You need Confidence 1 John 5:14 15

Hebrews [redacted] 13:6
[redacted] Hebrews 10:35, 36

I will pray
Watch Act on it

Dream & Vision

Num 12:6
12:8

[redacted] true vision

Prov. 29:18
Lam 2:9

Is 6:1-5
Ez 1:1-10
Ez 1:22
26
Ez 3:15
Daniel 1:1 28
[redacted] 8:15
Heba 2:1
Prayer is the Key

Heba 2:3
1 Sam 3:1

THE CONTEMPORARY PARALLEL NEW TESTAMENT

THE CONTEMPORARY PARALLEL NEW TESTAMENT

King James Version

New American Standard Bible
Updated Edition

New International Version

New Living Translation

New Century Version

Contemporary English Version

New King James Version

The Message

John R. Kohlenberger III
General Editor

New York Oxford
OXFORD UNIVERSITY PRESS

OXFORD UNIVERSITY PRESS

Oxford New York

Athens Auckland Bangkok Bogota Bombay
Buenos Aires Calcutta Cape Town Dar es Salaam
Delhi Florence Hong Kong Istanbul Karachi
Kuala Lumpur Madras Madrid Melbourne
Mexico City Nairobi Paris Singapore
Taipei Tokyo Toronto

and associated companies in

Berlin Ibadan

Published by Oxford University Press, Inc.
198 Madison Avenue, New York, NY 10016

Oxford is a registered trademark of Oxford University Press

Design and Typesetting by

John R. Kohlenberger III and Multnomah Graphics

Troutdale, Oregon

COPYRIGHT NOTICES

Printed in the United States of America
1 3 5 7 9 8 6 4 2

Table of Contents

The Books of the New Testament

The Books of the New Testament in Alphabetical Order

Acknowledgments

The Publisher wishes to thank all those who have contributed to this volume:

Peachtree Editorial and Proofreading Service, who proofread the entire volume.

The translation owners, particularly of the New Living Translation, who allowed modification of the apparatus and text of their Bible in Mark 16 to better fit the parallel format.

Introduction to *The Contemporary Parallel New Testament*

Whenever a new translation of the Bible is published, people ask, "Why are there so many translations of the Bible?" or, "What's the point of all these new translations?" The book you are holding in your hands—*The Contemporary Parallel New Testament*—is an answer to those questions. Within its covers are eight of the most popular translations of the present day: popular as best sellers, and popular as readable, friendly, open versions of a great treasure house of writings. They have been deliberately chosen because they are already known to a great many people and because each one of them has dealt in a creative way with the difficulties of translating the New Testament. In comparing them you will be able to see how gifted translators try in various ways to help the writers of the New Testament speak to men and women today.

Most people know that the Bible was not originally written in English. The New Testament was written in Greek, the ancient language of an empire that stretched from the western Mediterranean east almost to the borders of India. Even after that empire was taken over by the Romans, who spoke Latin, the Greek language continued to be the speech that people used to communicate with others from different countries in different parts of the ancient world. It was everybody's second language. The New Testament was written on purpose to speak to every human being in the known inhabited world. The language that would reach the widest circle of people was Greek—so the New Testament writers used it.

Nobody speaks ancient Greek today, and the inhabited world is a much wider place than it was twenty centuries ago, so it has been necessary to translate the New Testament into many other languages over the centuries. People first began translating it into English in the fifteenth and sixteenth centuries, and there have been more translations of the Bible into English than into any other language. The translations in this parallel New Testament are all English translations from the original Greek, and all are within the broad stream of the classic tradition of English translations that began with John Wycliffe and his followers in the 1380s and 1390s, and continued with William Tyndale in 1526.

As you read these paralleled texts in concert, you will find that they usually blend and harmonize. Like the members of a great choir, they sing the same song in different ways. At times you will notice clashes of dissonance, even unusual solos. The harmonies come from the different styles and vocabularies of each translation; the clashes come from different opinions about the original Greek text[1], or the different understanding of the meaning of Greek words and phrases. But like a grand oratorio, the differences work together to give you a larger, clearer, more vibrant experience of the great teachings of the New Testament.

1. See "Note on the Text" immediately following this introduction.

The Different Styles of Translation

For as long as there have been translations from one language to another, there have been two basic styles of translation. John Purvey, who translated the second Wycliffe Bible in the 1390s, tells us about these styles in his *General Prologue*:

> . . . the best translating . . . is to translate after the sentence and not only after the words . . . for the words ought to serve to the intent and sentence . . . [2]

These two translation styles—"after the word" and "after the sentence"—remain with us to this day and are reflected in the translations in *The Contemporary Parallel New Testament*. Word-for-word translation, often called "literal" in popular literature and "formal equivalent" by experts, is the style many scholars and students prefer. Phrase-for-phrase or meaning-for-meaning translation, an "idiomatic" style sometimes incorrectly referred to as "paraphrase" and called "dynamic equivalent" by experts, is the style most readers prefer.

Actually, no Bible translation is exclusively one style or the other. These labels represent "pure" or ideal versions, but the realities of language and the needs of readers mean that each translation is a mixture of both, with a primary emphasis towards one end of the spectrum or the other. The King James Version, which is closer to the "word-for-word" end, regularly uses idiomatic translation, as in the phrase "God forbid!" This phrase appears twenty-four times in the King James (for instance, Gen. 44:7, 17; Rom. 3:4, 6, 31), but it never translates Greek or Hebrew words meaning "God" or "forbid." It stands for a Hebrew word and a Greek phrase that mean, "This should never, ever happen!" In the same way, a translation that is idiomatic will use word-for-word renderings when the underlying Greek results in a good plain English style. Thus the New Living Translation renders John 3:16, in an almost perfect word-for-word style, as follows: "For God so loved the world that he gave his only Son, so that everyone who believes in him will not perish but have eternal life."

The eight translations in *The Contemporary Parallel New Testament* can be arranged roughly in order, from the most "word-for-word" style to the most "idiomatic" style. First are the three translations that are regularly word-for-word: the New American Standard Bible (NASB), the closest to a word-for-word translation; the New King James Version (NKJV), regularly word-for-word; and the King James Version (KJV), regularly word-for-word but often idiomatic as well. These three translations use italics to indicate words that are not present in the Greek text but that need to be supplied to make sense in English.

The New International Version [NIV] is often word-for-word but regularly idiomatic.

The next three translations are regularly idiomatic but sometimes word-for-word: the New Century Version (NCV), the New Living Translation (NLT), and the Contemporary English Version (CEV). All three translations make a strong effort to communicate in simpler language, and the CEV tries to use present-day vocabulary rather than traditional language.

Finally, *The Message* [TM] is regularly idiomatic and rarely word-for-word, with a very distinct character of its own.

For more information on each translation, especially regarding the translators' own presentation of their styles, we invite you to read the various Prefaces following this introduction.

The Vocabulary of Translation

When translators sit down to their work of expressing an ancient Greek document in modern American English, they have to make some decisions in advance. They have to agree on the

2. Quoted in F.F. Bruce, *History of the Bible in English*, Oxford, 1978.

level of the translation—will it use a complex or simple English style?—and the difficulty of the vocabulary. They have to decide how they are going to translate the same Greek word when in occurs in different contexts—will they try to use the same English word, or will they choose the English word that best fits its meaning in each passage? And they have to decide what kind of English they want to translate into. If their translation is meant to be read aloud in church, for instance, they might want to use a more formal style than they would for a translation that teenagers would like to read.

Some of these issues are reflected in the translations in *The Contemporary Parallel New Testament.*

The effort to use the same English word to represent the same Greek word is called *consistency*. Translations on the word-for-word end of the spectrum tend to be the most consistent. Of course, this cannot be an absolute rule. If you look at the NASB, NKJV, KJV, and NIV, you will notice that key words tend to be used consistently. By using a concordance (a word index to a translation), you can see all of the occurrences of any given word in a translation. But even these translations will translate common Greek words with a variety of English words. For instance, the Greek word *legō*, in general meaning "say," is translated not only "say," but "speak," "ask," "answer," and other terms as well. The King James Version translators wrote:

> We have not tied ourselves to an uniformity of phrasing, or to an identity of words, as some peradventure would wish that we had done.[3]

One of the major insights you can gain from *The Contemporary Parallel New Testament* is that the same message can be communicated clearly and accurately in a variety of phrasing. As the great Christian thinker Augustine said, "Variety of translations is profitable for finding out the sense of the Scriptures."

Another issue that translators have to deal with is one of traditional versus contemporary vocabulary. In addition to many unusual proper names and place names, the text of the Bible contains many specialized terms. These include objects unfamiliar to us, like "winnowing forks" and "phylacteries," unfamiliar names for familiar objects, such as Noah's "ark" (boat) and the "ark (chest) of the covenant," and the terms for theological ideas, like "grace," "propitiation," and "righteousness."

The more traditional versions, the KJV, NKJV, NASB, and NIV, assume that you know this vocabulary. The translations that use present-day language try to avoid these technical terms and often include footnotes that explain biblical terms, objects, and practices. For instance, look at Romans 3:24 in the New King James Version:

> Being justified freely by his grace through the redemption that is in Christ Jesus.

Now read the same verse in the Contemporary English Version:

> But God treats us much better than we deserve,[a] and because of Christ Jesus, he freely accepts us and sets us free from our sins.
>
> [a] *treats us much better than we deserve*: The Greek word *charis*, traditionally rendered "grace," is translated here and other places in the CEV to express the overwhelming kindness of God.

---

3. "The Translators to the Reader"

In Matthew 6:16, the New Century Version translates "fasting" as "giving up eating," and explains this custom in a footnote: "This is called 'fasting.' The people would give up eating for a special time of prayer and worship to God. It was also done to show sadness and disappointment." In the area of traditional terminology, *The Contemporary Parallel New Testament* offers the best of both worlds: classic church vocabulary beside modern English terms, often with additional information in footnotes.

How to Study the New Testament in Eight Translations

As you read through *The Contemporary Parallel New Testament* you will certainly notice great differences in style and choices of words and phrases. But you can also be reassured that these translations clearly communicate the same message in different words. Take advantage of stylistic differences as you are reading to gain insight into the meaning of passages that may have become over-familiar in one translation. You can also use the variety to guard against coming to a conclusion too quickly: where there is a difference, you may have to dig before you dogmatize.

The narrative portions of the New Testament, the Gospels and Acts, will come alive in the modern, easy-reading translations. But when you have read through the accounts of these great events, you may want to return to them to study the particular teachings of Jesus in their traditional wording. In the parallel format you will find it easy to move quickly among the translations in this way. Likewise, the logical discussions in the Letters are best analyzed in the word-for-word translations, but the modern translations will give you the feeling that the early Christians had, that of reading or hearing a letter from a close friend. No matter which translation you are reading, remember to consult the footnotes of the other translations for cultural insights and word meanings.

When there are differences among the translations that are not just matters of style, this is a signal that the meaning of the verse is difficult, or that two or more meanings are possible and even scholars cannot agree. You may need to consult a wise teacher or a commentary or other reference books.[4]

The New Testament reflects what surpasses all time and space in the terms of a particular place and time. It is both timeless and timely. The eight translations in *The Contemporary Parallel New Testament* exist in that tension, a tension that is part of the condition of being human. For we too live in passing time, yet we can at moments apprehend the eternal. As you study and live with the texts in this volume you will learn from these gifted translators, in the words of the poet William Blake:

> To see a world in a grain of sand,
> And heaven in a wild flower,
> To hold infinity in the palm of your hand,
> And eternity in an hour.[5]

JOHN R. KOHLENBERGER III
General Editor

4. See "For Further Study" immediately following this introduction.
5. "Auguries of Innocence"

For Further Study

The Contemporary Parallel New Testament provides eight English versions that can be used to explore issues of text, word meanings, interpretation and communication. If you wish to go deeper in your studies, the following are some leading resources.

Bible concordances are word indexes to a specific translation of the Bible and are invaluable for word studies. There are a variety of time-honored concordances to the King James Version from a variety of publishers; the notable editions are by Cruden, Young, and Strong. The New International Version has seven concordances of different size and organization, all published by Zondervan Publishing House (Grand Rapids, MI). Several concordances to the New King James Version are published by Thomas Nelson Publishers (Nashville, TN). *The NLT Complete Concordance* is published by Tyndale House Publishers (Wheaton, IL) An exhaustive concordance to the New American Standard Bible is available from Broadman & Holman (Nashville, TN). Although it is based on the earlier editions than the 1995 revision included here, most of the key words are the same. Strong's and Young's *Concordances* to the KJV, the *Exhaustive Concordance* to the NASB, and *The NIV Exhaustive Concordance* also show you what Greek words underlie the English words of these three translations.

More thorough definitions of Greek words may be found in Greek lexicons and word study books. The latest and most useful Greek lexicons are *A Greek-English Lexicon of the New Testament*, Bauer, Arndt, Gingrich and Danker (Chicago: University of Chicago and Grand Rapids: Zondervan, 1979) and *Greek-English Lexicon of the New Testament Based on Semantic Domains*, Louw and Nida (New York: United Bible Societies, 1988). More thorough in three volumes is the *Exegetical Dictionary of the New Testament*, Balz and Schneider (Grand Rapids: Eerdmans, 1990–93). The most thorough word study books include the ten-volume *Theological Dictionary of the New Testament*, Kittel and Friedrich (Grand Rapids: Eerdmans, 1964–76), its one-volume abridgment by Geoffrey W. Bromiley (Grand Rapids: Eerdmans, 1985), and the four-volume *New International Dictionary of New Testament Theology*, Brown (Grand Rapids: Zondervan, 1975–86).

Bible commentaries are the most handy, and often the most thorough, source for analyzing any passage of the New Testament and for explaining differences in its textual base and interpretation. Among the best series of critical commentaries for detailed study are the Anchor Bible (New York: Doubleday), Hermeneia (Philadelphia: Fortress), the New International Greek Testament (Grand Rapids: Eerdmans), and the Word Biblical Commentary (Dallas: Word). Expository commentaries, which are not as academic or detailed, but are more accessible to the general reader, include the Expositor's Bible Commentary (Grand Rapids: Eerdmans), the New International Commentary (Grand Rapids: Eerdmans), and the New American Commentary (Nashville: Broadman & Holman).

J.R.K.

Note on the Text

The New Testament writings appeared many centuries before the invention of the printing press, and therefore all of the early copies of them had to be written out by hand. What we have now are copies of the original writings—in fact, copies of copies. Each copy has slight variations in it, the result of both minor errors by the copiers and intentional changes where the copiers thought that they were restoring what the original text must have been. These variations are called *variant readings*. Many hundreds of these manuscript copies have survived, and modern scholars have compared the variant readings carefully in an effort to determine, as far as possible, what the original manuscripts said. (No original manuscripts are known to have survived.) These scholars, called *textual critics*, publish their results in what is called a *critical text*. This is a printed edition of the Greek New Testament with the most likely readings in the text and other significant variants in footnotes. The two critical texts generally used are one published by the United Bible Societies and one edited by Nestle and Aland. These critical texts generally rely on the oldest Greek manuscripts, only a few of which have survived, and consequently pay less attention to the many manuscripts from later centuries, of which hundreds and even thousands of copies exist.

Before these texts were published, however, there was a Greek New Testament available to translators. It is popularly called the "*Textus Receptus*," since it was the "text received" by most scholars in the sixteeneth and seventeenth centuries. It is also called the "Majority Text," since it uses the large number of Greek manuscripts that are from later centuries. This Majority tradition is the one that was used in translating the King James Version, and is also used by the New King James Version. The NKJV has very helpful footnotes that point out the differences between the Majority Text (which it calls the "M-Text") and the Nestle and United Bible Societies texts ("NU-Text").

The other translations in *The Contemporary Parallel New Testament* for the most part use the critical texts. The Message uses both the Majority Text and the critical texts.

Differences between texts may affect the way you interpret a specific passage, but they will not affect your overall theology. No major doctrine stands or falls on a variant reading. In fact, most differences between manuscripts are relatively minor, such as in spelling or word order. For example, in 2 Timothy 1:1 the KJV and NKJV read "Jesus Christ," while the other translations have "Christ Jesus." In other places variants may have synonyms rather than identical words, such as at 2 Timothy 2:19, where the KJV and NKJV have "the name of Christ" and the other translations have "the name of the Lord."

In many places in the Gospels, the Majority Text has more words than the ancient texts. Textual critics believe that in the course of copying, scribes would add words from one Gospel to make the other Gospels identical. For a major example of this, compare Matthew 6:9–13 with Luke 11:2–4, the two accounts of "the Lord's Prayer." In the KJV and NKJV they are nearly identical; in the other versions Luke's prayer is much shorter.

There are sixteen verses in KJV and NKJV that are not included in the text of most modern versions. Note that ten of these verses are still in the New Testament—at their original location. For example, Matthew 23:14, omitted from most modern translations of Matthew, still appears in Mark 12:40 and Luke 20:47. Nine other such duplicates are:

Matthew 17:21	=	Mark 9:29
Matthew 18:11	=	Luke 19:10
Mark 7:16	=	Mark 4:9, 21

Mark 9:44, 46	=	Mark 9:48
Mark 11:26	=	Matthew 6:15
Mark 15:28	=	Luke 22:37
Luke 17:36	=	Matthew 24:40
Luke 23:16	=	Matthew 27:15; Mark 15:6; John 18:39
Romans 16:24	=	Romans 16:20; 1 Corinthians 16:23; etc.

There are six more verses that do not appear in most modern translations. Acts 8:37 and 1 John 5:7b–8a were copied from an early Latin translation. John 5:3b–4, Acts 24:6b–7, 15:34 and 28:29 are not in the oldest manuscripts, and seem to be explanations added by later scribes.

Two larger sections and three individual verses of the Gospels are also not found in the most ancient manuscripts. They are included in the Greek texts and in modern translations, but there is usually a note that explains their textual status. The passages are Mark 16:9–20 (the "Longer Ending") and John 7:53–8:11. The verses are Luke 22:43–44 and 23:34.

Because of the diversity of ancient manuscripts, there are two endings to the Gospel of Mark. These are known as the "Shorter Ending" and the "Longer Ending." Both of these endings are included among the translations in *The Contemporary Parallel New Testament.* All of the translations have the traditional Longer Ending; the NASB, CEV, and NLT include the Shorter Ending as well. (The NLT usually prints the Shorter Ending after verse 8. The copyright holder graciously allowed the transposition of these materials to the end of the chapter in order to match the order in the NASB and CEV.)

For other word and phrase differences, please consult the textual notes in the various translations. For more information on the textual base of any particular translation, please consult the prefaces that follow.

J.R.K.

New American Standard Bible

Foreword

SCRIPTURAL PROMISE

"The grass withers, the flower fades, but the word of our God stands forever."
Isaiah 40:8

The New American Standard Bible has been produced with the conviction that the words of Scripture as originally penned in the Hebrew, Aramaic, and Greek were inspired by God. Since they are the eternal Word of God, the Holy Scriptures speak with fresh power to each generation, to give wisdom that leads to salvation, that men may serve Christ to the glory of God.

The purpose of the Editorial Board in making this translation was to adhere as closely as possible to the original languages of the Holy Scriptures, and to make the translation in a fluent and readable style according to current English usage.

THE FOURFOLD AIM OF THE LOCKMAN FOUNDATION

1. These publications shall be true to the original Hebrew, Aramaic, and Greek.
2. They shall be grammatically correct.
3. They shall be understandable.
4. They shall give the Lord Jesus Christ His proper place, the place which the Word gives Him; therefore, no work will ever be personalized.

Preface to the
New American Standard Bible

In the history of English Bible translations, the King James Version is the most prestigious. This time-honored version of 1611, itself a revision of the Bishops' Bible of 1568, became the basis for the English Revised Version appearing in 1881 (New Testament) and 1885 (Old Testament). The American counterpart of this last work was published in 1901 as the American Standard Version. The ASV, a product of both British and American scholarship, has been highly regarded for its scholarship and accuracy. Recognizing the values of the American Standard Version, The Lockman Foundation felt an urgency to preserve these and other lasting values of the ASV by incorporating recent discoveries of Hebrew and Greek textual sources and by rendering it into more current English. Therefore, in 1959 a new translation project was launched, based on the time-honored principles of translation of the ASV and KJV. The result is the New American Standard Bible.

Translation work for the NASB was begun in 1959. In the preparation of this work numerous other translations have been consulted along with the linguistic tools and literature of biblical scholarship. Decisions about English renderings were made by consensus of a team composed of educators and pastors. Subsequently, review and evaluation by other Hebrew and Greek scholars outside the Editorial Board were sought and carefully considered.

The Editorial Board has continued to function since publication of the complete Bible in 1971. This edition of the NASB represents revisions and refinements recommended over the last several years as well as thorough research based on modern English usage.

Principles of Translation

MODERN ENGLISH USAGE: The attempt has been made to render the grammar and terminology in contemporary English. When it was felt that the word-for-word literalness was unacceptable to the modern reader, a change was made in the direction of a more current English idiom. In the instances where this has been done, the more literal rendering has been indicated in the notes.

GREEK TEXT: Consideration was given to the latest available manuscripts with a view to determining the best Greek text. In most instances the 26th edition of Eberhard Nestle's NOVUM TESTAMENTUM GRAECE was followed.

GREEK TENSES: A careful distinction has been made in the treatment of the Greek aorist tense (usually translated as the English past, "He did") and the Greek imperfect tense (normally rendered either as English past progressive, "He was doing"; or, if inceptive, as "He began to do" or "He started to do"; or else if customary past, as "He used to do"). "Began" is italicized if it renders an imperfect tense, in order to distinguish it from the Greek verb for "begin." In some contexts the difference between the Greek imperfect and the English past is conveyed better by the choice of vocabulary or by other words in the context, and in such cases the Greek imperfect may be rendered as a simple past tense (e.g. "had an illness for many years" would be preferable to "was having an illness for many years" and would be understood in the same way).

On the other hand, not all aorists have been rendered as English pasts ("He did"), for some of them are clearly to be rendered as English perfects ("He has done"), or even as past perfects ("He had done"), judging from the context in which they occur. Such aorists have been rendered as perfects or past perfects in this translation.

As for the distinction between aorist and present imperatives, the translators have usually rendered these imperatives in the customary manner, rather than attempting any such fine distinction as "Begin to do!" (for the aorist imperative), or, "Continually do!" (for the present imperative).

As for sequence of tenses, the translators took care to follow English rules rather than Greek in translating Greek presents, imperfects and aorists. Thus, where English says, "We knew that he was doing," Greek puts it, "We knew that he does"; similarly, "We knew that he had done" is the Greek, "We knew that he did." Likewise, the English, "When he had come, they met him," is represented in Greek by: "When he came, they met him." In all cases a consistent transfer has been made from the Greek tense in the subordinate clause to the appropriate tense in English.

In the rendering of negative questions introduced by the particle *mē* (which always expects the answer "No") the wording has been altered from a mere, "Will he not do this?" to a more accurate, "He will not do this, will he?"

Editorial Board, THE LOCKMAN FOUNDATION

Explanation of General Format

FOOTNOTES are used only where the text especially requires them for clarification. Marginal notes and cross references have been removed from this edition.

PARAGRAPHS are designated by bold face verse numbers or letters.

QUOTATION MARKS are used in the text in accordance with modern English usage.

"THOU," "THEE" and "THY" are not used in this edition and have been rendered as "YOU" and "YOUR."

PERSONAL PRONOUNS are capitalized when pertaining to Deity.

ITALICS are used in the text to indicate words which are not found in the original Hebrew, Aramaic, or Greek but implied by it. Italics are used in the notes to signify alternate readings for the text. Roman text in the alternate note readings is the same as italics in the Bible text.

SMALL CAPS in the New Testament are used in the text to indicate Old Testament quotations or obvious references to Old Testament texts. Variations of Old Testament wording are found in New Testament citations depending on whether the New Testament writer translated from a Hebrew text, used existing Greek or Aramaic translations, or paraphrased the material. It should be noted that modern rules for the indication of direct quotation were not used in biblical times; thus, the ancient writer would use exact quotations or references to quotation without specific indication of such.

ASTERISKS are used to mark verbs that are historical presents in the Greek which have been translated with an English past tense in order to conform to modern usage. The translators recognized that in some contexts the present tense seems more unexpected and unjustified to the English reader than a past tense would have been. But Greek authors frequently used the present tense for the sake of heightened vividness, thereby transporting their readers in imagination to the actual scene at the time of occurrence. However, the translators felt that it would be wise to change these historical presents to English past tenses.

Preface to the New International Version

This New Testament of the *New International Version* of the Holy Bible is a completely new translation made by over a hundred scholars working directly from the best available Greek texts. It had its beginning in 1965 when, after several years of exploratory study by committees from the Christian Reformed Church and the National Association of Evangelicals, a group of scholars met at Palos Heights, Illinois, and concurred in the need for a new translation of the Bible in contemporary English. This group, though not made up of official church representatives, was transdenominational. Its conclusion was endorsed by a large number of leaders from many denominations who met in Chicago in 1966.

Responsibility for the new version was delegated by the Palos Heights group to a self-governing body of fifteen, the Committee on Bible Translation, composed for the most part of biblical scholars from colleges, universities and seminaries. In 1967 the New York Bible Society (now the International Bible Society) generously undertook the financial sponsorship of the project—a sponsorship that made it possible to enlist the help of many distinguished scholars. The fact that participants from the United States, Great Britain, Canada, Australia and New Zealand worked together gave the project its international scope. That they were from many denominations—including Anglican, Assemblies of God, Baptist, Brethren, Christian Reformed, Church of Christ, Evangelical Free, Lutheran, Mennonite, Methodist, Nazarene, Presbyterian, Wesleyan and other churches—helped to safeguard the translation from sectarian bias.

How it was made helps to give the New International Version its distinctiveness. The translation of each book was assigned to a team of scholars. Next, one of the Intermediate Editorial Committees revised the initial translation, with constant reference to the Hebrew, Aramaic or Greek. Their work then went to one of the General Editorial Committees, which checked it in detail and made another thorough revision. This revision in turn was carefully reviewed by the Committee on Bible Translation, which made further changes and then released the final version for publication. In this way the entire Bible underwent three revisions, during each of which the translation was examined for its faithfulness to the original languages and for its English style.

All this involved many thousands of hours of research and discussion regarding the meaning of the texts and the precise way of putting them into English. It may well be that no other translation has been made by a more thorough process of review and revision from committee to committee than this one.

From the beginning of the project, the Committee on Bible Translation held to certain goals for the New International Version: that it would be an accurate translation and one that would have clarity and literary quality and so prove suitable for public and private reading, teaching, preaching, memorizing and liturgical use. The Committee also sought to preserve some measure of continuity with the long tradition of translating the Scriptures into English.

In working toward these goals, the translators were united in their commitment to the authority and infallibility of the Bible as God's Word in written form. They believe that it contains the divine answer to the deepest needs of humanity, that it sheds unique light on our path in a dark world, and that it sets forth the way to our eternal well-being.

The first concern of the translators has been the accuracy of the translation and its fidelity to the thought of the biblical writers. They have striven for more than a word-for-word translation. Because thought patterns and syntax differ from language to language, faithful communication of the meaning of the writers of the Bible demands frequent modifications in sentence structure and constant regard for the contextual meanings of words.

The Committee on Bible Translation submitted the developing version to a number of stylistic consultants. Samples of the translation were tested for clarity and ease of reading by various kinds of people—young and old, highly educated and less well educated, ministers and laymen. Concern for clear and natural English motivated the translators and consultants. In view of the international use of English, the translators sought to avoid obvious Americanisms on the one hand and obvious Anglicisms on the other. A British edition reflects the comparatively few differences of significant idiom and of spelling.

As for the traditional pronouns "thou," "thee" and "thine" in reference to the Deity, the translators judged that to use these archaisms (along with the old verb forms such as "doest," "wouldest" and "hadst") would violate accuracy in translation. Greek does not use special pronouns for the persons of the Godhead. A present-day translation is not enhanced by forms that in the time of the King James Version were used in everyday speech, whether referring to God or man.

The Greek text used in translating the New Testament was an eclectic one. No other piece of ancient literature has such an abundance of manuscript witnesses as does the New Testament. Where existing manuscripts differ, the translators made their choice of readings according to accepted principles of New Testament textual criticism. Footnotes call attention to places where there was uncertainty about what the original text was. The best current printed texts of the Greek New Testament were used.

There is a sense in which the work of translation is never wholly finished. This applies to all great literature and uniquely so to the Bible. In 1973 the New Testament in the New International Version was published. Since then, suggestions for corrections and revisions have been received from various sources. The Committee on Bible Translation carefully considered the suggestions and adopted a number of them. These were incorporated in the first printing of the entire Bible in 1978. Additional revisions were made by the Committee on Bible Translation in 1983 and appear in printings after that date.

To achieve clarity the translators sometimes supplied words not in the original texts but required by the context. If there was uncertainty about such material, it is enclosed in brackets. Also for the sake of clarity or style, nouns, including some proper nouns, are sometimes substituted for pronouns, and vice versa. As an aid to the reader, italicized sectional headings are inserted in most of the books. They are not to be regarded as part of the

NIV text, are not for oral reading, and are not intended to dictate the interpretation of the sections they head.

The footnotes in this version are of several kinds, most of which need no explanation. Those giving alternative translations begin with "Or" and generally introduce the alternative with the last word preceding it in the text, except when it is a single-word alternative; in poetry quoted in a footnote a slant mark indicates a line division. Footnotes introduced by "Or" do not have uniform significance. In some cases two possible translations were considered to have about equal validity. In other cases, though the translators were convinced that the translation in the text was correct, they judged that another interpretation was possible and of sufficient importance to be represented in a footnote. In the New Testament, footnotes that refer to uncertainty regarding the original text are introduced by "Some manuscripts" or similar expressions.

It should be noted that minerals, flora and fauna, architectural details, articles of clothing and jewelry, musical instruments and other articles cannot always be identified with precision. Also measures of capacity in the biblical period are particularly uncertain.

Like all translations of the Bible, made as they are by imperfect man, this one undoubtedly falls short of its goals. Yet we are grateful to God for the extent to which he has enabled us to realize these goals and for the strength he has given us and our colleagues to complete our task. We offer this version of the Bible to him in whose name and for whose glory it has been made. We pray that it will lead many into a better understanding of the Holy Scriptures and a fuller knowledge of Jesus Christ the incarnate Word, of whom the Scriptures so faithfully testify.

The Committee on Bible Translation

June 1978
(Revised August 1983)

Names of the translators and editors may be secured
from the International Bible Society,
translation sponsors of the New International Version,
1820 Jet Stream Drive, Colorado Springs, Colorado
80921-3696 U.S.A.

Introduction to the New Living Translation

Translation Philosophy and Methodology

There are two general theories or methods of Bible translation. The first has been called "formal equivalence." According to this theory, the translator attempts to render each word of the original language into the receptor language and seeks to preserve the original word order and sentence structure as much as possible. The second has been called "dynamic equivalence" or "functional equivalence." The goal of this translation theory is to produce in the receptor language the closest natural equivalent of the message expressed by the original-language text—both in meaning and in style. Such a translation attempts to have the same impact on modern readers as the original had on its own audience.

A dynamic-equivalence translation can also be called a thought-for-thought translation, as contrasted with a formal-equivalence or word-for-word translation. Of course, to translate the thought of the original language requires that the text be interpreted accurately and then be rendered in understandable idiom. So the goal of any thought-for-thought translation is to be both reliable and eminently readable. Thus, as a thought-for-thought translation, the New Living Translation seeks to be both exegetically accurate and idiomatically powerful.

In making a thought-for-thought translation, the translators must do their best to enter into the thought patterns of the ancient authors and to present the same ideas, connotations, and effects in the receptor language. In order to guard against personal biases and to ensure the accuracy of the message, a thought-for-thought translation should be created by a group of scholars who employ the best exegetical tools and who also understand the receptor language very well. With these concerns in mind, the Bible Translation Committee assigned each book of the Bible to three different scholars. Each scholar made a thorough review of the assigned book and submitted suggested revisions to the appropriate general reviewer. The general reviewer reviewed and summarized these suggestions and then proposed a first-draft revision of the text. This draft served as the basis for several additional phases of exegetical and stylistic committee review. Then the Bible Translation Committee jointly reviewed and approved every verse in the final translation.

A thought-for-thought translation prepared by a group of capable scholars has the potential to represent the intended meaning of the original text even more accurately than a word-for-word translation. This is illustrated by the various renderings of the Hebrew word *hesed*. This term cannot be adequately translated by any single English word because it can connote love, mercy, grace, kindness, faithfulness, and loyalty. The context—not the lexicon—must determine which English term is selected for translation.

The value of a thought-for-thought translation can be illustrated by comparing 1 Kings 2:10 in the King James Version, the New International Version, and the New Living Translation. "So David slept with his fathers, and was buried in the city of David" (KJV). "Then David rested with his fathers and was buried in the City of David" (NIV). "Then David died and was buried in the City of David" (NLT). Only the New Living Translation clearly translates the real meaning of the Hebrew idiom "slept with his fathers" into contemporary English.

Written to Be Read Aloud

It is evident in Scripture that the biblical documents were written to be read aloud, often in public worship (see Nehemiah 8; Luke 4:16-20; 1 Timothy 4:13; Revelation 1:3). It is still the case today that more people will hear the Bible read aloud in church than are likely to read it for themselves. Therefore, a new translation must communicate with clarity and power when it is read aloud. For this reason, the New Living Translation is recommended as a Bible to be used for public reading. Its living language is not only easy to understand, but it also has an emotive quality that will make an impact on the listener.

The Texts behind the New Living Translation

The translators of the Old Testament used the Masoretic Text of the Hebrew Bible as their standard text. They used the edition known as *Biblia Hebraica Stuttgartensia* (1977) with its up-to-date textual apparatus, a revision of Rudolf Kittel's *Biblia Hebraica* (Stuttgart, 1937). The translators also compared the Dead Sea Scrolls, the Septuagint and other Greek manuscripts, the Samaritan Pentateuch, the Syriac Peshitta, the Latin Vulgate, and any other versions or manuscripts that shed light on textual problems.

The translators of the New Testament used the two standard editions of the Greek New Testament: the *Greek New Testament,* published by the United Bible Societies (fourth revised edition, 1993), and *Novum Testamentum Graece,* edited by Nestle and Aland (twenty-seventh edition, 1993). These two editions, which have the same text but differ in punctuation and textual notes, represent the best in modern textual scholarship.

Translation Issues

The translators have made a conscious effort to provide a text that can be easily understood by the average reader of modern English. To this end, we have used the vocabulary and language structures commonly used by the average person. The result is a translation of the Scriptures written generally at the reading level of a junior high school student. We have avoided using language that is likely to become quickly dated or that reflects a narrow subdialect of English, with the goal of making the New Living Translation as broadly useful as possible.

But our concern for readability goes beyond the concerns of vocabulary and sentence structure. We are also concerned about historical and cultural barriers to understanding the Bible, and we have sought to translate terms shrouded in history or culture in ways that can be immediately understood by the contemporary reader. Thus, our goal of easy readability expresses itself in a number of other ways:

- Rather than translating ancient weights and measures literally, which communicates little to the modern reader, we have expressed them by means of recognizable contemporary equivalents. We have converted ancient weights and measures to modern English (American) equivalents, and we have rendered the literal Hebrew or Greek measures, along with metric equivalents, in textual footnotes.
- Instead of translating ancient currency values literally, we have generally expressed them in terms of weights in precious metals. In some cases we have used other common

terms to communicate the message effectively. For example, "three shekels of silver" might become "three silver coins" or "three pieces of silver" to convey the intended message. Again, a rendering of the literal Hebrew or Greek is given in textual footnotes.

- Since the Hebrew lunar calendar fluctuates from year to year in relation to the solar calendar used today, we have translated Hebrew dates in a way that communicates with our modern readership. It was clear that we could not use the names of the Hebrew months, such as Abib, which are meaningless to the modern reader. Nor could we use a simple designation such as "first month," because the months of the Hebrew lunar calendar do not correspond with the months of our calendar. Thus, we have often used seasonal references to communicate the time of year when something happened. For example, "the first month" (which occurs in March and April) might be translated "early spring." Where it is possible to define a specific ancient date in terms of our modern calendar, we use modern dates in the text. Textual footnotes then give the literal Hebrew date and state the rationale for our rendering. For example, Ezra 7:9 pinpoints the date when Ezra arrived in Jerusalem: "the first day of the fifth month." This was during the seventh year of King Artaxerxes' reign (Ezra 7:7). We translate that lunar date as August 4, with a footnote giving the Hebrew and identifying the year as 458 B.C.
- Since ancient references to the time of day differ from our modern methods of denoting time, we used renderings that are instantly understandable to the modern reader. Accordingly, we have rendered specific times of day by using approximate equivalents in terms of our common "o'clock" system. On occasion, translations such as "at dawn the next morning" or "as the sun began to set" have been used when the biblical reference is general.
- Many words in the original texts made sense to the original audience but communicate something quite different to the modern reader. In such cases, some liberty must be allowed in translation to communicate what was intended. Places identified by the term normally translated "city," for example, are often better identified as "towns" or "villages." Similarly, the term normally translated "mountain" is often better rendered "hill."
- Many words and phrases carry a great deal of cultural meaning that was obvious to the original readers but needs explanation in our own culture. For example, the phrase "they beat their breasts" (Luke 23:48) in ancient times meant that people were very upset. In our translation we chose to translate this phrase dynamically: "They went home in deep sorrow." In some cases, however, we have simply illuminated the existing expression to make it immediately understandable. For example, we might have expanded the literal phrase to read "they beat their breasts in sorrow."
- Metaphorical language is often difficult for contemporary readers to understand, so at times we have chosen to translate or illuminate the metaphor. For example, the ancient poet writes, "Your eyes are doves" (Song of Songs 1:15). To help the modern reader, who might be confused or distracted by a literal visualization of this image, we converted the metaphor to a simile to make the meaning immediately clear: "Your eyes are soft like doves." Here we also added the modifier "soft" to help the modern reader catch the significance of the metaphoric expression. A few chapters later, the poet writes, "Your neck is like the tower of David" (Song of Songs 4:4). We rendered it "Your neck is as stately as the tower of David" to clarify the intended positive meaning of the metaphor.
- We did not feel obligated to display all Hebrew poetry in English poetic form. Only the

book of Psalms is set entirely in poetic lines. Other books, though poetic in nature, are set in prose for the sake of easier reading. Nonetheless, these prose renderings reflect the poetic language of the original Hebrew. Where a portion of text is explicitly said to be a poem or song, however, it has usually been set as such.

- One challenge we faced was in determining how to translate accurately the ancient biblical text that was originally written in a context where male-oriented terms were used to refer to humanity generally. We needed to respect the nature of the ancient context while also trying to make the translation clear to a modern audience that tends to read male-oriented language as applying only to males. Often the original text, though using masculine nouns and pronouns, clearly intends that the message be applied to both men and women. One example is found in the New Testament epistles, where the believers are called "brothers" (adelphoi). Yet it is clear that these epistles were addressed to all the believers—male and female. Thus, we have usually translated this Greek word "brothers and sisters" in order to represent the historical situation more accurately.
- We have also been sensitive to passages where the text applies generally to human beings or to the human condition. In many instances we have used plural pronouns (they, them) in place of the masculine singular (he, him). For example, a traditional rendering of Proverbs 22:6 is: "Train up a child in the way he should go, and when he is old he will not turn from it." We have rendered it: "Teach your children to choose the right path, and when they are older, they will remain upon it." At times, we have also replaced third person pronouns with the second person to ensure clarity. A traditional rendering of Proverbs 26:27 is: "He who digs a pit will fall into it, and he who rolls a stone, it will come back on him." We have rendered it: "If you set a trap for others, you will get caught in it yourself. If you roll a boulder down on others, it will roll back on you." All such decisions were driven by the concern to reflect accurately the intended meaning of the original texts of Scripture.
- We should emphasize, however, that all masculine nouns and pronouns used to represent God (for example, "Father") have been maintained without exception. We believe that essential traits of God's revealed character can only be conveyed through the masculine language expressed in the original texts of Scripture.

Lexical Consistency in Terminology

For the sake of clarity, we have maintained lexical consistency in areas such as divine names, synoptic passages, rhetorical structures, and nontheological technical terms (i.e., liturgical, cultic, zoological, botanical, cultural, and legal terms). For theological terms, we have allowed a greater semantic range of acceptable English words or phrases for a single Hebrew or Greek word. We avoided weighty theological terms that do not readily communicate to many modern readers. For example, we avoided using words such as "justification," "sanctification," and "regeneration." In place of these words (which are carryovers from Latin), we provided renderings such as "we are made right with God," "we are made holy," and "we are born anew."

The Spelling of Proper Names

Many individuals in the Bible, especially the Old Testament, are known by more than one name or by a number of variant names (e.g., Uzziah/Azariah). For the sake of clarity, we have tried to use a single spelling for any one individual, footnoting the literal spelling whenever we differ from it. This is especially helpful in delineating the kings of Israel and Judah. King Joash/Jehoash of Israel has been consistently called Jehoash, while King Joash/Jehoash of Judah is called Joash. A similar distinction has been used to distinguish between Joram/Jehoram of Israel and Joram/Jehoram of Judah. All such decisions were made with the goal of clarifying the text for the reader. When the ancient biblical writers clearly had a theological purpose in their choice of a variant name (e.g., Eshbaal/Ishbosheth), the different names have been maintained with an explanatory footnote.

The Rendering of Divine Names

All appearances of *'el, 'elohim,* or *'eloah* have been translated "God," except where the context demands the translation "god(s)." We have rendered the tetragrammaton *(YHWH)* consistently as "the LORD," utilizing a form with small capitals that is common among English translations. This will distinguish it from the name *'adonai,* which we render "Lord." When *'adonai* and *YHWH* appear in conjunction, we have rendered it "Sovereign LORD." This also distinguishes *'adonai YHWH* from cases where *YHWH* appears with *'elohim,* which is rendered "LORD God." When *YH* (the short form of *YHWH*) and *YHWH* appear together, we have rendered it "LORD GOD." The Hebrew word *'adon* is rendered "lord," or "master," or sometimes "sir."

In the New Testament, the Greek word *Christos* has been translated as "Messiah" when the context assumes a Jewish audience. When a Gentile audience can be assumed, *Christos* has been translated as "Christ." The Greek word *kurios* is consistently translated "Lord," except in four quotations of Psalm 110:1, where it is translated "LORD."

Textual Footnotes

The New Living Translation provides several kinds of textual footnotes:

- All Old Testament passages that are clearly quoted in the New Testament are identified in a textual footnote in the New Testament.
- Some textual footnotes provide cultural and historical information on places, things, and people in the Bible that are probably obscure to modern readers. Such notes should aid the reader in understanding the message of the text. For example, in Acts 12:1, "King Herod" is named in this translation as "King Herod Agrippa" and is identified in a footnote as being "the nephew of Herod Antipas and a grandson of Herod the Great."
- When various ancient manuscripts contain different readings, these differences are often documented in footnotes. For instance, textual variants are footnoted when the variant reading is very familiar (usually through the King James Version). We have used footnotes when we have selected variant readings that differ from the Hebrew and Greek editions normally followed.
- When the meaning of a proper name (or a wordplay inherent in a proper name) is relevant to the meaning of the text, it is illuminated with a textual footnote. For example, the footnote at Genesis 3:20 reads: *"Eve* sounds like a Hebrew term that means 'to give life.' " This wordplay in the Hebrew illuminates the meaning of the text, which goes on to say that Eve "would be the mother of all people everywhere." If the meaning of the name is more certain, it is stated more simply. For example, the footnote at Genesis 16:11 reads: *"Ishmael* means 'God hears.' " In this case, Hagar named her son Ishmael after realizing that God had heard her cry for help.
- When we translate the meaning of a place-name that is often simply transliterated from

the Hebrew or Greek, we provide a textual footnote showing the transliteration that appears in many English translations. For example, the name usually transliterated "Havvoth-jair" in Judges 10:4 has been translated "the Towns of Jair," with a footnote that gives the traditional transliteration: "Hebrew *Havvoth-jair.*"

- Textual footnotes are also used to show alternative renderings. These are prefaced with the word "Or." On occasion, we also provide notes on words or phrases that represent a translation that departs from long-standing tradition. These notes are prefaced with the words "traditionally rendered." For example, a footnote to the translation "contagious skin disease" at Leviticus 13:2 says, "Traditionally rendered *leprosy.*"

AS WE SUBMIT this translation of the Bible for publication, we recognize that any translation of the Scriptures is subject to limitations and imperfections. Anyone who has attempted to communicate the richness of God's Word into another language will realize it is impossible to make a perfect translation. Recognizing these limitations, we sought God's guidance and wisdom throughout this project. Now we pray that he will accept our efforts and use this translation for the benefit of the Church and of all people.

We pray that the New Living Translation will overcome some of the barriers of history, culture, and language that have kept people from reading and understanding God's Word. We hope that readers unfamiliar with the Bible will find the words clear and easy to understand, and that readers well versed in the Scriptures will gain a fresh perspective. We pray that readers will gain insight and wisdom for living, but most of all that they will meet the God of the Bible and be forever changed by knowing him.

The Bible Translation Committee
JULY 1996

Preface to the New Century Version

The Bible is God's message to humanity. He has spoken to all peoples and all generations. Of course, God first accomplished this by directly addressing his people, the Israelites in the Old Testament and the young church in the New Testament, in a language they could understand.

The original text of the Bible was written in Hebrew, Aramaic, and Greek—languages of the people. Since God intends to address all people of all ages through his Word, each generation and language group must translate the Bible into its own language.

These facts, that the Bible is God's message and that it is ultimately addressed to all people in every age, require that a translation be both accurate and clear. These are the two overarching principles that stand behind the *New Century Version*.

An Accurate Translation

The first concern of the *New Century Version* is that the translation be faithful to the manuscripts in the original languages. A team composed of the World Bible Translation Center and fifty additional, highly qualified and experienced Bible scholars and translators was assembled. This team included people with experience on the *New International Version,* the *New American Standard Bible,* and the *New King James Version.* The scholars came from a variety of theological colleges, universities, and seminaries in the United States, Canada, Australia, and Great Britain.

These translators recognize that the most accurate translations are those which pay close attention to the meanings of words in their broader context, rather than those which simply treat words as isolated entities. They understand that a contemporary English translation must sometimes depart from the word order of the original languages to reflect accurately the meaning of God's Word to a modern English-speaking audience.

Further, it is true that translation involves interpretive decisions. With this in mind, it is important to note that the breadth of scholarship which stands behind the *New Century Version* ensures an unbiased translation.

Last, it should be mentioned that the best available Hebrew and Greek texts were used, principally the third edition of the United Bible Societies' Greek text and the latest edition of the Biblia Hebraica, along with the Septuagint.

A Clear Translation

The second concern was to make the language clear enough for all people to read the Bible and understand it for themselves. In maintaining clear language, several guidelines were followed. Vocabulary choice has been based upon *The Living Word Vocabulary* by Dr. Edgar Dale and Dr. Joseph O'Rourke (Worldbook-Childcraft International, 1981), which is the standard used by the editors of *The World Book Encyclopedia* to determine appropriate vocabulary. For difficult words that have no simpler synonyms, footnotes and dictionary references are provided. Footnotes appear at the bottom of the page and are indicated in the text by a raised letter (^{n}) for "note."

The *New Century Version* aids understanding by using contemporary references for measurements and geographical locations when it is feasible. For instance, terms such as "shekels," "cubits," "omer," and "hin" have been converted to modern equivalents. Where geographical references are identical, the modern name has been used, such as the "Mediterranean Sea" instead of "Great Sea" or "Western Sea." Also, to minimize confusion, the most familiar name for a place is used consistently, instead of using variant names for the same place. "Lake Galilee" is used throughout rather than its variant forms, "Sea of Kinnereth," "Lake Gennesaret," and "Sea of Tiberias."

Ancient customs are often unfamiliar to modern readers. Customs such as shaving a man's beard to shame him or ritually walking between the halves of a dead animal to seal an agreement are meaningless to many modern-day readers. So these are clarified either in the text or in a footnote.

Since *meanings* of words change with time, care has been taken to avoid potential misunderstandings. To do so, the *New Century Version* uses contemporary language in place of the archaic language often found in translations. Frequently in the Old Testament God tells his people to "devote" something to him, as when he tells the Israelites to devote Jericho and everything in it to him. While we might understand this to mean he is telling them to keep it safe and holy, the exact opposite is true. He is telling them to destroy it totally as an offering to him. The *New Century Version* communicates the idea clearly by translating "devoted," in these situations, as "destroyed as an offering to the Lord."

Where there was potential for confusion, *rhetorical questions* have been stated according to their implied answer. The psalmist's question, "Who, O God, is like you?" has been stated more directly as, "God, there is no one like you."

Figures of speech have been translated according to their meanings. For instance, the expression, "the Virgin Daughter of Zion," which is frequently used in the Old Testament, is simply and accurately translated "the people of Jerusalem" so that the meaning is not obscured by the figure of speech.

Idiomatic expressions of the biblical languages are translated to communicate the same meaning to today's reader that would have been understood by the original audience. For example, the Hebrew idiom "he rested with his fathers" is translated by its meaning— "he died."

Obscure terms have been clarified. Terms are often obscure in the Bible because they are part of the ancient culture which God directly addressed in his revelation. In the Old Testament, for instance, God frequently condemns the people for their "high places" and "Asherah poles." The *New Century Version* translates these according to their meanings, which would have been understood by the Hebrews. "High places" is translated "places where gods were worshiped" and "Asherah poles" is translated "Asherah idols."

Gender language has also been translated with a concern for clarity. To avoid the misconception that "man," "mankind," and "he" are exclusively masculine when they are being used in a generic sense, this translation has chosen to use less ambiguous language, such as "people," "humans," and "human beings," and has carefully worked throughout to choose gender language that would accurately convey the intent of the original writers. Specifically and exclusively masculine and feminine references in the text have been retained.

Following in the tradition of other English versions, the *New Century Version* indicates the divine name YHWH, the Tetragrammaton, by putting LORD, and sometimes GOD, in capital letters. This is to distinguish it from Adonai, another Hebrew word that is translated "Lord."

Every attempt has been made to maintain proper English style, while clarifying concepts and communication. The beauty of Hebrew parallelism in poetry has been retained, and the images of the ancient languages have been captured in equivalent English images wherever possible, but in all cases, clarity of communication with the modern reader has taken precedence over preservation of the ancient form.

Our Prayer

It is with great humility and prayerfulness that this Bible is presented. We acknowledge the infallibility of God's Word and yet our own human frailty. We pray that God has worked through us as his vessels so that we all might better learn his truth for ourselves and that it might richly grow in our lives. It is to his glory that this Bible is given.

THE PUBLISHER

Preface to the Contemporary English Version

Translation it is that opens the window, to let in the light; that breaks the shell, that we may eat the kernel; that puts aside the curtain, that we may look into the most holy place; that removes the cover of the well, that we may come by the water ("The Translators to the Reader," King James Version, 1611).

The most important document in the history of the English language is the *King James Version* of the Bible. To measure its spiritual impact on the English speaking world would be more impossible than counting the grains of sand along the ocean shores. Historically, many Bible translators have attempted in some measure to *retain the form* of the *King James Version*. But the translators of the *Contemporary English Version* of the Bible have diligently sought to *capture the spirit* of the *King James Version* by following certain principles set forth by its translators in the document "The Translators to the Reader," which was printed in the earliest editions.

This is the Word of God, which we translate

Accuracy, beauty, clarity, and dignity—all of these can and must be achieved in the translation of the Bible. After all, as the translators of the *King James Version* stated, "This is the Word of God, which we translate."

Every attempt has been made to produce a text that is faithful to the *meaning* of the original. In order to assure the *accuracy* of the *Contemporary English Version*, the New Testament was translated directly from the Greek text published by the United Bible Societies (third edition corrected and compared with the fourth revised edition).

The drafts in their earliest stages were sent for review and comment to a number of biblical scholars, theologians, and educators representing a wide variety of church traditions. In addition, drafts were sent for review and comment to all English-speaking Bible Societies and to more than forty United Bible Societies translation consultants around the world. Final approval of the text was given by the American Bible Society Board of Trustees on the recommendation of its Translations Subcommittee.

We desire that the Scripture . . . may be understood

That the Scripture may be understood even by ordinary people was a primary goal of the translators of the *King James Version*. And they raised the question, "What can be more available thereto than to deliver God's book unto God's people in a tongue which they understand?" Martin Luther also did his translation for the common people, and he established the following guidelines:

> We do not have to inquire of the literal Latin, how we are to speak German . . . Rather we must inquire about this of the mother in the home, the children on

> the street, the common man in the marketplace. *We must be guided by their language, the way they speak, and do our translating accordingly.*

Today more people *hear* the Bible read aloud then read it for themselves! And statistics released by the National Center for Education indicate that "almost half of U.S. adults have very limited reading and writing skills." If this is the case, a contemporary translation must be a text that an inexperienced reader can *read aloud* without stumbling, that someone unfamiliar with traditional biblical terminology can *hear without misunderstanding,* and that everyone can *listen to with enjoyment* because the style is lucid and lyrical.

In order to attain these goals of clarity, beauty, and dignity, the translators of the *Contemporary English Version* carefully studied every word, phrase, clause, and paragraph of the original. Then, with equal care, they struggled to discover the best way to translate the text, so that it would be suitable both for *private* and *public* reading, and for *memorizing.* The result is an English text that is enjoyable and easily understood by the vast majority of English speakers, regardless of their religious or educational background.

In the *hearing* of a translation, even the inclusion of a simple word like "and" can make a significant difference. Matthew 2.9 of the *Contemporary English Version* reads as follows: "The wise men listened to what the king said and then left. *And* the star they had seen in the east went on ahead of them until it stopped over the place where the child was."

"And" at the beginning of the second sentence assists both the person who reads the text aloud and those who must depend upon hearing it read. Like all other punctuation marks, the period after "left" is silent, and so the text without "And" could possibly be *heard* as, "The wise men listened to what the king said and then left the star they had seen in the east." However, as the text now stands, the oral reader must pause briefly for a breath before "And," which will signal the hearer that a new sentence has begun.

As another example, try reading the following two sentences aloud: "You yourselves admit, then, that you agree with what your ancestors did" and "for it was better with me then than now." Both suffer from potential tongue twisters ("admit, then, that" and "then than"). But the first is doubly difficult because it consists of a lengthy series of unaccented syllables that do not allow the reader to take a breath. In the *Contemporary English Version* every attempt has been made to avoid these and other kinds of constructions that could possibly prove problematic for oral reading.

According to the rules of English grammar, the pronoun *he* must refer back to *God* in the following sentence: "The other, however, rebuked him saying, 'Don't you fear *God?* You received the same sentence *he* did.'" But the reference is actually to Jesus, who is mentioned earlier in the passage. Traditional translations assume that the reader can study the printed text and finally figure out the meaning, but the *Contemporary English Version* is concerned equally with the reader and the *hearer.* And in many situations, the hearer may have only *one* chance to understand what is read aloud.

In poetry, the *appearance of the text on the page* is important, since in oral reading there is a tendency to stress the last word on a line and to pause momentarily before going to the next line, especially if the second line is indented. Compare the three following examples, where the lines of the same text have been broken improperly (left column) and properly (right column):

He brought me out into a broad place.	He brought me out into a broad place.

With the loyal you show yourself
    loyal.
The Lord my God lights up
    my darkness.
	With the loyal
	    you show yourself loyal.
	The Lord my God
	    lights up my darkness.

No fault is to be found with the translation itself. Yet there is a significant difference in the *appearance* of the text on the page, because the lines on the right have been *measured,* in order to prevent unfortunate runovers. In this form, the text not only looks better on the page, but it is easier to read and memorize, and it avoids such disastrous combinations as "He brought me out into a broad" or "With the loyal you show yourself" or "The Lord my God lights up." Moreover, both formats require exactly the same amount of lines.

The first translation in the history of the English Bible to develop a text with measured poetry lines is the *Contemporary English Version*, in which the translators have consciously created a text that will not suffer from unfortunate line breaks when published in double columns. *Accuracy* is the main concern of translators, but it must be realized that in the translation of biblical poetry, what the reader *sees* is what will be *said,* and what others will *hear.* This means that lines improperly broken can easily lead to a misunderstanding of the text, especially for those who must depend upon *hearing* the Scriptures read.

Hebrew poetry has its own systems of sound, rhyme, and rhythm, as well as a *form* that involves much repetition. It is impossible in English to retain the sounds, rhymes, and rhythms of the Hebrew text, but traditional translations have attempted to reproduce the frequent repetition, in which a second line will repeat or expand, either negatively or positively, the thoughts of the previous line. However, this repetition is often ineffective for those English speakers who are unaccustomed to the poetic style of the biblical authors. And so, the translators of the *Contemporary English Version* have followed the example of Martin Luther in the translation of poetry:

> Whoever would speak German *must not use Hebrew style.* Rather he must see to it—once he understands the Hebrew author—that he concentrates on the *sense* of the text, asking himself, "Pray tell, what do the Germans say in such a situation?" Once he has the German words to serve his purpose, let him drop the Hebrew words and *express the meaning freely* in the best German he knows.

The qualities that many critics value most in modern poetry are effortless *economy* and *exactness* of language. It is hoped that readers will discover similar features in the poetry of the *Contemporary English Version*, which strives for beauty and dignity, as much as for accuracy and clarity. In this translation, the poetry often requires fewer lines than do traditional translations, but the *integrity, intent,* and *impact* of the original are consistently maintained. Note, for example, the rendering of Job 38.14,15:

> Early dawn outlines the hills
> like stitches on clothing
>   or sketches on clay.
> But its light is too much
> for those who are evil,
>   and their power is broken.

Whenever the contents of two or more verses have been joined together and rearranged in the poetic sections of the *Contemporary English Version*, this is signaled by an asterisk (*) before the first verse number in the series.

In everyday speech, "gender generic" or "inclusive" language is used, because it sounds most natural to people today. This means that where the biblical languages require masculine nouns or pronouns when both men and women are intended, this intention must be reflected in translation, though the English *form* may be very different from that of the original. The Greek text of Matthew 16.24 is literally, "If anyone wants to follow me, *he* must deny *himself* and take up *his* cross and follow me." The *Contemporary English Version* shifts to a form which is still accurate, and at the same time more effective in English: "If any of *you* want to be my followers, *you* must forget about *yourself. You* must take up *your* cross and follow me."

Variety of translations is profitable

The translators of the *King James Version* said, " . . . variety of translations is profitable for the finding out of the sense of the Scriptures" and "We affirm and avow that the very meanest translation of the Bible in English, set forth by men of our profession . . . contains the Word of God, nay is the Word of God." They even stated, "No cause therefore why the Word translated should be denied to be the Word, or forbidden to be current, notwithstanding that some imperfections and blemishes may be noted in the setting forth of it."

Each English translation is, in its own right, the Word of God, yet each translation serves to meet the needs of a different audience. In this regard, the *Contemporary English Version* should be considered a *companion*—the *mission* arm—of traditional translations, because it takes seriously the words of the apostle Paul that "faith comes by *hearing.*"

It has pleased God in his divine providence

Translating the Bible may be compared to living the life of faith. God has not given us all the answers for our pilgrim journey, but we have been provided with all that we need to know in order to be saved. As the translators of the *King James Version* observed:

> . . . it has pleased God in His divine providence here and there to scatter those words and sentences of that difficulty and doubtfulness, not in doctrinal points that concern salvation (for in such it has been vouched that the Scriptures are plain), but in matters of less moment, that fearfulness would better beseem us than confidence . . .
>
> For as it is a fault of incredulity, to doubt of those things that are evident; so to determine of such things that the Spirit of God has left (even in the mind of the judicious) questionable, can be no less than presumption.

Bible translators do not have the privilege and luxury of working from the original manuscripts of either the Old or New Testament. Indeed, there are numerous difficult passages where decisions must be made concerning what word or words actually belong in the text, and what these words may, in fact, mean. At such places, the best a translator can do is to give what seems to be one possible meaning for the difficult text and to indicate this by a note, which was also what the King James translators did: ". . . so diversity of signification and sense in the margin, where the text is not clear, must needs be good; yea, is necessary, as we are persuaded." Fortunately, these "words and sentences of that difficulty and doubtfulness" do not in any way leave unclear the central message of the Bible or any of its major doctrines.

Having and using as great helps as were needful

The translators of the *Contemporary English Version* have not created new or novel interpretations of the text. Rather, it was their goal to express mainstream interpretations of the text in current, everyday English. To do so required *listening* carefully to each word of the biblical text, to the way in which English is spoken today, to the remarks of their reviewers, and especially to the Spirit of God. Once again the comments of the translators of the *King James Version* are appropriate:

> Neither did we think much to consult the translators or commentators . . . but neither did we disdain to revise that which we had done, and to bring to the anvil that which we had hammered; but having and using as great helps as were needful, and fearing no reproach for slowness, nor coveting praise for expedition, we have at the length, through the good hand of the Lord upon us, brought forth the work to that pass that you see.

Accordingly, the translators of the *Contemporary English Version* are indebted to all translators and biblical scholars who have gone before them and have made it possible to understand something of the languages, cultures, and history of biblical times. And, together with the apostle Paul, they confess: *We don't have the right to claim that we have done anything on our own. God gives us what it takes to do all that we do.* (2 Corinthians 3.5)

Offer praise to God our Savior because of our Lord Jesus Christ!
(Jude 24,25)

Preface to the New King James Version

Purpose

In the preface to the 1611 edition, the translators of the Authorized Version, known popularly as the King James Bible, state that it was not their purpose "to make a new translation . . . but to make a good one better." Indebted to the earlier work of William Tyndale and others, they saw their best contribution to consist in revising and enhancing the excellence of the English versions which had sprung from the Reformation of the sixteenth century. In harmony with the purpose of the King James scholars, the translators and editors of the present work have not pursued a goal of innovation. They have perceived the Holy Bible, New King James Version, as a continuation of the labors of the earlier translators, thus unlocking for today's readers the spiritual treasures found especially in the Authorized Version of the Holy Scriptures.

A Living Legacy

For nearly four hundred years, and throughout several revisions of its English form, the King James Bible has been deeply revered among the English-speaking peoples of the world. The precision of translation for which it is historically renowned, and its majesty of style, have enabled that monumental version of the Word of God to become the mainspring of the religion, language, and legal foundations of our civilization.

Although the Elizabethan period and our own era share in zeal for technical advance, the former period was more aggressively devoted to classical learning. Along with this awakened concern for the classics came a flourishing companion interest in the Scriptures, an interest that was enlivened by the conviction that the manuscripts were providentially handed down and were a trustworthy record of the inspired Word of God. The King James translators were committed to producing an English Bible that would be a precise translation, and by no means a paraphrase or a broadly approximate rendering. On the one hand, the scholars were almost as familiar with the original languages of the Bible as with their native English. On the other hand, their reverence for the divine Author and His Word assured a translation of the Scriptures in which only a principle of utmost accuracy could be accepted.

In 1786 Catholic scholar Alexander Geddes said of the King James Bible, "If accuracy and strictest attention to the letter of the text be supposed to constitute an excellent version, this is of all versions the most excellent." George Bernard Shaw became a literary legend in our century because of his severe and often humorous criticisms of our most cherished values. Surprisingly, however, Shaw pays the following tribute to the scholars commissioned by King James: "The translation was extraordinarily well done because to the translators what they were translating was not merely a curious collection of ancient books written by different authors in different stages of culture, but the Word of God divinely revealed through His chosen and expressly inspired scribes. In this conviction they carried out their work with boundless reverence and care and achieved a beautifully artistic result." History agrees with these estimates. Therefore, while seeking to unveil the excellent *form* of the traditional English Bible, special care has also been taken in the present edition to preserve the work of *precision* which is the legacy of the 1611 translators.

Complete Equivalence in Translation

Where new translation has been necessary in the New King James Version, the most complete representation of the original has been rendered by considering the history of usage and etymology of words in their contexts. This principle of complete equivalence seeks to preserve *all* of the information in the text, while presenting it in good literary form. Dynamic equivalence, a recent procedure in Bible translation, commonly results in paraphrasing where a more literal rendering is needed to reflect a specific and vital sense. For example, complete equivalence truly renders the original text in expressions such as "Jesus met them, saying, 'Rejoice!'" (Matt. 28:9); and "'Woman, what does your concern have to do with Me?'" (John 2:4). Complete equivalence translates fully, in order to provide an English text that is both accurate and readable.

In keeping with the principle of complete equivalence, it is the policy to translate interjections which are commonly omitted in modern language renderings of the Bible. As an example, the interjection *behold*, in the older King James editions, continues to have a place in English usage, especially in dramatically calling attention to a spectacular scene, or an event of profound importance such as the Immanuel prophecy of Isaiah 7:14. Consequently, *behold* is retained for these occasions in the present edition. However, the Greek originals for this word can be translated variously, depending on the circumstances in the passage. Therefore, in addition to *behold*, words such as *indeed, look, see*, and *surely* are also rendered to convey the appropriate sense suggested by the context in each case.

In faithfulness to God and to our readers, it was deemed appropriate that all participating scholars sign a statement affirming their belief in the verbal and plenary inspiration of Scripture, and in the inerrancy of the original autographs.

Devotional Quality

The King James scholars readily appreciated the intrinsic beauty of divine revelation. They accordingly disciplined their talents to render well-chosen English words of their time, as well as a graceful, often musical arrangement of language, which has stirred the hearts of Bible readers through the years. The translators, the committees, and the editors of the present edition, while sensitive to the late-twentieth-century English idiom, and while adhering faithfully to the Greek texts, have sought to maintain those lyrical and devotional qualities that are so highly regarded in the Authorized Version. This devotional quality is especially apparent in the poetic and prophetic books, although even the relatively plain style of the Gospels and Epistles cannot strictly be likened, as sometimes suggested, to modern newspaper style. The Koine Greek of the New Testament is influenced by the Hebrew background of the writers, for whom even the gospel narratives were not merely flat utterance, but often song in various degrees of rhythm.

The Style

Students of the Bible applaud the timeless devotional character of our historic Bible. Yet it is also universally understood that our language, like all living languages, has undergone profound change since 1611. Subsequent revisions of the King James Bible have sought to keep abreast of changes in English speech. The present work is a further step toward this objective. Where obsolescence and other reading difficulties exist, present-day vocabulary, punctuation, and grammar have been carefully integrated. Words representing ancient objects, such as *chariot* and *phylactery*, have no modern substitutes and are therefore retained.

A special feature of the New King James Version is its conformity to the thought flow of the 1611 Bible. The reader discovers that the sequence and selection of words, phrases, and clauses of the new edition, while much clearer, are so close to the traditional that there is remarkable ease in listening to the reading of either edition while following with the other.

In the discipline of translating biblical and other ancient languages, a standard method of transliteration, that is, the English spelling of untranslated words, such as names of persons and places, has never been commonly adopted. In keeping with the design of the present work, the King James spelling of untranslated words is retained, although made uniform throughout.

King James doctrinal and theological terms, for example, *propitiation*, *justification*, and *sanctification*, are generally familiar to English-speaking peoples. Such terms have been retained except where the original language indicates need for a more precise translation.

Readers of the Authorized Version will immediately be struck by the absence of several pronouns: *thee, thou*, and *ye* are replaced by the simple *you*, while *your* and *yours* are substituted for *thy* and *thine* as applicable. *Thee, thou, thy,* and *thine* were once forms of address to express a special relationship to human as well as divine persons. These pronouns are no longer part of our language. However, reverence for God in the present work is preserved by capitalizing pronouns, including *You, Your*, and *Yours*, which refer to Him. Additionally, capitalization of these pronouns benefits the reader by clearly distinguishing divine and human persons referred to in a passage. Without such capitalization the distinction is often obscure, because the antecedent of a pronoun is not always clear in the English translation.

In addition to the pronoun usages of the seventeenth century, the *-eth* and *-est* verb endings, so familiar in the earlier King James editions, are now obsolete. Unless a speaker is schooled in these verb endings, there is common difficulty in selecting the correct form to be used with a given subject of the verb in vocal prayer. That is, should we use *love, loveth*, or *lovest*? *do, doeth, doest*, or *dost*? *have, hath*, or *hast*? Because these forms are obsolete, contemporary English usage has been substituted for the previous verb endings.

In older editions of the King James Version, the frequency of the connective *and* far exceeded the limits of present English usage. Also, biblical linguists agree that the Greek original words for this conjunction may commonly be translated otherwise, depending on the immediate context. Therefore, instead of *and*, alternatives such as *also, but, however, now, so, then*, and *thus* are accordingly rendered in the present edition, when the original language permits.

The real character of the Authorized Version does not reside in its archaic pronouns or verbs or other grammatical forms of the seventeenth century, but rather in the care taken by its scholars to impart the letter and spirit of the original text in a majestic and reverent style.

The Format

The format of the New King James Version is designed to enhance the vividness and devotional quality of the Holy Scriptures:

• Subject headings assist the reader to identify topics and transitions in the biblical content.
• Words or phrases in *italics* indicate expressions in the original language which require clarification by additional English words, as also done throughout the history of the King James Bible.
• *Oblique* type in the New Testament indicates a quotation from the Old Testament.
• Prose is divided into paragraphs to indicate the structure of thought.
• Poetry is structured as contemporary verse to reflect the poetic form and beauty of the passage in the original language.
• The covenant name of God was usually translated from the Hebrew as "LORD" or "GOD" (using capital letters as shown) in the King James Old Testament. This tradition is maintained. In the present edition the name is so capitalized whenever the covenant name is quoted in the New Testament from a passage in the Old Testament.

The New Testament Text

There is more manuscript support for the New Testament than for any other body of ancient literature. Over five thousand Greek, eight thousand Latin, and many more manuscripts in other languages attest the integrity of the New Testament. There is only one basic New Testament used by Protestants, Roman Catholics, and Orthodox, by conservatives and liberals. Minor variations in hand copying have appeared through the centuries, before mechanical printing began about A.D. 1450.

Some variations exist in the spelling of Greek words, in word order, and in similar details. These ordinarily do not show up in translation and do not affect the sense of the text in any way.

Other manuscript differences such as omission or inclusion of a word or a clause, and two paragraphs in the Gospels, should not overshadow the overwhelming degree of *agreement* which exists among the ancient records. Bible readers may be assured that the most important differences in English New Testaments of today are due, not to manuscript divergence, but to the way in which translators view the task of translation: How literally should the text be rendered? How does the translator view the matter of biblical inspiration? Does the translator adopt a paraphrase when a literal rendering would be quite clear and more to the point? The New King James Version follows the historic precedent of the Authorized Version in maintaining a literal approach to translation, except where the idiom of the original language cannot be translated directly into our tongue.

The King James New Testament was based on the traditional text of the Greek-speaking churches, first published in 1516, and later called the Textus Receptus or Received Text. Although based on the relatively few available manuscripts, these were representative of many more which existed at the time but only became known later. In the late nineteenth century, B. Westcott and F. Hort taught that this text had been officially edited by the fourth-century church, but a total lack of historical evidence for this event has forced a revision of the theory. It is now widely held that the Byzantine Text that largely supports the Textus Receptus has as much right as the Alexandrian or any other tradition to be weighed in determining the text of the New Testament. Those readings in the Textus Receptus which have weak support are indicated in the footnotes as being opposed by both Critical and Majority Texts.

Since the 1880s most contemporary translations of the New Testament have relied upon a relatively few manuscripts discovered chiefly in the late nineteenth and early twentieth centuries. Such translations depend primarily on two manuscripts, Codex Vaticanus and Codex Sinaiticus, because of their greater age. The Greek text obtained by using these sources and the related papyri (our most ancient manuscripts) is known as the Alexandrian Text. However, some scholars have grounds for doubting the faithfulness of Vaticanus and Sinaiticus, since they often disagree with one another, and Sinaiticus exhibits excessive omission.

A third viewpoint of New Testament scholarship holds that the best text is based on the consensus of the majority of existing Greek manuscripts. This text is called the Majority Text. Most of these manuscripts are in substantial agreement. Even though many are late, and none is earlier than the fifth century, usually their readings are verified by papyri, ancient versions, quotations from the early church fathers, or a combination of these. The Majority Text is similar to the Textus Receptus, but it corrects those readings which have little or no support in the Greek manuscript tradition.

Today, scholars agree that the science of New Testament textual criticism is in a state of flux. Very few scholars still favor the Textus Receptus as such, and then often for its historical prestige as the text of Luther, Calvin, Tyndale, and the King James Version. For about a century most have followed a Critical Text (so called because it is edited according to specific principles of textual criticism) which depends heavily upon the Alexandrian type of text. More recently many have abandoned this Critical Text (which is quite similar to the one edited by Westcott and Hort) for one that is more eclectic. Finally, a small but growing number of scholars prefer the Majority Text, which is close to the traditional text except in the Revelation.

In light of these facts, and also because the New King James Version is the fifth revision of a historic document translated from specific Greek texts, the editors decided to retain the traditional text in the body of the New Testament. Although variations are duly indicated in the footnotes, it is most important to emphasize that fully eighty-five percent of the New Testament text is the same in the Textus Receptus, the Alexandrian Text, and the Majority Text. Notes in the present edition of the New Testament make no evaluation of readings, but do clearly indicate the manuscript sources of readings. They objectively present the facts without such tendentious remarks as "the best manuscripts omit" or "the most reliable manuscripts read." Such notes are value judgments that differ according to varying viewpoints on the text. By giving a clearly defined set of variants the New King James Version benefits readers of all textual persuasions.

Where significant variations occur in the New Testament Greek manuscripts, textual notes are classified as follows:

NU-Text

These variations from the traditional text generally represent the Alexandrian or Egyptian type of text described previously in "The New Testament Text." They are found in the Critical Text published in the twenty-seventh edition of the Nestle-Aland Greek New Testament (N) and in the United Bible Societies' fourth edition (U), hence the acronym, "NU-Text."

M-Text

This symbol indicates points of variation in the Majority Text from the traditional text, as also previously discussed in "The New Testament Text." It should be noted that M stands for whatever reading is printed in the published *Greek New Testament According to the Majority Text*, whether supported by overwhelming, strong, or only a divided majority textual tradition.

The textual notes reflect the scholarship of the past 150 years and will assist the reader to observe the variations between the different manuscript traditions of the New Testament. Such information is generally not available in English translations of the New Testament.

Introduction to The Message

The arrival of Jesus signaled the beginning of a new era. God entered history in a personal way, and made it unmistakably clear that he is on our side, doing everything possible to save us. It was all presented and worked out in the life, death, and resurrection of Jesus. It was, and is, hard to believe—seemingly too good to be true.

But one by one, men and women did believe it, believed Jesus was God alive among them and for them. Soon they would realize that he also lived in them. To their great surprise they found themselves living in a world where God called all the shots—had the first word on everything; had the last word on everything. That meant that everything, quite literally every thing, had to be re-centered, re-imagined, and re-thought.

They went at it with immense gusto. They told stories of Jesus and arranged his teachings in memorable form. They wrote letters. They sang songs. They prayed. One of them wrote an extraordinary poem based on holy visions. There was no apparent organization to any of this; it was all more or less spontaneous and, to the eye of the casual observer, haphazard. Over the course of about fifty years, these writings added up to what would later be compiled by the followers of Jesus and designated "The New Testament."

Three kinds of writing—eyewitness stories, personal letters, and a visionary poem—make up the book. Five stories, twenty-one letters, one poem.

In the course of this writing and reading, collecting and arranging, with no one apparently in charge, the early Christians, whose lives were being changed and shaped by what they were reading, arrived at the conviction that there was, in fact, someone in charge—God's Holy Spirit was behind and in it all. In retrospect, they could see that it was not at all random or haphazard, that every word worked with every other word, and that all the separate documents worked in intricate harmony. There was nothing accidental in any of this, nothing merely circumstantial. They were bold to call what had been written "God's Word," and trusted their lives to it. They accepted its authority over their lives. Most of its readers since have been similarly convinced.

A striking feature in all this writing is that it was done in the street language of the day, the idiom of the playground and marketplace. In the Greek-speaking world of that day, there were two levels of language: formal and informal. Formal language was used to write philosophy and history, government decrees and epic poetry. If someone were to sit down and consciously write for posterity, it would of course be written in this formal language with its learned vocabulary and precise diction. But if the writing was routine—shopping lists, family letters, bills and receipts—it was written in the common, informal idiom of everyday speech, street language.

And this is the language used throughout the New Testament. Some people are taken aback by this, supposing that language dealing with a holy God and holy things should be elevated—stately and ceremonial. But one good look at Jesus—his preference for down-to-earth stories and easy association with common people—gets rid of that supposition. For Jesus is the descent of God to our lives, just as they are, not the ascent of our lives to God, hoping he might approve when he sees how hard we try.

And that is why the followers of Jesus in their witness and preaching, translating and teaching, have always done their best to get the Message—the "good news"—into the language of whatever streets they happen to be living on. In order to understand the Message right, the language must be right—not a refined language that appeals to our aspirations after the best but a rough and earthy language that reveals God's presence and action where we least expect it, catching us when we are up to our elbows in the soiled ordinariness of our lives and God is the furthest thing from our minds.

This version of the New Testament in a contemporary idiom keeps the language of the Message current and fresh and understandable in the same language in which we do our shopping, talk with our friends, worry about world affairs, and teach our children their table manners. The goal is not to render a word-for-word conversion of Greek into English, but rather to convert the tone, the rhythm, the events, the ideas, into the way we actually think and speak.

In the midst of doing this work, I realized that this is exactly what I have been doing all my vocational life. For thirty-five years as a pastor I stood at the border between two languages, biblical Greek and everyday English, acting as a translator, providing the right phrases, getting the right words so that the men and women to whom I was pastor could find their way around and get along in this world where God has spoken so decisively and clearly in Jesus. I did it from the pulpit and in the kitchen, in hospitals and restaurants, on parking lots and at picnics, always looking for an English way to make the biblical text relevant to the conditions of the people.

THE CONTEMPORARY PARALLEL NEW TESTAMENT

KING JAMES VERSION

THE GOSPEL ACCORDING TO
ST. MATTHEW

1 The book of the generation of Jesus Christ, the son of David, the son of Abraham.
2 Abraham begat Isaac; and Isaac begat Jacob; and Jacob begat Judas and his brethren;
3 And Judas begat Phares and Zara of Thamar; and Phares begat Esrom; and Esrom begat Aram;
4 And Aram begat Aminadab; and Aminadab begat Naasson; and Naasson begat Salmon;
5 And Salmon begat Booz of Rachab; and Booz begat Obed of Ruth; and Obed begat Jesse;
6 And Jesse begat David the king; and David the king begat Solomon of her *that had been the wife* of Urias;

NEW AMERICAN STANDARD BIBLE

THE GOSPEL ACCORDING TO
MATTHEW

The Genealogy of Jesus the Messiah

1 The record of the genealogy of Jesus the Messiah, the son of David, the son of Abraham:
2 Abraham was the father of Isaac, Isaac the father of Jacob, and Jacob the father of [1]Judah and his brothers.
3 Judah was the father of Perez and Zerah by Tamar, Perez was the father of Hezron, and Hezron the father of Ram.
4 Ram was the father of Amminadab, Amminadab the father of Nahshon, and Nahshon the father of Salmon.
5 Salmon was the father of Boaz by Rahab, Boaz was the father of Obed by Ruth, and Obed the father of Jesse.
6 Jesse was the father of David the king.
David was the father of Solomon by [2]Bathsheba who had been the wife of Uriah.

1:2 [1] Gr *Judas;* names of people in the Old Testament are given in their Old Testament form **1:6** [2] Lit *her of Uriah*

NEW CENTURY VERSION

MATTHEW

The Family History of Jesus

1 This is the family history of Jesus Christ. He came from the family of David, and David came from the family of Abraham.

2 Abraham was the father[a] of Isaac.
Isaac was the father of Jacob.
Jacob was the father of Judah and his brothers.
3 Judah was the father of Perez and Zerah.
(Their mother was Tamar.)
Perez was the father of Hezron.
Hezron was the father of Ram.
4 Ram was the father of Amminadab.
Amminadab was the father of Nahshon.
Nahshon was the father of Salmon.
5 Salmon was the father of Boaz.
(Boaz's mother was Rahab.)
Boaz was the father of Obed.
(Obed's mother was Ruth.)
Obed was the father of Jesse.
6 Jesse was the father of King David.
David was the father of Solomon.
(Solomon's mother had been Uriah's wife.)

1:2 [a] **father** "Father" in Jewish lists of ancestors can sometimes mean grandfather or more distant relative.

CONTEMPORARY ENGLISH VERSION

MATTHEW

The Ancestors of Jesus (Luke 3.23-38)

1 Jesus Christ came from the family of King David and
also from the family of Abraham. And this is a list of
his ancestors. 2-6a From Abraham to King David, his ances-
tors were:
Abraham, Isaac, Jacob, Judah and his brothers (Judah's sons were Perez and Zerah, and their mother was Tamar), Hezron;
Ram, Amminadab, Nahshon, Salmon, Boaz (his mother was Rahab), Obed (his mother was Ruth), Jesse, and King David.
6b-11 From David to the time of the exile in Babylonia, the ancestors of Jesus were:
David, Solomon (his mother had been Uriah's wife), Rehoboam, Abijah, Asa, Jehoshaphat, Jehoram;

NEW INTERNATIONAL VERSION

MATTHEW

The Genealogy of Jesus

1 A record of the genealogy of Jesus Christ the son of David, the son of Abraham:

2 Abraham was the father of Isaac,
Isaac the father of Jacob,
Jacob the father of Judah and his brothers,
3 Judah the father of Perez and Zerah, whose mother was Tamar,
Perez the father of Hezron,
Hezron the father of Ram,
4 Ram the father of Amminadab,
Amminadab the father of Nahshon,
Nahshon the father of Salmon,
5 Salmon the father of Boaz, whose mother was Rahab,
Boaz the father of Obed, whose mother was Ruth,
Obed the father of Jesse,
6 and Jesse the father of King David.

David was the father of Solomon, whose mother had been Uriah's wife,

NEW LIVING TRANSLATION

MATTHEW

The Record of Jesus' Ancestors

1 This is a record of the ancestors of Jesus the Messiah, a descendant of King David and of Abraham:

2 Abraham was the father of Isaac.
Isaac was the father of Jacob.
Jacob was the father of Judah and his brothers.
3 Judah was the father of Perez and Zerah (their mother was Tamar).
Perez was the father of Hezron.
Hezron was the father of Ram.*
4 Ram was the father of Amminadab.
Amminadab was the father of Nahshon.
Nahshon was the father of Salmon.
5 Salmon was the father of Boaz (his mother was Rahab).
Boaz was the father of Obed (his mother was Ruth).
Obed was the father of Jesse.
6 Jesse was the father of King David.
David was the father of Solomon (his mother was Bathsheba, the widow of Uriah).

1:3 Greek *Aram;* also in 1:4. See 1 Chr 2:9-10.

NEW KING JAMES VERSION

THE GOSPEL ACCORDING TO

MATTHEW

The Genealogy of Jesus Christ

1 The book of the genealogy of Jesus Christ, the Son of David, the Son of Abraham:

2 Abraham begot Isaac, Isaac begot Jacob, and Jacob
begot Judah and his brothers. 3 Judah begot Perez and
Zerah by Tamar, Perez begot Hezron, and Hezron begot
Ram. 4 Ram begot Amminadab, Amminadab begot Nah-
shon, and Nahshon begot Salmon. 5 Salmon begot Boaz by
Rahab, Boaz begot Obed by Ruth, Obed begot Jesse, 6 and
Jesse begot David the king.

David the king begot Solomon by her *who had been the
wife*[a] of Uriah. 7 Solomon begot Rehoboam, Rehoboam

1:6 [a] Words in italic type have been added for clarity. They are not found in the original Greek.

THE MESSAGE

MATTHEW

1 The family tree of Jesus Christ, David's son, Abraham's son:

Abraham had Isaac,
Isaac had Jacob,
Jacob had Judah and his brothers,
Judah had Perez and Zerah (the mother was Tamar),
Perez had Hezron,
Hezron had Aram,
Aram had Amminadab,
Amminadab had Nahshon,
Nahshon had Salmon,
Salmon had Boaz (his mother was Rahab),
Boaz had Obed (Ruth was the mother),
Obed had Jesse,
Jesse had David,
and David became king.

David had Solomon (Uriah's wife was the mother),

KING JAMES VERSION

7 And Solomon begat Roboam; and Roboam begat Abia; and Abia begat Asa;
8 And Asa begat Josaphat; and Josaphat begat Joram; and Joram begat Ozias;
9 And Ozias begat Joatham; and Joatham begat Achaz; and Achaz begat Ezekias;
10 And Ezekias begat Manasses; and Manasses begat Amon; and Amon begat Josias;
11 And Josias begat Jechonias and his brethren, about the time they were carried away to Babylon:
12 And after they were brought to Babylon, Jechonias begat Salathiel; and Salathiel begat Zorobabel;
13 And Zorobabel begat Abiud; and Abiud begat Eliakim; and Eliakim begat Azor;
14 And Azor begat Sadoc; and Sadoc begat Achim; and Achim begat Eliud;
15 And Eliud begat Eleazar; and Eleazar begat

NEW AMERICAN STANDARD BIBLE

7 Solomon was the father of Rehoboam, Rehoboam the father of Abijah, and Abijah the father of Asa.
8 Asa was the father of Jehoshaphat, Jehoshaphat the father of Joram, and Joram the father of Uzziah.
9 Uzziah was the father of Jotham, Jotham the father of Ahaz, and Ahaz the father of Hezekiah.
10 Hezekiah was the father of Manasseh, Manasseh the father of Amon, and Amon the father of Josiah.
11 Josiah became the father of Jeconiah and his brothers, at the time of the deportation to Babylon.
12 After the deportation to Babylon: Jeconiah became the father of Shealtiel, and Shealtiel the father of Zerubbabel.
13 Zerubbabel was the father of Abihud, Abihud the father of Eliakim, and Eliakim the father of Azor.
14 Azor was the father of Zadok, Zadok the father of Achim, and Achim the father of Eliud.
15 Eliud was the father of Eleazar, Eleazar the father of

NEW CENTURY VERSION

7 Solomon was the father of Rehoboam.
Rehoboam was the father of Abijah.
Abijah was the father of Asa.
8 Asa was the father of Jehoshaphat.
Jehoshaphat was the father of Jehoram.
Jehoram was the ancestor of Uzziah.
9 Uzziah was the father of Jotham.
Jotham was the father of Ahaz.
Ahaz was the father of Hezekiah.
10 Hezekiah was the father of Manasseh.
Manasseh was the father of Amon.
Amon was the father of Josiah.
11 Josiah was the grandfather of Jehoiachin and his brothers.
(This was at the time that the people were taken to Babylon.)
12 After they were taken to Babylon:
Jehoiachin was the father of Shealtiel.
Shealtiel was the grandfather of Zerubbabel.
13 Zerubbabel was the father of Abiud.
Abiud was the father of Eliakim.
Eliakim was the father of Azor.
14 Azor was the father of Zadok.
Zadok was the father of Akim.
Akim was the father of Eliud.
15 Eliud was the father of Eleazar.
Eleazar was the father of Matthan.

CONTEMPORARY ENGLISH VERSION

Uzziah, Jotham, Ahaz, Hezekiah, Manasseh, Amon, Josiah, and Jehoiachin and his brothers.
12-16 From the exile to the birth of Jesus, his ancestors were:
Jehoiachin, Shealtiel, Zerubbabel, Abiud, Eliakim, Azor, Zadok, Achim;

NEW INTERNATIONAL VERSION

7 Solomon the father of Rehoboam,
Rehoboam the father of Abijah,
Abijah the father of Asa,
8 Asa the father of Jehoshaphat,
Jehoshaphat the father of Jehoram,
Jehoram the father of Uzziah,
9 Uzziah the father of Jotham,
Jotham the father of Ahaz,
Ahaz the father of Hezekiah,
10 Hezekiah the father of Manasseh,
Manasseh the father of Amon,
Amon the father of Josiah,
11 and Josiah the father of Jeconiah[a] and his brothers at the time of the exile to Babylon.

12 After the exile to Babylon:
Jeconiah was the father of Shealtiel,
Shealtiel the father of Zerubbabel,
13 Zerubbabel the father of Abiud,
Abiud the father of Eliakim,
Eliakim the father of Azor,
14 Azor the father of Zadok,
Zadok the father of Akim,
Akim the father of Eliud,
15 Eliud the father of Eleazar,
Eleazar the father of Matthan,

[a] *11* That is, Jehoiachin; also in verse 12

NEW LIVING TRANSLATION

7 Solomon was the father of Rehoboam.
Rehoboam was the father of Abijah.
Abijah was the father of Asaph.*
8 Asaph was the father of Jehoshaphat.
Jehoshaphat was the father of Jehoram.*
Jehoram was the father* of Uzziah.
9 Uzziah was the father of Jotham.
Jotham was the father of Ahaz.
Ahaz was the father of Hezekiah.
10 Hezekiah was the father of Manasseh.
Manasseh was the father of Amos.*
Amos was the father of Josiah.
11 Josiah was the father of Jehoiachin* and his brothers (born at the time of the exile to Babylon).
12 After the Babylonian exile:
Jehoiachin was the father of Shealtiel.
Shealtiel was the father of Zerubbabel.
13 Zerubbabel was the father of Abiud.
Abiud was the father of Eliakim.
Eliakim was the father of Azor.
14 Azor was the father of Zadok.
Zadok was the father of Akim.
Akim was the father of Eliud.
15 Eliud was the father of Eleazar.
Eleazar was the father of Matthan.

1:7 *Asaph* is the same person as Asa; also in 1:8. See 1 Chr 3:10. **1:8a** Greek *Joram.* See 1 Kgs 22:50 and note at 1 Chr 3:11. **1:8b** Or *ancestor;* also in 1:11. **1:10** *Amos* is the same person as Amon. See 1 Chr 3:14. **1:11** Greek *Jeconiah;* also in 1:12. See 2 Kgs 24:6 and note at 1 Chr 3:16.

NEW KING JAMES VERSION

begot Abijah, and Abijah begot Asa.[b] 8Asa begot Jehosha-
phat, Jehoshaphat begot Joram, and Joram begot Uzziah.
9Uzziah begot Jotham, Jotham begot Ahaz, and Ahaz begot
Hezekiah. 10Hezekiah begot Manasseh, Manasseh begot
Amon,[c] and Amon begot Josiah. 11Josiah begot Jeconiah
and his brothers about the time they were carried away to
Babylon.

12And after they were brought to Babylon, Jeconiah
begot Shealtiel, and Shealtiel begot Zerubbabel. 13Ze-
rubbabel begot Abiud, Abiud begot Eliakim, and Eliakim
begot Azor. 14Azor begot Zadok, Zadok begot Achim, and
Achim begot Eliud. 15Eliud begot Eleazar, Eleazar begot

1:7 [b] NU-Text reads *Asaph.* 1:10 [c] NU-Text reads *Amos.*

THE MESSAGE

Solomon had Rehoboam,
Rehoboam had Abijah,
Abijah had Asa,
Asa had Jehoshaphat,
Jehoshaphat had Joram,
Joram had Uzziah,
Uzziah had Jotham,
Jotham had Ahaz,
Ahaz had Hezekiah,
Hezekiah had Manasseh,
Manasseh had Amon,
Amon had Josiah,
Josiah had Jehoiachin and his brothers,
and then the people were taken into the Babylonian exile.

When the Babylonian exile ended,
Jehoiachin had Shealtiel,
Shealtiel had Zerubbabel,
Zerubbabel had Abiud,
Abiud had Eliakim,
Eliakim had Azor,
Azor had Zadok,
Zadok had Achim,
Achim had Eliud,
Eliud had Eleazar,
Eleazar had Matthan,

KING JAMES VERSION

Matthan; and Matthan begat Jacob;

16 And Jacob begat Joseph the husband of Mary, of whom was born Jesus, who is called Christ.

17 So all the generations from Abraham to David *are* fourteen generations; and from David until the carrying away into Babylon *are* fourteen generations; and from the carrying away into Babylon unto Christ *are* fourteen generations.

18 ¶ Now the birth of Jesus Christ was on this wise: When as his mother Mary was espoused to Joseph, before they came together, she was found with child of the Holy Ghost.

19 Then Joseph her husband, being a just *man*, and not willing to make her a publick example, was minded to put her away privily.

20 But while he thought on these things, behold, the angel of the Lord appeared unto him in a dream, saying, Joseph, thou son of David, fear not to take unto thee Mary thy wife: for that which is conceived in her is of the Holy Ghost.

21 And she shall bring forth a son, and thou shalt call his name JESUS: for he shall save his people from their sins.

22 Now all this was done, that it might be fulfilled which was spoken of the Lord by the prophet, saying,

23 Behold, a virgin shall be with child, and shall bring

NEW AMERICAN STANDARD BIBLE

Matthan, and Matthan the father of Jacob.

16 Jacob was the father of Joseph the husband of Mary, by whom Jesus was born, who is called the Messiah.

17 So all the generations from Abraham to David are fourteen generations; from David to the deportation to Babylon, fourteen generations; and from the deportation to Babylon to the Messiah, fourteen generations.

Conception and Birth of Jesus

18 Now the birth of Jesus Christ was as follows: when His mother Mary had been betrothed to Joseph, before they came together she was found to be with child by the Holy Spirit.

19 And Joseph her husband, being a righteous man and not wanting to disgrace her, planned [3]to send her away secretly.

20 But when he had considered this, behold, an angel of the Lord appeared to him in a dream, saying, "Joseph, son of David, do not be afraid to take Mary as your wife; for the Child who has been [4]conceived in her is of the Holy Spirit.

21 "She will bear a Son; and you shall call His name Jesus, for He will save His people from their sins."

22 Now all this took place to fulfill what was spoken by the Lord through the prophet:

23 "BEHOLD, THE VIRGIN SHALL BE WITH CHILD AND SHALL

1:19 [3] Or *to divorce her* 1:20 [4] Lit *begotten*

NEW CENTURY VERSION

Matthan was the father of Jacob.
16 Jacob was the father of Joseph.
Joseph was the husband of Mary,
and Mary was the mother of Jesus.
Jesus is called the Christ.

17 So there were fourteen generations from Abraham to David. And there were fourteen generations from David until the people were taken to Babylon. And there were fourteen generations from the time when the people were taken to Babylon until Christ was born.

The Birth of Jesus Christ

18 This is how the birth of Jesus Christ came about. His mother Mary was engaged[b] to marry Joseph, but before they married, she learned she was pregnant by the power of the Holy Spirit. 19 Because Mary's husband, Joseph, was a good man, he did not want to disgrace her in public, so he planned to divorce her secretly.

20 While Joseph thought about these things, an angel of the Lord came to him in a dream. The angel said, "Joseph, descendant of David, don't be afraid to take Mary as your wife, because the baby in her is from the Holy Spirit. 21 She will give birth to a son, and you will name him Jesus,[c] because he will save his people from their sins."

22 All this happened to bring about what the Lord had said through the prophet: 23 "The virgin will be pregnant.

1:18 [b] **engaged** For the Jewish people an engagement was a lasting agreement, which could only be broken by a divorce. If a bride was unfaithful, it was considered adultery, and she could be put to death.
1:21 [c] **Jesus** The name Jesus means "salvation."

CONTEMPORARY ENGLISH VERSION

Eliud, Eleazar, Matthan, Jacob, and Joseph, the husband of Mary, the mother of Jesus, who is called the Messiah.

17 There were fourteen generations from Abraham to David. There were also fourteen from David to the exile in Babylonia and fourteen more to the birth of the Messiah.

The Birth of Jesus (Luke 2.1-7)

18 This is how Jesus Christ was born. A young woman named Mary was engaged to Joseph from King David's family. But before they were married, she learned that she was going to have a baby by God's Holy Spirit. 19 Joseph was a good man[a] and did not want to embarrass Mary in front of everyone. So he decided to quietly call off the wedding.

20 While Joseph was thinking about this, an angel from the Lord came to him in a dream. The angel said, "Joseph, the baby that Mary will have is from the Holy Spirit. Go ahead and marry her. 21 Then after her baby is born, name him Jesus,[b] because he will save his people from their sins."

22 So the Lord's promise came true, just as the prophet had said, 23 "A virgin will have a baby boy, and he will be

[a] 1.19 *good man*: Or "kind man," or "man who always did the right thing." [b] 1.21 *name him Jesus*: In Hebrew the name "Jesus" means "the Lord saves."

NEW INTERNATIONAL VERSION

Matthan the father of Jacob,
16 and Jacob the father of Joseph, the husband of Mary, of whom was born Jesus, who is called Christ.

17 Thus there were fourteen generations in all from Abraham to David, fourteen from David to the exile to Babylon, and fourteen from the exile to the Christ.[b]

The Birth of Jesus Christ

18 This is how the birth of Jesus Christ came about: His mother Mary was pledged to be married to Joseph, but before they came together, she was found to be with child through the Holy Spirit. 19 Because Joseph her husband was a righteous man and did not want to expose her to public disgrace, he had in mind to divorce her quietly.

20 But after he had considered this, an angel of the Lord appeared to him in a dream and said, "Joseph son of David, do not be afraid to take Mary home as your wife, because what is conceived in her is from the Holy Spirit. 21 She will give birth to a son, and you are to give him the name Jesus,[c] because he will save his people from their sins."

22 All this took place to fulfill what the Lord had said through the prophet: 23 "The virgin will be with child and

[b] 17 Or *Messiah.* "The Christ" (Greek) and "the Messiah" (Hebrew) both mean "the Anointed One." [c] 21 *Jesus* is the Greek form of *Joshua,* which means *the LORD saves.*

NEW LIVING TRANSLATION

Matthan was the father of Jacob.
16 Jacob was the father of Joseph, the husband of Mary.
Mary was the mother of Jesus, who is called the Messiah.

17 All those listed above include fourteen generations from Abraham to King David, and fourteen from David's time to the Babylonian exile, and fourteen from the Babylonian exile to the Messiah.

The Birth of Jesus the Messiah

18 Now this is how Jesus the Messiah was born. His mother, Mary, was engaged to be married to Joseph. But while she was still a virgin, she became pregnant by the Holy Spirit. 19 Joseph, her fiancé, being a just man, decided to break the engagement quietly, so as not to disgrace her publicly.

20 As he considered this, he fell asleep, and an angel of the Lord appeared to him in a dream. "Joseph, son of David," the angel said, "do not be afraid to go ahead with your marriage to Mary. For the child within her has been conceived by the Holy Spirit. 21 And she will have a son, and you are to name him Jesus,* for he will save his people from their sins." 22 All of this happened to fulfill the Lord's message through his prophet:

23 "Look! The virgin will conceive a child!

1:21 *Jesus* means "The LORD saves."

NEW KING JAMES VERSION

Matthan, and Matthan begot Jacob. 16 And Jacob begot Joseph the husband of Mary, of whom was born Jesus who is called Christ.

17 So all the generations from Abraham to David *are* fourteen generations, from David until the captivity in Babylon *are* fourteen generations, and from the captivity in Babylon until the Christ *are* fourteen generations.

Christ Born of Mary

18 Now the birth of Jesus Christ was as follows: After His mother Mary was betrothed to Joseph, before they came together, she was found with child of the Holy Spirit. 19 Then Joseph her husband, being a just *man,* and not wanting to make her a public example, was minded to put her away secretly. 20 But while he thought about these things, behold, an angel of the Lord appeared to him in a dream, saying, "Joseph, son of David, do not be afraid to take to you Mary your wife, for that which is conceived in her is of the Holy Spirit. 21 And she will bring forth a Son, and you shall call His name JESUS, for He will save His people from their sins."

22 So all this was done that it might be fulfilled which was spoken by the Lord through the prophet, saying: 23 *"Behold, the virgin shall be with child, and bear a Son,*

THE MESSAGE

Matthan had Jacob,
Jacob had Joseph, Mary's husband,
the Mary who gave birth to Jesus,
the Jesus who was called Christ.

There were fourteen generations from Abraham to David,
another fourteen from David to the Babylonian exile,
and yet another fourteen from the Babylonian exile to Christ.

The Birth of Jesus

The birth of Jesus took place like this. His mother, Mary, was engaged to be married to Joseph. Before they came to the marriage bed, Joseph discovered she was pregnant. (It was by the Holy Spirit, but he didn't know that.) Joseph, chagrined but noble, determined to take care of things quietly so Mary would not be disgraced.

While he was trying to figure a way out, he had a dream. God's angel spoke in the dream: "Joseph, son of David, don't hesitate to get married. Mary's pregnancy is Spirit-conceived. God's Holy Spirit has made her pregnant. She will bring a son to birth, and when she does, you, Joseph, will name him Jesus—'God saves'—because he will save his people from their sins." This would bring the prophet's embryonic sermon to full term:

"Watch for this—a virgin will get pregnant and bear
a son;

KING JAMES VERSION

forth a son, and they shall call his name Emmanuel, which being interpreted is, God with us.

24 Then Joseph being raised from sleep did as the angel of the Lord had bidden him, and took unto him his wife:

25 And knew her not till she had brought forth her firstborn son: and he called his name JESUS.

2 Now when Jesus was born in Bethlehem of Judaea in the days of Herod the king, behold, there came wise men from the east to Jerusalem,

2 Saying, Where is he that is born King of the Jews? for we have seen his star in the east, and are come to worship him.

3 When Herod the king had heard *these things*, he was troubled, and all Jerusalem with him.

4 And when he had gathered all the chief priests and scribes of the people together, he demanded of them where Christ should be born.

5 And they said unto him, In Bethlehem of Judaea: for thus it is written by the prophet,

6 And thou Bethlehem, *in* the land of Juda, art not the least among the princes of Juda: for out of thee shall come a Governor, that shall rule my people Israel.

NEW AMERICAN STANDARD BIBLE

BEAR A SON, AND THEY SHALL CALL HIS NAME IMMANUEL," which translated means, "GOD WITH US."

24 And Joseph awoke from his sleep and did as the angel of the Lord commanded him, and took *Mary* as his wife,

25 [5]but kept her a virgin until she gave birth to a Son; and he called His name Jesus.

The Visit of the Magi

2 Now after Jesus was born in Bethlehem of Judea in the days of Herod the king, [1]magi from the east arrived in Jerusalem, saying,

2 "Where is He who has been born King of the Jews? For we saw His star in the east and have come to worship Him."

3 When Herod the king heard *this*, he was troubled, and all Jerusalem with him.

4 Gathering together all the chief priests and scribes of the people, he inquired of them where the Messiah was to be born.

5 They said to him, "In Bethlehem of Judea; for this is what has been written by the prophet:

6 'AND YOU, BETHLEHEM, LAND OF JUDAH,
ARE BY NO MEANS LEAST AMONG THE LEADERS OF JUDAH;
FOR OUT OF YOU SHALL COME FORTH A RULER
WHO WILL SHEPHERD MY PEOPLE ISRAEL.' "

1:25 [5] Lit *and was not knowing her* 2:1 [1] A caste of wise men specializing in astronomy, astrology, and natural science

NEW CENTURY VERSION

She will have a son, and they will name him Immanuel,"[d] which means "God is with us."

24When Joseph woke up, he did what the Lord's angel had told him to do. Joseph took Mary as his wife, 25but he did not have sexual relations with her until she gave birth to the son. And Joseph named him Jesus.

Wise Men Come to Visit Jesus

2 Jesus was born in the town of Bethlehem in Judea during the time when Herod was king. When Jesus was born, some wise men from the east came to Jerusalem. 2They asked, "Where is the baby who was born to be the king of the Jews? We saw his star in the east and have come to worship him."

3When King Herod heard this, he was troubled, as well as all the people in Jerusalem. 4Herod called a meeting of all the leading priests and teachers of the law and asked them where the Christ would be born. 5They answered, "In the town of Bethlehem in Judea. The prophet wrote about this in the Scriptures:

6'But you, Bethlehem, in the land of Judah,
are important among the tribes of Judah.
A ruler will come from you
who will be like a shepherd for my people Israel.' "
Micah 5:2

1:23 [d] **"The virgin...Immanuel"** Quotation from Isaiah 7:14.

CONTEMPORARY ENGLISH VERSION

called Immanuel," which means "God is with us."

24After Joseph woke up, he and Mary were soon married, just as the Lord's angel had told him to do. 25But they did not sleep together before her baby was born. Then Joseph named him Jesus.

The Wise Men

2 When Jesus was born in the village of Bethlehem in Judea, Herod was king. During this time some wise men[a] from the east came to Jerusalem 2and said, "Where is the child born to be king of the Jews? We saw his star in the east[b] and have come to worship him."

3When King Herod heard about this, he was worried, and so was everyone else in Jerusalem. 4Herod brought together the chief priests and the teachers of the Law of Moses and asked them, "Where will the Messiah be born?"

5They told him, "He will be born in Bethlehem, just as the prophet wrote,

6'Bethlehem in the land
of Judea,
you are very important
among the towns of Judea.
From your town
will come a leader,
who will be like a shepherd
for my people Israel.' "

[a] 2.1 *wise men*: People famous for studying the stars. [b] 2.2 *his star in the east*: Or "his star rise."

NEW INTERNATIONAL VERSION

will give birth to a son, and they will call him Immanuel"[d]—which means, "God with us."

24When Joseph woke up, he did what the angel of the Lord had commanded him and took Mary home as his wife. 25But he had no union with her until she gave birth to a son. And he gave him the name Jesus.

The Visit of the Magi

2 After Jesus was born in Bethlehem in Judea, during the time of King Herod, Magi[a] from the east came to Jerusalem 2and asked, "Where is the one who has been born king of the Jews? We saw his star in the east[b] and have come to worship him."

3When King Herod heard this he was disturbed, and all Jerusalem with him. 4When he had called together all the people's chief priests and teachers of the law, he asked them where the Christ[c] was to be born. 5"In Bethlehem in Judea," they replied, "for this is what the prophet has written:

6" 'But you, Bethlehem, in the land of Judah,
are by no means least among the rulers of Judah;
for out of you will come a ruler
who will be the shepherd of my people Israel.'[d]"

d 23 Isaiah 7:14 *a 1* Traditionally *Wise Men* *b 2* Or *star when it rose* *c 4* Or *Messiah* *d 6* Micah 5:2

NEW LIVING TRANSLATION

She will give birth to a son,
and he will be called Immanuel*
(meaning, God is with us)."

24When Joseph woke up, he did what the angel of the Lord commanded. He brought Mary home to be his wife, 25but she remained a virgin until her son was born. And Joseph named him Jesus.

The Visit of the Wise Men

2 Jesus was born in the town of Bethlehem in Judea, during the reign of King Herod. About that time some wise men* from eastern lands arrived in Jerusalem, asking, 2"Where is the newborn king of the Jews? We have seen his star as it arose,* and we have come to worship him."

3Herod was deeply disturbed by their question, as was all of Jerusalem. 4He called a meeting of the leading priests and teachers of religious law. "Where did the prophets say the Messiah would be born?" he asked them.

5"In Bethlehem," they said, "for this is what the prophet wrote:

6 'O Bethlehem of Judah,
you are not just a lowly village in Judah,
for a ruler will come from you
who will be the shepherd for my people Israel.'* "

1:23 Isa 7:14; 8:8, 10. 2:1 Or *royal astrologers;* Greek reads *magi;* also in 2:7, 16. 2:2 Or *in the east.* 2:6 Mic 5:2; 2 Sam 5:2.

NEW KING JAMES VERSION

and they shall call His name Immanuel,"[d] which is translated, "God with us."

24Then Joseph, being aroused from sleep, did as the angel of the Lord commanded him and took to him his wife, 25and did not know her till she had brought forth her firstborn Son.[e] And he called His name JESUS.

Wise Men from the East

2 Now after Jesus was born in Bethlehem of Judea in the days of Herod the king, behold, wise men from the East came to Jerusalem, 2saying, "Where is He who has been born King of the Jews? For we have seen His star in the East and have come to worship Him."

3When Herod the king heard *this,* he was troubled, and all Jerusalem with him. 4And when he had gathered all the chief priests and scribes of the people together, he inquired of them where the Christ was to be born.

5So they said to him, "In Bethlehem of Judea, for thus it is written by the prophet:

6 *'But you, Bethlehem, in the land of Judah,*
Are not the least among the rulers of Judah;
For out of you shall come a Ruler
Who will shepherd My people Israel.' "[a]

1:23 [d] Isaiah 7:14. Words in oblique type in the New Testament are quoted from the Old Testament. 1:25 [e] NU-Text reads *a Son.*
2:6 [a] Micah 5:2

THE MESSAGE

They will name him Emmanuel" (Hebrew for "God is with us").

Then Joseph woke up. He did exactly what God's angel commanded in the dream: He married Mary. But he did not consummate the marriage until she had the baby. He named the baby Jesus.

Scholars From the East

2 After Jesus was born in Bethlehem village, Judah territory—this was during Herod's kingship—a band of scholars arrived in Jerusalem from the East. They asked around, "Where can we find and pay homage to the newborn King of the Jews? We observed a star in the eastern sky that signaled his birth. We're on pilgrimage to worship him."

When word of their inquiry got to Herod, he was terrified—and not Herod alone, but most of Jerusalem as well. Herod lost no time. He gathered all the high priests and religion scholars in the city together and asked, "Where is the Messiah supposed to be born?"

They told him, "Bethlehem, Judah territory. The prophet Micah wrote it plainly:

'It's you, Bethlehem, in Judah's land,
no longer bringing up the rear.
From you will come the leader
who will shepherd-rule my people, my Israel.' "

KING JAMES VERSION

7 Then Herod, when he had privily called the wise men, enquired of them diligently what time the star appeared.

8 And he sent them to Bethlehem, and said, Go and search diligently for the young child; and when ye have found *him*, bring me word again, that I may come and worship him also.

9 ¶ When they had heard the king, they departed; and, lo, the star, which they saw in the east, went before them, till it came and stood over where the young child was.

10 When they saw the star, they rejoiced with exceeding great joy.

11 And when they were come into the house, they saw the young child with Mary his mother, and fell down, and worshipped him: and when they had opened their treasures, they presented unto him gifts; gold, and frankincense, and myrrh.

12 And being warned of God in a dream that they should not return to Herod, they departed into their own country another way.

13 ¶ And when they were departed, behold, the angel of the Lord appeareth to Joseph in a dream, saying, Arise, and take the young child and his mother, and flee into Egypt, and be thou there until I bring thee word: for Herod will seek the young child to destroy him.

14 When he arose, he took the young child and his mother by night, and departed into Egypt:

15 And was there until the death of Herod: that it might be fulfilled which was spoken of the Lord by the prophet, saying, Out of Egypt have I called my son.

NEW AMERICAN STANDARD BIBLE

7 Then Herod secretly called the magi and determined from them the exact time the star appeared.

8 And he sent them to Bethlehem and said, "Go and search carefully for the Child; and when you have found *Him,* report to me, so that I too may come and worship Him."

9 After hearing the king, they went their way; and the star, which they had seen in the east, went on before them until it came and stood over *the place* where the Child was.

10 When they saw the star, they rejoiced exceedingly with great joy.

11 After coming into the house they saw the Child with Mary His mother; and they fell to the ground and worshiped Him. Then, opening their treasures, they presented to Him gifts of gold, frankincense, and myrrh.

12 And having been warned *by God* in a dream not to return to Herod, the magi left for their own country by another way.

The Flight to Egypt

13 Now when they had gone, behold, an angel of the Lord *appeared to Joseph in a dream and said, "Get up! Take the Child and His mother and flee to Egypt, and remain there until I tell you; for Herod is going to search for the Child to destroy Him."

14 So Joseph got up and took the Child and His mother while it was still night, and left for Egypt.

15 He remained there until the death of Herod. *This was* to fulfill what had been spoken by the Lord through the prophet: "OUT OF EGYPT I CALLED MY SON."

NEW CENTURY VERSION

7 Then Herod had a secret meeting with the wise men
and learned from them the exact time they first saw the
star. 8 He sent the wise men to Bethlehem, saying, "Look
carefully for the child. When you find him, come tell me so
I can worship him too."
9 After the wise men heard the king, they left. The star
that they had seen in the east went before them until it
stopped above the place where the child was. 10 When the
wise men saw the star, they were filled with joy. 11 They
came to the house where the child was and saw him with
his mother, Mary, and they bowed down and worshiped
him. They opened their gifts and gave him treasures of
gold, frankincense, and myrrh. 12 But God warned the wise
men in a dream not to go back to Herod, so they returned
to their own country by a different way.

Jesus' Parents Take Him to Egypt

13 After they left, an angel of the Lord came to Joseph in
a dream and said, "Get up! Take the child and his mother
and escape to Egypt, because Herod is starting to look for
the child so he can kill him. Stay in Egypt until I tell you to
return."
14 So Joseph got up and left for Egypt during the night
with the child and his mother. 15 And Joseph stayed in
Egypt until Herod died. This happened to bring about what
the Lord had said through the prophet: "I called my son
out of Egypt."[a]

2:15 [a] "I called...Egypt." Quotation from Hosea 11:1.

CONTEMPORARY ENGLISH VERSION

7 Herod secretly called in the wise men and asked them
when they had first seen the star. 8 He told them, "Go to
Bethlehem and search carefully for the child. As soon as
you find him, let me know. I want to go and worship him
too."
9 The wise men listened to what the king said and then
left. And the star they had seen in the east went on ahead
of them until it stopped over the place where the child was.
10 They were thrilled and excited to see the star.
11 When the men went into the house and saw the child
with Mary, his mother, they knelt down and worshiped
him. They took out their gifts of gold, frankincense, and
myrrh[c] and gave them to him. 12 Later they were warned in
a dream not to return to Herod, and they went back home
by another road.

The Escape to Egypt

13 After the wise men had gone, an angel from the Lord
appeared to Joseph in a dream and said, "Get up! Hurry
and take the child and his mother to Egypt! Stay there
until I tell you to return, because Herod is looking for the
child and wants to kill him."
14 That night, Joseph got up and took his wife and the
child to Egypt, 15 where they stayed until Herod died. So
the Lord's promise came true, just as the prophet had said,
"I called my son out of Egypt."

[c] 2.11 *frankincense, and myrrh*: Frankincense was a valuable powder that was burned to make a sweet smell. Myrrh was a valuable sweet-smelling powder often used in perfume.

NEW INTERNATIONAL VERSION

[7]Then Herod called the Magi secretly and found out from
them the exact time the star had appeared. [8]He sent them
to Bethlehem and said, "Go and make a careful search for
the child. As soon as you find him, report to me, so that I
too may go and worship him."
[9]After they had heard the king, they went on their way,
and the star they had seen in the east[e] went ahead of them
until it stopped over the place where the child was. [10]When
they saw the star, they were overjoyed. [11]On coming to the
house, they saw the child with his mother Mary, and they
bowed down and worshiped him. Then they opened their
treasures and presented him with gifts of gold and of
incense and of myrrh. [12]And having been warned in a
dream not to go back to Herod, they returned to their coun-
try by another route.

The Escape to Egypt

[13]When they had gone, an angel of the Lord appeared to
Joseph in a dream. "Get up," he said, "take the child and
his mother and escape to Egypt. Stay there until I tell you,
for Herod is going to search for the child to kill him."
[14]So he got up, took the child and his mother during the
night and left for Egypt, [15]where he stayed until the death
of Herod. And so was fulfilled what the Lord had said
through the prophet: "Out of Egypt I called my son."[f]

[e] *9* Or *seen when it rose* [f] *15* Hosea 11:1

NEW LIVING TRANSLATION

[7]Then Herod sent a private message to the wise men,
asking them to come see him. At this meeting he learned
the exact time when they first saw the star. [8]Then he told
them, "Go to Bethlehem and search carefully for the child.
And when you find him, come back and tell me so that I
can go and worship him, too!"
[9]After this interview the wise men went their way. Once
again the star appeared to them, guiding them to
Bethlehem. It went ahead of them and stopped over the
place where the child was. [10]When they saw the star, they
were filled with joy! [11]They entered the house where the
child and his mother, Mary, were, and they fell down
before him and worshiped him. Then they opened their
treasure chests and gave him gifts of gold, frankincense,
and myrrh. [12]But when it was time to leave, they went
home another way, because God had warned them in a
dream not to return to Herod.

The Escape to Egypt

[13]After the wise men were gone, an angel of the Lord
appeared to Joseph in a dream. "Get up and flee to Egypt
with the child and his mother," the angel said. "Stay there
until I tell you to return, because Herod is going to try to
kill the child." [14]That night Joseph left for Egypt with the
child and Mary, his mother, [15]and they stayed there until
Herod's death. This fulfilled what the Lord had spoken
through the prophet: "I called my Son out of Egypt."*

2:15 Hos 11:1.

NEW KING JAMES VERSION

[7]Then Herod, when he had secretly called the wise men,
determined from them what time the star appeared. [8]And he
sent them to Bethlehem and said, "Go and search carefully
for the young Child, and when you have found *Him,* bring
back word to me, that I may come and worship Him also."
[9]When they heard the king, they departed; and behold, the
star which they had seen in the East went before them, till it
came and stood over where the young Child was. [10]When
they saw the star, they rejoiced with exceedingly great joy.
[11]And when they had come into the house, they saw the
young Child with Mary His mother, and fell down and wor-
shiped Him. And when they had opened their treasures, they
presented gifts to Him: gold, frankincense, and myrrh.
[12]Then, being divinely warned in a dream that they
should not return to Herod, they departed for their own
country another way.

The Flight into Egypt

[13]Now when they had departed, behold, an angel of the
Lord appeared to Joseph in a dream, saying, "Arise, take
the young Child and His mother, flee to Egypt, and stay
there until I bring you word; for Herod will seek the young
Child to destroy Him."
[14]When he arose, he took the young Child and His moth-
er by night and departed for Egypt, [15]and was there until
the death of Herod, that it might be fulfilled which was
spoken by the Lord through the prophet, saying, *"Out of
Egypt I called My Son."*[b]

2:15 [b] Hosea 11:1

THE MESSAGE

Herod then arranged a secret meeting with the scholars from the East. Pretending to be as devout as they were, he got them to tell him exactly when the birth-announcement star appeared. Then he told them the prophecy about Bethlehem, and said, "Go find this child. Leave no stone unturned. As soon as you find him, send word and I'll join you at once in your worship."

Instructed by the king, they set off. Then the star appeared again, the same star they had seen in the eastern skies. It led them on until it hovered over the place of the child. They could hardly contain themselves: They were in the right place! They had arrived at the right time!

They entered the house and saw the child in the arms of Mary, his mother. Overcome, they kneeled and worshiped him. Then they opened their luggage and presented gifts: gold, frankincense, myrrh.

In a dream, they were warned not to report back to Herod. So they worked out another route, left the territory without being seen, and returned to their own country.

✠

After the scholars were gone, God's angel showed up again in Joseph's dream and commanded, "Get up. Take the child and his mother and flee to Egypt. Stay until further notice. Herod is on the hunt for this child, and wants to kill him."

Joseph obeyed. He got up, took the child and his mother under cover of darkness. They were out of town and well on their way by daylight. They lived in Egypt until Herod's death. This Egyptian exile fulfilled what Hosea had preached: "I called my son out of Egypt."

KING JAMES VERSION

16 ¶ Then Herod, when he saw that he was mocked of the wise men, was exceeding wroth, and sent forth, and slew all the children that were in Bethlehem, and in all the coasts thereof, from two years old and under, according to the time which he had diligently enquired of the wise men.

17 Then was fulfilled that which was spoken by Jeremy the prophet, saying,

18 In Rama was there a voice heard, lamentation, and weeping, and great mourning, Rachel weeping *for* her children, and would not be comforted, because they are not.

19 ¶ But when Herod was dead, behold, an angel of the Lord appeareth in a dream to Joseph in Egypt,

20 Saying, Arise, and take the young child and his mother, and go into the land of Israel: for they are dead which sought the young child's life.

21 And he arose, and took the young child and his mother, and came into the land of Israel.

22 But when he heard that Archelaus did reign in Judaea in the room of his father Herod, he was afraid to go thither: notwithstanding, being warned of God in a dream, he turned aside into the parts of Galilee:

23 And he came and dwelt in a city called Nazareth: that it might be fulfilled which was spoken by the prophets, He shall be called a Nazarene.

NEW AMERICAN STANDARD BIBLE

Herod Slaughters Babies

16 Then when Herod saw that he had been tricked by the magi, he became very enraged, and sent and slew all the male children who were in Bethlehem and all its vicinity, from two years old and under, according to the time which he had determined from the magi.

17 Then what had been spoken through Jeremiah the prophet was fulfilled:

18 "A VOICE WAS HEARD IN RAMAH,
WEEPING AND GREAT MOURNING,
RACHEL WEEPING FOR HER CHILDREN;
AND SHE REFUSED TO BE COMFORTED,
BECAUSE THEY WERE NO MORE."

19 But when Herod died, behold, an angel of the Lord *appeared in a dream to Joseph in Egypt, and said,

20 "Get up, take the Child and His mother, and go into the land of Israel; for those who sought the Child's life are dead."

21 So Joseph got up, took the Child and His mother, and came into the land of Israel.

22 But when he heard that Archelaus was reigning over Judea in place of his father Herod, he was afraid to go there. Then after being warned *by God* in a dream, he left for the regions of Galilee,

23 and came and lived in a city called Nazareth. *This was* to fulfill what was spoken through the prophets: "He shall be called a Nazarene."

NEW CENTURY VERSION

Herod Kills the Baby Boys

16 When Herod saw that the wise men had tricked him, he was furious. So he gave an order to kill all the baby boys in Bethlehem and in the surrounding area who were two years old or younger. This was in keeping with the time he learned from the wise men. 17 So what God had said through the prophet Jeremiah came true:

18 "A voice was heard in Ramah
of painful crying and deep sadness:
Rachel crying for her children.
She refused to be comforted,
because her children are dead." *Jeremiah 31:15*

Joseph and Mary Return

19 After Herod died, an angel of the Lord spoke to Joseph in a dream while he was in Egypt. 20 The angel said, "Get up! Take the child and his mother and go to the land of Israel, because the people who were trying to kill the child are now dead."

21 So Joseph took the child and his mother and went to Israel. 22 But he heard that Archelaus was now king in Judea since his father Herod had died. So Joseph was afraid to go there. After being warned in a dream, he went to the area of Galilee, 23 to a town called Nazareth, and lived there. And so what God had said through the prophets came true: "He will be called a Nazarene."[b]

2:23 [b] **Nazarene** A person from the city of Nazareth, a name probably meaning "branch" (see Isaiah 11:1).

CONTEMPORARY ENGLISH VERSION

The Killing of the Children

16 When Herod found out that the wise men from the east had tricked him, he was very angry. He gave orders for his men to kill all the boys who lived in or near Bethlehem and were two years old and younger. This was based on what he had learned from the wise men.

17 So the Lord's promise came true, just as the prophet Jeremiah had said,

18 "In Ramah a voice was heard
crying and weeping loudly.
Rachel was mourning
for her children,
and she refused
to be comforted,
because they were dead."

The Return from Egypt

19 After King Herod died, an angel from the Lord appeared in a dream to Joseph while he was still in Egypt. 20 The angel said, "Get up and take the child and his mother back to Israel. The people who wanted to kill him are now dead."

21 Joseph got up and left with them for Israel. 22 But when he heard that Herod's son Archelaus was now ruler of Judea, he was afraid to go there. Then in a dream he was told to go to Galilee, 23 and they went to live there in the town of Nazareth. So the Lord's promise came true, just as the prophet had said, "He will be called a Nazarene."[d]

[d] **2.23** *He will be called a Nazarene*: The prophet who said this is not known.

NEW INTERNATIONAL VERSION

16When Herod realized that he had been outwitted by the Magi, he was furious, and he gave orders to kill all the boys in Bethlehem and its vicinity who were two years old and under, in accordance with the time he had learned from the Magi. 17Then what was said through the prophet Jeremiah was fulfilled:

18 "A voice is heard in Ramah,
weeping and great mourning,
Rachel weeping for her children
and refusing to be comforted,
because they are no more."[g]

The Return to Nazareth

19After Herod died, an angel of the Lord appeared in a dream to Joseph in Egypt 20and said, "Get up, take the child and his mother and go to the land of Israel, for those who were trying to take the child's life are dead."

21So he got up, took the child and his mother and went to the land of Israel. 22But when he heard that Archelaus was reigning in Judea in place of his father Herod, he was afraid to go there. Having been warned in a dream, he withdrew to the district of Galilee, 23and he went and lived in a town called Nazareth. So was fulfilled what was said through the prophets: "He will be called a Nazarene."

g *18* Jer. 31:15

NEW LIVING TRANSLATION

16Herod was furious when he learned that the wise men had outwitted him. He sent soldiers to kill all the boys in and around Bethlehem who were two years old and under, because the wise men had told him the star first appeared to them about two years earlier.* 17Herod's brutal action fulfilled the prophecy of Jeremiah:

18 "A cry of anguish is heard in Ramah—
weeping and mourning unrestrained.
Rachel weeps for her children,
refusing to be comforted—for they are dead."*

The Return to Nazareth

19When Herod died, an angel of the Lord appeared in a dream to Joseph in Egypt and told him, 20"Get up and take the child and his mother back to the land of Israel, because those who were trying to kill the child are dead." 21So Joseph returned immediately to Israel with Jesus and his mother. 22But when he learned that the new ruler was Herod's son Archelaus, he was afraid. Then, in another dream, he was warned to go to Galilee. 23So they went and lived in a town called Nazareth. This fulfilled what was spoken by the prophets concerning the Messiah: "He will be called a Nazarene."

2:16 Or *according to the time he calculated from the wise men.*
2:18 Jer 31:15.

NEW KING JAMES VERSION

Massacre of the Innocents

16Then Herod, when he saw that he was deceived by the wise men, was exceedingly angry; and he sent forth and put to death all the male children who were in Bethlehem and in all its districts, from two years old and under, according to the time which he had determined from the wise men. 17Then was fulfilled what was spoken by Jeremiah the prophet, saying:

18 *"A voice was heard in Ramah,*
Lamentation, weeping, and great mourning,
Rachel weeping for her children,
Refusing to be comforted,
Because they are no more."[c]

The Home in Nazareth

19Now when Herod was dead, behold, an angel of the Lord appeared in a dream to Joseph in Egypt, 20saying, "Arise, take the young Child and His mother, and go to the land of Israel, for those who sought the young Child's life are dead." 21Then he arose, took the young Child and His mother, and came into the land of Israel.

22But when he heard that Archelaus was reigning over Judea instead of his father Herod, he was afraid to go there. And being warned by God in a dream, he turned aside into the region of Galilee. 23And he came and dwelt in a city called Nazareth, that it might be fulfilled which was spoken by the prophets, "He shall be called a Nazarene."

2:18 c Jeremiah 31:15

THE MESSAGE

Herod, when he realized that the scholars had tricked him, flew into a rage. He commanded the murder of every little boy two years old and under who lived in Bethlehem and its surrounding hills. (He determined that age from information he'd gotten from the scholars.) That's when Jeremiah's sermon was fulfilled:

"A sound was heard in Ramah,
weeping and much lament.
Rachel weeping for her children,
Rachel refusing all solace,
Her children gone,
dead and buried."

Later, when Herod died, God's angel appeared in a dream to Joseph in Egypt: "Up, take the child and his mother and return to Israel. All those out to murder the child are dead."

Joseph obeyed. He got up, took the child and his mother, and reentered Israel. When he heard, though, that Archelaus had succeeded his father, Herod, as king in Judea, he was afraid to go there. But then Joseph was directed in a dream to go to the hills of Galilee. On arrival, he settled in the village of Nazareth. This move was a fulfillment of the prophetic words, "He shall be called a Nazarene."

KING JAMES VERSION

3 In those days came John the Baptist, preaching in the wilderness of Judaea,

2 And saying, Repent ye: for the kingdom of heaven is at hand.

3 For this is he that was spoken of by the prophet Esaias, saying, The voice of one crying in the wilderness, Prepare ye the way of the Lord, make his paths straight.

4 And the same John had his raiment of camel's hair, and a leathern girdle about his loins; and his meat was locusts and wild honey.

5 Then went out to him Jerusalem, and all Judaea, and all the region round about Jordan,

6 And were baptized of him in Jordan, confessing their sins.

7 ¶ But when he saw many of the Pharisees and Sadducees come to his baptism, he said unto them, O generation of vipers, who hath warned you to flee from the wrath to come?

8 Bring forth therefore fruits meet for repentance:

9 And think not to say within yourselves, We have Abraham to *our* father: for I say unto you, that God is able of these stones to raise up children unto Abraham.

NEW AMERICAN STANDARD BIBLE

The Preaching of John the Baptist

3 Now in those days John the Baptist *came, preaching in the wilderness of Judea, saying,

2 "Repent, for the kingdom of heaven is at hand."

3 For this is the one referred to by Isaiah the prophet when he said,

"THE VOICE OF ONE CRYING IN THE WILDERNESS,
'MAKE READY THE WAY OF THE LORD,
MAKE HIS PATHS STRAIGHT!' "

4 Now John himself had a garment of camel's hair and a leather belt around his waist; and his food was locusts and wild honey.

5 Then Jerusalem was going out to him, and all Judea and all the district around the Jordan;

6 and they were being baptized by him in the Jordan River, as they confessed their sins.

7 But when he saw many of the Pharisees and Sadducees coming for baptism, he said to them, "You brood of vipers, who warned you to flee from the wrath to come?

8 "Therefore bear fruit in keeping with repentance;

9 and do not suppose that you can say to yourselves, 'We have Abraham for our father'; for I say to you that from these stones God is able to raise up children to Abraham.

NEW CENTURY VERSION

The Work of John the Baptist

3 About that time John the Baptist began preaching in the desert area of Judea. 2John said, "Change your hearts and lives because the kingdom of heaven is near." 3John the Baptist is the one Isaiah the prophet was talking about when he said:

"This is a voice of one
who calls out in the desert:
'Prepare the way for the Lord.
Make the road straight for him.' " *Isaiah 40:3*

4John's clothes were made from camel's hair, and he wore a leather belt around his waist. For food, he ate locusts and wild honey. 5Many people came from Jerusalem and Judea and all the area around the Jordan River to hear John. 6They confessed their sins, and he baptized them in the Jordan River.

7Many of the Pharisees and Sadducees came to the place where John was baptizing people. When John saw them, he said, "You are all snakes! Who warned you to run away from God's coming punishment? 8Do the things that show you really have changed your hearts and lives. 9And don't think you can say to yourselves, 'Abraham is our father.' I tell you that God could make children for Abraham from

CONTEMPORARY ENGLISH VERSION

The Preaching of John the Baptist

(Mark 1.1-8; Luke 3.1-18; John 1.19-28)

3 Years later, John the Baptist started preaching in the desert of Judea. 2He said, "Turn back to God! The kingdom of heaven[a] will soon be here."[b] 3John was the one the prophet Isaiah was talking about, when he said,

"In the desert someone
is shouting,
'Get the road ready
for the Lord!
Make a straight path
for him.' "

4John wore clothes made of camel's hair. He had a leather strap around his waist and ate grasshoppers and wild honey. 5From Jerusalem and all Judea and from the Jordan River Valley crowds of people went to John. 6They told how sorry they were for their sins, and he baptized them in the river.

7Many Pharisees and Sadducees also came to be baptized. But John said to them:

You bunch of snakes! Who warned you to run from the coming judgment? 8Do something to show that you have really given up your sins. 9And don't start telling yourselves that you belong to Abraham's family. I tell you that God can turn these stones into children for

[a] 3.2 *kingdom of heaven*: In the Gospel of Matthew "kingdom of heaven" is used with the same meaning as "God's kingdom" in Mark and Luke.
[b] 3.2 *will soon be here*: Or "is already here."

NEW INTERNATIONAL VERSION

John the Baptist Prepares the Way

3 In those days John the Baptist came, preaching in the
Desert of Judea [2]and saying, "Repent, for the kingdom
of heaven is near." [3]This is he who was spoken of through
the prophet Isaiah:

"A voice of one calling in the desert,
'Prepare the way for the Lord,
make straight paths for him.' "[a]

[4]John's clothes were made of camel's hair, and he had a
leather belt around his waist. His food was locusts and
wild honey. [5]People went out to him from Jerusalem and
all Judea and the whole region of the Jordan. [6]Confessing
their sins, they were baptized by him in the Jordan River.
[7]But when he saw many of the Pharisees and Sadducees
coming to where he was baptizing, he said to them: "You
brood of vipers! Who warned you to flee from the coming
wrath? [8]Produce fruit in keeping with repentance. [9]And do
not think you can say to yourselves, 'We have Abraham as
our father.' I tell you that out of these stones God can raise

[a] *3* Isaiah 40:3

NEW LIVING TRANSLATION

John the Baptist Prepares the Way

3 In those days John the Baptist began preaching in the
Judean wilderness. His message was, [2]"Turn from
your sins and turn to God, because the Kingdom of Heaven
is near.*" [3]Isaiah had spoken of John when he said,

"He is a voice shouting in the wilderness:
'Prepare a pathway for the Lord's coming!
Make a straight road for him!' "*

[4]John's clothes were woven from camel hair, and he wore a
leather belt; his food was locusts and wild honey. [5]People
from Jerusalem and from every section of Judea and from
all over the Jordan Valley went out to the wilderness to
hear him preach. [6]And when they confessed their sins, he
baptized them in the Jordan River.
[7]But when he saw many Pharisees and Sadducees com-
ing to be baptized, he denounced them. "You brood of
snakes!" he exclaimed. "Who warned you to flee God's
coming judgment? [8]Prove by the way you live that you
have really turned from your sins and turned to God. [9]Don't
just say, 'We're safe—we're the descendants of Abraham.'
That proves nothing. God can change these stones here into

3:2 Or *has come* or *is coming soon.* 3:3 Isa 40:3.

NEW KING JAMES VERSION

John the Baptist Prepares the Way

3 In those days John the Baptist came preaching in the
wilderness of Judea, [2]and saying, "Repent, for the
kingdom of heaven is at hand!" [3]For this is he who was
spoken of by the prophet Isaiah, saying:

"The voice of one crying in the wilderness:
'Prepare the way of the LORD;
Make His paths straight.' "[a]

[4]Now John himself was clothed in camel's hair, with a
leather belt around his waist; and his food was locusts and
wild honey. [5]Then Jerusalem, all Judea, and all the region
around the Jordan went out to him [6]and were baptized by
him in the Jordan, confessing their sins.
[7]But when he saw many of the Pharisees and Sadducees
coming to his baptism, he said to them, "Brood of vipers!
Who warned you to flee from the wrath to come? [8]There-
fore bear fruits worthy of repentance, [9]and do not think to
say to yourselves, 'We have Abraham as *our* father.' For I
say to you that God is able to raise up children to Abraham

3:3 [a] Isaiah 40:3

THE MESSAGE

Thunder in the Desert!

3 While Jesus was living in the Galilean hills, John,
called "the Baptizer," was preaching in the desert
country of Judea. His message was simple and austere, like
his desert surroundings: "Change your life. God's kingdom
is here."
John and his message were authorized by Isaiah's
prophecy:

"Thunder in the desert!
Prepare for God's arrival!
Make the road smooth and straight!"

John dressed in a camel-hair habit tied at the waist by a
leather strap. He lived on a diet of locusts and wild field
honey. People poured out of Jerusalem, Judea, and the
Jordanian countryside to hear and see him in action. There
at the Jordan River those who came to confess their sins
were baptized into a changed life.
When John realized that a lot of Pharisees and
Sadducees were showing up for a baptismal experience
because it was becoming the popular thing to do, he
exploded: "Brood of snakes! What do you think you're
doing slithering down here to the river? Do you think a lit-
tle water on your snakeskins is going to make any differ-
ence? It's your life that must change, not your skin! And
don't think you can pull rank by claiming Abraham as
father. Being a descendant of Abraham is neither here nor
there. Descendants of Abraham are a dime a dozen. What

KING JAMES VERSION

10 And now also the axe is laid unto the root of the trees: therefore every tree which bringeth not forth good fruit is hewn down, and cast into the fire.

11 I indeed baptize you with water unto repentance: but he that cometh after me is mightier than I, whose shoes I am not worthy to bear: he shall baptize you with the Holy Ghost, and *with* fire:

12 Whose fan *is* in his hand, and he will throughly purge his floor, and gather his wheat into the garner; but he will burn up the chaff with unquenchable fire.

13 ¶ Then cometh Jesus from Galilee to Jordan unto John, to be baptized of him.

14 But John forbad him, saying, I have need to be baptized of thee, and comest thou to me?

15 And Jesus answering said unto him, Suffer *it to be so* now: for thus it becometh us to fulfil all righteousness. Then he suffered him.

16 And Jesus, when he was baptized, went up straightway out of the water: and, lo, the heavens were opened unto him, and he saw the Spirit of God descending like a dove, and lighting upon him:

17 And lo a voice from heaven, saying, This is my beloved Son, in whom I am well pleased.

NEW AMERICAN STANDARD BIBLE

10 "The axe is already laid at the root of the trees; therefore every tree that does not bear good fruit is cut down and thrown into the fire.

11 "As for me, I baptize you [1]with water for repentance, but He who is coming after me is mightier than I, and I am not fit to remove His sandals; He will baptize you with the Holy Spirit and fire.

12 "His winnowing fork is in His hand, and He will thoroughly clear His threshing floor; and He will gather His wheat into the barn, but He will burn up the chaff with unquenchable fire."

The Baptism of Jesus

13 Then Jesus *arrived from Galilee at the Jordan *coming* to John, to be baptized by him.

14 But John tried to prevent Him, saying, "I have need to be baptized by You, and do You come to me?"

15 But Jesus answering said to him, "Permit *it* at this time; for in this way it is fitting for us to fulfill all righteousness." Then he *permitted Him.

16 After being baptized, Jesus came up immediately from the water; and behold, the heavens were opened, and he saw the Spirit of God descending as a dove *and* lighting on Him,

17 and behold, a voice out of the heavens said, "This is [2]My beloved Son, in whom I am well-pleased."

3:11 [1] The Gr here can be translated *in, with* or *by* 3:17 [2] Or *My Son, the Beloved*

NEW CENTURY VERSION

these rocks. 10The ax is now ready to cut down the trees, and every tree that does not produce good fruit will be cut down and thrown into the fire.[a]

11"I baptize you with water to show that your hearts and lives have changed. But there is one coming after me who is greater than I am, whose sandals I am not good enough to carry. He will baptize you with the Holy Spirit and fire. 12He will come ready to clean the grain, separating the good grain from the chaff. He will put the good part of the grain into his barn, but he will burn the chaff with a fire that cannot be put out."[b]

Jesus Is Baptized by John

13At that time Jesus came from Galilee to the Jordan River and wanted John to baptize him. 14But John tried to stop him, saying, "Why do you come to me to be baptized? I need to be baptized by you!"

15Jesus answered, "Let it be this way for now. We should do all things that are God's will." So John agreed to baptize Jesus.

16As soon as Jesus was baptized, he came up out of the water. Then heaven opened, and he saw God's Spirit coming down on him like a dove. 17And a voice from heaven said, "This is my Son, whom I love, and I am very pleased with him."

3:10 [a] **The ax…fire.** This means that God is ready to punish his people who do not obey him. 3:12 [b] **He will…out.** This means that Jesus will come to separate good people from bad people, saving the good and punishing the bad.

CONTEMPORARY ENGLISH VERSION

Abraham. 10An ax is ready to cut the trees down at their roots. Any tree that doesn't produce good fruit will be chopped down and thrown into a fire.

11I baptize you with water so that you will give up your sins.[c] But someone more powerful is going to come, and I am not good enough even to carry his sandals.[d] He will baptize you with the Holy Spirit and with fire. 12His threshing fork is in his hand, and he is ready to separate the wheat from the husks.[e] He will store the wheat in a barn and burn the husks in a fire that never goes out.

The Baptism of Jesus (Mark 1.9-11; Luke 3.21, 22)

13Jesus left Galilee and went to the Jordan River to be baptized by John. 14But John kept objecting and said, "I ought to be baptized by you. Why have you come to me?"

15Jesus answered, "For now this is how it should be, because we must do all that God wants us to do." Then John agreed.

16So Jesus was baptized. And as soon as he came out of the water, the sky opened, and he saw the Spirit of God coming down on him like a dove. 17Then a voice from heaven said, "This is my own dear Son, and I am pleased with him."

[c] **3.11** *so that you will give up your sins*: Or "because you have given up your sins." [d] **3.11** *carry his sandals*: This was one of the duties of a slave. [e] **3.12** *His threshing fork is in his hand, and he is ready to separate the wheat from the husks*: After Jewish farmers had trampled out the grain, they used a large fork to pitch the grain and the husks into the air. Wind would blow away the light husks, and the grain would fall back to the ground, where it could be gathered up.

NEW INTERNATIONAL VERSION

up children for Abraham. [10]The ax is already at the root of the trees, and every tree that does not produce good fruit will be cut down and thrown into the fire.

[11]"I baptize you with[b] water for repentance. But after me will come one who is more powerful than I, whose sandals I am not fit to carry. He will baptize you with the Holy Spirit and with fire. [12]His winnowing fork is in his hand, and he will clear his threshing floor, gathering his wheat into the barn and burning up the chaff with unquenchable fire."

The Baptism of Jesus

[13]Then Jesus came from Galilee to the Jordan to be baptized by John. [14]But John tried to deter him, saying, "I need to be baptized by you, and do you come to me?"

[15]Jesus replied, "Let it be so now; it is proper for us to do this to fulfill all righteousness." Then John consented.

[16]As soon as Jesus was baptized, he went up out of the water. At that moment heaven was opened, and he saw the Spirit of God descending like a dove and lighting on him. [17]And a voice from heaven said, "This is my Son, whom I love; with him I am well pleased."

[b] *11* Or *in*

NEW LIVING TRANSLATION

children of Abraham. [10]Even now the ax of God's judgment is poised, ready to sever your roots. Yes, every tree that does not produce good fruit will be chopped down and thrown into the fire.

[11]"I baptize with* water those who turn from their sins and turn to God. But someone is coming soon who is far greater than I am—so much greater that I am not even worthy to be his slave.* He will baptize you with the Holy Spirit and with fire.* [12]He is ready to separate the chaff from the grain with his winnowing fork. Then he will clean up the threshing area, storing the grain in his barn but burning the chaff with never-ending fire."

The Baptism of Jesus

[13]Then Jesus went from Galilee to the Jordan River to be baptized by John. [14]But John didn't want to baptize him. "I am the one who needs to be baptized by you," he said, "so why are you coming to me?"

[15]But Jesus said, "It must be done, because we must do everything that is right.*" So then John baptized him.

[16]After his baptism, as Jesus came up out of the water, the heavens were opened and he saw the Spirit of God descending like a dove and settling on him. [17]And a voice from heaven said, "This is my beloved Son, and I am fully pleased with him."

3:11a Or *in.* **3:11b** Greek *to carry his sandals.* **3:11c** Or *in the Holy Spirit and in fire.* **3:15** Or *we must fulfill all righteousness.*

NEW KING JAMES VERSION

from these stones. [10]And even now the ax is laid to the root of the trees. Therefore every tree which does not bear good fruit is cut down and thrown into the fire. [11]I indeed baptize you with water unto repentance, but He who is coming after me is mightier than I, whose sandals I am not worthy to carry. He will baptize you with the Holy Spirit and fire.[b] [12]His winnowing fan *is* in His hand, and He will thoroughly clean out His threshing floor, and gather His wheat into the barn; but He will burn up the chaff with unquenchable fire."

John Baptizes Jesus

[13]Then Jesus came from Galilee to John at the Jordan to be baptized by him. [14]And John *tried to* prevent Him, saying, "I need to be baptized by You, and are You coming to me?"

[15]But Jesus answered and said to him, "Permit *it to be so* now, for thus it is fitting for us to fulfill all righteousness." Then he allowed Him.

[16]When He had been baptized, Jesus came up immediately from the water; and behold, the heavens were opened to Him, and He[c] saw the Spirit of God descending like a dove and alighting upon Him. [17]And suddenly a voice *came* from heaven, saying, "This is My beloved Son, in whom I am well pleased."

3:11 [b] M-Text omits *and fire.* **3:16** [c] Or *he*

THE MESSAGE

counts is your life. Is it green and blossoming? Because if it's deadwood, it goes on the fire.

"I'm baptizing you here in the river, turning your old life in for a kingdom life. The real action comes next: The main character in this drama—compared to him I'm a mere stagehand—will ignite the kingdom life within you, a fire within you, the Holy Spirit within you, changing you from the inside out. He's going to clean house—make a clean sweep of your lives. He'll place everything true in its proper place before God; everything false he'll put out with the trash to be burned."

Jesus then appeared, arriving at the Jordan River from Galilee. He wanted John to baptize him. John objected, "I'm the one who needs to be baptized, not *you*!"

But Jesus insisted. "Do it. God's work, putting things right all these centuries, is coming together right now in this baptism." So John did it.

The moment Jesus came up out of the baptismal waters, the skies opened up and he saw God's Spirit—it looked like a dove—descending and landing on him. And along with the Spirit, a voice: "This is my Son, chosen and marked by my love, delight of my life."

KING JAMES VERSION

4 Then was Jesus led up of the Spirit into the wilderness to be tempted of the devil.

2 And when he had fasted forty days and forty nights, he was afterward an hungred.

3 And when the tempter came to him, he said, If thou be the Son of God, command that these stones be made bread.

4 But he answered and said, It is written, Man shall not live by bread alone, but by every word that proceedeth out of the mouth of God.

5 Then the devil taketh him up into the holy city, and setteth him on a pinnacle of the temple,

6 And saith unto him, If thou be the Son of God, cast thyself down: for it is written, He shall give his angels charge concerning thee: and in *their* hands they shall bear thee up, lest at any time thou dash thy foot against a stone.

7 Jesus said unto him, It is written again, Thou shalt not tempt the Lord thy God.

8 Again, the devil taketh him up into an exceeding high mountain, and sheweth him all the kingdoms of the world, and the glory of them;

NEW AMERICAN STANDARD BIBLE

The Temptation of Jesus

4 Then Jesus was led up by the Spirit into the wilderness to be tempted by the devil.

2 And after He had fasted forty days and forty nights, He [1]then became hungry.

3 And the tempter came and said to Him, "If You are the Son of God, command that these stones become bread."

4 But He answered and said, "It is written, 'MAN SHALL NOT LIVE ON BREAD ALONE, BUT ON EVERY WORD THAT PROCEEDS OUT OF THE MOUTH OF GOD.' "

5 Then the devil *took Him into the holy city and had Him stand on the pinnacle of the temple,

6 and *said to Him, "If You are the Son of God, throw Yourself down; for it is written,

'HE WILL COMMAND HIS ANGELS CONCERNING YOU';
and
'ON *their* HANDS THEY WILL BEAR YOU UP,
SO THAT YOU WILL NOT STRIKE YOUR FOOT AGAINST A STONE.' "

7 Jesus said to him, "On the other hand, it is written, 'YOU SHALL NOT PUT THE LORD YOUR GOD TO THE TEST.' "

8 Again, the devil *took Him to a very high mountain and *showed Him all the kingdoms of the world and their glory;

4:2 [1] Lit *later became;* or *afterward became*

NEW CENTURY VERSION

The Temptation of Jesus

4 Then the Spirit led Jesus into the desert to be tempted
by the devil. 2Jesus ate nothing for forty days and
nights. After this, he was very hungry. 3The devil came to
Jesus to tempt him, saying, "If you are the Son of God, tell
these rocks to become bread."
4Jesus answered, "It is written in the Scriptures, 'A person does not live by eating only bread, but by everything God says.' "[a]
5Then the devil led Jesus to the holy city of Jerusalem
and put him on a high place of the Temple. 6The devil said,
"If you are the Son of God, jump down, because it is written in the Scriptures:

'He has put his angels in charge of you.
They will catch you in their hands
so that you will not hit your foot on a rock.' "
Psalm 91:11–12

7Jesus answered him, "It also says in the Scriptures, 'Do not test the Lord your God.' "[b]
8Then the devil led Jesus to the top of a very high mountain and showed him all the kingdoms of the world and all

4:4 [a] 'A person...says.' Quotation from Deuteronomy 8:3.
4:7 [b] 'Do...God.' Quotation from Deuteronomy 6:16.

CONTEMPORARY ENGLISH VERSION

Jesus and the Devil (Mark 1.12, 13; Luke 4.1-13)

4 The Holy Spirit led Jesus into the desert, so that the
devil could test him. 2After Jesus had gone without
eating[a] for forty days and nights, he was very hungry.
3Then the devil came to him and said, "If you are God's
Son, tell these stones to turn into bread."
4Jesus answered, "The Scriptures say:

'No one can live only on food.
People need every word
that God has spoken.' "

5Next, the devil took Jesus to the holy city and had him
stand on the highest part of the temple. 6The devil said, "If
you are God's Son, jump off. The Scriptures say:

'God will give his angels
orders about you.
They will catch you
in their arms,
and you won't hurt
your feet on the stones.' "

7Jesus answered, "The Scriptures also say, 'Don't try to test the Lord your God!' "
8Finally, the devil took Jesus up on a very high mountain and showed him all the kingdoms on earth and their

[a] 4.2 *without eating*: The Jewish people sometimes went without eating (also called "fasting") to show their love for God or to show sorrow for their sins.

NEW INTERNATIONAL VERSION

The Temptation of Jesus

4 Then Jesus was led by the Spirit into the desert to be tempted by the devil. 2After fasting forty days and forty nights, he was hungry. 3The tempter came to him and said, "If you are the Son of God, tell these stones to become bread."

4Jesus answered, "It is written: 'Man does not live on bread alone, but on every word that comes from the mouth of God.'[a]"

5Then the devil took him to the holy city and had him stand on the highest point of the temple. 6"If you are the Son of God," he said, "throw yourself down. For it is written:

" 'He will command his angels concerning you,
and they will lift you up in their hands,
so that you will not strike your foot against a stone.'[b]"

7Jesus answered him, "It is also written: 'Do not put the Lord your God to the test.'[c]"

8Again, the devil took him to a very high mountain and showed him all the kingdoms of the world and their

[a] *4* Deut. 8:3 [b] *6* Psalm 91:11,12 [c] *7* Deut. 6:16

NEW LIVING TRANSLATION

The Temptation of Jesus

4 Then Jesus was led out into the wilderness by the Holy Spirit to be tempted there by the Devil. 2For forty days and forty nights he ate nothing and became very hungry. 3Then the Devil* came and said to him, "If you are the Son of God, change these stones into loaves of bread."

4But Jesus told him, "No! The Scriptures say,

'People need more than bread for their life;
they must feed on every word of God.'* "

5Then the Devil took him to Jerusalem, to the highest point of the Temple, 6and said, "If you are the Son of God, jump off! For the Scriptures say,

'He orders his angels to protect you.
And they will hold you with their hands
to keep you from striking your foot on a stone.'* "

7Jesus responded, "The Scriptures also say, 'Do not test the Lord your God.'* "

8Next the Devil took him to the peak of a very high mountain and showed him the nations of the world and all

4:3 Greek *the tempter.* **4:4** Deut 8:3. **4:6** Ps 91:11-12. **4:7** Deut 6:16.

NEW KING JAMES VERSION

Satan Tempts Jesus

4 Then Jesus was led up by the Spirit into the wilderness to be tempted by the devil. 2And when He had fasted forty days and forty nights, afterward He was hungry. 3Now when the tempter came to Him, he said, "If You are the Son of God, command that these stones become bread."

4But He answered and said, "It is written, *'Man shall not live by bread alone, but by every word that proceeds from the mouth of God.'* "[a]

5Then the devil took Him up into the holy city, set Him on the pinnacle of the temple, 6and said to Him, "If You are the Son of God, throw Yourself down. For it is written:

'He shall give His angels charge over you,'

and,

'In their hands they shall bear you up,
Lest you dash your foot against a stone.' "[b]

7Jesus said to him, "It is written again, *'You shall not tempt the LORD your God.'* "[c]

8Again, the devil took Him up on an exceedingly high mountain, and showed Him all the kingdoms of the world

4:4 [a] Deuteronomy 8:3 **4:6** [b] Psalm 91:11, 12
4:7 [c] Deuteronomy 6:16

THE MESSAGE

The Test

4 Next Jesus was taken into the wild by the Spirit for the Test. The Devil was ready to give it. Jesus prepared for the Test by fasting forty days and forty nights. That left him, of course, in a state of extreme hunger, which the Devil took advantage of in the first test: "Since you are God's Son, speak the word that will turn these stones into loaves of bread."

Jesus answered by quoting Deuteronomy: "It takes more than bread to stay alive. It takes a steady stream of words from God's mouth."

For the second test the Devil took him to the Holy City. He sat him on top of the Temple and said, "Since you are God's Son, jump." The Devil goaded him by quoting Psalm 91: "He has placed you in the care of angels. They will catch you so that you won't so much as stub your toe on a stone."

Jesus countered with another citation from Deuteronomy: "Don't you dare test the Lord your God."

For the third test, the Devil took him on the peak of a huge mountain. He gestured expansively, pointing out all the earth's kingdoms, how glorious they all were. Then he

KING JAMES VERSION

9 And saith unto him, All these things will I give thee, if thou wilt fall down and worship me.

10 Then saith Jesus unto him, Get thee hence, Satan: for it is written, Thou shalt worship the Lord thy God, and him only shalt thou serve.

11 Then the devil leaveth him, and, behold, angels came and ministered unto him.

12 ¶ Now when Jesus had heard that John was cast into prison, he departed into Galilee;

13 And leaving Nazareth, he came and dwelt in Capernaum, which is upon the sea coast, in the borders of Zabulon and Nephthalim:

14 That it might be fulfilled which was spoken by Esaias the prophet, saying,

15 The land of Zabulon, and the land of Nephthalim, *by* the way of the sea, beyond Jordan, Galilee of the Gentiles;

16 The people which sat in darkness saw great light;

NEW AMERICAN STANDARD BIBLE

9 and he said to Him, "All these things I will give You, if You fall down and worship me."

10 Then Jesus *said to him, "Go, Satan! For it is written, 'YOU SHALL WORSHIP THE LORD YOUR GOD, AND SERVE HIM ONLY.' "

11 Then the devil *left Him; and behold, angels came and *began* to minister to Him.

Jesus Begins His Ministry

12 Now when Jesus heard that John had been taken into custody, He withdrew into Galilee;

13 and leaving Nazareth, He came and settled in Capernaum, which is by the sea, in the region of Zebulun and Naphtali.

14 *This was* to fulfill what was spoken through Isaiah the prophet:

15 "THE LAND OF ZEBULUN AND THE LAND OF NAPHTALI,
BY THE WAY OF THE SEA, BEYOND THE JORDAN, GALILEE OF
THE [2]GENTILES—

16 "THE PEOPLE WHO WERE SITTING IN DARKNESS SAW A GREAT
LIGHT,

4:15 [2] Lit *nations*, usually non-Jewish

NEW CENTURY VERSION

their splendor. 9The devil said, "If you will bow down and worship me, I will give you all these things."

10Jesus said to the devil, "Go away from me, Satan! It is written in the Scriptures, 'You must worship the Lord your God and serve only him.' "[c]

11So the devil left Jesus, and angels came and took care of him.

Jesus Begins Work in Galilee

12When Jesus heard that John had been put in prison, he went back to Galilee. 13He left Nazareth and went to live in Capernaum, a town near Lake Galilee, in the area near Zebulun and Naphtali. 14Jesus did this to bring about what the prophet Isaiah had said:

15 "Land of Zebulun and land of Naphtali
along the sea,
beyond the Jordan River.
This is Galilee where the non-Jewish people live.
16 These people who live in darkness
will see a great light.

4:10 [c] 'You...him.' Quotation from Deuteronomy 6:13.

CONTEMPORARY ENGLISH VERSION

power. 9The devil said to him, "I will give all this to you, if you will bow down and worship me."

10Jesus answered, "Go away Satan! The Scriptures say:

'Worship the Lord your God
and serve only him.' "

11Then the devil left Jesus, and angels came to help him.

Jesus Begins His Work (Mark 1.14, 15; Luke 4.14, 15)

12When Jesus heard that John had been put in prison, he went to Galilee. 13But instead of staying in Nazareth, Jesus moved to Capernaum. This town was beside Lake Galilee in the territory of Zebulun and Naphtali.[b] 14So God's promise came true, just as the prophet Isaiah had said,

15 "Listen, lands of Zebulun
and Naphtali,
lands along the road
to the sea and east
of the Jordan!
Listen Galilee,
land of the Gentiles!
16 Although your people
live in darkness,
they will see
a bright light.

[b] 4.13 *Zebulun and Naphtali*: In Old Testament times these tribes were in northern Palestine, and in New Testament times many Gentiles lived where these tribes had once been.

NEW INTERNATIONAL VERSION

splendor. 9“All this I will give you,” he said, “if you will
bow down and worship me.”
10Jesus said to him, “Away from me, Satan! For it is
written: ‘Worship the Lord your God, and serve him
only.’[d]”
11Then the devil left him, and angels came and attended
him.

Jesus Begins to Preach

12When Jesus heard that John had been put in prison, he
returned to Galilee. 13Leaving Nazareth, he went and lived
in Capernaum, which was by the lake in the area of
Zebulun and Naphtali— 14to fulfill what was said through
the prophet Isaiah:

15“Land of Zebulun and land of Naphtali,
the way to the sea, along the Jordan,
Galilee of the Gentiles—
16the people living in darkness
have seen a great light;

[d] *10* Deut. 6:13

NEW LIVING TRANSLATION

their glory. 9“I will give it all to you,” he said, “if you will
only kneel down and worship me.”
10“Get out of here, Satan,” Jesus told him. “For the
Scriptures say,

‘You must worship the Lord your God;
serve only him.’* ”

11Then the Devil went away, and angels came and cared
for Jesus.

The Ministry of Jesus Begins

12When Jesus heard that John had been arrested, he left
Judea and returned to Galilee. 13But instead of going to
Nazareth, he went to Capernaum, beside the Sea of Galilee,
in the region of Zebulun and Naphtali. 14This fulfilled
Isaiah’s prophecy:

15 “In the land of Zebulun and of Naphtali,
beside the sea, beyond the Jordan River—
in Galilee where so many Gentiles live—
16 the people who sat in darkness
have seen a great light.

4:10 Deut 6:13.

NEW KING JAMES VERSION

and their glory. 9And he said to Him, “All these things I
will give You if You will fall down and worship me.”
10Then Jesus said to him, “Away with you,[d] Satan! For it
is written, *‘You shall worship the* LORD *your God, and Him
only you shall serve.’* ”[e]
11Then the devil left Him, and behold, angels came and
ministered to Him.

Jesus Begins His Galilean Ministry

12Now when Jesus heard that John had been put in
prison, He departed to Galilee. 13And leaving Nazareth, He
came and dwelt in Capernaum, which is by the sea, in the
regions of Zebulun and Naphtali, 14that it might be ful-
filled which was spoken by Isaiah the prophet, saying:

15 *“The land of Zebulun and the land of Naphtali,
By the way of the sea, beyond the Jordan,
Galilee of the Gentiles:*
16 *The people who sat in darkness have seen a great
light,*

4:10 [d] M-Text reads *Get behind Me.* [e] Deuteronomy 6:13

THE MESSAGE

said, “They’re yours—lock, stock, and barrel. Just go down
on your knees and worship me, and they’re yours.”

Jesus’ refusal was curt: “Beat it, Satan!” He backed his
rebuke with a third quotation from Deuteronomy:
“Worship the Lord your God, and only him. Serve him with
absolute single-heartedness.”

The Test was over. The Devil left. And in his place,
angels! Angels came and took care of Jesus’ needs.

Teaching and Healing

When Jesus got word that John had been arrested, he
returned to Galilee. He moved from his hometown,
Nazareth, to the lakeside village Capernaum, nestled at the
base of the Zebulun and Naphtali hills. This move complet-
ed Isaiah’s sermon:

“Land of Zebulun, land of Naphtali,
road to the sea, over Jordan,
Galilee, crossroads for the nations.
People sitting out their lives in the dark
saw a huge light;

KING JAMES VERSION

and to them which sat in the region and shadow of death light is sprung up.

17 From that time Jesus began to preach, and to say, Repent: for the kingdom of heaven is at hand.

18 ¶ And Jesus, walking by the sea of Galilee, saw two brethren, Simon called Peter, and Andrew his brother, casting a net into the sea: for they were fishers.

19 And he saith unto them, Follow me, and I will make you fishers of men.

20 And they straightway left *their* nets, and followed him.

21 And going on from thence, he saw other two brethren, James *the son* of Zebedee, and John his brother, in a ship with Zebedee their father, mending their nets; and he called them.

22 And they immediately left the ship and their father, and followed him.

23 ¶ And Jesus went about all Galilee, teaching in their synagogues, and preaching the gospel of the kingdom, and healing all manner of sickness and all manner of disease among the people.

24 And his fame went throughout all Syria: and they brought unto him all sick people that were taken with divers diseases and torments, and those which were possessed

NEW AMERICAN STANDARD BIBLE

AND THOSE WHO WERE SITTING IN THE LAND AND SHADOW
OF DEATH,
UPON THEM A LIGHT DAWNED."

17 From that time Jesus began to preach and say, "Repent, for the kingdom of heaven is at hand."

The First Disciples

18 Now as Jesus was walking by the Sea of Galilee, He saw two brothers, Simon who was called Peter, and Andrew his brother, casting a net into the sea; for they were fishermen.

19 And He *said to them, "Follow Me, and I will make you fishers of men."

20 Immediately they left their nets and followed Him.

21 Going on from there He saw two other brothers, James the *son* of Zebedee, and John his brother, in the boat with Zebedee their father, mending their nets; and He called them.

22 Immediately they left the boat and their father, and followed Him.

Ministry in Galilee

23 Jesus was going throughout all Galilee, teaching in their synagogues and proclaiming the gospel of the kingdom, and healing every kind of disease and every kind of sickness among the people.

24 The news about Him spread throughout all Syria; and they brought to Him all who were ill, those suffering

NEW CENTURY VERSION

They live in a place covered with the shadows of death,
but a light will shine on them." *Isaiah 9:1–2*

Jesus Chooses Some Followers

17From that time Jesus began to preach, saying, "Change your hearts and lives, because the kingdom of heaven is near."

18As Jesus was walking by Lake Galilee, he saw two brothers, Simon (called Peter) and his brother Andrew. They were throwing a net into the lake because they were fishermen. 19Jesus said, "Come follow me, and I will make you fish for people." 20So Simon and Andrew immediately left their nets and followed him.

21As Jesus continued walking by Lake Galilee, he saw two other brothers, James and John, the sons of Zebedee. They were in a boat with their father Zebedee, mending their nets. Jesus told them to come with him. 22Immediately they left the boat and their father, and they followed Jesus.

Jesus Teaches and Heals People

23Jesus went everywhere in Galilee, teaching in the synagogues, preaching the Good News about the kingdom of heaven, and healing all the people's diseases and sicknesses. 24The news about Jesus spread all over Syria, and people brought all the sick to him. They were suffering from different kinds of diseases. Some were in great pain,

CONTEMPORARY ENGLISH VERSION

Although they live
in the shadow of death,
a light will shine
on them."

17Then Jesus started preaching, "Turn back to God! The kingdom of heaven will soon be here."[c]

Jesus Chooses Four Fishermen (Mark 1.16-20; Luke 5.1-11)

18While Jesus was walking along the shore of Lake Galilee, he saw two brothers. One was Simon, also known as Peter, and the other was Andrew. They were fishermen, and they were casting their net into the lake. 19Jesus said to them, "Come with me! I will teach you how to bring in people instead of fish." 20Right then the two brothers dropped their nets and went with him.

21Jesus walked on until he saw James and John, the sons of Zebedee. They were in a boat with their father, mending their nets. Jesus asked them to come with him too. 22Right away they left the boat and their father and went with Jesus.

Jesus Teaches, Preaches, and Heals (Luke 6.17-19)

23Jesus went all over Galilee, teaching in the Jewish meeting places and preaching the good news about God's kingdom. He also healed every kind of disease and sickness. 24News about him spread all over Syria, and people with every kind of sickness or disease were brought to him. Some of them had a lot of demons in them, others

[c] **4.17** *The kingdom of heaven will soon be here*: See the two notes at 3.2.

NEW INTERNATIONAL VERSION

on those living in the land of the shadow of death
a light has dawned."[e]

[17]From that time on Jesus began to preach, "Repent, for the kingdom of heaven is near."

The Calling of the First Disciples

[18]As Jesus was walking beside the Sea of Galilee, he saw two brothers, Simon called Peter and his brother Andrew. They were casting a net into the lake, for they were fishermen. [19]"Come, follow me," Jesus said, "and I will make you fishers of men." [20]At once they left their nets and followed him.

[21]Going on from there, he saw two other brothers, James son of Zebedee and his brother John. They were in a boat with their father Zebedee, preparing their nets. Jesus called them, [22]and immediately they left the boat and their father and followed him.

Jesus Heals the Sick

[23]Jesus went throughout Galilee, teaching in their synagogues, preaching the good news of the kingdom, and healing every disease and sickness among the people. [24]News about him spread all over Syria, and people brought to him all who were ill with various diseases, those suffering severe pain, the demon-possessed, those

[e] *16* Isaiah 9:1,2

NEW LIVING TRANSLATION

And for those who lived in the land where death casts
its shadow,
a light has shined."*

[17]From then on, Jesus began to preach, "Turn from your sins and turn to God, because the Kingdom of Heaven is near.*"

The First Disciples

[18]One day as Jesus was walking along the shore beside the Sea of Galilee, he saw two brothers—Simon, also called Peter, and Andrew—fishing with a net, for they were commercial fishermen. [19]Jesus called out to them, "Come, be my disciples, and I will show you how to fish for people!" [20]And they left their nets at once and went with him.

[21]A little farther up the shore he saw two other brothers, James and John, sitting in a boat with their father, Zebedee, mending their nets. And he called them to come, too. [22]They immediately followed him, leaving the boat and their father behind.

The Ministry of Jesus in Galilee

[23]Jesus traveled throughout Galilee teaching in the synagogues, preaching everywhere the Good News about the Kingdom. And he healed people who had every kind of sickness and disease. [24]News about him spread far beyond the borders of Galilee so that the sick were soon coming to be healed from as far away as Syria. And whatever their illness and pain, or if they were possessed by demons, or

4:15-16 Isa 9:1-2. **4:17** Or *has come* or *is coming soon.*

NEW KING JAMES VERSION

And upon those who sat in the region and shadow of death
Light has dawned."[f]

[17]From that time Jesus began to preach and to say, "Repent, for the kingdom of heaven is at hand."

Four Fishermen Called as Disciples

[18]And Jesus, walking by the Sea of Galilee, saw two brothers, Simon called Peter, and Andrew his brother, casting a net into the sea; for they were fishermen. [19]Then He said to them, "Follow Me, and I will make you fishers of men." [20]They immediately left *their* nets and followed Him.

[21]Going on from there, He saw two other brothers, James *the son* of Zebedee, and John his brother, in the boat with Zebedee their father, mending their nets. He called them, [22]and immediately they left the boat and their father, and followed Him.

Jesus Heals a Great Multitude

[23]And Jesus went about all Galilee, teaching in their synagogues, preaching the gospel of the kingdom, and healing all kinds of sickness and all kinds of disease among the people. [24]Then His fame went throughout all Syria; and they brought to Him all sick people who were afflicted with various diseases and torments, and those who were

4:16 [f] Isaiah 9:1, 2

THE MESSAGE

Sitting in that dark, dark country of death,
they watched the sun come up."

This Isaiah-prophesied sermon came to life in Galilee the moment Jesus started preaching. He picked up where John left off: "Change your life. God's kingdom is here."

Walking along the beach of Lake Galilee, Jesus saw two brothers: Simon (later called Peter) and Andrew. They were fishing, throwing their nets into the lake. It was their regular work. Jesus said to them, "Come with me. I'll make a new kind of fisherman out of you. I'll show you how to catch men and women instead of perch and bass." They didn't ask questions, but simply dropped their nets and followed.

A short distance down the beach they came upon another pair of brothers, James and John, Zebedee's sons. These two were sitting in a boat with their father, Zebedee, mending their fishnets. Jesus made the same offer to them, and they were just as quick to follow, abandoning boat and father.

From there he went all over Galilee. He used synagogues for meeting places and taught people the truth of God. God's kingdom was his theme—that beginning right now they were under God's government, a good government! He also healed people of their diseases and of the bad effects of their bad lives. Word got around the entire Roman province of Syria. People brought anybody with an

KING JAMES VERSION

with devils, and those which were lunatick, and those that had the palsy; and he healed them.

25 And there followed him great multitudes of people from Galilee, and *from* Decapolis, and *from* Jerusalem, and *from* Judaea, and *from* beyond Jordan.

5 And seeing the multitudes, he went up into a mountain: and when he was set, his disciples came unto him:

2 And he opened his mouth, and taught them, saying,

3 ¶ Blessed *are* the poor in spirit: for theirs is the kingdom of heaven.

4 Blessed *are* they that mourn: for they shall be comforted.

5 Blessed *are* the meek: for they shall inherit the earth.

NEW AMERICAN STANDARD BIBLE

with various diseases and pains, demoniacs, epileptics, paralytics; and He healed them.

25 Large crowds followed Him from Galilee and *the* Decapolis and Jerusalem and Judea and *from* beyond the Jordan.

The Sermon on the Mount; The Beatitudes

5 When Jesus saw the crowds, He went up on the mountain; and after He sat down, His disciples came to Him.

2 He opened His mouth and *began* to teach them, saying,

3 "Blessed are the poor in spirit, for theirs is the kingdom of heaven.

4 "Blessed are those who mourn, for they shall be comforted.

5 "Blessed are the [1]gentle, for they shall inherit the earth.

5:5 [1] Or *humble, meek*

NEW CENTURY VERSION

some had demons, some were epileptics,[d] and some were paralyzed. Jesus healed all of them. 25 Many people from Galilee, the Ten Towns,[e] Jerusalem, Judea, and the land across the Jordan River followed him.

Jesus Teaches the People

5 When Jesus saw the crowds, he went up on a hill and sat down. His followers came to him, 2 and he began to teach them, saying:

3 "Those people who know they have great spiritual
needs are happy,
because the kingdom of heaven belongs to them.
4 Those who are sad now are happy,
because God will comfort them.
5 Those who are humble are happy,

4:24 [d] **epileptics** People with a disease that causes them sometimes to lose control of their bodies and maybe faint, shake strongly, or not be able to move. 4:25 [e] **Ten Towns** In Greek, called "Decapolis." It was an area east of Lake Galilee that once had ten main towns.

CONTEMPORARY ENGLISH VERSION

were thought to be crazy,[d] and still others could not walk. But Jesus healed them all.

25 Large crowds followed Jesus from Galilee and the region around the ten cities known as Decapolis.[e] They also came from Jerusalem, Judea, and from across the Jordan River.

The Sermon on the Mount

5 When Jesus saw the crowds, he went up on the side of a mountain and sat down.[a]

Blessings (Luke 6.20-23)

Jesus' disciples gathered around him, 2 and he taught them:

3 God blesses those people
who depend only on him.
They belong to the kingdom
of heaven![b]
4 God blesses those people
who grieve.
They will find comfort!
5 God blesses those people
who are humble.

[d] 4.24 *thought to be crazy*: In ancient times people with epilepsy were thought to be crazy. [e] 4.25 *the ten cities known as Decapolis*: A group of ten cities east of Samaria and Galilee, where the people followed the Greek way of life. [a] 5.1 *sat down*: Teachers in the ancient world, including Jewish teachers, usually sat down when they taught. [b] 5.3 *They belong to the kingdom of heaven*: Or "The kingdom of heaven belongs to them."

NEW INTERNATIONAL VERSION

having seizures, and the paralyzed, and he healed them.
25Large crowds from Galilee, the Decapolis,[f] Jerusalem,
Judea and the region across the Jordan followed him.

The Beatitudes

5 Now when he saw the crowds, he went up on a moun-
tainside and sat down. His disciples came to him,
2and he began to teach them, saying:

3 "Blessed are the poor in spirit,
for theirs is the kingdom of heaven.
4 Blessed are those who mourn,
for they will be comforted.
5 Blessed are the meek,

[f] *25* That is, the Ten Cities

NEW LIVING TRANSLATION

were epileptics, or were paralyzed—he healed them all.
25Large crowds followed him wherever he went—people
from Galilee, the Ten Towns,* Jerusalem, from all over
Judea, and from east of the Jordan River.

The Sermon on the Mount

5 One day as the crowds were gathering, Jesus went up
the mountainside with his disciples and sat down to
teach them.

The Beatitudes

2This is what he taught them:

3 "God blesses those who realize their need for him,*
for the Kingdom of Heaven is given to them.
4 God blesses those who mourn,
for they will be comforted.
5 God blesses those who are gentle and lowly,

4:25 Greek *Decapolis.* **5:3** Greek *the poor in spirit.*

NEW KING JAMES VERSION

demon-possessed, epileptics, and paralytics; and He healed
them. 25Great multitudes followed Him—from Galilee, and
from Decapolis, Jerusalem, Judea, and beyond the Jordan.

The Beatitudes

5 And seeing the multitudes, He went up on a moun-
tain, and when He was seated His disciples came to
Him. 2Then He opened His mouth and taught them, say-
ing:

3 "Blessed *are* the poor in spirit,
For theirs is the kingdom of heaven.
4 Blessed *are* those who mourn,
For they shall be comforted.
5 Blessed *are* the meek,

THE MESSAGE

ailment, whether mental, emotional, or physical. Jesus healed them, one and all. More and more people came, the momentum gathering. Besides those from Galilee, crowds came from the "Ten Towns" across the lake, others up from Jerusalem and Judea, still others from across the Jordan.

You're Blessed

5 When Jesus saw his ministry drawing huge crowds, he climbed a hillside. Those who were apprenticed to him, the committed, climbed with him. Arriving at a quiet place, he sat down and taught his climbing companions. This is what he said:

"You're blessed when you're at the end of your rope. With less of you there is more of God and his rule.

"You're blessed when you feel you've lost what is most dear to you. Only then can you be embraced by the One most dear to you.

"You're blessed when you're content with just who you

KING JAMES VERSION

6 Blessed *are* they which do hunger and thirst after righteousness: for they shall be filled.

7 Blessed *are* the merciful: for they shall obtain mercy.

8 Blessed *are* the pure in heart: for they shall see God.

9 Blessed *are* the peacemakers: for they shall be called the children of God.

10 Blessed *are* they which are persecuted for righteousness' sake: for theirs is the kingdom of heaven.

11 Blessed are ye, when *men* shall revile you, and persecute *you*, and shall say all manner of evil against you falsely, for my sake.

12 Rejoice, and be exceeding glad: for great *is* your

NEW AMERICAN STANDARD BIBLE

6 "Blessed are those who hunger and thirst for righteousness, for they shall be satisfied.

7 "Blessed are the merciful, for they shall receive mercy.

8 "Blessed are the pure in heart, for they shall see God.

9 "Blessed are the peacemakers, for they shall be called sons of God.

10 "Blessed are those who have been persecuted for the sake of righteousness, for theirs is the kingdom of heaven.

11 "Blessed are you when *people* insult you and persecute you, and falsely say all kinds of evil against you because of Me.

12 "Rejoice and be glad, for your reward in heaven is

NEW CENTURY VERSION

because the earth will belong to them.
6 Those who want to do right more than anything else are happy,
because God will fully satisfy them.
7 Those who show mercy to others are happy,
because God will show mercy to them.

8 Those who are pure in their thinking are happy,
because they will be with God.
9 Those who work to bring peace are happy,
because God will call them his children.
10 Those who are treated badly for doing good are happy,
because the kingdom of heaven belongs to them.

11 "People will insult you and hurt you. They will lie and
say all kinds of evil things about you because you follow
me. But when they do, you will be happy. 12 Rejoice and be
glad, because you have a great reward waiting for you in

CONTEMPORARY ENGLISH VERSION

The earth will belong
to them!
6 God blesses those people
who want to obey him[c]
more than to eat or drink.
They will be given
what they want!
7 God blesses those people
who are merciful.
They will be treated
with mercy!
8 God blesses those people
whose hearts are pure.
They will see him!
9 God blesses those people
who make peace.
They will be called
his children!
10 God blesses those people
who are treated badly
for doing right.
They belong to the kingdom
of heaven.[d]

11 God will bless you when people insult you, mistreat
you, and tell all kinds of evil lies about you because of
me. 12 Be happy and excited! You will have a great

[c] **5.6** *who want to obey him*: Or "who want to do right" or "who want everyone to be treated right." [d] **5.10** *They belong to the kingdom of heaven*: See the note at 5.3.

NEW INTERNATIONAL VERSION

for they will inherit the earth.
6 Blessed are those who hunger and thirst for righteousness,
for they will be filled.
7 Blessed are the merciful,
for they will be shown mercy.
8 Blessed are the pure in heart,
for they will see God.
9 Blessed are the peacemakers,
for they will be called sons of God.
10 Blessed are those who are persecuted because of righteousness,
for theirs is the kingdom of heaven.

11 "Blessed are you when people insult you, persecute
you and falsely say all kinds of evil against you because of
me. 12 Rejoice and be glad, because great is your reward in

NEW LIVING TRANSLATION

for the whole earth will belong to them.
6 God blesses those who are hungry and thirsty for justice,
for they will receive it in full.
7 God blesses those who are merciful,
for they will be shown mercy.
8 God blesses those whose hearts are pure,
for they will see God.
9 God blesses those who work for peace,
for they will be called the children of God.
10 God blesses those who are persecuted because they live for God,
for the Kingdom of Heaven is theirs.

11 "God blesses you when you are mocked and persecut-
ed and lied about because you are my followers. 12 Be
happy about it! Be very glad! For a great reward awaits

NEW KING JAMES VERSION

For they shall inherit the earth.
6 Blessed *are* those who hunger and thirst for righteousness,
For they shall be filled.
7 Blessed *are* the merciful,
For they shall obtain mercy.
8 Blessed *are* the pure in heart,
For they shall see God.
9 Blessed *are* the peacemakers,
For they shall be called sons of God.
10 Blessed are those who are persecuted for righteousness' sake,
For theirs is the kingdom of heaven.

11 "Blessed are you when they revile and persecute you,
and say all kinds of evil against you falsely for My sake.
12 Rejoice and be exceedingly glad, for great *is* your reward

THE MESSAGE

are—no more, no less. That's the moment you find yourselves proud owners of everything that can't be bought.

"You're blessed when you've worked up a good appetite for God. He's food and drink in the best meal you'll ever eat.

"You're blessed when you care. At the moment of being 'care-full,' you find yourselves cared for.

"You're blessed when you get your inside world—your mind and heart—put right. Then you can see God in the outside world.

"You're blessed when you can show people how to cooperate instead of compete or fight. That's when you discover who you really are, and your place in God's family.

"You're blessed when your commitment to God provokes persecution. The persecution drives you even deeper into God's kingdom.

"Not only that—count yourselves blessed every time people put you down or throw you out or speak lies about you to discredit me. What it means is that the truth is too close for comfort and they are uncomfortable. You can be glad when that happens—give a cheer, even!—for though they don't like it, *I* do! And all heaven applauds. And know

KING JAMES VERSION

reward in heaven: for so persecuted they the prophets which were before you.

13 ¶ Ye are the salt of the earth: but if the salt have lost his savour, wherewith shall it be salted? it is thenceforth good for nothing, but to be cast out, and to be trodden under foot of men.

14 Ye are the light of the world. A city that is set on an hill cannot be hid.

15 Neither do men light a candle, and put it under a bushel, but on a candlestick; and it giveth light unto all that are in the house.

16 Let your light so shine before men, that they may see your good works, and glorify your Father which is in heaven.

17 ¶ Think not that I am come to destroy the law, or the prophets: I am not come to destroy, but to fulfil.

18 For verily I say unto you, Till heaven and earth pass, one jot or one tittle shall in no wise pass from the law, till all be fulfilled.

19 Whosoever therefore shall break one of these least commandments, and shall teach men so, he shall be called the least in the kingdom of heaven: but whosoever shall do and teach *them*, the same shall be called great in the kingdom of heaven.

20 For I say unto you, That except your righteousness

NEW AMERICAN STANDARD BIBLE

great; for in the same way they persecuted the prophets who were before you.

Disciples and the World

13 "You are the salt of the earth; but if the salt has become tasteless, how can it be made salty *again?* It is no longer good for anything, except to be thrown out and trampled under foot by men.

14 "You are the light of the world. A city set on a hill cannot be hidden;

15 nor does *anyone* light a lamp and put it under a basket, but on the lampstand, and it gives light to all who are in the house.

16 "Let your light shine before men in such a way that they may see your good works, and glorify your Father who is in heaven.

17 "Do not think that I came to abolish the Law or the Prophets; I did not come to abolish but to fulfill.

18 "For truly I say to you, until heaven and earth pass away, not the smallest letter or stroke shall pass from the Law until all is accomplished.

19 "Whoever then annuls one of the least of these commandments, and teaches others *to do* the same, shall be called least in the kingdom of heaven; but whoever keeps and teaches *them,* he shall be called great in the kingdom of heaven.

20 "For I say to you that unless your righteousness sur-

NEW CENTURY VERSION

heaven. People did the same evil things to the prophets who lived before you.

You Are like Salt and Light

13 "You are the salt of the earth. But if the salt loses its salty taste, it cannot be made salty again. It is good for nothing, except to be thrown out and walked on.
14 "You are the light that gives light to the world. A city
that is built on a hill cannot be hidden. 15 And people don't
hide a light under a bowl. They put it on a lampstand so
the light shines for all the people in the house. 16 In the
same way, you should be a light for other people. Live so
that they will see the good things you do and will praise
your Father in heaven.

The Importance of the Law

17 "Don't think that I have come to destroy the law of
Moses or the teaching of the prophets. I have not come to
destroy them but to bring about what they said. 18 I tell you
the truth, nothing will disappear from the law until heaven
and earth are gone. Not even the smallest letter or the
smallest part of a letter will be lost until everything has
happened. 19 Whoever refuses to obey any command and
teaches other people not to obey that command will be the
least important in the kingdom of heaven. But whoever
obeys the commands and teaches other people to obey
them will be great in the kingdom of heaven. 20 I tell you
that if you are no more obedient than the teachers of the

CONTEMPORARY ENGLISH VERSION

reward in heaven. People did these same things to the prophets who lived long ago.

Salt and Light (Mark 9.50; Luke 14.34, 35)

13 You are like salt for everyone on earth. But if salt no longer tastes like salt, how can it make food salty? All it is good for is to be thrown out and walked on.

14 You are like light for the whole world. A city built on
top of a hill cannot be hidden, 15 and no one would light a
lamp and put it under a clay pot. A lamp is placed on a
lampstand, where it can give light to everyone in the
house. 16 Make your light shine, so that others will see the
good that you do and will praise your Father in heaven.

The Law of Moses

17 Don't suppose that I came to do away with the Law
and the Prophets.[e] I did not come to do away with them,
but to give them their full meaning. 18 Heaven and earth
may disappear. But I promise you that not even a period
or comma will ever disappear from the Law. Everything
written in it must happen.

19 If you reject even the least important command in
the Law and teach others to do the same, you will be the
least important person in the kingdom of heaven. But if
you obey and teach others its commands, you will have
an important place in the kingdom. 20 You must obey
God's commands better than the Pharisees and the

[e] 5.17 *the Law and the Prophets*: The Jewish Scriptures, that is, the Old Testament.

NEW INTERNATIONAL VERSION

heaven, for in the same way they persecuted the prophets who were before you.

Salt and Light

[13]"You are the salt of the earth. But if the salt loses its saltiness, how can it be made salty again? It is no longer good for anything, except to be thrown out and trampled by men.

[14]"You are the light of the world. A city on a hill cannot be hidden. [15]Neither do people light a lamp and put it under a bowl. Instead they put it on its stand, and it gives light to everyone in the house. [16]In the same way, let your light shine before men, that they may see your good deeds and praise your Father in heaven.

The Fulfillment of the Law

[17]"Do not think that I have come to abolish the Law or the Prophets; I have not come to abolish them but to fulfill them. [18]I tell you the truth, until heaven and earth disappear, not the smallest letter, not the least stroke of a pen, will by any means disappear from the Law until everything is accomplished. [19]Anyone who breaks one of the least of these commandments and teaches others to do the same will be called least in the kingdom of heaven, but whoever practices and teaches these commands will be called great in the kingdom of heaven. [20]For I tell you that unless your righteousness surpasses that of the Pharisees and the

NEW LIVING TRANSLATION

you in heaven. And remember, the ancient prophets were persecuted, too.

Teaching about Salt and Light

[13]"You are the salt of the earth. But what good is salt if it has lost its flavor? Can you make it useful again? It will be thrown out and trampled underfoot as worthless. [14]You are the light of the world—like a city on a mountain, glowing in the night for all to see. [15]Don't hide your light under a basket! Instead, put it on a stand and let it shine for all. [16]In the same way, let your good deeds shine out for all to see, so that everyone will praise your heavenly Father.

Teaching about the Law

[17]"Don't misunderstand why I have come. I did not come to abolish the law of Moses or the writings of the prophets. No, I came to fulfill them. [18]I assure you, until heaven and earth disappear, even the smallest detail of God's law will remain until its purpose is achieved. [19]So if you break the smallest commandment and teach others to do the same, you will be the least in the Kingdom of Heaven. But anyone who obeys God's laws and teaches them will be great in the Kingdom of Heaven.

[20]"But I warn you—unless you obey God better than the

NEW KING JAMES VERSION

in heaven, for so they persecuted the prophets who were before you.

Believers Are Salt and Light

[13]"You are the salt of the earth; but if the salt loses its flavor, how shall it be seasoned? It is then good for nothing but to be thrown out and trampled underfoot by men.

[14]"You are the light of the world. A city that is set on a hill cannot be hidden. [15]Nor do they light a lamp and put it under a basket, but on a lampstand, and it gives light to all *who are* in the house. [16]Let your light so shine before men, that they may see your good works and glorify your Father in heaven.

Christ Fulfills the Law

[17]"Do not think that I came to destroy the Law or the Prophets. I did not come to destroy but to fulfill. [18]For assuredly, I say to you, till heaven and earth pass away, one jot or one tittle will by no means pass from the law till all is fulfilled. [19]Whoever therefore breaks one of the least of these commandments, and teaches men so, shall be called least in the kingdom of heaven; but whoever does and teaches *them,* he shall be called great in the kingdom of heaven. [20]For I say to you, that unless your righteous-

THE MESSAGE

that you are in good company. My prophets and witnesses have always gotten into this kind of trouble.

Salt and Light

"Let me tell you why you are here. You're here to be salt-seasoning that brings out the God-flavors of this earth. If you lose your saltiness, how will people taste godliness? You've lost your usefulness and will end up in the garbage.

"Here's another way to put it: You're here to be light, bringing out the God-colors in the world. God is not a secret to be kept. We're going public with this, as public as a city on a hill. If I make you light-bearers, you don't think I'm going to hide you under a bucket, do you? I'm putting you on a light stand. Now that I've put you there on a hilltop, on a light stand—shine! Keep open house; be generous with your lives. By opening up to others, you'll prompt people to open up with God, this generous Father in heaven.

Completing God's Law

"Don't suppose for a minute that I have come to demolish the Scriptures—either God's Law or the Prophets. I'm not here to demolish but to complete. I am going to put it all together, pull it all together in a vast panorama. God's Law is more real and lasting than the stars in the sky and the ground at your feet. Long after stars burn out and earth wears out, God's Law will be alive and working.

"Trivialize even the smallest item in God's Law and you will only have trivialized yourself. But take it seriously, show the way for others, and you will find honor in the kingdom. Unless you do far better than the Pharisees in

KING JAMES VERSION

shall exceed *the righteousness* of the scribes and Phari-
sees, ye shall in no case enter into the kingdom of heaven.
21 ¶ Ye have heard that it was said by them of old time,
Thou shalt not kill; and whosoever shall kill shall be in
danger of the judgment:
22 But I say unto you, That whosoever is angry with his
brother without a cause shall be in danger of the judg-
ment: and whosoever shall say to his brother, Raca, shall
be in danger of the council: but whosoever shall say, Thou
fool, shall be in danger of hell fire.
23 Therefore if thou bring thy gift to the altar, and there
rememberest that thy brother hath ought against thee;
24 Leave there thy gift before the altar, and go thy way;
first be reconciled to thy brother, and then come and offer
thy gift.
25 Agree with thine adversary quickly, whiles thou art
in the way with him; lest at any time the adversary deliver
thee to the judge, and the judge deliver thee to the officer,
and thou be cast into prison.
26 Verily I say unto thee, Thou shalt by no means come
out thence, till thou hast paid the uttermost farthing.
27 ¶ Ye have heard that it was said by them of old time,
Thou shalt not commit adultery:
28 But I say unto you, That whosoever looketh on a

NEW AMERICAN STANDARD BIBLE

passes *that* of the scribes and Pharisees, you will not enter
the kingdom of heaven.

Personal Relationships

21 "You have heard that the ancients were told, 'YOU
SHALL NOT COMMIT MURDER' and 'Whoever commits murder
shall be [2]liable to the court.'
22 "But I say to you that everyone who is angry with his
brother shall be guilty before the court; and whoever says
to his brother, '[3]You good-for-nothing,' shall be guilty
before [4]the supreme court; and whoever says, 'You fool,'
shall be guilty *enough to go* into the [5]fiery hell.
23 "Therefore if you are presenting your offering at the
altar, and there remember that your brother has something
against you,
24 leave your offering there before the altar and go; first
be reconciled to your brother, and then come and present
your offering.
25 "Make friends quickly with your opponent at law
while you are with him on the way, so that your opponent
may not hand you over to the judge, and the judge to the
officer, and you be thrown into prison.
26 "Truly I say to you, you will not come out of there
until you have paid up the last [6]cent.
27 "You have heard that it was said, 'YOU SHALL NOT COM-
MIT ADULTERY';
28 but I say to you that everyone who looks at a woman

5:21 [2] Or *guilty before* 5:22 [3] Or *empty-head;* Gr *Raka (Raca)* fr Aram *reqa* 5:22 [4] Lit *the Sanhedrin* 5:22 [5] Lit *Gehenna of fire*
5:26 [6] Lit *quadrans* (equaling two mites); i.e. 1/64 of a daily wage

NEW CENTURY VERSION

law and the Pharisees, you will never enter the kingdom of
heaven.

Jesus Teaches About Anger

21 "You have heard that it was said to our people long
ago, 'You must not murder anyone.[a] Anyone who murders
another will be judged.'
22 But I tell you, if you are angry
with a brother or sister,[b] you will be judged. If you say bad
things to a brother or sister, you will be judged by the
council. And if you call someone a fool, you will be in dan-
ger of the fire of hell.
23 "So when you offer your gift to God at the altar, and
you remember that your brother or sister has something
against you,
24 leave your gift there at the altar. Go and
make peace with that person, and then come and offer
your gift.
25 "If your enemy is taking you to court, become friends
quickly, before you go to court. Otherwise, your enemy
might turn you over to the judge, and the judge might give
you to a guard to put you in jail.
26 I tell you the truth, you
will not leave there until you have paid everything you owe.

Jesus Teaches About Sexual Sin

27 "You have heard that it was said, 'You must not be
guilty of adultery.'[c]
28 But I tell you that if anyone looks at

5:21 [a] **You...anyone.** Quotation from Exodus 20:13; Deuteronomy 5:17.
5:22 [b] **brother...sister** Although the Greek text reads "brother" here and throughout this book, Jesus' words were meant for the entire church, including men and women. 5:27 [c] **'You...adultery.'** Quotation from Exodus 20:14; Deuteronomy 5:18.

CONTEMPORARY ENGLISH VERSION

teachers of the Law obey them. If you don't, I promise
you that you will never get into the kingdom of heaven.

Anger

21 You know that our ancestors were told, "Do not
murder" and "A murderer must be brought to trial."
22 But I promise you that if you are angry with someone,[f]
you will have to stand trial. If you call someone a fool,
you will be taken to court. And if you say that someone
is worthless, you will be in danger of the fires of hell.
23 So if you are about to place your gift on the altar
and remember that someone is angry with you,
24 leave
your gift there in front of the altar. Make peace with that
person, then come back and offer your gift to God.
25 Before you are dragged into court, make friends
with the person who has accused you of doing wrong. If
you don't, you will be handed over to the judge and then
to the officer who will put you in jail.
26 I promise you
that you will not get out until you have paid the last
cent you owe.

Marriage

27 You know the commandment which says, "Be faith-
ful in marriage."
28 But I tell you that if you look at

[f] **5.22** *someone*: In verses 22-24 the Greek text has "brother," which may refer to people in general or to other followers.

NEW INTERNATIONAL VERSION

teachers of the law, you will certainly not enter the kingdom of heaven.

Murder

[21]"You have heard that it was said to the people long ago, 'Do not murder,[a] and anyone who murders will be subject to judgment.' [22]But I tell you that anyone who is angry with his brother[b] will be subject to judgment. Again, anyone who says to his brother, 'Raca,[c]' is answerable to the Sanhedrin. But anyone who says, 'You fool!' will be in danger of the fire of hell.

[23]"Therefore, if you are offering your gift at the altar and there remember that your brother has something against you, [24]leave your gift there in front of the altar. First go and be reconciled to your brother; then come and offer your gift.

[25]"Settle matters quickly with your adversary who is taking you to court. Do it while you are still with him on the way, or he may hand you over to the judge, and the judge may hand you over to the officer, and you may be thrown into prison. [26]I tell you the truth, you will not get out until you have paid the last penny.[d]

Adultery

[27]"You have heard that it was said, 'Do not commit adultery.'[e] [28]But I tell you that anyone who looks at a

[a] *21* Exodus 20:13 [b] *22* Some manuscripts *brother without cause*
[c] *22* An Aramaic term of contempt [d] *26* Greek *kodrantes*
[e] *27* Exodus 20:14

NEW LIVING TRANSLATION

teachers of religious law and the Pharisees do, you can't enter the Kingdom of Heaven at all!

Teaching about Anger

[21]"You have heard that the law of Moses says, 'Do not murder. If you commit murder, you are subject to judgment.'* [22]But I say, if you are angry with someone,* you are subject to judgment! If you call someone an idiot,* you are in danger of being brought before the high council. And if you curse someone,* you are in danger of the fires of hell.

[23]"So if you are standing before the altar in the Temple, offering a sacrifice to God, and you suddenly remember that someone has something against you, [24]leave your sacrifice there beside the altar. Go and be reconciled to that person. Then come and offer your sacrifice to God. [25]Come to terms quickly with your enemy before it is too late and you are dragged into court, handed over to an officer, and thrown in jail. [26]I assure you that you won't be free again until you have paid the last penny.

Teaching about Adultery

[27]"You have heard that the law of Moses says, 'Do not commit adultery.'* [28]But I say, anyone who even looks at a

5:21 Exod 20:13; Deut 5:17. **5:22a** Greek *your brother*; also in 5:23. Some manuscripts add *without cause.* **5:22b** Greek uses an Aramaic term of contempt: *If you say to your brother, 'Raca.'* **5:22c** Greek *if you say, 'You fool.'* **5:27** Exod 20:14; Deut 5:18.

NEW KING JAMES VERSION

ness exceeds *the righteousness* of the scribes and Pharisees, you will by no means enter the kingdom of heaven.

Murder Begins in the Heart

[21]"You have heard that it was said to those of old, *'You shall not murder,*[a] and whoever murders will be in danger of the judgment.' [22]But I say to you that whoever is angry with his brother without a cause[b] shall be in danger of the judgment. And whoever says to his brother, 'Raca!' shall be in danger of the council. But whoever says, 'You fool!' shall be in danger of hell fire. [23]Therefore if you bring your gift to the altar, and there remember that your brother has something against you, [24]leave your gift there before the altar, and go your way. First be reconciled to your brother, and then come and offer your gift. [25]Agree with your adversary quickly, while you are on the way with him, lest your adversary deliver you to the judge, the judge hand you over to the officer, and you be thrown into prison. [26]Assuredly, I say to you, you will by no means get out of there till you have paid the last penny.

Adultery in the Heart

[27]"You have heard that it was said to those of old,[c] *'You shall not commit adultery.'*[d] [28]But I say to you that who-

5:21 [a] Exodus 20:13; Deuteronomy 5:17 **5:22** [b] NU-Text omits *without a cause.* **5:27** [c] NU-Text and M-Text omit *to those of old.* [d] Exodus 20:14; Deuteronomy 5:18

THE MESSAGE

the matters of right living, you won't know the first thing about entering the kingdom.

Murder

"You're familiar with the command to the ancients, 'Do not murder.' I'm telling you that anyone who is so much as angry with a brother or sister is guilty of murder. Carelessly call a brother 'idiot!' and you just might find yourself hauled into court. Thoughtlessly yell 'stupid!' at a sister and you are on the brink of hellfire. The simple moral fact is that words kill.

"This is how I want you to conduct yourself in these matters. If you enter your place of worship and, about to make an offering, you suddenly remember a grudge a friend has against you, abandon your offering, leave immediately, go to this friend and make things right. Then and only then, come back and work things out with God.

"Or say you're out on the street and an old enemy accosts you. Don't lose a minute. Make the first move; make things right with him. After all, if you leave the first move to him, knowing his track record, you're likely to end up in court, maybe even jail. If that happens, you won't get out without a stiff fine.

Adultery and Divorce

"You know the next commandment pretty well, too: 'Don't go to bed with another's spouse.' But don't think you've preserved your virtue simply by staying out of bed.

KING JAMES VERSION

woman to lust after her hath committed adultery with her already in his heart.

29 And if thy right eye offend thee, pluck it out, and cast *it* from thee: for it is profitable for thee that one of thy members should perish, and not *that* thy whole body should be cast into hell.

30 And if thy right hand offend thee, cut it off, and cast *it* from thee: for it is profitable for thee that one of thy members should perish, and not *that* thy whole body should be cast into hell.

31 It hath been said, Whosoever shall put away his wife, let him give her a writing of divorcement:

32 But I say unto you, That whosoever shall put away his wife, saving for the cause of fornication, causeth her to commit adultery: and whosoever shall marry her that is divorced committeth adultery.

33 ¶ Again, ye have heard that it hath been said by them of old time, Thou shalt not forswear thyself, but shalt perform unto the Lord thine oaths:

34 But I say unto you, Swear not at all; neither by heaven; for it is God's throne:

35 Nor by the earth; for it is his footstool: neither by Jerusalem; for it is the city of the great King.

36 Neither shalt thou swear by thy head, because thou

NEW AMERICAN STANDARD BIBLE

with lust for her has already committed adultery with her in his heart.

29 "If your right eye makes you stumble, tear it out and throw it from you; for it is better for you to lose one of the parts of your body, than for your whole body to be thrown into hell.

30 "If your right hand makes you stumble, cut it off and throw it from you; for it is better for you to lose one of the parts of your body, than for your whole body to go into hell.

31 "It was said, 'WHOEVER SENDS HIS WIFE AWAY, LET HIM GIVE HER A CERTIFICATE OF DIVORCE';

32 but I say to you that everyone who divorces his wife, except for *the* reason of unchastity, makes her commit adultery; and whoever marries a divorced woman commits adultery.

33 "Again, you have heard that the ancients were told, 'YOU SHALL NOT MAKE FALSE VOWS, BUT SHALL FULFILL YOUR VOWS TO THE LORD.'

34 "But I say to you, make no oath at all, either by heaven, for it is the throne of God,

35 or by the earth, for it is the footstool of His feet, or by Jerusalem, for it is THE CITY OF THE GREAT KING.

36 "Nor shall you make an oath by your head, for you

NEW CENTURY VERSION

a woman and wants to sin sexually with her, in his mind
he has already done that sin with the woman. 29 If your
right eye causes you to sin, take it out and throw it away.
It is better to lose one part of your body than to have your
whole body thrown into hell. 30 If your right hand causes
you to sin, cut it off and throw it away. It is better to lose
one part of your body than for your whole body to go into
hell.

Jesus Teaches About Divorce

31 "It was also said, 'Anyone who divorces his wife must
give her a written divorce paper.'[d] 32 But I tell you that any-
one who divorces his wife forces her to be guilty of adul-
tery. The only reason for a man to divorce his wife is if she
has sexual relations with another man. And anyone who
marries that divorced woman is guilty of adultery.

Make Promises Carefully

33 "You have heard that it was said to our people long
ago, 'Don't break your promises, but keep the promises
you make to the Lord.'[e] 34 But I tell you, never swear an
oath. Don't swear an oath using the name of heaven,
because heaven is God's throne. 35 Don't swear an oath
using the name of the earth, because the earth belongs to
God. Don't swear an oath using the name of Jerusalem,
because that is the city of the great King. 36 Don't even
swear by your own head, because you cannot make one

5:31 [d] **'Anyone...divorce paper.'** Quotation from Deuteronomy 24:1.
5:33 [e] **'Don't...Lord.'** This refers to Leviticus 19:12; Numbers 30:2; Deuteronomy 23:21.

CONTEMPORARY ENGLISH VERSION

another woman and want her, you are already unfaith-
ful in your thoughts. 29 If your right eye causes you to
sin, poke it out and throw it away. It is better to lose one
part of your body, than for your whole body to end up in
hell. 30 If your right hand causes you to sin, chop it off
and throw it away! It is better to lose one part of your
body, than for your whole body to be thrown into hell.

Divorce (Matthew 19.9; Mark 10.11, 12; Luke 16.18)

31 You have been taught that a man who divorces his
wife must write out divorce papers for her.[g] 32 But I tell
you not to divorce your wife unless she has committed
some terrible sexual sin.[h] If you divorce her, you will
cause her to be unfaithful, just as any man who marries
her is guilty of taking another man's wife.

Promises

33 You know that our ancestors were told, "Don't use
the Lord's name to make a promise unless you are going
to keep it." 34 But I tell you not to swear by anything
when you make a promise! Heaven is God's throne, so
don't swear by heaven. 35 The earth is God's footstool, so
don't swear by the earth. Jerusalem is the city of the
great king, so don't swear by it. 36 Don't swear by your

[g] **5.31** *write out divorce papers for her*: Jewish men could divorce their wives, but the women could not divorce their husbands. The purpose of writing these papers was to make it harder for a man to divorce his wife. Before this law was made, all a man had to do was to send his wife away and say that she was no longer his wife. [h] **5.32** *some terrible sexual sin*: This probably refers to the laws about the wrong kinds of marriages that are forbidden in Leviticus 18.6-18 or to some serious sexual sin.

NEW INTERNATIONAL VERSION

woman lustfully has already committed adultery with her in his heart. [29]If your right eye causes you to sin, gouge it out and throw it away. It is better for you to lose one part of your body than for your whole body to be thrown into hell. [30]And if your right hand causes you to sin, cut it off and throw it away. It is better for you to lose one part of your body than for your whole body to go into hell.

Divorce

[31]"It has been said, 'Anyone who divorces his wife must give her a certificate of divorce.'[f] [32]But I tell you that anyone who divorces his wife, except for marital unfaithfulness, causes her to become an adulteress, and anyone who marries the divorced woman commits adultery.

Oaths

[33]"Again, you have heard that it was said to the people long ago, 'Do not break your oath, but keep the oaths you have made to the Lord.' [34]But I tell you, Do not swear at all: either by heaven, for it is God's throne; [35]or by the earth, for it is his footstool; or by Jerusalem, for it is the city of the Great King. [36]And do not swear by your head,

[f] *31* Deut. 24:1

NEW LIVING TRANSLATION

woman with lust in his eye has already committed adultery with her in his heart. [29]So if your eye—even if it is your good eye*—causes you to lust, gouge it out and throw it away. It is better for you to lose one part of your body than for your whole body to be thrown into hell. [30]And if your hand—even if it is your stronger hand*—causes you to sin, cut it off and throw it away. It is better for you to lose one part of your body than for your whole body to be thrown into hell.

Teaching about Divorce

[31]"You have heard that the law of Moses says, 'A man can divorce his wife by merely giving her a letter of divorce.'* [32]But I say that a man who divorces his wife, unless she has been unfaithful, causes her to commit adultery. And anyone who marries a divorced woman commits adultery.

Teaching about Vows

[33]"Again, you have heard that the law of Moses says, 'Do not break your vows; you must carry out the vows you have made to the Lord.'* [34]But I say, don't make any vows! If you say, 'By heaven!' it is a sacred vow because heaven is God's throne. [35]And if you say, 'By the earth!' it is a sacred vow because the earth is his footstool. And don't swear, 'By Jerusalem!' for Jerusalem is the city of the great King. [36]Don't even swear, 'By my head!' for you can't

5:29 Greek *your right eye.* 5:30 Greek *your right hand.* 5:31 Deut 24:1. 5:33 Num 30:2.

NEW KING JAMES VERSION

ever looks at a woman to lust for her has already committed adultery with her in his heart. [29]If your right eye causes you to sin, pluck it out and cast *it* from you; for it is more profitable for you that one of your members perish, than for your whole body to be cast into hell. [30]And if your right hand causes you to sin, cut it off and cast *it* from you; for it is more profitable for you that one of your members perish, than for your whole body to be cast into hell.

Marriage Is Sacred and Binding

[31]"Furthermore it has been said, 'Whoever divorces his wife, let him give her a certificate of divorce.' [32]But I say to you that whoever divorces his wife for any reason except sexual immorality[e] causes her to commit adultery; and whoever marries a woman who is divorced commits adultery.

Jesus Forbids Oaths

[33]"Again you have heard that it was said to those of old, 'You shall not swear falsely, but shall perform your oaths to the Lord.' [34]But I say to you, do not swear at all: neither by heaven, for it is God's throne; [35]nor by the earth, for it is His footstool; nor by Jerusalem, for it is the city of the great King. [36]Nor shall you swear by your head, because

5:32 [e] Or *fornication*

THE MESSAGE

Your *heart* can be corrupted by lust even quicker than your *body*. Those leering looks you think nobody notices—they also corrupt.

"Let's not pretend this is easier than it really is. If you want to live a morally pure life, here's what you have to do: You have to blind your right eye the moment you catch it in a lustful leer. You have to choose to live one-eyed or else be dumped on a moral trash pile. And you have to chop off your right hand the moment you notice it raised threateningly. Better a bloody stump than your entire being discarded for good in the dump.

"Remember the Scripture that says, 'Whoever divorces his wife, let him do it legally, giving her divorce papers and her legal rights'? Too many of you are using that as a cover for selfishness and whim, pretending to be righteous just because you are 'legal.' Please, no more pretending. If you divorce your wife, you're responsible for making her an adulteress (unless she has already made herself that by sexual promiscuity). And if you marry such a divorced adulteress, you're automatically an adulterer yourself. You can't use legal cover to mask a moral failure.

Empty Promises

"And don't say anything you don't mean. This counsel is embedded deep in our traditions. You only make things worse when you lay down a smoke screen of pious talk, saying, 'I'll pray for you,' and never doing it, or saying, 'God be with you,' and not meaning it. You don't make your words true by embellishing them with religious lace. In making your speech sound more religious, it becomes

KING JAMES VERSION

canst not make one hair white or black.
37 But let your communication be, Yea, yea; Nay, nay:
for whatsoever is more than these cometh of evil.
38 ¶ Ye have heard that it hath been said, An eye for an
eye, and a tooth for a tooth:
39 But I say unto you, That ye resist not evil: but
whosoever shall smite thee on thy right cheek, turn to him
the other also.
40 And if any man will sue thee at the law, and take
away thy coat, let him have *thy* cloke also.
41 And whosoever shall compel thee to go a mile, go
with him twain.
42 Give to him that asketh thee, and from him that
would borrow of thee turn not thou away.
43 ¶ Ye have heard that it hath been said, Thou shalt
love thy neighbour, and hate thine enemy.
44 But I say unto you, Love your enemies, bless them
that curse you, do good to them that hate you, and pray
for them which despitefully use you, and persecute you;
45 That ye may be the children of your Father which is
in heaven: for he maketh his sun to rise on the evil and on
the good, and sendeth rain on the just and on the unjust.
46 For if ye love them which love you, what reward
have ye? do not even the publicans the same?
47 And if ye salute your brethren only, what do ye more

NEW AMERICAN STANDARD BIBLE

cannot make one hair white or black.
37 "But let your statement be, 'Yes, yes' *or* 'No, no'; any-
thing beyond these is of evil.
38 "You have heard that it was said, 'AN EYE FOR AN EYE,
AND A TOOTH FOR A TOOTH.'
39 "But I say to you, do not resist an evil person; but
whoever slaps you on your right cheek, turn the other to
him also.
40 "If anyone wants to sue you and take your [7]shirt, let
him have your [8]coat also.
41 "Whoever forces you to go one mile, go with him two.
42 "Give to him who asks of you, and do not turn away
from him who wants to borrow from you.
43 "You have heard that it was said, 'YOU SHALL LOVE
YOUR NEIGHBOR and hate your enemy.'
44 "But I say to you, love your enemies and pray for
those who persecute you,
45 so that you may be sons of your Father who is in
heaven; for He causes His sun to rise on *the* evil and *the*
good, and sends rain on *the* righteous and *the* unrigh-
teous.
46 "For if you love those who love you, what reward do
you have? Do not even the tax collectors do the same?
47 "If you greet only your brothers, what more are you

5:40 [7] Lit *tunic;* i.e. a garment worn next to the body 5:40 [8] Lit *cloak;* i.e. an outer garment

NEW CENTURY VERSION

hair on your head become white or black. 37Say only yes if
you mean yes, and no if you mean no. If you say more
than yes or no, it is from the Evil One.

Don't Fight Back

38"You have heard that it was said, 'An eye for an eye,
and a tooth for a tooth.'[f] 39But I tell you, don't stand up
against an evil person. If someone slaps you on the right
cheek, turn to him the other cheek also. 40If someone
wants to sue you in court and take your shirt, let him have
your coat also. 41If someone forces you to go with him one
mile, go with him two miles. 42If a person asks you for
something, give it to him. Don't refuse to give to someone
who wants to borrow from you.

Love All People

43"You have heard that it was said, 'Love your neighbor[g]
and hate your enemies.' 44But I say to you, love your ene-
mies. Pray for those who hurt you. 45If you do this, you
will be true children of your Father in heaven. He causes
the sun to rise on good people and on evil people, and he
sends rain to those who do right and to those who do
wrong. 46If you love only the people who love you, you will
get no reward. Even the tax collectors do that. 47And if you
are nice only to your friends, you are no better than other
people. Even those who don't know God are nice to their

5:38 [f] **'An eye...tooth.'** Quotation from Exodus 21:24; Leviticus 24:20; Deuteronomy 19:21. 5:43 [g] **Love your neighbor** Quotation from Leviticus 19:18.

CONTEMPORARY ENGLISH VERSION

own head. You cannot make one hair white or black.
37When you make a promise, say only "Yes" or "No."
Anything else comes from the devil.

Revenge (Luke 6.29, 30)

38You know that you have been taught, "An eye for an
eye and a tooth for a tooth." 39But I tell you not to try to
get even with a person who has done something to you.
When someone slaps your right cheek,[i] turn and let that
person slap your other cheek. 40If someone sues you for
your shirt, give up your coat as well. 41If a soldier forces
you to carry his pack one mile, carry it two miles.[j]
42When people ask you for something, give it to them.
When they want to borrow money, lend it to them.

Love (Luke 6.27, 28, 32-36)

43You have heard people say, "Love your neighbors
and hate your enemies." 44But I tell you to love your
enemies and pray for anyone who mistreats you. 45Then
you will be acting like your Father in heaven. He makes
the sun rise on both good and bad people. And he sends
rain for the ones who do right and for the ones who do
wrong. 46If you love only those people who love you, will
God reward you for that? Even tax collectors[k] love their
friends. 47If you greet only your friends, what's so great

[i] **5.39** *right cheek*: A slap on the right cheek was a bad insult.
[j] **5.41** *two miles*: A Roman soldier had the right to force a person to carry his pack as far as one mile. [k] **5.46** *tax collectors*: These were usually Jewish people who paid the Romans for the right to collect taxes. They were hated by other Jews who thought of them as traitors to their country and to their religion.

NEW INTERNATIONAL VERSION

for you cannot make even one hair white or black. 37Simply let your 'Yes' be 'Yes,' and your 'No,' 'No'; anything beyond this comes from the evil one.

An Eye for an Eye

38"You have heard that it was said, 'Eye for eye, and tooth for tooth.'[g] 39But I tell you, Do not resist an evil person. If someone strikes you on the right cheek, turn to him the other also. 40And if someone wants to sue you and take your tunic, let him have your cloak as well. 41If someone forces you to go one mile, go with him two miles. 42Give to the one who asks you, and do not turn away from the one who wants to borrow from you.

Love for Enemies

43"You have heard that it was said, 'Love your neighbor[h] and hate your enemy.' 44But I tell you: Love your enemies[i] and pray for those who persecute you, 45that you may be sons of your Father in heaven. He causes his sun to rise on the evil and the good, and sends rain on the righteous and the unrighteous. 46If you love those who love you, what reward will you get? Are not even the tax collectors doing that? 47And if you greet only your brothers, what are you

[g] *38* Exodus 21:24; Lev. 24:20; Deut. 19:21 [h] *43* Lev. 19:18
[i] *44* Some late manuscripts *enemies, bless those who curse you, do good to those who hate you*

NEW LIVING TRANSLATION

turn one hair white or black. 37Just say a simple, 'Yes, I will,' or 'No, I won't.' Your word is enough. To strengthen your promise with a vow shows that something is wrong.*

Teaching about Revenge

38"You have heard that the law of Moses says, 'If an eye is injured, injure the eye of the person who did it. If a tooth gets knocked out, knock out the tooth of the person who did it.'* 39But I say, don't resist an evil person! If you are slapped on the right cheek, turn the other, too. 40If you are ordered to court and your shirt is taken from you, give your coat, too. 41If a soldier demands that you carry his gear for a mile,* carry it two miles. 42Give to those who ask, and don't turn away from those who want to borrow.

Teaching about Love for Enemies

43"You have heard that the law of Moses says, 'Love your neighbor'* and hate your enemy. 44But I say, love your enemies!* Pray for those who persecute you! 45In that way, you will be acting as true children of your Father in heaven. For he gives his sunlight to both the evil and the good, and he sends rain on the just and on the unjust, too. 46If you love only those who love you, what good is that? Even corrupt tax collectors do that much. 47If you are kind only to your friends,* how are you different from anyone

5:37 Or *Anything beyond this is from the evil one.* **5:38** Greek *'An eye for an eye and a tooth for a tooth.'* Exod 21:24; Lev 24:20; Deut 19:21. **5:41** Greek *milion* [4,854 feet or 1,478 meters]. **5:43** Lev 19:18. **5:44** Some manuscripts add *Bless those who curse you, do good to those who hate you.* **5:47** Greek *your brothers.*

NEW KING JAMES VERSION

you cannot make one hair white or black. 37But let your 'Yes' be 'Yes,' and your 'No,' 'No.' For whatever is more than these is from the evil one.

Go the Second Mile

38"You have heard that it was said, *'An eye for an eye and a tooth for a tooth.'*[f] 39But I tell you not to resist an evil person. But whoever slaps you on your right cheek, turn the other to him also. 40If anyone wants to sue you and take away your tunic, let him have *your* cloak also. 41And whoever compels you to go one mile, go with him two. 42Give to him who asks you, and from him who wants to borrow from you do not turn away.

Love Your Enemies

43"You have heard that it was said, *'You shall love your neighbor*[g] and hate your enemy.' 44But I say to you, love your enemies, bless those who curse you, do good to those who hate you, and pray for those who spitefully use you and persecute you,[h] 45that you may be sons of your Father in heaven; for He makes His sun rise on the evil and on the good, and sends rain on the just and on the unjust. 46For if you love those who love you, what reward have you? Do not even the tax collectors do the same? 47And if you greet your brethren[i] only, what do you do more *than*

5:38 [f] Exodus 21:24; Leviticus 24:20; Deuteronomy 19:21
5:43 [g] Compare Leviticus 19:18 **5:44** [h] NU-Text omits three clauses from this verse, leaving, *"But I say to you, love your enemies and pray for those who persecute you."* **5:47** [i] M-Text reads *friends.*

THE MESSAGE

less true. Just say 'yes' and 'no.' When you manipulate words to get your own way, you go wrong.

Love Your Enemies

"Here's another old saying that deserves a second look: 'Eye for eye, tooth for tooth.' Is that going to get us anywhere? Here's what I propose: 'Don't hit back at all.' If someone strikes you, stand there and take it. If someone drags you into court and sues for the shirt off your back, giftwrap your best coat and make a present of it. And if someone takes unfair advantage of you, use the occasion to practice the servant life. No more tit-for-tat stuff. Live generously.

"You're familiar with the old written law, 'Love your friend,' and its unwritten companion, 'Hate your enemy.' I'm challenging that. I'm telling you to love your enemies. Let them bring out the best in you, not the worst. When someone gives you a hard time, respond with the energies of prayer, for then you are working out of your true selves, your God-created selves. This is what God does. He gives his best—the sun to warm and the rain to nourish—to everyone, regardless: the good and bad, the nice and nasty. If all you do is love the lovable, do you expect a bonus? Anybody can do that. If you simply say hello to

KING JAMES VERSION

than others? do not even the publicans so?

48 Be ye therefore perfect, even as your Father which is in heaven is perfect.

6 Take heed that ye do not your alms before men, to be seen of them: otherwise ye have no reward of your Father which is in heaven.

2 Therefore when thou doest *thine* alms, do not sound a trumpet before thee, as the hypocrites do in the synagogues and in the streets, that they may have glory of men. Verily I say unto you, They have their reward.

3 But when thou doest alms, let not thy left hand know what thy right hand doeth:

4 That thine alms may be in secret: and thy Father which seeth in secret himself shall reward thee openly.

5 ¶ And when thou prayest, thou shalt not be as the hypocrites *are*: for they love to pray standing in the synagogues and in the corners of the streets, that they may be seen of men. Verily I say unto you, They have their reward.

6 But thou, when thou prayest, enter into thy closet, and when thou hast shut thy door, pray to thy Father which is in secret; and thy Father which seeth in secret shall reward thee openly.

NEW AMERICAN STANDARD BIBLE

doing *than others?* Do not even the Gentiles do the same?

48 "Therefore you are to be perfect, as your heavenly Father is perfect.

Giving to the Poor and Prayer

6 "Beware of practicing your righteousness before men to be noticed by them; otherwise you have no reward with your Father who is in heaven.

2 "So when you give to the poor, do not sound a trumpet before you, as the hypocrites do in the synagogues and in the streets, so that they may be honored by men. Truly I say to you, they have their reward in full.

3 "But when you give to the poor, do not let your left hand know what your right hand is doing,

4 so that your giving will be in secret; and your Father who sees *what is done* in secret will reward you.

5 "When you pray, you are not to be like the hypocrites; for they love to stand and pray in the synagogues and on the street corners so that they may be seen by men. Truly I say to you, they have their reward in full.

6 "But you, when you pray, go into your inner room, close your door and pray to your Father who is in secret, and your Father who sees *what is done* in secret will reward you.

NEW CENTURY VERSION

friends. 48So you must be perfect, just as your Father in heaven is perfect.

Jesus Teaches About Giving

6 "Be careful! When you do good things, don't do them in front of people to be seen by them. If you do that, you will have no reward from your Father in heaven.

2"When you give to the poor, don't be like the hypocrites. They blow trumpets in the synagogues and on the streets so that people will see them and honor them. I tell you the truth, those hypocrites already have their full reward. 3So when you give to the poor, don't let anyone know what you are doing. 4Your giving should be done in secret. Your Father can see what is done in secret, and he will reward you.

Jesus Teaches About Prayer

5"When you pray, don't be like the hypocrites. They love to stand in the synagogues and on the street corners and pray so people will see them. I tell you the truth, they already have their full reward. 6When you pray, you should go into your room and close the door and pray to your Father who cannot be seen. Your Father can see what is done in secret, and he will reward you.

CONTEMPORARY ENGLISH VERSION

about that? Don't even unbelievers do that? 48But you must always act like your Father in heaven.

Giving

6 When you do good deeds, don't try to show off. If you do, you won't get a reward from your Father in heaven.

2When you give to the poor, don't blow a loud horn. That's what show-offs do in the meeting places and on the street corners, because they are always looking for praise. I can assure you that they already have their reward.

3When you give to the poor, don't let anyone know about it.[a] 4Then your gift will be given in secret. Your Father knows what is done in secret, and he will reward you.

Prayer (Luke 11.2-4)

5When you pray, don't be like those show-offs who love to stand up and pray in the meeting places and on the street corners. They do this just to look good. I can assure you that they already have their reward.

6When you pray, go into a room alone and close the door. Pray to your Father in private. He knows what is done in private, and he will reward you.

[a] 6.3 *don't let anyone know about it*: The Greek text has, "Don't let your left hand know what your right hand is doing."

NEW INTERNATIONAL VERSION

doing more than others? Do not even pagans do that? 48 Be
perfect, therefore, as your heavenly Father is perfect.

Giving to the Needy

6 "Be careful not to do your 'acts of righteousness'
before men, to be seen by them. If you do, you will
have no reward from your Father in heaven.

2 "So when you give to the needy, do not announce it
with trumpets, as the hypocrites do in the synagogues and
on the streets, to be honored by men. I tell you the truth,
they have received their reward in full. 3 But when you give
to the needy, do not let your left hand know what your
right hand is doing, 4 so that your giving may be in secret.
Then your Father, who sees what is done in secret, will
reward you.

Prayer

5 "And when you pray, do not be like the hypocrites, for
they love to pray standing in the synagogues and on the
street corners to be seen by men. I tell you the truth, they
have received their reward in full. 6 But when you pray, go
into your room, close the door and pray to your Father,
who is unseen. Then your Father, who sees what is done
in secret, will reward you. 7 And when you pray, do not

NEW LIVING TRANSLATION

else? Even pagans do that. 48 But you are to be perfect,
even as your Father in heaven is perfect.

Teaching about Giving to the Needy

6 "Take care! Don't do your good deeds publicly, to be
admired, because then you will lose the reward from
your Father in heaven. 2 When you give a gift to someone
in need, don't shout about it as the hypocrites do—blow-
ing trumpets in the synagogues and streets to call atten-
tion to their acts of charity! I assure you, they have
received all the reward they will ever get. 3 But when you
give to someone, don't tell your left hand what your right
hand is doing. 4 Give your gifts in secret, and your Father,
who knows all secrets, will reward you.

Teaching about Prayer and Fasting

5 "And now about prayer. When you pray, don't be like
the hypocrites who love to pray publicly on street corners
and in the synagogues where everyone can see them. I
assure you, that is all the reward they will ever get. 6 But
when you pray, go away by yourself, shut the door behind
you, and pray to your Father secretly. Then your Father,
who knows all secrets, will reward you.

NEW KING JAMES VERSION

others? Do not even the tax collectors[j] do so? 48 Therefore
you shall be perfect, just as your Father in heaven is per-
fect.

Do Good to Please God

6 "Take heed that you do not do your charitable deeds
before men, to be seen by them. Otherwise you have
no reward from your Father in heaven. 2 Therefore, when
you do a charitable deed, do not sound a trumpet before
you as the hypocrites do in the synagogues and in the
streets, that they may have glory from men. Assuredly, I
say to you, they have their reward. 3 But when you do a
charitable deed, do not let your left hand know what your
right hand is doing, 4 that your charitable deed may be in
secret; and your Father who sees in secret will Himself
reward you openly.[a]

The Model Prayer

5 "And when you pray, you shall not be like the hypo-
crites. For they love to pray standing in the synagogues
and on the corners of the streets, that they may be seen by
men. Assuredly, I say to you, they have their reward. 6 But
you, when you pray, go into your room, and when you
have shut your door, pray to your Father who *is* in the
secret *place;* and your Father who sees in secret will

5:47 [j] NU-Text reads *Gentiles.* 6:4 [a] NU-Text omits *openly.*

THE MESSAGE

those who greet you, do you expect a medal? Any run-of-the-mill sinner does that.

"In a word, what I'm saying is, *Grow up.* You're kingdom subjects. Now live like it. Live out your God-created identity. Live generously and graciously toward others, the way God lives toward you.

The World Is Not a Stage

6 "Be especially careful when you are trying to be good so that you don't make a performance out of it. It might be good theater, but the God who made you won't be applauding.

"When you do something for someone else, don't call attention to yourself. You've seen them in action, I'm sure—'playactors' I call them—treating prayer meeting and street corner alike as a stage, acting compassionate as long as someone is watching, playing to the crowds. They get applause, true, but that's all they get. When you help someone out, don't think about how it looks. Just do it—quietly and unobtrusively. That is the way your God, who conceived you in love, working behind the scenes, helps you out.

Pray With Simplicity

"And when you come before God, don't turn that into a theatrical production either. All these people making a regular show out of their prayers, hoping for stardom! Do you think God sits in a box seat?

"Here's what I want you to do: Find a quiet, secluded place so you won't be tempted to role-play before God. Just be there as simply and honestly as you can manage. The

KING JAMES VERSION

7 But when ye pray, use not vain repetitions, as the heathen *do*: for they think that they shall be heard for their much speaking.

8 Be not ye therefore like unto them: for your Father knoweth what things ye have need of, before ye ask him.

9 ¶ After this manner therefore pray ye: Our Father which art in heaven, Hallowed be thy name.

10 Thy kingdom come. Thy will be done in earth, as *it is* in heaven.

11 Give us this day our daily bread.

12 And forgive us our debts, as we forgive our debtors.

13 And lead us not into temptation, but deliver us from evil: For thine is the kingdom, and the power, and the glory, for ever. Amen.

14 For if ye forgive men their trespasses, your heavenly Father will also forgive you:

15 But if ye forgive not men their trespasses, neither will your Father forgive your trespasses.

NEW AMERICAN STANDARD BIBLE

7 "And when you are praying, do not use meaningless repetition as the Gentiles do, for they suppose that they will be heard for their many words.

8 "So do not be like them; for your Father knows what you need before you ask Him.

9 "Pray, then, in this way:
'Our Father who is in heaven,
Hallowed be Your name.
10 'Your kingdom come.
Your will be done,
On earth as it is in heaven.
11 'Give us this day our daily bread.
12 'And forgive us our debts, as we also have forgiven
our debtors.
13 'And do not lead us into temptation, but deliver us
from evil. [For Yours is the kingdom and the
power and the glory forever. Amen.]'

14 "For if you forgive others for their transgressions, your heavenly Father will also forgive you.

15 "But if you do not forgive others, then your Father will not forgive your transgressions.

NEW CENTURY VERSION

7 "And when you pray, don't be like those people who
don't know God. They continue saying things that mean
nothing, thinking that God will hear them because of their
many words. 8 Don't be like them, because your Father
knows the things you need before you ask him. 9 So when
you pray, you should pray like this:
'Our Father in heaven,
may your name always be kept holy.
10 May your kingdom come
and what you want be done,
here on earth as it is in heaven.
11 Give us the food we need for each day.
12 Forgive us for our sins,
just as we have forgiven those who sinned
against us.
13 And do not cause us to be tempted,
but save us from the Evil One.'
14 Yes, if you forgive others for their sins, your Father in
heaven will also forgive you for your sins. 15 But if you
don't forgive others, your Father in heaven will not forgive
your sins.

CONTEMPORARY ENGLISH VERSION

7 When you pray, don't talk on and on as people do
who don't know God. They think God likes to hear long
prayers. 8 Don't be like them. Your Father knows what
you need before you ask.
9 You should pray like this:

Our Father in heaven,
help us to honor
your name.
10 Come and set up
your kingdom,
so that everyone on earth
will obey you,
as you are obeyed
in heaven.
11 Give us our food for today.[b]
12 Forgive us for doing wrong,
as we forgive others.
13 Keep us from being tempted
and protect us from evil.[c]

14 If you forgive others for the wrongs they do to you,
your Father in heaven will forgive you. 15 But if you
don't forgive others, your Father will not forgive your
sins.

[b] 6.11 *our food for today*: Or "the food that we need" or "our food for the coming day." [c] 6.13 *evil*: Or "the evil one," that is, the devil. Some manuscripts add, "The kingdom, the power, and the glory are yours forever. Amen."

NEW INTERNATIONAL VERSION

keep on babbling like pagans, for they think they will be heard because of their many words. 8Do not be like them, for your Father knows what you need before you ask him.
9"This, then, is how you should pray:

" 'Our Father in heaven,
hallowed be your name,
10your kingdom come,
your will be done
on earth as it is in heaven.
11Give us today our daily bread.
12Forgive us our debts,
as we also have forgiven our debtors.
13And lead us not into temptation,
but deliver us from the evil one.[a]'

14For if you forgive men when they sin against you, your heavenly Father will also forgive you. 15But if you do not forgive men their sins, your Father will not forgive your sins.

[a] *13* Or *from evil*; some late manuscripts *one, / for yours is the kingdom and the power and the glory forever. Amen.*

NEW LIVING TRANSLATION

7"When you pray, don't babble on and on as people of other religions do. They think their prayers are answered only by repeating their words again and again. 8Don't be like them, because your Father knows exactly what you need even before you ask him! 9Pray like this:

Our Father in heaven,
may your name be honored.
10 May your Kingdom come soon.
May your will be done here on earth,
just as it is in heaven.
11 Give us our food for today,*
12 and forgive us our sins,
just as we have forgiven those who have sinned against us.
13 And don't let us yield to temptation,
but deliver us from the evil one.*

14"If you forgive those who sin against you, your heavenly Father will forgive you. 15But if you refuse to forgive others, your Father will not forgive your sins.

6:11 Or *for tomorrow.* 6:13 Or *from evil.* Some manuscripts add *For yours is the kingdom and the power and the glory forever. Amen.*

NEW KING JAMES VERSION

reward you openly.[b] 7And when you pray, do not use vain repetitions as the heathen *do.* For they think that they will be heard for their many words.
8"Therefore do not be like them. For your Father knows the things you have need of before you ask Him. 9In this manner, therefore, pray:

Our Father in heaven,
Hallowed be Your name.
10 Your kingdom come.
Your will be done
On earth as *it is* in heaven.
11 Give us this day our daily bread.
12 And forgive us our debts,
As we forgive our debtors.
13 And do not lead us into temptation,
But deliver us from the evil one.
For Yours is the kingdom and the power and the glory forever. Amen.[c]

14"For if you forgive men their trespasses, your heavenly Father will also forgive you. 15But if you do not forgive men their trespasses, neither will your Father forgive your trespasses.

6:6 [b] NU-Text omits *openly.* 6:13 [c] NU-Text omits *For Yours* through *Amen.*

THE MESSAGE

focus will shift from you to God, and you will begin to sense his grace.

"The world is full of so-called prayer warriors who are prayer-ignorant. They're full of formulas and programs and advice, peddling techniques for getting what you want from God. Don't fall for that nonsense. This is your Father you are dealing with, and he knows better than you what you need. With a God like this loving you, you can pray very simply. Like this:

'Our Father in heaven,
Reveal who you are.
Set the world right;
Do what's best—
as above, so below.
Keep us alive with three square meals.
Keep us forgiven with you and forgiving others.
Keep us safe from ourselves and the Devil.
You're in charge!
You can do anything you want!
You're ablaze in beauty!
Yes. Yes. Yes.'

"In prayer there is a connection between what God does and what you do. You can't get forgiveness from God, for instance, without also forgiving others. If you refuse to do your part, you cut yourself off from God's part.

KING JAMES VERSION

16 ¶ Moreover when ye fast, be not, as the hypocrites, of a sad countenance: for they disfigure their faces, that they may appear unto men to fast. Verily I say unto you, They have their reward.

17 But thou, when thou fastest, anoint thine head, and wash thy face;

18 That thou appear not unto men to fast, but unto thy Father which is in secret: and thy Father, which seeth in secret, shall reward thee openly.

19 ¶ Lay not up for yourselves treasures upon earth, where moth and rust doth corrupt, and where thieves break through and steal:

20 But lay up for yourselves treasures in heaven, where neither moth nor rust doth corrupt, and where thieves do not break through nor steal:

21 For where your treasure is, there will your heart be also.

22 The light of the body is the eye: if therefore thine eye be single, thy whole body shall be full of light.

23 But if thine eye be evil, thy whole body shall be full of darkness. If therefore the light that is in thee be darkness, how great *is* that darkness!

24 No man can serve two masters: for either he will hate the one, and love the other; or else he will hold to the one, and despise the other. Ye cannot serve God and mammon.

NEW AMERICAN STANDARD BIBLE

Fasting; The True Treasure; Wealth (Mammon)

16 "Whenever you fast, do not put on a gloomy face as the hypocrites *do,* for they neglect their appearance so that they will be noticed by men when they are fasting. Truly I say to you, they have their reward in full.

17 "But you, when you fast, anoint your head and wash your face

18 so that your fasting will not be noticed by men, but by your Father who is in secret; and your Father who sees *what is done* in secret will reward you.

19 "Do not store up for yourselves treasures on earth, where moth and rust destroy, and where thieves break in and steal.

20 "But store up for yourselves treasures in heaven, where neither moth nor rust destroys, and where thieves do not break in or steal;

21 for where your treasure is, there your heart will be also.

22 "The eye is the lamp of the body; so then if your eye is clear, your whole body will be full of light.

23 "But if your eye is bad, your whole body will be full of darkness. If then the light that is in you is darkness, how great is the darkness!

24 "No one can serve two masters; for either he will hate the one and love the other, or he will be devoted to one and despise the other. You cannot serve God and [1]wealth.

6:24 [1] *mamona,* Gr for Ara *mammon;* i.e. wealth, etc, personified as an object of worship

NEW CENTURY VERSION

Jesus Teaches About Worship

16"When you give up eating,[a] don't put on a sad face like the hypocrites. They make their faces look sad to show people they are giving up eating. I tell you the truth, those hypocrites already have their full reward. 17So when you give up eating, comb your hair and wash your face. 18Then people will not know that you are giving up eating, but your Father, whom you cannot see, will see you. Your Father sees what is done in secret, and he will reward you.

God Is More Important than Money

19"Don't store treasures for yourselves here on earth where moths and rust will destroy them and thieves can break in and steal them. 20But store your treasures in heaven where they cannot be destroyed by moths or rust and where thieves cannot break in and steal them. 21Your heart will be where your treasure is.

22"The eye is a light for the body. If your eyes are good, your whole body will be full of light. 23But if your eyes are evil, your whole body will be full of darkness. And if the only light you have is really darkness, then you have the worst darkness.

24"No one can serve two masters. The person will hate one master and love the other, or will follow one master and refuse to follow the other. You cannot serve both God and worldly riches.

6:16 [a] **give up eating** This is called "fasting." The people would give up eating for a special time of prayer and worship to God. It was also done to show sadness and disappointment.

CONTEMPORARY ENGLISH VERSION

Worshiping God by Going without Eating

16When you go without eating,[d] don't try to look gloomy as those show-offs do when they go without eating. I can assure you that they already have their reward. 17Instead, comb your hair and wash your face. 18Then others won't know that you are going without eating. But your Father sees what is done in private, and he will reward you.

Treasures in Heaven (Luke 12.33, 34)

19Don't store up treasures on earth! Moths and rust can destroy them, and thieves can break in and steal them. 20Instead, store up your treasures in heaven, where moths and rust cannot destroy them, and thieves cannot break in and steal them. 21Your heart will always be where your treasure is.

Light (Luke 11.34-36)

22Your eyes are like a window for your body. When they are good, you have all the light you need. 23But when your eyes are bad, everything is dark. If the light inside you is dark, you surely are in the dark.

Money (Luke 16.13)

24You cannot be the slave of two masters! You will like one more than the other or be more loyal to one than the other. You cannot serve both God and money.

[d] **6.16** *without eating*: See the note at 4.2.

NEW INTERNATIONAL VERSION

Fasting

16"When you fast, do not look somber as the hypocrites do, for they disfigure their faces to show men they are fasting. I tell you the truth, they have received their reward in full. 17But when you fast, put oil on your head and wash your face, 18so that it will not be obvious to men that you are fasting, but only to your Father, who is unseen; and your Father, who sees what is done in secret, will reward you.

Treasures in Heaven

19"Do not store up for yourselves treasures on earth, where moth and rust destroy, and where thieves break in and steal. 20But store up for yourselves treasures in heaven, where moth and rust do not destroy, and where thieves do not break in and steal. 21For where your treasure is, there your heart will be also.

22"The eye is the lamp of the body. If your eyes are good, your whole body will be full of light. 23But if your eyes are bad, your whole body will be full of darkness. If then the light within you is darkness, how great is that darkness!

24"No one can serve two masters. Either he will hate the one and love the other, or he will be devoted to the one and despise the other. You cannot serve both God and Money.

NEW LIVING TRANSLATION

16"And when you fast, don't make it obvious, as the hypocrites do, who try to look pale and disheveled so people will admire them for their fasting. I assure you, that is the only reward they will ever get. 17But when you fast, comb your hair and wash your face. 18Then no one will suspect you are fasting, except your Father, who knows what you do in secret. And your Father, who knows all secrets, will reward you.

Teaching about Money and Possessions

19"Don't store up treasures here on earth, where they can be eaten by moths and get rusty, and where thieves break in and steal. 20Store your treasures in heaven, where they will never become moth-eaten or rusty and where they will be safe from thieves. 21Wherever your treasure is, there your heart and thoughts will also be.

22"Your eye is a lamp for your body. A pure eye lets sunshine into your soul. 23But an evil eye shuts out the light and plunges you into darkness. If the light you think you have is really darkness, how deep that darkness will be!

24"No one can serve two masters. For you will hate one and love the other, or be devoted to one and despise the other. You cannot serve both God and money.

NEW KING JAMES VERSION

Fasting to Be Seen Only by God

16"Moreover, when you fast, do not be like the hypocrites, with a sad countenance. For they disfigure their faces that they may appear to men to be fasting. Assuredly, I say to you, they have their reward. 17But you, when you fast, anoint your head and wash your face, 18so that you do not appear to men to be fasting, but to your Father who *is* in the secret *place;* and your Father who sees in secret will reward you openly.[d]

Lay Up Treasures in Heaven

19"Do not lay up for yourselves treasures on earth, where moth and rust destroy and where thieves break in and steal; 20but lay up for yourselves treasures in heaven, where neither moth nor rust destroys and where thieves do not break in and steal. 21For where your treasure is, there your heart will be also.

The Lamp of the Body

22"The lamp of the body is the eye. If therefore your eye is good, your whole body will be full of light. 23But if your eye is bad, your whole body will be full of darkness. If therefore the light that is in you is darkness, how great *is* that darkness!

You Cannot Serve God and Riches

24"No one can serve two masters; for either he will hate the one and love the other, or else he will be loyal to the one and despise the other. You cannot serve God and mammon.

6:18 [d] NU-Text and M-Text omit *openly.*

THE MESSAGE

"When you practice some appetite-denying discipline to better concentrate on God, don't make a production out of it. It might turn you into a small-time celebrity but it won't make you a saint. If you 'go into training' inwardly, act normal outwardly. Shampoo and comb your hair, brush your teeth, wash your face. God doesn't require attention-getting devices. He won't overlook what you are doing; he'll reward you well.

A Life of God-Worship

"Don't hoard treasure down here where it gets eaten by moths and corroded by rust or—worse!—stolen by burglars. Stockpile treasure in heaven, where it's safe from moth and rust and burglars. It's obvious, isn't it? The place where your treasure is, is the place you will most want to be, and end up being.

"Your eyes are windows into your body. If you open your eyes wide in wonder and belief, your body fills up with light. If you live squinty-eyed in greed and distrust, your body is a dank cellar. If you pull the blinds on your windows, what a dark life you will have!

"You can't worship two gods at once. Loving one god, you'll end up hating the other. Adoration of one feeds contempt for the other. You can't worship God and Money both.

KING JAMES VERSION

25 ¶ Therefore I say unto you, Take no thought for your life, what ye shall eat, or what ye shall drink; nor yet for your body, what ye shall put on. Is not the life more than meat, and the body than raiment?

26 Behold the fowls of the air: for they sow not, neither do they reap, nor gather into barns; yet your heavenly Father feedeth them. Are ye not much better than they?

27 Which of you by taking thought can add one cubit unto his stature?

28 And why take ye thought for raiment? Consider the lilies of the field, how they grow; they toil not, neither do they spin:

29 And yet I say unto you, That even Solomon in all his glory was not arrayed like one of these.

30 Wherefore, if God so clothe the grass of the field, which to day is, and to morrow is cast into the oven, *shall he* not much more *clothe* you, O ye of little faith?

31 Therefore take no thought, saying, What shall we eat? or, What shall we drink? or, Wherewithal shall we be clothed?

32 (For after all these things do the Gentiles seek:) for your heavenly Father knoweth that ye have need of all these things.

33 But seek ye first the kingdom of God, and his righteousness; and all these things shall be added unto you.

34 Take therefore no thought for the morrow: for the morrow shall take thought for the things of itself. Sufficient unto the day *is* the evil thereof.

NEW AMERICAN STANDARD BIBLE

The Cure for Anxiety

25 "For this reason I say to you, do not be worried about your life, *as to* what you will eat or what you will drink; nor for your body, *as to* what you will put on. Is not life more than food, and the body more than clothing?

26 "Look at the birds of the air, that they do not sow, nor reap nor gather into barns, and *yet* your heavenly Father feeds them. Are you not worth much more than they?

27 "And who of you by being worried can add a *single* hour to his life?

28 "And why are you worried about clothing? Observe how the lilies of the field grow; they do not toil nor do they spin,

29 yet I say to you that not even Solomon in all his glory clothed himself like one of these.

30 "But if God so clothes the grass of the field, which is *alive* today and tomorrow is thrown into the furnace, *will He* not much more *clothe* you? You of little faith!

31 "Do not worry then, saying, 'What will we eat?' or 'What will we drink?' or 'What will we wear for clothing?'

32 "For the Gentiles eagerly seek all these things; for your heavenly Father knows that you need all these things.

33 "But seek first His kingdom and His righteousness, and all these things will be added to you.

34 "So do not worry about tomorrow; for tomorrow will care for itself. Each day has enough trouble of its own.

NEW CENTURY VERSION

Don't Worry

25"So I tell you, don't worry about the food or drink you need to live, or about the clothes you need for your body. Life is more than food, and the body is more than clothes.
26Look at the birds in the air. They don't plant or harvest or store food in barns, but your heavenly Father feeds them. And you know that you are worth much more than the birds. 27You cannot add any time to your life by worrying about it.

28"And why do you worry about clothes? Look at how the lilies in the field grow. They don't work or make clothes for themselves. 29But I tell you that even Solomon with his riches was not dressed as beautifully as one of these flowers. 30God clothes the grass in the field, which is alive today but tomorrow is thrown into the fire. So you can be even more sure that God will clothe you. Don't have so little faith! 31Don't worry and say, 'What will we eat?' or 'What will we drink?' or 'What will we wear?' 32The people who don't know God keep trying to get these things, and your Father in heaven knows you need them.
33The thing you should want most is God's kingdom and doing what God wants. Then all these other things you need will be given to you. 34So don't worry about tomorrow, because tomorrow will have its own worries. Each day has enough trouble of its own.

CONTEMPORARY ENGLISH VERSION

Worry (Luke 12.22-31)

25I tell you not to worry about your life. Don't worry about having something to eat, drink, or wear. Isn't life more than food or clothing? 26Look at the birds in the sky! They don't plant or harvest. They don't even store grain in barns. Yet your Father in heaven takes care of them. Aren't you worth more than birds?

27Can worry make you live longer?[e] 28Why worry about clothes? Look how the wild flowers grow. They don't work hard to make their clothes. 29But I tell you that Solomon with all his wealth[f] wasn't as well clothed as one of them. 30God gives such beauty to everything that grows in the fields, even though it is here today and thrown into a fire tomorrow. He will surely do even more for you! Why do you have such little faith?

31Don't worry and ask yourselves, "Will we have anything to eat? Will we have anything to drink? Will we have any clothes to wear?" 32Only people who don't know God are always worrying about such things. Your Father in heaven knows that you need all of these. 33But more than anything else, put God's work first and do what he wants. Then the other things will be yours as well.

34Don't worry about tomorrow. It will take care of itself. You have enough to worry about today.

[e] 6.27 *live longer*: Or "grow taller." [f] 6.29 *Solomon with all his wealth*: The Jewish people thought that Solomon was the richest person who had ever lived.

NEW INTERNATIONAL VERSION

Do Not Worry

25 “Therefore I tell you, do not worry about your life, what you will eat or drink; or about your body, what you will wear. Is not life more important than food, and the body more important than clothes? 26 Look at the birds of the air; they do not sow or reap or store away in barns, and yet your heavenly Father feeds them. Are you not much more valuable than they? 27 Who of you by worrying can add a single hour to his life[b]?

28 “And why do you worry about clothes? See how the lilies of the field grow. They do not labor or spin. 29 Yet I tell you that not even Solomon in all his splendor was dressed like one of these. 30 If that is how God clothes the grass of the field, which is here today and tomorrow is thrown into the fire, will he not much more clothe you, O you of little faith? 31 So do not worry, saying, ‘What shall we eat?’ or ‘What shall we drink?’ or ‘What shall we wear?’ 32 For the pagans run after all these things, and your heavenly Father knows that you need them. 33 But seek first his kingdom and his righteousness, and all these things will be given to you as well. 34 Therefore do not worry about tomorrow, for tomorrow will worry about itself. Each day has enough trouble of its own.

[b] 27 Or *single cubit to his height*

NEW LIVING TRANSLATION

25 “So I tell you, don’t worry about everyday life—whether you have enough food, drink, and clothes. Doesn’t life consist of more than food and clothing? 26 Look at the birds. They don’t need to plant or harvest or put food in barns because your heavenly Father feeds them. And you are far more valuable to him than they are. 27 Can all your worries add a single moment to your life? Of course not.

28 “And why worry about your clothes? Look at the lilies and how they grow. They don’t work or make their clothing, 29 yet Solomon in all his glory was not dressed as beautifully as they are. 30 And if God cares so wonderfully for flowers that are here today and gone tomorrow, won’t he more surely care for you? You have so little faith!

31 “So don’t worry about having enough food or drink or clothing. 32 Why be like the pagans who are so deeply concerned about these things? Your heavenly Father already knows all your needs, 33 and he will give you all you need from day to day if you live for him and make the Kingdom of God your primary concern.

34 “So don’t worry about tomorrow, for tomorrow will bring its own worries. Today’s trouble is enough for today.

NEW KING JAMES VERSION

Do Not Worry

25 “Therefore I say to you, do not worry about your life, what you will eat or what you will drink; nor about your body, what you will put on. Is not life more than food and the body more than clothing? 26 Look at the birds of the air, for they neither sow nor reap nor gather into barns; yet your heavenly Father feeds them. Are you not of more value than they? 27 Which of you by worrying can add one cubit to his stature?

28 “So why do you worry about clothing? Consider the lilies of the field, how they grow: they neither toil nor spin; 29 and yet I say to you that even Solomon in all his glory was not arrayed like one of these. 30 Now if God so clothes the grass of the field, which today is, and tomorrow is thrown into the oven, *will He* not much more *clothe* you, O you of little faith?

31 “Therefore do not worry, saying, ‘What shall we eat?’ or ‘What shall we drink?’ or ‘What shall we wear?’ 32 For after all these things the Gentiles seek. For your heavenly Father knows that you need all these things. 33 But seek first the kingdom of God and His righteousness, and all these things shall be added to you. 34 Therefore do not worry about tomorrow, for tomorrow will worry about its own things. Sufficient for the day *is* its own trouble.

THE MESSAGE

“If you decide for God, living a life of God-worship, it follows that you don’t fuss about what’s on the table at mealtimes or whether the clothes in your closet are in fashion. There is far more to your life than the food you put in your stomach, more to your outer appearance than the clothes you hang on your body. Look at the birds, free and unfettered, not tied down to a job description, careless in the care of God. And you count far more to him than birds.

“Has anyone by fussing in front of the mirror ever gotten taller by so much as an inch? All this time and money wasted on fashion—do you think it makes that much difference? Instead of looking at the fashions, walk out into the fields and look at the wildflowers. They never primp or shop, but have you ever seen color and design quite like it? The ten best-dressed men and women in the country look shabby alongside them.

“If God gives such attention to the appearance of wildflowers—most of which are never even seen—don’t you think he’ll attend to you, take pride in you, do his best for you? What I’m trying to do here is to get you to relax, to not be so preoccupied with *getting*, so you can respond to God’s *giving*. People who don’t know God and the way he works fuss over these things, but you know both God and how he works. Steep your life in God-reality, God-initiative, God-provisions. Don’t worry about missing out. You’ll find all your everyday human concerns will be met.

“Give your entire attention to what God is doing right now, and don’t get worked up about what may or may not happen tomorrow. God will help you deal with whatever hard things come up when the time comes.

KING JAMES VERSION

7 Judge not, that ye be not judged.

2 For with what judgment ye judge, ye shall be judged: and with what measure ye mete, it shall be measured to you again.

3 And why beholdest thou the mote that is in thy brother's eye, but considerest not the beam that is in thine own eye?

4 Or how wilt thou say to thy brother, Let me pull out the mote out of thine eye; and, behold, a beam *is* in thine own eye?

5 Thou hypocrite, first cast out the beam out of thine own eye; and then shalt thou see clearly to cast out the mote out of thy brother's eye.

6 Give not that which is holy unto the dogs, neither cast ye your pearls before swine, lest they trample them under their feet, and turn again and rend you.

7 ¶ Ask, and it shall be given you; seek, and ye shall find; knock, and it shall be opened unto you:

8 For every one that asketh receiveth; and he that seeketh findeth; and to him that knocketh it shall be opened.

9 Or what man is there of you, whom if his son ask bread, will he give him a stone?

10 Or if he ask a fish, will he give him a serpent?

11 If ye then, being evil, know how to give good gifts unto your children, how much more shall your Father which is in heaven give good things to them that ask him?

NEW AMERICAN STANDARD BIBLE

Judging Others

7 "Do not judge so that you will not be judged.

2 "For in the way you judge, you will be judged; and by your standard of measure, it will be measured to you.

3 "Why do you look at the speck that is in your brother's eye, but do not notice the log that is in your own eye?

4 "Or how can you say to your brother, 'Let me take the speck out of your eye,' and behold, the log is in your own eye?

5 "You hypocrite, first take the log out of your own eye, and then you will see clearly to take the speck out of your brother's eye.

6 "Do not give what is holy to dogs, and do not throw your pearls before swine, or they will trample them under their feet, and turn and tear you to pieces.

Prayer and the Golden Rule

7 "Ask, and it will be given to you; seek, and you will find; knock, and it will be opened to you.

8 "For everyone who asks receives, and he who seeks finds, and to him who knocks it will be opened.

9 "Or what man is there among you who, when his son asks for a loaf, will give him a stone?

10 "Or if he asks for a fish, he will not give him a snake, will he?

11 "If you then, being evil, know how to give good gifts to your children, how much more will your Father who is in heaven give what is good to those who ask Him!

NEW CENTURY VERSION

Be Careful About Judging Others

7 "Don't judge other people, or you will be judged. 2You
will be judged in the same way that you judge others,
and the amount you give to others will be given to you.
3"Why do you notice the little piece of dust in your
friend's eye, but you don't notice the big piece of wood in
your own eye? 4How can you say to your friend, 'Let me
take that little piece of dust out of your eye'? Look at yourself! You still have that big piece of wood in your own eye.
5You hypocrite! First, take the wood out of your own eye.
Then you will see clearly to take the dust out of your
friend's eye.
6"Don't give holy things to dogs, and don't throw your
pearls before pigs. Pigs will only trample on them, and
dogs will turn to attack you.

Ask God for What You Need

7"Ask, and God will give to you. Search, and you will
find. Knock, and the door will open for you. 8Yes, everyone
who asks will receive. Everyone who searches will find.
And everyone who knocks will have the door opened.
9"If your children ask for bread, which of you would give
them a stone? 10Or if your children ask for a fish, would
you give them a snake? 11Even though you are bad, you
know how to give good gifts to your children. How much
more your heavenly Father will give good things to those
who ask him!

CONTEMPORARY ENGLISH VERSION

Judging Others (Luke 6.37, 38, 41, 42)

7 Don't condemn others, and God won't condemn you.
2God will be as hard on you as you are on others! He
will treat you exactly as you treat them.
3You can see the speck in your friend's eye, but you
don't notice the log in your own eye. 4How can you say,
"My friend, let me take the speck out of your eye," when
you don't see the log in your own eye? 5You're nothing
but show-offs! First, take the log out of your own eye.
Then you can see how to take the speck out of your
friend's eye.
6Don't give to dogs what belongs to God. They will
only turn and attack you. Don't throw pearls down in
front of pigs. They will trample all over them.

Ask, Search, Knock (Luke 11.9-13)

7Ask, and you will receive. Search, and you will find.
Knock, and the door will be opened for you. 8Everyone
who asks will receive. Everyone who searches will find.
And the door will be opened for everyone who knocks.
9Would any of you give your hungry child a stone, if the
child asked for some bread? 10Would you give your child
a snake if the child asked for a fish? 11As bad as you
are, you still know how to give good gifts to your children. But your heavenly Father is even more ready to
give good things to people who ask.

NEW INTERNATIONAL VERSION

Judging Others

7 "Do not judge, or you too will be judged. 2For in the same way you judge others, you will be judged, and with the measure you use, it will be measured to you.

3"Why do you look at the speck of sawdust in your brother's eye and pay no attention to the plank in your own eye? 4How can you say to your brother, 'Let me take the speck out of your eye,' when all the time there is a plank in your own eye? 5You hypocrite, first take the plank out of your own eye, and then you will see clearly to remove the speck from your brother's eye.

6"Do not give dogs what is sacred; do not throw your pearls to pigs. If you do, they may trample them under their feet, and then turn and tear you to pieces.

Ask, Seek, Knock

7"Ask and it will be given to you; seek and you will find; knock and the door will be opened to you. 8For everyone who asks receives; he who seeks finds; and to him who knocks, the door will be opened.

9"Which of you, if his son asks for bread, will give him a stone? 10Or if he asks for a fish, will give him a snake? 11If you, then, though you are evil, know how to give good gifts to your children, how much more will your Father in heaven give good gifts to those who ask him!

NEW LIVING TRANSLATION

Don't Condemn Others

7 "Stop judging others, and you will not be judged. 2For others will treat you as you treat them.* Whatever measure you use in judging others, it will be used to measure how you are judged. 3And why worry about a speck in your friend's eye* when you have a log in your own? 4How can you think of saying, 'Let me help you get rid of that speck in your eye,' when you can't see past the log in your own eye? 5Hypocrite! First get rid of the log from your own eye; then perhaps you will see well enough to deal with the speck in your friend's eye.

6"Don't give what is holy to unholy people.* Don't give pearls to swine! They will trample the pearls, then turn and attack you.

Effective Prayer

7"Keep on asking, and you will be given what you ask for. Keep on looking, and you will find. Keep on knocking, and the door will be opened. 8For everyone who asks, receives. Everyone who seeks, finds. And the door is opened to everyone who knocks. 9You parents—if your children ask for a loaf of bread, do you give them a stone instead? 10Or if they ask for a fish, do you give them a snake? Of course not! 11If you sinful people know how to give good gifts to your children, how much more will your heavenly Father give good gifts to those who ask him.

7:2 Or *For God will treat you as you treat others;* Greek reads *For with the judgment you judge you will be judged.* 7:3 Greek *your brother's eye;* also in 7:5. 7:6 Greek *Don't give the sacred to dogs.*

NEW KING JAMES VERSION

Do Not Judge

7 "Judge not, that you be not judged. 2For with what judgment you judge, you will be judged; and with the measure you use, it will be measured back to you. 3And why do you look at the speck in your brother's eye, but do not consider the plank in your own eye? 4Or how can you say to your brother, 'Let me remove the speck from your eye'; and look, a plank *is* in your own eye? 5Hypocrite! First remove the plank from your own eye, and then you will see clearly to remove the speck from your brother's eye.

6"Do not give what is holy to the dogs; nor cast your pearls before swine, lest they trample them under their feet, and turn and tear you in pieces.

Keep Asking, Seeking, Knocking

7"Ask, and it will be given to you; seek, and you will find; knock, and it will be opened to you. 8For everyone who asks receives, and he who seeks finds, and to him who knocks it will be opened. 9Or what man is there among you who, if his son asks for bread, will give him a stone? 10Or if he asks for a fish, will he give him a serpent? 11If you then, being evil, know how to give good gifts to your children, how much more will your Father who is in heaven give good things to those who ask Him!

THE MESSAGE

A Simple Guide for Behavior

7 "Don't pick on people, jump on their failures, criticize their faults—unless, of course, you want the same treatment. That critical spirit has a way of boomeranging. It's easy to see a smudge on your neighbor's face and be oblivious to the ugly sneer on your own. Do you have the nerve to say, 'Let me wash your face for you,' when your own face is distorted by contempt? It's this whole traveling road-show mentality all over again, playing a holier-than-thou part instead of just living your part. Wipe that ugly sneer off your own face, and you might be fit to offer a washcloth to your neighbor.

"Don't be flip with the sacred. Banter and silliness give no honor to God. Don't reduce holy mysteries to slogans. In trying to be relevant, you're only being cute and inviting sacrilege.

"Don't bargain with God. Be direct. Ask for what you need. This isn't a cat-and-mouse, hide-and-seek game we're in. If your child asks for bread, do you trick him with sawdust? If he asks for fish, do you scare him with a live snake on his plate? As bad as you are, you wouldn't think of such a thing. You're at least decent to your own children. So don't you think the God who conceived you in love will be even better?

KING JAMES VERSION

12 ¶ Therefore all things whatsoever ye would that men should do to you, do ye even so to them: for this is the law and the prophets.

13 Enter ye in at the strait gate: for wide *is* the gate, and broad *is* the way, that leadeth to destruction, and many there be which go in thereat:

14 Because strait *is* the gate, and narrow *is* the way, which leadeth unto life, and few there be that find it.

15 ¶ Beware of false prophets, which come to you in sheep's clothing, but inwardly they are ravening wolves.

16 Ye shall know them by their fruits. Do men gather grapes of thorns, or figs of thistles?

17 Even so every good tree bringeth forth good fruit; but a corrupt tree bringeth forth evil fruit.

18 A good tree cannot bring forth evil fruit, neither *can* a corrupt tree bring forth good fruit.

19 Every tree that bringeth not forth good fruit is hewn down, and cast into the fire.

20 Wherefore by their fruits ye shall know them.

21 ¶ Not every one that saith unto me, Lord, Lord, shall enter into the kingdom of heaven; but he that doeth the will of my Father which is in heaven.

NEW AMERICAN STANDARD BIBLE

12 "In everything, therefore, treat people the same way you want them to treat you, for this is the Law and the Prophets.

The Narrow and Wide Gates

13 "Enter through the narrow gate; for the gate is wide and the way is broad that leads to destruction, and there are many who enter through it.

14 "For the gate is small and the way is narrow that leads to life, and there are few who find it.

A Tree and Its Fruit

15 "Beware of the false prophets, who come to you in sheep's clothing, but inwardly are ravenous wolves.

16 "You will know them by their fruits. Grapes are not gathered from thorn *bushes* nor figs from thistles, are they?

17 "So every good tree bears good fruit, but the bad tree bears bad fruit.

18 "A good tree cannot produce bad fruit, nor can a bad tree produce good fruit.

19 "Every tree that does not bear good fruit is cut down and thrown into the fire.

20 "So then, you will know them by their fruits.

21 "Not everyone who says to Me, 'Lord, Lord,' will enter the kingdom of heaven, but he who does the will of My Father who is in heaven *will enter*.

NEW CENTURY VERSION

The Most Important Rule

12"Do to others what you want them to do to you. This is the meaning of the law of Moses and the teaching of the prophets.

The Way to Heaven Is Hard

13"Enter through the narrow gate. The gate is wide and the road is wide that leads to hell, and many people enter through that gate. 14But the gate is small and the road is narrow that leads to true life. Only a few people find that road.

People Know You by Your Actions

15"Be careful of false prophets. They come to you looking gentle like sheep, but they are really dangerous like wolves. 16You will know these people by what they do. Grapes don't come from thornbushes, and figs don't come from thorny weeds. 17In the same way, every good tree produces good fruit, but a bad tree produces bad fruit. 18A good tree cannot produce bad fruit, and a bad tree cannot produce good fruit. 19Every tree that does not produce good fruit is cut down and thrown into the fire. 20In the same way, you will know these false prophets by what they do.

21"Not all those who say that I am their Lord will enter the kingdom of heaven. The only people who will enter the kingdom of heaven are those who do what my Father in

CONTEMPORARY ENGLISH VERSION

12Treat others as you want them to treat you. This is what the Law and the Prophets[a] are all about.

The Narrow Gate (Luke 13.24)

13Go in through the narrow gate. The gate to destruction is wide, and the road that leads there is easy to follow. A lot of people go through that gate. 14But the gate to life is very narrow. The road that leads there is so hard to follow that only a few people find it.

A Tree and Its Fruit (Luke 6.43-45)

15Watch out for false prophets! They dress up like sheep, but inside they are wolves who have come to attack you. 16You can tell what they are by what they do. No one picks grapes or figs from thornbushes. 17A good tree produces good fruit, and a bad tree produces bad fruit. 18A good tree cannot produce bad fruit, and a bad tree cannot produce good fruit. 19Every tree that produces bad fruit will be chopped down and burned. 20You can tell who the false prophets are by their deeds.

A Warning (Luke 13.26, 27)

21Not everyone who calls me their Lord will get into the kingdom of heaven. Only the ones who obey my

[a] 7.12 *the Law and the Prophets*: See the note at 5.17.

NEW INTERNATIONAL VERSION

[12]So in everything, do to others what you would have
them do to you, for this sums up the Law and the
Prophets.

The Narrow and Wide Gates

[13]"Enter through the narrow gate. For wide is the gate
and broad is the road that leads to destruction, and many
enter through it. [14]But small is the gate and narrow the
road that leads to life, and only a few find it.

A Tree and Its Fruit

[15]"Watch out for false prophets. They come to you in
sheep's clothing, but inwardly they are ferocious wolves.
[16]By their fruit you will recognize them. Do people pick
grapes from thornbushes, or figs from thistles? [17]Likewise
every good tree bears good fruit, but a bad tree bears bad
fruit. [18]A good tree cannot bear bad fruit, and a bad tree
cannot bear good fruit. [19]Every tree that does not bear
good fruit is cut down and thrown into the fire. [20]Thus, by
their fruit you will recognize them.

[21]"Not everyone who says to me, 'Lord, Lord,' will enter
the kingdom of heaven, but only he who does the will of

NEW LIVING TRANSLATION

The Golden Rule

[12]"Do for others what you would like them to do for you.
This is a summary of all that is taught in the law and the
prophets.

The Narrow Gate

[13]"You can enter God's Kingdom only through the narrow
gate. The highway to hell* is broad, and its gate is wide for
the many who choose the easy way. [14]But the gateway to life
is small, and the road is narrow, and only a few ever find it.

The Tree and Its Fruit

[15]"Beware of false prophets who come disguised as
harmless sheep, but are really wolves that will tear you
apart. [16]You can detect them by the way they act, just as
you can identify a tree by its fruit. You don't pick grapes
from thornbushes, or figs from thistles. [17]A healthy tree
produces good fruit, and an unhealthy tree produces bad
fruit. [18]A good tree can't produce bad fruit, and a bad tree
can't produce good fruit. [19]So every tree that does not pro-
duce good fruit is chopped down and thrown into the fire.
[20]Yes, the way to identify a tree or a person is by the kind
of fruit that is produced.

True Disciples

[21]"Not all people who sound religious are really godly.
They may refer to me as 'Lord,' but they still won't enter
the Kingdom of Heaven. The decisive issue is whether they

7:13 Greek *The way that leads to destruction.*

NEW KING JAMES VERSION

[12]Therefore, whatever you want men to do to you, do also
to them, for this is the Law and the Prophets.

The Narrow Way

[13]"Enter by the narrow gate; for wide *is* the gate and
broad *is* the way that leads to destruction, and there are
many who go in by it. [14]Because[a] narrow *is* the gate and
difficult *is* the way which leads to life, and there are few
who find it.

You Will Know Them by Their Fruits

[15]"Beware of false prophets, who come to you in sheep's
clothing, but inwardly they are ravenous wolves. [16]You
will know them by their fruits. Do men gather grapes from
thornbushes or figs from thistles? [17]Even so, every good
tree bears good fruit, but a bad tree bears bad fruit. [18]A
good tree cannot bear bad fruit, nor *can* a bad tree bear
good fruit. [19]Every tree that does not bear good fruit is cut
down and thrown into the fire. [20]Therefore by their fruits
you will know them.

I Never Knew You

[21]"Not everyone who says to Me, 'Lord, Lord,' shall enter
the kingdom of heaven, but he who does the will of My

7:14 [a] NU-Text and M-Text read *How . . . !*

THE MESSAGE

"Here is a simple, rule-of-thumb guide for behavior: Ask yourself what you want people to do for you, then grab the initiative and do it for *them*. Add up God's Law and Prophets and this is what you get.

Being and Doing

"Don't look for shortcuts to God. The market is flooded with surefire, easygoing formulas for a successful life that can be practiced in your spare time. Don't fall for that stuff, even though crowds of people do. The way to life—to God!—is vigorous and requires total attention.

"Be wary of false preachers who smile a lot, dripping with practiced sincerity. Chances are they are out to rip you off some way or other. Don't be impressed with charisma; look for character. Who preachers *are* is the main thing, not what they say. A genuine leader will never exploit your emotions or your pocketbook. These diseased trees with their bad apples are going to be chopped down and burned.

"Knowing the correct password—saying 'Master, Master,' for instance—isn't going to get you anywhere with me. What is required is serious obedience—*doing*

KING JAMES VERSION

22 Many will say to me in that day, Lord, Lord, have we not prophesied in thy name? and in thy name have cast out devils? and in thy name done many wonderful works?

23 And then will I profess unto them, I never knew you: depart from me, ye that work iniquity.

24 Therefore whosoever heareth these sayings of mine, and doeth them, I will liken him unto a wise man, which built his house upon a rock:

25 And the rain descended, and the floods came, and the winds blew, and beat upon that house; and it fell not: for it was founded upon a rock.

26 And every one that heareth these sayings of mine, and doeth them not, shall be likened unto a foolish man, which built his house upon the sand:

27 And the rain descended, and the floods came, and the winds blew, and beat upon that house; and it fell: and great was the fall of it.

28 And it came to pass, when Jesus had ended these sayings, the people were astonished at his doctrine:

29 For he taught them as *one* having authority, and not as the scribes.

8 When he was come down from the mountain, great multitudes followed him.

2 And, behold, there came a leper and worshipped him, saying, Lord, if thou wilt, thou canst make me clean.

NEW AMERICAN STANDARD BIBLE

22 "Many will say to Me on that day, 'Lord, Lord, did we not prophesy in Your name, and in Your name cast out demons, and in Your name perform many miracles?'

23 "And then I will declare to them, 'I never knew you; DEPART FROM ME, YOU WHO PRACTICE LAWLESSNESS.'

The Two Foundations

24 "Therefore everyone who hears these words of Mine and acts on them, may be compared to a wise man who built his house on the rock.

25 "And the rain fell, and the floods came, and the winds blew and slammed against that house; and *yet* it did not fall, for it had been founded on the rock.

26 "Everyone who hears these words of Mine and does not act on them, will be like a foolish man who built his house on the sand.

27 "The rain fell, and the floods came, and the winds blew and slammed against that house; and it fell—and great was its fall."

28 When Jesus had finished these words, the crowds were amazed at His teaching;

29 for He was teaching them as *one* having authority, and not as their scribes.

Jesus Cleanses a Leper; The Centurion's Faith

8 When Jesus came down from the mountain, large crowds followed Him.

2 And a leper came to Him and bowed down before Him, and said, "Lord, if You are willing, You can make me clean."

NEW CENTURY VERSION

heaven wants. 22On the last day many people will say to me, 'Lord, Lord, we spoke for you, and through you we forced out demons and did many miracles.' 23Then I will tell them clearly, 'Get away from me, you who do evil. I never knew you.'

Two Kinds of People

24"Everyone who hears my words and obeys them is like a wise man who built his house on rock. 25It rained hard, the floods came, and the winds blew and hit that house. But it did not fall, because it was built on rock. 26Everyone who hears my words and does not obey them is like a foolish man who built his house on sand. 27It rained hard, the floods came, and the winds blew and hit that house, and it fell with a big crash."

28When Jesus finished saying these things, the people were amazed at his teaching, 29because he did not teach like their teachers of the law. He taught like a person who had authority.

Jesus Heals a Sick Man

8 When Jesus came down from the hill, great crowds followed him. 2Then a man with a skin disease came to Jesus. The man bowed down before him and said, "Lord, you can heal me if you will."

CONTEMPORARY ENGLISH VERSION

Father in heaven will get in. 22On the day of judgment many will call me their Lord. They will say, "We preached in your name, and in your name we forced out demons and worked many miracles." 23But I will tell them, "I will have nothing to do with you! Get out of my sight, you evil people!"

Two Builders (Luke 6.47-49)

24Anyone who hears and obeys these teachings of mine is like a wise person who built a house on solid rock. 25Rain poured down, rivers flooded, and winds beat against that house. But it did not fall, because it was built on solid rock.

26Anyone who hears my teachings and doesn't obey them is like a foolish person who built a house on sand. 27The rain poured down, the rivers flooded, and the winds blew and beat against that house. Finally, it fell with a crash.

28When Jesus finished speaking, the crowds were surprised at his teaching. 29He taught them like someone with authority, and not like their teachers of the Law of Moses.

Jesus Heals a Man (Mark 1.40-45; Luke 5.12-16)

8 As Jesus came down the mountain, he was followed by large crowds. 2Suddenly a man with leprosy[a] came and knelt in front of Jesus. He said, "Lord, you have the power to make me well, if only you wanted to."

[a] **8.2** *leprosy*: In biblical times the word "leprosy" was used for many different kinds of skin diseases.

NEW INTERNATIONAL VERSION

my Father who is in heaven. 22Many will say to me on that day, 'Lord, Lord, did we not prophesy in your name, and in your name drive out demons and perform many miracles?' 23Then I will tell them plainly, 'I never knew you. Away from me, you evildoers!'

The Wise and Foolish Builders

24"Therefore everyone who hears these words of mine and puts them into practice is like a wise man who built his house on the rock. 25The rain came down, the streams rose, and the winds blew and beat against that house; yet it did not fall, because it had its foundation on the rock. 26But everyone who hears these words of mine and does not put them into practice is like a foolish man who built his house on sand. 27The rain came down, the streams rose, and the winds blew and beat against that house, and it fell with a great crash."

28When Jesus had finished saying these things, the crowds were amazed at his teaching, 29because he taught as one who had authority, and not as their teachers of the law.

The Man With Leprosy

8 When he came down from the mountainside, large crowds followed him. 2A man with leprosy[a] came and knelt before him and said, "Lord, if you are willing, you can make me clean."

[a] *2* The Greek word was used for various diseases affecting the skin—not necessarily leprosy.

NEW LIVING TRANSLATION

obey my Father in heaven. 22On judgment day many will tell me, 'Lord, Lord, we prophesied in your name and cast out demons in your name and performed many miracles in your name.' 23But I will reply, 'I never knew you. Go away; the things you did were unauthorized.*'

Building on a Solid Foundation

24"Anyone who listens to my teaching and obeys me is wise, like a person who builds a house on solid rock. 25Though the rain comes in torrents and the floodwaters rise and the winds beat against that house, it won't collapse, because it is built on rock. 26But anyone who hears my teaching and ignores it is foolish, like a person who builds a house on sand. 27When the rains and floods come and the winds beat against that house, it will fall with a mighty crash."

28After Jesus finished speaking, the crowds were amazed at his teaching, 29for he taught as one who had real authority—quite unlike the teachers of religious law.

Jesus Heals a Man with Leprosy

8 Large crowds followed Jesus as he came down the mountainside. 2Suddenly, a man with leprosy approached Jesus. He knelt before him, worshiping. "Lord," the man said, "if you want to, you can make me well again."

7:23 Or *unlawful.*

NEW KING JAMES VERSION

Father in heaven. 22Many will say to Me in that day, 'Lord, Lord, have we not prophesied in Your name, cast out demons in Your name, and done many wonders in Your name?' 23And then I will declare to them, 'I never knew you; depart from Me, you who practice lawlessness!'

Build on the Rock

24"Therefore whoever hears these sayings of Mine, and does them, I will liken him to a wise man who built his house on the rock: 25and the rain descended, the floods came, and the winds blew and beat on that house; and it did not fall, for it was founded on the rock.

26"But everyone who hears these sayings of Mine, and does not do them, will be like a foolish man who built his house on the sand: 27and the rain descended, the floods came, and the winds blew and beat on that house; and it fell. And great was its fall."

28And so it was, when Jesus had ended these sayings, that the people were astonished at His teaching, 29for He taught them as one having authority, and not as the scribes.

Jesus Cleanses a Leper

8 When He had come down from the mountain, great multitudes followed Him. 2And behold, a leper came and worshiped Him, saying, "Lord, if You are willing, You can make me clean."

THE MESSAGE

what my Father wills. I can see it now—at the Final Judgment thousands strutting up to me and saying, 'Master, we preached the Message, we bashed the demons, our God-sponsored projects had everyone talking.' And do you know what I am going to say? 'You missed the boat. All you did was use me to make yourselves important. You don't impress me one bit. You're out of here.'

"These words I speak to you are not incidental additions to your life, homeowner improvements to your standard of living. They are foundational words, words to build a life on. If you work these words into your life, you are like a smart carpenter who built his house on solid rock. Rain poured down, the river flooded, a tornado hit—but nothing moved that house. It was fixed to the rock.

"But if you just use my words in Bible studies and don't work them into your life, you are like a stupid carpenter who built his house on the sandy beach. When a storm rolled in and the waves came up, it collapsed like a house of cards."

When Jesus concluded his address, the crowd burst into applause. They had never heard teaching like this. It was apparent that he was living everything he was saying—quite a contrast to their religion teachers! This was the best teaching they had ever heard.

He Carried Our Diseases

8 Jesus came down the mountain with the cheers of the crowd still ringing in his ears. Then a leper appeared and went to his knees before Jesus, praying, "Master, if you want to, you can heal my body."

KING JAMES VERSION

3 And Jesus put forth *his* hand, and touched him, saying, I will; be thou clean. And immediately his leprosy was cleansed.

4 And Jesus saith unto him, See thou tell no man; but go thy way, shew thyself to the priest, and offer the gift that Moses commanded, for a testimony unto them.

5 ¶ And when Jesus was entered into Capernaum, there came unto him a centurion, beseeching him,

6 And saying, Lord, my servant lieth at home sick of the palsy, grievously tormented.

7 And Jesus saith unto him, I will come and heal him.

8 The centurion answered and said, Lord, I am not worthy that thou shouldest come under my roof: but speak the word only, and my servant shall be healed.

9 For I am a man under authority, having soldiers under me: and I say to this *man*, Go, and he goeth; and to another, Come, and he cometh; and to my servant, Do this, and he doeth *it*.

10 When Jesus heard *it*, he marvelled, and said to them that followed, Verily I say unto you, I have not found so great faith, no, not in Israel.

11 And I say unto you, That many shall come from the east and west, and shall sit down with Abraham, and Isaac, and Jacob, in the kingdom of heaven.

12 But the children of the kingdom shall be cast out

NEW AMERICAN STANDARD BIBLE

3 Jesus stretched out His hand and touched him, saying, "I am willing; be cleansed." And immediately his leprosy was cleansed.

4 And Jesus *said to him, "See that you tell no one; but go, show yourself to the priest and present the offering that Moses commanded, as a testimony to them."

5 And when Jesus entered Capernaum, a centurion came to Him, imploring Him,

6 and saying, "Lord, my servant is lying paralyzed at home, fearfully tormented."

7 Jesus *said to him, "I will come and heal him."

8 But the centurion said, "Lord, I am not worthy for You to come under my roof, but just say the word, and my servant will be healed.

9 "For I also am a man under authority, with soldiers under me; and I say to this one, 'Go!' and he goes, and to another, 'Come!' and he comes, and to my slave, 'Do this!' and he does *it*."

10 Now when Jesus heard *this*, He marveled and said to those who were following, "Truly I say to you, I have not found such great faith with anyone in Israel.

11 "I say to you that many will come from east and west, and [l]recline *at the table* with Abraham, Isaac and Jacob in the kingdom of heaven;

12 but the sons of the kingdom will be cast out into the

8:11 [l] Or *dine*

NEW CENTURY VERSION

[3]Jesus reached out his hand and touched the man and
said, "I will. Be healed!" And immediately the man was
healed from his disease. [4]Then Jesus said to him, "Don't
tell anyone about this. But go and show yourself to the
priest[a] and offer the gift Moses commanded[b] for people
who are made well. This will show the people what I have
done."

Jesus Heals a Soldier's Servant

[5]When Jesus entered the city of Capernaum, an army
officer came to him, begging for help. [6]The officer said,
"Lord, my servant is at home in bed. He can't move his
body and is in much pain."

[7]Jesus said to the officer, "I will go and heal him."

[8]The officer answered, "Lord, I am not worthy for you to
come into my house. You only need to command it, and my
servant will be healed. [9]I, too, am a man under the author-
ity of others, and I have soldiers under my command. I tell
one soldier, 'Go,' and he goes. I tell another soldier,
'Come,' and he comes. I say to my servant, 'Do this,' and
my servant does it.

[10]When Jesus heard this, he was amazed. He said to
those who were following him, "I tell you the truth, this is
the greatest faith I have found, even in Israel. [11]Many peo-
ple will come from the east and from the west and will sit
and eat with Abraham, Isaac, and Jacob in the kingdom of
heaven. [12]But those people who should be in the kingdom

8:4 [a] **show...priest** The law of Moses said a priest must say when a Jewish person with a skin disease was well. **8:4** [b] **Moses commanded** Read about this in Leviticus 14:1–32.

CONTEMPORARY ENGLISH VERSION

[3]Jesus put his hand on the man and said, "I want to!
Now you are well." At once the man's leprosy disappeared.
[4]Jesus told him, "Don't tell anyone about this, but go and
show the priest that you are well. Then take a gift to the
temple just as Moses commanded, and everyone will know
that you have been healed."[b]

Jesus Heals an Army Officer's Servant

(Luke 7.1-10; John 4.43-54)

[5]When Jesus was going into the town of Capernaum, an
army officer came up to him and said, [6]"Lord, my servant
is at home in such terrible pain that he can't even move."
[7]"I will go and heal him," Jesus replied.

[8]But the officer said, "Lord, I'm not good enough for you
to come into my house. Just give the order, and my servant
will get well. [9]I have officers who give orders to me, and I
have soldiers who take orders from me. I can say to one of
them, 'Go!' and he goes. I can say to another, 'Come!' and he
comes. I can say to my servant, 'Do this!' and he will do it."

[10]When Jesus heard this, he was so surprised that he
turned and said to the crowd following him, "I tell you that
in all of Israel I've never found anyone with this much
faith! [11]Many people will come from everywhere to enjoy
the feast in the kingdom of heaven with Abraham, Isaac,
and Jacob. [12]But the ones who should have been in the

[b] **8.4** *everyone will know that you have been healed*: People with leprosy had to be examined by a priest and told that they were well (that is "clean") before they could once again live a normal life in the Jewish community. The gift that Moses commanded was the sacrifice of some lambs together with flour mixed with olive oil.

NEW INTERNATIONAL VERSION

3Jesus reached out his hand and touched the man. "I am willing," he said. "Be clean!" Immediately he was cured[b] of his leprosy. 4Then Jesus said to him, "See that you don't tell anyone. But go, show yourself to the priest and offer the gift Moses commanded, as a testimony to them."

The Faith of the Centurion

5When Jesus had entered Capernaum, a centurion came to him, asking for help. 6"Lord," he said, "my servant lies at home paralyzed and in terrible suffering."

7Jesus said to him, "I will go and heal him."

8The centurion replied, "Lord, I do not deserve to have you come under my roof. But just say the word, and my servant will be healed. 9For I myself am a man under authority, with soldiers under me. I tell this one, 'Go,' and he goes; and that one, 'Come,' and he comes. I say to my servant, 'Do this,' and he does it."

10When Jesus heard this, he was astonished and said to those following him, "I tell you the truth, I have not found anyone in Israel with such great faith. 11I say to you that many will come from the east and the west, and will take their places at the feast with Abraham, Isaac and Jacob in the kingdom of heaven. 12But the subjects of the kingdom

[b] 3 Greek *made clean*

NEW LIVING TRANSLATION

3Jesus touched him. "I want to," he said. "Be healed!" And instantly the leprosy disappeared. 4Then Jesus said to him, "Go right over to the priest and let him examine you. Don't talk to anyone along the way. Take along the offering required in the law of Moses for those who have been healed of leprosy, so everyone will have proof of your healing."

Faith of the Roman Officer

5When Jesus arrived in Capernaum, a Roman officer came and pleaded with him, 6"Lord, my young servant lies in bed, paralyzed and racked with pain."

7Jesus said, "I will come and heal him."

8Then the officer said, "Lord, I am not worthy to have you come into my home. Just say the word from where you are, and my servant will be healed! 9I know, because I am under the authority of my superior officers and I have authority over my soldiers. I only need to say, 'Go,' and they go, or 'Come,' and they come. And if I say to my slaves, 'Do this or that,' they do it."

10When Jesus heard this, he was amazed. Turning to the crowd, he said, "I tell you the truth, I haven't seen faith like this in all the land of Israel! 11And I tell you this, that many Gentiles will come from all over the world and sit down with Abraham, Isaac, and Jacob at the feast in the Kingdom of Heaven. 12But many Israelites—those for

NEW KING JAMES VERSION

3Then Jesus put out *His* hand and touched him, saying, "I am willing; be cleansed." Immediately his leprosy was cleansed.

4And Jesus said to him, "See that you tell no one; but go your way, show yourself to the priest, and offer the gift that Moses commanded, as a testimony to them."

Jesus Heals a Centurion's Servant

5Now when Jesus had entered Capernaum, a centurion came to Him, pleading with Him, 6saying, "Lord, my servant is lying at home paralyzed, dreadfully tormented."

7And Jesus said to him, "I will come and heal him."

8The centurion answered and said, "Lord, I am not worthy that You should come under my roof. But only speak a word, and my servant will be healed. 9For I also am a man under authority, having soldiers under me. And I say to this *one,* 'Go,' and he goes; and to another, 'Come,' and he comes; and to my servant, 'Do this,' and he does *it.*"

10When Jesus heard *it,* He marveled, and said to those who followed, "Assuredly, I say to you, I have not found such great faith, not even in Israel! 11And I say to you that many will come from east and west, and sit down with Abraham, Isaac, and Jacob in the kingdom of heaven. 12But the sons of the kingdom will be cast out into outer

THE MESSAGE

Jesus reached out and touched him, saying, "I want to. Be clean." Then and there, all signs of the leprosy were gone. Jesus said, "Don't talk about this all over town. Just quietly present your healed body to the priest, along with the appropriate expressions of thanks to God. Your cleansed and grateful life, not your words, will bear witness to what I have done."

As Jesus entered the village of Capernaum, a Roman captain came up in a panic and said, "Master, my servant is sick. He can't walk. He's in terrible pain."

Jesus said, "I'll come and heal him."

"Oh, no," said the captain. "I don't want to put you to all that trouble. Just give the order and my servant will be fine. I'm a man who takes orders and gives orders. I tell one soldier, 'Go,' and he goes; to another, 'Come,' and he comes; to my slave, 'Do this,' and he does it."

Taken aback, Jesus said, "I've yet to come across this kind of simple trust in Israel, the very people who are supposed to know all about God and how he works. This man is the vanguard of many outsiders who will soon be coming from all directions—streaming in from the east, pouring in from the west, sitting down at God's kingdom banquet alongside Abraham, Isaac, and Jacob. Then those who grew up 'in the faith' but had no faith will find themselves

KING JAMES VERSION

into outer darkness: there shall be weeping and gnashing of teeth.

13 And Jesus said unto the centurion, Go thy way; and as thou hast believed, *so* be it done unto thee. And his servant was healed in the selfsame hour.

14 ¶ And when Jesus was come into Peter's house, he saw his wife's mother laid, and sick of a fever.

15 And he touched her hand, and the fever left her: and she arose, and ministered unto them.

16 When the even was come, they brought unto him many that were possessed with devils: and he cast out the spirits with *his* word, and healed all that were sick:

17 That it might be fulfilled which was spoken by Esaias the prophet, saying, Himself took our infirmities, and bare *our* sicknesses.

18 ¶ Now when Jesus saw great multitudes about him, he gave commandment to depart unto the other side.

19 And a certain scribe came, and said unto him, Master, I will follow thee whithersoever thou goest.

20 And Jesus saith unto him, The foxes have holes, and the birds of the air *have* nests; but the Son of man hath not where to lay *his* head.

NEW AMERICAN STANDARD BIBLE

outer darkness; in that place there will be weeping and gnashing of teeth."

13 And Jesus said to the centurion, "Go; it shall be done for you as you have believed." And the servant was healed that *very* moment.

Peter's Mother-in-law Healed; Many Healed

14 When Jesus came into Peter's home, He saw his mother-in-law lying sick in bed with a fever.

15 He touched her hand, and the fever left her; and she got up and waited on Him.

16 When evening came, they brought to Him many who were demon-possessed; and He cast out the spirits with a word, and healed all who were ill.

17 *This was* to fulfill what was spoken through Isaiah the prophet: "HE HIMSELF TOOK OUR INFIRMITIES AND CARRIED AWAY OUR DISEASES."

Discipleship Tested

18 Now when Jesus saw a crowd around Him, He gave orders to depart to the other side *of the sea*.

19 Then a scribe came and said to Him, "Teacher, I will follow You wherever You go."

20 Jesus *said to him, "The foxes have holes and the birds of the air *have* nests, but the Son of Man has nowhere to lay His head."

NEW CENTURY VERSION

will be thrown outside into the darkness, where people will cry and grind their teeth with pain."

13Then Jesus said to the officer, "Go home. Your servant will be healed just as you believed he would." And his servant was healed that same hour.

Jesus Heals Many People

14When Jesus went to Peter's house, he saw that Peter's mother-in-law was sick in bed with a fever. 15Jesus touched her hand, and the fever left her. Then she stood up and began to serve Jesus.

16That evening people brought to Jesus many who had demons. Jesus spoke and the demons left them, and he healed all the sick. 17He did these things to bring about what Isaiah the prophet had said:

"He took our suffering on him
 and carried our diseases." *Isaiah 53:4*

People Want to Follow Jesus

18When Jesus saw the crowd around him, he told his followers to go to the other side of the lake. 19Then a teacher of the law came to Jesus and said, "Teacher, I will follow you any place you go."

20Jesus said to him, "The foxes have holes to live in, and the birds have nests, but the Son of Man has no place to rest his head."

CONTEMPORARY ENGLISH VERSION

kingdom will be thrown out into the dark. They will cry and grit their teeth in pain."

13Then Jesus said to the officer, "You may go home now. Your faith has made it happen."

Right then his servant was healed.

Jesus Heals Many People (Mark 1.29-34; Luke 4.38-41)

14Jesus went to the home of Peter, where he found that Peter's mother-in-law was sick in bed with fever. 15He took her by the hand, and the fever left her. Then she got up and served Jesus a meal.

16That evening many people with demons in them were brought to Jesus. And with only a word he forced out the evil spirits and healed everyone who was sick. 17So God's promise came true, just as the prophet Isaiah had said,

"He healed our diseases
 and made us well."

Some Who Wanted To Go with Jesus (Luke 9.57-62)

18When Jesus saw the crowd,[c] he went across Lake Galilee. 19A teacher of the Law of Moses came up to him and said, "Teacher, I'll go anywhere with you!"

20Jesus replied, "Foxes have dens, and birds have nests. But the Son of Man doesn't have a place to call his own."

[c] **8.18** *saw the crowd*: Some manuscripts have "large crowd." Others have "large crowds."

NEW INTERNATIONAL VERSION

will be thrown outside, into the darkness, where there will be weeping and gnashing of teeth."
13Then Jesus said to the centurion, "Go! It will be done just as you believed it would." And his servant was healed at that very hour.

Jesus Heals Many

14When Jesus came into Peter's house, he saw Peter's mother-in-law lying in bed with a fever. 15He touched her hand and the fever left her, and she got up and began to wait on him.
16When evening came, many who were demon-possessed were brought to him, and he drove out the spirits with a word and healed all the sick. 17This was to fulfill what was spoken through the prophet Isaiah:

"He took up our infirmities
and carried our diseases."[c]

The Cost of Following Jesus

18When Jesus saw the crowd around him, he gave orders to cross to the other side of the lake. 19Then a teacher of the law came to him and said, "Teacher, I will follow you wherever you go."
20Jesus replied, "Foxes have holes and birds of the air have nests, but the Son of Man has no place to lay his head."

[c] *17* Isaiah 53:4

NEW LIVING TRANSLATION

whom the Kingdom was prepared—will be cast into outer darkness, where there will be weeping and gnashing of teeth."
13Then Jesus said to the Roman officer, "Go on home. What you have believed has happened." And the young servant was healed that same hour.

Jesus Heals Many People

14When Jesus arrived at Peter's house, Peter's mother-in-law was in bed with a high fever. 15But when Jesus touched her hand, the fever left her. Then she got up and prepared a meal for him.
16That evening many demon-possessed people were brought to Jesus. All the spirits fled when he commanded them to leave; and he healed all the sick. 17This fulfilled the word of the Lord through Isaiah, who said, "He took our sicknesses and removed our diseases."*

The Cost of Following Jesus

18When Jesus noticed how large the crowd was growing, he instructed his disciples to cross to the other side of the lake.
19Then one of the teachers of religious law said to him, "Teacher, I will follow you no matter where you go!"
20But Jesus said, "Foxes have dens to live in, and birds have nests, but I, the Son of Man, have no home of my own, not even a place to lay my head."

8:17 Isa 53:4.

NEW KING JAMES VERSION

darkness. There will be weeping and gnashing of teeth."
13Then Jesus said to the centurion, "Go your way; and as you have believed, *so* let it be done for you." And his servant was healed that same hour.

Peter's Mother-in-Law Healed

14Now when Jesus had come into Peter's house, He saw his wife's mother lying sick with a fever. 15So He touched her hand, and the fever left her. And she arose and served them.[a]

Many Healed After Sabbath Sunset

16When evening had come, they brought to Him many who were demon-possessed. And He cast out the spirits with a word, and healed all who were sick, 17that it might be fulfilled which was spoken by Isaiah the prophet, saying:

*"He Himself took our infirmities
And bore our sicknesses."*[b]

The Cost of Discipleship

18And when Jesus saw great multitudes about Him, He gave a command to depart to the other side. 19Then a certain scribe came and said to Him, "Teacher, I will follow You wherever You go."
20And Jesus said to him, "Foxes have holes and birds of the air *have* nests, but the Son of Man has nowhere to lay *His* head."

8:15 [a] NU-Text and M-Text read *Him*. 8:17 [b] Isaiah 53:4

THE MESSAGE

out in the cold, outsiders to grace and wondering what happened."

Then Jesus turned to the captain and said, "Go. What you believed could happen has happened." At that moment his servant became well.

By this time they were in front of Peter's house. On entering, Jesus found Peter's mother-in-law sick in bed, burning up with fever. He touched her hand and the fever was gone. No sooner was she up on her feet than she was fixing dinner for him.

That evening a lot of demon-afflicted people were brought to him. He relieved the inwardly tormented. He cured the bodily ill. He fulfilled Isaiah's well-known sermon:

"He took our illnesses,
He carried our diseases."

Your Business Is Life, Not Death

When Jesus saw that a curious crowd was growing by the minute, he told his disciples to get him out of there to the other side of the lake. As they left, a religion scholar asked if he could go along. "I'll go with you, wherever," he said.

Jesus was curt: "Are you ready to rough it? We're not staying in the best inns, you know."

KING JAMES VERSION

21 And another of his disciples said unto him, Lord, suffer me first to go and bury my father.

22 But Jesus said unto him, Follow me; and let the dead bury their dead.

23 ¶ And when he was entered into a ship, his disciples followed him.

24 And, behold, there arose a great tempest in the sea, insomuch that the ship was covered with the waves: but he was asleep.

25 And his disciples came to *him*, and awoke him, saying, Lord, save us: we perish.

26 And he saith unto them, Why are ye fearful, O ye of little faith? Then he arose, and rebuked the winds and the sea; and there was a great calm.

27 But the men marvelled, saying, What manner of man is this, that even the winds and the sea obey him!

28 ¶ And when he was come to the other side into the country of the Gergesenes, there met him two possessed with devils, coming out of the tombs, exceeding fierce, so that no man might pass by that way.

29 And, behold, they cried out, saying, What have we to do with thee, Jesus, thou Son of God? art thou come hither to torment us before the time?

NEW AMERICAN STANDARD BIBLE

21 Another of the disciples said to Him, "Lord, permit me first to go and bury my father."

22 But Jesus *said to him, "Follow Me, and allow the dead to bury their own dead."

23 When He got into the boat, His disciples followed Him.

24 And behold, there arose a great storm on the sea, so that the boat was being covered with the waves; but Jesus Himself was asleep.

25 And they came to *Him* and woke Him, saying, "Save *us,* Lord; we are perishing!"

26 He *said to them, "Why are you afraid, you men of little faith?" Then He got up and rebuked the winds and the sea, and it became perfectly calm.

27 The men were amazed, and said, "What kind of a man is this, that even the winds and the sea obey Him?"

Jesus Casts Out Demons

28 When He came to the other side into the country of the Gadarenes, two men who were demon-possessed met Him as they were coming out of the tombs. *They were* so extremely violent that no one could pass by that way.

29 And they cried out, saying, "What business do we have with each other, Son of God? Have You come here to torment us before the time?"

NEW CENTURY VERSION

21Another man, one of Jesus' followers, said to him, "Lord, first let me go and bury my father."

22But Jesus told him, "Follow me, and let the people who are dead bury their own dead."

Jesus Calms a Storm

23Jesus got into a boat, and his followers went with him.
24A great storm arose on the lake so that waves covered the boat, but Jesus was sleeping. 25His followers went to him and woke him, saying, "Lord, save us! We will drown!"

26Jesus answered, "Why are you afraid? You don't have enough faith." Then Jesus got up and gave a command to the wind and the waves, and it became completely calm.

27The men were amazed and said, "What kind of man is this? Even the wind and the waves obey him!"

Jesus Heals Two Men with Demons

28When Jesus arrived at the other side of the lake in the area of the Gadarene[c] people, two men who had demons in them met him. These men lived in the burial caves and were so dangerous that people could not use the road by those caves. 29They shouted, "What do you want with us, Son of God? Did you come here to torture us before the right time?"

8:28 [c] **Gadarene** From Gadara, an area southeast of Lake Galilee.

CONTEMPORARY ENGLISH VERSION

21Another disciple said to Jesus, "Lord, let me wait till I bury my father."

22Jesus answered, "Come with me, and let the dead bury their dead."[d]

A Storm (Mark 4.35-41; Luke 8.22-25)

23After Jesus left in a boat with his disciples, 24a terrible storm suddenly struck the lake, and waves started splashing into their boat.

Jesus was sound asleep, 25so the disciples went over to him and woke him up. They said, "Lord, save us! We're going to drown!"

26But Jesus replied, "Why are you so afraid? You surely don't have much faith." Then he got up and ordered the wind and the waves to calm down. And everything was calm.

27The men in the boat were amazed and said, "Who is this? Even the wind and the waves obey him."

Two Men with Demons in Them (Mark 5.1-20; Luke 8.26-39)

28After Jesus had crossed the lake, he came to shore near the town of Gadara[e] and started down the road. Two men with demons in them came to him from the tombs.[f] They were so fierce that no one could travel that way. 29Suddenly they shouted, "Jesus, Son of God, what do you want with us? Have you come to punish us before our time?"

[d] **8.22** *let the dead bury their dead*: For the Jewish people a proper burial of their dead was a very important duty. But Jesus teaches that following him is even more important. [e] **8.28** *Gadara*: Some manuscripts have "Gergesa." Others have "Gerasa." [f] **8.28** *tombs*: It was thought that demons and evil spirits lived in tombs and in caves that were used for burying the dead.

NEW INTERNATIONAL VERSION

21Another disciple said to him, "Lord, first let me go and bury my father."

22But Jesus told him, "Follow me, and let the dead bury their own dead."

Jesus Calms the Storm

23Then he got into the boat and his disciples followed him. 24Without warning, a furious storm came up on the lake, so that the waves swept over the boat. But Jesus was sleeping. 25The disciples went and woke him, saying, "Lord, save us! We're going to drown!"

26He replied, "You of little faith, why are you so afraid?" Then he got up and rebuked the winds and the waves, and it was completely calm.

27The men were amazed and asked, "What kind of man is this? Even the winds and the waves obey him!"

The Healing of Two Demon-possessed Men

28When he arrived at the other side in the region of the Gadarenes,[d] two demon-possessed men coming from the tombs met him. They were so violent that no one could pass that way. 29"What do you want with us, Son of God?" they shouted. "Have you come here to torture us before the appointed time?"

[d] *28* Some manuscripts *Gergesenes*; others *Gerasenes*

NEW LIVING TRANSLATION

21Another of his disciples said, "Lord, first let me return home and bury my father."

22But Jesus told him, "Follow me now! Let those who are spiritually dead care for their own dead."*

Jesus Calms the Storm

23Then Jesus got into the boat and started across the lake with his disciples. 24Suddenly, a terrible storm came up, with waves breaking into the boat. But Jesus was sleeping. 25The disciples went to him and woke him up, shouting, "Lord, save us! We're going to drown!"

26And Jesus answered, "Why are you afraid? You have so little faith!" Then he stood up and rebuked the wind and waves, and suddenly all was calm. 27The disciples just sat there in awe. "Who is this?" they asked themselves. "Even the wind and waves obey him!"

Jesus Heals Two Demon-Possessed Men

28When Jesus arrived on the other side of the lake in the land of the Gadarenes,* two men who were possessed by demons met him. They lived in a cemetery and were so dangerous that no one could go through that area. 29They began screaming at him, "Why are you bothering us, Son of God? You have no right to torture us before God's

8:22 Greek *Let the dead bury their own dead.* 8:28 Some manuscripts read *Gerasenes;* other manuscripts read *Gergesenes.* See Mark 5:1; Luke 8:26.

NEW KING JAMES VERSION

21Then another of His disciples said to Him, "Lord, let me first go and bury my father."

22But Jesus said to him, "Follow Me, and let the dead bury their own dead."

Wind and Wave Obey Jesus

23Now when He got into a boat, His disciples followed Him. 24And suddenly a great tempest arose on the sea, so that the boat was covered with the waves. But He was asleep. 25Then His disciples came to *Him* and awoke Him, saying, "Lord, save us! We are perishing!"

26But He said to them, "Why are you fearful, O you of little faith?" Then He arose and rebuked the winds and the sea, and there was a great calm. 27So the men marveled, saying, "Who can this be, that even the winds and the sea obey Him?"

Two Demon-Possessed Men Healed

28When He had come to the other side, to the country of the Gergesenes,[c] there met Him two demon-possessed *men,* coming out of the tombs, exceedingly fierce, so that no one could pass that way. 29And suddenly they cried out, saying, "What have we to do with You, Jesus, You Son of God? Have You come here to torment us before the time?"

8:28 [c] NU-Text reads *Gadarenes.*

THE MESSAGE

Another follower said, "Master, excuse me for a couple of days, please. I have my father's funeral to take care of."

Jesus refused. "First things first. Your business is life, not death. Follow me. Pursue life."

Then he got in the boat, his disciples with him. The next thing they knew, they were in a severe storm. Waves were crashing into the boat—and he was sound asleep! They roused him, pleading, "Master, save us! We're going down!"

Jesus reprimanded them. "Why are you such cowards, such faint-hearts?" Then he stood up and told the wind to be silent, the sea to quiet down: "Silence!" The sea became smooth as glass.

The men rubbed their eyes, astonished. "What's going on here? Wind and sea come to heel at his command!"

The Madmen and the Pigs

They landed in the country of the Gadarenes and were met by two madmen, victims of demons, coming out of the cemetery. The men had terrorized the region for so long that no one considered it safe to walk down that stretch of road anymore. Seeing Jesus, the madmen screamed out, "What business do you have giving us a hard time? You're the Son of God! You weren't supposed to show up here

KING JAMES VERSION

30 And there was a good way off from them an herd of many swine feeding.

31 So the devils besought him, saying, If thou cast us out, suffer us to go away into the herd of swine.

32 And he said unto them, Go. And when they were come out, they went into the herd of swine: and, behold, the whole herd of swine ran violently down a steep place into the sea, and perished in the waters.

33 And they that kept them fled, and went their ways into the city, and told every thing, and what was befallen to the possessed of the devils.

34 And, behold, the whole city came out to meet Jesus: and when they saw him, they besought *him* that he would depart out of their coasts.

9 And he entered into a ship, and passed over, and came into his own city.

2 And, behold, they brought to him a man sick of the palsy, lying on a bed: and Jesus seeing their faith said unto the sick of the palsy; Son, be of good cheer; thy sins be forgiven thee.

3 And, behold, certain of the scribes said within themselves, This *man* blasphemeth.

4 And Jesus knowing their thoughts said, Wherefore think ye evil in your hearts?

5 For whether is easier, to say, *Thy* sins be forgiven thee; or to say, Arise, and walk?

6 But that ye may know that the Son of man hath power on earth to forgive sins, (then saith he to the sick of the palsy,) Arise, take up thy bed, and go unto thine house.

7 And he arose, and departed to his house.

NEW AMERICAN STANDARD BIBLE

30 Now there was a herd of many swine feeding at a distance from them.

31 The demons *began* to entreat Him, saying, "If You *are going to* cast us out, send us into the herd of swine."

32 And He said to them, "Go!" And they came out and went into the swine, and the whole herd rushed down the steep bank into the sea and perished in the waters.

33 The herdsmen ran away, and went to the city and reported everything, including what had happened to the demoniacs.

34 And behold, the whole city came out to meet Jesus; and when they saw Him, they implored Him to leave their region.

A Paralytic Healed

9 Getting into a boat, Jesus crossed over *the sea* and came to His own city.

2 And they brought to Him a paralytic lying on a bed. Seeing their faith, Jesus said to the paralytic, "Take courage, son; your sins are forgiven."

3 And some of the scribes said to themselves, "This *fellow* blasphemes."

4 And Jesus knowing their thoughts said, "Why are you thinking evil in your hearts?

5 "Which is easier, to say, 'Your sins are forgiven,' or to say, 'Get up, and walk'?

6 "But so that you may know that the Son of Man has authority on earth to forgive sins"—then He *said to the paralytic, "Get up, pick up your bed and go home."

7 And he got up and went home.

NEW CENTURY VERSION

30 Near that place there was a large herd of pigs feeding. 31 The demons begged Jesus, "If you make us leave these men, please send us into that herd of pigs."

32 Jesus said to them, "Go!" So the demons left the men and went into the pigs. Then the whole herd rushed down the hill into the lake and were drowned. 33 The herdsmen ran away and went into town, where they told about all of this and what had happened to the men who had demons. 34 Then the whole town went out to see Jesus. When they saw him, they begged him to leave their area.

Jesus Heals a Paralyzed Man

9 Jesus got into a boat and went back across the lake to his own town. 2 Some people brought to Jesus a man who was paralyzed and lying on a mat. When Jesus saw the faith of these people, he said to the paralyzed man, "Be encouraged, young man. Your sins are forgiven."

3 Some of the teachers of the law said to themselves, "This man speaks as if he were God. That is blasphemy!"[a]

4 Knowing their thoughts, Jesus said, "Why are you thinking evil thoughts? 5 Which is easier: to say, 'Your sins are forgiven,' or to tell him, 'Stand up and walk'? 6 But I will prove to you that the Son of Man has authority on earth to forgive sins." Then Jesus said to the paralyzed man, "Stand up, take your mat, and go home." 7 And the man stood up and went home. 8 When the people saw this,

9:3 [a] **blasphemy** Saying things against God or not showing respect for God.

CONTEMPORARY ENGLISH VERSION

30 Not far from there a large herd of pigs was feeding. 31 So the demons begged Jesus, "If you force us out, please send us into those pigs!" 32 Jesus told them to go, and they went out of the men and into the pigs. All at once the pigs rushed down the steep bank into the lake and drowned.

33 The people taking care of the pigs ran to the town and told everything, especially what had happened to the two men. 34 Everyone in town came out to meet Jesus. When they saw him, they begged him to leave their part of the country.

Jesus Heals a Crippled Man (Mark 2.1-12; Luke 5.17-26)

9 Jesus got into a boat and crossed back over to the town where he lived.[a] 2 Some people soon brought to him a crippled man lying on a mat. When Jesus saw how much faith they had, he said to the crippled man, "My friend, don't worry! Your sins are forgiven."

3 Some teachers of the Law of Moses said to themselves, "Jesus must think he is God!"

4 But Jesus knew what was in their minds, and he said, "Why are you thinking such evil things? 5 Is it easier for me to tell this crippled man that his sins are forgiven or to tell him to get up and walk? 6 But I will show you that the Son of Man has the right to forgive sins here on earth." So Jesus said to the man, "Get up! Pick up your mat and go on home." 7 The man got up and went home. 8 When the

[a] **9.1** *where he lived*: Capernaum (see 4.13).

NEW INTERNATIONAL VERSION

30Some distance from them a large herd of pigs was feeding. 31The demons begged Jesus, "If you drive us out, send us into the herd of pigs."

32He said to them, "Go!" So they came out and went into the pigs, and the whole herd rushed down the steep bank into the lake and died in the water. 33Those tending the pigs ran off, went into the town and reported all this, including what had happened to the demon-possessed men. 34Then the whole town went out to meet Jesus. And when they saw him, they pleaded with him to leave their region.

Jesus Heals a Paralytic

9 Jesus stepped into a boat, crossed over and came to his own town. 2Some men brought to him a paralytic, lying on a mat. When Jesus saw their faith, he said to the paralytic, "Take heart, son; your sins are forgiven."

3At this, some of the teachers of the law said to themselves, "This fellow is blaspheming!"

4Knowing their thoughts, Jesus said, "Why do you entertain evil thoughts in your hearts? 5Which is easier: to say, 'Your sins are forgiven,' or to say, 'Get up and walk'? 6But so that you may know that the Son of Man has authority on earth to forgive sins. . . ." Then he said to the paralytic, "Get up, take your mat and go home." 7And the man got up

NEW LIVING TRANSLATION

appointed time!" 30A large herd of pigs was feeding in the distance, 31so the demons begged, "If you cast us out, send us into that herd of pigs."

32"All right, go!" Jesus commanded them. So the demons came out of the men and entered the pigs, and the whole herd plunged down the steep hillside into the lake and drowned in the water. 33The herdsmen fled to the nearby city, telling everyone what happened to the demon-possessed men. 34The entire town came out to meet Jesus, but they begged him to go away and leave them alone.

Jesus Heals a Paralyzed Man

9 Jesus climbed into a boat and went back across the lake to his own town. 2Some people brought to him a paralyzed man on a mat. Seeing their faith, Jesus said to the paralyzed man, "Take heart, son! Your sins are forgiven."

3"Blasphemy! This man talks like he is God!" some of the teachers of religious law said among themselves.

4Jesus knew what they were thinking, so he asked them, "Why are you thinking such evil thoughts? 5Is it easier to say, 'Your sins are forgiven' or 'Get up and walk'? 6I will prove that I, the Son of Man, have the authority on earth to forgive sins." Then Jesus turned to the paralyzed man and said, "Stand up, take your mat, and go on home, because you are healed!"

7And the man jumped up and went home! 8Fear swept

NEW KING JAMES VERSION

30Now a good way off from them there was a herd of many swine feeding. 31So the demons begged Him, saying, "If You cast us out, permit us to go away[d] into the herd of swine."

32And He said to them, "Go." So when they had come out, they went into the herd of swine. And suddenly the whole herd of swine ran violently down the steep place into the sea, and perished in the water.

33Then those who kept *them* fled; and they went away into the city and told everything, including what *had happened* to the demon-possessed *men.* 34And behold, the whole city came out to meet Jesus. And when they saw Him, they begged *Him* to depart from their region.

Jesus Forgives and Heals a Paralytic

9 So He got into a boat, crossed over, and came to His own city. 2Then behold, they brought to Him a paralytic lying on a bed. When Jesus saw their faith, He said to the paralytic, "Son, be of good cheer; your sins are forgiven you."

3And at once some of the scribes said within themselves, "This Man blasphemes!"

4But Jesus, knowing their thoughts, said, "Why do you think evil in your hearts? 5For which is easier, to say, *'Your* sins are forgiven you,' or to say, 'Arise and walk'? 6But that you may know that the Son of Man has power on earth to forgive sins"—then He said to the paralytic, "Arise, take up your bed, and go to your house." 7And he arose and departed to his house.

8:31 [d] NU-Text reads *send us.*

THE MESSAGE

yet!" Off in the distance a herd of pigs was browsing and rooting. The evil spirits begged Jesus, "If you kick us out of these men, let us live in the pigs."

Jesus said, "Go ahead, but get out of here!" Crazed, the pigs stampeded over a cliff into the sea and drowned. Scared to death, the swineherds bolted. They told everyone back in town what had happened to the madmen and the pigs. Those who heard about it were angry about the drowned pigs. A mob formed and demanded that Jesus get out and not come back.

Who Needs a Doctor?

9 Back in the boat, Jesus and the disciples recrossed the sea to Jesus' hometown. They were hardly out of the boat when some men carried a paraplegic on a stretcher and set him down in front of them. Jesus, impressed by their bold belief, said to the paraplegic, "Cheer up, son. I forgive your sins." Some religion scholars whispered, "Why, that's blasphemy!"

Jesus knew what they were thinking, and said, "Why this gossipy whispering? Which do you think is simpler: to say, 'I forgive your sins,' or, 'Get up and walk'? Well, just so it's clear that I'm the Son of Man and authorized to do either, or both. . . ." At this he turned to the paraplegic and said, "Get up. Take your bed and go home." And the man

KING JAMES VERSION

8 But when the multitudes saw *it*, they marvelled, and glorified God, which had given such power unto men.

9 ¶ And as Jesus passed forth from thence, he saw a man, named Matthew, sitting at the receipt of custom: and he saith unto him, Follow me. And he arose, and followed him.

10 And it came to pass, as Jesus sat at meat in the house, behold, many publicans and sinners came and sat down with him and his disciples.

11 And when the Pharisees saw *it*, they said unto his disciples, Why eateth your Master with publicans and sinners?

12 But when Jesus heard *that*, he said unto them, They that be whole need not a physician, but they that are sick.

13 But go ye and learn what *that* meaneth, I will have mercy, and not sacrifice: for I am not come to call the righteous, but sinners to repentance.

14 ¶ Then came to him the disciples of John, saying, Why do we and the Pharisees fast oft, but thy disciples fast not?

15 And Jesus said unto them, Can the children of the bridechamber mourn, as long as the bridegroom is with

NEW AMERICAN STANDARD BIBLE

8 But when the crowds saw *this,* they were awestruck, and glorified God, who had given such authority to men.

Matthew Called

9 As Jesus went on from there, He saw a man called Matthew, sitting in the tax collector's booth; and He *said to him, "Follow Me!" And he got up and followed Him.

10 Then it happened that as Jesus was reclining *at the table* in the house, behold, many tax collectors and sinners came and were dining with Jesus and His disciples.

11 When the Pharisees saw *this,* they said to His disciples, "Why is your Teacher eating with the tax collectors and sinners?"

12 But when Jesus heard *this*, He said, "*It is* not those who are healthy who need a physician, but those who are sick.

13 "But go and learn what this means: 'I DESIRE COMPASSION, [l]AND NOT SACRIFICE,' for I did not come to call the righteous, but sinners."

The Question about Fasting

14 Then the disciples of John *came to Him, asking, "Why do we and the Pharisees fast, but Your disciples do not fast?"

15 And Jesus said to them, "The attendants of the bridegroom cannot mourn as long as the bridegroom is with

9:13 [l] I.e. more than

NEW CENTURY VERSION

they were amazed and praised God for giving power like this to human beings.

Jesus Chooses Matthew

9When Jesus was leaving, he saw a man named Matthew sitting in the tax collector's booth. Jesus said to him, "Follow me," and he stood up and followed Jesus.

10As Jesus was having dinner at Matthew's house, many tax collectors and "sinners" came and ate with Jesus and his followers. 11When the Pharisees saw this, they asked Jesus' followers, "Why does your teacher eat with tax collectors and sinners?"

12When Jesus heard them, he said, "It is not the healthy people who need a doctor, but the sick. 13Go and learn what this means: 'I want kindness more than I want animal sacrifices.'[b] I did not come to invite good people but to invite sinners."

Jesus' Followers Are Criticized

14Then the followers of John[c] came to Jesus and said, "Why do we and the Pharisees often give up eating for a certain time,[d] but your followers don't?"

15Jesus answered, "The friends of the bridegroom are not sad while he is with them. But the time will come when

9:13 [b] **'I want...sacrifices.'** Quotation from Hosea 6:6. 9:14 [c] **John** John the Baptist, who preached to people about Christ's coming (Matthew 3, Luke 3). 9:14 [d] **give up...time** This is called "fasting." The people would give up eating for a special time of prayer and worship to God. It was also done to show sadness and disappointment.

CONTEMPORARY ENGLISH VERSION

crowds saw this, they were afraid[b] and praised God for giving such authority to people.

Jesus Chooses Matthew (Mark 2.13-17; Luke 5.27-32)

9As Jesus was leaving, he saw a tax collector[c] named Matthew sitting at the place for paying taxes. Jesus said to him, "Come with me." Matthew got up and went with him.

10Later, Jesus and his disciples were having dinner at Matthew's house.[d] Many tax collectors and other sinners were also there. 11Some Pharisees asked Jesus' disciples, "Why does your teacher eat with tax collectors and other sinners?"

12Jesus heard them and answered, "Healthy people don't need a doctor, but sick people do. 13Go and learn what the Scriptures mean when they say, 'Instead of offering sacrifices to me, I want you to be merciful to others.' I didn't come to invite good people to be my followers. I came to invite sinners."

People Ask about Going without Eating
(Mark 2.18-22; Luke 5.33-39)

14One day some followers of John the Baptist came and asked Jesus, "Why do we and the Pharisees often go without eating,[e] while your disciples never do?"

15Jesus answered:

The friends of a bridegroom don't go without eating
while he is still with them. But the time will come when he

[b] **9.8** *afraid*: Some manuscripts have "amazed." [c] **9.9** *tax collector*: See the note at 5.46. [d] **9.10** *Matthew's house*: Or "Jesus' house." [e] **9.14** *without eating*: See the note at 4.2.

NEW INTERNATIONAL VERSION

and went home. 8When the crowd saw this, they were filled
with awe; and they praised God, who had given such
authority to men.

The Calling of Matthew

9As Jesus went on from there, he saw a man named
Matthew sitting at the tax collector's booth. "Follow me,"
he told him, and Matthew got up and followed him.

10While Jesus was having dinner at Matthew's house,
many tax collectors and "sinners" came and ate with him
and his disciples. 11When the Pharisees saw this, they
asked his disciples, "Why does your teacher eat with tax
collectors and 'sinners'?"

12On hearing this, Jesus said, "It is not the healthy who
need a doctor, but the sick. 13But go and learn what this
means: 'I desire mercy, not sacrifice.'[a] For I have not come
to call the righteous, but sinners."

Jesus Questioned About Fasting

14Then John's disciples came and asked him, "How is it
that we and the Pharisees fast, but your disciples do not
fast?"

15Jesus answered, "How can the guests of the bride-
groom mourn while he is with them? The time will come

[a] *13* Hosea 6:6

NEW LIVING TRANSLATION

through the crowd as they saw this happen right before
their eyes. They praised God for sending a man with such
great authority.

Jesus Calls Matthew

9As Jesus was going down the road, he saw Matthew sit-
ting at his tax-collection booth. "Come, be my disciple,"
Jesus said to him. So Matthew got up and followed him.

10That night Matthew invited Jesus and his disciples to
be his dinner guests, along with his fellow tax collectors
and many other notorious sinners. 11The Pharisees were
indignant. "Why does your teacher eat with such scum*?"
they asked his disciples.

12When he heard this, Jesus replied, "Healthy people
don't need a doctor—sick people do." 13Then he added,
"Now go and learn the meaning of this Scripture: 'I want
you to be merciful; I don't want your sacrifices.'* For I
have come to call sinners, not those who think they are
already good enough."

A Discussion about Fasting

14One day the disciples of John the Baptist came to Jesus
and asked him, "Why do we and the Pharisees fast, but
your disciples don't fast?"

15Jesus responded, "Should the wedding guests mourn
while celebrating with the groom? Someday he will be

9:11 Greek *with tax collectors and sinners.* 9:13 Hos 6:6.

NEW KING JAMES VERSION

8Now when the multitudes saw *it,* they marveled[a] and
glorified God, who had given such power to men.

Matthew the Tax Collector

9As Jesus passed on from there, He saw a man named
Matthew sitting at the tax office. And He said to him, "Fol-
low Me." So he arose and followed Him.

10Now it happened, as Jesus sat at the table in the
house, *that* behold, many tax collectors and sinners came
and sat down with Him and His disciples. 11And when the
Pharisees saw *it,* they said to His disciples, "Why does
your Teacher eat with tax collectors and sinners?"

12When Jesus heard *that,* He said to them, "Those who
are well have no need of a physician, but those who are
sick. 13But go and learn what *this* means: *'I desire mercy
and not sacrifice.'*[b] For I did not come to call the righteous,
but sinners, to repentance."[c]

Jesus Is Questioned About Fasting

14Then the disciples of John came to Him, saying, "Why
do we and the Pharisees fast often,[d] but Your disciples do
not fast?"

15And Jesus said to them, "Can the friends of the bride-
groom mourn as long as the bridegroom is with them? But
the days will come when the bridegroom will be taken

9:8 [a] NU-Text reads *were afraid.* **9:13** [b] Hosea 6:6 [c] NU-Text omits *to repentance.* **9:14** [d] NU-Text brackets *often* as disputed.

THE MESSAGE

did it. The crowd was awestruck, amazed and pleased that God had authorized Jesus to work among them this way.

Passing along, Jesus saw a man at his work collecting taxes. His name was Matthew. Jesus said, "Come along with me." Matthew stood up and followed him.

Later when Jesus was eating supper at Matthew's house with his close followers, a lot of disreputable characters came and joined them. When the Pharisees saw him keeping this kind of company, they had a fit, and lit into Jesus' followers. "What kind of example is this from your Teacher, acting cozy with crooks and riffraff?"

Jesus, overhearing, shot back, "Who needs a doctor: the healthy or the sick? Go figure out what this Scripture means: 'I'm after mercy, not religion.' I'm here to invite outsiders, not coddle insiders."

Kingdom Come

A little later John's followers approached, asking, "Why is it that we and the Pharisees rigorously discipline body and spirit by fasting, but your followers don't?"

Jesus told them, "When you're celebrating a wedding, you don't skimp on the cake and wine. You feast. Later you may need to pull in your belt, but not now. No one

KING JAMES VERSION

them? but the days will come, when the bridegroom shall be taken from them, and then shall they fast.

16 No man putteth a piece of new cloth unto an old garment, for that which is put in to fill it up taketh from the garment, and the rent is made worse.

17 Neither do men put new wine into old bottles: else the bottles break, and the wine runneth out, and the bottles perish: but they put new wine into new bottles, and both are preserved.

18 ¶ While he spake these things unto them, behold, there came a certain ruler, and worshipped him, saying, My daughter is even now dead: but come and lay thy hand upon her, and she shall live.

19 And Jesus arose, and followed him, and *so did* his disciples.

20 And, behold, a woman, which was diseased with an issue of blood twelve years, came behind *him*, and touched the hem of his garment:

21 For she said within herself, If I may but touch his garment, I shall be whole.

22 But Jesus turned him about, and when he saw her, he said, Daughter, be of good comfort; thy faith hath made thee whole. And the woman was made whole from that hour.

23 And when Jesus came into the ruler's house, and saw the minstrels and the people making a noise,

24 He said unto them, Give place: for the maid is not dead, but sleepeth. And they laughed him to scorn.

NEW AMERICAN STANDARD BIBLE

them, can they? But the days will come when the bridegroom is taken away from them, and then they will fast.

16 "But no one puts a patch of unshrunk cloth on an old garment; for the patch pulls away from the garment, and a worse tear results.

17 "Nor do *people* put new wine into old wineskins; otherwise the wineskins burst, and the wine pours out and the wineskins are ruined; but they put new wine into fresh wineskins, and both are preserved."

Miracles of Healing

18 While He was saying these things to them, a *synagogue* official came and bowed down before Him, and said, "My daughter has just died; but come and lay Your hand on her, and she will live."

19 Jesus got up and *began* to follow him, and *so did* His disciples.

20 And a woman who had been suffering from a hemorrhage for twelve years, came up behind Him and touched the fringe of His cloak;

21 for she was saying to herself, "If I only touch His garment, I will get well."

22 But Jesus turning and seeing her said, "Daughter, take courage; your faith has made you well." At once the woman was made well.

23 When Jesus came into the official's house, and saw the flute-players and the crowd in noisy disorder,

24 He said, "Leave; for the girl has not died, but is asleep." And they *began* laughing at Him.

NEW CENTURY VERSION

the bridegroom will be taken from them, and then they will give up eating.

16"No one sews a patch of unshrunk cloth over a hole in an old coat. If he does, the patch will shrink and pull away from the coat, making the hole worse. 17Also, people never pour new wine into old leather bags. Otherwise, the bags will break, the wine will spill, and the wine bags will be ruined. But people always pour new wine into new wine bags. Then both will continue to be good."

Jesus Gives Life to a Dead Girl and Heals a Sick Woman

18While Jesus was saying these things, a leader of the synagogue came to him. He bowed down before Jesus and said, "My daughter has just died. But if you come and lay your hand on her, she will live again." 19So Jesus and his followers stood up and went with the leader.

20Then a woman who had been bleeding for twelve years came behind Jesus and touched the edge of his coat. 21She was thinking, "If I can just touch his clothes, I will be healed."

22Jesus turned and saw the woman and said, "Be encouraged, dear woman. You are made well because you believed." And the woman was healed from that moment on.

23Jesus continued along with the leader and went into his house. There he saw the funeral musicians and many people crying. 24Jesus said, "Go away. The girl is not dead, only asleep." But the people laughed at him. 25After the

CONTEMPORARY ENGLISH VERSION

will be taken from them. Then they will go without eating.

16No one uses a new piece of cloth to patch old
clothes. The patch would shrink and tear a bigger hole.

17No one pours new wine into old wineskins. The
wine would swell and burst the old skins.[f] Then the
wine would be lost, and the skins would be ruined. New
wine must be put into new wineskins. Both the skins
and the wine will then be safe.

A Dying Girl and a Sick Woman

(Mark 5.21-43; Luke 8.40-56)

18While Jesus was still speaking, an official came and knelt in front of him. The man said, "My daughter has just now died! Please come and place your hand on her. Then she will live again."

19Jesus and his disciples got up and went with the man.

20A woman who had been bleeding for twelve years came up behind Jesus and barely touched his clothes. 21She had said to herself, "If I can just touch his clothes, I will get well."

22Jesus turned. He saw the woman and said, "Don't worry! You are now well because of your faith." At that moment she was healed.

23When Jesus went into the home of the official and saw the musicians and the crowd of mourners,[g] 24he said, "Get out of here! The little girl isn't dead. She is just asleep." Everyone started laughing at Jesus. 25But after the crowd

[f] **9.17** *swell and burst the old skins*: While the juice from grapes was becoming wine, it would swell and stretch the skins in which it had been stored. If the skins were old and stiff, they would burst. [g] **9.23** *the crowd of mourners*: The Jewish people often hired mourners for funerals.

NEW INTERNATIONAL VERSION

when the bridegroom will be taken from them; then they will fast.

16"No one sews a patch of unshrunk cloth on an old garment, for the patch will pull away from the garment, making the tear worse. 17Neither do men pour new wine into old wineskins. If they do, the skins will burst, the wine will run out and the wineskins will be ruined. No, they pour new wine into new wineskins, and both are preserved."

A Dead Girl and a Sick Woman

18While he was saying this, a ruler came and knelt before him and said, "My daughter has just died. But come and put your hand on her, and she will live." 19Jesus got up and went with him, and so did his disciples.

20Just then a woman who had been subject to bleeding for twelve years came up behind him and touched the edge of his cloak. 21She said to herself, "If I only touch his cloak, I will be healed."

22Jesus turned and saw her. "Take heart, daughter," he said, "your faith has healed you." And the woman was healed from that moment.

23When Jesus entered the ruler's house and saw the flute players and the noisy crowd, 24he said, "Go away. The girl is not dead but asleep." But they laughed at him.

NEW LIVING TRANSLATION

taken from them, and then they will fast. 16And who would patch an old garment with unshrunk cloth? For the patch shrinks and pulls away from the old cloth, leaving an even bigger hole than before. 17And no one puts new wine into old wineskins. The old skins would burst from the pressure, spilling the wine and ruining the skins. New wine must be stored in new wineskins. That way both the wine and the wineskins are preserved."

Jesus Heals in Response to Faith

18As Jesus was saying this, the leader of a synagogue came and knelt down before him. "My daughter has just died," he said, "but you can bring her back to life again if you just come and lay your hand upon her."

19As Jesus and the disciples were going to the official's home, 20a woman who had had a hemorrhage for twelve years came up behind him. She touched the fringe of his robe, 21for she thought, "If I can just touch his robe, I will be healed."

22Jesus turned around and said to her, "Daughter, be encouraged! Your faith has made you well." And the woman was healed at that moment.

23When Jesus arrived at the official's home, he noticed the noisy crowds and heard the funeral music. 24He said, "Go away, for the girl isn't dead; she's only asleep." But the crowd laughed at him. 25When the crowd was finally

NEW KING JAMES VERSION

away from them, and then they will fast. 16No one puts a piece of unshrunk cloth on an old garment; for the patch pulls away from the garment, and the tear is made worse. 17Nor do they put new wine into old wineskins, or else the wineskins break, the wine is spilled, and the wineskins are ruined. But they put new wine into new wineskins, and both are preserved."

A Girl Restored to Life and a Woman Healed

18While He spoke these things to them, behold, a ruler came and worshiped Him, saying, "My daughter has just died, but come and lay Your hand on her and she will live." 19So Jesus arose and followed him, and so *did* His disciples.

20And suddenly, a woman who had a flow of blood for twelve years came from behind and touched the hem of His garment. 21For she said to herself, "If only I may touch His garment, I shall be made well." 22But Jesus turned around, and when He saw her He said, "Be of good cheer, daughter; your faith has made you well." And the woman was made well from that hour.

23When Jesus came into the ruler's house, and saw the flute players and the noisy crowd wailing, 24He said to them, "Make room, for the girl is not dead, but sleeping." And they ridiculed Him. 25But when the crowd was put

THE MESSAGE

throws cold water on a friendly bonfire. This is Kingdom Come!"

He went on, "No one cuts up a fine silk scarf to patch old work clothes; you want fabrics that match. And you don't put your wine in cracked bottles."

Just a Touch

As he finished saying this, a local official appeared, bowed politely, and said, "My daughter has just now died. If you come and touch her, she will live." Jesus got up and went with him, his disciples following along.

Just then a woman who had hemorrhaged for twelve years slipped in from behind and lightly touched his robe. She was thinking to herself, "If I can just put a finger on his robe, I'll get well." Jesus turned—caught her at it. Then he reassured her: "Courage, daughter. You took a risk of faith, and now you're well." The woman was well from then on.

By now they had arrived at the house of the town official, and pushed their way through the gossips looking for a story and the neighbors bringing in casseroles. Jesus was abrupt: "Clear out! This girl isn't dead. She's sleeping." They told him he didn't know what he was talking about.

KING JAMES VERSION

25 But when the people were put forth, he went in, and took her by the hand, and the maid arose.

26 And the fame hereof went abroad into all that land.

27 ¶ And when Jesus departed thence, two blind men followed him, crying, and saying, *Thou* Son of David, have mercy on us.

28 And when he was come into the house, the blind men came to him: and Jesus saith unto them, Believe ye that I am able to do this? They said unto him, Yea, Lord.

29 Then touched he their eyes, saying, According to your faith be it unto you.

30 And their eyes were opened; and Jesus straitly charged them, saying, See *that* no man know *it*.

31 But they, when they were departed, spread abroad his fame in all that country.

32 As they went out, behold, they brought to him a dumb man possessed with a devil.

33 And when the devil was cast out, the dumb spake: and the multitudes marvelled, saying, It was never so seen in Israel.

34 But the Pharisees said, He casteth out devils through the prince of the devils.

NEW AMERICAN STANDARD BIBLE

25 But when the crowd had been sent out, He entered and took her by the hand, and the girl got up.

26 This news spread throughout all that land.

27 As Jesus went on from there, two blind men followed Him, crying out, "Have mercy on us, Son of David!"

28 When He entered the house, the blind men came up to Him, and Jesus *said to them, "Do you believe that I am able to do this?" They *said to Him, "Yes, Lord."

29 Then He touched their eyes, saying, "It shall be done to you according to your faith."

30 And their eyes were opened. And Jesus sternly warned them: "See that no one knows *about this!*"

31 But they went out and spread the news about Him throughout all that land.

32 As they were going out, a mute, demon-possessed man was brought to Him.

33 After the demon was cast out, the mute man spoke; and the crowds were amazed, *and were* saying, "Nothing like this has ever been seen in Israel."

34 But the Pharisees were saying, "He casts out the demons by the ruler of the demons."

NEW CENTURY VERSION

crowd had been thrown out of the house, Jesus went into the girl's room and took hold of her hand, and she stood up. 26The news about this spread all around the area.

Jesus Heals More People

27When Jesus was leaving there, two blind men followed him. They cried out, "Have mercy on us, Son of David!"

28After Jesus went inside, the blind men went with him. He asked the men, "Do you believe that I can make you see again?"

They answered, "Yes, Lord."

29Then Jesus touched their eyes and said, "Because you believe I can make you see again, it will happen." 30Then the men were able to see. But Jesus warned them strongly, saying, "Don't tell anyone about this." 31But the blind men left and spread the news about Jesus all around that area.

32When the two men were leaving, some people brought another man to Jesus. This man could not talk because he had a demon in him. 33After Jesus forced the demon to leave the man, he was able to speak. The crowd was amazed and said, "We have never seen anything like this in Israel."

34But the Pharisees said, "The prince of demons is the one that gives him power to force demons out."

CONTEMPORARY ENGLISH VERSION

had been sent out of the house, Jesus went to the girl's bedside. He took her by the hand and helped her up.

26News about this spread all over that part of the country.

Jesus Heals Two Blind Men

27As Jesus was walking along, two blind men began following him and shouting, "Son of David,[h] have pity on us!"

28After Jesus had gone indoors, the two blind men came up to him. He asked them, "Do you believe I can make you well?"

"Yes, Lord," they answered.

29Jesus touched their eyes and said, "Because of your faith, you will be healed." 30They were able to see, and Jesus strictly warned them not to tell anyone about him. 31But they left and talked about him to everyone in that part of the country.

Jesus Heals a Man Who Could Not Talk

32As Jesus and his disciples were on their way, some people brought to him a man who could not talk because a demon was in him. 33After Jesus had forced the demon out, the man started talking. The crowds were so amazed that they began saying, "Nothing like this has ever happened in Israel!"

34But the Pharisees said, "The leader of the demons gives him the power to force out demons."

[h] **9.27** *Son of David*: The Jewish people expected the Messiah to be from the family of King David, and for this reason the Messiah was often called the "Son of David."

NEW INTERNATIONAL VERSION

25After the crowd had been put outside, he went in and took the girl by the hand, and she got up. 26News of this spread through all that region.

Jesus Heals the Blind and Mute

27As Jesus went on from there, two blind men followed him, calling out, "Have mercy on us, Son of David!"

28When he had gone indoors, the blind men came to him, and he asked them, "Do you believe that I am able to do this?"

"Yes, Lord," they replied.

29Then he touched their eyes and said, "According to your faith will it be done to you"; 30and their sight was restored. Jesus warned them sternly, "See that no one knows about this." 31But they went out and spread the news about him all over that region.

32While they were going out, a man who was demon-possessed and could not talk was brought to Jesus. 33And when the demon was driven out, the man who had been mute spoke. The crowd was amazed and said, "Nothing like this has ever been seen in Israel."

34But the Pharisees said, "It is by the prince of demons that he drives out demons."

NEW LIVING TRANSLATION

outside, Jesus went in and took the girl by the hand, and she stood up! 26The report of this miracle swept through the entire countryside.

Jesus Heals the Blind and Mute

27After Jesus left the girl's home, two blind men followed along behind him, shouting, "Son of David, have mercy on us!"

28They went right into the house where he was staying, and Jesus asked them, "Do you believe I can make you see?"

"Yes, Lord," they told him, "we do."

29Then he touched their eyes and said, "Because of your faith, it will happen." 30And suddenly they could see! Jesus sternly warned them, "Don't tell anyone about this." 31But instead, they spread his fame all over the region.

32When they left, some people brought to him a man who couldn't speak because he was possessed by a demon. 33So Jesus cast out the demon, and instantly the man could talk. The crowds marveled. "Nothing like this has ever happened in Israel!" they exclaimed.

34But the Pharisees said, "He can cast out demons because he is empowered by the prince of demons."

NEW KING JAMES VERSION

outside, He went in and took her by the hand, and the girl arose. 26And the report of this went out into all that land.

Two Blind Men Healed

27When Jesus departed from there, two blind men followed Him, crying out and saying, "Son of David, have mercy on us!"

28And when He had come into the house, the blind men came to Him. And Jesus said to them, "Do you believe that I am able to do this?"

They said to Him, "Yes, Lord."

29Then He touched their eyes, saying, "According to your faith let it be to you." 30And their eyes were opened. And Jesus sternly warned them, saying, "See *that* no one knows *it.*" 31But when they had departed, they spread the news about Him in all that country.

A Mute Man Speaks

32As they went out, behold, they brought to Him a man, mute and demon-possessed. 33And when the demon was cast out, the mute spoke. And the multitudes marveled, saying, "It was never seen like this in Israel!"

34But the Pharisees said, "He casts out demons by the ruler of the demons."

THE MESSAGE

But when Jesus had gotten rid of the crowd, he went in, took the girl's hand, and pulled her to her feet—alive. The news was soon out, and traveled throughout the region.

Become What You Believe

As Jesus left the house, he was followed by two blind men crying out, "Mercy, Son of David! Mercy on us!" When Jesus got home, the blind men went in with him. Jesus said to them, "Do you really believe I can do this?" They said, "Why, yes, Master!"

He touched their eyes and said, "Become what you believe." It happened. They saw. Then Jesus became very stern. "Don't let a soul know how this happened." But they were hardly out the door before they started blabbing it to everyone they met.

Right after that, as the blind men were leaving, a man who had been struck speechless by an evil spirit was brought to Jesus. As soon as Jesus threw the evil tormenting spirit out, the man talked away just as if he'd been talking all his life. The people were up on their feet applauding: "There's never been anything like this in Israel!"

The Pharisees were left sputtering, "Hocus pocus. It's nothing but hocus pocus. He's probably made a pact with the Devil."

KING JAMES VERSION

35 ¶ And Jesus went about all the cities and villages, teaching in their synagogues, and preaching the gospel of the kingdom, and healing every sickness and every disease among the people.

36 But when he saw the multitudes, he was moved with compassion on them, because they fainted, and were scattered abroad, as sheep having no shepherd.

37 Then saith he unto his disciples, The harvest truly *is* plenteous, but the labourers *are* few;

38 Pray ye therefore the Lord of the harvest, that he will send forth labourers into his harvest.

10 And when he had called unto *him* his twelve disciples, he gave them power *against* unclean spirits, to cast them out, and to heal all manner of sickness and all manner of disease.

2 Now the names of the twelve apostles are these; The first, Simon, who is called Peter, and Andrew his brother; James *the son* of Zebedee, and John his brother;

3 Philip, and Bartholomew; Thomas, and Matthew the publican; James *the son* of Alphaeus, and Lebbaeus, whose surname was Thaddaeus;

4 Simon the Canaanite, and Judas Iscariot, who also betrayed him.

NEW AMERICAN STANDARD BIBLE

35 Jesus was going through all the cities and villages, teaching in their synagogues and proclaiming the gospel of the kingdom, and healing every kind of disease and every kind of sickness.

36 Seeing the people, He felt compassion for them, because they were distressed and dispirited like sheep without a shepherd.

37 Then He *said to His disciples, "The harvest is plentiful, but the workers are few.

38 "Therefore beseech the Lord of the harvest to send out workers into His harvest."

The Twelve Disciples; Instructions for Service

10 Jesus summoned His twelve disciples and gave them authority over unclean spirits, to cast them out, and to heal every kind of disease and every kind of sickness.

2 Now the names of the twelve apostles are these: The first, Simon, who is called Peter, and Andrew his brother; and James the son of Zebedee, and John his brother;

3 Philip and Bartholomew; Thomas and Matthew the tax collector; James the son of Alphaeus, and Thaddaeus;

4 Simon the Zealot, and Judas Iscariot, the one who betrayed Him.

NEW CENTURY VERSION

35Jesus traveled through all the towns and villages, teaching in their synagogues, preaching the Good News about the kingdom, and healing all kinds of diseases and sicknesses. 36When he saw the crowds, he felt sorry for them because they were hurting and helpless, like sheep without a shepherd. 37Jesus said to his followers, "There are many people to harvest but only a few workers to help harvest them. 38Pray to the Lord, who owns the harvest, that he will send more workers to gather his harvest."[e]

Jesus Sends Out His Apostles

10 Jesus called his twelve followers together and gave them authority to drive out evil spirits and to heal every kind of disease and sickness. 2These are the names of the twelve apostles: Simon (also called Peter) and his brother Andrew; James son of Zebedee, and his brother John; 3Philip and Bartholomew; Thomas and Matthew, the tax collector; James son of Alphaeus, and Thaddaeus; 4Simon the Zealot and Judas Iscariot, who turned against Jesus.

9:38 [e] **"There are...harvest."** As a farmer sends workers to harvest the grain, Jesus sends his followers to bring people to God.

CONTEMPORARY ENGLISH VERSION

Jesus Has Pity on People

35Jesus went to every town and village. He taught in their meeting places and preached the good news about God's kingdom. Jesus also healed every kind of disease and sickness. 36When he saw the crowds, he felt sorry for them. They were confused and helpless, like sheep without a shepherd. 37He said to his disciples, "A large crop is in the fields, but there are only a few workers. 38Ask the Lord in charge of the harvest to send out workers to bring it in."

Jesus Chooses His Twelve Apostles

(Mark 3.13-19; Luke 6.12-16)

10 Jesus called together his twelve disciples. He gave them the power to force out evil spirits and to heal every kind of disease and sickness. 2The first of the twelve apostles was Simon, better known as Peter. His brother Andrew was an apostle, and so were James and John, the two sons of Zebedee. 3Philip, Bartholomew, Thomas, Matthew the tax collector,[a] James the son of Alphaeus, and Thaddaeus were also apostles. 4The others were Simon, known as the Eager One,[b] and Judas Iscariot,[c] who later betrayed Jesus.

[a] **10.3** *tax collector*: See the note at 5.46. [b] **10.4** *known as the Eager One*: The Greek text has "Cananaean," which probably comes from a Hebrew word meaning "zealous" (see Luke 6.15). "Zealot" was the name later given to the members of a Jewish group that resisted and fought against the Romans. [c] **10.4** *Iscariot*: This may mean "a man from Kerioth" (a place in Judea). But more probably it means "a man who was a liar" or "a man who was a betrayer."

NEW INTERNATIONAL VERSION

The Workers Are Few

35Jesus went through all the towns and villages, teach-
ing in their synagogues, preaching the good news of the
kingdom and healing every disease and sickness. 36When
he saw the crowds, he had compassion on them, because
they were harassed and helpless, like sheep without a
shepherd. 37Then he said to his disciples, "The harvest is
plentiful but the workers are few. 38Ask the Lord of the
harvest, therefore, to send out workers into his harvest
field."

Jesus Sends Out the Twelve

10 He called his twelve disciples to him and gave
them authority to drive out evil[a] spirits and to heal
every disease and sickness.

2These are the names of the twelve apostles: first, Simon
(who is called Peter) and his brother Andrew; James son of
Zebedee, and his brother John; 3Philip and Bartholomew;
Thomas and Matthew the tax collector; James son of
Alphaeus, and Thaddaeus; 4Simon the Zealot and Judas
Iscariot, who betrayed him.

[a] *1* Greek *unclean*

NEW LIVING TRANSLATION

The Need for Workers

35Jesus traveled through all the cities and villages of
that area, teaching in the synagogues and announcing the
Good News about the Kingdom. And wherever he went, he
healed people of every sort of disease and illness. 36He felt
great pity for the crowds that came, because their problems
were so great and they didn't know where to go for help.
They were like sheep without a shepherd. 37He said to his
disciples, "The harvest is so great, but the workers are so
few. 38So pray to the Lord who is in charge of the harvest;
ask him to send out more workers for his fields."

Jesus Sends Out the Twelve Apostles

10 Jesus called his twelve disciples to him and gave
them authority to cast out evil spirits and to heal
every kind of disease and illness. 2Here are the names of
the twelve apostles:

first Simon (also called Peter),
then Andrew (Peter's brother),
James (son of Zebedee),
John (James's brother),
3 Philip,
Bartholomew,
Thomas,
Matthew (the tax collector),
James (son of Alphaeus),
Thaddaeus,
4 Simon (the Zealot*),
Judas Iscariot (who later betrayed him).

10:4 Greek *the Cananean.*

NEW KING JAMES VERSION

The Compassion of Jesus

35Then Jesus went about all the cities and villages,
teaching in their synagogues, preaching the gospel of the
kingdom, and healing every sickness and every disease
among the people.[e] 36But when He saw the multitudes, He
was moved with compassion for them, because they were
weary[f] and scattered, like sheep having no shepherd.
37Then He said to His disciples, "The harvest truly *is* plen-
tiful, but the laborers *are* few. 38Therefore pray the Lord of
the harvest to send out laborers into His harvest."

The Twelve Apostles

10 And when He had called His twelve disciples to
Him, He gave them power *over* unclean spirits, to
cast them out, and to heal all kinds of sickness and all
kinds of disease. 2Now the names of the twelve apostles
are these: first, Simon, who is called Peter, and Andrew his
brother; James the *son* of Zebedee, and John his brother;
3Philip and Bartholomew; Thomas and Matthew the tax
collector; James the *son* of Alphaeus, and Lebbaeus, whose
surname was[a] Thaddaeus; 4Simon the Cananite,[b] and Ju-
das Iscariot, who also betrayed Him.

9:35 [e] NU-Text omits *among the people.* **9:36** [f] NU-Text and M-Text read *harassed.* **10:3** [a] NU-Text omits *Lebbaeus, whose surname was.* **10:4** [b] NU-Text reads *Cananaean.*

THE MESSAGE

Then Jesus made a circuit of all the towns and villages.
He taught in their meeting places, reported kingdom news,
and healed their diseased bodies, healed their bruised and
hurt lives. When he looked out over the crowds, his heart
broke. So confused and aimless they were, like sheep with
no shepherd. "What a huge harvest!" he said to his disci-
ples. "How few workers! On your knees and pray for har-
vest hands!"

The Twelve Harvest Hands

10 The prayer was no sooner prayed than it was
answered. Jesus called twelve of his followers and
sent them into the ripe fields. He gave them power to kick
out the evil spirits, and to tenderly care for the bruised and
hurt lives. This is the list of the twelve he sent:

Simon (they called him Peter, or "Rock"),
Andrew, his brother,
James, Zebedee's son,
John, his brother,
Philip,
Bartholomew,
Thomas,
Matthew, the tax man,
James, son of Alphaeus,
Thaddaeus,
Simon, the Canaanite,
Judas Iscariot (who later turned on him).

KING JAMES VERSION

5 ¶ These twelve Jesus sent forth, and commanded them, saying, Go not into the way of the Gentiles, and into *any* city of the Samaritans enter ye not:

6 But go rather to the lost sheep of the house of Israel.

7 And as ye go, preach, saying, The kingdom of heaven is at hand.

8 Heal the sick, cleanse the lepers, raise the dead, cast out devils: freely ye have received, freely give.

9 Provide neither gold, nor silver, nor brass in your purses,

10 Nor scrip for *your* journey, neither two coats, neither shoes, nor yet staves: for the workman is worthy of his meat.

11 And into whatsoever city or town ye shall enter, enquire who in it is worthy; and there abide till ye go thence.

12 And when ye come into an house, salute it.

13 And if the house be worthy, let your peace come upon it: but if it be not worthy, let your peace return to you.

14 And whosoever shall not receive you, nor hear your words, when ye depart out of that house or city, shake off the dust of your feet.

15 Verily I say unto you, It shall be more tolerable for the land of Sodom and Gomorrha in the day of judgment, than for that city.

NEW AMERICAN STANDARD BIBLE

5 These twelve Jesus sent out after instructing them: "Do not go in *the* way of *the* Gentiles, and do not enter *any* city of the Samaritans;

6 but rather go to the lost sheep of the house of Israel.

7 "And as you go, preach, saying, 'The kingdom of heaven is at hand.'

8 "Heal *the* sick, raise *the* dead, cleanse *the* lepers, cast out demons. Freely you received, freely give.

9 "Do not acquire gold, or silver, or copper for your money belts,

10 or a bag for *your* journey, or even two coats, or sandals, or a staff; for the worker is worthy of his support.

11 "And whatever city or village you enter, inquire who is worthy in it, and stay at his house until you leave *that city*.

12 "As you enter the house, give it your greeting.

13 "If the house is worthy, give it your *blessing of* peace. But if it is not worthy, take back your *blessing of* peace.

14 "Whoever does not receive you, nor heed your words, as you go out of that house or that city, shake the dust off your feet.

15 "Truly I say to you, it will be more tolerable for *the* land of Sodom and Gomorrah in the day of judgment than for that city.

NEW CENTURY VERSION

5 Jesus sent out these twelve men with the following order: "Don't go to the non-Jewish people or to any town where the Samaritans live. 6 But go to the people of Israel, who are like lost sheep. 7 When you go, preach this: 'The kingdom of heaven is near.' 8 Heal the sick, raise the dead to life again, heal those who have skin diseases, and force demons out of people. I give you these powers freely, so help other people freely. 9 Don't carry any money with you—gold or silver or copper. 10 Don't carry a bag or extra clothes or sandals or a walking stick. Workers should be given what they need.

11 "When you enter a city or town, find some worthy person there and stay in that home until you leave. 12 When you enter that home, say, 'Peace be with you.' 13 If the people there welcome you, let your peace stay there. But if they don't welcome you, take back the peace you wished for them. 14 And if a home or town refuses to welcome you or listen to you, leave that place and shake its dust off your feet.[a] 15 I tell you the truth, on the Judgment Day it will be better for the towns of Sodom and Gomorrah[b] than for the people of that town.

10:14 [a] **shake...feet.** A warning. It showed that they had rejected these people. 10:15 [b] **Sodom and Gomorrah** Two cities that God destroyed because the people were so evil.

CONTEMPORARY ENGLISH VERSION

Instructions for the Twelve Apostles

(Mark 6.7-13; Luke 9.1-6)

5 Jesus sent out the twelve apostles with these instructions:

Stay away from the Gentiles and don't go to any Samaritan town. 6 Go only to the people of Israel, because they are like a flock of lost sheep. 7 As you go, announce that the kingdom of heaven will soon be here.[d] 8 Heal the sick, raise the dead to life, heal people who have leprosy,[e] and force out demons. You received without paying, now give without being paid. 9 Don't take along any gold, silver, or copper coins. 10 And don't carry[f] a traveling bag or an extra shirt or sandals or a walking stick.

Workers deserve their food. 11 So when you go to a town or a village, find someone worthy enough to have you as their guest and stay with them until you leave. 12 When you go to a home, give it your blessing of peace. 13 If the home is deserving, let your blessing remain with them. But if the home isn't deserving, take back your blessing of peace. 14 If someone won't welcome you or listen to your message, leave their home or town. And shake the dust from your feet at them.[g] 15 I promise you that the day of judgment will be easier for the towns of Sodom and Gomorrah[h] than for that town.

[d] **10.7** *will soon be here*: Or "is already here." [e] **10.8** *leprosy*: See the note at 8.2. [f] **10.9,10** *Don't take along . . . don't carry*: Or "Don't accept . . . don't accept." [g] **10.14** *shake the dust from your feet at them*: This was a way of showing rejection (see Acts 13.51).
[h] **10.15** *Sodom and Gomorrah*: During the time of Abraham the Lord destroyed these towns because the people there were so evil.

NEW INTERNATIONAL VERSION

5 These twelve Jesus sent out with the following instructions: "Do not go among the Gentiles or enter any town of the Samaritans. 6 Go rather to the lost sheep of Israel. 7 As you go, preach this message: 'The kingdom of heaven is near.' 8 Heal the sick, raise the dead, cleanse those who have leprosy,[b] drive out demons. Freely you have received, freely give. 9 Do not take along any gold or silver or copper in your belts; 10 take no bag for the journey, or extra tunic, or sandals or a staff; for the worker is worth his keep.

11 "Whatever town or village you enter, search for some worthy person there and stay at his house until you leave. 12 As you enter the home, give it your greeting. 13 If the home is deserving, let your peace rest on it; if it is not, let your peace return to you. 14 If anyone will not welcome you or listen to your words, shake the dust off your feet when you leave that home or town. 15 I tell you the truth, it will be more bearable for Sodom and Gomorrah on the day of judgment than for that town. 16 I am sending you out like

b *8* The Greek word was used for various diseases affecting the skin—not necessarily leprosy.

NEW LIVING TRANSLATION

5 Jesus sent the twelve disciples out with these instructions: "Don't go to the Gentiles or the Samaritans, 6 but only to the people of Israel—God's lost sheep. 7 Go and announce to them that the Kingdom of Heaven is near.* 8 Heal the sick, raise the dead, cure those with leprosy, and cast out demons. Give as freely as you have received!

9 "Don't take any money with you. 10 Don't carry a traveler's bag with an extra coat and sandals or even a walking stick. Don't hesitate to accept hospitality, because those who work deserve to be fed.* 11 Whenever you enter a city or village, search for a worthy man and stay in his home until you leave for the next town. 12 When you are invited into someone's home, give it your blessing. 13 If it turns out to be a worthy home, let your blessing stand; if it is not, take back the blessing. 14 If a village doesn't welcome you or listen to you, shake off the dust of that place from your feet as you leave. 15 I assure you, the wicked cities of Sodom and Gomorrah will be better off on the judgment day than that place will be.

10:7 Or *has come* or *is coming soon.* **10:10** Or *the worker is worthy of support.*

NEW KING JAMES VERSION

Sending Out the Twelve

5 These twelve Jesus sent out and commanded them, saying: "Do not go into the way of the Gentiles, and do not enter a city of the Samaritans. 6 But go rather to the lost sheep of the house of Israel. 7 And as you go, preach, saying, 'The kingdom of heaven is at hand.' 8 Heal the sick, cleanse the lepers, raise the dead,[c] cast out demons. Freely you have received, freely give. 9 Provide neither gold nor silver nor copper in your money belts, 10 nor bag for *your* journey, nor two tunics, nor sandals, nor staffs; for a worker is worthy of his food.

11 "Now whatever city or town you enter, inquire who in it is worthy, and stay there till you go out. 12 And when you go into a household, greet it. 13 If the household is worthy, let your peace come upon it. But if it is not worthy, let your peace return to you. 14 And whoever will not receive you nor hear your words, when you depart from that house or city, shake off the dust from your feet. 15 Assuredly, I say to you, it will be more tolerable for the land of Sodom and Gomorrah in the day of judgment than for that city!

10:8 [c] NU-Text reads *raise the dead, cleanse the lepers;* M-Text omits *raise the dead.*

THE MESSAGE

Jesus sent his twelve harvest hands out with this charge:

"Don't begin by traveling to some faroff place to convert unbelievers. And don't try to be dramatic by tackling some public enemy. Go to the lost, confused people right here in the neighborhood. Tell them that the kingdom is here. Bring health to the sick. Raise the dead. Touch the untouchables. Kick out the demons. You have been treated generously, so live generously.

"Don't think you have to put on a fund-raising campaign before you start. You don't need a lot of equipment. *You* are the equipment, and all you need to keep that going is three meals a day. Travel light.

"When you enter a town or village, don't insist on staying in a luxury inn. Get a modest place with some modest people, and be content there until you leave.

"When you knock on a door, be courteous in your greeting. If they welcome you, be gentle in your conversation. If they don't welcome you, quietly withdraw. Don't make a scene. Shrug your shoulders and be on your way. You can be sure that on Judgment Day they'll be mighty sorry—but it's no concern of yours now.

KING JAMES VERSION

16 ¶ Behold, I send you forth as sheep in the midst of wolves: be ye therefore wise as serpents, and harmless as doves.

17 But beware of men: for they will deliver you up to the councils, and they will scourge you in their synagogues;

18 And ye shall be brought before governors and kings for my sake, for a testimony against them and the Gentiles.

19 But when they deliver you up, take no thought how or what ye shall speak: for it shall be given you in that same hour what ye shall speak.

20 For it is not ye that speak, but the Spirit of your Father which speaketh in you.

21 And the brother shall deliver up the brother to death, and the father the child: and the children shall rise up against *their* parents, and cause them to be put to death.

22 And ye shall be hated of all *men* for my name's sake: but he that endureth to the end shall be saved.

23 But when they persecute you in this city, flee ye into another: for verily I say unto you, Ye shall not have gone over the cities of Israel, till the Son of man be come.

24 The disciple is not above *his* master, nor the servant above his lord.

25 It is enough for the disciple that he be as his master, and the servant as his lord. If they have called the master of the house Beelzebub, how much more *shall they call* them of his household?

26 Fear them not therefore: for there is nothing covered,

NEW AMERICAN STANDARD BIBLE

A Hard Road before Them

16 "Behold, I send you out as sheep in the midst of wolves; so be shrewd as serpents and innocent as doves.

17 "But beware of men, for they will hand you over to *the* courts and scourge you in their synagogues;

18 and you will even be brought before governors and kings for My sake, as a testimony to them and to the Gentiles.

19 "But when they hand you over, do not worry about how or what you are to say; for it will be given you in that hour what you are to say.

20 "For it is not you who speak, but *it is* the Spirit of your Father who speaks in you.

21 "Brother will betray brother to death, and a father *his* child; and children will rise up against parents and cause them to be put to death.

22 "You will be hated by all because of My name, but it is the one who has endured to the end who will be saved.

23 "But whenever they persecute you in one city, flee to the next; for truly I say to you, you will not finish *going through* the cities of Israel until the Son of Man comes.

The Meaning of Discipleship

24 "A disciple is not above his teacher, nor a slave above his master.

25 "It is enough for the disciple that he become like his teacher, and the slave like his master. If they have called the head of the house Beelzebul, how much more *will they malign* the members of his household!

26 "Therefore do not fear them, for there is nothing

NEW CENTURY VERSION

Jesus Warns His Apostles

16 "Listen, I am sending you out like sheep among wolves. So be as smart as snakes and as innocent as doves. 17 Be careful of people, because they will arrest you and take you to court and whip you in their synagogues.
18 Because of me you will be taken to stand before governors and kings, and you will tell them and the non-Jewish people about me. 19 When you are arrested, don't worry about what to say or how to say it. At that time you will be given the things to say. 20 It will not really be you speaking but the Spirit of your Father speaking through you.
21 "Brothers will give their own brothers to be killed, and fathers will give their own children to be killed. Children will fight against their own parents and have them put to death. 22 All people will hate you because you follow me, but those people who keep their faith until the end will be saved. 23 When you are treated badly in one city, run to another city. I tell you the truth, you will not finish going through all the cities of Israel before the Son of Man comes.
24 "A student is not better than his teacher, and a servant is not better than his master. 25 A student should be satisfied to become like his teacher; a servant should be satisfied to become like his master. If the head of the family is called Beelzebul, then the other members of the family will be called worse names!

Fear God, Not People

26 "So don't be afraid of those people, because everything

CONTEMPORARY ENGLISH VERSION

Warning about Trouble (Mark 13.9-13; Luke 21.12-17)

16 I am sending you like lambs into a pack of wolves. So be as wise as snakes and as innocent as doves.
17 Watch out for people who will take you to court and have you beaten in their meeting places. 18 Because of me, you will be dragged before rulers and kings to tell them and the Gentiles about your faith. 19 But when someone arrests you, don't worry about what you will say or how you will say it. At that time you will be given the words to say. 20 But you will not really be the one speaking. The Spirit from your Father will tell you what to say.
21 Brothers and sisters will betray one another and have each other put to death. Parents will betray their own children, and children will turn against their parents and have them killed. 22 Everyone will hate you because of me. But if you remain faithful until the end, you will be saved. 23 When people mistreat you in one town, hurry to another one. I promise you that before you have gone to all the towns of Israel, the Son of Man will come.
24 Disciples are not better than their teacher, and slaves are not better than their master. 25 It is enough for disciples to be like their teacher and for slaves to be like their master. If people call the head of the family Satan, what will they say about the rest of the family?

The One To Fear (Luke 12.2-7)

26 Don't be afraid of anyone! Everything that is hidden

NEW INTERNATIONAL VERSION

sheep among wolves. Therefore be as shrewd as snakes
and as innocent as doves.
17“Be on your guard against men; they will hand you
over to the local councils and flog you in their synagogues.
18On my account you will be brought before governors and
kings as witnesses to them and to the Gentiles. 19But
when they arrest you, do not worry about what to say or
how to say it. At that time you will be given what to say,
20for it will not be you speaking, but the Spirit of your
Father speaking through you.
21“Brother will betray brother to death, and a father his
child; children will rebel against their parents and have
them put to death. 22All men will hate you because of me,
but he who stands firm to the end will be saved. 23When
you are persecuted in one place, flee to another. I tell you
the truth, you will not finish going through the cities of
Israel before the Son of Man comes.
24“A student is not above his teacher, nor a servant
above his master. 25It is enough for the student to be like
his teacher, and the servant like his master. If the head of
the house has been called Beelzebub,[c] how much more the
members of his household!
26“So do not be afraid of them. There is nothing concealed

[c] *25* Greek *Beezeboul* or *Beelzeboul*

NEW LIVING TRANSLATION

16“Look, I am sending you out as sheep among wolves.
Be as wary as snakes and harmless as doves. 17But
beware! For you will be handed over to the courts and
beaten in the synagogues. 18And you must stand trial
before governors and kings because you are my followers.
This will be your opportunity to tell them about me—yes,
to witness to the world. 19When you are arrested, don't
worry about what to say in your defense, because you will
be given the right words at the right time. 20For it won't be
you doing the talking—it will be the Spirit of your Father
speaking through you.
21“Brother will betray brother to death, fathers will
betray their own children, and children will rise against
their parents and cause them to be killed. 22And everyone
will hate you because of your allegiance to me. But those
who endure to the end will be saved. 23When you are per-
secuted in one town, flee to the next. I assure you that I,
the Son of Man, will return before you have reached all the
towns of Israel.
24“A student is not greater than the teacher. A servant is
not greater than the master. 25The student shares the
teacher's fate. The servant shares the master's fate. And
since I, the master of the household, have been called the
prince of demons,* how much more will it happen to you,
the members of the household! 26But don't be afraid of
those who threaten you. For the time is coming when

10:25 Greek *Beelzeboul.*

NEW KING JAMES VERSION

Persecutions Are Coming

16“Behold, I send you out as sheep in the midst of
wolves. Therefore be wise as serpents and harmless as
doves. 17But beware of men, for they will deliver you up to
councils and scourge you in their synagogues. 18You will
be brought before governors and kings for My sake, as a
testimony to them and to the Gentiles. 19But when they
deliver you up, do not worry about how or what you
should speak. For it will be given to you in that hour what
you should speak; 20for it is not you who speak, but the
Spirit of your Father who speaks in you.
21“Now brother will deliver up brother to death, and a
father *his* child; and children will rise up against parents
and cause them to be put to death. 22And you will be hated
by all for My name's sake. But he who endures to the end
will be saved. 23When they persecute you in this city, flee
to another. For assuredly, I say to you, you will not have
gone through the cities of Israel before the Son of Man
comes.
24“A disciple is not above *his* teacher, nor a servant
above his master. 25It is enough for a disciple that he be
like his teacher, and a servant like his master. If they have
called the master of the house Beelzebub,[d] how much more
will they call those of his household! 26Therefore do not

10:25 [d] NU-Text and M-Text read *Beelzebul.*

THE MESSAGE

“Stay alert. This is hazardous work I'm assigning you.
You're going to be like sheep running through a wolf pack,
so don't call attention to yourselves. Be as cunning as a
snake, inoffensive as a dove.

“Don't be naive. Some people will impugn your motives,
others will smear your reputation—just because you
believe in me. Don't be upset when they haul you before
the civil authorities. Without knowing it, they've done
you—and me—a favor, given you a platform for preaching
the kingdom news! And don't worry about what you'll say
or how you'll say it. The right words will be there; the
Spirit of your Father will supply the words.

“When people realize it is the living God you are pre-
senting and not some idol that makes them feel good, they
are going to turn on you, even people in your own family.
There is a great irony here: proclaiming so much love,
experiencing so much hate! But don't quit. Don't cave in. It
is all well worth it in the end. It is not success you are
after in such times but survival. Be survivors! Before
you've run out of options, the Son of Man will have
arrived.

“A student doesn't get a better desk than her teacher. A
laborer doesn't make more money than his boss. Be con-
tent—pleased, even—when you, my students, my harvest
hands, get the same treatment I get. If they call me, the
Master, ‘Dungface,’ what can the workers expect?

“Don't be intimidated. Eventually everything is going to

KING JAMES VERSION

that shall not be revealed; and hid, that shall not be known.

27 What I tell you in darkness, *that* speak ye in light: and what ye hear in the ear, *that* preach ye upon the housetops.

28 And fear not them which kill the body, but are not able to kill the soul: but rather fear him which is able to destroy both soul and body in hell.

29 Are not two sparrows sold for a farthing? and one of them shall not fall on the ground without your Father.

30 But the very hairs of your head are all numbered.

31 Fear ye not therefore, ye are of more value than many sparrows.

32 Whosoever therefore shall confess me before men, him will I confess also before my Father which is in heaven.

33 But whosoever shall deny me before men, him will I also deny before my Father which is in heaven.

34 Think not that I am come to send peace on earth: I came not to send peace, but a sword.

35 For I am come to set a man at variance against his father, and the daughter against her mother, and the daughter in law against her mother in law.

36 And a man's foes *shall be* they of his own household.

37 He that loveth father or mother more than me is not worthy of me: and he that loveth son or daughter more than me is not worthy of me.

NEW AMERICAN STANDARD BIBLE

concealed that will not be revealed, or hidden that will not be known.

27 "What I tell you in the darkness, speak in the light; and what you hear *whispered* in *your* ear, proclaim upon the housetops.

28 "Do not fear those who kill the body but are unable to kill the soul; but rather fear Him who is able to destroy both soul and body in hell.

29 "Are not two sparrows sold for a [1]cent? And *yet* not one of them will fall to the ground apart from your Father.

30 "But the very hairs of your head are all numbered.

31 "So do not fear; you are more valuable than many sparrows.

32 "Therefore everyone who confesses Me before men, I will also confess him before My Father who is in heaven.

33 "But whoever denies Me before men, I will also deny him before My Father who is in heaven.

34 "Do not think that I came to bring peace on the earth; I did not come to bring peace, but a sword.

35 "For I came to SET A MAN AGAINST HIS FATHER, AND A DAUGHTER AGAINST HER MOTHER, AND A DAUGHTER-IN-LAW AGAINST HER MOTHER-IN-LAW;

36 and A MAN'S ENEMIES WILL BE THE MEMBERS OF HIS HOUSEHOLD.

37 "He who loves father or mother more than Me is not worthy of Me; and he who loves son or daughter more than Me is not worthy of Me.

10:29 [1] Gr *assarion*, the smallest copper coin

NEW CENTURY VERSION

that is hidden will be shown. Everything that is secret will be made known. [27]I tell you these things in the dark, but I want you to tell them in the light. What you hear whispered in your ear you should shout from the housetops. [28]Don't be afraid of people, who can kill the body but cannot kill the soul. The only one you should fear is the one who can destroy the soul and the body in hell. [29]Two sparrows cost only a penny, but not even one of them can die without your Father's knowing it. [30]God even knows how many hairs are on your head. [31]So don't be afraid. You are worth much more than many sparrows.

Tell People About Your Faith

[32]"All those who stand before others and say they believe in me, I will say before my Father in heaven that they belong to me. [33]But all who stand before others and say they do not believe in me, I will say before my Father in heaven that they do not belong to me.

[34]"Don't think that I came to bring peace to the earth. I did not come to bring peace, but a sword. [35]I have come so that

'a son will be against his father,
a daughter will be against her mother,
a daughter-in-law will be against her mother-in-law.
[36] A person's enemies will be members of his own
family.' *Micah 7:6*

[37]"Those who love their father or mother more than they love me are not worthy to be my followers. Those who love their son or daughter more than they love me are not worthy

CONTEMPORARY ENGLISH VERSION

will be found out, and every secret will be known. [27]Whatever I say to you in the dark, you must tell in the light. And you must announce from the housetops whatever I have whispered to you. [28]Don't be afraid of people. They can kill you, but they cannot harm your soul. Instead, you should fear God who can destroy both your body and your soul in hell. [29]Aren't two sparrows sold for only a penny? But your Father knows when any one of them falls to the ground. [30]Even the hairs on your head are counted. [31]So don't be afraid! You are worth much more than many sparrows.

Telling Others about Christ (Luke 12.8, 9)

[32]If you tell others that you belong to me, I will tell my Father in heaven that you are my followers. [33]But if you reject me, I will tell my Father in heaven that you don't belong to me.

Not Peace, but Trouble (Luke 12.51-53; 14.26, 27)

[34]Don't think that I came to bring peace to the earth! I came to bring trouble, not peace. [35]I came to turn sons against their fathers, daughters against their mothers, and daughters-in-law against their mothers-in-law. [36]Your worst enemies will be in your own family.

[37]If you love your father or mother or even your sons and daughters more than me, you are not fit to be my

NEW INTERNATIONAL VERSION

that will not be disclosed, or hidden that will not be made known. 27What I tell you in the dark, speak in the daylight; what is whispered in your ear, proclaim from the roofs. 28Do not be afraid of those who kill the body but cannot kill the soul. Rather, be afraid of the One who can destroy both soul and body in hell. 29Are not two sparrows sold for a penny[d]? Yet not one of them will fall to the ground apart from the will of your Father. 30And even the very hairs of your head are all numbered. 31So don't be afraid; you are worth more than many sparrows.

32"Whoever acknowledges me before men, I will also acknowledge him before my Father in heaven. 33But whoever disowns me before men, I will disown him before my Father in heaven.

34"Do not suppose that I have come to bring peace to the earth. I did not come to bring peace, but a sword. 35For I have come to turn

" 'a man against his father,
a daughter against her mother,
a daughter-in-law against her mother-in-law—
36 a man's enemies will be the members of his own household.'[e]

37"Anyone who loves his father or mother more than me is not worthy of me; anyone who loves his son or daughter more than me is not worthy of me; 38and anyone who does

[d] 29 Greek *an assarion* [e] 36 Micah 7:6

NEW LIVING TRANSLATION

everything will be revealed; all that is secret will be made public. 27What I tell you now in the darkness, shout abroad when daybreak comes. What I whisper in your ears, shout from the housetops for all to hear!

28"Don't be afraid of those who want to kill you. They can only kill your body; they cannot touch your soul. Fear only God, who can destroy both soul and body in hell. 29Not even a sparrow, worth only half a penny, can fall to the ground without your Father knowing it. 30And the very hairs on your head are all numbered. 31So don't be afraid; you are more valuable to him than a whole flock of sparrows.

32"If anyone acknowledges me publicly here on earth, I will openly acknowledge that person before my Father in heaven. 33But if anyone denies me here on earth, I will deny that person before my Father in heaven.

34"Don't imagine that I came to bring peace to the earth! No, I came to bring a sword. 35I have come to set a man against his father, and a daughter against her mother, and a daughter-in-law against her mother-in-law. 36Your enemies will be right in your own household! 37If you love your father or mother more than you love me, you are not worthy of being mine; or if you love your son or daughter more than me, you are not worthy of being mine. 38If you

NEW KING JAMES VERSION

fear them. For there is nothing covered that will not be revealed, and hidden that will not be known.

Jesus Teaches the Fear of God

27"Whatever I tell you in the dark, speak in the light; and what you hear in the ear, preach on the housetops. 28And do not fear those who kill the body but cannot kill the soul. But rather fear Him who is able to destroy both soul and body in hell. 29Are not two sparrows sold for a copper coin? And not one of them falls to the ground apart from your Father's will. 30But the very hairs of your head are all numbered. 31Do not fear therefore; you are of more value than many sparrows.

Confess Christ Before Men

32"Therefore whoever confesses Me before men, him I will also confess before My Father who is in heaven. 33But whoever denies Me before men, him I will also deny before My Father who is in heaven.

Christ Brings Division

34"Do not think that I came to bring peace on earth. I did not come to bring peace but a sword. 35For I have come to *'set a man against his father, a daughter against her mother, and a daughter-in-law against her mother-in-law'*; 36and *'a man's enemies will be those of his own household.'*[e] 37He who loves father or mother more than Me is not worthy of Me. And he who loves son or daughter more

10:36 [e] Micah 7:6

THE MESSAGE

be out in the open, and everyone will know how things really are. So don't hesitate to go public now.

"Don't be bluffed into silence by the threats of bullies. There's nothing they can do to your soul, your core being. Save your fear for God, who holds your entire life—body and soul—in his hands.

Forget About Yourself

"What's the price of a pet canary? Some loose change, right? And God cares what happens to it even more than you do. He pays even greater attention to you, down to the last detail—even numbering the hairs on your head! So don't be intimidated by all this bully talk. You're worth more than a million canaries.

"Stand up for me against world opinion and I'll stand up for you before my Father in heaven. If you turn tail and run, do you think I'll cover for you?

"Don't think I've come to make life cozy. I've come to cut—make a sharp knife-cut between son and father, daughter and mother, bride and mother-in-law—cut through these cozy domestic arrangements and free you for God. Well-meaning family members can be your worst enemies. If you prefer father or mother over me, you don't deserve me. If you prefer son or daughter over me, you don't deserve me.

KING JAMES VERSION

38 And he that taketh not his cross, and followeth after me, is not worthy of me.

39 He that findeth his life shall lose it: and he that loseth his life for my sake shall find it.

40 He that receiveth you receiveth me, and he that receiveth me receiveth him that sent me.

41 He that receiveth a prophet in the name of a prophet shall receive a prophet's reward; and he that receiveth a righteous man in the name of a righteous man shall receive a righteous man's reward.

42 And whosoever shall give to drink unto one of these little ones a cup of cold *water* only in the name of a disciple, verily I say unto you, he shall in no wise lose his reward.

11 And it came to pass, when Jesus had made an end of commanding his twelve disciples, he departed thence to teach and to preach in their cities.

2 Now when John had heard in the prison the works of Christ, he sent two of his disciples,

3 And said unto him, Art thou he that should come, or do we look for another?

4 Jesus answered and said unto them, Go and shew John again those things which ye do hear and see:

5 The blind receive their sight, and the lame walk, the

NEW AMERICAN STANDARD BIBLE

38 "And he who does not take his cross and follow after Me is not worthy of Me.

39 "He who has found his life will lose it, and he who has lost his life for My sake will find it.

The Reward of Service

40 "He who receives you receives Me, and he who receives Me receives Him who sent Me.

41 "He who receives a prophet in *the* name of a prophet shall receive a prophet's reward; and he who receives a righteous man in the name of a righteous man shall receive a righteous man's reward.

42 "And whoever in the name of a disciple gives to one of these little ones even a cup of cold water to drink, truly I say to you, he shall not lose his reward."

John's Questions

11 When Jesus had finished giving instructions to His twelve disciples, He departed from there to teach and preach in their cities.

2 Now when John, while imprisoned, heard of the works of Christ, he sent *word* by his disciples

3 and said to Him, "Are You the Expected One, or shall we look for someone else?"

4 Jesus answered and said to them, "Go and report to John what you hear and see:

5 *the* BLIND RECEIVE SIGHT and *the* lame walk, *the* lepers

NEW CENTURY VERSION

to be my followers. [38]Whoever is not willing to carry the cross and follow me is not worthy of me. [39]Those who try to hold on to their lives will give up true life. Those who give up their lives for me will hold on to true life. [40]Whoever accepts you also accepts me, and whoever accepts me also accepts the One who sent me. [41]Whoever meets a prophet and accepts him will receive the reward of a prophet. And whoever accepts a good person because that person is good will receive the reward of a good person. [42]Those who give one of these little ones a cup of cold water because they are my followers will truly get their reward."

Jesus and John the Baptist

11 After Jesus finished telling these things to his twelve followers, he left there and went to the towns in Galilee to teach and preach.

[2]John the Baptist was in prison, but he heard about what Christ was doing. So John sent some of his followers to Jesus. [3]They asked him, "Are you the One who is to come, or should we wait for someone else?"

[4]Jesus answered them, "Go tell John what you hear and see: [5]The blind can see, the crippled can walk, and people with skin diseases are healed. The deaf can hear, the dead

CONTEMPORARY ENGLISH VERSION

disciples. [38]And unless you are willing to take up your cross and come with me, you are not fit to be my disciples. [39]If you try to save your life, you will lose it. But if you give it up for me, you will surely find it.

Rewards (Mark 9.41)

[40]Anyone who welcomes you welcomes me. And anyone who welcomes me also welcomes the one who sent me. [41]Anyone who welcomes a prophet, just because that person is a prophet, will be given the same reward as a prophet. Anyone who welcomes a good person, just because that person is good, will be given the same reward as a good person. [42]And anyone who gives one of my most humble followers a cup of cool water, just because that person is my follower, will surely be rewarded.

John the Baptist (Luke 7.18-35)

11 After Jesus had finished instructing his twelve disciples, he left and began teaching and preaching in the towns.[a]

[2]John was in prison when he heard what Christ was doing. So John sent some of his followers [3]to ask Jesus, "Are you the one we should be looking for? Or must we wait for someone else?"

[4]Jesus answered, "Go and tell John what you have heard and seen. [5]The blind are now able to see, and the lame can walk. People with leprosy[b] are being healed, and the deaf

[a] 11.1 *the towns*: The Greek text has "their towns," which may refer to the towns of Galilee or to the towns where Jesus' disciples had lived.
[b] 11.5 *leprosy*: See the note at 8.2.

NEW INTERNATIONAL VERSION

not take his cross and follow me is not worthy of me. 39Whoever finds his life will lose it, and whoever loses his life for my sake will find it.

40"He who receives you receives me, and he who receives me receives the one who sent me. 41Anyone who receives a prophet because he is a prophet will receive a prophet's reward, and anyone who receives a righteous man because he is a righteous man will receive a righteous man's reward. 42And if anyone gives even a cup of cold water to one of these little ones because he is my disciple, I tell you the truth, he will certainly not lose his reward."

Jesus and John the Baptist

11 After Jesus had finished instructing his twelve disciples, he went on from there to teach and preach in the towns of Galilee.[a]

2When John heard in prison what Christ was doing, he sent his disciples 3to ask him, "Are you the one who was to come, or should we expect someone else?"

4Jesus replied, "Go back and report to John what you hear and see: 5The blind receive sight, the lame walk, those who have leprosy[b] are cured, the deaf hear, the dead

[a] *1* Greek *in their towns* [b] *5* The Greek word was used for various diseases affecting the skin—not necessarily leprosy.

NEW LIVING TRANSLATION

refuse to take up your cross and follow me, you are not worthy of being mine. 39If you cling to your life, you will lose it; but if you give it up for me, you will find it.

40"Anyone who welcomes you is welcoming me, and anyone who welcomes me is welcoming the Father who sent me. 41If you welcome a prophet as one who speaks for God,* you will receive the same reward a prophet gets. And if you welcome good and godly people because of their godliness, you will be given a reward like theirs. 42And if you give even a cup of cold water to one of the least of my followers, you will surely be rewarded."

Jesus and John the Baptist

11 When Jesus had finished giving these instructions to his twelve disciples, he went off teaching and preaching in towns throughout the country.

2John the Baptist, who was now in prison, heard about all the things the Messiah was doing. So he sent his disciples to ask Jesus, 3"Are you really the Messiah we've been waiting for, or should we keep looking for someone else?"

4Jesus told them, "Go back to John and tell him about what you have heard and seen—5the blind see, the lame walk, the lepers are cured, the deaf hear, the dead are

10:41 Greek *welcome a prophet in the name of a prophet.*

NEW KING JAMES VERSION

than Me is not worthy of Me. 38And he who does not take his cross and follow after Me is not worthy of Me. 39He who finds his life will lose it, and he who loses his life for My sake will find it.

A Cup of Cold Water

40"He who receives you receives Me, and he who receives Me receives Him who sent Me. 41He who receives a prophet in the name of a prophet shall receive a prophet's reward. And he who receives a righteous man in the name of a righteous man shall receive a righteous man's reward. 42And whoever gives one of these little ones only a cup of cold *water* in the name of a disciple, assuredly, I say to you, he shall by no means lose his reward."

John the Baptist Sends Messengers to Jesus

11 Now it came to pass, when Jesus finished commanding His twelve disciples, that He departed from there to teach and to preach in their cities.

2And when John had heard in prison about the works of Christ, he sent two of[a] his disciples 3and said to Him, "Are You the Coming One, or do we look for another?"

4Jesus answered and said to them, "Go and tell John the things which you hear and see: 5*The* blind see and *the* lame walk; *the* lepers are cleansed and *the* deaf hear; *the*

11:2 [a] NU-Text reads *by* for *two of.*

THE MESSAGE

"If you don't go all the way with me, through thick and thin, you don't deserve me. If your first concern is to look after yourself, you'll never find yourself. But if you forget about yourself and look to me, you'll find both yourself and me.

"We are intimately linked in this harvest work. Anyone who accepts what you do, accepts me, the One who sent you. Anyone who accepts what I do accepts my Father, who sent me. Accepting a messenger of God is as good as being God's messenger. Accepting someone's help is as good as giving someone help. This is a large work I've called you into, but don't be overwhelmed by it. It's best to start small. Give a cool cup of water to someone who is thirsty, for instance. The smallest act of giving or receiving makes you a true apprentice. You won't lose out on a thing."

John the Baptizer

11 When Jesus finished placing this charge before his twelve disciples, he went on to teach and preach in their villages.

John, meanwhile, had been locked up in prison. When he got wind of what Jesus was doing, he sent his own disciples to ask, "Are you the One we've been expecting, or are we still waiting?"

Jesus told them, "Go back and tell John what's going on:

The blind see,
The lame walk,
Lepers are cleansed,
The deaf hear,

KING JAMES VERSION

lepers are cleansed, and the deaf hear, the dead are raised up, and the poor have the gospel preached to them.

6 And blessed is *he*, whosoever shall not be offended in me.

7 ¶ And as they departed, Jesus began to say unto the multitudes concerning John, What went ye out into the wilderness to see? A reed shaken with the wind?

8 But what went ye out for to see? A man clothed in soft raiment? behold, they that wear soft *clothing* are in kings' houses.

9 But what went ye out for to see? A prophet? yea, I say unto you, and more than a prophet.

10 For this is *he*, of whom it is written, Behold, I send my messenger before thy face, which shall prepare thy way before thee.

11 Verily I say unto you, Among them that are born of women there hath not risen a greater than John the Baptist: notwithstanding he that is least in the kingdom of heaven is greater than he.

12 And from the days of John the Baptist until now the kingdom of heaven suffereth violence, and the violent take it by force.

13 For all the prophets and the law prophesied until John.

14 And if ye will receive *it*, this is Elias, which was for to come.

15 He that hath ears to hear, let him hear.

NEW AMERICAN STANDARD BIBLE

are cleansed and *the* deaf hear, *the* dead are raised up, and *the* POOR HAVE THE GOSPEL PREACHED TO THEM.

6 "And blessed is he who does not take offense at Me."

Jesus' Tribute to John

7 As these men were going *away,* Jesus began to speak to the crowds about John, "What did you go out into the wilderness to see? A reed shaken by the wind?

8 "But what did you go out to see? A man dressed in soft *clothing?* Those who wear soft *clothing* are in kings' palaces!

9 "But what did you go out to see? A prophet? Yes, I tell you, and one who is more than a prophet.

10 "This is the one about whom it is written,

'BEHOLD, I SEND MY MESSENGER AHEAD OF YOU,
WHO WILL PREPARE YOUR WAY BEFORE YOU.'

11 "Truly I say to you, among those born of women there has not arisen *anyone* greater than John the Baptist! Yet the one who is least in the kingdom of heaven is greater than he.

12 "From the days of John the Baptist until now the kingdom of heaven suffers violence, and violent men take it by force.

13 "For all the prophets and the Law prophesied until John.

14 "And if you are willing to accept *it,* John himself is Elijah who was to come.

15 "He who has ears to hear, let him hear.

NEW CENTURY VERSION

are raised to life, and the Good News is preached to the
poor. [6]Those who do not stumble in their faith because of
me are blessed."
[7]As John's followers were leaving, Jesus began talking to
the people about John. Jesus said, "What did you go out
into the desert to see? A reed[a] blown by the wind? [8]What
did you go out to see? A man dressed in fine clothes? No,
those who wear fine clothes live in kings' palaces. [9]So why
did you go out? To see a prophet? Yes, and I tell you, John
is more than a prophet. [10]This was written about him:

'I will send my messenger ahead of you,
who will prepare the way for you.' *Malachi 3:1*

[11]I tell you the truth, John the Baptist is greater than any
other person ever born, but even the least important per-
son in the kingdom of heaven is greater than John. [12]Since
the time John the Baptist came until now, the kingdom of
heaven has been going forward in strength, and people
have been trying to take it by force. [13]All the prophets and
the law of Moses told about what would happen until the
time John came. [14]And if you will believe what they said,
you will believe that John is Elijah, whom they said would
come. [15]You people who can hear me, listen!

11:7 [a] **reed** It means that John was not ordinary or weak like grass blown by the wind.

CONTEMPORARY ENGLISH VERSION

can hear. The dead are raised to life, and the poor are
hearing the good news. [6]God will bless everyone who
doesn't reject me because of what I do."
[7]As John's followers were going away, Jesus spoke to the
crowds about John:

What sort of person did you go out into the desert to
see? Was he like tall grass blown about by the wind?
[8]What kind of man did you go out to see? Was he some-
one dressed in fine clothes? People who dress like that
live in the king's palace. [9]What did you really go out to
see? Was he a prophet? He certainly was. I tell you that
he was more than a prophet. [10]In the Scriptures God
says about him, "I am sending my messenger ahead of
you to get things ready for you." [11]I tell you that no one
ever born on this earth is greater than John the Baptist.
But whoever is least in the kingdom of heaven is greater
than John.
[12]From the time of John the Baptist until now, violent
people have been trying to take over the kingdom of
heaven by force. [13]All the Books of the Prophets and the
Law of Moses[c] told what was going to happen up to the
time of John. [14]And if you believe them, John is Elijah,
the prophet you are waiting for. [15]If you have ears, pay
attention!

[c] 11.13 *the Books of the Prophets and the Law of Moses*: The Jewish Scriptures, that is, the Old Testament.

NEW INTERNATIONAL VERSION

are raised, and the good news is preached to the poor. 6Blessed is the man who does not fall away on account of me."

7As John's disciples were leaving, Jesus began to speak to the crowd about John: "What did you go out into the desert to see? A reed swayed by the wind? 8If not, what did you go out to see? A man dressed in fine clothes? No, those who wear fine clothes are in kings' palaces. 9Then what did you go out to see? A prophet? Yes, I tell you, and more than a prophet. 10This is the one about whom it is written:

" 'I will send my messenger ahead of you,
who will prepare your way before you.'[c]

11I tell you the truth: Among those born of women there has not risen anyone greater than John the Baptist; yet he who is least in the kingdom of heaven is greater than he. 12From the days of John the Baptist until now, the kingdom of heaven has been forcefully advancing, and forceful men lay hold of it. 13For all the Prophets and the Law prophesied until John. 14And if you are willing to accept it, he is the Elijah who was to come. 15He who has ears, let him hear.

[c] *10* Mal. 3:1

NEW LIVING TRANSLATION

raised to life, and the Good News is being preached to the poor. 6And tell him: 'God blesses those who are not offended by me.*' "

7When John's disciples had gone, Jesus began talking about him to the crowds. "Who is this man in the wilderness that you went out to see? Did you find him weak as a reed, moved by every breath of wind? 8Or were you expecting to see a man dressed in expensive clothes? Those who dress like that live in palaces, not out in the wilderness. 9Were you looking for a prophet? Yes, and he is more than a prophet. 10John is the man to whom the Scriptures refer when they say,

'Look, I am sending my messenger before you,
and he will prepare your way before you.'*

11"I assure you, of all who have ever lived, none is greater than John the Baptist. Yet even the most insignificant person in the Kingdom of Heaven is greater than he is! 12And from the time John the Baptist began preaching and baptizing until now, the Kingdom of Heaven has been forcefully advancing, and violent people attack it.* 13For before John came, all the teachings of the Scriptures looked forward to this present time. 14And if you are willing to accept what I say, he is Elijah, the one the prophets said would come.* 15Anyone who is willing to hear should listen and understand!

11:6 Or *who don't fall away because of me.* **11:10** Mal 3:1. **11:12** Or *until now, eager multitudes have been pressing into the Kingdom of Heaven.* **11:14** See Mal 4:5.

NEW KING JAMES VERSION

dead are raised up and *the* poor have the gospel preached to them. 6And blessed is he who is not offended because of Me."

7As they departed, Jesus began to say to the multitudes concerning John: "What did you go out into the wilderness to see? A reed shaken by the wind? 8But what did you go out to see? A man clothed in soft garments? Indeed, those who wear soft *clothing* are in kings' houses. 9But what did you go out to see? A prophet? Yes, I say to you, and more than a prophet. 10For this is *he* of whom it is written:

*'Behold, I send My messenger before Your face,
Who will prepare Your way before You.'*[b]

11"Assuredly, I say to you, among those born of women there has not risen one greater than John the Baptist; but he who is least in the kingdom of heaven is greater than he. 12And from the days of John the Baptist until now the kingdom of heaven suffers violence, and the violent take it by force. 13For all the prophets and the law prophesied until John. 14And if you are willing to receive *it,* he is Elijah who is to come. 15He who has ears to hear, let him hear!

11:10 [b] Malachi 3:1

THE MESSAGE

The dead are raised,
The wretched of the earth learn that God is on their side.

Is this what you were expecting? Then count yourselves most blessed!"

When John's disciples left to report, Jesus started talking to the crowd about John. "What did you expect when you went out to see him in the wild? A weekend camper? Hardly. What then? A sheik in silk pajamas? Not in the wilderness, not by a long shot. What then? A prophet? That's right, a prophet! Probably the best prophet you'll ever hear. He is the prophet that Malachi announced when he wrote, 'I'm sending my prophet ahead of you, to make the road smooth for you.'

"Let me tell you what's going on here: No one in history surpasses John the Baptizer; but in the kingdom he prepared you for, the lowliest person is ahead of him. For a long time now people have tried to force themselves into God's kingdom. But if you read the books of the Prophets and God's Law closely, you will see them culminate in John, teaming up with him in preparing the way for the Messiah of the kingdom. Looked at it this way, John is the 'Elijah' you've all been expecting to arrive and introduce the Messiah.

"Are you listening to me?
"Really listening?

KING JAMES VERSION

16 ¶ But whereunto shall I liken this generation? It is like unto children sitting in the markets, and calling unto their fellows,

17 And saying, We have piped unto you, and ye have not danced; we have mourned unto you, and ye have not lamented.

18 For John came neither eating nor drinking, and they say, He hath a devil.

19 The Son of man came eating and drinking, and they say, Behold a man gluttonous, and a winebibber, a friend of publicans and sinners. But wisdom is justified of her children.

20 Then began he to upbraid the cities wherein most of his mighty works were done, because they repented not:

21 Woe unto thee, Chorazin! woe unto thee, Bethsaida! for if the mighty works, which were done in you, had been done in Tyre and Sidon, they would have repented long ago in sackcloth and ashes.

22 But I say unto you, It shall be more tolerable for Tyre and Sidon at the day of judgment, than for you.

23 And thou, Capernaum, which art exalted unto heaven,

NEW AMERICAN STANDARD BIBLE

16 "But to what shall I compare this generation? It is like children sitting in the market places, who call out to the other *children*,

17 and say, 'We played the flute for you, and you did not dance; we sang a dirge, and you did not mourn.'

18 "For John came neither eating nor drinking, and they say, 'He has a demon!'

19 "The Son of Man came eating and drinking, and they say, 'Behold, a gluttonous man and a drunkard, a friend of tax collectors and sinners!' Yet wisdom is vindicated by her deeds."

The Unrepenting Cities

20 Then He began to denounce the cities in which most of His miracles were done, because they did not repent.

21 "Woe to you, Chorazin! Woe to you, Bethsaida! For if the miracles had occurred in Tyre and Sidon which occurred in you, they would have repented long ago in sackcloth and ashes.

22 "Nevertheless I say to you, it will be more tolerable for Tyre and Sidon in *the* day of judgment than for you.

23 "And you, Capernaum, will not be exalted to heaven,

NEW CENTURY VERSION

16"What can I say about the people of this time? What are they like? They are like children sitting in the marketplace, who call out to each other,

17'We played music for you, but you did not dance;
we sang a sad song, but you did not cry.'

18John came and did not eat or drink like other people. So people say, 'He has a demon.'
19The Son of Man came, eating and drinking, and people say, 'Look at him! He eats too much and drinks too much wine, and he is a friend of tax collectors and sinners.' But wisdom is proved to be right by what it does."

Jesus Warns Unbelievers

20Then Jesus criticized the cities where he did most of his miracles, because the people did not change their lives and stop sinning.
21He said, "How terrible for you, Korazin! How terrible for you, Bethsaida! If the same miracles I did in you had happened in Tyre and Sidon,[b] those people would have changed their lives a long time ago. They would have worn rough cloth and put ashes on themselves to show they had changed.
22But I tell you, on the Judgment Day it will be better for Tyre and Sidon than for you.
23And you, Capernaum,[c] will you be lifted up to

11:21 [b] **Tyre and Sidon** Towns where wicked people lived.
11:23 [c] **Korazin...Bethsaida...Capernaum** Towns by Lake Galilee where Jesus preached to the people.

CONTEMPORARY ENGLISH VERSION

16You people are like children sitting in the market and shouting to each other,

17"We played the flute,
but you would not dance!
We sang a funeral song,
but you would not mourn!"

18John the Baptist did not go around eating and drinking, and you said, "That man has a demon in him!"
19But the Son of Man goes around eating and drinking, and you say, "That man eats and drinks too much! He is even a friend of tax collectors[d] and sinners." Yet Wisdom is shown to be right by what it does.

The Unbelieving Towns (Luke 10.13-15)

20In the towns where Jesus had worked most of his miracles, the people refused to turn to God. So Jesus was upset with them and said:

21You people of Chorazin are in for trouble! You people of Bethsaida are in for trouble too! If the miracles that took place in your towns had happened in Tyre and Sidon, the people there would have turned to God long ago. They would have dressed in sackcloth and put ashes on their heads.[e]
22I tell you that on the day of judgment the people of Tyre and Sidon will get off easier than you will.

23People of Capernaum, do you think you will be hon-

[d] 11.19 *tax collectors*: See the note at 5.46. [e] 11.21 *sackcloth . . . ashes on their heads*: This was one way that people showed how sorry they were for their sins.

NEW INTERNATIONAL VERSION

16 “To what can I compare this generation? They are like
children sitting in the marketplaces and calling out to oth-
ers:

17 “ ‘We played the flute for you,
and you did not dance;
we sang a dirge,
and you did not mourn.’

18 For John came neither eating nor drinking, and they say,
‘He has a demon.’ 19 The Son of Man came eating and
drinking, and they say, ‘Here is a glutton and a drunkard,
a friend of tax collectors and “sinners.” ’ But wisdom is
proved right by her actions.”

Woe on Unrepentant Cities

20 Then Jesus began to denounce the cities in which most
of his miracles had been performed, because they did not
repent. 21 “Woe to you, Korazin! Woe to you, Bethsaida! If
the miracles that were performed in you had been per-
formed in Tyre and Sidon, they would have repented long
ago in sackcloth and ashes. 22 But I tell you, it will be more
bearable for Tyre and Sidon on the day of judgment than
for you. 23 And you, Capernaum, will you be lifted up to the

NEW LIVING TRANSLATION

16 “How shall I describe this generation? These people
are like a group of children playing a game in the public
square. They complain to their friends, 17 ‘We played wed-
ding songs, and you weren’t happy, so we played funeral
songs, but you weren’t sad.’ 18 For John the Baptist didn’t
drink wine and he often fasted, and you say, ‘He’s demon
possessed.’ 19 And I, the Son of Man, feast and drink, and
you say, ‘He’s a glutton and a drunkard, and a friend of
the worst sort of sinners!’ But wisdom is shown to be right
by what results from it.”

Judgment for the Unbelievers

20 Then Jesus began to denounce the cities where he had
done most of his miracles, because they hadn’t turned
from their sins and turned to God. 21 “What horrors await
you, Korazin and Bethsaida! For if the miracles I did in
you had been done in wicked Tyre and Sidon, their people
would have sat in deep repentance long ago, clothed in
sackcloth and throwing ashes on their heads to show their
remorse. 22 I assure you, Tyre and Sidon will be better off
on the judgment day than you! 23 And you people of
Capernaum, will you be exalted to heaven? No, you will be

NEW KING JAMES VERSION

16 “But to what shall I liken this generation? It is like
children sitting in the marketplaces and calling to their
companions, 17 and saying:

‘We played the flute for you,
And you did not dance;
We mourned to you,
And you did not lament.’

18 For John came neither eating nor drinking, and they say,
‘He has a demon.’ 19 The Son of Man came eating and
drinking, and they say, ‘Look, a glutton and a winebibber,
a friend of tax collectors and sinners!’ But wisdom is justi-
fied by her children.”[c]

Woe to the Impenitent Cities

20 Then He began to rebuke the cities in which most of
His mighty works had been done, because they did not
repent: 21 “Woe to you, Chorazin! Woe to you, Bethsaida!
For if the mighty works which were done in you had been
done in Tyre and Sidon, they would have repented long
ago in sackcloth and ashes. 22 But I say to you, it will be
more tolerable for Tyre and Sidon in the day of judgment
than for you. 23 And you, Capernaum, who are exalted to

11:19 [c] NU-Text reads *works.*

THE MESSAGE

“How can I account for this generation? The people have been like spoiled children whining to their parents, ‘We wanted to skip rope, and you were always too tired; we wanted to talk, but you were always too busy.’ John came fasting and they called him crazy. I came feasting and they called me a lush, a friend of the riffraff. Opinion polls don’t count for much, do they? The proof of the pudding is in the eating.”

The Unforced Rhythms of Grace

Next Jesus let fly on the cities where he had worked the hardest but whose people had responded the least, shrugging their shoulders and going their own way.

“Doom to you, Chorazin! Doom, Bethsaida! If Tyre and Sidon had seen half of the powerful miracles you have seen, they would have been on their knees in a minute. At Judgment Day they’ll get off easy compared to you. And Capernaum! With all your peacock strutting, you are going

KING JAMES VERSION

shalt be brought down to hell: for if the mighty works, which have been done in thee, had been done in Sodom, it would have remained until this day.

24 But I say unto you, That it shall be more tolerable for the land of Sodom in the day of judgment, than for thee.

25 ¶ At that time Jesus answered and said, I thank thee, O Father, Lord of heaven and earth, because thou hast hid these things from the wise and prudent, and hast revealed them unto babes.

26 Even so, Father: for so it seemed good in thy sight.

27 All things are delivered unto me of my Father: and no man knoweth the Son, but the Father; neither knoweth any man the Father, save the Son, and *he* to whomsoever the Son will reveal *him*.

28 Come unto me, all *ye* that labour and are heavy laden, and I will give you rest.

29 Take my yoke upon you, and learn of me; for I am meek and lowly in heart: and ye shall find rest unto your souls.

30 For my yoke *is* easy, and my burden is light.

12 At that time Jesus went on the sabbath day through the corn; and his disciples were an hungred, and began to pluck the ears of corn, and to eat.

NEW AMERICAN STANDARD BIBLE

will you? You will descend to Hades; for if the miracles had occurred in Sodom which occurred in you, it would have remained to this day.

24 "Nevertheless I say to you that it will be more tolerable for the land of Sodom in *the* day of judgment, than for you."

Come to Me

25 At that time Jesus said, "I praise You, Father, Lord of heaven and earth, that You have hidden these things from *the* wise and intelligent and have revealed them to infants.

26 "Yes, Father, for this way was well-pleasing in Your sight.

27 "All things have been handed over to Me by My Father; and no one knows the Son except the Father; nor does anyone know the Father except the Son, and anyone to whom the Son wills to reveal *Him*.

28 "Come to Me, all who are weary and heavy-laden, and I will give you rest.

29 "Take My yoke upon you and learn from Me, for I am gentle and humble in heart, and YOU WILL FIND REST FOR YOUR SOULS.

30 "For My yoke is easy and My burden is light."

Sabbath Questions

12 At that time Jesus went through the grainfields on the Sabbath, and His disciples became hungry and began to pick the heads *of grain* and eat.

NEW CENTURY VERSION

heaven? No, you will be thrown down to the depths. If the miracles I did in you had happened in Sodom,[d] its people would have stopped sinning, and it would still be a city today. 24 But I tell you, on the Judgment Day it will be better for Sodom than for you."

Jesus Offers Rest to People

25 At that time Jesus said, "I praise you, Father, Lord of heaven and earth, because you have hidden these things from the people who are wise and smart. But you have shown them to those who are like little children. 26 Yes, Father, this is what you really wanted.

27 "My Father has given me all things. No one knows the Son, except the Father. And no one knows the Father, except the Son and those whom the Son chooses to tell.

28 "Come to me, all of you who are tired and have heavy loads, and I will give you rest. 29 Accept my teachings and learn from me, because I am gentle and humble in spirit, and you will find rest for your lives. 30 The teaching that I ask you to accept is easy; the load I give you to carry is light."

Jesus Is Lord of the Sabbath

12 At that time Jesus was walking through some fields of grain on a Sabbath day. His followers were hungry, so they began to pick the grain and eat it.

11:23 [d] **Sodom** A city that God destroyed because the people were so evil.

CONTEMPORARY ENGLISH VERSION

ored in heaven? You will go down to hell! If the miracles that took place in your town had happened in Sodom, that town would still be standing. 24 So I tell you that on the day of judgment the people of Sodom will get off easier than you.

Come to Me and Rest (Luke 10.21, 22)

25 At that moment Jesus said:

My Father, Lord of heaven and earth, I am grateful that you hid all this from wise and educated people and showed it to ordinary people. 26 Yes, Father, that is what pleased you.

27 My Father has given me everything, and he is the only one who knows the Son. The only one who truly knows the Father is the Son. But the Son wants to tell others about the Father, so that they can know him too.

28 If you are tired from carrying heavy burdens, come to me and I will give you rest. 29 Take the yoke[f] I give you. Put it on your shoulders and learn from me. I am gentle and humble, and you will find rest. 30 This yoke is easy to bear, and this burden is light.

A Question about the Sabbath (Mark 2.23-28; Luke 6.1-5)

12 One Sabbath, Jesus and his disciples were walking through some wheat fields.[a] His disciples were hungry and began picking and eating grains of wheat.

[f] 11.29 *yoke*: Yokes were put on the necks of animals, so that they could pull a plow or wagon. A yoke was a symbol of obedience and hard work.
[a] 12.1 *walking through some wheat fields*: It was the custom to let hungry travelers pick grains of wheat.

NEW INTERNATIONAL VERSION

skies? No, you will go down to the depths.[d] If the miracles
that were performed in you had been performed in Sodom,
it would have remained to this day. 24But I tell you that it
will be more bearable for Sodom on the day of judgment
than for you."

Rest for the Weary

25At that time Jesus said, "I praise you, Father, Lord of
heaven and earth, because you have hidden these things
from the wise and learned, and revealed them to little chil-
dren. 26Yes, Father, for this was your good pleasure.

27"All things have been committed to me by my Father.
No one knows the Son except the Father, and no one
knows the Father except the Son and those to whom the
Son chooses to reveal him.

28"Come to me, all you who are weary and burdened, and
I will give you rest. 29Take my yoke upon you and learn
from me, for I am gentle and humble in heart, and you will
find rest for your souls. 30For my yoke is easy and my bur-
den is light."

Lord of the Sabbath

12 At that time Jesus went through the grainfields on
the Sabbath. His disciples were hungry and began
to pick some heads of grain and eat them. 2When the

[d] 23 Greek *Hades*

NEW LIVING TRANSLATION

brought down to the place of the dead.* For if the miracles
I did for you had been done in Sodom, it would still be
here today. 24I assure you, Sodom will be better off on the
judgment day than you."

Jesus' Prayer of Thanksgiving

25Then Jesus prayed this prayer: "O Father, Lord of
heaven and earth, thank you for hiding the truth from
those who think themselves so wise and clever, and for
revealing it to the childlike. 26Yes, Father, it pleased you to
do it this way!

27"My Father has given me authority over everything.
No one really knows the Son except the Father, and no one
really knows the Father except the Son and those to whom
the Son chooses to reveal him."

28Then Jesus said, "Come to me, all of you who are
weary and carry heavy burdens, and I will give you rest.
29Take my yoke upon you. Let me teach you, because I am
humble and gentle, and you will find rest for your souls.
30For my yoke fits perfectly, and the burden I give you is
light."

Controversy about the Sabbath

12 At about that time Jesus was walking through
some grainfields on the Sabbath. His disciples
were hungry, so they began breaking off heads of wheat

11:23 Greek *to Hades.*

NEW KING JAMES VERSION

heaven, will be[d] brought down to Hades; for if the mighty
works which were done in you had been done in Sodom, it
would have remained until this day. 24But I say to you
that it shall be more tolerable for the land of Sodom in the
day of judgment than for you."

Jesus Gives True Rest

25At that time Jesus answered and said, "I thank You,
Father, Lord of heaven and earth, that You have hidden
these things from *the* wise and prudent and have revealed
them to babes. 26Even so, Father, for so it seemed good in
Your sight. 27All things have been delivered to Me by My
Father, and no one knows the Son except the Father. Nor
does anyone know the Father except the Son, and *the one*
to whom the Son wills to reveal *Him*. 28Come to Me, all
you who labor and are heavy laden, and I will give you
rest. 29Take My yoke upon you and learn from Me, for I am
gentle and lowly in heart, and you will find rest for your
souls. 30For My yoke *is* easy and My burden is light."

Jesus Is Lord of the Sabbath

12 At that time Jesus went through the grainfields on
the Sabbath. And His disciples were hungry, and
began to pluck heads of grain and to eat. 2And when the

11:23 [d] NU-Text reads *will you be exalted to heaven? No, you will be.*

THE MESSAGE

to end up in the abyss. If the people of Sodom had had
your chances, the city would still be around. At Judgment
Day they'll get off easy compared to you."

Abruptly Jesus broke into prayer: "Thank you, Father,
Lord of heaven and earth. You've concealed your ways
from sophisticates and know-it-alls, but spelled them out
clearly to ordinary people. Yes, Father, that's the way you
like to work."

Jesus resumed talking to the people, but now tenderly.
"The Father has given me all these things to do and say.
This is a unique Father-Son operation, coming out of
Father and Son intimacies and knowledge. No one knows
the Son the way the Father does, nor the Father the way
the Son does. But I'm not keeping it to myself; I'm ready to
go over it line by line with anyone willing to listen.

"Are you tired? Worn out? Burned out on religion? Come
to me. Get away with me and you'll recover your life. I'll
show you how to take a real rest. Walk with me and work
with me—watch how I do it. Learn the unforced rhythms
of grace. I won't lay anything heavy or ill-fitting on you.
Keep company with me and you'll learn to live freely and
lightly."

In Charge of the Sabbath

12 One Sabbath, Jesus was strolling with his disciples
through a field of ripe grain. Hungry, the disciples
were pulling off the heads of grain and munching on them.

KING JAMES VERSION

2 But when the Pharisees saw *it*, they said unto him, Behold, thy disciples do that which is not lawful to do upon the sabbath day.

3 But he said unto them, Have ye not read what David did, when he was an hungred, and they that were with him;

4 How he entered into the house of God, and did eat the shewbread, which was not lawful for him to eat, neither for them which were with him, but only for the priests?

5 Or have ye not read in the law, how that on the sabbath days the priests in the temple profane the sabbath, and are blameless?

6 But I say unto you, That in this place is *one* greater than the temple.

7 But if ye had known what *this* meaneth, I will have mercy, and not sacrifice, ye would not have condemned the guiltless.

8 For the Son of man is Lord even of the sabbath day.

9 And when he was departed thence, he went into their synagogue:

10 And, behold, there was a man which had *his* hand withered. And they asked him, saying, Is it lawful to heal on the sabbath days? that they might accuse him.

11 And he said unto them, What man shall there be among you, that shall have one sheep, and if it fall into a pit on the sabbath day, will he not lay hold on it, and lift *it* out?

12 How much then is a man better than a sheep? Wherefore it is lawful to do well on the sabbath days.

13 Then saith he to the man, Stretch forth thine hand.

NEW AMERICAN STANDARD BIBLE

2 But when the Pharisees saw *this*, they said to Him, "Look, Your disciples do what is not lawful to do on a Sabbath."

3 But He said to them, "Have you not read what David did when he became hungry, he and his companions,

4 how he entered the house of God, and they ate the consecrated bread, which was not lawful for him to eat nor for those with him, but for the priests alone?

5 "Or have you not read in the Law, that on the Sabbath the priests in the temple break the Sabbath and are innocent?

6 "But I say to you that something greater than the temple is here.

7 "But if you had known what this means, 'I DESIRE COMPASSION, AND NOT A SACRIFICE,' you would not have condemned the innocent.

Lord of the Sabbath

8 "For the Son of Man is Lord of the Sabbath."

9 Departing from there, He went into their synagogue.

10 And a man *was there* whose hand was withered. And they questioned Jesus, asking, "Is it lawful to heal on the Sabbath?"—so that they might accuse Him.

11 And He said to them, "What man is there among you who has a sheep, and if it falls into a pit on the Sabbath, will he not take hold of it and lift it out?

12 "How much more valuable then is a man than a sheep! So then, it is lawful to do good on the Sabbath."

13 Then He *said to the man, "Stretch out your hand!"

NEW CENTURY VERSION

2When the Pharisees saw this, they said to Jesus, "Look!
Your followers are doing what is unlawful to do on the
Sabbath day."

3Jesus answered, "Have you not read what David did
when he and the people with him were hungry? 4He went
into God's house, and he and those with him ate the holy
bread, which was lawful only for priests to eat. 5And have
you not read in the law of Moses that on every Sabbath
day the priests in the Temple break this law about the
Sabbath day? But the priests are not wrong for doing that.
6I tell you that there is something here that is greater than
the Temple. 7The Scripture says, 'I want kindness more
than I want animal sacrifices.'[a] You don't really know
what those words mean. If you understood them, you
would not judge those who have done nothing wrong.

8"So the Son of Man is Lord of the Sabbath day."

Jesus Heals a Man's Hand

9Jesus left there and went into their synagogue, 10where
there was a man with a crippled hand. They were looking
for a reason to accuse Jesus, so they asked him, "Is it right
to heal on the Sabbath day?"[b]

11Jesus answered, "If any of you has a sheep, and it falls
into a ditch on the Sabbath day, you will help it out of the
ditch. 12Surely a human being is more important than a
sheep. So it is lawful to do good things on the Sabbath
day."

13Then Jesus said to the man with the crippled hand,

12:7 [a] **'I...sacrifices.'** Quotation from Hosea 6:6. 12:10 [b] **"Is it right...day?"** It was against Jewish law to work on the Sabbath day.

CONTEMPORARY ENGLISH VERSION

2Some Pharisees noticed this and said to Jesus, "Why are
your disciples picking grain on the Sabbath? They are not
supposed to do that!"

3Jesus answered:

You surely must have read what David did when he
and his followers were hungry. 4He went into the house
of God, and then they ate the sacred loaves of bread that
only priests are supposed to eat. 5Haven't you read in
the Law of Moses that the priests are allowed to work in
the temple on the Sabbath? But no one says that they
are guilty of breaking the law of the Sabbath. 6I tell you
that there is something here greater than the temple.
7Don't you know what the Scriptures mean when they
say, "Instead of offering sacrifices to me, I want you to
be merciful to others?" If you knew what this means,
you would not condemn these innocent disciples of
mine. 8So the Son of Man is Lord over the Sabbath.

A Man with a Crippled Hand (Mark 3.1-6; Luke 6.6-11)

9Jesus left and went into one of the Jewish meeting
places, 10where there was a man whose hand was crippled.
Some Pharisees wanted to accuse Jesus of doing something
wrong, and they asked him, "Is it right to heal someone on
the Sabbath?"

11Jesus answered, "If you had a sheep that fell into a
ditch on the Sabbath, wouldn't you lift it out? 12People are
worth much more than sheep, and so it is right to do good
on the Sabbath." 13Then Jesus told the man, "Hold out

NEW INTERNATIONAL VERSION

Pharisees saw this, they said to him, "Look! Your disciples
are doing what is unlawful on the Sabbath."
3He answered, "Haven't you read what David did when
he and his companions were hungry? 4He entered the
house of God, and he and his companions ate the conse-
crated bread—which was not lawful for them to do, but
only for the priests. 5Or haven't you read in the Law that
on the Sabbath the priests in the temple desecrate the day
and yet are innocent? 6I tell you that one[a] greater than the
temple is here. 7If you had known what these words mean,
'I desire mercy, not sacrifice,'[b] you would not have con-
demned the innocent. 8For the Son of Man is Lord of the
Sabbath."
9Going on from that place, he went into their synagogue,
10and a man with a shriveled hand was there. Looking for
a reason to accuse Jesus, they asked him, "Is it lawful to
heal on the Sabbath?"
11He said to them, "If any of you has a sheep and it falls
into a pit on the Sabbath, will you not take hold of it and
lift it out? 12How much more valuable is a man than a
sheep! Therefore it is lawful to do good on the Sabbath."
13Then he said to the man, "Stretch out your hand." So

[a] 6 Or *something*; also in verses 41 and 42 [b] 7 Hosea 6:6

NEW LIVING TRANSLATION

and eating the grain. 2Some Pharisees saw them do it and
protested, "Your disciples shouldn't be doing that! It's
against the law to work by harvesting grain on the
Sabbath."
3But Jesus said to them, "Haven't you ever read in the
Scriptures what King David did when he and his compan-
ions were hungry? 4He went into the house of God, and
they ate the special bread reserved for the priests alone.
That was breaking the law, too. 5And haven't you ever
read in the law of Moses that the priests on duty in the
Temple may work on the Sabbath? 6I tell you, there is one
here who is even greater than the Temple! 7But you would
not have condemned those who aren't guilty if you knew
the meaning of this Scripture: 'I want you to be merciful; I
don't want your sacrifices.'* 8For I, the Son of Man, am
master even of the Sabbath."
9Then he went over to the synagogue, 10where he
noticed a man with a deformed hand. The Pharisees asked
Jesus, "Is it legal to work by healing on the Sabbath day?"
(They were, of course, hoping he would say yes, so they
could bring charges against him.)
11And he answered, "If you had one sheep, and it fell
into a well on the Sabbath, wouldn't you get to work and
pull it out? Of course you would. 12And how much more
valuable is a person than a sheep! Yes, it is right to do good
on the Sabbath." 13Then he said to the man, "Reach out

12:7 Hos 6:6.

NEW KING JAMES VERSION

Pharisees saw *it,* they said to Him, "Look, Your disciples
are doing what is not lawful to do on the Sabbath!"
3But He said to them, "Have you not read what David
did when he was hungry, he and those who were with him:
4how he entered the house of God and ate the showbread
which was not lawful for him to eat, nor for those who
were with him, but only for the priests? 5Or have you not
read in the law that on the Sabbath the priests in the tem-
ple profane the Sabbath, and are blameless? 6Yet I say to
you that in this place there is *One* greater than the temple.
7But if you had known what *this* means, *'I desire mercy
and not sacrifice,'*[a] you would not have condemned the
guiltless. 8For the Son of Man is Lord even[b] of the
Sabbath."

Healing on the Sabbath

9Now when He had departed from there, He went into
their synagogue. 10And behold, there was a man who had
a withered hand. And they asked Him, saying, "Is it lawful
to heal on the Sabbath?"—that they might accuse Him.
11Then He said to them, "What man is there among you
who has one sheep, and if it falls into a pit on the
Sabbath, will not lay hold of it and lift *it* out? 12Of how
much more value then is a man than a sheep? Therefore it
is lawful to do good on the Sabbath." 13Then He said to

12:7 [a] Hosea 6:6 12:8 [b] NU-Text and M-Text omit *even.*

THE MESSAGE

Some Pharisees reported them to Jesus: "Your disciples are
breaking the Sabbath rules!"

Jesus said, "Really? Didn't you ever read what David and his companions did when they were hungry, how they entered the sanctuary and ate fresh bread off the altar, bread that no one but priests were allowed to eat? And didn't you ever read in God's Law that priests carrying out their Temple duties break Sabbath rules all the time and it's not held against them?

"There is far more at stake here than religion. If you had any idea what this Scripture meant—'I prefer a flexible heart to an inflexible ritual'—you wouldn't be nitpicking like this. The Son of Man is no lackey to the Sabbath; he's in charge."

When Jesus left the field, he entered their meeting place. There was a man there with a crippled hand. They said to Jesus, "Is it legal to heal on the Sabbath?" They were baiting him.

He replied, "Is there a person here who, finding one of your lambs fallen into a ravine, wouldn't, even though it was a Sabbath, pull it out? Surely kindness to people is as legal as kindness to animals!" Then he said to the man,

KING JAMES VERSION

And he stretched *it* forth; and it was restored whole, like as the other.

14 ¶ Then the Pharisees went out, and held a council against him, how they might destroy him.

15 But when Jesus knew *it*, he withdrew himself from thence: and great multitudes followed him, and he healed them all;

16 And charged them that they should not make him known:

17 That it might be fulfilled which was spoken by Esaias the prophet, saying,

18 Behold my servant, whom I have chosen; my beloved, in whom my soul is well pleased: I will put my spirit upon him, and he shall shew judgment to the Gentiles.

19 He shall not strive, nor cry; neither shall any man hear his voice in the streets.

20 A bruised reed shall he not break, and smoking flax shall he not quench, till he send forth judgment unto victory.

21 And in his name shall the Gentiles trust.

22 ¶ Then was brought unto him one possessed with a devil, blind, and dumb: and he healed him, insomuch that the blind and dumb both spake and saw.

NEW AMERICAN STANDARD BIBLE

He stretched it out, and it was restored to normal, like the other.

14 But the Pharisees went out and conspired against Him, *as to* how they might destroy Him.

15 But Jesus, aware of *this,* withdrew from there. Many followed Him, and He healed them all,

16 and warned them not to tell who He was.

17 *This was* to fulfill what was spoken through Isaiah the prophet:

18 "BEHOLD, MY SERVANT WHOM I HAVE CHOSEN;
MY BELOVED IN WHOM MY SOUL IS WELL-PLEASED;
I WILL PUT MY SPIRIT UPON HIM,
AND HE SHALL PROCLAIM JUSTICE TO THE GENTILES.

19 "HE WILL NOT QUARREL, NOR CRY OUT;
NOR WILL ANYONE HEAR HIS VOICE IN THE STREETS.

20 "A BATTERED REED HE WILL NOT BREAK OFF,
AND A SMOLDERING WICK HE WILL NOT PUT OUT,
UNTIL HE LEADS JUSTICE TO VICTORY.

21 "AND IN HIS NAME THE GENTILES WILL HOPE."

The Pharisees Rebuked

22 Then a demon-possessed man *who was* blind and mute was brought to Jesus, and He healed him, so that the mute man spoke and saw.

NEW CENTURY VERSION

"Hold out your hand." The man held out his hand, and it
became well again, like the other hand. 14But the Phari-
sees left and made plans to kill Jesus.

Jesus Is God's Chosen Servant

15Jesus knew what the Pharisees were doing, so he left
that place. Many people followed him, and he healed all
who were sick. 16But Jesus warned the people not to tell
who he was. 17He did these things to bring about what
Isaiah the prophet had said:

18 "Here is my servant whom I have chosen.
I love him, and I am pleased with him.
I will put my Spirit upon him,
and he will tell of my justice to all people.
19 He will not argue or cry out;
no one will hear his voice in the streets.
20 He will not break a crushed blade of grass
or put out even a weak flame
until he makes justice win the victory.
21 In him will the non-Jewish people find hope."

Isaiah 42:1–4

Jesus' Power Is from God

22Then some people brought to Jesus a man who was
blind and could not talk, because he had a demon. Jesus
healed the man so that he could talk and see. 23All the

CONTEMPORARY ENGLISH VERSION

your hand." The man did, and it became as healthy as the other one.

14The Pharisees left and started making plans to kill Jesus.

God's Chosen Servant

15When Jesus found out what was happening, he left there
and large crowds followed him. He healed all of their sick,
16but warned them not to tell anyone about him. 17So God's
promise came true, just as Isaiah the prophet had said,

18 "Here is my chosen servant!
I love him,
and he pleases me.
I will give him my Spirit,
and he will bring justice
to the nations.
19 He won't shout or yell
or call out in the streets.
20 He won't break off a bent reed
or put out a dying flame,
but he will make sure
that justice is done.
21 All nations will place
their hope in him."

Jesus and the Ruler of the Demons

(Mark 3.20-30; Luke 11.14-23; 12.10)

22Some people brought to Jesus a man who was blind and could not talk because he had a demon in him. Jesus healed the man, and then he was able to talk and see.

NEW INTERNATIONAL VERSION

he stretched it out and it was completely restored, just as sound as the other. 14But the Pharisees went out and plotted how they might kill Jesus.

God's Chosen Servant

15Aware of this, Jesus withdrew from that place. Many followed him, and he healed all their sick, 16warning them not to tell who he was. 17This was to fulfill what was spoken through the prophet Isaiah:

18 "Here is my servant whom I have chosen,
the one I love, in whom I delight;
I will put my Spirit on him,
and he will proclaim justice to the nations.
19 He will not quarrel or cry out;
no one will hear his voice in the streets.
20 A bruised reed he will not break,
and a smoldering wick he will not snuff out,
till he leads justice to victory.
21 In his name the nations will put their hope."[c]

Jesus and Beelzebub

22Then they brought him a demon-possessed man who was blind and mute, and Jesus healed him, so that he

[c] *21* Isaiah 42:1–4

NEW LIVING TRANSLATION

your hand." The man reached out his hand, and it became normal, just like the other one. 14Then the Pharisees called a meeting and discussed plans for killing Jesus.

Jesus, God's Chosen Servant

15But Jesus knew what they were planning. He left that area, and many people followed him. He healed all the sick among them, 16but he warned them not to say who he was. 17This fulfilled the prophecy of Isaiah concerning him:

18 "Look at my Servant,
whom I have chosen.
He is my Beloved,
and I am very pleased with him.
I will put my Spirit upon him,
and he will proclaim justice to the nations.
19 He will not fight or shout;
he will not raise his voice in public.
20 He will not crush those who are weak,
or quench the smallest hope,
until he brings full justice with his final victory.
21 And his name will be the hope
of all the world."*

Jesus and the Prince of Demons

22Then a demon-possessed man, who was both blind and unable to talk, was brought to Jesus. He healed the man so that he could both speak and see. 23The crowd was

12:18-21 Isa 42:1-4.

NEW KING JAMES VERSION

the man, "Stretch out your hand." And he stretched *it* out, and it was restored as whole as the other. 14Then the Pharisees went out and plotted against Him, how they might destroy Him.

Behold, My Servant

15But when Jesus knew *it,* He withdrew from there. And great multitudes[c] followed Him, and He healed them all. 16Yet He warned them not to make Him known, 17that it might be fulfilled which was spoken by Isaiah the prophet, saying:

18 *"Behold! My Servant whom I have chosen,*
My Beloved in whom My soul is well pleased!
I will put My Spirit upon Him,
And He will declare justice to the Gentiles.
19 *He will not quarrel nor cry out,*
Nor will anyone hear His voice in the streets.
20 *A bruised reed He will not break,*
And smoking flax He will not quench,
Till He sends forth justice to victory;
21 *And in His name Gentiles will trust."*[d]

A House Divided Cannot Stand

22Then one was brought to Him who was demon-possessed, blind and mute; and He healed him, so that the blind and[e] mute man both spoke and saw. 23And all the

12:15 [c] NU-Text brackets *multitudes* as disputed. 12:21 [d] Isaiah 42:1–4 12:22 [e] NU-Text omits *blind and.*

THE MESSAGE

"Hold out your hand." He held it out and it was healed. The Pharisees walked out furious, sputtering about how they were going to ruin Jesus.

In Charge of Everything

Jesus, knowing they were out to get him, moved on. A lot of people followed him, and he healed them all. He also cautioned them to keep it quiet, following guidelines set down by Isaiah:

"Look well at my handpicked servant;
I love him so much, take such delight in him.
I've placed my Spirit on him;
he'll decree justice to the nations.
But he won't yell, won't raise his voice;
there'll be no commotion in the streets.
He won't walk over anyone's feelings,
won't push you into a corner.
Before you know it, his justice will triumph;
the mere sound of his name will signal hope, even
among faroff unbelievers."

No Neutral Ground

Next a poor demon-afflicted wretch, both blind and deaf, was set down before him. Jesus healed him, gave him his

KING JAMES VERSION

23 And all the people were amazed, and said, Is not this the son of David?

24 But when the Pharisees heard *it*, they said, This *fellow* doth not cast out devils, but by Beelzebub the prince of the devils.

25 And Jesus knew their thoughts, and said unto them, Every kingdom divided against itself is brought to desolation; and every city or house divided against itself shall not stand:

26 And if Satan cast out Satan, he is divided against himself; how shall then his kingdom stand?

27 And if I by Beelzebub cast out devils, by whom do your children cast *them* out? therefore they shall be your judges.

28 But if I cast out devils by the Spirit of God, then the kingdom of God is come unto you.

29 Or else how can one enter into a strong man's house, and spoil his goods, except he first bind the strong man? and then he will spoil his house.

30 He that is not with me is against me; and he that gathereth not with me scattereth abroad.

31 Wherefore I say unto you, All manner of sin and blasphemy shall be forgiven unto men: but the blasphemy *against* the *Holy* Ghost shall not be forgiven unto men.

32 And whosoever speaketh a word against the Son of man, it shall be forgiven him: but whosoever speaketh against the Holy Ghost, it shall not be forgiven him, neither in this world, neither in the *world* to come.

NEW AMERICAN STANDARD BIBLE

23 All the crowds were amazed, and were saying, "This man cannot be the Son of David, can he?"

24 But when the Pharisees heard *this*, they said, "This man casts out demons only by Beelzebul the ruler of the demons."

25 And knowing their thoughts Jesus said to them, "Any kingdom divided against itself is laid waste; and any city or house divided against itself will not stand.

26 "If Satan casts out Satan, he is divided against himself; how then will his kingdom stand?

27 "If I by Beelzebul cast out demons, by whom do your sons cast *them* out? For this reason they will be your judges.

28 "But if I cast out demons by the Spirit of God, then the kingdom of God has come upon you.

29 "Or how can anyone enter the strong man's house and carry off his property, unless he first binds the strong *man?* And then he will plunder his house.

The Unpardonable Sin

30 "He who is not with Me is against Me; and he who does not gather with Me scatters.

31 "Therefore I say to you, any sin and blasphemy shall be forgiven people, but blasphemy against the Spirit shall not be forgiven.

32 "Whoever speaks a word against the Son of Man, it shall be forgiven him; but whoever speaks against the Holy Spirit, it shall not be forgiven him, either in this age or in the *age* to come.

NEW CENTURY VERSION

people were amazed and said, "Perhaps this man is the Son of David!"

24When the Pharisees heard this, they said, "Jesus uses the power of Beelzebul, the ruler of demons, to force demons out of people."

25Jesus knew what the Pharisees were thinking, so he said to them, "Every kingdom that is divided against itself will be destroyed. And any city or family that is divided against itself will not continue. 26And if Satan forces out himself, then Satan is divided against himself, and his kingdom will not continue. 27You say that I use the power of Beelzebul to force out demons. If that is true, then what power do your people use to force out demons? So they will be your judges. 28But if I use the power of God's Spirit to force out demons, then the kingdom of God has come to you.

29"If anyone wants to enter a strong person's house and steal his things, he must first tie up the strong person. Then he can steal the things from the house.

30"Whoever is not with me is against me. Whoever does not work with me is working against me. 31So I tell you, people can be forgiven for every sin and everything they say against God. But whoever speaks against the Holy Spirit will not be forgiven. 32Anyone who speaks against the Son of Man can be forgiven, but anyone who speaks against the Holy Spirit will not be forgiven, now or in the future.

CONTEMPORARY ENGLISH VERSION

23The crowds were so amazed that they asked, "Could Jesus be the Son of David?"[b]

24When the Pharisees heard this, they said, "He forces out demons by the power of Beelzebul, the ruler of the demons!"

25Jesus knew what they were thinking, and he said to them:

Any kingdom where people fight each other will end up ruined. And a town or family that fights will soon destroy itself. 26So if Satan fights against himself, how can his kingdom last? 27If I use the power of Beelzebul to force out demons, whose power do your own followers use to force them out? Your followers are the ones who will judge you. 28But when I force out demons by the power of God's Spirit, it proves that God's kingdom has already come to you. 29How can anyone break into a strong man's house and steal his things, unless he first ties up the strong man? Then he can take everything.

30If you are not on my side, you are against me. If you don't gather in the harvest with me, you scatter it. 31-32I tell you that any sinful thing you do or say can be forgiven. Even if you speak against the Son of Man, you can be forgiven. But if you speak against the Holy Spirit, you can never be forgiven, either in this life or in the life to come.

[b] 12.23 *Could Jesus be the Son of David*: Or "Does Jesus think he is the Son of David?" See the note at 9.27.

NEW INTERNATIONAL VERSION

could both talk and see. 23All the people were astonished and said, "Could this be the Son of David?"

24But when the Pharisees heard this, they said, "It is only by Beelzebub,[d] the prince of demons, that this fellow drives out demons."

25Jesus knew their thoughts and said to them, "Every kingdom divided against itself will be ruined, and every city or household divided against itself will not stand. 26If Satan drives out Satan, he is divided against himself. How then can his kingdom stand? 27And if I drive out demons by Beelzebub, by whom do your people drive them out? So then, they will be your judges. 28But if I drive out demons by the Spirit of God, then the kingdom of God has come upon you.

29"Or again, how can anyone enter a strong man's house and carry off his possessions unless he first ties up the strong man? Then he can rob his house.

30"He who is not with me is against me, and he who does not gather with me scatters. 31And so I tell you, every sin and blasphemy will be forgiven men, but the blasphemy against the Spirit will not be forgiven. 32Anyone who speaks a word against the Son of Man will be forgiven, but anyone who speaks against the Holy Spirit will not be forgiven, either in this age or in the age to come.

[d] *24* Greek *Beezeboul* or *Beelzeboul*; also in verse 27

NEW LIVING TRANSLATION

amazed. "Could it be that Jesus is the Son of David, the Messiah?" they wondered out loud.

24But when the Pharisees heard about the miracle, they said, "No wonder he can cast out demons. He gets his power from Satan,* the prince of demons."

25Jesus knew their thoughts and replied, "Any kingdom at war with itself is doomed. A city or home divided against itself is doomed. 26And if Satan is casting out Satan, he is fighting against himself. His own kingdom will not survive. 27And if I am empowered by the prince of demons,* what about your own followers? They cast out demons, too, so they will judge you for what you have said. 28But if I am casting out demons by the Spirit of God, then the Kingdom of God has arrived among you. 29Let me illustrate this. You can't enter a strong man's house and rob him without first tying him up. Only then can his house be robbed!* 30Anyone who isn't helping me opposes me, and anyone who isn't working with me is actually working against me.

31"Every sin or blasphemy can be forgiven—except blasphemy against the Holy Spirit, which can never be forgiven. 32Anyone who blasphemes against me, the Son of Man, can be forgiven, but blasphemy against the Holy Spirit will never be forgiven, either in this world or in the world to come.

12:24 Greek *Beelzeboul.* **12:27** Greek *by Beelzeboul.* **12:29** Or *One cannot rob Satan's kingdom without first tying him up. Only then can his demons be cast out.*

NEW KING JAMES VERSION

multitudes were amazed and said, "Could this be the Son of David?"

24Now when the Pharisees heard *it* they said, "This *fellow* does not cast out demons except by Beelzebub,[f] the ruler of the demons."

25But Jesus knew their thoughts, and said to them: "Every kingdom divided against itself is brought to desolation, and every city or house divided against itself will not stand. 26If Satan casts out Satan, he is divided against himself. How then will his kingdom stand? 27And if I cast out demons by Beelzebub, by whom do your sons cast *them* out? Therefore they shall be your judges. 28But if I cast out demons by the Spirit of God, surely the kingdom of God has come upon you. 29Or how can one enter a strong man's house and plunder his goods, unless he first binds the strong man? And then he will plunder his house. 30He who is not with Me is against Me, and he who does not gather with Me scatters abroad.

The Unpardonable Sin

31"Therefore I say to you, every sin and blasphemy will be forgiven men, but the blasphemy *against* the Spirit will not be forgiven men. 32Anyone who speaks a word against the Son of Man, it will be forgiven him; but whoever speaks against the Holy Spirit, it will not be forgiven him, either in this age or in the *age* to come.

12:24 [f] NU-Text and M-Text read *Beelzebul.*

THE MESSAGE

sight and hearing. The people who saw it were impressed—"This has to be the Son of David!"

But the Pharisees, when they heard the report, were cynical. "Black magic," they said. "Some devil trick he's pulled from his sleeve."

Jesus confronted their slander. "A judge who gives opposite verdicts on the same person cancels himself out; a family that's in a constant squabble disintegrates; if Satan banishes Satan, is there any Satan left? If you're slinging devil mud at me, calling me a devil kicking out devils, doesn't the same mud stick to your own exorcists?

"But if it's by *God's* power that I am sending the evil spirits packing, then God's kingdom is here for sure. How in the world do you think it's possible in broad daylight to enter the house of an awake, able-bodied man and walk off with his possessions unless you tie him up first? Tie him up, though, and you can clean him out.

"This is war, and there is no neutral ground. If you're not on my side, you're the enemy; if you're not helping, you're making things worse.

"There's nothing done or said that can't be forgiven. But if you deliberately persist in your slanders against God's Spirit, you are repudiating the very One who forgives. If you reject the Son of Man out of some misunderstanding, the Holy Spirit can forgive you, but when you reject the Holy Spirit, you're sawing off the branch on which you're sitting, severing by your own perversity all connection with the One who forgives.

KING JAMES VERSION

33 Either make the tree good, and his fruit good; or else make the tree corrupt, and his fruit corrupt: for the tree is known by *his* fruit.

34 O generation of vipers, how can ye, being evil, speak good things? for out of the abundance of the heart the mouth speaketh.

35 A good man out of the good treasure of the heart bringeth forth good things: and an evil man out of the evil treasure bringeth forth evil things.

36 But I say unto you, That every idle word that men shall speak, they shall give account thereof in the day of judgment.

37 For by thy words thou shalt be justified, and by thy words thou shalt be condemned.

38 ¶ Then certain of the scribes and of the Pharisees answered, saying, Master, we would see a sign from thee.

39 But he answered and said unto them, An evil and adulterous generation seeketh after a sign; and there shall no sign be given to it, but the sign of the prophet Jonas:

40 For as Jonas was three days and three nights in the whale's belly; so shall the Son of man be three days and three nights in the heart of the earth.

41 The men of Nineveh shall rise in judgment with this generation, and shall condemn it: because they repented at the preaching of Jonas; and, behold, a greater than Jonas *is* here.

NEW AMERICAN STANDARD BIBLE

Words Reveal Character

33 "Either make the tree good and its fruit good, or make the tree bad and its fruit bad; for the tree is known by its fruit.

34 "You brood of vipers, how can you, being evil, speak what is good? For the mouth speaks out of that which fills the heart.

35 "The good man brings out of *his* good treasure what is good; and the evil man brings out of *his* evil treasure what is evil.

36 "But I tell you that every careless word that people speak, they shall give an accounting for it in the day of judgment.

37 "For by your words you will be justified, and by your words you will be condemned."

The Desire for Signs

38 Then some of the scribes and Pharisees said to Him, "Teacher, we want to see a sign from You."

39 But He answered and said to them, "An evil and adulterous generation craves for a sign; and *yet* no sign will be given to it but the sign of Jonah the prophet;

40 for just as JONAH WAS THREE DAYS AND THREE NIGHTS IN THE BELLY OF THE SEA MONSTER, so will the Son of Man be three days and three nights in the heart of the earth.

41 "The men of Nineveh will stand up with this generation at the judgment, and will condemn it because they repented at the preaching of Jonah; and behold, something greater than Jonah is here.

NEW CENTURY VERSION

People Know You by Your Words

33 "If you want good fruit, you must make the tree good.
If your tree is not good, it will have bad fruit. A tree is
known by the kind of fruit it produces. 34 You snakes! You
are evil people, so how can you say anything good? The
mouth speaks the things that are in the heart. 35 Good peo-
ple have good things in their hearts, and so they say good
things. But evil people have evil in their hearts, so they
say evil things. 36 And I tell you that on the Judgment Day
people will be responsible for every careless thing they
have said. 37 The words you have said will be used to judge
you. Some of your words will prove you right, but some of
your words will prove you guilty."

The People Ask for a Miracle

38 Then some of the Pharisees and teachers of the law
answered Jesus, saying, "Teacher, we want to see you
work a miracle as a sign."

39 Jesus answered, "Evil and sinful people are the ones
who want to see a miracle for a sign. But no sign will be
given to them, except the sign of the prophet Jonah.
40 Jonah was in the stomach of the big fish for three days
and three nights. In the same way, the Son of Man will be
in the grave three days and three nights. 41 On the
Judgment Day the people from Nineveh[c] will stand up with
you people who live now, and they will show that you are
guilty. When Jonah preached to them, they were sorry and
changed their lives. And I tell you that someone greater

12:41 [c] **Nineveh** The city where Jonah preached to warn the people. Read Jonah 3.

CONTEMPORARY ENGLISH VERSION

A Tree and Its Fruit (Luke 6.43-45)

33 A good tree produces only good fruit, and a bad tree
produces bad fruit. You can tell what a tree is like by the
fruit it produces. 34 You are a bunch of evil snakes, so
how can you say anything good? Your words show what
is in your hearts. 35 Good people bring good things out of
their hearts, but evil people bring evil things out of their
hearts. 36 I promise you that on the day of judgment,
everyone will have to account for every careless word
they have spoken. 37 On that day they will be told that
they are either innocent or guilty because of the things
they have said.

A Sign from Heaven (Mark 8.11, 12; Luke 11.29-32)

38 Some Pharisees and teachers of the Law of Moses said,
"Teacher, we want you to show us a sign from heaven."
39 But Jesus replied:

You want a sign because you are evil and won't
believe! But the only sign you will get is the sign of the
prophet Jonah. 40 He was in the stomach of a big fish for
three days and nights, just as the Son of Man will be
deep in the earth for three days and nights. 41 On the day
of judgment the people of Nineveh[c] will stand there with
you and condemn you. They turned to God when Jonah
preached, and yet here is something far greater than

[c] 12.41 *Nineveh*: During the time of Jonah this city was the capital of the Assyrian Empire, which was Israel's worst enemy. But Jonah was sent there to preach, so that the people would turn to the Lord and be saved.

NEW INTERNATIONAL VERSION

33“Make a tree good and its fruit will be good, or make a
tree bad and its fruit will be bad, for a tree is recognized by
its fruit. 34You brood of vipers, how can you who are evil
say anything good? For out of the overflow of the heart the
mouth speaks. 35The good man brings good things out of
the good stored up in him, and the evil man brings evil
things out of the evil stored up in him. 36But I tell you that
men will have to give account on the day of judgment for
every careless word they have spoken. 37For by your words
you will be acquitted, and by your words you will be con-
demned.”

The Sign of Jonah

38Then some of the Pharisees and teachers of the law
said to him, “Teacher, we want to see a miraculous sign
from you.”

39He answered, “A wicked and adulterous generation
asks for a miraculous sign! But none will be given it
except the sign of the prophet Jonah. 40For as Jonah was
three days and three nights in the belly of a huge fish, so
the Son of Man will be three days and three nights in the
heart of the earth. 41The men of Nineveh will stand up at
the judgment with this generation and condemn it; for
they repented at the preaching of Jonah, and now one[e]

[e] *41* Or *something*; also in verse 42

NEW LIVING TRANSLATION

33“A tree is identified by its fruit. Make a tree good, and
its fruit will be good. Make a tree bad, and its fruit will be
bad. 34You brood of snakes! How could evil men like you
speak what is good and right? For whatever is in your
heart determines what you say. 35A good person produces
good words from a good heart, and an evil person pro-
duces evil words from an evil heart. 36And I tell you this,
that you must give an account on judgment day of every
idle word you speak. 37The words you say now reflect your
fate then; either you will be justified by them or you will
be condemned.”

The Sign of Jonah

38One day some teachers of religious law and Pharisees
came to Jesus and said, “Teacher, we want you to show us
a miraculous sign to prove that you are from God.”

39But Jesus replied, “Only an evil, faithless generation
would ask for a miraculous sign; but the only sign I will
give them is the sign of the prophet Jonah. 40For as Jonah
was in the belly of the great fish for three days and three
nights, so I, the Son of Man, will be in the heart of the
earth for three days and three nights. 41The people of
Nineveh will rise up against this generation on judgment
day and condemn it, because they repented at the preach-
ing of Jonah. And now someone greater than Jonah is

NEW KING JAMES VERSION

A Tree Known by Its Fruit

33“Either make the tree good and its fruit good, or else
make the tree bad and its fruit bad; for a tree is known by
its fruit. 34Brood of vipers! How can you, being evil, speak
good things? For out of the abundance of the heart the
mouth speaks. 35A good man out of the good treasure of
his heart[g] brings forth good things, and an evil man out of
the evil treasure brings forth evil things. 36But I say to you
that for every idle word men may speak, they will give
account of it in the day of judgment. 37For by your words
you will be justified, and by your words you will be con-
demned.”

The Scribes and Pharisees Ask for a Sign

38Then some of the scribes and Pharisees answered, say-
ing, “Teacher, we want to see a sign from You.”

39But He answered and said to them, “An evil and adul-
terous generation seeks after a sign, and no sign will be
given to it except the sign of the prophet Jonah. 40For as
Jonah was three days and three nights in the belly of the
great fish, so will the Son of Man be three days and three
nights in the heart of the earth. 41The men of Nineveh will
rise up in the judgment with this generation and condemn
it, because they repented at the preaching of Jonah; and
indeed a greater than Jonah *is* here. 42The queen of the

12:35 [g] NU-Text and M-Text omit *of his heart.*

THE MESSAGE

“If you grow a healthy tree, you'll pick healthy fruit. If you grow a diseased tree, you'll pick worm-eaten fruit. The fruit tells you about the tree.

“You have minds like a snake pit! How do you suppose what you say is worth anything when you are so foul-minded? It's your heart, not the dictionary, that gives meaning to your words. A good person produces good deeds and words season after season. An evil person is a blight on the orchard. Let me tell you something: Every one of these careless words is going to come back to haunt you. There will be a time of Reckoning. Words are powerful; take them seriously. Words can be your salvation. Words can also be your damnation.”

Jonah-Evidence

Later a few religion scholars and Pharisees got on him. “Teacher, we want to see your credentials. Give us some hard evidence that God is in this. How about a miracle?”

Jesus said, “You're looking for proof, but you're looking for the wrong kind. All you want is something to titillate your curiosity, satisfy your lust for miracles. The only proof you're going to get is what looks like the absence of proof: Jonah-evidence. Like Jonah, three days and nights in the fish's belly, the Son of Man will be gone three days and nights in a deep grave.

“On Judgment Day, the Ninevites will stand up and give evidence that will condemn this generation, because when Jonah preached to them they changed their lives. A far greater preacher than Jonah is here, and you squabble about

KING JAMES VERSION

42 The queen of the south shall rise up in the judgment with this generation, and shall condemn it: for she came from the uttermost parts of the earth to hear the wisdom of Solomon; and, behold, a greater than Solomon *is* here.

43 When the unclean spirit is gone out of a man, he walketh through dry places, seeking rest, and findeth none.

44 Then he saith, I will return into my house from whence I came out; and when he is come, he findeth *it* empty, swept, and garnished.

45 Then goeth he, and taketh with himself seven other spirits more wicked than himself, and they enter in and dwell there: and the last *state* of that man is worse than the first. Even so shall it be also unto this wicked generation.

46 ¶ While he yet talked to the people, behold, *his* mother and his brethren stood without, desiring to speak with him.

47 Then one said unto him, Behold, thy mother and thy brethren stand without, desiring to speak with thee.

48 But he answered and said unto him that told him, Who is my mother? and who are my brethren?

49 And he stretched forth his hand toward his disciples, and said, Behold my mother and my brethren!

50 For whosoever shall do the will of my Father which is in heaven, the same is my brother, and sister, and mother.

NEW AMERICAN STANDARD BIBLE

42 "*The* Queen of *the* South will rise up with this generation at the judgment and will condemn it, because she came from the ends of the earth to hear the wisdom of Solomon; and behold, something greater than Solomon is here.

43 "Now when the unclean spirit goes out of a man, it passes through waterless places seeking rest, and does not find *it*.

44 "Then it says, 'I will return to my house from which I came'; and when it comes, it finds *it* unoccupied, swept, and put in order.

45 "Then it goes and takes along with it seven other spirits more wicked than itself, and they go in and live there; and the last state of that man becomes worse than the first. That is the way it will also be with this evil generation."

Changed Relationships

46 While He was still speaking to the crowds, behold, His mother and brothers were standing outside, seeking to speak to Him.

47 Someone said to Him, "Behold, Your mother and Your brothers are standing outside seeking to speak to You."

48 But Jesus answered the one who was telling Him and said, "Who is My mother and who are My brothers?"

49 And stretching out His hand toward His disciples, He said, "Behold My mother and My brothers!

50 "For whoever does the will of My Father who is in heaven, he is My brother and sister and mother."

NEW CENTURY VERSION

than Jonah is here. 42On the Judgment Day, the Queen of the South[d] will stand up with you people who live today. She will show that you are guilty, because she came from far away to listen to Solomon's wise teaching. And I tell you that someone greater than Solomon is here.

People Today Are Full of Evil

43"When an evil spirit comes out of a person, it travels through dry places, looking for a place to rest, but it doesn't find it. 44So the spirit says, 'I will go back to the house I left.' When the spirit comes back, it finds the house still empty, swept clean, and made neat. 45Then the evil spirit goes out and brings seven other spirits even more evil than it is, and they go in and live there. So the person has even more trouble than before. It is the same way with the evil people who live today."

Jesus' True Family

46While Jesus was talking to the people, his mother and brothers stood outside, trying to find a way to talk to him. 47Someone told Jesus, "Your mother and brothers are standing outside, and they want to talk to you."

48He answered, "Who is my mother? Who are my brothers?" 49Then he pointed to his followers and said, "Here are my mother and my brothers. 50My true brother and sister and mother are those who do what my Father in heaven wants."

12:42 [d] **Queen of the South** The Queen of Sheba. She traveled a thousand miles to learn God's wisdom from Solomon. Read 1 Kings 10:1–13.

CONTEMPORARY ENGLISH VERSION

Jonah. 42The Queen of the South[d] will also stand there with you and condemn you. She traveled a long way to hear Solomon's wisdom, and yet here is something much greater than Solomon.

Return of an Evil Spirit (Luke 11.24-26)

43When an evil spirit leaves a person, it travels through the desert, looking for a place to rest. But when the demon doesn't find a place, 44it says, "I will go back to the home I left." When it gets there and finds the place empty, clean, and fixed up, 45it goes off and finds seven other evil spirits even worse than itself. They all come and make their home there, and the person ends up in worse shape than before. That's how it will be with you evil people of today.

Jesus' Mother and Brothers (Mark 3.31-35; Luke 8.19-21)

46While Jesus was still speaking to the crowds, his mother and brothers came and stood outside because they wanted to talk with him. 47Someone told Jesus, "Your mother and brothers are standing outside and want to talk with you."[e]

48Jesus answered, "Who is my mother and who are my brothers?" 49Then he pointed to his disciples and said, "These are my mother and my brothers! 50Anyone who obeys my Father in heaven is my brother or sister or mother."

[d] 12.42 *Queen of the South*: Sheba, probably a country in southern Arabia.
[e] 12.47 *with you*: Some manuscripts do not have verse 47.

NEW INTERNATIONAL VERSION

greater than Jonah is here. 42 The Queen of the South will rise at the judgment with this generation and condemn it; for she came from the ends of the earth to listen to Solomon's wisdom, and now one greater than Solomon is here.

43 "When an evil[f] spirit comes out of a man, it goes through arid places seeking rest and does not find it. 44 Then it says, 'I will return to the house I left.' When it arrives, it finds the house unoccupied, swept clean and put in order. 45 Then it goes and takes with it seven other spirits more wicked than itself, and they go in and live there. And the final condition of that man is worse than the first. That is how it will be with this wicked generation."

Jesus' Mother and Brothers

46 While Jesus was still talking to the crowd, his mother and brothers stood outside, wanting to speak to him. 47 Someone told him, "Your mother and brothers are standing outside, wanting to speak to you."[g]

48 He replied to him, "Who is my mother, and who are my brothers?" 49 Pointing to his disciples, he said, "Here are my mother and my brothers. 50 For whoever does the will of my Father in heaven is my brother and sister and mother."

[f] 43 Greek *unclean* [g] 47 Some manuscripts do not have verse 47.

NEW LIVING TRANSLATION

here—and you refuse to repent. 42 The queen of Sheba* will also rise up against this generation on judgment day and condemn it, because she came from a distant land to hear the wisdom of Solomon. And now someone greater than Solomon is here—and you refuse to listen to him.

43 "When an evil spirit leaves a person, it goes into the desert, seeking rest but finding none. 44 Then it says, 'I will return to the person I came from.' So it returns and finds its former home empty, swept, and clean. 45 Then the spirit finds seven other spirits more evil than itself, and they all enter the person and live there. And so that person is worse off than before. That will be the experience of this evil generation."

The True Family of Jesus

46 As Jesus was speaking to the crowd, his mother and brothers were outside, wanting to talk with him. 47 Someone told Jesus, "Your mother and your brothers are outside, and they want to speak to you."

48 Jesus asked, "Who is my mother? Who are my brothers?" 49 Then he pointed to his disciples and said, "These are my mother and brothers. 50 Anyone who does the will of my Father in heaven is my brother and sister and mother!"

12:42 Greek *The queen of the south.*

NEW KING JAMES VERSION

South will rise up in the judgment with this generation and condemn it, for she came from the ends of the earth to hear the wisdom of Solomon; and indeed a greater than Solomon *is* here.

An Unclean Spirit Returns

43 "When an unclean spirit goes out of a man, he goes through dry places, seeking rest, and finds none. 44 Then he says, 'I will return to my house from which I came.' And when he comes, he finds *it* empty, swept, and put in order. 45 Then he goes and takes with him seven other spirits more wicked than himself, and they enter and dwell there; and the last *state* of that man is worse than the first. So shall it also be with this wicked generation."

Jesus' Mother and Brothers Send for Him

46 While He was still talking to the multitudes, behold, His mother and brothers stood outside, seeking to speak with Him. 47 Then one said to Him, "Look, Your mother and Your brothers are standing outside, seeking to speak with You."

48 But He answered and said to the one who told Him, "Who is My mother and who are My brothers?" 49 And He stretched out His hand toward His disciples and said, "Here are My mother and My brothers! 50 For whoever does the will of My Father in heaven is My brother and sister and mother."

THE MESSAGE

'proofs.' On Judgment Day, the Queen of Sheba will come forward and bring evidence that will condemn this generation, because she traveled from a far corner of the earth to listen to wise Solomon. Wisdom far greater than Solomon's is right in front of you, and you quibble over 'evidence.'

"When a defiling evil spirit is expelled from someone, it drifts along through the desert looking for an oasis, some unsuspecting soul it can bedevil. When it doesn't find anyone, it says, 'I'll go back to my old haunt.' On return it finds the person spotlessly clean, but vacant. It then runs out and rounds up seven other spirits more evil than itself and they all move in, whooping it up. That person ends up far worse off than if he'd never gotten cleaned up in the first place.

"That's what this generation is like: You may think you have cleaned out the junk from your lives and gotten ready for God, but you weren't hospitable to my kingdom message, and now all the devils are moving back in."

Obedience Is Thicker Than Blood

While he was still talking to the crowd, his mother and brothers showed up. They were outside trying to get a message to him. Someone told Jesus, "Your mother and brothers are out here, wanting to speak with you."

Jesus didn't respond directly, but said, "Who do you think my mother and brothers are?" He then stretched out his hand toward his disciples. "Look closely. These are my mother and brothers. Obedience is thicker than blood. The person who obeys my heavenly Father's will is my brother and sister and mother."

KING JAMES VERSION

13 The same day went Jesus out of the house, and sat by the sea side.

2 And great multitudes were gathered together unto him, so that he went into a ship, and sat; and the whole multitude stood on the shore.

3 And he spake many things unto them in parables, saying, Behold, a sower went forth to sow;

4 And when he sowed, some *seeds* fell by the way side, and the fowls came and devoured them up:

5 Some fell upon stony places, where they had not much earth: and forthwith they sprung up, because they had no deepness of earth:

6 And when the sun was up, they were scorched; and because they had no root, they withered away.

7 And some fell among thorns; and the thorns sprung up, and choked them:

8 But other fell into good ground, and brought forth fruit, some an hundredfold, some sixtyfold, some thirtyfold.

9 Who hath ears to hear, let him hear.

10 And the disciples came, and said unto him, Why speakest thou unto them in parables?

11 He answered and said unto them, Because it is given unto you to know the mysteries of the kingdom of heaven, but to them it is not given.

12 For whosoever hath, to him shall be given, and he shall have more abundance: but whosoever hath not, from him shall be taken away even that he hath.

NEW AMERICAN STANDARD BIBLE

Jesus Teaches in Parables

13 That day Jesus went out of the house and was sitting by the sea.

2 And large crowds gathered to Him, so He got into a boat and sat down, and the whole crowd was standing on the beach.

3 And He spoke many things to them in parables, saying, "Behold, the sower went out to sow;

4 and as he sowed, some *seeds* fell beside the road, and the birds came and ate them up.

5 "Others fell on the rocky places, where they did not have much soil; and immediately they sprang up, because they had no depth of soil.

6 "But when the sun had risen, they were scorched; and because they had no root, they withered away.

7 "Others fell among the thorns, and the thorns came up and choked them out.

8 "And others fell on the good soil and *yielded a crop, some a hundredfold, some sixty, and some thirty.

9 "He who has ears, let him hear."

An Explanation

10 And the disciples came and said to Him, "Why do You speak to them in parables?"

11 Jesus answered them, "To you it has been granted to know the mysteries of the kingdom of heaven, but to them it has not been granted.

12 "For whoever has, to him *more* shall be given, and he will have an abundance; but whoever does not have, even what he has shall be taken away from him.

NEW CENTURY VERSION

A Story About Planting Seed

13 That same day Jesus went out of the house and sat
by the lake. 2Large crowds gathered around him,
so he got into a boat and sat down, while the people stood
on the shore. 3Then Jesus used stories to teach them many
things. He said: "A farmer went out to plant his seed.
4While he was planting, some seed fell by the road, and
the birds came and ate it all up. 5Some seed fell on rocky
ground, where there wasn't much dirt. That seed grew very
fast, because the ground was not deep. 6But when the sun
rose, the plants dried up, because they did not have deep
roots. 7Some other seed fell among thorny weeds, which
grew and choked the good plants. 8Some other seed fell on
good ground where it grew and produced a crop. Some
plants made a hundred times more, some made sixty times
more, and some made thirty times more. 9You people who
can hear me, listen."

Why Jesus Used Stories to Teach

10The followers came to Jesus and asked, "Why do you
use stories to teach the people?"

11Jesus answered, "You have been chosen to know the
secrets about the kingdom of heaven, but others cannot
know these secrets. 12Those who have understanding will
be given more, and they will have all they need. But those
who do not have understanding, even what they have will
be taken away from them. 13This is why I use stories to

CONTEMPORARY ENGLISH VERSION

A Story about a Farmer (Mark 4.1-9; Luke 8.4-8)

13 That same day Jesus left the house and went out
beside Lake Galilee, where he sat down to teach.[a]
2Such large crowds gathered around him that he had to sit
in a boat, while the people stood on the shore. 3Then he
taught them many things by using stories. He said:

> A farmer went out to scatter seed in a field. 4While the
> farmer was scattering the seed, some of it fell along the
> road and was eaten by birds. 5Other seeds fell on thin,
> rocky ground and quickly started growing because the
> soil wasn't very deep. 6But when the sun came up, the
> plants were scorched and dried up, because they did not
> have enough roots. 7Some other seeds fell where thorn-
> bushes grew up and choked the plants. 8But a few seeds
> did fall on good ground where the plants produced a
> hundred or sixty or thirty times as much as was scat-
> tered. 9If you have ears, pay attention!

Why Jesus Used Stories (Mark 4.10-12; Luke 8.9, 10)

10Jesus' disciples came to him and asked, "Why do you
use nothing but stories when you speak to the people?"
11Jesus answered:

> I have explained the secrets about the kingdom of
> heaven to you, but not to others. 12Everyone who has
> something will be given more. But people who don't
> have anything will lose even what little they have.

[a] 13.1 *sat down to teach*: See the note at 5.1.

NEW INTERNATIONAL VERSION

The Parable of the Sower

13 That same day Jesus went out of the house and sat
by the lake. [2]Such large crowds gathered around
him that he got into a boat and sat in it, while all the peo-
ple stood on the shore. [3]Then he told them many things in
parables, saying: "A farmer went out to sow his seed. [4]As
he was scattering the seed, some fell along the path, and
the birds came and ate it up. [5]Some fell on rocky places,
where it did not have much soil. It sprang up quickly,
because the soil was shallow. [6]But when the sun came up,
the plants were scorched, and they withered because they
had no root. [7]Other seed fell among thorns, which grew up
and choked the plants. [8]Still other seed fell on good soil,
where it produced a crop—a hundred, sixty or thirty times
what was sown. [9]He who has ears, let him hear."

[10]The disciples came to him and asked, "Why do you
speak to the people in parables?"

[11]He replied, "The knowledge of the secrets of the king-
dom of heaven has been given to you, but not to them.
[12]Whoever has will be given more, and he will have an
abundance. Whoever does not have, even what he has will

NEW LIVING TRANSLATION

Story of the Farmer Scattering Seed

13 Later that same day, Jesus left the house and went
down to the shore, [2]where an immense crowd soon
gathered. He got into a boat, where he sat and taught as
the people listened on the shore. [3]He told many stories
such as this one:

"A farmer went out to plant some seed. [4]As he scattered
it across his field, some seeds fell on a footpath, and the
birds came and ate them. [5]Other seeds fell on shallow soil
with underlying rock. The plants sprang up quickly, [6]but
they soon wilted beneath the hot sun and died because the
roots had no nourishment in the shallow soil. [7]Other seeds
fell among thorns that shot up and choked out the tender
blades. [8]But some seeds fell on fertile soil and produced a
crop that was thirty, sixty, and even a hundred times as
much as had been planted. [9]Anyone who is willing to hear
should listen and understand!"

[10]His disciples came and asked him, "Why do you
always tell stories when you talk to the people?"

[11]Then he explained to them, "You have been permitted
to understand the secrets of the Kingdom of Heaven, but
others have not. [12]To those who are open to my teaching,
more understanding will be given, and they will have an
abundance of knowledge. But to those who are not listen-
ing, even what they have will be taken away from them.

NEW KING JAMES VERSION

The Parable of the Sower

13 On the same day Jesus went out of the house and
sat by the sea. [2]And great multitudes were gath-
ered together to Him, so that He got into a boat and sat;
and the whole multitude stood on the shore.

[3]Then He spoke many things to them in parables, say-
ing: "Behold, a sower went out to sow. [4]And as he sowed,
some *seed* fell by the wayside; and the birds came and
devoured them. [5]Some fell on stony places, where they did
not have much earth; and they immediately sprang up
because they had no depth of earth. [6]But when the sun
was up they were scorched, and because they had no root
they withered away. [7]And some fell among thorns, and the
thorns sprang up and choked them. [8]But others fell on
good ground and yielded a crop: some a hundredfold, some
sixty, some thirty. [9]He who has ears to hear, let him
hear!"

The Purpose of Parables

[10]And the disciples came and said to Him, "Why do You
speak to them in parables?"

[11]He answered and said to them, "Because it has been
given to you to know the mysteries of the kingdom of
heaven, but to them it has not been given. [12]For whoever
has, to him more will be given, and he will have abun-
dance; but whoever does not have, even what he has will
be taken away from him. [13]Therefore I speak to them in

THE MESSAGE

A Harvest Story

13 At about that same time Jesus left the house and
sat on the beach. In no time at all a crowd gath-
ered along the shoreline, forcing him to get into a boat.
Using the boat as a pulpit, he addressed his congregation,
telling stories.

"What do you make of this? A farmer planted seed. As
he scattered the seed, some of it fell on the road, and birds
ate it. Some fell in the gravel; it sprouted quickly but
didn't put down roots, so when the sun came up it with-
ered just as quickly. Some fell in the weeds; as it came up,
it was strangled by the weeds. Some fell on good earth,
and produced a harvest beyond his wildest dreams.

"Are you listening to this?
"Really listening?"

Why Tell Stories?

The disciples came up and asked, "Why do you tell sto-
ries?"

He replied, "You've been given insight into God's king-
dom. You know how it works. Not everybody has this gift,
this insight; it hasn't been given to them. Whenever
someone has a ready heart for this, the insights and
understandings flow freely. But if there is no readiness,
any trace of receptivity soon disappears. That's why I tell

KING JAMES VERSION

13 Therefore speak I to them in parables: because they seeing see not; and hearing they hear not, neither do they understand.
14 And in them is fulfilled the prophecy of Esaias, which saith, By hearing ye shall hear, and shall not understand; and seeing ye shall see, and shall not perceive:
15 For this people's heart is waxed gross, and *their* ears are dull of hearing, and their eyes they have closed; lest at any time they should see with *their* eyes, and hear with *their* ears, and should understand with *their* heart, and should be converted, and I should heal them.
16 But blessed *are* your eyes, for they see: and your ears, for they hear.
17 For verily I say unto you, That many prophets and righteous *men* have desired to see *those things* which ye see, and have not seen *them*; and to hear *those things* which ye hear, and have not heard *them*.
18 Hear ye therefore the parable of the sower.
19 When any one heareth the word of the kingdom, and

NEW AMERICAN STANDARD BIBLE

13 "Therefore I speak to them in parables; because while seeing they do not see, and while hearing they do not hear, nor do they understand.
14 "In their case the prophecy of Isaiah is being fulfilled, which says,

'YOU WILL KEEP ON HEARING, BUT WILL NOT UNDERSTAND;
YOU WILL KEEP ON SEEING, BUT WILL NOT PERCEIVE;
15 FOR THE HEART OF THIS PEOPLE HAS BECOME DULL,
WITH THEIR EARS THEY SCARCELY HEAR,
AND THEY HAVE CLOSED THEIR EYES,
OTHERWISE THEY WOULD SEE WITH THEIR EYES,
HEAR WITH THEIR EARS,
AND UNDERSTAND WITH THEIR HEART AND RETURN,
AND I WOULD HEAL THEM.'

16 "But blessed are your eyes, because they see; and your ears, because they hear.
17 "For truly I say to you that many prophets and righteous men desired to see what you see, and did not see *it*, and to hear what you hear, and did not hear *it*.

The Sower Explained

18 "Hear then the parable of the sower.
19 "When anyone hears the word of the kingdom and

NEW CENTURY VERSION

teach the people: They see, but they don't really see. They hear, but they don't really hear or understand. 14So they
show that the things Isaiah said about them are true:

'You will listen and listen, but you will not understand.
You will look and look, but you will not learn.
15 For the minds of these people have become stubborn.
They do not hear with their ears,
and they have closed their eyes.
Otherwise they might really understand
what they see with their eyes
and hear with their ears.
They might really understand in their minds
and come back to me and be healed.' *Isaiah 6:9–10*

16But you are blessed, because you see with your eyes and hear with your ears. 17I tell you the truth, many prophets
and good people wanted to see the things that you now see, but they did not see them. And they wanted to hear the things that you now hear, but they did not hear them.

Jesus Explains the Seed Story

18"So listen to the meaning of that story about the farmer. 19What is the seed that fell by the road? That seed

CONTEMPORARY ENGLISH VERSION

13I use stories when I speak to them because when they look, they cannot see, and when they listen, they cannot hear or understand. 14So God's promise came true, just
as the prophet Isaiah had said,

"These people will listen
and listen,
but never understand.
They will look and look,
but never see.
15 All of them have
stubborn minds!
Their ears are stopped up,
and their eyes are covered.
They cannot see or hear
or understand.
If they could,
they would turn to me,
and I would heal them."

16But God has blessed you, because your eyes can see and your ears can hear! 17Many prophets and good people were eager to see what you see and to hear what you hear. But I tell you that they did not see or hear.

Jesus Explains the Story about the Farmer

(Mark 4.13-20; Luke 8.11-15)

18Now listen to the meaning of the story about the farmer:
19The seeds that fell along the road are the people

NEW INTERNATIONAL VERSION

be taken from him. 13 This is why I speak to them in para-
bles:

"Though seeing, they do not see;
though hearing, they do not hear or understand.

14 In them is fulfilled the prophecy of Isaiah:

" 'You will be ever hearing but never understanding;
you will be ever seeing but never perceiving.
15 For this people's heart has become calloused;
they hardly hear with their ears,
and they have closed their eyes.
Otherwise they might see with their eyes,
hear with their ears,
understand with their hearts
and turn, and I would heal them.'[a]

16 But blessed are your eyes because they see, and your
ears because they hear. 17 For I tell you the truth, many
prophets and righteous men longed to see what you see
but did not see it, and to hear what you hear but did not
hear it.

18 "Listen then to what the parable of the sower means:
19 When anyone hears the message about the kingdom and

[a] *15* Isaiah 6:9,10

NEW LIVING TRANSLATION

13 That is why I tell these stories, because people see what I
do, but they don't really see. They hear what I say, but
they don't really hear, and they don't understand. 14 This
fulfills the prophecy of Isaiah, which says:

'You will hear my words,
but you will not understand;
you will see what I do,
but you will not perceive its meaning.
15 For the hearts of these people are hardened,
and their ears cannot hear,
and they have closed their eyes—
so their eyes cannot see,
and their ears cannot hear,
and their hearts cannot understand,
and they cannot turn to me
and let me heal them.'*

16 "But blessed are your eyes, because they see; and your
ears, because they hear. 17 I assure you, many prophets
and godly people have longed to see and hear what you
have seen and heard, but they could not.

18 "Now here is the explanation of the story I told about
the farmer sowing grain: 19 The seed that fell on the hard
path represents those who hear the Good News about the

13:14-15 Isa 6:9-10.

NEW KING JAMES VERSION

parables, because seeing they do not see, and hearing they
do not hear, nor do they understand. 14 And in them the
prophecy of Isaiah is fulfilled, which says:

'Hearing you will hear and shall not understand,
And seeing you will see and not perceive;
15 *For the hearts of this people have grown dull.*
Their ears are hard of hearing,
And their eyes they have closed,
Lest they should see with their eyes and hear with
their ears,
Lest they should understand with their *hearts and*
turn,
So that I should[a] *heal them.'*[b]

16 But blessed *are* your eyes for they see, and your ears for
they hear; 17 for assuredly, I say to you that many prophets
and righteous *men* desired to see what you see, and did
not see *it,* and to hear what you hear, and did not hear *it.*

The Parable of the Sower Explained

18 "Therefore hear the parable of the sower: 19 When any-
one hears the word of the kingdom, and does not under-

13:15 [a] NU-Text and M-Text read *would.* [b] Isaiah 6:9, 10

THE MESSAGE

stories: to create readiness, to nudge the people toward receptive insight. In their present state they can stare till doomsday and not see it, listen till they're blue in the face and not get it. I don't want Isaiah's forecast repeated all over again:

'Your ears are open but you don't hear a thing.
Your eyes are awake but you don't see a thing.
The people are blockheads!
They stick their fingers in their ears
so they won't have to listen;
They screw their eyes shut
so they won't have to look,
so they won't have to deal with me face-to-face
and let me heal them.'

"But you have God-blessed eyes—eyes that see! And God-blessed ears—ears that hear! A lot of people, prophets and humble believers among them, would have given anything to see what you are seeing, to hear what you are hearing, but never had the chance.

The Meaning of the Harvest Story

"Study this story of the farmer planting seed. When anyone hears news of the kingdom and doesn't take it in, it

KING JAMES VERSION

understandeth *it* not, then cometh the wicked *one*, and catcheth away that which was sown in his heart. This is he which received seed by the way side.

20 But he that received the seed into stony places, the same is he that heareth the word, and anon with joy receiveth it;

21 Yet hath he not root in himself, but dureth for a while: for when tribulation or persecution ariseth because of the word, by and by he is offended.

22 He also that received seed among the thorns is he that heareth the word; and the care of this world, and the deceitfulness of riches, choke the word, and he becometh unfruitful.

23 But he that received seed into the good ground is he that heareth the word, and understandeth *it*; which also beareth fruit, and bringeth forth, some an hundredfold, some sixty, some thirty.

24 ¶ Another parable put he forth unto them, saying, The kingdom of heaven is likened unto a man which sowed good seed in his field:

25 But while men slept, his enemy came and sowed tares among the wheat, and went his way.

26 But when the blade was sprung up, and brought forth fruit, then appeared the tares also.

27 So the servants of the householder came and said unto him, Sir, didst not thou sow good seed in thy field? from whence then hath it tares?

NEW AMERICAN STANDARD BIBLE

does not understand it, the evil *one* comes and snatches away what has been sown in his heart. This is the one on whom seed was sown beside the road.

20 "The one on whom seed was sown on the rocky places, this is the man who hears the word and immediately receives it with joy;

21 yet he has no *firm* root in himself, but is *only* temporary, and when affliction or persecution arises because of the word, immediately he falls away.

22 "And the one on whom seed was sown among the thorns, this is the man who hears the word, and the worry of the world and the deceitfulness of wealth choke the word, and it becomes unfruitful.

23 "And the one on whom seed was sown on the good soil, this is the man who hears the word and understands it; who indeed bears fruit and brings forth, some a hundredfold, some sixty, and some thirty."

Tares among Wheat

24 Jesus presented another parable to them, saying, "The kingdom of heaven may be compared to a man who sowed good seed in his field.

25 "But while his men were sleeping, his enemy came and sowed [7]tares among the wheat, and went away.

26 "But when the wheat sprouted and bore grain, then the tares became evident also.

27 "The slaves of the landowner came and said to him, 'Sir, did you not sow good seed in your field? How then does it have tares?'

13:25 [7] Or *darnel*, a weed resembling wheat

NEW CENTURY VERSION

is like the person who hears the message about the king-
dom but does not understand it. The Evil One comes and
takes away what was planted in that person's heart. 20And
what is the seed that fell on rocky ground? That seed is
like the person who hears the teaching and quickly accepts
it with joy. 21But he does not let the teaching go deep into
his life, so he keeps it only a short time. When trouble or
persecution comes because of the teaching he accepted, he
quickly gives up. 22And what is the seed that fell among
the thorny weeds? That seed is like the person who hears
the teaching but lets worries about this life and the temp-
tation of wealth stop that teaching from growing. So the
teaching does not produce fruit[a] in that person's life. 23But
what is the seed that fell on the good ground? That seed is
like the person who hears the teaching and understands it.
That person grows and produces fruit, sometimes a hun-
dred times more, sometimes sixty times more, and some-
times thirty times more."

A Story About Wheat and Weeds

24Then Jesus told them another story: "The kingdom of
heaven is like a man who planted good seed in his field.
25That night, when everyone was asleep, his enemy came
and planted weeds among the wheat and then left. 26Later,
the wheat sprouted and the heads of grain grew, but the
weeds also grew. 27Then the man's servants came to him
and said, 'You planted good seed in your field. Where did
the weeds come from?' 28The man answered, 'An enemy

13:22 [a] **produce fruit** To produce fruit means to have in your life the good things God wants.

CONTEMPORARY ENGLISH VERSION

who hear the message about the kingdom, but don't
understand it. Then the evil one comes and snatches the
message from their hearts. 20The seeds that fell on rocky
ground are the people who gladly hear the message and
accept it right away. 21But they don't have deep roots,
and they don't last very long. As soon as life gets hard
or the message gets them in trouble, they give up.

22The seeds that fell among the thornbushes are also
people who hear the message. But they start worrying
about the needs of this life and are fooled by the desire
to get rich. So the message gets choked out, and they
never produce anything. 23The seeds that fell on good
ground are the people who hear and understand the
message. They produce as much as a hundred or sixty or
thirty times what was planted.

Weeds among the Wheat

24Jesus then told them this story:

The kingdom of heaven is like what happened when a
farmer scattered good seed in a field. 25But while every-
one was sleeping, an enemy came and scattered weed
seeds in the field and then left.

26When the plants came up and began to ripen, the
farmer's servants could see the weeds. 27The servants
came and asked, "Sir, didn't you scatter good seed in
your field? Where did these weeds come from?"

NEW INTERNATIONAL VERSION

does not understand it, the evil one comes and snatches away what was sown in his heart. This is the seed sown along the path. 20The one who received the seed that fell on rocky places is the man who hears the word and at once receives it with joy. 21But since he has no root, he lasts only a short time. When trouble or persecution comes because of the word, he quickly falls away. 22The one who received the seed that fell among the thorns is the man who hears the word, but the worries of this life and the deceitfulness of wealth choke it, making it unfruitful. 23But the one who received the seed that fell on good soil is the man who hears the word and understands it. He produces a crop, yielding a hundred, sixty or thirty times what was sown."

The Parable of the Weeds

24Jesus told them another parable: "The kingdom of heaven is like a man who sowed good seed in his field. 25But while everyone was sleeping, his enemy came and sowed weeds among the wheat, and went away. 26When the wheat sprouted and formed heads, then the weeds also appeared.

27"The owner's servants came to him and said, 'Sir, didn't you sow good seed in your field? Where then did the weeds come from?'

NEW LIVING TRANSLATION

Kingdom and don't understand it. Then the evil one comes and snatches the seed away from their hearts. 20The rocky soil represents those who hear the message and receive it with joy. 21But like young plants in such soil, their roots don't go very deep. At first they get along fine, but they wilt as soon as they have problems or are persecuted because they believe the word. 22The thorny ground represents those who hear and accept the Good News, but all too quickly the message is crowded out by the cares of this life and the lure of wealth, so no crop is produced. 23The good soil represents the hearts of those who truly accept God's message and produce a huge harvest—thirty, sixty, or even a hundred times as much as had been planted."

Story of the Wheat and Weeds

24Here is another story Jesus told: "The Kingdom of Heaven is like a farmer who planted good seed in his field. 25But that night as everyone slept, his enemy came and planted weeds among the wheat. 26When the crop began to grow and produce grain, the weeds also grew. 27The farmer's servants came and told him, 'Sir, the field where you planted that good seed is full of weeds!'

NEW KING JAMES VERSION

stand *it,* then the wicked *one* comes and snatches away what was sown in his heart. This is he who received seed by the wayside. 20But he who received the seed on stony places, this is he who hears the word and immediately receives it with joy; 21yet he has no root in himself, but endures only for a while. For when tribulation or persecution arises because of the word, immediately he stumbles. 22Now he who received seed among the thorns is he who hears the word, and the cares of this world and the deceitfulness of riches choke the word, and he becomes unfruitful. 23But he who received seed on the good ground is he who hears the word and understands *it,* who indeed bears fruit and produces: some a hundredfold, some sixty, some thirty."

The Parable of the Wheat and the Tares

24Another parable He put forth to them, saying: "The kingdom of heaven is like a man who sowed good seed in his field; 25but while men slept, his enemy came and sowed tares among the wheat and went his way. 26But when the grain had sprouted and produced a crop, then the tares also appeared. 27So the servants of the owner came and said to him, 'Sir, did you not sow good seed in your field? How then does it have tares?' 28He said to them, 'An enemy has

THE MESSAGE

just remains on the surface, and so the Evil One comes along and plucks it right out of that person's heart. This is the seed the farmer scatters on the road.

"The seed cast in the gravel—this is the person who hears and instantly responds with enthusiasm. But there is no soil of character, and so when the emotions wear off and some difficulty arrives, there is nothing to show for it.

"The seed cast in the weeds is the person who hears the kingdom news, but weeds of worry and illusions about getting more and wanting everything under the sun strangle what was heard, and nothing comes of it.

"The seed cast on good earth is the person who hears and takes in the News, and then produces a harvest beyond his wildest dreams."

✢

He told another story. "God's kingdom is like a farmer who planted good seed in his field. That night, while his hired men were asleep, his enemy sowed thistles all through the wheat and slipped away before dawn. When the first green shoots appeared and the grain began to form, the thistles showed up, too.

"The farmhands came to the farmer and said, 'Master, that was clean seed you planted, wasn't it? Where did these thistles come from?'

KING JAMES VERSION

28 He said unto them, An enemy hath done this. The servants said unto him, Wilt thou then that we go and gather them up?

29 But he said, Nay; lest while ye gather up the tares, ye root up also the wheat with them.

30 Let both grow together until the harvest: and in the time of harvest I will say to the reapers, Gather ye together first the tares, and bind them in bundles to burn them: but gather the wheat into my barn.

31 Another parable put he forth unto them, saying, The kingdom of heaven is like to a grain of mustard seed, which a man took, and sowed in his field:

32 Which indeed is the least of all seeds: but when it is grown, it is the greatest among herbs, and becometh a tree, so that the birds of the air come and lodge in the branches thereof.

33 Another parable spake he unto them; The kingdom of heaven is like unto leaven, which a woman took, and hid in three measures of meal, till the whole was leavened.

34 All these things spake Jesus unto the multitude in parables; and without a parable spake he not unto them:

35 That it might be fulfilled which was spoken by the prophet, saying, I will open my mouth in parables; I will

NEW AMERICAN STANDARD BIBLE

28 "And he said to them, 'An enemy has done this!' The slaves *said to him, 'Do you want us, then, to go and gather them up?'

29 "But he *said, 'No; for while you are gathering up the tares, you may uproot the wheat with them.

30 'Allow both to grow together until the harvest; and in the time of the harvest I will say to the reapers, "First gather up the tares and bind them in bundles to burn them up; but gather the wheat into my barn." ' "

The Mustard Seed

31 He presented another parable to them, saying, "The kingdom of heaven is like a mustard seed, which a man took and sowed in his field;

32 and this is smaller than all *other* seeds, but when it is full grown, it is larger than the garden plants and becomes a tree, so that THE BIRDS OF THE AIR come and NEST IN ITS BRANCHES."

The Leaven

33 He spoke another parable to them, "The kingdom of heaven is like leaven, which a woman took and hid in three pecks of flour until it was all leavened."

34 All these things Jesus spoke to the crowds in parables, and He did not speak to them without a parable.

35 *This was* to fulfill what was spoken through the prophet:

"I WILL OPEN MY MOUTH IN PARABLES;

NEW CENTURY VERSION

planted weeds.' The servants asked, 'Do you want us to pull up the weeds?'
29The man answered, 'No, because when you pull up the weeds, you might also pull up the wheat.
30Let the weeds and the wheat grow together until the harvest time. At harvest time I will tell the workers, "First gather the weeds and tie them together to be burned. Then gather the wheat and bring it to my barn." ' "

Stories of Mustard Seed and Yeast

31Then Jesus told another story: "The kingdom of heaven is like a mustard seed that a man planted in his field.
32That seed is the smallest of all seeds, but when it grows, it is one of the largest garden plants. It becomes big enough for the wild birds to come and build nests in its branches."

33Then Jesus told another story: "The kingdom of heaven is like yeast that a woman took and hid in a large tub of flour until it made all the dough rise."

34Jesus used stories to tell all these things to the people; he always used stories to teach them.
35This is as the prophet said:

"I will speak using stories;

CONTEMPORARY ENGLISH VERSION

28"An enemy did this," he replied.

His servants then asked, "Do you want us to go out and pull up the weeds?"

29"No!" he answered. "You might also pull up the wheat.
30Leave the weeds alone until harvest time. Then I'll tell my workers to gather the weeds and tie them up and burn them. But I'll have them store the wheat in my barn."

Stories about a Mustard Seed and Yeast

(Mark 4.30-32; Luke 13.18-21)

31Jesus told them another story:

The kingdom of heaven is like what happens when a farmer plants a mustard seed in a field.
32Although it is the smallest of all seeds, it grows larger than any garden plant and becomes a tree. Birds even come and nest on its branches.

33Jesus also said:

The kingdom of heaven is like what happens when a woman mixes a little yeast into three big batches of flour. Finally, all the dough rises.

The Reason for Teaching with Stories (Mark 4.33, 34)

34Jesus used stories when he spoke to the people. In fact, he did not tell them anything without using stories.
35So God's promise came true, just as the prophet[b] had said,

"I will use stories

[b] 13.35 *the prophet*: Some manuscripts have "the prophet Isaiah."

NEW INTERNATIONAL VERSION

28" 'An enemy did this,' he replied.

"The servants asked him, 'Do you want us to go and pull them up?'

29" 'No,' he answered, 'because while you are pulling the weeds, you may root up the wheat with them. 30Let both grow together until the harvest. At that time I will tell the harvesters: First collect the weeds and tie them in bundles to be burned; then gather the wheat and bring it into my barn.' "

The Parables of the Mustard Seed and the Yeast

31He told them another parable: "The kingdom of heaven is like a mustard seed, which a man took and planted in his field. 32Though it is the smallest of all your seeds, yet when it grows, it is the largest of garden plants and becomes a tree, so that the birds of the air come and perch in its branches."

33He told them still another parable: "The kingdom of heaven is like yeast that a woman took and mixed into a large amount[b] of flour until it worked all through the dough."

34Jesus spoke all these things to the crowd in parables; he did not say anything to them without using a parable. 35So was fulfilled what was spoken through the prophet:

"I will open my mouth in parables,

[b] *33* Greek *three satas* (probably about 1/2 bushel or 22 liters)

NEW LIVING TRANSLATION

28" 'An enemy has done it!' the farmer exclaimed.

" 'Shall we pull out the weeds?' they asked.

29"He replied, 'No, you'll hurt the wheat if you do. 30Let both grow together until the harvest. Then I will tell the harvesters to sort out the weeds and burn them and to put the wheat in the barn.' "

Illustration of the Mustard Seed

31Here is another illustration Jesus used: "The Kingdom of Heaven is like a mustard seed planted in a field. 32It is the smallest of all seeds, but it becomes the largest of garden plants and grows into a tree where birds can come and find shelter in its branches."

Illustration of the Yeast

33Jesus also used this illustration: "The Kingdom of Heaven is like yeast used by a woman making bread. Even though she used a large amount* of flour, the yeast permeated every part of the dough."

34Jesus always used stories and illustrations like these when speaking to the crowds. In fact, he never spoke to them without using such parables. 35This fulfilled the prophecy that said,

"I will speak to you in parables.

13:33 Greek *3 measures.*

NEW KING JAMES VERSION

done this.' The servants said to him, 'Do you want us then to go and gather them up?' 29But he said, 'No, lest while you gather up the tares you also uproot the wheat with them. 30Let both grow together until the harvest, and at the time of harvest I will say to the reapers, "First gather together the tares and bind them in bundles to burn them, but gather the wheat into my barn." ' "

The Parable of the Mustard Seed

31Another parable He put forth to them, saying: "The kingdom of heaven is like a mustard seed, which a man took and sowed in his field, 32which indeed is the least of all the seeds; but when it is grown it is greater than the herbs and becomes a tree, so that the birds of the air come and nest in its branches."

The Parable of the Leaven

33Another parable He spoke to them: "The kingdom of heaven is like leaven, which a woman took and hid in three measures[c] of meal till it was all leavened."

Prophecy and the Parables

34All these things Jesus spoke to the multitude in parables; and without a parable He did not speak to them, 35that it might be fulfilled which was spoken by the prophet, saying:

"*I will open My mouth in parables;*

13:33 [c] Greek *sata,* approximately two pecks in all

THE MESSAGE

"He answered, 'Some enemy did this.'

"The farmhands asked, 'Should we weed out the thistles?'

"He said, 'No, if you weed the thistles, you'll pull up the wheat, too. Let them grow together until harvest time. Then I'll instruct the harvesters to pull up the thistles and tie them in bundles for the fire, then gather the wheat and put it in the barn.' "

Another story. "God's kingdom is like a pine nut that a farmer plants. It is quite small as seeds go, but in the course of years it grows into a huge pine tree, and eagles build nests in it."

Another story. "God's kingdom is like yeast that a woman works into the dough for dozens of loaves of barley bread—and waits while the dough rises."

All Jesus did that day was tell stories—a long storytelling afternoon. His storytelling fulfilled the prophecy:

"I will open my mouth and tell stories;

KING JAMES VERSION

utter things which have been kept secret from the founda-
tion of the world.
36 Then Jesus sent the multitude away, and went into
the house: and his disciples came unto him, saying,
Declare unto us the parable of the tares of the field.
37 He answered and said unto them, He that soweth
the good seed is the Son of man;
38 The field is the world; the good seed are the children
of the kingdom; but the tares are the children of the
wicked *one*;
39 The enemy that sowed them is the devil; the harvest
is the end of the world; and the reapers are the angels.
40 As therefore the tares are gathered and burned in the
fire; so shall it be in the end of this world.
41 The Son of man shall send forth his angels, and they
shall gather out of his kingdom all things that offend, and
them which do iniquity;
42 And shall cast them into a furnace of fire: there shall
be wailing and gnashing of teeth.
43 Then shall the righteous shine forth as the sun in
the kingdom of their Father. Who hath ears to hear, let
him hear.
44 ¶ Again, the kingdom of heaven is like unto treasure

NEW AMERICAN STANDARD BIBLE

I WILL UTTER THINGS HIDDEN SINCE THE FOUNDATION OF
THE WORLD."

The Tares Explained

36 Then He left the crowds and went into the house.
And His disciples came to Him and said, "Explain to us the
parable of the tares of the field."
37 And He said, "The one who sows the good seed is the
Son of Man,
38 and the field is the world; and *as for* the good seed,
these are the sons of the kingdom; and the tares are the
sons of the evil *one;*
39 and the enemy who sowed them is the devil, and the
harvest is the end of the age; and the reapers are angels.
40 "So just as the tares are gathered up and burned with
fire, so shall it be at the end of the age.
41 "The Son of Man will send forth His angels, and they
will gather out of His kingdom all stumbling blocks, and
those who commit lawlessness,
42 and will throw them into the furnace of fire; in that
place there will be weeping and gnashing of teeth.
43 "Then THE RIGHTEOUS WILL SHINE FORTH AS THE SUN in
the kingdom of their Father. He who has ears, let him
hear.

Hidden Treasure

44 "The kingdom of heaven is like a treasure hidden in

NEW CENTURY VERSION

I will tell things that have been secret since the world
was made." *Psalm 78:2*

Jesus Explains About the Weeds

36Then Jesus left the crowd and went into the house. His
followers came to him and said, "Explain to us the mean-
ing of the story about the weeds in the field."
37Jesus answered, "The man who planted the good seed
in the field is the Son of Man. 38The field is the world, and
the good seed are all of God's children who belong to the
kingdom. The weeds are those people who belong to the
Evil One. 39And the enemy who planted the bad seed is
the devil. The harvest time is the end of the world, and
the workers who gather are God's angels.
40"Just as the weeds are pulled up and burned in the
fire, so it will be at the end of the world. 41The Son of Man
will send out his angels, and they will gather out of his
kingdom all who cause sin and all who do evil. 42The
angels will throw them into the blazing furnace, where the
people will cry and grind their teeth with pain. 43Then the
good people will shine like the sun in the kingdom of their
Father. You people who can hear me, listen.

Stories of a Treasure and a Pearl

44"The kingdom of heaven is like a treasure hidden in a

CONTEMPORARY ENGLISH VERSION

to speak my message
and to explain things
that have been hidden
since the creation
of the world."

Jesus Explains the Story about the Weeds

36After Jesus left the crowd and went inside,[c] his disci-
ples came to him and said, "Explain to us the story about
the weeds in the wheat field."
37Jesus answered:
The one who scattered the good seed is the Son of
Man. 38The field is the world, and the good seeds are the
people who belong to the kingdom. The weed seeds are
those who belong to the evil one, 39and the one who
scattered them is the devil. The harvest is the end of
time, and angels are the ones who bring in the harvest.
40Weeds are gathered and burned. That's how it will
be at the end of time. 41The Son of Man will send out his
angels, and they will gather from his kingdom everyone
who does wrong or causes others to sin. 42Then he will
throw them into a flaming furnace, where people will cry
and grit their teeth in pain. 43But everyone who has
done right will shine like the sun in their Father's king-
dom. If you have ears, pay attention!

A Hidden Treasure

44The kingdom of heaven is like what happens when

c 13.36 *went inside:* Or "went home."

NEW INTERNATIONAL VERSION

I will utter things hidden since the creation of the
world."[c]

The Parable of the Weeds Explained

36 Then he left the crowd and went into the house. His
disciples came to him and said, "Explain to us the parable
of the weeds in the field."
37 He answered, "The one who sowed the good seed is
the Son of Man. 38 The field is the world, and the good seed
stands for the sons of the kingdom. The weeds are the
sons of the evil one, 39 and the enemy who sows them is
the devil. The harvest is the end of the age, and the harvesters are angels.
40 "As the weeds are pulled up and burned in the fire, so
it will be at the end of the age. 41 The Son of Man will send
out his angels, and they will weed out of his kingdom
everything that causes sin and all who do evil. 42 They will
throw them into the fiery furnace, where there will be
weeping and gnashing of teeth. 43 Then the righteous will
shine like the sun in the kingdom of their Father. He who
has ears, let him hear.

The Parables of the Hidden Treasure and the Pearl

44 "The kingdom of heaven is like treasure hidden in a

[c] *35* Psalm 78:2

NEW LIVING TRANSLATION

I will explain mysteries hidden since the creation of
the world."*

The Wheat and Weeds Explained

36 Then, leaving the crowds outside, Jesus went into the
house. His disciples said, "Please explain the story of the
weeds in the field."
37 "All right," he said. "I, the Son of Man, am the farmer
who plants the good seed. 38 The field is the world, and the
good seed represents the people of the Kingdom. The weeds
are the people who belong to the evil one. 39 The enemy who
planted the weeds among the wheat is the Devil. The harvest is the end of the world, and the harvesters are the
angels.
40 "Just as the weeds are separated out and burned, so it
will be at the end of the world. 41 I, the Son of Man, will
send my angels, and they will remove from my Kingdom
everything that causes sin and all who do evil, 42 and they
will throw them into the furnace and burn them. There will
be weeping and gnashing of teeth. 43 Then the godly will
shine like the sun in their Father's Kingdom. Anyone who
is willing to hear should listen and understand!

Illustration of the Hidden Treasure

44 "The Kingdom of Heaven is like a treasure that a man

13:35 Ps 78:2.

NEW KING JAMES VERSION

*I will utter things kept secret from the foundation of
the world."*[d]

The Parable of the Tares Explained

36 Then Jesus sent the multitude away and went into the
house. And His disciples came to Him, saying, "Explain to
us the parable of the tares of the field."
37 He answered and said to them: "He who sows the
good seed is the Son of Man. 38 The field is the world, the
good seeds are the sons of the kingdom, but the tares are
the sons of the wicked *one.* 39 The enemy who sowed them
is the devil, the harvest is the end of the age, and the
reapers are the angels. 40 Therefore as the tares are gathered and burned in the fire, so it will be at the end of this
age. 41 The Son of Man will send out His angels, and they
will gather out of His kingdom all things that offend, and
those who practice lawlessness, 42 and will cast them into
the furnace of fire. There will be wailing and gnashing of
teeth. 43 Then the righteous will shine forth as the sun in
the kingdom of their Father. He who has ears to hear, let
him hear!

The Parable of the Hidden Treasure

44 "Again, the kingdom of heaven is like treasure hidden

13:35 [d] Psalm 78:2

THE MESSAGE

I will bring out into the open
things hidden since the world's first day."

The Curtain of History

Jesus dismissed the congregation and went into the house. His disciples came in and said, "Explain to us that story of the thistles in the field."

So he explained. "The farmer who sows the pure seed is the Son of Man. The field is the world, the pure seeds are subjects of the kingdom, the thistles are subjects of the Devil, and the enemy who sows them is the Devil. The harvest is the end of the age, the curtain of history. The harvest hands are angels.

"The picture of thistles pulled up and burned is a scene from the final act. The Son of Man will send his angels, weed out the thistles from his kingdom, pitch them in the trash, and be done with them. They are going to complain to high heaven, but nobody is going to listen. At the same time, ripe, holy lives will mature and adorn the kingdom of their Father.

"Are you listening to this?
"Really listening?

"God's kingdom is like a treasure hidden in a field for

KING JAMES VERSION

hid in a field; the which when a man hath found, he hideth, and for joy thereof goeth and selleth all that he hath, and buyeth that field.
45 Again, the kingdom of heaven is like unto a merchant man, seeking goodly pearls:
46 Who, when he had found one pearl of great price, went and sold all that he had, and bought it.
47 Again, the kingdom of heaven is like unto a net, that was cast into the sea, and gathered of every kind:
48 Which, when it was full, they drew to shore, and sat down, and gathered the good into vessels, but cast the bad away.
49 So shall it be at the end of the world: the angels shall come forth, and sever the wicked from among the just,
50 And shall cast them into the furnace of fire: there shall be wailing and gnashing of teeth.
51 Jesus saith unto them, Have ye understood all these things? They say unto him, Yea, Lord.
52 Then said he unto them, Therefore every scribe *which is* instructed unto the kingdom of heaven is like unto a man *that is* an householder, which bringeth forth out of his treasure *things* new and old.

NEW AMERICAN STANDARD BIBLE

the field, which a man found and hid *again;* and from joy over it he goes and sells all that he has and buys that field.

A Costly Pearl

45 "Again, the kingdom of heaven is like a merchant seeking fine pearls,
46 and upon finding one pearl of great value, he went and sold all that he had and bought it.

A Dragnet

47 "Again, the kingdom of heaven is like a dragnet cast into the sea, and gathering *fish* of every kind;
48 and when it was filled, they drew it up on the beach; and they sat down and gathered the good *fish* into containers, but the bad they threw away.
49 "So it will be at the end of the age; the angels will come forth and take out the wicked from among the righteous,
50 and will throw them into the furnace of fire; in that place there will be weeping and gnashing of teeth.
51 "Have you understood all these things?" They *said to Him, "Yes."
52 And Jesus said to them, "Therefore every scribe who has become a disciple of the kingdom of heaven is like a head of a household, who brings out of his treasure things new and old."

NEW CENTURY VERSION

field. One day a man found the treasure, and then he hid it in the field again. He was so happy that he went and sold everything he owned to buy that field.

45 "Also, the kingdom of heaven is like a man looking for fine pearls. 46 When he found a very valuable pearl, he went and sold everything he had and bought it.

A Story of a Fishing Net

47 "Also, the kingdom of heaven is like a net that was put into the lake and caught many different kinds of fish. 48 When it was full, the fishermen pulled the net to the shore. They sat down and put all the good fish in baskets and threw away the bad fish. 49 It will be this way at the end of the world. The angels will come and separate the evil people from the good people. 50 The angels will throw the evil people into the blazing furnace, where people will cry and grind their teeth with pain."

51 Jesus asked his followers, "Do you understand all these things?"

They answered, "Yes, we understand."

52 Then Jesus said to them, "So every teacher of the law who has been taught about the kingdom of heaven is like the owner of a house. He brings out both new things and old things he has saved."

CONTEMPORARY ENGLISH VERSION

someone finds treasure hidden in a field and buries it again. A person like that is happy and goes and sells everything in order to buy that field.

A Valuable Pearl

45 The kingdom of heaven is like what happens when a shop owner is looking for fine pearls. 46 After finding a very valuable one, the owner goes and sells everything in order to buy that pearl.

A Fish Net

47 The kingdom of heaven is like what happens when a net is thrown into a lake and catches all kinds of fish. 48 When the net is full, it is dragged to the shore, and the fishermen sit down to separate the fish. They keep the good ones, but throw the bad ones away. 49 That's how it will be at the end of time. Angels will come and separate the evil people from the ones who have done right. 50 Then those evil people will be thrown into a flaming furnace, where they will cry and grit their teeth in pain.

New and Old Treasures

51 Jesus asked his disciples if they understood all these things. They said, "Yes, we do."

52 So he told them, "Every student of the Scriptures who becomes a disciple in the kingdom of heaven is like someone who brings out new and old treasures from the storeroom."

NEW INTERNATIONAL VERSION

field. When a man found it, he hid it again, and then in his joy went and sold all he had and bought that field.

45 "Again, the kingdom of heaven is like a merchant looking for fine pearls. 46 When he found one of great value, he went away and sold everything he had and bought it.

The Parable of the Net

47 "Once again, the kingdom of heaven is like a net that was let down into the lake and caught all kinds of fish. 48 When it was full, the fishermen pulled it up on the shore. Then they sat down and collected the good fish in baskets, but threw the bad away. 49 This is how it will be at the end of the age. The angels will come and separate the wicked from the righteous 50 and throw them into the fiery furnace, where there will be weeping and gnashing of teeth.

51 "Have you understood all these things?" Jesus asked.

"Yes," they replied.

52 He said to them, "Therefore every teacher of the law who has been instructed about the kingdom of heaven is like the owner of a house who brings out of his storeroom new treasures as well as old."

NEW LIVING TRANSLATION

discovered hidden in a field. In his excitement, he hid it again and sold everything he owned to get enough money to buy the field—and to get the treasure, too!

Illustration of the Pearl Merchant

45 "Again, the Kingdom of Heaven is like a pearl merchant on the lookout for choice pearls. 46 When he discovered a pearl of great value, he sold everything he owned and bought it!

Illustration of the Fishing Net

47 "Again, the Kingdom of Heaven is like a fishing net that is thrown into the water and gathers fish of every kind. 48 When the net is full, they drag it up onto the shore, sit down, sort the good fish into crates, and throw the bad ones away. 49 That is the way it will be at the end of the world. The angels will come and separate the wicked people from the godly, 50 throwing the wicked into the fire. There will be weeping and gnashing of teeth. 51 Do you understand?"

"Yes," they said, "we do."

52 Then he added, "Every teacher of religious law who has become a disciple in the Kingdom of Heaven is like a person who brings out of the storehouse the new teachings as well as the old."

NEW KING JAMES VERSION

in a field, which a man found and hid; and for joy over it he goes and sells all that he has and buys that field.

The Parable of the Pearl of Great Price

45 "Again, the kingdom of heaven is like a merchant seeking beautiful pearls, 46 who, when he had found one pearl of great price, went and sold all that he had and bought it.

The Parable of the Dragnet

47 "Again, the kingdom of heaven is like a dragnet that was cast into the sea and gathered some of every kind, 48 which, when it was full, they drew to shore; and they sat down and gathered the good into vessels, but threw the bad away. 49 So it will be at the end of the age. The angels will come forth, separate the wicked from among the just, 50 and cast them into the furnace of fire. There will be wailing and gnashing of teeth."

51 Jesus said to them,[e] "Have you understood all these things?"

They said to Him, "Yes, Lord."[f]

52 Then He said to them, "Therefore every scribe instructed concerning[g] the kingdom of heaven is like a householder who brings out of his treasure *things* new and old."

13:51 [e] NU-Text omits *Jesus said to them.* [f] NU-Text omits *Lord.*
13:52 [g] Or *for*

THE MESSAGE

years and then accidently found by a trespasser. The finder is ecstatic—what a find!—and proceeds to sell everything he owns to raise money and buy that field.

"Or, God's kingdom is like a jewel merchant on the hunt for excellent pearls. Finding one that is flawless, he immediately sells everything and buys it.

"Or, God's kingdom is like a fishnet cast into the sea, catching all kinds of fish. When it is full, it is hauled onto the beach. The good fish are picked out and put in a tub; those unfit to eat are thrown away. That's how it will be when the curtain comes down on history. The angels will come and cull the bad fish and throw them in the garbage. There will be a lot of desperate complaining, but it won't do any good."

Jesus asked, "Are you starting to get a handle on all this?"

They answered, "Yes."

He said, "Then you see how every student well-trained in God's kingdom is like the owner of a general store who can put his hands on anything you need, old or new, exactly when you need it."

KING JAMES VERSION

53 ¶ And it came to pass, *that* when Jesus had finished these parables, he departed thence.

54 And when he was come into his own country, he taught them in their synagogue, insomuch that they were astonished, and said, Whence hath this *man* this wisdom, and *these* mighty works?

55 Is not this the carpenter's son? is not his mother called Mary? and his brethren, James, and Joses, and Simon, and Judas?

56 And his sisters, are they not all with us? Whence then hath this *man* all these things?

57 And they were offended in him. But Jesus said unto them, A prophet is not without honour, save in his own country, and in his own house.

58 And he did not many mighty works there because of their unbelief.

14 At that time Herod the tetrarch heard of the fame of Jesus,

2 And said unto his servants, This is John the Baptist; he is risen from the dead; and therefore mighty works do shew forth themselves in him.

3 For Herod had laid hold on John, and bound him, and put *him* in prison for Herodias' sake, his brother Philip's wife.

4 For John said unto him, It is not lawful for thee to have her.

NEW AMERICAN STANDARD BIBLE

Jesus Revisits Nazareth

53 When Jesus had finished these parables, He departed from there.

54 He came to His hometown and *began* teaching them in their synagogue, so that they were astonished, and said, "Where *did* this man *get* this wisdom and *these* miraculous powers?

55 "Is not this the carpenter's son? Is not His mother called Mary, and His brothers, James and Joseph and Simon and Judas?

56 "And His sisters, are they not all with us? Where then *did* this man *get* all these things?"

57 And they took offense at Him. But Jesus said to them, "A prophet is not without honor except in his hometown and in his *own* household."

58 And He did not do many miracles there because of their unbelief.

John the Baptist Beheaded

14 At that time Herod the tetrarch heard the news about Jesus,

2 and said to his servants, "This is John the Baptist; he has risen from the dead, and that is why miraculous powers are at work in him."

3 For when Herod had John arrested, he bound him and put him in prison because of Herodias, the wife of his brother Philip.

4 For John had been saying to him, "It is not lawful for you to have her."

NEW CENTURY VERSION

Jesus Goes to His Hometown

53 When Jesus finished teaching with these stories, he
left there. 54 He went to his hometown and taught the peo-
ple in the synagogue, and they were amazed. They said,
"Where did this man get this wisdom and this power to do
miracles? 55 He is just the son of a carpenter. His mother is
Mary, and his brothers are James, Joseph, Simon, and
Judas. 56 And all his sisters are here with us. Where then
does this man get all these things?" 57 So the people were
upset with Jesus.

But Jesus said to them, "A prophet is honored everywhere except in his hometown and in his own home."

58 So he did not do many miracles there because they
had no faith.

How John the Baptist Was Killed

14 At that time Herod, the ruler of Galilee, heard the
reports about Jesus. 2 So he said to his servants,
"Jesus is John the Baptist, who has risen from the dead.
That is why he can work these miracles."

3 Sometime before this, Herod had arrested John, tied
him up, and put him into prison. Herod did this because of
Herodias, who had been the wife of Philip, Herod's brother.
4 John had been telling Herod, "It is not lawful for you to be

CONTEMPORARY ENGLISH VERSION

The People of Nazareth Turn against Jesus

(Mark 6.1-6; Luke 4.16-30)

53 When Jesus had finished telling these stories, he left
54 and went to his hometown. He taught in their meeting
place, and the people were so amazed that they asked,
"Where does he get all this wisdom and the power to work
these miracles? 55 Isn't he the son of the carpenter? Isn't
Mary his mother, and aren't James, Joseph, Simon, and
Judas his brothers? 56 Don't his sisters still live here in our
town? How can he do all this?" 57 So the people were very
unhappy because of what he was doing.

But Jesus said, "Prophets are honored by everyone,
except the people of their hometown and their own fami-
ly." 58 And because the people did not have any faith, Jesus
did not work many miracles there.

The Death of John the Baptist (Mark 6.14-29; Luke 9.7-9)

14 About this time Herod the ruler[a] heard the news
about Jesus 2 and told his officials, "This is John
the Baptist! He has come back from death, and that's why
he has the power to work these miracles."

3-4 Herod had earlier arrested John and had him chained
and put in prison. He did this because John had told him,
"It isn't right for you to take Herodias, the wife of your

[a] 14.1 *Herod the ruler*: Herod Antipas, the son of Herod the Great (see 2.1).

NEW INTERNATIONAL VERSION

A Prophet Without Honor

53When Jesus had finished these parables, he moved on
from there. 54Coming to his hometown, he began teaching
the people in their synagogue, and they were amazed.
"Where did this man get this wisdom and these miracu-
lous powers?" they asked. 55"Isn't this the carpenter's
son? Isn't his mother's name Mary, and aren't his brothers
James, Joseph, Simon and Judas? 56Aren't all his sisters
with us? Where then did this man get all these things?"
57And they took offense at him.

But Jesus said to them, "Only in his hometown and in
his own house is a prophet without honor."
58And he did not do many miracles there because of
their lack of faith.

John the Baptist Beheaded

14 At that time Herod the tetrarch heard the reports
about Jesus, 2and he said to his attendants, "This
is John the Baptist; he has risen from the dead! That is
why miraculous powers are at work in him."
3Now Herod had arrested John and bound him and put
him in prison because of Herodias, his brother Philip's
wife, 4for John had been saying to him: "It is not lawful

NEW LIVING TRANSLATION

Jesus Rejected at Nazareth

53When Jesus had finished telling these stories, he left
that part of the country. 54He returned to Nazareth, his
hometown. When he taught there in the synagogue, every-
one was astonished and said, "Where does he get his wis-
dom and his miracles? 55He's just a carpenter's son, and
we know Mary, his mother, and his brothers—James,
Joseph, Simon, and Judas. 56All his sisters live right here
among us. What makes him so great?" 57And they were
deeply offended and refused to believe in him.

Then Jesus told them, "A prophet is honored everywhere
except in his own hometown and among his own family."
58And so he did only a few miracles there because of their
unbelief.

The Death of John the Baptist

14 When Herod Antipas* heard about Jesus, 2he said
to his advisers, "This must be John the Baptist
come back to life again! That is why he can do such mira-
cles." 3For Herod had arrested and imprisoned John as a
favor to his wife Herodias (the former wife of Herod's
brother Philip). 4John kept telling Herod, "It is illegal for

14:1 Greek *Herod the tetrarch.* He was a son of King Herod and was ruler over one of the four districts in Palestine.

NEW KING JAMES VERSION

Jesus Rejected at Nazareth

53Now it came to pass, when Jesus had finished these
parables, that He departed from there. 54When He had
come to His own country, He taught them in their syna-
gogue, so that they were astonished and said, "Where did
this *Man* get this wisdom and *these* mighty works? 55Is
this not the carpenter's son? Is not His mother called
Mary? And His brothers James, Joses,[h] Simon, and Judas?
56And His sisters, are they not all with us? Where then did
this *Man* get all these things?" 57So they were offended at
Him.

But Jesus said to them, "A prophet is not without honor
except in his own country and in his own house." 58Now
He did not do many mighty works there because of their
unbelief.

John the Baptist Beheaded

14 At that time Herod the tetrarch heard the report
about Jesus 2and said to his servants, "This is John
the Baptist; he is risen from the dead, and therefore these
powers are at work in him." 3For Herod had laid hold of
John and bound him, and put *him* in prison for the sake of
Herodias, his brother Philip's wife. 4Because John had said
to him, "It is not lawful for you to have her." 5And

13:55 [h] NU-Text reads *Joseph.*

THE MESSAGE

When Jesus finished telling these stories, he left there, returned to his hometown, and gave a lecture in the meeting house. He made a real hit, impressing everyone. "We had no idea he was this good!" they said. "How did he get so wise, get such ability?" But in the next breath they were cutting him down: "We've known him since he was a kid; he's the carpenter's son. We know his mother, Mary. We know his brothers James and Joseph, Simon and Judas. All his sisters live here. Who does he think he is?" They got their noses all out of joint.

But Jesus said, "A prophet is taken for granted in his hometown and his family." He didn't do many miracles there because of their hostile indifference.

The Death of John

14 At about this time, Herod, the regional ruler, heard what was being said about Jesus. He said to his servants, "This has to be John the Baptizer come back from the dead. That's why he's able to work miracles!"

Herod had arrested John, put him in chains, and sent him to prison to placate Herodias, his brother Philip's wife. John had provoked Herod by naming his relationship with

KING JAMES VERSION

5 And when he would have put him to death, he feared the multitude, because they counted him as a prophet.

6 But when Herod's birthday was kept, the daughter of Herodias danced before them, and pleased Herod.

7 Whereupon he promised with an oath to give her whatsoever she would ask.

8 And she, being before instructed of her mother, said, Give me here John Baptist's head in a charger.

9 And the king was sorry: nevertheless for the oath's sake, and them which sat with him at meat, he commanded *it* to be given *her.*

10 And he sent, and beheaded John in the prison.

11 And his head was brought in a charger, and given to the damsel: and she brought *it* to her mother.

12 And his disciples came, and took up the body, and buried it, and went and told Jesus.

13 ¶ When Jesus heard *of it,* he departed thence by ship into a desert place apart: and when the people had heard *thereof,* they followed him on foot out of the cities.

14 And Jesus went forth, and saw a great multitude, and was moved with compassion toward them, and he healed their sick.

15 And when it was evening, his disciples came to him, saying, This is a desert place, and the time is now past; send the multitude away, that they may go into the villages, and buy themselves victuals.

16 But Jesus said unto them, They need not depart; give ye them to eat.

NEW AMERICAN STANDARD BIBLE

5 Although Herod wanted to put him to death, he feared the crowd, because they regarded John as a prophet.

6 But when Herod's birthday came, the daughter of Herodias danced before *them* and pleased Herod,

7 so *much* that he promised with an oath to give her whatever she asked.

8 Having been prompted by her mother, she *said, "Give me here on a platter the head of John the Baptist."

9 Although he was grieved, the king commanded *it* to be given because of his oaths, and because of his dinner guests.

10 He sent and had John beheaded in the prison.

11 And his head was brought on a platter and given to the girl, and she brought it to her mother.

12 His disciples came and took away the body and buried it; and they went and reported to Jesus.

Five Thousand Fed

13 Now when Jesus heard *about John,* He withdrew from there in a boat to a secluded place by Himself; and when the people heard *of this,* they followed Him on foot from the cities.

14 When He went ashore, He saw a large crowd, and felt compassion for them and healed their sick.

15 When it was evening, the disciples came to Him and said, "This place is desolate and the hour is already late; so send the crowds away, that they may go into the villages and buy food for themselves."

16 But Jesus said to them, "They do not need to go away; you give them *something* to eat!"

NEW CENTURY VERSION

married to Herodias." [5]Herod wanted to kill John, but he was afraid of the people, because they believed John was a prophet.

[6]On Herod's birthday, the daughter of Herodias danced for Herod and his guests, and she pleased him. [7]So he promised with an oath to give her anything she wanted. [8]Herodias told her daughter what to ask for, so she said to Herod, "Give me the head of John the Baptist here on a platter." [9]Although King Herod was very sad, he had made a promise, and his dinner guests had heard him. So Herod ordered that what she asked for be done. [10]He sent soldiers to the prison to cut off John's head. [11]And they brought it on a platter and gave it to the girl, and she took it to her mother. [12]John's followers came and got his body and buried it. Then they went and told Jesus.

More than Five Thousand Fed

[13]When Jesus heard what had happened to John, he left in a boat and went to a lonely place by himself. But the crowds heard about it and followed him on foot from the towns. [14]When he arrived, he saw a great crowd waiting. He felt sorry for them and healed those who were sick.

[15]When it was evening, his followers came to him and said, "No one lives in this place, and it is already late. Send the people away so they can go to the towns and buy food for themselves."

[16]But Jesus answered, "They don't need to go away. You give them something to eat."

CONTEMPORARY ENGLISH VERSION

brother Philip." [5]Herod wanted to kill John. But the people thought John was a prophet, and Herod was afraid of what they might do.

[6]When Herod's birthday came, the daughter of Herodias danced for the guests. She pleased Herod [7]so much that he swore to give her whatever she wanted. [8]But the girl's mother told her to say, "Here on a platter I want the head of John the Baptist!"

[9]The king was sorry for what he had said. But he did not want to break the promise he had made in front of his guests. So he ordered a guard [10]to go to the prison and cut off John's head. [11]It was taken on a platter to the girl, and she gave it to her mother. [12]John's followers took his body and buried it. Then they told Jesus what had happened.

Jesus Feeds Five Thousand

(Mark 6.30-44; Luke 9.10-17; John 6.1-14)

[13]After Jesus heard about John, he crossed Lake Galilee[b] to go to some place where he could be alone. But the crowds found out and followed him on foot from the towns. [14]When Jesus got out of the boat, he saw the large crowd. He felt sorry for them and healed everyone who was sick.

[15]That evening the disciples came to Jesus and said, "This place is like a desert, and it is already late. Let the crowds leave, so they can go to the villages and buy some food."

[16]Jesus replied, "They don't have to leave. Why don't you give them something to eat?"

[b] 14.13 *crossed Lake Galilee*: To the east side.

NEW INTERNATIONAL VERSION

for you to have her." 5Herod wanted to kill John, but he was afraid of the people, because they considered him a prophet.

6On Herod's birthday the daughter of Herodias danced for them and pleased Herod so much 7that he promised with an oath to give her whatever she asked. 8Prompted by her mother, she said, "Give me here on a platter the head of John the Baptist." 9The king was distressed, but because of his oaths and his dinner guests, he ordered that her request be granted 10and had John beheaded in the prison. 11His head was brought in on a platter and given to the girl, who carried it to her mother. 12John's disciples came and took his body and buried it. Then they went and told Jesus.

Jesus Feeds the Five Thousand

13When Jesus heard what had happened, he withdrew by boat privately to a solitary place. Hearing of this, the crowds followed him on foot from the towns. 14When Jesus landed and saw a large crowd, he had compassion on them and healed their sick.

15As evening approached, the disciples came to him and said, "This is a remote place, and it's already getting late. Send the crowds away, so they can go to the villages and buy themselves some food."

16Jesus replied, "They do not need to go away. You give them something to eat."

NEW LIVING TRANSLATION

you to marry her." 5Herod would have executed John, but he was afraid of a riot, because all the people believed John was a prophet.

6But at a birthday party for Herod, Herodias's daughter performed a dance that greatly pleased him, 7so he promised with an oath to give her anything she wanted. 8At her mother's urging, the girl asked, "I want the head of John the Baptist on a tray!" 9The king was sorry, but because of his oath and because he didn't want to back down in front of his guests, he issued the necessary orders. 10So John was beheaded in the prison, 11and his head was brought on a tray and given to the girl, who took it to her mother. 12John's disciples came for his body and buried it. Then they told Jesus what had happened.

Jesus Feeds Five Thousand

13As soon as Jesus heard the news, he went off by himself in a boat to a remote area to be alone. But the crowds heard where he was headed and followed by land from many villages. 14A vast crowd was there as he stepped from the boat, and he had compassion on them and healed their sick.

15That evening the disciples came to him and said, "This is a desolate place, and it is getting late. Send the crowds away so they can go to the villages and buy food for themselves."

16But Jesus replied, "That isn't necessary—you feed them."

NEW KING JAMES VERSION

although he wanted to put him to death, he feared the multitude, because they counted him as a prophet.

6But when Herod's birthday was celebrated, the daughter of Herodias danced before them and pleased Herod. 7Therefore he promised with an oath to give her whatever she might ask.

8So she, having been prompted by her mother, said, "Give me John the Baptist's head here on a platter."

9And the king was sorry; nevertheless, because of the oaths and because of those who sat with him, he commanded *it* to be given to *her.* 10So he sent and had John beheaded in prison. 11And his head was brought on a platter and given to the girl, and she brought *it* to her mother. 12Then his disciples came and took away the body and buried it, and went and told Jesus.

Feeding the Five Thousand

13When Jesus heard *it,* He departed from there by boat to a deserted place by Himself. But when the multitudes heard it, they followed Him on foot from the cities. 14And when Jesus went out He saw a great multitude; and He was moved with compassion for them, and healed their sick. 15When it was evening, His disciples came to Him, saying, "This is a deserted place, and the hour is already late. Send the multitudes away, that they may go into the villages and buy themselves food."

16But Jesus said to them, "They do not need to go away. You give them something to eat."

THE MESSAGE

Herodias "adultery." Herod wanted to kill him, but he was afraid because so many people revered John as a prophet of God.

But at his birthday celebration, he got his chance. Herodias's daughter provided the entertainment, dancing for the guests. She swept Herod away. In his drunken enthusiasm, he promised her on oath anything she wanted. Already coached by her mother, she was ready: "Give me, served up on a platter, the head of John the Baptizer." That sobered the king up fast. Unwilling to lose face with his guests, he did it—ordered John's head cut off and presented to the girl on a platter. She in turn gave it to her mother. Later, John's disciples got the body, gave it a reverent burial, and reported to Jesus.

Supper for Five Thousand

When Jesus got the news, he slipped away by boat to an out-of-the-way place by himself. But unsuccessfully—someone saw him and the word got around. Soon a lot of people from the nearby villages walked around the lake to where he was. When he saw them coming, he was overcome with pity and healed their sick.

Toward evening the disciples approached him. "We're out in the country and it's getting late. Dismiss the people so they can go to the villages and get some supper."

But Jesus said, "There is no need to dismiss them. You give them supper."

KING JAMES VERSION

17 And they say unto him, We have here but five loaves, and two fishes.

18 He said, Bring them hither to me.

19 And he commanded the multitude to sit down on the grass, and took the five loaves, and the two fishes, and looking up to heaven, he blessed, and brake, and gave the loaves to *his* disciples, and the disciples to the multitude.

20 And they did all eat, and were filled: and they took up of the fragments that remained twelve baskets full.

21 And they that had eaten were about five thousand men, beside women and children.

22 ¶ And straightway Jesus constrained his disciples to get into a ship, and to go before him unto the other side, while he sent the multitudes away.

23 And when he had sent the multitudes away, he went up into a mountain apart to pray: and when the evening was come, he was there alone.

24 But the ship was now in the midst of the sea, tossed with waves: for the wind was contrary.

25 And in the fourth watch of the night Jesus went unto them, walking on the sea.

26 And when the disciples saw him walking on the sea, they were troubled, saying, It is a spirit; and they cried out for fear.

NEW AMERICAN STANDARD BIBLE

17 They *said to Him, "We have here only five loaves and two fish."

18 And He said, "Bring them here to Me."

19 Ordering the people to sit down on the grass, He took the five loaves and the two fish, and looking up toward heaven, He blessed *the food,* and breaking the loaves He gave them to the disciples, and the disciples *gave them* to the crowds,

20 and they all ate and were satisfied. They picked up what was left over of the broken pieces, twelve full baskets.

21 There were about five thousand men who ate, besides women and children.

Jesus Walks on the Water

22 Immediately He made the disciples get into the boat and go ahead of Him to the other side, while He sent the crowds away.

23 After He had sent the crowds away, He went up on the mountain by Himself to pray; and when it was evening, He was there alone.

24 But the boat was already [1]a long distance from the land, battered by the waves; for the wind was contrary.

25 And in the [2]fourth watch of the night He came to them, walking on the sea.

26 When the disciples saw Him walking on the sea, they were terrified, and said, "It is a ghost!" And they cried out in fear.

14:24 [1] Lit *many stadia from;* a stadion was about 600 feet or about 182 meters 14:25 [2] I.e. 3-6 a.m.

NEW CENTURY VERSION

17They said to him, "But we have only five loaves of bread and two fish."

18Jesus said, "Bring the bread and the fish to me."
19Then he told the people to sit down on the grass. He took the five loaves and the two fish and, looking to heaven, he thanked God for the food. Jesus divided the bread and gave it to his followers, who gave it to the people. 20All the people ate and were satisfied. Then the followers filled twelve baskets with the leftover pieces of food. 21There were about five thousand men there who ate, not counting women and children.

Jesus Walks on the Water

22Immediately Jesus told his followers to get into the boat and go ahead of him across the lake. He stayed there to send the people home. 23After he had sent them away, he went by himself up into the hills to pray. It was late, and Jesus was there alone. 24By this time, the boat was already far away from land. It was being hit by waves, because the wind was blowing against it.

25Between three and six o'clock in the morning, Jesus came to them, walking on the water. 26When his followers saw him walking on the water, they were afraid. They said, "It's a ghost!" and cried out in fear.

CONTEMPORARY ENGLISH VERSION

17But they said, "We have only five small loaves of bread[c] and two fish." 18Jesus asked his disciples to bring the food to him, 19and he told the crowd to sit down on the grass. Jesus took the five loaves and the two fish. He looked up toward heaven and blessed the food. Then he broke the bread and handed it to his disciples, and they gave it to the people.

20After everyone had eaten all they wanted, Jesus' disciples picked up twelve large baskets of leftovers.

21There were about five thousand men who ate, not counting the women and children.

Jesus Walks on the Water (Mark 6.45-52; John 6.15-21)

22Right away, Jesus made his disciples get into a boat and start back across the lake.[d] But he stayed until he had sent the crowds away. 23Then he went up on a mountain where he could be alone and pray. Later that evening, he was still there.

24By this time the boat was a long way from the shore. It was going against the wind and was being tossed around by the waves. 25A little while before morning, Jesus came walking on the water toward his disciples. 26When they saw him, they thought he was a ghost. They were terrified and started screaming.

[c] 14.17 *small loaves of bread*: These would have been flat and round or in the shape of a bun. [d] 14.22 *back across the lake*: To the west side.

NEW INTERNATIONAL VERSION

17"We have here only five loaves of bread and two fish,"
they answered.
18"Bring them here to me," he said. 19And he directed
the people to sit down on the grass. Taking the five loaves
and the two fish and looking up to heaven, he gave
thanks and broke the loaves. Then he gave them to the
disciples, and the disciples gave them to the people.
20They all ate and were satisfied, and the disciples picked
up twelve basketfuls of broken pieces that were left over.
21The number of those who ate was about five thousand
men, besides women and children.

Jesus Walks on the Water

22Immediately Jesus made the disciples get into the boat
and go on ahead of him to the other side, while he dis-
missed the crowd. 23After he had dismissed them, he went
up on a mountainside by himself to pray. When evening
came, he was there alone, 24but the boat was already a
considerable distance[a] from land, buffeted by the waves
because the wind was against it.
25During the fourth watch of the night Jesus went out to
them, walking on the lake. 26When the disciples saw him
walking on the lake, they were terrified. "It's a ghost,"
they said, and cried out in fear.

[a] *24* Greek *many stadia*

NEW LIVING TRANSLATION

17"Impossible!" they exclaimed. "We have only five
loaves of bread and two fish!"
18"Bring them here," he said. 19Then he told the people
to sit down on the grass. And he took the five loaves and
two fish, looked up toward heaven, and asked God's bless-
ing on the food. Breaking the loaves into pieces, he gave
some of the bread and fish to each disciple, and the disci-
ples gave them to the people. 20They all ate as much as
they wanted, and they picked up twelve baskets of left-
overs. 21About five thousand men had eaten from those
five loaves, in addition to all the women and children!

Jesus Walks on Water

22Immediately after this, Jesus made his disciples get
back into the boat and cross to the other side of the lake
while he sent the people home. 23Afterward he went up
into the hills by himself to pray. Night fell while he was
there alone. 24Meanwhile, the disciples were in trouble far
away from land, for a strong wind had risen, and they
were fighting heavy waves.
25About three o'clock in the morning* Jesus came to
them, walking on the water. 26When the disciples saw him,
they screamed in terror, thinking he was a ghost. 27But

14:25 Greek *In the fourth watch of the night.*

NEW KING JAMES VERSION

17And they said to Him, "We have here only five loaves
and two fish."
18He said, "Bring them here to Me." 19Then He com-
manded the multitudes to sit down on the grass. And He
took the five loaves and the two fish, and looking up to
heaven, He blessed and broke and gave the loaves to the
disciples; and the disciples gave to the multitudes. 20So
they all ate and were filled, and they took up twelve bas-
kets full of the fragments that remained. 21Now those who
had eaten were about five thousand men, besides women
and children.

Jesus Walks on the Sea

22Immediately Jesus made His disciples get into the boat
and go before Him to the other side, while He sent the
multitudes away. 23And when He had sent the multitudes
away, He went up on the mountain by Himself to pray.
Now when evening came, He was alone there. 24But the
boat was now in the middle of the sea,[a] tossed by the
waves, for the wind was contrary.
25Now in the fourth watch of the night Jesus went to
them, walking on the sea. 26And when the disciples saw
Him walking on the sea, they were troubled, saying, "It is
a ghost!" And they cried out for fear.

14:24 [a] NU-Text reads *many furlongs away from the land.*

THE MESSAGE

"All we have are five loaves of bread and two fish," they said.

Jesus said, "Bring them here." Then he had the people sit on the grass. He took the five loaves and two fish, lifted his face to heaven in prayer, blessed, broke, and gave the bread to the disciples. The disciples then gave the food to the congregation. They all ate their fill. They gathered twelve baskets of leftovers. About five thousand were fed.

Walking on the Water

As soon as the meal was finished, he insisted that the disciples get in the boat and go on ahead to the other side while he dismissed the people. With the crowd dispersed, he climbed the mountain so he could be by himself and pray. He stayed there alone, late into the night.

Meanwhile, the boat was far out to sea when the wind came up against them and they were battered by the waves. At about four o'clock in the morning, Jesus came toward them walking on the water. They were scared out of their wits. "A ghost!" they said, crying out in terror.

KING JAMES VERSION

27 But straightway Jesus spake unto them, saying, Be of good cheer; it is I; be not afraid.
28 And Peter answered him and said, Lord, if it be thou, bid me come unto thee on the water.
29 And he said, Come. And when Peter was come down out of the ship, he walked on the water, to go to Jesus.
30 But when he saw the wind boisterous, he was afraid; and beginning to sink, he cried, saying, Lord, save me.
31 And immediately Jesus stretched forth *his* hand, and caught him, and said unto him, O thou of little faith, wherefore didst thou doubt?
32 And when they were come into the ship, the wind ceased.
33 Then they that were in the ship came and worshipped him, saying, Of a truth thou art the Son of God.
34 ¶ And when they were gone over, they came into the land of Gennesaret.
35 And when the men of that place had knowledge of him, they sent out into all that country round about, and brought unto him all that were diseased;
36 And besought him that they might only touch the hem of his garment: and as many as touched were made perfectly whole.

15 Then came to Jesus scribes and Pharisees, which were of Jerusalem, saying,
2 Why do thy disciples transgress the tradition of the elders? for they wash not their hands when they eat bread.

NEW AMERICAN STANDARD BIBLE

27 But immediately Jesus spoke to them, saying, "Take courage, it is I; do not be afraid."
28 Peter said to Him, "Lord, if it is You, command me to come to You on the water."
29 And He said, "Come!" And Peter got out of the boat, and walked on the water and came toward Jesus.
30 But seeing the wind, he became frightened, and beginning to sink, he cried out, "Lord, save me!"
31 Immediately Jesus stretched out His hand and took hold of him, and *said to him, "You of little faith, why did you doubt?"
32 When they got into the boat, the wind stopped.
33 And those who were in the boat worshiped Him, saying, "You are certainly God's Son!"
34 When they had crossed over, they came to land at Gennesaret.
35 And when the men of that place recognized Him, they sent *word* into all that surrounding district and brought to Him all who were sick;
36 and they implored Him that they might just touch the fringe of His cloak; and as many as touched *it* were cured.

Tradition and Commandment

15 Then some Pharisees and scribes *came to Jesus from Jerusalem and said,
2 "Why do Your disciples break the tradition of the elders? For they do not wash their hands when they eat bread."

NEW CENTURY VERSION

27But Jesus quickly spoke to them, "Have courage! It is I. Do not be afraid."
28Peter said, "Lord, if it is really you, then command me to come to you on the water."
29Jesus said, "Come."
And Peter left the boat and walked on the water to Jesus.
30But when Peter saw the wind and the waves, he became afraid and began to sink. He shouted, "Lord, save me!"
31Immediately Jesus reached out his hand and caught Peter. Jesus said, "Your faith is small. Why did you doubt?"
32After they got into the boat, the wind became calm.
33Then those who were in the boat worshiped Jesus and said, "Truly you are the Son of God!"
34When they had crossed the lake, they came to shore at
Gennesaret. 35When the people there recognized Jesus,
they told people all around there that Jesus had come, and
they brought all their sick to him. 36They begged Jesus to
let them touch just the edge of his coat, and all who touched it were healed.

Obey God's Law

15 Then some Pharisees and teachers of the law came to Jesus from Jerusalem. They asked him, 2"Why don't your followers obey the unwritten laws which have been handed down to us? They don't wash their hands before they eat."

CONTEMPORARY ENGLISH VERSION

27At once, Jesus said to them, "Don't worry! I am Jesus. Don't be afraid."
28Peter replied, "Lord, if it is really you, tell me to come to you on the water."
29"Come on!" Jesus said. Peter then got out of the boat and started walking on the water toward him.
30But when Peter saw how strong the wind was, he was afraid and started sinking. "Save me, Lord!" he shouted.
31Right away, Jesus reached out his hand. He helped Peter up and said, "You surely don't have much faith. Why do you doubt?"
32When Jesus and Peter got into the boat, the wind died
down. 33The men in the boat worshiped Jesus and said, "You really are the Son of God!"

Jesus Heals Sick People in Gennesaret (Mark 6.53-56)

34Jesus and his disciples crossed the lake and came to
shore near the town of Gennesaret. 35The people found out
that he was there, and they sent word to everyone who lived in that part of the country. So they brought all the
sick people to Jesus. 36They begged him just to let them touch his clothes, and everyone who did was healed.

The Teaching of the Ancestors (Mark 7.1-13)

15 About this time some Pharisees and teachers of the Law of Moses came from Jerusalem. They asked
Jesus, 2"Why don't your disciples obey what our ancestors taught us to do? They don't even wash their hands[a] before they eat."

[a] 15.2 *wash their hands*: The Jewish people had strict laws about washing their hands before eating, especially if they had been out in public.

NEW INTERNATIONAL VERSION

[27]But Jesus immediately said to them: "Take courage! It is I. Don't be afraid."

[28]"Lord, if it's you," Peter replied, "tell me to come to you on the water."

[29]"Come," he said.

Then Peter got down out of the boat, walked on the water and came toward Jesus. [30]But when he saw the wind, he was afraid and, beginning to sink, cried out, "Lord, save me!"

[31]Immediately Jesus reached out his hand and caught him. "You of little faith," he said, "why did you doubt?"

[32]And when they climbed into the boat, the wind died down. [33]Then those who were in the boat worshiped him, saying, "Truly you are the Son of God."

[34]When they had crossed over, they landed at Gennesaret. [35]And when the men of that place recognized Jesus, they sent word to all the surrounding country. People brought all their sick to him [36]and begged him to let the sick just touch the edge of his cloak, and all who touched him were healed.

Clean and Unclean

15 Then some Pharisees and teachers of the law came to Jesus from Jerusalem and asked, [2]"Why do your disciples break the tradition of the elders? They don't wash their hands before they eat!"

NEW LIVING TRANSLATION

Jesus spoke to them at once. "It's all right," he said. "I am here! Don't be afraid."

[28]Then Peter called to him, "Lord, if it's really you, tell me to come to you by walking on water."

[29]"All right, come," Jesus said.

So Peter went over the side of the boat and walked on the water toward Jesus. [30]But when he looked around at the high waves, he was terrified and began to sink. "Save me, Lord!" he shouted.

[31]Instantly Jesus reached out his hand and grabbed him. "You don't have much faith," Jesus said. "Why did you doubt me?" [32]And when they climbed back into the boat, the wind stopped.

[33]Then the disciples worshiped him. "You really are the Son of God!" they exclaimed.

[34]After they had crossed the lake, they landed at Gennesaret. [35]The news of their arrival spread quickly throughout the whole surrounding area, and soon people were bringing all their sick to be healed. [36]The sick begged him to let them touch even the fringe of his robe, and all who touched it were healed.

Jesus Teaches about Inner Purity

15 Some Pharisees and teachers of religious law now arrived from Jerusalem to interview Jesus. [2]"Why do your disciples disobey our age-old traditions?" they demanded. "They ignore our tradition of ceremonial hand washing before they eat."

NEW KING JAMES VERSION

[27]But immediately Jesus spoke to them, saying, "Be of good cheer! It is I; do not be afraid."

[28]And Peter answered Him and said, "Lord, if it is You, command me to come to You on the water."

[29]So He said, "Come." And when Peter had come down out of the boat, he walked on the water to go to Jesus. [30]But when he saw that the wind *was* boisterous,[b] he was afraid; and beginning to sink he cried out, saying, "Lord, save me!"

[31]And immediately Jesus stretched out *His* hand and caught him, and said to him, "O you of little faith, why did you doubt?" [32]And when they got into the boat, the wind ceased.

[33]Then those who were in the boat came and[c] worshiped Him, saying, "Truly You are the Son of God."

Many Touch Him and Are Made Well

[34]When they had crossed over, they came to the land of[d] Gennesaret. [35]And when the men of that place recognized Him, they sent out into all that surrounding region, brought to Him all who were sick, [36]and begged Him that they might only touch the hem of His garment. And as many as touched *it* were made perfectly well.

Defilement Comes from Within

15 Then the scribes and Pharisees who were from Jerusalem came to Jesus, saying, [2]"Why do Your disciples transgress the tradition of the elders? For they do not wash their hands when they eat bread."

14:30 [b] NU-Text brackets *that* and *boisterous* as disputed.
14:33 [c] NU-Text omits *came and.* **14:34** [d] NU-Text reads *came to land at.*

THE MESSAGE

But Jesus was quick to comfort them. "Courage, it's me. Don't be afraid."

Peter, suddenly bold, said, "Master, if it's really you, call me to come to you on the water."

He said, "Come ahead."

Jumping out of the boat, Peter walked on the water to Jesus. But when he looked down at the waves churning beneath his feet, he lost his nerve and started to sink. He cried, "Master, save me!"

Jesus didn't hesitate. He reached down and grabbed his hand. Then he said, "Faint-heart, what got into you?"

The two of them climbed into the boat, and the wind died down. The disciples in the boat, having watched the whole thing, worshiped Jesus, saying, "This is it! You are God's Son for sure!"

On return, they beached the boat at Gennesaret. When the people got wind that he was back, they sent out word through the neighborhood and rounded up all the sick, who asked for permission to touch the edge of his coat. And whoever touched him was healed.

What Pollutes Your Life

15 After that, Pharisees and religion scholars came to Jesus all the way from Jerusalem, criticizing, "Why do your disciples play fast and loose with the rules?"

KING JAMES VERSION

3 But he answered and said unto them, Why do ye also transgress the commandment of God by your tradition?
4 For God commanded, saying, Honour thy father and mother: and, He that curseth father or mother, let him die the death.
5 But ye say, Whosoever shall say to *his* father or *his* mother, *It is* a gift, by whatsoever thou mightest be profited by me;
6 And honour not his father or his mother, *he shall be free*. Thus have ye made the commandment of God of none effect by your tradition.
7 *Ye* hypocrites, well did Esaias prophesy of you, saying,
8 This people draweth nigh unto me with their mouth, and honoureth me with *their* lips; but their heart is far from me.
9 But in vain they do worship me, teaching *for* doctrines the commandments of men.
10 ¶ And he called the multitude, and said unto them, Hear, and understand:
11 Not that which goeth into the mouth defileth a man; but that which cometh out of the mouth, this defileth a man.

NEW AMERICAN STANDARD BIBLE

3 And He answered and said to them, "Why do you yourselves transgress the commandment of God for the sake of your tradition?
4 "For God said, 'HONOR YOUR FATHER AND MOTHER,' and, 'HE WHO SPEAKS EVIL OF FATHER OR MOTHER IS TO BE PUT TO DEATH.'
5 "But you say, 'Whoever says to *his* father or mother, "Whatever I have that would help you has been given *to God*,"
6 he is not to honor his father or his mother[1].' And *by this* you invalidated the word of God for the sake of your tradition.
7 "You hypocrites, rightly did Isaiah prophesy of you:
8 'THIS PEOPLE HONORS ME WITH THEIR LIPS,
BUT THEIR HEART IS FAR AWAY FROM ME.
9 'BUT IN VAIN DO THEY WORSHIP ME,
TEACHING AS DOCTRINES THE PRECEPTS OF MEN.' "
10 After Jesus called the crowd to Him, He said to them, "Hear and understand.
11 "*It is* not what enters into the mouth *that* defiles the man, but what proceeds out of the mouth, this defiles the man."

15:6 [1] I.e. by supporting them with it

NEW CENTURY VERSION

3 Jesus answered, "And why do you refuse to obey God's command so that you can follow your own teachings? 4 God said, 'Honor your father and your mother,'[a] and 'Anyone who says cruel things to his father or mother must be put to death.'[b] 5 But you say a person can tell his father or mother, 'I have something I could use to help you, but I have given it to God already.' 6 You teach that person not to honor his father or his mother. You rejected what God said for the sake of your own rules. 7 You are hypocrites! Isaiah was right when he said about you:

8 'These people show honor to me with words,
but their hearts are far from me.
9 Their worship of me is worthless.
The things they teach are nothing but human rules.' "
Isaiah 29:13

10 After Jesus called the crowd to him, he said, "Listen and understand what I am saying. 11 It is not what people put into their mouths that makes them unclean. It is what comes out of their mouths that makes them unclean."

15:4 [a] **'Honor...mother.'** Quotation from Exodus 20:12; Deuteronomy 5:16. 15:4 [b] **'Anyone...death.'** Quotation from Exodus 21:17.

CONTEMPORARY ENGLISH VERSION

3 Jesus answered:
Why do you disobey God and follow your own teaching? 4 Didn't God command you to respect your father and mother? Didn't he tell you to put to death all who curse their parents? 5 But you let people get by without helping their parents when they should. You let them say that what they have has been offered to God.[b] 6 Is this any way to show respect to your parents? You ignore God's commands in order to follow your own teaching. 7 And you are nothing but show-offs! Isaiah the prophet was right when he wrote that God had said,

8 "All of you praise me
with your words,
but you never really
think about me.
9 It is useless for you
to worship me,
when you teach rules
made up by humans."

What Really Makes People Unclean (Mark 7.14-23)

10 Jesus called the crowd together and said, "Pay attention and try to understand what I mean. 11 The food that you put into your mouth doesn't make you unclean and unfit to worship God. The bad words that come out of your mouth are what make you unclean."

[b] 15.5 *has been offered to God*: According to Jewish custom, when people said something was offered to God, it belonged to him and could not be used for anyone else, not even for their own parents.

NEW INTERNATIONAL VERSION

[3]Jesus replied, "And why do you break the command of God for the sake of your tradition? [4]For God said, 'Honor your father and mother'[a] and 'Anyone who curses his father or mother must be put to death.'[b] [5]But you say that if a man says to his father or mother, 'Whatever help you might otherwise have received from me is a gift devoted to God,' [6]he is not to 'honor his father[c]' with it. Thus you nullify the word of God for the sake of your tradition. [7]You hypocrites! Isaiah was right when he prophesied about you:

[8]" 'These people honor me with their lips,
but their hearts are far from me.
[9]They worship me in vain;
their teachings are but rules taught by men.'[d]"

[10]Jesus called the crowd to him and said, "Listen and understand. [11]What goes into a man's mouth does not make him 'unclean,' but what comes out of his mouth, that is what makes him 'unclean.' "

[a] *4* Exodus 20:12; Deut. 5:16 [b] *4* Exodus 21:17; Lev. 20:9
[c] *6* Some manuscripts *father or his mother* [d] *9* Isaiah 29:13

NEW LIVING TRANSLATION

[3]Jesus replied, "And why do you, by your traditions, violate the direct commandments of God? [4]For instance, God says, 'Honor your father and mother,' and 'Anyone who speaks evil of father or mother must be put to death.'* [5]But you say, 'You don't need to honor your parents by caring for their needs if you give the money to God instead.' [6]And so, by your own tradition, you nullify the direct commandment of God. [7]You hypocrites! Isaiah was prophesying about you when he said,

[8] 'These people honor me with their lips,
but their hearts are far away.
[9] Their worship is a farce,
for they replace God's commands with their own
man-made teachings.'* "

[10]Then Jesus called to the crowds and said, "Listen to what I say and try to understand. [11]You are not defiled by what you eat; you are defiled by what you say and do.*"

15:4 Exod 20:12; 21:17; Lev 20:9; Deut 5:16. **15:8-9** Isa 29:13.
15:11 Or *what comes out of the mouth defiles a person.*

NEW KING JAMES VERSION

[3]He answered and said to them, "Why do you also transgress the commandment of God because of your tradition? [4]For God commanded, saying, *'Honor your father and your mother'*;[a] and, *'He who curses father or mother, let him be put to death.'*[b] [5]But you say, 'Whoever says to his father or mother, "Whatever profit you might have received from me *is* a gift *to God*"— [6]then he need not honor his father or mother.'[c] Thus you have made the commandment[d] of God of no effect by your tradition. [7]Hypocrites! Well did Isaiah prophesy about you, saying:

[8] *'These people draw near to Me with their mouth,*
And[e] honor Me with their lips,
But their heart is far from Me.
[9] *And in vain they worship Me,*
Teaching as doctrines the commandments of men.' "[f]

[10]When He had called the multitude to *Himself*, He said to them, "Hear and understand: [11]Not what goes into the mouth defiles a man; but what comes out of the mouth, this defiles a man."

15:4 [a] Exodus 20:12; Deuteronomy 5:16 [b] Exodus 21:17
15:6 [c] NU-Text omits *or mother.* [d] NU-Text reads *word.*
15:8 [e] NU-Text omits *draw near to Me with their mouth, And.*
15:9 [f] Isaiah 29:13

THE MESSAGE

But Jesus put it right back on them. "Why do you use your rules to play fast and loose with God's commands? God clearly says, 'Respect your father and mother,' and, 'Anyone denouncing father or mother should be killed.' But you weasel around that by saying, 'Whoever wants to, can say to father and mother, "What I owed to you I've given to God."' That can hardly be called respecting a parent. You cancel God's command by your rules. Frauds! Isaiah's prophecy of you hit the bull's-eye:

'These people make a big show of saying the right thing,
but their heart isn't in it.
They act like they're worshiping me,
but they don't mean it.
They just use me as a cover
for teaching whatever suits their fancy.'"

He then called the crowd together and said, "Listen, and take this to heart. It's not what you swallow that pollutes your life, but what you vomit up."

KING JAMES VERSION

12 Then came his disciples, and said unto him, Knowest thou that the Pharisees were offended, after they heard this saying?

13 But he answered and said, Every plant, which my heavenly Father hath not planted, shall be rooted up.

14 Let them alone: they be blind leaders of the blind. And if the blind lead the blind, both shall fall into the ditch.

15 Then answered Peter and said unto him, Declare unto us this parable.

16 And Jesus said, Are ye also yet without understanding?

17 Do not ye yet understand, that whatsoever entereth in at the mouth goeth into the belly, and is cast out into the draught?

18 But those things which proceed out of the mouth come forth from the heart; and they defile the man.

19 For out of the heart proceed evil thoughts, murders, adulteries, fornications, thefts, false witness, blasphemies:

20 These are *the things* which defile a man: but to eat with unwashen hands defileth not a man.

21 ¶ Then Jesus went thence, and departed into the coasts of Tyre and Sidon.

22 And, behold, a woman of Canaan came out of the same coasts, and cried unto him, saying, Have mercy on me, O Lord, *thou* Son of David; my daughter is grievously vexed with a devil.

NEW AMERICAN STANDARD BIBLE

12 Then the disciples *came and *said to Him, "Do You know that the Pharisees were offended when they heard this statement?"

13 But He answered and said, "Every plant which My heavenly Father did not plant shall be uprooted.

14 "Let them alone; they are blind guides [2]of the blind. And if a blind man guides a blind man, both will fall into a pit."

The Heart of Man

15 Peter said to Him, "Explain the parable to us."

16 Jesus said, "Are you still lacking in understanding also?

17 "Do you not understand that everything that goes into the mouth passes into the stomach, and is eliminated?

18 "But the things that proceed out of the mouth come from the heart, and those defile the man.

19 "For out of the heart come evil thoughts, murders, adulteries, fornications, thefts, false witness, slanders.

20 "These are the things which defile the man; but to eat with unwashed hands does not defile the man."

The Syrophoenician Woman

21 Jesus went away from there, and withdrew into the district of Tyre and Sidon.

22 And a Canaanite woman from that region came out and *began* to cry out, saying, "Have mercy on me, Lord, Son of David; my daughter is cruelly demon-possessed."

15:14 [2] Later mss add *of the blind*

NEW CENTURY VERSION

12Then his followers came to him and asked, "Do you know that the Pharisees are angry because of what you said?"

13Jesus answered, "Every plant that my Father in heaven has not planted himself will be pulled up by the roots. 14Stay away from the Pharisees; they are blind leaders. And if a blind person leads a blind person, both will fall into a ditch."

15Peter said, "Explain the example to us."

16Jesus said, "Do you still not understand? 17Surely you know that all the food that enters the mouth goes into the stomach and then goes out of the body. 18But what people say with their mouths comes from the way they think; these are the things that make people unclean. 19Out of the mind come evil thoughts, murder, adultery, sexual sins, stealing, lying, and speaking evil of others. 20These things make people unclean; eating with unwashed hands does not make them unclean."

Jesus Helps a Non-Jewish Woman

21Jesus left that place and went to the area of Tyre and Sidon. 22A Canaanite woman from that area came to Jesus and cried out, "Lord, Son of David, have mercy on me! My daughter has a demon, and she is suffering very much."

CONTEMPORARY ENGLISH VERSION

12Then his disciples came over to him and asked, "Do you know that you insulted the Pharisees by what you said?"

13Jesus answered, "Every plant that my Father in heaven did not plant will be pulled up by the roots. 14Stay away from those Pharisees! They are like blind people leading other blind people, and all of them will fall into a ditch."

15Peter replied, "What did you mean when you talked about the things that make people unclean?"

16Jesus then said:

Don't any of you know what I am talking about by now? 17Don't you know that the food you put into your mouth goes into your stomach and then out of your body? 18But the words that come out of your mouth come from your heart. And they are what make you unfit to worship God. 19Out of your heart come evil thoughts, murder, unfaithfulness in marriage, vulgar deeds, stealing, telling lies, and insulting others. 20These are what make you unclean. Eating without washing your hands will not make you unfit to worship God.

A Woman's Faith (Mark 7.24-30)

21Jesus left and went to the territory near the cities of Tyre and Sidon. 22Suddenly a Canaanite woman[c] from there came out shouting, "Lord and Son of David,[d] have pity on me! My daughter is full of demons." 23Jesus did not say a

[c] 15.22 *Canaanite woman*: This woman was not Jewish. [d] 15.22 *Son of David*: See the note at 9.27.

NEW INTERNATIONAL VERSION

12Then the disciples came to him and asked, "Do you know that the Pharisees were offended when they heard this?"

13He replied, "Every plant that my heavenly Father has not planted will be pulled up by the roots. 14Leave them; they are blind guides.[e] If a blind man leads a blind man, both will fall into a pit."

15Peter said, "Explain the parable to us."

16"Are you still so dull?" Jesus asked them. 17"Don't you see that whatever enters the mouth goes into the stomach and then out of the body? 18But the things that come out of the mouth come from the heart, and these make a man 'unclean.' 19For out of the heart come evil thoughts, murder, adultery, sexual immorality, theft, false testimony, slander. 20These are what make a man 'unclean'; but eating with unwashed hands does not make him 'unclean.'"

The Faith of the Canaanite Woman

21Leaving that place, Jesus withdrew to the region of Tyre and Sidon. 22A Canaanite woman from that vicinity came to him, crying out, "Lord, Son of David, have mercy on me! My daughter is suffering terribly from demon-possession."

[e] *14* Some manuscripts *guides of the blind*

NEW LIVING TRANSLATION

12Then the disciples came to him and asked, "Do you realize you offended the Pharisees by what you just said?"

13Jesus replied, "Every plant not planted by my heavenly Father will be rooted up, 14so ignore them. They are blind guides leading the blind, and if one blind person guides another, they will both fall into a ditch."

15Then Peter asked Jesus, "Explain what you meant when you said people aren't defiled by what they eat."

16"Don't you understand?" Jesus asked him. 17"Anything you eat passes through the stomach and then goes out of the body. 18But evil words come from an evil heart and defile the person who says them. 19For from the heart come evil thoughts, murder, adultery, all other sexual immorality, theft, lying, and slander. 20These are what defile you. Eating with unwashed hands could never defile you and make you unacceptable to God!"

The Faith of a Gentile Woman

21Jesus then left Galilee and went north to the region of Tyre and Sidon. 22A Gentile* woman who lived there came to him, pleading, "Have mercy on me, O Lord, Son of David! For my daughter has a demon in her, and it is severely tormenting her."

15:22 Greek *Canaanite.*

NEW KING JAMES VERSION

12Then His disciples came and said to Him, "Do You know that the Pharisees were offended when they heard this saying?"

13But He answered and said, "Every plant which My heavenly Father has not planted will be uprooted. 14Let them alone. They are blind leaders of the blind. And if the blind leads the blind, both will fall into a ditch."

15Then Peter answered and said to Him, "Explain this parable to us."

16So Jesus said, "Are you also still without understanding? 17Do you not yet understand that whatever enters the mouth goes into the stomach and is eliminated? 18But those things which proceed out of the mouth come from the heart, and they defile a man. 19For out of the heart proceed evil thoughts, murders, adulteries, fornications, thefts, false witness, blasphemies. 20These are *the things* which defile a man, but to eat with unwashed hands does not defile a man."

A Gentile Shows Her Faith

21Then Jesus went out from there and departed to the region of Tyre and Sidon. 22And behold, a woman of Canaan came from that region and cried out to Him, saying, "Have mercy on me, O Lord, Son of David! My daughter is severely demon-possessed."

THE MESSAGE

Later his disciples came and told him, "Did you know how upset the Pharisees were when they heard what you said?"

Jesus shrugged it off. "Every tree that wasn't planted by my Father in heaven will be pulled up by its roots. Forget them. They are blind men leading blind men. When a blind man leads a blind man, they both end up in the ditch."

Peter said, "I don't get it. Put it in plain language."

Jesus replied, "You too? Are you being willfully stupid? Don't you know that anything that is swallowed works its way through the intestines and is finally defecated. But what comes out of the mouth gets its start in the heart. It's from the heart that we vomit up evil arguments, murders, adulteries, fornications, thefts, lies, and cussing. That's what pollutes. Eating or not eating certain foods, washing or not washing your hands—that's neither here nor there."

Healing the People

From there Jesus took a trip to Tyre and Sidon. They had hardly arrived when a Canaanite woman came down from the hills and pleaded, "Mercy, Master, Son of David! My daughter is cruelly afflicted by an evil spirit."

KING JAMES VERSION

23 But he answered her not a word. And his disciples came and besought him, saying, Send her away; for she crieth after us.

24 But he answered and said, I am not sent but unto the lost sheep of the house of Israel.

25 Then came she and worshipped him, saying, Lord, help me.

26 But he answered and said, It is not meet to take the children's bread, and to cast *it* to dogs.

27 And she said, Truth, Lord: yet the dogs eat of the crumbs which fall from their masters' table.

28 Then Jesus answered and said unto her, O woman, great *is* thy faith: be it unto thee even as thou wilt. And her daughter was made whole from that very hour.

29 ¶ And Jesus departed from thence, and came nigh unto the sea of Galilee; and went up into a mountain, and sat down there.

30 And great multitudes came unto him, having with them *those that were* lame, blind, dumb, maimed, and many others, and cast them down at Jesus' feet; and he healed them:

31 Insomuch that the multitude wondered, when they saw the dumb to speak, the maimed to be whole, the lame to walk, and the blind to see: and they glorified the God of Israel.

32 Then Jesus called his disciples *unto him*, and said, I have compassion on the multitude, because they continue

NEW AMERICAN STANDARD BIBLE

23 But He did not answer her a word. And His disciples came and implored Him, saying, "Send her away, because she keeps shouting at us."

24 But He answered and said, "I was sent only to the lost sheep of the house of Israel."

25 But she came and *began* to bow down before Him, saying, "Lord, help me!"

26 And He answered and said, "It is not good to take the children's bread and throw it to the dogs."

27 But she said, "Yes, Lord; but even the dogs feed on the crumbs which fall from their masters' table."

28 Then Jesus said to her, "O woman, your faith is great; it shall be done for you as you wish." And her daughter was healed at once.

Healing Crowds

29 Departing from there, Jesus went along by the Sea of Galilee, and having gone up on the mountain, He was sitting there.

30 And large crowds came to Him, bringing with them *those who were* lame, crippled, blind, mute, and many others, and they laid them down at His feet; and He healed them.

31 So the crowd marveled as they saw the mute speaking, the crippled restored, and the lame walking, and the blind seeing; and they glorified the God of Israel.

Four Thousand Fed

32 And Jesus called His disciples to Him, and said, "I feel compassion for the people, because they have

NEW CENTURY VERSION

23But Jesus did not answer the woman. So his followers came to Jesus and begged him, "Tell the woman to go away. She is following us and shouting."

24Jesus answered, "God sent me only to the lost sheep, the people of Israel."

25Then the woman came to Jesus again and bowed before him and said, "Lord, help me!"

26Jesus answered, "It is not right to take the children's bread and give it to the dogs."

27The woman said, "Yes, Lord, but even the dogs eat the crumbs that fall from their masters' table."

28Then Jesus answered, "Woman, you have great faith! I will do what you asked." And at that moment the woman's daughter was healed.

Jesus Heals Many People

29After leaving there, Jesus went along the shore of Lake Galilee. He went up on a hill and sat there.

30Great crowds came to Jesus, bringing with them the
lame, the blind, the crippled, those who could not speak,
and many others. They put them at Jesus' feet, and he
healed them. 31The crowd was amazed when they saw that
people who could not speak before were now able to speak.
The crippled were made strong. The lame could walk, and
the blind could see. And they praised the God of Israel for
this.

More than Four Thousand Fed

32Jesus called his followers to him and said, "I feel sorry for these people, because they have already been with me

CONTEMPORARY ENGLISH VERSION

word. But the woman kept following along and shouting, so his disciples came up and asked him to send her away.

24Jesus said, "I was sent only to the people of Israel! They are like a flock of lost sheep."

25The woman came closer. Then she knelt down and begged, "Please help me, Lord!"

26Jesus replied, "It isn't right to take food away from children and feed it to dogs."[e]

27"Lord, that's true," the woman said, "but even dogs get the crumbs that fall from their owner's table."

28Jesus answered, "Dear woman, you really do have a lot of faith, and you will be given what you want." At that moment her daughter was healed.

Jesus Heals Many People

29From there, Jesus went along Lake Galilee. Then he
climbed a hill and sat down. 30Large crowds came and
brought many people who were crippled or blind or lame or
unable to talk. They placed them, and many others, in
front of Jesus, and he healed them all. 31Everyone was
amazed at what they saw and heard. People who had
never spoken could now speak. The lame were healed, the
crippled could walk, and the blind were able to see.
Everyone was praising the God of Israel.

Jesus Feeds Four Thousand (Mark 8.1-10)

32Jesus called his disciples together and told them, "I feel sorry for these people. They have been with me for

[e] 15.26 *feed it to dogs*: The Jewish people sometimes referred to Gentiles as dogs.

NEW INTERNATIONAL VERSION

23Jesus did not answer a word. So his disciples came to him and urged him, "Send her away, for she keeps crying out after us."

24He answered, "I was sent only to the lost sheep of Israel."

25The woman came and knelt before him. "Lord, help me!" she said.

26He replied, "It is not right to take the children's bread and toss it to their dogs."

27"Yes, Lord," she said, "but even the dogs eat the crumbs that fall from their masters' table."

28Then Jesus answered, "Woman, you have great faith! Your request is granted." And her daughter was healed from that very hour.

Jesus Feeds the Four Thousand

29Jesus left there and went along the Sea of Galilee.
Then he went up on a mountainside and sat down. 30Great
crowds came to him, bringing the lame, the blind, the crippled, the mute and many others, and laid them at his feet;
and he healed them. 31The people were amazed when they
saw the mute speaking, the crippled made well, the lame walking and the blind seeing. And they praised the God of Israel.

32Jesus called his disciples to him and said, "I have compassion for these people; they have already been with me

NEW LIVING TRANSLATION

23But Jesus gave her no reply—not even a word. Then his disciples urged him to send her away. "Tell her to leave," they said. "She is bothering us with all her begging."

24Then he said to the woman, "I was sent only to help the people of Israel—God's lost sheep—not the Gentiles."

25But she came and worshiped him and pleaded again, "Lord, help me!"

26"It isn't right to take food from the children and throw it to the dogs," he said.

27"Yes, Lord," she replied, "but even dogs are permitted to eat crumbs that fall beneath their master's table."

28"Woman," Jesus said to her, "your faith is great. Your request is granted." And her daughter was instantly healed.

Jesus Heals Many People

29Jesus returned to the Sea of Galilee and climbed a hill
and sat down. 30A vast crowd brought him the lame, blind, crippled, mute, and many others with physical difficulties, and they laid them before Jesus. And he healed them all.
31The crowd was amazed! Those who hadn't been able to speak were talking, the crippled were made well, the lame were walking around, and those who had been blind could see again! And they praised the God of Israel.

Jesus Feeds Four Thousand

32Then Jesus called his disciples to him and said, "I feel sorry for these people. They have been here with me for

NEW KING JAMES VERSION

23But He answered her not a word.

And His disciples came and urged Him, saying, "Send her away, for she cries out after us."

24But He answered and said, "I was not sent except to the lost sheep of the house of Israel."

25Then she came and worshiped Him, saying, "Lord, help me!"

26But He answered and said, "It is not good to take the children's bread and throw *it* to the little dogs."

27And she said, "Yes, Lord, yet even the little dogs eat the crumbs which fall from their masters' table."

28Then Jesus answered and said to her, "O woman, great *is* your faith! Let it be to you as you desire." And her daughter was healed from that very hour.

Jesus Heals Great Multitudes

29Jesus departed from there, skirted the Sea of Galilee,
and went up on the mountain and sat down there. 30Then
great multitudes came to Him, having with them *the* lame, blind, mute, maimed, and many others; and they laid them
down at Jesus' feet, and He healed them. 31So the multitude marveled when they saw *the* mute speaking, *the* maimed made whole, *the* lame walking, and *the* blind seeing; and they glorified the God of Israel.

Feeding the Four Thousand

32Now Jesus called His disciples to *Himself* and said, "I have compassion on the multitude, because they have now

THE MESSAGE

Jesus ignored her. The disciples came and complained, "Now she's bothering us. Would you please take care of her? She's driving us crazy."

Jesus refused, telling them, "I've got my hands full dealing with the lost sheep of Israel."

Then the woman came back to Jesus, went to her knees and begged. "Master, help me."

He said, "It's not right to take bread out of children's mouths and throw it to dogs."

She was quick: "You're right, Master, but beggar dogs do get scraps from the master's table."

Jesus gave in. "Oh, woman, your faith is something else. What you want is what you get!" Right then her daughter became well.

After Jesus returned, he walked along Lake Galilee and then climbed a mountain and took his place, ready to receive visitors. They came, tons of them, bringing along the paraplegic, the blind, the maimed, the mute—all sorts of people in need—and more or less threw them down at Jesus' feet to see what he would do with them. He healed them. When the people saw the mutes speaking, the maimed healthy, the paraplegics walking around, the blind looking around, they were astonished and let everyone know that God was blazingly alive among them.

✠

But Jesus wasn't finished with them. He called his disciples and said, "I hurt for these people. For three days now

KING JAMES VERSION

with me now three days, and have nothing to eat: and I
will not send them away fasting, lest they faint in the way.
33 And his disciples say unto him, Whence should we
have so much bread in the wilderness, as to fill so great a
multitude?
34 And Jesus saith unto them, How many loaves have
ye? And they said, Seven, and a few little fishes.
35 And he commanded the multitude to sit down on the
ground.
36 And he took the seven loaves and the fishes, and
gave thanks, and brake *them*, and gave to his disciples,
and the disciples to the multitude.
37 And they did all eat, and were filled: and they took
up of the broken *meat* that was left seven baskets full.
38 And they that did eat were four thousand men,
beside women and children.
39 And he sent away the multitude, and took ship, and
came into the coasts of Magdala.
16 The Pharisees also with the Sadducees came, and
tempting desired him that he would shew them a
sign from heaven.
2 He answered and said unto them, When it is evening,
ye say, *It will be* fair weather: for the sky is red.
3 And in the morning, *It will be* foul weather to day: for
the sky is red and lowring. O *ye* hypocrites, ye can discern

NEW AMERICAN STANDARD BIBLE

remained with Me now three days and have nothing to eat;
and I do not want to send them away hungry, for they
might faint on the way."
33 The disciples *said to Him, "Where would we get so
many loaves in *this* desolate place to satisfy such a large
crowd?"
34 And Jesus *said to them, "How many loaves do you
have?" And they said, "Seven, and a few small fish."
35 And He directed the people to sit down on the
ground;
36 and He took the seven loaves and the fish; and giv-
ing thanks, He broke them and started giving them to the
disciples, and the disciples *gave them* to the people.
37 And they all ate and were satisfied, and they picked
up what was left over of the broken pieces, seven large
baskets full.
38 And those who ate were four thousand men, besides
women and children.
39 And sending away the crowds, Jesus got into the boat
and came to the region of Magadan.

Pharisees Test Jesus

16 The Pharisees and Sadducees came up, and testing
Jesus, they asked Him to show them a sign from
heaven.
2 But He replied to them, "When it is evening, you say,
'*It will be* fair weather, for the sky is red.'
3 "And in the morning, '*There will be* a storm today, for
the sky is red and threatening.' Do you know how to discern

NEW CENTURY VERSION

three days, and they have nothing to eat. I don't want to
send them away hungry. They might faint while going
home."
33 His followers asked him, "How can we get enough
bread to feed all these people? We are far away from any
town."
34 Jesus asked, "How many loaves of bread do you
have?"
They answered, "Seven, and a few small fish."
35 Jesus told the people to sit on the ground. 36 He took
the seven loaves of bread and the fish and gave thanks to
God. Then he divided the food and gave it to his followers,
and they gave it to the people. 37 All the people ate and
were satisfied. Then his followers filled seven baskets with
the leftover pieces of food. 38 There were about four thou-
sand men there who ate, besides women and children.
39 After sending the people home, Jesus got into the boat
and went to the area of Magadan.

The Leaders Ask for a Miracle

16 The Pharisees and Sadducees came to Jesus, want-
ing to trick him. So they asked him to show them a
miracle from God.
2 Jesus answered, "At sunset you say we will have good
weather, because the sky is red. 3 And in the morning you
say that it will be a rainy day, because the sky is dark and
red. You see these signs in the sky and know what they

CONTEMPORARY ENGLISH VERSION

three days, and they don't have anything to eat. I don't
want to send them away hungry. They might faint on their
way home."
33 His disciples said, "This place is like a desert. Where
can we find enough food to feed such a crowd?"
34 Jesus asked them how much food they had. They
replied, "Seven small loaves of bread[f] and a few little fish."
35 After Jesus had told the people to sit down, 36 he took
the seven loaves of bread and the fish and gave thanks. He
then broke them and handed them to his disciples, who
passed them around to the crowds.
37 Everyone ate all they wanted, and the leftovers filled
seven large baskets.
38 There were four thousand men who ate, not counting
the women and children.
39 After Jesus had sent the crowds away, he got into a
boat and sailed across the lake. He came to shore near the
town of Magadan.[g]

A Demand for a Sign from Heaven
(Mark 8.11-13; Luke 12.54-56)

16 The Pharisees and Sadducees came to Jesus and
tried to test him by asking for a sign from heaven.
2 He told them:
If the sky is red in the evening, you say the weather
will be good. 3 But if the sky is red and gloomy in the
morning, you say it is going to rain. You can tell what
the weather will be like by looking at the sky. But you

[f] 15.34 *small loaves of bread*: See the note at 14.17.
[g] 15.39 *Magadan*: The location is unknown.

NEW INTERNATIONAL VERSION

three days and have nothing to eat. I do not want to send
them away hungry, or they may collapse on the way."
33His disciples answered, "Where could we get enough
bread in this remote place to feed such a crowd?"
34"How many loaves do you have?" Jesus asked.
"Seven," they replied, "and a few small fish."
35He told the crowd to sit down on the ground. 36Then
he took the seven loaves and the fish, and when he had
given thanks, he broke them and gave them to the disci-
ples, and they in turn to the people. 37They all ate and
were satisfied. Afterward the disciples picked up seven
basketfuls of broken pieces that were left over. 38The num-
ber of those who ate was four thousand, besides women
and children. 39After Jesus had sent the crowd away, he
got into the boat and went to the vicinity of Magadan.

The Demand for a Sign

16 The Pharisees and Sadducees came to Jesus and
tested him by asking him to show them a sign
from heaven.
2He replied,[a] "When evening comes, you say, 'It will be
fair weather, for the sky is red,' 3and in the morning,
'Today it will be stormy, for the sky is red and overcast.'
You know how to interpret the appearance of the sky, but

[a] *2* Some early manuscripts do not have the rest of verse 2 and all of verse 3.

NEW LIVING TRANSLATION

three days, and they have nothing left to eat. I don't want
to send them away hungry, or they will faint along the
road."
33The disciples replied, "And where would we get
enough food out here in the wilderness for all of them to
eat?"
34Jesus asked, "How many loaves of bread do you
have?"
They replied, "Seven, and a few small fish." 35So Jesus
told all the people to sit down on the ground. 36Then he
took the seven loaves and the fish, thanked God for them,
broke them into pieces, and gave them to the disciples,
who distributed the food to the crowd.
37They all ate until they were full, and when the scraps
were picked up, there were seven large baskets of food left
over! 38There were four thousand men who were fed that
day, in addition to all the women and children. 39Then
Jesus sent the people home, and he got into a boat and
crossed over to the region of Magadan.

Leaders Demand a Miraculous Sign

16 One day the Pharisees and Sadducees came to test
Jesus' claims by asking him to show them a mirac-
ulous sign from heaven.
2He replied, "You know the saying, 'Red sky at night
means fair weather tomorrow, 3red sky in the morning
means foul weather all day.' You are good at reading the

NEW KING JAMES VERSION

continued with Me three days and have nothing to eat.
And I do not want to send them away hungry, lest they
faint on the way."
33Then His disciples said to Him, "Where could we get
enough bread in the wilderness to fill such a great multi-
tude?"
34Jesus said to them, "How many loaves do you have?"
And they said, "Seven, and a few little fish."
35So He commanded the multitude to sit down on the
ground. 36And He took the seven loaves and the fish and
gave thanks, broke *them* and gave *them* to His disciples;
and the disciples *gave* to the multitude. 37So they all ate
and were filled, and they took up seven large baskets full
of the fragments that were left. 38Now those who ate were
four thousand men, besides women and children. 39And He
sent away the multitude, got into the boat, and came to
the region of Magdala.[g]

The Pharisees and Sadducees Seek a Sign

16 Then the Pharisees and Sadducees came, and test-
ing Him asked that He would show them a sign
from heaven. 2He answered and said to them, "When it is
evening you say, '*It will be* fair weather, for the sky is red';
3and in the morning, '*It will be* foul weather today, for the
sky is red and threatening.' Hypocrites![a] You know how to
discern the face of the sky, but you cannot *discern* the

15:39 [g] NU-Text reads *Magadan.* 16:3 [a] NU-Text omits *Hypocrites.*

THE MESSAGE

they've been with me, and now they have nothing to eat. I
can't send them away without a meal—they'd probably
collapse on the road."
His disciples said, "But where in this deserted place are
you going to dig up enough food for a meal?"
Jesus asked, "How much bread do you have?"
"Seven loaves," they said, "plus a few fish." At that,
Jesus directed the people to sit down. He took the seven
loaves and the fish. After giving thanks, he divided it up
and gave it to the people. Everyone ate. They had all they
wanted. It took seven large baskets to collect the leftovers.
Over four thousand people ate their fill at that meal. After
Jesus sent them away, he climbed in the boat and crossed
over to the Magadan hills.

Some Bad Yeast

16 Some Pharisees and Sadducees were on him again,
pressing him to prove himself to them. He told
them, "You have a saying that goes, 'Red sky at night,
sailor's delight; red sky at morning, sailors take warning.'
You find it easy enough to forecast the weather—why

KING JAMES VERSION

the face of the sky; but can ye not *discern* the signs of the times?

4 A wicked and adulterous generation seeketh after a sign; and there shall no sign be given unto it, but the sign of the prophet Jonas. And he left them, and departed.

5 ¶ And when his disciples were come to the other side, they had forgotten to take bread.

6 Then Jesus said unto them, Take heed and beware of the leaven of the Pharisees and of the Sadducees.

7 And they reasoned among themselves, saying, *It is* because we have taken no bread.

8 *Which* when Jesus perceived, he said unto them, O ye of little faith, why reason ye among yourselves, because ye have brought no bread?

9 Do ye not yet understand, neither remember the five loaves of the five thousand, and how many baskets ye took up?

10 Neither the seven loaves of the four thousand, and how many baskets ye took up?

11 How is it that ye do not understand that I spake *it* not to you concerning bread, that ye should beware of the leaven of the Pharisees and of the Sadducees?

12 Then understood they how that he bade *them* not beware of the leaven of bread, but of the doctrine of the Pharisees and of the Sadducees.

NEW AMERICAN STANDARD BIBLE

the appearance of the sky, but cannot *discern* the signs of the times?

4 "An evil and adulterous generation seeks after a sign; and a sign will not be given it, except the sign of Jonah." And He left them and went away.

5 And the disciples came to the other side *of the sea*, but they had forgotten to bring *any* bread.

6 And Jesus said to them, "Watch out and beware of the leaven of the Pharisees and Sadducees."

7 They began to discuss *this* among themselves, saying, "*He said that* because we did not bring *any* bread."

8 But Jesus, aware of this, said, "You men of little faith, why do you discuss among yourselves that you have no bread?

9 "Do you not yet understand or remember the five loaves of the five thousand, and how many baskets *full* you picked up?

10 "Or the seven loaves of the four thousand, and how many large baskets *full* you picked up?

11 "How is it that you do not understand that I did not speak to you concerning bread? But beware of the leaven of the Pharisees and Sadducees."

12 Then they understood that He did not say to beware of the leaven of bread, but of the teaching of the Pharisees and Sadducees.

NEW CENTURY VERSION

mean. In the same way, you see the things that I am doing
now, but you don't know their meaning. 4Evil and sinful
people ask for a miracle as a sign, but they will not be
given any sign, except the sign of Jonah."[a] Then Jesus left
them and went away.

Guard Against Wrong Teachings

5Jesus' followers went across the lake, but they had for-
gotten to bring bread. 6Jesus said to them, "Be careful!
Beware of the yeast of the Pharisees and the Sadducees."
7His followers discussed the meaning of this, saying,
"He said this because we forgot to bring bread."
8Knowing what they were talking about, Jesus asked
them, "Why are you talking about not having bread? Your
faith is small. 9Do you still not understand? Remember the
five loaves of bread that fed the five thousand? And
remember that you filled many baskets with the leftovers?
10Or the seven loaves of bread that fed the four thousand
and the many baskets you filled then also? 11I was not
talking to you about bread. Why don't you understand
that? I am telling you to beware of the yeast of the
Pharisees and the Sadducees." 12Then the followers under-
stood that Jesus was not telling them to beware of the
yeast used in bread but to beware of the teaching of the
Pharisees and the Sadducees.

16:4 [a] **sign of Jonah** Jonah's three days in the fish are like Jesus' three days in the tomb. The story about Jonah is in the book of Jonah.

CONTEMPORARY ENGLISH VERSION

don't understand what is happening now.[a] 4You want a
sign because you are evil and won't believe! But the
only sign you will be given is what happened to Jonah.[b]
Then Jesus left.

The Yeast of the Pharisees and Sadducees (Mark 8.14-21)

5The disciples had forgotten to bring any bread when they
crossed the lake.[c] 6Jesus then warned them, "Watch out!
Guard against the yeast of the Pharisees and Sadducees."
7The disciples talked this over and said to each other,
"He must be saying this because we didn't bring along any
bread."
8Jesus knew what they were thinking and said:

You surely don't have much faith! Why are you talk-
ing about not having any bread? 9Don't you under-
stand? Have you forgotten about the five thousand peo-
ple and all those baskets of leftovers from just five
loaves of bread? 10And what about the four thousand
people and all those baskets of leftovers from only seven
loaves of bread? 11Don't you know by now that I am not
talking to you about bread? Watch out for the yeast of
the Pharisees and Sadducees!

12Finally, the disciples understood that Jesus wasn't
talking about the yeast used to make bread, but about the
teaching of the Pharisees and Sadducees.

[a] **16.2,3** *If the sky is red . . . what is happening now*: The words of Jesus in verses 2 and 3 are not in some manuscripts. [b] **16.4** *what happened to Jonah*: Jonah was in the stomach of a big fish for three days and nights (see 12.40). [c] **16.5** *crossed the lake*: To the east side.

NEW INTERNATIONAL VERSION

you cannot interpret the signs of the times. 4A wicked and adulterous generation looks for a miraculous sign, but none will be given it except the sign of Jonah." Jesus then left them and went away.

The Yeast of the Pharisees and Sadducees

5When they went across the lake, the disciples forgot to take bread. 6"Be careful," Jesus said to them. "Be on your guard against the yeast of the Pharisees and Sadducees."

7They discussed this among themselves and said, "It is because we didn't bring any bread."

8Aware of their discussion, Jesus asked, "You of little faith, why are you talking among yourselves about having no bread? 9Do you still not understand? Don't you remember the five loaves for the five thousand, and how many basketfuls you gathered? 10Or the seven loaves for the four thousand, and how many basketfuls you gathered? 11How is it you don't understand that I was not talking to you about bread? But be on your guard against the yeast of the Pharisees and Sadducees." 12Then they understood that he was not telling them to guard against the yeast used in bread, but against the teaching of the Pharisees and Sadducees.

NEW LIVING TRANSLATION

weather signs in the sky, but you can't read the obvious signs of the times!* 4Only an evil, faithless generation would ask for a miraculous sign, but the only sign I will give them is the sign of the prophet Jonah." Then Jesus left them and went away.

Yeast of the Pharisees and Sadducees

5Later, after they crossed to the other side of the lake, the disciples discovered they had forgotten to bring any food. 6"Watch out!" Jesus warned them. "Beware of the yeast of the Pharisees and Sadducees."

7They decided he was saying this because they hadn't brought any bread. 8Jesus knew what they were thinking, so he said, "You have so little faith! Why are you worried about having no food? 9Won't you ever understand? Don't you remember the five thousand I fed with five loaves, and the baskets of food that were left over? 10Don't you remember the four thousand I fed with seven loaves, with baskets of food left over? 11How could you even think I was talking about food? So again I say, 'Beware of the yeast of the Pharisees and Sadducees.' "

12Then at last they understood that he wasn't speaking about yeast or bread but about the false teaching of the Pharisees and Sadducees.

16:2-3 Several manuscripts do not include any of the words in 16:2-3 after *He replied.*

NEW KING JAMES VERSION

signs of the times. 4A wicked and adulterous generation seeks after a sign, and no sign shall be given to it except the sign of the prophet[b] Jonah." And He left them and departed.

The Leaven of the Pharisees and Sadducees

5Now when His disciples had come to the other side, they had forgotten to take bread. 6Then Jesus said to them, "Take heed and beware of the leaven of the Pharisees and the Sadducees."

7And they reasoned among themselves, saying, "*It is* because we have taken no bread."

8But Jesus, being aware of *it,* said to them, "O you of little faith, why do you reason among yourselves because you have brought no bread?[c] 9Do you not yet understand, or remember the five loaves of the five thousand and how many baskets you took up? 10Nor the seven loaves of the four thousand and how many large baskets you took up? 11How is it you do not understand that I did not speak to you concerning bread?—*but* to beware of the leaven of the Pharisees and Sadducees." 12Then they understood that He did not tell *them* to beware of the leaven of bread, but of the doctrine of the Pharisees and Sadducees.

16:4 [b] NU-Text omits *the prophet.* **16:8** [c] NU-Text reads *you have no bread.*

THE MESSAGE

can't you read the signs of the times? An evil and wanton generation is always wanting signs and wonders. The only sign you'll get is the Jonah sign." Then he turned on his heel and walked away.

On their way to the other side of the lake, the disciples discovered they had forgotten to bring along bread. In the meantime, Jesus said to them, "Keep a sharp eye out for Pharisee-Sadducee yeast."

Thinking he was scolding them for forgetting bread, they discussed in whispers what to do. Jesus knew what they were doing and said, "Why all these worried whispers about forgetting the bread? Runt believers! Haven't you caught on yet? Don't you remember the five loaves of bread and the five thousand people, and how many baskets of fragments you picked up? Or the seven loaves that fed four thousand, and how many baskets of leftovers you collected? Haven't you realized yet that bread isn't the problem? The problem is yeast, Pharisee-Sadducee yeast." Then they got it: that he wasn't concerned about eating, but teaching—the Pharisee-Sadducee kind of teaching.

KING JAMES VERSION

13 ¶ When Jesus came into the coasts of Caesarea Philippi, he asked his disciples, saying, Whom do men say that I the Son of man am?

14 And they said, Some *say that thou art* John the Baptist: some, Elias; and others, Jeremias, or one of the prophets.

15 He saith unto them, But whom say ye that I am?

16 And Simon Peter answered and said, Thou art the Christ, the Son of the living God.

17 And Jesus answered and said unto him, Blessed art thou, Simon Barjona: for flesh and blood hath not revealed *it* unto thee, but my Father which is in heaven.

18 And I say also unto thee, That thou art Peter, and upon this rock I will build my church; and the gates of hell shall not prevail against it.

19 And I will give unto thee the keys of the kingdom of heaven: and whatsoever thou shalt bind on earth shall be bound in heaven: and whatsoever thou shalt loose on earth shall be loosed in heaven.

20 Then charged he his disciples that they should tell no man that he was Jesus the Christ.

21 ¶ From that time forth began Jesus to shew unto his disciples, how that he must go unto Jerusalem, and suffer

NEW AMERICAN STANDARD BIBLE

Peter's Confession of Christ

13 Now when Jesus came into the district of Caesarea Philippi, He was asking His disciples, "Who do people say that the Son of Man is?"

14 And they said, "Some *say* John the Baptist; and others, Elijah; but still others, Jeremiah, or one of the prophets."

15 He *said to them, "But who do you say that I am?"

16 Simon Peter answered, "You are the Christ, the Son of the living God."

17 And Jesus said to him, "Blessed are you, Simon Barjona, because flesh and blood did not reveal *this* to you, but My Father who is in heaven.

18 "I also say to you that you are Peter, and upon this rock I will build My church; and the gates of Hades will not overpower it.

19 "I will give you the keys of the kingdom of heaven; and whatever you bind on earth shall have been bound in heaven, and whatever you loose on earth shall have been loosed in heaven."

20 Then He warned the disciples that they should tell no one that He was the Christ.

Jesus Foretells His Death

21 From that time Jesus began to show His disciples that He must go to Jerusalem, and suffer many things from

NEW CENTURY VERSION

Peter Says Jesus Is the Christ

13 When Jesus came to the area of Caesarea Philippi, he
asked his followers, "Who do people say the Son of Man is?"
14 They answered, "Some say you are John the Baptist.
Others say you are Elijah, and still others say you are
Jeremiah or one of the prophets."
15 Then Jesus asked them, "And who do you say I am?"
16 Simon Peter answered, "You are the Christ, the Son of
the living God."
17 Jesus answered, "You are blessed, Simon son of Jonah,
because no person taught you that. My Father in heaven
showed you who I am. 18 So I tell you, you are Peter.[b] On
this rock I will build my church, and the power of death
will not be able to defeat it. 19 I will give you the keys of
the kingdom of heaven; the things you don't allow on
earth will be the things that God does not allow, and the
things you allow on earth will be the things that God
allows." 20 Then Jesus warned his followers not to tell any-
one he was the Christ.

Jesus Says that He Must Die

21 From that time on Jesus began telling his followers
that he must go to Jerusalem, where the older Jewish lead-
ers, the leading priests, and the teachers of the law would

16:18 [b] **Peter** The Greek name "Peter," like the Aramaic name "Cephas," means "rock."

CONTEMPORARY ENGLISH VERSION

Who Is Jesus? (Mark 8.27-30; Luke 9.18-21)

13 When Jesus and his disciples were near the town of
Caesarea Philippi, he asked them, "What do people say
about the Son of Man?"
14 The disciples answered, "Some people say you are
John the Baptist or maybe Elijah[d] or Jeremiah or some
other prophet."
15 Then Jesus asked them, "But who do you say I am?"
16 Simon Peter spoke up, "You are the Messiah, the Son
of the living God."
17 Jesus told him:

Simon, son of Jonah, you are blessed! You didn't dis-
cover this on your own. It was shown to you by my
Father in heaven. 18 So I will call you Peter, which means
"a rock." On this rock I will build my church, and death
itself will not have any power over it. 19 I will give you
the keys to the kingdom of heaven, and God in heaven
will allow whatever you allow on earth. But he will not
allow anything that you don't allow.

20 Jesus told his disciples not to tell anyone that he was
the Messiah.

Jesus Speaks about His Suffering and Death
(Mark 8.31—9.1; Luke 9.22-27)

21 From then on, Jesus began telling his disciples what
would happen to him. He said, "I must go to Jerusalem.
There the nation's leaders, the chief priests, and the

[d] **16.14** *Elijah*: Many of the Jewish people expected the prophet Elijah to come and prepare the way for the Messiah.

NEW INTERNATIONAL VERSION

Peter's Confession of Christ

13 When Jesus came to the region of Caesarea Philippi, he asked his disciples, "Who do people say the Son of Man is?"

14 They replied, "Some say John the Baptist; others say Elijah; and still others, Jeremiah or one of the prophets."

15 "But what about you?" he asked. "Who do you say I am?"

16 Simon Peter answered, "You are the Christ,[b] the Son of the living God."

17 Jesus replied, "Blessed are you, Simon son of Jonah, for this was not revealed to you by man, but by my Father in heaven. 18 And I tell you that you are Peter,[c] and on this rock I will build my church, and the gates of Hades[d] will not overcome it.[e] 19 I will give you the keys of the kingdom of heaven; whatever you bind on earth will be[f] bound in heaven, and whatever you loose on earth will be[f] loosed in heaven." 20 Then he warned his disciples not to tell anyone that he was the Christ.

Jesus Predicts His Death

21 From that time on Jesus began to explain to his disciples that he must go to Jerusalem and suffer many things at the hands of the elders, chief priests and teachers of the

[b] *16* Or *Messiah*; also in verse 20 [c] *18* *Peter* means *rock.*
[d] *18* Or *hell* [e] *18* Or *not prove stronger than it* [f] *19* Or *have been*

NEW LIVING TRANSLATION

Peter's Declaration about Jesus

13 When Jesus came to the region of Caesarea Philippi, he asked his disciples, "Who do people say that the Son of Man is?"

14 "Well," they replied, "some say John the Baptist, some say Elijah, and others say Jeremiah or one of the other prophets."

15 Then he asked them, "Who do you say I am?"

16 Simon Peter answered, "You are the Messiah, the Son of the living God."

17 Jesus replied, "You are blessed, Simon son of John,* because my Father in heaven has revealed this to you. You did not learn this from any human being. 18 Now I say to you that you are Peter,* and upon this rock I will build my church, and all the powers of hell* will not conquer it. 19 And I will give you the keys of the Kingdom of Heaven. Whatever you lock on earth will be locked in heaven, and whatever you open on earth will be opened in heaven." 20 Then he sternly warned them not to tell anyone that he was the Messiah.

Jesus Predicts His Death

21 From then on Jesus began to tell his disciples plainly that he had to go to Jerusalem, and he told them what would happen to him there. He would suffer at the hands of the leaders and the leading priests and the teachers of

16:17 Greek *Simon son of Jonah;* see John 1:42; 21:15-17.
16:18a *Peter* means "stone" or "rock." **16:18b** Greek *and the gates of Hades.*

NEW KING JAMES VERSION

Peter Confesses Jesus as the Christ

13 When Jesus came into the region of Caesarea Philippi, He asked His disciples, saying, "Who do men say that I, the Son of Man, am?"

14 So they said, "Some *say* John the Baptist, some Elijah, and others Jeremiah or one of the prophets."

15 He said to them, "But who do you say that I am?"

16 Simon Peter answered and said, "You are the Christ, the Son of the living God."

17 Jesus answered and said to him, "Blessed are you, Simon Bar-Jonah, for flesh and blood has not revealed *this* to you, but My Father who is in heaven. 18 And I also say to you that you are Peter, and on this rock I will build My church, and the gates of Hades shall not prevail against it. 19 And I will give you the keys of the kingdom of heaven, and whatever you bind on earth will be bound in heaven, and whatever you loose on earth will be loosed[d] in heaven."

20 Then He commanded His disciples that they should tell no one that He was Jesus the Christ.

Jesus Predicts His Death and Resurrection

21 From that time Jesus began to show to His disciples that He must go to Jerusalem, and suffer many things from

16:19 [d] Or *will have been bound . . . will have been loosed*

THE MESSAGE

Son of Man, Son of God

When Jesus arrived in the villages of Caesarea Philippi, he asked his disciples, "What are people saying about who the Son of Man is?"

They replied, "Some think he is John the Baptizer, some say Elijah, some Jeremiah or one of the other prophets."

He pressed them, "And how about you? Who do you say I am?"

Simon Peter said, "You're the Christ, the Messiah, the Son of the living God."

Jesus came back, "God bless you, Simon, son of Jonah! You didn't get that answer out of books or from teachers. My Father in heaven, God himself, let you in on this secret of who I really am. And now I'm going to tell you who you are, *really* are. You are Peter, a rock. This is the rock on which I will put together my church, a church so expansive with energy that not even the gates of hell will be able to keep it out.

"And that's not all. You will have complete and free access to God's kingdom, keys to open any and every door: no more barriers between heaven and earth, earth and heaven. A yes on earth is yes in heaven. A no on earth is no in heaven."

He swore the disciples to secrecy. He made them promise they would tell no one that he was the Messiah.

You're Not in the Driver's Seat

Then Jesus made it clear to his disciples that it was now necessary for him to go to Jerusalem, submit to an ordeal

KING JAMES VERSION

many things of the elders and chief priests and scribes, and be killed, and be raised again the third day.

22 Then Peter took him, and began to rebuke him, saying, Be it far from thee, Lord: this shall not be unto thee.

23 But he turned, and said unto Peter, Get thee behind me, Satan: thou art an offence unto me: for thou savourest not the things that be of God, but those that be of men.

24 ¶ Then said Jesus unto his disciples, If any *man* will come after me, let him deny himself, and take up his cross, and follow me.

25 For whosoever will save his life shall lose it: and whosoever will lose his life for my sake shall find it.

26 For what is a man profited, if he shall gain the whole world, and lose his own soul? or what shall a man give in exchange for his soul?

27 For the Son of man shall come in the glory of his Father with his angels; and then he shall reward every man according to his works.

28 Verily I say unto you, There be some standing here, which shall not taste of death, till they see the Son of man coming in his kingdom.

17 And after six days Jesus taketh Peter, James, and John his brother, and bringeth them up into an high mountain apart,

2 And was transfigured before them: and his face did shine as the sun, and his raiment was white as the light.

NEW AMERICAN STANDARD BIBLE

the elders and chief priests and scribes, and be killed, and be raised up on the third day.

22 Peter took Him aside and began to rebuke Him, saying, "God forbid *it,* Lord! This shall never happen to You."

23 But He turned and said to Peter, "Get behind Me, Satan! You are a stumbling block to Me; for you are not setting your mind on God's interests, but man's."

Discipleship Is Costly

24 Then Jesus said to His disciples, "If anyone wishes to come after Me, he must deny himself, and take up his cross and follow Me.

25 "For whoever wishes to save his life will lose it; but whoever loses his life for My sake will find it.

26 "For what will it profit a man if he gains the whole world and forfeits his soul? Or what will a man give in exchange for his soul?

27 "For the Son of Man is going to come in the glory of His Father with His angels, and WILL THEN REPAY EVERY MAN ACCORDING TO HIS DEEDS.

28 "Truly I say to you, there are some of those who are standing here who will not taste death until they see the Son of Man coming in His kingdom."

The Transfiguration

17 Six days later Jesus *took with Him Peter and James and John his brother, and *led them up on a high mountain by themselves.

2 And He was transfigured before them; and His face shone like the sun, and His garments became as white as light.

NEW CENTURY VERSION

make him suffer many things. He told them he must be killed and then be raised from the dead on the third day.

22 Peter took Jesus aside and told him not to talk like that. He said, "God save you from those things, Lord! Those things will never happen to you!"

23 Then Jesus said to Peter, "Go away from me, Satan![c] You are not helping me! You don't care about the things of God, but only about the things people think are important."

24 Then Jesus said to his followers, "If people want to follow me, they must give up the things they want. They must be willing even to give up their lives to follow me. 25 Those who want to save their lives will give up true life, and those who give up their lives for me will have true life. 26 It is worth nothing for them to have the whole world if they lose their souls. They could never pay enough to buy back their souls. 27 The Son of Man will come again with his Father's glory and with his angels. At that time, he will reward them for what they have done. 28 I tell you the truth, some people standing here will see the Son of Man coming with his kingdom before they die."

Jesus Talks with Moses and Elijah

17 Six days later, Jesus took Peter, James, and John, the brother of James, up on a high mountain by themselves. 2 While they watched, Jesus' appearance was changed; his face became bright like the sun, and his

16:23 [c] Satan Name for the devil, meaning "the enemy." Jesus means that Peter was talking like Satan.

CONTEMPORARY ENGLISH VERSION

teachers of the Law of Moses will make me suffer terribly. I will be killed, but three days later I will rise to life."

22 Peter took Jesus aside and told him to stop talking like that. He said, "God would never let this happen to you, Lord!"

23 Jesus turned to Peter and said, "Satan, get away from me! You're in my way because you think like everyone else and not like God."

24 Then Jesus said to his disciples:

If any of you want to be my followers, you must forget about yourself. You must take up your cross and follow me. 25 If you want to save your life,[e] you will destroy it. But if you give up your life for me, you will find it. 26 What will you gain, if you own the whole world but destroy yourself? What would you give to get back your soul?

27 The Son of Man will soon come in the glory of his Father and with his angels to reward all people for what they have done. 28 I promise you that some of those standing here will not die before they see the Son of Man coming with his kingdom.

The True Glory of Jesus (Mark 9.2-13; Luke 9.28-36)

17 Six days later Jesus took Peter and the brothers James and John with him. They went up on a very high mountain where they could be alone. 2 There in front of the disciples, Jesus was completely changed. His face was shining like the sun, and his clothes became white as light.

[e] 16.25 *life*: In verses 25 and 26 the same Greek word is translated "life," "yourself," and "soul."

NEW INTERNATIONAL VERSION

law, and that he must be killed and on the third day be raised to life.

[22]Peter took him aside and began to rebuke him. "Never, Lord!" he said. "This shall never happen to you!"

[23]Jesus turned and said to Peter, "Get behind me, Satan! You are a stumbling block to me; you do not have in mind the things of God, but the things of men."

[24]Then Jesus said to his disciples, "If anyone would come after me, he must deny himself and take up his cross and follow me. [25]For whoever wants to save his life[g] will lose it, but whoever loses his life for me will find it. [26]What good will it be for a man if he gains the whole world, yet forfeits his soul? Or what can a man give in exchange for his soul? [27]For the Son of Man is going to come in his Father's glory with his angels, and then he will reward each person according to what he has done. [28]I tell you the truth, some who are standing here will not taste death before they see the Son of Man coming in his kingdom."

The Transfiguration

17 After six days Jesus took with him Peter, James and John the brother of James, and led them up a high mountain by themselves. [2]There he was transfigured before them. His face shone like the sun, and his clothes

g 25 The Greek word means either *life* or *soul*; also in verse 26.

NEW LIVING TRANSLATION

religious law. He would be killed, and he would be raised on the third day.

[22]But Peter took him aside and corrected him. "Heaven forbid, Lord," he said. "This will never happen to you!"

[23]Jesus turned to Peter and said, "Get away from me, Satan! You are a dangerous trap to me. You are seeing things merely from a human point of view, and not from God's."

[24]Then Jesus said to the disciples, "If any of you wants to be my follower, you must put aside your selfish ambition, shoulder your cross, and follow me. [25]If you try to keep your life for yourself, you will lose it. But if you give up your life for me, you will find true life. [26]And how do you benefit if you gain the whole world but lose your own soul* in the process? Is anything worth more than your soul? [27]For I, the Son of Man, will come in the glory of my Father with his angels and will judge all people according to their deeds. [28]And I assure you that some of you standing here right now will not die before you see me, the Son of Man, coming in my Kingdom."

The Transfiguration

17 Six days later Jesus took Peter and the two brothers, James and John, and led them up a high mountain. [2]As the men watched, Jesus' appearance changed so that his face shone like the sun, and his clothing became

16:26 Or *your life*.

NEW KING JAMES VERSION

the elders and chief priests and scribes, and be killed, and be raised the third day.

[22]Then Peter took Him aside and began to rebuke Him, saying, "Far be it from You, Lord; this shall not happen to You!"

[23]But He turned and said to Peter, "Get behind Me, Satan! You are an offense to Me, for you are not mindful of the things of God, but the things of men."

Take Up the Cross and Follow Him

[24]Then Jesus said to His disciples, "If anyone desires to come after Me, let him deny himself, and take up his cross, and follow Me. [25]For whoever desires to save his life will lose it, but whoever loses his life for My sake will find it. [26]For what profit is it to a man if he gains the whole world, and loses his own soul? Or what will a man give in exchange for his soul? [27]For the Son of Man will come in the glory of His Father with His angels, and then He will reward each according to his works.

Jesus Transfigured on the Mount

"[28]Assuredly, I say to you, there are some standing here who shall not taste death till they see the Son of Man coming in His kingdom."

17 Now after six days Jesus took Peter, James, and John his brother, led them up on a high mountain by themselves; [2]and He was transfigured before them. His face shone like the sun, and His clothes became as white

THE MESSAGE

of suffering at the hands of the religious leaders, be killed, and then on the third day be raised up alive. Peter took him in hand, protesting, "Impossible, Master! That can never be!"

But Jesus didn't swerve. "Peter, get out of my way. Satan, get lost. You have no idea how God works."

Then Jesus went to work on his disciples. "Anyone who intends to come with me has to let me lead. You're not in the driver's seat; *I* am. Don't run from suffering; embrace it. Follow me and I'll show you how. Self-help is no help at all. Self-sacrifice is the way, my way, to finding yourself, your true self. What kind of deal is it to get everything you want but lose yourself? What could you ever trade your soul for?

"Don't be in such a hurry to go into business for yourself. Before you know it the Son of Man will arrive with all the splendor of his Father, accompanied by an army of angels. You'll get everything you have coming to you, a personal gift. This isn't pie in the sky by and by. Some of you standing here are going to see it take place, see the Son of Man in kingdom glory."

Sunlight Poured From His Face

17 Six days later, three of them saw that glory. Jesus took Peter and the brothers, James and John, and led them up a high mountain. His appearance changed from the inside out, right before their eyes. Sunlight poured from his face. His clothes were filled with light.

KING JAMES VERSION

3 And, behold, there appeared unto them Moses and Elias talking with him.

4 Then answered Peter, and said unto Jesus, Lord, it is good for us to be here: if thou wilt, let us make here three tabernacles; one for thee, and one for Moses, and one for Elias.

5 While he yet spake, behold, a bright cloud overshadowed them: and behold a voice out of the cloud, which said, This is my beloved Son, in whom I am well pleased; hear ye him.

6 And when the disciples heard *it*, they fell on their face, and were sore afraid.

7 And Jesus came and touched them, and said, Arise, and be not afraid.

8 And when they had lifted up their eyes, they saw no man, save Jesus only.

9 And as they came down from the mountain, Jesus charged them, saying, Tell the vision to no man, until the Son of man be risen again from the dead.

10 And his disciples asked him, saying, Why then say the scribes that Elias must first come?

11 And Jesus answered and said unto them, Elias truly shall first come, and restore all things.

12 But I say unto you, That Elias is come already, and they knew him not, but have done unto him whatsoever they listed. Likewise shall also the Son of man suffer of them.

13 Then the disciples understood that he spake unto them of John the Baptist.

NEW AMERICAN STANDARD BIBLE

3 And behold, Moses and Elijah appeared to them, talking with Him.

4 Peter said to Jesus, "Lord, it is good for us to be here; if You wish, I will make three tabernacles here, one for You, and one for Moses, and one for Elijah."

5 While he was still speaking, a bright cloud overshadowed them, and behold, a voice out of the cloud said, "This is My beloved Son, with whom I am well-pleased; listen to Him!"

6 When the disciples heard *this,* they fell face down to the ground and were terrified.

7 And Jesus came to *them* and touched them and said, "Get up, and do not be afraid."

8 And lifting up their eyes, they saw no one except Jesus Himself alone.

9 As they were coming down from the mountain, Jesus commanded them, saying, "Tell the vision to no one until the Son of Man has risen from the dead."

10 And His disciples asked Him, "Why then do the scribes say that Elijah must come first?"

11 And He answered and said, "Elijah is coming and will restore all things;

12 but I say to you that Elijah already came, and they did not recognize him, but did to him whatever they wished. So also the Son of Man is going to suffer at their hands."

13 Then the disciples understood that He had spoken to them about John the Baptist.

NEW CENTURY VERSION

clothes became white as light. [3]Then Moses and Elijah[a]
appeared to them, talking with Jesus.
[4]Peter said to Jesus, "Lord, it is good that we are here. If
you want, I will put up three tents here—one for you, one
for Moses, and one for Elijah."
[5]While Peter was talking, a bright cloud covered them. A
voice came from the cloud and said, "This is my Son,
whom I love, and I am very pleased with him. Listen to
him!"
[6]When his followers heard the voice, they were so fright-
ened they fell to the ground. [7]But Jesus went to them and
touched them and said, "Stand up. Don't be afraid."
[8]When they looked up, they saw Jesus was now alone.
[9]As they were coming down the mountain, Jesus com-
manded them not to tell anyone about what they had seen
until the Son of Man had risen from the dead.
[10]Then his followers asked him, "Why do the teachers of
the law say that Elijah must come first?"
[11]Jesus answered, "They are right to say that Elijah is
coming and that he will make everything the way it should
be. [12]But I tell you that Elijah has already come, and they
did not recognize him. They did to him whatever they
wanted to do. It will be the same with the Son of Man;
those same people will make the Son of Man suffer."
[13]Then the followers understood that Jesus was talking
about John the Baptist.

17:3 [a] **Moses and Elijah** Two of the most important Jewish leaders in the past. Moses had given them the law, and Elijah was an important prophet.

CONTEMPORARY ENGLISH VERSION

[3]All at once Moses and Elijah were there talking with
Jesus. [4]So Peter said to him, "Lord, it is good for us to be
here! Let us make three shelters, one for you, one for
Moses, and one for Elijah."
[5]While Peter was still speaking, the shadow of a bright
cloud passed over them. From the cloud a voice said, "This
is my own dear Son, and I am pleased with him. Listen to
what he says!" [6]When the disciples heard the voice, they
were so afraid that they fell flat on the ground. [7]But Jesus
came over and touched them. He said, "Get up and don't
be afraid!" [8]When they opened their eyes, they saw only
Jesus.
[9]On their way down from the mountain, Jesus warned
his disciples not to tell anyone what they had seen until
after the Son of Man had been raised from death.
[10]The disciples asked Jesus, "Don't the teachers of the
Law of Moses say that Elijah must come before the
Messiah does?"
[11]Jesus told them, "Elijah certainly will come and get
everything ready. [12]In fact, he has already come. But the
people did not recognize him and treated him just as they
wanted to. They will soon make the Son of Man suffer in
the same way." [13]Then the disciples understood that Jesus
was talking to them about John the Baptist.

NEW INTERNATIONAL VERSION

became as white as the light. 3 Just then there appeared before them Moses and Elijah, talking with Jesus.

4 Peter said to Jesus, "Lord, it is good for us to be here. If you wish, I will put up three shelters—one for you, one for Moses and one for Elijah."

5 While he was still speaking, a bright cloud enveloped them, and a voice from the cloud said, "This is my Son, whom I love; with him I am well pleased. Listen to him!"

6 When the disciples heard this, they fell facedown to the ground, terrified. 7 But Jesus came and touched them. "Get up," he said. "Don't be afraid." 8 When they looked up, they saw no one except Jesus.

9 As they were coming down the mountain, Jesus instructed them, "Don't tell anyone what you have seen, until the Son of Man has been raised from the dead."

10 The disciples asked him, "Why then do the teachers of the law say that Elijah must come first?"

11 Jesus replied, "To be sure, Elijah comes and will restore all things. 12 But I tell you, Elijah has already come, and they did not recognize him, but have done to him everything they wished. In the same way the Son of Man is going to suffer at their hands." 13 Then the disciples understood that he was talking to them about John the Baptist.

NEW LIVING TRANSLATION

dazzling white. 3 Suddenly, Moses and Elijah appeared and began talking with Jesus. 4 Peter blurted out, "Lord, this is wonderful! If you want me to, I'll make three shrines,* one for you, one for Moses, and one for Elijah."

5 But even as he said it, a bright cloud came over them, and a voice from the cloud said, "This is my beloved Son, and I am fully pleased with him. Listen to him." 6 The disciples were terrified and fell face down on the ground.

7 Jesus came over and touched them. "Get up," he said, "don't be afraid." 8 And when they looked, they saw only Jesus with them. 9 As they descended the mountain, Jesus commanded them, "Don't tell anyone what you have seen until I, the Son of Man, have been raised from the dead."

10 His disciples asked, "Why do the teachers of religious law insist that Elijah must return before the Messiah comes*?"

11 Jesus replied, "Elijah is indeed coming first to set everything in order. 12 But I tell you, he has already come, but he wasn't recognized, and he was badly mistreated. And soon the Son of Man will also suffer at their hands." 13 Then the disciples realized he had been speaking of John the Baptist.

17:4 Or *shelters;* Greek reads *tabernacles.* 17:10 Greek *that Elijah must come first.*

NEW KING JAMES VERSION

as the light. 3 And behold, Moses and Elijah appeared to them, talking with Him. 4 Then Peter answered and said to Jesus, "Lord, it is good for us to be here; if You wish, let us[a] make here three tabernacles: one for You, one for Moses, and one for Elijah."

5 While he was still speaking, behold, a bright cloud overshadowed them; and suddenly a voice came out of the cloud, saying, "This is My beloved Son, in whom I am well pleased. Hear Him!" 6 And when the disciples heard *it,* they fell on their faces and were greatly afraid. 7 But Jesus came and touched them and said, "Arise, and do not be afraid." 8 When they had lifted up their eyes, they saw no one but Jesus only.

9 Now as they came down from the mountain, Jesus commanded them, saying, "Tell the vision to no one until the Son of Man is risen from the dead."

10 And His disciples asked Him, saying, "Why then do the scribes say that Elijah must come first?"

11 Jesus answered and said to them, "Indeed, Elijah is coming first[b] and will restore all things. 12 But I say to you that Elijah has come already, and they did not know him but did to him whatever they wished. Likewise the Son of Man is also about to suffer at their hands." 13 Then the disciples understood that He spoke to them of John the Baptist.

17:4 [a] NU-Text reads *I will.* 17:11 [b] NU-Text omits *first.*

THE MESSAGE

Then they realized that Moses and Elijah were also there in deep conversation with him.

Peter broke in, "Master, this is a great moment! What would you think if I built three memorials here on the mountain—one for you, one for Moses, one for Elijah?"

While he was going on like this, babbling, a light-radiant cloud enveloped them, and sounding from deep in the cloud a voice: "This is my Son, marked by my love, focus of my delight. Listen to him."

When the disciples heard it, they fell flat on their faces, scared to death. But Jesus came over and touched them. "Don't be afraid." When they opened their eyes and looked around all they saw was Jesus, only Jesus.

Coming down the mountain, Jesus swore them to secrecy. "Don't breathe a word of what you've seen. After the Son of Man is raised from the dead, you are free to talk."

The disciples, meanwhile, were asking questions. "Why do the religion scholars say that Elijah has to come first?"

Jesus answered, "Elijah does come and get everything ready. I'm telling you, Elijah has already come but they didn't know him when they saw him. They treated him like dirt, the same way they are about to treat the Son of Man." That's when the disciples realized that all along he had been talking about John the Baptizer.

KING JAMES VERSION

14 ¶ And when they were come to the multitude, there came to him a *certain* man, kneeling down to him, and saying,

15 Lord, have mercy on my son: for he is lunatick, and sore vexed: for ofttimes he falleth into the fire, and oft into the water.

16 And I brought him to thy disciples, and they could not cure him.

17 Then Jesus answered and said, O faithless and perverse generation, how long shall I be with you? how long shall I suffer you? bring him hither to me.

18 And Jesus rebuked the devil; and he departed out of him: and the child was cured from that very hour.

19 Then came the disciples to Jesus apart, and said, Why could not we cast him out?

20 And Jesus said unto them, Because of your unbelief: for verily I say unto you, If ye have faith as a grain of mustard seed, ye shall say unto this mountain, Remove hence to yonder place; and it shall remove; and nothing shall be impossible unto you.

21 Howbeit this kind goeth not out but by prayer and fasting.

22 ¶ And while they abode in Galilee, Jesus said unto them, The Son of man shall be betrayed into the hands of men:

23 And they shall kill him, and the third day he shall be raised again. And they were exceeding sorry.

NEW AMERICAN STANDARD BIBLE

The Demoniac

14 When they came to the crowd, a man came up to Jesus, falling on his knees before Him and saying,

15 "Lord, have mercy on my son, for he is a lunatic and is very ill; for he often falls into the fire and often into the water.

16 "I brought him to Your disciples, and they could not cure him."

17 And Jesus answered and said, "You unbelieving and perverted generation, how long shall I be with you? How long shall I put up with you? Bring him here to Me."

18 And Jesus rebuked him, and the demon came out of him, and the boy was cured at once.

19 Then the disciples came to Jesus privately and said, "Why could we not drive it out?"

20 And He *said to them, "Because of the littleness of your faith; for truly I say to you, if you have faith the size of a mustard seed, you will say to this mountain, 'Move from here to there,' and it will move; and nothing will be impossible to you.

21 ["[1]But this kind does not go out except by prayer and fasting."]

22 And while they were gathering together in Galilee, Jesus said to them, "The Son of Man is going to be delivered into the hands of men;

23 and they will kill Him, and He will be raised on the third day." And they were deeply grieved.

17:21 [1] Early mss do not contain this v

NEW CENTURY VERSION

Jesus Heals a Sick Boy

14When Jesus and his followers came back to the crowd,
a man came to Jesus and bowed before him. 15The man
said, "Lord, have mercy on my son. He has epilepsy[b] and
is suffering very much, because he often falls into the fire
or into the water. 16I brought him to your followers, but
they could not cure him."
17Jesus answered, "You people have no faith, and your
lives are all wrong. How long must I put up with you? How
long must I continue to be patient with you? Bring the boy
here." 18Jesus commanded the demon inside the boy. Then
the demon came out, and the boy was healed from that
time on.
19The followers came to Jesus when he was alone and
asked, "Why couldn't we force the demon out?"
20Jesus answered, "Because your faith is too small. I tell
you the truth, if your faith is as big as a mustard seed, you
can say to this mountain, 'Move from here to there,' and it
will move. All things will be possible for you." 21[c]

Jesus Talks About His Death

22While Jesus' followers were gathering in Galilee, he
said to them, "The Son of Man will be handed over to peo-
ple, 23and they will kill him. But on the third day he will
be raised from the dead." And the followers were filled
with sadness.

17:15 [b] **epilepsy** A disease that causes a person sometimes to lose control of his body and maybe faint, shake strongly, or not be able to move. 17:21 [c] **Verse 21** Some Greek copies add verse 21: "That kind of spirit comes out only if you use prayer and give up eating."

CONTEMPORARY ENGLISH VERSION

Jesus Heals a Boy (Mark 9.14-29; Luke 9.37-43a)

14Jesus and his disciples returned to the crowd. A man
knelt in front of him 15and said, "Lord, have pity on my
son! He has a bad case of epilepsy and often falls into a
fire or into water. 16I brought him to your disciples, but
none of them could heal him."
17Jesus said, "You people are too stubborn to have any
faith! How much longer must I be with you? Why do I have
to put up with you? Bring the boy here." 18Then Jesus
spoke sternly to the demon. It went out of the boy, and
right then he was healed.
19Later the disciples went to Jesus in private and asked
him, "Why couldn't we force out the demon?"
20-21Jesus replied:

It is because you don't have enough faith! But I can promise you this. If you had faith no larger than a mustard seed, you could tell this mountain to move from here to there. And it would. Everything would be possible for you.[a]

Jesus Again Speaks about His Death
(Mark 9.30-32; Luke 9.43b-45)

22While Jesus and his disciples were going from place to
place in Galilee, he told them, "The Son of Man will be
handed over to people 23who will kill him. But three days
later he will rise to life." All of this made the disciples very
sad.

[a] 17.20,21 *for you*: Some manuscripts add, "But the only way to force out that kind of demon is by praying and going without eating."

NEW INTERNATIONAL VERSION

The Healing of a Boy With a Demon

14When they came to the crowd, a man approached Jesus and knelt before him. 15"Lord, have mercy on my son," he said. "He has seizures and is suffering greatly. He often falls into the fire or into the water. 16I brought him to your disciples, but they could not heal him."

17"O unbelieving and perverse generation," Jesus replied, "how long shall I stay with you? How long shall I put up with you? Bring the boy here to me." 18Jesus rebuked the demon, and it came out of the boy, and he was healed from that moment.

19Then the disciples came to Jesus in private and asked, "Why couldn't we drive it out?"

20He replied, "Because you have so little faith. I tell you the truth, if you have faith as small as a mustard seed, you can say to this mountain, 'Move from here to there' and it will move. Nothing will be impossible for you.[a]"

22When they came together in Galilee, he said to them, "The Son of Man is going to be betrayed into the hands of men. 23They will kill him, and on the third day he will be raised to life." And the disciples were filled with grief.

[a] 20 Some manuscripts *you.* [21]*But this kind does not go out except by prayer and fasting.*

NEW LIVING TRANSLATION

Jesus Heals a Demon-Possessed Boy

14When they arrived at the foot of the mountain, a huge crowd was waiting for them. A man came and knelt before Jesus and said, 15"Lord, have mercy on my son, because he has seizures and suffers terribly. He often falls into the fire or into the water. 16So I brought him to your disciples, but they couldn't heal him."

17Jesus replied, "You stubborn, faithless people! How long must I be with you until you believe? How long must I put up with you? Bring the boy to me." 18Then Jesus rebuked the demon in the boy, and it left him. From that moment the boy was well.

19Afterward the disciples asked Jesus privately, "Why couldn't we cast out that demon?"

20"You didn't have enough faith," Jesus told them. "I assure you, even if you had faith as small as a mustard seed you could say to this mountain, 'Move from here to there,' and it would move. Nothing would be impossible."*

Jesus Again Predicts His Death

22One day after they had returned to Galilee, Jesus told them, "The Son of Man is going to be betrayed. 23He will be killed, but three days later he will be raised from the dead." And the disciples' hearts were filled with grief.

17:20 Some manuscripts add verse 21, *But this kind of demon won't leave unless you have prayed and fasted.*

NEW KING JAMES VERSION

A Boy Is Healed

14And when they had come to the multitude, a man came to Him, kneeling down to Him and saying, 15"Lord, have mercy on my son, for he is an epileptic[c] and suffers severely; for he often falls into the fire and often into the water. 16So I brought him to Your disciples, but they could not cure him."

17Then Jesus answered and said, "O faithless and perverse generation, how long shall I be with you? How long shall I bear with you? Bring him here to Me." 18And Jesus rebuked the demon, and it came out of him; and the child was cured from that very hour.

19Then the disciples came to Jesus privately and said, "Why could we not cast it out?"

20So Jesus said to them, "Because of your unbelief;[d] for assuredly, I say to you, if you have faith as a mustard seed, you will say to this mountain, 'Move from here to there,' and it will move; and nothing will be impossible for you. 21However, this kind does not go out except by prayer and fasting."[e]

Jesus Again Predicts His Death and Resurrection

22Now while they were staying[f] in Galilee, Jesus said to them, "The Son of Man is about to be betrayed into the hands of men, 23and they will kill Him, and the third day He will be raised up." And they were exceedingly sorrowful.

17:15 [c] Literally *moonstruck* 17:20 [d] NU-Text reads *little faith.* 17:21 [e] NU-Text omits this verse. 17:22 [f] NU-Text reads *gathering together.*

THE MESSAGE

With a Mere Kernel of Faith

At the bottom of the mountain, they were met by a crowd of waiting people. As they approached, a man came out of the crowd and fell to his knees begging, "Master, have mercy on my son. He goes out of his mind and suffers terribly, falling into seizures. Frequently he is pitched into the fire, other times into the river. I brought him to your disciples, but they could do nothing for him."

Jesus said, "What a generation! No sense of God! No focus to your lives! How many times do I have to go over these things? How much longer do I have to put up with this? Bring the boy here." He ordered the afflicting demon out—and it was out, gone. From that moment on the boy was well.

When the disciples had Jesus off to themselves, they asked, "Why couldn't we throw it out?"

"Because you're not yet taking *God* seriously," said Jesus. "The simple truth is that if you had a mere kernel of faith, a poppy seed, say, you would tell this mountain, 'Move!' and it would move. There is nothing you wouldn't be able to tackle."

As they were regrouping in Galilee, Jesus told them, "The Son of Man is about to be betrayed to some people who want nothing to do with God. They will murder him—and three days later he will be raised alive." The disciples felt terrible.

KING JAMES VERSION

24 ¶ And when they were come to Capernaum, they that
received tribute *money* came to Peter, and said, Doth not
your master pay tribute?
25 He saith, Yes. And when he was come into the
house, Jesus prevented him, saying, What thinkest thou,
Simon? of whom do the kings of the earth take custom or
tribute? of their own children, or of strangers?
26 Peter saith unto him, Of strangers. Jesus saith unto
him, Then are the children free.
27 Notwithstanding, lest we should offend them, go
thou to the sea, and cast an hook, and take up the fish
that first cometh up; and when thou hast opened his
mouth, thou shalt find a piece of money: that take, and
give unto them for me and thee.

18 At the same time came the disciples unto Jesus,
saying, Who is the greatest in the kingdom of
heaven?
2 And Jesus called a little child unto him, and set him in
the midst of them,
3 And said, Verily I say unto you, Except ye be convert-
ed, and become as little children, ye shall not enter into
the kingdom of heaven.
4 Whosoever therefore shall humble himself as this lit-
tle child, the same is greatest in the kingdom of heaven.
5 And whoso shall receive one such little child in my
name receiveth me.

NEW AMERICAN STANDARD BIBLE

The Tribute Money

24 When they came to Capernaum, those who collected
the [2]two-drachma *tax* came to Peter and said, "Does your
teacher not pay the [2]two-drachma *tax?*"
25 He *said, "Yes." And when he came into the house,
Jesus spoke to him first, saying, "What do you think,
Simon? From whom do the kings of the earth collect cus-
toms or poll-tax, from their sons or from strangers?"
26 When Peter said, "From strangers," Jesus said to him,
"Then the sons are exempt.
27 "However, so that we do not offend them, go to the
sea and throw in a hook, and take the first fish that comes
up; and when you open its mouth, you will find [3]a shekel.
Take that and give it to them for you and Me."

Rank in the Kingdom

18 At that time the disciples came to Jesus and said,
"Who then is greatest in the kingdom of heaven?"
2 And He called a child to Himself and set him before
them,
3 and said, "Truly I say to you, unless you are convert-
ed and become like children, you will not enter the king-
dom of heaven.
4 "Whoever then humbles himself as this child, he is the
greatest in the kingdom of heaven.
5 "And whoever receives one such child in My name
receives Me;

17:24 [2] Equivalent to two denarii or two days' wages, paid as a temple
tax 17:27 [3] Lit *standard coin,* which was a shekel

NEW CENTURY VERSION

Jesus Talks About Paying Taxes

24 When Jesus and his followers came to Capernaum, the
men who collected the Temple tax came to Peter. They
asked, "Does your teacher pay the Temple tax?"
25 Peter answered, "Yes, Jesus pays the tax."
Peter went into the house, but before he could speak,
Jesus said to him, "What do you think? The kings of the
earth collect different kinds of taxes. But who pays the
taxes—the king's children or others?"
26 Peter answered, "Other people pay the taxes."
Jesus said to Peter, "Then the children of the king don't
have to pay taxes. 27 But we don't want to upset these tax
collectors. So go to the lake and fish. After you catch the
first fish, open its mouth and you will find a coin. Take
that coin and give it to the tax collectors for you and me."

Who Is the Greatest?

18 At that time the followers came to Jesus and
asked, "Who is greatest in the kingdom of heav-
en?"
2 Jesus called a little child to him and stood the child
before his followers. 3 Then he said, "I tell you the truth,
you must change and become like little children.
Otherwise, you will never enter the kingdom of heaven.
4 The greatest person in the kingdom of heaven is the one
who makes himself humble like this child.
5 "Whoever accepts a child in my name accepts me. 6 If

CONTEMPORARY ENGLISH VERSION

Paying the Temple Tax

24 When Jesus and the others arrived in Capernaum, the
collectors for the temple tax came to Peter and asked,
"Does your teacher pay the temple tax?"
25 "Yes, he does," Peter answered.
After they had returned home, Jesus went up to Peter
and asked him, "Simon, what do you think? Do the kings
of this earth collect taxes and fees from their own people
or from foreigners?"[b]
26 Peter answered, "From foreigners."
Jesus replied, "Then their own people[c] don't have to pay.
27 But we don't want to cause trouble. So go cast a line into
the lake and pull out the first fish you hook. Open its
mouth, and you will find a coin. Use it to pay your taxes
and mine."

Who Is the Greatest? (Mark 9.33-37; Luke 9.46-48)

18 About this time the disciples came to Jesus and
asked him who would be the greatest in the king-
dom of heaven. 2 Jesus called a child over and had the child
stand near him. 3 Then he said:

I promise you this. If you don't change and become like
a child, you will never get into the kingdom of heaven.
4 But if you are as humble as this child, you are the great-
est in the kingdom of heaven. 5 And when you welcome
one of these children because of me, you welcome me.

[b] 17.25 *from their own people or from foreigners*: Or "from their children
or from others." [c] 17.26 *From foreigners . . . their own people*: Or
"From other people . . . their children."

NEW INTERNATIONAL VERSION

The Temple Tax

24 After Jesus and his disciples arrived in Capernaum, the collectors of the two-drachma tax came to Peter and asked, "Doesn't your teacher pay the temple tax[b]?"

25 "Yes, he does," he replied.

When Peter came into the house, Jesus was the first to speak. "What do you think, Simon?" he asked. "From whom do the kings of the earth collect duty and taxes—from their own sons or from others?"

26 "From others," Peter answered.

"Then the sons are exempt," Jesus said to him. 27 "But so that we may not offend them, go to the lake and throw out your line. Take the first fish you catch; open its mouth and you will find a four-drachma coin. Take it and give it to them for my tax and yours."

The Greatest in the Kingdom of Heaven

18 At that time the disciples came to Jesus and asked, "Who is the greatest in the kingdom of heaven?"

2 He called a little child and had him stand among them. 3 And he said: "I tell you the truth, unless you change and become like little children, you will never enter the kingdom of heaven. 4 Therefore, whoever humbles himself like this child is the greatest in the kingdom of heaven.

5 "And whoever welcomes a little child like this in my

[b] 24 Greek *the two drachmas*

NEW LIVING TRANSLATION

Payment of the Temple Tax

24 On their arrival in Capernaum, the tax collectors for the Temple tax came to Peter and asked him, "Doesn't your teacher pay the Temple tax?"

25 "Of course he does," Peter replied. Then he went into the house to talk to Jesus about it.

But before he had a chance to speak, Jesus asked him, "What do you think, Peter*? Do kings tax their own people or the foreigners they have conquered?"

26 "They tax the foreigners," Peter replied.

"Well, then," Jesus said, "the citizens are free! 27 However, we don't want to offend them, so go down to the lake and throw in a line. Open the mouth of the first fish you catch, and you will find a coin. Take the coin and pay the tax for both of us."

The Greatest in the Kingdom

18 About that time the disciples came to Jesus and asked, "Which of us is greatest in the Kingdom of Heaven?"

2 Jesus called a small child over to him and put the child among them. 3 Then he said, "I assure you, unless you turn from your sins and become as little children, you will never get into the Kingdom of Heaven. 4 Therefore, anyone who becomes as humble as this little child is the greatest in the Kingdom of Heaven. 5 And anyone who welcomes a little child like this on my behalf is welcoming me. 6 But if

17:25 Greek *Simon.*

NEW KING JAMES VERSION

Peter and His Master Pay Their Taxes

24 When they had come to Capernaum,[g] those who received the *temple* tax came to Peter and said, "Does your Teacher not pay the *temple* tax?"

25 He said, "Yes."

And when he had come into the house, Jesus anticipated him, saying, "What do you think, Simon? From whom do the kings of the earth take customs or taxes, from their sons or from strangers?"

26 Peter said to Him, "From strangers."

Jesus said to him, "Then the sons are free. 27 Nevertheless, lest we offend them, go to the sea, cast in a hook, and take the fish that comes up first. And when you have opened its mouth, you will find a piece of money;[h] take that and give it to them for Me and you."

Who Is the Greatest?

18 At that time the disciples came to Jesus, saying, "Who then is greatest in the kingdom of heaven?"

2 Then Jesus called a little child to Him, set him in the midst of them, 3 and said, "Assuredly, I say to you, unless you are converted and become as little children, you will by no means enter the kingdom of heaven. 4 Therefore whoever humbles himself as this little child is the greatest in the kingdom of heaven. 5 Whoever receives one little child like this in My name receives Me.

17:24 [g] NU-Text reads *Capharnaum* (here and elsewhere).
17:27 [h] Greek *stater,* the exact amount to pay the temple tax (didrachma) for two

THE MESSAGE

When they arrived at Capernaum, the tax men came to Peter and asked, "Does your teacher pay taxes?"

Peter said, "Of course."

But as soon as they were in the house, Jesus confronted him. "Simon, what do you think? When a king levies taxes, who pays—his children or his subjects?"

He answered, "His subjects."

Jesus said, "Then the children get off free, right? But so we don't upset them needlessly, go down to the lake, cast a hook, and pull in the first fish that bites. Open its mouth and you'll find a coin. Take it and give it to the tax men. It will be enough for both of us."

Whoever Becomes Simple Again

18 At about the same time, the disciples came to Jesus asking, "Who gets the highest rank in God's kingdom?"

For an answer Jesus called over a child, whom he stood in the middle of the room, and said, "I'm telling you, once and for all, that unless you return to square one and start over like children, you're not even going to get a look at the kingdom, let alone get in. Whoever becomes simple and elemental again, like this child, will rank high in God's kingdom. What's more, when you receive the childlike on my account, it's the same as receiving me.

KING JAMES VERSION

6 But whoso shall offend one of these little ones which believe in me, it were better for him that a millstone were hanged about his neck, and *that* he were drowned in the depth of the sea.

7 ¶ Woe unto the world because of offences! for it must needs be that offences come; but woe to that man by whom the offence cometh!

8 Wherefore if thy hand or thy foot offend thee, cut them off, and cast *them* from thee: it is better for thee to enter into life halt or maimed, rather than having two hands or two feet to be cast into everlasting fire.

9 And if thine eye offend thee, pluck it out, and cast *it* from thee: it is better for thee to enter into life with one eye, rather than having two eyes to be cast into hell fire.

10 Take heed that ye despise not one of these little ones; for I say unto you, That in heaven their angels do always behold the face of my Father which is in heaven.

11 For the Son of man is come to save that which was lost.

12 How think ye? if a man have an hundred sheep, and one of them be gone astray, doth he not leave the ninety and nine, and goeth into the mountains, and seeketh that which is gone astray?

13 And if so be that he find it, verily I say unto you, he

NEW AMERICAN STANDARD BIBLE

6 but whoever causes one of these little ones who believe in Me to stumble, it would be better for him to have a heavy millstone hung around his neck, and to be drowned in the depth of the sea.

Stumbling Blocks

7 "Woe to the world because of *its* stumbling blocks! For it is inevitable that stumbling blocks come; but woe to that man through whom the stumbling block comes!

8 "If your hand or your foot causes you to stumble, cut it off and throw it from you; it is better for you to enter life crippled or lame, than to have two hands or two feet and be cast into the eternal fire.

9 "If your eye causes you to stumble, pluck it out and throw it from you. It is better for you to enter life with one eye, than to have two eyes and be cast into the fiery hell.

10 "See that you do not despise one of these little ones, for I say to you that their angels in heaven continually see the face of My Father who is in heaven.

11 ["[1]For the Son of Man has come to save that which was lost.]

Ninety-nine Plus One

12 "What do you think? If any man has a hundred sheep, and one of them has gone astray, does he not leave the ninety-nine on the mountains and go and search for the one that is straying?

13 "If it turns out that he finds it, truly I say to you, he

18:11 [1] Early mss do not contain this v

NEW CENTURY VERSION

one of these little children believes in me, and someone causes that child to sin, it would be better for that person to have a large stone tied around the neck and be drowned in the sea. [7]How terrible for the people of the world because of the things that cause them to sin. Such things will happen, but how terrible for the one who causes them to happen! [8]If your hand or your foot causes you to sin, cut it off and throw it away. It is better for you to lose part of your body and live forever than to have two hands and two feet and be thrown into the fire that burns forever. [9]If your eye causes you to sin, take it out and throw it away. It is better for you to have only one eye and live forever than to have two eyes and be thrown into the fire of hell.

A Lost Sheep

[10]"Be careful. Don't think these little children are worth nothing. I tell you that they have angels in heaven who are always with my Father in heaven. [11a]

[12]"If a man has a hundred sheep but one of the sheep gets lost, he will leave the other ninety-nine on the hill and go to look for the lost sheep. [13]I tell you the truth, he

18:11 [a] **Verse 11** Some Greek copies add verse 11: "The Son of Man came to save lost people."

CONTEMPORARY ENGLISH VERSION

Temptations To Sin (Mark 9.42-48; Luke 17.1, 2)

[6]It will be terrible for people who cause even one of my little followers to sin. Those people would be better off thrown into the deepest part of the ocean with a heavy stone tied around their necks! [7]The world is in for trouble because of the way it causes people to sin. There will always be something to cause people to sin, but anyone who does this will be in for trouble.

[8]If your hand or foot causes you to sin, chop it off and throw it away! You would be better off to go into life crippled or lame than to have two hands or two feet and be thrown into the fire that never goes out. [9]If your eye causes you to sin, poke it out and get rid of it. You would be better off to go into life with only one eye than to have two eyes and be thrown into the fires of hell.

The Lost Sheep (Luke 15.3-7)

[10-11]Don't be cruel to any of these little ones! I promise you that their angels are always with my Father in heaven.[a] [12]Let me ask you this. What would you do if you had a hundred sheep and one of them wandered off? Wouldn't you leave the ninety-nine on the hillside and go look for the one that had wandered away? [13]I am sure that finding it would make you happier than having

[a] **18.10,11** *in heaven*: Some manuscripts add, "The Son of Man came to save people who are lost."

NEW INTERNATIONAL VERSION

name welcomes me. 6But if anyone causes one of these lit-
tle ones who believe in me to sin, it would be better for
him to have a large millstone hung around his neck and to
be drowned in the depths of the sea.
7"Woe to the world because of the things that cause peo-
ple to sin! Such things must come, but woe to the man
through whom they come! 8If your hand or your foot
causes you to sin, cut it off and throw it away. It is better
for you to enter life maimed or crippled than to have two
hands or two feet and be thrown into eternal fire. 9And if
your eye causes you to sin, gouge it out and throw it away.
It is better for you to enter life with one eye than to have
two eyes and be thrown into the fire of hell.

The Parable of the Lost Sheep

10"See that you do not look down on one of these little
ones. For I tell you that their angels in heaven always see
the face of my Father in heaven.[a]
12"What do you think? If a man owns a hundred sheep,
and one of them wanders away, will he not leave the nine-
ty-nine on the hills and go to look for the one that wan-
dered off? 13And if he finds it, I tell you the truth, he is

[a] *10* Some manuscripts *heaven.* [11]*The Son of Man came to save what was lost.*

NEW LIVING TRANSLATION

anyone causes one of these little ones who trusts in me to
lose faith, it would be better for that person to be thrown
into the sea with a large millstone tied around the neck.
7"How terrible it will be for anyone who causes others to
sin. Temptation to do wrong is inevitable, but how terrible
it will be for the person who does the tempting. 8So if your
hand or foot causes you to sin, cut it off and throw it
away. It is better to enter heaven* crippled or lame than to
be thrown into the unquenchable fire with both of your
hands and feet. 9And if your eye causes you to sin, gouge
it out and throw it away. It is better to enter heaven half
blind than to have two eyes and be thrown into hell.
10"Beware that you don't despise a single one of these
little ones. For I tell you that in heaven their angels are
always in the presence of my heavenly Father.*

Story of the Lost Sheep

12"If a shepherd has one hundred sheep, and one wan-
ders away and is lost, what will he do? Won't he leave the
ninety-nine others and go out into the hills to search for
the lost one? 13And if he finds it, he will surely rejoice over

18:8 Greek *enter life;* also in 18:9. **18:10** Some manuscripts add verse 11, *And I, the Son of Man, have come to save the lost.*

NEW KING JAMES VERSION

Jesus Warns of Offenses

6"Whoever causes one of these little ones who believe in
Me to sin, it would be better for him if a millstone were
hung around his neck, and he were drowned in the depth
of the sea. 7Woe to the world because of offenses! For of-
fenses must come, but woe to that man by whom the
offense comes!
8"If your hand or foot causes you to sin, cut it off and
cast *it* from you. It is better for you to enter into life lame
or maimed, rather than having two hands or two feet, to
be cast into the everlasting fire. 9And if your eye causes
you to sin, pluck it out and cast *it* from you. It is better for
you to enter into life with one eye, rather than having two
eyes, to be cast into hell fire.

The Parable of the Lost Sheep

10"Take heed that you do not despise one of these little
ones, for I say to you that in heaven their angels always
see the face of My Father who is in heaven. 11For the Son
of Man has come to save that which was lost.[a]
12"What do you think? If a man has a hundred sheep,
and one of them goes astray, does he not leave the ninety-
nine and go to the mountains to seek the one that is stray-
ing? 13And if he should find it, assuredly, I say to you, he

18:11 [a] NU-Text omits this verse.

THE MESSAGE

"But if you give them a hard time, bullying or taking advantage of their simple trust, you'll soon wish you hadn't. You'd be better off dropped in the middle of the lake with a millstone around your neck. Doom to the world for giving these God-believing children a hard time! Hard times are inevitable, but you don't have to make it worse—and it's doomsday to you if you do.

"If your hand or your foot gets in the way of God, chop it off and throw it away. You're better off maimed or lame and alive than the proud owners of two hands and two feet, godless in a furnace of eternal fire. And if your eye distracts you from God, pull it out and throw it away. You're better off one-eyed and alive than exercising your twenty-twenty vision from inside the fire of hell.

"Watch that you don't treat a single one of these childlike believers arrogantly. You realize, don't you, that their personal angels are constantly in touch with my Father in heaven?

Work It Out Between You

"Look at it this way. If someone has a hundred sheep and one of them wanders off, doesn't he leave the ninety-nine and go after the one? And if he finds it, doesn't he

KING JAMES VERSION

rejoiceth more of that *sheep*, than of the ninety and nine which went not astray.

14 Even so it is not the will of your Father which is in heaven, that one of these little ones should perish.

15 ¶ Moreover if thy brother shall trespass against thee, go and tell him his fault between thee and him alone: if he shall hear thee, thou hast gained thy brother.

16 But if he will not hear *thee, then* take with thee one or two more, that in the mouth of two or three witnesses every word may be established.

17 And if he shall neglect to hear them, tell *it* unto the church: but if he neglect to hear the church, let him be unto thee as an heathen man and a publican.

18 Verily I say unto you, Whatsoever ye shall bind on earth shall be bound in heaven: and whatsoever ye shall loose on earth shall be loosed in heaven.

19 Again I say unto you, That if two of you shall agree on earth as touching any thing that they shall ask, it shall be done for them of my Father which is in heaven.

20 For where two or three are gathered together in my name, there am I in the midst of them.

NEW AMERICAN STANDARD BIBLE

rejoices over it more than over the ninety-nine which have not gone astray.

14 "So it is not *the* will of your Father who is in heaven that one of these little ones perish.

Discipline and Prayer

15 "If your brother sins[2], go and show him his fault in private; if he listens to you, you have won your brother.

16 "But if he does not listen *to you,* take one or two more with you, so that BY THE MOUTH OF TWO OR THREE WITNESSES EVERY FACT MAY BE CONFIRMED.

17 "If he refuses to listen to them, tell it to the church; and if he refuses to listen even to the church, let him be to you as a Gentile and a tax collector.

18 "Truly I say to you, whatever you bind on earth shall have been bound in heaven; and whatever you loose on earth shall have been loosed in heaven.

19 "Again I say to you, that if two of you agree on earth about anything that they may ask, it shall be done for them by My Father who is in heaven.

20 "For where two or three have gathered together in My name, I am there in their midst."

18:15 [2] Late mss add *against you*

NEW CENTURY VERSION

is happier about that one sheep than about the ninety-nine
that were never lost. 14 In the same way, your Father in
heaven does not want any of these little children to be lost.

When a Person Sins Against You

15 "If your fellow believer sins against you, go and tell
him in private what he did wrong. If he listens to you, you
have helped that person to be your brother or sister again.
16 But if he refuses to listen, go to him again and take one
or two other people with you. 'Every case may be proved
by two or three witnesses.'[b] 17 If he refuses to listen to
them, tell the church. If he refuses to listen to the church,
then treat him like a person who does not believe in God or
like a tax collector.

18 "I tell you the truth, the things you don't allow on
earth will be the things God does not allow. And the things
you allow on earth will be the things that God allows.

19 "Also, I tell you that if two of you on earth agree about
something and pray for it, it will be done for you by my
Father in heaven. 20 This is true because if two or three
people come together in my name, I am there with them."

18:16 [b] **'Every...witnesses.'** Quotation from Deuteronomy 19:15.

CONTEMPORARY ENGLISH VERSION

the ninety-nine that never wandered off. 14 That's how it
is with your Father in heaven. He doesn't want any of
these little ones to be lost.

When Someone Sins (Luke 17.3)

15 If one of my followers[b] sins against you, go and
point out what was wrong. But do it in private, just
between the two of you. If that person listens, you have
won back a follower. 16 But if that one refuses to listen,
take along one or two others. The Scriptures teach that
every complaint must be proven true by two or more wit-
nesses. 17 If the follower refuses to listen to them, report
the matter to the church. Anyone who refuses to listen
to the church must be treated like an unbeliever or a tax
collector.[c]

Allowing and Not Allowing

18 I promise you that God in heaven will allow whatev-
er you allow on earth, but he will not allow anything
you don't allow. 19 I promise that when any two of you
on earth agree about something you are praying for, my
Father in heaven will do it for you. 20 Whenever two or
three of you come together in my name,[d] I am there with
you.

[b] **18.15** *followers*: The Greek text has "brother," which is used here and elsewhere in this chapter to refer to a follower of Christ. [c] **18.17** *tax collector*: See the note at 5.46. [d] **18.20** *in my name*: Or "as my followers."

NEW INTERNATIONAL VERSION

happier about that one sheep than about the ninety-nine that did not wander off. 14In the same way your Father in heaven is not willing that any of these little ones should be lost.

A Brother Who Sins Against You

15"If your brother sins against you,[b] go and show him his fault, just between the two of you. If he listens to you, you have won your brother over. 16But if he will not listen, take one or two others along, so that 'every matter may be established by the testimony of two or three witnesses.'[c] 17If he refuses to listen to them, tell it to the church; and if he refuses to listen even to the church, treat him as you would a pagan or a tax collector.

18"I tell you the truth, whatever you bind on earth will be[d] bound in heaven, and whatever you loose on earth will be[d] loosed in heaven.

19"Again, I tell you that if two of you on earth agree about anything you ask for, it will be done for you by my Father in heaven. 20For where two or three come together in my name, there am I with them."

[b] *15* Some manuscripts do not have *against you.* [c] *16* Deut. 19:15
[d] *18* Or *have been*

NEW LIVING TRANSLATION

it more than over the ninety-nine that didn't wander away! 14In the same way, it is not my heavenly Father's will that even one of these little ones should perish.

Correcting a Fellow Believer

15"If another believer* sins against you, go privately and point out the fault. If the other person listens and confesses it, you have won that person back. 16But if you are unsuccessful, take one or two others with you and go back again, so that everything you say may be confirmed by two or three witnesses. 17If that person still refuses to listen, take your case to the church. If the church decides you are right, but the other person won't accept it, treat that person as a pagan or a corrupt tax collector. 18I tell you this: Whatever you prohibit on earth is prohibited in heaven, and whatever you allow on earth is allowed in heaven.

19"I also tell you this: If two of you agree down here on earth concerning anything you ask, my Father in heaven will do it for you. 20For where two or three gather together because they are mine,* I am there among them."

18:15 Greek *your brother.* 18:20 Greek *gather together in my name.*

NEW KING JAMES VERSION

rejoices more over that *sheep* than over the ninety-nine that did not go astray. 14Even so it is not the will of your Father who is in heaven that one of these little ones should perish.

Dealing with a Sinning Brother

15"Moreover if your brother sins against you, go and tell him his fault between you and him alone. If he hears you, you have gained your brother. 16But if he will not hear, take with you one or two more, that *'by the mouth of two or three witnesses every word may be established.'*[b] 17And if he refuses to hear them, tell *it* to the church. But if he refuses even to hear the church, let him be to you like a heathen and a tax collector.

18"Assuredly, I say to you, whatever you bind on earth will be bound in heaven, and whatever you loose on earth will be loosed in heaven.

19"Again I say[c] to you that if two of you agree on earth concerning anything that they ask, it will be done for them by My Father in heaven. 20For where two or three are gathered together in My name, I am there in the midst of them."

18:16 [b] Deuteronomy 19:15 18:19 [c] NU-Text and M-Text read *Again, assuredly, I say.*

THE MESSAGE

make far more over it than over the ninety-nine who stay put? Your Father in heaven feels the same way. He doesn't want to lose even one of these simple believers.

"If a fellow believer hurts you, go and tell him—work it out between the two of you. If he listens, you've made a friend. If he won't listen, take one or two others along so that the presence of witnesses will keep things honest, and try again. If he still won't listen, tell the church. If he won't listen to the church, you'll have to start over from scratch, confront him with the need for repentance, and offer again God's forgiving love.

"Take this most seriously: A yes on earth is yes in heaven; a no on earth is no in heaven. What you say to one another is eternal. I mean this. When two of you get together on anything at all on earth and make a prayer of it, my Father in heaven goes into action. And when two or three of you are together because of me, you can be sure that I'll be there."

KING JAMES VERSION

21 ¶ Then came Peter to him, and said, Lord, how oft shall my brother sin against me, and I forgive him? till seven times?

22 Jesus saith unto him, I say not unto thee, Until seven times: but, Until seventy times seven.

23 Therefore is the kingdom of heaven likened unto a certain king, which would take account of his servants.

24 And when he had begun to reckon, one was brought unto him, which owed him ten thousand talents.

25 But forasmuch as he had not to pay, his lord commanded him to be sold, and his wife, and children, and all that he had, and payment to be made.

26 The servant therefore fell down, and worshipped him, saying, Lord, have patience with me, and I will pay thee all.

27 Then the lord of that servant was moved with compassion, and loosed him, and forgave him the debt.

28 But the same servant went out, and found one of his fellowservants, which owed him an hundred pence: and he laid hands on him, and took *him* by the throat, saying, Pay me that thou owest.

29 And his fellowservant fell down at his feet, and besought him, saying, Have patience with me, and I will pay thee all.

30 And he would not: but went and cast him into prison, till he should pay the debt.

NEW AMERICAN STANDARD BIBLE

Forgiveness

21 Then Peter came and said to Him, "Lord, how often shall my brother sin against me and I forgive him? Up to seven times?"

22 Jesus *said to him, "I do not say to you, up to seven times, but up to seventy times seven.

23 "For this reason the kingdom of heaven may be compared to a king who wished to settle accounts with his slaves.

24 "When he had begun to settle *them,* one who owed him [3]ten thousand talents was brought to him.

25 "But since he did not have *the means* to repay, his lord commanded him to be sold, along with his wife and children and all that he had, and repayment to be made.

26 "So the slave fell *to the ground* and prostrated himself before him, saying, 'Have patience with me and I will repay you everything.'

27 "And the lord of that slave felt compassion and released him and forgave him the debt.

28 "But that slave went out and found one of his fellow slaves who owed him a hundred [4]denarii; and he seized him and *began* to choke *him,* saying, 'Pay back what you owe.'

29 "So his fellow slave fell *to the ground* and *began* to plead with him, saying, 'Have patience with me and I will repay you.'

30 "But he was unwilling and went and threw him in prison until he should pay back what was owed.

18:24 [3] A talent was worth more than fifteen years' wages of a laborer
18:28 [4] The denarius was a day's wages

NEW CENTURY VERSION

An Unforgiving Servant

21 Then Peter came to Jesus and asked, "Lord, when my fellow believer sins against me, how many times must I forgive him? Should I forgive him as many as seven times?"

22 Jesus answered, "I tell you, you must forgive him more than seven times. You must forgive him even if he does wrong to you seventy-seven times.

23 "The kingdom of heaven is like a king who decided to collect the money his servants owed him. 24 When the king began to collect his money, a servant who owed him several million dollars was brought to him. 25 But the servant did not have enough money to pay his master, the king. So the master ordered that everything the servant owned should be sold, even the servant's wife and children. Then the money would be used to pay the king what the servant owed.

26 "But the servant fell on his knees and begged, 'Be patient with me, and I will pay you everything I owe.' 27 The master felt sorry for his servant and told him he did not have to pay it back. Then he let the servant go free.

28 "Later, that same servant found another servant who owed him a few dollars. The servant grabbed him around the neck and said, 'Pay me the money you owe me!'

29 "The other servant fell on his knees and begged him, 'Be patient with me, and I will pay you everything I owe.'

30 "But the first servant refused to be patient. He threw the other servant into prison until he could pay everything

CONTEMPORARY ENGLISH VERSION

An Official Who Refused To Forgive

21 Peter came up to the Lord and asked, "How many times should I forgive someone[e] who does something wrong to me? Is seven times enough?"

22 Jesus answered:

Not just seven times, but seventy-seven times![f] 23 This story will show you what the kingdom of heaven is like:

One day a king decided to call in his officials and ask them to give an account of what they owed him. 24 As he was doing this, one official was brought in who owed him fifty million silver coins. 25 But he didn't have any money to pay what he owed. The king ordered him to be sold, along with his wife and children and all he owned, in order to pay the debt.

26 The official got down on his knees and began begging, "Have pity on me, and I will pay you every cent I owe!" 27 The king felt sorry for him and let him go free. He even told the official that he did not have to pay back the money.

28 As the official was leaving, he happened to meet another official, who owed him a hundred silver coins. So he grabbed the man by the throat. He started choking him and said, "Pay me what you owe!"

29 The man got down on his knees and began begging, "Have pity on me, and I will pay you back." 30 But the first official refused to have pity. Instead, he went and had the other official put in jail until he could pay what he owed.

[e] **18.21** *someone*: Or "a follower." See the note at 18.15.
[f] **18.22** *seventy-seven times*: Or "seventy times seven." The large number means that one follower should never stop forgiving another.

NEW INTERNATIONAL VERSION

The Parable of the Unmerciful Servant

21 Then Peter came to Jesus and asked, "Lord, how many
times shall I forgive my brother when he sins against me?
Up to seven times?"
22 Jesus answered, "I tell you, not seven times, but sev-
enty-seven times.[e]
23 "Therefore, the kingdom of heaven is like a king who
wanted to settle accounts with his servants. 24 As he began
the settlement, a man who owed him ten thousand talents[f]
was brought to him. 25 Since he was not able to pay, the
master ordered that he and his wife and his children and
all that he had be sold to repay the debt.
26 "The servant fell on his knees before him. 'Be patient
with me,' he begged, 'and I will pay back everything.'
27 The servant's master took pity on him, canceled the debt
and let him go.
28 "But when that servant went out, he found one of his
fellow servants who owed him a hundred denarii.[g] He
grabbed him and began to choke him. 'Pay back what you
owe me!' he demanded.
29 "His fellow servant fell to his knees and begged him,
'Be patient with me, and I will pay you back.'
30 "But he refused. Instead, he went off and had the man
thrown into prison until he could pay the debt. 31 When the

[e] *22* Or *seventy times seven* [f] *24* That is, millions of dollars
[g] *28* That is, a few dollars

NEW LIVING TRANSLATION

Story of the Unforgiving Debtor

21 Then Peter came to him and asked, "Lord, how often
should I forgive someone* who sins against me? Seven
times?"
22 "No!" Jesus replied, "seventy times seven!*
23 "For this reason, the Kingdom of Heaven can be com-
pared to a king who decided to bring his accounts up to
date with servants who had borrowed money from him.
24 In the process, one of his debtors was brought in who
owed him millions of dollars.* 25 He couldn't pay, so the
king ordered that he, his wife, his children, and everything
he had be sold to pay the debt. 26 But the man fell down
before the king and begged him, 'Oh, sir, be patient with
me, and I will pay it all.' 27 Then the king was filled with
pity for him, and he released him and forgave his debt.
28 "But when the man left the king, he went to a fellow
servant who owed him a few thousand dollars.* He
grabbed him by the throat and demanded instant payment.
29 His fellow servant fell down before him and begged for a
little more time. 'Be patient and I will pay it,' he pleaded.
30 But his creditor wouldn't wait. He had the man arrested
and jailed until the debt could be paid in full.

18:21 Greek *my brother.* **18:22** Or *77 times.* **18:24** Greek *10,000 talents.* **18:28** Greek *100 denarii.* A denarius was the equivalent of a full day's wage.

NEW KING JAMES VERSION

The Parable of the Unforgiving Servant

21 Then Peter came to Him and said, "Lord, how often
shall my brother sin against me, and I forgive him? Up to
seven times?"
22 Jesus said to him, "I do not say to you, up to seven
times, but up to seventy times seven. 23 Therefore the king-
dom of heaven is like a certain king who wanted to settle
accounts with his servants. 24 And when he had begun to
settle accounts, one was brought to him who owed him ten
thousand talents. 25 But as he was not able to pay, his
master commanded that he be sold, with his wife and chil-
dren and all that he had, and that payment be made. 26 The
servant therefore fell down before him, saying, 'Master,
have patience with me, and I will pay you all.' 27 Then the
master of that servant was moved with compassion,
released him, and forgave him the debt.
28 "But that servant went out and found one of his fellow
servants who owed him a hundred denarii; and he laid
hands on him and took *him* by the throat, saying, 'Pay me
what you owe!' 29 So his fellow servant fell down at his
feet[d] and begged him, saying, 'Have patience with me, and
I will pay you all.'[e] 30 And he would not, but went and
threw him into prison till he should pay the debt. 31 So

18:29 [d] NU-Text omits *at his feet.* [e] NU-Text and M-Text omit *all.*

THE MESSAGE

A Story About Forgiveness

At that point Peter got up the nerve to ask, "Master, how many times do I forgive a brother or sister who hurts me? Seven?"

Jesus replied, "Seven! Hardly. Try seventy times seven.

"The kingdom of God is like a king who decided to square accounts with his servants. As he got under way, one servant was brought before him who had run up a debt of a hundred thousand dollars. He couldn't pay up, so the king ordered the man, along with his wife, children, and goods, to be auctioned off at the slave market.

"The poor wretch threw himself at the king's feet and begged, 'Give me a chance and I'll pay it all back.' Touched by his plea, the king let him off, erasing the debt.

"The servant was no sooner out of the room when he came upon one of his fellow servants who owed him ten dollars. He seized him by the throat and demanded, 'Pay up. Now!'

"The poor wretch threw himself down and begged, 'Give me a chance and I'll pay it all back.' But he wouldn't do it. He had him arrested and put in jail until the debt was

KING JAMES VERSION

31 So when his fellowservants saw what was done, they were very sorry, and came and told unto their lord all that was done.

32 Then his lord, after that he had called him, said unto him, O thou wicked servant, I forgave thee all that debt, because thou desiredst me:

33 Shouldest not thou also have had compassion on thy fellowservant, even as I had pity on thee?

34 And his lord was wroth, and delivered him to the tormentors, till he should pay all that was due unto him.

35 So likewise shall my heavenly Father do also unto you, if ye from your hearts forgive not every one his brother their trespasses.

19 And it came to pass, *that* when Jesus had finished these sayings, he departed from Galilee, and came into the coasts of Judaea beyond Jordan;

2 And great multitudes followed him; and he healed them there.

3 ¶ The Pharisees also came unto him, tempting him, and saying unto him, Is it lawful for a man to put away his wife for every cause?

4 And he answered and said unto them, Have ye not read, that he which made *them* at the beginning made them male and female,

5 And said, For this cause shall a man leave father and mother, and shall cleave to his wife: and they twain shall be one flesh?

6 Wherefore they are no more twain, but one flesh. What therefore God hath joined together, let not man put asunder.

NEW AMERICAN STANDARD BIBLE

31 "So when his fellow slaves saw what had happened, they were deeply grieved and came and reported to their lord all that had happened.

32 "Then summoning him, his lord *said to him, 'You wicked slave, I forgave you all that debt because you pleaded with me.

33 'Should you not also have had mercy on your fellow slave, in the same way that I had mercy on you?'

34 "And his lord, moved with anger, handed him over to the torturers until he should repay all that was owed him.

35 "My heavenly Father will also do the same to you, if each of you does not forgive his brother from your heart."

Concerning Divorce

19 When Jesus had finished these words, He departed from Galilee and came into the region of Judea beyond the Jordan;

2 and large crowds followed Him, and He healed them there.

3 *Some* Pharisees came to Jesus, testing Him and asking, "Is it lawful *for a man* to divorce his wife for any reason at all?"

4 And He answered and said, "Have you not read that He who created *them* from the beginning MADE THEM MALE AND FEMALE,

5 and said, 'FOR THIS REASON A MAN SHALL LEAVE HIS FATHER AND MOTHER AND BE JOINED TO HIS WIFE, AND THE TWO SHALL BECOME ONE FLESH'?

6 "So they are no longer two, but one flesh. What therefore God has joined together, let no man separate."

NEW CENTURY VERSION

he owed. 31When the other servants saw what had happened, they were very sorry. So they went and told their master all that had happened.

32"Then the master called his servant in and said, 'You evil servant! Because you begged me to forget what you owed, I told you that you did not have to pay anything. 33You should have showed mercy to that other servant, just as I showed mercy to you.' 34The master was very angry and put the servant in prison to be punished until he could pay everything he owed.

35"This king did what my heavenly Father will do to you if you do not forgive your brother or sister from your heart."

Jesus Teaches About Divorce

19 After Jesus said all these things, he left Galilee and went into the area of Judea on the other side of the Jordan River. 2Large crowds followed him, and he healed them there.

3Some Pharisees came to Jesus and tried to trick him. They asked, "Is it right for a man to divorce his wife for any reason he chooses?"

4Jesus answered, "Surely you have read in the Scriptures: When God made the world, 'he made them male and female.'[a] 5And God said, 'So a man will leave his father and mother and be united with his wife, and the two will become one body.'[b] 6So there are not two, but one. God has joined the two together, so no one should separate them."

19:4 [a] **'he made...female.'** Quotation from Genesis 1:27 or 5:2.
19:5 [b] **'So...body.'** Quotation from Genesis 2:24.

CONTEMPORARY ENGLISH VERSION

31When some other officials found out what had happened, they felt sorry for the man who had been put in jail. Then they told the king what had happened. 32The king called the first official back in and said, "You're an evil man! When you begged for mercy, I said you did not have to pay back a cent. 33Don't you think you should show pity to someone else, as I did to you?" 34The king was so angry that he ordered the official to be tortured until he could pay back everything he owed. 35That is how my Father in heaven will treat you, if you don't forgive each of my followers with all your heart.

Teaching about Divorce (Mark 10.1-12)

19 When Jesus finished teaching, he left Galilee and went to the part of Judea that is east of the Jordan River. 2Large crowds followed him, and he healed their sick people.

3Some Pharisees wanted to test Jesus. They came up to him and asked, "Is it right for a man to divorce his wife for just any reason?"

4Jesus answered, "Don't you know that in the beginning the Creator made a man and a woman? 5That's why a man leaves his father and mother and gets married. He becomes like one person with his wife. 6Then they are no longer two people, but one. And no one should separate a couple that God has joined together."

NEW INTERNATIONAL VERSION

other servants saw what had happened, they were greatly distressed and went and told their master everything that had happened.

32"Then the master called the servant in. 'You wicked servant,' he said, 'I canceled all that debt of yours because you begged me to. 33Shouldn't you have had mercy on your fellow servant just as I had on you?' 34In anger his master turned him over to the jailers to be tortured, until he should pay back all he owed.

35"This is how my heavenly Father will treat each of you unless you forgive your brother from your heart."

Divorce

19 When Jesus had finished saying these things, he left Galilee and went into the region of Judea to the other side of the Jordan. 2Large crowds followed him, and he healed them there.

3Some Pharisees came to him to test him. They asked, "Is it lawful for a man to divorce his wife for any and every reason?"

4"Haven't you read," he replied, "that at the beginning the Creator 'made them male and female,'[a] 5and said, 'For this reason a man will leave his father and mother and be united to his wife, and the two will become one flesh'[b]? 6So they are no longer two, but one. Therefore what God has joined together, let man not separate."

[a] *4* Gen. 1:27 [b] *5* Gen. 2:24

NEW LIVING TRANSLATION

31"When some of the other servants saw this, they were very upset. They went to the king and told him what had happened. 32Then the king called in the man he had forgiven and said, 'You evil servant! I forgave you that tremendous debt because you pleaded with me. 33Shouldn't you have mercy on your fellow servant, just as I had mercy on you?' 34Then the angry king sent the man to prison until he had paid every penny.

35"That's what my heavenly Father will do to you if you refuse to forgive your brothers and sisters* in your heart."

Discussion about Divorce and Marriage

19 After Jesus had finished saying these things, he left Galilee and went southward to the region of Judea and into the area east of the Jordan River. 2Vast crowds followed him there, and he healed their sick.

3Some Pharisees came and tried to trap him with this question: "Should a man be allowed to divorce his wife for any reason?"

4"Haven't you read the Scriptures?" Jesus replied. "They record that from the beginning 'God made them male and female.'* 5And he said, 'This explains why a man leaves his father and mother and is joined to his wife, and the two are united into one.'* 6Since they are no longer two but one, let no one separate them, for God has joined them together."

18:35 Greek *your brother.* **19:4** Gen 1:27; 5:2. **19:5** Gen 2:24.

NEW KING JAMES VERSION

when his fellow servants saw what had been done, they were very grieved, and came and told their master all that had been done. 32Then his master, after he had called him, said to him, 'You wicked servant! I forgave you all that debt because you begged me. 33Should you not also have had compassion on your fellow servant, just as I had pity on you?' 34And his master was angry, and delivered him to the torturers until he should pay all that was due to him.

35"So My heavenly Father also will do to you if each of you, from his heart, does not forgive his brother his trespasses."[f]

Marriage and Divorce

19 Now it came to pass, when Jesus had finished these sayings, *that* He departed from Galilee and came to the region of Judea beyond the Jordan. 2And great multitudes followed Him, and He healed them there.

3The Pharisees also came to Him, testing Him, and saying to Him, "Is it lawful for a man to divorce his wife for *just* any reason?"

4And He answered and said to them, "Have you not read that He who made[a] *them* at the beginning *'made them male and female,'*[b] 5and said, *'For this reason a man shall leave his father and mother and be joined to his wife, and the two shall become one flesh'*?[c] 6So then, they are no longer two but one flesh. Therefore what God has joined together, let not man separate."

18:35 [f] NU-Text omits *his trespasses.* **19:4** [a] NU-Text reads *created.* [b] Genesis 1:27; 5:2 **19:5** [c] Genesis 2:24

THE MESSAGE

paid. When the other servants saw this going on, they were outraged and brought a detailed report to the king.

"The king summoned the man and said, 'You evil servant! I forgave your entire debt when you begged me for mercy. Shouldn't you be compelled to be merciful to your fellow servant who asked for mercy?' The king was furious and put the screws to the man until he paid back his entire debt. And that's exactly what my Father in heaven is going to do to each one of you who doesn't forgive unconditionally anyone who asks for mercy."

Divorce

19 When Jesus had completed these teachings, he left Galilee and crossed the region of Judea on the other side of the Jordan. Great crowds followed him there, and he healed them.

One day the Pharisees were badgering him: "Is it legal for a man to divorce his wife for any reason?"

He answered, "Haven't you read in your Bible that the Creator originally made man and woman for each other, male and female? And because of this, a man leaves father and mother and is firmly bonded to his wife, becoming one flesh—no longer two bodies but one. Because God created this organic union of the two sexes, no one should desecrate his art by cutting them apart."

KING JAMES VERSION

7 They say unto him, Why did Moses then command to give a writing of divorcement, and to put her away?

8 He saith unto them, Moses because of the hardness of your hearts suffered you to put away your wives: but from the beginning it was not so.

9 And I say unto you, Whosoever shall put away his wife, except *it be* for fornication, and shall marry another, committeth adultery: and whoso marrieth her which is put away doth commit adultery.

10 His disciples say unto him, If the case of the man be so with *his* wife, it is not good to marry.

11 But he said unto them, All *men* cannot receive this saying, save *they* to whom it is given.

12 For there are some eunuchs, which were so born from *their* mother's womb: and there are some eunuchs, which were made eunuchs of men: and there be eunuchs, which have made themselves eunuchs for the kingdom of heaven's sake. He that is able to receive *it*, let him receive *it*.

13 ¶ Then were there brought unto him little children, that he should put *his* hands on them, and pray: and the disciples rebuked them.

14 But Jesus said, Suffer little children, and forbid them not, to come unto me: for of such is the kingdom of heaven.

15 And he laid *his* hands on them, and departed thence.

NEW AMERICAN STANDARD BIBLE

7 They *said to Him, "Why then did Moses command to GIVE HER A CERTIFICATE OF DIVORCE AND SEND *HER* AWAY?"

8 He *said to them, "Because of your hardness of heart Moses permitted you to divorce your wives; but from the beginning it has not been this way.

9 "And I say to you, whoever divorces his wife, except for immorality, and marries another woman commits adultery."

10 The disciples *said to Him, "If the relationship of the man with his wife is like this, it is better not to marry."

11 But He said to them, "Not all men *can* accept this statement, but *only* those to whom it has been given.

12 "For there are eunuchs who were born that way from their mother's womb; and there are eunuchs who were made eunuchs by men; and there are *also* eunuchs who made themselves eunuchs for the sake of the kingdom of heaven. He who is able to accept *this,* let him accept *it.*"

Jesus Blesses Little Children

13 Then *some* children were brought to Him so that He might lay His hands on them and pray; and the disciples rebuked them.

14 But Jesus said, "Let the children alone, and do not hinder them from coming to Me; for the kingdom of heaven belongs to such as these."

15 After laying His hands on them, He departed from there.

NEW CENTURY VERSION

7 The Pharisees asked, "Why then did Moses give a command for a man to divorce his wife by giving her divorce papers?"

8 Jesus answered, "Moses allowed you to divorce your wives because you refused to accept God's teaching, but divorce was not allowed in the beginning. 9 I tell you that anyone who divorces his wife and marries another woman is guilty of adultery. The only reason for a man to divorce his wife is if his wife has sexual relations with another man."

10 The followers said to him, "If that is the only reason a man can divorce his wife, it is better not to marry."

11 Jesus answered, "Not everyone can accept this teaching, but God has made some able to accept it. 12 There are different reasons why some men cannot marry. Some men were born without the ability to become fathers. Others were made that way later in life by other people. And some men have given up marriage because of the kingdom of heaven. But the person who can marry should accept this teaching about marriage."[c]

Jesus Welcomes Children

13 Then the people brought their little children to Jesus so he could put his hands on them[d] and pray for them. His followers told them to stop, 14 but Jesus said, "Let the little children come to me. Don't stop them, because the kingdom of heaven belongs to people who are like these children." 15 After Jesus put his hands on the children, he left there.

19:12 [c] **But...marriage.** This may also mean, "The person who can accept this teaching about not marrying should accept it." **19:13** [d] **put his hands on them** Showing that Jesus gave special blessings to these children.

CONTEMPORARY ENGLISH VERSION

7 The Pharisees asked Jesus, "Why did Moses say that a man could write out divorce papers and send his wife away?"

8 Jesus replied, "You are so heartless! That's why Moses allowed you to divorce your wife. But from the beginning God did not intend it to be that way. 9 I say that if your wife has not committed some terrible sexual sin,[a] you must not divorce her to marry someone else. If you do, you are unfaithful."

10 The disciples said, "If that's how it is between a man and a woman, it's better not to get married."

11 Jesus told them, "Only those people who have been given the gift of staying single can accept this teaching. 12 Some people are unable to marry because of birth defects or because of what someone has done to their bodies. Others stay single for the sake of the kingdom of heaven. Anyone who can accept this teaching should do so."

Jesus Blesses Little Children (Mark 10.13-16; Luke 18.15-17)

13 Some people brought their children to Jesus, so that he could place his hands on them and pray for them. His disciples told the people to stop bothering him. 14 But Jesus said, "Let the children come to me, and don't try to stop them! People who are like these children belong to God's kingdom."[b] 15 After Jesus had placed his hands on the children, he left.

[a] **19.9** *some terrible sexual sin*: See the note at 5.32. [b] **19.14** *People who are like these children belong to God's kingdom*: Or "God's kingdom belongs to people who are like these children."

NEW INTERNATIONAL VERSION

7"Why then," they asked, "did Moses command that a man give his wife a certificate of divorce and send her away?"

8Jesus replied, "Moses permitted you to divorce your wives because your hearts were hard. But it was not this way from the beginning. 9I tell you that anyone who divorces his wife, except for marital unfaithfulness, and marries another woman commits adultery."

10The disciples said to him, "If this is the situation between a husband and wife, it is better not to marry."

11Jesus replied, "Not everyone can accept this word, but only those to whom it has been given. 12For some are eunuchs because they were born that way; others were made that way by men; and others have renounced marriage[c] because of the kingdom of heaven. The one who can accept this should accept it."

The Little Children and Jesus

13Then little children were brought to Jesus for him to place his hands on them and pray for them. But the disciples rebuked those who brought them.

14Jesus said, "Let the little children come to me, and do not hinder them, for the kingdom of heaven belongs to such as these." 15When he had placed his hands on them, he went on from there.

[c] *12* Or *have made themselves eunuchs*

NEW LIVING TRANSLATION

7"Then why did Moses say a man could merely write an official letter of divorce and send her away?"* they asked.

8Jesus replied, "Moses permitted divorce as a concession to your hard-hearted wickedness, but it was not what God had originally intended. 9And I tell you this, a man who divorces his wife and marries another commits adultery—unless his wife has been unfaithful.*"

10Jesus' disciples then said to him, "Then it is better not to marry!"

11"Not everyone can accept this statement," Jesus said. "Only those whom God helps. 12Some are born as eunuchs, some have been made that way by others, and some choose not to marry for the sake of the Kingdom of Heaven. Let anyone who can, accept this statement."

Jesus Blesses the Children

13Some children were brought to Jesus so he could lay his hands on them and pray for them. The disciples told them not to bother him. 14But Jesus said, "Let the children come to me. Don't stop them! For the Kingdom of Heaven belongs to such as these." 15And he put his hands on their heads and blessed them before he left.

19:7 Deut 24:1. **19:9** Some manuscripts add *And the man who marries a divorced woman commits adultery.*

NEW KING JAMES VERSION

7They said to Him, "Why then did Moses command to give a certificate of divorce, and to put her away?"

8He said to them, "Moses, because of the hardness of your hearts, permitted you to divorce your wives, but from the beginning it was not so. 9And I say to you, whoever divorces his wife, except for sexual immorality,[d] and marries another, commits adultery; and whoever marries her who is divorced commits adultery."

10His disciples said to Him, "If such is the case of the man with *his* wife, it is better not to marry."

Jesus Teaches on Celibacy

11But He said to them, "All cannot accept this saying, but only *those* to whom it has been given: 12For there are eunuchs who were born thus from *their* mother's womb, and there are eunuchs who were made eunuchs by men, and there are eunuchs who have made themselves eunuchs for the kingdom of heaven's sake. He who is able to accept *it,* let him accept *it.*"

Jesus Blesses Little Children

13Then little children were brought to Him that He might put *His* hands on them and pray, but the disciples rebuked them. 14But Jesus said, "Let the little children come to Me, and do not forbid them; for of such is the kingdom of heaven." 15And He laid *His* hands on them and departed from there.

19:9 [d] Or *fornication*

THE MESSAGE

They shot back in rebuttal, "If that's so, why did Moses give instructions for divorce papers and divorce procedures?"

Jesus said, "Moses provided for divorce as a concession to your hardheartedness, but it is not part of God's original plan. I'm holding you to the original plan, and holding you liable for adultery if you divorce your faithful wife and then marry someone else. I make an exception in cases where the spouse has committed adultery."

Jesus' disciples objected, "If those are the terms of marriage, we're stuck. Why get married?"

But Jesus said, "Not everyone is mature enough to live a married life. It requires a certain aptitude and grace. Marriage isn't for everyone. Some, from birth seemingly, never give marriage a thought. Others never get asked—or accepted. And some decide not to get married for kingdom reasons. But if you're capable of growing into the largeness of marriage, do it."

To Enter God's Kingdom

One day children were brought to Jesus in the hope that he would lay hands on them and pray over them. The disciples shooed them off. But Jesus intervened: "Let the children alone, don't prevent them from coming to me. God's kingdom is made up of people like these." After laying hands on them, he left.

KING JAMES VERSION

16 ¶ And, behold, one came and said unto him, Good Master, what good thing shall I do, that I may have eternal life?

17 And he said unto him, Why callest thou me good? *there is* none good but one, *that is*, God: but if thou wilt enter into life, keep the commandments.

18 He saith unto him, Which? Jesus said, Thou shalt do no murder, Thou shalt not commit adultery, Thou shalt not steal, Thou shalt not bear false witness,

19 Honour thy father and *thy* mother: and, Thou shalt love thy neighbour as thyself.

20 The young man saith unto him, All these things have I kept from my youth up: what lack I yet?

21 Jesus said unto him, If thou wilt be perfect, go *and* sell that thou hast, and give to the poor, and thou shalt have treasure in heaven: and come *and* follow me.

22 But when the young man heard that saying, he went away sorrowful: for he had great possessions.

23 ¶ Then said Jesus unto his disciples, Verily I say unto you, That a rich man shall hardly enter into the kingdom of heaven.

24 And again I say unto you, It is easier for a camel to go through the eye of a needle, than for a rich man to enter into the kingdom of God.

NEW AMERICAN STANDARD BIBLE

The Rich Young Ruler

16 And someone came to Him and said, "Teacher, what good thing shall I do that I may obtain eternal life?"

17 And He said to him, "Why are you asking Me about what is good? There is *only* One who is good; but if you wish to enter into life, keep the commandments."

18 *Then* he *said to Him, "Which ones?" And Jesus said, "YOU SHALL NOT COMMIT MURDER; YOU SHALL NOT COMMIT ADULTERY; YOU SHALL NOT STEAL; YOU SHALL NOT BEAR FALSE WITNESS;

19 HONOR YOUR FATHER AND MOTHER; and YOU SHALL LOVE YOUR NEIGHBOR AS YOURSELF."

20 The young man *said to Him, "All these things I have kept; what am I still lacking?"

21 Jesus said to him, "If you wish to be complete, go *and* sell your possessions and give to *the* poor, and you will have treasure in heaven; and come, follow Me."

22 But when the young man heard this statement, he went away grieving; for he was one who owned much property.

23 And Jesus said to His disciples, "Truly I say to you, it is hard for a rich man to enter the kingdom of heaven.

24 "Again I say to you, it is easier for a camel to go through the eye of a needle, than for a rich man to enter the kingdom of God."

NEW CENTURY VERSION

A Rich Young Man's Question

16 A man came to Jesus and asked, "Teacher, what good thing must I do to have life forever?"

17 Jesus answered, "Why do you ask me about what is good? Only God is good. But if you want to have life forever, obey the commands."

18 The man asked, "Which commands?"

Jesus answered, " 'You must not murder anyone; you must not be guilty of adultery; you must not steal; you must not tell lies about your neighbor; 19 honor your father and mother;[e] and love your neighbor as you love yourself.' "[f]

20 The young man said, "I have obeyed all these things. What else do I need to do?"

21 Jesus answered, "If you want to be perfect, then go and sell your possessions and give the money to the poor. If you do this, you will have treasure in heaven. Then come and follow me."

22 But when the young man heard this, he left sorrowfully, because he was rich.

23 Then Jesus said to his followers, "I tell you the truth, it will be hard for a rich person to enter the kingdom of heaven. 24 Yes, I tell you that it is easier for a camel to go through the eye of a needle than for a rich person to enter the kingdom of God."

19:19 [e] **'You...mother.'** Quotation from Exodus 20:12–16; Deuteronomy 5:16–20. **19:19** [f] **'love...yourself.'** Quotation from Leviticus 19:18.

CONTEMPORARY ENGLISH VERSION

A Rich Young Man (Mark 10.17-31; Luke 18.18-30)

16 A man came to Jesus and asked, "Teacher, what good thing must I do to have eternal life?"

17 Jesus said to him, "Why do you ask me about what is good? Only God is good. If you want to have eternal life, you must obey his commandments."

18 "Which ones?" the man asked.

Jesus answered, "Do not murder. Be faithful in marriage. Do not steal. Do not tell lies about others. 19 Respect your father and mother. And love others as much as you love yourself." 20 The young man said, "I have obeyed all of these. What else must I do?"

21 Jesus replied, "If you want to be perfect, go sell everything you own! Give the money to the poor, and you will have riches in heaven. Then come and be my follower." 22 When the young man heard this, he was sad, because he was very rich.

23 Jesus said to his disciples, "It's terribly hard for rich people to get into the kingdom of heaven! 24 In fact, it's easier for a camel to go through the eye of a needle than for a rich person to get into God's kingdom."

NEW INTERNATIONAL VERSION

The Rich Young Man

16Now a man came up to Jesus and asked, "Teacher, what good thing must I do to get eternal life?"

17"Why do you ask me about what is good?" Jesus replied. "There is only One who is good. If you want to enter life, obey the commandments."

18"Which ones?" the man inquired.

Jesus replied, " 'Do not murder, do not commit adultery, do not steal, do not give false testimony, 19honor your father and mother,'[d] and 'love your neighbor as yourself.'[e]"

20"All these I have kept," the young man said. "What do I still lack?"

21Jesus answered, "If you want to be perfect, go, sell your possessions and give to the poor, and you will have treasure in heaven. Then come, follow me."

22When the young man heard this, he went away sad, because he had great wealth.

23Then Jesus said to his disciples, "I tell you the truth, it is hard for a rich man to enter the kingdom of heaven. 24Again I tell you, it is easier for a camel to go through the eye of a needle than for a rich man to enter the kingdom of God."

[d] *19* Exodus 20:12–16; Deut. 5:16–20 [e] *19* Lev. 19:18

NEW LIVING TRANSLATION

The Rich Young Man

16Someone came to Jesus with this question: "Teacher,* what good things must I do to have eternal life?"

17"Why ask me about what is good?" Jesus replied. "Only God is good. But to answer your question, you can receive eternal life if you keep the commandments."

18"Which ones?" the man asked.

And Jesus replied: " 'Do not murder. Do not commit adultery. Do not steal. Do not testify falsely. 19Honor your father and mother. Love your neighbor as yourself.'* "

20"I've obeyed all these commandments," the young man replied. "What else must I do?"

21Jesus told him, "If you want to be perfect, go and sell all you have and give the money to the poor, and you will have treasure in heaven. Then come, follow me." 22But when the young man heard this, he went sadly away because he had many possessions.

23Then Jesus said to his disciples, "I tell you the truth, it is very hard for a rich person to get into the Kingdom of Heaven. 24I say it again—it is easier for a camel to go through the eye of a needle than for a rich person to enter the Kingdom of God!"

19:16 Some manuscripts read *Good Teacher.* 19:18-19 Exod 20:12-16; Lev 19:18; Deut 5:16-20.

NEW KING JAMES VERSION

Jesus Counsels the Rich Young Ruler

16Now behold, one came and said to Him, "Good[e] Teacher, what good thing shall I do that I may have eternal life?"

17So He said to him, "Why do you call Me good?[f] No one *is* good but One, *that is,* God.[g] But if you want to enter into life, keep the commandments."

18He said to Him, "Which ones?"

Jesus said, " *'You shall not murder,' 'You shall not commit adultery,' 'You shall not steal,' 'You shall not bear false witness,'* 19*'Honor your father and your mother,'*[h] and, *'You shall love your neighbor as yourself.'* "[i]

20The young man said to Him, "All these things I have kept from my youth.[j] What do I still lack?"

21Jesus said to him, "If you want to be perfect, go, sell what you have and give to the poor, and you will have treasure in heaven; and come, follow Me."

22But when the young man heard that saying, he went away sorrowful, for he had great possessions.

With God All Things Are Possible

23Then Jesus said to His disciples, "Assuredly, I say to you that it is hard for a rich man to enter the kingdom of heaven. 24And again I say to you, it is easier for a camel to go through the eye of a needle than for a rich man to enter the kingdom of God."

19:16 [e] NU-Text omits *Good.* 19:17 [f] NU-Text reads *Why do you ask Me about what is good?* [g] NU-Text reads *There is One who is good.*
19:19 [h] Exodus 20:12–16; Deuteronomy 5:16–20 [i] Leviticus 19:18
19:20 [j] NU-Text omits *from my youth.*

THE MESSAGE

Another day, a man stopped Jesus and asked, "Teacher, what good thing must I do to get eternal life?"

Jesus said, "Why do you question me about what's good? *God* is the One who is good. If you want to enter the life of God, just do what he tells you."

The man asked, "What in particular?"

Jesus said, "Don't murder, don't commit adultery, don't steal, don't lie, honor your father and mother, and love your neighbor as you do yourself."

The young man said, "I've done all that. What's left?"

"If you want to give it all you've got," Jesus replied, "go sell your possessions; give everything to the poor. All your wealth will then be in heaven. Then come follow me."

That was the last thing the young man expected to hear. And so, crestfallen, he walked away. He was holding on tight to a lot of things, and he couldn't bear to let go.

As he watched him go, Jesus told his disciples, "Do you have any idea how difficult it is for the rich to enter God's kingdom? Let me tell you, it's easier to gallop a camel through a needle's eye than for the rich to enter God's kingdom."

KING JAMES VERSION

25 When his disciples heard *it*, they were exceedingly amazed, saying, Who then can be saved?

26 But Jesus beheld *them*, and said unto them, With men this is impossible; but with God all things are possible.

27 Then answered Peter and said unto him, Behold, we have forsaken all, and followed thee; what shall we have therefore?

28 And Jesus said unto them, Verily I say unto you, That ye which have followed me, in the regeneration when the Son of man shall sit in the throne of his glory, ye also shall sit upon twelve thrones, judging the twelve tribes of Israel.

29 And every one that hath forsaken houses, or brethren, or sisters, or father, or mother, or wife, or children, or lands, for my name's sake, shall receive an hundredfold, and shall inherit everlasting life.

30 But many *that are* first shall be last; and the last *shall be* first.

20 For the kingdom of heaven is like unto a man *that is* an householder, which went out early in the morning to hire labourers into his vineyard.

2 And when he had agreed with the labourers for a penny a day, he sent them into his vineyard.

3 And he went out about the third hour, and saw others standing idle in the marketplace,

4 And said unto them; Go ye also into the vineyard, and whatsoever is right I will give you. And they went their way.

NEW AMERICAN STANDARD BIBLE

25 When the disciples heard *this,* they were very astonished and said, "Then who can be saved?"

26 And looking at *them* Jesus said to them, "With people this is impossible, but with God all things are possible."

The Disciples' Reward

27 Then Peter said to Him, "Behold, we have left everything and followed You; what then will there be for us?"

28 And Jesus said to them, "Truly I say to you, that you who have followed Me, in the regeneration when the Son of Man will sit on His glorious throne, you also shall sit upon twelve thrones, judging the twelve tribes of Israel.

29 "And everyone who has left houses or brothers or sisters or father or mother [1]or children or farms for My name's sake, will receive many times as much, and will inherit eternal life.

30 "But many *who are* first will be last; and *the* last, first.

Laborers in the Vineyard

20 "For the kingdom of heaven is like a landowner who went out early in the morning to hire laborers for his vineyard.

2 "When he had agreed with the laborers for a [1]denarius for the day, he sent them into his vineyard.

3 "And he went out about the [2]third hour and saw others standing idle in the market place;

4 and to those he said, 'You also go into the vineyard, and whatever is right I will give you.' And *so* they went.

19:29 [1] One early ms adds *or wife* 20:2 [1] The denarius was a day's wages 20:3 [2] I.e. 9 a.m.

NEW CENTURY VERSION

25 When Jesus' followers heard this, they were very surprised and asked, "Then who can be saved?"

26 Jesus looked at them and said, "This is something people cannot do, but God can do all things."

27 Peter said to Jesus, "Look, we have left everything and followed you. So what will we have?"

28 Jesus said to them, "I tell you the truth, when the age
to come has arrived, the Son of Man will sit on his great
throne. All of you who followed me will also sit on twelve
thrones, judging the twelve tribes of Israel. 29 And all those
who have left houses, brothers, sisters, father, mother,
children, or farms to follow me will get much more than
they left, and they will have life forever. 30 Many who have
the highest place now will have the lowest place in the
future. And many who have the lowest place now will have
the highest place in the future.

A Story About Workers

20 "The kingdom of heaven is like a person who
owned some land. One morning, he went out very
early to hire some people to work in his vineyard. 2 The
man agreed to pay the workers one coin[a] for working that
day. Then he sent them into the vineyard to work. 3 About
nine o'clock the man went to the marketplace and saw
some other people standing there, doing nothing. 4 So he
said to them, 'If you go and work in my vineyard, I will
pay you what your work is worth.' 5 So they went to work

20:2 [a] **coin** A Roman denarius. One coin was the average pay for one day's work.

CONTEMPORARY ENGLISH VERSION

25 When the disciples heard this, they were greatly surprised and asked, "How can anyone ever be saved?"

26 Jesus looked straight at them and said, "There are some things that people cannot do, but God can do anything."

27 Peter replied, "Remember, we have left everything to be your followers! What will we get?"

28 Jesus answered:

Yes, all of you have become my followers. And so in
the future world, when the Son of Man sits on his glorious
throne, I promise that you will sit on twelve thrones
to judge the twelve tribes of Israel. 29 All who have given
up home or brothers and sisters or father and mother or
children or land for me will be given a hundred times as
much. They will also have eternal life. 30 But many who
are now first will be last, and many who are last will be
first.

Workers in a Vineyard

20 As Jesus was telling what the kingdom of heaven would be like, he said:

Early one morning a man went out to hire some workers
for his vineyard. 2 After he had agreed to pay them
the usual amount for a day's work, he sent them off to
his vineyard.

3 About nine that morning, the man saw some other
people standing in the market with nothing to do. 4 He
said he would pay them what was fair, if they would
work in his vineyard. 5 So they went.

NEW INTERNATIONAL VERSION

25 When the disciples heard this, they were greatly astonished and asked, "Who then can be saved?"

26 Jesus looked at them and said, "With man this is impossible, but with God all things are possible."

27 Peter answered him, "We have left everything to follow you! What then will there be for us?"

28 Jesus said to them, "I tell you the truth, at the renewal of all things, when the Son of Man sits on his glorious throne, you who have followed me will also sit on twelve thrones, judging the twelve tribes of Israel. 29 And everyone who has left houses or brothers or sisters or father or mother[f] or children or fields for my sake will receive a hundred times as much and will inherit eternal life. 30 But many who are first will be last, and many who are last will be first.

The Parable of the Workers in the Vineyard

20 "For the kingdom of heaven is like a landowner who went out early in the morning to hire men to work in his vineyard. 2 He agreed to pay them a denarius for the day and sent them into his vineyard.

3 "About the third hour he went out and saw others standing in the marketplace doing nothing. 4 He told them, 'You also go and work in my vineyard, and I will pay you whatever is right.' 5 So they went.

[f] 29 Some manuscripts *mother or wife*

NEW LIVING TRANSLATION

25 The disciples were astounded. "Then who in the world can be saved?" they asked.

26 Jesus looked at them intently and said, "Humanly speaking, it is impossible. But with God everything is possible."

27 Then Peter said to him, "We've given up everything to follow you. What will we get out of it?"

28 And Jesus replied, "I assure you that when I, the Son of Man, sit upon my glorious throne in the Kingdom,* you who have been my followers will also sit on twelve thrones, judging the twelve tribes of Israel. 29 And everyone who has given up houses or brothers or sisters or father or mother or children or property, for my sake, will receive a hundred times as much in return and will have eternal life. 30 But many who seem to be important now will be the least important then, and those who are considered least here will be the greatest then.*

Story of the Vineyard Workers

20 "For the Kingdom of Heaven is like the owner of an estate who went out early one morning to hire workers for his vineyard. 2 He agreed to pay the normal daily wage* and sent them out to work.

3 "At nine o'clock in the morning he was passing through the marketplace and saw some people standing around doing nothing. 4 So he hired them, telling them he would pay them whatever was right at the end of the day. 5 At

19:28 Greek *in the regeneration.* **19:30** Greek *But many who are first will be last; and the last, first.* **20:2** Greek *a denarius,* the payment for a full day's labor; also in 20:9, 10, 13.

NEW KING JAMES VERSION

25 When His disciples heard *it,* they were greatly astonished, saying, "Who then can be saved?"

26 But Jesus looked at *them* and said to them, "With men this is impossible, but with God all things are possible."

27 Then Peter answered and said to Him, "See, we have left all and followed You. Therefore what shall we have?"

28 So Jesus said to them, "Assuredly I say to you, that in the regeneration, when the Son of Man sits on the throne of His glory, you who have followed Me will also sit on twelve thrones, judging the twelve tribes of Israel. 29 And everyone who has left houses or brothers or sisters or father or mother or wife[k] or children or lands, for My name's sake, shall receive a hundredfold, and inherit eternal life. 30 But many *who are* first will be last, and the last first.

The Parable of the Workers in the Vineyard

20 "For the kingdom of heaven is like a landowner who went out early in the morning to hire laborers for his vineyard. 2 Now when he had agreed with the laborers for a denarius a day, he sent them into his vineyard. 3 And he went out about the third hour and saw others standing idle in the marketplace, 4 and said to them, 'You also go into the vineyard, and whatever is right I will give

19:29 [k] NU-Text omits *or wife.*

THE MESSAGE

The disciples were staggered. "Then who has any chance at all?"

Jesus looked hard at them and said, "No chance at all if you think you can pull it off yourself. Every chance in the world if you trust God to do it."

Then Peter chimed in, "We left everything and followed you. What do we get out of it?"

Jesus replied, "Yes, you have followed me. In the re-creation of the world, when the Son of Man will rule gloriously, you who have followed me will also rule, starting with the twelve tribes of Israel. And not only you, but anyone who sacrifices home, family, fields—whatever—because of me will get it all back a hundred times over, not to mention the considerable bonus of eternal life. This is the Great Reversal: many of the first ending up last, and the last first.

A Story About Workers

20 "God's kingdom is like an estate manager who went out early in the morning to hire workers for his vineyard. They agreed on a wage of a dollar a day, and went to work.

"Later, about nine o'clock, the manager saw some other men hanging around the town square unemployed. He told them to go to work in his vineyard and he would pay them a fair wage. They went.

KING JAMES VERSION

5 Again he went out about the sixth and ninth hour, and did likewise.

6 And about the eleventh hour he went out, and found others standing idle, and saith unto them, Why stand ye here all the day idle?

7 They say unto him, Because no man hath hired us. He saith unto them, Go ye also into the vineyard; and whatsoever is right, *that* shall ye receive.

8 So when even was come, the lord of the vineyard saith unto his steward, Call the labourers, and give them *their* hire, beginning from the last unto the first.

9 And when they came that *were hired* about the eleventh hour, they received every man a penny.

10 But when the first came, they supposed that they should have received more; and they likewise received every man a penny.

11 And when they had received *it*, they murmured against the goodman of the house,

12 Saying, These last have wrought *but* one hour, and thou hast made them equal unto us, which have borne the burden and heat of the day.

13 But he answered one of them, and said, Friend, I do thee no wrong: didst not thou agree with me for a penny?

14 Take *that* thine *is*, and go thy way: I will give unto this last, even as unto thee.

15 Is it not lawful for me to do what I will with mine own? Is thine eye evil, because I am good?

NEW AMERICAN STANDARD BIBLE

5 "Again he went out about the [3]sixth and the ninth hour, and did the same thing.

6 "And about the [4]eleventh *hour* he went out and found others standing *around;* and he *said to them, 'Why have you been standing here idle all day long?'

7 "They *said to him, 'Because no one hired us.' He *said to them, 'You go into the vineyard too.'

8 "When evening came, the owner of the vineyard *said to his foreman, 'Call the laborers and pay them their wages, beginning with the last *group* to the first.'

9 "When those *hired* about the eleventh hour came, each one received a [5]denarius.

10 "When those *hired* first came, they thought that they would receive more; but each of them also received a denarius.

11 "When they received it, they grumbled at the landowner,

12 saying, 'These last men have worked *only* one hour, and you have made them equal to us who have borne the burden and the scorching heat of the day.'

13 "But he answered and said to one of them, 'Friend, I am doing you no wrong; did you not agree with me for a denarius?

14 'Take what is yours and go, but I wish to give to this last man the same as to you.

15 'Is it not lawful for me to do what I wish with what is my own? Or is your eye envious because I am generous?'

20:5 [3] I.e. noon and 3 p.m. **20:6** [4] I.e. 5 p.m. **20:9** [5] The denarius was a day's wages

NEW CENTURY VERSION

in the vineyard. The man went out again about twelve o'clock and three o'clock and did the same thing. [6]About five o'clock the man went to the marketplace again and saw others standing there. He asked them, 'Why did you stand here all day doing nothing?' [7]They answered, 'No one gave us a job.' The man said to them, 'Then you can go and work in my vineyard.'

[8]"At the end of the day, the owner of the vineyard said to the boss of all the workers, 'Call the workers and pay them. Start with the last people I hired and end with those I hired first.'

[9]"When the workers who were hired at five o'clock came to get their pay, each received one coin. [10]When the workers who were hired first came to get their pay, they thought they would be paid more than the others. But each one of them also received one coin. [11]When they got their coin, they complained to the man who owned the land. [12]They said, 'Those people were hired last and worked only one hour. But you paid them the same as you paid us who worked hard all day in the hot sun.' [13]But the man who owned the vineyard said to one of those workers, 'Friend, I am being fair to you. You agreed to work for one coin. [14]So take your pay and go. I want to give the man who was hired last the same pay that I gave you. [15]I can do what I want with my own money. Are you jealous because I am good to those people?'

CONTEMPORARY ENGLISH VERSION

At noon and again about three in the afternoon he returned to the market. And each time he made the same agreement with others who were loafing around with nothing to do.

[6]Finally, about five in the afternoon the man went back and found some others standing there. He asked them, "Why have you been standing here all day long doing nothing?"

[7]"Because no one has hired us," they answered. Then he told them to go work in his vineyard.

[8]That evening the owner of the vineyard told the man in charge of the workers to call them in and give them their money. He also told the man to begin with the ones who were hired last. [9]When the workers arrived, the ones who had been hired at five in the afternoon were given a full day's pay.

[10]The workers who had been hired first thought they would be given more than the others. But when they were given the same, [11]they began complaining to the owner of the vineyard. [12]They said, "The ones who were hired last worked for only one hour. But you paid them the same that you did us. And we worked in the hot sun all day long!"

[13]The owner answered one of them, "Friend, I didn't cheat you. I paid you exactly what we agreed on. [14]Take your money now and go! What business is it of yours if I want to pay them the same that I paid you? [15]Don't I have the right to do what I want with my own money? Why should you be jealous, if I want to be generous?"

NEW INTERNATIONAL VERSION

"He went out again about the sixth hour and the ninth hour and did the same thing. [6]About the eleventh hour he went out and found still others standing around. He asked them, 'Why have you been standing here all day long doing nothing?'

[7]" 'Because no one has hired us,' they answered.

"He said to them, 'You also go and work in my vineyard.'

[8]"When evening came, the owner of the vineyard said to his foreman, 'Call the workers and pay them their wages, beginning with the last ones hired and going on to the first.'

[9]"The workers who were hired about the eleventh hour came and each received a denarius. [10]So when those came who were hired first, they expected to receive more. But each one of them also received a denarius. [11]When they received it, they began to grumble against the landowner. [12]'These men who were hired last worked only one hour,' they said, 'and you have made them equal to us who have borne the burden of the work and the heat of the day.'

[13]"But he answered one of them, 'Friend, I am not being unfair to you. Didn't you agree to work for a denarius? [14]Take your pay and go. I want to give the man who was hired last the same as I gave you. [15]Don't I have the right to do what I want with my own money? Or are you envious because I am generous?'

NEW LIVING TRANSLATION

noon and again around three o'clock he did the same thing. [6]At five o'clock that evening he was in town again and saw some more people standing around. He asked them, 'Why haven't you been working today?'

[7]"They replied, 'Because no one hired us.'

"The owner of the estate told them, 'Then go on out and join the others in my vineyard.'

[8]"That evening he told the foreman to call the workers in and pay them, beginning with the last workers first. [9]When those hired at five o'clock were paid, each received a full day's wage. [10]When those hired earlier came to get their pay, they assumed they would receive more. But they, too, were paid a day's wage. [11]When they received their pay, they protested, [12]'Those people worked only one hour, and yet you've paid them just as much as you paid us who worked all day in the scorching heat.'

[13]"He answered one of them, 'Friend, I haven't been unfair! Didn't you agree to work all day for the usual wage? [14]Take it and go. I wanted to pay this last worker the same as you. [15]Is it against the law for me to do what I want with my money? Should you be angry because I am kind?'

NEW KING JAMES VERSION

you.' So they went. [5]Again he went out about the sixth and the ninth hour, and did likewise. [6]And about the eleventh hour he went out and found others standing idle,[a] and said to them, 'Why have you been standing here idle all day?' [7]They said to him, 'Because no one hired us.' He said to them, 'You also go into the vineyard, and whatever is right you will receive.'[b]

[8]"So when evening had come, the owner of the vineyard said to his steward, 'Call the laborers and give them *their* wages, beginning with the last to the first.' [9]And when those came who *were hired* about the eleventh hour, they each received a denarius. [10]But when the first came, they supposed that they would receive more; and they likewise received each a denarius. [11]And when they had received *it,* they complained against the landowner, [12]saying, 'These last *men* have worked *only* one hour, and you made them equal to us who have borne the burden and the heat of the day.' [13]But he answered one of them and said, 'Friend, I am doing you no wrong. Did you not agree with me for a denarius? [14]Take *what is* yours and go your way. I wish to give to this last man *the same* as to you. [15]Is it not lawful for me to do what I wish with my own things? Or is your eye evil because I am good?' [16]So the

20:6 [a] NU-Text omits *idle.* 20:7 [b] NU-Text omits the last clause of this verse.

THE MESSAGE

"He did the same thing at noon, and again at three o'clock. At five o'clock he went back and found still others standing around. He said, 'Why are you standing around all day doing nothing?'

"They said, 'Because no one hired us.'

"He told them to go to work in his vineyard.

"When the day's work was over, the owner of the vineyard instructed his foreman, 'Call the workers in and pay them their wages. Start with the last hired and go on to the first.'

"Those hired at five o'clock came up and were each given a dollar. When those who were hired first saw that, they assumed they would get far more. But they got the same, each of them one dollar. Taking the dollar, they groused angrily to the manager, 'These last workers put in only one easy hour, and you just made them equal to us, who slaved all day under a scorching sun.'

"He replied to the one speaking for the rest, 'Friend, I haven't been unfair. We agreed on the wage of a dollar, didn't we? So take it and go. I decided to give to the one who came last the same as you. Can't I do what I want with my own money? Are you going to get stingy because I am generous?'

KING JAMES VERSION

16 So the last shall be first, and the first last: for many
be called, but few chosen.
17 ¶ And Jesus going up to Jerusalem took the twelve
disciples apart in the way, and said unto them,
18 Behold, we go up to Jerusalem; and the Son of man
shall be betrayed unto the chief priests and unto the
scribes, and they shall condemn him to death,
19 And shall deliver him to the Gentiles to mock, and to
scourge, and to crucify *him*: and the third day he shall rise
again.
20 ¶ Then came to him the mother of Zebedee's chil-
dren with her sons, worshipping *him*, and desiring a cer-
tain thing of him.
21 And he said unto her, What wilt thou? She saith
unto him, Grant that these my two sons may sit, the one
on thy right hand, and the other on the left, in thy king-
dom.
22 But Jesus answered and said, Ye know not what ye
ask. Are ye able to drink of the cup that I shall drink of,
and to be baptized with the baptism that I am baptized
with? They say unto him, We are able.
23 And he saith unto them, Ye shall drink indeed of my
cup, and be baptized with the baptism that I am baptized

NEW AMERICAN STANDARD BIBLE

16 "So the last shall be first, and the first last."

Death, Resurrection Foretold

17 As Jesus was about to go up to Jerusalem, He took
the twelve *disciples* aside by themselves, and on the way
He said to them,
18 "Behold, we are going up to Jerusalem; and the Son of
Man will be delivered to the chief priests and scribes, and
they will condemn Him to death,
19 and will hand Him over to the Gentiles to mock and
scourge and crucify *Him*, and on the third day He will be
raised up."

Preferment Asked

20 Then the mother of the sons of Zebedee came to Jesus
with her sons, bowing down and making a request of Him.
21 And He said to her, "What do you wish?" She *said
to Him, "Command that in Your kingdom these two sons of
mine may sit one on Your right and one on Your left."
22 But Jesus answered, "You do not know what you are
asking. Are you able to drink the cup that I am about to
drink?" They *said to Him, "We are able."
23 He *said to them, "My cup you shall drink; but to sit

NEW CENTURY VERSION

16 "So those who have the last place now will have the
first place in the future, and those who have the first place
now will have the last place in the future."

Jesus Talks About His Own Death

17 While Jesus was going to Jerusalem, he took his twelve
followers aside privately and said to them, 18 "Look, we are
going to Jerusalem. The Son of Man will be turned over to
the leading priests and the teachers of the law, and they
will say that he must die. 19 They will give the Son of Man
to the non-Jewish people to laugh at him and beat him
with whips and crucify him. But on the third day, he will
be raised to life again."

A Mother Asks Jesus a Favor

20 Then the wife of Zebedee came to Jesus with her sons.
She bowed before him and asked him to do something for
her.
21 Jesus asked, "What do you want?"
She said, "Promise that one of my sons will sit at your
right side and the other will sit at your left side in your
kingdom."
22 But Jesus said, "You don't understand what you are
asking. Can you drink the cup that I am about to drink?"[b]
The sons answered, "Yes, we can."
23 Jesus said to them, "You will drink from my cup. But I

20:22 [b] **drink...drink** Jesus used the idea of drinking from a cup to ask if they could accept the same terrible things that would happen to him.

CONTEMPORARY ENGLISH VERSION

16 Jesus then said, "So it is. Everyone who is now first
will be last, and everyone who is last will be first."

Jesus Again Tells about His Death

(Mark 10.32-34; Luke 18.31-34)

17 As Jesus was on his way to Jerusalem, he took his
twelve disciples aside and told them in private:
18 We are now on our way to Jerusalem, where the Son
of Man will be handed over to the chief priests and the
teachers of the Law of Moses. They will sentence him to
death, 19 and then they will hand him over to foreigners[a]
who will make fun of him. They will beat him and nail him
to a cross. But on the third day he will rise from death.

A Mother's Request (Mark 10.35-45)

20 The mother of James and John[b] came to Jesus with her
two sons. She knelt down and started begging him to do
something for her. 21 Jesus asked her what she wanted, and
she said, "When you come into your kingdom, please let one
of my sons sit at your right side and the other at your left."[c]
22 Jesus answered, "Not one of you knows what you are
asking. Are you able to drink from the cup[d] that I must
soon drink from?"
James and John said, "Yes, we are!"
23 Jesus replied, "You certainly will drink from my cup!

[a] 20.19 *foreigners*: The Romans, who ruled Judea at this time.
[b] 20.20 *mother of James and John*: The Greek text has "mother of the sons of Zebedee" (see 26.37). [c] 20.21 *right side . . . left*: The most powerful people in a kingdom sat at the right and left side of the king.
[d] 20.22 *drink from the cup*: In the Scriptures a cup is sometimes used as a symbol of suffering. To "drink from the cup" is to suffer.

NEW INTERNATIONAL VERSION

16"So the last will be first, and the first will be last."

Jesus Again Predicts His Death

17Now as Jesus was going up to Jerusalem, he took the twelve disciples aside and said to them, 18"We are going up to Jerusalem, and the Son of Man will be betrayed to the chief priests and the teachers of the law. They will condemn him to death 19and will turn him over to the Gentiles to be mocked and flogged and crucified. On the third day he will be raised to life!"

A Mother's Request

20Then the mother of Zebedee's sons came to Jesus with her sons and, kneeling down, asked a favor of him.

21"What is it you want?" he asked.

She said, "Grant that one of these two sons of mine may sit at your right and the other at your left in your kingdom."

22"You don't know what you are asking," Jesus said to them. "Can you drink the cup I am going to drink?"

"We can," they answered.

23Jesus said to them, "You will indeed drink from my

NEW LIVING TRANSLATION

16"And so it is, that many who are first now will be last then; and those who are last now will be first then."

Jesus Again Predicts His Death

17As Jesus was on the way to Jerusalem, he took the twelve disciples aside privately and told them what was going to happen to him. 18"When we get to Jerusalem," he said, "the Son of Man will be betrayed to the leading priests and the teachers of religious law. They will sentence him to die. 19Then they will hand him over to the Romans to be mocked, whipped, and crucified. But on the third day he will be raised from the dead."

Jesus Teaches about Serving Others

20Then the mother of James and John, the sons of Zebedee, came to Jesus with her sons. She knelt respectfully to ask a favor. 21"What is your request?" he asked.

She replied, "In your Kingdom, will you let my two sons sit in places of honor next to you, one at your right and the other at your left?"

22But Jesus told them, "You don't know what you are asking! Are you able to drink from the bitter cup of sorrow I am about to drink?"

"Oh yes," they replied, "we are able!"

23"You will indeed drink from it," he told them. "But I

NEW KING JAMES VERSION

last will be first, and the first last. For many are called, but few chosen."[c]

Jesus a Third Time Predicts His Death and Resurrection

17Now Jesus, going up to Jerusalem, took the twelve disciples aside on the road and said to them, 18"Behold, we are going up to Jerusalem, and the Son of Man will be betrayed to the chief priests and to the scribes; and they will condemn Him to death, 19and deliver Him to the Gentiles to mock and to scourge and to crucify. And the third day He will rise again."

Greatness Is Serving

20Then the mother of Zebedee's sons came to Him with her sons, kneeling down and asking something from Him.

21And He said to her, "What do you wish?"

She said to Him, "Grant that these two sons of mine may sit, one on Your right hand and the other on the left, in Your kingdom."

22But Jesus answered and said, "You do not know what you ask. Are you able to drink the cup that I am about to drink, and be baptized with the baptism that I am baptized with?"[d]

They said to Him, "We are able."

23So He said to them, "You will indeed drink My cup, and be baptized with the baptism that I am baptized with;[e]

20:16 [c] NU-Text omits the last sentence of this verse.
20:22 [d] NU-Text omits *and be baptized with the baptism that I am baptized with.* **20:23** [e] NU-Text omits *and be baptized with the baptism that I am baptized with.*

THE MESSAGE

"Here it is again, the Great Reversal: many of the first ending up last, and the last first."

To Drink From the Cup

Jesus, now well on the way up to Jerusalem, took the Twelve off to the side of the road and said, "Listen to me carefully. We are on our way up to Jerusalem. When we get there, the Son of Man will be betrayed to the religious leaders and scholars. They will sentence him to death. They will then hand him over to the Romans for mockery and torture and crucifixion. On the third day he will be raised up alive."

It was about that time that the mother of the Zebedee brothers came with her two sons and knelt before Jesus with a request.

"What do you want?" Jesus asked.

She said, "Give your word that these two sons of mine will be awarded the highest places of honor in your kingdom, one at your right hand, one at your left hand."

Jesus responded, "You have no idea what you're asking." And he said to James and John, "Are you capable of drinking the cup that I'm about to drink?"

They said, "Sure, why not?"

Jesus said, "Come to think of it, you *are* going to drink

KING JAMES VERSION

with: but to sit on my right hand, and on my left, is not mine to give, but *it shall be given to them* for whom it is prepared of my Father.

24 And when the ten heard *it*, they were moved with indignation against the two brethren.

25 But Jesus called them *unto him*, and said, Ye know that the princes of the Gentiles exercise dominion over them, and they that are great exercise authority upon them.

26 But it shall not be so among you: but whosoever will be great among you, let him be your minister;

27 And whosoever will be chief among you, let him be your servant:

28 Even as the Son of man came not to be ministered unto, but to minister, and to give his life a ransom for many.

29 ¶ And as they departed from Jericho, a great multitude followed him.

30 And, behold, two blind men sitting by the way side, when they heard that Jesus passed by, cried out, saying, Have mercy on us, O Lord, *thou* Son of David.

31 And the multitude rebuked them, because they should hold their peace: but they cried the more, saying, Have mercy on us, O Lord, *thou* Son of David.

32 And Jesus stood still, and called them, and said, What will ye that I shall do unto you?

33 They say unto him, Lord, that our eyes may be opened.

34 So Jesus had compassion *on them*, and touched their eyes: and immediately their eyes received sight, and they followed him.

NEW AMERICAN STANDARD BIBLE

on My right and on *My* left, this is not Mine to give, but it is for those for whom it has been prepared by My Father."

24 And hearing *this*, the ten became indignant with the two brothers.

25 But Jesus called them to Himself and said, "You know that the rulers of the Gentiles lord it over them, and *their* great men exercise authority over them.

26 "It is not this way among you, but whoever wishes to become great among you shall be your servant,

27 and whoever wishes to be first among you shall be your slave;

28 just as the Son of Man did not come to be served, but to serve, and to give His life a ransom for many."

Sight for the Blind

29 As they were leaving Jericho, a large crowd followed Him.

30 And two blind men sitting by the road, hearing that Jesus was passing by, cried out, "Lord, have mercy on us, Son of David!"

31 The crowd sternly told them to be quiet, but they cried out all the more, "Lord, Son of David, have mercy on us!"

32 And Jesus stopped and called them, and said, "What do you want Me to do for you?"

33 They *said to Him, "Lord, *we want* our eyes to be opened."

34 Moved with compassion, Jesus touched their eyes; and immediately they regained their sight and followed Him.

NEW CENTURY VERSION

cannot choose who will sit at my right or my left; those places belong to those for whom my Father has prepared them."

24When the other ten followers heard this, they were angry with the two brothers.

25Jesus called all the followers together and said, "You know that the rulers of the non-Jewish people love to show their power over the people. And their important leaders love to use all their authority. 26But it should not be that way among you. Whoever wants to become great among you must serve the rest of you like a servant. 27Whoever wants to become first among you must serve the rest of you like a slave. 28In the same way, the Son of Man did not come to be served. He came to serve others and to give his life as a ransom for many people."

Jesus Heals Two Blind Men

29When Jesus and his followers were leaving Jericho, a great many people followed him. 30Two blind men sitting by the road heard that Jesus was going by, so they shouted, "Lord, Son of David, have mercy on us!"

31The people warned the blind men to be quiet, but they shouted even more, "Lord, Son of David, have mercy on us!"

32Jesus stopped and said to the blind men, "What do you want me to do for you?"

33They answered, "Lord, we want to see."

34Jesus felt sorry for the blind men and touched their eyes, and at once they could see. Then they followed Jesus.

CONTEMPORARY ENGLISH VERSION

But it isn't for me to say who will sit at my right side and at my left. That is for my Father to say."

24When the ten other disciples heard this, they were angry with the two brothers. 25But Jesus called the disciples together and said:

You know that foreign rulers like to order their people around. And their great leaders have full power over everyone they rule. 26But don't act like them. If you want to be great, you must be the servant of all the others. 27And if you want to be first, you must be the slave of the rest. 28The Son of Man did not come to be a slave master, but a slave who will give his life to rescue[e] many people.

Jesus Heals Two Blind Men (Mark 10.46-52; Luke 18.35-43)

29Jesus was followed by a large crowd as he and his disciples were leaving Jericho. 30Two blind men were sitting beside the road. And when they heard that Jesus was coming their way, they shouted, "Lord and Son of David,[f] have pity on us!"

31The crowd told them to be quiet, but they shouted even louder, "Lord and Son of David, have pity on us!"

32When Jesus heard them, he stopped and asked, "What do you want me to do for you?"

33They answered, "Lord, we want to see!"

34Jesus felt sorry for them and touched their eyes. Right away they could see, and they became his followers.

[e] 20.28 *rescue*: The Greek word often, though not always, means the payment of a price to free a slave or a prisoner. [f] 20.30 *Son of David*: See the note at 9.27.

NEW INTERNATIONAL VERSION

cup, but to sit at my right or left is not for me to grant. These places belong to those for whom they have been prepared by my Father."

24 When the ten heard about this, they were indignant with the two brothers. 25 Jesus called them together and said, "You know that the rulers of the Gentiles lord it over them, and their high officials exercise authority over them. 26 Not so with you. Instead, whoever wants to become great among you must be your servant, 27 and whoever wants to be first must be your slave— 28 just as the Son of Man did not come to be served, but to serve, and to give his life as a ransom for many."

Two Blind Men Receive Sight

29 As Jesus and his disciples were leaving Jericho, a large crowd followed him. 30 Two blind men were sitting by the roadside, and when they heard that Jesus was going by, they shouted, "Lord, Son of David, have mercy on us!"

31 The crowd rebuked them and told them to be quiet, but they shouted all the louder, "Lord, Son of David, have mercy on us!"

32 Jesus stopped and called them. "What do you want me to do for you?" he asked.

33 "Lord," they answered, "we want our sight."

34 Jesus had compassion on them and touched their eyes. Immediately they received their sight and followed him.

NEW LIVING TRANSLATION

have no right to say who will sit on the thrones next to mine. My Father has prepared those places for the ones he has chosen."

24 When the ten other disciples heard what James and John had asked, they were indignant. 25 But Jesus called them together and said, "You know that in this world kings are tyrants, and officials lord it over the people beneath them. 26 But among you it should be quite different. Whoever wants to be a leader among you must be your servant, 27 and whoever wants to be first must become your slave. 28 For even I, the Son of Man, came here not to be served but to serve others, and to give my life as a ransom for many."

Jesus Heals Two Blind Men

29 As Jesus and the disciples left the city of Jericho, a huge crowd followed behind. 30 Two blind men were sitting beside the road. When they heard that Jesus was coming that way, they began shouting, "Lord, Son of David, have mercy on us!" 31 The crowd told them to be quiet, but they only shouted louder, "Lord, Son of David, have mercy on us!"

32 Jesus stopped in the road and called, "What do you want me to do for you?"

33 "Lord," they said, "we want to see!" 34 Jesus felt sorry for them and touched their eyes. Instantly they could see! Then they followed him.

NEW KING JAMES VERSION

but to sit on My right hand and on My left is not Mine to give, but *it is for those* for whom it is prepared by My Father."

24 And when the ten heard *it,* they were greatly displeased with the two brothers. 25 But Jesus called them to *Himself* and said, "You know that the rulers of the Gentiles lord it over them, and those who are great exercise authority over them. 26 Yet it shall not be so among you; but whoever desires to become great among you, let him be your servant. 27 And whoever desires to be first among you, let him be your slave— 28 just as the Son of Man did not come to be served, but to serve, and to give His life a ransom for many."

Two Blind Men Receive Their Sight

29 Now as they went out of Jericho, a great multitude followed Him. 30 And behold, two blind men sitting by the road, when they heard that Jesus was passing by, cried out, saying, "Have mercy on us, O Lord, Son of David!"

31 Then the multitude warned them that they should be quiet; but they cried out all the more, saying, "Have mercy on us, O Lord, Son of David!"

32 So Jesus stood still and called them, and said, "What do you want Me to do for you?"

33 They said to Him, "Lord, that our eyes may be opened." 34 So Jesus had compassion and touched their eyes. And immediately their eyes received sight, and they followed Him.

THE MESSAGE

my cup. But as to awarding places of honor, that's not my business. My Father is taking care of that."

When the ten others heard about this, they lost their tempers, thoroughly disgusted with the two brothers. So Jesus got them together to settle things down. He said, "You've observed how godless rulers throw their weight around, how quickly a little power goes to their heads. It's not going to be that way with you. Whoever wants to be great must become a servant. Whoever wants to be first among you must be your slave. That is what the Son of Man has done: He came to serve, not be served—and then to give away his life in exchange for the many who are held hostage."

✣

As they were leaving Jericho, a huge crowd followed. Suddenly they came upon two blind men sitting alongside the road. When they heard it was Jesus passing, they cried out, "Master, have mercy on us! Mercy, Son of David!" The crowd tried to hush them up, but they got all the louder, crying, "Master, have mercy on us! Mercy, Son of David!"

Jesus stopped and called over, "What do you want from me?"

They said, "Master, we want our eyes opened. We want to see!"

Deeply moved, Jesus touched their eyes. They had their sight back that very instant, and joined the procession.

KING JAMES VERSION

21 And when they drew nigh unto Jerusalem, and were come to Bethphage, unto the mount of Olives, then sent Jesus two disciples,

2 Saying unto them, Go into the village over against you, and straightway ye shall find an ass tied, and a colt with her: loose *them*, and bring *them* unto me.

3 And if any *man* say ought unto you, ye shall say, The Lord hath need of them; and straightway he will send them.

4 All this was done, that it might be fulfilled which was spoken by the prophet, saying,

5 Tell ye the daughter of Sion, Behold, thy King cometh unto thee, meek, and sitting upon an ass, and a colt the foal of an ass.

6 And the disciples went, and did as Jesus commanded them,

7 And brought the ass, and the colt, and put on them their clothes, and they set *him* thereon.

8 And a very great multitude spread their garments in the way; others cut down branches from the trees, and strawed *them* in the way.

9 And the multitudes that went before, and that followed,

NEW AMERICAN STANDARD BIBLE

The Triumphal Entry

21 When they had approached Jerusalem and had come to Bethphage, at the Mount of Olives, then Jesus sent two disciples,

2 saying to them, "Go into the village opposite you, and immediately you will find a donkey tied *there* and a colt with her; untie them and bring them to Me.

3 "If anyone says anything to you, you shall say, 'The Lord has need of them,' and immediately he will send them."

4 This took place to fulfill what was spoken through the prophet:

5 "SAY TO THE DAUGHTER OF ZION,
'BEHOLD YOUR KING IS COMING TO YOU,
GENTLE, AND MOUNTED ON A DONKEY,
EVEN ON A COLT, THE FOAL OF A BEAST OF BURDEN.' "

6 The disciples went and did just as Jesus had instructed them,

7 and brought the donkey and the colt, and laid their coats on them; and He sat on the coats.

8 Most of the crowd spread their coats in the road, and others were cutting branches from the trees and spreading them in the road.

9 The crowds going ahead of Him, and those who followed, were shouting,

NEW CENTURY VERSION

Jesus Enters Jerusalem as a King

21 As Jesus and his followers were coming closer to
Jerusalem, they stopped at Bethphage at the hill
called the Mount of Olives. From there Jesus sent two of
his followers 2 and said to them, "Go to the town you can
see there. When you enter it, you will quickly find a don-
key tied there with its colt. Untie them and bring them to
me. 3 If anyone asks you why you are taking the donkeys,
say that the Master needs them, and he will send them at
once."
4 This was to bring about what the prophet had said:
5 "Tell the people of Jerusalem,
'Your king is coming to you.
He is gentle and riding on a donkey,
on the colt of a donkey.' " *Isaiah 62:11; Zechariah 9:9*
6 The followers went and did what Jesus told them to do.
7 They brought the donkey and the colt to Jesus and laid
their coats on them, and Jesus sat on them. 8 Many people
spread their coats on the road. Others cut branches from
the trees and spread them on the road. 9 The people were
walking ahead of Jesus and behind him, shouting,

CONTEMPORARY ENGLISH VERSION

Jesus Enters Jerusalem

(Mark 11.1-11; Luke 19.28-38; John 12.12-19)

21 When Jesus and his disciples came near Jerusalem,
he went to Bethphage on the Mount of Olives and
sent two of them on ahead. 2 He told them, "Go into the
next village, where you will at once find a donkey and her
colt. Untie the two donkeys and bring them to me. 3 If any-
one asks why you are doing that, just say, 'The Lord[a] needs
them.' Right away he will let you have the donkeys."
4 So God's promise came true, just as the prophet had
said,

5 "Announce to the people
of Jerusalem:
'Your king is coming to you!
He is humble
and rides on a donkey.
He comes on the colt
of a donkey.' "

6 The disciples left and did what Jesus had told them to
do. 7 They brought the donkey and its colt and laid some
clothes on their backs. Then Jesus got on.
8 Many people spread clothes in the road, while others
put down branches[b] which they had cut from trees. 9 Some
people walked ahead of Jesus and others followed behind.
They were all shouting,

[a] 21.3 *The Lord*: Or "The master of the donkeys." [b] 21.8 *spread clothes . . . put down branches*: This was one way that the Jewish people welcomed a famous person.

NEW INTERNATIONAL VERSION

The Triumphal Entry

21 As they approached Jerusalem and came to Bethphage on the Mount of Olives, Jesus sent two disciples, 2saying to them, "Go to the village ahead of you, and at once you will find a donkey tied there, with her colt by her. Untie them and bring them to me. 3If anyone says anything to you, tell him that the Lord needs them, and he will send them right away."

4This took place to fulfill what was spoken through the prophet:

5 "Say to the Daughter of Zion,
'See, your king comes to you,
gentle and riding on a donkey,
on a colt, the foal of a donkey.' "[a]

6The disciples went and did as Jesus had instructed them. 7They brought the donkey and the colt, placed their cloaks on them, and Jesus sat on them. 8A very large crowd spread their cloaks on the road, while others cut branches from the trees and spread them on the road. 9The crowds that went ahead of him and those that followed shouted,

[a] *5* Zech. 9:9

NEW LIVING TRANSLATION

The Triumphal Entry

21 As Jesus and the disciples approached Jerusalem, they came to the town of Bethphage on the Mount of Olives. Jesus sent two of them on ahead. 2"Go into the village over there," he said, "and you will see a donkey tied there, with its colt beside it. Untie them and bring them here. 3If anyone asks what you are doing, just say, 'The Lord needs them,' and he will immediately send them." 4This was done to fulfill the prophecy,

5 "Tell the people of Israel,*
'Look, your King is coming to you.
He is humble, riding on a donkey—
even on a donkey's colt.' "*

6The two disciples did as Jesus said. 7They brought the animals to him and threw their garments over the colt, and he sat on it.*

8Most of the crowd spread their coats on the road ahead of Jesus, and others cut branches from the trees and spread them on the road. 9He was in the center of the procession, and the crowds all around him were shouting,

21:5a Greek *Tell the daughter of Zion.* Isa 62:11. 21:5b Zech 9:9.
21:7 Greek *over them, and he sat on them.*

NEW KING JAMES VERSION

The Triumphal Entry

21 Now when they drew near Jerusalem, and came to Bethphage,[a] at the Mount of Olives, then Jesus sent two disciples, 2saying to them, "Go into the village opposite you, and immediately you will find a donkey tied, and a colt with her. Loose *them* and bring *them* to Me. 3And if anyone says anything to you, you shall say, 'The Lord has need of them,' and immediately he will send them."

4All[b] this was done that it might be fulfilled which was spoken by the prophet, saying:

5 "*Tell the daughter of Zion,*
'Behold, your King is coming to you,
Lowly, and sitting on a donkey,
A colt, the foal of a donkey.' "[c]

6So the disciples went and did as Jesus commanded them. 7They brought the donkey and the colt, laid their clothes on them, and set *Him*[d] on them. 8And a very great multitude spread their clothes on the road; others cut down branches from the trees and spread *them* on the road. 9Then the multitudes who went before and those who followed cried out, saying:

21:1 [a] M-Text reads *Bethsphage.* 21:4 [b] NU-Text omits *All.*
21:5 [c] Zechariah 9:9 21:7 [d] NU-Text reads *and He sat.*

THE MESSAGE

The Royal Welcome

21 When they neared Jerusalem, having arrived at Bethphage on Mount Olives, Jesus sent two disciples with these instructions: "Go over to the village across from you. You'll find a donkey tethered there, her colt with her. Untie her and bring them to me. If anyone asks what you're doing, say, 'The Master needs them!' He will send them with you."

This is the full story of what was sketched earlier by the prophet:

"Tell Zion's daughter,
'Look, your king's on his way,
poised and ready, mounted
On a donkey, on a colt,
foal of a pack animal.' "

The disciples went and did exactly what Jesus told them to do. They led the donkey and colt out, laid some of their clothes on them, and Jesus mounted. Nearly all the people in the crowd threw their garments down on the road, giving him a royal welcome. Others cut branches from the trees and threw them down as a welcome mat. Crowds went ahead and crowds followed, all of them calling out,

KING JAMES VERSION

cried, saying, Hosanna to the Son of David: Blessed *is* he that cometh in the name of the Lord; Hosanna in the highest.

10 And when he was come into Jerusalem, all the city was moved, saying, Who is this?

11 And the multitude said, This is Jesus the prophet of Nazareth of Galilee.

12 ¶ And Jesus went into the temple of God, and cast out all them that sold and bought in the temple, and overthrew the tables of the moneychangers, and the seats of them that sold doves,

13 And said unto them, It is written, My house shall be called the house of prayer; but ye have made it a den of thieves.

14 And the blind and the lame came to him in the temple; and he healed them.

15 And when the chief priests and scribes saw the wonderful things that he did, and the children crying in the temple, and saying, Hosanna to the Son of David; they were sore displeased,

16 And said unto him, Hearest thou what these say?

NEW AMERICAN STANDARD BIBLE

"Hosanna to the Son of David;
BLESSED IS HE WHO COMES IN THE NAME OF THE LORD;
Hosanna in the highest!"

10 When He had entered Jerusalem, all the city was stirred, saying, "Who is this?"

11 And the crowds were saying, "This is the prophet Jesus, from Nazareth in Galilee."

Cleansing the Temple

12 And Jesus entered the temple and drove out all those who were buying and selling in the temple, and overturned the tables of the money changers and the seats of those who were selling doves.

13 And He *said to them, "It is written, 'MY HOUSE SHALL BE CALLED A HOUSE OF PRAYER'; but you are making it a ROBBERS' DEN."

14 And *the* blind and *the* lame came to Him in the temple, and He healed them.

15 But when the chief priests and the scribes saw the wonderful things that He had done, and the children who were shouting in the temple, "Hosanna to the Son of David," they became indignant

16 and said to Him, "Do You hear what these *children*

NEW CENTURY VERSION

"Praise[a] to the Son of David!
God bless the One who comes in the name
of the Lord! *Psalm 118:26*
Praise to God in heaven!"

10When Jesus entered Jerusalem, all the city was filled
with excitement. The people asked, "Who is this man?"
11The crowd said, "This man is Jesus, the prophet from
the town of Nazareth in Galilee."

Jesus Goes to the Temple

12Jesus went into the Temple and threw out all the people
who were buying and selling there. He turned over the tables
of those who were exchanging different kinds of money, and
he upset the benches of those who were selling doves.
13Jesus said to all the people there, "It is written in the
Scriptures, 'My Temple will be called a house for prayer.'[b]
But you are changing it into a 'hideout for robbers.' "[c]
14The blind and crippled people came to Jesus in the
Temple, and he healed them. 15The leading priests and the
teachers of the law saw that Jesus was doing wonderful
things and that the children were praising him in the Temple,
saying, "Praise[a] to the Son of David." All these things made
the priests and the teachers of the law very angry.
16They asked Jesus, "Do you hear the things these children are saying?"

21:9,15 [a] **Praise** Literally, "Hosanna," a Hebrew word used at first in praying to God for help. At this time it was probably a shout of joy used in praising God or his Messiah. 21:13 [b] **'My Temple...prayer.'** Quotation from Isaiah 56:7. 21:13 [c] **'hideout for robbers.'** Quotation from Jeremiah 7:11.

CONTEMPORARY ENGLISH VERSION

"Hooray[c] for the Son of David![d]
God bless the one who comes
in the name of the Lord.
Hooray for God
in heaven above!"

10When Jesus came to Jerusalem, everyone in the city
was excited and asked, "Who can this be?"
11The crowd answered, "This is Jesus, the prophet from
Nazareth in Galilee."

Jesus in the Temple
(Mark 11.15-19; Luke 19.45-48; John 2.13-22)

12Jesus went into the temple and chased out everyone
who was selling or buying. He turned over the tables of the
moneychangers and the benches of the ones who were selling doves. 13He told them, "The Scriptures say, 'My house
should be called a place of worship.' But you have turned
it into a place where robbers hide."
14Blind and lame people came to Jesus in the temple,
and he healed them. 15But the chief priests and the teachers of the Law of Moses were angry when they saw his
miracles and heard the children shouting praises to the
Son of David.[d] 16The men said to Jesus, "Don't you hear
what those children are saying?"

[c] **21.9** *Hooray*: This translates a word that can mean "please save us." But it is most often used as a shout of praise to God. [d] **21.9,15** *Son of David*: See the note at 9.27.

NEW INTERNATIONAL VERSION

"Hosanna[b] to the Son of David!"

"Blessed is he who comes in the name of the Lord!"[c]

"Hosanna[b] in the highest!"

10When Jesus entered Jerusalem, the whole city was stirred and asked, "Who is this?"
11The crowds answered, "This is Jesus, the prophet from Nazareth in Galilee."

Jesus at the Temple

12Jesus entered the temple area and drove out all who were buying and selling there. He overturned the tables of the money changers and the benches of those selling doves. 13"It is written," he said to them, " 'My house will be called a house of prayer,'[d] but you are making it a 'den of robbers.'[e]"
14The blind and the lame came to him at the temple, and he healed them. 15But when the chief priests and the teachers of the law saw the wonderful things he did and the children shouting in the temple area, "Hosanna to the Son of David," they were indignant.
16"Do you hear what these children are saying?" they asked him.

[b] *9* A Hebrew expression meaning "Save!" which became an exclamation of praise; also in verse 15 [c] *9* Psalm 118:26 [d] *13* Isaiah 56:7 [e] *13* Jer. 7:11

NEW LIVING TRANSLATION

"Praise God* for the Son of David!
Bless the one who comes in the name of the Lord!
Praise God in highest heaven!"*

10The entire city of Jerusalem was stirred as he entered. "Who is this?" they asked.
11And the crowds replied, "It's Jesus, the prophet from Nazareth in Galilee."

Jesus Clears the Temple

12Jesus entered the Temple and began to drive out the merchants and their customers. He knocked over the tables of the money changers and the stalls of those selling doves. 13He said, "The Scriptures declare, 'My Temple will be called a place of prayer,' but you have turned it into a den of thieves!"*
14The blind and the lame came to him, and he healed them there in the Temple. 15The leading priests and the teachers of religious law saw these wonderful miracles and heard even the little children in the Temple shouting, "Praise God for the Son of David." But they were indignant
16and asked Jesus, "Do you hear what these children are saying?"

21:9a Greek *Hosanna,* an exclamation of praise that literally means "save now"; also in 21:9b, 15. **21:9b** Pss 118:25-26; 148:1. **21:13** Isa 56:7; Jer 7:11.

NEW KING JAMES VERSION

"Hosanna to the Son of David!
'*Blessed is He who comes in the name of the* LORD!'[e]
Hosanna in the highest!"

10And when He had come into Jerusalem, all the city was moved, saying, "Who is this?"
11So the multitudes said, "This is Jesus, the prophet from Nazareth of Galilee."

Jesus Cleanses the Temple

12Then Jesus went into the temple of God[f] and drove out all those who bought and sold in the temple, and overturned the tables of the money changers and the seats of those who sold doves. 13And He said to them, "It is written, '*My house shall be called a house of prayer,*'[g] but you have made it a '*den of thieves.*' "[h]
14Then *the* blind and *the* lame came to Him in the temple, and He healed them. 15But when the chief priests and scribes saw the wonderful things that He did, and the children crying out in the temple and saying, "Hosanna to the Son of David!" they were indignant 16and said to Him, "Do You hear what these are saying?"

21:9 [e] Psalm 118:26 **21:12** [f] NU-Text omits *of God.*
21:13 [g] Isaiah 56:7 [h] Jeremiah 7:11

THE MESSAGE

"Hosanna to David's son!" "Blessed is he who comes in God's name!" "Hosanna in highest heaven!"
As he made his entrance into Jerusalem, the whole city was shaken. Unnerved, people were asking, "What's going on here? Who is this?"
The parade crowd answered, "This is the prophet Jesus, the one from Nazareth in Galilee."

He Kicked Over the Tables

Jesus went straight to the Temple and threw out everyone who had set up shop, buying and selling. He kicked over the tables of loan sharks and the stalls of dove merchants. He quoted this text:

"My house was designated a house of prayer;
You have made it a hangout for thieves."

Now there was room for the blind and crippled to get in. They came to Jesus and he healed them.
When the religious leaders saw the outrageous things he was doing, and heard all the children running and shouting through the Temple, "Hosanna to David's Son!" they were up in arms and took him to task. "Do you hear what these children are saying?"

KING JAMES VERSION

And Jesus saith unto them, Yea; have ye never read, Out of the mouth of babes and sucklings thou hast perfected praise?

17 And he left them, and went out of the city into Bethany; and he lodged there.

18 ¶ Now in the morning as he returned into the city, he hungered.

19 And when he saw a fig tree in the way, he came to it, and found nothing thereon, but leaves only, and said unto it, Let no fruit grow on thee henceforward for ever. And presently the fig tree withered away.

20 And when the disciples saw *it*, they marvelled, saying, How soon is the fig tree withered away!

21 Jesus answered and said unto them, Verily I say unto you, If ye have faith, and doubt not, ye shall not only do this *which is done* to the fig tree, but also if ye shall say unto this mountain, Be thou removed, and be thou cast into the sea; it shall be done.

22 And all things, whatsoever ye shall ask in prayer, believing, ye shall receive.

23 ¶ And when he was come into the temple, the chief priests and the elders of the people came unto him as he

NEW AMERICAN STANDARD BIBLE

are saying?" And Jesus *said to them, "Yes; have you never read, 'OUT OF THE MOUTH OF INFANTS AND NURSING BABIES YOU HAVE PREPARED PRAISE FOR YOURSELF'?"

17 And He left them and went out of the city to Bethany, and spent the night there.

The Barren Fig Tree

18 Now in the morning, when He was returning to the city, He became hungry.

19 Seeing a lone fig tree by the road, He came to it and found nothing on it except leaves only; and He *said to it, "No longer shall there ever be *any* fruit from you." And at once the fig tree withered.

20 Seeing *this,* the disciples were amazed and asked, "How did the fig tree wither *all* at once?"

21 And Jesus answered and said to them, "Truly I say to you, if you have faith and do not doubt, you will not only do what was done to the fig tree, but even if you say to this mountain, 'Be taken up and cast into the sea,' it will happen.

22 "And all things you ask in prayer, believing, you will receive."

Authority Challenged

23 When He entered the temple, the chief priests and the elders of the people came to Him while He was teaching,

NEW CENTURY VERSION

Jesus answered, "Yes. Haven't you read in the Scriptures, 'You have taught children and babies to sing praises'?"[e]

17 Then Jesus left and went out of the city to Bethany, where he spent the night.

The Power of Faith

18 Early the next morning, as Jesus was going back to the city, he became hungry. 19 Seeing a fig tree beside the road, Jesus went to it, but there were no figs on the tree, only leaves. So Jesus said to the tree, "You will never again have fruit." The tree immediately dried up.

20 When his followers saw this, they were amazed. They asked, "How did the fig tree dry up so quickly?"

21 Jesus answered, "I tell you the truth, if you have faith and do not doubt, you will be able to do what I did to this tree and even more. You will be able to say to this mountain, 'Go, fall into the sea.' And if you have faith, it will happen. 22 If you believe, you will get anything you ask for in prayer."

Leaders Doubt Jesus' Authority

23 Jesus went to the Temple, and while he was teaching there, the leading priests and the older leaders of the people

21:16 [e] **'You...praises'** Quotation from the Septuagint (Greek) version of Psalm 8:2.

CONTEMPORARY ENGLISH VERSION

"Yes, I do!" Jesus answered. "Don't you know that the Scriptures say, 'Children and infants will sing praises'?"
17 Then Jesus left the city and went out to the village of Bethany, where he spent the night.

Jesus Puts a Curse on a Fig Tree (Mark 11.12-14, 20-24)

18 When Jesus got up the next morning, he was hungry. He started out for the city, 19 and along the way he saw a fig tree. But when he came to it, he found only leaves and no figs. So he told the tree, "You will never again grow any fruit!" Right then the fig tree dried up.

20 The disciples were shocked when they saw how quickly the tree had dried up. 21 But Jesus said to them, "If you have faith and don't doubt, I promise that you can do what I did to this tree. And you will be able to do even more. You can tell this mountain to get up and jump into the sea, and it will. 22 If you have faith when you pray, you will be given whatever you ask for."

A Question about Jesus' Authority
(Mark 11.27-33; Luke 20.1-8)

23 Jesus had gone into the temple and was teaching when the chief priests and the leaders of the people came

NEW INTERNATIONAL VERSION

"Yes," replied Jesus, "have you never read,

" 'From the lips of children and infants
you have ordained praise'[g]?"

17And he left them and went out of the city to Bethany, where he spent the night.

The Fig Tree Withers

18Early in the morning, as he was on his way back to the city, he was hungry. 19Seeing a fig tree by the road, he went up to it but found nothing on it except leaves. Then he said to it, "May you never bear fruit again!" Immediately the tree withered.

20When the disciples saw this, they were amazed. "How did the fig tree wither so quickly?" they asked.

21Jesus replied, "I tell you the truth, if you have faith and do not doubt, not only can you do what was done to the fig tree, but also you can say to this mountain, 'Go, throw yourself into the sea,' and it will be done. 22If you believe, you will receive whatever you ask for in prayer."

The Authority of Jesus Questioned

23Jesus entered the temple courts, and, while he was teaching, the chief priests and the elders of the people

[g] *16* Psalm 8:2

NEW LIVING TRANSLATION

"Yes," Jesus replied. "Haven't you ever read the Scriptures? For they say, 'You have taught children and infants to give you praise.'* " 17Then he returned to Bethany, where he stayed overnight.

Jesus Curses the Fig Tree

18In the morning, as Jesus was returning to Jerusalem, he was hungry, 19and he noticed a fig tree beside the road. He went over to see if there were any figs on it, but there were only leaves. Then he said to it, "May you never bear fruit again!" And immediately the fig tree withered up.

20The disciples were amazed when they saw this and asked, "How did the fig tree wither so quickly?"

21Then Jesus told them, "I assure you, if you have faith and don't doubt, you can do things like this and much more. You can even say to this mountain, 'May God lift you up and throw you into the sea,' and it will happen. 22If you believe, you will receive whatever you ask for in prayer."

The Authority of Jesus Challenged

23When Jesus returned to the Temple and began teaching, the leading priests and other leaders came up to him.

21:16 Ps 8:2.

NEW KING JAMES VERSION

And Jesus said to them, "Yes. Have you never read,

'Out of the mouth of babes and nursing infants
You have perfected praise'? "[i]

17Then He left them and went out of the city to Bethany, and He lodged there.

The Fig Tree Withered

18Now in the morning, as He returned to the city, He was hungry. 19And seeing a fig tree by the road, He came to it and found nothing on it but leaves, and said to it, "Let no fruit grow on you ever again." Immediately the fig tree withered away.

The Lesson of the Withered Fig Tree

20And when the disciples saw *it,* they marveled, saying, "How did the fig tree wither away so soon?"

21So Jesus answered and said to them, "Assuredly, I say to you, if you have faith and do not doubt, you will not only do what was done to the fig tree, but also if you say to this mountain, 'Be removed and be cast into the sea,' it will be done. 22And whatever things you ask in prayer, believing, you will receive."

Jesus' Authority Questioned

23Now when He came into the temple, the chief priests and the elders of the people confronted Him as He was

21:16 [i] Psalm 8:2

THE MESSAGE

Jesus said, "Yes, I hear them. And haven't you read in God's Word, 'From the mouths of children and babies I'll furnish a place of praise'?"

Fed up, Jesus turned on his heel and left the city for Bethany, where he spent the night.

The Withered Fig Tree

Early the next morning Jesus was returning to the city. He was hungry. Seeing a lone fig tree alongside the road, he approached it anticipating a breakfast of figs. When he got to the tree, there was nothing but fig leaves. He said, "No more figs from this tree—ever!" The fig tree withered on the spot, a dry stick. The disciples saw it happen. They rubbed their eyes, saying, "Did we really see this? A leafy tree one minute, a dry stick the next?"

But Jesus was matter-of-fact: "Yes—and if you embrace this kingdom life and don't doubt God, you'll not only do minor feats like I did to the fig tree, but also triumph over huge obstacles. This mountain, for instance, you'll tell, 'Go jump in the lake,' and it will jump. Absolutely everything, ranging from small to large, as you make it a part of your believing prayer, gets included as you lay hold of God."

True Authority

Then he was back in the Temple, teaching. The high priests and leaders of the people came up and demanded,

KING JAMES VERSION

was teaching, and said, By what authority doest thou these things? and who gave thee this authority?

24 And Jesus answered and said unto them, I also will ask you one thing, which if ye tell me, I in like wise will tell you by what authority I do these things.

25 The baptism of John, whence was it? from heaven, or of men? And they reasoned with themselves, saying, If we shall say, From heaven; he will say unto us, Why did ye not then believe him?

26 But if we shall say, Of men; we fear the people; for all hold John as a prophet.

27 And they answered Jesus, and said, We cannot tell. And he said unto them, Neither tell I you by what authority I do these things.

28 ¶ But what think ye? A *certain* man had two sons; and he came to the first, and said, Son, go work to day in my vineyard.

29 He answered and said, I will not: but afterward he repented, and went.

30 And he came to the second, and said likewise. And he answered and said, I *go*, sir: and went not.

31 Whether of them twain did the will of *his* father? They say unto him, The first. Jesus saith unto them, Verily I say unto you, That the publicans and the harlots go into the kingdom of God before you.

NEW AMERICAN STANDARD BIBLE

and said, "By what authority are You doing these things, and who gave You this authority?"

24 Jesus said to them, "I will also ask you one thing, which if you tell Me, I will also tell you by what authority I do these things.

25 "The baptism of John was from what *source,* from heaven or from men?" And they *began* reasoning among themselves, saying, "If we say, 'From heaven,' He will say to us, 'Then why did you not believe him?'

26 "But if we say, 'From men,' we fear the people; for they all regard John as a prophet."

27 And answering Jesus, they said, "We do not know." He also said to them, "Neither will I tell you by what authority I do these things.

Parable of Two Sons

28 "But what do you think? A man had two sons, and he came to the first and said, 'Son, go work today in the vineyard.'

29 "And he answered, 'I will not'; but afterward he regretted it and went.

30 "The man came to the second and said the same thing; and he answered, 'I *will*, sir'; but he did not go.

31 "Which of the two did the will of his father?" They *said, "The first." Jesus *said to them, "Truly I say to you that the tax collectors and prostitutes will get into the kingdom of God before you.

NEW CENTURY VERSION

came to him. They said, "What authority do you have to do these things? Who gave you this authority?"

24 Jesus answered, "I also will ask you a question. If you answer me, then I will tell you what authority I have to do these things. 25 Tell me: When John baptized people, did that come from God or just from other people?"

They argued about Jesus' question, saying, "If we answer, 'John's baptism was from God,' Jesus will say, 'Then why didn't you believe him?' 26 But if we say, 'It was from people,' we are afraid of what the crowd will do because they all believe that John was a prophet."

27 So they answered Jesus, "We don't know."

Jesus said to them, "Then I won't tell you what authority I have to do these things.

A Story About Two Sons

28 "Tell me what you think about this: A man had two sons. He went to the first son and said, 'Son, go and work today in my vineyard.' 29 The son answered, 'I will not go.' But later the son changed his mind and went. 30 Then the father went to the other son and said, 'Son, go and work today in my vineyard.' The son answered, 'Yes, sir, I will go and work,' but he did not go. 31 Which of the two sons obeyed his father?"

The priests and leaders answered, "The first son."

Jesus said to them, "I tell you the truth, the tax collectors and the prostitutes will enter the kingdom of God

CONTEMPORARY ENGLISH VERSION

up to him. They asked, "What right do you have to do these things? Who gave you this authority?"

24 Jesus answered, "I have just one question to ask you. If you answer it, I will tell you where I got the right to do these things. 25 Who gave John the right to baptize? Was it God in heaven or merely some human being?"

They thought it over and said to each other, "We can't say that God gave John this right. Jesus will ask us why we didn't believe John. 26 On the other hand, these people think that John was a prophet, and we are afraid of what they might do to us. That's why we can't say that it was merely some human who gave John the right to baptize." 27 So they told Jesus, "We don't know."

Jesus said, "Then I won't tell you who gave me the right to do what I do."

A Story about Two Sons

28 Jesus said:

I will tell you a story about a man who had two sons. Then you can tell me what you think. The father went to the older son and said, "Go work in the vineyard today!" 29 His son told him that he would not do it, but later he changed his mind and went. 30 The man then told his younger son to go work in the vineyard. The boy said he would, but he didn't go. 31 Which one of the sons obeyed his father?

"The older one," the chief priests and leaders answered. Then Jesus told them:

You can be sure that tax collectors[e] and prostitutes

[e] 21.31 *tax collectors*: See the note at 5.46.

NEW INTERNATIONAL VERSION

came to him. "By what authority are you doing these
things?" they asked. "And who gave you this authority?"
24Jesus replied, "I will also ask you one question. If you
answer me, I will tell you by what authority I am doing
these things. 25John's baptism—where did it come from?
Was it from heaven, or from men?"

They discussed it among themselves and said, "If we
say, 'From heaven,' he will ask, 'Then why didn't you
believe him?' 26But if we say, 'From men'—we are afraid
of the people, for they all hold that John was a prophet."
27So they answered Jesus, "We don't know."

Then he said, "Neither will I tell you by what authority I
am doing these things.

The Parable of the Two Sons

28"What do you think? There was a man who had two
sons. He went to the first and said, 'Son, go and work
today in the vineyard.'
29" 'I will not,' he answered, but later he changed his
mind and went.
30"Then the father went to the other son and said the
same thing. He answered, 'I will, sir,' but he did not go.
31"Which of the two did what his father wanted?"

"The first," they answered.

Jesus said to them, "I tell you the truth, the tax collectors and the prostitutes are entering the kingdom of God

NEW LIVING TRANSLATION

They demanded, "By whose authority did you drive out
the merchants from the Temple?* Who gave you such
authority?"
24"I'll tell you who gave me the authority to do these
things if you answer one question," Jesus replied. 25"Did
John's baptism come from heaven or was it merely
human?"

They talked it over among themselves. "If we say it was
from heaven, he will ask why we didn't believe him. 26But
if we say it was merely human, we'll be mobbed, because
the people think he was a prophet." 27So they finally
replied, "We don't know."

And Jesus responded, "Then I won't answer your question either.

Story of the Two Sons

28"But what do you think about this? A man with two
sons told the older boy, 'Son, go out and work in the vine-
yard today.' 29The son answered, 'No, I won't go,' but later
he changed his mind and went anyway. 30Then the father
told the other son, 'You go,' and he said, 'Yes, sir, I will.'
But he didn't go. 31Which of the two was obeying his
father?"

They replied, "The first, of course."

Then Jesus explained his meaning: "I assure you, corrupt tax collectors and prostitutes will get into the

21:23 Or *By whose authority do you do these things?*

NEW KING JAMES VERSION

teaching, and said, "By what authority are You doing these
things? And who gave You this authority?"
24But Jesus answered and said to them, "I also will ask
you one thing, which if you tell Me, I likewise will tell you
by what authority I do these things: 25The baptism of
John—where was it from? From heaven or from men?"

And they reasoned among themselves, saying, "If we
say, 'From heaven,' He will say to us, 'Why then did you
not believe him?' 26But if we say, 'From men,' we fear the
multitude, for all count John as a prophet." 27So they
answered Jesus and said, "We do not know."

And He said to them, "Neither will I tell you by what
authority I do these things.

The Parable of the Two Sons

28"But what do you think? A man had two sons, and he
came to the first and said, 'Son, go, work today in my
vineyard.' 29He answered and said, 'I will not,' but after-
ward he regretted it and went. 30Then he came to the sec-
ond and said likewise. And he answered and said, 'I *go*,
sir,' but he did not go. 31Which of the two did the will of
his father?"

They said to Him, "The first."

Jesus said to them, "Assuredly, I say to you that tax collectors and harlots enter the kingdom of God before you.

THE MESSAGE

"Show us your credentials. Who authorized you to teach here?"

Jesus responded, "First let me ask you a question. You answer my question and I'll answer yours. About the baptism of John—who authorized it: heaven or humans?"

They were on the spot and knew it. They pulled back into a huddle and whispered, "If we say 'heaven,' he'll ask us why we didn't believe him; if we say 'humans,' we're up against it with the people because they all hold John up as a prophet." They decided to concede that round to Jesus. "We don't know," they answered.

Jesus said, "Then neither will I answer your question.

The Story of Two Sons

"Tell me what you think of this story: A man had two sons. He went up to the first and said, 'Son, go out for the day and work in the vineyard.'

"The son answered, 'I don't want to.' Later on he thought better of it and went.

"The father gave the same command to the second son. He answered, 'Sure, glad to.' But he never went.

"Which of the two sons did what the father asked?"

They said, "The first."

Jesus said, "Yes, and I tell you that crooks and whores are going to precede you into God's kingdom. John came to

KING JAMES VERSION

32 For John came unto you in the way of righteousness, and ye believed him not: but the publicans and the harlots believed him: and ye, when ye had seen *it*, repented not afterward, that ye might believe him.

33 ¶ Hear another parable: There was a certain householder, which planted a vineyard, and hedged it round about, and digged a winepress in it, and built a tower, and let it out to husbandmen, and went into a far country:

34 And when the time of the fruit drew near, he sent his servants to the husbandmen, that they might receive the fruits of it.

35 And the husbandmen took his servants, and beat one, and killed another, and stoned another.

36 Again, he sent other servants more than the first: and they did unto them likewise.

37 But last of all he sent unto them his son, saying, They will reverence my son.

38 But when the husbandmen saw the son, they said among themselves, This is the heir; come, let us kill him, and let us seize on his inheritance.

39 And they caught him, and cast *him* out of the vineyard, and slew *him*.

40 When the lord therefore of the vineyard cometh, what will he do unto those husbandmen?

41 They say unto him, He will miserably destroy those wicked men, and will let out *his* vineyard unto other

NEW AMERICAN STANDARD BIBLE

32 "For John came to you in the way of righteousness and you did not believe him; but the tax collectors and prostitutes did believe him; and you, seeing *this*, did not even feel remorse afterward so as to believe him.

Parable of the Landowner

33 "Listen to another parable. There was a landowner who PLANTED A VINEYARD AND PUT A WALL AROUND IT AND DUG A WINE PRESS IN IT, AND BUILT A TOWER, and rented it out to vine-growers and went on a journey.

34 "When the harvest time approached, he sent his slaves to the vine-growers to receive his produce.

35 "The vine-growers took his slaves and beat one, and killed another, and stoned a third.

36 "Again he sent another group of slaves larger than the first; and they did the same thing to them.

37 "But afterward he sent his son to them, saying, 'They will respect my son.'

38 "But when the vine-growers saw the son, they said among themselves, 'This is the heir; come, let us kill him and seize his inheritance.'

39 "They took him, and threw him out of the vineyard and killed him.

40 "Therefore when the owner of the vineyard comes, what will he do to those vine-growers?"

41 They *said to Him, "He will bring those wretches to a wretched end, and will rent out the vineyard to other

NEW CENTURY VERSION

before you do. 32John came to show you the right way to
live. You did not believe him, but the tax collectors and
prostitutes believed him. Even after seeing this, you still
refused to change your ways and believe him.

A Story About God's Son

33"Listen to this story: There was a man who owned a
vineyard. He put a wall around it and dug a hole for a
winepress and built a tower. Then he leased the land to
some farmers and left for a trip. 34When it was time for the
grapes to be picked, he sent his servants to the farmers to
get his share of the grapes. 35But the farmers grabbed the
servants, beat one, killed another, and then killed a third
servant with stones. 36So the man sent some other ser-
vants to the farmers, even more than he sent the first time.
But the farmers did the same thing to the servants that
they had done before. 37So the man decided to send his
son to the farmers. He said, 'They will respect my son.'
38But when the farmers saw the son, they said to each
other, 'This son will inherit the vineyard. If we kill him, it
will be ours!' 39Then the farmers grabbed the son, threw
him out of the vineyard, and killed him. 40So what will the
owner of the vineyard do to these farmers when he
comes?"

41The priests and leaders said, "He will surely kill those
evil men. Then he will lease the vineyard to some other

CONTEMPORARY ENGLISH VERSION

will get into the kingdom of God before you ever will!

32When John the Baptist showed you how to do right,
you would not believe him. But these evil people did
believe. And even when you saw what they did, you still
would not change your minds and believe.

Renters of a Vineyard (Mark 12.1-12; Luke 20.9-19)

33Jesus told the chief priests and leaders to listen to this
story:

A land owner once planted a vineyard. He built a wall
around it and dug a pit to crush the grapes in. He also
built a lookout tower. Then he rented out his vineyard
and left the country.

34When it was harvest time, the owner sent some ser-
vants to get his share of the grapes. 35But the renters
grabbed those servants. They beat up one, killed one,
and stoned one of them to death. 36He then sent more
servants than he did the first time. But the renters treat-
ed them in the same way.

37Finally, the owner sent his own son to the renters,
because he thought they would respect him. 38But when
they saw the man's son, they said, "Someday he will
own the vineyard. Let's kill him! Then we can have it all
for ourselves." 39So they grabbed him, threw him out of
the vineyard, and killed him.

40Jesus asked, "When the owner of that vineyard comes,
what do you suppose he will do to those renters?"

41The chief priests and leaders answered, "He will kill
them in some horrible way. Then he will rent out his

NEW INTERNATIONAL VERSION

ahead of you. 32For John came to you to show you the way of righteousness, and you did not believe him, but the tax collectors and the prostitutes did. And even after you saw this, you did not repent and believe him.

The Parable of the Tenants

33"Listen to another parable: There was a landowner who planted a vineyard. He put a wall around it, dug a winepress in it and built a watchtower. Then he rented the vineyard to some farmers and went away on a journey. 34When the harvest time approached, he sent his servants to the tenants to collect his fruit.

35"The tenants seized his servants; they beat one, killed another, and stoned a third. 36Then he sent other servants to them, more than the first time, and the tenants treated them the same way. 37Last of all, he sent his son to them. 'They will respect my son,' he said.

38"But when the tenants saw the son, they said to each other, 'This is the heir. Come, let's kill him and take his inheritance.' 39So they took him and threw him out of the vineyard and killed him.

40"Therefore, when the owner of the vineyard comes, what will he do to those tenants?"

41"He will bring those wretches to a wretched end," they

NEW LIVING TRANSLATION

Kingdom of God before you do. 32For John the Baptist came and showed you the way to life, and you didn't believe him, while tax collectors and prostitutes did. And even when you saw this happening, you refused to turn from your sins and believe him.

Story of the Evil Farmers

33"Now listen to this story. A certain landowner planted a vineyard, built a wall around it, dug a pit for pressing out the grape juice, and built a lookout tower. Then he leased the vineyard to tenant farmers and moved to another country. 34At the time of the grape harvest he sent his servants to collect his share of the crop. 35But the farmers grabbed his servants, beat one, killed one, and stoned another. 36So the landowner sent a larger group of his servants to collect for him, but the results were the same.

37"Finally, the owner sent his son, thinking, 'Surely they will respect my son.'

38"But when the farmers saw his son coming, they said to one another, 'Here comes the heir to this estate. Come on, let's kill him and get the estate for ourselves!' 39So they grabbed him, took him out of the vineyard, and murdered him.

40"When the owner of the vineyard returns," Jesus asked, "what do you think he will do to those farmers?"

41The religious leaders replied, "He will put the wicked men to a horrible death and lease the vineyard to others

NEW KING JAMES VERSION

32For John came to you in the way of righteousness, and you did not believe him; but tax collectors and harlots believed him; and when you saw *it,* you did not afterward relent and believe him.

The Parable of the Wicked Vinedressers

33"Hear another parable: There was a certain landowner who planted a vineyard and set a hedge around it, dug a winepress in it and built a tower. And he leased it to vinedressers and went into a far country. 34Now when vintage-time drew near, he sent his servants to the vinedressers, that they might receive its fruit. 35And the vinedressers took his servants, beat one, killed one, and stoned another. 36Again he sent other servants, more than the first, and they did likewise to them. 37Then last of all he sent his son to them, saying, 'They will respect my son.' 38But when the vinedressers saw the son, they said among themselves, 'This is the heir. Come, let us kill him and seize his inheritance.' 39So they took him and cast *him* out of the vineyard and killed *him.*

40"Therefore, when the owner of the vineyard comes, what will he do to those vinedressers?"

41They said to Him, "He will destroy those wicked men miserably, and lease *his* vineyard to other vinedressers

THE MESSAGE

you showing you the right road. You turned up your noses at him, but the crooks and whores believed him. Even when you saw their changed lives, you didn't care enough to change and believe him.

The Story of the Greedy Farmhands

"Here's another story. Listen closely. There was once a man, a wealthy farmer, who planted a vineyard. He fenced it, dug a winepress, put up a watchtower, then turned it over to the farmhands and went off on a trip. When it was time to harvest the grapes, he sent his servants back to collect his profits.

"The farmhands grabbed the first servant and beat him up. The next one they murdered. They threw stones at the third but he got away. The owner tried again, sending more servants. They got the same treatment. The owner was at the end of his rope. He decided to send his son. 'Surely,' he thought, 'they will respect my son.'

"But when the farmhands saw the son arrive, they rubbed their hands in greed. 'This is the heir! Let's kill him and have it all for ourselves.' They grabbed him, threw him out, and killed him.

"Now, when the owner of the vineyard arrives home from his trip, what do you think he will do to the farmhands?"

"He'll kill them—a rotten bunch, and good riddance," they answered. "Then he'll assign the vineyard to

KING JAMES VERSION

husbandmen, which shall render him the fruits in their seasons.

42 Jesus saith unto them, Did ye never read in the scriptures, The stone which the builders rejected, the same is become the head of the corner: this is the Lord's doing, and it is marvellous in our eyes?

43 Therefore say I unto you, The kingdom of God shall be taken from you, and given to a nation bringing forth the fruits thereof.

44 And whosoever shall fall on this stone shall be broken: but on whomsoever it shall fall, it will grind him to powder.

45 And when the chief priests and Pharisees had heard his parables, they perceived that he spake of them.

46 But when they sought to lay hands on him, they feared the multitude, because they took him for a prophet.

22 And Jesus answered and spake unto them again by parables, and said,

2 The kingdom of heaven is like unto a certain king, which made a marriage for his son,

3 And sent forth his servants to call them that were bidden to the wedding: and they would not come.

4 Again, he sent forth other servants, saying, Tell them which are bidden, Behold, I have prepared my dinner: my

NEW AMERICAN STANDARD BIBLE

vine-growers who will pay him the proceeds at the *proper* seasons."

42 Jesus *said to them, "Did you never read in the Scriptures,

'THE STONE WHICH THE BUILDERS REJECTED,
THIS BECAME THE CHIEF CORNER *stone;*
THIS CAME ABOUT FROM THE LORD,
AND IT IS MARVELOUS IN OUR EYES'?

43 "Therefore I say to you, the kingdom of God will be taken away from you and given to a people, producing the fruit of it.

44 "And he who falls on this stone will be broken to pieces; but on whomever it falls, it will scatter him like dust."

45 When the chief priests and the Pharisees heard His parables, they understood that He was speaking about them.

46 When they sought to seize Him, they feared the people, because they considered Him to be a prophet.

Parable of the Marriage Feast

22 Jesus spoke to them again in parables, saying,
2 "The kingdom of heaven may be compared to a king who gave a wedding feast for his son.

3 "And he sent out his slaves to call those who had been invited to the wedding feast, and they were unwilling to come.

4 "Again he sent out other slaves saying, 'Tell those who have been invited, "Behold, I have prepared my

NEW CENTURY VERSION

farmers who will give him his share of the crop at harvest time."

42 Jesus said to them, "Surely you have read this in the Scriptures:

'The stone that the builders rejected
became the cornerstone.
The Lord did this,
and it is wonderful to us.' *Psalm 118:22–23*

43 "So I tell you that the kingdom of God will be taken away from you and given to people who do the things God wants in his kingdom. 44 The person who falls on this stone will be broken, and on whomever that stone falls, that person will be crushed."[f]

45 When the leading priests and the Pharisees heard these stories, they knew Jesus was talking about them. 46 They wanted to arrest him, but they were afraid of the people, because the people believed that Jesus was a prophet.

A Story About a Wedding Feast

22 Jesus again used stories to teach the people. He said, 2 "The kingdom of heaven is like a king who prepared a wedding feast for his son. 3 The king invited some people to the feast. When the feast was ready, the king sent his servants to tell the people, but they refused to come.

4 "Then the king sent other servants, saying, 'Tell those who have been invited that my feast is ready. I have killed

21:44 [f] **Verse 44** Some copies do not have verse 44.

CONTEMPORARY ENGLISH VERSION

vineyard to people who will give him his share of grapes at harvest time."

42 Jesus replied, "You surely know that the Scriptures say,

'The stone that the builders
tossed aside
is now the most important
stone of all.
This is something
the Lord has done,
and it is amazing to us.'

43 I tell you that God's kingdom will be taken from you and given to people who will do what he demands. 44 Anyone who stumbles over this stone will be crushed, and anyone it falls on will be smashed to pieces."[f]

45 When the chief priests and the Pharisees heard these stories, they knew that Jesus was talking about them. 46 So they looked for a way to arrest Jesus. But they were afraid to, because the people thought he was a prophet.

The Great Banquet (Luke 14.15-24)

22 Once again Jesus used stories to teach the people:
2 The kingdom of heaven is like what happened when a king gave a wedding banquet for his son. 3 The king sent some servants to tell the invited guests to come to the banquet, but the guests refused. 4 He sent other servants to say to the guests, "The banquet is

[f] **21.44** *pieces*: Verse 44 is not in some manuscripts.

NEW INTERNATIONAL VERSION

replied, "and he will rent the vineyard to other tenants, who will give him his share of the crop at harvest time."

42 Jesus said to them, "Have you never read in the Scriptures:

" 'The stone the builders rejected
has become the capstone[g];
the Lord has done this,
and it is marvelous in our eyes'[h]?

43 "Therefore I tell you that the kingdom of God will be taken away from you and given to a people who will produce its fruit. 44 He who falls on this stone will be broken to pieces, but he on whom it falls will be crushed."[i]

45 When the chief priests and the Pharisees heard Jesus' parables, they knew he was talking about them. 46 They looked for a way to arrest him, but they were afraid of the crowd because the people held that he was a prophet.

The Parable of the Wedding Banquet

22 Jesus spoke to them again in parables, saying: 2 "The kingdom of heaven is like a king who prepared a wedding banquet for his son. 3 He sent his servants to those who had been invited to the banquet to tell them to come, but they refused to come.

4 "Then he sent some more servants and said, 'Tell those who have been invited that I have prepared my dinner: My

g 42 Or *cornerstone* h 42 Psalm 118:22,23 i 44 Some manuscripts do not have verse 44.

NEW LIVING TRANSLATION

who will give him his share of the crop after each harvest."

42 Then Jesus asked them, "Didn't you ever read this in the Scriptures?

'The stone rejected by the builders
has now become the cornerstone.
This is the Lord's doing,
and it is marvelous to see.'*

43 What I mean is that the Kingdom of God will be taken away from you and given to a nation that will produce the proper fruit. 44 Anyone who stumbles over that stone will be broken to pieces, and it will crush anyone on whom it falls.*"

45 When the leading priests and Pharisees heard Jesus, they realized he was pointing at them—that they were the farmers in his story. 46 They wanted to arrest him, but they were afraid to try because the crowds considered Jesus to be a prophet.

Story of the Great Feast

22 Jesus told them several other stories to illustrate the Kingdom. He said, 2 "The Kingdom of Heaven can be illustrated by the story of a king who prepared a great wedding feast for his son. 3 Many guests were invited, and when the banquet was ready, he sent his servants to notify everyone that it was time to come. But they all refused! 4 So he sent other servants to tell them, 'The feast

21:42 Ps 118:22-23. **21:44** This verse is omitted in some early manuscripts.

NEW KING JAMES VERSION

who will render to him the fruits in their seasons."

42 Jesus said to them, "Have you never read in the Scriptures:

'*The stone which the builders rejected*
Has become the chief cornerstone.
This was the LORD*'s doing,*
And it is marvelous in our eyes'?[j]

43 "Therefore I say to you, the kingdom of God will be taken from you and given to a nation bearing the fruits of it. 44 And whoever falls on this stone will be broken; but on whomever it falls, it will grind him to powder."

45 Now when the chief priests and Pharisees heard His parables, they perceived that He was speaking of them. 46 But when they sought to lay hands on Him, they feared the multitudes, because they took Him for a prophet.

The Parable of the Wedding Feast

22 And Jesus answered and spoke to them again by parables and said: 2 "The kingdom of heaven is like a certain king who arranged a marriage for his son, 3 and sent out his servants to call those who were invited to the wedding; and they were not willing to come. 4 Again, he sent out other servants, saying, 'Tell those who are invited, "See, I have prepared my dinner; my oxen and fatted

21:42 j Psalm 118:22, 23

THE MESSAGE

farmhands who will hand over the profits when it's time."

Jesus said, "Right—and you can read it for yourselves in your Bibles:

'The stone the masons threw out
is now the cornerstone.
This is God's work;
we rub our eyes, we can hardly believe it!'

This is the way it is with you. God's kingdom will be taken back from you and handed over to a people who will live out a kingdom life. Whoever stumbles on this Stone gets shattered; whoever the Stone falls on gets smashed."

When the religious leaders heard this story, they knew it was aimed at them. They wanted to arrest Jesus and put him in jail, but, intimidated by public opinion, they held back. Most people held him to be a prophet of God.

The Story of the Wedding Banquet

22 Jesus responded by telling still more stories. "God's kingdom," he said, "is like a king who threw a wedding banquet for his son. He sent out servants to call in all the invited guests. And they wouldn't come!

"He sent out another round of servants, instructing them to tell the guests, 'Look, everything is on the table, the prime rib is ready for carving. Come to the feast!'

KING JAMES VERSION

oxen and *my* fatlings *are* killed, and all things *are* ready: come unto the marriage.

5 But they made light of *it*, and went their ways, one to his farm, another to his merchandise:

6 And the remnant took his servants, and entreated *them* spitefully, and slew *them*.

7 But when the king heard *thereof*, he was wroth: and he sent forth his armies, and destroyed those murderers, and burned up their city.

8 Then saith he to his servants, The wedding is ready, but they which were bidden were not worthy.

9 Go ye therefore into the highways, and as many as ye shall find, bid to the marriage.

10 So those servants went out into the highways, and gathered together all as many as they found, both bad and good: and the wedding was furnished with guests.

11 And when the king came in to see the guests, he saw there a man which had not on a wedding garment:

12 And he saith unto him, Friend, how camest thou in hither not having a wedding garment? And he was speechless.

13 Then said the king to the servants, Bind him hand and foot, and take him away, and cast *him* into outer darkness; there shall be weeping and gnashing of teeth.

14 For many are called, but few *are* chosen.

15 ¶ Then went the Pharisees, and took counsel how they might entangle him in *his* talk.

16 And they sent out unto him their disciples with the

NEW AMERICAN STANDARD BIBLE

dinner; my oxen and my fattened livestock are *all* butchered and everything is ready; come to the wedding feast." '

5 "But they paid no attention and went their way, one to his own farm, another to his business,

6 and the rest seized his slaves and mistreated them and killed them.

7 "But the king was enraged, and he sent his armies and destroyed those murderers and set their city on fire.

8 "Then he *said to his slaves, 'The wedding is ready, but those who were invited were not worthy.

9 'Go therefore to the main highways, and as many as you find *there,* invite to the wedding feast.'

10 "Those slaves went out into the streets and gathered together all they found, both evil and good; and the wedding hall was filled with dinner guests.

11 "But when the king came in to look over the dinner guests, he saw a man there who was not dressed in wedding clothes,

12 and he *said to him, 'Friend, how did you come in here without wedding clothes?' And the man was speechless.

13 "Then the king said to the servants, 'Bind him hand and foot, and throw him into the outer darkness; in that place there will be weeping and gnashing of teeth.'

14 "For many are called, but few *are* chosen."

Tribute to Caesar

15 Then the Pharisees went and plotted together how they might trap Him in what He said.

16 And they *sent their disciples to Him, along with the

NEW CENTURY VERSION

my best bulls and calves for the dinner, and everything is
ready. Come to the wedding feast.'
5"But the people refused to listen to the servants and
left to do other things. One went to work in his field, and
another went to his business. 6Some of the other people
grabbed the servants, beat them, and killed them. 7The
king was furious and sent his army to kill the murderers
and burn their city.
8"After that, the king said to his servants, 'The wedding
feast is ready. I invited those people, but they were not wor-
thy to come. 9So go to the street corners and invite everyone
you find to come to my feast.' 10So the servants went into
the streets and gathered all the people they could find, both
good and bad. And the wedding hall was filled with guests.
11"When the king came in to see the guests, he saw a
man who was not dressed for a wedding. 12The king said,
'Friend, how were you allowed to come in here? You are
not dressed for a wedding.' But the man said nothing. 13So
the king told some servants, 'Tie this man's hands and
feet. Throw him out into the darkness, where people will
cry and grind their teeth with pain.'
14"Yes, many people are invited, but only a few are cho-
sen."

Is It Right to Pay Taxes or Not?

15Then the Pharisees left that place and made plans to
trap Jesus in saying something wrong. 16They sent some of
their own followers and some people from the group called
Herodians.[a] They said, "Teacher, we know that you are an

22:16 [a] **Herodians** A political group that followed Herod and his family.

CONTEMPORARY ENGLISH VERSION

ready! My cattle and prize calves have all been prepared.
Everything is ready. Come to the banquet!"
5But the guests did not pay any attention. Some of
them left for their farms, and some went to their places
of business. 6Others grabbed the servants, then beat
them up and killed them.
7This made the king so furious that he sent an army
to kill those murderers and burn down their city. 8Then
he said to the servants, "It is time for the wedding ban-
quet, and the invited guests don't deserve to come. 9Go
out to the street corners and tell everyone you meet to
come to the banquet." 10They went out on the streets
and brought in everyone they could find, good and bad
alike. And the banquet room was filled with guests.
11When the king went in to meet the guests, he found
that one of them wasn't wearing the right kind of clothes
for the wedding. 12The king asked, "Friend, why didn't
you wear proper clothes for the wedding?" But the guest
had no excuse. 13So the king gave orders for that person
to be tied hand and foot and to be thrown outside into
the dark. That's where people will cry and grit their teeth
in pain. 14Many are invited, but only a few are chosen.

Paying Taxes (Mark 12.13-17; Luke 20.20-26)

15The Pharisees got together and planned how they
could trick Jesus into saying something wrong. 16They sent
some of their followers and some of Herod's followers[a] to

[a] 22.16 *Herod's followers*: People who were political followers of the family of Herod the Great (see 2.1) and his son Herod Antipas (see 14.1), and who wanted Herod to be king in Jerusalem.

NEW INTERNATIONAL VERSION

oxen and fattened cattle have been butchered, and every-
thing is ready. Come to the wedding banquet.'
5"But they paid no attention and went off—one to his
field, another to his business. 6The rest seized his ser-
vants, mistreated them and killed them. 7The king was
enraged. He sent his army and destroyed those murderers
and burned their city.
8"Then he said to his servants, 'The wedding banquet is
ready, but those I invited did not deserve to come. 9Go to
the street corners and invite to the banquet anyone you
find.' 10So the servants went out into the streets and gath-
ered all the people they could find, both good and bad, and
the wedding hall was filled with guests.
11"But when the king came in to see the guests, he
noticed a man there who was not wearing wedding
clothes. 12'Friend,' he asked, 'how did you get in here
without wedding clothes?' The man was speechless.
13"Then the king told the attendants, 'Tie him hand and
foot, and throw him outside, into the darkness, where
there will be weeping and gnashing of teeth.'
14"For many are invited, but few are chosen."

Paying Taxes to Caesar

15Then the Pharisees went out and laid plans to trap him
in his words. 16They sent their disciples to him along with

NEW LIVING TRANSLATION

has been prepared, and choice meats have been cooked.
Everything is ready. Hurry!' 5But the guests he had invited
ignored them and went about their business, one to his
farm, another to his store. 6Others seized his messengers
and treated them shamefully, even killing some of them.
7"Then the king became furious. He sent out his army to
destroy the murderers and burn their city. 8And he said to
his servants, 'The wedding feast is ready, and the guests I
invited aren't worthy of the honor. 9Now go out to the
street corners and invite everyone you see.'
10"So the servants brought in everyone they could find,
good and bad alike, and the banquet hall was filled with
guests. 11But when the king came in to meet the guests, he
noticed a man who wasn't wearing the proper clothes for a
wedding. 12'Friend,' he asked, 'how is it that you are here
without wedding clothes?' And the man had no reply.
13Then the king said to his aides, 'Bind him hand and foot
and throw him out into the outer darkness, where there is
weeping and gnashing of teeth.' 14For many are called, but
few are chosen."

Taxes for Caesar

15Then the Pharisees met together to think of a way to
trap Jesus into saying something for which they could
accuse him. 16They decided to send some of their disci-
ples, along with the supporters of Herod, to ask him this

NEW KING JAMES VERSION

cattle *are* killed, and all things *are* ready. Come to the wed-
ding." ' 5But they made light of it and went their ways,
one to his own farm, another to his business. 6And the rest
seized his servants, treated *them* spitefully, and killed
them. 7But when the king heard *about it,* he was furious.
And he sent out his armies, destroyed those murderers,
and burned up their city. 8Then he said to his servants,
'The wedding is ready, but those who were invited were
not worthy. 9Therefore go into the highways, and as many
as you find, invite to the wedding.' 10So those servants
went out into the highways and gathered together all
whom they found, both bad and good. And the wedding
hall was filled with guests.
11"But when the king came in to see the guests, he saw
a man there who did not have on a wedding garment. 12So
he said to him, 'Friend, how did you come in here without
a wedding garment?' And he was speechless. 13Then the
king said to the servants, 'Bind him hand and foot, take
him away, and[a] cast *him* into outer darkness; there will be
weeping and gnashing of teeth.'
14"For many are called, but few *are* chosen."

The Pharisees: Is It Lawful to Pay Taxes to Caesar?

15Then the Pharisees went and plotted how they might
entangle Him in *His* talk. 16And they sent to Him their

22:13 [a] NU-Text omits *take him away, and.*

THE MESSAGE

"They only shrugged their shoulders and went off, one
to weed his garden, another to work in his shop. The rest,
with nothing better to do, beat up on the messengers and
then killed them. The king was outraged and sent his sol-
diers to destroy those thugs and level their city.

"Then he told his servants, 'We have a wedding banquet
all prepared but no guests. The ones I invited weren't up to
it. Go out into the busiest intersections in town and invite
anyone you find to the banquet.' The servants went out on
the streets and rounded up everyone they laid eyes on,
good and bad, regardless. And so the banquet was on—
every place filled.

"When the king entered and looked over the scene, he
spotted a man who wasn't properly dressed. He said to
him, 'Friend, how dare you come in here looking like that!'
The man was speechless. Then the king told his servants,
'Get him out of here—fast. Tie him up and ship him to
hell. And make sure he doesn't get back in.'

"That's what I mean when I say, 'Many get invited; only
a few make it.' "

Paying Taxes

That's when the Pharisees plotted a way to trap him into
saying something damaging. They sent their disciples,

KING JAMES VERSION

Herodians, saying, Master, we know that thou art true, and teachest the way of God in truth, neither carest thou for any *man*: for thou regardest not the person of men.

17 Tell us therefore, What thinkest thou? Is it lawful to give tribute unto Caesar, or not?

18 But Jesus perceived their wickedness, and said, Why tempt ye me, *ye* hypocrites?

19 Shew me the tribute money. And they brought unto him a penny.

20 And he saith unto them, Whose *is* this image and superscription?

21 They say unto him, Caesar's. Then saith he unto them, Render therefore unto Caesar the things which are Caesar's; and unto God the things that are God's.

22 When they had heard *these words*, they marvelled, and left him, and went their way.

23 ¶ The same day came to him the Sadducees, which say that there is no resurrection, and asked him,

24 Saying, Master, Moses said, If a man die, having no children, his brother shall marry his wife, and raise up seed unto his brother.

25 Now there were with us seven brethren: and the first, when he had married a wife, deceased, and, having no issue, left his wife unto his brother:

26 Likewise the second also, and the third, unto the seventh.

27 And last of all the woman died also.

28 Therefore in the resurrection whose wife shall she be of the seven? for they all had her.

NEW AMERICAN STANDARD BIBLE

Herodians, saying, "Teacher, we know that You are truthful and teach the way of God in truth, and defer to no one; for You are not partial to any.

17 "Tell us then, what do You think? Is it lawful to give a poll-tax to Caesar, or not?"

18 But Jesus perceived their malice, and said, "Why are you testing Me, you hypocrites?

19 "Show Me the coin *used* for the poll-tax." And they brought Him a denarius.

20 And He *said to them, "Whose likeness and inscription is this?"

21 They *said to Him, "Caesar's." Then He *said to them, "Then render to Caesar the things that are Caesar's; and to God the things that are God's."

22 And hearing *this,* they were amazed, and leaving Him, they went away.

Jesus Answers the Sadducees

23 On that day *some* Sadducees (who say there is no resurrection) came to Jesus and questioned Him,

24 asking, "Teacher, Moses said, 'IF A MAN DIES HAVING NO CHILDREN, HIS BROTHER AS NEXT OF KIN SHALL MARRY HIS WIFE, AND RAISE UP CHILDREN FOR HIS BROTHER.'

25 "Now there were seven brothers with us; and the first married and died, and having no children left his wife to his brother;

26 so also the second, and the third, down to the seventh.

27 "Last of all, the woman died.

28 "In the resurrection, therefore, whose wife of the seven will she be? For they all had *married* her."

NEW CENTURY VERSION

honest man and that you teach the truth about God's way.
You are not afraid of what other people think about you,
because you pay no attention to who they are. 17So tell us
what you think. Is it right to pay taxes to Caesar or not?"
18But knowing that these leaders were trying to trick
him, Jesus said, "You hypocrites! Why are you trying to
trap me? 19Show me a coin used for paying the tax." So
the men showed him a coin.[b] 20Then Jesus asked, "Whose
image and name are on the coin?"
21The men answered, "Caesar's."

Then Jesus said to them, "Give to Caesar the things that are Caesar's, and give to God the things that are God's."

22When the men heard what Jesus said, they were
amazed and left him and went away.

Some Sadducees Try to Trick Jesus

23That same day some Sadducees came to Jesus and
asked him a question. (Sadducees believed that people
would not rise from the dead.) 24They said, "Teacher,
Moses said if a married man dies without having children,
his brother must marry the widow and have children for
him. 25Once there were seven brothers among us. The first
one married and died. Since he had no children, his broth-
er married the widow. 26Then the second brother also died.
The same thing happened to the third brother and all the
other brothers. 27Finally, the woman died. 28Since all
seven men had married her, when people rise from the
dead, whose wife will she be?"

22:19 [b] **coin** A Roman denarius. One coin was the average pay for one day's work.

CONTEMPORARY ENGLISH VERSION

say to him, "Teacher, we know that you are honest. You
teach the truth about what God wants people to do. And
you treat everyone with the same respect, no matter who
they are. 17Tell us what you think! Should we pay taxes to
the Emperor or not?"
18Jesus knew their evil thoughts and said, "Why are you
trying to test me? You show-offs! 19Let me see one of the
coins used for paying taxes." They brought him a silver
coin, 20and he asked, "Whose picture and name are on it?"
21"The Emperor's," they answered.

Then Jesus told them, "Give the Emperor what belongs
to him and give God what belongs to God." 22His answer
surprised them so much that they walked away.

Life in the Future World (Mark 12.18-27; Luke 20.27-40)

23The Sadducees did not believe that people would rise
to life after death. So that same day some of the Sadducees
came to Jesus and said:

24Teacher, Moses wrote that if a married man dies and
has no children, his brother should marry the widow.
Their first son would then be thought of as the son of
the dead brother.

25Once there were seven brothers who lived here. The
first one married, but died without having any children.
So his wife was left to his brother. 26The same thing
happened to the second and third brothers and finally to
all seven of them. 27At last the woman died. 28When God
raises people from death, whose wife will this woman
be? She had been married to all seven brothers.

NEW INTERNATIONAL VERSION

the Herodians. "Teacher," they said, "we know you are a
man of integrity and that you teach the way of God in
accordance with the truth. You aren't swayed by men,
because you pay no attention to who they are. 17Tell us
then, what is your opinion? Is it right to pay taxes to
Caesar or not?"

18But Jesus, knowing their evil intent, said, "You hypo-
crites, why are you trying to trap me? 19Show me the coin
used for paying the tax." They brought him a denarius,
20and he asked them, "Whose portrait is this? And whose
inscription?"

21"Caesar's," they replied.

Then he said to them, "Give to Caesar what is Caesar's,
and to God what is God's."

22When they heard this, they were amazed. So they left
him and went away.

Marriage at the Resurrection

23That same day the Sadducees, who say there is no res-
urrection, came to him with a question. 24"Teacher," they
said, "Moses told us that if a man dies without having
children, his brother must marry the widow and have chil-
dren for him. 25Now there were seven brothers among us.
The first one married and died, and since he had no chil-
dren, he left his wife to his brother. 26The same thing hap-
pened to the second and third brother, right on down to
the seventh. 27Finally, the woman died. 28Now then, at the
resurrection, whose wife will she be of the seven, since all
of them were married to her?"

NEW LIVING TRANSLATION

question: "Teacher, we know how honest you are. You
teach about the way of God regardless of the conse-
quences. You are impartial and don't play favorites.
17Now tell us what you think about this: Is it right to pay
taxes to the Roman government or not?"

18But Jesus knew their evil motives. "You hypocrites!"
he said. "Whom are you trying to fool with your trick ques-
tions? 19Here, show me the Roman coin used for the tax."
When they handed him the coin,* 20he asked, "Whose pic-
ture and title are stamped on it?"

21"Caesar's," they replied.

"Well, then," he said, "give to Caesar what belongs to
him. But everything that belongs to God must be given to
God." 22His reply amazed them, and they went away.

Discussion about Resurrection

23That same day some Sadducees stepped forward—a
group of Jews who say there is no resurrection after death.
They posed this question: 24"Teacher, Moses said, 'If a
man dies without children, his brother should marry the
widow and have a child who will be the brother's heir.'*
25Well, there were seven brothers. The oldest married and
then died without children, so the second brother married
the widow. 26This brother also died without children, and
the wife was married to the next brother, and so on until
she had been the wife of each of them. 27And then she also
died. 28So tell us, whose wife will she be in the resurrec-
tion? For she was the wife of all seven of them!"

22:19 Greek *a denarius.* **22:24** Deut 25:5-6.

NEW KING JAMES VERSION

disciples with the Herodians, saying, "Teacher, we know
that You are true, and teach the way of God in truth; nor
do You care about anyone, for You do not regard the per-
son of men. 17Tell us, therefore, what do You think? Is it
lawful to pay taxes to Caesar, or not?"

18But Jesus perceived their wickedness, and said, "Why
do you test Me, *you* hypocrites? 19Show Me the tax
money."

So they brought Him a denarius.

20And He said to them, "Whose image and inscription *is*
this?"

21They said to Him, "Caesar's."

And He said to them, "Render therefore to Caesar the
things that are Caesar's, and to God the things that are
God's." 22When they had heard *these words,* they mar-
veled, and left Him and went their way.

The Sadducees: What About the Resurrection?

23The same day the Sadducees, who say there is no res-
urrection, came to Him and asked Him, 24saying: "Teacher,
Moses said that if a man dies, having no children, his
brother shall marry his wife and raise up offspring for his
brother. 25Now there were with us seven brothers. The first
died after he had married, and having no offspring, left his
wife to his brother. 26Likewise the second also, and the
third, even to the seventh. 27Last of all the woman died
also. 28Therefore, in the resurrection, whose wife of the
seven will she be? For they all had her."

THE MESSAGE

with a few of Herod's followers mixed in, to ask, "Teacher,
we know you have integrity, teach the way of God accu-
rately, are indifferent to popular opinion, and don't pander
to your students. So tell us honestly: Is it right to pay
taxes to Caesar or not?"

Jesus knew they were up to no good. He said, "Why are
you playing these games with me? Why are you trying to
trap me? Do you have a coin? Let me see it." They handed
him a silver piece.

"This engraving—who does it look like? And whose
name is on it?"

They said, "Caesar."

"Then give Caesar what is his, and give God what is
his."

The Pharisees were speechless. They went off shaking
their heads.

Marriage and Resurrection

That same day, Sadducees approached him. This is the
party that denies any possibility of resurrection. They
asked, "Teacher, Moses said that if a man dies childless,
his brother is obligated to marry his widow and get her
with child. Here's a case where there were seven brothers.
The first brother married and died, leaving no child, and
his wife passed to his brother. The second brother also left
her childless, then the third—and on and on, all seven.
Eventually the wife died. Now here's our question: At the
resurrection, whose wife is she? She was a wife to each of
them."

KING JAMES VERSION

29 Jesus answered and said unto them, Ye do err, not knowing the scriptures, nor the power of God.

30 For in the resurrection they neither marry, nor are given in marriage, but are as the angels of God in heaven.

31 But as touching the resurrection of the dead, have ye not read that which was spoken unto you by God, saying,

32 I am the God of Abraham, and the God of Isaac, and the God of Jacob? God is not the God of the dead, but of the living.

33 And when the multitude heard *this*, they were astonished at his doctrine.

34 ¶ But when the Pharisees had heard that he had put the Sadducees to silence, they were gathered together.

35 Then one of them, *which was* a lawyer, asked *him a question*, tempting him, and saying,

36 Master, which *is* the great commandment in the law?

37 Jesus said unto him, Thou shalt love the Lord thy God with all thy heart, and with all thy soul, and with all thy mind.

38 This is the first and great commandment.

39 And the second *is* like unto it, Thou shalt love thy neighbour as thyself.

40 On these two commandments hang all the law and the prophets.

NEW AMERICAN STANDARD BIBLE

29 But Jesus answered and said to them, "You are mistaken, not understanding the Scriptures nor the power of God.

30 "For in the resurrection they neither marry nor are given in marriage, but are like angels in heaven.

31 "But regarding the resurrection of the dead, have you not read what was spoken to you by God:

32 'I AM THE GOD OF ABRAHAM, AND THE GOD OF ISAAC, AND THE GOD OF JACOB'? He is not the God of the dead but of the living."

33 When the crowds heard *this,* they were astonished at His teaching.

34 But when the Pharisees heard that Jesus had silenced the Sadducees, they gathered themselves together.

35 One of them, [1]a lawyer, asked Him *a question,* testing Him,

36 "Teacher, which is the great commandment in the Law?"

37 And He said to him, " 'YOU SHALL LOVE THE LORD YOUR GOD WITH ALL YOUR HEART, AND WITH ALL YOUR SOUL, AND WITH ALL YOUR MIND.'

38 "This is the great and foremost commandment.

39 "The second is like it, 'YOU SHALL LOVE YOUR NEIGHBOR AS YOURSELF.'

40 "On these two commandments depend the whole Law and the Prophets."

22:35 [1] I.e. an expert in the Mosaic Law

NEW CENTURY VERSION

29 Jesus answered, "You don't understand, because you
don't know what the Scriptures say, and you don't know
about the power of God. 30 When people rise from the dead,
they will not marry, nor will they be given to someone to
marry. They will be like the angels in heaven. 31 Surely you
have read what God said to you about rising from the
dead. 32 God said, 'I am the God of Abraham, the God of
Isaac, and the God of Jacob.'[c] God is the God of the living,
not the dead."
33 When the people heard this, they were amazed at
Jesus' teaching.

The Most Important Command

34 When the Pharisees learned that the Sadducees could
not argue with Jesus' answers to them, the Pharisees met
together. 35 One Pharisee, who was an expert on the law of
Moses, asked Jesus this question to test him: 36 "Teacher,
which command in the law is the most important?"
37 Jesus answered, " 'Love the Lord your God with all
your heart, all your soul, and all your mind.'[d] 38 This is the
first and most important command. 39 And the second command
is like the first: 'Love your neighbor as you love
yourself.'[e] 40 All the law and the writings of the prophets
depend on these two commands."

22:32 [c] **'I am...Jacob.'** Quotation from Exodus 3:6.
22:37 [d] **'Love...mind.'** Quotation from Deuteronomy 6:5.
22:39 [e] **'Love...yourself.'** Quotation from Leviticus 19:18.

CONTEMPORARY ENGLISH VERSION

29 Jesus answered:
You are completely wrong! You don't know what the
Scriptures teach. And you don't know anything about
the power of God. 30 When God raises people to life, they
won't marry. They will be like the angels in heaven.
31 And as for people being raised to life, God was speaking
to you when he said, 32 "I am the God worshiped by
Abraham, Isaac, and Jacob."[b] He isn't the God of the
dead, but of the living.
33 The crowds were surprised to hear what Jesus was
teaching.

The Most Important Commandment

(Mark 12.28-34; Luke 10.25-28)

34 After Jesus had made the Sadducees look foolish, the
Pharisees heard about it and got together. 35 One of them
was an expert in the Jewish Law. So he tried to test Jesus
by asking, 36 "Teacher, what is the most important commandment
in the Law?"
37 Jesus answered:
Love the Lord your God with all your heart, soul, and
mind. 38 This is the first and most important commandment.
39 The second most important commandment is
like this one. And it is, "Love others as much as you love
yourself." 40 All the Law of Moses and the Books of the
Prophets[c] are based on these two commandments.

[b] 22.32 *I am the God worshiped by Abraham, Isaac, and Jacob*: Jesus argues that if God is worshiped by these three, they must still be alive, because he is the God of the living. [c] 22.40 *the Law of Moses and the Books of the Prophets*: The Jewish Scriptures, that is, the Old Testament.

NEW INTERNATIONAL VERSION

29Jesus replied, "You are in error because you do not
know the Scriptures or the power of God. 30At the resurrec-
tion people will neither marry nor be given in marriage;
they will be like the angels in heaven. 31But about the res-
urrection of the dead—have you not read what God said to
you, 32'I am the God of Abraham, the God of Isaac, and the
God of Jacob'[a]? He is not the God of the dead but of the liv-
ing."
33When the crowds heard this, they were astonished at
his teaching.

The Greatest Commandment

34Hearing that Jesus had silenced the Sadducees, the
Pharisees got together. 35One of them, an expert in the
law, tested him with this question: 36"Teacher, which is
the greatest commandment in the Law?"
37Jesus replied: " 'Love the Lord your God with all your
heart and with all your soul and with all your mind.'[b]
38This is the first and greatest commandment. 39And the
second is like it: 'Love your neighbor as yourself.'[c] 40All
the Law and the Prophets hang on these two command-
ments."

[a] *32* Exodus 3:6 [b] *37* Deut. 6:5 [c] *39* Lev. 19:18

NEW LIVING TRANSLATION

29Jesus replied, "Your problem is that you don't know
the Scriptures, and you don't know the power of God. 30For
when the dead rise, they won't be married. They will be
like the angels in heaven. 31But now, as to whether there
will be a resurrection of the dead—haven't you ever read
about this in the Scriptures? Long after Abraham, Isaac,
and Jacob had died, God said,* 32'I am the God of Abra-
ham, the God of Isaac, and the God of Jacob.'* So he is the
God of the living, not the dead."
33When the crowds heard him, they were impressed with
his teaching.

The Most Important Commandment

34But when the Pharisees heard that he had silenced the
Sadducees with his reply, they thought up a fresh question
of their own to ask him. 35One of them, an expert in reli-
gious law, tried to trap him with this question: 36"Teacher,
which is the most important commandment in the law of
Moses?"
37Jesus replied, " 'You must love the Lord your God with
all your heart, all your soul, and all your mind.'* 38This is
the first and greatest commandment. 39A second is equally
important: 'Love your neighbor as yourself.'* 40All the
other commandments and all the demands of the prophets
are based on these two commandments."

22:31 Greek *in the Scriptures? God said.* **22:32** Exod 3:6.
22:37 Deut 6:5. **22:39** Lev 19:18.

NEW KING JAMES VERSION

29Jesus answered and said to them, "You are mistaken,
not knowing the Scriptures nor the power of God. 30For in
the resurrection they neither marry nor are given in mar-
riage, but are like angels of God[b] in heaven. 31But concern-
ing the resurrection of the dead, have you not read what
was spoken to you by God, saying, 32*'I am the God of
Abraham, the God of Isaac, and the God of Jacob'* ?[c] God is
not the God of the dead, but of the living." 33And when the
multitudes heard *this,* they were astonished at His teach-
ing.

The Scribes: Which Is the First Commandment of All?

34But when the Pharisees heard that He had silenced the
Sadducees, they gathered together. 35Then one of them, a
lawyer, asked *Him a question,* testing Him, and saying,
36"Teacher, which *is* the great commandment in the law?"
37Jesus said to him, " *'You shall love the LORD your God
with all your heart, with all your soul, and with all your
mind.'*[d] 38This is *the* first and great commandment. 39And
the second *is* like it: *'You shall love your neighbor as your-
self.'*[e] 40On these two commandments hang all the Law
and the Prophets."

22:30 [b] NU-Text omits *of God.* **22:32** [c] Exodus 3:6, 15
22:37 [d] Deuteronomy 6:5 **22:39** [e] Leviticus 19:18

THE MESSAGE

Jesus answered, "You're off base on two counts: You don't know your Bibles, and you don't know how God works. At the resurrection we're beyond marriage. As with the angels, all our ecstasies and intimacies then will be with God. And regarding your speculation on whether the dead are raised or not, don't you read your Bibles? The grammar is clear: God says, 'I am—not *was*—the God of Abraham, the God of Isaac, the God of Jacob.' The living God defines himself not as the God of dead men, but of the *living*." Hearing this exchange the crowd was much impressed.

The Most Important Command

When the Pharisees heard how he had bested the Sadducees, they gathered their forces for an assault. One of their religion scholars spoke for them, posing a question they hoped would show him up: "Teacher, which command in God's Law is the most important?"

Jesus said, " 'Love the Lord your God with all your passion and prayer and intelligence.' This is the most important, the first on any list. But there is a second to set alongside it: 'Love others as well as you love yourself.' These two commands are pegs; everything in God's Law and the Prophets hangs from them."

KING JAMES VERSION

41 ¶ While the Pharisees were gathered together, Jesus asked them,

42 Saying, What think ye of Christ? whose son is he? They say unto him, *The Son* of David.

43 He saith unto them, How then doth David in spirit call him Lord, saying,

44 The Lord said unto my Lord, Sit thou on my right hand, till I make thine enemies thy footstool?

45 If David then call him Lord, how is he his son?

46 And no man was able to answer him a word, neither durst any *man* from that day forth ask him any more *questions*.

23 Then spake Jesus to the multitude, and to his disciples,

2 Saying, The scribes and the Pharisees sit in Moses' seat:

3 All therefore whatsoever they bid you observe, *that* observe and do; but do not ye after their works: for they say, and do not.

4 For they bind heavy burdens and grievous to be borne, and lay *them* on men's shoulders; but they *themselves* will not move them with one of their fingers.

NEW AMERICAN STANDARD BIBLE

41 Now while the Pharisees were gathered together, Jesus asked them a question:

42 "What do you think about the Christ, whose son is He?" They *said to Him, "*The son* of David."

43 He *said to them, "Then how does David in the Spirit call Him 'Lord,' saying,

44 'THE LORD SAID TO MY LORD,
"SIT AT MY RIGHT HAND,
UNTIL I PUT YOUR ENEMIES BENEATH YOUR FEET" '?

45 "If David then calls Him 'Lord,' how is He his son?"

46 No one was able to answer Him a word, nor did anyone dare from that day on to ask Him another question.

Pharisaism Exposed

23 Then Jesus spoke to the crowds and to His disciples,

2 saying: "The scribes and the Pharisees have seated themselves in the chair of Moses;

3 therefore all that they tell you, do and observe, but do not do according to their deeds; for they say *things* and do not do *them*.

4 "They tie up heavy burdens and lay them on men's shoulders, but they themselves are unwilling to move them with *so much as* a finger.

NEW CENTURY VERSION

Jesus Questions the Pharisees

41 While the Pharisees were together, Jesus asked them,
42 "What do you think about the Christ? Whose son is he?"
They answered, "The Christ is the Son of David."
43 Then Jesus said to them, "Then why did David call him 'Lord'? David, speaking by the power of the Holy Spirit, said,

44 'The Lord said to my Lord:
Sit by me at my right side,
until I put your enemies under your control.'
Psalm 110:1

45 David calls the Christ 'Lord,' so how can the Christ be his son?"

46 None of the Pharisees could answer Jesus' question, and after that day no one was brave enough to ask him any more questions.

Jesus Accuses Some Leaders

23 Then Jesus said to the crowds and to his followers,
2 "The teachers of the law and the Pharisees have
the authority to tell you what the law of Moses says. 3 So
you should obey and follow whatever they tell you, but their lives are not good examples for you to follow. They tell you to do things, but they themselves don't do them.
4 They make strict rules and try to force people to obey them, but they are unwilling to help those who struggle under the weight of their rules.

CONTEMPORARY ENGLISH VERSION

About David's Son (Mark 12.35-37; Luke 20.41-44)

41 While the Pharisees were still there, Jesus asked them,
42 "What do you think about the Messiah? Whose family will he come from?"
They answered, "He will be a son of King David."[d]
43 Jesus replied, "How then could the Spirit lead David to call the Messiah his Lord? David said,

44 'The Lord said to my Lord:
Sit at my right side[e]
until I make your enemies
into a footstool for you.'

45 If David called the Messiah his Lord, how can the
Messiah be a son of King David?" 46 No one was able to
give Jesus an answer, and from that day on, no one dared ask him any more questions.

Jesus Condemns the Pharisees and the Teachers of the Law of Moses
(Mark 12.38-40; Luke 11.37-52; 20.45-47)

23 Jesus said to the crowds and to his disciples:
2 The Pharisees and the teachers of the Law are
experts in the Law of Moses. 3 So obey everything they teach you, but don't do as they do. After all, they say one thing and do something else.
4 They pile heavy burdens on people's shoulders and

[d] 22.42 *son of King David*: See the note at 9.27. [e] 22.44 *right side*: The place of power and honor.

NEW INTERNATIONAL VERSION

Whose Son Is the Christ?

41While the Pharisees were gathered together, Jesus asked them, 42"What do you think about the Christ[d]? Whose son is he?"

"The son of David," they replied.

43He said to them, "How is it then that David, speaking by the Spirit, calls him 'Lord'? For he says,

44" 'The Lord said to my Lord:
"Sit at my right hand
until I put your enemies
under your feet." '[e]

45If then David calls him 'Lord,' how can he be his son?" 46No one could say a word in reply, and from that day on no one dared to ask him any more questions.

Seven Woes

23 Then Jesus said to the crowds and to his disciples: 2"The teachers of the law and the Pharisees sit in Moses' seat. 3So you must obey them and do everything they tell you. But do not do what they do, for they do not practice what they preach. 4They tie up heavy loads and put them on men's shoulders, but they themselves are not willing to lift a finger to move them.

[d] *42* Or *Messiah* [e] *44* Psalm 110:1

NEW LIVING TRANSLATION

Whose Son Is the Messiah?

41Then, surrounded by the Pharisees, Jesus asked them a question: 42"What do you think about the Messiah? Whose son is he?"

They replied, "He is the son of David."

43Jesus responded, "Then why does David, speaking under the inspiration of the Holy Spirit, call him Lord? For David said,

44 'The LORD said to my Lord,
Sit in honor at my right hand
until I humble your enemies beneath your feet.'*

45Since David called him Lord, how can he be his son at the same time?"

46No one could answer him. And after that, no one dared to ask him any more questions.

Jesus Warns the Religious Leaders

23 Then Jesus said to the crowds and to his disciples, 2"The teachers of religious law and the Pharisees are the official interpreters of the Scriptures. 3So practice and obey whatever they say to you, but don't follow their example. For they don't practice what they teach. 4They crush you with impossible religious demands and never lift a finger to help ease the burden.

22:44 Ps 110:1.

NEW KING JAMES VERSION

Jesus: How Can David Call His Descendant Lord?

41While the Pharisees were gathered together, Jesus asked them, 42saying, "What do you think about the Christ? Whose Son is He?"

They said to Him, *"The Son* of David."

43He said to them, "How then does David in the Spirit call Him *'Lord,'* saying:

44 *'The LORD said to my Lord,*
"Sit at My right hand,
Till I make Your enemies Your footstool" '?[f]

45If David then calls Him *'Lord,'* how is He his Son?" 46And no one was able to answer Him a word, nor from that day on did anyone dare question Him anymore.

Woe to the Scribes and Pharisees

23 Then Jesus spoke to the multitudes and to His disciples, 2saying: "The scribes and the Pharisees sit in Moses' seat. 3Therefore whatever they tell you to observe,[a] *that* observe and do, but do not do according to their works; for they say, and do not do. 4For they bind heavy burdens, hard to bear, and lay *them* on men's shoulders; but they *themselves* will not move them with one of

22:44 [f] Psalm 110:1 23:3 [a] NU-Text omits *to observe.*

THE MESSAGE

David's Son and Master

As the Pharisees were regrouping, Jesus caught them off balance with his own test question: "What do you think about the Christ? Whose son is he?" They said, "David's son."

Jesus replied, "Well, if the Christ is David's son, how do you explain that David, under inspiration, named Christ his 'Master'?

'God said to my Master,
"Sit here at my right hand
until I make your enemies your footstool." '

Now if David calls him 'Master,' how can he at the same time be his son?"

That stumped them, literalists that they were. Unwilling to risk losing face again in one of these public verbal exchanges, they quit asking questions for good.

Religious Fashion Shows

23 Now Jesus turned to address his disciples, along with the crowd that had gathered with them. "The religion scholars and Pharisees are competent teachers in God's Law. You won't go wrong in following their teachings on Moses. But be careful about following *them*. They talk a good line, but they don't live it. They don't take it into their hearts and live it out in their behavior. It's all spit-and-polish veneer.

"Instead of giving you God's Law as food and drink by which you can banquet on God, they package it in bundles of rules, loading you down like pack animals. They seem

KING JAMES VERSION

5 But all their works they do for to be seen of men: they make broad their phylacteries, and enlarge the borders of their garments,

6 And love the uppermost rooms at feasts, and the chief seats in the synagogues,

7 And greetings in the markets, and to be called of men, Rabbi, Rabbi.

8 But be not ye called Rabbi: for one is your Master, *even* Christ; and all ye are brethren.

9 And call no *man* your father upon the earth: for one is your Father, which is in heaven.

10 Neither be ye called masters: for one is your Master, *even* Christ.

11 But he that is greatest among you shall be your servant.

12 And whosoever shall exalt himself shall be abased; and he that shall humble himself shall be exalted.

13 ¶ But woe unto you, scribes and Pharisees, hypocrites! for ye shut up the kingdom of heaven against men: for ye neither go in *yourselves*, neither suffer ye them that are entering to go in.

14 Woe unto you, scribes and Pharisees, hypocrites! for ye devour widows' houses, and for a pretence make long prayer: therefore ye shall receive the greater damnation.

15 Woe unto you, scribes and Pharisees, hypocrites! for ye compass sea and land to make one proselyte, and when

NEW AMERICAN STANDARD BIBLE

5 "But they do all their deeds to be noticed by men; for they broaden their [1]phylacteries and lengthen the tassels *of their garments.*

6 "They love the place of honor at banquets and the chief seats in the synagogues,

7 and respectful greetings in the market places, and being called Rabbi by men.

8 "But do not be called Rabbi; for One is your Teacher, and you are all brothers.

9 "Do not call *anyone* on earth your father; for One is your Father, He who is in heaven.

10 "Do not be called leaders; for One is your Leader, *that is,* Christ.

11 "But the greatest among you shall be your servant.

12 "Whoever exalts himself shall be humbled; and whoever humbles himself shall be exalted.

Eight Woes

13 "But woe to you, scribes and Pharisees, hypocrites, because you shut off the kingdom of heaven from people; for you do not enter in yourselves, nor do you allow those who are entering to go in.

14 ["[2]Woe to you, scribes and Pharisees, hypocrites, because you devour widows' houses, and for a pretense you make long prayers; therefore you will receive greater condemnation.]

15 "Woe to you, scribes and Pharisees, hypocrites, because you travel around on sea and land to make one

23:5 [1] I.e. small cases containing Scripture texts worn on the left arm and forehead for religious purposes 23:14 [2] This v not found in early mss

NEW CENTURY VERSION

5 "They do good things so that other people will see them. They make the boxes[a] of Scriptures that they wear bigger, and they make their special prayer clothes very long. 6 Those Pharisees and teachers of the law love to have the most important seats at feasts and in the synagogues. 7 They love people to greet them with respect in the marketplaces, and they love to have people call them 'Teacher.'

8 "But you must not be called 'Teacher,' because you have only one Teacher, and you are all brothers and sisters together. 9 And don't call any person on earth 'Father,' because you have one Father, who is in heaven. 10 And you should not be called 'Master,' because you have only one Master, the Christ. 11 Whoever is your servant is the greatest among you. 12 Whoever makes himself great will be made humble. Whoever makes himself humble will be made great.

13 "How terrible for you, teachers of the law and Pharisees! You are hypocrites! You close the door for people to enter the kingdom of heaven. You yourselves don't enter, and you stop others who are trying to enter. 14[b]

15 "How terrible for you, teachers of the law and Pharisees! You are hypocrites! You travel across land and sea to find one person who will change to your ways.

23:5 [a] **boxes** Small leather boxes containing four important Scriptures. Some Jews tied these to the forehead and left arm, probably to show they were very religious. 23:14 [b] **Verse 14** Some Greek copies add verse 14: "How terrible for you, teachers of the law and Pharisees. You are hypocrites. You take away widows' houses, and you say long prayers so that people will notice you. So you will have a worse punishment."

CONTEMPORARY ENGLISH VERSION

won't lift a finger to help. 5 Everything they do is just to show off in front of others. They even make a big show of wearing Scripture verses on their foreheads and arms, and they wear big tassels[a] for everyone to see. 6 They love the best seats at banquets and the front seats in the meeting places. 7 And when they are in the market, they like to have people greet them as their teachers.

8 But none of you should be called a teacher. You have only one teacher, and all of you are like brothers and sisters. 9 Don't call anyone on earth your father. All of you have the same Father in heaven. 10 None of you should be called the leader. The Messiah is your only leader. 11 Whoever is the greatest should be the servant of the others. 12 If you put yourself above others, you will be put down. But if you humble yourself, you will be honored.

13-14 You Pharisees and teachers of the Law of Moses are in for trouble! You're nothing but show-offs. You lock people out of the kingdom of heaven. You won't go in yourselves, and you keep others from going in.[b]

15 You Pharisees and teachers of the Law of Moses are in for trouble! You're nothing but show-offs. You travel over land and sea to win one follower. And when you

[a] **23.5** *wearing Scripture verses on their foreheads and arms . . . tassels*: As a sign of their love for the Lord and his teachings, the Jewish people had started wearing Scripture verses in small leather boxes. But the Pharisees tried to show off by making the boxes bigger than necessary. The Jewish people were also taught to wear tassels on the four corners of their robes to show their love for God. [b] **23.13,14** *from going in*: Some manuscripts add, "You Pharisees and teachers are in for trouble! And you're nothing but show-offs! You cheat widows out of their homes and then pray long prayers just to show off. So you will be punished most of all."

NEW INTERNATIONAL VERSION

5"Everything they do is done for men to see: They make their phylacteries[a] wide and the tassels on their garments long; 6they love the place of honor at banquets and the most important seats in the synagogues; 7they love to be greeted in the marketplaces and to have men call them 'Rabbi.'

8"But you are not to be called 'Rabbi,' for you have only one Master and you are all brothers. 9And do not call anyone on earth 'father,' for you have one Father, and he is in heaven. 10Nor are you to be called 'teacher,' for you have one Teacher, the Christ.[b] 11The greatest among you will be your servant. 12For whoever exalts himself will be humbled, and whoever humbles himself will be exalted.

13"Woe to you, teachers of the law and Pharisees, you hypocrites! You shut the kingdom of heaven in men's faces. You yourselves do not enter, nor will you let those enter who are trying to.[c]

15"Woe to you, teachers of the law and Pharisees, you hypocrites! You travel over land and sea to win a single

[a] *5* That is, boxes containing Scripture verses, worn on forehead and arm
[b] *10* Or *Messiah* [c] *13* Some manuscripts *to.* *14Woe to you, teachers of the law and Pharisees, you hypocrites! You devour widows' houses and for a show make lengthy prayers. Therefore you will be punished more severely.*

NEW LIVING TRANSLATION

5"Everything they do is for show. On their arms they wear extra wide prayer boxes with Scripture verses inside,* and they wear extra long tassels on their robes. 6And how they love to sit at the head table at banquets and in the most prominent seats in the synagogue! 7They enjoy the attention they get on the streets, and they enjoy being called 'Rabbi.'* 8Don't ever let anyone call you 'Rabbi,' for you have only one teacher, and all of you are on the same level as brothers and sisters.* 9And don't address anyone here on earth as 'Father,' for only God in heaven is your spiritual Father. 10And don't let anyone call you 'Master,' for there is only one master, the Messiah. 11The greatest among you must be a servant. 12But those who exalt themselves will be humbled, and those who humble themselves will be exalted.

13"How terrible it will be for you teachers of religious law and you Pharisees. Hypocrites! For you won't let others enter the Kingdom of Heaven, and you won't go in yourselves.* 15Yes, how terrible it will be for you teachers of religious law and you Pharisees. For you cross land and

23:5 Greek *They enlarge their phylacteries.* 23:7 *Rabbi,* from Aramaic, means "master" or "teacher." 23:8 Greek *brothers.* 23:13 Some manuscripts add verse 14, *How terrible it will be for you teachers of religious law and you Pharisees. Hypocrites! You shamelessly cheat widows out of their property, and then, to cover up the kind of people you really are, you make long prayers in public. Because of this, your punishment will be the greater.*

NEW KING JAMES VERSION

their fingers. 5But all their works they do to be seen by men. They make their phylacteries broad and enlarge the borders of their garments. 6They love the best places at feasts, the best seats in the synagogues, 7greetings in the marketplaces, and to be called by men, 'Rabbi, Rabbi.' 8But you, do not be called 'Rabbi'; for One is your Teacher, the Christ,[b] and you are all brethren. 9Do not call anyone on earth your father; for One is your Father, He who is in heaven. 10And do not be called teachers; for One is your Teacher, the Christ. 11But he who is greatest among you shall be your servant. 12And whoever exalts himself will be humbled, and he who humbles himself will be exalted.

13"But woe to you, scribes and Pharisees, hypocrites! For you shut up the kingdom of heaven against men; for you neither go in *yourselves,* nor do you allow those who are entering to go in. 14Woe to you, scribes and Pharisees, hypocrites! For you devour widows' houses, and for a pretense make long prayers. Therefore you will receive greater condemnation.[c]

15"Woe to you, scribes and Pharisees, hypocrites! For you travel land and sea to win one proselyte, and when he

23:8 [b] NU-Text omits *the Christ.* 23:14 [c] NU-Text omits this verse.

THE MESSAGE

to take pleasure in watching you stagger under these loads, and wouldn't think of lifting a finger to help. Their lives are perpetual fashion shows, embroidered prayer shawls one day and flowery prayers the next. They love to sit at the head table at church dinners, basking in the most prominent positions, preening in the radiance of public flattery, receiving honorary degrees, and getting called 'Doctor' and 'Reverend.'

"Don't let people do that to *you,* put you on a pedestal like that. You all have a single Teacher, and you are all classmates. Don't set people up as experts over your life, letting them tell you what to do. Save that authority for God; let *him* tell you what to do. No one else should carry the title of 'Father'; you have only one Father, and he's in heaven. And don't let people maneuver you into taking charge of them. There is only one Life-Leader for you and them—Christ.

"Do you want to stand out? Then step down. Be a servant. If you puff yourself up, you'll get the wind knocked out of you. But if you're content to simply be yourself, your life will count for plenty.

Frauds!

"I've had it with you! You're hopeless, you religion scholars, you Pharisees! Frauds! Your lives are roadblocks to God's kingdom. You refuse to enter, and won't let anyone else in either.

"You're hopeless, you religion scholars and Pharisees! Frauds! You go halfway around the world to make a

KING JAMES VERSION

he is made, ye make him twofold more the child of hell than yourselves.

16 Woe unto you, *ye* blind guides, which say, Whosoever shall swear by the temple, it is nothing; but whosoever shall swear by the gold of the temple, he is a debtor!

17 *Ye* fools and blind: for whether is greater, the gold, or the temple that sanctifieth the gold?

18 And, Whosoever shall swear by the altar, it is nothing; but whosoever sweareth by the gift that is upon it, he is guilty.

19 *Ye* fools and blind: for whether *is* greater, the gift, or the altar that sanctifieth the gift?

20 Whoso therefore shall swear by the altar, sweareth by it, and by all things thereon.

21 And whoso shall swear by the temple, sweareth by it, and by him that dwelleth therein.

22 And he that shall swear by heaven, sweareth by the throne of God, and by him that sitteth thereon.

23 Woe unto you, scribes and Pharisees, hypocrites! for ye pay tithe of mint and anise and cummin, and have omitted the weightier *matters* of the law, judgment, mercy, and faith: these ought ye to have done, and not to leave the other undone.

24 *Ye* blind guides, which strain at a gnat, and swallow a camel.

NEW AMERICAN STANDARD BIBLE

proselyte; and when he becomes one, you make him twice as much a son of hell as yourselves.

16 "Woe to you, blind guides, who say, 'Whoever swears by the temple, *that* is nothing; but whoever swears by the gold of the temple is obligated.'

17 "You fools and blind men! Which is more important, the gold or the temple that sanctified the gold?

18 "And, 'Whoever swears by the altar, *that* is nothing, but whoever swears by the offering on it, he is obligated.'

19 "You blind men, which is more important, the offering, or the altar that sanctifies the offering?

20 "Therefore, whoever swears by the altar, swears *both* by the altar and by everything on it.

21 "And whoever swears by the temple, swears *both* by the temple and by Him who dwells within it.

22 "And whoever swears by heaven, swears *both* by the throne of God and by Him who sits upon it.

23 "Woe to you, scribes and Pharisees, hypocrites! For you tithe the mint and dill and cummin, and have neglected the weightier provisions of the law: justice and mercy and faithfulness; but these are the things you should have done without neglecting the others.

24 "You blind guides, who strain out a gnat and swallow a camel!

NEW CENTURY VERSION

When you find that person, you make him more fit for hell than you are.
16"How terrible for you! You guide the people, but you
are blind. You say, 'If people swear by the Temple when
they make a promise, that means nothing. But if they
swear by the gold that is in the Temple, they must keep
that promise.' 17You are blind fools! Which is greater: the
gold or the Temple that makes that gold holy? 18And you
say, 'If people swear by the altar when they make a promise, that means nothing. But if they swear by the gift on
the altar, they must keep that promise.' 19You are blind!
Which is greater: the gift or the altar that makes the gift
holy? 20The person who swears by the altar is really using
the altar and also everything on the altar. 21And the person who swears by the Temple is really using the Temple
and also everything in the Temple. 22The person who
swears by heaven is also using God's throne and the One who sits on that throne.
23"How terrible for you, teachers of the law and Pharisees! You are hypocrites! You give to God one-tenth of everything you earn—even your mint, dill, and cumin.[c] But you don't obey the really important teachings of the law—justice, mercy, and being loyal. These are the things
you should do, as well as those other things. 24You guide
the people, but you are blind! You are like a person who picks a fly out of a drink and then swallows a camel![d]

23:23 [c] **mint, dill, and cumin** Small plants grown in gardens and used for spices. Only very religious people would be careful enough to give a tenth of these plants. **23:24** [d] **You...camel!** Meaning, "You worry about the smallest mistakes but commit the biggest sin."

CONTEMPORARY ENGLISH VERSION

have done so, you make that person twice as fit for hell as you are.
16You are in for trouble! You are supposed to lead others, but you are blind. You teach that it doesn't matter if a person swears by the temple. But you say that it does matter if someone swears by the gold in the temple.
17You blind fools! Which is greater, the gold or the temple that makes the gold sacred?
18You also teach that it doesn't matter if a person swears by the altar. But you say that it does matter if
someone swears by the gift on the altar. 19Are you
blind? Which is more important, the gift or the altar that
makes the gift sacred? 20Anyone who swears by the
altar also swears by everything on it. 21And anyone who
swears by the temple also swears by God, who lives
there. 22To swear by heaven is the same as swearing by God's throne and by the one who sits on that throne.
23You Pharisees and teachers are show-offs, and you're in for trouble! You give God a tenth of the spices from your garden, such as mint, dill, and cumin. Yet you neglect the more important matters of the Law, such as justice, mercy, and faithfulness. These are the important things you should have done, though you should not
have left the others undone either. 24You blind leaders!
You strain out a small fly but swallow a camel.

NEW INTERNATIONAL VERSION

convert, and when he becomes one, you make him twice as much a son of hell as you are.

16"Woe to you, blind guides! You say, 'If anyone swears by the temple, it means nothing; but if anyone swears by the gold of the temple, he is bound by his oath.' 17You blind fools! Which is greater: the gold, or the temple that makes the gold sacred? 18You also say, 'If anyone swears by the altar, it means nothing; but if anyone swears by the gift on it, he is bound by his oath.' 19You blind men! Which is greater: the gift, or the altar that makes the gift sacred? 20Therefore, he who swears by the altar swears by it and by everything on it. 21And he who swears by the temple swears by it and by the one who dwells in it. 22And he who swears by heaven swears by God's throne and by the one who sits on it.

23"Woe to you, teachers of the law and Pharisees, you hypocrites! You give a tenth of your spices—mint, dill and cummin. But you have neglected the more important matters of the law—justice, mercy and faithfulness. You should have practiced the latter, without neglecting the former. 24You blind guides! You strain out a gnat but swallow a camel.

NEW LIVING TRANSLATION

sea to make one convert, and then you turn him into twice the son of hell as you yourselves are.

16"Blind guides! How terrible it will be for you! For you say that it means nothing to swear 'by God's Temple'—you can break that oath. But then you say that it is binding to swear 'by the gold in the Temple.' 17Blind fools! Which is greater, the gold, or the Temple that makes the gold sacred? 18And you say that to take an oath 'by the altar' can be broken, but to swear 'by the gifts on the altar' is binding! 19How blind! For which is greater, the gift on the altar, or the altar that makes the gift sacred? 20When you swear 'by the altar,' you are swearing by it and by everything on it. 21And when you swear 'by the Temple,' you are swearing by it and by God, who lives in it. 22And when you swear 'by heaven,' you are swearing by the throne of God and by God, who sits on the throne.

23"How terrible it will be for you teachers of religious law and you Pharisees. Hypocrites! For you are careful to tithe even the tiniest part of your income,* but you ignore the important things of the law—justice, mercy, and faith. You should tithe, yes, but you should not leave undone the more important things. 24Blind guides! You strain your water so you won't accidentally swallow a gnat; then you swallow a camel!

23:23 Greek *to tithe the mint, the dill, and the cumin.*

NEW KING JAMES VERSION

is won, you make him twice as much a son of hell as yourselves.

16"Woe to you, blind guides, who say, 'Whoever swears by the temple, it is nothing; but whoever swears by the gold of the temple, he is obliged *to perform it.*' 17Fools and blind! For which is greater, the gold or the temple that sanctifies[d] the gold? 18And, 'Whoever swears by the altar, it is nothing; but whoever swears by the gift that is on it, he is obliged *to perform it.*' 19Fools and blind! For which is greater, the gift or the altar that sanctifies the gift? 20Therefore he who swears by the altar, swears by it and by all things on it. 21He who swears by the temple, swears by it and by Him who dwells[e] in it. 22And he who swears by heaven, swears by the throne of God and by Him who sits on it.

23"Woe to you, scribes and Pharisees, hypocrites! For you pay tithe of mint and anise and cummin, and have neglected the weightier *matters* of the law: justice and mercy and faith. These you ought to have done, without leaving the others undone. 24Blind guides, who strain out a gnat and swallow a camel!

23:17 [d] NU-Text reads *sanctified.* 23:21 [e] M-Text reads *dwelt.*

THE MESSAGE

convert, but once you get him you make him into a replica of yourselves, double-damned.

"You're hopeless! What arrogant stupidity! You say, 'If someone makes a promise with his fingers crossed, that's nothing; but if he swears with his hand on the Bible, that's serious.' What ignorance! Does the leather on the Bible carry more weight than the skin on your hands? And what about this piece of trivia: 'If you shake hands on a promise, that's nothing; but if you raise your hand that God is your witness, that's serious'? What ridiculous hairsplitting! What difference does it make whether you shake hands or raise hands? A promise is a promise. What difference does it make if you make your promise inside or outside a house of worship? A promise is a promise. God is present, watching and holding you to account regardless.

"You're hopeless, you religion scholars and Pharisees! Frauds! You keep meticulous account books, tithing on every nickel and dime you get, but on the meat of God's Law, things like fairness and compassion and commitment—the absolute basics!—you carelessly take it or leave it. Careful bookkeeping is commendable, but the basics are required. Do you have any idea how silly you look, writing a life story that's wrong from start to finish, nitpicking over commas and semicolons?

KING JAMES VERSION

25 Woe unto you, scribes and Pharisees, hypocrites! for ye make clean the outside of the cup and of the platter, but within they are full of extortion and excess.

26 *Thou* blind Pharisee, cleanse first that *which is* within the cup and platter, that the outside of them may be clean also.

27 Woe unto you, scribes and Pharisees, hypocrites! for ye are like unto whited sepulchres, which indeed appear beautiful outward, but are within full of dead *men's* bones, and of all uncleanness.

28 Even so ye also outwardly appear righteous unto men, but within ye are full of hypocrisy and iniquity.

29 Woe unto you, scribes and Pharisees, hypocrites! because ye build the tombs of the prophets, and garnish the sepulchres of the righteous,

30 And say, If we had been in the days of our fathers, we would not have been partakers with them in the blood of the prophets.

31 Wherefore ye be witnesses unto yourselves, that ye are the children of them which killed the prophets.

32 Fill ye up then the measure of your fathers.

33 *Ye* serpents, *ye* generation of vipers, how can ye escape the damnation of hell?

34 ¶ Wherefore, behold, I send unto you prophets, and wise men, and scribes: and *some* of them ye shall kill and crucify; and *some* of them shall ye scourge in your synagogues, and persecute *them* from city to city:

35 That upon you may come all the righteous blood shed upon the earth, from the blood of righteous Abel unto

NEW AMERICAN STANDARD BIBLE

25 "Woe to you, scribes and Pharisees, hypocrites! For you clean the outside of the cup and of the dish, but inside they are full of robbery and self-indulgence.

26 "You blind Pharisee, first clean the inside of the cup and of the dish, so that the outside of it may become clean also.

27 "Woe to you, scribes and Pharisees, hypocrites! For you are like whitewashed tombs which on the outside appear beautiful, but inside they are full of dead men's bones and all uncleanness.

28 "So you, too, outwardly appear righteous to men, but inwardly you are full of hypocrisy and lawlessness.

29 "Woe to you, scribes and Pharisees, hypocrites! For you build the tombs of the prophets and adorn the monuments of the righteous,

30 and say, 'If we had been *living* in the days of our fathers, we would not have been partners with them in *shedding* the blood of the prophets.'

31 "So you testify against yourselves, that you are sons of those who murdered the prophets.

32 "Fill up, then, the measure *of the guilt* of your fathers.

33 "You serpents, you brood of vipers, how will you escape the sentence of hell?

34 "Therefore, behold, I am sending you prophets and wise men and scribes; some of them you will kill and crucify, and some of them you will scourge in your synagogues, and persecute from city to city,

35 so that upon you may fall *the guilt of* all the righteous blood shed on earth, from the blood of righteous

NEW CENTURY VERSION

25 "How terrible for you, teachers of the law and
Pharisees! You are hypocrites! You wash the outside of
your cups and dishes, but inside they are full of things you
got by cheating others and by pleasing only yourselves.
26 Pharisees, you are blind! First make the inside of the cup
clean, and then the outside of the cup can be truly clean.
27 "How terrible for you, teachers of the law and
Pharisees! You are hypocrites! You are like tombs that are
painted white. Outside, those tombs look fine, but inside,
they are full of the bones of dead people and all kinds of
unclean things. 28 It is the same with you. People look at
you and think you are good, but on the inside you are full
of hypocrisy and evil.
29 "How terrible for you, teachers of the law and
Pharisees! You are hypocrites! You build tombs for the
prophets, and you show honor to the graves of those who
lived good lives. 30 You say, 'If we had lived during the
time of our ancestors, we would not have helped them kill
the prophets.' 31 But you give proof that you are children of
those who murdered the prophets. 32 And you will complete
the sin that your ancestors started.
33 "You are snakes! A family of poisonous snakes! How
are you going to escape God's judgment? 34 So I tell you
this: I am sending to you prophets and wise men and
teachers. Some of them you will kill and crucify. Some of
them you will beat in your synagogues and chase from
town to town. 35 So you will be guilty for the death of all
the good people who have been killed on earth—from the

CONTEMPORARY ENGLISH VERSION

25 You Pharisees and teachers are show-offs, and
you're in for trouble! You wash the outside of your cups
and dishes, while inside there is nothing but greed and
selfishness. 26 You blind Pharisee! First clean the inside
of a cup, and then the outside will also be clean.
27 You Pharisees and teachers are in for trouble!
You're nothing but show-offs. You're like tombs that
have been whitewashed.[c] On the outside they are beau-
tiful, but inside they are full of bones and filth. 28 That's
what you are like. Outside you look good, but inside you
are evil and only pretend to be good.
29 You Pharisees and teachers are nothing but show-
offs, and you're in for trouble! You build monuments for
the prophets and decorate the tombs of good people.
30 And you claim that you would not have taken part
with your ancestors in killing the prophets. 31 But you
prove that you really are the relatives of the ones who
killed the prophets. 32 So keep on doing everything they
did. 33 You are nothing but snakes and the children of
snakes! How can you escape going to hell?
34 I will send prophets and wise people and experts in
the Law of Moses to you. But you will kill them or nail
them to a cross or beat them in your meeting places or
chase them from town to town. 35 That's why you will be
held guilty for the murder of every good person, beginning
with the good man Abel. This also includes Barachiah's

[c] 23.27 *whitewashed*: Tombs were whitewashed to keep anyone from accidentally touching them. A person who touched a dead body or a tomb was considered unclean and could not worship with the rest of the Jewish people.

NEW INTERNATIONAL VERSION

25"Woe to you, teachers of the law and Pharisees, you hypocrites! You clean the outside of the cup and dish, but inside they are full of greed and self-indulgence. 26Blind Pharisee! First clean the inside of the cup and dish, and then the outside also will be clean.

27"Woe to you, teachers of the law and Pharisees, you hypocrites! You are like whitewashed tombs, which look beautiful on the outside but on the inside are full of dead men's bones and everything unclean. 28In the same way, on the outside you appear to people as righteous but on the inside you are full of hypocrisy and wickedness.

29"Woe to you, teachers of the law and Pharisees, you hypocrites! You build tombs for the prophets and decorate the graves of the righteous. 30And you say, 'If we had lived in the days of our forefathers, we would not have taken part with them in shedding the blood of the prophets.' 31So you testify against yourselves that you are the descendants of those who murdered the prophets. 32Fill up, then, the measure of the sin of your forefathers!

33"You snakes! You brood of vipers! How will you escape being condemned to hell? 34Therefore I am sending you prophets and wise men and teachers. Some of them you will kill and crucify; others you will flog in your synagogues and pursue from town to town. 35And so upon you will come all the righteous blood that has been shed on earth, from the blood of righteous Abel to the blood of

NEW LIVING TRANSLATION

25"How terrible it will be for you teachers of religious law and you Pharisees. Hypocrites! You are so careful to clean the outside of the cup and the dish, but inside you are filthy—full of greed and self-indulgence! 26Blind Pharisees! First wash the inside of the cup, and then the outside will become clean, too.

27"How terrible it will be for you teachers of religious law and you Pharisees. Hypocrites! You are like whitewashed tombs—beautiful on the outside but filled on the inside with dead people's bones and all sorts of impurity. 28You try to look like upright people outwardly, but inside your hearts are filled with hypocrisy and lawlessness.

29"How terrible it will be for you teachers of religious law and you Pharisees. Hypocrites! For you build tombs for the prophets your ancestors killed and decorate the graves of the godly people your ancestors destroyed. 30Then you say, 'We never would have joined them in killing the prophets.'

31"In saying that, you are accusing yourselves of being the descendants of those who murdered the prophets. 32Go ahead. Finish what they started. 33Snakes! Sons of vipers! How will you escape the judgment of hell? 34I will send you prophets and wise men and teachers of religious law. You will kill some by crucifixion and whip others in your synagogues, chasing them from city to city. 35As a result, you will become guilty of murdering all the godly people

NEW KING JAMES VERSION

25"Woe to you, scribes and Pharisees, hypocrites! For you cleanse the outside of the cup and dish, but inside they are full of extortion and self-indulgence.[f] 26Blind Pharisee, first cleanse the inside of the cup and dish, that the outside of them may be clean also.

27"Woe to you, scribes and Pharisees, hypocrites! For you are like whitewashed tombs which indeed appear beautiful outwardly, but inside are full of dead *men's* bones and all uncleanness. 28Even so you also outwardly appear righteous to men, but inside you are full of hypocrisy and lawlessness.

29"Woe to you, scribes and Pharisees, hypocrites! Because you build the tombs of the prophets and adorn the monuments of the righteous, 30and say, 'If we had lived in the days of our fathers, we would not have been partakers with them in the blood of the prophets.'

31"Therefore you are witnesses against yourselves that you are sons of those who murdered the prophets. 32Fill up, then, the measure of your fathers' *guilt.* 33Serpents, brood of vipers! How can you escape the condemnation of hell? 34Therefore, indeed, I send you prophets, wise men, and scribes: *some* of them you will kill and crucify, and *some* of them you will scourge in your synagogues and persecute from city to city, 35that on you may come all the righteous blood shed on the earth, from the blood of righteous Abel to

23:25 [f] M-Text reads *unrighteousness.*

THE MESSAGE

"You're hopeless, you religion scholars and Pharisees! Frauds! You burnish the surface of your cups and bowls so they sparkle in the sun, while the insides are maggoty with your greed and gluttony. Stupid Pharisee! Scour the insides, and then the gleaming surface will mean something.

"You're hopeless, you religion scholars and Pharisees! Frauds! You're like manicured grave plots, grass clipped and the flowers bright, but six feet down it's all rotting bones and worm-eaten flesh. People look at you and think you're saints, but beneath the skin you're total frauds.

"You're hopeless, you religion scholars and Pharisees! Frauds! You build granite tombs for your prophets and marble monuments for your saints. And you say that if you had lived in the days of your ancestors, no blood would have been on your hands. You protest too much! You're cut from the same cloth as those murderers, and daily add to the death count.

"Snakes! Reptilian sneaks! Do you think you can worm your way out of this? Never have to pay the piper? It's on account of people like you that I send prophets and wise guides and scholars generation after generation—and generation after generation you treat them like dirt, greeting them with lynch mobs, hounding them with abuse.

"You can't squirm out of this: Every drop of righteous blood ever spilled on this earth, beginning with the blood

KING JAMES VERSION

the blood of Zacharias son of Barachias, whom ye slew
between the temple and the altar.
36 Verily I say unto you, All these things shall come
upon this generation.
37 O Jerusalem, Jerusalem, *thou* that killest the proph-
ets, and stonest them which are sent unto thee, how often
would I have gathered thy children together, even as a hen
gathereth her chickens under *her* wings, and ye would not!
38 Behold, your house is left unto you desolate.
39 For I say unto you, Ye shall not see me henceforth,
till ye shall say, Blessed *is* he that cometh in the name of
the Lord.

24 And Jesus went out, and departed from the temple:
and his disciples came to *him* for to shew him the
buildings of the temple.
2 And Jesus said unto them, See ye not all these things?
verily I say unto you, There shall not be left here one stone
upon another, that shall not be thrown down.
3 And as he sat upon the mount of Olives, the disciples
came unto him privately, saying, Tell us, when shall these
things be? and what *shall be* the sign of thy coming, and
of the end of the world?

NEW AMERICAN STANDARD BIBLE

Abel to the blood of Zechariah, the son of Berechiah,
whom you murdered between the temple and the altar.
36 "Truly I say to you, all these things will come upon
this generation.

Lament over Jerusalem

37 "Jerusalem, Jerusalem, who kills the prophets and
stones those who are sent to her! How often I wanted to
gather your children together, the way a hen gathers her
chicks under her wings, and you were unwilling.
38 "Behold, your house is being left to you desolate!
39 "For I say to you, from now on you will not see Me
until you say, 'BLESSED IS HE WHO COMES IN THE NAME OF THE
LORD!' "

Signs of Christ's Return

24 Jesus came out from the temple and was going
away when His disciples came up to point out the
temple buildings to Him.
2 And He said to them, "Do you not see all these
things? Truly I say to you, not one stone here will be left
upon another, which will not be torn down."
3 As He was sitting on the Mount of Olives, the disci-
ples came to Him privately, saying, "Tell us, when will
these things happen, and what *will be* the sign of Your
coming, and of the end of the age?"

NEW CENTURY VERSION

murder of that good man Abel to the murder of Zechariah[e]
son of Berakiah, whom you murdered between the Temple
and the altar. [36]I tell you the truth, all of these things will
happen to you people who are living now.

Jesus Feels Sorry for Jerusalem

[37]"Jerusalem, Jerusalem! You kill the prophets and stone
to death those who are sent to you. Many times I wanted
to gather your people as a hen gathers her chicks under
her wings, but you did not let me. [38]Now your house will
be left completely empty. [39]I tell you, you will not see me
again until that time when you will say, 'God bless the
One who comes in the name of the Lord.' "[f]

The Temple Will Be Destroyed

24 As Jesus left the Temple and was walking away,
his followers came up to show him the Temple's
buildings. [2]Jesus asked, "Do you see all these buildings? I
tell you the truth, not one stone will be left on another.
Every stone will be thrown down to the ground."
[3]Later, as Jesus was sitting on the Mount of Olives, his
followers came to be alone with him. They said, "Tell us,
when will these things happen? And what will be the sign
that it is time for you to come again and for this age to
end?"

23:35 [e] **Abel...Zechariah** In the order of the books of the Hebrew Old Testament, the first and last men to be murdered.
23:39 [f] **'God...Lord.'** Quotation from Psalm 118:26.

CONTEMPORARY ENGLISH VERSION

son Zechariah,[d] the man you murdered between the tem-
ple and the altar. [36]I can promise that you people living
today will be punished for all these things!

Jesus Loves Jerusalem (Luke 13.34, 35)

[37]Jerusalem, Jerusalem! Your people have killed the
prophets and have stoned the messengers who were
sent to you. I have often wanted to gather your people,
as a hen gathers her chicks under her wings. But you
wouldn't let me. [38]And now your temple will be desert-
ed. [39]You won't see me again until you say,

"Blessed is the one who comes
in the name of the Lord."

The Temple Will Be Destroyed (Mark 13.1, 2; Luke 21.5, 6)

24 After Jesus left the temple, his disciples came over
and said, "Look at all these buildings!"
[2]Jesus replied, "Do you see these buildings? They will
certainly be torn down! Not one stone will be left in place."

Warning about Trouble (Mark 13.3-13; Luke 21.7-19)

[3]Later, as Jesus was sitting on the Mount of Olives, his
disciples came to him in private and asked, "When will
this happen? What will be the sign of your coming and of
the end of the world?"

[d] 23.35 *Zechariah*: Genesis is the first book in the Jewish Scriptures, and it tells that Abel was the first person to be murdered. Second Chronicles is the last book in the Jewish Scriptures, and the last murder that it tells about is that of Zechariah.

NEW INTERNATIONAL VERSION

Zechariah son of Berekiah, whom you murdered between the temple and the altar. 36I tell you the truth, all this will come upon this generation.

37"O Jerusalem, Jerusalem, you who kill the prophets and stone those sent to you, how often I have longed to gather your children together, as a hen gathers her chicks under her wings, but you were not willing. 38Look, your house is left to you desolate. 39For I tell you, you will not see me again until you say, 'Blessed is he who comes in the name of the Lord.'[d]"

Signs of the End of the Age

24 Jesus left the temple and was walking away when his disciples came up to him to call his attention to its buildings. 2"Do you see all these things?" he asked. "I tell you the truth, not one stone here will be left on another; every one will be thrown down."

3As Jesus was sitting on the Mount of Olives, the disciples came to him privately. "Tell us," they said, "when will this happen, and what will be the sign of your coming and of the end of the age?"

[d] *39* Psalm 118:26

NEW LIVING TRANSLATION

from righteous Abel to Zechariah son of Barachiah, whom you murdered in the Temple between the altar and the sanctuary. 36I assure you, all the accumulated judgment of the centuries will break upon the heads of this very generation.

Jesus Grieves over Jerusalem

37"O Jerusalem, Jerusalem, the city that kills the prophets and stones God's messengers! How often I have wanted to gather your children together as a hen protects her chicks beneath her wings, but you wouldn't let me. 38And now look, your house is left to you, empty and desolate. 39For I tell you this, you will never see me again until you say, 'Bless the one who comes in the name of the Lord!'*"

Jesus Foretells the Future

24 As Jesus was leaving the Temple grounds, his disciples pointed out to him the various Temple buildings. 2But he told them, "Do you see all these buildings? I assure you, they will be so completely demolished that not one stone will be left on top of another!"

3Later, Jesus sat on the slopes of the Mount of Olives. His disciples came to him privately and asked, "When will all this take place? And will there be any sign ahead of time to signal your return and the end of the world*?"

23:39 Ps 118:26. **24:3** Or *the age.*

NEW KING JAMES VERSION

the blood of Zechariah, son of Berechiah, whom you murdered between the temple and the altar. 36Assuredly, I say to you, all these things will come upon this generation.

Jesus Laments over Jerusalem

37"O Jerusalem, Jerusalem, the one who kills the prophets and stones those who are sent to her! How often I wanted to gather your children together, as a hen gathers her chicks under *her* wings, but you were not willing! 38See! Your house is left to you desolate; 39for I say to you, you shall see Me no more till you say, *'Blessed is He who comes in the name of the* LORD!'"[g]

Jesus Predicts the Destruction of the Temple

24 Then Jesus went out and departed from the temple, and His disciples came up to show Him the buildings of the temple. 2And Jesus said to them, "Do you not see all these things? Assuredly, I say to you, not *one* stone shall be left here upon another, that shall not be thrown down."

The Signs of the Times and the End of the Age

3Now as He sat on the Mount of Olives, the disciples came to Him privately, saying, "Tell us, when will these things be? And what *will be* the sign of Your coming, and of the end of the age?"

23:39 [g] Psalm 118:26

THE MESSAGE

of that good man Abel right down to the blood of Zechariah, Barachiah's son, whom you murdered at his prayers, is on your head. All this, I'm telling you, is coming down on you, on your generation.

"Jerusalem! Jerusalem! Murderer of prophets! Killer of the ones who brought you God's news! How often I've ached to embrace your children, the way a hen gathers her chicks under her wings, and you wouldn't let me. And now you're so desolate, nothing but a ghost town. What is there left to say? Only this: I'm out of here soon. The next time you see me you'll say, 'Oh, God has blessed him! He's come, bringing God's rule!'"

Routine History

24 Jesus then left the Temple. As he walked away, his disciples pointed out how very impressive the Temple architecture was. Jesus said, "You're not impressed by all this sheer *size,* are you? The truth of the matter is that there's not a stone in that building that is not going to end up in a pile of rubble."

Later as he was sitting on Mount Olives, his disciples approached and asked him, "Tell us, when are these things going to happen? What will be the sign of your coming, that the time's up?"

KING JAMES VERSION

4 ¶ And Jesus answered and said unto them, Take heed that no man deceive you.

5 For many shall come in my name, saying, I am Christ; and shall deceive many.

6 And ye shall hear of wars and rumours of wars: see that ye be not troubled: for all *these things* must come to pass, but the end is not yet.

7 For nation shall rise against nation, and kingdom against kingdom: and there shall be famines, and pestilences, and earthquakes, in divers places.

8 All these *are* the beginning of sorrows.

9 Then shall they deliver you up to be afflicted, and shall kill you: and ye shall be hated of all nations for my name's sake.

10 And then shall many be offended, and shall betray one another, and shall hate one another.

11 And many false prophets shall rise, and shall deceive many.

12 And because iniquity shall abound, the love of many shall wax cold.

13 But he that shall endure unto the end, the same shall be saved.

14 And this gospel of the kingdom shall be preached in all the world for a witness unto all nations; and then shall the end come.

15 When ye therefore shall see the abomination of desolation, spoken of by Daniel the prophet, stand in the holy place, (whoso readeth, let him understand:)

16 Then let them which be in Judaea flee into the mountains:

NEW AMERICAN STANDARD BIBLE

4 And Jesus answered and said to them, "See to it that no one misleads you.

5 "For many will come in My name, saying, 'I am the Christ,' and will mislead many.

6 "You will be hearing of wars and rumors of wars. See that you are not frightened, for *those things* must take place, but *that* is not yet the end.

7 "For nation will rise against nation, and kingdom against kingdom, and in various places there will be famines and earthquakes.

8 "But all these things are *merely* the beginning of birth pangs.

9 "Then they will deliver you to tribulation, and will kill you, and you will be hated by all nations because of My name.

10 "At that time many will fall away and will betray one another and hate one another.

11 "Many false prophets will arise and will mislead many.

12 "Because lawlessness is increased, most people's love will grow cold.

13 "But the one who endures to the end, he will be saved.

14 "This gospel of the kingdom shall be preached in the whole world as a testimony to all the nations, and then the end will come.

Perilous Times

15 "Therefore when you see the ABOMINATION OF DESOLATION which was spoken of through Daniel the prophet, standing in the holy place (let the reader understand),

16 then those who are in Judea must flee to the mountains.

NEW CENTURY VERSION

4 Jesus answered, "Be careful that no one fools you.
5 Many will come in my name, saying, 'I am the Christ,'
and they will fool many people. 6 You will hear about wars
and stories of wars that are coming, but don't be afraid.
These things must happen before the end comes. 7 Nations
will fight against other nations; kingdoms will fight
against other kingdoms. There will be times when there is
no food for people to eat, and there will be earthquakes in
different places. 8 These things are like the first pains when
something new is about to be born.
9 "Then people will arrest you, hand you over to be hurt,
and kill you. They will hate you because you believe in me.
10 At that time, many will lose their faith, and they will
turn against each other and hate each other. 11 Many false
prophets will come and cause many people to believe lies.
12 There will be more and more evil in the world, so most
people will stop showing their love for each other. 13 But
those people who keep their faith until the end will be
saved. 14 The Good News about God's kingdom will be
preached in all the world, to every nation. Then the end
will come.
15 "Daniel the prophet spoke about 'the destroying terror.'[a] You will see this standing in the holy place." (You
who read this should understand what it means.) 16 "At
that time, the people in Judea should run away to the

24:15 [a] **'the destroying terror'** Mentioned in Daniel 9:27; 12:11 (see also Daniel 11:31).

CONTEMPORARY ENGLISH VERSION

4 Jesus answered:
Don't let anyone fool you. 5 Many will come and claim
to be me. They will say that they are the Messiah, and
they will fool many people.
6 You will soon hear about wars and threats of wars,
but don't be afraid. These things will have to happen
first, but that isn't the end. 7 Nations and kingdoms will
go to war against each other. People will starve to death,
and in some places there will be earthquakes. 8 But this
is just the beginning of troubles.
9 You will be arrested, punished, and even killed.
Because of me, you will be hated by people of all
nations. 10 Many will give up and will betray and hate
each other. 11 Many false prophets will come and fool a
lot of people. 12 Evil will spread and cause many people
to stop loving others. 13 But if you keep on being faithful
right to the end, you will be saved. 14 When the good
news about the kingdom has been preached all over the
world and told to all nations, the end will come.

The Horrible Thing (Mark 13.14-23; Luke 21.20-24)

15 Someday you will see that "Horrible Thing" in the
holy place, just as the prophet Daniel said. Everyone
who reads this must try to understand! 16 If you are
living in Judea at that time, run to the mountains.

NEW INTERNATIONAL VERSION

4Jesus answered: "Watch out that no one deceives you. 5For many will come in my name, claiming, 'I am the Christ,[a]' and will deceive many. 6You will hear of wars and rumors of wars, but see to it that you are not alarmed. Such things must happen, but the end is still to come. 7Nation will rise against nation, and kingdom against kingdom. There will be famines and earthquakes in various places. 8All these are the beginning of birth pains.

9"Then you will be handed over to be persecuted and put to death, and you will be hated by all nations because of me. 10At that time many will turn away from the faith and will betray and hate each other, 11and many false prophets will appear and deceive many people. 12Because of the increase of wickedness, the love of most will grow cold, 13but he who stands firm to the end will be saved. 14And this gospel of the kingdom will be preached in the whole world as a testimony to all nations, and then the end will come.

15"So when you see standing in the holy place 'the abomination that causes desolation,'[b] spoken of through the prophet Daniel—let the reader understand— 16then let those who are in Judea flee to the mountains. 17Let no one

[a] *5* Or *Messiah*; also in verse 23 [b] *15* Daniel 9:27; 11:31; 12:11

NEW LIVING TRANSLATION

4Jesus told them, "Don't let anyone mislead you. 5For many will come in my name, saying, 'I am the Messiah.' They will lead many astray. 6And wars will break out near and far, but don't panic. Yes, these things must come, but the end won't follow immediately. 7The nations and kingdoms will proclaim war against each other, and there will be famines and earthquakes in many parts of the world. 8But all this will be only the beginning of the horrors to come.

9"Then you will be arrested, persecuted, and killed. You will be hated all over the world because of your allegiance to me. 10And many will turn away from me and betray and hate each other. 11And many false prophets will appear and will lead many people astray. 12Sin will be rampant everywhere, and the love of many will grow cold. 13But those who endure to the end will be saved. 14And the Good News about the Kingdom will be preached throughout the whole world, so that all nations will hear it; and then, finally, the end will come.

15"The time will come when you will see what Daniel the prophet spoke about: the sacrilegious object that causes desecration* standing in the Holy Place"—reader, pay attention! 16"Then those in Judea must flee to the hills.

24:15 Greek *the abomination of desolation.* See Dan 9:27; 11:31; 12:11.

NEW KING JAMES VERSION

4And Jesus answered and said to them: "Take heed that no one deceives you. 5For many will come in My name, saying, 'I am the Christ,' and will deceive many. 6And you will hear of wars and rumors of wars. See that you are not troubled; for all[a] *these things* must come to pass, but the end is not yet. 7For nation will rise against nation, and kingdom against kingdom. And there will be famines, pestilences,[b] and earthquakes in various places. 8All these *are* the beginning of sorrows.

9"Then they will deliver you up to tribulation and kill you, and you will be hated by all nations for My name's sake. 10And then many will be offended, will betray one another, and will hate one another. 11Then many false prophets will rise up and deceive many. 12And because lawlessness will abound, the love of many will grow cold. 13But he who endures to the end shall be saved. 14And this gospel of the kingdom will be preached in all the world as a witness to all the nations, and then the end will come.

The Great Tribulation

15"Therefore when you see the *'abomination of desolation,'*[c] spoken of by Daniel the prophet, standing in the holy place" (whoever reads, let him understand), 16"then let those who are in Judea flee to the mountains. 17Let him

24:6 [a] NU-Text omits *all.* 24:7 [b] NU-Text omits *pestilences.*
24:15 [c] Daniel 11:31; 12:11

THE MESSAGE

Jesus said, "Watch out for doomsday deceivers. Many leaders are going to show up with forged identities, claiming, 'I am Christ, the Messiah.' They will deceive a lot of people. When reports come in of wars and rumored wars, keep your head and don't panic. This is routine history; this is no sign of the end. Nation will fight nation and ruler fight ruler, over and over. Famines and earthquakes will occur in various places. This is nothing compared to what is coming.

"They are going to throw you to the wolves and kill you, everyone hating you because you carry my name. And then, going from bad to worse, it will be dog-eat-dog, everyone at each other's throat, everyone hating each other.

"In the confusion, lying preachers will come forward and deceive a lot of people. For many others, the overwhelming spread of evil will do them in—nothing left of their love but a mound of ashes.

"Staying with it—that's what God requires. Stay with it to the end. You won't be sorry, and you'll be saved. All during this time, the good news—the Message of the kingdom—will be preached all over the world, a witness staked out in every country. And then the end will come.

The Monster of Desecration

"But be ready to run for it when you see the monster of desecration set up in the Temple sanctuary. The prophet Daniel described this. If you've read Daniel, you'll know what I'm talking about. If you're living in Judea at the time,

KING JAMES VERSION

17 Let him which is on the housetop not come down to take any thing out of his house:

18 Neither let him which is in the field return back to take his clothes.

19 And woe unto them that are with child, and to them that give suck in those days!

20 But pray ye that your flight be not in the winter, neither on the sabbath day:

21 For then shall be great tribulation, such as was not since the beginning of the world to this time, no, nor ever shall be.

22 And except those days should be shortened, there should no flesh be saved: but for the elect's sake those days shall be shortened.

23 Then if any man shall say unto you, Lo, here *is* Christ, or there; believe *it* not.

24 For there shall arise false Christs, and false prophets, and shall shew great signs and wonders; insomuch that, if *it were* possible, they shall deceive the very elect.

25 Behold, I have told you before.

26 Wherefore if they shall say unto you, Behold, he is in the desert; go not forth: behold, *he is* in the secret chambers; believe *it* not.

27 For as the lightning cometh out of the east, and shineth even unto the west; so shall also the coming of the Son of man be.

28 For wheresoever the carcase is, there will the eagles be gathered together.

NEW AMERICAN STANDARD BIBLE

17 "Whoever is on the housetop must not go down to get the things out that are in his house.

18 "Whoever is in the field must not turn back to get his cloak.

19 "But woe to those who are pregnant and to those who are nursing babies in those days!

20 "But pray that your flight will not be in the winter, or on a Sabbath.

21 "For then there will be a great tribulation, such as has not occurred since the beginning of the world until now, nor ever will.

22 "Unless those days had been cut short, no life would have been saved; but for the sake of the elect those days will be cut short.

23 "Then if anyone says to you, 'Behold, here is the Christ,' or 'There *He is,*' do not believe *him.*

24 "For false Christs and false prophets will arise and will show great signs and wonders, so as to mislead, if possible, even the elect.

25 "Behold, I have told you in advance.

26 "So if they say to you, 'Behold, He is in the wilderness,' do not go out, *or,* 'Behold, He is in the inner rooms,' do not believe *them.*

27 "For just as the lightning comes from the east and flashes even to the west, so will the coming of the Son of Man be.

28 "Wherever the corpse is, there the vultures will gather.

NEW CENTURY VERSION

mountains. 17If people are on the roofs[b] of their houses,
they must not go down to get anything out of their houses.
18If people are in the fields, they must not go back to get
their coats. 19At that time, how terrible it will be for
women who are pregnant or have nursing babies! 20Pray
that it will not be winter or a Sabbath day when these
things happen and you have to run away, 21because at
that time there will be much trouble. There will be more
trouble than there has ever been since the beginning of the
world until now, and nothing as bad will ever happen
again. 22God has decided to make that terrible time short.
Otherwise, no one would go on living. But God will make
that time short to help the people he has chosen. 23At that
time, someone might say to you, 'Look, there is the Christ!'
Or another person might say, 'There he is!' But don't
believe them. 24False Christs and false prophets will come
and perform great wonders and miracles. They will try to
fool even the people God has chosen, if that is possible.
25Now I have warned you about this before it happens.

26"If people tell you, 'The Christ is in the desert,' don't
go there. If they say, 'The Christ is in the inner room,'
don't believe it. 27When the Son of Man comes, he will be
seen by everyone, like lightning flashing from the east to
the west. 28Wherever the dead body is, there the vultures
will gather.

24:17 [b] **roof** In Bible times houses were built with flat roofs. The roof was used for drying things such as flax and fruit. And it was used as an extra room, as a place for worship, and as a place to sleep in the summer.

CONTEMPORARY ENGLISH VERSION

17If you are on the roof[a] of your house, don't go inside
to get anything. 18If you are out in the field, don't go
back for your coat. 19It will be a terrible time for women
who are expecting babies or nursing young children.
20And pray that you won't have to escape in winter or
on a Sabbath.[b] 21This will be the worst time of suffering
since the beginning of the world, and nothing this terrible will ever happen again. 22If God doesn't make the
time shorter, no one will be left alive. But because of
God's chosen ones, he will make the time shorter.
23Someone may say, "Here is the Messiah!" or "There
he is!" But don't believe it. 24False messiahs and false
prophets will come and work great miracles and signs.
They will even try to fool God's chosen ones. 25But I
have warned you ahead of time. 26If you are told that
the Messiah is out in the desert, don't go there! And if
you are told that he is in some secret place, don't believe
it! 27The coming of the Son of Man will be like lightning
that can be seen from east to west. 28Where there is a
corpse, there will always be buzzards.[c]

[a] **24.17** *roof*: In Palestine the houses usually had a flat roof. Stairs on the outside led up to the roof, which was made of beams and boards covered with packed earth. [b] **24.20** *in winter or on a Sabbath*: In Palestine the winters are cold and rainy and make travel difficult. The Jewish people were not allowed to travel much more than half a mile on the Sabbath. For these reasons it was hard for them to escape from their enemies in the winter or on a Sabbath. [c] **24.28** *Where there is a corpse, there will always be buzzards*: This saying may mean that when anything important happens, people soon know about it. Or the saying may mean that whenever something bad happens, curious people gather around and stare. But the word translated "buzzard" also means "eagle" and may refer to the Roman army, which had an eagle as its symbol.

NEW INTERNATIONAL VERSION

on the roof of his house go down to take anything out of the house. [18]Let no one in the field go back to get his cloak. [19]How dreadful it will be in those days for pregnant women and nursing mothers! [20]Pray that your flight will not take place in winter or on the Sabbath. [21]For then there will be great distress, unequaled from the beginning of the world until now—and never to be equaled again. [22]If those days had not been cut short, no one would survive, but for the sake of the elect those days will be shortened. [23]At that time if anyone says to you, 'Look, here is the Christ!' or, 'There he is!' do not believe it. [24]For false Christs and false prophets will appear and perform great signs and miracles to deceive even the elect—if that were possible. [25]See, I have told you ahead of time.

[26]"So if anyone tells you, 'There he is, out in the desert,' do not go out; or, 'Here he is, in the inner rooms,' do not believe it. [27]For as lightning that comes from the east is visible even in the west, so will be the coming of the Son of Man. [28]Wherever there is a carcass, there the vultures will gather.

NEW LIVING TRANSLATION

[17]A person outside the house* must not go inside to pack. [18]A person in the field must not return even to get a coat. [19]How terrible it will be for pregnant women and for mothers nursing their babies in those days. [20]And pray that your flight will not be in winter or on the Sabbath. [21]For that will be a time of greater horror than anything the world has ever seen or will ever see again. [22]In fact, unless that time of calamity is shortened, the entire human race will be destroyed. But it will be shortened for the sake of God's chosen ones.

[23]"Then if anyone tells you, 'Look, here is the Messiah,' or 'There he is,' don't pay any attention. [24]For false messiahs and false prophets will rise up and perform great miraculous signs and wonders so as to deceive, if possible, even God's chosen ones. [25]See, I have warned you.

[26]"So if someone tells you, 'Look, the Messiah is out in the desert,' don't bother to go and look. Or, 'Look, he is hiding here,' don't believe it! [27]For as the lightning lights up the entire sky, so it will be when the Son of Man comes. [28]Just as the gathering of vultures shows there is a carcass nearby, so these signs indicate that the end is near.*

24:17 Greek *on the roof.* **24:28** Greek *Wherever the carcass is, the vultures gather.*

NEW KING JAMES VERSION

who is on the housetop not go down to take anything out of his house. [18]And let him who is in the field not go back to get his clothes. [19]But woe to those who are pregnant and to those who are nursing babies in those days! [20]And pray that your flight may not be in winter or on the Sabbath. [21]For then there will be great tribulation, such as has not been since the beginning of the world until this time, no, nor ever shall be. [22]And unless those days were shortened, no flesh would be saved; but for the elect's sake those days will be shortened.

[23]"Then if anyone says to you, 'Look, here *is* the Christ!' or 'There!' do not believe *it.* [24]For false christs and false prophets will rise and show great signs and wonders to deceive, if possible, even the elect. [25]See, I have told you beforehand.

[26]"Therefore if they say to you, 'Look, He is in the desert!' do not go out; *or* 'Look, *He is* in the inner rooms!' do not believe *it.* [27]For as the lightning comes from the east and flashes to the west, so also will the coming of the Son of Man be. [28]For wherever the carcass is, there the eagles will be gathered together.

THE MESSAGE

run for the hills; if you're working in the yard, don't return to the house to get anything; if you're out in the field, don't go back and get your coat. Pregnant and nursing mothers will have it especially hard. Hope and pray this won't happen during the winter or on a Sabbath.

"This is going to be trouble on a scale beyond what the world has ever seen, or will see again. If these days of trouble were left to run their course, nobody would make it. But on account of God's chosen people, the trouble will be cut short.

The Arrival of the Son of Man

"If anyone tries to flag you down, calling out, 'Here's the Messiah!' or points, 'There he is!' don't fall for it. Fake Messiahs and lying preachers are going to pop up everywhere. Their impressive credentials and dazzling performances will pull the wool over the eyes of even those who ought to know better. But I've given you fair warning.

"So if they say, 'Run to the country and see him arrive!' or, 'Quick, get downtown, see him come!' don't give them the time of day. The Arrival of the Son of Man isn't something you go to see. He comes like swift lightning to you! Whenever you see crowds gathering, think of carrion vultures circling, moving in, hovering over a rotting carcass. You can be quite sure that it's not the living Son of Man pulling in those crowds.

KING JAMES VERSION

29 Immediately after the tribulation of those days shall the sun be darkened, and the moon shall not give her light, and the stars shall fall from heaven, and the powers of the heavens shall be shaken:

30 And then shall appear the sign of the Son of man in heaven: and then shall all the tribes of the earth mourn, and they shall see the Son of man coming in the clouds of heaven with power and great glory.

31 And he shall send his angels with a great sound of a trumpet, and they shall gather together his elect from the four winds, from one end of heaven to the other.

32 ¶ Now learn a parable of the fig tree; When his branch is yet tender, and putteth forth leaves, ye know that summer *is* nigh:

33 So likewise ye, when ye shall see all these things, know that it is near, *even* at the doors.

34 Verily I say unto you, This generation shall not pass, till all these things be fulfilled.

35 Heaven and earth shall pass away, but my words shall not pass away.

NEW AMERICAN STANDARD BIBLE

The Glorious Return

29 "But immediately after the tribulation of those days THE SUN WILL BE DARKENED, AND THE MOON WILL NOT GIVE ITS LIGHT, AND THE STARS WILL FALL from the sky, and the powers of the heavens will be shaken.

30 "And then the sign of the Son of Man will appear in the sky, and then all the tribes of the earth will mourn, and they will see the SON OF MAN COMING ON THE CLOUDS OF THE SKY with power and great glory.

31 "And He will send forth His angels with A GREAT TRUMPET and THEY WILL GATHER TOGETHER His elect from the four winds, from one end of the sky to the other.

Parable of the Fig Tree

32 "Now learn the parable from the fig tree: when its branch has already become tender and puts forth its leaves, you know that summer is near;

33 So, you too, when you see all these things, recognize that He is near, *right* at the door.

34 "Truly I say to you, this generation will not pass away until all these things take place.

35 "Heaven and earth will pass away, but My words will not pass away.

NEW CENTURY VERSION

29 "Soon after the trouble of those days,
'the sun will grow dark,
and the moon will not give its light.
The stars will fall from the sky.
And the powers of the heavens will be shaken.'
Isaiah 13:10; 34:4

30 "At that time, the sign of the Son of Man will appear in the sky. Then all the peoples of the world will cry. They will see the Son of Man coming on clouds in the sky with great power and glory. 31 He will use a loud trumpet to send his angels all around the earth, and they will gather his chosen people from every part of the world.

32 "Learn a lesson from the fig tree: When its branches become green and soft and new leaves appear, you know summer is near. 33 In the same way, when you see all these things happening, you will know that the time is near, ready to come. 34 I tell you the truth, all these things will happen while the people of this time are still living. 35 Earth and sky will be destroyed, but the words I have said will never be destroyed.

CONTEMPORARY ENGLISH VERSION

When the Son of Man Appears
(Mark 13.24-27; Luke 21.25-28)

29 Right after those days of suffering,

"The sun will become dark,
and the moon
will no longer shine.
The stars will fall,
and the powers in the sky[d]
will be shaken."

30 Then a sign will appear in the sky. And there will be the Son of Man.[e] All nations on earth will weep when they see the Son of Man coming on the clouds of heaven with power and great glory. 31 At the sound of a loud trumpet, he will send his angels to bring his chosen ones together from all over the earth.

A Lesson from a Fig Tree (Mark 13.28-31; Luke 21.29-33)

32 Learn a lesson from a fig tree. When its branches sprout and start putting out leaves, you know that summer is near. 33 So when you see all these things happening, you will know that the time has almost come.[f] 34 I can promise you that some of the people of this generation will still be alive when all this happens. 35 The sky and the earth won't last forever, but my words will.

[d] 24.29 *the powers in the sky*: In ancient times people thought that the stars were spiritual powers. [e] 24.30 *And there will be the Son of Man*: Or "And it will be the Son of Man." [f] 24.33 *the time has almost come*: Or "he (that is, the Son of Man) will soon be here."

NEW INTERNATIONAL VERSION

29"Immediately after the distress of those days

" 'the sun will be darkened,
and the moon will not give its light;
the stars will fall from the sky,
and the heavenly bodies will be shaken.'[c]

30"At that time the sign of the Son of Man will appear in the sky, and all the nations of the earth will mourn. They will see the Son of Man coming on the clouds of the sky, with power and great glory. 31And he will send his angels with a loud trumpet call, and they will gather his elect from the four winds, from one end of the heavens to the other.

32"Now learn this lesson from the fig tree: As soon as its twigs get tender and its leaves come out, you know that summer is near. 33Even so, when you see all these things, you know that it[d] is near, right at the door. 34I tell you the truth, this generation[e] will certainly not pass away until all these things have happened. 35Heaven and earth will pass away, but my words will never pass away.

[c] *29* Isaiah 13:10; 34:4 [d] *33* Or *he* [e] *34* Or *race*

NEW LIVING TRANSLATION

29"Immediately after those horrible days end,

the sun will be darkened,
the moon will not give light,
the stars will fall from the sky,
and the powers of heaven will be shaken.*

30And then at last, the sign of the coming of the Son of Man will appear in the heavens, and there will be deep mourning among all the nations of the earth. And they will see the Son of Man arrive on the clouds of heaven with power and great glory.* 31And he will send forth his angels with the sound of a mighty trumpet blast, and they will gather together his chosen ones from the farthest ends of the earth and heaven.

32"Now learn a lesson from the fig tree. When its buds become tender and its leaves begin to sprout, you know without being told that summer is near. 33Just so, when you see the events I've described beginning to happen, you can know his return is very near, right at the door. 34I assure you, this generation* will not pass from the scene before all these things take place. 35Heaven and earth will disappear, but my words will remain forever.

24:29 See Isa 13:10; 34:4; Joel 2:10. 24:30 See Dan 7:13. 24:34 Or *this age,* or *this nation.*

NEW KING JAMES VERSION

The Coming of the Son of Man

29"Immediately after the tribulation of those days the sun will be darkened, and the moon will not give its light; the stars will fall from heaven, and the powers of the heavens will be shaken. 30Then the sign of the Son of Man will appear in heaven, and then all the tribes of the earth will mourn, and they will see the Son of Man coming on the clouds of heaven with power and great glory. 31And He will send His angels with a great sound of a trumpet, and they will gather together His elect from the four winds, from one end of heaven to the other.

The Parable of the Fig Tree

32"Now learn this parable from the fig tree: When its branch has already become tender and puts forth leaves, you know that summer *is* near. 33So you also, when you see all these things, know that it[d] is near—at the doors! 34Assuredly, I say to you, this generation will by no means pass away till all these things take place. 35Heaven and earth will pass away, but My words will by no means pass away.

24:33 [d] Or *He*

THE MESSAGE

"Following those hard times,

'Sun will fade out,
moon cloud over,
Stars fall out of the sky,
cosmic powers tremble.'

"Then, the Arrival of the Son of Man! It will fill the skies—no one will miss it. Unready people all over the world, outsiders to the splendor and power, will raise a huge lament as they watch the Son of Man blazing out of heaven. At that same moment, he'll dispatch his angels with a trumpet-blast summons, pulling in God's chosen from the four winds, from pole to pole.

"Take a lesson from the fig tree. From the moment you notice its buds form, the merest hint of green, you know summer's just around the corner. So it is with you: When you see all these things, you'll know he's at the door. Don't take this lightly. I'm not just saying this for some future generation, but for all of you. This age continues until all these things take place. Sky and earth will wear out; my words won't wear out.

KING JAMES VERSION

36 But of that day and hour knoweth no *man*, no, not the angels of heaven, but my Father only.

37 But as the days of Noe *were*, so shall also the coming of the Son of man be.

38 For as in the days that were before the flood they were eating and drinking, marrying and giving in marriage, until the day that Noe entered into the ark,

39 And knew not until the flood came, and took them all away; so shall also the coming of the Son of man be.

40 Then shall two be in the field; the one shall be taken, and the other left.

41 Two *women shall be* grinding at the mill; the one shall be taken, and the other left.

42 Watch therefore: for ye know not what hour your Lord doth come.

43 But know this, that if the goodman of the house had known in what watch the thief would come, he would have watched, and would not have suffered his house to be broken up.

44 Therefore be ye also ready: for in such an hour as ye think not the Son of man cometh.

45 Who then is a faithful and wise servant, whom his lord hath made ruler over his household, to give them meat in due season?

46 Blessed *is* that servant, whom his lord when he cometh shall find so doing.

47 Verily I say unto you, That he shall make him ruler over all his goods.

NEW AMERICAN STANDARD BIBLE

36 "But of that day and hour no one knows, not even the angels of heaven, nor the Son, but the Father alone.

37 "For the coming of the Son of Man will be just like the days of Noah.

38 "For as in those days before the flood they were eating and drinking, marrying and giving in marriage, until the day that Noah entered the ark,

39 and they did not understand until the flood came and took them all away; so will the coming of the Son of Man be.

40 "Then there will be two men in the field; one will be taken and one will be left.

41 "Two women *will be* grinding at the mill; one will be taken and one will be left.

Be Ready for His Coming

42 "Therefore be on the alert, for you do not know which day your Lord is coming.

43 "But be sure of this, that if the head of the house had known at what time of the night the thief was coming, he would have been on the alert and would not have allowed his house to be broken into.

44 "For this reason you also must be ready; for the Son of Man is coming at an hour when you do not think *He will.*

45 "Who then is the faithful and sensible slave whom his master put in charge of his household to give them their food at the proper time?

46 "Blessed is that slave whom his master finds so doing when he comes.

47 "Truly I say to you that he will put him in charge of all his possessions.

NEW CENTURY VERSION

When Will Jesus Come Again?

36"No one knows when that day or time will be, not the angels in heaven, not even the Son. Only the Father knows. 37When the Son of Man comes, it will be like what happened during Noah's time. 38In those days before the flood, people were eating and drinking, marrying and giving their children to be married, until the day Noah entered the boat. 39They knew nothing about what was happening until the flood came and destroyed them. It will be the same when the Son of Man comes. 40Two men will be in the field. One will be taken, and the other will be left. 41Two women will be grinding grain with a mill.[c] One will be taken, and the other will be left.

42"So always be ready, because you don't know the day your Lord will come. 43Remember this: If the owner of the house knew what time of night a thief was coming, the owner would watch and not let the thief break in. 44So you also must be ready, because the Son of Man will come at a time you don't expect him.

45"Who is the wise and loyal servant that the master trusts to give the other servants their food at the right time? 46When the master comes and finds the servant doing his work, the servant will be blessed. 47I tell you the truth, the master will choose that servant to take care of

24:41 [c] **mill** Two large, round, flat rocks used for grinding grain to make flour.

CONTEMPORARY ENGLISH VERSION

No One Knows the Day or Time
(Mark 13.32-37; Luke 17.26-30, 34-36)

36No one knows the day or hour. The angels in heaven don't know, and the Son himself doesn't know.[g] Only the Father knows. 37When the Son of Man appears, things will be just as they were when Noah lived. 38People were eating, drinking, and getting married right up to the day that the flood came and Noah went into the big boat. 39They didn't know anything was happening until the flood came and swept them all away. That is how it will be when the Son of Man appears.

40Two men will be in the same field, but only one will be taken. The other will be left. 41Two women will be together grinding grain, but only one will be taken. The other will be left. 42So be on your guard! You don't know when your Lord will come. 43Homeowners never know when a thief is coming, and they are always on guard to keep one from breaking in. 44Always be ready! You don't know when the Son of Man will come.

Faithful and Unfaithful Servants (Luke 12.35-48)

45Who are faithful and wise servants? Who are the ones the master will put in charge of giving the other servants their food supplies at the proper time? 46Servants are fortunate if their master comes and finds them doing their job. 47You may be sure that a servant who is always faithful will be put in charge of everything the master

[g] 24.36 *and the Son himself doesn't know*: These words are not in some manuscripts.

NEW INTERNATIONAL VERSION

The Day and Hour Unknown

36"No one knows about that day or hour, not even the angels in heaven, nor the Son,[f] but only the Father. 37As it was in the days of Noah, so it will be at the coming of the Son of Man. 38For in the days before the flood, people were eating and drinking, marrying and giving in marriage, up to the day Noah entered the ark; 39and they knew nothing about what would happen until the flood came and took them all away. That is how it will be at the coming of the Son of Man. 40Two men will be in the field; one will be taken and the other left. 41Two women will be grinding with a hand mill; one will be taken and the other left.

42"Therefore keep watch, because you do not know on what day your Lord will come. 43But understand this: If the owner of the house had known at what time of night the thief was coming, he would have kept watch and would not have let his house be broken into. 44So you also must be ready, because the Son of Man will come at an hour when you do not expect him.

45"Who then is the faithful and wise servant, whom the master has put in charge of the servants in his household to give them their food at the proper time? 46It will be good for that servant whose master finds him doing so when he returns. 47I tell you the truth, he will put him in charge of

[f] *36* Some manuscripts do not have *nor the Son.*

NEW LIVING TRANSLATION

36"However, no one knows the day or the hour when these things will happen, not even the angels in heaven or the Son himself.* Only the Father knows.

37"When the Son of Man returns, it will be like it was in Noah's day. 38In those days before the Flood, the people were enjoying banquets and parties and weddings right up to the time Noah entered his boat. 39People didn't realize what was going to happen until the Flood came and swept them all away. That is the way it will be when the Son of Man comes.

40"Two men will be working together in the field; one will be taken, the other left. 41Two women will be grinding flour at the mill; one will be taken, the other left. 42So be prepared, because you don't know what day your Lord is coming.

43"Know this: A homeowner who knew exactly when a burglar was coming would stay alert and not permit the house to be broken into. 44You also must be ready all the time. For the Son of Man will come when least expected.

45"Who is a faithful, sensible servant, to whom the master can give the responsibility of managing his household and feeding his family? 46If the master returns and finds that the servant has done a good job, there will be a reward. 47I assure you, the master will put that servant in

24:36 Some manuscripts omit the phrase *or the Son himself.*

NEW KING JAMES VERSION

No One Knows the Day or Hour

36"But of that day and hour no one knows, not even the angels of heaven,[e] but My Father only. 37But as the days of Noah *were,* so also will the coming of the Son of Man be. 38For as in the days before the flood, they were eating and drinking, marrying and giving in marriage, until the day that Noah entered the ark, 39and did not know until the flood came and took them all away, so also will the coming of the Son of Man be. 40Then two *men* will be in the field: one will be taken and the other left. 41Two *women will be* grinding at the mill: one will be taken and the other left. 42Watch therefore, for you do not know what hour[f] your Lord is coming. 43But know this, that if the master of the house had known what hour the thief would come, he would have watched and not allowed his house to be broken into. 44Therefore you also be ready, for the Son of Man is coming at an hour you do not expect.

The Faithful Servant and the Evil Servant

45"Who then is a faithful and wise servant, whom his master made ruler over his household, to give them food in due season? 46Blessed *is* that servant whom his master, when he comes, will find so doing. 47Assuredly, I say to you that he will make him ruler over all his goods. 48But if

24:36 [e] NU-Text adds *nor the Son.* **24:42** [f] NU-Text reads *day.*

THE MESSAGE

"But the exact day and hour? No one knows that, not even heaven's angels, not even the Son. Only the Father knows.

"The Arrival of the Son of Man will take place in times like Noah's. Before the great flood everyone was carrying on as usual, having a good time right up to the day Noah boarded the ark. They knew nothing—until the flood hit and swept everything away.

"The Son of Man's Arrival will be like that: Two men will be working in the field—one will be taken, one left behind; two women will be grinding at the mill—one will be taken, one left behind. So stay awake, alert. You have no idea what day your Master will show up. But you do know this: You know that if the homeowner had known what time of night the burglar would arrive, he would have been there with his dogs to prevent the break-in. Be vigilant just like that. You have no idea when the Son of Man is going to show up.

"Who here qualifies for the job of overseeing the kitchen? A person the Master can depend on to feed the workers on time each day. Someone the Master can drop in on unannounced and always find him doing his job. A God-blessed man or woman, I tell you. It won't be long before the Master will put this person in charge of the whole operation.

KING JAMES VERSION

48 But and if that evil servant shall say in his heart, My lord delayeth his coming;

49 And shall begin to smite *his* fellowservants, and to eat and drink with the drunken;

50 The lord of that servant shall come in a day when he looketh not for *him*, and in an hour that he is not aware of,

51 And shall cut him asunder, and appoint *him* his portion with the hypocrites: there shall be weeping and gnashing of teeth.

25 Then shall the kingdom of heaven be likened unto ten virgins, which took their lamps, and went forth to meet the bridegroom.

2 And five of them were wise, and five *were* foolish.

3 They that *were* foolish took their lamps, and took no oil with them:

4 But the wise took oil in their vessels with their lamps.

5 While the bridegroom tarried, they all slumbered and slept.

6 And at midnight there was a cry made, Behold, the bridegroom cometh; go ye out to meet him.

7 Then all those virgins arose, and trimmed their lamps.

8 And the foolish said unto the wise, Give us of your oil; for our lamps are gone out.

9 But the wise answered, saying, *Not so*; lest there be not enough for us and you: but go ye rather to them that sell, and buy for yourselves.

NEW AMERICAN STANDARD BIBLE

48 "But if that evil slave says in his heart, 'My master is not coming for a long time,'

49 and begins to beat his fellow slaves and eat and drink with drunkards;

50 the master of that slave will come on a day when he does not expect *him* and at an hour which he does not know,

51 and will cut him in pieces and assign him a place with the hypocrites; in that place there will be weeping and gnashing of teeth.

Parable of Ten Virgins

25 "Then the kingdom of heaven will be comparable to ten virgins, who took their lamps and went out to meet the bridegroom.

2 "Five of them were foolish, and five were prudent.

3 "For when the foolish took their lamps, they took no oil with them,

4 but the prudent took oil in flasks along with their lamps.

5 "Now while the bridegroom was delaying, they all got drowsy and *began* to sleep.

6 "But at midnight there was a shout, 'Behold, the bridegroom! Come out to meet *him*.'

7 "Then all those virgins rose and trimmed their lamps.

8 "The foolish said to the prudent, 'Give us some of your oil, for our lamps are going out.'

9 "But the prudent answered, 'No, there will not be enough for us and you *too;* go instead to the dealers and buy *some* for yourselves.'

NEW CENTURY VERSION

everything he owns. 48But suppose that evil servant thinks
to himself, 'My master will not come back soon,' 49and he
begins to beat the other servants and eat and get drunk
with others like him? 50The master will come when that
servant is not ready and is not expecting him. 51Then the
master will cut him in pieces and send him away to be
with the hypocrites, where people will cry and grind their
teeth with pain.

A Story About Ten Bridesmaids

25 "At that time the kingdom of heaven will be like
ten bridesmaids who took their lamps and went to
wait for the bridegroom. 2Five of them were foolish and
five were wise. 3The five foolish bridesmaids took their
lamps, but they did not take more oil for the lamps to
burn. 4The wise bridesmaids took their lamps and more oil
in jars. 5Because the bridegroom was late, they became
sleepy and went to sleep.

6"At midnight someone cried out, 'The bridegroom is
coming! Come and meet him!' 7Then all the bridesmaids
woke up and got their lamps ready. 8But the foolish ones
said to the wise, 'Give us some of your oil, because our
lamps are going out.' 9The wise bridesmaids answered,
'No, the oil we have might not be enough for all of us. Go
to the people who sell oil and buy some for yourselves.'

CONTEMPORARY ENGLISH VERSION

owns. 48But suppose one of the servants thinks that the
master won't return until late. 49Suppose that evil ser-
vant starts beating the other servants and eats and
drinks with people who are drunk. 50If that happens, the
master will surely come on a day and at a time when the
servant least expects him. 51That servant will then be
punished and thrown out with the ones who only pre-
tended to serve their master. There they will cry and grit
their teeth in pain.

A Story about Ten Girls

25 The kingdom of heaven is like what happened one
night when ten girls took their oil lamps and went
to a wedding to meet the groom.[a] 2Five of the girls were
foolish and five were wise. 3The foolish ones took their
lamps, but no extra oil. 4The ones who were wise took
along extra oil for their lamps.

5The groom was late arriving, and the girls became
drowsy and fell asleep. 6Then in the middle of the night
someone shouted, "Here's the groom! Come to meet
him!"

7When the girls got up and started getting their lamps
ready, 8the foolish ones said to the others, "Let us have
some of your oil! Our lamps are going out."

9The girls who were wise answered, "There's not
enough oil for all of us! Go and buy some for yourselves."

[a] 25.1 *to meet the groom*: Some manuscripts add "and the bride." It was the custom for the groom to go to the home of the bride's parents to get his bride. Young girls and other guests would then go with them to the home of the groom's parents, where the wedding feast would take place.

NEW INTERNATIONAL VERSION

all his possessions. 48But suppose that servant is wicked
and says to himself, 'My master is staying away a long
time,' 49and he then begins to beat his fellow servants and
to eat and drink with drunkards. 50The master of that ser-
vant will come on a day when he does not expect him and
at an hour he is not aware of. 51He will cut him to pieces
and assign him a place with the hypocrites, where there
will be weeping and gnashing of teeth.

The Parable of the Ten Virgins

25 "At that time the kingdom of heaven will be like
ten virgins who took their lamps and went out to
meet the bridegroom. 2Five of them were foolish and five
were wise. 3The foolish ones took their lamps but did not
take any oil with them. 4The wise, however, took oil in jars
along with their lamps. 5The bridegroom was a long time
in coming, and they all became drowsy and fell asleep.

6"At midnight the cry rang out: 'Here's the bridegroom!
Come out to meet him!'

7"Then all the virgins woke up and trimmed their lamps.
8The foolish ones said to the wise, 'Give us some of your
oil; our lamps are going out.'

9" 'No,' they replied, 'there may not be enough for both
us and you. Instead, go to those who sell oil and buy some
for yourselves.'

NEW LIVING TRANSLATION

charge of all he owns. 48But if the servant is evil and
thinks, 'My master won't be back for a while,' 49and
begins oppressing the other servants, partying, and getting
drunk—50well, the master will return unannounced and
unexpected. 51He will tear the servant apart and banish
him with the hypocrites. In that place there will be weep-
ing and gnashing of teeth.

Story of the Ten Bridesmaids

25 "The Kingdom of Heaven can be illustrated by the
story of ten bridesmaids* who took their lamps
and went to meet the bridegroom. 2Five of them were fool-
ish, and five were wise. 3The five who were foolish took no
oil for their lamps, 4but the other five were wise enough to
take along extra oil. 5When the bridegroom was delayed,
they all lay down and slept. 6At midnight they were roused
by the shout, 'Look, the bridegroom is coming! Come out
and welcome him!'

7"All the bridesmaids got up and prepared their lamps.
8Then the five foolish ones asked the others, 'Please give
us some of your oil because our lamps are going out.' 9But
the others replied, 'We don't have enough for all of us. Go
to a shop and buy some for yourselves.'

25:1 Or *virgins;* also in 25:7, 11.

NEW KING JAMES VERSION

that evil servant says in his heart, 'My master is delaying
his coming,' [g] 49and begins to beat *his* fellow servants, and
to eat and drink with the drunkards, 50the master of that
servant will come on a day when he is not looking for *him*
and at an hour that he is not aware of, 51and will cut him
in two and appoint *him* his portion with the hypocrites.
There shall be weeping and gnashing of teeth.

The Parable of the Wise and Foolish Virgins

25 "Then the kingdom of heaven shall be likened to
ten virgins who took their lamps and went out to
meet the bridegroom. 2Now five of them were wise, and
five *were* foolish. 3Those who *were* foolish took their lamps
and took no oil with them, 4but the wise took oil in their
vessels with their lamps. 5But while the bridegroom was
delayed, they all slumbered and slept.

6"And at midnight a cry was *heard:* 'Behold, the bride-
groom is coming;[a] go out to meet him!' 7Then all those vir-
gins arose and trimmed their lamps. 8And the foolish said
to the wise, 'Give us *some* of your oil, for our lamps are
going out.' 9But the wise answered, saying, '*No,* lest there
should not be enough for us and you; but go rather to
those who sell, and buy for yourselves.' 10And while they

24:48 [g] NU-Text omits *his coming.* 25:6 [a] NU-Text omits *is coming.*

THE MESSAGE

"But if that person only looks out for himself, and the
minute the Master is away does what he pleases—abusing
the help and throwing drunken parties for his friends—the
Master is going to show up when he least expects it and
make hash of him. He'll end up in the dump with the hyp-
ocrites, out in the cold shivering, teeth chattering.

The Story of the Virgins

25 "God's kingdom is like ten young virgins who took
oil lamps and went out to greet the bridegroom.
Five were silly and five were smart. The silly virgins took
lamps, but no extra oil. The smart virgins took jars of oil to
feed their lamps. The bridegroom didn't show up when
they expected him, and they all fell asleep.

"In the middle of the night someone yelled out, 'He's
here! The bridegroom's here! Go out and greet him!'

"The ten virgins got up and got their lamps ready. The
silly virgins said to the smart ones, 'Our lamps are going
out; lend us some of your oil.'

"They answered, 'There might not be enough to go
around; go buy your own.'

KING JAMES VERSION

10 And while they went to buy, the bridegroom came; and they that were ready went in with him to the marriage: and the door was shut.

11 Afterward came also the other virgins, saying, Lord, Lord, open to us.

12 But he answered and said, Verily I say unto you, I know you not.

13 Watch therefore, for ye know neither the day nor the hour wherein the Son of man cometh.

14 ¶ For *the kingdom of heaven is* as a man travelling into a far country, *who* called his own servants, and delivered unto them his goods.

15 And unto one he gave five talents, to another two, and to another one; to every man according to his several ability; and straightway took his journey.

16 Then he that had received the five talents went and traded with the same, and made *them* other five talents.

17 And likewise he that *had received* two, he also gained other two.

18 But he that had received one went and digged in the earth, and hid his lord's money.

19 After a long time the lord of those servants cometh, and reckoneth with them.

20 And so he that had received five talents came and brought other five talents, saying, Lord, thou deliveredst unto me five talents: behold, I have gained beside them five talents more.

NEW AMERICAN STANDARD BIBLE

10 "And while they were going away to make the purchase, the bridegroom came, and those who were ready went in with him to the wedding feast; and the door was shut.

11 "Later the other virgins also came, saying, 'Lord, lord, open up for us.'

12 "But he answered, 'Truly I say to you, I do not know you.'

13 "Be on the alert then, for you do not know the day nor the hour.

Parable of the Talents

14 "For *it is* just like a man *about* to go on a journey, who called his own slaves and entrusted his possessions to them.

15 "To one he gave five talents, to another, two, and to another, one, each according to his own ability; and he went on his journey.

16 "Immediately the one who had received the five talents went and traded with them, and gained five more talents.

17 "In the same manner the one who *had received* the two *talents* gained two more.

18 "But he who received the one *talent* went away, and dug *a hole* in the ground and hid his master's money.

19 "Now after a long time the master of those slaves *came and *settled accounts with them.

20 "The one who had received the five talents came up and brought five more talents, saying, 'Master, you entrusted five talents to me. See, I have gained five more talents.'

NEW CENTURY VERSION

10 "So while the five foolish bridesmaids went to buy oil, the bridegroom came. The bridesmaids who were ready went in with the bridegroom to the wedding feast. Then the door was closed and locked.

11 "Later the others came back and said, 'Sir, sir, open the door to let us in.' 12 But the bridegroom answered, 'I tell you the truth, I don't want to know you.'

13 "So always be ready, because you don't know the day or the hour the Son of Man will come.

A Story About Three Servants

14 "The kingdom of heaven is like a man who was going to another place for a visit. Before he left, he called for his servants and told them to take care of his things while he was gone. 15 He gave one servant five bags of gold, another servant two bags of gold, and a third servant one bag of gold, to each one as much as he could handle. Then he left. 16 The servant who got five bags went quickly to invest the money and earned five more bags. 17 In the same way, the servant who had two bags invested them and earned two more. 18 But the servant who got one bag went out and dug a hole in the ground and hid the master's money.

19 "After a long time the master came home and asked the servants what they did with his money. 20 The servant who was given five bags of gold brought five more bags to the master and said, 'Master, you trusted me to care for five bags of gold, so I used your five bags to earn five

CONTEMPORARY ENGLISH VERSION

10 While the foolish girls were on their way to get some oil, the groom arrived. The girls who were ready went into the wedding, and the doors were closed.
11 Later the other girls returned and shouted, "Sir, sir! Open the door for us!"
12 But the groom replied, "I don't even know you!"
13 So, my disciples, always be ready! You don't know the day or the time when all this will happen.

A Story about Three Servants (Luke 19.11-27)

14 The kingdom is also like what happened when a man went away and put his three servants in charge of all he owned. 15 The man knew what each servant could do. So he handed five thousand coins to the first servant, two thousand to the second, and one thousand to the third. Then he left the country.

16 As soon as the man had gone, the servant with the five thousand coins used them to earn five thousand more. 17 The servant who had two thousand coins did the same with his money and earned two thousand more. 18 But the servant with one thousand coins dug a hole and hid his master's money in the ground.

19 Some time later the master of those servants returned. He called them in and asked what they had done with his money. 20 The servant who had been given five thousand coins brought them in with the five thousand that he had earned. He said, "Sir, you gave me five thousand coins, and I have earned five thousand more."

NEW INTERNATIONAL VERSION

10"But while they were on their way to buy the oil, the bridegroom arrived. The virgins who were ready went in with him to the wedding banquet. And the door was shut.

11"Later the others also came. 'Sir! Sir!' they said. 'Open the door for us!'

12"But he replied, 'I tell you the truth, I don't know you.'

13"Therefore keep watch, because you do not know the day or the hour.

The Parable of the Talents

14"Again, it will be like a man going on a journey, who called his servants and entrusted his property to them.
15To one he gave five talents[a] of money, to another two talents, and to another one talent, each according to his ability. Then he went on his journey. 16The man who had received the five talents went at once and put his money to work and gained five more. 17So also, the one with the two talents gained two more. 18But the man who had received the one talent went off, dug a hole in the ground and hid his master's money.

19"After a long time the master of those servants returned and settled accounts with them. 20The man who had received the five talents brought the other five. 'Master,' he said, 'you entrusted me with five talents. See, I have gained five more.'

[a] *15* A talent was worth more than a thousand dollars.

NEW LIVING TRANSLATION

10"But while they were gone to buy oil, the bridegroom came, and those who were ready went in with him to the marriage feast, and the door was locked. 11Later, when the other five bridesmaids returned, they stood outside, calling, 'Sir, open the door for us!' 12But he called back, 'I don't know you!'

13"So stay awake and be prepared, because you do not know the day or hour of my return.

Story of the Three Servants

14"Again, the Kingdom of Heaven can be illustrated by the story of a man going on a trip. He called together his servants and gave them money to invest for him while he was gone. 15He gave five bags of gold* to one, two bags of gold to another, and one bag of gold to the last—dividing it in proportion to their abilities—and then left on his trip.
16The servant who received the five bags of gold began immediately to invest the money and soon doubled it.
17The servant with two bags of gold also went right to work and doubled the money. 18But the servant who received the one bag of gold dug a hole in the ground and hid the master's money for safekeeping.

19"After a long time their master returned from his trip and called them to give an account of how they had used his money. 20The servant to whom he had entrusted the five bags of gold said, 'Sir, you gave me five bags of gold to invest, and I have doubled the amount.' 21The master

25:15 Greek *talents;* also throughout the story. A talent is equal to 75 pounds or 34 kilograms.

NEW KING JAMES VERSION

went to buy, the bridegroom came, and those who were ready went in with him to the wedding; and the door was shut.

11"Afterward the other virgins came also, saying, 'Lord, Lord, open to us!' 12But he answered and said, 'Assuredly, I say to you, I do not know you.'

13"Watch therefore, for you know neither the day nor the hour[b] in which the Son of Man is coming.

The Parable of the Talents

14"For *the kingdom of heaven is* like a man traveling to a far country, *who* called his own servants and delivered his goods to them. 15And to one he gave five talents, to another two, and to another one, to each according to his own ability; and immediately he went on a journey. 16Then he who had received the five talents went and traded with them, and made another five talents. 17And likewise he who *had received* two gained two more also. 18But he who had received one went and dug in the ground, and hid his lord's money. 19After a long time the lord of those servants came and settled accounts with them.

20"So he who had received five talents came and brought five other talents, saying, 'Lord, you delivered to me five talents; look, I have gained five more talents besides

25:13 [b] NU-Text omits the rest of this verse.

THE MESSAGE

"They did, but while they were out buying oil, the bridegroom arrived. When everyone who was there to greet him had gone into the wedding feast, the door was locked.

"Much later, the other virgins, the silly ones, showed up and knocked on the door, saying, 'Master, we're here. Let us in.'

"He answered, 'Do I know you? I don't think I know you.'

"So stay alert. You have no idea when he might arrive.

The Story About Investment

"It's also like a man going off on an extended trip. He called his servants together and delegated responsibilities. To one he gave five thousand dollars, to another two thousand, to a third one thousand, depending on their abilities. Then he left. Right off, the first servant went to work and doubled his master's investment. The second did the same. But the man with the single thousand dug a hole and carefully buried his master's money.

"After a long absence, the master of those three servants came back and settled up with them. The one given five thousand dollars showed him how he had doubled his

KING JAMES VERSION

21 His lord said unto him, Well done, *thou* good and faithful servant: thou hast been faithful over a few things, I will make thee ruler over many things: enter thou into the joy of thy lord.

22 He also that had received two talents came and said, Lord, thou deliveredst unto me two talents: behold, I have gained two other talents beside them.

23 His lord said unto him, Well done, good and faithful servant; thou hast been faithful over a few things, I will make thee ruler over many things: enter thou into the joy of thy lord.

24 Then he which had received the one talent came and said, Lord, I knew thee that thou art an hard man, reaping where thou hast not sown, and gathering where thou hast not strawed:

25 And I was afraid, and went and hid thy talent in the earth: lo, *there* thou hast *that is* thine.

26 His lord answered and said unto him, *Thou* wicked and slothful servant, thou knewest that I reap where I sowed not, and gather where I have not strawed:

27 Thou oughtest therefore to have put my money to the exchangers, and *then* at my coming I should have received mine own with usury.

28 Take therefore the talent from him, and give *it* unto him which hath ten talents.

29 For unto every one that hath shall be given, and he shall have abundance: but from him that hath not shall be taken away even that which he hath.

30 And cast ye the unprofitable servant into outer darkness: there shall be weeping and gnashing of teeth.

NEW AMERICAN STANDARD BIBLE

21 "His master said to him, 'Well done, good and faithful slave. You were faithful with a few things, I will put you in charge of many things; enter into the joy of your master.'

22 "Also the one who *had received* the two talents came up and said, 'Master, you entrusted two talents to me. See, I have gained two more talents.'

23 "His master said to him, 'Well done, good and faithful slave. You were faithful with a few things, I will put you in charge of many things; enter into the joy of your master.'

24 "And the one also who had received the one talent came up and said, 'Master, I knew you to be a hard man, reaping where you did not sow and gathering where you scattered no *seed*.

25 'And I was afraid, and went away and hid your talent in the ground. See, you have what is yours.'

26 "But his master answered and said to him, 'You wicked, lazy slave, you knew that I reap where I did not sow and gather where I scattered no *seed*.

27 'Then you ought to have put my money in the bank, and on my arrival I would have received my *money* back with interest.

28 'Therefore take away the talent from him, and give it to the one who has the ten talents.'

29 "For to everyone who has, *more* shall be given, and he will have an abundance; but from the one who does not have, even what he does have shall be taken away.

30 "Throw out the worthless slave into the outer darkness; in that place there will be weeping and gnashing of teeth.

NEW CENTURY VERSION

more.' 21The master answered, 'You did well. You are a
good and loyal servant. Because you were loyal with small
things, I will let you care for much greater things. Come
and share my joy with me.'
22"Then the servant who had been given two bags of
gold came to the master and said, 'Master, you gave me
two bags of gold to care for, so I used your two bags to
earn two more.' 23The master answered, 'You did well. You
are a good and loyal servant. Because you were loyal with
small things, I will let you care for much greater things.
Come and share my joy with me.'
24"Then the servant who had been given one bag of gold
came to the master and said, 'Master, I knew that you
were a hard man. You harvest things you did not plant.
You gather crops where you did not sow any seed. 25So I
was afraid and went and hid your money in the ground.
Here is your bag of gold.' 26The master answered, 'You are
a wicked and lazy servant! You say you knew that I har-
vest things I did not plant and that I gather crops where I
did not sow any seed. 27So you should have put my gold in
the bank. Then, when I came home, I would have received
my gold back with interest.'
28"So the master told his other servants, 'Take the bag
of gold from that servant and give it to the servant who
has ten bags of gold. 29Those who have much will get
more, and they will have much more than they need. But
those who do not have much will have everything taken
away from them.' 30Then the master said, 'Throw that use-
less servant outside, into the darkness where people will
cry and grind their teeth with pain.'

CONTEMPORARY ENGLISH VERSION

21"Wonderful!" his master replied. "You are a good
and faithful servant. I left you in charge of only a little,
but now I will put you in charge of much more. Come
and share in my happiness!"
22Next, the servant who had been given two thousand
coins came in and said, "Sir, you gave me two thousand
coins, and I have earned two thousand more."
23"Wonderful!" his master replied. "You are a good
and faithful servant. I left you in charge of only a little,
but now I will put you in charge of much more. Come
and share in my happiness!"
24The servant who had been given one thousand coins
then came in and said, "Sir, I know that you are hard to
get along with. You harvest what you don't plant and
gather crops where you haven't scattered seed. 25I was
frightened and went out and hid your money in the
ground. Here is every single coin!"
26The master of the servant told him, "You are lazy
and good-for-nothing! You know that I harvest what I
don't plant and gather crops where I haven't scattered
seed. 27You could have at least put my money in the
bank, so that I could have earned interest on it."
28Then the master said, "Now your money will be
taken away and given to the servant with ten thousand
coins! 29Everyone who has something will be given
more, and they will have more than enough. But every-
thing will be taken from those who don't have anything.
30You are a worthless servant, and you will be thrown
out into the dark where people will cry and grit their
teeth in pain."

NEW INTERNATIONAL VERSION

21“His master replied, ‘Well done, good and faithful ser-
vant! You have been faithful with a few things; I will put
you in charge of many things. Come and share your mas-
ter’s happiness!’
22“The man with the two talents also came. ‘Master,’ he
said, ‘you entrusted me with two talents; see, I have
gained two more.’
23“His master replied, ‘Well done, good and faithful ser-
vant! You have been faithful with a few things; I will put
you in charge of many things. Come and share your mas-
ter’s happiness!’
24“Then the man who had received the one talent came.
‘Master,’ he said, ‘I knew that you are a hard man, har-
vesting where you have not sown and gathering where you
have not scattered seed. 25So I was afraid and went out
and hid your talent in the ground. See, here is what
belongs to you.’
26“His master replied, ‘You wicked, lazy servant! So you
knew that I harvest where I have not sown and gather
where I have not scattered seed? 27Well then, you should
have put my money on deposit with the bankers, so that
when I returned I would have received it back with inter-
est.
28“ ‘Take the talent from him and give it to the one who
has the ten talents. 29For everyone who has will be given
more, and he will have an abundance. Whoever does not
have, even what he has will be taken from him. 30And
throw that worthless servant outside, into the darkness,
where there will be weeping and gnashing of teeth.’

NEW LIVING TRANSLATION

was full of praise. ‘Well done, my good and faithful ser-
vant. You have been faithful in handling this small
amount, so now I will give you many more responsibilities.
Let’s celebrate together!’
22“Next came the servant who had received the two bags
of gold, with the report, ‘Sir, you gave me two bags of gold
to invest, and I have doubled the amount.’ 23The master
said, ‘Well done, my good and faithful servant. You have
been faithful in handling this small amount, so now I will
give you many more responsibilities. Let’s celebrate
together!’
24“Then the servant with the one bag of gold came and
said, ‘Sir, I know you are a hard man, harvesting crops you
didn’t plant and gathering crops you didn’t cultivate. 25I
was afraid I would lose your money, so I hid it in the earth
and here it is.’
26“But the master replied, ‘You wicked and lazy servant!
You think I’m a hard man, do you, harvesting crops I
didn’t plant and gathering crops I didn’t cultivate? 27Well,
you should at least have put my money into the bank so I
could have some interest. 28Take the money from this ser-
vant and give it to the one with the ten bags of gold. 29To
those who use well what they are given, even more will be
given, and they will have an abundance. But from those
who are unfaithful,* even what little they have will be
taken away. 30Now throw this useless servant into outer
darkness, where there will be weeping and gnashing of
teeth.’

25:29 Or *who have nothing.*

NEW KING JAMES VERSION

them.’ 21His lord said to him, ‘Well *done,* good and faithful
servant; you were faithful over a few things, I will make
you ruler over many things. Enter into the joy of your
lord.’ 22He also who had received two talents came and
said, ‘Lord, you delivered to me two talents; look, I have
gained two more talents besides them.’ 23His lord said to
him, ‘Well *done,* good and faithful servant; you have been
faithful over a few things, I will make you ruler over many
things. Enter into the joy of your lord.’
24“Then he who had received the one talent came and
said, ‘Lord, I knew you to be a hard man, reaping where
you have not sown, and gathering where you have not
scattered seed. 25And I was afraid, and went and hid your
talent in the ground. Look, *there* you have *what is* yours.’
26“But his lord answered and said to him, ‘You wicked
and lazy servant, you knew that I reap where I have not
sown, and gather where I have not scattered seed. 27So
you ought to have deposited my money with the bankers,
and at my coming I would have received back my own with
interest. 28So take the talent from him, and give *it* to him
who has ten talents.
29‘For to everyone who has, more will be given, and he
will have abundance; but from him who does not have,
even what he has will be taken away. 30And cast the
unprofitable servant into the outer darkness. There will be
weeping and gnashing of teeth.’

THE MESSAGE

investment. His master commended him: ‘Good work! You did your job well. From now on be my partner.’

“The servant with the two thousand showed how he also had doubled his master’s investment. His master commended him: ‘Good work! You did your job well. From now on be my partner.’

“The servant given one thousand said, ‘Master, I know you have high standards and hate careless ways, that you demand the best and make no allowances for error. I was afraid I might disappoint you, so I found a good hiding place and secured your money. Here it is, safe and sound down to the last cent.’

“The master was furious. ‘That’s a terrible way to live! It’s criminal to live cautiously like that! If you knew I was after the best, why did you do less than the least? The least you could have done would have been to invest the sum with the bankers, where at least I would have gotten a little interest.

“ ‘Take the thousand and give it to the one who risked the most. And get rid of this “play-it-safe” who won’t go out on a limb. Throw him out into utter darkness.’

KING JAMES VERSION

31 ¶ When the Son of man shall come in his glory, and
all the holy angels with him, then shall he sit upon the
throne of his glory:
32 And before him shall be gathered all nations: and he
shall separate them one from another, as a shepherd
divideth *his* sheep from the goats:
33 And he shall set the sheep on his right hand, but the
goats on the left.
34 Then shall the King say unto them on his right hand,
Come, ye blessed of my Father, inherit the kingdom pre-
pared for you from the foundation of the world:
35 For I was an hungred, and ye gave me meat: I was
thirsty, and ye gave me drink: I was a stranger, and ye
took me in:
36 Naked, and ye clothed me: I was sick, and ye visited
me: I was in prison, and ye came unto me.
37 Then shall the righteous answer him, saying, Lord,
when saw we thee an hungred, and fed *thee*? or thirsty,
and gave *thee* drink?
38 When saw we thee a stranger, and took *thee* in? or
naked, and clothed *thee*?
39 Or when saw we thee sick, or in prison, and came
unto thee?
40 And the King shall answer and say unto them, Verily
I say unto you, Inasmuch as ye have done *it* unto one of
the least of these my brethren, ye have done *it* unto me.
41 Then shall he say also unto them on the left hand,
Depart from me, ye cursed, into everlasting fire, prepared
for the devil and his angels:

NEW AMERICAN STANDARD BIBLE

The Judgment

31 "But when the Son of Man comes in His glory, and all
the angels with Him, then He will sit on His glorious
throne.
32 "All the nations will be gathered before Him; and He
will separate them from one another, as the shepherd sep-
arates the sheep from the goats;
33 and He will put the sheep on His right, and the goats
on the left.
34 "Then the King will say to those on His right, 'Come,
you who are blessed of My Father, inherit the kingdom
prepared for you from the foundation of the world.
35 'For I was hungry, and you gave Me *something* to eat;
I was thirsty, and you gave Me *something* to drink; I was a
stranger, and you invited Me in;
36 naked, and you clothed Me; I was sick, and you visit-
ed Me; I was in prison, and you came to Me.'
37 "Then the righteous will answer Him, 'Lord, when did
we see You hungry, and feed You, or thirsty, and give You
something to drink?
38 'And when did we see You a stranger, and invite You
in, or naked, and clothe You?
39 'When did we see You sick, or in prison, and come to
You?'
40 "The King will answer and say to them, 'Truly I say to
you, to the extent that you did it to one of these brothers
of Mine, *even* the least *of them,* you did it to Me.'
41 "Then He will also say to those on His left, 'Depart
from Me, accursed ones, into the eternal fire which has
been prepared for the devil and his angels;

NEW CENTURY VERSION

The King Will Judge All People

31"The Son of Man will come again in his great glory,
with all his angels. He will be King and sit on his great
throne. 32All the nations of the world will be gathered
before him, and he will separate them into two groups as a
shepherd separates the sheep from the goats. 33The Son of
Man will put the sheep on his right and the goats on his
left.
34"Then the King will say to the people on his right,
'Come, my Father has given you his blessing. Receive the
kingdom God has prepared for you since the world was
made. 35I was hungry, and you gave me food. I was
thirsty, and you gave me something to drink. I was alone
and away from home, and you invited me into your house.
36I was without clothes, and you gave me something to
wear. I was sick, and you cared for me. I was in prison,
and you visited me.'
37"Then the good people will answer, 'Lord, when did we
see you hungry and give you food, or thirsty and give you
something to drink? 38When did we see you alone and
away from home and invite you into our house? When did
we see you without clothes and give you something to
wear? 39When did we see you sick or in prison and care for
you?'
40"Then the King will answer, 'I tell you the truth, any-
thing you did for even the least of my people here, you
also did for me.'
41"Then the King will say to those on his left, 'Go away
from me. You will be punished. Go into the fire that burns
forever that was prepared for the devil and his angels.

CONTEMPORARY ENGLISH VERSION

The Final Judgment

31When the Son of Man comes in his glory with all of
his angels, he will sit on his royal throne. 32The people
of all nations will be brought before him, and he will
separate them, as shepherds separate their sheep from
their goats.
33He will place the sheep on his right and the goats on
his left. 34Then the king will say to those on his right,
"My father has blessed you! Come and receive the king-
dom that was prepared for you before the world was cre-
ated. 35When I was hungry, you gave me something to
eat, and when I was thirsty, you gave me something to
drink. When I was a stranger, you welcomed me, 36and
when I was naked, you gave me clothes to wear. When I
was sick, you took care of me, and when I was in jail,
you visited me."
37Then the ones who pleased the Lord will ask, "When
did we give you something to eat or drink? 38When did
we welcome you as a stranger or give you clothes to
wear 39or visit you while you were sick or in jail?"
40The king will answer, "Whenever you did it for any
of my people, no matter how unimportant they seemed,
you did it for me."
41Then the king will say to those on his left, "Get
away from me! You are under God's curse. Go into the
everlasting fire prepared for the devil and his angels!

NEW INTERNATIONAL VERSION

The Sheep and the Goats

31 “When the Son of Man comes in his glory, and all the angels with him, he will sit on his throne in heavenly glory. 32 All the nations will be gathered before him, and he will separate the people one from another as a shepherd separates the sheep from the goats. 33 He will put the sheep on his right and the goats on his left.

34 “Then the King will say to those on his right, ‘Come, you who are blessed by my Father; take your inheritance, the kingdom prepared for you since the creation of the world. 35 For I was hungry and you gave me something to eat, I was thirsty and you gave me something to drink, I was a stranger and you invited me in, 36 I needed clothes and you clothed me, I was sick and you looked after me, I was in prison and you came to visit me.’

37 “Then the righteous will answer him, ‘Lord, when did we see you hungry and feed you, or thirsty and give you something to drink? 38 When did we see you a stranger and invite you in, or needing clothes and clothe you? 39 When did we see you sick or in prison and go to visit you?’

40 “The King will reply, ‘I tell you the truth, whatever you did for one of the least of these brothers of mine, you did for me.’

41 “Then he will say to those on his left, ‘Depart from me, you who are cursed, into the eternal fire prepared for the devil and his angels. 42 For I was hungry and you gave me

NEW LIVING TRANSLATION

The Final Judgment

31 “But when the Son of Man comes in his glory, and all the angels with him, then he will sit upon his glorious throne. 32 All the nations will be gathered in his presence, and he will separate them as a shepherd separates the sheep from the goats. 33 He will place the sheep at his right hand and the goats at his left. 34 Then the King will say to those on the right, ‘Come, you who are blessed by my Father, inherit the Kingdom prepared for you from the foundation of the world. 35 For I was hungry, and you fed me. I was thirsty, and you gave me a drink. I was a stranger, and you invited me into your home. 36 I was naked, and you gave me clothing. I was sick, and you cared for me. I was in prison, and you visited me.’

37 “Then these righteous ones will reply, ‘Lord, when did we ever see you hungry and feed you? Or thirsty and give you something to drink? 38 Or a stranger and show you hospitality? Or naked and give you clothing? 39 When did we ever see you sick or in prison, and visit you?’ 40 And the King will tell them, ‘I assure you, when you did it to one of the least of these my brothers and sisters,* you were doing it to me!’

41 “Then the King will turn to those on the left and say, ‘Away with you, you cursed ones, into the eternal fire prepared for the Devil and his demons! 42 For I was hungry,

25:40 Greek *my brothers.*

NEW KING JAMES VERSION

The Son of Man Will Judge the Nations

31 “When the Son of Man comes in His glory, and all the holy[c] angels with Him, then He will sit on the throne of His glory. 32 All the nations will be gathered before Him, and He will separate them one from another, as a shepherd divides *his* sheep from the goats. 33 And He will set the sheep on His right hand, but the goats on the left. 34 Then the King will say to those on His right hand, ‘Come, you blessed of My Father, inherit the kingdom prepared for you from the foundation of the world: 35 for I was hungry and you gave Me food; I was thirsty and you gave Me drink; I was a stranger and you took Me in; 36 I *was* naked and you clothed Me; I was sick and you visited Me; I was in prison and you came to Me.’

37 “Then the righteous will answer Him, saying, ‘Lord, when did we see You hungry and feed *You,* or thirsty and give *You* drink? 38 When did we see You a stranger and take *You* in, or naked and clothe *You?* 39 Or when did we see You sick, or in prison, and come to You?’ 40 And the King will answer and say to them, ‘Assuredly, I say to you, inasmuch as you did *it* to one of the least of these My brethren, you did *it* to Me.’

41 “Then He will also say to those on the left hand, ‘Depart from Me, you cursed, into the everlasting fire prepared for the devil and his angels: 42 for I was hungry and you

25:31 [c] NU-Text omits *holy.*

THE MESSAGE

The Sheep and the Goats

“When he finally arrives, blazing in beauty and all his angels with him, the Son of Man will take his place on his glorious throne. Then all the nations will be arranged before him and he will sort the people out, much as a shepherd sorts out sheep and goats, putting sheep to his right and goats to his left.

“Then the King will say to those on his right, ‘Enter, you who are blessed by my Father! Take what’s coming to you in this kingdom. It’s been ready for you since the world’s foundation. And here’s why:

I was hungry and you fed me,
I was thirsty and you gave me a drink,
I was homeless and you gave me a room,
I was shivering and you gave me clothes,
I was sick and you stopped to visit,
I was in prison and you came to me.’

“Then those ‘sheep’ are going to say, ‘Master, what are you talking about? When did we ever see you hungry and feed you, thirsty and give you a drink? And when did we ever see you sick or in prison and come to you?’ Then the King will say, ‘I’m telling the solemn truth: Whenever you did one of these things to someone overlooked or ignored, that was me—you did it to me.’

“Then he will turn to the ‘goats,’ the ones on his left, and say, ‘Get out, worthless goats! You’re good for nothing but the fires of hell. And why? Because—

KING JAMES VERSION

42 For I was an hungred, and ye gave me no meat: I was thirsty, and ye gave me no drink:
43 I was a stranger, and ye took me not in: naked, and ye clothed me not: sick, and in prison, and ye visited me not.
44 Then shall they also answer him, saying, Lord, when saw we thee an hungred, or athirst, or a stranger, or naked, or sick, or in prison, and did not minister unto thee?
45 Then shall he answer them, saying, Verily I say unto you, Inasmuch as ye did *it* not to one of the least of these, ye did *it* not to me.
46 And these shall go away into everlasting punishment: but the righteous into life eternal.
26 And it came to pass, when Jesus had finished all these sayings, he said unto his disciples,
2 Ye know that after two days is *the feast of* the passover, and the Son of man is betrayed to be crucified.
3 Then assembled together the chief priests, and the scribes, and the elders of the people, unto the palace of the high priest, who was called Caiaphas,
4 And consulted that they might take Jesus by subtilty, and kill *him*.
5 But they said, Not on the feast *day*, lest there be an uproar among the people.
6 ¶ Now when Jesus was in Bethany, in the house of Simon the leper,

NEW AMERICAN STANDARD BIBLE

42 for I was hungry, and you gave Me *nothing* to eat; I was thirsty, and you gave Me nothing to drink;
43 I was a stranger, and you did not invite Me in; naked, and you did not clothe Me; sick, and in prison, and you did not visit Me.'
44 "Then they themselves also will answer, 'Lord, when did we see You hungry, or thirsty, or a stranger, or naked, or sick, or in prison, and did not take care of You?'
45 "Then He will answer them, 'Truly I say to you, to the extent that you did not do it to one of the least of these, you did not do it to Me.'
46 "These will go away into eternal punishment, but the righteous into eternal life."

The Plot to Kill Jesus

26 When Jesus had finished all these words, He said to His disciples,
2 "You know that after two days the Passover is coming, and the Son of Man is *to be* handed over for crucifixion."
3 Then the chief priests and the elders of the people were gathered together in the court of the high priest, named Caiaphas;
4 and they plotted together to seize Jesus by stealth and kill Him.
5 But they were saying, "Not during the festival, otherwise a riot might occur among the people."

The Precious Ointment

6 Now when Jesus was in Bethany, at the home of Simon the leper,

NEW CENTURY VERSION

42I was hungry, and you gave me nothing to eat. I was thirsty, and you gave me nothing to drink. 43I was alone and away from home, and you did not invite me into your house. I was without clothes, and you gave me nothing to wear. I was sick and in prison, and you did not care for me.'
44"Then those people will answer, 'Lord, when did we see you hungry or thirsty or alone and away from home or without clothes or sick or in prison? When did we see these things and not help you?'
45"Then the King will answer, 'I tell you the truth, anything you refused to do for even the least of my people here, you refused to do for me.'
46"These people will go off to be punished forever, but the good people will go to live forever."

The Plan to Kill Jesus

26 After Jesus finished saying all these things, he told his followers, 2"You know that the day after tomorrow is the day of the Passover Feast. On that day the Son of Man will be given to his enemies to be crucified."
3Then the leading priests and the older Jewish leaders had a meeting at the palace of the high priest, named Caiaphas. 4At the meeting, they planned to set a trap to arrest Jesus and kill him. 5But they said, "We must not do it during the feast, because the people might cause a riot."

Perfume for Jesus' Burial

6Jesus was in Bethany at the house of Simon, who had a skin disease. 7While Jesus was there, a woman approached

CONTEMPORARY ENGLISH VERSION

42I was hungry, but you did not give me anything to eat, and I was thirsty, but you did not give me anything to drink. 43I was a stranger, but you did not welcome me, and I was naked, but you did not give me any clothes to wear. I was sick and in jail, but you did not take care of me."
44Then the people will ask, "Lord, when did we fail to help you when you were hungry or thirsty or a stranger or naked or sick or in jail?"
45The king will say to them, "Whenever you failed to help any of my people, no matter how unimportant they seemed, you failed to do it for me."
46Then Jesus said, "Those people will be punished forever. But the ones who pleased God will have eternal life."

The Plot To Kill Jesus
(Mark 14.1, 2; Luke 22.1, 2; John 11.45-53)

26 When Jesus had finished teaching, he told his disciples, 2"You know that two days from now will be Passover. That is when the Son of Man will be handed over to his enemies and nailed to a cross."
3At that time the chief priests and the nation's leaders were meeting at the home of Caiaphas the high priest. 4They planned how they could sneak around and have Jesus arrested and put to death. 5But they said, "We must not do it during Passover, because the people will riot."

At Bethany (Mark 14.3-9; John 12.1-8)

6Jesus was in the town of Bethany, eating at the home of Simon, who had leprosy.[a] 7A woman came in with a

[a] 26.6 *leprosy*: See the note at 8.2.

NEW INTERNATIONAL VERSION

nothing to eat, I was thirsty and you gave me nothing to drink, 43I was a stranger and you did not invite me in, I needed clothes and you did not clothe me, I was sick and in prison and you did not look after me.'

44"They also will answer, 'Lord, when did we see you hungry or thirsty or a stranger or needing clothes or sick or in prison, and did not help you?'

45"He will reply, 'I tell you the truth, whatever you did not do for one of the least of these, you did not do for me.'

46"Then they will go away to eternal punishment, but the righteous to eternal life."

The Plot Against Jesus

26 When Jesus had finished saying all these things, he said to his disciples, 2"As you know, the Passover is two days away—and the Son of Man will be handed over to be crucified."

3Then the chief priests and the elders of the people assembled in the palace of the high priest, whose name was Caiaphas, 4and they plotted to arrest Jesus in some sly way and kill him. 5"But not during the Feast," they said, "or there may be a riot among the people."

Jesus Anointed at Bethany

6While Jesus was in Bethany in the home of a man known as Simon the Leper, 7a woman came to him with an

NEW LIVING TRANSLATION

and you didn't feed me. I was thirsty, and you didn't give me anything to drink. 43I was a stranger, and you didn't invite me into your home. I was naked, and you gave me no clothing. I was sick and in prison, and you didn't visit me.'

44"Then they will reply, 'Lord, when did we ever see you hungry or thirsty or a stranger or naked or sick or in prison, and not help you?' 45And he will answer, 'I assure you, when you refused to help the least of these my brothers and sisters, you were refusing to help me.' 46And they will go away into eternal punishment, but the righteous will go into eternal life."

The Plot to Kill Jesus

26 When Jesus had finished saying these things, he said to his disciples, 2"As you know, the Passover celebration begins in two days, and I, the Son of Man, will be betrayed and crucified."

3At that same time the leading priests and other leaders were meeting at the residence of Caiaphas, the high priest, 4to discuss how to capture Jesus secretly and put him to death. 5"But not during the Passover," they agreed, "or there will be a riot."

Jesus Anointed at Bethany

6Meanwhile, Jesus was in Bethany at the home of Simon, a man who had leprosy. 7During supper, a woman

NEW KING JAMES VERSION

gave Me no food; I was thirsty and you gave Me no drink; 43I was a stranger and you did not take Me in, naked and you did not clothe Me, sick and in prison and you did not visit Me.'

44"Then they also will answer Him,[d] saying, 'Lord, when did we see You hungry or thirsty or a stranger or naked or sick or in prison, and did not minister to You?' 45Then He will answer them, saying, 'Assuredly, I say to you, inasmuch as you did not do *it* to one of the least of these, you did not do *it* to Me.' 46And these will go away into everlasting punishment, but the righteous into eternal life."

The Plot to Kill Jesus

26 Now it came to pass, when Jesus had finished all these sayings, *that* He said to His disciples, 2"You know that after two days is the Passover, and the Son of Man will be delivered up to be crucified."

3Then the chief priests, the scribes,[a] and the elders of the people assembled at the palace of the high priest, who was called Caiaphas, 4and plotted to take Jesus by trickery and kill *Him.* 5But they said, "Not during the feast, lest there be an uproar among the people."

The Anointing at Bethany

6And when Jesus was in Bethany at the house of Simon

25:44 [d] NU-Text and M-Text omit *Him.* 26:3 [a] NU-Text omits *the scribes.*

THE MESSAGE

I was hungry and you gave me no meal,
I was thirsty and you gave me no drink,
I was homeless and you gave me no bed,
I was shivering and you gave me no clothes,
Sick and in prison, and you never visited.'

"Then those 'goats' are going to say, 'Master, what are you talking about? When did we ever see you hungry or thirsty or homeless or shivering or sick or in prison and didn't help?'

"He will answer them, 'I'm telling the solemn truth: Whenever you failed to do one of these things to someone who was being overlooked or ignored, that was me—you failed to do it to me.'

"Then those 'goats' will be herded to their eternal doom, but the 'sheep' to their eternal reward."

Anointed for Burial

26 When Jesus finished saying these things, he told his disciples, "You know that Passover comes in two days. That's when the Son of Man will be betrayed and handed over for crucifixion."

At that very moment, the party of high priests and religious leaders was meeting in the chambers of the Chief Priest named Caiaphas, conspiring to seize Jesus by stealth and kill him. They agreed that it should not be done during Passover Week. "We don't want a riot on our hands," they said.

When Jesus was at Bethany, a guest of Simon the Leper,

KING JAMES VERSION

7 There came unto him a woman having an alabaster box of very precious ointment, and poured it on his head, as he sat *at meat*.

8 But when his disciples saw *it*, they had indignation, saying, To what purpose *is* this waste?

9 For this ointment might have been sold for much, and given to the poor.

10 When Jesus understood *it*, he said unto them, Why trouble ye the woman? for she hath wrought a good work upon me.

11 For ye have the poor always with you; but me ye have not always.

12 For in that she hath poured this ointment on my body, she did *it* for my burial.

13 Verily I say unto you, Wheresoever this gospel shall be preached in the whole world, *there* shall also this, that this woman hath done, be told for a memorial of her.

14 ¶ Then one of the twelve, called Judas Iscariot, went unto the chief priests,

15 And said *unto them*, What will ye give me, and I will deliver him unto you? And they covenanted with him for thirty pieces of silver.

16 And from that time he sought opportunity to betray him.

17 ¶ Now the first *day* of the *feast of* unleavened bread the disciples came to Jesus, saying unto him, Where wilt thou that we prepare for thee to eat the passover?

18 And he said, Go into the city to such a man, and say unto him, The Master saith, My time is at hand; I will keep the passover at thy house with my disciples.

NEW AMERICAN STANDARD BIBLE

7 a woman came to Him with an alabaster vial of very costly perfume, and she poured it on His head as He reclined *at the table*.

8 But the disciples were indignant when they saw *this*, and said, "Why this waste?

9 "For this *perfume* might have been sold for a high price and *the money* given to the poor."

10 But Jesus, aware of this, said to them, "Why do you bother the woman? For she has done a good deed to Me.

11 "For you always have the poor with you; but you do not always have Me.

12 "For when she poured this perfume on My body, she did it to prepare Me for burial.

13 "Truly I say to you, wherever this gospel is preached in the whole world, what this woman has done will also be spoken of in memory of her."

Judas' Bargain

14 Then one of the twelve, named Judas Iscariot, went to the chief priests

15 and said, "What are you willing to give me to betray Him to you?" And they weighed out thirty pieces of silver to him.

16 From then on he *began* looking for a good opportunity to betray Jesus.

17 Now on the first *day* of Unleavened Bread the disciples came to Jesus and asked, "Where do You want us to prepare for You to eat the Passover?"

18 And He said, "Go into the city to a certain man, and say to him, 'The Teacher says, "My time is near; I *am to* keep the Passover at your house with My disciples." ' "

NEW CENTURY VERSION

him with an alabaster jar filled with expensive perfume.
She poured this perfume on Jesus' head while he was eat-
ing.
8His followers were upset when they saw the woman do
this. They asked, "Why waste that perfume? 9It could have
been sold for a great deal of money and the money given
to the poor."
10Knowing what had happened, Jesus said, "Why are
you troubling this woman? She did an excellent thing for
me. 11You will always have the poor with you, but you will
not always have me. 12This woman poured perfume on my
body to prepare me for burial. 13I tell you the truth, wher-
ever the Good News is preached in all the world, what this
woman has done will be told, and people will remember
her."

Judas Becomes an Enemy of Jesus

14Then one of the twelve apostles, Judas Iscariot, went
to talk to the leading priests. 15He said, "What will you
pay me for giving Jesus to you?" And they gave him thirty
silver coins. 16After that, Judas watched for the best time
to turn Jesus in.

Jesus Eats the Passover Meal

17On the first day of the Feast of Unleavened Bread, the
followers came to Jesus. They said, "Where do you want us
to prepare for you to eat the Passover meal?"
18Jesus answered, "Go into the city to a certain man and
tell him, 'The Teacher says: The chosen time is near. I will
have the Passover with my followers at your house.' "

CONTEMPORARY ENGLISH VERSION

bottle of expensive perfume and poured it on Jesus' head.
8But when his disciples saw this, they became angry and
complained, "Why such a waste? 9We could have sold this
perfume for a lot of money and given it to the poor."
10Jesus knew what they were thinking, and he said:

Why are you bothering this woman? She has done a
beautiful thing for me. 11You will always have the poor
with you, but you won't always have me. 12She has
poured perfume on my body to prepare it for burial.[b]
13You may be sure that wherever the good news is told
all over the world, people will remember what she has
done. And they will tell others.

Judas and the Chief Priests (Mark 14.10, 11; Luke 22.3-6)

14Judas Iscariot[c] was one of the twelve disciples. He
went to the chief priests 15and asked, "How much will you
give me if I help you arrest Jesus?" They paid Judas thirty
silver coins, 16and from then on he started looking for a
good chance to betray Jesus.

Jesus Eats the Passover Meal with His Disciples
(Mark 14.12-21; Luke 22.7-13; John 13.21-30)

17On the first day of the Festival of Thin Bread, Jesus'
disciples came to him and asked, "Where do you want us
to prepare the Passover meal?"
18Jesus told them to go to a certain man in the city and
tell him, "Our teacher says, 'My time has come! I want to
eat the Passover meal with my disciples in your home.' "

[b] 26.12 *poured perfume on my body to prepare it for burial*: The Jewish people taught that giving someone a proper burial was even more important than helping the poor. [c] 26.14 *Iscariot*: See the note at 10.4.

NEW INTERNATIONAL VERSION

alabaster jar of very expensive perfume, which she poured on his head as he was reclining at the table.

8When the disciples saw this, they were indignant. "Why this waste?" they asked. 9"This perfume could have been sold at a high price and the money given to the poor."

10Aware of this, Jesus said to them, "Why are you bothering this woman? She has done a beautiful thing to me. 11The poor you will always have with you, but you will not always have me. 12When she poured this perfume on my body, she did it to prepare me for burial. 13I tell you the truth, wherever this gospel is preached throughout the world, what she has done will also be told, in memory of her."

Judas Agrees to Betray Jesus

14Then one of the Twelve—the one called Judas Iscariot—went to the chief priests 15and asked, "What are you willing to give me if I hand him over to you?" So they counted out for him thirty silver coins. 16From then on Judas watched for an opportunity to hand him over.

The Lord's Supper

17On the first day of the Feast of Unleavened Bread, the disciples came to Jesus and asked, "Where do you want us to make preparations for you to eat the Passover?"

18He replied, "Go into the city to a certain man and tell him, 'The Teacher says: My appointed time is near. I am going to celebrate the Passover with my disciples at your

NEW LIVING TRANSLATION

came in with a beautiful jar* of expensive perfume and poured it over his head. 8The disciples were indignant when they saw this. "What a waste of money," they said. 9"She could have sold it for a fortune and given the money to the poor."

10But Jesus replied, "Why berate her for doing such a good thing to me? 11You will always have the poor among you, but I will not be here with you much longer. 12She has poured this perfume on me to prepare my body for burial. 13I assure you, wherever the Good News is preached throughout the world, this woman's deed will be talked about in her memory."

Judas Agrees to Betray Jesus

14Then Judas Iscariot, one of the twelve disciples, went to the leading priests 15and asked, "How much will you pay me to betray Jesus to you?" And they gave him thirty pieces of silver. 16From that time on, Judas began looking for the right time and place to betray Jesus.

The Last Supper

17On the first day of the Festival of Unleavened Bread, the disciples came to Jesus and asked, "Where do you want us to prepare the Passover supper?"

18"As you go into the city," he told them, "you will see a certain man. Tell him, 'The Teacher says, My time has come, and I will eat the Passover meal with my disciples at

26:7 Greek *an alabaster jar.*

NEW KING JAMES VERSION

the leper, 7a woman came to Him having an alabaster flask of very costly fragrant oil, and she poured *it* on His head as He sat *at the table.* 8But when His disciples saw *it,* they were indignant, saying, "Why this waste? 9For this fragrant oil might have been sold for much and given to *the* poor."

10But when Jesus was aware of *it,* He said to them, "Why do you trouble the woman? For she has done a good work for Me. 11For you have the poor with you always, but Me you do not have always. 12For in pouring this fragrant oil on My body, she did *it* for My burial. 13Assuredly, I say to you, wherever this gospel is preached in the whole world, what this woman has done will also be told as a memorial to her."

Judas Agrees to Betray Jesus

14Then one of the twelve, called Judas Iscariot, went to the chief priests 15and said, "What are you willing to give me if I deliver Him to you?" And they counted out to him thirty pieces of silver. 16So from that time he sought opportunity to betray Him.

Jesus Celebrates Passover with His Disciples

17Now on the first *day of the Feast* of Unleavened Bread the disciples came to Jesus, saying to Him, "Where do You want us to prepare for You to eat the Passover?"

18And He said, "Go into the city to a certain man, and say to him, 'The Teacher says, "My time is at hand; I will keep the Passover at your house with My disciples." ' "

THE MESSAGE

a woman came up to him as he was eating dinner and anointed him with a bottle of very expensive perfume. When the disciples saw what was happening, they were furious. "That's criminal! This could have been sold for a lot and the money handed out to the poor."

When Jesus realized what was going on, he intervened. "Why are you giving this woman a hard time? She has just done something wonderfully significant for me. You will have the poor with you every day for the rest of your lives, but not me. When she poured this perfume on my body, what she really did was anoint me for burial. You can be sure that wherever in the whole world the Message is preached, what she has just done is going to be remembered and admired."

That is when one of the Twelve, the one named Judas Iscariot, went to the cabal of high priests and said, "What will you give me if I hand him over to you?" They settled on thirty silver pieces. He began looking for just the right moment to hand him over.

The Traitor

On the first of the Days of Unleavened Bread, the disciples came to Jesus and said, "Where do you want us to prepare your Passover meal?"

He said, "Enter the city. Go up to a certain man and say, 'The Teacher says, "My time is near. I and my disciples plan to celebrate the Passover meal at your house." ' " The

KING JAMES VERSION

19 And the disciples did as Jesus had appointed them; and they made ready the passover.

20 Now when the even was come, he sat down with the twelve.

21 And as they did eat, he said, Verily I say unto you, that one of you shall betray me.

22 And they were exceeding sorrowful, and began every one of them to say unto him, Lord, is it I?

23 And he answered and said, He that dippeth *his* hand with me in the dish, the same shall betray me.

24 The Son of man goeth as it is written of him: but woe unto that man by whom the Son of man is betrayed! it had been good for that man if he had not been born.

25 Then Judas, which betrayed him, answered and said, Master, is it I? He said unto him, Thou hast said.

26 ¶ And as they were eating, Jesus took bread, and blessed *it*, and brake *it*, and gave *it* to the disciples, and said, Take, eat; this is my body.

27 And he took the cup, and gave thanks, and gave *it* to them, saying, Drink ye all of it;

28 For this is my blood of the new testament, which is shed for many for the remission of sins.

NEW AMERICAN STANDARD BIBLE

19 The disciples did as Jesus had directed them; and they prepared the Passover.

The Last Passover

20 Now when evening came, Jesus was reclining *at the table* with the twelve disciples.

21 As they were eating, He said, "Truly I say to you that one of you will betray Me."

22 Being deeply grieved, they each one began to say to Him, "Surely not I, Lord?"

23 And He answered, "He who dipped his hand with Me in the bowl is the one who will betray Me.

24 "The Son of Man *is to* go, just as it is written of Him; but woe to that man by whom the Son of Man is betrayed! It would have been good for that man if he had not been born."

25 And Judas, who was betraying Him, said, "Surely it is not I, Rabbi?" Jesus *said to him, "You have said *it* yourself."

The Lord's Supper Instituted

26 While they were eating, Jesus took *some* bread, and after a blessing, He broke *it* and gave *it* to the disciples, and said, "Take, eat; this is My body."

27 And when He had taken a cup and given thanks, He gave *it* to them, saying, "Drink from it, all of you;

28 for this is My blood of the covenant, which is poured out for many for forgiveness of sins.

NEW CENTURY VERSION

19 The followers did what Jesus told them to do, and they prepared the Passover meal.

20 In the evening Jesus was sitting at the table with his
twelve followers. 21 As they were eating, Jesus said, "I tell
you the truth, one of you will turn against me."

22 This made the followers very sad. Each one began to say to Jesus, "Surely, Lord, I am not the one who will turn against you, am I?"

23 Jesus answered, "The man who has dipped his hand
with me into the bowl is the one who will turn against me.
24 The Son of Man will die, just as the Scriptures say. But how terrible it will be for the person who hands the Son of Man over to be killed. It would be better for him if he had never been born."

25 Then Judas, who would give Jesus to his enemies, said to Jesus, "Teacher, surely I am not the one, am I?"

Jesus answered, "Yes, it is you."

The Lord's Supper

26 While they were eating, Jesus took some bread and thanked God for it and broke it. Then he gave it to his followers and said, "Take this bread and eat it; this is my body."

27 Then Jesus took a cup and thanked God for it and gave
it to the followers. He said, "Every one of you drink this.
28 This is my blood which is the new agreement that God makes with his people. This blood is poured out for many

CONTEMPORARY ENGLISH VERSION

19 They did as Jesus told them and prepared the meal.

20-21 When Jesus was eating with his twelve disciples that evening, he said, "One of you will surely hand me over to my enemies."

22 The disciples were very sad, and each one said to Jesus, "Lord, you can't mean me!"

23 He answered, "One of you men who has eaten with me
from this dish will betray me. 24 The Son of Man will die,
as the Scriptures say. But it's going to be terrible for the one who betrays me! That man would be better off if he had never been born."

25 Judas said, "Teacher, you surely don't mean me!"

"That's what you say!" Jesus replied. But later, Judas did betray him.

The Lord's Supper

(Mark 14.22-26; Luke 22.14-23; 1 Corinthians 11.23-25)

26 During the meal Jesus took some bread in his hands. He blessed the bread and broke it. Then he gave it to his disciples and said, "Take this and eat it. This is my body."

27 Jesus picked up a cup of wine and gave thanks to God.
He then gave it to his disciples and said, "Take this and
drink it. 28 This is my blood, and with it God makes his
agreement with you. It will be poured out, so that many

NEW INTERNATIONAL VERSION

house.' " [19]So the disciples did as Jesus had directed them and prepared the Passover.

[20]When evening came, Jesus was reclining at the table with the Twelve. [21]And while they were eating, he said, "I tell you the truth, one of you will betray me."

[22]They were very sad and began to say to him one after the other, "Surely not I, Lord?"

[23]Jesus replied, "The one who has dipped his hand into the bowl with me will betray me. [24]The Son of Man will go just as it is written about him. But woe to that man who betrays the Son of Man! It would be better for him if he had not been born."

[25]Then Judas, the one who would betray him, said, "Surely not I, Rabbi?"

Jesus answered, "Yes, it is you."[a]

[26]While they were eating, Jesus took bread, gave thanks and broke it, and gave it to his disciples, saying, "Take and eat; this is my body."

[27]Then he took the cup, gave thanks and offered it to them, saying, "Drink from it, all of you. [28]This is my blood of the[b] covenant, which is poured out for many for

[a] *25* Or *"You yourself have said it"* [b] *28* Some manuscripts *the new*

NEW LIVING TRANSLATION

your house.' " [19]So the disciples did as Jesus told them and prepared the Passover supper there.

[20]When it was evening, Jesus sat down at the table with the twelve disciples. [21]While they were eating, he said, "The truth is, one of you will betray me."

[22]Greatly distressed, one by one they began to ask him, "I'm not the one, am I, Lord?"

[23]He replied, "One of you who is eating with me now* will betray me. [24]For I, the Son of Man, must die, as the Scriptures declared long ago. But how terrible it will be for my betrayer. Far better for him if he had never been born!"

[25]Judas, the one who would betray him, also asked, "Teacher, I'm not the one, am I?"

And Jesus told him, "You have said it yourself."

[26]As they were eating, Jesus took a loaf of bread and asked God's blessing on it. Then he broke it in pieces and gave it to the disciples, saying, "Take it and eat it, for this is my body." [27]And he took a cup of wine and gave thanks to God for it. He gave it to them and said, "Each of you drink from it, [28]for this is my blood, which seals the covenant* between God and his people. It is poured out to

26:23 Or *The one who has dipped his hand in the bowl with me.*
26:28 Some manuscripts read *the new covenant.*

NEW KING JAMES VERSION

[19]So the disciples did as Jesus had directed them; and they prepared the Passover.

[20]When evening had come, He sat down with the twelve. [21]Now as they were eating, He said, "Assuredly, I say to you, one of you will betray Me."

[22]And they were exceedingly sorrowful, and each of them began to say to Him, "Lord, is it I?"

[23]He answered and said, "He who dipped *his* hand with Me in the dish will betray Me. [24]The Son of Man indeed goes just as it is written of Him, but woe to that man by whom the Son of Man is betrayed! It would have been good for that man if he had not been born."

[25]Then Judas, who was betraying Him, answered and said, "Rabbi, is it I?"

He said to him, "You have said it."

Jesus Institutes the Lord's Supper

[26]And as they were eating, Jesus took bread, blessed[b] and broke *it,* and gave *it* to the disciples and said, "Take, eat; this is My body."

[27]Then He took the cup, and gave thanks, and gave *it* to them, saying, "Drink from it, all of you. [28]For this is My blood of the new[c] covenant, which is shed for many for the

26:26 [b] M-Text reads *gave thanks for.* **26:28** [c] NU-Text omits *new.*

THE MESSAGE

disciples followed Jesus' instructions to the letter, and prepared the Passover meal.

After sunset, he and the Twelve were sitting around the table. During the meal, he said, "I have something hard but important to say to you: One of you is going to hand me over to the conspirators."

They were stunned, and then began to ask, one after another, "It isn't me, is it, Master?"

Jesus answered, "The one who hands me over is someone I eat with daily, one who passes me food at the table. In one sense the Son of Man is entering into a way of treachery well-marked by the Scriptures—no surprises here. In another sense that man who turns him in, turns traitor to the Son of Man—better never to have been born than do this!"

Then Judas, already turned traitor, said, "It isn't me, is it, Rabbi?"

Jesus said, "Don't play games with me, Judas."

The Bread and the Cup

During the meal, Jesus took and blessed the bread, broke it, and gave it to his disciples:

"Take, eat.
This is my body."

Taking the cup and thanking God, he gave it to them:

"Drink this, all of you.
This is my blood,
God's new covenant poured out for many people

KING JAMES VERSION

29 But I say unto you, I will not drink henceforth of this fruit of the vine, until that day when I drink it new with you in my Father's kingdom.
30 And when they had sung an hymn, they went out into the mount of Olives.
31 ¶ Then saith Jesus unto them, All ye shall be offended because of me this night: for it is written, I will smite the shepherd, and the sheep of the flock shall be scattered abroad.
32 But after I am risen again, I will go before you into Galilee.
33 Peter answered and said unto him, Though all *men* shall be offended because of thee, *yet* will I never be offended.
34 Jesus said unto him, Verily I say unto thee, That this night, before the cock crow, thou shalt deny me thrice.
35 Peter said unto him, Though I should die with thee, yet will I not deny thee. Likewise also said all the disciples.
36 ¶ Then cometh Jesus with them unto a place called Gethsemane, and saith unto the disciples, Sit ye here, while I go and pray yonder.
37 And he took with him Peter and the two sons of Zebedee, and began to be sorrowful and very heavy.

NEW AMERICAN STANDARD BIBLE

29 "But I say to you, I will not drink of this fruit of the vine from now on until that day when I drink it new with you in My Father's kingdom."
30 After singing a hymn, they went out to the Mount of Olives.
31 Then Jesus *said to them, "You will all fall away because of Me this night, for it is written, 'I WILL STRIKE DOWN THE SHEPHERD, AND THE SHEEP OF THE FLOCK SHALL BE SCATTERED.'
32 "But after I have been raised, I will go ahead of you to Galilee."
33 But Peter said to Him, "*Even* though all may fall away because of You, I will never fall away."
34 Jesus said to him, "Truly I say to you that this *very* night, before a rooster crows, you will deny Me three times."
35 Peter *said to Him, "Even if I have to die with You, I will not deny You." All the disciples said the same thing too.

The Garden of Gethsemane

36 Then Jesus *came with them to a place called Gethsemane, and *said to His disciples, "Sit here while I go over there and pray."
37 And He took with Him Peter and the two sons of Zebedee, and began to be grieved and distressed.

NEW CENTURY VERSION

to forgive their sins. 29I tell you this: I will not drink of this fruit of the vine[a] again until that day when I drink it new with you in my Father's kingdom."
30After singing a hymn, they went out to the Mount of Olives.

Jesus' Followers Will Leave Him

31Jesus told his followers, "Tonight you will all stumble in your faith on account of me, because it is written in the Scriptures:

'I will kill the shepherd,
and the sheep will scatter.' *Zechariah 13:7*

32But after I rise from the dead, I will go ahead of you into Galilee."
33Peter said, "Everyone else may stumble in their faith because of you, but I will not."
34Jesus said, "I tell you the truth, tonight before the rooster crows you will say three times that you don't know me."
35But Peter said, "I will never say that I don't know you! I will even die with you!" And all the other followers said the same thing.

Jesus Prays Alone

36Then Jesus went with his followers to a place called Gethsemane. He said to them, "Sit here while I go over there and pray." 37He took Peter and the two sons of Zebedee with him, and he began to be very sad and troubled.

26:29 [a] **fruit of the vine** Product of the grapevine; this may also be translated "wine."

CONTEMPORARY ENGLISH VERSION

people will have their sins forgiven. 29From now on I am not going to drink any wine, until I drink new wine with you in my Father's kingdom." 30Then they sang a hymn and went out to the Mount of Olives.

Peter's Promise
(Mark 14.27-31; Luke 22.31-34; John 13.36-38)

31Jesus said to his disciples, "During this very night, all of you will reject me, as the Scriptures say,

'I will strike down
the shepherd,
and the sheep
will be scattered.'

32But after I am raised to life, I will go to Galilee ahead of you."
33Peter spoke up, "Even if all the others reject you, I never will!"
34Jesus replied, "I promise you that before a rooster crows tonight, you will say three times that you don't know me." 35But Peter said, "Even if I have to die with you, I will never say I don't know you."
All the others said the same thing.

Jesus Prays (Mark 14.32-42; Luke 22.39-46)

36Jesus went with his disciples to a place called Gethsemane. When they got there, he told them, "Sit here while I go over there and pray."
37Jesus took along Peter and the two brothers, James

NEW INTERNATIONAL VERSION

the forgiveness of sins. 29I tell you, I will not drink of this fruit of the vine from now on until that day when I drink it anew with you in my Father's kingdom."

30When they had sung a hymn, they went out to the Mount of Olives.

Jesus Predicts Peter's Denial

31Then Jesus told them, "This very night you will all fall away on account of me, for it is written:

" 'I will strike the shepherd,
and the sheep of the flock will be scattered.'[c]

32But after I have risen, I will go ahead of you into Galilee."

33Peter replied, "Even if all fall away on account of you, I never will."

34"I tell you the truth," Jesus answered, "this very night, before the rooster crows, you will disown me three times."

35But Peter declared, "Even if I have to die with you, I will never disown you." And all the other disciples said the same.

Gethsemane

36Then Jesus went with his disciples to a place called Gethsemane, and he said to them, "Sit here while I go over there and pray." 37He took Peter and the two sons of Zebedee along with him, and he began to be sorrowful and

c *31* Zech. 13:7

NEW LIVING TRANSLATION

forgive the sins of many. 29Mark my words—I will not drink wine again until the day I drink it new with you in my Father's Kingdom." 30Then they sang a hymn and went out to the Mount of Olives.

Jesus Predicts Peter's Denial

31"Tonight all of you will desert me," Jesus told them. "For the Scriptures say,

'God* will strike the Shepherd,
and the sheep of the flock will be scattered.'*

32But after I have been raised from the dead, I will go ahead of you to Galilee and meet you there."

33Peter declared, "Even if everyone else deserts you, I never will."

34"Peter," Jesus replied, "the truth is, this very night, before the rooster crows, you will deny me three times."

35"No!" Peter insisted. "Not even if I have to die with you! I will never deny you!" And all the other disciples vowed the same.

Jesus Prays in Gethsemane

36Then Jesus brought them to an olive grove called Gethsemane, and he said, "Sit here while I go on ahead to pray." 37He took Peter and Zebedee's two sons, James and John, and he began to be filled with anguish and deep

26:31a Greek *I.* **26:31b** Zech 13:7.

NEW KING JAMES VERSION

remission of sins. 29But I say to you, I will not drink of this fruit of the vine from now on until that day when I drink it new with you in My Father's kingdom."

30And when they had sung a hymn, they went out to the Mount of Olives.

Jesus Predicts Peter's Denial

31Then Jesus said to them, "All of you will be made to stumble because of Me this night, for it is written:

'I will strike the Shepherd,
And the sheep of the flock will be scattered.'[d]

32But after I have been raised, I will go before you to Galilee."

33Peter answered and said to Him, "Even if all are made to stumble because of You, I will never be made to stumble."

34Jesus said to him, "Assuredly, I say to you that this night, before the rooster crows, you will deny Me three times."

35Peter said to Him, "Even if I have to die with You, I will not deny You!"

And so said all the disciples.

The Prayer in the Garden

36Then Jesus came with them to a place called Gethsemane, and said to the disciples, "Sit here while I go and pray over there." 37And He took with Him Peter and the two sons of Zebedee, and He began to be sorrowful and

26:31 d Zechariah 13:7

THE MESSAGE

for the forgiveness of sins.

I'll not be drinking wine from this cup again until that new day when I'll drink with you in the kingdom of my Father."

They sang a hymn and went directly to Mount Olives.

Gethsemane

Then Jesus told them, "Before the night's over, you're going to fall to pieces because of what happens to me. There is a Scripture that says,

'I'll strike the shepherd;
helter-skelter the sheep will be scattered.'

But after I am raised up, I, your Shepherd, will go ahead of you, leading the way to Galilee."

Peter broke in, "Even if everyone else falls to pieces on account of you, I won't."

"Don't be so sure," Jesus said. "This very night, before the rooster crows up the dawn, you will deny me three times."

Peter protested, "Even if I had to die with you, I would never deny you." All the others said the same thing.

Then Jesus went with them to a garden called Gethsemane and told his disciples, "Stay here while I go over there and pray." Taking along Peter and the two sons of Zebedee, he plunged into an agonizing sorrow. Then he

KING JAMES VERSION

38 Then saith he unto them, My soul is exceeding sorrowful, even unto death: tarry ye here, and watch with me.

39 And he went a little further, and fell on his face, and prayed, saying, O my Father, if it be possible, let this cup pass from me: nevertheless not as I will, but as thou *wilt*.

40 And he cometh unto the disciples, and findeth them asleep, and saith unto Peter, What, could ye not watch with me one hour?

41 Watch and pray, that ye enter not into temptation: the spirit indeed *is* willing, but the flesh *is* weak.

42 He went away again the second time, and prayed, saying, O my Father, if this cup may not pass away from me, except I drink it, thy will be done.

43 And he came and found them asleep again: for their eyes were heavy.

44 And he left them, and went away again, and prayed the third time, saying the same words.

45 Then cometh he to his disciples, and saith unto them, Sleep on now, and take *your* rest: behold, the hour is at hand, and the Son of man is betrayed into the hands of sinners.

46 Rise, let us be going: behold, he is at hand that doth betray me.

47 ¶ And while he yet spake, lo, Judas, one of the twelve, came, and with him a great multitude with

NEW AMERICAN STANDARD BIBLE

38 Then He *said to them, "My soul is deeply grieved, to the point of death; remain here and keep watch with Me."

39 And He went a little beyond *them,* and fell on His face and prayed, saying, "My Father, if it is possible, let this cup pass from Me; yet not as I will, but as You will."

40 And He *came to the disciples and *found them sleeping, and *said to Peter, "So, you *men* could not keep watch with Me for one hour?

41 "Keep watching and praying that you may not enter into temptation; the spirit is willing, but the flesh is weak."

42 He went away again a second time and prayed, saying, "My Father, if this cannot pass away unless I drink it, Your will be done."

43 Again He came and found them sleeping, for their eyes were heavy.

44 And He left them again, and went away and prayed a third time, saying the same thing once more.

45 Then He *came to the disciples and *said to them, "Are you still sleeping and resting? Behold, the hour is at hand and the Son of Man is being betrayed into the hands of sinners.

46 "Get up, let us be going; behold, the one who betrays Me is at hand!"

Jesus' Betrayal and Arrest

47 While He was still speaking, behold, Judas, one of the twelve, came up accompanied by a large crowd with

NEW CENTURY VERSION

38He said to them, "My heart is full of sorrow, to the point
of death. Stay here and watch with me."
39After walking a little farther away from them, Jesus
fell to the ground and prayed, "My Father, if it is possible,
do not give me this cup[b] of suffering. But do what you
want, not what I want." 40Then Jesus went back to his fol-
lowers and found them asleep. He said to Peter, "You men
could not stay awake with me for one hour? 41Stay awake
and pray for strength against temptation. The spirit wants
to do what is right, but the body is weak."
42Then Jesus went away a second time and prayed, "My
Father, if it is not possible for this painful thing to be
taken from me, and if I must do it, I pray that what you
want will be done."
43Then he went back to his followers, and again he
found them asleep, because their eyes were heavy. 44So
Jesus left them and went away and prayed a third time,
saying the same thing.
45Then Jesus went back to his followers and said, "Are
you still sleeping and resting? The time has come for the
Son of Man to be handed over to sinful people. 46Get up,
we must go. Look, here comes the man who has turned
against me."

Jesus Is Arrested

47While Jesus was still speaking, Judas, one of the twelve
apostles, came up. With him were many people carrying

26:39 [b] **cup** Jesus is talking about the terrible things that will happen to him. Accepting these things will be very hard, like drinking a cup of something bitter.

CONTEMPORARY ENGLISH VERSION

and John.[d] He was very sad and troubled, 38and he said to
them, "I am so sad that I feel as if I am dying. Stay here
and keep awake with me."
39Jesus walked on a little way. Then he knelt with his
face to the ground and prayed, "My Father, if it is possible,
don't make me suffer by having me drink from this cup.[e]
But do what you want, and not what I want."
40He came back and found his disciples sleeping. So he
said to Peter, "Can't any of you stay awake with me for
just one hour? 41Stay awake and pray that you won't be
tested. You want to do what is right, but you are weak."
42Again Jesus went to pray and said, "My Father, if there
is no other way, and I must suffer, I will still do what you
want."
43Jesus came back and found them sleeping again. They
simply could not keep their eyes open. 44He left them and
prayed the same prayer once more.
45Finally, Jesus returned to his disciples and said, "Are
you still sleeping and resting?[f] The time has come for the
Son of Man to be handed over to sinners. 46Get up! Let's
go. The one who will betray me is already here."

Jesus Is Arrested

(Mark 14.43-50; Luke 22.47-53; John 18.3-12)

47Jesus was still speaking, when Judas the betrayer
came up. He was one of the twelve disciples, and a large

[d] **26.37** *the two brothers, James and John*: The Greek text has "the two sons of Zebedee" (see 27.56). [e] **26.39** *having me drink from this cup*: In the Scriptures "to drink from a cup" sometimes means to suffer (see the note at 20.22). [f] **26.45** *Are you still sleeping and resting?*: Or "You may as well keep on sleeping and resting."

NEW INTERNATIONAL VERSION

troubled. 38Then he said to them, "My soul is overwhelmed with sorrow to the point of death. Stay here and keep watch with me."

39Going a little farther, he fell with his face to the ground and prayed, "My Father, if it is possible, may this cup be taken from me. Yet not as I will, but as you will."

40Then he returned to his disciples and found them sleeping. "Could you men not keep watch with me for one
hour?" he asked Peter. 41"Watch and pray so that you will not fall into temptation. The spirit is willing, but the body is weak."

42He went away a second time and prayed, "My Father, if it is not possible for this cup to be taken away unless I drink it, may your will be done."

43When he came back, he again found them sleeping,
because their eyes were heavy. 44So he left them and went away once more and prayed the third time, saying the same thing.

45Then he returned to the disciples and said to them, "Are you still sleeping and resting? Look, the hour is near, and the Son of Man is betrayed into the hands of sinners.
46Rise, let us go! Here comes my betrayer!"

Jesus Arrested

47While he was still speaking, Judas, one of the Twelve, arrived. With him was a large crowd armed with swords

NEW LIVING TRANSLATION

distress. 38He told them, "My soul is crushed with grief to the point of death. Stay here and watch with me."

39He went on a little farther and fell face down on the ground, praying, "My Father! If it is possible, let this cup of suffering be taken away from me. Yet I want your will,
not mine." 40Then he returned to the disciples and found them asleep. He said to Peter, "Couldn't you stay awake
and watch with me even one hour? 41Keep alert and pray. Otherwise temptation will overpower you. For though the spirit is willing enough, the body is weak!"

42Again he left them and prayed, "My Father! If this cup cannot be taken away until I drink it, your will be done."
43He returned to them again and found them sleeping, for they just couldn't keep their eyes open.

44So he went back to pray a third time, saying the same
things again. 45Then he came to the disciples and said, "Still sleeping? Still resting?* Look, the time has come. I, the Son of Man, am betrayed into the hands of sinners.
46Up, let's be going. See, my betrayer is here!"

Jesus Is Arrested

47And even as he said this, Judas, one of the twelve disciples, arrived with a mob that was armed with swords

26:45 Or *Sleep on, take your rest.*

NEW KING JAMES VERSION

deeply distressed. 38Then He said to them, "My soul is exceedingly sorrowful, even to death. Stay here and watch with Me."

39He went a little farther and fell on His face, and prayed, saying, "O My Father, if it is possible, let this cup pass from Me; nevertheless, not as I will, but as You *will.*"

40Then He came to the disciples and found them sleeping, and said to Peter, "What! Could you not watch with
Me one hour? 41Watch and pray, lest you enter into temptation. The spirit indeed *is* willing, but the flesh *is* weak."

42Again, a second time, He went away and prayed, saying, "O My Father, if this cup cannot pass away from Me
unless[e] I drink it, Your will be done." 43And He came and found them asleep again, for their eyes were heavy.

44So He left them, went away again, and prayed the
third time, saying the same words. 45Then He came to His disciples and said to them, "Are *you* still sleeping and resting? Behold, the hour is at hand, and the Son of Man is
being betrayed into the hands of sinners. 46Rise, let us be going. See, My betrayer is at hand."

Betrayal and Arrest in Gethsemane

47And while He was still speaking, behold, Judas, one of the twelve, with a great multitude with swords and

26:42 [e] NU-Text reads *if this may not pass away unless.*

THE MESSAGE

said, "This sorrow is crushing my life out. Stay here and keep vigil with me."

Going a little ahead, he fell on his face, praying, "My Father, if there is any way, get me out of this. But please, not what I want. You, what do *you* want?"

When he came back to his disciples, he found them sound asleep. He said to Peter, "Can't you stick it out with me a single hour? Stay alert; be in prayer so you don't wander into temptation without even knowing you're in danger. There is a part of you that is eager, ready for anything in God. But there's another part that's as lazy as an old dog sleeping by the fire."

He then left them a second time. Again he prayed, "My Father, if there is no other way than this, drinking this cup to the dregs, I'm ready. Do it your way."

When he came back, he again found them sound asleep. They simply couldn't keep their eyes open. This time he let them sleep on, and went back a third time to pray, going over the same ground one last time.

When he came back the next time, he said, "Are you going to sleep on and make a night of it? My time is up, the Son of Man is about to be handed over to the hands of sinners. Get up! Let's get going! My betrayer is here."

With Swords and Clubs

The words were barely out of his mouth when Judas (the one from the Twelve) showed up, and with him a gang

KING JAMES VERSION

swords and staves, from the chief priests and elders of the people.

48 Now he that betrayed him gave them a sign, saying, Whomsoever I shall kiss, that same is he: hold him fast.

49 And forthwith he came to Jesus, and said, Hail, master; and kissed him.

50 And Jesus said unto him, Friend, wherefore art thou come? Then came they, and laid hands on Jesus, and took him.

51 And, behold, one of them which were with Jesus stretched out *his* hand, and drew his sword, and struck a servant of the high priest's, and smote off his ear.

52 Then said Jesus unto him, Put up again thy sword into his place: for all they that take the sword shall perish with the sword.

53 Thinkest thou that I cannot now pray to my Father, and he shall presently give me more than twelve legions of angels?

54 But how then shall the scriptures be fulfilled, that thus it must be?

55 In that same hour said Jesus to the multitudes, Are ye come out as against a thief with swords and staves for to take me? I sat daily with you teaching in the temple, and ye laid no hold on me.

56 But all this was done, that the scriptures of the prophets might be fulfilled. Then all the disciples forsook him, and fled.

57 ¶ And they that had laid hold on Jesus led *him* away

NEW AMERICAN STANDARD BIBLE

swords and clubs, *who came* from the chief priests and elders of the people.

48 Now he who was betraying Him gave them a sign, saying, "Whomever I kiss, He is the one; seize Him."

49 Immediately Judas went to Jesus and said, "Hail, Rabbi!" and kissed Him.

50 And Jesus said to him, "Friend, *do* what you have come for." Then they came and laid hands on Jesus and seized Him.

51 And behold, one of those who were with Jesus reached and drew out his sword, and struck the slave of the high priest and cut off his ear.

52 Then Jesus *said to him, "Put your sword back into its place; for all those who take up the sword shall perish by the sword.

53 "Or do you think that I cannot appeal to My Father, and He will at once put at My disposal more than twelve [1]legions of angels?

54 "How then will the Scriptures be fulfilled, *which say* that it must happen this way?"

55 At that time Jesus said to the crowds, "Have you come out with swords and clubs to arrest Me as *you would* against a robber? Every day I used to sit in the temple teaching and you did not seize Me.

56 "But all this has taken place to fulfill the Scriptures of the prophets." Then all the disciples left Him and fled.

Jesus before Caiaphas

57 Those who had seized Jesus led Him away to

26:53 [1] A legion equaled 6,000 troops

NEW CENTURY VERSION

swords and clubs who had been sent from the leading priests and the older Jewish leaders of the people. 48Judas had planned to give them a signal, saying, "The man I kiss is Jesus. Arrest him." 49At once Judas went to Jesus and said, "Greetings, Teacher!" and kissed him.

50Jesus answered, "Friend, do what you came to do."

Then the people came and grabbed Jesus and arrested him. 51When that happened, one of Jesus' followers reached for his sword and pulled it out. He struck the servant of the high priest and cut off his ear.

52Jesus said to the man, "Put your sword back in its place. All who use swords will be killed with swords. 53Surely you know I could ask my Father, and he would give me more than twelve armies of angels. 54But it must happen this way to bring about what the Scriptures say."

55Then Jesus said to the crowd, "You came to get me with swords and clubs as if I were a criminal. Every day I sat in the Temple teaching, and you did not arrest me there. 56But all these things have happened so that it will come about as the prophets wrote." Then all of Jesus' followers left him and ran away.

Jesus Before the Leaders

57Those people who arrested Jesus led him to the house

CONTEMPORARY ENGLISH VERSION

mob armed with swords and clubs was with him. They had been sent by the chief priests and the nation's leaders. 48Judas had told them ahead of time, "Arrest the man I greet with a kiss."[g]

49Judas walked right up to Jesus and said, "Hello, teacher." Then Judas kissed him.

50Jesus replied, "My friend, why are you here?"[h]

The men grabbed Jesus and arrested him. 51One of Jesus' followers pulled out a sword. He struck the servant of the high priest and cut off his ear.

52But Jesus told him, "Put your sword away. Anyone who lives by fighting will die by fighting. 53Don't you know that I could ask my Father, and right away he would send me more than twelve armies of angels? 54But then, how could the words of the Scriptures come true, which say that this must happen?"

55Jesus said to the mob, "Why do you come with swords and clubs to arrest me like a criminal? Day after day I sat and taught in the temple, and you didn't arrest me. 56But all this happened, so that what the prophets wrote would come true."

All of Jesus' disciples left him and ran away.

Jesus Is Questioned by the Council

(Mark 14.53-65; Luke 22.54, 55, 63-71; John 18.13, 14, 19-24)

57After Jesus had been arrested, he was led off to the

[g] 26.48 *the man I greet with a kiss*: It was the custom for people to greet each other with a kiss on the cheek. [h] 26.50 *why are you here?*: Or "do what you came for."

NEW INTERNATIONAL VERSION

and clubs, sent from the chief priests and the elders of the
people. 48Now the betrayer had arranged a signal with
them: "The one I kiss is the man; arrest him." 49Going at
once to Jesus, Judas said, "Greetings, Rabbi!" and kissed
him.
50Jesus replied, "Friend, do what you came for."[d]
Then the men stepped forward, seized Jesus and arrested
him. 51With that, one of Jesus' companions reached for his
sword, drew it out and struck the servant of the high
priest, cutting off his ear.
52"Put your sword back in its place," Jesus said to him,
"for all who draw the sword will die by the sword. 53Do
you think I cannot call on my Father, and he will at once
put at my disposal more than twelve legions of angels?
54But how then would the Scriptures be fulfilled that say it
must happen in this way?"
55At that time Jesus said to the crowd, "Am I leading a
rebellion, that you have come out with swords and clubs to
capture me? Every day I sat in the temple courts teaching,
and you did not arrest me. 56But this has all taken place
that the writings of the prophets might be fulfilled." Then
all the disciples deserted him and fled.

Before the Sanhedrin

57Those who had arrested Jesus took him to Caiaphas,

[d] *50* Or *"Friend, why have you come?"*

NEW LIVING TRANSLATION

and clubs. They had been sent out by the leading priests
and other leaders of the people. 48Judas had given them a
prearranged signal: "You will know which one to arrest
when I go over and give him the kiss of greeting." 49So
Judas came straight to Jesus. "Greetings, Teacher!" he
exclaimed and gave him the kiss.
50Jesus said, "My friend, go ahead and do what you have
come for." Then the others grabbed Jesus and arrested
him. 51One of the men with Jesus pulled out a sword and
slashed off an ear of the high priest's servant.
52"Put away your sword," Jesus told him. "Those who
use the sword will be killed by the sword. 53Don't you real-
ize that I could ask my Father for thousands* of angels to
protect us, and he would send them instantly? 54But if I
did, how would the Scriptures be fulfilled that describe
what must happen now?"
55Then Jesus said to the crowd, "Am I some dangerous
criminal, that you have come armed with swords and clubs
to arrest me? Why didn't you arrest me in the Temple? I
was there teaching every day. 56But this is all happening
to fulfill the words of the prophets as recorded in the
Scriptures." At that point, all the disciples deserted him
and fled.

Jesus before the Council

57Then the people who had arrested Jesus led him to the

26:53 Greek *12 legions.*

NEW KING JAMES VERSION

clubs, came from the chief priests and elders of the peo-
ple.
48Now His betrayer had given them a sign, saying,
"Whomever I kiss, He is the One; seize Him." 49Immedi-
ately he went up to Jesus and said, "Greetings, Rabbi!"
and kissed Him.
50But Jesus said to him, "Friend, why have you come?"
Then they came and laid hands on Jesus and took Him.
51And suddenly, one of those *who were* with Jesus
stretched out *his* hand and drew his sword, struck the ser-
vant of the high priest, and cut off his ear.
52But Jesus said to him, "Put your sword in its place, for
all who take the sword will perish[f] by the sword. 53Or do
you think that I cannot now pray to My Father, and He will
provide Me with more than twelve legions of angels?
54How then could the Scriptures be fulfilled, that it must
happen thus?"
55In that hour Jesus said to the multitudes, "Have you
come out, as against a robber, with swords and clubs to
take Me? I sat daily with you, teaching in the temple, and
you did not seize Me. 56But all this was done that the
Scriptures of the prophets might be fulfilled."
Then all the disciples forsook Him and fled.

Jesus Faces the Sanhedrin

57And those who had laid hold of Jesus led *Him* away to

26:52 [f] M-Text reads *die.*

THE MESSAGE

from the high priests and religious leaders brandishing
swords and clubs. The betrayer had worked out a sign with
them: "The one I kiss, that's the one—seize him." He went
straight to Jesus, greeted him, "How are you, Rabbi?" and
kissed him.

Jesus said, "Friend, why this charade?"

Then they came on him—grabbed him and roughed him
up. One of those with Jesus pulled his sword and, taking a
swing at the Chief Priest's servant, cut off his ear.

Jesus said, "Put your sword back where it belongs. All
who use swords are destroyed by swords. Don't you realize
that I am able right now to call to my Father, and twelve
companies—more, if I want them—of fighting angels
would be here, battle-ready? But if I did that, how would
the Scriptures come true that say this is the way it has to
be?"

Then Jesus addressed the mob: "What is this—coming
out after me with swords and clubs as if I were a danger-
ous criminal? Day after day I have been sitting in the
Temple teaching, and you never so much as lifted a hand
against me. You've done it this way to confirm and fulfill
the prophetic writings."

Then all the disciples cut and ran.

False Charges

The gang that had seized Jesus led him before Caiaphas

KING JAMES VERSION

to Caiaphas the high priest, where the scribes and the elders were assembled.

58 But Peter followed him afar off unto the high priest's palace, and went in, and sat with the servants, to see the end.

59 Now the chief priests, and elders, and all the council, sought false witness against Jesus, to put him to death;

60 But found none: yea, though many false witnesses came, *yet* found they none. At the last came two false witnesses,

61 And said, This *fellow* said, I am able to destroy the temple of God, and to build it in three days.

62 And the high priest arose, and said unto him, Answerest thou nothing? what *is it which* these witness against thee?

63 But Jesus held his peace. And the high priest answered and said unto him, I adjure thee by the living God, that thou tell us whether thou be the Christ, the Son of God.

64 Jesus saith unto him, Thou hast said: nevertheless I say unto you, Hereafter shall ye see the Son of man sitting on the right hand of power, and coming in the clouds of heaven.

NEW AMERICAN STANDARD BIBLE

Caiaphas, the high priest, where the scribes and the elders were gathered together.

58 But Peter was following Him at a distance as far as the courtyard of the high priest, and entered in, and sat down with the officers to see the outcome.

59 Now the chief priests and the whole Council kept trying to obtain false testimony against Jesus, so that they might put Him to death.

60 They did not find *any,* even though many false witnesses came forward. But later on two came forward,

61 and said, "This man stated, 'I am able to destroy the temple of God and to rebuild it in three days.' "

62 The high priest stood up and said to Him, "Do You not answer? What is it that these men are testifying against You?"

63 But Jesus kept silent. And the high priest said to Him, "I adjure You by the living God, that You tell us whether You are the Christ, the Son of God."

64 Jesus *said to him, "You have said it *yourself;* nevertheless I tell you, hereafter you will see THE SON OF MAN SITTING AT THE RIGHT HAND OF POWER, and COMING ON THE CLOUDS OF HEAVEN."

NEW CENTURY VERSION

of Caiaphas, the high priest, where the teachers of the law and the older Jewish leaders were gathered. 58 Peter followed far behind to the courtyard of the high priest's house, and he sat down with the guards to see what would happen to Jesus.

59 The leading priests and the whole Jewish council tried to find something false against Jesus so they could kill him. 60 Many people came and told lies about him, but the council could find no real reason to kill him. Then two people came and said, 61 "This man said, 'I can destroy the Temple of God and build it again in three days.' "

62 Then the high priest stood up and said to Jesus, "Aren't you going to answer? Don't you have something to say about their charges against you?" 63 But Jesus said nothing.

Again the high priest said to Jesus, "I command you by the power of the living God: Tell us if you are the Christ, the Son of God."

64 Jesus answered, "Those are your words. But I tell you, in the future you will see the Son of Man sitting at the right hand of God, the Powerful One, and coming on clouds in the sky."

CONTEMPORARY ENGLISH VERSION

house of Caiaphas the high priest. The nation's leaders and the teachers of the Law of Moses were meeting there. 58 But Peter followed along at a distance and came to the courtyard of the high priest's palace. He went in and sat down with the guards to see what was going to happen.

59 The chief priests and the whole council wanted to put Jesus to death. So they tried to find some people who would tell lies about him in court.[i] 60 But they could not find any, even though many did come and tell lies. At last, two men came forward 61 and said, "This man claimed that he would tear down God's temple and build it again in three days."

62 The high priest stood up and asked Jesus, "Why don't you say something in your own defense? Don't you hear the charges they are making against you?" 63 But Jesus did not answer. So the high priest said, "With the living God looking on, you must tell the truth. Tell us, are you the Messiah, the Son of God?"[j]

64 "That is what you say!" Jesus answered. "But I tell all of you,

'Soon you will see
the Son of Man
sitting at the right side[k]
of God All-Powerful
and coming on the clouds
of heaven.' "

[i] 26.59 *some people who would tell lies about him in court*: The Law of Moses taught that two witnesses were necessary before a person could be put to death (see verse 60). [j] 26.63 *Son of God*: One of the titles used for the kings of Israel. [k] 26.64 *right side*: See the note at 22.44.

NEW INTERNATIONAL VERSION

the high priest, where the teachers of the law and the
elders had assembled. 58But Peter followed him at a dis-
tance, right up to the courtyard of the high priest. He
entered and sat down with the guards to see the outcome.
59The chief priests and the whole Sanhedrin were look-
ing for false evidence against Jesus so that they could put
him to death. 60But they did not find any, though many
false witnesses came forward.
Finally two came forward 61and declared, "This fellow
said, 'I am able to destroy the temple of God and rebuild it
in three days.' "
62Then the high priest stood up and said to Jesus, "Are
you not going to answer? What is this testimony that
these men are bringing against you?" 63But Jesus
remained silent.
The high priest said to him, "I charge you under oath by
the living God: Tell us if you are the Christ,[e] the Son of
God."
64"Yes, it is as you say," Jesus replied. "But I say to all
of you: In the future you will see the Son of Man sitting at
the right hand of the Mighty One and coming on the clouds
of heaven."

[e] *63* Or *Messiah*; also in verse 68

NEW LIVING TRANSLATION

home of Caiaphas, the high priest, where the teachers of
religious law and other leaders had gathered.
58Meanwhile, Peter was following far behind and eventual-
ly came to the courtyard of the high priest's house. He
went in, sat with the guards, and waited to see what was
going to happen to Jesus.
59Inside, the leading priests and the entire high council*
were trying to find witnesses who would lie about Jesus,
so they could put him to death. 60But even though they
found many who agreed to give false witness, there was
no testimony they could use. Finally, two men were found
61who declared, "This man said, 'I am able to destroy the
Temple of God and rebuild it in three days.' "
62Then the high priest stood up and said to Jesus, "Well,
aren't you going to answer these charges? What do you
have to say for yourself?" 63But Jesus remained silent.
Then the high priest said to him, "I demand in the name of
the living God that you tell us whether you are the
Messiah, the Son of God."
64Jesus replied, "Yes, it is as you say. And in the future
you will see me, the Son of Man, sitting at God's right
hand in the place of power and coming back on the clouds
of heaven."*

26:59 Greek *the Sanhedrin.* 26:64 See Ps 110:1; Dan 7:13.

NEW KING JAMES VERSION

Caiaphas the high priest, where the scribes and the elders
were assembled. 58But Peter followed Him at a distance to
the high priest's courtyard. And he went in and sat with
the servants to see the end.
59Now the chief priests, the elders,[g] and all the council
sought false testimony against Jesus to put Him to death,
60but found none. Even though many false witnesses came
forward, they found none.[h] But at last two false witnesses[i]
came forward 61and said, "This *fellow* said, 'I am able to
destroy the temple of God and to build it in three days.' "
62And the high priest arose and said to Him, "Do You
answer nothing? What *is it* these men testify against
You?" 63But Jesus kept silent. And the high priest
answered and said to Him, "I put You under oath by the
living God: Tell us if You are the Christ, the Son of God!"
64Jesus said to him, "*It is as* you said. Nevertheless, I
say to you, hereafter you will see the Son of Man sitting at
the right hand of the Power, and coming on the clouds of
heaven."

26:59 [g] NU-Text omits *the elders.* 26:60 [h] NU-Text puts a comma after *but found none,* does not capitalize *Even,* and omits *they found none.* [i] NU-Text omits *false witnesses.*

THE MESSAGE

the Chief Priest, where the religion scholars and leaders
had assembled. Peter followed at a safe distance until they
got to the Chief Priest's courtyard. Then he slipped in and
mingled with the servants, watching to see how things
would turn out.
The high priests, conspiring with the Jewish Council,
tried to cook up charges against Jesus in order to sentence
him to death. But even though many stepped up, making
up one false accusation after another, nothing was believ-
able.
Finally two men came forward with this: "He said, 'I can
tear down this Temple of God and after three days rebuild
it.' "
The Chief Priest stood up and said, "What do you have
to say to the accusation?"
Jesus kept silent.
Then the Chief Priest said, "I command you by the
authority of the living God to say if you are the Messiah,
the Son of God."
Jesus was curt: "You yourself said it. And that's not all.
Soon you'll see it for yourself:

The Son of Man seated at the right hand of the Mighty
One,
Arriving on the clouds of heaven."

KING JAMES VERSION

65 Then the high priest rent his clothes, saying, He hath spoken blasphemy; what further need have we of witnesses? behold, now ye have heard his blasphemy.

66 What think ye? They answered and said, He is guilty of death.

67 Then did they spit in his face, and buffeted him; and others smote *him* with the palms of their hands,

68 Saying, Prophesy unto us, thou Christ, Who is he that smote thee?

69 ¶ Now Peter sat without in the palace: and a damsel came unto him, saying, Thou also wast with Jesus of Galilee.

70 But he denied before *them* all, saying, I know not what thou sayest.

71 And when he was gone out into the porch, another *maid* saw him, and said unto them that were there, This *fellow* was also with Jesus of Nazareth.

72 And again he denied with an oath, I do not know the man.

73 And after a while came unto *him* they that stood by, and said to Peter, Surely thou also art *one* of them; for thy speech bewrayeth thee.

74 Then began he to curse and to swear, *saying*, I know not the man. And immediately the cock crew.

75 And Peter remembered the word of Jesus, which said unto him, Before the cock crow, thou shalt deny me thrice. And he went out, and wept bitterly.

NEW AMERICAN STANDARD BIBLE

65 Then the high priest tore his robes and said, "He has blasphemed! What further need do we have of witnesses? Behold, you have now heard the blasphemy;

66 what do you think?" They answered, "He deserves death!"

67 Then they spat in His face and beat Him with their fists; and others slapped Him,

68 and said, "Prophesy to us, You Christ; who is the one who hit You?"

Peter's Denials

69 Now Peter was sitting outside in the courtyard, and a servant-girl came to him and said, "You too were with Jesus the Galilean."

70 But he denied *it* before them all, saying, "I do not know what you are talking about."

71 When he had gone out to the gateway, another *servant-girl* saw him and *said to those who were there, "This man was with Jesus of Nazareth."

72 And again he denied *it* with an oath, "I do not know the man."

73 A little later the bystanders came up and said to Peter, "Surely you too are *one* of them; for even the way you talk gives you away."

74 Then he began to curse and swear, "I do not know the man!" And immediately a rooster crowed.

75 And Peter remembered the word which Jesus had said, "Before a rooster crows, you will deny Me three times." And he went out and wept bitterly.

NEW CENTURY VERSION

65When the high priest heard this, he tore his clothes and said, "This man has said things that are against God! We don't need any more witnesses; you all heard him say these things against God. 66What do you think?"

The people answered, "He should die."

67Then the people there spat in Jesus' face and beat him with their fists. Others slapped him. 68They said, "Prove to us that you are a prophet, you Christ! Tell us who hit you!"

Peter Says He Doesn't Know Jesus

69At that time, as Peter was sitting in the courtyard, a servant girl came to him and said, "You also were with Jesus of Galilee."

70But Peter said to all the people there that he was never with Jesus. He said, "I don't know what you are talking about."

71When he left the courtyard and was at the gate, another girl saw him. She said to the people there, "This man was with Jesus of Nazareth."

72Again, Peter said he was never with him, saying, "I swear I don't know this man Jesus!"

73A short time later, some people standing there went to Peter and said, "Surely you are one of those who followed Jesus. The way you talk shows it."

74Then Peter began to place a curse on himself and swear, "I don't know the man." At once, a rooster crowed. 75And Peter remembered what Jesus had told him: "Before the rooster crows, you will say three times that you don't know me." Then Peter went outside and cried painfully.

CONTEMPORARY ENGLISH VERSION

65The high priest then tore his robe and said, "This man claims to be God! We don't need any more witnesses! You have heard what he said. 66What do you think?"

They answered, "He is guilty and deserves to die!" 67Then they spit in his face and hit him with their fists. Others slapped him 68and said, "You think you are the Messiah! So tell us who hit you!"

Peter Says He Doesn't Know Jesus

(Mark 14.66-72; Luke 22.56-62; John 18.15-18, 25-27)

69While Peter was sitting out in the courtyard, a servant girl came up to him and said, "You were with Jesus from Galilee."

70But in front of everyone Peter said, "That isn't so! I don't know what you are talking about!"

71When Peter had gone out to the gate, another servant girl saw him and said to some people there, "This man was with Jesus from Nazareth."

72Again Peter denied it, and this time he swore, "I don't even know that man!"

73A little while later some people standing there walked over to Peter and said, "We know that you are one of them. We can tell it because you talk like someone from Galilee."

74Peter began to curse and swear, "I don't know that man!"

Right then a rooster crowed, 75and Peter remembered that Jesus had said, "Before a rooster crows, you will say three times that you don't know me." Then Peter went out and cried hard.

NEW INTERNATIONAL VERSION

65 Then the high priest tore his clothes and said, "He has
spoken blasphemy! Why do we need any more witnesses?
Look, now you have heard the blasphemy. 66 What do you
think?"
"He is worthy of death," they answered.
67 Then they spit in his face and struck him with their
fists. Others slapped him 68 and said, "Prophesy to us,
Christ. Who hit you?"

Peter Disowns Jesus

69 Now Peter was sitting out in the courtyard, and a ser-
vant girl came to him. "You also were with Jesus of
Galilee," she said.
70 But he denied it before them all. "I don't know what
you're talking about," he said.
71 Then he went out to the gateway, where another girl
saw him and said to the people there, "This fellow was
with Jesus of Nazareth."
72 He denied it again, with an oath: "I don't know the
man!"
73 After a little while, those standing there went up to
Peter and said, "Surely you are one of them, for your
accent gives you away."
74 Then he began to call down curses on himself and he
swore to them, "I don't know the man!"
Immediately a rooster crowed. 75 Then Peter remembered
the word Jesus had spoken: "Before the rooster crows, you
will disown me three times." And he went outside and
wept bitterly.

NEW LIVING TRANSLATION

65 Then the high priest tore his clothing to show his hor-
ror, shouting, "Blasphemy! Why do we need other wit-
nesses? You have all heard his blasphemy. 66 What is your
verdict?"
"Guilty!" they shouted. "He must die!"
67 Then they spit in Jesus' face and hit him with their
fists. And some slapped him, 68 saying, "Prophesy to us,
you Messiah! Who hit you that time?"

Peter Denies Jesus

69 Meanwhile, as Peter was sitting outside in the court-
yard, a servant girl came over and said to him, "You were
one of those with Jesus the Galilean."
70 But Peter denied it in front of everyone. "I don't know
what you are talking about," he said.
71 Later, out by the gate, another servant girl noticed him
and said to those standing around, "This man was with
Jesus of Nazareth."
72 Again Peter denied it, this time with an oath. "I don't
even know the man," he said.
73 A little later some other bystanders came over to him
and said, "You must be one of them; we can tell by your
Galilean accent."
74 Peter said, "I swear by God, I don't know the man."
And immediately the rooster crowed. 75 Suddenly, Jesus'
words flashed through Peter's mind: "Before the rooster
crows, you will deny me three times." And he went away,
crying bitterly.

NEW KING JAMES VERSION

65 Then the high priest tore his clothes, saying, "He has
spoken blasphemy! What further need do we have of wit-
nesses? Look, now you have heard His blasphemy! 66 What
do you think?"
They answered and said, "He is deserving of death."
67 Then they spat in His face and beat Him; and others
struck *Him* with the palms of their hands, 68 saying,
"Prophesy to us, Christ! Who is the one who struck You?"

Peter Denies Jesus, and Weeps Bitterly

69 Now Peter sat outside in the courtyard. And a servant
girl came to him, saying, "You also were with Jesus of Gal-
ilee."
70 But he denied it before *them* all, saying, "I do not
know what you are saying."
71 And when he had gone out to the gateway, another
girl saw him and said to those *who were* there, "This *fel-
low* also was with Jesus of Nazareth."
72 But again he denied with an oath, "I do not know the
Man!"
73 And a little later those who stood by came up and said
to Peter, "Surely you also are *one* of them, for your speech
betrays you."
74 Then he began to curse and swear, *saying,* "I do not
know the Man!"
Immediately a rooster crowed. 75 And Peter remembered
the word of Jesus who had said to him, "Before the rooster
crows, you will deny Me three times." So he went out and
wept bitterly.

THE MESSAGE

At that, the Chief Priest lost his temper, ripping his robes, yelling, "He blasphemed! Why do we need witnesses to accuse him? You all heard him blaspheme! Are you going to stand for such blasphemy?"

They all said, "Death! That seals his death sentence."

Then they were spitting in his face and banging him around. They jeered as they slapped him: "Prophesy, Messiah: Who hit you that time?"

Denial in the Courtyard

All this time, Peter was sitting out in the courtyard. One servant girl came up to him and said, "You were with Jesus the Galilean."

In front of everybody there, he denied it. "I don't know what you're talking about."

As he moved over toward the gate, someone else said to the people there, "This man was with Jesus the Nazarene."

Again he denied it, salting his denial with an oath: "I swear, I never laid eyes on the man."

Shortly after that, some bystanders approached Peter. "You've got to be one of them. Your accent gives you away."

Then he got really nervous and swore. "I don't know the man!"

Just then a rooster crowed. Peter remembered what Jesus had said: "Before the rooster crows, you will deny me three times." He went out and cried and cried and cried.

KING JAMES VERSION

27 When the morning was come, all the chief priests
and elders of the people took counsel against Jesus
to put him to death:
2 And when they had bound him, they led *him* away,
and delivered him to Pontius Pilate the governor.
3 Then Judas, which had betrayed him, when he saw
that he was condemned, repented himself, and brought
again the thirty pieces of silver to the chief priests and
elders,
4 Saying, I have sinned in that I have betrayed the
innocent blood. And they said, What *is that* to us? see
thou *to that*.
5 And he cast down the pieces of silver in the temple,
and departed, and went and hanged himself.
6 And the chief priests took the silver pieces, and said,
It is not lawful for to put them into the treasury, because it
is the price of blood.
7 And they took counsel, and bought with them the pot-
ter's field, to bury strangers in.
8 Wherefore that field was called, The field of blood,
unto this day.
9 Then was fulfilled that which was spoken by Jeremy
the prophet, saying, And they took the thirty pieces of sil-
ver, the price of him that was valued, whom they of the
children of Israel did value;

NEW AMERICAN STANDARD BIBLE

Judas' Remorse

27 Now when morning came, all the chief priests and
the elders of the people conferred together against
Jesus to put Him to death;
2 and they bound Him, and led Him away and deliv-
ered Him to Pilate the governor.
3 Then when Judas, who had betrayed Him, saw that
He had been condemned, he felt remorse and returned the
thirty pieces of silver to the chief priests and elders,
4 saying, "I have sinned by betraying innocent blood."
But they said, "What is that to us? See *to that* yourself!"
5 And he threw the pieces of silver into the temple
sanctuary and departed; and he went away and hanged
himself.
6 The chief priests took the pieces of silver and said, "It
is not lawful to put them into the temple treasury, since it
is the price of blood."
7 And they conferred together and with the money
bought the Potter's Field as a burial place for strangers.
8 For this reason that field has been called the Field of
Blood to this day.
9 Then that which was spoken through Jeremiah the
prophet was fulfilled: "AND THEY TOOK THE THIRTY PIECES OF
SILVER, THE PRICE OF THE ONE WHOSE PRICE HAD BEEN SET by
the sons of Israel;

NEW CENTURY VERSION

Jesus Is Taken to Pilate

27 Early the next morning, all the leading priests and
older leaders of the people decided that Jesus
should die. 2 They tied him, led him away, and turned him
over to Pilate, the governor.

Judas Kills Himself

3 Judas, the one who had given Jesus to his enemies, saw
that they had decided to kill Jesus. Then he was very sorry
for what he had done. So he took the thirty silver coins
back to the priests and the leaders, 4 saying, "I sinned; I
handed over to you an innocent man."
The leaders answered, "What is that to us? That's your
problem, not ours."
5 So Judas threw the money into the Temple. Then he
went off and hanged himself.
6 The leading priests picked up the silver coins in the
Temple and said, "Our law does not allow us to keep this
money with the Temple money, because it has paid for a
man's death." 7 So they decided to use the coins to buy
Potter's Field as a place to bury strangers who died in
Jerusalem. 8 That is why that field is still called the Field of
Blood. 9 So what Jeremiah the prophet had said came true:
"They took thirty silver coins. That is how little the
Israelites thought he was worth. 10 They used those thirty

CONTEMPORARY ENGLISH VERSION

Jesus Is Taken to Pilate

(Mark 15.1; Luke 23.1, 2; John 18.28-32)

27 Early the next morning all the chief priests and the
nation's leaders met and decided that Jesus should
be put to death. 2 They tied him up and led him away to
Pilate the governor.

The Death of Judas (Acts 1.18, 19)

3 Judas had betrayed Jesus, but when he learned that
Jesus had been sentenced to death, he was sorry for what
he had done. He returned the thirty silver coins to the chief
priests and leaders 4 and said, "I have sinned by betraying
a man who has never done anything wrong."
"So what? That's your problem," they replied. 5 Judas
threw the money into the temple and then went out and
hanged himself.
6 The chief priests picked up the money and said, "This
money was paid to have a man killed. We can't put it in
the temple treasury." 7 Then they had a meeting and decid-
ed to buy a field that belonged to someone who made clay
pots. They wanted to use it as a graveyard for foreigners.
8 That's why people still call that place "Field of Blood."
9 So the words of the prophet Jeremiah came true,

"They took
the thirty silver coins,
the price of a person
among the people of Israel.

NEW INTERNATIONAL VERSION

Judas Hangs Himself

27 Early in the morning, all the chief priests and the elders of the people came to the decision to put Jesus to death. 2They bound him, led him away and handed him over to Pilate, the governor.

3When Judas, who had betrayed him, saw that Jesus was condemned, he was seized with remorse and returned the thirty silver coins to the chief priests and the elders. 4"I have sinned," he said, "for I have betrayed innocent blood."

"What is that to us?" they replied. "That's your responsibility."

5So Judas threw the money into the temple and left. Then he went away and hanged himself.

6The chief priests picked up the coins and said, "It is against the law to put this into the treasury, since it is blood money." 7So they decided to use the money to buy the potter's field as a burial place for foreigners. 8That is why it has been called the Field of Blood to this day. 9Then what was spoken by Jeremiah the prophet was fulfilled: "They took the thirty silver coins, the price set on him by

NEW LIVING TRANSLATION

Judas Hangs Himself

27 Very early in the morning, the leading priests and other leaders met again to discuss how to persuade the Roman government to sentence Jesus to death. 2Then they bound him and took him to Pilate, the Roman governor.

3When Judas, who had betrayed him, realized that Jesus had been condemned to die, he was filled with remorse. So he took the thirty pieces of silver back to the leading priests and other leaders. 4"I have sinned," he declared, "for I have betrayed an innocent man."

"What do we care?" they retorted. "That's your problem." 5Then Judas threw the money onto the floor of the Temple and went out and hanged himself. 6The leading priests picked up the money. "We can't put it in the Temple treasury," they said, "since it's against the law to accept money paid for murder." 7After some discussion they finally decided to buy the potter's field, and they made it into a cemetery for foreigners. 8That is why the field is still called the Field of Blood. 9This fulfilled the prophecy of Jeremiah that says,

"They took* the thirty pieces of silver—
the price at which he was valued by the people of Israel—

27:9 Or *I took.*

NEW KING JAMES VERSION

Jesus Handed Over to Pontius Pilate

27 When morning came, all the chief priests and elders of the people plotted against Jesus to put Him to death. 2And when they had bound Him, they led Him away and delivered Him to Pontius[a] Pilate the governor.

Judas Hangs Himself

3Then Judas, His betrayer, seeing that He had been condemned, was remorseful and brought back the thirty pieces of silver to the chief priests and elders, 4saying, "I have sinned by betraying innocent blood."

And they said, "What *is that* to us? You see *to it!*"

5Then he threw down the pieces of silver in the temple and departed, and went and hanged himself.

6But the chief priests took the silver pieces and said, "It is not lawful to put them into the treasury, because they are the price of blood." 7And they consulted together and bought with them the potter's field, to bury strangers in. 8Therefore that field has been called the Field of Blood to this day.

9Then was fulfilled what was spoken by Jeremiah the prophet, saying, *"And they took the thirty pieces of silver, the value of Him who was priced,* whom they of the children

27:2 [a] NU-Text omits *Pontius.*

THE MESSAGE

Thirty Silver Coins

27 In the first light of dawn, all the high priests and religious leaders met and put the finishing touches on their plot to kill Jesus. Then they tied him up and paraded him to Pilate, the governor.

Judas, the one who betrayed him, realized that Jesus was doomed. Overcome with remorse, he gave back the thirty silver coins to the high priests, saying, "I've sinned. I've betrayed an innocent man."

They said, "What do we care? That's *your* problem!"

Judas threw the silver coins into the Temple and left. Then he went out and hung himself.

The high priests picked up the silver pieces, but then didn't know what to do with them. "It wouldn't be right to give this—a payment for murder!—as an offering in the Temple." They decided to get rid of it by buying the "Potter's Field" and use it as a burial place for the homeless. That's how the field got called "Murder Meadow," a name that has stuck to this day. Then Jeremiah's words became history:

"They took the thirty silver pieces,
The price of the one priced by some sons of Israel,

KING JAMES VERSION

10 And gave them for the potter's field, as the Lord appointed me.

11 ¶ And Jesus stood before the governor: and the governor asked him, saying, Art thou the King of the Jews? And Jesus said unto him, Thou sayest.

12 And when he was accused of the chief priests and elders, he answered nothing.

13 Then said Pilate unto him, Hearest thou not how many things they witness against thee?

14 And he answered him to never a word; insomuch that the governor marvelled greatly.

15 Now at *that* feast the governor was wont to release unto the people a prisoner, whom they would.

16 And they had then a notable prisoner, called Barabbas.

17 Therefore when they were gathered together, Pilate said unto them, Whom will ye that I release unto you? Barabbas, or Jesus which is called Christ?

18 For he knew that for envy they had delivered him.

19 When he was set down on the judgment seat, his

NEW AMERICAN STANDARD BIBLE

10 AND THEY GAVE THEM FOR THE POTTER'S FIELD, AS THE LORD DIRECTED ME."

Jesus before Pilate

11 Now Jesus stood before the governor, and the governor questioned Him, saying, "Are You the King of the Jews?" And Jesus said to him, "*It is as* you say."

12 And while He was being accused by the chief priests and elders, He did not answer.

13 Then Pilate *said to Him, "Do You not hear how many things they testify against You?"

14 And He did not answer him with regard to even a *single* charge, so the governor was quite amazed.

15 Now at *the* feast the governor was accustomed to release for the people *any* one prisoner whom they wanted.

16 At that time they were holding a notorious prisoner, called Barabbas.

17 So when the people gathered together, Pilate said to them, "Whom do you want me to release for you? Barabbas, or Jesus who is called Christ?"

18 For he knew that because of envy they had handed Him over.

19 While he was sitting on the judgment seat, his wife

NEW CENTURY VERSION

silver coins to buy the potter's field, as the Lord commanded me."[a]

Pilate Questions Jesus

11Jesus stood before Pilate the governor, and Pilate asked him, "Are you the king of the Jews?"

Jesus answered, "Those are your words."

12When the leading priests and the older leaders accused Jesus, he said nothing.

13So Pilate said to Jesus, "Don't you hear them accusing you of all these things?"

14But Jesus said nothing in answer to Pilate, and Pilate was very surprised at this.

Pilate Tries to Free Jesus

15Every year at the time of Passover the governor would free one prisoner whom the people chose. 16At that time there was a man in prison, named Barabbas, who was known to be very bad. 17When the people gathered at Pilate's house, Pilate said, "Whom do you want me to set free: Barabbas or Jesus who is called the Christ?" 18Pilate knew that the people turned Jesus in to him because they were jealous.

19While Pilate was sitting there on the judge's seat, his

27:10 [a] **"They...commanded me."** See Zechariah 11:12–13 and Jeremiah 32:6–9.

CONTEMPORARY ENGLISH VERSION

10They paid it
for a potter's field,[a]
as the Lord
had commanded me."

Pilate Questions Jesus

(Mark 15.2-5; Luke 23.3-5; John 18.33-38)

11Jesus was brought before Pilate the governor, who asked him, "Are you the king of the Jews?"

"Those are your words!" Jesus answered. 12And when the chief priests and leaders brought their charges against him, he did not say a thing.

13Pilate asked him, "Don't you hear what crimes they say you have done?" 14But Jesus did not say anything, and the governor was greatly amazed.

The Death Sentence

(Mark 15.6-15; Luke 23.13-26; John 18.39—19.16)

15During Passover the governor always freed a prisoner chosen by the people. 16At that time a well-known terrorist named Jesus Barabbas [b] was in jail. 17So when the crowd came together, Pilate asked them, "Which prisoner do you want me to set free? Do you want Jesus Barabbas or Jesus who is called the Messiah?" 18Pilate knew that the leaders had brought Jesus to him because they were jealous.

19While Pilate was judging the case, his wife sent him a

[a] **27.10** *a potter's field*: Perhaps a field owned by someone who made clay pots. But it may have been a field where potters came to get clay or to make pots or to throw away their broken pieces of pottery.

[b] **27.16** *Jesus Barabbas*: Here and in verse 17 many manuscripts have "Barabbas."

NEW INTERNATIONAL VERSION

the people of Israel, 10and they used them to buy the potter's field, as the Lord commanded me."[a]

Jesus Before Pilate

11Meanwhile Jesus stood before the governor, and the governor asked him, "Are you the king of the Jews?"

"Yes, it is as you say," Jesus replied.

12When he was accused by the chief priests and the elders, he gave no answer. 13Then Pilate asked him, "Don't you hear the testimony they are bringing against you?" 14But Jesus made no reply, not even to a single charge—to the great amazement of the governor.

15Now it was the governor's custom at the Feast to release a prisoner chosen by the crowd. 16At that time they had a notorious prisoner, called Barabbas. 17So when the crowd had gathered, Pilate asked them, "Which one do you want me to release to you: Barabbas, or Jesus who is called Christ?" 18For he knew it was out of envy that they had handed Jesus over to him.

19While Pilate was sitting on the judge's seat, his wife

[a] *10* See Zech. 11:12,13; Jer. 19:1–13; 32:6–9.

NEW LIVING TRANSLATION

10 and purchased the potter's field,
as the Lord directed.*"

Jesus' Trial before Pilate

11Now Jesus was standing before Pilate, the Roman governor. "Are you the King of the Jews?" the governor asked him.

Jesus replied, "Yes, it is as you say."

12But when the leading priests and other leaders made their accusations against him, Jesus remained silent. 13"Don't you hear their many charges against you?" Pilate demanded. 14But Jesus said nothing, much to the governor's great surprise.

15Now it was the governor's custom to release one prisoner to the crowd each year during the Passover celebration—anyone they wanted. 16This year there was a notorious criminal in prison, a man named Barabbas.* 17As the crowds gathered before Pilate's house that morning, he asked them, "Which one do you want me to release to you—Barabbas, or Jesus who is called the Messiah?" 18(He knew very well that the Jewish leaders had arrested Jesus out of envy.)

19Just then, as Pilate was sitting on the judgment seat,

27:9-10 Greek *as the Lord directed me.* Zech 11:12-13; Jer 32:6-9.
27:16 Some manuscripts read *Jesus Barabbas;* also in 27:17.

NEW KING JAMES VERSION

of Israel priced, 10*and gave them for the potter's field, as the* LORD *directed me."*[b]

Jesus Faces Pilate

11Now Jesus stood before the governor. And the governor asked Him, saying, "Are You the King of the Jews?"

Jesus said to him, "*It is as* you say." 12And while He was being accused by the chief priests and elders, He answered nothing.

13Then Pilate said to Him, "Do You not hear how many things they testify against You?" 14But He answered him not one word, so that the governor marveled greatly.

Taking the Place of Barabbas

15Now at the feast the governor was accustomed to releasing to the multitude one prisoner whom they wished. 16And at that time they had a notorious prisoner called Barabbas.[c] 17Therefore, when they had gathered together, Pilate said to them, "Whom do you want me to release to you? Barabbas, or Jesus who is called Christ?" 18For he knew that they had handed Him over because of envy.

19While he was sitting on the judgment seat, his wife

27:10 [b] Jeremiah 32:6–9 **27:16** [c] NU-Text reads *Jesus Barabbas.*

THE MESSAGE

And they purchased the potter's field."

And so they unwittingly followed the divine instructions to the letter.

Pilate

Jesus was placed before the governor, who questioned him: "Are you the 'King of the Jews'?"

Jesus said, "If you say so."

But when the accusations rained down hot and heavy from the high priests and religious leaders, he said nothing. Pilate asked him, "Do you hear that long list of accusations? Aren't you going to say something?" Jesus kept silence—not a word from his mouth. The governor was impressed, really impressed.

It was an old custom during the Feast for the governor to pardon a single prisoner named by the crowd. At the time, they had the infamous Jesus Barabbas in prison. With the crowd before him, Pilate said, "Which prisoner do you want me to pardon: Jesus Barabbas, or Jesus the so-called Christ?" He knew it was through sheer spite that they had turned Jesus over to him.

While court was still in session, Pilate's wife sent him a

KING JAMES VERSION

wife sent unto him, saying, Have thou nothing to do with that just man: for I have suffered many things this day in a dream because of him.

20 But the chief priests and elders persuaded the multitude that they should ask Barabbas, and destroy Jesus.

21 The governor answered and said unto them, Whether of the twain will ye that I release unto you? They said, Barabbas.

22 Pilate saith unto them, What shall I do then with Jesus which is called Christ? *They* all say unto him, Let him be crucified.

23 And the governor said, Why, what evil hath he done? But they cried out the more, saying, Let him be crucified.

24 When Pilate saw that he could prevail nothing, but *that* rather a tumult was made, he took water, and washed *his* hands before the multitude, saying, I am innocent of the blood of this just person: see ye *to it*.

25 Then answered all the people, and said, His blood *be* on us, and on our children.

26 ¶ Then released he Barabbas unto them: and when he had scourged Jesus, he delivered *him* to be crucified.

27 Then the soldiers of the governor took Jesus into the common hall, and gathered unto him the whole band *of soldiers*.

NEW AMERICAN STANDARD BIBLE

sent him *a message*, saying, "Have nothing to do with that righteous Man; for last night I suffered greatly in a dream because of Him."

20 But the chief priests and the elders persuaded the crowds to ask for Barabbas and to put Jesus to death.

21 But the governor said to them, "Which of the two do you want me to release for you?" And they said, "Barabbas."

22 Pilate *said to them, "Then what shall I do with Jesus who is called Christ?" They all *said, "Crucify Him!"

23 And he said, "Why, what evil has He done?" But they kept shouting all the more, saying, "Crucify Him!"

24 When Pilate saw that he was accomplishing nothing, but rather that a riot was starting, he took water and washed his hands in front of the crowd, saying, "I am innocent of this Man's blood; see *to that* yourselves."

25 And all the people said, "His blood shall be on us and on our children!"

26 Then he released Barabbas for them; but after having Jesus scourged, he handed Him over to be crucified.

Jesus Is Mocked

27 Then the soldiers of the governor took Jesus into the Praetorium and gathered the whole *Roman* cohort around Him.

NEW CENTURY VERSION

wife sent this message to him: "Don't do anything to that man, because he is innocent. Today I had a dream about him, and it troubled me very much."

20But the leading priests and older leaders convinced the crowd to ask for Barabbas to be freed and for Jesus to be killed.

21Pilate said, "I have Barabbas and Jesus. Which do you want me to set free for you?"

The people answered, "Barabbas."

22Pilate asked, "So what should I do with Jesus, the one called the Christ?"

They all answered, "Crucify him!"

23Pilate asked, "Why? What wrong has he done?"

But they shouted louder, "Crucify him!"

24When Pilate saw that he could do nothing about this and that a riot was starting, he took some water and washed his hands[b] in front of the crowd. Then he said, "I am not guilty of this man's death. You are the ones who are causing it!"

25All the people answered, "We and our children will be responsible for his death."

26Then he set Barabbas free. But Jesus was beaten with whips and handed over to the soldiers to be crucified.

27The governor's soldiers took Jesus into the governor's palace, and they all gathered around him. 28They took off

27:24 [b] **washed his hands** He did this as a sign to show that he wanted no part in what the people did.

CONTEMPORARY ENGLISH VERSION

message. It said, "Don't have anything to do with that innocent man. I have had nightmares because of him."

20But the chief priests and the leaders convinced the crowds to ask for Barabbas to be set free and for Jesus to be killed. 21Pilate asked the crowd again, "Which of these two men do you want me to set free?"

"Barabbas!" they replied.

22Pilate asked them, "What am I to do with Jesus, who is called the Messiah?"

They all yelled, "Nail him to a cross!"

23Pilate answered, "But what crime has he done?"

"Nail him to a cross!" they yelled even louder.

24Pilate saw that there was nothing he could do and that the people were starting to riot. So he took some water and washed his hands[c] in front of them and said, "I won't have anything to do with killing this man. You are the ones doing it!"

25Everyone answered, "We and our own families will take the blame for his death!"

26Pilate set Barabbas free. Then he ordered his soldiers to beat Jesus with a whip and nail him to a cross.

Soldiers Make Fun of Jesus (Mark 15.16-21; John 19.2, 3)

27The governor's soldiers led Jesus into the fortress[d] and brought together the rest of the troops. 28They stripped off

[c] 27.24 *washed his hands*: To show that he was innocent.
[d] 27.27 *fortress*: The place where the Roman governor stayed. It was probably at Herod's palace west of Jerusalem, though it may have been Fortress Antonia north of the temple, where the Roman troops were stationed.

NEW INTERNATIONAL VERSION

sent him this message: "Don't have anything to do with that innocent man, for I have suffered a great deal today in a dream because of him."

20But the chief priests and the elders persuaded the crowd to ask for Barabbas and to have Jesus executed.

21"Which of the two do you want me to release to you?" asked the governor.

"Barabbas," they answered.

22"What shall I do, then, with Jesus who is called Christ?" Pilate asked.

They all answered, "Crucify him!"

23"Why? What crime has he committed?" asked Pilate.

But they shouted all the louder, "Crucify him!"

24When Pilate saw that he was getting nowhere, but that instead an uproar was starting, he took water and washed his hands in front of the crowd. "I am innocent of this man's blood," he said. "It is your responsibility!"

25All the people answered, "Let his blood be on us and on our children!"

26Then he released Barabbas to them. But he had Jesus flogged, and handed him over to be crucified.

The Soldiers Mock Jesus

27Then the governor's soldiers took Jesus into the Praetorium and gathered the whole company of soldiers

NEW LIVING TRANSLATION

his wife sent him this message: "Leave that innocent man alone, because I had a terrible nightmare about him last night."

20Meanwhile, the leading priests and other leaders persuaded the crowds to ask for Barabbas to be released and for Jesus to be put to death. 21So when the governor asked again, "Which of these two do you want me to release to you?" the crowd shouted back their reply: "Barabbas!"

22"But if I release Barabbas," Pilate asked them, "what should I do with Jesus who is called the Messiah?"

And they all shouted, "Crucify him!"

23"Why?" Pilate demanded. "What crime has he committed?"

But the crowd only roared the louder, "Crucify him!"

24Pilate saw that he wasn't getting anywhere and that a riot was developing. So he sent for a bowl of water and washed his hands before the crowd, saying, "I am innocent of the blood of this man. The responsibility is yours!"

25And all the people yelled back, "We will take responsibility for his death—we and our children!"*

26So Pilate released Barabbas to them. He ordered Jesus flogged with a lead-tipped whip, then turned him over to the Roman soldiers to crucify him.

The Soldiers Mock Jesus

27Some of the governor's soldiers took Jesus into their headquarters and called out the entire battalion. 28They

27:25 Greek *"His blood be on us and on our children."*

NEW KING JAMES VERSION

sent to him, saying, "Have nothing to do with that just Man, for I have suffered many things today in a dream because of Him."

20But the chief priests and elders persuaded the multitudes that they should ask for Barabbas and destroy Jesus. 21The governor answered and said to them, "Which of the two do you want me to release to you?"

They said, "Barabbas!"

22Pilate said to them, "What then shall I do with Jesus who is called Christ?"

They all said to him, "Let Him be crucified!"

23Then the governor said, "Why, what evil has He done?"

But they cried out all the more, saying, "Let Him be crucified!"

24When Pilate saw that he could not prevail at all, but rather *that* a tumult was rising, he took water and washed *his* hands before the multitude, saying, "I am innocent of the blood of this just Person.[d] You see *to it.*"

25And all the people answered and said, "His blood *be* on us and on our children."

26Then he released Barabbas to them; and when he had scourged Jesus, he delivered *Him* to be crucified.

The Soldiers Mock Jesus

27Then the soldiers of the governor took Jesus into the Praetorium and gathered the whole garrison around Him.

27:24 [d] NU-Text omits *just.*

THE MESSAGE

message: "Don't get mixed up in judging this noble man. I've just been through a long and troubled night because of a dream about him."

Meanwhile, the high priests and religious leaders had talked the crowd into asking for the pardon of Barabbas and the execution of Jesus.

The governor asked, "Which of the two do you want me to pardon?"

They said, "Barabbas!"

"Then what do I do with Jesus, the so-called Christ?"

They all shouted, "Nail him to a cross!"

He objected, "But for what crime?"

But they yelled all the louder, "Nail him to a cross!"

When Pilate saw that he was getting nowhere and that a riot was imminent, he took a basin of water and washed his hands in full sight of the crowd, saying, "I'm washing my hands of responsibility for this man's death. From now on, it's in your hands. You're judge and jury."

The crowd answered, "We'll take the blame, we and our children after us."

Then he pardoned Barabbas. But he had Jesus whipped, and then handed over for crucifixion.

The Crucifixion

The soldiers assigned to the governor took Jesus into the governor's palace and got the entire brigade together for

KING JAMES VERSION

28 And they stripped him, and put on him a scarlet robe.

29 And when they had platted a crown of thorns, they put *it* upon his head, and a reed in his right hand: and they bowed the knee before him, and mocked him, saying, Hail, King of the Jews!

30 And they spit upon him, and took the reed, and smote him on the head.

31 And after that they had mocked him, they took the robe off from him, and put his own raiment on him, and led him away to crucify *him*.

32 And as they came out, they found a man of Cyrene, Simon by name: him they compelled to bear his cross.

33 ¶ And when they were come unto a place called Golgotha, that is to say, a place of a skull,

34 They gave him vinegar to drink mingled with gall: and when he had tasted *thereof*, he would not drink.

35 And they crucified him, and parted his garments, casting lots: that it might be fulfilled which was spoken by the prophet, They parted my garments among them, and upon my vesture did they cast lots.

36 And sitting down they watched him there;

37 And set up over his head his accusation written, THIS IS JESUS THE KING OF THE JEWS.

NEW AMERICAN STANDARD BIBLE

28 They stripped Him and put a scarlet robe on Him.

29 And after twisting together a crown of thorns, they put it on His head, and a reed in His right hand; and they knelt down before Him and mocked Him, saying, "Hail, King of the Jews!"

30 They spat on Him, and took the reed and *began* to beat Him on the head.

31 After they had mocked Him, they took the *scarlet* robe off Him and put His *own* garments back on Him, and led Him away to crucify Him.

32 As they were coming out, they found a man of Cyrene named Simon, whom they pressed into service to bear His cross.

The Crucifixion

33 And when they came to a place called Golgotha, which means Place of a Skull,

34 they gave Him wine to drink mixed with gall; and after tasting *it,* He was unwilling to drink.

35 And when they had crucified Him, they divided up His garments among themselves by casting lots.

36 And sitting down, they *began* to keep watch over Him there.

37 And above His head they put up the charge against Him which read, "THIS IS JESUS THE KING OF THE JEWS."

NEW CENTURY VERSION

his clothes and put a red robe on him. 29Using thorny
branches, they made a crown, put it on his head, and put a
stick in his right hand. Then the soldiers bowed before
Jesus and made fun of him, saying, "Hail, King of the
Jews!" 30They spat on Jesus. Then they took his stick and
began to beat him on the head. 31After they finished, the
soldiers took off the robe and put his own clothes on him
again. Then they led him away to be crucified.

Jesus Is Crucified

32As the soldiers were going out of the city with Jesus,
they forced a man from Cyrene, named Simon, to carry the
cross for Jesus. 33They all came to the place called
Golgotha, which means the Place of the Skull. 34The sol-
diers gave Jesus wine mixed with gall[c] to drink. He tasted
the wine but refused to drink it. 35When the soldiers had
crucified him, they threw lots to decide who would get his
clothes. 36The soldiers sat there and continued watching
him. 37They put a sign above Jesus' head with a charge
against him. It said: THIS IS JESUS, THE KING OF THE JEWS.

27:34 [c] **gall** Probably a drink of wine mixed with drugs to help a person feel less pain.

CONTEMPORARY ENGLISH VERSION

Jesus' clothes and put a scarlet robe[e] on him. 29They made
a crown out of thorn branches and placed it on his head,
and they put a stick in his right hand. The soldiers knelt
down and pretended to worship him. They made fun of
him and shouted, "Hey, you king of the Jews!" 30Then they
spit on him. They took the stick from him and beat him on
the head with it.

Jesus Is Nailed to a Cross

(Mark 15.22-32; Luke 23.27-43; John 19.17-27)

31When the soldiers had finished making fun of Jesus,
they took off the robe. They put his own clothes back on
him and led him off to be nailed to a cross. 32On the way
they met a man from Cyrene named Simon, and they
forced him to carry Jesus' cross.

33They came to a place named Golgotha, which means
"Place of a Skull."[f] 34There they gave Jesus some wine
mixed with a drug to ease the pain. But when Jesus tasted
what it was, he refused to drink it.

35The soldiers nailed Jesus to a cross and gambled to see
who would get his clothes. 36Then they sat down to guard
him. 37Above his head they put a sign that told why he
was nailed there. It read, "This is Jesus, the King of the

[e] 27.28 *scarlet robe*: This was probably a Roman soldier's robe.
[f] 27.33 *Place of a Skull*: The place was probably given this name because it was near a large rock in the shape of a human skull.

NEW INTERNATIONAL VERSION

around him. [28]They stripped him and put a scarlet robe on him, [29]and then twisted together a crown of thorns and set it on his head. They put a staff in his right hand and knelt in front of him and mocked him. "Hail, king of the Jews!" they said. [30]They spit on him, and took the staff and struck him on the head again and again. [31]After they had mocked him, they took off the robe and put his own clothes on him. Then they led him away to crucify him.

The Crucifixion

[32]As they were going out, they met a man from Cyrene, named Simon, and they forced him to carry the cross. [33]They came to a place called Golgotha (which means The Place of the Skull). [34]There they offered Jesus wine to drink, mixed with gall; but after tasting it, he refused to drink it. [35]When they had crucified him, they divided up his clothes by casting lots.[b] [36]And sitting down, they kept watch over him there. [37]Above his head they placed the written charge against him: THIS IS JESUS, THE KING OF THE

[b] *35* A few late manuscripts *lots that the word spoken by the prophet might be fulfilled: "They divided my garments among themselves and cast lots for my clothing"* (Psalm 22:18)

NEW LIVING TRANSLATION

stripped him and put a scarlet robe on him. [29]They made a crown of long, sharp thorns and put it on his head, and they placed a stick in his right hand as a scepter. Then they knelt before him in mockery, yelling, "Hail! King of the Jews!" [30]And they spit on him and grabbed the stick and beat him on the head with it. [31]When they were finally tired of mocking him, they took off the robe and put his own clothes on him again. Then they led him away to be crucified.

The Crucifixion

[32]As they were on the way, they came across a man named Simon, who was from Cyrene,* and they forced him to carry Jesus' cross. [33]Then they went out to a place called Golgotha (which means Skull Hill). [34]The soldiers gave him wine mixed with bitter gall, but when he had tasted it, he refused to drink it.

[35]After they had nailed him to the cross, the soldiers gambled for his clothes by throwing dice.* [36]Then they sat around and kept guard as he hung there. [37]A signboard was fastened to the cross above Jesus' head, announcing the charge against him. It read: "This is Jesus, the King of the Jews."

27:32 *Cyrene* was a city in northern Africa. 27:35 Greek *by casting lots.* A few late manuscripts add *This fulfilled the word of the prophet: "They divided my clothes among themselves and cast lots for my robe."* See Ps 22:18.

NEW KING JAMES VERSION

[28]And they stripped Him and put a scarlet robe on Him. [29]When they had twisted a crown of thorns, they put *it* on His head, and a reed in His right hand. And they bowed the knee before Him and mocked Him, saying, "Hail, King of the Jews!" [30]Then they spat on Him, and took the reed and struck Him on the head. [31]And when they had mocked Him, they took the robe off Him, put His *own* clothes on Him, and led Him away to be crucified.

The King on a Cross

[32]Now as they came out, they found a man of Cyrene, Simon by name. Him they compelled to bear His cross. [33]And when they had come to a place called Golgotha, that is to say, Place of a Skull, [34]they gave Him sour[e] wine mingled with gall to drink. But when He had tasted *it,* He would not drink.

[35]Then they crucified Him, and divided His garments, casting lots,[f] that it might be fulfilled which was spoken by the prophet:

> *"They divided My garments among them,*
> *And for My clothing they cast lots."*[g]

[36]Sitting down, they kept watch over Him there. [37]And they put up over His head the accusation written against Him:

THIS IS JESUS THE KING OF THE JEWS.

27:34 [e] NU-Text omits *sour.* **27:35** [f] NU-Text and M-Text omit the rest of this verse. [g] Psalm 22:18

THE MESSAGE

some fun. They stripped him and dressed him in a red toga. They plaited a crown from branches of a thorn bush and set it on his head. They put a stick in his right hand for a scepter. Then they knelt before him in mocking reverence: "Bravo, King of the Jews!" they said. "Bravo!" Then they spit on him and hit him on the head with the stick. When they had had their fun, they took off the toga and put his own clothes back on him. Then they proceeded out to the crucifixion.

Along the way they came on a man from Cyrene named Simon and made him carry Jesus' cross. Arriving at Golgotha, the place they call "Skull Hill," they offered him a mild painkiller (a mixture of wine and myrrh), but when he tasted it he wouldn't drink it.

After they had finished nailing him to the cross and were waiting for him to die, they whiled away the time by throwing dice for his clothes. Above his head they had posted the criminal charge against him: THIS IS JESUS, THE KING OF THE JEWS. Along with him, they also crucified two

KING JAMES VERSION

38 Then were there two thieves crucified with him, one on the right hand, and another on the left.

39 And they that passed by reviled him, wagging their heads,

40 And saying, Thou that destroyest the temple, and buildest *it* in three days, save thyself. If thou be the Son of God, come down from the cross.

41 Likewise also the chief priests mocking *him*, with the scribes and elders, said,

42 He saved others; himself he cannot save. If he be the King of Israel, let him now come down from the cross, and we will believe him.

43 He trusted in God; let him deliver him now, if he will have him: for he said, I am the Son of God.

44 The thieves also, which were crucified with him, cast the same in his teeth.

45 Now from the sixth hour there was darkness over all the land unto the ninth hour.

46 And about the ninth hour Jesus cried with a loud voice, saying, Eli, Eli, lama sabachthani? that is to say, My God, my God, why hast thou forsaken me?

47 Some of them that stood there, when they heard *that*, said, This *man* calleth for Elias.

48 And straightway one of them ran, and took a spunge, and filled *it* with vinegar, and put *it* on a reed, and gave him to drink.

NEW AMERICAN STANDARD BIBLE

38 At that time two robbers *were crucified with Him, one on the right and one on the left.

39 And those passing by were hurling abuse at Him, wagging their heads

40 and saying, "You who *are going to* destroy the temple and rebuild it in three days, save Yourself! If You are the Son of God, come down from the cross."

41 In the same way the chief priests also, along with the scribes and elders, were mocking *Him* and saying,

42 "He saved others; He cannot save Himself. He is the King of Israel; let Him now come down from the cross, and we will believe in Him.

43 "HE TRUSTS IN GOD; LET GOD RESCUE *Him* NOW, IF HE DELIGHTS IN HIM; for He said, 'I am the Son of God.' "

44 The robbers who had been crucified with Him were also insulting Him with the same words.

45 Now from the [1]sixth hour darkness fell upon all the land until the [2]ninth hour.

46 About the ninth hour Jesus cried out with a loud voice, saying, "ELI, ELI, LAMA SABACHTHANI?" that is, "MY GOD, MY GOD, WHY HAVE YOU FORSAKEN ME?"

47 And some of those who were standing there, when they heard it, *began* saying, "This man is calling for Elijah."

48 Immediately one of them ran, and taking a sponge, he filled it with sour wine and put it on a reed, and gave Him a drink.

27:45 [1] I.e. noon 27:45 [2] I.e. 3 p.m.

NEW CENTURY VERSION

38 Two robbers were crucified beside Jesus, one on the right and the other on the left. 39 People walked by and insulted Jesus and shook their heads, 40 saying, "You said you could destroy the Temple and build it again in three days. So save yourself! Come down from that cross if you are really the Son of God!"

41 The leading priests, the teachers of the law, and the older Jewish leaders were also making fun of Jesus. 42 They said, "He saved others, but he can't save himself! He says he is the king of Israel! If he is the king, let him come down now from the cross. Then we will believe in him. 43 He trusts in God, so let God save him now, if God really wants him. He himself said, 'I am the Son of God.' " 44 And in the same way, the robbers who were being crucified beside Jesus also insulted him.

Jesus Dies

45 At noon the whole country became dark, and the darkness lasted for three hours. 46 About three o'clock Jesus cried out in a loud voice, "Eli, Eli, lama sabachthani?" This means, "My God, my God, why have you rejected me?"

47 Some of the people standing there who heard this said, "He is calling Elijah."

48 Quickly one of them ran and got a sponge and filled it with vinegar and tied it to a stick and gave it to Jesus to

CONTEMPORARY ENGLISH VERSION

Jews." 38 The soldiers also nailed two criminals on crosses, one to the right of Jesus and the other to his left.

39 People who passed by said terrible things about Jesus. They shook their heads and 40 shouted, "So you're the one who claimed you could tear down the temple and build it again in three days! If you are God's Son, save yourself and come down from the cross!"

41 The chief priests, the leaders, and the teachers of the Law of Moses also made fun of Jesus. They said, 42 "He saved others, but he can't save himself. If he is the king of Israel, he should come down from the cross! Then we will believe him. 43 He trusted God, so let God save him, if he wants to. He even said he was God's Son." 44 The two criminals also said cruel things to Jesus.

The Death of Jesus

(Mark 15.33-41; Luke 23.44-49; John 19.28-30)

45 At noon the sky turned dark and stayed that way until three o'clock. 46 Then about that time Jesus shouted, "Eli, Eli, lema sabachthani?"[g] which means, "My God, my God, why have you deserted me?"

47 Some of the people standing there heard Jesus and said, "He's calling for Elijah."[h] 48 One of them at once ran and grabbed a sponge. He soaked it in wine, then put it on a stick and held it up to Jesus.

[g] 27.46 *Eli . . . sabachthani*: These words are in Hebrew.
[h] 27.47 *Elijah*: In Aramaic the name "Elijah" sounds like "Eli," which means "my God."

NEW INTERNATIONAL VERSION

JEWS. 38Two robbers were crucified with him, one on his
right and one on his left. 39Those who passed by hurled
insults at him, shaking their heads 40and saying, "You
who are going to destroy the temple and build it in three
days, save yourself! Come down from the cross, if you are
the Son of God!"
41In the same way the chief priests, the teachers of the
law and the elders mocked him. 42"He saved others," they
said, "but he can't save himself! He's the King of Israel!
Let him come down now from the cross, and we will
believe in him. 43He trusts in God. Let God rescue him now
if he wants him, for he said, 'I am the Son of God.' " 44In
the same way the robbers who were crucified with him
also heaped insults on him.

The Death of Jesus

45From the sixth hour until the ninth hour darkness
came over all the land. 46About the ninth hour Jesus cried
out in a loud voice, *"Eloi, Eloi,*[c] *lama sabachthani?"*—
which means, "My God, my God, why have you forsaken
me?"[d]
47When some of those standing there heard this, they
said, "He's calling Elijah."
48Immediately one of them ran and got a sponge. He
filled it with wine vinegar, put it on a stick, and offered it

[c] *46* Some manuscripts *Eli, Eli* [d] *46* Psalm 22:1

NEW LIVING TRANSLATION

38Two criminals were crucified with him, their crosses
on either side of his. 39And the people passing by shouted
abuse, shaking their heads in mockery. 40"So! You can
destroy the Temple and build it again in three days, can
you? Well then, if you are the Son of God, save yourself
and come down from the cross!"
41The leading priests, the teachers of religious law, and
the other leaders also mocked Jesus. 42"He saved others,"
they scoffed, "but he can't save himself! So he is the king
of Israel, is he? Let him come down from the cross, and we
will believe in him! 43He trusted God—let God show his
approval by delivering him! For he said, 'I am the Son of
God.' " 44And the criminals who were crucified with him
also shouted the same insults at him.

The Death of Jesus

45At noon, darkness fell across the whole land until
three o'clock. 46At about three o'clock, Jesus called out
with a loud voice, *"Eli, Eli, lema sabachthani?"* which
means, "My God, my God, why have you forsaken me?"*
47Some of the bystanders misunderstood and thought he
was calling for the prophet Elijah. 48One of them ran and
filled a sponge with sour wine, holding it up to him on a

27:46 Ps 22:1.

NEW KING JAMES VERSION

38Then two robbers were crucified with Him, one on the
right and another on the left.
39And those who passed by blasphemed Him, wagging
their heads 40and saying, "You who destroy the temple and
build *it* in three days, save Yourself! If You are the Son of
God, come down from the cross."
41Likewise the chief priests also, mocking with the
scribes and elders,[h] said, 42"He saved others; Himself He
cannot save. If He is the King of Israel,[i] let Him now come
down from the cross, and we will believe Him.[j] 43He trust-
ed in God; let Him deliver Him now if He will have Him;
for He said, 'I am the Son of God.' "
44Even the robbers who were crucified with Him reviled
Him with the same thing.

Jesus Dies on the Cross

45Now from the sixth hour until the ninth hour there
was darkness over all the land. 46And about the ninth hour
Jesus cried out with a loud voice, saying, "Eli, Eli, lama
sabachthani?" that is, *"My God, My God, why have You
forsaken Me?"*[k]
47Some of those who stood there, when they heard *that,*
said, "This Man is calling for Elijah!" 48Immediately one of
them ran and took a sponge, filled *it* with sour wine and
put *it* on a reed, and offered it to Him to drink.

27:41 [h] M-Text reads *with the scribes, the Pharisees, and the elders.*
27:42 [i] NU-Text reads *He is the King of Israel!* [j] NU-Text and M-Text read *we will believe in Him.* **27:46** [k] Psalm 22:1

THE MESSAGE

criminals, one to his right, the other to his left. People passing along the road jeered, shaking their heads in mock lament: "You bragged that you could tear down the Temple and then rebuild it in three days—so show us your stuff! Save yourself! If you're really God's Son, come down from that cross!"

The high priests, along with the religion scholars and leaders, were right there mixing it up with the rest of them, having a great time poking fun at him: "He saved others—he can't save himself! King of Israel, is he? Then let him get down from that cross. We'll *all* become believers then! He was so sure of God—well, let him rescue his 'Son' now—if he wants him! He did claim to be God's Son, didn't he?" Even the two criminals crucified next to him joined in the mockery.

From noon to three, the whole earth was dark. Around mid-afternoon Jesus groaned out of the depths, crying loudly, *"Eli, Eli, lama sabachthani?"* which means "My God, my God, why have you abandoned me?"

Some bystanders who heard him said, "He's calling for Elijah." One of them ran and got a sponge soaked in sour wine and lifted it on a stick so he could drink. The others

KING JAMES VERSION

49 The rest said, Let be, let us see whether Elias will come to save him.

50 ¶ Jesus, when he had cried again with a loud voice, yielded up the ghost.

51 And, behold, the veil of the temple was rent in twain from the top to the bottom; and the earth did quake, and the rocks rent;

52 And the graves were opened; and many bodies of the saints which slept arose,

53 And came out of the graves after his resurrection, and went into the holy city, and appeared unto many.

54 Now when the centurion, and they that were with him, watching Jesus, saw the earthquake, and those things that were done, they feared greatly, saying, Truly this was the Son of God.

55 And many women were there beholding afar off, which followed Jesus from Galilee, ministering unto him:

56 Among which was Mary Magdalene, and Mary the mother of James and Joses, and the mother of Zebedee's children.

57 ¶ When the even was come, there came a rich man of Arimathaea, named Joseph, who also himself was Jesus' disciple:

58 He went to Pilate, and begged the body of Jesus. Then Pilate commanded the body to be delivered.

NEW AMERICAN STANDARD BIBLE

49 But the rest *of them* said, "Let us see whether Elijah will come to save Him."[3]

50 And Jesus cried out again with a loud voice, and yielded up His spirit.

51 And behold, the veil of the temple was torn in two from top to bottom; and the earth shook and the rocks were split.

52 The tombs were opened, and many bodies of the saints who had fallen asleep were raised;

53 and coming out of the tombs after His resurrection they entered the holy city and appeared to many.

54 Now the centurion, and those who were with him keeping guard over Jesus, when they saw the earthquake and the things that were happening, became very frightened and said, "Truly this was the Son of God!"

55 Many women were there looking on from a distance, who had followed Jesus from Galilee while ministering to Him.

56 Among them was Mary Magdalene, and Mary the mother of James and Joseph, and the mother of the sons of Zebedee.

Jesus Is Buried

57 When it was evening, there came a rich man from Arimathea, named Joseph, who himself had also become a disciple of Jesus.

58 This man went to Pilate and asked for the body of Jesus. Then Pilate ordered it to be given *to him.*

27:49 [3] Some early mss read *And another took a spear and pierced His side, and there came out water and blood* (cf John 19:34)

NEW CENTURY VERSION

drink. 49But the others said, "Don't bother him. We want to see if Elijah will come to save him."
50But Jesus cried out again in a loud voice and died.
51Then the curtain in the Temple[d] was torn into two pieces, from the top to the bottom. Also, the earth shook and rocks broke apart. 52The graves opened, and many of God's people who had died were raised from the dead.
53They came out of the graves after Jesus was raised from the dead and went into the holy city, where they appeared to many people.
54When the army officer and the soldiers guarding Jesus saw this earthquake and everything else that happened, they were very frightened and said, "He really was the Son of God!"
55Many women who had followed Jesus from Galilee to help him were standing at a distance from the cross, watching. 56Mary Magdalene, and Mary the mother of James and Joseph, and the mother of James and John were there.

Jesus Is Buried

57That evening a rich man named Joseph, a follower of Jesus from the town of Arimathea, came to Jerusalem.
58Joseph went to Pilate and asked to have Jesus' body. So Pilate gave orders for the soldiers to give it to Joseph.

27:51 [d] **curtain in the Temple** A curtain divided the Most Holy Place from the other part of the Temple. That was the special building in Jerusalem where God commanded the Jewish people to worship him.

CONTEMPORARY ENGLISH VERSION

49Others said, "Wait! Let's see if Elijah will come[i] and save him." 50Once again Jesus shouted, and then he died.
51At once the curtain in the temple[j] was torn in two from top to bottom. The earth shook, and rocks split apart.
52Graves opened, and many of God's people were raised to life. 53Then after Jesus had risen to life, they came out of their graves and went into the holy city, where they were seen by many people.
54The officer and the soldiers guarding Jesus felt the earthquake and saw everything else that happened. They were frightened and said, "This man really was God's Son!"
55Many women had come with Jesus from Galilee to be of help to him, and they were there, looking on at a distance. 56Mary Magdalene, Mary the mother of James and Joseph, and the mother of James and John[k] were some of these women.

Jesus Is Buried

(Mark 15.42-47; Luke 23.50-56; John 19.38-42)

57That evening a rich disciple named Joseph from the town of Arimathea 58went and asked for Jesus' body. Pilate gave orders for it to be given to Joseph, 59who took the

[i] 27.49 *Elijah will come*: See the note at 16.14. [j] 27.51 *curtain in the temple*: There were two curtains in the temple. One was at the entrance, and the other separated the holy place from the most holy place that the Jewish people thought of as God's home on earth. The second curtain is probably the one that is meant. [k] 27.56 *of James and John*: The Greek text has "of Zebedee's sons" (see 26.37).

NEW INTERNATIONAL VERSION

to Jesus to drink. 49The rest said, "Now leave him alone. Let's see if Elijah comes to save him."

50And when Jesus had cried out again in a loud voice, he gave up his spirit.

51At that moment the curtain of the temple was torn in two from top to bottom. The earth shook and the rocks split. 52The tombs broke open and the bodies of many holy people who had died were raised to life. 53They came out of the tombs, and after Jesus' resurrection they went into the holy city and appeared to many people.

54When the centurion and those with him who were guarding Jesus saw the earthquake and all that had happened, they were terrified, and exclaimed, "Surely he was the Son[e] of God!"

55Many women were there, watching from a distance. They had followed Jesus from Galilee to care for his needs. 56Among them were Mary Magdalene, Mary the mother of James and Joses, and the mother of Zebedee's sons.

The Burial of Jesus

57As evening approached, there came a rich man from Arimathea, named Joseph, who had himself become a disciple of Jesus. 58Going to Pilate, he asked for Jesus' body, and Pilate ordered that it be given to him. 59Joseph took

e *54* Or *a son*

NEW LIVING TRANSLATION

stick so he could drink. 49But the rest said, "Leave him alone. Let's see whether Elijah will come and save him."*

50Then Jesus shouted out again, and he gave up his spirit. 51At that moment the curtain in the Temple was torn in two, from top to bottom. The earth shook, rocks split apart, 52and tombs opened. The bodies of many godly men and women who had died were raised from the dead 53after Jesus' resurrection. They left the cemetery, went into the holy city of Jerusalem, and appeared to many people.*

54The Roman officer and the other soldiers at the crucifixion were terrified by the earthquake and all that had happened. They said, "Truly, this was the Son of God!"

55And many women who had come from Galilee with Jesus to care for him were watching from a distance. 56Among them were Mary Magdalene, Mary (the mother of James and Joseph), and Zebedee's wife, the mother of James and John.

The Burial of Jesus

57As evening approached, Joseph, a rich man from Arimathea who was one of Jesus' followers, 58went to Pilate and asked for Jesus' body. And Pilate issued an order to release it to him. 59Joseph took the body and

27:49 Some manuscripts add *And another took a spear and pierced his side, and out came water and blood.* 27:51-53 Or *The earth shook, rocks split apart, tombs opened, and the bodies of many godly men and women who had died were raised from the dead. After Jesus' resurrection, they left the cemetery, went into the holy city of Jerusalem, and appeared to many people.*

NEW KING JAMES VERSION

49The rest said, "Let Him alone; let us see if Elijah will come to save Him."

50And Jesus cried out again with a loud voice, and yielded up His spirit.

51Then, behold, the veil of the temple was torn in two from top to bottom; and the earth quaked, and the rocks were split, 52and the graves were opened; and many bodies of the saints who had fallen asleep were raised; 53and coming out of the graves after His resurrection, they went into the holy city and appeared to many.

54So when the centurion and those with him, who were guarding Jesus, saw the earthquake and the things that had happened, they feared greatly, saying, "Truly this was the Son of God!"

55And many women who followed Jesus from Galilee, ministering to Him, were there looking on from afar, 56among whom were Mary Magdalene, Mary the mother of James and Joses,[l] and the mother of Zebedee's sons.

Jesus Buried in Joseph's Tomb

57Now when evening had come, there came a rich man from Arimathea, named Joseph, who himself had also become a disciple of Jesus. 58This man went to Pilate and asked for the body of Jesus. Then Pilate commanded the body to be given to him. 59When Joseph had taken the

27:56 l NU-Text reads *Joseph.*

THE MESSAGE

joked, "Don't be in such a hurry. Let's see if Elijah comes and saves him."

But Jesus, again crying out loudly, breathed his last.

At that moment, the Temple curtain was ripped in two, top to bottom. There was an earthquake, and rocks were split in pieces. What's more, tombs were opened up, and many bodies of believers asleep in their graves were raised. (After Jesus' resurrection, they left the tombs, entered the holy city, and appeared to many.)

The captain of the guard and those with him, when they saw the earthquake and everything else that was happening, were scared to death. They said, "This has to be the Son of God!"

There were also quite a few women watching from a distance, women who had followed Jesus from Galilee in order to serve him. Among them were Mary Magdalene, Mary the mother of James and Joseph, and the mother of the Zebedee brothers.

The Tomb

Late in the afternoon a wealthy man from Arimathea, a disciple of Jesus, arrived. His name was Joseph. He went to Pilate and asked for Jesus' body. Pilate granted his request. Joseph took the body and wrapped it in clean

KING JAMES VERSION

59 And when Joseph had taken the body, he wrapped it in a clean linen cloth,

60 And laid it in his own new tomb, which he had hewn out in the rock: and he rolled a great stone to the door of the sepulchre, and departed.

61 And there was Mary Magdalene, and the other Mary, sitting over against the sepulchre.

62 Now the next day, that followed the day of the preparation, the chief priests and Pharisees came together unto Pilate,

63 Saying, Sir, we remember that that deceiver said, while he was yet alive, After three days I will rise again.

64 Command therefore that the sepulchre be made sure until the third day, lest his disciples come by night, and steal him away, and say unto the people, He is risen from the dead: so the last error shall be worse than the first.

65 Pilate said unto them, Ye have a watch: go your way, make *it* as sure as ye can.

66 So they went, and made the sepulchre sure, sealing the stone, and setting a watch.

28 In the end of the sabbath, as it began to dawn toward the first *day* of the week, came Mary Magdalene and the other Mary to see the sepulchre.

2 And, behold, there was a great earthquake: for the angel of the Lord descended from heaven, and came and rolled back the stone from the door, and sat upon it.

NEW AMERICAN STANDARD BIBLE

59 And Joseph took the body and wrapped it in a clean linen cloth,

60 and laid it in his own new tomb, which he had hewn out in the rock; and he rolled a large stone against the entrance of the tomb and went away.

61 And Mary Magdalene was there, and the other Mary, sitting opposite the grave.

62 Now on the next day, the day after the preparation, the chief priests and the Pharisees gathered together with Pilate,

63 and said, "Sir, we remember that when He was still alive that deceiver said, 'After three days I *am to* rise again.'

64 "Therefore, give orders for the grave to be made secure until the third day, otherwise His disciples may come and steal Him away and say to the people, 'He has risen from the dead,' and the last deception will be worse than the first."

65 Pilate said to them, "You have a guard; go, make it *as* secure as you know how."

66 And they went and made the grave secure, and along with the guard they set a seal on the stone.

Jesus Is Risen!

28 Now after the Sabbath, as it began to dawn toward the first *day* of the week, Mary Magdalene and the other Mary came to look at the grave.

2 And behold, a severe earthquake had occurred, for an angel of the Lord descended from heaven and came and rolled away the stone and sat upon it.

NEW CENTURY VERSION

59Then Joseph took the body and wrapped it in a clean
linen cloth. 60He put Jesus' body in a new tomb that he
had cut out of a wall of rock, and he rolled a very large
stone to block the entrance of the tomb. Then Joseph went
away. 61Mary Magdalene and the other woman named
Mary were sitting near the tomb.

The Tomb of Jesus Is Guarded

62The next day, the day after Preparation Day, the lead-
ing priests and the Pharisees went to Pilate. 63They said,
"Sir, we remember that while that liar was still alive he
said, 'After three days I will rise from the dead.' 64So give
the order for the tomb to be guarded closely till the third
day. Otherwise, his followers might come and steal the
body and tell people that he has risen from the dead. That
lie would be even worse than the first one."
65Pilate said, "Take some soldiers and go guard the
tomb the best way you know." 66So they all went to the
tomb and made it safe from thieves by sealing the stone in
the entrance and putting soldiers there to guard it.

Jesus Rises from the Dead

28 The day after the Sabbath day was the first day of
the week. At dawn on the first day, Mary Mag-
dalene and another woman named Mary went to look at
the tomb.
2At that time there was a strong earthquake. An angel of
the Lord came down from heaven, went to the tomb, and
rolled the stone away from the entrance. Then he sat on

CONTEMPORARY ENGLISH VERSION

body and wrapped it in a clean linen cloth. 60Then Joseph
put the body in his own tomb that had been cut into solid
rock[l] and had never been used. He rolled a big stone
against the entrance to the tomb and went away.
61All this time Mary Magdalene and the other Mary were
sitting across from the tomb.
62On the next day, which was a Sabbath, the chief
priests and the Pharisees went together to Pilate. 63They
said, "Sir, we remember what that liar said while he was
still alive. He claimed that in three days he would come
back from death. 64So please order the tomb to be carefully
guarded for three days. If you don't, his disciples may
come and steal his body. They will tell the people that he
has been raised to life, and this last lie will be worse than
the first one."[m]
65Pilate said to them, "All right, take some of your sol-
diers and guard the tomb as well as you know how." 66So
they sealed it tight and placed soldiers there to guard it.

Jesus Is Alive (Mark 16.1-8; Luke 24.1-12; John 20.1-10)

28 The Sabbath was over, and it was almost daybreak
on Sunday when Mary Magdalene and the other
Mary went to see the tomb. 2Suddenly a strong earthquake
struck, and the Lord's angel came down from heaven. He
rolled away the stone and sat on it. 3The angel looked as

[l] 27.60 *tomb . . . solid rock*: Some of the Jewish people buried their dead in rooms carved into solid rock. A heavy stone was rolled against the entrance. [m] 27.64 *the first one*: Probably the belief that Jesus is the Messiah.

NEW INTERNATIONAL VERSION

the body, wrapped it in a clean linen cloth, 60and placed it
in his own new tomb that he had cut out of the rock. He
rolled a big stone in front of the entrance to the tomb and
went away. 61Mary Magdalene and the other Mary were
sitting there opposite the tomb.

The Guard at the Tomb

62The next day, the one after Preparation Day, the chief
priests and the Pharisees went to Pilate. 63"Sir," they said,
"we remember that while he was still alive that deceiver
said, 'After three days I will rise again.' 64So give the order
for the tomb to be made secure until the third day.
Otherwise, his disciples may come and steal the body and
tell the people that he has been raised from the dead. This
last deception will be worse than the first."

65"Take a guard," Pilate answered. "Go, make the tomb
as secure as you know how." 66So they went and made the
tomb secure by putting a seal on the stone and posting the
guard.

The Resurrection

28 After the Sabbath, at dawn on the first day of the
week, Mary Magdalene and the other Mary went to
look at the tomb.

2There was a violent earthquake, for an angel of the
Lord came down from heaven and, going to the tomb,
rolled back the stone and sat on it. 3His appearance was

NEW LIVING TRANSLATION

wrapped it in a long linen cloth. 60He placed it in his own
new tomb, which had been carved out of the rock. Then he
rolled a great stone across the entrance as he left. 61Both
Mary Magdalene and the other Mary were sitting nearby
watching.

The Guard at the Tomb

62The next day—on the first day of the Passover cere-
monies*—the leading priests and Pharisees went to see
Pilate. 63They told him, "Sir, we remember what that
deceiver once said while he was still alive: 'After three
days I will be raised from the dead.' 64So we request that
you seal the tomb until the third day. This will prevent his
disciples from coming and stealing his body and then
telling everyone he came back to life! If that happens, we'll
be worse off than we were at first."

65Pilate replied, "Take guards and secure it the best you
can." 66So they sealed the tomb and posted guards to pro-
tect it.

The Resurrection

28 Early on Sunday morning,* as the new day was
dawning, Mary Magdalene and the other Mary
went out to see the tomb. 2Suddenly there was a great
earthquake, because an angel of the Lord came down from
heaven and rolled aside the stone and sat on it. 3His face

27:62 Or *On the next day, which is after the Preparation.* 28:1 Greek *After the Sabbath, on the first day of the week.*

NEW KING JAMES VERSION

body, he wrapped it in a clean linen cloth, 60and laid it in
his new tomb which he had hewn out of the rock; and he
rolled a large stone against the door of the tomb, and
departed. 61And Mary Magdalene was there, and the other
Mary, sitting opposite the tomb.

Pilate Sets a Guard

62On the next day, which followed the Day of
Preparation, the chief priests and Pharisees gathered
together to Pilate, 63saying, "Sir, we remember, while He
was still alive, how that deceiver said, 'After three days I
will rise.' 64Therefore command that the tomb be made
secure until the third day, lest His disciples come by
night[m] and steal Him *away*, and say to the people, 'He has
risen from the dead.' So the last deception will be worse
than the first."

65Pilate said to them, "You have a guard; go your way,
make *it* as secure as you know how." 66So they went and
made the tomb secure, sealing the stone and setting the
guard.

He Is Risen

28 Now after the Sabbath, as the first *day* of the week
began to dawn, Mary Magdalene and the other
Mary came to see the tomb. 2And behold, there was a great
earthquake; for an angel of the Lord descended from heav-
en, and came and rolled back the stone from the door,[a]

27:64 [m] NU-Text omits *by night.* 28:2 [a] NU-Text omits *from the door.*

THE MESSAGE

linens, put it in his own tomb, a new tomb only recently
cut into the rock, and rolled a large stone across the
entrance. Then he went off. But Mary Magdalene and the
other Mary stayed, sitting in plain view of the tomb.

After sundown, the high priests and Pharisees arranged
a meeting with Pilate. They said, "Sir, we just remembered
that that liar announced while he was still alive, 'After
three days I will be raised.' We've got to get that tomb
sealed until the third day. There's a good chance his disci-
ples will come and steal the corpse and then go around
saying, 'He's risen from the dead.' Then we'll be worse off
than before, the final deceit surpassing the first."

Pilate told them, "You will have a guard. Go ahead and
secure it the best you can." So they went out and secured
the tomb, sealing the stone and posting guards.

Risen From the Dead

28 After the Sabbath, as the first light of the new
week dawned, Mary Magdalene and the other Mary
came to keep vigil at the tomb. Suddenly the earth reeled
and rocked under their feet as God's angel came down
from heaven, came right up to where they were standing.
He rolled back the stone and then sat on it. Shafts of light-

KING JAMES VERSION

3 His countenance was like lightning, and his raiment white as snow:

4 And for fear of him the keepers did shake, and became as dead *men*.

5 And the angel answered and said unto the women, Fear not ye: for I know that ye seek Jesus, which was crucified.

6 He is not here: for he is risen, as he said. Come, see the place where the Lord lay.

7 And go quickly, and tell his disciples that he is risen from the dead; and, behold, he goeth before you into Galilee; there shall ye see him: lo, I have told you.

8 And they departed quickly from the sepulchre with fear and great joy; and did run to bring his disciples word.

9 And as they went to tell his disciples, behold, Jesus met them, saying, All hail. And they came and held him by the feet, and worshipped him.

10 Then said Jesus unto them, Be not afraid: go tell my brethren that they go into Galilee, and there shall they see me.

11 ¶ Now when they were going, behold, some of the watch came into the city, and shewed unto the chief priests all the things that were done.

12 And when they were assembled with the elders, and had taken counsel, they gave large money unto the soldiers,

13 Saying, Say ye, His disciples came by night, and stole him *away* while we slept.

14 And if this come to the governor's ears, we will persuade him, and secure you.

NEW AMERICAN STANDARD BIBLE

3 And his appearance was like lightning, and his clothing as white as snow.

4 The guards shook for fear of him and became like dead men.

5 The angel said to the women, "Do not be afraid; for I know that you are looking for Jesus who has been crucified.

6 "He is not here, for He has risen, just as He said. Come, see the place where He was lying.

7 "Go quickly and tell His disciples that He has risen from the dead; and behold, He is going ahead of you into Galilee, there you will see Him; behold, I have told you."

8 And they left the tomb quickly with fear and great joy and ran to report it to His disciples.

9 And behold, Jesus met them and greeted them. And they came up and took hold of His feet and worshiped Him.

10 Then Jesus *said to them, "Do not be afraid; go and take word to My brethren to leave for Galilee, and there they will see Me."

11 Now while they were on their way, some of the guard came into the city and reported to the chief priests all that had happened.

12 And when they had assembled with the elders and consulted together, they gave a large sum of money to the soldiers,

13 and said, "You are to say, 'His disciples came by night and stole Him away while we were asleep.'

14 "And if this should come to the governor's ears, we will win him over and keep you out of trouble."

NEW CENTURY VERSION

the stone. 3He was shining as bright as lightning, and his
clothes were white as snow. 4The soldiers guarding the
tomb shook with fear because of the angel, and they
became like dead men.
5The angel said to the women, "Don't be afraid. I know
that you are looking for Jesus, who has been crucified. 6He
is not here. He has risen from the dead as he said he
would. Come and see the place where his body was. 7And
go quickly and tell his followers, 'Jesus has risen from the
dead. He is going into Galilee ahead of you, and you will
see him there.' " Then the angel said, "Now I have told
you."
8The women left the tomb quickly. They were afraid, but
they were also very happy. They ran to tell Jesus' followers
what had happened. 9Suddenly, Jesus met them and said,
"Greetings." The women came up to him, took hold of his
feet, and worshiped him. 10Then Jesus said to them, "Don't
be afraid. Go and tell my followers to go on to Galilee, and
they will see me there."

The Soldiers Report to the Leaders

11While the women went to tell Jesus' followers, some of
the soldiers who had been guarding the tomb went into the
city to tell the leading priests everything that had hap-
pened. 12Then the priests met with the older Jewish leaders
and made a plan. They paid the soldiers a large amount of
money 13and said to them, "Tell the people that Jesus' fol-
lowers came during the night and stole the body while you
were asleep. 14If the governor hears about this, we will

CONTEMPORARY ENGLISH VERSION

bright as lightning, and his clothes were white as snow.
4The guards shook from fear and fell down, as though they
were dead.
5The angel said to the women, "Don't be afraid! I know
you are looking for Jesus, who was nailed to a cross. 6He
isn't here! God has raised him to life, just as Jesus said he
would. Come, see the place where his body was lying.
7Now hurry! Tell his disciples that he has been raised to
life and is on his way to Galilee. Go there, and you will see
him. That is what I came to tell you."
8The women were frightened and yet very happy, as they
hurried from the tomb and ran to tell his disciples.
9Suddenly Jesus met them and greeted them. They went
near him, held on to his feet, and worshiped him. 10Then
Jesus said, "Don't be afraid! Tell my followers to go to
Galilee. They will see me there."

Report of the Guard

11While the women were on their way, some soldiers
who had been guarding the tomb went into the city. They
told the chief priests everything that had happened. 12So
the chief priests met with the leaders and decided to bribe
the soldiers with a lot of money. 13They said to the sol-
diers, "Tell everyone that Jesus' disciples came during the
night and stole his body while you were asleep. 14If the
governor[a] hears about this, we will talk to him. You won't

[a] **28.14** *governor*: Pontius Pilate.

NEW INTERNATIONAL VERSION

like lightning, and his clothes were white as snow. 4The guards were so afraid of him that they shook and became like dead men.

5The angel said to the women, "Do not be afraid, for I know that you are looking for Jesus, who was crucified. 6He is not here; he has risen, just as he said. Come and see the place where he lay. 7Then go quickly and tell his disciples: 'He has risen from the dead and is going ahead of you into Galilee. There you will see him.' Now I have told you."

8So the women hurried away from the tomb, afraid yet filled with joy, and ran to tell his disciples. 9Suddenly Jesus met them. "Greetings," he said. They came to him, clasped his feet and worshiped him. 10Then Jesus said to them, "Do not be afraid. Go and tell my brothers to go to Galilee; there they will see me."

The Guards' Report

11While the women were on their way, some of the guards went into the city and reported to the chief priests everything that had happened. 12When the chief priests had met with the elders and devised a plan, they gave the soldiers a large sum of money, 13telling them, "You are to say, 'His disciples came during the night and stole him away while we were asleep.' 14If this report gets to the governor, we will satisfy him and keep you out of trouble."

NEW LIVING TRANSLATION

shone like lightning, and his clothing was as white as snow. 4The guards shook with fear when they saw him, and they fell into a dead faint.

5Then the angel spoke to the women. "Don't be afraid!" he said. "I know you are looking for Jesus, who was crucified. 6He isn't here! He has been raised from the dead, just as he said would happen. Come, see where his body was lying. 7And now, go quickly and tell his disciples he has been raised from the dead, and he is going ahead of you to Galilee. You will see him there. Remember, I have told you."

8The women ran quickly from the tomb. They were very frightened but also filled with great joy, and they rushed to find the disciples to give them the angel's message. 9And as they went, Jesus met them. "Greetings!" he said. And they ran to him, held his feet, and worshiped him. 10Then Jesus said to them, "Don't be afraid! Go tell my brothers to leave for Galilee, and they will see me there."

The Report of the Guard

11As the women were on their way into the city, some of the men who had been guarding the tomb went to the leading priests and told them what had happened. 12A meeting of all the religious leaders was called, and they decided to bribe the soldiers. 13They told the soldiers, "You must say, 'Jesus' disciples came during the night while we were sleeping, and they stole his body.' 14If the governor hears about it, we'll stand up for you and everything will

NEW KING JAMES VERSION

and sat on it. 3His countenance was like lightning, and his clothing as white as snow. 4And the guards shook for fear of him, and became like dead *men*.

5But the angel answered and said to the women, "Do not be afraid, for I know that you seek Jesus who was crucified. 6He is not here; for He is risen, as He said. Come, see the place where the Lord lay. 7And go quickly and tell His disciples that He is risen from the dead, and indeed He is going before you into Galilee; there you will see Him. Behold, I have told you."

8So they went out quickly from the tomb with fear and great joy, and ran to bring His disciples word.

The Women Worship the Risen Lord

9And as they went to tell His disciples,[b] behold, Jesus met them, saying, "Rejoice!" So they came and held Him by the feet and worshiped Him. 10Then Jesus said to them, "Do not be afraid. Go *and* tell My brethren to go to Galilee, and there they will see Me."

The Soldiers Are Bribed

11Now while they were going, behold, some of the guard came into the city and reported to the chief priests all the things that had happened. 12When they had assembled with the elders and consulted together, they gave a large sum of money to the soldiers, 13saying, "Tell them, 'His disciples came at night and stole Him *away* while we slept.' 14And if this comes to the governor's ears, we will

28:9 [b] NU-Text omits the first clause of this verse.

THE MESSAGE

ning blazed from him. His garments shimmered snow-white. The guards at the tomb were scared to death. They were so frightened, they couldn't move.

The angel spoke to the women: "There is nothing to fear here. I know you're looking for Jesus, the One they nailed to the cross. He is not here. He was raised, just as he said. Come and look at the place where he was placed.

"Now, get on your way quickly and tell his disciples, 'He is risen from the dead. He is going on ahead of you to Galilee. You will see him there.' That's the message."

The women, deep in wonder and full of joy, lost no time in leaving the tomb. They ran to tell the disciples. Then Jesus met them, stopping them in their tracks. "Good morning!" he said. They fell to their knees, embraced his feet, and worshiped him. Jesus said, "You're holding on to me for dear life! Don't be frightened like that. Go tell my brothers that they are to go to Galilee, and that I'll meet them there."

Meanwhile, the guards had scattered, but a few of them went into the city and told the high priests everything that had happened. They called a meeting of the religious leaders and came up with a plan: They took a large sum of money and gave it to the soldiers, bribing them to say, "His disciples came in the night and stole the body while we were sleeping." They assured them, "If the governor hears about your sleeping on duty, we will make sure you

KING JAMES VERSION

15 So they took the money, and did as they were taught: and this saying is commonly reported among the Jews until this day.

16 ¶ Then the eleven disciples went away into Galilee, into a mountain where Jesus had appointed them.

17 And when they saw him, they worshipped him: but some doubted.

18 And Jesus came and spake unto them, saying, All power is given unto me in heaven and in earth.

19 Go ye therefore, and teach all nations, baptizing them in the name of the Father, and of the Son, and of the Holy Ghost:

20 Teaching them to observe all things whatsoever I have commanded you: and, lo, I am with you alway, *even* unto the end of the world. Amen.

NEW AMERICAN STANDARD BIBLE

15 And they took the money and did as they had been instructed; and this story was widely spread among the Jews, *and is* to this day.

The Great Commission

16 But the eleven disciples proceeded to Galilee, to the mountain which Jesus had designated.

17 When they saw Him, they worshiped *Him;* but some were doubtful.

18 And Jesus came up and spoke to them, saying, "All authority has been given to Me in heaven and on earth.

19 "Go therefore and make disciples of all the nations, baptizing them in the name of the Father and the Son and the Holy Spirit,

20 teaching them to observe all that I commanded you; and lo, I am with you always, even to the end of the age."

NEW CENTURY VERSION

satisfy him and save you from trouble." 15So the soldiers kept the money and did as they were told. And that story is still spread among the Jewish people even today.

Jesus Talks to His Followers

16The eleven followers went to Galilee to the mountain where Jesus had told them to go. 17On the mountain they saw Jesus and worshiped him, but some of them did not believe it was really Jesus. 18Then Jesus came to them and said, "All power in heaven and on earth is given to me. 19So go and make followers of all people in the world. Baptize them in the name of the Father and the Son and the Holy Spirit. 20Teach them to obey everything that I have taught you, and I will be with you always, even until the end of this age."

CONTEMPORARY ENGLISH VERSION

have anything to worry about." 15The soldiers took the money and did what they were told. The people of Judea still tell each other this story.

What Jesus' Followers Must Do

(Mark 16.14-18; Luke 24.36-49; John 20.19-23; Acts 1.6-8)

16Jesus' eleven disciples went to a mountain in Galilee, where Jesus had told them to meet him. 17They saw him and worshiped him, but some of them doubted.

18Jesus came to them and said:

I have been given all authority in heaven and on earth! 19Go to the people of all nations and make them my disciples. Baptize them in the name of the Father, the Son, and the Holy Spirit, 20and teach them to do everything I have told you. I will be with you always, even until the end of the world.

NEW INTERNATIONAL VERSION

15So the soldiers took the money and did as they were instructed. And this story has been widely circulated among the Jews to this very day.

The Great Commission

16Then the eleven disciples went to Galilee, to the mountain where Jesus had told them to go. 17When they saw him, they worshiped him; but some doubted. 18Then Jesus came to them and said, "All authority in heaven and on earth has been given to me. 19Therefore go and make disciples of all nations, baptizing them in[a] the name of the Father and of the Son and of the Holy Spirit, 20and teaching them to obey everything I have commanded you. And surely I am with you always, to the very end of the age."

[a] *19* Or *into*; see Acts 8:16; 19:5; Romans 6:3; 1 Cor. 1:13; 10:2 and Gal. 3:27.

NEW LIVING TRANSLATION

be all right." 15So the guards accepted the bribe and said what they were told to say. Their story spread widely among the Jews, and they still tell it today.

The Great Commission

16Then the eleven disciples left for Galilee, going to the mountain where Jesus had told them to go. 17When they saw him, they worshiped him—but some of them still doubted!

18Jesus came and told his disciples, "I have been given complete authority in heaven and on earth. 19Therefore, go and make disciples of all the nations, baptizing them in the name of the Father and the Son and the Holy Spirit. 20Teach these new disciples to obey all the commands I have given you. And be sure of this: I am with you always, even to the end of the age."

NEW KING JAMES VERSION

appease him and make you secure." 15So they took the money and did as they were instructed; and this saying is commonly reported among the Jews until this day.

The Great Commission

16Then the eleven disciples went away into Galilee, to the mountain which Jesus had appointed for them. 17When they saw Him, they worshiped Him; but some doubted.

18And Jesus came and spoke to them, saying, "All authority has been given to Me in heaven and on earth. 19Go therefore[c] and make disciples of all the nations, baptizing them in the name of the Father and of the Son and of the Holy Spirit, 20teaching them to observe all things that I have commanded you; and lo, I am with you always, *even* to the end of the age." Amen.[d]

28:19 [c] M-Text omits *therefore*. 28:20 [d] NU-Text omits *Amen*.

THE MESSAGE

don't get blamed." The soldiers took the bribe and did as they were told. That story, cooked up in the Jewish High Council, is still going around.

✢

Meanwhile, the eleven disciples were on their way to Galilee, headed for the mountain Jesus had set for their reunion. The moment they saw him they worshiped him. Some, though, held back, not sure about *worship*, about risking themselves totally.

Jesus, undeterred, went right ahead and gave his charge: "God authorized and commanded me to commission you: Go out and train everyone you meet, far and near, in this way of life, marking them by baptism in the threefold name: Father, Son, and Holy Spirit. Then instruct them in the practice of all I have commanded you. I'll be with you as you do this, day after day after day, right up to the end of the age."

KING JAMES VERSION

THE GOSPEL ACCORDING TO
ST. MARK

1 The beginning of the gospel of Jesus Christ, the Son of God;
2 As it is written in the prophets, Behold, I send my messenger before thy face, which shall prepare thy way before thee.
3 The voice of one crying in the wilderness, Prepare ye the way of the Lord, make his paths straight.
4 John did baptize in the wilderness, and preach the baptism of repentance for the remission of sins.
5 And there went out unto him all the land of Judaea, and they of Jerusalem, and were all baptized of him in the river of Jordan, confessing their sins.
6 And John was clothed with camel's hair, and with a

NEW AMERICAN STANDARD BIBLE

THE GOSPEL ACCORDING TO
MARK

Preaching of John the Baptist

1 The beginning of the gospel of Jesus Christ, the Son of God.
2 As it is written in Isaiah the prophet:
"BEHOLD, I SEND MY MESSENGER AHEAD OF YOU,
WHO WILL PREPARE YOUR WAY;
3 THE VOICE OF ONE CRYING IN THE WILDERNESS,
'MAKE READY THE WAY OF THE LORD,
MAKE HIS PATHS STRAIGHT.' "
4 John the Baptist appeared in the wilderness [1]preaching a baptism of repentance for the forgiveness of sins.
5 And all the country of Judea was going out to him, and all the people of Jerusalem; and they were being baptized by him in the Jordan River, confessing their sins.
6 John was clothed with camel's hair and *wore* a

1:4 [1] Or *proclaiming*

NEW CENTURY VERSION

MARK

John Prepares for Jesus

1 This is the beginning of the Good News about Jesus Christ, the Son of God,[a] 2as the prophet Isaiah wrote:
"I will send my messenger ahead of you,
who will prepare your way." *Malachi 3:1*
3 "This is a voice of one
who calls out in the desert:
'Prepare the way for the Lord.
Make the road straight for him.' " *Isaiah 40:3*
4John was baptizing people in the desert and preaching a baptism of changed hearts and lives for the forgiveness of sins. 5All the people from Judea and Jerusalem were going out to him. They confessed their sins and were baptized by him in the Jordan River. 6John wore clothes made

1:1 [a] **the Son of God** Some Greek copies omit these words.

CONTEMPORARY ENGLISH VERSION

MARK

The Preaching of John the Baptist
(Matthew 3.1-12; Luke 3.1-18; John 1.19-28)

1 This is the good news about Jesus Christ, the Son of God.[a] 2It began just as God had said in the book written by Isaiah the prophet,

"I am sending my messenger
to get the way ready
for you.
3 In the desert
someone is shouting,
'Get the road ready
for the Lord!
Make a straight path
for him.' "

4So John the Baptist showed up in the desert and told everyone, "Turn back to God and be baptized! Then your sins will be forgiven."

5From all Judea and Jerusalem crowds of people went to John. They told how sorry they were for their sins, and he baptized them in the Jordan River.

6John wore clothes made of camel's hair. He had a

[a] 1.1 *the Son of God*: These words are not in some manuscripts.

NEW INTERNATIONAL VERSION

MARK

John the Baptist Prepares the Way

1 The beginning of the gospel about Jesus Christ, the Son of God.[a]

2It is written in Isaiah the prophet:

"I will send my messenger ahead of you,
who will prepare your way"[b]—
3 "a voice of one calling in the desert,
'Prepare the way for the Lord,
make straight paths for him.' "[c]

4And so John came, baptizing in the desert region and preaching a baptism of repentance for the forgiveness of sins. 5The whole Judean countryside and all the people of Jerusalem went out to him. Confessing their sins, they were baptized by him in the Jordan River. 6John wore

[a] *1* Some manuscripts do not have *the Son of God.* [b] *2* Mal. 3:1
[c] *3* Isaiah 40:3

NEW LIVING TRANSLATION

MARK

John the Baptist Prepares the Way

1 Here begins the Good News about Jesus the Messiah, the Son of God.*

2In the book of the prophet Isaiah, God said,

"Look, I am sending my messenger before you,
and he will prepare your way.*
3 He is a voice shouting in the wilderness:
'Prepare a pathway for the Lord's coming!
Make a straight road for him!'* "

4This messenger was John the Baptist. He lived in the wilderness and was preaching that people should be baptized to show that they had turned from their sins and turned to God to be forgiven.* 5People from Jerusalem and from all over Judea traveled out into the wilderness to see and hear John. And when they confessed their sins, he baptized them in the Jordan River. 6His clothes were

1:1 Some manuscripts do not include *the Son of God.* 1:2 Mal 3:1.
1:3 Isa 40:3. 1:4 Greek *preaching a baptism of repentance for the forgiveness of sins.*

NEW KING JAMES VERSION

THE GOSPEL ACCORDING TO

MARK

John the Baptist Prepares the Way

1 The beginning of the gospel of Jesus Christ, the Son of God. 2As it is written in the Prophets:[a]

"Behold, I send My messenger before Your face,
Who will prepare Your way before You."[b]
3 *"The voice of one crying in the wilderness:*
'Prepare the way of the LORD;
Make His paths straight.' "[c]

4John came baptizing in the wilderness and preaching a baptism of repentance for the remission of sins. 5Then all the land of Judea, and those from Jerusalem, went out to him and were all baptized by him in the Jordan River, confessing their sins.

6Now John was clothed with camel's hair and with a

1:2 [a] NU-Text reads *Isaiah the prophet.* [b] Malachi 3:1
1:3 [c] Isaiah 40:3

THE MESSAGE

MARK

John the Baptizer

1 The good news of Jesus Christ—the Message!—begins here, following to the letter the scroll of the prophet Isaiah.

"Watch closely: I'm sending my preacher ahead of you;
He'll make the road smooth for you.
Thunder in the desert!
Prepare for God's arrival!
Make the road smooth and straight!"

John the Baptizer appeared in the wild, preaching a baptism of life-change that leads to forgiveness of sins. People thronged to him from Judea and Jerusalem and, as they confessed their sins, were baptized by him in the Jordan River into a changed life. John wore a camel-hair habit,

KING JAMES VERSION

girdle of a skin about his loins; and he did eat locusts and wild honey;

7 And preached, saying, There cometh one mightier than I after me, the latchet of whose shoes I am not worthy to stoop down and unloose.

8 I indeed have baptized you with water: but he shall baptize you with the Holy Ghost.

9 ¶ And it came to pass in those days, that Jesus came from Nazareth of Galilee, and was baptized of John in Jordan.

10 And straightway coming up out of the water, he saw the heavens opened, and the Spirit like a dove descending upon him:

11 And there came a voice from heaven, *saying*, Thou art my beloved Son, in whom I am well pleased.

12 And immediately the Spirit driveth him into the wilderness.

13 And he was there in the wilderness forty days, tempted of Satan; and was with the wild beasts; and the angels ministered unto him.

14 ¶ Now after that John was put in prison, Jesus came into Galilee, preaching the gospel of the kingdom of God,

15 And saying, The time is fulfilled, and the kingdom of God is at hand: repent ye, and believe the gospel.

NEW AMERICAN STANDARD BIBLE

leather belt around his waist, and his diet was locusts and wild honey.

7 And he was preaching, and saying, "After me One is coming who is mightier than I, and I am not fit to stoop down and untie the thong of His sandals.

8 "I baptized you [2]with water; but He will baptize you [2]with the Holy Spirit."

The Baptism of Jesus

9 In those days Jesus came from Nazareth in Galilee and was baptized by John in the Jordan.

10 Immediately coming up out of the water, He saw the heavens opening, and the Spirit like a dove descending upon Him;

11 and a voice came out of the heavens: "You are My beloved Son, in You I am well-pleased."

12 Immediately the Spirit *impelled Him *to go* out into the wilderness.

13 And He was in the wilderness forty days being tempted by Satan; and He was with the wild beasts, and the angels were ministering to Him.

Jesus Preaches in Galilee

14 Now after John had been taken into custody, Jesus came into Galilee, preaching the gospel of God,

15 and saying, "The time is fulfilled, and the kingdom of God is at hand; repent and believe in the gospel."

1:8 [2] The Gr here can be translated *in, with* or *by*

NEW CENTURY VERSION

from camel's hair, had a leather belt around his waist, and ate locusts and wild honey. [7]This is what John preached to the people: "There is one coming after me who is greater than I; I am not good enough even to kneel down and untie his sandals. [8]I baptize you with water, but he will baptize you with the Holy Spirit."

Jesus Is Baptized

[9]At that time Jesus came from the town of Nazareth in Galilee and was baptized by John in the Jordan River. [10]Immediately, as Jesus was coming up out of the water, he saw heaven open. The Holy Spirit came down on him like a dove, [11]and a voice came from heaven: "You are my Son, whom I love, and I am very pleased with you."

[12]Then the Spirit sent Jesus into the desert. [13]He was in the desert forty days and was tempted by Satan. He was with the wild animals, and the angels came and took care of him.

Jesus Chooses Some Followers

[14]After John was put in prison, Jesus went into Galilee, preaching the Good News from God. [15]He said, "The right time has come. The kingdom of God is near. Change your hearts and lives and believe the Good News!"

CONTEMPORARY ENGLISH VERSION

leather strap around his waist and ate grasshoppers and wild honey.

[7]John also told the people, "Someone more powerful is going to come. And I am not good enough even to stoop down and untie his sandals.[b] [8]I baptize you with water, but he will baptize you with the Holy Spirit!"

The Baptism of Jesus (Matthew 3.13-17; Luke 3.21, 22)

[9]About that time Jesus came from Nazareth in Galilee, and John baptized him in the Jordan River. [10]As soon as Jesus came out of the water, he saw the sky open and the Holy Spirit coming down to him like a dove. [11]A voice from heaven said, "You are my own dear Son, and I am pleased with you."

Jesus and Satan (Matthew 4.1-11; Luke 4.1-13)

[12]Right away God's Spirit made Jesus go into the desert. [13]He stayed there for forty days while Satan tested him. Jesus was with the wild animals, but angels took care of him.

Jesus Begins His Work (Matthew 4.12-17; Luke 4.14, 15)

[14]After John was arrested, Jesus went to Galilee and told the good news that comes from God.[c] [15]He said, "The time has come! God's kingdom will soon be here.[d] Turn back to God and believe the good news!"

[b] 1.7 *untie his sandals*: This was the duty of a slave. [c] 1.14 *that comes from God*: Or "that is about God." [d] 1.15 *will soon be here*: Or "is already here."

NEW INTERNATIONAL VERSION

clothing made of camel's hair, with a leather belt around his waist, and he ate locusts and wild honey. 7And this was his message: "After me will come one more powerful than I, the thongs of whose sandals I am not worthy to stoop down and untie. 8I baptize you with[d] water, but he will baptize you with the Holy Spirit."

The Baptism and Temptation of Jesus

9At that time Jesus came from Nazareth in Galilee and was baptized by John in the Jordan. 10As Jesus was coming up out of the water, he saw heaven being torn open and the Spirit descending on him like a dove. 11And a voice came from heaven: "You are my Son, whom I love; with you I am well pleased."

12At once the Spirit sent him out into the desert, 13and he was in the desert forty days, being tempted by Satan. He was with the wild animals, and angels attended him.

The Calling of the First Disciples

14After John was put in prison, Jesus went into Galilee, proclaiming the good news of God. 15"The time has come," he said. "The kingdom of God is near. Repent and believe the good news!"

[d] 8 Or *in*

NEW LIVING TRANSLATION

woven from camel hair, and he wore a leather belt; his food was locusts and wild honey. 7He announced: "Someone is coming soon who is far greater than I am—so much greater that I am not even worthy to be his slave.* 8I baptize you with* water, but he will baptize you with the Holy Spirit!"

The Baptism of Jesus

9One day Jesus came from Nazareth in Galilee, and he was baptized by John in the Jordan River. 10And when Jesus came up out of the water, he saw the heavens split open and the Holy Spirit descending like a dove on him. 11And a voice came from heaven saying, "You are my beloved Son, and I am fully pleased with you."

The Temptation of Jesus

12Immediately the Holy Spirit compelled Jesus to go into the wilderness. 13He was there for forty days, being tempted by Satan. He was out among the wild animals, and angels took care of him.

The First Disciples

14Later on, after John was arrested by Herod Antipas, Jesus went to Galilee to preach God's Good News. 15"At last the time has come!" he announced. "The Kingdom of God is near! Turn from your sins and believe this Good News!"

1:7 Greek *to stoop down and untie his sandals.* 1:8 Or *in.*

NEW KING JAMES VERSION

leather belt around his waist, and he ate locusts and wild honey. 7And he preached, saying, "There comes One after me who is mightier than I, whose sandal strap I am not worthy to stoop down and loose. 8I indeed baptized you with water, but He will baptize you with the Holy Spirit."

John Baptizes Jesus

9It came to pass in those days *that* Jesus came from Nazareth of Galilee, and was baptized by John in the Jordan. 10And immediately, coming up from[d] the water, He saw the heavens parting and the Spirit descending upon Him like a dove. 11Then a voice came from heaven, "You are My beloved Son, in whom I am well pleased."

Satan Tempts Jesus

12Immediately the Spirit drove Him into the wilderness. 13And He was there in the wilderness forty days, tempted by Satan, and was with the wild beasts; and the angels ministered to Him.

Jesus Begins His Galilean Ministry

14Now after John was put in prison, Jesus came to Galilee, preaching the gospel of the kingdom[e] of God, 15and saying, "The time is fulfilled, and the kingdom of God is at hand. Repent, and believe in the gospel."

1:10 [d] NU-Text reads *out of.* 1:14 [e] NU-Text omits *of the kingdom.*

THE MESSAGE

tied at the waist with a leather belt. He ate locusts and wild field honey.

As he preached he said, "The real action comes next: The star in this drama, to whom I'm a mere stagehand, will change your life. I'm baptizing you here in the river, turning your old life in for a kingdom life. His baptism—a holy baptism by the Holy Spirit—will change you from the inside out."

At this time, Jesus came from Nazareth in Galilee and was baptized by John in the Jordan. The moment he came out of the water, he saw the sky split open and God's Spirit, looking like a dove, come down on him. Along with the Spirit, a voice: "You are my Son, chosen and marked by my love, pride of my life."

God's Kingdom Is Here

At once, this same Spirit pushed Jesus out into the wild. For forty wilderness days and nights he was tested by Satan. Wild animals were his companions, and angels took care of him.

After John was arrested, Jesus went to Galilee preaching the Message of God: "Time's up! God's kingdom is here. Change your life and believe the Message."

KING JAMES VERSION

16 Now as he walked by the sea of Galilee, he saw Simon and Andrew his brother casting a net into the sea: for they were fishers.

17 And Jesus said unto them, Come ye after me, and I will make you to become fishers of men.

18 And straightway they forsook their nets, and followed him.

19 And when he had gone a little further thence, he saw James the *son* of Zebedee, and John his brother, who also were in the ship mending their nets.

20 And straightway he called them: and they left their father Zebedee in the ship with the hired servants, and went after him.

21 And they went into Capernaum; and straightway on the sabbath day he entered into the synagogue, and taught.

22 And they were astonished at his doctrine: for he taught them as one that had authority, and not as the scribes.

23 ¶ And there was in their synagogue a man with an unclean spirit; and he cried out,

24 Saying, Let *us* alone; what have we to do with thee, thou Jesus of Nazareth? art thou come to destroy us? I know thee who thou art, the Holy One of God.

25 And Jesus rebuked him, saying, Hold thy peace, and come out of him.

26 And when the unclean spirit had torn him, and cried with a loud voice, he came out of him.

NEW AMERICAN STANDARD BIBLE

16 As He was going along by the Sea of Galilee, He saw Simon and Andrew, the brother of Simon, casting a net in the sea; for they were fishermen.

17 And Jesus said to them, "Follow Me, and I will make you become fishers of men."

18 Immediately they left their nets and followed Him.

19 Going on a little farther, He saw James the son of Zebedee, and John his brother, who were also in the boat mending the nets.

20 Immediately He called them; and they left their father Zebedee in the boat with the hired servants, and went away to follow Him.

21 They *went into Capernaum; and immediately on the Sabbath He entered the synagogue and *began* to teach.

22 They were amazed at His teaching; for He was teaching them as *one* having authority, and not as the scribes.

23 Just then there was a man in their synagogue with an unclean spirit; and he cried out,

24 saying, "What business do we have with each other, Jesus [3]of Nazareth? Have You come to destroy us? I know who You are—the Holy One of God!"

25 And Jesus rebuked him, saying, "Be quiet, and come out of him!"

26 Throwing him into convulsions, the unclean spirit cried out with a loud voice and came out of him.

1:24 [3] Lit *the Nazarene*

NEW CENTURY VERSION

16When Jesus was walking by Lake Galilee, he saw Simon[b] and his brother Andrew throwing a net into the lake because they were fishermen. 17Jesus said to them, "Come follow me, and I will make you fish for people." 18So Simon and Andrew immediately left their nets and followed him.

19Going a little farther, Jesus saw two more brothers, James and John, the sons of Zebedee. They were in a boat, mending their nets. 20Jesus immediately called them, and they left their father in the boat with the hired workers and followed Jesus.

Jesus Forces Out an Evil Spirit

21Jesus and his followers went to Capernaum. On the Sabbath day He went to the synagogue and began to teach. 22The people were amazed at his teaching, because he taught like a person who had authority, not like their teachers of the law. 23Just then, a man was there in the synagogue who had an evil spirit in him. He shouted, 24"Jesus of Nazareth! What do you want with us? Did you come to destroy us? I know who you are—God's Holy One!"

25Jesus commanded the evil spirit, "Be quiet! Come out of the man!" 26The evil spirit shook the man violently, gave a loud cry, and then came out of him.

1:16 [b] **Simon** Simon's other name was Peter.

CONTEMPORARY ENGLISH VERSION

Jesus Chooses Four Fishermen

(Matthew 4.18-22; Luke 5.1-11)

16As Jesus was walking along the shore of Lake Galilee, he saw Simon and his brother Andrew. They were fishermen and were casting their nets into the lake. 17Jesus said to them, "Come with me! I will teach you how to bring in people instead of fish." 18Right then the two brothers dropped their nets and went with him.

19Jesus walked on and soon saw James and John, the sons of Zebedee. They were in a boat, mending their nets. 20At once Jesus asked them to come with him. They left their father in the boat with the hired workers and went with him.

A Man with an Evil Spirit (Luke 4.31-37)

21Jesus and his disciples went to the town of Capernaum. Then on the next Sabbath he went into the Jewish meeting place and started teaching. 22Everyone was amazed at his teaching. He taught with authority, and not like the teachers of the Law of Moses. 23Suddenly a man with an evil spirit[e] in him entered the meeting place and yelled, 24"Jesus from Nazareth, what do you want with us? Have you come to destroy us? I know who you are! You are God's Holy One."

25Jesus told the evil spirit, "Be quiet and come out of the man!" 26The spirit shook him. Then it gave a loud shout and left.

[e] **1.23** *evil spirit*: A Jewish person who had an evil spirit was considered "unclean" and was not allowed to eat or worship with other Jewish people.

NEW INTERNATIONAL VERSION

16As Jesus walked beside the Sea of Galilee, he saw
Simon and his brother Andrew casting a net into the lake,
for they were fishermen. 17"Come, follow me," Jesus said,
"and I will make you fishers of men." 18At once they left
their nets and followed him.
19When he had gone a little farther, he saw James son of
Zebedee and his brother John in a boat, preparing their
nets. 20Without delay he called them, and they left their
father Zebedee in the boat with the hired men and fol-
lowed him.

Jesus Drives Out an Evil Spirit

21They went to Capernaum, and when the Sabbath came,
Jesus went into the synagogue and began to teach. 22The
people were amazed at his teaching, because he taught
them as one who had authority, not as the teachers of the
law. 23Just then a man in their synagogue who was pos-
sessed by an evil[e] spirit cried out, 24"What do you want
with us, Jesus of Nazareth? Have you come to destroy us?
I know who you are—the Holy One of God!"
25"Be quiet!" said Jesus sternly. "Come out of him!"
26The evil spirit shook the man violently and came out of
him with a shriek.

e *23* Greek *unclean*; also in verses 26 and 27

NEW LIVING TRANSLATION

16One day as Jesus was walking along the shores of the
Sea of Galilee, he saw Simon* and his brother, Andrew,
fishing with a net, for they were commercial fishermen.
17Jesus called out to them, "Come, be my disciples, and I
will show you how to fish for people!" 18And they left their
nets at once and went with him.
19A little farther up the shore Jesus saw Zebedee's sons,
James and John, in a boat mending their nets. 20He called
them, too, and immediately they left their father, Zebedee,
in the boat with the hired men and went with him.

Jesus Casts Out an Evil Spirit

21Jesus and his companions went to the town of
Capernaum, and every Sabbath day he went into the syna-
gogue and taught the people. 22They were amazed at his
teaching, for he taught as one who had real authority—
quite unlike the teachers of religious law.
23A man possessed by an evil spirit was in the syna-
gogue, 24and he began shouting, "Why are you bothering
us, Jesus of Nazareth? Have you come to destroy us? I
know who you are—the Holy One sent from God!"
25Jesus cut him short. "Be silent! Come out of the man."
26At that, the evil spirit screamed and threw the man into
a convulsion, but then he left him.

1:16 *Simon* is called *Peter* in 3:16 and thereafter.

NEW KING JAMES VERSION

Four Fishermen Called as Disciples

16And as He walked by the Sea of Galilee, He saw Simon
and Andrew his brother casting a net into the sea; for they
were fishermen. 17Then Jesus said to them, "Follow Me,
and I will make you become fishers of men." 18They imme-
diately left their nets and followed Him.
19When He had gone a little farther from there, He saw
James the *son* of Zebedee, and John his brother, who also
were in the boat mending their nets. 20And immediately He
called them, and they left their father Zebedee in the boat
with the hired servants, and went after Him.

Jesus Casts Out an Unclean Spirit

21Then they went into Capernaum, and immediately on
the Sabbath He entered the synagogue and taught. 22And
they were astonished at His teaching, for He taught them
as one having authority, and not as the scribes.
23Now there was a man in their synagogue with an un-
clean spirit. And he cried out, 24saying, "Let *us* alone!
What have we to do with You, Jesus of Nazareth? Did You
come to destroy us? I know who You are—the Holy One of
God!"
25But Jesus rebuked him, saying, "Be quiet, and come
out of him!" 26And when the unclean spirit had convulsed
him and cried out with a loud voice, he came out of him.

THE MESSAGE

Passing along the beach of Lake Galilee, he saw Simon and his brother Andrew net-fishing. Fishing was their regular work. Jesus said to them, "Come with me. I'll make a new kind of fisherman out of you. I'll show you how to catch men and women instead of perch and bass." They didn't ask questions. They dropped their nets and followed.

A dozen yards or so down the beach, he saw the brothers James and John, Zebedee's sons. They were in the boat, mending their fishnets. Right off, he made the same offer. Immediately, they left their father Zebedee, the boat, and the hired hands, and followed.

Confident Teaching

Then they entered Capernaum. When the Sabbath arrived, Jesus lost no time in getting to the meeting place. He spent the day there teaching. They were surprised at his teaching—so forthright, so confident—not quibbling and quoting like the religion scholars.

Suddenly, while still in the meeting place, he was interrupted by a man who was deeply disturbed and yelling out, "What business do you have here with us, Jesus? Nazarene! I know what you're up to! You're the Holy One of God, and you've come to destroy us!"

Jesus shut him up: "Quiet! Get out of him!" The afflicting spirit threw the man into spasms, protesting loudly—and got out.

KING JAMES VERSION

27 And they were all amazed, insomuch that they questioned among themselves, saying, What thing is this? what new doctrine *is* this? for with authority commandeth he even the unclean spirits, and they do obey him.

28 And immediately his fame spread abroad throughout all the region round about Galilee.

29 ¶ And forthwith, when they were come out of the synagogue, they entered into the house of Simon and Andrew, with James and John.

30 But Simon's wife's mother lay sick of a fever, and anon they tell him of her.

31 And he came and took her by the hand, and lifted her up; and immediately the fever left her, and she ministered unto them.

32 And at even, when the sun did set, they brought unto him all that were diseased, and them that were possessed with devils.

33 And all the city was gathered together at the door.

34 And he healed many that were sick of divers diseases, and cast out many devils; and suffered not the devils to speak, because they knew him.

35 And in the morning, rising up a great while before day, he went out, and departed into a solitary place, and there prayed.

36 And Simon and they that were with him followed after him.

37 And when they had found him, they said unto him, All *men* seek for thee.

NEW AMERICAN STANDARD BIBLE

27 They were all amazed, so that they debated among themselves, saying, "What is this? A new teaching with authority! He commands even the unclean spirits, and they obey Him."

28 Immediately the news about Him spread everywhere into all the surrounding district of Galilee.

Crowds Healed

29 And immediately after they came out of the synagogue, they came into the house of Simon and Andrew, with James and John.

30 Now Simon's mother-in-law was lying sick with a fever; and immediately they *spoke to Jesus about her.

31 And He came to her and raised her up, taking her by the hand, and the fever left her, and she [4]waited on them.

32 When evening came, after the sun had set, they *began* bringing to Him all who were ill and those who were demon-possessed.

33 And the whole city had gathered at the door.

34 And He healed many who were ill with various diseases, and cast out many demons; and He was not permitting the demons to speak, because they knew who He was.

35 In the early morning, while it was still dark, Jesus got up, left *the house*, and went away to a secluded place, and was praying there.

36 Simon and his companions searched for Him;

37 they found Him, and *said to Him, "Everyone is looking for You."

1:31 [4] Or *served*

NEW CENTURY VERSION

27The people were so amazed they asked each other, "What is happening here? This man is teaching something new, and with authority. He even gives commands to evil spirits, and they obey him." 28And the news about Jesus spread quickly everywhere in the area of Galilee.

Jesus Heals Many People

29As soon as Jesus and his followers left the synagogue, they went with James and John to the home of Simon[c] and Andrew. 30Simon's mother-in-law was sick in bed with a fever, and the people told Jesus about her. 31So Jesus went to her bed, took her hand, and helped her up. The fever left her, and she began serving them.

32That evening, after the sun went down, the people brought to Jesus all who were sick and had demons in them. 33The whole town gathered at the door. 34Jesus healed many who had different kinds of sicknesses, and he forced many demons to leave people. But he would not allow the demons to speak, because they knew who he was.

35Early the next morning, while it was still dark, Jesus woke and left the house. He went to a lonely place, where he prayed. 36Simon and his friends went to look for Jesus. 37When they found him, they said, "Everyone is looking for you!"

1:29 [c] **Simon** Simon's other name was Peter.

CONTEMPORARY ENGLISH VERSION

27Everyone was completely surprised and kept saying to each other, "What is this? It must be some new kind of powerful teaching! Even the evil spirits obey him." 28News about Jesus quickly spread all over Galilee.

Jesus Heals Many People (Matthew 8.14-17; Luke 4.38-41)

29As soon as Jesus left the meeting place with James and John, they went home with Simon and Andrew. 30When they got there, Jesus was told that Simon's mother-in-law was sick in bed with fever. 31Jesus went to her. He took hold of her hand and helped her up. The fever left her, and she served them a meal.

32That evening after sunset,[f] all who were sick or had demons in them were brought to Jesus. 33In fact, the whole town gathered around the door of the house. 34Jesus healed all kinds of terrible diseases and forced out a lot of demons. But the demons knew who he was, and he did not let them speak.

35Very early the next morning, Jesus got up and went to a place where he could be alone and pray. 36Simon and the others started looking for him. 37And when they found him, they said, "Everyone is looking for you!"

[f] **1.32** *after sunset*: The Sabbath was over, and a new day began at sunset.

NEW INTERNATIONAL VERSION

27 The people were all so amazed that they asked each
other, "What is this? A new teaching—and with authority!
He even gives orders to evil spirits and they obey him."
28 News about him spread quickly over the whole region of
Galilee.

Jesus Heals Many

29 As soon as they left the synagogue, they went with
James and John to the home of Simon and Andrew.
30 Simon's mother-in-law was in bed with a fever, and they
told Jesus about her. 31 So he went to her, took her hand
and helped her up. The fever left her and she began to wait
on them.
32 That evening after sunset the people brought to Jesus
all the sick and demon-possessed. 33 The whole town gath-
ered at the door, 34 and Jesus healed many who had vari-
ous diseases. He also drove out many demons, but he
would not let the demons speak because they knew who he
was.

Jesus Prays in a Solitary Place

35 Very early in the morning, while it was still dark, Jesus
got up, left the house and went off to a solitary place,
where he prayed. 36 Simon and his companions went to
look for him, 37 and when they found him, they exclaimed:
"Everyone is looking for you!"

NEW LIVING TRANSLATION

27 Amazement gripped the audience, and they began to
discuss what had happened. "What sort of new teaching is
this?" they asked excitedly. "It has such authority! Even
evil spirits obey his orders!" 28 The news of what he had
done spread quickly through that entire area of Galilee.

Jesus Heals Many People

29 After Jesus and his disciples left the synagogue, they
went over to Simon and Andrew's home, and James and
John were with them. 30 Simon's mother-in-law was sick in
bed with a high fever. They told Jesus about her right
away. 31 He went to her bedside, and as he took her by the
hand and helped her to sit up, the fever suddenly left, and
she got up and prepared a meal for them.
32 That evening at sunset, many sick and demon-pos-
sessed people were brought to Jesus. 33 And a huge crowd
of people from all over Capernaum gathered outside the
door to watch. 34 So Jesus healed great numbers of sick
people who had many different kinds of diseases, and he
ordered many demons to come out of their victims. But
because they knew who he was, he refused to allow the
demons to speak.

Jesus Preaches in Galilee

35 The next morning Jesus awoke long before daybreak
and went out alone into the wilderness to pray. 36 Later
Simon and the others went out to find him. 37 They said,
"Everyone is asking for you."

NEW KING JAMES VERSION

27 Then they were all amazed, so that they questioned
among themselves, saying, "What is this? What new doc-
trine *is* this? For with authority[f] He commands even the
unclean spirits, and they obey Him." 28 And immediately
His fame spread throughout all the region around Galilee.

Peter's Mother-in-Law Healed

29 Now as soon as they had come out of the synagogue,
they entered the house of Simon and Andrew, with James
and John. 30 But Simon's wife's mother lay sick with a
fever, and they told Him about her at once. 31 So He came
and took her by the hand and lifted her up, and immedi-
ately the fever left her. And she served them.

Many Healed After Sabbath Sunset

32 At evening, when the sun had set, they brought to Him
all who were sick and those who were demon-possessed.
33 And the whole city was gathered together at the door.
34 Then He healed many who were sick with various dis-
eases, and cast out many demons; and He did not allow
the demons to speak, because they knew Him.

Preaching in Galilee

35 Now in the morning, having risen a long while before
daylight, He went out and departed to a solitary place; and
there He prayed. 36 And Simon and those *who were* with
Him searched for Him. 37 When they found Him, they said
to Him, "Everyone is looking for You."

1:27 [f] NU-Text reads *What is this? A new doctrine with authority.*

THE MESSAGE

Everyone there was incredulous, buzzing with curiosity. "What's going on here? A new teaching that does what it says? He shuts up defiling, demonic spirits and sends them packing!" News of this traveled fast and was soon all over Galilee.

Directly on leaving the meeting place, they came to Simon and Andrew's house, accompanied by James and John. Simon's mother-in-law was sick in bed, burning up with fever. They told Jesus. He went to her, took her hand, and raised her up. No sooner had the fever left than she was up fixing dinner for them.

That evening, after the sun was down, they brought sick and evil-afflicted people to him, the whole city lined up at his door! He cured their sick bodies and tormented spirits. Because the demons knew his true identity, he didn't let them say a word.

The Leper

While it was still night, way before dawn, he got up and went out to a secluded spot and prayed. Simon and those with him went looking for him. They found him and said, "Everybody's looking for you."

KING JAMES VERSION

38 And he said unto them, Let us go into the next towns, that I may preach there also: for therefore came I forth.

39 And he preached in their synagogues throughout all Galilee, and cast out devils.

40 ¶ And there came a leper to him, beseeching him, and kneeling down to him, and saying unto him, If thou wilt, thou canst make me clean.

41 And Jesus, moved with compassion, put forth *his* hand, and touched him, and saith unto him, I will; be thou clean.

42 And as soon as he had spoken, immediately the leprosy departed from him, and he was cleansed.

43 And he straitly charged him, and forthwith sent him away;

44 And saith unto him, See thou say nothing to any man: but go thy way, shew thyself to the priest, and offer for thy cleansing those things which Moses commanded, for a testimony unto them.

45 But he went out, and began to publish *it* much, and to blaze abroad the matter, insomuch that Jesus could no more openly enter into the city, but was without in desert places: and they came to him from every quarter.

NEW AMERICAN STANDARD BIBLE

38 He *said to them, "Let us go somewhere else to the towns nearby, so that I may preach there also; for that is what I came for."

39 And He went into their synagogues throughout all Galilee, preaching and casting out the demons.

40 And a leper *came to Jesus, beseeching Him and falling on his knees before Him, and saying, "If You are willing, You can make me clean."

41 Moved with compassion, Jesus stretched out His hand and touched him, and *said to him, "I am willing; be cleansed."

42 Immediately the leprosy left him and he was cleansed.

43 And He sternly warned him and immediately sent him away,

44 and He *said to him, "See that you say nothing to anyone; but go, show yourself to the priest and offer for your cleansing what Moses commanded, as a testimony to them."

45 But he went out and began to proclaim it freely and to spread the news around, to such an extent that Jesus could no longer publicly enter a city, but [5]stayed out in unpopulated areas; and they were coming to Him from everywhere.

1:45 [5] Lit *was*

NEW CENTURY VERSION

38Jesus answered, "We should go to other towns around here so I can preach there too. That is the reason I came." 39So he went everywhere in Galilee, preaching in the synagogues and forcing out demons.

Jesus Heals a Sick Man

40A man with a skin disease came to Jesus. He fell to his knees and begged Jesus, "You can heal me if you will." 41Jesus felt sorry for the man, so he reached out his hand and touched him and said, "I will. Be healed!" 42Immediately the disease left the man, and he was healed.

43Jesus told the man to go away at once, but he warned him strongly, 44"Don't tell anyone about this. But go and show yourself to the priest. And offer the gift Moses commanded for people who are made well.[d] This will show the people what I have done." 45The man left there, but he began to tell everyone that Jesus had healed him, and so he spread the news about Jesus. As a result, Jesus could not enter a town if people saw him. He stayed in places where nobody lived, but people came to him from everywhere.

1:44 [d] **Moses...well** Read about this in Leviticus 14:1–32.

CONTEMPORARY ENGLISH VERSION

38Jesus replied, "We must go to the nearby towns, so that I can tell the good news to those people. This is why I have come." 39Then Jesus went to Jewish meeting places everywhere in Galilee, where he preached and forced out demons.

Jesus Heals a Man (Matthew 8.1-4; Luke 5.12-16)

40A man with leprosy[g] came to Jesus and knelt down.[h] He begged, "You have the power to make me well, if only you wanted to."

41Jesus felt sorry for[i] the man. So he put his hand on him and said, "I want to! Now you are well." 42At once the man's leprosy disappeared, and he was well.

43After Jesus strictly warned the man, he sent him on his way. 44He said, "Don't tell anyone about this. Just go and show the priest that you are well. Then take a gift to the temple as Moses commanded, and everyone will know that you have been healed."[j]

45The man talked about it so much and told so many people, that Jesus could no longer go openly into a town. He had to stay away from the towns, but people still came to him from everywhere.

[g] 1.40 *leprosy*: In biblical times the word "leprosy" was used for many different kinds of skin diseases. [h] 1.40 *and knelt down*: These words are not in some manuscripts. [i] 1.41 *felt sorry for*: Some manuscripts have "was angry with." [j] 1.44 *everyone will know that you have been healed*: People with leprosy had to be examined by a priest and told that they were well (that is, "clean") before they could once again live a normal life in the Jewish community. The gift that Moses commanded was the sacrifice of some lambs together with flour mixed with olive oil.

NEW INTERNATIONAL VERSION

38Jesus replied, "Let us go somewhere else—to the nearby villages—so I can preach there also. That is why I have come." 39So he traveled throughout Galilee, preaching in their synagogues and driving out demons.

A Man With Leprosy

40A man with leprosy[f] came to him and begged him on his knees, "If you are willing, you can make me clean."

41Filled with compassion, Jesus reached out his hand and touched the man. "I am willing," he said. "Be clean!" 42Immediately the leprosy left him and he was cured.

43Jesus sent him away at once with a strong warning: 44"See that you don't tell this to anyone. But go, show yourself to the priest and offer the sacrifices that Moses commanded for your cleansing, as a testimony to them." 45Instead he went out and began to talk freely, spreading the news. As a result, Jesus could no longer enter a town openly but stayed outside in lonely places. Yet the people still came to him from everywhere.

[f] *40* The Greek word was used for various diseases affecting the skin—not necessarily leprosy.

NEW LIVING TRANSLATION

38But he replied, "We must go on to other towns as well, and I will preach to them, too, because that is why I came." 39So he traveled throughout the region of Galilee, preaching in the synagogues and expelling demons from many people.

Jesus Heals a Man with Leprosy

40A man with leprosy came and knelt in front of Jesus, begging to be healed. "If you want to, you can make me well again," he said.

41Moved with pity,* Jesus touched him. "I want to," he said. "Be healed!" 42Instantly the leprosy disappeared—the man was healed. 43Then Jesus sent him on his way and told him sternly, 44"Go right over to the priest and let him examine you. Don't talk to anyone along the way. Take along the offering required in the law of Moses for those who have been healed of leprosy, so everyone will have proof of your healing."

45But as the man went on his way, he spread the news, telling everyone what had happened to him. As a result, such crowds soon surrounded Jesus that he couldn't enter a town anywhere publicly. He had to stay out in the secluded places, and people from everywhere came to him there.

1:41 Some manuscripts read *Moved with anger.*

NEW KING JAMES VERSION

38But He said to them, "Let us go into the next towns, that I may preach there also, because for this purpose I have come forth."

39And He was preaching in their synagogues throughout all Galilee, and casting out demons.

Jesus Cleanses a Leper

40Now a leper came to Him, imploring Him, kneeling down to Him and saying to Him, "If You are willing, You can make me clean."

41Then Jesus, moved with compassion, stretched out *His* hand and touched him, and said to him, "I am willing; be cleansed." 42As soon as He had spoken, immediately the leprosy left him, and he was cleansed. 43And He strictly warned him and sent him away at once, 44and said to him, "See that you say nothing to anyone; but go your way, show yourself to the priest, and offer for your cleansing those things which Moses commanded, as a testimony to them."

45However, he went out and began to proclaim *it* freely, and to spread the matter, so that Jesus could no longer openly enter the city, but was outside in deserted places; and they came to Him from every direction.

THE MESSAGE

Jesus said, "Let's go to the rest of the villages so I can preach there also. This is why I've come." He went to their meeting places all through Galilee, preaching and throwing out the demons.

A leper came to him, begging on his knees, "If you want to, you can cleanse me."

Deeply moved, Jesus put out his hand, touched him, and said, "I want to. Be clean." Then and there the leprosy was gone, his skin smooth and healthy. Jesus dismissed him with strict orders: "Say nothing to anyone. Take the offering for cleansing that Moses prescribed and present yourself to the priest. This will validate your healing to the people." But as soon as the man was out of earshot, he told everyone he met what had happened, spreading the news all over town. So Jesus kept to out-of-the-way places, no longer able to move freely in and out of the city. But people found him, and came from all over.

KING JAMES VERSION

2 And again he entered into Capernaum after *some* days; and it was noised that he was in the house.

2 And straightway many were gathered together, insomuch that there was no room to receive *them*, no, not so much as about the door: and he preached the word unto them.

3 And they come unto him, bringing one sick of the palsy, which was borne of four.

4 And when they could not come nigh unto him for the press, they uncovered the roof where he was: and when they had broken *it* up, they let down the bed wherein the sick of the palsy lay.

5 When Jesus saw their faith, he said unto the sick of the palsy, Son, thy sins be forgiven thee.

6 But there were certain of the scribes sitting there, and reasoning in their hearts,

7 Why doth this *man* thus speak blasphemies? who can forgive sins but God only?

8 And immediately when Jesus perceived in his spirit that they so reasoned within themselves, he said unto them, Why reason ye these things in your hearts?

9 Whether is it easier to say to the sick of the palsy, *Thy* sins be forgiven thee; or to say, Arise, and take up thy bed, and walk?

10 But that ye may know that the Son of man hath power on earth to forgive sins, (he saith to the sick of the palsy,)

11 I say unto thee, Arise, and take up thy bed, and go thy way into thine house.

NEW AMERICAN STANDARD BIBLE

The Paralytic Healed

2 When He had come back to Capernaum several days afterward, it was heard that He was at home.

2 And many were gathered together, so that there was no longer room, not even near the door; and He was speaking the word to them.

3 And they *came, bringing to Him a paralytic, carried by four men.

4 Being unable to get to Him because of the crowd, they removed the roof above Him; and when they had dug an opening, they let down the pallet on which the paralytic was lying.

5 And Jesus seeing their faith *said to the paralytic, "[1]Son, your sins are forgiven."

6 But some of the scribes were sitting there and reasoning in their hearts,

7 "Why does this man speak that way? He is blaspheming; who can forgive sins but God alone?"

8 Immediately Jesus, aware in His spirit that they were reasoning that way within themselves, *said to them, "Why are you reasoning about these things in your hearts?

9 "Which is easier, to say to the paralytic, 'Your sins are forgiven'; or to say, 'Get up, and pick up your pallet and walk'?

10 "But so that you may know that the Son of Man has authority on earth to forgive sins"—He *said to the paralytic,

11 "I say to you, get up, pick up your pallet and go home."

2:5 [1] Lit *child*

NEW CENTURY VERSION

Jesus Heals a Paralyzed Man

2 A few days later, when Jesus came back to Capernaum, the news spread that he was at home.
2Many people gathered together so that there was no room in the house, not even outside the door. And Jesus was teaching them God's message. 3Four people came, carrying a paralyzed man. 4Since they could not get to Jesus because of the crowd, they dug a hole in the roof right above where he was speaking. When they got through, they lowered the mat with the paralyzed man on it. 5When Jesus saw the faith of these people, he said to the paralyzed man, "Young man, your sins are forgiven."
6Some of the teachers of the law were sitting there, thinking to themselves, 7"Why does this man say things like that? He is speaking as if he were God. Only God can forgive sins."
8Jesus knew immediately what these teachers of the law were thinking. So he said to them, "Why are you thinking these things? 9Which is easier: to tell this paralyzed man, 'Your sins are forgiven,' or to tell him, 'Stand up. Take your mat and walk'? 10But I will prove to you that the Son of Man has authority on earth to forgive sins." So Jesus said to the paralyzed man, 11"I tell you, stand up, take your mat, and go home." 12Immediately the paralyzed man

CONTEMPORARY ENGLISH VERSION

Jesus Heals a Crippled Man (Matthew 9.1-8; Luke 5.17-26)

2 Jesus went back to Capernaum, and a few days later people heard that he was at home.[a] 2Then so many of them came to the house that there wasn't even standing room left in front of the door.
Jesus was still teaching 3when four people came up, carrying a crippled man on a mat. 4But because of the crowd, they could not get him to Jesus. So they made a hole in the roof[b] above him and let the man down in front of everyone.
5When Jesus saw how much faith they had, he said to the crippled man, "My friend, your sins are forgiven."
6Some of the teachers of the Law of Moses were sitting there. They started wondering, 7"Why would he say such a thing? He must think he is God! Only God can forgive sins."
8Right away, Jesus knew what they were thinking, and he said, "Why are you thinking such things? 9Is it easier for me to tell this crippled man that his sins are forgiven or to tell him to get up and pick up his mat and go on home? 10I will show you that the Son of Man has the right to forgive sins here on earth." So Jesus said to the man, 11"Get up! Pick up your mat and go on home."

[a] 2.1 *at home*: Or "in the house" (perhaps Simon Peter's home).
[b] 2.4 *roof*: In Palestine the houses usually had a flat roof. Stairs on the outside led up to the roof that was made of beams and boards covered with packed earth.

NEW INTERNATIONAL VERSION

Jesus Heals a Paralytic

2 A few days later, when Jesus again entered Capernaum, the people heard that he had come home. 2So many gathered that there was no room left, not even outside the door, and he preached the word to them. 3Some men came, bringing to him a paralytic, carried by four of them. 4Since they could not get him to Jesus because of the crowd, they made an opening in the roof above Jesus and, after digging through it, lowered the mat the paralyzed man was lying on. 5When Jesus saw their faith, he said to the paralytic, "Son, your sins are forgiven."

6Now some teachers of the law were sitting there, thinking to themselves, 7"Why does this fellow talk like that? He's blaspheming! Who can forgive sins but God alone?"

8Immediately Jesus knew in his spirit that this was what they were thinking in their hearts, and he said to them, "Why are you thinking these things? 9Which is easier: to say to the paralytic, 'Your sins are forgiven,' or to say, 'Get up, take your mat and walk'? 10But that you may know that the Son of Man has authority on earth to forgive sins . . . ." He said to the paralytic, 11"I tell you, get up, take your mat and go home." 12He got up, took his mat and

NEW LIVING TRANSLATION

Jesus Heals a Paralyzed Man

2 Several days later Jesus returned to Capernaum, and the news of his arrival spread quickly through the town. 2Soon the house where he was staying was so packed with visitors that there wasn't room for one more person, not even outside the door. And he preached the word to them. 3Four men arrived carrying a paralyzed man on a mat. 4They couldn't get to Jesus through the crowd, so they dug through the clay roof above his head. Then they lowered the sick man on his mat, right down in front of Jesus. 5Seeing their faith, Jesus said to the paralyzed man, "My son, your sins are forgiven."

6But some of the teachers of religious law who were sitting there said to themselves, 7"What? This is blasphemy! Who but God can forgive sins!"

8Jesus knew what they were discussing among themselves, so he said to them, "Why do you think this is blasphemy? 9Is it easier to say to the paralyzed man, 'Your sins are forgiven' or 'Get up, pick up your mat, and walk'? 10I will prove that I, the Son of Man, have the authority on earth to forgive sins." Then Jesus turned to the paralyzed man and said, 11"Stand up, take your mat, and go on home, because you are healed!"

NEW KING JAMES VERSION

Jesus Forgives and Heals a Paralytic

2 And again He entered Capernaum after *some* days, and it was heard that He was in the house. 2Immediately[a] many gathered together, so that there was no longer room to receive *them,* not even near the door. And He preached the word to them. 3Then they came to Him, bringing a paralytic who was carried by four *men.* 4And when they could not come near Him because of the crowd, they uncovered the roof where He was. So when they had broken through, they let down the bed on which the paralytic was lying.

5When Jesus saw their faith, He said to the paralytic, "Son, your sins are forgiven you."

6And some of the scribes were sitting there and reasoning in their hearts, 7"Why does this *Man* speak blasphemies like this? Who can forgive sins but God alone?"

8But immediately, when Jesus perceived in His spirit that they reasoned thus within themselves, He said to them, "Why do you reason about these things in your hearts? 9Which is easier, to say to the paralytic, '*Your* sins are forgiven you,' or to say, 'Arise, take up your bed and walk'? 10But that you may know that the Son of Man has power on earth to forgive sins"—He said to the paralytic, 11"I say to you, arise, take up your bed, and go to your

2:2 [a] NU-Text omits *Immediately.*

THE MESSAGE

A Paraplegic

2 After a few days, Jesus returned to Capernaum, and word got around that he was back home. A crowd gathered, jamming the entrance so no one could get in or out. He was teaching the Word. They brought a paraplegic to him, carried by four men. When they weren't able to get in because of the crowd, they removed part of the roof and lowered the paraplegic on his stretcher. Impressed by their bold belief, Jesus said to the paraplegic, "Son, I forgive your sins."

Some religion scholars sitting there started whispering among themselves, "He can't talk that way! That's blasphemy! God and only God can forgive sins."

Jesus knew right away what they were thinking, and said, "Why are you so skeptical? Which is simpler: to say to the paraplegic, 'I forgive your sins,' or say, 'Get up, take your stretcher, and start walking'? Well, just so it's clear that I'm the Son of Man and authorized to do either, or both . . ." (he looked now at the paraplegic), "Get up. Pick up your stretcher and go home." And the man did it—got

KING JAMES VERSION

12 And immediately he arose, took up the bed, and went forth before them all; insomuch that they were all amazed, and glorified God, saying, We never saw it on this fashion.

13 ¶ And he went forth again by the sea side; and all the multitude resorted unto him, and he taught them.

14 And as he passed by, he saw Levi the *son* of Alphaeus sitting at the receipt of custom, and said unto him, Follow me. And he arose and followed him.

15 And it came to pass, that, as Jesus sat at meat in his house, many publicans and sinners sat also together with Jesus and his disciples: for there were many, and they followed him.

16 And when the scribes and Pharisees saw him eat with publicans and sinners, they said unto his disciples, How is it that he eateth and drinketh with publicans and sinners?

17 When Jesus heard *it*, he saith unto them, They that are whole have no need of the physician, but they that are sick: I came not to call the righteous, but sinners to repentance.

18 ¶ And the disciples of John and of the Pharisees used

NEW AMERICAN STANDARD BIBLE

12 And he got up and immediately picked up the pallet and went out in the sight of everyone, so that they were all amazed and were glorifying God, saying, "We have never seen anything like this."

13 And He went out again by the seashore; and all the people were coming to Him, and He was teaching them.

Levi (Matthew) Called

14 As He passed by, He saw Levi the *son* of Alphaeus sitting in the tax booth, and He *said to him, "Follow Me!" And he got up and followed Him.

15 And it *happened that He was reclining *at the table* in his house, and many tax collectors and sinners were dining with Jesus and His disciples; for there were many of them, and they were following Him.

16 When the scribes of the Pharisees saw that He was eating with the sinners and tax collectors, they said to His disciples, "Why is He eating and drinking with tax collectors and sinners?"

17 And hearing *this*, Jesus *said to them, "*It is* not those who are healthy who need a physician, but those who are sick; I did not come to call the righteous, but sinners."

18 John's disciples and the Pharisees were fasting; and

NEW CENTURY VERSION

stood up, took his mat, and walked out while everyone was watching him.

The people were amazed and praised God. They said, "We have never seen anything like this!"

[13]Jesus went to the lake again. The whole crowd followed him there, and he taught them. [14]While he was walking along, he saw a man named Levi son of Alphaeus, sitting in the tax collector's booth. Jesus said to him, "Follow me," and he stood up and followed Jesus.

[15]Later, as Jesus was having dinner at Levi's house, many tax collectors and "sinners" were eating there with Jesus and his followers. Many people like this followed Jesus. [16]When the teachers of the law who were Pharisees saw Jesus eating with the tax collectors and "sinners," they asked his followers, "Why does he eat with tax collectors and sinners?"

[17]Jesus heard this and said to them, "It is not the healthy people who need a doctor, but the sick. I did not come to invite good people but to invite sinners."

Jesus' Followers Are Criticized

[18]Now the followers of John[a] and the Pharisees often

2:18 [a] **John** John the Baptist, who preached to the Jewish people about Christ's coming (Mark 1:4–8).

CONTEMPORARY ENGLISH VERSION

[12]The man got right up. He picked up his mat and went out while everyone watched in amazement. They praised God and said, "We have never seen anything like this!"

Jesus Chooses Levi (Matthew 9.9-13; Luke 5.27-32)

[13]Once again, Jesus went to the shore of Lake Galilee. A large crowd gathered around him, and he taught them. [14]As he walked along, he saw Levi, the son of Alphaeus. Levi was sitting at the place for paying taxes, and Jesus said to him, "Come with me!" So he got up and went with Jesus.

[15]Later, Jesus and his disciples were having dinner at Levi's house.[c] Many tax collectors[d] and other sinners had become followers of Jesus, and they were also guests at the dinner.

[16]Some of the teachers of the Law of Moses were Pharisees, and they saw that Jesus was eating with sinners and tax collectors. So they asked his disciples, "Why does he eat with tax collectors and sinners?"

[17]Jesus heard them and answered, "Healthy people don't need a doctor, but sick people do. I didn't come to invite good people to be my followers. I came to invite sinners."

People Ask about Going without Eating
(Matthew 9.14-17; Luke 5.33-39)

[18]The followers of John the Baptist and the Pharisees often

[c] **2.15** *Levi's house*: Or "Jesus' house." [d] **2.15** *tax collectors*: These were usually Jewish people who paid the Romans for the right to collect taxes. They were hated by other Jews who thought of them as traitors to their country and to their religion.

NEW INTERNATIONAL VERSION

walked out in full view of them all. This amazed everyone and they praised God, saying, "We have never seen anything like this!"

The Calling of Levi

13Once again Jesus went out beside the lake. A large crowd came to him, and he began to teach them. 14As he walked along, he saw Levi son of Alphaeus sitting at the tax collector's booth. "Follow me," Jesus told him, and Levi got up and followed him.

15While Jesus was having dinner at Levi's house, many tax collectors and "sinners" were eating with him and his disciples, for there were many who followed him. 16When the teachers of the law who were Pharisees saw him eating with the "sinners" and tax collectors, they asked his disciples: "Why does he eat with tax collectors and 'sinners'?"

17On hearing this, Jesus said to them, "It is not the healthy who need a doctor, but the sick. I have not come to call the righteous, but sinners."

Jesus Questioned About Fasting

18Now John's disciples and the Pharisees were fasting.

NEW LIVING TRANSLATION

12The man jumped up, took the mat, and pushed his way through the stunned onlookers. Then they all praised God. "We've never seen anything like this before!" they exclaimed.

Jesus Calls Levi (Matthew)

13Then Jesus went out to the lakeshore again and taught the crowds that gathered around him. 14As he walked along, he saw Levi son of Alphaeus sitting at his tax-collection booth. "Come, be my disciple," Jesus said to him. So Levi got up and followed him.

15That night Levi invited Jesus and his disciples to be his dinner guests, along with his fellow tax collectors and many other notorious sinners. (There were many people of this kind among the crowds that followed Jesus.) 16But when some of the teachers of religious law who were Pharisees* saw him eating with people like that, they said to his disciples, "Why does he eat with such scum*?"

17When Jesus heard this, he told them, "Healthy people don't need a doctor—sick people do. I have come to call sinners, not those who think they are already good enough."

A Discussion about Fasting

18John's disciples and the Pharisees sometimes fasted.

2:16a Greek *the scribes of the Pharisees.* **2:16b** Greek *with tax collectors and sinners.*

NEW KING JAMES VERSION

house." 12Immediately he arose, took up the bed, and went out in the presence of them all, so that all were amazed and glorified God, saying, "We never saw *anything* like this!"

Matthew the Tax Collector

13Then He went out again by the sea; and all the multitude came to Him, and He taught them. 14As He passed by, He saw Levi the *son* of Alphaeus sitting at the tax office. And He said to him, "Follow Me." So he arose and followed Him.

15Now it happened, as He was dining in *Levi's* house, that many tax collectors and sinners also sat together with Jesus and His disciples; for there were many, and they followed Him. 16And when the scribes and[b] Pharisees saw Him eating with the tax collectors and sinners, they said to His disciples, "How *is it* that He eats and drinks with tax collectors and sinners?"

17When Jesus heard *it,* He said to them, "Those who are well have no need of a physician, but those who are sick. I did not come to call *the* righteous, but sinners, to repentance."[c]

Jesus Is Questioned About Fasting

18The disciples of John and of the Pharisees were fasting.

2:16 [b] NU-Text reads *of the.* **2:17** [c] NU-Text omits *to repentance.*

THE MESSAGE

up, grabbed his stretcher, and walked out, with everyone there watching him. They rubbed their eyes, incredulous—and then praised God, saying, "We've never seen anything like this!"

The Tax Collector

Then Jesus went again to walk alongside the lake. Again a crowd came to him, and he taught them. Strolling along, he saw Levi, son of Alphaeus, at his work collecting taxes. Jesus said, "Come along with me." He came.

Later Jesus and his disciples were at home having supper with a collection of disreputable guests. Unlikely as it seems, more than a few of them had become followers. The religion scholars and Pharisees saw him keeping this kind of company and lit into his disciples: "What kind of example is this, acting cozy with the riffraff?"

Jesus, overhearing, shot back, "Who needs a doctor: the healthy or the sick? I'm here inviting the sin-sick, not the spiritually-fit."

Feasting or Fasting?

The disciples of John and the disciples of the Pharisees

KING JAMES VERSION

to fast: and they come and say unto him, Why do the disciples of John and of the Pharisees fast, but thy disciples fast not?

19 And Jesus said unto them, Can the children of the bridechamber fast, while the bridegroom is with them? as long as they have the bridegroom with them, they cannot fast.

20 But the days will come, when the bridegroom shall be taken away from them, and then shall they fast in those days.

21 No man also seweth a piece of new cloth on an old garment: else the new piece that filled it up taketh away from the old, and the rent is made worse.

22 And no man putteth new wine into old bottles: else the new wine doth burst the bottles, and the wine is spilled, and the bottles will be marred: but new wine must be put into new bottles.

23 And it came to pass, that he went through the corn fields on the sabbath day; and his disciples began, as they went, to pluck the ears of corn.

24 And the Pharisees said unto him, Behold, why do they on the sabbath day that which is not lawful?

25 And he said unto them, Have ye never read what David did, when he had need, and was an hungred, he, and they that were with him?

NEW AMERICAN STANDARD BIBLE

they *came and *said to Him, "Why do John's disciples and the disciples of the Pharisees fast, but Your disciples do not fast?"

19 And Jesus said to them, "While the bridegroom is with them, the attendants of the bridegroom cannot fast, can they? So long as they have the bridegroom with them, they cannot fast.

20 "But the days will come when the bridegroom is taken away from them, and then they will fast in that day.

21 "No one sews a patch of unshrunk cloth on an old garment; otherwise the patch pulls away from it, the new from the old, and a worse tear results.

22 "No one puts new wine into old wineskins; otherwise the wine will burst the skins, and the wine is lost and the skins *as well;* but *one puts* new wine into fresh wineskins."

Question of the Sabbath

23 And it happened that He was passing through the grainfields on the Sabbath, and His disciples began to make their way along while picking the heads *of grain.*

24 The Pharisees were saying to Him, "Look, why are they doing what is not lawful on the Sabbath?"

25 And He *said to them, "Have you never read what David did when he was in need and he and his companions became hungry;

NEW CENTURY VERSION

gave up eating for a certain time.[b] Some people came to
Jesus and said, "Why do John's followers and the followers
of the Pharisees often give up eating, but your followers
don't?"
19Jesus answered, "The friends of the bridegroom do not
give up eating while the bridegroom is still with them. As
long as the bridegroom is with them, they cannot give up
eating. 20But the time will come when the bridegroom will
be taken from them, and then they will give up eating.
21"No one sews a patch of unshrunk cloth over a hole in
an old coat. Otherwise, the patch will shrink and pull
away—the new patch will pull away from the old coat.
Then the hole will be worse. 22Also, no one ever pours new
wine into old leather bags. Otherwise, the new wine will
break the bags, and the wine will be ruined along with the
bags. But new wine should be put into new leather bags."

Jesus Is Lord of the Sabbath

23One Sabbath day, as Jesus was walking through some
fields of grain, his followers began to pick some grain to
eat. 24The Pharisees said to Jesus, "Why are your followers
doing what is not lawful on the Sabbath day?"
25Jesus answered, "Have you never read what David did
when he and those with him were hungry and needed

2:18 [b] **gave...time** This is called "fasting." The people would give up eating for a special time of prayer and worship to God. It was also done to show sadness and disappointment.

CONTEMPORARY ENGLISH VERSION

went without eating.[e] Some people came and asked Jesus,
"Why do the followers of John and those of the Pharisees
often go without eating, while your disciples never do?"
19Jesus answered:
The friends of a bridegroom don't go without eating
while he is still with them. 20But the time will come
when he will be taken from them. Then they will go
without eating.
21No one patches old clothes by sewing on a piece of new
cloth. The new piece would shrink and tear a bigger hole.
22No one pours new wine into old wineskins. The
wine would swell and burst the old skins.[f] Then the
wine would be lost, and the skins would be ruined. New
wine must be put into new wineskins.

A Question about the Sabbath (Matthew 12.1-8; Luke 6.1-5)

23One Sabbath Jesus and his disciples were walking
through some wheat fields. His disciples were picking
grains of wheat as they went along.[g] 24Some Pharisees
asked Jesus, "Why are your disciples picking grain on the
Sabbath? They are not supposed to do that!"
25Jesus answered, "Haven't you read what David did
when he and his followers were hungry and in need? 26It

[e] 2.18 *without eating*: The Jewish people sometimes went without eating (also called "fasting") to show their love for God or to show sorrow for their sins. [f] 2.22 *swell and burst the old skins*: While the juice from grapes was becoming wine, it would swell and stretch the skins in which it had been stored. If the skins were old and stiff, they would burst.
[g] 2.23 *went along*: It was the custom to let hungry travelers pick grains of wheat.

NEW INTERNATIONAL VERSION

Some people came and asked Jesus, "How is it that John's disciples and the disciples of the Pharisees are fasting, but yours are not?"

19Jesus answered, "How can the guests of the bridegroom fast while he is with them? They cannot, so long as they have him with them. 20But the time will come when the bridegroom will be taken from them, and on that day they will fast.

21"No one sews a patch of unshrunk cloth on an old garment. If he does, the new piece will pull away from the old, making the tear worse. 22And no one pours new wine into old wineskins. If he does, the wine will burst the skins, and both the wine and the wineskins will be ruined. No, he pours new wine into new wineskins."

Lord of the Sabbath

23One Sabbath Jesus was going through the grainfields, and as his disciples walked along, they began to pick some heads of grain. 24The Pharisees said to him, "Look, why are they doing what is unlawful on the Sabbath?"

25He answered, "Have you never read what David did when he and his companions were hungry and in need?

NEW LIVING TRANSLATION

One day some people came to Jesus and asked, "Why do John's disciples and the Pharisees fast, but your disciples don't fast?"

19Jesus replied, "Do wedding guests fast while celebrating with the groom? Of course not. They can't fast while they are with the groom. 20But someday he will be taken away from them, and then they will fast. 21And who would patch an old garment with unshrunk cloth? For the new patch shrinks and pulls away from the old cloth, leaving an even bigger hole than before. 22And no one puts new wine into old wineskins. The wine would burst the wineskins, spilling the wine and ruining the skins. New wine needs new wineskins."

A Discussion about the Sabbath

23One Sabbath day as Jesus was walking through some grainfields, his disciples began breaking off heads of wheat. 24But the Pharisees said to Jesus, "They shouldn't be doing that! It's against the law to work by harvesting grain on the Sabbath."

25But Jesus replied, "Haven't you ever read in the Scriptures what King David did when he and his companions

NEW KING JAMES VERSION

Then they came and said to Him, "Why do the disciples of John and of the Pharisees fast, but Your disciples do not fast?"

19And Jesus said to them, "Can the friends of the bridegroom fast while the bridegroom is with them? As long as they have the bridegroom with them they cannot fast. 20But the days will come when the bridegroom will be taken away from them, and then they will fast in those days. 21No one sews a piece of unshrunk cloth on an old garment; or else the new piece pulls away from the old, and the tear is made worse. 22And no one puts new wine into old wineskins; or else the new wine bursts the wineskins, the wine is spilled, and the wineskins are ruined. But new wine must be put into new wineskins."

Jesus Is Lord of the Sabbath

23Now it happened that He went through the grainfields on the Sabbath; and as they went His disciples began to pluck the heads of grain. 24And the Pharisees said to Him, "Look, why do they do what is not lawful on the Sabbath?"

25But He said to them, "Have you never read what David did when he was in need and hungry, he and those with

THE MESSAGE

made a practice of fasting. Some people confronted Jesus: "Why do the followers of John and the Pharisees take on the discipline of fasting, but your followers don't?"

Jesus said, "When you're celebrating a wedding, you don't skimp on the cake and wine. You feast. Later you may need to pull in your belt, but not now. As long as the bride and groom are with you, you have a good time. No one throws cold water on a friendly bonfire. This is Kingdom Come!"

He went on, "No one cuts up a fine silk scarf to patch old work clothes; you want fabrics that match. And you don't put your wine in cracked bottles."

One Sabbath day he was walking through a field of ripe grain. As his disciples made a path, they pulled off heads of grain. The Pharisees told on them to Jesus: "Look, your disciples are breaking Sabbath rules!"

Jesus said, "Really? Haven't you ever read what David did when he was hungry, along with those who were with

KING JAMES VERSION

26 How he went into the house of God in the days of
Abiathar the high priest, and did eat the shewbread, which
is not lawful to eat but for the priests, and gave also to
them which were with him?
27 And he said unto them, The sabbath was made for
man, and not man for the sabbath:
28 Therefore the Son of man is Lord also of the sab-
bath.
3 And he entered again into the synagogue; and there
was a man there which had a withered hand.
2 And they watched him, whether he would heal him on
the sabbath day; that they might accuse him.
3 And he saith unto the man which had the withered
hand, Stand forth.
4 And he saith unto them, Is it lawful to do good on the
sabbath days, or to do evil? to save life, or to kill? But they
held their peace.
5 And when he had looked round about on them with
anger, being grieved for the hardness of their hearts, he
saith unto the man, Stretch forth thine hand. And he
stretched *it* out: and his hand was restored whole as the
other.
6 And the Pharisees went forth, and straightway took
counsel with the Herodians against him, how they might
destroy him.

NEW AMERICAN STANDARD BIBLE

26 how he entered the house of God in the time of
Abiathar *the* high priest, and ate the consecrated bread,
which is not lawful for *anyone* to eat except the priests,
and he also gave it to those who were with him?"
27 Jesus said to them, "The Sabbath was made for man,
and not man for the Sabbath.
28 "So the Son of Man is Lord even of the Sabbath."

Jesus Heals on the Sabbath

3 He entered again into a synagogue; and a man was
there whose hand was withered.
2 They were watching Him *to see* if He would heal him
on the Sabbath, so that they might accuse Him.
3 He *said to the man with the withered hand, "Get up
and come forward!"
4 And He *said to them, "Is it lawful to do good or to
do harm on the Sabbath, to save a life or to kill?" But they
kept silent.
5 After looking around at them with anger, grieved at
their hardness of heart, He *said to the man, "Stretch out
your hand." And he stretched it out, and his hand was
restored.
6 The Pharisees went out and immediately *began* con-
spiring with the Herodians against Him, *as to* how they
might destroy Him.

NEW CENTURY VERSION

food? 26 During the time of Abiathar the high priest, David
went into God's house and ate the holy bread, which is
lawful only for priests to eat. And David also gave some of
the bread to those who were with him."
27 Then Jesus said to the Pharisees, "The Sabbath day
was made to help people; they were not made to be ruled
by the Sabbath day. 28 So then, the Son of Man is Lord
even of the Sabbath day."

Jesus Heals a Man's Hand

3 Another time when Jesus went into a synagogue, a
man with a crippled hand was there. 2 Some people
watched Jesus closely to see if he would heal the man on
the Sabbath day so they could accuse him.
3 Jesus said to the man with the crippled hand, "Stand up
here in the middle of everyone."
4 Then Jesus asked the people, "Which is lawful on the
Sabbath day: to do good or to do evil, to save a life or to
kill?" But they said nothing to answer him.
5 Jesus was angry as he looked at the people, and he felt
very sad because they were stubborn. Then he said to the
man, "Hold out your hand." The man held out his hand
and it was healed. 6 Then the Pharisees left and began
making plans with the Herodians[a] about a way to kill
Jesus.

3:6 [a] **Herodians** A political group that followed Herod and his family.

CONTEMPORARY ENGLISH VERSION

was during the time of Abiathar the high priest. David
went into the house of God and ate the sacred loaves of
bread that only priests are allowed to eat. He also gave
some to his followers."
27 Jesus finished by saying, "People were not made for
the good of the Sabbath. The Sabbath was made for the
good of people. 28 So the Son of Man is Lord over the
Sabbath."

A Man with a Crippled Hand (Matthew 12.9-14; Luke 6.6-11)

3 The next time that Jesus went into the meeting place,
a man with a crippled hand was there. 2 The Phari-
sees[a] wanted to accuse Jesus of doing something wrong,
and they kept watching to see if Jesus would heal him on
the Sabbath.
3 Jesus told the man to stand up where everyone could
see him. 4 Then he asked, "On the Sabbath should we do
good deeds or evil deeds? Should we save someone's life or
destroy it?" But no one said a word.
5 Jesus was angry as he looked around at the people. Yet
he felt sorry for them because they were so stubborn. Then
he told the man, "Stretch out your hand." He did, and his
bad hand was healed.
6 The Pharisees left. And right away they started making
plans with Herod's followers[b] to kill Jesus.

[a] **3.2** *Pharisees*: The Greek text has "they" (but see verse 6).
[b] **3.6** *Herod's followers*: People who were political followers of the family
of Herod the Great and his son Herod Antipas.

NEW INTERNATIONAL VERSION

26 In the days of Abiathar the high priest, he entered the house of God and ate the consecrated bread, which is lawful only for priests to eat. And he also gave some to his companions."

27 Then he said to them, "The Sabbath was made for man, not man for the Sabbath. 28 So the Son of Man is Lord even of the Sabbath."

3 Another time he went into the synagogue, and a man with a shriveled hand was there. 2 Some of them were looking for a reason to accuse Jesus, so they watched him closely to see if he would heal him on the Sabbath. 3 Jesus said to the man with the shriveled hand, "Stand up in front of everyone."

4 Then Jesus asked them, "Which is lawful on the Sabbath: to do good or to do evil, to save life or to kill?" But they remained silent.

5 He looked around at them in anger and, deeply distressed at their stubborn hearts, said to the man, "Stretch out your hand." He stretched it out, and his hand was completely restored. 6 Then the Pharisees went out and began to plot with the Herodians how they might kill Jesus.

NEW LIVING TRANSLATION

were hungry? 26 He went into the house of God (during the days when Abiathar was high priest), ate the special bread reserved for the priests alone, and then gave some to his companions. That was breaking the law, too." 27 Then he said to them, "The Sabbath was made to benefit people, and not people to benefit the Sabbath. 28 And I, the Son of Man, am master even of the Sabbath!"

Jesus Heals on the Sabbath

3 Jesus went into the synagogue again and noticed a man with a deformed hand. 2 Since it was the Sabbath, Jesus' enemies watched him closely. Would he heal the man's hand on the Sabbath? If he did, they planned to condemn him. 3 Jesus said to the man, "Come and stand in front of everyone." 4 Then he turned to his critics and asked, "Is it legal to do good deeds on the Sabbath, or is it a day for doing harm? Is this a day to save life or to destroy it?" But they wouldn't answer him. 5 He looked around at them angrily, because he was deeply disturbed by their hard hearts. Then he said to the man, "Reach out your hand." The man reached out his hand, and it became normal again! 6 At once the Pharisees went away and met with the supporters of Herod to discuss plans for killing Jesus.

NEW KING JAMES VERSION

him: 26 how he went into the house of God *in the days* of Abiathar the high priest, and ate the showbread, which is not lawful to eat except for the priests, and also gave some to those who were with him?"

27 And He said to them, "The Sabbath was made for man, and not man for the Sabbath. 28 Therefore the Son of Man is also Lord of the Sabbath."

Healing on the Sabbath

3 And He entered the synagogue again, and a man was there who had a withered hand. 2 So they watched Him closely, whether He would heal him on the Sabbath, so that they might accuse Him. 3 And He said to the man who had the withered hand, "Step forward." 4 Then He said to them, "Is it lawful on the Sabbath to do good or to do evil, to save life or to kill?" But they kept silent. 5 And when He had looked around at them with anger, being grieved by the hardness of their hearts, He said to the man, "Stretch out your hand." And he stretched *it* out, and his hand was restored as whole as the other.[a] 6 Then the Pharisees went out and immediately plotted with the Herodians against Him, how they might destroy Him.

3:5 [a] NU-Text omits *as whole as the other.*

THE MESSAGE

him? How he entered the sanctuary and ate fresh bread off the altar, with the Chief Priest Abiathar right there watching—holy bread that no one but priests were allowed to eat—and handed it out to his companions?" Then Jesus said, "The Sabbath was made to serve us; we weren't made to serve the Sabbath. The Son of Man is no lackey to the Sabbath. He's in charge!"

Doing Good on the Sabbath

3 Then he went back in the meeting place where he found a man with a crippled hand. The Pharisees had their eyes on Jesus to see if he would heal him, hoping to catch him in a Sabbath infraction. He said to the man with the crippled hand, "Stand here where we can see you."

Then he spoke to the people: "What kind of action suits the Sabbath best? Doing good or doing evil? Helping people or leaving them helpless?" No one said a word.

He looked them in the eye, one after another, angry now, furious at their hard-nosed religion. He said to the man, "Hold out your hand." He held it out—it was as good as new! The Pharisees got out as fast as they could, sputtering about how they would join forces with Herod's followers and ruin him.

KING JAMES VERSION

7 But Jesus withdrew himself with his disciples to the sea: and a great multitude from Galilee followed him, and from Judaea,

8 And from Jerusalem, and from Idumaea, and *from* beyond Jordan; and they about Tyre and Sidon, a great multitude, when they had heard what great things he did, came unto him.

9 And he spake to his disciples, that a small ship should wait on him because of the multitude, lest they should throng him.

10 For he had healed many; insomuch that they pressed upon him for to touch him, as many as had plagues.

11 And unclean spirits, when they saw him, fell down before him, and cried, saying, Thou art the Son of God.

12 And he straitly charged them that they should not make him known.

13 ¶ And he goeth up into a mountain, and calleth *unto him* whom he would: and they came unto him.

14 And he ordained twelve, that they should be with him, and that he might send them forth to preach,

15 And to have power to heal sicknesses, and to cast out devils:

16 And Simon he surnamed Peter;

17 And James the *son* of Zebedee, and John the brother of James; and he surnamed them Boanerges, which is, The sons of thunder:

NEW AMERICAN STANDARD BIBLE

7 Jesus withdrew to the sea with His disciples; and a great multitude from Galilee followed; and *also* from Judea,

8 and from Jerusalem, and from Idumea, and beyond the Jordan, and the vicinity of Tyre and Sidon, a great number of people heard of all that He was doing and came to Him.

9 And He told His disciples that a boat should stand ready for Him because of the crowd, so that they would not crowd Him;

10 for He had healed many, with the result that all those who had afflictions pressed around Him in order to touch Him.

11 Whenever the unclean spirits saw Him, they would fall down before Him and shout, "You are the Son of God!"

12 And He earnestly warned them not to tell who He was.

The Twelve Are Chosen

13 And He *went up on the mountain and *summoned those whom He Himself wanted, and they came to Him.

14 And He appointed twelve, so that they would be with Him and that He *could* send them out to preach,

15 and to have authority to cast out the demons.

16 And He appointed the twelve: Simon (to whom He gave the name Peter),

17 and James, the *son* of Zebedee, and John the brother of James (to them He gave the name Boanerges, which means, "Sons of Thunder");

NEW CENTURY VERSION

Many People Follow Jesus

[7]Jesus left with his followers for the lake, and a large
crowd from Galilee followed him. [8]Also many people came
from Judea, from Jerusalem, from Idumea, from the lands
across the Jordan River, and from the area of Tyre and
Sidon. When they heard what Jesus was doing, many peo-
ple came to him. [9]When Jesus saw the crowds, he told his
followers to get a boat ready for him to keep people from
crowding against him. [10]He had healed many people, so all
the sick were pushing toward him to touch him. [11]When
evil spirits saw Jesus, they fell down before him and shout-
ed, "You are the Son of God!" [12]But Jesus strongly warned
them not to tell who he was.

Jesus Chooses His Twelve Apostles

[13]Then Jesus went up on a mountain and called to him
the men he wanted, and they came to him. [14]Jesus chose
twelve men and called them apostles. He wanted them to
be with him, and he wanted to send them out to preach
[15]and to have the authority to force demons out of people.
[16]These are the twelve men he chose: Simon (Jesus named
him Peter), [17]James and John, the sons of Zebedee (Jesus
named them Boanerges, which means "Sons of Thunder"),

CONTEMPORARY ENGLISH VERSION

Large Crowds Come to Jesus

[7]Jesus led his disciples down to the shore of the lake.
Large crowds followed him from Galilee, Judea, [8]and
Jerusalem. People came from Idumea, as well as other
places east of the Jordan River. They also came from the
region around the cities of Tyre and Sidon. All of these
crowds came because they had heard what Jesus was
doing. [9]He even had to tell his disciples to get a boat ready
to keep him from being crushed by the crowds.
[10]After Jesus had healed many people, the other sick
people begged him to let them touch him. [11]And whenever
any evil spirits saw Jesus, they would fall to the ground
and shout, "You are the Son of God!" [12]But Jesus warned
the spirits not to tell who he was.

Jesus Chooses His Twelve Apostles

(Matthew 10.1-4; Luke 6.12-16)

[13]Jesus decided to ask some of his disciples to go up on
a mountain with him, and they went. [14]Then he chose
twelve of them to be his apostles,[c] so that they could be
with him. He also wanted to send them out to preach
[15]and to force out demons. [16]Simon was one of the twelve,
and Jesus named him Peter. [17]There were also James and
John, the two sons of Zebedee. Jesus called them
Boanerges, which means "Thunderbolts." [18]Andrew,

[c] **3.14** *to be his apostles*: These words are not in some manuscripts.

NEW INTERNATIONAL VERSION

Crowds Follow Jesus

[7]Jesus withdrew with his disciples to the lake, and a large crowd from Galilee followed. [8]When they heard all he was doing, many people came to him from Judea, Jerusalem, Idumea, and the regions across the Jordan and around Tyre and Sidon. [9]Because of the crowd he told his disciples to have a small boat ready for him, to keep the people from crowding him. [10]For he had healed many, so that those with diseases were pushing forward to touch him. [11]Whenever the evil[a] spirits saw him, they fell down before him and cried out, "You are the Son of God." [12]But he gave them strict orders not to tell who he was.

The Appointing of the Twelve Apostles

[13]Jesus went up on a mountainside and called to him those he wanted, and they came to him. [14]He appointed twelve—designating them apostles[b]—that they might be with him and that he might send them out to preach [15]and to have authority to drive out demons. [16]These are the twelve he appointed: Simon (to whom he gave the name Peter); [17]James son of Zebedee and his brother John (to them he gave the name Boanerges, which means Sons of

[a] *11* Greek *unclean*; also in verse 30 [b] *14* Some manuscripts do not have *designating them apostles.*

NEW LIVING TRANSLATION

Crowds Follow Jesus

[7]Jesus and his disciples went out to the lake, followed by a huge crowd from all over Galilee, Judea, [8]Jerusalem, Idumea, from east of the Jordan River, and even from as far away as Tyre and Sidon. The news about his miracles had spread far and wide, and vast numbers of people came to see him for themselves.

[9]Jesus instructed his disciples to bring around a boat and to have it ready in case he was crowded off the beach. [10]There had been many healings that day. As a result, many sick people were crowding around him, trying to touch him. [11]And whenever those possessed by evil spirits caught sight of him, they would fall down in front of him shrieking, "You are the Son of God!" [12]But Jesus strictly warned them not to say who he was.

Jesus Chooses the Twelve Apostles

[13]Afterward Jesus went up on a mountain and called the ones he wanted to go with him. And they came to him. [14]Then he selected twelve of them to be his regular companions, calling them apostles.* He sent them out to preach, [15]and he gave them authority to cast out demons. [16]These are the names of the twelve he chose:

Simon (he renamed him Peter),
[17] James and John (the sons of Zebedee, but Jesus
nicknamed them "Sons of Thunder"*),

3:14 Some manuscripts do not include *calling them apostles.*
3:17 Greek *whom he named Boanerges, which means Sons of Thunder.*

NEW KING JAMES VERSION

A Great Multitude Follows Jesus

[7]But Jesus withdrew with His disciples to the sea. And a great multitude from Galilee followed Him, and from Judea [8]and Jerusalem and Idumea and beyond the Jordan; and those from Tyre and Sidon, a great multitude, when they heard how many things He was doing, came to Him. [9]So He told His disciples that a small boat should be kept ready for Him because of the multitude, lest they should crush Him. [10]For He healed many, so that as many as had afflictions pressed about Him to touch Him. [11]And the unclean spirits, whenever they saw Him, fell down before Him and cried out, saying, "You are the Son of God." [12]But He sternly warned them that they should not make Him known.

The Twelve Apostles

[13]And He went up on the mountain and called to *Him* those He Himself wanted. And they came to Him. [14]Then He appointed twelve,[b] that they might be with Him and that He might send them out to preach, [15]and to have power to heal sicknesses and[c] to cast out demons: [16]Simon,[d] to whom He gave the name Peter; [17]James the *son* of Zebedee and John the brother of James, to whom He gave the name Boanerges, that is, "Sons of Thunder";

3:14 [b] NU-Text adds *whom He also named apostles.* 3:15 [c] NU-Text omits *to heal sicknesses and.* 3:16 [d] NU-Text reads *and He appointed the twelve: Simon . . .*

THE MESSAGE

The Twelve Apostles

Jesus went off with his disciples to the sea to get away. But a huge crowd from Galilee trailed after them—also from Judea, Jerusalem, Idumea, across the Jordan, and around Tyre and Sidon—swarms of people who had heard the reports and had come to see for themselves. He told his disciples to get a boat ready so he wouldn't be trampled by the crowd. He had healed many people, and now everyone who had something wrong was pushing and shoving to get near and touch him.

Evil spirits, when they recognized him, fell down and cried out, "You are the Son of God!" But Jesus would have none of it. He shut them up, forbidding them to identify him in public.

He climbed a mountain and invited those he wanted with him. They climbed together. He settled on twelve, and designated them apostles. The plan was that they would be with him, and he would send them out to proclaim the Word and give them authority to banish demons. These are the Twelve:

Simon (Jesus later named him Peter, meaning "Rock"),
James, son of Zebedee,
John, brother of James (Jesus nicknamed the Zebedee
brothers Boanerges, meaning "Sons of Thunder"),

KING JAMES VERSION

18 And Andrew, and Philip, and Bartholomew, and Matthew, and Thomas, and James the *son* of Alphaeus, and Thaddaeus, and Simon the Canaanite,

19 And Judas Iscariot, which also betrayed him: and they went into an house.

20 And the multitude cometh together again, so that they could not so much as eat bread.

21 And when his friends heard *of it*, they went out to lay hold on him: for they said, He is beside himself.

22 ¶ And the scribes which came down from Jerusalem said, He hath Beelzebub, and by the prince of the devils casteth he out devils.

23 And he called them *unto him*, and said unto them in parables, How can Satan cast out Satan?

24 And if a kingdom be divided against itself, that kingdom cannot stand.

25 And if a house be divided against itself, that house cannot stand.

26 And if Satan rise up against himself, and be divided, he cannot stand, but hath an end.

27 No man can enter into a strong man's house, and

NEW AMERICAN STANDARD BIBLE

18 and Andrew, and Philip, and Bartholomew, and Matthew, and Thomas, and James the son of Alphaeus, and Thaddaeus, and Simon the Zealot;

19 and Judas Iscariot, who betrayed Him.

20 And He *came [1]home, and the crowd *gathered again, to such an extent that they could not even eat a meal.

21 When His own [2]people heard *of this,* they went out to take custody of Him; for they were saying, "He has lost His senses."

22 The scribes who came down from Jerusalem were saying, "He is possessed by Beelzebul," and "He casts out the demons by the ruler of the demons."

23 And He called them to Himself and began speaking to them in parables, "How can Satan cast out Satan?

24 "If a kingdom is divided against itself, that kingdom cannot stand.

25 "If a house is divided against itself, that house will not be able to stand.

26 "If Satan has risen up against himself and is divided, he cannot stand, but he is finished!

27 "But no one can enter the strong man's house and

3:20 [1] Lit *into a house* 3:21 [2] Or *kinsmen*

NEW CENTURY VERSION

18Andrew, Philip, Bartholomew, Matthew, Thomas, James
the son of Alphaeus, Thaddaeus, Simon the Zealot, 19and
Judas Iscariot, who later turned against Jesus.

Some People Say Jesus Has a Devil

20Then Jesus went home, but again a crowd gathered.
There were so many people that Jesus and his followers
could not eat. 21When his family heard this, they went to
get him because they thought he was out of his mind.
22But the teachers of the law from Jerusalem were saying,
"Beelzebul is living inside him! He uses power from the
ruler of demons to force demons out of people."
23So Jesus called the people together and taught them
with stories. He said, "Satan will not force himself out of
people. 24A kingdom that is divided cannot continue, 25and
a family that is divided cannot continue. 26And if Satan is
against himself and fights against his own people, he can-
not continue; that is the end of Satan. 27No one can enter
a strong person's house and steal his things unless he first

CONTEMPORARY ENGLISH VERSION

Philip, Bartholomew, Matthew, Thomas, James son of
Alphaeus, and Thaddaeus were also apostles. The others
were Simon, known as the Eager One,[d] 19and Judas
Iscariot,[e] who later betrayed Jesus.

Jesus and the Ruler of Demons

(Matthew 12.22-32; Luke 11.14-23; 12.10)

20Jesus went back home,[f] and once again such a large
crowd gathered that there was no chance even to eat.
21When Jesus' family heard what he was doing, they
thought he was crazy and went to get him under control.
22Some teachers of the Law of Moses came from
Jerusalem and said, "This man is under the power of
Beelzebul, the ruler of demons! He is even forcing out
demons with the help of Beelzebul."
23Jesus told the people to gather around him. Then he
spoke to them in riddles and said:

How can Satan force himself out? 24A nation whose
people fight each other won't last very long. 25And a
family that fights won't last long either. 26So if Satan
fights against himself, that will be the end of him.
27How can anyone break into the house of a strong

[d] **3.18** *known as the Eager One*: The Greek text has "Cananaean," which probably comes from a Hebrew word meaning "zealous" (see Luke 6.15). "Zealot" was the name later given to the members of a Jewish group that resisted and fought against the Romans. [e] **3.19** *Iscariot*: This may mean "a man from Kerioth" (a place in Judea). But more probably it means "a man who was a liar" or "a man who was a betrayer."
[f] **3.20** *went back home*: Or "entered a house" (perhaps the home of Simon Peter).

NEW INTERNATIONAL VERSION

Thunder); [18]Andrew, Philip, Bartholomew, Matthew, Thomas, James son of Alphaeus, Thaddaeus, Simon the Zealot [19]and Judas Iscariot, who betrayed him.

Jesus and Beelzebub

[20]Then Jesus entered a house, and again a crowd gathered, so that he and his disciples were not even able to eat. [21]When his family heard about this, they went to take charge of him, for they said, "He is out of his mind."

[22]And the teachers of the law who came down from Jerusalem said, "He is possessed by Beelzebub[c]! By the prince of demons he is driving out demons."

[23]So Jesus called them and spoke to them in parables: "How can Satan drive out Satan? [24]If a kingdom is divided against itself, that kingdom cannot stand. [25]If a house is divided against itself, that house cannot stand. [26]And if Satan opposes himself and is divided, he cannot stand; his end has come. [27]In fact, no one can enter a strong man's

c 22 Greek *Beezeboul* or *Beelzeboul*

NEW LIVING TRANSLATION

[18] Andrew,
Philip,
Bartholomew,
Matthew,
Thomas,
James (son of Alphaeus),
Thaddaeus,
Simon (the Zealot*),
[19] Judas Iscariot (who later betrayed him).

Jesus and the Prince of Demons

[20]When Jesus returned to the house where he was staying, the crowds began to gather again, and soon he and his disciples couldn't even find time to eat. [21]When his family heard what was happening, they tried to take him home with them. "He's out of his mind," they said.

[22]But the teachers of religious law who had arrived from Jerusalem said, "He's possessed by Satan,* the prince of demons. That's where he gets the power to cast out demons."

[23]Jesus called them over and said to them by way of illustration, "How can Satan cast out Satan? [24]A kingdom at war with itself will collapse. [25]A home divided against itself is doomed. [26]And if Satan is fighting against himself, how can he stand? He would never survive. [27]Let me illustrate this. You can't enter a strong man's house and rob

3:18 Greek *the Cananean.* 3:22 Greek *Beelzeboul.*

NEW KING JAMES VERSION

[18]Andrew, Philip, Bartholomew, Matthew, Thomas, James the *son* of Alphaeus, Thaddaeus, Simon the Cananite; [19]and Judas Iscariot, who also betrayed Him. And they went into a house.

A House Divided Cannot Stand

[20]Then the multitude came together again, so that they could not so much as eat bread. [21]But when His own people heard *about this,* they went out to lay hold of Him, for they said, "He is out of His mind."

[22]And the scribes who came down from Jerusalem said, "He has Beelzebub," and, "By the ruler of the demons He casts out demons."

[23]So He called them to *Himself* and said to them in parables: "How can Satan cast out Satan? [24]If a kingdom is divided against itself, that kingdom cannot stand. [25]And if a house is divided against itself, that house cannot stand. [26]And if Satan has risen up against himself, and is divided, he cannot stand, but has an end. [27]No one can enter a

THE MESSAGE

Andrew,
Philip,
Bartholomew,
Matthew,
Thomas,
James, son of Alphaeus,
Thaddaeus,
Simon the Canaanite,
Judas Iscariot (who betrayed him).

Satan Fighting Satan?

Jesus came home and, as usual, a crowd gathered—so many making demands on him that there wasn't even time to eat. His friends heard what was going on and went to rescue him, by force if necessary. They suspected he was getting carried away with himself.

The religion scholars from Jerusalem came down spreading rumors that he was working black magic, using devil tricks to impress them with spiritual power. Jesus confronted their slander with a story: "Does it make sense to send a devil to catch a devil, to use Satan to get rid of Satan? A constantly squabbling family disintegrates. If Satan were fighting Satan, there soon wouldn't be any Satan left. Do you think it's possible in broad daylight to enter the house of an awake, able-bodied man, and walk

KING JAMES VERSION

spoil his goods, except he will first bind the strong man; and then he will spoil his house.

28 Verily I say unto you, All sins shall be forgiven unto the sons of men, and blasphemies wherewith soever they shall blaspheme:

29 But he that shall blaspheme against the Holy Ghost hath never forgiveness, but is in danger of eternal damnation:

30 Because they said, He hath an unclean spirit.

31 ¶ There came then his brethren and his mother, and, standing without, sent unto him, calling him.

32 And the multitude sat about him, and they said unto him, Behold, thy mother and thy brethren without seek for thee.

33 And he answered them, saying, Who is my mother, or my brethren?

34 And he looked round about on them which sat about him, and said, Behold my mother and my brethren!

35 For whosoever shall do the will of God, the same is my brother, and my sister, and mother.

4 And he began again to teach by the sea side: and there was gathered unto him a great multitude, so that he entered into a ship, and sat in the sea; and the whole multitude was by the sea on the land.

2 And he taught them many things by parables, and said unto them in his doctrine,

NEW AMERICAN STANDARD BIBLE

plunder his property unless he first binds the strong man, and then he will plunder his house.

28 "Truly I say to you, all sins shall be forgiven the sons of men, and whatever blasphemies they utter;

29 but whoever blasphemes against the Holy Spirit never has forgiveness, but is guilty of an eternal sin"—

30 because they were saying, "He has an unclean spirit."

31 Then His mother and His brothers *arrived, and standing outside they sent *word* to Him and called Him.

32 A crowd was sitting around Him, and they *said to Him, "Behold, Your mother and Your brothers are outside looking for You."

33 Answering them, He *said, "Who are My mother and My brothers?"

34 Looking about at those who were sitting around Him, He *said, "Behold My mother and My brothers!

35 "For whoever does the will of God, he is My brother and sister and mother."

Parable of the Sower and Soils

4 He began to teach again by the sea. And such a very large crowd gathered to Him that He got into a boat in the sea and sat down; and the whole crowd was by the sea on the land.

2 And He was teaching them many things in parables, and was saying to them in His teaching,

NEW CENTURY VERSION

ties up the strong person. Then he can steal things from the house. 28I tell you the truth, all sins that people do and all the things people say against God can be forgiven. 29But anyone who speaks against the Holy Spirit will never be forgiven; he is guilty of a sin that continues forever."

30Jesus said this because the teachers of the law said that he had an evil spirit inside him.

Jesus' True Family

31Then Jesus' mother and brothers arrived. Standing outside, they sent someone in to tell him to come out. 32Many people were sitting around Jesus, and they said to him, "Your mother and brothers are waiting for you outside."

33Jesus asked, "Who are my mother and my brothers?" 34Then he looked at those sitting around him and said, "Here are my mother and my brothers! 35My true brother and sister and mother are those who do what God wants."

A Story About Planting Seed

4 Again Jesus began teaching by the lake. A great crowd gathered around him, so he sat down in a boat near the shore. All the people stayed on the shore close to the water. 2Jesus taught them many things, using stories. He

CONTEMPORARY ENGLISH VERSION

man and steal his things, unless he first ties up the strong man? Then he can take everything.

28I promise you that any of the sinful things you say or do can be forgiven, no matter how terrible those things are.

29But if you speak against the Holy Spirit, you can never be forgiven. That sin will be held against you forever.

30Jesus said this because the people were saying that he had an evil spirit in him.

Jesus' Mother and Brothers
(Matthew 12.46-50; Luke 8.19-21)

31Jesus' mother and brothers came and stood outside. Then they sent someone with a message for him to come out to them. 32The crowd that was sitting around Jesus told him, "Your mother and your brothers and sisters[g] are outside and want to see you."

33Jesus asked, "Who is my mother and who are my brothers?" 34Then he looked at the people sitting around him and said, "Here are my mother and my brothers. 35Anyone who obeys God is my brother or sister or mother."

A Story about a Farmer (Matthew 13.1-9; Luke 8.4-8)

4 The next time Jesus taught beside Lake Galilee, a big crowd gathered. It was so large that he had to sit in a boat out on the lake, while the people stood on the shore. 2He used stories to teach them many things, and this is part of what he taught:

[g] 3.32 *and sisters*: These words are not in some manuscripts.

NEW INTERNATIONAL VERSION

house and carry off his possessions unless he first ties up the strong man. Then he can rob his house. 28I tell you the truth, all the sins and blasphemies of men will be forgiven them. 29But whoever blasphemes against the Holy Spirit will never be forgiven; he is guilty of an eternal sin."

30He said this because they were saying, "He has an evil spirit."

Jesus' Mother and Brothers

31Then Jesus' mother and brothers arrived. Standing outside, they sent someone in to call him. 32A crowd was sitting around him, and they told him, "Your mother and brothers are outside looking for you."

33"Who are my mother and my brothers?" he asked.

34Then he looked at those seated in a circle around him and said, "Here are my mother and my brothers! 35Whoever does God's will is my brother and sister and mother."

The Parable of the Sower

4 Again Jesus began to teach by the lake. The crowd that gathered around him was so large that he got into a boat and sat in it out on the lake, while all the people were along the shore at the water's edge. 2He taught them many things by parables, and in his teaching said:

NEW LIVING TRANSLATION

him without first tying him up. Only then can his house be robbed!*

28"I assure you that any sin can be forgiven, including blasphemy; 29but anyone who blasphemes against the Holy Spirit will never be forgiven. It is an eternal sin." 30He told them this because they were saying he had an evil spirit.

The True Family of Jesus

31Jesus' mother and brothers arrived at the house where he was teaching. They stood outside and sent word for him to come out and talk with them. 32There was a crowd around Jesus, and someone said, "Your mother and your brothers and sisters* are outside, asking for you."

33Jesus replied, "Who is my mother? Who are my brothers?" 34Then he looked at those around him and said, "These are my mother and brothers. 35Anyone who does God's will is my brother and sister and mother."

Story of the Farmer Scattering Seed

4 Once again Jesus began teaching by the lakeshore. There was such a large crowd along the shore that he got into a boat and sat down and spoke from there. 2He began to teach the people by telling many stories such as this one:

3:27 Or *One cannot rob Satan's kingdom without first tying him up. Only then can his demons be cast out.* 3:32 Some manuscripts do not include *and sisters.*

NEW KING JAMES VERSION

strong man's house and plunder his goods, unless he first binds the strong man. And then he will plunder his house.

The Unpardonable Sin

28"Assuredly, I say to you, all sins will be forgiven the sons of men, and whatever blasphemies they may utter; 29but he who blasphemes against the Holy Spirit never has forgiveness, but is subject to eternal condemnation"— 30because they said, "He has an unclean spirit."

Jesus' Mother and Brothers Send for Him

31Then His brothers and His mother came, and standing outside they sent to Him, calling Him. 32And a multitude was sitting around Him; and they said to Him, "Look, Your mother and Your brothers[e] are outside seeking You."

33But He answered them, saying, "Who is My mother, or My brothers?" 34And He looked around in a circle at those who sat about Him, and said, "Here are My mother and My brothers! 35For whoever does the will of God is My brother and My sister and mother."

The Parable of the Sower

4 And again He began to teach by the sea. And a great multitude was gathered to Him, so that He got into a boat and sat *in it* on the sea; and the whole multitude was on the land facing the sea. 2Then He taught them many things by parables, and said to them in His teaching:

3:32 [e] NU-Text and M-Text add *and Your sisters.*

THE MESSAGE

off with his possessions unless you tie him up first? Tie him up, though, and you can clean him out.

"Listen to this carefully. I'm warning you. There's nothing done or said that can't be forgiven. But if you persist in your slanders against God's Holy Spirit, you are repudiating the very One who forgives, sawing off the branch on which you're sitting, severing by your own perversity all connection with the One who forgives." He gave this warning because they were accusing him of being in league with Evil.

Jesus' Mother and Brothers

Just then his mother and brothers showed up. Standing outside, they relayed a message that they wanted a word with him. He was surrounded by the crowd when he was given the message, "Your mother and brothers and sisters are outside looking for you."

Jesus responded, "Who do you think are my mother and brothers?" Looking around, taking in everyone seated around him, he said, "Right here, right in front of you— my mother and my brothers. Obedience is thicker than blood. The person who obeys God's will is my brother and sister and mother."

The Story of the Scattered Seed

4 He went back to teaching by the sea. A crowd built up to such a great size that he had to get into an offshore boat, using the boat as a pulpit as the people pushed to the water's edge. He taught by using stories, many stories.

KING JAMES VERSION

3 Hearken; Behold, there went out a sower to sow:

4 And it came to pass, as he sowed, some fell by the way side, and the fowls of the air came and devoured it up.

5 And some fell on stony ground, where it had not much earth; and immediately it sprang up, because it had no depth of earth:

6 But when the sun was up, it was scorched; and because it had no root, it withered away.

7 And some fell among thorns, and the thorns grew up, and choked it, and it yielded no fruit.

8 And other fell on good ground, and did yield fruit that sprang up and increased; and brought forth, some thirty, and some sixty, and some an hundred.

9 And he said unto them, He that hath ears to hear, let him hear.

10 And when he was alone, they that were about him with the twelve asked of him the parable.

11 And he said unto them, Unto you it is given to know the mystery of the kingdom of God: but unto them that are without, all *these* things are done in parables:

12 That seeing they may see, and not perceive; and hearing they may hear, and not understand; lest at any time they should be converted, and *their* sins should be forgiven them.

NEW AMERICAN STANDARD BIBLE

3 "Listen *to this!* Behold, the sower went out to sow;

4 as he was sowing, some *seed* fell beside the road, and the birds came and ate it up.

5 "Other *seed* fell on the rocky *ground* where it did not have much soil; and immediately it sprang up because it had no depth of soil.

6 "And after the sun had risen, it was scorched; and because it had no root, it withered away.

7 "Other *seed* fell among the thorns, and the thorns came up and choked it, and it yielded no crop.

8 "Other *seeds* fell into the good soil, and as they grew up and increased, they yielded a crop and produced thirty, sixty, and a hundredfold."

9 And He was saying, "He who has ears to hear, let him hear."

10 As soon as He was alone, His followers, along with the twelve, *began* asking Him *about* the parables.

11 And He was saying to them, "To you has been given the mystery of the kingdom of God, but those who are outside get everything in parables,

12 so that WHILE SEEING, THEY MAY SEE AND NOT PERCEIVE, AND WHILE HEARING, THEY MAY HEAR AND NOT UNDERSTAND, OTHERWISE THEY MIGHT RETURN AND BE FORGIVEN."

NEW CENTURY VERSION

said, 3"Listen! A farmer went out to plant his seed. 4While
he was planting, some seed fell by the road, and the birds
came and ate it up. 5Some seed fell on rocky ground where
there wasn't much dirt. That seed grew very fast, because
the ground was not deep. 6But when the sun rose, the
plants dried up because they did not have deep roots.
7Some other seed fell among thorny weeds, which grew
and choked the good plants. So those plants did not produce a crop. 8Some other seed fell on good ground and
began to grow. It got taller and produced a crop. Some
plants made thirty times more, some made sixty times
more, and some made a hundred times more."

9Then Jesus said, "You people who can hear me, listen!"

Jesus Tells Why He Used Stories

10Later, when Jesus was alone, the twelve apostles and others around him asked him about the stories.

11Jesus said, "You can know the secret about the kingdom of God. But to other people I tell everything by using
stories 12so that:

'They will look and look, but they will not learn.
They will listen and listen, but they will not
understand.
If they did learn and understand,
they would come back to me and be
forgiven.' " *Isaiah 6:9–10*

CONTEMPORARY ENGLISH VERSION

3Now listen! A farmer went out to scatter seed in a
field. 4While the farmer was scattering the seed, some of
it fell along the road and was eaten by birds. 5Other
seeds fell on thin, rocky ground and quickly started
growing because the soil wasn't very deep. 6But when
the sun came up, the plants were scorched and dried up,
because they did not have enough roots. 7Some other
seeds fell where thornbushes grew up and choked out
the plants. So they did not produce any grain. 8But a few
seeds did fall on good ground where the plants grew and
produced thirty or sixty or even a hundred times as
much as was scattered.

9Then Jesus said, "If you have ears, pay attention."

Why Jesus Used Stories (Matthew 13.10-17; Luke 8.9, 10)

10When Jesus was alone with the twelve apostles and
some others, they asked him about these stories. 11He
answered:

I have explained the secret about God's kingdom to
you, but for others I can use only stories. 12The reason is,

"These people will look
and look, but never see.
They will listen and listen,
but never understand.
If they did,
they would turn to God,
and he would forgive them."

NEW INTERNATIONAL VERSION

3“Listen! A farmer went out to sow his seed. 4As he was
scattering the seed, some fell along the path, and the birds
came and ate it up. 5Some fell on rocky places, where it did
not have much soil. It sprang up quickly, because the soil
was shallow. 6But when the sun came up, the plants were
scorched, and they withered because they had no root.
7Other seed fell among thorns, which grew up and choked
the plants, so that they did not bear grain. 8Still other seed
fell on good soil. It came up, grew and produced a crop,
multiplying thirty, sixty, or even a hundred times.”

9Then Jesus said, “He who has ears to hear, let him
hear.”

10When he was alone, the Twelve and the others around
him asked him about the parables. 11He told them, “The
secret of the kingdom of God has been given to you. But to
those on the outside everything is said in parables 12so
that,

“ ‘they may be ever seeing but never perceiving,
and ever hearing but never understanding;
otherwise they might turn and be forgiven!’[a]”

[a] *12* Isaiah 6:9,10

NEW LIVING TRANSLATION

3“Listen! A farmer went out to plant some seed. 4As he
scattered it across his field, some seed fell on a footpath,
and the birds came and ate it. 5Other seed fell on shallow
soil with underlying rock. The plant sprang up quickly,
6but it soon wilted beneath the hot sun and died because
the roots had no nourishment in the shallow soil. 7Other
seed fell among thorns that shot up and choked out the
tender blades so that it produced no grain. 8Still other seed
fell on fertile soil and produced a crop that was thirty,
sixty, and even a hundred times as much as had been
planted.” Then he said, 9“Anyone who is willing to hear
should listen and understand!”

10Later, when Jesus was alone with the twelve disciples
and with the others who were gathered around, they asked
him, “What do your stories mean?”

11He replied, “You are permitted to understand the
secret about the Kingdom of God. But I am using these sto-
ries to conceal everything about it from outsiders, 12so
that the Scriptures might be fulfilled:

‘They see what I do,
but they don’t perceive its meaning.
They hear my words,
but they don’t understand.
So they will not turn from their sins
and be forgiven.’*

4:12 Isa 6:9-10.

NEW KING JAMES VERSION

3“Listen! Behold, a sower went out to sow. 4And it hap-
pened, as he sowed, *that* some *seed* fell by the wayside;
and the birds of the air[a] came and devoured it. 5Some fell
on stony ground, where it did not have much earth; and
immediately it sprang up because it had no depth of earth.
6But when the sun was up it was scorched, and because it
had no root it withered away. 7And some *seed* fell among
thorns; and the thorns grew up and choked it, and it yield-
ed no crop. 8But other *seed* fell on good ground and yielded
a crop that sprang up, increased and produced: some thir-
tyfold, some sixty, and some a hundred.”

9And He said to them,[b] “He who has ears to hear, let
him hear!”

The Purpose of Parables

10But when He was alone, those around Him with the
twelve asked Him about the parable. 11And He said to
them, “To you it has been given to know the mystery of
the kingdom of God; but to those who are outside, all
things come in parables, 12so that

‘Seeing they may see and not perceive,
And hearing they may hear and not understand;
Lest they should turn,
And their sins be forgiven them.’ ”[c]

4:4 [a] NU-Text and M-Text omit *of the air.* 4:9 [b] NU-Text and M-Text omit *to them.* 4:12 [c] Isaiah 6:9, 10

THE MESSAGE

“Listen. What do you make of this? A farmer planted seed. As he scattered the seed, some of it fell on the road and birds ate it. Some fell in the gravel; it sprouted quickly but didn’t put down roots, so when the sun came up it withered just as quickly. Some fell in the weeds; as it came up, it was strangled among the weeds and nothing came of it. Some fell on good earth and came up with a flourish, producing a harvest exceeding his wildest dreams.

“Are you listening to this?

“Really listening?”

When they were off by themselves, those who were close to him, along with the Twelve, asked about the stories. He told them, “You’ve been given insight into God’s kingdom—you know how it works. But to those who can’t see it yet, everything comes in stories, creating readiness, nudging them toward receptive insight. These are people—

‘Whose eyes are open but don’t see a thing,
Whose ears are open but don’t understand a word,
Who avoid making an about-face and getting
forgiven.’ ”

KING JAMES VERSION

13 And he said unto them, Know ye not this parable? and how then will ye know all parables?

14 The sower soweth the word.

15 And these are they by the way side, where the word is sown; but when they have heard, Satan cometh immediately, and taketh away the word that was sown in their hearts.

16 And these are they likewise which are sown on stony ground; who, when they have heard the word, immediately receive it with gladness;

17 And have no root in themselves, and so endure but for a time: afterward, when affliction or persecution ariseth for the word's sake, immediately they are offended.

18 And these are they which are sown among thorns; such as hear the word,

19 And the cares of this world, and the deceitfulness of riches, and the lusts of other things entering in, choke the word, and it becometh unfruitful.

20 And these are they which are sown on good ground; such as hear the word, and receive *it*, and bring forth fruit, some thirtyfold, some sixty, and some an hundred.

21 ¶ And he said unto them, Is a candle brought to be put under a bushel, or under a bed? and not to be set on a candlestick?

22 For there is nothing hid, which shall not be manifested; neither was any thing kept secret, but that it should come abroad.

NEW AMERICAN STANDARD BIBLE

Explanation

13 And He *said to them, "Do you not understand this parable? How will you understand all the parables?

14 "The sower sows the word.

15 "These are the ones who are beside the road where the word is sown; and when they hear, immediately Satan comes and takes away the word which has been sown in them.

16 "In a similar way these are the ones on whom seed was sown on the rocky *places,* who, when they hear the word, immediately receive it with joy;

17 and they have no *firm* root in themselves, but are *only* temporary; then, when affliction or persecution arises because of the word, immediately they fall away.

18 "And others are the ones on whom seed was sown among the thorns; these are the ones who have heard the word,

19 but the worries of the [1]world, and the deceitfulness of riches, and the desires for other things enter in and choke the word, and it becomes unfruitful.

20 "And those are the ones on whom seed was sown on the good soil; and they hear the word and accept it and bear fruit, thirty, sixty, and a hundredfold."

21 And He was saying to them, "A lamp is not brought to be put under a basket, is it, or under a bed? Is it not *brought* to be put on the lampstand?

22 "For nothing is hidden, except to be revealed; nor has *anything* been secret, but that it would come to light.

4:19 [1] Or *age*

NEW CENTURY VERSION

Jesus Explains the Seed Story

13Then Jesus said to his followers, "Don't you understand this story? If you don't, how will you understand any story? 14The farmer is like a person who plants God's message in people. 15Sometimes the teaching falls on the road. This is like the people who hear the teaching of God, but Satan quickly comes and takes away the teaching that was planted in them. 16Others are like the seed planted on rocky ground. They hear the teaching and quickly accept it with joy. 17But since they don't allow the teaching to go deep into their lives, they keep it only a short time. When trouble or persecution comes because of the teaching they accepted, they quickly give up. 18Others are like the seed planted among the thorny weeds. They hear the teaching, 19but the worries of this life, the temptation of wealth, and many other evil desires keep the teaching from growing and producing fruit[a] in their lives. 20Others are like the seed planted in the good ground. They hear the teaching and accept it. Then they grow and produce fruit—sometimes thirty times more, sometimes sixty times more, and sometimes a hundred times more."

Use What You Have

21Then Jesus said to them, "Do you hide a lamp under a bowl or under a bed? No! You put the lamp on a lampstand. 22Everything that is hidden will be made clear and every

4:19 [a] **producing fruit** To produce fruit means to have in your life the good things God wants.

CONTEMPORARY ENGLISH VERSION

Jesus Explains the Story about the Farmer
(Matthew 13.18-23; Luke 8.11-15)

13Jesus told them:

If you don't understand this story, you won't understand any others. 14What the farmer is spreading is really the message about the kingdom. 15The seeds that fell along the road are the people who hear the message. But Satan soon comes and snatches it away from them. 16The seeds that fell on rocky ground are the people who gladly hear the message and accept it right away. 17But they don't have any roots, and they don't last very long. As soon as life gets hard or the message gets them in trouble, they give up.

18The seeds that fell among the thornbushes are also people who hear the message. 19But they start worrying about the needs of this life. They are fooled by the desire to get rich and to have all kinds of other things. So the message gets choked out, and they never produce anything. 20The seeds that fell on good ground are the people who hear and welcome the message. They produce thirty or sixty or even a hundred times as much as was planted.

Light (Luke 8.16-18)

21Jesus also said:

You don't light a lamp and put it under a clay pot or under a bed. Don't you put a lamp on a lampstand? 22There is nothing hidden that will not be made public.

NEW INTERNATIONAL VERSION

13Then Jesus said to them, "Don't you understand this parable? How then will you understand any parable? 14The farmer sows the word. 15Some people are like seed along the path, where the word is sown. As soon as they hear it, Satan comes and takes away the word that was sown in them. 16Others, like seed sown on rocky places, hear the word and at once receive it with joy. 17But since they have no root, they last only a short time. When trouble or persecution comes because of the word, they quickly fall away. 18Still others, like seed sown among thorns, hear the word; 19but the worries of this life, the deceitfulness of wealth and the desires for other things come in and choke the word, making it unfruitful. 20Others, like seed sown on good soil, hear the word, accept it, and produce a crop—thirty, sixty or even a hundred times what was sown."

A Lamp on a Stand

21He said to them, "Do you bring in a lamp to put it under a bowl or a bed? Instead, don't you put it on its stand? 22For whatever is hidden is meant to be disclosed,

NEW LIVING TRANSLATION

13"But if you can't understand this story, how will you understand all the others I am going to tell? 14The farmer I talked about is the one who brings God's message to others. 15The seed that fell on the hard path represents those who hear the message, but then Satan comes at once and takes it away from them. 16The rocky soil represents those who hear the message and receive it with joy. 17But like young plants in such soil, their roots don't go very deep. At first they get along fine, but they wilt as soon as they have problems or are persecuted because they believe the word. 18The thorny ground represents those who hear and accept the Good News, 19but all too quickly the message is crowded out by the cares of this life, the lure of wealth, and the desire for nice things, so no crop is produced. 20But the good soil represents those who hear and accept God's message and produce a huge harvest—thirty, sixty, or even a hundred times as much as had been planted."

Illustration of the Lamp

21Then Jesus asked them, "Would anyone light a lamp and then put it under a basket or under a bed to shut out the light? Of course not! A lamp is placed on a stand, where its light will shine.

22"Everything that is now hidden or secret will eventually

NEW KING JAMES VERSION

The Parable of the Sower Explained

13And He said to them, "Do you not understand this parable? How then will you understand all the parables? 14The sower sows the word. 15And these are the ones by the wayside where the word is sown. When they hear, Satan comes immediately and takes away the word that was sown in their hearts. 16These likewise are the ones sown on stony ground who, when they hear the word, immediately receive it with gladness; 17and they have no root in themselves, and so endure only for a time. Afterward, when tribulation or persecution arises for the word's sake, immediately they stumble. 18Now these are the ones sown among thorns; *they are* the ones who hear the word, 19and the cares of this world, the deceitfulness of riches, and the desires for other things entering in choke the word, and it becomes unfruitful. 20But these are the ones sown on good ground, those who hear the word, accept *it,* and bear fruit: some thirtyfold, some sixty, and some a hundred."

Light Under a Basket

21Also He said to them, "Is a lamp brought to be put under a basket or under a bed? Is it not to be set on a lampstand? 22For there is nothing hidden which will not be revealed, nor has anything been kept secret but that it

THE MESSAGE

He continued, "Do you see how this story works? All my stories work this way.

"The farmer plants the Word. Some people are like the seed that falls on the hardened soil of the road. No sooner do they hear the Word than Satan snatches away what has been planted in them.

"And some are like the seed that lands in the gravel. When they first hear the Word, they respond with great enthusiasm. But there is such shallow soil of character that when the emotions wear off and some difficulty arrives, there is nothing to show for it.

"The seed cast in the weeds represents the ones who hear the kingdom news but are overwhelmed with worries about all the things they have to do and all the things they want to get. The stress strangles what they heard, and nothing comes of it.

"But the seed planted in the good earth represents those who hear the Word, embrace it, and produce a harvest beyond their wildest dreams."

Giving, Not Getting

Jesus went on: "Does anyone bring a lamp home and put it under a washtub or beneath the bed? Don't you put it up on a table or on the mantel? We're not keeping secrets, we're telling them; we're not hiding things, we're bringing them out into the open.

KING JAMES VERSION

23 If any man have ears to hear, let him hear.
24 And he said unto them, Take heed what ye hear: with what measure ye mete, it shall be measured to you: and unto you that hear shall more be given.
25 For he that hath, to him shall be given: and he that hath not, from him shall be taken even that which he hath.
26 And he said, So is the kingdom of God, as if a man should cast seed into the ground;
27 And should sleep, and rise night and day, and the seed should spring and grow up, he knoweth not how.
28 For the earth bringeth forth fruit of herself; first the blade, then the ear, after that the full corn in the ear.
29 But when the fruit is brought forth, immediately he putteth in the sickle, because the harvest is come.
30 And he said, Whereunto shall we liken the kingdom of God? or with what comparison shall we compare it?
31 *It is* like a grain of mustard seed, which, when it is sown in the earth, is less than all the seeds that be in the earth:
32 But when it is sown, it groweth up, and becometh greater than all herbs, and shooteth out great branches; so that the fowls of the air may lodge under the shadow of it.

NEW AMERICAN STANDARD BIBLE

23 "If anyone has ears to hear, let him hear."
24 And He was saying to them, "Take care what you listen to. By your standard of measure it will be measured to you; and more will be given you besides.
25 "For whoever has, to him *more* shall be given; and whoever does not have, even what he has shall be taken away from him."

Parable of the Seed

26 And He was saying, "The kingdom of God is like a man who casts seed upon the soil;
27 and he goes to bed at night and gets up by day, and the seed sprouts and grows—how, he himself does not know.
28 "The soil produces crops by itself; first the blade, then the head, then the mature grain in the head.
29 "But when the crop permits, he immediately puts in the sickle, because the harvest has come."

Parable of the Mustard Seed

30 And He said, "How shall we [2]picture the kingdom of God, or by what parable shall we present it?
31 "*It is* like a mustard seed, which, when sown upon the soil, though it is smaller than all the seeds that are upon the soil,
32 yet when it is sown, it grows up and becomes larger than all the garden plants and forms large branches; so that THE BIRDS OF THE [3]AIR can NEST UNDER ITS SHADE."

4:30 [2] Lit *compare* 4:32 [3] Or *sky*

NEW CENTURY VERSION

secret thing will be made known. 23You people who can hear me, listen!
24"Think carefully about what you hear. The way you give to others is the way God will give to you, but God will give you even more. 25Those who have understanding will be given more. But those who do not have understanding, even what they have will be taken away from them."

Jesus Uses a Story About Seed

26Then Jesus said, "The kingdom of God is like someone who plants seed in the ground. 27Night and day, whether the person is asleep or awake, the seed still grows, but the person does not know how it grows. 28By itself the earth produces grain. First the plant grows, then the head, and then all the grain in the head. 29When the grain is ready, the farmer cuts it, because this is the harvest time."

A Story About Mustard Seed

30Then Jesus said, "How can I show you what the kingdom of God is like? What story can I use to explain it? 31The kingdom of God is like a mustard seed, the smallest seed you plant in the ground. 32But when planted, this seed grows and becomes the largest of all garden plants. It produces large branches, and the wild birds can make nests in its shade."

CONTEMPORARY ENGLISH VERSION

There is no secret that will not be well known. 23If you have ears, pay attention!
24Listen carefully to what you hear! The way you treat others will be the way you will be treated—and even worse. 25Everyone who has something will be given more. But people who don't have anything will lose what little they have.

Another Story about Seeds

26Again Jesus said:
God's kingdom is like what happens when a farmer scatters seed in a field. 27The farmer sleeps at night and is up and around during the day. Yet the seeds keep sprouting and growing, and he doesn't understand how. 28It is the ground that makes the seeds sprout and grow into plants that produce grain. 29Then when harvest season comes and the grain is ripe, the farmer cuts it with a sickle.[a]

A Mustard Seed (Matthew 13.31, 32; Luke 13.18, 19)

30Finally, Jesus said:
What is God's kingdom like? What story can I use to explain it? 31It is like what happens when a mustard seed is planted in the ground. It is the smallest seed in all the world. 32But once it is planted, it grows larger than any garden plant. It even puts out branches that are big enough for birds to nest in its shade.

[a] **4.29** *sickle:* A knife with a long curved blade, used to cut grain and other crops.

NEW INTERNATIONAL VERSION

and whatever is concealed is meant to be brought out into the open. [23]If anyone has ears to hear, let him hear."

[24]"Consider carefully what you hear," he continued. "With the measure you use, it will be measured to you—and even more. [25]Whoever has will be given more; whoever does not have, even what he has will be taken from him."

The Parable of the Growing Seed

[26]He also said, "This is what the kingdom of God is like. A man scatters seed on the ground. [27]Night and day, whether he sleeps or gets up, the seed sprouts and grows, though he does not know how. [28]All by itself the soil produces grain—first the stalk, then the head, then the full kernel in the head. [29]As soon as the grain is ripe, he puts the sickle to it, because the harvest has come."

The Parable of the Mustard Seed

[30]Again he said, "What shall we say the kingdom of God is like, or what parable shall we use to describe it? [31]It is like a mustard seed, which is the smallest seed you plant in the ground. [32]Yet when planted, it grows and becomes the largest of all garden plants, with such big branches that the birds of the air can perch in its shade."

NEW LIVING TRANSLATION

be brought to light. [23]Anyone who is willing to hear should listen and understand! [24]And be sure to pay attention to what you hear. The more you do this, the more you will understand—and even more, besides. [25]To those who are open to my teaching, more understanding will be given. But to those who are not listening, even what they have will be taken away from them."

Illustration of the Growing Seed

[26]Jesus also said, "Here is another illustration of what the Kingdom of God is like: A farmer planted seeds in a field, [27]and then he went on with his other activities. As the days went by, the seeds sprouted and grew without the farmer's help, [28]because the earth produces crops on its own. First a leaf blade pushes through, then the heads of wheat are formed, and finally the grain ripens. [29]And as soon as the grain is ready, the farmer comes and harvests it with a sickle."

Illustration of the Mustard Seed

[30]Jesus asked, "How can I describe the Kingdom of God? What story should I use to illustrate it? [31]It is like a tiny mustard seed. Though this is one of the smallest of seeds, [32]it grows to become one of the largest of plants, with long branches where birds can come and find shelter."

NEW KING JAMES VERSION

should come to light. [23]If anyone has ears to hear, let him hear."

[24]Then He said to them, "Take heed what you hear. With the same measure you use, it will be measured to you; and to you who hear, more will be given. [25]For whoever has, to him more will be given; but whoever does not have, even what he has will be taken away from him."

The Parable of the Growing Seed

[26]And He said, "The kingdom of God is as if a man should scatter seed on the ground, [27]and should sleep by night and rise by day, and the seed should sprout and grow, he himself does not know how. [28]For the earth yields crops by itself: first the blade, then the head, after that the full grain in the head. [29]But when the grain ripens, immediately he puts in the sickle, because the harvest has come."

The Parable of the Mustard Seed

[30]Then He said, "To what shall we liken the kingdom of God? Or with what parable shall we picture it? [31]*It is* like a mustard seed which, when it is sown on the ground, is smaller than all the seeds on earth; [32]but when it is sown, it grows up and becomes greater than all herbs, and shoots out large branches, so that the birds of the air may nest under its shade."

THE MESSAGE

"Are you listening to this?

"Really listening?

"Listen carefully to what I am saying—and be wary of the shrewd advice that tells you how to get ahead in the world on your own. Giving, not getting, is the way. Generosity begets generosity. Stinginess impoverishes."

Never Without a Story

Then Jesus said, "God's kingdom is like seed thrown on a field by a man who then goes to bed and forgets about it. The seed sprouts and grows—he has no idea how it happens. The earth does it all without his help: first a green stem of grass, then a bud, then the ripened grain. When the grain is fully formed, he reaps—harvest time!

"How can we picture God's kingdom? What kind of story can we use? It's like a pine nut. When it lands on the ground it is quite small as seeds go, yet once it is planted it grows into a huge pine tree with thick branches. Eagles nest in it."

KING JAMES VERSION

33 And with many such parables spake he the word unto them, as they were able to hear *it*.

34 But without a parable spake he not unto them: and when they were alone, he expounded all things to his disciples.

35 ¶ And the same day, when the even was come, he saith unto them, Let us pass over unto the other side.

36 And when they had sent away the multitude, they took him even as he was in the ship. And there were also with him other little ships.

37 And there arose a great storm of wind, and the waves beat into the ship, so that it was now full.

38 And he was in the hinder part of the ship, asleep on a pillow: and they awake him, and say unto him, Master, carest thou not that we perish?

39 And he arose, and rebuked the wind, and said unto the sea, Peace, be still. And the wind ceased, and there was a great calm.

40 And he said unto them, Why are ye so fearful? how is it that ye have no faith?

41 And they feared exceedingly, and said one to another, What manner of man is this, that even the wind and the sea obey him?

5 And they came over unto the other side of the sea, into the country of the Gadarenes.

NEW AMERICAN STANDARD BIBLE

33 With many such parables He was speaking the word to them, so far as they were able to hear it;

34 and He did not speak to them without a parable; but He was explaining everything privately to His own disciples.

Jesus Stills the Sea

35 On that day, when evening came, He *said to them, "Let us go over to the other side."

36 Leaving the crowd, they *took Him along with them in the boat, just as He was; and other boats were with Him.

37 And there *arose a fierce gale of wind, and the waves were breaking over the boat so much that the boat was already filling up.

38 Jesus Himself was in the stern, asleep on the cushion; and they *woke Him and *said to Him, "Teacher, do You not care that we are perishing?"

39 And He got up and rebuked the wind and said to the sea, "Hush, be still." And the wind died down and it became perfectly calm.

40 And He said to them, "Why are you afraid? How is it that you have no faith?"

41 They became very much afraid and said to one another, "Who then is this, that even the wind and the sea obey Him?"

The Gerasene Demoniac

5 They came to the other side of the sea, into the country of the Gerasenes.

NEW CENTURY VERSION

33 Jesus used many stories like these to teach the crowd God's message—as much as they could understand. 34 He always used stories to teach them. But when he and his followers were alone, Jesus explained everything to them.

Jesus Calms a Storm

35 That evening, Jesus said to his followers, "Let's go across the lake." 36 Leaving the crowd behind, they took him in the boat just as he was. There were also other boats with them. 37 A very strong wind came up on the lake. The waves came over the sides and into the boat so that it was already full of water. 38 Jesus was at the back of the boat, sleeping with his head on a cushion. His followers woke him and said, "Teacher, don't you care that we are drowning!"

39 Jesus stood up and commanded the wind and said to the waves, "Quiet! Be still!" Then the wind stopped, and it became completely calm.

40 Jesus said to his followers, "Why are you afraid? Do you still have no faith?"

41 The followers were very afraid and asked each other, "Who is this? Even the wind and the waves obey him!"

A Man with Demons Inside Him

5 Jesus and his followers went to the other side of the lake to the area of the Gerasene people. 2 When Jesus

CONTEMPORARY ENGLISH VERSION

The Reason for Teaching with Stories (Matthew 13.34, 35)

33 Jesus used many other stories when he spoke to the people, and he taught them as much as they could understand. 34 He did not tell them anything without using stories. But when he was alone with his disciples, he explained everything to them.

A Storm (Matthew 8.23-27; Luke 8.22-25)

35 That evening, Jesus said to his disciples, "Let's cross to the east side." 36 So they left the crowd, and his disciples started across the lake with him in the boat. Some other boats followed along. 37 Suddenly a windstorm struck the lake. Waves started splashing into the boat, and it was about to sink.

38 Jesus was in the back of the boat with his head on a pillow, and he was asleep. His disciples woke him and said, "Teacher, don't you care that we're about to drown?"

39 Jesus got up and ordered the wind and the waves to be quiet. The wind stopped, and everything was calm.

40 Jesus asked his disciples, "Why were you afraid? Don't you have any faith?"

41 Now they were more afraid than ever and said to each other, "Who is this? Even the wind and the waves obey him!"

A Man with Evil Spirits (Matthew 8.28-34; Luke 8.26-39)

5 Jesus and his disciples crossed Lake Galilee and came to shore near the town of Gerasa.[a] 2 When he was

[a] 5.1 *Gerasa*: Some manuscripts have "Gadara," and others have "Gergesa."

NEW INTERNATIONAL VERSION

33With many similar parables Jesus spoke the word to them, as much as they could understand. 34He did not say anything to them without using a parable. But when he was alone with his own disciples, he explained everything.

Jesus Calms the Storm

35That day when evening came, he said to his disciples, "Let us go over to the other side." 36Leaving the crowd behind, they took him along, just as he was, in the boat. There were also other boats with him. 37A furious squall came up, and the waves broke over the boat, so that it was nearly swamped. 38Jesus was in the stern, sleeping on a cushion. The disciples woke him and said to him, "Teacher, don't you care if we drown?"

39He got up, rebuked the wind and said to the waves, "Quiet! Be still!" Then the wind died down and it was completely calm.

40He said to his disciples, "Why are you so afraid? Do you still have no faith?"

41They were terrified and asked each other, "Who is this? Even the wind and the waves obey him!"

The Healing of a Demon-possessed Man

5 They went across the lake to the region of the Gerasenes.[a] 2When Jesus got out of the boat, a man

[a] *1* Some manuscripts *Gadarenes*; other manuscripts *Gergesenes*

NEW LIVING TRANSLATION

33He used many such stories and illustrations to teach the people as much as they were able to understand. 34In fact, in his public teaching he taught only with parables, but afterward when he was alone with his disciples, he explained the meaning to them.

Jesus Calms the Storm

35As evening came, Jesus said to his disciples, "Let's cross to the other side of the lake." 36He was already in the boat, so they started out, leaving the crowds behind (although other boats followed). 37But soon a fierce storm arose. High waves began to break into the boat until it was nearly full of water.

38Jesus was sleeping at the back of the boat with his head on a cushion. Frantically they woke him up, shouting, "Teacher, don't you even care that we are going to drown?"

39When he woke up, he rebuked the wind and said to the water, "Quiet down!" Suddenly the wind stopped, and there was a great calm. 40And he asked them, "Why are you so afraid? Do you still not have faith in me?"

41And they were filled with awe and said among themselves, "Who is this man, that even the wind and waves obey him?"

Jesus Heals a Demon-Possessed Man

5 So they arrived at the other side of the lake, in the land of the Gerasenes.* 2Just as Jesus was climbing

5:1 Some manuscripts read *Gadarenes;* others read *Gergesenes.* See Matt 8:28; Luke 8:26.

NEW KING JAMES VERSION

Jesus' Use of Parables

33And with many such parables He spoke the word to them as they were able to hear *it.* 34But without a parable He did not speak to them. And when they were alone, He explained all things to His disciples.

Wind and Wave Obey Jesus

35On the same day, when evening had come, He said to them, "Let us cross over to the other side." 36Now when they had left the multitude, they took Him along in the boat as He was. And other little boats were also with Him. 37And a great windstorm arose, and the waves beat into the boat, so that it was already filling. 38But He was in the stern, asleep on a pillow. And they awoke Him and said to Him, "Teacher, do You not care that we are perishing?"

39Then He arose and rebuked the wind, and said to the sea, "Peace, be still!" And the wind ceased and there was a great calm. 40But He said to them, "Why are you so fearful? How *is it* that you have no faith?"[d] 41And they feared exceedingly, and said to one another, "Who can this be, that even the wind and the sea obey Him!"

A Demon-Possessed Man Healed

5 Then they came to the other side of the sea, to the country of the Gadarenes.[a] 2And when He had come

4:40 [d] NU-Text reads *Have you still no faith?* **5:1** [a] NU-Text reads *Gerasenes.*

THE MESSAGE

With many stories like these, he presented his message to them, fitting the stories to their experience and maturity. He was never without a story when he spoke. When he was alone with his disciples, he went over everything, sorting out the tangles, untying the knots.

The Wind Ran Out of Breath

Late that day he said to them, "Let's go across to the other side." They took him in the boat as he was. Other boats came along. A huge storm came up. Waves poured into the boat, threatening to sink it. And Jesus was in the stern, head on a pillow, sleeping! They roused him, saying, "Teacher, is it nothing to you that we're going down?"

Awake now, he told the wind to pipe down and said to the sea, "Quiet! Settle down!" The wind ran out of breath; the sea became smooth as glass. Jesus reprimanded the disciples: "Why are you such cowards? Don't you have any faith at all?"

They were in absolute awe, staggered. "Who is this, anyway?" they asked. "Wind and sea at his beck and call!"

The Madman

5 They arrived on the other side of the sea in the country of the Gerasenes. As Jesus got out of the boat, a

KING JAMES VERSION

2 And when he was come out of the ship, immediately there met him out of the tombs a man with an unclean spirit,

3 Who had *his* dwelling among the tombs; and no man could bind him, no, not with chains:

4 Because that he had been often bound with fetters and chains, and the chains had been plucked asunder by him, and the fetters broken in pieces: neither could any *man* tame him.

5 And always, night and day, he was in the mountains, and in the tombs, crying, and cutting himself with stones.

6 But when he saw Jesus afar off, he ran and worshipped him,

7 And cried with a loud voice, and said, What have I to do with thee, Jesus, *thou* Son of the most high God? I adjure thee by God, that thou torment me not.

8 For he said unto him, Come out of the man, *thou* unclean spirit.

9 And he asked him, What *is* thy name? And he answered, saying, My name *is* Legion: for we are many.

10 And he besought him much that he would not send them away out of the country.

11 Now there was there nigh unto the mountains a great herd of swine feeding.

12 And all the devils besought him, saying, Send us into the swine, that we may enter into them.

13 And forthwith Jesus gave them leave. And the unclean spirits went out, and entered into the swine: and

NEW AMERICAN STANDARD BIBLE

2 When He got out of the boat, immediately a man from the tombs with an unclean spirit met Him,

3 and he had his dwelling among the tombs. And no one was able to bind him anymore, even with a chain;

4 because he had often been bound with shackles and chains, and the chains had been torn apart by him and the shackles broken in pieces, and no one was strong enough to subdue him.

5 Constantly, night and day, he was screaming among the tombs and in the mountains, and gashing himself with stones.

6 Seeing Jesus from a distance, he ran up and bowed down before Him;

7 and shouting with a loud voice, he *said, "What business do we have with each other, Jesus, Son of the Most High God? I implore You by God, do not torment me!"

8 For He had been saying to him, "Come out of the man, you unclean spirit!"

9 And He was asking him, "What is your name?" And he *said to Him, "My name is Legion; for we are many."

10 And he *began* to implore Him earnestly not to send them out of the country.

11 Now there was a large herd of swine feeding nearby on the mountain.

12 *The demons* implored Him, saying, "Send us into the swine so that we may enter them."

13 Jesus gave them permission. And coming out, the unclean spirits entered the swine; and the herd rushed

NEW CENTURY VERSION

got out of the boat, instantly a man with an evil spirit
came to him from the burial caves. 3This man lived in the
caves, and no one could tie him up, not even with a chain.
4Many times people had used chains to tie the man's
hands and feet, but he always broke them off. No one was
strong enough to control him. 5Day and night he would
wander around the burial caves and on the hills, screaming and cutting himself with stones. 6While Jesus was still
far away, the man saw him, ran to him, and fell down
before him.

7The man shouted in a loud voice, "What do you want
with me, Jesus, Son of the Most High God? I command you
in God's name not to torture me!" 8He said this because
Jesus was saying to him, "You evil spirit, come out of the
man."

9Then Jesus asked him, "What is your name?"

He answered, "My name is Legion,[a] because we are
many spirits." 10He begged Jesus again and again not to
send them out of that area.

11A large herd of pigs was feeding on a hill near there.
12The demons begged Jesus, "Send us into the pigs; let us
go into them." 13So Jesus allowed them to do this. The evil
spirits left the man and went into the pigs. Then the herd

5:9 [a] **Legion** Means very many. A legion was about five thousand men in the Roman army.

CONTEMPORARY ENGLISH VERSION

getting out of the boat, a man with an evil spirit quickly
ran to him 3from the graveyard[b] where he had been living.
No one was able to tie the man up anymore, not even with
a chain. 4He had often been put in chains and leg irons,
but he broke the chains and smashed the leg irons. No one
could control him. 5Night and day he was in the graveyard
or on the hills, yelling and cutting himself with stones.

6When the man saw Jesus in the distance, he ran up to
him and knelt down. 7He shouted, "Jesus, Son of God in
heaven, what do you want with me? Promise me in God's
name that you won't torture me!" 8The man said this
because Jesus had already told the evil spirit to come out
of him.

9Jesus asked, "What is your name?"

The man answered, "My name is Lots, because I have
'lots' of evil spirits." 10He then begged Jesus not to send
them away.

11Over on the hillside a large herd of pigs was feeding.
12So the evil spirits begged Jesus, "Send us into those pigs!
Let us go into them." 13Jesus let them go, and they went
out of the man and into the pigs. The whole herd of about

[b] 5.3 *graveyard*: It was thought that demons and evil spirits lived in graveyards.

NEW INTERNATIONAL VERSION

with an evil[b] spirit came from the tombs to meet him. 3 This man lived in the tombs, and no one could bind him any more, not even with a chain. 4 For he had often been chained hand and foot, but he tore the chains apart and broke the irons on his feet. No one was strong enough to subdue him. 5 Night and day among the tombs and in the hills he would cry out and cut himself with stones.

6 When he saw Jesus from a distance, he ran and fell on his knees in front of him. 7 He shouted at the top of his voice, "What do you want with me, Jesus, Son of the Most High God? Swear to God that you won't torture me!" 8 For Jesus had said to him, "Come out of this man, you evil spirit!"

9 Then Jesus asked him, "What is your name?"

"My name is Legion," he replied, "for we are many." 10 And he begged Jesus again and again not to send them out of the area.

11 A large herd of pigs was feeding on the nearby hillside. 12 The demons begged Jesus, "Send us among the pigs; allow us to go into them." 13 He gave them permission, and the evil spirits came out and went into the pigs.

[b] 2 Greek *unclean*; also in verses 8 and 13

NEW LIVING TRANSLATION

from the boat, a man possessed by an evil spirit ran out from a cemetery to meet him. 3 This man lived among the tombs and could not be restrained, even with a chain. 4 Whenever he was put into chains and shackles—as he often was—he snapped the chains from his wrists and smashed the shackles. No one was strong enough to control him. 5 All day long and throughout the night, he would wander among the tombs and in the hills, screaming and hitting himself with stones.

6 When Jesus was still some distance away, the man saw him. He ran to meet Jesus and fell down before him. 7 He gave a terrible scream, shrieking, "Why are you bothering me, Jesus, Son of the Most High God? For God's sake, don't torture me!" 8 For Jesus had already said to the spirit, "Come out of the man, you evil spirit."

9 Then Jesus asked, "What is your name?"

And the spirit replied, "Legion, because there are many of us here inside this man." 10 Then the spirits begged him again and again not to send them to some distant place. 11 There happened to be a large herd of pigs feeding on the hillside nearby. 12 "Send us into those pigs," the evil spirits begged. 13 Jesus gave them permission. So the evil spirits came out of the man and entered the pigs, and the entire

NEW KING JAMES VERSION

out of the boat, immediately there met Him out of the tombs a man with an unclean spirit, 3 who had *his* dwelling among the tombs; and no one could bind him,[b] not even with chains, 4 because he had often been bound with shackles and chains. And the chains had been pulled apart by him, and the shackles broken in pieces; neither could anyone tame him. 5 And always, night and day, he was in the mountains and in the tombs, crying out and cutting himself with stones.

6 When he saw Jesus from afar, he ran and worshiped Him. 7 And he cried out with a loud voice and said, "What have I to do with You, Jesus, Son of the Most High God? I implore You by God that You do not torment me."

8 For He said to him, "Come out of the man, unclean spirit!" 9 Then He asked him, "What *is* your name?"

And he answered, saying, "My name *is* Legion; for we are many." 10 Also he begged Him earnestly that He would not send them out of the country.

11 Now a large herd of swine was feeding there near the mountains. 12 So all the demons begged Him, saying, "Send us to the swine, that we may enter them." 13 And at once Jesus[c] gave them permission. Then the unclean spirits went out and entered the swine (there were about two

5:3 [b] NU-Text adds *anymore.* 5:13 [c] NU-Text reads *And He gave.*

THE MESSAGE

madman from the cemetery came up to him. He lived there among the tombs and graves. No one could restrain him—he couldn't be chained, couldn't be tied down. He had been tied up many times with chains and ropes, but he broke the chains, snapped the ropes. No one was strong enough to tame him. Night and day he roamed through the graves and the hills, screaming out and slashing himself with sharp stones.

When he saw Jesus a long way off, he ran and bowed in worship before him—then bellowed in protest, "What business do you have, Jesus, Son of the High God, messing with me? I swear to God, don't give me a hard time!" (Jesus had just commanded the tormenting evil spirit, "Out! Get out of the man!")

Jesus asked him, "Tell me your name."

He replied, "My name is Mob. I'm a rioting mob." Then he desperately begged Jesus not to banish them from the country.

A large herd of pigs was browsing and rooting on a nearby hill. The demons begged him, "Send us to the pigs so we can live in them." Jesus gave the order. But it was

KING JAMES VERSION

the herd ran violently down a steep place into the sea, (they were about two thousand;) and were choked in the sea.

14 And they that fed the swine fled, and told *it* in the city, and in the country. And they went out to see what it was that was done.

15 And they come to Jesus, and see him that was possessed with the devil, and had the legion, sitting, and clothed, and in his right mind: and they were afraid.

16 And they that saw *it* told them how it befell to him that was possessed with the devil, and *also* concerning the swine.

17 And they began to pray him to depart out of their coasts.

18 And when he was come into the ship, he that had been possessed with the devil prayed him that he might be with him.

19 Howbeit Jesus suffered him not, but saith unto him, Go home to thy friends, and tell them how great things the Lord hath done for thee, and hath had compassion on thee.

20 And he departed, and began to publish in Decapolis how great things Jesus had done for him: and all *men* did marvel.

21 ¶ And when Jesus was passed over again by ship unto the other side, much people gathered unto him: and he was nigh unto the sea.

NEW AMERICAN STANDARD BIBLE

down the steep bank into the sea, about two thousand *of them;* and they were drowned in the sea.

14 Their herdsmen ran away and reported it in the city and in the country. And *the people* came to see what it was that had happened.

15 They *came to Jesus and *observed the man who had been demon-possessed sitting down, clothed and in his right mind, the very man who had had the "legion"; and they became frightened.

16 Those who had seen it described to them how it had happened to the demon-possessed man, and *all* about the swine.

17 And they began to implore Him to leave their region.

18 As He was getting into the boat, the man who had been demon-possessed was imploring Him that he might accompany Him.

19 And He did not let him, but He *said to him, "Go home to your people and report to them [1]what great things the Lord has done for you, and *how* He had mercy on you."

20 And he went away and began to proclaim in Decapolis what great things Jesus had done for him; and everyone was amazed.

Miracles and Healing

21 When Jesus had crossed over again in the boat to the other side, a large crowd gathered around Him; and so He stayed by the seashore.

5:19 [1] Or *everything that*

NEW CENTURY VERSION

of pigs—about two thousand of them—rushed down the hill into the lake and were drowned.

14The herdsmen ran away and went to the town and to the countryside, telling everyone about this. So people went out to see what had happened. 15They came to Jesus and saw the man who used to have the many evil spirits, sitting, clothed, and in his right mind. And they were frightened. 16The people who saw this told the others what had happened to the man who had the demons living in him, and they told about the pigs. 17Then the people began to beg Jesus to leave their area.

18As Jesus was getting back into the boat, the man who was freed from the demons begged to go with him.

19But Jesus would not let him. He said, "Go home to your family and tell them how much the Lord has done for you and how he has had mercy on you." 20So the man left and began to tell the people in the Ten Towns[b] about what Jesus had done for him. And everyone was amazed.

Jesus Gives Life to a Dead Girl and Heals a Sick Woman

21When Jesus went in the boat back to the other side of the lake, a large crowd gathered around him there. 22A

5:20 [b] **Ten Towns** In Greek, called "Decapolis." It was an area east of Lake Galilee that once had ten main towns.

CONTEMPORARY ENGLISH VERSION

two thousand pigs rushed down the steep bank into the lake and drowned.

14The men taking care of the pigs ran to the town and the farms to spread the news. Then the people came out to see what had happened. 15When they came to Jesus, they saw the man who had once been full of demons. He was sitting there with his clothes on and in his right mind, and they were terrified.

16Everyone who had seen what had happened told about the man and the pigs. 17Then the people started begging Jesus to leave their part of the country.

18When Jesus was getting into the boat, the man begged to go with him. 19But Jesus would not let him. Instead, he said, "Go home to your family and tell them how much the Lord has done for you and how good he has been to you."

20The man went away into the region near the ten cities known as Decapolis[c] and began telling everyone how much Jesus had done for him. Everyone who heard what had happened was amazed.

A Dying Girl and a Sick Woman

(Matthew 9.18-26; Luke 8.40-56)

21Once again Jesus got into the boat and crossed Lake Galilee.[d] Then as he stood on the shore, a large crowd

[c] **5.20** *the ten cities known as Decapolis*: A group of ten cities east of Samaria and Galilee, where the people followed the Greek way of life.
[d] **5.21** *crossed Lake Galilee*: To the west side.

NEW INTERNATIONAL VERSION

The herd, about two thousand in number, rushed down the steep bank into the lake and were drowned.

14Those tending the pigs ran off and reported this in the town and countryside, and the people went out to see what had happened. 15When they came to Jesus, they saw the man who had been possessed by the legion of demons, sitting there, dressed and in his right mind; and they were afraid. 16Those who had seen it told the people what had happened to the demon-possessed man—and told about the pigs as well. 17Then the people began to plead with Jesus to leave their region.

18As Jesus was getting into the boat, the man who had been demon-possessed begged to go with him. 19Jesus did not let him, but said, "Go home to your family and tell them how much the Lord has done for you, and how he has had mercy on you." 20So the man went away and began to tell in the Decapolis[c] how much Jesus had done for him. And all the people were amazed.

A Dead Girl and a Sick Woman

21When Jesus had again crossed over by boat to the other side of the lake, a large crowd gathered around him

[c] *20* That is, the Ten Cities

NEW LIVING TRANSLATION

herd of two thousand pigs plunged down the steep hillside into the lake, where they drowned.

14The herdsmen fled to the nearby city and the surrounding countryside, spreading the news as they ran. Everyone rushed out to see for themselves. 15A crowd soon gathered around Jesus, but they were frightened when they saw the man who had been demon possessed, for he was sitting there fully clothed and perfectly sane. 16Those who had seen what happened to the man and to the pigs told everyone about it, 17and the crowd began pleading with Jesus to go away and leave them alone.

18When Jesus got back into the boat, the man who had been demon possessed begged to go, too. 19But Jesus said, "No, go home to your friends, and tell them what wonderful things the Lord has done for you and how merciful he has been." 20So the man started off to visit the Ten Towns* of that region and began to tell everyone about the great things Jesus had done for him; and everyone was amazed at what he told them.

Jesus Heals in Response to Faith

21When Jesus went back across to the other side of the lake, a large crowd gathered around him on the shore. 22A

5:20 Greek *Decapolis.*

NEW KING JAMES VERSION

thousand); and the herd ran violently down the steep place into the sea, and drowned in the sea.

14So those who fed the swine fled, and they told *it* in the city and in the country. And they went out to see what it was that had happened. 15Then they came to Jesus, and saw the one *who had been* demon-possessed and had the legion, sitting and clothed and in his right mind. And they were afraid. 16And those who saw it told them how it happened to him *who had been* demon-possessed, and about the swine. 17Then they began to plead with Him to depart from their region.

18And when He got into the boat, he who had been demon-possessed begged Him that he might be with Him. 19However, Jesus did not permit him, but said to him, "Go home to your friends, and tell them what great things the Lord has done for you, and how He has had compassion on you." 20And he departed and began to proclaim in Decapolis all that Jesus had done for him; and all marveled.

A Girl Restored to Life and a Woman Healed

21Now when Jesus had crossed over again by boat to the other side, a great multitude gathered to Him; and He was

THE MESSAGE

even worse for the pigs than for the man. Crazed, they stampeded over a cliff into the sea and drowned.

Those tending the pigs, scared to death, bolted and told their story in town and country. Everyone wanted to see what had happened. They came up to Jesus, and saw the madman sitting there wearing decent clothes and making sense, no longer a walking madhouse of a man.

Those who had seen it told the others what had happened to the demon-possessed man and the pigs. At first they were in awe—and then they were upset, upset over the drowned pigs. They demanded that Jesus leave and not come back.

As Jesus was getting into the boat, the demon-delivered man begged to go along, but he wouldn't let him. Jesus said, "Go home to your own people. Tell them your story—what the Master did, how he had mercy on you." The man went back and began to preach in the Ten Towns area about what Jesus had done for him. He was the talk of the town.

A Risk of Faith

After Jesus crossed over by boat, a large crowd met him at the seaside. One of the meeting-place leaders named

KING JAMES VERSION

22 And, behold, there cometh one of the rulers of the synagogue, Jairus by name; and when he saw him, he fell at his feet,

23 And besought him greatly, saying, My little daughter lieth at the point of death: *I pray thee*, come and lay thy hands on her, that she may be healed; and she shall live.

24 And *Jesus* went with him; and much people followed him, and thronged him.

25 And a certain woman, which had an issue of blood twelve years,

26 And had suffered many things of many physicians, and had spent all that she had, and was nothing bettered, but rather grew worse,

27 When she had heard of Jesus, came in the press behind, and touched his garment.

28 For she said, If I may touch but his clothes, I shall be whole.

29 And straightway the fountain of her blood was dried up; and she felt in *her* body that she was healed of that plague.

30 And Jesus, immediately knowing in himself that virtue had gone out of him, turned him about in the press, and said, Who touched my clothes?

31 And his disciples said unto him, Thou seest the multitude thronging thee, and sayest thou, Who touched me?

32 And he looked round about to see her that had done this thing.

33 But the woman fearing and trembling, knowing

NEW AMERICAN STANDARD BIBLE

22 One of the synagogue officials named Jairus *came up, and on seeing Him, *fell at His feet

23 and *implored Him earnestly, saying, "My little daughter is at the point of death; *please* come and lay Your hands on her, so that she will get well and live."

24 And He went off with him; and a large crowd was following Him and pressing in on Him.

25 A woman who had had a hemorrhage for twelve years,

26 and had endured much at the hands of many physicians, and had spent all that she had and was not helped at all, but rather had grown worse—

27 after hearing about Jesus, she came up in the crowd behind *Him* and touched His cloak.

28 For she thought, "If I just touch His garments, I will get well."

29 Immediately the flow of her blood was dried up; and she felt in her body that she was healed of her affliction.

30 Immediately Jesus, perceiving in Himself that the power *proceeding* from Him had gone forth, turned around in the crowd and said, "Who touched My garments?"

31 And His disciples said to Him, "You see the crowd pressing in on You, and You say, 'Who touched Me?' "

32 And He looked around to see the woman who had done this.

33 But the woman fearing and trembling, aware of what

NEW CENTURY VERSION

leader of the synagogue, named Jairus, came there, saw
Jesus, and fell at his feet. 23He begged Jesus, saying again
and again, "My daughter is dying. Please come and put
your hands on her so she will be healed and will live."
24So Jesus went with him.

A large crowd followed Jesus and pushed very close
around him. 25Among them was a woman who had been
bleeding for twelve years. 26She had suffered very much
from many doctors and had spent all the money she had,
but instead of improving, she was getting worse. 27When
the woman heard about Jesus, she came up behind him in
the crowd and touched his coat. 28She thought, "If I can
just touch his clothes, I will be healed." 29Instantly her
bleeding stopped, and she felt in her body that she was
healed from her disease.

30At once Jesus felt power go out from him. So he turned
around in the crowd and asked, "Who touched my
clothes?"

31His followers said, "Look at how many people are
pushing against you! And you ask, 'Who touched me?' "

32But Jesus continued looking around to see who had
touched him. 33The woman, knowing that she was healed,

CONTEMPORARY ENGLISH VERSION

gathered around him. 22The person in charge of the Jewish
meeting place was also there. His name was Jairus, and
when he saw Jesus, he went over to him. He knelt at Jesus'
feet 23and started begging him for help. He said, "My
daughter is about to die! Please come and touch her, so
she will get well and live." 24Jesus went with Jairus. Many
people followed along and kept crowding around.

25In the crowd was a woman who had been bleeding for
twelve years. 26She had gone to many doctors, and they
had not done anything except cause her a lot of pain. She
had paid them all the money she had. But instead of getting better, she only got worse.

27The woman had heard about Jesus, so she came up
behind him in the crowd and barely touched his clothes.
28She had said to herself, "If I can just touch his clothes, I
will get well." 29As soon as she touched them, her bleeding
stopped, and she knew she was well.

30At that moment Jesus felt power go out from him. He
turned to the crowd and asked, "Who touched my
clothes?"

31His disciples said to him, "Look at all these people
crowding around you! How can you ask who touched
you?" 32But Jesus turned to see who had touched him.

33The woman knew what had happened to her. She

NEW INTERNATIONAL VERSION

while he was by the lake. 22 Then one of the synagogue rulers, named Jairus, came there. Seeing Jesus, he fell at his feet 23 and pleaded earnestly with him, "My little daughter is dying. Please come and put your hands on her so that she will be healed and live." 24 So Jesus went with him.

A large crowd followed and pressed around him. 25 And a woman was there who had been subject to bleeding for twelve years. 26 She had suffered a great deal under the care of many doctors and had spent all she had, yet instead of getting better she grew worse. 27 When she heard about Jesus, she came up behind him in the crowd and touched his cloak, 28 because she thought, "If I just touch his clothes, I will be healed." 29 Immediately her bleeding stopped and she felt in her body that she was freed from her suffering.

30 At once Jesus realized that power had gone out from him. He turned around in the crowd and asked, "Who touched my clothes?"

31 "You see the people crowding against you," his disciples answered, "and yet you can ask, 'Who touched me?' "

32 But Jesus kept looking around to see who had done it. 33 Then the woman, knowing what had happened to her,

NEW LIVING TRANSLATION

leader of the local synagogue, whose name was Jairus, came and fell down before him, 23 pleading with him to heal his little daughter. "She is about to die," he said in desperation. "Please come and place your hands on her; heal her so she can live."

24 Jesus went with him, and the crowd thronged behind. 25 And there was a woman in the crowd who had had a hemorrhage for twelve years. 26 She had suffered a great deal from many doctors through the years and had spent everything she had to pay them, but she had gotten no better. In fact, she was worse. 27 She had heard about Jesus, so she came up behind him through the crowd and touched the fringe of his robe. 28 For she thought to herself, "If I can just touch his clothing, I will be healed." 29 Immediately the bleeding stopped, and she could feel that she had been healed!

30 Jesus realized at once that healing power had gone out from him, so he turned around in the crowd and asked, "Who touched my clothes?"

31 His disciples said to him, "All this crowd is pressing around you. How can you ask, 'Who touched me?' "

32 But he kept on looking around to see who had done it. 33 Then the frightened woman, trembling at the realization

NEW KING JAMES VERSION

by the sea. 22 And behold, one of the rulers of the synagogue came, Jairus by name. And when he saw Him, he fell at His feet 23 and begged Him earnestly, saying, "My little daughter lies at the point of death. Come and lay Your hands on her, that she may be healed, and she will live." 24 So *Jesus* went with him, and a great multitude followed Him and thronged Him.

25 Now a certain woman had a flow of blood for twelve years, 26 and had suffered many things from many physicians. She had spent all that she had and was no better, but rather grew worse. 27 When she heard about Jesus, she came behind *Him* in the crowd and touched His garment. 28 For she said, "If only I may touch His clothes, I shall be made well."

29 Immediately the fountain of her blood was dried up, and she felt in *her* body that she was healed of the affliction. 30 And Jesus, immediately knowing in Himself that power had gone out of Him, turned around in the crowd and said, "Who touched My clothes?"

31 But His disciples said to Him, "You see the multitude thronging You, and You say, 'Who touched Me?' "

32 And He looked around to see her who had done this thing. 33 But the woman, fearing and trembling, knowing

THE MESSAGE

Jairus came. When he saw Jesus, he fell to his knees, beside himself as he begged, "My dear daughter is at death's door. Come and lay hands on her so she will get well and live." Jesus went with him, the whole crowd tagging along, pushing and jostling him.

A woman who had suffered a condition of hemorrhaging for twelve years—a long succession of physicians had treated her, and treated her badly, taking all her money and leaving her worse off than before—had heard about Jesus. She slipped in from behind and touched his robe. She was thinking to herself, "If I can put a finger on his robe, I can get well." The moment she did it, the flow of blood dried up. She could feel the change, and knew her plague was over and done with.

At the same moment, Jesus felt energy discharging from him. He turned around to the crowd and asked, "Who touched my robe?"

His disciples said, "What are you talking about? With this crowd pushing and jostling you, you're asking, 'Who touched me?' Dozens have touched you!"

But he went on asking, looking around to see who had done it. The woman, knowing what had happened, knowing

KING JAMES VERSION

what was done in her, came and fell down before him, and told him all the truth.

34 And he said unto her, Daughter, thy faith hath made thee whole; go in peace, and be whole of thy plague.

35 ¶ While he yet spake, there came from the ruler of the synagogue's *house certain* which said, Thy daughter is dead: why troublest thou the Master any further?

36 As soon as Jesus heard the word that was spoken, he saith unto the ruler of the synagogue, Be not afraid, only believe.

37 And he suffered no man to follow him, save Peter, and James, and John the brother of James.

38 And he cometh to the house of the ruler of the synagogue, and seeth the tumult, and them that wept and wailed greatly.

39 And when he was come in, he saith unto them, Why make ye this ado, and weep? the damsel is not dead, but sleepeth.

40 And they laughed him to scorn. But when he had put them all out, he taketh the father and the mother of the damsel, and them that were with him, and entereth in where the damsel was lying.

41 And he took the damsel by the hand, and said unto her, Talitha cumi; which is, being interpreted, Damsel, I say unto thee, arise.

42 And straightway the damsel arose, and walked; for she was *of the age* of twelve years. And they were astonished with a great astonishment.

43 And he charged them straitly that no man should

NEW AMERICAN STANDARD BIBLE

had happened to her, came and fell down before Him and told Him the whole truth.

34 And He said to her, "Daughter, your faith has made you well; go in peace and be healed of your affliction."

35 While He was still speaking, they *came from the *house of* the synagogue official, saying, "Your daughter has died; why trouble the Teacher anymore?"

36 But Jesus, overhearing what was being spoken, *said to the synagogue official, "Do not be afraid *any longer,* only believe."

37 And He allowed no one to accompany Him, except Peter and James and John the brother of James.

38 They *came to the house of the synagogue official; and He *saw a commotion, and *people* loudly weeping and wailing.

39 And entering in, He *said to them, "Why make a commotion and weep? The child has not died, but is asleep."

40 They *began* laughing at Him. But putting them all out, He *took along the child's father and mother and His own companions, and *entered *the room* where the child was.

41 Taking the child by the hand, He *said to her, "Talitha kum!" (which translated means, "Little girl, I say to you, get up!").

42 Immediately the girl got up and *began* to walk, for she was twelve years old. And immediately they were completely astounded.

43 And He gave them strict orders that no one should

NEW CENTURY VERSION

came and fell at Jesus' feet. Shaking with fear, she told him the whole truth. [34]Jesus said to her, "Dear woman, you are made well because you believed. Go in peace; be healed of your disease."

[35]While Jesus was still speaking, some people came from the house of the synagogue leader. They said, "Your daughter is dead. There is no need to bother the teacher anymore."

[36]But Jesus paid no attention to what they said. He told the synagogue leader, "Don't be afraid; just believe."

[37]Jesus let only Peter, James, and John the brother of James go with him. [38]When they came to the house of the synagogue leader, Jesus found many people there making lots of noise and crying loudly. [39]Jesus entered the house and said to them, "Why are you crying and making so much noise? The child is not dead, only asleep." [40]But they laughed at him. So, after throwing them out of the house, Jesus took the child's father and mother and his three followers into the room where the child was. [41]Taking hold of the girl's hand, he said to her, "Talitha, koum!" (This means, "Young girl, I tell you to stand up!") [42]At once the girl stood right up and began walking. (She was twelve years old.) Everyone was completely amazed.

CONTEMPORARY ENGLISH VERSION

came shaking with fear and knelt down in front of Jesus. Then she told him the whole story.

[34]Jesus said to the woman, "You are now well because of your faith. May God give you peace! You are healed, and you will no longer be in pain."

[35]While Jesus was still speaking, some men came from Jairus' home and said, "Your daughter has died! Why bother the teacher anymore?"

[36]Jesus heard[e] what they said, and he said to Jairus, "Don't worry. Just have faith!"

[37]Jesus did not let anyone go with him except Peter and the two brothers, James and John. [38]They went home with Jairus and saw the people crying and making a lot of noise.[f] [39]Then Jesus went inside and said to them, "Why are you crying and carrying on like this? The child isn't dead. She is just asleep." [40]But the people laughed at him.

After Jesus had sent them all out of the house, he took the girl's father and mother and his three disciples and went to where she was. [41-42]He took the twelve-year-old girl by the hand and said, "Talitha, koum!"[g] which means, "Little girl, get up!" The girl got right up and started walking around.

Everyone was greatly surprised. [43]But Jesus ordered

[e] 5.36 *heard*: Or "ignored." [f] 5.38 *crying and making a lot of noise*: The Jewish people often hired mourners for funerals.
[g] 5.41,42 *Talitha, koum*: These words are in Aramaic, a language spoken in Palestine during the time of Jesus.

NEW INTERNATIONAL VERSION

came and fell at his feet and, trembling with fear, told him the whole truth. 34He said to her, "Daughter, your faith has healed you. Go in peace and be freed from your suffering."

35While Jesus was still speaking, some men came from the house of Jairus, the synagogue ruler. "Your daughter is dead," they said. "Why bother the teacher any more?"

36Ignoring what they said, Jesus told the synagogue ruler, "Don't be afraid; just believe."

37He did not let anyone follow him except Peter, James and John the brother of James. 38When they came to the home of the synagogue ruler, Jesus saw a commotion, with people crying and wailing loudly. 39He went in and said to them, "Why all this commotion and wailing? The child is not dead but asleep." 40But they laughed at him.

After he put them all out, he took the child's father and mother and the disciples who were with him, and went in where the child was. 41He took her by the hand and said to her, *"Talitha koum!"* (which means, "Little girl, I say to you, get up!"). 42Immediately the girl stood up and walked around (she was twelve years old). At this they were completely astonished. 43He gave strict orders not to

NEW LIVING TRANSLATION

of what had happened to her, came and fell at his feet and told him what she had done. 34And he said to her, "Daughter, your faith has made you well. Go in peace. You have been healed."

35While he was still speaking to her, messengers arrived from Jairus's home with the message, "Your daughter is dead. There's no use troubling the Teacher now."

36But Jesus ignored their comments and said to Jairus, "Don't be afraid. Just trust me." 37Then Jesus stopped the crowd and wouldn't let anyone go with him except Peter and James and John. 38When they came to the home of the synagogue leader, Jesus saw the commotion and the weeping and wailing. 39He went inside and spoke to the people. "Why all this weeping and commotion?" he asked. "The child isn't dead; she is only asleep."

40The crowd laughed at him, but he told them all to go outside. Then he took the girl's father and mother and his three disciples into the room where the girl was lying. 41Holding her hand, he said to her, "Get up, little girl!"* 42And the girl, who was twelve years old, immediately stood up and walked around! Her parents were absolutely overwhelmed. 43Jesus commanded them not to tell anyone

5:41 Greek text uses Aramaic *"Talitha cumi"* and then translates it as "Get up, little girl."

NEW KING JAMES VERSION

what had happened to her, came and fell down before Him and told Him the whole truth. 34And He said to her, "Daughter, your faith has made you well. Go in peace, and be healed of your affliction."

35While He was still speaking, *some* came from the ruler of the synagogue's *house* who said, "Your daughter is dead. Why trouble the Teacher any further?"

36As soon as Jesus heard the word that was spoken, He said to the ruler of the synagogue, "Do not be afraid; only believe." 37And He permitted no one to follow Him except Peter, James, and John the brother of James. 38Then He came to the house of the ruler of the synagogue, and saw a tumult and those who wept and wailed loudly. 39When He came in, He said to them, "Why make this commotion and weep? The child is not dead, but sleeping."

40And they ridiculed Him. But when He had put them all outside, He took the father and the mother of the child, and those *who were* with Him, and entered where the child was lying. 41Then He took the child by the hand, and said to her, "Talitha, cumi," which is translated, "Little girl, I say to you, arise." 42Immediately the girl arose and walked, for she was twelve years *of age.* And they were overcome with great amazement. 43But He commanded

THE MESSAGE

she was the one, stepped up in fear and trembling, knelt before him, and gave him the whole story.

Jesus said to her, "Daughter, you took a risk of faith, and now you're healed and whole. Live well, live blessed! Be healed of your plague."

✠

While he was still talking, some people came from the leader's house and told him, "Your daughter is dead. Why bother the Teacher any more?"

Jesus overheard what they were talking about and said to the leader, "Don't listen to them; just trust me."

He permitted no one to go in with him except Peter, James, and John. They entered the leader's house and pushed their way through the gossips looking for a story and neighbors bringing in casseroles. Jesus was abrupt: "Why all this busybody grief and gossip? This child isn't dead; she's sleeping." Provoked to sarcasm, they told him he didn't know what he was talking about.

But when he had sent them all out, he took the child's father and mother, along with his companions, and entered the child's room. He clasped the girl's hand and said, "*Talitha koum*," which means "Little girl, get up." At that, she was up and walking around! This girl was twelve years of age. They, of course, were all beside themselves with joy. He gave them strict orders that no one was to

KING JAMES VERSION

know it; and commanded that something should be given her to eat.

6 And he went out from thence, and came into his own country; and his disciples follow him.

2 And when the sabbath day was come, he began to teach in the synagogue: and many hearing *him* were astonished, saying, From whence hath this *man* these things? and what wisdom *is* this which is given unto him, that even such mighty works are wrought by his hands?

3 Is not this the carpenter, the son of Mary, the brother of James, and Joses, and of Juda, and Simon? and are not his sisters here with us? And they were offended at him.

4 But Jesus said unto them, A prophet is not without honour, but in his own country, and among his own kin, and in his own house.

5 And he could there do no mighty work, save that he laid his hands upon a few sick folk, and healed *them*.

6 And he marvelled because of their unbelief. And he went round about the villages, teaching.

7 ¶ And he called *unto him* the twelve, and began to send them forth by two and two; and gave them power over unclean spirits;

8 And commanded them that they should take nothing for *their* journey, save a staff only; no scrip, no bread, no money in *their* purse:

NEW AMERICAN STANDARD BIBLE

know about this, and He said that *something* should be given her to eat.

Teaching at Nazareth

6 Jesus went out from there and *came into His hometown; and His disciples *followed Him.

2 When the Sabbath came, He began to teach in the synagogue; and the many listeners were astonished, saying, "Where did this man *get* these things, and what is *this* wisdom given to Him, and such miracles as these performed by His hands?

3 "Is not this the carpenter, the son of Mary, and brother of James and Joses and Judas and Simon? Are not His sisters here with us?" And they took offense at Him.

4 Jesus said to them, "A prophet is not without honor except in his hometown and among his *own* relatives and in his *own* household."

5 And He could do no miracle there except that He laid His hands on a few sick people and healed them.

6 And He wondered at their unbelief.

And He was going around the villages teaching.

The Twelve Sent Out

7 And He *summoned the twelve and began to send them out in pairs, and gave them authority over the unclean spirits;

8 and He instructed them that they should take nothing for *their* journey, except a mere staff—no bread, no bag, no money in their belt—

NEW CENTURY VERSION

[43]Jesus gave them strict orders not to tell people about
this. Then he told them to give the girl something to eat.

Jesus Goes to His Hometown

6 Jesus left there and went to his hometown, and his
followers went with him. [2]On the Sabbath day he
taught in the synagogue. Many people heard him and were
amazed, saying, "Where did this man get these teachings?
What is this wisdom that has been given to him? And
where did he get the power to do miracles? [3]He is just the
carpenter, the son of Mary and the brother of James,
Joseph, Judas, and Simon. And his sisters are here with
us." So the people were upset with Jesus.
[4]Jesus said to them, "A prophet is honored everywhere
except in his hometown and with his own people and in
his own home." [5]So Jesus was not able to work any mira-
cles there except to heal a few sick people by putting his
hands on them. [6]He was amazed at how many people had
no faith.
Then Jesus went to other villages in that area and
taught. [7]He called his twelve followers together and got
ready to send them out two by two and gave them author-
ity over evil spirits. [8]This is what Jesus commanded them:
"Take nothing for your trip except a walking stick. Take
no bread, no bag, and no money in your pockets. [9]Wear

CONTEMPORARY ENGLISH VERSION

them not to tell anyone what had happened. Then he said, "Give her something to eat."

The People of Nazareth Turn against Jesus

(Matthew 13.53-58; Luke 4.16-30)

6 Jesus left and returned to his hometown[a] with his dis-
ciples. [2]The next Sabbath he taught in the Jewish
meeting place. Many of the people who heard him were
amazed and asked, "How can he do all this? Where did he
get such wisdom and the power to work these miracles?
[3]Isn't he the carpenter,[b] the son of Mary? Aren't James,
Joseph, Judas, and Simon his brothers? Don't his sisters
still live here in our town?" The people were very unhappy
because of what he was doing.
[4]But Jesus said, "Prophets are honored by everyone,
except the people of their hometown and their relatives
and their own family." [5]Jesus could not work any miracles
there, except to heal a few sick people by placing his hands
on them. [6]He was surprised that the people did not have
any faith.

Instructions for the Twelve Apostles

(Matthew 10.5-15; Luke 9.1-6)

Jesus taught in all the neighboring villages. [7]Then he
called together his twelve apostles and sent them out two
by two with power over evil spirits. [8]He told them, "You
may take along a walking stick. But don't carry food or a

[a] 6.1 *hometown*: Nazareth. [b] 6.3 *carpenter*: The Greek word may also mean someone who builds or works with stone or brick.

NEW INTERNATIONAL VERSION

let anyone know about this, and told them to give her something to eat.

A Prophet Without Honor

6 Jesus left there and went to his hometown, accompanied by his disciples. 2When the Sabbath came, he began to teach in the synagogue, and many who heard him were amazed.

"Where did this man get these things?" they asked. "What's this wisdom that has been given him, that he even does miracles! 3Isn't this the carpenter? Isn't this Mary's son and the brother of James, Joseph,[a] Judas and Simon? Aren't his sisters here with us?" And they took offense at him.

4Jesus said to them, "Only in his hometown, among his relatives and in his own house is a prophet without honor." 5He could not do any miracles there, except lay his hands on a few sick people and heal them. 6And he was amazed at their lack of faith.

Jesus Sends Out the Twelve

Then Jesus went around teaching from village to village. 7Calling the Twelve to him, he sent them out two by two and gave them authority over evil[b] spirits.

8These were his instructions: "Take nothing for the journey except a staff—no bread, no bag, no money in your

[a] *3* Greek *Joses*, a variant of *Joseph* [b] *7* Greek *unclean*

NEW LIVING TRANSLATION

what had happened, and he told them to give her something to eat.

Jesus Rejected at Nazareth

6 Jesus left that part of the country and returned with his disciples to Nazareth, his hometown. 2The next Sabbath he began teaching in the synagogue, and many who heard him were astonished. They asked, "Where did he get all his wisdom and the power to perform such miracles? 3He's just the carpenter, the son of Mary and brother of James, Joseph,* Judas, and Simon. And his sisters live right here among us." They were deeply offended and refused to believe in him.

4Then Jesus told them, "A prophet is honored everywhere except in his own hometown and among his relatives and his own family." 5And because of their unbelief, he couldn't do any mighty miracles among them except to place his hands on a few sick people and heal them. 6And he was amazed at their unbelief.

Jesus Sends Out the Twelve Apostles

Then Jesus went out from village to village, teaching. 7And he called his twelve disciples together and sent them out two by two, with authority to cast out evil spirits. 8He told them to take nothing with them except a walking stick—no food, no traveler's bag, no money. 9He told them

6:3 Greek *Joses;* see Matt 13:55.

NEW KING JAMES VERSION

them strictly that no one should know it, and said that *something* should be given her to eat.

Jesus Rejected at Nazareth

6 Then He went out from there and came to His own country, and His disciples followed Him. 2And when the Sabbath had come, He began to teach in the synagogue. And many hearing *Him* were astonished, saying, "Where *did* this Man *get* these things? And what wisdom *is* this which is given to Him, that such mighty works are performed by His hands! 3Is this not the carpenter, the Son of Mary, and brother of James, Joses, Judas, and Simon? And are not His sisters here with us?" So they were offended at Him.

4But Jesus said to them, "A prophet is not without honor except in his own country, among his own relatives, and in his own house." 5Now He could do no mighty work there, except that He laid His hands on a few sick people and healed *them.* 6And He marveled because of their unbelief. Then He went about the villages in a circuit, teaching.

Sending Out the Twelve

7And He called the twelve to *Himself,* and began to send them out two *by* two, and gave them power over unclean spirits. 8He commanded them to take nothing for the journey except a staff—no bag, no bread, no copper in *their*

THE MESSAGE

know what had taken place in that room. Then he said, "Give her something to eat."

Just a Carpenter

6 He left there and returned to his hometown. His disciples came along. On the Sabbath, he gave a lecture in the meeting place. He made a real hit, impressing everyone. "We had no idea he was this good!" they said. "How did he get so wise all of a sudden, get such ability?"

But in the next breath they were cutting him down: "He's just a carpenter—Mary's boy. We've known him since he was a kid. We know his brothers, James, Justus, Jude, and Simon, and his sisters. Who does he think he is?" They tripped over what little they knew about him and fell, sprawling. And they never got any further.

Jesus told them, "A prophet has little honor in his hometown, among his relatives, on the streets he played in as a child." Jesus wasn't able to do much of anything there—he laid hands on a few sick people and healed them, that's all. He couldn't get over their stubbornness. He left and made a circuit of the other villages, teaching.

The Twelve

Jesus called the Twelve to him, and sent them out in pairs. He gave them authority and power to deal with the evil opposition. He sent them off with these instructions:

"Don't think you need a lot of extra equipment for this. *You* are the equipment. No special appeals for funds. Keep it simple.

KING JAMES VERSION

9 But *be* shod with sandals; and not put on two coats.

10 And he said unto them, In what place soever ye enter into an house, there abide till ye depart from that place.

11 And whosoever shall not receive you, nor hear you, when ye depart thence, shake off the dust under your feet for a testimony against them. Verily I say unto you, It shall be more tolerable for Sodom and Gomorrha in the day of judgment, than for that city.

12 And they went out, and preached that men should repent.

13 And they cast out many devils, and anointed with oil many that were sick, and healed *them*.

14 ¶ And king Herod heard *of him*; (for his name was spread abroad:) and he said, That John the Baptist was risen from the dead, and therefore mighty works do shew forth themselves in him.

15 Others said, That it is Elias. And others said, That it is a prophet, or as one of the prophets.

16 But when Herod heard *thereof*, he said, It is John, whom I beheaded: he is risen from the dead.

17 For Herod himself had sent forth and laid hold upon John, and bound him in prison for Herodias' sake, his brother Philip's wife: for he had married her.

18 For John had said unto Herod, It is not lawful for thee to have thy brother's wife.

19 Therefore Herodias had a quarrel against him, and would have killed him; but she could not:

NEW AMERICAN STANDARD BIBLE

9 but *to* wear sandals; and *He added*, "Do not put on two [1]tunics."

10 And He said to them, "Wherever you enter a house, stay there until you leave town.

11 "Any place that does not receive you or listen to you, as you go out from there, shake the dust off the soles of your feet for a testimony against them."

12 They went out and preached that *men* should repent.

13 And they were casting out many demons and were anointing with oil many sick people and healing them.

John's Fate Recalled

14 And King Herod heard *of it,* for His name had become well known; and *people* were saying, "John the Baptist has risen from the dead, and that is why these miraculous powers are at work in Him."

15 But others were saying, "He is Elijah." And others were saying, "*He is* a prophet, like one of the prophets *of old.*"

16 But when Herod heard *of it,* he kept saying, "John, whom I beheaded, has risen!"

17 For Herod himself had sent and had John arrested and bound in prison on account of Herodias, the wife of his brother Philip, because he had married her.

18 For John had been saying to Herod, "It is not lawful for you to have your brother's wife."

19 Herodias had a grudge against him and wanted to put him to death and could not *do so;*

6:9 [1] Or *inner garments*

NEW CENTURY VERSION

sandals, but take only the clothes you are wearing. 10When you enter a house, stay there until you leave that town. 11If the people in a certain place refuse to welcome you or listen to you, leave that place. Shake its dust off your feet[a] as a warning to them."

12So the followers went out and preached that people should change their hearts and lives. 13They forced many demons out and put olive oil on many sick people and healed them.

How John the Baptist Was Killed

14King Herod heard about Jesus, because he was now well known. Some people said, "He is John the Baptist, who has risen from the dead. That is why he can work these miracles."

15Others said, "He is Elijah."[b]

Other people said, "Jesus is a prophet, like the prophets who lived long ago."

16When Herod heard this, he said, "I killed John by cutting off his head. Now he has risen from the dead!"

17Herod himself had ordered his soldiers to arrest John and put him in prison in order to please his wife, Herodias. She had been the wife of Philip, Herod's brother, but then Herod had married her. 18John had been telling Herod, "It is not lawful for you to be married to your brother's wife." 19So Herodias hated John and wanted to kill him. But she

6:11 [a] **Shake...feet** A warning. It showed that they were rejecting these people. **6:15** [b] **Elijah** A man who spoke for God and who lived hundreds of years before Christ. See 1 Kings 17.

CONTEMPORARY ENGLISH VERSION

traveling bag or any money. 9It's all right to wear sandals, but don't take along a change of clothes. 10When you are welcomed into a home, stay there until you leave that town. 11If any place won't welcome you or listen to your message, leave and shake the dust from your feet[c] as a warning to them."

12The apostles left and started telling everyone to turn to God. 13They forced out many demons and healed a lot of sick people by putting olive oil[d] on them.

The Death of John the Baptist (Matthew 14.1-12; Luke 9.7-9)

14Jesus became so well-known that Herod the ruler[e] heard about him. Some people thought he was John the Baptist, who had come back to life with the power to work miracles. 15Others thought he was Elijah[f] or some other prophet who had lived long ago. 16But when Herod heard about Jesus, he said, "This must be John! I had his head cut off, and now he has come back to life."

17-18Herod had earlier married Herodias, the wife of his brother Philip. But John had told him, "It isn't right for you to take your brother's wife!" So, in order to please Herodias, Herod arrested John and put him in prison.

19Herodias had a grudge against John and wanted to kill

[c] **6.11** *shake the dust from your feet*: This was a way of showing rejection. [d] **6.13** *olive oil*: The Jewish people used olive oil as a way of healing people. Sometimes olive oil is a symbol for healing by means of a miracle (see James 5.14). [e] **6.14** *Herod the ruler*: Herod Antipas, the son of Herod the Great. [f] **6.15** *Elijah*: Many of the Jewish people expected the prophet Elijah to come and prepare the way for the Messiah.

NEW INTERNATIONAL VERSION

belts. 9Wear sandals but not an extra tunic. 10Whenever
you enter a house, stay there until you leave that town.
11And if any place will not welcome you or listen to you,
shake the dust off your feet when you leave, as a testimo-
ny against them."

12They went out and preached that people should repent.
13They drove out many demons and anointed many sick
people with oil and healed them.

John the Baptist Beheaded

14King Herod heard about this, for Jesus' name had
become well known. Some were saying,[c] "John the Baptist
has been raised from the dead, and that is why miraculous
powers are at work in him."

15Others said, "He is Elijah."

And still others claimed, "He is a prophet, like one of the
prophets of long ago."

16But when Herod heard this, he said, "John, the man I
beheaded, has been raised from the dead!"

17For Herod himself had given orders to have John
arrested, and he had him bound and put in prison. He did
this because of Herodias, his brother Philip's wife, whom
he had married. 18For John had been saying to Herod, "It is
not lawful for you to have your brother's wife." 19So
Herodias nursed a grudge against John and wanted to kill

c 14 Some early manuscripts *He was saying*

NEW LIVING TRANSLATION

to wear sandals but not to take even an extra coat.
10"When you enter each village, be a guest in only one
home," he said. 11"And if a village won't welcome you or
listen to you, shake off its dust from your feet as you
leave. It is a sign that you have abandoned that village to
its fate."

12So the disciples went out, telling all they met to turn
from their sins. 13And they cast out many demons and
healed many sick people, anointing them with olive oil.

The Death of John the Baptist

14Herod Antipas, the king, soon heard about Jesus,
because people everywhere were talking about him. Some
were saying,* "This must be John the Baptist come back to
life again. That is why he can do such miracles." 15Others
thought Jesus was the ancient prophet Elijah. Still others
thought he was a prophet like the other great prophets of
the past. 16When Herod heard about Jesus, he said, "John,
the man I beheaded, has come back from the dead." 17For
Herod had sent soldiers to arrest and imprison John as a
favor to Herodias. She had been his brother Philip's wife,
but Herod had married her. 18John kept telling Herod, "It is
illegal for you to marry your brother's wife." 19Herodias
was enraged and wanted John killed in revenge, but with-

6:14 Some manuscripts read *He was saying.*

NEW KING JAMES VERSION

money belts— 9but to wear sandals, and not to put on two
tunics.

10Also He said to them, "In whatever place you enter a
house, stay there till you depart from that place. 11And
whoever[a] will not receive you nor hear you, when you
depart from there, shake off the dust under your feet as a
testimony against them.[b] Assuredly, I say to you, it will be
more tolerable for Sodom and Gomorrah in the day of judg-
ment than for that city!"

12So they went out and preached that *people* should
repent. 13And they cast out many demons, and anointed
with oil many who were sick, and healed *them.*

John the Baptist Beheaded

14Now King Herod heard *of Him,* for His name had become
well known. And he said, "John the Baptist is risen from the
dead, and therefore these powers are at work in him."

15Others said, "It is Elijah."

And others said, "It is the Prophet, or[c] like one of the
prophets."

16But when Herod heard, he said, "This is John, whom I
beheaded; he has been raised from the dead!" 17For Herod
himself had sent and laid hold of John, and bound him in
prison for the sake of Herodias, his brother Philip's wife;
for he had married her. 18Because John had said to Herod,
"It is not lawful for you to have your brother's wife."

19Therefore Herodias held it against him and wanted to

6:11 *a* NU-Text reads *whatever place.* *b* NU-Text omits the rest of this verse. 6:15 *c* NU-Text and M-Text omit *or.*

THE MESSAGE

"And no luxury inns. Get a modest place and be content
there until you leave.

"If you're not welcomed, not listened to, quietly with-
draw. Don't make a scene. Shrug your shoulders and be on
your way."

Then they were on the road. They preached with joyful
urgency that life can be radically different; right and left
they sent the demons packing; they brought wellness to
the sick, anointing their bodies, healing their spirits.

The Death of John

King Herod heard of all this, for by this time the name of
Jesus was on everyone's lips. He said, "This has to be John
the Baptizer come back from the dead—that's why he's
able to work miracles!"

Others said, "No, it's Elijah."

Others said, "He's a prophet, just like one of the old-time
prophets."

But Herod wouldn't budge: "It's John, sure enough. I cut
off his head, and now he's back, alive."

Herod was the one who had ordered the arrest of John,
put him in chains, and sent him to prison at the nagging
of Herodias, his brother Philip's wife. For John had pro-
voked Herod by naming his relationship with Herodias
"adultery." Herodias, smoldering with hate, wanted to kill

KING JAMES VERSION

20 For Herod feared John, knowing that he was a just man and an holy, and observed him; and when he heard him, he did many things, and heard him gladly.

21 And when a convenient day was come, that Herod on his birthday made a supper to his lords, high captains, and chief *estates* of Galilee;

22 And when the daughter of the said Herodias came in, and danced, and pleased Herod and them that sat with him, the king said unto the damsel, Ask of me whatsoever thou wilt, and I will give *it* thee.

23 And he sware unto her, Whatsoever thou shalt ask of me, I will give *it* thee, unto the half of my kingdom.

24 And she went forth, and said unto her mother, What shall I ask? And she said, The head of John the Baptist.

25 And she came in straightway with haste unto the king, and asked, saying, I will that thou give me by and by in a charger the head of John the Baptist.

26 And the king was exceeding sorry; *yet* for his oath's sake, and for their sakes which sat with him, he would not reject her.

27 And immediately the king sent an executioner, and commanded his head to be brought: and he went and beheaded him in the prison,

28 And brought his head in a charger, and gave it to the damsel: and the damsel gave it to her mother.

29 And when his disciples heard *of it*, they came and took up his corpse, and laid it in a tomb.

NEW AMERICAN STANDARD BIBLE

20 for Herod was afraid of John, knowing that he was a righteous and holy man, and he kept him safe. And when he heard him, he was very perplexed; but he used to enjoy listening to him.

21 A strategic day came when Herod on his birthday gave a banquet for his lords and military commanders and the leading men of Galilee;

22 and when the daughter of Herodias herself came in and danced, she pleased Herod and his dinner guests; and the king said to the girl, "Ask me for whatever you want and I will give it to you."

23 And he swore to her, "Whatever you ask of me, I will give it to you; up to half of my kingdom."

24 And she went out and said to her mother, "What shall I ask for?" And she said, "The head of John the Baptist."

25 Immediately she came in a hurry to the king and asked, saying, "I want you to give me at once the head of John the Baptist on a platter."

26 And although the king was very sorry, *yet* because of his oaths and because of his dinner guests, he was unwilling to refuse her.

27 Immediately the king sent an executioner and commanded *him* to bring *back* his head. And he went and had him beheaded in the prison,

28 and brought his head on a platter, and gave it to the girl; and the girl gave it to her mother.

29 When his disciples heard *about this,* they came and took away his body and laid it in a tomb.

NEW CENTURY VERSION

couldn't, 20because Herod was afraid of John and protected
him. He knew John was a good and holy man. Also,
though John's preaching always bothered him, he enjoyed
listening to John.
21Then the perfect time came for Herodias to cause
John's death. On Herod's birthday, he gave a dinner party
for the most important government leaders, the command-
ers of his army, and the most important people in Galilee.
22When the daughter of Herodias came in and danced, she
pleased Herod and the people eating with him.
So King Herod said to the girl, "Ask me for anything you
want, and I will give it to you." 23He promised her,
"Anything you ask for I will give to you—up to half of my
kingdom."
24The girl went to her mother and asked, "What should I
ask for?"
Her mother answered, "Ask for the head of John the
Baptist."
25At once the girl went back to the king and said to him,
"I want the head of John the Baptist right now on a plat-
ter."
26Although the king was very sad, he had made a prom-
ise, and his dinner guests had heard it. So he did not want
to refuse what she asked. 27Immediately the king sent a
soldier to bring John's head. The soldier went and cut off
John's head in the prison 28and brought it back on a plat-
ter. He gave it to the girl, and the girl gave it to her moth-
er. 29When John's followers heard this, they came and got
John's body and put it in a tomb.

CONTEMPORARY ENGLISH VERSION

him. But she could not do it 20because Herod was afraid of
John and protected him. He knew that John was a good
and holy man. Even though Herod was confused by what
John said,[g] he was glad to listen to him. And he often did.
21Finally, Herodias got her chance when Herod gave a
great birthday celebration for himself and invited his offi-
cials, his army officers, and the leaders of Galilee. 22The
daughter of Herodias[h] came in and danced for Herod and
his guests. She pleased them so much that Herod said,
"Ask for anything, and it's yours! 23I swear that I will give
you as much as half of my kingdom, if you want it."
24The girl left and asked her mother, "What do you
think I should ask for?"
Her mother answered, "The head of John the Baptist!"
25The girl hurried back and told Herod, "Right now on a
platter I want the head of John the Baptist!"
26The king was very sorry for what he had said. But he
did not want to break the promise he had made in front of
his guests. 27At once he ordered a guard to cut off John's
head there in prison. 28The guard put the head on a platter
and took it to the girl. Then she gave it to her mother.
29When John's followers learned that he had been killed,
they took his body and put it in a tomb.

[g] 6.20 *was confused by what John said*: Some manuscripts have "did many things because of what John said." [h] 6.22 *Herodias*: Some manuscripts have "Herod."

NEW INTERNATIONAL VERSION

him. But she was not able to, 20because Herod feared John and protected him, knowing him to be a righteous and holy man. When Herod heard John, he was greatly puzzled[d]; yet he liked to listen to him.

21Finally the opportune time came. On his birthday Herod gave a banquet for his high officials and military commanders and the leading men of Galilee. 22When the daughter of Herodias came in and danced, she pleased Herod and his dinner guests.

The king said to the girl, "Ask me for anything you want, and I'll give it to you." 23And he promised her with an oath, "Whatever you ask I will give you, up to half my kingdom."

24She went out and said to her mother, "What shall I ask for?"

"The head of John the Baptist," she answered.

25At once the girl hurried in to the king with the request: "I want you to give me right now the head of John the Baptist on a platter."

26The king was greatly distressed, but because of his oaths and his dinner guests, he did not want to refuse her. 27So he immediately sent an executioner with orders to bring John's head. The man went, beheaded John in the prison, 28and brought back his head on a platter. He presented it to the girl, and she gave it to her mother. 29On hearing of this, John's disciples came and took his body and laid it in a tomb.

[d] *20* Some early manuscripts *he did many things*

NEW LIVING TRANSLATION

out Herod's approval she was powerless. 20And Herod respected John, knowing that he was a good and holy man, so he kept him under his protection. Herod was disturbed whenever he talked with John, but even so, he liked to listen to him.

21Herodias's chance finally came. It was Herod's birthday, and he gave a party for his palace aides, army officers, and the leading citizens of Galilee. 22Then his daughter, also named Herodias,* came in and performed a dance that greatly pleased them all. "Ask me for anything you like," the king said to the girl, "and I will give it to you." 23Then he promised, "I will give you whatever you ask, up to half of my kingdom!"

24She went out and asked her mother, "What should I ask for?"

Her mother told her, "Ask for John the Baptist's head!"

25So the girl hurried back to the king and told him, "I want the head of John the Baptist, right now, on a tray!"

26Then the king was very sorry, but he was embarrassed to break his oath in front of his guests. 27So he sent an executioner to the prison to cut off John's head and bring it to him. The soldier beheaded John in the prison, 28brought his head on a tray, and gave it to the girl, who took it to her mother. 29When John's disciples heard what had happened, they came for his body and buried it in a tomb.

6:22 Some manuscripts read *the daughter of Herodias herself.*

NEW KING JAMES VERSION

kill him, but she could not; 20for Herod feared John, knowing that he *was* a just and holy man, and he protected him. And when he heard him, he did many things, and heard him gladly.

21Then an opportune day came when Herod on his birthday gave a feast for his nobles, the high officers, and the chief *men* of Galilee. 22And when Herodias' daughter herself came in and danced, and pleased Herod and those who sat with him, the king said to the girl, "Ask me whatever you want, and I will give *it* to you." 23He also swore to her, "Whatever you ask me, I will give you, up to half my kingdom."

24So she went out and said to her mother, "What shall I ask?"

And she said, "The head of John the Baptist!"

25Immediately she came in with haste to the king and asked, saying, "I want you to give me at once the head of John the Baptist on a platter."

26And the king was exceedingly sorry; *yet,* because of the oaths and because of those who sat with him, he did not want to refuse her. 27Immediately the king sent an executioner and commanded his head to be brought. And he went and beheaded him in prison, 28brought his head on a platter, and gave it to the girl; and the girl gave it to her mother. 29When his disciples heard *of it,* they came and took away his corpse and laid it in a tomb.

THE MESSAGE

him, but didn't dare because Herod was in awe of John. Convinced that he was a holy man, he gave him special treatment. Whenever he listened to him he was miserable with guilt—and yet he couldn't stay away. Something in John kept pulling him back.

But a portentous day arrived when Herod threw a birthday party, inviting all the brass and bluebloods in Galilee. Herodias's daughter entered the banquet hall and danced for the guests. She dazzled Herod and the guests.

The king said to the girl, "Ask me anything. I'll give you anything you want." Carried away, he kept on, "I swear, I'll split my kingdom with you if you say so!"

She went back to her mother and said, "What should I ask for?"

"Ask for the head of John the Baptizer."

Excited, she ran back to the king and said, "I want the head of John the Baptizer served up on a platter. And I want it now!"

That sobered the king up fast. But unwilling to lose face with his guests, he caved in and let her have her wish. The king sent the executioner off to the prison with orders to bring back John's head. He went, cut off John's head, brought it back on a platter, and presented it to the girl, who gave it to her mother. When John's disciples heard about this, they came and got the body and gave it a decent burial.

KING JAMES VERSION

30 ¶ And the apostles gathered themselves together unto Jesus, and told him all things, both what they had done, and what they had taught.

31 And he said unto them, Come ye yourselves apart into a desert place, and rest a while: for there were many coming and going, and they had no leisure so much as to eat.

32 And they departed into a desert place by ship privately.

33 And the people saw them departing, and many knew him, and ran afoot thither out of all cities, and outwent them, and came together unto him.

34 And Jesus, when he came out, saw much people, and was moved with compassion toward them, because they were as sheep not having a shepherd: and he began to teach them many things.

35 And when the day was now far spent, his disciples came unto him, and said, This is a desert place, and now the time *is* far passed:

36 Send them away, that they may go into the country round about, and into the villages, and buy themselves bread: for they have nothing to eat.

37 He answered and said unto them, Give ye them to eat. And they say unto him, Shall we go and buy two hundred pennyworth of bread, and give them to eat?

38 He saith unto them, How many loaves have ye? go and see. And when they knew, they say, Five, and two fishes.

NEW AMERICAN STANDARD BIBLE

30 The apostles *gathered together with Jesus; and they reported to Him all that they had done and taught.

31 And He *said to them, "Come away by yourselves to a secluded place and rest a while." (For there were many *people* coming and going, and they did not even have time to eat.)

32 They went away in the boat to a secluded place by themselves.

Five Thousand Fed

33 *The people* saw them going, and many recognized *them* and ran there together on foot from all the cities, and got there ahead of them.

34 When Jesus went ashore, He saw a large crowd, and He felt compassion for them because they were like sheep without a shepherd; and He began to teach them many things.

35 When it was already quite late, His disciples came to Him and said, "This place is desolate and it is already quite late;

36 send them away so that they may go into the surrounding countryside and villages and buy themselves something to eat."

37 But He answered them, "You give them *something* to eat!" And they *said to Him, "Shall we go and spend two hundred [2]denarii on bread and give them *something* to eat?"

38 And He *said to them, "How many loaves do you have? Go look!" And when they found out, they *said, "Five, and two fish."

6:37 [2] The denarius was equivalent to one day's wage

NEW CENTURY VERSION

More than Five Thousand Fed

[30]The apostles gathered around Jesus and told him about all the things they had done and taught. [31]Crowds of people were coming and going so that Jesus and his followers did not even have time to eat. He said to them, "Come away by yourselves, and we will go to a lonely place to get some rest."

[32]So they went in a boat by themselves to a lonely place. [33]But many people saw them leave and recognized them. So from all the towns they ran to the place where Jesus was going, and they got there before him. [34]When he arrived, he saw a great crowd waiting. He felt sorry for them, because they were like sheep without a shepherd. So he began to teach them many things.

[35]When it was late in the day, his followers came to him and said, "No one lives in this place, and it is already very late. [36]Send the people away so they can go to the countryside and towns around here to buy themselves something to eat."

[37]But Jesus answered, "You give them something to eat."

They said to him, "We would all have to work a month to earn enough money to buy that much bread!"

[38]Jesus asked them, "How many loaves of bread do you have? Go and see."

When they found out, they said, "Five loaves and two fish."

CONTEMPORARY ENGLISH VERSION

Jesus Feeds Five Thousand

(Matthew 14.13-21; Luke 9.10-17; John 6.1-14)

[30]After the apostles returned to Jesus,[i] they told him everything they had done and taught. [31]But so many people were coming and going that Jesus and the apostles did not even have a chance to eat. Then Jesus said, "Let's go to a place[j] where we can be alone and get some rest." [32]They left in a boat for a place where they could be alone. [33]But many people saw them leave and figured out where they were going. So people from every town ran on ahead and got there first.

[34]When Jesus got out of the boat, he saw the large crowd that was like sheep without a shepherd. He felt sorry for the people and started teaching them many things.

[35]That evening the disciples came to Jesus and said, "This place is like a desert, and it is already late. [36]Let the crowds leave, so they can go to the farms and villages near here and buy something to eat."

[37]Jesus replied, "You give them something to eat."

But they asked him, "Don't you know that it would take almost a year's wages[k] to buy all of these people something to eat?"

[38]Then Jesus said, "How much bread do you have? Go and see!"

They found out and answered, "We have five small

[i] 6.30 *the apostles returned to Jesus*: From the mission on which he had sent them (see 6.7, 12, 13). [j] 6.31 *a place*: This was probably northeast of Lake Galilee (see verse 45). [k] 6.37 *almost a year's wages*: The Greek text has "two hundred silver coins." Each coin was the average day's wage for a worker.

NEW INTERNATIONAL VERSION

Jesus Feeds the Five Thousand

30The apostles gathered around Jesus and reported to him all they had done and taught. 31Then, because so many people were coming and going that they did not even have a chance to eat, he said to them, "Come with me by yourselves to a quiet place and get some rest."

32So they went away by themselves in a boat to a solitary place. 33But many who saw them leaving recognized them and ran on foot from all the towns and got there ahead of them. 34When Jesus landed and saw a large crowd, he had compassion on them, because they were like sheep without a shepherd. So he began teaching them many things.

35By this time it was late in the day, so his disciples came to him. "This is a remote place," they said, "and it's already very late. 36Send the people away so they can go to the surrounding countryside and villages and buy themselves something to eat."

37But he answered, "You give them something to eat."

They said to him, "That would take eight months of a man's wages[e]! Are we to go and spend that much on bread and give it to them to eat?"

38"How many loaves do you have?" he asked. "Go and see."

When they found out, they said, "Five—and two fish."

[e] 37 Greek *take two hundred denarii*

NEW LIVING TRANSLATION

Jesus Feeds Five Thousand

30The apostles returned to Jesus from their ministry tour and told him all they had done and what they had taught. 31Then Jesus said, "Let's get away from the crowds for a while and rest." There were so many people coming and going that Jesus and his apostles didn't even have time to eat. 32They left by boat for a quieter spot. 33But many people saw them leaving, and people from many towns ran ahead along the shore and met them as they landed. 34A vast crowd was there as he stepped from the boat, and he had compassion on them because they were like sheep without a shepherd. So he taught them many things.

35Late in the afternoon his disciples came to him and said, "This is a desolate place, and it is getting late. 36Send the crowds away so they can go to the nearby farms and villages and buy themselves some food."

37But Jesus said, "You feed them."

"With what?" they asked. "It would take a small fortune* to buy food for all this crowd!"

38"How much food do you have?" he asked. "Go and find out."

They came back and reported, "We have five loaves of

6:37 Greek *200 denarii.* A denarius was the equivalent of a full day's wage.

NEW KING JAMES VERSION

Feeding the Five Thousand

30Then the apostles gathered to Jesus and told Him all things, both what they had done and what they had taught. 31And He said to them, "Come aside by yourselves to a deserted place and rest a while." For there were many coming and going, and they did not even have time to eat. 32So they departed to a deserted place in the boat by themselves.

33But the multitudes[d] saw them departing, and many knew Him and ran there on foot from all the cities. They arrived before them and came together to Him. 34And Jesus, when He came out, saw a great multitude and was moved with compassion for them, because they were like sheep not having a shepherd. So He began to teach them many things. 35When the day was now far spent, His disciples came to Him and said, "This is a deserted place, and already the hour *is* late. 36Send them away, that they may go into the surrounding country and villages and buy themselves bread;[e] for they have nothing to eat."

37But He answered and said to them, "You give them something to eat."

And they said to Him, "Shall we go and buy two hundred denarii worth of bread and give them *something* to eat?"

38But He said to them, "How many loaves do you have? Go and see."

And when they found out they said, "Five, and two fish."

6:33 [d] NU-Text and M-Text read *they.* 6:36 [e] NU-Text reads *something to eat* and omits the rest of this verse.

THE MESSAGE

Supper for Five Thousand

The apostles then rendezvoused with Jesus and reported on all that they had done and taught. Jesus said, "Come off by yourselves; let's take a break and get a little rest." For there was constant coming and going. They didn't even have time to eat.

So they got in the boat and went off to a remote place by themselves. Someone saw them going and the word got around. From the surrounding towns people went out on foot, running, and got there ahead of them. When Jesus arrived, he saw this huge crowd. At the sight of them, his heart broke—like sheep with no shepherd they were. He went right to work teaching them.

When his disciples thought this had gone on long enough—it was now quite late in the day—they interrupted: "We are a long way out in the country, and it's very late. Pronounce a benediction and send these folks off so they can get some supper."

Jesus said, "You do it. Fix supper for them."

They replied, "Are you serious? You want us to go spend a fortune on food for their supper?"

But he was quite serious. "How many loaves of bread do you have? Take an inventory."

That didn't take long. "Five," they said, "plus two fish."

KING JAMES VERSION

39 And he commanded them to make all sit down by companies upon the green grass.

40 And they sat down in ranks, by hundreds, and by fifties.

41 And when he had taken the five loaves and the two fishes, he looked up to heaven, and blessed, and brake the loaves, and gave *them* to his disciples to set before them; and the two fishes divided he among them all.

42 And they did all eat, and were filled.

43 And they took up twelve baskets full of the fragments, and of the fishes.

44 And they that did eat of the loaves were about five thousand men.

45 ¶ And straightway he constrained his disciples to get into the ship, and to go to the other side before unto Bethsaida, while he sent away the people.

46 And when he had sent them away, he departed into a mountain to pray.

47 And when even was come, the ship was in the midst of the sea, and he alone on the land.

48 And he saw them toiling in rowing; for the wind was contrary unto them: and about the fourth watch of the night he cometh unto them, walking upon the sea, and would have passed by them.

49 But when they saw him walking upon the sea, they supposed it had been a spirit, and cried out:

50 For they all saw him, and were troubled. And immediately he talked with them, and saith unto them, Be of good cheer: it is I; be not afraid.

NEW AMERICAN STANDARD BIBLE

39 And He commanded them all to sit down by groups on the green grass.

40 They sat down in groups of hundreds and of fifties.

41 And He took the five loaves and the two fish, and looking up toward heaven, He blessed *the food* and broke the loaves and He kept giving *them* to the disciples to set before them; and He divided up the two fish among them all.

42 They all ate and were satisfied,

43 and they picked up twelve full baskets of the broken pieces, and also of the fish.

44 There were five thousand men who ate the loaves.

Jesus Walks on the Water

45 Immediately Jesus made His disciples get into the boat and go ahead of *Him* to the other side to Bethsaida, while He Himself was sending the crowd away.

46 After bidding them farewell, He left for the mountain to pray.

47 When it was evening, the boat was in the middle of the sea, and He was alone on the land.

48 Seeing them straining at the oars, for the wind was against them, at about the fourth watch of the night He *came to them, walking on the sea; and He intended to pass by them.

49 But when they saw Him walking on the sea, they supposed that it was a ghost, and cried out;

50 for they all saw Him and were terrified. But immediately He spoke with them and *said to them, "Take courage; it is I, do not be afraid."

NEW CENTURY VERSION

[39]Then Jesus told his followers to have the people sit in groups on the green grass. [40]So they sat in groups of fifty or a hundred. [41]Jesus took the five loaves and two fish and, looking up to heaven, he thanked God for the food. He divided the bread and gave it to his followers for them to give to the people. Then he divided the two fish among them all. [42]All the people ate and were satisfied. [43]The followers filled twelve baskets with the leftover pieces of bread and fish. [44]There were five thousand men who ate.

Jesus Walks on the Water

[45]Immediately Jesus told his followers to get into the boat and go ahead of him to Bethsaida across the lake. He stayed there to send the people home. [46]After sending them away, he went into the hills to pray.

[47]That night, the boat was in the middle of the lake, and Jesus was alone on the land. [48]He saw his followers struggling hard to row the boat, because the wind was blowing against them. Between three and six o'clock in the morning, Jesus came to them, walking on the water, and he wanted to walk past the boat. [49]But when they saw him walking on the water, they thought he was a ghost and cried out. [50]They all saw him and were afraid. But quickly Jesus spoke to them and said, "Have courage! It is I. Do not be afraid." [51]Then he got into the boat with them, and

CONTEMPORARY ENGLISH VERSION

loaves of bread[l] and two fish." [39]Jesus told his disciples to have the people sit down on the green grass. [40]They sat down in groups of a hundred and groups of fifty.

[41]Jesus took the five loaves and the two fish. He looked up toward heaven and blessed the food. Then he broke the bread and handed it to his disciples to give to the people. He also divided the two fish, so that everyone could have some.

[42]After everyone had eaten all they wanted, [43]Jesus' disciples picked up twelve large baskets of leftover bread and fish.

[44]There were five thousand men who ate the food.

Jesus Walks on the Water (Matthew 14.22-33; John 6.15-21)

[45]Right away, Jesus made his disciples get into the boat and start back across to Bethsaida. But he stayed until he had sent the crowds away. [46]Then he told them good-by and went up on the side of a mountain to pray.

[47]Later that evening he was still there by himself, and the boat was somewhere in the middle of the lake. [48]He could see that the disciples were struggling hard, because they were rowing against the wind. Not long before morning, Jesus came toward them. He was walking on the water and was about to pass the boat.

[49]When the disciples saw Jesus walking on the water, they thought he was a ghost, and they started screaming. [50]All of them saw him and were terrified. But at that same time he said, "Don't worry! I am Jesus. Don't be afraid."

[l] 6.38 *small loaves of bread*: These would have been flat and round or in the shape of a bun.

NEW INTERNATIONAL VERSION

39Then Jesus directed them to have all the people sit down in groups on the green grass. 40So they sat down in groups of hundreds and fifties. 41Taking the five loaves and the two fish and looking up to heaven, he gave thanks and broke the loaves. Then he gave them to his disciples to set before the people. He also divided the two fish among them all. 42They all ate and were satisfied, 43and the disciples picked up twelve basketfuls of broken pieces of bread and fish. 44The number of the men who had eaten was five thousand.

Jesus Walks on the Water

45Immediately Jesus made his disciples get into the boat and go on ahead of him to Bethsaida, while he dismissed the crowd. 46After leaving them, he went up on a mountainside to pray.

47When evening came, the boat was in the middle of the lake, and he was alone on land. 48He saw the disciples straining at the oars, because the wind was against them. About the fourth watch of the night he went out to them, walking on the lake. He was about to pass by them, 49but when they saw him walking on the lake, they thought he was a ghost. They cried out, 50because they all saw him and were terrified.

Immediately he spoke to them and said, "Take courage! It is I. Don't be afraid." 51Then he climbed into the boat

NEW LIVING TRANSLATION

bread and two fish." 39Then Jesus told the crowd to sit down in groups on the green grass. 40So they sat in groups of fifty or a hundred.

41Jesus took the five loaves and two fish, looked up toward heaven, and asked God's blessing on the food. Breaking the loaves into pieces, he kept giving the bread and fish to the disciples to give to the people. 42They all ate as much as they wanted, 43and they picked up twelve baskets of leftover bread and fish. 44Five thousand men had eaten from those five loaves!

Jesus Walks on Water

45Immediately after this, Jesus made his disciples get back into the boat and head out across the lake to Bethsaida, while he sent the people home. 46Afterward he went up into the hills by himself to pray.

47During the night, the disciples were in their boat out in the middle of the lake, and Jesus was alone on land. 48He saw that they were in serious trouble, rowing hard and struggling against the wind and waves. About three o'clock in the morning* he came to them, walking on the water. He started to go past them, 49but when they saw him walking on the water, they screamed in terror, thinking he was a ghost. 50They were all terrified when they saw him. But Jesus spoke to them at once. "It's all right," he said. "I am here! Don't be afraid." 51Then he climbed

6:48 Greek *About the fourth watch of the night.*

NEW KING JAMES VERSION

39Then He commanded them to make them all sit down in groups on the green grass. 40So they sat down in ranks, in hundreds and in fifties. 41And when He had taken the five loaves and the two fish, He looked up to heaven, blessed and broke the loaves, and gave *them* to His disciples to set before them; and the two fish He divided among *them* all. 42So they all ate and were filled. 43And they took up twelve baskets full of fragments and of the fish. 44Now those who had eaten the loaves were about[f] five thousand men.

Jesus Walks on the Sea

45Immediately He made His disciples get into the boat and go before Him to the other side, to Bethsaida, while He sent the multitude away. 46And when He had sent them away, He departed to the mountain to pray. 47Now when evening came, the boat was in the middle of the sea; and He *was* alone on the land. 48Then He saw them straining at rowing, for the wind was against them. Now about the fourth watch of the night He came to them, walking on the sea, and would have passed them by. 49And when they saw Him walking on the sea, they supposed it was a ghost, and cried out; 50for they all saw Him and were troubled. But immediately He talked with them and said to them, "Be of good cheer! It is I; do not be afraid." 51Then He

6:44 [f] NU-Text and M-Text omit *about.*

THE MESSAGE

Jesus got them all to sit down in groups of fifty or a hundred—they looked like a patchwork quilt of wildflowers spread out on the green grass! He took the five loaves and two fish, lifted his face to heaven in prayer, blessed, broke, and gave the bread to the disciples, and the disciples in turn gave it to the people. He did the same with the fish. They all ate their fill. The disciples gathered twelve baskets of leftovers. More than five thousand were at the supper.

Walking on the Sea

As soon as the meal was finished, Jesus insisted that the disciples get in the boat and go on ahead across to Bethsaida while he dismissed the congregation. After sending them off, he climbed a mountain to pray.

Late at night, the boat was far out at sea; Jesus was still by himself on land. He could see his men struggling with the oars, the wind having come up against them. At about four o'clock in the morning, Jesus came toward them, walking on the sea. He intended to go right by them. But when they saw him walking on the sea, they thought it was a ghost and screamed, scared out of their wits.

Jesus was quick to comfort them: "Courage! It's me. Don't be afraid." As soon as he climbed into the boat, the

KING JAMES VERSION

51 And he went up unto them into the ship; and the wind ceased: and they were sore amazed in themselves beyond measure, and wondered.
52 For they considered not *the miracle* of the loaves: for their heart was hardened.
53 And when they had passed over, they came into the land of Gennesaret, and drew to the shore.
54 And when they were come out of the ship, straightway they knew him,
55 And ran through that whole region round about, and began to carry about in beds those that were sick, where they heard he was.
56 And whithersoever he entered, into villages, or cities, or country, they laid the sick in the streets, and besought him that they might touch if it were but the border of his garment: and as many as touched him were made whole.

7 Then came together unto him the Pharisees, and certain of the scribes, which came from Jerusalem.
2 And when they saw some of his disciples eat bread with defiled, that is to say, with unwashen, hands, they found fault.
3 For the Pharisees, and all the Jews, except they wash *their* hands oft, eat not, holding the tradition of the elders.
4 And *when they come* from the market, except they wash, they eat not. And many other things there be, which

NEW AMERICAN STANDARD BIBLE

51 Then He got into the boat with them, and the wind stopped; and they were utterly astonished,
52 for they had not gained any insight from the *incident of* the loaves, but their heart was hardened.

Healing at Gennesaret

53 When they had crossed over they came to land at Gennesaret, and moored to the shore.
54 When they got out of the boat, immediately *the people* recognized Him,
55 and ran about that whole country and began to carry here and there on their pallets those who were sick, to the place they heard He was.
56 Wherever He entered villages, or cities, or countryside, they were laying the sick in the market places, and imploring Him that they might just touch the fringe of His cloak; and as many as touched it were being cured.

Followers of Tradition

7 The Pharisees and some of the scribes gathered around Him when they had come from Jerusalem,
2 and had seen that some of His disciples were eating their bread with impure hands, that is, unwashed.
3 (For the Pharisees and all the Jews do not eat unless they carefully wash their hands, *thus* observing the traditions of the elders;
4 and *when they come* from the market place, they do not eat unless they cleanse themselves; and there are

NEW CENTURY VERSION

the wind became calm. The followers were greatly amazed.
52They did not understand about the miracle of the five loaves, because their minds were closed.
53When they had crossed the lake, they came to shore at Gennesaret and tied the boat there. 54When they got out of the boat, people immediately recognized Jesus. 55They ran everywhere in that area and began to bring sick people on mats wherever they heard he was. 56And everywhere he went—into towns, cities, or countryside—the people brought the sick to the marketplaces. They begged him to let them touch just the edge of his coat, and all who touched it were healed.

Obey God's Law

7 When some Pharisees and some teachers of the law came from Jerusalem, they gathered around Jesus.
2They saw that some of Jesus' followers ate food with hands that were not clean, that is, they hadn't washed them. 3(The Pharisees and all the Jews never eat before washing their hands in a special way according to their unwritten laws. 4And when they buy something in the market, they never eat it until they wash themselves in a

CONTEMPORARY ENGLISH VERSION

51He then got into the boat with them, and the wind died down. The disciples were completely confused. 52Their minds were closed, and they could not understand the true meaning of the loaves of bread.

Jesus Heals Sick People in Gennesaret (Matthew 14.34-36)

53Jesus and his disciples crossed the lake and brought the boat to shore near the town of Gennesaret. 54As soon as they got out of the boat, the people recognized Jesus. 55So they ran all over that part of the country to bring their sick people to him on mats. They brought them each time they heard where he was. 56In every village or farm or marketplace where Jesus went, the people brought their sick to him. They begged him to let them just touch his clothes, and everyone who did was healed.

The Teaching of the Ancestors (Matthew 15.1-9)

7 Some Pharisees and several teachers of the Law of Moses from Jerusalem came and gathered around Jesus. 2They noticed that some of his disciples ate without first washing their hands.[a]
3The Pharisees and many other Jewish people obey the teachings of their ancestors. They always wash their hands in the proper way[b] before eating. 4None of them will eat anything they buy in the market until it is washed.

[a] 7.2 *without first washing their hands*: The Jewish people had strict laws about washing their hands before eating, especially if they had been out in public. [b] 7.3 *in the proper way*: The Greek text has "with the fist," but the exact meaning is not clear. It could mean "to the wrist" or "to the elbow."

NEW INTERNATIONAL VERSION

with them, and the wind died down. They were completely amazed, [52]for they had not understood about the loaves; their hearts were hardened.

[53]When they had crossed over, they landed at Gennesaret and anchored there. [54]As soon as they got out of the boat, people recognized Jesus. [55]They ran throughout that whole region and carried the sick on mats to wherever they heard he was. [56]And wherever he went—into villages, towns or countryside—they placed the sick in the marketplaces. They begged him to let them touch even the edge of his cloak, and all who touched him were healed.

Clean and Unclean

7 The Pharisees and some of the teachers of the law who had come from Jerusalem gathered around Jesus and [2]saw some of his disciples eating food with hands that were "unclean," that is, unwashed. [3](The Pharisees and all the Jews do not eat unless they give their hands a ceremonial washing, holding to the tradition of the elders. [4]When they come from the marketplace they do not eat unless

NEW LIVING TRANSLATION

into the boat, and the wind stopped. They were astonished at what they saw. [52]They still didn't understand the significance of the miracle of the multiplied loaves, for their hearts were hard and they did not believe.

[53]When they arrived at Gennesaret on the other side of the lake, they anchored the boat [54]and climbed out. The people standing there recognized him at once, [55]and they ran throughout the whole area and began carrying sick people to him on mats. [56]Wherever he went—in villages and cities and out on the farms—they laid the sick in the market plazas and streets. The sick begged him to let them at least touch the fringe of his robe, and all who touched it were healed.

Jesus Teaches about Inner Purity

7 One day some Pharisees and teachers of religious law arrived from Jerusalem to confront Jesus. [2]They noticed that some of Jesus' disciples failed to follow the usual Jewish ritual of hand washing before eating. [3](The Jews, especially the Pharisees, do not eat until they have poured water over their cupped hands,* as required by their ancient traditions. [4]Similarly, they eat nothing bought from the market unless they have immersed their hands in water. This is but one of many traditions they

7:3 Greek *washed with the fist.*

NEW KING JAMES VERSION

went up into the boat to them, and the wind ceased. And they were greatly amazed in themselves beyond measure, and marveled. [52]For they had not understood about the loaves, because their heart was hardened.

Many Touch Him and Are Made Well

[53]When they had crossed over, they came to the land of Gennesaret and anchored there. [54]And when they came out of the boat, immediately the people recognized Him, [55]ran through that whole surrounding region, and began to carry about on beds those who were sick to wherever they heard He was. [56]Wherever He entered, into villages, cities, or the country, they laid the sick in the marketplaces, and begged Him that they might just touch the hem of His garment. And as many as touched Him were made well.

Defilement Comes from Within

7 Then the Pharisees and some of the scribes came together to Him, having come from Jerusalem. [2]Now when[a] they saw some of His disciples eat bread with defiled, that is, with unwashed hands, they found fault. [3]For the Pharisees and all the Jews do not eat unless they wash *their* hands in a special way, holding the tradition of the elders. [4]*When they come* from the marketplace, they do not eat unless they wash. And there are many other things

7:2 [a] NU-Text omits *when* and *they found fault.*

THE MESSAGE

wind died down. They were stunned, shaking their heads, wondering what was going on. They didn't understand what he had done at the supper. None of this had yet penetrated their hearts.

They beached the boat at Gennesaret and tied up at the landing. As soon as they got out of the boat, word got around fast. People ran this way and that, bringing their sick on stretchers to where they heard he was. Wherever he went, village or town or country crossroads, they brought their sick to the marketplace and begged him to let them touch the edge of his coat—that's all. And whoever touched him became well.

The Source of Your Pollution

7 The Pharisees, along with some religion scholars who had come from Jerusalem, gathered around him. They noticed that some of his disciples weren't being careful with ritual washings before meals. The Pharisees—Jews in general, in fact—would never eat a meal without going through the motions of a ritual hand-washing, with an especially vigorous scrubbing if they had just come from

KING JAMES VERSION

they have received to hold, *as* the washing of cups, and
pots, brasen vessels, and of tables.
5 Then the Pharisees and scribes asked him, Why walk
not thy disciples according to the tradition of the elders,
but eat bread with unwashen hands?
6 He answered and said unto them, Well hath Esaias
prophesied of you hypocrites, as it is written, This people
honoureth me with *their* lips, but their heart is far from
me.
7 Howbeit in vain do they worship me, teaching *for*
doctrines the commandments of men.
8 For laying aside the commandment of God, ye hold
the tradition of men, *as* the washing of pots and cups: and
many other such like things ye do.
9 And he said unto them, Full well ye reject the com-
mandment of God, that ye may keep your own tradition.
10 For Moses said, Honour thy father and thy mother;
and, Whoso curseth father or mother, let him die the
death:
11 But ye say, If a man shall say to his father or moth-
er, *It is* Corban, that is to say, a gift, by whatsoever thou
mightest be profited by me; *he shall be free*.

NEW AMERICAN STANDARD BIBLE

many other things which they have received in order to
observe, such as the washing of cups and pitchers and
copper pots.)
5 The Pharisees and the scribes *asked Him, "Why do
Your disciples not walk according to the tradition of the
elders, but eat their bread with impure hands?"
6 And He said to them, "Rightly did Isaiah prophesy of
you hypocrites, as it is written:
'THIS PEOPLE HONORS ME WITH THEIR LIPS,
BUT THEIR HEART IS FAR AWAY FROM ME.
7 'BUT IN VAIN DO THEY WORSHIP ME,
TEACHING AS DOCTRINES THE PRECEPTS OF MEN.'
8 "Neglecting the commandment of God, you hold to the
tradition of men."
9 He was also saying to them, "You are experts at set-
ting aside the commandment of God in order to keep your
tradition.
10 "For Moses said, 'HONOR YOUR FATHER AND YOUR
MOTHER'; and, 'HE WHO SPEAKS EVIL OF FATHER OR MOTHER, IS
TO BE PUT TO DEATH';
11 but you say, 'If a man says to *his* father or *his* moth-
er, whatever I have that would help you is Corban (that is
to say, [1]given *to God),*'

7:11 [1] Or *a gift,* i.e. *an offering*

NEW CENTURY VERSION

special way. They also follow many other unwritten laws,
such as the washing of cups, pitchers, and pots.)
5The Pharisees and the teachers of the law said to Jesus,
"Why don't your followers obey the unwritten laws which
have been handed down to us? Why do your followers eat
their food with hands that are not clean?"
6Jesus answered, "Isaiah was right when he spoke about
you hypocrites. He wrote,
'These people show honor to me with words,
but their hearts are far from me.
7Their worship of me is worthless.
The things they teach are nothing but human rules.'
Isaiah 29:13
8You have stopped following the commands of God, and
you follow only human teachings."
9Then Jesus said to them, "You cleverly ignore the com-
mands of God so you can follow your own teachings.
10Moses said, 'Honor your father and your mother,'[a] and
'Anyone who says cruel things to his father or mother
must be put to death.'[b] 11But you say a person can tell his
father or mother, 'I have something I could use to help
you, but it is Corban—a gift to God.' 12You no longer let

7:10 [a] **'Honor...mother'** Quotation from Exodus 20:12; Deuteronomy
5:16. 7:10 [b] **'Anyone...death.'** Quotation from Exodus 21:17.

CONTEMPORARY ENGLISH VERSION

They also follow a lot of other teachings, such as washing
cups, pitchers, and bowls.[c]
5The Pharisees and teachers asked Jesus, "Why don't
your disciples obey what our ancestors taught us to do?
Why do they eat without washing their hands?"
6Jesus replied:
You are nothing but show-offs! The prophet Isaiah
was right when he wrote that God had said,
"All of you praise me
with your words,
but you never really
think about me.
7It is useless for you
to worship me,
when you teach rules
made up by humans."

8You disobey God's commands in order to obey what
humans have taught. 9You are good at rejecting God's
commands so that you can follow your own teachings!
10Didn't Moses command you to respect your father and
mother? Didn't he tell you to put to death all who curse
their parents? 11But you let people get by without help-
ing their parents when they should. You let them say
that what they own has been offered to God.[d] 12You

[c] **7.4** *bowls*: Some manuscripts add "and sleeping mats." [d] **7.11** *has
been offered to God*: According to Jewish custom, when anything was
offered to God, it could not be used for anyone else, not even for a
person's parents.

NEW INTERNATIONAL VERSION

they wash. And they observe many other traditions, such as the washing of cups, pitchers and kettles.[a])

5 So the Pharisees and teachers of the law asked Jesus, "Why don't your disciples live according to the tradition of the elders instead of eating their food with 'unclean' hands?"

6 He replied, "Isaiah was right when he prophesied about you hypocrites; as it is written:

" 'These people honor me with their lips,
but their hearts are far from me.
7 They worship me in vain;
their teachings are but rules taught by men.'[b]

8 You have let go of the commands of God and are holding on to the traditions of men."

9 And he said to them: "You have a fine way of setting aside the commands of God in order to observe[c] your own traditions! 10 For Moses said, 'Honor your father and your mother,'[d] and, 'Anyone who curses his father or mother must be put to death.'[e] 11 But you say that if a man says to his father or mother: 'Whatever help you might otherwise have received from me is Corban' (that is, a gift devoted to

[a] *4* Some early manuscripts *pitchers, kettles and dining couches*
[b] *6,7* Isaiah 29:13 [c] *9* Some manuscripts *set up* [d] *10* Exodus 20:12; Deut. 5:16 [e] *10* Exodus 21:17; Lev. 20:9

NEW LIVING TRANSLATION

have clung to—such as their ceremony of washing cups, pitchers, and kettles.*) 5 So the Pharisees and teachers of religious law asked him, "Why don't your disciples follow our age-old customs? For they eat without first performing the hand-washing ceremony."

6 Jesus replied, "You hypocrites! Isaiah was prophesying about you when he said,

7 'These people honor me with their lips,
but their hearts are far away.
Their worship is a farce,
for they replace God's commands with their own
man-made teachings.'*

8 For you ignore God's specific laws and substitute your own traditions."

9 Then he said, "You reject God's laws in order to hold on to your own traditions. 10 For instance, Moses gave you this law from God: 'Honor your father and mother,' and 'Anyone who speaks evil of father or mother must be put to death.'* 11 But you say it is all right for people to say to their parents, 'Sorry, I can't help you. For I have vowed to give to God what I could have given to you.'* 12 You let

7:4 Some Greek manuscripts add *and dining couches.* 7:7 Isa 29:13. 7:10 Exod 20:12; 21:17; Lev 20:9; Deut 5:16. 7:11 Greek *'What I could have given to you is Corban' (that is, a gift).*

NEW KING JAMES VERSION

which they have received and hold, *like* the washing of cups, pitchers, copper vessels, and couches.

5 Then the Pharisees and scribes asked Him, "Why do Your disciples not walk according to the tradition of the elders, but eat bread with unwashed hands?"

6 He answered and said to them, "Well did Isaiah prophesy of you hypocrites, as it is written:

'This people honors Me with their lips,
But their heart is far from Me.
7 *And in vain they worship Me,*
Teaching as doctrines the commandments of men.'[b]

8 For laying aside the commandment of God, you hold the tradition of men[c]—the washing of pitchers and cups, and many other such things you do."

9 He said to them, "*All too* well you reject the commandment of God, that you may keep your tradition. 10 For Moses said, *'Honor your father and your mother'*;[d] and, *'He who curses father or mother, let him be put to death.'*[e] 11 But you say, 'If a man says to his father or mother, "Whatever profit you might have received from me *is* Corban"—' (that is, a gift *to God*), 12 then you no longer let

7:7 [b] Isaiah 29:13 7:8 [c] NU-Text omits the rest of this verse.
7:10 [d] Exodus 20:12; Deuteronomy 5:16 [e] Exodus 21:17

THE MESSAGE

the market (to say nothing of the scourings they'd give jugs and pots and pans).

The Pharisees and religion scholars asked, "Why do your disciples flout the rules, showing up at meals without washing their hands?"

Jesus answered, "Isaiah was right about frauds like you, hit the bull's-eye in fact:

'These people make a big show of saying the right
thing,
but their heart isn't in it.
They act like they are worshiping me,
but they don't mean it.
They just use me as a cover
for teaching whatever suits their fancy,
Ditching God's command
and taking up the latest fads.' "

He went on, "Well, good for you. You get rid of God's command so you won't be inconvenienced in following the religious fashions! Moses said, 'Respect your father and mother,' and, 'Anyone denouncing father or mother should be killed.' But you weasel out of that by saying that it's perfectly acceptable to say to father or mother, 'Gift! What I owed you I've given as a gift to God,' thus

KING JAMES VERSION

12 And ye suffer him no more to do ought for his father or his mother;

13 Making the word of God of none effect through your tradition, which ye have delivered: and many such like things do ye.

14 And when he had called all the people *unto him*, he said unto them, Hearken unto me every one *of you*, and understand:

15 There is nothing from without a man, that entering into him can defile him: but the things which come out of him, those are they that defile the man.

16 If any man have ears to hear, let him hear.

17 And when he was entered into the house from the people, his disciples asked him concerning the parable.

18 And he saith unto them, Are ye so without understanding also? Do ye not perceive, that whatsoever thing from without entereth into the man, *it* cannot defile him;

19 Because it entereth not into his heart, but into the belly, and goeth out into the draught, purging all meats?

20 And he said, That which cometh out of the man, that defileth the man.

21 For from within, out of the heart of men, proceed evil thoughts, adulteries, fornications, murders,

22 Thefts, covetousness, wickedness, deceit, lasciviousness, an evil eye, blasphemy, pride, foolishness:

23 All these evil things come from within, and defile the man.

NEW AMERICAN STANDARD BIBLE

12 you no longer permit him to do anything for *his* father or *his* mother;

13 *thus* invalidating the word of God by your tradition which you have handed down; and you do many things such as that."

The Heart of Man

14 After He called the crowd to Him again, He *began* saying to them, "Listen to Me, all of you, and understand:

15 there is nothing outside the man which can defile him if it goes into him; but the things which proceed out of the man are what defile the man.

16 ["[2]If anyone has ears to hear, let him hear."]

17 When he had left the crowd *and* entered the house, His disciples questioned Him about the parable.

18 And He *said to them, "Are you so lacking in understanding also? Do you not understand that whatever goes into the man from outside cannot defile him,

19 because it does not go into his heart, but into his stomach, and is eliminated?" (*Thus He* declared all foods clean.)

20 And He was saying, "That which proceeds out of the man, that is what defiles the man.

21 "For from within, out of the heart of men, proceed the evil thoughts, fornications, thefts, murders, adulteries,

22 deeds of coveting *and* wickedness, *as well as* deceit, sensuality, envy, slander, pride *and* foolishness.

23 "All these evil things proceed from within and defile the man."

7:16 [2] Early mss do not contain this verse

NEW CENTURY VERSION

that person use that money for his father or his mother.
[13]By your own rules, which you teach people, you are
rejecting what God said. And you do many things like
that."
[14]After Jesus called the crowd to him again, he said,
"Every person should listen to me and understand what I
am saying. [15]There is nothing people put into their bodies
that makes them unclean. People are made unclean by the
things that come out of them." [16][c]
[17]When Jesus left the people and went into the house,
his followers asked him about this story. [18]Jesus said, "Do
you still not understand? Surely you know that nothing
that enters someone from the outside can make that person unclean. [19]It does not go into the mind, but into the
stomach. Then it goes out of the body." (When Jesus said
this, he meant that no longer was any food unclean for
people to eat.)
[20]And Jesus said, "The things that come out of people
are the things that make them unclean. [21]All these evil
things begin inside people, in the mind: evil thoughts, sexual sins, stealing, murder, adultery, [22]greed, evil actions,
lying, doing sinful things, jealousy, speaking evil of others, pride, and foolish living. [23]All these evil things come
from inside and make people unclean."

7:16 [c] **Verse 16** Some Greek copies add verse 16: "You people who can hear me, listen!"

CONTEMPORARY ENGLISH VERSION

won't let those people help their parents. [13]And you
ignore God's commands in order to follow your own
teaching. You do a lot of other things that are just as
bad.

What Really Makes People Unclean (Matthew 15.10-20)

[14]Jesus called the crowd together again and said, "Pay
attention and try to understand what I mean. [15-16]The food
that you put into your mouth doesn't make you unclean
and unfit to worship God. The bad words that come out of
your mouth are what make you unclean."[e]
[17]After Jesus and his disciples had left the crowd and
had gone into the house, they asked him what these sayings meant. [18]He answered, "Don't you know what I am
talking about by now? You surely know that the food you
put into your mouth cannot make you unclean. [19]It doesn't
go into your heart, but into your stomach, and then out of
your body." By saying this, Jesus meant that all foods were
fit to eat.
[20]Then Jesus said:

What comes from your heart is what makes you
unclean. [21]Out of your heart come evil thoughts, vulgar
deeds, stealing, murder, [22]unfaithfulness in marriage,
greed, meanness, deceit, indecency, envy, insults, pride,
and foolishness. [23]All of these come from your heart,
and they are what make you unfit to worship God.

[e] **7.15,16** *unclean*: Some manuscripts add, "If you have ears, pay attention."

NEW INTERNATIONAL VERSION

God), [12]then you no longer let him do anything for his father or mother. [13]Thus you nullify the word of God by your tradition that you have handed down. And you do many things like that."

[14]Again Jesus called the crowd to him and said, "Listen to me, everyone, and understand this. [15]Nothing outside a man can make him 'unclean' by going into him. Rather, it is what comes out of a man that makes him 'unclean.'[f]"

[17]After he had left the crowd and entered the house, his disciples asked him about this parable. [18]"Are you so dull?" he asked. "Don't you see that nothing that enters a man from the outside can make him 'unclean'? [19]For it doesn't go into his heart but into his stomach, and then out of his body." (In saying this, Jesus declared all foods "clean.")

[20]He went on: "What comes out of a man is what makes him 'unclean.' [21]For from within, out of men's hearts, come evil thoughts, sexual immorality, theft, murder, adultery, [22]greed, malice, deceit, lewdness, envy, slander, arrogance and folly. [23]All these evils come from inside and make a man 'unclean.' "

[f] *15* Some early manuscripts *'unclean.'* [16]*If anyone has ears to hear, let him hear.*

NEW LIVING TRANSLATION

them disregard their needy parents. [13]As such, you break the law of God in order to protect your own tradition. And this is only one example. There are many, many others."

[14]Then Jesus called to the crowd to come and hear. "All of you listen," he said, "and try to understand. [15]You are not defiled by what you eat; you are defiled by what you say and do!*"

[17]Then Jesus went into a house to get away from the crowds, and his disciples asked him what he meant by the statement he had made. [18]"Don't you understand either?" he asked. "Can't you see that what you eat won't defile you? [19]Food doesn't come in contact with your heart, but only passes through the stomach and then comes out again." (By saying this, he showed that every kind of food is acceptable.)

[20]And then he added, "It is the thought-life that defiles you. [21]For from within, out of a person's heart, come evil thoughts, sexual immorality, theft, murder, [22]adultery, greed, wickedness, deceit, eagerness for lustful pleasure, envy, slander, pride, and foolishness. [23]All these vile things come from within; they are what defile you and make you unacceptable to God."

7:15 Some manuscripts add verse 16, *Anyone who is willing to hear should listen and understand.*

NEW KING JAMES VERSION

him do anything for his father or his mother, [13]making the word of God of no effect through your tradition which you have handed down. And many such things you do."

[14]When He had called all the multitude to *Himself,* He said to them, "Hear Me, everyone, and understand: [15]There is nothing that enters a man from outside which can defile him; but the things which come out of him, those are the things that defile a man. [16]If anyone has ears to hear, let him hear!"[f]

[17]When He had entered a house away from the crowd, His disciples asked Him concerning the parable. [18]So He said to them, "Are you thus without understanding also? Do you not perceive that whatever enters a man from outside cannot defile him, [19]because it does not enter his heart but his stomach, and is eliminated, *thus* purifying all foods?"[g] [20]And He said, "What comes out of a man, that defiles a man. [21]For from within, out of the heart of men, proceed evil thoughts, adulteries, fornications, murders, [22]thefts, covetousness, wickedness, deceit, lewdness, an evil eye, blasphemy, pride, foolishness. [23]All these evil things come from within and defile a man."

7:16 [f] NU-Text omits this verse. 7:19 [g] NU-Text ends quotation with *eliminated,* setting off the final clause as Mark's comment that Jesus has declared all foods clean.

THE MESSAGE

relieving yourselves of obligation to father or mother. You scratch out God's Word and scrawl a whim in its place. You do a lot of things like this."

Jesus called the crowd together again and said, "Listen now, all of you—take this to heart. It's not what you swallow that pollutes your life; it's what you vomit—that's the real pollution."

When he was back home after being with the crowd, his disciples said, "We don't get it. Put it in plain language."

Jesus said, "Are you being willfully stupid? Don't you see that what you swallow can't contaminate you? It doesn't enter your heart but your stomach, works its way through the intestines, and is finally flushed." (That took care of dietary quibbling; Jesus was saying that *all* foods are fit to eat.)

He went on: "It's what comes out of a person that pollutes: obscenities, lusts, thefts, murders, adulteries, greed, depravity, deceptive dealings, carousing, mean looks, slander, arrogance, foolishness—all these are vomit from the heart. *There* is the source of your pollution."

KING JAMES VERSION

24 ¶ And from thence he arose, and went into the borders of Tyre and Sidon, and entered into an house, and would have no man know *it*: but he could not be hid.

25 For a *certain* woman, whose young daughter had an unclean spirit, heard of him, and came and fell at his feet:

26 The woman was a Greek, a Syrophenician by nation; and she besought him that he would cast forth the devil out of her daughter.

27 But Jesus said unto her, Let the children first be filled: for it is not meet to take the children's bread, and to cast *it* unto the dogs.

28 And she answered and said unto him, Yes, Lord: yet the dogs under the table eat of the children's crumbs.

29 And he said unto her, For this saying go thy way; the devil is gone out of thy daughter.

30 And when she was come to her house, she found the devil gone out, and her daughter laid upon the bed.

31 ¶ And again, departing from the coasts of Tyre and Sidon, he came unto the sea of Galilee, through the midst of the coasts of Decapolis.

32 And they bring unto him one that was deaf, and had an impediment in his speech; and they beseech him to put his hand upon him.

33 And he took him aside from the multitude, and put his fingers into his ears, and he spit, and touched his tongue;

NEW AMERICAN STANDARD BIBLE

The Syrophoenician Woman

24 Jesus got up and went away from there to the region of Tyre[3]. And when He had entered a house, He wanted no one to know *of it;* yet He could not escape notice.

25 But after hearing of Him, a woman whose little daughter had an unclean spirit immediately came and fell at His feet.

26 Now the woman was a [4]Gentile, of the Syrophoenician race. And she kept asking Him to cast the demon out of her daughter.

27 And He was saying to her, "Let the children be satisfied first, for it is not good to take the children's bread and throw it to the dogs."

28 But she answered and *said to Him, "Yes, Lord, *but* even the dogs under the table feed on the children's crumbs."

29 And He said to her, "Because of this answer go; the demon has gone out of your daughter."

30 And going back to her home, she found the child lying on the bed, the demon having left.

31 Again He went out from the region of Tyre, and came through Sidon to the Sea of Galilee, within the region of Decapolis.

32 They *brought to Him one who was deaf and spoke with difficulty, and they *implored Him to lay His hand on him.

33 Jesus took him aside from the crowd, by himself, and put His fingers into his ears, and after spitting, He touched his tongue *with the saliva;*

7:24 [3] Two early mss add *and Sidon* **7:26** [4] Lit *Greek*

NEW CENTURY VERSION

Jesus Helps a Non-Jewish Woman

24 Jesus left that place and went to the area around Tyre.
When he went into a house, he did not want anyone to
know he was there, but he could not stay hidden. 25 A
woman whose daughter had an evil spirit in her heard that
he was there. So she quickly came to Jesus and fell at his
feet. 26 She was Greek, born in Phoenicia, in Syria. She
begged Jesus to force the demon out of her daughter.

27 Jesus told the woman, "It is not right to take the children's bread and give it to the dogs. First let the children eat all they want."

28 But she answered, "Yes, Lord, but even the dogs under the table can eat the children's crumbs."

29 Then Jesus said, "Because of your answer, you may go. The demon has left your daughter."

30 The woman went home and found her daughter lying in bed; the demon was gone.

Jesus Heals a Deaf Man

31 Then Jesus left the area around Tyre and went through
Sidon to Lake Galilee, to the area of the Ten Towns.[d]
32 While he was there, some people brought a man to him
who was deaf and could not talk plainly. The people
begged Jesus to put his hand on the man to heal him.

33 Jesus led the man away from the crowd, by himself. He put his fingers in the man's ears and then spit and

7:31 [d] **Ten Towns** In Greek, called "Decapolis." It was an area east of Lake Galilee that once had ten main towns.

CONTEMPORARY ENGLISH VERSION

A Woman's Faith (Matthew 15.21-28)

24 Jesus left and went to the region near the city of Tyre,
where he stayed in someone's home. He did not want peo-
ple to know he was there, but they found out anyway. 25 A
woman whose daughter had an evil spirit in her heard
where Jesus was. And right away she came and knelt down
at his feet. 26 The woman was Greek and had been born in
the part of Syria known as Phoenicia. She begged Jesus to
force the demon out of her daughter. 27 But Jesus said,
"The children must first be fed! It isn't right to take away
their food and feed it to dogs."[f]

28 The woman replied, "Lord, even dogs eat the crumbs that children drop from the table."

29 Jesus answered, "That's true! You may go now. The
demon has left your daughter." 30 When the woman got
back home, she found her child lying on the bed. The
demon had gone.

Jesus Heals a Man Who Was Deaf and Could Hardly Talk

31 Jesus left the region around Tyre and went by way of
Sidon toward Lake Galilee. He went through the land near
the ten cities known as Decapolis.[g] 32 Some people brought
to him a man who was deaf and could hardly talk. They
begged Jesus just to touch him.

33 After Jesus had taken him aside from the crowd, he stuck his fingers in the man's ears. Then he spit and put it

[f] 7.27 *feed it to dogs*: The Jewish people often referred to Gentiles as dogs. [g] 7.31 *the ten cities known as Decapolis*: See the note at 5.20.

NEW INTERNATIONAL VERSION

The Faith of a Syrophoenician Woman

24Jesus left that place and went to the vicinity of Tyre.[g]
He entered a house and did not want anyone to know it;
yet he could not keep his presence secret. 25In fact, as soon
as she heard about him, a woman whose little daughter
was possessed by an evil[h] spirit came and fell at his feet.
26The woman was a Greek, born in Syrian Phoenicia. She
begged Jesus to drive the demon out of her daughter.

27"First let the children eat all they want," he told her,
"for it is not right to take the children's bread and toss it
to their dogs."

28"Yes, Lord," she replied, "but even the dogs under the
table eat the children's crumbs."

29Then he told her, "For such a reply, you may go; the
demon has left your daughter."

30She went home and found her child lying on the bed,
and the demon gone.

The Healing of a Deaf and Mute Man

31Then Jesus left the vicinity of Tyre and went through
Sidon, down to the Sea of Galilee and into the region of the
Decapolis.[i] 32There some people brought to him a man who
was deaf and could hardly talk, and they begged him to
place his hand on the man.

33After he took him aside, away from the crowd, Jesus
put his fingers into the man's ears. Then he spit and
touched the man's tongue. 34He looked up to heaven and

[g] *24* Many early manuscripts *Tyre and Sidon* [h] *25* Greek *unclean*
[i] *31* That is, the Ten Cities

NEW LIVING TRANSLATION

The Faith of a Gentile Woman

24Then Jesus left Galilee and went north to the region of
Tyre.* He tried to keep it secret that he was there, but he
couldn't. As usual, the news of his arrival spread fast.
25Right away a woman came to him whose little girl was
possessed by an evil spirit. She had heard about Jesus, and
now she came and fell at his feet. 26She begged him to
release her child from the demon's control.

Since she was a Gentile, born in Syrian Phoenicia,
27Jesus told her, "First I should help my own family, the
Jews.* It isn't right to take food from the children and
throw it to the dogs."

28She replied, "That's true, Lord, but even the dogs under
the table are given some crumbs from the children's plates."

29"Good answer!" he said. "And because you have
answered so well, I have healed your daughter." 30And
when she arrived home, her little girl was lying quietly in
bed, and the demon was gone.

Jesus Heals a Deaf and Mute Man

31Jesus left Tyre and went to Sidon, then back to the Sea
of Galilee and the region of the Ten Towns.* 32A deaf man
with a speech impediment was brought to him, and the
people begged Jesus to lay his hands on the man to heal
him. 33Jesus led him to a private place away from the
crowd. He put his fingers into the man's ears. Then, spit-
ting onto his own fingers, he touched the man's tongue

7:24 Some Greek manuscripts add *and Sidon.* 7:27 Greek *Let the children eat first.* 7:31 Greek *Decapolis.*

NEW KING JAMES VERSION

A Gentile Shows Her Faith

24From there He arose and went to the region of Tyre and
Sidon.[h] And He entered a house and wanted no one to
know *it,* but He could not be hidden. 25For a woman whose
young daughter had an unclean spirit heard about Him,
and she came and fell at His feet. 26The woman was a
Greek, a Syro-Phoenician by birth, and she kept asking Him
to cast the demon out of her daughter. 27But Jesus said to
her, "Let the children be filled first, for it is not good to take
the children's bread and throw *it* to the little dogs."

28And she answered and said to Him, "Yes, Lord, yet
even the little dogs under the table eat from the children's
crumbs."

29Then He said to her, "For this saying go your way; the
demon has gone out of your daughter."

30And when she had come to her house, she found the
demon gone out, and her daughter lying on the bed.

Jesus Heals a Deaf-Mute

31Again, departing from the region of Tyre and Sidon, He
came through the midst of the region of Decapolis to the
Sea of Galilee. 32Then they brought to Him one who was
deaf and had an impediment in his speech, and they
begged Him to put His hand on him. 33And He took him
aside from the multitude, and put His fingers in his ears,
and He spat and touched his tongue. 34Then, looking up to

7:24 [h] NU-Text omits *and Sidon.*

THE MESSAGE

From there Jesus set out for the vicinity of Tyre. He entered a house there where he didn't think he would be found, but he couldn't escape notice. He was barely inside when a woman who had a disturbed daughter heard where he was. She came and knelt at his feet, begging for help. The woman was Greek, Syro-Phoenician by birth. She asked him to cure her daughter.

He said, "Stand in line and take your turn. The children get fed first. If there's any left over, the dogs get it."

She said, "Of course, Master. But don't dogs under the table get scraps dropped by the children?"

Jesus was impressed. "You're right! On your way! Your daughter is no longer disturbed. The demonic affliction is gone." She went home and found her daughter relaxed on the bed, the torment gone for good.

Then he left the region of Tyre, went through Sidon back to Galilee Lake and over to the district of the Ten Towns. Some people brought a man who could neither hear nor speak and asked Jesus to lay a healing hand on him. He took the man off by himself, put his fingers in the man's ears and some spit on the man's tongue. Then Jesus

KING JAMES VERSION

34 And looking up to heaven, he sighed, and saith unto him, Ephphatha, that is, Be opened.

35 And straightway his ears were opened, and the string of his tongue was loosed, and he spake plain.

36 And he charged them that they should tell no man: but the more he charged them, so much the more a great deal they published *it*;

37 And were beyond measure astonished, saying, He hath done all things well: he maketh both the deaf to hear, and the dumb to speak.

8 In those days the multitude being very great, and having nothing to eat, Jesus called his disciples *unto him*, and saith unto them,

2 I have compassion on the multitude, because they have now been with me three days, and have nothing to eat:

3 And if I send them away fasting to their own houses, they will faint by the way: for divers of them came from far.

4 And his disciples answered him, From whence can a man satisfy these *men* with bread here in the wilderness?

5 And he asked them, How many loaves have ye? And they said, Seven.

6 And he commanded the people to sit down on the ground: and he took the seven loaves, and gave thanks, and brake, and gave to his disciples to set before *them*; and they did set *them* before the people.

NEW AMERICAN STANDARD BIBLE

34 and looking up to heaven with a deep sigh, He *said to him, "Ephphatha!" that is, "Be opened!"

35 And his ears were opened, and the impediment of his tongue was removed, and he *began* speaking plainly.

36 And He gave them orders not to tell anyone; but the more He ordered them, the more widely they continued to proclaim it.

37 They were utterly astonished, saying, "He has done all things well; He makes even the deaf to hear and the mute to speak."

Four Thousand Fed

8 In those days, when there was again a large crowd and they had nothing to eat, Jesus called His disciples and *said to them,

2 "I feel compassion for the people because they have remained with Me now three days and have nothing to eat.

3 "If I send them away hungry to their homes, they will faint on the way; and some of them have come from a great distance."

4 And His disciples answered Him, "Where will anyone be able *to find enough* bread here in *this* desolate place to satisfy these people?"

5 And He was asking them, "How many loaves do you have?" And they said, "Seven."

6 And He *directed the people to sit down on the ground; and taking the seven loaves, He gave thanks and broke them, and started giving them to His disciples to serve to them, and they served them to the people.

NEW CENTURY VERSION

touched the man's tongue. 34Looking up to heaven, he
sighed and said to the man, "Ephphatha!" (This means,
"Be opened.") 35Instantly the man was able to hear and to
use his tongue so that he spoke clearly.
36Jesus commanded the people not to tell anyone about
what happened. But the more he commanded them, the
more they told about it. 37They were completely amazed
and said, "Jesus does everything well. He makes the deaf
hear! And those who can't talk he makes able to speak."

More than Four Thousand People Fed

8 Another time there was a great crowd with Jesus that
had nothing to eat. So Jesus called his followers and
said, 2"I feel sorry for these people, because they have
already been with me for three days, and they have noth-
ing to eat. 3If I send them home hungry, they will faint on
the way. Some of them live a long way from here."
4Jesus' followers answered, "How can we get enough
bread to feed all these people? We are far away from any
town."
5Jesus asked, "How many loaves of bread do you have?"
They answered, "Seven."
6Jesus told the people to sit on the ground. Then he took
the seven loaves, gave thanks to God, and divided the bread.
He gave the pieces to his followers to give to the people, and

CONTEMPORARY ENGLISH VERSION

on the man's tongue. 34Jesus looked up toward heaven,
and with a groan he said, "Effatha!"[h] which means "Open
up!" 35At once the man could hear, and he had no more
trouble talking clearly.
36Jesus told the people not to say anything about what
he had done. But the more he told them, the more they
talked about it. 37They were completely amazed and said,
"Everything he does is good! He even heals people who
cannot hear or talk."

Jesus Feeds Four Thousand (Matthew 15.32-39)

8 One day another large crowd gathered around Jesus.
They had not brought along anything to eat. So Jesus
called his disciples together and said, 2"I feel sorry for
these people. They have been with me for three days, and
they don't have anything to eat. 3Some of them live a long
way from here. If I send them away hungry, they might
faint on their way home."
4The disciples said, "This place is like a desert. Where
can we find enough food to feed such a crowd?"
5Jesus asked them how much food they had. They
replied, "Seven small loaves of bread."[a]
6After Jesus told the crowd to sit down, he took the
seven loaves and blessed them. He then broke the loaves
and handed them to his disciples, who passed them out to

[h] 7.34 *Effatha*: This word is in Aramaic, a language spoken in Palestine during the time of Jesus. [a] 8.5 *small loaves of bread*: See the note at 6.38.

NEW INTERNATIONAL VERSION

with a deep sigh said to him, *"Ephphatha!"* (which means,
"Be opened!"). 35At this, the man's ears were opened, his
tongue was loosened and he began to speak plainly.

36Jesus commanded them not to tell anyone. But the
more he did so, the more they kept talking about it.
37People were overwhelmed with amazement. "He has
done everything well," they said. "He even makes the deaf
hear and the mute speak."

Jesus Feeds the Four Thousand

8 During those days another large crowd gathered.
Since they had nothing to eat, Jesus called his disci-
ples to him and said, 2"I have compassion for these peo-
ple; they have already been with me three days and have
nothing to eat. 3If I send them home hungry, they will col-
lapse on the way, because some of them have come a long
distance."

4His disciples answered, "But where in this remote place
can anyone get enough bread to feed them?"

5"How many loaves do you have?" Jesus asked.

"Seven," they replied.

6He told the crowd to sit down on the ground. When he
had taken the seven loaves and given thanks, he broke them
and gave them to his disciples to set before the people, and

NEW LIVING TRANSLATION

with the spittle. 34And looking up to heaven, he sighed and
commanded, "Be opened!"* 35Instantly the man could hear
perfectly and speak plainly!

36Jesus told the crowd not to tell anyone, but the more
he told them not to, the more they spread the news, 37for
they were completely amazed. Again and again they said,
"Everything he does is wonderful. He even heals those
who are deaf and mute."

Jesus Feeds Four Thousand

8 About this time another great crowd had gathered,
and the people ran out of food again. Jesus called his
disciples and told them, 2"I feel sorry for these people.
They have been here with me for three days, and they have
nothing left to eat. 3And if I send them home without feed-
ing them, they will faint along the road. For some of them
have come a long distance."

4"How are we supposed to find enough food for them
here in the wilderness?" his disciples asked.

5"How many loaves of bread do you have?" he asked.

"Seven," they replied. 6So Jesus told all the people to sit
down on the ground. Then he took the seven loaves,
thanked God for them, broke them into pieces, and gave
them to his disciples, who distributed the bread to the

7:34 Greek text uses Aramaic *"Ephphatha"* and then translates it as
"Be opened."

NEW KING JAMES VERSION

heaven, He sighed, and said to him, "Ephphatha," that is,
"Be opened."

35Immediately his ears were opened, and the impedi-
ment of his tongue was loosed, and he spoke plainly.
36Then He commanded them that they should tell no one;
but the more He commanded them, the more widely they
proclaimed *it.* 37And they were astonished beyond mea-
sure, saying, "He has done all things well. He makes both
the deaf to hear and the mute to speak."

Feeding the Four Thousand

8 In those days, the multitude being very great and hav-
ing nothing to eat, Jesus called His disciples *to Him*
and said to them, 2"I have compassion on the multitude,
because they have now continued with Me three days and
have nothing to eat. 3And if I send them away hungry to
their own houses, they will faint on the way; for some of
them have come from afar."

4Then His disciples answered Him, "How can one satisfy
these people with bread here in the wilderness?"

5He asked them, "How many loaves do you have?"

And they said, "Seven."

6So He commanded the multitude to sit down on the
ground. And He took the seven loaves and gave thanks,
broke *them* and gave *them* to His disciples to set before
them; and they set *them* before the multitude. 7They also

THE MESSAGE

looked up in prayer, groaned mightily, and commanded,
"*Ephphatha!*—Open up!" And it happened. The man's
hearing was clear and his speech plain—just like that.

Jesus urged them to keep it quiet, but they talked it up
all the more, beside themselves with excitement. "He's
done it all and done it well. He gives hearing to the deaf,
speech to the speechless."

A Meal for Four Thousand

8 At about this same time he again found himself with
a hungry crowd on his hands. He called his disciples
together and said, "This crowd is breaking my heart. They
have stuck with me for three days, and now they have
nothing to eat. If I send them home hungry, they'll faint
along the way—some of them have come a long distance."

His disciples responded, "What do you expect us to do
about it? Buy food out here in the desert?"

He asked, "How much bread do you have?"

"Seven loaves," they said.

So Jesus told the crowd to sit down on the ground. After
giving thanks, he took the seven bread loaves, broke them
into pieces, and gave them to his disciples so they could
hand them out to the crowd. They also had a few fish. He

KING JAMES VERSION

7 And they had a few small fishes: and he blessed, and commanded to set them also before *them*.

8 So they did eat, and were filled: and they took up of the broken *meat* that was left seven baskets.

9 And they that had eaten were about four thousand: and he sent them away.

10 ¶ And straightway he entered into a ship with his disciples, and came into the parts of Dalmanutha.

11 And the Pharisees came forth, and began to question with him, seeking of him a sign from heaven, tempting him.

12 And he sighed deeply in his spirit, and saith, Why doth this generation seek after a sign? verily I say unto you, There shall no sign be given unto this generation.

13 And he left them, and entering into the ship again departed to the other side.

14 Now *the disciples* had forgotten to take bread, neither had they in the ship with them more than one loaf.

15 And he charged them, saying, Take heed, beware of the leaven of the Pharisees, and *of* the leaven of Herod.

16 And they reasoned among themselves, saying, *It is* because we have no bread.

17 And when Jesus knew *it*, he saith unto them, Why reason ye, because ye have no bread? perceive ye not yet, neither understand? have ye your heart yet hardened?

NEW AMERICAN STANDARD BIBLE

7 They also had a few small fish; and after He had blessed them, He ordered these to be served as well.

8 And they ate and were satisfied; and they picked up seven large baskets full of what was left over of the broken pieces.

9 About four thousand were *there;* and He sent them away.

10 And immediately He entered the boat with His disciples and came to the district of Dalmanutha.

11 The Pharisees came out and began to argue with Him, seeking from Him a sign from heaven, to test Him.

12 Sighing deeply in His spirit, He *said, "Why does this generation seek for a sign? Truly I say to you, no sign will be given to this generation."

13 Leaving them, He again embarked and went away to the other side.

14 And they had forgotten to take bread, and did not have more than one loaf in the boat with them.

15 And He was giving orders to them, saying, "Watch out! Beware of the leaven of the Pharisees and the leaven of Herod."

16 They *began* to discuss with one another *the fact* that they had no bread.

17 And Jesus, aware of this, *said to them, "Why do you discuss *the fact* that you have no bread? Do you not yet see or understand? Do you have a hardened heart?

NEW CENTURY VERSION

they did so. 7The followers also had a few small fish. After
Jesus gave thanks for the fish, he told his followers to give
them to the people also. 8All the people ate and were satis-
fied. Then his followers filled seven baskets with the leftover
pieces of food. 9There were about four thousand people who
ate. After they had eaten, Jesus sent them home. 10Then
right away he got into a boat with his followers and went to
the area of Dalmanutha.

The Leaders Ask for a Miracle

11The Pharisees came to Jesus and began to ask him
questions. Hoping to trap him, they asked Jesus for a mira-
cle from God. 12Jesus sighed deeply and said, "Why do you
people ask for a miracle as a sign? I tell you the truth, no
sign will be given to you." 13Then Jesus left the Pharisees
and went in the boat to the other side of the lake.

Guard Against Wrong Teachings

14His followers had only one loaf of bread with them in
the boat; they had forgotten to bring more. 15Jesus warned
them, "Be careful! Beware of the yeast of the Pharisees
and the yeast of Herod."

16His followers discussed the meaning of this, saying,
"He said this because we have no bread."

17Knowing what they were talking about, Jesus asked
them, "Why are you talking about not having bread? Do
you still not see or understand? Are your minds closed?

CONTEMPORARY ENGLISH VERSION

the crowd. 7They also had a few little fish, and after Jesus
had blessed these, he told the disciples to pass them
around.

8-9The crowd of about four thousand people ate all they
wanted, and the leftovers filled seven large baskets.

As soon as Jesus had sent the people away, 10he got into
the boat with the disciples and crossed to the territory near
Dalmanutha.[b]

A Sign from Heaven (Matthew 16.1-4)

11The Pharisees came out and started an argument with
Jesus. They wanted to test him by asking for a sign from
heaven. 12Jesus groaned and said, "Why are you always
looking for a sign? I can promise you that you will not be
given one!" 13Then he left them. He again got into a boat
and crossed over to the other side of the lake.

The Yeast of the Pharisees and of Herod (Matthew 16.5-12)

14The disciples had forgotten to bring any bread, and
they had only one loaf with them in the boat. 15Jesus
warned them, "Watch out! Guard against the yeast of the
Pharisees and of Herod."[c]

16The disciples talked this over and said to each other,
"He must be saying this because we don't have any bread."

17Jesus knew what they were thinking and asked, "Why
are you talking about not having any bread? Don't you
understand? Are your minds still closed? 18Are your eyes

[b] **8.10** *Dalmanutha*: The place is unknown. [c] **8.15** *Herod*: Herod Antipas, the son of Herod the Great.

NEW INTERNATIONAL VERSION

they did so. 7They had a few small fish as well; he gave thanks for them also and told the disciples to distribute them. 8The people ate and were satisfied. Afterward the disciples picked up seven basketfuls of broken pieces that were left over. 9About four thousand men were present. And having sent them away, 10he got into the boat with his disciples and went to the region of Dalmanutha.

11The Pharisees came and began to question Jesus. To test him, they asked him for a sign from heaven. 12He sighed deeply and said, "Why does this generation ask for a miraculous sign? I tell you the truth, no sign will be given to it." 13Then he left them, got back into the boat and crossed to the other side.

The Yeast of the Pharisees and Herod

14The disciples had forgotten to bring bread, except for one loaf they had with them in the boat. 15"Be careful," Jesus warned them. "Watch out for the yeast of the Pharisees and that of Herod."

16They discussed this with one another and said, "It is because we have no bread."

17Aware of their discussion, Jesus asked them: "Why are you talking about having no bread? Do you still not see or understand? Are your hearts hardened? 18Do you have

NEW LIVING TRANSLATION

crowd. 7A few small fish were found, too, so Jesus also blessed these and told the disciples to pass them out.

8They ate until they were full, and when the scraps were picked up, there were seven large baskets of food left over! 9There were about four thousand people in the crowd that day, and he sent them home after they had eaten. 10Immediately after this, he got into a boat with his disciples and crossed over to the region of Dalmanutha.

Pharisees Demand a Miraculous Sign

11When the Pharisees heard that Jesus had arrived, they came to argue with him. Testing him to see if he was from God, they demanded, "Give us a miraculous sign from heaven to prove yourself."

12When he heard this, he sighed deeply and said, "Why do you people keep demanding a miraculous sign? I assure you, I will not give this generation any such sign." 13So he got back into the boat and left them, and he crossed to the other side of the lake.

Yeast of the Pharisees and Herod

14But the disciples discovered they had forgotten to bring any food, so there was only one loaf of bread with them in the boat. 15As they were crossing the lake, Jesus warned them, "Beware of the yeast of the Pharisees and of Herod."

16They decided he was saying this because they hadn't brought any bread. 17Jesus knew what they were thinking, so he said, "Why are you so worried about having no food? Won't you ever learn or understand? Are your hearts too

NEW KING JAMES VERSION

had a few small fish; and having blessed them, He said to set them also before *them.* 8So they ate and were filled, and they took up seven large baskets of leftover fragments. 9Now those who had eaten were about four thousand. And He sent them away, 10immediately got into the boat with His disciples, and came to the region of Dalmanutha.

The Pharisees Seek a Sign

11Then the Pharisees came out and began to dispute with Him, seeking from Him a sign from heaven, testing Him. 12But He sighed deeply in His spirit, and said, "Why does this generation seek a sign? Assuredly, I say to you, no sign shall be given to this generation."

Beware of the Leaven of the Pharisees and Herod

13And He left them, and getting into the boat again, departed to the other side. 14Now the disciples[a] had forgotten to take bread, and they did not have more than one loaf with them in the boat. 15Then He charged them, saying, "Take heed, beware of the leaven of the Pharisees and the leaven of Herod."

16And they reasoned among themselves, saying, *"It is* because we have no bread."

17But Jesus, being aware of *it,* said to them, "Why do you reason because you have no bread? Do you not yet perceive nor understand? Is your heart still[b] hardened?

8:14 [a] NU-Text and M-Text read *they.* 8:17 [b] NU-Text omits *still.*

THE MESSAGE

pronounced a blessing over the fish and told his disciples to hand them out as well. The crowd ate its fill. Seven sacks of leftovers were collected. There were well over four thousand at the meal. Then he sent them home. He himself went straight to the boat with his disciples and set out for Dalmanoutha.

When they arrived, the Pharisees came out and started in on him, badgering him to prove himself, pushing him up against the wall. Provoked, he said, "Why does this generation clamor for miraculous guarantees? If I have anything to say about it, you'll not get so much as a hint of a guarantee."

Contaminating Yeast

He then left them, got back in the boat and headed for the other side. But the disciples forgot to pack a lunch. Except for a single loaf of bread, there wasn't a crumb in the boat. Jesus warned, "Be very careful. Keep a sharp eye out for the contaminating yeast of Pharisees and the followers of Herod."

Meanwhile, the disciples were finding fault with each other because they had forgotten to bring bread. Jesus overheard and said, "Why are you fussing because you forgot bread? Don't you see the point of all this? Don't you

KING JAMES VERSION

18 Having eyes, see ye not? and having ears, hear ye not? and do ye not remember?

19 When I brake the five loaves among five thousand, how many baskets full of fragments took ye up? They say unto him, Twelve.

20 And when the seven among four thousand, how many baskets full of fragments took ye up? And they said, Seven.

21 And he said unto them, How is it that ye do not understand?

22 ¶ And he cometh to Bethsaida; and they bring a blind man unto him, and besought him to touch him.

23 And he took the blind man by the hand, and led him out of the town; and when he had spit on his eyes, and put his hands upon him, he asked him if he saw ought.

24 And he looked up, and said, I see men as trees, walking.

25 After that he put *his* hands again upon his eyes, and made him look up: and he was restored, and saw every man clearly.

26 And he sent him away to his house, saying, Neither go into the town, nor tell *it* to any in the town.

27 ¶ And Jesus went out, and his disciples, into the

NEW AMERICAN STANDARD BIBLE

18 "HAVING EYES, DO YOU NOT SEE? AND HAVING EARS, DO YOU NOT HEAR? And do you not remember,

19 when I broke the five loaves for the five thousand, how many baskets full of broken pieces you picked up?" They *said to Him, "Twelve."

20 "When *I broke* the seven for the four thousand, how many large baskets full of broken pieces did you pick up?" And they *said to Him, "Seven."

21 And He was saying to them, "Do you not yet understand?"

22 And they *came to Bethsaida. And they *brought a blind man to Jesus and *implored Him to touch him.

23 Taking the blind man by the hand, He brought him out of the village; and after spitting on his eyes and laying His hands on him, He asked him, "Do you see anything?"

24 And he looked up and said, "I see men, for I see *them* like trees, walking around."

25 Then again He laid His hands on his eyes; and he looked intently and was restored, and *began* to see everything clearly.

26 And He sent him to his home, saying, "Do not even enter the village."

Peter's Confession of Christ

27 Jesus went out, along with His disciples, to the villages

NEW CENTURY VERSION

[18]You have eyes, but you don't really see. You have ears, but you don't really listen. Remember when [19]I divided five loaves of bread for the five thousand? How many baskets did you fill with leftover pieces of food?"

They answered, "Twelve."

[20]"And when I divided seven loaves of bread for the four thousand, how many baskets did you fill with leftover pieces of food?"

They answered, "Seven."

[21]Then Jesus said to them, "Don't you understand yet?"

Jesus Heals a Blind Man

[22]Jesus and his followers came to Bethsaida. There some people brought a blind man to Jesus and begged him to touch the man. [23]So Jesus took the blind man's hand and led him out of the village. Then he spit on the man's eyes and put his hands on the man and asked, "Can you see now?"

[24]The man looked up and said, "Yes, I see people, but they look like trees walking around."

[25]Again Jesus put his hands on the man's eyes. Then the man opened his eyes wide and they were healed, and he was able to see everything clearly. [26]Jesus told him to go home, saying, "Don't go into the town."

Peter Says Jesus Is the Christ

[27]Jesus and his followers went to the towns around

CONTEMPORARY ENGLISH VERSION

blind and your ears deaf? Don't you remember [19]how many baskets of leftovers you picked up when I fed those five thousand people with only five small loaves of bread?"

"Yes," the disciples answered. "There were twelve baskets."

[20]Jesus then asked, "And how many baskets of leftovers did you pick up when I broke seven small loaves of bread for those four thousand people?"

"Seven," they answered.

[21]"Don't you know what I am talking about by now?" Jesus asked.

Jesus Heals a Blind Man at Bethsaida

[22]As Jesus and his disciples were going into Bethsaida, some people brought a blind man to him and begged him to touch the man. [23]Jesus took him by the hand and led him out of the village, where he spit into the man's eyes. He placed his hands on the blind man and asked him if he could see anything. [24]The man looked up and said, "I see people, but they look like trees walking around."

[25]Once again Jesus placed his hands on the man's eyes, and this time the man stared. His eyes were healed, and he saw everything clearly. [26]Jesus said to him, "You may return home now, but don't go into the village."

Who Is Jesus? (Matthew 16.13-20; Luke 9.18-21)

[27]Jesus and his disciples went to the villages near the

NEW INTERNATIONAL VERSION

eyes but fail to see, and ears but fail to hear? And don't you remember? [19]When I broke the five loaves for the five thousand, how many basketfuls of pieces did you pick up?"

"Twelve," they replied.

[20]"And when I broke the seven loaves for the four thousand, how many basketfuls of pieces did you pick up?"

They answered, "Seven."

[21]He said to them, "Do you still not understand?"

The Healing of a Blind Man at Bethsaida

[22]They came to Bethsaida, and some people brought a blind man and begged Jesus to touch him. [23]He took the blind man by the hand and led him outside the village. When he had spit on the man's eyes and put his hands on him, Jesus asked, "Do you see anything?"

[24]He looked up and said, "I see people; they look like trees walking around."

[25]Once more Jesus put his hands on the man's eyes. Then his eyes were opened, his sight was restored, and he saw everything clearly. [26]Jesus sent him home, saying, "Don't go into the village.[a]"

Peter's Confession of Christ

[27]Jesus and his disciples went on to the villages around

[a] 26 Some manuscripts *Don't go and tell anyone in the village*

NEW LIVING TRANSLATION

hard to take it in? [18]'You have eyes—can't you see? You have ears—can't you hear?'* Don't you remember anything at all? [19]What about the five thousand men I fed with five loaves of bread? How many baskets of leftovers did you pick up afterward?"

"Twelve," they said.

[20]"And when I fed the four thousand with seven loaves, how many large baskets of leftovers did you pick up?"

"Seven," they said.

[21]"Don't you understand even yet?" he asked them.

Jesus Heals a Blind Man

[22]When they arrived at Bethsaida, some people brought a blind man to Jesus, and they begged him to touch and heal the man. [23]Jesus took the blind man by the hand and led him out of the village. Then, spitting on the man's eyes, he laid his hands on him and asked, "Can you see anything now?"

[24]The man looked around. "Yes," he said, "I see people, but I can't see them very clearly. They look like trees walking around."

[25]Then Jesus placed his hands over the man's eyes again. As the man stared intently, his sight was completely restored, and he could see everything clearly. [26]Jesus sent him home, saying, "Don't go back into the village on your way home."

Peter's Declaration about Jesus

[27]Jesus and his disciples left Galilee and went up to the

8:18 Jer 5:21.

NEW KING JAMES VERSION

[18]Having eyes, do you not see? And having ears, do you not hear? And do you not remember? [19]When I broke the five loaves for the five thousand, how many baskets full of fragments did you take up?"

They said to Him, "Twelve."

[20]"Also, when I broke the seven for the four thousand, how many large baskets full of fragments did you take up?"

And they said, "Seven."

[21]So He said to them, "How *is it* you do not understand?"

A Blind Man Healed at Bethsaida

[22]Then He came to Bethsaida; and they brought a blind man to Him, and begged Him to touch him. [23]So He took the blind man by the hand and led him out of the town. And when He had spit on his eyes and put His hands on him, He asked him if he saw anything.

[24]And he looked up and said, "I see men like trees, walking."

[25]Then He put *His* hands on his eyes again and made him look up. And he was restored and saw everyone clearly. [26]Then He sent him away to his house, saying, "Neither go into the town, nor tell anyone in the town."[c]

Peter Confesses Jesus as the Christ

[27]Now Jesus and His disciples went out to the towns of

8:26 [c] NU-Text reads *"Do not even go into the town."*

THE MESSAGE

get it at all? Remember the five loaves I broke for the five thousand? How many baskets of leftovers did you pick up?"

They said, "Twelve."

"And the seven loaves for the four thousand—how many bags full of leftovers did you get?"

"Seven."

He said, "Do you still not get it?"

They arrived at Bethsaida. Some people brought a sightless man and begged Jesus to give him a healing touch. Taking him by the hand, he led him out of the village. He put spit in the man's eyes, laid hands on him, and asked, "Do you see anything?"

He looked up. "I see men. They look like walking trees." So Jesus laid hands on his eyes again. The man looked hard and realized that he had recovered perfect sight, saw everything in bright, twenty-twenty focus. Jesus sent him straight home, telling him, "Don't enter the village."

The Messiah

Jesus and his disciples headed out for the villages

KING JAMES VERSION

towns of Caesarea Philippi: and by the way he asked his disciples, saying unto them, Whom do men say that I am?

28 And they answered, John the Baptist: but some *say*, Elias; and others, One of the prophets.

29 And he saith unto them, But whom say ye that I am? And Peter answereth and saith unto him, Thou art the Christ.

30 And he charged them that they should tell no man of him.

31 And he began to teach them, that the Son of man must suffer many things, and be rejected of the elders, and *of* the chief priests, and scribes, and be killed, and after three days rise again.

32 And he spake that saying openly. And Peter took him, and began to rebuke him.

33 But when he had turned about and looked on his disciples, he rebuked Peter, saying, Get thee behind me, Satan: for thou savourest not the things that be of God, but the things that be of men.

34 And when he had called the people *unto him* with his disciples also, he said unto them, Whosoever will come after me, let him deny himself, and take up his cross, and follow me.

35 For whosoever will save his life shall lose it; but

NEW AMERICAN STANDARD BIBLE

of Caesarea Philippi; and on the way He questioned His disciples, saying to them, "Who do people say that I am?"

28 They told Him, saying, "John the Baptist; and others *say* Elijah; but others, one of the prophets."

29 And He *continued* by questioning them, "But who do you say that I am?" Peter *answered and *said to Him, "You are the Christ."

30 And He warned them to tell no one about Him.

31 And He began to teach them that the Son of Man must suffer many things and be rejected by the elders and the chief priests and the scribes, and be killed, and after three days rise again.

32 And He was stating the matter plainly. And Peter took Him aside and began to rebuke Him.

33 But turning around and seeing His disciples, He rebuked Peter and *said, "Get behind Me, Satan; for you are not setting your mind on [1]God's interests, but man's."

34 And He summoned the crowd with His disciples, and said to them, "If anyone wishes to come after Me, he must deny himself, and take up his cross and follow Me.

35 "For whoever wishes to save his life will lose it, but

8:33 [1] Lit *the things of God*

NEW CENTURY VERSION

Caesarea Philippi. While they were traveling, Jesus asked them, "Who do people say I am?"

28They answered, "Some say you are John the Baptist. Others say you are Elijah,[a] and others say you are one of the prophets."

29Then Jesus asked, "But who do you say I am?"
Peter answered, "You are the Christ."

30Jesus warned his followers not to tell anyone who he was.

31Then Jesus began to teach them that the Son of Man
must suffer many things and that he would be rejected by
the older Jewish leaders, the leading priests, and the teach-
ers of the law. He told them that the Son of Man must be
killed and then rise from the dead after three days. 32Jesus
told them plainly what would happen. Then Peter took
Jesus aside and began to tell him not to talk like that.
33But Jesus turned and looked at his followers. Then he
told Peter not to talk that way. He said, "Go away from me,
Satan![b] You don't care about the things of God, but only
about things people think are important."

34Then Jesus called the crowd to him, along with his fol-
lowers. He said, "If people want to follow me, they must
give up the things they want. They must be willing even to
give up their lives to follow me. 35Those who want to save
their lives will give up true life. But those who give up

8:28 [a] **Elijah** A man who spoke for God and who lived hundreds of years before Christ. See 1 Kings 17. 8:33 [b] **Satan** Name for the devil meaning "the enemy." Jesus means that Peter was talking like Satan.

CONTEMPORARY ENGLISH VERSION

town of Caesarea Philippi. As they were walking along, he asked them, "What do people say about me?"

28The disciples answered, "Some say you are John the
Baptist or maybe Elijah.[d] Others say you are one of the
prophets."

29Then Jesus asked them, "But who do you say I am?"
"You are the Messiah!" Peter replied.

30Jesus warned the disciples not to tell anyone about him.

Jesus Speaks about His Suffering and Death

(Matthew 16.21-28; Luke 9.22-27)

31Jesus began telling his disciples what would happen to
him. He said, "The nation's leaders, the chief priests, and
the teachers of the Law of Moses will make the Son of Man
suffer terribly. He will be rejected and killed, but three
days later he will rise to life." 32Then Jesus explained
clearly what he meant.

Peter took Jesus aside and told him to stop talking like
that. 33But when Jesus turned and saw the disciples, he
corrected Peter. He said to him, "Satan, get away from me!
You are thinking like everyone else and not like God."

34Jesus then told the crowd and the disciples to come closer, and he said:

If any of you want to be my followers, you must forget
about yourself. You must take up your cross and follow
me. 35If you want to save your life,[e] you will destroy it.
But if you give up your life for me and for the good

[d] 8.28 *Elijah*: See the note at 6.15. [e] 8.35 *life*: In verses 35-37 the same Greek word is translated "life," "yourself," and "soul."

NEW INTERNATIONAL VERSION

Caesarea Philippi. On the way he asked them, "Who do people say I am?"

[28]They replied, "Some say John the Baptist; others say Elijah; and still others, one of the prophets."

[29]"But what about you?" he asked. "Who do you say I am?"

Peter answered, "You are the Christ.[b]"

[30]Jesus warned them not to tell anyone about him.

Jesus Predicts His Death

[31]He then began to teach them that the Son of Man must suffer many things and be rejected by the elders, chief priests and teachers of the law, and that he must be killed and after three days rise again. [32]He spoke plainly about this, and Peter took him aside and began to rebuke him.

[33]But when Jesus turned and looked at his disciples, he rebuked Peter. "Get behind me, Satan!" he said. "You do not have in mind the things of God, but the things of men."

[34]Then he called the crowd to him along with his disciples and said: "If anyone would come after me, he must deny himself and take up his cross and follow me. [35]For whoever wants to save his life[c] will lose it, but whoever

[b] *29* Or *Messiah.* "The Christ" (Greek) and "the Messiah" (Hebrew) both mean "the Anointed One." [c] *35* The Greek word means either *life* or *soul;* also in verse 36.

NEW LIVING TRANSLATION

villages of Caesarea Philippi. As they were walking along, he asked them, "Who do people say I am?"

[28]"Well," they replied, "some say John the Baptist, some say Elijah, and others say you are one of the other prophets."

[29]Then Jesus asked, "Who do you say I am?"

Peter replied, "You are the Messiah." [30]But Jesus warned them not to tell anyone about him.

Jesus Predicts His Death

[31]Then Jesus began to tell them that he, the Son of Man, would suffer many terrible things and be rejected by the leaders, the leading priests, and the teachers of religious law. He would be killed, and three days later he would rise again. [32]As he talked about this openly with his disciples, Peter took him aside and told him he shouldn't say things like that.*

[33]Jesus turned and looked at his disciples and then said to Peter very sternly, "Get away from me, Satan! You are seeing things merely from a human point of view, not from God's."

[34]Then he called his disciples and the crowds to come over and listen. "If any of you wants to be my follower," he told them, "you must put aside your selfish ambition, shoulder your cross, and follow me. [35]If you try to keep your life for yourself, you will lose it. But if you give up

8:32 Or *and began to correct him.*

NEW KING JAMES VERSION

Caesarea Philippi; and on the road He asked His disciples, saying to them, "Who do men say that I am?"

[28]So they answered, "John the Baptist; but some *say,* Elijah; and others, one of the prophets."

[29]He said to them, "But who do you say that I am?"

Peter answered and said to Him, "You are the Christ."

[30]Then He strictly warned them that they should tell no one about Him.

Jesus Predicts His Death and Resurrection

[31]And He began to teach them that the Son of Man must suffer many things, and be rejected by the elders and chief priests and scribes, and be killed, and after three days rise again. [32]He spoke this word openly. Then Peter took Him aside and began to rebuke Him. [33]But when He had turned around and looked at His disciples, He rebuked Peter, saying, "Get behind Me, Satan! For you are not mindful of the things of God, but the things of men."

Take Up the Cross and Follow Him

[34]When He had called the people to *Himself,* with His disciples also, He said to them, "Whoever desires to come after Me, let him deny himself, and take up his cross, and follow Me. [35]For whoever desires to save his life will lose

THE MESSAGE

around Caesarea Philippi. As they walked, he asked, "Who do the people say I am?"

"Some say 'John the Baptizer,'" they said. "Others say 'Elijah.' Still others say 'one of the prophets.'"

He then asked, "And you—what are you saying about me? Who am I?"

Peter gave the answer: "You are the Christ, the Messiah."

Jesus warned them to keep it quiet, not to breathe a word of it to anyone. He then began explaining things to them: "It is necessary that the Son of Man proceed to an ordeal of suffering, be tried and found guilty by the elders, high priests, and religion scholars, be killed, and after three days rise up alive." He said this simply and clearly so they couldn't miss it.

But Peter grabbed him in protest. Turning and seeing his disciples wavering, wondering what to believe, Jesus confronted Peter. "Peter, get out of my way! Satan, get lost! You have no idea how God works."

Calling the crowd to join his disciples, he said, "Anyone who intends to come with me has to let me lead. You're not in the driver's seat; *I* am. Don't run from suffering; embrace it. Follow me and I'll show you how. Self-help is no help at all. Self-sacrifice is the way, my way, to saving

KING JAMES VERSION

whosoever shall lose his life for my sake and the gospel's, the same shall save it.

36 For what shall it profit a man, if he shall gain the whole world, and lose his own soul?

37 Or what shall a man give in exchange for his soul?

38 Whosoever therefore shall be ashamed of me and of my words in this adulterous and sinful generation; of him also shall the Son of man be ashamed, when he cometh in the glory of his Father with the holy angels.

9 And he said unto them, Verily I say unto you, That there be some of them that stand here, which shall not taste of death, till they have seen the kingdom of God come with power.

2 And after six days Jesus taketh *with him* Peter, and James, and John, and leadeth them up into an high mountain apart by themselves: and he was transfigured before them.

3 And his raiment became shining, exceeding white as snow; so as no fuller on earth can white them.

4 And there appeared unto them Elias with Moses: and they were talking with Jesus.

5 And Peter answered and said to Jesus, Master, it is good for us to be here: and let us make three tabernacles; one for thee, and one for Moses, and one for Elias.

6 For he wist not what to say; for they were sore afraid.

7 And there was a cloud that overshadowed them: and

NEW AMERICAN STANDARD BIBLE

whoever loses his life for My sake and the gospel's will save it.

36 "For what does it profit a man to gain the whole world, and forfeit his soul?

37 "For what will a man give in exchange for his soul?

38 "For whoever is ashamed of Me and My words in this adulterous and sinful generation, the Son of Man will also be ashamed of him when He comes in the glory of His Father with the holy angels."

The Transfiguration

9 And Jesus was saying to them, "Truly I say to you, there are some of those who are standing here who will not taste death until they see the kingdom of God after it has come with power."

2 Six days later, Jesus *took with Him Peter and James and John, and *brought them up on a high mountain by themselves. And He was transfigured before them;

3 and His garments became radiant and exceedingly white, as no launderer on earth can whiten them.

4 Elijah appeared to them along with Moses; and they were talking with Jesus.

5 Peter *said to Jesus, "Rabbi, it is good for us to be here; let us make three tabernacles, one for You, and one for Moses, and one for Elijah."

6 For he did not know what to answer; for they became terrified.

7 Then a cloud formed, overshadowing them, and a

NEW CENTURY VERSION

their lives for me and for the Good News will have true life. 36It is worth nothing for them to have the whole world if they lose their souls. 37They could never pay enough to buy back their souls. 38The people who live now are living in a sinful and evil time. If people are ashamed of me and my teaching, the Son of Man will be ashamed of them when he comes with his Father's glory and with the holy angels."

9 Then Jesus said to the people, "I tell you the truth, some people standing here will see the kingdom of God come with power before they die."

Jesus Talks with Moses and Elijah

2Six days later, Jesus took Peter, James, and John up on a high mountain by themselves. While they watched, Jesus' appearance was changed. 3His clothes became shining white, whiter than any person could make them. 4Then Elijah and Moses[a] appeared to them, talking with Jesus.

5Peter said to Jesus, "Teacher, it is good that we are here. Let us make three tents—one for you, one for Moses, and one for Elijah." 6Peter did not know what to say, because he and the others were so frightened.

7Then a cloud came and covered them, and a voice came

9:4 [a] **Elijah and Moses** Two of the most important Jewish leaders in the past. Moses had given them the law, and Elijah was an important prophet.

CONTEMPORARY ENGLISH VERSION

news, you will save it. 36What will you gain, if you own the whole world but destroy yourself? 37What could you give to get back your soul?

38Don't be ashamed of me and my message among these unfaithful and sinful people! If you are, the Son of Man will be ashamed of you when he comes in the glory of his Father with the holy angels.

9 I can assure you that some of the people standing here will not die before they see God's kingdom come with power.

The True Glory of Jesus (Matthew 17.1-13; Luke 9.28-36)

2Six days later Jesus took Peter, James, and John with him. They went up on a high mountain, where they could be alone. There in front of the disciples, Jesus was completely changed. 3And his clothes became much whiter than any bleach on earth could make them. 4Then Moses and Elijah were there talking with Jesus.

5Peter said to Jesus, "Teacher, it is good for us to be here! Let us make three shelters, one for you, one for Moses, and one for Elijah." 6But Peter and the others were terribly frightened, and he did not know what he was talking about.

7The shadow of a cloud passed over and covered them.

NEW INTERNATIONAL VERSION

loses his life for me and for the gospel will save it. [36]What good is it for a man to gain the whole world, yet forfeit his soul? [37]Or what can a man give in exchange for his soul? [38]If anyone is ashamed of me and my words in this adulterous and sinful generation, the Son of Man will be ashamed of him when he comes in his Father's glory with the holy angels."

9 And he said to them, "I tell you the truth, some who are standing here will not taste death before they see the kingdom of God come with power."

The Transfiguration

[2]After six days Jesus took Peter, James and John with him and led them up a high mountain, where they were all alone. There he was transfigured before them. [3]His clothes became dazzling white, whiter than anyone in the world could bleach them. [4]And there appeared before them Elijah and Moses, who were talking with Jesus.

[5]Peter said to Jesus, "Rabbi, it is good for us to be here. Let us put up three shelters—one for you, one for Moses and one for Elijah." [6](He did not know what to say, they were so frightened.)

[7]Then a cloud appeared and enveloped them, and a voice

NEW LIVING TRANSLATION

your life for my sake and for the sake of the Good News, you will find true life. [36]And how do you benefit if you gain the whole world but lose your own soul* in the process? [37]Is anything worth more than your soul? [38]If a person is ashamed of me and my message in these adulterous and sinful days, I, the Son of Man, will be ashamed of that person when I return in the glory of my Father with the holy angels."

9 Jesus went on to say, "I assure you that some of you standing here right now will not die before you see the Kingdom of God arrive in great power!"

The Transfiguration

[2]Six days later Jesus took Peter, James, and John to the top of a mountain. No one else was there. As the men watched, Jesus' appearance changed, [3]and his clothing became dazzling white, far whiter than any earthly process could ever make it. [4]Then Elijah and Moses appeared and began talking with Jesus.

[5]"Teacher, this is wonderful!" Peter exclaimed. "We will make three shrines*—one for you, one for Moses, and one for Elijah." [6]He didn't really know what to say, for they were all terribly afraid.

[7]Then a cloud came over them, and a voice from the

8:36 Or *your life;* also in 8:37. **9:5** Or *shelters;* Greek reads *tabernacles.*

NEW KING JAMES VERSION

it, but whoever loses his life for My sake and the gospel's will save it. [36]For what will it profit a man if he gains the whole world, and loses his own soul? [37]Or what will a man give in exchange for his soul? [38]For whoever is ashamed of Me and My words in this adulterous and sinful generation, of him the Son of Man also will be ashamed when He comes in the glory of His Father with the holy angels."

Jesus Transfigured on the Mount

9 And He said to them, "Assuredly, I say to you that there are some standing here who will not taste death till they see the kingdom of God present with power."

[2]Now after six days Jesus took Peter, James, and John, and led them up on a high mountain apart by themselves; and He was transfigured before them. [3]His clothes became shining, exceedingly white, like snow, such as no launderer on earth can whiten them. [4]And Elijah appeared to them with Moses, and they were talking with Jesus. [5]Then Peter answered and said to Jesus, "Rabbi, it is good for us to be here; and let us make three tabernacles: one for You, one for Moses, and one for Elijah"— [6]because he did not know what to say, for they were greatly afraid.

[7]And a cloud came and overshadowed them; and a voice

THE MESSAGE

yourself, your true self. What good would it do to get everything you want and lose you, the real you? What could you ever trade your soul for?

"If any of you are embarrassed over me and the way I'm leading you when you get around your fickle and unfocused friends, know that you'll be an even greater embarrassment to the Son of Man when he arrives in all the splendor of God, his Father, with an army of the holy angels."

9 Then he drove it home by saying, "This isn't pie in the sky by and by. Some of you who are standing here are going to see it happen, see the kingdom of God arrive in full force."

In a Light-Radiant Cloud

Six days later, three of them *did* see it. Jesus took Peter, James, and John and led them up a high mountain. His appearance changed from the inside out, right before their eyes. His clothes shimmered, glistening white, whiter than any bleach could make them. Elijah, along with Moses, came into view, in deep conversation with Jesus.

Peter interrupted, "Rabbi, this is a great moment! Let's build three memorials—one for you, one for Moses, one for Elijah." He blurted this out without thinking, stunned as they all were by what they were seeing.

Just then a light-radiant cloud enveloped them, and from

KING JAMES VERSION

a voice came out of the cloud, saying, This is my beloved Son: hear him.

8 And suddenly, when they had looked round about, they saw no man any more, save Jesus only with themselves.

9 And as they came down from the mountain, he charged them that they should tell no man what things they had seen, till the Son of man were risen from the dead.

10 And they kept that saying with themselves, questioning one with another what the rising from the dead should mean.

11 And they asked him, saying, Why say the scribes that Elias must first come?

12 And he answered and told them, Elias verily cometh first, and restoreth all things; and how it is written of the Son of man, that he must suffer many things, and be set at nought.

13 But I say unto you, That Elias is indeed come, and they have done unto him whatsoever they listed, as it is written of him.

14 ¶ And when he came to *his* disciples, he saw a great multitude about them, and the scribes questioning with them.

15 And straightway all the people, when they beheld him, were greatly amazed, and running to *him* saluted him.

16 And he asked the scribes, What question ye with them?

17 And one of the multitude answered and said, Master, I have brought unto thee my son, which hath a dumb spirit;

NEW AMERICAN STANDARD BIBLE

voice came out of the cloud, "This is My beloved Son, listen to Him!"

8 All at once they looked around and saw no one with them anymore, except Jesus alone.

9 As they were coming down from the mountain, He gave them orders not to relate to anyone what they had seen, until the Son of Man rose from the dead.

10 They seized upon that statement, discussing with one another what rising from the dead meant.

11 They asked Him, saying, "*Why is it* that the scribes say that Elijah must come first?"

12 And He said to them, "Elijah does first come and restore all things. And *yet* how is it written of the Son of Man that He will suffer many things and be treated with contempt?

13 "But I say to you that Elijah has indeed come, and they did to him whatever they wished, just as it is written of him."

All Things Possible

14 When they came *back* to the disciples, they saw a large crowd around them, and *some* scribes arguing with them.

15 Immediately, when the entire crowd saw Him, they were amazed and *began* running up to greet Him.

16 And He asked them, "What are you discussing with them?"

17 And one of the crowd answered Him, "Teacher, I brought You my son, possessed with a spirit which makes him mute;

NEW CENTURY VERSION

from the cloud, saying, "This is my Son, whom I love. Listen to him!"

8Suddenly Peter, James, and John looked around, but they saw only Jesus there alone with them.

9As they were coming down the mountain, Jesus commanded them not to tell anyone about what they had seen until the Son of Man had risen from the dead.

10So the followers obeyed Jesus, but they discussed what he meant about rising from the dead.

11Then they asked Jesus, "Why do the teachers of the law say that Elijah must come first?"

12Jesus answered, "They are right to say that Elijah must come first and make everything the way it should be. But why does the Scripture say that the Son of Man will suffer much and that people will treat him as if he were nothing? 13I tell you that Elijah has already come. And people did to him whatever they wanted to do, just as the Scriptures said it would happen."

Jesus Heals a Sick Boy

14When Jesus, Peter, James, and John came back to the other followers, they saw a great crowd around them and the teachers of the law arguing with them. 15But as soon as the crowd saw Jesus, the people were surprised and ran to welcome him.

16Jesus asked, "What are you arguing about?"

17A man answered, "Teacher, I brought my son to you. He has an evil spirit in him that stops him from talking.

CONTEMPORARY ENGLISH VERSION

From the cloud a voice said, "This is my Son, and I love him. Listen to what he says!" 8At once the disciples looked around, but they saw only Jesus.

9As Jesus and his disciples were coming down the mountain, he told them not to say a word about what they had seen, until the Son of Man had been raised from death. 10So they kept it to themselves. But they wondered what he meant by the words "raised from death."

11The disciples asked Jesus, "Don't the teachers of the Law of Moses say that Elijah must come before the Messiah does?"

12Jesus answered:

> Elijah certainly will come[a] to get everything ready. But don't the Scriptures also say that the Son of Man must suffer terribly and be rejected? 13I can assure you that Elijah has already come. And people treated him just as they wanted to, as the Scriptures say they would.

Jesus Heals a Boy (Matthew 17.14-20; Luke 9.37-43a)

14When Jesus and his three disciples came back down, they saw a large crowd around the other disciples. The teachers of the Law of Moses were arguing with them.

15The crowd was really surprised to see Jesus, and everyone hurried over to greet him.

16Jesus asked, "What are you arguing about?"

17Someone from the crowd answered, "Teacher, I brought my son to you. A demon keeps him from talking.

[a] **9.12** *Elijah certainly will come*: See the note at 6.15.

NEW INTERNATIONAL VERSION

came from the cloud: "This is my Son, whom I love. Listen to him!"

8Suddenly, when they looked around, they no longer saw anyone with them except Jesus.

9As they were coming down the mountain, Jesus gave them orders not to tell anyone what they had seen until the Son of Man had risen from the dead. 10They kept the matter to themselves, discussing what "rising from the dead" meant.

11And they asked him, "Why do the teachers of the law say that Elijah must come first?"

12Jesus replied, "To be sure, Elijah does come first, and restores all things. Why then is it written that the Son of Man must suffer much and be rejected? 13But I tell you, Elijah has come, and they have done to him everything they wished, just as it is written about him."

The Healing of a Boy With an Evil Spirit

14When they came to the other disciples, they saw a large crowd around them and the teachers of the law arguing with them. 15As soon as all the people saw Jesus, they were overwhelmed with wonder and ran to greet him.

16"What are you arguing with them about?" he asked.

17A man in the crowd answered, "Teacher, I brought you my son, who is possessed by a spirit that has robbed him

NEW LIVING TRANSLATION

cloud said, "This is my beloved Son. Listen to him."
8Suddenly they looked around, and Moses and Elijah were gone, and only Jesus was with them. 9As they descended the mountainside, he told them not to tell anyone what they had seen until he, the Son of Man, had risen from the dead. 10So they kept it to themselves, but they often asked each other what he meant by "rising from the dead."

11Now they began asking him, "Why do the teachers of religious law insist that Elijah must return before the Messiah comes?"

12Jesus responded, "Elijah is indeed coming first to set everything in order. Why then is it written in the Scriptures that the Son of Man must suffer and be treated with utter contempt? 13But I tell you, Elijah has already come, and he was badly mistreated, just as the Scriptures predicted."

Jesus Heals a Boy Possessed by an Evil Spirit

14At the foot of the mountain they found a great crowd surrounding the other disciples, as some teachers of religious law were arguing with them. 15The crowd watched Jesus in awe as he came toward them, and then they ran to greet him. 16"What is all this arguing about?" he asked.

17One of the men in the crowd spoke up and said, "Teacher, I brought my son for you to heal him. He can't speak because he is possessed by an evil spirit that won't let

NEW KING JAMES VERSION

came out of the cloud, saying, "This is My beloved Son. Hear Him!" 8Suddenly, when they had looked around, they saw no one anymore, but only Jesus with themselves.

9Now as they came down from the mountain, He commanded them that they should tell no one the things they had seen, till the Son of Man had risen from the dead. 10So they kept this word to themselves, questioning what the rising from the dead meant.

11And they asked Him, saying, "Why do the scribes say that Elijah must come first?"

12Then He answered and told them, "Indeed, Elijah is coming first and restores all things. And how is it written concerning the Son of Man, that He must suffer many things and be treated with contempt? 13But I say to you that Elijah has also come, and they did to him whatever they wished, as it is written of him."

A Boy Is Healed

14And when He came to the disciples, He saw a great multitude around them, and scribes disputing with them. 15Immediately, when they saw Him, all the people were greatly amazed, and running to *Him,* greeted Him. 16And He asked the scribes, "What are you discussing with them?"

17Then one of the crowd answered and said, "Teacher, I brought You my son, who has a mute spirit. 18And wherever

THE MESSAGE

deep in the cloud, a voice: "This is my Son, marked by my love. Listen to him."

The next minute the disciples were looking around, rubbing their eyes, seeing nothing but Jesus, only Jesus.

Coming down the mountain, Jesus swore them to secrecy. "Don't tell a soul what you saw. After the Son of Man rises from the dead, you're free to talk." They puzzled over that, wondering what on earth "rising from the dead" meant.

Meanwhile they were asking, "Why do the religion scholars say that Elijah has to come first?"

Jesus replied, "Elijah does come first and get everything ready for the coming of the Son of Man. They treated this Elijah like dirt, much like they will treat the Son of Man, who will, according to Scripture, suffer terribly and be kicked around contemptibly."

There Are No Ifs

When they came back down the mountain to the other disciples, they saw a huge crowd around them, and the religion scholars cross-examining them. As soon as the people in the crowd saw Jesus, admiring excitement stirred them. They ran and greeted him. He asked, "What's going on? What's all the commotion?"

A man out of the crowd answered, "Teacher, I brought my mute son, made speechless by a demon, to you.

KING JAMES VERSION

18 And wheresoever he taketh him, he teareth him: and he foameth, and gnasheth with his teeth, and pineth away: and I spake to thy disciples that they should cast him out; and they could not.

19 He answereth him, and saith, O faithless generation, how long shall I be with you? how long shall I suffer you? bring him unto me.

20 And they brought him unto him: and when he saw him, straightway the spirit tare him; and he fell on the ground, and wallowed foaming.

21 And he asked his father, How long is it ago since this came unto him? And he said, Of a child.

22 And ofttimes it hath cast him into the fire, and into the waters, to destroy him: but if thou canst do any thing, have compassion on us, and help us.

23 Jesus said unto him, If thou canst believe, all things *are* possible to him that believeth.

24 And straightway the father of the child cried out, and said with tears, Lord, I believe; help thou mine unbelief.

25 When Jesus saw that the people came running together, he rebuked the foul spirit, saying unto him, *Thou* dumb and deaf spirit, I charge thee, come out of him, and enter no more into him.

26 And *the spirit* cried, and rent him sore, and came out of him: and he was as one dead; insomuch that many said, He is dead.

27 But Jesus took him by the hand, and lifted him up; and he arose.

NEW AMERICAN STANDARD BIBLE

18 and whenever it seizes him, it slams him *to the ground* and he foams *at the mouth,* and grinds his teeth and stiffens out. I told Your disciples to cast it out, and they could not *do it.*"

19 And He *answered them and *said, "O unbelieving generation, how long shall I be with you? How long shall I put up with you? Bring him to Me!"

20 They brought the boy to Him. When he saw Him, immediately the spirit threw him into a convulsion, and falling to the ground, he *began* rolling around and foaming *at the mouth.*

21 And He asked his father, "How long has this been happening to him?" And he said, "From childhood.

22 "It has often thrown him both into the fire and into the water to destroy him. But if You can do anything, take pity on us and help us!"

23 And Jesus said to him, " 'If You can?' All things are possible to him who believes."

24 Immediately the boy's father cried out and said, "I do believe; help my unbelief."

25 When Jesus saw that a crowd was rapidly gathering, He rebuked the unclean spirit, saying to it, "You deaf and mute spirit, I command you, come out of him and do not enter him again."

26 After crying out and throwing him into terrible convulsions, it came out; and *the boy* became so much like a corpse that most *of them* said, "He is dead!"

27 But Jesus took him by the hand and raised him; and he got up.

NEW CENTURY VERSION

18When the spirit attacks him, it throws him on the
ground. Then my son foams at the mouth, grinds his teeth,
and becomes very stiff. I asked your followers to force the
evil spirit out, but they couldn't."

19Jesus answered, "You people have no faith. How long
must I stay with you? How long must I put up with you?
Bring the boy to me."

20So the followers brought him to Jesus. As soon as the
evil spirit saw Jesus, it made the boy lose control of him-
self, and he fell down and rolled on the ground, foaming at
the mouth.

21Jesus asked the boy's father, "How long has this been
happening?"

The father answered, "Since he was very young. 22The spir-
it often throws him into a fire or into water to kill him. If you
can do anything for him, please have pity on us and help us."

23Jesus said to the father, "You said, 'If you can!' All
things are possible for the one who believes."

24Immediately the father cried out, "I do believe! Help
me to believe more!"

25When Jesus saw that a crowd was quickly gathering,
he ordered the evil spirit, saying, "You spirit that makes
people unable to hear or speak, I command you to come
out of this boy and never enter him again!"

26The evil spirit screamed and caused the boy to fall on
the ground again. Then the spirit came out. The boy looked
as if he were dead, and many people said, "He is dead!"
27But Jesus took hold of the boy's hand and helped him to
stand up.

CONTEMPORARY ENGLISH VERSION

18Whenever the demon attacks my son, it throws him to
the ground and makes him foam at the mouth and grit his
teeth in pain. Then he becomes stiff. I asked your disciples
to force out the demon, but they couldn't do it."

19Jesus said, "You people don't have any faith! How
much longer must I be with you? Why do I have to put up
with you? Bring the boy to me."

20They brought the boy, and as soon as the demon saw
Jesus, it made the boy shake all over. He fell down and
began rolling on the ground and foaming at the mouth.

21Jesus asked the boy's father, "How long has he been
like this?"

The man answered, "Ever since he was a child. 22The
demon has often tried to kill him by throwing him into a
fire or into water. Please have pity and help us if you can!"

23Jesus replied, "Why do you say 'if you can'? Anything
is possible for someone who has faith!"

24Right away the boy's father shouted, "I do have faith!
Please help me to have even more."

25When Jesus saw that a crowd was gathering fast, he
spoke sternly to the evil spirit that had kept the boy from
speaking or hearing. He said, "I order you to come out of
the boy! Don't ever bother him again."

26The spirit screamed and made the boy shake all over.
Then it went out of him. The boy looked dead, and almost
everyone said he was. 27But Jesus took hold of his hand
and helped him stand up.

NEW INTERNATIONAL VERSION

of speech. [18]Whenever it seizes him, it throws him to the ground. He foams at the mouth, gnashes his teeth and becomes rigid. I asked your disciples to drive out the spirit, but they could not."

[19]"O unbelieving generation," Jesus replied, "how long shall I stay with you? How long shall I put up with you? Bring the boy to me."

[20]So they brought him. When the spirit saw Jesus, it immediately threw the boy into a convulsion. He fell to the ground and rolled around, foaming at the mouth.

[21]Jesus asked the boy's father, "How long has he been like this?"

"From childhood," he answered. [22]"It has often thrown him into fire or water to kill him. But if you can do anything, take pity on us and help us."

[23]" 'If you can'?" said Jesus. "Everything is possible for him who believes."

[24]Immediately the boy's father exclaimed, "I do believe; help me overcome my unbelief!"

[25]When Jesus saw that a crowd was running to the scene, he rebuked the evil[a] spirit. "You deaf and mute spirit," he said, "I command you, come out of him and never enter him again."

[26]The spirit shrieked, convulsed him violently and came out. The boy looked so much like a corpse that many said, "He's dead." [27]But Jesus took him by the hand and lifted him to his feet, and he stood up.

[a] *25* Greek *unclean*

NEW LIVING TRANSLATION

him talk. [18]And whenever this evil spirit seizes him, it throws him violently to the ground and makes him foam at the mouth and grind his teeth and become rigid.* So I asked your disciples to cast out the evil spirit, but they couldn't do it."

[19]Jesus said to them, "You faithless people! How long must I be with you until you believe? How long must I put up with you? Bring the boy to me." [20]So they brought the boy. But when the evil spirit saw Jesus, it threw the child into a violent convulsion, and he fell to the ground, writhing and foaming at the mouth. [21]"How long has this been happening?" Jesus asked the boy's father.

He replied, "Since he was very small. [22]The evil spirit often makes him fall into the fire or into water, trying to kill him. Have mercy on us and help us. Do something if you can."

[23]"What do you mean, 'If I can'?" Jesus asked. "Anything is possible if a person believes."

[24]The father instantly replied, "I do believe, but help me not to doubt!"

[25]When Jesus saw that the crowd of onlookers was growing, he rebuked the evil spirit. "Spirit of deafness and muteness," he said, "I command you to come out of this child and never enter him again!" [26]Then the spirit screamed and threw the boy into another violent convulsion and left him. The boy lay there motionless, and he appeared to be dead. A murmur ran through the crowd, "He's dead." [27]But Jesus took him by the hand and helped him to his feet, and he stood up.

9:18 Or *become weak.*

NEW KING JAMES VERSION

it seizes him, it throws him down; he foams at the mouth, gnashes his teeth, and becomes rigid. So I spoke to Your disciples, that they should cast it out, but they could not."

[19]He answered him and said, "O faithless generation, how long shall I be with you? How long shall I bear with you? Bring him to Me." [20]Then they brought him to Him. And when he saw Him, immediately the spirit convulsed him, and he fell on the ground and wallowed, foaming at the mouth.

[21]So He asked his father, "How long has this been happening to him?"

And he said, "From childhood. [22]And often he has thrown him both into the fire and into the water to destroy him. But if You can do anything, have compassion on us and help us."

[23]Jesus said to him, "If you can believe,[a] all things *are* possible to him who believes."

[24]Immediately the father of the child cried out and said with tears, "Lord, I believe; help my unbelief!"

[25]When Jesus saw that the people came running together, He rebuked the unclean spirit, saying to it, "Deaf and dumb spirit, I command you, come out of him and enter him no more!" [26]Then *the spirit* cried out, convulsed him greatly, and came out of him. And he became as one dead, so that many said, "He is dead." [27]But Jesus took him by the hand and lifted him up, and he arose.

9:23 [a] NU-Text reads " *'If You can!' All things. . . .*"

THE MESSAGE

Whenever it seizes him, it throws him to the ground. He foams at the mouth, grinds his teeth, and goes stiff as a board. I told your disciples, hoping they could deliver him, but they couldn't."

Jesus said, "What a generation! No sense of God! How many times do I have to go over these things? How much longer do I have to put up with this? Bring the boy here." They brought him. When the demon saw Jesus, it threw the boy into a seizure, causing him to writhe on the ground and foam at the mouth.

He asked the boy's father, "How long has this been going on?"

"Ever since he was a little boy. Many times it pitches him into fire or the river to do away with him. If you can do anything, do it. Have a heart and help us!"

Jesus said, "If? There are no 'ifs' among believers. Anything can happen."

No sooner were the words out of his mouth than the father cried, "Then I believe. Help me with my doubts!"

Seeing that the crowd was forming fast, Jesus gave the vile spirit its marching orders: "Dumb and deaf spirit, I command you— Out of him, and stay out!" Screaming, and with much thrashing about, it left. The boy was pale as a corpse, so people started saying, "He's dead." But Jesus, taking his hand, raised him. The boy stood up.

KING JAMES VERSION

28 And when he was come into the house, his disciples asked him privately, Why could not we cast him out?

29 And he said unto them, This kind can come forth by nothing, but by prayer and fasting.

30 ¶ And they departed thence, and passed through Galilee; and he would not that any man should know *it*.

31 For he taught his disciples, and said unto them, The Son of man is delivered into the hands of men, and they shall kill him; and after that he is killed, he shall rise the third day.

32 But they understood not that saying, and were afraid to ask him.

33 And he came to Capernaum: and being in the house he asked them, What was it that ye disputed among yourselves by the way?

34 But they held their peace: for by the way they had disputed among themselves, who *should be* the greatest.

35 And he sat down, and called the twelve, and saith unto them, If any man desire to be first, *the same* shall be last of all, and servant of all.

36 And he took a child, and set him in the midst of them: and when he had taken him in his arms, he said unto them,

37 Whosoever shall receive one of such children in my name, receiveth me: and whosoever shall receive me, receiveth not me, but him that sent me.

NEW AMERICAN STANDARD BIBLE

28 When He came into *the* house, His disciples *began* questioning Him privately, "Why could we not drive it out?"

29 And He said to them, "This kind cannot come out by anything but prayer."

Death and Resurrection Foretold

30 From there they went out and *began* to go through Galilee, and He did not want anyone to know *about it.*

31 For He was teaching His disciples and telling them, "The Son of Man is to be [1]delivered into the hands of men, and they will kill Him; and when He has been killed, He will rise three days later."

32 But they did not understand *this* statement, and they were afraid to ask Him.

33 They came to Capernaum; and when He was in the house, He *began* to question them, "What were you discussing on the way?"

34 But they kept silent, for on the way they had discussed with one another which *of them was* the greatest.

35 Sitting down, He called the twelve and *said to them, "If anyone wants to be first, he shall be last of all and servant of all."

36 Taking a child, He set him before them, and taking him in His arms, He said to them,

37 "Whoever receives one child like this in My name receives Me; and whoever receives Me does not receive Me, but Him who sent Me."

9:31 [1] Or *betrayed*

NEW CENTURY VERSION

28 When Jesus went into the house, his followers began asking him privately, "Why couldn't we force that evil spirit out?"

29 Jesus answered, "That kind of spirit can only be forced out by prayer."

Jesus Talks About His Death

30 Then Jesus and his followers left that place and went through Galilee. He didn't want anyone to know where he was, 31 because he was teaching his followers. He said to them, "The Son of Man will be handed over to people, and they will kill him. After three days, he will rise from the dead." 32 But the followers did not understand what Jesus meant, and they were afraid to ask him.

Who Is the Greatest?

33 Jesus and his followers went to Capernaum. When they went into a house there, he asked them, "What were you arguing about on the road?" 34 But the followers did not answer, because their argument on the road was about which one of them was the greatest.

35 Jesus sat down and called the twelve apostles to him. He said, "Whoever wants to be the most important must be last of all and servant of all."

36 Then Jesus took a small child and had him stand among them. Taking the child in his arms, he said, 37 "Whoever accepts a child like this in my name accepts me. And whoever accepts me accepts the One who sent me."

CONTEMPORARY ENGLISH VERSION

28 After Jesus and the disciples had gone back home and were alone, they asked him, "Why couldn't we force out that demon?"

29 Jesus answered, "Only prayer can force out that kind of demon."

Jesus Again Speaks about His Death
(Matthew 17.22, 23; Luke 9.43b-45)

30 Jesus left with his disciples and started through Galilee. He did not want anyone to know about it, 31 because he was teaching the disciples that the Son of Man would be handed over to people who would kill him. But three days later he would rise to life. 32 The disciples did not understand what Jesus meant, and they were afraid to ask.

Who Is the Greatest? (Matthew 18.1-5; Luke 9.46-48)

33 Jesus and his disciples went to his home in Capernaum. After they were inside the house, Jesus asked them, "What were you arguing about along the way?" 34 They had been arguing about which one of them was the greatest, and so they did not answer.

35 After Jesus sat down and told the twelve disciples to gather around him, he said, "If you want the place of honor, you must become a slave and serve others!"

36 Then Jesus had a child stand near him. He put his arm around the child and said, 37 "When you welcome even a child because of me, you welcome me. And when you welcome me, you welcome the one who sent me."

NEW INTERNATIONAL VERSION

28After Jesus had gone indoors, his disciples asked him privately, "Why couldn't we drive it out?"

29He replied, "This kind can come out only by prayer.[b]"

30They left that place and passed through Galilee. Jesus did not want anyone to know where they were, 31because he was teaching his disciples. He said to them, "The Son of Man is going to be betrayed into the hands of men. They will kill him, and after three days he will rise." 32But they did not understand what he meant and were afraid to ask him about it.

Who Is the Greatest?

33They came to Capernaum. When he was in the house, he asked them, "What were you arguing about on the road?" 34But they kept quiet because on the way they had argued about who was the greatest.

35Sitting down, Jesus called the Twelve and said, "If anyone wants to be first, he must be the very last, and the servant of all."

36He took a little child and had him stand among them. Taking him in his arms, he said to them, 37"Whoever welcomes one of these little children in my name welcomes me; and whoever welcomes me does not welcome me but the one who sent me."

[b] *29* Some manuscripts *prayer and fasting*

NEW LIVING TRANSLATION

28Afterward, when Jesus was alone in the house with his disciples, they asked him, "Why couldn't we cast out that evil spirit?"

29Jesus replied, "This kind can be cast out only by prayer.*"

Jesus Again Predicts His Death

30Leaving that region, they traveled through Galilee. Jesus tried to avoid all publicity 31in order to spend more time with his disciples and teach them. He said to them, "The Son of Man is going to be betrayed. He will be killed, but three days later he will rise from the dead." 32But they didn't understand what he was saying, and they were afraid to ask him what he meant.

The Greatest in the Kingdom

33After they arrived at Capernaum, Jesus and his disciples settled in the house where they would be staying. Jesus asked them, "What were you discussing out on the road?" 34But they didn't answer, because they had been arguing about which of them was the greatest. 35He sat down and called the twelve disciples over to him. Then he said, "Anyone who wants to be the first must take last place and be the servant of everyone else."

36Then he put a little child among them. Taking the child in his arms, he said to them, 37"Anyone who welcomes a little child like this on my behalf welcomes me, and anyone who welcomes me welcomes my Father who sent me."

9:29 Some manuscripts add *and fasting.*

NEW KING JAMES VERSION

28And when He had come into the house, His disciples asked Him privately, "Why could we not cast it out?"

29So He said to them, "This kind can come out by nothing but prayer and fasting."[b]

Jesus Again Predicts His Death and Resurrection

30Then they departed from there and passed through Galilee, and He did not want anyone to know *it.* 31For He taught His disciples and said to them, "The Son of Man is being betrayed into the hands of men, and they will kill Him. And after He is killed, He will rise the third day." 32But they did not understand this saying, and were afraid to ask Him.

Who Is the Greatest?

33Then He came to Capernaum. And when He was in the house He asked them, "What was it you disputed among yourselves on the road?" 34But they kept silent, for on the road they had disputed among themselves who *would be the* greatest. 35And He sat down, called the twelve, and said to them, "If anyone desires to be first, he shall be last of all and servant of all." 36Then He took a little child and set him in the midst of them. And when He had taken him in His arms, He said to them, 37"Whoever receives one of these little children in My name receives Me; and whoever receives Me, receives not Me but Him who sent Me."

9:29 [b] NU-Text omits *and fasting.*

THE MESSAGE

After arriving back home, his disciples cornered Jesus and asked, "Why couldn't we throw the demon out?"

He answered, "There is no way to get rid of this kind of demon except by prayer."

Leaving there, they went through Galilee. He didn't want anyone to know their whereabouts, for he wanted to teach his disciples. He told them, "The Son of Man is about to be betrayed to some people who want nothing to do with God. They will murder him. Three days after his murder, he will rise, alive." They didn't know what he was talking about, but were afraid to ask him about it.

So You Want First Place?

They came to Capernaum. When he was safe at home, he asked them, "What were you discussing on the road?"

The silence was deafening—they had been arguing with one another over who among them was greatest.

He sat down and summoned the Twelve. "So you want first place? Then take the last place. Be the servant of all."

He put a child in the middle of the room. Then, cradling the little one in his arms, he said, "Whoever embraces one of these children as I do embraces me, and far more than me—God who sent me."

KING JAMES VERSION

38 And John answered him, saying, Master, we saw one casting out devils in thy name, and he followeth not us: and we forbad him, because he followeth not us.

39 But Jesus said, Forbid him not: for there is no man which shall do a miracle in my name, that can lightly speak evil of me.

40 For he that is not against us is on our part.

41 ¶ For whosoever shall give you a cup of water to drink in my name, because ye belong to Christ, verily I say unto you, he shall not lose his reward.

42 And whosoever shall offend one of *these* little ones that believe in me, it is better for him that a millstone were hanged about his neck, and he were cast into the sea.

43 And if thy hand offend thee, cut it off: it is better for thee to enter into life maimed, than having two hands to go into hell, into the fire that never shall be quenched:

44 Where their worm dieth not, and the fire is not quenched.

45 And if thy foot offend thee, cut it off: it is better for thee to enter halt into life, than having two feet to be cast into hell, into the fire that never shall be quenched:

NEW AMERICAN STANDARD BIBLE

Dire Warnings

38 John said to Him, "Teacher, we saw someone casting out demons in Your name, and we tried to prevent him because he was not following us."

39 But Jesus said, "Do not hinder him, for there is no one who will perform a miracle in My name, and be able soon afterward to speak evil of Me.

40 "For he who is not against us is [2]for us.

41 "For whoever gives you a cup of water to drink because of your name as *followers* of Christ, truly I say to you, he will not lose his reward.

42 "Whoever causes one of these little ones who believe to stumble, it would be better for him if, with a heavy millstone hung around his neck, he had been cast into the sea.

43 "If your hand causes you to stumble, cut it off; it is better for you to enter life crippled, than, having your two hands, to go into hell, into the unquenchable fire,

44 [[3]where THEIR WORM DOES NOT DIE, AND THE FIRE IS NOT QUENCHED.]

45 "If your foot causes you to stumble, cut it off; it is better for you to enter life lame, than, having your two feet, to be cast into hell,

9:40 [2] Or *on our side* 9:44 [3] Vv 44 and 46, which are identical to v 48, are not found in the early mss

NEW CENTURY VERSION

Anyone Not Against Us Is for Us

38Then John said, "Teacher, we saw someone using your
name to force demons out of a person. We told him to stop,
because he does not belong to our group."
39But Jesus said, "Don't stop him, because anyone who
uses my name to do powerful things will not easily say
evil things about me. 40Whoever is not against us is with
us. 41I tell you the truth, whoever gives you a drink of
water because you belong to the Christ will truly get his
reward.
42"If one of these little children believes in me, and
someone causes that child to sin, it would be better for
that person to have a large stone tied around his neck and
be drowned in the sea. 43If your hand causes you to sin,
cut it off. It is better for you to lose part of your body and
live forever than to have two hands and go to hell, where
the fire never goes out. 44[b] 45If your foot causes you to sin,
cut it off. It is better for you to lose part of your body and
to live forever than to have two feet and be thrown into

9:44 [b] **Verse 44** Some Greek copies of Mark add verse 44, which is the same as verse 48.

CONTEMPORARY ENGLISH VERSION

For or against Jesus (Luke 9.49, 50)

38John said, "Teacher, we saw a man using your name
to force demons out of people. But he wasn't one of us,
and we told him to stop."
39Jesus said to his disciples:
Don't stop him! No one who works miracles in my
name will soon turn and say something bad about me.
40Anyone who isn't against us is for us. 41And anyone
who gives you a cup of water in my name, just because
you belong to me, will surely be rewarded.

Temptations To Sin (Matthew 18.6-9; Luke 17.1, 2)

42It will be terrible for people who cause even one of
my little followers to sin. Those people would be better
off thrown into the ocean with a heavy stone tied
around their necks. 43-44So if your hand causes you to
sin, cut it off! You would be better off to go into life crip-
pled than to have two hands and be thrown into the
fires of hell that never go out.[b] 45-46If your foot causes
you to sin, chop it off. You would be better off to go into
life lame than to have two feet and be thrown into hell.[c]

[b] **9.43,44** *never go out*: Some manuscripts add, "The worms there never die, and the fire never stops burning." [c] **9.45,46** *thrown into hell*: Some manuscripts add, "The worms there never die, and the fire never stops burning."

NEW INTERNATIONAL VERSION

Whoever Is Not Against Us Is for Us

38"Teacher," said John, "we saw a man driving out
demons in your name and we told him to stop, because he
was not one of us."

39"Do not stop him," Jesus said. "No one who does a
miracle in my name can in the next moment say anything
bad about me, 40for whoever is not against us is for us. 41I
tell you the truth, anyone who gives you a cup of water in
my name because you belong to Christ will certainly not
lose his reward.

Causing to Sin

42"And if anyone causes one of these little ones who
believe in me to sin, it would be better for him to be
thrown into the sea with a large millstone tied around his
neck. 43If your hand causes you to sin, cut it off. It is better for you to enter life maimed than with two hands to go
into hell, where the fire never goes out.[c] 45And if your foot
causes you to sin, cut it off. It is better for you to enter life crippled than to have two feet and be thrown into hell.[d]

[c] *43* Some manuscripts *out, 44where / " 'their worm does not die, / and the fire is not quenched.'* [d] *45* Some manuscripts *hell, 46where / " 'their worm does not die, / and the fire is not quenched.'*

NEW LIVING TRANSLATION

Using the Name of Jesus

38John said to Jesus, "Teacher, we saw a man using your name to cast out demons, but we told him to stop because he isn't one of our group."

39"Don't stop him!" Jesus said. "No one who performs
miracles in my name will soon be able to speak evil of me.
40Anyone who is not against us is for us. 41If anyone gives
you even a cup of water because you belong to the Messiah, I assure you, that person will be rewarded.

42"But if anyone causes one of these little ones who trusts in me to lose faith, it would be better for that person to be thrown into the sea with a large millstone tied
around the neck. 43If your hand causes you to sin, cut it
off. It is better to enter heaven* with only one hand than to
go into the unquenchable fires of hell with two hands.* 45If
your foot causes you to sin, cut it off. It is better to enter heaven with only one foot than to be thrown into hell with

9:43a Greek *enter life;* also in 9:45. **9:43b** Some manuscripts add verse 44 (which is identical with 9:48).

NEW KING JAMES VERSION

Jesus Forbids Sectarianism

38Now John answered Him, saying, "Teacher, we saw someone who does not follow us casting out demons in Your name, and we forbade him because he does not follow us."

39But Jesus said, "Do not forbid him, for no one who
works a miracle in My name can soon afterward speak evil
of Me. 40For he who is not against us is on our[c] side. 41For
whoever gives you a cup of water to drink in My name, because you belong to Christ, assuredly, I say to you, he will by no means lose his reward.

Jesus Warns of Offenses

42"But whoever causes one of these little ones who believe in Me to stumble, it would be better for him if a millstone were hung around his neck, and he were thrown
into the sea. 43If your hand causes you to sin, cut it off. It
is better for you to enter into life maimed, rather than having two hands, to go to hell, into the fire that shall never
be quenched— 44where

'Their worm does not die
And the fire is not quenched.'[d]

45And if your foot causes you to sin, cut it off. It is better
for you to enter life lame, rather than having two feet, to be cast into hell, into the fire that shall never be
quenched— 46where

9:40 [c] M-Text reads *against you is on your side.* **9:44** [d] NU-Text omits this verse.

THE MESSAGE

John spoke up, "Teacher, we saw a man using your name to expel demons and we stopped him because he wasn't in our group."

Jesus wasn't pleased. "Don't stop him. No one can use my name to do something good and powerful, and in the next breath cut me down. If he's not an enemy, he's an ally. Why, anyone by just giving you a cup of water in my name is on our side. Count on it that God will notice.

"On the other hand, if you give one of these simple, childlike believers a hard time, bullying or taking advantage of their simple trust, you'll soon wish you hadn't. You'd be better off dropped in the middle of the lake with a millstone around your neck.

"If your hand or your foot gets in God's way, chop it off and throw it away. You're better off maimed or lame and alive than the proud owner of two hands and two feet,

KING JAMES VERSION

46 Where their worm dieth not, and the fire is not quenched.

47 And if thine eye offend thee, pluck it out: it is better for thee to enter into the kingdom of God with one eye, than having two eyes to be cast into hell fire:

48 Where their worm dieth not, and the fire is not quenched.

49 For every one shall be salted with fire, and every sacrifice shall be salted with salt.

50 Salt *is* good: but if the salt have lost his saltness, wherewith will ye season it? Have salt in yourselves, and have peace one with another.

10 And he arose from thence, and cometh into the coasts of Judaea by the farther side of Jordan: and the people resort unto him again; and, as he was wont, he taught them again.

2 And the Pharisees came to him, and asked him, Is it lawful for a man to put away *his* wife? tempting him.

3 And he answered and said unto them, What did Moses command you?

4 And they said, Moses suffered to write a bill of divorcement, and to put *her* away.

NEW AMERICAN STANDARD BIBLE

46 [[4]where THEIR WORM DOES NOT DIE, AND THE FIRE IS NOT QUENCHED.]

47 "If your eye causes you to stumble, throw it out; it is better for you to enter the kingdom of God with one eye, than, having two eyes, to be cast into hell,

48 where THEIR WORM DOES NOT DIE, AND THE FIRE IS NOT QUENCHED.

49 "For everyone will be salted with fire.

50 "Salt is good; but if the salt becomes unsalty, with what will you make it salty *again?* Have salt in yourselves, and be at peace with one another."

Jesus' Teaching about Divorce

10 Getting up, He *went from there to the region of Judea and beyond the Jordan; crowds *gathered around Him again, and, according to His custom, He once more *began* to teach them.

2 *Some* Pharisees came up to Jesus, testing Him, and *began* to question Him whether it was lawful for a man to divorce a wife.

3 And He answered and said to them, "What did Moses command you?"

4 They said, "Moses permitted *a man* TO WRITE A CERTIFICATE OF DIVORCE AND SEND *her* AWAY."

9:46 [4] See v 44 note

NEW CENTURY VERSION

hell. 46[c] 47If your eye causes you to sin, take it out. It is
better for you to enter the kingdom of God with only one
eye than to have two eyes and be thrown into hell. 48In
hell the worm does not die; the fire is never put out.
49Every person will be salted with fire.

50"Salt is good, but if the salt loses its salty taste, you
cannot make it salty again. So, be full of salt, and have
peace with each other."

Jesus Teaches About Divorce

10 Then Jesus left that place and went into the area of Judea and across the Jordan River. Again, crowds came to him, and he taught them as he usually did.

2Some Pharisees came to Jesus and tried to trick him. They asked, "Is it right for a man to divorce his wife?"

3Jesus answered, "What did Moses command you to do?"

4They said, "Moses allowed a man to write out divorce papers and send her away."[a]

9:46 [c] **Verse 46** Some Greek copies of Mark add verse 46, which is the same as verse 48. **10:4** [a] **"Moses...away."** Quotation from Deuteronomy 24:1.

CONTEMPORARY ENGLISH VERSION

47If your eye causes you to sin, get rid of it. You would
be better off to go into God's kingdom with only one eye
than to have two eyes and be thrown into hell. 48The
worms there never die, and the fire never stops burning.

49Everyone must be salted with fire.[d]

50Salt is good. But if it no longer tastes like salt, how can it be made salty again? Have salt among you and live at peace with each other.[e]

Teaching about Divorce (Matthew 19.1-12; Luke 16.18)

10 After Jesus left, he went to Judea and then on to the other side of the Jordan River. Once again large crowds came to him, and as usual, he taught them.

2Some Pharisees wanted to test Jesus. So they came up to him and asked if it was right for a man to divorce his wife. 3Jesus asked them, "What does the Law of Moses say about that?"

4They answered, "Moses allows a man to write out divorce papers and send his wife away."

[d] **9.49** *salted with fire*: Some manuscripts add "and every sacrifice will be seasoned with salt." The verse may mean that Christ's followers must suffer because of their faith. [e] **9.50** *Have salt among you and live at peace with each other*: This may mean that when Christ's followers have to suffer because of their faith, they must still try to live at peace with each other.

NEW INTERNATIONAL VERSION

47And if your eye causes you to sin, pluck it out. It is better for you to enter the kingdom of God with one eye than to have two eyes and be thrown into hell, 48where

" 'their worm does not die,
and the fire is not quenched.'[e]

49Everyone will be salted with fire.

50"Salt is good, but if it loses its saltiness, how can you make it salty again? Have salt in yourselves, and be at peace with each other."

Divorce

10 Jesus then left that place and went into the region of Judea and across the Jordan. Again crowds of people came to him, and as was his custom, he taught them.

2Some Pharisees came and tested him by asking, "Is it lawful for a man to divorce his wife?"

3"What did Moses command you?" he replied.

4They said, "Moses permitted a man to write a certificate of divorce and send her away."

[e] *48* Isaiah 66:24

NEW LIVING TRANSLATION

two feet.* 47And if your eye causes you to sin, gouge it out. It is better to enter the Kingdom of God half blind than to have two eyes and be thrown into hell, 48'where the worm never dies and the fire never goes out.'*

49"For everyone will be purified with fire.* 50Salt is good for seasoning. But if it loses its flavor, how do you make it salty again? You must have the qualities of salt among yourselves and live in peace with each other."

Discussion about Divorce and Marriage

10 Then Jesus left Capernaum and went southward to the region of Judea and into the area east of the Jordan River. As always there were the crowds, and as usual he taught them.

2Some Pharisees came and tried to trap him with this question: "Should a man be allowed to divorce his wife?"

3"What did Moses say about divorce?" Jesus asked them.

4"Well, he permitted it," they replied. "He said a man merely has to write his wife an official letter of divorce and send her away."*

9:45 Some manuscripts add verse 46 (which is identical with 9:48).
9:48 Isa 66:24. 9:49 Greek *salted with fire.* Some manuscripts add *and every sacrifice will be salted with salt.* 10:4 Deut 24:1.

NEW KING JAMES VERSION

*'Their worm does not die
And the fire is not quenched.'*[e]

47And if your eye causes you to sin, pluck it out. It is better for you to enter the kingdom of God with one eye, rather than having two eyes, to be cast into hell fire— 48where

*'Their worm does not die
And the fire is not quenched.'*[f]

Tasteless Salt Is Worthless

49"For everyone will be seasoned with fire,[g] and every sacrifice will be seasoned with salt. 50Salt *is* good, but if the salt loses its flavor, how will you season it? Have salt in yourselves, and have peace with one another."

Marriage and Divorce

10 Then He arose from there and came to the region of Judea by the other side of the Jordan. And multitudes gathered to Him again, and as He was accustomed, He taught them again.

2The Pharisees came and asked Him, "Is it lawful for a man to divorce *his* wife?" testing Him.

3And He answered and said to them, "What did Moses command you?"

4They said, "Moses permitted *a man* to write a certificate of divorce, and to dismiss *her*."

9:46 [e] NU-Text omits the last clause of verse 45 and all of verse 46.
9:48 [f] Isaiah 66:24 9:49 [g] NU-Text omits the rest of this verse.

THE MESSAGE

godless in a furnace of eternal fire. And if your eye distracts you from God, pull it out and throw it away. You're better off one-eyed and alive than exercising your twenty-twenty vision from inside the fire of hell.

"Everyone's going through a refining fire sooner or later, but you'll be well-preserved, protected from the *eternal* flames. Be preservatives yourselves. Preserve the peace."

Divorce

10 From there he went to the area of Judea across the Jordan. A crowd of people, as was so often the case, went along, and he, as he so often did, taught them. Pharisees came up, intending to give him a hard time. They asked, "Is it legal for a man to divorce his wife?"

Jesus said, "What did Moses command?"

They answered, "Moses gave permission to fill out a certificate of dismissal and divorce her."

KING JAMES VERSION

5 And Jesus answered and said unto them, For the hardness of your heart he wrote you this precept.

6 But from the beginning of the creation God made them male and female.

7 For this cause shall a man leave his father and mother, and cleave to his wife;

8 And they twain shall be one flesh: so then they are no more twain, but one flesh.

9 What therefore God hath joined together, let not man put asunder.

10 And in the house his disciples asked him again of the same *matter*.

11 And he saith unto them, Whosoever shall put away his wife, and marry another, committeth adultery against her.

12 And if a woman shall put away her husband, and be married to another, she committeth adultery.

13 ¶ And they brought young children to him, that he should touch them: and *his* disciples rebuked those that brought *them*.

14 But when Jesus saw *it*, he was much displeased, and said unto them, Suffer the little children to come unto me, and forbid them not: for of such is the kingdom of God.

15 Verily I say unto you, Whosoever shall not receive the kingdom of God as a little child, he shall not enter therein.

16 And he took them up in his arms, put *his* hands upon them, and blessed them.

NEW AMERICAN STANDARD BIBLE

5 But Jesus said to them, "Because of your hardness of heart he wrote you this commandment.

6 "But from the beginning of creation, *God* MADE THEM MALE AND FEMALE.

7 "FOR THIS REASON A MAN SHALL LEAVE HIS FATHER AND MOTHER,[1]

8 AND THE TWO SHALL BECOME ONE FLESH; so they are no longer two, but one flesh.

9 "What therefore God has joined together, let no man separate."

10 In the house the disciples *began* questioning Him about this again.

11 And He *said to them, "Whoever divorces his wife and marries another woman commits adultery against her;

12 and if she herself divorces her husband and marries another man, she is committing adultery."

Jesus Blesses Little Children

13 And they were bringing children to Him so that He might touch them; but the disciples rebuked them.

14 But when Jesus saw this, He was indignant and said to them, "Permit the children to come to Me; do not hinder them; for the kingdom of God belongs to such as these.

15 "Truly I say to you, whoever does not receive the kingdom of God like a child will not enter it *at all*."

16 And He took them in His arms and *began* blessing them, laying His hands on them.

10:7 [1] Many late mss add *and shall cling to his wife*

NEW CENTURY VERSION

[5]Jesus said, "Moses wrote that command for you because you were stubborn. [6]But when God made the world, 'he made them male and female.'[b] [7]'So a man will leave his father and mother and be united with his wife, [8]and the two will become one body.'[c] So there are not two, but one. [9]God has joined the two together, so no one should separate them."

[10]Later, in the house, his followers asked Jesus again about the question of divorce. [11]He answered, "Anyone who divorces his wife and marries another woman is guilty of adultery against her. [12]And the woman who divorces her husband and marries another man is also guilty of adultery."

Jesus Accepts Children

[13]Some people brought their little children to Jesus so he could touch them, but his followers told them to stop. [14]When Jesus saw this, he was upset and said to them, "Let the little children come to me. Don't stop them, because the kingdom of God belongs to people who are like these children. [15]I tell you the truth, you must accept the kingdom of God as if you were a little child, or you will never enter it." [16]Then Jesus took the children in his arms, put his hands on them, and blessed them.

10:6 [b] **'he made...female.'** Quotation from Genesis 1:27.
10:8 [c] **'So...body.'** Quotation from Genesis 2:24.

CONTEMPORARY ENGLISH VERSION

[5]Jesus replied, "Moses gave you this law because you are so heartless. [6]But in the beginning God made a man and a woman. [7]That's why a man leaves his father and mother and gets married. [8]He becomes like one person with his wife. Then they are no longer two people, but one. [9]And no one should separate a couple that God has joined together."

[10]When Jesus and his disciples were back in the house, they asked him about what he had said. [11]He told them, "A man who divorces his wife and marries someone else is unfaithful to his wife. [12]A woman who divorces her husband[a] and marries again is also unfaithful."

Jesus Blesses Little Children

(Matthew 19.13-15; Luke 18.15-17)

[13]Some people brought their children to Jesus so that he could bless them by placing his hands on them. But his disciples told the people to stop bothering him.

[14]When Jesus saw this, he became angry and said, "Let the children come to me! Don't try to stop them. People who are like these little children belong to the kingdom of God.[b] [15]I promise you that you cannot get into God's kingdom, unless you accept it the way a child does." [16]Then Jesus took the children in his arms and blessed them by placing his hands on them.

[a] **10.12** *A woman who divorces her husband*: Roman law let a woman divorce her husband, but Jewish law did not let a woman do this.
[b] **10.14** *People who are like these little children belong to the kingdom of God*: Or "The kingdom of God belongs to people who are like these little children."

NEW INTERNATIONAL VERSION

5"It was because your hearts were hard that Moses wrote you this law," Jesus replied. 6"But at the beginning of creation God 'made them male and female.'[a] 7'For this reason a man will leave his father and mother and be united to his wife,[b] 8and the two will become one flesh.'[c] So they are no longer two, but one. 9Therefore what God has joined together, let man not separate."

10When they were in the house again, the disciples asked Jesus about this. 11He answered, "Anyone who divorces his wife and marries another woman commits adultery against her. 12And if she divorces her husband and marries another man, she commits adultery."

The Little Children and Jesus

13People were bringing little children to Jesus to have him touch them, but the disciples rebuked them. 14When Jesus saw this, he was indignant. He said to them, "Let the little children come to me, and do not hinder them, for the kingdom of God belongs to such as these. 15I tell you the truth, anyone who will not receive the kingdom of God like a little child will never enter it." 16And he took the children in his arms, put his hands on them and blessed them.

[a] *6* Gen. 1:27 [b] *7* Some early manuscripts do not have *and be united to his wife.* [c] *8* Gen. 2:24

NEW LIVING TRANSLATION

5But Jesus responded, "He wrote those instructions only as a concession to your hard-hearted wickedness. 6But God's plan was seen from the beginning of creation, for 'He made them male and female.'* 7'This explains why a man leaves his father and mother and is joined to his wife,* 8and the two are united into one.'* Since they are no longer two but one, 9let no one separate them, for God has joined them together."

10Later, when he was alone with his disciples in the house, they brought up the subject again. 11He told them, "Whoever divorces his wife and marries someone else commits adultery against her. 12And if a woman divorces her husband and remarries, she commits adultery."

Jesus Blesses the Children

13One day some parents brought their children to Jesus so he could touch them and bless them, but the disciples told them not to bother him. 14But when Jesus saw what was happening, he was very displeased with his disciples. He said to them, "Let the children come to me. Don't stop them! For the Kingdom of God belongs to such as these. 15I assure you, anyone who doesn't have their kind of faith will never get into the Kingdom of God." 16Then he took the children into his arms and placed his hands on their heads and blessed them.

10:6 Gen 1:27; 5:2. **10:7** Some manuscripts do not include *and is joined to his wife.* **10:7-8** Gen 2:24.

NEW KING JAMES VERSION

5And Jesus answered and said to them, "Because of the hardness of your heart he wrote you this precept. 6But from the beginning of the creation, God *'made them male and female.'*[a] 7*'For this reason a man shall leave his father and mother and be joined to his wife, 8and the two shall become one flesh'*;[b] so then they are no longer two, but one flesh. 9Therefore what God has joined together, let not man separate."

10In the house His disciples also asked Him again about the same *matter.* 11So He said to them, "Whoever divorces his wife and marries another commits adultery against her. 12And if a woman divorces her husband and marries another, she commits adultery."

Jesus Blesses Little Children

13Then they brought little children to Him, that He might touch them; but the disciples rebuked those who brought *them.* 14But when Jesus saw *it,* He was greatly displeased and said to them, "Let the little children come to Me, and do not forbid them; for of such is the kingdom of God. 15Assuredly, I say to you, whoever does not receive the kingdom of God as a little child will by no means enter it." 16And He took them up in His arms, laid *His* hands on them, and blessed them.

10:6 [a] Genesis 1:27; 5:2 **10:8** [b] Genesis 2:24

THE MESSAGE

Jesus said, "Moses wrote this command only as a concession to your hardhearted ways. In the original creation, God made male and female to be together. Because of this, a man leaves father and mother, and in marriage he becomes one flesh with a woman—no longer two individuals, but forming a new unity. Because God created this organic union of the two sexes, no one should desecrate his art by cutting them apart."

When they were back home, the disciples brought it up again. Jesus gave it to them straight: "A man who divorces his wife so he can marry someone else commits adultery against her. And a woman who divorces her husband so she can marry someone else commits adultery."

✠

The people brought children to Jesus, hoping he might touch them. The disciples shooed them off. But Jesus was irate and let them know it: "Don't push these children away. Don't ever get between them and me. These children are at the very center of life in the kingdom. Mark this: Unless you accept God's kingdom in the simplicity of a child, you'll never get in." Then, gathering the children up in his arms, he laid his hands of blessing on them.

KING JAMES VERSION

17 ¶ And when he was gone forth into the way, there came one running, and kneeled to him, and asked him, Good Master, what shall I do that I may inherit eternal life?

18 And Jesus said unto him, Why callest thou me good? *there is* none good but one, *that is*, God.

19 Thou knowest the commandments, Do not commit adultery, Do not kill, Do not steal, Do not bear false witness, Defraud not, Honour thy father and mother.

20 And he answered and said unto him, Master, all these have I observed from my youth.

21 Then Jesus beholding him loved him, and said unto him, One thing thou lackest: go thy way, sell whatsoever thou hast, and give to the poor, and thou shalt have treasure in heaven: and come, take up the cross, and follow me.

22 And he was sad at that saying, and went away grieved: for he had great possessions.

23 And Jesus looked round about, and saith unto his disciples, How hardly shall they that have riches enter into the kingdom of God!

24 And the disciples were astonished at his words. But Jesus answereth again, and saith unto them, Children, how hard is it for them that trust in riches to enter into the kingdom of God!

25 It is easier for a camel to go through the eye of a needle, than for a rich man to enter into the kingdom of God.

NEW AMERICAN STANDARD BIBLE

The Rich Young Ruler

17 As He was setting out on a journey, a man ran up to Him and knelt before Him, and asked Him, "Good Teacher, what shall I do to inherit eternal life?"

18 And Jesus said to him, "Why do you call Me good? No one is good except God alone.

19 "You know the commandments, 'DO NOT MURDER, DO NOT COMMIT ADULTERY, DO NOT STEAL, DO NOT BEAR FALSE WITNESS, Do not defraud, HONOR YOUR FATHER AND MOTHER.' "

20 And he said to Him, "Teacher, I have kept all these things from my youth up."

21 Looking at him, Jesus felt a love for him and said to him, "One thing you lack: go and sell all you possess and give to the poor, and you will have treasure in heaven; and come, follow Me."

22 But at these words he was saddened, and he went away grieving, for he was one who owned much property.

23 And Jesus, looking around, *said to His disciples, "How hard it will be for those who are wealthy to enter the kingdom of God!"

24 The disciples were amazed at His words. But Jesus *answered again and *said to them, "Children, how hard it is to enter the kingdom of God!

25 "It is easier for a camel to go through the eye of a needle than for a rich man to enter the kingdom of God."

NEW CENTURY VERSION

A Rich Young Man's Question

17 As Jesus started to leave, a man ran to him and fell on his knees before Jesus. The man asked, "Good teacher, what must I do to have life forever?"

18 Jesus answered, "Why do you call me good? Only God is good. 19 You know the commands: 'You must not murder anyone. You must not be guilty of adultery. You must not steal. You must not tell lies about your neighbor. You must not cheat. Honor your father and mother.' "[d]

20 The man said, "Teacher, I have obeyed all these things since I was a boy."

21 Jesus, looking at the man, loved him and said, "There is one more thing you need to do. Go and sell everything you have, and give the money to the poor, and you will have treasure in heaven. Then come and follow me."

22 He was very sad to hear Jesus say this, and he left sorrowfully, because he was rich.

23 Then Jesus looked at his followers and said, "How hard it will be for the rich to enter the kingdom of God!"

24 The followers were amazed at what Jesus said. But he said again, "My children, it is very hard to enter the kingdom of God! 25 It is easier for a camel to go through the eye of a needle than for a rich person to enter the kingdom of God."

10:19 [d] **'You...mother.'** Quotation from Exodus 20:12–16; Deuteronomy 5:16–20.

CONTEMPORARY ENGLISH VERSION

A Rich Man (Matthew 19.16-30; Luke 18.18-30)

17 As Jesus was walking down a road, a man ran up to him. He knelt down, and asked, "Good teacher, what can I do to have eternal life?"

18 Jesus replied, "Why do you call me good? Only God is good. 19 You know the commandments. 'Do not murder. Be faithful in marriage. Do not steal. Do not tell lies about others. Do not cheat. Respect your father and mother.' "

20 The man answered, "Teacher, I have obeyed all these commandments since I was a young man."

21 Jesus looked closely at the man. He liked him and said, "There's one thing you still need to do. Go sell everything you own. Give the money to the poor, and you will have riches in heaven. Then come with me."

22 When the man heard Jesus say this, he went away gloomy and sad because he was very rich.

23 Jesus looked around and said to his disciples, "It's hard for rich people to get into God's kingdom!" 24 The disciples were shocked to hear this. So Jesus told them again, "It's terribly hard[c] to get into God's kingdom! 25 In fact, it's easier for a camel to go through the eye of a needle than for a rich person to get into God's kingdom."

[c] **10.24** *hard*: Some manuscripts add "for people who trust in their wealth." Others add "for the rich."

NEW INTERNATIONAL VERSION

The Rich Young Man

17As Jesus started on his way, a man ran up to him and fell on his knees before him. "Good teacher," he asked, "what must I do to inherit eternal life?"

18"Why do you call me good?" Jesus answered. "No one is good—except God alone. 19You know the commandments: 'Do not murder, do not commit adultery, do not steal, do not give false testimony, do not defraud, honor your father and mother.'[d]"

20"Teacher," he declared, "all these I have kept since I was a boy."

21Jesus looked at him and loved him. "One thing you lack," he said. "Go, sell everything you have and give to the poor, and you will have treasure in heaven. Then come, follow me."

22At this the man's face fell. He went away sad, because he had great wealth.

23Jesus looked around and said to his disciples, "How hard it is for the rich to enter the kingdom of God!"

24The disciples were amazed at his words. But Jesus said again, "Children, how hard it is[e] to enter the kingdom of God! 25It is easier for a camel to go through the eye of a needle than for a rich man to enter the kingdom of God."

[d] *19* Exodus 20:12-16; Deut. 5:16-20 [e] *24* Some manuscripts *is for those who trust in riches*

NEW LIVING TRANSLATION

The Rich Man

17As he was starting out on a trip, a man came running up to Jesus, knelt down, and asked, "Good Teacher, what should I do to get eternal life?"

18"Why do you call me good?" Jesus asked. "Only God is truly good. 19But as for your question, you know the commandments: 'Do not murder. Do not commit adultery. Do not steal. Do not testify falsely. Do not cheat. Honor your father and mother.'* "

20"Teacher," the man replied, "I've obeyed all these commandments since I was a child."

21Jesus felt genuine love for this man as he looked at him. "You lack only one thing," he told him. "Go and sell all you have and give the money to the poor, and you will have treasure in heaven. Then come, follow me." 22At this, the man's face fell, and he went sadly away because he had many possessions.

23Jesus looked around and said to his disciples, "How hard it is for rich people to get into the Kingdom of God!" 24This amazed them. But Jesus said again, "Dear children, it is very hard* to get into the Kingdom of God. 25It is easier for a camel to go through the eye of a needle than for a rich person to enter the Kingdom of God!"

10:19 Exod 20:12-16; Deut 5:16-20. 10:24 Some manuscripts add *for those who trust in riches.*

NEW KING JAMES VERSION

Jesus Counsels the Rich Young Ruler

17Now as He was going out on the road, one came running, knelt before Him, and asked Him, "Good Teacher, what shall I do that I may inherit eternal life?"

18So Jesus said to him, "Why do you call Me good? No one *is* good but One, *that is,* God. 19You know the commandments: *'Do not commit adultery,' 'Do not murder,' 'Do not steal,' 'Do not bear false witness,'* 'Do not defraud,' *'Honor your father and your mother.'* "[c]

20And he answered and said to Him, "Teacher, all these things I have kept from my youth."

21Then Jesus, looking at him, loved him, and said to him, "One thing you lack: Go your way, sell whatever you have and give to the poor, and you will have treasure in heaven; and come, take up the cross, and follow Me."

22But he was sad at this word, and went away sorrowful, for he had great possessions.

With God All Things Are Possible

23Then Jesus looked around and said to His disciples, "How hard it is for those who have riches to enter the kingdom of God!" 24And the disciples were astonished at His words. But Jesus answered again and said to them, "Children, how hard it is for those who trust in riches[d] to enter the kingdom of God! 25It is easier for a camel to go through the eye of a needle than for a rich man to enter the kingdom of God."

10:19 [c] Exodus 20:12-16; Deuteronomy 5:16-20 10:24 [d] NU-Text omits *for those who trust in riches.*

THE MESSAGE

To Enter God's Kingdom

As he went out into the street, a man came running up, greeted him with great reverence, and asked, "Good Teacher, what must I do to get eternal life?"

Jesus said, "Why are you calling me good? No one is good, only God. You know the commandments: Don't murder, don't commit adultery, don't steal, don't lie, don't cheat, honor your father and mother."

He said, "Teacher, I have—from my youth—kept them all!"

Jesus looked him hard in the eye—and loved him! He said, "There's one thing left: Go sell whatever you own and give it to the poor. All your wealth will then be heavenly wealth. And come follow me."

The man's face clouded over. This was the last thing he expected to hear, and he walked off with a heavy heart. He was holding on tight to a lot of things, and not about to let go.

Looking at his disciples, Jesus said, "Do you have any idea how difficult it is for people who 'have it all' to enter God's kingdom?" The disciples couldn't believe what they were hearing, but Jesus kept on: "You can't imagine how difficult. I'd say it's easier for a camel to go through a needle's eye than for the rich to get into God's kingdom."

KING JAMES VERSION

26 And they were astonished out of measure, saying among themselves, Who then can be saved?

27 And Jesus looking upon them saith, With men *it is* impossible, but not with God: for with God all things are possible.

28 Then Peter began to say unto him, Lo, we have left all, and have followed thee.

29 And Jesus answered and said, Verily I say unto you, There is no man that hath left house, or brethren, or sisters, or father, or mother, or wife, or children, or lands, for my sake, and the gospel's,

30 But he shall receive an hundredfold now in this time, houses, and brethren, and sisters, and mothers, and children, and lands, with persecutions; and in the world to come eternal life.

31 But many *that are* first shall be last; and the last first.

32 ¶ And they were in the way going up to Jerusalem; and Jesus went before them: and they were amazed; and as they followed, they were afraid. And he took again the twelve, and began to tell them what things should happen unto him,

33 *Saying*, Behold, we go up to Jerusalem; and the Son of man shall be delivered unto the chief priests, and unto the scribes; and they shall condemn him to death, and shall deliver him to the Gentiles:

NEW AMERICAN STANDARD BIBLE

26 They were even more astonished and said to Him, "Then who can be saved?"

27 Looking at them, Jesus *said, "With people it is impossible, but not with God; for all things are possible with God."

28 Peter began to say to Him, "Behold, we have left everything and followed You."

29 Jesus said, "Truly I say to you, there is no one who has left house or brothers or sisters or mother or father or children or farms, for My sake and for the gospel's sake,

30 but that he will receive a hundred times as much now in the present age, houses and brothers and sisters and mothers and children and farms, along with persecutions; and in the age to come, eternal life.

31 "But many *who are* first will be last, and the last, first."

Jesus' Sufferings Foretold

32 They were on the road going up to Jerusalem, and Jesus was walking on ahead of them; and they were amazed, and those who followed were fearful. And again He took the twelve aside and began to tell them what was going to happen to Him,

33 *saying*, "Behold, we are going up to Jerusalem, and the Son of Man will be [2]delivered to the chief priests and the scribes; and they will condemn Him to death and will hand Him over to the Gentiles.

10:33 [2] Or *betrayed*

NEW CENTURY VERSION

26The followers were even more surprised and said to each other, "Then who can be saved?"

27Jesus looked at them and said, "This is something people cannot do, but God can. God can do all things."

28Peter said to Jesus, "Look, we have left everything and followed you."

29Jesus said, "I tell you the truth, all those who have left houses, brothers, sisters, mother, father, children, or farms for me and for the Good News 30will get more than they left. Here in this world they will have a hundred times more homes, brothers, sisters, mothers, children, and fields. And with those things, they will also suffer for their belief. But in the age that is coming they will have life forever. 31Many who have the highest place now will have the lowest place in the future. And many who have the lowest place now will have the highest place in the future."

Jesus Talks About His Death

32As Jesus and the people with him were on the road to Jerusalem, he was leading the way. His followers were amazed, but others in the crowd who followed were afraid. Again Jesus took the twelve apostles aside and began to tell them what was about to happen in Jerusalem. 33He said, "Look, we are going to Jerusalem. The Son of Man will be turned over to the leading priests and the teachers of the law. They will say that he must die, and they will turn him over to the non-Jewish people, 34who will laugh at him and

CONTEMPORARY ENGLISH VERSION

26Jesus' disciples were even more amazed. They asked each other, "How can anyone ever be saved?"

27Jesus looked at them and said, "There are some things that people cannot do, but God can do anything."

28Peter replied, "Remember, we left everything to be your followers!"

29Jesus told him:

You can be sure that anyone who gives up home or brothers or sisters or mother or father or children or land for me and for the good news 30will be rewarded. In this world they will be given a hundred times as many houses and brothers and sisters and mothers and children and pieces of land, though they will also be mistreated. And in the world to come, they will have eternal life. 31But many who are now first will be last, and many who are now last will be first.

Jesus Again Tells about His Death

(Matthew 20.17-19; Luke 18.31-34)

32The disciples were confused as Jesus led them toward Jerusalem, and his other followers were afraid. Once again, Jesus took the twelve disciples aside and told them what was going to happen to him. He said:

33We are now on our way to Jerusalem where the Son of Man will be handed over to the chief priests and the teachers of the Law of Moses. They will sentence him to death and hand him over to foreigners,[d] 34who will

[d] 10.33 *foreigners*: The Romans who ruled Judea at this time.

NEW INTERNATIONAL VERSION

26The disciples were even more amazed, and said to each other, "Who then can be saved?"

27Jesus looked at them and said, "With man this is impossible, but not with God; all things are possible with God."

28Peter said to him, "We have left everything to follow you!"

29"I tell you the truth," Jesus replied, "no one who has left home or brothers or sisters or mother or father or children or fields for me and the gospel 30will fail to receive a hundred times as much in this present age (homes, brothers, sisters, mothers, children and fields—and with them, persecutions) and in the age to come, eternal life. 31But many who are first will be last, and the last first."

Jesus Again Predicts His Death

32They were on their way up to Jerusalem, with Jesus leading the way, and the disciples were astonished, while those who followed were afraid. Again he took the Twelve aside and told them what was going to happen to him. 33"We are going up to Jerusalem," he said, "and the Son of Man will be betrayed to the chief priests and teachers of the law. They will condemn him to death and will hand

NEW LIVING TRANSLATION

26The disciples were astounded. "Then who in the world can be saved?" they asked.

27Jesus looked at them intently and said, "Humanly speaking, it is impossible. But not with God. Everything is possible with God."

28Then Peter began to mention all that he and the other disciples had left behind. "We've given up everything to follow you," he said.

29And Jesus replied, "I assure you that everyone who has given up house or brothers or sisters or mother or father or children or property, for my sake and for the Good News, 30will receive now in return, a hundred times over, houses, brothers, sisters, mothers, children, and property—with persecutions. And in the world to come they will have eternal life. 31But many who seem to be important now will be the least important then, and those who are considered least here will be the greatest then.*"

Jesus Again Predicts His Death

32They were now on the way to Jerusalem, and Jesus was walking ahead of them. The disciples were filled with dread and the people following behind were overwhelmed with fear. Taking the twelve disciples aside, Jesus once more began to describe everything that was about to happen to him in Jerusalem. 33"When we get to Jerusalem," he told them, "the Son of Man will be betrayed to the leading priests and the teachers of religious law. They will sentence

10:31 Greek *But many who are first will be last; and the last, first.*

NEW KING JAMES VERSION

26And they were greatly astonished, saying among themselves, "Who then can be saved?"

27But Jesus looked at them and said, "With men *it is* impossible, but not with God; for with God all things are possible."

28Then Peter began to say to Him, "See, we have left all and followed You."

29So Jesus answered and said, "Assuredly, I say to you, there is no one who has left house or brothers or sisters or father or mother or wife[e] or children or lands, for My sake and the gospel's, 30who shall not receive a hundredfold now in this time—houses and brothers and sisters and mothers and children and lands, with persecutions—and in the age to come, eternal life. 31But many *who are* first will be last, and the last first."

Jesus a Third Time Predicts His Death and Resurrection

32Now they were on the road, going up to Jerusalem, and Jesus was going before them; and they were amazed. And as they followed they were afraid. Then He took the twelve aside again and began to tell them the things that would happen to Him: 33"Behold, we are going up to Jerusalem, and the Son of Man will be betrayed to the chief priests and to the scribes; and they will condemn Him to death and deliver Him to the Gentiles; 34and they will mock Him,

10:29 [e] NU-Text omits *or wife.*

THE MESSAGE

That set the disciples back on their heels. "Then who has any chance at all?" they asked.

Jesus was blunt: "No chance at all if you think you can pull it off by yourself. Every chance in the world if you let God do it."

Peter tried another angle: "We left everything and followed you."

Jesus said, "Mark my words, no one who sacrifices house, brothers, sisters, mother, father, children, land—whatever—because of me and the Message will lose out. They'll get it all back, but multiplied many times in homes, brothers, sisters, mothers, children, and land—but also in troubles. And then the bonus of eternal life! This is once again the Great Reversal: Many who are first will end up last, and the last first."

Back on the road, they set out for Jerusalem. Jesus had a head start on them, and they were following, puzzled and not just a little afraid. He took the Twelve and began again to go over what to expect next. "Listen to me carefully. We're on our way up to Jerusalem. When we get there, the Son of Man will be betrayed to the religious leaders and scholars. They will sentence him to death. Then they will hand him over to the Romans, who will mock and spit on

KING JAMES VERSION

34 And they shall mock him, and shall scourge him, and shall spit upon him, and shall kill him: and the third day he shall rise again.

35 And James and John, the sons of Zebedee, come unto him, saying, Master, we would that thou shouldest do for us whatsoever we shall desire.

36 And he said unto them, What would ye that I should do for you?

37 They said unto him, Grant unto us that we may sit, one on thy right hand, and the other on thy left hand, in thy glory.

38 But Jesus said unto them, Ye know not what ye ask: can ye drink of the cup that I drink of? and be baptized with the baptism that I am baptized with?

39 And they said unto him, We can. And Jesus said unto them, Ye shall indeed drink of the cup that I drink of; and with the baptism that I am baptized withal shall ye be baptized:

40 But to sit on my right hand and on my left hand is not mine to give; but *it shall be given to them* for whom it is prepared.

41 And when the ten heard *it*, they began to be much displeased with James and John.

42 But Jesus called them *to him*, and saith unto them, Ye know that they which are accounted to rule over the Gentiles exercise lordship over them; and their great ones exercise authority upon them.

43 But so shall it not be among you: but whosoever will be great among you, shall be your minister:

NEW AMERICAN STANDARD BIBLE

34 "They will mock Him and spit on Him, and scourge Him and kill *Him*, and three days later He will rise again."

35 James and John, the two sons of Zebedee, *came up to Jesus, saying, "Teacher, we want You to do for us whatever we ask of You."

36 And He said to them, "What do you want Me to do for you?"

37 They said to Him, "Grant that we may sit, one on Your right and one on *Your* left, in Your glory."

38 But Jesus said to them, "You do not know what you are asking. Are you able to drink the cup that I drink, or to be baptized with the baptism with which I am baptized?"

39 They said to Him, "We are able." And Jesus said to them, "The cup that I drink you shall drink; and you shall be baptized with the baptism with which I am baptized.

40 "But to sit on My right or on *My* left, this is not Mine to give; but it is for those for whom it has been prepared."

41 Hearing *this*, the ten began to feel indignant with James and John.

42 Calling them to Himself, Jesus *said to them, "You know that those who are recognized as rulers of the Gentiles lord it over them; and their great men exercise authority over them.

43 "But it is not this way among you, but whoever wishes to become great among you shall be your servant;

NEW CENTURY VERSION

spit on him. They will beat him with whips and crucify him. But on the third day, he will rise to life again."

Two Followers Ask Jesus a Favor

35 Then James and John, sons of Zebedee, came to Jesus and said, "Teacher, we want to ask you to do something for us."

36 Jesus asked, "What do you want me to do for you?"

37 They answered, "Let one of us sit at your right side and one of us sit at your left side in your glory in your kingdom."

38 Jesus said, "You don't understand what you are asking. Can you drink the cup that I must drink? And can you be baptized with the same kind of baptism that I must go through?"[e]

39 They answered, "Yes, we can."

Jesus said to them, "You will drink the same cup that I will drink, and you will be baptized with the same baptism that I must go through. 40 But I cannot choose who will sit at my right or my left; those places belong to those for whom they have been prepared."

41 When the other ten followers heard this, they began to be angry with James and John.

42 Jesus called them together and said, "The non-Jewish people have rulers. You know that those rulers love to show their power over the people, and their important leaders love to use all their authority. 43 But it should not be that way among you. Whoever wants to become great among you

10:38 [e] **Can you...through?** Jesus was asking if they could suffer the same terrible things that would happen to him.

CONTEMPORARY ENGLISH VERSION

make fun of him and spit on him. They will beat him and kill him. But three days later he will rise to life.

The Request of James and John (Matthew 20.20-28)

35 James and John, the sons of Zebedee, came up to Jesus and asked, "Teacher, will you do us a favor?"

36 Jesus asked them what they wanted, 37 and they answered, "When you come into your glory, please let one of us sit at your right side and the other at your left."[e]

38 Jesus told them, "You don't really know what you're asking! Are you able to drink from the cup[f] that I must soon drink from or be baptized as I must be baptized?"[g]

39 "Yes, we are!" James and John answered.

Then Jesus replied, "You certainly will drink from the cup from which I must drink. And you will be baptized just as I must! 40 But it isn't for me to say who will sit at my right side and at my left. That is for God to decide."

41 When the ten other disciples heard this, they were angry with James and John. 42 But Jesus called the disciples together and said:

You know that those foreigners who call themselves kings like to order their people around. And their great leaders have full power over the people they rule. 43 But don't act like them. If you want to be great, you must be the servant of all the others. 44 And if you want to be

[e] **10.37** *right side . . . left*: The most powerful people in a kingdom sat at the right and left side of the king. [f] **10.38** *drink from the cup*: In the Scriptures a "cup" is sometimes used as a symbol of suffering. To "drink from the cup" would be to suffer. [g] **10.38** *as I must be baptized*: Baptism is used with the same meaning that "cup" has in this verse.

NEW INTERNATIONAL VERSION

him over to the Gentiles, 34who will mock him and spit on him, flog him and kill him. Three days later he will rise."

The Request of James and John

35Then James and John, the sons of Zebedee, came to him. "Teacher," they said, "we want you to do for us whatever we ask."

36"What do you want me to do for you?" he asked.

37They replied, "Let one of us sit at your right and the other at your left in your glory."

38"You don't know what you are asking," Jesus said. "Can you drink the cup I drink or be baptized with the baptism I am baptized with?"

39"We can," they answered.

Jesus said to them, "You will drink the cup I drink and be baptized with the baptism I am baptized with, 40but to sit at my right or left is not for me to grant. These places belong to those for whom they have been prepared."

41When the ten heard about this, they became indignant with James and John. 42Jesus called them together and said, "You know that those who are regarded as rulers of the Gentiles lord it over them, and their high officials exercise authority over them. 43Not so with you. Instead, whoever wants to become great among you must be your servant,

NEW LIVING TRANSLATION

him to die and hand him over to the Romans. 34They will mock him, spit on him, beat him with their whips, and kill him, but after three days he will rise again."

Jesus Teaches about Serving Others

35Then James and John, the sons of Zebedee, came over and spoke to him. "Teacher," they said, "we want you to do us a favor."

36"What is it?" he asked.

37"In your glorious Kingdom, we want to sit in places of honor next to you," they said, "one at your right and the other at your left."

38But Jesus answered, "You don't know what you are asking! Are you able to drink from the bitter cup of sorrow I am about to drink? Are you able to be baptized with the baptism of suffering I must be baptized with?"

39"Oh yes," they said, "we are able!"

And Jesus said, "You will indeed drink from my cup and be baptized with my baptism, 40but I have no right to say who will sit on the thrones next to mine. God has prepared those places for the ones he has chosen."

41When the ten other disciples discovered what James and John had asked, they were indignant. 42So Jesus called them together and said, "You know that in this world kings are tyrants, and officials lord it over the people beneath them. 43But among you it should be quite different. Whoever wants to be a leader among you must be your servant,

NEW KING JAMES VERSION

and scourge Him, and spit on Him, and kill Him. And the third day He will rise again."

Greatness Is Serving

35Then James and John, the sons of Zebedee, came to Him, saying, "Teacher, we want You to do for us whatever we ask."

36And He said to them, "What do you want Me to do for you?"

37They said to Him, "Grant us that we may sit, one on Your right hand and the other on Your left, in Your glory."

38But Jesus said to them, "You do not know what you ask. Are you able to drink the cup that I drink, and be baptized with the baptism that I am baptized with?"

39They said to Him, "We are able."

So Jesus said to them, "You will indeed drink the cup that I drink, and with the baptism I am baptized with you will be baptized; 40but to sit on My right hand and on My left is not Mine to give, but *it is for those* for whom it is prepared."

41And when the ten heard *it,* they began to be greatly displeased with James and John. 42But Jesus called them to *Himself* and said to them, "You know that those who are considered rulers over the Gentiles lord it over them, and their great ones exercise authority over them. 43Yet it shall not be so among you; but whoever desires to become great among you shall be your servant. 44And whoever of you

THE MESSAGE

him, give him the third degree, and kill him. After three days he will rise alive."

The Highest Places of Honor

James and John, Zebedee's sons, came up to him. "Teacher, we have something we want you to do for us."

"What is it? I'll see what I can do."

"Arrange it," they said, "so that we will be awarded the highest places of honor in your glory—one of us at your right, the other at your left."

Jesus said, "You have no idea what you're asking. Are you capable of drinking the cup I drink, of being baptized in the baptism I'm about to be plunged into?"

"Sure," they said. "Why not?"

Jesus said, "Come to think of it, you *will* drink the cup I drink, and be baptized in my baptism. But as to awarding places of honor, that's not my business. There are other arrangements for that."

When the other ten heard of this conversation, they lost their tempers with James and John. Jesus got them together to settle things down. "You've observed how godless rulers throw their weight around," he said, "and when people get a little power how quickly it goes to their heads. It's not going to be that way with you. Whoever wants to be great must become a servant. Whoever wants to be first

KING JAMES VERSION

44 And whosoever of you will be the chiefest, shall be servant of all.

45 For even the Son of man came not to be ministered unto, but to minister, and to give his life a ransom for many.

46 ¶ And they came to Jericho: and as he went out of Jericho with his disciples and a great number of people, blind Bartimaeus, the son of Timaeus, sat by the highway side begging.

47 And when he heard that it was Jesus of Nazareth, he began to cry out, and say, Jesus, *thou* Son of David, have mercy on me.

48 And many charged him that he should hold his peace: but he cried the more a great deal, *Thou* Son of David, have mercy on me.

49 And Jesus stood still, and commanded him to be called. And they call the blind man, saying unto him, Be of good comfort, rise; he calleth thee.

50 And he, casting away his garment, rose, and came to Jesus.

51 And Jesus answered and said unto him, What wilt thou that I should do unto thee? The blind man said unto him, Lord, that I might receive my sight.

52 And Jesus said unto him, Go thy way; thy faith hath made thee whole. And immediately he received his sight, and followed Jesus in the way.

NEW AMERICAN STANDARD BIBLE

44 and whoever wishes to be first among you shall be slave of all.

45 "For even the Son of Man did not come to be served, but to serve, and to give His life a ransom for many."

Bartimaeus Receives His Sight

46 Then they *came to Jericho. And as He was leaving Jericho with His disciples and a large crowd, a blind beggar *named* Bartimaeus, the son of Timaeus, was sitting by the road.

47 When he heard that it was Jesus the Nazarene, he began to cry out and say, "Jesus, Son of David, have mercy on me!"

48 Many were sternly telling him to be quiet, but he kept crying out all the more, "Son of David, have mercy on me!"

49 And Jesus stopped and said, "Call him *here*." So they *called the blind man, saying to him, "Take courage, stand up! He is calling for you."

50 Throwing aside his cloak, he jumped up and came to Jesus.

51 And answering him, Jesus said, "What do you want Me to do for you?" And the blind man said to Him, "[3]Rabboni, *I want* to regain my sight!"

52 And Jesus said to him, "Go; your faith has made you well." Immediately he regained his sight and *began* following Him on the road.

10:51 [3] I.e. My Master

NEW CENTURY VERSION

must serve the rest of you like a servant. 44Whoever wants to become the first among you must serve all of you like a slave. 45In the same way, the Son of Man did not come to be served. He came to serve others and to give his life as a ransom for many people."

Jesus Heals a Blind Man

46Then they came to the town of Jericho. As Jesus was leaving there with his followers and a great many people, a blind beggar named Bartimaeus son of Timaeus was sitting by the road. 47When he heard that Jesus from Nazareth was walking by, he began to shout, "Jesus, Son of David, have mercy on me!"

48Many people warned the blind man to be quiet, but he shouted even more, "Son of David, have mercy on me!"

49Jesus stopped and said, "Tell the man to come here."

So they called the blind man, saying, "Cheer up! Get to your feet. Jesus is calling you." 50The blind man jumped up, left his coat there, and went to Jesus.

51Jesus asked him, "What do you want me to do for you?"

The blind man answered, "Teacher, I want to see."

52Jesus said, "Go, you are healed because you believed." At once the man could see, and he followed Jesus on the road.

CONTEMPORARY ENGLISH VERSION

first, you must be everyone's slave. 45The Son of Man did not come to be a slave master, but a slave who will give his life to rescue[h] many people.

Jesus Heals Blind Bartimaeus

(Matthew 20.29-34; Luke 18.35-43)

46Jesus and his disciples went to Jericho. And as they were leaving, they were followed by a large crowd. A blind beggar by the name of Bartimaeus son of Timaeus was sitting beside the road. 47When he heard that it was Jesus from Nazareth, he shouted, "Jesus, Son of David,[i] have pity on me!" 48Many people told the man to stop, but he shouted even louder, "Son of David, have pity on me!"

49Jesus stopped and said, "Call him over!"

They called out to the blind man and said, "Don't be afraid! Come on! He is calling for you." 50The man threw off his coat as he jumped up and ran to Jesus.

51Jesus asked, "What do you want me to do for you?"

The blind man answered, "Master,[j] I want to see!"

52Jesus told him, "You may go. Your eyes are healed because of your faith."

Right away the man could see, and he went down the road with Jesus.

[h] 10.45 *rescue*: The Greek word often, though not always, means the payment of a price to free a slave or a prisoner. [i] 10.47 *Son of David*: The Jewish people expected the Messiah to be from the family of King David, and for this reason the Messiah was often called the "Son of David." [j] 10.51 *Master*: A Hebrew word that may also mean "Teacher."

NEW INTERNATIONAL VERSION

44and whoever wants to be first must be slave of all. 45For even the Son of Man did not come to be served, but to serve, and to give his life as a ransom for many."

Blind Bartimaeus Receives His Sight

46Then they came to Jericho. As Jesus and his disciples, together with a large crowd, were leaving the city, a blind man, Bartimaeus (that is, the Son of Timaeus), was sitting by the roadside begging. 47When he heard that it was Jesus of Nazareth, he began to shout, "Jesus, Son of David, have mercy on me!"

48Many rebuked him and told him to be quiet, but he shouted all the more, "Son of David, have mercy on me!"

49Jesus stopped and said, "Call him."

So they called to the blind man, "Cheer up! On your feet! He's calling you." 50Throwing his cloak aside, he jumped to his feet and came to Jesus.

51"What do you want me to do for you?" Jesus asked him.

The blind man said, "Rabbi, I want to see."

52"Go," said Jesus, "your faith has healed you." Immediately he received his sight and followed Jesus along the road.

NEW LIVING TRANSLATION

44and whoever wants to be first must be the slave of all. 45For even I, the Son of Man, came here not to be served but to serve others, and to give my life as a ransom for many."

Jesus Heals Blind Bartimaeus

46And so they reached Jericho. Later, as Jesus and his disciples left town, a great crowd was following. A blind beggar named Bartimaeus (son of Timaeus) was sitting beside the road as Jesus was going by. 47When Bartimaeus heard that Jesus from Nazareth was nearby, he began to shout out, "Jesus, Son of David, have mercy on me!"

48"Be quiet!" some of the people yelled at him.

But he only shouted louder, "Son of David, have mercy on me!"

49When Jesus heard him, he stopped and said, "Tell him to come here."

So they called the blind man. "Cheer up," they said. "Come on, he's calling you!" 50Bartimaeus threw aside his coat, jumped up, and came to Jesus.

51"What do you want me to do for you?" Jesus asked.

"Teacher," the blind man said, "I want to see!"

52And Jesus said to him, "Go your way. Your faith has healed you." And instantly the blind man could see! Then he followed Jesus down the road.*

10:52 Or *on the way.*

NEW KING JAMES VERSION

desires to be first shall be slave of all. 45For even the Son of Man did not come to be served, but to serve, and to give His life a ransom for many."

Jesus Heals Blind Bartimaeus

46Now they came to Jericho. As He went out of Jericho with His disciples and a great multitude, blind Bartimaeus, the son of Timaeus, sat by the road begging. 47And when he heard that it was Jesus of Nazareth, he began to cry out and say, "Jesus, Son of David, have mercy on me!"

48Then many warned him to be quiet; but he cried out all the more, "Son of David, have mercy on me!"

49So Jesus stood still and commanded him to be called.

Then they called the blind man, saying to him, "Be of good cheer. Rise, He is calling you."

50And throwing aside his garment, he rose and came to Jesus.

51So Jesus answered and said to him, "What do you want Me to do for you?"

The blind man said to Him, "Rabboni, that I may receive my sight."

52Then Jesus said to him, "Go your way; your faith has made you well." And immediately he received his sight and followed Jesus on the road.

THE MESSAGE

among you must be your slave. That is what the Son of Man has done: He came to serve, not to be served—and then to give away his life in exchange for many who are held hostage."

✠

They spent some time in Jericho. As Jesus was leaving town, trailed by his disciples and a parade of people, a blind beggar by the name of Bartimaeus, son of Timaeus, was sitting alongside the road. When he heard that Jesus the Nazarene was passing by, he began to cry out, "Son of David, Jesus! Mercy, have mercy on me!" Many tried to hush him up, but he yelled all the louder, "Son of David! Mercy, have mercy on me!"

Jesus stopped in his tracks. "Call him over."

They called him. "It's your lucky day! Get up! He's calling you to come!" Throwing off his coat, he was on his feet at once, and came to Jesus.

Jesus said, "What can I do for you?"

The blind man said, "Rabbi, I want to see."

"On your way," said Jesus. "Your faith has saved and healed you."

In that very instant he recovered his sight and followed Jesus down the road.

KING JAMES VERSION

11 And when they came nigh to Jerusalem, unto Bethphage and Bethany, at the mount of Olives, he sendeth forth two of his disciples,

2 And saith unto them, Go your way into the village over against you: and as soon as ye be entered into it, ye shall find a colt tied, whereon never man sat; loose him, and bring *him*.

3 And if any man say unto you, Why do ye this? say ye that the Lord hath need of him; and straightway he will send him hither.

4 And they went their way, and found the colt tied by the door without in a place where two ways met; and they loose him.

5 And certain of them that stood there said unto them, What do ye, loosing the colt?

6 And they said unto them even as Jesus had commanded: and they let them go.

7 And they brought the colt to Jesus, and cast their garments on him; and he sat upon him.

8 And many spread their garments in the way: and others cut down branches off the trees, and strawed *them* in the way.

9 And they that went before, and they that followed, cried, saying, Hosanna; Blessed *is* he that cometh in the name of the Lord:

NEW AMERICAN STANDARD BIBLE

The Triumphal Entry

11 As they *approached Jerusalem, at Bethphage and Bethany, near the Mount of Olives, He *sent two of His disciples,

2 and *said to them, "Go into the village opposite you, and immediately as you enter it, you will find a colt tied *there,* on which no one yet has ever sat; untie it and bring it *here.*

3 "If anyone says to you, 'Why are you doing this?' you say, 'The Lord has need of it'; and immediately he will send it back here."

4 They went away and found a colt tied at the door, outside in the street; and they *untied it.

5 Some of the bystanders were saying to them, "What are you doing, untying the colt?"

6 They spoke to them just as Jesus had told *them,* and they gave them permission.

7 They *brought the colt to Jesus and put their coats on it; and He sat on it.

8 And many spread their coats in the road, and others *spread* leafy branches which they had cut from the fields.

9 Those who went in front and those who followed were shouting:

"Hosanna!
BLESSED IS HE WHO COMES IN THE NAME OF THE LORD;

NEW CENTURY VERSION

Jesus Enters Jerusalem as a King

11 As Jesus and his followers were coming closer to Jerusalem, they came to the towns of Bethphage and Bethany near the Mount of Olives. From there Jesus sent two of his followers
2 and said to them, "Go to the town you can see there. When you enter it, you will quickly find a colt tied, which no one has ever ridden. Untie it and bring it here to me.
3 If anyone asks you why you are doing this, tell him its Master needs the colt, and he will send it at once."

4 The followers went into the town, found a colt tied in the street near the door of a house, and untied it.
5 Some people were standing there and asked, "What are you doing? Why are you untying that colt?"
6 The followers answered the way Jesus told them to answer, and the people let them take the colt.

7 They brought the colt to Jesus and put their coats on it, and Jesus sat on it.
8 Many people spread their coats on the road. Others cut branches in the fields and spread them on the road.
9 The people were walking ahead of Jesus and behind him, shouting,

"Praise[a] God!
God bless the One who comes in the name
of the Lord! *Psalm 118:26*

11:9 [a] **Praise** Literally, "Hosanna," a Hebrew word used at first in praying to God for help, but at this time it was probably a shout of joy used in praising God or his Messiah.

CONTEMPORARY ENGLISH VERSION

Jesus Enters Jerusalem

(Matthew 21.1-11; Luke 19.28-40; John 12.12-19)

11 Jesus and his disciples reached Bethphage and Bethany near the Mount of Olives. When they were getting close to Jerusalem, Jesus sent two of them on ahead.
2 He told them, "Go into the next village. As soon as you enter it, you will find a young donkey that has never been ridden. Untie the donkey and bring it here.
3 If anyone asks why you are doing that, say, 'The Lord[a] needs it and will soon bring it back.' "

4 The disciples left and found the donkey tied near a door that faced the street. While they were untying it,
5 some of the people standing there asked, "Why are you untying the donkey?"
6 They told them what Jesus had said, and the people let them take it.

7 The disciples led the donkey to Jesus. They put some of their clothes on its back, and Jesus got on.
8 Many people spread clothes on the road, while others went to cut branches from the fields.[b]

9 In front of Jesus and behind him, people went along shouting,

"Hooray![c]
God bless the one who comes
in the name of the Lord!

[a] 11.3 *The Lord*: Or "The master of the donkey." [b] 11.8 *spread . . . branches from the fields*: This was one way that the Jewish people welcomed a famous person. [c] 11.9 *Hooray*: This translates a word that can mean "please save us." But it is most often used as a shout of praise to God.

NEW INTERNATIONAL VERSION

The Triumphal Entry

11 As they approached Jerusalem and came to Bethphage and Bethany at the Mount of Olives, Jesus sent two of his disciples, [2]saying to them, "Go to the village ahead of you, and just as you enter it, you will find a colt tied there, which no one has ever ridden. Untie it and bring it here. [3]If anyone asks you, 'Why are you doing this?' tell him, 'The Lord needs it and will send it back here shortly.' "

[4]They went and found a colt outside in the street, tied at a doorway. As they untied it, [5]some people standing there asked, "What are you doing, untying that colt?" [6]They answered as Jesus had told them to, and the people let them go. [7]When they brought the colt to Jesus and threw their cloaks over it, he sat on it. [8]Many people spread their cloaks on the road, while others spread branches they had cut in the fields. [9]Those who went ahead and those who followed shouted,

"Hosanna![a]"

"Blessed is he who comes in the name of the Lord!"[b]

[a] *9* A Hebrew expression meaning "Save!" which became an exclamation of praise; also in verse 10 [b] *9* Psalm 118:25,26

NEW LIVING TRANSLATION

The Triumphal Entry

11 As Jesus and his disciples approached Jerusalem, they came to the towns of Bethphage and Bethany, on the Mount of Olives. Jesus sent two of them on ahead. [2]"Go into that village over there," he told them, "and as soon as you enter it, you will see a colt tied there that has never been ridden. Untie it and bring it here. [3]If anyone asks what you are doing, just say, 'The Lord needs it and will return it soon.' "

[4]The two disciples left and found the colt standing in the street, tied outside a house. [5]As they were untying it, some bystanders demanded, "What are you doing, untying that colt?" [6]They said what Jesus had told them to say, and they were permitted to take it. [7]Then they brought the colt to Jesus and threw their garments over it, and he sat on it.

[8]Many in the crowd spread their coats on the road ahead of Jesus, and others cut leafy branches in the fields and spread them along the way. [9]He was in the center of the procession, and the crowds all around him were shouting,

"Praise God!*
Bless the one who comes in the name of the Lord!

11:9 Greek *Hosanna,* an exclamation of praise that literally means "save now"; also in 11:10.

NEW KING JAMES VERSION

The Triumphal Entry

11 Now when they drew near Jerusalem, to Bethphage[a] and Bethany, at the Mount of Olives, He sent two of His disciples; [2]and He said to them, "Go into the village opposite you; and as soon as you have entered it you will find a colt tied, on which no one has sat. Loose it and bring *it.* [3]And if anyone says to you, 'Why are you doing this?' say, 'The Lord has need of it,' and immediately he will send it here."

[4]So they went their way, and found the[b] colt tied by the door outside on the street, and they loosed it. [5]But some of those who stood there said to them, "What are you doing, loosing the colt?"

[6]And they spoke to them just as Jesus had commanded. So they let them go. [7]Then they brought the colt to Jesus and threw their clothes on it, and He sat on it. [8]And many spread their clothes on the road, and others cut down leafy branches from the trees and spread *them* on the road. [9]Then those who went before and those who followed cried out, saying:

"Hosanna!
'Blessed is He who comes in the name of the L*ORD*!'[c]

11:1 [a] M-Text reads *Bethsphage.* 11:4 [b] NU-Text and M-Text read *a.*
11:9 [c] Psalm 118:26

THE MESSAGE

Entering Jerusalem on a Colt

11 When they were nearing Jerusalem, at Bethphage and Bethany on Mount Olives, he sent off two of the disciples with instructions: "Go to the village across from you. As soon as you enter, you'll find a colt tethered, one that has never yet been ridden. Untie it and bring it. If anyone asks, 'What are you doing?' say, 'The Master needs him, and will return him right away.' "

They went and found a colt tied to a door at the street corner and untied it. Some of those standing there said, "What are you doing untying that colt?" The disciples replied exactly as Jesus had instructed them, and the people let them alone. They brought the colt to Jesus, spread their coats on it, and he mounted.

The people gave him a wonderful welcome, some throwing their coats on the street, others spreading out rushes they had cut in the fields. Running ahead and following after, they were calling out,

"Hosanna!"
"Blessed is he who comes in God's name!"

KING JAMES VERSION

10 Blessed *be* the kingdom of our father David, that cometh in the name of the Lord: Hosanna in the highest.

11 And Jesus entered into Jerusalem, and into the temple: and when he had looked round about upon all things, and now the eventide was come, he went out unto Bethany with the twelve.

12 ¶ And on the morrow, when they were come from Bethany, he was hungry:

13 And seeing a fig tree afar off having leaves, he came, if haply he might find any thing thereon: and when he came to it, he found nothing but leaves; for the time of figs was not *yet*.

14 And Jesus answered and said unto it, No man eat fruit of thee hereafter for ever. And his disciples heard *it*.

15 And they come to Jerusalem: and Jesus went into the temple, and began to cast out them that sold and bought in the temple, and overthrew the tables of the moneychangers, and the seats of them that sold doves;

16 And would not suffer that any man should carry *any* vessel through the temple.

17 And he taught, saying unto them, Is it not written, My house shall be called of all nations the house of prayer? but ye have made it a den of thieves.

NEW AMERICAN STANDARD BIBLE

10 Blessed *is* the coming kingdom of our father David;
Hosanna in the highest!"

11 Jesus entered Jerusalem *and came* into the temple; and after looking around at everything, He left for Bethany with the twelve, since it was already late.

12 On the next day, when they had left Bethany, He became hungry.

13 Seeing at a distance a fig tree in leaf, He went *to see* if perhaps He would find anything on it; and when He came to it, He found nothing but leaves, for it was not the season for figs.

14 He said to it, "May no one ever eat fruit from you again!" And His disciples were listening.

Jesus Drives Money Changers from the Temple

15 Then they *came to Jerusalem. And He entered the temple and began to drive out those who were buying and selling in the temple, and overturned the tables of the money changers and the seats of those who were selling doves;

16 and He would not permit anyone to carry merchandise through the temple.

17 And He *began* to teach and say to them, "Is it not written, 'MY HOUSE SHALL BE CALLED A HOUSE OF PRAYER FOR ALL THE NATIONS'? But you have made it a ROBBERS' DEN."

NEW CENTURY VERSION

10 God bless the kingdom of our father David!
That kingdom is coming!
Praise to God in heaven!"

11 Jesus entered Jerusalem and went into the Temple. After he had looked at everything, since it was already late, he went out to Bethany with the twelve apostles.

12 The next day as Jesus was leaving Bethany, he became hungry. 13 Seeing a fig tree in leaf from far away, he went to see if it had any figs on it. But he found no figs, only leaves, because it was not the right season for figs. 14 So Jesus said to the tree, "May no one ever eat fruit from you again." And Jesus' followers heard him say this.

Jesus Goes to the Temple

15 When Jesus returned to Jerusalem, he went into the Temple and began to throw out those who were buying and selling there. He turned over the tables of those who were exchanging different kinds of money, and he upset the benches of those who were selling doves. 16 Jesus refused to allow anyone to carry goods through the Temple courts. 17 Then he taught the people, saying, "It is written in the Scriptures, 'My Temple will be called a house for prayer for people from all nations.'[b] But you are changing God's house into a 'hideout for robbers.' "[c]

11:17 [b] **'My Temple...nations.'** Quotation from Isaiah 56:7.
11:17 [c] **'hideout for robbers.'** Quotation from Jeremiah 7:11.

CONTEMPORARY ENGLISH VERSION

10 God bless the coming kingdom
of our ancestor David.
Hooray for God
in heaven above!"

11 After Jesus had gone to Jerusalem, he went into the temple and looked around at everything. But since it was already late in the day, he went back to Bethany with the twelve disciples.

Jesus Puts a Curse on a Fig Tree (Matthew 21.18, 19)

12 When Jesus and his disciples left Bethany the next morning, he was hungry. 13 From a distance Jesus saw a fig tree covered with leaves, and he went to see if there were any figs on the tree. But there were not any, because it wasn't the season for figs. 14 So Jesus said to the tree, "Never again will anyone eat fruit from this tree!" The disciples heard him say this.

Jesus in the Temple

(Matthew 21.12-17; Luke 19.45-48; John 2.13-22)

15 After Jesus and his disciples reached Jerusalem, he went into the temple and began chasing out everyone who was selling and buying. He turned over the tables of the moneychangers and the benches of those who were selling doves. 16 Jesus would not let anyone carry things through the temple. 17 Then he taught the people and said, "The Scriptures say, 'My house should be called a place of worship for all nations.' But you have made it a place where robbers hide!"

NEW INTERNATIONAL VERSION

10 "Blessed is the coming kingdom of our father David!"
"Hosanna in the highest!"

11 Jesus entered Jerusalem and went to the temple. He looked around at everything, but since it was already late, he went out to Bethany with the Twelve.

Jesus Clears the Temple

12 The next day as they were leaving Bethany, Jesus was hungry.
13 Seeing in the distance a fig tree in leaf, he went to find out if it had any fruit. When he reached it, he found nothing but leaves, because it was not the season for figs.
14 Then he said to the tree, "May no one ever eat fruit from you again." And his disciples heard him say it.
15 On reaching Jerusalem, Jesus entered the temple area and began driving out those who were buying and selling there. He overturned the tables of the money changers and the benches of those selling doves,
16 and would not allow anyone to carry merchandise through the temple courts.
17 And as he taught them, he said, "Is it not written:

" 'My house will be called
a house of prayer for all nations'[c]?

But you have made it 'a den of robbers.'[d]"

[c] *17* Isaiah 56:7 [d] *17* Jer. 7:11

NEW LIVING TRANSLATION

10 Bless the coming kingdom of our ancestor David!
Praise God in highest heaven!"*

11 So Jesus came to Jerusalem and went into the Temple. He looked around carefully at everything, and then he left because it was late in the afternoon. Then he went out to Bethany with the twelve disciples.

Jesus Curses the Fig Tree

12 The next morning as they were leaving Bethany, Jesus felt hungry.
13 He noticed a fig tree a little way off that was in full leaf, so he went over to see if he could find any figs on it. But there were only leaves because it was too early in the season for fruit.
14 Then Jesus said to the tree, "May no one ever eat your fruit again!" And the disciples heard him say it.

Jesus Clears the Temple

15 When they arrived back in Jerusalem, Jesus entered the Temple and began to drive out the merchants and their customers. He knocked over the tables of the money changers and the stalls of those selling doves,
16 and he stopped everyone from bringing in merchandise.
17 He taught them, "The Scriptures declare, 'My Temple will be called a place of prayer for all nations,' but you have turned it into a den of thieves."*

11:9-10 Pss 118:25-26; 148:1. **11:17** Isa 56:7; Jer 7:11.

NEW KING JAMES VERSION

10 Blessed *is* the kingdom of our father David
That comes in the name of the Lord![d]
Hosanna in the highest!"

11 And Jesus went into Jerusalem and into the temple. So when He had looked around at all things, as the hour was already late, He went out to Bethany with the twelve.

The Fig Tree Withered

12 Now the next day, when they had come out from Bethany, He was hungry.
13 And seeing from afar a fig tree having leaves, He went to see if perhaps He would find something on it. When He came to it, He found nothing but leaves, for it was not the season for figs.
14 In response Jesus said to it, "Let no one eat fruit from you ever again."
And His disciples heard *it.*

Jesus Cleanses the Temple

15 So they came to Jerusalem. Then Jesus went into the temple and began to drive out those who bought and sold in the temple, and overturned the tables of the money changers and the seats of those who sold doves.
16 And He would not allow anyone to carry wares through the temple.
17 Then He taught, saying to them, "Is it not written, *'My house shall be called a house of prayer for all nations'*?[e] But you have made it a *'den of thieves.'* "[f]

11:10 [d] NU-Text omits *in the name of the Lord.* **11:17** [e] Isaiah 56:7 [f] Jeremiah 7:11

THE MESSAGE

"Blessed the coming kingdom of our father David!"
"Hosanna in highest heaven!"

He entered Jerusalem, then entered the Temple. He looked around, taking it all in. But by now it was late, so he went back to Bethany with the Twelve.

The Cursed Fig Tree

As they left Bethany the next day, he was hungry. Off in the distance he saw a fig tree in full leaf. He came up to it expecting to find something for breakfast, but found nothing but fig leaves. (It wasn't yet the season for figs.) He addressed the tree: "No one is going to eat fruit from you again—ever!" And his disciples overheard him.

They arrived at Jerusalem. Immediately on entering the Temple Jesus started throwing out everyone who had set up shop there, buying and selling. He kicked over the tables of the bankers and the stalls of the pigeon merchants. He didn't let anyone even carry a basket through the Temple. And then he taught them, quoting this text:

"My house was designated a house of prayer for the nations;
You've turned it into a hangout for thieves."

KING JAMES VERSION

18 And the scribes and chief priests heard *it*, and sought how they might destroy him: for they feared him, because all the people was astonished at his doctrine.

19 And when even was come, he went out of the city.

20 And in the morning, as they passed by, they saw the fig tree dried up from the roots.

21 And Peter calling to remembrance saith unto him, Master, behold, the fig tree which thou cursedst is withered away.

22 And Jesus answering saith unto them, Have faith in God.

23 For verily I say unto you, That whosoever shall say unto this mountain, Be thou removed, and be thou cast into the sea; and shall not doubt in his heart, but shall believe that those things which he saith shall come to pass; he shall have whatsoever he saith.

24 Therefore I say unto you, What things soever ye desire, when ye pray, believe that ye receive *them*, and ye shall have *them*.

25 And when ye stand praying, forgive, if ye have ought against any: that your Father also which is in heaven may forgive you your trespasses.

26 But if ye do not forgive, neither will your Father which is in heaven forgive your trespasses.

27 ¶ And they come again to Jerusalem: and as he was walking in the temple, there come to him the chief priests, and the scribes, and the elders,

28 And say unto him, By what authority doest thou

NEW AMERICAN STANDARD BIBLE

18 The chief priests and the scribes heard *this*, and *began* seeking how to destroy Him; for they were afraid of Him, for the whole crowd was astonished at His teaching.

19 When evening came, they would go out of the city.

20 As they were passing by in the morning, they saw the fig tree withered from the roots *up*.

21 Being reminded, Peter *said to Him, "Rabbi, look, the fig tree which You cursed has withered."

22 And Jesus *answered saying to them, "Have faith in God.

23 "Truly I say to you, whoever says to this mountain, 'Be taken up and cast into the sea,' and does not doubt in his heart, but believes that what he says is going to happen, it will be *granted* him.

24 "Therefore I say to you, all things for which you pray and ask, believe that you have received them, and they will be *granted* you.

25 "Whenever you stand praying, forgive, if you have anything against anyone, so that your Father who is in heaven will also forgive you your transgressions.

26 ["[l]But if you do not forgive, neither will your Father who is in heaven forgive your transgressions."]

Jesus' Authority Questioned

27 They *came again to Jerusalem. And as He was walking in the temple, the chief priests and the scribes and the elders *came to Him,

28 and *began* saying to Him, "By what authority are

11:26 [l] Early mss do not contain this v

NEW CENTURY VERSION

18The leading priests and the teachers of the law heard all this and began trying to find a way to kill Jesus. They were afraid of him, because all the people were amazed at his teaching. 19That evening, Jesus and his followers left the city.

The Power of Faith

20The next morning as Jesus was passing by with his followers, they saw the fig tree dry and dead, even to the roots. 21Peter remembered the tree and said to Jesus, "Teacher, look! The fig tree you cursed is dry and dead!"

22Jesus answered, "Have faith in God. 23I tell you the truth, you can say to this mountain, 'Go, fall into the sea.' And if you have no doubts in your mind and believe that what you say will happen, God will do it for you. 24So I tell you to believe that you have received the things you ask for in prayer, and God will give them to you. 25When you are praying, if you are angry with someone, forgive him so that your Father in heaven will also forgive your sins." 26[d]

Leaders Doubt Jesus' Authority

27Jesus and his followers went again to Jerusalem. As Jesus was walking in the Temple, the leading priests, the teachers of the law, and the older leaders came to him.

11:26 [d] **Verse 26** Some early Greek copies add verse 26: "But if you don't forgive other people, then your Father in heaven will not forgive your sins."

CONTEMPORARY ENGLISH VERSION

18The chief priests and the teachers of the Law of Moses heard what Jesus said, and they started looking for a way to kill him. They were afraid of him, because the crowds were completely amazed at his teaching.

19That evening, Jesus and the disciples went outside the city.

A Lesson from the Fig Tree (Matthew 21.20-22)

20As the disciples walked past the fig tree the next morning, they noticed that it was completely dried up, roots and all. 21Peter remembered what Jesus had said to the tree. Then Peter said, "Teacher, look! The tree you put a curse on has dried up."

22Jesus told his disciples:

Have faith in God! 23If you have faith in God and don't doubt, you can tell this mountain to get up and jump into the sea, and it will. 24Everything you ask for in prayer will be yours, if you only have faith.

25-26Whenever you stand up to pray, you must forgive what others have done to you. Then your Father in heaven will forgive your sins.[d]

A Question about Jesus' Authority
(Matthew 21.23-27; Luke 20.1-8)

27Jesus and his disciples returned to Jerusalem. And as he was walking through the temple, the chief priests, the nation's leaders, and the teachers of the Law of Moses

[d] 11.25,26 *your sins*: Some manuscripts add, "But if you do not forgive others, God will not forgive you."

NEW INTERNATIONAL VERSION

18The chief priests and the teachers of the law heard this
and began looking for a way to kill him, for they feared
him, because the whole crowd was amazed at his teaching.
19When evening came, they[e] went out of the city.

The Withered Fig Tree

20In the morning, as they went along, they saw the fig
tree withered from the roots. 21Peter remembered and said
to Jesus, "Rabbi, look! The fig tree you cursed has with-
ered!"
22"Have[f] faith in God," Jesus answered. 23"I tell you the
truth, if anyone says to this mountain, 'Go, throw yourself
into the sea,' and does not doubt in his heart but believes
that what he says will happen, it will be done for him.
24Therefore I tell you, whatever you ask for in prayer,
believe that you have received it, and it will be yours.
25And when you stand praying, if you hold anything
against anyone, forgive him, so that your Father in heaven
may forgive you your sins.[g]"

The Authority of Jesus Questioned

27They arrived again in Jerusalem, and while Jesus was
walking in the temple courts, the chief priests, the teach-
ers of the law and the elders came to him. 28"By what

[e] *19* Some early manuscripts *he* [f] *22* Some early manuscripts *If you have* [g] *25* Some manuscripts *sins. 26But if you do not forgive, neither will your Father who is in heaven forgive your sins.*

NEW LIVING TRANSLATION

18When the leading priests and teachers of religious law
heard what Jesus had done, they began planning how to
kill him. But they were afraid of him because the people
were so enthusiastic about Jesus' teaching. 19That evening
Jesus and the disciples* left the city.
20The next morning as they passed by the fig tree he had
cursed, the disciples noticed it was withered from the
roots. 21Peter remembered what Jesus had said to the tree
on the previous day and exclaimed, "Look, Teacher! The
fig tree you cursed has withered!"
22Then Jesus said to the disciples, "Have faith in God. 23I
assure you that you can say to this mountain, 'May God
lift you up and throw you into the sea,' and your command
will be obeyed. All that's required is that you really believe
and do not doubt in your heart. 24Listen to me! You can
pray for anything, and if you believe, you will have it.
25But when you are praying, first forgive anyone you are
holding a grudge against, so that your Father in heaven
will forgive your sins, too.*"

The Authority of Jesus Challenged

27By this time they had arrived in Jerusalem again. As
Jesus was walking through the Temple area, the leading
priests, the teachers of religious law, and the other leaders
came up to him. They demanded, 28"By whose authority

11:19 Greek *they;* some manuscripts read *he.* **11:25** Some manuscripts add verse 26, *But if you do not forgive, neither will your Father who is in heaven forgive your sins.*

NEW KING JAMES VERSION

18And the scribes and chief priests heard it and sought
how they might destroy Him; for they feared Him, because
all the people were astonished at His teaching. 19When
evening had come, He went out of the city.

The Lesson of the Withered Fig Tree

20Now in the morning, as they passed by, they saw the
fig tree dried up from the roots. 21And Peter, remembering,
said to Him, "Rabbi, look! The fig tree which You cursed
has withered away."
22So Jesus answered and said to them, "Have faith in
God. 23For assuredly, I say to you, whoever says to this
mountain, 'Be removed and be cast into the sea,' and does
not doubt in his heart, but believes that those things he
says will be done, he will have whatever he says. 24There-
fore I say to you, whatever things you ask when you pray,
believe that you receive *them,* and you will have *them.*

Forgiveness and Prayer

25"And whenever you stand praying, if you have any-
thing against anyone, forgive him, that your Father in
heaven may also forgive you your trespasses. 26But if you
do not forgive, neither will your Father in heaven forgive
your trespasses."[g]

Jesus' Authority Questioned

27Then they came again to Jerusalem. And as He was
walking in the temple, the chief priests, the scribes, and

11:26 [g] NU-Text omits this verse.

THE MESSAGE

The high priests and religion scholars heard what was going on and plotted how they might get rid of him. They panicked, for the entire crowd was carried away by his teaching.

At evening, Jesus and his disciples left the city.

In the morning, walking along the road, they saw the fig tree, shriveled to a dry stick. Peter, remembering what had happened the previous day, said to him, "Rabbi, look—the fig tree you cursed is shriveled up!"

Jesus was matter-of-fact: "Embrace this God-life. Really embrace it, and nothing will be too much for you. This mountain, for instance: Just say, 'Go jump in the lake'—no shuffling or shilly-shallying—and it's as good as done. That's why I urge you to pray for absolutely everything, ranging from small to large. Include everything as you embrace this God-life, and you'll get God's everything. And when you assume the posture of prayer, remember that it's not all *asking*. If you have anything against someone, *forgive*—only then will your heavenly Father be inclined to also wipe your slate clean of sins."

His Credentials

Then when they were back in Jerusalem once again, as they were walking through the Temple, the high priests, religion scholars, and leaders came up and demanded,

KING JAMES VERSION

these things? and who gave thee this authority to do these things?

29 And Jesus answered and said unto them, I will also ask of you one question, and answer me, and I will tell you by what authority I do these things.

30 The baptism of John, was *it* from heaven, or of men? answer me.

31 And they reasoned with themselves, saying, If we shall say, From heaven; he will say, Why then did ye not believe him?

32 But if we shall say, Of men; they feared the people: for all *men* counted John, that he was a prophet indeed.

33 And they answered and said unto Jesus, We cannot tell. And Jesus answering saith unto them, Neither do I tell you by what authority I do these things.

12 And he began to speak unto them by parables. A *certain* man planted a vineyard, and set an hedge about *it*, and digged *a place for* the winefat, and built a tower, and let it out to husbandmen, and went into a far country.

2 And at the season he sent to the husbandmen a servant, that he might receive from the husbandmen of the fruit of the vineyard.

3 And they caught *him*, and beat him, and sent *him* away empty.

4 And again he sent unto them another servant; and at him they cast stones, and wounded *him* in the head, and sent *him* away shamefully handled.

NEW AMERICAN STANDARD BIBLE

You doing these things, or who gave You this authority to do these things?"

29 And Jesus said to them, "I will ask you one question, and you answer Me, and *then* I will tell you by what authority I do these things.

30 "Was the baptism of John from heaven, or from men? Answer Me."

31 They *began* reasoning among themselves, saying, "If we say, 'From heaven,' He will say, 'Then why did you not believe him?'

32 "But shall we say, 'From men'?"—they were afraid of the people, for everyone considered John to have been a real prophet.

33 Answering Jesus, they *said, "We do not know." And Jesus *said to them, "Nor will I tell you by what authority I do these things."

Parable of the Vine-growers

12 And He began to speak to them in parables: "A man PLANTED A VINEYARD AND PUT A WALL AROUND IT, AND DUG A VAT UNDER THE WINE PRESS AND BUILT A TOWER, and rented it out to [1]vine-growers and went on a journey.

2 "At the *harvest* time he sent a slave to the vine-growers, in order to receive *some* of the produce of the vineyard from the vine-growers.

3 "They took him, and beat him and sent him away empty-handed.

4 "Again he sent them another slave, and they wounded him in the head, and treated him shamefully.

12:1 [1] Or *tenant farmers,* also vv 2, 7, 9

NEW CENTURY VERSION

28They said to him, "What authority do you have to do these things? Who gave you this authority?"

29Jesus answered, "I will ask you one question. If you answer me, I will tell you what authority I have to do these things. 30Tell me: When John baptized people, was that authority from God or just from other people?"

31They argued about Jesus' question, saying, "If we answer, 'John's baptism was from God,' Jesus will say, 'Then why didn't you believe him?' 32But if we say, 'It was from other people,' the crowd will be against us." (These leaders were afraid of the people, because all the people believed that John was a prophet.)

33So they answered Jesus, "We don't know."

Jesus said to them, "Then I won't tell you what authority I have to do these things."

A Story About God's Son

12 Jesus began to use stories to teach the people. He said, "A man planted a vineyard. He put a wall around it and dug a hole for a winepress and built a tower. Then he leased the land to some farmers and left for a trip. 2When it was time for the grapes to be picked, he sent a servant to the farmers to get his share of the grapes. 3But the farmers grabbed the servant and beat him and sent him away empty-handed. 4Then the man sent another servant. They hit him on the head and showed no respect for

CONTEMPORARY ENGLISH VERSION

came over to him. 28They asked, "What right do you have to do these things? Who gave you this authority?"

29Jesus answered, "I have just one question to ask you. If you answer it, I will tell you where I got the right to do these things. 30Who gave John the right to baptize? Was it God in heaven or merely some human being?"

31They thought it over and said to each other, "We can't say that God gave John this right. Jesus will ask us why we didn't believe John. 32On the other hand, these people think that John was a prophet. So we can't say that it was merely some human who gave John the right to baptize."

They were afraid of the crowd 33and told Jesus, "We don't know."

Jesus replied, "Then I won't tell you who gave me the right to do what I do."

Renters of a Vineyard (Matthew 21.33-46; Luke 20.9-19)

12 Jesus then told them this story:

A farmer once planted a vineyard. He built a wall around it and dug a pit to crush the grapes in. He also built a lookout tower. Then he rented out his vineyard and left the country.

2When it was harvest time, he sent a servant to get his share of the grapes. 3The renters grabbed the servant. They beat him up and sent him away without a thing.

4The owner sent another servant, but the renters beat him on the head and insulted him terribly. 5Then the

NEW INTERNATIONAL VERSION

authority are you doing these things?" they asked. "And
who gave you authority to do this?"
[29]Jesus replied, "I will ask you one question. Answer me,
and I will tell you by what authority I am doing these
things. [30]John's baptism—was it from heaven, or from
men? Tell me!"
[31]They discussed it among themselves and said, "If we
say, 'From heaven,' he will ask, 'Then why didn't you
believe him?' [32]But if we say, 'From men' . . . ." (They
feared the people, for everyone held that John really was a
prophet.)
[33]So they answered Jesus, "We don't know."
Jesus said, "Neither will I tell you by what authority I
am doing these things."

The Parable of the Tenants

12 He then began to speak to them in parables: "A
man planted a vineyard. He put a wall around it,
dug a pit for the winepress and built a watchtower. Then
he rented the vineyard to some farmers and went away on
a journey. [2]At harvest time he sent a servant to the ten-
ants to collect from them some of the fruit of the vineyard.
[3]But they seized him, beat him and sent him away empty-
handed. [4]Then he sent another servant to them; they
struck this man on the head and treated him shamefully.

NEW LIVING TRANSLATION

did you drive out the merchants from the Temple?* Who
gave you such authority?"
[29]"I'll tell who gave me authority to do these things if
you answer one question," Jesus replied. [30]"Did John's
baptism come from heaven or was it merely human?
Answer me!"
[31]They talked it over among themselves. "If we say it
was from heaven, he will ask why we didn't believe him.
[32]But do we dare say it was merely human?" For they were
afraid that the people would start a riot, since everyone
thought that John was a prophet. [33]So they finally replied,
"We don't know."
And Jesus responded, "Then I won't answer your ques-
tion either."

Story of the Evil Farmers

12 Then Jesus began telling them stories: "A man
planted a vineyard, built a wall around it, dug a
pit for pressing out the grape juice, and built a lookout
tower. Then he leased the vineyard to tenant farmers and
moved to another country. [2]At grape-picking time he sent
one of his servants to collect his share of the crop. [3]But the
farmers grabbed the servant, beat him up, and sent him
back empty-handed.
[4]"The owner then sent another servant, but they beat
him over the head and treated him shamefully. [5]The next

11:28 Or *By whose authority do you do these things?*

NEW KING JAMES VERSION

the elders came to Him. [28]And they said to Him, "By what
authority are You doing these things? And who gave You
this authority to do these things?"
[29]But Jesus answered and said to them, "I also will ask
you one question; then answer Me, and I will tell you by
what authority I do these things: [30]The baptism of John—
was it from heaven or from men? Answer Me."
[31]And they reasoned among themselves, saying, "If we
say, 'From heaven,' He will say, 'Why then did you not
believe him?' [32]But if we say, 'From men' "—they feared
the people, for all counted John to have been a prophet
indeed. [33]So they answered and said to Jesus, "We do not
know."
And Jesus answered and said to them, "Neither will I tell
you by what authority I do these things."

The Parable of the Wicked Vinedressers

12 Then He began to speak to them in parables: "A
man planted a vineyard and set a hedge around *it,*
dug *a place for* the wine vat and built a tower. And he
leased it to vinedressers and went into a far country. [2]Now
at vintage-time he sent a servant to the vinedressers, that
he might receive some of the fruit of the vineyard from the
vinedressers. [3]And they took *him* and beat him and sent
him away empty-handed. [4]Again he sent them another ser-
vant, and at him they threw stones,[a] wounded *him* in the
head, and sent *him* away shamefully treated. [5]And again

12:4 [a] NU-Text omits *and at him they threw stones.*

THE MESSAGE

"Show us your credentials. Who authorized you to speak
and act like this?"
Jesus responded, "First let me ask you a question.
Answer my question and then I'll present my credentials.
About the baptism of John—who authorized it: heaven or
humans? Tell me."
They were on the spot, and knew it. They pulled back
into a huddle and whispered, "If we say 'heaven,' he'll ask
us why we didn't believe John; if we say 'humans,' we'll be
up against it with the people because they all hold John up
as a prophet." They decided to concede that round to Jesus.
"We don't know," they said.
Jesus replied, "Then I won't answer your question
either."

The Story About a Vineyard

12 Then Jesus started telling them stories. "A man
planted a vineyard. He fenced it, dug a winepress,
erected a watchtower, turned it over to the farmhands, and
went off on a trip. At the time for harvest, he sent a ser-
vant back to the farmhands to collect his profits.
"They grabbed him, beat him up, and sent him off
empty-handed. So he sent another servant. That one they

KING JAMES VERSION

5 And again he sent another; and him they killed, and
many others; beating some, and killing some.
6 Having yet therefore one son, his wellbeloved, he sent
him also last unto them, saying, They will reverence my
son.
7 But those husbandmen said among themselves, This
is the heir; come, let us kill him, and the inheritance shall
be ours.
8 And they took him, and killed *him*, and cast *him* out
of the vineyard.
9 What shall therefore the lord of the vineyard do? he
will come and destroy the husbandmen, and will give the
vineyard unto others.
10 And have ye not read this scripture; The stone which
the builders rejected is become the head of the corner:
11 This was the Lord's doing, and it is marvellous in
our eyes?
12 And they sought to lay hold on him, but feared the
people: for they knew that he had spoken the parable
against them: and they left him, and went their way.

NEW AMERICAN STANDARD BIBLE

5 "And he sent another, and that one they killed; and *so*
with many others, beating some and killing others.
6 "He had one more *to send,* a beloved son; he sent him
last *of all* to them, saying, 'They will respect my son.'
7 "But those vine-growers said to one another, 'This is
the heir; come, let us kill him, and the inheritance will be
ours!'
8 "They took him, and killed him and threw him out of
the vineyard.
9 "What will the owner of the vineyard do? He will come
and destroy the vine-growers, and will give the vineyard to
others.
10 "Have you not even read this Scripture:

'THE STONE WHICH THE BUILDERS REJECTED,
THIS BECAME THE CHIEF CORNER *stone;*
11 THIS CAME ABOUT FROM THE LORD,
AND IT IS MARVELOUS IN OUR EYES'?"

12 And they were seeking to seize Him, and *yet* they
feared the people, for they understood that He spoke the
parable against them. And *so* they left Him and went
away.

NEW CENTURY VERSION

him. 5 So the man sent another servant, whom they killed.
The man sent many other servants; the farmers beat some
of them and killed others.
6 "The man had one person left to send, his son whom he
loved. He sent him last of all, saying, 'They will respect my
son.'
7 "But the farmers said to each other, 'This son will
inherit the vineyard. If we kill him, it will be ours.' 8 So
they took the son, killed him, and threw him out of the
vineyard.
9 "So what will the owner of the vineyard do? He will
come and kill those farmers and will give the vineyard to
other farmers. 10 Surely you have read this Scripture:

'The stone that the builders rejected
became the cornerstone.
11 The Lord did this,
and it is wonderful to us.' " *Psalm 118:22–23*

12 The Jewish leaders knew that the story was about
them. So they wanted to find a way to arrest Jesus, but
they were afraid of the people. So the leaders left him and
went away.

CONTEMPORARY ENGLISH VERSION

man sent another servant, and they killed him. He kept
sending servant after servant. They beat some of them
and killed others.
6 The owner had a son he loved very much. Finally, he
sent his son to the renters because he thought they
would respect him. 7 But they said to themselves,
"Someday he will own this vineyard. Let's kill him! That
way we can have it all for ourselves." 8 So they grabbed
the owner's son and killed him. Then they threw his
body out of the vineyard.
9 Jesus asked, "What do you think the owner of the vine-
yard will do? He will come and kill those renters and let
someone else have his vineyard. 10 You surely know that
the Scriptures say,

'The stone that the builders
tossed aside
is now the most important
stone of all.
11 This is something
the Lord has done,
and it is amazing to us.' "

12 The leaders knew that Jesus was really talking about
them, and they wanted to arrest him. But because they
were afraid of the crowd, they let him alone and left.

NEW INTERNATIONAL VERSION

5He sent still another, and that one they killed. He sent many others; some of them they beat, others they killed.

6"He had one left to send, a son, whom he loved. He sent him last of all, saying, 'They will respect my son.'

7"But the tenants said to one another, 'This is the heir. Come, let's kill him, and the inheritance will be ours.' 8So they took him and killed him, and threw him out of the vineyard.

9"What then will the owner of the vineyard do? He will come and kill those tenants and give the vineyard to others. 10Haven't you read this scripture:

" 'The stone the builders rejected
has become the capstone[a];
11 the Lord has done this,
and it is marvelous in our eyes'[b]?"

12Then they looked for a way to arrest him because they knew he had spoken the parable against them. But they were afraid of the crowd; so they left him and went away.

[a] *10* Or *cornerstone* [b] *11* Psalm 118:22,23

NEW LIVING TRANSLATION

servant he sent was killed. Others who were sent were either beaten or killed, 6until there was only one left—his son whom he loved dearly. The owner finally sent him, thinking, 'Surely they will respect my son.'

7"But the farmers said to one another, 'Here comes the heir to this estate. Let's kill him and get the estate for ourselves!' 8So they grabbed him and murdered him and threw his body out of the vineyard.

9"What do you suppose the owner of the vineyard will do?" Jesus asked. "I'll tell you—he will come and kill them all and lease the vineyard to others. 10Didn't you ever read this in the Scriptures?

'The stone rejected by the builders
has now become the cornerstone.
11 This is the Lord's doing,
and it is marvelous to see.'* "

12The Jewish leaders wanted to arrest him for using this illustration because they realized he was pointing at them—they were the wicked farmers in his story. But they were afraid to touch him because of the crowds. So they left him and went away.

12:10-11 Ps 118:22-23.

NEW KING JAMES VERSION

he sent another, and him they killed; and many others, beating some and killing some. 6Therefore still having one son, his beloved, he also sent him to them last, saying, 'They will respect my son.' 7But those vinedressers said among themselves, 'This is the heir. Come, let us kill him, and the inheritance will be ours.' 8So they took him and killed *him* and cast *him* out of the vineyard.

9"Therefore what will the owner of the vineyard do? He will come and destroy the vinedressers, and give the vineyard to others. 10Have you not even read this Scripture:

'*The stone which the builders rejected*
Has become the chief cornerstone.
11 *This was the LORD's doing,*
And it is marvelous in our eyes'?"[b]

12And they sought to lay hands on Him, but feared the multitude, for they knew He had spoken the parable against them. So they left Him and went away.

12:11 [b] Psalm 118:22, 23

THE MESSAGE

tarred and feathered. He sent another and that one they killed. And on and on, many others. Some they beat up, some they killed.

"Finally there was only one left: a beloved son. In a last-ditch effort, he sent him, thinking, 'Surely they will respect my son.'

"But those farmhands saw their chance. They rubbed their hands together in greed and said, 'This is the heir! Let's kill him and have it all for ourselves.' They grabbed him, killed him, and threw him over the fence.

"What do you think the owner of the vineyard will do? Right. He'll come and clean house. Then he'll assign the care of the vineyard to others. Read it for yourselves in Scripture:

'That stone the masons threw out
is now the cornerstone!
This is God's work;
we rub our eyes—we can hardly believe it!' "

They wanted to lynch him then and there but, intimidated by public opinion, held back. They knew the story was about them. They got away from there as fast as they could.

KING JAMES VERSION

13 ¶ And they send unto him certain of the Pharisees and of the Herodians, to catch him in *his* words.

14 And when they were come, they say unto him, Master, we know that thou art true, and carest for no man: for thou regardest not the person of men, but teachest the way of God in truth: Is it lawful to give tribute to Caesar, or not?

15 Shall we give, or shall we not give? But he, knowing their hypocrisy, said unto them, Why tempt ye me? bring me a penny, that I may see *it*.

16 And they brought *it*. And he saith unto them, Whose *is* this image and superscription? And they said unto him, Caesar's.

17 And Jesus answering said unto them, Render to Caesar the things that are Caesar's, and to God the things that are God's. And they marvelled at him.

18 ¶ Then come unto him the Sadducees, which say there is no resurrection; and they asked him, saying,

19 Master, Moses wrote unto us, If a man's brother die, and leave *his* wife *behind him*, and leave no children, that his brother should take his wife, and raise up seed unto his brother.

20 Now there were seven brethren: and the first took a wife, and dying left no seed.

21 And the second took her, and died, neither left he any seed: and the third likewise.

NEW AMERICAN STANDARD BIBLE

Jesus Answers the Pharisees, Sadducees and Scribes

13 Then they *sent some of the Pharisees and Herodians to Him in order to trap Him in a statement.

14 They *came and *said to Him, "Teacher, we know that You are truthful and defer to no one; for You are not partial to any, but teach the way of God in truth. Is it lawful to pay a poll-tax to Caesar, or not?

15 "Shall we pay or shall we not pay?" But He, knowing their hypocrisy, said to them, "Why are you testing Me? Bring Me a [2]denarius to look at."

16 They brought *one*. And He *said to them, "Whose likeness and inscription is this?" And they said to Him, "Caesar's."

17 And Jesus said to them, "Render to Caesar the things that are Caesar's, and to God the things that are God's." And they were amazed at Him.

18 *Some* Sadducees (who say that there is no resurrection) *came to Jesus, and *began* questioning Him, saying,

19 "Teacher, Moses wrote for us that IF A MAN'S BROTHER DIES and leaves behind a wife AND LEAVES NO CHILD, HIS BROTHER SHOULD MARRY THE WIFE AND RAISE UP CHILDREN TO HIS BROTHER.

20 "There were seven brothers; and the first took a wife, and died leaving no children.

21 "The second one married her, and died leaving behind no children; and the third likewise;

12:15 [2] The denarius was a day's wages

NEW CENTURY VERSION

Is It Right to Pay Taxes or Not?

[13]Later, the Jewish leaders sent some Pharisees and Herodians[a] to Jesus to trap him in saying something wrong. [14]They came to him and said, "Teacher, we know that you are an honest man. You are not afraid of what other people think about you, because you pay no attention to who they are. And you teach the truth about God's way. Tell us: Is it right to pay taxes to Caesar or not? [15]Should we pay them, or not?"

But knowing what these men were really trying to do, Jesus said to them, "Why are you trying to trap me? Bring me a coin to look at." [16]They gave Jesus a coin, and he asked, "Whose image and name are on the coin?"

They answered, "Caesar's."

[17]Then Jesus said to them, "Give to Caesar the things that are Caesar's, and give to God the things that are God's." The men were amazed at what Jesus said.

Some Sadducees Try to Trick Jesus

[18]Then some Sadducees came to Jesus and asked him a question. (Sadducees believed that people would not rise from the dead.) [19]They said, "Teacher, Moses wrote that if a man's brother dies, leaving a wife but no children, then that man must marry the widow and have children for his brother. [20]Once there were seven brothers. The first brother married and died, leaving no children. [21]So the second brother married the widow, but he also died and had no children. The same thing happened with the third brother.

12:13 [a] **Herodians** A political group that followed Herod and his family.

CONTEMPORARY ENGLISH VERSION

Paying Taxes (Matthew 22.15-22; Luke 20.20-26)

[13]The Pharisees got together with Herod's followers.[a] Then they sent some men to trick Jesus into saying something wrong. [14]They went to him and said, "Teacher, we know that you are honest. You treat everyone with the same respect, no matter who they are. And you teach the truth about what God wants people to do. Tell us, should we pay taxes to the Emperor or not?"

[15]Jesus knew what they were up to, and he said, "Why are you trying to test me? Show me a coin!"

[16]They brought him a silver coin, and he asked, "Whose picture and name are on it?"

"The Emperor's," they answered.

[17]Then Jesus told them, "Give the Emperor what belongs to him and give God what belongs to God." The men were amazed at Jesus.

Life in the Future World (Matthew 22.23-33; Luke 20.27-40)

[18]The Sadducees did not believe that people would rise to life after death. So some of them came to Jesus and said:

[19]Teacher, Moses wrote that if a married man dies and has no children, his brother should marry the widow. Their first son would then be thought of as the son of the dead brother. [20]There were once seven brothers. The first one married, but died without having any children. [21]The second brother married his brother's widow, and he also died without having children. The same thing

[a] 12.13 *Herod's followers*: People who were political followers of the family of Herod the Great and his son Herod Antipas.

NEW INTERNATIONAL VERSION

Paying Taxes to Caesar

13 Later they sent some of the Pharisees and Herodians
to Jesus to catch him in his words. 14 They came to him and
said, "Teacher, we know you are a man of integrity. You
aren't swayed by men, because you pay no attention to
who they are; but you teach the way of God in accordance
with the truth. Is it right to pay taxes to Caesar or not?
15 Should we pay or shouldn't we?"

But Jesus knew their hypocrisy. "Why are you trying to
trap me?" he asked. "Bring me a denarius and let me look
at it." 16 They brought the coin, and he asked them,
"Whose portrait is this? And whose inscription?"

"Caesar's," they replied.

17 Then Jesus said to them, "Give to Caesar what is
Caesar's and to God what is God's."

And they were amazed at him.

Marriage at the Resurrection

18 Then the Sadducees, who say there is no resurrection,
came to him with a question. 19 "Teacher," they said,
"Moses wrote for us that if a man's brother dies and leaves
a wife but no children, the man must marry the widow and
have children for his brother. 20 Now there were seven
brothers. The first one married and died without leaving
any children. 21 The second one married the widow, but he
also died, leaving no child. It was the same with the third.

NEW LIVING TRANSLATION

Taxes for Caesar

13 The leaders sent some Pharisees and supporters of
Herod to try to trap Jesus into saying something for which
he could be arrested. 14 "Teacher," these men said, "we
know how honest you are. You are impartial and don't
play favorites. You sincerely teach the ways of God. Now
tell us—is it right to pay taxes to the Roman government
or not? 15 Should we pay them, or should we not?"

Jesus saw through their hypocrisy and said, "Whom are
you trying to fool with your trick questions? Show me a
Roman coin,* and I'll tell you." 16 When they handed it to
him, he asked, "Whose picture and title are stamped on it?"

"Caesar's," they replied.

17 "Well, then," Jesus said, "give to Caesar what belongs
to him. But everything that belongs to God must be given
to God." This reply completely amazed them.

Discussion about Resurrection

18 Then the Sadducees stepped forward—a group of Jews
who say there is no resurrection after death. They posed
this question: 19 "Teacher, Moses gave us a law that if a
man dies, leaving a wife without children, his brother
should marry the widow and have a child who will be the
brother's heir.* 20 Well, there were seven brothers. The old-
est of them married and then died without children. 21 So
the second brother married the widow, but soon he too
died and left no children. Then the next brother married

12:15 Greek *a denarius*. 12:19 Deut 25:5-6.

NEW KING JAMES VERSION

The Pharisees: Is It Lawful to Pay Taxes to Caesar?

13 Then they sent to Him some of the Pharisees and the
Herodians, to catch Him in *His* words. 14 When they had
come, they said to Him, "Teacher, we know that You are
true, and care about no one; for You do not regard the per-
son of men, but teach the way of God in truth. Is it lawful
to pay taxes to Caesar, or not? 15 Shall we pay, or shall we
not pay?"

But He, knowing their hypocrisy, said to them, "Why do
you test Me? Bring Me a denarius that I may see *it*." 16 So
they brought *it*.

And He said to them, "Whose image and inscription *is*
this?" They said to Him, "Caesar's."

17 And Jesus answered and said to them, "Render to Cae-
sar the things that are Caesar's, and to God the things that
are God's."

And they marveled at Him.

The Sadducees: What About the Resurrection?

18 Then *some* Sadducees, who say there is no resurrec-
tion, came to Him; and they asked Him, saying:
19 "Teacher, Moses wrote to us that if a man's brother dies,
and leaves *his* wife behind, and leaves no children, his
brother should take his wife and raise up offspring for his
brother. 20 Now there were seven brothers. The first took a
wife; and dying, he left no offspring. 21 And the second
took her, and he died; nor did he leave any offspring. And

THE MESSAGE

Paying Taxes to Caesar

They sent some Pharisees and followers of Herod to bait him, hoping to catch him saying something incriminating. They came up and said, "Teacher, we know you have integrity, that you are indifferent to public opinion, don't pander to your students, and teach the way of God accurately. Tell us: Is it lawful to pay taxes to Caesar or not?"

He knew it was a trick question, and said, "Why are you playing these games with me? Bring me a coin and let me look at it." They handed him one.

"This engraving—who does it look like? And whose name is on it?"

"Caesar," they said.

Jesus said, "Give Caesar what is his, and give God what is his."

Their mouths hung open, speechless.

Our Intimacies Will Be With God

Some Sadducees, the party that denies any possibility of resurrection, came up and asked, "Teacher, Moses wrote that if a man dies and leaves a wife but no child, his brother is obligated to marry the widow and have children. Well, there once were seven brothers. The first took a wife. He died childless. The second married her. He died, and

KING JAMES VERSION

22 And the seven had her, and left no seed: last of all the woman died also.

23 In the resurrection therefore, when they shall rise, whose wife shall she be of them? for the seven had her to wife.

24 And Jesus answering said unto them, Do ye not therefore err, because ye know not the scriptures, neither the power of God?

25 For when they shall rise from the dead, they neither marry, nor are given in marriage; but are as the angels which are in heaven.

26 And as touching the dead, that they rise: have ye not read in the book of Moses, how in the bush God spake unto him, saying, I *am* the God of Abraham, and the God of Isaac, and the God of Jacob?

27 He is not the God of the dead, but the God of the living: ye therefore do greatly err.

28 ¶ And one of the scribes came, and having heard them reasoning together, and perceiving that he had answered them well, asked him, Which is the first commandment of all?

29 And Jesus answered him, The first of all the commandments *is*, Hear, O Israel; The Lord our God is one Lord:

30 And thou shalt love the Lord thy God with all thy heart, and with all thy soul, and with all thy mind, and with all thy strength: this *is* the first commandment.

31 And the second *is* like, *namely* this, Thou shalt love thy neighbour as thyself. There is none other commandment greater than these.

NEW AMERICAN STANDARD BIBLE

22 and *so* all seven left no children. Last of all the woman died also.

23 "In the resurrection, [3]when they rise again, which one's wife will she be? For all seven had married her."

24 Jesus said to them, "Is this not the reason you are mistaken, that you do not understand the Scriptures or the power of God?

25 "For when they rise from the dead, they neither marry nor are given in marriage, but are like angels in heaven.

26 "But regarding the fact that the dead rise again, have you not read in the book of Moses, in the *passage* about *the burning* bush, how God spoke to him, saying, 'I AM THE GOD OF ABRAHAM, AND THE GOD OF ISAAC, and the God of Jacob'?

27 "He is not the God of the dead, but of the living; you are greatly mistaken."

28 One of the scribes came and heard them arguing, and recognizing that He had answered them well, asked Him, "What commandment is the foremost of all?"

29 Jesus answered, "The foremost is, 'HEAR, O ISRAEL! THE LORD OUR GOD IS ONE LORD;

30 AND YOU SHALL LOVE THE LORD YOUR GOD WITH ALL YOUR HEART, AND WITH ALL YOUR SOUL, AND WITH ALL YOUR MIND, AND WITH ALL YOUR STRENGTH.'

31 "The second is this, 'YOU SHALL LOVE YOUR NEIGHBOR AS YOURSELF.' There is no other commandment greater than these."

12:23 [3] Early mss do not contain *when they rise again*

NEW CENTURY VERSION

22 All seven brothers married her and died, and none of the
brothers had any children. Finally the woman died too.
23 Since all seven brothers had married her, when people
rise from the dead, whose wife will she be?"
24 Jesus answered, "Why don't you understand? Don't
you know what the Scriptures say, and don't you know
about the power of God? 25 When people rise from the dead,
they will not marry, nor will they be given to someone to
marry. They will be like the angels in heaven. 26 Surely you
have read what God said about people rising from the dead.
In the book in which Moses wrote about the burning bush,[b]
it says that God told Moses, 'I am the God of Abraham, the
God of Isaac, and the God of Jacob.'[c] 27 God is the God of the
living, not the dead. You Sadducees are wrong!"

The Most Important Command

28 One of the teachers of the law came and heard Jesus
arguing with the Sadducees. Seeing that Jesus gave good
answers to their questions, he asked Jesus, "Which of the
commands is most important?"
29 Jesus answered, "The most important command is this:
'Listen, people of Israel! The Lord our God is the only Lord.
30 Love the Lord your God with all your heart, all your soul,
all your mind, and all your strength.'[d] 31 The second com-
mand is this: 'Love your neighbor as you love yourself.'[e]
There are no commands more important than these."

12:26 [b] **burning bush** Read Exodus 3:1–12 in the Old Testament.
12:26 [c] **'I am…Jacob.'** Quotation from Exodus 3:6.
12:30 [d] **'Listen…strength.'** Quotation from Deuteronomy 6:4–5.
12:31 [e] **'Love…yourself.'** Quotation from Leviticus 19:18.

CONTEMPORARY ENGLISH VERSION

happened to the third brother, 22 and finally to all seven
brothers. At last the woman died. 23 When God raises
people from death, whose wife will this woman be? After
all, she had been married to all seven brothers.
24 Jesus answered:
You are completely wrong! You don't know what the
Scriptures teach. And you don't know anything about
the power of God. 25 When God raises people to life, they
won't marry. They will be like the angels in heaven.
26 You surely know about people being raised to life. You
know that in the story about Moses and the burning
bush, God said, "I am the God worshiped by Abraham,
Isaac, and Jacob."[b] 27 He isn't the God of the dead, but of
the living. You Sadducees are all wrong.

The Most Important Commandment

(Matthew 22.34-40; Luke 10.25-28)

28 One of the teachers of the Law of Moses came up while
Jesus and the Sadducees were arguing. When he heard
Jesus give a good answer, he asked him, "What is the most
important commandment?"
29 Jesus answered, "The most important one says:
'People of Israel, you have only one Lord and God. 30 You
must love him with all your heart, soul, mind, and
strength.' 31 The second most important commandment
says: 'Love others as much as you love yourself.' No other
commandment is more important than these."

[b] 12.26 *"I am the God worshiped by Abraham, Isaac, and Jacob"*: Jesus argues that if God is worshiped by these three, they must still be alive, because he is the God of the living.

NEW INTERNATIONAL VERSION

22In fact, none of the seven left any children. Last of all, the woman died too. 23At the resurrection[c] whose wife will she be, since the seven were married to her?"

24Jesus replied, "Are you not in error because you do not know the Scriptures or the power of God? 25When the dead rise, they will neither marry nor be given in marriage; they will be like the angels in heaven. 26Now about the dead rising—have you not read in the book of Moses, in the account of the bush, how God said to him, 'I am the God of Abraham, the God of Isaac, and the God of Jacob'[d]? 27He is not the God of the dead, but of the living. You are badly mistaken!"

The Greatest Commandment

28One of the teachers of the law came and heard them debating. Noticing that Jesus had given them a good answer, he asked him, "Of all the commandments, which is the most important?"

29"The most important one," answered Jesus, "is this: 'Hear, O Israel, the Lord our God, the Lord is one.[e] 30Love the Lord your God with all your heart and with all your soul and with all your mind and with all your strength.'[f] 31The second is this: 'Love your neighbor as yourself.'[g] There is no commandment greater than these."

[c] *23* Some manuscripts *resurrection, when men rise from the dead,*
[d] *26* Exodus 3:6 [e] *29* Or *the Lord our God is one Lord*
[f] *30* Deut. 6:4,5 [g] *31* Lev. 19:18

NEW LIVING TRANSLATION

her and died without children. 22This continued until all the brothers had married her and died, and still there were no children. Last of all, the woman died, too. 23So tell us, whose wife will she be in the resurrection? For all seven were married to her."

24Jesus replied, "Your problem is that you don't know the Scriptures, and you don't know the power of God. 25For when the dead rise, they won't be married. They will be like the angels in heaven. 26But now, as to whether the dead will be raised—haven't you ever read about this in the writings of Moses, in the story of the burning bush? Long after Abraham, Isaac, and Jacob had died, God said to Moses,* 'I am the God of Abraham, the God of Isaac, and the God of Jacob.'* 27So he is the God of the living, not the dead. You have made a serious error."

The Most Important Commandment

28One of the teachers of religious law was standing there listening to the discussion. He realized that Jesus had answered well, so he asked, "Of all the commandments, which is the most important?"

29Jesus replied, "The most important commandment is this: 'Hear, O Israel! The Lord our God is the one and only Lord. 30And you must love the Lord your God with all your heart, all your soul, all your mind, and all your strength.'* 31The second is equally important: 'Love your neighbor as yourself.'* No other commandment is greater than these."

12:26a Greek *in the story of the bush? God said to him.* **12:26b** Exod 3:6. **12:29-30** Deut 6:4-5. **12:31** Lev 19:18.

NEW KING JAMES VERSION

the third likewise. 22So the seven had her and left no offspring. Last of all the woman died also. 23Therefore, in the resurrection, when they rise, whose wife will she be? For all seven had her as wife."

24Jesus answered and said to them, "Are you not therefore mistaken, because you do not know the Scriptures nor the power of God? 25For when they rise from the dead, they neither marry nor are given in marriage, but are like angels in heaven. 26But concerning the dead, that they rise, have you not read in the book of Moses, in the *burning* bush *passage,* how God spoke to him, saying, *'I am the God of Abraham, the God of Isaac, and the God of Jacob'*?[c] 27He is not the God of the dead, but the God of the living. You are therefore greatly mistaken."

The Scribes: Which Is the First Commandment of All?

28Then one of the scribes came, and having heard them reasoning together, perceiving[d] that He had answered them well, asked Him, "Which is the first commandment of all?"

29Jesus answered him, "The first of all the commandments *is: 'Hear, O Israel, the LORD our God, the LORD is one.* 30*And you shall love the LORD your God with all your heart, with all your soul, with all your mind, and with all your strength.'*[e] This *is* the first commandment.[f] 31And the second, like *it, is* this: *'You shall love your neighbor as yourself.'*[g] There is no other commandment greater than these."

12:26 [c] Exodus 3:6, 15 **12:28** [d] NU-Text reads *seeing.*
12:30 [e] Deuteronomy 6:4, 5 [f] NU-Text omits this sentence.
12:31 [g] Leviticus 19:18

THE MESSAGE

still no child. The same with the third. All seven took their turn, but no child. Finally the wife died. When they are raised at the resurrection, whose wife is she? All seven were her husband."

Jesus said, "You're way off base, and here's why: One, you don't know your Bibles; two, you don't know how God works. After the dead are raised up, we're past the marriage business. As it is with angels now, all our ecstasies and intimacies then will be with God. And regarding the dead, whether or not they are raised, don't you ever read the Bible? How God at the bush said to Moses, 'I am—not *was*—the God of Abraham, the God of Isaac, and the God of Jacob'? The living God is God of the *living*, not the dead. You're way, way off base."

The Most Important Commandment

One of the religion scholars came up. Hearing the lively exchanges of question and answer and seeing how sharp Jesus was in his answers, he put in his question: "Which is most important of all the commandments?"

Jesus said, "The first in importance is, 'Listen, Israel: The Lord your God is one; so love the Lord God with all your passion and prayer and intelligence and energy.' And here is the second: 'Love others as well as you love yourself.' There is no other commandment that ranks with these."

KING JAMES VERSION

32 And the scribe said unto him, Well, Master, thou hast said the truth: for there is one God; and there is none other but he:
33 And to love him with all the heart, and with all the understanding, and with all the soul, and with all the strength, and to love *his* neighbour as himself, is more than all whole burnt offerings and sacrifices.
34 And when Jesus saw that he answered discreetly, he said unto him, Thou art not far from the kingdom of God. And no man after that durst ask him *any question*.
35 ¶ And Jesus answered and said, while he taught in the temple, How say the scribes that Christ is the Son of David?
36 For David himself said by the Holy Ghost, The Lord said to my Lord, Sit thou on my right hand, till I make thine enemies thy footstool.
37 David therefore himself calleth him Lord; and whence is he *then* his son? And the common people heard him gladly.
38 And he said unto them in his doctrine, Beware of the

NEW AMERICAN STANDARD BIBLE

32 The scribe said to Him, "Right, Teacher; You have truly stated that HE IS ONE, AND THERE IS NO ONE ELSE BESIDES HIM;
33 AND TO LOVE HIM WITH ALL THE HEART AND WITH ALL THE UNDERSTANDING AND WITH ALL THE STRENGTH, AND TO LOVE ONE'S NEIGHBOR AS HIMSELF, is much more than all burnt offerings and sacrifices."
34 When Jesus saw that he had answered intelligently, He said to him, "You are not far from the kingdom of God." After that, no one would venture to ask Him any more questions.
35 And Jesus *began* to say, as He taught in the temple, "How *is it that* the scribes say that the Christ is the son of David?
36 "David himself said in the Holy Spirit,

'THE LORD SAID TO MY LORD,
"SIT AT MY RIGHT HAND,
UNTIL I PUT YOUR ENEMIES BENEATH YOUR FEET." '

37 "David himself calls Him 'Lord'; so in what sense is He his son?" And the large crowd enjoyed listening to Him.
38 In His teaching He was saying: "Beware of the

NEW CENTURY VERSION

32The man answered, "That was a good answer, Teacher. You were right when you said God is the only Lord and there is no other God besides him. 33One must love God with all his heart, all his mind, and all his strength. And one must love his neighbor as he loves himself. These commands are more important than all the animals and sacrifices we offer to God."

34When Jesus saw that the man answered him wisely, Jesus said to him, "You are close to the kingdom of God." And after that, no one was brave enough to ask Jesus any more questions.

35As Jesus was teaching in the Temple, he asked, "Why do the teachers of the law say that the Christ is the son of David? 36David himself, speaking by the Holy Spirit, said:

'The Lord said to my Lord:
Sit by me at my right side,
until I put your enemies under your control.'
Psalm 110:1

37David himself calls the Christ 'Lord,' so how can the Christ be his son?" The large crowd listened to Jesus with pleasure.

38Jesus continued teaching and said, "Beware of the

CONTEMPORARY ENGLISH VERSION

32The man replied, "Teacher, you are certainly right to say there is only one God. 33It is also true that we must love God with all our heart, mind, and strength, and that we must love others as much as we love ourselves. These commandments are more important than all the sacrifices and offerings that we could possibly make."

34When Jesus saw that the man had given a sensible answer, he told him, "You are not far from God's kingdom." After this, no one dared ask Jesus any more questions.

About David's Son (Matthew 22.41-46; Luke 20.41-44)

35As Jesus was teaching in the temple, he said, "How can the teachers of the Law of Moses say that the Messiah will come from the family of King David? 36The Holy Spirit led David to say,

'The Lord said to my Lord:
Sit at my right side[c]
until I make your enemies
into a footstool for you.'

37If David called the Messiah his Lord, how can the Messiah be his son?"[d]

The large crowd enjoyed listening to Jesus teach.

Jesus Condemns the Pharisees and the Teachers of the Law of Moses (Matthew 23.1-36; Luke 20.45-47)

38As Jesus was teaching, he said:

[c] 12.36 *right side*: The place of power and honor. [d] 12.37 *David . . . his son*: See the note at 10.47.

NEW INTERNATIONAL VERSION

32"Well said, teacher," the man replied. "You are right in saying that God is one and there is no other but him. 33To love him with all your heart, with all your understanding and with all your strength, and to love your neighbor as yourself is more important than all burnt offerings and sacrifices."

34When Jesus saw that he had answered wisely, he said to him, "You are not far from the kingdom of God." And from then on no one dared ask him any more questions.

Whose Son Is the Christ?

35While Jesus was teaching in the temple courts, he asked, "How is it that the teachers of the law say that the Christ[h] is the son of David? 36David himself, speaking by the Holy Spirit, declared:

" 'The Lord said to my Lord:
"Sit at my right hand
until I put your enemies
under your feet." '[i]

37David himself calls him 'Lord.' How then can he be his son?"

The large crowd listened to him with delight.

38As he taught, Jesus said, "Watch out for the teachers

[h] 35 Or *Messiah* [i] 36 Psalm 110:1

NEW LIVING TRANSLATION

32The teacher of religious law replied, "Well said, Teacher. You have spoken the truth by saying that there is only one God and no other. 33And I know it is important to love him with all my heart and all my understanding and all my strength, and to love my neighbors as myself. This is more important than to offer all of the burnt offerings and sacrifices required in the law."

34Realizing this man's understanding, Jesus said to him, "You are not far from the Kingdom of God." And after that, no one dared to ask him any more questions.

Whose Son Is the Messiah?

35Later, as Jesus was teaching the people in the Temple, he asked, "Why do the teachers of religious law claim that the Messiah will be the son of David? 36For David himself, speaking under the inspiration of the Holy Spirit, said,

'The LORD said to my Lord,
Sit in honor at my right hand
until I humble your enemies beneath your feet.'*

37Since David himself called him Lord, how can he be his son at the same time?" And the crowd listened to him with great interest.

38Here are some of the other things he taught them at

12:36 Ps 110:1.

NEW KING JAMES VERSION

32So the scribe said to Him, "Well *said,* Teacher. You have spoken the truth, for there is one God, and there is no other but He. 33And to love Him with all the heart, with all the understanding, with all the soul,[h] and with all the strength, and to love one's neighbor as oneself, is more than all the whole burnt offerings and sacrifices."

34Now when Jesus saw that he answered wisely, He said to him, "You are not far from the kingdom of God."

But after that no one dared question Him.

Jesus: How Can David Call His Descendant Lord?

35Then Jesus answered and said, while He taught in the temple, "How *is it* that the scribes say that the Christ is the Son of David? 36For David himself said by the Holy Spirit:

'The LORD said to my Lord,
"Sit at My right hand,
Till I make Your enemies Your footstool." '[i]

37Therefore David himself calls Him *'Lord'*; how is He *then* his Son?"

And the common people heard Him gladly.

Beware of the Scribes

38Then He said to them in His teaching, "Beware of the

12:33 [h] NU-Text omits *with all the soul.* 12:36 [i] Psalm 110:1

THE MESSAGE

The religion scholar said, "A wonderful answer, Teacher! So lucid and accurate—that God is one and there is no other. And loving him with all passion and intelligence and energy, and loving others as well as you love yourself. Why, that's better than all offerings and sacrifices put together!"

When Jesus realized how insightful he was, he said, "You're almost there, right on the border of God's kingdom."

After that, no one else dared ask a question.

✢

While he was teaching in the Temple, Jesus asked, "How is it that the religion scholars say that the Messiah is David's 'son,' when we all know that David, inspired by the Holy Spirit, said,

'God said to my Master,
"Sit here at my right hand
until I put your enemies under your feet." '

David here designates the Messiah 'my Master'—so how can the Messiah also be his 'son'?"

The large crowd was delighted with what they heard.

He continued teaching. "Watch out for the religion

KING JAMES VERSION

scribes, which love to go in long clothing, and *love* salutations in the marketplaces,

39 And the chief seats in the synagogues, and the uppermost rooms at feasts:

40 Which devour widows' houses, and for a pretence make long prayers: these shall receive greater damnation.

41 ¶ And Jesus sat over against the treasury, and beheld how the people cast money into the treasury: and many that were rich cast in much.

42 And there came a certain poor widow, and she threw in two mites, which make a farthing.

43 And he called *unto him* his disciples, and saith unto them, Verily I say unto you, That this poor widow hath cast more in, than all they which have cast into the treasury:

44 For all *they* did cast in of their abundance; but she of her want did cast in all that she had, *even* all her living.

13 And as he went out of the temple, one of his disciples saith unto him, Master, see what manner of stones and what buildings *are here*!

2 And Jesus answering said unto him, Seest thou these great buildings? there shall not be left one stone upon another, that shall not be thrown down.

3 And as he sat upon the mount of Olives over against the temple, Peter and James and John and Andrew asked him privately,

NEW AMERICAN STANDARD BIBLE

scribes who like to walk around in long robes, and *like* respectful greetings in the market places,

39 and chief seats in the synagogues and places of honor at banquets,

40 who devour widows' houses, and for appearance's sake offer long prayers; these will receive greater condemnation."

The Widow's Mite

41 And He sat down opposite the treasury, and *began* observing how the people were putting money into the treasury; and many rich people were putting in large sums.

42 A poor widow came and put in two small copper coins, which amount to a cent.

43 Calling His disciples to Him, He said to them, "Truly I say to you, this poor widow put in more than all the contributors to the treasury;

44 for they all put in out of their surplus, but she, out of her poverty, put in all she owned, all she had to live on."

Things to Come

13 As He was going out of the temple, one of His disciples *said to Him, "Teacher, behold [1]what wonderful stones and what wonderful buildings!"

2 And Jesus said to him, "Do you see these great buildings? Not one stone will be left upon another which will not be torn down."

3 As He was sitting on the Mount of Olives opposite the temple, Peter and James and John and Andrew were questioning Him privately,

13:1 [1] Lit *how great*

NEW CENTURY VERSION

teachers of the law. They like to walk around wearing fancy clothes, and they love for people to greet them with respect in the marketplaces. 39They love to have the most important seats in the synagogues and at feasts. 40But they cheat widows and steal their houses and then try to make themselves look good by saying long prayers. They will receive a greater punishment."

True Giving

41Jesus sat near the Temple money box and watched the people put in their money. Many rich people gave large sums of money. 42Then a poor widow came and put in two small copper coins, which were only worth a few cents.

43Calling his followers to him, Jesus said, "I tell you the truth, this poor widow gave more than all those rich people. 44They gave only what they did not need. This woman is very poor, but she gave all she had; she gave all she had to live on."

The Temple Will Be Destroyed

13 As Jesus was leaving the Temple, one of his followers said to him, "Look, Teacher! How beautiful the buildings are! How big the stones are!"

2Jesus said, "Do you see all these great buildings? Not one stone will be left on another. Every stone will be thrown down to the ground."

3Later, as Jesus was sitting on the Mount of Olives, opposite the Temple, he was alone with Peter, James, John,

CONTEMPORARY ENGLISH VERSION

Guard against the teachers of the Law of Moses! They love to walk around in long robes and be greeted in the market. 39They like the front seats in the meeting places and the best seats at banquets. 40But they cheat widows out of their homes and pray long prayers just to show off. They will be punished most of all.

A Widow's Offering (Luke 21.1-4)

41Jesus was sitting in the temple near the offering box and watching people put in their gifts. He noticed that many rich people were giving a lot of money. 42Finally, a poor widow came up and put in two coins that were worth only a few pennies. 43Jesus told his disciples to gather around him. Then he said:

I tell you that this poor widow has put in more than all the others. 44Everyone else gave what they didn't need. But she is very poor and gave everything she had. Now she doesn't have a cent to live on.

The Temple Will Be Destroyed (Matthew 24.1, 2; Luke 21.5, 6)

13 As Jesus was leaving the temple, one of his disciples said to him, "Teacher, look at these beautiful stones and wonderful buildings!"

2Jesus replied, "Do you see these huge buildings? They will certainly be torn down! Not one stone will be left in place."

Warning about Trouble (Matthew 24.3-14; Luke 21.7-19)

3Later, as Jesus was sitting on the Mount of Olives across from the temple, Peter, James, John, and Andrew

NEW INTERNATIONAL VERSION

of the law. They like to walk around in flowing robes and be greeted in the marketplaces, [39]and have the most important seats in the synagogues and the places of honor at banquets. [40]They devour widows' houses and for a show make lengthy prayers. Such men will be punished most severely."

The Widow's Offering

[41]Jesus sat down opposite the place where the offerings were put and watched the crowd putting their money into the temple treasury. Many rich people threw in large amounts. [42]But a poor widow came and put in two very small copper coins,[j] worth only a fraction of a penny.[k]

[43]Calling his disciples to him, Jesus said, "I tell you the truth, this poor widow has put more into the treasury than all the others. [44]They all gave out of their wealth; but she, out of her poverty, put in everything—all she had to live on."

Signs of the End of the Age

13 As he was leaving the temple, one of his disciples said to him, "Look, Teacher! What massive stones! What magnificent buildings!"

[2]"Do you see all these great buildings?" replied Jesus. "Not one stone here will be left on another; every one will be thrown down."

[3]As Jesus was sitting on the Mount of Olives opposite the temple, Peter, James, John and Andrew asked him privately,

[j] 42 Greek *two lepta* [k] 42 Greek *kodrantes*

NEW LIVING TRANSLATION

this time: "Beware of these teachers of religious law! For they love to parade in flowing robes and to have everyone bow to them as they walk in the marketplaces. [39]And how they love the seats of honor in the synagogues and at banquets. [40]But they shamelessly cheat widows out of their property, and then, to cover up the kind of people they really are, they make long prayers in public. Because of this, their punishment will be the greater."

The Widow's Offering

[41]Jesus went over to the collection box in the Temple and sat and watched as the crowds dropped in their money. Many rich people put in large amounts. [42]Then a poor widow came and dropped in two pennies.* [43]He called his disciples to him and said, "I assure you, this poor widow has given more than all the others have given. [44]For they gave a tiny part of their surplus, but she, poor as she is, has given everything she has."

Jesus Foretells the Future

13 As Jesus was leaving the Temple that day, one of his disciples said, "Teacher, look at these tremendous buildings! Look at the massive stones in the walls!"

[2]Jesus replied, "These magnificent buildings will be so completely demolished that not one stone will be left on top of another."

[3]Later, Jesus sat on the slopes of the Mount of Olives across the valley from the Temple. Peter, James, John, and

12:42 Greek *2 lepta, which is a kodrantes.*

NEW KING JAMES VERSION

scribes, who desire to go around in long robes, *love* greetings in the marketplaces, [39]the best seats in the synagogues, and the best places at feasts, [40]who devour widows' houses, and for a pretense make long prayers. These will receive greater condemnation."

The Widow's Two Mites

[41]Now Jesus sat opposite the treasury and saw how the people put money into the treasury. And many *who were* rich put in much. [42]Then one poor widow came and threw in two mites,[j] which make a quadrans. [43]So He called His disciples to *Himself* and said to them, "Assuredly, I say to you that this poor widow has put in more than all those who have given to the treasury; [44]for they all put in out of their abundance, but she out of her poverty put in all that she had, her whole livelihood."

Jesus Predicts the Destruction of the Temple

13 Then as He went out of the temple, one of His disciples said to Him, "Teacher, see what manner of stones and what buildings *are here!*"

[2]And Jesus answered and said to him, "Do you see these great buildings? Not *one* stone shall be left upon another, that shall not be thrown down."

The Signs of the Times and the End of the Age

[3]Now as He sat on the Mount of Olives opposite the temple, Peter, James, John, and Andrew asked Him privately,

12:42 [j] Greek *lepta,* very small copper coins worth a fraction of a penny

THE MESSAGE

scholars. They love to walk around in academic gowns, preening in the radiance of public flattery, basking in prominent positions, sitting at the head table at every church function. And all the time they are exploiting the weak and helpless. The longer their prayers, the worse they get. But they'll pay for it in the end."

Sitting across from the offering box, he was observing how the crowd tossed money in for the collection. Many of the rich were making large contributions. One poor widow came up and put in two small coins—a measly two cents. Jesus called his disciples over and said, "The truth is that this poor widow gave more to the collection than all the others put together. All the others gave what they'll never miss; she gave extravagantly what she couldn't afford—she gave her all."

Doomsday Deceivers

13 As he walked away from the Temple, one of his disciples said, "Teacher, look at that stonework! Those buildings!"

Jesus said, "You're impressed by this grandiose architecture? There's not a stone in the whole works that is not going to end up in a heap of rubble."

Later, as he was sitting on Mount Olives in full view of the Temple, Peter, James, John, and Andrew got him off by

KING JAMES VERSION

4 Tell us, when shall these things be? and what *shall be* the sign when all these things shall be fulfilled?

5 ¶ And Jesus answering them began to say, Take heed lest any *man* deceive you:

6 For many shall come in my name, saying, I am *Christ*; and shall deceive many.

7 And when ye shall hear of wars and rumours of wars, be ye not troubled: for *such things* must needs be; but the end *shall* not *be* yet.

8 For nation shall rise against nation, and kingdom against kingdom: and there shall be earthquakes in divers places, and there shall be famines and troubles: these *are* the beginnings of sorrows.

9 But take heed to yourselves: for they shall deliver you up to councils; and in the synagogues ye shall be beaten: and ye shall be brought before rulers and kings for my sake, for a testimony against them.

10 And the gospel must first be published among all nations.

11 But when they shall lead *you*, and deliver you up, take no thought beforehand what ye shall speak, neither do ye premeditate: but whatsoever shall be given you in that hour, that speak ye: for it is not ye that speak, but the Holy Ghost.

12 Now the brother shall betray the brother to death, and the father the son; and children shall rise up against *their* parents, and shall cause them to be put to death.

13 And ye shall be hated of all *men* for my name's sake: but he that shall endure unto the end, the same shall be saved.

NEW AMERICAN STANDARD BIBLE

4 "Tell us, when will these things be, and what *will be* the sign when all these things are going to be fulfilled?"

5 And Jesus began to say to them, "See to it that no one misleads you.

6 "Many will come in My name, saying, 'I am *He!*' and will mislead many.

7 "When you hear of wars and rumors of wars, do not be frightened; *those things* must take place; but *that is* not yet the end.

8 "For nation will rise up against nation, and kingdom against kingdom; there will be earthquakes in various places; there will *also* be famines. These things are *merely* the beginning of birth pangs.

9 "But be on your guard; for they will deliver you to *the* courts, and you will be flogged in *the* synagogues, and you will stand before governors and kings for My sake, as a testimony to them.

10 "The gospel must first be preached to all the nations.

11 "When they arrest you and hand you over, do not worry beforehand about what you are to say, but say whatever is given you in that hour; for it is not you who speak, but *it is* the Holy Spirit.

12 "Brother will betray brother to death, and a father *his* child; and children will rise up against parents and have them put to death.

13 "You will be hated by all because of My name, but the one who endures to the end, he will be saved.

NEW CENTURY VERSION

and Andrew. They asked Jesus, 4"Tell us, when will these
things happen? And what will be the sign that they are
going to happen?"
5Jesus began to answer them, "Be careful that no one
fools you. 6Many people will come in my name, saying, 'I
am the One,' and they will fool many people. 7When you
hear about wars and stories of wars that are coming, don't
be afraid. These things must happen before the end comes.
8Nations will fight against other nations, and kingdoms
against other kingdoms. There will be earthquakes in different places, and there will be times when there is no food
for people to eat. These things are like the first pains when
something new is about to be born.
9"You must be careful. People will arrest you and take
you to court and beat you in their synagogues. You will be
forced to stand before kings and governors, to tell them
about me. This will happen to you because you follow me.
10But before these things happen, the Good News must be
told to all people. 11When you are arrested and judged,
don't worry ahead of time about what you should say. Say
whatever is given you to say at that time, because it will
not really be you speaking; it will be the Holy Spirit.
12"Brothers will give their own brothers to be killed, and
fathers will give their own children to be killed. Children
will fight against their own parents and cause them to be
put to death. 13All people will hate you because you follow
me, but those people who keep their faith until the end will
be saved.

CONTEMPORARY ENGLISH VERSION

came to him in private. 4They asked, "When will these
things happen? What will be the sign that they are about
to take place?"
5Jesus answered:

Watch out and don't let anyone fool you! 6Many will
come and claim to be me. They will use my name and
fool many people.
7When you hear about wars and threats of wars, don't
be afraid. These things will have to happen first, but
that isn't the end. 8Nations and kingdoms will go to war
against each other. There will be earthquakes in many
places, and people will starve to death. But this is just
the beginning of troubles.
9Be on your guard! You will be taken to courts and
beaten with whips in their meeting places. And because
of me, you will have to stand before rulers and kings to
tell about your faith. 10But before the end comes, the
good news must be preached to all nations.
11When you are arrested, don't worry about what you
will say. You will be given the right words when the
time comes. But you will not really be the ones speaking. Your words will come from the Holy Spirit.
12Brothers and sisters will betray each other and have
each other put to death. Parents will betray their own
children, and children will turn against their parents
and have them killed. 13Everyone will hate you because
of me. But if you keep on being faithful right to the end,
you will be saved.

NEW INTERNATIONAL VERSION

4"Tell us, when will these things happen? And what will be the sign that they are all about to be fulfilled?"

5Jesus said to them: "Watch out that no one deceives you. 6Many will come in my name, claiming, 'I am he,' and will deceive many. 7When you hear of wars and rumors of wars, do not be alarmed. Such things must happen, but the end is still to come. 8Nation will rise against nation, and kingdom against kingdom. There will be earthquakes in various places, and famines. These are the beginning of birth pains.

9"You must be on your guard. You will be handed over to the local councils and flogged in the synagogues. On account of me you will stand before governors and kings as witnesses to them. 10And the gospel must first be preached to all nations. 11Whenever you are arrested and brought to trial, do not worry beforehand about what to say. Just say whatever is given you at the time, for it is not you speaking, but the Holy Spirit.

12"Brother will betray brother to death, and a father his child. Children will rebel against their parents and have them put to death. 13All men will hate you because of me, but he who stands firm to the end will be saved.

NEW LIVING TRANSLATION

Andrew came to him privately and asked him, 4"When will all this take place? And will there be any sign ahead of time to show us when all this will be fulfilled?"

5Jesus replied, "Don't let anyone mislead you, 6because many will come in my name, claiming to be the Messiah.* They will lead many astray. 7And wars will break out near and far, but don't panic. Yes, these things must come, but the end won't follow immediately. 8Nations and kingdoms will proclaim war against each other, and there will be earthquakes in many parts of the world, and famines. But all this will be only the beginning of the horrors to come. 9But when these things begin to happen, watch out! You will be handed over to the courts and beaten in the synagogues. You will be accused before governors and kings of being my followers. This will be your opportunity to tell them about me.* 10And the Good News must first be preached to every nation. 11But when you are arrested and stand trial, don't worry about what to say in your defense. Just say what God tells you to. Then it is not you who will be speaking, but the Holy Spirit.

12"Brother will betray brother to death, fathers will betray their own children, and children will rise against their parents and cause them to be killed. 13And everyone will hate you because of your allegiance to me. But those who endure to the end will be saved.

13:6 Greek *name, saying, 'I am.'* **13:9** Or *This will be your testimony against them.*

NEW KING JAMES VERSION

4"Tell us, when will these things be? And what *will be* the sign when all these things will be fulfilled?"

5And Jesus, answering them, began to say: "Take heed that no one deceives you. 6For many will come in My name, saying, 'I am *He,*' and will deceive many. 7But when you hear of wars and rumors of wars, do not be troubled; for *such things* must happen, but the end *is* not yet. 8For nation will rise against nation, and kingdom against kingdom. And there will be earthquakes in various places, and there will be famines and troubles.[a] These *are* the beginnings of sorrows.

9"But watch out for yourselves, for they will deliver you up to councils, and you will be beaten in the synagogues. You will be brought[b] before rulers and kings for My sake, for a testimony to them. 10And the gospel must first be preached to all the nations. 11But when they arrest *you* and deliver you up, do not worry beforehand, or premeditate[c] what you will speak. But whatever is given you in that hour, speak that; for it is not you who speak, but the Holy Spirit. 12Now brother will betray brother to death, and a father *his* child; and children will rise up against parents and cause them to be put to death. 13And you will be hated by all for My name's sake. But he who endures to the end shall be saved.

13:8 [a] NU-Text omits *and troubles.* **13:9** [b] NU-Text and M-Text read *will stand.* **13:11** [c] NU-Text omits *or premeditate.*

THE MESSAGE

himself and asked, "Tell us, when is this going to happen? What sign will we get that things are coming to a head?"

Jesus began, "Watch out for doomsday deceivers. Many leaders are going to show up with forged identities claiming, 'I'm the One.' They will deceive a lot of people. When you hear of wars and rumored wars, keep your head and don't panic. This is routine history, and no sign of the end. Nation will fight nation and ruler fight ruler, over and over. Earthquakes will occur in various places. There will be famines. But these things are nothing compared to what's coming.

"And watch out! They're going to drag you into court. And then it will go from bad to worse, dog-eat-dog, everyone at your throat because you carry my name. You're placed there as sentinels to truth. The Message has to be preached all across the world.

"When they bring you, betrayed, into court, don't worry about what you'll say. When the time comes, say what's on your heart—the Holy Spirit will make his witness in and through you.

"It's going to be brother killing brother, father killing child, children killing parents. There's no telling who will hate you because of me.

"Stay with it—that's what is required. Stay with it to the end. You won't be sorry; you'll be saved.

KING JAMES VERSION

14 ¶ But when ye shall see the abomination of desolation, spoken of by Daniel the prophet, standing where it ought not, (let him that readeth understand,) then let them that be in Judaea flee to the mountains:

15 And let him that is on the housetop not go down into the house, neither enter *therein*, to take any thing out of his house:

16 And let him that is in the field not turn back again for to take up his garment.

17 But woe to them that are with child, and to them that give suck in those days!

18 And pray ye that your flight be not in the winter.

19 For *in* those days shall be affliction, such as was not from the beginning of the creation which God created unto this time, neither shall be.

20 And except that the Lord had shortened those days, no flesh should be saved: but for the elect's sake, whom he hath chosen, he hath shortened the days.

21 And then if any man shall say to you, Lo, here *is* Christ; or, lo, *he is* there; believe *him* not:

22 For false Christs and false prophets shall rise, and shall shew signs and wonders, to seduce, if *it were* possible, even the elect.

23 But take ye heed: behold, I have foretold you all things.

24 ¶ But in those days, after that tribulation, the sun shall be darkened, and the moon shall not give her light,

NEW AMERICAN STANDARD BIBLE

14 "But when you see the ABOMINATION OF DESOLATION standing where it should not be (let the reader understand), then those who are in Judea must flee to the mountains.

15 "The one who is on the housetop must not go down, or go in to get anything out of his house;

16 and the one who is in the field must not turn back to get his coat.

17 "But woe to those who are pregnant and to those who are nursing babies in those days!

18 "But pray that it may not happen in the winter.

19 "For those days will be a *time of* tribulation such as has not occurred since the beginning of the creation which God created until now, and never will.

20 "Unless the Lord had shortened *those* days, no life would have been saved; but for the sake of the elect, whom He chose, He shortened the days.

21 "And then if anyone says to you, 'Behold, here is the Christ'; or, 'Behold, *He is* there'; do not believe *him;*

22 for false Christs and false prophets will arise, and will show signs and wonders, in order to lead astray, if possible, the elect.

23 "But take heed; behold, I have told you everything in advance.

The Return of Christ

24 "But in those days, after that tribulation, THE SUN WILL BE DARKENED AND THE MOON WILL NOT GIVE ITS LIGHT,

NEW CENTURY VERSION

14 "You will see 'the destroying terror'[a] standing where it should not be." (You who read this should understand what it means.) "At that time, the people in Judea should run away to the mountains. 15 If people are on the roofs[b] of their houses, they must not go down or go inside to get anything out of their houses. 16 If people are in the fields, they must not go back to get their coats. 17 At that time, how terrible it will be for women who are pregnant or have nursing babies! 18 Pray that these things will not happen in winter, 19 because those days will be full of trouble. There will be more trouble than there has ever been since the beginning, when God made the world, until now, and nothing as bad will ever happen again. 20 God has decided to make that terrible time short. Otherwise, no one would go on living. But God will make that time short to help the people he has chosen. 21 At that time, someone might say to you, 'Look, there is the Christ!' Or another person might say, 'There he is!' But don't believe them. 22 False Christs and false prophets will come and perform great wonders and miracles. They will try to fool even the people God has chosen, if that is possible. 23 So be careful. I have warned you about all this before it happens.

24 "During the days after this trouble comes,
'the sun will grow dark,
and the moon will not give its light.

13:14 [a] **'the destroying terror'** Mentioned in Daniel 9:27; 12:11 (cf. Daniel 11:31). 13:15 [b] **roofs** In Bible times houses were built with flat roofs. The roof was used for drying things such as flax and fruit. And it was used as an extra room, as a place for worship, and as a place to sleep in the summer.

CONTEMPORARY ENGLISH VERSION

The Horrible Thing (Matthew 24.15-21; Luke 21.20-24)

14 Someday you will see that "Horrible Thing" where it should not be.[a] Everyone who reads this must try to understand! If you are living in Judea at that time, run to the mountains. 15 If you are on the roof[b] of your house, don't go inside to get anything. 16 If you are out in the field, don't go back for your coat. 17 It will be an awful time for women who are expecting babies or nursing young children. 18 Pray that it won't happen in winter.[c] 19 This will be the worst time of suffering since God created the world, and nothing this terrible will ever happen again. 20 If the Lord doesn't make the time shorter, no one will be left alive. But because of his chosen and special ones, he will make the time shorter.

21 If someone should say, "Here is the Messiah!" or "There he is!" don't believe it. 22 False messiahs and false prophets will come and work miracles and signs. They will even try to fool God's chosen ones. 23 But be on your guard! That's why I am telling you these things now.

When the Son of Man Appears
(Matthew 24.29-31; Luke 21.25-28)

24 In those days, right after that time of suffering,

"The sun will become dark,
and the moon
will no longer shine.

[a] 13.14 *where it should not be*: Probably the holy place in the temple. [b] 13.15 *roof*: See the note at 2.4. [c] 13.18 *in winter*: In Palestine the winters are cold and rainy and make travel difficult.

NEW INTERNATIONAL VERSION

14“When you see ‘the abomination that causes desola-
tion’[a] standing where it[b] does not belong—let the reader
understand—then let those who are in Judea flee to the
mountains. 15Let no one on the roof of his house go down
or enter the house to take anything out. 16Let no one in
the field go back to get his cloak. 17How dreadful it will be
in those days for pregnant women and nursing mothers!
18Pray that this will not take place in winter, 19because
those will be days of distress unequaled from the begin-
ning, when God created the world, until now—and never
to be equaled again. 20If the Lord had not cut short those
days, no one would survive. But for the sake of the elect,
whom he has chosen, he has shortened them. 21At that
time if anyone says to you, ‘Look, here is the Christ[c]!’ or,
‘Look, there he is!’ do not believe it. 22For false Christs and
false prophets will appear and perform signs and miracles
to deceive the elect—if that were possible. 23So be on your
guard; I have told you everything ahead of time.
24“But in those days, following that distress,

“ ‘the sun will be darkened,
and the moon will not give its light;

[a] *14* Daniel 9:27; 11:31; 12:11 [b] *14* Or *he*; also in verse 29
[c] *21* Or *Messiah*

NEW LIVING TRANSLATION

14“The time will come when you will see the sacrilegious
object that causes desecration* standing where it should
not be”—reader, pay attention! “Then those in Judea must
flee to the hills. 15A person outside the house* must not go
back into the house to pack. 16A person in the field must
not return even to get a coat. 17How terrible it will be for
pregnant women and for mothers nursing their babies in
those days. 18And pray that your flight will not be in win-
ter. 19For those will be days of greater horror than at any
time since God created the world. And it will never happen
again. 20In fact, unless the Lord shortens that time of
calamity, the entire human race will be destroyed. But for
the sake of his chosen ones he has shortened those days.
21“And then if anyone tells you, ‘Look, here is the
Messiah,’ or, ‘There he is,’ don’t pay any attention. 22For
false messiahs and false prophets will rise up and perform
miraculous signs and wonders so as to deceive, if possible,
even God’s chosen ones. 23Watch out! I have warned you!
24“At that time, after those horrible days end,

the sun will be darkened,
the moon will not give light,

13:14 Greek *the abomination of desolation.* See Dan 9:27; 11:31; 12:11.
13:15 Greek *on the roof.*

NEW KING JAMES VERSION

The Great Tribulation

14“So when you see the *‘abomination of desolation,’*[d]
spoken of by Daniel the prophet,[e] standing where it ought
not” (let the reader understand), “then let those who are in
Judea flee to the mountains. 15Let him who is on the
housetop not go down into the house, nor enter to take
anything out of his house. 16And let him who is in the
field not go back to get his clothes. 17But woe to those who
are pregnant and to those who are nursing babies in those
days! 18And pray that your flight may not be in winter.
19For *in* those days there will be tribulation, such as has
not been since the beginning of the creation which God
created until this time, nor ever shall be. 20And unless the
Lord had shortened those days, no flesh would be saved;
but for the elect’s sake, whom He chose, He shortened the
days.
21“Then if anyone says to you, ‘Look, here *is* the Christ!’
or, ‘Look, *He is* there!’ do not believe it. 22For false christs
and false prophets will rise and show signs and wonders
to deceive, if possible, even the elect. 23But take heed; see,
I have told you all things beforehand.

The Coming of the Son of Man

24“But in those days, after that tribulation, the sun will
be darkened, and the moon will not give its light; 25the

13:14 [d] Daniel 11:31; 12:11 [e] NU-Text omits *spoken of by Daniel the prophet.*

THE MESSAGE

Run for the Hills

“But be ready to run for it when you see the monster of desecration set up where it should *never* be. You who can read, make sure you understand what I’m talking about. If you’re living in Judea at the time, run for the hills; if you’re working in the yard, don’t go back to the house to get anything; if you’re out in the field, don’t go back to get your coat. Pregnant and nursing mothers will have it especially hard. Hope and pray this won’t happen in the middle of winter.

“These are going to be hard days—nothing like it from the time God made the world right up to the present. And there’ll be nothing like it again. If he let the days of trouble run their course, nobody would make it. But because of God’s chosen people, those he personally chose, he has already intervened.

No One Knows the Day or Hour

“If anyone tries to flag you down, calling out, ‘Here’s the Messiah!’ or points, ‘There he is!’ don’t fall for it. Fake Messiahs and lying preachers are going to pop up everywhere. Their impressive credentials and dazzling performances will pull the wool over the eyes of even those who ought to know better. So watch out. I’ve given you fair warning.

“Following those hard times,

‘Sun will fade out,
moon cloud over,

KING JAMES VERSION

25 And the stars of heaven shall fall, and the powers that are in heaven shall be shaken.

26 And then shall they see the Son of man coming in the clouds with great power and glory.

27 And then shall he send his angels, and shall gather together his elect from the four winds, from the uttermost part of the earth to the uttermost part of heaven.

28 ¶ Now learn a parable of the fig tree; When her branch is yet tender, and putteth forth leaves, ye know that summer is near:

29 So ye in like manner, when ye shall see these things come to pass, know that it is nigh, *even* at the doors.

30 Verily I say unto you, that this generation shall not pass, till all these things be done.

31 Heaven and earth shall pass away: but my words shall not pass away.

32 But of that day and *that* hour knoweth no man, no, not the angels which are in heaven, neither the Son, but the Father.

33 Take ye heed, watch and pray: for ye know not when the time is.

34 *For the Son of man is* as a man taking a far journey, who left his house, and gave authority to his servants, and to every man his work, and commanded the porter to watch.

35 Watch ye therefore: for ye know not when the master

NEW AMERICAN STANDARD BIBLE

25 AND THE STARS WILL BE FALLING from heaven, and the powers that are in the heavens will be shaken.

26 "Then they will see THE SON OF MAN COMING IN CLOUDS with great power and glory.

27 "And then He will send forth the angels, and will gather together His elect from the four winds, from the farthest end of the earth to the farthest end of heaven.

28 "Now learn the parable from the fig tree: when its branch has already become tender and puts forth its leaves, you know that summer is near.

29 "Even so, you too, when you see these things happening, recognize that He is near, *right* at the door.

30 "Truly I say to you, this [2]generation will not pass away until all these things take place.

31 "Heaven and earth will pass away, but My words will not pass away.

32 "But of that day or hour no one knows, not even the angels in heaven, nor the Son, but the Father *alone.*

33 "Take heed, keep on the alert; for you do not know when the *appointed* time will come.

34 "*It is* like a man away on a journey, *who* upon leaving his house and putting his slaves in charge, *assigning* to each one his task, also commanded the doorkeeper to stay on the alert.

35 "Therefore, be on the alert—for you do not know when

13:30 [2] Or *race*

NEW CENTURY VERSION

25 The stars will fall from the sky.
And the powers of the heavens will be shaken.'
Isaiah 13:10; 34:4

26 "Then people will see the Son of Man coming in clouds with great power and glory. 27 Then he will send his angels all around the earth to gather his chosen people from every part of the earth and from every part of heaven.

28 "Learn a lesson from the fig tree: When its branches become green and soft and new leaves appear, you know summer is near. 29 In the same way, when you see these things happening, you will know that the time is near, ready to come. 30 I tell you the truth, all these things will happen while the people of this time are still living. 31 Earth and sky will be destroyed, but the words I have said will never be destroyed.

32 "No one knows when that day or time will be, not the angels in heaven, not even the Son. Only the Father knows. 33 Be careful! Always be ready, because you don't know when that time will be. 34 It is like a man who goes on a trip. He leaves his house and lets his servants take care of it, giving each one a special job to do. The man tells the servant guarding the door always to be watchful. 35 So always be ready, because you don't know when the owner

CONTEMPORARY ENGLISH VERSION

25 The stars will fall,
and the powers in the sky[d]
will be shaken."

26 Then the Son of Man will be seen coming in the clouds with great power and glory. 27 He will send his angels to gather his chosen ones from all over the earth.

A Lesson from a Fig Tree (Matthew 24.32-35; Luke 21.29-33)

28 Learn a lesson from a fig tree. When its branches sprout and start putting out leaves, you know summer is near. 29 So when you see all these things happening, you will know that the time has almost come.[e] 30 You can be sure that some of the people of this generation will still be alive when all this happens. 31 The sky and the earth will not last forever, but my words will.

No One Knows the Day or Time (Matthew 24.36-44)

32 No one knows the day or the time. The angels in heaven don't know, and the Son himself doesn't know. Only the Father knows. 33 So watch out and be ready! You don't know when the time will come. 34 It is like what happens when a man goes away for a while and places his servants in charge of everything. He tells each of them what to do, and he orders the guard to keep alert. 35 So be alert! You don't know when the master of

[d] 13.25 *the powers in the sky*: In ancient times people thought that the stars were spiritual powers. [e] 13.29 *the time has almost come*: Or "he (that is, the Son of Man) will soon be here."

NEW INTERNATIONAL VERSION

25 the stars will fall from the sky,
and the heavenly bodies will be shaken.'[d]

26 "At that time men will see the Son of Man coming in clouds with great power and glory. 27 And he will send his angels and gather his elect from the four winds, from the ends of the earth to the ends of the heavens.
28 "Now learn this lesson from the fig tree: As soon as its twigs get tender and its leaves come out, you know that summer is near. 29 Even so, when you see these things happening, you know that it is near, right at the door. 30 I tell you the truth, this generation[e] will certainly not pass away until all these things have happened. 31 Heaven and earth will pass away, but my words will never pass away.

The Day and Hour Unknown

32 "No one knows about that day or hour, not even the angels in heaven, nor the Son, but only the Father. 33 Be on guard! Be alert[f]! You do not know when that time will come. 34 It's like a man going away: He leaves his house and puts his servants in charge, each with his assigned task, and tells the one at the door to keep watch.
35 "Therefore keep watch because you do not know when

[d] *25* Isaiah 13:10; 34:4 [e] *30* Or *race* [f] *33* Some manuscripts *alert and pray*

NEW LIVING TRANSLATION

25 the stars will fall from the sky,
and the powers of heaven will be shaken.*

26 Then everyone will see the Son of Man arrive on the clouds with great power and glory.* 27 And he will send forth his angels to gather together his chosen ones from all over the world—from the farthest ends of the earth and heaven.
28 "Now, learn a lesson from the fig tree. When its buds become tender and its leaves begin to sprout, you know without being told that summer is near. 29 Just so, when you see the events I've described beginning to happen, you can be sure that his return is very near, right at the door. 30 I assure you, this generation* will not pass from the scene until all these events have taken place. 31 Heaven and earth will disappear, but my words will remain forever.
32 "However, no one knows the day or hour when these things will happen, not even the angels in heaven or the Son himself. Only the Father knows. 33 And since you don't know when they will happen, stay alert and keep watch.*
34 "The coming of the Son of Man can be compared with that of a man who left home to go on a trip. He gave each of his employees instructions about the work they were to do, and he told the gatekeeper to watch for his return. 35 So keep a sharp lookout! For you do not know when the

13:24-25 See Isa 13:10; 34:4; Joel 2:10. **13:26** See Dan 7:13. **13:30** Or *this age,* or *this nation.* **13:33** Some manuscripts add *and pray.*

NEW KING JAMES VERSION

stars of heaven will fall, and the powers in the heavens will be shaken. 26 Then they will see the Son of Man coming in the clouds with great power and glory. 27 And then He will send His angels, and gather together His elect from the four winds, from the farthest part of earth to the farthest part of heaven.

The Parable of the Fig Tree

28 "Now learn this parable from the fig tree: When its branch has already become tender, and puts forth leaves, you know that summer is near. 29 So you also, when you see these things happening, know that it[f] is near—at the doors! 30 Assuredly, I say to you, this generation will by no means pass away till all these things take place. 31 Heaven and earth will pass away, but My words will by no means pass away.

No One Knows the Day or Hour

32 "But of that day and hour no one knows, not even the angels in heaven, nor the Son, but only the Father. 33 Take heed, watch and pray; for you do not know when the time is. 34 *It is* like a man going to a far country, who left his house and gave authority to his servants, and to each his work, and commanded the doorkeeper to watch. 35 Watch therefore, for you do not know when the master of the

13:29 [f] Or *He*

THE MESSAGE

Stars fall out of the sky,
cosmic powers tremble.'

"And then they'll see the Son of Man enter in grand style, his Arrival filling the sky—no one will miss it! He'll dispatch the angels; they will pull in the chosen from the four winds, from pole to pole.
"Take a lesson from the fig tree. From the moment you notice its buds form, the merest hint of green, you know summer's just around the corner. And so it is with you. When you see all these things, you know he is at the door. Don't take this lightly. I'm not just saying this for some future generation, but for this one, too—these things will happen. Sky and earth will wear out; my words won't wear out.
"But the exact day and hour? No one knows that, not even heaven's angels, not even the Son. Only the Father. So keep a sharp lookout, for you don't know the timetable. It's like a man who takes a trip, leaving home and putting his servants in charge, each assigned a task, and commanding the gatekeeper to stand watch. So, stay at your post, watching. You have no idea when the homeowner is

KING JAMES VERSION

of the house cometh, at even, or at midnight, or at the cockcrowing, or in the morning:

36 Lest coming suddenly he find you sleeping.

37 And what I say unto you I say unto all, Watch.

14 After two days was *the feast of* the passover, and of unleavened bread: and the chief priests and the scribes sought how they might take him by craft, and put *him* to death.

2 But they said, Not on the feast *day*, lest there be an uproar of the people.

3 And being in Bethany in the house of Simon the leper, as he sat at meat, there came a woman having an alabaster box of ointment of spikenard very precious; and she brake the box, and poured *it* on his head.

4 And there were some that had indignation within themselves, and said, Why was this waste of the ointment made?

5 For it might have been sold for more than three hundred pence, and have been given to the poor. And they murmured against her.

6 And Jesus said, Let her alone; why trouble ye her? she hath wrought a good work on me.

7 For ye have the poor with you always, and whensoever

NEW AMERICAN STANDARD BIBLE

the master of the house is coming, whether in the evening, at midnight, or when the rooster crows, or in the morning—

36 in case he should come suddenly and find you asleep.

37 "What I say to you I say to all, 'Be on the alert!' "

Death Plot and Anointing

14 Now the Passover and Unleavened Bread were two days away; and the chief priests and the scribes were seeking how to seize Him by stealth and kill *Him;*

2 for they were saying, "Not during the festival, otherwise there might be a riot of the people."

3 While He was in Bethany at the home of Simon the leper, and reclining *at the table,* there came a woman with an alabaster vial of very costly perfume of pure nard; *and* she broke the vial and poured it over His head.

4 But some were indignantly *remarking* to one another, "Why has this perfume been wasted?

5 "For this perfume might have been sold for over three hundred [1]denarii, and *the money* given to the poor." And they were scolding her.

6 But Jesus said, "Let her alone; why do you bother her? She has done a good deed to Me.

7 "For you always have the poor with you, and whenever

14:5 [1] The denarius was equivalent to a day's wages

NEW CENTURY VERSION

of the house will come back. It might be in the evening, or at midnight, or in the morning while it is still dark, or when the sun rises. [36]Always be ready. Otherwise he might come back suddenly and find you sleeping. [37]I tell you this, and I say this to everyone: 'Be ready!' "

The Plan to Kill Jesus

14 It was now only two days before the Passover and the Feast of Unleavened Bread. The leading priests and teachers of the law were trying to find a trick to arrest Jesus and kill him. [2]But they said, "We must not do it during the feast, because the people might cause a riot."

A Woman with Perfume for Jesus

[3]Jesus was in Bethany at the house of Simon, who had a skin disease. While Jesus was eating there, a woman approached him with an alabaster jar filled with very expensive perfume, made of pure nard. She opened the jar and poured the perfume on Jesus' head.

[4]Some who were there became upset and said to each other, "Why waste that perfume? [5]It was worth a full year's work. It could have been sold and the money given to the poor." And they got very angry with the woman.

[6]Jesus said, "Leave her alone. Why are you troubling her? She did an excellent thing for me. [7]You will always

CONTEMPORARY ENGLISH VERSION

the house will come back. It could be in the evening or at midnight or before dawn or in the morning. [36]But if he comes suddenly, don't let him find you asleep. [37]I tell everyone just what I have told you. Be alert!

A Plot To Kill Jesus

(Matthew 26.1-5; Luke 22.1, 2; John 11.45-53)

14 It was now two days before Passover and the Festival of Thin Bread. The chief priests and the teachers of the Law of Moses were planning how they could sneak around and have Jesus arrested and put to death. [2]They were saying, "We must not do it during the festival, because the people will riot."

At Bethany (Matthew 26.6-13; John 12.1-8)

[3]Jesus was eating in Bethany at the home of Simon, who once had leprosy,[a] when a woman came in with a very expensive bottle of sweet-smelling perfume.[b] After breaking it open, she poured the perfume on Jesus' head. [4]This made some of the guests angry, and they complained, "Why such a waste? [5]We could have sold this perfume for more than three hundred silver coins and given the money to the poor!" So they started saying cruel things to the woman.

[6]But Jesus said:

Leave her alone! Why are you bothering her? She has done a beautiful thing for me. [7]You will always have the

[a] 14.3 *leprosy*: In biblical times the word "leprosy" was used for many different skin diseases. [b] 14.3 *sweet-smelling perfume*: The Greek text has "perfume made of pure spikenard," a plant used to make perfume.

NEW INTERNATIONAL VERSION

the owner of the house will come back—whether in the evening, or at midnight, or when the rooster crows, or at dawn. 36If he comes suddenly, do not let him find you sleeping. 37What I say to you, I say to everyone: 'Watch!' "

Jesus Anointed at Bethany

14 Now the Passover and the Feast of Unleavened Bread were only two days away, and the chief priests and the teachers of the law were looking for some sly way to arrest Jesus and kill him. 2"But not during the Feast," they said, "or the people may riot."

3While he was in Bethany, reclining at the table in the home of a man known as Simon the Leper, a woman came with an alabaster jar of very expensive perfume, made of pure nard. She broke the jar and poured the perfume on his head.

4Some of those present were saying indignantly to one another, "Why this waste of perfume? 5It could have been sold for more than a year's wages[a] and the money given to the poor." And they rebuked her harshly.

6"Leave her alone," said Jesus. "Why are you bothering her? She has done a beautiful thing to me. 7The poor you

[a] 5 Greek *than three hundred denarii*

NEW LIVING TRANSLATION

homeowner will return—at evening, midnight, early dawn, or late daybreak. 36Don't let him find you sleeping when he arrives without warning. 37What I say to you I say to everyone: Watch for his return!"

Jesus Anointed at Bethany

14 It was now two days before the Passover celebration and the Festival of Unleavened Bread. The leading priests and the teachers of religious law were still looking for an opportunity to capture Jesus secretly and put him to death. 2"But not during the Passover," they agreed, "or there will be a riot."

3Meanwhile, Jesus was in Bethany at the home of Simon, a man who had leprosy. During supper, a woman came in with a beautiful jar of expensive perfume.* She broke the seal and poured the perfume over his head. 4Some of those at the table were indignant. "Why was this expensive perfume wasted?" they asked. 5"She could have sold it for a small fortune* and given the money to the poor!" And they scolded her harshly.

6But Jesus replied, "Leave her alone. Why berate her for doing such a good thing to me? 7You will always have the

14:3 Greek *an alabaster jar of expensive ointment, pure nard.*
14:5 Greek *300 denarii.* A denarius was the equivalent of a full day's wage.

NEW KING JAMES VERSION

house is coming—in the evening, at midnight, at the crowing of the rooster, or in the morning— 36lest, coming suddenly, he find you sleeping. 37And what I say to you, I say to all: Watch!"

The Plot to Kill Jesus

14 After two days it was the Passover and *the Feast* of Unleavened Bread. And the chief priests and the scribes sought how they might take Him by trickery and put *Him* to death. 2But they said, "Not during the feast, lest there be an uproar of the people."

The Anointing at Bethany

3And being in Bethany at the house of Simon the leper, as He sat at the table, a woman came having an alabaster flask of very costly oil of spikenard. Then she broke the flask and poured *it* on His head. 4But there were some who were indignant among themselves, and said, "Why was this fragrant oil wasted? 5For it might have been sold for more than three hundred denarii and given to the poor." And they criticized her sharply.

6But Jesus said, "Let her alone. Why do you trouble her? She has done a good work for Me. 7For you have the poor

THE MESSAGE

returning, whether evening, midnight, cockcrow, or morning. You don't want him showing up unannounced, with you asleep on the job. I say it to you, and I'm saying it to all: Stay at your post. Keep watch."

Anointing His Head

14 In only two days the eight-day Festival of Passover and the Feast of Unleavened Bread would begin. The high priests and religion scholars were looking for a way they could seize Jesus by stealth and kill him. They agreed that it should not be done during Passover Week. "We don't want the crowds up in arms," they said.

Jesus was at Bethany, a guest of Simon the Leper. While he was eating dinner, a woman came up carrying a bottle of very expensive perfume. Opening the bottle, she poured it on his head. Some of the guests became furious among themselves. "That's criminal! A sheer waste! This perfume could have been sold for well over a year's wages and handed out to the poor." They swelled up in anger, nearly bursting with indignation over her.

But Jesus said, "Let her alone. Why are you giving her a hard time? She has just done something wonderfully significant for me. You will have the poor with you every day

KING JAMES VERSION

ye will ye may do them good: but me ye have not always.
8 She hath done what she could: she is come aforehand to anoint my body to the burying.
9 Verily I say unto you, Wheresoever this gospel shall be preached throughout the whole world, *this* also that she hath done shall be spoken of for a memorial of her.
10 And Judas Iscariot, one of the twelve, went unto the chief priests, to betray him unto them.
11 And when they heard *it*, they were glad, and promised to give him money. And he sought how he might conveniently betray him.
12 ¶ And the first day of unleavened bread, when they killed the passover, his disciples said unto him, Where wilt thou that we go and prepare that thou mayest eat the passover?
13 And he sendeth forth two of his disciples, and saith unto them, Go ye into the city, and there shall meet you a man bearing a pitcher of water: follow him.
14 And wheresoever he shall go in, say ye to the goodman of the house, The Master saith, Where is the guestchamber, where I shall eat the passover with my disciples?
15 And he will shew you a large upper room furnished *and* prepared: there make ready for us.

NEW AMERICAN STANDARD BIBLE

you wish you can do good to them; but you do not always have Me.
8 "She has done what she could; she has anointed My body beforehand for the burial.
9 "Truly I say to you, wherever the gospel is preached in the whole world, what this woman has done will also be spoken of in memory of her."
10 Then Judas Iscariot, who was one of the twelve, went off to the chief priests in order to betray Him to them.
11 They were glad when they heard *this,* and promised to give him money. And he *began* seeking how to betray Him at an opportune time.

The Last Passover

12 On the first day of Unleavened Bread, when the Passover *lamb* was being sacrificed, His disciples *said to Him, "Where do You want us to go and prepare for You to eat the Passover?"
13 And He *sent two of His disciples and *said to them, "Go into the city, and a man will meet you carrying a pitcher of water; follow him;
14 and wherever he enters, say to the owner of the house, 'The Teacher says, "Where is My guest room in which I may eat the Passover with My disciples?" '
15 "And he himself will show you a large upper room furnished *and* ready; prepare for us there."

NEW CENTURY VERSION

have the poor with you, and you can help them anytime
you want. But you will not always have me. 8This woman
did the only thing she could do for me; she poured perfume
on my body to prepare me for burial. 9I tell you the truth,
wherever the Good News is preached in all the world, what this woman has done will be told, and people will remember her."

Judas Becomes an Enemy of Jesus

10One of the twelve apostles, Judas Iscariot, went to talk
to the leading priests to offer to hand Jesus over to them.
11These priests were pleased about this and promised to
pay Judas money. So he watched for the best time to turn Jesus in.

Jesus Eats the Passover Meal

12It was now the first day of the Feast of Unleavened Bread when the Passover lamb was sacrificed. Jesus' followers said to him, "Where do you want us to go and prepare for you to eat the Passover meal?"
13Jesus sent two of his followers and said to them, "Go
into the city and a man carrying a jar of water will meet
you. Follow him. 14When he goes into a house, tell the
owner of the house, 'The Teacher says: Where is my guest
room in which I can eat the Passover meal with my followers?' 15The owner will show you a large room upstairs that
is furnished and ready. Prepare the food for us there."

CONTEMPORARY ENGLISH VERSION

poor with you. And whenever you want to, you can give to them. But you won't always have me here with you.
8She has done all she could by pouring perfume on my
body to prepare it for burial. 9You may be sure that wherever the good news is told all over the world, people will remember what she has done. And they will tell others.

Judas and the Chief Priests (Matthew 26.14-16; Luke 22.3-6)

10Judas Iscariot[c] was one of the twelve disciples. He went to the chief priests and offered to help them arrest
Jesus. 11They were glad to hear this, and they promised to pay him. So Judas started looking for a good chance to betray Jesus.

Jesus Eats with His Disciples

(Matthew 26.17-25; Luke 22.7-14, 21-23; John 13.21-30)

12It was the first day of the Festival of Thin Bread, and the Passover lambs were being killed. Jesus' disciples asked him, "Where do you want us to prepare the Passover meal?"
13Jesus said to two of the disciples, "Go into the city,
where you will meet a man carrying a jar of water.[d] Follow
him, 14and when he goes into a house, say to the owner,
'Our teacher wants to know if you have a room where he
can eat the Passover meal with his disciples.' 15The owner
will take you upstairs and show you a large room furnished and ready for you to use. Prepare the meal there."

[c] 14.10 *Iscariot*: See the note at 3.19. [d] 14.13 *a man carrying a jar of water*: A male slave carrying water could mean that the family was rich.

NEW INTERNATIONAL VERSION

will always have with you, and you can help them any time you want. But you will not always have me. 8She did what she could. She poured perfume on my body beforehand to prepare for my burial. 9I tell you the truth, wherever the gospel is preached throughout the world, what she has done will also be told, in memory of her."

10Then Judas Iscariot, one of the Twelve, went to the chief priests to betray Jesus to them. 11They were delighted to hear this and promised to give him money. So he watched for an opportunity to hand him over.

The Lord's Supper

12On the first day of the Feast of Unleavened Bread, when it was customary to sacrifice the Passover lamb, Jesus' disciples asked him, "Where do you want us to go and make preparations for you to eat the Passover?"

13So he sent two of his disciples, telling them, "Go into the city, and a man carrying a jar of water will meet you. Follow him. 14Say to the owner of the house he enters, 'The Teacher asks: Where is my guest room, where I may eat the Passover with my disciples?' 15He will show you a large upper room, furnished and ready. Make preparations for us there."

NEW LIVING TRANSLATION

poor among you, and you can help them whenever you want to. But I will not be here with you much longer. 8She has done what she could and has anointed my body for burial ahead of time. 9I assure you, wherever the Good News is preached throughout the world, this woman's deed will be talked about in her memory."

Judas Agrees to Betray Jesus

10Then Judas Iscariot, one of the twelve disciples, went to the leading priests to arrange to betray Jesus to them. 11The leading priests were delighted when they heard why he had come, and they promised him a reward. So he began looking for the right time and place to betray Jesus.

The Last Supper

12On the first day of the Festival of Unleavened Bread (the day the Passover lambs were sacrificed), Jesus' disciples asked him, "Where do you want us to go to prepare the Passover supper?"

13So Jesus sent two of them into Jerusalem to make the arrangements. "As you go into the city," he told them, "a man carrying a pitcher of water will meet you. Follow him. 14At the house he enters, say to the owner, 'The Teacher asks, Where is the guest room where I can eat the Passover meal with my disciples?' 15He will take you upstairs to a large room that is already set up. That is the place; go ahead and prepare our supper there." 16So the

NEW KING JAMES VERSION

with you always, and whenever you wish you may do them good; but Me you do not have always. 8She has done what she could. She has come beforehand to anoint My body for burial. 9Assuredly, I say to you, wherever this gospel is preached in the whole world, what this woman has done will also be told as a memorial to her."

Judas Agrees to Betray Jesus

10Then Judas Iscariot, one of the twelve, went to the chief priests to betray Him to them. 11And when they heard *it,* they were glad, and promised to give him money. So he sought how he might conveniently betray Him.

Jesus Celebrates the Passover with His Disciples

12Now on the first day of Unleavened Bread, when they killed the Passover *lamb,* His disciples said to Him, "Where do You want us to go and prepare, that You may eat the Passover?"

13And He sent out two of His disciples and said to them, "Go into the city, and a man will meet you carrying a pitcher of water; follow him. 14Wherever he goes in, say to the master of the house, 'The Teacher says, "Where is the guest room in which I may eat the Passover with My disciples?" ' 15Then he will show you a large upper room, furnished *and* prepared; there make ready for us."

THE MESSAGE

for the rest of your lives. Whenever you feel like it, you can do something for them. Not so with me. She did what she could when she could—she pre-anointed my body for burial. And you can be sure that wherever in the whole world the Message is preached, what she just did is going to be talked about admiringly."

Judas Iscariot, one of the Twelve, went to the cabal of high priests, determined to betray him. They couldn't believe their ears, and promised to pay him well. He started looking for just the right moment to hand him over.

Traitor to the Son of Man

On the first of the Days of Unleavened Bread, the day they prepare the Passover sacrifice, his disciples asked him, "Where do you want us to go and make preparations so you can eat the Passover meal?"

He directed two of his disciples, "Go into the city. A man carrying a water jug will meet you. Follow him. Ask the owner of whichever house he enters, 'The Teacher wants to know, "Where is my guest room where I can eat the Passover meal with my disciples?"' He will show you a spacious second-story room, swept and ready. Prepare for us there."

KING JAMES VERSION

16 And his disciples went forth, and came into the city, and found as he had said unto them: and they made ready the passover.

17 And in the evening he cometh with the twelve.

18 And as they sat and did eat, Jesus said, Verily I say unto you, One of you which eateth with me shall betray me.

19 And they began to be sorrowful, and to say unto him one by one, *Is* it I? and another *said, Is* it I?

20 And he answered and said unto them, *It is* one of the twelve, that dippeth with me in the dish.

21 The Son of man indeed goeth, as it is written of him: but woe to that man by whom the Son of man is betrayed! good were it for that man if he had never been born.

22 And as they did eat, Jesus took bread, and blessed, and brake *it*, and gave to them, and said, Take, eat: this is my body.

23 And he took the cup, and when he had given thanks, he gave *it* to them: and they all drank of it.

24 And he said unto them, This is my blood of the new testament, which is shed for many.

25 Verily I say unto you, I will drink no more of the fruit of the vine, until that day that I drink it new in the kingdom of God.

NEW AMERICAN STANDARD BIBLE

16 The disciples went out and came to the city, and found *it* just as He had told them; and they prepared the Passover.

17 When it was evening He *came with the twelve.

18 As they were reclining *at the table* and eating, Jesus said, "Truly I say to you that one of you will betray Me—one who is eating with Me."

19 They began to be grieved and to say to Him one by one, "Surely not I?"

20 And He said to them, "*It is* one of the twelve, one who dips with Me in the bowl.

21 "For the Son of Man *is to* go just as it is written of Him; but woe to that man by whom the Son of Man is betrayed! *It would have been* good for that man if he had not been born."

The Lord's Supper

22 While they were eating, He took *some* bread, and after a blessing He broke *it*, and gave *it* to them, and said, "Take *it;* this is My body."

23 And when He had taken a cup *and* given thanks, He gave *it* to them, and they all drank from it.

24 And He said to them, "This is My blood of the covenant, which is poured out for many.

25 "Truly I say to you, I will never again drink of the fruit of the vine until that day when I drink it new in the kingdom of God."

NEW CENTURY VERSION

16So the followers left and went into the city. Everything happened as Jesus had said, so they prepared the Passover meal.

17In the evening, Jesus went to that house with the twelve. 18While they were all eating, Jesus said, "I tell you the truth, one of you will turn against me—one of you eating with me now."

19The followers were very sad to hear this. Each one began to say to Jesus, "I am not the one, am I?"

20Jesus answered, "It is one of the twelve—the one who dips his bread into the bowl with me. 21The Son of Man will die, just as the Scriptures say. But how terrible it will be for the person who hands the Son of Man over to be killed. It would be better for him if he had never been born."

The Lord's Supper

22While they were eating, Jesus took some bread and thanked God for it and broke it. Then he gave it to his followers and said, "Take it; this is my body."

23Then Jesus took a cup and thanked God for it and gave it to the followers, and they all drank from the cup.

24Then Jesus said, "This is my blood which is the new agreement that God makes with his people. This blood is poured out for many. 25I tell you the truth, I will not drink of this fruit of the vine[a] again until that day when I drink it new in the kingdom of God."

14:25 [a] **fruit of the vine** Product of the grapevine; this may also be translated "wine."

CONTEMPORARY ENGLISH VERSION

16The two disciples went into the city and found everything just as Jesus had told them. So they prepared the Passover meal.

17-18While Jesus and the twelve disciples were eating together that evening, he said, "The one who will betray me is now eating with me."

19This made the disciples sad, and one after another they said to Jesus, "You surely don't mean me!"

20He answered, "It is one of you twelve men who is eating from this dish with me. 21The Son of Man will die, just as the Scriptures say. But it is going to be terrible for the one who betrays me. That man would be better off if he had never been born."

The Lord's Supper

(Matthew 26.26-30; Luke 22.14-23; 1 Corinthians 11.23-25)

22During the meal Jesus took some bread in his hands. He blessed the bread and broke it. Then he gave it to his disciples and said, "Take this. It is my body."

23Jesus picked up a cup of wine and gave thanks to God. He gave it to his disciples, and they all drank some. 24Then he said, "This is my blood, which is poured out for many people, and with it God makes his agreement. 25From now on I will not drink any wine, until I drink new wine in God's

NEW INTERNATIONAL VERSION

16 The disciples left, went into the city and found things just as Jesus had told them. So they prepared the Passover.

17 When evening came, Jesus arrived with the Twelve. 18 While they were reclining at the table eating, he said, "I tell you the truth, one of you will betray me—one who is eating with me."

19 They were saddened, and one by one they said to him, "Surely not I?"

20 "It is one of the Twelve," he replied, "one who dips bread into the bowl with me. 21 The Son of Man will go just as it is written about him. But woe to that man who betrays the Son of Man! It would be better for him if he had not been born."

22 While they were eating, Jesus took bread, gave thanks and broke it, and gave it to his disciples, saying, "Take it; this is my body."

23 Then he took the cup, gave thanks and offered it to them, and they all drank from it.

24 "This is my blood of the[b] covenant, which is poured out for many," he said to them. 25 "I tell you the truth, I will not drink again of the fruit of the vine until that day when I drink it anew in the kingdom of God."

[b] *24* Some manuscripts *the new*

NEW LIVING TRANSLATION

two disciples went on ahead into the city and found everything just as Jesus had said, and they prepared the Passover supper there.

17 In the evening Jesus arrived with the twelve disciples. 18 As they were sitting around the table eating, Jesus said, "The truth is, one of you will betray me, one of you who is here eating with me."

19 Greatly distressed, one by one they began to ask him, "I'm not the one, am I?"

20 He replied, "It is one of you twelve, one who is eating with me now.* 21 For I, the Son of Man, must die, as the Scriptures declared long ago. But how terrible it will be for my betrayer. Far better for him if he had never been born!"

22 As they were eating, Jesus took a loaf of bread and asked God's blessing on it. Then he broke it in pieces and gave it to the disciples, saying, "Take it, for this is my body."

23 And he took a cup of wine and gave thanks to God for it. He gave it to them, and they all drank from it. 24 And he said to them, "This is my blood, poured out for many, sealing the covenant* between God and his people. 25 I solemnly declare that I will not drink wine again until that day when I drink it new in the Kingdom of God."

14:20 Or *one who is dipping bread into the bowl with me.* **14:24** Some manuscripts read *the new covenant.*

NEW KING JAMES VERSION

16 So His disciples went out, and came into the city, and found it just as He had said to them; and they prepared the Passover.

17 In the evening He came with the twelve. 18 Now as they sat and ate, Jesus said, "Assuredly, I say to you, one of you who eats with Me will betray Me."

19 And they began to be sorrowful, and to say to Him one by one, "*Is* it I?" And another *said,* "*Is* it I?"[a]

20 He answered and said to them, "*It is* one of the twelve, who dips with Me in the dish. 21 The Son of Man indeed goes just as it is written of Him, but woe to that man by whom the Son of Man is betrayed! It would have been good for that man if he had never been born."

Jesus Institutes the Lord's Supper

22 And as they were eating, Jesus took bread, blessed and broke *it,* and gave *it* to them and said, "Take, eat;[b] this is My body."

23 Then He took the cup, and when He had given thanks He gave *it* to them, and they all drank from it. 24 And He said to them, "This is My blood of the new[c] covenant, which is shed for many. 25 Assuredly, I say to you, I will no longer drink of the fruit of the vine until that day when I drink it new in the kingdom of God."

14:19 [a] NU-Text omits this sentence. **14:22** [b] NU-Text omits *eat.*
14:24 [c] NU-Text omits *new.*

THE MESSAGE

The disciples left, came to the city, found everything just as he had told them, and prepared the Passover meal.

After sunset he came with the Twelve. As they were at the supper table eating, Jesus said, "I have something hard but important to say to you: One of you is going to hand me over to the conspirators, one who at this moment is eating with me."

Stunned, they started asking, one after another, "It isn't me, is it?"

He said, "It's one of the Twelve, one who eats with me out of the same bowl. In one sense, it turns out that the Son of Man is entering into a way of treachery well-marked by the Scriptures—no surprises here. In another sense, the man who turns him in, turns traitor to the Son of Man—better never to have been born than do this!"

"This Is My Body"

In the course of their meal, having taken and blessed the bread, he broke it and gave it to them. Then he said,

"Take, this is my body."

Taking the chalice, he gave it to them, thanking God, and they all drank from it. He said,

"This is my blood,
God's new covenant,
Poured out for many people.

"I'll not be drinking wine again until the new day when I drink it in the kingdom of God."

KING JAMES VERSION

26 And when they had sung an hymn, they went out into the mount of Olives.

27 And Jesus saith unto them, All ye shall be offended because of me this night: for it is written, I will smite the shepherd, and the sheep shall be scattered.

28 But after that I am risen, I will go before you into Galilee.

29 But Peter said unto him, Although all shall be offended, yet *will* not I.

30 And Jesus saith unto him, Verily I say unto thee, That this day, *even* in this night, before the cock crow twice, thou shalt deny me thrice.

31 But he spake the more vehemently, If I should die with thee, I will not deny thee in any wise. Likewise also said they all.

32 ¶ And they came to a place which was named Gethsemane: and he saith to his disciples, Sit ye here, while I shall pray.

33 And he taketh with him Peter and James and John, and began to be sore amazed, and to be very heavy;

34 And saith unto them, My soul is exceeding sorrowful unto death: tarry ye here, and watch.

NEW AMERICAN STANDARD BIBLE

26 After singing a hymn, they went out to the Mount of Olives.

27 And Jesus *said to them, "You will all fall away, because it is written, 'I WILL STRIKE DOWN THE SHEPHERD, AND THE SHEEP SHALL BE SCATTERED.'

28 "But after I have been raised, I will go ahead of you to Galilee."

29 But Peter said to Him, "*Even* though all may fall away, yet I will not."

30 And Jesus *said to him, "Truly I say to you, that this very night, before a rooster crows twice, you yourself will deny Me three times."

31 But *Peter* kept saying insistently, "*Even* if I have to die with You, I will not deny You!" And they all were saying the same thing also.

Jesus in Gethsemane

32 They *came to a place named Gethsemane; and He *said to His disciples, "Sit here until I have prayed."

33 And He *took with Him Peter and James and John, and began to be very distressed and troubled.

34 And He *said to them, "My soul is deeply grieved to the point of death; remain here and keep watch."

NEW CENTURY VERSION

26After singing a hymn, they went out to the Mount of Olives.

Jesus' Followers Will Leave Him

27Then Jesus told the followers, "You will all stumble in your faith, because it is written in the Scriptures:

'I will kill the shepherd,
and the sheep will scatter.' *Zechariah 13:7*

28But after I rise from the dead, I will go ahead of you into Galilee."

29Peter said, "Everyone else may stumble in their faith, but I will not."

30Jesus answered, "I tell you the truth, tonight before the rooster crows twice you will say three times you don't know me."

31But Peter insisted, "I will never say that I don't know you! I will even die with you!" And all the other followers said the same thing.

Jesus Prays Alone

32Jesus and his followers went to a place called Gethsemane. He said to them, "Sit here while I pray." 33Jesus took Peter, James, and John with him, and he began to be very sad and troubled. 34He said to them, "My heart is full of sorrow, to the point of death. Stay here and watch."

CONTEMPORARY ENGLISH VERSION

kingdom." 26Then they sang a hymn and went out to the Mount of Olives.

Peter's Promise
(Matthew 26.31-35; Luke 22.31-34; John 13.36-38)

27Jesus said to his disciples, "All of you will reject me, as the Scriptures say,

'I will strike down
the shepherd,
and the sheep
will be scattered.'

28But after I am raised to life, I will go ahead of you to Galilee."

29Peter spoke up, "Even if all the others reject you, I never will!"

30Jesus replied, "This very night before a rooster crows twice, you will say three times that you don't know me."

31But Peter was so sure of himself that he said, "Even if I have to die with you, I will never say that I don't know you!" All the others said the same thing.

Jesus Prays (Matthew 26.36-46; Luke 22.39-46)

32Jesus went with his disciples to a place called Gethsemane, and he told them, "Sit here while I pray."

33Jesus took along Peter, James, and John. He was sad and troubled and 34told them, "I am so sad that I feel as if I am dying. Stay here and keep awake with me."

NEW INTERNATIONAL VERSION

26When they had sung a hymn, they went out to the Mount of Olives.

Jesus Predicts Peter's Denial

27"You will all fall away," Jesus told them, "for it is written:

" 'I will strike the shepherd,
and the sheep will be scattered.'[c]

28But after I have risen, I will go ahead of you into Galilee."

29Peter declared, "Even if all fall away, I will not."

30"I tell you the truth," Jesus answered, "today—yes, tonight—before the rooster crows twice[d] you yourself will disown me three times."

31But Peter insisted emphatically, "Even if I have to die with you, I will never disown you." And all the others said the same.

Gethsemane

32They went to a place called Gethsemane, and Jesus said to his disciples, "Sit here while I pray." 33He took Peter, James and John along with him, and he began to be deeply distressed and troubled. 34"My soul is overwhelmed with sorrow to the point of death," he said to them. "Stay here and keep watch."

[c] *27* Zech. 13:7 [d] *30* Some early manuscripts do not have *twice*.

NEW LIVING TRANSLATION

26Then they sang a hymn and went out to the Mount of Olives.

Jesus Predicts Peter's Denial

27"All of you will desert me," Jesus told them. "For the Scriptures say,

'God* will strike the Shepherd,
and the sheep will be scattered.'*

28But after I am raised from the dead, I will go ahead of you to Galilee and meet you there."

29Peter said to him, "Even if everyone else deserts you, I never will."

30"Peter," Jesus replied, "the truth is, this very night, before the rooster crows twice, you will deny me three times."

31"No!" Peter insisted. "Not even if I have to die with you! I will never deny you!" And all the others vowed the same.

Jesus Prays in Gethsemane

32And they came to an olive grove called Gethsemane, and Jesus said, "Sit here while I go and pray." 33He took Peter, James, and John with him, and he began to be filled with horror and deep distress. 34He told them, "My soul is crushed with grief to the point of death. Stay here and watch with me."

14:27a Greek *I.* **14:27b** Zech 13:7.

NEW KING JAMES VERSION

26And when they had sung a hymn, they went out to the Mount of Olives.

Jesus Predicts Peter's Denial

27Then Jesus said to them, "All of you will be made to stumble because of Me this night,[d] for it is written:

*'I will strike the Shepherd,
And the sheep will be scattered.'*[e]

28"But after I have been raised, I will go before you to Galilee."

29Peter said to Him, "Even if all are made to stumble, yet I *will* not *be*."

30Jesus said to him, "Assuredly, I say to you that today, *even* this night, before the rooster crows twice, you will deny Me three times."

31But he spoke more vehemently, "If I have to die with You, I will not deny You!"

And they all said likewise.

The Prayer in the Garden

32Then they came to a place which was named Gethsemane; and He said to His disciples, "Sit here while I pray." 33And He took Peter, James, and John with Him, and He began to be troubled and deeply distressed. 34Then He said to them, "My soul is exceedingly sorrowful, *even* to death. Stay here and watch."

14:27 [d] NU-Text omits *because of Me this night.* [e] Zechariah 13:7

THE MESSAGE

They sang a hymn and then went directly to Mount Olives.

✠

Jesus told them, "You're all going to feel that your world is falling apart and that it's my fault. There's a Scripture that says,

'I will strike the shepherd;
The sheep will go helter-skelter.'

But after I am raised up, I will go ahead of you, leading the way to Galilee."

Peter blurted out, "Even if everyone else is ashamed of you when things fall to pieces, I won't be."

Jesus said, "Don't be so sure. Today, this very night in fact, before the rooster crows twice, you will deny me three times."

He blustered in protest, "Even if I have to die with you, I will never deny you." All the others said the same thing.

Gethsemane

They came to an area called Gethsemane. Jesus told his disciples, "Sit here while I pray." He took Peter, James, and John with him. He plunged into a sinkhole of dreadful agony. He told them, "I feel bad enough right now to die. Stay here and keep vigil with me."

KING JAMES VERSION

35 And he went forward a little, and fell on the ground, and prayed that, if it were possible, the hour might pass from him.

36 And he said, Abba, Father, all things *are* possible unto thee; take away this cup from me: nevertheless not what I will, but what thou wilt.

37 And he cometh, and findeth them sleeping, and saith unto Peter, Simon, sleepest thou? couldest not thou watch one hour?

38 Watch ye and pray, lest ye enter into temptation. The spirit truly *is* ready, but the flesh *is* weak.

39 And again he went away, and prayed, and spake the same words.

40 And when he returned, he found them asleep again, (for their eyes were heavy,) neither wist they what to answer him.

41 And he cometh the third time, and saith unto them, Sleep on now, and take *your* rest: it is enough, the hour is come; behold, the Son of man is betrayed into the hands of sinners.

42 Rise up, let us go; lo, he that betrayeth me is at hand.

43 ¶ And immediately, while he yet spake, cometh Judas, one of the twelve, and with him a great multitude with swords and staves, from the chief priests and the scribes and the elders.

NEW AMERICAN STANDARD BIBLE

35 And He went a little beyond *them,* and fell to the ground and *began* to pray that if it were possible, the hour might pass Him by.

36 And He was saying, "Abba! Father! All things are possible for You; remove this cup from Me; yet not what I will, but what You will."

37 And He *came and *found them sleeping, and *said to Peter, "Simon, are you asleep? Could you not keep watch for one hour?

38 "Keep watching and praying that you may not come into temptation; the spirit is willing, but the flesh is weak."

39 Again He went away and prayed, saying the same words.

40 And again He came and found them sleeping, for their eyes were very heavy; and they did not know what to answer Him.

41 And He *came the third time, and *said to them, "Are you still sleeping and resting? It is enough; the hour has come; behold, the Son of Man is being betrayed into the hands of sinners.

42 "Get up, let us be going; behold, the one who betrays Me is at hand!"

Betrayal and Arrest

43 Immediately while He was still speaking, Judas, one of the twelve, *came up accompanied by a crowd with swords and clubs, *who were* from the chief priests and the scribes and the elders.

NEW CENTURY VERSION

35After walking a little farther away from them, Jesus fell to the ground and prayed that, if possible, he would not have this time of suffering. 36He prayed, "Abba,[b] Father! You can do all things. Take away this cup[c] of suffering. But do what you want, not what I want."

37Then Jesus went back to his followers and found them asleep. He said to Peter, "Simon, are you sleeping? Couldn't you stay awake with me for one hour? 38Stay awake and pray for strength against temptation. The spirit wants to do what is right, but the body is weak."

39Again Jesus went away and prayed the same thing. 40Then he went back to his followers, and again he found them asleep, because their eyes were very heavy. And they did not know what to say to him.

41After Jesus prayed a third time, he went back to his followers and said to them, "Are you still sleeping and resting? That's enough. The time has come for the Son of Man to be handed over to sinful people. 42Get up, we must go. Look, here comes the man who has turned against me."

Jesus Is Arrested

43At once, while Jesus was still speaking, Judas, one of the twelve apostles, came up. With him were many people carrying swords and clubs who had been sent from the leading priests, the teachers of the law, and the older Jewish leaders.

14:36 [b] **Abba** Name that a child called his father. 14:36 [c] **cup** Jesus is talking about the terrible things that will happen to him. Accepting these things will be very hard, like drinking a cup of something bitter.

CONTEMPORARY ENGLISH VERSION

35-36Jesus walked on a little way. Then he knelt down on the ground and prayed, "Father,[e] if it is possible, don't let this happen to me! Father, you can do anything. Don't make me suffer by having me drink from this cup.[f] But do what you want, and not what I want."

37When Jesus came back and found the disciples sleeping, he said to Simon Peter, "Are you asleep? Can't you stay awake for just one hour? 38Stay awake and pray that you won't be tested. You want to do what is right, but you are weak."

39Jesus went back and prayed the same prayer. 40But when he returned to the disciples, he found them sleeping again. They simply could not keep their eyes open, and they did not know what to say.

41When Jesus returned to the disciples the third time, he said, "Are you still sleeping and resting?[g] Enough of that! The time has come for the Son of Man to be handed over to sinners. 42Get up! Let's go. The one who will betray me is already here."

Jesus Is Arrested

(Matthew 26.47-56; Luke 22.47-53; John 18.3-12)

43Jesus was still speaking, when Judas the betrayer came up. He was one of the twelve disciples, and a mob of men armed with swords and clubs were with him. They had been sent by the chief priests, the nation's leaders,

[e] **14.35,36** *Father*: The Greek text has "Abba," which is an Aramaic word meaning "father." [f] **14.35,36** *by having me drink from this cup*: See the note at 10.38. [g] **14.41** *Are you still sleeping and resting?*: Or "You may as well keep on sleeping and resting."

NEW INTERNATIONAL VERSION

[35]Going a little farther, he fell to the ground and prayed that if possible the hour might pass from him. [36]*"Abba,*[e] Father," he said, "everything is possible for you. Take this cup from me. Yet not what I will, but what you will."

[37]Then he returned to his disciples and found them sleeping. "Simon," he said to Peter, "are you asleep? Could you not keep watch for one hour? [38]Watch and pray so that you will not fall into temptation. The spirit is willing, but the body is weak."

[39]Once more he went away and prayed the same thing. [40]When he came back, he again found them sleeping, because their eyes were heavy. They did not know what to say to him.

[41]Returning the third time, he said to them, "Are you still sleeping and resting? Enough! The hour has come. Look, the Son of Man is betrayed into the hands of sinners. [42]Rise! Let us go! Here comes my betrayer!"

Jesus Arrested

[43]Just as he was speaking, Judas, one of the Twelve, appeared. With him was a crowd armed with swords and clubs, sent from the chief priests, the teachers of the law, and the elders.

[e] *36* Aramaic for *Father*

NEW LIVING TRANSLATION

[35]He went on a little farther and fell face down on the ground. He prayed that, if it were possible, the awful hour awaiting him might pass him by. [36]"Abba,* Father," he said, "everything is possible for you. Please take this cup of suffering away from me. Yet I want your will, not mine."

[37]Then he returned and found the disciples asleep. "Simon!" he said to Peter. "Are you asleep? Couldn't you stay awake and watch with me even one hour? [38]Keep alert and pray. Otherwise temptation will overpower you. For though the spirit is willing enough, the body is weak."

[39]Then Jesus left them again and prayed, repeating his pleadings. [40]Again he returned to them and found them sleeping, for they just couldn't keep their eyes open. And they didn't know what to say.

[41]When he returned to them the third time, he said, "Still sleeping? Still resting?* Enough! The time has come. I, the Son of Man, am betrayed into the hands of sinners. [42]Up, let's be going. See, my betrayer is here!"

Jesus Is Betrayed and Arrested

[43]And immediately, as he said this, Judas, one of the twelve disciples, arrived with a mob that was armed with swords and clubs. They had been sent out by the leading priests, the teachers of religious law, and the other leaders.

14:36 *Abba* is an Aramaic term for "father." **14:41** Or *Sleep on, take your rest.*

NEW KING JAMES VERSION

[35]He went a little farther, and fell on the ground, and prayed that if it were possible, the hour might pass from Him. [36]And He said, "Abba, Father, all things *are* possible for You. Take this cup away from Me; nevertheless, not what I will, but what You *will.*"

[37]Then He came and found them sleeping, and said to Peter, "Simon, are you sleeping? Could you not watch one hour? [38]Watch and pray, lest you enter into temptation. The spirit indeed *is* willing, but the flesh *is* weak."

[39]Again He went away and prayed, and spoke the same words. [40]And when He returned, He found them asleep again, for their eyes were heavy; and they did not know what to answer Him.

[41]Then He came the third time and said to them, "Are you still sleeping and resting? It is enough! The hour has come; behold, the Son of Man is being betrayed into the hands of sinners. [42]Rise, let us be going. See, My betrayer is at hand."

Betrayal and Arrest in Gethsemane

[43]And immediately, while He was still speaking, Judas, one of the twelve, with a great multitude with swords and clubs, came from the chief priests and the scribes and the

THE MESSAGE

Going a little ahead, he fell to the ground and prayed for a way out: "Papa, Father, you can—can't you?—get me out of this. Take this cup away from me. But please, not what I want—what do *you* want?"

He came back and found them sound asleep. He said to Peter, "Simon, you went to sleep on me? Can't you stick it out with me a single hour? Stay alert, be in prayer, so you don't enter the danger zone without even knowing it. Don't be naive. Part of you is eager, ready for anything in God; but another part is as lazy as an old dog sleeping by the fire."

He then went back and prayed the same prayer. Returning, he again found them sound asleep. They simply couldn't keep their eyes open, and they didn't have a plausible excuse.

He came back a third time and said, "Are you going to sleep all night? No—you've slept long enough. Time's up. The Son of Man is about to be betrayed into the hands of sinners. Get up. Let's get going. My betrayer has arrived."

A Gang of Ruffians

No sooner were the words out of his mouth when Judas, the one out of the Twelve, showed up, and with him a gang of ruffians, sent by the high priests, religion scholars, and leaders, brandishing swords and clubs. The

KING JAMES VERSION

44 And he that betrayed him had given them a token, saying, Whomsoever I shall kiss, that same is he; take him, and lead *him* away safely.

45 And as soon as he was come, he goeth straightway to him, and saith, Master, master; and kissed him.

46 And they laid their hands on him, and took him.

47 And one of them that stood by drew a sword, and smote a servant of the high priest, and cut off his ear.

48 And Jesus answered and said unto them, Are ye come out, as against a thief, with swords and *with* staves to take me?

49 I was daily with you in the temple teaching, and ye took me not: but the scriptures must be fulfilled.

50 And they all forsook him, and fled.

51 And there followed him a certain young man, having a linen cloth cast about *his* naked *body*; and the young men laid hold on him:

52 And he left the linen cloth, and fled from them naked.

53 ¶ And they led Jesus away to the high priest: and with him were assembled all the chief priests and the elders and the scribes.

54 And Peter followed him afar off, even into the palace of the high priest: and he sat with the servants, and warmed himself at the fire.

NEW AMERICAN STANDARD BIBLE

44 Now he who was betraying Him had given them a signal, saying, "Whomever I kiss, He is the one; seize Him and lead Him away under guard."

45 After coming, Judas immediately went to Him, saying, "Rabbi!" and kissed Him.

46 They laid hands on Him and seized Him.

47 But one of those who stood by drew his sword, and struck the slave of the high priest and cut off his ear.

48 And Jesus said to them, "Have you come out with swords and clubs to arrest Me, as *you would* against a robber?

49 "Every day I was with you in the temple teaching, and you did not seize Me; but *this has taken place* to fulfill the Scriptures."

50 And they all left Him and fled.

51 A young man was following Him, wearing *nothing but* a linen sheet over *his* naked *body;* and they *seized him.

52 But he pulled free of the linen sheet and escaped naked.

Jesus before His Accusers

53 They led Jesus away to the high priest; and all the chief priests and the elders and the scribes *gathered together.

54 Peter had followed Him at a distance, right into the courtyard of the high priest; and he was sitting with the officers and warming himself at the fire.

NEW CENTURY VERSION

44Judas had planned a signal for them, saying, "The man I kiss is Jesus. Arrest him and guard him while you lead him away." 45So Judas went straight to Jesus and said, "Teacher!" and kissed him. 46Then the people grabbed Jesus and arrested him. 47One of his followers standing nearby pulled out his sword and struck the servant of the high priest and cut off his ear.

48Then Jesus said, "You came to get me with swords and clubs as if I were a criminal. 49Every day I was with you teaching in the Temple, and you did not arrest me there. But all these things have happened to make the Scriptures come true." 50Then all of Jesus' followers left him and ran away.

51A young man, wearing only a linen cloth, was following Jesus, and the people also grabbed him. 52But the cloth he was wearing came off, and he ran away naked.

Jesus Before the Leaders

53The people who arrested Jesus led him to the house of the high priest, where all the leading priests, the older Jewish leaders, and the teachers of the law were gathered. 54Peter followed far behind and entered the courtyard of the high priest's house. There he sat with the guards, warming himself by the fire.

CONTEMPORARY ENGLISH VERSION

and the teachers of the Law of Moses. 44Judas had told them ahead of time, "Arrest the man I greet with a kiss.[h] Tie him up tight and lead him away."

45Judas walked right up to Jesus and said, "Teacher!" Then Judas kissed him, 46and the men grabbed Jesus and arrested him.

47Someone standing there pulled out a sword. He struck the servant of the high priest and cut off his ear.

48Jesus said to the mob, "Why do you come with swords and clubs to arrest me like a criminal? 49Day after day I was with you and taught in the temple, and you didn't arrest me. But what the Scriptures say must come true."

50All of Jesus' disciples ran off and left him. 51One of them was a young man who was wearing only a linen cloth. And when the men grabbed him, 52he left the cloth behind and ran away naked.

Jesus Is Questioned by the Council

(Matthew 26.57-68; Luke 22.54, 55, 63-71; John 18.13, 14, 19-24)

53Jesus was led off to the high priest. Then the chief priests, the nation's leaders, and the teachers of the Law of Moses all met together. 54Peter had followed at a distance. And when he reached the courtyard of the high priest's house, he sat down with the guards to warm himself beside a fire.

[h] **14.44** *greet with a kiss*: It was the custom for people to greet each other with a kiss on the cheek.

NEW INTERNATIONAL VERSION

44Now the betrayer had arranged a signal with them: "The one I kiss is the man; arrest him and lead him away under guard." 45Going at once to Jesus, Judas said, "Rabbi!" and kissed him. 46The men seized Jesus and arrested him. 47Then one of those standing near drew his sword and struck the servant of the high priest, cutting off his ear.

48"Am I leading a rebellion," said Jesus, "that you have come out with swords and clubs to capture me? 49Every day I was with you, teaching in the temple courts, and you did not arrest me. But the Scriptures must be fulfilled." 50Then everyone deserted him and fled.

51A young man, wearing nothing but a linen garment, was following Jesus. When they seized him, 52he fled naked, leaving his garment behind.

Before the Sanhedrin

53They took Jesus to the high priest, and all the chief priests, elders and teachers of the law came together. 54Peter followed him at a distance, right into the courtyard of the high priest. There he sat with the guards and warmed himself at the fire.

NEW LIVING TRANSLATION

44Judas had given them a prearranged signal: "You will know which one to arrest when I go over and give him the kiss of greeting. Then you can take him away under guard."

45As soon as they arrived, Judas walked up to Jesus. "Teacher!" he exclaimed, and gave him the kiss. 46Then the others grabbed Jesus and arrested him. 47But someone pulled out a sword and slashed off an ear of the high priest's servant.

48Jesus asked them, "Am I some dangerous criminal, that you come armed with swords and clubs to arrest me? 49Why didn't you arrest me in the Temple? I was there teaching every day. But these things are happening to fulfill what the Scriptures say about me."

50Meanwhile, all his disciples deserted him and ran away. 51There was a young man following along behind, clothed only in a linen nightshirt. When the mob tried to grab him, 52they tore off his clothes, but he escaped and ran away naked.

Jesus before the Council

53Jesus was led to the high priest's home where the leading priests, other leaders, and teachers of religious law had gathered. 54Meanwhile, Peter followed far behind and then slipped inside the gates of the high priest's courtyard. For a while he sat with the guards, warming himself by the fire.

NEW KING JAMES VERSION

elders. 44Now His betrayer had given them a signal, saying, "Whomever I kiss, He is the One; seize Him and lead *Him* away safely."

45As soon as he had come, immediately he went up to Him and said to Him, "Rabbi, Rabbi!" and kissed Him.

46Then they laid their hands on Him and took Him. 47And one of those who stood by drew his sword and struck the servant of the high priest, and cut off his ear.

48Then Jesus answered and said to them, "Have you come out, as against a robber, with swords and clubs to take Me? 49I was daily with you in the temple teaching, and you did not seize Me. But the Scriptures must be fulfilled."

50Then they all forsook Him and fled.

A Young Man Flees Naked

51Now a certain young man followed Him, having a linen cloth thrown around *his* naked *body.* And the young men laid hold of him, 52and he left the linen cloth and fled from them naked.

Jesus Faces the Sanhedrin

53And they led Jesus away to the high priest; and with him were assembled all the chief priests, the elders, and the scribes. 54But Peter followed Him at a distance, right into the courtyard of the high priest. And he sat with the servants and warmed himself at the fire.

THE MESSAGE

betrayer had worked out a signal with them: "The one I kiss, that's the one—seize him. Make sure he doesn't get away." He went straight to Jesus and said, "Rabbi!" and kissed him. The others then grabbed him and roughed him up. One of the men standing there unsheathed his sword, swung, and came down on the Chief Priest's servant, lopping off the man's ear.

Jesus said to them, "What is this, coming after me with swords and clubs as if I were a dangerous criminal? Day after day I've been sitting in the Temple teaching, and you never so much as lifted a hand against me. What you in fact have done is confirm the prophetic writings." All the disciples cut and ran.

A young man was following along. All he had on was a bedsheet. Some of the men grabbed him but he got away, running off naked, leaving them holding the sheet.

Condemned to Death

They led Jesus to the Chief Priest, where the high priests, religious leaders, and scholars had gathered together. Peter followed at a safe distance until they got to the Chief Priest's courtyard, where he mingled with the servants and warmed himself at the fire.

KING JAMES VERSION

55 And the chief priests and all the council sought for witness against Jesus to put him to death; and found none.
56 For many bare false witness against him, but their witness agreed not together.
57 And there arose certain, and bare false witness against him, saying,
58 We heard him say, I will destroy this temple that is made with hands, and within three days I will build another made without hands.
59 But neither so did their witness agree together.
60 And the high priest stood up in the midst, and asked Jesus, saying, Answerest thou nothing? what *is it which* these witness against thee?
61 But he held his peace, and answered nothing. Again the high priest asked him, and said unto him, Art thou the Christ, the Son of the Blessed?
62 And Jesus said, I am: and ye shall see the Son of man sitting on the right hand of power, and coming in the clouds of heaven.
63 Then the high priest rent his clothes, and saith, What need we any further witnesses?
64 Ye have heard the blasphemy: what think ye? And they all condemned him to be guilty of death.

NEW AMERICAN STANDARD BIBLE

55 Now the chief priests and the whole [2]Council kept trying to obtain testimony against Jesus to put Him to death, and they were not finding any.
56 For many were giving false testimony against Him, but their testimony was not consistent.
57 Some stood up and *began* to give false testimony against Him, saying,
58 "We heard Him say, 'I will destroy this temple made with hands, and in three days I will build another made without hands.' "
59 Not even in this respect was their testimony consistent.
60 The high priest stood up *and came* forward and questioned Jesus, saying, "Do You not answer? What is it that these men are testifying against You?"
61 But He kept silent and did not answer. Again the high priest was questioning Him, and saying to Him, "Are You the Christ, the Son of the Blessed *One?*"
62 And Jesus said, "I am; and you shall see THE SON OF MAN SITTING AT THE RIGHT HAND OF POWER, and COMING WITH THE CLOUDS OF HEAVEN."
63 Tearing his clothes, the high priest *said, "What further need do we have of witnesses?
64 "You have heard the blasphemy; how does it seem to you?" And they all condemned Him to be deserving of death.

14:55 [2] Or *Sanhedrin*

NEW CENTURY VERSION

55The leading priests and the whole Jewish council tried to find something that Jesus had done wrong so they could kill him. But the council could find no proof of anything.
56Many people came and told false things about him, but all said different things—none of them agreed.
57Then some people stood up and lied about Jesus, saying, 58"We heard this man say, 'I will destroy this Temple that people made. And three days later, I will build another Temple not made by people.' " 59But even the things these people said did not agree.
60Then the high priest stood before them and asked Jesus, "Aren't you going to answer? Don't you have something to say about their charges against you?" 61But Jesus said nothing; he did not answer.
The high priest asked Jesus another question: "Are you the Christ, the Son of the blessed God?"
62Jesus answered, "I am. And in the future you will see the Son of Man sitting at the right hand of God, the Powerful One, and coming on clouds in the sky."
63When the high priest heard this, he tore his clothes and said, "We don't need any more witnesses! 64You all heard him say these things against God. What do you think?"
They all said that Jesus was guilty and should die. 65Some

CONTEMPORARY ENGLISH VERSION

55The chief priests and the whole council tried to find someone to accuse Jesus of a crime, so they could put him to death. But they could not find anyone to accuse him.
56Many people did tell lies against Jesus, but they did not agree on what they said. 57Finally, some men stood up and lied about him. They said, 58"We heard him say he would tear down this temple that we built. He also claimed that in three days he would build another one without any help."
59But even then they did not agree on what they said.
60The high priest stood up in the council and asked Jesus, "Why don't you say something in your own defense? Don't you hear the charges they are making against you?" 61But Jesus kept quiet and did not say a word. The high priest asked him another question, "Are you the Messiah, the Son of the glorious God?"[i]
62"Yes, I am!" Jesus answered.

"Soon you will see
the Son of Man
sitting at the right side[j]
of God All-Powerful,
and coming with the clouds
of heaven."

63At once the high priest ripped his robe apart and shouted, "Why do we need more witnesses? 64You heard him claim to be God! What is your decision?" They all agreed that he should be put to death.

[i] 14.61 *Son of the glorious God*: "Son of God" was one of the titles used for the kings of Israel. [j] 14.62 *right side*: See the note at 12.36.

NEW INTERNATIONAL VERSION

55 The chief priests and the whole Sanhedrin were look-
ing for evidence against Jesus so that they could put him
to death, but they did not find any. 56 Many testified falsely
against him, but their statements did not agree.
57 Then some stood up and gave this false testimony
against him: 58 "We heard him say, 'I will destroy this
man-made temple and in three days will build another, not
made by man.' " 59 Yet even then their testimony did not
agree.
60 Then the high priest stood up before them and asked
Jesus, "Are you not going to answer? What is this testimo-
ny that these men are bringing against you?" 61 But Jesus
remained silent and gave no answer.
Again the high priest asked him, "Are you the Christ,[f]
the Son of the Blessed One?"
62 "I am," said Jesus. "And you will see the Son of Man
sitting at the right hand of the Mighty One and coming on
the clouds of heaven."
63 The high priest tore his clothes. "Why do we need any
more witnesses?" he asked. 64 "You have heard the blas-
phemy. What do you think?"
They all condemned him as worthy of death. 65 Then

f 61 Or *Messiah*

NEW LIVING TRANSLATION

55 Inside, the leading priests and the entire high council*
were trying to find witnesses who would testify against
Jesus, so they could put him to death. But their efforts
were in vain. 56 Many false witnesses spoke against him,
but they contradicted each other. 57 Finally, some men
stood up to testify against him with this lie: 58 "We heard
him say, 'I will destroy this Temple made with human
hands, and in three days I will build another, made with-
out human hands.' " 59 But even then they didn't get their
stories straight!
60 Then the high priest stood up before the others and
asked Jesus, "Well, aren't you going to answer these
charges? What do you have to say for yourself?" 61 Jesus
made no reply. Then the high priest asked him, "Are you
the Messiah, the Son of the blessed God?"
62 Jesus said, "I am, and you will see me, the Son of Man,
sitting at God's right hand in the place of power and com-
ing back on the clouds of heaven."*
63 Then the high priest tore his clothing to show his hor-
ror and said, "Why do we need other witnesses? 64 You
have all heard his blasphemy. What is your verdict?" And
they all condemned him to death.

14:55 Greek *the Sanhedrin.* 14:62 See Ps 110:1; Dan 7:13.

NEW KING JAMES VERSION

55 Now the chief priests and all the council sought testi-
mony against Jesus to put Him to death, but found none.
56 For many bore false witness against Him, but their testi-
monies did not agree.
57 Then some rose up and bore false witness against
Him, saying, 58 "We heard Him say, 'I will destroy this tem-
ple made with hands, and within three days I will build
another made without hands.' " 59 But not even then did
their testimony agree.
60 And the high priest stood up in the midst and asked
Jesus, saying, "Do You answer nothing? What *is it* these
men testify against You?" 61 But He kept silent and
answered nothing.
Again the high priest asked Him, saying to Him, "Are
You the Christ, the Son of the Blessed?"
62 Jesus said, "I am. And you will see the Son of Man sit-
ting at the right hand of the Power, and coming with the
clouds of heaven."
63 Then the high priest tore his clothes and said, "What
further need do we have of witnesses? 64 You have heard
the blasphemy! What do you think?"
And they all condemned Him to be deserving of death.

THE MESSAGE

The high priests conspiring with the Jewish Council looked high and low for evidence against Jesus by which they could sentence him to death. They found nothing. Plenty of people were willing to bring in false charges, but nothing added up, and they ended up canceling each other out. Then a few of them stood up and lied: "We heard him say, 'I am going to tear down this Temple, built by hard labor, and in three days build another without lifting a hand.'" But even they couldn't agree exactly.

In the middle of this, the Chief Priest stood up and asked Jesus, "What do you have to say to the accusation?" Jesus was silent. He said nothing.

The Chief Priest tried again, this time asking, "Are you the Messiah, the Son of the Blessed?"

Jesus said, "Yes, I am, and you'll see it yourself:

The Son of Man seated
At the right hand of the Mighty One,
Arriving on the clouds of heaven."

The Chief Priest lost his temper. Ripping his clothes, he yelled, "Did you hear that? After that do we need witnesses? You heard the blasphemy. Are you going to stand for it?"

They condemned him, one and all. The sentence: death.

KING JAMES VERSION

65 And some began to spit on him, and to cover his face, and to buffet him, and to say unto him, Prophesy: and the servants did strike him with the palms of their hands.

66 ¶ And as Peter was beneath in the palace, there cometh one of the maids of the high priest:

67 And when she saw Peter warming himself, she looked upon him, and said, And thou also wast with Jesus of Nazareth.

68 But he denied, saying, I know not, neither understand I what thou sayest. And he went out into the porch; and the cock crew.

69 And a maid saw him again, and began to say to them that stood by, This is *one* of them.

70 And he denied it again. And a little after, they that stood by said again to Peter, Surely thou art *one* of them: for thou art a Galilaean, and thy speech agreeth *thereto*.

71 But he began to curse and to swear, *saying*, I know not this man of whom ye speak.

72 And the second time the cock crew. And Peter called to mind the word that Jesus said unto him, Before the cock crow twice, thou shalt deny me thrice. And when he thought thereon, he wept.

NEW AMERICAN STANDARD BIBLE

65 Some began to spit at Him, and to blindfold Him, and to beat Him with their fists, and to say to Him, "Prophesy!" And the officers received Him with slaps *in the face.*

Peter's Denials

66 As Peter was below in the courtyard, one of the servant-girls of the high priest *came,

67 and seeing Peter warming himself, she looked at him and *said, "You also were with Jesus the Nazarene."

68 But he denied *it,* saying, "I neither know nor understand what you are talking about." And he went out onto the porch, and a rooster crowed.[3]

69 The servant-girl saw him, and began once more to say to the bystanders, "This is *one* of them!"

70 But again he denied it. And after a little while the bystanders were again saying to Peter, "Surely you are *one* of them, for you are a Galilean too."

71 But he began to curse and swear, "I do not know this man you are talking about!"

72 Immediately a rooster crowed a second time. And Peter remembered how Jesus had made the remark to him, "Before a rooster crows twice, you will deny Me three times." And he began to weep.

14:68 [3] Later mss add *and a rooster crowed*

NEW CENTURY VERSION

of the people there began to spit at Jesus. They blindfolded him and beat him with their fists and said, "Prove you are a prophet!" Then the guards led Jesus away and beat him.

Peter Says He Doesn't Know Jesus

66 While Peter was in the courtyard, a servant girl of the
high priest came there. 67 She saw Peter warming himself
at the fire and looked closely at him.

Then she said, "You also were with Jesus, that man from Nazareth."

68 But Peter said that he was never with Jesus. He said, "I don't know or understand what you are talking about." Then Peter left and went toward the entrance of the courtyard. And the rooster crowed.[d]

69 The servant girl saw Peter there, and again she said to
the people who were standing nearby, "This man is one of
those who followed Jesus." 70 Again Peter said that it was
not true.

A short time later, some people were standing near Peter saying, "Surely you are one of those who followed Jesus, because you are from Galilee, too."

71 Then Peter began to place a curse on himself and swear, "I don't know this man you're talking about!"

72 At once, the rooster crowed the second time. Then Peter remembered what Jesus had told him: "Before the rooster crows twice, you will say three times that you don't know me." Then Peter lost control of himself and began to cry.

14:68 [d] **And...crowed.** A few, early Greek copies leave out this phrase.

CONTEMPORARY ENGLISH VERSION

65 Some of the people started spitting on Jesus. They blindfolded him, hit him with their fists, and said, "Tell us who hit you!" Then the guards took charge of Jesus and beat him.

Peter Says He Doesn't Know Jesus

(Matthew 26.69-75; Luke 22.56-62; John 18.15-18, 25-27)

66 While Peter was still in the courtyard, a servant girl of
the high priest came up 67 and saw Peter warming himself
by the fire. She stared at him and said, "You were with
Jesus from Nazareth!"

68 Peter replied, "That isn't true! I don't know what you're talking about. I don't have any idea what you mean." He went out to the gate, and a rooster crowed.[k]

69 The servant girl saw Peter again and said to the people standing there, "This man is one of them!"

70 "No, I'm not!" Peter replied.

A little while later some of the people said to Peter, "You certainly are one of them. You're a Galilean!"

71 This time Peter began to curse and swear, "I don't even know the man you're talking about!"

72 Right away the rooster crowed a second time. Then Peter remembered that Jesus had told him, "Before a rooster crows twice, you will say three times that you don't know me." So Peter started crying.

[k] **14.68** *a rooster crowed*: These words are not in some manuscripts.

NEW INTERNATIONAL VERSION

some began to spit at him; they blindfolded him, struck him with their fists, and said, "Prophesy!" And the guards took him and beat him.

Peter Disowns Jesus

66While Peter was below in the courtyard, one of the servant girls of the high priest came by. 67When she saw Peter warming himself, she looked closely at him.

"You also were with that Nazarene, Jesus," she said.

68But he denied it. "I don't know or understand what you're talking about," he said, and went out into the entryway.[g]

69When the servant girl saw him there, she said again to those standing around, "This fellow is one of them." 70Again he denied it.

After a little while, those standing near said to Peter, "Surely you are one of them, for you are a Galilean."

71He began to call down curses on himself, and he swore to them, "I don't know this man you're talking about."

72Immediately the rooster crowed the second time.[h] Then Peter remembered the word Jesus had spoken to him: "Before the rooster crows twice[i] you will disown me three times." And he broke down and wept.

[g] 68 Some early manuscripts *entryway and the rooster crowed*
[h] 72 Some early manuscripts do not have *the second time*. [i] 72 Some early manuscripts do not have *twice*.

NEW LIVING TRANSLATION

65Then some of them began to spit at him, and they blindfolded him and hit his face with their fists. "Who hit you that time, you prophet?" they jeered. And even the guards were hitting him as they led him away.

Peter Denies Jesus

66Meanwhile, Peter was below in the courtyard. One of the servant girls who worked for the high priest 67noticed Peter warming himself at the fire. She looked at him closely and then said, "You were one of those with Jesus, the Nazarene."

68Peter denied it. "I don't know what you're talking about," he said, and he went out into the entryway. Just then, a rooster crowed.*

69The servant girl saw him standing there and began telling the others, "That man is definitely one of them!" 70Peter denied it again.

A little later some other bystanders began saying to Peter, "You must be one of them because you are from Galilee."

71Peter said, "I swear by God, I don't know this man you're talking about." 72And immediately the rooster crowed the second time. Suddenly, Jesus' words flashed through Peter's mind: "Before the rooster crows twice, you will deny me three times." And he broke down and cried.

14:68 Some manuscripts do not include *Just then, a rooster crowed.*

NEW KING JAMES VERSION

65Then some began to spit on Him, and to blindfold Him, and to beat Him, and to say to Him, "Prophesy!" And the officers struck Him with the palms of their hands.[f]

Peter Denies Jesus, and Weeps

66Now as Peter was below in the courtyard, one of the servant girls of the high priest came. 67And when she saw Peter warming himself, she looked at him and said, "You also were with Jesus of Nazareth."

68But he denied it, saying, "I neither know nor understand what you are saying." And he went out on the porch, and a rooster crowed.

69And the servant girl saw him again, and began to say to those who stood by, "This is one of them." 70But he denied it again.

And a little later those who stood by said to Peter again, "Surely you are *one* of them; for you are a Galilean, and your speech shows *it*."[g]

71Then he began to curse and swear, "I do not know this Man of whom you speak!"

72A second time *the* rooster crowed. Then Peter called to mind the word that Jesus had said to him, "Before the rooster crows twice, you will deny Me three times." And when he thought about it, he wept.

14:65 [f] NU-Text reads *received Him with slaps*. 14:70 [g] NU-Text omits *and your speech shows it*.

THE MESSAGE

Some of them started spitting at him. They blindfolded his eyes, then hit him, saying, "Who hit you? Prophesy!" The guards, punching and slapping, took him away.

The Rooster Crowed

While all this was going on, Peter was down in the courtyard. One of the Chief Priest's servant girls came in and, seeing Peter warming himself there, looked hard at him and said, "You were with the Nazarene, Jesus."

He denied it: "I don't know what you're talking about." He went out on the porch. A rooster crowed.

The girl spotted him and began telling the people standing around, "He's one of them." He denied it again.

After a little while, the bystanders brought it up again. "You've *got* to be one of them. You've got 'Galilean' written all over you."

Now Peter got really nervous and swore, "I never laid eyes on this man you're talking about." Just then the rooster crowed a second time. Peter remembered how Jesus had said, "Before a rooster crows twice, you'll deny me three times." He collapsed in tears.

KING JAMES VERSION

15 And straightway in the morning the chief priests held a consultation with the elders and scribes and the whole council, and bound Jesus, and carried *him* away, and delivered *him* to Pilate.

2 And Pilate asked him, Art thou the King of the Jews? And he answering said unto him, Thou sayest *it*.

3 And the chief priests accused him of many things: but he answered nothing.

4 And Pilate asked him again, saying, Answerest thou nothing? behold how many things they witness against thee.

5 But Jesus yet answered nothing; so that Pilate marvelled.

6 Now at *that* feast he released unto them one prisoner, whomsoever they desired.

7 And there was *one* named Barabbas, *which lay* bound with them that had made insurrection with him, who had committed murder in the insurrection.

8 And the multitude crying aloud began to desire *him to do* as he had ever done unto them.

9 But Pilate answered them, saying, Will ye that I release unto you the King of the Jews?

10 For he knew that the chief priests had delivered him for envy.

11 But the chief priests moved the people, that he should rather release Barabbas unto them.

12 And Pilate answered and said again unto them, What will ye then that I shall do *unto him* whom ye call the King of the Jews?

NEW AMERICAN STANDARD BIBLE

Jesus before Pilate

15 Early in the morning the chief priests with the elders and scribes and the whole [1]Council, immediately held a consultation; and binding Jesus, they led Him away and delivered Him to Pilate.

2 Pilate questioned Him, "Are You the King of the Jews?" And He *answered him, "*It is as* you say."

3 The chief priests *began* to accuse Him harshly.

4 Then Pilate questioned Him again, saying, "Do You not answer? See how many charges they bring against You!"

5 But Jesus made no further answer; so Pilate was amazed.

6 Now at *the* feast he used to release for them *any* one prisoner whom they requested.

7 The man named Barabbas had been imprisoned with the insurrectionists who had committed murder in the insurrection.

8 The crowd went up and began asking him *to do* as he had been accustomed to do for them.

9 Pilate answered them, saying, "Do you want me to release for you the King of the Jews?"

10 For he was aware that the chief priests had handed Him over because of envy.

11 But the chief priests stirred up the crowd *to ask* him to release Barabbas for them instead.

12 Answering again, Pilate said to them, "Then what shall I do with Him whom you call the King of the Jews?"

15:1 [1] Or *Sanhedrin*

NEW CENTURY VERSION

Pilate Questions Jesus

15 Very early in the morning, the leading priests, the older leaders, the teachers of the law, and all the Jewish council decided what to do with Jesus. They tied him, led him away, and turned him over to Pilate, the governor.

2 Pilate asked Jesus, "Are you the king of the Jews?"

Jesus answered, "Those are your words."

3 The leading priests accused Jesus of many things. 4 So Pilate asked Jesus another question, "You can see that they are accusing you of many things. Aren't you going to answer?"

5 But Jesus still said nothing, so Pilate was very surprised.

Pilate Tries to Free Jesus

6 Every year at the time of the Passover the governor would free one prisoner whom the people chose. 7 At that time, there was a man named Barabbas in prison who was a rebel and had committed murder during a riot. 8 The crowd came to Pilate and began to ask him to free a prisoner as he always did.

9 So Pilate asked them, "Do you want me to free the king of the Jews?" 10 Pilate knew that the leading priests had turned Jesus in to him because they were jealous. 11 But the leading priests had persuaded the people to ask Pilate to free Barabbas, not Jesus.

12 Then Pilate asked the crowd again, "So what should I do with this man you call the king of the Jews?"

CONTEMPORARY ENGLISH VERSION

Pilate Questions Jesus

(Matthew 27.1, 2, 11-14; Luke 23.1-5; John 18.28-38)

15 Early the next morning the chief priests, the nation's leaders, and the teachers of the Law of Moses met together with the whole Jewish council. They tied up Jesus and led him off to Pilate.

2 He asked Jesus, "Are you the king of the Jews?"

"Those are your words," Jesus answered.

3 The chief priests brought many charges against Jesus. 4 Then Pilate questioned him again, "Don't you have anything to say? Don't you hear what crimes they say you have done?" 5 But Jesus did not answer, and Pilate was amazed.

The Death Sentence

(Matthew 27.15-26; Luke 23.13-25; John 18.39—19.16)

6 During Passover, Pilate always freed one prisoner chosen by the people. 7 And at that time there was a prisoner named Barabbas. He and some others had been arrested for murder during a riot. 8 The crowd now came and asked Pilate to set a prisoner free, just as he usually did.

9 Pilate asked them, "Do you want me to free the king of the Jews?" 10 Pilate knew that the chief priests had brought Jesus to him because they were jealous.

11 But the chief priests told the crowd to ask Pilate to free Barabbas.

12 Then Pilate asked the crowd, "What do you want me to do with this man you say is[a] the king of the Jews?"

[a] 15.12 *this man you say is*: These words are not in some manuscripts.

NEW INTERNATIONAL VERSION

Jesus Before Pilate

15 Very early in the morning, the chief priests, with the elders, the teachers of the law and the whole Sanhedrin, reached a decision. They bound Jesus, led him away and handed him over to Pilate.

2“Are you the king of the Jews?” asked Pilate.

“Yes, it is as you say,” Jesus replied.

3The chief priests accused him of many things. 4So again Pilate asked him, “Aren't you going to answer? See how many things they are accusing you of.”

5But Jesus still made no reply, and Pilate was amazed.

6Now it was the custom at the Feast to release a prisoner whom the people requested. 7A man called Barabbas was in prison with the insurrectionists who had committed murder in the uprising. 8The crowd came up and asked Pilate to do for them what he usually did.

9“Do you want me to release to you the king of the Jews?” asked Pilate, 10knowing it was out of envy that the chief priests had handed Jesus over to him. 11But the chief priests stirred up the crowd to have Pilate release Barabbas instead.

12“What shall I do, then, with the one you call the king of the Jews?” Pilate asked them.

NEW LIVING TRANSLATION

Jesus' Trial before Pilate

15 Very early in the morning the leading priests, other leaders, and teachers of religious law—the entire high council*—met to discuss their next step. They bound Jesus and took him to Pilate, the Roman governor.

2Pilate asked Jesus, “Are you the King of the Jews?”

Jesus replied, “Yes, it is as you say.”

3Then the leading priests accused him of many crimes, 4and Pilate asked him, “Aren't you going to say something? What about all these charges against you?” 5But Jesus said nothing, much to Pilate's surprise.

6Now it was the governor's custom to release one prisoner each year at Passover time—anyone the people requested. 7One of the prisoners at that time was Barabbas, convicted along with others for murder during an insurrection. 8The mob began to crowd in toward Pilate, asking him to release a prisoner as usual. 9“Should I give you the King of the Jews?” Pilate asked. 10(For he realized by now that the leading priests had arrested Jesus out of envy.) 11But at this point the leading priests stirred up the mob to demand the release of Barabbas instead of Jesus. 12“But if I release Barabbas,” Pilate asked them, “what should I do with this man you call the King of the Jews?”

15:1 Greek *the Sanhedrin;* also in 15:43.

NEW KING JAMES VERSION

Jesus Faces Pilate

15 Immediately, in the morning, the chief priests held a consultation with the elders and scribes and the whole council; and they bound Jesus, led *Him* away, and delivered *Him* to Pilate. 2Then Pilate asked Him, “Are You the King of the Jews?”

He answered and said to him, “*It is as* you say.”

3And the chief priests accused Him of many things, but He answered nothing. 4Then Pilate asked Him again, saying, “Do You answer nothing? See how many things they testify against You!”[a] 5But Jesus still answered nothing, so that Pilate marveled.

Taking the Place of Barabbas

6Now at the feast he was accustomed to releasing one prisoner to them, whomever they requested. 7And there was one named Barabbas, *who was* chained with his fellow rebels; they had committed murder in the rebellion. 8Then the multitude, crying aloud,[b] began to ask *him to do* just as he had always done for them. 9But Pilate answered them, saying, “Do you want me to release to you the King of the Jews?” 10For he knew that the chief priests had handed Him over because of envy.

11But the chief priests stirred up the crowd, so that he should rather release Barabbas to them. 12Pilate answered and said to them again, “What then do you want me to do *with Him* whom you call the King of the Jews?”

15:4 [a] NU-Text reads *of which they accuse You.* **15:8** [b] NU-Text reads *going up.*

THE MESSAGE

Standing Before Pilate

15 At dawn's first light, the high priests, with the religious leaders and scholars, arranged a conference with the entire Jewish Council. After tying Jesus securely, they took him out and presented him to Pilate.

Pilate asked him, “Are you the ‘King of the Jews’?”

He answered, “If you say so.” The high priests let loose a barrage of accusations.

Pilate asked again, “Aren't you going to answer anything? That's quite a list of accusations.” Still, he said nothing. Pilate was impressed, really impressed.

It was a custom at the Feast to release a prisoner, anyone the people asked for. There was one prisoner called Barabbas, locked up with the insurrectionists who had committed murder during the uprising against Rome. As the crowd came up and began to present its petition for him to release a prisoner, Pilate anticipated them: “Do you want me to release the King of the Jews to you?” Pilate knew by this time that it was through sheer spite that the high priests had turned Jesus over to him.

But the high priests by then had worked up the crowd to ask for the release of Barabbas. Pilate came back, “So what do I do with this man you call King of the Jews?”

KING JAMES VERSION

13 And they cried out again, Crucify him.
14 Then Pilate said unto them, Why, what evil hath he done? And they cried out the more exceedingly, Crucify him.
15 ¶ And *so* Pilate, willing to content the people, released Barabbas unto them, and delivered Jesus, when he had scourged *him*, to be crucified.
16 And the soldiers led him away into the hall, called Praetorium; and they call together the whole band.
17 And they clothed him with purple, and platted a crown of thorns, and put it about his *head*,
18 And began to salute him, Hail, King of the Jews!
19 And they smote him on the head with a reed, and did spit upon him, and bowing *their* knees worshipped him.
20 And when they had mocked him, they took off the purple from him, and put his own clothes on him, and led him out to crucify him.
21 And they compel one Simon a Cyrenian, who passed by, coming out of the country, the father of Alexander and Rufus, to bear his cross.
22 ¶ And they bring him unto the place Golgotha, which is, being interpreted, The place of a skull.

NEW AMERICAN STANDARD BIBLE

13 They shouted back, "Crucify Him!"
14 But Pilate said to them, "Why, what evil has He done?" But they shouted all the more, "Crucify Him!"
15 Wishing to satisfy the crowd, Pilate released Barabbas for them, and after having Jesus scourged, he handed Him over to be crucified.

Jesus Is Mocked

16 The soldiers took Him away into the palace (that is, the Praetorium), and they *called together the whole *Roman* [2]cohort.
17 They *dressed Him up in purple, and after twisting a crown of thorns, they put it on Him;
18 and they began to acclaim Him, "Hail, King of the Jews!"
19 They kept beating His head with a [3]reed, and spitting on Him, and kneeling and bowing before Him.
20 After they had mocked Him, they took the purple robe off Him and put His *own* garments on Him. And they *led Him out to crucify Him.
21 They *pressed into service a passer-by coming from the country, Simon of Cyrene (the father of Alexander and Rufus), to bear His cross.

The Crucifixion

22 Then they *brought Him to the place Golgotha, which is translated, Place of a Skull.

15:16 [2] Or *battalion* 15:19 [3] Or *staff* (made of a reed)

NEW CENTURY VERSION

13They shouted, "Crucify him!"
14Pilate asked, "Why? What wrong has he done?"
But they shouted even louder, "Crucify him!"
15Pilate wanted to please the crowd, so he freed
Barabbas for them. After having Jesus beaten with whips,
he handed Jesus over to the soldiers to be crucified.

16The soldiers took Jesus into the governor's palace
(called the Praetorium) and called all the other soldiers
together. 17They put a purple robe on Jesus and used
thorny branches to make a crown for his head. 18They
began to call out to him, "Hail, King of the Jews!" 19The
soldiers beat Jesus on the head many times with a stick.
They spit on him and made fun of him by bowing on their
knees and worshiping him. 20After they finished, the sol-
diers took off the purple robe and put his own clothes on
him again. Then they led him out of the palace to be cruci-
fied.

Jesus Is Crucified

21A man named Simon from Cyrene, the father of
Alexander and Rufus, was coming from the fields to the
city. The soldiers forced Simon to carry the cross for Jesus.
22They led Jesus to the place called Golgotha, which means

CONTEMPORARY ENGLISH VERSION

13They yelled, "Nail him to a cross!"
14Pilate asked, "But what crime has he done?"
"Nail him to a cross!" they yelled even louder.
15Pilate wanted to please the crowd. So he set Barabbas
free. Then he ordered his soldiers to beat Jesus with a whip
and nail him to a cross.

Soldiers Make Fun of Jesus (Matthew 27.27-30; John 19.2, 3)

16The soldiers led Jesus inside the courtyard of the
fortress[b] and called together the rest of the troops. 17They
put a purple robe[c] on him, and on his head they placed a
crown that they had made out of thorn branches. 18They
made fun of Jesus and shouted, "Hey, you king of the
Jews!" 19Then they beat him on the head with a stick. They
spit on him and knelt down and pretended to worship him.
20When the soldiers had finished making fun of Jesus,
they took off the purple robe. They put his own clothes
back on him and led him off to be nailed to a cross.
21Simon from Cyrene happened to be coming in from a
farm, and they forced him to carry Jesus' cross. Simon was
the father of Alexander and Rufus.

Jesus Is Nailed to a Cross
(Matthew 27.31-44; Luke 23.27-43; John 19.17-27)

22The soldiers took Jesus to Golgotha, which means

[b] 15.16 *fortress*: The place where the Roman governor stayed. It was probably at Herod's palace west of Jerusalem, though it may have been Fortress Antonia, north of the temple, where the Roman troops were stationed. [c] 15.17 *purple robe*: This was probably a Roman soldier's robe.

NEW INTERNATIONAL VERSION

13"Crucify him!" they shouted.
14"Why? What crime has he committed?" asked Pilate.
But they shouted all the louder, "Crucify him!"
15Wanting to satisfy the crowd, Pilate released Barabbas to them. He had Jesus flogged, and handed him over to be crucified.

The Soldiers Mock Jesus

16The soldiers led Jesus away into the palace (that is, the Praetorium) and called together the whole company of soldiers. 17They put a purple robe on him, then twisted together a crown of thorns and set it on him. 18And they began to call out to him, "Hail, king of the Jews!" 19Again and again they struck him on the head with a staff and spit on him. Falling on their knees, they paid homage to him. 20And when they had mocked him, they took off the purple robe and put his own clothes on him. Then they led him out to crucify him.

The Crucifixion

21A certain man from Cyrene, Simon, the father of Alexander and Rufus, was passing by on his way in from the country, and they forced him to carry the cross. 22They brought Jesus to the place called Golgotha (which means

NEW LIVING TRANSLATION

13They shouted back, "Crucify him!"
14"Why?" Pilate demanded. "What crime has he committed?"
But the crowd only roared the louder, "Crucify him!"
15So Pilate, anxious to please the crowd, released Barabbas to them. He ordered Jesus flogged with a lead-tipped whip, then turned him over to the Roman soldiers to crucify him.

The Soldiers Mock Jesus

16The soldiers took him into their headquarters* and called out the entire battalion. 17They dressed him in a purple robe and made a crown of long, sharp thorns and put it on his head. 18Then they saluted, yelling, "Hail! King of the Jews!" 19And they beat him on the head with a stick, spit on him, and dropped to their knees in mock worship. 20When they were finally tired of mocking him, they took off the purple robe and put his own clothes on him again. Then they led him away to be crucified.

The Crucifixion

21A man named Simon, who was from Cyrene,* was coming in from the country just then, and they forced him to carry Jesus' cross. (Simon is the father of Alexander and Rufus.) 22And they brought Jesus to a place called Golgotha

15:16 Greek *the courtyard, which is the praetorium.* 15:21 *Cyrene* was a city in northern Africa.

NEW KING JAMES VERSION

13So they cried out again, "Crucify Him!"
14Then Pilate said to them, "Why, what evil has He done?"
But they cried out all the more, "Crucify Him!"
15So Pilate, wanting to gratify the crowd, released Barabbas to them; and he delivered Jesus, after he had scourged *Him,* to be crucified.

The Soldiers Mock Jesus

16Then the soldiers led Him away into the hall called Praetorium, and they called together the whole garrison.
17And they clothed Him with purple; and they twisted a crown of thorns, put it on His *head,* 18and began to salute Him, "Hail, King of the Jews!" 19Then they struck Him on the head with a reed and spat on Him; and bowing the knee, they worshiped Him. 20And when they had mocked Him, they took the purple off Him, put His own clothes on Him, and led Him out to crucify Him.

The King on a Cross

21Then they compelled a certain man, Simon a Cyrenian, the father of Alexander and Rufus, as he was coming out of the country and passing by, to bear His cross.
22And they brought Him to the place Golgotha, which is

THE MESSAGE

They yelled, "Nail him to a cross!"
Pilate objected, "But for what crime?"
But they yelled all the louder, "Nail him to a cross!"
Pilate gave the crowd what it wanted, set Barabbas free and turned Jesus over for whipping and crucifixion.
The soldiers took Jesus into the palace (called Praetorium) and called together the entire brigade. They dressed him up in purple and put a crown plaited from a thorn bush on his head. Then they began their mockery: "Bravo, King of the Jews!" They banged on his head with a club, spit on him, and knelt down in mock worship. After they had had their fun, they took off the purple cape and put his own clothes back on him. Then they marched out to nail him to the cross.

The Crucifixion

There was a man walking by, coming from work, Simon from Cyrene, the father of Alexander and Rufus. They made him carry Jesus' cross.
The soldiers brought Jesus to Golgotha, meaning "Skull

KING JAMES VERSION

23 And they gave him to drink wine mingled with myrrh: but he received *it* not.

24 And when they had crucified him, they parted his garments, casting lots upon them, what every man should take.

25 And it was the third hour, and they crucified him.

26 And the superscription of his accusation was written over, THE KING OF THE JEWS.

27 And with him they crucify two thieves; the one on his right hand, and the other on his left.

28 And the scripture was fulfilled, which saith, And he was numbered with the transgressors.

29 And they that passed by railed on him, wagging their heads, and saying, Ah, thou that destroyest the temple, and buildest *it* in three days,

30 Save thyself, and come down from the cross.

31 Likewise also the chief priests mocking said among themselves with the scribes, He saved others; himself he cannot save.

32 Let Christ the King of Israel descend now from the cross, that we may see and believe. And they that were crucified with him reviled him.

33 ¶ And when the sixth hour was come, there was darkness over the whole land until the ninth hour.

34 And at the ninth hour Jesus cried with a loud voice,

NEW AMERICAN STANDARD BIBLE

23 They tried to give Him wine mixed with myrrh; but He did not take it.

24 And they *crucified Him, and *divided up His garments among themselves, casting lots for them *to decide* what each man should take.

25 It was the [4]third hour when they crucified Him.

26 The inscription of the charge against Him read, "THE KING OF THE JEWS."

27 They *crucified two robbers with Him, one on His right and one on His left.

28 [[5]And the Scripture was fulfilled which says, "And He was numbered with transgressors."]

29 Those passing by were hurling abuse at Him, wagging their heads, and saying, "Ha! You who *are going to* destroy the temple and rebuild it in three days,

30 save Yourself, and come down from the cross!"

31 In the same way the chief priests also, along with the scribes, were mocking *Him* among themselves and saying, "He saved others; He cannot save Himself.

32 "Let *this* Christ, the King of Israel, now come down from the cross, so that we may see and believe!" Those who were crucified with Him were also insulting Him.

33 When the [6]sixth hour came, darkness fell over the whole land until the [7]ninth hour.

34 At the ninth hour Jesus cried out with a loud voice,

15:25 [4] I.e. 9 a.m. **15:28** [5] Early mss do not contain this v
15:33 [6] I.e. noon **15:33** [7] I.e. 3 p.m.

NEW CENTURY VERSION

the Place of the Skull. 23The soldiers tried to give Jesus wine mixed with myrrh to drink, but he refused. 24The soldiers crucified Jesus and divided his clothes among themselves, throwing lots to decide what each soldier would get.

25It was nine o'clock in the morning when they crucified Jesus. 26There was a sign with this charge against Jesus written on it: THE KING OF THE JEWS. 27They also put two robbers on crosses beside Jesus, one on the right, and the other on the left. 28[a] 29People walked by and insulted Jesus and shook their heads, saying, "You said you could destroy the Temple and build it again in three days. 30So save yourself! Come down from that cross!"

31The leading priests and the teachers of the law were also making fun of Jesus. They said to each other, "He saved other people, but he can't save himself. 32If he is really the Christ, the king of Israel, let him come down now from the cross. When we see this, we will believe in him." The robbers who were being crucified beside Jesus also insulted him.

Jesus Dies

33At noon the whole country became dark, and the darkness lasted for three hours. 34At three o'clock Jesus cried in

15:28 [a] **Verse 28** Some Greek copies add verse 28: "And the Scripture came true that says, 'They put him with criminals.' "

CONTEMPORARY ENGLISH VERSION

"Place of a Skull."[d] 23There they gave him some wine mixed with a drug to ease the pain, but he refused to drink it.

24They nailed Jesus to a cross and gambled to see who would get his clothes. 25It was about nine o'clock in the morning when they nailed him to the cross. 26On it was a sign that told why he was nailed there. It read, "This is the King of the Jews." 27-28The soldiers also nailed two criminals on crosses, one to the right of Jesus and the other to his left.[e]

29People who passed by said terrible things about Jesus. They shook their heads and shouted, "Ha! So you're the one who claimed you could tear down the temple and build it again in three days. 30Save yourself and come down from the cross!"

31The chief priests and the teachers of the Law of Moses also made fun of Jesus. They said to each other, "He saved others, but he can't save himself. 32If he is the Messiah, the king of Israel, let him come down from the cross! Then we will see and believe." The two criminals also said cruel things to Jesus.

The Death of Jesus
(Matthew 27.45-56; Luke 23.44-49; John 19.28-30)

33About noon the sky turned dark and stayed that way until around three o'clock. 34Then about that time Jesus

[d] **15.22** *Place of a Skull*: The place was probably given this name because it was near a large rock in the shape of a human skull.
[e] **15.27-28** *left*: Some manuscripts add, "So the Scriptures came true which say, 'He was accused of being a criminal.' "

NEW INTERNATIONAL VERSION

The Place of the Skull). 23Then they offered him wine
mixed with myrrh, but he did not take it. 24And they cruci-
fied him. Dividing up his clothes, they cast lots to see what
each would get.
25It was the third hour when they crucified him. 26The
written notice of the charge against him read: THE KING OF
THE JEWS. 27They crucified two robbers with him, one on his
right and one on his left.[a] 29Those who passed by hurled
insults at him, shaking their heads and saying, "So! You
who are going to destroy the temple and build it in three
days, 30come down from the cross and save yourself!"
31In the same way the chief priests and the teachers of
the law mocked him among themselves. "He saved oth-
ers," they said, "but he can't save himself! 32Let this
Christ,[b] this King of Israel, come down now from the cross,
that we may see and believe." Those crucified with him
also heaped insults on him.

The Death of Jesus

33At the sixth hour darkness came over the whole land
until the ninth hour. 34And at the ninth hour Jesus cried

[a] *27* Some manuscripts *left,* [28]*and the scripture was fulfilled which says, "He was counted with the lawless ones"* (Isaiah 53:12) [b] *32* Or *Messiah*

NEW LIVING TRANSLATION

(which means Skull Hill). 23They offered him wine drugged
with myrrh, but he refused it. 24Then they nailed him to the
cross. They gambled for his clothes, throwing dice* to
decide who would get them.
25It was nine o'clock in the morning when the crucifix-
ion took place. 26A signboard was fastened to the cross
above Jesus' head, announcing the charge against him. It
read: "The King of the Jews." 27Two criminals were cruci-
fied with him, their crosses on either side of his.* 29And
the people passing by shouted abuse, shaking their heads
in mockery. "Ha! Look at you now!" they yelled at him.
"You can destroy the Temple and rebuild it in three days,
can you? 30Well then, save yourself and come down from
the cross!"
31The leading priests and teachers of religious law also
mocked Jesus. "He saved others," they scoffed, "but he
can't save himself! 32Let this Messiah, this king of Israel,
come down from the cross so we can see it and believe
him!" Even the two criminals who were being crucified
with Jesus ridiculed him.

The Death of Jesus

33At noon, darkness fell across the whole land until
three o'clock. 34Then, at that time Jesus called out with a

15:24 Greek *casting lots.* See Ps 22:18. **15:27** Some manuscripts add verse 28, *And the Scripture was fulfilled that said, "He was counted among those who were rebels."* See Isa 53:12.

NEW KING JAMES VERSION

translated, Place of a Skull. 23Then they gave Him wine
mingled with myrrh to drink, but He did not take *it.* 24And
when they crucified Him, they divided His garments, cast-
ing lots for them to determine what every man should
take.
25Now it was the third hour, and they crucified Him.
26And the inscription of His accusation was written above:

THE KING OF THE JEWS.

27With Him they also crucified two robbers, one on His
right and the other on His left. 28So the Scripture was ful-
filled[c] which says, *"And He was numbered with the trans-
gressors."*[d]
29And those who passed by blasphemed Him, wagging
their heads and saying, "Aha! *You* who destroy the temple
and build *it* in three days, 30save Yourself, and come down
from the cross!"
31Likewise the chief priests also, mocking among them-
selves with the scribes, said, "He saved others; Himself He
cannot save. 32Let the Christ, the King of Israel, descend
now from the cross, that we may see and believe."[e]
Even those who were crucified with Him reviled Him.

Jesus Dies on the Cross

33Now when the sixth hour had come, there was dark-
ness over the whole land until the ninth hour. 34And at the

15:28 [c] Isaiah 53:12 [d] NU-Text omits this verse. **15:32** [e] M-Text reads *believe Him.*

THE MESSAGE

Hill." They offered him a mild painkiller (wine mixed with
myrrh), but he wouldn't take it. And they nailed him to the
cross. They divided up his clothes and threw dice to see
who would get them.
They nailed him up at nine o'clock in the morning. The
charge against him—THE KING OF THE JEWS—was printed on
a poster. Along with him, they crucified two criminals, one
to his right, the other to his left. People passing along the
road jeered, shaking their heads in mock lament: "You
bragged that you could tear down the Temple and then
rebuild it in three days—so show us your stuff! Save your-
self! If you're really God's Son, come down from that
cross!"
The high priests, along with the religion scholars, were
right there mixing it up with the rest of them, having a
great time poking fun at him: "He saved others—but he
can't save himself! Messiah, is he? King of Israel? Then let
him climb down from that cross. We'll *all* become believers
then!" Even the men crucified alongside him joined in the
mockery.
At noon the sky became extremely dark. The darkness
lasted three hours. At three o'clock, Jesus groaned out of

KING JAMES VERSION

saying, Eloi, Eloi, lama sabachthani? which is, being inter-
preted, My God, my God, why hast thou forsaken me?
35 And some of them that stood by, when they heard *it*,
said, Behold, he calleth Elias.
36 And one ran and filled a spunge full of vinegar, and
put *it* on a reed, and gave him to drink, saying, Let alone;
let us see whether Elias will come to take him down.
37 And Jesus cried with a loud voice, and gave up the
ghost.
38 And the veil of the temple was rent in twain from the
top to the bottom.
39 And when the centurion, which stood over against
him, saw that he so cried out, and gave up the ghost, he
said, Truly this man was the Son of God.
40 There were also women looking on afar off: among
whom was Mary Magdalene, and Mary the mother of
James the less and of Joses, and Salome;
41 (Who also, when he was in Galilee, followed him,
and ministered unto him;) and many other women which
came up with him unto Jerusalem.
42 ¶ And now when the even was come, because it was
the preparation, that is, the day before the sabbath,

NEW AMERICAN STANDARD BIBLE

"Eloi, Eloi, lama sabachthani?" which is translated, "My
God, My God, why have You forsaken Me?"
35 When some of the bystanders heard it, they *began*
saying, "Behold, He is calling for Elijah."
36 Someone ran and filled a sponge with sour wine, put
it on a reed, and gave Him a drink, saying, "Let us see
whether Elijah will come to take Him down."
37 And Jesus uttered a loud cry, and breathed His last.
38 And the veil of the temple was torn in two from top
to bottom.
39 When the centurion, who was standing right in front
of Him, saw the way He breathed His last, he said, "Truly
this man was the Son of God!"
40 There were also *some* women looking on from a dis-
tance, among whom *were* Mary Magdalene, and Mary the
mother of James the Less and Joses, and Salome.
41 When He was in Galilee, they used to follow Him and
minister to Him; and *there were* many other women who
came up with Him to Jerusalem.

Jesus Is Buried

42 When evening had already come, because it was the
preparation day, that is, the day before the Sabbath,

NEW CENTURY VERSION

a loud voice, "Eloi, Eloi, lama sabachthani." This means,
"My God, my God, why have you rejected me?"
35When some of the people standing there heard this,
they said, "Listen! He is calling Elijah."
36Someone there ran and got a sponge, filled it with
vinegar, tied it to a stick, and gave it to Jesus to drink. He
said, "We want to see if Elijah will come to take him down
from the cross."
37Then Jesus cried in a loud voice and died.
38The curtain in the Temple[b] was torn into two pieces,
from the top to the bottom. 39When the army officer who
was standing in front of the cross saw what happened
when Jesus died, he said, "This man really was the Son of
God!"
40Some women were standing at a distance from the
cross, watching; among them were Mary Magdalene,
Salome, and Mary the mother of James and Joseph. (James
was her youngest son.) 41These women had followed Jesus
in Galilee and helped him. Many other women were also
there who had come with Jesus to Jerusalem.

Jesus Is Buried

42This was Preparation Day. (That means the day before

15:38 [b] **curtain in the Temple** A curtain divided the Most Holy Place from the other part of the Temple. That was the special building in Jerusalem where God commanded the Jewish people to worship him.

CONTEMPORARY ENGLISH VERSION

shouted, "Eloi, Eloi, lema sabachthani?"[f] which means,
"My God, my God, why have you deserted me?"
35Some of the people standing there heard Jesus and
said, "He is calling for Elijah."[g] 36One of them ran and
grabbed a sponge. After he had soaked it in wine, he put it
on a stick and held it up to Jesus. He said, "Let's wait and
see if Elijah will come[h] and take him down!" 37Jesus
shouted and then died.
38At once the curtain in the temple[i] tore in two from top
to bottom.
39A Roman army officer was standing in front of Jesus.
When the officer saw how Jesus died, he said, "This man
really was the Son of God!"
40-41Some women were looking on from a distance. They
had come with Jesus to Jerusalem. But even before this
they had been his followers and had helped him while he
was in Galilee. Mary Magdalene and Mary the mother of
the younger James and of Joseph were two of these
women. Salome was also one of them.

Jesus Is Buried

(Matthew 27.57-61; Luke 23.50-56; John 19.38-42)

42It was now the evening before the Sabbath, and the

[f] 15.34 *Eloi . . . sabachthani*: These words are in Aramaic, a language spoken in Palestine during the time of Jesus. [g] 15.35 *Elijah*: The name "Elijah" sounds something like "Eloi," which means "my God." [h] 15.36 *see if Elijah will come*: See the note at 6.15. [i] 15.38 *curtain in the temple*: There were two curtains in the temple. One was at the entrance, and the other separated the holy place from the most holy place that the Jewish people thought of as God's home on earth. The second curtain is probably the one which is meant.

NEW INTERNATIONAL VERSION

out in a loud voice, *"Eloi, Eloi, lama sabachthani?"*—which means, "My God, my God, why have you forsaken me?"[c]

[35]When some of those standing near heard this, they said, "Listen, he's calling Elijah."

[36]One man ran, filled a sponge with wine vinegar, put it on a stick, and offered it to Jesus to drink. "Now leave him alone. Let's see if Elijah comes to take him down," he said.

[37]With a loud cry, Jesus breathed his last.

[38]The curtain of the temple was torn in two from top to bottom. [39]And when the centurion, who stood there in front of Jesus, heard his cry and[d] saw how he died, he said, "Surely this man was the Son[e] of God!"

[40]Some women were watching from a distance. Among them were Mary Magdalene, Mary the mother of James the younger and of Joses, and Salome. [41]In Galilee these women had followed him and cared for his needs. Many other women who had come up with him to Jerusalem were also there.

The Burial of Jesus

[42]It was Preparation Day (that is, the day before the

[c] *34* Psalm 22:1 [d] *39* Some manuscripts do not have *heard his cry and* [e] *39* Or *a son*

NEW LIVING TRANSLATION

loud voice, *"Eloi, Eloi, lema sabachthani?"* which means, "My God, my God, why have you forsaken me?"*

[35]Some of the bystanders misunderstood and thought he was calling for the prophet Elijah. [36]One of them ran and filled a sponge with sour wine, holding it up to him on a stick so he could drink. "Leave him alone. Let's see whether Elijah will come and take him down!" he said.

[37]Then Jesus uttered another loud cry and breathed his last. [38]And the curtain in the Temple was torn in two, from top to bottom. [39]When the Roman officer who stood facing him saw how he had died, he exclaimed, "Truly, this was the Son of God!"

[40]Some women were there, watching from a distance, including Mary Magdalene, Mary (the mother of James the younger and of Joseph*), and Salome. [41]They had been followers of Jesus and had cared for him while he was in Galilee. Then they and many other women had come with him to Jerusalem.

The Burial of Jesus

[42]This all happened on Friday, the day of preparation,*

15:34 Ps 22:1. 15:40 Greek *Joses;* also in 15:47. See Matt 27:56. 15:42 Greek *on the day of preparation.*

NEW KING JAMES VERSION

ninth hour Jesus cried out with a loud voice, saying, "Eloi, Eloi, lama sabachthani?" which is translated, *"My God, My God, why have You forsaken Me?"*[f]

[35]Some of those who stood by, when they heard *that,* said, "Look, He is calling for Elijah!" [36]Then someone ran and filled a sponge full of sour wine, put *it* on a reed, and offered *it* to Him to drink, saying, "Let Him alone; let us see if Elijah will come to take Him down."

[37]And Jesus cried out with a loud voice, and breathed His last.

[38]Then the veil of the temple was torn in two from top to bottom. [39]So when the centurion, who stood opposite Him, saw that He cried out like this and breathed His last,[g] he said, "Truly this Man was the Son of God!"

[40]There were also women looking on from afar, among whom were Mary Magdalene, Mary the mother of James the Less and of Joses, and Salome, [41]who also followed Him and ministered to Him when He was in Galilee, and many other women who came up with Him to Jerusalem.

Jesus Buried in Joseph's Tomb

[42]Now when evening had come, because it was the

15:34 [f] Psalm 22:1 15:39 [g] NU-Text reads *that He thus breathed His last.*

THE MESSAGE

the depths, crying loudly, *"Eloi, Eloi, lama sabachthani?"* which means, "My God, my God, why have you abandoned me?"

Some of the bystanders who heard him said, "Listen, he's calling for Elijah." Someone ran off, soaked a sponge in sour wine, put it on a stick, and gave it to him to drink, saying, "Let's see if Elijah comes to take him down."

But Jesus, with a loud cry, gave his last breath. At that moment the Temple curtain ripped right down the middle. When the Roman captain standing guard in front of him saw that he had quit breathing, he said, "This has to be the Son of God!"

Taken to a Tomb

There were women watching from a distance, among them Mary Magdalene, Mary the mother of the younger James and Joses, and Salome. When Jesus was in Galilee, these women followed and served him, and had come up with him to Jerusalem.

Late in the afternoon, since it was the Day of Preparation

KING JAMES VERSION

43 Joseph of Arimathaea, an honourable counsellor, which also waited for the kingdom of God, came, and went in boldly unto Pilate, and craved the body of Jesus.

44 And Pilate marvelled if he were already dead: and calling *unto him* the centurion, he asked him whether he had been any while dead.

45 And when he knew *it* of the centurion, he gave the body to Joseph.

46 And he bought fine linen, and took him down, and wrapped him in the linen, and laid him in a sepulchre which was hewn out of a rock, and rolled a stone unto the door of the sepulchre.

47 And Mary Magdalene and Mary *the mother* of Joses beheld where he was laid.

16 And when the sabbath was past, Mary Magdalene, and Mary the *mother* of James, and Salome, had bought sweet spices, that they might come and anoint him.

2 And very early in the morning the first *day* of the week, they came unto the sepulchre at the rising of the sun.

3 And they said among themselves, Who shall roll us away the stone from the door of the sepulchre?

4 And when they looked, they saw that the stone was rolled away: for it was very great.

5 And entering into the sepulchre, they saw a young man sitting on the right side, clothed in a long white garment; and they were affrighted.

6 And he saith unto them, Be not affrighted: Ye seek

NEW AMERICAN STANDARD BIBLE

43 Joseph of Arimathea came, a prominent member of the Council, who himself was waiting for the kingdom of God; and he gathered up courage and went in before Pilate, and asked for the body of Jesus.

44 Pilate wondered if He was dead by this time, and summoning the centurion, he questioned him as to whether He was already dead.

45 And ascertaining this from the centurion, he granted the body to Joseph.

46 Joseph bought a linen cloth, took Him down, wrapped Him in the linen cloth and laid Him in a tomb which had been hewn out in the rock; and he rolled a stone against the entrance of the tomb.

47 Mary Magdalene and Mary the *mother* of Joses were looking on *to see* where He was laid.

The Resurrection

16 When the Sabbath was over, Mary Magdalene, and Mary the *mother* of James, and Salome, bought spices, so that they might come and anoint Him.

2 Very early on the first day of the week, they *came to the tomb when the sun had risen.

3 They were saying to one another, "Who will roll away the stone for us from the entrance of the tomb?"

4 Looking up, they *saw that the stone had been rolled away, although it was extremely large.

5 Entering the tomb, they saw a young man sitting at the right, wearing a white robe; and they were amazed.

6 And he *said to them, "Do not be amazed; you are

NEW CENTURY VERSION

the Sabbath day.) That evening, 43 Joseph from Arimathea was brave enough to go to Pilate and ask for Jesus' body. Joseph, an important member of the Jewish council, was one of the people who was waiting for the kingdom of God to come. 44 Pilate was amazed that Jesus would have already died, so he called the army officer who had guarded Jesus and asked him if Jesus had already died. 45 The officer told Pilate that he was dead, so Pilate told Joseph he could have the body. 46 Joseph bought some linen cloth, took the body down from the cross, and wrapped it in the linen. He put the body in a tomb that was cut out of a wall of rock. Then he rolled a very large stone to block the entrance of the tomb. 47 And Mary Magdalene and Mary the mother of Joseph saw the place where Jesus was laid.

Jesus Rises from the Dead

16 The day after the Sabbath day, Mary Magdalene, Mary the mother of James, and Salome bought some sweet-smelling spices to put on Jesus' body. 2 Very early on that day, the first day of the week, soon after sunrise, the women were on their way to the tomb. 3 They said to each other, "Who will roll away for us the stone that covers the entrance of the tomb?"

4 Then the women looked and saw that the stone had already been rolled away, even though it was very large. 5 The women entered the tomb and saw a young man wearing a white robe and sitting on the right side, and they were afraid.

6 But the man said, "Don't be afraid. You are looking for

CONTEMPORARY ENGLISH VERSION

Jewish people were getting ready for that sacred day. 43 A man named Joseph from Arimathea was brave enough to ask Pilate for the body of Jesus. Joseph was a highly respected member of the Jewish council, and he was also waiting for God's kingdom to come.

44 Pilate was surprised to hear that Jesus was already dead, and he called in the army officer to find out if Jesus had been dead very long. 45 After the officer told him, Pilate let Joseph have Jesus' body.

46 Joseph bought a linen cloth and took the body down from the cross. He had it wrapped in the cloth, and he put it in a tomb that had been cut into solid rock. Then he rolled a big stone against the entrance to the tomb.

47 Mary Magdalene and Mary the mother of Joseph were watching and saw where the body was placed.

Jesus Is Alive (Matthew 28.1-8; Luke 24.1-12; John 20.1-10)

16 After the Sabbath, Mary Magdalene, Salome, and Mary the mother of James bought some spices to put on Jesus' body. 2 Very early on Sunday morning, just as the sun was coming up, they went to the tomb. 3 On their way, they were asking one another, "Who will roll the stone away from the entrance for us?" 4 But when they looked, they saw that the stone had already been rolled away. And it was a huge stone!

5 The women went into the tomb, and on the right side they saw a young man in a white robe sitting there. They were alarmed.

6 The man said, "Don't be alarmed! You are looking for

NEW INTERNATIONAL VERSION

Sabbath). So as evening approached, 43Joseph of Arimathea, a prominent member of the Council, who was himself waiting for the kingdom of God, went boldly to Pilate and asked for Jesus' body. 44Pilate was surprised to hear that he was already dead. Summoning the centurion, he asked him if Jesus had already died. 45When he learned from the centurion that it was so, he gave the body to Joseph. 46So Joseph bought some linen cloth, took down the body, wrapped it in the linen, and placed it in a tomb cut out of rock. Then he rolled a stone against the entrance of the tomb. 47Mary Magdalene and Mary the mother of Joses saw where he was laid.

The Resurrection

16 When the Sabbath was over, Mary Magdalene, Mary the mother of James, and Salome bought spices so that they might go to anoint Jesus' body. 2Very early on the first day of the week, just after sunrise, they were on their way to the tomb 3and they asked each other, "Who will roll the stone away from the entrance of the tomb?"

4But when they looked up, they saw that the stone, which was very large, had been rolled away. 5As they entered the tomb, they saw a young man dressed in a white robe sitting on the right side, and they were alarmed.

6"Don't be alarmed," he said. "You are looking for Jesus

NEW LIVING TRANSLATION

the day before the Sabbath. As evening approached, 43an honored member of the high council, Joseph from Arimathea (who was waiting for the Kingdom of God to come), gathered his courage and went to Pilate to ask for Jesus' body. 44Pilate couldn't believe that Jesus was already dead, so he called for the Roman military officer in charge and asked him. 45The officer confirmed the fact, and Pilate told Joseph he could have the body. 46Joseph bought a long sheet of linen cloth, and taking Jesus' body down from the cross, he wrapped it in the cloth and laid it in a tomb that had been carved out of the rock. Then he rolled a stone in front of the entrance. 47Mary Magdalene and Mary the mother of Joseph saw where Jesus' body was laid.

The Resurrection

16 The next evening, when the Sabbath ended, Mary Magdalene and Salome and Mary the mother of James went out and purchased burial spices to put on Jesus' body. 2Very early on Sunday morning,* just at sunrise, they came to the tomb. 3On the way they were discussing who would roll the stone away from the entrance to the tomb. 4But when they arrived, they looked up and saw that the stone—a very large one—had already been rolled aside. 5So they entered the tomb, and there on the right sat a young man clothed in a white robe. The women

16:2 Greek *on the first day of the week;* also in 16:9.

NEW KING JAMES VERSION

Preparation Day, that is, the day before the Sabbath, 43Joseph of Arimathea, a prominent council member, who was himself waiting for the kingdom of God, coming and taking courage, went in to Pilate and asked for the body of Jesus. 44Pilate marveled that He was already dead; and summoning the centurion, he asked him if He had been dead for some time. 45So when he found out from the centurion, he granted the body to Joseph. 46Then he bought fine linen, took Him down, and wrapped Him in the linen. And he laid Him in a tomb which had been hewn out of the rock, and rolled a stone against the door of the tomb. 47And Mary Magdalene and Mary *the mother* of Joses observed where He was laid.

He Is Risen

16 Now when the Sabbath was past, Mary Magdalene, Mary *the mother* of James, and Salome bought spices, that they might come and anoint Him. 2Very early in the morning, on the first *day* of the week, they came to the tomb when the sun had risen. 3And they said among themselves, "Who will roll away the stone from the door of the tomb for us?" 4But when they looked up, they saw that the stone had been rolled away—for it was very large. 5And entering the tomb, they saw a young man clothed in a long white robe sitting on the right side; and they were alarmed.

6But he said to them, "Do not be alarmed. You seek

THE MESSAGE

(that is, Sabbath eve), Joseph of Arimathea, a highly respected member of the Jewish Council, came. He was one who lived expectantly, on the lookout for the kingdom of God. Working up his courage, he went to Pilate and asked for Jesus' body. Pilate questioned whether he could be dead that soon and called for the captain to verify that he was really dead. Assured by the captain, he gave Joseph the corpse.

Having already purchased a linen shroud, Joseph took him down, wrapped him in the shroud, placed him in a tomb that had been cut into the rock, and rolled a large stone across the opening. Mary Magdalene and Mary, mother of Joses, watched the burial.

The Resurrection

16 When the Sabbath was over, Mary Magdalene, Mary the mother of James, and Salome bought spices so they could embalm him. Very early on Sunday morning, as the sun rose, they went to the tomb. They worried out loud to each other, "Who will roll back the stone from the tomb for us?"

Then they looked up, saw that it had been rolled back—it was a huge stone—and walked right in. They saw a young man sitting on the right side, dressed all in white. They were completely taken aback, astonished.

He said, "Don't be afraid. I know you're looking for

KING JAMES VERSION

Jesus of Nazareth, which was crucified: he is risen; he is not here: behold the place where they laid him.

7 But go your way, tell his disciples and Peter that he goeth before you into Galilee: there shall ye see him, as he said unto you.

8 And they went out quickly, and fled from the sepulchre; for they trembled and were amazed: neither said they any thing to any *man*; for they were afraid.

9 ¶ Now when *Jesus* was risen early the first *day* of the week, he appeared first to Mary Magdalene, out of whom he had cast seven devils.

10 *And* she went and told them that had been with him, as they mourned and wept.

11 And they, when they had heard that he was alive, and had been seen of her, believed not.

12 After that he appeared in another form unto two of them, as they walked, and went into the country.

13 And they went and told *it* unto the residue: neither believed they them.

14 ¶ Afterward he appeared unto the eleven as they sat

NEW AMERICAN STANDARD BIBLE

looking for Jesus the Nazarene, who has been crucified. He has risen; He is not here; behold, *here is* the place where they laid Him.

7 "But go, tell His disciples and Peter, 'He is going ahead of you to Galilee; there you will see Him, just as He told you.' "

8 They went out and fled from the tomb, for trembling and astonishment had gripped them; and they said nothing to anyone, for they were afraid.

9 [[1]Now after He had risen early on the first day of the week, He first appeared to Mary Magdalene, from whom He had cast out seven demons.

10 She went and reported to those who had been with Him, while they were mourning and weeping.

11 When they heard that He was alive and had been seen by her, they refused to believe it.

12 After that, He appeared in a different form to two of them while they were walking along on their way to the country.

13 They went away and reported it to the others, but they did not believe them either.

The Disciples Commissioned

14 Afterward He appeared to the eleven themselves as

16:9 [1] Later mss add vv 9-20

NEW CENTURY VERSION

Jesus from Nazareth, who has been crucified. He has risen from the dead; he is not here. Look, here is the place they laid him. [7]Now go and tell his followers and Peter, 'Jesus is going into Galilee ahead of you, and you will see him there as he told you before.' "

[8]The women were confused and shaking with fear, so they left the tomb and ran away. They did not tell anyone about what happened, because they were afraid.

Verses 9–20 are not included in two of the best and oldest Greek manuscripts of Mark.

Some Followers See Jesus

[[9]After Jesus rose from the dead early on the first day of the week, he showed himself first to Mary Magdalene. One time in the past, he had forced seven demons out of her. [10]After Mary saw Jesus, she went and told his followers, who were very sad and were crying. [11]But Mary told them that Jesus was alive. She said that she had seen him, but the followers did not believe her.

[12]Later, Jesus showed himself to two of his followers while they were walking in the country, but he did not look the same as before. [13]These followers went back to the others and told them what had happened, but again, the followers did not believe them.

Jesus Talks to the Apostles

[14]Later Jesus showed himself to the eleven apostles

CONTEMPORARY ENGLISH VERSION

Jesus from Nazareth, who was nailed to a cross. God has raised him to life, and he isn't here. You can see the place where they put his body. [7]Now go and tell his disciples, and especially Peter, that he will go ahead of you to Galilee. You will see him there, just as he told you."

[8]When the women ran from the tomb, they were confused and shaking all over. They were too afraid to tell anyone what had happened.

ONE OLD ENDING TO MARK'S GOSPEL[a]

Jesus Appears to Mary Magdalene
(Matthew 28.9, 10; John 20.11-18)

[9]Very early on the first day of the week, after Jesus had risen to life, he appeared to Mary Magdalene. Earlier he had forced seven demons out of her. [10]She left and told his friends, who were crying and mourning. [11]Even though they heard that Jesus was alive and that Mary had seen him, they would not believe it.

Jesus Appears to Two Disciples (Luke 24.13-35)

[12]Later, Jesus appeared in another form to two disciples, as they were on their way out of the city. [13]But when these disciples told what had happened, the others would not believe.

What Jesus' Followers Must Do
(Matthew 28.16-20; Luke 24.36-49; John 20.19-23; Acts 1.6-8)

[14]Afterwards, Jesus appeared to his eleven disciples as

[a] 16.9 *One Old Ending to Mark's Gospel*: Verses 9-20 are not in some manuscripts.

NEW INTERNATIONAL VERSION

the Nazarene, who was crucified. He has risen! He is not here. See the place where they laid him. 7But go, tell his disciples and Peter, 'He is going ahead of you into Galilee. There you will see him, just as he told you.' "
8Trembling and bewildered, the women went out and fled from the tomb. They said nothing to anyone, because they were afraid.

[The earliest manuscripts and some other ancient witnesses do not have Mark 16:9–20.]

9When Jesus rose early on the first day of the week, he appeared first to Mary Magdalene, out of whom he had driven seven demons. 10She went and told those who had been with him and who were mourning and weeping.
11When they heard that Jesus was alive and that she had seen him, they did not believe it.
12Afterward Jesus appeared in a different form to two of them while they were walking in the country. 13These returned and reported it to the rest; but they did not believe them either.
14Later Jesus appeared to the Eleven as they were eating;

NEW LIVING TRANSLATION

were startled, 6but the angel said, "Do not be so surprised. You are looking for Jesus, the Nazarene, who was crucified. He isn't here! He has been raised from the dead! Look, this is where they laid his body. 7Now go and give this message to his disciples, including Peter: Jesus is going ahead of you to Galilee. You will see him there, just as he told you before he died!" 8The women fled from the tomb, trembling and bewildered, saying nothing to anyone because they were too frightened to talk.*

[*Longer Ending of Mark*]

9It was early on Sunday morning when Jesus rose from the dead, and the first person who saw him was Mary Magdalene, the woman from whom he had cast out seven demons. 10She went and found the disciples, who were grieving and weeping. 11But when she told them that Jesus was alive and she had seen him, they didn't believe her.
12Afterward he appeared to two who were walking from Jerusalem into the country, but they didn't recognize him at first because he had changed his appearance. 13When they realized who he was, they rushed back to tell the others, but no one believed them.
14Still later he appeared to the eleven disciples as they

16:8 The most reliable early manuscripts conclude the Gospel of Mark at verse 8. Other manuscripts include various endings to the Gospel. Two of the more noteworthy endings are printed here.

NEW KING JAMES VERSION

Jesus of Nazareth, who was crucified. He is risen! He is not here. See the place where they laid Him. 7But go, tell His disciples—and Peter—that He is going before you into Galilee; there you will see Him, as He said to you."
8So they went out quickly[a] and fled from the tomb, for they trembled and were amazed. And they said nothing to anyone, for they were afraid.

Mary Magdalene Sees the Risen Lord

9Now when *He* rose early on the first *day* of the week, He appeared first to Mary Magdalene, out of whom He had cast seven demons. 10She went and told those who had been with Him, as they mourned and wept. 11And when they heard that He was alive and had been seen by her, they did not believe.

Jesus Appears to Two Disciples

12After that, He appeared in another form to two of them as they walked and went into the country. 13And they went and told *it* to the rest, *but* they did not believe them either.

The Great Commission

14Later He appeared to the eleven as they sat at the

16:8 [a] NU-Text and M-Text omit *quickly.*

THE MESSAGE

Jesus the Nazarene, the one they nailed on the cross. He's been raised up; he's here no longer. You can see for yourselves that the place is empty. Now—on your way. Tell his disciples and Peter that he is going on ahead of you to Galilee. You'll see him there, exactly as he said."

They got out as fast as they could, beside themselves, their heads swimming. Stunned, they said nothing to anyone.

[After rising from the dead, Jesus appeared early on Sunday morning to Mary Magdalene, whom he had delivered from seven demons. She went to his former companions, now weeping and carrying on, and told them. When they heard her report that she had seen him alive and well, they didn't believe her.

Later he appeared, but in a different form, to two of them out walking in the countryside. They went back and told the rest, but they weren't believed either.

Still later, as the Eleven were eating supper, he appeared

KING JAMES VERSION

at meat, and upbraided them with their unbelief and hardness of heart, because they believed not them which had seen him after he was risen.

15 And he said unto them, Go ye into all the world, and preach the gospel to every creature.

16 He that believeth and is baptized shall be saved; but he that believeth not shall be damned.

17 And these signs shall follow them that believe; In my name shall they cast out devils; they shall speak with new tongues;

18 They shall take up serpents; and if they drink any deadly thing, it shall not hurt them; they shall lay hands on the sick, and they shall recover.

19 ¶ So then after the Lord had spoken unto them, he was received up into heaven, and sat on the right hand of God.

20 And they went forth, and preached every where, the Lord working with *them*, and confirming the word with signs following. Amen.

NEW AMERICAN STANDARD BIBLE

they were reclining *at the table;* and He reproached them for their unbelief and hardness of heart, because they had not believed those who had seen Him after He had risen.

15 And He said to them, "Go into all the world and preach the gospel to all creation.

16 "He who has believed and has been baptized shall be saved; but he who has disbelieved shall be condemned.

17 "These signs will accompany those who have believed: in My name they will cast out demons, they will speak with new tongues;

18 they will pick up serpents, and if they drink any deadly *poison,* it will not hurt them; they will lay hands on the sick, and they will recover."

19 So then, when the Lord Jesus had spoken to them, He was received up into heaven and sat down at the right hand of God.

20 And they went out and preached everywhere, while the Lord worked with them, and confirmed the word by the signs that followed.]

[[2]*And they promptly reported all these instructions to Peter and his companions. And after that, Jesus Himself sent out through them from east to west the sacred and imperishable proclamation of eternal salvation.*]

16:20 [2] A few late mss and versions contain this paragraph, usually after v 8; a few have it at the end of ch

NEW CENTURY VERSION

while they were eating, and he criticized them because they had no faith. They were stubborn and refused to believe those who had seen him after he had risen from the dead.

15 Jesus said to his followers, "Go everywhere in the world, and tell the Good News to everyone. 16 Anyone who believes and is baptized will be saved, but anyone who does not believe will be punished. 17 And those who believe will be able to do these things as proof: They will use my name to force out demons. They will speak in new languages.[a] 18 They will pick up snakes and drink poison without being hurt. They will touch the sick, and the sick will be healed."

19 After the Lord Jesus said these things to his followers, he was carried up into heaven, and he sat at the right side of God. 20 The followers went everywhere in the world and told the Good News to people, and the Lord helped them. The Lord proved that the Good News they told was true by giving them power to work miracles.]

16:17 [a] **languages** This can also be translated "tongues."

CONTEMPORARY ENGLISH VERSION

they were eating. He scolded them because they were too stubborn to believe the ones who had seen him after he had been raised to life. 15 Then he told them:

> Go and preach the good news to everyone in the world. 16 Anyone who believes me and is baptized will be saved. But anyone who refuses to believe me will be condemned. 17 Everyone who believes me will be able to do wonderful things. By using my name they will force out demons, and they will speak new languages. 18 They will handle snakes and will drink poison and not be hurt. They will also heal sick people by placing their hands on them.

Jesus Returns to Heaven (Luke 24.50-53; Acts 1.9-11)

19 After the Lord Jesus had said these things to the disciples, he was taken back up to heaven where he sat down at the right side[b] of God. 20 Then the disciples left and preached everywhere. The Lord was with them, and the miracles they worked proved that their message was true.

ANOTHER OLD ENDING TO MARK'S GOSPEL[c]

9-10 The women quickly told Peter and his friends what had happened. Later, Jesus sent the disciples to the east and to the west with his sacred and everlasting message of how people can be saved forever.

[b] **16.19** *right side*: See the note at 12.36. [c] **16.9,10** *Another Old Ending to Mark's Gospel*: Some manuscripts and early translations have both this shorter ending and the longer one (verses 9-20).

NEW INTERNATIONAL VERSION

he rebuked them for their lack of faith and their stubborn refusal to believe those who had seen him after he had risen.

15He said to them, "Go into all the world and preach the good news to all creation. 16Whoever believes and is baptized will be saved, but whoever does not believe will be condemned. 17And these signs will accompany those who believe: In my name they will drive out demons; they will speak in new tongues; 18they will pick up snakes with their hands; and when they drink deadly poison, it will not hurt them at all; they will place their hands on sick people, and they will get well."

19After the Lord Jesus had spoken to them, he was taken up into heaven and he sat at the right hand of God. 20Then the disciples went out and preached everywhere, and the Lord worked with them and confirmed his word by the signs that accompanied it.

NEW LIVING TRANSLATION

were eating together. He rebuked them for their unbelief—their stubborn refusal to believe those who had seen him after he had risen.

15And then he told them, "Go into all the world and preach the Good News to everyone, everywhere. 16Anyone who believes and is baptized will be saved. But anyone who refuses to believe will be condemned. 17These signs will accompany those who believe: They will cast out demons in my name, and they will speak new languages.* 18They will be able to handle snakes with safety, and if they drink anything poisonous, it won't hurt them. They will be able to place their hands on the sick and heal them."

19When the Lord Jesus had finished talking with them, he was taken up into heaven and sat down in the place of honor at God's right hand. 20And the disciples went everywhere and preached, and the Lord worked with them, confirming what they said by many miraculous signs.

[Shorter Ending of Mark]

Then they reported all these instructions briefly to Peter and his companions. Afterward Jesus himself sent them out from east to west with the sacred and unfailing message of salvation that gives eternal life. Amen.

16:17 Or *new tongues.* Some manuscripts omit *new.*

NEW KING JAMES VERSION

table; and He rebuked their unbelief and hardness of heart, because they did not believe those who had seen Him after He had risen. 15And He said to them, "Go into all the world and preach the gospel to every creature. 16He who believes and is baptized will be saved; but he who does not believe will be condemned. 17And these signs will follow those who believe: In My name they will cast out demons; they will speak with new tongues; 18they[b] will take up serpents; and if they drink anything deadly, it will by no means hurt them; they will lay hands on the sick, and they will recover."

Christ Ascends to God's Right Hand

19So then, after the Lord had spoken to them, He was received up into heaven, and sat down at the right hand of God. 20And they went out and preached everywhere, the Lord working with *them* and confirming the word through the accompanying signs. Amen.[c]

16:18 [b] NU-Text reads *and in their hands they will.* **16:20** [c] Verses 9–20 are bracketed in NU-Text as not original. They are lacking in Codex Sinaiticus and Codex Vaticanus, although nearly all other manuscripts of Mark contain them.

THE MESSAGE

and took them to task most severely for their stubborn unbelief, refusing to believe those who had seen him raised up. Then he said, "Go into the world. Go everywhere and announce the Message of God's good news to one and all. Whoever believes and is baptized is saved; whoever refuses to believe is damned.

"These are some of the signs that will accompany believers: They will throw out demons in my name, they will speak in new tongues, they will take snakes in their hands, they will drink poison and not be hurt, they will lay hands on the sick and make them well."

Then the Master Jesus, after briefing them, was taken up to heaven, and he sat down beside God in the place of honor. And the disciples went everywhere preaching, the Master working right with them, validating the Message with indisputable evidence.]

Note: Mark 16:9-20 [the portion in brackets] is contained only in later manuscripts.

KING JAMES VERSION

THE GOSPEL ACCORDING TO

ST. LUKE

1 Forasmuch as many have taken in hand to set forth in order a declaration of those things which are most surely believed among us,

2 Even as they delivered them unto us, which from the beginning were eyewitnesses, and ministers of the word;

3 It seemed good to me also, having had perfect understanding of all things from the very first, to write unto thee in order, most excellent Theophilus,

4 That thou mightest know the certainty of those things, wherein thou hast been instructed.

5 ¶ There was in the days of Herod, the king of Judaea, a certain priest named Zacharias, of the course of Abia: and his wife *was* of the daughters of Aaron, and her name *was* Elisabeth.

6 And they were both righteous before God, walking in all the commandments and ordinances of the Lord blameless.

7 And they had no child, because that Elisabeth was barren, and they both were *now* well stricken in years.

8 And it came to pass, that while he executed the

NEW AMERICAN STANDARD BIBLE

THE GOSPEL ACCORDING TO

LUKE

Introduction

1 In as much as many have undertaken to compile an account of the things accomplished among us,

2 just as they were handed down to us by those who from the beginning were eyewitnesses and servants of the [1]word,

3 it seemed fitting for me as well, having investigated everything carefully from the beginning, to write *it* out for you in consecutive order, most excellent Theophilus;

4 so that you may know the exact truth about the things you have been taught.

Birth of John the Baptist Foretold

5 In the days of Herod, king of Judea, there was a priest named Zacharias, of the division of [2]Abijah; and he had a wife [3]from the daughters of Aaron, and her name was Elizabeth.

6 They were both righteous in the sight of God, walking blamelessly in all the commandments and requirements of the Lord.

7 But they had no child, because Elizabeth was barren, and they were both advanced in years.

8 Now it happened *that* while he was performing his

1:2 [1] I.e. gospel 1:5 [2] Gr *Abia* 1:5 [3] I.e. of priestly descent

NEW CENTURY VERSION

LUKE

Luke Writes About Jesus' Life

1 Many have tried to report on the things that happened among us. 2They have written the same things that we learned from others—the people who saw those things from the beginning and served God by telling people his message. 3Since I myself have studied everything carefully from the beginning, most excellent[a] Theophilus, it seemed good for me to write it out for you. I arranged it in order 4to help you know that what you have been taught is true.

Zechariah and Elizabeth

5During the time Herod ruled Judea, there was a priest named Zechariah who belonged to Abijah's group.[b] Zechariah's wife, Elizabeth, came from the family of Aaron. 6Zechariah and Elizabeth truly did what God said was good. They did everything the Lord commanded and were without fault in keeping his law. 7But they had no children, because Elizabeth could not have a baby, and both of them were very old.

8One day Zechariah was serving as a priest before God,

1:3 [a] **excellent** This word was used to show respect to an important person like a king or ruler. 1:5 [b] **Abijah's group** The Jewish priests were divided into twenty-four groups. See 1 Chronicles 24.

CONTEMPORARY ENGLISH VERSION

LUKE

1 Many people have tried to tell the story of what God has done among us. 2They wrote what we had been told by the ones who were there in the beginning and saw what happened. 3So I made a careful study[a] of everything and then decided to write and tell you exactly what took place. Honorable Theophilus, 4I have done this to let you know the truth about what you have heard.

An Angel Tells about the Birth of John

5When Herod was king of Judea, there was a priest by the name of Zechariah from the priestly group of Abijah. His wife Elizabeth was from the family of Aaron.[b] 6Both of them were good people and pleased the Lord God by obeying all that he had commanded. 7But they did not have children. Elizabeth could not have any, and both Zechariah and Elizabeth were already old.

8One day Zechariah's group of priests were on duty, and

[a] 1.3 *a careful study*: Or "a study from the beginning." [b] 1.5 *Aaron*: The brother of Moses and the first priest.

NEW INTERNATIONAL VERSION

LUKE

Introduction

1 Many have undertaken to draw up an account of the things that have been fulfilled[a] among us, 2just as they were handed down to us by those who from the first were eyewitnesses and servants of the word. 3Therefore, since I myself have carefully investigated everything from the beginning, it seemed good also to me to write an orderly account for you, most excellent Theophilus, 4so that you may know the certainty of the things you have been taught.

The Birth of John the Baptist Foretold

5In the time of Herod king of Judea there was a priest named Zechariah, who belonged to the priestly division of Abijah; his wife Elizabeth was also a descendant of Aaron. 6Both of them were upright in the sight of God, observing all the Lord's commandments and regulations blamelessly. 7But they had no children, because Elizabeth was barren; and they were both well along in years.

8Once when Zechariah's division was on duty and he

[a] *1* Or *been surely believed*

NEW LIVING TRANSLATION

LUKE

Introduction

1 Most honorable Theophilus:

Many people have written accounts about the events that took place* among us. 2They used as their source material the reports circulating among us from the early disciples and other eyewitnesses of what God has done in fulfillment of his promises. 3Having carefully investigated all of these accounts from the beginning, I have decided to write a careful summary for you, 4to reassure you of the truth of all you were taught.

The Birth of John the Baptist Foretold

5It all begins with a Jewish priest, Zechariah, who lived when Herod was king of Judea. Zechariah was a member of the priestly order of Abijah. His wife, Elizabeth, was also from the priestly line of Aaron. 6Zechariah and Elizabeth were righteous in God's eyes, careful to obey all of the Lord's commandments and regulations. 7They had no children because Elizabeth was barren, and now they were both very old.

8One day Zechariah was serving God in the Temple, for

1:1 Or *have been fulfilled.*

NEW KING JAMES VERSION

THE GOSPEL ACCORDING TO

LUKE

Dedication to Theophilus

1 Inasmuch as many have taken in hand to set in order a narrative of those things which have been fulfilled[a] among us, 2just as those who from the beginning were eyewitnesses and ministers of the word delivered them to us, 3it seemed good to me also, having had perfect understanding of all things from the very first, to write to you an orderly account, most excellent Theophilus, 4that you may know the certainty of those things in which you were instructed.

John's Birth Announced to Zacharias

5There was in the days of Herod, the king of Judea, a certain priest named Zacharias, of the division of Abijah. His wife *was* of the daughters of Aaron, and her name *was* Elizabeth. 6And they were both righteous before God, walking in all the commandments and ordinances of the Lord blameless. 7But they had no child, because Elizabeth was barren, and they were both well advanced in years.

8So it was, that while he was serving as priest before

1:1 [a] Or *are most surely believed*

THE MESSAGE

LUKE

1 So many others have tried their hand at putting together a story of the wonderful harvest of Scripture and history that took place among us, using reports handed down by the original eyewitnesses who served this Word with their very lives. Since I have investigated all the reports in close detail, starting from the story's beginning, I decided to write it all out for you, most honorable Theophilus, so you can know beyond the shadow of a doubt the reliability of what you were taught.

A Childless Couple Conceives

During the rule of Herod, King of Judea, there was a priest assigned service in the regiment of Abijah. His name was Zachariah. His wife was descended from the daughters of Aaron. Her name was Elizabeth. Together they lived honorably before God, careful in keeping to the ways of the commandments and enjoying a clear conscience before God. But they were childless because Elizabeth could never conceive, and now they were quite old.

It so happened that as Zachariah was carrying out his

KING JAMES VERSION

priest's office before God in the order of his course,

9 According to the custom of the priest's office, his lot was to burn incense when he went into the temple of the Lord.

10 And the whole multitude of the people were praying without at the time of incense.

11 And there appeared unto him an angel of the Lord standing on the right side of the altar of incense.

12 And when Zacharias saw *him*, he was troubled, and fear fell upon him.

13 But the angel said unto him, Fear not, Zacharias: for thy prayer is heard; and thy wife Elisabeth shall bear thee a son, and thou shalt call his name John.

14 And thou shalt have joy and gladness; and many shall rejoice at his birth.

15 For he shall be great in the sight of the Lord, and shall drink neither wine nor strong drink; and he shall be filled with the Holy Ghost, even from his mother's womb.

16 And many of the children of Israel shall he turn to the Lord their God.

17 And he shall go before him in the spirit and power of Elias, to turn the hearts of the fathers to the children, and the disobedient to the wisdom of the just; to make ready a people prepared for the Lord.

18 And Zacharias said unto the angel, Whereby shall I know this? for I am an old man, and my wife well stricken in years.

NEW AMERICAN STANDARD BIBLE

priestly service before God in the *appointed* order of his division,

9 according to the custom of the priestly office, he was chosen by lot to enter the temple of the Lord and burn incense.

10 And the whole multitude of the people were in prayer outside at the hour of the incense offering.

11 And an angel of the Lord appeared to him, standing to the right of the altar of incense.

12 Zacharias was troubled when he saw *the angel,* and fear gripped him.

13 But the angel said to him, "Do not be afraid, Zacharias, for your petition has been heard, and your wife Elizabeth will bear you a son, and you will give him the name John.

14 "You will have joy and gladness, and many will rejoice at his birth.

15 "For he will be great in the sight of the Lord; and he will drink no wine or liquor, and he will be filled with the Holy Spirit while yet in his mother's womb.

16 "And he will turn many of the sons of Israel back to the Lord their God.

17 "It is he who will go *as a forerunner* before Him in the spirit and power of Elijah, TO TURN THE HEARTS OF THE FATHERS BACK TO THE CHILDREN, and the disobedient to the attitude of the righteous, so as to make ready a people prepared for the Lord."

18 Zacharias said to the angel, "How will I know this *for certain?* For I am an old man and my wife is advanced in years."

NEW CENTURY VERSION

because his group was on duty. 9According to the custom
of the priests, he was chosen by lot to go into the Temple
of the Lord and burn incense. 10There were a great many
people outside praying at the time the incense was offered.
11Then an angel of the Lord appeared to Zechariah, stand-
ing on the right side of the incense table. 12When he saw
the angel, Zechariah was startled and frightened. 13But the
angel said to him, "Zechariah, don't be afraid. God has
heard your prayer. Your wife, Elizabeth, will give birth to a
son, and you will name him John. 14He will bring you joy
and gladness, and many people will be happy because of
his birth. 15John will be a great man for the Lord. He will
never drink wine or beer, and even from birth, he will be
filled with the Holy Spirit. 16He will help many people of
Israel return to the Lord their God. 17He will go before the
Lord in spirit and power like Elijah. He will make peace
between parents and their children and will bring those
who are not obeying God back to the right way of thinking,
to make a people ready for the coming of the Lord."
18Zechariah said to the angel, "How can I know that
what you say is true? I am an old man, and my wife is old,
too."

CONTEMPORARY ENGLISH VERSION

he was serving God as a priest. 9According to the custom
of the priests, he had been chosen to go into the Lord's
temple that day and to burn incense,[c] 10while the people
stood outside praying.
11All at once an angel from the Lord appeared to
Zechariah at the right side of the altar. 12Zechariah was
confused and afraid when he saw the angel. 13But the
angel told him:

Don't be afraid, Zechariah! God has heard your
prayers. Your wife Elizabeth will have a son, and you
must name him John. 14His birth will make you very
happy, and many people will be glad. 15Your son will be
a great servant of the Lord. He must never drink wine or
beer, and the power of the Holy Spirit will be with him
from the time he is born.
16John will lead many people in Israel to turn back to
the Lord their God. 17He will go ahead of the Lord with
the same power and spirit that Elijah[d] had. And because
of John, parents will be more thoughtful of their chil-
dren. And people who now disobey God will begin to
think as they ought to. That is how John will get people
ready for the Lord.

18Zechariah said to the angel, "How will I know this is
going to happen? My wife and I are both very old."

[c] 1.9 *burn incense*: This was done twice a day, once in the morning and again in the late afternoon. [d] 1.17 *Elijah*: The prophet Elijah was known for his power to work miracles.

NEW INTERNATIONAL VERSION

was serving as priest before God, 9he was chosen by lot, according to the custom of the priesthood, to go into the temple of the Lord and burn incense. 10And when the time for the burning of incense came, all the assembled worshipers were praying outside.

11Then an angel of the Lord appeared to him, standing at the right side of the altar of incense. 12When Zechariah saw him, he was startled and was gripped with fear. 13But the angel said to him: "Do not be afraid, Zechariah; your prayer has been heard. Your wife Elizabeth will bear you a son, and you are to give him the name John. 14He will be a joy and delight to you, and many will rejoice because of his birth, 15for he will be great in the sight of the Lord. He is never to take wine or other fermented drink, and he will be filled with the Holy Spirit even from birth.[b] 16Many of the people of Israel will he bring back to the Lord their God. 17And he will go on before the Lord, in the spirit and power of Elijah, to turn the hearts of the fathers to their children and the disobedient to the wisdom of the righteous—to make ready a people prepared for the Lord."

18Zechariah asked the angel, "How can I be sure of this? I am an old man and my wife is well along in years."

[b] *15* Or *from his mother's womb*

NEW LIVING TRANSLATION

his order was on duty that week. 9As was the custom of the priests, he was chosen by lot to enter the sanctuary and burn incense in the Lord's presence. 10While the incense was being burned, a great crowd stood outside, praying.

11Zechariah was in the sanctuary when an angel of the Lord appeared, standing to the right of the incense altar. 12Zechariah was overwhelmed with fear. 13But the angel said, "Don't be afraid, Zechariah! For God has heard your prayer, and your wife, Elizabeth, will bear you a son! And you are to name him John. 14You will have great joy and gladness, and many will rejoice with you at his birth, 15for he will be great in the eyes of the Lord. He must never touch wine or hard liquor, and he will be filled with the Holy Spirit, even before his birth.* 16And he will persuade many Israelites to turn to the Lord their God. 17He will be a man with the spirit and power of Elijah, the prophet of old. He will precede the coming of the Lord, preparing the people for his arrival. He will turn the hearts of the fathers to their children, and he will change disobedient minds to accept godly wisdom."*

18Zechariah said to the angel, "How can I know this will happen? I'm an old man now, and my wife is also well along in years."

1:15 Or *even from birth.* 1:17 See Mal 4:5-6.

NEW KING JAMES VERSION

God in the order of his division, 9according to the custom of the priesthood, his lot fell to burn incense when he went into the temple of the Lord. 10And the whole multitude of the people was praying outside at the hour of incense. 11Then an angel of the Lord appeared to him, standing on the right side of the altar of incense. 12And when Zacharias saw *him,* he was troubled, and fear fell upon him.

13But the angel said to him, "Do not be afraid, Zacharias, for your prayer is heard; and your wife Elizabeth will bear you a son, and you shall call his name John. 14And you will have joy and gladness, and many will rejoice at his birth. 15For he will be great in the sight of the Lord, and shall drink neither wine nor strong drink. He will also be filled with the Holy Spirit, even from his mother's womb. 16And he will turn many of the children of Israel to the Lord their God. 17He will also go before Him in the spirit and power of Elijah, *'to turn the hearts of the fathers to the children,'*[b] and the disobedient to the wisdom of the just, to make ready a people prepared for the Lord."

18And Zacharias said to the angel, "How shall I know this? For I am an old man, and my wife is well advanced in years."

1:17 [b] Malachi 4:5, 6

THE MESSAGE

priestly duties before God, working the shift assigned to his regiment, it came his one turn in life to enter the sanctuary of God and burn incense. The congregation was gathered and praying outside the Temple at the hour of the incense offering. Unannounced, an angel of God appeared just to the right of the altar of incense. Zachariah was paralyzed in fear.

But the angel reassured him, "Don't fear, Zachariah. Your prayer has been heard. Elizabeth, your wife, will bear a son by you. You are to name him John. You're going to leap like a gazelle for joy, and not only you—many will delight in his birth. He'll achieve great stature with God.

"He'll drink neither wine nor beer. He'll be filled with the Holy Spirit from the moment he leaves his mother's womb. He will turn many sons and daughters of Israel back to their God. He will herald God's arrival in the style and strength of Elijah, soften the hearts of parents to children, and kindle devout understanding among hardened skeptics—he'll get the people ready for God."

Zachariah said to the angel, "Do you expect me to believe this? I'm an old man and my wife is an old woman."

KING JAMES VERSION

19 And the angel answering said unto him, I am Gabriel, that stand in the presence of God; and am sent to speak unto thee, and to shew thee these glad tidings.

20 And, behold, thou shalt be dumb, and not able to speak, until the day that these things shall be performed, because thou believest not my words, which shall be fulfilled in their season.

21 And the people waited for Zacharias, and marvelled that he tarried so long in the temple.

22 And when he came out, he could not speak unto them: and they perceived that he had seen a vision in the temple: for he beckoned unto them, and remained speechless.

23 And it came to pass, that, as soon as the days of his ministration were accomplished, he departed to his own house.

24 And after those days his wife Elisabeth conceived, and hid herself five months, saying,

25 Thus hath the Lord dealt with me in the days wherein he looked on *me*, to take away my reproach among men.

26 ¶ And in the sixth month the angel Gabriel was sent from God unto a city of Galilee, named Nazareth,

27 To a virgin espoused to a man whose name was Joseph, of the house of David; and the virgin's name *was* Mary.

28 And the angel came in unto her, and said, Hail, *thou that art* highly favoured, the Lord *is* with thee: blessed *art* thou among women.

29 And when she saw *him*, she was troubled at his saying, and cast in her mind what manner of salutation this should be.

NEW AMERICAN STANDARD BIBLE

19 The angel answered and said to him, "I am Gabriel, who stands in the presence of God, and I have been sent to speak to you and to bring you this good news.

20 "And behold, you shall be silent and unable to speak until the day when these things take place, because you did not believe my words, which will be fulfilled in their proper time."

21 The people were waiting for Zacharias, and were wondering at his delay in the temple.

22 But when he came out, he was unable to speak to them; and they realized that he had seen a vision in the temple; and he kept making signs to them, and remained mute.

23 When the days of his priestly service were ended, he went back home.

24 After these days Elizabeth his wife became pregnant, and she kept herself in seclusion for five months, saying,

25 "This is the way the Lord has dealt with me in the days when He looked *with favor* upon *me,* to take away my disgrace among men."

Jesus' Birth Foretold

26 Now in the sixth month the angel Gabriel was sent from God to a city in Galilee called Nazareth,

27 to a virgin engaged to a man whose name was Joseph, of the descendants of David; and the virgin's name was Mary.

28 And coming in, he said to her, "Greetings, favored one! The Lord *is* with you."

29 But she was very perplexed at *this* statement, and kept pondering what kind of salutation this was.

NEW CENTURY VERSION

19The angel answered him, "I am Gabriel. I stand before God, who sent me to talk to you and to tell you this good news. 20Now, listen! You will not be able to speak until the day these things happen, because you did not believe what I told you. But they will really happen."

21Outside, the people were still waiting for Zechariah and were surprised that he was staying so long in the Temple. 22When Zechariah came outside, he could not speak to them, and they knew he had seen a vision in the Temple. He could only make signs to them and remained unable to speak. 23When his time of service at the Temple was finished, he went home.

24Later, Zechariah's wife, Elizabeth, became pregnant and did not go out of her house for five months. Elizabeth said, 25"Look what the Lord has done for me! My people were ashamed[c] of me, but now the Lord has taken away that shame."

An Angel Appears to Mary

26During Elizabeth's sixth month of pregnancy, God sent the angel Gabriel to Nazareth, a town in Galilee, 27to a virgin. She was engaged to marry a man named Joseph from the family of David. Her name was Mary. 28The angel came to her and said, "Greetings! The Lord has blessed you and is with you."

29But Mary was very startled by what the angel said and wondered what this greeting might mean.

1:25 [c] **ashamed** The Jewish people thought it was a disgrace for women not to have children.

CONTEMPORARY ENGLISH VERSION

19The angel answered, "I am Gabriel, God's servant, and I was sent to tell you this good news. 20You have not believed what I have said. So you will not be able to say a thing until all this happens. But everything will take place when it is supposed to."

21The crowd was waiting for Zechariah and kept wondering why he was staying so long in the temple. 22When he did come out, he could not speak, and they knew he had seen a vision. He motioned to them with his hands, but did not say a thing.

23When Zechariah's time of service in the temple was over, he went home. 24Soon after that, his wife was expecting a baby, and for five months she did not leave the house. She said to herself, 25"What the Lord has done for me will keep people from looking down on me."[e]

An Angel Tells about the Birth of Jesus

26One month later God sent the angel Gabriel to the town of Nazareth in Galilee 27with a message for a virgin named Mary. She was engaged to Joseph from the family of King David. 28The angel greeted Mary and said, "You are truly blessed! The Lord is with you."

29Mary was confused by the angel's words and wondered

[e] 1.25 *keep people from looking down on me*: When a married woman could not have children, it was thought that the Lord was punishing her.

NEW INTERNATIONAL VERSION

19 The angel answered, "I am Gabriel. I stand in the presence of God, and I have been sent to speak to you and to tell you this good news. 20 And now you will be silent and not able to speak until the day this happens, because you did not believe my words, which will come true at their proper time."

21 Meanwhile, the people were waiting for Zechariah and wondering why he stayed so long in the temple. 22 When he came out, he could not speak to them. They realized he had seen a vision in the temple, for he kept making signs to them but remained unable to speak.

23 When his time of service was completed, he returned home. 24 After this his wife Elizabeth became pregnant and for five months remained in seclusion. 25 "The Lord has done this for me," she said. "In these days he has shown his favor and taken away my disgrace among the people."

The Birth of Jesus Foretold

26 In the sixth month, God sent the angel Gabriel to Nazareth, a town in Galilee, 27 to a virgin pledged to be married to a man named Joseph, a descendant of David. The virgin's name was Mary. 28 The angel went to her and said, "Greetings, you who are highly favored! The Lord is with you."

29 Mary was greatly troubled at his words and wondered what kind of greeting this might be. 30 But the angel said

NEW LIVING TRANSLATION

19 Then the angel said, "I am Gabriel! I stand in the very presence of God. It was he who sent me to bring you this good news! 20 And now, since you didn't believe what I said, you won't be able to speak until the child is born. For my words will certainly come true at the proper time."

21 Meanwhile, the people were waiting for Zechariah to come out, wondering why he was taking so long. 22 When he finally did come out, he couldn't speak to them. Then they realized from his gestures that he must have seen a vision in the Temple sanctuary.

23 He stayed at the Temple until his term of service was over, and then he returned home. 24 Soon afterward his wife, Elizabeth, became pregnant and went into seclusion for five months. 25 "How kind the Lord is!" she exclaimed. "He has taken away my disgrace of having no children!"

The Birth of Jesus Foretold

26 In the sixth month of Elizabeth's pregnancy, God sent the angel Gabriel to Nazareth, a village in Galilee, 27 to a virgin named Mary. She was engaged to be married to a man named Joseph, a descendant of King David. 28 Gabriel appeared to her and said, "Greetings, favored woman! The Lord is with you!*"

29 Confused and disturbed, Mary tried to think what the

1:28 Some manuscripts add *Blessed are you among women.*

NEW KING JAMES VERSION

19 And the angel answered and said to him, "I am Gabriel, who stands in the presence of God, and was sent to speak to you and bring you these glad tidings. 20 But behold, you will be mute and not able to speak until the day these things take place, because you did not believe my words which will be fulfilled in their own time."

21 And the people waited for Zacharias, and marveled that he lingered so long in the temple. 22 But when he came out, he could not speak to them; and they perceived that he had seen a vision in the temple, for he beckoned to them and remained speechless.

23 So it was, as soon as the days of his service were completed, that he departed to his own house. 24 Now after those days his wife Elizabeth conceived; and she hid herself five months, saying, 25 "Thus the Lord has dealt with me, in the days when He looked on *me,* to take away my reproach among people."

Christ's Birth Announced to Mary

26 Now in the sixth month the angel Gabriel was sent by God to a city of Galilee named Nazareth, 27 to a virgin betrothed to a man whose name was Joseph, of the house of David. The virgin's name *was* Mary. 28 And having come in, the angel said to her, "Rejoice, highly favored *one,* the Lord *is* with you; blessed *are* you among women!"[c]

29 But when she saw *him,*[d] she was troubled at his saying, and considered what manner of greeting this was.

1:28 [c] NU-Text omits *blessed are you among women.* 1:29 [d] NU-Text omits *when she saw him.*

THE MESSAGE

But the angel said, "I am Gabriel, the sentinel of God, sent especially to bring you this glad news. But because you won't believe me, you'll be unable to say a word until the day of your son's birth. Every word I've spoken to you will come true on time—*God's* time."

Meanwhile, the congregation waiting for Zachariah was getting restless, wondering what was keeping him so long in the sanctuary. When he came out and couldn't speak, they knew he had seen a vision. He continued speechless and had to use sign language with the people.

When the course of his priestly assignment was completed, he went back home. It wasn't long before his wife, Elizabeth, conceived. She went off by herself for five months, relishing her pregnancy. "So, this is how God acts to remedy my unfortunate condition!" she said.

A Virgin Conceives

In the sixth month of Elizabeth's pregnancy, God sent the angel Gabriel to the Galilean village of Nazareth to a virgin engaged to be married to a man descended from David. His name was Joseph, and the virgin's name, Mary. Upon entering, Gabriel greeted her:

"Good morning!
You're beautiful with God's beauty,
Beautiful inside and out!
God be with you."

She was thoroughly shaken, wondering what was behind a greeting like that. But the angel assured her,

KING JAMES VERSION

30 And the angel said unto her, Fear not, Mary: for thou hast found favour with God.

31 And, behold, thou shalt conceive in thy womb, and bring forth a son, and shalt call his name JESUS.

32 He shall be great, and shall be called the Son of the Highest: and the Lord God shall give unto him the throne of his father David:

33 And he shall reign over the house of Jacob for ever; and of his kingdom there shall be no end.

34 Then said Mary unto the angel, How shall this be, seeing I know not a man?

35 And the angel answered and said unto her, The Holy Ghost shall come upon thee, and the power of the Highest shall overshadow thee: therefore also that holy thing which shall be born of thee shall be called the Son of God.

36 And, behold, thy cousin Elisabeth, she hath also conceived a son in her old age: and this is the sixth month with her, who was called barren.

37 For with God nothing shall be impossible.

38 And Mary said, Behold the handmaid of the Lord; be it unto me according to thy word. And the angel departed from her.

NEW AMERICAN STANDARD BIBLE

30 The angel said to her, "Do not be afraid, Mary; for you have found favor with God.

31 "And behold, you will conceive in your womb and bear a son, and you shall name Him Jesus.

32 "He will be great and will be called the Son of the Most High; and the Lord God will give Him the throne of His father David;

33 and He will reign over the house of Jacob forever, and His kingdom will have no end."

34 Mary said to the angel, "How can this be, since I am a virgin?"

35 The angel answered and said to her, "The Holy Spirit will come upon you, and the power of the Most High will overshadow you; and for that reason the holy Child shall be called the Son of God.

36 "And behold, even your relative Elizabeth has also conceived a son in her old age; and she who was called barren is now in her sixth month.

37 "For nothing will be impossible with God."

38 And Mary said, "Behold, the [4]bondslave of the Lord; may it be done to me according to your word." And the angel departed from her.

1:38 [4] I.e. female slave

NEW CENTURY VERSION

30The angel said to her, "Don't be afraid, Mary; God has
shown you his grace. 31Listen! You will become pregnant
and give birth to a son, and you will name him Jesus. 32He
will be great and will be called the Son of the Most High.
The Lord God will give him the throne of King David, his
ancestor. 33He will rule over the people of Jacob forever,
and his kingdom will never end."

34Mary said to the angel, "How will this happen since I
am a virgin?"

35The angel said to Mary, "The Holy Spirit will come
upon you, and the power of the Most High will cover you.
For this reason the baby will be holy and will be called the
Son of God. 36Now Elizabeth, your relative, is also preg-
nant with a son though she is very old. Everyone thought
she could not have a baby, but she has been pregnant for
six months. 37God can do anything!"

38Mary said, "I am the servant of the Lord. Let this hap-
pen to me as you say!" Then the angel went away.

CONTEMPORARY ENGLISH VERSION

what they meant. 30Then the angel told Mary, "Don't be
afraid! God is pleased with you, 31and you will have a son.
His name will be Jesus. 32He will be great and will be called
the Son of God Most High. The Lord God will make him
king, as his ancestor David was. 33He will rule the people of
Israel forever, and his kingdom will never end."

34Mary asked the angel, "How can this happen? I am
not married!"

35The angel answered, "The Holy Spirit will come down
to you, and God's power will come over you. So your child
will be called the holy Son of God. 36Your relative
Elizabeth is also going to have a son, even though she is
old. No one thought she could ever have a baby, but in
three months she will have a son. 37Nothing is impossible
for God!"

38Mary said, "I am the Lord's servant! Let it happen as
you have said." And the angel left her.

NEW INTERNATIONAL VERSION

to her, "Do not be afraid, Mary, you have found favor with
God. 31You will be with child and give birth to a son, and
you are to give him the name Jesus. 32He will be great and
will be called the Son of the Most High. The Lord God will
give him the throne of his father David, 33and he will reign
over the house of Jacob forever; his kingdom will never
end."
34"How will this be," Mary asked the angel, "since I am
a virgin?"
35The angel answered, "The Holy Spirit will come upon
you, and the power of the Most High will overshadow you.
So the holy one to be born will be called[c] the Son of God.
36Even Elizabeth your relative is going to have a child in
her old age, and she who was said to be barren is in her
sixth month. 37For nothing is impossible with God."
38"I am the Lord's servant," Mary answered. "May it be
to me as you have said." Then the angel left her.

c 35 Or *So the child to be born will be called holy,*

NEW LIVING TRANSLATION

angel could mean. 30"Don't be frightened, Mary," the angel
told her, "for God has decided to bless you! 31You will
become pregnant and have a son, and you are to name him
Jesus. 32He will be very great and will be called the Son of
the Most High. And the Lord God will give him the throne
of his ancestor David. 33And he will reign over Israel* for-
ever; his Kingdom will never end!"
34Mary asked the angel, "But how can I have a baby? I
am a virgin."
35The angel replied, "The Holy Spirit will come upon
you, and the power of the Most High will overshadow you.
So the baby born to you will be holy, and he will be called
the Son of God. 36What's more, your relative Elizabeth has
become pregnant in her old age! People used to say she
was barren, but she's already in her sixth month. 37For
nothing is impossible with God."
38Mary responded, "I am the Lord's servant, and I am
willing to accept whatever he wants. May everything you
have said come true." And then the angel left.

1:33 Greek *over the house of Jacob.*

NEW KING JAMES VERSION

30Then the angel said to her, "Do not be afraid, Mary, for
you have found favor with God. 31And behold, you will
conceive in your womb and bring forth a Son, and shall
call His name Jesus. 32He will be great, and will be called
the Son of the Highest; and the Lord God will give Him the
throne of His father David. 33And He will reign over the
house of Jacob forever, and of His kingdom there will be no
end."
34Then Mary said to the angel, "How can this be, since I
do not know a man?"
35And the angel answered and said to her, "*The* Holy
Spirit will come upon you, and the power of the Highest
will overshadow you; therefore, also, that Holy One who is
to be born will be called the Son of God. 36Now indeed,
Elizabeth your relative has also conceived a son in her old
age; and this is now the sixth month for her who was
called barren. 37For with God nothing will be impossible."
38Then Mary said, "Behold the maidservant of the Lord!
Let it be to me according to your word." And the angel
departed from her.

THE MESSAGE

"Mary, you have nothing to fear. God has a surprise for
you: You will become pregnant and give birth to a son and
call his name Jesus.

He will be great,
  be called 'Son of the Highest.'
The Lord God will give him
  the throne of his father David;
He will rule Jacob's house forever—
  no end, ever, to his kingdom."

Mary said to the angel, "But how? I've never slept with a
man."

The angel answered,

"The Holy Spirit will come upon you,
  the power of the Highest hover over you;
Therefore, the child you bring to birth
  will be called Holy, Son of God.

"And did you know that your cousin Elizabeth conceived
a son, old as she is? Everyone called her barren, and here
she is six months pregnant! Nothing, you see, is impossi-
ble with God."

And Mary said,

"Yes, I see it all now:
  I'm the Lord's maid, ready to serve.
Let it be with me
  just as you say."

Then the angel left her.

KING JAMES VERSION

39 ¶ And Mary arose in those days, and went into the
hill country with haste, into a city of Juda;
40 And entered into the house of Zacharias, and saluted
Elisabeth.
41 And it came to pass, that, when Elisabeth heard the
salutation of Mary, the babe leaped in her womb; and
Elisabeth was filled with the Holy Ghost:
42 And she spake out with a loud voice, and said,
Blessed *art* thou among women, and blessed *is* the fruit of
thy womb.
43 And whence *is* this to me, that the mother of my
Lord should come to me?
44 For, lo, as soon as the voice of thy salutation sound-
ed in mine ears, the babe leaped in my womb for joy.
45 And blessed *is* she that believed: for there shall be a
performance of those things which were told her from the
Lord.
46 And Mary said, My soul doth magnify the Lord,
47 And my spirit hath rejoiced in God my Saviour.
48 For he hath regarded the low estate of his hand-
maiden: for, behold, from henceforth all generations shall
call me blessed.
49 For he that is mighty hath done to me great things;
and holy *is* his name.

NEW AMERICAN STANDARD BIBLE

Mary Visits Elizabeth

39 Now at this time Mary arose and went in a hurry to
the hill country, to a city of Judah,
40 and entered the house of Zacharias and greeted
Elizabeth.
41 When Elizabeth heard Mary's greeting, the baby
leaped in her womb; and Elizabeth was filled with the Holy
Spirit.
42 And she cried out with a loud voice and said,
"Blessed *are* you among women, and blessed *is* the fruit of
your womb!
43 "And how has it *happened* to me, that the mother of
my Lord would come to me?
44 "For behold, when the sound of your greeting reached
my ears, the baby leaped in my womb for joy.
45 "And blessed *is* she who believed that there would be
a fulfillment of what had been spoken to her by the Lord."

The Magnificat

46 And Mary said:
"My soul exalts the Lord,
47 And my spirit has rejoiced in God my Savior.
48 "For He has had regard for the humble state of His
bondslave;
For behold, from this time on all generations will
count me blessed.
49 "For the Mighty One has done great things for me;
And holy is His name.

NEW CENTURY VERSION

Mary Visits Elizabeth

39 Mary got up and went quickly to a town in the hills of
Judea. 40 She came to Zechariah's house and greeted
Elizabeth. 41 When Elizabeth heard Mary's greeting, the
unborn baby inside her jumped, and Elizabeth was filled
with the Holy Spirit. 42 She cried out in a loud voice, "God
has blessed you more than any other woman, and he has
blessed the baby to which you will give birth. 43 Why has
this good thing happened to me, that the mother of my
Lord comes to me? 44 When I heard your voice, the baby
inside me jumped with joy. 45 You are blessed because you
believed that what the Lord said to you would really hap-
pen."

Mary Praises God

46 Then Mary said,
"My soul praises the Lord;
47 my heart rejoices in God my Savior,
48 because he has shown his concern for his humble
servant girl.
From now on, all people will say that I am blessed,
49 because the Powerful One has done great things
for me.
His name is holy.

CONTEMPORARY ENGLISH VERSION

Mary Visits Elizabeth

39 A short time later Mary hurried to a town in the hill
country of Judea. 40 She went into Zechariah's home, where
she greeted Elizabeth. 41 When Elizabeth heard Mary's
greeting, her baby moved within her.
The Holy Spirit came upon Elizabeth. 42 Then in a loud
voice she said to Mary:
God has blessed you more than any other woman! He
has also blessed the child you will have. 43 Why should
the mother of my Lord come to me? 44 As soon as I heard
your greeting, my baby became happy and moved within
me. 45 The Lord has blessed you because you believed
that he will keep his promise.

Mary's Song of Praise

46 Mary said:

With all my heart
I praise the Lord,
47 and I am glad
because of God my Savior.
48 He cares for me,
his humble servant.
From now on,
all people will say
God has blessed me.
49 God All-Powerful has done
great things for me,
and his name is holy.

NEW INTERNATIONAL VERSION

Mary Visits Elizabeth

39 At that time Mary got ready and hurried to a town in
the hill country of Judea, 40 where she entered Zechariah's
home and greeted Elizabeth. 41 When Elizabeth heard
Mary's greeting, the baby leaped in her womb, and
Elizabeth was filled with the Holy Spirit. 42 In a loud voice
she exclaimed: "Blessed are you among women, and
blessed is the child you will bear! 43 But why am I so
favored, that the mother of my Lord should come to me?
44 As soon as the sound of your greeting reached my ears,
the baby in my womb leaped for joy. 45 Blessed is she who
has believed that what the Lord has said to her will be
accomplished!"

Mary's Song

46 And Mary said:

"My soul glorifies the Lord
47 and my spirit rejoices in God my Savior,
48 for he has been mindful
of the humble state of his servant.
From now on all generations will call me blessed,
49 for the Mighty One has done great things for me—
holy is his name.

NEW LIVING TRANSLATION

Mary Visits Elizabeth

39 A few days later Mary hurried to the hill country of
Judea, to the town 40 where Zechariah lived. She entered
the house and greeted Elizabeth. 41 At the sound of Mary's
greeting, Elizabeth's child leaped within her, and Elizabeth
was filled with the Holy Spirit.
42 Elizabeth gave a glad cry and exclaimed to Mary, "You
are blessed by God above all other women, and your child
is blessed. 43 What an honor this is, that the mother of my
Lord should visit me! 44 When you came in and greeted me,
my baby jumped for joy the instant I heard your voice!
45 You are blessed, because you believed that the Lord
would do what he said."

The Magnificat: Mary's Song of Praise

46 Mary responded,

"Oh, how I praise the Lord.
47 How I rejoice in God my Savior!
48 For he took notice of his lowly servant girl,
and now generation after generation
will call me blessed.
49 For he, the Mighty One, is holy,
and he has done great things for me.

NEW KING JAMES VERSION

Mary Visits Elizabeth

39 Now Mary arose in those days and went into the hill
country with haste, to a city of Judah, 40 and entered the
house of Zacharias and greeted Elizabeth. 41 And it hap-
pened, when Elizabeth heard the greeting of Mary, that the
babe leaped in her womb; and Elizabeth was filled with the
Holy Spirit. 42 Then she spoke out with a loud voice and
said, "Blessed *are* you among women, and blessed *is* the
fruit of your womb! 43 But why *is* this *granted* to me, that
the mother of my Lord should come to me? 44 For indeed,
as soon as the voice of your greeting sounded in my ears,
the babe leaped in my womb for joy. 45 Blessed *is* she who
believed, for there will be a fulfillment of those things
which were told her from the Lord."

The Song of Mary

46 And Mary said:

"My soul magnifies the Lord,
47 And my spirit has rejoiced in God my Savior.
48 For He has regarded the lowly state of His
maidservant;
For behold, henceforth all generations will call me
blessed.
49 For He who is mighty has done great things for me,
And holy *is* His name.

THE MESSAGE

Blessed Among Women

Mary didn't waste a minute. She got up and traveled to a town in Judah in the hill country, straight to Zachariah's house, and greeted Elizabeth. When Elizabeth heard Mary's greeting, the baby in her womb leaped. She was filled with the Holy Spirit, and sang out exuberantly,

"You're so blessed among women,
and the babe in your womb, also blessed!
And why am I so blessed that
the mother of my Lord visits me?
The moment the sound of your
greeting entered my ears,
The babe in my womb
skipped like a lamb for sheer joy.
Blessed woman, who believed what God said,
believed every word would come true!"

And Mary said,

"I'm bursting with God-news;
I'm dancing the song of my Savior God.
God took one good look at me, and look what
happened—
I'm the most fortunate woman on earth!
What God has done for me will never be forgotten,
the God whose very name is holy, set apart from all
others.

KING JAMES VERSION

50 And his mercy *is* on them that fear him from generation to generation.

51 He hath shewed strength with his arm; he hath scattered the proud in the imagination of their hearts.

52 He hath put down the mighty from *their* seats, and exalted them of low degree.

53 He hath filled the hungry with good things; and the rich he hath sent empty away.

54 He hath holpen his servant Israel, in remembrance of *his* mercy;

55 As he spake to our fathers, to Abraham, and to his seed for ever.

56 And Mary abode with her about three months, and returned to her own house.

57 ¶ Now Elisabeth's full time came that she should be delivered; and she brought forth a son.

58 And her neighbours and her cousins heard how the Lord had shewed great mercy upon her; and they rejoiced with her.

NEW AMERICAN STANDARD BIBLE

50 "AND HIS MERCY IS UPON GENERATION AFTER GENERATION
TOWARD THOSE WHO FEAR HIM.
51 "He has done mighty deeds with His arm;
He has scattered *those who were* proud in the thoughts of their heart.
52 "He has brought down rulers from *their* thrones,
And has exalted those who were humble.
53 "HE HAS FILLED THE HUNGRY WITH GOOD THINGS;
And sent away the rich empty-handed.
54 "He has given help to Israel His servant,
In remembrance of His mercy,
55 As He spoke to our fathers,
To Abraham and his descendants forever."

56 And Mary stayed with her about three months, and *then* returned to her home.

John Is Born

57 Now the time had come for Elizabeth to give birth, and she gave birth to a son.

58 Her neighbors and her relatives heard that the Lord had displayed His great mercy toward her; and they were rejoicing with her.

NEW CENTURY VERSION

50 God will show his mercy forever and ever
to those who worship and serve him.
51 He has done mighty deeds by his power.
He has scattered the people who are proud
and think great things about themselves.
52 He has brought down rulers from their thrones
and raised up the humble.
53 He has filled the hungry with good things
and sent the rich away with nothing.
54 He has helped his servant, the people of Israel,
remembering to show them mercy
55 as he promised to our ancestors,
to Abraham and to his children forever."

56 Mary stayed with Elizabeth for about three months and then returned home.

The Birth of John

57 When it was time for Elizabeth to give birth, she had a boy. 58 Her neighbors and relatives heard how good the Lord was to her, and they rejoiced with her.

CONTEMPORARY ENGLISH VERSION

50 He always shows mercy
to everyone
who worships him.
51 The Lord has used
his powerful arm
to scatter those
who are proud.
52 He drags strong rulers
from their thrones
and puts humble people
in places of power.
53 God gives the hungry
good things to eat,
and sends the rich away
with nothing.
54 He helps his servant Israel
and is always merciful
to his people.
55 The Lord made this promise
to our ancestors,
to Abraham and his family
forever!

56 Mary stayed with Elizabeth about three months. Then she went back home.

The Birth of John the Baptist

57 When Elizabeth's son was born, 58 her neighbors and relatives heard how kind the Lord had been to her, and they too were glad.

NEW INTERNATIONAL VERSION

50 His mercy extends to those who fear him,
from generation to generation.
51 He has performed mighty deeds with his arm;
he has scattered those who are proud in their inmost thoughts.
52 He has brought down rulers from their thrones
but has lifted up the humble.
53 He has filled the hungry with good things
but has sent the rich away empty.
54 He has helped his servant Israel,
remembering to be merciful
55 to Abraham and his descendants forever,
even as he said to our fathers."

56 Mary stayed with Elizabeth for about three months and then returned home.

The Birth of John the Baptist

57 When it was time for Elizabeth to have her baby, she gave birth to a son. 58 Her neighbors and relatives heard that the Lord had shown her great mercy, and they shared her joy.

NEW LIVING TRANSLATION

50 His mercy goes on from generation to generation,
to all who fear him.
51 His mighty arm does tremendous things!
How he scatters the proud and haughty ones!
52 He has taken princes from their thrones
and exalted the lowly.
53 He has satisfied the hungry with good things
and sent the rich away with empty hands.
54 And how he has helped his servant Israel!
He has not forgotten his promise to be merciful.
55 For he promised our ancestors—Abraham and his children—
to be merciful to them forever."

56 Mary stayed with Elizabeth about three months and then went back to her own home.

The Birth of John the Baptist

57 Now it was time for Elizabeth's baby to be born, and it was a boy. 58 The word spread quickly to her neighbors and relatives that the Lord had been very kind to her, and everyone rejoiced with her.

NEW KING JAMES VERSION

50 And His mercy *is* on those who fear Him
From generation to generation.
51 He has shown strength with His arm;
He has scattered *the* proud in the imagination of their hearts.
52 He has put down the mighty from *their* thrones,
And exalted *the* lowly.
53 He has filled *the* hungry with good things,
And *the* rich He has sent away empty.
54 He has helped His servant Israel,
In remembrance of *His* mercy,
55 As He spoke to our fathers,
To Abraham and to his seed forever."

56 And Mary remained with her about three months, and returned to her house.

Birth of John the Baptist

57 Now Elizabeth's full time came for her to be delivered, and she brought forth a son. 58 When her neighbors and relatives heard how the Lord had shown great mercy to her, they rejoiced with her.

THE MESSAGE

His mercy flows in wave after wave
on those who are in awe before him.
He bared his arm and showed his strength,
scattered the bluffing braggarts.
He knocked tyrants off their high horses,
pulled victims out of the mud.
The starving poor sat down to a banquet;
the callous rich were left out in the cold.
He embraced his chosen child, Israel;
he remembered and piled on the mercies, piled them high.
It's exactly what he promised,
beginning with Abraham and right up to now."

Mary stayed with Elizabeth for three months and then went back to her own home.

The Birth of John

When Elizabeth was full-term in her pregnancy, she bore a son. Her neighbors and relatives, seeing that God had overwhelmed her with mercy, celebrated with her.

KING JAMES VERSION

59 And it came to pass, that on the eighth day they came to circumcise the child; and they called him Zacharias, after the name of his father.

60 And his mother answered and said, Not *so*; but he shall be called John.

61 And they said unto her, There is none of thy kindred that is called by this name.

62 And they made signs to his father, how he would have him called.

63 And he asked for a writing table, and wrote, saying, His name is John. And they marvelled all.

64 And his mouth was opened immediately, and his tongue *loosed*, and he spake, and praised God.

65 And fear came on all that dwelt round about them: and all these sayings were noised abroad throughout all the hill country of Judaea.

66 And all they that heard *them* laid *them* up in their hearts, saying, What manner of child shall this be! And the hand of the Lord was with him.

67 ¶ And his father Zacharias was filled with the Holy Ghost, and prophesied, saying,

68 Blessed *be* the Lord God of Israel; for he hath visited and redeemed his people,

69 And hath raised up an horn of salvation for us in

NEW AMERICAN STANDARD BIBLE

59 And it happened that on the eighth day they came to circumcise the child, and they were going to call him Zacharias, after his father.

60 But his mother answered and said, "No indeed; but he shall be called John."

61 And they said to her, "There is no one among your relatives who is called by that name."

62 And they made signs to his father, as to what he wanted him called.

63 And he asked for a tablet and wrote as follows, "His name is John." And they were all astonished.

64 And at once his mouth was opened and his tongue *loosed,* and he *began* to speak in praise of God.

65 Fear came on all those living around them; and all these matters were being talked about in all the hill country of Judea.

66 All who heard them kept them in mind, saying, "What then will this child *turn out to* be?" For the hand of the Lord was certainly with him.

Zacharias' Prophecy

67 And his father Zacharias was filled with the Holy Spirit, and prophesied, saying:

68 "Blessed *be* the Lord God of Israel,
For He has visited us and accomplished redemption
for His people,
69 And has raised up a horn of salvation for us

NEW CENTURY VERSION

59 When the baby was eight days old, they came to circumcise him. They wanted to name him Zechariah because this was his father's name, 60 but his mother said, "No! He will be named John."

61 The people said to Elizabeth, "But no one in your family has this name." 62 Then they made signs to his father to find out what he would like to name him.

63 Zechariah asked for a writing tablet and wrote, "His name is John," and everyone was surprised. 64 Immediately Zechariah could talk again, and he began praising God. 65 All their neighbors became alarmed, and in all the mountains of Judea people continued talking about all these things. 66 The people who heard about them wondered, saying, "What will this child be?" because the Lord was with him.

Zechariah Praises God

67 Then Zechariah, John's father, was filled with the Holy Spirit and prophesied:

68 "Let us praise the Lord, the God of Israel,
because he has come to help his people and has given them freedom.
69 He has given us a powerful Savior

CONTEMPORARY ENGLISH VERSION

59 Eight days later they did for the child what the Law of Moses commands.[f] They were going to name him Zechariah, after his father. 60 But Elizabeth said, "No! His name is John."

61 The people argued, "No one in your family has ever been named John." 62 So they motioned to Zechariah to find out what he wanted to name his son.

63 Zechariah asked for a writing tablet. Then he wrote, "His name is John." Everyone was amazed. 64 Right away, Zechariah started speaking and praising God.

65 All the neighbors were frightened because of what had happened, and everywhere in the hill country people kept talking about these things. 66 Everyone who heard about this wondered what this child would grow up to be. They knew that the Lord was with him.

Zechariah Praises the Lord

67 The Holy Spirit came upon Zechariah, and he began to speak:

68 Praise the Lord,
the God of Israel!
He has come
to save his people.
69 Our God has given us
a mighty Savior[g]

[f] **1.59** *what the Law of Moses commands*: This refers to circumcision. It is the cutting off of skin from the private part of Jewish boys eight days after birth to show that they belong to the Lord. [g] **1.69** *a mighty Savior*: The Greek text has "a horn of salvation." In the Scriptures animal horns are often a symbol of great strength.

NEW INTERNATIONAL VERSION

59 On the eighth day they came to circumcise the child,
and they were going to name him after his father
Zechariah, 60 but his mother spoke up and said, "No! He is
to be called John."

61 They said to her, "There is no one among your relatives who has that name."

62 Then they made signs to his father, to find out what
he would like to name the child. 63 He asked for a writing
tablet, and to everyone's astonishment he wrote, "His
name is John." 64 Immediately his mouth was opened and
his tongue was loosed, and he began to speak, praising
God. 65 The neighbors were all filled with awe, and
throughout the hill country of Judea people were talking
about all these things. 66 Everyone who heard this wondered about it, asking, "What then is this child going to
be?" For the Lord's hand was with him.

Zechariah's Song

67 His father Zechariah was filled with the Holy Spirit
and prophesied:

68 "Praise be to the Lord, the God of Israel,
because he has come and has redeemed his people.
69 He has raised up a horn[d] of salvation for us

[d] 69 *Horn* here symbolizes strength.

NEW LIVING TRANSLATION

59 When the baby was eight days old, all the relatives
and friends came for the circumcision ceremony. They
wanted to name him Zechariah, after his father. 60 But
Elizabeth said, "No! His name is John!"

61 "What?" they exclaimed. "There is no one in all your
family by that name." 62 So they asked the baby's father,
communicating to him by making gestures. 63 He motioned
for a writing tablet, and to everyone's surprise he wrote,
"His name is John!" 64 Instantly Zechariah could speak
again, and he began praising God.

65 Wonder fell upon the whole neighborhood, and the
news of what had happened spread throughout the Judean
hills. 66 Everyone who heard about it reflected on these
events and asked, "I wonder what this child will turn out
to be? For the hand of the Lord is surely upon him in a
special way."

Zechariah's Prophecy

67 Then his father, Zechariah, was filled with the Holy
Spirit and gave this prophecy:

68 "Praise the Lord, the God of Israel,
because he has visited his people and redeemed them.
69 He has sent us a mighty Savior

NEW KING JAMES VERSION

Circumcision of John the Baptist

59 So it was, on the eighth day, that they came to circumcise the child; and they would have called him by the name
of his father, Zacharias. 60 His mother answered and said,
"No; he shall be called John."

61 But they said to her, "There is no one among your relatives who is called by this name." 62 So they made signs
to his father—what he would have him called.

63 And he asked for a writing tablet, and wrote, saying,
"His name is John." So they all marveled. 64 Immediately
his mouth was opened and his tongue *loosed,* and he
spoke, praising God. 65 Then fear came on all who dwelt
around them; and all these sayings were discussed
throughout all the hill country of Judea. 66 And all those
who heard *them* kept *them* in their hearts, saying, "What
kind of child will this be?" And the hand of the Lord was
with him.

Zacharias' Prophecy

67 Now his father Zacharias was filled with the Holy
Spirit, and prophesied, saying:

68 "Blessed *is* the Lord God of Israel,
For He has visited and redeemed His people,
69 And has raised up a horn of salvation for us

THE MESSAGE

On the eighth day, they came to circumcise the child and were calling him Zachariah after his father. But his mother intervened: "No. He is to be called John."

"But," they said, "no one in your family is named that." They used sign language to ask Zachariah what he wanted him named.

Asking for a tablet, Zachariah wrote, "His name is to be John." That took everyone by surprise. Surprise followed surprise—Zachariah's mouth was now open, his tongue loose, and he was talking, praising God!

A deep, reverential fear settled over the neighborhood, and in all that Judean hill country people talked about nothing else. Everyone who heard about it took it to heart, wondering, "What will become of this child? Clearly, God has his hand in this."

Then Zachariah was filled with the Holy Spirit and prophesied,

"Blessed be the Lord, the God of Israel;
he came and set his people free.
He set the power of salvation in the center of our lives,

KING JAMES VERSION

the house of his servant David;
70 As he spake by the mouth of his holy prophets,
which have been since the world began:
71 That we should be saved from our enemies, and from
the hand of all that hate us;
72 To perform the mercy *promised* to our fathers, and to
remember his holy covenant;
73 The oath which he sware to our father Abraham,
74 That he would grant unto us, that we being delivered
out of the hand of our enemies might serve him without
fear,
75 In holiness and righteousness before him, all the
days of our life.
76 And thou, child, shalt be called the prophet of the
Highest: for thou shalt go before the face of the Lord to
prepare his ways;
77 To give knowledge of salvation unto his people by
the remission of their sins,

NEW AMERICAN STANDARD BIBLE

In the house of David His servant—
70 As He spoke by the mouth of His holy prophets from of old—
71 Salvation FROM OUR ENEMIES,
And FROM THE HAND OF ALL WHO HATE US;
72 To show mercy toward our fathers,
And to remember His holy covenant,
73 The oath which He swore to Abraham our father,
74 To grant us that we, being rescued from the hand of our enemies,
Might serve Him without fear,
75 In holiness and righteousness before Him all our days.
76 "And you, child, will be called the prophet of the Most High;
For you will go on BEFORE THE LORD TO PREPARE HIS WAYS;
77 To give to His people *the* knowledge of salvation
By the forgiveness of their sins,

NEW CENTURY VERSION

from the family of God's servant David.
70 He said that he would do this
through his holy prophets who lived long ago:
71 He promised he would save us from our enemies
and from the power of all those who hate us.
72 He said he would give mercy to our fathers
and that he would remember his holy promise.
73 God promised Abraham, our father,
74 that he would save us from the power of our enemies
so we could serve him without fear,
75 being holy and good before God as long as we live.

76 "Now you, child, will be called a prophet of the Most High God.
You will go before the Lord to prepare his way.
77 You will make his people know that they will be saved
by having their sins forgiven.

CONTEMPORARY ENGLISH VERSION

from the family
of David his servant.
70 Long ago the Lord promised
by the words
of his holy prophets
71 to save us from our enemies
and from everyone
who hates us.
72 God said he would be kind
to our people and keep
his sacred promise.
73 He told our ancestor Abraham
74 that he would rescue us
from our enemies.
Then we could serve him
without fear,
75 by being holy and good
as long as we live.

76 You, my son, will be called
a prophet of God
in heaven above.
You will go ahead of the Lord
to get everything ready
for him.
77 You will tell his people
that they can be saved
when their sins
are forgiven.

NEW INTERNATIONAL VERSION

in the house of his servant David
70 (as he said through his holy prophets of long ago),
71 salvation from our enemies
and from the hand of all who hate us—
72 to show mercy to our fathers
and to remember his holy covenant,
73 the oath he swore to our father Abraham:
74 to rescue us from the hand of our enemies,
and to enable us to serve him without fear
75 in holiness and righteousness before him all our days.

76 And you, my child, will be called a prophet of the Most High;
for you will go on before the Lord to prepare the way for him,
77 to give his people the knowledge of salvation
through the forgiveness of their sins,

NEW LIVING TRANSLATION

from the royal line of his servant David,
70 just as he promised
through his holy prophets long ago.
71 Now we will be saved from our enemies
and from all who hate us.
72 He has been merciful to our ancestors
by remembering his sacred covenant with them,
73 the covenant he gave to our ancestor Abraham.
74 We have been rescued from our enemies,
so we can serve God without fear,
75 in holiness and righteousness forever.

76 "And you, my little son,
will be called the prophet of the Most High,
because you will prepare the way for the Lord.
77 You will tell his people how to find salvation
through forgiveness of their sins.

NEW KING JAMES VERSION

In the house of His servant David,
70 As He spoke by the mouth of His holy prophets,
Who *have been* since the world began,
71 That we should be saved from our enemies
And from the hand of all who hate us,
72 To perform the mercy *promised* to our fathers
And to remember His holy covenant,
73 The oath which He swore to our father Abraham:
74 To grant us that we,
Being delivered from the hand of our enemies,
Might serve Him without fear,
75 In holiness and righteousness before Him all the days of our life.

76 "And you, child, will be called the prophet of the Highest;
For you will go before the face of the Lord to prepare His ways,
77 To give knowledge of salvation to His people
By the remission of their sins,

THE MESSAGE

and in the very house of David his servant,
Just as he promised long ago
through the preaching of his holy prophets:
Deliverance from our enemies
and every hateful hand;
Mercy to our fathers,
as he remembers to do what he said he'd do,
What he swore to our father Abraham—
a clean rescue from the enemy camp,
So we can worship him without a care in the world,
made holy before him as long as we live.

"And you, my child, 'Prophet of the Highest,'
will go ahead of the Master to prepare his ways,
Present the offer of salvation to his people,
the forgiveness of their sins.

KING JAMES VERSION

78 Through the tender mercy of our God; whereby the dayspring from on high hath visited us,

79 To give light to them that sit in darkness and *in* the shadow of death, to guide our feet into the way of peace.

80 And the child grew, and waxed strong in spirit, and was in the deserts till the day of his shewing unto Israel.

2 And it came to pass in those days, that there went out a decree from Caesar Augustus, that all the world should be taxed.

2 (*And* this taxing was first made when Cyrenius was governor of Syria.)

3 And all went to be taxed, every one into his own city.

4 And Joseph also went up from Galilee, out of the city of Nazareth, into Judaea, unto the city of David, which is called Bethlehem; (because he was of the house and lineage of David:)

NEW AMERICAN STANDARD BIBLE

78 Because of the tender mercy of our God,
With which the Sunrise from on high will visit us,
79 TO SHINE UPON THOSE WHO SIT IN DARKNESS AND THE SHADOW OF DEATH,
To guide our feet into the way of peace."

80 And the child continued to grow and to become strong in spirit, and he lived in the deserts until the day of his public appearance to Israel.

Jesus' Birth in Bethlehem

2 Now in those days a decree went out from Caesar Augustus, that a census be taken of all [1]the inhabited earth.

2 This was the first census taken while [2]Quirinius was governor of Syria.

3 And everyone was on his way to register for the census, each to his own city.

4 Joseph also went up from Galilee, from the city of Nazareth, to Judea, to the city of David which is called Bethlehem, because he was of the house and family of David,

2:1 [1] I.e. the Roman empire   2:2 [2] Gr *Kyrenios*

NEW CENTURY VERSION

78 With the loving mercy of our God,
a new day from heaven will dawn upon us.
79 It will shine on those who live in darkness,
in the shadow of death.
It will guide us into the path of peace."

80 And so the child grew up and became strong in spirit. John lived in the desert until the time when he came out to preach to Israel.

The Birth of Jesus

2 At that time, Augustus Caesar sent an order that all people in the countries under Roman rule must list their names in a register. 2 This was the first registration;[a] it was taken while Quirinius was governor of Syria. 3 And all went to their own towns to be registered.

4 So Joseph left Nazareth, a town in Galilee, and went to the town of Bethlehem in Judea, known as the town of David. Joseph went there because he was from the family

2:2 [a] **registration** Census. A counting of all the people and the things they own.

CONTEMPORARY ENGLISH VERSION

78 God's love and kindness
will shine upon us
like the sun that rises
in the sky.[h]
79 On us who live
in the dark shadow
of death
this light will shine
to guide us
into a life of peace.

80 As John grew up, God's Spirit gave him great power. John lived in the desert until the time he was sent to the people of Israel.

The Birth of Jesus (Matthew 1.18-25)

2 About that time Emperor Augustus gave orders for the names of all the people to be listed in record books.[a]
2 These first records were made when Quirinius was governor of Syria.[b]

3 Everyone had to go to their own hometown to be listed.
4 So Joseph had to leave Nazareth in Galilee and go to Bethlehem in Judea. Long ago Bethlehem had been King David's hometown, and Joseph went there because he was from David's family.

[h] 1.78 *like the sun that rises in the sky*: Or "like the Messiah coming from heaven."   [a] 2.1 *names . . . listed in record books*: This was done so that everyone could be made to pay taxes to the Emperor.
[b] 2.2 *Quirinius was governor of Syria*: It is known that Quirinius made a record of the people in A.D. 6 or 7. But the exact date of the record taking that Luke mentions is not known.

NEW INTERNATIONAL VERSION

78 because of the tender mercy of our God,
by which the rising sun will come to us from heaven
79 to shine on those living in darkness
and in the shadow of death,
to guide our feet into the path of peace."

80 And the child grew and became strong in spirit; and he lived in the desert until he appeared publicly to Israel.

The Birth of Jesus

2 In those days Caesar Augustus issued a decree that a census should be taken of the entire Roman world.
2 (This was the first census that took place while Quirinius
was governor of Syria.) 3 And everyone went to his own
town to register.
4 So Joseph also went up from the town of Nazareth in Galilee to Judea, to Bethlehem the town of David, because he belonged to the house and line of David.
5 He went there

NEW LIVING TRANSLATION

78 Because of God's tender mercy,
the light from heaven is about to break upon us,
79 to give light to those who sit in darkness and in the
shadow of death,
and to guide us to the path of peace."

80 John grew up and became strong in spirit. Then he lived out in the wilderness until he began his public ministry to Israel.

The Birth of Jesus

2 At that time the Roman emperor, Augustus, decreed that a census should be taken throughout the Roman
Empire. 2 (This was the first census taken when Quirinius
was governor of Syria.) 3 All returned to their own towns to
register for this census. 4 And because Joseph was a descendant of King David, he had to go to Bethlehem in Judea, David's ancient home. He traveled there from the village of

NEW KING JAMES VERSION

78 Through the tender mercy of our God,
With which the Dayspring from on high has visited[e] us;
79 To give light to those who sit in darkness and the
shadow of death,
To guide our feet into the way of peace."

80 So the child grew and became strong in spirit, and was in the deserts till the day of his manifestation to Israel.

Christ Born of Mary

2 And it came to pass in those days *that* a decree went out from Caesar Augustus that all the world should be
registered. 2 This census first took place while Quirinius
was governing Syria. 3 So all went to be registered, everyone to his own city.
4 Joseph also went up from Galilee, out of the city of Nazareth, into Judea, to the city of David, which is called Bethlehem, because he was of the house and lineage of David,

1:78 [e] NU-Text reads *shall visit.*

THE MESSAGE

Through the heartfelt mercies of our God,
God's Sunrise will break in upon us,
Shining on those in the darkness,
those sitting in the shadow of death,
Then showing us the way, one foot at a time,
down the path of peace."

The child grew up, healthy and spirited. He lived out in the desert until the day he made his prophetic debut in Israel.

The Birth of Jesus

2 About that time Caesar Augustus ordered a census to be taken throughout the Empire. This was the first census when Quirinius was governor of Syria. Everyone had to travel to his own ancestral hometown to be accounted for. So Joseph went from the Galilean town of Nazareth up to Bethlehem in Judah, David's town, for the census. As

KING JAMES VERSION

5 To be taxed with Mary his espoused wife, being great with child.

6 And so it was, that, while they were there, the days were accomplished that she should be delivered.

7 And she brought forth her firstborn son, and wrapped him in swaddling clothes, and laid him in a manger; because there was no room for them in the inn.

8 ¶ And there were in the same country shepherds abiding in the field, keeping watch over their flock by night.

9 And, lo, the angel of the Lord came upon them, and the glory of the Lord shone round about them: and they were sore afraid.

10 And the angel said unto them, Fear not: for, behold, I bring you good tidings of great joy, which shall be to all people.

11 For unto you is born this day in the city of David a Saviour, which is Christ the Lord.

12 And this *shall be* a sign unto you; Ye shall find the babe wrapped in swaddling clothes, lying in a manger.

13 And suddenly there was with the angel a multitude of the heavenly host praising God, and saying,

14 Glory to God in the highest, and on earth peace, good will toward men.

15 And it came to pass, as the angels were gone away from them into heaven, the shepherds said one to another,

NEW AMERICAN STANDARD BIBLE

5 in order to register along with Mary, who was engaged to him, and was with child.

6 While they were there, the days were completed for her to give birth.

7 And she gave birth to her firstborn son; and she wrapped Him in cloths, and laid Him in a manger, because there was no room for them in the inn.

8 In the same region there were *some* shepherds staying out in the fields and keeping watch over their flock by night.

9 And an angel of the Lord suddenly stood before them, and the glory of the Lord shone around them; and they were terribly frightened.

10 But the angel said to them, "Do not be afraid; for behold, I bring you good news of great joy which will be for all the people;

11 for today in the city of David there has been born for you a Savior, who is [3]Christ the Lord.

12 "This *will be* a sign for you: you will find a baby wrapped in cloths and lying in a manger."

13 And suddenly there appeared with the angel a multitude of the heavenly host praising God and saying,

14 "Glory to God in the highest,
And on earth peace among men [4]with whom He is pleased."

15 When the angels had gone away from them into heaven, the shepherds *began* saying to one another, "Let

2:11 [3] I.e. Messiah 2:14 [4] Lit *of good pleasure;* or *of good will*

NEW CENTURY VERSION

of David. [5]Joseph registered with Mary, to whom he was engaged[b] and who was now pregnant. [6]While they were in Bethlehem, the time came for Mary to have the baby, [7]and she gave birth to her first son. Because there were no rooms left in the inn, she wrapped the baby with pieces of cloth and laid him in a box where animals are fed.

Shepherds Hear About Jesus

[8]That night, some shepherds were in the fields nearby watching their sheep. [9]Then an angel of the Lord stood before them. The glory of the Lord was shining around them, and they became very frightened. [10]The angel said to them, "Do not be afraid. I am bringing you good news that will be a great joy to all the people. [11]Today your Savior was born in the town of David. He is Christ, the Lord. [12]This is how you will know him: You will find a baby wrapped in pieces of cloth and lying in a feeding box."

[13]Then a very large group of angels from heaven joined the first angel, praising God and saying:

[14] "Give glory to God in heaven,
and on earth let there be peace among the people who please God."

[15]When the angels left them and went back to heaven, the shepherds said to each other, "Let's go to Bethlehem.

2:5 [b] **engaged** For the Jewish people, an engagement was a lasting agreement. It could only be broken by divorce.

CONTEMPORARY ENGLISH VERSION

[5]Mary was engaged to Joseph and traveled with him to Bethlehem. She was soon going to have a baby, [6]and while they were there, [7]she gave birth to her first-born[c] son. She dressed him in baby clothes[d] and laid him on a bed of hay, because there was no room for them in the inn.

The Shepherds

[8]That night in the fields near Bethlehem some shepherds were guarding their sheep. [9]All at once an angel came down to them from the Lord, and the brightness of the Lord's glory flashed around them. The shepherds were frightened. [10]But the angel said, "Don't be afraid! I have good news for you, which will make everyone happy. [11]This very day in King David's hometown a Savior was born for you. He is Christ the Lord. [12]You will know who he is, because you will find him dressed in baby clothes and lying on a bed of hay."

[13]Suddenly many other angels came down from heaven and joined in praising God. They said:

[14] "Praise God in heaven!
Peace on earth to everyone
who pleases God."

[15]After the angels had left and gone back to heaven, the shepherds said to each other, "Let's go to Bethlehem and

[c] **2.7** *first-born*: The Jewish people said that the first-born son in each of their families belonged to the Lord. [d] **2.7** *dressed him in baby clothes*: The Greek text has "wrapped him in wide strips of cloth," which was how young babies were dressed.

NEW INTERNATIONAL VERSION

to register with Mary, who was pledged to be married to
him and was expecting a child. [6]While they were there, the
time came for the baby to be born, [7]and she gave birth to
her firstborn, a son. She wrapped him in cloths and placed
him in a manger, because there was no room for them in
the inn.

The Shepherds and the Angels

[8]And there were shepherds living out in the fields near-
by, keeping watch over their flocks at night. [9]An angel of
the Lord appeared to them, and the glory of the Lord shone
around them, and they were terrified. [10]But the angel said
to them, "Do not be afraid. I bring you good news of great
joy that will be for all the people. [11]Today in the town of
David a Savior has been born to you; he is Christ[a] the
Lord. [12]This will be a sign to you: You will find a baby
wrapped in cloths and lying in a manger."

[13]Suddenly a great company of the heavenly host
appeared with the angel, praising God and saying,

[14] "Glory to God in the highest,
and on earth peace to men on whom his favor rests."

[15]When the angels had left them and gone into heaven,
the shepherds said to one another, "Let's go to Bethlehem

[a] *11* Or *Messiah.* "The Christ" (Greek) and "the Messiah" (Hebrew) both mean "the Anointed One"; also in verse 26.

NEW LIVING TRANSLATION

Nazareth in Galilee. [5]He took with him Mary, his fiancée,
who was obviously pregnant by this time.

[6]And while they were there, the time came for her baby
to be born. [7]She gave birth to her first child, a son. She
wrapped him snugly in strips of cloth and laid him in a
manger, because there was no room for them in the village
inn.

The Shepherds and Angels

[8]That night some shepherds were in the fields outside
the village, guarding their flocks of sheep. [9]Suddenly, an
angel of the Lord appeared among them, and the radiance
of the Lord's glory surrounded them. They were terribly
frightened, [10]but the angel reassured them. "Don't be
afraid!" he said. "I bring you good news of great joy for
everyone! [11]The Savior—yes, the Messiah, the Lord—has
been born tonight in Bethlehem, the city of David! [12]And
this is how you will recognize him: You will find a baby
lying in a manger, wrapped snugly in strips of cloth!"

[13]Suddenly, the angel was joined by a vast host of oth-
ers—the armies of heaven—praising God:

[14] "Glory to God in the highest heaven,
and peace on earth to all whom God favors.*"

[15]When the angels had returned to heaven, the shep-
herds said to each other, "Come on, let's go to Bethlehem!

2:14 Or *and peace on earth for all those pleasing God.* Some manuscripts read *and peace on earth, goodwill among people.*

NEW KING JAMES VERSION

[5]to be registered with Mary, his betrothed wife,[a] who was
with child. [6]So it was, that while they were there, the days
were completed for her to be delivered. [7]And she brought
forth her firstborn Son, and wrapped Him in swaddling
cloths, and laid Him in a manger, because there was no
room for them in the inn.

Glory in the Highest

[8]Now there were in the same country shepherds living
out in the fields, keeping watch over their flock by night.
[9]And behold,[b] an angel of the Lord stood before them, and
the glory of the Lord shone around them, and they were
greatly afraid. [10]Then the angel said to them, "Do not be
afraid, for behold, I bring you good tidings of great joy
which will be to all people. [11]For there is born to you this
day in the city of David a Savior, who is Christ the Lord.
[12]And this *will be* the sign to you: You will find a Babe
wrapped in swaddling cloths, lying in a manger."

[13]And suddenly there was with the angel a multitude of
the heavenly host praising God and saying:

[14] "Glory to God in the highest,
And on earth peace, goodwill toward men!"[c]

[15]So it was, when the angels had gone away from them
into heaven, that the shepherds said to one another, "Let
us now go to Bethlehem and see this thing that has come

2:5 [a] NU-Text omits *wife.* 2:9 [b] NU-Text omits *behold.*
2:14 [c] NU-Text reads *toward men of goodwill.*

THE MESSAGE

a descendant of David, he had to go there. He went with
Mary, his fiancée, who was pregnant.

While they were there, the time came for her to give
birth. She gave birth to a son, her firstborn. She wrapped
him in a blanket and laid him in a manger, because there
was no room in the hostel.

An Event for Everyone

There were sheepherders camping in the neighborhood.
They had set night watches over their sheep. Suddenly,
God's angel stood among them and God's glory blazed
around them. They were terrified. The angel said, "Don't
be afraid. I'm here to announce a great and joyful event
that is meant for everybody, worldwide: A Savior has just
been born in David's town, a Savior who is Messiah and
Master. This is what you're to look for: a baby wrapped in
a blanket and lying in a manger."

At once the angel was joined by a huge angelic choir
singing God's praises:

"Glory to God in the heavenly heights,
Peace to all men and women on earth who please him."

As the angel choir withdrew into heaven, the sheep-
herders talked it over. "Let's get over to Bethlehem as fast

KING JAMES VERSION

Let us now go even unto Bethlehem, and see this thing
which is come to pass, which the Lord hath made known
unto us.
16 And they came with haste, and found Mary, and
Joseph, and the babe lying in a manger.
17 And when they had seen *it*, they made known
abroad the saying which was told them concerning this
child.
18 And all they that heard *it* wondered at those things
which were told them by the shepherds.
19 But Mary kept all these things, and pondered *them*
in her heart.
20 And the shepherds returned, glorifying and praising
God for all the things that they had heard and seen, as it
was told unto them.
21 ¶ And when eight days were accomplished for the
circumcising of the child, his name was called JESUS,
which was so named of the angel before he was conceived
in the womb.
22 And when the days of her purification according to
the law of Moses were accomplished, they brought him to
Jerusalem, to present *him* to the Lord;
23 (As it is written in the law of the Lord, Every male
that openeth the womb shall be called holy to the Lord;)
24 And to offer a sacrifice according to that which is

NEW AMERICAN STANDARD BIBLE

us go straight to Bethlehem then, and see this thing that
has happened which the Lord has made known to us."
16 So they came in a hurry and found their way to Mary
and Joseph, and the baby as He lay in the manger.
17 When they had seen this, they made known the
statement which had been told them about this Child.
18 And all who heard it wondered at the things which
were told them by the shepherds.
19 But Mary treasured all these things, pondering them
in her heart.
20 The shepherds went back, glorifying and praising
God for all that they had heard and seen, just as had been
told them.

Jesus Presented at the Temple

21 And when eight days had passed, before His circum-
cision, His name was *then* called Jesus, the name given by
the angel before He was conceived in the womb.
22 And when the days for their purification according to
the law of Moses were completed, they brought Him up to
Jerusalem to present Him to the Lord
23 (as it is written in the Law of the Lord, "EVERY *first-
born* MALE THAT OPENS THE WOMB SHALL BE CALLED HOLY TO
THE LORD"),
24 and to offer a sacrifice according to what was said in

NEW CENTURY VERSION

Let's see this thing that has happened which the Lord has
told us about."
16 So the shepherds went quickly and found Mary and
Joseph and the baby, who was lying in a feeding box.
17 When they had seen him, they told what the angels had
said about this child. 18 Everyone was amazed at what the
shepherds said to them. 19 But Mary treasured these things
and continued to think about them. 20 Then the shepherds
went back to their sheep, praising God and thanking him
for everything they had seen and heard. It had been just as
the angel had told them.
21 When the baby was eight days old, he was circumcised
and was named Jesus, the name given by the angel before
the baby began to grow inside Mary.

Jesus Is Presented in the Temple

22 When the time came for Mary and Joseph to do what
the law of Moses taught about being made pure,[c] they took
Jesus to Jerusalem to present him to the Lord. 23 (It is writ-
ten in the law of the Lord: "Every firstborn male shall be
given to the Lord.")[d] 24 Mary and Joseph also went to offer

2:22 [c] **pure** The law of Moses said that forty days after a Jewish woman gave birth to a son, she must be cleansed by a ceremony at the Temple. Read Leviticus 12:2–8. 2:23 [d] **"Every...Lord."** Quotation from Exodus 13:2.

CONTEMPORARY ENGLISH VERSION

see what the Lord has told us about." 16 They hurried off
and found Mary and Joseph, and they saw the baby lying
on a bed of hay.
17 When the shepherds saw Jesus, they told his parents
what the angel had said about him. 18 Everyone listened
and was surprised. 19 But Mary kept thinking about all this
and wondering what it meant.
20 As the shepherds returned to their sheep, they were
praising God and saying wonderful things about him.
Everything they had seen and heard was just as the angel
had said.
21 Eight days later Jesus' parents did for him what the
Law of Moses commands.[e] And they named him Jesus, just
as the angel had told Mary when he promised she would
have a baby.

Simeon Praises the Lord

22 The time came for Mary and Joseph to do what the
Law of Moses says a mother is supposed to do after her
baby is born.[f]
They took Jesus to the temple in Jerusalem and present-
ed him to the Lord, 23 just as the Law of the Lord says,
"Each first-born[g] baby boy belongs to the Lord." 24 The Law
of the Lord also says that parents have to offer a sacrifice,

[e] **2.21** *what the Law of Moses commands*: See the note at 1.59.
[f] **2.22** *after her baby is born*: After a Jewish mother gave birth to a son, she was considered "unclean" and had to stay home until he was circumcised (see the note at 1.59). Then she had to stay home for another 33 days, before offering a sacrifice to the Lord. [g] **2.23** *first-born*: See the note at 2.7.

NEW INTERNATIONAL VERSION

and see this thing that has happened, which the Lord has
told us about."
[16]So they hurried off and found Mary and Joseph, and
the baby, who was lying in the manger. [17]When they had
seen him, they spread the word concerning what had been
told them about this child, [18]and all who heard it were
amazed at what the shepherds said to them. [19]But Mary
treasured up all these things and pondered them in her
heart. [20]The shepherds returned, glorifying and praising
God for all the things they had heard and seen, which were
just as they had been told.

Jesus Presented in the Temple

[21]On the eighth day, when it was time to circumcise
him, he was named Jesus, the name the angel had given
him before he had been conceived.
[22]When the time of their purification according to the
Law of Moses had been completed, Joseph and Mary took
him to Jerusalem to present him to the Lord [23](as it is writ-
ten in the Law of the Lord, "Every firstborn male is to be
consecrated to the Lord"[b]), [24]and to offer a sacrifice in

[b] *23* Exodus 13:2,12

NEW LIVING TRANSLATION

Let's see this wonderful thing that has happened, which
the Lord has told us about."
[16]They ran to the village and found Mary and Joseph.
And there was the baby, lying in the manger. [17]Then the
shepherds told everyone what had happened and what the
angel had said to them about this child. [18]All who heard
the shepherds' story were astonished, [19]but Mary quietly
treasured these things in her heart and thought about
them often. [20]The shepherds went back to their fields and
flocks, glorifying and praising God for what the angels had
told them, and because they had seen the child, just as the
angel had said.

Jesus Is Presented in the Temple

[21]Eight days later, when the baby was circumcised, he
was named Jesus, the name given him by the angel even
before he was conceived.
[22]Then it was time for the purification offering, as
required by the law of Moses after the birth of a child; so
his parents took him to Jerusalem to present him to the
Lord. [23]The law of the Lord says, "If a woman's first child
is a boy, he must be dedicated to the Lord."* [24]So they
offered a sacrifice according to what was required in the

2:23 Exod 13:2.

NEW KING JAMES VERSION

to pass, which the Lord has made known to us." [16]And
they came with haste and found Mary and Joseph, and the
Babe lying in a manger. [17]Now when they had seen *Him,*
they made widely[d] known the saying which was told them
concerning this Child. [18]And all those who heard *it* mar-
veled at those things which were told them by the shep-
herds. [19]But Mary kept all these things and pondered *them*
in her heart. [20]Then the shepherds returned, glorifying and
praising God for all the things that they had heard and
seen, as it was told them.

Circumcision of Jesus

[21]And when eight days were completed for the circumci-
sion of the Child,[e] His name was called JESUS, the name
given by the angel before He was conceived in the womb.

Jesus Presented in the Temple

[22]Now when the days of her purification according to the
law of Moses were completed, they brought Him to Jerusa-
lem to present *Him* to the Lord [23](as it is written in the law
of the Lord, *"Every male who opens the womb shall be
called holy to the LORD"*),[f] [24]and to offer a sacrifice accord-

2:17 [d] NU-Text omits *widely.* 2:21 [e] NU-Text reads *for His
circumcision.* 2:23 [f] Exodus 13:2, 12, 15

THE MESSAGE

as we can and see for ourselves what God has revealed to
us." They left, running, and found Mary and Joseph, and
the baby lying in the manger. Seeing was believing. They
told everyone they met what the angels had said about
this child. All who heard the sheepherders were impressed.

Mary kept all these things to herself, holding them dear, deep within herself. The sheepherders returned and let loose, glorifying and praising God for everything they had heard and seen. It turned out exactly the way they'd been told!

Blessings

When the eighth day arrived, the day of circumcision, the child was named Jesus, the name given by the angel before he was conceived.

Then when the days stipulated by Moses for purification were complete, they took him up to Jerusalem to offer him to God as commanded in God's Law: "Every male who opens the womb shall be a holy offering to God," and also

KING JAMES VERSION

said in the law of the Lord, A pair of turtledoves, or two young pigeons.

25 ¶ And, behold, there was a man in Jerusalem, whose name *was* Simeon; and the same man *was* just and devout, waiting for the consolation of Israel: and the Holy Ghost was upon him.

26 And it was revealed unto him by the Holy Ghost, that he should not see death, before he had seen the Lord's Christ.

27 And he came by the Spirit into the temple: and when the parents brought in the child Jesus, to do for him after the custom of the law,

28 Then took he him up in his arms, and blessed God, and said,

29 Lord, now lettest thou thy servant depart in peace, according to thy word:

30 For mine eyes have seen thy salvation,

31 Which thou hast prepared before the face of all people;

32 A light to lighten the Gentiles, and the glory of thy people Israel.

33 And Joseph and his mother marvelled at those things which were spoken of him.

34 And Simeon blessed them, and said unto Mary his mother, Behold, this *child* is set for the fall and rising

NEW AMERICAN STANDARD BIBLE

the Law of the Lord, "A PAIR OF TURTLEDOVES OR TWO YOUNG PIGEONS."

25 And there was a man in Jerusalem whose name was Simeon; and this man was righteous and devout, looking for the consolation of Israel; and the Holy Spirit was upon him.

26 And it had been revealed to him by the Holy Spirit that he would not see death before he had seen the Lord's Christ.

27 And he came in the Spirit into the temple; and when the parents brought in the child Jesus, to carry out for Him the custom of the Law,

28 then he took Him into his arms, and blessed God, and said,

29 "Now Lord, You are releasing Your bond-servant to
depart in peace,
According to Your word;
30 For my eyes have seen Your salvation,
31 Which You have prepared in the presence of all
peoples,
32 A LIGHT OF REVELATION TO THE GENTILES,
And the glory of Your people Israel."

33 And His father and mother were amazed at the things which were being said about Him.

34 And Simeon blessed them and said to Mary His mother, "Behold, this *Child* is appointed for the fall and

NEW CENTURY VERSION

a sacrifice, as the law of the Lord says: "You must sacrifice two doves or two young pigeons."[e]

Simeon Sees Jesus

25 In Jerusalem lived a man named Simeon who was a good man and godly. He was waiting for the time when God would take away Israel's sorrow, and the Holy Spirit was in him. 26 Simeon had been told by the Holy Spirit that he would not die before he saw the Christ promised by the Lord. 27 The Spirit led Simeon to the Temple. When Mary and Joseph brought the baby Jesus to the Temple to do what the law said they must do, 28 Simeon took the baby in his arms and thanked God:

29 "Now, Lord, you can let me, your servant,
die in peace as you said.
30 With my own eyes I have seen your salvation,
31 which you prepared before all people.
32 It is a light for the non-Jewish people to see
and an honor for your people, the Israelites."

33 Jesus' father and mother were amazed at what Simeon had said about him. 34 Then Simeon blessed them and said to Mary, "God has chosen this child to cause the fall and

2:24 [e] **"You...pigeons."** Quotation from Leviticus 12:8.

CONTEMPORARY ENGLISH VERSION

giving at least a pair of doves or two young pigeons. So that is what Mary and Joseph did.

25 At this time a man named Simeon was living in Jerusalem. Simeon was a good man. He loved God and was waiting for God to save the people of Israel. God's Spirit came to him 26 and told him that he would not die until he had seen Christ the Lord.

27 When Mary and Joseph brought Jesus to the temple to do what the Law of Moses says should be done for a new baby, the Spirit told Simeon to go into the temple. 28 Simeon took the baby Jesus in his arms and praised God,

29 "Lord, I am your servant,
and now can die in peace,
because you have kept
your promise to me.
30 With my own eyes I have seen
what you have done
to save your people,
31 and foreign nations
will also see this.
32 Your mighty power is a light
for all nations,
and it will bring honor
to your people Israel."

33 Jesus' parents were surprised at what Simeon had said. 34 Then he blessed them and told Mary, "This child of yours will cause many people in Israel to fall and others to

NEW INTERNATIONAL VERSION

keeping with what is said in the Law of the Lord: "a pair of doves or two young pigeons."[c]

25 Now there was a man in Jerusalem called Simeon, who was righteous and devout. He was waiting for the consolation of Israel, and the Holy Spirit was upon him. 26 It had been revealed to him by the Holy Spirit that he would not die before he had seen the Lord's Christ. 27 Moved by the Spirit, he went into the temple courts. When the parents brought in the child Jesus to do for him what the custom of the Law required, 28 Simeon took him in his arms and praised God, saying:

29 "Sovereign Lord, as you have promised,
you now dismiss[d] your servant in peace.
30 For my eyes have seen your salvation,
31 which you have prepared in the sight of all people,
32 a light for revelation to the Gentiles
and for glory to your people Israel."

33 The child's father and mother marveled at what was said about him. 34 Then Simeon blessed them and said to Mary, his mother: "This child is destined to cause the falling and rising of many in Israel, and to be a sign that

[c] *24* Lev. 12:8 [d] *29* Or *promised, / now dismiss*

NEW LIVING TRANSLATION

law of the Lord—"either a pair of turtledoves or two young pigeons."*

The Prophecy of Simeon

25 Now there was a man named Simeon who lived in Jerusalem. He was a righteous man and very devout. He was filled with the Holy Spirit, and he eagerly expected the Messiah to come and rescue Israel. 26 The Holy Spirit had revealed to him that he would not die until he had seen the Lord's Messiah. 27 That day the Spirit led him to the Temple. So when Mary and Joseph came to present the baby Jesus to the Lord as the law required, 28 Simeon was there. He took the child in his arms and praised God, saying,

29 "Lord, now I can die in peace!
As you promised me,
30 I have seen the Savior
31 you have given to all people.
32 He is a light to reveal God to the nations,
and he is the glory of your people Israel!"

33 Joseph and Mary were amazed at what was being said about Jesus. 34 Then Simeon blessed them, and he said to Mary, "This child will be rejected by many in Israel, and it will be their undoing. But he will be the greatest joy to

2:24 Lev 12:8.

NEW KING JAMES VERSION

ing to what is said in the law of the Lord, *"A pair of turtledoves or two young pigeons."*[g]

Simeon Sees God's Salvation

25 And behold, there was a man in Jerusalem whose name was Simeon, and this man was just and devout, waiting for the Consolation of Israel, and the Holy Spirit was upon him. 26 And it had been revealed to him by the Holy Spirit that he would not see death before he had seen the Lord's Christ. 27 So he came by the Spirit into the temple. And when the parents brought in the Child Jesus, to do for Him according to the custom of the law, 28 he took Him up in his arms and blessed God and said:

29 "Lord, now You are letting Your servant depart in peace,
According to Your word;
30 For my eyes have seen Your salvation
31 Which You have prepared before the face of all peoples,
32 A light to *bring* revelation to the Gentiles,
And the glory of Your people Israel."

33 And Joseph and His mother[h] marveled at those things which were spoken of Him. 34 Then Simeon blessed them, and said to Mary His mother, "Behold, this *Child* is destined for the fall and rising of many in Israel, and for a

2:24 [g] Leviticus 12:8 **2:33** [h] NU-Text reads *And His father and mother.*

THE MESSAGE

to sacrifice the "pair of doves or two young pigeons" prescribed in God's Law.

In Jerusalem at the time, there was a man, Simeon by name, a good man, a man who lived in the prayerful expectancy of help for Israel. And the Holy Spirit was on him. The Holy Spirit had shown him that he would see the Messiah of God before he died. Led by the Spirit, he entered the Temple. As the parents of the child Jesus brought him in to carry out the rituals of the Law, Simeon took him into his arms and blessed God:

"God, you can now release your servant;
release me in peace as you promised.
With my own eyes I've seen your salvation;
it's now out in the open for everyone to see:
A God-revealing light to the non-Jewish nations,
and of glory for your people Israel."

Jesus' father and mother were speechless with surprise at these words. Simeon went on to bless them, and said to Mary his mother,

"This child marks both the failure and
the recovery of many in Israel,

KING JAMES VERSION

again of many in Israel; and for a sign which shall be spoken against;

35 (Yea, a sword shall pierce through thy own soul also,) that the thoughts of many hearts may be revealed.

36 And there was one Anna, a prophetess, the daughter of Phanuel, of the tribe of Aser: she was of a great age, and had lived with an husband seven years from her virginity;

37 And she *was* a widow of about fourscore and four years, which departed not from the temple, but served *God* with fastings and prayers night and day.

38 And she coming in that instant gave thanks likewise unto the Lord, and spake of him to all them that looked for redemption in Jerusalem.

39 And when they had performed all things according to the law of the Lord, they returned into Galilee, to their own city Nazareth.

40 And the child grew, and waxed strong in spirit, filled with wisdom: and the grace of God was upon him.

41 ¶ Now his parents went to Jerusalem every year at the feast of the passover.

42 And when he was twelve years old, they went up to Jerusalem after the custom of the feast.

NEW AMERICAN STANDARD BIBLE

rise of many in Israel, and for a sign to be opposed—

35 and a sword will pierce even your own soul—to the end that thoughts from many hearts may be revealed."

36 And there was a prophetess, Anna the daughter of Phanuel, of the tribe of Asher. She was advanced in years and had lived with *her* husband seven years after her marriage,

37 and then as a widow to the age of eighty-four. She never left the temple, serving night and day with fastings and prayers.

38 At that very moment she came up and *began* giving thanks to God, and continued to speak of Him to all those who were looking for the redemption of Jerusalem.

Return to Nazareth

39 When they had performed everything according to the Law of the Lord, they returned to Galilee, to their own city of Nazareth.

40 The Child continued to grow and become strong, increasing in wisdom; and the grace of God was upon Him.

Visit to Jerusalem

41 Now His parents went to Jerusalem every year at the Feast of the Passover.

42 And when He became twelve, they went up *there* according to the custom of the Feast;

NEW CENTURY VERSION

rise of many in Israel. He will be a sign from God that many people will not accept 35 so that the thoughts of many will be made known. And the things that will happen will make your heart sad, too."

Anna Sees Jesus

36 There was a prophetess, Anna, from the family of Phanuel in the tribe of Asher. Anna was very old. She had once been married for seven years. 37 Then her husband died, and she was a widow for eighty-four years. Anna never left the Temple but worshiped God, going without food and praying day and night. 38 Standing there at that time, she thanked God and spoke about Jesus to all who were waiting for God to free Jerusalem.

Joseph and Mary Return Home

39 When Joseph and Mary had done everything the law of the Lord commanded, they went home to Nazareth, their own town in Galilee. 40 The little child grew and became strong. He was filled with wisdom, and God's goodness was upon him.

Jesus As a Boy

41 Every year Jesus' parents went to Jerusalem for the Passover Feast. 42 When he was twelve years old, they went to the feast as they always did. 43 After the feast days were

CONTEMPORARY ENGLISH VERSION

stand. The child will be like a warning sign. Many people will reject him, 35 and you, Mary, will suffer as though you had been stabbed by a dagger. But all this will show what people are really thinking."

Anna Speaks about the Child Jesus

36 The prophet Anna was also there in the temple. She was the daughter of Phanuel from the tribe of Asher, and she was very old. In her youth she had been married for seven years, but her husband died. 37 And now she was eighty-four years old.[h] Night and day she served God in the temple by praying and often going without eating.[i]

38 At that time Anna came in and praised God. She spoke about the child Jesus to everyone who hoped for Jerusalem to be set free.

The Return to Nazareth

39 After Joseph and Mary had done everything that the Law of the Lord commands, they returned home to Nazareth in Galilee. 40 The child Jesus grew. He became strong and wise, and God blessed him.

The Boy Jesus in the Temple

41 Every year Jesus' parents went to Jerusalem for Passover. 42 And when Jesus was twelve years old, they all went there as usual for the celebration. 43 After Passover

[h] 2.37 *And now she was eighty-four years old*: Or "And now she had been a widow for eighty-four years." [i] 2.37 *without eating*: The Jewish people sometimes went without eating (also called "fasting") to show their love for God or to show sorrow for their sins.

NEW INTERNATIONAL VERSION

will be spoken against, 35so that the thoughts of many hearts will be revealed. And a sword will pierce your own soul too."

36There was also a prophetess, Anna, the daughter of Phanuel, of the tribe of Asher. She was very old; she had lived with her husband seven years after her marriage, 37and then was a widow until she was eighty-four.[e] She never left the temple but worshiped night and day, fasting and praying. 38Coming up to them at that very moment, she gave thanks to God and spoke about the child to all who were looking forward to the redemption of Jerusalem.

39When Joseph and Mary had done everything required by the Law of the Lord, they returned to Galilee to their own town of Nazareth. 40And the child grew and became strong; he was filled with wisdom, and the grace of God was upon him.

The Boy Jesus at the Temple

41Every year his parents went to Jerusalem for the Feast of the Passover. 42When he was twelve years old, they went up to the Feast, according to the custom. 43After the

[e] *37* Or *widow for eighty-four years*

NEW LIVING TRANSLATION

many others. 35Thus, the deepest thoughts of many hearts will be revealed. And a sword will pierce your very soul."

The Prophecy of Anna

36Anna, a prophet, was also there in the Temple. She was the daughter of Phanuel, of the tribe of Asher, and was very old. She was a widow, for her husband had died when they had been married only seven years. 37She was now eighty-four years old. She never left the Temple but stayed there day and night, worshiping God with fasting and prayer. 38She came along just as Simeon was talking with Mary and Joseph, and she began praising God. She talked about Jesus to everyone who had been waiting for the promised King to come and deliver Jerusalem.

39When Jesus' parents had fulfilled all the requirements of the law of the Lord, they returned home to Nazareth in Galilee. 40There the child grew up healthy and strong. He was filled with wisdom beyond his years, and God placed his special favor upon him.

Jesus Speaks with the Teachers

41Every year Jesus' parents went to Jerusalem for the Passover festival. 42When Jesus was twelve years old, they attended the festival as usual. 43After the celebration was

NEW KING JAMES VERSION

sign which will be spoken against 35(yes, a sword will pierce through your own soul also), that the thoughts of many hearts may be revealed."

Anna Bears Witness to the Redeemer

36Now there was one, Anna, a prophetess, the daughter of Phanuel, of the tribe of Asher. She was of a great age, and had lived with a husband seven years from her virginity; 37and this woman *was* a widow of about eighty-four years,[i] who did not depart from the temple, but served *God* with fastings and prayers night and day. 38And coming in that instant she gave thanks to the Lord,[j] and spoke of Him to all those who looked for redemption in Jerusalem.

The Family Returns to Nazareth

39So when they had performed all things according to the law of the Lord, they returned to Galilee, to their *own* city, Nazareth. 40And the Child grew and became strong in spirit,[k] filled with wisdom; and the grace of God was upon Him.

The Boy Jesus Amazes the Scholars

41His parents went to Jerusalem every year at the Feast of the Passover. 42And when He was twelve years old, they went up to Jerusalem according to the custom of the feast.

2:37 [i] NU-Text reads *a widow until she was eighty-four.*
2:38 [j] NU-Text reads *to God.* 2:40 [k] NU-Text omits *in spirit.*

THE MESSAGE

A figure misunderstood and contradicted—
the pain of a sword-thrust through you—
But the rejection will force honesty,
as God reveals who they really are."

Anna the prophetess was also there, a daughter of Phanuel from the tribe of Asher. She was by now a very old woman. She had been married seven years and a widow for eighty-four. She never left the Temple area, worshiping night and day with her fastings and prayers. At the very time Simeon was praying, she showed up, broke into an anthem of praise to God, and talked about the child to all who were waiting expectantly for the freeing of Jerusalem.

When they finished everything required by God in the Law, they returned to Galilee and their own town, Nazareth. There the child grew strong in body and wise in spirit. And the grace of God was on him.

They Found Him in the Temple

Every year Jesus' parents traveled to Jerusalem for the Feast of Passover. When he was twelve years old, they went up as they always did for the Feast. When it was over

KING JAMES VERSION

43 And when they had fulfilled the days, as they returned, the child Jesus tarried behind in Jerusalem; and Joseph and his mother knew not *of it*.

44 But they, supposing him to have been in the company, went a day's journey; and they sought him among *their* kinsfolk and acquaintance.

45 And when they found him not, they turned back again to Jerusalem, seeking him.

46 And it came to pass, that after three days they found him in the temple, sitting in the midst of the doctors, both hearing them, and asking them questions.

47 And all that heard him were astonished at his understanding and answers.

48 And when they saw him, they were amazed: and his mother said unto him, Son, why hast thou thus dealt with us? behold, thy father and I have sought thee sorrowing.

49 And he said unto them, How is it that ye sought me? wist ye not that I must be about my Father's business?

50 And they understood not the saying which he spake unto them.

51 And he went down with them, and came to Nazareth, and was subject unto them: but his mother kept all these sayings in her heart.

52 And Jesus increased in wisdom and stature, and in favour with God and man.

NEW AMERICAN STANDARD BIBLE

43 and as they were returning, after spending the full number of days, the boy Jesus stayed behind in Jerusalem. But His parents were unaware of it,

44 but supposed Him to be in the caravan, and went a day's journey; and they *began* looking for Him among their relatives and acquaintances.

45 When they did not find Him, they returned to Jerusalem looking for Him.

46 Then, after three days they found Him in the temple, sitting in the midst of the teachers, both listening to them and asking them questions.

47 And all who heard Him were amazed at His understanding and His answers.

48 When they saw Him, they were astonished; and His mother said to Him, "Son, why have You treated us this way? Behold, Your father and I have been anxiously looking for You."

49 And He said to them, "Why is it that you were looking for Me? Did you not know that I had to be in My Father's *house?*"

50 But they did not understand the statement which He had made to them.

51 And He went down with them and came to Nazareth, and He continued in subjection to them; and His mother treasured all *these* things in her heart.

52 And Jesus kept increasing in wisdom and stature, and in favor with God and men.

NEW CENTURY VERSION

over, they started home. The boy Jesus stayed behind in
Jerusalem, but his parents did not know it. 44Thinking that
Jesus was with them in the group, they traveled for a
whole day. Then they began to look for him among their
family and friends. 45When they did not find him, they
went back to Jerusalem to look for him there. 46After three
days they found Jesus sitting in the Temple with the teach-
ers, listening to them and asking them questions. 47All
who heard him were amazed at his understanding and
answers. 48When Jesus' parents saw him, they were aston-
ished. His mother said to him, "Son, why did you do this
to us? Your father and I were very worried about you and
have been looking for you."

49Jesus said to them, "Why were you looking for me?
Didn't you know that I must be in my Father's house?"
50But they did not understand the meaning of what he
said.

51Jesus went with them to Nazareth and was obedient to
them. But his mother kept in her mind all that had hap-
pened. 52Jesus became wiser and grew physically. People
liked him, and he pleased God.

CONTEMPORARY ENGLISH VERSION

his parents left, but they did not know that Jesus had
stayed on in the city. 44They thought he was traveling with
some other people, and they went a whole day before they
started looking for him. 45When they could not find him
with their relatives and friends, they went back to
Jerusalem and started looking for him there.

46Three days later they found Jesus sitting in the temple,
listening to the teachers and asking them questions.
47Everyone who heard him was surprised at how much he
knew and at the answers he gave.

48When his parents found him, they were amazed. His
mother said, "Son, why have you done this to us? Your
father and I have been very worried, and we have been
searching for you!"

49Jesus answered, "Why did you have to look for me?
Didn't you know that I would be in my Father's house?"[j]
50But they did not understand what he meant.

51Jesus went back to Nazareth with his parents and
obeyed them. His mother kept on thinking about all that
had happened.

52Jesus became wise, and he grew strong. God was
pleased with him and so were the people.

[j] **2.49** *in my Father's house*: Or "doing my Father's work."

NEW INTERNATIONAL VERSION

Feast was over, while his parents were returning home, the
boy Jesus stayed behind in Jerusalem, but they were
unaware of it. 44 Thinking he was in their company, they
traveled on for a day. Then they began looking for him
among their relatives and friends. 45 When they did not
find him, they went back to Jerusalem to look for him.
46 After three days they found him in the temple courts, sit-
ting among the teachers, listening to them and asking
them questions. 47 Everyone who heard him was amazed at
his understanding and his answers. 48 When his parents
saw him, they were astonished. His mother said to him,
"Son, why have you treated us like this? Your father and I
have been anxiously searching for you."

49 "Why were you searching for me?" he asked. "Didn't
you know I had to be in my Father's house?" 50 But they
did not understand what he was saying to them.

51 Then he went down to Nazareth with them and was
obedient to them. But his mother treasured all these things
in her heart. 52 And Jesus grew in wisdom and stature, and
in favor with God and men.

NEW LIVING TRANSLATION

over, they started home to Nazareth, but Jesus stayed
behind in Jerusalem. His parents didn't miss him at first,
44 because they assumed he was with friends among the
other travelers. But when he didn't show up that evening,
they started to look for him among their relatives and
friends. 45 When they couldn't find him, they went back to
Jerusalem to search for him there. 46 Three days later they
finally discovered him. He was in the Temple, sitting
among the religious teachers, discussing deep questions
with them. 47 And all who heard him were amazed at his
understanding and his answers.

48 His parents didn't know what to think. "Son!" his
mother said to him. "Why have you done this to us? Your
father and I have been frantic, searching for you every-
where."

49 "But why did you need to search?" he asked. "You
should have known that I would be in my Father's
house."* 50 But they didn't understand what he meant.

51 Then he returned to Nazareth with them and was obe-
dient to them; and his mother stored all these things in her
heart. 52 So Jesus grew both in height and in wisdom, and
he was loved by God and by all who knew him.

2:49 Or *"Didn't you realize that I should be involved with my Father's affairs?"*

NEW KING JAMES VERSION

43 When they had finished the days, as they returned, the
Boy Jesus lingered behind in Jerusalem. And Joseph and
His mother[l] did not know *it;* 44 but supposing Him to have
been in the company, they went a day's journey, and
sought Him among *their* relatives and acquaintances. 45 So
when they did not find Him, they returned to Jerusalem,
seeking Him. 46 Now so it was *that* after three days they
found Him in the temple, sitting in the midst of the teach-
ers, both listening to them and asking them questions.
47 And all who heard Him were astonished at His under-
standing and answers. 48 So when they saw Him, they were
amazed; and His mother said to Him, "Son, why have You
done this to us? Look, Your father and I have sought You
anxiously."

49 And He said to them, "Why did you seek Me? Did you
not know that I must be about My Father's business?"
50 But they did not understand the statement which He
spoke to them.

Jesus Advances in Wisdom and Favor

51 Then He went down with them and came to Nazareth,
and was subject to them, but His mother kept all these
things in her heart. 52 And Jesus increased in wisdom and
stature, and in favor with God and men.

2:43 [l] NU-Text reads *And His parents.*

THE MESSAGE

and they left for home, the child Jesus stayed behind in Jerusalem, but his parents didn't know it. Thinking he was somewhere in the company of pilgrims, they journeyed for a whole day and then began looking for him among relatives and neighbors. When they didn't find him, they went back to Jerusalem looking for him.

The next day they found him in the Temple seated among the teachers, listening to them and asking questions. The teachers were all quite taken with him, impressed with the sharpness of his answers. But his parents were not impressed; they were upset and hurt.

His mother said, "Young man, why have you done this to us? Your father and I have been half out of our minds looking for you."

He said, "Why were you looking for me? Didn't you know that I had to be here, dealing with the things of my Father?" But they had no idea what he was talking about.

So he went back to Nazareth with them, and lived obediently with them. His mother held these things dearly, deep within herself. And Jesus matured, growing up in both body and spirit, blessed by both God and people.

KING JAMES VERSION

3 Now in the fifteenth year of the reign of Tiberius
Caesar, Pontius Pilate being governor of Judaea, and
Herod being tetrarch of Galilee, and his brother Philip
tetrarch of Ituraea and of the region of Trachonitis, and
Lysanias the tetrarch of Abilene,

2 Annas and Caiaphas being the high priests, the word
of God came unto John the son of Zacharias in the wilder-
ness.

3 And he came into all the country about Jordan,
preaching the baptism of repentance for the remission of
sins;

4 As it is written in the book of the words of Esaias the
prophet, saying, The voice of one crying in the wilderness,
Prepare ye the way of the Lord, make his paths straight.

5 Every valley shall be filled, and every mountain and
hill shall be brought low; and the crooked shall be made
straight, and the rough ways *shall be* made smooth;

NEW AMERICAN STANDARD BIBLE

John the Baptist Preaches

3 Now in the fifteenth year of the reign of Tiberius
Caesar, when Pontius Pilate was governor of Judea,
and Herod was tetrarch of Galilee, and his brother Philip
was tetrarch of the region of Ituraea and Trachonitis, and
Lysanias was tetrarch of Abilene,

2 in the high priesthood of Annas and Caiaphas, the
word of God came to John, the son of Zacharias, in the
wilderness.

3 And he came into all the district around the Jordan,
preaching a baptism of repentance for the forgiveness of
sins;

4 as it is written in the book of the words of Isaiah the
prophet,

"THE VOICE OF ONE CRYING IN THE WILDERNESS,
'MAKE READY THE WAY OF THE LORD,
MAKE HIS PATHS STRAIGHT.
5 'EVERY RAVINE WILL BE FILLED,
AND EVERY MOUNTAIN AND HILL WILL BE BROUGHT LOW;
THE CROOKED WILL BECOME STRAIGHT,
AND THE ROUGH ROADS SMOOTH;

NEW CENTURY VERSION

The Preaching of John

3 It was the fifteenth year of the rule of Tiberius Caesar.
These men were under Caesar: Pontius Pilate, the
ruler of Judea; Herod, the ruler of Galilee; Philip, Herod's
brother, the ruler of Iturea and Trachonitis; and Lysanias,
the ruler of Abilene. 2Annas and Caiaphas were the high
priests. At this time, the word of God came to John son of
Zechariah in the desert. 3He went all over the area around
the Jordan River preaching a baptism of changed hearts
and lives for the forgiveness of sins. 4As it is written in the
book of Isaiah the prophet:

"This is a voice of one
who calls out in the desert:
'Prepare the way for the Lord.
Make the road straight for him.
5 Every valley should be filled in,
and every mountain and hill should be made flat.
Roads with turns should be made straight,
and rough roads should be made smooth.

CONTEMPORARY ENGLISH VERSION

The Preaching of John the Baptist
(Matthew 3.1-12; Mark 1.1-8; John 1.19-28)

3 For fifteen years[a] Emperor Tiberius had ruled that part
of the world. Pontius Pilate was governor of Judea,
and Herod[b] was the ruler of Galilee. Herod's brother,
Philip, was the ruler in the countries of Iturea and
Trachonitis, and Lysanias was the ruler of Abilene. 2Annas
and Caiaphas were the Jewish high priests.[c]

At that time God spoke to Zechariah's son John, who
was living in the desert. 3So John went along the Jordan
Valley, telling the people, "Turn back to God and be bap-
tized! Then your sins will be forgiven." 4Isaiah the prophet
wrote about John when he said,

"In the desert
someone is shouting,
'Get the road ready
for the Lord!
Make a straight path
for him.
5 Fill up every valley
and level every mountain
and hill.
Straighten the crooked paths
and smooth out
the rough roads.

[a] 3.1 *For fifteen years*: This was either A.D. 28 or 29, and Jesus was about thirty years old (see 3.23). [b] 3.1 *Herod*: Herod Antipas, the son of Herod the Great. [c] 3.2 *Annas and Caiaphas . . . high priests*: Annas was high priest from A.D. 6 until 15. His son-in-law Caiaphas was high priest from A.D. 18 until 37.

NEW INTERNATIONAL VERSION

John the Baptist Prepares the Way

3 In the fifteenth year of the reign of Tiberius Caesar—
when Pontius Pilate was governor of Judea, Herod
tetrarch of Galilee, his brother Philip tetrarch of Iturea and
Traconitis, and Lysanias tetrarch of Abilene— 2during the
high priesthood of Annas and Caiaphas, the word of God
came to John son of Zechariah in the desert. 3He went into
all the country around the Jordan, preaching a baptism of
repentance for the forgiveness of sins. 4As is written in the
book of the words of Isaiah the prophet:

"A voice of one calling in the desert,
'Prepare the way for the Lord,
make straight paths for him.
5 Every valley shall be filled in,
every mountain and hill made low.
The crooked roads shall become straight,
the rough ways smooth.

NEW LIVING TRANSLATION

John the Baptist Prepares the Way

3 It was now the fifteenth year of the reign of Tiberius,
the Roman emperor. Pilate was governor over Judea;
Herod Antipas was ruler* over Galilee; his brother Philip
was ruler* over Iturea and Traconitis; Lysanias was ruler
over Abilene. 2Annas and Caiaphas were the high priests.
At this time a message from God came to John son of
Zechariah, who was living out in the wilderness. 3Then
John went from place to place on both sides of the Jordan
River, preaching that people should be baptized to show
that they had turned from their sins and turned to God to
be forgiven.* 4Isaiah had spoken of John when he said,

"He is a voice shouting in the wilderness:
'Prepare a pathway for the Lord's coming!
Make a straight road for him!
5 Fill in the valleys,
and level the mountains and hills!
Straighten the curves,
and smooth out the rough places!

3:1a Greek *Herod was tetrarch.* Herod Antipas was a son of King Herod.
3:1b Greek *tetrarch;* also in 3:19. 3:3 Greek *preaching a baptism of repentance for the forgiveness of sins.*

NEW KING JAMES VERSION

John the Baptist Prepares the Way

3 Now in the fifteenth year of the reign of Tiberius Cae-
sar, Pontius Pilate being governor of Judea, Herod
being tetrarch of Galilee, his brother Philip tetrarch of Itu-
rea and the region of Trachonitis, and Lysanias tetrarch of
Abilene, 2while Annas and Caiaphas were high priests,[a]
the word of God came to John the son of Zacharias in the
wilderness. 3And he went into all the region around the
Jordan, preaching a baptism of repentance for the remis-
sion of sins, 4as it is written in the book of the words of
Isaiah the prophet, saying:

"The voice of one crying in the wilderness:
'Prepare the way of the Lord;
Make His paths straight.
5 *Every valley shall be filled*
And every mountain and hill brought low;
The crooked places shall be made straight
And the rough ways smooth;

3:2 [a] NU-Text and M-Text read *in the high priesthood of Annas and Caiaphas.*

THE MESSAGE

A Baptism of Life-Change

3 In the fifteenth year of the rule of Caesar Tiberius—it
was while Pontius Pilate was governor of Judea; Herod,
ruler of Galilee; his brother Philip, ruler of Iturea and
Trachonitis; Lysanias, ruler of Abilene; during the Chief-
Priesthood of Annas and Caiaphas—John, Zachariah's son,
out in the desert at the time, received a message from God.
He went all through the country around the Jordan River
preaching a baptism of life-change leading to forgiveness of
sins, as described in the words of Isaiah the prophet:

"Thunder in the desert!
'Prepare God's arrival!
Make the road smooth and straight!
Every ditch will be filled in,
Every bump smoothed out,
The detours straightened out,
All the ruts paved over.

KING JAMES VERSION

6 And all flesh shall see the salvation of God.

7 Then said he to the multitude that came forth to be baptized of him, O generation of vipers, who hath warned you to flee from the wrath to come?

8 Bring forth therefore fruits worthy of repentance, and begin not to say within yourselves, We have Abraham to *our* father: for I say unto you, That God is able of these stones to raise up children unto Abraham.

9 And now also the axe is laid unto the root of the trees: every tree therefore which bringeth not forth good fruit is hewn down, and cast into the fire.

10 And the people asked him, saying, What shall we do then?

11 He answereth and saith unto them, He that hath two coats, let him impart to him that hath none; and he that hath meat, let him do likewise.

12 Then came also publicans to be baptized, and said unto him, Master, what shall we do?

13 And he said unto them, Exact no more than that which is appointed you.

14 And the soldiers likewise demanded of him, saying, And what shall we do? And he said unto them, Do violence to no man, neither accuse *any* falsely; and be content with your wages.

15 ¶ And as the people were in expectation, and all men mused in their hearts of John, whether he were the Christ, or not;

NEW AMERICAN STANDARD BIBLE

6 AND ALL FLESH WILL SEE THE SALVATION OF GOD.' "

7 So he *began* saying to the crowds who were going out to be baptized by him, "You brood of vipers, who warned you to flee from the wrath to come?

8 "Therefore bear fruits in keeping with repentance, and do not begin to say to yourselves, 'We have Abraham for our father,' for I say to you that from these stones God is able to raise up children to Abraham.

9 "Indeed the axe is already laid at the root of the trees; so every tree that does not bear good fruit is cut down and thrown into the fire."

10 And the crowds were questioning him, saying, "Then what shall we do?"

11 And he would answer and say to them, "The man who has two tunics is to share with him who has none; and he who has food is to do likewise."

12 And *some* tax collectors also came to be baptized, and they said to him, "Teacher, what shall we do?"

13 And he said to them, "Collect no more than what you have been ordered to."

14 *Some* soldiers were questioning him, saying, "And *what about* us, what shall we do?" And he said to them, "Do not take money from anyone by force, or accuse *anyone* falsely, and be content with your wages."

15 Now while the people were in a state of expectation and all were wondering in their hearts about John, as to whether he was the Christ,

NEW CENTURY VERSION

6 And all people will know about the salvation of God!' "

Isaiah 40:3–5

7 To the crowds of people who came to be baptized by John, he said, "You are all snakes! Who warned you to run away from God's coming punishment? 8 Do the things that show you really have changed your hearts and lives. Don't begin to say to yourselves, 'Abraham is our father.' I tell you that God could make children for Abraham from these rocks. 9 The ax is now ready to cut down the trees, and every tree that does not produce good fruit will be cut down and thrown into the fire."[a]

10 The people asked John, "Then what should we do?"

11 John answered, "If you have two shirts, share with the person who does not have one. If you have food, share that also."

12 Even tax collectors came to John to be baptized. They said to him, "Teacher, what should we do?"

13 John said to them, "Don't take more taxes from people than you have been ordered to take."

14 The soldiers asked John, "What about us? What should we do?"

John said to them, "Don't force people to give you money, and don't lie about them. Be satisfied with the pay you get."

15 Since the people were hoping for the Christ to come, they wondered if John might be the one.

3:9 [a] **The ax...fire.** This means that God is ready to punish his people who do not obey him.

CONTEMPORARY ENGLISH VERSION

6 Then everyone will see
the saving power of God.' "

7 Crowds of people came out to be baptized, but John said to them, "You bunch of snakes! Who warned you to run from the coming judgment? 8 Do something to show that you really have given up your sins. Don't start saying that you belong to Abraham's family. God can turn these stones into children for Abraham.[d] 9 An ax is ready to cut the trees down at their roots. Any tree that doesn't produce good fruit will be cut down and thrown into a fire."

10 The crowds asked John, "What should we do?"

11 John told them, "If you have two coats, give one to someone who doesn't have any. If you have food, share it with someone else."

12 When tax collectors[e] came to be baptized, they asked John, "Teacher, what should we do?"

13 John told them, "Don't make people pay more than they owe."

14 Some soldiers asked him, "And what about us? What do we have to do?"

John told them, "Don't force people to pay money to make you leave them alone. Be satisfied with your pay."

15 Everyone became excited and wondered, "Could John be the Messiah?"

[d] **3.8** *children for Abraham*: The Jewish people thought they were God's chosen people because of God's promises to their ancestor Abraham.
[e] **3.12** *tax collectors*: These were usually Jewish people who paid the Romans for the right to collect taxes. They were hated by other Jews who thought of them as traitors to their country and to their religion.

NEW INTERNATIONAL VERSION

6 And all mankind will see God's salvation.' "[a]

7 John said to the crowds coming out to be baptized by him, "You brood of vipers! Who warned you to flee from the coming wrath? 8 Produce fruit in keeping with repentance. And do not begin to say to yourselves, 'We have Abraham as our father.' For I tell you that out of these stones God can raise up children for Abraham. 9 The ax is already at the root of the trees, and every tree that does not produce good fruit will be cut down and thrown into the fire."

10 "What should we do then?" the crowd asked.

11 John answered, "The man with two tunics should share with him who has none, and the one who has food should do the same."

12 Tax collectors also came to be baptized. "Teacher," they asked, "what should we do?"

13 "Don't collect any more than you are required to," he told them.

14 Then some soldiers asked him, "And what should we do?"

He replied, "Don't extort money and don't accuse people falsely—be content with your pay."

15 The people were waiting expectantly and were all wondering in their hearts if John might possibly be the Christ.[b]

[a] *6* Isaiah 40:3–5 [b] *15* Or *Messiah*

NEW LIVING TRANSLATION

6 And then all people will see
the salvation sent from God.' "*

7 Here is a sample of John's preaching to the crowds that came for baptism: "You brood of snakes! Who warned you to flee God's coming judgment? 8 Prove by the way you live that you have really turned from your sins and turned to God. Don't just say, 'We're safe—we're the descendants of Abraham.' That proves nothing. God can change these stones here into children of Abraham. 9 Even now the ax of God's judgment is poised, ready to sever your roots. Yes, every tree that does not produce good fruit will be chopped down and thrown into the fire."

10 The crowd asked, "What should we do?"

11 John replied, "If you have two coats, give one to the poor. If you have food, share it with those who are hungry."

12 Even corrupt tax collectors came to be baptized and asked, "Teacher, what should we do?"

13 "Show your honesty," he replied. "Make sure you collect no more taxes than the Roman government requires you to."

14 "What should we do?" asked some soldiers.

John replied, "Don't extort money, and don't accuse people of things you know they didn't do. And be content with your pay."

15 Everyone was expecting the Messiah to come soon, and they were eager to know whether John might be the

3:4-6 Isa 40:3-5.

NEW KING JAMES VERSION

6 *And all flesh shall see the salvation of God.' "*[b]

John Preaches to the People

7 Then he said to the multitudes that came out to be baptized by him, "Brood of vipers! Who warned you to flee from the wrath to come? 8 Therefore bear fruits worthy of repentance, and do not begin to say to yourselves, 'We have Abraham as *our* father.' For I say to you that God is able to raise up children to Abraham from these stones. 9 And even now the ax is laid to the root of the trees. Therefore every tree which does not bear good fruit is cut down and thrown into the fire."

10 So the people asked him, saying, "What shall we do then?"

11 He answered and said to them, "He who has two tunics, let him give to him who has none; and he who has food, let him do likewise."

12 Then tax collectors also came to be baptized, and said to him, "Teacher, what shall we do?"

13 And he said to them, "Collect no more than what is appointed for you."

14 Likewise the soldiers asked him, saying, "And what shall we do?"

So he said to them, "Do not intimidate anyone or accuse falsely, and be content with your wages."

15 Now as the people were in expectation, and all reasoned in their hearts about John, whether he was the

3:6 [b] Isaiah 40:3–5

THE MESSAGE

Everyone will be there to see
The parade of God's salvation.' "

When crowds of people came out for baptism because it was the popular thing to do, John exploded: "Brood of snakes! What do you think you're doing slithering down here to the river? Do you think a little water on your snakeskins is going to deflect God's judgment? It's your *life* that must change, not your skin. And don't think you can pull rank by claiming Abraham as 'father.' Being a child of Abraham is neither here nor there—children of Abraham are a dime a dozen. God can make children from stones if he wants. What counts is your life. Is it green and blossoming? Because if it's deadwood, it goes on the fire."

The crowd asked him, "Then what are we supposed to do?"

"If you have two coats, give one away," he said. "Do the same with your food."

Tax men also came to be baptized and said, "Teacher, what should we do?"

He told them, "No more extortion—collect only what is required by law."

Soldiers asked him, "And what should we do?"

He told them, "No shakedowns, no blackmail—and be content with your rations."

The interest of the people by now was building. They were all beginning to wonder, "Could this John be the Messiah?"

KING JAMES VERSION

16 John answered, saying unto *them* all, I indeed baptize you with water; but one mightier than I cometh, the latchet of whose shoes I am not worthy to unloose: he shall baptize you with the Holy Ghost and with fire:

17 Whose fan *is* in his hand, and he will throughly purge his floor, and will gather the wheat into his garner; but the chaff he will burn with fire unquenchable.

18 And many other things in his exhortation preached he unto the people.

19 But Herod the tetrarch, being reproved by him for Herodias his brother Philip's wife, and for all the evils which Herod had done,

20 Added yet this above all, that he shut up John in prison.

21 ¶ Now when all the people were baptized, it came to pass, that Jesus also being baptized, and praying, the heaven was opened,

22 And the Holy Ghost descended in a bodily shape like a dove upon him, and a voice came from heaven, which said, Thou art my beloved Son; in thee I am well pleased.

23 And Jesus himself began to be about thirty years of age, being (as was supposed) the son of Joseph, which was *the son* of Heli,

NEW AMERICAN STANDARD BIBLE

16 John answered and said to them all, "As for me, I baptize you with water; but One is coming who is mightier than I, and I am not fit to untie the thong of His sandals; He will baptize you with the Holy Spirit and fire.

17 "His winnowing fork is in His hand to thoroughly clear His threshing floor, and to gather the wheat into His barn; but He will burn up the chaff with unquenchable fire."

18 So with many other exhortations he preached the gospel to the people.

19 But when Herod the tetrarch was reprimanded by him because of Herodias, his brother's wife, and because of all the wicked things which Herod had done,

20 Herod also added this to them all: he locked John up in prison.

Jesus Is Baptized

21 Now when all the people were baptized, Jesus was also baptized, and while He was praying, heaven was opened,

22 and the Holy Spirit descended upon Him in bodily form like a dove, and a voice came out of heaven, "You are My beloved Son, in You I am well-pleased."

Genealogy of Jesus

23 When He began His ministry, Jesus Himself was about thirty years of age, being, as was supposed, the son of Joseph, the son of Eli,

NEW CENTURY VERSION

16John answered everyone, "I baptize you with water,
but there is one coming who is greater than I am. I am not
good enough to untie his sandals. He will baptize you with
the Holy Spirit and fire. 17He will come ready to clean the
grain, separating the good grain from the chaff. He will
put the good part of the grain into his barn, but he will
burn the chaff with a fire that cannot be put out."[b] 18And
John continued to preach the Good News, saying many
other things to encourage the people.

19But John spoke against Herod, the governor, because
of his sin with Herodias, the wife of Herod's brother, and
because of the many other evil things Herod did. 20So
Herod did something even worse: He put John in prison.

Jesus Is Baptized by John

21When all the people were being baptized by John, Jesus
also was baptized. While Jesus was praying, heaven
opened 22and the Holy Spirit came down on him in the
form of a dove. Then a voice came from heaven, saying,
"You are my Son, whom I love, and I am very pleased with
you."

The Family History of Jesus

23When Jesus began his ministry, he was about thirty
years old. People thought that Jesus was Joseph's son.

3:17 [b] **He will...out.** This means that Jesus will come to separate good people from bad people, saving the good and punishing the bad.

CONTEMPORARY ENGLISH VERSION

16John said, "I am just baptizing with water. But some-
one more powerful is going to come, and I am not good
enough even to untie his sandals.[f] He will baptize you
with the Holy Spirit and with fire. 17His threshing fork[g] is
in his hand, and he is ready to separate the wheat from
the husks. He will store the wheat in his barn and burn the
husks with a fire that never goes out."

18In many different ways John preached the good news
to the people. 19But to Herod the ruler, he said, "It was
wrong for you to take Herodias, your brother's wife." John
also said that Herod had done many other bad things.
20Finally, Herod put John in jail, and this was the worst
thing he had done.

The Baptism of Jesus (Matthew 3.13-17; Mark 1.9-11)

21While everyone else was being baptized, Jesus himself
was baptized. Then as he prayed, the sky opened up, 22and
the Holy Spirit came down upon him in the form of a dove.
A voice from heaven said, "You are my own dear Son, and
I am pleased with you."

The Ancestors of Jesus (Matthew 1.1-17)

23When Jesus began to preach, he was about thirty years
old. Everyone thought he was the son of Joseph. But his

[f] **3.16** *untie his sandals*: This was the duty of a slave.

[g] **3.17** *threshing fork*: After Jewish farmers had trampled out the grain, they used a large fork to pitch the grain and the husks into the air. Wind would blow away the light husks, and the grain would fall back to the ground, where it could be gathered up.

NEW INTERNATIONAL VERSION

[16]John answered them all, "I baptize you with[c] water. But one more powerful than I will come, the thongs of whose sandals I am not worthy to untie. He will baptize you with the Holy Spirit and with fire. [17]His winnowing fork is in his hand to clear his threshing floor and to gather the wheat into his barn, but he will burn up the chaff with unquenchable fire." [18]And with many other words John exhorted the people and preached the good news to them.

[19]But when John rebuked Herod the tetrarch because of Herodias, his brother's wife, and all the other evil things he had done, [20]Herod added this to them all: He locked John up in prison.

The Baptism and Genealogy of Jesus

[21]When all the people were being baptized, Jesus was baptized too. And as he was praying, heaven was opened [22]and the Holy Spirit descended on him in bodily form like a dove. And a voice came from heaven: "You are my Son, whom I love; with you I am well pleased."

[23]Now Jesus himself was about thirty years old when he began his ministry. He was the son, so it was thought, of Joseph,

c *16* Or *in*

NEW LIVING TRANSLATION

Messiah. [16]John answered their questions by saying, "I baptize with* water; but someone is coming soon who is greater than I am—so much greater that I am not even worthy to be his slave.* He will baptize you with the Holy Spirit and with fire.* [17]He is ready to separate the chaff from the grain with his winnowing fork. Then he will clean up the threshing area, storing the grain in his barn but burning the chaff with never-ending fire." [18]John used many such warnings as he announced the Good News to the people.

[19]John also publicly criticized Herod Antipas, ruler of Galilee, for marrying Herodias, his brother's wife, and for many other wrongs he had done. [20]So Herod put John in prison, adding this sin to his many others.

The Baptism of Jesus

[21]One day when the crowds were being baptized, Jesus himself was baptized. As he was praying, the heavens opened, [22]and the Holy Spirit descended on him in the form of a dove. And a voice from heaven said, "You are my beloved Son, and I am fully pleased with you.*"

The Record of Jesus' Ancestors

[23]Jesus was about thirty years old when he began his public ministry.

Jesus was known as the son of Joseph.

3:16a Or *in.* **3:16b** Greek *to untie his sandals.* **3:16c** Or *in the Holy Spirit and in fire.* **3:22** Some manuscripts read *and today I have become your Father.*

NEW KING JAMES VERSION

Christ *or* not, [16]John answered, saying to all, "I indeed baptize you with water; but One mightier than I is coming, whose sandal strap I am not worthy to loose. He will baptize you with the Holy Spirit and fire. [17]His winnowing fan *is* in His hand, and He will thoroughly clean out His threshing floor, and gather the wheat into His barn; but the chaff He will burn with unquenchable fire."

[18]And with many other exhortations he preached to the people. [19]But Herod the tetrarch, being rebuked by him concerning Herodias, his brother Philip's wife,[c] and for all the evils which Herod had done, [20]also added this, above all, that he shut John up in prison.

John Baptizes Jesus

[21]When all the people were baptized, it came to pass that Jesus also was baptized; and while He prayed, the heaven was opened. [22]And the Holy Spirit descended in bodily form like a dove upon Him, and a voice came from heaven which said, "You are My beloved Son; in You I am well pleased."

The Genealogy of Jesus Christ

[23]Now Jesus Himself began *His ministry at* about thirty years of age, being (as was supposed) *the* son of Joseph,

3:19 c NU-Text reads *his brother's wife.*

THE MESSAGE

But John intervened: "I'm baptizing you here in the river. The main character in this drama, to whom I'm a mere stagehand, will ignite the kingdom life, a fire, the Holy Spirit within you, changing you from the inside out. He's going to clean house—make a clean sweep of your lives. He'll place everything true in its proper place before God; everything false he'll put out with the trash to be burned."

There was a lot more of this—words that gave strength to the people, words that put heart in them. The Message! But Herod, the ruler, stung by John's rebuke in the matter of Herodias, his brother Philip's wife, capped his long string of evil deeds with this outrage: He put John in jail.

After all the people were baptized, Jesus was baptized. As he was praying, the sky opened up and the Holy Spirit, like a dove descending, came down on him. And along with the Spirit, a voice: "You are my Son, chosen and marked by my love, pride of my life."

Son of Adam, Son of God

When Jesus entered public life he was about thirty years old, the son (in public perception) of Joseph, who was—

KING JAMES VERSION

24 Which was *the son* of Matthat, which was *the son* of Levi, which was *the son* of Melchi, which was *the son* of Janna, which was *the son* of Joseph,
25 Which was *the son* of Mattathias, which was *the son* of Amos, which was *the son* of Naum, which was *the son* of Esli, which was *the son* of Nagge,
26 Which was *the son* of Maath, which was *the son* of Mattathias, which was *the son* of Semei, which was *the son* of Joseph, which was *the son* of Juda,
27 Which was *the son* of Joanna, which was *the son* of Rhesa, which was *the son* of Zorobabel, which was *the son* of Salathiel, which was *the son* of Neri,
28 Which was *the son* of Melchi, which was *the son* of Addi, which was *the son* of Cosam, which was *the son* of Elmodam, which was *the son* of Er,

NEW AMERICAN STANDARD BIBLE

24 the son of Matthat, the son of Levi, the son of Melchi, the son of Jannai, the son of Joseph,
25 the son of Mattathias, the son of Amos, the son of Nahum, the son of Hesli, the son of Naggai,
26 the son of Maath, the son of Mattathias, the son of Semein, the son of Josech, the son of Joda,
27 the son of Joanan, the son of Rhesa, the son of Zerubbabel, the son of Shealtiel, the son of Neri,
28 the son of Melchi, the son of Addi, the son of Cosam, the son of Elmadam, the son of Er,

NEW CENTURY VERSION

Joseph was the son[c] of Heli.
24 Heli was the son of Matthat.
Matthat was the son of Levi.
Levi was the son of Melki.
Melki was the son of Jannai.
Jannai was the son of Joseph.
25 Joseph was the son of Mattathias.
Mattathias was the son of Amos.
Amos was the son of Nahum.
Nahum was the son of Esli.
Esli was the son of Naggai.
26 Naggai was the son of Maath.
Maath was the son of Mattathias.
Mattathias was the son of Semein.
Semein was the son of Josech.
Josech was the son of Joda.
27 Joda was the son of Joanan.
Joanan was the son of Rhesa.
Rhesa was the son of Zerubbabel.
Zerubbabel was the grandson of Shealtiel.
Shealtiel was the son of Neri.
28 Neri was the son of Melchi.
Melchi was the son of Addi.
Addi was the son of Cosam.
Cosam was the son of Elmadam.
Elmadam was the son of Er.
29 Er was the son of Joshua.

3:23 [c] **son** "Son" in Jewish lists of ancestors can sometimes mean grandson or more distant relative.

CONTEMPORARY ENGLISH VERSION

family went back through Heli, 24 Matthat, Levi, Melchi,
Jannai, Joseph, 25 Mattathias, Amos, Nahum, Esli, Naggai,
26 Maath, Mattathias, Semein, Josech, Joda;
27 Joanan, Rhesa, Zerubbabel, Shealtiel, Neri, 28 Melchi,
Addi, Cosam, Elmadam, Er, 29 Joshua, Eliezer, Jorim,

NEW INTERNATIONAL VERSION

the son of Heli, [24]the son of Matthat,
the son of Levi, the son of Melki,
the son of Jannai, the son of Joseph,
25 the son of Mattathias, the son of Amos,
the son of Nahum, the son of Esli,
the son of Naggai, [26]the son of Maath,
the son of Mattathias, the son of Semein,
the son of Josech, the son of Joda,
27 the son of Joanan, the son of Rhesa,
the son of Zerubbabel, the son of Shealtiel,
the son of Neri, [28]the son of Melki,
the son of Addi, the son of Cosam,
the son of Elmadam, the son of Er,
29 the son of Joshua, the son of Eliezer,

NEW LIVING TRANSLATION

Joseph was the son of Heli.
24 Heli was the son of Matthat.
Matthat was the son of Levi.
Levi was the son of Melki.
Melki was the son of Jannai.
Jannai was the son of Joseph.
25 Joseph was the son of Mattathias.
Mattathias was the son of Amos.
Amos was the son of Nahum.
Nahum was the son of Esli.
Esli was the son of Naggai.
26 Naggai was the son of Maath.
Maath was the son of Mattathias.
Mattathias was the son of Semein.
Semein was the son of Josech.
Josech was the son of Joda.
27 Joda was the son of Joanan.
Joanan was the son of Rhesa.
Rhesa was the son of Zerubbabel.
Zerubbabel was the son of Shealtiel.
Shealtiel was the son of Neri.
28 Neri was the son of Melki.
Melki was the son of Addi.
Addi was the son of Cosam.
Cosam was the son of Elmadam.
Elmadam was the son of Er.
29 Er was the son of Joshua.

NEW KING JAMES VERSION

the son of Heli, [24]*the son* of Matthat,[d] *the son* of Levi, *the*
son of Melchi, *the son* of Janna, *the son* of Joseph, [25]*the*
son of Mattathiah, *the son* of Amos, *the son* of Nahum, *the*
son of Esli, *the son* of Naggai, [26]*the son* of Maath, *the son*
of Mattathiah, *the son* of Semei, *the son* of Joseph, *the son*
of Judah, [27]*the son* of Joannas, *the son* of Rhesa, *the son* of
Zerubbabel, *the son* of Shealtiel, *the son* of Neri, [28]*the son*
of Melchi, *the son* of Addi, *the son* of Cosam, *the son* of El-
modam, *the son* of Er, [29]*the son* of Jose, *the son* of Eliezer,

3:24 [d] This and several other names in the genealogy are spelled somewhat differently in the NU-Text. Since the New King James Version uses the Old Testament spelling for persons mentioned in the New Testament, these variations, which come from the Greek, have not been footnoted.

THE MESSAGE

son of Heli,
son of Matthat,
son of Levi,
son of Melchi,
son of Jannai,
son of Joseph,
son of Mattathias,
son of Amos,
son of Nahum,
son of Esli,
son of Naggai,
son of Maath,
son of Mattathias,
son of Semein,
son of Josech,
son of Joda,
son of Joanan,
son of Rhesa,
son of Zerubbabel,
son of Shealtiel,
son of Neri,
son of Melchi,
son of Addi,
son of Cosam,
son of Elmadam,
son of Er,
son of Joshua,

KING JAMES VERSION

29 Which was *the son* of Jose, which was *the son* of
Eliezer, which was *the son* of Jorim, which was *the son* of
Matthat, which was *the son* of Levi,
30 Which was *the son* of Simeon, which was *the son* of
Juda, which was *the son* of Joseph, which was *the son* of
Jonan, which was *the son* of Eliakim,
31 Which was *the son* of Melea, which was *the son* of
Menan, which was *the son* of Mattatha, which was *the son*
of Nathan, which was *the son* of David,
32 Which was *the son* of Jesse, which was *the son* of
Obed, which was *the son* of Booz, which was *the son* of
Salmon, which was *the son* of Naasson,
33 Which was *the son* of Aminadab, which was *the son*
of Aram, which was *the son* of Esrom, which was *the son*
of Phares, which was *the son* of Juda,
34 Which was *the son* of Jacob, which was *the son* of
Isaac, which was *the son* of Abraham, which was *the son*

NEW AMERICAN STANDARD BIBLE

29 the son of Joshua, the son of Eliezer, the son of
Jorim, the son of Matthat, the son of Levi,
30 the son of Simeon, the son of Judah, the son of
Joseph, the son of Jonam, the son of Eliakim,
31 the son of Melea, the son of Menna, the son of
Mattatha, the son of Nathan, the son of David,
32 the son of Jesse, the son of Obed, the son of Boaz, the
son of Salmon, the son of Nahshon,
33 the son of Amminadab, the son of Admin, the son of
Ram, the son of Hezron, the son of Perez, the son of Judah,
34 the son of Jacob, the son of Isaac, the son of Abraham,

NEW CENTURY VERSION

Joshua was the son of Eliezer.
Eliezer was the son of Jorim.
Jorim was the son of Matthat.
Matthat was the son of Levi.
30 Levi was the son of Simeon.
Simeon was the son of Judah.
Judah was the son of Joseph.
Joseph was the son of Jonam.
Jonam was the son of Eliakim.
31 Eliakim was the son of Melea.
Melea was the son of Menna.
Menna was the son of Mattatha.
Mattatha was the son of Nathan.
Nathan was the son of David.
32 David was the son of Jesse.
Jesse was the son of Obed.
Obed was the son of Boaz.
Boaz was the son of Salmon.
Salmon was the son of Nahshon.
33 Nahshon was the son of Amminadab.
Amminadab was the son of Admin.
Admin was the son of Arni.
Arni was the son of Hezron.
Hezron was the son of Perez.
Perez was the son of Judah.
34 Judah was the son of Jacob.
Jacob was the son of Isaac.
Isaac was the son of Abraham.

CONTEMPORARY ENGLISH VERSION

Matthat, Levi;
30 Simeon, Judah, Joseph, Jonam, Eliakim, 31 Melea,
Menna, Mattatha, Nathan, David, 32 Jesse, Obed, Boaz,
Salmon, Nahshon;
33 Amminadab, Admin, Arni, Hezron, Perez, Judah,
34 Jacob, Isaac, Abraham, Terah, Nahor, 35 Serug, Reu,

NEW INTERNATIONAL VERSION

the son of Jorim, the son of Matthat,
the son of Levi, [30]the son of Simeon,
the son of Judah, the son of Joseph,
the son of Jonam, the son of Eliakim,
[31] the son of Melea, the son of Menna,
the son of Mattatha, the son of Nathan,
the son of David, [32]the son of Jesse,
the son of Obed, the son of Boaz,
the son of Salmon,[d] the son of Nahshon,
[33] the son of Amminadab, the son of Ram,[e]
the son of Hezron, the son of Perez,
the son of Judah, [34]the son of Jacob,
the son of Isaac, the son of Abraham,

[d] *32* Some early manuscripts *Sala* [e] *33* Some manuscripts *Amminadab, the son of Admin, the son of Arni*; other manuscripts vary widely.

NEW LIVING TRANSLATION

Joshua was the son of Eliezer.
Eliezer was the son of Jorim.
Jorim was the son of Matthat.
Matthat was the son of Levi.
[30] Levi was the son of Simeon.
Simeon was the son of Judah.
Judah was the son of Joseph.
Joseph was the son of Jonam.
Jonam was the son of Eliakim.
[31] Eliakim was the son of Melea.
Melea was the son of Menna.
Menna was the son of Mattatha.
Mattatha was the son of Nathan.
Nathan was the son of David.
[32] David was the son of Jesse.
Jesse was the son of Obed.
Obed was the son of Boaz.
Boaz was the son of Salmon.*
Salmon was the son of Nahshon.
[33] Nahshon was the son of Amminadab.
Amminadab was the son of Admin.
Admin was the son of Arni.*
Arni was the son of Hezron.
Hezron was the son of Perez.
Perez was the son of Judah.
[34] Judah was the son of Jacob.
Jacob was the son of Isaac.
Isaac was the son of Abraham.

3:32 Greek *Sala;* see Ruth 4:22. 3:33 *Arni* is the same person as Ram; see 1 Chr 2:9-10.

NEW KING JAMES VERSION

the son of Jorim, *the son* of Matthat, *the son* of Levi, [30]*the*
son of Simeon, *the son* of Judah, *the son* of Joseph, *the son*
of Jonan, *the son* of Eliakim, [31]*the son* of Melea, *the son* of
Menan, *the son* of Mattathah, *the son* of Nathan, *the son*
of David, [32]*the son* of Jesse, *the son* of Obed, *the son* of
Boaz, *the son* of Salmon, *the son* of Nahshon, [33]*the son* of
Amminadab, *the son* of Ram, *the son* of Hezron, *the son*
of Perez, *the son* of Judah, [34]*the son* of Jacob, *the son* of
Isaac, *the son* of Abraham, *the son* of Terah, *the son* of

THE MESSAGE

son of Eliezer,
son of Jorim,
son of Matthat,
son of Levi,
son of Simeon,
son of Judah,
son of Joseph,
son of Jonam,
son of Eliakim,
son of Melea,
son of Menna,
son of Mattatha,
son of Nathan,
son of David,
son of Jesse,
son of Obed,
son of Boaz,
son of Sala,
son of Nahshon,
son of Amminadab,
son of Admin,
son of Arni,
son of Hezron,
son of Perez,
son of Judah,
son of Jacob,
son of Isaac,
son of Abraham,

KING JAMES VERSION

of Thara, which was *the son* of Nachor,
35 Which was *the son* of Saruch, which was *the son* of
Ragau, which was *the son* of Phalec, which was *the son* of
Heber, which was *the son* of Sala,
36 Which was *the son* of Cainan, which was *the son* of
Arphaxad, which was *the son* of Sem, which was *the son*
of Noe, which was *the son* of Lamech,
37 Which was *the son* of Mathusala, which was *the son*
of Enoch, which was *the son* of Jared, which was *the son* of
Maleleel, which was *the son* of Cainan,
38 Which was *the son* of Enos, which was *the son* of
Seth, which was *the son* of Adam, which was *the son* of
God.
4 And Jesus being full of the Holy Ghost returned from
Jordan, and was led by the Spirit into the wilderness,
2 Being forty days tempted of the devil. And in those
days he did eat nothing: and when they were ended, he
afterward hungered.

NEW AMERICAN STANDARD BIBLE

the son of Terah, the son of Nahor,
35 the son of Serug, the son of Reu, the son of Peleg, the
son of Heber, the son of Shelah,
36 the son of Cainan, the son of Arphaxad, the son of
Shem, the son of Noah, the son of Lamech,
37 the son of Methuselah, the son of Enoch, the son of
Jared, the son of Mahalaleel, the son of Cainan,
38 the son of Enosh, the son of Seth, the son of Adam,
the son of God.

The Temptation of Jesus

4 Jesus, full of the Holy Spirit, returned from the Jordan
and was led around by the Spirit in the wilderness
2 for forty days, being tempted by the devil. And He ate
nothing during those days, and when they had ended, He
became hungry.

NEW CENTURY VERSION

Abraham was the son of Terah.
Terah was the son of Nahor.
35 Nahor was the son of Serug.
Serug was the son of Reu.
Reu was the son of Peleg.
Peleg was the son of Eber.
Eber was the son of Shelah.
36 Shelah was the son of Cainan.
Cainan was the son of Arphaxad.
Arphaxad was the son of Shem.
Shem was the son of Noah.
Noah was the son of Lamech.
37 Lamech was the son of Methuselah.
Methuselah was the son of Enoch.
Enoch was the son of Jared.
Jared was the son of Mahalalel.
Mahalalel was the son of Kenan.
38 Kenan was the son of Enosh.
Enosh was the son of Seth.
Seth was the son of Adam.
Adam was the son of God.

Jesus Is Tempted by the Devil

4 Jesus, filled with the Holy Spirit, returned from the
Jordan River. The Spirit led Jesus into the desert
2 where the devil tempted Jesus for forty days. Jesus ate
nothing during that time, and when those days were
ended, he was very hungry.

CONTEMPORARY ENGLISH VERSION

Peleg, Eber, Shelah;
36 Cainan, Arphaxad, Shem, Noah, Lamech, 37 Methu-
selah, Enoch, Jared, Mahalaleel, Kenan, 38 Enosh, and Seth.
The family of Jesus went all the way back to Adam and
then to God.

Jesus and the Devil (Matthew 4.1-11; Mark 1.12, 13)

4 When Jesus returned from the Jordan River, the power
of the Holy Spirit was with him, and the Spirit led him
into the desert. 2 For forty days Jesus was tested by the
devil, and during that time he went without eating.[a] When
it was all over, he was hungry.

[a] 4.2 *went without eating*: See the note at 2.37.

NEW INTERNATIONAL VERSION

the son of Terah, the son of Nahor,
35 the son of Serug, the son of Reu,
the son of Peleg, the son of Eber,
the son of Shelah, 36 the son of Cainan,
the son of Arphaxad, the son of Shem,
the son of Noah, the son of Lamech,
37 the son of Methuselah, the son of Enoch,
the son of Jared, the son of Mahalalel,
the son of Kenan, 38 the son of Enosh,
the son of Seth, the son of Adam,
the son of God.

The Temptation of Jesus

4 Jesus, full of the Holy Spirit, returned from the Jordan
and was led by the Spirit in the desert, 2 where for
forty days he was tempted by the devil. He ate nothing
during those days, and at the end of them he was hungry.

NEW LIVING TRANSLATION

Abraham was the son of Terah.
Terah was the son of Nahor.
35 Nahor was the son of Serug.
Serug was the son of Reu.
Reu was the son of Peleg.
Peleg was the son of Eber.
Eber was the son of Shelah.
36 Shelah was the son of Cainan.
Cainan was the son of Arphaxad.
Arphaxad was the son of Shem.
Shem was the son of Noah.
Noah was the son of Lamech.
37 Lamech was the son of Methuselah.
Methuselah was the son of Enoch.
Enoch was the son of Jared.
Jared was the son of Mahalalel.
Mahalalel was the son of Kenan.
38 Kenan was the son of Enosh.*
Enosh was the son of Seth.
Seth was the son of Adam.
Adam was the son of God.

The Temptation of Jesus

4 Then Jesus, full of the Holy Spirit, left the Jordan
River. He was led by the Spirit to go out into the
wilderness, 2 where the Devil tempted him for forty days.
He ate nothing all that time and was very hungry.

3:38 Greek *Enos;* see Gen 5:6.

NEW KING JAMES VERSION

Nahor, 35 *the son* of Serug, *the son* of Reu, *the son* of Peleg,
the son of Eber, *the son* of Shelah, 36 *the son* of Cainan, *the*
son of Arphaxad, *the son* of Shem, *the son* of Noah, *the*
son of Lamech, 37 *the son* of Methuselah, *the son* of Enoch,
the son of Jared, *the son* of Mahalalel, *the son* of Cainan,
38 *the son* of Enosh, *the son* of Seth, *the son* of Adam, *the*
son of God.

Satan Tempts Jesus

4 Then Jesus, being filled with the Holy Spirit, returned
from the Jordan and was led by the Spirit into[a] the
wilderness, 2 being tempted for forty days by the devil. And
in those days He ate nothing, and afterward, when they
had ended, He was hungry.

4:1 [a] NU-Text reads *in.*

THE MESSAGE

son of Terah,
son of Nahor,
son of Serug,
son of Reu,
son of Peleg,
son of Eber,
son of Shelah,
son of Cainan,
son of Arphaxad,
son of Shem,
son of Noah,
son of Lamech,
son of Methuselah,
son of Enoch,
son of Jared,
son of Mahalaleel,
son of Cainan,
son of Enos,
son of Seth,
son of Adam,
son of God.

Tested by the Devil

4 Now Jesus, full of the Holy Spirit, left the Jordan and
was led by the Spirit into the wild. For forty wilder-
ness days and nights he was tested by the Devil. He ate
nothing during those days, and when the time was up he
was hungry.

KING JAMES VERSION

3 And the devil said unto him, If thou be the Son of God, command this stone that it be made bread.

4 And Jesus answered him, saying, It is written, That man shall not live by bread alone, but by every word of God.

5 And the devil, taking him up into an high mountain, shewed unto him all the kingdoms of the world in a moment of time.

6 And the devil said unto him, All this power will I give thee, and the glory of them: for that is delivered unto me; and to whomsoever I will I give it.

7 If thou therefore wilt worship me, all shall be thine.

8 And Jesus answered and said unto him, Get thee behind me, Satan: for it is written, Thou shalt worship the Lord thy God, and him only shalt thou serve.

9 And he brought him to Jerusalem, and set him on a pinnacle of the temple, and said unto him, If thou be the Son of God, cast thyself down from hence:

10 For it is written, He shall give his angels charge over thee, to keep thee:

11 And in *their* hands they shall bear thee up, lest at any time thou dash thy foot against a stone.

12 And Jesus answering said unto him, It is said, Thou shalt not tempt the Lord thy God.

NEW AMERICAN STANDARD BIBLE

3 And the devil said to Him, "If You are the Son of God, tell this stone to become bread."

4 And Jesus answered him, "It is written, 'MAN SHALL NOT LIVE ON BREAD ALONE.' "

5 And he led Him up and showed Him all the kingdoms of the world in a moment of time.

6 And the devil said to Him, "I will give You all this domain and its glory; for it has been handed over to me, and I give it to whomever I wish.

7 "Therefore if You worship before me, it shall all be Yours."

8 Jesus answered him, "It is written, 'YOU SHALL WORSHIP THE LORD YOUR GOD AND SERVE HIM ONLY.' "

9 And he led Him to Jerusalem and had Him stand on the pinnacle of the temple, and said to Him, "If You are the Son of God, throw Yourself down from here;

10 for it is written,

'HE WILL COMMAND HIS ANGELS CONCERNING YOU TO GUARD YOU,'

11 and,

'ON *their* HANDS THEY WILL BEAR YOU UP,
SO THAT YOU WILL NOT STRIKE YOUR FOOT AGAINST A STONE.' "

12 And Jesus answered and said to him, "It is said, 'YOU SHALL NOT PUT THE LORD YOUR GOD TO THE TEST.' "

NEW CENTURY VERSION

3The devil said to Jesus, "If you are the Son of God, tell this rock to become bread."

4Jesus answered, "It is written in the Scriptures: 'A person does not live by eating only bread.' "[a]

5Then the devil took Jesus and showed him all the kingdoms of the world in an instant. 6The devil said to Jesus, "I will give you all these kingdoms and all their power and glory. It has all been given to me, and I can give it to anyone I wish. 7If you worship me, then it will all be yours."

8Jesus answered, "It is written in the Scriptures: 'You must worship the Lord your God and serve only him.' "[b]

9Then the devil led Jesus to Jerusalem and put him on a high place of the Temple. He said to Jesus, "If you are the Son of God, jump down. 10It is written in the Scriptures:

'He has put his angels in charge of you
to watch over you.' *Psalm 91:11*

11It is also written:

'They will catch you in their hands
so that you will not hit your foot on a rock.' " *Psalm 91:12*

12Jesus answered, "But it also says in the Scriptures: 'Do not test the Lord your God.' "[c]

4:4 [a] 'A person...bread.' Quotation from Deuteronomy 8:3.
4:8 [b] 'You...him.' Quotation from Deuteronomy 6:13.
4:12 [c] 'Do...God.' Quotation from Deuteronomy 6:16.

CONTEMPORARY ENGLISH VERSION

3The devil said to Jesus, "If you are God's Son, tell this stone to turn into bread."

4Jesus answered, "The Scriptures say, 'No one can live only on food.' "

5Then the devil led Jesus up to a high place and quickly showed him all the nations on earth. 6The devil said, "I will give all this power and glory to you. It has been given to me, and I can give it to anyone I want to. 7Just worship me, and you can have it all."

8Jesus answered, "The Scriptures say:

'Worship the Lord your God
and serve only him!' "

9Finally, the devil took Jesus to Jerusalem and had him stand on top of the temple. The devil said, "If you are God's Son, jump off. 10-11The Scriptures say:

'God will tell his angels
to take care of you.
They will catch you
in their arms,
and you will not hurt
your feet on the stones.' "

12Jesus answered, "The Scriptures also say, 'Don't try to test the Lord your God!' "

NEW INTERNATIONAL VERSION

3The devil said to him, "If you are the Son of God, tell this stone to become bread."

4Jesus answered, "It is written: 'Man does not live on bread alone.'[a]"

5The devil led him up to a high place and showed him in an instant all the kingdoms of the world. 6And he said to him, "I will give you all their authority and splendor, for it has been given to me, and I can give it to anyone I want to. 7So if you worship me, it will all be yours."

8Jesus answered, "It is written: 'Worship the Lord your God and serve him only.'[b]"

9The devil led him to Jerusalem and had him stand on the highest point of the temple. "If you are the Son of God," he said, "throw yourself down from here. 10For it is written:

" 'He will command his angels concerning you
to guard you carefully;
11 they will lift you up in their hands,
so that you will not strike your foot against a
stone.'[c]"

12Jesus answered, "It says: 'Do not put the Lord your God to the test.'[d]"

[a] *4* Deut. 8:3 [b] *8* Deut. 6:13 [c] *11* Psalm 91:11,12
[d] *12* Deut. 6:16

NEW LIVING TRANSLATION

3Then the Devil said to him, "If you are the Son of God, change this stone into a loaf of bread."

4But Jesus told him, "No! The Scriptures say, 'People need more than bread for their life.'* "

5Then the Devil took him up and revealed to him all the kingdoms of the world in a moment of time. 6The Devil told him, "I will give you the glory of these kingdoms and authority over them—because they are mine to give to anyone I please. 7I will give it all to you if you will bow down and worship me."

8Jesus replied, "The Scriptures say,

'You must worship the Lord your God;
serve only him.'* "

9Then the Devil took him to Jerusalem, to the highest point of the Temple, and said, "If you are the Son of God, jump off! 10For the Scriptures say,

'He orders his angels to protect and guard you.
11 And they will hold you with their hands
to keep you from striking your foot on a stone.'* "

12Jesus responded, "The Scriptures also say, 'Do not test the Lord your God.'* "

4:4 Deut 8:3. **4:8** Deut 6:13. **4:10-11** Ps 91:11-12.
4:12 Deut 6:16.

NEW KING JAMES VERSION

3And the devil said to Him, "If You are the Son of God, command this stone to become bread."

4But Jesus answered him, saying,[b] "It is written, *'Man shall not live by bread alone, but by every word of God.'* "[c]

5Then the devil, taking Him up on a high mountain, showed Him[d] all the kingdoms of the world in a moment of time. 6And the devil said to Him, "All this authority I will give You, and their glory; for *this* has been delivered to me, and I give it to whomever I wish. 7Therefore, if You will worship before me, all will be Yours."

8And Jesus answered and said to him, "Get behind Me, Satan![e] For[f] it is written, *'You shall worship the LORD your God, and Him only you shall serve.'* "[g]

9Then he brought Him to Jerusalem, set Him on the pinnacle of the temple, and said to Him, "If You are the Son of God, throw Yourself down from here. 10For it is written:

'He shall give His angels charge over you,
To keep you,'

11and,

'In their hands they shall bear you up,
Lest you dash your foot against a stone.' "[h]

12And Jesus answered and said to him, "It has been said, *'You shall not tempt the LORD your God.'* "[i]

4:4 [b] Deuteronomy 8:3 [c] NU-Text omits *but by every word of God.*
4:5 [d] NU-Text reads *And taking Him up, he showed Him.* **4:8** [e] NU-Text omits *Get behind Me, Satan.* [f] NU-Text and M-Text omit *For.*
[g] Deuteronomy 6:13 **4:11** [h] Psalm 91:11, 12 **4:12** [i] Deuteronomy 6:16

THE MESSAGE

The Devil, playing on his hunger, gave the first test: "Since you're God's Son, command this stone to turn into a loaf of bread."

Jesus answered by quoting Deuteronomy: "It takes more than bread to really live."

For the second test he led him up and spread out all the kingdoms of the earth on display at once. Then the Devil said, "They're yours in all their splendor to serve your pleasure. I'm in charge of them all and can turn them over to whomever I wish. Worship me and they're yours, the whole works."

Jesus refused, again backing his refusal with Deuteronomy: "Worship the Lord your God and only the Lord your God. Serve him with absolute single-heartedness."

For the third test the Devil took him to Jerusalem and put him on top of the Temple. He said, "If you are God's Son, jump. It's written, isn't it, that 'he has placed you in the care of angels to protect you; they will catch you; you won't so much as stub your toe on a stone'?"

"Yes," said Jesus, "and it's also written, 'Don't you dare tempt the Lord your God.'"

KING JAMES VERSION

13 And when the devil had ended all the temptation, he departed from him for a season.

14 ¶ And Jesus returned in the power of the Spirit into Galilee: and there went out a fame of him through all the region round about.

15 And he taught in their synagogues, being glorified of all.

16 And he came to Nazareth, where he had been brought up: and, as his custom was, he went into the synagogue on the sabbath day, and stood up for to read.

17 And there was delivered unto him the book of the prophet Esaias. And when he had opened the book, he found the place where it was written,

18 The Spirit of the Lord *is* upon me, because he hath anointed me to preach the gospel to the poor; he hath sent me to heal the brokenhearted, to preach deliverance to the captives, and recovering of sight to the blind, to set at liberty them that are bruised,

19 To preach the acceptable year of the Lord.

NEW AMERICAN STANDARD BIBLE

13 When the devil had finished every temptation, he left Him until an opportune time.

Jesus' Public Ministry

14 And Jesus returned to Galilee in the power of the Spirit, and news about Him spread through all the surrounding district.

15 And He *began* teaching in their synagogues and was praised by all.

16 And He came to Nazareth, where He had been brought up; and as was His custom, He entered the synagogue on the Sabbath, and stood up to read.

17 And the book of the prophet Isaiah was handed to Him. And He opened the book and found the place where it was written,

18 "THE SPIRIT OF THE LORD IS UPON ME,
BECAUSE HE ANOINTED ME TO PREACH THE GOSPEL TO THE POOR.
HE HAS SENT ME TO PROCLAIM RELEASE TO THE CAPTIVES,
AND RECOVERY OF SIGHT TO THE BLIND,
TO SET FREE THOSE WHO ARE OPPRESSED,
19 TO PROCLAIM THE FAVORABLE YEAR OF THE LORD."

NEW CENTURY VERSION

13 After the devil had tempted Jesus in every way, he left him to wait until a better time.

Jesus Teaches the People

14 Jesus returned to Galilee in the power of the Holy Spirit, and stories about him spread all through the area. 15 He began to teach in their synagogues, and everyone praised him.

16 Jesus traveled to Nazareth, where he had grown up. On the Sabbath day he went to the synagogue, as he always did, and stood up to read. 17 The book of Isaiah the prophet was given to him. He opened the book and found the place where this is written:

18 "The Lord has put his Spirit in me,
because he appointed me to tell the Good News
to the poor.
He has sent me to tell the captives they are free
and to tell the blind that they can see
again. *Isaiah 61:1*
God sent me to free those who have been treated
unfairly *Isaiah 58:6*
19 and to announce the time when the Lord will show
his kindness." *Isaiah 61:2*

CONTEMPORARY ENGLISH VERSION

13 After the devil had finished testing Jesus in every way possible, he left him for a while.

Jesus Begins His Work (Matthew 4.12-17; Mark 1.14, 15)

14 Jesus returned to Galilee with the power of the Spirit. News about him spread everywhere. 15 He taught in the Jewish meeting places, and everyone praised him.

The People of Nazareth Turn against Jesus
(Matthew 13.53-58; Mark 6.1-6)

16 Jesus went back to Nazareth, where he had been brought up, and as usual he went to the meeting place on the Sabbath. When he stood up to read from the Scriptures, 17 he was given the book of Isaiah the prophet. He opened it and read,

18 "The Lord's Spirit
has come to me,
because he has chosen me
to tell the good news
to the poor.
The Lord has sent me
to announce freedom
for prisoners,
to give sight to the blind,
to free everyone
who suffers,
19 and to say, 'This is the year
the Lord has chosen.' "

NEW INTERNATIONAL VERSION

13When the devil had finished all this tempting, he left him until an opportune time.

Jesus Rejected at Nazareth

14Jesus returned to Galilee in the power of the Spirit, and news about him spread through the whole countryside.
15He taught in their synagogues, and everyone praised him.
16He went to Nazareth, where he had been brought up, and on the Sabbath day he went into the synagogue, as was his custom. And he stood up to read.
17The scroll of the prophet Isaiah was handed to him. Unrolling it, he found the place where it is written:

18 "The Spirit of the Lord is on me,
because he has anointed me
to preach good news to the poor.
He has sent me to proclaim freedom for the prisoners
and recovery of sight for the blind,
to release the oppressed,
19 to proclaim the year of the Lord's favor."[e]

[e] *19* Isaiah 61:1,2

NEW LIVING TRANSLATION

13When the Devil had finished tempting Jesus, he left him until the next opportunity came.

Jesus Rejected at Nazareth

14Then Jesus returned to Galilee, filled with the Holy Spirit's power. Soon he became well known throughout the surrounding country.
15He taught in their synagogues and was praised by everyone.
16When he came to the village of Nazareth, his boyhood home, he went as usual to the synagogue on the Sabbath and stood up to read the Scriptures.
17The scroll containing the messages of Isaiah the prophet was handed to him, and he unrolled the scroll to the place where it says:

18 "The Spirit of the Lord is upon me,
for he has appointed me to preach Good News to the poor.
He has sent me to proclaim
that captives will be released,
that the blind will see,
that the downtrodden will be freed from their oppressors,
19 and that the time of the Lord's favor has come.*"

4:18-19 Or *and to proclaim the acceptable year of the Lord.* Isa 61:1-2.

NEW KING JAMES VERSION

13Now when the devil had ended every temptation, he departed from Him until an opportune time.

Jesus Begins His Galilean Ministry

14Then Jesus returned in the power of the Spirit to Galilee, and news of Him went out through all the surrounding region.
15And He taught in their synagogues, being glorified by all.

Jesus Rejected at Nazareth

16So He came to Nazareth, where He had been brought up. And as His custom was, He went into the synagogue on the Sabbath day, and stood up to read.
17And He was handed the book of the prophet Isaiah. And when He had opened the book, He found the place where it was written:

18 "*The Spirit of the* LORD *is upon Me,*
Because He has anointed Me
To preach the gospel to the poor;
He has sent Me to heal the brokenhearted,[j]
To proclaim liberty to the captives
And recovery of sight to the blind,
To set at liberty those who are oppressed;
19 *To proclaim the acceptable year of the* LORD."[k]

4:18 [j] NU-Text omits *to heal the brokenhearted.* 4:19 [k] Isaiah 61:1, 2

THE MESSAGE

That completed the testing. The Devil retreated temporarily, lying in wait for another opportunity.

To Set the Burdened Free

Jesus returned to Galilee powerful in the Spirit. News that he was back spread through the countryside. He taught in their meeting places to everyone's acclaim and pleasure.

He came to Nazareth where he had been reared. As he always did on the Sabbath, he went to the meeting place. When he stood up to read, he was handed the scroll of the prophet Isaiah. Unrolling the scroll, he found the place where it was written,

"God's Spirit is on me;
he's chosen me to preach the Message of good news to the poor,
Sent me to announce pardon to prisoners and
recovery of sight to the blind,
To set the burdened and battered free,
to announce, 'This is God's year to act!'"

KING JAMES VERSION

20 And he closed the book, and he gave *it* again to the minister, and sat down. And the eyes of all them that were in the synagogue were fastened on him.

21 And he began to say unto them, This day is this scripture fulfilled in your ears.

22 And all bare him witness, and wondered at the gracious words which proceeded out of his mouth. And they said, Is not this Joseph's son?

23 And he said unto them, Ye will surely say unto me this proverb, Physician, heal thyself: whatsoever we have heard done in Capernaum, do also here in thy country.

24 And he said, Verily I say unto you, No prophet is accepted in his own country.

25 But I tell you of a truth, many widows were in Israel in the days of Elias, when the heaven was shut up three years and six months, when great famine was throughout all the land;

26 But unto none of them was Elias sent, save unto Sarepta, *a city* of Sidon, unto a woman *that was* a widow.

27 And many lepers were in Israel in the time of Eliseus the prophet; and none of them was cleansed, saving Naaman the Syrian.

28 And all they in the synagogue, when they heard these things, were filled with wrath,

29 And rose up, and thrust him out of the city, and led him unto the brow of the hill whereon their city was built, that they might cast him down headlong.

30 But he passing through the midst of them went his way,

NEW AMERICAN STANDARD BIBLE

20 And He closed the book, gave it back to the attendant and sat down; and the eyes of all in the synagogue were fixed on Him.

21 And He began to say to them, "Today this Scripture has been fulfilled in your hearing."

22 And all were speaking well of Him, and wondering at the gracious words which were falling from His lips; and they were saying, "Is this not Joseph's son?"

23 And He said to them, "No doubt you will quote this proverb to Me, 'Physician, heal yourself! Whatever we heard was done at Capernaum, do here in your hometown as well.' "

24 And He said, "Truly I say to you, no prophet is welcome in his hometown.

25 "But I say to you in truth, there were many widows in Israel in the days of Elijah, when the sky was shut up for three years and six months, when a great famine came over all the land;

26 and yet Elijah was sent to none of them, but only to Zarephath, *in the land* of Sidon, to a woman who was a widow.

27 "And there were many lepers in Israel in the time of Elisha the prophet; and none of them was cleansed, but only Naaman the Syrian."

28 And all *the people* in the synagogue were filled with rage as they heard these things;

29 and they got up and drove Him out of the city, and led Him to the brow of the hill on which their city had been built, in order to throw Him down the cliff.

30 But passing through their midst, He went His way.

NEW CENTURY VERSION

20 Jesus closed the book, gave it back to the assistant,
and sat down. Everyone in the synagogue was watching
Jesus closely. 21 He began to say to them, "While you heard
these words just now, they were coming true!"

22 All the people spoke well of Jesus and were amazed at
the words of grace he spoke. They asked, "Isn't this
Joseph's son?"

23 Jesus said to them, "I know that you will tell me the
old saying: 'Doctor, heal yourself.' You want to say, 'We
heard about the things you did in Capernaum. Do those
things here in your own town!' " 24 Then Jesus said, "I tell
you the truth, a prophet is not accepted in his hometown.
25 But I tell you the truth, there were many widows in
Israel during the time of Elijah. It did not rain in Israel for
three and one-half years, and there was no food anywhere
in the whole country. 26 But Elijah was sent to none of
those widows, only to a widow in Zarephath, a town in
Sidon. 27 And there were many with skin diseases living in
Israel during the time of the prophet Elisha. But none of
them were healed, only Naaman, who was from the country of Syria."

28 When all the people in the synagogue heard these
things, they became very angry. 29 They got up, forced
Jesus out of town, and took him to the edge of the cliff on
which the town was built. They planned to throw him off
the edge, 30 but Jesus walked through the crowd and went
on his way.

CONTEMPORARY ENGLISH VERSION

20 Jesus closed the book, then handed it back to the man
in charge and sat down. Everyone in the meeting place
looked straight at Jesus.

21 Then Jesus said to them, "What you have just heard
me read has come true today."

22 All the people started talking about Jesus and were
amazed at the wonderful things he said. They kept on asking, "Isn't he Joseph's son?"

23 Jesus answered:

You will certainly want to tell me this saying, "Doctor,
first make yourself well." You will tell me to do the same
things here in my own hometown that you heard I did in
Capernaum. 24 But you can be sure that no prophets are
liked by the people of their own hometown.

25 Once during the time of Elijah there was no rain for
three and a half years, and people everywhere were
starving. There were many widows in Israel, 26 but Elijah
was sent only to a widow in the town of Zarephath near
the city of Sidon. 27 During the time of the prophet
Elisha, many men in Israel had leprosy.[b] But no one was
healed, except Naaman who lived in Syria.

28 When the people in the meeting place heard Jesus say
this, they became so angry 29 that they got up and threw
him out of town. They dragged him to the edge of the cliff
on which the town was built, because they wanted to
throw him down from there. 30 But Jesus slipped through
the crowd and got away.

[b] **4.27** *leprosy*: In biblical times the word "leprosy" was used for many different kinds of skin diseases.

NEW INTERNATIONAL VERSION

20 Then he rolled up the scroll, gave it back to the attendant and sat down. The eyes of everyone in the synagogue were fastened on him, 21 and he began by saying to them, "Today this scripture is fulfilled in your hearing."

22 All spoke well of him and were amazed at the gracious words that came from his lips. "Isn't this Joseph's son?" they asked.

23 Jesus said to them, "Surely you will quote this proverb to me: 'Physician, heal yourself! Do here in your hometown what we have heard that you did in Capernaum.' "

24 "I tell you the truth," he continued, "no prophet is accepted in his hometown. 25 I assure you that there were many widows in Israel in Elijah's time, when the sky was shut for three and a half years and there was a severe famine throughout the land. 26 Yet Elijah was not sent to any of them, but to a widow in Zarephath in the region of Sidon. 27 And there were many in Israel with leprosy[f] in the time of Elisha the prophet, yet not one of them was cleansed—only Naaman the Syrian."

28 All the people in the synagogue were furious when they heard this. 29 They got up, drove him out of the town, and took him to the brow of the hill on which the town was built, in order to throw him down the cliff. 30 But he walked right through the crowd and went on his way.

f 27 The Greek word was used for various diseases affecting the skin—not necessarily leprosy.

NEW LIVING TRANSLATION

20 He rolled up the scroll, handed it back to the attendant, and sat down. Everyone in the synagogue stared at him intently. 21 Then he said, "This Scripture has come true today before your very eyes!"

22 All who were there spoke well of him and were amazed by the gracious words that fell from his lips. "How can this be?" they asked. "Isn't this Joseph's son?"

23 Then he said, "Probably you will quote me that proverb, 'Physician, heal yourself'—meaning, 'Why don't you do miracles here in your hometown like those you did in Capernaum?' 24 But the truth is, no prophet is accepted in his own hometown.

25 "Certainly there were many widows in Israel who needed help in Elijah's time, when there was no rain for three and a half years and hunger stalked the land. 26 Yet Elijah was not sent to any of them. He was sent instead to a widow of Zarephath—a foreigner in the land of Sidon. 27 Or think of the prophet Elisha, who healed Naaman, a Syrian, rather than the many lepers in Israel who needed help."

28 When they heard this, the people in the synagogue were furious. 29 Jumping up, they mobbed him and took him to the edge of the hill on which the city was built. They intended to push him over the cliff, 30 but he slipped away through the crowd and left them.

NEW KING JAMES VERSION

20 Then He closed the book, and gave *it* back to the attendant and sat down. And the eyes of all who were in the synagogue were fixed on Him. 21 And He began to say to them, "Today this Scripture is fulfilled in your hearing." 22 So all bore witness to Him, and marveled at the gracious words which proceeded out of His mouth. And they said, "Is this not Joseph's son?"

23 He said to them, "You will surely say this proverb to Me, 'Physician, heal yourself! Whatever we have heard done in Capernaum,[l] do also here in Your country.' " 24 Then He said, "Assuredly, I say to you, no prophet is accepted in his own country. 25 But I tell you truly, many widows were in Israel in the days of Elijah, when the heaven was shut up three years and six months, and there was a great famine throughout all the land; 26 but to none of them was Elijah sent except to Zarephath,[m] *in the region* of Sidon, to a woman *who was* a widow. 27 And many lepers were in Israel in the time of Elisha the prophet, and none of them was cleansed except Naaman the Syrian."

28 So all those in the synagogue, when they heard these things, were filled with wrath, 29 and rose up and thrust Him out of the city; and they led Him to the brow of the hill on which their city was built, that they might throw Him down over the cliff. 30 Then passing through the midst of them, He went His way.

4:23 *l* Here and elsewhere the NU-Text spelling is *Capharnaum.*
4:26 *m* Greek *Sarepta*

THE MESSAGE

He rolled up the scroll, handed it back to the assistant, and sat down. Every eye in the place was on him, intent. Then he started in, "You've just heard Scripture make history. It came true just now in this place."

All who were there, watching and listening, were surprised at how well he spoke. But they also said, "Isn't this Joseph's son, the one we've known since he was a youngster?"

He answered, "I suppose you're going to quote the proverb, '"Doctor, go heal yourself." Do here in your hometown what we heard you did in Capernaum.' Well, let me tell you something: No prophet is ever welcomed in his hometown. Isn't it a fact that there were many widows in Israel at the time of Elijah during that three and a half years of drought when famine devastated the land, but the only widow to whom Elijah was sent was in Sarepta in Sidon? And there were many lepers in Israel at the time of the prophet Elisha but the only one cleansed was Naaman the Syrian."

That set everyone in the meeting place seething with anger. They threw him out, banishing him from the village, then took him to a mountain cliff at the edge of the village to throw him to his doom, but he gave them the slip and was on his way.

KING JAMES VERSION

31 ¶ And came down to Capernaum, a city of Galilee, and taught them on the sabbath days.

32 And they were astonished at his doctrine: for his word was with power.

33 And in the synagogue there was a man, which had a spirit of an unclean devil, and cried out with a loud voice,

34 Saying, Let *us* alone; what have we to do with thee, *thou* Jesus of Nazareth? art thou come to destroy us? I know thee who thou art; the Holy One of God.

35 And Jesus rebuked him, saying, Hold thy peace, and come out of him. And when the devil had thrown him in the midst, he came out of him, and hurt him not.

36 And they were all amazed, and spake among themselves, saying, What a word *is* this! for with authority and power he commandeth the unclean spirits, and they come out.

37 And the fame of him went out into every place of the country round about.

38 And he arose out of the synagogue, and entered into Simon's house. And Simon's wife's mother was taken with a great fever; and they besought him for her.

39 And he stood over her, and rebuked the fever; and it left her: and immediately she arose and ministered unto them.

40 Now when the sun was setting, all they that had any sick with divers diseases brought them unto him; and he

NEW AMERICAN STANDARD BIBLE

31 And He came down to Capernaum, a city of Galilee, and He was teaching them on the Sabbath;

32 and they were amazed at His teaching, for His message was with authority.

33 In the synagogue there was a man possessed by the spirit of an unclean demon, and he cried out with a loud voice,

34 "Let us alone! What business do we have with each other, Jesus of Nazareth? Have You come to destroy us? I know who You are—the Holy One of God!"

35 But Jesus rebuked him, saying, "Be quiet and come out of him!" And when the demon had thrown him down in the midst *of the people*, he came out of him without doing him any harm.

36 And amazement came upon them all, and they *began* talking with one another saying, "What is this message? For with authority and power He commands the unclean spirits and they come out."

37 And the report about Him was spreading into every locality in the surrounding district.

Many Are Healed

38 Then He got up and *left* the synagogue, and entered Simon's home. Now Simon's mother-in-law was suffering from a high fever, and they asked Him to help her.

39 And standing over her, He rebuked the fever, and it left her; and she immediately got up and waited on them.

40 While the sun was setting, all those who had any *who were* sick with various diseases brought them to Him;

NEW CENTURY VERSION

Jesus Forces Out an Evil Spirit

31 Jesus went to Capernaum, a city in Galilee, and on the
Sabbath day, he taught the people. 32 They were amazed at
his teaching, because he spoke with authority. 33 In the
synagogue a man who had within him an evil spirit shout-
ed in a loud voice, 34 "Jesus of Nazareth! What do you want
with us? Did you come to destroy us? I know who you
are—God's Holy One!"

35 Jesus commanded the evil spirit, "Be quiet! Come out
of the man!" The evil spirit threw the man down to the
ground before all the people and then left the man without
hurting him.

36 The people were amazed and said to each other, "What
does this mean? With authority and power he commands
evil spirits, and they come out." 37 And so the news about
Jesus spread to every place in the whole area.

Jesus Heals Many People

38 Jesus left the synagogue and went to the home of
Simon.[d] Simon's mother-in-law was sick with a high fever,
and they asked Jesus to help her. 39 He came to her side
and commanded the fever to leave. It left her, and immedi-
ately she got up and began serving them.

40 When the sun went down, the people brought those
who were sick to Jesus. Putting his hands on each sick per-

4:38 [d] **Simon** Simon's other name was Peter.

CONTEMPORARY ENGLISH VERSION

A Man with an Evil Spirit (Mark 1.21-28)

31 Jesus went to the town of Capernaum in Galilee and
taught the people on the Sabbath. 32 His teaching amazed
them because he spoke with power. 33 There in the Jewish
meeting place was a man with an evil spirit. He yelled out,
34 "Hey, Jesus of Nazareth, what do you want with us? Are
you here to get rid of us? I know who you are! You are
God's Holy One."

35 Jesus ordered the evil spirit to be quiet and come out.
The demon threw the man to the ground in front of every-
one and left without harming him.

36 They all were amazed and kept saying to each other,
"What kind of teaching is this? He has power to order evil
spirits out of people!" 37 News about Jesus spread all over
that part of the country.

Jesus Heals Many People (Matthew 8.14-17; Mark 1.29-34)

38 Jesus left the meeting place and went to Simon's
home. When Jesus got there, he was told that Simon's
mother-in-law was sick with a high fever. 39 So Jesus went
over to her and ordered the fever to go away. Right then
she was able to get up and serve them a meal.

40 After the sun had set, people with all kinds of diseases
were brought to Jesus. He put his hands on each one of

NEW INTERNATIONAL VERSION

Jesus Drives Out an Evil Spirit

31Then he went down to Capernaum, a town in Galilee,
and on the Sabbath began to teach the people. 32They
were amazed at his teaching, because his message had
authority.

33In the synagogue there was a man possessed by a
demon, an evil[g] spirit. He cried out at the top of his voice,
34"Ha! What do you want with us, Jesus of Nazareth?
Have you come to destroy us? I know who you are—the
Holy One of God!"

35"Be quiet!" Jesus said sternly. "Come out of him!"
Then the demon threw the man down before them all and
came out without injuring him.

36All the people were amazed and said to each other,
"What is this teaching? With authority and power he gives
orders to evil spirits and they come out!" 37And the news
about him spread throughout the surrounding area.

Jesus Heals Many

38Jesus left the synagogue and went to the home of
Simon. Now Simon's mother-in-law was suffering from a
high fever, and they asked Jesus to help her. 39So he bent
over her and rebuked the fever, and it left her. She got up
at once and began to wait on them.

40When the sun was setting, the people brought to Jesus
all who had various kinds of sickness, and laying his

g 33 Greek *unclean*; also in verse 36

NEW LIVING TRANSLATION

Jesus Casts Out a Demon

31Then Jesus went to Capernaum, a town in Galilee, and
taught there in the synagogue every Sabbath day. 32There,
too, the people were amazed at the things he said, because
he spoke with authority.

33Once when he was in the synagogue, a man possessed
by a demon began shouting at Jesus, 34"Go away! Why are
you bothering us, Jesus of Nazareth? Have you come to
destroy us? I know who you are—the Holy One sent from
God."

35Jesus cut him short. "Be silent!" he told the demon.
"Come out of the man!" The demon threw the man to the
floor as the crowd watched; then it left him without hurt-
ing him further.

36Amazed, the people exclaimed, "What authority and
power this man's words possess! Even evil spirits obey
him and flee at his command!" 37The story of what he had
done spread like wildfire throughout the whole region.

Jesus Heals Many People

38After leaving the synagogue that day, Jesus went to
Simon's home, where he found Simon's mother-in-law
very sick with a high fever. "Please heal her," everyone
begged. 39Standing at her bedside, he spoke to the fever,
rebuking it, and immediately her temperature returned to
normal. She got up at once and prepared a meal for them.

40As the sun went down that evening, people through-
out the village brought sick family members to Jesus. No

NEW KING JAMES VERSION

Jesus Casts Out an Unclean Spirit

31Then He went down to Capernaum, a city of Galilee,
and was teaching them on the Sabbaths. 32And they were
astonished at His teaching, for His word was with authori-
ty. 33Now in the synagogue there was a man who had a
spirit of an unclean demon. And he cried out with a loud
voice, 34saying, "Let *us* alone! What have we to do with
You, Jesus of Nazareth? Did You come to destroy us? I
know who You are—the Holy One of God!"

35But Jesus rebuked him, saying, "Be quiet, and come
out of him!" And when the demon had thrown him in *their*
midst, it came out of him and did not hurt him. 36Then
they were all amazed and spoke among themselves, say-
ing, "What a word this *is!* For with authority and power He
commands the unclean spirits, and they come out." 37And
the report about Him went out into every place in the sur-
rounding region.

Peter's Mother-in-Law Healed

38Now He arose from the synagogue and entered Si-
mon's house. But Simon's wife's mother was sick with a
high fever, and they made request of Him concerning her.
39So He stood over her and rebuked the fever, and it left
her. And immediately she arose and served them.

Many Healed After Sabbath Sunset

40When the sun was setting, all those who had any that
were sick with various diseases brought them to Him; and

THE MESSAGE

He went down to Capernaum, a village in Galilee. He was teaching the people on the Sabbath. They were surprised and impressed—his teaching was so forthright, so confident, so authoritative, not the quibbling and quoting they were used to.

In the meeting place that day there was a man demonically disturbed. He screamed, "Ho! What business do you have here with us, Jesus? Nazarene! I know what you're up to. You're the Holy One of God and you've come to destroy us!"

Jesus shut him up: "Quiet! Get out of him!" The demonic spirit threw the man down in front of them all and left. The demon didn't hurt him.

That set everyone back on their heels, whispering and wondering, "What's going on here? Someone whose words make things happen? Someone who orders demonic spirits to get out and they go?" Jesus was the talk of the town.

He Healed Them All

He left the meeting place and went to Simon's house. Simon's mother-in-law was running a high fever and they asked him to do something for her. He stood over her, told the fever to leave—and it left. Before they knew it, she was up getting dinner for them.

When the sun went down, everyone who had anyone sick with some ailment or other brought them to him. One

KING JAMES VERSION

laid his hands on every one of them, and healed them.

41 And devils also came out of many, crying out, and saying, Thou art Christ the Son of God. And he rebuking *them* suffered them not to speak: for they knew that he was Christ.

42 And when it was day, he departed and went into a desert place: and the people sought him, and came unto him, and stayed him, that he should not depart from them.

43 And he said unto them, I must preach the kingdom of God to other cities also: for therefore am I sent.

44 And he preached in the synagogues of Galilee.

5 And it came to pass, that, as the people pressed upon him to hear the word of God, he stood by the lake of Gennesaret,

2 And saw two ships standing by the lake: but the fishermen were gone out of them, and were washing *their* nets.

3 And he entered into one of the ships, which was Simon's, and prayed him that he would thrust out a little from the land. And he sat down, and taught the people out of the ship.

4 Now when he had left speaking, he said unto Simon, Launch out into the deep, and let down your nets for a draught.

NEW AMERICAN STANDARD BIBLE

and laying His hands on each one of them, He was healing them.

41 Demons also were coming out of many, shouting, "You are the Son of God!" But rebuking them, He would not allow them to speak, because they knew Him to be the Christ.

42 When day came, Jesus left and went to a secluded place; and the crowds were searching for Him, and came to Him and tried to keep Him from going away from them.

43 But He said to them, "I must preach the kingdom of God to the other cities also, for I was sent for this purpose."

44 So He kept on preaching in the synagogues of [1]Judea.

The First Disciples

5 Now it happened that while the crowd was pressing around Him and listening to the word of God, He was standing by the lake of Gennesaret;

2 and He saw two boats lying at the edge of the lake; but the fishermen had gotten out of them and were washing their nets.

3 And He got into one of the boats, which was Simon's, and asked him to put out a little way from the land. And He sat down and *began* teaching the people from the boat.

4 When He had finished speaking, He said to Simon, "Put out into the deep water and let down your nets for a catch."

4:44 [1] I.e. the country of the Jews (including Galilee)

NEW CENTURY VERSION

son, he healed every one of them. [41]Demons came out of many people, shouting, "You are the Son of God." But Jesus commanded the demons and would not allow them to speak, because they knew Jesus was the Christ.

[42]At daybreak, Jesus went to a lonely place, but the people looked for him. When they found him, they tried to keep him from leaving. [43]But Jesus said to them, "I must preach about God's kingdom to other towns, too. This is why I was sent."

[44]Then he kept on preaching in the synagogues of Judea.

Jesus' First Followers

5 One day while Jesus was standing beside Lake Galilee, many people were pressing all around him to hear the word of God. [2]Jesus saw two boats at the shore of the lake. The fishermen had left them and were washing their nets. [3]Jesus got into one of the boats, the one that belonged to Simon,[a] and asked him to push off a little from the land. Then Jesus sat down and continued to teach the people from the boat.

[4]When Jesus had finished speaking, he said to Simon, "Take the boat into deep water, and put your nets in the water to catch some fish."

5:3 [a] **Simon** Simon's other name was Peter.

CONTEMPORARY ENGLISH VERSION

them and healed them. [41]Demons went out of many people and shouted, "You are the Son of God!" But Jesus ordered the demons not to speak because they knew he was the Messiah.

[42]The next morning Jesus went out to a place where he could be alone, and crowds came looking for him. When they found him, they tried to stop him from leaving. [43]But Jesus said, "People in other towns must hear the good news about God's kingdom. That's why I was sent." [44]So he kept on preaching in the Jewish meeting places in Judea.[c]

Jesus Chooses His First Disciples

(Matthew 4.18-22; Mark 1.16-20)

5 Jesus was standing on the shore of Lake Gennesaret,[a] teaching the people as they crowded around him to hear God's message. [2]Near the shore he saw two boats left there by some fishermen who had gone to wash their nets. [3]Jesus got into the boat that belonged to Simon and asked him to row it out a little way from the shore. Then Jesus sat down[b] in the boat to teach the crowd.

[4]When Jesus had finished speaking, he told Simon, "Row the boat out into the deep water and let your nets down to catch some fish."

[c] 4.44 *Judea*: Some manuscripts have "Galilee." [a] 5.1 *Lake Gennesaret*: Another name for Lake Galilee. [b] 5.3 *sat down*: Teachers in the ancient world, including Jewish teachers, usually sat down when they taught.

NEW INTERNATIONAL VERSION

hands on each one, he healed them. [41]Moreover, demons came out of many people, shouting, "You are the Son of God!" But he rebuked them and would not allow them to speak, because they knew he was the Christ.[h]

[42]At daybreak Jesus went out to a solitary place. The people were looking for him and when they came to where he was, they tried to keep him from leaving them. [43]But he said, "I must preach the good news of the kingdom of God to the other towns also, because that is why I was sent." [44]And he kept on preaching in the synagogues of Judea.[i]

The Calling of the First Disciples

5 One day as Jesus was standing by the Lake of Gennesaret,[a] with the people crowding around him and listening to the word of God, [2]he saw at the water's edge two boats, left there by the fishermen, who were washing their nets. [3]He got into one of the boats, the one belonging to Simon, and asked him to put out a little from shore. Then he sat down and taught the people from the boat.

[4]When he had finished speaking, he said to Simon, "Put out into deep water, and let down[b] the nets for a catch."

[h] *41* Or *Messiah* [i] *44* Or *the land of the Jews*; some manuscripts *Galilee* [a] *1* That is, Sea of Galilee [b] *4* The Greek verb is plural.

NEW LIVING TRANSLATION

matter what their diseases were, the touch of his hand healed every one. [41]Some were possessed by demons; and the demons came out at his command, shouting, "You are the Son of God." But because they knew he was the Messiah, he stopped them and told them to be silent.

Jesus Continues to Preach

[42]Early the next morning Jesus went out into the wilderness. The crowds searched everywhere for him, and when they finally found him, they begged him not to leave them. [43]But he replied, "I must preach the Good News of the Kingdom of God in other places, too, because that is why I was sent." [44]So he continued to travel around, preaching in synagogues throughout Judea.*

The First Disciples

5 One day as Jesus was preaching on the shore of the Sea of Galilee,* great crowds pressed in on him to listen to the word of God. [2]He noticed two empty boats at the water's edge, for the fishermen had left them and were washing their nets. [3]Stepping into one of the boats, Jesus asked Simon,* its owner, to push it out into the water. So he sat in the boat and taught the crowds from there.

[4]When he had finished speaking, he said to Simon, "Now go out where it is deeper and let down your nets, and you will catch many fish."

4:44 Some manuscripts read *Galilee.* 5:1 Greek *Lake Gennesaret,* another name for the Sea of Galilee. 5:3 *Simon* is called *Peter* in 6:14 and thereafter.

NEW KING JAMES VERSION

He laid His hands on every one of them and healed them. [41]And demons also came out of many, crying out and saying, "You are the Christ,[n] the Son of God!"

And He, rebuking *them,* did not allow them to speak, for they knew that He was the Christ.

Jesus Preaches in Galilee

[42]Now when it was day, He departed and went into a deserted place. And the crowd sought Him and came to Him, and tried to keep Him from leaving them; [43]but He said to them, "I must preach the kingdom of God to the other cities also, because for this purpose I have been sent." [44]And He was preaching in the synagogues of Galilee.[o]

Four Fishermen Called as Disciples

5 So it was, as the multitude pressed about Him to hear the word of God, that He stood by the Lake of Gennesaret, [2]and saw two boats standing by the lake; but the fishermen had gone from them and were washing *their* nets. [3]Then He got into one of the boats, which was Simon's, and asked him to put out a little from the land. And He sat down and taught the multitudes from the boat.

[4]When He had stopped speaking, He said to Simon, "Launch out into the deep and let down your nets for a catch."

4:41 [n] NU-Text omits *the Christ.* 4:44 [o] NU-Text reads *Judea.*

THE MESSAGE

by one he placed his hands on them and healed them. Demons left in droves, screaming, "Son of God! You're the Son of God!" But he shut them up, refusing to let them speak because they knew too much, knew him to be the Messiah.

He left the next day for open country. But the crowds went looking and, when they found him, clung to him so he couldn't go on. He told them, "Don't you realize that there are yet other villages where I have to tell the Message of God's kingdom, that this is the work God sent me to do?" Meanwhile he continued preaching in the meeting places of Galilee.

Push Out Into Deep Water

5 Once when he was standing on the shore of Lake Gennesaret, the crowd was pushing in on him to better hear the Word of God. He noticed two boats tied up. The fishermen had just left them and were out scrubbing their nets. He climbed into the boat that was Simon's and asked him to put out a little from the shore. Sitting there, using the boat for a pulpit, he taught the crowd.

When he finished teaching, he said to Simon, "Push out into deep water and let your nets out for a catch."

KING JAMES VERSION

5 And Simon answering said unto him, Master, we have toiled all the night, and have taken nothing: nevertheless at thy word I will let down the net.

6 And when they had this done, they inclosed a great multitude of fishes: and their net brake.

7 And they beckoned unto *their* partners, which were in the other ship, that they should come and help them. And they came, and filled both the ships, so that they began to sink.

8 When Simon Peter saw *it*, he fell down at Jesus' knees, saying, Depart from me; for I am a sinful man, O Lord.

9 For he was astonished, and all that were with him, at the draught of the fishes which they had taken:

10 And so *was* also James, and John, the sons of Zebedee, which were partners with Simon. And Jesus said unto Simon, Fear not; from henceforth thou shalt catch men.

11 And when they had brought their ships to land, they forsook all, and followed him.

12 ¶ And it came to pass, when he was in a certain city, behold a man full of leprosy: who seeing Jesus fell on *his* face, and besought him, saying, Lord, if thou wilt, thou canst make me clean.

13 And he put forth *his* hand, and touched him, saying, I will: be thou clean. And immediately the leprosy departed from him.

14 And he charged him to tell no man: but go, and shew thyself to the priest, and offer for thy cleansing,

NEW AMERICAN STANDARD BIBLE

5 Simon answered and said, "Master, we worked hard all night and caught nothing, but I will do as You say *and* let down the nets."

6 When they had done this, they enclosed a great quantity of fish, and their nets *began* to break;

7 so they signaled to their partners in the other boat for them to come and help them. And they came and filled both of the boats, so that they began to sink.

8 But when Simon Peter saw *that,* he fell down at Jesus' feet, saying, "Go away from me Lord, for I am a sinful man, O Lord!"

9 For amazement had seized him and all his companions because of the catch of fish which they had taken;

10 and so also *were* James and John, sons of Zebedee, who were partners with Simon. And Jesus said to Simon, "Do not fear, from now on you will be catching men."

11 When they had brought their boats to land, they left everything and followed Him.

The Leper and the Paralytic

12 While He was in one of the cities, behold, *there was* a man covered with leprosy; and when he saw Jesus, he fell on his face and implored Him, saying, "Lord, if You are willing, You can make me clean."

13 And He stretched out His hand and touched him, saying, "I am willing; be cleansed." And immediately the leprosy left him.

14 And He ordered him to tell no one, "But go and show

NEW CENTURY VERSION

5Simon answered, "Master, we worked hard all night trying to catch fish, and we caught nothing. But you say to put the nets in the water, so I will." 6When the fishermen did as Jesus told them, they caught so many fish that the nets began to break. 7They called to their partners in the other boat to come and help them. They came and filled both boats so full that they were almost sinking.

8When Simon Peter saw what had happened, he bowed down before Jesus and said, "Go away from me, Lord. I am a sinful man!" 9He and the other fishermen were amazed at the many fish they caught, as were 10James and John, the sons of Zebedee, Simon's partners.

Jesus said to Simon, "Don't be afraid. From now on you will fish for people." 11When the men brought their boats to the shore, they left everything and followed Jesus.

Jesus Heals a Sick Man

12When Jesus was in one of the towns, there was a man covered with a skin disease. When he saw Jesus, he bowed before him and begged him, "Lord, you can heal me if you will."

13Jesus reached out his hand and touched the man and said, "I will. Be healed!" Immediately the disease disappeared. 14Then Jesus said, "Don't tell anyone about this, but go and show yourself to the priest[b] and offer a gift for

5:14 [b] **show...priest** The law of Moses said a priest must say when a Jewish person with a skin disease was well.

CONTEMPORARY ENGLISH VERSION

5"Master," Simon answered, "we have worked hard all night long and have not caught a thing. But if you tell me to, I will let the nets down." 6They did it and caught so many fish that their nets began ripping apart. 7Then they signaled for their partners in the other boat to come and help them. The men came, and together they filled the two boats so full that they both began to sink.

8When Simon Peter saw this happen, he knelt down in front of Jesus and said, "Lord, don't come near me! I am a sinner." 9Peter and everyone with him were completely surprised at all the fish they had caught. 10His partners James and John, the sons of Zebedee, were surprised too.

Jesus told Simon, "Don't be afraid! From now on you will bring in people instead of fish." 11The men pulled their boats up on the shore. Then they left everything and went with Jesus.

Jesus Heals a Man (Matthew 8.1-4; Mark 1.40-45)

12Jesus came to a town where there was a man who had leprosy.[c] When the man saw Jesus, he knelt down to the ground in front of Jesus and begged, "Lord, you have the power to make me well, if only you wanted to."

13Jesus put his hand on him and said, "I want to! Now you are well." At once the man's leprosy disappeared. 14Jesus told him, "Don't tell anyone about this, but go and show yourself to the priest. Offer a gift to the priest, just

[c] 5.12 *leprosy*: See the note at 4.27.

NEW INTERNATIONAL VERSION

5 Simon answered, "Master, we've worked hard all night
and haven't caught anything. But because you say so, I
will let down the nets."
6 When they had done so, they caught such a large num-
ber of fish that their nets began to break. 7 So they signaled
their partners in the other boat to come and help them,
and they came and filled both boats so full that they began
to sink.
8 When Simon Peter saw this, he fell at Jesus' knees and
said, "Go away from me, Lord; I am a sinful man!" 9 For he
and all his companions were astonished at the catch of
fish they had taken, 10 and so were James and John, the
sons of Zebedee, Simon's partners.
Then Jesus said to Simon, "Don't be afraid; from now on
you will catch men." 11 So they pulled their boats up on
shore, left everything and followed him.

The Man With Leprosy

12 While Jesus was in one of the towns, a man came
along who was covered with leprosy.[c] When he saw Jesus,
he fell with his face to the ground and begged him, "Lord,
if you are willing, you can make me clean."
13 Jesus reached out his hand and touched the man. "I
am willing," he said. "Be clean!" And immediately the lep-
rosy left him.
14 Then Jesus ordered him, "Don't tell anyone, but go,

c *12* The Greek word was used for various diseases affecting the skin—not necessarily leprosy.

NEW LIVING TRANSLATION

5 "Master," Simon replied, "we worked hard all last night
and didn't catch a thing. But if you say so, we'll try
again." 6 And this time their nets were so full they began to
tear! 7 A shout for help brought their partners in the other
boat, and soon both boats were filled with fish and on the
verge of sinking.
8 When Simon Peter realized what had happened, he fell
to his knees before Jesus and said, "Oh, Lord, please leave
me—I'm too much of a sinner to be around you." 9 For he
was awestruck by the size of their catch, as were the oth-
ers with him. 10 His partners, James and John, the sons of
Zebedee, were also amazed.
Jesus replied to Simon, "Don't be afraid! From now on
you'll be fishing for people!" 11 And as soon as they landed,
they left everything and followed Jesus.

Jesus Heals a Man with Leprosy

12 In one of the villages, Jesus met a man with an
advanced case of leprosy. When the man saw Jesus, he fell
to the ground, face down in the dust, begging to be healed.
"Lord," he said, "if you want to, you can make me well
again."
13 Jesus reached out and touched the man. "I want to,"
he said. "Be healed!" And instantly the leprosy disap-
peared. 14 Then Jesus instructed him not to tell anyone
what had happened. He said, "Go right to the priest and let

NEW KING JAMES VERSION

5 But Simon answered and said to Him, "Master, we have
toiled all night and caught nothing; nevertheless at Your
word I will let down the net." 6 And when they had done
this, they caught a great number of fish, and their net was
breaking. 7 So they signaled to *their* partners in the other
boat to come and help them. And they came and filled both
the boats, so that they began to sink. 8 When Simon Peter
saw *it,* he fell down at Jesus' knees, saying, "Depart from
me, for I am a sinful man, O Lord!"
9 For he and all who were with him were astonished at
the catch of fish which they had taken; 10 and so also *were*
James and John, the sons of Zebedee, who were partners
with Simon. And Jesus said to Simon, "Do not be afraid.
From now on you will catch men." 11 So when they had
brought their boats to land, they forsook all and followed
Him.

Jesus Cleanses a Leper

12 And it happened when He was in a certain city, that
behold, a man who was full of leprosy saw Jesus; and he
fell on *his* face and implored Him, saying, "Lord, if You are
willing, You can make me clean."
13 Then He put out *His* hand and touched him, saying, "I
am willing; be cleansed." Immediately the leprosy left him.
14 And He charged him to tell no one, "But go and show
yourself to the priest, and make an offering for your

THE MESSAGE

Simon said, "Master, we've been fishing hard all night and haven't caught even a minnow. But if you say so, I'll let out the nets." It was no sooner said than done—a huge haul of fish, straining the nets past capacity. They waved to their partners in the other boat to come help them. They filled both boats, nearly swamping them with the catch.

Simon Peter, when he saw it, fell to his knees before Jesus. "Master, leave. I'm a sinner and can't handle this holiness. Leave me to myself." When they pulled in that catch of fish, awe overwhelmed Simon and everyone with him. It was the same with James and John, Zebedee's sons, coworkers with Simon.

Jesus said to Simon, "There is nothing to fear. From now on you'll be fishing for men and women." They pulled their boats up on the beach, left them, nets and all, and followed him.

Invitation to a Changed Life

One day in one of the villages there was a man covered with leprosy. When he saw Jesus he fell down before him in prayer and said, "If you want to, you can cleanse me."

Jesus put out his hand, touched him, and said, "I want to. Be clean." Then and there his skin was smooth, the leprosy gone.

Jesus instructed him, "Don't talk about this all over town. Just quietly present your healed self to the priest,

KING JAMES VERSION

according as Moses commanded, for a testimony unto them.

15 But so much the more went there a fame abroad of him: and great multitudes came together to hear, and to be healed by him of their infirmities.

16 And he withdrew himself into the wilderness, and prayed.

17 ¶ And it came to pass on a certain day, as he was teaching, that there were Pharisees and doctors of the law sitting by, which were come out of every town of Galilee, and Judaea, and Jerusalem: and the power of the Lord was *present* to heal them.

18 And, behold, men brought in a bed a man which was taken with a palsy: and they sought *means* to bring him in, and to lay *him* before him.

19 And when they could not find by what *way* they might bring him in because of the multitude, they went upon the housetop, and let him down through the tiling with *his* couch into the midst before Jesus.

20 And when he saw their faith, he said unto him, Man, thy sins are forgiven thee.

21 And the scribes and the Pharisees began to reason, saying, Who is this which speaketh blasphemies? Who can forgive sins, but God alone?

22 But when Jesus perceived their thoughts, he answering said unto them, What reason ye in your hearts?

NEW AMERICAN STANDARD BIBLE

yourself to the priest and make an offering for your cleansing, just as Moses commanded, as a testimony to them."

15 But the news about Him was spreading even farther, and large crowds were gathering to hear *Him* and to be healed of their sicknesses.

16 But Jesus Himself would *often* slip away to the wilderness and pray.

17 One day He was teaching; and there were *some* Pharisees and teachers of the law sitting *there,* who had come from every village of Galilee and Judea and *from* Jerusalem; and the power of the Lord was *present* for Him to perform healing.

18 And *some* men *were* carrying on a bed a man who was paralyzed; and they were trying to bring him in and to set him down in front of Him.

19 But not finding any *way* to bring him in because of the crowd, they went up on the roof and let him down through the tiles with his stretcher, into the middle *of the crowd*, in front of Jesus.

20 Seeing their faith, He said, "Friend, your sins are forgiven you."

21 The scribes and the Pharisees began to reason, saying, "Who is this *man* who speaks blasphemies? Who can forgive sins, but God alone?"

22 But Jesus, aware of their reasonings, answered and said to them, "Why are you reasoning in your hearts?

NEW CENTURY VERSION

your healing, as Moses commanded.[c] This will show the people what I have done."

[15]But the news about Jesus spread even more. Many people came to hear Jesus and to be healed of their sicknesses, [16]but Jesus often slipped away to be alone so he could pray.

Jesus Heals a Paralyzed Man

[17]One day as Jesus was teaching the people, the Pharisees and teachers of the law from every town in Galilee and Judea and from Jerusalem were there. The Lord was giving Jesus the power to heal people. [18]Just then, some men were carrying on a mat a man who was paralyzed. They tried to bring him in and put him down before Jesus. [19]But because there were so many people there, they could not find a way in. So they went up on the roof and lowered the man on his mat through the ceiling into the middle of the crowd right before Jesus. [20]Seeing their faith, Jesus said, "Friend, your sins are forgiven."

[21]The Jewish teachers of the law and the Pharisees thought to themselves, "Who is this man who is speaking as if he were God? Only God can forgive sins."

[22]But Jesus knew what they were thinking and said,

5:14 [c] **Moses commanded** Read about this in Leviticus 14:1–32.

CONTEMPORARY ENGLISH VERSION

as Moses commanded, and everyone will know that you have been healed."[d]

[15]News about Jesus kept spreading. Large crowds came to listen to him teach and to be healed of their diseases. [16]But Jesus would often go to some place where he could be alone and pray.

Jesus Heals a Crippled Man (Matthew 9.1-8; Mark 2.1-12)

[17]One day some Pharisees and experts in the Law of Moses sat listening to Jesus teach. They had come from every village in Galilee and Judea and from Jerusalem.

God had given Jesus the power to heal the sick, [18]and some people came carrying a crippled man on a mat. They tried to take him inside the house and put him in front of Jesus. [19]But because of the crowd, they could not get him to Jesus. So they went up on the roof,[e] where they removed some tiles and let the mat down in the middle of the room.

[20]When Jesus saw how much faith they had, he said to the crippled man, "My friend, your sins are forgiven."

[21]The Pharisees and the experts began arguing, "Jesus must think he is God! Only God can forgive sins."

[22]Jesus knew what they were thinking, and he said,

[d] **5.14** *everyone will know that you have been healed*: People with leprosy had to be examined by a priest and told that they were well (that is, "clean") before they could once again live a normal life in the Jewish community. The gift that Moses commanded was the sacrifice of some lambs together with flour mixed with olive oil. [e] **5.19** *roof*: In Palestine the houses usually had a flat roof. Stairs on the outside led up to the roof, which was made of beams and boards covered with packed earth. Luke says that the roof was made of (clay) tiles, which were also used for making roofs in New Testament times.

NEW INTERNATIONAL VERSION

show yourself to the priest and offer the sacrifices that Moses commanded for your cleansing, as a testimony to them."

[15]Yet the news about him spread all the more, so that crowds of people came to hear him and to be healed of their sicknesses. [16]But Jesus often withdrew to lonely places and prayed.

Jesus Heals a Paralytic

[17]One day as he was teaching, Pharisees and teachers of the law, who had come from every village of Galilee and from Judea and Jerusalem, were sitting there. And the power of the Lord was present for him to heal the sick. [18]Some men came carrying a paralytic on a mat and tried to take him into the house to lay him before Jesus. [19]When they could not find a way to do this because of the crowd, they went up on the roof and lowered him on his mat through the tiles into the middle of the crowd, right in front of Jesus.

[20]When Jesus saw their faith, he said, "Friend, your sins are forgiven."

[21]The Pharisees and the teachers of the law began thinking to themselves, "Who is this fellow who speaks blasphemy? Who can forgive sins but God alone?"

[22]Jesus knew what they were thinking and asked, "Why

NEW LIVING TRANSLATION

him examine you. Take along the offering required in the law of Moses for those who have been healed of leprosy, so everyone will have proof of your healing." [15]Yet despite Jesus' instructions, the report of his power spread even faster, and vast crowds came to hear him preach and to be healed of their diseases. [16]But Jesus often withdrew to the wilderness for prayer.

Jesus Heals a Paralyzed Man

[17]One day while Jesus was teaching, some Pharisees and teachers of religious law were sitting nearby. (It seemed that these men showed up from every village in all Galilee and Judea, as well as from Jerusalem.) And the Lord's healing power was strongly with Jesus. [18]Some men came carrying a paralyzed man on a sleeping mat. They tried to push through the crowd to Jesus, [19]but they couldn't reach him. So they went up to the roof, took off some tiles, and lowered the sick man down into the crowd, still on his mat, right in front of Jesus. [20]Seeing their faith, Jesus said to the man, "Son, your sins are forgiven."

[21]"Who does this man think he is?" the Pharisees and teachers of religious law said to each other. "This is blasphemy! Who but God can forgive sins?"

[22]Jesus knew what they were thinking, so he asked

NEW KING JAMES VERSION

cleansing, as a testimony to them, just as Moses commanded."

[15]However, the report went around concerning Him all the more; and great multitudes came together to hear, and to be healed by Him of their infirmities. [16]So He Himself *often* withdrew into the wilderness and prayed.

Jesus Forgives and Heals a Paralytic

[17]Now it happened on a certain day, as He was teaching, that there were Pharisees and teachers of the law sitting by, who had come out of every town of Galilee, Judea, and Jerusalem. And the power of the Lord was *present* to heal them.[a] [18]Then behold, men brought on a bed a man who was paralyzed, whom they sought to bring in and lay before Him. [19]And when they could not find how they might bring him in, because of the crowd, they went up on the housetop and let him down with *his* bed through the tiling into the midst before Jesus.

[20]When He saw their faith, He said to him, "Man, your sins are forgiven you."

[21]And the scribes and the Pharisees began to reason, saying, "Who is this who speaks blasphemies? Who can forgive sins but God alone?"

[22]But when Jesus perceived their thoughts, He answered

5:17 [a] NU-Text reads *present with Him to heal.*

THE MESSAGE

along with the offering ordered by Moses. Your cleansed and obedient life, not your words, will bear witness to what I have done." But the man couldn't keep it to himself, and the word got out. Soon a large crowd of people had gathered to listen and be healed of their ailments. As often as possible Jesus withdrew to out-of-the-way places for prayer.

One day as he was teaching, Pharisees and religion teachers were sitting around. They had come from nearly every village in Galilee and Judea, even as far away as Jerusalem, to be there. The healing power of God was on him.

Some men arrived carrying a paraplegic on a stretcher. They were looking for a way to get into the house and set him before Jesus. When they couldn't find a way in because of the crowd, they went up on the roof, removed some tiles, and let him down in the middle of everyone, right in front of Jesus. Impressed by their bold belief, he said, "Friend, I forgive your sins."

That set the religion scholars and Pharisees buzzing. "Who does he think he is? That's blasphemous talk! God and only God can forgive sins."

Jesus knew exactly what they were thinking and said,

KING JAMES VERSION

23 Whether is easier, to say, Thy sins be forgiven thee; or to say, Rise up and walk?

24 But that ye may know that the Son of man hath power upon earth to forgive sins, (he said unto the sick of the palsy,) I say unto thee, Arise, and take up thy couch, and go into thine house.

25 And immediately he rose up before them, and took up that whereon he lay, and departed to his own house, glorifying God.

26 And they were all amazed, and they glorified God, and were filled with fear, saying, We have seen strange things to day.

27 ¶ And after these things he went forth, and saw a publican, named Levi, sitting at the receipt of custom: and he said unto him, Follow me.

28 And he left all, rose up, and followed him.

29 And Levi made him a great feast in his own house: and there was a great company of publicans and of others that sat down with them.

30 But their scribes and Pharisees murmured against his disciples, saying, Why do ye eat and drink with publicans and sinners?

31 And Jesus answering said unto them, They that are whole need not a physician; but they that are sick.

32 I came not to call the righteous, but sinners to repentance.

NEW AMERICAN STANDARD BIBLE

23 "Which is easier, to say, 'Your sins have been forgiven you,' or to say, 'Get up and walk'?

24 "But, so that you may know that the Son of Man has authority on earth to forgive sins,"—He said to the paralytic—"I say to you, get up, and pick up your stretcher and go home."

25 Immediately he got up before them, and picked up what he had been lying on, and went home glorifying God.

26 They were all struck with astonishment and *began* glorifying God; and they were filled with fear, saying, "We have seen remarkable things today."

Call of Levi (Matthew)

27 After that He went out and noticed a tax collector named Levi sitting in the tax booth, and He said to him, "Follow Me."

28 And he left everything behind, and got up and *began* to follow Him.

29 And Levi gave a big reception for Him in his house; and there was a great crowd of tax collectors and other *people* who were reclining *at the table* with them.

30 The Pharisees and their scribes *began* grumbling at His disciples, saying, "Why do you eat and drink with the tax collectors and sinners?"

31 And Jesus answered and said to them, "*It is* not those who are well who need a physician, but those who are sick.

32 "I have not come to call the righteous but sinners to repentance."

NEW CENTURY VERSION

"Why are you thinking these things? 23Which is easier: to say, 'Your sins are forgiven,' or to say, 'Stand up and walk'? 24But I will prove to you that the Son of Man has authority on earth to forgive sins." So Jesus said to the paralyzed man, "I tell you, stand up, take your mat, and go home."

25At once the man stood up before them, picked up his mat, and went home, praising God. 26All the people were fully amazed and began to praise God. They were filled with much respect and said, "Today we have seen amazing things!"

Levi Follows Jesus

27After this, Jesus went out and saw a tax collector named Levi sitting in the tax collector's booth. Jesus said to him, "Follow me!" 28So Levi got up, left everything, and followed him.

29Then Levi gave a big dinner for Jesus at his house. Many tax collectors and other people were eating there, too. 30But the Pharisees and the men who taught the law for the Pharisees began to complain to Jesus' followers, "Why do you eat and drink with tax collectors and sinners?"

31Jesus answered them, "It is not the healthy people who need a doctor, but the sick. 32I have not come to invite good people but sinners to change their hearts and lives."

CONTEMPORARY ENGLISH VERSION

"Why are you thinking that? 23Is it easier for me to tell this crippled man that his sins are forgiven or to tell him to get up and walk? 24But now you will see that the Son of Man has the right to forgive sins here on earth." Jesus then said to the man, "Get up! Pick up your mat and walk home."

25At once the man stood up in front of everyone. He picked up his mat and went home, giving thanks to God. 26Everyone was amazed and praised God. What they saw surprised them, and they said, "We have seen a great miracle today!"

Jesus Chooses Levi (Matthew 9.9-13; Mark 2.13-17)

27Later, Jesus went out and saw a tax collector[f] named Levi sitting at the place for paying taxes. Jesus said to him, "Come with me." 28Levi left everything and went with Jesus.

29In his home Levi gave a big dinner for Jesus. Many tax collectors and other guests were also there.

30The Pharisees and some of their teachers of the Law of Moses grumbled to Jesus' disciples, "Why do you eat and drink with those tax collectors and other sinners?"

31Jesus answered, "Healthy people don't need a doctor, but sick people do. 32I didn't come to invite good people to turn to God. I came to invite sinners."

[f] 5.27 *tax collector*: See the note at 3.12.

NEW INTERNATIONAL VERSION

are you thinking these things in your hearts? 23 Which is easier: to say, 'Your sins are forgiven,' or to say, 'Get up and walk'? 24 But that you may know that the Son of Man has authority on earth to forgive sins. . . ." He said to the paralyzed man, "I tell you, get up, take your mat and go home." 25 Immediately he stood up in front of them, took what he had been lying on and went home praising God. 26 Everyone was amazed and gave praise to God. They were filled with awe and said, "We have seen remarkable things today."

The Calling of Levi

27 After this, Jesus went out and saw a tax collector by the name of Levi sitting at his tax booth. "Follow me," Jesus said to him, 28 and Levi got up, left everything and followed him.

29 Then Levi held a great banquet for Jesus at his house, and a large crowd of tax collectors and others were eating with them. 30 But the Pharisees and the teachers of the law who belonged to their sect complained to his disciples, "Why do you eat and drink with tax collectors and 'sinners'?"

31 Jesus answered them, "It is not the healthy who need a doctor, but the sick. 32 I have not come to call the righteous, but sinners to repentance."

NEW LIVING TRANSLATION

them, "Why do you think this is blasphemy? 23 Is it easier to say, 'Your sins are forgiven' or 'Get up and walk'? 24 I will prove that I, the Son of Man, have the authority on earth to forgive sins." Then Jesus turned to the paralyzed man and said, "Stand up, take your mat, and go on home, because you are healed!"

25 And immediately, as everyone watched, the man jumped to his feet, picked up his mat, and went home praising God. 26 Everyone was gripped with great wonder and awe. And they praised God, saying over and over again, "We have seen amazing things today."

Jesus Calls Levi (Matthew)

27 Later, as Jesus left the town, he saw a tax collector named Levi sitting at his tax-collection booth. "Come, be my disciple!" Jesus said to him. 28 So Levi got up, left everything, and followed him.

29 Soon Levi held a banquet in his home with Jesus as the guest of honor. Many of Levi's fellow tax collectors and other guests were there. 30 But the Pharisees and their teachers of religious law complained bitterly to Jesus' disciples, "Why do you eat and drink with such scum*?"

31 Jesus answered them, "Healthy people don't need a doctor—sick people do. 32 I have come to call sinners to turn from their sins, not to spend my time with those who think they are already good enough."

5:30 Greek *with tax collectors and sinners.*

NEW KING JAMES VERSION

and said to them, "Why are you reasoning in your hearts? 23 Which is easier, to say, 'Your sins are forgiven you,' or to say, 'Rise up and walk'? 24 But that you may know that the Son of Man has power on earth to forgive sins"—He said to the man who was paralyzed, "I say to you, arise, take up your bed, and go to your house."

25 Immediately he rose up before them, took up what he had been lying on, and departed to his own house, glorifying God. 26 And they were all amazed, and they glorified God and were filled with fear, saying, "We have seen strange things today!"

Matthew the Tax Collector

27 After these things He went out and saw a tax collector named Levi, sitting at the tax office. And He said to him, "Follow Me." 28 So he left all, rose up, and followed Him.

29 Then Levi gave Him a great feast in his own house. And there were a great number of tax collectors and others who sat down with them. 30 And their scribes and the Pharisees[b] complained against His disciples, saying, "Why do You eat and drink with tax collectors and sinners?"

31 Jesus answered and said to them, "Those who are well have no need of a physician, but those who are sick. 32 I have not come to call *the* righteous, but sinners, to repentance."

5:30 [b] NU-Text reads *But the Pharisees and their scribes.*

THE MESSAGE

"Why all this gossipy whispering? Which is simpler: to say 'I forgive your sins,' or to say 'Get up and start walking'? Well, just so it's clear that I'm the Son of Man and authorized to do either, or both. . . ." He now spoke directly to the paraplegic: "Get up. Take your bedroll and go home." Without a moment's hesitation, he did it—got up, took his blanket, and left for home, giving glory to God all the way. The people rubbed their eyes, incredulous—and then also gave glory to God. Awestruck, they said, "We've never seen anything like that!"

After this he went out and saw a man named Levi at his work collecting taxes. Jesus said, "Come along with me." And he did—walked away from everything and went with him.

Levi gave a large dinner at his home for Jesus. Everybody was there, tax men and other disreputable characters as guests at the dinner. The Pharisees and their religion scholars came to his disciples greatly offended. "What is he doing eating and drinking with crooks and 'sinners'?"

Jesus heard about it and spoke up, "Who needs a doctor: the healthy or the sick? I'm here inviting outsiders, not insiders—an invitation to a changed life, changed inside and out."

KING JAMES VERSION

33 And they said unto him, Why do the disciples of John fast often, and make prayers, and likewise *the disciples* of the Pharisees; but thine eat and drink?

34 And he said unto them, Can ye make the children of the bridechamber fast, while the bridegroom is with them?

35 But the days will come, when the bridegroom shall be taken away from them, and then shall they fast in those days.

36 And he spake also a parable unto them; No man putteth a piece of a new garment upon an old; if otherwise, then both the new maketh a rent, and the piece that was *taken* out of the new agreeth not with the old.

37 And no man putteth new wine into old bottles; else the new wine will burst the bottles, and be spilled, and the bottles shall perish.

38 But new wine must be put into new bottles; and both are preserved.

39 No man also having drunk old *wine* straightway desireth new: for he saith, The old is better.

6 And it came to pass on the second sabbath after the first, that he went through the corn fields; and his

NEW AMERICAN STANDARD BIBLE

33 And they said to Him, "The disciples of John often fast and offer prayers, the *disciples* of the Pharisees also do the same, but Yours eat and drink."

34 And Jesus said to them, "You cannot make the attendants of the bridegroom fast while the bridegroom is with them, can you?

35 "But *the* days will come; and when the bridegroom is taken away from them, then they will fast in those days."

36 And He was also telling them a parable: "No one tears a piece of cloth from a new garment and puts it on an old garment; otherwise he will both tear the new, and the piece from the new will not match the old.

37 "And no one puts new wine into old wineskins; otherwise the new wine will burst the skins and it will be spilled out, and the skins will be ruined.

38 "But new wine must be put into fresh wineskins.

39 "And no one, after drinking old *wine* wishes for new; for he says, 'The old is good *enough*.' "

Jesus Is Lord of the Sabbath

6 Now it happened that He was passing through *some* grainfields on a Sabbath; and His disciples were pick-

NEW CENTURY VERSION

Jesus Answers a Question

33 They said to Jesus, "John's followers often give up eating[d] for a certain time and pray, just as the Pharisees do. But your followers eat and drink all the time."

34 Jesus said to them, "You cannot make the friends of the bridegroom give up eating while he is still with them. 35 But the time will come when the bridegroom will be taken away from them, and then they will give up eating."

36 Jesus told them this story: "No one takes cloth off a new coat to cover a hole in an old coat. Otherwise, he ruins the new coat, and the cloth from the new coat will not be the same as the old cloth. 37 Also, no one ever pours new wine into old leather bags. Otherwise, the new wine will break the bags, the wine will spill out, and the leather bags will be ruined. 38 New wine must be put into new leather bags. 39 No one after drinking old wine wants new wine, because he says, 'The old wine is better.' "

Jesus Is Lord over the Sabbath

6 One Sabbath day Jesus was walking through some fields of grain. His followers picked the heads of

5:33 [d] **give up eating** This is called "fasting." The people would give up eating for a special time of prayer and worship to God. It was also done to show sadness and disappointment.

CONTEMPORARY ENGLISH VERSION

People Ask about Going without Eating

(Matthew 9.14-17; Mark 2.18-22)

33 Some people said to Jesus, "John's followers often pray and go without eating,[g] and so do the followers of the Pharisees. But your disciples never go without eating or drinking."

34 Jesus told them, "The friends of a bridegroom don't go without eating while he is still with them. 35 But the time will come when he will be taken from them. Then they will go without eating."

36 Jesus then told them these sayings:

No one uses a new piece of cloth to patch old clothes.
The patch would shrink and make the hole even bigger.
37 No one pours new wine into old wineskins. The new wine would swell and burst the old skins.[h] Then the wine would be lost, and the skins would be ruined.
38 New wine must be put only into new wineskins.
39 No one wants new wine after drinking old wine.
They say, "The old wine is better."

A Question about the Sabbath

(Matthew 12.1-8; Mark 2.23-28)

6 One Sabbath when Jesus and his disciples were walking through some wheat fields,[a] the disciples picked

[g] 5.33 *without eating*: See the note at 2.37. [h] 5.37 *swell and burst the old skins*: While the juice from grapes was becoming wine, it would swell and stretch the skins in which it had been stored. If the skins were old and stiff, they would burst. [a] 6.1 *walking through some wheat fields*: It was the custom to let hungry travelers pick grains of wheat.

NEW INTERNATIONAL VERSION

Jesus Questioned About Fasting

33 They said to him, "John's disciples often fast and pray, and so do the disciples of the Pharisees, but yours go on eating and drinking."

34 Jesus answered, "Can you make the guests of the bridegroom fast while he is with them? 35 But the time will come when the bridegroom will be taken from them; in those days they will fast."

36 He told them this parable: "No one tears a patch from a new garment and sews it on an old one. If he does, he will have torn the new garment, and the patch from the new will not match the old. 37 And no one pours new wine into old wineskins. If he does, the new wine will burst the skins, the wine will run out and the wineskins will be ruined. 38 No, new wine must be poured into new wineskins. 39 And no one after drinking old wine wants the new, for he says, 'The old is better.'"

Lord of the Sabbath

6 One Sabbath Jesus was going through the grainfields, and his disciples began to pick some heads of grain,

NEW LIVING TRANSLATION

A Discussion about Fasting

33 The religious leaders complained that Jesus' disciples were feasting instead of fasting. "John the Baptist's disciples always fast and pray," they declared, "and so do the disciples of the Pharisees. Why are yours always feasting?"

34 Jesus asked, "Do wedding guests fast while celebrating with the groom? 35 Someday he will be taken away from them, and then they will fast."

36 Then Jesus gave them this illustration: "No one tears a piece of cloth from a new garment and uses it to patch an old garment. For then the new garment would be torn, and the patch wouldn't even match the old garment. 37 And no one puts new wine into old wineskins. The new wine would burst the old skins, spilling the wine and ruining the skins. 38 New wine must be put into new wineskins. 39 But no one who drinks the old wine seems to want the fresh and the new. 'The old is better,' they say."

A Discussion about the Sabbath

6 One Sabbath day as Jesus was walking through some grainfields, his disciples broke off heads of wheat,

NEW KING JAMES VERSION

Jesus Is Questioned About Fasting

33 Then they said to Him, "Why do[c] the disciples of John fast often and make prayers, and likewise those of the Pharisees, but Yours eat and drink?"

34 And He said to them, "Can you make the friends of the bridegroom fast while the bridegroom is with them? 35 But the days will come when the bridegroom will be taken away from them; then they will fast in those days."

36 Then He spoke a parable to them: "No one puts a piece from a new garment on an old one;[d] otherwise the new makes a tear, and also the piece that was *taken* out of the new does not match the old. 37 And no one puts new wine into old wineskins; or else the new wine will burst the wineskins and be spilled, and the wineskins will be ruined. 38 But new wine must be put into new wineskins, and both are preserved.[e] 39 And no one, having drunk old *wine,* immediately[f] desires new; for he says, 'The old is better.'"[g]

Jesus Is Lord of the Sabbath

6 Now it happened on the second Sabbath after the first[a] that He went through the grainfields. And His

5:33 [c] NU-Text omits *Why do,* making the verse a statement.
5:36 [d] NU-Text reads *No one tears a piece from a new garment and puts it on an old one.* **5:38** [e] NU-Text omits *and both are preserved.*
5:39 [f] NU-Text omits *immediately.* [g] NU-Text reads *good.*
6:1 [a] NU-Text reads *on a Sabbath.*

THE MESSAGE

They asked him, "John's disciples are well-known for keeping fasts and saying prayers. Also the Pharisees. But you seem to spend most of your time at parties. Why?"

Jesus said, "When you're celebrating a wedding, you don't skimp on the cake and wine. You feast. Later you may need to pull in your belt, but this isn't the time. As long as the bride and groom are with you, you have a good time. When the groom is gone, the fasting can begin. No one throws cold water on a friendly bonfire. This is Kingdom Come!

"No one cuts up a fine silk scarf to patch old work clothes; you want fabrics that match. And you don't put wine in old, cracked bottles; you get strong, clean bottles for your fresh vintage wine. And no one who has ever tasted fine aged wine prefers unaged wine."

In Charge of the Sabbath

6 On a certain Sabbath Jesus was walking through a field of ripe grain. His disciples were pulling off heads

KING JAMES VERSION

disciples plucked the ears of corn, and did eat, rubbing *them* in *their* hands.

2 And certain of the Pharisees said unto them, Why do ye that which is not lawful to do on the sabbath days?

3 And Jesus answering them said, Have ye not read so much as this, what David did, when himself was an hungred, and they which were with him;

4 How he went into the house of God, and did take and eat the shewbread, and gave also to them that were with him; which it is not lawful to eat but for the priests alone?

5 And he said unto them, That the Son of man is Lord also of the sabbath.

6 And it came to pass also on another sabbath, that he entered into the synagogue and taught: and there was a man whose right hand was withered.

7 And the scribes and Pharisees watched him, whether he would heal on the sabbath day; that they might find an accusation against him.

8 But he knew their thoughts, and said to the man which had the withered hand, Rise up, and stand forth in the midst. And he arose and stood forth.

9 Then said Jesus unto them, I will ask you one thing; Is it lawful on the sabbath days to do good, or to do evil? to save life, or to destroy *it?*

10 And looking round about upon them all, he said

NEW AMERICAN STANDARD BIBLE

ing the heads of grain, rubbing them in their hands, and eating *the grain*.

2 But some of the Pharisees said, "Why do you do what is not lawful on the Sabbath?"

3 And Jesus answering them said, "Have you not even read what David did when he was hungry, he and those who were with him,

4 how he entered the house of God, and took and ate the [1]consecrated bread which is not lawful for any to eat except the priests alone, and gave it to his companions?"

5 And He was saying to them, "The Son of Man is Lord of the Sabbath."

6 On another Sabbath He entered the synagogue and was teaching; and there was a man there whose right hand was withered.

7 The scribes and the Pharisees were watching Him closely *to see* if He healed on the Sabbath, so that they might find *reason* to accuse Him.

8 But He knew what they were thinking, and He said to the man with the withered hand, "Get up and come forward!" And he got up and came forward.

9 And Jesus said to them, "I ask you, is it lawful to do good or to do harm on the Sabbath, to save a life or to destroy it?"

10 After looking around at them all, He said to him,

6:4 [1] Or *showbread;* lit *loaves of presentation*

NEW CENTURY VERSION

grain, rubbed them in their hands, and ate them. [2]Some
Pharisees said, "Why do you do what is not lawful on the
Sabbath day?"
[3]Jesus answered, "Have you not read what David did
when he and those with him were hungry? [4]He went into
God's house and took and ate the holy bread, which is
lawful only for priests to eat. And he gave some to the peo-
ple who were with him." [5]Then Jesus said to the Pharisees,
"The Son of Man is Lord of the Sabbath day."

Jesus Heals a Man's Hand

[6]On another Sabbath day Jesus went into the synagogue
and was teaching, and a man with a crippled right hand
was there. [7]The teachers of the law and the Pharisees were
watching closely to see if Jesus would heal on the Sabbath
day so they could accuse him. [8]But he knew what they
were thinking, and he said to the man with the crippled
hand, "Stand up here in the middle of everyone." The man
got up and stood there. [9]Then Jesus said to them, "I ask
you, which is lawful on the Sabbath day: to do good or to
do evil, to save a life or to destroy it?" [10]Jesus looked

CONTEMPORARY ENGLISH VERSION

some wheat. They rubbed the husks off with their hands
and started eating the grain.
[2]Some Pharisees said, "Why are you picking grain on
the Sabbath? You're not supposed to do that!"
[3]Jesus answered, "You surely have read what David did
when he and his followers were hungry. [4]He went into the
house of God and took the sacred loaves of bread that only
priests were supposed to eat. He not only ate some him-
self, but even gave some to his followers."
[5]Jesus finished by saying, "The Son of Man is Lord over
the Sabbath."

A Man with a Crippled Hand (Matthew 12.9-14; Mark 3.1-6)

[6]On another Sabbath[b] Jesus was teaching in a Jewish
meeting place, and a man with a crippled right hand was
there. [7]Some Pharisees and teachers of the Law of Moses
kept watching Jesus to see if he would heal the man. They
did this because they wanted to accuse Jesus of doing
something wrong.
[8]Jesus knew what they were thinking. So he told the
man to stand up where everyone could see him. And the
man stood up. [9]Then Jesus asked, "On the Sabbath should
we do good deeds or evil deeds? Should we save someone's
life or destroy it?"
[10]After he had looked around at everyone, he told the

[b] **6.6** *On another Sabbath*: Some manuscripts have a reading which may mean "the Sabbath after the next."

NEW INTERNATIONAL VERSION

rub them in their hands and eat the kernels. 2Some of the Pharisees asked, "Why are you doing what is unlawful on the Sabbath?"

3Jesus answered them, "Have you never read what David did when he and his companions were hungry? 4He entered the house of God, and taking the consecrated bread, he ate what is lawful only for priests to eat. And he also gave some to his companions." 5Then Jesus said to them, "The Son of Man is Lord of the Sabbath."

6On another Sabbath he went into the synagogue and was teaching, and a man was there whose right hand was shriveled. 7The Pharisees and the teachers of the law were looking for a reason to accuse Jesus, so they watched him closely to see if he would heal on the Sabbath. 8But Jesus knew what they were thinking and said to the man with the shriveled hand, "Get up and stand in front of everyone." So he got up and stood there.

9Then Jesus said to them, "I ask you, which is lawful on the Sabbath: to do good or to do evil, to save life or to destroy it?"

10He looked around at them all, and then said to the

NEW LIVING TRANSLATION

rubbed off the husks in their hands, and ate the grains. 2But some Pharisees said, "You shouldn't be doing that! It's against the law to work by harvesting grain on the Sabbath."

3Jesus replied, "Haven't you ever read in the Scriptures what King David did when he and his companions were hungry? 4He went into the house of God, ate the special bread reserved for the priests alone, and then gave some to his friends. That was breaking the law, too." 5And Jesus added, "I, the Son of Man, am master even of the Sabbath."

Jesus Heals on the Sabbath

6On another Sabbath day, a man with a deformed right hand was in the synagogue while Jesus was teaching. 7The teachers of religious law and the Pharisees watched closely to see whether Jesus would heal the man on the Sabbath, because they were eager to find some legal charge to bring against him. 8But Jesus knew their thoughts. He said to the man with the deformed hand, "Come and stand here where everyone can see." So the man came forward. 9Then Jesus said to his critics, "I have a question for you. Is it legal to do good deeds on the Sabbath, or is it a day for doing harm? Is this a day to save life or to destroy it?" 10He looked around at them one by one and then said to the man, "Reach out

NEW KING JAMES VERSION

disciples plucked the heads of grain and ate *them,* rubbing *them* in *their* hands. 2And some of the Pharisees said to them, "Why are you doing what is not lawful to do on the Sabbath?"

3But Jesus answering them said, "Have you not even read this, what David did when he was hungry, he and those who were with him: 4how he went into the house of God, took and ate the showbread, and also gave some to those with him, which is not lawful for any but the priests to eat?" 5And He said to them, "The Son of Man is also Lord of the Sabbath."

Healing on the Sabbath

6Now it happened on another Sabbath, also, that He entered the synagogue and taught. And a man was there whose right hand was withered. 7So the scribes and Pharisees watched Him closely, whether He would heal on the Sabbath, that they might find an accusation against Him. 8But He knew their thoughts, and said to the man who had the withered hand, "Arise and stand here." And he arose and stood. 9Then Jesus said to them, "I will ask you one thing: Is it lawful on the Sabbath to do good or to do evil, to save life or to destroy?"[b] 10And when He had looked

6:9 [b] M-Text reads *to kill.*

THE MESSAGE

of grain, rubbing them in their hands to get rid of the chaff, and eating them. Some Pharisees said, "Why are you doing that, breaking a Sabbath rule?"

But Jesus stood up for them. "Have you never read what David and those with him did when they were hungry? How he entered the sanctuary and ate fresh bread off the altar, bread that no one but priests were allowed to eat? He also handed it out to his companions."

Then he said, "The Son of Man is no slave to the Sabbath; he's in charge."

On another Sabbath he went to the meeting place and taught. There was a man there with a crippled right hand. The religion scholars and Pharisees had their eye on Jesus to see if he would heal the man, hoping to catch him in a Sabbath infraction. He knew what they were up to and spoke to the man with the crippled hand: "Get up and stand here before us." He did.

Then Jesus addressed them, "Let me ask you something: What kind of action suits the Sabbath best? Doing good or doing evil? Helping people or leaving them helpless?"

He looked around, looked each one in the eye. He said to

KING JAMES VERSION

unto the man, Stretch forth thy hand. And he did so: and his hand was restored whole as the other.

11 And they were filled with madness; and communed one with another what they might do to Jesus.

12 ¶ And it came to pass in those days, that he went out into a mountain to pray, and continued all night in prayer to God.

13 And when it was day, he called *unto him* his disciples: and of them he chose twelve, whom also he named apostles;

14 Simon, (whom he also named Peter,) and Andrew his brother, James and John, Philip and Bartholomew,

15 Matthew and Thomas, James the *son* of Alphaeus, and Simon called Zelotes,

16 And Judas *the brother* of James, and Judas Iscariot, which also was the traitor.

17 And he came down with them, and stood in the plain, and the company of his disciples, and a great multitude of people out of all Judaea and Jerusalem, and from the sea coast of Tyre and Sidon, which came to hear him,

NEW AMERICAN STANDARD BIBLE

"Stretch out your hand!" And he did *so;* and his hand was restored.

11 But they themselves were filled with rage, and discussed together what they might do to Jesus.

Choosing the Twelve

12 It was at this time that He went off to the mountain to pray, and He spent the whole night in prayer to God.

13 And when day came, He called His disciples to Him and chose twelve of them, whom He also named as apostles:

14 Simon, whom He also named Peter, and Andrew his brother; and James and John; and Philip and Bartholomew;

15 and Matthew and Thomas; James *the son* of Alphaeus, and Simon who was called the Zealot;

16 Judas *the son* of James, and Judas Iscariot, who became a traitor.

17 Jesus came down with them and stood on a level place; and *there was* a large crowd of His disciples, and a great throng of people from all Judea and Jerusalem and the coastal region of Tyre and Sidon,

NEW CENTURY VERSION

around at all of them and said to the man, "Hold out your hand." The man held out his hand, and it was healed.

11But the Pharisees and the teachers of the law were very angry and discussed with each other what they could do to Jesus.

Jesus Chooses His Apostles

12At that time Jesus went off to a mountain to pray, and
he spent the night praying to God. 13The next morning,
Jesus called his followers to him and chose twelve of them,
whom he named apostles: 14Simon (Jesus named him
Peter), his brother Andrew, James, John, Philip, Bartholo-
mew, 15Matthew, Thomas, James son of Alphaeus, Simon
(called the Zealot), 16Judas son of James, and Judas
Iscariot, who later turned Jesus over to his enemies.

Jesus Teaches and Heals

17Jesus and the apostles came down from the mountain,
and he stood on level ground. A large group of his followers
was there, as well as many people from all around Judea,
Jerusalem, and the seacoast cities of Tyre and Sidon. 18They

CONTEMPORARY ENGLISH VERSION

man, "Stretch out your hand." He did, and his bad hand became completely well.

11The teachers and the Pharisees were furious and started saying to each other, "What can we do about Jesus?"

Jesus Chooses His Twelve Apostles

(Matthew 10.1-4; Mark 3.13-19)

12About that time Jesus went off to a mountain to pray,
and he spent the whole night there. 13The next morning he
called his disciples together and chose twelve of them to be
his apostles. 14One was Simon, and Jesus named him
Peter. Another was Andrew, Peter's brother. There were
also James, John, Philip, Bartholomew, 15Matthew,
Thomas, and James the son of Alphaeus. The rest of the
apostles were Simon, known as the Eager One,[c] 16Jude,
who was the son of James, and Judas Iscariot,[d] who later
betrayed Jesus.

Jesus Teaches, Preaches, and Heals (Matthew 4.23-25)

17Jesus and his apostles went down from the mountain
and came to some flat, level ground. Many other disciples
were there to meet him. Large crowds of people from all
over Judea, Jerusalem, and the coastal cities of Tyre and
Sidon were there too. 18These people had come to listen to

[c] **6.15** *known as the Eager One*: The word "eager" translates the Greek word "zealot," which was a name later given to the members of a Jewish group that resisted and fought against the Romans. [d] **6.16** *Iscariot*: This may mean "a man from Kerioth" (a place in Judea). But more probably it means "a man who was a liar" or "a man who was a betrayer."

NEW INTERNATIONAL VERSION

man, "Stretch out your hand." He did so, and his hand was completely restored. 11But they were furious and began to discuss with one another what they might do to Jesus.

The Twelve Apostles

12One of those days Jesus went out to a mountainside to pray, and spent the night praying to God. 13When morning came, he called his disciples to him and chose twelve of them, whom he also designated apostles: 14Simon (whom he named Peter), his brother Andrew, James, John, Philip, Bartholomew, 15Matthew, Thomas, James son of Alphaeus, Simon who was called the Zealot, 16Judas son of James, and Judas Iscariot, who became a traitor.

Blessings and Woes

17He went down with them and stood on a level place. A large crowd of his disciples was there and a great number of people from all over Judea, from Jerusalem, and from the coast of Tyre and Sidon, 18who had come to hear him and

NEW LIVING TRANSLATION

your hand." The man reached out his hand, and it became normal again! 11At this, the enemies of Jesus were wild with rage and began to discuss what to do with him.

Jesus Chooses the Twelve Apostles

12One day soon afterward Jesus went to a mountain to pray, and he prayed to God all night. 13At daybreak he called together all of his disciples and chose twelve of them to be apostles. Here are their names:

14 Simon (he also called him Peter),
Andrew (Peter's brother),
James,
John,
Philip,
Bartholomew,
15 Matthew,
Thomas,
James (son of Alphaeus),
Simon (the Zealot),
16 Judas (son of James),
Judas Iscariot (who later betrayed him).

Crowds Follow Jesus

17When they came down the slopes of the mountain, the disciples stood with Jesus on a large, level area, surrounded by many of his followers and by the crowds. There were people from all over Judea and from Jerusalem and from as far north as the seacoasts of Tyre and Sidon. 18They had

NEW KING JAMES VERSION

around at them all, He said to the man,[c] "Stretch out your hand." And he did so, and his hand was restored as whole as the other.[d] 11But they were filled with rage, and discussed with one another what they might do to Jesus.

The Twelve Apostles

12Now it came to pass in those days that He went out to the mountain to pray, and continued all night in prayer to God. 13And when it was day, He called His disciples to *Himself;* and from them He chose twelve whom He also named apostles: 14Simon, whom He also named Peter, and Andrew his brother; James and John; Philip and Bartholomew; 15Matthew and Thomas; James the *son* of Alphaeus, and Simon called the Zealot; 16Judas *the son* of James, and Judas Iscariot who also became a traitor.

Jesus Heals a Great Multitude

17And He came down with them and stood on a level place with a crowd of His disciples and a great multitude of people from all Judea and Jerusalem, and from the seacoast of Tyre and Sidon, who came to hear Him and be

6:10 [c] NU-Text and M-Text read *to him.* [d] NU-Text omits *as whole as the other.*

THE MESSAGE

the man, "Hold out your hand." He held it out—it was as good as new! They were beside themselves with anger, and started plotting how they might get even with him.

The Twelve Apostles

At about that same time he climbed a mountain to pray. He was there all night in prayer before God. The next day he summoned his disciples; from them he selected twelve he designated as apostles:

Simon, whom he named Peter,
Andrew, his brother,
James,
John,
Philip,
Bartholomew,
Matthew,
Thomas,
James, son of Alphaeus,
Simon, called the Zealot,
Judas, son of James,
Judas Iscariot, who betrayed him.

You're Blessed

Coming down off the mountain with them, he stood on a plain surrounded by disciples, and was soon joined by a huge congregation from all over Judea and Jerusalem, even from the seaside towns of Tyre and Sidon. They had come

KING JAMES VERSION

and to be healed of their diseases;
18 And they that were vexed with unclean spirits: and they were healed.
19 And the whole multitude sought to touch him: for there went virtue out of him, and healed *them* all.
20 ¶ And he lifted up his eyes on his disciples, and said, Blessed *be ye* poor: for yours is the kingdom of God.
21 Blessed *are ye* that hunger now: for ye shall be filled. Blessed *are ye* that weep now: for ye shall laugh.
22 Blessed are ye, when men shall hate you, and when they shall separate you *from their company*, and shall reproach *you*, and cast out your name as evil, for the Son of man's sake.
23 Rejoice ye in that day, and leap for joy: for, behold, your reward *is* great in heaven: for in the like manner did their fathers unto the prophets.
24 But woe unto you that are rich! for ye have received your consolation.

NEW AMERICAN STANDARD BIBLE

18 who had come to hear Him and to be healed of their diseases; and those who were troubled with unclean spirits were being cured.
19 And all the people were trying to touch Him, for power was coming from Him and healing *them* all.

The Beatitudes

20 And turning His gaze toward His disciples, He *began* to say, "Blessed *are* you *who are* poor, for yours is the kingdom of God.
21 "Blessed *are* you who hunger now, for you shall be satisfied. Blessed *are* you who weep now, for you shall laugh.
22 "Blessed are you when men hate you, and ostracize you, and insult you, and scorn your name as evil, for the sake of the Son of Man.
23 "Be glad in that day and leap *for joy*, for behold, your reward is great in heaven. For in the same way their fathers used to treat the prophets.
24 "But woe to you who are rich, for you are receiving your comfort in full.

NEW CENTURY VERSION

all came to hear Jesus teach and to be healed of their sicknesses, and he healed those who were troubled by evil spirits. 19All the people were trying to touch Jesus, because power was coming from him and healing them all.

20Jesus looked at his followers and said,

"You people who are poor are happy,
because the kingdom of God belongs to you.
21 You people who are now hungry are happy,
because you will be satisfied.
You people who are now crying are happy,
because you will laugh with joy.

22"People will hate you, shut you out, insult you, and say you are evil because you follow the Son of Man. But when they do, you will be happy. 23Be full of joy at that time, because you have a great reward waiting for you in heaven. Their ancestors did the same things to the prophets.

24 "But how terrible it will be for you who are rich,
because you have had your easy life.

CONTEMPORARY ENGLISH VERSION

Jesus and to be healed of their diseases. All who were troubled by evil spirits were also healed. 19Everyone was trying to touch Jesus, because power was going out from him and healing them all.

Blessings and Troubles (Matthew 5.1-12)

20Jesus looked at his disciples and said:

God will bless you people
who are poor.
His kingdom belongs to you!
21 God will bless
you hungry people.
You will have plenty
to eat!
God will bless you people
who are crying.
You will laugh!

22God will bless you when others hate you and won't have anything to do with you. God will bless you when people insult you and say cruel things about you, all because you are a follower of the Son of Man. 23Long ago your own people did these same things to the prophets. So when this happens to you, be happy and jump for joy! You will have a great reward in heaven.

24 But you rich people
are in for trouble.
You have already had
an easy life!

NEW INTERNATIONAL VERSION

to be healed of their diseases. Those troubled by evil[a] spir-
its were cured, 19 and the people all tried to touch him,
because power was coming from him and healing them all.
20 Looking at his disciples, he said:

"Blessed are you who are poor,
for yours is the kingdom of God.
21 Blessed are you who hunger now,
for you will be satisfied.
Blessed are you who weep now,
for you will laugh.
22 Blessed are you when men hate you,
when they exclude you and insult you
and reject your name as evil,
because of the Son of Man.

23 "Rejoice in that day and leap for joy, because great is
your reward in heaven. For that is how their fathers treat-
ed the prophets.

24 "But woe to you who are rich,
for you have already received your comfort.

[a] *18* Greek *unclean*

NEW LIVING TRANSLATION

come to hear him and to be healed, and Jesus cast out
many evil spirits. 19 Everyone was trying to touch him,
because healing power went out from him, and they were
all cured.

The Beatitudes

20 Then Jesus turned to his disciples and said,

"God blesses you who are poor,
for the Kingdom of God is given to you.
21 God blesses you who are hungry now,
for you will be satisfied.
God blesses you who weep now,
for the time will come when you will laugh with joy.
22 God blesses you who are hated and excluded and
mocked and cursed
because you are identified with me, the Son of Man.

23 "When that happens, rejoice! Yes, leap for joy! For a
great reward awaits you in heaven. And remember, the
ancient prophets were also treated that way by your ances-
tors.

Sorrows Foretold

24 "What sorrows await you who are rich,
for you have your only happiness now.

NEW KING JAMES VERSION

healed of their diseases, 18 as well as those who were tor-
mented with unclean spirits. And they were healed. 19 And
the whole multitude sought to touch Him, for power went
out from Him and healed *them* all.

The Beatitudes

20 Then He lifted up His eyes toward His disciples, and
said:

"Blessed *are you* poor,
For yours is the kingdom of God.
21 Blessed *are you* who hunger now,
For you shall be filled.
Blessed *are you* who weep now,
For you shall laugh.
22 Blessed are you when men hate you,
And when they exclude you,
And revile *you,* and cast out your name as evil,
For the Son of Man's sake.
23 Rejoice in that day and leap for joy!
For indeed your reward *is* great in heaven,
For in like manner their fathers did to the
prophets.

Jesus Pronounces Woes

24 "But woe to you who are rich,
For you have received your consolation.

THE MESSAGE

both to hear him and to be cured of their ailments. Those disturbed by evil spirits were healed. Everyone was trying to touch him—so much energy surging from him, so many people healed! Then he spoke:

"You're blessed when you've lost it all.
God's kingdom is there for the finding.

"You're blessed when you're ravenously hungry.
Then you're ready for the Messianic meal.

"You're blessed when the tears flow freely.
Joy comes with the morning.

"Count yourself blessed every time someone cuts you down or throws you out, every time someone smears or blackens your name to discredit me. What it means is that the truth is too close for comfort and that that person is uncomfortable. You can be glad when that happens—skip like a lamb, if you like!—for even though they don't like it, I do . . . and all heaven applauds. And know that you are in good company; my preachers and witnesses have always been treated like this.

Give Away Your Life

"But it's trouble ahead if you think you have it made.
What you have is all you'll ever get.

KING JAMES VERSION

25 Woe unto you that are full! for ye shall hunger. Woe unto you that laugh now! for ye shall mourn and weep.

26 Woe unto you, when all men shall speak well of you! for so did their fathers to the false prophets.

27 ¶ But I say unto you which hear, Love your enemies, do good to them which hate you,

28 Bless them that curse you, and pray for them which despitefully use you.

29 And unto him that smiteth thee on the *one* cheek offer also the other; and him that taketh away thy cloke forbid not *to take thy* coat also.

30 Give to every man that asketh of thee; and of him that taketh away thy goods ask *them* not again.

31 And as ye would that men should do to you, do ye also to them likewise.

32 For if ye love them which love you, what thank have ye? for sinners also love those that love them.

33 And if ye do good to them which do good to you, what thank have ye? for sinners also do even the same.

NEW AMERICAN STANDARD BIBLE

25 "Woe to you who are well-fed now, for you shall be hungry. Woe *to you* who laugh now, for you shall mourn and weep.

26 "Woe *to you* when all men speak well of you, for their fathers used to treat the false prophets in the same way.

27 "But I say to you who hear, love your enemies, do good to those who hate you,

28 bless those who curse you, pray for those who mistreat you.

29 "Whoever hits you on the cheek, offer him the other also; and whoever takes away your coat, do not withhold your shirt from him either.

30 "Give to everyone who asks of you, and whoever takes away what is yours, do not demand it back.

31 "Treat others the same way you want them to treat you.

32 "If you love those who love you, what credit is *that* to you? For even sinners love those who love them.

33 "If you do good to those who do good to you, what credit is *that* to you? For even sinners do the same.

NEW CENTURY VERSION

25 How terrible it will be for you who are full now,
because you will be hungry.
How terrible it will be for you who are laughing now,
because you will be sad and cry.

26 "How terrible when everyone says only good things about you, because their ancestors said the same things about the false prophets.

Love Your Enemies

27 "But I say to you who are listening, love your enemies. Do good to those who hate you, 28 bless those who curse you, pray for those who are cruel to you. 29 If anyone slaps you on one cheek, offer him the other cheek, too. If someone takes your coat, do not stop him from taking your shirt. 30 Give to everyone who asks you, and when someone takes something that is yours, don't ask for it back. 31 Do to others what you would want them to do to you. 32 If you love only the people who love you, what praise should you get? Even sinners love the people who love them. 33 If you do good only to those who do good to you, what praise should you get? Even sinners do that! 34 If you lend things

CONTEMPORARY ENGLISH VERSION

25 You well-fed people
are in for trouble.
You will go hungry!
You people
who are laughing now
are in for trouble.
You are going to cry
and weep!

26 You are in for trouble when everyone says good things about you. That is what your own people said about those prophets who told lies.

Love for Enemies (Matthew 5.38-48; 7.12a)

27 This is what I say to all who will listen to me:

Love your enemies, and be good to everyone who hates you. 28 Ask God to bless anyone who curses you, and pray for everyone who is cruel to you. 29 If someone slaps you on one cheek, don't stop that person from slapping you on the other cheek. If someone wants to take your coat, don't try to keep back your shirt. 30 Give to everyone who asks and don't ask people to return what they have taken from you. 31 Treat others just as you want to be treated.

32 If you love only someone who loves you, will God praise you for that? Even sinners love people who love them. 33 If you are kind only to someone who is kind to you, will God be pleased with you for that? Even sinners are kind to people who are kind to them. 34 If you lend

NEW INTERNATIONAL VERSION

25 Woe to you who are well fed now,
for you will go hungry.
Woe to you who laugh now,
for you will mourn and weep.
26 Woe to you when all men speak well of you,
for that is how their fathers treated the false
prophets.

Love for Enemies

27 "But I tell you who hear me: Love your enemies, do good to those who hate you, 28 bless those who curse you, pray for those who mistreat you. 29 If someone strikes you on one cheek, turn to him the other also. If someone takes your cloak, do not stop him from taking your tunic. 30 Give to everyone who asks you, and if anyone takes what belongs to you, do not demand it back. 31 Do to others as you would have them do to you.

32 "If you love those who love you, what credit is that to you? Even 'sinners' love those who love them. 33 And if you do good to those who are good to you, what credit is that to you? Even 'sinners' do that. 34 And if you lend to those

NEW LIVING TRANSLATION

25 What sorrows await you who are satisfied and
prosperous now,
for a time of awful hunger is before you.
What sorrows await you who laugh carelessly,
for your laughing will turn to mourning and sorrow.
26 What sorrows await you who are praised by the crowds,
for their ancestors also praised false prophets.

Love for Enemies

27 "But if you are willing to listen, I say, love your enemies. Do good to those who hate you. 28 Pray for the happiness of those who curse you. Pray for those who hurt you. 29 If someone slaps you on one cheek, turn the other cheek. If someone demands your coat, offer your shirt also. 30 Give what you have to anyone who asks you for it; and when things are taken away from you, don't try to get them back. 31 Do for others as you would like them to do for you.

32 "Do you think you deserve credit merely for loving those who love you? Even the sinners do that! 33 And if you do good only to those who do good to you, is that so wonderful? Even sinners do that much! 34 And if you lend

NEW KING JAMES VERSION

25 Woe to you who are full,
For you shall hunger.
Woe to you who laugh now,
For you shall mourn and weep.
26 Woe to you[e] when all[f] men speak well of you,
For so did their fathers to the false prophets.

Love Your Enemies

27 "But I say to you who hear: Love your enemies, do good to those who hate you, 28 bless those who curse you, and pray for those who spitefully use you. 29 To him who strikes you on the *one* cheek, offer the other also. And from him who takes away your cloak, do not withhold *your* tunic either. 30 Give to everyone who asks of you. And from him who takes away your goods do not ask *them* back. 31 And just as you want men to do to you, you also do to them likewise.

32 "But if you love those who love you, what credit is that to you? For even sinners love those who love them. 33 And if you do good to those who do good to you, what credit is that to you? For even sinners do the same. 34 And

6:26 [e] NU-Text and M-Text omit *to you.* [f] M-Text omits *all.*

THE MESSAGE

"And it's trouble ahead if you're satisfied with yourself.
Your *self* will not satisfy you for long.
"And it's trouble ahead if you think life's all fun and
games.
There's suffering to be met, and you're going to meet it.

"There's trouble ahead when you live only for the approval of others, saying what flatters them, doing what indulges them. Popularity contests are not truth contests—look how many scoundrel preachers were approved by your ancestors! Your task is to be true, not popular.

"To you who are ready for the truth, I say this: Love your enemies. Let them bring out the best in you, not the worst. When someone gives you a hard time, respond with the energies of prayer for that person. If someone slaps you in the face, stand there and take it. If someone grabs your shirt, giftwrap your best coat and make a present of it. If someone takes unfair advantage of you, use the occasion to practice the servant life. No more tit-for-tat stuff. Live generously.

"Here is a simple rule of thumb for behavior: Ask yourself what you want people to do for you; then grab the initiative and do it for *them*! If you only love the lovable, do you expect a pat on the back? Run-of-the-mill sinners do that. If you only help those who help you, do you expect a medal? Garden-variety sinners do that. If you only give for

KING JAMES VERSION

34 And if ye lend *to them* of whom ye hope to receive, what thank have ye? for sinners also lend to sinners, to receive as much again.

35 But love ye your enemies, and do good, and lend, hoping for nothing again; and your reward shall be great, and ye shall be the children of the Highest: for he is kind unto the unthankful and *to* the evil.

36 Be ye therefore merciful, as your Father also is merciful.

37 ¶ Judge not, and ye shall not be judged: condemn not, and ye shall not be condemned: forgive, and ye shall be forgiven:

38 Give, and it shall be given unto you; good measure, pressed down, and shaken together, and running over, shall men give into your bosom. For with the same measure that ye mete withal it shall be measured to you again.

39 And he spake a parable unto them, Can the blind lead the blind? shall they not both fall into the ditch?

40 The disciple is not above his master: but every one that is perfect shall be as his master.

41 And why beholdest thou the mote that is in thy brother's eye, but perceivest not the beam that is in thine own eye?

42 Either how canst thou say to thy brother, Brother, let me pull out the mote that is in thine eye, when thou thyself beholdest not the beam that is in thine own eye? Thou

NEW AMERICAN STANDARD BIBLE

34 "If you lend to those from whom you expect to receive, what credit is *that* to you? Even sinners lend to sinners in order to receive back the same *amount.*

35 "But love your enemies, and do good, and lend, expecting nothing in return; and your reward will be great, and you will be sons of the Most High; for He Himself is kind to ungrateful and evil *men.*

36 "Be merciful, just as your Father is merciful.

37 "Do not judge, and you will not be judged; and do not condemn, and you will not be condemned; pardon, and you will be pardoned.

38 "Give, and it will be given to you. They will pour into your lap a good measure—pressed down, shaken together, *and* running over. For by your standard of measure it will be measured to you in return."

39 And He also spoke a parable to them: "A blind man cannot guide a blind man, can he? Will they not both fall into a pit?

40 "A pupil is not above his teacher; but everyone, after he has been fully trained, will be like his teacher.

41 "Why do you look at the speck that is in your brother's eye, but do not notice the log that is in your own eye?

42 "Or how can you say to your brother, 'Brother, let me take out the speck that is in your eye,' when you yourself do not see the log that is in your own eye? You hypocrite,

NEW CENTURY VERSION

to people, always hoping to get something back, what
praise should you get? Even sinners lend to other sinners
so that they can get back the same amount! 35 But love
your enemies, do good to them, and lend to them without
hoping to get anything back. Then you will have a great
reward, and you will be children of the Most High God,
because he is kind even to people who are ungrateful and
full of sin. 36 Show mercy, just as your Father shows mercy.

Look at Yourselves

37 "Don't judge other people, and you will not be judged.
Don't accuse others of being guilty, and you will not be
accused of being guilty. Forgive, and you will be forgiven.
38 Give, and you will receive. You will be given much.
Pressed down, shaken together, and running over, it will
spill into your lap. The way you give to others is the way
God will give to you."

39 Jesus told them this story: "Can a blind person lead
another blind person? No! Both of them will fall into a
ditch. 40 A student is not better than the teacher, but the
student who has been fully trained will be like the teacher.

41 "Why do you notice the little piece of dust in your
friend's eye, but you don't notice the big piece of wood in
your own eye? 42 How can you say to your friend, 'Friend,
let me take that little piece of dust out of your eye' when
you cannot see that big piece of wood in your own eye!

CONTEMPORARY ENGLISH VERSION

money only to someone you think will pay you back,
will God be pleased with you for that? Even sinners lend
to sinners because they think they will get it all back.

35 But love your enemies and be good to them. Lend with-
out expecting to be paid back.[e] Then you will get a great
reward, and you will be the true children of God in heaven.
He is good even to people who are unthankful and cruel.
36 Have pity on others, just as your Father has pity on you.

Judging Others (Matthew 7.1-5)

37 Jesus said:

Don't judge others, and God won't judge you. Don't be
hard on others, and God won't be hard on you. Forgive
others, and God will forgive you. 38 If you give to others,
you will be given a full amount in return. It will be packed
down, shaken together, and spilling over into your lap.
The way you treat others is the way you will be treated.

39 Jesus also used some sayings as he spoke to the peo-
ple. He said:

Can one blind person lead another blind person?
Won't they both fall into a ditch? 40 Are students better
than their teacher? But when they are fully trained, they
will be like their teacher.

41 You can see the speck in your friend's eye. But you
don't notice the log in your own eye. 42 How can you say,
"My friend, let me take the speck out of your eye," when
you don't see the log in your own eye? You show-offs!

[e] 6.35 *without expecting to be paid back*: Some manuscripts have "without giving up on anyone."

NEW INTERNATIONAL VERSION

from whom you expect repayment, what credit is that to you? Even 'sinners' lend to 'sinners,' expecting to be repaid in full. [35]But love your enemies, do good to them, and lend to them without expecting to get anything back. Then your reward will be great, and you will be sons of the Most High, because he is kind to the ungrateful and wicked. [36]Be merciful, just as your Father is merciful.

Judging Others

[37]"Do not judge, and you will not be judged. Do not condemn, and you will not be condemned. Forgive, and you will be forgiven. [38]Give, and it will be given to you. A good measure, pressed down, shaken together and running over, will be poured into your lap. For with the measure you use, it will be measured to you."

[39]He also told them this parable: "Can a blind man lead a blind man? Will they not both fall into a pit? [40]A student is not above his teacher, but everyone who is fully trained will be like his teacher.

[41]"Why do you look at the speck of sawdust in your brother's eye and pay no attention to the plank in your own eye? [42]How can you say to your brother, 'Brother, let me take the speck out of your eye,' when you yourself fail to see the plank in your own eye? You hypocrite, first take

NEW LIVING TRANSLATION

money only to those who can repay you, what good is that? Even sinners will lend to their own kind for a full return.

[35]"Love your enemies! Do good to them! Lend to them! And don't be concerned that they might not repay. Then your reward from heaven will be very great, and you will truly be acting as children of the Most High, for he is kind to the unthankful and to those who are wicked. [36]You must be compassionate, just as your Father is compassionate.

Don't Condemn Others

[37]"Stop judging others, and you will not be judged. Stop criticizing others, or it will all come back on you. If you forgive others, you will be forgiven. [38]If you give, you will receive. Your gift will return to you in full measure, pressed down, shaken together to make room for more, and running over. Whatever measure you use in giving—large or small—it will be used to measure what is given back to you."

[39]Then Jesus gave the following illustration: "What good is it for one blind person to lead another? The first one will fall into a ditch and pull the other down also. [40]A student is not greater than the teacher. But the student who works hard will become like the teacher.

[41]"And why worry about a speck in your friend's eye* when you have a log in your own? [42]How can you think of saying, 'Friend,* let me help you get rid of that speck in your eye,' when you can't see past the log in your own

6:41 Greek *your brother's eye;* also in 6:42. 6:42 Greek *Brother.*

NEW KING JAMES VERSION

if you lend *to those* from whom you hope to receive back, what credit is that to you? For even sinners lend to sinners to receive as much back. [35]But love your enemies, do good, and lend, hoping for nothing in return; and your reward will be great, and you will be sons of the Most High. For He is kind to the unthankful and evil. [36]Therefore be merciful, just as your Father also is merciful.

Do Not Judge

[37]"Judge not, and you shall not be judged. Condemn not, and you shall not be condemned. Forgive, and you will be forgiven. [38]Give, and it will be given to you: good measure, pressed down, shaken together, and running over will be put into your bosom. For with the same measure that you use, it will be measured back to you."

[39]And He spoke a parable to them: "Can the blind lead the blind? Will they not both fall into the ditch? [40]A disciple is not above his teacher, but everyone who is perfectly trained will be like his teacher. [41]And why do you look at the speck in your brother's eye, but do not perceive the plank in your own eye? [42]Or how can you say to your brother, 'Brother, let me remove the speck that *is* in your eye,' when you yourself do not see the plank that *is* in

THE MESSAGE

what you hope to get out of it, do you think that's charity? The stingiest of pawnbrokers does that.

"I tell you, love your enemies. Help and give without expecting a return. You'll never—I promise—regret it. Live out this God-created identity the way our Father lives toward us, generously and graciously, even when we're at our worst. Our Father is kind; you be kind.

"Don't pick on people, jump on their failures, criticize their faults—unless, of course, you want the same treatment. Don't condemn those who are down; that hardness can boomerang. Be easy on people; you'll find life a lot easier. Give away your life; you'll find life given back, but not merely given back—given back with bonus and blessing. Giving, not getting, is the way. Generosity begets generosity."

He quoted a proverb: "'Can a blind man guide a blind man?' Wouldn't they both end up in the ditch? An apprentice doesn't lecture the master. The point is to be careful who you follow as your teacher.

"It's easy to see a smudge on your neighbor's face and be oblivious to the ugly sneer on your own. Do you have the nerve to say, 'Let me wash your face for you,' when your own face is distorted by contempt? It's this I-know-better-than-you mentality again, playing a holier-than-thou part

KING JAMES VERSION

hypocrite, cast out first the beam out of thine own eye, and then shalt thou see clearly to pull out the mote that is in thy brother's eye.

43 For a good tree bringeth not forth corrupt fruit; neither doth a corrupt tree bring forth good fruit.

44 For every tree is known by his own fruit. For of thorns men do not gather figs, nor of a bramble bush gather they grapes.

45 A good man out of the good treasure of his heart bringeth forth that which is good; and an evil man out of the evil treasure of his heart bringeth forth that which is evil: for of the abundance of the heart his mouth speaketh.

46 And why call ye me, Lord, Lord, and do not the things which I say?

47 Whosoever cometh to me, and heareth my sayings, and doeth them, I will shew you to whom he is like:

48 He is like a man which built an house, and digged deep, and laid the foundation on a rock: and when the flood arose, the stream beat vehemently upon that house, and could not shake it: for it was founded upon a rock.

49 But he that heareth, and doeth not, is like a man that without a foundation built an house upon the earth; against which the stream did beat vehemently, and immediately it fell; and the ruin of that house was great.

NEW AMERICAN STANDARD BIBLE

first take the log out of your own eye, and then you will see clearly to take out the speck that is in your brother's eye.

43 "For there is no good tree which produces bad fruit, nor, on the other hand, a bad tree which produces good fruit.

44 "For each tree is known by its own fruit. For men do not gather figs from thorns, nor do they pick grapes from a briar bush.

45 "The good man out of the good treasure of his heart brings forth what is good; and the evil *man* out of the evil *treasure* brings forth what is evil; for his mouth speaks from that which fills his heart.

Builders and Foundations

46 "Why do you call Me, 'Lord, Lord,' and do not do what I say?

47 "Everyone who comes to Me and hears My words and acts on them, I will show you whom he is like:

48 he is like a man building a house, who dug deep and laid a foundation on the rock; and when a flood occurred, the torrent burst against that house and could not shake it, because it had been well built.

49 "But the one who has heard and has not acted *accordingly,* is like a man who built a house on the ground without any foundation; and the torrent burst against it and immediately it collapsed, and the ruin of that house was great."

NEW CENTURY VERSION

You hypocrite! First, take the wood out of your own eye. Then you will see clearly to take the dust out of your friend's eye.

Two Kinds of Fruit

43"A good tree does not produce bad fruit, nor does a bad tree produce good fruit. 44Each tree is known by its own fruit. People don't gather figs from thornbushes, and they don't get grapes from bushes. 45Good people bring good things out of the good they stored in their hearts. But evil people bring evil things out of the evil they stored in their hearts. People speak the things that are in their hearts.

Two Kinds of People

46"Why do you call me, 'Lord, Lord,' but do not do what I say? 47I will show you what everyone is like who comes to me and hears my words and obeys. 48That person is like a man building a house who dug deep and laid the foundation on rock. When the floods came, the water tried to wash the house away, but it could not shake it, because the house was built well. 49But the one who hears my words and does not obey is like a man who built his house on the ground without a foundation. When the floods came, the house quickly fell and was completely destroyed."

CONTEMPORARY ENGLISH VERSION

First, get the log out of your own eye. Then you can see how to take the speck out of your friend's eye.

A Tree and Its Fruit (Matthew 7.17-20; 12.34b, 35)

43A good tree cannot produce bad fruit, and a bad tree cannot produce good fruit. 44You can tell what a tree is like by the fruit it produces. You cannot pick figs or grapes from thornbushes. 45Good people do good things because of the good in their hearts. Bad people do bad things because of the evil in their hearts. Your words show what is in your heart.

Two Builders (Matthew 7.24-27)

46Why do you keep on saying that I am your Lord, when you refuse to do what I say? 47Anyone who comes and listens to me and obeys me 48is like someone who dug down deep and built a house on solid rock. When the flood came and the river rushed against the house, it was built so well that it didn't even shake. 49But anyone who hears what I say and doesn't obey me is like someone whose house wasn't built on solid rock. As soon as the river rushed against that house, it was smashed to pieces!

NEW INTERNATIONAL VERSION

the plank out of your eye, and then you will see clearly to remove the speck from your brother's eye.

A Tree and Its Fruit

43"No good tree bears bad fruit, nor does a bad tree bear good fruit. 44Each tree is recognized by its own fruit. People do not pick figs from thornbushes, or grapes from briers. 45The good man brings good things out of the good stored up in his heart, and the evil man brings evil things out of the evil stored up in his heart. For out of the overflow of his heart his mouth speaks.

The Wise and Foolish Builders

46"Why do you call me, 'Lord, Lord,' and do not do what I say? 47I will show you what he is like who comes to me and hears my words and puts them into practice. 48He is like a man building a house, who dug down deep and laid the foundation on rock. When a flood came, the torrent struck that house but could not shake it, because it was well built. 49But the one who hears my words and does not put them into practice is like a man who built a house on the ground without a foundation. The moment the torrent struck that house, it collapsed and its destruction was complete."

NEW LIVING TRANSLATION

eye? Hypocrite! First get rid of the log from your own eye; then perhaps you will see well enough to deal with the speck in your friend's eye.

The Tree and Its Fruit

43"A good tree can't produce bad fruit, and a bad tree can't produce good fruit. 44A tree is identified by the kind of fruit it produces. Figs never grow on thornbushes or grapes on bramble bushes. 45A good person produces good deeds from a good heart, and an evil person produces evil deeds from an evil heart. Whatever is in your heart determines what you say.

Building on a Solid Foundation

46"So why do you call me 'Lord,' when you won't obey me? 47I will show you what it's like when someone comes to me, listens to my teaching, and then obeys me. 48It is like a person who builds a house on a strong foundation laid upon the underlying rock. When the floodwaters rise and break against the house, it stands firm because it is well built. 49But anyone who listens and doesn't obey is like a person who builds a house without a foundation. When the floods sweep down against that house, it will crumble into a heap of ruins."

NEW KING JAMES VERSION

your own eye? Hypocrite! First remove the plank from your own eye, and then you will see clearly to remove the speck that is in your brother's eye.

A Tree Is Known by Its Fruit

43"For a good tree does not bear bad fruit, nor does a bad tree bear good fruit. 44For every tree is known by its own fruit. For *men* do not gather figs from thorns, nor do they gather grapes from a bramble bush. 45A good man out of the good treasure of his heart brings forth good; and an evil man out of the evil treasure of his heart[g] brings forth evil. For out of the abundance of the heart his mouth speaks.

Build on the Rock

46"But why do you call Me 'Lord, Lord,' and not do the things which I say? 47Whoever comes to Me, and hears My sayings and does them, I will show you whom he is like: 48He is like a man building a house, who dug deep and laid the foundation on the rock. And when the flood arose, the stream beat vehemently against that house, and could not shake it, for it was founded on the rock.[h] 49But he who heard and did nothing is like a man who built a house on the earth without a foundation, against which the stream beat vehemently; and immediately it fell.[i] And the ruin of that house was great."

6:45 [g] NU-Text omits *treasure of his heart.* **6:48** [h] NU-Text reads *for it was well built.* **6:49** [i] NU-Text reads *collapsed.*

THE MESSAGE

instead of just living your own part. Wipe that ugly sneer off your own face and you might be fit to offer a washcloth to your neighbor.

Work the Words Into Your Life

"You don't get wormy apples off a healthy tree, nor good apples off a diseased tree. The health of the apple tells the health of the tree. You must begin with your own life-giving lives. It's who you are, not what you say and do, that counts. Your true being brims over into true words and deeds.

"Why are you so polite with me, always saying 'Yes, sir,' and 'That's right, sir,' but never doing a thing I tell you? These words I speak to you are not mere additions to your life, homeowner improvements to your standard of living. They are foundation words, words to build a life on.

"If you work the words into your life, you are like a smart carpenter who dug deep and laid the foundation of his house on bedrock. When the river burst its banks and crashed against the house, nothing could shake it; it was built to last. But if you just use my words in Bible studies and don't work them into your life, you are like a dumb carpenter who built a house but skipped the foundation. When the swollen river came crashing in, it collapsed like a house of cards. It was a total loss."

KING JAMES VERSION

7 Now when he had ended all his sayings in the audience of the people, he entered into Capernaum.

2 And a certain centurion's servant, who was dear unto him, was sick, and ready to die.

3 And when he heard of Jesus, he sent unto him the elders of the Jews, beseeching him that he would come and heal his servant.

4 And when they came to Jesus, they besought him instantly, saying, That he was worthy for whom he should do this:

5 For he loveth our nation, and he hath built us a synagogue.

6 Then Jesus went with them. And when he was now not far from the house, the centurion sent friends to him, saying unto him, Lord, trouble not thyself: for I am not worthy that thou shouldest enter under my roof:

7 Wherefore neither thought I myself worthy to come unto thee: but say in a word, and my servant shall be healed.

8 For I also am a man set under authority, having under me soldiers, and I say unto one, Go, and he goeth; and to another, Come, and he cometh; and to my servant, Do this, and he doeth *it*.

9 When Jesus heard these things, he marvelled at him, and turned him about, and said unto the people that followed him, I say unto you, I have not found so great faith, no, not in Israel.

10 And they that were sent, returning to the house, found the servant whole that had been sick.

NEW AMERICAN STANDARD BIBLE

Jesus Heals a Centurion's Servant

7 When He had completed all His discourse in the hearing of the people, He went to Capernaum.

2 And a centurion's slave, who was highly regarded by him, was sick and about to die.

3 When he heard about Jesus, he sent some Jewish elders asking Him to come and save the life of his slave.

4 When they came to Jesus, they earnestly implored Him, saying, "He is worthy for You to grant this to him;

5 for he loves our nation and it was he who built us our synagogue."

6 Now Jesus *started* on His way with them; and when He was not far from the house, the centurion sent friends, saying to Him, "Lord, do not trouble Yourself further, for I am not worthy for You to come under my roof;

7 for this reason I did not even consider myself worthy to come to You, but *just* say the word, and my servant will be healed.

8 "For I also am a man placed under authority, with soldiers under me; and I say to this one, 'Go!' and he goes, and to another, 'Come!' and he comes, and to my slave, 'Do this!' and he does it."

9 Now when Jesus heard this, He marveled at him, and turned and said to the crowd that was following Him, "I say to you, not even in Israel have I found such great faith."

10 When those who had been sent returned to the house, they found the slave in good health.

NEW CENTURY VERSION

Jesus Heals a Soldier's Servant

7 When Jesus finished saying all these things to the
people, he went to Capernaum. [2]There was an army
officer who had a servant who was very important to him.
The servant was so sick he was nearly dead. [3]When the
officer heard about Jesus, he sent some older Jewish lead-
ers to him to ask Jesus to come and heal his servant. [4]The
men went to Jesus and begged him, saying, "This officer is
worthy of your help. [5]He loves our people, and he built us
a synagogue."
[6]So Jesus went with the men. He was getting near the
officer's house when the officer sent friends to say, "Lord,
don't trouble yourself, because I am not worthy to have
you come into my house. [7]That is why I did not come to
you myself. But you only need to command it, and my ser-
vant will be healed. [8]I, too, am a man under the authority
of others, and I have soldiers under my command. I tell
one soldier, 'Go,' and he goes. I tell another soldier,
'Come,' and he comes. I say to my servant, 'Do this,' and
my servant does it."
[9]When Jesus heard this, he was amazed. Turning to the
crowd that was following him, he said, "I tell you, this is
the greatest faith I have found anywhere, even in Israel."
[10]Those who had been sent to Jesus went back to the
house where they found the servant in good health.

CONTEMPORARY ENGLISH VERSION

Jesus Heals an Army Officer's Servant

(Matthew 8.5-13; John 4.43-54)

7 After Jesus had finished teaching the people, he went
to Capernaum. [2]In that town an army officer's servant
was sick and about to die. The officer liked this servant
very much. [3]And when he heard about Jesus, he sent some
Jewish leaders to ask him to come and heal the servant.
[4]The leaders went to Jesus and begged him to do some-
thing. They said, "This man deserves your help! [5]He loves
our nation and even built us a meeting place." [6]So Jesus
went with them.
When Jesus wasn't far from the house, the officer sent
some friends to tell him, "Lord, don't go to any trouble for
me! I am not good enough for you to come into my house.
[7]And I am certainly not worthy to come to you. Just say
the word, and my servant will get well. [8]I have officers
who give orders to me, and I have soldiers who take orders
from me. I can say to one of them, 'Go!' and he goes. I can
say to another, 'Come!' and he comes. I can say to my ser-
vant, 'Do this!' and he will do it."
[9]When Jesus heard this, he was so surprised that he
turned and said to the crowd following him, "In all of
Israel I've never found anyone with this much faith!"
[10]The officer's friends returned and found the servant
well.

NEW INTERNATIONAL VERSION

The Faith of the Centurion

7 When Jesus had finished saying all this in the hearing of the people, he entered Capernaum. 2There a centurion's servant, whom his master valued highly, was sick and about to die. 3The centurion heard of Jesus and sent some elders of the Jews to him, asking him to come and heal his servant. 4When they came to Jesus, they pleaded earnestly with him, "This man deserves to have you do this, 5because he loves our nation and has built our synagogue." 6So Jesus went with them.

He was not far from the house when the centurion sent friends to say to him: "Lord, don't trouble yourself, for I do not deserve to have you come under my roof. 7That is why I did not even consider myself worthy to come to you. But say the word, and my servant will be healed. 8For I myself am a man under authority, with soldiers under me. I tell this one, 'Go,' and he goes; and that one, 'Come,' and he comes. I say to my servant, 'Do this,' and he does it."

9When Jesus heard this, he was amazed at him, and turning to the crowd following him, he said, "I tell you, I have not found such great faith even in Israel." 10Then the men who had been sent returned to the house and found the servant well.

NEW LIVING TRANSLATION

Faith of the Roman Officer

7 When Jesus had finished saying all this, he went back to Capernaum. 2Now the highly valued slave of a Roman officer was sick and near death. 3When the officer heard about Jesus, he sent some respected Jewish leaders to ask him to come and heal his slave. 4So they earnestly begged Jesus to come with them and help the man. "If anyone deserves your help, it is he," they said, 5"for he loves the Jews and even built a synagogue for us."

6So Jesus went with them. But just before they arrived at the house, the officer sent some friends to say, "Lord, don't trouble yourself by coming to my home, for I am not worthy of such an honor. 7I am not even worthy to come and meet you. Just say the word from where you are, and my servant will be healed. 8I know because I am under the authority of my superior officers, and I have authority over my soldiers. I only need to say, 'Go,' and they go, or 'Come,' and they come. And if I say to my slaves, 'Do this or that,' they do it."

9When Jesus heard this, he was amazed. Turning to the crowd, he said, "I tell you, I haven't seen faith like this in all the land of Israel!" 10And when the officer's friends returned to his house, they found the slave completely healed.

NEW KING JAMES VERSION

Jesus Heals a Centurion's Servant

7 Now when He concluded all His sayings in the hearing of the people, He entered Capernaum. 2And a certain centurion's servant, who was dear to him, was sick and ready to die. 3So when he heard about Jesus, he sent elders of the Jews to Him, pleading with Him to come and heal his servant. 4And when they came to Jesus, they begged Him earnestly, saying that the one for whom He should do this was deserving, 5"for he loves our nation, and has built us a synagogue."

6Then Jesus went with them. And when He was already not far from the house, the centurion sent friends to Him, saying to Him, "Lord, do not trouble Yourself, for I am not worthy that You should enter under my roof. 7Therefore I did not even think myself worthy to come to You. But say the word, and my servant will be healed. 8For I also am a man placed under authority, having soldiers under me. And I say to one, 'Go,' and he goes; and to another, 'Come,' and he comes; and to my servant, 'Do this,' and he does *it*."

9When Jesus heard these things, He marveled at him, and turned around and said to the crowd that followed Him, "I say to you, I have not found such great faith, not even in Israel!" 10And those who were sent, returning to the house, found the servant well who had been sick.[a]

7:10 [a] NU-Text omits *who had been sick.*

THE MESSAGE

A Place of Holy Mystery

7 When he finished speaking to the people, he entered Capernaum. A Roman captain there had a servant who was on his deathbed. He prized him highly and didn't want to lose him. When he heard Jesus was back, he sent leaders from the Jewish community asking him to come and heal his servant. They came to Jesus and urged him to do it, saying, "He deserves this. He loves our people. He even built our meeting place."

Jesus went with them. When he was still quite far from the house, the captain sent friends to tell him, "Master, you don't have to go to all this trouble. I'm not that good a person, you know. I'd be embarrassed for you to come to my house, even embarrassed to come to you in person. Just give the order and my servant will get well. I'm a man under orders; I also give orders. I tell one soldier, 'Go,' and he goes; another, 'Come,' and he comes; my slave, 'Do this,' and he does it."

Taken aback, Jesus addressed the accompanying crowd: "I've yet to come across this kind of simple trust anywhere in Israel, the very people who are supposed to know about God and how he works." When the messengers got back home, they found the servant up and well.

KING JAMES VERSION

11 ¶ And it came to pass the day after, that he went into a city called Nain; and many of his disciples went with him, and much people.

12 Now when he came nigh to the gate of the city, behold, there was a dead man carried out, the only son of his mother, and she was a widow: and much people of the city was with her.

13 And when the Lord saw her, he had compassion on her, and said unto her, Weep not.

14 And he came and touched the bier: and they that bare *him* stood still. And he said, Young man, I say unto thee, Arise.

15 And he that was dead sat up, and began to speak. And he delivered him to his mother.

16 And there came a fear on all: and they glorified God, saying, That a great prophet is risen up among us; and, That God hath visited his people.

17 And this rumour of him went forth throughout all Judaea, and throughout all the region round about.

18 And the disciples of John shewed him of all these things.

19 ¶ And John calling *unto him* two of his disciples sent *them* to Jesus, saying, Art thou he that should come? or look we for another?

20 When the men were come unto him, they said, John Baptist hath sent us unto thee, saying, Art thou he that should come? or look we for another?

NEW AMERICAN STANDARD BIBLE

11 Soon afterwards He went to a city called Nain; and His disciples were going along with Him, accompanied by a large crowd.

12 Now as He approached the gate of the city, a dead man was being carried out, the only son of his mother, and she was a widow; and a sizeable crowd from the city was with her.

13 When the Lord saw her, He felt compassion for her, and said to her, "Do not weep."

14 And He came up and touched the coffin; and the bearers came to a halt. And He said, "Young man, I say to you, arise!"

15 The dead man sat up and began to speak. And *Jesus* gave him back to his mother.

16 Fear gripped them all, and they *began* glorifying God, saying, "A great prophet has arisen among us!" and, "God has visited His people!"

17 This report concerning Him went out all over Judea and in all the surrounding district.

A Deputation from John

18 The disciples of John reported to him about all these things.

19 Summoning two of his disciples, John sent them to the Lord, saying, "Are You the Expected One, or do we look for someone else?"

20 When the men came to Him, they said, "John the Baptist has sent us to You, to ask, 'Are You the Expected One, or do we look for someone else?' "

NEW CENTURY VERSION

Jesus Brings a Man Back to Life

11 Soon afterwards Jesus went to a town called Nain, and
his followers and a large crowd traveled with him. 12 When
he came near the town gate, he saw a funeral. A mother,
who was a widow, had lost her only son. A large crowd
from the town was with the mother while her son was
being carried out. 13 When the Lord saw her, he felt very
sorry for her and said, "Don't cry." 14 He went up and
touched the coffin, and the people who were carrying it
stopped. Jesus said, "Young man, I tell you, get up!" 15 And
the son sat up and began to talk. Then Jesus gave him
back to his mother.

16 All the people were amazed and began praising God,
saying, "A great prophet has come to us! God has come to
help his people."

17 This news about Jesus spread through all Judea and
into all the places around there.

John Asks a Question

18 John's followers told him about all these things. He
called for two of his followers 19 and sent them to the Lord
to ask, "Are you the One who is to come, or should we wait
for someone else?"

20 When the men came to Jesus, they said, "John the
Baptist sent us to you with this question: 'Are you the One
who is to come, or should we wait for someone else?' "

CONTEMPORARY ENGLISH VERSION

A Widow's Son

11 Soon Jesus and his disciples were on their way to the
town of Nain, and a big crowd was going along with them.
12 As they came near the gate of the town, they saw people
carrying out the body of a widow's only son. Many people
from the town were walking along with her.

13 When the Lord saw the woman, he felt sorry for her
and said, "Don't cry!"

14 Jesus went over and touched the stretcher on which
the people were carrying the dead boy. They stopped, and
Jesus said, "Young man, get up!" 15 The boy sat up and
began to speak. Jesus then gave him back to his mother.

16 Everyone was frightened and praised God. They said, "A
great prophet is here with us! God has come to his people."

17 News about Jesus spread all over Judea and every-
where else in that part of the country.

John the Baptist (Matthew 11.1-19)

18-19 John's followers told John everything that was being
said about Jesus. So he sent two of them to ask the Lord,
"Are you the one we should be looking for? Or must we
wait for someone else?"

20 When these messengers came to Jesus, they said,
"John the Baptist sent us to ask, 'Are you the one we
should be looking for? Or are we supposed to wait for
someone else?' "

NEW INTERNATIONAL VERSION

Jesus Raises a Widow's Son

11 Soon afterward, Jesus went to a town called Nain, and his disciples and a large crowd went along with him. 12 As he approached the town gate, a dead person was being carried out—the only son of his mother, and she was a widow. And a large crowd from the town was with her. 13 When the Lord saw her, his heart went out to her and he said, "Don't cry."

14 Then he went up and touched the coffin, and those carrying it stood still. He said, "Young man, I say to you, get up!" 15 The dead man sat up and began to talk, and Jesus gave him back to his mother.

16 They were all filled with awe and praised God. "A great prophet has appeared among us," they said. "God has come to help his people." 17 This news about Jesus spread throughout Judea[a] and the surrounding country.

Jesus and John the Baptist

18 John's disciples told him about all these things. Calling two of them, 19 he sent them to the Lord to ask, "Are you the one who was to come, or should we expect someone else?"

20 When the men came to Jesus, they said, "John the Baptist sent us to you to ask, 'Are you the one who was to come, or should we expect someone else?' "

[a] *17* Or *the land of the Jews*

NEW LIVING TRANSLATION

Jesus Raises a Widow's Son

11 Soon afterward Jesus went with his disciples to the village of Nain, with a great crowd following him. 12 A funeral procession was coming out as he approached the village gate. The boy who had died was the only son of a widow, and many mourners from the village were with her. 13 When the Lord saw her, his heart overflowed with compassion. "Don't cry!" he said. 14 Then he walked over to the coffin and touched it, and the bearers stopped. "Young man," he said, "get up." 15 Then the dead boy sat up and began to talk to those around him! And Jesus gave him back to his mother.

16 Great fear swept the crowd, and they praised God, saying, "A mighty prophet has risen among us," and "We have seen the hand of God at work today." 17 The report of what Jesus had done that day spread all over Judea and even out across its borders.

Jesus and John the Baptist

18 The disciples of John the Baptist told John about everything Jesus was doing. So John called for two of his disciples, 19 and he sent them to the Lord to ask him, "Are you the Messiah we've been expecting, or should we keep looking for someone else?"

20 John's two disciples found Jesus and said to him, "John the Baptist sent us to ask, 'Are you the Messiah we've been expecting, or should we keep looking for someone else?' "

NEW KING JAMES VERSION

Jesus Raises the Son of the Widow of Nain

11 Now it happened, the day after, *that* He went into a city called Nain; and many of His disciples went with Him, and a large crowd. 12 And when He came near the gate of the city, behold, a dead man was being carried out, the only son of his mother; and she was a widow. And a large crowd from the city was with her. 13 When the Lord saw her, He had compassion on her and said to her, "Do not weep." 14 Then He came and touched the open coffin, and those who carried *him* stood still. And He said, "Young man, I say to you, arise." 15 So he who was dead sat up and began to speak. And He presented him to his mother.

16 Then fear came upon all, and they glorified God, saying, "A great prophet has risen up among us"; and, "God has visited His people." 17 And this report about Him went throughout all Judea and all the surrounding region.

John the Baptist Sends Messengers to Jesus

18 Then the disciples of John reported to him concerning all these things. 19 And John, calling two of his disciples to *him,* sent *them* to Jesus,[b] saying, "Are You the Coming One, or do we look for another?"

20 When the men had come to Him, they said, "John the Baptist has sent us to You, saying, 'Are You the Coming One, or do we look for another?' " 21 And that very hour He

7:19 [b] NU-Text reads *the Lord.*

THE MESSAGE

Not long after that, Jesus went to the village Nain. His disciples were with him, along with quite a large crowd. As they approached the village gate, they met a funeral procession—a woman's only son was being carried out for burial. And the mother was a widow. When Jesus saw her, his heart broke. He said to her, "Don't cry." Then he went over and touched the coffin. The pallbearers stopped. He said, "Young man, I tell you: Get up." The dead son sat up and began talking. Jesus presented him to his mother.

They all realized they were in a place of holy mystery, that God was at work among them. They were quietly worshipful—and then noisily grateful, calling out among themselves, "God is back, looking to the needs of his people!" The news of Jesus spread all through the country.

Is This What You Were Expecting?

John's disciples reported back to him the news of all these events taking place. He sent two of them to the Master to ask the question, "Are you the One we've been expecting, or are we still waiting?"

The men showed up before Jesus and said, "John the Baptizer sent us to ask you, 'Are you the One we've been expecting, or are we still waiting?' "

KING JAMES VERSION

21 And in that same hour he cured many of *their* infirmities and plagues, and of evil spirits; and unto many *that were* blind he gave sight.

22 Then Jesus answering said unto them, Go your way, and tell John what things ye have seen and heard; how that the blind see, the lame walk, the lepers are cleansed, the deaf hear, the dead are raised, to the poor the gospel is preached.

23 And blessed is *he*, whosoever shall not be offended in me.

24 And when the messengers of John were departed, he began to speak unto the people concerning John, What went ye out into the wilderness for to see? A reed shaken with the wind?

25 But what went ye out for to see? A man clothed in soft raiment? Behold, they which are gorgeously apparelled, and live delicately, are in kings' courts.

26 But what went ye out for to see? A prophet? Yea, I say unto you, and much more than a prophet.

27 This is *he*, of whom it is written, Behold, I send my messenger before thy face, which shall prepare thy way before thee.

28 For I say unto you, Among those that are born of women there is not a greater prophet than John the Baptist: but he that is least in the kingdom of God is greater than he.

NEW AMERICAN STANDARD BIBLE

21 At that very time He cured many *people* of diseases and afflictions and evil spirits; and He gave sight to many *who were* blind.

22 And He answered and said to them, "Go and report to John what you have seen and heard: *the* BLIND RECEIVE SIGHT, *the* lame walk, *the* lepers are cleansed, and *the* deaf hear, *the* dead are raised up, *the* POOR HAVE THE GOSPEL PREACHED TO THEM.

23 "Blessed is he who does not take offense at Me."

24 When the messengers of John had left, He began to speak to the crowds about John, "What did you go out into the wilderness to see? A reed shaken by the wind?

25 "But what did you go out to see? A man dressed in soft clothing? Those who are splendidly clothed and live in luxury are *found* in royal palaces!

26 "But what did you go out to see? A prophet? Yes, I say to you, and one who is more than a prophet.

27 "This is the one about whom it is written,

'BEHOLD, I SEND MY MESSENGER AHEAD OF YOU,
WHO WILL PREPARE YOUR WAY BEFORE YOU.'

28 "I say to you, among those born of women there is no one greater than John; yet he who is least in the kingdom of God is greater than he."

NEW CENTURY VERSION

21 At that time, Jesus healed many people of their sicknesses, diseases, and evil spirits, and he gave sight to many blind people. 22 Then Jesus answered John's followers, "Go tell John what you saw and heard here. The blind can see, the crippled can walk, and people with skin diseases are healed. The deaf can hear, the dead are raised to life, and the Good News is preached to the poor. 23 Those who do not stumble in their faith because of me are blessed!"

24 When John's followers left, Jesus began talking to the people about John: "What did you go out into the desert to see? A reed[a] blown by the wind? 25 What did you go out to see? A man dressed in fine clothes? No, people who have fine clothes and much wealth live in kings' palaces. 26 But what did you go out to see? A prophet? Yes, and I tell you, John is more than a prophet. 27 This was written about him:

'I will send my messenger ahead of you,
who will prepare the way for you.' *Malachi 3:1*

28 I tell you, John is greater than any other person ever born, but even the least important person in the kingdom of God is greater than John."

7:24 [a] **reed** It means that John was not ordinary or weak like grass blown by the wind.

CONTEMPORARY ENGLISH VERSION

21 At that time Jesus was healing many people who were sick or in pain or were troubled by evil spirits, and he was giving sight to a lot of blind people. 22 Jesus said to the messengers sent by John, "Go and tell John what you have seen and heard. Blind people are now able to see, and the lame can walk. People who have leprosy[a] are being healed, and the deaf can now hear. The dead are raised to life, and the poor are hearing the good news. 23 God will bless everyone who doesn't reject me because of what I do."

24 After John's messengers had gone, Jesus began speaking to the crowds about John:

What kind of person did you go out to the desert to see? Was he like tall grass blown about by the wind? 25 What kind of man did you really go out to see? Was he someone dressed in fine clothes? People who wear expensive clothes and live in luxury are in the king's palace. 26 What then did you go out to see? Was he a prophet? He certainly was! I tell you that he was more than a prophet. 27 In the Scriptures, God calls John his messenger and says, "I am sending my messenger ahead of you to get things ready for you." 28 No one ever born on this earth is greater than John. But whoever is least important in God's kingdom is greater than John.

[a] 7.22 *leprosy*: See the note at 4.27.

NEW INTERNATIONAL VERSION

[21]At that very time Jesus cured many who had diseases, sicknesses and evil spirits, and gave sight to many who were blind. [22]So he replied to the messengers, "Go back and report to John what you have seen and heard: The blind receive sight, the lame walk, those who have leprosy[b] are cured, the deaf hear, the dead are raised, and the good news is preached to the poor. [23]Blessed is the man who does not fall away on account of me."

[24]After John's messengers left, Jesus began to speak to the crowd about John: "What did you go out into the desert to see? A reed swayed by the wind? [25]If not, what did you go out to see? A man dressed in fine clothes? No, those who wear expensive clothes and indulge in luxury are in palaces. [26]But what did you go out to see? A prophet? Yes, I tell you, and more than a prophet. [27]This is the one about whom it is written:

" 'I will send my messenger ahead of you,
who will prepare your way before you.'[c]

[28]I tell you, among those born of women there is no one greater than John; yet the one who is least in the kingdom of God is greater than he."

[b] *22* The Greek word was used for various diseases affecting the skin—not necessarily leprosy. [c] *27* Mal. 3:1

NEW LIVING TRANSLATION

[21]At that very time, he cured many people of their various diseases, and he cast out evil spirits and restored sight to the blind. [22]Then he told John's disciples, "Go back to John and tell him what you have seen and heard—the blind see, the lame walk, the lepers are cured, the deaf hear, the dead are raised to life, and the Good News is being preached to the poor. [23]And tell him, 'God blesses those who are not offended by me.*' "

[24]After they left, Jesus talked to the crowd about John. "Who is this man in the wilderness that you went out to see? Did you find him weak as a reed, moved by every breath of wind? [25]Or were you expecting to see a man dressed in expensive clothes? No, people who wear beautiful clothes and live in luxury are found in palaces, not in the wilderness. [26]Were you looking for a prophet? Yes, and he is more than a prophet. [27]John is the man to whom the Scriptures refer when they say,

'Look, I am sending my messenger before you,
and he will prepare your way before you.'*

[28]I tell you, of all who have ever lived, none is greater than John. Yet even the most insignificant person in the Kingdom of God is greater than he is!"

7:23 Or *who don't fall away because of me.* 7:27 Mal 3:1.

NEW KING JAMES VERSION

cured many of infirmities, afflictions, and evil spirits; and to many blind He gave sight.

[22]Jesus answered and said to them, "Go and tell John the things you have seen and heard: that *the* blind see, *the* lame walk, *the* lepers are cleansed, *the* deaf hear, *the* dead are raised, *the* poor have the gospel preached to them. [23]And blessed is *he* who is not offended because of Me."

[24]When the messengers of John had departed, He began to speak to the multitudes concerning John: "What did you go out into the wilderness to see? A reed shaken by the wind? [25]But what did you go out to see? A man clothed in soft garments? Indeed those who are gorgeously appareled and live in luxury are in kings' courts. [26]But what did you go out to see? A prophet? Yes, I say to you, and more than a prophet. [27]This is *he* of whom it is written:

'Behold, I send My messenger before Your face,
Who will prepare Your way before You.'[c]

[28]For I say to you, among those born of women there is not a greater prophet than John the Baptist;[d] but he who is least in the kingdom of God is greater than he."

7:27 [c] Malachi 3:1 7:28 [d] NU-Text reads *there is none greater than John.*

THE MESSAGE

In the next two or three hours Jesus healed many from diseases, distress, and evil spirits. To many of the blind he gave the gift of sight. Then he gave his answer: "Go back and tell John what you have just seen and heard:

The blind see,
The lame walk,
Lepers are cleansed,
The deaf hear,
The dead are raised,
The wretched of the earth
have God's salvation hospitality extended to them.

Is this what you were expecting? Then count yourselves fortunate!"

After John's messengers left to make their report, Jesus said more about John to the crowd of people. "What did you expect when you went out to see him in the wild? A weekend camper? Hardly. What then? A sheik in silk pajamas? Not in the wilderness, not by a long shot. What then? A messenger from God? That's right, a messenger! Probably the greatest messenger you'll ever hear. He is the messenger Malachi announced when he wrote,

'I'm sending my messenger on ahead
To make the road smooth for you.'

"Let me lay it out for you as plainly as I can: No one in history surpasses John the Baptizer, but in the kingdom he prepared you for, the lowliest person is ahead of him. The

KING JAMES VERSION

29 And all the people that heard *him*, and the publicans, justified God, being baptized with the baptism of John.

30 But the Pharisees and lawyers rejected the counsel of God against themselves, being not baptized of him.

31 And the Lord said, Whereunto then shall I liken the men of this generation? and to what are they like?

32 They are like unto children sitting in the marketplace, and calling one to another, and saying, We have piped unto you, and ye have not danced; we have mourned to you, and ye have not wept.

33 For John the Baptist came neither eating bread nor drinking wine; and ye say, He hath a devil.

34 The Son of man is come eating and drinking; and ye say, Behold a gluttonous man, and a winebibber, a friend of publicans and sinners!

35 But wisdom is justified of all her children.

36 ¶ And one of the Pharisees desired him that he would eat with him. And he went into the Pharisee's house, and sat down to meat.

NEW AMERICAN STANDARD BIBLE

29 When all the people and the tax collectors heard *this,* they acknowledged God's justice, having been baptized with the baptism of John.

30 But the Pharisees and the [1]lawyers rejected God's purpose for themselves, not having been baptized by John.

31 "To what then shall I compare the men of this generation, and what are they like?

32 "They are like children who sit in the market place and call to one another, and they say, 'We played the flute for you, and you did not dance; we sang a dirge, and you did not weep.'

33 "For John the Baptist has come eating no bread and drinking no wine, and you say, 'He has a demon!'

34 "The Son of Man has come eating and drinking, and you say, 'Behold, a gluttonous man and a drunkard, a friend of tax collectors and sinners!'

35 "Yet wisdom is vindicated by all her children."

36 Now one of the Pharisees was requesting Him to dine with him, and He entered the Pharisee's house and reclined *at the table.*

7:30 [1] I.e. experts in the Mosaic Law

NEW CENTURY VERSION

29(When the people, including the tax collectors, heard this, they all agreed that God's teaching was good, because they had been baptized by John. 30But the Pharisees and experts on the law refused to accept God's plan for themselves; they did not let John baptize them.)

31Then Jesus said, "What shall I say about the people of this time? What are they like? 32They are like children sitting in the marketplace, calling to one another and saying,

'We played music for you, but you did not dance;
we sang a sad song, but you did not cry.'

33John the Baptist came and did not eat bread or drink wine, and you say, 'He has a demon in him.' 34The Son of Man came eating and drinking, and you say, 'Look at him! He eats too much and drinks too much wine, and he is a friend of tax collectors and sinners!' 35But wisdom is proved to be right by what it does."

A Woman Washes Jesus' Feet

36One of the Pharisees asked Jesus to eat with him, so Jesus went into the Pharisee's house and sat at the table.

CONTEMPORARY ENGLISH VERSION

29Everyone had been listening to John. Even the tax collectors[b] had obeyed God and had done what was right by letting John baptize them. 30But the Pharisees and the experts in the Law of Moses refused to obey God and be baptized by John.

31Jesus went on to say:

What are you people like? What kind of people are you? 32You are like children sitting in the market and shouting to each other,

"We played the flute,
but you would not dance!
We sang a funeral song,
but you would not cry!"

33John the Baptist did not go around eating and drinking, and you said, "John has a demon in him!" 34But because the Son of Man goes around eating and drinking, you say, "Jesus eats and drinks too much! He is even a friend of tax collectors and sinners." 35Yet Wisdom is shown to be right by what its followers do.

Simon the Pharisee

36A Pharisee invited Jesus to have dinner with him. So Jesus went to the Pharisee's home and got ready to eat.[c]

[b] 7.29 *tax collectors*: See the note at 3.12. [c] 7.36 *got ready to eat*: On special occasions the Jewish people often followed the Greek and Roman custom of lying down on their left side and leaning on their left elbow, while eating with their right hand. This is how the woman could come up behind Jesus and wash his feet (see verse 38).

NEW INTERNATIONAL VERSION

29(All the people, even the tax collectors, when they heard Jesus' words, acknowledged that God's way was right, because they had been baptized by John. 30But the Pharisees and experts in the law rejected God's purpose for themselves, because they had not been baptized by John.)

31"To what, then, can I compare the people of this generation? What are they like? 32They are like children sitting in the marketplace and calling out to each other:

" 'We played the flute for you,
and you did not dance;
we sang a dirge,
and you did not cry.'

33For John the Baptist came neither eating bread nor drinking wine, and you say, 'He has a demon.' 34The Son of Man came eating and drinking, and you say, 'Here is a glutton and a drunkard, a friend of tax collectors and "sinners." ' 35But wisdom is proved right by all her children."

Jesus Anointed by a Sinful Woman

36Now one of the Pharisees invited Jesus to have dinner with him, so he went to the Pharisee's house and reclined

NEW LIVING TRANSLATION

29When they heard this, all the people, including the unjust tax collectors, agreed that God's plan was right,* for they had been baptized by John. 30But the Pharisees and experts in religious law had rejected God's plan for them, for they had refused John's baptism.

31"How shall I describe this generation?" Jesus asked. "With what will I compare them? 32They are like a group of children playing a game in the public square. They complain to their friends, 'We played wedding songs, and you weren't happy, so we played funeral songs, but you weren't sad.' 33For John the Baptist didn't drink wine and he often fasted, and you say, 'He's demon possessed.' 34And I, the Son of Man, feast and drink, and you say, 'He's a glutton and a drunkard, and a friend of the worst sort of sinners!' 35But wisdom is shown to be right by the lives of those who follow it.*"

Jesus Anointed by a Sinful Woman

36One of the Pharisees asked Jesus to come to his home for a meal, so Jesus accepted the invitation and sat down

7:29 Or *praised God.* 7:35 Or *But wisdom is justified by all her children.*

NEW KING JAMES VERSION

29And when all the people heard *Him,* even the tax collectors justified God, having been baptized with the baptism of John. 30But the Pharisees and lawyers rejected the will of God for themselves, not having been baptized by him.

31And the Lord said,[e] "To what then shall I liken the men of this generation, and what are they like? 32They are like children sitting in the marketplace and calling to one another, saying:

'We played the flute for you,
And you did not dance;
We mourned to you,
And you did not weep.'

33For John the Baptist came neither eating bread nor drinking wine, and you say, 'He has a demon.' 34The Son of Man has come eating and drinking, and you say, 'Look, a glutton and a winebibber, a friend of tax collectors and sinners!' 35But wisdom is justified by all her children."

A Sinful Woman Forgiven

36Then one of the Pharisees asked Him to eat with him. And He went to the Pharisee's house, and sat down to eat.

7:31 [e] NU-Text and M-Text omit *And the Lord said.*

THE MESSAGE

ordinary and disreputable people who heard John, by being baptized by him into the kingdom, are the clearest evidence; the Pharisees and religious officials would have nothing to do with such a baptism, wouldn't think of giving up their place in line to their inferiors.

"How can I account for the people of this generation? They're like spoiled children complaining to their parents, 'We wanted to skip rope and you were always too tired; we wanted to talk but you were always too busy.' John the Baptizer came fasting and you called him crazy. The Son of Man came feasting and you called him a lush. Opinion polls don't count for much, do they? The proof of the pudding is in the eating."

Anointing His Feet

One of the Pharisees asked him over for a meal. He went to the Pharisee's house and sat down at the dinner table.

KING JAMES VERSION

37 And, behold, a woman in the city, which was a sin-
ner, when she knew that *Jesus* sat at meat in the
Pharisee's house, brought an alabaster box of ointment,
38 And stood at his feet behind *him* weeping, and
began to wash his feet with tears, and did wipe *them* with
the hairs of her head, and kissed his feet, and anointed
them with the ointment.
39 Now when the Pharisee which had bidden him saw
it, he spake within himself, saying, This man, if he were a
prophet, would have known who and what manner of
woman *this is* that toucheth him: for she is a sinner.
40 And Jesus answering said unto him, Simon, I have
somewhat to say unto thee. And he saith, Master, say on.
41 There was a certain creditor which had two debtors:
the one owed five hundred pence, and the other fifty.
42 And when they had nothing to pay, he frankly for-
gave them both. Tell me therefore, which of them will love
him most?
43 Simon answered and said, I suppose that *he*, to
whom he forgave most. And he said unto him, Thou hast
rightly judged.
44 And he turned to the woman, and said unto Simon,
Seest thou this woman? I entered into thine house, thou
gavest me no water for my feet: but she hath washed my
feet with tears, and wiped *them* with the hairs of her head.

NEW AMERICAN STANDARD BIBLE

37 And there was a woman in the city who was a sinner;
and when she learned that He was reclining *at the table* in
the Pharisee's house, she brought an alabaster vial of per-
fume,
38 and standing behind *Him* at His feet, weeping, she
began to wet His feet with her tears, and kept wiping them
with the hair of her head, and kissing His feet and anoint-
ing them with the perfume.
39 Now when the Pharisee who had invited Him saw
this, he said to himself, "If this man were a prophet He
would know who and what sort of person this woman is
who is touching Him, that she is a sinner."

Parable of Two Debtors

40 And Jesus answered him, "Simon, I have something
to say to you." And he replied, "Say it, Teacher."
41 "A moneylender had two debtors: one owed five hun-
dred [2]denarii, and the other fifty.
42 "When they were unable to repay, he graciously for-
gave them both. So which of them will love him more?"
43 Simon answered and said, "I suppose the one whom
he forgave more." And He said to him, "You have judged
correctly."
44 Turning toward the woman, He said to Simon, "Do
you see this woman? I entered your house; you gave Me no
water for My feet, but she has wet My feet with her tears
and wiped them with her hair.

7:41 [2] The denarius was equivalent to a day's wages

NEW CENTURY VERSION

37A sinful woman in the town learned that Jesus was eat-
ing at the Pharisee's house. So she brought an alabaster
jar of perfume 38and stood behind Jesus at his feet, crying.
She began to wash his feet with her tears, and she dried
them with her hair, kissing them many times and rubbing
them with the perfume. 39When the Pharisee who asked
Jesus to come to his house saw this, he thought to himself,
"If Jesus were a prophet, he would know that the woman
touching him is a sinner!"
40Jesus said to the Pharisee, "Simon, I have something
to say to you."
Simon said, "Teacher, tell me."
41Jesus said, "Two people owed money to the same
banker. One owed five hundred coins[b] and the other owed
fifty. 42They had no money to pay what they owed, but the
banker told both of them they did not have to pay him.
Which person will love the banker more?"
43Simon, the Pharisee, answered, "I think it would be
the one who owed him the most money."
Jesus said to Simon, "You are right." 44Then Jesus
turned toward the woman and said to Simon, "Do you see
this woman? When I came into your house, you gave me
no water for my feet, but she washed my feet with her
tears and dried them with her hair. 45You gave me no kiss

7:41 [b] **coins** Roman denarii. One coin was the average pay for one day's work.

CONTEMPORARY ENGLISH VERSION

37When a sinful woman in that town found out that
Jesus was there, she bought an expensive bottle of per-
fume. 38Then she came and stood behind Jesus. She cried
and started washing his feet with her tears and drying
them with her hair. The woman kissed his feet and poured
the perfume on them.
39The Pharisee who had invited Jesus saw this and said
to himself, "If this man really were a prophet, he would
know what kind of woman is touching him! He would
know that she is a sinner."
40Jesus said to the Pharisee, "Simon, I have something
to say to you."
"Teacher, what is it?" Simon replied.
41Jesus told him, "Two people were in debt to a money-
lender. One of them owed him five hundred silver coins,
and the other owed him fifty. 42Since neither of them could
pay him back, the moneylender said that they didn't have
to pay him anything. Which one of them will like him
more?"
43Simon answered, "I suppose it would be the one who
had owed more and didn't have to pay it back."
"You are right," Jesus said.
44He turned toward the woman and said to Simon,
"Have you noticed this woman? When I came into your
home, you didn't give me any water so I could wash my
feet. But she has washed my feet with her tears and dried
them with her hair. 45You didn't greet me with a kiss, but

NEW INTERNATIONAL VERSION

at the table. 37When a woman who had lived a sinful life in that town learned that Jesus was eating at the Pharisee's house, she brought an alabaster jar of perfume, 38and as she stood behind him at his feet weeping, she began to wet his feet with her tears. Then she wiped them with her hair, kissed them and poured perfume on them.

39When the Pharisee who had invited him saw this, he said to himself, "If this man were a prophet, he would know who is touching him and what kind of woman she is—that she is a sinner."

40Jesus answered him, "Simon, I have something to tell you."

"Tell me, teacher," he said.

41"Two men owed money to a certain moneylender. One owed him five hundred denarii,[d] and the other fifty. 42Neither of them had the money to pay him back, so he canceled the debts of both. Now which of them will love him more?"

43Simon replied, "I suppose the one who had the bigger debt canceled."

"You have judged correctly," Jesus said.

44Then he turned toward the woman and said to Simon, "Do you see this woman? I came into your house. You did not give me any water for my feet, but she wet my feet with her tears and wiped them with her hair. 45You did not

d 41 A denarius was a coin worth about a day's wages.

NEW LIVING TRANSLATION

to eat. 37A certain immoral woman heard he was there and brought a beautiful jar* filled with expensive perfume. 38Then she knelt behind him at his feet, weeping. Her tears fell on his feet, and she wiped them off with her hair. Then she kept kissing his feet and putting perfume on them.

39When the Pharisee who was the host saw what was happening and who the woman was, he said to himself, "This proves that Jesus is no prophet. If God had really sent him, he would know what kind of woman is touching him. She's a sinner!"

40Then Jesus spoke up and answered his thoughts. "Simon," he said to the Pharisee, "I have something to say to you."

"All right, Teacher," Simon replied, "go ahead."

41Then Jesus told him this story: "A man loaned money to two people—five hundred pieces of silver* to one and fifty pieces to the other. 42But neither of them could repay him, so he kindly forgave them both, canceling their debts. Who do you suppose loved him more after that?"

43Simon answered, "I suppose the one for whom he canceled the larger debt."

"That's right," Jesus said. 44Then he turned to the woman and said to Simon, "Look at this woman kneeling here. When I entered your home, you didn't offer me water to wash the dust from my feet, but she has washed them with her tears and wiped them with her hair. 45You didn't

7:37 Greek *an alabaster jar.* **7:41** Greek *500 denarii.* A denarius was the equivalent of a full day's wage.

NEW KING JAMES VERSION

37And behold, a woman in the city who was a sinner, when she knew that *Jesus* sat at the table in the Pharisee's house, brought an alabaster flask of fragrant oil, 38and stood at His feet behind *Him* weeping; and she began to wash His feet with her tears, and wiped *them* with the hair of her head; and she kissed His feet and anointed *them* with the fragrant oil. 39Now when the Pharisee who had invited Him saw *this,* he spoke to himself, saying, "This Man, if He were a prophet, would know who and what manner of woman *this is* who is touching Him, for she is a sinner."

40And Jesus answered and said to him, "Simon, I have something to say to you."

So he said, "Teacher, say it."

41"There was a certain creditor who had two debtors. One owed five hundred denarii, and the other fifty. 42And when they had nothing with which to repay, he freely forgave them both. Tell Me, therefore, which of them will love him more?"

43Simon answered and said, "I suppose the *one* whom he forgave more."

And He said to him, "You have rightly judged." 44Then He turned to the woman and said to Simon, "Do you see this woman? I entered your house; you gave Me no water for My feet, but she has washed My feet with her tears and wiped *them* with the hair of her head. 45You gave Me no

THE MESSAGE

Just then a woman of the village, the town harlot, having learned that Jesus was a guest in the home of the Pharisee, came with a bottle of very expensive perfume and stood at his feet, weeping, raining tears on his feet. Letting down her hair, she dried his feet, kissed them, and anointed them with the perfume. When the Pharisee who had invited him saw this, he said to himself, "If this man was the prophet I thought he was, he would have known what kind of woman this is who is falling all over him."

Jesus said to him, "Simon, I have something to tell you."

"Oh? Tell me."

"Two men were in debt to a banker. One owed five hundred silver pieces, the other fifty. Neither of them could pay up, and so the banker canceled both debts. Which of the two would be more grateful?"

Simon answered, "I suppose the one who was forgiven the most."

"That's right," said Jesus. Then turning to the woman, but speaking to Simon, he said, "Do you see this woman? I came to your home; you provided no water for my feet, but she rained tears on my feet and dried them with her hair.

KING JAMES VERSION

45 Thou gavest me no kiss: but this woman since the time I came in hath not ceased to kiss my feet.

46 My head with oil thou didst not anoint: but this woman hath anointed my feet with ointment.

47 Wherefore I say unto thee, Her sins, which are many, are forgiven; for she loved much: but to whom little is forgiven, *the same* loveth little.

48 And he said unto her, Thy sins are forgiven.

49 And they that sat at meat with him began to say within themselves, Who is this that forgiveth sins also?

50 And he said to the woman, Thy faith hath saved thee; go in peace.

8 And it came to pass afterward, that he went throughout every city and village, preaching and shewing the glad tidings of the kingdom of God: and the twelve *were* with him,

2 And certain women, which had been healed of evil spirits and infirmities, Mary called Magdalene, out of whom went seven devils,

NEW AMERICAN STANDARD BIBLE

45 "You gave Me no kiss; but she, since the time I came in, has not ceased to kiss My feet.

46 "You did not anoint My head with oil, but she anointed My feet with perfume.

47 "For this reason I say to you, her sins, which are many, have been forgiven, for she loved much; but he who is forgiven little, loves little."

48 Then He said to her, "Your sins have been forgiven."

49 Those who were reclining *at the table* with Him began to say to themselves, "Who is this *man* who even forgives sins?"

50 And He said to the woman, "Your faith has saved you; go in peace."

Ministering Women

8 Soon afterwards, He *began* going around from one city and village to another, proclaiming and preaching the kingdom of God. The twelve were with Him,

2 and *also* some women who had been healed of evil spirits and sicknesses: Mary who was called Magdalene, from whom seven demons had gone out,

NEW CENTURY VERSION

of greeting, but she has been kissing my feet since I came
in. 46You did not put oil on my head, but she poured per-
fume on my feet. 47I tell you that her many sins are forgiv-
en, so she showed great love. But the person who is forgiv-
en only a little will love only a little."

48Then Jesus said to her, "Your sins are forgiven."

49The people sitting at the table began to say among
themselves, "Who is this who even forgives sins?"

50Jesus said to the woman, "Because you believed, you
are saved from your sins. Go in peace."

The Group with Jesus

8 After this, while Jesus was traveling through some cit-
ies and small towns, he preached and told the Good
News about God's kingdom. The twelve apostles were with
him, 2and also some women who had been healed of sick-
nesses and evil spirits: Mary, called Magdalene, from
whom seven demons had gone out; 3Joanna, the wife of

CONTEMPORARY ENGLISH VERSION

from the time I came in, she has not stopped kissing my
feet. 46You didn't even pour olive oil on my head,[d] but she
has poured expensive perfume on my feet. 47So I tell you
that all her sins are forgiven, and that is why she has
shown great love. But anyone who has been forgiven for
only a little will show only a little love."

48Then Jesus said to the woman, "Your sins are forgiven."

49Some other guests started saying to one another,
"Who is this who dares to forgive sins?"

50But Jesus told the woman, "Because of your faith, you
are now saved.[e] May God give you peace!"

Women Who Helped Jesus

8 Soon after this, Jesus was going through towns and vil-
lages, telling the good news about God's kingdom. His
twelve apostles were with him, 2and so were some women
who had been healed of evil spirits and all sorts of diseases.
One of the women was Mary Magdalene,[a] who once had
seven demons in her. 3Joanna, Susanna, and many others

[d] 7.44-46 *washed my feet . . . greet me with a kiss . . . pour olive oil on my head*: Guests in a home were usually offered water so they could wash their feet, because most people either went barefoot or wore sandals and would come in the house with very dusty feet. Guests were also greeted with a kiss on the cheek, and special ones often had sweet-smelling olive oil poured on their head. [e] 7.50 *saved*: Or "healed." The Greek word may have either meaning. [a] 8.2 *Magdalene*: Meaning "from Magdala," a small town on the western shore of Lake Galilee. There is no hint that she is the sinful woman in 7.36-50.

NEW INTERNATIONAL VERSION

give me a kiss, but this woman, from the time I entered, has not stopped kissing my feet. [46]You did not put oil on my head, but she has poured perfume on my feet. [47]Therefore, I tell you, her many sins have been forgiven—for she loved much. But he who has been forgiven little loves little."

[48]Then Jesus said to her, "Your sins are forgiven."

[49]The other guests began to say among themselves, "Who is this who even forgives sins?"

[50]Jesus said to the woman, "Your faith has saved you; go in peace."

The Parable of the Sower

8 After this, Jesus traveled about from one town and village to another, proclaiming the good news of the kingdom of God. The Twelve were with him, [2]and also some women who had been cured of evil spirits and diseases: Mary (called Magdalene) from whom seven demons

NEW LIVING TRANSLATION

give me a kiss of greeting, but she has kissed my feet again and again from the time I first came in. [46]You neglected the courtesy of olive oil to anoint my head, but she has anointed my feet with rare perfume. [47]I tell you, her sins—and they are many—have been forgiven, so she has shown me much love. But a person who is forgiven little shows only little love." [48]Then Jesus said to the woman, "Your sins are forgiven."

[49]The men at the table said among themselves, "Who does this man think he is, going around forgiving sins?" [50]And Jesus said to the woman, "Your faith has saved you; go in peace."

Women Who Followed Jesus

8 Not long afterward Jesus began a tour of the nearby cities and villages to announce the Good News concerning the Kingdom of God. He took his twelve disciples with him, [2]along with some women he had healed and from whom he had cast out evil spirits. Among them were Mary Magdalene, from whom he had cast out seven

NEW KING JAMES VERSION

kiss, but this woman has not ceased to kiss My feet since the time I came in. [46]You did not anoint My head with oil, but this woman has anointed My feet with fragrant oil. [47]Therefore I say to you, her sins, *which are* many, are forgiven, for she loved much. But to whom little is forgiven, *the same* loves little."

[48]Then He said to her, "Your sins are forgiven."

[49]And those who sat at the table with Him began to say to themselves, "Who is this who even forgives sins?"

[50]Then He said to the woman, "Your faith has saved you. Go in peace."

Many Women Minister to Jesus

8 Now it came to pass, afterward, that He went through every city and village, preaching and bringing the glad tidings of the kingdom of God. And the twelve *were* with Him, [2]and certain women who had been healed of evil spirits and infirmities—Mary called Magdalene, out of whom had come seven demons, [3]and Joanna the wife of

THE MESSAGE

You gave me no greeting, but from the time I arrived she hasn't quit kissing my feet. You provided nothing for freshening up, but she has soothed my feet with perfume. Impressive, isn't it? She was forgiven many, many sins, and so she is very, very grateful. If the forgiveness is minimal, the gratitude is minimal."

Then he spoke to her: "I forgive your sins."

That set the dinner guests talking behind his back: "Who does he think he is, forgiving sins!"

He ignored them and said to the woman, "Your faith has saved you. Go in peace."

8 He continued according to plan, traveled to town after town, village after village, preaching God's kingdom, spreading the Message. The Twelve were with him. There were also some women in their company who had been healed of various evil afflictions and illnesses: Mary, the one called Magdalene, from whom seven demons had gone

KING JAMES VERSION

3 And Joanna the wife of Chuza Herod's steward, and Susanna, and many others, which ministered unto him of their substance.

4 ¶ And when much people were gathered together, and were come to him out of every city, he spake by a parable:

5 A sower went out to sow his seed: and as he sowed, some fell by the way side; and it was trodden down, and the fowls of the air devoured it.

6 And some fell upon a rock; and as soon as it was sprung up, it withered away, because it lacked moisture.

7 And some fell among thorns; and the thorns sprang up with it, and choked it.

8 And other fell on good ground, and sprang up, and bare fruit an hundredfold. And when he had said these things, he cried, He that hath ears to hear, let him hear.

9 And his disciples asked him, saying, What might this parable be?

10 And he said, Unto you it is given to know the mysteries of the kingdom of God: but to others in parables; that seeing they might not see, and hearing they might not understand.

11 Now the parable is this: The seed is the word of God.

NEW AMERICAN STANDARD BIBLE

3 and Joanna the wife of Chuza, Herod's steward, and Susanna, and many others who were contributing to their support out of their private means.

Parable of the Sower

4 When a large crowd was coming together, and those from the various cities were journeying to Him, He spoke by way of a parable:

5 "The sower went out to sow his seed; and as he sowed, some fell beside the road, and it was trampled under foot and the birds of the air ate it up.

6 "Other *seed* fell on rocky *soil,* and as soon as it grew up, it withered away, because it had no moisture.

7 "Other *seed* fell among the thorns; and the thorns grew up with it and choked it out.

8 "Other *seed* fell into the good soil, and grew up, and produced a crop a hundred times as great." As He said these things, He would call out, "He who has ears to hear, let him hear."

9 His disciples *began* questioning Him as to what this parable meant.

10 And He said, "To you it has been granted to know the mysteries of the kingdom of God, but to the rest *it is* in parables, so that SEEING THEY MAY NOT SEE, AND HEARING THEY MAY NOT UNDERSTAND.

11 "Now the parable is this: the seed is the word of God.

NEW CENTURY VERSION

Chuza (the manager of Herod's house); Susanna; and many others. These women used their own money to help Jesus and his apostles.

A Story About Planting Seed

4 When a great crowd was gathered, and people were
coming to Jesus from every town, he told them this story:
5 "A farmer went out to plant his seed. While he was
planting, some seed fell by the road. People walked on the
seed, and the birds ate it up. 6 Some seed fell on rock, and
when it began to grow, it died because it had no water.
7 Some seed fell among thorny weeds, but the weeds grew
up with it and choked the good plants. 8 And some seed fell
on good ground and grew and made a hundred times
more."

As Jesus finished the story, he called out, "You people who can hear me, listen!"

9 Jesus' followers asked him what this story meant.

10 Jesus said, "You have been chosen to know the secrets about the kingdom of God. But I use stories to speak to other people so that:

'They will look, but they may not see.
They will listen, but they may not
understand.' *Isaiah 6:9*

11 "This is what the story means: The seed is God's mes-

CONTEMPORARY ENGLISH VERSION

had also used what they owned to help Jesus[b] and his disciples. Joanna's husband Chuza was one of Herod's officials.[c]

A Story about a Farmer (Matthew 13.1-9; Mark 4.1-9)

4 When a large crowd from several towns had gathered around Jesus, he told them this story:

5 A farmer went out to scatter seed in a field. While the
farmer was doing it, some of the seeds fell along the road
and were stepped on or eaten by birds. 6 Other seeds fell
on rocky ground and started growing. But the plants did
not have enough water and soon dried up. 7 Some other
seeds fell where thornbushes grew up and choked the
plants. 8 The rest of the seeds fell on good ground where
they grew and produced a hundred times as many seeds.

When Jesus had finished speaking, he said, "If you have ears, pay attention!"

Why Jesus Used Stories (Matthew 13.10-17; Mark 4.10-12)

9 Jesus' disciples asked him what the story meant. 10 So
he answered:

I have explained the secrets about God's kingdom to you, but for others I can only use stories. These people look, but they don't see, and they hear, but they don't understand.

Jesus Explains the Story about a Farmer (Matthew 13.18-23; Mark 4.13-20)

11 This is what the story means: The seed is God's

[b] **8.3** *used what they owned to help Jesus*: Women often helped Jewish teachers by giving them money. [c] **8.3** *Herod's officials*: Herod Antipas, the son of Herod the Great.

NEW INTERNATIONAL VERSION

had come out; 3Joanna the wife of Cuza, the manager of
Herod's household; Susanna; and many others. These
women were helping to support them out of their own
means.

4While a large crowd was gathering and people were
coming to Jesus from town after town, he told this parable:
5"A farmer went out to sow his seed. As he was scattering
the seed, some fell along the path; it was trampled on, and
the birds of the air ate it up. 6Some fell on rock, and when
it came up, the plants withered because they had no mois-
ture. 7Other seed fell among thorns, which grew up with it
and choked the plants. 8Still other seed fell on good soil. It
came up and yielded a crop, a hundred times more than
was sown."

When he said this, he called out, "He who has ears to hear, let him hear."

9His disciples asked him what this parable meant. 10He
said, "The knowledge of the secrets of the kingdom of God
has been given to you, but to others I speak in parables, so
that,

" 'though seeing, they may not see;
though hearing, they may not understand.'[a]

11"This is the meaning of the parable: The seed is the

[a] *10* Isaiah 6:9

NEW LIVING TRANSLATION

demons; 3Joanna, the wife of Chuza, Herod's business manager; Susanna; and many others who were contributing from their own resources to support Jesus and his disciples.

Story of the Farmer Scattering Seed

4One day Jesus told this story to a large crowd that had
gathered from many towns to hear him: 5"A farmer went out
to plant some seed. As he scattered it across his field, some
seed fell on a footpath, where it was stepped on, and the
birds came and ate it. 6Other seed fell on shallow soil with
underlying rock. This seed began to grow, but soon it with-
ered and died for lack of moisture. 7Other seed fell among
thorns that shot up and choked out the tender blades. 8Still
other seed fell on fertile soil. This seed grew and produced a
crop one hundred times as much as had been planted." When
he had said this, he called out, "Anyone who is willing to
hear should listen and understand!"

9His disciples asked him what the story meant. 10He
replied, "You have been permitted to understand the
secrets of the Kingdom of God. But I am using these stories
to conceal everything about it from outsiders, so that the
Scriptures might be fulfilled:

'They see what I do,
but they don't really see;
they hear what I say,
but they don't understand.'*

11"This is the meaning of the story: The seed is God's

8:10 Isa 6:9.

NEW KING JAMES VERSION

Chuza, Herod's steward, and Susanna, and many others who provided for Him[a] from their substance.

The Parable of the Sower

4And when a great multitude had gathered, and they
had come to Him from every city, He spoke by a parable:
5"A sower went out to sow his seed. And as he sowed,
some fell by the wayside; and it was trampled down, and
the birds of the air devoured it. 6Some fell on rock; and as
soon as it sprang up, it withered away because it lacked
moisture. 7And some fell among thorns, and the thorns
sprang up with it and choked it. 8But others fell on good
ground, sprang up, and yielded a crop a hundredfold."
When He had said these things He cried, "He who has ears
to hear, let him hear!"

The Purpose of Parables

9Then His disciples asked Him, saying, "What does this parable mean?"

10And He said, "To you it has been given to know the
mysteries of the kingdom of God, but to the rest *it is given*
in parables, that

'*Seeing they may not see,*
And hearing they may not understand.'[b]

The Parable of the Sower Explained

11"Now the parable is this: The seed is the word of God.

8:3 [a] NU-Text and M-Text read *them*. **8:10** [b] Isaiah 6:9

THE MESSAGE

out; Joanna, wife of Chuza, Herod's manager; and Susanna—along with many others who used their considerable means to provide for the company.

The Story of the Seeds

As they went from town to town, a lot of people joined in and traveled along. He addressed them, using this story: "A farmer went out to sow his seed. Some of it fell on the road; it was tramped down and the birds ate it. Other seed fell in the gravel; it sprouted, but withered because it didn't have good roots. Other seed fell in the weeds; the weeds grew with it and strangled it. Other seed fell in rich earth and produced a bumper crop.

"Are you listening to this?

"Really listening?"

His disciples asked, "Why did you tell this story?"

He said, "You've been given insight into God's kingdom—you know how it works. There are others who need stories. But even with stories some of them aren't going to get it:

'Their eyes are open but don't see a thing,
Their ears are open but don't hear a thing.'

"This story is about some of those people. The seed is

KING JAMES VERSION

12 Those by the way side are they that hear; then cometh the devil, and taketh away the word out of their hearts, lest they should believe and be saved.

13 They on the rock *are they*, which, when they hear, receive the word with joy; and these have no root, which for a while believe, and in time of temptation fall away.

14 And that which fell among thorns are they, which, when they have heard, go forth, and are choked with cares and riches and pleasures of *this* life, and bring no fruit to perfection.

15 But that on the good ground are they, which in an honest and good heart, having heard the word, keep *it*, and bring forth fruit with patience.

16 No man, when he hath lighted a candle, covereth it with a vessel, or putteth *it* under a bed; but setteth *it* on a candlestick, that they which enter in may see the light.

17 For nothing is secret, that shall not be made manifest; neither *any thing* hid, that shall not be known and come abroad.

18 Take heed therefore how ye hear: for whosoever hath, to him shall be given; and whosoever hath not, from him shall be taken even that which he seemeth to have.

19 Then came to him *his* mother and his brethren, and could not come at him for the press.

NEW AMERICAN STANDARD BIBLE

12 "Those beside the road are those who have heard; then the devil comes and takes away the word from their heart, so that they will not believe and be saved.

13 "Those on the rocky *soil are* those who, when they hear, receive the word with joy; and these have no *firm* root; they believe for a while, and in time of temptation fall away.

14 "The *seed* which fell among the thorns, these are the ones who have heard, and as they go on their way they are choked with worries and riches and pleasures of *this* life, and bring no fruit to maturity.

15 "But the *seed* in the good soil, these are the ones who have heard the word in an honest and good heart, and hold it fast, and bear fruit with perseverance.

Parable of the Lamp

16 "Now no one after lighting a lamp covers it over with a container, or puts it under a bed; but he puts it on a lampstand, so that those who come in may see the light.

17 "For nothing is hidden that will not become evident, nor *anything* secret that will not be known and come to light.

18 "So take care how you listen; for whoever has, to him *more* shall be given; and whoever does not have, even what he thinks he has shall be taken away from him."

19 And His mother and brothers came to Him, and they were unable to get to Him because of the crowd.

NEW CENTURY VERSION

sage. 12The seed that fell beside the road is like the people
who hear God's teaching, but the devil comes and takes it
away from them so they cannot believe it and be saved.
13The seed that fell on rock is like those who hear God's
teaching and accept it gladly, but they don't allow the
teaching to go deep into their lives. They believe for a
while, but when trouble comes, they give up. 14The seed
that fell among the thorny weeds is like those who hear
God's teaching, but they let the worries, riches, and plea-
sures of this life keep them from growing and producing
good fruit. 15And the seed that fell on the good ground is
like those who hear God's teaching with good, honest
hearts and obey it and patiently produce good fruit.

Use What You Have

16"No one after lighting a lamp covers it with a bowl or
hides it under a bed. Instead, the person puts it on a lamp-
stand so those who come in will see the light. 17Everything
that is hidden will become clear, and every secret thing
will be made known. 18So be careful how you listen. Those
who have understanding will be given more. But those
who do not have understanding, even what they think they
have will be taken away from them."

Jesus' True Family

19Jesus' mother and brothers came to see him, but there
was such a crowd they could not get to him. 20Someone

CONTEMPORARY ENGLISH VERSION

message, 12and the seeds that fell along the road are the
people who hear the message. But the devil comes and
snatches the message out of their hearts, so that they
will not believe and be saved. 13The seeds that fell on
rocky ground are the people who gladly hear the mes-
sage and accept it. But they don't have deep roots, and
they believe only for a little while. As soon as life gets
hard, they give up.

14The seeds that fell among the thornbushes are also
people who hear the message. But they are so eager for
riches and pleasures that they never produce anything.
15Those seeds that fell on good ground are the people
who listen to the message and keep it in good and hon-
est hearts. They last and produce a harvest.

Light (Mark 4.21-25)

16No one lights a lamp and puts it under a bowl or
under a bed. A lamp is always put on a lampstand, so
that people who come into a house will see the light.
17There is nothing hidden that will not be found. There
is no secret that will not be well known. 18Pay attention
to how you listen! Everyone who has something will be
given more, but people who have nothing will lose what
little they think they have.

Jesus' Mother and Brothers
(Matthew 12.46-50; Mark 3.31-35)

19Jesus' mother and brothers went to see him, but
because of the crowd they could not get near him.

NEW INTERNATIONAL VERSION

word of God. 12Those along the path are the ones who
hear, and then the devil comes and takes away the word
from their hearts, so that they may not believe and be
saved. 13Those on the rock are the ones who receive the
word with joy when they hear it, but they have no root.
They believe for a while, but in the time of testing they fall
away. 14The seed that fell among thorns stands for those
who hear, but as they go on their way they are choked by
life's worries, riches and pleasures, and they do not
mature. 15But the seed on good soil stands for those with a
noble and good heart, who hear the word, retain it, and by
persevering produce a crop.

A Lamp on a Stand

16"No one lights a lamp and hides it in a jar or puts it
under a bed. Instead, he puts it on a stand, so that those
who come in can see the light. 17For there is nothing hid-
den that will not be disclosed, and nothing concealed that
will not be known or brought out into the open.
18Therefore consider carefully how you listen. Whoever has
will be given more; whoever does not have, even what he
thinks he has will be taken from him."

Jesus' Mother and Brothers

19Now Jesus' mother and brothers came to see him, but
they were not able to get near him because of the crowd.

NEW LIVING TRANSLATION

message. 12The seed that fell on the hard path represents
those who hear the message, but then the Devil comes and
steals it away and prevents them from believing and being
saved. 13The rocky soil represents those who hear the mes-
sage with joy. But like young plants in such soil, their
roots don't go very deep. They believe for a while, but they
wilt when the hot winds of testing blow. 14The thorny
ground represents those who hear and accept the message,
but all too quickly the message is crowded out by the cares
and riches and pleasures of this life. And so they never
grow into maturity. 15But the good soil represents honest,
good-hearted people who hear God's message, cling to it,
and steadily produce a huge harvest.

Illustration of the Lamp

16"No one would light a lamp and then cover it up or put
it under a bed. No, lamps are mounted in the open, where
they can be seen by those entering the house. 17For every-
thing that is hidden or secret will eventually be brought to
light and made plain to all. 18So be sure to pay attention to
what you hear. To those who are open to my teaching,
more understanding will be given. But to those who are
not listening, even what they think they have will be taken
away from them."

The True Family of Jesus

19Once when Jesus' mother and brothers came to see
him, they couldn't get to him because of the crowds.

NEW KING JAMES VERSION

12Those by the wayside are the ones who hear; then the
devil comes and takes away the word out of their hearts,
lest they should believe and be saved. 13But the ones on
the rock *are those* who, when they hear, receive the word
with joy; and these have no root, who believe for a while
and in time of temptation fall away. 14Now the ones *that*
fell among thorns are those who, when they have heard,
go out and are choked with cares, riches, and pleasures of
life, and bring no fruit to maturity. 15But the ones *that* fell
on the good ground are those who, having heard the word
with a noble and good heart, keep *it* and bear fruit with
patience.

The Parable of the Revealed Light

16"No one, when he has lit a lamp, covers it with a ves-
sel or puts *it* under a bed, but sets *it* on a lampstand, that
those who enter may see the light. 17For nothing is secret
that will not be revealed, nor *anything* hidden that will not
be known and come to light. 18Therefore take heed how
you hear. For whoever has, to him *more* will be given; and
whoever does not have, even what he seems to have will
be taken from him."

Jesus' Mother and Brothers Come to Him

19Then His mother and brothers came to Him, and could
not approach Him because of the crowd. 20And it was told

THE MESSAGE

the Word of God. The seeds on the road are those who hear
the Word, but no sooner do they hear it than the Devil
snatches it from them so they won't believe and be saved.

"The seeds in the gravel are those who hear with enthu-
siasm, but the enthusiasm doesn't go very deep. It's only
another fad, and the moment there's trouble it's gone.

"And the seed that fell in the weeds—well, these are the
ones who hear, but then the seed is crowded out and noth-
ing comes of it as they go about their lives worrying about
tomorrow, making money and having fun.

"But the seed in the good earth—these are the good-
hearts who seize the Word and hold on no matter what,
sticking with it until there's a harvest.

Misers of What You Hear

"No one lights a lamp and then covers it with a washtub
or shoves it under the bed. No, you set it up on a lamp
stand so those who enter the room can see their way. We're
not keeping secrets; we're telling them. We're not hiding
things; we're bringing *everything* out into the open. So be
careful that you don't become misers of what you hear.
Generosity begets generosity. Stinginess impoverishes."

His mother and brothers showed up but couldn't get
through to him because of the crowd. He was given the

KING JAMES VERSION

20 And it was told him *by certain* which said, Thy mother and thy brethren stand without, desiring to see thee.

21 And he answered and said unto them, My mother and my brethren are these which hear the word of God, and do it.

22 ¶ Now it came to pass on a certain day, that he went into a ship with his disciples: and he said unto them, Let us go over unto the other side of the lake. And they launched forth.

23 But as they sailed he fell asleep: and there came down a storm of wind on the lake; and they were filled *with water*, and were in jeopardy.

24 And they came to him, and awoke him, saying, Master, master, we perish. Then he arose, and rebuked the wind and the raging of the water: and they ceased, and there was a calm.

25 And he said unto them, Where is your faith? And they being afraid wondered, saying one to another, What manner of man is this! for he commandeth even the winds and water, and they obey him.

26 And they arrived at the country of the Gadarenes, which is over against Galilee.

27 And when he went forth to land, there met him out of the city a certain man, which had devils long time, and ware no clothes, neither abode in *any* house, but in the tombs.

NEW AMERICAN STANDARD BIBLE

20 And it was reported to Him, "Your mother and Your brothers are standing outside, wishing to see You."

21 But He answered and said to them, "My mother and My brothers are these who hear the word of God and do it."

Jesus Stills the Sea

22 Now on one of *those* days Jesus and His disciples got into a boat, and He said to them, "Let us go over to the other side of the lake." So they launched out.

23 But as they were sailing along He fell asleep; and a fierce gale of wind descended on the lake, and they *began* to be swamped and to be in danger.

24 They came to Jesus and woke Him up, saying, "Master, Master, we are perishing!" And He got up and rebuked the wind and the surging waves, and they stopped, and it became calm.

25 And He said to them, "Where is your faith?" They were fearful and amazed, saying to one another, "Who then is this, that He commands even the winds and the water, and they obey Him?"

The Demoniac Cured

26 Then they sailed to the country of the Gerasenes, which is opposite Galilee.

27 And when He came out onto the land, He was met by a man from the city who was possessed with demons; and who had not put on any clothing for a long time, and was not living in a house, but in the tombs.

NEW CENTURY VERSION

said to Jesus, "Your mother and your brothers are standing
outside, wanting to see you."
[21]Jesus answered them, "My mother and my brothers are
those who listen to God's teaching and obey it!"

Jesus Calms a Storm

[22]One day Jesus and his followers got into a boat, and
he said to them, "Let's go across the lake." And so they
started across. [23]While they were sailing, Jesus fell asleep.
A very strong wind blew up on the lake, causing the boat
to fill with water, and they were in danger.
[24]The followers went to Jesus and woke him, saying,
"Master! Master! We will drown!"
Jesus got up and gave a command to the wind and the
waves. They stopped, and it became calm. [25]Jesus said to
his followers, "Where is your faith?"
The followers were afraid and amazed and said to each
other, "Who is this that commands even the wind and the
water, and they obey him?"

A Man with Demons Inside Him

[26]Jesus and his followers sailed across the lake from
Galilee to the area of the Gerasene people. [27]When Jesus
got out on the land, a man from the town who had demons
inside him came to Jesus. For a long time he had worn no
clothes and had lived in the burial caves, not in a house.

CONTEMPORARY ENGLISH VERSION

[20]Someone told Jesus, "Your mother and brothers are
standing outside and want to see you."
[21]Jesus answered, "My mother and my brothers are
those people who hear and obey God's message."

A Storm (Matthew 8.23-27; Mark 4.35-41)

[22]One day, Jesus and his disciples got into a boat, and
he said, "Let's cross the lake."[d] They started out, [23]and
while they were sailing across, he went to sleep.
Suddenly a windstorm struck the lake, and the boat start-
ed sinking. They were in danger. [24]So they went to Jesus
and woke him up, "Master, Master! We are about to drown!"
Jesus got up and ordered the wind and waves to stop.
They obeyed, and everything was calm. [25]Then Jesus asked
the disciples, "Don't you have any faith?"
But they were frightened and amazed. They said to each
other, "Who is this? He can give orders to the wind and
the waves, and they obey him!"

A Man with Demons in Him (Matthew 8.28-34; Mark 5.1-20)

[26]Jesus and his disciples sailed across Lake Galilee and
came to shore near the town of Gerasa.[e] [27]As Jesus was get-
ting out of the boat, he was met by a man from that town.
The man had demons in him. He had gone naked for a long
time and no longer lived in a house, but in the graveyard.[f]

[d] **8.22** *cross the lake*: To the eastern shore of Lake Galilee, where most of the people were not Jewish. [e] **8.26** *Gerasa*: Some manuscripts have "Gergesa." [f] **8.27** *graveyard*: It was thought that demons and evil spirits lived in graveyards.

NEW INTERNATIONAL VERSION

20Someone told him, "Your mother and brothers are stand-
ing outside, wanting to see you."
21He replied, "My mother and brothers are those who
hear God's word and put it into practice."

Jesus Calms the Storm

22One day Jesus said to his disciples, "Let's go over to
the other side of the lake." So they got into a boat and set
out. 23As they sailed, he fell asleep. A squall came down
on the lake, so that the boat was being swamped, and they
were in great danger.
24The disciples went and woke him, saying, "Master,
Master, we're going to drown!"
He got up and rebuked the wind and the raging waters;
the storm subsided, and all was calm. 25"Where is your
faith?" he asked his disciples.
In fear and amazement they asked one another, "Who is
this? He commands even the winds and the water, and
they obey him."

The Healing of a Demon-possessed Man

26They sailed to the region of the Gerasenes,[b] which is
across the lake from Galilee. 27When Jesus stepped ashore,
he was met by a demon-possessed man from the town. For
a long time this man had not worn clothes or lived in a
house, but had lived in the tombs. 28When he saw Jesus,

[b] *26* Some manuscripts *Gadarenes*; other manuscripts *Gergesenes*; also in verse 37

NEW LIVING TRANSLATION

20Someone told Jesus, "Your mother and your brothers are
outside, and they want to see you."
21Jesus replied, "My mother and my brothers are all
those who hear the message of God and obey it."

Jesus Calms the Storm

22One day Jesus said to his disciples, "Let's cross over to
the other side of the lake." So they got into a boat and
started out. 23On the way across, Jesus lay down for a nap,
and while he was sleeping the wind began to rise. A fierce
storm developed that threatened to swamp them, and they
were in real danger.
24The disciples woke him up, shouting, "Master, Master,
we're going to drown!"
So Jesus rebuked the wind and the raging waves. The
storm stopped and all was calm! 25Then he asked them,
"Where is your faith?"
And they were filled with awe and amazement. They
said to one another, "Who is this man, that even the winds
and waves obey him?"

Jesus Heals a Demon-Possessed Man

26So they arrived in the land of the Gerasenes,* across
the lake from Galilee. 27As Jesus was climbing out of the
boat, a man who was possessed by demons came out to
meet him. Homeless and naked, he had lived in a cemetery

8:26 Some manuscripts read *Gadarenes;* other manuscripts read *Gergesenes.* See Matt 8:28; Mark 5:1.

NEW KING JAMES VERSION

Him *by some,* who said, "Your mother and Your brothers
are standing outside, desiring to see You."
21But He answered and said to them, "My mother and My
brothers are these who hear the word of God and do it."

Wind and Wave Obey Jesus

22Now it happened, on a certain day, that He got into a
boat with His disciples. And He said to them, "Let us cross
over to the other side of the lake." And they launched out.
23But as they sailed He fell asleep. And a windstorm came
down on the lake, and they were filling *with water,* and
were in jeopardy. 24And they came to Him and awoke Him,
saying, "Master, Master, we are perishing!"
Then He arose and rebuked the wind and the raging of
the water. And they ceased, and there was a calm. 25But
He said to them, "Where is your faith?"
And they were afraid, and marveled, saying to one
another, "Who can this be? For He commands even the
winds and water, and they obey Him!"

A Demon-Possessed Man Healed

26Then they sailed to the country of the Gadarenes,[c]
which is opposite Galilee. 27And when He stepped out on
the land, there met Him a certain man from the city who
had demons for a long time. And he wore no clothes,[d] nor
did he live in a house but in the tombs. 28When he saw

8:26 [c] NU-Text reads *Gerasenes.* **8:27** [d] NU-Text reads *who had demons and for a long time wore no clothes.*

THE MESSAGE

message, "Your mother and brothers are standing outside
wanting to see you."
He replied, "My mother and brothers are the ones who
hear and do God's Word. Obedience is thicker than blood."
One day he and his disciples got in a boat. "Let's cross
the lake," he said. And off they went. It was smooth sail-
ing, and he fell asleep. A terrific storm came up suddenly
on the lake. Water poured in, and they were about to cap-
size. They woke Jesus: "Master, Master, we're going to
drown!"
Getting to his feet, he told the wind, "Silence!" and the
waves, "Quiet down!" They did it. The lake became smooth
as glass.
Then he said to his disciples, "Why can't you trust me?"
They were in absolute awe, staggered and stammering,
"Who is this, anyway? He calls out to the winds and sea,
and they do what he tells them!"

The Madman and the Pigs

They sailed on to the country of the Gerasenes, directly
opposite Galilee. As he stepped out onto land, a madman
from town met him; he was a victim of demons. He hadn't
worn clothes for a long time, nor lived at home; he lived in

KING JAMES VERSION

28 When he saw Jesus, he cried out, and fell down before him, and with a loud voice said, What have I to do with thee, Jesus, *thou* Son of God most high? I beseech thee, torment me not.

29 (For he had commanded the unclean spirit to come out of the man. For oftentimes it had caught him: and he was kept bound with chains and in fetters; and he brake the bands, and was driven of the devil into the wilderness.)

30 And Jesus asked him, saying, What is thy name? And he said, Legion: because many devils were entered into him.

31 And they besought him that he would not command them to go out into the deep.

32 And there was there an herd of many swine feeding on the mountain: and they besought him that he would suffer them to enter into them. And he suffered them.

33 Then went the devils out of the man, and entered into the swine: and the herd ran violently down a steep place into the lake, and were choked.

34 When they that fed *them* saw what was done, they fled, and went and told *it* in the city and in the country.

35 Then they went out to see what was done; and came to Jesus, and found the man, out of whom the devils were departed, sitting at the feet of Jesus, clothed, and in his right mind: and they were afraid.

36 They also which saw *it* told them by what means he that was possessed of the devils was healed.

NEW AMERICAN STANDARD BIBLE

28 Seeing Jesus, he cried out and fell before Him, and said in a loud voice, "What business do we have with each other, Jesus, Son of the Most High God? I beg You, do not torment me."

29 For He had commanded the unclean spirit to come out of the man. For it had seized him many times; and he was bound with chains and shackles and kept under guard, and *yet* he would break his bonds and be driven by the demon into the desert.

30 And Jesus asked him, "What is your name?" And he said, "Legion"; for many demons had entered him.

31 They were imploring Him not to command them to go away into the abyss.

32 Now there was a herd of many swine feeding there on the mountain; and *the demons* implored Him to permit them to enter the swine. And He gave them permission.

33 And the demons came out of the man and entered the swine; and the herd rushed down the steep bank into the lake and was drowned.

34 When the herdsmen saw what had happened, they ran away and reported it in the city and *out* in the country.

35 *The people* went out to see what had happened; and they came to Jesus, and found the man from whom the demons had gone out, sitting down at the feet of Jesus, clothed and in his right mind; and they became frightened.

36 Those who had seen it reported to them how the man who was demon-possessed had been made well.

NEW CENTURY VERSION

[28]When he saw Jesus, he cried out and fell down before him. He said with a loud voice, "What do you want with me, Jesus, Son of the Most High God? I beg you, don't torture me!" [29]He said this because Jesus was commanding the evil spirit to come out of the man. Many times it had taken hold of him. Though he had been kept under guard and chained hand and foot, he had broken his chains and had been forced by the demon out into a lonely place.

[30]Jesus asked him, "What is your name?"

He answered, "Legion,"[a] because many demons were in him. [31]The demons begged Jesus not to send them into eternal darkness.[b] [32]A large herd of pigs was feeding on a hill, and the demons begged Jesus to allow them to go into the pigs. So Jesus allowed them to do this. [33]When the demons came out of the man, they went into the pigs, and the herd ran down the hill into the lake and was drowned.

[34]When the herdsmen saw what had happened, they ran away and told about this in the town and the countryside. [35]And people went to see what had happened. When they came to Jesus, they found the man sitting at Jesus' feet, clothed and in his right mind, because the demons were gone. But the people were frightened. [36]The people who saw this happen told the others how Jesus had made the

8:30 [a] **"Legion"** Means very many. A legion was about five thousand men in the Roman army. **8:31** [b] **eternal darkness** Literally, "the abyss," something like a pit or a hole that has no end.

CONTEMPORARY ENGLISH VERSION

[28]The man saw Jesus and screamed. He knelt down in front of him and shouted, "Jesus, Son of God in heaven, what do you want with me? I beg you not to torture me!" [29]He said this because Jesus had already told the evil spirit to go out of him.

The man had often been attacked by the demon. And even though he had been bound with chains and leg irons and kept under guard, he smashed whatever bound him. Then the demon would force him out into lonely places.

[30]Jesus asked the man, "What is your name?"

He answered, "My name is Lots." He said this because there were 'lots' of demons in him. [31]They begged Jesus not to send them to the deep pit,[g] where they would be punished. [32]A large herd of pigs was feeding there on the hillside. So the demons begged Jesus to let them go into the pigs, and Jesus let them go. [33]Then the demons left the man and went into the pigs. The whole herd rushed down the steep bank into the lake and drowned.

[34]When the men taking care of the pigs saw this, they ran to spread the news in the town and on the farms. [35]The people went out to see what had happened, and when they came to Jesus, they also found the man. The demons had gone out of him, and he was sitting there at the feet of Jesus. He had clothes on and was in his right mind. But the people were terrified.

[36]Then all who had seen the man healed told about it.

[g] **8.31** *deep pit*: The place where evil spirits are kept and punished.

NEW INTERNATIONAL VERSION

he cried out and fell at his feet, shouting at the top of his voice, "What do you want with me, Jesus, Son of the Most High God? I beg you, don't torture me!" 29For Jesus had commanded the evil[c] spirit to come out of the man. Many times it had seized him, and though he was chained hand and foot and kept under guard, he had broken his chains and had been driven by the demon into solitary places.

30Jesus asked him, "What is your name?"

"Legion," he replied, because many demons had gone into him. 31And they begged him repeatedly not to order them to go into the Abyss.

32A large herd of pigs was feeding there on the hillside. The demons begged Jesus to let them go into them, and he gave them permission. 33When the demons came out of the man, they went into the pigs, and the herd rushed down the steep bank into the lake and was drowned.

34When those tending the pigs saw what had happened, they ran off and reported this in the town and countryside, 35and the people went out to see what had happened. When they came to Jesus, they found the man from whom the demons had gone out, sitting at Jesus' feet, dressed and in his right mind; and they were afraid. 36Those who had seen it told the people how the demon-possessed man

c 29 Greek *unclean*

NEW LIVING TRANSLATION

for a long time. 28As soon as he saw Jesus, he shrieked and fell to the ground before him, screaming, "Why are you bothering me, Jesus, Son of the Most High God? Please, I beg you, don't torture me!" 29For Jesus had already commanded the evil spirit to come out of him. This spirit had often taken control of the man. Even when he was shackled with chains, he simply broke them and rushed out into the wilderness, completely under the demon's power.

30"What is your name?" Jesus asked.

"Legion," he replied—for the man was filled with many demons. 31The demons kept begging Jesus not to send them into the Bottomless Pit. 32A large herd of pigs was feeding on the hillside nearby, and the demons pleaded with him to let them enter into the pigs. Jesus gave them permission. 33So the demons came out of the man and entered the pigs, and the whole herd plunged down the steep hillside into the lake, where they drowned.

34When the herdsmen saw it, they fled to the nearby city and the surrounding countryside, spreading the news as they ran. 35A crowd soon gathered around Jesus, for they wanted to see for themselves what had happened. And they saw the man who had been possessed by demons sitting quietly at Jesus' feet, clothed and sane. And the whole crowd was afraid. 36Then those who had seen what happened told the others how the demon-possessed man had

NEW KING JAMES VERSION

Jesus, he cried out, fell down before Him, and with a loud voice said, "What have I to do with You, Jesus, Son of the Most High God? I beg You, do not torment me!" 29For He had commanded the unclean spirit to come out of the man. For it had often seized him, and he was kept under guard, bound with chains and shackles; and he broke the bonds and was driven by the demon into the wilderness.

30Jesus asked him, saying, "What is your name?"

And he said, "Legion," because many demons had entered him. 31And they begged Him that He would not command them to go out into the abyss.

32Now a herd of many swine was feeding there on the mountain. So they begged Him that He would permit them to enter them. And He permitted them. 33Then the demons went out of the man and entered the swine, and the herd ran violently down the steep place into the lake and drowned.

34When those who fed *them* saw what had happened, they fled and told *it* in the city and in the country. 35Then they went out to see what had happened, and came to Jesus, and found the man from whom the demons had departed, sitting at the feet of Jesus, clothed and in his right mind. And they were afraid. 36They also who had seen *it* told them by what means he who had been demon-

THE MESSAGE

the cemetery. When he saw Jesus he screamed, fell before him, and bellowed, "What business do you have messing with me? You're Jesus, Son of the High God, but don't give me a hard time!" (The man said this because Jesus had started to order the unclean spirit out of him.) Time after time the demon threw the man into convulsions. He had been placed under constant guard and tied with chains and shackles, but crazed and driven wild by the demon, he would shatter the bonds.

Jesus asked him, "What is your name?"

"Mob. My name is Mob," he said, because many demons afflicted him. And they begged Jesus desperately not to order them to the bottomless pit.

A large herd of pigs was browsing and rooting on a nearby hill. The demons begged Jesus to order them into the pigs. He gave the order. It was even worse for the pigs than for the man. Crazed, they stampeded over a cliff into the lake and drowned.

Those tending the pigs, scared to death, bolted and told their story in town and country. People went out to see what had happened. They came to Jesus and found the man from whom the demons had been sent, sitting there at Jesus' feet, wearing decent clothes and making sense. It was a holy moment, and for a short time they were more reverent than curious. Then those who had seen it happen told how the demoniac had been saved.

KING JAMES VERSION

37 Then the whole multitude of the country of the Gadarenes round about besought him to depart from them; for they were taken with great fear: and he went up into the ship, and returned back again.

38 Now the man out of whom the devils were departed besought him that he might be with him: but Jesus sent him away, saying,

39 Return to thine own house, and shew how great things God hath done unto thee. And he went his way, and published throughout the whole city how great things Jesus had done unto him.

40 ¶ And it came to pass, that, when Jesus was returned, the people *gladly* received him: for they were all waiting for him.

41 And, behold, there came a man named Jairus, and he was a ruler of the synagogue: and he fell down at Jesus' feet, and besought him that he would come into his house:

42 For he had one only daughter, about twelve years of age, and she lay a dying. But as he went the people thronged him.

43 And a woman having an issue of blood twelve years, which had spent all her living upon physicians, neither could be healed of any,

44 Came behind *him*, and touched the border of his garment: and immediately her issue of blood stanched.

45 And Jesus said, Who touched me? When all denied, Peter and they that were with him said, Master, the multitude throng thee and press *thee*, and sayest thou, Who touched me?

NEW AMERICAN STANDARD BIBLE

37 And all the people of the country of the Gerasenes and the surrounding district asked Him to leave them, for they were gripped with great fear; and He got into a boat and returned.

38 But the man from whom the demons had gone out was begging Him that he might accompany Him; but He sent him away, saying,

39 "Return to your house and describe what great things God has done for you." So he went away, proclaiming throughout the whole city what great things Jesus had done for him.

Miracles of Healing

40 And as Jesus returned, the people welcomed Him, for they had all been waiting for Him.

41 And there came a man named Jairus, and he was an official of the synagogue; and he fell at Jesus' feet, and *began* to implore Him to come to his house;

42 for he had an only daughter, about twelve years old, and she was dying. But as He went, the crowds were pressing against Him.

43 And a woman who had a hemorrhage for twelve years, and could not be healed by anyone,

44 came up behind Him and touched the fringe of His cloak, and immediately her hemorrhage stopped.

45 And Jesus said, "Who is the one who touched Me?" And while they were all denying it, Peter said, "Master, the people are crowding and pressing in on You."

NEW CENTURY VERSION

man well. 37All the people of the Gerasene country asked
Jesus to leave, because they were all very afraid. So Jesus
got into the boat and went back to Galilee.
38The man whom Jesus had healed begged to go with
him, but Jesus sent him away, saying, 39"Go back home
and tell people how much God has done for you." So the
man went all over town telling how much Jesus had done
for him.

Jesus Gives Life to a Dead Girl and Heals a Sick Woman

40When Jesus got back to Galilee, a crowd welcomed
him, because everyone was waiting for him. 41A man
named Jairus, a leader of the synagogue, came to Jesus
and fell at his feet, begging him to come to his house.
42Jairus' only daughter, about twelve years old, was dying.
While Jesus was on his way to Jairus' house, the people
were crowding all around him. 43A woman was in the
crowd who had been bleeding for twelve years, but no one
was able to heal her. 44She came up behind Jesus and
touched the edge of his coat, and instantly her bleeding
stopped. 45Then Jesus said, "Who touched me?"
When all the people said they had not touched him,
Peter said, "Master, the people are all around you and are
pushing against you."

CONTEMPORARY ENGLISH VERSION

37Everyone from around Gerasa[h] begged Jesus to leave,
because they were so frightened.
When Jesus got into the boat to start back, 38the man
who had been healed begged to go with him. But Jesus
sent him off and said, 39"Go back home and tell everyone
how much God has done for you." The man then went all
over town, telling everything that Jesus had done for him.

A Dying Girl and a Sick Woman

(Matthew 9.18-26; Mark 5.21-43)

40Everyone had been waiting for Jesus, and when he
came back, a crowd was there to welcome him. 41Just then
the man in charge of the Jewish meeting place came and
knelt down in front of Jesus. His name was Jairus, and he
begged Jesus to come to his home 42because his twelve-
year-old child was dying. She was his only daughter.
While Jesus was on his way, people were crowding all
around him. 43In the crowd was a woman who had been
bleeding for twelve years. She had spent everything she
had on doctors,[i] but none of them could make her well.
44As soon as she came up behind Jesus and barely
touched his clothes, her bleeding stopped.
45"Who touched me?" Jesus asked.
While everyone was denying it, Peter said, "Master, people
are crowding all around and pushing you from every side."[j]

[h] **8.37** *Gerasa*: See the note at 8.26. [i] **8.43** *She had spent everything she had on doctors*: Some manuscripts do not have these words.
[j] **8.45** *from every side*: Some manuscripts add "and you ask, 'Who touched me?' "

NEW INTERNATIONAL VERSION

had been cured. [37]Then all the people of the region of the Gerasenes asked Jesus to leave them, because they were overcome with fear. So he got into the boat and left.

[38]The man from whom the demons had gone out begged to go with him, but Jesus sent him away, saying, [39]"Return home and tell how much God has done for you." So the man went away and told all over town how much Jesus had done for him.

A Dead Girl and a Sick Woman

[40]Now when Jesus returned, a crowd welcomed him, for they were all expecting him. [41]Then a man named Jairus, a ruler of the synagogue, came and fell at Jesus' feet, pleading with him to come to his house [42]because his only daughter, a girl of about twelve, was dying.

As Jesus was on his way, the crowds almost crushed him. [43]And a woman was there who had been subject to bleeding for twelve years,[d] but no one could heal her. [44]She came up behind him and touched the edge of his cloak, and immediately her bleeding stopped.

[45]"Who touched me?" Jesus asked.

When they all denied it, Peter said, "Master, the people are crowding and pressing against you."

[d] *43* Many manuscripts *years, and she had spent all she had on doctors*

NEW LIVING TRANSLATION

been healed. [37]And all the people in that region begged Jesus to go away and leave them alone, for a great wave of fear swept over them.

So Jesus returned to the boat and left, crossing back to the other side of the lake. [38]The man who had been demon possessed begged to go, too, but Jesus said, [39]"No, go back to your family and tell them all the wonderful things God has done for you." So he went all through the city telling about the great thing Jesus had done for him.

Jesus Heals in Response to Faith

[40]On the other side of the lake the crowds received Jesus with open arms because they had been waiting for him. [41]And now a man named Jairus, a leader of the local synagogue, came and fell down at Jesus' feet, begging him to come home with him. [42]His only child was dying, a little girl twelve years old.

As Jesus went with him, he was surrounded by the crowds. [43]And there was a woman in the crowd who had had a hemorrhage for twelve years. She had spent everything she had on doctors* and still could find no cure. [44]She came up behind Jesus and touched the fringe of his robe. Immediately, the bleeding stopped.

[45]"Who touched me?" Jesus asked.

Everyone denied it, and Peter said, "Master, this whole crowd is pressing up against you."

8:43 Some manuscripts omit *She had spent everything she had on doctors.*

NEW KING JAMES VERSION

possessed was healed. [37]Then the whole multitude of the surrounding region of the Gadarenes[e] asked Him to depart from them, for they were seized with great fear. And He got into the boat and returned.

[38]Now the man from whom the demons had departed begged Him that he might be with Him. But Jesus sent him away, saying, [39]"Return to your own house, and tell what great things God has done for you." And he went his way and proclaimed throughout the whole city what great things Jesus had done for him.

A Girl Restored to Life and a Woman Healed

[40]So it was, when Jesus returned, that the multitude welcomed Him, for they were all waiting for Him. [41]And behold, there came a man named Jairus, and he was a ruler of the synagogue. And he fell down at Jesus' feet and begged Him to come to his house, [42]for he had an only daughter about twelve years of age, and she was dying.

But as He went, the multitudes thronged Him. [43]Now a woman, having a flow of blood for twelve years, who had spent all her livelihood on physicians and could not be healed by any, [44]came from behind and touched the border of His garment. And immediately her flow of blood stopped.

[45]And Jesus said, "Who touched Me?"

When all denied it, Peter and those with him[f] said, "Master, the multitudes throng and press You, and You say, 'Who touched Me?' "[g]

8:37 [e] NU-Text reads *Gerasenes.* **8:45** [f] NU-Text omits *and those with him.* [g] NU-Text omits *and You say, 'Who touched Me?'*

THE MESSAGE

Later, a great many people from the Gerasene countryside got together and asked Jesus to leave—too much change, too fast, and they were scared. So Jesus got back in the boat and set off. The man whom he had delivered from the demons asked to go with him, but he sent him back, saying, "Go home and tell everything God did in you." So he went back and preached all over town everything Jesus had done in him.

His Touch

On his return, Jesus was welcomed by a crowd. They were all there expecting him. A man came up, Jairus by name. He was president of the meeting place. He fell at Jesus' feet and begged him to come to his home because his twelve-year-old daughter, his only child, was dying. Jesus went with him, making his way through the pushing, jostling crowd.

In the crowd that day there was a woman who for twelve years had been afflicted with hemorrhages. She had spent every penny she had on doctors but not one had been able to help her. She slipped in from behind and touched the edge of Jesus' robe. At that very moment her hemorrhaging stopped. Jesus said, "Who touched me?"

When no one stepped forward, Peter said, "But Master, we've got crowds of people on our hands. Dozens have touched you."

KING JAMES VERSION

46 And Jesus said, Somebody hath touched me: for I perceive that virtue is gone out of me.

47 And when the woman saw that she was not hid, she came trembling, and falling down before him, she declared unto him before all the people for what cause she had touched him, and how she was healed immediately.

48 And he said unto her, Daughter, be of good comfort: thy faith hath made thee whole; go in peace.

49 While he yet spake, there cometh one from the ruler of the synagogue's *house*, saying to him, Thy daughter is dead; trouble not the Master.

50 But when Jesus heard *it*, he answered him, saying, Fear not: believe only, and she shall be made whole.

51 And when he came into the house, he suffered no man to go in, save Peter, and James, and John, and the father and the mother of the maiden.

52 And all wept, and bewailed her: but he said, Weep not; she is not dead, but sleepeth.

53 And they laughed him to scorn, knowing that she was dead.

54 And he put them all out, and took her by the hand, and called, saying, Maid, arise.

55 And her spirit came again, and she arose straightway: and he commanded to give her meat.

56 And her parents were astonished: but he charged them that they should tell no man what was done.

NEW AMERICAN STANDARD BIBLE

46 But Jesus said, "Someone did touch Me, for I was aware that power had gone out of Me."

47 When the woman saw that she had not escaped notice, she came trembling and fell down before Him, and declared in the presence of all the people the reason why she had touched Him, and how she had been immediately healed.

48 And He said to her, "Daughter, your faith has made you well; go in peace."

49 While He was still speaking, someone *came from *the house of* the synagogue official, saying, "Your daughter has died; do not trouble the Teacher anymore."

50 But when Jesus heard *this,* He answered him, "Do not be afraid *any longer;* only believe, and she will be made well."

51 When He came to the house, He did not allow anyone to enter with Him, except Peter and John and James, and the girl's father and mother.

52 Now they were all weeping and lamenting for her; but He said, "Stop weeping, for she has not died, but is asleep."

53 And they *began* laughing at Him, knowing that she had died.

54 He, however, took her by the hand and called, saying, "Child, arise!"

55 And her spirit returned, and she got up immediately; and He gave orders for *something* to be given her to eat.

56 Her parents were amazed; but He instructed them to tell no one what had happened.

NEW CENTURY VERSION

46 But Jesus said, "Someone did touch me, because I felt
power go out from me." 47 When the woman saw she could
not hide, she came forward, shaking, and fell down before
Jesus. While all the people listened, she told why she had
touched him and how she had been instantly healed.
48 Jesus said to her, "Dear woman, you are made well
because you believed. Go in peace."
49 While Jesus was still speaking, someone came from
the house of the synagogue leader and said to him, "Your
daughter is dead. Don't bother the teacher anymore."
50 When Jesus heard this, he said to Jairus, "Don't be
afraid. Just believe, and your daughter will be well."
51 When Jesus went to the house, he let only Peter, John,
James, and the girl's father and mother go inside with him.
52 All the people were crying and feeling sad because the
girl was dead, but Jesus said, "Stop crying. She is not
dead, only asleep."
53 The people laughed at Jesus because they knew the
girl was dead. 54 But Jesus took hold of her hand and called
to her, "My child, stand up!" 55 Her spirit came back into
her, and she stood up at once. Then Jesus ordered that she
be given something to eat. 56 The girl's parents were
amazed, but Jesus told them not to tell anyone what had
happened.

CONTEMPORARY ENGLISH VERSION

46 But Jesus answered, "Someone touched me, because I
felt power going out from me." 47 The woman knew that
she could not hide, so she came trembling and knelt down
in front of Jesus. She told everyone why she had touched
him and that she had been healed right away.
48 Jesus said to the woman, "You are now well because
of your faith. May God give you peace!"
49 While Jesus was speaking, someone came from Jairus'
home and said, "Your daughter has died! Why bother the
teacher anymore?"
50 When Jesus heard this, he told Jairus, "Don't worry!
Have faith, and your daughter will get well."
51 Jesus went into the house, but he did not let anyone
else go with him, except Peter, John, James, and the girl's
father and mother. 52 Everyone was crying and weeping for
the girl. But Jesus said, "The child isn't dead. She is just
asleep." 53 The people laughed at him because they knew
she was dead.
54 Jesus took hold of the girl's hand and said, "Child, get
up!" 55 She came back to life and got right up. Jesus told
them to give her something to eat. 56 Her parents were sur-
prised, but Jesus ordered them not to tell anyone what had
happened.

NEW INTERNATIONAL VERSION

46But Jesus said, "Someone touched me; I know that
power has gone out from me."
47Then the woman, seeing that she could not go unno-
ticed, came trembling and fell at his feet. In the presence of
all the people, she told why she had touched him and how
she had been instantly healed. 48Then he said to her,
"Daughter, your faith has healed you. Go in peace."
49While Jesus was still speaking, someone came from
the house of Jairus, the synagogue ruler. "Your daughter is
dead," he said. "Don't bother the teacher any more."
50Hearing this, Jesus said to Jairus, "Don't be afraid; just
believe, and she will be healed."
51When he arrived at the house of Jairus, he did not let
anyone go in with him except Peter, John and James, and
the child's father and mother. 52Meanwhile, all the people
were wailing and mourning for her. "Stop wailing," Jesus
said. "She is not dead but asleep."
53They laughed at him, knowing that she was dead.
54But he took her by the hand and said, "My child, get
up!" 55Her spirit returned, and at once she stood up. Then
Jesus told them to give her something to eat. 56Her parents
were astonished, but he ordered them not to tell anyone
what had happened.

NEW LIVING TRANSLATION

46But Jesus told him, "No, someone deliberately touched
me, for I felt healing power go out from me." 47When the
woman realized that Jesus knew, she began to tremble and
fell to her knees before him. The whole crowd heard her
explain why she had touched him and that she had been
immediately healed. 48"Daughter," he said to her, "your
faith has made you well. Go in peace."
49While he was still speaking to her, a messenger
arrived from Jairus's home with the message, "Your little
girl is dead. There's no use troubling the Teacher now."
50But when Jesus heard what had happened, he said to
Jairus, "Don't be afraid. Just trust me, and she will be all
right."
51When they arrived at the house, Jesus wouldn't let
anyone go in with him except Peter, James, John, and the
little girl's father and mother. 52The house was filled with
people weeping and wailing, but he said, "Stop the weep-
ing! She isn't dead; she is only asleep."
53But the crowd laughed at him because they all knew
she had died. 54Then Jesus took her by the hand and said
in a loud voice, "Get up, my child!" 55And at that moment
her life returned, and she immediately stood up! Then
Jesus told them to give her something to eat. 56Her parents
were overwhelmed, but Jesus insisted that they not tell
anyone what had happened.

NEW KING JAMES VERSION

46But Jesus said, "Somebody touched Me, for I perceived
power going out from Me." 47Now when the woman saw
that she was not hidden, she came trembling; and falling
down before Him, she declared to Him in the presence of
all the people the reason she had touched Him and how
she was healed immediately.
48And He said to her, "Daughter, be of good cheer;[h] your
faith has made you well. Go in peace."
49While He was still speaking, someone came from the
ruler of the synagogue's *house,* saying to him, "Your
daughter is dead. Do not trouble the Teacher."[i]
50But when Jesus heard *it,* He answered him, saying,
"Do not be afraid; only believe, and she will be made well."
51When He came into the house, He permitted no one to go
in[j] except Peter, James, and John,[k] and the father and
mother of the girl. 52Now all wept and mourned for her;
but He said, "Do not weep; she is not dead, but sleeping."
53And they ridiculed Him, knowing that she was dead.
54But He put them all outside,[l] took her by the hand and
called, saying, "Little girl, arise." 55Then her spirit
returned, and she arose immediately. And He commanded
that she be given *something* to eat. 56And her parents were
astonished, but He charged them to tell no one what had
happened.

8:48 [h] NU-Text omits *be of good cheer.* **8:49** [i] NU-Text adds *anymore.*
8:51 [j] NU-Text adds *with Him.* [k] NU-Text and M-Text read *Peter, John,
and James.* **8:54** [l] NU-Text omits *put them all outside.*

THE MESSAGE

Jesus insisted, "Someone touched me. I felt power discharging from me."

When the woman realized that she couldn't remain hidden, she knelt trembling before him. In front of all the people, she blurted out her story—why she touched him and how at that same moment she was healed.

Jesus said, "Daughter, you took a risk trusting me, and now you're healed and whole. Live well, live blessed!"

While he was still talking, someone from the leader's house came up and told him, "Your daughter died. No need now to bother the Teacher."

Jesus overheard and said, "Don't be upset. Just trust me and everything will be all right." Going into the house, he wouldn't let anyone enter with him except Peter, John, James, and the child's parents.

Everyone was crying and carrying on over her. Jesus said, "Don't cry. She didn't die; she's sleeping." They laughed at him. They knew she was dead.

Then Jesus, gripping her hand, called, "My dear child, get up." She was up in an instant, up and breathing again! He told them to give her something to eat. Her parents were ecstatic, but Jesus warned them to keep quiet. "Don't tell a soul what happened in this room."

KING JAMES VERSION

9 Then he called his twelve disciples together, and gave them power and authority over all devils, and to cure diseases.

2 And he sent them to preach the kingdom of God, and to heal the sick.

3 And he said unto them, Take nothing for *your* journey, neither staves, nor scrip, neither bread, neither money; neither have two coats apiece.

4 And whatsoever house ye enter into, there abide, and thence depart.

5 And whosoever will not receive you, when ye go out of that city, shake off the very dust from your feet for a testimony against them.

6 And they departed, and went through the towns, preaching the gospel, and healing every where.

7 Now Herod the tetrarch heard of all that was done by him: and he was perplexed, because that it was said of some, that John was risen from the dead;

8 And of some, that Elias had appeared; and of others, that one of the old prophets was risen again.

9 And Herod said, John have I beheaded: but who is this, of whom I hear such things? And he desired to see him.

10 ¶ And the apostles, when they were returned, told

NEW AMERICAN STANDARD BIBLE

Ministry of the Twelve

9 And He called the twelve together, and gave them power and authority over all the demons and to heal diseases.

2 And He sent them out to proclaim the kingdom of God and to perform healing.

3 And He said to them, "Take nothing for *your* journey, neither a staff, nor a bag, nor bread, nor money; and do not *even* have two tunics apiece.

4 "Whatever house you enter, stay there until you leave that city.

5 "And as for those who do not receive you, as you go out from that city, shake the dust off your feet as a testimony against them."

6 Departing, they *began* going throughout the villages, preaching the gospel and healing everywhere.

7 Now Herod the tetrarch heard of all that was happening; and he was greatly perplexed, because it was said by some that John had risen from the dead,

8 and by some that Elijah had appeared, and by others that one of the prophets of old had risen again.

9 Herod said, "I myself had John beheaded; but who is this man about whom I hear such things?" And he kept trying to see Him.

10 When the apostles returned, they gave an account to

NEW CENTURY VERSION

Jesus Sends Out the Apostles

9 Jesus called the twelve apostles together and gave them power and authority over all demons and the ability to heal sicknesses. 2He sent the apostles out to tell about God's kingdom and to heal the sick. 3He said to them, "Take nothing for your trip, neither a walking stick, bag, bread, money, or extra clothes. 4When you enter a house, stay there until it is time to leave. 5If people do not welcome you, shake the dust off of your feet[a] as you leave the town, as a warning to them."

6So the apostles went out and traveled through all the towns, preaching the Good News and healing people everywhere.

Herod Is Confused About Jesus

7Herod, the governor, heard about all the things that were happening and was confused, because some people said, "John the Baptist has risen from the dead." 8Others said, "Elijah has come to us." And still others said, "One of the prophets who lived long ago has risen from the dead." 9Herod said, "I cut off John's head, so who is this man I hear such things about?" And Herod kept trying to see Jesus.

More than Five Thousand Fed

10When the apostles returned, they told Jesus everything

9:5 [a] **shake...feet** A warning. It showed that they had rejected these people.

CONTEMPORARY ENGLISH VERSION

Instructions for the Twelve Apostles

(Matthew 10.5-15; Mark 6.7-13)

9 Jesus called together his twelve apostles and gave them complete power over all demons and diseases. 2Then he sent them to tell about God's kingdom and to heal the sick. 3He told them, "Don't take anything with you! Don't take a walking stick or a traveling bag or food or money or even a change of clothes. 4When you are welcomed into a home, stay there until you leave that town. 5If people won't welcome you, leave the town and shake the dust from your feet[a] as a warning to them."

6The apostles left and went from village to village, telling the good news and healing people everywhere.

Herod Is Worried (Matthew 14.1-12; Mark 6.14-29)

7Herod[b] the ruler heard about all that was happening, and he was worried. Some people were saying that John the Baptist had come back to life. 8Others were saying that Elijah had come[c] or that one of the prophets from long ago had come back to life. 9But Herod said, "I had John's head cut off! Who is this I hear so much about?" Herod was eager to meet Jesus.

Jesus Feeds Five Thousand

(Matthew 14.13-21; Mark 6.30-44; John 6.1-14)

10The apostles came back and told Jesus everything they

[a] 9.5 *shake the dust from your feet*: This was a way of showing rejection. [b] 9.7 *Herod*: Herod Antipas, the son of Herod the Great. [c] 9.8 *Elijah had come*: Many of the Jewish people expected the prophet Elijah to come and prepare the way for the Messiah.

NEW INTERNATIONAL VERSION

Jesus Sends Out the Twelve

9 When Jesus had called the Twelve together, he gave them power and authority to drive out all demons and to cure diseases, [2]and he sent them out to preach the kingdom of God and to heal the sick. [3]He told them: "Take nothing for the journey—no staff, no bag, no bread, no money, no extra tunic. [4]Whatever house you enter, stay there until you leave that town. [5]If people do not welcome you, shake the dust off your feet when you leave their town, as a testimony against them." [6]So they set out and went from village to village, preaching the gospel and healing people everywhere.

[7]Now Herod the tetrarch heard about all that was going on. And he was perplexed, because some were saying that John had been raised from the dead, [8]others that Elijah had appeared, and still others that one of the prophets of long ago had come back to life. [9]But Herod said, "I beheaded John. Who, then, is this I hear such things about?" And he tried to see him.

Jesus Feeds the Five Thousand

[10]When the apostles returned, they reported to Jesus

NEW LIVING TRANSLATION

Jesus Sends Out the Twelve Apostles

9 One day Jesus called together his twelve apostles and gave them power and authority to cast out demons and to heal all diseases. [2]Then he sent them out to tell everyone about the coming of the Kingdom of God and to heal the sick. [3]"Don't even take along a walking stick," he instructed them, "nor a traveler's bag, nor food, nor money. Not even an extra coat. [4]When you enter each village, be a guest in only one home. [5]If the people of the village won't receive your message when you enter it, shake off its dust from your feet as you leave. It is a sign that you have abandoned that village to its fate."

[6]So they began their circuit of the villages, preaching the Good News and healing the sick.

Herod's Confusion

[7]When reports of Jesus' miracles reached Herod Antipas,* he was worried and puzzled because some were saying, "This is John the Baptist come back to life again." [8]Others were saying, "It is Elijah or some other ancient prophet risen from the dead."

[9]"I beheaded John," Herod said, "so who is this man about whom I hear such strange stories?" And he tried to see him.

Jesus Feeds Five Thousand

[10]When the apostles returned, they told Jesus everything

9:7 Greek *Herod the tetrarch.* He was a son of King Herod and was ruler over one of the four districts in Palestine.

NEW KING JAMES VERSION

Sending Out the Twelve

9 Then He called His twelve disciples together and gave them power and authority over all demons, and to cure diseases. [2]He sent them to preach the kingdom of God and to heal the sick. [3]And He said to them, "Take nothing for the journey, neither staffs nor bag nor bread nor money; and do not have two tunics apiece.

[4]"Whatever house you enter, stay there, and from there depart. [5]And whoever will not receive you, when you go out of that city, shake off the very dust from your feet as a testimony against them."

[6]So they departed and went through the towns, preaching the gospel and healing everywhere.

Herod Seeks to See Jesus

[7]Now Herod the tetrarch heard of all that was done by Him; and he was perplexed, because it was said by some that John had risen from the dead, [8]and by some that Elijah had appeared, and by others that one of the old prophets had risen again. [9]Herod said, "John I have beheaded, but who is this of whom I hear such things?" So he sought to see Him.

Feeding the Five Thousand

[10]And the apostles, when they had returned, told Him all

THE MESSAGE

Keep It Simple

9 Jesus now called the Twelve and gave them authority and power to deal with all the demons and cure diseases. He commissioned them to preach the news of God's kingdom and heal the sick. He said, "Don't load yourselves up with equipment. Keep it simple; *you* are the equipment. And no luxury inns—get a modest place and be content there until you leave. If you're not welcomed, leave town. Don't make a scene. Shrug your shoulders and move on."

Commissioned, they left. They traveled from town to town telling the latest news of God, the Message, and curing people everywhere they went.

Herod, the ruler, heard of these goings on and didn't know what to think. There were people saying John had come back from the dead, others that Elijah had appeared, still others that some prophet of long ago had shown up. Herod said, "But I killed John—took off his head. So who is this that I keep hearing about?" Curious, he looked for a chance to see him in action.

The apostles returned and reported on what they had

KING JAMES VERSION

him all that they had done. And he took them, and went aside privately into a desert place belonging to the city called Bethsaida.

11 And the people, when they knew *it*, followed him: and he received them, and spake unto them of the kingdom of God, and healed them that had need of healing.

12 And when the day began to wear away, then came the twelve, and said unto him, Send the multitude away, that they may go into the towns and country round about, and lodge, and get victuals: for we are here in a desert place.

13 But he said unto them, Give ye them to eat. And they said, We have no more but five loaves and two fishes; except we should go and buy meat for all this people.

14 For they were about five thousand men. And he said to his disciples, Make them sit down by fifties in a company.

15 And they did so, and made them all sit down.

16 Then he took the five loaves and the two fishes, and looking up to heaven, he blessed them, and brake, and gave to the disciples to set before the multitude.

17 And they did eat, and were all filled: and there was taken up of fragments that remained to them twelve baskets.

18 ¶ And it came to pass, as he was alone praying, his disciples were with him: and he asked them, saying, Whom say the people that I am?

NEW AMERICAN STANDARD BIBLE

Him of all that they had done. Taking them with Him, He withdrew by Himself to a city called Bethsaida.

11 But the crowds were aware of this and followed Him; and welcoming them, He *began* speaking to them about the kingdom of God and curing those who had need of healing.

Five Thousand Fed

12 Now the day was ending, and the twelve came and said to Him, "Send the crowd away, that they may go into the surrounding villages and countryside and find lodging and get something to eat; for here we are in a desolate place."

13 But He said to them, "You give them *something* to eat!" And they said, "We have no more than five loaves and two fish, unless perhaps we go and buy food for all these people."

14 (For there were about five thousand men.) And He said to His disciples, "Have them sit down *to eat* in groups of about fifty each."

15 They did so, and had them all sit down.

16 Then He took the five loaves and the two fish, and looking up to heaven, He blessed them, and broke *them,* and kept giving *them* to the disciples to set before the people.

17 And they all ate and were satisfied; and the broken pieces which they had left over were picked up, twelve baskets *full.*

18 And it happened that while He was praying alone, the disciples were with Him, and He questioned them, saying, "Who do the people say that I am?"

NEW CENTURY VERSION

they had done. Then Jesus took them with him to a town
called Bethsaida where they could be alone together. [11]But
the people learned where Jesus went and followed him. He
welcomed them and talked with them about God's kingdom and healed those who needed to be healed.

[12]Late in the afternoon, the twelve apostles came to
Jesus and said, "Send the people away. They need to go to
the towns and countryside around here and find places to
sleep and something to eat, because no one lives in this
place."

[13]But Jesus said to them, "You give them something to
eat."

They said, "We have only five loaves of bread and two
fish, unless we go buy food for all these people." [14](There
were about five thousand men there.)

Jesus said to his followers, "Tell the people to sit in
groups of about fifty people."

[15]So the followers did this, and all the people sat down.
[16]Then Jesus took the five loaves of bread and two fish,
and looking up to heaven, he thanked God for the food.
Then he divided the food and gave it to the followers to
give to the people. [17]They all ate and were satisfied, and
what was left over was gathered up, filling twelve baskets.

Jesus Is the Christ

[18]One time when Jesus was praying alone, his followers
were with him, and he asked them, "Who do the people
say I am?"

CONTEMPORARY ENGLISH VERSION

had done. He then took them with him to the village of
Bethsaida, where they could be alone. [11]But a lot of people
found out about this and followed him. Jesus welcomed
them. He spoke to them about God's kingdom and healed
everyone who was sick.

[12]Late in the afternoon the twelve apostles came to Jesus
and said, "Send the crowd to the villages and farms around
here. They need to find a place to stay and something to
eat. There is nothing in this place. It is like a desert!"

[13]Jesus answered, "You give them something to eat."

But they replied, "We have only five small loaves of
bread[d] and two fish. If we are going to feed all these people, we will have to go and buy food." [14]There were about
five thousand men in the crowd.

Jesus said to his disciples, "Have the people sit in groups
of fifty." [15]They did this, and all the people sat down.
[16]Jesus took the five loaves and the two fish. He looked up
toward heaven and blessed the food. Then he broke the
bread and fish and handed them to his disciples to give to
the people.

[17]Everyone ate all they wanted. What was left over filled
twelve baskets.

Who Is Jesus? (Matthew 16.13-19; Mark 8.27-29)

[18]When Jesus was alone praying, his disciples came to
him, and he asked them, "What do people say about me?"

[d] **9.13** *small loaves of bread*: These would have been flat and round or in the shape of a bun.

NEW INTERNATIONAL VERSION

what they had done. Then he took them with him and they withdrew by themselves to a town called Bethsaida, [11]but the crowds learned about it and followed him. He welcomed them and spoke to them about the kingdom of God, and healed those who needed healing.

[12]Late in the afternoon the Twelve came to him and said, "Send the crowd away so they can go to the surrounding villages and countryside and find food and lodging, because we are in a remote place here."

[13]He replied, "You give them something to eat."

They answered, "We have only five loaves of bread and two fish—unless we go and buy food for all this crowd." [14](About five thousand men were there.)

But he said to his disciples, "Have them sit down in groups of about fifty each." [15]The disciples did so, and everybody sat down. [16]Taking the five loaves and the two fish and looking up to heaven, he gave thanks and broke them. Then he gave them to the disciples to set before the people. [17]They all ate and were satisfied, and the disciples picked up twelve basketfuls of broken pieces that were left over.

Peter's Confession of Christ

[18]Once when Jesus was praying in private and his disciples were with him, he asked them, "Who do the crowds say I am?"

NEW LIVING TRANSLATION

they had done. Then he slipped quietly away with them toward the town of Bethsaida. [11]But the crowds found out where he was going, and they followed him. And he welcomed them, teaching them about the Kingdom of God and curing those who were ill. [12]Late in the afternoon the twelve disciples came to him and said, "Send the crowds away to the nearby villages and farms, so they can find food and lodging for the night. There is nothing to eat here in this deserted place."

[13]But Jesus said, "You feed them."

"Impossible!" they protested. "We have only five loaves of bread and two fish. Or are you expecting us to go and buy enough food for this whole crowd?" [14]For there were about five thousand men there.

"Just tell them to sit down on the ground in groups of about fifty each," Jesus replied. [15]So the people all sat down. [16]Jesus took the five loaves and two fish, looked up toward heaven, and asked God's blessing on the food. Breaking the loaves into pieces, he kept giving the bread and fish to the disciples to give to the people. [17]They all ate as much as they wanted, and they picked up twelve baskets of leftovers!

Peter's Declaration about Jesus

[18]One day as Jesus was alone, praying, he came over to his disciples and asked them, "Who do people say I am?"

NEW KING JAMES VERSION

that they had done. Then He took them and went aside privately into a deserted place belonging to the city called Bethsaida. [11]But when the multitudes knew *it,* they followed Him; and He received them and spoke to them about the kingdom of God, and healed those who had need of healing. [12]When the day began to wear away, the twelve came and said to Him, "Send the multitude away, that they may go into the surrounding towns and country, and lodge and get provisions; for we are in a deserted place here."

[13]But He said to them, "You give them something to eat."

And they said, "We have no more than five loaves and two fish, unless we go and buy food for all these people." [14]For there were about five thousand men.

Then He said to His disciples, "Make them sit down in groups of fifty." [15]And they did so, and made them all sit down.

[16]Then He took the five loaves and the two fish, and looking up to heaven, He blessed and broke *them,* and gave *them* to the disciples to set before the multitude. [17]So they all ate and were filled, and twelve baskets of the leftover fragments were taken up by them.

Peter Confesses Jesus as the Christ

[18]And it happened, as He was alone praying, *that* His disciples joined Him, and He asked them, saying, "Who do the crowds say that I am?"

THE MESSAGE

done. Jesus took them away, off by themselves, near the town called Bethsaida. But the crowds got wind of it and followed. Jesus graciously welcomed them and talked to them about the kingdom of God. Those who needed healing, he healed.

Bread and Fish for Five Thousand

As the day declined, the Twelve said, "Dismiss the crowd so they can go to the farms or villages around here and get a room for the night and a bite to eat. We're out in the middle of nowhere."

"You feed them," Jesus said.

They said, "We couldn't scrape up more than five loaves of bread and a couple of fish—unless, of course, you want us to go to town ourselves and buy food for everybody." (There were more than five thousand people in the crowd.)

But he went ahead and directed his disciples, "Sit them down in groups of about fifty." They did what he said, and soon had everyone seated. He took the five loaves and two fish, lifted his face to heaven in prayer, blessed, broke, and gave the bread and fish to the disciples to hand out to the crowd. After the people had all eaten their fill, twelve baskets of leftovers were gathered up.

Don't Run From Suffering

One time when Jesus was off praying by himself, his disciples nearby, he asked them, "What are the crowds saying about me, about who I am?"

KING JAMES VERSION

19 They answering said, John the Baptist; but some *say*, Elias; and others *say*, that one of the old prophets is risen again.

20 He said unto them, But whom say ye that I am? Peter answering said, The Christ of God.

21 And he straitly charged them, and commanded *them* to tell no man that thing;

22 Saying, The Son of man must suffer many things, and be rejected of the elders and chief priests and scribes, and be slain, and be raised the third day.

23 And he said to *them* all, If any *man* will come after me, let him deny himself, and take up his cross daily, and follow me.

24 For whosoever will save his life shall lose it: but whosoever will lose his life for my sake, the same shall save it.

25 For what is a man advantaged, if he gain the whole world, and lose himself, or be cast away?

26 For whosoever shall be ashamed of me and of my words, of him shall the Son of man be ashamed, when he shall come in his own glory, and *in his* Father's, and of the holy angels.

27 But I tell you of a truth, there be some standing here, which shall not taste of death, till they see the kingdom of God.

NEW AMERICAN STANDARD BIBLE

19 They answered and said, "John the Baptist, and others *say* Elijah; but others, that one of the prophets of old has risen again."

20 And He said to them, "But who do you say that I am?" And Peter answered and said, "The Christ of God."

21 But He warned them and instructed *them* not to tell this to anyone,

22 saying, "The Son of Man must suffer many things and be rejected by the elders and chief priests and scribes, and be killed and be raised up on the third day."

23 And He was saying to *them* all, "If anyone wishes to come after Me, he must deny himself, and take up his cross daily and follow Me.

24 "For whoever wishes to save his life will lose it, but whoever loses his life for My sake, he is the one who will save it.

25 "For what is a man profited if he gains the whole world, and loses or forfeits himself?

26 "For whoever is ashamed of Me and My words, the Son of Man will be ashamed of him when He comes in His glory, and *the glory* of the Father and of the holy angels.

27 "But I say to you truthfully, there are some of those standing here who will not taste death until they see the kingdom of God."

NEW CENTURY VERSION

19 They answered, "Some say you are John the Baptist. Others say you are Elijah.[b] And others say you are one of the prophets from long ago who has come back to life."

20 Then Jesus asked, "But who do you say I am?"

Peter answered, "You are the Christ from God."

21 Jesus warned them not to tell anyone, saying, 22 "The Son of Man must suffer many things. He will be rejected by the older Jewish leaders, the leading priests, and the teachers of the law. He will be killed and after three days will be raised from the dead."

23 Jesus said to all of them, "If people want to follow me, they must give up the things they want. They must be willing to give up their lives daily to follow me. 24 Those who want to save their lives will give up true life. But those who give up their lives for me will have true life. 25 It is worth nothing for them to have the whole world if they themselves are destroyed or lost. 26 If people are ashamed of me and my teaching, then the Son of Man will be ashamed of them when he comes in his glory and with the glory of the Father and the holy angels. 27 I tell you the truth, some people standing here will see the kingdom of God before they die."

9:19 [b] **Elijah** A man who spoke for God and who lived hundreds of years before Christ. See 1 Kings 17.

CONTEMPORARY ENGLISH VERSION

19 They answered, "Some say that you are John the Baptist or Elijah[e] or a prophet from long ago who has come back to life."

20 Jesus then asked them, "But who do you say I am?"

Peter answered, "You are the Messiah sent from God."

21 Jesus strictly warned his disciples not to tell anyone about this.

Jesus Speaks about His Suffering and Death

(Matthew 16.20-28; Mark 8.30—9.1)

22 Jesus told his disciples, "The nation's leaders, the chief priests, and the teachers of the Law of Moses will make the Son of Man suffer terribly. They will reject him and kill him, but three days later he will rise to life."

23 Then Jesus said to all the people:

If any of you want to be my followers, you must forget about yourself. You must take up your cross each day and follow me. 24 If you want to save your life,[f] you will destroy it. But if you give up your life for me, you will save it. 25 What will you gain, if you own the whole world but destroy yourself or waste your life? 26 If you are ashamed of me and my message, the Son of Man will be ashamed of you when he comes in his glory and in the glory of his Father and the holy angels. 27 You can be sure that some of the people standing here will not die before they see God's kingdom.

[e] **9.19** *Elijah*: See the note at 9.8. [f] **9.24** *life*: In verses 24, 25 a Greek word which often means "soul" is translated "life" and "yourself."

NEW INTERNATIONAL VERSION

[19]They replied, "Some say John the Baptist; others say
Elijah; and still others, that one of the prophets of long
ago has come back to life."

[20]"But what about you?" he asked. "Who do you say
I am?"

Peter answered, "The Christ[a] of God."

[21]Jesus strictly warned them not to tell this to anyone.
[22]And he said, "The Son of Man must suffer many things
and be rejected by the elders, chief priests and teachers of
the law, and he must be killed and on the third day be
raised to life."

[23]Then he said to them all: "If anyone would come after
me, he must deny himself and take up his cross daily and
follow me. [24]For whoever wants to save his life will lose it,
but whoever loses his life for me will save it. [25]What good
is it for a man to gain the whole world, and yet lose or for-
feit his very self? [26]If anyone is ashamed of me and my
words, the Son of Man will be ashamed of him when he
comes in his glory and in the glory of the Father and of the
holy angels. [27]I tell you the truth, some who are standing
here will not taste death before they see the kingdom of
God."

[a] 20 Or *Messiah*

NEW LIVING TRANSLATION

[19]"Well," they replied, "some say John the Baptist, some
say Elijah, and others say you are one of the other ancient
prophets risen from the dead."

[20]Then he asked them, "Who do you say I am?"

Peter replied, "You are the Messiah sent from God!"

Jesus Predicts His Death

[21]Jesus warned them not to tell anyone about this.
[22]"For I, the Son of Man, must suffer many terrible
things," he said. "I will be rejected by the leaders, the lead-
ing priests, and the teachers of religious law. I will be
killed, but three days later I will be raised from the dead."

[23]Then he said to the crowd, "If any of you wants to be
my follower, you must put aside your selfish ambition,
shoulder your cross daily, and follow me. [24]If you try to
keep your life for yourself, you will lose it. But if you give
up your life for me, you will find true life. [25]And how do
you benefit if you gain the whole world but lose or forfeit
your own soul in the process? [26]If a person is ashamed of
me and my message, I, the Son of Man, will be ashamed of
that person when I return in my glory and in the glory of
the Father and the holy angels. [27]And I assure you that
some of you standing here right now will not die before
you see the Kingdom of God."

NEW KING JAMES VERSION

[19]So they answered and said, "John the Baptist, but
some *say* Elijah; and others *say* that one of the old proph-
ets has risen again."

[20]He said to them, "But who do you say that I am?"
Peter answered and said, "The Christ of God."

Jesus Predicts His Death and Resurrection

[21]And He strictly warned and commanded them to tell
this to no one, [22]saying, "The Son of Man must suffer
many things, and be rejected by the elders and chief
priests and scribes, and be killed, and be raised the third
day."

Take Up the Cross and Follow Him

[23]Then He said to *them* all, "If anyone desires to come
after Me, let him deny himself, and take up his cross
daily,[a] and follow Me. [24]For whoever desires to save his
life will lose it, but whoever loses his life for My sake will
save it. [25]For what profit is it to a man if he gains the
whole world, and is himself destroyed or lost? [26]For who-
ever is ashamed of Me and My words, of him the Son of
Man will be ashamed when He comes in His *own* glory,
and *in His* Father's, and of the holy angels.

Jesus Transfigured on the Mount

[27]But I tell you truly, there are some standing here who
shall not taste death till they see the kingdom of God."

9:23 [a] M-Text omits *daily.*

THE MESSAGE

They said, "John the Baptizer. Others say Elijah. Still others say that one of the prophets from long ago has come back."

He then asked, "And you—what are you saying about me? Who am I?"

Peter answered, "The Messiah of God." Jesus then warned them to keep it quiet. They were to tell no one what Peter had said.

He went on, "It is necessary that the Son of Man proceed to an ordeal of suffering, be tried and found guilty by the religious leaders, high priests, and religion scholars, be killed, and on the third day be raised up alive."

Then he told them what they could expect for themselves: "Anyone who intends to come with me has to let me lead. You're not in the driver's seat—I am. Don't run from suffering; embrace it. Follow me and I'll show you how. Self-help is no help at all. Self-sacrifice is the way, *my* way, to finding yourself, your true self. What good would it do to get everything you want and lose you, the real you? If any of you is embarrassed with me and the way I'm leading you, know that the Son of Man will be far more embarrassed with you when he arrives in all his splendor in company with the Father and the holy angels. This isn't, you realize, pie in the sky by and by. Some who have taken their stand right here are going to see it happen, see with their own eyes the kingdom of God."

KING JAMES VERSION

28 ¶ And it came to pass about an eight days after these sayings, he took Peter and John and James, and went up into a mountain to pray.

29 And as he prayed, the fashion of his countenance was altered, and his raiment *was* white *and* glistering.

30 And, behold, there talked with him two men, which were Moses and Elias:

31 Who appeared in glory, and spake of his decease which he should accomplish at Jerusalem.

32 But Peter and they that were with him were heavy with sleep: and when they were awake, they saw his glory, and the two men that stood with him.

33 And it came to pass, as they departed from him, Peter said unto Jesus, Master, it is good for us to be here: and let us make three tabernacles; one for thee, and one for Moses, and one for Elias: not knowing what he said.

34 While he thus spake, there came a cloud, and overshadowed them: and they feared as they entered into the cloud.

35 And there came a voice out of the cloud, saying, This is my beloved Son: hear him.

36 And when the voice was past, Jesus was found alone. And they kept *it* close, and told no man in those days any of those things which they had seen.

37 ¶ And it came to pass, that on the next day, when they were come down from the hill, much people met him.

NEW AMERICAN STANDARD BIBLE

The Transfiguration

28 Some eight days after these sayings, He took along Peter and John and James, and went up on the mountain to pray.

29 And while He was praying, the appearance of His face became different, and His clothing *became* white *and* gleaming.

30 And behold, two men were talking with Him; and they were Moses and Elijah,

31 who, appearing in glory, were speaking of His departure which He was about to accomplish at Jerusalem.

32 Now Peter and his companions had been overcome with sleep; but when they were fully awake, they saw His glory and the two men standing with Him.

33 And as these were leaving Him, Peter said to Jesus, "Master, it is good for us to be here; let us make three tabernacles: one for You, and one for Moses, and one for Elijah"—not realizing what he was saying.

34 While he was saying this, a cloud formed and *began* to overshadow them; and they were afraid as they entered the cloud.

35 Then a voice came out of the cloud, saying, "This is My Son, *My* Chosen One; listen to Him!"

36 And when the voice had spoken, Jesus was found alone. And they kept silent, and reported to no one in those days any of the things which they had seen.

37 On the next day, when they came down from the mountain, a large crowd met Him.

NEW CENTURY VERSION

Jesus Talks with Moses and Elijah

28About eight days after Jesus said these things, he took Peter, John, and James and went up on a mountain to pray.
29While Jesus was praying, the appearance of his face changed, and his clothes became shining white. 30Then two men, Moses and Elijah,[c] were talking with Jesus.
31They appeared in heavenly glory, talking about his departure which he would soon bring about in Jerusalem.
32Peter and the others were very sleepy, but when they awoke fully, they saw the glory of Jesus and the two men standing with him. 33When Moses and Elijah were about to leave, Peter said to Jesus, "Master, it is good that we are here. Let us make three tents—one for you, one for Moses, and one for Elijah." (Peter did not know what he was talking about.)

34While he was saying these things, a cloud came and covered them, and they became afraid as the cloud covered them. 35A voice came from the cloud, saying, "This is my Son, whom I have chosen. Listen to him!"

36When the voice finished speaking, only Jesus was there. Peter, John, and James said nothing and told no one at that time what they had seen.

Jesus Heals a Sick Boy

37The next day, when they came down from the mountain, a large crowd met Jesus. 38A man in the crowd shout-

9:30 [c] **Moses and Elijah** Two of the most important Jewish leaders in the past. Moses had given them the law, and Elijah was an important prophet.

CONTEMPORARY ENGLISH VERSION

The True Glory of Jesus (Matthew 17.1-8; Mark 9.2-8)

28About eight days later Jesus took Peter, John, and James with him and went up on a mountain to pray.
29While he was praying, his face changed, and his clothes became shining white. 30Suddenly Moses and Elijah were there speaking with him. 31They appeared in heavenly glory and talked about all that Jesus' death[g] in Jerusalem would mean.

32Peter and the other two disciples had been sound asleep. All at once they woke up and saw how glorious Jesus was. They also saw the two men who were with him.

33Moses and Elijah were about to leave, when Peter said to Jesus, "Master, it is good for us to be here! Let us make three shelters, one for you, one for Moses, and one for Elijah." But Peter did not know what he was talking about.

34While Peter was still speaking, a shadow from a cloud passed over them, and they were frightened as the cloud covered them. 35From the cloud a voice spoke, "This is my chosen Son. Listen to what he says!"

36After the voice had spoken, Peter, John, and James saw only Jesus. For some time they kept quiet and did not say anything about what they had seen.

Jesus Heals a Boy (Matthew 17.14-18; Mark 9.14-27)

37The next day Jesus and his three disciples came down from the mountain and were met by a large crowd. 38Just

[g] 9.31 *Jesus' death*: In Greek this is "his departure," which probably includes his rising to life and his return to heaven.

NEW INTERNATIONAL VERSION

The Transfiguration

28 About eight days after Jesus said this, he took Peter, John and James with him and went up onto a mountain to pray. 29 As he was praying, the appearance of his face changed, and his clothes became as bright as a flash of lightning. 30 Two men, Moses and Elijah, 31 appeared in glorious splendor, talking with Jesus. They spoke about his departure, which he was about to bring to fulfillment at Jerusalem. 32 Peter and his companions were very sleepy, but when they became fully awake, they saw his glory and the two men standing with him. 33 As the men were leaving Jesus, Peter said to him, "Master, it is good for us to be here. Let us put up three shelters—one for you, one for Moses and one for Elijah." (He did not know what he was saying.)

34 While he was speaking, a cloud appeared and enveloped them, and they were afraid as they entered the cloud. 35 A voice came from the cloud, saying, "This is my Son, whom I have chosen; listen to him." 36 When the voice had spoken, they found that Jesus was alone. The disciples kept this to themselves, and told no one at that time what they had seen.

The Healing of a Boy With an Evil Spirit

37 The next day, when they came down from the mountain, a large crowd met him. 38 A man in the crowd called

NEW LIVING TRANSLATION

The Transfiguration

28 About eight days later Jesus took Peter, James, and John to a mountain to pray. 29 And as he was praying, the appearance of his face changed, and his clothing became dazzling white. 30 Then two men, Moses and Elijah, appeared and began talking with Jesus. 31 They were glorious to see. And they were speaking of how he was about to fulfill God's plan by dying in Jerusalem.

32 Peter and the others were very drowsy and had fallen asleep. Now they woke up and saw Jesus' glory and the two men standing with him. 33 As Moses and Elijah were starting to leave, Peter, not even knowing what he was saying, blurted out, "Master, this is wonderful! We will make three shrines*—one for you, one for Moses, and one for Elijah." 34 But even as he was saying this, a cloud came over them; and terror gripped them as it covered them.

35 Then a voice from the cloud said, "This is my Son, my Chosen One.* Listen to him." 36 When the voice died away, Jesus was there alone. They didn't tell anyone what they had seen until long after this happened.

Jesus Heals a Demon-Possessed Boy

37 The next day, after they had come down the mountain, a huge crowd met Jesus. 38 A man in the crowd called out

9:33 Or *shelters;* Greek reads *tabernacles.* 9:35 Some manuscripts read *This is my beloved Son.*

NEW KING JAMES VERSION

28 Now it came to pass, about eight days after these sayings, that He took Peter, John, and James and went up on the mountain to pray. 29 As He prayed, the appearance of His face was altered, and His robe *became* white *and* glistening. 30 And behold, two men talked with Him, who were Moses and Elijah, 31 who appeared in glory and spoke of His decease which He was about to accomplish at Jerusalem. 32 But Peter and those with him were heavy with sleep; and when they were fully awake, they saw His glory and the two men who stood with Him. 33 Then it happened, as they were parting from Him, *that* Peter said to Jesus, "Master, it is good for us to be here; and let us make three tabernacles: one for You, one for Moses, and one for Elijah"—not knowing what he said.

34 While he was saying this, a cloud came and overshadowed them; and they were fearful as they entered the cloud. 35 And a voice came out of the cloud, saying, "This is My beloved Son.[b] Hear Him!" 36 When the voice had ceased, Jesus was found alone. But they kept quiet, and told no one in those days any of the things they had seen.

A Boy Is Healed

37 Now it happened on the next day, when they had come down from the mountain, that a great multitude met Him.

9:35 [b] NU-Text reads *This is My Son, the Chosen One.*

THE MESSAGE

Jesus in His Glory

About eight days after saying this, he climbed the mountain to pray, taking Peter, John, and James along. While he was in prayer, the appearance of his face changed and his clothes became blinding white. At once two men were there talking with him. They turned out to be Moses and Elijah—and what a glorious appearance they made! They talked over his exodus, the one Jesus was about to complete in Jerusalem.

Meanwhile, Peter and those with him were slumped over in sleep. When they came to, rubbing their eyes, they saw Jesus in his glory and the two men standing with him. When Moses and Elijah had left, Peter said to Jesus, "Master, this is a great moment! Let's build three memorials: one for you, one for Moses, and one for Elijah." He blurted this out without thinking.

While he was babbling on like this, a light-radiant cloud enveloped them. As they found themselves buried in the cloud, they became deeply aware of God. Then there was a voice out of the cloud: "This is my Son, the Chosen! Listen to him."

When the sound of the voice died away, they saw Jesus there alone. They were speechless. And they continued speechless, said not one thing to anyone during those days of what they had seen.

✣

When they came down off the mountain the next day, a big crowd was there to meet them. A man called from out

KING JAMES VERSION

38 And, behold, a man of the company cried out, saying, Master, I beseech thee, look upon my son: for he is mine only child.

39 And, lo, a spirit taketh him, and he suddenly crieth out; and it teareth him that he foameth again, and bruising him hardly departeth from him.

40 And I besought thy disciples to cast him out; and they could not.

41 And Jesus answering said, O faithless and perverse generation, how long shall I be with you, and suffer you? Bring thy son hither.

42 And as he was yet a coming, the devil threw him down, and tare *him*. And Jesus rebuked the unclean spirit, and healed the child, and delivered him again to his father.

43 ¶ And they were all amazed at the mighty power of God. But while they wondered every one at all things which Jesus did, he said unto his disciples,

44 Let these sayings sink down into your ears: for the Son of man shall be delivered into the hands of men.

45 But they understood not this saying, and it was hid from them, that they perceived it not: and they feared to ask him of that saying.

46 Then there arose a reasoning among them, which of them should be greatest.

47 And Jesus, perceiving the thought of their heart, took a child, and set him by him,

NEW AMERICAN STANDARD BIBLE

38 And a man from the crowd shouted, saying, "Teacher, I beg You to look at my son, for he is my only *boy*,

39 and a spirit seizes him, and he suddenly screams, and it throws him into a convulsion with foaming *at the mouth;* and only with difficulty does it leave him, mauling him *as it leaves*.

40 "I begged Your disciples to cast it out, and they could not."

41 And Jesus answered and said, "You unbelieving and perverted generation, how long shall I be with you and put up with you? Bring your son here."

42 While he was still approaching, the demon slammed him *to the ground* and threw him into a convulsion. But Jesus rebuked the unclean spirit, and healed the boy and gave him back to his father.

43 And they were all amazed at the greatness of God.

But while everyone was marveling at all that He was doing, He said to His disciples,

44 "Let these words sink into your ears; for the Son of Man is going to be delivered into the hands of men."

45 But they did not understand this statement, and it was concealed from them so that they would not perceive it; and they were afraid to ask Him about this statement.

The Test of Greatness

46 An argument started among them as to which of them might be the greatest.

47 But Jesus, knowing what they were thinking in their heart, took a child and stood him by His side,

NEW CENTURY VERSION

ed to him, "Teacher, please come and look at my son, because he is my only child. 39An evil spirit seizes my son, and suddenly he screams. It causes him to lose control of himself and foam at the mouth. The evil spirit keeps on hurting him and almost never leaves him. 40I begged your followers to force the evil spirit out, but they could not do it."

41Jesus answered, "You people have no faith, and your lives are all wrong. How long must I stay with you and put up with you? Bring your son here."

42While the boy was coming, the demon threw him on the ground and made him lose control of himself. But Jesus gave a strong command to the evil spirit and healed the boy and gave him back to his father. 43All the people were amazed at the great power of God.

Jesus Talks About His Death

While everyone was wondering about all that Jesus did, he said to his followers, 44"Don't forget what I tell you now: The Son of Man will be handed over to people." 45But the followers did not understand what this meant; the meaning was hidden from them so they could not understand. But they were afraid to ask Jesus about it.

Who Is the Greatest?

46Jesus' followers began to have an argument about which one of them was the greatest. 47Jesus knew what they were thinking, so he took a little child and stood the

CONTEMPORARY ENGLISH VERSION

then someone in the crowd shouted, "Teacher, please do something for my son! He is my only child! 39A demon often attacks him and makes him scream. It shakes him until he foams at the mouth, and it won't leave him until it has completely worn the boy out. 40I begged your disciples to force out the demon, but they couldn't do it."

41Jesus said to them, "You people are stubborn and don't have any faith! How much longer must I be with you? Why do I have to put up with you?"

Then Jesus said to the man, "Bring your son to me." 42While the boy was being brought, the demon attacked him and made him shake all over. Jesus ordered the demon to stop. Then he healed the boy and gave him back to his father. 43Everyone was amazed at God's great power.

Jesus Again Speaks about His Death

(Matthew 17.22, 23; Mark 9.30-32)

While everyone was still amazed at what Jesus was doing, he said to his disciples, 44"Pay close attention to what I am telling you! The Son of Man will be handed over to his enemies." 45But the disciples did not know what he meant. The meaning was hidden from them. They could not understand it, and they were afraid to ask.

Who Is the Greatest? (Matthew 18.1-5; Mark 9.33-37)

46Jesus' disciples were arguing about which one of them was the greatest. 47Jesus knew what they were thinking, and he had a child stand there beside him. 48Then he said

NEW INTERNATIONAL VERSION

out, "Teacher, I beg you to look at my son, for he is my only child. [39]A spirit seizes him and he suddenly screams; it throws him into convulsions so that he foams at the mouth. It scarcely ever leaves him and is destroying him. [40]I begged your disciples to drive it out, but they could not."

[41]"O unbelieving and perverse generation," Jesus replied, "how long shall I stay with you and put up with you? Bring your son here."

[42]Even while the boy was coming, the demon threw him to the ground in a convulsion. But Jesus rebuked the evil[b] spirit, healed the boy and gave him back to his father. [43]And they were all amazed at the greatness of God.

While everyone was marveling at all that Jesus did, he said to his disciples, [44]"Listen carefully to what I am about to tell you: The Son of Man is going to be betrayed into the hands of men." [45]But they did not understand what this meant. It was hidden from them, so that they did not grasp it, and they were afraid to ask him about it.

Who Will Be the Greatest?

[46]An argument started among the disciples as to which of them would be the greatest. [47]Jesus, knowing their thoughts, took a little child and had him stand beside him.

[b] *42* Greek *unclean*

NEW LIVING TRANSLATION

to him, "Teacher, look at my boy, who is my only son. [39]An evil spirit keeps seizing him, making him scream. It throws him into convulsions so that he foams at the mouth. It is always hitting and injuring him. It hardly ever leaves him alone. [40]I begged your disciples to cast the spirit out, but they couldn't do it."

[41]"You stubborn, faithless people," Jesus said, "how long must I be with you and put up with you? Bring him here." [42]As the boy came forward, the demon knocked him to the ground and threw him into a violent convulsion. But Jesus rebuked the evil spirit and healed the boy. Then he gave him back to his father. [43]Awe gripped the people as they saw this display of God's power.

Jesus Again Predicts His Death

While everyone was marveling over all the wonderful things he was doing, Jesus said to his disciples, [44]"Listen to me and remember what I say. The Son of Man is going to be betrayed." [45]But they didn't know what he meant. Its significance was hidden from them, so they could not understand it, and they were afraid to ask him about it.

The Greatest in the Kingdom

[46]Then there was an argument among them as to which of them would be the greatest. [47]But Jesus knew their thoughts, so he brought a little child to his side. [48]Then he

NEW KING JAMES VERSION

[38]Suddenly a man from the multitude cried out, saying, "Teacher, I implore You, look on my son, for he is my only child. [39]And behold, a spirit seizes him, and he suddenly cries out; it convulses him so that he foams *at the mouth;* and it departs from him with great difficulty, bruising him. [40]So I implored Your disciples to cast it out, but they could not."

[41]Then Jesus answered and said, "O faithless and perverse generation, how long shall I be with you and bear with you? Bring your son here." [42]And as he was still coming, the demon threw him down and convulsed *him.* Then Jesus rebuked the unclean spirit, healed the child, and gave him back to his father.

Jesus Again Predicts His Death

[43]And they were all amazed at the majesty of God.

But while everyone marveled at all the things which Jesus did, He said to His disciples, [44]"Let these words sink down into your ears, for the Son of Man is about to be betrayed into the hands of men." [45]But they did not understand this saying, and it was hidden from them so that they did not perceive it; and they were afraid to ask Him about this saying.

Who Is the Greatest?

[46]Then a dispute arose among them as to which of them would be greatest. [47]And Jesus, perceiving the thought of their heart, took a little child and set him by Him, [48]and

THE MESSAGE

of the crowd, "Please, please, Teacher, take a look at my son. He's my only child. Often a spirit seizes him. Suddenly he's screaming, thrown into convulsions, his mouth foaming. And then it beats him black and blue before it leaves. I asked your disciples to deliver him but they couldn't."

Jesus said, "What a generation! No sense of God! No focus to your lives! How many times do I have to go over these things? How much longer do I have to put up with this? Bring your son here."

While he was coming, the demon slammed him to the ground and threw him into convulsions. Jesus stepped in, ordered the vile spirit gone, healed the boy, and handed him back to his father. They all shook their heads in wonder, astonished at God's greatness, God's majestic greatness.

Your Business Is Life

While they continued to stand around exclaiming over all the things he was doing, Jesus said to his disciples, "Treasure and ponder each of these next words: The Son of Man is about to be betrayed into human hands."

They didn't get what he was saying. It was like he was speaking a foreign language and they couldn't make heads or tails of it. But they were embarrassed to ask him what he meant.

They started arguing over which of them would be most famous. When Jesus realized how much this mattered to them, he brought a child to his side. "Whoever accepts this

KING JAMES VERSION

48 And said unto them, Whosoever shall receive this child in my name receiveth me: and whosoever shall receive me receiveth him that sent me: for he that is least among you all, the same shall be great.

49 And John answered and said, Master, we saw one casting out devils in thy name; and we forbad him, because he followeth not with us.

50 And Jesus said unto him, Forbid *him* not: for he that is not against us is for us.

51 ¶ And it came to pass, when the time was come that he should be received up, he stedfastly set his face to go to Jerusalem,

52 And sent messengers before his face: and they went, and entered into a village of the Samaritans, to make ready for him.

53 And they did not receive him, because his face was as though he would go to Jerusalem.

54 And when his disciples James and John saw *this*, they said, Lord, wilt thou that we command fire to come down from heaven, and consume them, even as Elias did?

55 But he turned, and rebuked them, and said, Ye know not what manner of spirit ye are of.

56 For the Son of man is not come to destroy men's lives, but to save *them*. And they went to another village.

NEW AMERICAN STANDARD BIBLE

48 and said to them, "Whoever receives this child in My name receives Me, and whoever receives Me receives Him who sent Me; for the one who is least among all of you, this is the one who is great."

49 John answered and said, "Master, we saw someone casting out demons in Your name; and we tried to prevent him because he does not follow along with us."

50 But Jesus said to him, "Do not hinder *him;* for he who is not against you is for you."

51 When the days were approaching for His ascension, He was determined to go to Jerusalem;

52 and He sent messengers on ahead of Him, and they went and entered a village of the Samaritans to make arrangements for Him.

53 But they did not receive Him, because He was traveling toward Jerusalem.

54 When His disciples James and John saw *this,* they said, "Lord, do You want us to command fire to come down from heaven and consume them?"

55 But He turned and rebuked them, [and said, "You do not know what kind of spirit you are of;

56 for the Son of Man did not come to destroy men's lives, but to save them."] And they went on to another village.

NEW CENTURY VERSION

child beside him. 48Then Jesus said, "Whoever accepts this little child in my name accepts me. And whoever accepts me accepts the One who sent me, because whoever is least among you all is really the greatest."

Anyone Not Against Us Is for Us

49John answered, "Master, we saw someone using your name to force demons out of people. We told him to stop, because he does not belong to our group."

50But Jesus said to him, "Don't stop him, because whoever is not against you is for you."

A Town Rejects Jesus

51When the time was coming near for Jesus to depart, he was determined to go to Jerusalem. 52He sent some men ahead of him, who went into a town in Samaria to make everything ready for him. 53But the people there would not welcome him, because he was set on going to Jerusalem. 54When James and John, followers of Jesus, saw this, they said, "Lord, do you want us to call fire down from heaven and destroy those people?"[d]

55But Jesus turned and scolded them. 56Then[e] they went to another town.

9:54 [d] **Verse 54** Here, some Greek copies add: ". . . as Elijah did."
9:56 [e] **Verse 55–56** Some copies read: "But Jesus turned and scolded them. And Jesus said, 'You don't know what kind of spirit you belong to. 56The Son of Man did not come to destroy the souls of people but to save them.' Then"

CONTEMPORARY ENGLISH VERSION

to his disciples, "When you welcome even a child because of me, you welcome me. And when you welcome me, you welcome the one who sent me. Whichever one of you is the most humble is the greatest."

For or against Jesus (Mark 9.38-40)

49John said, "Master, we saw a man using your name to force demons out of people. But we told him to stop, because he isn't one of us."

50"Don't stop him!" Jesus said. "Anyone who isn't against you is for you."

A Samaritan Village Refuses To Receive Jesus

51Not long before it was time for Jesus to be taken up to heaven, he made up his mind to go to Jerusalem. 52He sent some messengers on ahead to a Samaritan village to get things ready for him. 53But he was on his way to Jerusalem, so the people there refused to welcome him. 54When the disciples James and John saw what was happening, they asked, "Lord, do you want us to call down fire from heaven to destroy these people?"[h]

55But Jesus turned and corrected them for what they had said.[i] 56Then they all went on to another village.

[h] **9.54** *to destroy these people*: Some manuscripts add "as Elijah did."
[i] **9.55** *what they had said*: Some manuscripts add, "and said, 'Don't you know what spirit you belong to? The Son of Man did not come to destroy people's lives, but to save them.' "

NEW INTERNATIONAL VERSION

48Then he said to them, "Whoever welcomes this little child in my name welcomes me; and whoever welcomes me welcomes the one who sent me. For he who is least among you all—he is the greatest."

49"Master," said John, "we saw a man driving out demons in your name and we tried to stop him, because he is not one of us."

50"Do not stop him," Jesus said, "for whoever is not against you is for you."

Samaritan Opposition

51As the time approached for him to be taken up to heaven, Jesus resolutely set out for Jerusalem. 52And he sent messengers on ahead, who went into a Samaritan village to get things ready for him; 53but the people there did not welcome him, because he was heading for Jerusalem. 54When the disciples James and John saw this, they asked, "Lord, do you want us to call fire down from heaven to destroy them[c]?" 55But Jesus turned and rebuked them, 56and[d] they went to another village.

[c] *54* Some manuscripts *them, even as Elijah did* [d] *55,56* Some manuscripts *them. And he said, "You do not know what kind of spirit you are of, for the Son of Man did not come to destroy men's lives, but to save them."* 56*And*

NEW LIVING TRANSLATION

said to them, "Anyone who welcomes a little child like this on my behalf welcomes me, and anyone who welcomes me welcomes my Father who sent me. Whoever is the least among you is the greatest."

Using the Name of Jesus

49John said to Jesus, "Master, we saw someone using your name to cast out demons. We tried to stop him because he isn't in our group."

50But Jesus said, "Don't stop him! Anyone who is not against you is for you."

Opposition from Samaritans

51As the time drew near for his return to heaven, Jesus resolutely set out for Jerusalem. 52He sent messengers ahead to a Samaritan village to prepare for his arrival. 53But they were turned away. The people of the village refused to have anything to do with Jesus because he had resolved to go to Jerusalem. 54When James and John heard about it, they said to Jesus, "Lord, should we order down fire from heaven to burn them up*?" 55But Jesus turned and rebuked them.* 56So they went on to another village.

9:54 Some manuscripts add *as Elijah did.* 9:55 Some manuscripts add *And he said, "You don't realize what your hearts are like.* 56*For the Son of Man has not come to destroy men's lives, but to save them."*

NEW KING JAMES VERSION

said to them, "Whoever receives this little child in My name receives Me; and whoever receives Me receives Him who sent Me. For he who is least among you all will be great."

Jesus Forbids Sectarianism

49Now John answered and said, "Master, we saw someone casting out demons in Your name, and we forbade him because he does not follow with us."

50But Jesus said to him, "Do not forbid *him,* for he who is not against us[c] is on our[d] side."

A Samaritan Village Rejects the Savior

51Now it came to pass, when the time had come for Him to be received up, that He steadfastly set His face to go to Jerusalem, 52and sent messengers before His face. And as they went, they entered a village of the Samaritans, to prepare for Him. 53But they did not receive Him, because His face was *set* for the journey to Jerusalem. 54And when His disciples James and John saw *this,* they said, "Lord, do You want us to command fire to come down from heaven and consume them, just as Elijah did?"[e]

55But He turned and rebuked them,[f] and said, "You do not know what manner of spirit you are of. 56For the Son of Man did not come to destroy men's lives but to save *them.*"[g] And they went to another village.

9:50 [c] NU-Text reads *you.* [d] NU-Text reads *your.* 9:54 [e] NU-Text omits *just as Elijah did.* 9:55 [f] NU-Text omits the rest of this verse. 9:56 [g] NU-Text omits the first sentence of this verse.

THE MESSAGE

child as if the child were me, accepts me," he said. "And whoever accepts me, accepts the One who sent me. You become great by accepting, not asserting. Your spirit, not your size, makes the difference."

John spoke up, "Master, we saw a man using your name to expel demons and we stopped him because he wasn't of our group."

Jesus said, "Don't stop him. If he's not an enemy, he's an ally."

When it came close to the time for his Ascension, he gathered up his courage and steeled himself for the journey to Jerusalem. He sent messengers on ahead. They came to a Samaritan village to make arrangements for his hospitality. But when the Samaritans learned that his destination was Jerusalem, they refused hospitality. When the disciples James and John learned of it, they said, "Master, do you want us to call a bolt of lightning down out of the sky and incinerate them?"

Jesus turned on them: "Of course not!" And they traveled on to another village.

KING JAMES VERSION

57 ¶ And it came to pass, that, as they went in the way, a certain *man* said unto him, Lord, I will follow thee whithersoever thou goest.

58 And Jesus said unto him, Foxes have holes, and birds of the air *have* nests; but the Son of man hath not where to lay *his* head.

59 And he said unto another, Follow me. But he said, Lord, suffer me first to go and bury my father.

60 Jesus said unto him, Let the dead bury their dead: but go thou and preach the kingdom of God.

61 And another also said, Lord, I will follow thee; but let me first go bid them farewell, which are at home at my house.

62 And Jesus said unto him, No man, having put his hand to the plough, and looking back, is fit for the kingdom of God.

10 After these things the Lord appointed other seventy also, and sent them two and two before his face into every city and place, whither he himself would come.

2 Therefore said he unto them, The harvest truly *is* great, but the labourers *are* few: pray ye therefore the Lord of the harvest, that he would send forth labourers into his harvest.

3 Go your ways: behold, I send you forth as lambs among wolves.

NEW AMERICAN STANDARD BIBLE

Exacting Discipleship

57 As they were going along the road, someone said to Him, "I will follow You wherever You go."

58 And Jesus said to him, "The foxes have holes and the birds of the air *have* nests, but the Son of Man has nowhere to lay His head."

59 And He said to another, "Follow Me." But he said, "Lord, permit me first to go and bury my father."

60 But He said to him, "Allow the dead to bury their own dead; but as for you, go and proclaim everywhere the kingdom of God."

61 Another also said, "I will follow You, Lord; but first permit me to say good-bye to those at home."

62 But Jesus said to him, "No one, after putting his hand to the plow and looking back, is fit for the kingdom of God."

The Seventy Sent Out

10 Now after this the Lord appointed seventy others, and sent them in pairs ahead of Him to every city and place where He Himself was going to come.

2 And He was saying to them, "The harvest is plentiful, but the laborers are few; therefore beseech the Lord of the harvest to send out laborers into His harvest.

3 "Go; behold, I send you out as lambs in the midst of wolves.

NEW CENTURY VERSION

Following Jesus

57As they were going along the road, someone said to Jesus, "I will follow you any place you go."

58Jesus said to them, "The foxes have holes to live in, and the birds have nests, but the Son of Man has no place to rest his head."

59Jesus said to another man, "Follow me!"

But he said, "Lord, first let me go and bury my father."

60But Jesus said to him, "Let the people who are dead bury their own dead. You must go and tell about the kingdom of God."

61Another man said, "I will follow you, Lord, but first let me go and say good-bye to my family."

62Jesus said, "Anyone who begins to plow a field but keeps looking back is of no use in the kingdom of God."

Jesus Sends Out the Seventy-Two

10 After this, the Lord chose seventy-two[a] others and sent them out in pairs ahead of him into every town and place where he planned to go. 2He said to them, "There are a great many people to harvest, but there are only a few workers. So pray to God, who owns the harvest, that he will send more workers to help gather his harvest. 3Go now, but listen! I am sending you out like sheep

10:1 [a] seventy-two Many Greek copies read seventy.

CONTEMPORARY ENGLISH VERSION

Three People Who Wanted To Be Followers

(Matthew 8.19-22)

57Along the way someone said to Jesus, "I'll go anywhere with you!"

58Jesus said, "Foxes have dens, and birds have nests, but the Son of Man doesn't have a place to call his own."

59Jesus told someone else to come with him. But the man said, "Lord, let me wait until I bury my father."[j]

60Jesus answered, "Let the dead take care of the dead, while you go and tell about God's kingdom."

61Then someone said to Jesus, "I want to go with you, Lord, but first let me go back and take care of things at home."

62Jesus answered, "Anyone who starts plowing and keeps looking back isn't worth a thing to God's kingdom!"

The Work of the Seventy-Two Followers

10 Later the Lord chose seventy-two[a] other followers and sent them out two by two to every town and village where he was about to go. 2He said to them:

A large crop is in the fields, but there are only a few workers. Ask the Lord in charge of the harvest to send out workers to bring it in. 3Now go, but remember, I am sending you like lambs into a pack of wolves. 4Don't

[j] **9.59** *bury my father*: The Jewish people taught that giving someone a proper burial was even more important than helping the poor.

[a] **10.1** *seventy-two*: Some manuscripts have "seventy." According to Jewish tradition, there were seventy nations on earth. But the ancient Greek translation of the Old Testament has "seventy-two" in place of "seventy." Jesus probably chose this number of followers to show that his message was for everyone in the world.

NEW INTERNATIONAL VERSION

The Cost of Following Jesus

57 As they were walking along the road, a man said to him, "I will follow you wherever you go."

58 Jesus replied, "Foxes have holes and birds of the air have nests, but the Son of Man has no place to lay his head."

59 He said to another man, "Follow me."

But the man replied, "Lord, first let me go and bury my father."

60 Jesus said to him, "Let the dead bury their own dead, but you go and proclaim the kingdom of God."

61 Still another said, "I will follow you, Lord; but first let me go back and say good-by to my family."

62 Jesus replied, "No one who puts his hand to the plow and looks back is fit for service in the kingdom of God."

Jesus Sends Out the Seventy-two

10 After this the Lord appointed seventy-two[a] others and sent them two by two ahead of him to every town and place where he was about to go. 2 He told them, "The harvest is plentiful, but the workers are few. Ask the Lord of the harvest, therefore, to send out workers into his harvest field. 3 Go! I am sending you out like lambs among

[a] *1* Some manuscripts *seventy*; also in verse 17

NEW LIVING TRANSLATION

The Cost of Following Jesus

57 As they were walking along someone said to Jesus, "I will follow you no matter where you go."

58 But Jesus replied, "Foxes have dens to live in, and birds have nests, but I, the Son of Man, have no home of my own, not even a place to lay my head."

59 He said to another person, "Come, be my disciple."

The man agreed, but he said, "Lord, first let me return home and bury my father."

60 Jesus replied, "Let those who are spiritually dead care for their own dead.* Your duty is to go and preach the coming of the Kingdom of God."

61 Another said, "Yes, Lord, I will follow you, but first let me say good-bye to my family."

62 But Jesus told him, "Anyone who puts a hand to the plow and then looks back is not fit for the Kingdom of God."

Jesus Sends Out His Disciples

10 The Lord now chose seventy-two* other disciples and sent them on ahead in pairs to all the towns and villages he planned to visit. 2 These were his instructions to them: "The harvest is so great, but the workers are so few. Pray to the Lord who is in charge of the harvest, and ask him to send out more workers for his fields. 3 Go now, and remember that I am sending you out as lambs

9:60 Greek *Let the dead bury their own dead.* **10:1** Some manuscripts read *70;* also in 10:17.

NEW KING JAMES VERSION

The Cost of Discipleship

57 Now it happened as they journeyed on the road, *that* someone said to Him, "Lord, I will follow You wherever You go."

58 And Jesus said to him, "Foxes have holes and birds of the air *have* nests, but the Son of Man has nowhere to lay *His* head."

59 Then He said to another, "Follow Me."

But he said, "Lord, let me first go and bury my father."

60 Jesus said to him, "Let the dead bury their own dead, but you go and preach the kingdom of God."

61 And another also said, "Lord, I will follow You, but let me first go *and* bid them farewell who are at my house."

62 But Jesus said to him, "No one, having put his hand to the plow, and looking back, is fit for the kingdom of God."

The Seventy Sent Out

10 After these things the Lord appointed seventy others also,[a] and sent them two by two before His face into every city and place where He Himself was about to go. 2 Then He said to them, "The harvest truly *is* great, but the laborers *are* few; therefore pray the Lord of the harvest to send out laborers into His harvest. 3 Go your way; behold, I send you out as lambs among wolves.

10:1 [a] NU-Text reads *seventy-two others.*

THE MESSAGE

On the road someone asked if he could go along. "I'll go with you, wherever," he said.

Jesus was curt: "Are you ready to rough it? We're not staying in the best inns, you know."

Jesus said to another, "Follow me."

He said, "Certainly, but first excuse me for a couple of days, please. I have to make arrangements for my father's funeral."

Jesus refused. "First things first. Your business is life, not death. And life is urgent: Announce God's kingdom!"

Then another said, "I'm ready to follow you, Master, but first excuse me while I get things straightened out at home."

Jesus said, "No procrastination. No backward looks. You can't put God's kingdom off till tomorrow. Seize the day."

Lambs in a Wolf Pack

10 Later the Master selected seventy and sent them ahead of him in pairs to every town and place where he intended to go. He gave them this charge:

"What a huge harvest! And how few the harvest hands. So on your knees; ask the God of the Harvest to send harvest hands.

"On your way! But be careful—this is hazardous work. You're like lambs in a wolf pack.

KING JAMES VERSION

4 Carry neither purse, nor scrip, nor shoes: and salute no man by the way.

5 And into whatsoever house ye enter, first say, Peace *be* to this house.

6 And if the son of peace be there, your peace shall rest upon it: if not, it shall turn to you again.

7 And in the same house remain, eating and drinking such things as they give: for the labourer is worthy of his hire. Go not from house to house.

8 And into whatsoever city ye enter, and they receive you, eat such things as are set before you:

9 And heal the sick that are therein, and say unto them, The kingdom of God is come nigh unto you.

10 But into whatsoever city ye enter, and they receive you not, go your ways out into the streets of the same, and say,

11 Even the very dust of your city, which cleaveth on us, we do wipe off against you: notwithstanding be ye sure of this, that the kingdom of God is come nigh unto you.

12 But I say unto you, that it shall be more tolerable in that day for Sodom, than for that city.

13 Woe unto thee, Chorazin! woe unto thee, Bethsaida! for if the mighty works had been done in Tyre and Sidon, which have been done in you, they had a great while ago repented, sitting in sackcloth and ashes.

NEW AMERICAN STANDARD BIBLE

4 "Carry no money belt, no bag, no shoes; and greet no one on the way.

5 "Whatever house you enter, first say, 'Peace *be* to this house.'

6 "If a man of peace is there, your peace will rest on him; but if not, it will return to you.

7 "Stay in that house, eating and drinking what they give you; for the laborer is worthy of his wages. Do not keep moving from house to house.

8 "Whatever city you enter and they receive you, eat what is set before you;

9 and heal those in it who are sick, and say to them, 'The kingdom of God has come near to you.'

10 "But whatever city you enter and they do not receive you, go out into its streets and say,

11 'Even the dust of your city which clings to our feet we wipe off *in protest* against you; yet be sure of this, that the kingdom of God has come near.'

12 "I say to you, it will be more tolerable in that day for Sodom than for that city.

13 "Woe to you, Chorazin! Woe to you, Bethsaida! For if the miracles had been performed in Tyre and Sidon which occurred in you, they would have repented long ago, sitting in sackcloth and ashes.

NEW CENTURY VERSION

among wolves. 4Don't carry a purse, a bag, or sandals, and
don't waste time talking with people on the road. 5Before
you go into a house, say, 'Peace be with this house.' 6If
peaceful people live there, your blessing of peace will stay
with them, but if not, then your blessing will come back to
you. 7Stay in the peaceful house, eating and drinking what
the people there give you. A worker should be given his
pay. Don't move from house to house. 8If you go into a
town and the people welcome you, eat what they give you.
9Heal the sick who live there, and tell them, 'The kingdom
of God is near you.' 10But if you go into a town, and the
people don't welcome you, then go into the streets and
say, 11'Even the dirt from your town that sticks to our feet
we wipe off against you.[b] But remember that the kingdom
of God is near.' 12I tell you, on the Judgment Day it will be
better for the people of Sodom[c] than for the people of that
town.

Jesus Warns Unbelievers

13"How terrible for you, Korazin! How terrible for you,
Bethsaida! If the miracles I did in you had happened in
Tyre and Sidon,[d] those people would have changed their
lives long ago. They would have worn rough cloth and put
ashes on themselves to show they had changed. 14But on

10:11 [b] **dirt...you** A warning. It showed that they had rejected these people. 10:12 [c] **Sodom** City that God destroyed because the people were so evil. 10:13 [d] **Tyre and Sidon** Towns where wicked people lived.

CONTEMPORARY ENGLISH VERSION

take along a moneybag or a traveling bag or sandals.
And don't waste time greeting people on the road.[b] 5As
soon as you enter a home, say, "God bless this home
with peace." 6If the people living there are peace-loving,
your prayer for peace will bless them. But if they are not
peace-loving, your prayer will return to you. 7Stay with
the same family, eating and drinking whatever they give
you, because workers are worth what they earn. Don't
move around from house to house.

8If the people of a town welcome you, eat whatever
they offer. 9Heal their sick and say, "God's kingdom will
soon be here!"[c]

10But if the people of a town refuse to welcome you,
go out into the street and say, 11"We are shaking the
dust from our feet[d] as a warning to you. And you can be
sure that God's kingdom will soon be here!"[e] 12I tell you
that on the day of judgment the people of Sodom will get
off easier than the people of that town!

The Unbelieving Towns (Matthew 11.20-24)

13You people of Chorazin are in for trouble! You peo-
ple of Bethsaida are also in for trouble! If the miracles
that took place in your towns had happened in Tyre and
Sidon, the people there would have turned to God long
ago. They would have dressed in sackcloth and put

[b] 10.4 *waste time greeting people on the road*: In those days a polite greeting could take a long time. [c] 10.9 *will soon be here*: Or "is already here." [d] 10.11 *shaking the dust from our feet*: This was a way of showing rejection. [e] 10.11 *will soon be here*: Or "is already here."

NEW INTERNATIONAL VERSION

wolves. 4 Do not take a purse or bag or sandals; and do not greet anyone on the road.

5 "When you enter a house, first say, 'Peace to this house.' 6 If a man of peace is there, your peace will rest on him; if not, it will return to you. 7 Stay in that house, eating and drinking whatever they give you, for the worker deserves his wages. Do not move around from house to house.

8 "When you enter a town and are welcomed, eat what is set before you. 9 Heal the sick who are there and tell them, 'The kingdom of God is near you.' 10 But when you enter a town and are not welcomed, go into its streets and say, 11 'Even the dust of your town that sticks to our feet we wipe off against you. Yet be sure of this: The kingdom of God is near.' 12 I tell you, it will be more bearable on that day for Sodom than for that town.

13 "Woe to you, Korazin! Woe to you, Bethsaida! For if the miracles that were performed in you had been performed in Tyre and Sidon, they would have repented long ago, sitting in sackcloth and ashes. 14 But it will be more

NEW LIVING TRANSLATION

among wolves. 4 Don't take along any money, or a traveler's bag, or even an extra pair of sandals. And don't stop to greet anyone on the road.

5 "Whenever you enter a home, give it your blessing. 6 If those who live there are worthy, the blessing will stand; if they are not, the blessing will return to you. 7 When you enter a town, don't move around from home to home. Stay in one place, eating and drinking what they provide you. Don't hesitate to accept hospitality, because those who work deserve their pay.

8 "If a town welcomes you, eat whatever is set before you 9 and heal the sick. As you heal them, say, 'The Kingdom of God is near you now.' 10 But if a town refuses to welcome you, go out into its streets and say, 11 'We wipe the dust of your town from our feet as a public announcement of your doom. And don't forget the Kingdom of God is near!' 12 The truth is, even wicked Sodom will be better off than such a town on the judgment day.

13 "What horrors await you, Korazin and Bethsaida! For if the miracles I did in you had been done in wicked Tyre and Sidon, their people would have sat in deep repentance long ago, clothed in sackcloth and throwing ashes on their

NEW KING JAMES VERSION

4 Carry neither money bag, knapsack, nor sandals; and greet no one along the road. 5 But whatever house you enter, first say, 'Peace to this house.' 6 And if a son of peace is there, your peace will rest on it; if not, it will return to you. 7 And remain in the same house, eating and drinking such things as they give, for the laborer is worthy of his wages. Do not go from house to house. 8 Whatever city you enter, and they receive you, eat such things as are set before you. 9 And heal the sick there, and say to them, 'The kingdom of God has come near to you.' 10 But whatever city you enter, and they do not receive you, go out into its streets and say, 11 'The very dust of your city which clings to us[b] we wipe off against you. Nevertheless know this, that the kingdom of God has come near you.' 12 But[c] I say to you that it will be more tolerable in that Day for Sodom than for that city.

Woe to the Impenitent Cities

13 "Woe to you, Chorazin! Woe to you, Bethsaida! For if the mighty works which were done in you had been done in Tyre and Sidon, they would have repented long ago, sitting in sackcloth and ashes. 14 But it will be more tolerable

10:11 [b] NU-Text reads *our feet.* 10:12 [c] NU-Text and M-Text omit *But.*

THE MESSAGE

"Travel light. Comb and toothbrush and no extra luggage.

"Don't loiter and make small talk with everyone you meet along the way.

"When you enter a home, greet the family, 'Peace.' If your greeting is received, then it's a good place to stay. But if it's not received, take it back and get out. Don't impose yourself.

"Stay at one home, taking your meals there, for a worker deserves three square meals. Don't move from house to house, looking for the best cook in town.

"When you enter a town and are received, eat what they set before you, heal anyone who is sick, and tell them, 'God's kingdom is right on your doorstep!'

"When you enter a town and are not received, go out in the street and say, 'The only thing we got from you is the dirt on our feet, and we're giving it back. Did you have any idea that God's kingdom was right on your doorstep?' Sodom will have it better on Judgment Day than the town that rejects you.

"Doom, Chorazin! Doom, Bethsaida! If Tyre and Sidon had been given half the chances given you, they'd have been on their knees long ago, repenting and crying for

KING JAMES VERSION

14 But it shall be more tolerable for Tyre and Sidon at the judgment, than for you.

15 And thou, Capernaum, which art exalted to heaven, shalt be thrust down to hell.

16 He that heareth you heareth me; and he that despiseth you despiseth me; and he that despiseth me despiseth him that sent me.

17 ¶ And the seventy returned again with joy, saying, Lord, even the devils are subject unto us through thy name.

18 And he said unto them, I beheld Satan as lightning fall from heaven.

19 Behold, I give unto you power to tread on serpents and scorpions, and over all the power of the enemy: and nothing shall by any means hurt you.

20 Notwithstanding in this rejoice not, that the spirits are subject unto you; but rather rejoice, because your names are written in heaven.

21 In that hour Jesus rejoiced in spirit, and said, I thank thee, O Father, Lord of heaven and earth, that thou hast hid these things from the wise and prudent, and hast

NEW AMERICAN STANDARD BIBLE

14 "But it will be more tolerable for Tyre and Sidon in the judgment than for you.

15 "And you, Capernaum, will not be exalted to heaven, will you? You will be brought down to Hades!

16 "The one who listens to you listens to Me, and the one who rejects you rejects Me; and he who rejects Me rejects the One who sent Me."

The Happy Results

17 The seventy returned with joy, saying, "Lord, even the demons are subject to us in Your name."

18 And He said to them, "I was watching Satan fall from heaven like lightning.

19 "Behold, I have given you authority to tread on serpents and scorpions, and over all the power of the enemy, and nothing will injure you.

20 "Nevertheless do not rejoice in this, that the spirits are subject to you, but rejoice that your names are recorded in heaven."

21 At that very time He rejoiced greatly in the Holy Spirit, and said, "I praise You, O Father, Lord of heaven and earth, that You have hidden these things from *the*

NEW CENTURY VERSION

the Judgment Day it will be better for Tyre and Sidon than for you. 15 And you, Capernaum,[e] will you be lifted up to heaven? No! You will be thrown down to the depths!

16 "Whoever listens to you listens to me, and whoever refuses to accept you refuses to accept me. And whoever refuses to accept me refuses to accept the One who sent me."

Satan Falls

17 When the seventy-two[f] came back, they were very happy and said, "Lord, even the demons obeyed us when we used your name!"

18 Jesus said, "I saw Satan fall like lightning from heaven. 19 Listen, I have given you power to walk on snakes and scorpions, power that is greater than the enemy has. So nothing will hurt you. 20 But you should not be happy because the spirits obey you but because your names are written in heaven."

Jesus Prays to the Father

21 Then Jesus rejoiced in the Holy Spirit and said, "I praise you, Father, Lord of heaven and earth, because you have hidden these things from the people who are wise

10:15 [e] **Korazin, Bethsaida, Capernaum** Towns by Lake Galilee where Jesus preached to the people. **10:17** [f] **seventy-two** Many Greek copies read seventy.

CONTEMPORARY ENGLISH VERSION

ashes on their heads.[f] 14 On the day of judgment the people of Tyre and Sidon will get off easier than you will. 15 People of Capernaum, do you think you will be honored in heaven? Well, you will go down to hell!

16 My followers, whoever listens to you is listening to me. Anyone who says "No" to you is saying "No" to me. And anyone who says "No" to me is really saying "No" to the one who sent me.

The Return of the Seventy-Two

17 When the seventy-two[g] followers returned, they were excited and said, "Lord, even the demons obeyed when we spoke in your name!"

18 Jesus told them:

I saw Satan fall from heaven like a flash of lightning. 19 I have given you the power to trample on snakes and scorpions and to defeat the power of your enemy Satan. Nothing can harm you. 20 But don't be happy because evil spirits obey you. Be happy that your names are written in heaven!

Jesus Thanks His Father (Matthew 11.25-27; 13.16, 17)

21 At that same time, Jesus felt the joy that comes from the Holy Spirit,[h] and he said:

My Father, Lord of heaven and earth, I am grateful that you hid all this from wise and educated people and

[f] **10.13** *dressed in sackcloth . . . ashes on their heads*: This was one way that people showed how sorry they were for their sins.
[g] **10.17** *seventy-two*: See the note at 10.1. [h] **10.21** *the Holy Spirit*: Some manuscripts have "his spirit."

NEW INTERNATIONAL VERSION

bearable for Tyre and Sidon at the judgment than for you. 15And you, Capernaum, will you be lifted up to the skies? No, you will go down to the depths.[b]

16"He who listens to you listens to me; he who rejects you rejects me; but he who rejects me rejects him who sent me."

17The seventy-two returned with joy and said, "Lord, even the demons submit to us in your name."

18He replied, "I saw Satan fall like lightning from heaven. 19I have given you authority to trample on snakes and scorpions and to overcome all the power of the enemy; nothing will harm you. 20However, do not rejoice that the spirits submit to you, but rejoice that your names are written in heaven."

21At that time Jesus, full of joy through the Holy Spirit, said, "I praise you, Father, Lord of heaven and earth, because you have hidden these things from the wise and

[b] *15* Greek *Hades*

NEW LIVING TRANSLATION

heads to show their remorse. 14Yes, Tyre and Sidon will be better off on the judgment day than you. 15And you people of Capernaum, will you be exalted to heaven? No, you will be brought down to the place of the dead.*"

16Then he said to the disciples, "Anyone who accepts your message is also accepting me. And anyone who rejects you is rejecting me. And anyone who rejects me is rejecting God who sent me."

17When the seventy-two disciples returned, they joyfully reported to him, "Lord, even the demons obey us when we use your name!"

18"Yes," he told them, "I saw Satan falling from heaven as a flash of lightning! 19And I have given you authority over all the power of the enemy, and you can walk among snakes and scorpions and crush them. Nothing will injure you. 20But don't rejoice just because evil spirits obey you; rejoice because your names are registered as citizens of heaven."

Jesus' Prayer of Thanksgiving

21Then Jesus was filled with the joy of the Holy Spirit and said, "O Father, Lord of heaven and earth, thank you for hiding the truth from those who think themselves so

10:15 Greek *to Hades.*

NEW KING JAMES VERSION

for Tyre and Sidon at the judgment than for you. 15And you, Capernaum, who are exalted to heaven, will be brought down to Hades.[d] 16He who hears you hears Me, he who rejects you rejects Me, and he who rejects Me rejects Him who sent Me."

The Seventy Return with Joy

17Then the seventy[e] returned with joy, saying, "Lord, even the demons are subject to us in Your name."

18And He said to them, "I saw Satan fall like lightning from heaven. 19Behold, I give you the authority to trample on serpents and scorpions, and over all the power of the enemy, and nothing shall by any means hurt you. 20Nevertheless do not rejoice in this, that the spirits are subject to you, but rather[f] rejoice because your names are written in heaven."

Jesus Rejoices in the Spirit

21In that hour Jesus rejoiced in the Spirit and said, "I thank You, Father, Lord of heaven and earth, that You have hidden these things from *the* wise and prudent and

10:15 [d] NU-Text reads *will you be exalted to heaven? You will be thrust down to Hades!* 10:17 [e] NU-Text reads *seventy-two.*
10:20 [f] NU-Text and M-Text omit *rather.*

THE MESSAGE

mercy. Tyre and Sidon will have it easy on Judgment Day compared to you.

"And you, Capernaum! Do you think you're about to be promoted to heaven? Think again. You're on a mud slide to hell.

"The one who listens to you, listens to me. The one who rejects you, rejects me. And rejecting me is the same as rejecting God, who sent me."

The seventy came back triumphant. "Master, even the demons danced to your tune!"

Jesus said, "I know. I saw Satan fall, a bolt of lightning out of the sky. See what I've given you? Safe passage as you walk on snakes and scorpions, and protection from every assault of the Enemy. No one can put a hand on you. All the same, the great triumph is not in your authority over evil, but in God's authority over you and presence with you. Not what you do for God but what God does for you—that's the agenda for rejoicing."

At that, Jesus rejoiced, exuberant in the Holy Spirit. "I thank you, Father, Master of heaven and earth, that you hid these things from the know-it-alls and showed them to

KING JAMES VERSION

revealed them unto babes: even so, Father; for so it seemed good in thy sight.

22 All things are delivered to me of my Father: and no man knoweth who the Son is, but the Father; and who the Father is, but the Son, and *he* to whom the Son will reveal *him*.

23 And he turned him unto *his* disciples, and said privately, Blessed *are* the eyes which see the things that ye see:

24 For I tell you, that many prophets and kings have desired to see those things which ye see, and have not seen *them*; and to hear those things which ye hear, and have not heard *them*.

25 ¶ And, behold, a certain lawyer stood up, and tempted him, saying, Master, what shall I do to inherit eternal life?

26 He said unto him, What is written in the law? how readest thou?

27 And he answering said, Thou shalt love the Lord thy God with all thy heart, and with all thy soul, and with all thy strength, and with all thy mind; and thy neighbour as thyself.

28 And he said unto him, Thou hast answered right: this do, and thou shalt live.

29 But he, willing to justify himself, said unto Jesus, And who is my neighbour?

30 And Jesus answering said, A certain *man* went down from Jerusalem to Jericho, and fell among thieves, which

NEW AMERICAN STANDARD BIBLE

wise and intelligent and have revealed them to infants. Yes, Father, for this way was well-pleasing in Your sight.

22 "All things have been handed over to Me by My Father, and no one knows who the Son is except the Father, and who the Father is except the Son, and anyone to whom the Son wills to reveal *Him*."

23 Turning to the disciples, He said privately, "Blessed *are* the eyes which see the things you see,

24 for I say to you, that many prophets and kings wished to see the things which you see, and did not see *them*, and to hear the things which you hear, and did not hear *them*."

25 And a lawyer stood up and put Him to the test, saying, "Teacher, what shall I do to inherit eternal life?"

26 And He said to him, "What is written in the Law? How does it read to you?"

27 And he answered, "YOU SHALL LOVE THE LORD YOUR GOD WITH ALL YOUR HEART, AND WITH ALL YOUR SOUL, AND WITH ALL YOUR STRENGTH, AND WITH ALL YOUR MIND; AND YOUR NEIGHBOR AS YOURSELF."

28 And He said to him, "You have answered correctly; DO THIS AND YOU WILL LIVE."

29 But wishing to justify himself, he said to Jesus, "And who is my neighbor?"

The Good Samaritan

30 Jesus replied and said, "A man was going down from Jerusalem to Jericho, and fell among robbers, and they

NEW CENTURY VERSION

and smart. But you have shown them to those who are like little children. Yes, Father, this is what you really wanted.

22"My Father has given me all things. No one knows who the Son is, except the Father. And no one knows who the Father is, except the Son and those whom the Son chooses to tell."

23Then Jesus turned to his followers and said privately, "You are blessed to see what you now see. 24I tell you, many prophets and kings wanted to see what you now see, but they did not, and they wanted to hear what you now hear, but they did not."

The Good Samaritan

25Then an expert on the law stood up to test Jesus, saying, "Teacher, what must I do to get life forever?"

26Jesus said, "What is written in the law? What do you read there?"

27The man answered, "Love the Lord your God with all your heart, all your soul, all your strength, and all your mind."[g] Also, "Love your neighbor as you love yourself."[h]

28Jesus said to him, "Your answer is right. Do this and you will live."

29But the man, wanting to show the importance of his question, said to Jesus, "And who is my neighbor?"

30Jesus answered, "As a man was going down from Jerusalem to Jericho, some robbers attacked him. They tore

10:27 [g] **"Love...mind."** Quotation from Deuteronomy 6:5.
10:27 [h] **"Love...yourself."** Quotation from Leviticus 19:18.

CONTEMPORARY ENGLISH VERSION

showed it to ordinary people. Yes, Father, that is what pleased you.

22My Father has given me everything, and he is the only one who knows the Son. The only one who really knows the Father is the Son. But the Son wants to tell others about the Father, so that they can know him too.

23Jesus then turned to his disciples and said to them in private, "You are really blessed to see what you see! 24Many prophets and kings were eager to see what you see and to hear what you hear. But I tell you that they did not see or hear."

The Good Samaritan

25An expert in the Law of Moses stood up and asked Jesus a question to see what he would say. "Teacher," he asked, "what must I do to have eternal life?"

26Jesus answered, "What is written in the Scriptures? How do you understand them?"

27The man replied, "The Scriptures say, 'Love the Lord your God with all your heart, soul, strength, and mind.' They also say, 'Love your neighbors as much as you love yourself.' "

28Jesus said, "You have given the right answer. If you do this, you will have eternal life."

29But the man wanted to show that he knew what he was talking about. So he asked Jesus, "Who are my neighbors?"

30Jesus replied:

As a man was going down from Jerusalem to Jericho,

NEW INTERNATIONAL VERSION

learned, and revealed them to little children. Yes, Father, for this was your good pleasure.

22“All things have been committed to me by my Father. No one knows who the Son is except the Father, and no one knows who the Father is except the Son and those to whom the Son chooses to reveal him.”

23Then he turned to his disciples and said privately, “Blessed are the eyes that see what you see. 24For I tell you that many prophets and kings wanted to see what you see but did not see it, and to hear what you hear but did not hear it.”

The Parable of the Good Samaritan

25On one occasion an expert in the law stood up to test Jesus. “Teacher,” he asked, “what must I do to inherit eternal life?”

26“What is written in the Law?” he replied. “How do you read it?”

27He answered: “ ‘Love the Lord your God with all your heart and with all your soul and with all your strength and with all your mind’[c]; and, ‘Love your neighbor as yourself.’[d]”

28“You have answered correctly,” Jesus replied. “Do this and you will live.”

29But he wanted to justify himself, so he asked Jesus, “And who is my neighbor?”

30In reply Jesus said: “A man was going down from Jerusalem to Jericho, when he fell into the hands of robbers.

[c] *27* Deut. 6:5   [d] *27* Lev. 19:18

NEW LIVING TRANSLATION

wise and clever, and for revealing it to the childlike. Yes, Father, it pleased you to do it this way.

22“My Father has given me authority over everything. No one really knows the Son except the Father, and no one really knows the Father except the Son and those to whom the Son chooses to reveal him.”

23Then when they were alone, he turned to the disciples and said, “How privileged you are to see what you have seen. 24I tell you, many prophets and kings have longed to see and hear what you have seen and heard, but they could not.”

The Most Important Commandment

25One day an expert in religious law stood up to test Jesus by asking him this question: “Teacher, what must I do to receive eternal life?”

26Jesus replied, “What does the law of Moses say? How do you read it?”

27The man answered, “ ‘You must love the Lord your God with all your heart, all your soul, all your strength, and all your mind.’ And, ‘Love your neighbor as yourself.’ ”*

28“Right!” Jesus told him. “Do this and you will live!”

29The man wanted to justify his actions, so he asked Jesus, “And who is my neighbor?”

Story of the Good Samaritan

30Jesus replied with an illustration: “A Jewish man was traveling on a trip from Jerusalem to Jericho, and he was

10:27 Deut 6:5; Lev 19:18.

NEW KING JAMES VERSION

revealed them to babes. Even so, Father, for so it seemed good in Your sight. 22All[g] things have been delivered to Me by My Father, and no one knows who the Son is except the Father, and who the Father is except the Son, and *the one* to whom the Son wills to reveal *Him.*”

23Then He turned to *His* disciples and said privately, “Blessed *are* the eyes which see the things you see; 24for I tell you that many prophets and kings have desired to see what you see, and have not seen *it,* and to hear what you hear, and have not heard *it.*”

The Parable of the Good Samaritan

25And behold, a certain lawyer stood up and tested Him, saying, “Teacher, what shall I do to inherit eternal life?”

26He said to him, “What is written in the law? What is your reading *of it?*”

27So he answered and said, “ *‘You shall love the* LORD *your God with all your heart, with all your soul, with all your strength, and with all your mind,’*[h] and *‘your neighbor as yourself.’* ”[i]

28And He said to him, “You have answered rightly; do this and you will live.”

29But he, wanting to justify himself, said to Jesus, “And who is my neighbor?”

30Then Jesus answered and said: “A certain *man* went down from Jerusalem to Jericho, and fell among thieves,

10:22 [g] M-Text reads *And turning to the disciples He said, “All . . . .*
10:27 [h] Deuteronomy 6:5   [i] Leviticus 19:18

THE MESSAGE

these innocent newcomers. Yes, Father, it pleased you to do it this way.

“I've been given it all by my Father! Only the Father knows who the Son is and only the Son knows who the Father is. The Son can introduce the Father to anyone he wants to.”

He then turned in a private aside to his disciples. “Fortunate the eyes that see what you're seeing! There are plenty of prophets and kings who would have given their right arm to see what you are seeing but never got so much as a glimpse, to hear what you are hearing but never got so much as a whisper.”

Defining “Neighbor”

Just then a religion scholar stood up with a question to test Jesus. “Teacher, what do I need to do to get eternal life?”

He answered, “What's written in God's Law? How do you interpret it?”

He said, “That you love the Lord your God with all your passion and prayer and muscle and intelligence—and that you love your neighbor as well as you do yourself.”

“Good answer!” said Jesus. “Do it and you'll live.”

Looking for a loophole, he asked, “And just how would you define ‘neighbor’?”

Jesus answered by telling a story. “There was once a man traveling from Jerusalem to Jericho. On the way he

KING JAMES VERSION

stripped him of his raiment, and wounded *him*, and departed, leaving *him* half dead.

31 And by chance there came down a certain priest that way: and when he saw him, he passed by on the other side.

32 And likewise a Levite, when he was at the place, came and looked *on him*, and passed by on the other side.

33 But a certain Samaritan, as he journeyed, came where he was: and when he saw him, he had compassion *on him*,

34 And went to *him*, and bound up his wounds, pouring in oil and wine, and set him on his own beast, and brought him to an inn, and took care of him.

35 And on the morrow when he departed, he took out two pence, and gave *them* to the host, and said unto him, Take care of him; and whatsoever thou spendest more, when I come again, I will repay thee.

36 Which now of these three, thinkest thou, was neighbour unto him that fell among the thieves?

37 And he said, He that shewed mercy on him. Then said Jesus unto him, Go, and do thou likewise.

NEW AMERICAN STANDARD BIBLE

stripped him and beat him, and went away leaving him half dead.

31 "And by chance a priest was going down on that road, and when he saw him, he passed by on the other side.

32 "Likewise a Levite also, when he came to the place and saw him, passed by on the other side.

33 "But a Samaritan, who was on a journey, came upon him; and when he saw him, he felt compassion,

34 and came to him and bandaged up his wounds, pouring oil and wine on *them;* and he put him on his own beast, and brought him to an inn and took care of him.

35 "On the next day he took out two [I]denarii and gave them to the innkeeper and said, 'Take care of him; and whatever more you spend, when I return I will repay you.'

36 "Which of these three do you think proved to be a neighbor to the man who fell into the robbers' *hands?*"

37 And he said, "The one who showed mercy toward him." Then Jesus said to him, "Go and do the same."

10:35 [I] The denarius was equivalent to a day's wages

NEW CENTURY VERSION

off his clothes, beat him, and left him lying there, almost dead. 31 It happened that a Jewish priest was going down that road. When he saw the man, he walked by on the other side. 32 Next, a Levite[i] came there, and after he went over and looked at the man, he walked by on the other side of the road. 33 Then a Samaritan[j] traveling down the road came to where the hurt man was. When he saw the man, he felt very sorry for him. 34 The Samaritan went to him, poured olive oil and wine[k] on his wounds, and bandaged them. Then he put the hurt man on his own donkey and took him to an inn where he cared for him. 35 The next day, the Samaritan brought out two coins,[l] gave them to the innkeeper, and said, 'Take care of this man. If you spend more money on him, I will pay it back to you when I come again.' "

36 Then Jesus said, "Which one of these three men do you think was a neighbor to the man who was attacked by the robbers?"

37 The expert on the law answered, "The one who showed him mercy."

Jesus said to him, "Then go and do what he did."

10:32 [i] **Levite** Levites were members of the tribe of Levi who helped the Jewish priests with their work in the Temple. Read 1 Chronicles 23:24–32. 10:33 [j] **Samaritan** Samaritans were people from Samaria. These people were part Jewish, but the Jews did not accept them as true Jews. Samaritans and Jews disliked each other. 10:34 [k] **olive oil and wine** Oil and wine were used like medicine to soften and clean wounds. 10:35 [l] **coins** Roman denarii. One coin was the average pay for one day's work.

CONTEMPORARY ENGLISH VERSION

robbers attacked him and grabbed everything he had. They beat him up and ran off, leaving him half dead.

31 A priest happened to be going down the same road. But when he saw the man, he walked by on the other side. 32 Later a temple helper[i] came to the same place. But when he saw the man who had been beaten up, he also went by on the other side.

33 A man from Samaria then came traveling along that road. When he saw the man, he felt sorry for him 34 and went over to him. He treated his wounds with olive oil and wine[j] and bandaged them. Then he put him on his own donkey and took him to an inn, where he took care of him. 35 The next morning he gave the innkeeper two silver coins and said, "Please take care of the man. If you spend more than this on him, I will pay you when I return."

36 Then Jesus asked, "Which one of these three people was a real neighbor to the man who was beaten up by robbers?"

37 The teacher answered, "The one who showed pity."

Jesus said, "Go and do the same!"

[i] 10.32 *temple helper*: A man from the tribe of Levi, whose job it was to work around the temple. [j] 10.34 *olive oil and wine*: In New Testament times these were used as medicine. Sometimes olive oil is a symbol for healing by means of a miracle (see James 5.14).

NEW INTERNATIONAL VERSION

They stripped him of his clothes, beat him and went away, leaving him half dead. 31 A priest happened to be going down the same road, and when he saw the man, he passed by on the other side. 32 So too, a Levite, when he came to the place and saw him, passed by on the other side. 33 But a Samaritan, as he traveled, came where the man was; and when he saw him, he took pity on him. 34 He went to him and bandaged his wounds, pouring on oil and wine. Then he put the man on his own donkey, took him to an inn and took care of him. 35 The next day he took out two silver coins[e] and gave them to the innkeeper. 'Look after him,' he said, 'and when I return, I will reimburse you for any extra expense you may have.'

36 "Which of these three do you think was a neighbor to the man who fell into the hands of robbers?"

37 The expert in the law replied, "The one who had mercy on him."

Jesus told him, "Go and do likewise."

[e] *35* Greek *two denarii*

NEW LIVING TRANSLATION

attacked by bandits. They stripped him of his clothes and money, beat him up, and left him half dead beside the road.

31 "By chance a Jewish priest came along; but when he saw the man lying there, he crossed to the other side of the road and passed him by. 32 A Temple assistant* walked over and looked at him lying there, but he also passed by on the other side.

33 "Then a despised Samaritan came along, and when he saw the man, he felt deep pity. 34 Kneeling beside him, the Samaritan soothed his wounds with medicine and bandaged them. Then he put the man on his own donkey and took him to an inn, where he took care of him. 35 The next day he handed the innkeeper two pieces of silver* and told him to take care of the man. 'If his bill runs higher than that,' he said, 'I'll pay the difference the next time I am here.'

36 "Now which of these three would you say was a neighbor to the man who was attacked by bandits?" Jesus asked.

37 The man replied, "The one who showed him mercy."

Then Jesus said, "Yes, now go and do the same."

10:32 Greek *A Levite.* 10:35 Greek *2 denarii.* A denarius was the equivalent of a full day's wage.

NEW KING JAMES VERSION

who stripped him of his clothing, wounded *him,* and departed, leaving *him* half dead. 31 Now by chance a certain priest came down that road. And when he saw him, he passed by on the other side. 32 Likewise a Levite, when he arrived at the place, came and looked, and passed by on the other side. 33 But a certain Samaritan, as he journeyed, came where he was. And when he saw him, he had compassion. 34 So he went to *him* and bandaged his wounds, pouring on oil and wine; and he set him on his own animal, brought him to an inn, and took care of him. 35 On the next day, when he departed,[j] he took out two denarii, gave *them* to the innkeeper, and said to him, 'Take care of him; and whatever more you spend, when I come again, I will repay you.' 36 So which of these three do you think was neighbor to him who fell among the thieves?"

37 And he said, "He who showed mercy on him."

Then Jesus said to him, "Go and do likewise."

10:35 [j] NU-Text omits *when he departed.*

THE MESSAGE

was attacked by robbers. They took his clothes, beat him up, and went off leaving him half-dead. Luckily, a priest was on his way down the same road, but when he saw him he angled across to the other side. Then a Levite religious man showed up; he also avoided the injured man.

"A Samaritan traveling the road came on him. When he saw the man's condition, his heart went out to him. He gave him first aid, disinfecting and bandaging his wounds. Then he lifted him on to his donkey, led him to an inn, and made him comfortable. In the morning he took out two silver coins and gave them to the innkeeper, saying, 'Take good care of him. If it costs any more, put it on my bill—I'll pay you on my way back.'

"What do you think? Which of the three became a neighbor to the man attacked by robbers?"

"The one who treated him kindly," the religion scholar responded.

Jesus said, "Go and do the same."

KING JAMES VERSION

38 ¶ Now it came to pass, as they went, that he entered into a certain village: and a certain woman named Martha received him into her house.

39 And she had a sister called Mary, which also sat at Jesus' feet, and heard his word.

40 But Martha was cumbered about much serving, and came to him, and said, Lord, dost thou not care that my sister hath left me to serve alone? bid her therefore that she help me.

41 And Jesus answered and said unto her, Martha, Martha, thou art careful and troubled about many things:

42 But one thing is needful: and Mary hath chosen that good part, which shall not be taken away from her.

11 And it came to pass, that, as he was praying in a certain place, when he ceased, one of his disciples said unto him, Lord, teach us to pray, as John also taught his disciples.

2 And he said unto them, When ye pray, say, Our Father which art in heaven, Hallowed be thy name. Thy kingdom come. Thy will be done, as in heaven, so in earth.

3 Give us day by day our daily bread.

NEW AMERICAN STANDARD BIBLE

Martha and Mary

38 Now as they were traveling along, He entered a village; and a woman named Martha welcomed Him into her home.

39 She had a sister called Mary, who was seated at the Lord's feet, listening to His word.

40 But Martha was distracted with all her preparations; and she came up *to Him* and said, "Lord, do You not care that my sister has left me to do all the serving alone? Then tell her to help me."

41 But the Lord answered and said to her, "Martha, Martha, you are worried and bothered about so many things;

42 but *only* one thing is necessary, for Mary has chosen the good part, which shall not be taken away from her."

Instruction about Prayer

11 It happened that while Jesus was praying in a certain place, after He had finished, one of His disciples said to Him, "Lord, teach us to pray just as John also taught his disciples."

2 And He said to them, "When you pray, say:
'[1]Father, hallowed be Your name.
Your kingdom come.
3 'Give us each day our daily bread.

11:2 [1] Later mss add phrases from Matt 6:9-13 to make the two passages closely similar

NEW CENTURY VERSION

Mary and Martha

38While Jesus and his followers were traveling, Jesus went into a town. A woman named Martha let Jesus stay at her house. 39Martha had a sister named Mary, who was sitting at Jesus' feet and listening to him teach. 40But Martha was busy with all the work to be done. She went in and said, "Lord, don't you care that my sister has left me alone to do all the work? Tell her to help me."

41But the Lord answered her, "Martha, Martha, you are worried and upset about many things. 42Only one thing is important. Mary has chosen the better thing, and it will never be taken away from her."

Jesus Teaches About Prayer

11 One time Jesus was praying in a certain place. When he finished, one of his followers said to him, "Lord, teach us to pray as John taught his followers."

2Jesus said to them, "When you pray, say:
'Father, may your name always be kept holy.
May your kingdom come.
3Give us the food we need for each day.

CONTEMPORARY ENGLISH VERSION

Martha and Mary

38The Lord and his disciples were traveling along and came to a village. When they got there, a woman named Martha welcomed him into her home. 39She had a sister named Mary, who sat down in front of the Lord and was listening to what he said. 40Martha was worried about all that had to be done. Finally, she went to Jesus and said, "Lord, doesn't it bother you that my sister has left me to do all the work by myself? Tell her to come and help me!"

41The Lord answered, "Martha, Martha! You are worried and upset about so many things, 42but only one thing is necessary. Mary has chosen what is best, and it will not be taken away from her."

Prayer (Matthew 6.9-13; 7.7-11)

11 When Jesus had finished praying, one of his disciples said to him, "Lord, teach us to pray, just as John taught his followers to pray."

2So Jesus told them, "Pray in this way:

'Father, help us
to honor your name.
Come and set up
your kingdom.
3Give us each day
the food we need.[a]

[a] 11.3 *the food we need*: Or "food for today" or "food for the coming day."

NEW INTERNATIONAL VERSION

At the Home of Martha and Mary

38 As Jesus and his disciples were on their way, he came to a village where a woman named Martha opened her home to him. 39 She had a sister called Mary, who sat at the Lord's feet listening to what he said. 40 But Martha was distracted by all the preparations that had to be made. She came to him and asked, "Lord, don't you care that my sister has left me to do the work by myself? Tell her to help me!"

41 "Martha, Martha," the Lord answered, "you are worried and upset about many things, 42 but only one thing is needed.[f] Mary has chosen what is better, and it will not be taken away from her."

Jesus' Teaching on Prayer

11 One day Jesus was praying in a certain place. When he finished, one of his disciples said to him, "Lord, teach us to pray, just as John taught his disciples."

2 He said to them, "When you pray, say:

" 'Father,[a]
hallowed be your name,
your kingdom come.[b]
3 Give us each day our daily bread.

[f] 42 Some manuscripts *but few things are needed—or only one*
[a] 2 Some manuscripts *Our Father in heaven* [b] 2 Some manuscripts *come. May your will be done on earth as it is in heaven.*

NEW LIVING TRANSLATION

Jesus Visits Martha and Mary

38 As Jesus and the disciples continued on their way to Jerusalem, they came to a village where a woman named Martha welcomed them into her home. 39 Her sister, Mary, sat at the Lord's feet, listening to what he taught. 40 But Martha was worrying over the big dinner she was preparing. She came to Jesus and said, "Lord, doesn't it seem unfair to you that my sister just sits here while I do all the work? Tell her to come and help me."

41 But the Lord said to her, "My dear Martha, you are so upset over all these details! 42 There is really only one thing worth being concerned about. Mary has discovered it—and I won't take it away from her."

Teaching about Prayer

11 Once when Jesus had been out praying, one of his disciples came to him as he finished and said, "Lord, teach us to pray, just as John taught his disciples."

2 He said, "This is how you should pray:

"Father, may your name be honored.
May your Kingdom come soon.
3 Give us our food day by day.

NEW KING JAMES VERSION

Mary and Martha Worship and Serve

38 Now it happened as they went that He entered a certain village; and a certain woman named Martha welcomed Him into her house. 39 And she had a sister called Mary, who also sat at Jesus'[k] feet and heard His word. 40 But Martha was distracted with much serving, and she approached Him and said, "Lord, do You not care that my sister has left me to serve alone? Therefore tell her to help me."

41 And Jesus[l] answered and said to her, "Martha, Martha, you are worried and troubled about many things. 42 But one thing is needed, and Mary has chosen that good part, which will not be taken away from her."

The Model Prayer

11 Now it came to pass, as He was praying in a certain place, when He ceased, *that* one of His disciples said to Him, "Lord, teach us to pray, as John also taught his disciples."

2 So He said to them, "When you pray, say:

Our Father in heaven,[a]
Hallowed be Your name.
Your kingdom come.[b]
Your will be done
On earth as *it is* in heaven.
3 Give us day by day our daily bread.

10:39 [k] NU-Text reads *the Lord's.* 10:41 [l] NU-Text reads *the Lord.*
11:2 [a] NU-Text omits *Our* and *in heaven.* [b] NU-Text omits the rest of this verse.

THE MESSAGE

Mary and Martha

As they continued their travel, Jesus entered a village. A woman by the name of Martha welcomed him and made him feel quite at home. She had a sister, Mary, who sat before the Master, hanging on every word he said. But Martha was pulled away by all she had to do in the kitchen. Later, she stepped in, interrupting them. "Master, don't you care that my sister has abandoned the kitchen to me? Tell her to lend me a hand."

The Master said, "Martha, dear Martha, you're fussing far too much and getting yourself worked up over nothing. One thing only is essential, and Mary has chosen it—it's the main course, and won't be taken from her."

Ask For What You Need

11 One day he was praying in a certain place. When he finished, one of his disciples said, "Master, teach us to pray just as John taught his disciples."

So he said, "When you pray, say,

'Father,
Reveal who you are.
Set the world right.
Keep us alive with three square meals.

KING JAMES VERSION

4 And forgive us our sins; for we also forgive every one that is indebted to us. And lead us not into temptation; but deliver us from evil.

5 And he said unto them, Which of you shall have a friend, and shall go unto him at midnight, and say unto him, Friend, lend me three loaves;

6 For a friend of mine in his journey is come to me, and I have nothing to set before him?

7 And he from within shall answer and say, Trouble me not: the door is now shut, and my children are with me in bed; I cannot rise and give thee.

8 I say unto you, Though he will not rise and give him, because he is his friend, yet because of his importunity he will rise and give him as many as he needeth.

9 And I say unto you, Ask, and it shall be given you; seek, and ye shall find; knock, and it shall be opened unto you.

10 For every one that asketh receiveth; and he that seeketh findeth; and to him that knocketh it shall be opened.

11 If a son shall ask bread of any of you that is a father, will he give him a stone? or if *he ask* a fish, will he for a fish give him a serpent?

12 Or if he shall ask an egg, will he offer him a scorpion?

13 If ye then, being evil, know how to give good gifts unto your children: how much more shall *your* heavenly Father give the Holy Spirit to them that ask him?

NEW AMERICAN STANDARD BIBLE

4 'And forgive us our sins,
For we ourselves also forgive everyone who is
indebted to us.
And lead us not into temptation.' "

5 Then He said to them, "Suppose one of you has a friend, and goes to him at midnight and says to him, 'Friend, lend me three loaves;

6 for a friend of mine has come to me from a journey, and I have nothing to set before him';

7 and from inside he answers and says, 'Do not bother me; the door has already been shut and my children and I are in bed; I cannot get up and give you *anything.*'

8 "I tell you, even though he will not get up and give him *anything* because he is his friend, yet because of his persistence he will get up and give him as much as he needs.

9 "So I say to you, ask, and it will be given to you; seek, and you will find; knock, and it will be opened to you.

10 "For everyone who asks, receives; and he who seeks, finds; and to him who knocks, it will be opened.

11 "Now suppose one of you fathers is asked by his son for a fish; he will not give him a snake instead of a fish, will he?

12 "Or *if* he is asked for an egg, he will not give him a scorpion, will he?

13 "If you then, being evil, know how to give good gifts to your children, how much more will *your* heavenly Father give the Holy Spirit to those who ask Him?"

NEW CENTURY VERSION

4 Forgive us for our sins,
because we forgive everyone who has done wrong
to us.
And do not cause us to be tempted.' "

Continue to Ask

5 Then Jesus said to them, "Suppose one of you went to
your friend's house at midnight and said to him, 'Friend,
loan me three loaves of bread. 6 A friend of mine has come
into town to visit me, but I have nothing for him to eat.'
7 Your friend inside the house answers, 'Don't bother me!
The door is already locked, and my children and I are in
bed. I cannot get up and give you anything.' 8 I tell you, if
friendship is not enough to make him get up to give you
the bread, your boldness will make him get up and give
you whatever you need. 9 So I tell you, ask, and God will
give to you. Search, and you will find. Knock, and the door
will open for you. 10 Yes, everyone who asks will receive.
The one who searches will find. And everyone who knocks
will have the door opened. 11 If your children ask for a fish,
which of you would give them a snake instead? 12 Or, if
your children ask for an egg, would you give them a scor-
pion? 13 Even though you are bad, you know how to give
good things to your children. How much more your heav-
enly Father will give the Holy Spirit to those who ask
him!"

CONTEMPORARY ENGLISH VERSION

4 Forgive our sins,
as we forgive everyone
who has done wrong to us.
And keep us
from being tempted.' "

5 Then Jesus went on to say:

Suppose one of you goes to a friend in the middle of the night and says, "Let me borrow three loaves of
bread. 6 A friend of mine has dropped in, and I don't have a thing for him to eat." 7 And suppose your friend answers, "Don't bother me! The door is bolted, and my children and I are in bed. I cannot get up to give you something."

8 He may not get up and give you the bread, just because you are his friend. But he will get up and give you as much as you need, simply because you are not ashamed to keep on asking.

9 So I tell you to ask and you will receive, search and you will find, knock and the door will be opened for you.
10 Everyone who asks will receive, everyone who searches will find, and the door will be opened for every-
one who knocks. 11 Which one of you fathers would give your hungry child a snake if the child asked for a fish?
12 Which one of you would give your child a scorpion if the child asked for an egg? 13 As bad as you are, you still know how to give good gifts to your children. But your heavenly Father is even more ready to give the Holy Spirit to anyone who asks.

NEW INTERNATIONAL VERSION

4 Forgive us our sins,
for we also forgive everyone who sins against us.[c]
And lead us not into temptation.[d] "

5 Then he said to them, "Suppose one of you has a
friend, and he goes to him at midnight and says, 'Friend,
lend me three loaves of bread, 6 because a friend of mine
on a journey has come to me, and I have nothing to set
before him.'
7 "Then the one inside answers, 'Don't bother me. The
door is already locked, and my children are with me in bed.
I can't get up and give you anything.' 8 I tell you, though
he will not get up and give him the bread because he is his
friend, yet because of the man's boldness[e] he will get up
and give him as much as he needs.
9 "So I say to you: Ask and it will be given to you; seek
and you will find; knock and the door will be opened to
you. 10 For everyone who asks receives; he who seeks
finds; and to him who knocks, the door will be opened.
11 "Which of you fathers, if your son asks for[f] a fish, will
give him a snake instead? 12 Or if he asks for an egg, will
give him a scorpion? 13 If you then, though you are evil,
know how to give good gifts to your children, how much
more will your Father in heaven give the Holy Spirit to
those who ask him!"

[c] *4* Greek *everyone who is indebted to us* [d] *4* Some manuscripts *temptation but deliver us from the evil one* [e] *8* Or *persistence*
[f] *11* Some manuscripts *for bread, will give him a stone; or if he asks for*

NEW LIVING TRANSLATION

4 And forgive us our sins—
just as we forgive those who have sinned against us.
And don't let us yield to temptation.*"

5 Then, teaching them more about prayer, he used this
illustration: "Suppose you went to a friend's house at mid-
night, wanting to borrow three loaves of bread. You would
say to him, 6 'A friend of mine has just arrived for a visit,
and I have nothing for him to eat.' 7 He would call out from
his bedroom, 'Don't bother me. The door is locked for the
night, and we are all in bed. I can't help you this time.'
8 But I tell you this—though he won't do it as a friend, if
you keep knocking long enough, he will get up and give
you what you want so his reputation won't be damaged.*
9 "And so I tell you, keep on asking, and you will be
given what you ask for. Keep on looking, and you will find.
Keep on knocking, and the door will be opened. 10 For
everyone who asks, receives. Everyone who seeks, finds.
And the door is opened to everyone who knocks.
11 "You fathers—if your children ask* for a fish, do you
give them a snake instead? 12 Or if they ask for an egg, do
you give them a scorpion? Of course not! 13 If you sinful
people know how to give good gifts to your children, how
much more will your heavenly Father give the Holy Spirit
to those who ask him."

11:2-4 Some manuscripts add additional portions of the Lord's Prayer as it reads in Matt 6:9-13. 11:8 Greek *in order to avoid shame,* or *because of [your] persistence.* 11:11 Some manuscripts add *for bread, do you give them a stone? Or if they ask.*

NEW KING JAMES VERSION

4 And forgive us our sins,
For we also forgive everyone who is indebted to us.
And do not lead us into temptation,
But deliver us from the evil one." [c]

A Friend Comes at Midnight

5 And He said to them, "Which of you shall have a friend,
and go to him at midnight and say to him, 'Friend, lend me
three loaves; 6 for a friend of mine has come to me on his
journey, and I have nothing to set before him'; 7 and he will
answer from within and say, 'Do not trouble me; the door is
now shut, and my children are with me in bed; I cannot rise
and give to you'? 8 I say to you, though he will not rise and
give to him because he is his friend, yet because of his per-
sistence he will rise and give him as many as he needs.

Keep Asking, Seeking, Knocking

9 "So I say to you, ask, and it will be given to you; seek,
and you will find; knock, and it will be opened to you. 10 For
everyone who asks receives, and he who seeks finds, and to
him who knocks it will be opened. 11 If a son asks for bread[d]
from any father among you, will he give him a stone? Or if
he asks for a fish, will he give him a serpent instead of a
fish? 12 Or if he asks for an egg, will he offer him a scorpi-
on? 13 If you then, being evil, know how to give good gifts
to your children, how much more will *your* heavenly Father
give the Holy Spirit to those who ask Him!"

11:4 [c] NU-Text omits *But deliver us from the evil one.* 11:11 [d] NU-Text omits the words from *bread* through *for* in the next sentence.

THE MESSAGE

Keep us forgiven with you and forgiving others.
Keep us safe from ourselves and the Devil.'"

Then he said, "Imagine what would happen if you went to a friend in the middle of the night and said, 'Friend, lend me three loaves of bread. An old friend traveling through just showed up, and I don't have a thing on hand.'

"The friend answers from his bed, 'Don't bother me. The door's locked; my children are all down for the night; I can't get up to give you anything.'

"But let me tell you, even if he won't get up because he's a friend, if you stand your ground, knocking and waking all the neighbors, he'll finally get up and get you whatever you need.

"Here's what I'm saying:

Ask and you'll get;
Seek and you'll find;
Knock and the door will open.

"Don't bargain with God. Be direct. Ask for what you need. This is not a cat-and-mouse, hide-and-seek game we're in. If your little boy asks for a serving of fish, do you scare him with a live snake on his plate? If your little girl asks for an egg, do you trick her with a spider? As bad as you are, you wouldn't think of such a thing—you're at least decent to your own children. And don't you think the Father who conceived you in love will give the Holy Spirit when you ask him?"

KING JAMES VERSION

14 ¶ And he was casting out a devil, and it was dumb. And it came to pass, when the devil was gone out, the dumb spake; and the people wondered.

15 But some of them said, He casteth out devils through Beelzebub the chief of the devils.

16 And others, tempting *him*, sought of him a sign from heaven.

17 But he, knowing their thoughts, said unto them, Every kingdom divided against itself is brought to desolation; and a house *divided* against a house falleth.

18 If Satan also be divided against himself, how shall his kingdom stand? because ye say that I cast out devils through Beelzebub.

19 And if I by Beelzebub cast out devils, by whom do your sons cast *them* out? therefore shall they be your judges.

20 But if I with the finger of God cast out devils, no doubt the kingdom of God is come upon you.

21 When a strong man armed keepeth his palace, his goods are in peace:

22 But when a stronger than he shall come upon him, and overcome him, he taketh from him all his armour wherein he trusted, and divideth his spoils.

23 He that is not with me is against me: and he that gathereth not with me scattereth.

NEW AMERICAN STANDARD BIBLE

Pharisees' Blasphemy

14 And He was casting out a demon, and it was mute; when the demon had gone out, the mute man spoke; and the crowds were amazed.

15 But some of them said, "He casts out demons by Beelzebul, the ruler of the demons."

16 Others, to test *Him*, were demanding of Him a sign from heaven.

17 But He knew their thoughts and said to them, "Any kingdom divided against itself is laid waste; and a house *divided* against itself falls.

18 "If Satan also is divided against himself, how will his kingdom stand? For you say that I cast out demons by Beelzebul.

19 "And if I by Beelzebul cast out demons, by whom do your sons cast them out? So they will be your judges.

20 "But if I cast out demons by the finger of God, then the kingdom of God has come upon you.

21 "When a strong *man*, fully armed, guards his own house, his possessions are undisturbed.

22 "But when someone stronger than he attacks him and overpowers him, he takes away from him all his armor on which he had relied and distributes his plunder.

23 "He who is not with Me is against Me; and he who does not gather with Me, scatters.

NEW CENTURY VERSION

Jesus' Power Is from God

14 One time Jesus was sending out a demon that could not talk. When the demon came out, the man who had been unable to speak, then spoke. The people were amazed. 15 But some of them said, "Jesus uses the power of Beelzebul, the ruler of demons, to force demons out of people."

16 Other people, wanting to test Jesus, asked him to give them a sign from heaven. 17 But knowing their thoughts, he said to them, "Every kingdom that is divided against itself will be destroyed. And a family that is divided against itself will not continue. 18 So if Satan is divided against himself, his kingdom will not continue. You say that I use the power of Beelzebul to force out demons. 19 But if I use the power of Beelzebul to force out demons, what power do your people use to force demons out? So they will be your judges. 20 But if I use the power of God to force out demons, then the kingdom of God has come to you.

21 "When a strong person with many weapons guards his own house, his possessions are safe. 22 But when someone stronger comes and defeats him, the stronger one will take away the weapons the first man trusted and will give away the possessions.

23 "Anyone who is not with me is against me, and anyone who does not work with me is working against me.

CONTEMPORARY ENGLISH VERSION

Jesus and the Ruler of Demons

(Matthew 12.22-30; Mark 3.20-27)

14 Jesus forced a demon out of a man who could not talk. And after the demon had gone out, the man started speaking, and the crowds were amazed. 15 But some people said, "He forces out demons by the power of Beelzebul, the ruler of the demons!"

16 Others wanted to put Jesus to the test. So they asked him to show them a sign from God. 17 Jesus knew what they were thinking, and he said:

A kingdom where people fight each other will end up in ruin. And a family that fights will break up. 18 If Satan fights against himself, how can his kingdom last? Yet you say that I force out demons by the power of Beelzebul. 19 If I use his power to force out demons, whose power do your own followers use to force them out? They are the ones who will judge you. 20 But if I use God's power to force out demons, it proves that God's kingdom has already come to you.

21 When a strong man arms himself and guards his home, everything he owns is safe. 22 But if a stronger man comes and defeats him, he will carry off the weapons in which the strong man trusted. Then he will divide with others what he has taken. 23 If you are not on my side, you are against me. If you don't gather in the crop with me, you scatter it.

NEW INTERNATIONAL VERSION

Jesus and Beelzebub

[14]Jesus was driving out a demon that was mute. When the demon left, the man who had been mute spoke, and the crowd was amazed. [15]But some of them said, "By Beelzebub,[g] the prince of demons, he is driving out demons." [16]Others tested him by asking for a sign from heaven.

[17]Jesus knew their thoughts and said to them: "Any kingdom divided against itself will be ruined, and a house divided against itself will fall. [18]If Satan is divided against himself, how can his kingdom stand? I say this because you claim that I drive out demons by Beelzebub. [19]Now if I drive out demons by Beelzebub, by whom do your followers drive them out? So then, they will be your judges. [20]But if I drive out demons by the finger of God, then the kingdom of God has come to you.

[21]"When a strong man, fully armed, guards his own house, his possessions are safe. [22]But when someone stronger attacks and overpowers him, he takes away the armor in which the man trusted and divides up the spoils.

[23]"He who is not with me is against me, and he who does not gather with me, scatters.

g *15* Greek *Beezeboul* or *Beelzeboul*; also in verses 18 and 19

NEW LIVING TRANSLATION

Jesus and the Prince of Demons

[14]One day Jesus cast a demon out of a man who couldn't speak, and the man's voice returned to him. The crowd was amazed, [15]but some said, "No wonder he can cast out demons. He gets his power from Satan,* the prince of demons!" [16]Trying to test Jesus, others asked for a miraculous sign from heaven to see if he was from God.

[17]He knew their thoughts, so he said, "Any kingdom at war with itself is doomed. A divided home is also doomed. [18]You say I am empowered by the prince of demons.* But if Satan is fighting against himself by empowering me to cast out his demons, how can his kingdom survive? [19]And if I am empowered by the prince of demons, what about your own followers? They cast out demons, too, so they will judge you for what you have said. [20]But if I am casting out demons by the power of God, then the Kingdom of God has arrived among you. [21]For when Satan,* who is completely armed, guards his palace, it is safe—[22]until someone who is stronger attacks and overpowers him, strips him of his weapons, and carries off his belongings.

[23]"Anyone who isn't helping me opposes me, and anyone who isn't working with me is actually working against me.

11:15 Greek *Beelzeboul.* 11:18 Greek *by Beelzeboul;* also in 11:19. 11:21 Greek *the strong one.*

NEW KING JAMES VERSION

A House Divided Cannot Stand

[14]And He was casting out a demon, and it was mute. So it was, when the demon had gone out, that the mute spoke; and the multitudes marveled. [15]But some of them said, "He casts out demons by Beelzebub,[e] the ruler of the demons."

[16]Others, testing *Him,* sought from Him a sign from heaven. [17]But He, knowing their thoughts, said to them: "Every kingdom divided against itself is brought to desolation, and a house *divided* against a house falls. [18]If Satan also is divided against himself, how will his kingdom stand? Because you say I cast out demons by Beelzebub. [19]And if I cast out demons by Beelzebub, by whom do your sons cast *them* out? Therefore they will be your judges. [20]But if I cast out demons with the finger of God, surely the kingdom of God has come upon you. [21]When a strong man, fully armed, guards his own palace, his goods are in peace. [22]But when a stronger than he comes upon him and overcomes him, he takes from him all his armor in which he trusted, and divides his spoils. [23]He who is not with Me is against Me, and he who does not gather with Me scatters.

11:15 e NU-Text and M-Text read *Beelzebul.*

THE MESSAGE

No Neutral Ground

Jesus delivered a man from a demon that had kept him speechless. The demon gone, the man started talking a blue streak, taking the crowd by complete surprise. But some from the crowd were cynical. "Black magic," they said. "Some devil trick he's pulled from his sleeve." Others were skeptical, waiting around for him to prove himself with a spectacular miracle.

Jesus knew what they were thinking and said, "Any country in civil war for very long is wasted. A constantly squabbling family falls to pieces. If Satan cancels Satan, is there any Satan left? You accuse me of ganging up with the Devil, the prince of demons, to cast out demons, but if you're slinging devil mud at me, calling me a devil who kicks out devils, doesn't the same mud stick to your own exorcists? But if it's *God's* finger I'm pointing that sends the demons on their way, then God's kingdom is here for sure.

"When a strong man, armed to the teeth, stands guard in his front yard, his property is safe and sound. But what if a stronger man comes along with superior weapons? Then he's beaten at his own game, the arsenal that gave him such confidence hauled off, and his precious possessions plundered.

"This is war, and there is no neutral ground. If you're not on my side, you're the enemy; if you're not helping, you're making things worse.

KING JAMES VERSION

24 When the unclean spirit is gone out of a man, he walketh through dry places, seeking rest; and finding none, he saith, I will return unto my house whence I came out.

25 And when he cometh, he findeth *it* swept and garnished.

26 Then goeth he, and taketh *to him* seven other spirits more wicked than himself; and they enter in, and dwell there: and the last *state* of that man is worse than the first.

27 ¶ And it came to pass, as he spake these things, a certain woman of the company lifted up her voice, and said unto him, Blessed *is* the womb that bare thee, and the paps which thou hast sucked.

28 But he said, Yea rather, blessed *are* they that hear the word of God, and keep it.

29 ¶ And when the people were gathered thick together, he began to say, This is an evil generation: they seek a sign; and there shall no sign be given it, but the sign of Jonas the prophet.

30 For as Jonas was a sign unto the Ninevites, so shall also the Son of man be to this generation.

NEW AMERICAN STANDARD BIBLE

24 "When the unclean spirit goes out of a man, it passes through waterless places seeking rest, and not finding any, it says, 'I will return to my house from which I came.'

25 "And when it comes, it finds it swept and put in order.

26 "Then it goes and takes *along* seven other spirits more evil than itself, and they go in and live there; and the last state of that man becomes worse than the first."

27 While Jesus was saying these things, one of the women in the crowd raised her voice and said to Him, "Blessed is the womb that bore You and the breasts at which You nursed."

28 But He said, "On the contrary, blessed are those who hear the word of God and observe it."

The Sign of Jonah

29 As the crowds were increasing, He began to say, "This generation is a wicked generation; it seeks for a sign, and *yet* no sign will be given to it but the sign of Jonah.

30 "For just as Jonah became a sign to the Ninevites, so will the Son of Man be to this generation.

NEW CENTURY VERSION

The Empty Person

24"When an evil spirit comes out of a person, it travels through dry places, looking for a place to rest. But when it finds no place, it says, 'I will go back to the house I left.' 25And when it comes back, it finds that house swept clean and made neat. 26Then the evil spirit goes out and brings seven other spirits more evil than it is, and they go in and live there. So the person has even more trouble than before."

People Who Are Truly Happy

27As Jesus was saying these things, a woman in the crowd called out to Jesus, "Happy is the mother who gave birth to you and nursed you."

28But Jesus said, "No, happy are those who hear the teaching of God and obey it."

The People Want a Miracle

29As the crowd grew larger, Jesus said, "The people who live today are evil. They want to see a miracle for a sign, but no sign will be given them, except the sign of Jonah.[a] 30As Jonah was a sign for those people who lived in Nineveh, the Son of Man will be a sign for the people of

11:29 [a] **sign of Jonah** Jonah's three days in the fish are like Jesus' three days in the tomb. See Matthew 12:40.

CONTEMPORARY ENGLISH VERSION

Return of an Evil Spirit (Matthew 12.43-45)

24When an evil spirit leaves a person, it travels through the desert, looking for a place to rest. But when it doesn't find a place, it says, "I will go back to the home I left." 25When it gets there and finds the place clean and fixed up, 26it goes off and finds seven other evil spirits even worse than itself. They all come and make their home there, and that person ends up in worse shape than before.

Being Really Blessed

27While Jesus was still talking, a woman in the crowd spoke up, "The woman who gave birth to you and nursed you is blessed!"

28Jesus replied, "That's true, but the people who are really blessed are the ones who hear and obey God's message!"[b]

A Sign from God (Matthew 12.38-42; Mark 8.12)

29As crowds were gathering around Jesus, he said:

You people of today are evil! You keep looking for a sign from God. But what happened to Jonah[c] is the only sign you will be given. 30Just as Jonah was a sign to the people of Nineveh, the Son of Man will be a sign to the people of today. 31When the judgment comes, the Queen

[b] **11.28** *"That's true, but the people who are really blessed . . . message"*: Or " 'That's not true, the people who are blessed . . . message.' "
[c] **11.29** *what happened to Jonah*: Jonah was in the stomach of a big fish for three days and nights (see Matthew 12.40).

NEW INTERNATIONAL VERSION

24"When an evil[h] spirit comes out of a man, it goes through arid places seeking rest and does not find it. Then it says, 'I will return to the house I left.' 25When it arrives, it finds the house swept clean and put in order. 26Then it goes and takes seven other spirits more wicked than itself, and they go in and live there. And the final condition of that man is worse than the first."

27As Jesus was saying these things, a woman in the crowd called out, "Blessed is the mother who gave you birth and nursed you."

28He replied, "Blessed rather are those who hear the word of God and obey it."

The Sign of Jonah

29As the crowds increased, Jesus said, "This is a wicked generation. It asks for a miraculous sign, but none will be given it except the sign of Jonah. 30For as Jonah was a sign to the Ninevites, so also will the Son of Man be to

[h] 24 Greek *unclean*

NEW LIVING TRANSLATION

24"When an evil spirit leaves a person, it goes into the desert, searching for rest. But when it finds none, it says, 'I will return to the person I came from.' 25So it returns and finds that its former home is all swept and clean. 26Then the spirit finds seven other spirits more evil than itself, and they all enter the person and live there. And so that person is worse off than before."

27As he was speaking, a woman in the crowd called out, "God bless your mother—the womb from which you came, and the breasts that nursed you!"

28He replied, "But even more blessed are all who hear the word of God and put it into practice."

The Sign of Jonah

29As the crowd pressed in on Jesus, he said, "These are evil times, and this evil generation keeps asking me to show them a miraculous sign. But the only sign I will give them is the sign of the prophet Jonah. 30What happened to him was a sign to the people of Nineveh that God had sent him. What happens to me will be a sign that God has sent me, the Son of Man, to these people.

NEW KING JAMES VERSION

An Unclean Spirit Returns

24"When an unclean spirit goes out of a man, he goes through dry places, seeking rest; and finding none, he says, 'I will return to my house from which I came.' 25And when he comes, he finds *it* swept and put in order. 26Then he goes and takes with *him* seven other spirits more wicked than himself, and they enter and dwell there; and the last *state* of that man is worse than the first."

Keeping the Word

27And it happened, as He spoke these things, that a certain woman from the crowd raised her voice and said to Him, "Blessed *is* the womb that bore You, and *the* breasts which nursed You!"

28But He said, "More than that, blessed *are* those who hear the word of God and keep it!"

Seeking a Sign

29And while the crowds were thickly gathered together, He began to say, "This is an evil generation. It seeks a sign, and no sign will be given to it except the sign of Jonah the prophet.[f] 30For as Jonah became a sign to the Ninevites, so also the Son of Man will be to this generation.

11:29 [f] NU-Text omits *the prophet.*

THE MESSAGE

"When a corrupting spirit is expelled from someone, it drifts along through the desert looking for an oasis, some unsuspecting soul it can bedevil. When it doesn't find anyone, it says, 'I'll go back to my old haunt.' On return, it finds the person swept and dusted, but vacant. It then runs out and rounds up seven other spirits dirtier than itself and they all move in, whooping it up. That person ends up far worse than if he'd never gotten cleaned up in the first place."

While he was saying these things, some woman lifted her voice above the murmur of the crowd: "Blessed the womb that carried you, and the breasts at which you nursed!"

Jesus commented, "Even more blessed are those who hear God's Word and guard it with their lives!"

Keep Your Eyes Open

As the crowd swelled, he took a fresh tack: "The mood of this age is all wrong. Everybody's looking for proof, but you're looking for the wrong kind. All you're looking for is something to titillate your curiosity, satisfy your lust for miracles. But the only proof you're going to get is the Jonah-proof given to the Ninevites, which looks like no proof at all. What Jonah was to Nineveh, the Son of Man is to this age.

"On Judgment Day the Ninevites will stand up and give evidence that will condemn this generation, because when Jonah preached to them they changed their lives. A far greater preacher than Jonah is here, and you squabble

KING JAMES VERSION

31 The queen of the south shall rise up in the judgment with the men of this generation, and condemn them: for she came from the utmost parts of the earth to hear the wisdom of Solomon; and, behold, a greater than Solomon *is* here.

32 The men of Nineve shall rise up in the judgment with this generation, and shall condemn it: for they repented at the preaching of Jonas; and, behold, a greater than Jonas *is* here.

33 No man, when he hath lighted a candle, putteth *it* in a secret place, neither under a bushel, but on a candlestick, that they which come in may see the light.

34 The light of the body is the eye: therefore when thine eye is single, thy whole body also is full of light; but when *thine eye* is evil, thy body also *is* full of darkness.

35 Take heed therefore that the light which is in thee be not darkness.

36 If thy whole body therefore *be* full of light, having no part dark, the whole shall be full of light, as when the bright shining of a candle doth give thee light.

37 ¶ And as he spake, a certain Pharisee besought him to dine with him: and he went in, and sat down to meat.

38 And when the Pharisee saw *it*, he marvelled that he had not first washed before dinner.

NEW AMERICAN STANDARD BIBLE

31 "The Queen of the South will rise up with the men of this generation at the judgment and condemn them, because she came from the ends of the earth to hear the wisdom of Solomon; and behold, something greater than Solomon is here.

32 "The men of Nineveh will stand up with this generation at the judgment and condemn it, because they repented at the preaching of Jonah; and behold, something greater than Jonah is here.

33 "No one, after lighting a lamp, puts it away in a cellar nor under a basket, but on the lampstand, so that those who enter may see the light.

34 "The eye is the lamp of your body; when your eye is clear, your whole body also is full of light; but when it is bad, your body also is full of darkness.

35 "Then watch out that the light in you is not darkness.

36 "If therefore your whole body is full of light, with no dark part in it, it will be wholly illumined, as when the lamp illumines you with its rays."

Woes upon the Pharisees

37 Now when He had spoken, a Pharisee *asked Him to have lunch with him; and He went in, and reclined *at the table.*

38 When the Pharisee saw it, he was surprised that He had not first ceremonially washed before the meal.

NEW CENTURY VERSION

this time. 31On the Judgment Day the Queen of the South[b]
will stand up with the people who live now. She will show
they are guilty, because she came from far away to listen
to Solomon's wise teaching. And I tell you that someone
greater than Solomon is here. 32On the Judgment Day the
people of Nineveh will stand up with the people who live
now, and they will show that you are guilty. When Jonah
preached to them, they were sorry and changed their lives.
And I tell you that someone greater than Jonah is here.

Be a Light for the World

33"No one lights a lamp and puts it in a secret place or
under a bowl, but on a lampstand so the people who come in
can see. 34Your eye is a light for the body. When your eyes
are good, your whole body will be full of light. But when
your eyes are evil, your whole body will be full of darkness.
35So be careful not to let the light in you become darkness.
36If your whole body is full of light, and none of it is dark,
then you will shine bright, as when a lamp shines on you."

Jesus Accuses the Pharisees

37After Jesus had finished speaking, a Pharisee asked
Jesus to eat with him. So Jesus went in and sat at the
table. 38But the Pharisee was surprised when he saw that
Jesus did not wash his hands[c] before the meal. 39The Lord

11:31 [b] **Queen of the South** The Queen of Sheba. She traveled a thousand miles to learn God's wisdom from Solomon. Read 1 Kings 10:1–3. 11:38 [c] **wash his hands** This was a Jewish religious custom that the Pharisees thought was very important.

CONTEMPORARY ENGLISH VERSION

of the South[d] will stand there with you and condemn
you. She traveled a long way to hear Solomon's wisdom,
and yet here is something far greater than Solomon.
32The people of Nineveh will also stand there with you
and condemn you. They turned to God when Jonah
preached, and yet here is something far greater than
Jonah.

Light (Matthew 5.15; 6.22, 23)

33No one lights a lamp and then hides it or puts it
under a clay pot. A lamp is put on a lampstand, so that
everyone who comes into the house can see the light.
34Your eyes are the lamp for your body. When your eyes
are good, you have all the light you need. But when your
eyes are bad, everything is dark. 35So be sure that your
light isn't darkness. 36If you have light, and nothing is
dark, then light will be everywhere, as when a lamp
shines brightly on you.

Jesus Condemns the Pharisees and Teachers of the Law of Moses (Matthew 23.1-36; Mark 12.38-40; Luke 20.45-47)

37When Jesus finished speaking, a Pharisee invited him
home for a meal. Jesus went and sat down to eat.[e] 38The
Pharisee was surprised that he did not wash his hands[f]
before eating. 39So the Lord said to him:

[d] 11.31 *Queen of the South*: Sheba, probably a country in southern Arabia. [e] 11.37 *sat down to eat*: See the note at 7.36. [f] 11.38 *did not wash his hands*: The Jewish people had strict laws about washing their hands before eating, especially if they had been out in public.

NEW INTERNATIONAL VERSION

this generation. [31]The Queen of the South will rise at the judgment with the men of this generation and condemn them; for she came from the ends of the earth to listen to Solomon's wisdom, and now one[i] greater than Solomon is here. [32]The men of Nineveh will stand up at the judgment with this generation and condemn it; for they repented at the preaching of Jonah, and now one greater than Jonah is here.

The Lamp of the Body

[33]"No one lights a lamp and puts it in a place where it will be hidden, or under a bowl. Instead he puts it on its stand, so that those who come in may see the light. [34]Your eye is the lamp of your body. When your eyes are good, your whole body also is full of light. But when they are bad, your body also is full of darkness. [35]See to it, then, that the light within you is not darkness. [36]Therefore, if your whole body is full of light, and no part of it dark, it will be completely lighted, as when the light of a lamp shines on you."

Six Woes

[37]When Jesus had finished speaking, a Pharisee invited him to eat with him; so he went in and reclined at the table. [38]But the Pharisee, noticing that Jesus did not first wash before the meal, was surprised.

i 31 Or *something*; also in verse 32

NEW LIVING TRANSLATION

[31]"The queen of Sheba* will rise up against this generation on judgment day and condemn it, because she came from a distant land to hear the wisdom of Solomon. And now someone greater than Solomon is here—and you refuse to listen to him. [32]The people of Nineveh, too, will rise up against this generation on judgment day and condemn it, because they repented at the preaching of Jonah. And now someone greater than Jonah is here—and you refuse to repent.

Receiving the Light

[33]"No one lights a lamp and then hides it or puts it under a basket. Instead, it is put on a lampstand to give light to all who enter the room. [34]Your eye is a lamp for your body. A pure eye lets sunshine into your soul. But an evil eye shuts out the light and plunges you into darkness. [35]Make sure that the light you think you have is not really darkness. [36]If you are filled with light, with no dark corners, then your whole life will be radiant, as though a floodlight is shining on you."

Jesus Criticizes the Religious Leaders

[37]As Jesus was speaking, one of the Pharisees invited him home for a meal. So he went in and took his place at the table. [38]His host was amazed to see that he sat down to eat without first performing the ceremonial washing required by Jewish custom. [39]Then the Lord said to him,

11:31 Greek *the queen of the south.*

NEW KING JAMES VERSION

[31]The queen of the South will rise up in the judgment with the men of this generation and condemn them, for she came from the ends of the earth to hear the wisdom of Solomon; and indeed a greater than Solomon *is* here. [32]The men of Nineveh will rise up in the judgment with this generation and condemn it, for they repented at the preaching of Jonah; and indeed a greater than Jonah *is* here.

The Lamp of the Body

[33]"No one, when he has lit a lamp, puts *it* in a secret place or under a basket, but on a lampstand, that those who come in may see the light. [34]The lamp of the body is the eye. Therefore, when your eye is good, your whole body also is full of light. But when *your eye* is bad, your body also *is* full of darkness. [35]Therefore take heed that the light which is in you is not darkness. [36]If then your whole body *is* full of light, having no part dark, *the* whole *body* will be full of light, as when the bright shining of a lamp gives you light."

Woe to the Pharisees and Lawyers

[37]And as He spoke, a certain Pharisee asked Him to dine with him. So He went in and sat down to eat. [38]When the Pharisee saw *it,* he marveled that He had not first washed before dinner.

THE MESSAGE

about 'proofs.' On Judgment Day the Queen of Sheba will come forward and bring evidence that condemns this generation, because she traveled from a far corner of the earth to listen to wise Solomon. Wisdom far greater than Solomon's is right in front of you, and you quibble over 'evidence.'

"No one lights a lamp, then hides it in a drawer. It's put on a lamp stand so those entering the room have light to see where they're going. Your eye is a lamp, lighting up your whole body. If you live wide-eyed in wonder and belief, your body fills up with light. If you live squinty-eyed in greed and distrust, your body is a dank cellar. Keep your eyes open, your lamp burning, so you don't get musty and murky. Keep your life as well-lighted as your best-lighted room."

Frauds!

When he finished that talk, a Pharisee asked him to dinner. He entered his house and sat right down at the table. The Pharisee was shocked and somewhat offended when he saw that Jesus didn't wash up before the meal. But the

KING JAMES VERSION

39 And the Lord said unto him, Now do ye Pharisees make clean the outside of the cup and the platter; but your inward part is full of ravening and wickedness.
40 *Ye* fools, did not he that made that which is without make that which is within also?
41 But rather give alms of such things as ye have; and, behold, all things are clean unto you.
42 But woe unto you, Pharisees! for ye tithe mint and rue and all manner of herbs, and pass over judgment and the love of God: these ought ye to have done, and not to leave the other undone.
43 Woe unto you, Pharisees! for ye love the uppermost seats in the synagogues, and greetings in the markets.
44 Woe unto you, scribes and Pharisees, hypocrites! for ye are as graves which appear not, and the men that walk over *them* are not aware *of them*.
45 Then answered one of the lawyers, and said unto him, Master, thus saying thou reproachest us also.
46 And he said, Woe unto you also, *ye* lawyers! for ye lade men with burdens grievous to be borne, and ye yourselves touch not the burdens with one of your fingers.
47 Woe unto you! for ye build the sepulchres of the prophets, and your fathers killed them.
48 Truly ye bear witness that ye allow the deeds of your fathers: for they indeed killed them, and ye build their sepulchres.

NEW AMERICAN STANDARD BIBLE

39 But the Lord said to him, "Now you Pharisees clean the outside of the cup and of the platter; but inside of you, you are full of robbery and wickedness.
40 "You foolish ones, did not He who made the outside make the inside also?
41 "But give that which is within as charity, and then all things are clean for you.
42 "But woe to you Pharisees! For you pay tithe of mint and rue and every *kind of* garden herb, and *yet* disregard justice and the love of God; but these are the things you should have done without neglecting the others.
43 "Woe to you Pharisees! For you love the chief seats in the synagogues and the respectful greetings in the market places.
44 "Woe to you! For you are like concealed tombs, and the people who walk over *them* are unaware *of it.*"
45 One of the [2]lawyers *said to Him in reply, "Teacher, when You say this, You insult us too."
46 But He said, "Woe to you lawyers as well! For you weigh men down with burdens hard to bear, while you yourselves will not even touch the burdens with one of your fingers.
47 "Woe to you! For you build the tombs of the prophets, and *it was* your fathers *who* killed them.
48 "So you are witnesses and approve the deeds of your fathers; because it was they who killed them, and you build *their tombs.*

11:45 [2] I.e. experts in the Mosaic Law

NEW CENTURY VERSION

said to him, "You Pharisees clean the outside of the cup
and the dish, but inside you are full of greed and evil.
40You foolish people! The same one who made what is out-
side also made what is inside. 41So give what is in your
dishes to the poor, and then you will be fully clean. 42How
terrible for you Pharisees! You give God one-tenth of even
your mint, your rue, and every other plant in your garden.
But you fail to be fair to others and to love God. These are
the things you should do while continuing to do those
other things. 43How terrible for you Pharisees, because you
love to have the most important seats in the synagogues,
and you love to be greeted with respect in the market-
places. 44How terrible for you, because you are like hidden
graves, which people walk on without knowing."

Jesus Talks to Experts on the Law

45One of the experts on the law said to Jesus, "Teacher,
when you say these things, you are insulting us, too."
46Jesus answered, "How terrible for you, you experts on
the law! You make strict rules that are very hard for people
to obey, but you yourselves don't even try to follow those
rules. 47How terrible for you, because you build tombs for
the prophets whom your ancestors killed! 48And now you
show that you approve of what your ancestors did. They
killed the prophets, and you build tombs for them! 49This

CONTEMPORARY ENGLISH VERSION

You Pharisees clean the outside of cups and dishes,
but on the inside you are greedy and evil. 40You fools!
Didn't God make both the outside and the inside?[g] 41If
you would only give what you have to the poor, every-
thing you do would please God.
42You Pharisees are in for trouble! You give God a tenth
of the spices from your gardens, such as mint and rue.
But you cheat people, and you don't love God. You should
be fair and kind to others and still give a tenth to God.
43You Pharisees are in for trouble! You love the front
seats in the meeting places, and you like to be greeted
with honor in the market. 44But you are in for trouble!
You are like unmarked graves[h] that people walk on
without even knowing it.
45A teacher of the Law of Moses spoke up, "Teacher, you
said cruel things about us."
46Jesus replied:
You teachers are also in for trouble! You load people
down with heavy burdens, but you won't lift a finger to
help them carry the loads. 47Yes, you are really in for
trouble. You build monuments to honor the prophets
your own people murdered long ago. 48You must think
that was the right thing for your people to do, or else
you would not have built monuments for the prophets
they murdered.

[g] **11.40** *Didn't God make both the outside and the inside?*: Or "Doesn't the person who washes the outside always wash the inside too?"
[h] **11.44** *unmarked graves*: Tombs were whitewashed to keep anyone from accidentally touching them. A person who touched a dead body or a tomb was considered unclean and could not worship with other Jewish people.

NEW INTERNATIONAL VERSION

39Then the Lord said to him, "Now then, you Pharisees clean the outside of the cup and dish, but inside you are full of greed and wickedness. 40You foolish people! Did not the one who made the outside make the inside also? 41But give what is inside ⌊the dish⌋[j] to the poor, and everything will be clean for you.

42"Woe to you Pharisees, because you give God a tenth of your mint, rue and all other kinds of garden herbs, but you neglect justice and the love of God. You should have practiced the latter without leaving the former undone.

43"Woe to you Pharisees, because you love the most important seats in the synagogues and greetings in the marketplaces.

44"Woe to you, because you are like unmarked graves, which men walk over without knowing it."

45One of the experts in the law answered him, "Teacher, when you say these things, you insult us also."

46Jesus replied, "And you experts in the law, woe to you, because you load people down with burdens they can hardly carry, and you yourselves will not lift one finger to help them.

47"Woe to you, because you build tombs for the prophets, and it was your forefathers who killed them. 48So you testify that you approve of what your forefathers did; they killed the prophets, and you build their tombs. 49Because

j 41 Or *what you have*

NEW LIVING TRANSLATION

"You Pharisees are so careful to clean the outside of the cup and the dish, but inside you are still filthy—full of greed and wickedness! 40Fools! Didn't God make the inside as well as the outside? 41So give to the needy what you greedily possess, and you will be clean all over.

42"But how terrible it will be for you Pharisees! For you are careful to tithe even the tiniest part of your income,* but you completely forget about justice and the love of God. You should tithe, yes, but you should not leave undone the more important things.

43"How terrible it will be for you Pharisees! For how you love the seats of honor in the synagogues and the respectful greetings from everyone as you walk through the markets! 44Yes, how terrible it will be for you. For you are like hidden graves in a field. People walk over them without knowing the corruption they are stepping on."

45"Teacher," said an expert in religious law, "you have insulted us, too, in what you just said."

46"Yes," said Jesus, "how terrible it will be for you experts in religious law! For you crush people beneath impossible religious demands, and you never lift a finger to help ease the burden. 47How terrible it will be for you! For you build tombs for the very prophets your ancestors killed long ago. 48Murderers! You agree with your ancestors that what they did was right. You would have done

11:42 Greek *to tithe the mint and the rue and every herb.*

NEW KING JAMES VERSION

39Then the Lord said to him, "Now you Pharisees make the outside of the cup and dish clean, but your inward part is full of greed and wickedness. 40Foolish ones! Did not He who made the outside make the inside also? 41But rather give alms of such things as you have; then indeed all things are clean to you.

42"But woe to you Pharisees! For you tithe mint and rue and all manner of herbs, and pass by justice and the love of God. These you ought to have done, without leaving the others undone. 43Woe to you Pharisees! For you love the best seats in the synagogues and greetings in the marketplaces. 44Woe to you, scribes and Pharisees, hypocrites![g] For you are like graves which are not seen, and the men who walk over *them* are not aware *of them.*"

45Then one of the lawyers answered and said to Him, "Teacher, by saying these things You reproach us also."

46And He said, "Woe to you also, lawyers! For you load men with burdens hard to bear, and you yourselves do not touch the burdens with one of your fingers. 47Woe to you! For you build the tombs of the prophets, and your fathers killed them. 48In fact, you bear witness that you approve the deeds of your fathers; for they indeed killed them, and

11:44 g NU-Text omits *scribes and Pharisees, hypocrites.*

THE MESSAGE

Master said to him, "I know you Pharisees burnish the surface of your cups and plates so they sparkle in the sun, but I also know your insides are maggoty with greed and secret evil. Stupid Pharisees! Didn't the One who made the outside also make the inside? Turn both your pockets and your hearts inside out and give generously to the poor; then your *lives* will be clean, not just your dishes and your hands.

"I've had it with you! You're hopeless, you Pharisees! Frauds! You keep meticulous account books, tithing on every nickel and dime you get, but manage to find loopholes for getting around basic matters of justice and God's love. Careful bookkeeping is commendable, but the basics are required.

"You're hopeless, you Pharisees! Frauds! You love sitting at the head table at church dinners, love preening yourselves in the radiance of public flattery. Frauds! You're just like unmarked graves: People walk over that nice, grassy surface, never suspecting the rot and corruption that is six feet under."

One of the religion scholars spoke up: "Teacher, do you realize that in saying these things you're insulting us?"

He said, "Yes, and I can be even more explicit. You're hopeless, you religion scholars! You load people down with rules and regulations, nearly breaking their backs, but never lift even a finger to help.

"You're hopeless! You build tombs for the prophets your ancestors killed. The tombs you build are monuments to your murdering ancestors more than to the murdered

KING JAMES VERSION

49 Therefore also said the wisdom of God, I will send them prophets and apostles, and *some* of them they shall slay and persecute:

50 That the blood of all the prophets, which was shed from the foundation of the world, may be required of this generation;

51 From the blood of Abel unto the blood of Zacharias, which perished between the altar and the temple: verily I say unto you, It shall be required of this generation.

52 Woe unto you, lawyers! for ye have taken away the key of knowledge: ye entered not in yourselves, and them that were entering in ye hindered.

53 And as he said these things unto them, the scribes and the Pharisees began to urge *him* vehemently, and to provoke him to speak of many things:

54 Laying wait for him, and seeking to catch something out of his mouth, that they might accuse him.

12 In the mean time, when there were gathered together an innumerable multitude of people, insomuch that they trode one upon another, he began to say unto his disciples first of all, Beware ye of the leaven of the Pharisees, which is hypocrisy.

2 For there is nothing covered, that shall not be revealed; neither hid, that shall not be known.

NEW AMERICAN STANDARD BIBLE

49 "For this reason also the wisdom of God said, 'I will send to them prophets and apostles, and *some* of them they will kill and *some* they will persecute,

50 so that the blood of all the prophets, shed since the foundation of the world, may be charged against this generation,

51 from the blood of Abel to the blood of Zechariah, who was killed between the altar and the house *of God;* yes, I tell you, it shall be charged against this generation.'

52 "Woe to you lawyers! For you have taken away the key of knowledge; you yourselves did not enter, and you hindered those who were entering."

53 When He left there, the scribes and the Pharisees began to be very hostile and to question Him closely on many subjects,

54 plotting against Him to catch *Him* in something He might say.

God Knows and Cares

12 Under these circumstances, after so many thousands of people had gathered together that they were stepping on one another, He began saying to His disciples first *of all,* "Beware of the leaven of the Pharisees, which is hypocrisy.

2 "But there is nothing covered up that will not be revealed, and hidden that will not be known.

NEW CENTURY VERSION

is why in his wisdom God said, 'I will send prophets and apostles to them. They will kill some, and they will treat others cruelly.' 50So you who live now will be punished for the deaths of all the prophets who were killed since the beginning of the world— 51from the killing of Abel to the killing of Zechariah,[d] who died between the altar and the Temple. Yes, I tell you that you who are alive now will be punished for them all.

52"How terrible for you, you experts on the law. You have taken away the key to learning about God. You yourselves would not learn, and you stopped others from learning, too."

53When Jesus left, the teachers of the law and the Pharisees began to give him trouble, asking him questions about many things, 54trying to catch him saying something wrong.

Don't Be Like the Pharisees

12 So many thousands of people had gathered that they were stepping on each other. Jesus spoke first to his followers, saying, "Beware of the yeast of the Pharisees, because they are hypocrites. 2Everything that is hidden will be shown, and everything that is secret will be

11:51 [d] **Abel...Zechariah** In the Hebrew Old Testament, the first and last men to be murdered.

CONTEMPORARY ENGLISH VERSION

49Because of your evil deeds, the Wisdom of God said, "I will send prophets and apostles to you. But you will murder some and mistreat others." 50You people living today will be punished for all the prophets who have been murdered since the beginning of the world. 51This includes every prophet from the time of Abel to the time of Zechariah,[i] who was murdered between the altar and the temple. You people will certainly be punished for all of this.

52You teachers of the Law of Moses are really in for trouble! You carry the keys to the door of knowledge about God. But you never go in, and you keep others from going in.

53Jesus was about to leave, but the teachers and the Pharisees wanted to get even with him. They tried to make him say what he thought about other things, 54so that they could catch him saying something wrong.

Warnings

12 As thousands of people crowded around Jesus and were stepping on each other, he told his disciples: Be sure to guard against the dishonest teaching[a] of the Pharisees! It is their way of fooling people. 2Everything that is hidden will be found out, and every

[i] 11.51 *from the time of Abel . . . Zechariah*: Genesis is the first book in the Jewish Scriptures, and it tells that Abel was the first person to be murdered. Second Chronicles is the last book in the Jewish Scriptures, and the last murder that it tells about is that of Zechariah.

[a] 12.1 *dishonest teaching*: The Greek text has "yeast," which is used here of a teaching that is not true (see Matthew 16.6, 12).

NEW INTERNATIONAL VERSION

of this, God in his wisdom said, 'I will send them prophets
and apostles, some of whom they will kill and others they
will persecute.' 50Therefore this generation will be held
responsible for the blood of all the prophets that has been
shed since the beginning of the world, 51from the blood of
Abel to the blood of Zechariah, who was killed between the
altar and the sanctuary. Yes, I tell you, this generation will
be held responsible for it all.

52"Woe to you experts in the law, because you have
taken away the key to knowledge. You yourselves have not
entered, and you have hindered those who were entering."

53When Jesus left there, the Pharisees and the teachers
of the law began to oppose him fiercely and to besiege him
with questions, 54waiting to catch him in something he
might say.

Warnings and Encouragements

12 Meanwhile, when a crowd of many thousands had
gathered, so that they were trampling on one
another, Jesus began to speak first to his disciples, saying:
"Be on your guard against the yeast of the Pharisees,
which is hypocrisy. 2There is nothing concealed that will
not be disclosed, or hidden that will not be made known.

NEW LIVING TRANSLATION

the same yourselves. 49This is what God in his wisdom
said about you:* 'I will send prophets and apostles to
them, and they will kill some and persecute the others.'

50"And you of this generation will be held responsible
for the murder of all God's prophets from the creation of
the world—51from the murder of Abel to the murder of
Zechariah, who was killed between the altar and the sanc-
tuary. Yes, it will surely be charged against you.

52"How terrible it will be for you experts in religious
law! For you hide the key to knowledge from the people.
You don't enter the Kingdom yourselves, and you prevent
others from entering."

53As Jesus finished speaking, the Pharisees and teachers
of religious law were furious. From that time on they
grilled him with many hostile questions, 54trying to trap
him into saying something they could use against him.

A Warning against Hypocrisy

12 Meanwhile, the crowds grew until thousands were
milling about and crushing each other. Jesus
turned first to his disciples and warned them, "Beware of
the yeast of the Pharisees—beware of their hypocrisy. 2The
time is coming when everything will be revealed; all that is

11:49 Greek *Therefore, the wisdom of God said.*

NEW KING JAMES VERSION

you build their tombs. 49Therefore the wisdom of God also
said, 'I will send them prophets and apostles, and *some* of
them they will kill and persecute,' 50that the blood of all
the prophets which was shed from the foundation of the
world may be required of this generation, 51from the blood
of Abel to the blood of Zechariah who perished between
the altar and the temple. Yes, I say to you, it shall be
required of this generation.

52"Woe to you lawyers! For you have taken away the key
of knowledge. You did not enter in yourselves, and those
who were entering in you hindered."

53And as He said these things to them,[h] the scribes and
the Pharisees began to assail *Him* vehemently, and to
cross-examine Him about many things, 54lying in wait for
Him, and seeking to catch Him in something He might say,
that they might accuse Him.[i]

Beware of Hypocrisy

12 In the meantime, when an innumerable multitude
of people had gathered together, so that they tram-
pled one another, He began to say to His disciples first *of
all,* "Beware of the leaven of the Pharisees, which is hypoc-
risy. 2For there is nothing covered that will not be
revealed, nor hidden that will not be known. 3Therefore

11:53 [h] NU-Text reads *And when He left there.* 11:54 [i] NU-Text omits *and seeking* and *that they might accuse Him.*

THE MESSAGE

prophets. That accounts for God's Wisdom saying, 'I will
send them prophets and apostles, but they'll kill them and
run them off.' What it means is that every drop of righ-
teous blood ever spilled from the time earth began until
now, from the blood of Abel to the blood of Zechariah, who
was struck down between altar and sanctuary, is on your
heads. Yes, it's on the bill of this generation and this gen-
eration will pay.

"You're hopeless, you religion scholars! You took the
key of knowledge, but instead of unlocking doors, you
locked them. You won't go in yourself, and won't let any-
one else in either."

As soon as Jesus left the table, the religion scholars and
Pharisees went into a rage. They went over and over every-
thing he said, plotting how they could trap him in some-
thing from his own mouth.

Can't Hide Behind a Religious Mask

12 By this time the crowd, unwieldy and stepping on
each other's toes, numbered into the thousands.
But Jesus' primary concern was his disciples. He said to
them, "Watch yourselves carefully so you don't get conta-
minated with Pharisee yeast, Pharisee phoniness. You
can't keep your true self hidden forever; before long you'll
be exposed. You can't hide behind a religious mask forev-
er; sooner or later the mask will slip and your true face

KING JAMES VERSION

3 Therefore whatsoever ye have spoken in darkness shall be heard in the light; and that which ye have spoken in the ear in closets shall be proclaimed upon the housetops.

4 And I say unto you my friends, Be not afraid of them that kill the body, and after that have no more that they can do.

5 But I will forewarn you whom ye shall fear: Fear him, which after he hath killed hath power to cast into hell; yea, I say unto you, Fear him.

6 Are not five sparrows sold for two farthings, and not one of them is forgotten before God?

7 But even the very hairs of your head are all numbered. Fear not therefore: ye are of more value than many sparrows.

8 Also I say unto you, Whosoever shall confess me before men, him shall the Son of man also confess before the angels of God:

9 But he that denieth me before men shall be denied before the angels of God.

10 And whosoever shall speak a word against the Son of man, it shall be forgiven him: but unto him that blasphemeth against the Holy Ghost it shall not be forgiven.

11 And when they bring you unto the synagogues, and *unto* magistrates, and powers, take ye no thought how or what thing ye shall answer, or what ye shall say:

12 For the Holy Ghost shall teach you in the same hour what ye ought to say.

NEW AMERICAN STANDARD BIBLE

3 "Accordingly, whatever you have said in the dark will be heard in the light, and what you have whispered in the inner rooms will be proclaimed upon the housetops.

4 "I say to you, My friends, do not be afraid of those who kill the body and after that have no more that they can do.

5 "But I will warn you whom to fear: fear the One who, after He has killed, has authority to cast into hell; yes, I tell you, fear Him!

6 "Are not five sparrows sold for two cents? *Yet* not one of them is forgotten before God.

7 "Indeed, the very hairs of your head are all numbered. Do not fear; you are more valuable than many sparrows.

8 "And I say to you, everyone who confesses Me before men, the Son of Man will confess him also before the angels of God;

9 but he who denies Me before men will be denied before the angels of God.

10 "And everyone who speaks a word against the Son of Man, it will be forgiven him; but he who blasphemes against the Holy Spirit, it will not be forgiven him.

11 "When they bring you before the synagogues and the rulers and the authorities, do not worry about how or what you are to speak in your defense, or what you are to say;

12 for the Holy Spirit will teach you in that very hour what you ought to say."

NEW CENTURY VERSION

made known. [3]What you have said in the dark will be heard in the light, and what you have whispered in an inner room will be shouted from the housetops.

[4]"I tell you, my friends, don't be afraid of people who can kill the body but after that can do nothing more to hurt you. [5]I will show you the one to fear. Fear the one who has the power to kill you and also to throw you into hell. Yes, this is the one you should fear.

[6]"Five sparrows are sold for only two pennies, and God does not forget any of them. [7]But God even knows how many hairs you have on your head. Don't be afraid. You are worth much more than many sparrows.

Don't Be Ashamed of Jesus

[8]"I tell you, all those who stand before others and say they believe in me, I, the Son of Man, will say before the angels of God that they belong to me. [9]But all who stand before others and say they do not believe in me, I will say before the angels of God that they do not belong to me.

[10]"Anyone who speaks against the Son of Man can be forgiven, but anyone who speaks against the Holy Spirit will not be forgiven.

[11]"When you are brought into the synagogues before the leaders and other powerful people, don't worry about how to defend yourself or what to say. [12]At that time the Holy Spirit will teach you what you must say."

CONTEMPORARY ENGLISH VERSION

secret will be known. [3]Whatever you say in the dark will be heard when it is day. Whatever you whisper in a closed room will be shouted from the housetops.

The One To Fear (Matthew 10.28-31)

[4]My friends, don't be afraid of people. They can kill you, but after that, there is nothing else they can do. [5]God is the one you must fear. Not only can he take your life, but he can throw you into hell. God is certainly the one you should fear!

[6]Five sparrows are sold for just two pennies, but God doesn't forget a one of them. [7]Even the hairs on your head are counted. So don't be afraid! You are worth much more than many sparrows.

Telling Others about Christ
(Matthew 10.32, 33; 12.32; 10.19, 20)

[8]If you tell others that you belong to me, the Son of Man will tell God's angels that you are my followers. [9]But if you reject me, you will be rejected in front of them. [10]If you speak against the Son of Man, you can be forgiven, but if you speak against the Holy Spirit, you cannot be forgiven.

[11]When you are brought to trial in the Jewish meeting places or before rulers or officials, don't worry about how you will defend yourselves or what you will say. [12]At that time the Holy Spirit will tell you what to say.

NEW INTERNATIONAL VERSION

3 What you have said in the dark will be heard in the daylight, and what you have whispered in the ear in the inner rooms will be proclaimed from the roofs.

4 "I tell you, my friends, do not be afraid of those who kill the body and after that can do no more. 5 But I will show you whom you should fear: Fear him who, after the killing of the body, has power to throw you into hell. Yes, I tell you, fear him. 6 Are not five sparrows sold for two pennies[a]? Yet not one of them is forgotten by God. 7 Indeed, the very hairs of your head are all numbered. Don't be afraid; you are worth more than many sparrows.

8 "I tell you, whoever acknowledges me before men, the Son of Man will also acknowledge him before the angels of God. 9 But he who disowns me before men will be disowned before the angels of God. 10 And everyone who speaks a word against the Son of Man will be forgiven, but anyone who blasphemes against the Holy Spirit will not be forgiven.

11 "When you are brought before synagogues, rulers and authorities, do not worry about how you will defend yourselves or what you will say, 12 for the Holy Spirit will teach you at that time what you should say."

a 6 Greek *two assaria*

NEW LIVING TRANSLATION

secret will be made public. 3 Whatever you have said in the dark will be heard in the light, and what you have whispered behind closed doors will be shouted from the housetops for all to hear!

4 "Dear friends, don't be afraid of those who want to kill you. They can only kill the body; they cannot do any more to you. 5 But I'll tell you whom to fear. Fear God, who has the power to kill people and then throw them into hell.

6 "What is the price of five sparrows? A couple of pennies? Yet God does not forget a single one of them. 7 And the very hairs on your head are all numbered. So don't be afraid; you are more valuable to him than a whole flock of sparrows.

8 "And I assure you of this: If anyone acknowledges me publicly here on earth, I, the Son of Man, will openly acknowledge that person in the presence of God's angels. 9 But if anyone denies me here on earth, I will deny that person before God's angels. 10 Yet those who speak against the Son of Man may be forgiven, but anyone who speaks blasphemies against the Holy Spirit will never be forgiven.

11 "And when you are brought to trial in the synagogues and before rulers and authorities, don't worry about what to say in your defense, 12 for the Holy Spirit will teach you what needs to be said even as you are standing there."

NEW KING JAMES VERSION

whatever you have spoken in the dark will be heard in the light, and what you have spoken in the ear in inner rooms will be proclaimed on the housetops.

Jesus Teaches the Fear of God

4 "And I say to you, My friends, do not be afraid of those who kill the body, and after that have no more that they can do. 5 But I will show you whom you should fear: Fear Him who, after He has killed, has power to cast into hell; yes, I say to you, fear Him!

6 "Are not five sparrows sold for two copper coins?[a] And not one of them is forgotten before God. 7 But the very hairs of your head are all numbered. Do not fear therefore; you are of more value than many sparrows.

Confess Christ Before Men

8 "Also I say to you, whoever confesses Me before men, him the Son of Man also will confess before the angels of God. 9 But he who denies Me before men will be denied before the angels of God.

10 "And anyone who speaks a word against the Son of Man, it will be forgiven him; but to him who blasphemes against the Holy Spirit, it will not be forgiven.

11 "Now when they bring you to the synagogues and magistrates and authorities, do not worry about how or what you should answer, or what you should say. 12 For

12:6 a Greek *assarion,* a coin of very small value

THE MESSAGE

will be known. You can't whisper one thing in private and preach the opposite in public; the day's coming when those whispers will be repeated all over town.

"I'm speaking to you as dear friends. Don't be bluffed into silence or insincerity by the threats of religious bullies. True, they can kill you, but *then* what can they do? There's nothing they can do to your soul, your core being. Save your fear for God, who holds your entire life—body and soul—in his hands.

"What's the price of two or three pet canaries? Some loose change, right? But God never overlooks a single one. And he pays even greater attention to you, down to the last detail—even numbering the hairs on your head! So don't be intimidated by all this bully talk. You're worth more than a million canaries.

"Stand up for me among the people you meet and the Son of Man will stand up for you before all God's angels. But if you pretend you don't know me, do you think I'll defend you before God's angels?

"If you bad-mouth the Son of Man out of misunderstanding or ignorance, that can be overlooked. But if you're knowingly attacking God himself, taking aim at the Holy Spirit, that won't be overlooked.

"When they drag you into their meeting places, or into police courts and before judges, don't worry about defending yourselves—what you'll say or how you'll say it. The right words will be there. The Holy Spirit will give you the right words when the time comes."

KING JAMES VERSION

13 ¶ And one of the company said unto him, Master, speak to my brother, that he divide the inheritance with me.

14 And he said unto him, Man, who made me a judge or a divider over you?

15 And he said unto them, Take heed, and beware of covetousness: for a man's life consisteth not in the abundance of the things which he possesseth.

16 And he spake a parable unto them, saying, The ground of a certain rich man brought forth plentifully:

17 And he thought within himself, saying, What shall I do, because I have no room where to bestow my fruits?

18 And he said, This will I do: I will pull down my barns, and build greater; and there will I bestow all my fruits and my goods.

19 And I will say to my soul, Soul, thou hast much goods laid up for many years; take thine ease, eat, drink, *and* be merry.

20 But God said unto him, *Thou* fool, this night thy soul shall be required of thee: then whose shall those things be, which thou hast provided?

21 So *is* he that layeth up treasure for himself, and is not rich toward God.

22 ¶ And he said unto his disciples, Therefore I say unto you, Take no thought for your life, what ye shall eat; neither for the body, what ye shall put on.

23 The life is more than meat, and the body *is more* than raiment.

24 Consider the ravens: for they neither sow nor reap;

NEW AMERICAN STANDARD BIBLE

Covetousness Denounced

13 Someone in the crowd said to Him, "Teacher, tell my brother to divide the *family* inheritance with me."

14 But He said to him, "Man, who appointed Me a judge or arbitrator over you?"

15 Then He said to them, "Beware, and be on your guard against every form of greed; for not *even* when one has an abundance does his life consist of his possessions."

16 And He told them a parable, saying, "The land of a rich man was very productive.

17 "And he began reasoning to himself, saying, 'What shall I do, since I have no place to store my crops?'

18 "Then he said, 'This is what I will do: I will tear down my barns and build larger ones, and there I will store all my grain and my goods.

19 'And I will say to my soul, "Soul, you have many goods laid up for many years *to come;* take your ease, eat, drink *and* be merry." '

20 "But God said to him, 'You fool! This *very* night your soul is required of you; and *now* who will own what you have prepared?'

21 "So is the man who stores up treasure for himself, and is not rich toward God."

22 And He said to His disciples, "For this reason I say to you, do not worry about *your* life, *as to* what you will eat; nor for your body, *as to* what you will put on.

23 "For life is more than food, and the body more than clothing.

24 "Consider the ravens, for they neither sow nor reap;

NEW CENTURY VERSION

Jesus Warns Against Selfishness

13Someone in the crowd said to Jesus, "Teacher, tell my brother to divide with me the property our father left us."
14But Jesus said to him, "Who said I should judge or decide between you?" 15Then Jesus said to them, "Be careful and guard against all kinds of greed. Life is not measured by how much one owns."
16Then Jesus told this story: "There was a rich man who had some land, which grew a good crop. 17He thought to himself, 'What will I do? I have no place to keep all my crops.' 18Then he said, 'This is what I will do: I will tear down my barns and build bigger ones, and there I will store all my grain and other goods. 19Then I can say to myself, "I have enough good things stored to last for many years. Rest, eat, drink, and enjoy life!" '
20"But God said to him, 'Foolish man! Tonight your life will be taken from you. So who will get those things you have prepared for yourself?'
21"This is how it will be for those who store up things for themselves and are not rich toward God."

Don't Worry

22Jesus said to his followers, "So I tell you, don't worry about the food you need to live, or about the clothes you need for your body. 23Life is more than food, and the body is more than clothes. 24Look at the birds. They don't plant or harvest, they don't have storerooms or barns, but God

CONTEMPORARY ENGLISH VERSION

A Rich Fool

13A man in a crowd said to Jesus, "Teacher, tell my brother to give me my share of what our father left us when he died."

14Jesus answered, "Who gave me the right to settle arguments between you and your brother?"
15Then he said to the crowd, "Don't be greedy! Owning a lot of things won't make your life safe."
16So Jesus told them this story:

A rich man's farm produced a big crop, 17and he said to himself, "What can I do? I don't have a place large enough to store everything."
18Later, he said, "Now I know what I'll do. I'll tear down my barns and build bigger ones, where I can store all my grain and other goods. 19Then I'll say to myself, 'You have stored up enough good things to last for years to come. Live it up! Eat, drink, and enjoy yourself.' "
20But God said to him, "You fool! Tonight you will die. Then who will get what you have stored up?"
21"This is what happens to people who store up everything for themselves, but are poor in the sight of God."

Worry (Matthew 6.25-34)

22Jesus said to his disciples:

I tell you not to worry about your life! Don't worry about having something to eat or wear. 23Life is more than food or clothing. 24Look at the crows! They don't plant or harvest, and they don't have storehouses or

NEW INTERNATIONAL VERSION

The Parable of the Rich Fool

13Someone in the crowd said to him, "Teacher, tell my brother to divide the inheritance with me."

14Jesus replied, "Man, who appointed me a judge or an arbiter between you?" 15Then he said to them, "Watch out! Be on your guard against all kinds of greed; a man's life does not consist in the abundance of his possessions."

16And he told them this parable: "The ground of a certain rich man produced a good crop. 17He thought to himself, 'What shall I do? I have no place to store my crops.'

18"Then he said, 'This is what I'll do. I will tear down my barns and build bigger ones, and there I will store all my grain and my goods. 19And I'll say to myself, "You have plenty of good things laid up for many years. Take life easy; eat, drink and be merry." '

20"But God said to him, 'You fool! This very night your life will be demanded from you. Then who will get what you have prepared for yourself?'

21"This is how it will be with anyone who stores up things for himself but is not rich toward God."

Do Not Worry

22Then Jesus said to his disciples: "Therefore I tell you, do not worry about your life, what you will eat; or about your body, what you will wear. 23Life is more than food, and the body more than clothes. 24Consider the ravens: They do not sow or reap, they have no storeroom or barn;

NEW LIVING TRANSLATION

Story of the Rich Fool

13Then someone called from the crowd, "Teacher, please tell my brother to divide our father's estate with me."

14Jesus replied, "Friend, who made me a judge over you to decide such things as that?" 15Then he said, "Beware! Don't be greedy for what you don't have. Real life is not measured by how much we own."

16And he gave an illustration: "A rich man had a fertile farm that produced fine crops. 17In fact, his barns were full to overflowing. 18So he said, 'I know! I'll tear down my barns and build bigger ones. Then I'll have room enough to store everything. 19And I'll sit back and say to myself, My friend, you have enough stored away for years to come. Now take it easy! Eat, drink, and be merry!'

20"But God said to him, 'You fool! You will die this very night. Then who will get it all?'

21"Yes, a person is a fool to store up earthly wealth but not have a rich relationship with God."

Teaching about Money and Possessions

22Then turning to his disciples, Jesus said, "So I tell you, don't worry about everyday life—whether you have enough food to eat or clothes to wear. 23For life consists of far more than food and clothing. 24Look at the ravens. They don't need to plant or harvest or put food in barns

NEW KING JAMES VERSION

the Holy Spirit will teach you in that very hour what you ought to say."

The Parable of the Rich Fool

13Then one from the crowd said to Him, "Teacher, tell my brother to divide the inheritance with me."

14But He said to him, "Man, who made Me a judge or an arbitrator over you?" 15And He said to them, "Take heed and beware of covetousness,[b] for one's life does not consist in the abundance of the things he possesses."

16Then He spoke a parable to them, saying: "The ground of a certain rich man yielded plentifully. 17And he thought within himself, saying, 'What shall I do, since I have no room to store my crops?' 18So he said, 'I will do this: I will pull down my barns and build greater, and there I will store all my crops and my goods. 19And I will say to my soul, "Soul, you have many goods laid up for many years; take your ease; eat, drink, *and* be merry." ' 20But God said to him, 'Fool! This night your soul will be required of you; then whose will those things be which you have provided?'

21"So *is* he who lays up treasure for himself, and is not rich toward God."

Do Not Worry

22Then He said to His disciples, "Therefore I say to you, do not worry about your life, what you will eat; nor about the body, what you will put on. 23Life is more than food, and the body *is more* than clothing. 24Consider the ravens,

12:15 [b] NU-Text reads *all covetousness.*

THE MESSAGE

The Story of the Greedy Farmer

Someone out of the crowd said, "Teacher, order my brother to give me a fair share of the family inheritance."

He replied, "Mister, what makes you think it's any of my business to be a judge or mediator for you?"

Speaking to the people, he went on, "Take care! Protect yourself against the least bit of greed. Life is not defined by what you have, even when you have a lot."

Then he told them this story: "The farm of a certain rich man produced a terrific crop. He talked to himself: 'What can I do? My barn isn't big enough for this harvest.' Then he said, 'Here's what I'll do: I'll tear down my barns and build bigger ones. Then I'll gather in all my grain and goods, and I'll say to myself, "Self, you've done well! You've got it made and can now retire. Take it easy and have the time of your life!" '

"Just then God showed up and said, 'Fool! Tonight you die. And your barnful of goods—who gets it?'

"That's what happens when you fill your barn with Self and not with God."

Steep Yourself in God-Reality

He continued this subject with his disciples. "Don't fuss about what's on the table at mealtimes or if the clothes in your closet are in fashion. There is far more to your inner life than the food you put in your stomach, more to your outer appearance than the clothes you hang on your body. Look at the ravens, free and unfettered, not tied down to a

KING JAMES VERSION

which neither have storehouse nor barn; and God feedeth them: how much more are ye better than the fowls?

25 And which of you with taking thought can add to his stature one cubit?

26 If ye then be not able to do that thing which is least, why take ye thought for the rest?

27 Consider the lilies how they grow: they toil not, they spin not; and yet I say unto you, that Solomon in all his glory was not arrayed like one of these.

28 If then God so clothe the grass, which is to day in the field, and to morrow is cast into the oven; how much more *will he clothe* you, O ye of little faith?

29 And seek not ye what ye shall eat, or what ye shall drink, neither be ye of doubtful mind.

30 For all these things do the nations of the world seek after: and your Father knoweth that ye have need of these things.

31 But rather seek ye the kingdom of God; and all these things shall be added unto you.

32 Fear not, little flock; for it is your Father's good pleasure to give you the kingdom.

33 Sell that ye have, and give alms; provide yourselves bags which wax not old, a treasure in the heavens that faileth not, where no thief approacheth, neither moth corrupteth.

34 For where your treasure is, there will your heart be also.

NEW AMERICAN STANDARD BIBLE

they have no storeroom nor barn, and *yet* God feeds them; how much more valuable you are than the birds!

25 "And which of you by worrying can add a *single* [1]hour to his [2]life's span?

26 "If then you cannot do even a very little thing, why do you worry about other matters?

27 "Consider the lilies, how they grow: they neither toil nor spin; but I tell you, not even Solomon in all his glory clothed himself like one of these.

28 "But if God so clothes the grass in the field, which is *alive* today and tomorrow is thrown into the furnace, how much more *will He clothe* you? You men of little faith!

29 "And do not seek what you will eat and what you will drink, and do not keep worrying.

30 "For all these things the nations of the world eagerly seek; but your Father knows that you need these things.

31 "But seek His kingdom, and these things will be added to you.

32 "Do not be afraid, little flock, for your Father has chosen gladly to give you the kingdom.

33 "Sell your possessions and give to charity; make yourselves money belts which do not wear out, an unfailing treasure in heaven, where no thief comes near nor moth destroys.

34 "For where your treasure is, there your heart will be also.

12:25 [1] Lit *cubit* (approx 18 in.) 12:25 [2] Or *height*

NEW CENTURY VERSION

feeds them. And you are worth much more than birds. 25You cannot add any time to your life by worrying about it. 26If you cannot do even the little things, then why worry about the big things? 27Consider how the lilies grow; they don't work or make clothes for themselves. But I tell you that even Solomon with his riches was not dressed as beautifully as one of these flowers. 28God clothes the grass in the field, which is alive today but tomorrow is thrown into the fire. So how much more will God clothe you? Don't have so little faith! 29Don't always think about what you will eat or what you will drink, and don't keep worrying. 30All the people in the world are trying to get these things, and your Father knows you need them. 31But seek God's kingdom, and all the other things you need will be given to you.

Don't Trust in Money

32"Don't fear, little flock, because your Father wants to give you the kingdom. 33Sell your possessions and give to the poor. Get for yourselves purses that will not wear out, the treasure in heaven that never runs out, where thieves can't steal and moths can't destroy. 34Your heart will be where your treasure is.

CONTEMPORARY ENGLISH VERSION

barns. But God takes care of them. You are much more important than any birds. 25Can worry make you live longer?[b] 26If you don't have power over small things, why worry about everything else?

27Look how the wild flowers grow! They don't work hard to make their clothes. But I tell you that Solomon with all his wealth[c] wasn't as well clothed as one of these flowers. 28God gives such beauty to everything that grows in the fields, even though it is here today and thrown into a fire tomorrow. Won't he do even more for you? You have such little faith!

29Don't keep worrying about having something to eat or drink. 30Only people who don't know God are always worrying about such things. Your Father knows what you need. 31But put God's work first, and these things will be yours as well.

Treasures in Heaven (Matthew 6.19-21)

32My little group of disciples, don't be afraid! Your Father wants to give you the kingdom. 33Sell what you have and give the money to the poor. Make yourselves moneybags that never wear out. Make sure your treasure is safe in heaven, where thieves cannot steal it and moths cannot destroy it. 34Your heart will always be where your treasure is.

[b] 12.25 *live longer*: Or "grow taller." [c] 12.27 *Solomon with all his wealth*: The Jewish people thought that Solomon was the richest person who had ever lived.

NEW INTERNATIONAL VERSION

yet God feeds them. And how much more valuable you are
than birds! 25Who of you by worrying can add a single
hour to his life[b]? 26Since you cannot do this very little
thing, why do you worry about the rest?
27"Consider how the lilies grow. They do not labor or
spin. Yet I tell you, not even Solomon in all his splendor
was dressed like one of these. 28If that is how God clothes
the grass of the field, which is here today, and tomorrow is
thrown into the fire, how much more will he clothe you,
O you of little faith! 29And do not set your heart on what
you will eat or drink; do not worry about it. 30For the
pagan world runs after all such things, and your Father
knows that you need them. 31But seek his kingdom, and
these things will be given to you as well.
32"Do not be afraid, little flock, for your Father has been
pleased to give you the kingdom. 33Sell your possessions
and give to the poor. Provide purses for yourselves that
will not wear out, a treasure in heaven that will not be
exhausted, where no thief comes near and no moth
destroys. 34For where your treasure is, there your heart
will be also.

[b] *25* Or *single cubit to his height*

NEW LIVING TRANSLATION

because God feeds them. And you are far more valuable to
him than any birds! 25Can all your worries add a single
moment to your life? Of course not! 26And if worry can't do
little things like that, what's the use of worrying over bigger things?
27"Look at the lilies and how they grow. They don't
work or make their clothing, yet Solomon in all his glory
was not dressed as beautifully as they are. 28And if God
cares so wonderfully for flowers that are here today and
gone tomorrow, won't he more surely care for you? You
have so little faith! 29And don't worry about food—what to
eat and drink. Don't worry whether God will provide it for
you. 30These things dominate the thoughts of most people,
but your Father already knows your needs. 31He will give
you all you need from day to day if you make the Kingdom
of God your primary concern.
32"So don't be afraid, little flock. For it gives your Father
great happiness to give you the Kingdom.
33"Sell what you have and give to those in need. This
will store up treasure for you in heaven! And the purses of
heaven have no holes in them. Your treasure will be safe—
no thief can steal it and no moth can destroy it.
34Wherever your treasure is, there your heart and thoughts
will also be.

NEW KING JAMES VERSION

for they neither sow nor reap, which have neither storehouse nor barn; and God feeds them. Of how much more
value are you than the birds? 25And which of you by worrying can add one cubit to his stature? 26If you then are
not able to do *the* least, why are you anxious for the rest?
27Consider the lilies, how they grow: they neither toil nor
spin; and yet I say to you, even Solomon in all his glory
was not arrayed like one of these. 28If then God so clothes
the grass, which today is in the field and tomorrow is
thrown into the oven, how much more *will He clothe* you,
O *you* of little faith?
29"And do not seek what you should eat or what you
should drink, nor have an anxious mind. 30For all these
things the nations of the world seek after, and your Father
knows that you need these things. 31But seek the kingdom
of God, and all these things[c] shall be added to you.
32"Do not fear, little flock, for it is your Father's good
pleasure to give you the kingdom. 33Sell what you have
and give alms; provide yourselves money bags which do
not grow old, a treasure in the heavens that does not fail,
where no thief approaches nor moth destroys. 34For where
your treasure is, there your heart will be also.

12:31 [c] NU-Text reads *His kingdom, and these things.*

THE MESSAGE

job description, carefree in the care of God. And you count far more.

"Has anyone by fussing before the mirror ever gotten taller by so much as an inch? If fussing can't even do that, why fuss at all? Walk into the fields and look at the wildflowers. They don't fuss with their appearance—but have you ever seen color and design quite like it? The ten best-dressed men and women in the country look shabby alongside them. If God gives such attention to the wildflowers, most of them never even seen, don't you think he'll attend to you, take pride in you, do his best for you?

"What I'm trying to do here is get you to relax, not be so preoccupied with *getting* so you can respond to God's *giving*. People who don't know God and the way he works fuss over these things, but you know both God and how he works. Steep yourself in God-reality, God-initiative, God-provisions. You'll find all your everyday human concerns will be met. Don't be afraid of missing out. You're my dearest friends! The Father wants to give you the very kingdom itself.

"Be generous. Give to the poor. Get yourselves a bank that can't go bankrupt, a bank in heaven far from bankrobbers, safe from embezzlers, a bank you can bank on. It's obvious, isn't it? The place where your treasure is, is the place you will most want to be, and end up being.

KING JAMES VERSION

35 Let your loins be girded about, and *your* lights burning;

36 And ye yourselves like unto men that wait for their lord, when he will return from the wedding; that when he cometh and knocketh, they may open unto him immediately.

37 Blessed *are* those servants, whom the lord when he cometh shall find watching: verily I say unto you, that he shall gird himself, and make them to sit down to meat, and will come forth and serve them.

38 And if he shall come in the second watch, or come in the third watch, and find *them* so, blessed are those servants.

39 And this know, that if the goodman of the house had known what hour the thief would come, he would have watched, and not have suffered his house to be broken through.

40 Be ye therefore ready also: for the Son of man cometh at an hour when ye think not.

41 ¶ Then Peter said unto him, Lord, speakest thou this parable unto us, or even to all?

42 And the Lord said, Who then is that faithful and wise steward, whom *his* lord shall make ruler over his household, to give *them their* portion of meat in due season?

43 Blessed *is* that servant, whom his lord when he cometh shall find so doing.

44 Of a truth I say unto you, that he will make him ruler over all that he hath.

45 But and if that servant say in his heart, My lord delayeth his coming; and shall begin to beat the menservants and maidens, and to eat and drink, and to be drunken;

NEW AMERICAN STANDARD BIBLE

Be in Readiness

35 "Be dressed in readiness, and *keep* your lamps lit.

36 "Be like men who are waiting for their master when he returns from the wedding feast, so that they may immediately open *the door* to him when he comes and knocks.

37 "Blessed are those slaves whom the master will find on the alert when he comes; truly I say to you, that he will gird himself *to serve,* and have them recline *at the table,* and will come up and wait on them.

38 "Whether he comes in the [3]second watch, or even in the [4]third, and finds *them* so, blessed are those *slaves.*

39 "But be sure of this, that if the head of the house had known at what hour the thief was coming, he would not have allowed his house to be broken into.

40 "You too, be ready; for the Son of Man is coming at an hour that you do not expect."

41 Peter said, "Lord, are You addressing this parable to us, or to everyone *else* as well?"

42 And the Lord said, "Who then is the faithful and sensible steward, whom his master will put in charge of his servants, to give them their rations at the proper time?

43 "Blessed is that slave whom his master finds so doing when he comes.

44 "Truly I say to you that he will put him in charge of all his possessions.

45 "But if that slave says in his heart, 'My master will be a long time in coming,' and begins to beat the slaves, *both* men and women, and to eat and drink and get drunk;

12:38 [3] I.e. 9 p.m. to midnight 12:38 [4] I.e. midnight to 3 a.m.

NEW CENTURY VERSION

Always Be Ready

35"Be dressed, ready for service, and have your lamps
shining. 36Be like servants who are waiting for their mas-
ter to come home from a wedding party. When he comes
and knocks, the servants immediately open the door for
him. 37They will be blessed when their master comes
home, because he sees that they were watching for him. I
tell you the truth, the master will dress himself to serve
and tell the servants to sit at the table, and he will serve
them. 38Those servants will be happy when he comes in
and finds them still waiting, even if it is midnight or later.

39"Remember this: If the owner of the house knew what
time a thief was coming, he would not allow the thief to
enter his house. 40So you also must be ready, because the
Son of Man will come at a time when you don't expect him!"

Who Is the Trusted Servant?

41Peter said, "Lord, did you tell this story to us or to all
people?"

42The Lord said, "Who is the wise and trusted servant
that the master trusts to give the other servants their food
at the right time? 43When the master comes and finds the
servant doing his work, the servant will be blessed. 44I tell
you the truth, the master will choose that servant to take
care of everything he owns. 45But suppose the servant
thinks to himself, 'My master will not come back soon,'
and he begins to beat the other servants, men and women,
and to eat and drink and get drunk. 46The master will

CONTEMPORARY ENGLISH VERSION

Faithful and Unfaithful Servants (Matthew 24.45-51)

35Be ready and keep your lamps burning 36just like
those servants who wait up for their master to return
from a wedding feast. As soon as he comes and knocks,
they open the door for him. 37Servants are fortunate if
their master finds them awake and ready when he
comes! I promise you that he will get ready and have his
servants sit down so he can serve them. 38Those ser-
vants are really fortunate if their master finds them
ready, even though he comes late at night or early in the
morning. 39You would surely not let a thief break into
your home, if you knew when the thief was coming. 40So
always be ready! You don't know when the Son of Man
will come.

41Peter asked Jesus, "Did you say this just for us or for
everyone?"

42The Lord answered:

Who are faithful and wise servants? Who are the ones
the master will put in charge of giving the other ser-
vants their food supplies at the proper time? 43Servants
are fortunate if their master comes and finds them doing
their job. 44A servant who is always faithful will surely
be put in charge of everything the master owns.

45But suppose one of the servants thinks that the
master won't return until late. Suppose that servant
starts beating all the other servants and eats and drinks

NEW INTERNATIONAL VERSION

Watchfulness

35“Be dressed ready for service and keep your lamps burning, 36like men waiting for their master to return from a wedding banquet, so that when he comes and knocks they can immediately open the door for him. 37It will be good for those servants whose master finds them watching when he comes. I tell you the truth, he will dress himself to serve, will have them recline at the table and will come and wait on them. 38It will be good for those servants whose master finds them ready, even if he comes in the second or third watch of the night. 39But understand this: If the owner of the house had known at what hour the thief was coming, he would not have let his house be broken into. 40You also must be ready, because the Son of Man will come at an hour when you do not expect him.”

41Peter asked, “Lord, are you telling this parable to us, or to everyone?”

42The Lord answered, “Who then is the faithful and wise manager, whom the master puts in charge of his servants to give them their food allowance at the proper time? 43It will be good for that servant whom the master finds doing so when he returns. 44I tell you the truth, he will put him in charge of all his possessions. 45But suppose the servant says to himself, ‘My master is taking a long time in coming,’ and he then begins to beat the menservants and maidservants and to eat and drink and get drunk. 46The

NEW LIVING TRANSLATION

Be Ready for the Lord’s Coming

35“Be dressed for service and well prepared, 36as though you were waiting for your master to return from the wedding feast. Then you will be ready to open the door and let him in the moment he arrives and knocks. 37There will be special favor for those who are ready and waiting for his return. I tell you, he himself will seat them, put on an apron, and serve them as they sit and eat! 38He may come in the middle of the night or just before dawn.* But whenever he comes, there will be special favor for his servants who are ready!

39“Know this: A homeowner who knew exactly when a burglar was coming would not permit the house to be broken into. 40You must be ready all the time, for the Son of Man will come when least expected.”

41Peter asked, “Lord, is this illustration just for us or for everyone?”

42And the Lord replied, “I’m talking to any faithful, sensible servant to whom the master gives the responsibility of managing his household and feeding his family. 43If the master returns and finds that the servant has done a good job, there will be a reward. 44I assure you, the master will put that servant in charge of all he owns. 45But if the servant thinks, ‘My master won’t be back for a while,’ and begins oppressing the other servants, partying, and getting

12:38 Greek *in the second or third watch.*

NEW KING JAMES VERSION

The Faithful Servant and the Evil Servant

35“Let your waist be girded and *your* lamps burning; 36and you yourselves be like men who wait for their master, when he will return from the wedding, that when he comes and knocks they may open to him immediately. 37Blessed *are* those servants whom the master, when he comes, will find watching. Assuredly, I say to you that he will gird himself and have them sit down *to eat,* and will come and serve them. 38And if he should come in the second watch, or come in the third watch, and find *them* so, blessed are those servants. 39But know this, that if the master of the house had known what hour the thief would come, he would have watched and[d] not allowed his house to be broken into. 40Therefore you also be ready, for the Son of Man is coming at an hour you do not expect.”

41Then Peter said to Him, “Lord, do You speak this parable *only* to us, or to all *people?*”

42And the Lord said, “Who then is that faithful and wise steward, whom *his* master will make ruler over his household, to give *them their* portion of food in due season? 43Blessed *is* that servant whom his master will find so doing when he comes. 44Truly, I say to you that he will make him ruler over all that he has. 45But if that servant says in his heart, ‘My master is delaying his coming,’ and begins to beat the male and female servants, and to eat and drink and be drunk, 46the master of that servant will

12:39 [d] NU-Text reads *he would not have allowed.*

THE MESSAGE

When the Master Shows Up

“Keep your shirts on; keep the lights on! Be like house servants waiting for their master to come back from his honeymoon, awake and ready to open the door when he arrives and knocks. Lucky the servants whom the master finds on watch! He’ll put on an apron, sit them at the table, and serve them a meal, sharing his wedding feast with them. It doesn’t matter what time of the night he arrives; they’re awake—and so blessed!

“You know that if the house owner had known what night the burglar was coming, he wouldn’t have stayed out late and left the place unlocked. So don’t you be slovenly and careless. Just when you don’t expect him, the Son of Man will show up.”

Peter said, “Master, are you telling this story just for us? Or is it for everybody?”

The Master said, “Let me ask you: Who is the dependable manager, full of common sense, that the master puts in charge of his staff to feed them well and on time? He is a blessed man if when the master shows up he’s doing his job. But if he says to himself, ‘The master is certainly taking his time,’ begins maltreating the servants and maids, throws parties for his friends, and gets drunk, the master

KING JAMES VERSION

46 The lord of that servant will come in a day when he looketh not for *him*, and at an hour when he is not aware, and will cut him in sunder, and will appoint him his portion with the unbelievers.

47 And that servant, which knew his lord's will, and prepared not *himself*, neither did according to his will, shall be beaten with many *stripes*.

48 But he that knew not, and did commit things worthy of stripes, shall be beaten with few *stripes*. For unto whomsoever much is given, of him shall be much required: and to whom men have committed much, of him they will ask the more.

49 I am come to send fire on the earth; and what will I, if it be already kindled?

50 But I have a baptism to be baptized with; and how am I straitened till it be accomplished!

51 Suppose ye that I am come to give peace on earth? I tell you, Nay; but rather division:

52 For from henceforth there shall be five in one house divided, three against two, and two against three.

53 The father shall be divided against the son, and the son against the father; the mother against the daughter, and the daughter against the mother; the mother in law against her daughter in law, and the daughter in law against her mother in law.

54 ¶ And he said also to the people, When ye see a cloud rise out of the west, straightway ye say, There cometh a shower; and so it is.

NEW AMERICAN STANDARD BIBLE

46 the master of that slave will come on a day when he does not expect *him* and at an hour he does not know, and will cut him in pieces, and assign him a place with the unbelievers.

47 "And that slave who knew his master's will and did not get ready or act in accord with his will, will receive many lashes,

48 but the one who did not know *it*, and committed deeds worthy of a flogging, will receive but few. From everyone who has been given much, much will be required; and to whom they entrusted much, of him they will ask all the more.

Christ Divides Men

49 "I have come to cast fire upon the earth; and how I wish it were already kindled!

50 "But I have a baptism to undergo, and how distressed I am until it is accomplished!

51 "Do you suppose that I came to grant peace on earth? I tell you, no, but rather division;

52 for from now on five *members* in one household will be divided, three against two and two against three.

53 "They will be divided, father against son and son against father, mother against daughter and daughter against mother, mother-in-law against daughter-in-law and daughter-in-law against mother-in-law."

54 And He was also saying to the crowds, "When you see a cloud rising in the west, immediately you say, 'A shower is coming,' and so it turns out.

NEW CENTURY VERSION

come when that servant is not ready and is not expecting
him. Then the master will cut him in pieces and send him
away to be with the others who don't obey.
47"The servant who knows what his master wants but is
not ready, or who does not do what the master wants, will
be beaten with many blows! 48But the servant who does
not know what his master wants and does things that
should be punished will be beaten with few blows. From
everyone who has been given much, much will be demand-
ed. And from the one trusted with much, much more will
be expected.

Jesus Causes Division

49"I came to set fire to the world, and I wish it were
already burning! 50I have a baptism[a] to suffer through,
and I feel very troubled until it is over. 51Do you think I
came to give peace to the earth? No, I tell you, I came to
divide it. 52From now on, a family with five people will be
divided, three against two, and two against three. 53They
will be divided: father against son and son against father,
mother against daughter and daughter against mother,
mother-in-law against daughter-in-law and daughter-in-
law against mother-in-law."

Understanding the Times

54Then Jesus said to the people, "When you see clouds
coming up in the west, you say, 'It's going to rain,' and it

12:50 [a] **I...baptism** Jesus was talking about the suffering he would soon go through.

CONTEMPORARY ENGLISH VERSION

and gets drunk. 46If that happens, the master will come
on a day and at a time when the servant least expects
him. That servant will then be punished and thrown out
with the servants who cannot be trusted.
47If servants are not ready or willing to do what their
master wants them to do, they will be beaten hard.
48But servants who don't know what their master wants
them to do will not be beaten so hard for doing wrong. If
God has been generous with you, he will expect you to
serve him well. But if he has been more than generous,
he will expect you to serve him even better.

Not Peace, but Trouble (Matthew 10.34-36)

49I came to set fire to the earth, and I wish it were
already on fire! 50I am going to be put to a hard test.
And I will have to suffer a lot of pain until it is over.
51Do you think that I came to bring peace to earth? No
indeed! I came to make people choose sides. 52A family
of five will be divided, with two of them against the
other three. 53Fathers and sons will turn against one
another, and mothers and daughters will do the same.
Mothers-in-law and daughters-in-law will also turn
against each other.

Knowing What To Do (Matthew 16.2, 3; 5.25, 26)

54Jesus said to all the people:
As soon as you see a cloud coming up in the west, you
say, "It's going to rain," and it does. 55When the south

NEW INTERNATIONAL VERSION

master of that servant will come on a day when he does not expect him and at an hour he is not aware of. He will cut him to pieces and assign him a place with the unbelievers.

47“That servant who knows his master’s will and does not get ready or does not do what his master wants will be beaten with many blows. 48But the one who does not know and does things deserving punishment will be beaten with few blows. From everyone who has been given much, much will be demanded; and from the one who has been entrusted with much, much more will be asked.

Not Peace but Division

49“I have come to bring fire on the earth, and how I wish it were already kindled! 50But I have a baptism to undergo, and how distressed I am until it is completed! 51Do you think I came to bring peace on earth? No, I tell you, but division. 52From now on there will be five in one family divided against each other, three against two and two against three. 53They will be divided, father against son and son against father, mother against daughter and daughter against mother, mother-in-law against daughter-in-law and daughter-in-law against mother-in-law.”

Interpreting the Times

54He said to the crowd: “When you see a cloud rising in the west, immediately you say, ‘It’s going to rain,’ and it

NEW LIVING TRANSLATION

drunk—46well, the master will return unannounced and unexpected. He will tear the servant apart and banish him with the unfaithful. 47The servant will be severely punished, for though he knew his duty, he refused to do it.

48“But people who are not aware that they are doing wrong will be punished only lightly. Much is required from those to whom much is given, and much more is required from those to whom much more is given.

Jesus Causes Division

49“I have come to bring fire to the earth, and I wish that my task were already completed! 50There is a terrible baptism ahead of me, and I am under a heavy burden until it is accomplished. 51Do you think I have come to bring peace to the earth? No, I have come to bring strife and division! 52From now on families will be split apart, three in favor of me, and two against—or the other way around. 53There will be a division between father and son, mother and daughter, mother-in-law and daughter-in-law.”

54Then Jesus turned to the crowd and said, “When you see clouds beginning to form in the west, you say, ‘Here comes a shower.’ And you are right. 55When the south

NEW KING JAMES VERSION

come on a day when he is not looking for *him,* and at an hour when he is not aware, and will cut him in two and appoint *him* his portion with the unbelievers. 47And that servant who knew his master’s will, and did not prepare *himself* or do according to his will, shall be beaten with many *stripes.* 48But he who did not know, yet committed things deserving of stripes, shall be beaten with few. For everyone to whom much is given, from him much will be required; and to whom much has been committed, of him they will ask the more.

Christ Brings Division

49“I came to send fire on the earth, and how I wish it were already kindled! 50But I have a baptism to be baptized with, and how distressed I am till it is accomplished! 51Do *you* suppose that I came to give peace on earth? I tell you, not at all, but rather division. 52For from now on five in one house will be divided: three against two, and two against three. 53Father will be divided against son and son against father, mother against daughter and daughter against mother, mother-in-law against her daughter-in-law and daughter-in-law against her mother-in-law.”

Discern the Time

54Then He also said to the multitudes, “Whenever *you see* a cloud rising out of the west, immediately you say, ‘A shower is coming’; and so it is. 55And when you see the

THE MESSAGE

will walk in when he least expects it, give him the thrashing of his life, and put him back in the kitchen peeling potatoes.

“The servant who knows what his master wants and ignores it, or insolently does whatever he pleases, will be thoroughly thrashed. But if he does a poor job through ignorance, he’ll get off with a slap on the hand. Great gifts mean great responsibilities; greater gifts, greater responsibilities!

To Start a Fire

“I’ve come to start a fire on this earth—how I wish it were blazing right now! I’ve come to change everything, turn everything rightside up—how I long for it to be finished! Do you think I came to smooth things over and make everything nice? Not so. I’ve come to disrupt and confront! From now on, when you find five in a house, it will be—

Three against two,
 and two against three;
Father against son,
 and son against father;
Mother against daughter,
 and daughter against mother;
Mother-in-law against bride,
 and bride against mother-in-law.”

Then he turned to the crowd: “When you see clouds coming in from the west, you say, ‘Storm’s coming’—and

KING JAMES VERSION

55 And when *ye see* the south wind blow, ye say, There will be heat; and it cometh to pass.

56 *Ye* hypocrites, ye can discern the face of the sky and of the earth; but how is it that ye do not discern this time?

57 Yea, and why even of yourselves judge ye not what is right?

58 When thou goest with thine adversary to the magistrate, *as thou art* in the way, give diligence that thou mayest be delivered from him; lest he hale thee to the judge, and the judge deliver thee to the officer, and the officer cast thee into prison.

59 I tell thee, thou shalt not depart thence, till thou hast paid the very last mite.

13 There were present at that season some that told him of the Galilaeans, whose blood Pilate had mingled with their sacrifices.

2 And Jesus answering said unto them, Suppose ye that these Galilaeans were sinners above all the Galilaeans, because they suffered such things?

3 I tell you, Nay: but, except ye repent, ye shall all likewise perish.

4 Or those eighteen, upon whom the tower in Siloam fell, and slew them, think ye that they were sinners above all men that dwelt in Jerusalem?

5 I tell you, Nay: but, except ye repent, ye shall all likewise perish.

NEW AMERICAN STANDARD BIBLE

55 "And when *you see* a south wind blowing, you say, 'It will be a hot day,' and it turns out *that way.*

56 "You hypocrites! You know how to analyze the appearance of the earth and the sky, but why do you not analyze this present time?

57 "And why do you not even on your own initiative judge what is right?

58 "For while you are going with your opponent to appear before the magistrate, on *your* way *there* make an effort to settle with him, so that he may not drag you before the judge, and the judge turn you over to the officer, and the officer throw you into prison.

59 "I say to you, you will not get out of there until you have paid the very last cent."

Call to Repent

13 Now on the same occasion there were some present who reported to Him about the Galileans whose blood Pilate had mixed with their sacrifices.

2 And Jesus said to them, "Do you suppose that these Galileans were *greater* sinners than all *other* Galileans because they suffered this *fate?*

3 "I tell you, no, but unless you repent, you will all likewise perish.

4 "Or do you suppose that those eighteen on whom the tower in Siloam fell and killed them were *worse* culprits than all the men who live in Jerusalem?

5 "I tell you, no, but unless you repent, you will all likewise perish."

NEW CENTURY VERSION

happens. 55 When you feel the wind begin to blow from the
south, you say, 'It will be a hot day,' and it happens.
56 Hypocrites! You know how to understand the appearance
of the earth and sky. Why don't you understand what is
happening now?

Settle Your Problems

57 "Why can't you decide for yourselves what is right? 58 If
your enemy is taking you to court, try hard to settle it on the
way. If you don't, your enemy might take you to the judge,
and the judge might turn you over to the officer, and the
officer might throw you into jail. 59 I tell you, you will not
get out of there until you have paid everything you owe."

Change Your Hearts

13 At that time some people were there who told Jesus
that Pilate[a] had killed some people from Galilee
while they were worshiping. He mixed their blood with the
blood of the animals they were sacrificing to God. 2 Jesus
answered, "Do you think this happened to them because
they were more sinful than all others from Galilee? 3 No, I
tell you. But unless you change your hearts and lives, you
will be destroyed as they were! 4 What about those eighteen
people who died when the tower of Siloam fell on them? Do
you think they were more sinful than all the others who
live in Jerusalem? 5 No, I tell you. But unless you change
your hearts and lives, you will all be destroyed too!"

13:1 [a] **Pilate** Pontius Pilate was the Roman governor of Judea from A.D. 26 to A.D. 36.

CONTEMPORARY ENGLISH VERSION

wind blows, you say, "It's going to get hot," and it does.
56 Are you trying to fool someone? You can predict the
weather by looking at the earth and sky, but you don't
really know what's going on right now. 57 Why don't you
understand the right thing to do? 58 When someone
accuses you of something, try to settle things before you
are taken to court. If you don't, you will be dragged
before the judge. Then the judge will hand you over to
the jailer, and you will be locked up. 59 You won't get out
until you have paid the last cent you owe.

Turn Back to God

13 About this same time Jesus was told that Pilate
had given orders for some people from Galilee to
be killed while they were offering sacrifices. 2 Jesus replied:
Do you think that these people were worse sinners
than everyone else in Galilee just because of what happened to them? 3 Not at all! But you can be sure that if
you don't turn back to God, every one of you will also be
killed. 4 What about those eighteen people who died
when the tower in Siloam fell on them? Do you think
they were worse than everyone else in Jerusalem? 5 Not
at all! But you can be sure that if you don't turn back to
God, every one of you will also die.

NEW INTERNATIONAL VERSION

does. 55And when the south wind blows, you say, 'It's going to be hot,' and it is. 56Hypocrites! You know how to interpret the appearance of the earth and the sky. How is it that you don't know how to interpret this present time?

57"Why don't you judge for yourselves what is right? 58As you are going with your adversary to the magistrate, try hard to be reconciled to him on the way, or he may drag you off to the judge, and the judge turn you over to the officer, and the officer throw you into prison. 59I tell you, you will not get out until you have paid the last penny.[c]"

Repent or Perish

13 Now there were some present at that time who told Jesus about the Galileans whose blood Pilate had mixed with their sacrifices. 2Jesus answered, "Do you think that these Galileans were worse sinners than all the other Galileans because they suffered this way? 3I tell you, no! But unless you repent, you too will all perish. 4Or those eighteen who died when the tower in Siloam fell on them—do you think they were more guilty than all the others living in Jerusalem? 5I tell you, no! But unless you repent, you too will all perish."

[c] *59* Greek *lepton*

NEW LIVING TRANSLATION

wind blows, you say, 'Today will be a scorcher.' And it is. 56You hypocrites! You know how to interpret the appearance of the earth and the sky, but you can't interpret these present times.

57"Why can't you decide for yourselves what is right? 58If you are on the way to court and you meet your accuser, try to settle the matter before it reaches the judge, or you may be sentenced and handed over to an officer and thrown in jail. 59And if that happens, you won't be free again until you have paid the last penny."

A Call to Repentance

13 About this time Jesus was informed that Pilate had murdered some people from Galilee as they were sacrificing at the Temple in Jerusalem. 2"Do you think those Galileans were worse sinners than other people from Galilee?" he asked. "Is that why they suffered? 3Not at all! And you will also perish unless you turn from your evil ways and turn to God. 4And what about the eighteen men who died when the Tower of Siloam fell on them? Were they the worst sinners in Jerusalem? 5No, and I tell you again that unless you repent, you will also perish."

NEW KING JAMES VERSION

south wind blow, you say, 'There will be hot weather'; and there is. 56Hypocrites! You can discern the face of the sky and of the earth, but how *is it* you do not discern this time?

Make Peace with Your Adversary

57"Yes, and why, even of yourselves, do you not judge what is right? 58When you go with your adversary to the magistrate, make every effort along the way to settle with him, lest he drag you to the judge, the judge deliver you to the officer, and the officer throw you into prison. 59I tell you, you shall not depart from there till you have paid the very last mite."

Repent or Perish

13 There were present at that season some who told Him about the Galileans whose blood Pilate had mingled with their sacrifices. 2And Jesus answered and said to them, "Do you suppose that these Galileans were worse sinners than all *other* Galileans, because they suffered such things? 3I tell you, no; but unless you repent you will all likewise perish. 4Or those eighteen on whom the tower in Siloam fell and killed them, do you think that they were worse sinners than all *other* men who dwelt in Jerusalem? 5I tell you, no; but unless you repent you will all likewise perish."

THE MESSAGE

you're right. And when the wind comes out of the south, you say, 'This'll be a hot one'—and you're right. Frauds! You know how to tell a change in the weather, so don't tell me you can't tell a change in the season, the God-season we're in right now.

"You don't have to be a genius to understand these things. Just use your common sense, the kind you'd use if, while being taken to court, you decided to settle up with your accuser on the way, knowing that if the case went to the judge you'd probably go to jail and pay every last penny of the fine. That's the kind of decision I'm asking you to make."

Unless You Turn to God

13 About that time some people came up and told him about the Galileans Pilate had killed while they were at worship, mixing their blood with the blood of the sacrifices on the altar. Jesus responded, "Do you think those murdered Galileans were worse sinners than all other Galileans? Not at all. Unless you turn to God, you too will die. And those eighteen in Jerusalem the other day, the ones crushed and killed when the Tower of Siloam collapsed and fell on them, do you think they were worse citizens than all other Jerusalemites? Not at all. Unless you turn to God, you too will die."

KING JAMES VERSION

6 ¶ He spake also this parable; A certain *man* had a fig tree planted in his vineyard; and he came and sought fruit thereon, and found none.

7 Then said he unto the dresser of his vineyard, Behold, these three years I come seeking fruit on this fig tree, and find none: cut it down; why cumbereth it the ground?

8 And he answering said unto him, Lord, let it alone this year also, till I shall dig about it, and dung *it*:

9 And if it bear fruit, *well*: and if not, *then* after that thou shalt cut it down.

10 ¶ And he was teaching in one of the synagogues on the sabbath.

11 And, behold, there was a woman which had a spirit of infirmity eighteen years, and was bowed together, and could in no wise lift up *herself*.

12 And when Jesus saw her, he called *her to him*, and said unto her, Woman, thou art loosed from thine infirmity.

13 And he laid *his* hands on her: and immediately she was made straight, and glorified God.

14 And the ruler of the synagogue answered with indignation, because that Jesus had healed on the sabbath day, and said unto the people, There are six days in which men ought to work: in them therefore come and be healed, and not on the sabbath day.

15 The Lord then answered him, and said, *Thou* hypocrite, doth not each one of you on the sabbath loose his ox or *his* ass from the stall, and lead *him* away to watering?

NEW AMERICAN STANDARD BIBLE

6 And He *began* telling this parable: "A man had a fig tree which had been planted in his vineyard; and he came looking for fruit on it and did not find any.

7 "And he said to the vineyard-keeper, 'Behold, for three years I have come looking for fruit on this fig tree without finding any. Cut it down! Why does it even use up the ground?'

8 "And he answered and said to him, 'Let it alone, sir, for this year too, until I dig around it and put in fertilizer;

9 and if it bears fruit next year, *fine;* but if not, cut it down.' "

Healing on the Sabbath

10 And He was teaching in one of the synagogues on the Sabbath.

11 And there was a woman who for eighteen years had had a sickness caused by a spirit; and she was bent double, and could not straighten up at all.

12 When Jesus saw her, He called her over and said to her, "Woman, you are freed from your sickness."

13 And He laid His hands on her; and immediately she was made erect again and *began* glorifying God.

14 But the synagogue official, indignant because Jesus had healed on the Sabbath, *began* saying to the crowd in response, "There are six days in which work should be done; so come during them and get healed, and not on the Sabbath day."

15 But the Lord answered him and said, "You hypocrites, does not each of you on the Sabbath untie his ox or his donkey from the stall and lead him away to water *him?*

NEW CENTURY VERSION

The Useless Tree

6Jesus told this story: "A man had a fig tree planted in his vineyard. He came looking for some fruit on the tree, but he found none. 7So the man said to his gardener, 'I have been looking for fruit on this tree for three years, but I never find any. Cut it down. Why should it waste the ground?' 8But the servant answered, 'Master, let the tree have one more year to produce fruit. Let me dig up the dirt around it and put on some fertilizer. 9If the tree produces fruit next year, good. But if not, you can cut it down.' "

Jesus Heals on the Sabbath

10Jesus was teaching in one of the synagogues on the Sabbath day. 11A woman was there who, for eighteen years, had an evil spirit in her that made her crippled. Her back was always bent; she could not stand up straight. 12When Jesus saw her, he called her over and said, "Woman, you are free from your sickness." 13Jesus put his hands on her, and immediately she was able to stand up straight and began praising God.

14The synagogue leader was angry because Jesus healed on the Sabbath day. He said to the people, "There are six days when one has to work. So come to be healed on one of those days, and not on the Sabbath day."

15The Lord answered, "You hypocrites! Doesn't each of you untie your work animals and lead them to drink water every day—even on the Sabbath day? 16This woman that I

CONTEMPORARY ENGLISH VERSION

A Story about a Fig Tree

6Jesus then told them this story:

A man had a fig tree growing in his vineyard. One day he went out to pick some figs, but he didn't find any.

7So he said to the gardener, "For three years I have come looking for figs on this tree, and I haven't found any yet. Chop it down! Why should it take up space?"

8The gardener answered, "Master, leave it for another year. I'll dig around it and put some manure on it to make it grow. 9Maybe it will have figs on it next year. If it doesn't, you can have it cut down."

Healing a Woman on the Sabbath

10One Sabbath, Jesus was teaching in a Jewish meeting place, 11and a woman was there who had been crippled by an evil spirit for eighteen years. She was completely bent over and could not straighten up. 12When Jesus saw the woman, he called her over and said, "You are now well." 13He placed his hands on her, and right away she stood up straight and praised God.

14The man in charge of the meeting place was angry because Jesus had healed someone on the Sabbath. So he said to the people, "Each week has six days when we can work. Come and be healed on one of those days, but not on the Sabbath."

15The Lord replied, "Are you trying to fool someone? Won't any one of you untie your ox or donkey and lead it out to drink on a Sabbath? 16This woman belongs to the

NEW INTERNATIONAL VERSION

6Then he told this parable: "A man had a fig tree, planted in his vineyard, and he went to look for fruit on it, but did not find any. 7So he said to the man who took care of the vineyard, 'For three years now I've been coming to look for fruit on this fig tree and haven't found any. Cut it down! Why should it use up the soil?'

8" 'Sir,' the man replied, 'leave it alone for one more year, and I'll dig around it and fertilize it. 9If it bears fruit next year, fine! If not, then cut it down.' "

A Crippled Woman Healed on the Sabbath

10On a Sabbath Jesus was teaching in one of the synagogues, 11and a woman was there who had been crippled by a spirit for eighteen years. She was bent over and could not straighten up at all. 12When Jesus saw her, he called her forward and said to her, "Woman, you are set free from your infirmity." 13Then he put his hands on her, and immediately she straightened up and praised God.

14Indignant because Jesus had healed on the Sabbath, the synagogue ruler said to the people, "There are six days for work. So come and be healed on those days, not on the Sabbath."

15The Lord answered him, "You hypocrites! Doesn't each of you on the Sabbath untie his ox or donkey from the stall and lead it out to give it water? 16Then should not this

NEW LIVING TRANSLATION

Illustration of the Barren Fig Tree

6Then Jesus used this illustration: "A man planted a fig tree in his garden and came again and again to see if there was any fruit on it, but he was always disappointed. 7Finally, he said to his gardener, 'I've waited three years, and there hasn't been a single fig! Cut it down. It's taking up space we can use for something else.'

8"The gardener answered, 'Give it one more chance. Leave it another year, and I'll give it special attention and plenty of fertilizer. 9If we get figs next year, fine. If not, you can cut it down.' "

Jesus Heals on the Sabbath

10One Sabbath day as Jesus was teaching in a synagogue, 11he saw a woman who had been crippled by an evil spirit. She had been bent double for eighteen years and was unable to stand up straight. 12When Jesus saw her, he called her over and said, "Woman, you are healed of your sickness!" 13Then he touched her, and instantly she could stand straight. How she praised and thanked God!

14But the leader in charge of the synagogue was indignant that Jesus had healed her on the Sabbath day. "There are six days of the week for working," he said to the crowd. "Come on those days to be healed, not on the Sabbath."

15But the Lord replied, "You hypocrite! You work on the Sabbath day! Don't you untie your ox or your donkey from their stalls on the Sabbath and lead them out for water?

NEW KING JAMES VERSION

The Parable of the Barren Fig Tree

6He also spoke this parable: "A certain *man* had a fig tree planted in his vineyard, and he came seeking fruit on it and found none. 7Then he said to the keeper of his vineyard, 'Look, for three years I have come seeking fruit on this fig tree and find none. Cut it down; why does it use up the ground?' 8But he answered and said to him, 'Sir, let it alone this year also, until I dig around it and fertilize *it*. 9And if it bears fruit, *well*. But if not, after that[a] you can cut it down.' "

A Spirit of Infirmity

10Now He was teaching in one of the synagogues on the Sabbath. 11And behold, there was a woman who had a spirit of infirmity eighteen years, and was bent over and could in no way raise *herself* up. 12But when Jesus saw her, He called *her* to *Him* and said to her, "Woman, you are loosed from your infirmity." 13And He laid *His* hands on her, and immediately she was made straight, and glorified God.

14But the ruler of the synagogue answered with indignation, because Jesus had healed on the Sabbath; and he said to the crowd, "There are six days on which men ought to work; therefore come and be healed on them, and not on the Sabbath day."

15The Lord then answered him and said, "Hypocrite![b] Does not each one of you on the Sabbath loose his ox or donkey from the stall, and lead *it* away to water it? 16So

13:9 [a] NU-Text reads *And if it bears fruit after that, well. But if not, you can cut it down.* 13:15 [b] NU-Text and M-Text read *Hypocrites.*

THE MESSAGE

Then he told them a story: "A man had an apple tree planted in his front yard. He came to it expecting to find apples, but there weren't any. He said to his gardener, 'What's going on here? For three years now I've come to this tree expecting apples and not one apple have I found. Chop it down! Why waste good ground with it any longer?'

"The gardener said, 'Let's give it another year. I'll dig around it and fertilize, and maybe it will produce next year; if it doesn't, then chop it down.' "

Healing on the Sabbath

He was teaching in one of the meeting places on the Sabbath. There was a woman present, so twisted and bent over with arthritis that she couldn't even look up. She had been afflicted with this for eighteen years. When Jesus saw her, he called her over. "Woman, you're free!" He laid hands on her and suddenly she was standing straight and tall, giving glory to God.

The meeting-place president, furious because Jesus had healed on the Sabbath, said to the congregation, "Six days have been defined as work days. Come on one of the six if you want to be healed, but not on the seventh, the Sabbath."

But Jesus shot back, "You frauds! Each Sabbath every one of you regularly unties your cow or donkey from its stall, leads it out for water, and thinks nothing of it. So

KING JAMES VERSION

16 And ought not this woman, being a daughter of Abraham, whom Satan hath bound, lo, these eighteen years, be loosed from this bond on the sabbath day?

17 And when he had said these things, all his adversaries were ashamed: and all the people rejoiced for all the glorious things that were done by him.

18 ¶ Then said he, Unto what is the kingdom of God like? and whereunto shall I resemble it?

19 It is like a grain of mustard seed, which a man took, and cast into his garden; and it grew, and waxed a great tree; and the fowls of the air lodged in the branches of it.

20 And again he said, Whereunto shall I liken the kingdom of God?

21 It is like leaven, which a woman took and hid in three measures of meal, till the whole was leavened.

22 And he went through the cities and villages, teaching, and journeying toward Jerusalem.

23 ¶ Then said one unto him, Lord, are there few that be saved? And he said unto them,

24 Strive to enter in at the strait gate: for many, I say unto you, will seek to enter in, and shall not be able.

25 When once the master of the house is risen up, and hath shut to the door, and ye begin to stand without, and to knock at the door, saying, Lord, Lord, open unto us; and he shall answer and say unto you, I know you not whence ye are:

NEW AMERICAN STANDARD BIBLE

16 "And this woman, a daughter of Abraham as she is, whom Satan has bound for eighteen long years, should she not have been released from this bond on the Sabbath day?"

17 As He said this, all His opponents were being humiliated; and the entire crowd was rejoicing over all the glorious things being done by Him.

Parables of Mustard Seed and Leaven

18 So He was saying, "What is the kingdom of God like, and to what shall I compare it?

19 "It is like a mustard seed, which a man took and threw into his own garden; and it grew and became a tree, and THE BIRDS OF THE AIR NESTED IN ITS BRANCHES."

20 And again He said, "To what shall I compare the kingdom of God?

21 "It is like leaven, which a woman took and hid in three pecks of flour until it was all leavened."

Teaching in the Villages

22 And He was passing through from one city and village to another, teaching, and proceeding on His way to Jerusalem.

23 And someone said to Him, "Lord, are there *just* a few who are being saved?" And He said to them,

24 "Strive to enter through the narrow door; for many, I tell you, will seek to enter and will not be able.

25 "Once the head of the house gets up and shuts the door, and you begin to stand outside and knock on the door, saying, 'Lord, open up to us!' then He will answer and say to you, 'I do not know where you are from.'

NEW CENTURY VERSION

healed, a daughter of Abraham, has been held by Satan for eighteen years. Surely it is not wrong for her to be freed from her sickness on a Sabbath day!" 17 When Jesus said this, all of those who were criticizing him were ashamed, but the entire crowd rejoiced at all the wonderful things Jesus was doing.

Stories of Mustard Seed and Yeast

18 Then Jesus said, "What is God's kingdom like? What can I compare it with? 19 It is like a mustard seed that a man plants in his garden. The seed grows and becomes a tree, and the wild birds build nests in its branches."

20 Jesus said again, "What can I compare God's kingdom with? 21 It is like yeast that a woman took and hid in a large tub of flour until it made all the dough rise."

The Narrow Door

22 Jesus was teaching in every town and village as he traveled toward Jerusalem. 23 Someone said to Jesus, "Lord, will only a few people be saved?"

Jesus said, 24 "Try hard to enter through the narrow door, because many people will try to enter there, but they will not be able. 25 When the owner of the house gets up and closes the door, you can stand outside and knock on the door and say, 'Sir, open the door for us.' But he will answer, 'I don't know you or where you come from.'

CONTEMPORARY ENGLISH VERSION

family of Abraham, but Satan has kept her bound for eighteen years. Isn't it right to set her free on the Sabbath?" 17 Jesus' words made his enemies ashamed. But everyone else in the crowd was happy about the wonderful things he was doing.

A Mustard Seed and Yeast (Matthew 13.31-33; Mark 4.30-32)

18 Jesus said, "What is God's kingdom like? What can I compare it with? 19 It is like what happens when someone plants a mustard seed in a garden. The seed grows as big as a tree, and birds nest in its branches."

20 Then Jesus said, "What can I compare God's kingdom with? 21 It is like what happens when a woman mixes yeast into three batches of flour. Finally, all the dough rises."

The Narrow Door (Matthew 7.13, 14, 21-23)

22 As Jesus was on his way to Jerusalem, he taught the people in the towns and villages. 23 Someone asked him, "Lord, are only a few people going to be saved?"

Jesus answered:

24 Do all you can to go in by the narrow door! A lot of people will try to get in, but will not be able to. 25 Once the owner of the house gets up and locks the door, you will be left standing outside. You will knock on the door and say, "Sir, open the door for us!"

But the owner will answer, "I don't know a thing about you!"

NEW INTERNATIONAL VERSION

woman, a daughter of Abraham, whom Satan has kept bound for eighteen long years, be set free on the Sabbath day from what bound her?"

[17]When he said this, all his opponents were humiliated, but the people were delighted with all the wonderful things he was doing.

The Parables of the Mustard Seed and the Yeast

[18]Then Jesus asked, "What is the kingdom of God like? What shall I compare it to? [19]It is like a mustard seed, which a man took and planted in his garden. It grew and became a tree, and the birds of the air perched in its branches."

[20]Again he asked, "What shall I compare the kingdom of God to? [21]It is like yeast that a woman took and mixed into a large amount[a] of flour until it worked all through the dough."

The Narrow Door

[22]Then Jesus went through the towns and villages, teaching as he made his way to Jerusalem. [23]Someone asked him, "Lord, are only a few people going to be saved?"

He said to them, [24]"Make every effort to enter through the narrow door, because many, I tell you, will try to enter and will not be able to. [25]Once the owner of the house gets up and closes the door, you will stand outside knocking and pleading, 'Sir, open the door for us.'

"But he will answer, 'I don't know you or where you come from.'

[a] *21* Greek *three satas* (probably about 1/2 bushel or 22 liters)

NEW LIVING TRANSLATION

[16]Wasn't it necessary for me, even on the Sabbath day, to free this dear woman* from the bondage in which Satan has held her for eighteen years?" [17]This shamed his enemies. And all the people rejoiced at the wonderful things he did.

Illustration of the Mustard Seed

[18]Then Jesus said, "What is the Kingdom of God like? How can I illustrate it? [19]It is like a tiny mustard seed planted in a garden; it grows and becomes a tree, and the birds come and find shelter among its branches."

Illustration of the Yeast

[20]He also asked, "What else is the Kingdom of God like? [21]It is like yeast used by a woman making bread. Even though she used a large amount* of flour, the yeast permeated every part of the dough."

The Narrow Door

[22]Jesus went through the towns and villages, teaching as he went, always pressing on toward Jerusalem. [23]Someone asked him, "Lord, will only a few be saved?"

He replied, [24]"The door to heaven is narrow. Work hard to get in, because many will try to enter, [25]but when the head of the house has locked the door, it will be too late. Then you will stand outside knocking and pleading, 'Lord, open the door for us!' But he will reply, 'I do not know

13:16 Greek *this woman, a daughter of Abraham.* 13:21 Greek *3 measures.*

NEW KING JAMES VERSION

ought not this woman, being a daughter of Abraham, whom Satan has bound—think of it—for eighteen years, be loosed from this bond on the Sabbath?" [17]And when He said these things, all His adversaries were put to shame; and all the multitude rejoiced for all the glorious things that were done by Him.

The Parable of the Mustard Seed

[18]Then He said, "What is the kingdom of God like? And to what shall I compare it? [19]It is like a mustard seed, which a man took and put in his garden; and it grew and became a large[c] tree, and the birds of the air nested in its branches."

The Parable of the Leaven

[20]And again He said, "To what shall I liken the kingdom of God? [21]It is like leaven, which a woman took and hid in three measures[d] of meal till it was all leavened."

The Narrow Way

[22]And He went through the cities and villages, teaching, and journeying toward Jerusalem. [23]Then one said to Him, "Lord, are there few who are saved?"

And He said to them, [24]"Strive to enter through the narrow gate, for many, I say to you, will seek to enter and will not be able. [25]When once the Master of the house has risen up and shut the door, and you begin to stand outside and knock at the door, saying, 'Lord, Lord, open for us,' and He will answer and say to you, 'I do not know you, where you

13:19 [c] NU-Text omits *large.* 13:21 [d] Greek *sata,* approximately two pecks in all

THE MESSAGE

why isn't it all right for me to untie this daughter of Abraham and lead her from the stall where Satan has had her tied these eighteen years?"

When he put it that way, his critics were left looking quite silly and red-faced. The congregation was delighted and cheered him on.

The Way to God

Then he said, "How can I picture God's kingdom for you? What kind of story can I use? It's like a pine nut that a man plants in his front yard. It grows into a huge pine tree with thick branches, and eagles build nests in it."

He tried again. "How can I picture God's kingdom? It's like yeast that a woman works into enough dough for three loaves of bread—and waits while the dough rises."

He went on teaching from town to village, village to town, but keeping on a steady course toward Jerusalem.

A bystander said, "Master, will only a few be saved?"

He said, "Whether few or many is none of your business. Put your mind on your life with God. The way to life—to God!—is vigorous and requires your total attention. A lot of you are going to assume that you'll sit down to God's salvation banquet just because you've been hanging around the neighborhood all your lives. Well, one day you're going to be banging on the door, wanting to get in, but you'll find the door locked and the Master saying, 'Sorry, you're not on my guest list.'

KING JAMES VERSION

26 Then shall ye begin to say, We have eaten and drunk in thy presence, and thou hast taught in our streets.

27 But he shall say, I tell you, I know you not whence ye are; depart from me, all *ye* workers of iniquity.

28 There shall be weeping and gnashing of teeth, when ye shall see Abraham, and Isaac, and Jacob, and all the prophets, in the kingdom of God, and you *yourselves* thrust out.

29 And they shall come from the east, and *from* the west, and from the north, and *from* the south, and shall sit down in the kingdom of God.

30 And, behold, there are last which shall be first, and there are first which shall be last.

31 ¶ The same day there came certain of the Pharisees, saying unto him, Get thee out, and depart hence: for Herod will kill thee.

32 And he said unto them, Go ye, and tell that fox, Behold, I cast out devils, and I do cures to day and to morrow, and the third *day* I shall be perfected.

33 Nevertheless I must walk to day, and to morrow, and the *day* following: for it cannot be that a prophet perish out of Jerusalem.

34 O Jerusalem, Jerusalem, which killest the prophets, and stonest them that are sent unto thee; how often would I have gathered thy children together, as a hen *doth gather* her brood under *her* wings, and ye would not!

NEW AMERICAN STANDARD BIBLE

26 "Then you will begin to say, 'We ate and drank in Your presence, and You taught in our streets';

27 and He will say, 'I tell you, I do not know where you are from; DEPART FROM ME, ALL YOU EVILDOERS.'

28 "In that place there will be weeping and gnashing of teeth when you see Abraham and Isaac and Jacob and all the prophets in the kingdom of God, but yourselves being thrown out.

29 "And they will come from east and west and from north and south, and will recline *at the table* in the kingdom of God.

30 "And behold, *some* are last who will be first and *some* are first who will be last."

31 Just at that time some Pharisees approached, saying to Him, "Go away, leave here, for Herod wants to kill You."

32 And He said to them, "Go and tell that fox, 'Behold, I cast out demons and perform cures today and tomorrow, and the third *day* I reach My goal.'

33 "Nevertheless I must journey on today and tomorrow and the next *day;* for it cannot be that a prophet would perish outside of Jerusalem.

34 "O Jerusalem, Jerusalem, *the city* that kills the prophets and stones those sent to her! How often I wanted to gather your children together, just as a hen *gathers* her brood under her wings, and you would not *have it!*

NEW CENTURY VERSION

26 Then you will say, 'We ate and drank with you, and you taught in the streets of our town.' 27 But he will say to you, 'I don't know you or where you come from. Go away from me, all you who do evil!' 28 You will cry and grind your teeth with pain when you see Abraham, Isaac, Jacob, and all the prophets in God's kingdom, but you yourselves thrown outside. 29 People will come from the east, west, north, and south and will sit down at the table in the kingdom of God. 30 There are those who have the lowest place in life now who will have the highest place in the future. And there are those who have the highest place now who will have the lowest place in the future."

Jesus Will Die in Jerusalem

31 At that time some Pharisees came to Jesus and said, "Go away from here! Herod wants to kill you!"

32 Jesus said to them, "Go tell that fox Herod, 'Today and tomorrow I am forcing demons out and healing people. Then, on the third day, I will reach my goal.' 33 Yet I must be on my way today and tomorrow and the next day. Surely it cannot be right for a prophet to be killed anywhere except in Jerusalem.

34 "Jerusalem, Jerusalem! You kill the prophets and stone to death those who are sent to you. Many times I wanted to gather your people as a hen gathers her chicks under her wings, but you would not let me. 35 Now your house is

CONTEMPORARY ENGLISH VERSION

26 Then you will start saying, "We dined with you, and you taught in our streets."

27 But he will say, "I really don't know who you are! Get away from me, you evil people!"

28 Then when you have been thrown outside, you will weep and grit your teeth because you will see Abraham, Isaac, Jacob, and all the prophets in God's kingdom. 29 People will come from all directions and sit down to feast in God's kingdom. 30 There the ones who are now least important will be the most important, and those who are now most important will be least important.

Jesus and Herod

31 At that time some Pharisees came to Jesus and said, "You had better get away from here! Herod[a] wants to kill you."

32 Jesus said to them:

Go tell that fox, "I am going to force out demons and heal people today and tomorrow, and three days later I'll be through." 33 But I am going on my way today and tomorrow and the next day. After all, Jerusalem is the place where prophets are killed.

Jesus Loves Jerusalem (Matthew 23.37-39)

34 Jerusalem, Jerusalem! Your people have killed the prophets and have stoned the messengers who were sent to you. I have often wanted to gather your people, as a hen gathers her chicks under her wings. But you wouldn't

[a] 13.31 *Herod:* Herod Antipas, the son of Herod the Great.

NEW INTERNATIONAL VERSION

26 “Then you will say, ‘We ate and drank with you, and
you taught in our streets.’
27 “But he will reply, ‘I don’t know you or where you
come from. Away from me, all you evildoers!’
28 “There will be weeping there, and gnashing of teeth,
when you see Abraham, Isaac and Jacob and all the proph-
ets in the kingdom of God, but you yourselves thrown out.
29 People will come from east and west and north and
south, and will take their places at the feast in the king-
dom of God. 30 Indeed there are those who are last who will
be first, and first who will be last.”

Jesus’ Sorrow for Jerusalem

31 At that time some Pharisees came to Jesus and said to
him, “Leave this place and go somewhere else. Herod
wants to kill you.”
32 He replied, “Go tell that fox, ‘I will drive out demons
and heal people today and tomorrow, and on the third day
I will reach my goal.’ 33 In any case, I must keep going
today and tomorrow and the next day—for surely no
prophet can die outside Jerusalem!
34 “O Jerusalem, Jerusalem, you who kill the prophets
and stone those sent to you, how often I have longed to
gather your children together, as a hen gathers her chicks
under her wings, but you were not willing! 35 Look, your

NEW LIVING TRANSLATION

you.’ 26 You will say, ‘But we ate and drank with you, and
you taught in our streets.’ 27 And he will reply, ‘I tell you, I
don’t know you. Go away, all you who do evil.’
28 “And there will be great weeping and gnashing of
teeth, for you will see Abraham, Isaac, Jacob, and all the
prophets within the Kingdom of God, but you will be
thrown out. 29 Then people will come from all over the
world to take their places in the Kingdom of God. 30 And
note this: Some who are despised now will be greatly hon-
ored then; and some who are greatly honored now will be
despised then.*”

Jesus Grieves over Jerusalem

31 A few minutes later some Pharisees said to him, “Get
out of here if you want to live, because Herod Antipas
wants to kill you!”
32 Jesus replied, “Go tell that fox that I will keep on cast-
ing out demons and doing miracles of healing today and
tomorrow; and the third day I will accomplish my purpose.
33 Yes, today, tomorrow, and the next day I must proceed
on my way. For it wouldn’t do for a prophet of God to be
killed except in Jerusalem!
34 “O Jerusalem, Jerusalem, the city that kills the proph-
ets and stones God’s messengers! How often I have wanted
to gather your children together as a hen protects her
chicks beneath her wings, but you wouldn’t let me. 35 And

13:30 Greek *Some are last who will be first, and some are first who will be last.*

NEW KING JAMES VERSION

are from,’ 26 then you will begin to say, ‘We ate and drank
in Your presence, and You taught in our streets.’ 27 But He
will say, ‘I tell you I do not know you, where you are from.
Depart from Me, all you workers of iniquity.’ 28 There will
be weeping and gnashing of teeth, when you see Abraham
and Isaac and Jacob and all the prophets in the kingdom of
God, and yourselves thrust out. 29 They will come from the
east and the west, from the north and the south, and sit
down in the kingdom of God. 30 And indeed there are last
who will be first, and there are first who will be last.”
31 On that very day[e] some Pharisees came, saying to
Him, “Get out and depart from here, for Herod wants to
kill You.”
32 And He said to them, “Go, tell that fox, ‘Behold, I cast
out demons and perform cures today and tomorrow, and
the third *day* I shall be perfected.’ 33 Nevertheless I must
journey today, tomorrow, and the *day* following; for it can-
not be that a prophet should perish outside of Jerusalem.

Jesus Laments over Jerusalem

34 “O Jerusalem, Jerusalem, the one who kills the proph-
ets and stones those who are sent to her! How often I
wanted to gather your children together, as a hen *gathers*
her brood under *her* wings, but you were not willing!

13:31 [e] NU-Text reads *In that very hour.*

THE MESSAGE

“You’ll protest, ‘But we’ve known you all our lives!’ only to be interrupted with his abrupt, ‘Your kind of knowing can hardly be called knowing. You don’t know the first thing about me.’

“That’s when you’ll find yourselves out in the cold, strangers to grace. You’ll watch Abraham, Isaac, Jacob, and all the prophets march into God’s kingdom. You’ll watch outsiders stream in from east, west, north, and south and sit down at the table of God’s kingdom. And all the time you’ll be outside looking in—and wondering what happened. This is the Great Reversal: the last in line put at the head of the line, and the so-called first ending up last.

✠

Just then some Pharisees came up and said, “Run for your life! Herod’s on the hunt. He’s out to kill you!”

Jesus said, “Tell that fox that I’ve no time for him right now. Today and tomorrow I’m busy clearing out the demons and healing the sick; the third day I’m wrapping things up. Besides, it’s not proper for a prophet to come to a bad end outside Jerusalem.

Jerusalem, Jerusalem, killer of prophets,
 abuser of the messengers of God!
How often I’ve longed to gather your children,
 gather your children like a hen,
Her brood safe under her wings—
 but you refused and turned away!

KING JAMES VERSION

35 Behold, your house is left unto you desolate: and verily I say unto you, Ye shall not see me, until *the time* come when ye shall say, Blessed *is* he that cometh in the name of the Lord.

14 And it came to pass, as he went into the house of one of the chief Pharisees to eat bread on the sabbath day, that they watched him.

2 And, behold, there was a certain man before him which had the dropsy.

3 And Jesus answering spake unto the lawyers and Pharisees, saying, Is it lawful to heal on the sabbath day?

4 And they held their peace. And he took *him*, and healed him, and let him go;

5 And answered them, saying, Which of you shall have an ass or an ox fallen into a pit, and will not straightway pull him out on the sabbath day?

6 And they could not answer him again to these things.

7 ¶ And he put forth a parable to those which were bidden, when he marked how they chose out the chief rooms; saying unto them,

8 When thou art bidden of any *man* to a wedding, sit not down in the highest room; lest a more honourable man than thou be bidden of him;

9 And he that bade thee and him come and say to thee, Give this man place; and thou begin with shame to take the lowest room.

NEW AMERICAN STANDARD BIBLE

35 "Behold, your house is left to you *desolate;* and I say to you, you will not see Me until *the time* comes when you say, 'BLESSED IS HE WHO COMES IN THE NAME OF THE LORD!' "

Jesus Heals on the Sabbath

14 It happened that when He went into the house of one of the leaders of the Pharisees on *the* Sabbath to eat bread, they were watching Him closely.

2 And there in front of Him was a man suffering from dropsy.

3 And Jesus answered and spoke to the lawyers and Pharisees, saying, "Is it lawful to heal on the Sabbath, or not?"

4 But they kept silent. And He took hold of him and healed him, and sent him away.

5 And He said to them, "Which one of you will have a son or an ox fall into a well, and will not immediately pull him out on a Sabbath day?"

6 And they could make no reply to this.

Parable of the Guests

7 And He *began* speaking a parable to the invited guests when He noticed how they had been picking out the places of honor *at the table,* saying to them,

8 "When you are invited by someone to a wedding feast, do not take the place of honor, for someone more distinguished than you may have been invited by him,

9 and he who invited you both will come and say to you, 'Give *your* place to this man,' and then in disgrace you proceed to occupy the last place.

NEW CENTURY VERSION

left completely empty. I tell you, you will not see me until that time when you will say, 'God bless the One who comes in the name of the Lord.' "[b]

Healing on the Sabbath

14 On a Sabbath day, when Jesus went to eat at the home of a leading Pharisee, the people were
watching Jesus very closely. 2And in front of him was a
man with dropsy.[a] 3Jesus said to the Pharisees and experts
on the law, "Is it right or wrong to heal on the Sabbath
day?" 4But they would not answer his question. So Jesus
took the man, healed him, and sent him away. 5Jesus said
to the Pharisees and teachers of the law, "If your child or
ox falls into a well on the Sabbath day, will you not pull
him out quickly?" 6And they could not answer him.

Don't Make Yourself Important

7When Jesus noticed that some of the guests were
choosing the best places to sit, he told this story: 8"When
someone invites you to a wedding feast, don't take the
most important seat, because someone more important
than you may have been invited. 9The host, who invited
both of you, will come to you and say, 'Give this person
your seat.' Then you will be embarrassed and will have to
move to the last place. 10So when you are invited, go sit in

13:35 [b] **'God...Lord.'** Quotation from Psalm 118:26. 14:2 [a] **dropsy** A sickness that causes the body to swell larger and larger.

CONTEMPORARY ENGLISH VERSION

let me. 35Now your temple will be deserted. You won't see me again until the time when you say,

"Blessed is the one who comes
in the name of the Lord."

Jesus Heals a Sick Man

14 One Sabbath, Jesus was having dinner in the home of an important Pharisee, and everyone was care-
fully watching Jesus. 2All of a sudden a man with swollen
legs stood up in front of him. 3Jesus turned and asked the
Pharisees and the teachers of the Law of Moses, "Is it right
to heal on the Sabbath?" 4But they did not say a word.

Jesus took hold of the man. Then he healed him and
sent him away. 5Afterwards, Jesus asked the people, "If
your son or ox falls into a well, wouldn't you pull him out
right away, even on the Sabbath?" 6There was nothing
they could say.

How To Be a Guest

7Jesus saw how the guests had tried to take the best seats. So he told them:

8When you are invited to a wedding feast, don't sit in
the best place. Someone more important may have been
invited. 9Then the one who invited you will come and
say, "Give your place to this other guest!" You will be
embarrassed and will have to sit in the worst place.

NEW INTERNATIONAL VERSION

house is left to you desolate. I tell you, you will not see me again until you say, 'Blessed is he who comes in the name of the Lord.'[b]"

Jesus at a Pharisee's House

14 One Sabbath, when Jesus went to eat in the house of a prominent Pharisee, he was being carefully watched. 2There in front of him was a man suffering from dropsy. 3Jesus asked the Pharisees and experts in the law, "Is it lawful to heal on the Sabbath or not?" 4But they remained silent. So taking hold of the man, he healed him and sent him away.

5Then he asked them, "If one of you has a son[a] or an ox that falls into a well on the Sabbath day, will you not immediately pull him out?" 6And they had nothing to say.

7When he noticed how the guests picked the places of honor at the table, he told them this parable: 8"When someone invites you to a wedding feast, do not take the place of honor, for a person more distinguished than you may have been invited. 9If so, the host who invited both of you will come and say to you, 'Give this man your seat.' Then, humiliated, you will have to take the least important

[b] *35* Psalm 118:26 [a] *5* Some manuscripts *donkey*

NEW LIVING TRANSLATION

now look, your house is left to you empty. And you will never see me again until you say, 'Bless the one who comes in the name of the Lord!'* "

Jesus Heals on the Sabbath

14 One Sabbath day Jesus was in the home of a leader of the Pharisees. The people were watching him closely, 2because there was a man there whose arms and legs were swollen.* 3Jesus asked the Pharisees and experts in religious law, "Well, is it permitted in the law to heal people on the Sabbath day, or not?" 4When they refused to answer, Jesus touched the sick man and healed him and sent him away. 5Then he turned to them and asked, "Which of you doesn't work on the Sabbath? If your son* or your cow falls into a pit, don't you proceed at once to get him out?" 6Again they had no answer.

Jesus Teaches about Humility

7When Jesus noticed that all who had come to the dinner were trying to sit near the head of the table, he gave them this advice: 8"If you are invited to a wedding feast, don't always head for the best seat. What if someone more respected than you has also been invited? 9The host will say, 'Let this person sit here instead.' Then you will be embarrassed and will have to take whatever seat is left at the foot of the table!

13:35 Ps 118:26. 14:2 Traditionally translated *who had dropsy.*
14:5 Some manuscripts read *donkey.*

NEW KING JAMES VERSION

35See! Your house is left to you desolate; and assuredly,[f] I say to you, you shall not see Me until *the time* comes when you say, *'Blessed is He who comes in the name of the* LORD!' "[g]

A Man with Dropsy Healed on the Sabbath

14 Now it happened, as He went into the house of one of the rulers of the Pharisees to eat bread on the Sabbath, that they watched Him closely. 2And behold, there was a certain man before Him who had dropsy. 3And Jesus, answering, spoke to the lawyers and Pharisees, saying, "Is it lawful to heal on the Sabbath?"[a]

4But they kept silent. And He took *him* and healed him, and let him go. 5Then He answered them, saying, "Which of you, having a donkey[b] or an ox that has fallen into a pit, will not immediately pull him out on the Sabbath day?" 6And they could not answer Him regarding these things.

Take the Lowly Place

7So He told a parable to those who were invited, when He noted how they chose the best places, saying to them: 8"When you are invited by anyone to a wedding feast, do not sit down in the best place, lest one more honorable than you be invited by him; 9and he who invited you and him come and say to you, 'Give place to this man,' and then you begin with shame to take the lowest place. 10But

13:35 [f] NU-Text and M-Text omit *assuredly.* [g] Psalm 118:26
14:3 [a] NU-Text adds *or not.* 14:5 [b] NU-Text and M-Text read *son.*

THE MESSAGE

And now it's too late: You won't see me again
until the day you say,
'Blessed is he
who comes in
the name of God.' "

14 One time when Jesus went for a Sabbath meal with one of the top leaders of the Pharisees, all the guests had their eyes on him, watching his every move. Right before him there was a man hugely swollen in his joints. So Jesus asked the religion scholars and Pharisees present, "Is it permitted to heal on the Sabbath? Yes or no?" They were silent. So he took the man, healed him, and sent him on his way. Then he said, "Is there anyone here who, if a child or animal fell down a well, wouldn't rush to pull him out immediately, not asking whether or not it was the Sabbath?" They were stumped. There was nothing they could say to that.

Invite the Misfits

He went on to tell a story to the guests around the table. Noticing how each had tried to elbow into the place of honor, he said, "When someone invites you to dinner, don't take the place of honor. Somebody more important than you might have been invited by the host. Then he'll come and call out in front of everybody, 'You're in the wrong place. The place of honor belongs to this man.' Red-faced, you'll have to make your way to the very last table, the only place left.

KING JAMES VERSION

10 But when thou art bidden, go and sit down in the lowest room; that when he that bade thee cometh, he may say unto thee, Friend, go up higher: then shalt thou have worship in the presence of them that sit at meat with thee.

11 For whosoever exalteth himself shall be abased; and he that humbleth himself shall be exalted.

12 Then said he also to him that bade him, When thou makest a dinner or a supper, call not thy friends, nor thy brethren, neither thy kinsmen, nor *thy* rich neighbours; lest they also bid thee again, and a recompence be made thee.

13 But when thou makest a feast, call the poor, the maimed, the lame, the blind:

14 And thou shalt be blessed; for they cannot recompense thee: for thou shalt be recompensed at the resurrection of the just.

15 ¶ And when one of them that sat at meat with him heard these things, he said unto him, Blessed *is* he that shall eat bread in the kingdom of God.

16 Then said he unto him, A certain man made a great supper, and bade many:

17 And sent his servant at supper time to say to them that were bidden, Come; for all things are now ready.

18 And they all with one *consent* began to make excuse. The first said unto him, I have bought a piece of ground, and I must needs go and see it: I pray thee have me excused.

NEW AMERICAN STANDARD BIBLE

10 "But when you are invited, go and recline at the last place, so that when the one who has invited you comes, he may say to you, 'Friend, move up higher'; then you will have honor in the sight of all who are at the table with you.

11 "For everyone who exalts himself will be humbled, and he who humbles himself will be exalted."

12 And He also went on to say to the one who had invited Him, "When you give a luncheon or a dinner, do not invite your friends or your brothers or your relatives or rich neighbors, otherwise they may also invite you in return and *that* will be your repayment.

13 "But when you give a reception, invite *the* poor, *the* crippled, *the* lame, *the* blind,

14 and you will be blessed, since they do not have *the means* to repay you; for you will be repaid at the resurrection of the righteous."

15 When one of those who were reclining *at the table* with Him heard this, he said to Him, "Blessed is everyone who will eat bread in the kingdom of God!"

Parable of the Dinner

16 But He said to him, "A man was giving a big dinner, and he invited many;

17 and at the dinner hour he sent his slave to say to those who had been invited, 'Come; for everything is ready now.'

18 "But they all alike began to make excuses. The first one said to him, 'I have bought a piece of land and I need to go out and look at it; please consider me excused.'

NEW CENTURY VERSION

a seat that is not important. When the host comes to you, he may say, 'Friend, move up here to a more important place.' Then all the other guests will respect you. 11 All who make themselves great will be made humble, but those who make themselves humble will be made great."

You Will Be Rewarded

12 Then Jesus said to the man who had invited him, "When you give a lunch or a dinner, don't invite only your friends, your family, your other relatives, and your rich neighbors. At another time they will invite you to eat with them, and you will be repaid. 13 Instead, when you give a feast, invite the poor, the crippled, the lame, and the blind. 14 Then you will be blessed, because they have nothing and cannot pay you back. But you will be repaid when the good people rise from the dead."

A Story About a Big Banquet

15 One of those at the table with Jesus heard these things and said to him, "Happy are the people who will share in the meal in God's kingdom."

16 Jesus said to him, "A man gave a big banquet and invited many people. 17 When it was time to eat, the man sent his servant to tell the guests, 'Come. Everything is ready.'

18 "But all the guests made excuses. The first one said, 'I have just bought a field, and I must go look at it. Please

CONTEMPORARY ENGLISH VERSION

10 When you are invited to be a guest, go and sit in the worst place. Then the one who invited you may come and say, "My friend, take a better seat!" You will then be honored in front of all the other guests. 11 If you put yourself above others, you will be put down. But if you humble yourself, you will be honored.

12 Then Jesus said to the man who had invited him:

When you give a dinner or a banquet, don't invite your friends and family and relatives and rich neighbors. If you do, they will invite you in return, and you will be paid back. 13 When you give a feast, invite the poor, the crippled, the lame, and the blind. 14 They cannot pay you back. But God will bless you and reward you when his people rise from death.

The Great Banquet (Matthew 22.1-10)

15 After Jesus had finished speaking, one of the guests said, "The greatest blessing of all is to be at the banquet in God's kingdom!"

16 Jesus told him:

A man once gave a great banquet and invited a lot of guests. 17 When the banquet was ready, he sent a servant to tell the guests, "Everything is ready! Please come."

18 One guest after another started making excuses. The first one said, "I bought some land, and I've got to look it over. Please excuse me."

NEW INTERNATIONAL VERSION

place. 10 But when you are invited, take the lowest place, so
that when your host comes, he will say to you, 'Friend,
move up to a better place.' Then you will be honored in the
presence of all your fellow guests. 11 For everyone who
exalts himself will be humbled, and he who humbles him-
self will be exalted."

12 Then Jesus said to his host, "When you give a lun-
cheon or dinner, do not invite your friends, your brothers
or relatives, or your rich neighbors; if you do, they may
invite you back and so you will be repaid. 13 But when you
give a banquet, invite the poor, the crippled, the lame, the
blind, 14 and you will be blessed. Although they cannot
repay you, you will be repaid at the resurrection of the
righteous."

The Parable of the Great Banquet

15 When one of those at the table with him heard this, he
said to Jesus, "Blessed is the man who will eat at the feast
in the kingdom of God."

16 Jesus replied: "A certain man was preparing a great
banquet and invited many guests. 17 At the time of the ban-
quet he sent his servant to tell those who had been invited,
'Come, for everything is now ready.'

18 "But they all alike began to make excuses. The first
said, 'I have just bought a field, and I must go and see it.
Please excuse me.'

NEW LIVING TRANSLATION

10 "Do this instead—sit at the foot of the table. Then
when your host sees you, he will come and say, 'Friend,
we have a better place than this for you!' Then you will be
honored in front of all the other guests. 11 For the proud
will be humbled, but the humble will be honored."

12 Then he turned to his host. "When you put on a lun-
cheon or a dinner," he said, "don't invite your friends,
brothers, relatives, and rich neighbors. For they will repay
you by inviting you back. 13 Instead, invite the poor, the
crippled, the lame, and the blind. 14 Then at the resurrec-
tion of the godly, God will reward you for inviting those
who could not repay you."

Story of the Great Feast

15 Hearing this, a man sitting at the table with Jesus
exclaimed, "What a privilege it would be to have a share in
the Kingdom of God!"

16 Jesus replied with this illustration: "A man prepared a
great feast and sent out many invitations. 17 When all was
ready, he sent his servant around to notify the guests that
it was time for them to come. 18 But they all began making
excuses. One said he had just bought a field and wanted to
inspect it, so he asked to be excused. 19 Another said he had

NEW KING JAMES VERSION

when you are invited, go and sit down in the lowest place,
so that when he who invited you comes he may say to you,
'Friend, go up higher.' Then you will have glory in the
presence of those who sit at the table with you. 11 For who-
ever exalts himself will be humbled, and he who humbles
himself will be exalted."

12 Then He also said to him who invited Him, "When you
give a dinner or a supper, do not ask your friends, your
brothers, your relatives, nor rich neighbors, lest they also
invite you back, and you be repaid. 13 But when you give a
feast, invite *the* poor, *the* maimed, *the* lame, *the* blind.
14 And you will be blessed, because they cannot repay you;
for you shall be repaid at the resurrection of the just."

The Parable of the Great Supper

15 Now when one of those who sat at the table with Him
heard these things, he said to Him, "Blessed *is* he who
shall eat bread[c] in the kingdom of God!"

16 Then He said to him, "A certain man gave a great sup-
per and invited many, 17 and sent his servant at supper
time to say to those who were invited, 'Come, for all things
are now ready.' 18 But they all with one *accord* began to
make excuses. The first said to him, 'I have bought a piece
of ground, and I must go and see it. I ask you to have me

14:15 [c] M-Text reads *dinner.*

THE MESSAGE

"When you're invited to dinner, go and sit at the last
place. Then when the host comes he may very well say,
'Friend, come up to the front.' That will give the dinner
guests something to talk about! What I'm saying is, If you
walk around with your nose in the air, you're going to end
up flat on your face. But if you're content to be simply
yourself, you will become more than yourself."

Then he turned to the host. "The next time you put on a
dinner, don't just invite your friends and family and rich
neighbors, the kind of people who will return the favor.
Invite some people who never get invited out, the misfits
from the wrong side of the tracks. You'll be—and experi-
ence—a blessing. They won't be able to return the favor,
but the favor will be returned—oh, how it will be
returned!—at the resurrection of God's people."

The Story of the Dinner Party

That triggered a response from one of the guests: "How
fortunate the one who gets to eat dinner in God's king-
dom!"

Jesus followed up. "Yes. For there was once a man who
threw a great dinner party and invited many. When it was
time for dinner, he sent out his servant to the invited
guests, saying, 'Come on in; the food's on the table.'

"Then they all began to beg off, one after another mak-
ing excuses. The first said, 'I bought a piece of property
and need to look it over. Send my regrets.'

KING JAMES VERSION

19 And another said, I have bought five yoke of oxen, and I go to prove them: I pray thee have me excused.

20 And another said, I have married a wife, and therefore I cannot come.

21 So that servant came, and shewed his lord these things. Then the master of the house being angry said to his servant, Go out quickly into the streets and lanes of the city, and bring in hither the poor, and the maimed, and the halt, and the blind.

22 And the servant said, Lord, it is done as thou hast commanded, and yet there is room.

23 And the lord said unto the servant, Go out into the highways and hedges, and compel *them* to come in, that my house may be filled.

24 For I say unto you, That none of those men which were bidden shall taste of my supper.

25 ¶ And there went great multitudes with him: and he turned, and said unto them,

26 If any *man* come to me, and hate not his father, and mother, and wife, and children, and brethren, and sisters, yea, and his own life also, he cannot be my disciple.

27 And whosoever doth not bear his cross, and come after me, cannot be my disciple.

28 For which of you, intending to build a tower, sitteth not down first, and counteth the cost, whether he have *sufficient* to finish *it?*

NEW AMERICAN STANDARD BIBLE

19 "Another one said, 'I have bought five yoke of oxen, and I am going to try them out; please consider me excused.'

20 "Another one said, 'I have married a wife, and for that reason I cannot come.'

21 "And the slave came *back* and reported this to his master. Then the head of the household became angry and said to his slave, 'Go out at once into the streets and lanes of the city and bring in here the poor and crippled and blind and lame.'

22 "And the slave said, 'Master, what you commanded has been done, and still there is room.'

23 "And the master said to the slave, 'Go out into the highways and along the hedges, and compel *them* to come in, so that my house may be filled.

24 'For I tell you, none of those men who were invited shall taste of my dinner.' "

Discipleship Tested

25 Now large crowds were going along with Him; and He turned and said to them,

26 "If anyone comes to Me, and does not [j]hate his own father and mother and wife and children and brothers and sisters, yes, and even his own life, he cannot be My disciple.

27 "Whoever does not carry his own cross and come after Me cannot be My disciple.

28 "For which one of you, when he wants to build a tower, does not first sit down and calculate the cost to see if he has enough to complete it?

14:26 [j] I.e. by comparison of his love for Me

NEW CENTURY VERSION

excuse me.' 19Another said, 'I have just bought five pairs of oxen; I must go and try them. Please excuse me.' 20A third person said, 'I just got married; I can't come.' 21So the servant returned and told his master what had happened. Then the master became angry and said, 'Go at once into the streets and alleys of the town, and bring in the poor, the crippled, the blind, and the lame.' 22Later the servant said to him, 'Master, I did what you commanded, but we still have room.' 23The master said to the servant, 'Go out to the roads and country lanes, and urge the people there to come so my house will be full. 24I tell you, none of those whom I invited first will eat with me.' "

The Cost of Being Jesus' Follower

25Large crowds were traveling with Jesus, and he turned and said to them, 26"If anyone comes to me but loves his father, mother, wife, children, brothers, or sisters—or even life—more than me, he cannot be my follower. 27Whoever is not willing to carry the cross and follow me cannot be my follower. 28If you want to build a tower, you first sit down and decide how much it will cost, to see if you have

CONTEMPORARY ENGLISH VERSION

19Another guest said, "I bought five teams of oxen, and I need to try them out. Please excuse me."

20Still another guest said, "I have just gotten married, and I can't be there."

21The servant told his master what happened, and the master became so angry that he said, "Go as fast as you can to every street and alley in town! Bring in everyone who is poor or crippled or blind or lame."

22When the servant returned, he said, "Master, I've done what you told me, and there is still plenty of room for more people."

23His master then told him, "Go out along the back roads and fence rows and make people come in, so that my house will be full. 24Not one of the guests I first invited will get even a bite of my food!"

Being a Disciple (Matthew 10.37, 38)

25Large crowds were walking along with Jesus, when he turned and said:

26You cannot be my disciple, unless you love me more than you love your father and mother, your wife and children, and your brothers and sisters. You cannot come with me unless you love me more than you love your own life.

27You cannot be my disciple unless you carry your own cross and come with me.

28Suppose one of you wants to build a tower. What is the first thing you will do? Won't you sit down and figure out how much it will cost and if you have enough

NEW INTERNATIONAL VERSION

19“Another said, ‘I have just bought five yoke of oxen,
and I'm on my way to try them out. Please excuse me.’
20“Still another said, ‘I just got married, so I can't come.’
21“The servant came back and reported this to his mas-
ter. Then the owner of the house became angry and
ordered his servant, ‘Go out quickly into the streets and
alleys of the town and bring in the poor, the crippled, the
blind and the lame.’
22“ ‘Sir,’ the servant said, ‘what you ordered has been
done, but there is still room.’
23“Then the master told his servant, ‘Go out to the roads
and country lanes and make them come in, so that my
house will be full. 24I tell you, not one of those men who
were invited will get a taste of my banquet.’ ”

The Cost of Being a Disciple

25Large crowds were traveling with Jesus, and turning to
them he said: 26“If anyone comes to me and does not hate
his father and mother, his wife and children, his brothers
and sisters—yes, even his own life—he cannot be my dis-
ciple. 27And anyone who does not carry his cross and fol-
low me cannot be my disciple.
28“Suppose one of you wants to build a tower. Will he
not first sit down and estimate the cost to see if he has

NEW LIVING TRANSLATION

just bought five pair of oxen and wanted to try them out.
20Another had just been married, so he said he couldn't
come.
21“The servant returned and told his master what they
had said. His master was angry and said, ‘Go quickly into
the streets and alleys of the city and invite the poor, the
crippled, the lame, and the blind.’ 22After the servant had
done this, he reported, ‘There is still room for more.’ 23So
his master said, ‘Go out into the country lanes and behind
the hedges and urge anyone you find to come, so that the
house will be full. 24For none of those I invited first will
get even the smallest taste of what I had prepared for
them.’ ”

The Cost of Being a Disciple

25Great crowds were following Jesus. He turned around
and said to them, 26“If you want to be my follower you
must love me more than* your own father and mother,
wife and children, brothers and sisters—yes, more than
your own life. Otherwise, you cannot be my disciple. 27And
you cannot be my disciple if you do not carry your own
cross and follow me.
28“But don't begin until you count the cost. For who
would begin construction of a building without first get-
ting estimates and then checking to see if there is enough

14:26 Greek *you must hate.*

NEW KING JAMES VERSION

excused.’ 19And another said, ‘I have bought five yoke of
oxen, and I am going to test them. I ask you to have me
excused.’ 20Still another said, ‘I have married a wife, and
therefore I cannot come.’ 21So that servant came and
reported these things to his master. Then the master of the
house, being angry, said to his servant, ‘Go out quickly
into the streets and lanes of the city, and bring in here *the*
poor and *the* maimed and *the* lame and *the* blind.’ 22And
the servant said, ‘Master, it is done as you commanded,
and still there is room.’ 23Then the master said to the ser-
vant, ‘Go out into the highways and hedges, and compel
them to come in, that my house may be filled. 24For I say
to you that none of those men who were invited shall taste
my supper.’ ”

Leaving All to Follow Christ

25Now great multitudes went with Him. And He turned
and said to them, 26“If anyone comes to Me and does not
hate his father and mother, wife and children, brothers
and sisters, yes, and his own life also, he cannot be My
disciple. 27And whoever does not bear his cross and come
after Me cannot be My disciple. 28For which of you, intend-
ing to build a tower, does not sit down first and count the

THE MESSAGE

“Another said, ‘I just bought five teams of oxen, and I
really need to check them out. Send my regrets.’

“And yet another said, ‘I just got married and need to
get home to my wife.’

“The servant went back and told the master what had
happened. He was outraged and told the servant, ‘Quickly,
get out into the city streets and alleys. Collect all who look
like they need a square meal, all the misfits and homeless
and wretched you can lay your hands on, and bring them
here.’

“The servant reported back, ‘Master, I did what you com-
manded—and there's still room.’

“The master said, ‘Then go to the country roads.
Whoever you find, drag them in. I want my house full! Let
me tell you, not one of those originally invited is going to
get so much as a bite at my dinner party.’ ”

Figure the Cost

One day when large groups of people were walking
along with him, Jesus turned and told them, “Anyone who
comes to me but refuses to let go of father, mother,
spouse, children, brothers, sisters—yes, even one's own
self!—can't be my disciple. Anyone who won't shoulder
his own cross and follow behind me can't be my disciple.

“Is there anyone here who, planning to build a new
house, doesn't first sit down and figure the cost so you'll

KING JAMES VERSION

29 Lest haply, after he hath laid the foundation, and is not able to finish *it*, all that behold *it* begin to mock him,

30 Saying, This man began to build, and was not able to finish.

31 Or what king, going to make war against another king, sitteth not down first, and consulteth whether he be able with ten thousand to meet him that cometh against him with twenty thousand?

32 Or else, while the other is yet a great way off, he sendeth an ambassage, and desireth conditions of peace.

33 So likewise, whosoever he be of you that forsaketh not all that he hath, he cannot be my disciple.

34 Salt *is* good: but if the salt have lost his savour, wherewith shall it be seasoned?

35 It is neither fit for the land, nor yet for the dunghill; *but* men cast it out. He that hath ears to hear, let him hear.

15 Then drew near unto him all the publicans and sinners for to hear him.

2 And the Pharisees and scribes murmured, saying, This man receiveth sinners, and eateth with them.

3 And he spake this parable unto them, saying,

4 What man of you, having an hundred sheep, if he lose one of them, doth not leave the ninety and nine in the wilderness, and go after that which is lost, until he find it?

NEW AMERICAN STANDARD BIBLE

29 "Otherwise, when he has laid a foundation and is not able to finish, all who observe it begin to ridicule him,

30 saying, 'This man began to build and was not able to finish.'

31 "Or what king, when he sets out to meet another king in battle, will not first sit down and consider whether he is strong enough with ten thousand *men* to encounter the one coming against him with twenty thousand?

32 "Or else, while the other is still far away, he sends a delegation and asks for terms of peace.

33 "So then, none of you can be My disciple who does not give up all his own possessions.

34 "Therefore, salt is good; but if even salt has become tasteless, with what will it be seasoned?

35 "It is useless either for the soil or for the manure pile; it is thrown out. He who has ears to hear, let him hear."

The Lost Sheep

15 Now all the tax collectors and the sinners were coming near Him to listen to Him.

2 Both the Pharisees and the scribes *began* to grumble, saying, "This man receives sinners and eats with them."

3 So He told them this parable, saying,

4 "What man among you, if he has a hundred sheep and has lost one of them, does not leave the ninety-nine in the open pasture and go after the one which is lost until he finds it?

NEW CENTURY VERSION

enough money to finish the job. 29If you don't, you might
lay the foundation, but you would not be able to finish.
Then all who would see it would make fun of you, 30say-
ing, 'This person began to build but was not able to finish.'
31"If a king is going to fight another king, first he will
sit down and plan. He will decide if he and his ten thou-
sand soldiers can defeat the other king who has twenty
thousand soldiers. 32If he can't, then while the other king
is still far away, he will send some people to speak to him
and ask for peace. 33In the same way, you must give up
everything you have to be my follower.

Don't Lose Your Influence

34"Salt is good, but if it loses its salty taste, you cannot
make it salty again. 35It is no good for the soil or for
manure; it is thrown away.

"You people who can hear me, listen."

A Lost Sheep, a Lost Coin

15 The tax collectors and sinners all came to listen to
Jesus. 2But the Pharisees and the teachers of the
law began to complain: "Look, this man welcomes sinners
and even eats with them."
3Then Jesus told them this story: 4"Suppose one of you
has a hundred sheep but loses one of them. Then he will
leave the other ninety-nine sheep in the open field and go
out and look for the lost sheep until he finds it. 5And when

CONTEMPORARY ENGLISH VERSION

money to pay for it? 29Otherwise, you will start building
the tower, but not be able to finish. Then everyone who
sees what is happening will laugh at you. 30They will
say, "You started building, but could not finish the job."
31What will a king do if he has only ten thousand sol-
diers to defend himself against a king who is about to
attack him with twenty thousand soldiers? Before he
goes out to battle, won't he first sit down and decide if he
can win? 32If he thinks he won't be able to defend him-
self, he will send messengers and ask for peace while the
other king is still a long way off. 33So then, you cannot
be my disciple unless you give away everything you own.

Salt and Light (Matthew 5.13; Mark 9.50)

34Salt is good, but if it no longer tastes like salt, how
can it be made to taste salty again? 35It is no longer
good for the soil or even for the manure pile. People sim-
ply throw it out. If you have ears, pay attention!

One Sheep (Matthew 18.12-14)

15 Tax collectors[a] and sinners were all crowding
around to listen to Jesus. 2So the Pharisees and
the teachers of the Law of Moses started grumbling, "This
man is friendly with sinners. He even eats with them."
3Then Jesus told them this story:
4If any of you has a hundred sheep, and one of them
gets lost, what will you do? Won't you leave the ninety-
nine in the field and go look for the lost sheep until you

[a] 15.1 *Tax collectors*: See the note at 3.12.

NEW INTERNATIONAL VERSION

enough money to complete it? 29For if he lays the founda-
tion and is not able to finish it, everyone who sees it will
ridicule him, 30saying, 'This fellow began to build and was
not able to finish.'

31"Or suppose a king is about to go to war against
another king. Will he not first sit down and consider
whether he is able with ten thousand men to oppose the
one coming against him with twenty thousand? 32If he is
not able, he will send a delegation while the other is still a
long way off and will ask for terms of peace. 33In the same
way, any of you who does not give up everything he has
cannot be my disciple.

34"Salt is good, but if it loses its saltiness, how can it be
made salty again? 35It is fit neither for the soil nor for the
manure pile; it is thrown out.

"He who has ears to hear, let him hear."

The Parable of the Lost Sheep

15 Now the tax collectors and "sinners" were all gath-
ering around to hear him. 2But the Pharisees and
the teachers of the law muttered, "This man welcomes sin-
ners and eats with them."

3Then Jesus told them this parable: 4"Suppose one of
you has a hundred sheep and loses one of them. Does he
not leave the ninety-nine in the open country and go after
the lost sheep until he finds it? 5And when he finds it, he

NEW LIVING TRANSLATION

money to pay the bills? 29Otherwise, you might complete
only the foundation before running out of funds. And then
how everyone would laugh at you! 30They would say,
'There's the person who started that building and ran out
of money before it was finished!'

31"Or what king would ever dream of going to war with-
out first sitting down with his counselors and discussing
whether his army of ten thousand is strong enough to
defeat the twenty thousand soldiers who are marching
against him? 32If he is not able, then while the enemy is
still far away, he will send a delegation to discuss terms of
peace. 33So no one can become my disciple without giving
up everything for me.

34"Salt is good for seasoning. But if it loses its flavor,
how do you make it salty again? 35Flavorless salt is good
neither for the soil nor for fertilizer. It is thrown away.
Anyone who is willing to hear should listen and under-
stand!"

Story of the Lost Sheep

15 Tax collectors and other notorious sinners often
came to listen to Jesus teach. 2This made the
Pharisees and teachers of religious law complain that he
was associating with such despicable people—even eating
with them!

3So Jesus used this illustration: 4"If you had one hun-
dred sheep, and one of them strayed away and was lost in
the wilderness, wouldn't you leave the ninety-nine others
to go and search for the lost one until you found it? 5And

NEW KING JAMES VERSION

cost, whether he has *enough* to finish *it*— 29lest, after he
has laid the foundation, and is not able to finish, all who
see *it* begin to mock him, 30saying, 'This man began to
build and was not able to finish.' 31Or what king, going to
make war against another king, does not sit down first
and consider whether he is able with ten thousand to meet
him who comes against him with twenty thousand? 32Or
else, while the other is still a great way off, he sends a del-
egation and asks conditions of peace. 33So likewise, who-
ever of you does not forsake all that he has cannot be My
disciple.

Tasteless Salt Is Worthless

34"Salt *is* good; but if the salt has lost its flavor, how
shall it be seasoned? 35It is neither fit for the land nor for
the dunghill, *but* men throw it out. He who has ears to
hear, let him hear!"

The Parable of the Lost Sheep

15 Then all the tax collectors and the sinners drew
near to Him to hear Him. 2And the Pharisees and
scribes complained, saying, "This Man receives sinners
and eats with them." 3So He spoke this parable to them,
saying:

4"What man of you, having a hundred sheep, if he loses
one of them, does not leave the ninety-nine in the wilder-
ness, and go after the one which is lost until he finds it?

THE MESSAGE

know if you can complete it? If you only get the founda-
tion laid and then run out of money, you're going to look
pretty foolish. Everyone passing by will poke fun at you:
'He started something he couldn't finish.'

"Or can you imagine a king going into battle against
another king without first deciding whether it is possible
with his ten thousand troops to face the twenty thousand
troops of the other? And if he decides he can't, won't he
send an emissary and work out a truce?

"Simply put, if you're not willing to take what is dearest
to you, whether plans or people, and kiss it goodbye, you
can't be my disciple.

"Salt is excellent. But if the salt goes flat, it's useless,
good for nothing.

"Are you listening to this?

"Really listening?"

The Story of the Lost Sheep

15 By this time a lot of men and women of doubtful
reputation were hanging around Jesus, listening
intently. The Pharisees and religion scholars were not
pleased, not at all pleased. They growled, "He takes in sin-
ners and eats meals with them, treating them like old
friends." Their grumbling triggered this story.

"Suppose one of you had a hundred sheep and lost one.
Wouldn't you leave the ninety-nine in the wilderness and
go after the lost one until you found it? When found, you

KING JAMES VERSION

5 And when he hath found *it*, he layeth *it* on his shoulders, rejoicing.

6 And when he cometh home, he calleth together *his* friends and neighbours, saying unto them, Rejoice with me; for I have found my sheep which was lost.

7 I say unto you, that likewise joy shall be in heaven over one sinner that repenteth, more than over ninety and nine just persons, which need no repentance.

8 Either what woman having ten pieces of silver, if she lose one piece, doth not light a candle, and sweep the house, and seek diligently till she find *it?*

9 And when she hath found *it*, she calleth *her* friends and *her* neighbours together, saying, Rejoice with me; for I have found the piece which I had lost.

10 Likewise, I say unto you, there is joy in the presence of the angels of God over one sinner that repenteth.

11 ¶ And he said, A certain man had two sons:

12 And the younger of them said to *his* father, Father, give me the portion of goods that falleth *to me*. And he divided unto them *his* living.

13 And not many days after the younger son gathered all together, and took his journey into a far country, and there wasted his substance with riotous living.

NEW AMERICAN STANDARD BIBLE

5 "When he has found it, he lays it on his shoulders, rejoicing.

6 "And when he comes home, he calls together his friends and his neighbors, saying to them, 'Rejoice with me, for I have found my sheep which was lost!'

7 "I tell you that in the same way, there will be *more* joy in heaven over one sinner who repents than over ninety-nine righteous persons who need no repentance.

The Lost Coin

8 "Or what woman, if she has ten silver coins and loses one coin, does not light a lamp and sweep the house and search carefully until she finds it?

9 "When she has found it, she calls together her friends and neighbors, saying, 'Rejoice with me, for I have found the coin which I had lost!'

10 "In the same way, I tell you, there is joy in the presence of the angels of God over one sinner who repents."

The Prodigal Son

11 And He said, "A man had two sons.

12 "The younger of them said to his father, 'Father, give me the share of the estate that falls to me.' So he divided his wealth between them.

13 "And not many days later, the younger son gathered everything together and went on a journey into a distant country, and there he squandered his estate with loose living.

NEW CENTURY VERSION

he finds it, he happily puts it on his shoulders 6and goes
home. He calls to his friends and neighbors and says, 'Be
happy with me because I found my lost sheep.' 7In the
same way, I tell you there is more joy in heaven over one
sinner who changes his heart and life, than over ninety-
nine good people who don't need to change.
8"Suppose a woman has ten silver coins,[a] but loses one.
She will light a lamp, sweep the house, and look carefully
for the coin until she finds it. 9And when she finds it, she
will call her friends and neighbors and say, 'Be happy with
me because I have found the coin that I lost.' 10In the same
way, there is joy in the presence of the angels of God when
one sinner changes his heart and life."

The Son Who Left Home

11Then Jesus said, "A man had two sons. 12The younger
son said to his father, 'Give me my share of the property.'
So the father divided the property between his two sons.
13Then the younger son gathered up all that was his and
traveled far away to another country. There he wasted his
money in foolish living. 14After he had spent everything, a

15:8 [a] **silver coins** Roman denarii. One coin was the average pay for one day's work.

CONTEMPORARY ENGLISH VERSION

find it? 5And when you find it, you will be so glad that
you will put it on your shoulder 6and carry it home.
Then you will call in your friends and neighbors and
say, "Let's celebrate! I've found my lost sheep."
7Jesus said, "In the same way there is more happiness in
heaven because of one sinner who turns to God than over
ninety-nine good people who don't need to."

One Coin

8Jesus told the people another story:
What will a woman do if she has ten silver coins and
loses one of them? Won't she light a lamp, sweep the
floor, and look carefully until she finds it? 9Then she
will call in her friends and neighbors and say, "Let's cel-
ebrate! I've found the coin I lost."
10Jesus said, "In the same way God's angels are happy
when even one person turns to him."

Two Sons

11Jesus also told them another story:
Once a man had two sons. 12The younger son said to
his father, "Give me my share of the property." So the
father divided his property between his two sons.
13Not long after that, the younger son packed up
everything he owned and left for a foreign country,
where he wasted all his money in wild living. 14He had

NEW INTERNATIONAL VERSION

joyfully puts it on his shoulders [6]and goes home. Then he calls his friends and neighbors together and says, 'Rejoice with me; I have found my lost sheep.' [7]I tell you that in the same way there will be more rejoicing in heaven over one sinner who repents than over ninety-nine righteous persons who do not need to repent.

The Parable of the Lost Coin

[8]"Or suppose a woman has ten silver coins[a] and loses one. Does she not light a lamp, sweep the house and search carefully until she finds it? [9]And when she finds it, she calls her friends and neighbors together and says, 'Rejoice with me; I have found my lost coin.' [10]In the same way, I tell you, there is rejoicing in the presence of the angels of God over one sinner who repents."

The Parable of the Lost Son

[11]Jesus continued: "There was a man who had two sons. [12]The younger one said to his father, 'Father, give me my share of the estate.' So he divided his property between them.

[13]"Not long after that, the younger son got together all he had, set off for a distant country and there squandered his wealth in wild living. [14]After he had spent everything,

[a] *8* Greek *ten drachmas,* each worth about a day's wages

NEW LIVING TRANSLATION

then you would joyfully carry it home on your shoulders. [6]When you arrived, you would call together your friends and neighbors to rejoice with you because your lost sheep was found. [7]In the same way, heaven will be happier over one lost sinner who returns to God than over ninety-nine others who are righteous and haven't strayed away!

Story of the Lost Coin

[8]"Or suppose a woman has ten valuable silver coins* and loses one. Won't she light a lamp and look in every corner of the house and sweep every nook and cranny until she finds it? [9]And when she finds it, she will call in her friends and neighbors to rejoice with her because she has found her lost coin. [10]In the same way, there is joy in the presence of God's angels when even one sinner repents."

Story of the Lost Son

[11]To illustrate the point further, Jesus told them this story: "A man had two sons. [12]The younger son told his father, 'I want my share of your estate now, instead of waiting until you die.' So his father agreed to divide his wealth between his sons.

[13]"A few days later this younger son packed all his belongings and took a trip to a distant land, and there he wasted all his money on wild living. [14]About the time his

15:8 Greek *10 drachmas.* A drachma was the equivalent of a full day's wage.

NEW KING JAMES VERSION

[5]And when he has found *it,* he lays *it* on his shoulders, rejoicing. [6]And when he comes home, he calls together *his* friends and neighbors, saying to them, 'Rejoice with me, for I have found my sheep which was lost!' [7]I say to you that likewise there will be more joy in heaven over one sinner who repents than over ninety-nine just persons who need no repentance.

The Parable of the Lost Coin

[8]"Or what woman, having ten silver coins,[a] if she loses one coin, does not light a lamp, sweep the house, and search carefully until she finds *it?* [9]And when she has found *it,* she calls *her* friends and neighbors together, saying, 'Rejoice with me, for I have found the piece which I lost!' [10]Likewise, I say to you, there is joy in the presence of the angels of God over one sinner who repents."

The Parable of the Lost Son

[11]Then He said: "A certain man had two sons. [12]And the younger of them said to *his* father, 'Father, give me the portion of goods that falls *to me.*' So he divided to them *his* livelihood. [13]And not many days after, the younger son gathered all together, journeyed to a far country, and there wasted his possessions with prodigal living. [14]But when

15:8 [a] Greek *drachma,* a valuable coin often worn in a ten-piece garland by married women

THE MESSAGE

can be sure you would put it across your shoulders, rejoicing, and when you got home call in your friends and neighbors, saying, 'Celebrate with me! I've found my lost sheep!' Count on it—there's more joy in heaven over one sinner's rescued life than over ninety-nine good people in no need of rescue.

The Story of the Lost Coin

"Or imagine a woman who has ten coins and loses one. Won't she light a lamp and scour the house, looking in every nook and cranny until she finds it? And when she finds it you can be sure she'll call her friends and neighbors: 'Celebrate with me! I found my lost coin!' Count on it—that's the kind of party God's angels throw every time one lost soul turns to God."

The Story of the Lost Son

Then he said, "There was once a man who had two sons. The younger said to his father, 'Father, I want right now what's coming to me.'

"So the father divided the property between them. It wasn't long before the younger son packed his bags and left for a distant country. There, undisciplined and dissipated, he wasted everything he had. After he had gone

KING JAMES VERSION

14 And when he had spent all, there arose a mighty famine in that land; and he began to be in want.

15 And he went and joined himself to a citizen of that country; and he sent him into his fields to feed swine.

16 And he would fain have filled his belly with the husks that the swine did eat: and no man gave unto him.

17 And when he came to himself, he said, How many hired servants of my father's have bread enough and to spare, and I perish with hunger!

18 I will arise and go to my father, and will say unto him, Father, I have sinned against heaven, and before thee,

19 And am no more worthy to be called thy son: make me as one of thy hired servants.

20 And he arose, and came to his father. But when he was yet a great way off, his father saw him, and had compassion, and ran, and fell on his neck, and kissed him.

21 And the son said unto him, Father, I have sinned against heaven, and in thy sight, and am no more worthy to be called thy son.

22 But the father said to his servants, Bring forth the best robe, and put *it* on him; and put a ring on his hand, and shoes on *his* feet:

23 And bring hither the fatted calf, and kill *it*; and let us eat, and be merry:

NEW AMERICAN STANDARD BIBLE

14 "Now when he had spent everything, a severe famine occurred in that country, and he began to be impoverished.

15 "So he went and hired himself out to one of the citizens of that country, and he sent him into his fields to feed swine.

16 "And he would have gladly filled his stomach with the pods that the swine were eating, and no one was giving *anything* to him.

17 "But when he came to his senses, he said, 'How many of my father's hired men have more than enough bread, but I am dying here with hunger!

18 'I will get up and go to my father, and will say to him, "Father, I have sinned against heaven, and in your sight;

19 I am no longer worthy to be called your son; make me as one of your hired men." '

20 "So he got up and came to his father. But while he was still a long way off, his father saw him and felt compassion *for him,* and ran and embraced him and kissed him.

21 "And the son said to him, 'Father, I have sinned against heaven and in your sight; I am no longer worthy to be called your son.'

22 "But the father said to his slaves, 'Quickly bring out the best robe and put it on him, and put a ring on his hand and sandals on his feet;

23 and bring the fattened calf, kill it, and let us eat and celebrate;

NEW CENTURY VERSION

time came when there was no food anywhere in the country, and the son was poor and hungry. 15So he got a job with one of the citizens there who sent the son into the fields to feed pigs. 16The son was so hungry that he wanted to eat the pods the pigs were eating, but no one gave him anything. 17When he realized what he was doing, he thought, 'All of my father's servants have plenty of food. But I am here, almost dying with hunger. 18I will leave and return to my father and say to him, "Father, I have sinned against God and have done wrong to you. 19I am no longer worthy to be called your son, but let me be like one of your servants." ' 20So the son left and went to his father.

"While the son was still a long way off, his father saw him and felt sorry for his son. So the father ran to him and hugged and kissed him. 21The son said, 'Father, I have sinned against God and have done wrong to you. I am no longer worthy to be called your son.' 22But the father said to his servants, 'Hurry! Bring the best clothes and put them on him. Also, put a ring on his finger and sandals on his feet. 23And get our fat calf and kill it so we can have a

CONTEMPORARY ENGLISH VERSION

spent everything, when a bad famine spread through that whole land. Soon he had nothing to eat.

15He went to work for a man in that country, and the man sent him out to take care of his pigs.[b] 16He would have been glad to eat what the pigs were eating,[c] but no one gave him a thing.

17Finally, he came to his senses and said, "My father's workers have plenty to eat, and here I am, starving to death! 18I will go to my father and say to him, 'Father, I have sinned against God in heaven and against you. 19I am no longer good enough to be called your son. Treat me like one of your workers.' "

20The younger son got up and started back to his father. But when he was still a long way off, his father saw him and felt sorry for him. He ran to his son and hugged and kissed him.

21The son said, "Father, I have sinned against God in heaven and against you. I am no longer good enough to be called your son."

22But his father said to the servants, "Hurry and bring the best clothes and put them on him. Give him a ring for his finger and sandals[d] for his feet. 23Get the best calf and

[b] 15.15 *pigs*: The Jewish religion taught that pigs were not fit to eat or even to touch. A Jewish man would have felt terribly insulted if he had to feed pigs, much less eat with them. [c] 15.16 *what the pigs were eating*: The Greek text has "(bean) pods," which came from a tree in Palestine. These were used to feed animals. Poor people sometimes ate them too. [d] 15.22 *ring . . . sandals*: These show that the young man's father fully accepted him as his son. A ring was a sign of high position in the family. Sandals showed that he was a son instead of a slave, since slaves did not usually wear sandals.

NEW INTERNATIONAL VERSION

there was a severe famine in that whole country, and he began to be in need. 15 So he went and hired himself out to a citizen of that country, who sent him to his fields to feed pigs. 16 He longed to fill his stomach with the pods that the pigs were eating, but no one gave him anything.

17 "When he came to his senses, he said, 'How many of my father's hired men have food to spare, and here I am starving to death! 18 I will set out and go back to my father and say to him: Father, I have sinned against heaven and against you. 19 I am no longer worthy to be called your son; make me like one of your hired men.' 20 So he got up and went to his father.

"But while he was still a long way off, his father saw him and was filled with compassion for him; he ran to his son, threw his arms around him and kissed him.

21 "The son said to him, 'Father, I have sinned against heaven and against you. I am no longer worthy to be called your son.[b]'

22 "But the father said to his servants, 'Quick! Bring the best robe and put it on him. Put a ring on his finger and sandals on his feet. 23 Bring the fattened calf and kill it.

[b] 21 Some early manuscripts *son. Make me like one of your hired men.*

NEW LIVING TRANSLATION

money ran out, a great famine swept over the land, and he began to starve. 15 He persuaded a local farmer to hire him to feed his pigs. 16 The boy became so hungry that even the pods he was feeding the pigs looked good to him. But no one gave him anything.

17 "When he finally came to his senses, he said to himself, 'At home even the hired men have food enough to spare, and here I am, dying of hunger! 18 I will go home to my father and say, "Father, I have sinned against both heaven and you, 19 and I am no longer worthy of being called your son. Please take me on as a hired man." '

20 "So he returned home to his father. And while he was still a long distance away, his father saw him coming. Filled with love and compassion, he ran to his son, embraced him, and kissed him. 21 His son said to him, 'Father, I have sinned against both heaven and you, and I am no longer worthy of being called your son.*'

22 "But his father said to the servants, 'Quick! Bring the finest robe in the house and put it on him. Get a ring for his finger, and sandals for his feet. 23 And kill the calf we have been fattening in the pen. We must celebrate with a

15:21 Some manuscripts add *Please take me on as a hired man.*

NEW KING JAMES VERSION

he had spent all, there arose a severe famine in that land, and he began to be in want. 15 Then he went and joined himself to a citizen of that country, and he sent him into his fields to feed swine. 16 And he would gladly have filled his stomach with the pods that the swine ate, and no one gave him *anything.*

17 "But when he came to himself, he said, 'How many of my father's hired servants have bread enough and to spare, and I perish with hunger! 18 I will arise and go to my father, and will say to him, "Father, I have sinned against heaven and before you, 19 and I am no longer worthy to be called your son. Make me like one of your hired servants." '

20 "And he arose and came to his father. But when he was still a great way off, his father saw him and had compassion, and ran and fell on his neck and kissed him. 21 And the son said to him, 'Father, I have sinned against heaven and in your sight, and am no longer worthy to be called your son.'

22 "But the father said to his servants, 'Bring[b] out the best robe and put *it* on him, and put a ring on his hand and sandals on *his* feet. 23 And bring the fatted calf here

15:22 [b] NU-Text reads *Quickly bring.*

THE MESSAGE

through all his money, there was a bad famine all through that country and he began to hurt. He signed on with a citizen there who assigned him to his fields to slop the pigs. He was so hungry he would have eaten the corncobs in the pig slop, but no one would give him any.

"That brought him to his senses. He said, 'All those farmhands working for my father sit down to three meals a day, and here I am starving to death. I'm going back to my father. I'll say to him, "Father, I've sinned against God, I've sinned before you; I don't deserve to be called your son. Take me on as a hired hand."' He got right up and went home to his father.

"When he was still a long way off, his father saw him. His heart pounding, he ran out, embraced him, and kissed him. The son started his speech: 'Father, I've sinned against God, I've sinned before you; I don't deserve to be called your son ever again.'

"But the father wasn't listening. He was calling to the servants, 'Quick. Bring a clean set of clothes and dress him. Put the family ring on his finger and sandals on his feet. Then get a grain-fed heifer and roast it. We're going

KING JAMES VERSION

24 For this my son was dead, and is alive again; he was lost, and is found. And they began to be merry.

25 Now his elder son was in the field: and as he came and drew nigh to the house, he heard musick and dancing.

26 And he called one of the servants, and asked what these things meant.

27 And he said unto him, Thy brother is come; and thy father hath killed the fatted calf, because he hath received him safe and sound.

28 And he was angry, and would not go in: therefore came his father out, and intreated him.

29 And he answering said to *his* father, Lo, these many years do I serve thee, neither transgressed I at any time thy commandment: and yet thou never gavest me a kid, that I might make merry with my friends:

30 But as soon as this thy son was come, which hath devoured thy living with harlots, thou hast killed for him the fatted calf.

31 And he said unto him, Son, thou art ever with me, and all that I have is thine.

32 It was meet that we should make merry, and be glad: for this thy brother was dead, and is alive again; and was lost, and is found.

16 And he said also unto his disciples, There was a certain rich man, which had a steward; and the same was accused unto him that he had wasted his goods.

NEW AMERICAN STANDARD BIBLE

24 for this son of mine was dead and has come to life again; he was lost and has been found.' And they began to celebrate.

25 "Now his older son was in the field, and when he came and approached the house, he heard music and dancing.

26 "And he summoned one of the servants and *began* inquiring what these things could be.

27 "And he said to him, 'Your brother has come, and your father has killed the fattened calf because he has received him back safe and sound.'

28 "But he became angry and was not willing to go in; and his father came out and *began* pleading with him.

29 "But he answered and said to his father, 'Look! For so many years I have been serving you and I have never neglected a command of yours; and *yet* you have never given me a young goat, so that I might celebrate with my friends;

30 but when this son of yours came, who has devoured your wealth with prostitutes, you killed the fattened calf for him.'

31 "And he said to him, 'Son, you have always been with me, and all that is mine is yours.

32 'But we had to celebrate and rejoice, for this brother of yours was dead and *has begun* to live, and *was* lost and has been found.' "

The Unrighteous Steward

16 Now He was also saying to the disciples, "There was a rich man who had a manager, and this *manager* was reported to him as squandering his possessions.

NEW CENTURY VERSION

feast and celebrate. 24 My son was dead, but now he is alive again! He was lost, but now he is found!' So they began to celebrate.

25 "The older son was in the field, and as he came closer to the house, he heard the sound of music and dancing. 26 So he called to one of the servants and asked what all this meant. 27 The servant said, 'Your brother has come back, and your father killed the fat calf, because your brother came home safely.' 28 The older son was angry and would not go in to the feast. So his father went out and begged him to come in. 29 But the older son said to his father, 'I have served you like a slave for many years and have always obeyed your commands. But you never gave me even a young goat to have at a feast with my friends. 30 But your other son, who wasted all your money on prostitutes, comes home, and you kill the fat calf for him!' 31 The father said to him, 'Son, you are always with me, and all that I have is yours. 32 We had to celebrate and be happy because your brother was dead, but now he is alive. He was lost, but now he is found.' "

True Wealth

16 Jesus also said to his followers, "Once there was a rich man who had a manager to take care of his business. This manager was accused of cheating him. 2 So

CONTEMPORARY ENGLISH VERSION

prepare it, so we can eat and celebrate. 24 This son of mine was dead, but has now come back to life. He was lost and has now been found." And they began to celebrate.

25 The older son had been out in the field. But when he came near the house, he heard the music and dancing. 26 So he called one of the servants over and asked, "What's going on here?"

27 The servant answered, "Your brother has come home safe and sound, and your father ordered us to kill the best calf." 28 The older brother got so angry that he would not even go into the house.

His father came out and begged him to go in. 29 But he said to his father, "For years I have worked for you like a slave and have always obeyed you. But you have never even given me a little goat, so that I could give a dinner for my friends. 30 This other son of yours wasted your money on prostitutes. And now that he has come home, you ordered the best calf to be killed for a feast."

31 His father replied, "My son, you are always with me, and everything I have is yours. 32 But we should be glad and celebrate! Your brother was dead, but he is now alive. He was lost and has now been found."

A Dishonest Manager

16 Jesus said to his disciples:

A rich man once had a manager to take care of his business. But he was told that his manager was wasting money. 2 So the rich man called him in and said,

NEW INTERNATIONAL VERSION

Let's have a feast and celebrate. 24For this son of mine was dead and is alive again; he was lost and is found.' So they began to celebrate.

25"Meanwhile, the older son was in the field. When he came near the house, he heard music and dancing. 26So he called one of the servants and asked him what was going on. 27'Your brother has come,' he replied, 'and your father has killed the fattened calf because he has him back safe and sound.'

28"The older brother became angry and refused to go in. So his father went out and pleaded with him. 29But he answered his father, 'Look! All these years I've been slaving for you and never disobeyed your orders. Yet you never gave me even a young goat so I could celebrate with my friends. 30But when this son of yours who has squandered your property with prostitutes comes home, you kill the fattened calf for him!'

31" 'My son,' the father said, 'you are always with me, and everything I have is yours. 32But we had to celebrate and be glad, because this brother of yours was dead and is alive again; he was lost and is found.' "

The Parable of the Shrewd Manager

16 Jesus told his disciples: "There was a rich man whose manager was accused of wasting his possessions. 2So he called him in and asked him, 'What is this

NEW LIVING TRANSLATION

feast, 24for this son of mine was dead and has now returned to life. He was lost, but now he is found.' So the party began.

25"Meanwhile, the older son was in the fields working. When he returned home, he heard music and dancing in the house, 26and he asked one of the servants what was going on. 27'Your brother is back,' he was told, 'and your father has killed the calf we were fattening and has prepared a great feast. We are celebrating because of his safe return.'

28"The older brother was angry and wouldn't go in. His father came out and begged him, 29but he replied, 'All these years I've worked hard for you and never once refused to do a single thing you told me to. And in all that time you never gave me even one young goat for a feast with my friends. 30Yet when this son of yours comes back after squandering your money on prostitutes, you celebrate by killing the finest calf we have.'

31"His father said to him, 'Look, dear son, you and I are very close, and everything I have is yours. 32We had to celebrate this happy day. For your brother was dead and has come back to life! He was lost, but now he is found!' "

Story of the Shrewd Manager

16 Jesus told this story to his disciples: "A rich man hired a manager to handle his affairs, but soon a rumor went around that the manager was thoroughly dishonest. 2So his employer called him in and said, 'What's

NEW KING JAMES VERSION

and kill *it,* and let us eat and be merry; 24for this my son was dead and is alive again; he was lost and is found.' And they began to be merry.

25"Now his older son was in the field. And as he came and drew near to the house, he heard music and dancing. 26So he called one of the servants and asked what these things meant. 27And he said to him, 'Your brother has come, and because he has received him safe and sound, your father has killed the fatted calf.'

28"But he was angry and would not go in. Therefore his father came out and pleaded with him. 29So he answered and said to *his* father, 'Lo, these many years I have been serving you; I never transgressed your commandment at any time; and yet you never gave me a young goat, that I might make merry with my friends. 30But as soon as this son of yours came, who has devoured your livelihood with harlots, you killed the fatted calf for him.'

31"And he said to him, 'Son, you are always with me, and all that I have is yours. 32It was right that we should make merry and be glad, for your brother was dead and is alive again, and was lost and is found.' "

The Parable of the Unjust Steward

16 He also said to His disciples: "There was a certain rich man who had a steward, and an accusation was brought to him that this man was wasting his goods.

THE MESSAGE

to feast! We're going to have a wonderful time! My son is here—given up for dead and now alive! Given up for lost and now found!' And they began to have a wonderful time.

"All this time his older son was out in the field. When the day's work was done he came in. As he approached the house, he heard the music and dancing. Calling over one of the houseboys, he asked what was going on. He told him, 'Your brother came home. Your father has ordered a feast—barbecued beef!—because he has him home safe and sound.'

"The older brother stalked off in an angry sulk and refused to join in. His father came out and tried to talk to him, but he wouldn't listen. The son said, 'Look how many years I've stayed here serving you, never giving you one moment of grief, but have you ever thrown a party for me and my friends? Then this son of yours who has thrown away your money on whores shows up and you go all out with a feast!'

"His father said, 'Son, you don't understand. You're with me all the time, and everything that is mine is yours—but this is a wonderful time, and we had to celebrate. This brother of yours was dead, and he's alive! He was lost, and he's found!' "

The Story of the Crooked Manager

16 Jesus said to his disciples, "There was once a rich man who had a manager. He got reports that the manager had been taking advantage of his position by running up huge personal expenses. So he called him in

KING JAMES VERSION

2 And he called him, and said unto him, How is it that I hear this of thee? give an account of thy stewardship; for thou mayest be no longer steward.

3 Then the steward said within himself, What shall I do? for my lord taketh away from me the stewardship: I cannot dig; to beg I am ashamed.

4 I am resolved what to do, that, when I am put out of the stewardship, they may receive me into their houses.

5 So he called every one of his lord's debtors *unto him*, and said unto the first, How much owest thou unto my lord?

6 And he said, An hundred measures of oil. And he said unto him, Take thy bill, and sit down quickly, and write fifty.

7 Then said he to another, And how much owest thou? And he said, An hundred measures of wheat. And he said unto him, Take thy bill, and write fourscore.

8 And the lord commended the unjust steward, because he had done wisely: for the children of this world are in their generation wiser than the children of light.

9 And I say unto you, Make to yourselves friends of the mammon of unrighteousness; that, when ye fail, they may receive you into everlasting habitations.

NEW AMERICAN STANDARD BIBLE

2 "And he called him and said to him, 'What is this I hear about you? Give an accounting of your management, for you can no longer be manager.'

3 "The manager said to himself, 'What shall I do, since my master is taking the management away from me? I am not strong enough to dig; I am ashamed to beg.

4 'I know what I shall do, so that when I am removed from the management people will welcome me into their homes.'

5 "And he summoned each one of his master's debtors, and he *began* saying to the first, 'How much do you owe my master?'

6 "And he said, 'A hundred measures of oil.' And he said to him, 'Take your bill, and sit down quickly and write fifty.'

7 "Then he said to another, 'And how much do you owe?' And he said, 'A hundred measures of wheat.' He *said to him, 'Take your bill, and write eighty.'

8 "And his master praised the unrighteous manager because he had acted shrewdly; for the sons of this age are more shrewd in relation to their own kind than the sons of light.

9 "And I say to you, make friends for yourselves by means of the [l]wealth of unrighteousness, so that when it fails, they will receive you into the eternal dwellings.

16:9 [l] Gr *mammon*, fr Aram *mamona*, signifying riches, wealth, etc, personified as an object of worship

NEW CENTURY VERSION

he called the manager in and said to him, 'What is this I
hear about you? Give me a report of what you have done
with my money, because you can't be my manager any
longer.' [3]The manager thought to himself, 'What will I do
since my master is taking my job away from me? I am not
strong enough to dig ditches, and I am ashamed to beg. [4]I
know what I'll do so that when I lose my job people will
welcome me into their homes.'
[5]"So the manager called in everyone who owed the mas-
ter any money. He asked the first one, 'How much do you
owe?' [6]He answered, 'Eight hundred gallons of olive oil.'
The manager said to him, 'Take your bill, sit down quickly,
and write four hundred gallons.' [7]Then the manager asked
another one, 'How much do you owe?' He answered, 'One
thousand bushels of wheat.' Then the manager said to
him, 'Take your bill and write eight hundred bushels.' [8]So,
the master praised the dishonest manager for being smart.
Yes, worldly people are smarter with their own kind than
spiritual people are.
[9]"I tell you, make friends for yourselves using worldly
riches so that when those riches are gone, you will be wel-
comed in those homes that continue forever. [10]Whoever

CONTEMPORARY ENGLISH VERSION

"What is this I hear about you? Tell me what you have
done! You are no longer going to work for me."
[3]The manager said to himself, "What shall I do now
that my master is going to fire me? I can't dig ditches, and
I'm ashamed to beg. [4]I know what I'll do, so that people
will welcome me into their homes after I've lost my job."
[5]Then one by one he called in the people who were in
debt to his master. He asked the first one, "How much
do you owe my master?"
[6]"A hundred barrels of olive oil," the man answered.
So the manager said, "Take your bill and sit down and
quickly write 'fifty'."
[7]The manager asked someone else who was in debt to
his master, "How much do you owe?"
"A thousand bushels[a] of wheat," the man replied.
The manager said, "Take your bill and write 'eight
hundred'."
[8]The master praised his dishonest manager for look-
ing out for himself so well. That's how it is! The people
of this world look out for themselves better than the
people who belong to the light.
[9]My disciples, I tell you to use wicked wealth to make
friends for yourselves. Then when it is gone, you will be
welcomed into an eternal home. [10]Anyone who can be

[a] 16.7 *A thousand bushels*: The Greek text has "A hundred measures," and each measure is about ten or twelve bushels.

NEW INTERNATIONAL VERSION

I hear about you? Give an account of your management, because you cannot be manager any longer.'

3"The manager said to himself, 'What shall I do now? My master is taking away my job. I'm not strong enough to dig, and I'm ashamed to beg— 4I know what I'll do so that, when I lose my job here, people will welcome me into their houses.'

5"So he called in each one of his master's debtors. He asked the first, 'How much do you owe my master?'

6" 'Eight hundred gallons[a] of olive oil,' he replied.

"The manager told him, 'Take your bill, sit down quickly, and make it four hundred.'

7"Then he asked the second, 'And how much do you owe?'

" 'A thousand bushels[b] of wheat,' he replied.

"He told him, 'Take your bill and make it eight hundred.'

8"The master commended the dishonest manager because he had acted shrewdly. For the people of this world are more shrewd in dealing with their own kind than are the people of the light. 9I tell you, use worldly wealth to gain friends for yourselves, so that when it is gone, you will be welcomed into eternal dwellings.

[a] *6* Greek *one hundred batous* (probably about 3 kiloliters) [b] *7* Greek *one hundred korous* (probably about 35 kiloliters)

NEW LIVING TRANSLATION

this I hear about your stealing from me? Get your report in order, because you are going to be dismissed.'

3"The manager thought to himself, 'Now what? I'm through here, and I don't have the strength to go out and dig ditches, and I'm too proud to beg. 4I know just the thing! And then I'll have plenty of friends to take care of me when I leave!'

5"So he invited each person who owed money to his employer to come and discuss the situation. He asked the first one, 'How much do you owe him?' 6The man replied, 'I owe him eight hundred gallons of olive oil.' So the manager told him, 'Tear up that bill and write another one for four hundred gallons.*'

7" 'And how much do you owe my employer?' he asked the next man. 'A thousand bushels of wheat,' was the reply. 'Here,' the manager said, 'take your bill and replace it with one for only eight hundred bushels.*'

8"The rich man had to admire the dishonest rascal for being so shrewd. And it is true that the citizens of this world are more shrewd than the godly are. 9I tell you, use your worldly resources to benefit others and make friends. In this way, your generosity stores up a reward for you in heaven.*

16:6 Greek *100 baths . . . 50 [baths].* **16:7** Greek *100 korous . . . 80 [korous].* **16:9** Or *Then when you run out at the end of this life, your friends will welcome you into eternal homes.*

NEW KING JAMES VERSION

2So he called him and said to him, 'What is this I hear about you? Give an account of your stewardship, for you can no longer be steward.'

3"Then the steward said within himself, 'What shall I do? For my master is taking the stewardship away from me. I cannot dig; I am ashamed to beg. 4I have resolved what to do, that when I am put out of the stewardship, they may receive me into their houses.'

5"So he called every one of his master's debtors to *him,* and said to the first, 'How much do you owe my master?' 6And he said, 'A hundred measures[a] of oil.' So he said to him, 'Take your bill, and sit down quickly and write fifty.' 7Then he said to another, 'And how much do you owe?' So he said, 'A hundred measures[b] of wheat.' And he said to him, 'Take your bill, and write eighty.' 8So the master commended the unjust steward because he had dealt shrewdly. For the sons of this world are more shrewd in their generation than the sons of light.

9"And I say to you, make friends for yourselves by unrighteous mammon, that when you fail,[c] they may receive you into an everlasting home. 10He who *is* faithful

16:6 [a] Greek *batos,* eight or nine gallons each (Old Testament *bath*)
16:7 [b] Greek *koros,* ten or twelve bushels each (Old Testament *kor*)
16:9 [c] NU-Text reads *it fails.*

THE MESSAGE

and said, 'What's this I hear about you? You're fired. And I want a complete audit of your books.'

"The manager said to himself, 'What am I going to do? I've lost my job as manager. I'm not strong enough for a laboring job, and I'm too proud to beg. . . . Ah, I've got a plan. Here's what I'll do . . . then when I'm turned out into the street, people will take me into their houses.'

"Then he went at it. One after another, he called in the people who were in debt to his master. He said to the first, 'How much do you owe my master?'

"He replied, 'A hundred jugs of olive oil.'

"The manager said, 'Here, take your bill, sit down here—quick now—write "fifty." '

"To the next he said, 'And you, what do you owe?'

"He answered, 'A hundred sacks of wheat.'

"He said, 'Take your bill, write in "eighty." '

"Now here's a surprise: The master praised the crooked manager! And why? Because he knew how to look after himself. Streetwise people are smarter in this regard than law-abiding citizens. They are on constant alert, looking for angles, surviving by their wits. I want you to be smart in the same way—but for what is *right*—using every adversity to stimulate you to creative survival, to concentrate your attention on the bare essentials, so you'll live, really live, and not complacently just get by on good behavior."

KING JAMES VERSION

10 He that is faithful in that which is least is faithful also in much: and he that is unjust in the least is unjust also in much.

11 If therefore ye have not been faithful in the unrighteous mammon, who will commit to your trust the true *riches?*

12 And if ye have not been faithful in that which is another man's, who shall give you that which is your own?

13 No servant can serve two masters: for either he will hate the one, and love the other; or else he will hold to the one, and despise the other. Ye cannot serve God and mammon.

14 And the Pharisees also, who were covetous, heard all these things: and they derided him.

15 And he said unto them, Ye are they which justify yourselves before men; but God knoweth your hearts: for that which is highly esteemed among men is abomination in the sight of God.

16 The law and the prophets *were* until John: since that time the kingdom of God is preached, and every man presseth into it.

NEW AMERICAN STANDARD BIBLE

10 "He who is faithful in a very little thing is faithful also in much; and he who is unrighteous in a very little thing is unrighteous also in much.

11 "Therefore if you have not been faithful in the *use of* unrighteous wealth, who will entrust the true *riches* to you?

12 "And if you have not been faithful in *the use of* that which is another's, who will give you that which is your own?

13 "No servant can serve two masters; for either he will hate the one and love the other, or else he will be devoted to one and despise the other. You cannot serve God and wealth."

14 Now the Pharisees, who were lovers of money, were listening to all these things and were scoffing at Him.

15 And He said to them, "You are those who justify yourselves in the sight of men, but God knows your hearts; for that which is highly esteemed among men is detestable in the sight of God.

16 "The Law and the Prophets *were proclaimed* until John; since that time the gospel of the kingdom of God has been preached, and everyone is forcing his way into it.

NEW CENTURY VERSION

can be trusted with a little can also be trusted with a lot,
and whoever is dishonest with a little is dishonest with a
lot. 11 If you cannot be trusted with worldly riches, then
who will trust you with true riches? 12 And if you cannot be
trusted with things that belong to someone else, who will
give you things of your own?

13 "No servant can serve two masters. The servant will
hate one master and love the other, or will follow one master and refuse to follow the other. You cannot serve both
God and worldly riches."

God's Law Cannot Be Changed

14 The Pharisees, who loved money, were listening to all
these things and made fun of Jesus. 15 He said to them,
"You make yourselves look good in front of people, but
God knows what is really in your hearts. What is important to people is hateful in God's sight.

16 "The law of Moses and the writings of the prophets
were preached until John[a] came. Since then the Good News
about the kingdom of God is being told, and everyone tries

16:16 [a] **John** John the Baptist, who preached to people about Christ's coming (Matthew 3, Luke 3).

CONTEMPORARY ENGLISH VERSION

trusted in little matters can also be trusted in important
matters. But anyone who is dishonest in little matters
will be dishonest in important matters. 11 If you cannot
be trusted with this wicked wealth, who will trust you
with true wealth? 12 And if you cannot be trusted with
what belongs to someone else, who will give you something that will be your own? 13 You cannot be the slave
of two masters. You will like one more than the other or
be more loyal to one than to the other. You cannot serve
God and money.

Some Sayings of Jesus

(Matthew 11.12, 13; 5.31, 32; Mark 10.11, 12)

14 The Pharisees really loved money. So when they heard
what Jesus said, they made fun of him. 15 But Jesus told
them:

You are always making yourselves look good, but God sees what is in your heart. The things that most people think are important are worthless as far as God is concerned.

16 Until the time of John the Baptist, people had to
obey the Law of Moses and the Books of the Prophets.[b]
But since God's kingdom has been preached, everyone is

[b] 16.16 *the Law of Moses and the Books of the Prophets*: The Jewish Scriptures, that is, the Old Testament.

NEW INTERNATIONAL VERSION

10"Whoever can be trusted with very little can also be trusted with much, and whoever is dishonest with very little will also be dishonest with much. 11So if you have not been trustworthy in handling worldly wealth, who will trust you with true riches? 12And if you have not been trustworthy with someone else's property, who will give you property of your own?

13"No servant can serve two masters. Either he will hate the one and love the other, or he will be devoted to the one and despise the other. You cannot serve both God and Money."

14The Pharisees, who loved money, heard all this and were sneering at Jesus. 15He said to them, "You are the ones who justify yourselves in the eyes of men, but God knows your hearts. What is highly valued among men is detestable in God's sight.

Additional Teachings

16"The Law and the Prophets were proclaimed until John. Since that time, the good news of the kingdom of God is being preached, and everyone is forcing his way

NEW LIVING TRANSLATION

10"Unless you are faithful in small matters, you won't be faithful in large ones. If you cheat even a little, you won't be honest with greater responsibilities. 11And if you are untrustworthy about worldly wealth, who will trust you with the true riches of heaven? 12And if you are not faithful with other people's money, why should you be trusted with money of your own?

13"No one can serve two masters. For you will hate one and love the other, or be devoted to one and despise the other. You cannot serve both God and money."

14The Pharisees, who dearly loved their money, naturally scoffed at all this. 15Then he said to them, "You like to look good in public, but God knows your evil hearts. What this world honors is an abomination in the sight of God.

16"Until John the Baptist began to preach, the laws of Moses and the messages of the prophets were your guides. But now the Good News of the Kingdom of God is preached, and eager multitudes are forcing their way in.

NEW KING JAMES VERSION

in *what is* least is faithful also in much; and he who is unjust in *what is* least is unjust also in much. 11Therefore if you have not been faithful in the unrighteous mammon, who will commit to your trust the true *riches?* 12And if you have not been faithful in what is another man's, who will give you what is your own?

13"No servant can serve two masters; for either he will hate the one and love the other, or else he will be loyal to the one and despise the other. You cannot serve God and mammon."

The Law, the Prophets, and the Kingdom

14Now the Pharisees, who were lovers of money, also heard all these things, and they derided Him. 15And He said to them, "You are those who justify yourselves before men, but God knows your hearts. For what is highly esteemed among men is an abomination in the sight of God.

16"The law and the prophets *were* until John. Since that time the kingdom of God has been preached, and everyone

THE MESSAGE

God Sees Behind Appearances

Jesus went on to make these comments:

"If you're honest in small things,
you'll be honest in big things;
If you're a crook in small things,
you'll be a crook in big things.
If you're not honest in small jobs,
who will put you in charge of the store?
No worker can serve two bosses:
He'll either hate the first and love the second
Or adore the first and despise the second.
You can't serve both God and the Bank."

When the Pharisees, a money-obsessed bunch, heard him say these things, they rolled their eyes, dismissing him as hopelessly out of touch. So Jesus spoke to them: "You are masters at making yourselves look good in front of others, but God knows what's behind the appearance.

What society sees and calls monumental,
God sees through and calls monstrous.
God's Law and the Prophets climaxed in John;
Now it's all kingdom of God—the glad news
and compelling invitation to every man and woman.

KING JAMES VERSION

17 And it is easier for heaven and earth to pass, than one tittle of the law to fail.

18 Whosoever putteth away his wife, and marrieth another, committeth adultery: and whosoever marrieth her that is put away from *her* husband committeth adultery.

19 ¶ There was a certain rich man, which was clothed in purple and fine linen, and fared sumptuously every day:

20 And there was a certain beggar named Lazarus, which was laid at his gate, full of sores,

21 And desiring to be fed with the crumbs which fell from the rich man's table: moreover the dogs came and licked his sores.

22 And it came to pass, that the beggar died, and was carried by the angels into Abraham's bosom: the rich man also died, and was buried;

23 And in hell he lift up his eyes, being in torments, and seeth Abraham afar off, and Lazarus in his bosom.

24 And he cried and said, Father Abraham, have mercy on me, and send Lazarus, that he may dip the tip of his finger in water, and cool my tongue; for I am tormented in this flame.

25 But Abraham said, Son, remember that thou in thy lifetime receivedst thy good things, and likewise Lazarus

NEW AMERICAN STANDARD BIBLE

17 "But it is easier for heaven and earth to pass away than for one stroke of a letter of the Law to fail.

18 "Everyone who divorces his wife and marries another commits adultery, and he who marries one who is divorced from a husband commits adultery.

The Rich Man and Lazarus

19 "Now there was a rich man, and he habitually dressed in purple and fine linen, joyously living in splendor every day.

20 "And a poor man named Lazarus was laid at his gate, covered with sores,

21 and longing to be fed with the *crumbs* which were falling from the rich man's table; besides, even the dogs were coming and licking his sores.

22 "Now the poor man died and was carried away by the angels to Abraham's bosom; and the rich man also died and was buried.

23 "In Hades he lifted up his eyes, being in torment, and *saw Abraham far away and Lazarus in his bosom.

24 "And he cried out and said, 'Father Abraham, have mercy on me, and send Lazarus so that he may dip the tip of his finger in water and cool off my tongue, for I am in agony in this flame.'

25 "But Abraham said, 'Child, remember that during your life you received your good things, and likewise Lazarus

NEW CENTURY VERSION

to enter it by force. 17 It would be easier for heaven and earth to pass away than for the smallest part of a letter in the law to be changed.

Divorce and Remarriage

18 "If a man divorces his wife and marries another woman, he is guilty of adultery, and the man who marries a divorced woman is also guilty of adultery."

The Rich Man and Lazarus

19 Jesus said, "There was a rich man who always dressed in the finest clothes and lived in luxury every day. 20 And a very poor man named Lazarus, whose body was covered with sores, was laid at the rich man's gate. 21 He wanted to eat only the small pieces of food that fell from the rich man's table. And the dogs would come and lick his sores. 22 Later, Lazarus died, and the angels carried him to the arms of Abraham. The rich man died, too, and was buried. 23 In the place of the dead, he was in much pain. The rich man saw Abraham far away with Lazarus at his side. 24 He called, 'Father Abraham, have mercy on me! Send Lazarus to dip his finger in water and cool my tongue, because I am suffering in this fire!' 25 But Abraham said, 'Child, remember when you were alive you had the good things in

CONTEMPORARY ENGLISH VERSION

trying hard to get in. 17 Heaven and earth will disappear before the smallest letter of the Law does.

18 It is a terrible sin[c] for a man to divorce his wife and marry another woman. It is also a terrible sin for a man to marry a divorced woman.

Lazarus and the Rich Man

19 There was once a rich man who wore expensive clothes and every day ate the best food. 20 But a poor beggar named Lazarus was brought to the gate of the rich man's house. 21 He was happy just to eat the scraps that fell from the rich man's table. His body was covered with sores, and dogs kept coming up to lick them. 22 The poor man died, and angels took him to the place of honor next to Abraham.[d]

The rich man also died and was buried. 23 He went to hell[e] and was suffering terribly. When he looked up and saw Abraham far off and Lazarus at his side, 24 he said to Abraham, "Have pity on me! Send Lazarus to dip his finger in water and touch my tongue. I'm suffering terribly in this fire."

25 Abraham answered, "My friend, remember that while you lived, you had everything good, and Lazarus

[c] 16.18 *a terrible sin*: The Greek text uses a word that means the sin of being unfaithful in marriage. [d] 16.22 *the place of honor next to Abraham*: The Jewish people thought that heaven would be a banquet that God would give for them. Abraham would be the most important person there, and the guest of honor would sit next to him.

[e] 16.23 *hell*: The Greek text has "hades," which the Jewish people often thought of as the place where the dead wait for the final judgment.

NEW INTERNATIONAL VERSION

into it. [17]It is easier for heaven and earth to disappear than for the least stroke of a pen to drop out of the Law.

[18]"Anyone who divorces his wife and marries another woman commits adultery, and the man who marries a divorced woman commits adultery.

The Rich Man and Lazarus

[19]"There was a rich man who was dressed in purple and fine linen and lived in luxury every day. [20]At his gate was laid a beggar named Lazarus, covered with sores [21]and longing to eat what fell from the rich man's table. Even the dogs came and licked his sores.

[22]"The time came when the beggar died and the angels carried him to Abraham's side. The rich man also died and was buried. [23]In hell,[c] where he was in torment, he looked up and saw Abraham far away, with Lazarus by his side. [24]So he called to him, 'Father Abraham, have pity on me and send Lazarus to dip the tip of his finger in water and cool my tongue, because I am in agony in this fire.'

[25]"But Abraham replied, 'Son, remember that in your lifetime you received your good things, while Lazarus

[c] *23* Greek *Hades*

NEW LIVING TRANSLATION

[17]But that doesn't mean that the law has lost its force in even the smallest point. It is stronger and more permanent than heaven and earth.

[18]"Anyone who divorces his wife and marries someone else commits adultery, and anyone who marries a divorced woman commits adultery."

The Rich Man and Lazarus

[19]Jesus said, "There was a certain rich man who was splendidly clothed and who lived each day in luxury. [20]At his door lay a diseased beggar named Lazarus. [21]As Lazarus lay there longing for scraps from the rich man's table, the dogs would come and lick his open sores. [22]Finally, the beggar died and was carried by the angels to be with Abraham.* The rich man also died and was buried, [23]and his soul went to the place of the dead.* There, in torment, he saw Lazarus in the far distance with Abraham.

[24]"The rich man shouted, 'Father Abraham, have some pity! Send Lazarus over here to dip the tip of his finger in water and cool my tongue, because I am in anguish in these flames.'

[25]"But Abraham said to him, 'Son, remember that during your lifetime you had everything you wanted, and Lazarus

16:22 Greek *into Abraham's bosom.* **16:23** Greek *to Hades.*

NEW KING JAMES VERSION

is pressing into it. [17]And it is easier for heaven and earth to pass away than for one tittle of the law to fail.

[18]"Whoever divorces his wife and marries another commits adultery; and whoever marries her who is divorced from *her* husband commits adultery.

The Rich Man and Lazarus

[19]"There was a certain rich man who was clothed in purple and fine linen and fared sumptuously every day. [20]But there was a certain beggar named Lazarus, full of sores, who was laid at his gate, [21]desiring to be fed with the crumbs which fell[d] from the rich man's table. Moreover the dogs came and licked his sores. [22]So it was that the beggar died, and was carried by the angels to Abraham's bosom. The rich man also died and was buried. [23]And being in torments in Hades, he lifted up his eyes and saw Abraham afar off, and Lazarus in his bosom.

[24]"Then he cried and said, 'Father Abraham, have mercy on me, and send Lazarus that he may dip the tip of his finger in water and cool my tongue; for I am tormented in this flame.' [25]But Abraham said, 'Son, remember that in your lifetime you received your good things, and likewise

16:21 [d] NU-Text reads *with what fell.*

THE MESSAGE

The sky will disintegrate and the earth dissolve
before a single letter of God's Law wears out.
Using the legalities of divorce
as a cover for lust is adultery;
Using the legalities of marriage
as a cover for lust is adultery.

The Rich Man and Lazarus

"There once was a rich man, expensively dressed in the latest fashions, wasting his days in conspicuous consumption. A poor man named Lazarus, covered with sores, had been dumped on his doorstep. All he lived for was to get a meal from scraps off the rich man's table. His best friends were the dogs who came and licked his sores.

"Then he died, this poor man, and was taken up by the angels to the lap of Abraham. The rich man also died and was buried. In hell and in torment, he looked up and saw Abraham in the distance and Lazarus in his lap. He called out, 'Father Abraham, mercy! Have mercy! Send Lazarus to dip his finger in water to cool my tongue. I'm in agony in this fire.'

"But Abraham said, 'Child, remember that in your lifetime you got the good things and Lazarus the bad things.

KING JAMES VERSION

evil things: but now he is comforted, and thou art tormented.

26 And beside all this, between us and you there is a great gulf fixed: so that they which would pass from hence to you cannot; neither can they pass to us, that *would come* from thence.

27 Then he said, I pray thee therefore, father, that thou wouldest send him to my father's house:

28 For I have five brethren; that he may testify unto them, lest they also come into this place of torment.

29 Abraham saith unto him, They have Moses and the prophets; let them hear them.

30 And he said, Nay, father Abraham: but if one went unto them from the dead, they will repent.

31 And he said unto him, If they hear not Moses and the prophets, neither will they be persuaded, though one rose from the dead.

17 Then said he unto the disciples, It is impossible but that offences will come: but woe *unto him*, through whom they come!

2 It were better for him that a millstone were hanged about his neck, and he cast into the sea, than that he should offend one of these little ones.

3 Take heed to yourselves: If thy brother trespass against thee, rebuke him; and if he repent, forgive him.

4 And if he trespass against thee seven times in a day,

NEW AMERICAN STANDARD BIBLE

bad things; but now he is being comforted here, and you are in agony.

26 'And besides all this, between us and you there is a great chasm fixed, so that those who wish to come over from here to you will not be able, and *that* none may cross over from there to us.'

27 "And he said, 'Then I beg you, father, that you send him to my father's house—

28 for I have five brothers—in order that he may warn them, so that they will not also come to this place of torment.'

29 "But Abraham *said, 'They have Moses and the Prophets; let them hear them.'

30 "But he said, 'No, father Abraham, but if someone goes to them from the dead, they will repent!'

31 "But he said to him, 'If they do not listen to Moses and the Prophets, they will not be persuaded even if someone rises from the dead.' "

Instructions

17 He said to His disciples, "It is inevitable that stumbling blocks come, but woe to him through whom they come!

2 "It would be better for him if a millstone were hung around his neck and he were thrown into the sea, than that he would cause one of these little ones to stumble.

3 "Be on your guard! If your brother sins, rebuke him; and if he repents, forgive him.

4 "And if he sins against you seven times a day, and

NEW CENTURY VERSION

life, but bad things happened to Lazarus. Now he is comforted here, and you are suffering. [26]Besides, there is a big pit between you and us, so no one can cross over to you, and no one can leave there and come here.' [27]The rich man said, 'Father, then please send Lazarus to my father's house. [28]I have five brothers, and Lazarus could warn them so that they will not come to this place of pain.' [29]But Abraham said, 'They have the law of Moses and the writings of the prophets; let them learn from them.' [30]The rich man said, 'No, father Abraham! If someone goes to them from the dead, they would believe and change their hearts and lives.' [31]But Abraham said to him, 'If they will not listen to Moses and the prophets, they will not listen to someone who comes back from the dead.' "

Sin and Forgiveness

17 Jesus said to his followers, "Things that cause people to sin will happen, but how terrible for the person who causes them to happen! [2]It would be better for you to be thrown into the sea with a large stone around your neck than to cause one of these little ones to sin. [3]So be careful!

"If another follower sins, warn him, and if he is sorry and stops sinning, forgive him. [4]If he sins against you

CONTEMPORARY ENGLISH VERSION

had everything bad. Now he is happy, and you are in pain. [26]And besides, there is a deep ditch between us, and no one from either side can cross over."

[27]But the rich man said, "Abraham, then please send Lazarus to my father's home. [28]Let him warn my five brothers, so they won't come to this horrible place."

[29]Abraham answered, "Your brothers can read what Moses and the prophets[f] wrote. They should pay attention to that."

[30]Then the rich man said, "No, that's not enough! If only someone from the dead would go to them, they would listen and turn to God."

[31]So Abraham said, "If they won't pay attention to Moses and the prophets, they won't listen even to someone who comes back from the dead."

Faith and Service (Matthew 18.6, 7, 21, 22; Mark 9.42)

17 Jesus said to his disciples:

There will always be something that causes people to sin. But anyone who causes them to sin is in for trouble. A person who causes even one of my little followers to sin [2]would be better off thrown into the ocean with a heavy stone tied around their neck. [3]So be careful what you do.

Correct any followers[a] of mine who sin, and forgive the ones who say they are sorry. [4]Even if one of them

[f] 16.29 *Moses and the prophets*: The Jewish Scriptures, that is, the Old Testament. [a] 17.3 *followers*: The Greek text has "brothers," which is often used in the New Testament for followers of Jesus.

NEW INTERNATIONAL VERSION

received bad things, but now he is comforted here and you are in agony. [26]And besides all this, between us and you a great chasm has been fixed, so that those who want to go from here to you cannot, nor can anyone cross over from there to us.'

[27]"He answered, 'Then I beg you, father, send Lazarus to my father's house, [28]for I have five brothers. Let him warn them, so that they will not also come to this place of torment.'

[29]"Abraham replied, 'They have Moses and the Prophets; let them listen to them.'

[30]" 'No, father Abraham,' he said, 'but if someone from the dead goes to them, they will repent.'

[31]"He said to him, 'If they do not listen to Moses and the Prophets, they will not be convinced even if someone rises from the dead.' "

Sin, Faith, Duty

17 Jesus said to his disciples: "Things that cause people to sin are bound to come, but woe to that person through whom they come. [2]It would be better for him to be thrown into the sea with a millstone tied around his neck than for him to cause one of these little ones to sin. [3]So watch yourselves.

"If your brother sins, rebuke him, and if he repents, forgive him. [4]If he sins against you seven times in a day, and

NEW LIVING TRANSLATION

had nothing. So now he is here being comforted, and you are in anguish. [26]And besides, there is a great chasm separating us. Anyone who wanted to cross over to you from here is stopped at its edge, and no one there can cross over to us.'

[27]"Then the rich man said, 'Please, Father Abraham, send him to my father's home. [28]For I have five brothers, and I want him to warn them about this place of torment so they won't have to come here when they die.'

[29]"But Abraham said, 'Moses and the prophets have warned them. Your brothers can read their writings anytime they want to.'

[30]"The rich man replied, 'No, Father Abraham! But if someone is sent to them from the dead, then they will turn from their sins.'

[31]"But Abraham said, 'If they won't listen to Moses and the prophets, they won't listen even if someone rises from the dead.' "

Teachings about Forgiveness and Faith

17 One day Jesus said to his disciples, "There will always be temptations to sin, but how terrible it will be for the person who does the tempting. [2]It would be better to be thrown into the sea with a large millstone tied around the neck than to face the punishment in store for harming one of these little ones. [3]I am warning you! If another believer* sins, rebuke him; then if he repents, forgive him. [4]Even if he wrongs you seven times a day and

17:3 Greek *your brother.*

NEW KING JAMES VERSION

Lazarus evil things; but now he is comforted and you are tormented. [26]And besides all this, between us and you there is a great gulf fixed, so that those who want to pass from here to you cannot, nor can those from there pass to us.'

[27]"Then he said, 'I beg you therefore, father, that you would send him to my father's house, [28]for I have five brothers, that he may testify to them, lest they also come to this place of torment.' [29]Abraham said to him, 'They have Moses and the prophets; let them hear them.' [30]And he said, 'No, father Abraham; but if one goes to them from the dead, they will repent.' [31]But he said to him, 'If they do not hear Moses and the prophets, neither will they be persuaded though one rise from the dead.' "

Jesus Warns of Offenses

17 Then He said to the disciples, "It is impossible that no offenses should come, but woe *to him* through whom they do come! [2]It would be better for him if a millstone were hung around his neck, and he were thrown into the sea, than that he should offend one of these little ones. [3]Take heed to yourselves. If your brother sins against you,[a] rebuke him; and if he repents, forgive him. [4]And if he sins against you seven times in a day, and seven times

17:3 [a] NU-Text omits *against you.*

THE MESSAGE

It's not like that here. Here he's consoled and you're tormented. Besides, in all these matters there is a huge chasm set between us so that no one can go from us to you even if he wanted to, nor can anyone cross over from you to us.'

"The rich man said, 'Then let me ask you, Father: Send him to the house of my father where I have five brothers, so he can tell them the score and warn them so they won't end up here in this place of torment.'

"Abraham answered, 'They have Moses and the Prophets to tell them the score. Let them listen to them.'

" 'I know, Father Abraham,' he said, 'but they're not listening. If someone came back to them from the dead, they would change their ways.'

"Abraham replied, 'If they won't listen to Moses and the Prophets, they're not going to be convinced by someone who rises from the dead.' "

A Kernel of Faith

17 He said to his disciples, "Hard trials and temptations are bound to come, but too bad for whoever brings them on! Better to wear a millstone necklace and take a swim in the deep blue sea than give even one of these dear little ones a hard time!

"Be alert. If you see your friend going wrong, correct him. If he responds, forgive him. Even if it's personal against you and repeated seven times through the day,

KING JAMES VERSION

and seven times in a day turn again to thee, saying, I repent; thou shalt forgive him.

5 And the apostles said unto the Lord, Increase our faith.

6 And the Lord said, If ye had faith as a grain of mustard seed, ye might say unto this sycamine tree, Be thou plucked up by the root, and be thou planted in the sea; and it should obey you.

7 But which of you, having a servant plowing or feeding cattle, will say unto him by and by, when he is come from the field, Go and sit down to meat?

8 And will not rather say unto him, Make ready wherewith I may sup, and gird thyself, and serve me, till I have eaten and drunken; and afterward thou shalt eat and drink?

9 Doth he thank that servant because he did the things that were commanded him? I trow not.

10 So likewise ye, when ye shall have done all those things which are commanded you, say, We are unprofitable servants: we have done that which was our duty to do.

11 ¶ And it came to pass, as he went to Jerusalem, that he passed through the midst of Samaria and Galilee.

12 And as he entered into a certain village, there met him ten men that were lepers, which stood afar off:

13 And they lifted up *their* voices, and said, Jesus, Master, have mercy on us.

NEW AMERICAN STANDARD BIBLE

returns to you seven times, saying, 'I repent,' forgive him."

5 The apostles said to the Lord, "Increase our faith!"

6 And the Lord said, "If you had faith like a mustard seed, you would say to this mulberry tree, 'Be uprooted and be planted in the sea'; and it would obey you.

7 "Which of you, having a slave plowing or tending sheep, will say to him when he has come in from the field, 'Come immediately and sit down to eat'?

8 "But will he not say to him, 'Prepare something for me to eat, and *properly* clothe yourself and serve me while I eat and drink; and afterward you may eat and drink'?

9 "He does not thank the slave because he did the things which were commanded, does he?

10 "So you too, when you do all the things which are commanded you, say, 'We are unworthy slaves; we have done *only* that which we ought to have done.' "

Ten Lepers Cleansed

11 While He was on the way to Jerusalem, He was passing between Samaria and Galilee.

12 As He entered a village, ten leprous men who stood at a distance met Him;

13 and they raised their voices, saying, "Jesus, Master, have mercy on us!"

NEW CENTURY VERSION

seven times in one day and says that he is sorry each time, forgive him."

How Big Is Your Faith?

5The apostles said to the Lord, "Give us more faith!"

6The Lord said, "If your faith were the size of a mustard seed, you could say to this mulberry tree, 'Dig yourself up and plant yourself in the sea,' and it would obey you.

Be Good Servants

7"Suppose one of you has a servant who has been plowing the ground or caring for the sheep. When the servant comes in from working in the field, would you say, 'Come in and sit down to eat'? 8No, you would say to him, 'Prepare something for me to eat. Then get yourself ready and serve me. After I finish eating and drinking, you can eat.' 9The servant does not get any special thanks for doing what his master commanded. 10It is the same with you. When you have done everything you are told to do, you should say, 'We are unworthy servants; we have only done the work we should do.' "

Be Thankful

11While Jesus was on his way to Jerusalem, he was going through the area between Samaria and Galilee. 12As he came into a small town, ten men who had a skin disease met him there. They did not come close to Jesus 13but called to him, "Jesus! Master! Have mercy on us!"

CONTEMPORARY ENGLISH VERSION

mistreats you seven times in one day and says, "I am sorry," you should still forgive that person.

5The apostles said to the Lord, "Make our faith stronger!"

6Jesus replied:

If you had faith no bigger than a tiny mustard seed, you could tell this mulberry tree to pull itself up, roots and all, and to plant itself in the ocean. And it would!

7If your servant comes in from plowing or from taking care of the sheep, would you say, "Welcome! Come on in and have something to eat"? 8No, you wouldn't say that. You would say, "Fix me something to eat. Get ready to serve me, so I can have my meal. Then later on you can eat and drink." 9Servants don't deserve special thanks for doing what they are supposed to do. 10And that's how it should be with you. When you've done all you should, then say, "We are merely servants, and we have simply done our duty."

Ten Men with Leprosy

11On his way to Jerusalem, Jesus went along the border between Samaria and Galilee. 12As he was going into a village, ten men with leprosy[b] came toward him. They stood at a distance 13and shouted, "Jesus, Master, have pity on us!"

[b] 17.12 *leprosy*: See the note at 4.27.

NEW INTERNATIONAL VERSION

seven times comes back to you and says, 'I repent,' forgive him."

5The apostles said to the Lord, "Increase our faith!"

6He replied, "If you have faith as small as a mustard seed, you can say to this mulberry tree, 'Be uprooted and planted in the sea,' and it will obey you.

7"Suppose one of you had a servant plowing or looking after the sheep. Would he say to the servant when he comes in from the field, 'Come along now and sit down to eat'? 8Would he not rather say, 'Prepare my supper, get yourself ready and wait on me while I eat and drink; after that you may eat and drink'? 9Would he thank the servant because he did what he was told to do? 10So you also, when you have done everything you were told to do, should say, 'We are unworthy servants; we have only done our duty.' "

Ten Healed of Leprosy

11Now on his way to Jerusalem, Jesus traveled along the border between Samaria and Galilee. 12As he was going into a village, ten men who had leprosy[a] met him. They stood at a distance 13and called out in a loud voice, "Jesus, Master, have pity on us!"

[a] *12* The Greek word was used for various diseases affecting the skin—not necessarily leprosy.

NEW LIVING TRANSLATION

each time turns again and asks forgiveness, forgive him."

5One day the apostles said to the Lord, "We need more faith; tell us how to get it."

6"Even if you had faith as small as a mustard seed," the Lord answered, "you could say to this mulberry tree, 'May God uproot you and throw you into the sea,' and it would obey you!

7"When a servant comes in from plowing or taking care of sheep, he doesn't just sit down and eat. 8He must first prepare his master's meal and serve him his supper before eating his own. 9And the servant is not even thanked, because he is merely doing what he is supposed to do. 10In the same way, when you obey me you should say, 'We are not worthy of praise. We are servants who have simply done our duty.' "

Ten Healed of Leprosy

11As Jesus continued on toward Jerusalem, he reached the border between Galilee and Samaria. 12As he entered a village there, ten lepers stood at a distance, 13crying out, "Jesus, Master, have mercy on us!"

NEW KING JAMES VERSION

in a day returns to you,[b] saying, 'I repent,' you shall forgive him."

Faith and Duty

5And the apostles said to the Lord, "Increase our faith."

6So the Lord said, "If you have faith as a mustard seed, you can say to this mulberry tree, 'Be pulled up by the roots and be planted in the sea,' and it would obey you. 7And which of you, having a servant plowing or tending sheep, will say to him when he has come in from the field, 'Come at once and sit down to eat'? 8But will he not rather say to him, 'Prepare something for my supper, and gird yourself and serve me till I have eaten and drunk, and afterward you will eat and drink'? 9Does he thank that servant because he did the things that were commanded him? I think not.[c] 10So likewise you, when you have done all those things which you are commanded, say, 'We are unprofitable servants. We have done what was our duty to do.' "

Ten Lepers Cleansed

11Now it happened as He went to Jerusalem that He passed through the midst of Samaria and Galilee. 12Then as He entered a certain village, there met Him ten men who were lepers, who stood afar off. 13And they lifted up *their* voices and said, "Jesus, Master, have mercy on us!"

17:4 [b] M-Text omits *to you.* 17:9 [c] NU-Text ends verse with *commanded;* M-Text omits *him.*

THE MESSAGE

and seven times he says, 'I'm sorry, I won't do it again,' forgive him."

The apostles came up and said to the Master, "Give us more faith."

But the Master said, "You don't need *more* faith. There is no 'more' or 'less' in faith. If you have a bare kernel of faith, say the size of a poppy seed, you could say to this sycamore tree, 'Go jump in the lake,' and it would do it.

"Suppose one of you has a servant who comes in from plowing the field or tending the sheep. Would you take his coat, set the table, and say, 'Sit down and eat'? Wouldn't you be more likely to say, 'Prepare dinner; change your clothes and wait table for me until I've finished my coffee; then go to the kitchen and have your supper'? Does the servant get special thanks for doing what's expected of him? It's the same with you. When you've done everything expected of you, be matter-of-fact and say, 'The work is done. What we were told to do, we did.' "

It happened that as he made his way toward Jerusalem, he crossed over the border between Samaria and Galilee. As he entered a village, ten men, all lepers, met him. They kept their distance but raised their voices, calling out, "Jesus, Master, have mercy on us!"

KING JAMES VERSION

14 And when he saw *them*, he said unto them, Go shew yourselves unto the priests. And it came to pass, that, as they went, they were cleansed.

15 And one of them, when he saw that he was healed, turned back, and with a loud voice glorified God,

16 And fell down on *his* face at his feet, giving him thanks: and he was a Samaritan.

17 And Jesus answering said, Were there not ten cleansed? but where *are* the nine?

18 There are not found that returned to give glory to God, save this stranger.

19 And he said unto him, Arise, go thy way: thy faith hath made thee whole.

20 ¶ And when he was demanded of the Pharisees, when the kingdom of God should come, he answered them and said, The kingdom of God cometh not with observation:

21 Neither shall they say, Lo here! or, lo there! for, behold, the kingdom of God is within you.

22 And he said unto the disciples, The days will come, when ye shall desire to see one of the days of the Son of man, and ye shall not see *it*.

23 And they shall say to you, See here; or, see there: go not after *them*, nor follow *them*.

24 For as the lightning, that lighteneth out of the one *part* under heaven, shineth unto the other *part* under heaven; so shall also the Son of man be in his day.

NEW AMERICAN STANDARD BIBLE

14 When He saw them, He said to them, "Go and show yourselves to the priests." And as they were going, they were cleansed.

15 Now one of them, when he saw that he had been healed, turned back, glorifying God with a loud voice,

16 and he fell on his face at His feet, giving thanks to Him. And he was a Samaritan.

17 Then Jesus answered and said, "Were there not ten cleansed? But the nine—where are they?

18 "Was no one found who returned to give glory to God, except this foreigner?"

19 And He said to him, "Stand up and go; your faith [1]has made you well."

20 Now having been questioned by the Pharisees as to when the kingdom of God was coming, He answered them and said, "The kingdom of God is not coming with signs to be observed;

21 nor will they say, 'Look, here *it is!*' or, 'There *it is!*' For behold, the kingdom of God is in your midst."

Second Coming Foretold

22 And He said to the disciples, "The days will come when you will long to see one of the days of the Son of Man, and you will not see it.

23 "They will say to you, 'Look there! Look here!' Do not go away, and do not run after *them*.

24 "For just like the lightning, when it flashes out of one part of the sky, shines to the other part of the sky, so will the Son of Man be in His day.

17:19 [1] Lit *has saved you*

NEW CENTURY VERSION

14 When Jesus saw the men, he said, "Go and show yourselves to the priests."[a]

As the ten men were going, they were healed. 15 When one of them saw that he was healed, he went back to Jesus, praising God in a loud voice. 16 Then he bowed down at Jesus' feet and thanked him. (And this man was a Samaritan.) 17 Jesus said, "Weren't ten men healed? Where are the other nine? 18 Is this Samaritan the only one who came back to thank God?" 19 Then Jesus said to him, "Stand up and go on your way. You were healed because you believed."

God's Kingdom Is Within You

20 Some of the Pharisees asked Jesus, "When will the kingdom of God come?"

Jesus answered, "God's kingdom is coming, but not in a way that you will be able to see with your eyes. 21 People will not say, 'Look, here it is!' or, 'There it is!' because God's kingdom is within[b] you."

22 Then Jesus said to his followers, "The time will come when you will want very much to see one of the days of the Son of Man. But you will not see it. 23 People will say to you, 'Look, there he is!' or, 'Look, here he is!' Stay where you are; don't go away and search.

When Jesus Comes Again

24 "When the Son of Man comes again, he will shine like lightning, which flashes across the sky and lights it up

17:14 [a] **show...priests** The law of Moses said a priest must say when a Jewish person with a skin disease became well. 17:21 [b] **within** Or "among."

CONTEMPORARY ENGLISH VERSION

14 Jesus looked at them and said, "Go show yourselves to the priests."[c]

On their way they were healed. 15 When one of them discovered that he was healed, he came back, shouting praises to God. 16 He bowed down at the feet of Jesus and thanked him. The man was from the country of Samaria.

17 Jesus asked, "Weren't ten men healed? Where are the other nine? 18 Why was this foreigner the only one who came back to thank God?" 19 Then Jesus told the man, "You may get up and go. Your faith has made you well."

God's Kingdom (Matthew 24.23-28, 37-41)

20 Some Pharisees asked Jesus when God's kingdom would come. He answered, "God's kingdom isn't something you can see. 21 There is no use saying, 'Look! Here it is' or 'Look! There it is.' God's kingdom is here with you."[d]

22 Jesus said to his disciples:

The time will come when you will long to see one of the days of the Son of Man, but you will not. 23 When people say to you, "Look there," or "Look here," don't go looking for him. 24 The day of the Son of Man will be like lightning flashing across the sky. 25 But first he must

[c] **17.14** *show yourselves to the priests*: See the note at 5.14.
[d] **17.21** *here with you*: Or "in your hearts."

NEW INTERNATIONAL VERSION

14When he saw them, he said, "Go, show yourselves to the priests." And as they went, they were cleansed.

15One of them, when he saw he was healed, came back, praising God in a loud voice. 16He threw himself at Jesus' feet and thanked him—and he was a Samaritan.

17Jesus asked, "Were not all ten cleansed? Where are the other nine? 18Was no one found to return and give praise to God except this foreigner?" 19Then he said to him, "Rise and go; your faith has made you well."

The Coming of the Kingdom of God

20Once, having been asked by the Pharisees when the kingdom of God would come, Jesus replied, "The kingdom of God does not come with your careful observation, 21nor will people say, 'Here it is,' or 'There it is,' because the kingdom of God is within[b] you."

22Then he said to his disciples, "The time is coming when you will long to see one of the days of the Son of Man, but you will not see it. 23Men will tell you, 'There he is!' or 'Here he is!' Do not go running off after them. 24For the Son of Man in his day[c] will be like the lightning, which flashes and lights up the sky from one end to the other.

[b] 21 Or *among* [c] 24 Some manuscripts do not have *in his day.*

NEW LIVING TRANSLATION

14He looked at them and said, "Go show yourselves to the priests." And as they went, their leprosy disappeared.

15One of them, when he saw that he was healed, came back to Jesus, shouting, "Praise God, I'm healed!" 16He fell face down on the ground at Jesus' feet, thanking him for what he had done. This man was a Samaritan.

17Jesus asked, "Didn't I heal ten men? Where are the other nine? 18Does only this foreigner return to give glory to God?" 19And Jesus said to the man, "Stand up and go. Your faith has made you well."

The Coming of the Kingdom

20One day the Pharisees asked Jesus, "When will the Kingdom of God come?"

Jesus replied, "The Kingdom of God isn't ushered in with visible signs.* 21You won't be able to say, 'Here it is!' or 'It's over there!' For the Kingdom of God is among you.*"

22Later he talked again about this with his disciples. "The time is coming when you will long to share in the days of the Son of Man, but you won't be able to," he said. 23"Reports will reach you that the Son of Man has returned and that he is in this place or that. Don't believe such reports or go out to look for him. 24For when the Son of Man returns, you will know it beyond all doubt. It will be as evident as the lightning that flashes across the sky.

17:20 Or *by your speculations.* 17:21 Or *within you.*

NEW KING JAMES VERSION

14So when He saw *them,* He said to them, "Go, show yourselves to the priests." And so it was that as they went, they were cleansed.

15And one of them, when he saw that he was healed, returned, and with a loud voice glorified God, 16and fell down on *his* face at His feet, giving Him thanks. And he was a Samaritan.

17So Jesus answered and said, "Were there not ten cleansed? But where *are* the nine? 18Were there not any found who returned to give glory to God except this foreigner?" 19And He said to him, "Arise, go your way. Your faith has made you well."

The Coming of the Kingdom

20Now when He was asked by the Pharisees when the kingdom of God would come, He answered them and said, "The kingdom of God does not come with observation; 21nor will they say, 'See here!' or 'See there!'[d] For indeed, the kingdom of God is within you."

22Then He said to the disciples, "The days will come when you will desire to see one of the days of the Son of Man, and you will not see *it.* 23And they will say to you, 'Look here!' or 'Look there!'[e] Do not go after *them* or follow *them.* 24For as the lightning that flashes out of one *part* under heaven shines to the other *part* under heaven, so also the Son of Man will be in His day. 25But first He

17:21 [d] NU-Text reverses *here* and *there.* 17:23 [e] NU-Text reverses *here* and *there.*

THE MESSAGE

Taking a good look at them, he said, "Go, show yourselves to the priests."

They went, and while still on their way, became clean. One of them, when he realized that he was healed, turned around and came back, shouting his gratitude, glorifying God. He kneeled at Jesus' feet, so grateful. He couldn't thank him enough—and he was a Samaritan.

Jesus said, "Were not ten healed? Where are the nine? Can none be found to come back and give glory to God except this outsider?" Then he said to him, "Get up. On your way. Your faith has healed and saved you."

When the Son of Man Arrives

Jesus, grilled by the Pharisees on when the kingdom of God would come, answered, "The kingdom of God doesn't come by counting the days on the calendar. Nor when someone says, 'Look here!' or, 'There it is!' And why? Because God's kingdom is already among you."

He went on to say to his disciples, "The days are coming when you are going to be desperately homesick for just a glimpse of one of the days of the Son of Man, and you won't see a thing. And they'll say to you, 'Look over there!' or, 'Look here!' Don't fall for any of that nonsense. The arrival of the Son of Man is not something you go out to see. He simply comes.

"You know how the whole sky lights up from a single flash of lightning? That's how it will be on the Day of the

KING JAMES VERSION

25 But first must he suffer many things, and be rejected of this generation.

26 And as it was in the days of Noe, so shall it be also in the days of the Son of man.

27 They did eat, they drank, they married wives, they were given in marriage, until the day that Noe entered into the ark, and the flood came, and destroyed them all.

28 Likewise also as it was in the days of Lot; they did eat, they drank, they bought, they sold, they planted, they builded;

29 But the same day that Lot went out of Sodom it rained fire and brimstone from heaven, and destroyed *them* all.

30 Even thus shall it be in the day when the Son of man is revealed.

31 In that day, he which shall be upon the housetop, and his stuff in the house, let him not come down to take it away: and he that is in the field, let him likewise not return back.

32 Remember Lot's wife.

33 Whosoever shall seek to save his life shall lose it; and whosoever shall lose his life shall preserve it.

34 I tell you, in that night there shall be two *men* in one bed; the one shall be taken, and the other shall be left.

35 Two *women* shall be grinding together; the one shall be taken, and the other left.

36 Two *men* shall be in the field; the one shall be taken, and the other left.

37 And they answered and said unto him, Where, Lord?

NEW AMERICAN STANDARD BIBLE

25 "But first He must suffer many things and be rejected by this generation.

26 "And just as it happened in the days of Noah, so it will be also in the days of the Son of Man:

27 they were eating, they were drinking, they were marrying, they were being given in marriage, until the day that Noah entered the ark, and the flood came and destroyed them all.

28 "It was the same as happened in the days of Lot: they were eating, they were drinking, they were buying, they were selling, they were planting, they were building;

29 but on the day that Lot went out from Sodom it rained fire and brimstone from heaven and destroyed them all.

30 "It will be just the same on the day that the Son of Man is revealed.

31 "On that day, the one who is on the housetop and whose goods are in the house must not go down to take them out; and likewise the one who is in the field must not turn back.

32 "Remember Lot's wife.

33 "Whoever seeks to keep his life will lose it, and whoever loses *his life* will preserve it.

34 "I tell you, on that night there will be two in one bed; one will be taken and the other will be left.

35 "There will be two women grinding at the same place; one will be taken and the other will be left.

36 ["[2]Two men will be in the field; one will be taken and the other will be left."]

37 And answering they *said to Him, "Where, Lord?"

17:36 [2] Early mss do not contain this v

NEW CENTURY VERSION

from one side to the other. 25But first he must suffer many
things and be rejected by the people of this time. 26When
the Son of Man comes again, it will be as it was when
Noah lived. 27People were eating, drinking, marrying, and
giving their children to be married until the day Noah
entered the boat. Then the flood came and killed them all.
28It will be the same as during the time of Lot. People were
eating, drinking, buying, selling, planting, and building.
29But the day Lot left Sodom,[c] fire and sulfur rained down
from the sky and killed them all. 30This is how it will be
when the Son of Man comes again.

31"On that day, a person who is on the roof and whose
belongings are in the house should not go inside to get
them. A person who is in the field should not go back
home. 32Remember Lot's wife.[d] 33Those who try to keep
their lives will lose them. But those who give up their lives
will save them. 34I tell you, on that night two people will
be sleeping in one bed; one will be taken and the other will
be left. 35There will be two women grinding grain together;
one will be taken, and the other will be left." 36[e]

37The followers asked Jesus, "Where will this be, Lord?"

17:29 [c] **Sodom** City that God destroyed because the people were so evil.
17:32 [d] **Lot's wife** A story about what happened to Lot's wife is found in Genesis 19:15–17, 26. 17:36 [e] **Verse 36** A few Greek copies add verse 36: "Two people will be in the field. One will be taken, and the other will be left."

CONTEMPORARY ENGLISH VERSION

suffer terribly and be rejected by the people of today.
26When the Son of Man comes, things will be just as
they were when Noah lived. 27People were eating, drink-
ing, and getting married right up to the day when Noah
went into the big boat. Then the flood came and
drowned everyone on earth.

28When Lot[e] lived, people were also eating and drink-
ing. They were buying, selling, planting, and building.
29But on the very day Lot left Sodom, fiery flames poured
down from the sky and killed everyone. 30The same will
happen on the day when the Son of Man appears.

31At that time no one on a rooftop[f] should go down
into the house to get anything. No one in a field should
go back to the house for anything. 32Remember what
happened to Lot's wife.[g]

33People who try to save their lives will lose them,
and those who lose their lives will save them. 34On that
night two people will be sleeping in the same bed, but
only one will be taken. The other will be left. 35-36Two
women will be together grinding wheat, but only one
will be taken. The other will be left.[h]

37Then Jesus' disciples spoke up, "But where will this
happen, Lord?"

[e] 17.27,28 *Noah . . . Lot*: When God destroyed the earth by a flood, he saved Noah and his family. And when God destroyed the cities of Sodom and Gomorrah and the evil people who lived there, he rescued Lot and his family (see Genesis 19.1-29). [f] 17.31 *rooftop*: See the note at 5.19. [g] 17.32 *what happened to Lot's wife*: She turned into a block of salt when she disobeyed God (see Genesis 19.26). [h] 17.35,36 *will be left*: Some manuscripts add, "Two men will be in the same field, but only one will be taken. The other will be left."

NEW INTERNATIONAL VERSION

25But first he must suffer many things and be rejected by this generation.

26"Just as it was in the days of Noah, so also will it be in the days of the Son of Man. 27People were eating, drinking, marrying and being given in marriage up to the day Noah entered the ark. Then the flood came and destroyed them all.

28"It was the same in the days of Lot. People were eating and drinking, buying and selling, planting and building. 29But the day Lot left Sodom, fire and sulfur rained down from heaven and destroyed them all.

30"It will be just like this on the day the Son of Man is revealed. 31On that day no one who is on the roof of his house, with his goods inside, should go down to get them. Likewise, no one in the field should go back for anything. 32Remember Lot's wife! 33Whoever tries to keep his life will lose it, and whoever loses his life will preserve it. 34I tell you, on that night two people will be in one bed; one will be taken and the other left. 35Two women will be grinding grain together; one will be taken and the other left.[d]"

37"Where, Lord?" they asked.

[d] 35 Some manuscripts *left.* 36*Two men will be in the field; one will be taken and the other left.*

NEW LIVING TRANSLATION

25But first the Son of Man must suffer terribly* and be rejected by this generation.

26"When the Son of Man returns, the world will be like the people were in Noah's day. 27In those days before the flood, the people enjoyed banquets and parties and weddings right up to the time Noah entered his boat and the flood came to destroy them all.

28"And the world will be as it was in the days of Lot. People went about their daily business—eating and drinking, buying and selling, farming and building—29until the morning Lot left Sodom. Then fire and burning sulfur rained down from heaven and destroyed them all. 30Yes, it will be 'business as usual' right up to the hour when the Son of Man returns.* 31On that day a person outside the house* must not go into the house to pack. A person in the field must not return to town. 32Remember what happened to Lot's wife! 33Whoever clings to this life will lose it, and whoever loses this life will save it. 34That night two people will be asleep in one bed; one will be taken away, and the other will be left. 35Two women will be grinding flour together at the mill; one will be taken, the other left.*"

37"Lord, where will this happen?" the disciples asked.

17:25 Or *suffer many things.* **17:30** Or *on the day the Son of Man is revealed.* **17:31** Greek *on the roof.* **17:35** Some manuscripts add verse 36, *Two men will be working in the field; one will be taken, the other left.*

NEW KING JAMES VERSION

must suffer many things and be rejected by this generation. 26And as it was in the days of Noah, so it will be also in the days of the Son of Man: 27They ate, they drank, they married wives, they were given in marriage, until the day that Noah entered the ark, and the flood came and destroyed them all. 28Likewise as it was also in the days of Lot: They ate, they drank, they bought, they sold, they planted, they built; 29but on the day that Lot went out of Sodom it rained fire and brimstone from heaven and destroyed *them* all. 30Even so will it be in the day when the Son of Man is revealed.

31"In that day, he who is on the housetop, and his goods *are* in the house, let him not come down to take them away. And likewise the one who is in the field, let him not turn back. 32Remember Lot's wife. 33Whoever seeks to save his life will lose it, and whoever loses his life will preserve it. 34I tell you, in that night there will be two *men* in one bed: the one will be taken and the other will be left. 35Two *women* will be grinding together: the one will be taken and the other left. 36Two *men* will be in the field: the one will be taken and the other left."[f]

37And they answered and said to Him, "Where, Lord?"

17:36 [f] NU-Text and M-Text omit verse 36.

THE MESSAGE

Son of Man. But first it's necessary that he suffer many things and be turned down by the people of today.

"The time of the Son of Man will be just like the time of Noah—everyone carrying on as usual, having a good time right up to the day Noah boarded the ship. They suspected nothing until the flood hit and swept everything away.

"It was the same in the time of Lot—the people carrying on, having a good time, business as usual right up to the day Lot walked out of Sodom and a firestorm swept down and burned everything to a crisp. That's how it will be—sudden, total—when the Son of Man is revealed.

"When the Day arrives and you're out working in the yard, don't run into the house to get anything. And if you're out in the field, don't go back and get your coat. Remember what happened to Lot's wife! If you grasp and cling to life on your terms, you'll lose it, but if you let that life go, you'll get life on God's terms.

"On that Day, two men will be in the same boat fishing—one taken, the other left. Two women will be working in the same kitchen—one taken, the other left."

Trying to take all this in, the disciples said, "Master, where?"

KING JAMES VERSION

And he said unto them, Wheresoever the body *is*, thither will the eagles be gathered together.

18 And he spake a parable unto them *to this end*, that men ought always to pray, and not to faint;

2 Saying, There was in a city a judge, which feared not God, neither regarded man:

3 And there was a widow in that city; and she came unto him, saying, Avenge me of mine adversary.

4 And he would not for a while: but afterward he said within himself, Though I fear not God, nor regard man;

5 Yet because this widow troubleth me, I will avenge her, lest by her continual coming she weary me.

6 And the Lord said, Hear what the unjust judge saith.

7 And shall not God avenge his own elect, which cry day and night unto him, though he bear long with them?

8 I tell you that he will avenge them speedily. Nevertheless when the Son of man cometh, shall he find faith on the earth?

9 ¶ And he spake this parable unto certain which trusted in themselves that they were righteous, and despised others:

NEW AMERICAN STANDARD BIBLE

And He said to them, "Where the body *is*, there also the vultures will be gathered."

Parables on Prayer

18 Now He was telling them a parable to show that at all times they ought to pray and not to lose heart,

2 saying, "In a certain city there was a judge who did not fear God and did not respect man.

3 "There was a widow in that city, and she kept coming to him, saying, 'Give me legal protection from my opponent.'

4 "For a while he was unwilling; but afterward he said to himself, 'Even though I do not fear God nor respect man,

5 yet because this widow bothers me, I will give her legal protection, otherwise by continually coming she will wear me out.' "

6 And the Lord said, "Hear what the unrighteous judge *said;

7 now, will not God bring about justice for His elect who cry to Him day and night, and will He delay long over them?

8 "I tell you that He will bring about justice for them quickly. However, when the Son of Man comes, will He find faith on the earth?"

The Pharisee and the Publican

9 And He also told this parable to some people who trusted in themselves that they were righteous, and viewed others with contempt:

NEW CENTURY VERSION

Jesus answered, "Where there is a dead body, there the vultures will gather."

God Will Answer His People

18 Then Jesus used this story to teach his followers that they should always pray and never lose hope.
2"In a certain town there was a judge who did not respect
God or care about people. 3In that same town there was a
widow who kept coming to this judge, saying, 'Give me my
rights against my enemy.' 4For a while the judge refused
to help her. But afterwards, he thought to himself, 'Even
though I don't respect God or care about people, 5I will see
that she gets her rights. Otherwise she will continue to
bother me until I am worn out.' "

6The Lord said, "Listen to what the unfair judge said.
7God will always give what is right to his people who cry
to him night and day, and he will not be slow to answer
them. 8I tell you, God will help his people quickly. But
when the Son of Man comes again, will he find those on
earth who believe in him?"

Being Right with God

9Jesus told this story to some people who thought they
were very good and looked down on everyone else: 10"A

CONTEMPORARY ENGLISH VERSION

Jesus said, "Where there is a corpse, there will always be buzzards."[i]

A Widow and a Judge

18 Jesus told his disciples a story about how they should keep on praying and never give up:
2In a town there was once a judge who didn't fear God
or care about people. 3In that same town there was a
widow who kept going to the judge and saying, "Make
sure that I get fair treatment in court."

4For a while the judge refused to do anything. Finally,
he said to himself, "Even though I don't fear God or care
about people, 5I will help this widow because she keeps on
bothering me. If I don't help her, she will wear me out."

6The Lord said:

Think about what that crooked judge said. 7Won't God
protect his chosen ones who pray to him day and night?
Won't he be concerned for them? 8He will surely hurry
and help them. But when the Son of Man comes, will he
find on this earth anyone with faith?

A Pharisee and a Tax Collector

9Jesus told a story to some people who thought they were
better than others and who looked down on everyone else:

[i] 17.37 *Where there is a corpse, there will always be buzzards*: This saying may mean that when anything important happens, people soon know about it. Or the saying may mean that whenever something bad happens, curious people gather around and stare. But the word translated "buzzard" also means "eagle" and may refer to the Roman army, which had an eagle as its symbol.

NEW INTERNATIONAL VERSION

He replied, "Where there is a dead body, there the vul-
tures will gather."

The Parable of the Persistent Widow

18 Then Jesus told his disciples a parable to show
them that they should always pray and not give
up. 2He said: "In a certain town there was a judge who
neither feared God nor cared about men. 3And there was a
widow in that town who kept coming to him with the plea,
'Grant me justice against my adversary.'

4"For some time he refused. But finally he said to him-
self, 'Even though I don't fear God or care about men, 5yet
because this widow keeps bothering me, I will see that she
gets justice, so that she won't eventually wear me out with
her coming!' "

6And the Lord said, "Listen to what the unjust judge
says. 7And will not God bring about justice for his chosen
ones, who cry out to him day and night? Will he keep
putting them off? 8I tell you, he will see that they get jus-
tice, and quickly. However, when the Son of Man comes,
will he find faith on the earth?"

The Parable of the Pharisee and the Tax Collector

9To some who were confident of their own righteousness
and looked down on everybody else, Jesus told this parable:

NEW LIVING TRANSLATION

Jesus replied, "Just as the gathering of vultures shows
there is a carcass nearby, so these signs indicate that the
end is near."*

Story of the Persistent Widow

18 One day Jesus told his disciples a story to illus-
trate their need for constant prayer and to show
them that they must never give up. 2"There was a judge in
a certain city," he said, "who was a godless man with
great contempt for everyone. 3A widow of that city came to
him repeatedly, appealing for justice against someone who
had harmed her. 4The judge ignored her for a while, but
eventually she wore him out. 'I fear neither God nor man,'
he said to himself, 5'but this woman is driving me crazy.
I'm going to see that she gets justice, because she is wear-
ing me out with her constant requests!' "

6Then the Lord said, "Learn a lesson from this evil
judge. 7Even he rendered a just decision in the end, so
don't you think God will surely give justice to his chosen
people who plead with him day and night? Will he keep
putting them off? 8I tell you, he will grant justice to them
quickly! But when I, the Son of Man, return, how many
will I find who have faith?"

Story of the Pharisee and Tax Collector

9Then Jesus told this story to some who had great self-
confidence and scorned everyone else: 10"Two men went to

17:37 Greek *Wherever the carcass is, the vultures gather.*

NEW KING JAMES VERSION

So He said to them, "Wherever the body is, there the
eagles will be gathered together."

The Parable of the Persistent Widow

18 Then He spoke a parable to them, that men always
ought to pray and not lose heart, 2saying: "There
was in a certain city a judge who did not fear God nor re-
gard man. 3Now there was a widow in that city; and she
came to him, saying, 'Get justice for me from my adver-
sary.' 4And he would not for a while; but afterward he said
within himself, 'Though I do not fear God nor regard man,
5yet because this widow troubles me I will avenge her, lest
by her continual coming she weary me.' "

6Then the Lord said, "Hear what the unjust judge said.
7And shall God not avenge His own elect who cry out day
and night to Him, though He bears long with them? 8I tell
you that He will avenge them speedily. Nevertheless, when
the Son of Man comes, will He really find faith on the
earth?"

The Parable of the Pharisee and the Tax Collector

9Also He spoke this parable to some who trusted in
themselves that they were righteous, and despised others:

THE MESSAGE

He told them, "Watch for the circling of the vultures.
They'll spot the corpse first. The action will begin around
my dead body."

The Story of the Persistent Widow

18 Jesus told them a story showing that it was neces-
sary for them to pray consistently and never quit.
He said, "There was once a judge in some city who never
gave God a thought and cared nothing for people. A widow
in that city kept after him: 'My rights are being violated.
Protect me!'

"He never gave her the time of day. But after this went
on and on he said to himself, 'I care nothing what God
thinks, even less what people think. But because this
widow won't quit badgering me, I'd better do something
and see that she gets justice—otherwise I'm going to end
up beaten black-and-blue by her pounding.'"

Then the Master said, "Do you hear what that judge, cor-
rupt as he is, is saying? So what makes you think God
won't step in and work justice for his chosen people, who
continue to cry out for help? Won't he stick up for them? I
assure you, he will. He will not drag his feet. But how
much of that kind of persistent faith will the Son of Man
find on the earth when he returns?"

The Story of the Tax Man and the Pharisee

He told his next story to some who were complacently
pleased with themselves over their moral performance and
looked down their noses at the common people: "Two men

KING JAMES VERSION

10 Two men went up into the temple to pray; the one a Pharisee, and the other a publican.

11 The Pharisee stood and prayed thus with himself, God, I thank thee, that I am not as other men *are*, extortioners, unjust, adulterers, or even as this publican.

12 I fast twice in the week, I give tithes of all that I possess.

13 And the publican, standing afar off, would not lift up so much as *his* eyes unto heaven, but smote upon his breast, saying, God be merciful to me a sinner.

14 I tell you, this man went down to his house justified *rather* than the other: for every one that exalteth himself shall be abased; and he that humbleth himself shall be exalted.

15 ¶ And they brought unto him also infants, that he would touch them: but when *his* disciples saw *it*, they rebuked them.

16 But Jesus called them *unto him*, and said, Suffer little children to come unto me, and forbid them not: for of such is the kingdom of God.

NEW AMERICAN STANDARD BIBLE

10 "Two men went up into the temple to pray, one a Pharisee and the other a tax collector.

11 "The Pharisee stood and was praying this to himself: 'God, I thank You that I am not like other people: swindlers, unjust, adulterers, or even like this tax collector.

12 'I fast twice a week; I pay tithes of all that I get.'

13 "But the tax collector, standing some distance away, was even unwilling to lift up his eyes to heaven, but was beating his breast, saying, 'God, be merciful to me, the sinner!'

14 "I tell you, this man went to his house justified rather than the other; for everyone who exalts himself will be humbled, but he who humbles himself will be exalted."

15 And they were bringing even their babies to Him so that He would touch them, but when the disciples saw it, they *began* rebuking them.

16 But Jesus called for them, saying, "Permit the children to come to Me, and do not hinder them, for the kingdom of God belongs to such as these.

NEW CENTURY VERSION

Pharisee and a tax collector both went to the Temple to
pray. 11The Pharisee stood alone and prayed, 'God, I thank
you that I am not like other people who steal, cheat, or
take part in adultery, or even like this tax collector. 12I
give up eating[a] twice a week, and I give one-tenth of everything I get!'

13"The tax collector, standing at a distance, would not
even look up to heaven. But he beat on his chest because
he was so sad. He said, 'God, have mercy on me, a sinner.'
14I tell you, when this man went home, he was right with
God, but the Pharisee was not. All who make themselves great will be made humble, but all who make themselves humble will be made great."

Who Will Enter God's Kingdom?

15Some people brought even their babies to Jesus so he
could touch them. When the followers saw this, they told
them to stop. 16But Jesus called for the children, saying,
"Let the little children come to me. Don't stop them, because the kingdom of God belongs to people who are like

18:12 [a] **give up eating** This is called "fasting." The people would give up eating for a special time of prayer and worship to God. It was also done to show sadness and disappointment.

CONTEMPORARY ENGLISH VERSION

10Two men went into the temple to pray.[a] One was a
Pharisee and the other a tax collector.[b] 11The Pharisee
stood over by himself and prayed,[c] "God, I thank you that I am not greedy, dishonest, and unfaithful in marriage like other people. And I am really glad that I am not like
that tax collector over there. 12I go without eating[d] for
two days a week, and I give you one tenth of all I earn."

13The tax collector stood off at a distance and did not think he was good enough even to look up toward heaven. He was so sorry for what he had done that he pounded his chest and prayed, "God, have pity on me! I am such a sinner."

14Then Jesus said, "When the two men went home, it was the tax collector and not the Pharisee who was pleasing to God. If you put yourself above others, you will be put down. But if you humble yourself, you will be honored."

Jesus Blesses Little Children

(Matthew 19.13-15; Mark 10.13-16)

15Some people brought their little children for Jesus to
bless. But when his disciples saw them doing this, they told
the people to stop bothering him. 16So Jesus called the children over to him and said, "Let the children come to me! Don't try to stop them. People who are like these children

[a] **18.10** *into the temple to pray*: Jewish people usually prayed there early in the morning and late in the afternoon. [b] **18.10** *tax collector*: See the note at 3.12. [c] **18.11** *stood over by himself and prayed*: Some manuscripts have "stood up and prayed to himself." [d] **18.12** *without eating*: See the note at 2.37.

NEW INTERNATIONAL VERSION

[10]"Two men went up to the temple to pray, one a Pharisee and the other a tax collector. [11]The Pharisee stood up and prayed about[a] himself: 'God, I thank you that I am not like other men—robbers, evildoers, adulterers—or even like this tax collector. [12]I fast twice a week and give a tenth of all I get.'

[13]"But the tax collector stood at a distance. He would not even look up to heaven, but beat his breast and said, 'God, have mercy on me, a sinner.'

[14]"I tell you that this man, rather than the other, went home justified before God. For everyone who exalts himself will be humbled, and he who humbles himself will be exalted."

The Little Children and Jesus

[15]People were also bringing babies to Jesus to have him touch them. When the disciples saw this, they rebuked them. [16]But Jesus called the children to him and said, "Let the little children come to me, and do not hinder them, for the kingdom of God belongs to such as these. [17]I tell you

[a] *11* Or *to*

NEW LIVING TRANSLATION

the Temple to pray. One was a Pharisee, and the other was a dishonest tax collector. [11]The proud Pharisee stood by himself and prayed this prayer: 'I thank you, God, that I am not a sinner like everyone else, especially like that tax collector over there! For I never cheat, I don't sin, I don't commit adultery, [12]I fast twice a week, and I give you a tenth of my income.'

[13]"But the tax collector stood at a distance and dared not even lift his eyes to heaven as he prayed. Instead, he beat his chest in sorrow, saying, 'O God, be merciful to me, for I am a sinner.' [14]I tell you, this sinner, not the Pharisee, returned home justified before God. For the proud will be humbled, but the humble will be honored."

Jesus Blesses the Children

[15]One day some parents brought their little children to Jesus so he could touch them and bless them, but the disciples told them not to bother him. [16]Then Jesus called for the children and said to the disciples, "Let the children come to me. Don't stop them! For the Kingdom of God belongs to

NEW KING JAMES VERSION

[10]"Two men went up to the temple to pray, one a Pharisee and the other a tax collector. [11]The Pharisee stood and prayed thus with himself, 'God, I thank You that I am not like other men—extortioners, unjust, adulterers, or even as this tax collector. [12]I fast twice a week; I give tithes of all that I possess.' [13]And the tax collector, standing afar off, would not so much as raise *his* eyes to heaven, but beat his breast, saying, 'God, be merciful to me a sinner!' [14]I tell you, this man went down to his house justified *rather* than the other; for everyone who exalts himself will be humbled, and he who humbles himself will be exalted."

Jesus Blesses Little Children

[15]Then they also brought infants to Him that He might touch them; but when the disciples saw *it,* they rebuked them. [16]But Jesus called them to *Him* and said, "Let the little children come to Me, and do not forbid them; for of such is the kingdom of God. [17]Assuredly, I say to you,

THE MESSAGE

went up to the Temple to pray, one a Pharisee, the other a tax man. The Pharisee posed and prayed like this: 'Oh, God, I thank you that I am not like other people—robbers, crooks, adulterers, or, heaven forbid, like this tax man. I fast twice a week and tithe on all my income.'

"Meanwhile the tax man, slumped in the shadows, his face in his hands, not daring to look up, said, 'God, give mercy. Forgive me, a sinner.'"

Jesus commented, "This tax man, not the other, went home made right with God. If you walk around with your nose in the air, you're going to end up flat on your face, but if you're content to be simply yourself, you will become more than yourself."

✢

People brought babies to Jesus, hoping he might touch them. When the disciples saw it, they shooed them off. Jesus called them back. "Let these children alone. Don't get between them and me. These children are the kingdom's

KING JAMES VERSION

17 Verily I say unto you, Whosoever shall not receive the kingdom of God as a little child shall in no wise enter therein.

18 ¶ And a certain ruler asked him, saying, Good Master, what shall I do to inherit eternal life?

19 And Jesus said unto him, Why callest thou me good? none *is* good, save one, *that is*, God.

20 Thou knowest the commandments, Do not commit adultery, Do not kill, Do not steal, Do not bear false witness, Honour thy father and thy mother.

21 And he said, All these have I kept from my youth up.

22 Now when Jesus heard these things, he said unto him, Yet lackest thou one thing: sell all that thou hast, and distribute unto the poor, and thou shalt have treasure in heaven: and come, follow me.

23 And when he heard this, he was very sorrowful: for he was very rich.

24 And when Jesus saw that he was very sorrowful, he said, How hardly shall they that have riches enter into the kingdom of God!

25 For it is easier for a camel to go through a needle's eye, than for a rich man to enter into the kingdom of God.

26 And they that heard *it* said, Who then can be saved?

NEW AMERICAN STANDARD BIBLE

17 "Truly I say to you, whoever does not receive the kingdom of God like a child will not enter it *at all*."

The Rich Young Ruler

18 A ruler questioned Him, saying, "Good Teacher, what shall I do to inherit eternal life?"

19 And Jesus said to him, "Why do you call Me good? No one is good except God alone.

20 "You know the commandments, 'DO NOT COMMIT ADULTERY, DO NOT MURDER, DO NOT STEAL, DO NOT BEAR FALSE WITNESS, HONOR YOUR FATHER AND MOTHER.' "

21 And he said, "All these things I have kept from *my* youth."

22 When Jesus heard *this*, He said to him, "One thing you still lack; sell all that you possess and distribute it to the poor, and you shall have treasure in heaven; and come, follow Me."

23 But when he had heard these things, he became very sad, for he was extremely rich.

24 And Jesus looked at him and said, "How hard it is for those who are wealthy to enter the kingdom of God!

25 "For it is easier for a camel to go through the eye of a needle than for a rich man to enter the kingdom of God."

26 They who heard it said, "Then who can be saved?"

NEW CENTURY VERSION

these children. 17I tell you the truth, you must accept the kingdom of God as if you were a child, or you will never enter it."

A Rich Man's Question

18A certain leader asked Jesus, "Good Teacher, what must I do to have life forever?"

19Jesus said to him, "Why do you call me good? Only God is good. 20You know the commands: 'You must not be guilty of adultery. You must not murder anyone. You must not steal. You must not tell lies about your neighbor. Honor your father and mother.' "[b]

21But the leader said, "I have obeyed all these commands since I was a boy."

22When Jesus heard this, he said to him, "There is still one more thing you need to do. Sell everything you have and give it to the poor, and you will have treasure in heaven. Then come and follow me." 23But when the man heard this, he became very sad, because he was very rich.

24Jesus looked at him and said, "It is very hard for rich people to enter the kingdom of God. 25It is easier for a camel to go through the eye of a needle than for a rich person to enter the kingdom of God."

Who Can Be Saved?

26When the people heard this, they asked, "Then who can be saved?"

18:20 [b] **'You...mother.'** Quotation from Exodus 20:12–16; Deuteronomy 5:16–20.

CONTEMPORARY ENGLISH VERSION

belong to God's kingdom.[e] 17You will never get into God's kingdom unless you enter it like a child!"

A Rich and Important Man

(Matthew 19.16-30; Mark 10.17-31)

18An important man asked Jesus, "Good Teacher, what must I do to have eternal life?"

19Jesus said, "Why do you call me good? Only God is good. 20You know the commandments: 'Be faithful in marriage. Do not murder. Do not steal. Do not tell lies about others. Respect your father and mother.' "

21He told Jesus, "I have obeyed all these commandments since I was a young man."

22When Jesus heard this, he said, "There is one thing you still need to do. Go and sell everything you own! Give the money to the poor, and you will have riches in heaven. Then come and be my follower." 23When the man heard this, he was sad, because he was very rich.

24Jesus saw how sad the man was. So he said, "It's terribly hard for rich people to get into God's kingdom! 25In fact, it's easier for a camel to go through the eye of a needle than for a rich person to get into God's kingdom."

26When the crowd heard this, they asked, "How can anyone ever be saved?"

[e] **18.16** *People who are like these children belong to God's kingdom*: Or "God's kingdom belongs to people who are like these children."

NEW INTERNATIONAL VERSION

the truth, anyone who will not receive the kingdom of God like a little child will never enter it."

The Rich Ruler

18A certain ruler asked him, "Good teacher, what must I do to inherit eternal life?"

19"Why do you call me good?" Jesus answered. "No one is good—except God alone. 20You know the commandments: 'Do not commit adultery, do not murder, do not steal, do not give false testimony, honor your father and mother.'[b]"

21"All these I have kept since I was a boy," he said.

22When Jesus heard this, he said to him, "You still lack one thing. Sell everything you have and give to the poor, and you will have treasure in heaven. Then come, follow me."

23When he heard this, he became very sad, because he was a man of great wealth. 24Jesus looked at him and said, "How hard it is for the rich to enter the kingdom of God! 25Indeed, it is easier for a camel to go through the eye of a needle than for a rich man to enter the kingdom of God."

26Those who heard this asked, "Who then can be saved?"

[b] *20* Exodus 20:12–16; Deut. 5:16–20

NEW LIVING TRANSLATION

such as these. 17I assure you, anyone who doesn't have their kind of faith will never get into the Kingdom of God."

The Rich Man

18Once a religious leader asked Jesus this question: "Good teacher, what should I do to get eternal life?"

19"Why do you call me good?" Jesus asked him. "Only God is truly good. 20But as for your question, you know the commandments: 'Do not commit adultery. Do not murder. Do not steal. Do not testify falsely. Honor your father and mother.'* "

21The man replied, "I've obeyed all these commandments since I was a child."

22"There is still one thing you lack," Jesus said. "Sell all you have and give the money to the poor, and you will have treasure in heaven. Then come, follow me." 23But when the man heard this, he became sad because he was very rich.

24Jesus watched him go and then said to his disciples, "How hard it is for rich people to get into the Kingdom of God! 25It is easier for a camel to go through the eye of a needle than for a rich person to enter the Kingdom of God!"

26Those who heard this said, "Then who in the world can be saved?"

18:20 Exod 20:12-16; Deut 5:16-20.

NEW KING JAMES VERSION

whoever does not receive the kingdom of God as a little child will by no means enter it."

Jesus Counsels the Rich Young Ruler

18Now a certain ruler asked Him, saying, "Good Teacher, what shall I do to inherit eternal life?"

19So Jesus said to him, "Why do you call Me good? No one *is* good but One, *that is,* God. 20You know the commandments: *'Do not commit adultery,' 'Do not murder,' 'Do not steal,' 'Do not bear false witness,' 'Honor your father and your mother.'* "[a]

21And he said, "All these things I have kept from my youth."

22So when Jesus heard these things, He said to him, "You still lack one thing. Sell all that you have and distribute to the poor, and you will have treasure in heaven; and come, follow Me."

23But when he heard this, he became very sorrowful, for he was very rich.

With God All Things Are Possible

24And when Jesus saw that he became very sorrowful, He said, "How hard it is for those who have riches to enter the kingdom of God! 25For it is easier for a camel to go through the eye of a needle than for a rich man to enter the kingdom of God."

26And those who heard it said, "Who then can be saved?"

18:20 [a] Exodus 20:12–16; Deuteronomy 5:16–20

THE MESSAGE

pride and joy. Mark this: Unless you accept God's kingdom in the simplicity of a child, you'll never get in."

The Rich Official

One day one of the local officials asked him, "Good Teacher, what must I do to deserve eternal life?"

Jesus said, "Why are you calling me good? No one is good—only God. You know the commandments, don't you? No illicit sex, no killing, no stealing, no lying, honor your father and mother."

He said, "I've kept them all for as long as I can remember."

When Jesus heard that, he said, "Then there's only one thing left to do: Sell everything you own and give it away to the poor. You will have riches in heaven. Then come, follow me."

This was the last thing the official expected to hear. He was very rich and became terribly sad. He was holding on tight to a lot of things and not about to let them go.

Seeing his reaction, Jesus said, "Do you have any idea how difficult it is for people who have it all to enter God's kingdom? I'd say it's easier to thread a camel through a needle's eye than get a rich person into God's kingdom."

"Then who has any chance at all?" the others asked.

KING JAMES VERSION

27 And he said, The things which are impossible with men are possible with God.

28 Then Peter said, Lo, we have left all, and followed thee.

29 And he said unto them, Verily I say unto you, There is no man that hath left house, or parents, or brethren, or wife, or children, for the kingdom of God's sake,

30 Who shall not receive manifold more in this present time, and in the world to come life everlasting.

31 ¶ Then he took *unto him* the twelve, and said unto them, Behold, we go up to Jerusalem, and all things that are written by the prophets concerning the Son of man shall be accomplished.

32 For he shall be delivered unto the Gentiles, and shall be mocked, and spitefully entreated, and spitted on:

33 And they shall scourge *him*, and put him to death: and the third day he shall rise again.

34 And they understood none of these things: and this saying was hid from them, neither knew they the things which were spoken.

35 ¶ And it came to pass, that as he was come nigh unto Jericho, a certain blind man sat by the way side begging:

36 And hearing the multitude pass by, he asked what it meant.

37 And they told him, that Jesus of Nazareth passeth by.

NEW AMERICAN STANDARD BIBLE

27 But He said, "The things that are impossible with people are possible with God."

28 Peter said, "Behold, we have left our own *homes* and followed You."

29 And He said to them, "Truly I say to you, there is no one who has left house or wife or brothers or parents or children, for the sake of the kingdom of God,

30 who will not receive many times as much at this time and in the age to come, eternal life."

31 Then He took the twelve aside and said to them, "Behold, we are going up to Jerusalem, and all things which are written through the prophets about the Son of Man will be accomplished.

32 "For He will be handed over to the Gentiles, and will be mocked and mistreated and spit upon,

33 and after they have scourged Him, they will kill Him; and the third day He will rise again."

34 But the disciples understood none of these things, and *the meaning of* this statement was hidden from them, and they did not comprehend the things that were said.

Bartimaeus Receives Sight

35 As Jesus was approaching Jericho, a blind man was sitting by the road begging.

36 Now hearing a crowd going by, he *began* to inquire what this was.

37 They told him that Jesus of Nazareth was passing by.

NEW CENTURY VERSION

27Jesus answered, "God can do things that are not possible for people to do."

28Peter said, "Look, we have left everything and followed you."

29Jesus said, "I tell you the truth, all those who have left houses, wives, brothers, parents, or children for the kingdom of God 30will get much more in this life. And in the age that is coming, they will have life forever."

Jesus Will Rise from the Dead

31Then Jesus took the twelve apostles aside and said to them, "We are going to Jerusalem. Everything the prophets wrote about the Son of Man will happen. 32He will be turned over to those who are not Jews. They will laugh at him, insult him, spit on him, 33beat him with whips, and kill him. But on the third day, he will rise to life again." 34The apostles did not understand this; the meaning was hidden from them, and they did not realize what was said.

Jesus Heals a Blind Man

35As Jesus came near the city of Jericho, a blind man was sitting beside the road, begging. 36When he heard the people coming down the road, he asked, "What is happening?"

37They told him, "Jesus, from Nazareth, is going by."

CONTEMPORARY ENGLISH VERSION

27Jesus replied, "There are some things that people cannot do, but God can do anything."

28Peter said, "Remember, we left everything to be your followers!"

29Jesus answered, "You can be sure that anyone who gives up home or wife or brothers or family or children because of God's kingdom 30will be given much more in this life. And in the future world they will have eternal life."

Jesus Again Tells about His Death

(Matthew 20.17-19; Mark 10.32-34)

31Jesus took the twelve apostles aside and said:

We are now on our way to Jerusalem. Everything that the prophets wrote about the Son of Man will happen there. 32He will be handed over to foreigners,[f] who will make fun of him, mistreat him, and spit on him. 33They will beat him and kill him, but three days later he will rise to life.

34The apostles did not understand what Jesus was talking about. They could not understand, because the meaning of what he said was hidden from them.

Jesus Heals a Blind Beggar

(Matthew 20.29-34; Mark 10.46-52)

35When Jesus was coming close to Jericho, a blind man sat begging beside the road. 36The man heard the crowd walking by and asked what was happening. 37Some people told him that Jesus from Nazareth was passing by. 38So

[f] 18.32 *foreigners*: The Romans, who ruled Judea at this time.

NEW INTERNATIONAL VERSION

27Jesus replied, "What is impossible with men is possible with God."

28Peter said to him, "We have left all we had to follow you!"

29"I tell you the truth," Jesus said to them, "no one who has left home or wife or brothers or parents or children for the sake of the kingdom of God 30will fail to receive many times as much in this age and, in the age to come, eternal life."

Jesus Again Predicts His Death

31Jesus took the Twelve aside and told them, "We are going up to Jerusalem, and everything that is written by the prophets about the Son of Man will be fulfilled. 32He will be handed over to the Gentiles. They will mock him, insult him, spit on him, flog him and kill him. 33On the third day he will rise again."

34The disciples did not understand any of this. Its meaning was hidden from them, and they did not know what he was talking about.

A Blind Beggar Receives His Sight

35As Jesus approached Jericho, a blind man was sitting by the roadside begging. 36When he heard the crowd going by, he asked what was happening. 37They told him, "Jesus of Nazareth is passing by."

NEW LIVING TRANSLATION

27He replied, "What is impossible from a human perspective is possible with God."

28Peter said, "We have left our homes and followed you."

29"Yes," Jesus replied, "and I assure you, everyone who has given up house or wife or brothers or parents or children, for the sake of the Kingdom of God, 30will be repaid many times over in this life, as well as receiving eternal life in the world to come."

Jesus Again Predicts His Death

31Gathering the twelve disciples around him, Jesus told them, "As you know, we are going to Jerusalem. And when we get there, all the predictions of the ancient prophets concerning the Son of Man will come true. 32He will be handed over to the Romans to be mocked, treated shamefully, and spit upon. 33They will whip him and kill him, but on the third day he will rise again."

34But they didn't understand a thing he said. Its significance was hidden from them, and they failed to grasp what he was talking about.

Jesus Heals a Blind Beggar

35As they approached Jericho, a blind beggar was sitting beside the road. 36When he heard the noise of a crowd going past, he asked what was happening. 37They told him that Jesus of Nazareth was going by. 38So he began

NEW KING JAMES VERSION

27But He said, "The things which are impossible with men are possible with God."

28Then Peter said, "See, we have left all[b] and followed You."

29So He said to them, "Assuredly, I say to you, there is no one who has left house or parents or brothers or wife or children, for the sake of the kingdom of God, 30who shall not receive many times more in this present time, and in the age to come eternal life."

Jesus a Third Time Predicts His Death and Resurrection

31Then He took the twelve aside and said to them, "Behold, we are going up to Jerusalem, and all things that are written by the prophets concerning the Son of Man will be accomplished. 32For He will be delivered to the Gentiles and will be mocked and insulted and spit upon. 33They will scourge *Him* and kill Him. And the third day He will rise again."

34But they understood none of these things; this saying was hidden from them, and they did not know the things which were spoken.

A Blind Man Receives His Sight

35Then it happened, as He was coming near Jericho, that a certain blind man sat by the road begging. 36And hearing a multitude passing by, he asked what it meant. 37So they told him that Jesus of Nazareth was passing by. 38And he

18:28 [b] NU-Text reads *our own.*

THE MESSAGE

"No chance at all," Jesus said, "if you think you can pull it off by yourself. Every chance in the world if you trust God to do it."

Peter tried to regain some initiative: "We left everything we owned and followed you, didn't we?"

"Yes," said Jesus, "and you won't regret it. No one who has sacrificed home, spouse, brothers and sisters, parents, children—whatever—will lose out. It will all come back multiplied many times over in your lifetime. And then the bonus of eternal life!"

I Want to See Again

Then Jesus took the Twelve off to the side and said, "Listen carefully. We're on our way up to Jerusalem. Everything written in the Prophets about the Son of Man will take place. He will be handed over to the Romans, jeered at, made sport of, and spit on. Then, after giving him the third degree, they will kill him. In three days he will rise, alive." But they didn't get it, could make neither heads nor tails of what he was talking about.

He came to the outskirts of Jericho. A blind man was sitting beside the road asking for handouts. When he heard the rustle of the crowd, he asked what was going on. They told him, "Jesus the Nazarene is going by."

KING JAMES VERSION

38 And he cried, saying, Jesus, *thou* Son of David, have mercy on me.

39 And they which went before rebuked him, that he should hold his peace: but he cried so much the more, *Thou* Son of David, have mercy on me.

40 And Jesus stood, and commanded him to be brought unto him: and when he was come near, he asked him,

41 Saying, What wilt thou that I shall do unto thee? And he said, Lord, that I may receive my sight.

42 And Jesus said unto him, Receive thy sight: thy faith hath saved thee.

43 And immediately he received his sight, and followed him, glorifying God: and all the people, when they saw *it*, gave praise unto God.

19 And *Jesus* entered and passed through Jericho.
2 And, behold, *there was* a man named Zacchaeus, which was the chief among the publicans, and he was rich.

3 And he sought to see Jesus who he was; and could not for the press, because he was little of stature.

4 And he ran before, and climbed up into a sycomore tree to see him: for he was to pass that *way*.

5 And when Jesus came to the place, he looked up, and saw him, and said unto him, Zacchaeus, make haste, and come down; for to day I must abide at thy house.

6 And he made haste, and came down, and received him joyfully.

NEW AMERICAN STANDARD BIBLE

38 And he called out, saying, "Jesus, Son of David, have mercy on me!"

39 Those who led the way were sternly telling him to be quiet; but he kept crying out all the more, "Son of David, have mercy on me!"

40 And Jesus stopped and commanded that he be brought to Him; and when he came near, He questioned him,

41 "What do you want Me to do for you?" And he said, "Lord, *I want* to regain my sight!"

42 And Jesus said to him, "Receive your sight; your faith has made you well."

43 Immediately he regained his sight and *began* following Him, glorifying God; and when all the people saw it, they gave praise to God.

Zaccheus Converted

19 He entered Jericho and was passing through.
2 And there was a man called by the name of Zaccheus; he was a chief tax collector and he was rich.

3 Zaccheus was trying to see who Jesus was, and was unable because of the crowd, for he was small in stature.

4 So he ran on ahead and climbed up into a sycamore tree in order to see Him, for He was about to pass through that way.

5 When Jesus came to the place, He looked up and said to him, "Zaccheus, hurry and come down, for today I must stay at your house."

6 And he hurried and came down and received Him gladly.

NEW CENTURY VERSION

38The blind man cried out, "Jesus, Son of David, have mercy on me!"

39The people leading the group warned the blind man to be quiet. But the blind man shouted even more, "Son of David, have mercy on me!"

40Jesus stopped and ordered the blind man to be brought to him. When he came near, Jesus asked him, 41"What do you want me to do for you?"

He said, "Lord, I want to see."

42Jesus said to him, "Then see. You are healed because you believed."

43At once the man was able to see, and he followed Jesus, thanking God. All the people who saw this praised God.

Zacchaeus Meets Jesus

19 Jesus was going through the city of Jericho. 2A man was there named Zacchaeus, who was a very important tax collector, and he was wealthy. 3He wanted to see who Jesus was, but he was not able because he was too short to see above the crowd. 4He ran ahead to a place where Jesus would come, and he climbed a sycamore tree so he could see him. 5When Jesus came to that place, he looked up and said to him, "Zacchaeus, hurry and come down! I must stay at your house today."

6Zacchaeus came down quickly and welcomed him gladly.

CONTEMPORARY ENGLISH VERSION

the blind man shouted, "Jesus, Son of David,[g] have pity on me!" 39The people who were going along with Jesus told the man to be quiet. But he shouted even louder, "Son of David, have pity on me!"

40Jesus stopped and told some people to bring the blind man over to him. When the blind man was getting near, Jesus asked, 41"What do you want me to do for you?"

"Lord, I want to see!" he answered.

42Jesus replied, "Look and you will see! Your eyes are healed because of your faith." 43Right away the man could see, and he went with Jesus and started thanking God. When the crowds saw what happened, they praised God.

Zacchaeus

19 Jesus was going through Jericho, 2where a man named Zacchaeus lived. He was in charge of collecting taxes[a] and was very rich. 3-4Jesus was heading his way, and Zacchaeus wanted to see what he was like. But Zacchaeus was a short man and could not see over the crowd. So he ran ahead and climbed up into a sycamore tree.

5When Jesus got there, he looked up and said, "Zacchaeus, hurry down! I want to stay with you today." 6Zacchaeus hurried down and gladly welcomed Jesus.

[g] 18.38 *Son of David*: The Jewish people expected the Messiah to be from the family of King David, and for this reason the Messiah was often called the "Son of David." [a] 19.2 *in charge of collecting taxes*: See the note at 3.12.

NEW INTERNATIONAL VERSION

38He called out, "Jesus, Son of David, have mercy on me!"

39Those who led the way rebuked him and told him to be quiet, but he shouted all the more, "Son of David, have mercy on me!"

40Jesus stopped and ordered the man to be brought to him. When he came near, Jesus asked him, 41"What do you want me to do for you?"

"Lord, I want to see," he replied.

42Jesus said to him, "Receive your sight; your faith has healed you." 43Immediately he received his sight and followed Jesus, praising God. When all the people saw it, they also praised God.

Zacchaeus the Tax Collector

19 Jesus entered Jericho and was passing through. 2A man was there by the name of Zacchaeus; he was a chief tax collector and was wealthy. 3He wanted to see who Jesus was, but being a short man he could not, because of the crowd. 4So he ran ahead and climbed a sycamore-fig tree to see him, since Jesus was coming that way.

5When Jesus reached the spot, he looked up and said to him, "Zacchaeus, come down immediately. I must stay at your house today." 6So he came down at once and welcomed him gladly.

NEW LIVING TRANSLATION

shouting, "Jesus, Son of David, have mercy on me!" 39The crowds ahead of Jesus tried to hush the man, but he only shouted louder, "Son of David, have mercy on me!"

40When Jesus heard him, he stopped and ordered that the man be brought to him. 41Then Jesus asked the man, "What do you want me to do for you?"

"Lord," he pleaded, "I want to see!"

42And Jesus said, "All right, you can see! Your faith has healed you." 43Instantly the man could see, and he followed Jesus, praising God. And all who saw it praised God, too.

Jesus and Zacchaeus

19 Jesus entered Jericho and made his way through the town. 2There was a man there named Zacchaeus. He was one of the most influential Jews in the Roman tax-collecting business, and he had become very rich. 3He tried to get a look at Jesus, but he was too short to see over the crowds. 4So he ran ahead and climbed a sycamore tree beside the road, so he could watch from there.

5When Jesus came by, he looked up at Zacchaeus and called him by name. "Zacchaeus!" he said. "Quick, come down! For I must be a guest in your home today."

6Zacchaeus quickly climbed down and took Jesus to his house in great excitement and joy. 7But the crowds were

NEW KING JAMES VERSION

cried out, saying, "Jesus, Son of David, have mercy on me!"

39Then those who went before warned him that he should be quiet; but he cried out all the more, "Son of David, have mercy on me!"

40So Jesus stood still and commanded him to be brought to Him. And when he had come near, He asked him, 41saying, "What do you want Me to do for you?"

He said, "Lord, that I may receive my sight."

42Then Jesus said to him, "Receive your sight; your faith has made you well." 43And immediately he received his sight, and followed Him, glorifying God. And all the people, when they saw *it,* gave praise to God.

Jesus Comes to Zacchaeus' House

19 Then *Jesus* entered and passed through Jericho. 2Now behold, *there was* a man named Zacchaeus who was a chief tax collector, and he was rich. 3And he sought to see who Jesus was, but could not because of the crowd, for he was of short stature. 4So he ran ahead and climbed up into a sycamore tree to see Him, for He was going to pass that *way.* 5And when Jesus came to the place, He looked up and saw him,[a] and said to him, "Zacchaeus, make haste and come down, for today I must stay at your house." 6So he made haste and came down, and received Him joyfully. 7But when they saw *it,* they all

19:5 [a] NU-Text omits *and saw him.*

THE MESSAGE

He yelled, "Jesus! Son of David! Mercy, have mercy on me!"

Those ahead of Jesus told the man to shut up, but he only yelled all the louder, "Son of David! Mercy, have mercy on me!"

Jesus stopped and ordered him to be brought over. When he had come near, Jesus asked, "What do you want from me?"

He said, "Master, I want to see again."

Jesus said, "Go ahead—see again! Your faith has saved and healed you!" The healing was instant: He looked up, seeing—and then followed Jesus, glorifying God. Everyone in the street joined in, shouting praise to God.

Zacchaeus

19 Then Jesus entered and walked through Jericho. There was a man there, his name Zacchaeus, the head tax man and quite rich. He wanted desperately to see Jesus, but the crowd was in his way—he was a short man and couldn't see over the crowd. So he ran on ahead and climbed up in a sycamore tree so he could see Jesus when he came by.

When Jesus got to the tree, he looked up and said, "Zacchaeus, hurry down. Today is my day to be a guest in your home." Zacchaeus scrambled out of the tree, hardly believing his good luck, delighted to take Jesus home with

KING JAMES VERSION

7 And when they saw *it*, they all murmured, saying, That he was gone to be guest with a man that is a sinner.

8 And Zacchaeus stood, and said unto the Lord; Behold, Lord, the half of my goods I give to the poor; and if I have taken any thing from any man by false accusation, I restore *him* fourfold.

9 And Jesus said unto him, This day is salvation come to this house, forsomuch as he also is a son of Abraham.

10 For the Son of man is come to seek and to save that which was lost.

11 ¶ And as they heard these things, he added and spake a parable, because he was nigh to Jerusalem, and because they thought that the kingdom of God should immediately appear.

12 He said therefore, A certain nobleman went into a far country to receive for himself a kingdom, and to return.

13 And he called his ten servants, and delivered them ten pounds, and said unto them, Occupy till I come.

14 But his citizens hated him, and sent a message after him, saying, We will not have this *man* to reign over us.

15 And it came to pass, that when he was returned, having received the kingdom, then he commanded these servants to be called unto him, to whom he had given the money, that he might know how much every man had gained by trading.

NEW AMERICAN STANDARD BIBLE

7 When they saw it, they all *began* to grumble, saying, "He has gone to be the guest of a man who is a sinner."

8 Zaccheus stopped and said to the Lord, "Behold, Lord, half of my possessions I will give to the poor, and if I have defrauded anyone of anything, I will give back four times as much."

9 And Jesus said to him, "Today salvation has come to this house, because he, too, is a son of Abraham.

10 "For the Son of Man has come to seek and to save that which was lost."

Parable of Money Usage

11 While they were listening to these things, Jesus went on to tell a parable, because He was near Jerusalem, and they supposed that the kingdom of God was going to appear immediately.

12 So He said, "A nobleman went to a distant country to receive a kingdom for himself, and *then* return.

13 "And he called ten of his slaves, and gave them ten [1]minas and said to them, 'Do business *with this* until I come *back*.'

14 "But his citizens hated him and sent a delegation after him, saying, 'We do not want this man to reign over us.'

15 "When he returned, after receiving the kingdom, he ordered that these slaves, to whom he had given the money, be called to him so that he might know what business they had done.

19:13 [1] A mina is equal to about 100 days' wages

NEW CENTURY VERSION

7All the people saw this and began to complain, "Jesus is
staying with a sinner!"
8But Zacchaeus stood and said to the Lord, "I will give
half of my possessions to the poor. And if I have cheated
anyone, I will pay back four times more."
9Jesus said to him, "Salvation has come to this house
today, because this man also belongs to the family of
Abraham. 10The Son of Man came to find lost people and
save them."

A Story About Three Servants

11As the people were listening to this, Jesus told them a
story because he was near Jerusalem and they thought
God's kingdom would appear immediately. 12He said: "A
very important man went to a country far away to be made
a king and then to return home. 13So he called ten of his
servants and gave a coin[a] to each servant. He said, 'Do
business with this money until I get back.' 14But the peo-
ple in the kingdom hated the man. So they sent a group to
follow him and say, 'We don't want this man to be our
king.'
15"But the man became king. When he returned home,
he said, 'Call those servants who have my money so I can
know how much they earned with it.'

19:13 [a] coin A Greek "mina." One mina was enough money to pay a person for working three months.

CONTEMPORARY ENGLISH VERSION

7Everyone who saw this started grumbling, "This man
Zacchaeus is a sinner! And Jesus is going home to eat with
him."
8Later that day Zacchaeus stood up and said to the Lord, "I
will give half of my property to the poor. And I will now pay
back four times as much[b] to everyone I have ever cheated."
9Jesus said to Zacchaeus, "Today you and your family have
been saved,[c] because you are a true son of Abraham.[d] 10The
Son of Man came to look for and to save people who are lost."

A Story about Ten Servants (Matthew 25.14-30)

11The crowd was still listening to Jesus as he was getting
close to Jerusalem. Many of them thought that God's king-
dom would soon appear, 12and Jesus told them this story:

A prince once went to a foreign country to be crowned
king and then to return. 13But before leaving, he called in
ten servants and gave each of them some money. He told
them, "Use this to earn more money until I get back."
14But the people of his country hated him, and they
sent messengers to the foreign country to say, "We don't
want this man to be our king."
15After the prince had been made king, he returned
and called in his servants. He asked them how much
they had earned with the money they had been given.

[b] 19.8 *pay back four times as much*: Both Jewish and Roman law said that a person must pay back four times the amount that was taken.
[c] 19.9 *saved*: Zacchaeus was Jewish, but it is only now that he is rescued from sin and placed under God's care. [d] 19.9 *son of Abraham*: As used in this verse, the words mean that Zacchaeus is truly one of God's special people.

NEW INTERNATIONAL VERSION

[7]All the people saw this and began to mutter, "He has gone to be the guest of a 'sinner.' "

[8]But Zacchaeus stood up and said to the Lord, "Look, Lord! Here and now I give half of my possessions to the poor, and if I have cheated anybody out of anything, I will pay back four times the amount."

[9]Jesus said to him, "Today salvation has come to this house, because this man, too, is a son of Abraham. [10]For the Son of Man came to seek and to save what was lost."

The Parable of the Ten Minas

[11]While they were listening to this, he went on to tell them a parable, because he was near Jerusalem and the people thought that the kingdom of God was going to appear at once. [12]He said: "A man of noble birth went to a distant country to have himself appointed king and then to return. [13]So he called ten of his servants and gave them ten minas.[a] 'Put this money to work,' he said, 'until I come back.'

[14]"But his subjects hated him and sent a delegation after him to say, 'We don't want this man to be our king.'

[15]"He was made king, however, and returned home. Then he sent for the servants to whom he had given the money, in order to find out what they had gained with it.

[a] *13* A mina was about three months' wages.

NEW LIVING TRANSLATION

displeased. "He has gone to be the guest of a notorious sinner," they grumbled.

[8]Meanwhile, Zacchaeus stood there and said to the Lord, "I will give half my wealth to the poor, Lord, and if I have overcharged people on their taxes, I will give them back four times as much!"

[9]Jesus responded, "Salvation has come to this home today, for this man has shown himself to be a son of Abraham. [10]And I, the Son of Man, have come to seek and save those like him who are lost."

Story of the Ten Servants

[11]The crowd was listening to everything Jesus said. And because he was nearing Jerusalem, he told a story to correct the impression that the Kingdom of God would begin right away. [12]He said, "A nobleman was called away to a distant empire to be crowned king and then return. [13]Before he left, he called together ten servants and gave them ten pounds of silver* to invest for him while he was gone. [14]But his people hated him and sent a delegation after him to say they did not want him to be their king.

[15]"When he returned, the king called in the servants to whom he had given the money. He wanted to find out what they had done with the money and what their profits

19:13 Greek *10 minas;* 1 mina was was worth about 3 months' wages.

NEW KING JAMES VERSION

complained, saying, "He has gone to be a guest with a man who is a sinner."

[8]Then Zacchaeus stood and said to the Lord, "Look, Lord, I give half of my goods to the poor; and if I have taken anything from anyone by false accusation, I restore fourfold."

[9]And Jesus said to him, "Today salvation has come to this house, because he also is a son of Abraham; [10]for the Son of Man has come to seek and to save that which was lost."

The Parable of the Minas

[11]Now as they heard these things, He spoke another parable, because He was near Jerusalem and because they thought the kingdom of God would appear immediately. [12]Therefore He said: "A certain nobleman went into a far country to receive for himself a kingdom and to return. [13]So he called ten of his servants, delivered to them ten minas,[b] and said to them, 'Do business till I come.' [14]But his citizens hated him, and sent a delegation after him, saying, 'We will not have this *man* to reign over us.'

[15]"And so it was that when he returned, having received the kingdom, he then commanded these servants, to whom he had given the money, to be called to him, that he might know how much every man had gained by trading. [16]Then

19:13 [b] The *mina* (Greek *mna,* Hebrew *minah*) was worth about three months' salary.

THE MESSAGE

him. Everyone who saw the incident was indignant and grumped, "What business does he have getting cozy with this crook?"

Zacchaeus just stood there, a little stunned. He stammered apologetically, "Master, I give away half my income to the poor—and if I'm caught cheating, I pay four times the damages."

Jesus said, "Today is salvation day in this home! Here he is: Zacchaeus, son of Abraham! For the Son of Man came to find and restore the lost."

The Story About Investment

While he had their attention, and because they were getting close to Jerusalem by this time and expectation was building that God's kingdom would appear any minute, he told this story:

"There was once a man descended from a royal house who needed to make a long trip back to headquarters to get authorization for his rule and then return. But first he called ten servants together, gave them each a sum of money, and instructed them, 'Operate with this until I return.'

"But the citizens there hated him. So they sent a commission with a signed petition to oppose his rule: 'We don't want this man to rule us.'

"When he came back bringing the authorization of his rule, he called those ten servants to whom he had given the money to find out how they had done.

KING JAMES VERSION

16 Then came the first, saying, Lord, thy pound hath gained ten pounds.

17 And he said unto him, Well, thou good servant: because thou hast been faithful in a very little, have thou authority over ten cities.

18 And the second came, saying, Lord, thy pound hath gained five pounds.

19 And he said likewise to him, Be thou also over five cities.

20 And another came, saying, Lord, behold, *here is* thy pound, which I have kept laid up in a napkin:

21 For I feared thee, because thou art an austere man: thou takest up that thou layedst not down, and reapest that thou didst not sow.

22 And he saith unto him, Out of thine own mouth will I judge thee, *thou* wicked servant. Thou knewest that I was an austere man, taking up that I laid not down, and reaping that I did not sow:

23 Wherefore then gavest not thou my money into the bank, that at my coming I might have required mine own with usury?

24 And he said unto them that stood by, Take from him the pound, and give *it* to him that hath ten pounds.

25 (And they said unto him, Lord, he hath ten pounds.)

26 For I say unto you, That unto every one which hath shall be given; and from him that hath not, even that he hath shall be taken away from him.

27 But those mine enemies, which would not that I should reign over them, bring hither, and slay *them* before me.

NEW AMERICAN STANDARD BIBLE

16 "The first appeared, saying, 'Master, your mina has made ten minas more.'

17 "And he said to him, 'Well done, good slave, because you have been faithful in a very little thing, you are to be in authority over ten cities.'

18 "The second came, saying, 'Your mina, master, has made five minas.'

19 "And he said to him also, 'And you are to be over five cities.'

20 "Another came, saying, 'Master, here is your mina, which I kept put away in a handkerchief;

21 for I was afraid of you, because you are an exacting man; you take up what you did not lay down and reap what you did not sow.'

22 "He *said to him, 'By your own words I will judge you, you worthless slave. Did you know that I am an exacting man, taking up what I did not lay down and reaping what I did not sow?

23 'Then why did you not put my money in the bank, and having come, I would have collected it with interest?'

24 "Then he said to the bystanders, 'Take the mina away from him and give it to the one who has the ten minas.'

25 "And they said to him, 'Master, he has ten minas *already.*'

26 "I tell you that to everyone who has, more shall be given, but from the one who does not have, even what he does have shall be taken away.

27 "But these enemies of mine, who did not want me to reign over them, bring them here and slay them in my presence."

NEW CENTURY VERSION

16"The first servant came and said, 'Sir, I earned ten coins with the one you gave me.' 17The king said to the servant, 'Excellent! You are a good servant. Since I can trust you with small things, I will let you rule over ten of my cities.'

18"The second servant said, 'Sir, I earned five coins with your one.' 19The king said to this servant, 'You can rule over five cities.'

20"Then another servant came in and said to the king, 'Sir, here is your coin which I wrapped in a piece of cloth and hid. 21I was afraid of you, because you are a hard man. You even take money that you didn't earn and gather food that you didn't plant.' 22Then the king said to the servant, 'I will condemn you by your own words, you evil servant. You knew that I am a hard man, taking money that I didn't earn and gathering food that I didn't plant. 23Why then didn't you put my money in the bank? Then when I came back, my money would have earned some interest.'

24"The king said to the men who were standing by, 'Take the coin away from this servant and give it to the servant who earned ten coins.' 25They said, 'But sir, that servant already has ten coins.' 26The king said, 'Those who have will be given more, but those who do not have anything will have everything taken away from them. 27Now where are my enemies who didn't want me to be king? Bring them here and kill them before me.' "

CONTEMPORARY ENGLISH VERSION

16The first servant came and said, "Sir, with the money you gave me I have earned ten times as much."

17"That's fine, my good servant!" the king said. "Since you have shown that you can be trusted with a small amount, you will be given ten cities to rule."

18The second one came and said, "Sir, with the money you gave me, I have earned five times as much."

19The king said, "You will be given five cities."

20Another servant came and said, "Sir, here is your money. I kept it safe in a handkerchief. 21You are a hard man, and I was afraid of you. You take what isn't yours, and you harvest crops you didn't plant."

22"You worthless servant!" the king told him. "You have condemned yourself by what you have just said. You knew that I am a hard man, taking what isn't mine and harvesting what I've not planted. 23Why didn't you put my money in the bank? On my return, I could have had the money together with interest."

24Then he said to some other servants standing there, "Take the money away from him and give it to the servant who earned ten times as much."

25But they said, "Sir, he already has ten times as much!"

26The king replied, "Those who have something will be given more. But everything will be taken away from those who don't have anything. 27Now bring me the enemies who didn't want me to be their king. Kill them while I watch!"

NEW INTERNATIONAL VERSION

16“The first one came and said, ‘Sir, your mina has earned ten more.’

17“ ‘Well done, my good servant!’ his master replied. ‘Because you have been trustworthy in a very small matter, take charge of ten cities.’

18“The second came and said, ‘Sir, your mina has earned five more.’

19“His master answered, ‘You take charge of five cities.’

20“Then another servant came and said, ‘Sir, here is your mina; I have kept it laid away in a piece of cloth. 21I was afraid of you, because you are a hard man. You take out what you did not put in and reap what you did not sow.’

22“His master replied, ‘I will judge you by your own words, you wicked servant! You knew, did you, that I am a hard man, taking out what I did not put in, and reaping what I did not sow? 23Why then didn’t you put my money on deposit, so that when I came back, I could have collected it with interest?’

24“Then he said to those standing by, ‘Take his mina away from him and give it to the one who has ten minas.’

25“ ‘Sir,’ they said, ‘he already has ten!’

26“He replied, ‘I tell you that to everyone who has, more will be given, but as for the one who has nothing, even what he has will be taken away. 27But those enemies of mine who did not want me to be king over them—bring them here and kill them in front of me.’ ”

NEW LIVING TRANSLATION

were. 16The first servant reported a tremendous gain—ten times as much as the original amount! 17‘Well done!’ the king exclaimed. ‘You are a trustworthy servant. You have been faithful with the little I entrusted to you, so you will be governor of ten cities as your reward.’

18“The next servant also reported a good gain—five times the original amount. 19‘Well done!’ the king said. ‘You can be governor over five cities.’

20“But the third servant brought back only the original amount of money and said, ‘I hid it and kept it safe. 21I was afraid because you are a hard man to deal with, taking what isn’t yours and harvesting crops you didn’t plant.’

22“ ‘You wicked servant!’ the king roared. ‘Hard, am I? If you knew so much about me and how tough I am, 23why didn’t you deposit the money in the bank so I could at least get some interest on it?’ 24Then turning to the others standing nearby, the king ordered, ‘Take the money from this servant, and give it to the one who earned the most.’

25“ ‘But, master,’ they said, ‘that servant has enough already!’

26“ ‘Yes,’ the king replied, ‘but to those who use well what they are given, even more will be given. But from those who are unfaithful,* even what little they have will be taken away. 27And now about these enemies of mine who didn’t want me to be their king—bring them in and execute them right here in my presence.’ ”

19:26 Or *who have nothing.*

NEW KING JAMES VERSION

came the first, saying, ‘Master, your mina has earned ten minas.’ 17And he said to him, ‘Well *done,* good servant; because you were faithful in a very little, have authority over ten cities.’ 18And the second came, saying, ‘Master, your mina has earned five minas.’ 19Likewise he said to him, ‘You also be over five cities.’

20“Then another came, saying, ‘Master, here is your mina, which I have kept put away in a handkerchief. 21For I feared you, because you are an austere man. You collect what you did not deposit, and reap what you did not sow.’ 22And he said to him, ‘Out of your own mouth I will judge you, *you* wicked servant. You knew that I was an austere man, collecting what I did not deposit and reaping what I did not sow. 23Why then did you not put my money in the bank, that at my coming I might have collected it with interest?’

24“And he said to those who stood by, ‘Take the mina from him, and give *it* to him who has ten minas.’ 25(But they said to him, ‘Master, he has ten minas.’) 26‘For I say to you, that to everyone who has will be given; and from him who does not have, even what he has will be taken away from him. 27But bring here those enemies of mine, who did not want me to reign over them, and slay *them* before me.’ ”

THE MESSAGE

“The first said, ‘Master, I doubled your money.’

“He said, ‘Good servant! Great work! Because you’ve been trustworthy in this small job, I’m making you governor of ten towns.’

“The second said, ‘Master, I made a fifty percent profit on your money.’

“He said, ‘I’m putting you in charge of five towns.’

“The next servant said, ‘Master, here’s your money safe and sound. I kept it hidden in the cellar. To tell you the truth, I was a little afraid. I know you have high standards and hate sloppiness, and don’t suffer fools gladly.’

“He said, ‘You’re right that I don’t suffer fools gladly—and you’ve acted the fool! Why didn’t you at least invest the money in securities so I would have gotten a little interest on it?’

“Then he said to those standing there, ‘Take the money from him and give it to the servant who doubled my stake.’

“They said, ‘But Master, he already has double . . .’

“He said, ‘That’s what I mean: Risk your life and get more than you ever dreamed of. Play it safe and end up holding the bag.

“ ‘As for these enemies of mine who petitioned against my rule, clear them out of here. I don’t want to see their faces around here again.’ ”

KING JAMES VERSION

28 ¶ And when he had thus spoken, he went before, ascending up to Jerusalem.

29 And it came to pass, when he was come nigh to Bethphage and Bethany, at the mount called *the mount* of Olives, he sent two of his disciples,

30 Saying, Go ye into the village over against *you*; in the which at your entering ye shall find a colt tied, whereon yet never man sat: loose him, and bring *him hither*.

31 And if any man ask you, Why do ye loose *him?* thus shall ye say unto him, Because the Lord hath need of him.

32 And they that were sent went their way, and found even as he had said unto them.

33 And as they were loosing the colt, the owners thereof said unto them, Why loose ye the colt?

34 And they said, The Lord hath need of him.

35 And they brought him to Jesus: and they cast their garments upon the colt, and they set Jesus thereon.

36 And as he went, they spread their clothes in the way.

37 And when he was come nigh, even now at the descent of the mount of Olives, the whole multitude of the disciples began to rejoice and praise God with a loud voice for all the mighty works that they had seen;

38 Saying, Blessed *be* the King that cometh in the name of the Lord: peace in heaven, and glory in the highest.

39 And some of the Pharisees from among the multitude said unto him, Master, rebuke thy disciples.

NEW AMERICAN STANDARD BIBLE

Triumphal Entry

28 After He had said these things, He was going on ahead, going up to Jerusalem.

29 When He approached Bethphage and Bethany, near the mount that is called Olivet, He sent two of the disciples,

30 saying, "Go into the village ahead of *you;* there, as you enter, you will find a colt tied on which no one yet has ever sat; untie it and bring it *here.*

31 "If anyone asks you, 'Why are you untying it?' you shall say, 'The Lord has need of it.' "

32 So those who were sent went away and found it just as He had told them.

33 As they were untying the colt, its owners said to them, "Why are you untying the colt?"

34 They said, "The Lord has need of it."

35 They brought it to Jesus, and they threw their coats on the colt and put Jesus *on it.*

36 As He was going, they were spreading their coats on the road.

37 As soon as He was approaching, near the descent of the Mount of Olives, the whole crowd of the disciples began to praise God joyfully with a loud voice for all the miracles which they had seen,

38 shouting:

" BLESSED IS THE KING WHO COMES IN THE NAME OF THE LORD;
Peace in heaven and glory in the highest!"

39 Some of the Pharisees in the crowd said to Him, "Teacher, rebuke Your disciples."

NEW CENTURY VERSION

Jesus Enters Jerusalem as a King

28After Jesus said this, he went on toward Jerusalem.
29As Jesus came near Bethphage and Bethany, towns near
the hill called the Mount of Olives, he sent out two of his
followers. 30He said, "Go to the town you can see there.
When you enter it, you will find a colt tied there, which no
one has ever ridden. Untie it and bring it here to me. 31If
anyone asks you why you are untying it, say that the
Master needs it."

32The two followers went into town and found the colt
just as Jesus had told them. 33As they were untying it, its
owners came out and asked the followers, "Why are you
untying our colt?"

34The followers answered, "The Master needs it." 35So
they brought it to Jesus, threw their coats on the colt's
back, and put Jesus on it. 36As Jesus rode toward Jerusalem, others spread their coats on the road before him.

37As he was coming close to Jerusalem, on the way
down the Mount of Olives, the whole crowd of followers
began joyfully shouting praise to God for all the miracles
they had seen. 38They said,

"God bless the king who comes in the name
of the Lord! *Psalm 118:26*
There is peace in heaven and glory to God!"

39Some of the Pharisees in the crowd said to Jesus,
"Teacher, tell your followers not to say these things."

CONTEMPORARY ENGLISH VERSION

Jesus Enters Jerusalem

(Matthew 21.1-11; Mark 11.1-11; John 12.12-19)

28When Jesus had finished saying all this, he went on
toward Jerusalem. 29As he was getting near Bethphage and
Bethany on the Mount of Olives, he sent two of his disciples on ahead. 30He told them, "Go into the next village,
where you will find a young donkey that has never been
ridden. Untie the donkey and bring it here. 31If anyone asks
why you are doing that, just say, 'The Lord[e] needs it.' "

32They went off and found everything just as Jesus had
said. 33While they were untying the donkey, its owners
asked, "Why are you doing that?"

34They answered, "The Lord[e] needs it."

35Then they led the donkey to Jesus. They put some of
their clothes on its back and helped Jesus get on. 36And as he
rode along, the people spread clothes on the road[f] in front of
him. 37When Jesus was starting down the Mount of Olives,
his large crowd of disciples were happy and praised God
because of all the miracles they had seen. 38They shouted,

"Blessed is the king who comes
in the name of the Lord!
Peace in heaven
and glory to God."

39Some Pharisees in the crowd said to Jesus, "Teacher,
make your disciples stop shouting!"

[e] 19.31,34 *The Lord*: Or "The master of the donkey." [f] 19.36 *spread clothes on the road*: This was one way that the Jewish people welcomed a famous person.

NEW INTERNATIONAL VERSION

The Triumphal Entry

[28]After Jesus had said this, he went on ahead, going up
to Jerusalem. [29]As he approached Bethphage and Bethany
at the hill called the Mount of Olives, he sent two of his
disciples, saying to them, [30]"Go to the village ahead of
you, and as you enter it, you will find a colt tied there,
which no one has ever ridden. Untie it and bring it here.
[31]If anyone asks you, 'Why are you untying it?' tell him,
'The Lord needs it.' "

[32]Those who were sent ahead went and found it just as
he had told them. [33]As they were untying the colt, its own-
ers asked them, "Why are you untying the colt?"

[34]They replied, "The Lord needs it."

[35]They brought it to Jesus, threw their cloaks on the colt
and put Jesus on it. [36]As he went along, people spread
their cloaks on the road.

[37]When he came near the place where the road goes
down the Mount of Olives, the whole crowd of disciples
began joyfully to praise God in loud voices for all the mira-
cles they had seen:

[38]"Blessed is the king who comes in the name of the
Lord!"[b]

"Peace in heaven and glory in the highest!"

[39]Some of the Pharisees in the crowd said to Jesus,
"Teacher, rebuke your disciples!"

[b] *38* Psalm 118:26

NEW LIVING TRANSLATION

The Triumphal Entry

[28]After telling this story, Jesus went on toward
Jerusalem, walking ahead of his disciples. [29]As they came
to the towns of Bethphage and Bethany, on the Mount of
Olives, he sent two disciples ahead. [30]"Go into that village
over there," he told them, "and as you enter it, you will see
a colt tied there that has never been ridden. Untie it and
bring it here. [31]If anyone asks what you are doing, just
say, 'The Lord needs it.' "

[32]So they went and found the colt, just as Jesus had
said. [33]And sure enough, as they were untying it, the own-
ers asked them, "Why are you untying our colt?"

[34]And the disciples simply replied, "The Lord needs it."
[35]So they brought the colt to Jesus and threw their gar-
ments over it for him to ride on.

[36]Then the crowds spread out their coats on the road
ahead of Jesus. [37]As they reached the place where the road
started down from the Mount of Olives, all of his followers
began to shout and sing as they walked along, praising
God for all the wonderful miracles they had seen.

[38] "Bless the King who comes in the name of the Lord!
Peace in heaven
and glory in highest heaven!"*

[39]But some of the Pharisees among the crowd said,
"Teacher, rebuke your followers for saying things like that!"

19:38 Pss 118:26; 148:1.

NEW KING JAMES VERSION

The Triumphal Entry

[28]When He had said this, He went on ahead, going up to
Jerusalem. [29]And it came to pass, when He drew near to
Bethphage[c] and Bethany, at the mountain called Olivet, *that*
He sent two of His disciples, [30]saying, "Go into the village
opposite *you,* where as you enter you will find a colt tied, on
which no one has ever sat. Loose it and bring *it here.* [31]And
if anyone asks you, 'Why are you loosing *it?'* thus you shall
say to him, 'Because the Lord has need of it.' "

[32]So those who were sent went their way and found *it*
just as He had said to them. [33]But as they were loosing the
colt, the owners of it said to them, "Why are you loosing
the colt?"

[34]And they said, "The Lord has need of him." [35]Then
they brought him to Jesus. And they threw their own
clothes on the colt, and they set Jesus on him. [36]And as He
went, *many* spread their clothes on the road.

[37]Then, as He was now drawing near the descent of the
Mount of Olives, the whole multitude of the disciples
began to rejoice and praise God with a loud voice for all
the mighty works they had seen, [38]saying:

" *'Blessed is the King who comes in the name of the
Lord!'*[d]
Peace in heaven and glory in the highest!"

[39]And some of the Pharisees called to Him from the
crowd, "Teacher, rebuke Your disciples."

19:29 [c] M-Text reads *Bethsphage.* **19:38** [d] Psalm 118:26

THE MESSAGE

God's Personal Visit

After saying these things, Jesus headed straight up to Jerusalem. When he got near Bethphage and Bethany at the mountain called Olives, he sent off two of the disciples with instructions: "Go to the village across from you. As soon as you enter, you'll find a colt tethered, one that has never been ridden. Untie it and bring it. If anyone says anything, asks, 'What are you doing?' say, 'His Master needs him.' "

The two left and found it just as he said. As they were untying the colt, its owners said, "What are you doing untying the colt?"

They said, "His Master needs him."

They brought the colt to Jesus. Then, throwing their coats on its back, they helped Jesus get on. As he rode, the people gave him a grand welcome, throwing their coats on the street.

Right at the crest, where Mount Olives begins its descent, the whole crowd of disciples burst into enthusiastic praise over all the mighty works they had witnessed:

"Blessed he who comes,
the king in God's name!
All's well in heaven!
Glory in the high places!"

Some Pharisees from the crowd told him, "Teacher, get your disciples under control!"

KING JAMES VERSION

40 And he answered and said unto them, I tell you that, if these should hold their peace, the stones would immediately cry out.

41 ¶ And when he was come near, he beheld the city, and wept over it,

42 Saying, If thou hadst known, even thou, at least in this thy day, the things *which belong* unto thy peace! but now they are hid from thine eyes.

43 For the days shall come upon thee, that thine enemies shall cast a trench about thee, and compass thee round, and keep thee in on every side,

44 And shall lay thee even with the ground, and thy children within thee; and they shall not leave in thee one stone upon another; because thou knewest not the time of thy visitation.

45 And he went into the temple, and began to cast out them that sold therein, and them that bought;

46 Saying unto them, It is written, My house is the house of prayer: but ye have made it a den of thieves.

47 And he taught daily in the temple. But the chief priests and the scribes and the chief of the people sought to destroy him,

48 And could not find what they might do: for all the people were very attentive to hear him.

NEW AMERICAN STANDARD BIBLE

40 But Jesus answered, "I tell you, if these become silent, the stones will cry out!"

41 When He approached *Jerusalem*, He saw the city and wept over it,

42 saying, "If you had known in this day, even you, the things which make for peace! But now they have been hidden from your eyes.

43 "For the days will come upon you when your enemies will throw up a barricade against you, and surround you and hem you in on every side,

44 and they will level you to the ground and your children within you, and they will not leave in you one stone upon another, because you did not recognize the time of your visitation."

Traders Driven from the Temple

45 Jesus entered the temple and began to drive out those who were selling,

46 saying to them, "It is written, 'AND MY HOUSE SHALL BE A HOUSE OF PRAYER,' but you have made it a ROBBERS' DEN."

47 And He was teaching daily in the temple; but the chief priests and the scribes and the leading men among the people were trying to destroy Him,

48 and they could not find anything that they might do, for all the people were hanging on to every word He said.

NEW CENTURY VERSION

40But Jesus answered, "I tell you, if my followers didn't say these things, then the stones would cry out."

Jesus Cries for Jerusalem

41As Jesus came near Jerusalem, he saw the city and cried for it, 42saying, "I wish you knew today what would bring you peace. But now it is hidden from you. 43The time is coming when your enemies will build a wall around you and will hold you in on all sides. 44They will destroy you and all your people, and not one stone will be left on another. All this will happen because you did not recognize the time when God came to save you."

Jesus Goes to the Temple

45Jesus went into the Temple and began to throw out the people who were selling things there. 46He said, "It is written in the Scriptures, 'My Temple will be a house for prayer.'[b] But you have changed it into a 'hideout for robbers'!"[c]

47Jesus taught in the Temple every day. The leading priests, the experts on the law, and some of the leaders of the people wanted to kill Jesus. 48But they did not know how they could do it, because all the people were listening closely to him.

19:46 [b] **'My Temple...prayer.'** Quotation from Isaiah 56:7.
19:46 [c] **'hideout for robbers'** Quotation from Jeremiah 7:11.

CONTEMPORARY ENGLISH VERSION

40But Jesus answered, "If they keep quiet, these stones will start shouting."

41When Jesus came closer and could see Jerusalem, he cried 42and said:

It is too bad that today your people don't know what will bring them peace! Now it is hidden from them. 43Jerusalem, the time will come when your enemies will build walls around you to attack you. Armies will surround you and close in on you from every side. 44They will level you to the ground and kill your people. Not one stone in your buildings will be left on top of another. This will happen because you did not see that God had come to save you.[g]

Jesus in the Temple

(Matthew 21.12-17; Mark 11.15-19; John 2.13-22)

45When Jesus entered the temple, he started chasing out the people who were selling things. 46He told them, "The Scriptures say, 'My house should be a place of worship.' But you have made it a place where robbers hide!"

47Each day, Jesus kept on teaching in the temple. So the chief priests, the teachers of the Law of Moses, and some other important people tried to have him killed. 48But they could not find a way to do it, because everyone else was eager to listen to him.

[g] **19.44** *that God had come to save you*: The Jewish people looked for the time when God would come and rescue them from their enemies. But when Jesus came, many of them refused to obey him.

NEW INTERNATIONAL VERSION

40 “I tell you,” he replied, “if they keep quiet, the stones will cry out.”

41 As he approached Jerusalem and saw the city, he wept over it 42 and said, “If you, even you, had only known on this day what would bring you peace—but now it is hidden from your eyes. 43 The days will come upon you when your enemies will build an embankment against you and encircle you and hem you in on every side. 44 They will dash you to the ground, you and the children within your walls. They will not leave one stone on another, because you did not recognize the time of God’s coming to you.”

Jesus at the Temple

45 Then he entered the temple area and began driving out those who were selling. 46 “It is written,” he said to them, “ ‘My house will be a house of prayer’[c]; but you have made it ‘a den of robbers.’[d]”

47 Every day he was teaching at the temple. But the chief priests, the teachers of the law and the leaders among the people were trying to kill him. 48 Yet they could not find any way to do it, because all the people hung on his words.

[c] *46* Isaiah 56:7 [d] *46* Jer. 7:11

NEW LIVING TRANSLATION

40 He replied, “If they kept quiet, the stones along the road would burst into cheers!”

Jesus Weeps over Jerusalem

41 But as they came closer to Jerusalem and Jesus saw the city ahead, he began to cry. 42 “I wish that even today you would find the way of peace. But now it is too late, and peace is hidden from you. 43 Before long your enemies will build ramparts against your walls and encircle you and close in on you. 44 They will crush you to the ground, and your children with you. Your enemies will not leave a single stone in place, because you have rejected the opportunity God offered you.”

Jesus Clears the Temple

45 Then Jesus entered the Temple and began to drive out the merchants from their stalls. 46 He told them, “The Scriptures declare, ‘My Temple will be a place of prayer,’ but you have turned it into a den of thieves.”*

47 After that, he taught daily in the Temple, but the leading priests, the teachers of religious law, and the other leaders of the people began planning how to kill him. 48 But they could think of nothing, because all the people hung on every word he said.

19:46 Isa 56:7; Jer 7:11.

NEW KING JAMES VERSION

40 But He answered and said to them, “I tell you that if these should keep silent, the stones would immediately cry out.”

Jesus Weeps over Jerusalem

41 Now as He drew near, He saw the city and wept over it, 42 saying, “If you had known, even you, especially in this your day, the things *that make* for your peace! But now they are hidden from your eyes. 43 For days will come upon you when your enemies will build an embankment around you, surround you and close you in on every side, 44 and level you, and your children within you, to the ground; and they will not leave in you one stone upon another, because you did not know the time of your visitation.”

Jesus Cleanses the Temple

45 Then He went into the temple and began to drive out those who bought and sold in it,[e] 46 saying to them, “It is written, *‘My house is[f] a house of prayer,’*[g] but you have made it a *‘den of thieves.’* ”[h]

47 And He was teaching daily in the temple. But the chief priests, the scribes, and the leaders of the people sought to destroy Him, 48 and were unable to do anything; for all the people were very attentive to hear Him.

19:45 [e] NU-Text reads *those who were selling.* **19:46** [f] NU-Text reads *shall be.* [g] Isaiah 56:7 [h] Jeremiah 7:11

THE MESSAGE

But he said, “If they kept quiet, the stones would do it for them, shouting praise.”

When the city came into view, he wept over it. “If you had only recognized this day, and everything that was good for you! But now it’s too late. In the days ahead your enemies are going to bring up their heavy artillery and surround you, pressing in from every side. They’ll smash you and your babies on the pavement. Not one stone will be left intact. All this because you didn’t recognize and welcome God’s personal visit.”

Going into the Temple he began to throw out everyone who had set up shop, selling everything and anything. He said, “It’s written in Scripture,

‘My house is a house of prayer;
You have turned it into a religious bazaar.’ ”

From then on he taught each day in the Temple. The high priests, religion scholars, and the leaders of the people were trying their best to find a way to get rid of him. But with the people hanging on every word he spoke, they couldn’t come up with anything.

KING JAMES VERSION

20 And it came to pass, *that* on one of those days, as
he taught the people in the temple, and preached
the gospel, the chief priests and the scribes came upon *him*
with the elders,
2 And spake unto him, saying, Tell us, by what authori-
ty doest thou these things? or who is he that gave thee
this authority?
3 And he answered and said unto them, I will also ask
you one thing; and answer me:
4 The baptism of John, was it from heaven, or of men?
5 And they reasoned with themselves, saying, If we
shall say, From heaven; he will say, Why then believed ye
him not?
6 But and if we say, Of men; all the people will stone
us: for they be persuaded that John was a prophet.
7 And they answered, that they could not tell whence *it*
was.
8 And Jesus said unto them, Neither tell I you by what
authority I do these things.
9 ¶ Then began he to speak to the people this parable; A
certain man planted a vineyard, and let it forth to hus-
bandmen, and went into a far country for a long time.
10 And at the season he sent a servant to the husband-
men, that they should give him of the fruit of the vineyard:
but the husbandmen beat him, and sent *him* away empty.
11 And again he sent another servant: and they beat

NEW AMERICAN STANDARD BIBLE

Jesus' Authority Questioned

20 On one of the days while He was teaching the peo-
ple in the temple and preaching the gospel, the
chief priests and the scribes with the elders confronted
Him,
2 and they spoke, saying to Him, "Tell us by what
authority You are doing these things, or who is the one
who gave You this authority?"
3 Jesus answered and said to them, "I will also ask you
a question, and you tell Me:
4 "Was the baptism of John from heaven or from men?"
5 They reasoned among themselves, saying, "If we say,
'From heaven,' He will say, 'Why did you not believe him?'
6 "But if we say, 'From men,' all the people will stone us
to death, for they are convinced that John was a prophet."
7 So they answered that they did not know where *it*
came from.
8 And Jesus said to them, "Nor will I tell you by what
authority I do these things."

Parable of the Vine-growers

9 And He began to tell the people this parable: "A man
planted a vineyard and rented it out to vine-growers, and
went on a journey for a long time.
10 "At the *harvest* time he sent a slave to the vine-grow-
ers, so that they would give him *some* of the produce of the
vineyard; but the vine-growers beat him and sent him
away empty-handed.
11 "And he proceeded to send another slave; and they

NEW CENTURY VERSION

Jewish Leaders Question Jesus

20 One day Jesus was in the Temple, teaching the peo-
ple and telling them the Good News. The leading
priests, teachers of the law, and older Jewish leaders came
up to talk with him, [2]saying, "Tell us what authority you
have to do these things? Who gave you this authority?"
[3]Jesus answered, "I will also ask you a question. Tell
me: [4]When John baptized people, was that authority from
God or just from other people?"
[5]They argued about this, saying, "If we answer, 'John's
baptism was from God,' Jesus will say, 'Then why did you
not believe him?' [6]But if we say, 'It was from other peo-
ple,' all the people will stone us to death, because they
believe John was a prophet." [7]So they answered that they
didn't know where it came from.
[8]Jesus said to them, "Then I won't tell you what authori-
ty I have to do these things."

A Story About God's Son

[9]Then Jesus told the people this story: "A man planted a
vineyard and leased it to some farmers. Then he went
away for a long time. [10]When it was time for the grapes to
be picked, he sent a servant to the farmers to get some of
the grapes. But they beat the servant and sent him away
empty-handed. [11]Then he sent another servant. They beat

CONTEMPORARY ENGLISH VERSION

A Question about Jesus' Authority
(Matthew 21.23-27; Mark 11.27-33)

20 One day, Jesus was teaching in the temple and
telling the good news. So the chief priests, the
teachers, and the nation's leaders [2]asked him, "What right
do you have to do these things? Who gave you this author-
ity?"
[3]Jesus replied, "I want to ask you a question. [4]Who gave
John the right to baptize? Was it God in heaven or merely
some human being?"
[5]They talked this over and said to each other, "We can't
say that God gave John this right. Jesus will ask us why we
didn't believe John. [6]And we can't say that it was merely
some human who gave John the right to baptize. The
crowd will stone us to death, because they think John was
a prophet."
[7]So they told Jesus, "We don't know who gave John the
right to baptize."
[8]Jesus replied, "Then I won't tell you who gave me the
right to do what I do."

Renters of a Vineyard (Matthew 21.33-46; Mark 12.1-12)

[9]Jesus told the people this story:
A man once planted a vineyard and rented it out. Then
he left the country for a long time. [10]When it was time to
harvest the crop, he sent a servant to ask the renters for
his share of the grapes. But they beat up the servant and
sent him away without anything. [11]So the owner sent

NEW INTERNATIONAL VERSION

The Authority of Jesus Questioned

20 One day as he was teaching the people in the temple courts and preaching the gospel, the chief priests and the teachers of the law, together with the elders, came up to him. 2"Tell us by what authority you are doing these things," they said. "Who gave you this authority?"

3He replied, "I will also ask you a question. Tell me, 4John's baptism—was it from heaven, or from men?"

5They discussed it among themselves and said, "If we say, 'From heaven,' he will ask, 'Why didn't you believe him?' 6But if we say, 'From men,' all the people will stone us, because they are persuaded that John was a prophet."

7So they answered, "We don't know where it was from."

8Jesus said, "Neither will I tell you by what authority I am doing these things."

The Parable of the Tenants

9He went on to tell the people this parable: "A man planted a vineyard, rented it to some farmers and went away for a long time. 10At harvest time he sent a servant to the tenants so they would give him some of the fruit of the vineyard. But the tenants beat him and sent him away empty-handed. 11He sent another servant, but that one

NEW LIVING TRANSLATION

The Authority of Jesus Challenged

20 One day as Jesus was teaching and preaching the Good News in the Temple, the leading priests and teachers of religious law and other leaders came up to him. 2They demanded, "By whose authority did you drive out the merchants from the Temple?* Who gave you such authority?"

3"Let me ask you a question first," he replied. 4"Did John's baptism come from heaven, or was it merely human?"

5They talked it over among themselves. "If we say it was from heaven, he will ask why we didn't believe him. 6But if we say it was merely human, the people will stone us, because they are convinced he was a prophet." 7Finally they replied, "We don't know."

8And Jesus responded, "Then I won't answer your question either."

Story of the Evil Farmers

9Now Jesus turned to the people again and told them this story: "A man planted a vineyard, leased it out to tenant farmers, and moved to another country to live for several years. 10At grape-picking time, he sent one of his servants to collect his share of the crop. But the farmers attacked the servant, beat him up, and sent him back empty-handed. 11So the owner sent another servant, but

20:2 Or *By whose authority do you do these things?*

NEW KING JAMES VERSION

Jesus' Authority Questioned

20 Now it happened on one of those days, as He taught the people in the temple and preached the gospel, *that* the chief priests and the scribes, together with the elders, confronted *Him* 2and spoke to Him, saying, "Tell us, by what authority are You doing these things? Or who is he who gave You this authority?"

3But He answered and said to them, "I also will ask you one thing, and answer Me: 4The baptism of John—was it from heaven or from men?"

5And they reasoned among themselves, saying, "If we say, 'From heaven,' He will say, 'Why then[a] did you not believe him?' 6But if we say, 'From men,' all the people will stone us, for they are persuaded that John was a prophet." 7So they answered that they did not know where *it was* from.

8And Jesus said to them, "Neither will I tell you by what authority I do these things."

The Parable of the Wicked Vinedressers

9Then He began to tell the people this parable: "A certain man planted a vineyard, leased it to vinedressers, and went into a far country for a long time. 10Now at vintage-time he sent a servant to the vinedressers, that they might give him some of the fruit of the vineyard. But the vinedressers beat him and sent *him* away empty-handed. 11Again he sent another servant; and they beat him also,

20:5 [a] NU-Text and M-Text omit *then.*

THE MESSAGE

20 One day he was teaching the people in the Temple, proclaiming the Message. The high priests, religion scholars, and leaders confronted him and demanded, "Show us your credentials. Who authorized you to speak and act like this?"

Jesus answered, "First, let me ask you a question: About the baptism of John—who authorized it, heaven or humans?"

They were on the spot, and knew it. They pulled back into a huddle and whispered, "If we say 'heaven,' he'll ask us why we didn't believe him; if we say 'humans,' the people will tear us limb from limb, convinced as they are that John was God's prophet." They agreed to concede that round to Jesus and said they didn't know.

Jesus said, "Then neither will I answer your question."

The Story of Corrupt Farmhands

Jesus told another story to the people: "A man planted a vineyard. He handed it over to farmhands and went off on a trip. He was gone a long time. In time he sent a servant back to the farmhands to collect the profits, but they beat him up and sent him off empty-handed. He decided to try

KING JAMES VERSION

him also, and entreated *him* shamefully, and sent *him* away empty.

12 And again he sent a third: and they wounded him also, and cast *him* out.

13 Then said the lord of the vineyard, What shall I do? I will send my beloved son: it may be they will reverence *him* when they see him.

14 But when the husbandmen saw him, they reasoned among themselves, saying, This is the heir: come, let us kill him, that the inheritance may be ours.

15 So they cast him out of the vineyard, and killed *him*. What therefore shall the lord of the vineyard do unto them?

16 He shall come and destroy these husbandmen, and shall give the vineyard to others. And when they heard *it*, they said, God forbid.

17 And he beheld them, and said, What is this then that is written, The stone which the builders rejected, the same is become the head of the corner?

18 Whosoever shall fall upon that stone shall be broken; but on whomsoever it shall fall, it will grind him to powder.

19 And the chief priests and the scribes the same hour sought to lay hands on him; and they feared the people: for they perceived that he had spoken this parable against them.

NEW AMERICAN STANDARD BIBLE

beat him also and treated him shamefully and sent him away empty-handed.

12 "And he proceeded to send a third; and this one also they wounded and cast out.

13 "The owner of the vineyard said, 'What shall I do? I will send my beloved son; perhaps they will respect him.'

14 "But when the vine-growers saw him, they reasoned with one another, saying, 'This is the heir; let us kill him so that the inheritance will be ours.'

15 "So they threw him out of the vineyard and killed him. What, then, will the owner of the vineyard do to them?

16 "He will come and destroy these vine-growers and will give the vineyard to others." When they heard it, they said, "May it never be!"

17 But Jesus looked at them and said, "What then is this that is written:

'THE STONE WHICH THE BUILDERS REJECTED,
THIS BECAME THE CHIEF CORNER *stone*'?

18 "Everyone who falls on that stone will be broken to pieces; but on whomever it falls, it will scatter him like dust."

Tribute to Caesar

19 The scribes and the chief priests tried to lay hands on Him that very hour, and they feared the people; for they understood that He spoke this parable against them.

NEW CENTURY VERSION

this servant also, and showed no respect for him, and sent him away empty-handed. 12So the man sent a third servant. The farmers wounded him and threw him out. 13The owner of the vineyard said, 'What will I do now? I will send my son whom I love. Maybe they will respect him.' 14But when the farmers saw the son, they said to each other, 'This son will inherit the vineyard. If we kill him, it will be ours.' 15So the farmers threw the son out of the vineyard and killed him.

"What will the owner of this vineyard do to them? 16He will come and kill those farmers and will give the vineyard to other farmers."

When the people heard this story, they said, "Let this never happen!"

17But Jesus looked at them and said, "Then what does this verse mean:

'The stone that the builders rejected
became the cornerstone'? *Psalm 118:22*

18Everyone who falls on that stone will be broken, and the person on whom it falls, that person will be crushed!"

19The teachers of the law and the leading priests wanted to arrest Jesus at once, because they knew the story was about them. But they were afraid of what the people would do.

CONTEMPORARY ENGLISH VERSION

another servant. The renters also beat him up. They insulted him terribly and sent him away without a thing. 12The owner sent a third servant. He was also beaten terribly and thrown out of the vineyard.

13The owner then said to himself, "What am I going to do? I know what. I'll send my son, the one I love so much. They will surely respect him!"

14When the renters saw the owner's son, they said to one another, "Someday he will own the vineyard. Let's kill him! Then we can have it all for ourselves." 15So they threw him out of the vineyard and killed him.

Jesus asked, "What do you think the owner of the vineyard will do? 16I'll tell you what. He will come and kill those renters and let someone else have his vineyard."

When the people heard this, they said, "This must never happen!"

17But Jesus looked straight at them and said, "Then what do the Scriptures mean when they say, 'The stone that the builders tossed aside is now the most important stone of all'? 18Anyone who stumbles over this stone will get hurt, and anyone it falls on will be smashed to pieces."

19The chief priests and the teachers of the Law of Moses knew that Jesus was talking about them when he was telling this story. They wanted to arrest him right then, but they were afraid of the people.

NEW INTERNATIONAL VERSION

also they beat and treated shamefully and sent away empty-handed. 12He sent still a third, and they wounded him and threw him out.

13"Then the owner of the vineyard said, 'What shall I do? I will send my son, whom I love; perhaps they will respect him.'

14"But when the tenants saw him, they talked the matter over. 'This is the heir,' they said. 'Let's kill him, and the inheritance will be ours.' 15So they threw him out of the vineyard and killed him.

"What then will the owner of the vineyard do to them? 16He will come and kill those tenants and give the vineyard to others."

When the people heard this, they said, "May this never be!"

17Jesus looked directly at them and asked, "Then what is the meaning of that which is written:

" 'The stone the builders rejected
has become the capstone'[a][b]?

18Everyone who falls on that stone will be broken to pieces, but he on whom it falls will be crushed."

19The teachers of the law and the chief priests looked for a way to arrest him immediately, because they knew he had spoken this parable against them. But they were afraid of the people.

[a] *17* Or *cornerstone* [b] *17* Psalm 118:22

NEW LIVING TRANSLATION

the same thing happened; he was beaten up and treated shamefully, and he went away empty-handed. 12A third man was sent and the same thing happened. He, too, was wounded and chased away.

13" 'What will I do?' the owner asked himself. 'I know! I'll send my cherished son. Surely they will respect him.'

14"But when the farmers saw his son, they said to each other, 'Here comes the heir to this estate. Let's kill him and get the estate for ourselves!' 15So they dragged him out of the vineyard and murdered him.

"What do you suppose the owner of the vineyard will do to those farmers?" Jesus asked. 16"I'll tell you—he will come and kill them all and lease the vineyard to others."

"But God forbid that such a thing should ever happen," his listeners protested.

17Jesus looked at them and said, "Then what do the Scriptures mean?

'The stone rejected by the builders
has now become the cornerstone.'*

18All who stumble over that stone will be broken to pieces, and it will crush anyone on whom it falls."

19When the teachers of religious law and the leading priests heard this story, they wanted to arrest Jesus immediately because they realized he was pointing at them—that they were the farmers in the story. But they were afraid there would be a riot if they arrested him.

20:17 Ps 118:22.

NEW KING JAMES VERSION

treated *him* shamefully, and sent *him* away empty-handed. 12And again he sent a third; and they wounded him also and cast *him* out.

13"Then the owner of the vineyard said, 'What shall I do? I will send my beloved son. Probably they will respect *him* when they see him.' 14But when the vinedressers saw him, they reasoned among themselves, saying, 'This is the heir. Come, let us kill him, that the inheritance may be ours.' 15So they cast him out of the vineyard and killed *him.* Therefore what will the owner of the vineyard do to them? 16He will come and destroy those vinedressers and give the vineyard to others."

And when they heard *it* they said, "Certainly not!"

17Then He looked at them and said, "What then is this that is written:

'The stone which the builders rejected
Has become the chief cornerstone'?[b]

18Whoever falls on that stone will be broken; but on whomever it falls, it will grind him to powder."

19And the chief priests and the scribes that very hour sought to lay hands on Him, but they feared the people[c]—for they knew He had spoken this parable against them.

20:17 [b] Psalm 118:22 20:19 [c] M-Text reads *but they were afraid.*

THE MESSAGE

again and sent another servant. That one they beat black-and-blue, and sent him off empty-handed. He tried a third time. They worked that servant over from head to foot and dumped him in the street.

"Then the owner of the vineyard said, 'I know what I'll do: I'll send my beloved son. They're bound to respect my son.'

"But when the farmhands saw him coming, they quickly put their heads together. 'This is our chance—this is the heir! Let's kill him and have it all to ourselves.' They killed him and threw him over the fence.

"What do you think the owner of the vineyard will do? Right. He'll come and clean house. Then he'll assign the care of the vineyard to others."

Those who were listening said, "Oh, no! He'd never do that!"

But Jesus didn't back down. "Why, then, do you think this was written:

'That stone the masons threw out—
It's now the cornerstone!'?

Anyone falling over that stone will break every bone in his body; if the stone falls on anyone, it will be a total smash-up."

The religion scholars and high priests wanted to lynch him on the spot, but they were intimidated by public opinion. They knew the story was about them.

KING JAMES VERSION

20 ¶ And they watched *him*, and sent forth spies, which should feign themselves just men, that they might take hold of his words, that so they might deliver him unto the power and authority of the governor.

21 And they asked him, saying, Master, we know that thou sayest and teachest rightly, neither acceptest thou the person *of any*, but teachest the way of God truly:

22 Is it lawful for us to give tribute unto Caesar, or no?

23 But he perceived their craftiness, and said unto them, Why tempt ye me?

24 Shew me a penny. Whose image and superscription hath it? They answered and said, Caesar's.

25 And he said unto them, Render therefore unto Caesar the things which be Caesar's, and unto God the things which be God's.

26 And they could not take hold of his words before the people: and they marvelled at his answer, and held their peace.

27 ¶ Then came to *him* certain of the Sadducees, which deny that there is any resurrection; and they asked him,

28 Saying, Master, Moses wrote unto us, If any man's brother die, having a wife, and he die without children, that his brother should take his wife, and raise up seed unto his brother.

29 There were therefore seven brethren: and the first took a wife, and died without children.

NEW AMERICAN STANDARD BIBLE

20 So they watched Him, and sent spies who pretended to be righteous, in order that they might catch Him in some statement, so that they *could* deliver Him to the rule and the authority of the governor.

21 They questioned Him, saying, "Teacher, we know that You speak and teach correctly, and You are not partial to any, but teach the way of God in truth.

22 "Is it lawful for us to pay taxes to Caesar, or not?"

23 But He detected their trickery and said to them,

24 "Show Me a [l]denarius. Whose likeness and inscription does it have?" They said, "Caesar's."

25 And He said to them, "Then render to Caesar the things that are Caesar's, and to God the things that are God's."

26 And they were unable to catch Him in a saying in the presence of the people; and being amazed at His answer, they became silent.

Is There a Resurrection?

27 Now there came to Him some of the Sadducees (who say that there is no resurrection),

28 and they questioned Him, saying, "Teacher, Moses wrote for us that IF A MAN'S BROTHER DIES, having a wife, AND HE IS CHILDLESS, HIS BROTHER SHOULD MARRY THE WIFE AND RAISE UP CHILDREN TO HIS BROTHER.

29 "Now there were seven brothers; and the first took a wife and died childless;

20:24 *l* The denarius was a day's wages

NEW CENTURY VERSION

Is It Right to Pay Taxes or Not?

20So they watched Jesus and sent some spies who acted as if they were sincere. They wanted to trap Jesus in saying something wrong so they could hand him over to the authority and power of the governor. 21So the spies asked Jesus, "Teacher, we know that what you say and teach is true. You pay no attention to who people are, and you always teach the truth about God's way. 22Tell us, is it right for us to pay taxes to Caesar or not?"

23But Jesus, knowing they were trying to trick him, said, 24"Show me a coin. Whose image and name are on it?"

They said, "Caesar's."

25Jesus said to them, "Then give to Caesar the things that are Caesar's, and give to God the things that are God's."

26So they were not able to trap Jesus in anything he said in the presence of the people. And being amazed at his answer, they became silent.

Some Sadducees Try to Trick Jesus

27Some Sadducees, who believed people would not rise from the dead, came to Jesus. 28They asked, "Teacher, Moses wrote that if a man's brother dies and leaves a wife but no children, then that man must marry the widow and have children for his brother. 29Once there were seven brothers. The first brother married and died, but had no

CONTEMPORARY ENGLISH VERSION

Paying Taxes (Matthew 22.15-22; Mark 12.13-17)

20Jesus' enemies kept watching him closely, because they wanted to hand him over to the Roman governor. So they sent some men who pretended to be good. But they were really spies trying to catch Jesus saying something wrong. 21The spies said to him, "Teacher, we know that you teach the truth about what God wants people to do. And you treat everyone with the same respect, no matter who they are. 22Tell us, should we pay taxes to the Emperor or not?"

23Jesus knew that they were trying to trick him. So he told them, 24"Show me a coin." Then he asked, "Whose picture and name are on it?"

"The Emperor's," they answered.

25Then he told them, "Give the Emperor what belongs to him and give God what belongs to God." 26Jesus' enemies could not catch him saying anything wrong there in front of the people. They were amazed at his answer and kept quiet.

Life in the Future World (Matthew 22.23-33; Mark 12.18-27)

27The Saddducees did not believe that people would rise to life after death. So some of them came to Jesus 28and said:

> Teacher, Moses wrote that if a married man dies and has no children, his brother should marry the widow. Their first son would then be thought of as the son of the dead brother.

29There were once seven brothers. The first one married, but died without having any children. 30The second

NEW INTERNATIONAL VERSION

Paying Taxes to Caesar

20 Keeping a close watch on him, they sent spies, who pretended to be honest. They hoped to catch Jesus in something he said so that they might hand him over to the power and authority of the governor. 21 So the spies questioned him: "Teacher, we know that you speak and teach what is right, and that you do not show partiality but teach the way of God in accordance with the truth. 22 Is it right for us to pay taxes to Caesar or not?"

23 He saw through their duplicity and said to them, 24 "Show me a denarius. Whose portrait and inscription are on it?"

25 "Caesar's," they replied.

He said to them, "Then give to Caesar what is Caesar's, and to God what is God's."

26 They were unable to trap him in what he had said there in public. And astonished by his answer, they became silent.

The Resurrection and Marriage

27 Some of the Sadducees, who say there is no resurrection, came to Jesus with a question. 28 "Teacher," they said, "Moses wrote for us that if a man's brother dies and leaves a wife but no children, the man must marry the widow and have children for his brother. 29 Now there were seven brothers. The first one married a woman and died childless.

NEW LIVING TRANSLATION

Taxes for Caesar

20 Watching for their opportunity, the leaders sent secret agents pretending to be honest men. They tried to get Jesus to say something that could be reported to the Roman governor so he would arrest Jesus. 21 They said, "Teacher, we know that you speak and teach what is right and are not influenced by what others think. You sincerely teach the ways of God. 22 Now tell us—is it right to pay taxes to the Roman government or not?"

23 He saw through their trickery and said, 24 "Show me a Roman coin.* Whose picture and title are stamped on it?"

"Caesar's," they replied.

25 "Well then," he said, "give to Caesar what belongs to him. But everything that belongs to God must be given to God." 26 So they failed to trap him in the presence of the people. Instead, they were amazed by his answer, and they were silenced.

Discussion about Resurrection

27 Then some Sadducees stepped forward—a group of Jews who say there is no resurrection after death. 28 They posed this question: "Teacher, Moses gave us a law that if a man dies, leaving a wife but no children, his brother should marry the widow and have a child who will be the brother's heir.* 29 Well, there were seven brothers. The oldest married and then died without children. 30 His brother

20:24 Greek *a denarius.* **20:28** Deut 25:5-6.

NEW KING JAMES VERSION

The Pharisees: Is It Lawful to Pay Taxes to Caesar?

20 So they watched *Him,* and sent spies who pretended to be righteous, that they might seize on His words, in order to deliver Him to the power and the authority of the governor.

21 Then they asked Him, saying, "Teacher, we know that You say and teach rightly, and You do not show personal favoritism, but teach the way of God in truth: 22 Is it lawful for us to pay taxes to Caesar or not?"

23 But He perceived their craftiness, and said to them, "Why do you test Me?[d] 24 Show Me a denarius. Whose image and inscription does it have?"

They answered and said, "Caesar's."

25 And He said to them, "Render therefore to Caesar the things that are Caesar's, and to God the things that are God's."

26 But they could not catch Him in His words in the presence of the people. And they marveled at His answer and kept silent.

The Sadducees: What About the Resurrection?

27 Then some of the Sadducees, who deny that there is a resurrection, came to *Him* and asked Him, 28 saying: "Teacher, Moses wrote to us *that* if a man's brother dies, having a wife, and he dies without children, his brother should take his wife and raise up offspring for his brother. 29 Now there were seven brothers. And the first took a wife,

20:23 [d] NU-Text omits *Why do you test Me?*

THE MESSAGE

Paying Taxes

Watching for a chance to get him, they sent spies who posed as honest inquirers, hoping to trick him into saying something that would get him in trouble with the law. So they asked him, "Teacher, we know that you're honest and straightforward when you teach, that you don't pander to anyone but teach the way of God accurately. Tell us: Is it lawful to pay taxes to Caesar or not?"

He knew they were laying for him and said, "Show me a coin. Now, this engraving, who does it look like and what does it say?"

"Caesar," they said.

Jesus said, "Then give Caesar what is his and give God what is his."

Try as they might, they couldn't trap him into saying anything incriminating. His answer caught them off guard and left them speechless.

All Intimacies Will Be With God

Some Sadducees came up. This is the Jewish party that denies any possibility of resurrection. They asked, "Teacher, Moses wrote us that if a man dies and leaves a wife but no child, his brother is obligated to take the widow to wife and get her with child. Well, there once were seven brothers. The first took a wife. He died childless. The

KING JAMES VERSION

30 And the second took her to wife, and he died child-
less.
31 And the third took her; and in like manner the seven
also: and they left no children, and died.
32 Last of all the woman died also.
33 Therefore in the resurrection whose wife of them is
she? for seven had her to wife.
34 And Jesus answering said unto them, The children of
this world marry, and are given in marriage:
35 But they which shall be accounted worthy to obtain
that world, and the resurrection from the dead, neither
marry, nor are given in marriage:
36 Neither can they die any more: for they are equal
unto the angels; and are the children of God, being the
children of the resurrection.
37 Now that the dead are raised, even Moses shewed at
the bush, when he calleth the Lord the God of Abraham,
and the God of Isaac, and the God of Jacob.
38 For he is not a God of the dead, but of the living: for
all live unto him.
39 ¶ Then certain of the scribes answering said, Master,
thou hast well said.
40 And after that they durst not ask him any *question
at all*.
41 And he said unto them, How say they that Christ is
David's son?
42 And David himself saith in the book of Psalms, The

NEW AMERICAN STANDARD BIBLE

30 and the second
31 and the third married her; and in the same way all
seven died, leaving no children.
32 "Finally the woman died also.
33 "In the resurrection therefore, which one's wife will
she be? For all seven had married her."
34 Jesus said to them, "The sons of this age marry and
are given in marriage,
35 but those who are considered worthy to attain to that
age and the resurrection from the dead, neither marry nor
are given in marriage;
36 for they cannot even die anymore, because they are
like angels, and are sons of God, being sons of the resur-
rection.
37 "But that the dead are raised, even Moses showed, in
the *passage about the burning* bush, where he calls the
Lord THE GOD OF ABRAHAM, AND THE GOD OF ISAAC, AND THE
GOD OF JACOB.
38 "Now He is not the God of the dead but of the living;
for all live to Him."
39 Some of the scribes answered and said, "Teacher,
You have spoken well."
40 For they did not have courage to question Him any
longer about anything.
41 Then He said to them, "How *is it that* they say [2]the
Christ is David's son?
42 "For David himself says in the book of Psalms,

20:41 [2] I.e. the Messiah

NEW CENTURY VERSION

children. 30Then the second brother married the widow,
and he died. 31And the third brother married the widow,
and he died. The same thing happened with all seven
brothers; they died and had no children. 32Finally, the
woman died also. 33Since all seven brothers had married
her, whose wife will she be when people rise from the
dead?"

34Jesus said to them, "On earth, people marry and are
given to someone to marry. 35But those who will be worthy
to be raised from the dead and live again will not marry,
nor will they be given to someone to marry. 36In that life
they are like angels and cannot die. They are children of
God, because they have been raised from the dead. 37Even
Moses clearly showed that the dead are raised to life.
When he wrote about the burning bush,[a] he said that the
Lord is 'the God of Abraham, the God of Isaac, and the God
of Jacob.'[b] 38God is the God of the living, not the dead,
because all people are alive to him."

39Some of the teachers of the law said, "Teacher, your
answer was good." 40No one was brave enough to ask him
another question.

Is the Christ the Son of David?

41Then Jesus said, "Why do people say that the Christ is
the Son of David? 42In the book of Psalms, David himself
says:

20:37 [a] **burning bush** Read Exodus 3:1–12 in the Old Testament.
20:37 [b] **'the God of...Jacob'** These words are taken from Exodus 3:6.

CONTEMPORARY ENGLISH VERSION

one married his brother's widow, and he also died with-
out having any children. 31The same thing happened to
the third one. Finally, all seven brothers married that
woman and died without having any children. 32At last
the woman died. 33When God raises people from death,
whose wife will this woman be? All seven brothers had
married her.
34Jesus answered:
The people in this world get married. 35But in the future
world no one who is worthy to rise from death will either
marry 36or die. They will be like the angels and will be
God's children, because they have been raised to life.
37In the story about the burning bush, Moses clearly
shows that people will live again. He said, "The Lord is
the God worshiped by Abraham, Isaac, and Jacob."[a] 38So
the Lord isn't the God of the dead, but of the living. This
means that everyone is alive as far as God is concerned.
39Some of the teachers of the Law of Moses said,
"Teacher, you have given a good answer!" 40From then on,
no one dared to ask Jesus any questions.

About David's Son (Matthew 22.41-46; Mark 12.35-37)

41Jesus asked, "Why do people say that the Messiah will
be the son of King David?[b] 42In the book of Psalms, David
himself says,

[a] **20.37** *"The Lord is the God worshiped by Abraham, Isaac, and Jacob"*: Jesus argues that if God is worshiped by these three, they must be alive, because he is the God of the living. [b] **20.41** *the son of King David*: See the note at 18.38.

NEW INTERNATIONAL VERSION

[30]The second [31]and then the third married her, and in the same way the seven died, leaving no children. [32]Finally, the woman died too. [33]Now then, at the resurrection whose wife will she be, since the seven were married to her?"

[34]Jesus replied, "The people of this age marry and are given in marriage. [35]But those who are considered worthy of taking part in that age and in the resurrection from the dead will neither marry nor be given in marriage, [36]and they can no longer die; for they are like the angels. They are God's children, since they are children of the resurrection. [37]But in the account of the bush, even Moses showed that the dead rise, for he calls the Lord 'the God of Abraham, and the God of Isaac, and the God of Jacob.'[c] [38]He is not the God of the dead, but of the living, for to him all are alive."

[39]Some of the teachers of the law responded, "Well said, teacher!" [40]And no one dared to ask him any more questions.

Whose Son Is the Christ?

[41]Then Jesus said to them, "How is it that they say the Christ[d] is the Son of David? [42]David himself declares in the Book of Psalms:

[c] *37* Exodus 3:6 [d] *41* Or *Messiah*

NEW LIVING TRANSLATION

married the widow, but he also died. Still no children. [31]And so it went, one after the other, until each of the seven had married her and died, leaving no children. [32]Finally, the woman died, too. [33]So tell us, whose wife will she be in the resurrection? For all seven were married to her!"

[34]Jesus replied, "Marriage is for people here on earth. [35]But that is not the way it will be in the age to come. For those worthy of being raised from the dead won't be married then. [36]And they will never die again. In these respects they are like angels. They are children of God raised up to new life. [37]But now, as to whether the dead will be raised—even Moses proved this when he wrote about the burning bush. Long after Abraham, Isaac, and Jacob had died, he referred to the Lord* as 'the God of Abraham, the God of Isaac, and the God of Jacob.'* [38]So he is the God of the living, not the dead. They are all alive to him."

[39]"Well said, Teacher!" remarked some of the teachers of religious law who were standing there. [40]And that ended their questions; no one dared to ask any more.

Whose Son Is the Messiah?

[41]Then Jesus presented them with a question. "Why is it," he asked, "that the Messiah is said to be the son of David? [42]For David himself wrote in the book of Psalms:

20:37a Greek *when he wrote about the bush. He referred to the Lord.*
20:37b Exod 3:6.

NEW KING JAMES VERSION

and died without children. [30]And the second[e] took her as wife, and he died childless. [31]Then the third took her, and in like manner the seven also; and they left no children,[f] and died. [32]Last of all the woman died also. [33]Therefore, in the resurrection, whose wife does she become? For all seven had her as wife."

[34]Jesus answered and said to them, "The sons of this age marry and are given in marriage. [35]But those who are counted worthy to attain that age, and the resurrection from the dead, neither marry nor are given in marriage; [36]nor can they die anymore, for they are equal to the angels and are sons of God, being sons of the resurrection. [37]But even Moses showed in the *burning* bush *passage* that the dead are raised, when he called the Lord *'the God of Abraham, the God of Isaac, and the God of Jacob.'*[g] [38]For He is not the God of the dead but of the living, for all live to Him."

[39]Then some of the scribes answered and said, "Teacher, You have spoken well." [40]But after that they dared not question Him anymore.

Jesus: How Can David Call His Descendant Lord?

[41]And He said to them, "How can they say that the Christ is the Son of David? [42]Now David himself said in the Book of Psalms:

20:30 [e] NU-Text ends verse 30 here. **20:31** [f] NU-Text and M-Text read *the seven also left no children.* **20:37** [g] Exodus 3:6, 15

THE MESSAGE

second married her and died, then the third, and eventually all seven had their turn, but no child. After all that, the wife died. That wife, now—in the resurrection whose wife is she? All seven married her."

Jesus said, "Marriage is a major preoccupation here, but not there. Those who are included in the resurrection of the dead will no longer be concerned with marriage nor, of course, with death. They will have better things to think about, if you can believe it. All ecstasies and intimacies then will be with God. Even Moses exclaimed about resurrection at the burning bush, saying, 'God: God of Abraham, God of Isaac, God of Jacob!' God isn't the God of dead men, but of the living. To him all are alive."

Some of the religion scholars said, "Teacher, that's a great answer!" For a while, anyway, no one dared put questions to him.

✣

Then he put a question to them: "How is it that they say that the Messiah is David's son? In the Book of Psalms, David clearly says,

KING JAMES VERSION

LORD said unto my Lord, Sit thou on my right hand,
43 Till I make thine enemies thy footstool.
44 David therefore calleth him Lord, how is he then his son?
45 Then in the audience of all the people he said unto his disciples,
46 Beware of the scribes, which desire to walk in long robes, and love greetings in the markets, and the highest seats in the synagogues, and the chief rooms at feasts;
47 Which devour widows' houses, and for a shew make long prayers: the same shall receive greater damnation.

21 And he looked up, and saw the rich men casting their gifts into the treasury.
2 And he saw also a certain poor widow casting in thither two mites.
3 And he said, Of a truth I say unto you, that this poor widow hath cast in more than they all:
4 For all these have of their abundance cast in unto the offerings of God: but she of her penury hath cast in all the living that she had.

NEW AMERICAN STANDARD BIBLE

'THE LORD SAID TO MY LORD,
"SIT AT MY RIGHT HAND,
43 UNTIL I MAKE YOUR ENEMIES A FOOTSTOOL FOR YOUR FEET." '
44 "Therefore David calls Him 'Lord,' and how is He his son?"
45 And while all the people were listening, He said to the disciples,
46 "Beware of the scribes, who like to walk around in long robes, and love respectful greetings in the market places, and chief seats in the synagogues and places of honor at banquets,
47 who devour widows' houses, and for appearance's sake offer long prayers. These will receive greater condemnation."

The Widow's Gift

21 And He looked up and saw the rich putting their gifts into the treasury.
2 And He saw a poor widow putting in two small copper coins.
3 And He said, "Truly I say to you, this poor widow put in more than all *of them;*
4 for they all out of their surplus put into the offering; but she out of her poverty put in all that she had to live on."

NEW CENTURY VERSION

'The Lord said to my Lord:
Sit by me at my right side,
43 until I put your enemies under your
control.'[c] *Psalm 110:1*

44 David calls the Christ 'Lord,' so how can the Christ be his son?"

Jesus Accuses Some Leaders

45 While all the people were listening, Jesus said to his followers, 46 "Beware of the teachers of the law. They like to walk around wearing fancy clothes, and they love for people to greet them with respect in the marketplaces. They love to have the most important seats in the synagogues and at feasts. 47 But they cheat widows and steal their houses and then try to make themselves look good by saying long prayers. They will receive a greater punishment."

True Giving

21 As Jesus looked up, he saw some rich people putting their gifts into the Temple money box.[a] 2 Then he saw a poor widow putting two small copper coins into the box. 3 He said, "I tell you the truth, this poor widow gave more than all those rich people. 4 They gave only what they did not need. This woman is very poor, but she gave all she had to live on."

20:43 [c] **until...control** Literally, "until I make your enemies a footstool for your feet." 21:1 [a] **money box** A special box in the Jewish place of worship where people put their gifts to God.

CONTEMPORARY ENGLISH VERSION

'The Lord said to my Lord,
Sit at my right side[c]
43 until I make your enemies
into a footstool for you.'

44 David spoke of the Messiah as his Lord, so how can the Messiah be his son?"

Jesus and the Teachers of the Law of Moses

(Matthew 23.1-36; Mark 12.38-40; Luke 11.37-54)

45 While everyone was listening to Jesus, he said to his disciples:

46 Guard against the teachers of the Law of Moses! They love to walk around in long robes, and they like to be greeted in the market. They want the front seats in the meeting places and the best seats at banquets. 47 But they cheat widows out of their homes and then pray long prayers just to show off. These teachers will be punished most of all.

A Widow's Offering (Mark 12.41-44)

21 Jesus looked up and saw some rich people tossing their gifts into the offering box. 2 He also saw a poor widow putting in two pennies. 3 And he said, "I tell you that this poor woman has put in more than all the others. 4 Everyone else gave what they didn't need. But she is very poor and gave everything she had."

[c] **20.42** *right side*: The place of power and honor.

NEW INTERNATIONAL VERSION

" 'The Lord said to my Lord:
"Sit at my right hand
43 until I make your enemies
a footstool for your feet." '[e]

44 David calls him 'Lord.' How then can he be his son?"
45 While all the people were listening, Jesus said to his
disciples, 46 "Beware of the teachers of the law. They like to
walk around in flowing robes and love to be greeted in the
marketplaces and have the most important seats in the
synagogues and the places of honor at banquets. 47 They
devour widows' houses and for a show make lengthy
prayers. Such men will be punished most severely."

The Widow's Offering

21 As he looked up, Jesus saw the rich putting their
gifts into the temple treasury. 2 He also saw a poor
widow put in two very small copper coins.[a] 3 "I tell you the
truth," he said, "this poor widow has put in more than all
the others. 4 All these people gave their gifts out of their
wealth; but she out of her poverty put in all she had to
live on."

[e] *43* Psalm 110:1 [a] *2* Greek *two lepta*

NEW LIVING TRANSLATION

'The LORD said to my Lord,
Sit in honor at my right hand
43 until I humble your enemies,
making them a footstool under your feet.'*

44 Since David called him Lord, how can he be his son at
the same time?"
45 Then, with the crowds listening, he turned to his disci-
ples and said, 46 "Beware of these teachers of religious law!
For they love to parade in flowing robes and to have every-
one bow to them as they walk in the marketplaces. And
how they love the seats of honor in the synagogues and at
banquets. 47 But they shamelessly cheat widows out of
their property, and then, to cover up the kind of people
they really are, they make long prayers in public. Because
of this, their punishment will be the greater."

The Widow's Offering

21 While Jesus was in the Temple, he watched the
rich people putting their gifts into the collection
box. 2 Then a poor widow came by and dropped in two pen-
nies.* 3 "I assure you," he said, "this poor widow has given
more than all the rest of them. 4 For they have given a tiny
part of their surplus, but she, poor as she is, has given
everything she has."

20:42-43 Ps 110:1. **21:2** Greek *2 lepta.*

NEW KING JAMES VERSION

'The LORD said to my Lord,
" Sit at My right hand,
43 *Till I make Your enemies Your footstool." '[h]*

44 Therefore David calls Him *'Lord'*; how is He then his
Son?"

Beware of the Scribes

45 Then, in the hearing of all the people, He said to His
disciples, 46 "Beware of the scribes, who desire to go
around in long robes, love greetings in the marketplaces,
the best seats in the synagogues, and the best places at
feasts, 47 who devour widows' houses, and for a pretense
make long prayers. These will receive greater condemna-
tion."

The Widow's Two Mites

21 And He looked up and saw the rich putting their
gifts into the treasury, 2 and He saw also a certain
poor widow putting in two mites. 3 So He said, "Truly I say
to you that this poor widow has put in more than all; 4 for
all these out of their abundance have put in offerings for
God,[a] but she out of her poverty put in all the livelihood
that she had."

20:43 [h] Psalm 110:1 **21:4** [a] NU-Text omits *for God.*

THE MESSAGE

'God said to my Master,
"Sit here at my right hand
until I put your enemies under your feet." '

David here designates the Messiah as 'my Master'—so
how can the Messiah also be his 'son'?"

With everybody listening, Jesus spoke to his disciples.
"Watch out for the religion scholars. They love to walk
around in academic gowns, preen in the radiance of public
flattery, bask in prominent positions, sit at the head table
at every church function. And all the time they are exploit-
ing the weak and helpless. The longer their prayers, the
worse they get. But they'll pay for it in the end."

21 Just then he looked up and saw the rich people
dropping offerings in the collection plate. Then
he saw a poor widow put in two pennies. He said, "The
plain truth is that this widow has given by far the largest
offering today. All these others made offerings that they'll
never miss; she gave extravagantly what she couldn't
afford—she gave her all!"

KING JAMES VERSION

5 ¶ And as some spake of the temple, how it was adorned with goodly stones and gifts, he said,

6 *As for* these things which ye behold, the days will come, in the which there shall not be left one stone upon another, that shall not be thrown down.

7 And they asked him, saying, Master, but when shall these things be? and what sign *will there be* when these things shall come to pass?

8 And he said, Take heed that ye be not deceived: for many shall come in my name, saying, I am *Christ*; and the time draweth near: go ye not therefore after them.

9 But when ye shall hear of wars and commotions, be not terrified: for these things must first come to pass; but the end *is* not by and by.

10 Then said he unto them, Nation shall rise against nation, and kingdom against kingdom:

11 And great earthquakes shall be in divers places, and famines, and pestilences; and fearful sights and great signs shall there be from heaven.

12 But before all these, they shall lay their hands on you, and persecute *you*, delivering *you* up to the synagogues, and into prisons, being brought before kings and rulers for my name's sake.

13 And it shall turn to you for a testimony.

14 Settle *it* therefore in your hearts, not to meditate before what ye shall answer:

NEW AMERICAN STANDARD BIBLE

5 And while some were talking about the temple, that it was adorned with beautiful stones and votive gifts, He said,

6 "*As for* these things which you are looking at, the days will come in which there will not be left one stone upon another which will not be torn down."

7 They questioned Him, saying, "Teacher, when therefore will these things happen? And what *will be* the sign when these things are about to take place?"

8 And He said, "See to it that you are not misled; for many will come in My name, saying, 'I am *He,*' and, 'The time is near.' Do not go after them.

9 "When you hear of wars and disturbances, do not be terrified; for these things must take place first, but the end *does* not *follow* immediately."

Things to Come

10 Then He continued by saying to them, "Nation will rise against nation and kingdom against kingdom,

11 and there will be great earthquakes, and in various places plagues and famines; and there will be terrors and great signs from heaven.

12 "But before all these things, they will lay their hands on you and will persecute you, delivering you to the synagogues and prisons, bringing you before kings and governors for My name's sake.

13 "It will lead to an opportunity for your testimony.

14 "So make up your minds not to prepare beforehand to defend yourselves;

NEW CENTURY VERSION

The Temple Will Be Destroyed

5Some people were talking about the Temple and how it was decorated with beautiful stones and gifts offered to God.

But Jesus said, 6"As for these things you are looking at, the time will come when not one stone will be left on another. Every stone will be thrown down."

7They asked Jesus, "Teacher, when will these things happen? What will be the sign that they are about to take place?"

8Jesus said, "Be careful so you are not fooled. Many people will come in my name, saying, 'I am the One' and, 'The time has come!' But don't follow them. 9When you hear about wars and riots, don't be afraid, because these things must happen first, but the end will come later."

10Then he said to them, "Nations will fight against other nations, and kingdoms against other kingdoms. 11In various places there will be great earthquakes, sicknesses, and a lack of food. Fearful events and great signs will come from heaven.

12"But before all these things happen, people will arrest you and treat you cruelly. They will judge you in their synagogues and put you in jail and force you to stand before kings and governors, because you follow me. 13But this will give you an opportunity to tell about me. 14Make up your minds not to worry ahead of time about what you will

CONTEMPORARY ENGLISH VERSION

The Temple Will Be Destroyed
(Matthew 24.1, 2; Mark 13.1, 2)

5Some people were talking about the beautiful stones used to build the temple and about the gifts that had been placed in it. Jesus said, 6"Do you see these stones? The time is coming when not one of them will be left in place. They will all be knocked down."

Warning about Trouble (Matthew 24.3-14; Mark 13.3-13)

7Some people asked, "Teacher, when will all this happen? How can we know when these things are about to take place?"

8Jesus replied:

Don't be fooled by those who will come and claim to be me. They will say, "I am Christ!" and "Now is the time!" But don't follow them. 9When you hear about wars and riots, don't be afraid. These things will have to happen first, but that isn't the end.

10Nations will go to war against one another, and kingdoms will attack each other. 11There will be great earthquakes, and in many places people will starve to death and suffer terrible diseases. All sorts of frightening things will be seen in the sky.

12Before all this happens, you will be arrested and punished. You will be tried in your meeting places and put in jail. Because of me you will be placed on trial before kings and governors. 13But this will be your chance to tell about your faith.

14Don't worry about what you will say to defend your-

NEW INTERNATIONAL VERSION

Signs of the End of the Age

5 Some of his disciples were remarking about how the temple was adorned with beautiful stones and with gifts dedicated to God. But Jesus said, 6 "As for what you see here, the time will come when not one stone will be left on another; every one of them will be thrown down."

7 "Teacher," they asked, "when will these things happen? And what will be the sign that they are about to take place?"

8 He replied: "Watch out that you are not deceived. For many will come in my name, claiming, 'I am he,' and, 'The time is near.' Do not follow them. 9 When you hear of wars and revolutions, do not be frightened. These things must happen first, but the end will not come right away."

10 Then he said to them: "Nation will rise against nation, and kingdom against kingdom. 11 There will be great earthquakes, famines and pestilences in various places, and fearful events and great signs from heaven.

12 "But before all this, they will lay hands on you and persecute you. They will deliver you to synagogues and prisons, and you will be brought before kings and governors, and all on account of my name. 13 This will result in your being witnesses to them. 14 But make up your mind not to worry beforehand how you will defend yourselves.

NEW LIVING TRANSLATION

Jesus Foretells the Future

5 Some of his disciples began talking about the beautiful stonework of the Temple and the memorial decorations on the walls. But Jesus said, 6 "The time is coming when all these things will be so completely demolished that not one stone will be left on top of another."

7 "Teacher," they asked, "when will all this take place? And will there be any sign ahead of time?"

8 He replied, "Don't let anyone mislead you. For many will come in my name, claiming to be the Messiah* and saying, 'The time has come!' But don't believe them. 9 And when you hear of wars and insurrections, don't panic. Yes, these things must come, but the end won't follow immediately." 10 Then he added, "Nations and kingdoms will proclaim war against each other. 11 There will be great earthquakes, and there will be famines and epidemics in many lands, and there will be terrifying things and great miraculous signs in the heavens.

12 "But before all this occurs, there will be a time of great persecution. You will be dragged into synagogues and prisons, and you will be accused before kings and governors of being my followers. 13 This will be your opportunity to tell them about me. 14 So don't worry about how to answer the

21:8 Greek *name, saying, 'I am.'*

NEW KING JAMES VERSION

Jesus Predicts the Destruction of the Temple

5 Then, as some spoke of the temple, how it was adorned with beautiful stones and donations, He said, 6 "These things which you see—the days will come in which not *one* stone shall be left upon another that shall not be thrown down."

The Signs of the Times and the End of the Age

7 So they asked Him, saying, "Teacher, but when will these things be? And what sign *will there be* when these things are about to take place?"

8 And He said: "Take heed that you not be deceived. For many will come in My name, saying, 'I am *He,*' and, 'The time has drawn near.' Therefore[b] do not go after them. 9 But when you hear of wars and commotions, do not be terrified; for these things must come to pass first, but the end *will not come* immediately."

10 Then He said to them, "Nation will rise against nation, and kingdom against kingdom. 11 And there will be great earthquakes in various places, and famines and pestilences; and there will be fearful sights and great signs from heaven. 12 But before all these things, they will lay their hands on you and persecute *you,* delivering *you* up to the synagogues and prisons. You will be brought before kings and rulers for My name's sake. 13 But it will turn out for you as an occasion for testimony. 14 Therefore settle *it* in your hearts not to meditate beforehand on what you

21:8 [b] NU-Text omits *Therefore.*

THE MESSAGE

Watch Out for Doomsday Deceivers

One day people were standing around talking about the Temple, remarking how beautiful it was, the splendor of its stonework and memorial gifts. Jesus said, "All this you're admiring so much—the time is coming when every stone in that building will end up in a heap of rubble."

They asked him, "Teacher, when is this going to happen? What clue will we get that it's about to take place?"

He said, "Watch out for the doomsday deceivers. Many leaders are going to show up with forged identities claiming, 'I'm the One,' or, 'The end is near.' Don't fall for any of that. When you hear of wars and uprisings, keep your head and don't panic. This is routine history and no sign of the end."

He went on, "Nation will fight nation and ruler fight ruler, over and over. Huge earthquakes will occur in various places. There will be famines. You'll think at times that the very sky is falling.

"But before any of this happens, they'll arrest you, hunt you down and drag you to court and jail. It will go from bad to worse, dog-eat-dog, everyone at your throat because you carry my name. You'll end up on the witness stand, called to testify. Make up your mind right now not to

KING JAMES VERSION

15 For I will give you a mouth and wisdom, which all your adversaries shall not be able to gainsay nor resist.

16 And ye shall be betrayed both by parents, and brethren, and kinsfolks, and friends; and *some* of you shall they cause to be put to death.

17 And ye shall be hated of all *men* for my name's sake.

18 But there shall not an hair of your head perish.

19 In your patience possess ye your souls.

20 ¶ And when ye shall see Jerusalem compassed with armies, then know that the desolation thereof is nigh.

21 Then let them which are in Judaea flee to the mountains; and let them which are in the midst of it depart out; and let not them that are in the countries enter thereinto.

22 For these be the days of vengeance, that all things which are written may be fulfilled.

23 But woe unto them that are with child, and to them that give suck, in those days! for there shall be great distress in the land, and wrath upon this people.

24 And they shall fall by the edge of the sword, and shall be led away captive into all nations: and Jerusalem shall be trodden down of the Gentiles, until the times of the Gentiles be fulfilled.

25 And there shall be signs in the sun, and in the moon, and in the stars; and upon the earth distress of nations, with perplexity; the sea and the waves roaring;

26 Men's hearts failing them for fear, and for looking

NEW AMERICAN STANDARD BIBLE

15 for I will give you utterance and wisdom which none of your opponents will be able to resist or refute.

16 "But you will be betrayed even by parents and brothers and relatives and friends, and they will put *some* of you to death,

17 and you will be hated by all because of My name.

18 "Yet not a hair of your head will perish.

19 "By your endurance you will gain your lives.

20 "But when you see Jerusalem surrounded by armies, then recognize that her desolation is near.

21 "Then those who are in Judea must flee to the mountains, and those who are in the midst of the city must leave, and those who are in the country must not enter the city;

22 because these are days of vengeance, so that all things which are written will be fulfilled.

23 "Woe to those who are pregnant and to those who are nursing babies in those days; for there will be great distress upon the land and wrath to this people;

24 and they will fall by the edge of the sword, and will be led captive into all the nations; and Jerusalem will be trampled under foot by the Gentiles until the times of the Gentiles are fulfilled.

The Return of Christ

25 "There will be signs in sun and moon and stars, and on the earth dismay among nations, in perplexity at the roaring of the sea and the waves,

26 men fainting from fear and the expectation of the

NEW CENTURY VERSION

say. 15I will give you the wisdom to say things that none
of your enemies will be able to stand against or prove
wrong. 16Even your parents, brothers, relatives, and
friends will turn against you, and they will kill some of
you. 17All people will hate you because you follow me.
18But none of these things can really harm you. 19By con-
tinuing to have faith you will save your lives.

Jerusalem Will Be Destroyed

20"When you see armies all around Jerusalem, you will
know it will soon be destroyed. 21At that time, the people
in Judea should run away to the mountains. The people in
Jerusalem must get out, and those who are near the city
should not go in. 22These are the days of punishment to
bring about all that is written in the Scriptures. 23How ter-
rible it will be for women who are pregnant or have nurs-
ing babies! Great trouble will come upon this land, and
God will be angry with these people. 24They will be killed
by the sword and taken as prisoners to all nations.
Jerusalem will be crushed by non-Jewish people until their
time is over.

Don't Fear

25"There will be signs in the sun, moon, and stars. On
earth, nations will be afraid and confused because of the
roar and fury of the sea. 26People will be so afraid they will

CONTEMPORARY ENGLISH VERSION

selves. 15I will give you the wisdom to know what to
say. None of your enemies will be able to oppose you or
to say that you are wrong. 16You will be betrayed by
your own parents, brothers, family, and friends. Some of
you will even be killed. 17Because of me, you will be
hated by everyone. 18But don't worry![a] 19You will be
saved by being faithful to me.

Jerusalem Will Be Destroyed

(Matthew 24.15-21; Mark 13.14-19)

20When you see Jerusalem surrounded by soldiers,
you will know that it will soon be destroyed. 21If you are
living in Judea at that time, run to the mountains. If you
are in the city, leave it. And if you are out in the coun-
try, don't go back into the city. 22This time of punish-
ment is what is written about in the Scriptures. 23It will
be an awful time for women who are expecting babies or
nursing young children! Everywhere in the land people
will suffer horribly and be punished. 24Some of them
will be killed by swords. Others will be carried off to for-
eign countries. Jerusalem will be overrun by foreign
nations until their time comes to an end.

When the Son of Man Appears

(Matthew 24.29-31; Mark 13.24-27)

25Strange things will happen to the sun, moon, and
stars. The nations on earth will be afraid of the roaring
sea and tides, and they won't know what to do. 26People

[a] 21.18 *But don't worry*: The Greek text has "Not a hair of your head will be lost," which means, "There's no need to worry."

NEW INTERNATIONAL VERSION

15For I will give you words and wisdom that none of your
adversaries will be able to resist or contradict. 16You will
be betrayed even by parents, brothers, relatives and
friends, and they will put some of you to death. 17All men
will hate you because of me. 18But not a hair of your head
will perish. 19By standing firm you will gain life.
20"When you see Jerusalem being surrounded by armies,
you will know that its desolation is near. 21Then let those
who are in Judea flee to the mountains, let those in the
city get out, and let those in the country not enter the city.
22For this is the time of punishment in fulfillment of all
that has been written. 23How dreadful it will be in those
days for pregnant women and nursing mothers! There will
be great distress in the land and wrath against this people.
24They will fall by the sword and will be taken as prisoners
to all the nations. Jerusalem will be trampled on by the
Gentiles until the times of the Gentiles are fulfilled.
25"There will be signs in the sun, moon and stars. On the
earth, nations will be in anguish and perplexity at the roar-
ing and tossing of the sea. 26Men will faint from terror,

NEW LIVING TRANSLATION

charges against you, 15for I will give you the right words
and such wisdom that none of your opponents will be able
to reply! 16Even those closest to you—your parents, broth-
ers, relatives, and friends—will betray you. And some of
you will be killed. 17And everyone will hate you because of
your allegiance to me. 18But not a hair of your head will
perish! 19By standing firm, you will win your souls.
20"And when you see Jerusalem surrounded by armies,
then you will know that the time of its destruction has
arrived. 21Then those in Judea must flee to the hills. Let
those in Jerusalem escape, and those outside the city
should not enter it for shelter. 22For those will be days of
God's vengeance, and the prophetic words of the Scriptures
will be fulfilled. 23How terrible it will be for pregnant
women and for mothers nursing their babies. For there will
be great distress in the land and wrath upon this people.
24They will be brutally killed by the sword or sent away as
captives to all the nations of the world. And Jerusalem will
be conquered and trampled down by the Gentiles until the
age of the Gentiles comes to an end.
25"And there will be strange events in the skies—signs
in the sun, moon, and stars. And down here on earth the
nations will be in turmoil, perplexed by the roaring seas
and strange tides. 26The courage of many people will falter

NEW KING JAMES VERSION

will answer; 15for I will give you a mouth and wisdom
which all your adversaries will not be able to contradict or
resist. 16You will be betrayed even by parents and broth-
ers, relatives and friends; and they will put *some* of you to
death. 17And you will be hated by all for My name's sake.
18But not a hair of your head shall be lost. 19By your
patience possess your souls.

The Destruction of Jerusalem

20"But when you see Jerusalem surrounded by armies,
then know that its desolation is near. 21Then let those who
are in Judea flee to the mountains, let those who are in the
midst of her depart, and let not those who are in the coun-
try enter her. 22For these are the days of vengeance, that
all things which are written may be fulfilled. 23But woe to
those who are pregnant and to those who are nursing
babies in those days! For there will be great distress in the
land and wrath upon this people. 24And they will fall by
the edge of the sword, and be led away captive into all
nations. And Jerusalem will be trampled by Gentiles until
the times of the Gentiles are fulfilled.

The Coming of the Son of Man

25"And there will be signs in the sun, in the moon, and
in the stars; and on the earth distress of nations, with per-
plexity, the sea and the waves roaring; 26men's hearts fail-
ing them from fear and the expectation of those things

THE MESSAGE

worry about it. I'll give you the words and wisdom that
will reduce all your accusers to stammers and stutters.

"You'll even be turned in by parents, brothers, relatives, and friends. Some of you will be killed. There's no telling who will hate you because of me. Even so, every detail of your body and soul—even the hairs of your head!—is in my care; nothing of you will be lost. Staying with it—that's what is required. Stay with it to the end. You won't be sorry; you'll be saved.

Vengeance Day

"When you see soldiers camped all around Jerusalem, then you'll know that she is about to be devastated. If you're living in Judea at the time, run for the hills. If you're in the city, get out quickly. If you're out in the fields, don't go home to get your coat. This is Vengeance Day—everything written about it will come to a head. Pregnant and nursing mothers will have it especially hard. Incredible misery! Torrential rage! People dropping like flies; people dragged off to prisons; Jerusalem under the boot of barbarians until the nations finish what was given them to do.

"It will seem like all hell has broken loose—sun, moon, stars, earth, sea, in an uproar and everyone all over the

KING JAMES VERSION

after those things which are coming on the earth: for the powers of heaven shall be shaken.
27 And then shall they see the Son of man coming in a cloud with power and great glory.
28 And when these things begin to come to pass, then look up, and lift up your heads; for your redemption draweth nigh.
29 ¶ And he spake to them a parable; Behold the fig tree, and all the trees;
30 When they now shoot forth, ye see and know of your own selves that summer is now nigh at hand.
31 So likewise ye, when ye see these things come to pass, know ye that the kingdom of God is nigh at hand.
32 Verily I say unto you, This generation shall not pass away, till all be fulfilled.
33 Heaven and earth shall pass away: but my words shall not pass away.
34 And take heed to yourselves, lest at any time your hearts be overcharged with surfeiting, and drunkenness, and cares of this life, and *so* that day come upon you unawares.
35 For as a snare shall it come on all them that dwell on the face of the whole earth.
36 Watch ye therefore, and pray always, that ye may be accounted worthy to escape all these things that shall come to pass, and to stand before the Son of man.
37 And in the day time he was teaching in the temple; and at night he went out, and abode in the mount that is called *the mount* of Olives.
38 And all the people came early in the morning to him in the temple, for to hear him.

NEW AMERICAN STANDARD BIBLE

things which are coming upon the world; for the powers of the heavens will be shaken.
27 "Then they will see THE SON OF MAN COMING IN A CLOUD with power and great glory.
28 "But when these things begin to take place, straighten up and lift up your heads, because your redemption is drawing near."
29 Then He told them a parable: "Behold the fig tree and all the trees;
30 as soon as they put forth *leaves,* you see it and know for yourselves that summer is now near.
31 "So you also, when you see these things happening, recognize that the kingdom of God is near.
32 "Truly I say to you, this generation will not pass away until all things take place.
33 "Heaven and earth will pass away, but My words will not pass away.
34 "Be on guard, so that your hearts will not be weighted down with dissipation and drunkenness and the worries of life, and that day will not come on you suddenly like a trap;
35 for it will come upon all those who dwell on the face of all the earth.
36 "But keep on the alert at all times, praying that you may have strength to escape all these things that are about to take place, and to stand before the Son of Man."
37 Now during the day He was teaching in the temple, but at evening He would go out and spend the night on the mount that is called Olivet.
38 And all the people would get up early in the morning *to come* to Him in the temple to listen to Him.

NEW CENTURY VERSION

faint, wondering what is happening to the world, because
the powers of the heavens will be shaken. [27]Then people
will see the Son of Man coming in a cloud with power and
great glory. [28]When these things begin to happen, look up
and hold your heads high, because the time when God will
free you is near!"

Jesus' Words Will Live Forever

[29]Then Jesus told this story: "Look at the fig tree and all
the other trees. [30]When their leaves appear, you know that
summer is near. [31]In the same way, when you see these
things happening, you will know that God's kingdom is
near.
[32]"I tell you the truth, all these things will happen while
the people of this time are still living. [33]Earth and sky will
be destroyed, but the words I have spoken will never be
destroyed.

Be Ready All the Time

[34]"Be careful not to spend your time feasting, drinking,
or worrying about worldly things. If you do, that day
might come on you suddenly, [35]like a trap on all people on
earth. [36]So be ready all the time. Pray that you will be
strong enough to escape all these things that will happen
and that you will be able to stand before the Son of Man."
[37]During the day, Jesus taught the people in the Temple,
and at night he went out of the city and stayed on the
Mount of Olives. [38]Every morning all the people got up
early to go to the Temple to listen to him.

CONTEMPORARY ENGLISH VERSION

will be so frightened that they will faint because of what
is happening to the world. Every power in the sky will be
shaken.[b] [27]Then the Son of Man will be seen, coming in
a cloud with great power and glory. [28]When all of this
starts happening, stand up straight and be brave. You
will soon be set free.

A Lesson from a Fig Tree (Matthew 24.32-35; Mark 13.28-31)

[29]Then Jesus told them a story:
When you see a fig tree or any other tree [30]putting out
leaves, you know that summer will soon come. [31]So,
when you see these things happening, you know that
God's kingdom will soon be here. [32]You can be sure that
some of the people of this generation will still be alive
when all of this takes place. [33]The sky and the earth
won't last forever, but my words will.

A Warning

[34]Don't spend all of your time thinking about eating
or drinking or worrying about life. If you do, the final
day will suddenly catch you [35]like a trap. That day will
surprise everyone on earth. [36]Watch out and keep pray-
ing that you can escape all that is going to happen and
that the Son of Man will be pleased with you.
[37]Jesus taught in the temple each day, and he spent
each night on the Mount of Olives. [38]Everyone got up early
and came to the temple to hear him teach.

b 21.26 *Every power in the sky will be shaken*: In ancient times people thought that the stars were spiritual powers.

NEW INTERNATIONAL VERSION

apprehensive of what is coming on the world, for the heav-
enly bodies will be shaken. [27]At that time they will see the
Son of Man coming in a cloud with power and great glory.
[28]When these things begin to take place, stand up and lift
up your heads, because your redemption is drawing near."

[29]He told them this parable: "Look at the fig tree and all
the trees. [30]When they sprout leaves, you can see for your-
selves and know that summer is near. [31]Even so, when
you see these things happening, you know that the king-
dom of God is near.

[32]"I tell you the truth, this generation[b] will certainly not
pass away until all these things have happened. [33]Heaven
and earth will pass away, but my words will never pass
away.

[34]"Be careful, or your hearts will be weighed down with
dissipation, drunkenness and the anxieties of life, and that
day will close on you unexpectedly like a trap. [35]For it will
come upon all those who live on the face of the whole
earth. [36]Be always on the watch, and pray that you may be
able to escape all that is about to happen, and that you
may be able to stand before the Son of Man."

[37]Each day Jesus was teaching at the temple, and each
evening he went out to spend the night on the hill called
the Mount of Olives, [38]and all the people came early in the
morning to hear him at the temple.

[b] *32* Or *race*

NEW LIVING TRANSLATION

because of the fearful fate they see coming upon the earth,
because the stability of the very heavens will be broken up.
[27]Then everyone will see the Son of Man arrive on the
clouds with power and great glory.* [28]So when all these
things begin to happen, stand straight and look up, for
your salvation is near!"

[29]Then he gave them this illustration: "Notice the fig
tree, or any other tree. [30]When the leaves come out, you
know without being told that summer is near. [31]Just so,
when you see the events I've described taking place, you
can be sure that the Kingdom of God is near. [32]I assure
you, this generation* will not pass from the scene until all
these events have taken place. [33]Heaven and earth will
disappear, but my words will remain forever.

[34]"Watch out! Don't let me find you living in careless
ease and drunkenness, and filled with the worries of this
life. Don't let that day catch you unaware, [35]as in a trap.
For that day will come upon everyone living on the earth.
[36]Keep a constant watch. And pray that, if possible, you
may escape these horrors and stand before the Son of
Man."

[37]Every day Jesus went to the Temple to teach, and each
evening he returned to spend the night on the Mount of
Olives. [38]The crowds gathered early each morning to hear
him.

21:27 See Dan 7:13. **21:32** Or *this age,* or *this nation.*

NEW KING JAMES VERSION

which are coming on the earth, for the powers of the heav-
ens will be shaken. [27]Then they will see the Son of Man
coming in a cloud with power and great glory. [28]Now when
these things begin to happen, look up and lift up your
heads, because your redemption draws near."

The Parable of the Fig Tree

[29]Then He spoke to them a parable: "Look at the fig tree,
and all the trees. [30]When they are already budding, you
see and know for yourselves that summer is now near.
[31]So you also, when you see these things happening, know
that the kingdom of God is near. [32]Assuredly, I say to you,
this generation will by no means pass away till all things
take place. [33]Heaven and earth will pass away, but My
words will by no means pass away.

The Importance of Watching

[34]"But take heed to yourselves, lest your hearts be
weighed down with carousing, drunkenness, and cares of
this life, and that Day come on you unexpectedly. [35]For it
will come as a snare on all those who dwell on the face of
the whole earth. [36]Watch therefore, and pray always that
you may be counted worthy[c] to escape all these things that
will come to pass, and to stand before the Son of Man."

[37]And in the daytime He was teaching in the temple, but
at night He went out and stayed on the mountain called
Olivet. [38]Then early in the morning all the people came to
Him in the temple to hear Him.

21:36 [c] NU-Text reads *may have strength.*

THE MESSAGE

world in a panic, the wind knocked out of them by the
threat of doom, the powers-that-be quaking.

"And then—then!—they'll see the Son of Man welcomed
in grand style—a glorious welcome! When all this starts to
happen, up on your feet. Stand tall with your heads high.
Help is on the way!"

He told them a story. "Look at a fig tree. Any tree for
that matter. When the leaves begin to show, one look tells
you that summer is right around the corner. The same
here—when you see these things happen, you know God's
kingdom is about here. Don't brush this off: I'm not just
saying this for some future generation, but for this one,
too—these things will happen. Sky and earth will wear
out; my words won't wear out.

"But be on your guard. Don't let the sharp edge of your
expectation get dulled by parties and drinking and shop-
ping. Otherwise, that Day is going to take you by complete
surprise, spring on you suddenly like a trap, for it's going
to come on everyone, everywhere, at once. So, whatever
you do, don't go to sleep at the switch. Pray constantly
that you will have the strength and wits to make it
through everything that's coming and end up on your feet
before the Son of Man."

He spent his days in the Temple teaching, but his nights
out on the mountain called Olives. All the people were up
at the crack of dawn to come to the Temple and listen to
him.

KING JAMES VERSION

22 Now the feast of unleavened bread drew nigh, which is called the Passover.

2 And the chief priests and scribes sought how they might kill him; for they feared the people.

3 Then entered Satan into Judas surnamed Iscariot, being of the number of the twelve.

4 And he went his way, and communed with the chief priests and captains, how he might betray him unto them.

5 And they were glad, and covenanted to give him money.

6 And he promised, and sought opportunity to betray him unto them in the absence of the multitude.

7 ¶ Then came the day of unleavened bread, when the passover must be killed.

8 And he sent Peter and John, saying, Go and prepare us the passover, that we may eat.

9 And they said unto him, Where wilt thou that we prepare?

10 And he said unto them, Behold, when ye are entered into the city, there shall a man meet you, bearing a pitcher of water; follow him into the house where he entereth in.

11 And ye shall say unto the goodman of the house, The Master saith unto thee, Where is the guestchamber, where I shall eat the passover with my disciples?

12 And he shall shew you a large upper room furnished: there make ready.

NEW AMERICAN STANDARD BIBLE

Preparing the Passover

22 Now the Feast of Unleavened Bread, which is called the Passover, was approaching.

2 The chief priests and the scribes were seeking how they might put Him to death; for they were afraid of the people.

3 And Satan entered into Judas who was called Iscariot, belonging to the number of the twelve.

4 And he went away and discussed with the chief priests and officers how he might betray Him to them.

5 They were glad and agreed to give him money.

6 So he consented, and *began* seeking a good opportunity to betray Him to them apart from the crowd.

7 Then came the *first* day of Unleavened Bread on which the Passover *lamb* had to be sacrificed.

8 And Jesus sent Peter and John, saying, "Go and prepare the Passover for us, so that we may eat it."

9 They said to Him, "Where do You want us to prepare it?"

10 And He said to them, "When you have entered the city, a man will meet you carrying a pitcher of water; follow him into the house that he enters.

11 "And you shall say to the owner of the house, 'The Teacher says to you, "Where is the guest room in which I may eat the Passover with My disciples?"'

12 "And he will show you a large, furnished upper room; prepare it there."

NEW CENTURY VERSION

Judas Becomes an Enemy of Jesus

22 It was almost time for the Feast of Unleavened Bread, called the Passover Feast. 2The leading priests and teachers of the law were trying to find a way to kill Jesus, because they were afraid of the people.

3Satan entered Judas Iscariot, one of Jesus' twelve apostles. 4Judas went to the leading priests and some of the soldiers who guarded the Temple and talked to them about a way to hand Jesus over to them. 5They were pleased and agreed to give Judas money. 6He agreed and watched for the best time to hand Jesus over to them when he was away from the crowd.

Jesus Eats the Passover Meal

7The Day of Unleavened Bread came when the Passover lambs had to be sacrificed. 8Jesus said to Peter and John, "Go and prepare the Passover meal for us to eat."

9They asked, "Where do you want us to prepare it?" 10Jesus said to them, "After you go into the city, a man carrying a jar of water will meet you. Follow him into the house that he enters, 11and tell the owner of the house, 'The Teacher says: Where is the guest room in which I may eat the Passover meal with my followers?' 12Then he will show you a large, furnished room upstairs. Prepare the Passover meal there."

CONTEMPORARY ENGLISH VERSION

A Plot To Kill Jesus

(Matthew 26.1-5, 14, 16; Mark 14.1, 2, 10, 11; John 11.45-53)

22 The Festival of Thin Bread, also called Passover, was near. 2The chief priests and the teachers of the Law of Moses were looking for a way to get rid of Jesus, because they were afraid of what the people might do. 3Then Satan entered the heart of Judas Iscariot,[a] who was one of the twelve apostles.

4Judas went to talk with the chief priests and the officers of the temple police about how he could help them arrest Jesus. 5They were very pleased and offered to pay Judas some money. 6He agreed and started looking for a good chance to betray Jesus when the crowds were not around.

Jesus Eats with His Disciples

(Matthew 26.17-25; Mark 14.12-21; John 13.21-30)

7The day had come for the Festival of Thin Bread, and it was time to kill the Passover lambs. 8So Jesus said to Peter and John, "Go and prepare the Passover meal for us to eat."

9But they asked, "Where do you want us to prepare it?"

10Jesus told them, "As you go into the city, you will meet a man carrying a jar of water.[b] Follow him into the house 11and say to the owner, 'Our teacher wants to know where he can eat the Passover meal with his disciples.' 12The owner will take you upstairs and show you a large room ready for you to use. Prepare the meal there."

[a] 22.3 *Iscariot*: See the note at 6.16. [b] 22.10 *a man carrying a jar of water*: A male slave carrying water would probably mean that the family was rich.

NEW INTERNATIONAL VERSION

Judas Agrees to Betray Jesus

22 Now the Feast of Unleavened Bread, called the Passover, was approaching, 2and the chief priests and the teachers of the law were looking for some way to get rid of Jesus, for they were afraid of the people. 3Then Satan entered Judas, called Iscariot, one of the Twelve. 4And Judas went to the chief priests and the officers of the temple guard and discussed with them how he might betray Jesus. 5They were delighted and agreed to give him money. 6He consented, and watched for an opportunity to hand Jesus over to them when no crowd was present.

The Last Supper

7Then came the day of Unleavened Bread on which the Passover lamb had to be sacrificed. 8Jesus sent Peter and John, saying, "Go and make preparations for us to eat the Passover."

9"Where do you want us to prepare for it?" they asked.

10He replied, "As you enter the city, a man carrying a jar of water will meet you. Follow him to the house that he enters, 11and say to the owner of the house, 'The Teacher asks: Where is the guest room, where I may eat the Passover with my disciples?' 12He will show you a large upper room, all furnished. Make preparations there."

NEW LIVING TRANSLATION

Judas Agrees to Betray Jesus

22 The Festival of Unleavened Bread, which begins with the Passover celebration, was drawing near. 2The leading priests and teachers of religious law were actively plotting Jesus' murder. But they wanted to kill him without starting a riot, a possibility they greatly feared.

3Then Satan entered into Judas Iscariot, who was one of the twelve disciples, 4and he went over to the leading priests and captains of the Temple guard to discuss the best way to betray Jesus to them. 5They were delighted that he was ready to help them, and they promised him a reward. 6So he began looking for an opportunity to betray Jesus so they could arrest him quietly when the crowds weren't around.

The Last Supper

7Now the Festival of Unleavened Bread arrived, when the Passover lambs were sacrificed. 8Jesus sent Peter and John ahead and said, "Go and prepare the Passover meal, so we can eat it together."

9"Where do you want us to go?" they asked him.

10He replied, "As soon as you enter Jerusalem, a man carrying a pitcher of water will meet you. Follow him. At the house he enters, 11say to the owner, 'The Teacher asks, Where is the guest room where I can eat the Passover meal with my disciples?' 12He will take you upstairs to a large room that is already set up. That is the place. Go ahead and prepare our supper there." 13They went off to the city

NEW KING JAMES VERSION

The Plot to Kill Jesus

22 Now the Feast of Unleavened Bread drew near, which is called Passover. 2And the chief priests and the scribes sought how they might kill Him, for they feared the people.

3Then Satan entered Judas, surnamed Iscariot, who was numbered among the twelve. 4So he went his way and conferred with the chief priests and captains, how he might betray Him to them. 5And they were glad, and agreed to give him money. 6So he promised and sought opportunity to betray Him to them in the absence of the multitude.

Jesus and His Disciples Prepare the Passover

7Then came the Day of Unleavened Bread, when the Passover must be killed. 8And He sent Peter and John, saying, "Go and prepare the Passover for us, that we may eat."

9So they said to Him, "Where do You want us to prepare?"

10And He said to them, "Behold, when you have entered the city, a man will meet you carrying a pitcher of water; follow him into the house which he enters. 11Then you shall say to the master of the house, 'The Teacher says to you, "Where is the guest room where I may eat the Passover with My disciples?" ' 12Then he will show you a large, furnished upper room; there make ready."

THE MESSAGE

The Passover Meal

22 The Feast of Unleavened Bread, also called Passover, drew near. The high priests and religion scholars were looking for a way to do away with Jesus but, fearful of the people, they were also looking for a way to cover their tracks.

That's when Satan entered Judas, the one called Iscariot. He was one of the Twelve. Leaving the others, he conferred with the high priests and the Temple guards about how he might betray Jesus to them. They couldn't believe their good luck and agreed to pay him well. He gave them his word and started looking for a way to betray Jesus, but out of sight of the crowd.

The Day of Unleavened Bread came, the day the Passover lamb was butchered. Jesus sent Peter and John off, saying, "Go prepare the Passover for us so we can eat it together."

They said, "Where do you want us to do this?"

He said, "Keep your eyes open as you enter the city. A man carrying a water jug will meet you. Follow him home. Then speak with the owner of the house: 'The Teacher wants to know, "Where is the guest room where I can eat the Passover meal with my disciples?"' He will show you a spacious second-story room, swept and ready. Prepare the meal there."

KING JAMES VERSION

13 And they went, and found as he had said unto them: and they made ready the passover.

14 And when the hour was come, he sat down, and the twelve apostles with him.

15 And he said unto them, With desire I have desired to eat this passover with you before I suffer:

16 For I say unto you, I will not any more eat thereof, until it be fulfilled in the kingdom of God.

17 And he took the cup, and gave thanks, and said, Take this, and divide *it* among yourselves:

18 For I say unto you, I will not drink of the fruit of the vine, until the kingdom of God shall come.

19 And he took bread, and gave thanks, and brake *it*, and gave unto them, saying, This is my body which is given for you: this do in remembrance of me.

20 Likewise also the cup after supper, saying, This cup *is* the new testament in my blood, which is shed for you.

21 ¶ But, behold, the hand of him that betrayeth me *is* with me on the table.

22 And truly the Son of man goeth, as it was determined: but woe unto that man by whom he is betrayed!

23 And they began to enquire among themselves, which of them it was that should do this thing.

NEW AMERICAN STANDARD BIBLE

13 And they left and found *everything* just as He had told them; and they prepared the Passover.

The Lord's Supper

14 When the hour had come, He reclined *at the table,* and the apostles with Him.

15 And He said to them, "I have earnestly desired to eat this Passover with you before I suffer;

16 for I say to you, I shall never again eat it until it is fulfilled in the kingdom of God."

17 And when He had taken a cup *and* given thanks, He said, "Take this and share it among yourselves;

18 for I say to you, I will not drink of the fruit of the vine from now on until the kingdom of God comes."

19 And when He had taken *some* bread *and* given thanks, He broke it and gave it to them, saying, "This is My body which is given for you; do this in remembrance of Me."

20 And in the same way *He took* the cup after they had eaten, saying, "This cup which is poured out for you is the new covenant in My blood.

21 "But behold, the hand of the one betraying Me is with Mine on the table.

22 "For indeed, the Son of Man is going as it has been determined; but woe to that man by whom He is betrayed!"

23 And they began to discuss among themselves which one of them it might be who was going to do this thing.

NEW CENTURY VERSION

13 So Peter and John left and found everything as Jesus had said. And they prepared the Passover meal.

The Lord's Supper

14 When the time came, Jesus and the apostles were sitting at the table. 15 He said to them, "I wanted very much to eat this Passover meal with you before I suffer. 16 I will not eat another Passover meal until it is given its true meaning in the kingdom of God."

17 Then Jesus took a cup, gave thanks, and said, "Take this cup and share it among yourselves. 18 I will not drink again from the fruit of the vine[a] until God's kingdom comes."

19 Then Jesus took some bread, gave thanks, broke it, and gave it to the apostles, saying, "This is my body, which I am giving for you. Do this to remember me." 20 In the same way, after supper, Jesus took the cup and said, "This cup is the new agreement that God makes with his people. This new agreement begins with my blood which is poured out for you.

Who Will Turn Against Jesus?

21 "But one of you will turn against me, and his hand is with mine on the table. 22 What God has planned for the Son of Man will happen, but how terrible it will be for that one who turns against the Son of Man."

23 Then the apostles asked each other which one of them would do that.

22:18 [a] **fruit of the vine** Product of the grapevine; this may also be translated "wine."

CONTEMPORARY ENGLISH VERSION

13 Peter and John left. They found everything just as Jesus had told them, and they prepared the Passover meal.

The Lord's Supper

(Matthew 26.26-30; Mark 14.22-26; 1 Corinthians 11.23-25)

14 When the time came for Jesus and the apostles to eat, 15 he said to them, "I have very much wanted to eat this Passover meal with you before I suffer. 16 I tell you that I will not eat another Passover meal until it is finally eaten in God's kingdom."

17 Jesus took a cup of wine in his hands and gave thanks to God. Then he told the apostles, "Take this wine and share it with each other. 18 I tell you that I will not drink any more wine until God's kingdom comes."

19 Jesus took some bread in his hands and gave thanks for it. He broke the bread and handed it to his apostles. Then he said, "This is my body, which is given for you. Eat this as a way of remembering me!"

20 After the meal he took another cup of wine in his hands. Then he said, "This is my blood. It is poured out for you, and with it God makes his new agreement. 21 The one who will betray me is here at the table with me! 22 The Son of Man will die in the way that has been decided for him, but it will be terrible for the one who betrays him!"

23 Then the apostles started arguing about who would ever do such a thing.

NEW INTERNATIONAL VERSION

[13]They left and found things just as Jesus had told them. So they prepared the Passover.

[14]When the hour came, Jesus and his apostles reclined at the table. [15]And he said to them, "I have eagerly desired to eat this Passover with you before I suffer. [16]For I tell you, I will not eat it again until it finds fulfillment in the kingdom of God."

[17]After taking the cup, he gave thanks and said, "Take this and divide it among you. [18]For I tell you I will not drink again of the fruit of the vine until the kingdom of God comes."

[19]And he took bread, gave thanks and broke it, and gave it to them, saying, "This is my body given for you; do this in remembrance of me."

[20]In the same way, after the supper he took the cup, saying, "This cup is the new covenant in my blood, which is poured out for you. [21]But the hand of him who is going to betray me is with mine on the table. [22]The Son of Man will go as it has been decreed, but woe to that man who betrays him." [23]They began to question among themselves which of them it might be who would do this.

NEW LIVING TRANSLATION

and found everything just as Jesus had said, and they prepared the Passover supper there.

[14]Then at the proper time Jesus and the twelve apostles sat down together at the table. [15]Jesus said, "I have looked forward to this hour with deep longing, anxious to eat this Passover meal with you before my suffering begins. [16]For I tell you now that I won't eat it again until it comes to fulfillment in the Kingdom of God."

[17]Then he took a cup of wine, and when he had given thanks for it, he said, "Take this and share it among yourselves. [18]For I will not drink wine again until the Kingdom of God has come."

[19]Then he took a loaf of bread; and when he had thanked God for it, he broke it in pieces and gave it to the disciples, saying, "This is my body, given for you. Do this in remembrance of me." [20]After supper he took another cup of wine and said, "This wine is the token of God's new covenant to save you—an agreement sealed with the blood I will pour out for you.*

[21]"But here at this table, sitting among us as a friend, is the man who will betray me. [22]For I, the Son of Man, must die since it is part of God's plan. But how terrible it will be for my betrayer!" [23]Then the disciples began to ask each other which of them would ever do such a thing.

22:19-20 Some manuscripts omit 22:19b-20, *given for you . . . I will pour out for you.*

NEW KING JAMES VERSION

[13]So they went and found it just as He had said to them, and they prepared the Passover.

Jesus Institutes the Lord's Supper

[14]When the hour had come, He sat down, and the twelve[a] apostles with Him. [15]Then He said to them, "With *fervent* desire I have desired to eat this Passover with you before I suffer; [16]for I say to you, I will no longer eat of it until it is fulfilled in the kingdom of God."

[17]Then He took the cup, and gave thanks, and said, "Take this and divide *it* among yourselves; [18]for I say to you,[b] I will not drink of the fruit of the vine until the kingdom of God comes."

[19]And He took bread, gave thanks and broke *it*, and gave *it* to them, saying, "This is My body which is given for you; do this in remembrance of Me."

[20]Likewise He also *took* the cup after supper, saying, "This cup *is* the new covenant in My blood, which is shed for you. [21]But behold, the hand of My betrayer *is* with Me on the table. [22]And truly the Son of Man goes as it has been determined, but woe to that man by whom He is betrayed!"

[23]Then they began to question among themselves, which of them it was who would do this thing.

22:14 [a] NU-Text omits *twelve.* 22:18 [b] NU-Text adds *from now on.*

THE MESSAGE

They left, found everything just as he told them, and prepared the Passover meal.

When it was time, he sat down, all the apostles with him, and said, "You've no idea how much I have looked forward to eating this Passover meal with you before I enter my time of suffering. It's the last one I'll eat until we all eat it together in the kingdom of God."

Taking the cup, he blessed it, then said, "Take this and pass it among you. As for me, I'll not drink wine again until the kingdom of God arrives."

Taking bread, he blessed it, broke it, and gave it to them, saying, "This is my body, given for you. Eat it in my memory."

He did the same with the cup after supper, saying, "This cup is the new covenant written in my blood, blood poured out for you.

"Do you realize that the hand of the one who is betraying me is at this moment on this table? It's true that the Son of Man is going down a path already marked out—no surprises there. But for the one who turns him in, turns traitor to the Son of Man, this is doomsday."

They immediately became suspicious of each other and began quizzing one another, wondering who might be about to do this.

KING JAMES VERSION

24 And there was also a strife among them, which of them should be accounted the greatest.

25 And he said unto them, The kings of the Gentiles exercise lordship over them; and they that exercise authority upon them are called benefactors.

26 But ye *shall* not *be* so: but he that is greatest among you, let him be as the younger; and he that is chief, as he that doth serve.

27 For whether *is* greater, he that sitteth at meat, or he that serveth? *is* not he that sitteth at meat? but I am among you as he that serveth.

28 Ye are they which have continued with me in my temptations.

29 And I appoint unto you a kingdom, as my Father hath appointed unto me;

30 That ye may eat and drink at my table in my kingdom, and sit on thrones judging the twelve tribes of Israel.

31 And the Lord said, Simon, Simon, behold, Satan hath desired *to have* you, that he may sift *you* as wheat:

32 But I have prayed for thee, that thy faith fail not: and when thou art converted, strengthen thy brethren.

33 And he said unto him, Lord, I am ready to go with thee, both into prison, and to death.

34 And he said, I tell thee, Peter, the cock shall not crow

NEW AMERICAN STANDARD BIBLE

Who Is Greatest

24 And there arose also a dispute among them *as to* which one of them was regarded to be greatest.

25 And He said to them, "The kings of the Gentiles lord it over them; and those who have authority over them are called 'Benefactors.'

26 "But *it is* not this way with you, but the one who is the greatest among you must become like the youngest, and the leader like the servant.

27 "For who is greater, the one who reclines *at the table* or the one who serves? Is it not the one who reclines *at the table?* But I am among you as the one who serves.

28 "You are those who have stood by Me in My trials;

29 and just as My Father has granted Me a kingdom, I grant you

30 that you may eat and drink at My table in My kingdom, and you will sit on thrones judging the twelve tribes of Israel.

31 "Simon, Simon, behold, Satan has demanded *permission* to sift you like wheat;

32 but I have prayed for you, that your faith may not fail; and you, when once you have turned again, strengthen your brothers."

33 But he said to Him, "Lord, with You I am ready to go both to prison and to death!"

34 And He said, "I say to you, Peter, the rooster will not

NEW CENTURY VERSION

Be Like a Servant

24 The apostles also began to argue about which one of
them was the most important. 25 But Jesus said to them,
"The kings of the non-Jewish people rule over them, and
those who have authority over others like to be called
'friends of the people.' 26 But you must not be like that.
Instead, the greatest among you should be like the
youngest, and the leader should be like the servant. 27 Who
is more important: the one sitting at the table or the one
serving? You think the one at the table is more important,
but I am like a servant among you.
28 "You have stayed with me through my struggles.
29 Just as my Father has given me a kingdom, I also give
you a kingdom 30 so you may eat and drink at my table in
my kingdom. And you will sit on thrones, judging the
twelve tribes of Israel.

Don't Lose Your Faith!

31 "Simon, Simon, Satan has asked to test all of you as a
farmer sifts his wheat. 32 I have prayed that you will not
lose your faith! Help your brothers be stronger when you
come back to me."
33 But Peter said to Jesus, "Lord, I am ready to go with
you to prison and even to die with you!"
34 But Jesus said, "Peter, before the rooster crows this

CONTEMPORARY ENGLISH VERSION

An Argument about Greatness

24 The apostles got into an argument about which one of
them was the greatest. 25 So Jesus told them:
Foreign kings order their people around, and powerful
rulers call themselves everyone's friends.[c] 26 But don't be
like them. The most important one of you should be like
the least important, and your leader should be like a servant. 27 Who do people think is the greatest, a person
who is served or one who serves? Isn't it the one who is
served? But I have been with you as a servant.
28 You have stayed with me in all my troubles. 29 So I
will give you the right to rule as kings, just as my Father
has given me the right to rule as a king. 30 You will eat
and drink with me in my kingdom, and you will each sit
on a throne to judge the twelve tribes of Israel.

Jesus' Disciples Will Be Tested

(Matthew 26.31-35; Mark 14.27-31; John 13.36-38)

31 Jesus said, "Simon, listen to me! Satan has demanded
the right to test each one of you, as a farmer does when he
separates wheat from the husks.[d] 32 But Simon, I have
prayed that your faith will be strong. And when you have
come back to me, help the others."
33 Peter said, "Lord, I am ready to go with you to jail and
even to die with you."
34 Jesus replied, "Peter, I tell you that before a rooster

[c] 22.25 *everyone's friends*: This translates a Greek word that rulers sometimes used as a title for themselves or for special friends.
[d] 22.31 *separates wheat from the husks*: See the note at 3.17.

NEW INTERNATIONAL VERSION

[24]Also a dispute arose among them as to which of them was considered to be greatest. [25]Jesus said to them, "The kings of the Gentiles lord it over them; and those who exercise authority over them call themselves Benefactors. [26]But you are not to be like that. Instead, the greatest among you should be like the youngest, and the one who rules like the one who serves. [27]For who is greater, the one who is at the table or the one who serves? Is it not the one who is at the table? But I am among you as one who serves. [28]You are those who have stood by me in my trials. [29]And I confer on you a kingdom, just as my Father conferred one on me, [30]so that you may eat and drink at my table in my kingdom and sit on thrones, judging the twelve tribes of Israel.

[31]"Simon, Simon, Satan has asked to sift you[a] as wheat. [32]But I have prayed for you, Simon, that your faith may not fail. And when you have turned back, strengthen your brothers."

[33]But he replied, "Lord, I am ready to go with you to prison and to death."

[34]Jesus answered, "I tell you, Peter, before the rooster

[a] *31* The Greek is plural.

NEW LIVING TRANSLATION

[24]And they began to argue among themselves as to who would be the greatest in the coming Kingdom. [25]Jesus told them, "In this world the kings and great men order their people around, and yet they are called 'friends of the people.' [26]But among you, those who are the greatest should take the lowest rank, and the leader should be like a servant. [27]Normally the master sits at the table and is served by his servants. But not here! For I am your servant. [28]You have remained true to me in my time of trial. [29]And just as my Father has granted me a Kingdom, I now grant you the right [30]to eat and drink at my table in that Kingdom. And you will sit on thrones, judging the twelve tribes of Israel.

Jesus Predicts Peter's Denial

[31]"Simon, Simon, Satan has asked to have all of you, to sift you like wheat. [32]But I have pleaded in prayer for you, Simon, that your faith should not fail. So when you have repented and turned to me again, strengthen and build up your brothers."

[33]Peter said, "Lord, I am ready to go to prison with you, and even to die with you."

[34]But Jesus said, "Peter, let me tell you something. The

NEW KING JAMES VERSION

The Disciples Argue About Greatness

[24]Now there was also a dispute among them, as to which of them should be considered the greatest. [25]And He said to them, "The kings of the Gentiles exercise lordship over them, and those who exercise authority over them are called 'benefactors.' [26]But not so *among* you; on the contrary, he who is greatest among you, let him be as the younger, and he who governs as he who serves. [27]For who *is* greater, he who sits at the table, or he who serves? *Is* it not he who sits at the table? Yet I am among you as the One who serves.

[28]"But you are those who have continued with Me in My trials. [29]And I bestow upon you a kingdom, just as My Father bestowed *one* upon Me, [30]that you may eat and drink at My table in My kingdom, and sit on thrones judging the twelve tribes of Israel."

Jesus Predicts Peter's Denial

[31]And the Lord said,[c] "Simon, Simon! Indeed, Satan has asked for you, that he may sift *you* as wheat. [32]But I have prayed for you, that your faith should not fail; and when you have returned to *Me,* strengthen your brethren."

[33]But he said to Him, "Lord, I am ready to go with You, both to prison and to death."

[34]Then He said, "I tell you, Peter, the rooster shall not

22:31 [c] NU-Text omits *And the Lord said.*

THE MESSAGE

Get Ready for Trouble

Within minutes they were bickering over who of them would end up the greatest. But Jesus intervened: "Kings like to throw their weight around and people in authority like to give themselves fancy titles. It's not going to be that way with you. Let the senior among you become like the junior; let the leader act the part of the servant.

"Who would you rather be: the one who eats the dinner or the one who serves the dinner? You'd rather eat and be served, right? But I've taken my place among you as the one who serves. And you've stuck with me through thick and thin. Now I confer on you the royal authority my Father conferred on me so you can eat and drink at my table in my kingdom and be strengthened as you take up responsibilities among the congregations of God's people.

"Simon, stay on your toes. Satan has tried his best to separate all of you from me, like chaff from wheat. Simon, I've prayed for you in particular that you not give in or give out. When you have come through the time of testing, turn to your companions and give them a fresh start."

Peter said, "Master, I'm ready for anything with you. I'd go to jail for you. I'd *die* for you!"

Jesus said, "I'm sorry to have to tell you this, Peter, but

KING JAMES VERSION

this day, before that thou shalt thrice deny that thou knowest me.

35 And he said unto them, When I sent you without purse, and scrip, and shoes, lacked ye any thing? And they said, Nothing.

36 Then said he unto them, But now, he that hath a purse, let him take *it*, and likewise *his* scrip: and he that hath no sword, let him sell his garment, and buy one.

37 For I say unto you, that this that is written must yet be accomplished in me, And he was reckoned among the transgressors: for the things concerning me have an end.

38 And they said, Lord, behold, here *are* two swords. And he said unto them, It is enough.

39 ¶ And he came out, and went, as he was wont, to the mount of Olives; and his disciples also followed him.

40 And when he was at the place, he said unto them, Pray that ye enter not into temptation.

41 And he was withdrawn from them about a stone's cast, and kneeled down, and prayed,

42 Saying, Father, if thou be willing, remove this cup from me: nevertheless not my will, but thine, be done.

NEW AMERICAN STANDARD BIBLE

crow today until you have denied three times that you know Me."

35 And He said to them, "When I sent you out without money belt and bag and sandals, you did not lack anything, did you?" They said, "*No,* nothing."

36 And He said to them, "But now, whoever has a money belt is to take it along, likewise also a bag, and whoever has no sword is to sell his coat and buy one.

37 "For I tell you that this which is written must be fulfilled in Me, 'AND HE WAS NUMBERED WITH TRANSGRESSORS'; for that which refers to Me has *its* fulfillment."

38 They said, "Lord, look, here are two swords." And He said to them, "It is enough."

The Garden of Gethsemane

39 And He came out and proceeded as was His custom to the Mount of Olives; and the disciples also followed Him.

40 When He arrived at the place, He said to them, "Pray that you may not enter into temptation."

41 And He withdrew from them about a stone's throw, and He knelt down and *began* to pray,

42 saying, "Father, if You are willing, remove this cup from Me; yet not My will, but Yours be done."

NEW CENTURY VERSION

day, you will say three times that you don't know me."

Be Ready for Trouble

35Then Jesus said to the apostles, "When I sent you out without a purse, a bag, or sandals, did you need anything?"

They said, "No."

36He said to them, "But now if you have a purse or a bag, carry that with you. If you don't have a sword, sell your coat and buy one. 37The Scripture says, 'He was treated like a criminal,'[b] and I tell you this scripture must have its full meaning. It was written about me, and it is happening now."

38His followers said, "Look, Lord, here are two swords."

He said to them, "That is enough."

Jesus Prays Alone

39Jesus left the city and went to the Mount of Olives, as he often did, and his followers went with him. 40When he reached the place, he said to them, "Pray for strength against temptation."

41Then Jesus went about a stone's throw away from them. He kneeled down and prayed, 42"Father, if you are willing, take away this cup[c] of suffering. But do what you want, not

22:37 [b] **'He...criminal'** Quotation from Isaiah 53:12. **22:42** [c] **cup** Jesus is talking about the painful things that will happen to him. Accepting these things will be hard, like drinking a cup of something bitter.

CONTEMPORARY ENGLISH VERSION

crows tomorrow morning, you will say three times that you don't know me."

Moneybags, Traveling Bags, and Swords

35Jesus asked his disciples, "When I sent you out without a moneybag or a traveling bag or sandals, did you need anything?"

"No!" they answered.

36Jesus told them, "But now, if you have a moneybag, take it with you. Also take a traveling bag, and if you don't have a sword,[e] sell some of your clothes and buy one. 37Do this because the Scriptures say, 'He was considered a criminal.' This was written about me, and it will soon come true."

38The disciples said, "Lord, here are two swords!"

"Enough of that!" Jesus replied.

Jesus Prays (Matthew 26.36-46; Mark 14.32-42)

39Jesus went out to the Mount of Olives, as he often did, and his disciples went with him. 40When they got there, he told them, "Pray that you won't be tested."

41Jesus walked on a little way before he knelt down and prayed, 42"Father, if you will, please don't make me suffer by having me drink from this cup.[f] But do what you want, and not what I want."

[e] **22.36** *moneybag . . . traveling bag . . . sword*: These were things that someone would take on a dangerous journey. Jesus was telling his disciples to be ready for anything that might happen. They seem to have understood what he meant (see 22.49-51). [f] **22.42** *having me drink from this cup*: In the Scriptures "to drink from a cup" sometimes means to suffer.

NEW INTERNATIONAL VERSION

crows today, you will deny three times that you know me."

[35]Then Jesus asked them, "When I sent you without purse, bag or sandals, did you lack anything?"

"Nothing," they answered.

[36]He said to them, "But now if you have a purse, take it, and also a bag; and if you don't have a sword, sell your cloak and buy one. [37]It is written: 'And he was numbered with the transgressors'[b]; and I tell you that this must be fulfilled in me. Yes, what is written about me is reaching its fulfillment."

[38]The disciples said, "See, Lord, here are two swords."

"That is enough," he replied.

Jesus Prays on the Mount of Olives

[39]Jesus went out as usual to the Mount of Olives, and his disciples followed him. [40]On reaching the place, he said to them, "Pray that you will not fall into temptation." [41]He withdrew about a stone's throw beyond them, knelt down and prayed, [42]"Father, if you are willing, take this cup from me; yet not my will, but yours be done." [43]An angel

[b] *37* Isaiah 53:12

NEW LIVING TRANSLATION

rooster will not crow tomorrow morning until you have denied three times that you even know me."

[35]Then Jesus asked them, "When I sent you out to preach the Good News and you did not have money, a traveler's bag, or extra clothing, did you lack anything?"

"No," they replied.

[36]"But now," he said, "take your money and a traveler's bag. And if you don't have a sword, sell your clothes and buy one! [37]For the time has come for this prophecy about me to be fulfilled: 'He was counted among those who were rebels.'* Yes, everything written about me by the prophets will come true."

[38]"Lord," they replied, "we have two swords among us."

"That's enough," he said.

Jesus Prays on the Mount of Olives

[39]Then, accompanied by the disciples, Jesus left the upstairs room and went as usual to the Mount of Olives. [40]There he told them, "Pray that you will not be overcome by temptation."

[41]He walked away, about a stone's throw, and knelt down and prayed, [42]"Father, if you are willing, please take this cup of suffering away from me. Yet I want your will,

22:37 Isa 53:12.

NEW KING JAMES VERSION

crow this day before you will deny three times that you know Me."

Supplies for the Road

[35]And He said to them, "When I sent you without money bag, knapsack, and sandals, did you lack anything?"

So they said, "Nothing."

[36]Then He said to them, "But now, he who has a money bag, let him take *it,* and likewise a knapsack; and he who has no sword, let him sell his garment and buy one. [37]For I say to you that this which is written must still be accomplished in Me: *'And He was numbered with the transgressors.'*[d] For the things concerning Me have an end."

[38]So they said, "Lord, look, here *are* two swords."

And He said to them, "It is enough."

The Prayer in the Garden

[39]Coming out, He went to the Mount of Olives, as He was accustomed, and His disciples also followed Him. [40]When He came to the place, He said to them, "Pray that you may not enter into temptation."

[41]And He was withdrawn from them about a stone's throw, and He knelt down and prayed, [42]saying, "Father, if it is Your will, take this cup away from Me; nevertheless not My will, but Yours, be done." [43]Then an angel

22:37 [d] Isaiah 53:12

THE MESSAGE

before the rooster crows you will have three times denied that you know me."

Then Jesus said, "When I sent you out and told you to travel light, to take only the bare necessities, did you get along all right?"

"Certainly," they said, "we got along just fine."

He said, "This is different. Get ready for trouble. Look to what you'll need; there are difficult times ahead. Pawn your coat and get a sword. What was written in Scripture, 'He was lumped in with the criminals,' gets its final meaning in me. Everything written about me is now coming to a conclusion."

They said, "Look, Master, two swords!"

But he said, "Enough of that; no more sword talk!"

A Dark Night

Leaving there, he went, as he so often did, to Mount Olives. The disciples followed him. When they arrived at the place, he said, "Pray that you don't give in to temptation."

He pulled away from them about a stone's throw, knelt down, and prayed, "Father, remove this cup from me. But please, not what I want. What do *you* want?" At once an

KING JAMES VERSION

43 And there appeared an angel unto him from heaven, strengthening him.

44 And being in an agony he prayed more earnestly: and his sweat was as it were great drops of blood falling down to the ground.

45 And when he rose up from prayer, and was come to his disciples, he found them sleeping for sorrow,

46 And said unto them, Why sleep ye? rise and pray, lest ye enter into temptation.

47 ¶ And while he yet spake, behold a multitude, and he that was called Judas, one of the twelve, went before them, and drew near unto Jesus to kiss him.

48 But Jesus said unto him, Judas, betrayest thou the Son of man with a kiss?

49 When they which were about him saw what would follow, they said unto him, Lord, shall we smite with the sword?

50 And one of them smote the servant of the high priest, and cut off his right ear.

51 And Jesus answered and said, Suffer ye thus far. And he touched his ear, and healed him.

52 Then Jesus said unto the chief priests, and captains of the temple, and the elders, which were come to him, Be ye come out, as against a thief, with swords and staves?

53 When I was daily with you in the temple, ye stretched forth no hands against me: but this is your hour, and the power of darkness.

NEW AMERICAN STANDARD BIBLE

43 Now an angel from heaven appeared to Him, strengthening Him.

44 And being in agony He was praying very fervently; and His sweat became like drops of blood, falling down upon the ground.

45 When He rose from prayer, He came to the disciples and found them sleeping from sorrow,

46 and said to them, "Why are you sleeping? Get up and pray that you may not enter into temptation."

Jesus Betrayed by Judas

47 While He was still speaking, behold, a crowd *came,* and the one called Judas, one of the twelve, was preceding them; and he approached Jesus to kiss Him.

48 But Jesus said to him, "Judas, are you betraying the Son of Man with a kiss?"

49 When those who were around Him saw what was going to happen, they said, "Lord, shall we strike with the sword?"

50 And one of them struck the slave of the high priest and cut off his right ear.

51 But Jesus answered and said, "Stop! No more of this." And He touched his ear and healed him.

52 Then Jesus said to the chief priests and officers of the temple and elders who had come against Him, "Have you come out with swords and clubs as you would against a robber?

53 "While I was with you daily in the temple, you did not lay hands on Me; but this hour and the power of darkness are yours."

NEW CENTURY VERSION

what I want." 43Then an angel from heaven appeared to him to strengthen him. 44Being full of pain, Jesus prayed even harder. His sweat was like drops of blood falling to the ground. 45When he finished praying, he went to his followers and found them asleep because of their sadness. 46Jesus said to them, "Why are you sleeping? Get up and pray for strength against temptation."

Jesus Is Arrested

47While Jesus was speaking, a crowd came up, and Judas, one of the twelve apostles, was leading them. He came close to Jesus so he could kiss him.

48But Jesus said to him, "Judas, are you using the kiss to give the Son of Man to his enemies?"

49When those who were standing around him saw what was happening, they said, "Lord, should we strike them with our swords?" 50And one of them struck the servant of the high priest and cut off his right ear.

51Jesus said, "Stop! No more of this." Then he touched the servant's ear and healed him.

52Those who came to arrest Jesus were the leading priests, the soldiers who guarded the Temple, and the older Jewish leaders. Jesus said to them, "You came out here with swords and clubs as though I were a criminal. 53I was with you every day in the Temple, and you didn't arrest me there. But this is your time—the time when darkness rules."

CONTEMPORARY ENGLISH VERSION

43Then an angel from heaven came to help him. 44Jesus was in great pain and prayed so sincerely that his sweat fell to the ground like drops of blood.[g]

45Jesus got up from praying and went over to his disciples. They were asleep and worn out from being so sad. 46He said to them, "Why are you asleep? Wake up and pray that you won't be tested."

Jesus Is Arrested

(Matthew 26.47-56; Mark 14.43-50; John 18.3-11)

47While Jesus was still speaking, a crowd came up. It was led by Judas, one of the twelve apostles. He went over to Jesus and greeted him with a kiss.[h]

48Jesus asked Judas, "Are you betraying the Son of Man with a kiss?"

49When Jesus' disciples saw what was about to happen, they asked, "Lord, should we attack them with a sword?" 50One of the disciples even struck at the high priest's servant with his sword and cut off the servant's right ear.

51"Enough of that!" Jesus said. Then he touched the servant's ear and healed it.

52Jesus spoke to the chief priests, the temple police, and the leaders who had come to arrest him. He said, "Why do you come out with swords and clubs and treat me like a criminal? 53I was with you every day in the temple, and you didn't arrest me. But this is your time, and darkness[i] is in control."

[g] 22.43, 44 *Then an angel . . . like drops of blood*: Verses 43, 44 are not in some manuscripts. [h] 22.47 *greeted him with a kiss*: It was the custom for people to greet each other with a kiss on the cheek.
[i] 22.53 *darkness*: Darkness stands for the power of the devil.

NEW INTERNATIONAL VERSION

from heaven appeared to him and strengthened him. 44And
being in anguish, he prayed more earnestly, and his sweat
was like drops of blood falling to the ground.[c]
45When he rose from prayer and went back to the disci-
ples, he found them asleep, exhausted from sorrow.
46"Why are you sleeping?" he asked them. "Get up and
pray so that you will not fall into temptation."

Jesus Arrested

47While he was still speaking a crowd came up, and the
man who was called Judas, one of the Twelve, was leading
them. He approached Jesus to kiss him, 48but Jesus asked
him, "Judas, are you betraying the Son of Man with a
kiss?"
49When Jesus' followers saw what was going to happen,
they said, "Lord, should we strike with our swords?"
50And one of them struck the servant of the high priest,
cutting off his right ear.
51But Jesus answered, "No more of this!" And he
touched the man's ear and healed him.
52Then Jesus said to the chief priests, the officers of the
temple guard, and the elders, who had come for him, "Am I
leading a rebellion, that you have come with swords and
clubs? 53Every day I was with you in the temple courts,
and you did not lay a hand on me. But this is your hour—
when darkness reigns."

[c] *44* Some early manuscripts do not have verses 43 and 44.

NEW LIVING TRANSLATION

not mine." 43Then an angel from heaven appeared and
strengthened him. 44He prayed more fervently, and he was
in such agony of spirit that his sweat fell to the ground like
great drops of blood.* 45At last he stood up again and
returned to the disciples, only to find them asleep, exhaust-
ed from grief. 46"Why are you sleeping?" he asked. "Get up
and pray. Otherwise temptation will overpower you."

Jesus Is Betrayed and Arrested

47But even as he said this, a mob approached, led by
Judas, one of his twelve disciples. Judas walked over to
Jesus and greeted him with a kiss. 48But Jesus said,
"Judas, how can you betray me, the Son of Man, with a
kiss?"
49When the other disciples saw what was about to hap-
pen, they exclaimed, "Lord, should we fight? We brought
the swords!" 50And one of them slashed at the high
priest's servant and cut off his right ear.
51But Jesus said, "Don't resist anymore." And he
touched the place where the man's ear had been and
healed him. 52Then Jesus spoke to the leading priests and
captains of the Temple guard and the other leaders who
headed the mob. "Am I some dangerous criminal," he
asked, "that you have come armed with swords and clubs
to arrest me? 53Why didn't you arrest me in the Temple?
I was there every day. But this is your moment, the time
when the power of darkness reigns."

22:43-44 These verses are not included in many ancient manuscripts.

NEW KING JAMES VERSION

appeared to Him from heaven, strengthening Him. 44And
being in agony, He prayed more earnestly. Then His sweat
became like great drops of blood falling down to the
ground.[e]
45When He rose up from prayer, and had come to His
disciples, He found them sleeping from sorrow. 46Then He
said to them, "Why do you sleep? Rise and pray, lest you
enter into temptation."

Betrayal and Arrest in Gethsemane

47And while He was still speaking, behold, a multitude;
and he who was called Judas, one of the twelve, went
before them and drew near to Jesus to kiss Him. 48But
Jesus said to him, "Judas, are you betraying the Son of
Man with a kiss?"
49When those around Him saw what was going to hap-
pen, they said to Him, "Lord, shall we strike with the
sword?" 50And one of them struck the servant of the high
priest and cut off his right ear.
51But Jesus answered and said, "Permit even this." And
He touched his ear and healed him.
52Then Jesus said to the chief priests, captains of the
temple, and the elders who had come to Him, "Have you
come out, as against a robber, with swords and clubs?
53When I was with you daily in the temple, you did not try
to seize Me. But this is your hour, and the power of dark-
ness."

22:44 [e] NU-Text brackets verses 43 and 44 as not in the original text.

THE MESSAGE

angel from heaven was at his side, strengthening him. He prayed on all the harder. Sweat, wrung from him like drops of blood, poured off his face.

He got up from prayer, went back to the disciples and found them asleep, drugged by grief. He said, "What business do you have sleeping? Get up. Pray so you won't give in to temptation."

No sooner were the words out of his mouth than a crowd showed up, Judas, the one from the Twelve, in the lead. He came right up to Jesus to kiss him. Jesus said, "Judas, you would betray the Son of Man with a kiss?"

When those with him saw what was happening, they said, "Master, shall we fight?" One of them took a swing at the Chief Priest's servant and cut off his right ear.

Jesus said, "Let them be. Even in this." Then, touching the servant's ear, he healed him.

Jesus spoke to those who had come—high priests, Temple police, religion leaders: "What is this, jumping me with swords and clubs as if I were a dangerous criminal? Day after day I've been with you in the Temple and you've not so much as lifted a hand against me. But do it your way—it's a dark night, a dark hour."

KING JAMES VERSION

54 ¶ Then took they him, and led *him*, and brought him into the high priest's house. And Peter followed afar off.

55 And when they had kindled a fire in the midst of the hall, and were set down together, Peter sat down among them.

56 But a certain maid beheld him as he sat by the fire, and earnestly looked upon him, and said, This man was also with him.

57 And he denied him, saying, Woman, I know him not.

58 And after a little while another saw him, and said, Thou art also of them. And Peter said, Man, I am not.

59 And about the space of one hour after another confidently affirmed, saying, Of a truth this *fellow* also was with him: for he is a Galilaean.

60 And Peter said, Man, I know not what thou sayest. And immediately, while he yet spake, the cock crew.

61 And the Lord turned, and looked upon Peter. And Peter remembered the word of the Lord, how he had said unto him, Before the cock crow, thou shalt deny me thrice.

62 And Peter went out, and wept bitterly.

63 ¶ And the men that held Jesus mocked him, and smote *him*.

64 And when they had blindfolded him, they struck him on the face, and asked him, saying, Prophesy, who is it that smote thee?

NEW AMERICAN STANDARD BIBLE

Jesus' Arrest

54 Having arrested Him, they led Him *away* and brought Him to the house of the high priest; but Peter was following at a distance.

55 After they had kindled a fire in the middle of the courtyard and had sat down together, Peter was sitting among them.

56 And a servant-girl, seeing him as he sat in the firelight and looking intently at him, said, "This man was with Him too."

57 But he denied *it,* saying, "Woman, I do not know Him."

58 A little later, another saw him and said, "You are *one* of them too!" But Peter said, "Man, I am not!"

59 After about an hour had passed, another man *began* to insist, saying, "Certainly this man also was with Him, for he is a Galilean too."

60 But Peter said, "Man, I do not know what you are talking about." Immediately, while he was still speaking, a rooster crowed.

61 The Lord turned and looked at Peter. And Peter remembered the word of the Lord, how He had told him, "Before a rooster crows today, you will deny Me three times."

62 And he went out and wept bitterly.

63 Now the men who were holding Jesus in custody were mocking Him and beating Him,

64 and they blindfolded Him and were asking Him, saying, "Prophesy, who is the one who hit You?"

NEW CENTURY VERSION

Peter Says He Doesn't Know Jesus

54 They arrested Jesus, and led him away, and brought
him into the house of the high priest. Peter followed far
behind them. 55 After the soldiers started a fire in the mid-
dle of the courtyard and sat together, Peter sat with them.
56 A servant girl saw Peter sitting there in the firelight, and
looking closely at him, she said, "This man was also with
him."

57 But Peter said this was not true; he said, "Woman, I
don't know him."

58 A short time later, another person saw Peter and said,
"You are also one of them."

But Peter said, "Man, I am not!"

59 About an hour later, another man insisted, "Certainly
this man was with him, because he is from Galilee, too."

60 But Peter said, "Man, I don't know what you are talk-
ing about!"

At once, while Peter was still speaking, a rooster crowed.
61 Then the Lord turned and looked straight at Peter. And
Peter remembered what the Lord had said: "Before the
rooster crows this day, you will say three times that you
don't know me." 62 Then Peter went outside and cried
painfully.

The People Make Fun of Jesus

63 The men who were guarding Jesus began making fun
of him and beating him.

64 They blindfolded him and said, "Prove that you are a

CONTEMPORARY ENGLISH VERSION

Peter Says He Doesn't Know Jesus

(Matthew 26.57, 58, 67-75; Mark 14.53, 54, 66-72; John 18.12-18, 25-27)

54 Jesus was arrested and led away to the house of the
high priest, while Peter followed at a distance. 55 Some peo-
ple built a fire in the middle of the courtyard and were sit-
ting around it. Peter sat there with them, 56 and a servant
girl saw him. Then after she had looked at him carefully,
she said, "This man was with Jesus!"

57 Peter said, "Woman, I don't even know that man!"

58 A little later someone else saw Peter and said, "You
are one of them!"

"No, I'm not!" Peter replied.

59 About an hour later another man insisted, "This man
must have been with Jesus. They both come from Galilee."

60 Peter replied, "I don't know what you are talking
about!" Right then, while Peter was still speaking, a roost-
er crowed.

61 The Lord turned and looked at Peter. And Peter
remembered that the Lord had said, "Before a rooster
crows tomorrow morning, you will say three times that
you don't know me." 62 Then Peter went out and cried hard.

63 The men who were guarding Jesus made fun of him
and beat him. 64 They put a blindfold on him and said,

NEW INTERNATIONAL VERSION

Peter Disowns Jesus

54Then seizing him, they led him away and took him into the house of the high priest. Peter followed at a distance. 55But when they had kindled a fire in the middle of the courtyard and had sat down together, Peter sat down with them. 56A servant girl saw him seated there in the firelight. She looked closely at him and said, "This man was with him."

57But he denied it. "Woman, I don't know him," he said.

58A little later someone else saw him and said, "You also are one of them."

"Man, I am not!" Peter replied.

59About an hour later another asserted, "Certainly this fellow was with him, for he is a Galilean."

60Peter replied, "Man, I don't know what you're talking about!" Just as he was speaking, the rooster crowed. 61The Lord turned and looked straight at Peter. Then Peter remembered the word the Lord had spoken to him: "Before the rooster crows today, you will disown me three times." 62And he went outside and wept bitterly.

The Guards Mock Jesus

63The men who were guarding Jesus began mocking and beating him. 64They blindfolded him and demanded,

NEW LIVING TRANSLATION

Peter Denies Jesus

54So they arrested him and led him to the high priest's residence, and Peter was following far behind. 55The guards lit a fire in the courtyard and sat around it, and Peter joined them there. 56A servant girl noticed him in the firelight and began staring at him. Finally she said, "This man was one of Jesus' followers!"

57Peter denied it. "Woman," he said, "I don't even know the man!"

58After a while someone else looked at him and said, "You must be one of them!"

"No, man, I'm not!" Peter replied.

59About an hour later someone else insisted, "This must be one of Jesus' disciples because he is a Galilean, too."

60But Peter said, "Man, I don't know what you are talking about." And as soon as he said these words, the rooster crowed. 61At that moment the Lord turned and looked at Peter. Then Peter remembered that the Lord had said, "Before the rooster crows tomorrow morning, you will deny me three times." 62And Peter left the courtyard, crying bitterly.

63Now the guards in charge of Jesus began mocking and beating him. 64They blindfolded him; then they hit him

NEW KING JAMES VERSION

Peter Denies Jesus, and Weeps Bitterly

54Having arrested Him, they led *Him* and brought Him into the high priest's house. But Peter followed at a distance. 55Now when they had kindled a fire in the midst of the courtyard and sat down together, Peter sat among them. 56And a certain servant girl, seeing him as he sat by the fire, looked intently at him and said, "This man was also with Him."

57But he denied Him,[f] saying, "Woman, I do not know Him."

58And after a little while another saw him and said, "You also are of them."

But Peter said, "Man, I am not!"

59Then after about an hour had passed, another confidently affirmed, saying, "Surely this *fellow* also was with Him, for he is a Galilean."

60But Peter said, "Man, I do not know what you are saying!"

Immediately, while he was still speaking, the rooster[g] crowed. 61And the Lord turned and looked at Peter. Then Peter remembered the word of the Lord, how He had said to him, "Before the rooster crows,[h] you will deny Me three times." 62So Peter went out and wept bitterly.

Jesus Mocked and Beaten

63Now the men who held Jesus mocked Him and beat Him. 64And having blindfolded Him, they struck Him on

22:57 [f] NU-Text reads *denied it.* 22:60 [g] NU-Text and M-Text read *a rooster.* 22:61 [h] NU-Text adds *today.*

THE MESSAGE

A Rooster Crowed

Arresting Jesus, they marched him off and took him into the house of the Chief Priest. Peter followed, but at a safe distance. In the middle of the courtyard some people had started a fire and were sitting around it, trying to keep warm. One of the serving maids sitting at the fire noticed him, then took a second look and said, "This man was with him!"

He denied it, "Woman, I don't even know him."

A short time later, someone else noticed him and said, "You're one of them."

But Peter denied it: "Man, I am not."

About an hour later, someone else spoke up, really adamant: "He's got to have been with him! He's got 'Galilean' written all over him."

Peter said, "Man, I don't know what you're talking about." At that very moment, the last word hardly off his lips, a rooster crowed. Just then, the Master turned and looked at Peter. Peter remembered what the Master had said to him: "Before the rooster crows, you will deny me three times." He went out and cried and cried and cried.

Slapping Him Around

The men in charge of Jesus began poking fun at him, slapping him around. They put a blindfold on him and

KING JAMES VERSION

65 And many other things blasphemously spake they against him.

66 And as soon as it was day, the elders of the people and the chief priests and the scribes came together, and led him into their council, saying,

67 Art thou the Christ? tell us. And he said unto them, If I tell you, ye will not believe:

68 And if I also ask *you*, ye will not answer me, nor let *me* go.

69 Hereafter shall the Son of man sit on the right hand of the power of God.

70 Then said they all, Art thou then the Son of God? And he said unto them, Ye say that I am.

71 And they said, What need we any further witness? for we ourselves have heard of his own mouth.

23 And the whole multitude of them arose, and led him unto Pilate.

2 And they began to accuse him, saying, We found this *fellow* perverting the nation, and forbidding to give tribute to Caesar, saying that he himself is Christ a King.

3 And Pilate asked him, saying, Art thou the King of the Jews? And he answered him and said, Thou sayest *it*.

NEW AMERICAN STANDARD BIBLE

65 And they were saying many other things against Him, blaspheming.

Jesus before the Sanhedrin

66 When it was day, the [1]Council of elders of the people assembled, both chief priests and scribes, and they led Him away to their council *chamber,* saying,

67 "If You are the Christ, tell us." But He said to them, "If I tell you, you will not believe;

68 and if I ask a question, you will not answer.

69 "But from now on THE SON OF MAN WILL BE SEATED AT THE RIGHT HAND of the power OF GOD."

70 And they all said, "Are You the Son of God, then?" And He said to them, "Yes, I am."

71 Then they said, "What further need do we have of testimony? For we have heard it ourselves from His own mouth."

Jesus before Pilate

23 Then the whole body of them got up and brought Him before Pilate.

2 And they began to accuse Him, saying, "We found this man misleading our nation and forbidding to pay taxes to Caesar, and saying that He Himself is Christ, a King."

3 So Pilate asked Him, saying, "Are You the King of the Jews?" And He answered him and said, "*It is as* you say."

22:66 [1] Or *Sanhedrin*

NEW CENTURY VERSION

prophet, and tell us who hit you." 65They said many cruel things to Jesus.

Jesus Before the Leaders

66When day came, the council of the older leaders of the people, both the leading priests and the teachers of the law, came together and led Jesus to their highest court. 67They said, "If you are the Christ, tell us."

Jesus said to them, "If I tell you, you will not believe me. 68And if I ask you, you will not answer. 69But from now on, the Son of Man will sit at the right hand of the powerful God."

70They all said, "Then are you the Son of God?"

Jesus said to them, "You say that I am."

71They said, "Why do we need witnesses now? We ourselves heard him say this."

Pilate Questions Jesus

23 Then the whole group stood up and led Jesus to Pilate.[a] 2They began to accuse Jesus, saying, "We caught this man telling things that mislead our people. He says that we should not pay taxes to Caesar, and he calls himself the Christ, a king."

3Pilate asked Jesus, "Are you the king of the Jews?"

Jesus answered, "Those are your words."

23:1 [a] **Pilate** Pontius Pilate was the Roman governor of Judea from A.D. 26 to A.D. 36.

CONTEMPORARY ENGLISH VERSION

"Tell us who struck you!" 65They kept on insulting Jesus in many other ways.

Jesus Is Questioned by the Council

(Matthew 26.59-66; Mark 14.55-64; John 18.19-24)

66At daybreak the nation's leaders, the chief priests, and the teachers of the Law of Moses got together and brought Jesus before their council. 67They said, "Tell us! Are you the Messiah?"

Jesus replied, "If I said so, you wouldn't believe me. 68And if I asked you a question, you wouldn't answer. 69But from now on, the Son of Man will be seated at the right side of God All-Powerful."

70Then they asked, "Are you the Son of God?"[j]

Jesus answered, "You say I am!"[k]

71They replied, "Why do we need more witnesses? He said it himself!"

Pilate Questions Jesus

(Matthew 27.1, 2, 11-14; Mark 15.1-5; John 18.28-38)

23 Everyone in the council got up and led Jesus off to Pilate. 2They started accusing him and said, "We caught this man trying to get our people to riot and to stop paying taxes to the Emperor. He also claims that he is the Messiah, our king."

3Pilate asked Jesus, "Are you the king of the Jews?"

"Those are your words," Jesus answered.

[j] 22.70 *Son of God*: This was one of the titles used for the kings of Israel.
[k] 22.70 *You say I am*: Or "That's what you say."

NEW INTERNATIONAL VERSION

"Prophesy! Who hit you?" 65And they said many other
insulting things to him.

Jesus Before Pilate and Herod

66At daybreak the council of the elders of the people,
both the chief priests and teachers of the law, met togeth-
er, and Jesus was led before them. 67"If you are the
Christ,[d]" they said, "tell us."
Jesus answered, "If I tell you, you will not believe me,
68and if I asked you, you would not answer. 69But from
now on, the Son of Man will be seated at the right hand of
the mighty God."
70They all asked, "Are you then the Son of God?"
He replied, "You are right in saying I am."
71Then they said, "Why do we need any more testimony?
We have heard it from his own lips."
23 Then the whole assembly rose and led him off to
Pilate. 2And they began to accuse him, saying,
"We have found this man subverting our nation. He
opposes payment of taxes to Caesar and claims to be
Christ,[a] a king."
3So Pilate asked Jesus, "Are you the king of the Jews?"
"Yes, it is as you say," Jesus replied.

[d] 67 Or *Messiah* [a] 2 Or *Messiah*; also in verses 35 and 39

NEW LIVING TRANSLATION

and asked, "Who hit you that time, you prophet?" 65And
they threw all sorts of terrible insults at him.

Jesus before the Council

66At daybreak all the leaders of the people assembled,
including the leading priests and the teachers of religious
law. Jesus was led before this high council,* 67and they
said, "Tell us if you are the Messiah."
But he replied, "If I tell you, you won't believe me. 68And
if I ask you a question, you won't answer. 69But the time is
soon coming when I, the Son of Man, will be sitting at
God's right hand in the place of power."*
70They all shouted, "Then you claim you are the Son of
God?"
And he replied, "You are right in saying that I am."
71"What need do we have for other witnesses?" they
shouted. "We ourselves heard him say it."

Jesus' Trial before Pilate

23 Then the entire council took Jesus over to Pilate,
the Roman governor. 2They began at once to state
their case: "This man has been leading our people to ruin
by telling them not to pay their taxes to the Roman gov-
ernment and by claiming he is the Messiah, a king."
3So Pilate asked him, "Are you the King of the Jews?"
Jesus replied, "Yes, it is as you say."

22:66 Greek *before their Sanhedrin.* 22:69 See Ps 110:1.

NEW KING JAMES VERSION

the face and asked Him,[i] saying, "Prophesy! Who is the
one who struck You?" 65And many other things they blas-
phemously spoke against Him.

Jesus Faces the Sanhedrin

66As soon as it was day, the elders of the people, both
chief priests and scribes, came together and led Him into
their council, saying, 67"If You are the Christ, tell us."
But He said to them, "If I tell you, you will by no means
believe. 68And if I also ask *you,* you will by no means
answer Me or let *Me* go.[j] 69Hereafter the Son of Man will
sit on the right hand of the power of God."
70Then they all said, "Are You then the Son of God?"
So He said to them, "You *rightly* say that I am."
71And they said, "What further testimony do we need?
For we have heard it ourselves from His own mouth."

Jesus Handed Over to Pontius Pilate

23 Then the whole multitude of them arose and led
Him to Pilate. 2And they began to accuse Him, say-
ing, "We found this *fellow* perverting the[a] nation, and for-
bidding to pay taxes to Caesar, saying that He Himself is
Christ, a King."
3Then Pilate asked Him, saying, "Are You the King of
the Jews?"
He answered him and said, "*It is as* you say."

22:64 [i] NU-Text reads *And having blindfolded Him, they asked Him.*
22:68 [j] NU-Text omits *also* and *Me or let Me go.* 23:2 [a] NU-Text reads *our.*

THE MESSAGE

taunted, "Who hit you that time?" They were having a
grand time with him.

When it was morning, the religious leaders of the people and the high priests and scholars all got together and brought him before their High Council. They said, "Are you the Messiah?"

He answered, "If I said yes, you wouldn't believe me. If I asked what you meant by your question, you wouldn't answer me. So here's what I have to say: From here on the Son of Man takes his place at God's right hand, the place of power."

They all said, "So you admit your claim to be the Son of God?"

"You're the ones who keep saying it," he said.

But they had made up their minds, "Why do we need any more evidence? We've all heard him as good as say it himself."

Pilate

23 Then they all took Jesus to Pilate and began to bring up charges against him. They said, "We found this man undermining our law and order, forbidding taxes to be paid to Caesar, setting himself up as Messiah-King."

Pilate asked him, "Is this true that you're 'King of the Jews'?"

"Those are your words, not mine," Jesus replied.

KING JAMES VERSION

4 Then said Pilate to the chief priests and *to* the people, I find no fault in this man.

5 And they were the more fierce, saying, He stirreth up the people, teaching throughout all Jewry, beginning from Galilee to this place.

6 When Pilate heard of Galilee, he asked whether the man were a Galilaean.

7 And as soon as he knew that he belonged unto Herod's jurisdiction, he sent him to Herod, who himself also was at Jerusalem at that time.

8 And when Herod saw Jesus, he was exceeding glad: for he was desirous to see him of a long *season*, because he had heard many things of him; and he hoped to have seen some miracle done by him.

9 Then he questioned with him in many words; but he answered him nothing.

10 And the chief priests and scribes stood and vehemently accused him.

11 And Herod with his men of war set him at nought, and mocked *him*, and arrayed him in a gorgeous robe, and sent him again to Pilate.

12 And the same day Pilate and Herod were made friends together: for before they were at enmity between themselves.

13 ¶ And Pilate, when he had called together the chief priests and the rulers and the people,

NEW AMERICAN STANDARD BIBLE

4 Then Pilate said to the chief priests and the crowds, "I find no guilt in this man."

5 But they kept on insisting, saying, "He stirs up the people, teaching all over Judea, starting from Galilee even as far as this place."

6 When Pilate heard it, he asked whether the man was a Galilean.

7 And when he learned that He belonged to Herod's jurisdiction, he sent Him to Herod, who himself also was in Jerusalem at that time.

Jesus before Herod

8 Now Herod was very glad when he saw Jesus; for he had wanted to see Him for a long time, because he had been hearing about Him and was hoping to see some sign performed by Him.

9 And he questioned Him at some length; but He answered him nothing.

10 And the chief priests and the scribes were standing there, accusing Him vehemently.

11 And Herod with his soldiers, after treating Him with contempt and mocking Him, dressed Him in a gorgeous robe and sent Him back to Pilate.

12 Now Herod and Pilate became friends with one another that very day; for before they had been enemies with each other.

Pilate Seeks Jesus' Release

13 Pilate summoned the chief priests and the rulers and the people,

NEW CENTURY VERSION

4 Pilate said to the leading priests and the people, "I find nothing against this man."

5 They were insisting, saying, "But Jesus makes trouble with the people, teaching all around Judea. He began in Galilee, and now he is here."

Pilate Sends Jesus to Herod

6 Pilate heard this and asked if Jesus was from Galilee. 7 Since Jesus was under Herod's authority, Pilate sent Jesus to Herod, who was in Jerusalem at that time. 8 When Herod saw Jesus, he was very glad, because he had heard about Jesus and had wanted to meet him for a long time. He was hoping to see Jesus work a miracle. 9 Herod asked Jesus many questions, but Jesus said nothing. 10 The leading priests and teachers of the law were standing there, strongly accusing Jesus. 11 After Herod and his soldiers had made fun of Jesus, they dressed him in a kingly robe and sent him back to Pilate. 12 In the past, Pilate and Herod had always been enemies, but on that day they became friends.

Jesus Must Die

13 Pilate called the people together with the leading

CONTEMPORARY ENGLISH VERSION

4 Pilate told the chief priests and the crowd, "I don't find him guilty of anything."

5 But they all kept on saying, "He has been teaching and causing trouble all over Judea. He started in Galilee and has now come all the way here."

Jesus Is Brought before Herod

6 When Pilate heard this, he asked, "Is this man from Galilee?" 7 After Pilate learned that Jesus came from the region ruled by Herod,[a] he sent him to Herod, who was in Jerusalem at that time.

8 For a long time Herod had wanted to see Jesus and was very happy because he finally had this chance. He had heard many things about Jesus and hoped to see him work a miracle.

9 Herod asked him a lot of questions, but Jesus did not answer. 10 Then the chief priests and the teachers of the Law of Moses stood up and accused him of all kinds of bad things.

11 Herod and his soldiers made fun of Jesus and insulted him. They put a fine robe on him and sent him back to Pilate. 12 That same day Herod and Pilate became friends, even though they had been enemies before this.

The Death Sentence

(Matthew 27.15-26; Mark 15.6-15; John 18.39—19.16)

13 Pilate called together the chief priests, the leaders, and

[a] 23.7 *Herod*: Herod Antipas, the son of Herod the Great.

NEW INTERNATIONAL VERSION

4Then Pilate announced to the chief priests and the crowd, "I find no basis for a charge against this man."

5But they insisted, "He stirs up the people all over Judea[b] by his teaching. He started in Galilee and has come all the way here."

6On hearing this, Pilate asked if the man was a Galilean.
7When he learned that Jesus was under Herod's jurisdiction, he sent him to Herod, who was also in Jerusalem at that time.

8When Herod saw Jesus, he was greatly pleased, because for a long time he had been wanting to see him. From what he had heard about him, he hoped to see him perform some miracle. 9He plied him with many questions, but Jesus gave him no answer. 10The chief priests and the teachers of the law were standing there, vehemently accusing him. 11Then Herod and his soldiers ridiculed and mocked him. Dressing him in an elegant robe, they sent him back to Pilate. 12That day Herod and Pilate became friends—before this they had been enemies.

13Pilate called together the chief priests, the rulers and

[b] 5 Or *over the land of the Jews*

NEW LIVING TRANSLATION

4Pilate turned to the leading priests and to the crowd and said, "I find nothing wrong with this man!"

5Then they became desperate. "But he is causing riots everywhere he goes, all over Judea, from Galilee to Jerusalem!"

6"Oh, is he a Galilean?" Pilate asked. 7When they answered that he was, Pilate sent him to Herod Antipas, because Galilee was under Herod's jurisdiction, and Herod happened to be in Jerusalem at the time.

8Herod was delighted at the opportunity to see Jesus, because he had heard about him and had been hoping for a long time to see him perform a miracle. 9He asked Jesus question after question, but Jesus refused to answer.
10Meanwhile, the leading priests and the teachers of religious law stood there shouting their accusations. 11Now Herod and his soldiers began mocking and ridiculing Jesus. Then they put a royal robe on him and sent him back to Pilate. 12Herod and Pilate, who had been enemies before, became friends that day.

13Then Pilate called together the leading priests and other religious leaders, along with the people, 14and he

NEW KING JAMES VERSION

4So Pilate said to the chief priests and the crowd, "I find no fault in this Man."

5But they were the more fierce, saying, "He stirs up the people, teaching throughout all Judea, beginning from Galilee to this place."

Jesus Faces Herod

6When Pilate heard of Galilee,[b] he asked if the Man were a Galilean. 7And as soon as he knew that He belonged to Herod's jurisdiction, he sent Him to Herod, who was also in Jerusalem at that time. 8Now when Herod saw Jesus, he was exceedingly glad; for he had desired for a long *time* to see Him, because he had heard many things about Him, and he hoped to see some miracle done by Him. 9Then he questioned Him with many words, but He answered him nothing. 10And the chief priests and scribes stood and vehemently accused Him. 11Then Herod, with his men of war, treated Him with contempt and mocked *Him*, arrayed Him in a gorgeous robe, and sent Him back to Pilate.
12That very day Pilate and Herod became friends with each other, for previously they had been at enmity with each other.

Taking the Place of Barabbas

13Then Pilate, when he had called together the chief priests, the rulers, and the people, 14said to them, "You

23:6 [b] NU-Text omits *of Galilee*.

THE MESSAGE

Pilate told the high priests and the accompanying crowd, "I find nothing wrong here. He seems harmless enough to me."

But they were vehement. "He's stirring up unrest among the people with his teaching, disturbing the peace everywhere, starting in Galilee and now all through Judea. He's a dangerous man, endangering the peace."

When Pilate heard that, he asked, "So, he's a Galilean?" Realizing that he properly came under Herod's jurisdiction, he passed the buck to Herod, who just happened to be in Jerusalem for a few days.

Herod was delighted when Jesus showed up. He had wanted for a long time to see him, he'd heard so much about him. He hoped to see him do something spectacular. He peppered him with questions. Jesus didn't answer—not one word. But the high priests and religion scholars were right there, saying their piece, strident and shrill in their accusations.

Mightily offended, Herod turned on Jesus. His soldiers joined in, taunting and jeering. Then they dressed him up in an elaborate king costume and sent him back to Pilate. That day Herod and Pilate became thick as thieves. Always before they had kept their distance.

Then Pilate called in the high priests, rulers, and the

KING JAMES VERSION

14 Said unto them, Ye have brought this man unto me, as one that perverteth the people: and, behold, I, having examined *him* before you, have found no fault in this man touching those things whereof ye accuse him:

15 No, nor yet Herod: for I sent you to him; and, lo, nothing worthy of death is done unto him.

16 I will therefore chastise him, and release *him*.

17 (For of necessity he must release one unto them at the feast.)

18 And they cried out all at once, saying, Away with this *man*, and release unto us Barabbas:

19 (Who for a certain sedition made in the city, and for murder, was cast into prison.)

20 Pilate therefore, willing to release Jesus, spake again to them.

21 But they cried, saying, Crucify *him*, crucify him.

22 And he said unto them the third time, Why, what evil hath he done? I have found no cause of death in him: I will therefore chastise him, and let *him* go.

23 And they were instant with loud voices, requiring that he might be crucified. And the voices of them and of the chief priests prevailed.

24 And Pilate gave sentence that it should be as they required.

25 And he released unto them him that for sedition and murder was cast into prison, whom they had desired; but he delivered Jesus to their will.

NEW AMERICAN STANDARD BIBLE

14 and said to them, "You brought this man to me as one who incites the people to rebellion, and behold, having examined Him before you, I have found no guilt in this man regarding the charges which you make against Him.

15 "No, nor has Herod, for he sent Him back to us; and behold, nothing deserving death has been done by Him.

16 "Therefore I will punish Him and release Him."

17 [[1]Now he was obliged to release to them at the feast one prisoner.]

18 But they cried out all together, saying, "Away with this man, and release for us Barabbas!"

19 (He was one who had been thrown into prison for an insurrection made in the city, and for murder.)

20 Pilate, wanting to release Jesus, addressed them again,

21 but they kept on calling out, saying, "Crucify, crucify Him!"

22 And he said to them the third time, "Why, what evil has this man done? I have found in Him no guilt *demanding* death; therefore I will punish Him and release Him."

23 But they were insistent, with loud voices asking that He be crucified. And their voices *began* to prevail.

24 And Pilate pronounced sentence that their demand be granted.

25 And he released the man they were asking for who had been thrown into prison for insurrection and murder, but he delivered Jesus to their will.

23:17 [1] Early mss do not contain this v

NEW CENTURY VERSION

priests and the Jewish leaders. 14He said to them, "You brought this man to me, saying he makes trouble among the people. But I have questioned him before you all, and I have not found him guilty of what you say. 15Also, Herod found nothing wrong with him; he sent him back to us. Look, he has done nothing for which he should die. 16So, after I punish him, I will let him go free." 17[b]

18But the people shouted together, "Take this man away! Let Barabbas go free!" 19(Barabbas was a man who was in prison for his part in a riot in the city and for murder.)

20Pilate wanted to let Jesus go free and told this to the crowd. 21But they shouted again, "Crucify him! Crucify him!"

22A third time Pilate said to them, "Why? What wrong has he done? I can find no reason to kill him. So I will have him punished and set him free."

23But they continued to shout, demanding that Jesus be crucified. Their yelling became so loud that 24Pilate decided to give them what they wanted. 25He set free the man who was in jail for rioting and murder, and he handed Jesus over to them to do with him as they wished.

23:17 [b] **Verse 17** A few Greek copies add verse 17: "Every year at the Passover Feast, Pilate had to release one prisoner to the people."

CONTEMPORARY ENGLISH VERSION

the people. 14He told them, "You brought Jesus to me and said he was a troublemaker. But I have questioned him here in front of you, and I have not found him guilty of anything that you say he has done. 15Herod didn't find him guilty either and sent him back. This man doesn't deserve to be put to death! 16-17I will just have him beaten with a whip and set free."[b]

18But the whole crowd shouted, "Kill Jesus! Give us Barabbas!" 19Now Barabbas was in jail because he had started a riot in the city and had murdered someone.

20Pilate wanted to set Jesus free, so he spoke again to the crowds. 21But they kept shouting, "Nail him to a cross! Nail him to a cross!"

22Pilate spoke to them a third time, "But what crime has he done? I have not found him guilty of anything for which he should be put to death. I will have him beaten with a whip and set free."

23The people kept on shouting as loud as they could for Jesus to be put to death. 24Finally, Pilate gave in. 25He freed the man who was in jail for rioting and murder, because he was the one the crowd wanted to be set free. Then Pilate handed Jesus over for them to do what they wanted with him.

[b] 23.16,17 *set free*: Some manuscripts add, "Pilate said this, because at every Passover he was supposed to set one prisoner free for the Jewish people."

NEW INTERNATIONAL VERSION

the people, 14and said to them, "You brought me this man as one who was inciting the people to rebellion. I have examined him in your presence and have found no basis for your charges against him. 15Neither has Herod, for he sent him back to us; as you can see, he has done nothing to deserve death. 16Therefore, I will punish him and then release him.[c]"

18With one voice they cried out, "Away with this man! Release Barabbas to us!" 19(Barabbas had been thrown into prison for an insurrection in the city, and for murder.)

20Wanting to release Jesus, Pilate appealed to them again. 21But they kept shouting, "Crucify him! Crucify him!"

22For the third time he spoke to them: "Why? What crime has this man committed? I have found in him no grounds for the death penalty. Therefore I will have him punished and then release him."

23But with loud shouts they insistently demanded that he be crucified, and their shouts prevailed. 24So Pilate decided to grant their demand. 25He released the man who had been thrown into prison for insurrection and murder, the one they asked for, and surrendered Jesus to their will.

[c] *16* Some manuscripts *him.*" 17*Now he was obliged to release one man to them at the Feast.*

NEW LIVING TRANSLATION

announced his verdict. "You brought this man to me, accusing him of leading a revolt. I have examined him thoroughly on this point in your presence and find him innocent. 15Herod came to the same conclusion and sent him back to us. Nothing this man has done calls for the death penalty. 16So I will have him flogged, but then I will release him."*

18Then a mighty roar rose from the crowd, and with one voice they shouted, "Kill him, and release Barabbas to us!" 19(Barabbas was in prison for murder and for taking part in an insurrection in Jerusalem against the government.) 20Pilate argued with them, because he wanted to release Jesus. 21But they shouted, "Crucify him! Crucify him!"

22For the third time he demanded, "Why? What crime has he committed? I have found no reason to sentence him to death. I will therefore flog him and let him go."

23But the crowd shouted louder and louder for Jesus' death, and their voices prevailed. 24So Pilate sentenced Jesus to die as they demanded. 25As they had requested, he released Barabbas, the man in prison for insurrection and murder. But he delivered Jesus over to them to do as they wished.

23:16 Some manuscripts add verse 17, *For it was necessary for him to release one [prisoner] for them during the feast.*

NEW KING JAMES VERSION

have brought this Man to me, as one who misleads the people. And indeed, having examined *Him* in your presence, I have found no fault in this Man concerning those things of which you accuse Him; 15no, neither did Herod, for I sent you back to him;[c] and indeed nothing deserving of death has been done by Him. 16I will therefore chastise Him and release *Him*" 17(for it was necessary for him to release one to them at the feast).[d]

18And they all cried out at once, saying, "Away with this *Man,* and release to us Barabbas"— 19who had been thrown into prison for a certain rebellion made in the city, and for murder.

20Pilate, therefore, wishing to release Jesus, again called out to them. 21But they shouted, saying, "Crucify *Him,* crucify Him!"

22Then he said to them the third time, "Why, what evil has He done? I have found no reason for death in Him. I will therefore chastise Him and let *Him* go."

23But they were insistent, demanding with loud voices that He be crucified. And the voices of these men and of the chief priests prevailed.[e] 24So Pilate gave sentence that it should be as they requested. 25And he released to them[f] the one they requested, who for rebellion and murder had been thrown into prison; but he delivered Jesus to their will.

23:15 [c] NU-Text reads *for he sent Him back to us.* 23:17 [d] NU-Text omits verse 17.

THE MESSAGE

others and said, "You brought this man to me as a disturber of the peace. I examined him in front of all of you and found there was nothing to your charge. And neither did Herod, for he has sent him back here with a clean bill of health. It's clear that he's done nothing wrong, let alone anything deserving death. I'm going to warn him to watch his step and let him go."

At that, the crowd went wild: "Kill him! Give us Barabbas!" (Barabbas had been thrown in prison for starting a riot in the city and for murder.) Pilate still wanted to let Jesus go, and so spoke out again.

But they kept shouting back, "Crucify! Crucify him!"

He tried a third time. "But for what crime? I've found nothing in him deserving death. I'm going to warn him to watch his step and let him go."

But they kept at it, a shouting mob, demanding that he be crucified. And finally they shouted him down. Pilate caved in and gave them what they wanted. He released the man thrown in prison for rioting and murder, and gave them Jesus to do whatever they wanted.

KING JAMES VERSION

26 ¶ And as they led him away, they laid hold upon one Simon, a Cyrenian, coming out of the country, and on him they laid the cross, that he might bear *it* after Jesus.

27 And there followed him a great company of people, and of women, which also bewailed and lamented him.

28 But Jesus turning unto them said, Daughters of Jerusalem, weep not for me, but weep for yourselves, and for your children.

29 For, behold, the days are coming, in the which they shall say, Blessed *are* the barren, and the wombs that never bare, and the paps which never gave suck.

30 Then shall they begin to say to the mountains, Fall on us; and to the hills, Cover us.

31 For if they do these things in a green tree, what shall be done in the dry?

32 ¶ And there were also two other, malefactors, led with him to be put to death.

33 And when they were come to the place, which is called Calvary, there they crucified him, and the malefactors, one on the right hand, and the other on the left.

34 Then said Jesus, Father, forgive them; for they know not what they do. And they parted his raiment, and cast lots.

35 And the people stood beholding. And the rulers also

NEW AMERICAN STANDARD BIBLE

Simon Bears the Cross

26 When they led Him away, they seized a man, Simon of Cyrene, coming in from the country, and placed on him the cross to carry behind Jesus.

27 And following Him was a large crowd of the people, and of women who were mourning and lamenting Him.

28 But Jesus turning to them said, "Daughters of Jerusalem, stop weeping for Me, but weep for yourselves and for your children.

29 "For behold, the days are coming when they will say, 'Blessed are the barren, and the wombs that never bore, and the breasts that never nursed.'

30 "Then they will begin TO SAY TO THE MOUNTAINS, 'FALL ON US,' AND TO THE HILLS, 'COVER US.'

31 "For if they do these things when the tree is green, what will happen when it is dry?"

32 Two others also, who were criminals, were being led away to be put to death with Him.

The Crucifixion

33 When they came to the place called The Skull, there they crucified Him and the criminals, one on the right and the other on the left.

34 But Jesus was saying, "Father, forgive them; for they do not know what they are doing." And they cast lots, dividing up His garments among themselves.

35 And the people stood by, looking on. And even the

NEW CENTURY VERSION

Jesus Is Crucified

26As they led Jesus away, Simon, a man from Cyrene, was coming in from the fields. They forced him to carry Jesus' cross and to walk behind him.

27A large crowd of people was following Jesus, including some women who were sad and crying for him. 28But Jesus turned and said to them, "Women of Jerusalem, don't cry for me. Cry for yourselves and for your children. 29The time is coming when people will say, 'Happy are the women who cannot have children and who have no babies to nurse.' 30Then people will say to the mountains, 'Fall on us!' And they will say to the hills, 'Cover us!' 31If they act like this now when life is good, what will happen when bad times come?"[c]

32There were also two criminals led out with Jesus to be put to death. 33When they came to a place called the Skull, the soldiers crucified Jesus and the criminals—one on his right and the other on his left. 34Jesus said, "Father, forgive them, because they don't know what they are doing."[d]

The soldiers threw lots to decide who would get his clothes. 35The people stood there watching. And the leaders

23:31 [c] **If...come?** Literally, "If they do these things in the green tree, what will happen in the dry?" 23:34 [d] **Verse 34** Some early Greek copies do not have this part of the verse.

CONTEMPORARY ENGLISH VERSION

Jesus Is Nailed to a Cross

(Matthew 27.31-44; Mark 15.21-32; John 19.17-27)

26As Jesus was being led away, some soldiers grabbed hold of a man from Cyrene named Simon. He was coming in from the fields, but they put the cross on him and made him carry it behind Jesus.

27A large crowd was following Jesus, and in the crowd a lot of women were crying and weeping for him. 28Jesus turned to the women and said:

> Women of Jerusalem, don't cry for me! Cry for yourselves and for your children. 29Someday people will say, "Women who never had children are really fortunate!" 30At that time everyone will say to the mountains, "Fall on us!" They will say to the hills, "Hide us!" 31If this can happen when the wood is green, what do you think will happen when it is dry?[c]

32Two criminals were led out to be put to death with Jesus. 33When the soldiers came to the place called "The Skull,"[d] they nailed Jesus to a cross. They also nailed the two criminals to crosses, one on each side of Jesus.

34-35Jesus said, "Father, forgive these people! They don't know what they're doing."[e]

While the crowd stood there watching Jesus, the soldiers gambled for his clothes. The leaders insulted him by saying,

[c] 23.31 *If this can happen when the wood is green, what do you think will happen when it is dry?*: This saying probably means, "If this can happen to an innocent person, what do you think will happen to one who is guilty?" [d] 23.33 *"The Skull"*: The place was probably given this name because it was near a large rock in the shape of a human skull.
[e] 23.34,35 *Jesus said, "Father, forgive these people! They don't know what they're doing."*: These words are not in some manuscripts.

NEW INTERNATIONAL VERSION

The Crucifixion

26As they led him away, they seized Simon from Cyrene,
who was on his way in from the country, and put the cross
on him and made him carry it behind Jesus. 27A large num-
ber of people followed him, including women who mourned
and wailed for him. 28Jesus turned and said to them,
"Daughters of Jerusalem, do not weep for me; weep for
yourselves and for your children. 29For the time will come
when you will say, 'Blessed are the barren women, the
wombs that never bore and the breasts that never nursed!'
30Then

" 'they will say to the mountains, "Fall on us!"
and to the hills, "Cover us!" '[d]

31For if men do these things when the tree is green, what
will happen when it is dry?"
32Two other men, both criminals, were also led out with
him to be executed. 33When they came to the place called
the Skull, there they crucified him, along with the crimi-
nals—one on his right, the other on his left. 34Jesus said,
"Father, forgive them, for they do not know what they are
doing."[e] And they divided up his clothes by casting lots.
35The people stood watching, and the rulers even

[d] *30* Hosea 10:8 [e] *34* Some early manuscripts do not have this sentence.

NEW LIVING TRANSLATION

The Crucifixion

26As they led Jesus away, Simon of Cyrene,* who was
coming in from the country just then, was forced to follow
Jesus and carry his cross. 27Great crowds trailed along
behind, including many grief-stricken women. 28But Jesus
turned and said to them, "Daughters of Jerusalem, don't
weep for me, but weep for yourselves and for your chil-
dren. 29For the days are coming when they will say,
'Fortunate indeed are the women who are childless, the
wombs that have not borne a child and the breasts that
have never nursed.' 30People will beg the mountains to fall
on them and the hills to bury them. 31For if these things
are done when the tree is green, what will happen when it
is dry?*"
32Two others, both criminals, were led out to be execut-
ed with him. 33Finally, they came to a place called The
Skull.* All three were crucified there—Jesus on the center
cross, and the two criminals on either side.
34Jesus said, "Father, forgive these people, because they
don't know what they are doing."* And the soldiers gam-
bled for his clothes by throwing dice.*
35The crowd watched, and the leaders laughed and

23:26 *Cyrene* was a city in northern Africa. **23:31** Or *If these things are done to me, the living tree, what will happen to you, the dry tree?* **23:33** Sometimes rendered *Calvary,* which comes from the Latin word for "skull." **23:34a** This sentence is not included in many ancient manuscripts. **23:34b** Greek *by casting lots.* See Ps 22:18.

NEW KING JAMES VERSION

The King on a Cross

26Now as they led Him away, they laid hold of a certain
man, Simon a Cyrenian, who was coming from the coun-
try, and on him they laid the cross that he might bear *it*
after Jesus.
27And a great multitude of the people followed Him, and
women who also mourned and lamented Him. 28But Jesus,
turning to them, said, "Daughters of Jerusalem, do not
weep for Me, but weep for yourselves and for your chil-
dren. 29For indeed the days are coming in which they will
say, 'Blessed *are* the barren, wombs that never bore, and
breasts which never nursed!' 30Then they will begin *'to say
to the mountains, "Fall on us!" and to the hills, "Cover
us!" '*[g] 31For if they do these things in the green wood,
what will be done in the dry?"
32There were also two others, criminals, led with Him to
be put to death. 33And when they had come to the place
called Calvary, there they crucified Him, and the criminals,
one on the right hand and the other on the left. 34Then
Jesus said, "Father, forgive them, for they do not know
what they do."[h]
And they divided His garments and cast lots. 35And the
people stood looking on. But even the rulers with them

23:23 [e] NU-Text omits *and of the chief priests.* **23:25** [f] NU-Text and M-Text omit *to them.* **23:30** [g] Hosea 10:8 **23:34** [h] NU-Text brackets the first sentence as a later addition.

THE MESSAGE

Skull Hill

As they led him off, they made Simon, a man from Cyrene who happened to be coming in from the countryside, carry the cross behind Jesus. A huge crowd of people followed, along with women weeping and carrying on. At one point Jesus turned to the women and said, "Daughters of Jerusalem, don't cry for me. Cry for yourselves and for your children. The time is coming when they'll say, 'Lucky the women who never conceived! Lucky the wombs that never gave birth! Lucky the breasts that never gave milk!' Then they'll start calling to the mountains, 'Fall down on us!' calling to the hills, 'Cover us up!' If people do these things to a live, green tree, can you imagine what they'll do with deadwood?"

Two others, both criminals, were taken along with him for execution.

When they got to the place called Skull Hill, they crucified him, along with the criminals, one on his right, the other on his left.

Jesus prayed, "Father, forgive them; they don't know what they're doing."

Dividing up his clothes, they threw dice for them. The people stood there staring at Jesus, and the ringleaders

KING JAMES VERSION

with them derided *him*, saying, He saved others; let him save himself, if he be Christ, the chosen of God.

36 And the soldiers also mocked him, coming to him, and offering him vinegar,

37 And saying, If thou be the king of the Jews, save thyself.

38 And a superscription also was written over him in letters of Greek, and Latin, and Hebrew, THIS IS THE KING OF THE JEWS.

39 And one of the malefactors which were hanged railed on him, saying, If thou be Christ, save thyself and us.

40 But the other answering rebuked him, saying, Dost not thou fear God, seeing thou art in the same condemnation?

41 And we indeed justly; for we receive the due reward of our deeds: but this man hath done nothing amiss.

42 And he said unto Jesus, Lord, remember me when thou comest into thy kingdom.

43 And Jesus said unto him, Verily I say unto thee, To day shalt thou be with me in paradise.

44 ¶ And it was about the sixth hour, and there was a darkness over all the earth until the ninth hour.

45 And the sun was darkened, and the veil of the temple was rent in the midst.

NEW AMERICAN STANDARD BIBLE

rulers were sneering at Him, saying, "He saved others; let Him save Himself if this is the Christ of God, His Chosen One."

36 The soldiers also mocked Him, coming up to Him, offering Him sour wine,

37 and saying, "If You are the King of the Jews, save Yourself!"

38 Now there was also an inscription above Him, "THIS IS THE KING OF THE JEWS."

39 One of the criminals who were hanged *there* was hurling abuse at Him, saying, "Are You not the Christ? Save Yourself and us!"

40 But the other answered, and rebuking him said, "Do you not even fear God, since you are under the same sentence of condemnation?

41 "And we indeed *are suffering* justly, for we are receiving what we deserve for our deeds; but this man has done nothing wrong."

42 And he was saying, "Jesus, remember me when You come in Your kingdom!"

43 And He said to him, "Truly I say to you, today you shall be with Me in Paradise."

44 It was now about [2]the sixth hour, and darkness fell over the whole land until [3]the ninth hour,

45 because the sun was obscured; and the veil of the temple was torn in two.

23:44 [2] I.e. noon 23:44 [3] I.e. 3 p.m.

NEW CENTURY VERSION

made fun of Jesus, saying, "He saved others. Let him save
himself if he is God's Chosen One, the Christ."
36The soldiers also made fun of him, coming to Jesus
and offering him some vinegar. 37They said, "If you are the
king of the Jews, save yourself!" 38At the top of the cross
these words were written: THIS IS THE KING OF THE JEWS.
39One of the criminals on a cross began to shout insults
at Jesus: "Aren't you the Christ? Then save yourself and us."
40But the other criminal stopped him and said, "You
should fear God! You are getting the same punishment he
is. 41We are punished justly, getting what we deserve for
what we did. But this man has done nothing wrong."
42Then he said, "Jesus, remember me when you come into
your kingdom."
43Jesus said to him, "I tell you the truth, today you will
be with me in paradise."[e]

Jesus Dies

44It was about noon, and the whole land became dark
until three o'clock in the afternoon, 45because the sun did
not shine. The curtain in the Temple[f] was torn in two.

23:43 [e] **paradise** A place where people who are obedient to God go when they die. 23:45 [f] **curtain in the Temple** A curtain divided the Most Holy Place from the other part of the Temple, the special building in Jerusalem where God commanded the Jewish people to worship him.

CONTEMPORARY ENGLISH VERSION

"He saved others. Now he should save himself, if he really is
God's chosen Messiah!"
36The soldiers made fun of Jesus and brought him some
wine. 37They said, "If you are the king of the Jews, save
yourself!"
38Above him was a sign that said, "This is the King of
the Jews."
39One of the criminals hanging there also insulted Jesus by
saying, "Aren't you the Messiah? Save yourself and save us!"
40But the other criminal told the first one off, "Don't you
fear God? Aren't you getting the same punishment as this
man? 41We got what was coming to us, but he didn't do
anything wrong." 42Then he said to Jesus, "Remember me
when you come into power!"
43Jesus replied, "I promise that today you will be with
me in paradise."[f]

The Death of Jesus

(Matthew 27.45-56; Mark 15.33-41; John 19.28-30)

44Around noon the sky turned dark and stayed that way
until the middle of the afternoon. 45The sun stopped shining, and the curtain in the temple[g] split down the middle.

[f] 23.43 *paradise*: In the Greek translation of the Old Testament, this word is used for the Garden of Eden. In New Testament times it was sometimes used for the place where God's people are happy and at rest, as they wait for the final judgment. [g] 23.45 *curtain in the temple*: There were two curtains in the temple. One was at the entrance, and the other separated the holy place from the most holy place that the Jewish people thought of as God's home on earth. The second curtain is probably the one which is meant.

NEW INTERNATIONAL VERSION

sneered at him. They said, "He saved others; let him save
himself if he is the Christ of God, the Chosen One."
36The soldiers also came up and mocked him. They
offered him wine vinegar 37and said, "If you are the king
of the Jews, save yourself."
38There was a written notice above him, which read: THIS
IS THE KING OF THE JEWS.
39One of the criminals who hung there hurled insults at
him: "Aren't you the Christ? Save yourself and us!"
40But the other criminal rebuked him. "Don't you fear
God," he said, "since you are under the same sentence?
41We are punished justly, for we are getting what our
deeds deserve. But this man has done nothing wrong."
42Then he said, "Jesus, remember me when you come
into your kingdom.[f]"
43Jesus answered him, "I tell you the truth, today you
will be with me in paradise."

Jesus' Death

44It was now about the sixth hour, and darkness came
over the whole land until the ninth hour, 45for the sun
stopped shining. And the curtain of the temple was torn in

[f] 42 Some manuscripts *come with your kingly power*

NEW LIVING TRANSLATION

scoffed. "He saved others," they said, "let him save him-
self if he is really God's Chosen One, the Messiah." 36The
soldiers mocked him, too, by offering him a drink of sour
wine. 37They called out to him, "If you are the King of the
Jews, save yourself!" 38A signboard was nailed to the cross
above him with these words: "This is the King of the
Jews."
39One of the criminals hanging beside him scoffed, "So
you're the Messiah, are you? Prove it by saving yourself—
and us, too, while you're at it!"
40But the other criminal protested, "Don't you fear God
even when you are dying? 41We deserve to die for our evil
deeds, but this man hasn't done anything wrong." 42Then
he said, "Jesus, remember me when you come into your
Kingdom."
43And Jesus replied, "I assure you, today you will be
with me in paradise."

The Death of Jesus

44By this time it was noon, and darkness fell across the
whole land until three o'clock. 45The light from the sun was
gone. And suddenly, the thick veil hanging in the Temple

NEW KING JAMES VERSION

sneered, saying, "He saved others; let Him save Himself if
He is the Christ, the chosen of God."
36The soldiers also mocked Him, coming and offering
Him sour wine, 37and saying, "If You are the King of the
Jews, save Yourself."
38And an inscription also was written over Him in letters
of Greek, Latin, and Hebrew:[i]

THIS IS THE KING OF THE JEWS.

39Then one of the criminals who were hanged blasphemed
Him, saying, "If You are the Christ,[j] save Yourself and us."
40But the other, answering, rebuked him, saying, "Do
you not even fear God, seeing you are under the same
condemnation? 41And we indeed justly, for we receive the
due reward of our deeds; but this Man has done nothing
wrong." 42Then he said to Jesus, "Lord,[k] remember me
when You come into Your kingdom."
43And Jesus said to him, "Assuredly, I say to you, today
you will be with Me in Paradise."

Jesus Dies on the Cross

44Now it was[l] about the sixth hour, and there was dark-
ness over all the earth until the ninth hour. 45Then the sun
was darkened,[m] and the veil of the temple was torn in two.

23:38 [i] NU-Text omits *written* and *in letters of Greek, Latin, and Hebrew.*
23:39 [j] NU-Text reads *Are You not the Christ?* **23:42** [k] NU-Text reads
And he said, "Jesus, remember me. **23:44** [l] NU-Text adds *already.*
23:45 [m] NU-Text reads *obscured.*

THE MESSAGE

made faces, taunting, "He saved others. Let's see him save
himself! The Messiah of God—ha! The Chosen—ha!"

The soldiers also came up and poked fun at him, making
a game of it. They toasted him with sour wine: "So you're
King of the Jews! Save yourself!"

Printed over him was a sign: THIS IS THE KING OF THE JEWS.

One of the criminals hanging alongside cursed him:
"Some Messiah you are! Save yourself! Save us!"

But the other one made him shut up: "Have you no fear
of God? You're getting the same as him. We deserve this,
but not him—he did nothing to deserve this."

Then he said, "Jesus, remember me when you enter your
kingdom."

He said, "Don't worry, I will. Today you will join me in
paradise."

By now it was noon. The whole earth became dark, the
darkness lasting three hours—a total blackout. The
Temple curtain split right down the middle. Jesus called

KING JAMES VERSION

46 And when Jesus had cried with a loud voice, he said, Father, into thy hands I commend my spirit: and having said thus, he gave up the ghost.

47 Now when the centurion saw what was done, he glorified God, saying, Certainly this was a righteous man.

48 And all the people that came together to that sight, beholding the things which were done, smote their breasts, and returned.

49 And all his acquaintance, and the women that followed him from Galilee, stood afar off, beholding these things.

50 ¶ And, behold, *there was* a man named Joseph, a counsellor; *and he was* a good man, and a just:

51 (The same had not consented to the counsel and deed of them;) *he was* of Arimathaea, a city of the Jews: who also himself waited for the kingdom of God.

52 This *man* went unto Pilate, and begged the body of Jesus.

53 And he took it down, and wrapped it in linen, and laid it in a sepulchre that was hewn in stone, wherein never man before was laid.

54 And that day was the preparation, and the sabbath drew on.

55 And the women also, which came with him from Galilee, followed after, and beheld the sepulchre, and how his body was laid.

56 And they returned, and prepared spices and ointments;

NEW AMERICAN STANDARD BIBLE

46 And Jesus, crying out with a loud voice, said, "Father, INTO YOUR HANDS I COMMIT MY SPIRIT." Having said this, He breathed His last.

47 Now when the centurion saw what had happened, he *began* praising God, saying, "Certainly this man was innocent."

48 And all the crowds who came together for this spectacle, when they observed what had happened, *began* to return, beating their breasts.

49 And all His acquaintances and the women who accompanied Him from Galilee were standing at a distance, seeing these things.

Jesus Is Buried

50 And a man named Joseph, who was a member of the Council, a good and righteous man

51 (he had not consented to their plan and action), *a man* from Arimathea, a city of the Jews, who was waiting for the kingdom of God;

52 this man went to Pilate and asked for the body of Jesus.

53 And he took it down and wrapped it in a linen cloth, and laid Him in a tomb cut into the rock, where no one had ever lain.

54 It was the preparation day, and the Sabbath was about to begin.

55 Now the women who had come with Him out of Galilee followed, and saw the tomb and how His body was laid.

56 Then they returned and prepared spices and perfumes.

NEW CENTURY VERSION

46Jesus cried out in a loud voice, "Father, I give you my life." After Jesus said this, he died.

47When the army officer there saw what happened, he praised God, saying, "Surely this was a good man!"

48When all the people who had gathered there to watch saw what happened, they returned home, beating their chests because they were so sad. 49But those who were close friends of Jesus, including the women who had followed him from Galilee, stood at a distance and watched.

Joseph Takes Jesus' Body

50There was a good and religious man named Joseph who was a member of the Jewish council. 51But he had not agreed to the other leaders' plans and actions against Jesus. He was from the Jewish town of Arimathea and was waiting for the kingdom of God to come. 52Joseph went to Pilate to ask for the body of Jesus. 53He took the body down from the cross, wrapped it in cloth, and put it in a tomb that was cut out of a wall of rock. This tomb had never been used before. 54This was late on Preparation Day, and when the sun went down, the Sabbath day would begin.

55The women who had come from Galilee with Jesus followed Joseph and saw the tomb and how Jesus' body was laid. 56Then the women left to prepare spices and perfumes.

CONTEMPORARY ENGLISH VERSION

46Jesus shouted, "Father, I put myself in your hands!" Then he died.

47When the Roman officer saw what had happened, he praised God and said, "Jesus must really have been a good man!"

48A crowd had gathered to see the terrible sight. Then after they had seen it, they felt brokenhearted and went home. 49All of Jesus' close friends and the women who had come with him from Galilee stood at a distance and watched.

Jesus Is Buried

(Matthew 27.57-61; Mark 15.42-47; John 19.38-42)

50-51There was a man named Joseph, who was from Arimathea in Judea. Joseph was a good and honest man, and he was eager for God's kingdom to come. He was also a member of the council, but he did not agree with what they had decided.

52Joseph went to Pilate and asked for Jesus' body. 53He took the body down from the cross and wrapped it in fine cloth. Then he put it in a tomb that had been cut out of solid rock and had never been used. 54It was Friday, and the Sabbath was about to begin.[h]

55The women who had come with Jesus from Galilee followed Joseph and watched how Jesus' body was placed in the tomb. 56Then they went to prepare some sweet-smelling

[h] 23.54 *the Sabbath was about to begin*: The Sabbath begins at sunset on Friday.

NEW INTERNATIONAL VERSION

two. 46 Jesus called out with a loud voice, "Father, into your hands I commit my spirit." When he had said this, he breathed his last.

47 The centurion, seeing what had happened, praised God and said, "Surely this was a righteous man." 48 When all the people who had gathered to witness this sight saw what took place, they beat their breasts and went away. 49 But all those who knew him, including the women who had followed him from Galilee, stood at a distance, watching these things.

Jesus' Burial

50 Now there was a man named Joseph, a member of the Council, a good and upright man, 51 who had not consented to their decision and action. He came from the Judean town of Arimathea and he was waiting for the kingdom of God. 52 Going to Pilate, he asked for Jesus' body. 53 Then he took it down, wrapped it in linen cloth and placed it in a tomb cut in the rock, one in which no one had yet been laid. 54 It was Preparation Day, and the Sabbath was about to begin.

55 The women who had come with Jesus from Galilee followed Joseph and saw the tomb and how his body was laid in it. 56 Then they went home and prepared spices and

NEW LIVING TRANSLATION

was torn apart. 46 Then Jesus shouted, "Father, I entrust my spirit into your hands!"* And with those words he breathed his last.

47 When the captain of the Roman soldiers handling the executions saw what had happened, he praised God and said, "Surely this man was innocent.*" 48 And when the crowd that came to see the crucifixion saw all that had happened, they went home in deep sorrow.* 49 But Jesus' friends, including the women who had followed him from Galilee, stood at a distance watching.

The Burial of Jesus

50 Now there was a good and righteous man named Joseph. He was a member of the Jewish high council, 51 but he had not agreed with the decision and actions of the other religious leaders. He was from the town of Arimathea in Judea, and he had been waiting for the Kingdom of God to come. 52 He went to Pilate and asked for Jesus' body. 53 Then he took the body down from the cross and wrapped it in a long linen cloth and laid it in a new tomb that had been carved out of rock. 54 This was done late on Friday afternoon, the day of preparation* for the Sabbath.

55 As his body was taken away, the women from Galilee followed and saw the tomb where they placed his body. 56 Then they went home and prepared spices and ointments

23:46 Ps 31:5. **23:47** Or *righteous.* **23:48** Greek *beating their breasts.* **23:54** Greek *on the day of preparation.*

NEW KING JAMES VERSION

46 And when Jesus had cried out with a loud voice, He said, "Father, *'into Your hands I commit My spirit.'* "[n] Having said this, He breathed His last.

47 So when the centurion saw what had happened, he glorified God, saying, "Certainly this was a righteous Man!"

48 And the whole crowd who came together to that sight, seeing what had been done, beat their breasts and returned. 49 But all His acquaintances, and the women who followed Him from Galilee, stood at a distance, watching these things.

Jesus Buried in Joseph's Tomb

50 Now behold, *there was* a man named Joseph, a council member, a good and just man. 51 He had not consented to their decision and deed. *He was* from Arimathea, a city of the Jews, who himself was also waiting[o] for the kingdom of God. 52 This man went to Pilate and asked for the body of Jesus. 53 Then he took it down, wrapped it in linen, and laid it in a tomb *that was* hewn out of the rock, where no one had ever lain before. 54 That day was the Preparation, and the Sabbath drew near.

55 And the women who had come with Him from Galilee followed after, and they observed the tomb and how His body was laid. 56 Then they returned and prepared spices

23:46 [n] Psalm 31:5 **23:51** [o] NU-Text reads *who was waiting.*

THE MESSAGE

loudly, "Father, I place my life in your hands!" Then he breathed his last.

✢

When the captain there saw what happened, he honored God: "This man was innocent! A good man, and innocent!"

All who had come around as spectators to watch the show, when they saw what actually happened, were overcome with grief and headed home. Those who knew Jesus well, along with the women who had followed him from Galilee, stood at a respectful distance and kept vigil.

There was a man by the name of Joseph, a member of the Jewish High Council, a man of good heart and good character. He had not gone along with the plans and actions of the council. His hometown was the Jewish village of Arimathea. He lived in alert expectation of the kingdom of God. He went to Pilate and asked for the body of Jesus. Taking him down, he wrapped him in a linen shroud and placed him in a tomb chiseled into the rock, a tomb never yet used. It was the day before Sabbath, the Sabbath just about to begin.

The women who had been companions of Jesus from Galilee followed along. They saw the tomb where Jesus' body was placed. Then they went back to prepare burial

KING JAMES VERSION

and rested the sabbath day according to the commandment.

24 Now upon the first *day* of the week, very early in the morning, they came unto the sepulchre, bringing the spices which they had prepared, and certain *others* with them.
2 And they found the stone rolled away from the sepulchre.
3 And they entered in, and found not the body of the Lord Jesus.
4 And it came to pass, as they were much perplexed thereabout, behold, two men stood by them in shining garments:
5 And as they were afraid, and bowed down *their* faces to the earth, they said unto them, Why seek ye the living among the dead?
6 He is not here, but is risen: remember how he spake unto you when he was yet in Galilee,
7 Saying, The Son of man must be delivered into the hands of sinful men, and be crucified, and the third day rise again.
8 And they remembered his words,
9 And returned from the sepulchre, and told all these things unto the eleven, and to all the rest.
10 It was Mary Magdalene, and Joanna, and Mary *the mother* of James, and other *women that were* with them, which told these things unto the apostles.
11 And their words seemed to them as idle tales, and they believed them not.
12 Then arose Peter, and ran unto the sepulchre; and

NEW AMERICAN STANDARD BIBLE

And on the Sabbath they rested according to the commandment.

The Resurrection

24 But on the first day of the week, at early dawn, they came to the tomb bringing the spices which they had prepared.
2 And they found the stone rolled away from the tomb,
3 but when they entered, they did not find the body of the Lord Jesus.
4 While they were perplexed about this, behold, two men suddenly stood near them in dazzling clothing;
5 and as *the women* were terrified and bowed their faces to the ground, *the men* said to them, "Why do you seek the living One among the dead?
6 "He is not here, but He has risen. Remember how He spoke to you while He was still in Galilee,
7 saying that the Son of Man must be delivered into the hands of sinful men, and be crucified, and the third day rise again."
8 And they remembered His words,
9 and returned from the tomb and reported all these things to the eleven and to all the rest.
10 Now they were Mary Magdalene and Joanna and Mary the *mother* of James; also the other women with them were telling these things to the apostles.
11 But these words appeared to them as nonsense, and they would not believe them.
12 But Peter got up and ran to the tomb; stooping and

NEW CENTURY VERSION

On the Sabbath day they rested, as the law of Moses commanded.

Jesus Rises from the Dead

24 Very early on the first day of the week, at dawn,
the women came to the tomb, bringing the spices
they had prepared. 2They found the stone rolled away from
the entrance of the tomb, 3but when they went in, they did
not find the body of the Lord Jesus. 4While they were won-
dering about this, two men in shining clothes suddenly
stood beside them. 5The women were very afraid and
bowed their heads to the ground. The men said to them,
"Why are you looking for a living person in this place for
the dead? 6He is not here; he has risen from the dead. Do
you remember what he told you in Galilee? 7He said the
Son of Man must be handed over to sinful people, be cruci-
fied, and rise from the dead on the third day." 8Then the
women remembered what Jesus had said.
9The women left the tomb and told all these things to
the eleven apostles and the other followers. 10It was Mary
Magdalene, Joanna, Mary the mother of James, and some
other women who told the apostles everything that had
happened at the tomb. 11But they did not believe the
women, because it sounded like nonsense. 12But Peter got
up and ran to the tomb. Bending down and looking in, he

CONTEMPORARY ENGLISH VERSION

spices for his burial. But on the Sabbath they rested, as the Law of Moses commands.

Jesus Is Alive (Matthew 28.1-10; Mark 16.1-8; John 20.1-10)

24 Very early on Sunday morning the women went to
the tomb, carrying the spices that they had pre-
pared. 2When they found the stone rolled away from the
entrance, 3they went in. But they did not find the body of
the Lord[a] Jesus, 4and they did not know what to think.
Suddenly two men in shining white clothes stood beside
them. 5The women were afraid and bowed to the ground.
But the men said, "Why are you looking in the place of the
dead for someone who is alive? 6Jesus isn't here! He has
been raised from death. Remember that while he was still
in Galilee, he told you, 7'The Son of Man will be handed
over to sinners who will nail him to a cross. But three days
later he will rise to life.' " 8Then they remembered what
Jesus had said.
9-10Mary Magdalene, Joanna, Mary the mother of James,
and some other women were the ones who had gone to the
tomb. When they returned, they told the eleven apostles
and the others what had happened. 11The apostles thought
it was all nonsense, and they would not believe.
12But Peter ran to the tomb. And when he stooped down

[a] 24.3 *the Lord*: These words are not in some manuscripts.

NEW INTERNATIONAL VERSION

perfumes. But they rested on the Sabbath in obedience to the commandment.

The Resurrection

24 On the first day of the week, very early in the morning, the women took the spices they had prepared and went to the tomb. 2They found the stone rolled away from the tomb, 3but when they entered, they did not find the body of the Lord Jesus. 4While they were wondering about this, suddenly two men in clothes that gleamed like lightning stood beside them. 5In their fright the women bowed down with their faces to the ground, but the men said to them, "Why do you look for the living among the dead? 6He is not here; he has risen! Remember how he told you, while he was still with you in Galilee: 7'The Son of Man must be delivered into the hands of sinful men, be crucified and on the third day be raised again.' " 8Then they remembered his words.

9When they came back from the tomb, they told all these things to the Eleven and to all the others. 10It was Mary Magdalene, Joanna, Mary the mother of James, and the others with them who told this to the apostles. 11But they did not believe the women, because their words seemed to them like nonsense. 12Peter, however, got up and ran to the tomb. Bending over, he saw the strips of linen lying by

NEW LIVING TRANSLATION

to embalm him. But by the time they were finished it was the Sabbath, so they rested all that day as required by the law.

The Resurrection

24 But very early on Sunday morning* the women came to the tomb, taking the spices they had prepared. 2They found that the stone covering the entrance had been rolled aside. 3So they went in, but they couldn't find the body of the Lord Jesus. 4They were puzzled, trying to think what could have happened to it. Suddenly, two men appeared to them, clothed in dazzling robes. 5The women were terrified and bowed low before them. Then the men asked, "Why are you looking in a tomb for someone who is alive? 6He isn't here! He has risen from the dead! Don't you remember what he told you back in Galilee, 7that the Son of Man must be betrayed into the hands of sinful men and be crucified, and that he would rise again the third day?"

8Then they remembered that he had said this. 9So they rushed back to tell his eleven disciples—and everyone else—what had happened. 10The women who went to the tomb were Mary Magdalene, Joanna, Mary the mother of James, and several others. They told the apostles what had happened, 11but the story sounded like nonsense, so they didn't believe it. 12However, Peter ran to the tomb to look.

24:1 Greek *But on the first day of the week, very early in the morning.*

NEW KING JAMES VERSION

and fragrant oils. And they rested on the Sabbath according to the commandment.

He Is Risen

24 Now on the first *day* of the week, very early in the morning, they, and certain *other women* with them,[a] came to the tomb bringing the spices which they had prepared. 2But they found the stone rolled away from the tomb. 3Then they went in and did not find the body of the Lord Jesus. 4And it happened, as they were greatly[b] perplexed about this, that behold, two men stood by them in shining garments. 5Then, as they were afraid and bowed *their* faces to the earth, they said to them, "Why do you seek the living among the dead? 6He is not here, but is risen! Remember how He spoke to you when He was still in Galilee, 7saying, 'The Son of Man must be delivered into the hands of sinful men, and be crucified, and the third day rise again.' "

8And they remembered His words. 9Then they returned from the tomb and told all these things to the eleven and to all the rest. 10It was Mary Magdalene, Joanna, Mary *the mother* of James, and the other *women* with them, who told these things to the apostles. 11And their words seemed to them like idle tales, and they did not believe them. 12But Peter arose and ran to the tomb; and stooping down,

24:1 [a] NU-Text omits *and certain other women with them.*
24:4 [b] NU-Text omits *greatly.*

THE MESSAGE

spices and perfumes. They rested quietly on the Sabbath, as commanded.

Looking for the Living One in a Cemetery

24 At the crack of dawn on Sunday, the women came to the tomb carrying the burial spices they had prepared. They found the entrance stone rolled back from the tomb, so they walked in. But once inside, they couldn't find the body of the Master Jesus.

They were puzzled, wondering what to make of this. Then, out of nowhere it seemed, two men, light cascading over them, stood there. The women were awestruck and bowed down in worship. The men said, "Why are you looking for the Living One in a cemetery? He is not here, but raised up. Remember how he told you when you were still back in Galilee that he had to be handed over to sinners, be killed on a cross, and in three days rise up?" Then they remembered Jesus' words.

They left the tomb and broke the news of all this to the Eleven and the rest. Mary Magdalene, Joanna, Mary the mother of James, and the other women with them kept telling these things to the apostles, but the apostles didn't believe a word of it, thought they were making it all up.

But Peter jumped to his feet and ran to the tomb. He

KING JAMES VERSION

stooping down, he beheld the linen clothes laid by themselves, and departed, wondering in himself at that which was come to pass.

13 ¶ And, behold, two of them went that same day to a village called Emmaus, which was from Jerusalem *about* threescore furlongs.

14 And they talked together of all these things which had happened.

15 And it came to pass, that, while they communed *together* and reasoned, Jesus himself drew near, and went with them.

16 But their eyes were holden that they should not know him.

17 And he said unto them, What manner of communications *are* these that ye have one to another, as ye walk, and are sad?

18 And the one of them, whose name was Cleopas, answering said unto him, Art thou only a stranger in Jerusalem, and hast not known the things which are come to pass there in these days?

19 And he said unto them, What things? And they said unto him, Concerning Jesus of Nazareth, which was a prophet mighty in deed and word before God and all the people:

20 And how the chief priests and our rulers delivered him to be condemned to death, and have crucified him.

21 But we trusted that it had been he which should have redeemed Israel: and beside all this, to day is the third day since these things were done.

NEW AMERICAN STANDARD BIBLE

looking in, he *saw the linen wrappings only; and he went away to his home, marveling at what had happened.

The Road to Emmaus

13 And behold, two of them were going that very day to a village named Emmaus, which was [1]about seven miles from Jerusalem.

14 And they were talking with each other about all these things which had taken place.

15 While they were talking and discussing, Jesus Himself approached and *began* traveling with them.

16 But their eyes were prevented from recognizing Him.

17 And He said to them, "What are these words that you are exchanging with one another as you are walking?" And they stood still, looking sad.

18 One *of them*, named Cleopas, answered and said to Him, "Are You the only one visiting Jerusalem and unaware of the things which have happened here in these days?"

19 And He said to them, "What things?" And they said to Him, "The things about Jesus the Nazarene, who was a prophet mighty in deed and word in the sight of God and all the people,

20 and how the chief priests and our rulers delivered Him to the sentence of death, and crucified Him.

21 "But we were hoping that it was He who was going to redeem Israel. Indeed, besides all this, it is the third day since these things happened.

24:13 [1] Lit *60 stadia;* one stadion was about 600 ft

NEW CENTURY VERSION

saw only the cloth that Jesus' body had been wrapped in. Peter went away to his home, wondering about what had happened.

Jesus on the Road to Emmaus

13That same day two of Jesus' followers were going to a town named Emmaus, about seven miles from Jerusalem. 14They were talking about everything that had happened. 15While they were talking and discussing, Jesus himself came near and began walking with them, 16but they were kept from recognizing him. 17Then he said, "What are these things you are talking about while you walk?"

The two followers stopped, looking very sad. 18The one named Cleopas answered, "Are you the only visitor in Jerusalem who does not know what just happened there?"

19Jesus said to them, "What are you talking about?"

They said, "About Jesus of Nazareth. He was a prophet who said and did many powerful things before God and all the people. 20Our leaders and the leading priests handed him over to be sentenced to death, and they crucified him. 21But we were hoping that he would free Israel. Besides this, it is now the third day since this happened. 22And

CONTEMPORARY ENGLISH VERSION

and looked in, he saw only the burial clothes. Then he returned, wondering what had happened.[b]

Jesus Appears to Two Disciples (Mark 16.12, 13)

13That same day two of Jesus' disciples were going to the village of Emmaus, which was about seven miles from Jerusalem. 14As they were talking and thinking about what had happened, 15Jesus came near and started walking along beside them. 16But they did not know who he was.

17Jesus asked them, "What were you talking about as you walked along?"

The two of them stood there looking sad and gloomy. 18Then the one named Cleopas asked Jesus, "Are you the only person from Jerusalem who didn't know what was happening there these last few days?"

19"What do you mean?" Jesus asked.

They answered:

Those things that happened to Jesus from Nazareth. By what he did and said he showed that he was a powerful prophet, who pleased God and all the people. 20Then the chief priests and our leaders had him arrested and sentenced to die on a cross. 21We had hoped that he would be the one to set Israel free! But it has already been three days since all this happened.

[b] 24.12 *what had happened*: Verse 12 is not in some manuscripts.

NEW INTERNATIONAL VERSION

themselves, and he went away, wondering to himself what had happened.

On the Road to Emmaus

13Now that same day two of them were going to a village called Emmaus, about seven miles[a] from Jerusalem. 14They were talking with each other about everything that had happened. 15As they talked and discussed these things with each other, Jesus himself came up and walked along with them; 16but they were kept from recognizing him.

17He asked them, "What are you discussing together as you walk along?"

They stood still, their faces downcast. 18One of them, named Cleopas, asked him, "Are you only a visitor to Jerusalem and do not know the things that have happened there in these days?"

19"What things?" he asked.

"About Jesus of Nazareth," they replied. "He was a prophet, powerful in word and deed before God and all the people. 20The chief priests and our rulers handed him over to be sentenced to death, and they crucified him; 21but we had hoped that he was the one who was going to redeem Israel. And what is more, it is the third day since all this

[a] *13* Greek *sixty stadia* (about 11 kilometers)

NEW LIVING TRANSLATION

Stooping, he peered in and saw the empty linen wrappings; then he went home again, wondering what had happened.*

The Walk to Emmaus

13That same day two of Jesus' followers were walking to the village of Emmaus, seven miles* out of Jerusalem. 14As they walked along they were talking about everything that had happened. 15Suddenly, Jesus himself came along and joined them and began walking beside them. 16But they didn't know who he was, because God kept them from recognizing him.

17"You seem to be in a deep discussion about something," he said. "What are you so concerned about?"

They stopped short, sadness written across their faces. 18Then one of them, Cleopas, replied, "You must be the only person in Jerusalem who hasn't heard about all the things that have happened there the last few days."

19"What things?" Jesus asked.

"The things that happened to Jesus, the man from Nazareth," they said. "He was a prophet who did wonderful miracles. He was a mighty teacher, highly regarded by both God and all the people. 20But our leading priests and other religious leaders arrested him and handed him over to be condemned to death, and they crucified him. 21We had thought he was the Messiah who had come to rescue Israel. That all happened three days ago. 22Then some

24:12 Some manuscripts do not include this verse. 24:13 Greek *60 stadia* [11.1 kilometers].

NEW KING JAMES VERSION

he saw the linen cloths lying[c] by themselves; and he departed, marveling to himself at what had happened.

The Road to Emmaus

13Now behold, two of them were traveling that same day to a village called Emmaus, which was seven miles[d] from Jerusalem. 14And they talked together of all these things which had happened. 15So it was, while they conversed and reasoned, that Jesus Himself drew near and went with them. 16But their eyes were restrained, so that they did not know Him.

17And He said to them, "What kind of conversation *is* this that you have with one another as you walk and are sad?"[e]

18Then the one whose name was Cleopas answered and said to Him, "Are You the only stranger in Jerusalem, and have You not known the things which happened there in these days?"

19And He said to them, "What things?"

So they said to Him, "The things concerning Jesus of Nazareth, who was a Prophet mighty in deed and word before God and all the people, 20and how the chief priests and our rulers delivered Him to be condemned to death, and crucified Him. 21But we were hoping that it was He who was going to redeem Israel. Indeed, besides all this, today is the third day since these things happened. 22Yes,

24:12 [c] NU-Text omits *lying.* 24:13 [d] Literally *sixty stadia*
24:17 [e] NU-Text reads *as you walk? And they stood still, looking sad.*

THE MESSAGE

stooped to look in and saw a few grave clothes, that's all. He walked away puzzled, shaking his head.

The Road to Emmaus

That same day two of them were walking to the village Emmaus, about seven miles out of Jerusalem. They were deep in conversation, going over all these things that had happened. In the middle of their talk and questions, Jesus came up and walked along with them. But they were not able to recognize who he was.

He asked, "What's this you're discussing so intently as you walk along?"

They just stood there, long-faced, like they had lost their best friend. Then one of them, his name was Cleopas, said, "Are you the only one in Jerusalem who hasn't heard what's happened during the last few days?"

He said, "What has happened?"

They said, "The things that happened to Jesus the Nazarene. He was a man of God, a prophet, dynamic in work and word, blessed by both God and all the people. Then our high priests and leaders betrayed him, got him sentenced to death, and crucified him. And we had our hopes up that he was the One, the One about to deliver Israel. And it is now the third day since it happened. But

KING JAMES VERSION

22 Yea, and certain women also of our company made us astonished, which were early at the sepulchre;

23 And when they found not his body, they came, saying, that they had also seen a vision of angels, which said that he was alive.

24 And certain of them which were with us went to the sepulchre, and found *it* even so as the women had said: but him they saw not.

25 Then he said unto them, O fools, and slow of heart to believe all that the prophets have spoken:

26 Ought not Christ to have suffered these things, and to enter into his glory?

27 And beginning at Moses and all the prophets, he expounded unto them in all the scriptures the things concerning himself.

28 And they drew nigh unto the village, whither they went: and he made as though he would have gone further.

29 But they constrained him, saying, Abide with us: for it is toward evening, and the day is far spent. And he went in to tarry with them.

30 And it came to pass, as he sat at meat with them, he took bread, and blessed *it*, and brake, and gave to them.

31 And their eyes were opened, and they knew him; and he vanished out of their sight.

32 And they said one to another, Did not our heart burn within us, while he talked with us by the way, and while he opened to us the scriptures?

33 And they rose up the same hour, and returned to

NEW AMERICAN STANDARD BIBLE

22 "But also some women among us amazed us. When they were at the tomb early in the morning,

23 and did not find His body, they came, saying that they had also seen a vision of angels who said that He was alive.

24 "Some of those who were with us went to the tomb and found it just exactly as the women also had said; but Him they did not see."

25 And He said to them, "O foolish men and slow of heart to believe in all that the prophets have spoken!

26 "Was it not necessary for the Christ to suffer these things and to enter into His glory?"

27 Then beginning with Moses and with all the prophets, He explained to them the things concerning Himself in all the Scriptures.

28 And they approached the village where they were going, and He acted as though He were going farther.

29 But they urged Him, saying, "Stay with us, for it is *getting* toward evening, and the day is now nearly over." So He went in to stay with them.

30 When He had reclined *at the table* with them, He took the bread and blessed *it,* and breaking *it,* He *began* giving *it* to them.

31 Then their eyes were opened and they recognized Him; and He vanished from their sight.

32 They said to one another, "Were not our hearts burning within us while He was speaking to us on the road, while He was explaining the Scriptures to us?"

33 And they got up that very hour and returned to

NEW CENTURY VERSION

today some women among us amazed us. Early this morning they went to the tomb, 23but they did not find his body there. They came and told us that they had seen a vision of angels who said that Jesus was alive! 24So some of our group went to the tomb, too. They found it just as the women said, but they did not see Jesus."

25Then Jesus said to them, "You are foolish and slow to believe everything the prophets said. 26They said that the Christ must suffer these things before he enters his glory." 27Then starting with what Moses and all the prophets had said about him, Jesus began to explain everything that had been written about himself in the Scriptures.

28They came near the town of Emmaus, and Jesus acted as if he were going farther. 29But they begged him, "Stay with us, because it is late; it is almost night." So he went in to stay with them.

30When Jesus was at the table with them, he took some bread, gave thanks, divided it, and gave it to them. 31And then, they were allowed to recognize Jesus. But when they saw who he was, he disappeared. 32They said to each other, "It felt like a fire burning in us when Jesus talked to us on the road and explained the Scriptures to us."

33So the two followers got up at once and went back to

CONTEMPORARY ENGLISH VERSION

22Some women in our group surprised us. They had gone to the tomb early in the morning, 23but did not find the body of Jesus. They came back, saying that they had seen a vision of angels who told them that he is alive. 24Some men from our group went to the tomb and found it just as the women had said. But they didn't see Jesus either.

25Then Jesus asked the two disciples, "Why can't you understand? How can you be so slow to believe all that the prophets said? 26Didn't you know that the Messiah would have to suffer before he was given his glory?" 27Jesus then explained everything written about himself in the Scriptures, beginning with the Law of Moses and the Books of the Prophets.[c]

28When the two of them came near the village where they were going, Jesus seemed to be going farther. 29They begged him, "Stay with us! It's already late, and the sun is going down." So Jesus went into the house to stay with them.

30After Jesus sat down to eat, he took some bread. He blessed it and broke it. Then he gave it to them. 31At once they knew who he was, but he disappeared. 32They said to each other, "When he talked with us along the road and explained the Scriptures to us, didn't it warm our hearts?" 33So they got right up and returned to Jerusalem.

[c] **24.27** *the Law of Moses and the Books of the Prophets*: See the note at 16.16.

NEW INTERNATIONAL VERSION

took place. 22In addition, some of our women amazed us.
They went to the tomb early this morning 23but didn't find
his body. They came and told us that they had seen a
vision of angels, who said he was alive. 24Then some of
our companions went to the tomb and found it just as the
women had said, but him they did not see."
25He said to them, "How foolish you are, and how slow
of heart to believe all that the prophets have spoken! 26Did
not the Christ[b] have to suffer these things and then enter
his glory?" 27And beginning with Moses and all the
Prophets, he explained to them what was said in all the
Scriptures concerning himself.
28As they approached the village to which they were
going, Jesus acted as if he were going farther. 29But they
urged him strongly, "Stay with us, for it is nearly evening;
the day is almost over." So he went in to stay with them.
30When he was at the table with them, he took bread,
gave thanks, broke it and began to give it to them. 31Then
their eyes were opened and they recognized him, and he
disappeared from their sight. 32They asked each other,
"Were not our hearts burning within us while he talked
with us on the road and opened the Scriptures to us?"
33They got up and returned at once to Jerusalem. There

[b] *26* Or *Messiah*; also in verse 46

NEW LIVING TRANSLATION

women from our group of his followers were at his tomb
early this morning, and they came back with an amazing
report. 23They said his body was missing, and they had
seen angels who told them Jesus is alive! 24Some of our
men ran out to see, and sure enough, Jesus' body was
gone, just as the women had said."
25Then Jesus said to them, "You are such foolish people!
You find it so hard to believe all that the prophets wrote in
the Scriptures. 26Wasn't it clearly predicted by the prophets
that the Messiah would have to suffer all these things
before entering his time of glory?" 27Then Jesus quoted
passages from the writings of Moses and all the prophets,
explaining what all the Scriptures said about himself.
28By this time they were nearing Emmaus and the end of
their journey. Jesus would have gone on, 29but they begged
him to stay the night with them, since it was getting late.
So he went home with them. 30As they sat down to eat, he
took a small loaf of bread, asked God's blessing on it,
broke it, then gave it to them. 31Suddenly, their eyes were
opened, and they recognized him. And at that moment he
disappeared!
32They said to each other, "Didn't our hearts feel
strangely warm as he talked with us on the road and
explained the Scriptures to us?" 33And within the hour
they were on their way back to Jerusalem, where the

NEW KING JAMES VERSION

and certain women of our company, who arrived at the
tomb early, astonished us. 23When they did not find His
body, they came saying that they had also seen a vision of
angels who said He was alive. 24And certain of those *who
were* with us went to the tomb and found *it* just as the
women had said; but Him they did not see."
25Then He said to them, "O foolish ones, and slow of
heart to believe in all that the prophets have spoken!
26Ought not the Christ to have suffered these things and to
enter into His glory?" 27And beginning at Moses and all
the Prophets, He expounded to them in all the Scriptures
the things concerning Himself.

The Disciples' Eyes Opened

28Then they drew near to the village where they were
going, and He indicated that He would have gone farther.
29But they constrained Him, saying, "Abide with us, for it
is toward evening, and the day is far spent." And He went
in to stay with them.
30Now it came to pass, as He sat at the table with them,
that He took bread, blessed and broke *it,* and gave it to
them. 31Then their eyes were opened and they knew Him;
and He vanished from their sight.
32And they said to one another, "Did not our heart burn
within us while He talked with us on the road, and while
He opened the Scriptures to us?" 33So they rose up that
very hour and returned to Jerusalem, and found the eleven

THE MESSAGE

now some of our women have completely confused us. Early this morning they were at the tomb and couldn't find his body. They came back with the story that they had seen a vision of angels who said he was alive. Some of our friends went off to the tomb to check and found it empty just as the women said, but they didn't see Jesus."

Then he said to them, "So thick-headed! So slow-hearted! Why can't you simply believe all that the prophets said? Don't you see that these things had to happen, that the Messiah had to suffer and only then enter into his glory?" Then he started at the beginning, with the Books of Moses, and went on through all the Prophets, pointing out everything in the Scriptures that referred to him.

They came to the edge of the village where they were headed. He acted as if he were going on but they pressed him: "Stay and have supper with us. It's nearly evening; the day is done." So he went in with them. And here is what happened: He sat down at the table with them. Taking the bread, he blessed and broke and gave it to them. At that moment, open-eyed, wide-eyed, they recognized him. And then he disappeared.

Back and forth they talked. "Didn't we feel on fire as he conversed with us on the road, as he opened up the Scriptures for us?"

A Ghost Doesn't Have Muscle and Bone

They didn't waste a minute. They were up and on their way back to Jerusalem. They found the Eleven and their

KING JAMES VERSION

Jerusalem, and found the eleven gathered together, and
them that were with them,
34 Saying, The Lord is risen indeed, and hath appeared
to Simon.
35 And they told what things *were done* in the way, and
how he was known of them in breaking of bread.
36 ¶ And as they thus spake, Jesus himself stood in the
midst of them, and saith unto them, Peace *be* unto you.
37 But they were terrified and affrighted, and supposed
that they had seen a spirit.
38 And he said unto them, Why are ye troubled? and
why do thoughts arise in your hearts?
39 Behold my hands and my feet, that it is I myself:
handle me, and see; for a spirit hath not flesh and bones,
as ye see me have.
40 And when he had thus spoken, he shewed them *his*
hands and *his* feet.
41 And while they yet believed not for joy, and won-
dered, he said unto them, Have ye here any meat?
42 And they gave him a piece of a broiled fish, and of
an honeycomb.
43 And he took *it*, and did eat before them.
44 And he said unto them, These *are* the words which I
spake unto you, while I was yet with you, that all things
must be fulfilled, which were written in the law of Moses,
and *in* the prophets, and *in* the psalms, concerning me.

NEW AMERICAN STANDARD BIBLE

Jerusalem, and found gathered together the eleven and
those who were with them,
34 saying, "The Lord has really risen and has appeared
to Simon."
35 They *began* to relate their experiences on the road
and how He was recognized by them in the breaking of the
bread.

Other Appearances

36 While they were telling these things, He Himself
stood in their midst.
37 But they were startled and frightened and thought
that they were seeing a spirit.
38 And He said to them, "Why are you troubled, and
why do doubts arise in your hearts?
39 "See My hands and My feet, that it is I Myself; touch
Me and see, for a spirit does not have flesh and bones as
you see that I have."
40 And when He had said this, He showed them His
hands and His feet.
41 While they still could not believe *it* because of their
joy and amazement, He said to them, "Have you anything
here to eat?"
42 They gave Him a piece of a broiled fish;
43 and He took it and ate *it* before them.
44 Now He said to them, "These are My words which I
spoke to you while I was still with you, that all things
which are written about Me in the Law of Moses and the
Prophets and the Psalms must be fulfilled."

NEW CENTURY VERSION

Jerusalem. There they found the eleven apostles and others
gathered. 34They were saying, "The Lord really has risen
from the dead! He showed himself to Simon."
35Then the two followers told what had happened on the
road and how they recognized Jesus when he divided the
bread.

Jesus Appears to His Followers

36While the two followers were telling this, Jesus himself
stood right in the middle of them and said, "Peace be with
you."
37They were fearful and terrified and thought they were
seeing a ghost. 38But Jesus said, "Why are you troubled?
Why do you doubt what you see? 39Look at my hands and
my feet. It is I myself! Touch me and see, because a ghost
does not have a living body as you see I have."
40After Jesus said this, he showed them his hands and
feet. 41While they still could not believe it because they were
amazed and happy, Jesus said to them, "Do you have any
food here?" 42They gave him a piece of broiled fish. 43While
the followers watched, Jesus took the fish and ate it.
44He said to them, "Remember when I was with you
before? I said that everything written about me must hap-
pen—everything in the law of Moses, the books of the
prophets, and the Psalms."

CONTEMPORARY ENGLISH VERSION

The two disciples found the eleven apostles and the oth-
ers gathered together. 34And they learned from the group
that the Lord was really alive and had appeared to Peter.
35Then the disciples from Emmaus told what happened on
the road and how they knew he was the Lord when he
broke the bread.

What Jesus' Followers Must Do

(Matthew 28.16-20; Mark 16.14-18; John 20.19-23; Acts 1.6-8)

36While Jesus' disciples were talking about what had
happened, Jesus appeared and greeted them. 37They were
frightened and terrified because they thought they were
seeing a ghost.
38But Jesus said, "Why are you so frightened? Why do
you doubt? 39Look at my hands and my feet and see who I
am! Touch me and find out for yourselves. Ghosts don't
have flesh and bones as you see I have."
40After Jesus said this, he showed them his hands and
his feet. 41The disciples were so glad and amazed that they
could not believe it. Jesus then asked them, "Do you have
something to eat?" 42They gave him a piece of baked fish.
43He took it and ate it as they watched.
44Jesus said to them, "While I was still with you, I told you
that everything written about me in the Law of Moses, the
Books of the Prophets, and in the Psalms[d] had to happen."

[d] 24.44 *Psalms*: The Jewish Scriptures were made up of three parts: (1) the Law of Moses, (2) the Books of the Prophets, (3) and the Writings, which included the Psalms. Sometimes the Scriptures were just called the Law or the Law (of Moses) and the Books of the Prophets.

NEW INTERNATIONAL VERSION

they found the Eleven and those with them, assembled together 34and saying, "It is true! The Lord has risen and has appeared to Simon." 35Then the two told what had happened on the way, and how Jesus was recognized by them when he broke the bread.

Jesus Appears to the Disciples

36While they were still talking about this, Jesus himself stood among them and said to them, "Peace be with you."

37They were startled and frightened, thinking they saw a ghost. 38He said to them, "Why are you troubled, and why do doubts rise in your minds? 39Look at my hands and my feet. It is I myself! Touch me and see; a ghost does not have flesh and bones, as you see I have."

40When he had said this, he showed them his hands and feet. 41And while they still did not believe it because of joy and amazement, he asked them, "Do you have anything here to eat?" 42They gave him a piece of broiled fish, 43and he took it and ate it in their presence.

44He said to them, "This is what I told you while I was still with you: Everything must be fulfilled that is written about me in the Law of Moses, the Prophets and the Psalms."

NEW LIVING TRANSLATION

eleven disciples and the other followers of Jesus were gathered. When they arrived, they were greeted with the report, 34"The Lord has really risen! He appeared to Peter*!"

Jesus Appears to the Disciples

35Then the two from Emmaus told their story of how Jesus had appeared to them as they were walking along the road and how they had recognized him as he was breaking the bread. 36And just as they were telling about it, Jesus himself was suddenly standing there among them. He said, "Peace be with you."* 37But the whole group was terribly frightened, thinking they were seeing a ghost! 38"Why are you frightened?" he asked. "Why do you doubt who I am? 39Look at my hands. Look at my feet. You can see that it's really me. Touch me and make sure that I am not a ghost, because ghosts don't have bodies, as you see that I do!" 40As he spoke, he held out his hands for them to see, and he showed them his feet.*

41Still they stood there doubting, filled with joy and wonder. Then he asked them, "Do you have anything here to eat?" 42They gave him a piece of broiled fish, 43and he ate it as they watched.

44Then he said, "When I was with you before, I told you that everything written about me by Moses and the prophets and in the Psalms must all come true." 45Then he

24:34 Greek *Simon.* **24:36** Some manuscripts do not include *He said, "Peace be with you."* **24:40** Some manuscripts do not include this verse.

NEW KING JAMES VERSION

and those *who were* with them gathered together, 34saying, "The Lord is risen indeed, and has appeared to Simon!" 35And they told about the things *that had happened* on the road, and how He was known to them in the breaking of bread.

Jesus Appears to His Disciples

36Now as they said these things, Jesus Himself stood in the midst of them, and said to them, "Peace to you." 37But they were terrified and frightened, and supposed they had seen a spirit. 38And He said to them, "Why are you troubled? And why do doubts arise in your hearts? 39Behold My hands and My feet, that it is I Myself. Handle Me and see, for a spirit does not have flesh and bones as you see I have."

40When He had said this, He showed them His hands and His feet.[f] 41But while they still did not believe for joy, and marveled, He said to them, "Have you any food here?" 42So they gave Him a piece of a broiled fish and some honeycomb.[g] 43And He took *it* and ate in their presence.

The Scriptures Opened

44Then He said to them, "These *are* the words which I spoke to you while I was still with you, that all things must be fulfilled which were written in the Law of Moses and *the* Prophets and *the* Psalms concerning Me." 45And

24:40 [f] Some printed New Testaments omit this verse. It is found in nearly all Greek manuscripts. **24:42** [g] NU-Text omits *and some honeycomb.*

THE MESSAGE

friends gathered together, talking away: "It's really happened! The Master has been raised up—Simon saw him!"

Then the two went over everything that happened on the road and how they recognized him when he broke the bread.

While they were saying all this, Jesus appeared to them and said, "Peace be with you." They thought they were seeing a ghost and were scared half to death. He continued with them, "Don't be upset, and don't let all these doubting questions take over. Look at my hands; look at my feet—it's really me. Touch me. Look me over from head to toe. A ghost doesn't have muscle and bone like this." As he said this, he showed them his hands and feet. They still couldn't believe what they were seeing. It was too much; it seemed too good to be true.

He asked, "Do you have any food here?" They gave him a piece of leftover fish they had cooked. He took it and ate it right before their eyes.

You're the Witnesses

Then he said, "Everything I told you while I was with you comes to this: All the things written about me in the Law of Moses, in the Prophets, and in the Psalms have to be fulfilled."

KING JAMES VERSION

45 Then opened he their understanding, that they might understand the scriptures,

46 And said unto them, Thus it is written, and thus it behoved Christ to suffer, and to rise from the dead the third day:

47 And that repentance and remission of sins should be preached in his name among all nations, beginning at Jerusalem.

48 And ye are witnesses of these things.

49 And, behold, I send the promise of my Father upon you: but tarry ye in the city of Jerusalem, until ye be endued with power from on high.

50 ¶ And he led them out as far as to Bethany, and he lifted up his hands, and blessed them.

51 And it came to pass, while he blessed them, he was parted from them, and carried up into heaven.

52 And they worshipped him, and returned to Jerusalem with great joy:

53 And were continually in the temple, praising and blessing God. Amen.

NEW AMERICAN STANDARD BIBLE

45 Then He opened their minds to understand the Scriptures,

46 and He said to them, "Thus it is written, that the Christ would suffer and rise again from the dead the third day,

47 and that repentance for forgiveness of sins would be proclaimed in His name to all the nations, beginning from Jerusalem.

48 "You are witnesses of these things.

49 "And behold, I am sending forth the promise of My Father upon you; but you are to stay in the city until you are clothed with power from on high."

The Ascension

50 And He led them out as far as Bethany, and He lifted up His hands and blessed them.

51 While He was blessing them, He parted from them and was carried up into heaven.

52 And they, after worshiping Him, returned to Jerusalem with great joy,

53 and were continually in the temple praising God.

NEW CENTURY VERSION

45Then Jesus opened their minds so they could under-
stand the Scriptures. 46He said to them, "It is written that
the Christ would suffer and rise from the dead on the third
day 47and that a change of hearts and lives and forgive-
ness of sins would be preached in his name to all nations,
starting at Jerusalem. 48You are witnesses of these things.
49I will send you what my Father has promised, but you
must stay in Jerusalem until you have received that power
from heaven."

Jesus Goes Back to Heaven

50Jesus led his followers as far as Bethany, and he
raised his hands and blessed them. 51While he was bless-
ing them, he was separated from them and carried into
heaven. 52They worshiped him and returned to Jerusalem
very happy. 53They stayed in the Temple all the time,
praising God.

CONTEMPORARY ENGLISH VERSION

45Then he helped them understand the Scriptures. 46He
told them:

The Scriptures say that the Messiah must suffer, then
three days later he will rise from death. 47They also say
that all people of every nation must be told in my name
to turn to God, in order to be forgiven. So beginning in
Jerusalem, 48you must tell everything that has hap-
pened. 49I will send you the one my Father has prom-
ised,[e] but you must stay in the city until you are given
power from heaven.

Jesus Returns to Heaven (Mark 16.19, 20; Acts 1.9-11)

50Jesus led his disciples out to Bethany, where he raised
his hands and blessed them. 51As he was doing this, he
left and was taken up to heaven.[f] 52After his disciples had
worshiped him,[g] they returned to Jerusalem and were very
happy. 53They spent their time in the temple, praising God.

[e] 24.49 *the one my Father has promised*: Jesus means the Holy Spirit.
[f] 24.51 *and was taken up to heaven*: These words are not in some manuscripts. [g] 24.52 *After his disciples had worshiped him*: These words are not in some manuscripts.

NEW INTERNATIONAL VERSION

45Then he opened their minds so they could understand
the Scriptures. 46He told them, "This is what is written:
The Christ will suffer and rise from the dead on the third
day, 47and repentance and forgiveness of sins will be
preached in his name to all nations, beginning at Jeru-
salem. 48You are witnesses of these things. 49I am going to
send you what my Father has promised; but stay in the
city until you have been clothed with power from on high."

The Ascension

50When he had led them out to the vicinity of Bethany,
he lifted up his hands and blessed them. 51While he was
blessing them, he left them and was taken up into heaven.
52Then they worshiped him and returned to Jerusalem with
great joy. 53And they stayed continually at the temple,
praising God.

NEW LIVING TRANSLATION

opened their minds to understand these many Scriptures.
46And he said, "Yes, it was written long ago that the
Messiah must suffer and die and rise again from the dead
on the third day. 47With my authority, take this message
of repentance to all the nations, beginning in Jerusalem:
'There is forgiveness of sins for all who turn to me.' 48You
are witnesses of all these things.

49"And now I will send the Holy Spirit, just as my Father
promised. But stay here in the city until the Holy Spirit
comes and fills you with power from heaven."

The Ascension

50Then Jesus led them to Bethany, and lifting his hands
to heaven, he blessed them. 51While he was blessing them,
he left them and was taken up to heaven.* 52They wor-
shiped him and* then returned to Jerusalem filled with
great joy. 53And they spent all of their time in the Temple,
praising God.

24:51 Some manuscripts do not include *and was taken up to heaven.*
24:52 Some manuscripts do not include *worshiped him and.*

NEW KING JAMES VERSION

He opened their understanding, that they might compre-
hend the Scriptures.

46Then He said to them, "Thus it is written, and thus it
was necessary for the Christ to suffer and to rise[h] from the
dead the third day, 47and that repentance and remission of
sins should be preached in His name to all nations, begin-
ning at Jerusalem. 48And you are witnesses of these
things. 49Behold, I send the Promise of My Father upon
you; but tarry in the city of Jerusalem[i] until you are
endued with power from on high."

The Ascension

50And He led them out as far as Bethany, and He lifted
up His hands and blessed them. 51Now it came to pass,
while He blessed them, that He was parted from them and
carried up into heaven. 52And they worshiped Him, and
returned to Jerusalem with great joy, 53and were continual-
ly in the temple praising and[j] blessing God. Amen.[k]

24:46 [h] NU-Text reads *written, that the Christ should suffer and rise.*
24:49 [i] NU-Text omits *of Jerusalem.* 24:53 [j] NU-Text omits *praising and.* [k] NU-Text omits *Amen.*

THE MESSAGE

He went on to open their understanding of the Word of God, showing them how to read their Bibles this way. He said, "You can see now how it is written that the Messiah suffers, rises from the dead on the third day, and then a total life-change through the forgiveness of sins is proclaimed in his name to all nations—starting from here, from Jerusalem! You're the first to hear and see it. You're the witnesses. What comes next is very important: I am sending what my Father promised to you, so stay here in the city until he arrives, until you're equipped with power from on high."

He then led them out of the city over to Bethany. Raising his hands he blessed them, and while blessing them, took his leave, being carried up to heaven.

And they were on their knees, worshiping him. They returned to Jerusalem bursting with joy. They spent all their time in the Temple praising God. Yes.

KING JAMES VERSION

THE GOSPEL ACCORDING TO ST. JOHN

1 In the beginning was the Word, and the Word was with God, and the Word was God.
2 The same was in the beginning with God.
3 All things were made by him; and without him was not any thing made that was made.
4 In him was life; and the life was the light of men.
5 ¶ And the light shineth in darkness; and the darkness comprehended it not.
6 There was a man sent from God, whose name *was* John.
7 The same came for a witness, to bear witness of the

NEW AMERICAN STANDARD BIBLE

THE GOSPEL ACCORDING TO JOHN

The Deity of Jesus Christ

1 In the beginning was the Word, and the Word was with God, and the Word was God.
2 He was in the beginning with God.
3 All things came into being through Him, and apart from Him nothing came into being that has come into being.
4 In Him was life, and the life was the Light of men.
5 The Light shines in the darkness, and the darkness did not [1]comprehend it.

The Witness John

6 There [2]came a man sent from God, whose name was John.
7 He came as a witness, to testify about the Light, so

1:5 [1] Or *overpower* 1:6 [2] Or *came into being*

NEW CENTURY VERSION

JOHN

Christ Comes to the World

1 In the beginning there was the Word.[a] The Word was with God, and the Word was God.
2He was with God
in the beginning.
3All things were made by him, and nothing was made without him.
4In him there was life, and that life was the light of all people.
5The Light shines in the darkness, and the darkness has not overpowered it.
6There was a man named John[b] who was sent by God.
7He came to tell people the truth about the Light so that

1:1 [a] **Word** The Greek word is "logos," meaning any kind of communication; it could be translated "message." Here, it means Christ, because Christ was the way God told people about himself. 1:6 [b] **John** John the Baptist, who preached to people about Christ's coming (Matthew 3, Luke 3).

CONTEMPORARY ENGLISH VERSION

JOHN

The Word of Life

1 In the beginning was the one
who is called the Word.
The Word was with God
and was truly God.
2 From the very beginning
the Word was with God.

3 And with this Word,
God created all things.
Nothing was made
without the Word.
Everything that was created
4 received its life from him,
and his life gave light
to everyone.
5 The light keeps shining
in the dark,
and darkness has never
put it out.[a]
6 God sent a man named John,
7 who came to tell
about the light

[a] 1.5 *put it out*: Or "understood it."

NEW INTERNATIONAL VERSION

JOHN

The Word Became Flesh

1 In the beginning was the Word, and the Word was
with God, and the Word was God. 2He was with God
in the beginning.
3Through him all things were made; without him noth-
ing was made that has been made. 4In him was life, and
that life was the light of men. 5The light shines in the
darkness, but the darkness has not understood[a] it.
6There came a man who was sent from God; his name
was John. 7He came as a witness to testify concerning that

[a] 5 Or *darkness, and the darkness has not overcome*

NEW LIVING TRANSLATION

JOHN

Christ, the Eternal Word

1 In the beginning the Word already existed. He was
with God, and he was God. 2He was in the beginning
with God. 3He created everything there is. Nothing exists
that he didn't make. 4Life itself was in him, and this life
gives light to everyone. 5The light shines through the dark-
ness, and the darkness can never extinguish it.
6God sent John the Baptist 7to tell everyone about the

NEW KING JAMES VERSION

THE GOSPEL ACCORDING TO

JOHN

The Eternal Word

1 In the beginning was the Word, and the Word was
with God, and the Word was God. 2He was in the
beginning with God. 3All things were made through Him,
and without Him nothing was made that was made. 4In
Him was life, and the life was the light of men. 5And the
light shines in the darkness, and the darkness did not
comprehend[a] it.

John's Witness: The True Light

6There was a man sent from God, whose name *was* John.
7This man came for a witness, to bear witness of the Light,

1:5 [a] Or *overcome*

THE MESSAGE

JOHN

The Life-Light

1 The Word was first,
the Word present to God,
God present to the Word.
The Word was God,
in readiness for God from day one.

Everything was created through him;
nothing—not one thing!—
came into being without him.
What came into existence was Life,
and the Life was Light to live by.
The Life-Light blazed out of the darkness;
the darkness couldn't put it out.

There once was a man, his name John, sent by God to
point out the way to the Life-Light. He came to show

KING JAMES VERSION

Light, that all *men* through him might believe.

8 He was not that Light, but *was sent* to bear witness of that Light.

9 *That* was the true Light, which lighteth every man that cometh into the world.

10 He was in the world, and the world was made by him, and the world knew him not.

11 He came unto his own, and his own received him not.

12 But as many as received him, to them gave he power to become the sons of God, *even* to them that believe on his name:

13 Which were born, not of blood, nor of the will of the flesh, nor of the will of man, but of God.

14 And the Word was made flesh, and dwelt among us,

NEW AMERICAN STANDARD BIBLE

that all might believe through him.

8 He was not the Light, but *he came* to testify about the Light.

9 There was the true Light [3]which, coming into the world, enlightens every man.

10 He was in the world, and the world was made through Him, and the world did not know Him.

11 He came to His [4]own, and those who were His own did not receive Him.

12 But as many as received Him, to them He gave the right to become children of God, *even* to those who believe in His name,

13 who were born, not of blood nor of the will of the flesh nor of the will of man, but of God.

The Word Made Flesh

14 And the Word became flesh, and dwelt among us,

1:9 [3] Or *which enlightens every person coming into the world*
1:11 [4] Or *own things, possessions, domain*

NEW CENTURY VERSION

through him all people could hear about the Light and
believe. 8John was not the Light, but he came to tell people
the truth about the Light. 9The true Light that gives light
to all was coming into the world!
10The Word was in the world, and the world was made
by him, but the world did not know him. 11He came to the
world that was his own, but his own people did not accept
him. 12But to all who did accept him and believe in him he
gave the right to become children of God. 13They did not
become his children in any human way—by any human
parents or human desire. They were born of God.
14The Word became a human and lived among us. We

CONTEMPORARY ENGLISH VERSION

and to lead all people
to have faith.
8 John wasn't that light.
He came only to tell
about the light.

9 The true light that shines
on everyone
was coming into the world.
10 The Word was in the world,
but no one knew him,
though God had made the world
with his Word.
11 He came into his own world,
but his own nation
did not welcome him.
12 Yet some people accepted him
and put their faith in him.
So he gave them the right
to be the children of God.
13 They were not God's children
by nature or because
of any human desires.
God himself was the one
who made them his children.

14 The Word became
a human being
and lived here with us.

NEW INTERNATIONAL VERSION

light, so that through him all men might believe. 8He himself was not the light; he came only as a witness to the light. 9The true light that gives light to every man was coming into the world.[b]

10He was in the world, and though the world was made through him, the world did not recognize him. 11He came to that which was his own, but his own did not receive him. 12Yet to all who received him, to those who believed in his name, he gave the right to become children of God— 13children born not of natural descent,[c] nor of human decision or a husband's will, but born of God.

14The Word became flesh and made his dwelling among

[b] 9 Or *This was the true light that gives light to every man who comes into the world* [c] 13 Greek *of bloods*

NEW LIVING TRANSLATION

light so that everyone might believe because of his testimony. 8John himself was not the light; he was only a witness to the light. 9The one who is the true light, who gives light to everyone, was going to come into the world.

10But although the world was made through him, the world didn't recognize him when he came. 11Even in his own land and among his own people, he was not accepted. 12But to all who believed him and accepted him, he gave the right to become children of God. 13They are reborn! This is not a physical birth resulting from human passion or plan—this rebirth comes from God.

14So the Word became human and lived here on earth

NEW KING JAMES VERSION

that all through him might believe. 8He was not that Light, but *was sent* to bear witness of that Light. 9That was the true Light which gives light to every man coming into the world.[b]

10He was in the world, and the world was made through Him, and the world did not know Him. 11He came to His own,[c] and His own[d] did not receive Him. 12But as many as received Him, to them He gave the right to become children of God, to those who believe in His name: 13who were born, not of blood, nor of the will of the flesh, nor of the will of man, but of God.

The Word Becomes Flesh

14And the Word became flesh and dwelt among us, and

1:9 [b] Or *That was the true Light which, coming into the world, gives light to every man.* 1:11 [c] That is, His own things or domain [d] That is, His own people

THE MESSAGE

everyone where to look, who to believe in. John was not himself the Light; he was there to show the way to the Light.

The Life-Light was the real thing:
  Every person entering Life
  he brings into Light.
He was in the world,
  the world was there through him,
  and yet the world didn't even notice.
He came to his own people,
  but they didn't want him.
But whoever did want him,
  who believed he was who he claimed
  and would do what he said,
He made to be their true selves,
  their child-of-God selves.
These are the God-begotten,
  not blood-begotten,
  not flesh-begotten,
  not sex-begotten.

The Word became flesh and blood,
  and moved into the neighborhood.

KING JAMES VERSION

(and we beheld his glory, the glory as of the only begotten of the Father,) full of grace and truth.

15 ¶ John bare witness of him, and cried, saying, This was he of whom I spake, He that cometh after me is preferred before me: for he was before me.

16 And of his fulness have all we received, and grace for grace.

17 For the law was given by Moses, *but* grace and truth came by Jesus Christ.

18 No man hath seen God at any time; the only begotten Son, which is in the bosom of the Father, he hath declared *him*.

19 ¶ And this is the record of John, when the Jews sent priests and Levites from Jerusalem to ask him, Who art thou?

20 And he confessed, and denied not; but confessed, I am not the Christ.

21 And they asked him, What then? Art thou Elias? And

NEW AMERICAN STANDARD BIBLE

and we saw His glory, glory as of the only begotten from the Father, full of grace and truth.

15 John *testified about Him and cried out, saying, "This was He of whom I said, 'He who comes after me has a higher rank than I, for He existed before me.' "

16 For of His fullness we have all received, and grace upon grace.

17 For the Law was given through Moses; grace and truth were realized through Jesus Christ.

18 No one has seen God at any time; the only begotten God who is in the bosom of the Father, He has explained *Him*.

The Testimony of John

19 This is the testimony of John, when the Jews sent to him priests and Levites from Jerusalem to ask him, "Who are you?"

20 And he confessed and did not deny, but confessed, "I am not the Christ."

21 They asked him, "What then? Are you Elijah?" And

NEW CENTURY VERSION

saw his glory—the glory that belongs to the only Son of the Father—and he was full of grace and truth.
15John tells the truth about him and cries out, saying, "This is the One I told you about: 'The One who comes after me is greater than I am, because he was living before me.' "
16Because he was full of grace and truth, from him we all received one gift after another.
17The law was given through Moses, but grace and truth came through Jesus Christ.
18No one has ever seen God. But God the only Son is very close to the Father,[c] and he has shown us what God is like.

John Tells People About Jesus

19Here is the truth John[d] told when the Jews in Jerusalem sent priests and Levites to ask him, "Who are you?"
20John spoke freely and did not refuse to answer. He said, "I am not the Christ."
21So they asked him, "Then who are you? Are you Elijah?"[e]

1:18 [c] **But...Father** This could be translated, "But the only God is very close to the Father." Also, some Greek copies say, "But the only Son is very close to the Father." 1:19 [d] **John** John the Baptist, who preached to people about Christ's coming (Matthew 3, Luke 3). 1:21 [e] **Elijah** A man who spoke for God. He lived hundreds of years before Christ and was expected to return before Christ (Malachi 4:5–6).

CONTEMPORARY ENGLISH VERSION

We saw his true glory,
the glory of the only Son
of the Father.
From him all the kindness
and all the truth of God
have come down to us.

15John spoke about him and shouted, "This is the one I told you would come! He is greater than I am, because he was alive before I was born."
16Because of all that the Son is, we have been given one blessing after another.[b]
17The Law was given by Moses, but Jesus Christ brought us undeserved kindness and truth.
18No one has ever seen God. The only Son, who is truly God and is closest to the Father, has shown us what God is like.

John the Baptist Tells about Jesus

(Matthew 3.1-12; Mark 1.1-8; Luke 3.15-17)

19-20The Jewish leaders in Jerusalem sent priests and temple helpers to ask John who he was. He told them plainly, "I am not the Messiah."
21Then when they asked him if he were Elijah, he said, "No, I am not!" And when

[b] 1.16 *one blessing after another*: Or "one blessing in place of another."

NEW INTERNATIONAL VERSION

us. We have seen his glory, the glory of the One and Only,[d]
who came from the Father, full of grace and truth.
15John testifies concerning him. He cries out, saying,
"This was he of whom I said, 'He who comes after me has
surpassed me because he was before me.' " 16From the
fullness of his grace we have all received one blessing after
another. 17For the law was given through Moses; grace
and truth came through Jesus Christ. 18No one has ever
seen God, but God the One and Only,[d,e] who is at the
Father's side, has made him known.

John the Baptist Denies Being the Christ

19Now this was John's testimony when the Jews of Jeru-
salem sent priests and Levites to ask him who he was.
20He did not fail to confess, but confessed freely, "I am not
the Christ.[f]"
21They asked him, "Then who are you? Are you Elijah?"

[d] *14,18* Or *the Only Begotten* [e] *18* Some manuscripts *but the only* (or *only begotten*) *Son* [f] *20* Or *Messiah.* "The Christ" (Greek) and "the Messiah" (Hebrew) both mean "the Anointed One"; also in verse 25.

NEW LIVING TRANSLATION

among us. He was full of unfailing love and faithfulness.*
And we have seen his glory, the glory of the only Son of
the Father.
15John pointed him out to the people. He shouted to the
crowds, "This is the one I was talking about when I said,
'Someone is coming who is far greater than I am, for he
existed long before I did.' "
16We have all benefited from the rich blessings he
brought to us—one gracious blessing after another.* 17For
the law was given through Moses; God's unfailing love
and faithfulness came through Jesus Christ. 18No one has
ever seen God. But his only Son, who is himself God,* is
near to the Father's heart; he has told us about him.

The Testimony of John the Baptist

19This was the testimony of John when the Jewish lead-
ers sent priests and Temple assistants* from Jerusalem to
ask John whether he claimed to be the Messiah. 20He flatly
denied it. "I am not the Messiah," he said.
21"Well then, who are you?" they asked. "Are you Elijah?"

1:14 Greek *grace and truth;* also in 1:17. 1:16 Greek *grace upon grace.* 1:18 Some manuscripts read *his one and only Son.* 1:19 Greek *and Levites.*

NEW KING JAMES VERSION

we beheld His glory, the glory as of the only begotten of
the Father, full of grace and truth.
15John bore witness of Him and cried out, saying, "This
was He of whom I said, 'He who comes after me is pre-
ferred before me, for He was before me.' "
16And[e] of His fullness we have all received, and grace
for grace. 17For the law was given through Moses, *but*
grace and truth came through Jesus Christ. 18No one has
seen God at any time. The only begotten Son,[f] who is in
the bosom of the Father, He has declared *Him.*

A Voice in the Wilderness

19Now this is the testimony of John, when the Jews sent
priests and Levites from Jerusalem to ask him, "Who are
you?"
20He confessed, and did not deny, but confessed, "I am
not the Christ."
21And they asked him, "What then? Are you Elijah?"

1:16 [e] NU-Text reads *For.* 1:18 [f] NU-Text reads *only begotten God.*

THE MESSAGE

We saw the glory with our own eyes,
the one-of-a-kind glory,
like Father, like Son,
Generous inside and out,
true from start to finish.

John pointed him out and called, "This is the One! The One I told you was coming after me but in fact was ahead of me. He has always been ahead of me, has always had the first word."

We all live off his generous bounty,
gift after gift after gift.
We got the basics from Moses,
and then this exuberant giving and receiving,
This endless knowing and understanding—
all this came through Jesus, the Messiah.
No one has ever seen God,
not so much as a glimpse.
This one-of-a-kind God-Expression,
who exists at the very heart of the Father,
has made him plain as day.

Thunder in the Desert

When Jews from Jerusalem sent a group of priests and officials to ask John who he was, he was completely honest. He didn't evade the question. He told the plain truth: "I am not the Messiah."
They pressed him, "Who, then? Elijah?"

KING JAMES VERSION

he saith, I am not. Art thou that prophet? And he answered, No.

22 Then said they unto him, Who art thou? that we may give an answer to them that sent us. What sayest thou of thyself?

23 He said, I *am* the voice of one crying in the wilderness, Make straight the way of the Lord, as said the prophet Esaias.

24 And they which were sent were of the Pharisees.

25 And they asked him, and said unto him, Why baptizest thou then, if thou be not that Christ, nor Elias, neither that prophet?

26 John answered them, saying, I baptize with water: but there standeth one among you, whom ye know not;

27 He it is, who coming after me is preferred before me, whose shoe's latchet I am not worthy to unloose.

28 These things were done in Bethabara beyond Jordan, where John was baptizing.

29 ¶ The next day John seeth Jesus coming unto him, and saith, Behold the Lamb of God, which taketh away the sin of the world.

30 This is he of whom I said, After me cometh a man which is preferred before me: for he was before me.

NEW AMERICAN STANDARD BIBLE

he *said, "I am not." "Are you the Prophet?" And he answered, "No."

22 Then they said to him, "Who are you, so that we may give an answer to those who sent us? What do you say about yourself?"

23 He said, "I am A VOICE OF ONE CRYING IN THE WILDERNESS, 'MAKE STRAIGHT THE WAY OF THE LORD,' as Isaiah the prophet said."

24 Now they had been sent from the Pharisees.

25 They asked him, and said to him, "Why then are you baptizing, if you are not the Christ, nor Elijah, nor the Prophet?"

26 John answered them saying, "I baptize [5]in water, *but* among you stands One whom you do not know.

27 "*It is* He who comes after me, the thong of whose sandal I am not worthy to untie."

28 These things took place in Bethany beyond the Jordan, where John was baptizing.

29 The next day he *saw Jesus coming to him and *said, "Behold, the Lamb of God who takes away the sin of the world!

30 "This is He on behalf of whom I said, 'After me comes a Man who has a higher rank than I, for He existed before me.'

1:26 [5] The Gr here can be translated *in, with* or *by*

NEW CENTURY VERSION

He answered, "No, I am not."
"Are you the Prophet?"[f] they asked.
He answered, "No."
22Then they said, "Who are you? Give us an answer to
tell those who sent us. What do you say about yourself?"
23John told them in the words of the prophet Isaiah:
"I am the voice of one
calling out in the desert:
'Make the road straight for the Lord.' " *Isaiah 40:3*
24Some Pharisees who had been sent asked John: 25"If
you are not the Christ or Elijah or the Prophet, why do you
baptize people?"
26John answered, "I baptize with water, but there is one
here with you that you don't know about. 27He is the One
who comes after me. I am not good enough to untie the
strings of his sandals."
28This all happened at Bethany on the other side of the
Jordan River, where John was baptizing people.
29The next day John saw Jesus coming toward him. John
said, "Look, the Lamb of God,[g] who takes away the sin of
the world! 30This is the One I was talking about when I
said, 'A man will come after me, but he is greater than I
am, because he was living before me.' 31Even I did not

1:21 [f] **Prophet** They probably meant the prophet that God told Moses he would send (Deuteronomy 18:15–19). 1:29 [g] **Lamb of God** Name for Jesus. Jesus is like the lambs that were offered for a sacrifice to God.

CONTEMPORARY ENGLISH VERSION

they asked if he were the Prophet,[c] he also said "No!"
22Finally, they said, "Who are you then? We have to give
an answer to the ones who sent us. Tell us who you are!"
23John answered in the words of the prophet Isaiah, "I
am only someone shouting in the desert, 'Get the road
ready for the Lord!' "
24Some Pharisees had also been sent to John. 25They
asked him, "Why are you baptizing people, if you are not
the Messiah or Elijah or the Prophet?"
26John told them, "I use water to baptize people. But
here with you is someone you don't know. 27Even though I
came first, I am not good enough to untie his sandals."
28John said this as he was baptizing east of the Jordan
River in Bethany.[d]

The Lamb of God

29The next day, John saw Jesus coming toward him and
said:
Here is the Lamb of God who takes away the sin of
the world! 30He is the one I told you about when I said,
"Someone else will come. He is greater than I am,
because he was alive before I was born." 31I didn't know

[c] 1.21 *the Prophet*: Many of the Jewish people expected God to send them a prophet who would be like Moses, but with even greater power (see Deuteronomy 18.15, 18). [d] 1.28 *Bethany*: An unknown village east of the Jordan with the same name as the village near Jerusalem.

NEW INTERNATIONAL VERSION

He said, "I am not."

"Are you the Prophet?"

He answered, "No."

22 Finally they said, "Who are you? Give us an answer to take back to those who sent us. What do you say about yourself?"

23 John replied in the words of Isaiah the prophet, "I am the voice of one calling in the desert, 'Make straight the way for the Lord.' "[g]

24 Now some Pharisees who had been sent 25 questioned him, "Why then do you baptize if you are not the Christ, nor Elijah, nor the Prophet?"

26 "I baptize with[h] water," John replied, "but among you stands one you do not know. 27 He is the one who comes after me, the thongs of whose sandals I am not worthy to untie."

28 This all happened at Bethany on the other side of the Jordan, where John was baptizing.

Jesus the Lamb of God

29 The next day John saw Jesus coming toward him and said, "Look, the Lamb of God, who takes away the sin of the world! 30 This is the one I meant when I said, 'A man who comes after me has surpassed me because he was

[g] *23* Isaiah 40:3 [h] *26* Or *in*; also in verses 31 and 33

NEW LIVING TRANSLATION

"No," he replied.

"Are you the Prophet?"*

"No."

22 "Then who are you? Tell us, so we can give an answer to those who sent us. What do you have to say about yourself?"

23 John replied in the words of Isaiah:

"I am a voice shouting in the wilderness,
'Prepare a straight pathway for the Lord's coming!' "*

24 Then those who were sent by the Pharisees 25 asked him, "If you aren't the Messiah or Elijah or the Prophet, what right do you have to baptize?"

26 John told them, "I baptize with* water, but right here in the crowd is someone you do not know, 27 who will soon begin his ministry. I am not even worthy to be his slave.*" 28 This incident took place at Bethany, a village east of the Jordan River, where John was baptizing.

Jesus, the Lamb of God

29 The next day John saw Jesus coming toward him and said, "Look! There is the Lamb of God who takes away the sin of the world! 30 He is the one I was talking about when I said, 'Soon a man is coming who is far greater than I am, for he existed long before I did.' 31 I didn't know he was the

1:21 See Deut 18:15, 18; Mal 4:5-6. 1:23 Isa 40:3. 1:26 Or *in;* also in 1:31, 33. 1:27 Greek *to untie his sandals.*

NEW KING JAMES VERSION

He said, "I am not."

"Are you the Prophet?"

And he answered, "No."

22 Then they said to him, "Who are you, that we may give an answer to those who sent us? What do you say about yourself?"

23 He said: "I *am*

'The voice of one crying in the wilderness:
"Make straight the way of the LORD,*"* '[g]

as the prophet Isaiah said."

24 Now those who were sent were from the Pharisees. 25 And they asked him, saying, "Why then do you baptize if you are not the Christ, nor Elijah, nor the Prophet?"

26 John answered them, saying, "I baptize with water, but there stands One among you whom you do not know. 27 It is He who, coming after me, is preferred before me, whose sandal strap I am not worthy to loose."

28 These things were done in Bethabara[h] beyond the Jordan, where John was baptizing.

The Lamb of God

29 The next day John saw Jesus coming toward him, and said, "Behold! The Lamb of God who takes away the sin of the world! 30 This is He of whom I said, 'After me comes a Man who is preferred before me, for He was before me.'

1:23 [g] Isaiah 40:3 1:28 [h] NU-Text and M-Text read *Bethany.*

THE MESSAGE

"I am not."

"The Prophet?"

"No."

Exasperated, they said, "Who, then? We need an answer for those who sent us. Tell us something—anything!—about yourself."

"I'm thunder in the desert: 'Make the road straight for God!' I'm doing what the prophet Isaiah preached."

Those sent to question him were from the Pharisee party. Now they had a question of their own: "If you're neither the Messiah, nor Elijah, nor the Prophet, why do you baptize?"

John answered, "I only baptize using water. A person you don't recognize has taken his stand in your midst. He comes after me, but he is not in second place to me. I'm not even worthy to hold his coat for him."

These conversations took place in Bethany on the other side of the Jordan, where John was baptizing at the time.

The God-Revealer

The very next day John saw Jesus coming toward him and yelled out, "Here he is, God's Passover Lamb! He forgives the sins of the world! This is the man I've been talking about, 'the One who comes after me but is really ahead

KING JAMES VERSION

31 And I knew him not: but that he should be made manifest to Israel, therefore am I come baptizing with water.

32 And John bare record, saying, I saw the Spirit descending from heaven like a dove, and it abode upon him.

33 And I knew him not: but he that sent me to baptize with water, the same said unto me, Upon whom thou shalt see the Spirit descending, and remaining on him, the same is he which baptizeth with the Holy Ghost.

34 And I saw, and bare record that this is the Son of God.

35 Again the next day after John stood, and two of his disciples;

36 And looking upon Jesus as he walked, he saith, Behold the Lamb of God!

37 ¶ And the two disciples heard him speak, and they followed Jesus.

38 Then Jesus turned, and saw them following, and saith unto them, What seek ye? They said unto him, Rabbi, (which is to say, being interpreted, Master,) where dwellest thou?

39 He saith unto them, Come and see. They came and saw where he dwelt, and abode with him that day: for it was about the tenth hour.

40 One of the two which heard John *speak*, and followed him, was Andrew, Simon Peter's brother.

NEW AMERICAN STANDARD BIBLE

31 "I did not recognize Him, but so that He might be manifested to Israel, I came baptizing [6]in water."

32 John testified saying, "I have seen the Spirit descending as a dove out of heaven, and He remained upon Him.

33 "I did not recognize Him, but He who sent me to baptize [6]in water said to me, 'He upon whom you see the Spirit descending and remaining upon Him, this is the One who baptizes in the Holy Spirit.'

34 "I myself have seen, and have testified that this is the Son of God."

Jesus' Public Ministry, First Converts

35 Again the next day John was standing with two of his disciples,

36 and he looked at Jesus as He walked, and *said, "Behold, the Lamb of God!"

37 The two disciples heard him speak, and they followed Jesus.

38 And Jesus turned and saw them following, and *said to them, "What do you seek?" They said to Him, "Rabbi (which translated means Teacher), where are You staying?"

39 He *said to them, "Come, and you will see." So they came and saw where He was staying; and they stayed with Him that day, for it was about the [7]tenth hour.

40 One of the two who heard John *speak* and followed Him, was Andrew, Simon Peter's brother.

1:31,33 [6] The Gr here can be translated *in, with* or *by* 1:39 [7] Perhaps 10 a.m. (Roman time)

NEW CENTURY VERSION

know who he was, although I came baptizing with water so that the people of Israel would know who he is."

[32–33]Then John said, "I saw the Spirit come down from heaven in the form of a dove and rest on him. Until then I did not know who the Christ was. But the God who sent me to baptize with water told me, 'You will see the Spirit come down and rest on a man; he is the One who will baptize with the Holy Spirit.' [34]I have seen this happen, and I tell you the truth: This man is the Son of God."

The First Followers of Jesus

[35]The next day John[h] was there again with two of his followers. [36]When he saw Jesus walking by, he said, "Look, the Lamb of God!"[i]

[37]The two followers heard John say this, so they followed Jesus. [38]When Jesus turned and saw them following him, he asked, "What are you looking for?"

They said, "Rabbi, where are you staying?" ("Rabbi" means "Teacher.")

[39]He answered, "Come and see." So the two men went with Jesus and saw where he was staying and stayed there with him that day. It was about four o'clock in the afternoon.

[40]One of the two men who followed Jesus after they heard John speak about him was Andrew, Simon Peter's

1:35 [h] **John** John the Baptist, who preached to people about Christ's coming (Matthew 3, Luke 3). 1:36 [i] **Lamb of God** Name for Jesus. Jesus is like the lambs that were offered for a sacrifice to God.

CONTEMPORARY ENGLISH VERSION

who he was. But I came to baptize you with water, so that everyone in Israel would see him.

[32]I was there and saw the Spirit come down on him like a dove from heaven. And the Spirit stayed on him. [33]Before this I didn't know who he was. But the one who sent me to baptize with water had told me, "You will see the Spirit come down and stay on someone. Then you will know that he is the one who will baptize with the Holy Spirit." [34]I saw this happen, and I tell you that he is the Son of God.

The First Disciples of Jesus

[35]The next day, John was there again, and two of his followers were with him. [36]When he saw Jesus walking by, he said, "Here is the Lamb of God!" [37]John's two followers heard him, and they went with Jesus.

[38]When Jesus turned and saw them, he asked, "What do you want?"

They answered, "Rabbi, where do you live?" The Hebrew word "Rabbi" means "Teacher."

[39]Jesus replied, "Come and see!" It was already about four o'clock in the afternoon when they went with him and saw where he lived. So they stayed on for the rest of the day.

[40]One of the two men who had heard John and had gone with Jesus was Andrew, the brother of Simon Peter. [41]The

NEW INTERNATIONAL VERSION

before me.' 31I myself did not know him, but the reason I came baptizing with water was that he might be revealed to Israel."

32Then John gave this testimony: "I saw the Spirit come down from heaven as a dove and remain on him. 33I would not have known him, except that the one who sent me to baptize with water told me, 'The man on whom you see the Spirit come down and remain is he who will baptize with the Holy Spirit.' 34I have seen and I testify that this is the Son of God."

Jesus' First Disciples

35The next day John was there again with two of his disciples. 36When he saw Jesus passing by, he said, "Look, the Lamb of God!"

37When the two disciples heard him say this, they followed Jesus. 38Turning around, Jesus saw them following and asked, "What do you want?"

They said, "Rabbi" (which means Teacher), "where are you staying?"

39"Come," he replied, "and you will see."

So they went and saw where he was staying, and spent that day with him. It was about the tenth hour.

40Andrew, Simon Peter's brother, was one of the two who heard what John had said and who had followed

NEW LIVING TRANSLATION

one, but I have been baptizing with water in order to point him out to Israel."

32Then John said, "I saw the Holy Spirit descending like a dove from heaven and resting upon him. 33I didn't know he was the one, but when God sent me to baptize with water, he told me, 'When you see the Holy Spirit descending and resting upon someone, he is the one you are looking for. He is the one who baptizes with the Holy Spirit.' 34I saw this happen to Jesus, so I testify that he is the Son of God.*"

The First Disciples

35The following day, John was again standing with two of his disciples. 36As Jesus walked by, John looked at him and then declared, "Look! There is the Lamb of God!" 37Then John's two disciples turned and followed Jesus.

38Jesus looked around and saw them following. "What do you want?" he asked them.

They replied, "Rabbi" (which means Teacher), "where are you staying?"

39"Come and see," he said. It was about four o'clock in the afternoon when they went with him to the place, and they stayed there the rest of the day.

40Andrew, Simon Peter's brother, was one of these men who had heard what John said and then followed Jesus.

1:34 Some manuscripts read *the chosen One of God.*

NEW KING JAMES VERSION

31I did not know Him; but that He should be revealed to Israel, therefore I came baptizing with water."

32And John bore witness, saying, "I saw the Spirit descending from heaven like a dove, and He remained upon Him. 33I did not know Him, but He who sent me to baptize with water said to me, 'Upon whom you see the Spirit descending, and remaining on Him, this is He who baptizes with the Holy Spirit.' 34And I have seen and testified that this is the Son of God."

The First Disciples

35Again, the next day, John stood with two of his disciples. 36And looking at Jesus as He walked, he said, "Behold the Lamb of God!"

37The two disciples heard him speak, and they followed Jesus. 38Then Jesus turned, and seeing them following, said to them, "What do you seek?"

They said to Him, "Rabbi" (which is to say, when translated, Teacher), "where are You staying?"

39He said to them, "Come and see." They came and saw where He was staying, and remained with Him that day (now it was about the tenth hour).

40One of the two who heard John *speak,* and followed Him, was Andrew, Simon Peter's brother. 41He first found

THE MESSAGE

of me.' I knew nothing about who he was—only this: that my task has been to get Israel ready to recognize him as the God-Revealer. That is why I came here baptizing with water, giving you a good bath and scrubbing sins from your life so you can get a fresh start with God."

John clinched his witness with this: "I watched the Spirit, like a dove flying down out of the sky, making himself at home in him. I repeat, I know nothing about him except this: The One who authorized me to baptize with water told me, 'The One on whom you see the Spirit come down and stay, this One will baptize with the Holy Spirit.' That's exactly what I saw happen, and I'm telling you, there's no question about it: *This* is the Son of God."

Come, See for Yourself

The next day John was back at his post with two disciples, who were watching. He looked up, saw Jesus walking nearby, and said, "Here he is, God's Passover Lamb."

The two disciples heard him and went after Jesus. Jesus looked over his shoulder and said to them, "What are you after?"

They said, "Rabbi" (which means "Teacher"), "where are you staying?"

He replied, "Come along and see for yourself."

They came, saw where he was living, and ended up staying with him for the day. It was late afternoon when this happened.

Andrew, Simon Peter's brother, was one of the two who heard John's witness and followed Jesus. The first thing he

KING JAMES VERSION

41 He first findeth his own brother Simon, and saith unto him, We have found the Messias, which is, being interpreted, the Christ.

42 And he brought him to Jesus. And when Jesus beheld him, he said, Thou art Simon the son of Jona: thou shalt be called Cephas, which is by interpretation, A stone.

43 ¶ The day following Jesus would go forth into Galilee, and findeth Philip, and saith unto him, Follow me.

44 Now Philip was of Bethsaida, the city of Andrew and Peter.

45 Philip findeth Nathanael, and saith unto him, We have found him, of whom Moses in the law, and the prophets, did write, Jesus of Nazareth, the son of Joseph.

46 And Nathanael said unto him, Can there any good thing come out of Nazareth? Philip saith unto him, Come and see.

47 Jesus saw Nathanael coming to him, and saith of him, Behold an Israelite indeed, in whom is no guile!

48 Nathanael saith unto him, Whence knowest thou me? Jesus answered and said unto him, Before that Philip called thee, when thou wast under the fig tree, I saw thee.

NEW AMERICAN STANDARD BIBLE

41 He *found first his own brother Simon and *said to him, "We have found the Messiah" (which translated means Christ).

42 He brought him to Jesus. Jesus looked at him and said, "You are Simon the son of John; you shall be called Cephas" (which is translated Peter).

43 The next day He purposed to go into Galilee, and He *found Philip. And Jesus *said to him, "Follow Me."

44 Now Philip was from Bethsaida, of the city of Andrew and Peter.

45 Philip *found Nathanael and *said to him, "We have found Him of whom Moses in the Law and *also* the Prophets wrote—Jesus of Nazareth, the son of Joseph."

46 Nathanael said to him, "Can any good thing come out of Nazareth?" Philip *said to him, "Come and see."

47 Jesus saw Nathanael coming to Him, and *said of him, "Behold, an Israelite indeed, in whom there is no deceit!"

48 Nathanael *said to Him, "How do You know me?" Jesus answered and said to him, "Before Philip called you, when you were under the fig tree, I saw you."

NEW CENTURY VERSION

brother. 41The first thing Andrew did was to find his brother Simon and say to him, "We have found the Messiah." ("Messiah" means "Christ.")

42Then Andrew took Simon to Jesus. Jesus looked at him and said, "You are Simon son of John. You will be called Cephas." ("Cephas" means "Peter."/)

43The next day Jesus decided to go to Galilee. He found Philip and said to him, "Follow me."

44Philip was from the town of Bethsaida, where Andrew and Peter lived. 45Philip found Nathanael and told him, "We have found the man that Moses wrote about in the law, and the prophets also wrote about him. He is Jesus, the son of Joseph, from Nazareth."

46But Nathanael said to Philip, "Can anything good come from Nazareth?"

Philip answered, "Come and see."

47As Jesus saw Nathanael coming toward him, he said, "Here is truly an Israelite. There is nothing false in him."

48Nathanael asked, "How do you know me?"

Jesus answered, "I saw you when you were under the fig tree, before Philip told you about me."

1:42 / **Peter** The Greek name "Peter," like the Aramaic name "Cephas," means "rock."

CONTEMPORARY ENGLISH VERSION

first thing Andrew did was to find his brother and tell him, "We have found the Messiah!" The Hebrew word "Messiah" means the same as the Greek word "Christ."

42Andrew brought his brother to Jesus. And when Jesus saw him, he said, "Simon son of John, you will be called Cephas." This name can be translated as "Peter."[e]

Jesus Chooses Philip and Nathanael

43-44The next day Jesus decided to go to Galilee. There he met Philip, who was from Bethsaida, the hometown of Andrew and Peter. Jesus said to Philip, "Come with me."

45Philip then found Nathanael and said, "We have found the one that Moses and the Prophets[f] wrote about. He is Jesus, the son of Joseph from Nazareth."

46Nathanael asked, "Can anything good come from Nazareth?"

Philip answered, "Come and see."

47When Jesus saw Nathanael coming toward him, he said, "Here is a true descendant of our ancestor Israel. And he isn't deceitful."[g]

48"How do you know me?" Nathanael asked.

Jesus answered, "Before Philip called you, I saw you under the fig tree."

[e] 1.42 *Peter*: The Aramaic name "Cephas" and the Greek name "Peter" each mean "rock." [f] 1.45 *Moses and the Prophets*: The Jewish Scriptures, that is, the Old Testament. [g] 1.47 *Israel . . . isn't deceitful*: Israel (meaning "a man who wrestled with God" or "a prince of God") was the name that the Lord gave to Jacob (meaning "cheater" or "deceiver"), the famous ancestor of the Jewish people.

NEW INTERNATIONAL VERSION

Jesus. 41The first thing Andrew did was to find his brother Simon and tell him, "We have found the Messiah" (that is, the Christ). 42And he brought him to Jesus.

Jesus looked at him and said, "You are Simon son of John. You will be called Cephas" (which, when translated, is Peter[j]).

Jesus Calls Philip and Nathanael

43The next day Jesus decided to leave for Galilee. Finding Philip, he said to him, "Follow me."

44Philip, like Andrew and Peter, was from the town of Bethsaida. 45Philip found Nathanael and told him, "We have found the one Moses wrote about in the Law, and about whom the prophets also wrote—Jesus of Nazareth, the son of Joseph."

46"Nazareth! Can anything good come from there?" Nathanael asked.

"Come and see," said Philip.

47When Jesus saw Nathanael approaching, he said of him, "Here is a true Israelite, in whom there is nothing false."

48"How do you know me?" Nathanael asked.

Jesus answered, "I saw you while you were still under the fig tree before Philip called you."

[j] *42* Both *Cephas* (Aramaic) and *Peter* (Greek) mean *rock*.

NEW LIVING TRANSLATION

41The first thing Andrew did was to find his brother, Simon, and tell him, "We have found the Messiah" (which means the Christ).

42Then Andrew brought Simon to meet Jesus. Looking intently at Simon, Jesus said, "You are Simon, the son of John—but you will be called Cephas" (which means Peter*).

43The next day Jesus decided to go to Galilee. He found Philip and said to him, "Come, be my disciple." 44Philip was from Bethsaida, Andrew and Peter's hometown.

45Philip went off to look for Nathanael and told him, "We have found the very person Moses and the prophets wrote about! His name is Jesus, the son of Joseph from Nazareth."

46"Nazareth!" exclaimed Nathanael. "Can anything good come from there?"

"Just come and see for yourself," Philip said.

47As they approached, Jesus said, "Here comes an honest man—a true son of Israel."

48"How do you know about me?" Nathanael asked.

And Jesus replied, "I could see you under the fig tree before Philip found you."

1:42 The names *Cephas* and *Peter* both mean "rock."

NEW KING JAMES VERSION

his own brother Simon, and said to him, "We have found the Messiah" (which is translated, the Christ). 42And he brought him to Jesus.

Now when Jesus looked at him, He said, "You are Simon the son of Jonah.[j] You shall be called Cephas" (which is translated, A Stone).

Philip and Nathanael

43The following day Jesus wanted to go to Galilee, and He found Philip and said to him, "Follow Me." 44Now Philip was from Bethsaida, the city of Andrew and Peter. 45Philip found Nathanael and said to him, "We have found Him of whom Moses in the law, and also the prophets, wrote—Jesus of Nazareth, the son of Joseph."

46And Nathanael said to him, "Can anything good come out of Nazareth?"

Philip said to him, "Come and see."

47Jesus saw Nathanael coming toward Him, and said of him, "Behold, an Israelite indeed, in whom is no deceit!"

48Nathanael said to Him, "How do You know me?"

Jesus answered and said to him, "Before Philip called you, when you were under the fig tree, I saw you."

1:42 [j] NU-Text reads *John*.

THE MESSAGE

did after finding where Jesus lived was find his own brother, Simon, telling him, "We've found the Messiah" (that is, "Christ"). He immediately led him to Jesus.

Jesus took one look up and said, "You're John's son, Simon? From now on your name is Cephas" (or Peter, which means "Rock").

The next day Jesus decided to go to Galilee. When he got there, he ran across Philip and said, "Come, follow me." (Philip's hometown was Bethsaida, the same as Andrew and Peter.)

Philip went and found Nathanael and told him, "We've found the One Moses wrote of in the Law, the One preached by the prophets. It's *Jesus*, Joseph's son, the one from Nazareth!" Nathanael said, "Nazareth? You've got to be kidding."

But Philip said, "Come, see for yourself."

When Jesus saw him coming he said, "There's a real Israelite, not a false bone in his body."

Nathanael said, "Where did you get that idea? You don't know me."

Jesus answered, "One day, long before Philip called you here, I saw you under the fig tree."

KING JAMES VERSION

49 Nathanael answered and saith unto him, Rabbi, thou art the Son of God; thou art the King of Israel.

50 Jesus answered and said unto him, Because I said unto thee, I saw thee under the fig tree, believest thou? thou shalt see greater things than these.

51 And he saith unto him, Verily, verily, I say unto you, Hereafter ye shall see heaven open, and the angels of God ascending and descending upon the Son of man.

2 And the third day there was a marriage in Cana of Galilee; and the mother of Jesus was there:

2 And both Jesus was called, and his disciples, to the marriage.

3 And when they wanted wine, the mother of Jesus saith unto him, They have no wine.

4 Jesus saith unto her, Woman, what have I to do with thee? mine hour is not yet come.

5 His mother saith unto the servants, Whatsoever he saith unto you, do *it*.

6 And there were set there six waterpots of stone, after the manner of the purifying of the Jews, containing two or three firkins apiece.

7 Jesus saith unto them, Fill the waterpots with water. And they filled them up to the brim.

8 And he saith unto them, Draw out now, and bear unto the governor of the feast. And they bare *it*.

NEW AMERICAN STANDARD BIBLE

49 Nathanael answered Him, "Rabbi, You are the Son of God; You are the King of Israel."

50 Jesus answered and said to him, "Because I said to you that I saw you under the fig tree, do you believe? You will see greater things than these."

51 And He *said to him, "Truly, truly, I say to you, you will see the heavens opened and the angels of God ascending and descending on the Son of Man."

Miracle at Cana

2 On the third day there was a wedding in Cana of Galilee, and the mother of Jesus was there;

2 and both Jesus and His disciples were invited to the wedding.

3 When the wine ran out, the mother of Jesus *said to Him, "They have no wine."

4 And Jesus *said to her, "Woman, what does that have to do with us? My hour has not yet come."

5 His mother *said to the servants, "Whatever He says to you, do it."

6 Now there were six stone waterpots set there for the Jewish custom of purification, containing twenty or thirty gallons each.

7 Jesus *said to them, "Fill the waterpots with water." So they filled them up to the brim.

8 And He *said to them, "Draw *some* out now and take it to the [1]headwaiter." So they took it *to him*.

2:8 [1] Or *steward*

NEW CENTURY VERSION

49Then Nathanael said to Jesus, "Teacher, you are the Son of God; you are the King of Israel."

50Jesus said to Nathanael, "Do you believe simply because I told you I saw you under the fig tree? You will see greater things than that." 51And Jesus said to them, "I tell you the truth, you will all see heaven open and 'angels of God going up and coming down'[k] on the Son of Man."

The Wedding at Cana

2 Two days later there was a wedding in the town of Cana in Galilee. Jesus' mother was there, 2and Jesus and his followers were also invited to the wedding. 3When all the wine was gone, Jesus' mother said to him, "They have no more wine."

4Jesus answered, "Dear woman, why come to me? My time has not yet come."

5His mother said to the servants, "Do whatever he tells you to do."

6In that place there were six stone water jars that the Jews used in their washing ceremony.[a] Each jar held about twenty or thirty gallons.

7Jesus said to the servants, "Fill the jars with water." So they filled the jars to the top.

8Then he said to them, "Now take some out and give it to the master of the feast."

1:51 [k] **'angels...down'** These words are from Genesis 28:12.
2:6 [a] **washing ceremony** The Jewish people washed themselves in special ways before eating, before worshiping in the Temple, and at other special times.

CONTEMPORARY ENGLISH VERSION

49Nathanael said, "Rabbi, you are the Son of God and the King of Israel!"

50Jesus answered, "Did you believe me just because I said that I saw you under the fig tree? You will see something even greater. 51I tell you for certain that you will see heaven open and God's angels going up and coming down on the Son of Man."[h]

Jesus at a Wedding in Cana

2 Three days later Mary, the mother of Jesus, was at a wedding feast in the village of Cana in Galilee. 2Jesus and his disciples had also been invited and were there.

3When the wine was all gone, Mary said to Jesus, "They don't have any more wine."

4Jesus replied, "Mother, my time hasn't yet come![a] You must not tell me what to do."

5Mary then said to the servants, "Do whatever Jesus tells you to do."

6At the feast there were six stone water jars that were used by the people for washing themselves in the way that their religion said they must. Each jar held about twenty or thirty gallons. 7Jesus told the servants to fill them to the top with water. Then after the jars had been filled, 8he said, "Now take some water and give it to the man in charge of the feast."

[h] 1.51 *going up and coming down on the Son of Man*: When Jacob (see the note at verse 47) was running from his brother Esau, he had a dream in which he saw angels going up and down on a ladder from earth to heaven (see Genesis 32.22-32). [a] 2.4 *my time hasn't yet come!*: The time when the true glory of Jesus would be seen, and he would be recognized as God's Son (see 12.23).

NEW INTERNATIONAL VERSION

49 Then Nathanael declared, "Rabbi, you are the Son of God; you are the King of Israel."
50 Jesus said, "You believe[j] because I told you I saw you under the fig tree. You shall see greater things than that."
51 He then added, "I tell you[k] the truth, you[k] shall see heaven open, and the angels of God ascending and descending on the Son of Man."

Jesus Changes Water to Wine

2 On the third day a wedding took place at Cana in Galilee. Jesus' mother was there,
2 and Jesus and his disciples had also been invited to the wedding.
3 When the wine was gone, Jesus' mother said to him, "They have no more wine."

4 "Dear woman, why do you involve me?" Jesus replied. "My time has not yet come."

5 His mother said to the servants, "Do whatever he tells you."

6 Nearby stood six stone water jars, the kind used by the Jews for ceremonial washing, each holding from twenty to thirty gallons.[a]

7 Jesus said to the servants, "Fill the jars with water"; so they filled them to the brim.

8 Then he told them, "Now draw some out and take it to the master of the banquet."

[j] 50 Or *Do you believe . . . ?* [k] 51 The Greek is plural. [a] 6 Greek *two to three metretes* (probably about 75 to 115 liters)

NEW LIVING TRANSLATION

49 Nathanael replied, "Teacher, you are the Son of God—the King of Israel!"

50 Jesus asked him, "Do you believe all this just because I told you I had seen you under the fig tree? You will see greater things than this."
51 Then he said, "The truth is, you will all see heaven open and the angels of God going up and down upon the Son of Man."*

The Wedding at Cana

2 The next day* Jesus' mother was a guest at a wedding celebration in the village of Cana in Galilee.
2 Jesus and his disciples were also invited to the celebration.
3 The wine supply ran out during the festivities, so Jesus' mother spoke to him about the problem. "They have no more wine," she told him.

4 "How does that concern you and me?" Jesus asked. "My time has not yet come."

5 But his mother told the servants, "Do whatever he tells you."

6 Six stone waterpots were standing there; they were used for Jewish ceremonial purposes and held twenty to thirty gallons* each.
7 Jesus told the servants, "Fill the jars with water." When the jars had been filled to the brim,
8 he said, "Dip some out and take it to the master of ceremonies." So they followed his instructions.

1:51 See Gen 28:10-17, the account of Jacob's ladder. 2:1 Greek *On the third day;* see 1:35, 43. 2:6 Greek *2 or 3 measures* [75 to 113 liters].

NEW KING JAMES VERSION

49 Nathanael answered and said to Him, "Rabbi, You are the Son of God! You are the King of Israel!"

50 Jesus answered and said to him, "Because I said to you, 'I saw you under the fig tree,' do you believe? You will see greater things than these."
51 And He said to him, "Most assuredly, I say to you, hereafter[l] you shall see heaven open, and the angels of God ascending and descending upon the Son of Man."

Water Turned to Wine

2 On the third day there was a wedding in Cana of Galilee, and the mother of Jesus was there.
2 Now both Jesus and His disciples were invited to the wedding.
3 And when they ran out of wine, the mother of Jesus said to Him, "They have no wine."

4 Jesus said to her, "Woman, what does your concern have to do with Me? My hour has not yet come."

5 His mother said to the servants, "Whatever He says to you, do *it*."

6 Now there were set there six waterpots of stone, according to the manner of purification of the Jews, containing twenty or thirty gallons apiece.
7 Jesus said to them, "Fill the waterpots with water." And they filled them up to the brim.
8 And He said to them, "Draw *some* out now, and take *it* to the master of the feast." And they took *it*.
9 When

1:51 [l] NU-Text omits *hereafter.*

THE MESSAGE

Nathanael exclaimed, "Rabbi! You are the Son of God, the King of Israel!"

Jesus said, "You've become a believer simply because I say I saw you one day sitting under the fig tree? You haven't seen anything yet! Before this is over you're going to see heaven open and God's angels descending to the Son of Man and ascending again."

From Water to Wine

2 Three days later there was a wedding in the village of Cana in Galilee. Jesus' mother was there. Jesus and his disciples were guests also. When they started running low on wine at the wedding banquet, Jesus' mother told him, "They're just about out of wine."

Jesus said, "Is that any of our business, Mother—yours or mine? This isn't my time. Don't push me."

She went ahead anyway, telling the servants, "Whatever he tells you, do it."

Six stoneware water pots were there, used by the Jews for ritual washings. Each held twenty to thirty gallons. Jesus ordered the servants, "Fill the pots with water." And they filled them to the brim.

"Now fill your pitchers and take them to the host," Jesus said, and they did.

KING JAMES VERSION

9 When the ruler of the feast had tasted the water that was made wine, and knew not whence it was: (but the servants which drew the water knew;) the governor of the feast called the bridegroom,

10 And saith unto him, Every man at the beginning doth set forth good wine; and when men have well drunk, then that which is worse: *but* thou hast kept the good wine until now.

11 This beginning of miracles did Jesus in Cana of Galilee, and manifested forth his glory; and his disciples believed on him.

12 ¶ After this he went down to Capernaum, he, and his mother, and his brethren, and his disciples: and they continued there not many days.

13 And the Jews' passover was at hand, and Jesus went up to Jerusalem,

14 And found in the temple those that sold oxen and sheep and doves, and the changers of money sitting:

15 And when he had made a scourge of small cords, he drove them all out of the temple, and the sheep, and the oxen; and poured out the changers' money, and overthrew the tables;

16 And said unto them that sold doves, Take these things hence; make not my Father's house an house of merchandise.

NEW AMERICAN STANDARD BIBLE

9 When the headwaiter tasted the water which had become wine, and did not know where it came from (but the servants who had drawn the water knew), the headwaiter *called the bridegroom,

10 and *said to him, "Every man serves the good wine first, and when *the people* have drunk freely, *then he serves* the poorer *wine; but* you have kept the good wine until now."

11 This beginning of *His* signs Jesus did in Cana of Galilee, and manifested His glory, and His disciples believed in Him.

12 After this He went down to Capernaum, He and His mother and *His* brothers and His disciples; and they stayed there a few days.

First Passover—Cleansing the Temple

13 The Passover of the Jews was near, and Jesus went up to Jerusalem.

14 And He found in the temple those who were selling oxen and sheep and doves, and the money changers seated *at their tables*.

15 And He made a scourge of cords, and drove *them* all out of the temple, with the sheep and the oxen; and He poured out the coins of the money changers and overturned their tables;

16 and to those who were selling the doves He said, "Take these things away; stop making My Father's house a place of business."

NEW CENTURY VERSION

So they took the water to the master. 9 When he tasted it,
the water had become wine. He did not know where the
wine came from, but the servants who had brought the
water knew. The master of the wedding called the bride-
groom 10 and said to him, "People always serve the best
wine first. Later, after the guests have been drinking
awhile, they serve the cheaper wine. But you have saved
the best wine till now."

11 So in Cana of Galilee Jesus did his first miracle. There
he showed his glory, and his followers believed in him.

Jesus in the Temple

12 After this, Jesus went to the town of Capernaum with
his mother, brothers, and followers. They stayed there for
just a few days. 13 When it was almost time for the Jewish
Passover Feast, Jesus went to Jerusalem. 14 In the Temple
he found people selling cattle, sheep, and doves. He saw
others sitting at tables, exchanging different kinds of
money. 15 Jesus made a whip out of cords and forced all of
them, both the sheep and cattle, to leave the Temple. He
turned over the tables and scattered the money of those
who were exchanging it. 16 Then he said to those who were
selling pigeons, "Take these things out of here! Don't
make my Father's house a place for buying and selling!"

CONTEMPORARY ENGLISH VERSION

The servants did as Jesus told them, 9 and the man in
charge drank some of the water that had now turned into
wine. He did not know where the wine had come from, but
the servants did. He called the bridegroom over 10 and said,
"The best wine is always served first. Then after the guests
have had plenty, the other wine is served. But you have
kept the best until last!"

11 This was Jesus' first miracle,[b] and he did it in the vil-
lage of Cana in Galilee. There Jesus showed his glory, and
his disciples put their faith in him. 12 After this, he went
with his mother, his brothers, and his disciples to the town
of Capernaum, where they stayed for a few days.

Jesus in the Temple

(Matthew 21.12, 13; Mark 11.15-17; Luke 19.45, 46)

13 Not long before the Jewish festival of Passover, Jesus
went to Jerusalem. 14 There he found people selling cattle,
sheep, and doves in the temple. He also saw moneychang-
ers sitting at their tables. 15 So he took some rope and
made a whip. Then he chased everyone out of the temple,
together with their sheep and cattle. He turned over the
tables of the moneychangers and scattered their coins.

16 Jesus said to the people who had been selling doves,
"Get those doves out of here! Don't make my Father's
house a marketplace."

[b] 2.11 *miracle*: The Greek text has "sign." In the Gospel of John the word "sign" is used for the miracle itself and as a way of pointing to Jesus as the Son of God.

NEW INTERNATIONAL VERSION

They did so, 9 and the master of the banquet tasted the
water that had been turned into wine. He did not realize
where it had come from, though the servants who had
drawn the water knew. Then he called the bridegroom
aside 10 and said, "Everyone brings out the choice wine
first and then the cheaper wine after the guests have had
too much to drink; but you have saved the best till now."
11 This, the first of his miraculous signs, Jesus performed
at Cana in Galilee. He thus revealed his glory, and his dis-
ciples put their faith in him.

Jesus Clears the Temple

12 After this he went down to Capernaum with his mother
and brothers and his disciples. There they stayed for a few
days.
13 When it was almost time for the Jewish Passover,
Jesus went up to Jerusalem. 14 In the temple courts he
found men selling cattle, sheep and doves, and others sit-
ting at tables exchanging money. 15 So he made a whip out
of cords, and drove all from the temple area, both sheep
and cattle; he scattered the coins of the money changers
and overturned their tables. 16 To those who sold doves he
said, "Get these out of here! How dare you turn my
Father's house into a market!"

NEW LIVING TRANSLATION

9 When the master of ceremonies tasted the water that
was now wine, not knowing where it had come from
(though, of course, the servants knew), he called the bride-
groom over. 10 "Usually a host serves the best wine first,"
he said. "Then, when everyone is full and doesn't care, he
brings out the less expensive wines. But you have kept the
best until now!"
11 This miraculous sign at Cana in Galilee was Jesus' first
display of his glory. And his disciples believed in him.
12 After the wedding he went to Capernaum for a few
days with his mother, his brothers, and his disciples.

Jesus Clears the Temple

13 It was time for the annual Passover celebration, and
Jesus went to Jerusalem. 14 In the Temple area he saw mer-
chants selling cattle, sheep, and doves for sacrifices; and
he saw money changers behind their counters. 15 Jesus
made a whip from some ropes and chased them all out of
the Temple. He drove out the sheep and oxen, scattered the
money changers' coins over the floor, and turned over their
tables. 16 Then, going over to the people who sold doves, he
told them, "Get these things out of here. Don't turn my
Father's house into a marketplace!"

NEW KING JAMES VERSION

the master of the feast had tasted the water that was made
wine, and did not know where it came from (but the ser-
vants who had drawn the water knew), the master of the
feast called the bridegroom. 10 And he said to him, "Every
man at the beginning sets out the good wine, and when
the *guests* have well drunk, then the inferior. You have
kept the good wine until now!"
11 This beginning of signs Jesus did in Cana of Galilee,
and manifested His glory; and His disciples believed in
Him.
12 After this He went down to Capernaum, He, His moth-
er, His brothers, and His disciples; and they did not stay
there many days.

Jesus Cleanses the Temple

13 Now the Passover of the Jews was at hand, and Jesus
went up to Jerusalem. 14 And He found in the temple those
who sold oxen and sheep and doves, and the money chan-
gers doing business. 15 When He had made a whip of cords,
He drove them all out of the temple, with the sheep and the
oxen, and poured out the changers' money and overturned
the tables. 16 And He said to those who sold doves, "Take
these things away! Do not make My Father's house a house

THE MESSAGE

When the host tasted the water that had become wine (he didn't know what had just happened but the servants, of course, knew), he called out to the bridegroom, "Everybody I know begins with their finest wines and after the guests have had their fill brings in the cheap stuff. But you've saved the best till now!"

This act in Cana of Galilee was the first sign Jesus gave, the first glimpse of his glory. And his disciples believed in him.

After this he went down to Capernaum along with his mother, brothers, and disciples, and stayed several days.

Tear Down This Temple . . .

When the Passover Feast, celebrated each spring by the Jews, was about to take place, Jesus traveled up to Jerusalem. He found the Temple teeming with people selling cattle and sheep and doves. The loan sharks were also there in full strength.

Jesus put together a whip out of strips of leather and chased them out of the Temple, stampeding the sheep and cattle, upending the tables of the loan sharks, spilling coins left and right. He told the dove merchants, "Get your things out of here! Stop turning my Father's house into a

KING JAMES VERSION

17 And his disciples remembered that it was written, The zeal of thine house hath eaten me up.

18 Then answered the Jews and said unto him, What sign shewest thou unto us, seeing that thou doest these things?

19 Jesus answered and said unto them, Destroy this temple, and in three days I will raise it up.

20 Then said the Jews, Forty and six years was this temple in building, and wilt thou rear it up in three days?

21 But he spake of the temple of his body.

22 When therefore he was risen from the dead, his disciples remembered that he had said this unto them; and they believed the scripture, and the word which Jesus had said.

23 ¶ Now when he was in Jerusalem at the passover, in the feast *day*, many believed in his name, when they saw the miracles which he did.

24 But Jesus did not commit himself unto them, because he knew all *men*,

25 And needed not that any should testify of man: for he knew what was in man.

3 There was a man of the Pharisees, named Nicodemus, a ruler of the Jews:

2 The same came to Jesus by night, and said unto him, Rabbi, we know that thou art a teacher come from God: for no man can do these miracles that thou doest, except God be with him.

NEW AMERICAN STANDARD BIBLE

17 His disciples remembered that it was written, "ZEAL FOR YOUR HOUSE WILL CONSUME ME."

18 The Jews then said to Him, "What sign do You show us as your authority for doing these things?"

19 Jesus answered them, "Destroy this temple, and in three days I will raise it up."

20 The Jews then said, "It took forty-six years to build this temple, and will You raise it up in three days?"

21 But He was speaking of the temple of His body.

22 So when He was raised from the dead, His disciples remembered that He said this; and they believed the Scripture and the word which Jesus had spoken.

23 Now when He was in Jerusalem at the Passover, during the feast, many believed in His name, observing His signs which He was doing.

24 But Jesus, on His part, was not entrusting Himself to them, for He knew all men,

25 and because He did not need anyone to testify concerning man, for He Himself knew what was in man.

The New Birth

3 Now there was a man of the Pharisees, named Nicodemus, a ruler of the Jews;

2 this man came to Jesus by night and said to Him, "Rabbi, we know that You have come from God *as* a teacher; for no one can do these signs that You do unless God is with him."

NEW CENTURY VERSION

17When this happened, the followers remembered what was written in the Scriptures: "My strong love for your Temple completely controls me."[b]

18The Jews said to Jesus, "Show us a miracle to prove you have the right to do these things."

19Jesus answered them, "Destroy this temple, and I will build it again in three days."

20The Jews answered, "It took forty-six years to build this Temple! Do you really believe you can build it again in three days?"

21(But the temple Jesus meant was his own body.
22After Jesus was raised from the dead, his followers remembered that Jesus had said this. Then they believed the Scripture and the words Jesus had said.)

23When Jesus was in Jerusalem for the Passover Feast, many people believed in him because they saw the miracles he did.
24But Jesus did not trust himself to them because he knew them all.
25He did not need anyone to tell him about people, because he knew what was in people's minds.

Nicodemus Comes to Jesus

3 There was a man named Nicodemus who was one of the Pharisees and an important Jewish leader.
2One night Nicodemus came to Jesus and said, "Teacher, we know you are a teacher sent from God, because no one can do the miracles you do unless God is with him."

2:17 [b] "My...me." Quotation from Psalm 69:9.

CONTEMPORARY ENGLISH VERSION

17The disciples then remembered that the Scriptures say, "My love for your house burns in me like a fire."

18The Jewish leaders asked Jesus, "What miracle[b] will you work to show us why you have done this?"

19"Destroy this temple," Jesus answered, "and in three days I will build it again!"

20The leaders replied, "It took forty-six years to build this temple. What makes you think you can rebuild it in three days?"

21But Jesus was talking about his body as a temple.
22And when he was raised from death, his disciples remembered what he had told them. Then they believed the Scriptures and the words of Jesus.

Jesus Knows What People Are Like

23In Jerusalem during Passover many people put their faith in Jesus, because they saw him work miracles.[b]
24But Jesus knew what was in their hearts, and he would not let them have power over him.
25No one had to tell him what people were like. He already knew.

Jesus and Nicodemus

3 There was a man named Nicodemus who was a Pharisee and a Jewish leader.
2One night he went to Jesus and said, "Sir, we know that God has sent you to teach us. You could not work these miracles, unless God were with you."

[b] 2.18,23 *miracle*: The Greek text has "sign." In the Gospel of John the word "sign" is used for the miracle itself and as a way of pointing to Jesus as the Son of God.

NEW INTERNATIONAL VERSION

17 His disciples remembered that it is written: "Zeal for
your house will consume me."[b]
18 Then the Jews demanded of him, "What miraculous
sign can you show us to prove your authority to do all
this?"
19 Jesus answered them, "Destroy this temple, and I will
raise it again in three days."
20 The Jews replied, "It has taken forty-six years to build
this temple, and you are going to raise it in three days?"
21 But the temple he had spoken of was his body. 22 After he
was raised from the dead, his disciples recalled what he
had said. Then they believed the Scripture and the words
that Jesus had spoken.
23 Now while he was in Jerusalem at the Passover Feast,
many people saw the miraculous signs he was doing and
believed in his name.[c] 24 But Jesus would not entrust him-
self to them, for he knew all men. 25 He did not need man's
testimony about man, for he knew what was in a man.

Jesus Teaches Nicodemus

3 Now there was a man of the Pharisees named
Nicodemus, a member of the Jewish ruling council.
2 He came to Jesus at night and said, "Rabbi, we know you
are a teacher who has come from God. For no one could
perform the miraculous signs you are doing if God were
not with him."

[b] *17* Psalm 69:9 [c] *23* Or *and believed in him*

NEW LIVING TRANSLATION

17 Then his disciples remembered this prophecy from the
Scriptures: "Passion for God's house burns within me."*
18 "What right do you have to do these things?" the
Jewish leaders demanded. "If you have this authority from
God, show us a miraculous sign to prove it."
19 "All right," Jesus replied. "Destroy this temple, and in
three days I will raise it up."
20 "What!" they exclaimed. "It took forty-six years to
build this Temple, and you can do it in three days?" 21 But
by "this temple," Jesus meant his body. 22 After he was
raised from the dead, the disciples remembered that he
had said this. And they believed both Jesus and the
Scriptures.
23 Because of the miraculous signs he did in Jerusalem at
the Passover celebration, many people were convinced that
he was indeed the Messiah. 24 But Jesus didn't trust them,
because he knew what people were really like. 25 No one
needed to tell him about human nature.

Jesus and Nicodemus

3 After dark one evening, a Jewish religious leader
named Nicodemus, a Pharisee, 2 came to speak with
Jesus. "Teacher," he said, "we all know that God has sent
you to teach us. Your miraculous signs are proof enough
that God is with you."

2:17 Or *"Concern for God's house will be my undoing."* Ps 69:9.

NEW KING JAMES VERSION

of merchandise!" 17 Then His disciples remembered that it
was written, *"Zeal for Your house has eaten[a] Me up."*[b]
18 So the Jews answered and said to Him, "What sign do
You show to us, since You do these things?"
19 Jesus answered and said to them, "Destroy this tem-
ple, and in three days I will raise it up."
20 Then the Jews said, "It has taken forty-six years to
build this temple, and will You raise it up in three days?"
21 But He was speaking of the temple of His body.
22 Therefore, when He had risen from the dead, His disci-
ples remembered that He had said this to them;[c] and they
believed the Scripture and the word which Jesus had said.

The Discerner of Hearts

23 Now when He was in Jerusalem at the Passover, dur-
ing the feast, many believed in His name when they saw
the signs which He did. 24 But Jesus did not commit Him-
self to them, because He knew all *men,* 25 and had no need
that anyone should testify of man, for He knew what was
in man.

The New Birth

3 There was a man of the Pharisees named Nicodemus,
a ruler of the Jews. 2 This man came to Jesus by night
and said to Him, "Rabbi, we know that You are a teacher
come from God; for no one can do these signs that You do
unless God is with him."

2:17 [a] NU-Text and M-Text read *will eat.* [b] Psalm 69:9
2:22 [c] NU-Text and M-Text omit *to them.*

THE MESSAGE

shopping mall!" That's when his disciples remembered the Scripture, "Zeal for your house consumes me."

But the Jews were upset. They asked, "What credentials can you present to justify this?" Jesus answered, "Tear down this Temple and in three days I'll put it back together."

They were indignant: "It took forty-six years to build this Temple, and you're going to rebuild it in three days?" But Jesus was talking about his body as the Temple. Later, after he was raised from the dead, his disciples remembered he had said this. They then put two and two together and believed both what was written in Scripture and what Jesus had said.

During the time he was in Jerusalem, those days of the Passover Feast, many people noticed the signs he was displaying and, seeing they pointed straight to God, entrusted their lives to him. But Jesus didn't entrust his life to them. He knew them inside and out, knew how untrustworthy they were. He didn't need any help in seeing right through them.

Born From Above

3 There was a man of the Pharisee sect, Nicodemus, a prominent leader among the Jews. Late one night he visited Jesus and said, "Rabbi, we all know you're a teacher straight from God. No one could do all the God-pointing, God-revealing acts you do if God weren't in on it."

KING JAMES VERSION

3 Jesus answered and said unto him, Verily, verily, I say unto thee, Except a man be born again, he cannot see the kingdom of God.

4 Nicodemus saith unto him, How can a man be born when he is old? can he enter the second time into his mother's womb, and be born?

5 Jesus answered, Verily, verily, I say unto thee, Except a man be born of water and *of* the Spirit, he cannot enter into the kingdom of God.

6 That which is born of the flesh is flesh; and that which is born of the Spirit is spirit.

7 Marvel not that I said unto thee, Ye must be born again.

8 The wind bloweth where it listeth, and thou hearest the sound thereof, but canst not tell whence it cometh, and whither it goeth: so is every one that is born of the Spirit.

9 Nicodemus answered and said unto him, How can these things be?

10 Jesus answered and said unto him, Art thou a master of Israel, and knowest not these things?

11 Verily, verily, I say unto thee, We speak that we do know, and testify that we have seen; and ye receive not our witness.

NEW AMERICAN STANDARD BIBLE

3 Jesus answered and said to him, "Truly, truly, I say to you, unless one is born again he cannot see the kingdom of God."

4 Nicodemus *said to Him, "How can a man be born when he is old? He cannot enter a second time into his mother's womb and be born, can he?"

5 Jesus answered, "Truly, truly, I say to you, unless one is born of water and the Spirit he cannot enter into the kingdom of God.

6 "That which is born of the flesh is flesh, and that which is born of the Spirit is spirit.

7 "Do not be amazed that I said to you, 'You must be born again.'

8 "The wind blows where it wishes and you hear the sound of it, but do not know where it comes from and where it is going; so is everyone who is born of the Spirit."

9 Nicodemus said to Him, "How can these things be?"

10 Jesus answered and said to him, "Are you the teacher of Israel and do not understand these things?

11 "Truly, truly, I say to you, we speak of what we know and testify of what we have seen, and you do not accept our testimony.

NEW CENTURY VERSION

3 Jesus answered, "I tell you the truth, unless one is born
again, he cannot be in God's kingdom."
4 Nicodemus said, "But if a person is already old, how
can he be born again? He cannot enter his mother's body
again. So how can a person be born a second time?"
5 But Jesus answered, "I tell you the truth, unless one is
born from water and the Spirit, he cannot enter God's
kingdom. 6 Human life comes from human parents, but
spiritual life comes from the Spirit. 7 Don't be surprised
when I tell you, 'You must all be born again.' 8 The wind
blows where it wants to and you hear the sound of it, but
you don't know where the wind comes from or where it is
going. It is the same with every person who is born from
the Spirit."
9 Nicodemus asked, "How can this happen?"
10 Jesus said, "You are an important teacher in Israel,
and you don't understand these things? 11 I tell you the
truth, we talk about what we know, and we tell about
what we have seen, but you don't accept what we tell you.

CONTEMPORARY ENGLISH VERSION

3 Jesus replied, "I tell you for certain that you must be
born from above[a] before you can see God's kingdom!"
4 Nicodemus asked, "How can a grown man ever be born
a second time?"
5 Jesus answered:

I tell you for certain that before you can get into God's
kingdom, you must be born not only by water, but by
the Spirit. 6 Humans give life to their children. Yet only
God's Spirit can change you into a child of God. 7 Don't
be surprised when I say that you must be born from
above. 8 Only God's Spirit gives new life. The Spirit is
like the wind that blows wherever it wants to. You can
hear the wind, but you don't know where it comes from
or where it is going.

9 "How can this be?" Nicodemus asked.
10 Jesus replied:

How can you be a teacher of Israel and not know
these things? 11 I tell you for certain that we know what
we are talking about because we have seen it ourselves.
But none of you will accept what we say. 12 If you don't

[a] 3.3 *from above*: Or "in a new way." The same Greek word is used in verses 7, 31.

NEW INTERNATIONAL VERSION

3 In reply Jesus declared, "I tell you the truth, no one can see the kingdom of God unless he is born again.[a]"

4 "How can a man be born when he is old?" Nicodemus asked. "Surely he cannot enter a second time into his mother's womb to be born!"

5 Jesus answered, "I tell you the truth, no one can enter the kingdom of God unless he is born of water and the Spirit. 6 Flesh gives birth to flesh, but the Spirit[b] gives birth to spirit. 7 You should not be surprised at my saying, 'You[c] must be born again.' 8 The wind blows wherever it pleases. You hear its sound, but you cannot tell where it comes from or where it is going. So it is with everyone born of the Spirit."

9 "How can this be?" Nicodemus asked.

10 "You are Israel's teacher," said Jesus, "and do you not understand these things? 11 I tell you the truth, we speak of what we know, and we testify to what we have seen, but still you people do not accept our testimony. 12 I have

[a] *3* Or *born from above*; also in verse 7 [b] *6* Or *but spirit* [c] *7* The Greek is plural.

NEW LIVING TRANSLATION

3 Jesus replied, "I assure you, unless you are born again,* you can never see the Kingdom of God."

4 "What do you mean?" exclaimed Nicodemus. "How can an old man go back into his mother's womb and be born again?"

5 Jesus replied, "The truth is, no one can enter the Kingdom of God without being born of water and the Spirit.* 6 Humans can reproduce only human life, but the Holy Spirit gives new life from heaven. 7 So don't be surprised at my statement that you* must be born again. 8 Just as you can hear the wind but can't tell where it comes from or where it is going, so you can't explain how people are born of the Spirit."

9 "What do you mean?" Nicodemus asked.

10 Jesus replied, "You are a respected Jewish teacher, and yet you don't understand these things? 11 I assure you, I am telling you what we know and have seen, and yet you won't

3:3 Or *born from above;* also in 3:7. 3:5 Or *spirit.* The Greek word for *Spirit* can also be translated *wind;* see 3:8. 3:7 The Greek word for *you* is plural; also in 3:12.

NEW KING JAMES VERSION

3 Jesus answered and said to him, "Most assuredly, I say to you, unless one is born again, he cannot see the kingdom of God."

4 Nicodemus said to Him, "How can a man be born when he is old? Can he enter a second time into his mother's womb and be born?"

5 Jesus answered, "Most assuredly, I say to you, unless one is born of water and the Spirit, he cannot enter the kingdom of God. 6 That which is born of the flesh is flesh, and that which is born of the Spirit is spirit. 7 Do not marvel that I said to you, 'You must be born again.' 8 The wind blows where it wishes, and you hear the sound of it, but cannot tell where it comes from and where it goes. So is everyone who is born of the Spirit."

9 Nicodemus answered and said to Him, "How can these things be?"

10 Jesus answered and said to him, "Are you the teacher of Israel, and do not know these things? 11 Most assuredly, I say to you, We speak what We know and testify what We have seen, and you do not receive Our witness. 12 If I have

THE MESSAGE

Jesus said, "You're absolutely right. Take it from me: Unless a person is born from above, it's not possible to see what I'm pointing to—to God's kingdom."

"How can anyone," said Nicodemus, "be born who has already been born and grown up? You can't re-enter your mother's womb and be born again. What are you saying with this 'born-from-above' talk?"

Jesus said, "You're not listening. Let me say it again. Unless a person submits to this original creation—the 'wind hovering over the water' creation, the invisible moving the visible, a baptism into a new life—it's not possible to enter God's kingdom. When you look at a baby, it's just that: a body you can look at and touch. But the person who takes shape within is formed by something you can't see and touch—the Spirit—and becomes a living spirit.

"So don't be so surprised when I tell you that you have to be 'born from above'—out of this world, so to speak. You know well enough how the wind blows this way and that. You hear it rustling through the trees, but you have no idea where it comes from or where it's headed next. That's the way it is with everyone 'born from above' by the wind of God, the Spirit of God."

Nicodemus asked, "What do you mean by this? How does this happen?"

Jesus said, "You're a respected teacher of Israel and you don't know these basics? Listen carefully. I'm speaking sober truth to you. I speak only of what I know by experience; I give witness only to what I have seen with my own eyes. There is nothing secondhand here, no hearsay. Yet

KING JAMES VERSION

12 If I have told you earthly things, and ye believe not, how shall ye believe, if I tell you *of* heavenly things?

13 And no man hath ascended up to heaven, but he that came down from heaven, *even* the Son of man which is in heaven.

14 And as Moses lifted up the serpent in the wilderness, even so must the Son of man be lifted up:

15 That whosoever believeth in him should not perish, but have eternal life.

16 For God so loved the world, that he gave his only begotten Son, that whosoever believeth in him should not perish, but have everlasting life.

17 For God sent not his Son into the world to condemn the world; but that the world through him might be saved.

18 He that believeth on him is not condemned: but he that believeth not is condemned already, because he hath not believed in the name of the only begotten Son of God.

19 And this is the condemnation, that light is come into the world, and men loved darkness rather than light, because their deeds were evil.

20 For every one that doeth evil hateth the light, neither cometh to the light, lest his deeds should be reproved.

NEW AMERICAN STANDARD BIBLE

12 "If I told you earthly things and you do not believe, how will you believe if I tell you heavenly things?

13 "No one has ascended into heaven, but He who descended from heaven: the Son of Man.

14 "As Moses lifted up the serpent in the wilderness, even so must the Son of Man be lifted up;

15 so that whoever [1]believes will in Him have eternal life.

16 "For God so loved the world, that He gave His only begotten Son, that whoever believes in Him shall not perish, but have eternal life.

17 "For God did not send the Son into the world to judge the world, but that the world might be saved through Him.

18 "He who believes in Him is not judged; he who does not believe has been judged already, because he has not believed in the name of the only begotten Son of God.

19 "This is the judgment, that the Light has come into the world, and men loved the darkness rather than the Light, for their deeds were evil.

20 "For everyone who does evil hates the Light, and does not come to the Light for fear that his deeds will be exposed.

3:15 [1] Or *believes in Him will have eternal life*

NEW CENTURY VERSION

12I have told you about things here on earth, and you do not believe me. So you will not believe me if I tell you about things of heaven. 13The only one who has ever gone up to heaven is the One who came down from heaven—the Son of Man.

14"Just as Moses lifted up the snake in the desert,[a] the Son of Man must also be lifted up. 15So that everyone who believes can have eternal life in him.

16"God loved the world so much that he gave his one and only Son so that whoever believes in him may not be lost, but have eternal life. 17God did not send his Son into the world to judge the world guilty, but to save the world through him. 18People who believe in God's Son are not judged guilty. Those who do not believe have already been judged guilty, because they have not believed in God's one and only Son. 19They are judged by this fact: The Light has come into the world, but they did not want light. They wanted darkness, because they were doing evil things. 20All who do evil hate the light and will not come to the light, because it will show all the evil things they do. 21But

3:14 [a] **Moses...desert** When the Israelites were dying from snake bites, God told Moses to put a brass snake on a pole. The people who looked at the snake were healed (Numbers 21:4–9).

CONTEMPORARY ENGLISH VERSION

believe when I talk to you about things on earth, how can you possibly believe if I talk to you about things in heaven?

13No one has gone up to heaven except the Son of Man, who came down from there. 14And the Son of Man must be lifted up, just as that metal snake was lifted up by Moses in the desert.[b] 15Then everyone who has faith in the Son of Man will have eternal life.

16God loved the people of this world so much that he gave his only Son, so that everyone who has faith in him will have eternal life and never really die. 17God did not send his Son into the world to condemn its people. He sent him to save them! 18No one who has faith in God's Son will be condemned. But everyone who doesn't have faith in him has already been condemned for not having faith in God's only Son.

19The light has come into the world, and people who do evil things are judged guilty because they love the dark more than the light. 20People who do evil hate the light and won't come to the light, because it clearly

[b] 3.14 *just as that metal snake was lifted up by Moses in the desert*: When the Lord punished the people of Israel by sending snakes to bite them, he told Moses to hold a metal snake up on a pole. Everyone who looked at the snake was cured of the snake bites (see Numbers 21.4-9).

NEW INTERNATIONAL VERSION

spoken to you of earthly things and you do not believe; how then will you believe if I speak of heavenly things? [13]No one has ever gone into heaven except the one who came from heaven—the Son of Man.[d] [14]Just as Moses lifted up the snake in the desert, so the Son of Man must be lifted up, [15]that everyone who believes in him may have eternal life.[e]

[16]"For God so loved the world that he gave his one and only Son,[f] that whoever believes in him shall not perish but have eternal life. [17]For God did not send his Son into the world to condemn the world, but to save the world through him. [18]Whoever believes in him is not condemned, but whoever does not believe stands condemned already because he has not believed in the name of God's one and only Son.[g] [19]This is the verdict: Light has come into the world, but men loved darkness instead of light because their deeds were evil. [20]Everyone who does evil hates the light, and will not come into the light for fear that his

[d] *13* Some manuscripts *Man, who is in heaven* [e] *15* Or *believes may have eternal life in him* [f] *16* Or *his only begotten Son* [g] *18* Or *God's only begotten Son*

NEW LIVING TRANSLATION

believe us. [12]But if you don't even believe me when I tell you about things that happen here on earth, how can you possibly believe if I tell you what is going on in heaven? [13]For only I, the Son of Man,* have come to earth and will return to heaven again. [14]And as Moses lifted up the bronze snake on a pole in the wilderness, so I, the Son of Man, must be lifted up on a pole,* [15]so that everyone who believes in me will have eternal life.

[16]"For God so loved the world that he gave his only Son, so that everyone who believes in him will not perish but have eternal life. [17]God did not send his Son into the world to condemn it, but to save it.

[18]"There is no judgment awaiting those who trust him. But those who do not trust him have already been judged for not believing in the only Son of God. [19]Their judgment is based on this fact: The light from heaven came into the world, but they loved the darkness more than the light, for their actions were evil. [20]They hate the light because they want to sin in the darkness. They stay away from the light for fear their sins will be exposed and they will be

3:13 Some manuscripts add *who lives in heaven.* 3:14 Greek *must be lifted up.*

NEW KING JAMES VERSION

told you earthly things and you do not believe, how will you believe if I tell you heavenly things? [13]No one has ascended to heaven but He who came down from heaven, *that is,* the Son of Man who is in heaven.[a] [14]And as Moses lifted up the serpent in the wilderness, even so must the Son of Man be lifted up, [15]that whoever believes in Him should not perish but[b] have eternal life. [16]For God so loved the world that He gave His only begotten Son, that whoever believes in Him should not perish but have everlasting life. [17]For God did not send His Son into the world to condemn the world, but that the world through Him might be saved.

[18]"He who believes in Him is not condemned; but he who does not believe is condemned already, because he has not believed in the name of the only begotten Son of God. [19]And this is the condemnation, that the light has come into the world, and men loved darkness rather than light, because their deeds were evil. [20]For everyone practicing evil hates the light and does not come to the light, lest

3:13 [a] NU-Text omits *who is in heaven.* 3:15 [b] NU-Text omits *not perish but.*

THE MESSAGE

instead of facing the evidence and accepting it, you procrastinate with questions. If I tell you things that are plain as the hand before your face and you don't believe me, what use is there in telling you of things you can't see, the things of God?

"No one has ever gone up into the presence of God except the One who came down from that Presence, the Son of Man. In the same way that Moses lifted the serpent in the desert so people could have something to see and then believe, it is necessary for the Son of Man to be lifted up—and everyone who looks up to him, trusting and expectant, will gain a real life, eternal life.

"This is how much God loved the world: He gave his Son, his one and only Son. And this is why: so that no one need be destroyed; by believing in him, anyone can have a whole and lasting life. God didn't go to all the trouble of sending his Son merely to point an accusing finger, telling the world how bad it was. He came to help, to put the world right again. Anyone who trusts in him is acquitted; anyone who refuses to trust him has long since been under the death sentence without knowing it. And why? Because of that person's failure to believe in the one-of-a-kind Son of God when introduced to him.

"This is the crisis we're in: God-light streamed into the world, but men and women everywhere ran for the darkness. They went for the darkness because they were not really interested in pleasing God. Everyone who makes a practice of doing evil, addicted to denial and illusion, hates God-light and won't come near it, fearing a painful

KING JAMES VERSION

21 But he that doeth truth cometh to the light, that his deeds may be made manifest, that they are wrought in God.
22 ¶ After these things came Jesus and his disciples into the land of Judaea; and there he tarried with them, and baptized.
23 And John also was baptizing in Aenon near to Salim, because there was much water there: and they came, and were baptized.
24 For John was not yet cast into prison.
25 Then there arose a question between *some* of John's disciples and the Jews about purifying.
26 And they came unto John, and said unto him, Rabbi, he that was with thee beyond Jordan, to whom thou barest witness, behold, the same baptizeth, and all *men* come to him.
27 John answered and said, A man can receive nothing, except it be given him from heaven.
28 Ye yourselves bear me witness, that I said, I am not the Christ, but that I am sent before him.
29 He that hath the bride is the bridegroom: but the friend of the bridegroom, which standeth and heareth him, rejoiceth greatly because of the bridegroom's voice: this my joy therefore is fulfilled.
30 He must increase, but I *must* decrease.

NEW AMERICAN STANDARD BIBLE

21 "But he who practices the truth comes to the Light, so that his deeds may be manifested as having been wrought in God."

John's Last Testimony

22 After these things Jesus and His disciples came into the land of Judea, and there He was spending time with them and baptizing.
23 John also was baptizing in Aenon near Salim, because there was much water there; and *people* were coming and were being baptized—
24 for John had not yet been thrown into prison.
25 Therefore there arose a discussion on the part of John's disciples with a Jew about purification.
26 And they came to John and said to him, "Rabbi, He who was with you beyond the Jordan, to whom you have testified, behold, He is baptizing and all are coming to Him."
27 John answered and said, "A man can receive nothing unless it has been given him from heaven.
28 "You yourselves are my witnesses that I said, 'I am not the Christ,' but, 'I have been sent ahead of Him.'
29 "He who has the bride is the bridegroom; but the friend of the bridegroom, who stands and hears him, rejoices greatly because of the bridegroom's voice. So this joy of mine has been made full.
30 "He must increase, but I must decrease.

NEW CENTURY VERSION

those who follow the true way come to the light, and it shows that the things they do were done through God."

Jesus and John the Baptist

22After this, Jesus and his followers went into the area of Judea, where he stayed with his followers and baptized
people. 23John was also baptizing in Aenon, near Salim, because there was plenty of water there. People were going
there to be baptized. 24(This was before John was put into prison.)
25Some of John's followers had an argument with a Jew
about religious washing.[b] 26So they came to John and said, "Teacher, remember the man who was with you on the other side of the Jordan River, the one you spoke about so much? He is baptizing, and everyone is going to him."
27John answered, "A man can get only what God gives
him. 28You yourselves heard me say, 'I am not the Christ,
but I am the one sent to prepare the way for him.' 29The bride belongs only to the bridegroom. But the friend who helps the bridegroom stands by and listens to him. He is thrilled that he gets to hear the bridegroom's voice. In the
same way, I am really happy. 30He must become greater, and I must become less important.

3:25 [b] **religious washing** The Jewish people washed themselves in special ways before eating, before worshiping in the Temple, and at other special times.

CONTEMPORARY ENGLISH VERSION

shows what they have done. 21But everyone who lives by the truth will come to the light, because they want others to know that God is really the one doing what they do.

Jesus and John the Baptist

22Later, Jesus and his disciples went to Judea, where he stayed with them for a while and was baptizing people.
23-24John had not yet been put in jail. He was at Aenon near Salim, where there was a lot of water, and people were coming there for John to baptize them.
25John's followers got into an argument with a Jewish
man[c] about a ceremony of washing.[d] 26They went to John and said, "Rabbi, you spoke about a man when you were with him east of the Jordan. He is now baptizing people, and everyone is going to him."
27John replied:

No one can do anything unless God in heaven allows
it. 28You surely remember how I told you that I am not the Messiah. I am only the one sent ahead of him.
29At a wedding the groom is the one who gets married. The best man is glad just to be there and to hear
the groom's voice. That's why I am so glad. 30Jesus must become more important, while I become less important.

[c] 3.25 *a Jewish man*: Some manuscripts have "some Jewish men."
[d] 3.25 *about a ceremony of washing*: The Jewish people had many rules about washing themselves and their dishes, in order to make themselves fit to worship God.

NEW INTERNATIONAL VERSION

deeds will be exposed. 21But whoever lives by the truth
comes into the light, so that it may be seen plainly that
what he has done has been done through God."[h]

John the Baptist's Testimony About Jesus

22After this, Jesus and his disciples went out into the
Judean countryside, where he spent some time with them,
and baptized. 23Now John also was baptizing at Aenon
near Salim, because there was plenty of water, and people
were constantly coming to be baptized. 24(This was before
John was put in prison.) 25An argument developed between
some of John's disciples and a certain Jew[i] over the matter
of ceremonial washing. 26They came to John and said to
him, "Rabbi, that man who was with you on the other side
of the Jordan—the one you testified about—well, he is
baptizing, and everyone is going to him."

27To this John replied, "A man can receive only what is
given him from heaven. 28You yourselves can testify that I
said, 'I am not the Christ[j] but am sent ahead of him.' 29The
bride belongs to the bridegroom. The friend who attends
the bridegroom waits and listens for him, and is full of joy
when he hears the bridegroom's voice. That joy is mine,
and it is now complete. 30He must become greater; I must
become less.

[h] *21* Some interpreters end the quotation after verse 15. [i] *25* Some manuscripts *and certain Jews* [j] *28* Or *Messiah*

NEW LIVING TRANSLATION

punished. 21But those who do what is right come to the
light gladly, so everyone can see that they are doing what
God wants."

John the Baptist Exalts Jesus

22Afterward Jesus and his disciples left Jerusalem, but
they stayed in Judea for a while and baptized there.

23At this time John the Baptist was baptizing at Aenon,
near Salim, because there was plenty of water there and
people kept coming to him for baptism. 24This was before
John was put into prison. 25At that time a certain Jew
began an argument with John's disciples over ceremonial
cleansing. 26John's disciples came to him and said,
"Teacher, the man you met on the other side of the Jordan
River, the one you said was the Messiah, is also baptizing
people. And everybody is going over there instead of com-
ing here to us."

27John replied, "God in heaven appoints each person's
work. 28You yourselves know how plainly I told you that I
am not the Messiah. I am here to prepare the way for
him—that is all. 29The bride will go where the bridegroom
is. A bridegroom's friend rejoices with him. I am the bride-
groom's friend, and I am filled with joy at his success.
30He must become greater and greater, and I must become
less and less.

NEW KING JAMES VERSION

his deeds should be exposed. 21But he who does the truth
comes to the light, that his deeds may be clearly seen, that
they have been done in God."

John the Baptist Exalts Christ

22After these things Jesus and His disciples came into
the land of Judea, and there He remained with them and
baptized. 23Now John also was baptizing in Aenon near
Salim, because there was much water there. And they
came and were baptized. 24For John had not yet been
thrown into prison.

25Then there arose a dispute between *some* of John's dis-
ciples and the Jews about purification. 26And they came to
John and said to him, "Rabbi, He who was with you
beyond the Jordan, to whom you have testified—behold,
He is baptizing, and all are coming to Him!"

27John answered and said, "A man can receive nothing
unless it has been given to him from heaven. 28You your-
selves bear me witness, that I said, 'I am not the Christ,'
but, 'I have been sent before Him.' 29He who has the bride
is the bridegroom; but the friend of the bridegroom, who
stands and hears him, rejoices greatly because of the
bridegroom's voice. Therefore this joy of mine is fulfilled.
30He must increase, but I *must* decrease. 31He who comes

THE MESSAGE

exposure. But anyone working and living in truth and reality welcomes God-light so the work can be seen for the God-work it is."

The Bridegroom's Friend

After this conversation, Jesus went on with his disciples into the Judean countryside and relaxed with them there. He was also baptizing. At the same time, John was baptizing over at Aenon near Salim, where water was abundant. This was before John was thrown into jail. John's disciples got into an argument with the establishment Jews over the nature of baptism. They came to John and said, "Rabbi, you know the one who was with you on the other side of the Jordan? The one you authorized with your witness? Well, he's now competing with us. He's baptizing, too, and everyone's going to him instead of us."

John answered, "It's not possible for a person to succeed—I'm talking about *eternal* success—without heaven's help. You yourselves were there when I made it public that I was not the Messiah but simply the one sent ahead of him to get things ready. The one who gets the bride is, by definition, the bridegroom. And the bridegroom's friend, his 'best man'—that's me—in place at his side where he can hear every word, is genuinely happy. How could he be jealous when he knows that the wedding is finished and the marriage is off to a good start?

"That's why my cup is running over. This is the assigned moment for him to move into the center, while I slip off to the sidelines.

KING JAMES VERSION

31 He that cometh from above is above all: he that is of the earth is earthly, and speaketh of the earth: he that cometh from heaven is above all.

32 And what he hath seen and heard, that he testifieth; and no man receiveth his testimony.

33 He that hath received his testimony hath set to his seal that God is true.

34 For he whom God hath sent speaketh the words of God: for God giveth not the Spirit by measure *unto him*.

35 The Father loveth the Son, and hath given all things into his hand.

36 He that believeth on the Son hath everlasting life: and he that believeth not the Son shall not see life; but the wrath of God abideth on him.

4 When therefore the Lord knew how the Pharisees had heard that Jesus made and baptized more disciples than John,

2 (Though Jesus himself baptized not, but his disciples,)

3 He left Judaea, and departed again into Galilee.

4 ¶ And he must needs go through Samaria.

5 Then cometh he to a city of Samaria, which is called Sychar, near to the parcel of ground that Jacob gave to his son Joseph.

6 Now Jacob's well was there. Jesus therefore, being wearied with *his* journey, sat thus on the well: *and* it was about the sixth hour.

NEW AMERICAN STANDARD BIBLE

31 "He who comes from above is above all, he who is of the earth is from the earth and speaks of the earth. He who comes from heaven is above all.

32 "What He has seen and heard, of that He testifies; and no one receives His testimony.

33 "He who has received His testimony has set his seal to *this,* that God is true.

34 "For He whom God has sent speaks the words of God; for He gives the Spirit without measure.

35 "The Father loves the Son and has given all things into His hand.

36 "He who believes in the Son has eternal life; but he who does not obey the Son will not see life, but the wrath of God abides on him."

Jesus Goes to Galilee

4 Therefore when the Lord knew that the Pharisees had heard that Jesus was making and baptizing more disciples than John

2 (although Jesus Himself was not baptizing, but His disciples were),

3 He left Judea and went away again into Galilee.

4 And He had to pass through Samaria.

5 So He *came to a city of Samaria called Sychar, near the parcel of ground that Jacob gave to his son Joseph;

6 and Jacob's well was there. So Jesus, being wearied from His journey, was sitting thus by the well. It was about [1]the sixth hour.

4:6 [1] Perhaps 6 p.m. Roman time or noon Jewish time

NEW CENTURY VERSION

The One Who Comes from Heaven

31"The One who comes from above is greater than all.
The one who is from the earth belongs to the earth and
talks about things on the earth. But the One who comes
from heaven is greater than all. 32He tells what he has
seen and heard, but no one accepts what he says.
33Whoever accepts what he says has proven that God is
true. 34The One whom God sent speaks the words of God,
because God gives him the Spirit fully. 35The Father loves
the Son and has given him power over everything. 36Those
who believe in the Son have eternal life, but those who do
not obey the Son will never have life. God's anger stays on
them."

Jesus and a Samaritan Woman

4 The Pharisees heard that Jesus was making and bap-
tizing more followers than John, 2although Jesus him-
self did not baptize people, but his followers did. 3Jesus
knew that the Pharisees had heard about him, so he left
Judea and went back to Galilee. 4But on the way he had to
go through the country of Samaria.

5In Samaria Jesus came to the town called Sychar, which
is near the field Jacob gave to his son Joseph. 6Jacob's well
was there. Jesus was tired from his long trip, so he sat
down beside the well. It was about twelve o'clock noon.

CONTEMPORARY ENGLISH VERSION

The One Who Comes from Heaven

31God's Son comes from heaven and is above all oth-
ers. Everyone who comes from the earth belongs to the
earth and speaks about earthly things. The one who
comes from heaven is above all others. 32He speaks
about what he has seen and heard, and yet no one
believes him. 33But everyone who does believe him has
shown that God is truthful. 34The Son was sent to speak
God's message, and he has been given the full power of
God's Spirit.

35The Father loves the Son and has given him every-
thing. 36Everyone who has faith in the Son has eternal
life. But no one who rejects him will ever share in that
life, and God will be angry with them forever.

4 Jesus knew that the Pharisees had heard that he was
winning and baptizing more followers than John was.
2But Jesus' disciples were really the ones doing the baptiz-
ing, and not Jesus himself.

Jesus and the Samaritan Woman

3Jesus left Judea and started for Galilee again. 4This
time he had to go through Samaria, 5and on his way he
came to the town of Sychar. It was near the field that Jacob
had long ago given to his son Joseph. 6-8The well that
Jacob had dug was still there, and Jesus sat down beside it
because he was tired from traveling. It was noon, and after

NEW INTERNATIONAL VERSION

[31]“The one who comes from above is above all; the one who is from the earth belongs to the earth, and speaks as one from the earth. The one who comes from heaven is above all. [32]He testifies to what he has seen and heard, but no one accepts his testimony. [33]The man who has accepted it has certified that God is truthful. [34]For the one whom God has sent speaks the words of God, for God[k] gives the Spirit without limit. [35]The Father loves the Son and has placed everything in his hands. [36]Whoever believes in the Son has eternal life, but whoever rejects the Son will not see life, for God’s wrath remains on him.”[l]

Jesus Talks With a Samaritan Woman

4 The Pharisees heard that Jesus was gaining and baptizing more disciples than John, [2]although in fact it was not Jesus who baptized, but his disciples. [3]When the Lord learned of this, he left Judea and went back once more to Galilee.

[4]Now he had to go through Samaria. [5]So he came to a town in Samaria called Sychar, near the plot of ground Jacob had given to his son Joseph. [6]Jacob’s well was there, and Jesus, tired as he was from the journey, sat down by the well. It was about the sixth hour.

[k] *34* Greek *he* [l] *36* Some interpreters end the quotation after verse 30.

NEW LIVING TRANSLATION

[31]“He has come from above and is greater than anyone else. I am of the earth, and my understanding is limited to the things of earth, but he has come from heaven.* [32]He tells what he has seen and heard, but how few believe what he tells them! [33]Those who believe him discover that God is true. [34]For he is sent by God. He speaks God’s words, for God’s Spirit is upon him without measure or limit. [35]The Father loves his Son, and he has given him authority over everything. [36]And all who believe in God’s Son have eternal life. Those who don’t obey the Son will never experience eternal life, but the wrath of God remains upon them.”

Jesus and the Samaritan Woman

4 Jesus* learned that the Pharisees had heard, “Jesus is baptizing and making more disciples than John” [2](though Jesus himself didn’t baptize them—his disciples did). [3]So he left Judea to return to Galilee.

[4]He had to go through Samaria on the way. [5]Eventually he came to the Samaritan village of Sychar, near the parcel of ground that Jacob gave to his son Joseph. [6]Jacob’s well was there; and Jesus, tired from the long walk, sat wearily beside the well about noontime. [7]Soon a Samaritan woman

3:31 Some manuscripts omit *but he has come from heaven.* 4:1 Some manuscripts read *The Lord.*

NEW KING JAMES VERSION

from above is above all; he who is of the earth is earthly and speaks of the earth. He who comes from heaven is above all. [32]And what He has seen and heard, that He testifies; and no one receives His testimony. [33]He who has received His testimony has certified that God is true. [34]For He whom God has sent speaks the words of God, for God does not give the Spirit by measure. [35]The Father loves the Son, and has given all things into His hand. [36]He who believes in the Son has everlasting life; and he who does not believe the Son shall not see life, but the wrath of God abides on him.”

A Samaritan Woman Meets Her Messiah

4 Therefore, when the Lord knew that the Pharisees had heard that Jesus made and baptized more disciples than John [2](though Jesus Himself did not baptize, but His disciples), [3]He left Judea and departed again to Galilee. [4]But He needed to go through Samaria.

[5]So He came to a city of Samaria which is called Sychar, near the plot of ground that Jacob gave to his son Joseph. [6]Now Jacob’s well was there. Jesus therefore, being wearied from *His* journey, sat thus by the well. It was about the sixth hour.

THE MESSAGE

“The One who comes from above is head and shoulders over other messengers from God. The earthborn is earthbound and speaks earth language; the heavenborn is in a league of his own. He sets out the evidence of what he saw and heard in heaven. No one wants to deal with these facts. But anyone who examines this evidence will come to stake his life on this: that God himself is the truth.

“The One that God sent speaks God’s words. And don’t think he rations out the Spirit in bits and pieces. The Father loves the Son extravagantly. He turned everything over to him so he could give it away—a lavish distribution of gifts. That is why whoever accepts and trusts the Son gets in on everything, life complete and forever! And that is also why the person who avoids and distrusts the Son is in the dark and doesn’t see life. All he experiences of God is darkness, and an angry darkness at that.”

The Woman at the Well

4 Jesus realized that the Pharisees were keeping count of the baptisms that he and John performed (although his disciples, not Jesus, did the actual baptizing). They had posted the score that Jesus was ahead, turning him and John into rivals in the eyes of the people. So Jesus left the Judean countryside and went back to Galilee.

To get there, he had to pass through Samaria. He came into Sychar, a Samaritan village that bordered the field Jacob had given his son Joseph. Jacob’s well was still there. Jesus, worn out by the trip, sat down at the well. It was noon.

KING JAMES VERSION

7 There cometh a woman of Samaria to draw water: Jesus saith unto her, Give me to drink.

8 (For his disciples were gone away unto the city to buy meat.)

9 Then saith the woman of Samaria unto him, How is it that thou, being a Jew, askest drink of me, which am a woman of Samaria? for the Jews have no dealings with the Samaritans.

10 Jesus answered and said unto her, If thou knewest the gift of God, and who it is that saith to thee, Give me to drink; thou wouldest have asked of him, and he would have given thee living water.

11 The woman saith unto him, Sir, thou hast nothing to draw with, and the well is deep: from whence then hast thou that living water?

12 Art thou greater than our father Jacob, which gave us the well, and drank thereof himself, and his children, and his cattle?

13 Jesus answered and said unto her, Whosoever drinketh of this water shall thirst again:

14 But whosoever drinketh of the water that I shall give him shall never thirst; but the water that I shall give him shall be in him a well of water springing up into everlasting life.

15 The woman saith unto him, Sir, give me this water, that I thirst not, neither come hither to draw.

16 Jesus saith unto her, Go, call thy husband, and come hither.

17 The woman answered and said, I have no husband.

NEW AMERICAN STANDARD BIBLE

The Woman of Samaria

7 There *came a woman of Samaria to draw water. Jesus *said to her, "Give Me a drink."

8 For His disciples had gone away into the city to buy food.

9 Therefore the Samaritan woman *said to Him, "How is it that You, being a Jew, ask me for a drink since I am a Samaritan woman?" (For Jews have no dealings with Samaritans.)

10 Jesus answered and said to her, "If you knew the gift of God, and who it is who says to you, 'Give Me a drink,' you would have asked Him, and He would have given you living water."

11 She *said to Him, "Sir, You have nothing to draw with and the well is deep; where then do You get that living water?

12 "You are not greater than our father Jacob, are You, who gave us the well, and drank of it himself and his sons and his cattle?"

13 Jesus answered and said to her, "Everyone who drinks of this water will thirst again;

14 but whoever drinks of the water that I will give him shall never thirst; but the water that I will give him will become in him a well of water springing up to eternal life."

15 The woman *said to Him, "Sir, give me this water, so I will not be thirsty nor come all the way here to draw."

16 He *said to her, "Go, call your husband and come here."

17 The woman answered and said, "I have no husband."

NEW CENTURY VERSION

7When a Samaritan woman came to the well to get some water, Jesus said to her, "Please give me a drink." 8(This happened while Jesus' followers were in town buying some food.)

9The woman said, "I am surprised that you ask me for a drink, since you are a Jewish man and I am a Samaritan woman." (Jewish people are not friends with Samaritans.[a])

10Jesus said, "If you only knew the free gift of God and who it is that is asking you for water, you would have asked him, and he would have given you living water."

11The woman said, "Sir, where will you get this living water? The well is very deep, and you have nothing to get water with. 12Are you greater than Jacob, our father, who gave us this well and drank from it himself along with his sons and flocks?"

13Jesus answered, "Everyone who drinks this water will be thirsty again, 14but whoever drinks the water I give will never be thirsty. The water I give will become a spring of water gushing up inside that person, giving eternal life."

15The woman said to him, "Sir, give me this water so I will never be thirsty again and will not have to come back here to get more water."

16Jesus told her, "Go get your husband and come back here."

17The woman answered, "I have no husband."

4:9 [a] **Jewish people...Samaritans.** This can also be translated "Jewish people don't use things that Samaritans have used."

CONTEMPORARY ENGLISH VERSION

Jesus' disciples had gone into town to buy some food, a Samaritan woman came to draw water from the well.

Jesus asked her, "Would you please give me a drink of water?"

9"You are a Jew," she replied, "and I am a Samaritan woman. How can you ask me for a drink of water when Jews and Samaritans won't have anything to do with each other?"[a]

10Jesus answered, "You don't know what God wants to give you, and you don't know who is asking you for a drink. If you did, you would ask me for the water that gives life."

11"Sir," the woman said, "you don't even have a bucket, and the well is deep. Where are you going to get this life-giving water? 12Our ancestor Jacob dug this well for us, and his family and animals got water from it. Are you greater than Jacob?"

13Jesus answered, "Everyone who drinks this water will get thirsty again. 14But no one who drinks the water I give will ever be thirsty again. The water I give is like a flowing fountain that gives eternal life."

15The woman replied, "Sir, please give me a drink of that water! Then I won't get thirsty and have to come to this well again."

16Jesus told her, "Go and bring your husband."

17-18The woman answered, "I don't have a husband."

[a] 4.9 *won't have anything to do with each other*: Or "won't use the same cups." The Samaritans lived in the land between Judea and Galilee. They worshiped God differently from the Jews and did not get along with them.

NEW INTERNATIONAL VERSION

7When a Samaritan woman came to draw water, Jesus said to her, "Will you give me a drink?" 8(His disciples had gone into the town to buy food.)

9The Samaritan woman said to him, "You are a Jew and I am a Samaritan woman. How can you ask me for a drink?" (For Jews do not associate with Samaritans.[a])

10Jesus answered her, "If you knew the gift of God and who it is that asks you for a drink, you would have asked him and he would have given you living water."

11"Sir," the woman said, "you have nothing to draw with and the well is deep. Where can you get this living water? 12Are you greater than our father Jacob, who gave us the well and drank from it himself, as did also his sons and his flocks and herds?"

13Jesus answered, "Everyone who drinks this water will be thirsty again, 14but whoever drinks the water I give him will never thirst. Indeed, the water I give him will become in him a spring of water welling up to eternal life."

15The woman said to him, "Sir, give me this water so that I won't get thirsty and have to keep coming here to draw water."

16He told her, "Go, call your husband and come back."

17"I have no husband," she replied.

[a] 9 Or *do not use dishes Samaritans have used*

NEW LIVING TRANSLATION

came to draw water, and Jesus said to her, "Please give me a drink." 8He was alone at the time because his disciples had gone into the village to buy some food.

9The woman was surprised, for Jews refuse to have anything to do with Samaritans. She said to Jesus, "You are a Jew, and I am a Samaritan woman. Why are you asking me for a drink?"

10Jesus replied, "If you only knew the gift God has for you and who I am, you would ask me, and I would give you living water."

11"But sir, you don't have a rope or a bucket," she said, "and this is a very deep well. Where would you get this living water? 12And besides, are you greater than our ancestor Jacob who gave us this well? How can you offer better water than he and his sons and his cattle enjoyed?"

13Jesus replied, "People soon become thirsty again after drinking this water. 14But the water I give them takes away thirst altogether. It becomes a perpetual spring within them, giving them eternal life."

15"Please, sir," the woman said, "give me some of that water! Then I'll never be thirsty again, and I won't have to come here to haul water."

16"Go and get your husband," Jesus told her.

17"I don't have a husband," the woman replied.

NEW KING JAMES VERSION

7A woman of Samaria came to draw water. Jesus said to her, "Give Me a drink." 8For His disciples had gone away into the city to buy food.

9Then the woman of Samaria said to Him, "How is it that You, being a Jew, ask a drink from me, a Samaritan woman?" For Jews have no dealings with Samaritans.

10Jesus answered and said to her, "If you knew the gift of God, and who it is who says to you, 'Give Me a drink,' you would have asked Him, and He would have given you living water."

11The woman said to Him, "Sir, You have nothing to draw with, and the well is deep. Where then do You get that living water? 12Are You greater than our father Jacob, who gave us the well, and drank from it himself, as well as his sons and his livestock?"

13Jesus answered and said to her, "Whoever drinks of this water will thirst again, 14but whoever drinks of the water that I shall give him will never thirst. But the water that I shall give him will become in him a fountain of water springing up into everlasting life."

15The woman said to Him, "Sir, give me this water, that I may not thirst, nor come here to draw."

16Jesus said to her, "Go, call your husband, and come here."

17The woman answered and said, "I have no husband."

THE MESSAGE

A woman, a Samaritan, came to draw water. Jesus said, "Would you give me a drink of water?" (His disciples had gone to the village to buy food for lunch.)

The Samaritan woman, taken aback, asked, "How come you, a Jew, are asking me, a Samaritan woman, for a drink?" (Jews in those days wouldn't be caught dead talking to Samaritans.)

Jesus answered, "If you knew the generosity of God and who I am, you would be asking *me* for a drink, and I would give you fresh, living water."

The woman said, "Sir, you don't even have a bucket to draw with, and this well is deep. So how are you going to get this 'living water'? Are you a better man than our ancestor Jacob, who dug this well and drank from it, he and his sons and livestock, and passed it down to us?"

Jesus said, "Everyone who drinks this water will get thirsty again and again. Anyone who drinks the water I give will never thirst—not ever. The water I give will be an artesian spring within, gushing fountains of endless life."

The woman said, "Sir, give me this water so I won't ever get thirsty, won't ever have to come back to this well again!"

He said, "Go call your husband and then come back."

"I have no husband," she said.

KING JAMES VERSION

Jesus said unto her, Thou hast well said, I have no husband:

18 For thou hast had five husbands; and he whom thou now hast is not thy husband: in that saidst thou truly.

19 The woman saith unto him, Sir, I perceive that thou art a prophet.

20 Our fathers worshipped in this mountain; and ye say, that in Jerusalem is the place where men ought to worship.

21 Jesus saith unto her, Woman, believe me, the hour cometh, when ye shall neither in this mountain, nor yet at Jerusalem, worship the Father.

22 Ye worship ye know not what: we know what we worship: for salvation is of the Jews.

23 But the hour cometh, and now is, when the true worshippers shall worship the Father in spirit and in truth: for the Father seeketh such to worship him.

24 God *is* a Spirit: and they that worship him must worship *him* in spirit and in truth.

25 The woman saith unto him, I know that Messias cometh, which is called Christ: when he is come, he will tell us all things.

26 Jesus saith unto her, I that speak unto thee am *he*.

27 ¶ And upon this came his disciples, and marvelled that he talked with the woman: yet no man said, What seekest thou? or, Why talkest thou with her?

NEW AMERICAN STANDARD BIBLE

Jesus *said to her, "You have correctly said, 'I have no husband';

18 for you have had five husbands, and the one whom you now have is not your husband; this you have said truly."

19 The woman *said to Him, "Sir, I perceive that You are a prophet.

20 "Our fathers worshiped in this mountain, and you *people* say that in Jerusalem is the place where men ought to worship."

21 Jesus *said to her, "Woman, believe Me, an hour is coming when neither in this mountain nor in Jerusalem will you worship the Father.

22 "You worship what you do not know; we worship what we know, for salvation is from the Jews.

23 "But an hour is coming, and now is, when the true worshipers will worship the Father in spirit and truth; for such people the Father seeks to be His worshipers.

24 "God is spirit, and those who worship Him must worship in spirit and truth."

25 The woman *said to Him, "I know that Messiah is coming (He who is called Christ); when that One comes, He will declare all things to us."

26 Jesus *said to her, "I who speak to you am *He.*"

27 At this point His disciples came, and they were amazed that He had been speaking with a woman, yet no one said, "What do You seek?" or, "Why do You speak with her?"

NEW CENTURY VERSION

Jesus said to her, "You are right to say you have no hus-
band. 18Really you have had five husbands, and the man
you live with now is not your husband. You told the
truth."
19The woman said, "Sir, I can see that you are a prophet.
20Our ancestors worshiped on this mountain, but you Jews
say that Jerusalem is the place where people must wor-
ship."
21Jesus said, "Believe me, woman. The time is coming
when neither in Jerusalem nor on this mountain will you
actually worship the Father. 22You Samaritans worship
something you don't understand. We understand what we
worship, because salvation comes from the Jews. 23The
time is coming when the true worshipers will worship the
Father in spirit and truth, and that time is here already.
You see, the Father too is actively seeking such people to
worship him. 24God is spirit, and those who worship him
must worship in spirit and truth."
25The woman said, "I know that the Messiah is coming."
(Messiah is the One called Christ.) "When the Messiah
comes, he will explain everything to us."
26Then Jesus said, "I am he—I, the one talking to you."
27Just then his followers came back from town and were
surprised to see him talking with a woman. But none of
them asked, "What do you want?" or "Why are you talking
with her?"

CONTEMPORARY ENGLISH VERSION

"That's right," Jesus replied, "you're telling the truth.
You don't have a husband. You have already been married
five times, and the man you are now living with isn't your
husband."
19The woman said, "Sir, I can see that you are a proph-
et. 20My ancestors worshiped on this mountain,[b] but you
Jews say Jerusalem is the only place to worship."
21Jesus said to her:

Believe me, the time is coming when you won't worship
the Father either on this mountain or in Jerusalem. 22You
Samaritans don't really know the one you worship. But
we Jews do know the God we worship, and by using us,
God will save the world. 23But a time is coming, and it is
already here! Even now the true worshipers are being led
by the Spirit to worship the Father according to the truth.
These are the ones the Father is seeking to worship him.
24God is Spirit, and those who worship God must be led
by the Spirit to worship him according to the truth.

25The woman said, "I know that the Messiah will come.
He is the one we call Christ. When he comes, he will
explain everything to us."
26"I am that one," Jesus told her, "and I am speaking to
you now."
27The disciples returned about this time and were sur-
prised to find Jesus talking with a woman. But none of
them asked him what he wanted or why he was talking
with her.

[b] **4.20** *this mountain*: Mount Gerizim, near the city of Shechem.

NEW INTERNATIONAL VERSION

Jesus said to her, "You are right when you say you have
no husband. [18]The fact is, you have had five husbands,
and the man you now have is not your husband. What you
have just said is quite true."
[19]"Sir," the woman said, "I can see that you are a proph-
et. [20]Our fathers worshiped on this mountain, but you
Jews claim that the place where we must worship is in
Jerusalem."
[21]Jesus declared, "Believe me, woman, a time is coming
when you will worship the Father neither on this mountain
nor in Jerusalem. [22]You Samaritans worship what you do
not know; we worship what we do know, for salvation is
from the Jews. [23]Yet a time is coming and has now come
when the true worshipers will worship the Father in spirit
and truth, for they are the kind of worshipers the Father
seeks. [24]God is spirit, and his worshipers must worship in
spirit and in truth."
[25]The woman said, "I know that Messiah" (called Christ)
"is coming. When he comes, he will explain everything
to us."
[26]Then Jesus declared, "I who speak to you am he."

The Disciples Rejoin Jesus

[27]Just then his disciples returned and were surprised to
find him talking with a woman. But no one asked, "What
do you want?" or "Why are you talking with her?"

NEW LIVING TRANSLATION

Jesus said, "You're right! You don't have a husband—
[18]for you have had five husbands, and you aren't even
married to the man you're living with now."
[19]"Sir," the woman said, "you must be a prophet. [20]So
tell me, why is it that you Jews insist that Jerusalem is the
only place of worship, while we Samaritans claim it is here
at Mount Gerizim,* where our ancestors worshiped?"
[21]Jesus replied, "Believe me, the time is coming when it
will no longer matter whether you worship the Father here
or in Jerusalem. [22]You Samaritans know so little about the
one you worship, while we Jews know all about him, for
salvation comes through the Jews. [23]But the time is com-
ing and is already here when true worshipers will worship
the Father in spirit and in truth. The Father is looking for
anyone who will worship him that way. [24]For God is Spirit,
so those who worship him must worship in spirit and in
truth."
[25]The woman said, "I know the Messiah will come—the
one who is called Christ. When he comes, he will explain
everything to us."
[26]Then Jesus told her, "I am the Messiah!"*
[27]Just then his disciples arrived. They were astonished to
find him talking to a woman, but none of them asked him
why he was doing it or what they had been discussing.

4:20 Greek *on this mountain.* **4:26** Greek *"I am, the one speaking to you."*

NEW KING JAMES VERSION

Jesus said to her, "You have well said, 'I have no hus-
band,' [18]for you have had five husbands, and the one
whom you now have is not your husband; in that you
spoke truly."
[19]The woman said to Him, "Sir, I perceive that You are a
prophet. [20]Our fathers worshiped on this mountain, and
you *Jews* say that in Jerusalem is the place where one
ought to worship."
[21]Jesus said to her, "Woman, believe Me, the hour is
coming when you will neither on this mountain, nor in Je-
rusalem, worship the Father. [22]You worship what you do
not know; we know what we worship, for salvation is of
the Jews. [23]But the hour is coming, and now is, when the
true worshipers will worship the Father in spirit and truth;
for the Father is seeking such to worship Him. [24]God *is*
Spirit, and those who worship Him must worship in spirit
and truth."
[25]The woman said to Him, "I know that Messiah is com-
ing" (who is called Christ). "When He comes, He will tell
us all things."
[26]Jesus said to her, "I who speak to you am *He*."

The Whitened Harvest

[27]And at this *point* His disciples came, and they mar-
veled that He talked with a woman; yet no one said, "What
do You seek?" or, "Why are You talking with her?"

THE MESSAGE

"That's nicely put: 'I have no husband.' You've had five husbands, and the man you're living with now isn't even your husband. You spoke the truth there, sure enough."

"Oh, so you're a prophet! Well, tell me this: Our ancestors worshiped God at this mountain, but you Jews insist that Jerusalem is the only place for worship, right?"

"Believe me, woman, the time is coming when you Samaritans will worship the Father neither here at this mountain nor there in Jerusalem. You worship guessing in the dark; we Jews worship in the clear light of day. God's way of salvation is made available through the Jews. But the time is coming—it has, in fact, come—when what you're called will not matter and where you go to worship will not matter.

"It's who you are and the way you live that count before God. Your worship must engage your spirit in the pursuit of truth. That's the kind of people the Father is out looking for: those who are simply and honestly *themselves* before him in their worship. God is sheer being itself—Spirit. Those who worship him must do it out of their very being, their spirits, their true selves, in adoration."

The woman said, "I don't know about that. I do know that the Messiah is coming. When he arrives, we'll get the whole story."

"I am he," said Jesus. "You don't have to wait any longer or look any further."

Just then his disciples came back. They were shocked. They couldn't believe he was talking with that kind of a woman. No one said what they were all thinking, but their faces showed it.

KING JAMES VERSION

28 The woman then left her waterpot, and went her way into the city, and saith to the men,

29 Come, see a man, which told me all things that ever I did: is not this the Christ?

30 Then they went out of the city, and came unto him.

31 In the mean while his disciples prayed him, saying, Master, eat.

32 But he said unto them, I have meat to eat that ye know not of.

33 Therefore said the disciples one to another, Hath any man brought him *ought* to eat?

34 Jesus saith unto them, My meat is to do the will of him that sent me, and to finish his work.

35 Say not ye, There are yet four months, and *then* cometh harvest? behold, I say unto you, Lift up your eyes, and look on the fields; for they are white already to harvest.

36 And he that reapeth receiveth wages, and gathereth fruit unto life eternal: that both he that soweth and he that reapeth may rejoice together.

37 And herein is that saying true, One soweth, and another reapeth.

38 I sent you to reap that whereon ye bestowed no labour: other men laboured, and ye are entered into their labours.

39 And many of the Samaritans of that city believed on him for the saying of the woman, which testified, He told me all that ever I did.

NEW AMERICAN STANDARD BIBLE

28 So the woman left her waterpot, and went into the city and *said to the men,

29 "Come, see a man who told me all the things that I *have* done; this is not the Christ, is it?"

30 They went out of the city, and were coming to Him.

31 Meanwhile the disciples were urging Him, saying, "Rabbi, eat."

32 But He said to them, "I have food to eat that you do not know about."

33 So the disciples were saying to one another, "No one brought Him *anything* to eat, did he?"

34 Jesus *said to them, "My food is to do the will of Him who sent Me and to accomplish His work.

35 "Do you not say, 'There are yet four months, and *then* comes the harvest'? Behold, I say to you, lift up your eyes and look on the fields, that they are white for harvest.

36 "Already he who reaps is receiving wages and is gathering fruit for life eternal; so that he who sows and he who reaps may rejoice together.

37 "For in this *case* the saying is true, 'One sows and another reaps.'

38 "I sent you to reap that for which you have not labored; others have labored and you have entered into their labor."

The Samaritans

39 From that city many of the Samaritans believed in Him because of the word of the woman who testified, "He told me all the things that I *have* done."

NEW CENTURY VERSION

28Then the woman left her water jar and went back to town. She said to the people, 29"Come and see a man who told me everything I ever did. Do you think he might be the Christ?" 30So the people left the town and went to see Jesus.

31Meanwhile, his followers were begging him, "Teacher, eat something."

32But Jesus answered, "I have food to eat that you know nothing about."

33So the followers asked themselves, "Did somebody already bring him food?"

34Jesus said, "My food is to do what the One who sent me wants me to do and to finish his work. 35You have a saying, 'Four more months till harvest.' But I tell you, open your eyes and look at the fields ready for harvest now. 36Already, the one who harvests is being paid and is gathering crops for eternal life. So the one who plants and the one who harvests celebrate at the same time. 37Here the saying is true, 'One person plants, and another harvests.' 38I sent you to harvest a crop that you did not work on. Others did the work, and you get to finish up their work."[b]

39Many of the Samaritans in that town believed in Jesus because of what the woman said: "He told me everything I

4:38 [b] **But I...their work.** As a farmer sends workers to harvest grain, Jesus sends his followers out to bring people to God.

CONTEMPORARY ENGLISH VERSION

28The woman left her water jar and ran back into town. She said to the people, 29"Come and see a man who told me everything I have ever done! Could he be the Messiah?" 30Everyone in town went out to see Jesus.

31While this was happening, Jesus' disciples were saying to him, "Teacher, please eat something."

32But Jesus told them, "I have food that you don't know anything about."

33His disciples started asking each other, "Has someone brought him something to eat?"

34Jesus said:

My food is to do what God wants! He is the one who sent me, and I must finish the work that he gave me to do. 35You may say that there are still four months until harvest time. But I tell you to look, and you will see that the fields are ripe and ready to harvest.

36Even now the harvest workers are receiving their reward by gathering a harvest that brings eternal life. Then everyone who planted the seed and everyone who harvests the crop will celebrate together. 37So the saying proves true, "Some plant the seed, and others harvest the crop." 38I am sending you to harvest crops in fields where others have done all the hard work.

39A lot of Samaritans in that town put their faith in Jesus because the woman had said, "This man told me

NEW INTERNATIONAL VERSION

[28]Then, leaving her water jar, the woman went back to
the town and said to the people, [29]"Come, see a man who
told me everything I ever did. Could this be the Christ[b]?"
[30]They came out of the town and made their way toward
him.
[31]Meanwhile his disciples urged him, "Rabbi, eat something."
[32]But he said to them, "I have food to eat that you know
nothing about."
[33]Then his disciples said to each other, "Could someone
have brought him food?"
[34]"My food," said Jesus, "is to do the will of him who
sent me and to finish his work. [35]Do you not say, 'Four
months more and then the harvest'? I tell you, open your
eyes and look at the fields! They are ripe for harvest.
[36]Even now the reaper draws his wages, even now he harvests the crop for eternal life, so that the sower and the
reaper may be glad together. [37]Thus the saying 'One sows
and another reaps' is true. [38]I sent you to reap what you
have not worked for. Others have done the hard work, and
you have reaped the benefits of their labor."

Many Samaritans Believe

[39]Many of the Samaritans from that town believed in him
because of the woman's testimony, "He told me everything

b 29 Or *Messiah*

NEW LIVING TRANSLATION

[28]The woman left her water jar beside the well and went
back to the village and told everyone, [29]"Come and meet a
man who told me everything I ever did! Can this be the
Messiah?" [30]So the people came streaming from the village
to see him.
[31]Meanwhile, the disciples were urging Jesus to eat.
[32]"No," he said, "I have food you don't know about."
[33]"Who brought it to him?" the disciples asked each
other.
[34]Then Jesus explained: "My nourishment comes from
doing the will of God, who sent me, and from finishing his
work. [35]Do you think the work of harvesting will not begin
until the summer ends four months from now? Look
around you! Vast fields are ripening all around us and are
ready now for the harvest. [36]The harvesters are paid good
wages, and the fruit they harvest is people brought to eternal life. What joy awaits both the planter and the harvester alike! [37]You know the saying, 'One person plants
and someone else harvests.' And it's true. [38]I sent you to
harvest where you didn't plant; others had already done
the work, and you will gather the harvest."

Many Samaritans Believe

[39]Many Samaritans from the village believed in Jesus
because the woman had said, "He told me everything I

NEW KING JAMES VERSION

[28]The woman then left her waterpot, went her way into
the city, and said to the men, [29]"Come, see a Man who told
me all things that I ever did. Could this be the Christ?"
[30]Then they went out of the city and came to Him.
[31]In the meantime His disciples urged Him, saying,
"Rabbi, eat."
[32]But He said to them, "I have food to eat of which you
do not know."
[33]Therefore the disciples said to one another, "Has anyone brought Him *anything* to eat?"
[34]Jesus said to them, "My food is to do the will of Him
who sent Me, and to finish His work. [35]Do you not say,
'There are still four months and *then* comes the harvest'?
Behold, I say to you, lift up your eyes and look at the
fields, for they are already white for harvest! [36]And he who
reaps receives wages, and gathers fruit for eternal life, that
both he who sows and he who reaps may rejoice together.
[37]For in this the saying is true: 'One sows and another
reaps.' [38]I sent you to reap that for which you have not
labored; others have labored, and you have entered into
their labors."

The Savior of the World

[39]And many of the Samaritans of that city believed in
Him because of the word of the woman who testified, "He

THE MESSAGE

The woman took the hint and left. In her confusion she left her water pot. Back in the village she told the people, "Come see a man who knew all about the things I did, who knows me inside and out. Do you think this could be the Messiah?" And they went out to see for themselves.

It's Harvest Time

In the meantime, the disciples pressed him, "Rabbi, eat. Aren't you going to eat?"

He told them, "I have food to eat you know nothing about."

The disciples were puzzled. "Who could have brought him food?"

Jesus said, "The food that keeps me going is that I do the will of the One who sent me, finishing the work he started. As you look around right now, wouldn't you say that in about four months it will be time to harvest? Well, I'm telling you to open your eyes and take a good look at what's right in front of you. These Samaritan fields are ripe. It's harvest time!

"The Harvester isn't waiting. He's taking his pay, gathering in this grain that's ripe for eternal life. Now the Sower is arm in arm with the Harvester, triumphant. That's the truth of the saying, 'This one sows, that one harvests.' I sent you to harvest a field you never worked. Without lifting a finger, you have walked in on a field worked long and hard by others."

Many of the Samaritans from that village committed themselves to him because of the woman's witness: "He knew all about the things I did. He knows me inside and

KING JAMES VERSION

40 So when the Samaritans were come unto him, they besought him that he would tarry with them: and he abode there two days.

41 And many more believed because of his own word;

42 And said unto the woman, Now we believe, not because of thy saying: for we have heard *him* ourselves, and know that this is indeed the Christ, the Saviour of the world.

43 ¶ Now after two days he departed thence, and went into Galilee.

44 For Jesus himself testified, that a prophet hath no honour in his own country.

45 Then when he was come into Galilee, the Galilaeans received him, having seen all the things that he did at Jerusalem at the feast: for they also went unto the feast.

46 So Jesus came again into Cana of Galilee, where he made the water wine. And there was a certain nobleman, whose son was sick at Capernaum.

47 When he heard that Jesus was come out of Judaea into Galilee, he went unto him, and besought him that he would come down, and heal his son: for he was at the point of death.

48 Then said Jesus unto him, Except ye see signs and wonders, ye will not believe.

49 The nobleman saith unto him, Sir, come down ere my child die.

NEW AMERICAN STANDARD BIBLE

40 So when the Samaritans came to Jesus, they were asking Him to stay with them; and He stayed there two days.

41 Many more believed because of His word;

42 and they were saying to the woman, "It is no longer because of what you said that we believe, for we have heard for ourselves and know that this One is indeed the Savior of the world."

43 After the two days He went forth from there into Galilee.

44 For Jesus Himself testified that a prophet has no honor in his own country.

45 So when He came to Galilee, the Galileans received Him, having seen all the things that He did in Jerusalem at the feast; for they themselves also went to the feast.

Healing a Nobleman's Son

46 Therefore He came again to Cana of Galilee where He had made the water wine. And there was a royal official whose son was sick at Capernaum.

47 When he heard that Jesus had come out of Judea into Galilee, he went to Him and was imploring *Him* to come down and heal his son; for he was at the point of death.

48 So Jesus said to him, "Unless you *people* see signs and wonders, you *simply* will not believe."

49 The royal official *said to Him, "Sir, come down before my child dies."

NEW CENTURY VERSION

ever did." 40When the Samaritans came to Jesus, they begged him to stay with them, so he stayed there two more days. 41And many more believed because of the things he said.

42They said to the woman, "First we believed in Jesus because of your speech, but now we believe because we heard him ourselves. We know that this man really is the Savior of the world."

Jesus Heals an Officer's Son

43Two days later, Jesus left and went to Galilee. 44(Jesus had said before that a prophet is not respected in his own country.) 45When Jesus arrived in Galilee, the people there welcomed him. They had seen all the things he did at the Passover Feast in Jerusalem, because they had been there, too.

46Jesus went again to visit Cana in Galilee where he had changed the water into wine. One of the king's important officers lived in the city of Capernaum, and his son was sick. 47When he heard that Jesus had come from Judea to Galilee, he went to Jesus and begged him to come to Capernaum and heal his son, because his son was almost dead. 48Jesus said to him, "You people must see signs and miracles before you will believe in me."

49The officer said, "Sir, come before my child dies."

CONTEMPORARY ENGLISH VERSION

everything I have ever done." 40They came and asked him to stay in their town, and he stayed on for two days.

41Many more Samaritans put their faith in Jesus because of what they heard him say. 42They told the woman, "We no longer have faith in Jesus just because of what you told us. We have heard him ourselves, and we are certain that he is the Savior of the world!"

Jesus Heals an Official's Son (Matthew 8.5-13; Luke 7.1-10)

43-44Jesus had said, "Prophets are honored everywhere, except in their own country." Then two days later he left 45and went to Galilee. The people there welcomed him, because they had gone to the festival in Jerusalem and had seen everything he had done.

46While Jesus was in Galilee, he returned to the village of Cana, where he had turned the water into wine. There was an official in Capernaum whose son was sick. 47And when the man heard that Jesus had come from Judea, he went and begged him to keep his son from dying.

48Jesus told the official, "You won't have faith unless you see miracles and wonders!"

49The man replied, "Lord, please come before my son dies!"

NEW INTERNATIONAL VERSION

I ever did." 40So when the Samaritans came to him, they urged him to stay with them, and he stayed two days. 41And because of his words many more became believers.

42They said to the woman, "We no longer believe just because of what you said; now we have heard for ourselves, and we know that this man really is the Savior of the world."

Jesus Heals the Official's Son

43After the two days he left for Galilee. 44(Now Jesus himself had pointed out that a prophet has no honor in his own country.) 45When he arrived in Galilee, the Galileans welcomed him. They had seen all that he had done in Jerusalem at the Passover Feast, for they also had been there.

46Once more he visited Cana in Galilee, where he had turned the water into wine. And there was a certain royal official whose son lay sick at Capernaum. 47When this man heard that Jesus had arrived in Galilee from Judea, he went to him and begged him to come and heal his son, who was close to death.

48"Unless you people see miraculous signs and wonders," Jesus told him, "you will never believe."

49The royal official said, "Sir, come down before my child dies."

NEW LIVING TRANSLATION

ever did!" 40When they came out to see him, they begged him to stay at their village. So he stayed for two days, 41long enough for many of them to hear his message and believe. 42Then they said to the woman, "Now we believe because we have heard him ourselves, not just because of what you told us. He is indeed the Savior of the world."

Jesus Heals an Official's Son

43At the end of the two days' stay, Jesus went on into Galilee. 44He had previously said, "A prophet is honored everywhere except in his own country." 45The Galileans welcomed him, for they had been in Jerusalem at the Passover celebration and had seen all his miraculous signs.

46In the course of his journey through Galilee, he arrived at the town of Cana, where he had turned the water into wine. There was a government official in the city of Capernaum whose son was very sick. 47When he heard that Jesus had come from Judea and was traveling in Galilee, he went over to Cana. He found Jesus and begged him to come to Capernaum with him to heal his son, who was about to die.

48Jesus asked, "Must I do miraculous signs and wonders before you people will believe in me?"

49The official pleaded, "Lord, please come now before my little boy dies."

NEW KING JAMES VERSION

told me all that I *ever* did." 40So when the Samaritans had come to Him, they urged Him to stay with them; and He stayed there two days. 41And many more believed because of His own word.

42Then they said to the woman, "Now we believe, not because of what you said, for we ourselves have heard *Him* and we know that this is indeed the Christ,[a] the Savior of the world."

Welcome at Galilee

43Now after the two days He departed from there and went to Galilee. 44For Jesus Himself testified that a prophet has no honor in his own country. 45So when He came to Galilee, the Galileans received Him, having seen all the things He did in Jerusalem at the feast; for they also had gone to the feast.

A Nobleman's Son Healed

46So Jesus came again to Cana of Galilee where He had made the water wine. And there was a certain nobleman whose son was sick at Capernaum. 47When he heard that Jesus had come out of Judea into Galilee, he went to Him and implored Him to come down and heal his son, for he was at the point of death. 48Then Jesus said to him, "Unless you *people* see signs and wonders, you will by no means believe."

49The nobleman said to Him, "Sir, come down before my child dies!"

4:42 [a] NU-Text omits *the Christ.*

THE MESSAGE

out!" They asked him to stay on, so Jesus stayed two days. A lot more people entrusted their lives to him when they heard what he had to say. They said to the woman, "We're no longer taking this on your say-so. We've heard it for ourselves and know it for sure. He's the Savior of the world!"

After the two days he left for Galilee. Now, Jesus knew well from experience that a prophet is not respected in the place where he grew up. So when he arrived in Galilee, the Galileans welcomed him, but only because they were impressed with what he had done in Jerusalem during the Passover Feast, not that they really had a clue about who he was or what he was up to.

Now he was back in Cana of Galilee, the place where he made the water into wine. Meanwhile in Capernaum, there was a certain official from the king's court whose son was sick. When he heard that Jesus had come from Judea to Galilee, he went and asked that he come down and heal his son, who was on the brink of death. Jesus put him off: "Unless you people are dazzled by a miracle, you refuse to believe."

But the court official wouldn't be put off. "Come down! It's life or death for my son."

KING JAMES VERSION

50 Jesus saith unto him, Go thy way; thy son liveth. And the man believed the word that Jesus had spoken unto him, and he went his way.

51 And as he was now going down, his servants met him, and told *him*, saying, Thy son liveth.

52 Then enquired he of them the hour when he began to amend. And they said unto him, Yesterday at the seventh hour the fever left him.

53 So the father knew that *it was* at the same hour, in the which Jesus said unto him, Thy son liveth: and himself believed, and his whole house.

54 This *is* again the second miracle *that* Jesus did, when he was come out of Judaea into Galilee.

5 After this there was a feast of the Jews; and Jesus went up to Jerusalem.

2 Now there is at Jerusalem by the sheep *market* a pool, which is called in the Hebrew tongue Bethesda, having five porches.

3 In these lay a great multitude of impotent folk, of blind, halt, withered, waiting for the moving of the water.

4 For an angel went down at a certain season into the pool, and troubled the water: whosoever then first after the troubling of the water stepped in was made whole of whatsoever disease he had.

5 And a certain man was there, which had an infirmity thirty and eight years.

6 When Jesus saw him lie, and knew that he had been

NEW AMERICAN STANDARD BIBLE

50 Jesus *said to him, "Go; your son lives." The man believed the word that Jesus spoke to him and started off.

51 As he was now going down, *his* slaves met him, saying that his son was living.

52 So he inquired of them the hour when he began to get better. Then they said to him, "Yesterday at the [2]seventh hour the fever left him."

53 So the father knew that *it was* at that hour in which Jesus said to him, "Your son lives"; and he himself believed and his whole household.

54 This is again a second sign that Jesus performed when He had come out of Judea into Galilee.

The Healing at Bethesda

5 After these things there was a feast of the Jews, and Jesus went up to Jerusalem.

2 Now there is in Jerusalem by the sheep *gate* a pool, which is called in Hebrew Bethesda, having five porticoes.

3 In these lay a multitude of those who were sick, blind, lame, and withered, [[1]waiting for the moving of the waters;

4 for an angel of the Lord went down at certain seasons into the pool and stirred up the water; whoever then first, after the stirring up of the water, stepped in was made well from whatever disease with which he was afflicted.]

5 A man was there who had been ill for thirty-eight years.

6 When Jesus saw him lying *there*, and knew that he

4:52 [2] Perhaps 7 p.m. Roman time or 1 p.m. Jewish time   5:3 [1] Early mss do not contain the remainder of v 3, nor v 4

NEW CENTURY VERSION

50 Jesus answered, "Go. Your son will live."

The man believed what Jesus told him and went home. 51 On the way the man's servants came and met him and told him, "Your son is alive."

52 The man asked, "What time did my son begin to get well?"

They answered, "Yesterday at one o'clock the fever left him."

53 The father knew that one o'clock was the exact time that Jesus had said, "Your son will live." So the man and all the people who lived in his house believed in Jesus.

54 That was the second miracle Jesus did after coming from Judea to Galilee.

Jesus Heals a Man at a Pool

5 Later Jesus went to Jerusalem for a special Jewish feast. 2 In Jerusalem there is a pool with five covered porches, which is called Bethzatha[a] in the Jewish language.[b] This pool is near the Sheep Gate. 3 Many sick people were lying on the porches beside the pool. Some were blind, some were crippled, and some were paralyzed.[c] 5 A man was lying there who had been sick for thirty-eight years. 6 When Jesus saw the man and knew that he had

5:2 [a] **Bethzatha** Also called Bethsaida or Bethesda, a pool of water north of the Temple in Jerusalem.   5:2 [b] **Jewish language** Hebrew or Aramaic, the languages of the Jewish people in the first century.
5:3 [c] **Verse 3** Some Greek copies add "and they waited for the water to move." A few later copies add verse 4: "Sometimes an angel of the Lord came down to the pool and stirred up the water. After the angel did this, the first person to go into the pool was healed from any sickness he had."

CONTEMPORARY ENGLISH VERSION

50 Jesus then said, "Your son will live. Go on home to him." The man believed Jesus and started back home.

51 Some of the official's servants met him along the road and told him, "Your son is better!" 52 He asked them when the boy got better, and they answered, "The fever left him yesterday at one o'clock."

53 The boy's father realized that at one o'clock the day before, Jesus had told him, "Your son will live!" So the man and everyone in his family put their faith in Jesus.

54 This was the second miracle[c] that Jesus worked after he left Judea and went to Galilee.

Jesus Heals a Sick Man

5 Later, Jesus went to Jerusalem for another Jewish festival.[a] 2 In the city near the sheep gate was a pool with five porches, and its name in Hebrew was Bethzatha.[b]

3-4 Many sick, blind, lame, and crippled people were lying close to the pool.[c]

5 Beside the pool was a man who had been sick for thirty-eight years. 6 When Jesus saw the man and realized that

[c] **4.54** *miracle*: See the note at 2.11.   [a] **5.1** *another Jewish festival*: Either the Festival of Shelters or Passover.   [b] **5.2** *Bethzatha*: Some manuscripts have "Bethesda" and others have "Bethsaida."
[c] **5.3,4** *pool*: Some manuscripts add, "They were waiting for the water to be stirred, because an angel from the Lord would sometimes come down and stir it. The first person to get into the pool after that would be healed."

NEW INTERNATIONAL VERSION

50 Jesus replied, "You may go. Your son will live."
The man took Jesus at his word and departed. 51 While
he was still on the way, his servants met him with the
news that his boy was living. 52 When he inquired as to the
time when his son got better, they said to him, "The fever
left him yesterday at the seventh hour."
53 Then the father realized that this was the exact time at
which Jesus had said to him, "Your son will live." So he
and all his household believed.
54 This was the second miraculous sign that Jesus per-
formed, having come from Judea to Galilee.

The Healing at the Pool

5 Some time later, Jesus went up to Jerusalem for a
feast of the Jews. 2 Now there is in Jerusalem near the
Sheep Gate a pool, which in Aramaic is called Bethesda[a]
and which is surrounded by five covered colonnades. 3 Here
a great number of disabled people used to lie—the blind,
the lame, the paralyzed.[b] 5 One who was there had been an
invalid for thirty-eight years. 6 When Jesus saw him lying

[a] *2* Some manuscripts *Bethzatha*; other manuscripts *Bethsaida*
[b] *3* Some less important manuscripts *paralyzed—and they waited for the moving of the waters. 4From time to time an angel of the Lord would come down and stir up the waters. The first one into the pool after each such disturbance would be cured of whatever disease he had.*

NEW LIVING TRANSLATION

50 Then Jesus told him, "Go back home. Your son will
live!" And the man believed Jesus' word and started home.
51 While he was on his way, some of his servants met
him with the news that his son was alive and well. 52 He
asked them when the boy had begun to feel better, and
they replied, "Yesterday afternoon at one o'clock his fever
suddenly disappeared!" 53 Then the father realized it was
the same time that Jesus had told him, "Your son will
live." And the officer and his entire household believed in
Jesus. 54 This was Jesus' second miraculous sign in Galilee
after coming from Judea.

Jesus Heals a Lame Man

5 Afterward Jesus returned to Jerusalem for one of the
Jewish holy days. 2 Inside the city, near the Sheep
Gate, was the pool of Bethesda,* with five covered porches.
3 Crowds of sick people—blind, lame, or paralyzed—lay on
the porches.* 5 One of the men lying there had been sick for
thirty-eight years. 6 When Jesus saw him and knew how

5:2 Some manuscripts read *Beth-zatha;* other manuscripts read *Bethsaida.* 5:3 Some manuscripts add *waiting for a certain movement of the water, 4for an angel of the Lord came from time to time and stirred up the water. And the first person to step down into it afterward was healed.*

NEW KING JAMES VERSION

50 Jesus said to him, "Go your way; your son lives." So
the man believed the word that Jesus spoke to him, and he
went his way. 51 And as he was now going down, his ser-
vants met him and told *him,* saying, "Your son lives!"
52 Then he inquired of them the hour when he got better.
And they said to him, "Yesterday at the seventh hour the
fever left him." 53 So the father knew that *it was* at the
same hour in which Jesus said to him, "Your son lives."
And he himself believed, and his whole household.
54 This again *is* the second sign Jesus did when He had
come out of Judea into Galilee.

A Man Healed at the Pool of Bethesda

5 After this there was a feast of the Jews, and Jesus
went up to Jerusalem. 2 Now there is in Jerusalem by
the Sheep *Gate* a pool, which is called in Hebrew, Be-
thesda,[a] having five porches. 3 In these lay a great multi-
tude of sick people, blind, lame, paralyzed, waiting for the
moving of the water. 4 For an angel went down at a certain
time into the pool and stirred up the water; then whoever
stepped in first, after the stirring of the water, was made
well of whatever disease he had.[b] 5 Now a certain man was
there who had an infirmity thirty-eight years. 6 When Jesus
saw him lying there, and knew that he already had been *in*

5:2 [a] NU-Text reads *Bethzatha.* 5:4 [b] NU-Text omits *waiting for the moving of the water* at the end of verse 3, and all of verse 4.

THE MESSAGE

Jesus simply replied, "Go home. Your son lives."
The man believed the bare word Jesus spoke and headed
home. On his way back, his servants intercepted him and
announced, "Your son lives!"
He asked them what time he began to get better. They
said, "The fever broke yesterday afternoon at one o'clock."
The father knew that that was the very moment Jesus had
said, "Your son lives."
That clinched it. Not only he but his entire household
believed. This was now the second sign Jesus gave after
having come from Judea into Galilee.

Even On the Sabbath

5 Soon another Feast came around and Jesus was back
in Jerusalem. Near the Sheep Gate in Jerusalem there
was a pool, in Hebrew called *Bethesda,* with five alcoves.
Hundreds of sick people—blind, crippled, paralyzed—were
in these alcoves. One man had been an invalid there for
thirty-eight years. When Jesus saw him stretched out by

KING JAMES VERSION

now a long time *in that case,* he saith unto him, Wilt thou be made whole?

7 The impotent man answered him, Sir, I have no man, when the water is troubled, to put me into the pool: but while I am coming, another steppeth down before me.

8 Jesus saith unto him, Rise, take up thy bed, and walk.

9 And immediately the man was made whole, and took up his bed, and walked: and on the same day was the sabbath.

10 The Jews therefore said unto him that was cured, It is the sabbath day: it is not lawful for thee to carry *thy* bed.

11 He answered them, He that made me whole, the same said unto me, Take up thy bed, and walk.

12 Then asked they him, What man is that which said unto thee, Take up thy bed, and walk?

13 And he that was healed wist not who it was: for Jesus had conveyed himself away, a multitude being in *that* place.

14 Afterward Jesus findeth him in the temple, and said unto him, Behold, thou art made whole: sin no more, lest a worse thing come unto thee.

15 The man departed, and told the Jews that it was Jesus, which had made him whole.

16 And therefore did the Jews persecute Jesus, and sought to slay him, because he had done these things on the sabbath day.

17 ¶ But Jesus answered them, My Father worketh hitherto, and I work.

NEW AMERICAN STANDARD BIBLE

had already been a long time *in that condition,* He *said to him, "Do you wish to get well?"

7 The sick man answered Him, "Sir, I have no man to put me into the pool when the water is stirred up, but while I am coming, another steps down before me."

8 Jesus *said to him, "Get up, pick up your pallet and walk."

9 Immediately the man became well, and picked up his pallet and *began* to walk.

Now it was the Sabbath on that day.

10 So the Jews were saying to the man who was cured, "It is the Sabbath, and it is not permissible for you to carry your pallet."

11 But he answered them, "He who made me well was the one who said to me, 'Pick up your pallet and walk.' "

12 They asked him, "Who is the man who said to you, 'Pick up *your pallet* and walk'?"

13 But the man who was healed did not know who it was, for Jesus had slipped away while there was a crowd in *that* place.

14 Afterward Jesus *found him in the temple and said to him, "Behold, you have become well; do not sin anymore, so that nothing worse happens to you."

15 The man went away, and told the Jews that it was Jesus who had made him well.

16 For this reason the Jews were persecuting Jesus, because He was doing these things on the Sabbath.

17 But He answered them, "My Father is working until now, and I Myself am working."

NEW CENTURY VERSION

been sick for such a long time, Jesus asked him, "Do you
want to be well?"

7 The sick man answered, "Sir, there is no one to help me
get into the pool when the water starts moving. While I am
coming to the water, someone else always gets in before
me."

8 Then Jesus said, "Stand up. Pick up your mat and
walk." 9 And immediately the man was well; he picked up
his mat and began to walk.

The day this happened was a Sabbath day. 10 So the Jews
said to the man who had been healed, "Today is the
Sabbath. It is against our law for you to carry your mat on
the Sabbath day."

11 But he answered, "The man who made me well told
me, 'Pick up your mat and walk.' "

12 Then they asked him, "Who is the man who told you
to pick up your mat and walk?"

13 But the man who had been healed did not know who it
was, because there were many people in that place, and
Jesus had left.

14 Later, Jesus found the man at the Temple and said to
him, "See, you are well now. Stop sinning so that something worse does not happen to you."

15 Then the man left and told the Jews that Jesus was the
one who had made him well.

16 Because Jesus was doing this on the Sabbath day, the
Jews began to persecute him. 17 But Jesus said to them,
"My Father never stops working, and so I keep working,
too."

CONTEMPORARY ENGLISH VERSION

he had been crippled for a long time, he asked him, "Do
you want to be healed?"

7 The man answered, "Lord, I don't have anyone to put
me in the pool when the water is stirred up. I try to get in,
but someone else always gets there first."

8 Jesus told him, "Pick up your mat and walk!" 9 Right
then the man was healed. He picked up his mat and started walking around. The day on which this happened was a
Sabbath.

10 When the Jewish leaders saw the man carrying his
mat, they said to him, "This is the Sabbath! No one is
allowed to carry a mat on the Sabbath."

11 But he replied, "The man who healed me told me to
pick up my mat and walk."

12 They asked him, "Who is this man that told you to
pick up your mat and walk?" 13 But he did not know who
Jesus was, and Jesus had left because of the crowd.

14 Later, Jesus met the man in the temple and told him,
"You are now well. But don't sin anymore or something
worse might happen to you." 15 The man left and told the
leaders that Jesus was the one who had healed him.
16 They started making a lot of trouble for Jesus because he
did things like this on the Sabbath.

17 But Jesus said, "My Father has never stopped working,
and that is why I keep on working." 18 Now the leaders

NEW INTERNATIONAL VERSION

there and learned that he had been in this condition for a long time, he asked him, "Do you want to get well?"

7"Sir," the invalid replied, "I have no one to help me into the pool when the water is stirred. While I am trying to get in, someone else goes down ahead of me."

8Then Jesus said to him, "Get up! Pick up your mat and walk." 9At once the man was cured; he picked up his mat and walked.

The day on which this took place was a Sabbath, 10and so the Jews said to the man who had been healed, "It is the Sabbath; the law forbids you to carry your mat."

11But he replied, "The man who made me well said to me, 'Pick up your mat and walk.' "

12So they asked him, "Who is this fellow who told you to pick it up and walk?"

13The man who was healed had no idea who it was, for Jesus had slipped away into the crowd that was there.

14Later Jesus found him at the temple and said to him, "See, you are well again. Stop sinning or something worse may happen to you." 15The man went away and told the Jews that it was Jesus who had made him well.

Life Through the Son

16So, because Jesus was doing these things on the Sabbath, the Jews persecuted him. 17Jesus said to them, "My Father is always at his work to this very day, and I,

NEW LIVING TRANSLATION

long he had been ill, he asked him, "Would you like to get well?"

7"I can't, sir," the sick man said, "for I have no one to help me into the pool when the water is stirred up. While I am trying to get there, someone else always gets in ahead of me."

8Jesus told him, "Stand up, pick up your sleeping mat, and walk!"

9Instantly, the man was healed! He rolled up the mat and began walking! But this miracle happened on the Sabbath day. 10So the Jewish leaders objected. They said to the man who was cured, "You can't work on the Sabbath! It's illegal to carry that sleeping mat!"

11He replied, "The man who healed me said to me, 'Pick up your sleeping mat and walk.' "

12"Who said such a thing as that?" they demanded.

13The man didn't know, for Jesus had disappeared into the crowd. 14But afterward Jesus found him in the Temple and told him, "Now you are well; so stop sinning, or something even worse may happen to you." 15Then the man went to find the Jewish leaders and told them it was Jesus who had healed him.

Jesus Claims to Be the Son of God

16So the Jewish leaders began harassing Jesus for breaking the Sabbath rules. 17But Jesus replied, "My Father never stops working, so why should I?" 18So the Jewish

NEW KING JAMES VERSION

that condition a long time, He said to him, "Do you want to be made well?"

7The sick man answered Him, "Sir, I have no man to put me into the pool when the water is stirred up; but while I am coming, another steps down before me."

8Jesus said to him, "Rise, take up your bed and walk."
9And immediately the man was made well, took up his bed, and walked.

And that day was the Sabbath. 10The Jews therefore said to him who was cured, "It is the Sabbath; it is not lawful for you to carry your bed."

11He answered them, "He who made me well said to me, 'Take up your bed and walk.' "

12Then they asked him, "Who is the Man who said to you, 'Take up your bed and walk'?" 13But the one who was healed did not know who it was, for Jesus had withdrawn, a multitude being in *that* place. 14Afterward Jesus found him in the temple, and said to him, "See, you have been made well. Sin no more, lest a worse thing come upon you."

15The man departed and told the Jews that it was Jesus who had made him well.

Honor the Father and the Son

16For this reason the Jews persecuted Jesus, and sought to kill Him,[c] because He had done these things on the Sabbath. 17But Jesus answered them, "My Father has been working until now, and I have been working."

5:16 [c] NU-Text omits *and sought to kill Him.*

THE MESSAGE

the pool and knew how long he had been there, he said, "Do you want to get well?"

The sick man said, "Sir, when the water is stirred, I don't have anybody to put me in the pool. By the time I get there, somebody else is already in."

Jesus said, "Get up, take your bedroll, start walking." The man was healed on the spot. He picked up his bedroll and walked off.

That day happened to be the Sabbath. The Jews stopped the healed man and said, "It's the Sabbath. You can't carry your bedroll around. It's against the rules."

But he told them, "The man who made me well told me to. He said, 'Take your bedroll and start walking.'"

They asked, "Who gave you the order to take it up and start walking?" But the healed man didn't know, for Jesus had slipped away into the crowd.

A little later Jesus found him in the Temple and said, "You look wonderful! You're well! Don't return to a sinning life or something worse might happen."

The man went back and told the Jews that it was Jesus who had made him well. That is why the Jews were out to get Jesus—because he did this kind of thing on the Sabbath.

But Jesus defended himself. "My Father is working straight through, even on the Sabbath. So am I."

KING JAMES VERSION

18 Therefore the Jews sought the more to kill him, because he not only had broken the sabbath, but said also that God was his Father, making himself equal with God.

19 Then answered Jesus and said unto them, Verily, verily, I say unto you, The Son can do nothing of himself, but what he seeth the Father do: for what things soever he doeth, these also doeth the Son likewise.

20 For the Father loveth the Son, and sheweth him all things that himself doeth: and he will shew him greater works than these, that ye may marvel.

21 For as the Father raiseth up the dead, and quickeneth *them*; even so the Son quickeneth whom he will.

22 For the Father judgeth no man, but hath committed all judgment unto the Son:

23 That all *men* should honour the Son, even as they honour the Father. He that honoureth not the Son honoureth not the Father which hath sent him.

24 Verily, verily, I say unto you, He that heareth my word, and believeth on him that sent me, hath everlasting life, and shall not come into condemnation; but is passed from death unto life.

25 Verily, verily, I say unto you, The hour is coming, and now is, when the dead shall hear the voice of the Son of God: and they that hear shall live.

26 For as the Father hath life in himself; so hath he given to the Son to have life in himself;

NEW AMERICAN STANDARD BIBLE

Jesus' Equality with God

18 For this reason therefore the Jews were seeking all the more to kill Him, because He not only was breaking the Sabbath, but also was calling God His own Father, making Himself equal with God.

19 Therefore Jesus answered and was saying to them, "Truly, truly, I say to you, the Son can do nothing of Himself, unless *it is* something He sees the Father doing; for whatever the Father does, these things the Son also does in like manner.

20 "For the Father loves the Son, and shows Him all things that He Himself is doing; and *the Father* will show Him greater works than these, so that you will marvel.

21 "For just as the Father raises the dead and gives them life, even so the Son also gives life to whom He wishes.

22 "For not even the Father judges anyone, but He has given all judgment to the Son,

23 so that all will honor the Son even as they honor the Father. He who does not honor the Son does not honor the Father who sent Him.

24 "Truly, truly, I say to you, he who hears My word, and believes Him who sent Me, has eternal life, and does not come into judgment, but has passed out of death into life.

Two Resurrections

25 "Truly, truly, I say to you, an hour is coming and now is, when the dead will hear the voice of the Son of God, and those who hear will live.

26 "For just as the Father has life in Himself, even so He gave to the Son also to have life in Himself;

NEW CENTURY VERSION

18 This made the Jews try still harder to kill him. They
said, "First Jesus was breaking the law about the Sabbath
day. Now he says that God is his own Father, making him-
self equal with God!"

Jesus Has God's Authority

19 But Jesus said, "I tell you the truth, the Son can do
nothing alone. The Son does only what he sees the Father
doing, because the Son does whatever the Father does.
20 The Father loves the Son and shows the Son all the
things he himself does. But the Father will show the Son
even greater things than this so that you can all be
amazed. 21 Just as the Father raises the dead and gives
them life, so also the Son gives life to those he wants to.
22 In fact, the Father judges no one, but he has given the
Son power to do all the judging 23 so that all people will
honor the Son as much as they honor the Father. Anyone
who does not honor the Son does not honor the Father
who sent him.

24 "I tell you the truth, whoever hears what I say and
believes in the One who sent me has eternal life. That per-
son will not be judged guilty but has already left death and
entered life. 25 I tell you the truth, the time is coming and is
already here when the dead will hear the voice of the Son
of God, and those who hear will have life. 26 Life comes
from the Father himself, and he has allowed the Son to
have life in himself as well. 27 And the Father has given the

CONTEMPORARY ENGLISH VERSION

wanted to kill Jesus for two reasons. First, he had broken the law of the Sabbath. But even worse, he had said that God was his Father, which made him equal with God.

The Son's Authority

19 Jesus told the people:

I tell you for certain that the Son cannot do anything
on his own. He can do only what he sees the Father
doing, and he does exactly what he sees the Father do.
20 The Father loves the Son and has shown him every-
thing he does. The Father will show him even greater
things, and you will be amazed. 21 Just as the Father
raises the dead and gives life, so the Son gives life to
anyone he wants to.

22 The Father doesn't judge anyone, but he has made
his Son the judge of everyone. 23 The Father wants all
people to honor the Son as much as they honor him.
When anyone refuses to honor the Son, that is the same
as refusing to honor the Father who sent him. 24 I tell
you for certain that everyone who hears my message
and has faith in the one who sent me has eternal life
and will never be condemned. They have already gone
from death to life.

25 I tell you for certain that the time will come, and it
is already here, when all of the dead will hear the voice
of the Son of God. And those who listen to it will live!
26 The Father has the power to give life, and he has given
that same power to the Son. 27 And he has given his Son

NEW INTERNATIONAL VERSION

too, am working." 18For this reason the Jews tried all the harder to kill him; not only was he breaking the Sabbath, but he was even calling God his own Father, making himself equal with God.

19Jesus gave them this answer: "I tell you the truth, the Son can do nothing by himself; he can do only what he sees his Father doing, because whatever the Father does the Son also does. 20For the Father loves the Son and shows him all he does. Yes, to your amazement he will show him even greater things than these. 21For just as the Father raises the dead and gives them life, even so the Son gives life to whom he is pleased to give it. 22Moreover, the Father judges no one, but has entrusted all judgment to the Son, 23that all may honor the Son just as they honor the Father. He who does not honor the Son does not honor the Father, who sent him.

24"I tell you the truth, whoever hears my word and believes him who sent me has eternal life and will not be condemned; he has crossed over from death to life. 25I tell you the truth, a time is coming and has now come when the dead will hear the voice of the Son of God and those who hear will live. 26For as the Father has life in himself, so he has granted the Son to have life in himself. 27And he

NEW LIVING TRANSLATION

leaders tried all the more to kill him. In addition to disobeying the Sabbath rules, he had spoken of God as his Father, thereby making himself equal with God.

19Jesus replied, "I assure you, the Son can do nothing by himself. He does only what he sees the Father doing. Whatever the Father does, the Son also does. 20For the Father loves the Son and tells him everything he is doing, and the Son will do far greater things than healing this man. You will be astonished at what he does. 21He will even raise from the dead anyone he wants to, just as the Father does. 22And the Father leaves all judgment to his Son, 23so that everyone will honor the Son, just as they honor the Father. But if you refuse to honor the Son, then you are certainly not honoring the Father who sent him.

24"I assure you, those who listen to my message and believe in God who sent me have eternal life. They will never be condemned for their sins, but they have already passed from death into life.

25"And I assure you that the time is coming, in fact it is here, when the dead will hear my voice—the voice of the Son of God. And those who listen will live. 26The Father has life in himself, and he has granted his Son to have life

NEW KING JAMES VERSION

18Therefore the Jews sought all the more to kill Him, because He not only broke the Sabbath, but also said that God was His Father, making Himself equal with God.
19Then Jesus answered and said to them, "Most assuredly, I say to you, the Son can do nothing of Himself, but what He sees the Father do; for whatever He does, the Son also does in like manner. 20For the Father loves the Son, and shows Him all things that He Himself does; and He will show Him greater works than these, that you may marvel.
21For as the Father raises the dead and gives life to *them,* even so the Son gives life to whom He will. 22For the Father judges no one, but has committed all judgment to the Son, 23that all should honor the Son just as they honor the Father. He who does not honor the Son does not honor the Father who sent Him.

Life and Judgment Are Through the Son

24"Most assuredly, I say to you, he who hears My word and believes in Him who sent Me has everlasting life, and shall not come into judgment, but has passed from death into life. 25Most assuredly, I say to you, the hour is coming, and now is, when the dead will hear the voice of the Son of God; and those who hear will live. 26For as the Father has life in Himself, so He has granted the Son to have life in

THE MESSAGE

That really set them off. The Jews were now not only out to expose him; they were out to *kill* him. Not only was he breaking the Sabbath, but he was calling God his own Father, putting himself on a level with God.

What the Father Does, The Son Does

So Jesus explained himself at length. "I'm telling you this straight. The Son can't independently do a thing, only what he sees the Father doing. What the Father does, the Son does. The Father loves the Son and includes him in everything he is doing.

"But you haven't seen the half of it yet, for in the same way that the Father raises the dead and creates life, so does the Son. The Son gives life to anyone he chooses. Neither he nor the Father shuts anyone out. The Father handed all authority to judge over to the Son so that the Son will be honored equally with the Father. Anyone who dishonors the Son, dishonors the Father, for it was the Father's decision to put the Son in the place of honor.

"It's urgent that you listen carefully to this: Anyone here who believes what I am saying right now and aligns himself with the Father, who has in fact put me in charge, has at this very moment the real, lasting life and is no longer condemned to be an outsider. This person has taken a giant step from the world of the dead to the world of the living.

"It's urgent that you get this right: The time has arrived—I mean right now!—when dead men and women will hear the voice of the Son of God and, hearing, will come alive. Just as the Father has life in himself, he has conferred on the Son life in himself. And he has given him

KING JAMES VERSION

27 And hath given him authority to execute judgment also, because he is the Son of man.

28 Marvel not at this: for the hour is coming, in the which all that are in the graves shall hear his voice,

29 And shall come forth; they that have done good, unto the resurrection of life; and they that have done evil, unto the resurrection of damnation.

30 I can of mine own self do nothing: as I hear, I judge: and my judgment is just; because I seek not mine own will, but the will of the Father which hath sent me.

31 ¶ If I bear witness of myself, my witness is not true.

32 There is another that beareth witness of me; and I know that the witness which he witnesseth of me is true.

33 Ye sent unto John, and he bare witness unto the truth.

34 But I receive not testimony from man: but these things I say, that ye might be saved.

35 He was a burning and a shining light: and ye were willing for a season to rejoice in his light.

36 But I have greater witness than *that* of John: for the works which the Father hath given me to finish, the same works that I do, bear witness of me, that the Father hath sent me.

37 And the Father himself, which hath sent me, hath

NEW AMERICAN STANDARD BIBLE

27 and He gave Him authority to execute judgment, because He is *the* Son of Man.

28 "Do not marvel at this; for an hour is coming, in which all who are in the tombs will hear His voice,

29 and will come forth; those who did the good *deeds* to a resurrection of life, those who committed the evil *deeds* to a resurrection of judgment.

30 "I can do nothing on My own initiative. As I hear, I judge; and My judgment is just, because I do not seek My own will, but the will of Him who sent Me.

31 "If I *alone* testify about Myself, My testimony is not true.

32 "There is another who testifies of Me, and I know that the testimony which He gives about Me is true.

Witness of John

33 "You have sent to John, and he has testified to the truth.

34 "But the testimony which I receive is not from man, but I say these things so that you may be saved.

35 "He was the lamp that was burning and was shining and you were willing to rejoice for a while in his light.

Witness of Works

36 "But the testimony which I have is greater than *the testimony of* John; for the works which the Father has given Me to accomplish—the very works that I do—testify about Me, that the Father has sent Me.

Witness of the Father

37 "And the Father who sent Me, He has testified of Me.

NEW CENTURY VERSION

Son the power to judge, because he is the Son of Man.
28Don't be surprised at this: A time is coming when all
who are dead and in their graves will hear his voice.
29Then they will come out of their graves. Those who did
good will rise and have life forever, but those who did evil
will rise to be judged guilty.

Jesus Is God's Son

30"I can do nothing alone. I judge only the way I am
told, so my judgment is fair. I don't try to please myself,
but I try to please the One who sent me.

31"If only I tell people about myself, what I say is not
true. 32But there is another who tells about me, and I
know that the things he says about me are true.

33"You have sent people to John, and he has told you the
truth. 34It is not that I accept such human telling; I tell you
this so you can be saved. 35John was like a burning and
shining lamp, and you were happy to enjoy his light for a
while.

36"But I have a proof about myself that is greater than
that of John. The things I do, which are the things my
Father gave me to do, prove that the Father sent me. 37And
the Father himself who sent me has given proof about me.

CONTEMPORARY ENGLISH VERSION

the right to judge everyone, because he is the Son of
Man.

28Don't be surprised! The time will come when all of
the dead will hear the voice of the Son of Man, 29and
they will come out of their graves. Everyone who has
done good things will rise to life, but everyone who has
done evil things will rise and be condemned.

30I cannot do anything on my own. The Father sent
me, and he is the one who told me how to judge. I judge
with fairness, because I obey him, and I don't just try to
please myself.

Witnesses to Jesus

31If I speak for myself, there is no way to prove I am
telling the truth. 32But there is someone else who speaks
for me, and I know what he says is true. 33You sent mes-
sengers to John, and he told them the truth. 34I don't
depend on what people say about me, but I tell you
these things so that you may be saved. 35John was a
lamp that gave a lot of light, and you were glad to enjoy
his light for a while.

36But something more important than John speaks for
me. I mean the things that the Father has given me to
do! All of these speak for me and prove that the Father
sent me.

37The Father who sent me also speaks for me, but you

NEW INTERNATIONAL VERSION

has given him authority to judge because he is the Son of
Man.
[28]"Do not be amazed at this, for a time is coming when
all who are in their graves will hear his voice [29]and come
out—those who have done good will rise to live, and those
who have done evil will rise to be condemned. [30]By myself
I can do nothing; I judge only as I hear, and my judgment
is just, for I seek not to please myself but him who
sent me.

Testimonies About Jesus

[31]"If I testify about myself, my testimony is not valid.
[32]There is another who testifies in my favor, and I know
that his testimony about me is valid.
[33]"You have sent to John and he has testified to the
truth. [34]Not that I accept human testimony; but I mention
it that you may be saved. [35]John was a lamp that burned
and gave light, and you chose for a time to enjoy his light.
[36]"I have testimony weightier than that of John. For the
very work that the Father has given me to finish, and which
I am doing, testifies that the Father has sent me. [37]And the
Father who sent me has himself testified concerning me.

NEW LIVING TRANSLATION

in himself. [27]And he has given him authority to judge all
mankind because he is the Son of Man. [28]Don't be so sur-
prised! Indeed, the time is coming when all the dead in
their graves will hear the voice of God's Son, [29]and they
will rise again. Those who have done good will rise to eter-
nal life, and those who have continued in evil will rise to
judgment. [30]But I do nothing without consulting the
Father. I judge as I am told. And my judgment is absolute-
ly just, because it is according to the will of God who sent
me; it is not merely my own.

Witnesses to Jesus

[31]"If I were to testify on my own behalf, my testimony
would not be valid. [32]But someone else is also testifying
about me, and I can assure you that everything he says
about me is true. [33]In fact, you sent messengers to listen
to John the Baptist, and he preached the truth. [34]But the
best testimony about me is not from a man, though I have
reminded you about John's testimony so you might be
saved. [35]John shone brightly for a while, and you benefited
and rejoiced. [36]But I have a greater witness than John—my
teachings and my miracles. They have been assigned to me
by the Father, and they testify that the Father has sent me.
[37]And the Father himself has also testified about me. You

NEW KING JAMES VERSION

Himself, [27]and has given Him authority to execute judg-
ment also, because He is the Son of Man. [28]Do not marvel
at this; for the hour is coming in which all who are in the
graves will hear His voice [29]and come forth—those who
have done good, to the resurrection of life, and those who
have done evil, to the resurrection of condemnation. [30]I can
of Myself do nothing. As I hear, I judge; and My judgment
is righteous, because I do not seek My own will but the will
of the Father who sent Me.

The Fourfold Witness

[31]"If I bear witness of Myself, My witness is not true.
[32]There is another who bears witness of Me, and I know
that the witness which He witnesses of Me is true. [33]You
have sent to John, and he has borne witness to the truth.
[34]Yet I do not receive testimony from man, but I say these
things that you may be saved. [35]He was the burning and
shining lamp, and you were willing for a time to rejoice in
his light. [36]But I have a greater witness than John's; for
the works which the Father has given Me to finish—the
very works that I do—bear witness of Me, that the Father
has sent Me. [37]And the Father Himself, who sent Me, has

THE MESSAGE

the authority, simply because he is the Son of Man, to
decide and carry out matters of Judgment.

"Don't act so surprised at all this. The time is coming when everyone dead and buried will hear his voice. Those who have lived the right way will walk out into a resurrection Life; those who have lived the wrong way, into a resurrection Judgment.

"I can't do a solitary thing on my own: I listen, then I decide. You can trust my decision because I'm not out to get my own way but only to carry out orders. If I were simply speaking on my own account, it would be an empty, self-serving witness. But an independent witness confirms me, the most reliable Witness of all. Furthermore, you all saw and heard John, and he gave expert and reliable testimony about me, didn't he?

"But my purpose is not to get your vote, and not to appeal to mere human testimony. I'm speaking to you this way so that you will be saved. John was a torch, blazing and bright, and you were glad enough to dance for an hour or so in his bright light. But the witness that really confirms me far exceeds John's witness. It's the work the Father gave me to complete. These very tasks, as I go about completing them, confirm that the Father, in fact, sent me. The Father who sent me, confirmed me. And you

KING JAMES VERSION

borne witness of me. Ye have neither heard his voice at any time, nor seen his shape.

38 And ye have not his word abiding in you: for whom he hath sent, him ye believe not.

39 Search the scriptures; for in them ye think ye have eternal life: and they are they which testify of me.

40 And ye will not come to me, that ye might have life.

41 I receive not honour from men.

42 But I know you, that ye have not the love of God in you.

43 I am come in my Father's name, and ye receive me not: if another shall come in his own name, him ye will receive.

44 How can ye believe, which receive honour one of another, and seek not the honour that *cometh* from God only?

45 Do not think that I will accuse you to the Father: there is *one* that accuseth you, *even* Moses, in whom ye trust.

46 For had ye believed Moses, ye would have believed me: for he wrote of me.

47 But if ye believe not his writings, how shall ye believe my words?

NEW AMERICAN STANDARD BIBLE

You have neither heard His voice at any time nor seen His form.

38 "You do not have His word abiding in you, for you do not believe Him whom He sent.

Witness of the Scripture

39 "[2]You search the Scriptures because you think that in them you have eternal life; it is these that testify about Me;

40 and you are unwilling to come to Me so that you may have life.

41 "I do not receive glory from men;

42 but I know you, that you do not have the love of God in yourselves.

43 "I have come in My Father's name, and you do not receive Me; if another comes in his own name, you will receive him.

44 "How can you believe, when you receive glory from one another and you do not seek the glory that is from the *one and* only God?

45 "Do not think that I will accuse you before the Father; the one who accuses you is Moses, in whom you have set your hope.

46 "For if you believed Moses, you would believe Me, for he wrote about Me.

47 "But if you do not believe his writings, how will you believe My words?"

5:39 [2] Or (a command) *Search the Scriptures!*

NEW CENTURY VERSION

You have never heard his voice or seen what he looks like.
38His teaching does not live in you, because you don't
believe in the One the Father sent. 39You carefully study
the Scriptures because you think they give you eternal life.
They do in fact tell about me, 40but you refuse to come to
me to have that life.
41"I don't need praise from people. 42But I know you—I
know that you don't have God's love in you. 43I have come
from my Father and speak for him, but you don't accept
me. But when another person comes, speaking only for
himself, you will accept him. 44You try to get praise from
each other, but you do not try to get the praise that comes
from the only God. So how can you believe? 45Don't think
that I will stand before the Father and say you are wrong.
The one who says you are wrong is Moses, the one you
hoped would save you. 46If you really believed Moses, you
would believe me, because Moses wrote about me. 47But if
you don't believe what Moses wrote, how can you believe
what I say?"

CONTEMPORARY ENGLISH VERSION

have never heard his voice or seen him face to face.
38You have not believed his message, because you
refused to have faith in the one he sent.
39You search the Scriptures, because you think you
will find eternal life in them. The Scriptures tell about
me, 40but you refuse to come to me for eternal life.
41I don't care about human praise, 42but I do know
that none of you love God. 43I have come with my
Father's authority, and you have not welcomed me. But
you will welcome people who come on their own. 44How
could you possibly believe? You like to have your friends
praise you, and you don't care about praise that the only
God can give!
45Don't think that I will be the one to accuse you to
the Father. You have put your hope in Moses, yet he is
the very one who will accuse you. 46Moses wrote about
me, and if you had believed Moses, you would have
believed me. 47But if you don't believe what Moses
wrote, how can you believe what I say?

NEW INTERNATIONAL VERSION

You have never heard his voice nor seen his form, [38]nor does his word dwell in you, for you do not believe the one he sent. [39]You diligently study[c] the Scriptures because you think that by them you possess eternal life. These are the Scriptures that testify about me, [40]yet you refuse to come to me to have life.

[41]"I do not accept praise from men, [42]but I know you. I know that you do not have the love of God in your hearts. [43]I have come in my Father's name, and you do not accept me; but if someone else comes in his own name, you will accept him. [44]How can you believe if you accept praise from one another, yet make no effort to obtain the praise that comes from the only God[d]?

[45]"But do not think I will accuse you before the Father. Your accuser is Moses, on whom your hopes are set. [46]If you believed Moses, you would believe me, for he wrote about me. [47]But since you do not believe what he wrote, how are you going to believe what I say?"

[c] *39* Or *Study diligently* (the imperative) [d] *44* Some early manuscripts *the Only One*

NEW LIVING TRANSLATION

have never heard his voice or seen him face to face, [38]and you do not have his message in your hearts, because you do not believe me—the one he sent to you.

[39]"You search the Scriptures because you believe they give you eternal life. But the Scriptures point to me! [40]Yet you refuse to come to me so that I can give you this eternal life.

[41]"Your approval or disapproval means nothing to me, [42]because I know you don't have God's love within you. [43]For I have come to you representing my Father, and you refuse to welcome me, even though you readily accept others who represent only themselves. [44]No wonder you can't believe! For you gladly honor each other, but you don't care about the honor that comes from God alone.

[45]"Yet it is not I who will accuse you of this before the Father. Moses will accuse you! Yes, Moses, on whom you set your hopes. [46]But if you had believed Moses, you would have believed me because he wrote about me. [47]And since you don't believe what he wrote, how will you believe what I say?"

NEW KING JAMES VERSION

testified of Me. You have neither heard His voice at any time, nor seen His form. [38]But you do not have His word abiding in you, because whom He sent, Him you do not believe. [39]You search the Scriptures, for in them you think you have eternal life; and these are they which testify of Me. [40]But you are not willing to come to Me that you may have life.

[41]"I do not receive honor from men. [42]But I know you, that you do not have the love of God in you. [43]I have come in My Father's name, and you do not receive Me; if another comes in his own name, him you will receive. [44]How can you believe, who receive honor from one another, and do not seek the honor that *comes* from the only God? [45]Do not think that I shall accuse you to the Father; there is *one* who accuses you—Moses, in whom you trust. [46]For if you believed Moses, you would believe Me; for he wrote about Me. [47]But if you do not believe his writings, how will you believe My words?"

THE MESSAGE

missed it. You never heard his voice, you never saw his appearance. There is nothing left in your memory of his Message because you do not take his Messenger seriously.

"You have your heads in your Bibles constantly because you think you'll find eternal life there. But you miss the forest for the trees. These Scriptures are all about *me*! And here I am, standing right before you, and you aren't willing to receive from me the life you say you want.

"I'm not interested in crowd approval. And do you know why? Because I know you and your crowds. I know that love, especially God's love, is not on your working agenda. I came with the authority of my Father, and you either dismiss me or avoid me. If another came, acting self-important, you would welcome him with open arms. How do you expect to get anywhere with God when you spend all your time jockeying for position with each other, ranking your rivals and ignoring God?

"But don't think I'm going to accuse you before my Father. Moses, in whom you put so much stock, is your accuser. If you believed, really believed, what Moses said, you would believe me. He wrote of me. If you won't take seriously what *he* wrote, how can I expect you to take seriously what *I* speak?"

KING JAMES VERSION

6 After these things Jesus went over the sea of Galilee, which is *the sea* of Tiberias.

2 And a great multitude followed him, because they saw his miracles which he did on them that were diseased.

3 And Jesus went up into a mountain, and there he sat with his disciples.

4 And the passover, a feast of the Jews, was nigh.

5 When Jesus then lifted up *his* eyes, and saw a great company come unto him, he saith unto Philip, Whence shall we buy bread, that these may eat?

6 And this he said to prove him: for he himself knew what he would do.

7 Philip answered him, Two hundred pennyworth of bread is not sufficient for them, that every one of them may take a little.

8 One of his disciples, Andrew, Simon Peter's brother, saith unto him,

9 There is a lad here, which hath five barley loaves, and two small fishes: but what are they among so many?

10 And Jesus said, Make the men sit down. Now there was much grass in the place. So the men sat down, in number about five thousand.

11 And Jesus took the loaves; and when he had given thanks, he distributed to the disciples, and the disciples to them that were set down; and likewise of the fishes as much as they would.

NEW AMERICAN STANDARD BIBLE

Five Thousand Fed

6 After these things Jesus went away to the other side of the Sea of Galilee (or Tiberias).

2 A large crowd followed Him, because they saw the signs which He was performing on those who were sick.

3 Then Jesus went up on the mountain, and there He sat down with His disciples.

4 Now the Passover, the feast of the Jews, was near.

5 Therefore Jesus, lifting up His eyes and seeing that a large crowd was coming to Him, *said to Philip, "Where are we to buy bread, so that these may eat?"

6 This He was saying to test him, for He Himself knew what He was intending to do.

7 Philip answered Him, "Two hundred [1]denarii worth of bread is not sufficient for them, for everyone to receive a little."

8 One of His disciples, Andrew, Simon Peter's brother, *said to Him,

9 "There is a lad here who has five barley loaves and two fish, but what are these for so many people?"

10 Jesus said, "Have the people sit down." Now there was much grass in the place. So the men sat down, in number about five thousand.

11 Jesus then took the loaves, and having given thanks, He distributed to those who were seated; likewise also of the fish as much as they wanted.

6:7 [1] The denarius was equivalent to a day's wages

NEW CENTURY VERSION

More than Five Thousand Fed

6 After this, Jesus went across Lake Galilee (or, Lake
Tiberias). 2Many people followed him because they
saw the miracles he did to heal the sick. 3Jesus went up on
a hill and sat down there with his followers. 4It was
almost the time for the Jewish Passover Feast.
5When Jesus looked up and saw a large crowd coming
toward him, he said to Philip, "Where can we buy enough
bread for all these people to eat?" 6(Jesus asked Philip this
question to test him, because Jesus already knew what he
planned to do.)
7Philip answered, "We would all have to work a month
to buy enough bread for each person to have only a little
piece."
8Another one of his followers, Andrew, Simon Peter's
brother, said, 9"Here is a boy with five loaves of barley
bread and two little fish, but that is not enough for so
many people."
10Jesus said, "Tell the people to sit down." This was a
very grassy place, and about five thousand men sat down
there. 11Then Jesus took the loaves of bread, thanked God
for them, and gave them to the people who were sitting
there. He did the same with the fish, giving as much as the
people wanted.

CONTEMPORARY ENGLISH VERSION

Feeding Five Thousand

(Matthew 14.13-21; Mark 6.30-44; Luke 9.10-17)

6 Jesus crossed Lake Galilee, which was also known as
Lake Tiberias. 2A large crowd had seen him work mira-
cles to heal the sick, and those people went with him. 3-4It
was almost time for the Jewish festival of Passover, and Jesus
went up on a mountain with his disciples and sat down.[a]
5When Jesus saw the large crowd coming toward him, he
asked Philip, "Where will we get enough food to feed all
these people?" 6He said this to test Philip, since he already
knew what he was going to do.
7Philip answered, "Don't you know that it would take
almost a year's wages[b] just to buy only a little bread for
each of these people?"
8Andrew, the brother of Simon Peter, was one of the dis-
ciples. He spoke up and said, 9"There is a boy here who
has five small loaves[c] of barley bread and two fish. But
what good is that with all these people?"
10The ground was covered with grass, and Jesus told his
disciples to have everyone sit down. About five thousand
men were in the crowd. 11Jesus took the bread in his hands
and gave thanks to God. Then he passed the bread to the
people, and he did the same with the fish, until everyone
had plenty to eat.

[a] 6.3,4 *sat down*: Possibly to teach. Teachers in the ancient world, including Jewish teachers, usually sat down to teach. [b] 6.7 *almost a year's wages*: The Greek text has "two hundred silver coins." Each coin was worth the average day's wages for a worker. [c] 6.9 *small loaves*: These would have been flat and round or in the shape of a bun.

NEW INTERNATIONAL VERSION

Jesus Feeds the Five Thousand

6 Some time after this, Jesus crossed to the far shore of the Sea of Galilee (that is, the Sea of Tiberias), 2and a great crowd of people followed him because they saw the miraculous signs he had performed on the sick. 3Then Jesus went up on a mountainside and sat down with his disciples. 4The Jewish Passover Feast was near.

5When Jesus looked up and saw a great crowd coming toward him, he said to Philip, "Where shall we buy bread for these people to eat?" 6He asked this only to test him, for he already had in mind what he was going to do.

7Philip answered him, "Eight months' wages[a] would not buy enough bread for each one to have a bite!"

8Another of his disciples, Andrew, Simon Peter's brother, spoke up, 9"Here is a boy with five small barley loaves and two small fish, but how far will they go among so many?"

10Jesus said, "Have the people sit down." There was plenty of grass in that place, and the men sat down, about five thousand of them. 11Jesus then took the loaves, gave thanks, and distributed to those who were seated as much as they wanted. He did the same with the fish.

[a] 7 Greek *two hundred denarii*

NEW LIVING TRANSLATION

Jesus Feeds Five Thousand

6 After this, Jesus crossed over the Sea of Galilee, also known as the Sea of Tiberias. 2And a huge crowd kept following him wherever he went, because they saw his miracles as he healed the sick. 3Then Jesus went up into the hills and sat down with his disciples around him. 4(It was nearly time for the annual Passover celebration.) 5Jesus soon saw a great crowd of people climbing the hill, looking for him. Turning to Philip, he asked, "Philip, where can we buy bread to feed all these people?" 6He was testing Philip, for he already knew what he was going to do.

7Philip replied, "It would take a small fortune* to feed them!"

8Then Andrew, Simon Peter's brother, spoke up. 9"There's a young boy here with five barley loaves and two fish. But what good is that with this huge crowd?"

10"Tell everyone to sit down," Jesus ordered. So all of them—the men alone numbered five thousand—sat down on the grassy slopes. 11Then Jesus took the loaves, gave thanks to God, and passed them out to the people. Afterward he did the same with the fish. And they all ate

6:7 Greek *200 denarii.* A denarius was the equivalent of a full day's wage.

NEW KING JAMES VERSION

Feeding the Five Thousand

6 After these things Jesus went over the Sea of Galilee, which is *the Sea* of Tiberias. 2Then a great multitude followed Him, because they saw His signs which He performed on those who were diseased. 3And Jesus went up on the mountain, and there He sat with His disciples.

4Now the Passover, a feast of the Jews, was near. 5Then Jesus lifted up *His* eyes, and seeing a great multitude coming toward Him, He said to Philip, "Where shall we buy bread, that these may eat?" 6But this He said to test him, for He Himself knew what He would do.

7Philip answered Him, "Two hundred denarii worth of bread is not sufficient for them, that every one of them may have a little."

8One of His disciples, Andrew, Simon Peter's brother, said to Him, 9"There is a lad here who has five barley loaves and two small fish, but what are they among so many?"

10Then Jesus said, "Make the people sit down." Now there was much grass in the place. So the men sat down, in number about five thousand. 11And Jesus took the loaves, and when He had given thanks He distributed *them* to the disciples, and the disciples[a] to those sitting down; and likewise of the fish, as much as they wanted. 12So

6:11 [a] NU-Text omits *to the disciples, and the disciples.*

THE MESSAGE

Bread and Fish for All

6 After this, Jesus went across the Sea of Galilee (some call it Tiberias). A huge crowd followed him, attracted by the miracles they had seen him do among the sick. When he got to the other side, he climbed a hill and sat down, surrounded by his disciples. It was nearly time for the Feast of Passover, kept annually by the Jews.

When Jesus looked out and saw that a large crowd had arrived, he said to Philip, "Where can we buy bread to feed these people?" He said this to stretch Philip's faith. He already knew what he was going to do.

Philip answered, "Two hundred silver pieces wouldn't be enough to buy bread for each person to get a piece."

One of the disciples—it was Andrew, brother to Simon Peter—said, "There's a little boy here who has five barley loaves and two fish. But that's a drop in the bucket for a crowd like this."

Jesus said, "Make the people sit down." There was a nice carpet of green grass in this place. They sat down, about five thousand of them. Then Jesus took the bread and, having given thanks, gave it to those who were seated. He did the same with the fish. All ate as much as they wanted.

KING JAMES VERSION

12 When they were filled, he said unto his disciples, Gather up the fragments that remain, that nothing be lost.

13 Therefore they gathered *them* together, and filled twelve baskets with the fragments of the five barley loaves, which remained over and above unto them that had eaten.

14 Then those men, when they had seen the miracle that Jesus did, said, This is of a truth that prophet that should come into the world.

15 ¶ When Jesus therefore perceived that they would come and take him by force, to make him a king, he departed again into a mountain himself alone.

16 And when even was *now* come, his disciples went down unto the sea,

17 And entered into a ship, and went over the sea toward Capernaum. And it was now dark, and Jesus was not come to them.

18 And the sea arose by reason of a great wind that blew.

19 So when they had rowed about five and twenty or thirty furlongs, they see Jesus walking on the sea, and drawing nigh unto the ship: and they were afraid.

20 But he saith unto them, It is I; be not afraid.

21 Then they willingly received him into the ship: and immediately the ship was at the land whither they went.

22 ¶ The day following, when the people which stood

NEW AMERICAN STANDARD BIBLE

12 When they were filled, He *said to His disciples, "Gather up the leftover fragments so that nothing will be lost."

13 So they gathered them up, and filled twelve baskets with fragments from the five barley loaves which were left over by those who had eaten.

14 Therefore when the people saw the sign which He had performed, they said, "This is truly the Prophet who is to come into the world."

Jesus Walks on the Water

15 So Jesus, perceiving that they were intending to come and take Him by force to make Him king, withdrew again to the mountain by Himself alone.

16 Now when evening came, His disciples went down to the sea,

17 and after getting into a boat, they *started to* cross the sea to Capernaum. It had already become dark, and Jesus had not yet come to them.

18 The sea *began* to be stirred up because a strong wind was blowing.

19 Then, when they had rowed about three or four miles, they *saw Jesus walking on the sea and drawing near to the boat; and they were frightened.

20 But He *said to them, "It is I; do not be afraid."

21 So they were willing to receive Him into the boat, and immediately the boat was at the land to which they were going.

22 The next day the crowd that stood on the other side of

NEW CENTURY VERSION

12When they had all had enough to eat, Jesus said to his followers, "Gather the leftover pieces of fish and bread so that nothing is wasted." 13So they gathered up the pieces and filled twelve baskets with the pieces left from the five barley loaves.

14When the people saw this miracle that Jesus did, they said, "He must truly be the Prophet[a] who is coming into the world."

15Jesus knew that the people planned to come and take him by force and make him their king, so he left and went into the hills alone.

Jesus Walks on the Water

16That evening Jesus' followers went down to Lake Galilee. 17It was dark now, and Jesus had not yet come to them. The followers got into a boat and started across the lake to Capernaum. 18By now a strong wind was blowing, and the waves on the lake were getting bigger. 19When they had rowed the boat about three or four miles, they saw Jesus walking on the water, coming toward the boat. The followers were afraid, 20but Jesus said to them, "It is I. Do not be afraid." 21Then they were glad to take him into the boat. At once the boat came to land at the place where they wanted to go.

The People Seek Jesus

22The next day the people who had stayed on the other

6:14 [a] **Prophet** They probably meant the prophet that God told Moses he would send (Deuteronomy 18:15–19).

CONTEMPORARY ENGLISH VERSION

12The people ate all they wanted, and Jesus told his disciples to gather up the leftovers, so that nothing would be wasted. 13The disciples gathered them up and filled twelve large baskets with what was left over from the five barley loaves.

14After the people had seen Jesus work this miracle,[d] they began saying, "This must be the Prophet[e] who is to come into the world!" 15Jesus realized that they would try to force him to be their king. So he went up on a mountain, where he could be alone.

Jesus Walks on the Water (Matthew 14.22-27; Mark 6.45-52)

16That evening, Jesus' disciples went down to the lake. 17They got into a boat and started across for Capernaum. Later that evening Jesus had still not come to them, 18and a strong wind was making the water rough.

19When the disciples had rowed for three or four miles, they saw Jesus walking on the water. He kept coming closer to the boat, and they were terrified. 20But he said, "I am Jesus![f] Don't be afraid!" 21The disciples wanted to take him into the boat, but suddenly the boat reached the shore where they were headed.

The Bread That Gives Life

22The people who had stayed on the east side of the lake

[d] **6.14** *miracle*: See the note at 2.11. [e] **6.14** *the Prophet*: See the note at 1.21. [f] **6.20** *I am Jesus*: The Greek text has "I am" (see the note at 8.24).

NEW INTERNATIONAL VERSION

[12]When they had all had enough to eat, he said to his disciples, "Gather the pieces that are left over. Let nothing be wasted." [13]So they gathered them and filled twelve baskets with the pieces of the five barley loaves left over by those who had eaten.

[14]After the people saw the miraculous sign that Jesus did, they began to say, "Surely this is the Prophet who is to come into the world." [15]Jesus, knowing that they intended to come and make him king by force, withdrew again to a mountain by himself.

Jesus Walks on the Water

[16]When evening came, his disciples went down to the lake, [17]where they got into a boat and set off across the lake for Capernaum. By now it was dark, and Jesus had not yet joined them. [18]A strong wind was blowing and the waters grew rough. [19]When they had rowed three or three and a half miles,[b] they saw Jesus approaching the boat, walking on the water; and they were terrified. [20]But he said to them, "It is I; don't be afraid." [21]Then they were willing to take him into the boat, and immediately the boat reached the shore where they were heading.

[22]The next day the crowd that had stayed on the opposite

[b] 19 Greek *rowed twenty-five or thirty stadia* (about 5 or 6 kilometers)

NEW LIVING TRANSLATION

until they were full. [12]"Now gather the leftovers," Jesus told his disciples, "so that nothing is wasted." [13]There were only five barley loaves to start with, but twelve baskets were filled with the pieces of bread the people did not eat!

[14]When the people saw this miraculous sign, they exclaimed, "Surely, he is the Prophet* we have been expecting!" [15]Jesus saw that they were ready to take him by force and make him king, so he went higher into the hills alone.

Jesus Walks on Water

[16]That evening his disciples went down to the shore to wait for him. [17]But as darkness fell and Jesus still hadn't come back, they got into the boat and headed out across the lake toward Capernaum. [18]Soon a gale swept down upon them as they rowed, and the sea grew very rough. [19]They were three or four miles* out when suddenly they saw Jesus walking on the water toward the boat. They were terrified, [20]but he called out to them, "I am here! Don't be afraid." [21]Then they were eager to let him in, and immediately the boat arrived at their destination!

Jesus, the Bread of Life

[22]The next morning, back across the lake, crowds began

6:14 See Deut 18:15, 18. **6:19** Greek *25 or 30 stadia* [4.6 or 5.5 kilometers].

NEW KING JAMES VERSION

when they were filled, He said to His disciples, "Gather up the fragments that remain, so that nothing is lost." [13]Therefore they gathered *them* up, and filled twelve baskets with the fragments of the five barley loaves which were left over by those who had eaten. [14]Then those men, when they had seen the sign that Jesus did, said, "This is truly the Prophet who is to come into the world."

Jesus Walks on the Sea

[15]Therefore when Jesus perceived that they were about to come and take Him by force to make Him king, He departed again to the mountain by Himself alone.

[16]Now when evening came, His disciples went down to the sea, [17]got into the boat, and went over the sea toward Capernaum. And it was already dark, and Jesus had not come to them. [18]Then the sea arose because a great wind was blowing. [19]So when they had rowed about three or four miles,[b] they saw Jesus walking on the sea and drawing near the boat; and they were afraid. [20]But He said to them, "It is I; do not be afraid." [21]Then they willingly received Him into the boat, and immediately the boat was at the land where they were going.

The Bread from Heaven

[22]On the following day, when the people who were

6:19 [b] Literally *twenty-five or thirty stadia*

THE MESSAGE

When the people had eaten their fill, he said to his disciples, "Gather the leftovers so nothing is wasted." They went to work and filled twelve large baskets with leftovers from the five barley loaves.

The people realized that God was at work among them in what Jesus had just done. They said, "This is the Prophet for sure, God's Prophet right here in Galilee!" Jesus saw that in their enthusiasm, they were about to grab him and make him king, so he slipped off and went back up the mountain to be by himself.

In the evening his disciples went down to the sea, got in the boat, and headed back across the water to Capernaum. It had grown quite dark and Jesus had not yet returned. A huge wind blew up, churning the sea. They were maybe three or four miles out when they saw Jesus walking on the sea, quite near the boat. They were scared senseless, but he reassured them, "It's me. It's all right. Don't be afraid." So they took him on board. In no time they reached land—the exact spot they were headed to.

The next day the crowd that was left behind realized that

KING JAMES VERSION

on the other side of the sea saw that there was none other boat there, save that one whereinto his disciples were entered, and that Jesus went not with his disciples into the boat, but *that* his disciples were gone away alone;

23 (Howbeit there came other boats from Tiberias nigh unto the place where they did eat bread, after that the Lord had given thanks:)

24 When the people therefore saw that Jesus was not there, neither his disciples, they also took shipping, and came to Capernaum, seeking for Jesus.

25 And when they had found him on the other side of the sea, they said unto him, Rabbi, when camest thou hither?

26 Jesus answered them and said, Verily, verily, I say unto you, Ye seek me, not because ye saw the miracles, but because ye did eat of the loaves, and were filled.

27 Labour not for the meat which perisheth, but for that meat which endureth unto everlasting life, which the Son of man shall give unto you: for him hath God the Father sealed.

28 ¶ Then said they unto him, What shall we do, that we might work the works of God?

29 Jesus answered and said unto them, This is the work of God, that ye believe on him whom he hath sent.

30 They said therefore unto him, What sign shewest thou then, that we may see, and believe thee? what dost thou work?

31 Our fathers did eat manna in the desert; as it is written, He gave them bread from heaven to eat.

NEW AMERICAN STANDARD BIBLE

the sea saw that there was no other small boat there, except one, and that Jesus had not entered with His disciples into the boat, but *that* His disciples had gone away alone.

23 There came other small boats from Tiberias near to the place where they ate the bread after the Lord had given thanks.

24 So when the crowd saw that Jesus was not there, nor His disciples, they themselves got into the small boats, and came to Capernaum seeking Jesus.

25 When they found Him on the other side of the sea, they said to Him, "Rabbi, when did You get here?"

Words to the People

26 Jesus answered them and said, "Truly, truly, I say to you, you seek Me, not because you saw signs, but because you ate of the loaves and were filled.

27 "Do not work for the food which perishes, but for the food which endures to eternal life, which the Son of Man will give to you, for on Him the Father, God, has set His seal."

28 Therefore they said to Him, "What shall we do, so that we may work the works of God?"

29 Jesus answered and said to them, "This is the work of God, that you believe in Him whom He has sent."

30 So they said to Him, "What then do You do for a sign, so that we may see, and believe You? What work do You perform?

31 "Our fathers ate the manna in the wilderness; as it is written, 'HE GAVE THEM BREAD OUT OF HEAVEN TO EAT.' "

NEW CENTURY VERSION

side of the lake knew that Jesus had not gone in the boat
with his followers but that they had left without him. And
they knew that only one boat had been there. 23But then
some boats came from Tiberias and landed near the place
where the people had eaten the bread after the Lord had
given thanks. 24When the people saw that Jesus and his
followers were not there now, they got into boats and went
to Capernaum to find Jesus.

Jesus, the Bread of Life

25When the people found Jesus on the other side of the
lake, they asked him, "Teacher, when did you come here?"
26Jesus answered, "I tell you the truth, you aren't look-
ing for me because you saw me do miracles. You are look-
ing for me because you ate the bread and were satisfied.
27Don't work for the food that spoils. Work for the food
that stays good always and gives eternal life. The Son of
Man will give you this food, because on him God the
Father has put his power."
28The people asked Jesus, "What are the things God
wants us to do?"
29Jesus answered, "The work God wants you to do is
this: Believe the One he sent."
30So the people asked, "What miracle will you do? If we
see a miracle, we will believe you. What will you do? 31Our
fathers ate the manna in the desert. This is written in the
Scriptures: 'He gave them bread from heaven to eat.' "[b]

6:31 [b] **'He gave...eat.'** Quotation from Psalm 78:24.

CONTEMPORARY ENGLISH VERSION

knew that only one boat had been there. They also knew
that Jesus had not left in it with his disciples. But the next
day 23some boats from Tiberias sailed near the place where
the crowd had eaten the bread for which the Lord had
given thanks. 24They saw that Jesus and his disciples had
left. Then they got into the boats and went to Capernaum
to look for Jesus. 25They found him on the west side of the
lake and asked, "Rabbi, when did you get here?"
26Jesus answered, "I tell you for certain that you are not
looking for me because you saw the miracles,[g] but because
you ate all the food you wanted. 27Don't work for food that
spoils. Work for food that gives eternal life. The Son of
Man will give you this food, because God the Father has
given him the right to do so."
28"What exactly does God want us to do?" the people
asked.
29Jesus answered, "God wants you to have faith in the
one he sent."
30They replied, "What miracle will you work, so that we
can have faith in you? What will you do? 31For example,
when our ancestors were in the desert, they were given
manna[h] to eat. It happened just as the Scriptures say, 'God
gave them bread from heaven to eat.' "

[g] **6.26** *miracles*: The Greek text has "signs" here and "sign" in verse 30 (see the note at 2.11). [h] **6.31** *manna*: When the people of Israel were wandering through the desert, the Lord gave them a special kind of food to eat. It tasted like a wafer and was called "manna," which in Hebrew means, "What is this?"

NEW INTERNATIONAL VERSION

shore of the lake realized that only one boat had been there, and that Jesus had not entered it with his disciples, but that they had gone away alone. 23Then some boats from Tiberias landed near the place where the people had eaten the bread after the Lord had given thanks. 24Once the crowd realized that neither Jesus nor his disciples were there, they got into the boats and went to Capernaum in search of Jesus.

Jesus the Bread of Life

25When they found him on the other side of the lake, they asked him, "Rabbi, when did you get here?"

26Jesus answered, "I tell you the truth, you are looking for me, not because you saw miraculous signs but because you ate the loaves and had your fill. 27Do not work for food that spoils, but for food that endures to eternal life, which the Son of Man will give you. On him God the Father has placed his seal of approval."

28Then they asked him, "What must we do to do the works God requires?"

29Jesus answered, "The work of God is this: to believe in the one he has sent."

30So they asked him, "What miraculous sign then will you give that we may see it and believe you? What will you do? 31Our forefathers ate the manna in the desert; as it is written: 'He gave them bread from heaven to eat.'[c]"

[c] *31* Exodus 16:4; Neh. 9:15; Psalm 78:24,25

NEW LIVING TRANSLATION

gathering on the shore, waiting to see Jesus. For they knew that he and his disciples had come over together and that the disciples had gone off in their boat, leaving him behind. 23Several boats from Tiberias landed near the place where the Lord had blessed the bread and the people had eaten. 24When the crowd saw that Jesus wasn't there, nor his disciples, they got into the boats and went across to Capernaum to look for him. 25When they arrived and found him, they asked, "Teacher, how did you get here?"

26Jesus replied, "The truth is, you want to be with me because I fed you, not because you saw the miraculous sign. 27But you shouldn't be so concerned about perishable things like food. Spend your energy seeking the eternal life that I, the Son of Man, can give you. For God the Father has sent me for that very purpose."

28They replied, "What does God want us to do?"

29Jesus told them, "This is what God wants you to do: Believe in the one he has sent."

30They replied, "You must show us a miraculous sign if you want us to believe in you. What will you do for us? 31After all, our ancestors ate manna while they journeyed through the wilderness! As the Scriptures say, 'Moses gave them bread from heaven to eat.'* "

6:31 Exod 16:4; Ps 78:24.

NEW KING JAMES VERSION

standing on the other side of the sea saw that there was no other boat there, except that one which His disciples had entered,[c] and that Jesus had not entered the boat with His disciples, but His disciples had gone away alone—23however, other boats came from Tiberias, near the place where they ate bread after the Lord had given thanks—24when the people therefore saw that Jesus was not there, nor His disciples, they also got into boats and came to Capernaum, seeking Jesus. 25And when they found Him on the other side of the sea, they said to Him, "Rabbi, when did You come here?"

26Jesus answered them and said, "Most assuredly, I say to you, you seek Me, not because you saw the signs, but because you ate of the loaves and were filled. 27Do not labor for the food which perishes, but for the food which endures to everlasting life, which the Son of Man will give you, because God the Father has set His seal on Him."

28Then they said to Him, "What shall we do, that we may work the works of God?"

29Jesus answered and said to them, "This is the work of God, that you believe in Him whom He sent."

30Therefore they said to Him, "What sign will You perform then, that we may see it and believe You? What work will You do? 31Our fathers ate the manna in the desert; as it is written, *'He gave them bread from heaven to eat.'* "[d]

6:22 [c] NU-Text omits *that* and *which His disciples had entered.*
6:31 [d] Exodus 16:4; Nehemiah 9:15; Psalm 78:24

THE MESSAGE

there had been only one boat, and that Jesus had not gotten into it with his disciples. They had seen them go off without him. By now boats from Tiberias had pulled up near where they had eaten the bread blessed by the Master. So when the crowd realized he was gone and wasn't coming back, they piled into the Tiberias boats and headed for Capernaum, looking for Jesus.

When they found him back across the sea, they said, "Rabbi, when did you get here?"

Jesus answered, "You've come looking for me not because you saw God in my actions but because I fed you, filled your stomachs—and for free.

The Bread of Life

"Don't waste your energy striving for perishable food like that. Work for the food that sticks with you, food that nourishes your lasting life, food the Son of Man provides. He and what he does are guaranteed by God the Father to last."

To that they said, "Well, what do we do then to get in on God's works?"

Jesus said, "Throw your lot in with the One that God has sent. That kind of a commitment gets you in on God's works."

They waffled: "Why don't you give us a clue about who you are, just a hint of what's going on? When we see what's up, we'll commit ourselves. Show us what you can do. Moses fed our ancestors with bread in the desert. It says so in the Scriptures: 'He gave them bread from heaven to eat.' "

KING JAMES VERSION

32 Then Jesus said unto them, Verily, verily, I say unto you, Moses gave you not that bread from heaven; but my Father giveth you the true bread from heaven.
33 For the bread of God is he which cometh down from heaven, and giveth life unto the world.
34 Then said they unto him, Lord, evermore give us this bread.
35 And Jesus said unto them, I am the bread of life: he that cometh to me shall never hunger; and he that believeth on me shall never thirst.
36 But I said unto you, That ye also have seen me, and believe not.
37 All that the Father giveth me shall come to me; and him that cometh to me I will in no wise cast out.
38 For I came down from heaven, not to do mine own will, but the will of him that sent me.
39 And this is the Father's will which hath sent me, that of all which he hath given me I should lose nothing, but should raise it up again at the last day.
40 And this is the will of him that sent me, that every one which seeth the Son, and believeth on him, may have everlasting life: and I will raise him up at the last day.
41 The Jews then murmured at him, because he said, I am the bread which came down from heaven.
42 And they said, Is not this Jesus, the son of Joseph, whose father and mother we know? how is it then that he saith, I came down from heaven?

NEW AMERICAN STANDARD BIBLE

32 Jesus then said to them, "Truly, truly, I say to you, it is not Moses who has given you the bread out of heaven, but it is My Father who gives you the true bread out of heaven.
33 "For the bread of God is [2]that which comes down out of heaven, and gives life to the world."
34 Then they said to Him, "Lord, always give us this bread."
35 Jesus said to them, "I am the bread of life; he who comes to Me will not hunger, and he who believes in Me will never thirst.
36 "But I said to you that you have seen Me, and yet do not believe.
37 "All that the Father gives Me will come to Me, and the one who comes to Me I will certainly not cast out.
38 "For I have come down from heaven, not to do My own will, but the will of Him who sent Me.
39 "This is the will of Him who sent Me, that of all that He has given Me I lose nothing, but raise it up on the last day.
40 "For this is the will of My Father, that everyone who beholds the Son and believes in Him will have eternal life, and I Myself will raise him up on the last day."

Words to the Jews

41 Therefore the Jews were grumbling about Him, because He said, "I am the bread that came down out of heaven."
42 They were saying, "Is not this Jesus, the son of Joseph, whose father and mother we know? How does He now say, 'I have come down out of heaven'?"

6:33 [2] Or *He who comes*

NEW CENTURY VERSION

32Jesus said, "I tell you the truth, it was not Moses who gave you bread from heaven; it is my Father who is giving you the true bread from heaven. 33God's bread is the One who comes down from heaven and gives life to the world."
34The people said, "Sir, give us this bread always."
35Then Jesus said, "I am the bread that gives life. Whoever comes to me will never be hungry, and whoever believes in me will never be thirsty. 36But as I told you before, you have seen me and still don't believe. 37The Father gives me my people. Every one of them will come to me, and I will always accept them. 38I came down from heaven to do what God wants me to do, not what I want to do. 39Here is what the One who sent me wants me to do: I must not lose even one whom God gave me, but I must raise them all on the last day. 40Those who see the Son and believe in him have eternal life, and I will raise them on the last day. This is what my Father wants."
41The Jews began to complain about Jesus because he said, "I am the bread that comes down from heaven." 42They said, "This is Jesus, the son of Joseph. We know his father and mother. How can he say, 'I came down from heaven'?"

CONTEMPORARY ENGLISH VERSION

32Jesus then told them, "I tell you for certain that Moses wasn't the one who gave you bread from heaven. My Father is the one who gives you the true bread from heaven. 33And the bread that God gives is the one who came down from heaven to give life to the world."
34The people said, "Lord, give us this bread and don't ever stop!"
35Jesus replied:

I am the bread that gives life! No one who comes to me will ever be hungry. No one who has faith in me will ever be thirsty. 36I have told you already that you have seen me and still do not have faith in me. 37Everything and everyone that the Father has given me will come to me, and I won't turn any of them away.

38I didn't come from heaven to do what I want! I came to do what the Father wants me to do. He sent me, 39and he wants to make certain that none of the ones he has given me will be lost. Instead, he wants me to raise them to life on the last day.[i] 40My Father wants everyone who sees the Son to have faith in him and to have eternal life. Then I will raise them to life on the last day.

41The people started grumbling because Jesus had said he was the bread that had come down from heaven. 42They were asking each other, "Isn't he Jesus, the son of Joseph? Don't we know his father and mother? How can he say that he has come down from heaven?"

[i] 6.39 *the last day*: When God will judge all people.

NEW INTERNATIONAL VERSION

32 Jesus said to them, "I tell you the truth, it is not Moses who has given you the bread from heaven, but it is my Father who gives you the true bread from heaven. 33 For the bread of God is he who comes down from heaven and gives life to the world."

34 "Sir," they said, "from now on give us this bread."

35 Then Jesus declared, "I am the bread of life. He who comes to me will never go hungry, and he who believes in me will never be thirsty. 36 But as I told you, you have seen me and still you do not believe. 37 All that the Father gives me will come to me, and whoever comes to me I will never drive away. 38 For I have come down from heaven not to do my will but to do the will of him who sent me. 39 And this is the will of him who sent me, that I shall lose none of all that he has given me, but raise them up at the last day. 40 For my Father's will is that everyone who looks to the Son and believes in him shall have eternal life, and I will raise him up at the last day."

41 At this the Jews began to grumble about him because he said, "I am the bread that came down from heaven." 42 They said, "Is this not Jesus, the son of Joseph, whose father and mother we know? How can he now say, 'I came down from heaven'?"

NEW LIVING TRANSLATION

32 Jesus said, "I assure you, Moses didn't give them bread from heaven. My Father did. And now he offers you the true bread from heaven. 33 The true bread of God is the one who comes down from heaven and gives life to the world."

34 "Sir," they said, "give us that bread every day of our lives."

35 Jesus replied, "I am the bread of life. No one who comes to me will ever be hungry again. Those who believe in me will never thirst. 36 But you haven't believed in me even though you have seen me. 37 However, those the Father has given me will come to me, and I will never reject them. 38 For I have come down from heaven to do the will of God who sent me, not to do what I want. 39 And this is the will of God, that I should not lose even one of all those he has given me, but that I should raise them to eternal life at the last day. 40 For it is my Father's will that all who see his Son and believe in him should have eternal life—that I should raise them at the last day."

41 Then the people* began to murmur in disagreement because he had said, "I am the bread from heaven." 42 They said, "This is Jesus, the son of Joseph. We know his father and mother. How can he say, 'I came down from heaven'?"

6:41 Greek *Jewish people;* also in 6:52.

NEW KING JAMES VERSION

32 Then Jesus said to them, "Most assuredly, I say to you, Moses did not give you the bread from heaven, but My Father gives you the true bread from heaven. 33 For the bread of God is He who comes down from heaven and gives life to the world."

34 Then they said to Him, "Lord, give us this bread always."

35 And Jesus said to them, "I am the bread of life. He who comes to Me shall never hunger, and he who believes in Me shall never thirst. 36 But I said to you that you have seen Me and yet do not believe. 37 All that the Father gives Me will come to Me, and the one who comes to Me I will by no means cast out. 38 For I have come down from heaven, not to do My own will, but the will of Him who sent Me. 39 This is the will of the Father who sent Me, that of all He has given Me I should lose nothing, but should raise it up at the last day. 40 And this is the will of Him who sent Me, that everyone who sees the Son and believes in Him may have everlasting life; and I will raise him up at the last day."

Rejected by His Own

41 The Jews then complained about Him, because He said, "I am the bread which came down from heaven." 42 And they said, "Is not this Jesus, the son of Joseph, whose father and mother we know? How is it then that He says, 'I have come down from heaven'?"

THE MESSAGE

Jesus responded, "The real significance of that Scripture is not that Moses gave you bread from heaven but that my Father is right now offering you bread from heaven, the *real* bread. The Bread of God came down out of heaven and is giving life to the world."

They jumped at that: "Master, give us this bread, now and forever!"

Jesus said, "I am the Bread of Life. The person who aligns with me hungers no more and thirsts no more, ever. I have told you this explicitly because even though you have seen me in action, you don't really believe me. Every person the Father gives me eventually comes running to me. And once that person is with me, I hold on and don't let go. I came down from heaven not to follow my own whim but to accomplish the will of the One who sent me.

"This, in a nutshell, is that will: that everything handed over to me by the Father be completed—not a single detail missed—and at the wrap-up of time I have everything and everyone put together, upright and whole. This is what my Father wants: that anyone who sees the Son and trusts who he is and what he does and then aligns with him will enter *real* life, *eternal* life. My part is to put them on their feet alive and whole at the completion of time."

At this, because he said "I am the Bread that came down from heaven," the Jews started arguing over him: "Isn't this the son of Joseph? Don't we know his father? Don't we know his mother? How can he now say 'I came down out of heaven' and expect anyone to believe him?"

KING JAMES VERSION

43 Jesus therefore answered and said unto them, Murmur not among yourselves.

44 No man can come to me, except the Father which hath sent me draw him: and I will raise him up at the last day.

45 It is written in the prophets, And they shall be all taught of God. Every man therefore that hath heard, and hath learned of the Father, cometh unto me.

46 Not that any man hath seen the Father, save he which is of God, he hath seen the Father.

47 Verily, verily, I say unto you, He that believeth on me hath everlasting life.

48 I am that bread of life.

49 Your fathers did eat manna in the wilderness, and are dead.

50 This is the bread which cometh down from heaven, that a man may eat thereof, and not die.

51 I am the living bread which came down from heaven: if any man eat of this bread, he shall live for ever: and the bread that I will give is my flesh, which I will give for the life of the world.

52 The Jews therefore strove among themselves, saying, How can this man give us *his* flesh to eat?

53 Then Jesus said unto them, Verily, verily, I say unto you, Except ye eat the flesh of the Son of man, and drink his blood, ye have no life in you.

54 Whoso eateth my flesh, and drinketh my blood, hath eternal life; and I will raise him up at the last day.

55 For my flesh is meat indeed, and my blood is drink indeed.

NEW AMERICAN STANDARD BIBLE

43 Jesus answered and said to them, "Do not grumble among yourselves.

44 "No one can come to Me unless the Father who sent Me draws him; and I will raise him up on the last day.

45 "It is written in the prophets, 'AND THEY SHALL ALL BE TAUGHT OF GOD.' Everyone who has heard and learned from the Father, comes to Me.

46 "Not that anyone has seen the Father, except the One who is from God; He has seen the Father.

47 "Truly, truly, I say to you, he who believes has eternal life.

48 "I am the bread of life.

49 "Your fathers ate the manna in the wilderness, and they died.

50 "This is the bread which comes down out of heaven, so that one may eat of it and not die.

51 "I am the living bread that came down out of heaven; if anyone eats of this bread, he will live forever; and the bread also which I will give for the life of the world is My flesh."

52 Then the Jews *began* to argue with one another, saying, "How can this man give us *His* flesh to eat?"

53 So Jesus said to them, "Truly, truly, I say to you, unless you eat the flesh of the Son of Man and drink His blood, you have no life in yourselves.

54 "He who eats My flesh and drinks My blood has eternal life, and I will raise him up on the last day.

55 "For My flesh is true food, and My blood is true drink.

NEW CENTURY VERSION

43 But Jesus answered, "Stop complaining to each other.
44 The Father is the One who sent me. No one can come to
me unless the Father draws him to me, and I will raise
that person up on the last day. 45 It is written in the proph-
ets, 'They will all be taught by God.'[c] Everyone who listens
to the Father and learns from him comes to me. 46 No one
has seen the Father except the One who is from God; only
he has seen the Father. 47 I tell you the truth, whoever
believes has eternal life. 48 I am the bread that gives life.
49 Your ancestors ate the manna in the desert, but still they
died. 50 Here is the bread that comes down from heaven.
Anyone who eats this bread will never die. 51 I am the liv-
ing bread that came down from heaven. Anyone who eats
this bread will live forever. This bread is my flesh, which I
will give up so that the world may have life."

52 Then the Jews began to argue among themselves, say-
ing, "How can this man give us his flesh to eat?"
53 Jesus said, "I tell you the truth, you must eat the flesh
of the Son of Man and drink his blood. Otherwise, you
won't have real life in you. 54 Those who eat my flesh and
drink my blood have eternal life, and I will raise them up
on the last day. 55 My flesh is true food, and my blood is

6:45 [c] 'They...God.' Quotation from Isaiah 54:13.

CONTEMPORARY ENGLISH VERSION

43 Jesus told them:
Stop grumbling! 44 No one can come to me, unless the
Father who sent me makes them want to come. But if
they do come, I will raise them to life on the last day.
45 One of the prophets wrote, "God will teach all of
them." And so everyone who listens to the Father and
learns from him will come to me.
46 The only one who has seen the Father is the one
who has come from him. No one else has ever seen the
Father. 47 I tell you for certain that everyone who has
faith in me has eternal life.
48 I am the bread that gives life! 49 Your ancestors ate
manna[j] in the desert, and later they died. 50 But the
bread from heaven has come down, so that no one who
eats it will ever die. 51 I am that bread from heaven!
Everyone who eats it will live forever. My flesh is the
life-giving bread that I give to the people of this world.
52 They started arguing with each other and asked, "How
can he give us his flesh to eat?"
53 Jesus answered:
I tell you for certain that you won't live unless you eat
the flesh and drink the blood of the Son of Man. 54 But if
you do eat my flesh and drink my blood, you will have
eternal life, and I will raise you to life on the last day.
55 My flesh is the true food, and my blood is the true

[j] 6.49 *manna*: See the note at 6.31.

NEW INTERNATIONAL VERSION

43"Stop grumbling among yourselves," Jesus answered. 44"No one can come to me unless the Father who sent me draws him, and I will raise him up at the last day. 45It is written in the Prophets: 'They will all be taught by God.'[d] Everyone who listens to the Father and learns from him comes to me. 46No one has seen the Father except the one who is from God; only he has seen the Father. 47I tell you the truth, he who believes has everlasting life. 48I am the bread of life. 49Your forefathers ate the manna in the desert, yet they died. 50But here is the bread that comes down from heaven, which a man may eat and not die. 51I am the living bread that came down from heaven. If anyone eats of this bread, he will live forever. This bread is my flesh, which I will give for the life of the world."

52Then the Jews began to argue sharply among themselves, "How can this man give us his flesh to eat?"

53Jesus said to them, "I tell you the truth, unless you eat the flesh of the Son of Man and drink his blood, you have no life in you. 54Whoever eats my flesh and drinks my blood has eternal life, and I will raise him up at the last day. 55For my flesh is real food and my blood is real drink.

[d] *45* Isaiah 54:13

NEW LIVING TRANSLATION

43But Jesus replied, "Don't complain about what I said. 44For people can't come to me unless the Father who sent me draws them to me, and at the last day I will raise them from the dead. 45As it is written in the Scriptures, 'They will all be taught by God.'* Everyone who hears and learns from the Father comes to me. 46(Not that anyone has ever seen the Father; only I, who was sent from God, have seen him.)

47"I assure you, anyone who believes in me already has eternal life. 48Yes, I am the bread of life! 49Your ancestors ate manna in the wilderness, but they all died. 50However, the bread from heaven gives eternal life to everyone who eats it. 51I am the living bread that came down out of heaven. Anyone who eats this bread will live forever; this bread is my flesh, offered so the world may live."

52Then the people began arguing with each other about what he meant. "How can this man give us his flesh to eat?" they asked.

53So Jesus said again, "I assure you, unless you eat the flesh of the Son of Man and drink his blood, you cannot have eternal life within you. 54But those who eat my flesh and drink my blood have eternal life, and I will raise them at the last day. 55For my flesh is the true food, and my blood

6:45 Isa 54:13.

NEW KING JAMES VERSION

43Jesus therefore answered and said to them, "Do not murmur among yourselves. 44No one can come to Me unless the Father who sent Me draws him; and I will raise him up at the last day. 45It is written in the prophets, *'And they shall all be taught by God.'*[e] Therefore everyone who has heard and learned[f] from the Father comes to Me. 46Not that anyone has seen the Father, except He who is from God; He has seen the Father. 47Most assuredly, I say to you, he who believes in Me[g] has everlasting life. 48I am the bread of life. 49Your fathers ate the manna in the wilderness, and are dead. 50This is the bread which comes down from heaven, that one may eat of it and not die. 51I am the living bread which came down from heaven. If anyone eats of this bread, he will live forever; and the bread that I shall give is My flesh, which I shall give for the life of the world."

52The Jews therefore quarreled among themselves, saying, "How can this Man give us *His* flesh to eat?"

53Then Jesus said to them, "Most assuredly, I say to you, unless you eat the flesh of the Son of Man and drink His blood, you have no life in you. 54Whoever eats My flesh and drinks My blood has eternal life, and I will raise him up at the last day. 55For My flesh is food indeed,[h] and My

6:45 [e] Isaiah 54:13 [f] M-Text reads *hears and has learned.*
6:47 [g] NU-Text omits *in Me.* **6:55** [h] NU-Text reads *true food* and *true drink.*

THE MESSAGE

Jesus said, "Don't bicker among yourselves over me. You're not in charge here. The Father who sent me is in charge. He draws people to me—that's the only way you'll ever come. Only then do I do my work, putting people together, setting them on their feet, ready for the End. This is what the prophets meant when they wrote, 'And then they will all be personally taught by God.' Anyone who has spent any time at all listening to the Father, really listening and therefore learning, comes to me to be taught personally—to see it with his own eyes, hear it with his own ears, from me, since I have it firsthand from the Father. No one has seen the Father except the One who has his Being alongside the Father—and you can see *me*.

"I'm telling you the most solemn and sober truth now: Whoever believes in me has real life, eternal life. I am the Bread of Life. Your ancestors ate the manna bread in the desert and died. But now here is Bread that truly comes down out of heaven. Anyone eating this Bread will not die, ever. I am the Bread—living Bread!—who came down out of heaven. Anyone who eats this Bread will live—and forever! The Bread that I present to the world so that it can eat and live is myself, this flesh-and-blood self."

At this, the Jews started fighting among themselves: "How can this man serve up his flesh for a meal?"

But Jesus didn't give an inch. "Only insofar as you eat and drink flesh and blood, the flesh and blood of the Son of Man, do you have life within you. The one who brings a hearty appetite to this eating and drinking has eternal life and will be fit and ready for the Final Day. My flesh is real

KING JAMES VERSION

56 He that eateth my flesh, and drinketh my blood, dwelleth in me, and I in him.

57 As the living Father hath sent me, and I live by the Father: so he that eateth me, even he shall live by me.

58 This is that bread which came down from heaven: not as your fathers did eat manna, and are dead: he that eateth of this bread shall live for ever.

59 These things said he in the synagogue, as he taught in Capernaum.

60 ¶ Many therefore of his disciples, when they had heard *this*, said, This is an hard saying; who can hear it?

61 When Jesus knew in himself that his disciples murmured at it, he said unto them, Doth this offend you?

62 *What* and if ye shall see the Son of man ascend up where he was before?

63 It is the spirit that quickeneth; the flesh profiteth nothing: the words that I speak unto you, *they* are spirit, and *they* are life.

64 But there are some of you that believe not. For Jesus knew from the beginning who they were that believed not, and who should betray him.

65 And he said, Therefore said I unto you, that no man can come unto me, except it were given unto him of my Father.

66 From that *time* many of his disciples went back, and walked no more with him.

NEW AMERICAN STANDARD BIBLE

56 "He who eats My flesh and drinks My blood abides in Me, and I in him.

57 "As the living Father sent Me, and I live because of the Father, so he who eats Me, he also will live because of Me.

58 "This is the bread which came down out of heaven; not as the fathers ate and died; he who eats this bread will live forever."

Words to the Disciples

59 These things He said in the synagogue as He taught in Capernaum.

60 Therefore many of His disciples, when they heard *this* said, "This is a difficult statement; who can listen to it?"

61 But Jesus, conscious that His disciples grumbled at this, said to them, "Does this cause you to stumble?

62 "*What* then if you see the Son of Man ascending to where He was before?

63 "It is the Spirit who gives life; the flesh profits nothing; the words that I have spoken to you are spirit and are life.

64 "But there are some of you who do not believe." For Jesus knew from the beginning who they were who did not believe, and who it was that would betray Him.

65 And He was saying, "For this reason I have said to you, that no one can come to Me unless it has been granted him from the Father."

Peter's Confession of Faith

66 As a result of this many of His disciples withdrew and were not walking with Him anymore.

NEW CENTURY VERSION

true drink. 56Those who eat my flesh and drink my blood
live in me, and I live in them. 57The living Father sent me,
and I live because of the Father. So whoever eats me will
live because of me. 58I am not like the bread your ances-
tors ate. They ate that bread and still died. I am the bread
that came down from heaven, and whoever eats this bread
will live forever." 59Jesus said all these things while he
was teaching in the synagogue in Capernaum.

The Words of Eternal Life

60When the followers of Jesus heard this, many of them
said, "This teaching is hard. Who can accept it?"

61Knowing that his followers were complaining about
this, Jesus said, "Does this teaching bother you? 62Then
will it also bother you to see the Son of Man going back to
the place where he came from? 63It is the Spirit that gives
life. The flesh doesn't give life. The words I told you are
spirit, and they give life. 64But some of you don't believe."
(Jesus knew from the beginning who did not believe and
who would turn against him.) 65Jesus said, "That is the
reason I said, 'If the Father does not bring a person to me,
that one cannot come.' "

66After Jesus said this, many of his followers left him
and stopped following him.

CONTEMPORARY ENGLISH VERSION

drink. 56If you eat my flesh and drink my blood, you are
one with me, and I am one with you.

57The living Father sent me, and I have life because of
him. Now everyone who eats my flesh will live because
of me. 58The bread that comes down from heaven isn't
like what your ancestors ate. They died, but whoever
eats this bread will live forever.

59Jesus was teaching in a Jewish place of worship in
Capernaum when he said these things.

The Words of Eternal Life

60Many of Jesus' disciples heard him and said, "This is
too hard for anyone to understand."

61Jesus knew that his disciples were grumbling. So he
asked, "Does this bother you? 62What if you should see the
Son of Man go up to heaven where he came from? 63The
Spirit is the one who gives life! Human strength can do
nothing. The words that I have spoken to you are from
that life-giving Spirit. 64But some of you refuse to have
faith in me." Jesus said this, because from the beginning
he knew who would have faith in him. He also knew which
one would betray him.

65Then Jesus said, "You cannot come to me, unless the
Father makes you want to come. That is why I have told
these things to all of you."

66Because of what Jesus said, many of his disciples
turned their backs on him and stopped following him.

NEW INTERNATIONAL VERSION

56Whoever eats my flesh and drinks my blood remains in me, and I in him. 57Just as the living Father sent me and I live because of the Father, so the one who feeds on me will live because of me. 58This is the bread that came down from heaven. Your forefathers ate manna and died, but he who feeds on this bread will live forever." 59He said this while teaching in the synagogue in Capernaum.

Many Disciples Desert Jesus

60On hearing it, many of his disciples said, "This is a hard teaching. Who can accept it?"

61Aware that his disciples were grumbling about this, Jesus said to them, "Does this offend you? 62What if you see the Son of Man ascend to where he was before! 63The Spirit gives life; the flesh counts for nothing. The words I have spoken to you are spirit[e] and they are life. 64Yet there are some of you who do not believe." For Jesus had known from the beginning which of them did not believe and who would betray him. 65He went on to say, "This is why I told you that no one can come to me unless the Father has enabled him."

66From this time many of his disciples turned back and no longer followed him.

[e] *63* Or *Spirit*

NEW LIVING TRANSLATION

is the true drink. 56All who eat my flesh and drink my blood remain in me, and I in them. 57I live by the power of the living Father who sent me; in the same way, those who partake of me will live because of me. 58I am the true bread from heaven. Anyone who eats this bread will live forever and not die as your ancestors did, even though they ate the manna."

59He said these things while he was teaching in the synagogue in Capernaum.

Many Disciples Desert Jesus

60Even his disciples said, "This is very hard to understand. How can anyone accept it?"

61Jesus knew within himself that his disciples were complaining, so he said to them, "Does this offend you? 62Then what will you think if you see me, the Son of Man, return to heaven again? 63It is the Spirit who gives eternal life. Human effort accomplishes nothing. And the very words I have spoken to you are spirit and life. 64But some of you don't believe me." (For Jesus knew from the beginning who didn't believe, and he knew who would betray him.) 65Then he said, "That is what I meant when I said that people can't come to me unless the Father brings them to me."

66At this point many of his disciples turned away and

NEW KING JAMES VERSION

blood is drink indeed. 56He who eats My flesh and drinks My blood abides in Me, and I in him. 57As the living Father sent Me, and I live because of the Father, so he who feeds on Me will live because of Me. 58This is the bread which came down from heaven—not as your fathers ate the manna, and are dead. He who eats this bread will live forever."

59These things He said in the synagogue as He taught in Capernaum.

Many Disciples Turn Away

60Therefore many of His disciples, when they heard *this,* said, "This is a hard saying; who can understand it?"

61When Jesus knew in Himself that His disciples complained about this, He said to them, "Does this offend you? 62*What* then if you should see the Son of Man ascend where He was before? 63It is the Spirit who gives life; the flesh profits nothing. The words that I speak to you are spirit, and *they* are life. 64But there are some of you who do not believe." For Jesus knew from the beginning who they were who did not believe, and who would betray Him. 65And He said, "Therefore I have said to you that no one can come to Me unless it has been granted to him by My Father."

66From that *time* many of His disciples went back and

THE MESSAGE

food and my blood is real drink. By eating my flesh and drinking my blood you enter into me and I into you. In the same way that the fully alive Father sent me here and I live because of him, so the one who makes a meal of me lives because of me. This is the Bread from heaven. Your ancestors ate bread, and later died. Whoever eats this Bread will live always."

He said these things while teaching in the meeting place in Capernaum.

Too Tough to Swallow

Many among his disciples heard this and said, "This is tough teaching, too tough to swallow."

Jesus sensed that his disciples were having a hard time with this and said, "Does this throw you completely? What would happen if you saw the Son of Man ascending to where he came from? The Spirit can make life. Sheer muscle and willpower don't make anything happen. Every word I've spoken to you is a Spirit-word, and so it is life-making. But some of you are resisting, refusing to have any part in this." (Jesus knew from the start that some weren't going to risk themselves with him. He knew also who would betray him.) He went on to say, "This is why I told you earlier that no one is capable of coming to me on his own. You get to me only as a gift from the Father."

After this a lot of his disciples left. They no longer wanted

KING JAMES VERSION

67 Then said Jesus unto the twelve, Will ye also go away?

68 Then Simon Peter answered him, Lord, to whom shall we go? thou hast the words of eternal life.

69 And we believe and are sure that thou art that Christ, the Son of the living God.

70 Jesus answered them, Have not I chosen you twelve, and one of you is a devil?

71 He spake of Judas Iscariot *the son* of Simon: for he it was that should betray him, being one of the twelve.

7 After these things Jesus walked in Galilee: for he would not walk in Jewry, because the Jews sought to kill him.

2 Now the Jews' feast of tabernacles was at hand.

3 His brethren therefore said unto him, Depart hence, and go into Judaea, that thy disciples also may see the works that thou doest.

4 For *there is* no man *that* doeth any thing in secret, and he himself seeketh to be known openly. If thou do these things, shew thyself to the world.

5 For neither did his brethren believe in him.

6 Then Jesus said unto them, My time is not yet come: but your time is alway ready.

7 The world cannot hate you; but me it hateth, because I testify of it, that the works thereof are evil.

NEW AMERICAN STANDARD BIBLE

67 So Jesus said to the twelve, "You do not want to go away also, do you?"

68 Simon Peter answered Him, "Lord, to whom shall we go? You have words of eternal life.

69 "We have believed and have come to know that You are the Holy One of God."

70 Jesus answered them, "Did I Myself not choose you, the twelve, and *yet* one of you is a devil?"

71 Now He meant Judas *the son* of Simon Iscariot, for he, one of the twelve, was going to betray Him.

Jesus Teaches at the Feast

7 After these things Jesus was walking in Galilee, for He was unwilling to walk in Judea because the Jews were seeking to kill Him.

2 Now the feast of the Jews, the Feast of Booths, was near.

3 Therefore His brothers said to Him, "Leave here and go into Judea, so that Your disciples also may see Your works which You are doing.

4 "For no one does anything in secret when he himself seeks to be *known* publicly. If You do these things, show Yourself to the world."

5 For not even His brothers were believing in Him.

6 So Jesus *said to them, "My time is not yet here, but your time is always opportune.

7 "The world cannot hate you, but it hates Me because I testify of it, that its deeds are evil.

NEW CENTURY VERSION

67Jesus asked the twelve followers, "Do you want to leave, too?"

68Simon Peter answered him, "Lord, where would we go? You have the words that give eternal life. 69We believe and know that you are the Holy One from God."

70Then Jesus answered, "I chose all twelve of you, but one of you is a devil."

71Jesus was talking about Judas, the son of Simon Iscariot. Judas was one of the twelve, but later he was going to turn against Jesus.

Jesus' Brothers Don't Believe

7 After this, Jesus traveled around Galilee. He did not want to travel in Judea, because the Jews there wanted to kill him. 2It was time for the Jewish Feast of Shelters. 3So Jesus' brothers said to him, "You should leave here and go to Judea so your followers there can see the miracles you do. 4Anyone who wants to be well known does not hide what he does. If you are doing these things, show yourself to the world." 5(Even Jesus' brothers did not believe in him.)

6Jesus said to his brothers, "The right time for me has not yet come, but any time is right for you. 7The world cannot hate you, but it hates me, because I tell it the evil

CONTEMPORARY ENGLISH VERSION

67Jesus then asked his twelve disciples if they were going to leave him. 68Simon Peter answered, "Lord, there is no one else that we can go to! Your words give eternal life. 69We have faith in you, and we are sure that you are God's Holy One."

70Jesus told his disciples, "I chose all twelve of you, but one of you is a demon!" 71Jesus was talking about Judas, the son of Simon Iscariot.[k] He would later betray Jesus, even though he was one of the twelve disciples.

Jesus' Brothers Don't Have Faith in Him

7 Jesus decided to leave Judea and to start going through Galilee because the Jewish leaders wanted to kill him. 2It was almost time for the Festival of Shelters, 3and Jesus' brothers said to him, "Why don't you go to Judea? Then your disciples can see what you are doing. 4No one does anything in secret, if they want others to know about them. So let the world know what you are doing!" 5Even Jesus' own brothers had not yet become his followers.

6Jesus answered, "My time hasn't yet come,[a] but your time is always here. 7The people of this world cannot hate you. They hate me, because I tell them that they do evil

[k] 6.71 *Iscariot*: This may mean "a man from Kerioth" (a place in Judea). But more probably it means "a man who was a liar" or "a man who was a betrayer." [a] 7.6 *My time hasn't yet come*: See the note at 2.4.

NEW INTERNATIONAL VERSION

67“You do not want to leave too, do you?” Jesus asked the Twelve.

68Simon Peter answered him, “Lord, to whom shall we go? You have the words of eternal life. 69We believe and know that you are the Holy One of God.”

70Then Jesus replied, “Have I not chosen you, the Twelve? Yet one of you is a devil!” 71(He meant Judas, the son of Simon Iscariot, who, though one of the Twelve, was later to betray him.)

Jesus Goes to the Feast of Tabernacles

7 After this, Jesus went around in Galilee, purposely staying away from Judea because the Jews there were waiting to take his life. 2But when the Jewish Feast of Tabernacles was near, 3Jesus' brothers said to him, “You ought to leave here and go to Judea, so that your disciples may see the miracles you do. 4No one who wants to become a public figure acts in secret. Since you are doing these things, show yourself to the world.” 5For even his own brothers did not believe in him.

6Therefore Jesus told them, “The right time for me has not yet come; for you any time is right. 7The world cannot hate you, but it hates me because I testify that what it

NEW LIVING TRANSLATION

deserted him. 67Then Jesus turned to the Twelve and asked, “Are you going to leave, too?”

68Simon Peter replied, “Lord, to whom would we go? You alone have the words that give eternal life. 69We believe them, and we know you are the Holy One of God.”

70Then Jesus said, “I chose the twelve of you, but one is a devil.” 71He was speaking of Judas, son of Simon Iscariot, one of the Twelve, who would betray him.

Jesus and His Brothers

7 After this, Jesus stayed in Galilee, going from village to village. He wanted to stay out of Judea where the Jewish leaders were plotting his death. 2But soon it was time for the Festival of Shelters, 3and Jesus' brothers urged him to go to Judea for the celebration. “Go where your followers can see your miracles!” they scoffed. 4“You can't become a public figure if you hide like this! If you can do such wonderful things, prove it to the world!” 5For even his brothers didn't believe in him.

6Jesus replied, “Now is not the right time for me to go. But you can go anytime, and it will make no difference. 7The world can't hate you, but it does hate me because I

NEW KING JAMES VERSION

walked with Him no more. 67Then Jesus said to the twelve, “Do you also want to go away?”

68But Simon Peter answered Him, “Lord, to whom shall we go? You have the words of eternal life. 69Also we have come to believe and know that You are the Christ, the Son of the living God.”[j]

70Jesus answered them, “Did I not choose you, the twelve, and one of you is a devil?” 71He spoke of Judas Iscariot, *the son* of Simon, for it was he who would betray Him, being one of the twelve.

Jesus' Brothers Disbelieve

7 After these things Jesus walked in Galilee; for He did not want to walk in Judea, because the Jews[a] sought to kill Him. 2Now the Jews' Feast of Tabernacles was at hand. 3His brothers therefore said to Him, “Depart from here and go into Judea, that Your disciples also may see the works that You are doing. 4For no one does anything in secret while he himself seeks to be known openly. If You do these things, show Yourself to the world.” 5For even His brothers did not believe in Him.

6Then Jesus said to them, “My time has not yet come, but your time is always ready. 7The world cannot hate you, but it hates Me because I testify of it that its works

6:69 [j] NU-Text reads *You are the Holy One of God.* 7:1 [a] That is, the ruling authorities

THE MESSAGE

to be associated with him. Then Jesus gave the Twelve their chance: “Do you also want to leave?”

Peter replied, “Master, to whom would we go? You have the words of real life, eternal life. We've already committed ourselves, confident that you are the Holy One of God.”

Jesus responded, “Haven't I handpicked you, the Twelve? Still, one of you is a devil!” He was referring to Judas, son of Simon Iscariot. This man—one from the Twelve!—was even then getting ready to betray him.

7 Later Jesus was going about his business in Galilee. He didn't want to travel in Judea because the Jews there were looking for a chance to kill him. It was near the time of Tabernacles, a feast observed annually by the Jews.

His brothers said, “Why don't you leave here and go up to the Feast so your disciples can get a good look at the works you do? No one who intends to be publicly known does everything behind the scenes. If you're serious about what you are doing, come out in the open and show the world.” His brothers were pushing him like this because they didn't believe in him either.

Jesus came back at them, “Don't crowd me. This isn't my time. It's your time—it's *always* your time; you have nothing to lose. The world has nothing against you, but it's up in arms against me. It's against me because I expose the

KING JAMES VERSION

8 Go ye up unto this feast: I go not up yet unto this feast; for my time is not yet full come.

9 When he had said these words unto them, he abode *still* in Galilee.

10 But when his brethren were gone up, then went he also up unto the feast, not openly, but as it were in secret.

11 Then the Jews sought him at the feast, and said, Where is he?

12 And there was much murmuring among the people concerning him: for some said, He is a good man: others said, Nay; but he deceiveth the people.

13 Howbeit no man spake openly of him for fear of the Jews.

14 ¶ Now about the midst of the feast Jesus went up into the temple, and taught.

15 And the Jews marvelled, saying, How knoweth this man letters, having never learned?

16 Jesus answered them, and said, My doctrine is not mine, but his that sent me.

17 If any man will do his will, he shall know of the doctrine, whether it be of God, or *whether* I speak of myself.

18 He that speaketh of himself seeketh his own glory: but he that seeketh his glory that sent him, the same is true, and no unrighteousness is in him.

19 Did not Moses give you the law, and *yet* none of you keepeth the law? Why go ye about to kill me?

NEW AMERICAN STANDARD BIBLE

8 "Go up to the feast yourselves; I do not go up to this feast because My time has not yet fully come."

9 Having said these things to them, He stayed in Galilee.

10 But when His brothers had gone up to the feast, then He Himself also went up, not publicly, but as if, in secret.

11 So the Jews were seeking Him at the feast and were saying, "Where is He?"

12 There was much grumbling among the crowds concerning Him; some were saying, "He is a good man"; others were saying, "No, on the contrary, He leads the people astray."

13 Yet no one was speaking openly of Him for fear of the Jews.

14 But when it was now the midst of the feast Jesus went up into the temple, and *began to* teach.

15 The Jews then were astonished, saying, "How has this man become learned, having never been educated?"

16 So Jesus answered them and said, "My teaching is not Mine, but His who sent Me.

17 "If anyone is willing to do His will, he will know of the teaching, whether it is of God or *whether* I speak from Myself.

18 "He who speaks from himself seeks his own glory; but He who is seeking the glory of the One who sent Him, He is true, and there is no unrighteousness in Him.

19 "Did not Moses give you the Law, and *yet* none of you carries out the Law? Why do you seek to kill Me?"

NEW CENTURY VERSION

things it does. 8So you go to the feast. I will not go yet to
this feast, because the right time for me has not yet come."
9After saying this, Jesus stayed in Galilee.
10But after Jesus' brothers had gone to the feast, Jesus went
also. But he did not let people see him. 11At the feast the Jews
were looking for him and saying, "Where is that man?"
12Within the large crowd there, many people were whispering to each other about Jesus. Some said, "He is a good man."

Others said, "No, he fools the people." 13But no one was
brave enough to talk about Jesus openly, because they were afraid of the Jews.

Jesus Teaches at the Feast

14When the feast was about half over, Jesus went to the
Temple and began to teach. 15The Jews were amazed and said, "This man has never studied in school. How did he learn so much?"

16Jesus answered, "The things I teach are not my own,
but they come from him who sent me. 17If people choose to
do what God wants, they will know that my teaching
comes from God and not from me. 18Those who teach their own ideas are trying to get honor for themselves. But those who try to bring honor to the one who sent him speak the truth, and there is nothing false in them.
19Moses gave you the law,[a] but none of you obeys that law. Why are you trying to kill me?"

7:19 [a] law Moses gave God's people the law that God gave him on Mount Sinai (Exodus 34:29–32).

CONTEMPORARY ENGLISH VERSION

things. 8Go on to the festival. My time hasn't yet come,
and I am not going." 9Jesus said this and stayed on in
Galilee.

Jesus at the Festival of Shelters

10After Jesus' brothers had gone to the festival, he went secretly, without telling anyone.

11During the festival the Jewish leaders looked for Jesus
and asked, "Where is he?" 12The crowds even got into an argument about him. Some were saying, "Jesus is a good man," while others were saying, "He is lying to everyone."
13But the people were afraid of their leaders, and none of them talked in public about him.

14When the festival was about half over, Jesus went into
the temple and started teaching. 15The leaders were surprised and said, "How does this man know so much? He has never been taught!"

16Jesus replied:

I am not teaching something that I thought up. What I
teach comes from the one who sent me. 17If you really
want to obey God, you will know if what I teach comes
from God or from me. 18If I wanted to bring honor to myself, I would speak for myself. But I want to honor the one who sent me. That is why I tell the truth and not a lie. 19Didn't Moses give you the Law? Yet none of you obey it! So why do you want to kill me?

NEW INTERNATIONAL VERSION

does is evil. 8You go to the Feast. I am not yet[a] going up to this Feast, because for me the right time has not yet come." 9Having said this, he stayed in Galilee.

10However, after his brothers had left for the Feast, he went also, not publicly, but in secret. 11Now at the Feast the Jews were watching for him and asking, "Where is that man?"

12Among the crowds there was widespread whispering about him. Some said, "He is a good man."

Others replied, "No, he deceives the people." 13But no one would say anything publicly about him for fear of the Jews.

Jesus Teaches at the Feast

14Not until halfway through the Feast did Jesus go up to the temple courts and begin to teach. 15The Jews were amazed and asked, "How did this man get such learning without having studied?"

16Jesus answered, "My teaching is not my own. It comes from him who sent me. 17If anyone chooses to do God's will, he will find out whether my teaching comes from God or whether I speak on my own. 18He who speaks on his own does so to gain honor for himself, but he who works for the honor of the one who sent him is a man of truth; there is nothing false about him. 19Has not Moses given you the law? Yet not one of you keeps the law. Why are you trying to kill me?"

[a] *8* Some early manuscripts do not have *yet.*

NEW LIVING TRANSLATION

accuse it of sin and evil. 8You go on. I am not yet* ready to go to this festival, because my time has not yet come." 9So Jesus remained in Galilee.

Jesus Teaches Openly at the Temple

10But after his brothers had left for the festival, Jesus also went, though secretly, staying out of public view. 11The Jewish leaders tried to find him at the festival and kept asking if anyone had seen him. 12There was a lot of discussion about him among the crowds. Some said, "He's a wonderful man," while others said, "He's nothing but a fraud, deceiving the people." 13But no one had the courage to speak favorably about him in public, for they were afraid of getting in trouble with the Jewish leaders.

14Then, midway through the festival, Jesus went up to the Temple and began to teach. 15The Jewish leaders were surprised when they heard him. "How does he know so much when he hasn't studied everything we've studied?" they asked.

16So Jesus told them, "I'm not teaching my own ideas, but those of God who sent me. 17Anyone who wants to do the will of God will know whether my teaching is from God or is merely my own. 18Those who present their own ideas are looking for praise for themselves, but those who seek to honor the one who sent them are good and genuine. 19None of you obeys the law of Moses! In fact, you are trying to kill me."

7:8 Some manuscripts omit *yet.*

NEW KING JAMES VERSION

are evil. 8You go up to this feast. I am not yet[b] going up to this feast, for My time has not yet fully come." 9When He had said these things to them, He remained in Galilee.

The Heavenly Scholar

10But when His brothers had gone up, then He also went up to the feast, not openly, but as it were in secret. 11Then the Jews sought Him at the feast, and said, "Where is He?" 12And there was much complaining among the people concerning Him. Some said, "He is good"; others said, "No, on the contrary, He deceives the people." 13However, no one spoke openly of Him for fear of the Jews.

14Now about the middle of the feast Jesus went up into the temple and taught. 15And the Jews marveled, saying, "How does this Man know letters, having never studied?"

16Jesus[c] answered them and said, "My doctrine is not Mine, but His who sent Me. 17If anyone wills to do His will, he shall know concerning the doctrine, whether it is from God or *whether* I speak on My own *authority.* 18He who speaks from himself seeks his own glory; but He who seeks the glory of the One who sent Him is true, and no unrighteousness is in Him. 19Did not Moses give you the law, yet none of you keeps the law? Why do you seek to kill Me?"

7:8 [b] NU-Text omits *yet.* 7:16 [c] NU-Text and M-Text read *So Jesus.*

THE MESSAGE

evil behind its pretensions. You go ahead, go up to the Feast. Don't wait for me. I'm not ready. It's not the right time for me."

He said this and stayed on in Galilee. But later, after his family had gone up to the Feast, he also went. But he kept out of the way, careful not to draw attention to himself. The Jews were already out looking for him, asking around, "Where is that man?"

There was a lot of contentious talk about him circulating through the crowds. Some were saying, "He's a good man." But others said, "Not so. He's selling snake oil." This kind of talk went on in guarded whispers because of the intimidating Jewish leaders.

Could It Be the Messiah?

With the Feast already half over, Jesus showed up in the Temple, teaching. The Jews were impressed, but puzzled: "How does he know so much without being schooled?"

Jesus said, "I didn't make this up. What I teach comes from the One who sent me. Anyone who wants to do his will can test this teaching and know whether it's from God or whether I'm making it up. A person making things up tries to make himself look good. But someone trying to honor the one who sent him sticks to the facts and doesn't tamper with reality. It was Moses, wasn't it, who gave you God's Law? But none of you are living it. So why are you trying to kill me?"

KING JAMES VERSION

20 The people answered and said, Thou hast a devil: who goeth about to kill thee?

21 Jesus answered and said unto them, I have done one work, and ye all marvel.

22 Moses therefore gave unto you circumcision; (not because it is of Moses, but of the fathers;) and ye on the sabbath day circumcise a man.

23 If a man on the sabbath day receive circumcision, that the law of Moses should not be broken; are ye angry at me, because I have made a man every whit whole on the sabbath day?

24 Judge not according to the appearance, but judge righteous judgment.

25 Then said some of them of Jerusalem, Is not this he, whom they seek to kill?

26 But, lo, he speaketh boldly, and they say nothing unto him. Do the rulers know indeed that this is the very Christ?

27 Howbeit we know this man whence he is: but when Christ cometh, no man knoweth whence he is.

28 Then cried Jesus in the temple as he taught, saying, Ye both know me, and ye know whence I am: and I am not come of myself, but he that sent me is true, whom ye know not.

29 But I know him: for I am from him, and he hath sent me.

30 Then they sought to take him: but no man laid hands on him, because his hour was not yet come.

31 And many of the people believed on him, and said,

NEW AMERICAN STANDARD BIBLE

20 The crowd answered, "You have a demon! Who seeks to kill You?"

21 Jesus answered them, "I did one deed, and you all marvel.

22 "For this reason Moses has given you circumcision (not because it is from Moses, but from the fathers), and on *the* Sabbath you circumcise a man.

23 "If a man receives circumcision on *the* Sabbath so that the Law of Moses will not be broken, are you angry with Me because I made an entire man well on *the* Sabbath?

24 "Do not judge according to appearance, but judge with righteous judgment."

25 So some of the people of Jerusalem were saying, "Is this not the man whom they are seeking to kill?

26 "Look, He is speaking publicly, and they are saying nothing to Him. The rulers do not really know that this is the Christ, do they?

27 "However, we know where this man is from; but whenever the Christ may come, no one knows where He is from."

28 Then Jesus cried out in the temple, teaching and saying, "You both know Me and know where I am from; and I have not come of Myself, but He who sent Me is true, whom you do not know.

29 "I know Him, because I am from Him, and He sent Me."

30 So they were seeking to seize Him; and no man laid his hand on Him, because His hour had not yet come.

31 But many of the crowd believed in Him; and they

NEW CENTURY VERSION

20 The people answered, "A demon has come into you.
We are not trying to kill you."

21 Jesus said to them, "I did one miracle, and you are all
amazed. 22 Moses gave you the law about circumcision.
(But really Moses did not give you circumcision; it came
from our ancestors.) And yet you circumcise a baby on a
Sabbath day. 23 If a baby can be circumcised on a Sabbath
day to obey the law of Moses, why are you angry at me for
healing a person's whole body on the Sabbath day? 24 Stop
judging by the way things look, but judge by what is really
right."

Is Jesus the Christ?

25 Then some of the people who lived in Jerusalem said,
"This is the man they are trying to kill. 26 But he is teach-
ing where everyone can see and hear him, and no one is
trying to stop him. Maybe the leaders have decided he real-
ly is the Christ. 27 But we know where this man is from.
And when the real Christ comes, no one will know where
he comes from."

28 Jesus, teaching in the Temple, cried out, "Yes, you
know me, and you know where I am from. But I have not
come by my own authority. I was sent by the One who is
true, whom you don't know. 29 But I know him, because I
am from him, and he sent me."

30 When Jesus said this, the people tried to take him. But
no one was able to touch him, because it was not yet the
right time. 31 But many of the people believed in Jesus.

CONTEMPORARY ENGLISH VERSION

20 The crowd replied, "You're crazy! What makes you
think someone wants to kill you?"

21 Jesus answered:

I worked one miracle,[b] and it amazed you. 22 Moses
commanded you to circumcise your sons. But it wasn't
really Moses who gave you this command. It was your
ancestors, and even on the Sabbath you circumcise your
sons 23 in order to obey the Law of Moses. Why are you
angry with me for making someone completely well on
the Sabbath? 24 Don't judge by appearances. Judge by
what is right.

25 Some of the people from Jerusalem were saying, "Isn't
this the man they want to kill? 26 Yet here he is, speaking
for everyone to hear. And no one is arguing with him. Do
you suppose the authorities know that he is the Messiah?
27 But how could that be? No one knows where the Messiah
will come from, but we know where this man comes from."

28 As Jesus was teaching in the temple, he shouted, "Do
you really think you know me and where I came from? I
didn't come on my own! The one who sent me is truthful,
and you don't know him. 29 But I know the one who sent
me, because I came from him."

30 Some of the people wanted to arrest Jesus right then.
But no one even laid a hand on him, because his time had
not yet come.[c] 31 A lot of people in the crowd put their faith

[b] 7.21 *one miracle*: The healing of the lame man (5.1-18; see also the note at 2.11). [c] 7.30 *his time had not yet come*: See the note at 2.4.

NEW INTERNATIONAL VERSION

20"You are demon-possessed," the crowd answered.
"Who is trying to kill you?"
21Jesus said to them, "I did one miracle, and you are all
astonished. 22Yet, because Moses gave you circumcision
(though actually it did not come from Moses, but from the
patriarchs), you circumcise a child on the Sabbath. 23Now
if a child can be circumcised on the Sabbath so that the
law of Moses may not be broken, why are you angry with
me for healing the whole man on the Sabbath? 24Stop
judging by mere appearances, and make a right judgment."

Is Jesus the Christ?

25At that point some of the people of Jerusalem began to
ask, "Isn't this the man they are trying to kill? 26Here he
is, speaking publicly, and they are not saying a word to
him. Have the authorities really concluded that he is the
Christ[b]? 27But we know where this man is from; when the
Christ comes, no one will know where he is from."
28Then Jesus, still teaching in the temple courts, cried
out, "Yes, you know me, and you know where I am from. I
am not here on my own, but he who sent me is true. You
do not know him, 29but I know him because I am from him
and he sent me."
30At this they tried to seize him, but no one laid a hand
on him, because his time had not yet come. 31Still, many
in the crowd put their faith in him. They said, "When the

[b] *26* Or *Messiah*; also in verses 27, 31, 41 and 42

NEW LIVING TRANSLATION

20The crowd replied, "You're demon possessed! Who's
trying to kill you?"
21Jesus replied, "I worked on the Sabbath by healing a
man, and you were offended. 22But you work on the
Sabbath, too, when you obey Moses' law of circumcision.
(Actually, this tradition of circumcision is older than the
law of Moses; it goes back to Abraham.) 23For if the correct
time for circumcising your son falls on the Sabbath, you go
ahead and do it, so as not to break the law of Moses. So
why should I be condemned for making a man completely
well on the Sabbath? 24Think this through and you will
see that I am right."

Is Jesus the Messiah?

25Some of the people who lived there in Jerusalem said
among themselves, "Isn't this the man they are trying to
kill? 26But here he is, speaking in public, and they say
nothing to him. Can it be that our leaders know that he
really is the Messiah? 27But how could he be? For we know
where this man comes from. When the Messiah comes, he
will simply appear; no one will know where he comes
from."
28While Jesus was teaching in the Temple, he called out,
"Yes, you know me, and you know where I come from. But
I represent one you don't know, and he is true. 29I know
him because I have come from him, and he sent me to
you." 30Then the leaders tried to arrest him; but no one
laid a hand on him, because his time had not yet come.
31Many among the crowds at the Temple believed in

NEW KING JAMES VERSION

20The people answered and said, "You have a demon.
Who is seeking to kill You?"
21Jesus answered and said to them, "I did one work, and
you all marvel. 22Moses therefore gave you circumcision
(not that it is from Moses, but from the fathers), and you
circumcise a man on the Sabbath. 23If a man receives cir-
cumcision on the Sabbath, so that the law of Moses should
not be broken, are you angry with Me because I made a
man completely well on the Sabbath? 24Do not judge
according to appearance, but judge with righteous judg-
ment."

Could This Be the Christ?

25Now some of them from Jerusalem said, "Is this not He
whom they seek to kill? 26But look! He speaks boldly, and
they say nothing to Him. Do the rulers know indeed that
this is truly[d] the Christ? 27However, we know where this
Man is from; but when the Christ comes, no one knows
where He is from."
28Then Jesus cried out, as He taught in the temple, say-
ing, "You both know Me, and you know where I am from;
and I have not come of Myself, but He who sent Me is true,
whom you do not know. 29But[e] I know Him, for I am from
Him, and He sent Me."
30Therefore they sought to take Him; but no one laid a
hand on Him, because His hour had not yet come. 31And
many of the people believed in Him, and said, "When the

7:26 [d] NU-Text omits *truly*. 7:29 [e] NU-Text and M-Text omit *But*.

THE MESSAGE

The crowd said, "You're crazy! Who's trying to kill you?
You're demon-possessed."

Jesus said, "I did one miraculous thing a few months ago, and you're still standing around getting all upset, wondering what I'm up to. Moses prescribed circumcision—originally it came not from Moses but from his ancestors—and so you circumcise a man, dealing with one part of his body, even if it's the Sabbath. You do this in order to preserve one item in the Law of Moses. So why are you upset with me because I made a man's whole body well on the Sabbath? Don't be nitpickers; use your head—and heart!—to discern what is right, to test what is authentically right."

That's when some of the people of Jerusalem said, "Isn't this the one they were out to kill? And here he is out in the open, saying whatever he pleases, and no one is stopping him. Could it be that the rulers know that he is, in fact, the Messiah? And yet we know where this man came from. The Messiah is going to come out of nowhere. Nobody is going to know where he comes from."

That provoked Jesus, who was teaching in the Temple, to cry out, "Yes, you think you know me and where I'm from, but that's not where I'm from. I didn't set myself up in business. My true origin is in the One who sent me, and you don't know him at all. I come from him—that's how I know him. He sent me here."

They were looking for a way to arrest him, but not a hand was laid on him because it wasn't yet God's time. Many from the crowd committed themselves in faith to

KING JAMES VERSION

When Christ cometh, will he do more miracles than these which this *man* hath done?

32 The Pharisees heard that the people murmured such things concerning him; and the Pharisees and the chief priests sent officers to take him.

33 Then said Jesus unto them, Yet a little while am I with you, and *then* I go unto him that sent me.

34 Ye shall seek me, and shall not find *me*: and where I am, *thither* ye cannot come.

35 Then said the Jews among themselves, Whither will he go, that we shall not find him? will he go unto the dispersed among the Gentiles, and teach the Gentiles?

36 What *manner of* saying is this that he said, Ye shall seek me, and shall not find *me*: and where I am, *thither* ye cannot come?

37 ¶ In the last day, that great *day* of the feast, Jesus stood and cried, saying, If any man thirst, let him come unto me, and drink.

38 He that believeth on me, as the scripture hath said, out of his belly shall flow rivers of living water.

39 (But this spake he of the Spirit, which they that believe on him should receive: for the Holy Ghost was not yet *given*; because that Jesus was not yet glorified.)

NEW AMERICAN STANDARD BIBLE

were saying, "When the Christ comes, He will not perform more signs than those which this man has, will He?"

32 The Pharisees heard the crowd muttering these things about Him, and the chief priests and the Pharisees sent officers to seize Him.

33 Therefore Jesus said, "For a little while longer I am with you, then I go to Him who sent Me.

34 "You will seek Me, and will not find Me; and where I am, you cannot come."

35 The Jews then said to one another, "Where does this man intend to go that we will not find Him? He is not intending to go to the Dispersion among the Greeks, and teach the Greeks, is He?

36 "What is this statement that He said, 'You will seek Me, and will not find Me; and where I am, you cannot come'?"

37 Now on the last day, the great *day* of the feast, Jesus stood and cried out, saying, "If anyone is thirsty, let him come to Me and drink.

38 "He who believes in Me, as the Scripture said, 'From his innermost being will flow rivers of living water.' "

39 But this He spoke of the Spirit, whom those who believed in Him were to receive; for the Spirit was not yet *given,* because Jesus was not yet glorified.

NEW CENTURY VERSION

They said, "When the Christ comes, will he do more miracles than this man has done?"

The Leaders Try to Arrest Jesus

32 The Pharisees heard the crowd whispering these
things about Jesus. So the leading priests and the
Pharisees sent some Temple guards to arrest him. 33 Jesus
said, "I will be with you a little while longer. Then I will go
back to the One who sent me. 34 You will look for me, but
you will not find me. And you cannot come where I am."
35 The Jews said to each other, "Where will this man go
so we cannot find him? Will he go to the Greek cities
where our people live and teach the Greek people there?
36 What did he mean when he said, 'You will look for me,
but you will not find me,' and 'You cannot come where I
am'?"

Jesus Talks About the Spirit

37 On the last and most important day of the feast Jesus
stood up and said in a loud voice, "Let anyone who is
thirsty come to me and drink. 38 If anyone believes in me,
rivers of living water will flow out from that person's
heart, as the Scripture says." 39 Jesus was talking about the
Holy Spirit. The Spirit had not yet been given, because
Jesus had not yet been raised to glory. But later, those who
believed in Jesus would receive the Spirit.

CONTEMPORARY ENGLISH VERSION

in him and said, "When the Messiah comes, he surely won't perform more miracles[d] than this man has done!"

Officers Sent To Arrest Jesus

32 When the Pharisees heard the crowd arguing about
Jesus, they got together with the chief priests and sent
some temple police to arrest him. 33 But Jesus told them, "I
will be with you a little while longer, and then I will return
to the one who sent me. 34 You will look for me, but you
won't find me. You cannot go where I am going."
35 The Jewish leaders asked each other, "Where can he go to
keep us from finding him? Is he going to some foreign country
where our people live? Is he going there to teach the Greeks?[e]
36 What did he mean by saying that we will look for him, but
won't find him? Why can't we go where he is going?"

Streams of Life-Giving Water

37 On the last and most important day of the festival,
Jesus stood up and shouted, "If you are thirsty, come to me
and drink! 38 Have faith in me, and you will have life-giv-
ing water flowing from deep inside you, just as the
Scriptures say." 39 Jesus was talking about the Holy Spirit,
who would be given to everyone that had faith in him. The
Spirit had not yet been given to anyone, since Jesus had
not yet been given his full glory.[f]

[d] 7.31 *miracles*: See the note at 2.11. [e] 7.35 *Greeks*: Perhaps Gentiles or Jews who followed Greek customs. [f] 7.39 *had not yet been given his full glory*: In the Gospel of John, Jesus is given his full glory both when he is nailed to the cross and when he is raised from death to sit beside his Father in heaven.

NEW INTERNATIONAL VERSION

Christ comes, will he do more miraculous signs than this man?"

[32]The Pharisees heard the crowd whispering such things about him. Then the chief priests and the Pharisees sent temple guards to arrest him.

[33]Jesus said, "I am with you for only a short time, and then I go to the one who sent me. [34]You will look for me, but you will not find me; and where I am, you cannot come."

[35]The Jews said to one another, "Where does this man intend to go that we cannot find him? Will he go where our people live scattered among the Greeks, and teach the Greeks? [36]What did he mean when he said, 'You will look for me, but you will not find me,' and 'Where I am, you cannot come'?"

[37]On the last and greatest day of the Feast, Jesus stood and said in a loud voice, "If anyone is thirsty, let him come to me and drink. [38]Whoever believes in me, as[c] the Scripture has said, streams of living water will flow from within him." [39]By this he meant the Spirit, whom those who believed in him were later to receive. Up to that time the Spirit had not been given, since Jesus had not yet been glorified.

[c] 37,38 Or / *If anyone is thirsty, let him come to me. / And let him drink,* [38]*who believes in me. / As*

NEW LIVING TRANSLATION

him. "After all," they said, "would you expect the Messiah to do more miraculous signs than this man has done?"

[32]When the Pharisees heard that the crowds were murmuring such things, they and the leading priests sent Temple guards to arrest Jesus. [33]But Jesus told them, "I will be here a little longer. Then I will return to the one who sent me. [34]You will search for me but not find me. And you won't be able to come where I am."

[35]The Jewish leaders were puzzled by this statement. "Where is he planning to go?" they asked. "Maybe he is thinking of leaving the country and going to the Jews in other lands, or maybe even to the Gentiles! [36]What does he mean when he says, 'You will search for me but not find me,' and 'You won't be able to come where I am'?"

Jesus Promises Living Water

[37]On the last day, the climax of the festival, Jesus stood and shouted to the crowds, "If you are thirsty, come to me! [38]If you believe in me, come and drink! For the Scriptures declare that rivers of living water will flow out from within."* [39](When he said "living water," he was speaking of the Spirit, who would be given to everyone believing in him. But the Spirit had not yet been given, because Jesus had not yet entered into his glory.)

7:37-38 Or *"Let anyone who is thirsty come to me and drink. [38]For the Scriptures declare that rivers of living water will flow from the heart of those who believe in me."*

NEW KING JAMES VERSION

Christ comes, will He do more signs than these which this *Man* has done?"

Jesus and the Religious Leaders

[32]The Pharisees heard the crowd murmuring these things concerning Him, and the Pharisees and the chief priests sent officers to take Him. [33]Then Jesus said to them,[f] "I shall be with you a little while longer, and *then* I go to Him who sent Me. [34]You will seek Me and not find *Me,* and where I am you cannot come."

[35]Then the Jews said among themselves, "Where does He intend to go that we shall not find Him? Does He intend to go to the Dispersion among the Greeks and teach the Greeks? [36]What is this thing that He said, 'You will seek Me and not find Me, and where I am you cannot come'?"

The Promise of the Holy Spirit

[37]On the last day, that great *day* of the feast, Jesus stood and cried out, saying, "If anyone thirsts, let him come to Me and drink. [38]He who believes in Me, as the Scripture has said, out of his heart will flow rivers of living water." [39]But this He spoke concerning the Spirit, whom those believing[g] in Him would receive; for the Holy[h] Spirit was not yet *given,* because Jesus was not yet glorified.

7:33 [f] NU-Text and M-Text omit *to them.* 7:39 [g] NU-Text reads *who believed.* [h] NU-Text omits *Holy.*

THE MESSAGE

him, saying, "Will the Messiah, when he comes, provide better or more convincing evidence than this?"

The Pharisees, alarmed at this seditious undertow going through the crowd, teamed up with the high priests and sent their police to arrest him. Jesus rebuffed them: "I am with you only a short time. Then I go on to the One who sent me. You will look for me, but you won't find me. Where I am, you can't come."

The Jews put their heads together. "Where do you think he is going that we won't be able to find him? Do you think he is about to travel to the Greek world to teach the Jews? What is he talking about, anyway: 'You will look for me, but you won't find me,' and 'Where I am, you can't come'?"

On the final and climactic day of the Feast, Jesus took his stand. He cried out, "If anyone thirsts, let him come to me and drink. Rivers of living water will brim and spill out of the depths of anyone who believes in me this way, just as the Scripture says." (He said this in regard to the Spirit, whom those who believed in him were about to receive. The Spirit had not yet been given because Jesus had not yet been glorified.)

KING JAMES VERSION

40 Many of the people therefore, when they heard this saying, said, Of a truth this is the Prophet.
41 Others said, This is the Christ. But some said, Shall Christ come out of Galilee?
42 Hath not the scripture said, That Christ cometh of the seed of David, and out of the town of Bethlehem, where David was?
43 So there was a division among the people because of him.
44 And some of them would have taken him; but no man laid hands on him.
45 ¶ Then came the officers to the chief priests and Pharisees; and they said unto them, Why have ye not brought him?
46 The officers answered, Never man spake like this man.
47 Then answered them the Pharisees, Are ye also deceived?
48 Have any of the rulers or of the Pharisees believed on him?
49 But this people who knoweth not the law are cursed.
50 Nicodemus saith unto them, (he that came to Jesus by night, being one of them,)
51 Doth our law judge *any* man, before it hear him, and know what he doeth?
52 They answered and said unto him, Art thou also of

NEW AMERICAN STANDARD BIBLE

Division of People over Jesus

40 *Some* of the people therefore, when they heard these words, were saying, "This certainly is the Prophet."
41 Others were saying, "This is the Christ." Still others were saying, "Surely the Christ is not going to come from Galilee, is He?
42 "Has not the Scripture said that the Christ comes from the descendants of David, and from Bethlehem, the village where David was?"
43 So a division occurred in the crowd because of Him.
44 Some of them wanted to seize Him, but no one laid hands on Him.
45 The officers then came to the chief priests and Pharisees, and they said to them, "Why did you not bring Him?"
46 The officers answered, "Never has a man spoken the way this man speaks."
47 The Pharisees then answered them, "You have not also been led astray, have you?
48 "No one of the rulers or Pharisees has believed in Him, has he?
49 "But this crowd which does not know the Law is accursed."
50 Nicodemus (he who came to Him before, being one of them) *said to them,
51 "Our Law does not judge a man unless it first hears from him and knows what he is doing, does it?"
52 They answered him, "You are not also from Galilee,

NEW CENTURY VERSION

The People Argue About Jesus

40When the people heard Jesus' words, some of them said, "This man really is the Prophet."[b]
41Others said, "He is the Christ."

Still others said, "The Christ will not come from Galilee.
42The Scripture says that the Christ will come from David's family and from Bethlehem, the town where David lived."
43So the people did not agree with each other about Jesus.
44Some of them wanted to arrest him, but no one was able to touch him.

Some Leaders Won't Believe

45The Temple guards went back to the leading priests and the Pharisees, who asked, "Why didn't you bring Jesus?"

46The guards answered, "The words he says are greater than the words of any other person who has ever spoken!"

47The Pharisees answered, "So Jesus has fooled you
also! 48Have any of the leaders or the Pharisees believed in
him? No! 49But these people, who know nothing about the law, are under God's curse."

50Nicodemus, who had gone to see Jesus before, was in
that group.[c] He said, 51"Our law does not judge a man without hearing him and knowing what he has done."

52They answered, "Are you from Galilee, too? Study the

7:40 [b] **Prophet** They probably meant the prophet God told Moses he would send (Deuteronomy 18:15–19). 7:50 [c] **Nicodemus...group.** The story about Nicodemus going and talking to Jesus is in John 3:1–21.

CONTEMPORARY ENGLISH VERSION

The People Take Sides

40When the crowd heard Jesus say this, some of them
said, "He must be the Prophet!"[g] 41Others said, "He is the
Messiah!" Others even said, "Can the Messiah come from
Galilee? 42The Scriptures say that the Messiah will come from the family of King David. Doesn't this mean that he
will be born in David's hometown of Bethlehem?" 43The
people started taking sides against each other because of
Jesus. 44Some of them wanted to arrest him, but no one laid a hand on him.

The Leaders Refuse To Have Faith in Jesus

45When the temple police returned to the chief priests and Pharisees, they were asked, "Why didn't you bring Jesus here?"

46They answered, "No one has ever spoken like that man!"
47The Pharisees said to them, "Have you also been
fooled? 48Not one of the chief priests or the Pharisees has
faith in him. 49And these people who don't know the Law are under God's curse anyway."

50Nicodemus was there at the time. He was a member of the council, and was the same one who had earlier come to
see Jesus.[h] He said, 51"Our Law doesn't let us condemn people before we hear what they have to say. We cannot judge them before we know what they have done."

52Then they said, "Nicodemus, you must be from

[g] 7.40 *the Prophet*: See the note at 1.21. [h] 7.50 *who had earlier come to see Jesus*: See 3.1-21.

NEW INTERNATIONAL VERSION

40On hearing his words, some of the people said, "Surely
this man is the Prophet."
41Others said, "He is the Christ."
Still others asked, "How can the Christ come from
Galilee? 42Does not the Scripture say that the Christ will
come from David's family[d] and from Bethlehem, the town
where David lived?" 43Thus the people were divided
because of Jesus. 44Some wanted to seize him, but no one
laid a hand on him.

Unbelief of the Jewish Leaders

45Finally the temple guards went back to the chief
priests and Pharisees, who asked them, "Why didn't you
bring him in?"
46"No one ever spoke the way this man does," the
guards declared.
47"You mean he has deceived you also?" the Pharisees
retorted. 48"Has any of the rulers or of the Pharisees
believed in him? 49No! But this mob that knows nothing of
the law—there is a curse on them."
50Nicodemus, who had gone to Jesus earlier and who
was one of their own number, asked, 51"Does our law con-
demn anyone without first hearing him to find out what he
is doing?"
52They replied, "Are you from Galilee, too? Look into it,

[d] *42* Greek *seed*

NEW LIVING TRANSLATION

Division and Unbelief

40When the crowds heard him say this, some of them
declared, "This man surely is the Prophet."* 41Others said,
"He is the Messiah." Still others said, "But he can't be!
Will the Messiah come from Galilee? 42For the Scriptures
clearly state that the Messiah will be born of the royal line
of David, in Bethlehem, the village where King David was
born."* 43So the crowd was divided in their opinion about
him. 44And some wanted him arrested, but no one touched
him.
45The Temple guards who had been sent to arrest him
returned to the leading priests and Pharisees. "Why didn't
you bring him in?" they demanded.
46"We have never heard anyone talk like this!" the
guards responded.
47"Have you been led astray, too?" the Pharisees
mocked. 48"Is there a single one of us rulers or Pharisees
who believes in him? 49These ignorant crowds do, but
what do they know about it? A curse on them anyway!"
50Nicodemus, the leader who had met with Jesus earlier,
then spoke up. 51"Is it legal to convict a man before he is
given a hearing?" he asked.
52They replied, "Are you from Galilee, too? Search the

7:40 See Deut 18:15, 18. **7:42** See Mic 5:2.

NEW KING JAMES VERSION

Who Is He?

40Therefore many[i] from the crowd, when they heard this
saying, said, "Truly this is the Prophet." 41Others said,
"This is the Christ."
But some said, "Will the Christ come out of Galilee?
42Has not the Scripture said that the Christ comes from the
seed of David and from the town of Bethlehem, where Da-
vid was?" 43So there was a division among the people
because of Him. 44Now some of them wanted to take Him,
but no one laid hands on Him.

Rejected by the Authorities

45Then the officers came to the chief priests and Phari-
sees, who said to them, "Why have you not brought Him?"
46The officers answered, "No man ever spoke like this
Man!"
47Then the Pharisees answered them, "Are you also
deceived? 48Have any of the rulers or the Pharisees
believed in Him? 49But this crowd that does not know the
law is accursed."
50Nicodemus (he who came to Jesus by night,[j] being one
of them) said to them, 51"Does our law judge a man before
it hears him and knows what he is doing?"
52They answered and said to him, "Are you also from

7:40 [i] NU-Text reads *some.* **7:50** [j] NU-Text reads *before.*

THE MESSAGE

Those in the crowd who heard these words were saying, "This has to be the Prophet." Others said, "He is the Messiah!" But others were saying, "The Messiah doesn't come from Galilee, does he? Don't the Scriptures tell us that the Messiah comes from David's line and from Bethlehem, David's village?" So there was a split in the crowd over him. Some went so far as wanting to arrest him, but no one laid a hand on him.

That's when the Temple police reported back to the high priests and Pharisees, who demanded, "Why didn't you bring him with you?"

The police answered, "Have you heard the way he talks? We've never heard anyone speak like this man."

The Pharisees said, "Are you carried away like the rest of the rabble? You don't see any of the leaders believing in him, do you? Or any from the Pharisees? It's only this crowd, ignorant of God's Law, that is taken in by him—and damned."

Nicodemus, the man who had come to Jesus earlier and was both a ruler and a Pharisee, spoke up. "Does our Law decide about a man's guilt without first listening to him and finding out what he is doing?"

But they cut him off. "Are you also campaigning for the

KING JAMES VERSION

Galilee? Search, and look: for out of Galilee ariseth no prophet.

53 And every man went unto his own house.

8 Jesus went unto the mount of Olives.

2 And early in the morning he came again into the temple, and all the people came unto him; and he sat down, and taught them.

3 And the scribes and Pharisees brought unto him a woman taken in adultery; and when they had set her in the midst,

4 They say unto him, Master, this woman was taken in adultery, in the very act.

5 Now Moses in the law commanded us, that such should be stoned: but what sayest thou?

6 This they said, tempting him, that they might have to accuse him. But Jesus stooped down, and with *his* finger wrote on the ground, *as though he heard them not*.

7 So when they continued asking him, he lifted up himself, and said unto them, He that is without sin among you, let him first cast a stone at her.

8 And again he stooped down, and wrote on the ground.

9 And they which heard *it*, being convicted by *their own* conscience, went out one by one, beginning at the eldest, *even* unto the last: and Jesus was left alone, and the woman standing in the midst.

NEW AMERICAN STANDARD BIBLE

are you? Search, and see that no prophet arises out of Galilee."

53 [[1]Everyone went to his home.

The Adulterous Woman

8 But Jesus went to the Mount of Olives.

2 Early in the morning He came again into the temple, and all the people were coming to Him; and He sat down and *began* to teach them.

3 The scribes and the Pharisees *brought a woman caught in adultery, and having set her in the center *of the court*,

4 they *said to Him, "Teacher, this woman has been caught in adultery, in the very act.

5 "Now in the Law Moses commanded us to stone such women; what then do You say?"

6 They were saying this, testing Him, so that they might have grounds for accusing Him. But Jesus stooped down and with His finger wrote on the ground.

7 But when they persisted in asking Him, He straightened up, and said to them, "He who is without sin among you, let him *be the* first to throw a stone at her."

8 Again He stooped down and wrote on the ground.

9 When they heard it, they *began* to go out one by one, beginning with the older ones, and He was left alone, and the woman, where she was, in the center *of the court*.

7:53 [1] Later mss add the story of the adulterous woman, numbering it as John 7:53-8:11

NEW CENTURY VERSION

Scriptures, and you will learn that no prophet comes from Galilee."

Some early Greek manuscripts do not contain 7:53–8:11.

[53And everyone left and went home.

The Woman Caught in Adultery

8 Jesus went to the Mount of Olives. 2But early in the
morning he went back to the Temple, and all the peo-
ple came to him, and he sat and taught them. 3The teach-
ers of the law and the Pharisees brought a woman who
had been caught in adultery. They forced her to stand
before the people. 4They said to Jesus, "Teacher, this
woman was caught having sexual relations with a man
who is not her husband. 5The law of Moses commands
that we stone to death every woman who does this. What
do you say we should do?" 6They were asking this to trick
Jesus so that they could have some charge against him.

But Jesus bent over and started writing on the ground
with his finger. 7When they continued to ask Jesus their
question, he raised up and said, "Anyone here who has
never sinned can throw the first stone at her." 8Then Jesus
bent over again and wrote on the ground.

9Those who heard Jesus began to leave one by one, first
the older men and then the others. Jesus was left there

CONTEMPORARY ENGLISH VERSION

Galilee! Read the Scriptures, and you will find that no prophet is to come from Galilee."

A Woman Caught in Sin

8 53Everyone else went home, 1but Jesus walked out to
the Mount of Olives. 2Then early the next morning he
went to the temple. The people came to him, and he sat
down[a] and started teaching them.

3The Pharisees and the teachers of the Law of Moses
brought in a woman who had been caught in bed with a
man who wasn't her husband. They made her stand in the
middle of the crowd. 4Then they said, "Teacher, this
woman was caught sleeping with a man who isn't her hus-
band. 5The Law of Moses teaches that a woman like this
should be stoned to death! What do you say?"

6They asked Jesus this question, because they wanted to
test him and bring some charge against him. But Jesus
simply bent over and started writing on the ground with
his finger.

7They kept on asking Jesus about the woman. Finally,
he stood up and said, "If any of you have never sinned,
then go ahead and throw the first stone at her!" 8Once
again he bent over and began writing on the ground. 9The
people left one by one, beginning with the oldest. Finally,
Jesus and the woman were there alone.

[a] 8.2 *sat down*: See the note at 6.3, 4.

NEW INTERNATIONAL VERSION

and you will find that a prophet[e] does not come out of Galilee."

[The earliest manuscripts and many other ancient witnesses do not have John 7:53–8:11.]

53Then each went to his own home.

8 But Jesus went to the Mount of Olives. 2At dawn he appeared again in the temple courts, where all the people gathered around him, and he sat down to teach them. 3The teachers of the law and the Pharisees brought in a woman caught in adultery. They made her stand before the group 4and said to Jesus, "Teacher, this woman was caught in the act of adultery. 5In the Law Moses commanded us to stone such women. Now what do you say?" 6They were using this question as a trap, in order to have a basis for accusing him.

But Jesus bent down and started to write on the ground with his finger. 7When they kept on questioning him, he straightened up and said to them, "If any one of you is without sin, let him be the first to throw a stone at her." 8Again he stooped down and wrote on the ground.

9At this, those who heard began to go away one at a time, the older ones first, until only Jesus was left, with

[e] *52* Two early manuscripts *the Prophet*

NEW LIVING TRANSLATION

Scriptures and see for yourself—no prophet ever comes from Galilee!"

[*The most ancient Greek manuscripts do not include John 7:53—8:11.*]

53Then the meeting broke up and everybody went home.

A Woman Caught in Adultery

8 Jesus returned to the Mount of Olives, 2but early the next morning he was back again at the Temple. A crowd soon gathered, and he sat down and taught them. 3As he was speaking, the teachers of religious law and Pharisees brought a woman they had caught in the act of adultery. They put her in front of the crowd.

4"Teacher," they said to Jesus, "this woman was caught in the very act of adultery. 5The law of Moses says to stone her. What do you say?"

6They were trying to trap him into saying something they could use against him, but Jesus stooped down and wrote in the dust with his finger. 7They kept demanding an answer, so he stood up again and said, "All right, stone her. But let those who have never sinned throw the first stones!" 8Then he stooped down again and wrote in the dust.

9When the accusers heard this, they slipped away one by one, beginning with the oldest, until only Jesus was left in

NEW KING JAMES VERSION

Galilee? Search and look, for no prophet has arisen[k] out of Galilee."

An Adulteress Faces the Light of the World

53And everyone went to his *own* house.[l]

8 But Jesus went to the Mount of Olives.

2Now early[a] in the morning He came again into the temple, and all the people came to Him; and He sat down and taught them. 3Then the scribes and Pharisees brought to Him a woman caught in adultery. And when they had set her in the midst, 4they said to Him, "Teacher, this woman was caught[b] in adultery, in the very act. 5Now Moses, in the law, commanded[c] us that such should be stoned.[d] But what do You say?"[e] 6This they said, testing Him, that they might have *something* of which to accuse Him. But Jesus stooped down and wrote on the ground with *His* finger, as though He did not hear.[f]

7So when they continued asking Him, He raised Himself up[g] and said to them, "He who is without sin among you, let him throw a stone at her first." 8And again He stooped down and wrote on the ground. 9Then those who heard *it*, being convicted by *their* conscience,[h] went out one by one, beginning with the oldest *even* to the last. And Jesus was

7:52 [k] NU-Text reads *is to rise.* **7:53** [l] The words *And everyone* through *sin no more* (8:11) are bracketed by NU-Text as not original. They are present in over 900 manuscripts. **8:2** [a] M-Text reads *very early.* **8:4** [b] M-Text reads *we found this woman.* **8:5** [c] M-Text reads *in our law Moses commanded.* [d] NU-Text and M-Text read *to stone such.* [e] M-Text adds *about her.* **8:6** [f] NU-Text and M-Text omit *as though He did not hear.* **8:7** [g] M-Text reads *He looked up.* **8:9** [h] NU-Text and M-Text omit *being convicted by their conscience.*

THE MESSAGE

Galilean? Examine the evidence. See if any prophet ever comes from Galilee."

Then they all went home.

To Throw the Stone

8 Jesus went across to Mount Olives, but he was soon back in the Temple again. Swarms of people came to him. He sat down and taught them.

The religion scholars and Pharisees led in a woman who had been caught in an act of adultery. They stood her in plain sight of everyone and said, "Teacher, this woman was caught red-handed in the act of adultery. Moses, in the Law, gives orders to stone such persons. What do you say?" They were trying to trap him into saying something incriminating so they could bring charges against him.

Jesus bent down and wrote with his finger in the dirt. They kept at him, badgering him. He straightened up and said, "The sinless one among you, go first: Throw the stone." Bending down again, he wrote some more in the dirt.

Hearing that, they walked away, one after another, beginning with the oldest. The woman was left alone.

KING JAMES VERSION

10 When Jesus had lifted up himself, and saw none but the woman, he said unto her, Woman, where are those thine accusers? hath no man condemned thee?

11 She said, No man, Lord. And Jesus said unto her, Neither do I condemn thee: go, and sin no more.

12 ¶ Then spake Jesus again unto them, saying, I am the light of the world: he that followeth me shall not walk in darkness, but shall have the light of life.

13 The Pharisees therefore said unto him, Thou bearest record of thyself; thy record is not true.

14 Jesus answered and said unto them, Though I bear record of myself, *yet* my record is true: for I know whence I came, and whither I go; but ye cannot tell whence I come, and whither I go.

15 Ye judge after the flesh; I judge no man.

16 And yet if I judge, my judgment is true: for I am not alone, but I and the Father that sent me.

17 It is also written in your law, that the testimony of two men is true.

18 I am one that bear witness of myself, and the Father that sent me beareth witness of me.

19 Then said they unto him, Where is thy Father? Jesus answered, Ye neither know me, nor my Father: if ye had known me, ye should have known my Father also.

NEW AMERICAN STANDARD BIBLE

10 Straightening up, Jesus said to her, "Woman, where are they? Did no one condemn you?"

11 She said, "No one, Lord." And Jesus said, "I do not condemn you, either. Go. From now on sin no more."]

Jesus Is the Light of the World

12 Then Jesus again spoke to them, saying, "I am the Light of the world; he who follows Me will not walk in the darkness, but will have the Light of life."

13 So the Pharisees said to Him, "You are testifying about Yourself; Your testimony is not true."

14 Jesus answered and said to them, "Even if I testify about Myself, My testimony is true, for I know where I came from and where I am going; but you do not know where I come from or where I am going.

15 "You judge according to the flesh; I am not judging anyone.

16 "But even if I do judge, My judgment is true; for I am not alone *in it,* but I and the Father who sent Me.

17 "Even in your law it has been written that the testimony of two men is true.

18 "I am He who testifies about Myself, and the Father who sent Me testifies about Me."

19 So they were saying to Him, "Where is Your Father?" Jesus answered, "You know neither Me nor My Father; if you knew Me, you would know My Father also."

NEW CENTURY VERSION

alone with the woman standing before him. 10Jesus raised
up again and asked her, "Woman, where are they? Has no
one judged you guilty?"
11She answered, "No one, sir."
Then Jesus said, "I also don't judge you guilty. You may
go now, but don't sin anymore."]

Jesus Is the Light of the World

12Later, Jesus talked to the people again, saying, "I am
the light of the world. The person who follows me will never
live in darkness but will have the light that gives life."
13The Pharisees said to Jesus, "When you talk about
yourself, you are the only one to say these things are true.
We cannot accept what you say."
14Jesus answered, "Yes, I am saying these things about
myself, but they are true. I know where I came from and
where I am going. But you don't know where I came from
or where I am going. 15You judge by human standards. I
am not judging anyone. 16But when I do judge, my judging
is true, because I am not alone. The Father who sent me is
with me. 17Your own law says that when two witnesses
say the same thing, you must accept what they say. 18I am
one of the witnesses who speaks about myself, and the
Father who sent me is the other witness."
19They asked, "Where is your father?"
Jesus answered, "You don't know me or my Father. If
you knew me, you would know my Father, too." 20Jesus

CONTEMPORARY ENGLISH VERSION

10Jesus stood up and asked her, "Where is everyone?
Isn't there anyone left to accuse you?"
11"No sir," the woman answered.
Then Jesus told her, "I am not going to accuse you
either. You may go now, but don't sin anymore."[b]

Jesus Is the Light for the World

12Once again Jesus spoke to the people. This time he
said, "I am the light for the world! Follow me, and you
won't be walking in the dark. You will have the light that
gives life."
13The Pharisees objected, "You are the only one speak-
ing for yourself, and what you say isn't true!"
14Jesus replied:
Even if I do speak for myself, what I say is true! I
know where I came from and where I am going. But you
don't know where I am from or where I am going. 15You
judge in the same way that everyone else does, but I
don't judge anyone. 16If I did judge, I would judge fairly,
because I would not be doing it alone. The Father who
sent me is here with me. 17Your Law requires two wit-
nesses to prove that something is true. 18I am one of my
witnesses, and the Father who sent me is the other one.
19"Where is your Father?" they asked.
"You don't know me or my Father!" Jesus answered. "If
you knew me, you would know my Father."

[b] 8.11 *don't sin anymore*: Verses 1-11 are not in some manuscripts. In other manuscripts these verses are placed after 7.36 or after 21.25 or after Luke 21.38, with some differences in the text.

NEW INTERNATIONAL VERSION

the woman still standing there. 10Jesus straightened up
and asked her, "Woman, where are they? Has no one con-
demned you?"

11"No one, sir," she said.

"Then neither do I condemn you," Jesus declared. "Go
now and leave your life of sin."

The Validity of Jesus' Testimony

12When Jesus spoke again to the people, he said, "I am
the light of the world. Whoever follows me will never walk
in darkness, but will have the light of life."

13The Pharisees challenged him, "Here you are, appear-
ing as your own witness; your testimony is not valid."

14Jesus answered, "Even if I testify on my own behalf,
my testimony is valid, for I know where I came from and
where I am going. But you have no idea where I come from
or where I am going. 15You judge by human standards; I
pass judgment on no one. 16But if I do judge, my decisions
are right, because I am not alone. I stand with the Father,
who sent me. 17In your own Law it is written that the testi-
mony of two men is valid. 18I am one who testifies for
myself; my other witness is the Father, who sent me."

19Then they asked him, "Where is your father?"

"You do not know me or my Father," Jesus replied. "If
you knew me, you would know my Father also." 20He

NEW LIVING TRANSLATION

the middle of the crowd with the woman. 10Then Jesus
stood up again and said to her, "Where are your accusers?
Didn't even one of them condemn you?"

11"No, Lord," she said.

And Jesus said, "Neither do I. Go and sin no more."

Jesus, the Light of the World

12Jesus said to the people, "I am the light of the world. If
you follow me, you won't be stumbling through the dark-
ness, because you will have the light that leads to life."

13The Pharisees replied, "You are making false claims
about yourself!"

14Jesus told them, "These claims are valid even though I
make them about myself. For I know where I came from
and where I am going, but you don't know this about me.
15You judge me with all your human limitations,* but I am
not judging anyone. 16And if I did, my judgment would be
correct in every respect because I am not alone—I have
with me the Father who sent me. 17Your own law says that
if two people agree about something, their witness is
accepted as fact.* 18I am one witness, and my Father who
sent me is the other."

19"Where is your father?" they asked.

Jesus answered, "Since you don't know who I am, you
don't know who my Father is. If you knew me, then you
would know my Father, too." 20Jesus made these statements

8:15 Or *judge me by human standards.* 8:17 See Deut 19:15.

NEW KING JAMES VERSION

left alone, and the woman standing in the midst. 10When
Jesus had raised Himself up and saw no one but the
woman, He said to her,[i] "Woman, where are those
accusers of yours?[j] Has no one condemned you?"

11She said, "No one, Lord."

And Jesus said to her, "Neither do I condemn you; go
and[k] sin no more."

12Then Jesus spoke to them again, saying, "I am the
light of the world. He who follows Me shall not walk in
darkness, but have the light of life."

Jesus Defends His Self-Witness

13The Pharisees therefore said to Him, "You bear witness
of Yourself; Your witness is not true."

14Jesus answered and said to them, "Even if I bear wit-
ness of Myself, My witness is true, for I know where I came
from and where I am going; but you do not know where I
come from and where I am going. 15You judge according to
the flesh; I judge no one. 16And yet if I do judge, My judg-
ment is true; for I am not alone, but I *am* with the Father
who sent Me. 17It is also written in your law that the testi-
mony of two men is true. 18I am One who bears witness of
Myself, and the Father who sent Me bears witness of Me."

19Then they said to Him, "Where is Your Father?"

Jesus answered, "You know neither Me nor My Father. If
you had known Me, you would have known My Father also."

8:10 [i] NU-Text omits *and saw no one but the woman;* M-Text reads *He saw her and said.* [j] NU-Text and M-Text omit *of yours.* 8:11 [k] NU-Text and M-Text add *from now on.*

THE MESSAGE

Jesus stood up and spoke to her. "Woman, where are they?
Does no one condemn you?"

"No one, Master."

"Neither do I," said Jesus. "Go on your way. From now
on, don't sin."

You're Missing God in All This

Jesus once again addressed them: "I am the world's Light. No one who follows me stumbles around in the darkness. I provide plenty of light to live in."

The Pharisees objected, "All we have is your word on this. We need more than this to go on."

Jesus replied, "You're right that you only have my word. But you can depend on it being true. I know where I've come from and where I go next. You don't know where I'm from or where I'm headed. You decide according to what you can see and touch. I don't make judgments like that. But even if I did, my judgment would be true because I wouldn't make it out of the narrowness of my experience but in the largeness of the One who sent me, the Father. That fulfills the conditions set down in God's Law: that you can count on the testimony of two witnesses. And that is what you have: You have my word and you have the word of the Father who sent me."

They said, "Where is this so-called Father of yours?"

Jesus said, "You're looking right at me and you don't see me. How do you expect to see the Father? If you knew me, you would at the same time know the Father."

KING JAMES VERSION

20 These words spake Jesus in the treasury, as he taught in the temple: and no man laid hands on him; for his hour was not yet come.

21 ¶ Then said Jesus again unto them, I go my way, and ye shall seek me, and shall die in your sins: whither I go, ye cannot come.

22 Then said the Jews, Will he kill himself? because he saith, Whither I go, ye cannot come.

23 And he said unto them, Ye are from beneath; I am from above: ye are of this world; I am not of this world.

24 I said therefore unto you, that ye shall die in your sins: for if ye believe not that I am *he*, ye shall die in your sins.

25 Then said they unto him, Who art thou? And Jesus saith unto them, Even *the same* that I said unto you from the beginning.

26 I have many things to say and to judge of you: but he that sent me is true; and I speak to the world those things which I have heard of him.

27 They understood not that he spake to them of the Father.

28 Then said Jesus unto them, When ye have lifted up the Son of man, then shall ye know that I am *he*, and *that*

NEW AMERICAN STANDARD BIBLE

20 These words He spoke in the treasury, as He taught in the temple; and no one seized Him, because His hour had not yet come.

21 Then He said again to them, "I go away, and you will seek Me, and will die in your sin; where I am going, you cannot come."

22 So the Jews were saying, "Surely He will not kill Himself, will He, since He says, 'Where I am going, you cannot come'?"

23 And He was saying to them, "You are from below, I am from above; you are of this world, I am not of this world.

24 "Therefore I said to you that you will die in your sins; for unless you believe that I am *He*, you will die in your sins."

25 So they were saying to Him, "Who are You?" Jesus said to them, "What have I been saying to you *from* the beginning?

26 "I have many things to speak and to judge concerning you, but He who sent Me is true; and the things which I heard from Him, these I speak to the world."

27 They did not realize that He had been speaking to them about the Father.

28 So Jesus said, "When you lift up the Son of Man, then you will know that I am *He*, and I do nothing on My

NEW CENTURY VERSION

said these things while he was teaching in the Temple, near where the money is kept. But no one arrested him, because the right time for him had not yet come.

The People Misunderstand Jesus

21 Again, Jesus said to the people, "I will leave you, and you will look for me, but you will die in your sins. You cannot come where I am going."

22 So the Jews asked, "Will Jesus kill himself? Is that why he said, 'You cannot come where I am going'?"

23 Jesus said, "You people are from here below, but I am from above. You belong to this world, but I don't belong to
this world. 24 So I told you that you would die in your sins.
Yes, you will die in your sins if you don't believe that I am he."

25 They asked, "Then who are you?"

Jesus answered, "I am what I have told you from the
beginning. 26 I have many things to say and decide about you. But I tell people only the things I have heard from the One who sent me, and he speaks the truth."

27 The people did not understand that he was talking to
them about the Father. 28 So Jesus said to them, "When you lift up the Son of Man, you will know that I am he.

CONTEMPORARY ENGLISH VERSION

20 Jesus said this while he was still teaching in the place where the temple treasures were stored. But no one arrested him, because his time had not yet come.[c]

You Cannot Go Where I Am Going

21 Jesus also told them, "I am going away, and you will look for me. But you cannot go where I am going, and you will die with your sins unforgiven."

22 The Jewish leaders asked, "Does he intend to kill himself? Is that what he means by saying we cannot go where he is going?"

23 Jesus answered, "You are from below, but I am from
above. You belong to this world, but I don't. 24 That is why
I said you will die with your sins unforgiven. If you don't have faith in me for who I am,[d] you will die, and your sins will not be forgiven."

25 "Who are you?" they asked Jesus.

Jesus answered, "I am exactly who I told you at the
beginning. 26 There is a lot more I could say to condemn you. But the one who sent me is truthful, and I tell the people of this world only what I have heard from him."

27 No one understood that Jesus was talking to them about the Father.

28 Jesus went on to say, "When you have lifted up the Son of Man,[e] you will know who I am. You will also know

[c] 8.20 *his time had not yet come*: See the note at 2.4. [d] 8.24 *I am*: For the Jewish people the most holy name of God is "Yahweh," which may be translated "I am." In the Gospel of John "I am" is sometimes used by Jesus to show that he is that one. [e] 8.28 *lifted up the Son of Man*: See the note at 7.39.

NEW INTERNATIONAL VERSION

spoke these words while teaching in the temple area near
the place where the offerings were put. Yet no one seized
him, because his time had not yet come.
21 Once more Jesus said to them, "I am going away, and
you will look for me, and you will die in your sin. Where I
go, you cannot come."
22 This made the Jews ask, "Will he kill himself? Is that
why he says, 'Where I go, you cannot come'?"
23 But he continued, "You are from below; I am from
above. You are of this world; I am not of this world. 24 I
told you that you would die in your sins; if you do not
believe that I am ⌊the one I claim to be⌋,[a] you will indeed
die in your sins."
25 "Who are you?" they asked.
"Just what I have been claiming all along," Jesus replied.
26 "I have much to say in judgment of you. But he who sent
me is reliable, and what I have heard from him I tell the
world."
27 They did not understand that he was telling them
about his Father. 28 So Jesus said, "When you have lifted
up the Son of Man, then you will know that I am ⌊the one I

[a] *24* Or *I am he*; also in verse 28

NEW LIVING TRANSLATION

while he was teaching in the section of the Temple known
as the Treasury. But he was not arrested, because his time
had not yet come.

The Unbelieving People Warned

21 Later Jesus said to them again, "I am going away. You
will search for me and die in your sin. You cannot come
where I am going."
22 The Jewish leaders asked, "Is he planning to commit
suicide? What does he mean, 'You cannot come where I am
going'?"
23 Then he said to them, "You are from below; I am from
above. You are of this world; I am not. 24 That is why I said
that you will die in your sins; for unless you believe that I
am who I say I am, you will die in your sins."
25 "Tell us who you are," they demanded.
Jesus replied, "I am the one I have always claimed to be.*
26 I have much to say about you and much to condemn, but
I won't. For I say only what I have heard from the one who
sent me, and he is true." 27 But they still didn't understand
that he was talking to them about his Father.
28 So Jesus said, "When you have lifted up the Son of
Man on the cross, then you will realize that I am he and

8:25 Or *"Why do I speak to you at all?"*

NEW KING JAMES VERSION

20 These words Jesus spoke in the treasury, as He taught
in the temple; and no one laid hands on Him, for His hour
had not yet come.

Jesus Predicts His Departure

21 Then Jesus said to them again, "I am going away, and
you will seek Me, and will die in your sin. Where I go you
cannot come."
22 So the Jews said, "Will He kill Himself, because He
says, 'Where I go you cannot come'?"
23 And He said to them, "You are from beneath; I am
from above. You are of this world; I am not of this world.
24 Therefore I said to you that you will die in your sins; for
if you do not believe that I am *He,* you will die in your
sins."
25 Then they said to Him, "Who are You?"
And Jesus said to them, "Just what I have been saying to
you from the beginning. 26 I have many things to say and
to judge concerning you, but He who sent Me is true; and I
speak to the world those things which I heard from Him."
27 They did not understand that He spoke to them of the
Father.
28 Then Jesus said to them, "When you lift up the Son of
Man, then you will know that I am *He,* and *that* I do nothing

THE MESSAGE

He gave this speech in the Treasury while teaching in the Temple. No one arrested him because his time wasn't yet up.

Then he went over the same ground again. "I'm leaving and you are going to look for me, but you're missing God in this and are headed for a dead end. There is no way you can come with me."

The Jews said, "So, is he going to kill himself? Is that what he means by 'You can't come with me'?"

Jesus said, "You're tied down to the mundane; I'm in touch with what is beyond your horizons. You live in terms of what you see and touch. I'm living on other terms. I told you that you were missing God in all this. You're at a dead end. If you won't believe I am who I say I am, you're at the dead end of sins. You're missing God in your lives."

They said to him, "Just who are you anyway?"

Jesus said, "What I've said from the start. I have so many things to say that concern you, judgments to make that affect you, but if you don't accept the trustworthiness of the One who commanded my words and acts, none of it matters. That is who you are questioning—not me but the One who sent me."

They still didn't get it, didn't realize that he was referring to the Father. So Jesus tried again. "When you raise up the Son of Man, then you will know who I am—that I'm

KING JAMES VERSION

I do nothing of myself; but as my Father hath taught me, I speak these things.

29 And he that sent me is with me: the Father hath not left me alone; for I do always those things that please him.

30 As he spake these words, many believed on him.

31 ¶ Then said Jesus to those Jews which believed on him, If ye continue in my word, *then* are ye my disciples indeed;

32 And ye shall know the truth, and the truth shall make you free.

33 They answered him, We be Abraham's seed, and were never in bondage to any man: how sayest thou, Ye shall be made free?

34 Jesus answered them, Verily, verily, I say unto you, Whosoever committeth sin is the servant of sin.

35 And the servant abideth not in the house for ever: *but* the Son abideth ever.

36 If the Son therefore shall make you free, ye shall be free indeed.

37 I know that ye are Abraham's seed; but ye seek to kill me, because my word hath no place in you.

38 ¶ I speak that which I have seen with my Father: and ye do that which ye have seen with your father.

39 They answered and said unto him, Abraham is our father. Jesus saith unto them, If ye were Abraham's children, ye would do the works of Abraham.

NEW AMERICAN STANDARD BIBLE

own initiative, but I speak these things as the Father taught Me.

29 "And He who sent Me is with Me; He has not left Me alone, for I always do the things that are pleasing to Him."

30 As He spoke these things, many came to believe in Him.

The Truth Will Make You Free

31 So Jesus was saying to those Jews who had believed Him, "If you continue in My word, *then* you are truly disciples of Mine;

32 and you will know the truth, and the truth will make you free."

33 They answered Him, "We are Abraham's descendants and have never yet been enslaved to anyone; how is it that You say, 'You will become free'?"

34 Jesus answered them, "Truly, truly, I say to you, everyone who commits sin is the slave of sin.

35 "The slave does not remain in the house forever; the son does remain forever.

36 "So if the Son makes you free, you will be free indeed.

37 "I know that you are Abraham's descendants; yet you seek to kill Me, because My word has no place in you.

38 "I speak the things which I have seen with *My* Father; therefore you also do the things which you heard from *your* father."

39 They answered and said to Him, "Abraham is our father." Jesus *said to them, "If you are Abraham's children, do the deeds of Abraham.

NEW CENTURY VERSION

You will know that these things I do are not by my own authority but that I say only what the Father has taught me. 29The One who sent me is with me. I always do what is pleasing to him, so he has not left me alone." 30While Jesus was saying these things, many people believed in him.

Freedom from Sin

31So Jesus said to the Jews who believed in him, "If you continue to obey my teaching, you are truly my followers. 32Then you will know the truth, and the truth will make you free."

33They answered, "We are Abraham's children, and we have never been anyone's slaves. So why do you say we will be free?"

34Jesus answered, "I tell you the truth, everyone who lives in sin is a slave to sin. 35A slave does not stay with a family forever, but a son belongs to the family forever. 36So if the Son makes you free, you will be truly free. 37I know you are Abraham's children, but you want to kill me because you don't accept my teaching. 38I am telling you what my Father has shown me, but you do what your father has told you."

39They answered, "Our father is Abraham."

Jesus said, "If you were really Abraham's children, you would do the things Abraham did. 40I am a man who has

CONTEMPORARY ENGLISH VERSION

that I don't do anything on my own. I say only what my Father taught me. 29The one who sent me is with me. I always do what pleases him, and he will never leave me."

30After Jesus said this, many of the people put their faith in him.

The Truth Will Set You Free

31Jesus told the people who had faith in him, "If you keep on obeying what I have said, you truly are my disciples. 32You will know the truth, and the truth will set you free."

33They answered, "We are Abraham's children! We have never been anyone's slaves. How can you say we will be set free?"

34Jesus replied:

I tell you for certain that anyone who sins is a slave of sin! 35And slaves don't stay in the family forever, though the Son will always remain in the family. 36If the Son gives you freedom, you are free! 37I know that you are from Abraham's family. Yet you want to kill me, because my message isn't really in your hearts. 38I am telling you what my Father has shown me, just as you are doing what your father has taught you.

Your Father Is the Devil

39The people said to Jesus, "Abraham is our father!"

Jesus replied, "If you were Abraham's children, you would do what Abraham did. 40Instead, you want to kill

NEW INTERNATIONAL VERSION

claim to be⌋ and that I do nothing on my own but speak
just what the Father has taught me. [29]The one who sent
me is with me; he has not left me alone, for I always do
what pleases him." [30]Even as he spoke, many put their
faith in him.

The Children of Abraham

[31]To the Jews who had believed him, Jesus said, "If you
hold to my teaching, you are really my disciples. [32]Then
you will know the truth, and the truth will set you free."
[33]They answered him, "We are Abraham's descendants[b]
and have never been slaves of anyone. How can you say
that we shall be set free?"
[34]Jesus replied, "I tell you the truth, everyone who sins
is a slave to sin. [35]Now a slave has no permanent place in
the family, but a son belongs to it forever. [36]So if the Son
sets you free, you will be free indeed. [37]I know you are
Abraham's descendants. Yet you are ready to kill me,
because you have no room for my word. [38]I am telling you
what I have seen in the Father's presence, and you do
what you have heard from your father.[c]"
[39]"Abraham is our father," they answered.
"If you were Abraham's children," said Jesus, "then you
would[d] do the things Abraham did. [40]As it is, you are

[b] *33* Greek *seed*; also in verse 37 [c] *38* Or *presence. Therefore do what you have heard from the Father.* [d] *39* Some early manuscripts *"If you are Abraham's children," said Jesus, "then*

NEW LIVING TRANSLATION

that I do nothing on my own, but I speak what the Father
taught me. [29]And the one who sent me is with me—he has
not deserted me. For I always do those things that are
pleasing to him." [30]Then many who heard him say these
things believed in him.

Jesus and Abraham

[31]Jesus said to the people* who believed in him, "You
are truly my disciples if you keep obeying my teachings.
[32]And you will know the truth, and the truth will set you
free."
[33]"But we are descendants of Abraham," they said. "We
have never been slaves to anyone on earth. What do you
mean, 'set free'?"
[34]Jesus replied, "I assure you that everyone who sins is
a slave of sin. [35]A slave is not a permanent member of the
family, but a son is part of the family forever. [36]So if the
Son sets you free, you will indeed be free. [37]Yes, I realize
that you are descendants of Abraham. And yet some of you
are trying to kill me because my message does not find a
place in your hearts. [38]I am telling you what I saw when I
was with my Father. But you are following the advice of
your father."
[39]"Our father is Abraham," they declared.
"No," Jesus replied, "for if you were children of
Abraham, you would follow his good example.* [40]I told

8:31 Greek *Jewish people;* also in 8:48, 52, 57. 8:39 Some manuscripts read *if you are children of Abraham, follow his example.*

NEW KING JAMES VERSION

of Myself; but as My Father taught Me, I speak these things.
[29]And He who sent Me is with Me. The Father has not left
Me alone, for I always do those things that please Him."
[30]As He spoke these words, many believed in Him.

The Truth Shall Make You Free

[31]Then Jesus said to those Jews who believed Him, "If you
abide in My word, you are My disciples indeed. [32]And you
shall know the truth, and the truth shall make you free."
[33]They answered Him, "We are Abraham's descendants,
and have never been in bondage to anyone. How *can* You
say, 'You will be made free'?"
[34]Jesus answered them, "Most assuredly, I say to you,
whoever commits sin is a slave of sin. [35]And a slave does
not abide in the house forever, *but* a son abides forever.
[36]Therefore if the Son makes you free, you shall be free
indeed.

Abraham's Seed and Satan's

[37]"I know that you are Abraham's descendants, but you
seek to kill Me, because My word has no place in you. [38]I
speak what I have seen with My Father, and you do what
you have seen with[l] your father."
[39]They answered and said to Him, "Abraham is our
father."
Jesus said to them, "If you were Abraham's children, you
would do the works of Abraham. [40]But now you seek to

8:38 [l] NU-Text reads *heard from.*

THE MESSAGE

not making this up, but speaking only what the Father
taught me. The One who sent me stays with me. He
doesn't abandon me. He sees how much joy I take in pleas-
ing him."

When he put it in these terms, many people decided to
believe.

If the Son Sets You Free

Then Jesus turned to the Jews who had claimed to
believe in him. "If you stick with this, living out what I tell
you, you are my disciples for sure. Then you will experi-
ence for yourselves the truth, and the truth will free you."

Surprised, they said, "But we're descendants of Abra-
ham. We've never been slaves to anyone. How can you
say, 'The truth will free you'?"

Jesus said, "I tell you most solemnly that anyone who
chooses a life of sin is trapped in a dead-end life and is, in
fact, a slave. A slave is a transient, who can't come and go
at will. The Son, though, has an established position, the
run of the house. So if the Son sets you free, you are free
through and through. I know you are Abraham's descen-
dants. But I also know that you are trying to kill me
because my message hasn't yet penetrated your thick
skulls. I'm talking about things I have seen while keeping
company with the Father, and you just go on doing what
you have heard from your father."

They were indignant. "Our father is Abraham!"

Jesus said, "If you were Abraham's children, you would
have been doing the things Abraham did. And yet here you

KING JAMES VERSION

40 But now ye seek to kill me, a man that hath told you the truth, which I have heard of God: this did not Abraham.

41 Ye do the deeds of your father. Then said they to him, We be not born of fornication; we have one Father, *even* God.

42 Jesus said unto them, If God were your Father, ye would love me: for I proceeded forth and came from God; neither came I of myself, but he sent me.

43 Why do ye not understand my speech? *even* because ye cannot hear my word.

44 Ye are of *your* father the devil, and the lusts of your father ye will do. He was a murderer from the beginning, and abode not in the truth, because there is no truth in him. When he speaketh a lie, he speaketh of his own: for he is a liar, and the father of it.

45 And because I tell *you* the truth, ye believe me not.

46 ¶ Which of you convinceth me of sin? And if I say the truth, why do ye not believe me?

47 He that is of God heareth God's words: ye therefore hear *them* not, because ye are not of God.

48 Then answered the Jews, and said unto him, Say we not well that thou art a Samaritan, and hast a devil?

49 Jesus answered, I have not a devil; but I honour my Father, and ye do dishonour me.

50 And I seek not mine own glory: there is one that seeketh and judgeth.

NEW AMERICAN STANDARD BIBLE

40 "But as it is, you are seeking to kill Me, a man who has told you the truth, which I heard from God; this Abraham did not do.

41 "You are doing the deeds of your father." They said to Him, "We were not born of fornication; we have one Father: God."

42 Jesus said to them, "If God were your Father, you would love Me, for I proceeded forth and have come from God, for I have not even come on My own initiative, but He sent Me.

43 "Why do you not understand what I am saying? *It is* because you cannot hear My word.

44 "You are of *your* father the devil, and you want to do the desires of your father. He was a murderer from the beginning, and does not stand in the truth because there is no truth in him. Whenever he speaks a lie, he speaks from his own *nature*, for he is a liar and the father of lies.

45 "But because I speak the truth, you do not believe Me.

46 "Which one of you convicts Me of sin? If I speak truth, why do you not believe Me?

47 "He who is of God hears the words of God; for this reason you do not hear *them*, because you are not of God."

48 The Jews answered and said to Him, "Do we not say rightly that You are a Samaritan and have a demon?"

49 Jesus answered, "I do not have a demon; but I honor My Father, and you dishonor Me.

50 "But I do not seek My glory; there is One who seeks and judges.

NEW CENTURY VERSION

told you the truth which I heard from God, but you are trying to kill me. Abraham did nothing like that. 41 So you are doing the things your own father did."

But they said, "We are not like children who never knew who their father was. God is our Father; he is the only Father we have."

42 Jesus said to them, "If God were really your Father, you would love me, because I came from God and now I am here. I did not come by my own authority; God sent me. 43 You don't understand what I say, because you cannot accept my teaching. 44 You belong to your father the devil, and you want to do what he wants. He was a murderer from the beginning and was against the truth, because there is no truth in him. When he tells a lie, he shows what he is really like, because he is a liar and the father of lies. 45 But because I speak the truth, you don't believe me. 46 Can any of you prove that I am guilty of sin? If I am telling the truth, why don't you believe me? 47 The person who belongs to God accepts what God says. But you don't accept what God says, because you don't belong to God."

Jesus Is Greater than Abraham

48 The Jews answered, "We say you are a Samaritan and have a demon in you. Are we not right?"

49 Jesus answered, "I have no demon in me. I give honor to my Father, but you dishonor me. 50 I am not trying to get honor for myself. There is One who wants this honor for

CONTEMPORARY ENGLISH VERSION

me for telling you the truth that God gave me. Abraham never did anything like that. 41 But you are doing exactly what your father does."

"Don't accuse us of having someone else as our father!" they said. "We just have one father, and he is God."

42 Jesus answered:

If God were your Father, you would love me, because I came from God and only from him. He sent me. I did not come on my own. 43 Why can't you understand what I am talking about? Can't you stand to hear what I am saying? 44 Your father is the devil, and you do exactly what he wants. He has always been a murderer and a liar. There is nothing truthful about him. He speaks on his own, and everything he says is a lie. Not only is he a liar himself, but he is also the father of all lies.

45 Everything I have told you is true, and you still refuse to have faith in me. 46 Can any of you accuse me of sin? If you cannot, why won't you have faith in me? After all, I am telling you the truth. 47 Anyone who belongs to God will listen to his message. But you refuse to listen, because you don't belong to God.

Jesus and Abraham

48 The people told Jesus, "We were right to say that you are a Samaritan[f] and that you have a demon in you!"

49 Jesus answered, "I don't have a demon in me. I honor my Father, and you refuse to honor me. 50 I don't want honor for myself. But there is one who wants me to be

[f] **8.48** *Samaritan*: See 4.9 and the note there.

NEW INTERNATIONAL VERSION

determined to kill me, a man who has told you the truth that I heard from God. Abraham did not do such things. 41You are doing the things your own father does."

"We are not illegitimate children," they protested. "The only Father we have is God himself."

The Children of the Devil

42Jesus said to them, "If God were your Father, you would love me, for I came from God and now am here. I have not come on my own; but he sent me. 43Why is my language not clear to you? Because you are unable to hear what I say. 44You belong to your father, the devil, and you want to carry out your father's desire. He was a murderer from the beginning, not holding to the truth, for there is no truth in him. When he lies, he speaks his native language, for he is a liar and the father of lies. 45Yet because I tell the truth, you do not believe me! 46Can any of you prove me guilty of sin? If I am telling the truth, why don't you believe me? 47He who belongs to God hears what God says. The reason you do not hear is that you do not belong to God."

The Claims of Jesus About Himself

48The Jews answered him, "Aren't we right in saying that you are a Samaritan and demon-possessed?"

49"I am not possessed by a demon," said Jesus, "but I honor my Father and you dishonor me. 50I am not seeking glory for myself; but there is one who seeks it, and he is

NEW LIVING TRANSLATION

you the truth I heard from God, but you are trying to kill me. Abraham wouldn't do a thing like that. 41No, you are obeying your real father when you act that way."

They replied, "We were not born out of wedlock! Our true Father is God himself."

42Jesus told them, "If God were your Father, you would love me, because I have come to you from God. I am not here on my own, but he sent me. 43Why can't you understand what I am saying? It is because you are unable to do so! 44For you are the children of your father the Devil, and you love to do the evil things he does. He was a murderer from the beginning and has always hated the truth. There is no truth in him. When he lies, it is consistent with his character; for he is a liar and the father of lies. 45So when I tell the truth, you just naturally don't believe me! 46Which of you can truthfully accuse me of sin? And since I am telling you the truth, why don't you believe me? 47Anyone whose Father is God listens gladly to the words of God. Since you don't, it proves you aren't God's children."

48The people retorted, "You Samaritan devil! Didn't we say all along that you were possessed by a demon?"

49"No," Jesus said, "I have no demon in me. For I honor my Father—and you dishonor me. 50And though I have no wish to glorify myself, God wants to glorify me. Let him be

NEW KING JAMES VERSION

kill Me, a Man who has told you the truth which I heard from God. Abraham did not do this. 41You do the deeds of your father."

Then they said to Him, "We were not born of fornication; we have one Father—God."

42Jesus said to them, "If God were your Father, you would love Me, for I proceeded forth and came from God; nor have I come of Myself, but He sent Me. 43Why do you not understand My speech? Because you are not able to listen to My word. 44You are of *your* father the devil, and the desires of your father you want to do. He was a murderer from the beginning, and does not stand in the truth, because there is no truth in him. When he speaks a lie, he speaks from his own *resources,* for he is a liar and the father of it. 45But because I tell the truth, you do not believe Me. 46Which of you convicts Me of sin? And if I tell the truth, why do you not believe Me? 47He who is of God hears God's words; therefore you do not hear, because you are not of God."

Before Abraham Was, I AM

48Then the Jews answered and said to Him, "Do we not say rightly that You are a Samaritan and have a demon?"

49Jesus answered, "I do not have a demon; but I honor My Father, and you dishonor Me. 50And I do not seek My *own* glory; there is One who seeks and judges. 51Most

THE MESSAGE

are trying to kill me, a man who has spoken to you the truth he got straight from God! Abraham never did that sort of thing. You persist in repeating the works of your father."

They said, "We're not bastards. We have a legitimate father: the one and only God."

"If God was your father," said Jesus, "you would love me, for I came from God and arrived here. I didn't come on my own. He sent me. Why can't you understand one word I say? Here's why: You can't handle it. You're from your father, the Devil, and all you want to do is please him. He was a killer from the very start. He couldn't stand the truth because there wasn't a shred of truth in him. When the Liar speaks, he makes it up out of his lying nature and fills the world with lies. I arrive on the scene, tell you the plain truth, and you refuse to have a thing to do with me. Can any one of you convict me of a single misleading word, a single sinful act? But if I'm telling the truth, why don't you believe me? Anyone on God's side listens to God's words. This is why you're not listening—because you're not on God's side."

I Am Who I Am

The Jews then said, "That clinches it. We were right all along when we called you a Samaritan and said you were crazy—demon-possessed!"

Jesus said, "I'm not crazy. I simply honor my Father, while you dishonor me. I am not trying to get anything for myself. God intends something gloriously grand here and is making the decisions that will bring it about. I say this

KING JAMES VERSION

51 ¶ Verily, verily, I say unto you, If a man keep my saying, he shall never see death.

52 Then said the Jews unto him, Now we know that thou hast a devil. Abraham is dead, and the prophets; and thou sayest, If a man keep my saying, he shall never taste of death.

53 Art thou greater than our father Abraham, which is dead? and the prophets are dead: whom makest thou thyself?

54 Jesus answered, If I honour myself, my honour is nothing: it is my Father that honoureth me; of whom ye say, that he is your God:

55 Yet ye have not known him; but I know him: and if I should say, I know him not, I shall be a liar like unto you: but I know him, and keep his saying.

56 Your father Abraham rejoiced to see my day: and he saw *it*, and was glad.

57 Then said the Jews unto him, Thou art not yet fifty years old, and hast thou seen Abraham?

58 Jesus said unto them, Verily, verily, I say unto you, Before Abraham was, I am.

59 Then took they up stones to cast at him: but Jesus hid himself, and went out of the temple, going through the midst of them, and so passed by.

9 And as *Jesus* passed by, he saw a man which was blind from *his* birth.

2 And his disciples asked him, saying, Master, who did sin, this man, or his parents, that he was born blind?

3 Jesus answered, Neither hath this man sinned, nor his

NEW AMERICAN STANDARD BIBLE

51 "Truly, truly, I say to you, if anyone keeps My word he will never see death."

52 The Jews said to Him, "Now we know that You have a demon. Abraham died, and the prophets *also;* and You say, 'If anyone keeps My word, he will never taste of death.'

53 "Surely You are not greater than our father Abraham, who died? The prophets died too; whom do You make Yourself out *to be?*"

54 Jesus answered, "If I glorify Myself, My glory is nothing; it is My Father who glorifies Me, of whom you say, 'He is our God';

55 and you have not come to know Him, but I know Him; and if I say that I do not know Him, I will be a liar like you, but I do know Him and keep His word.

56 "Your father Abraham rejoiced to see My day, and he saw *it* and was glad."

57 So the Jews said to Him, "You are not yet fifty years old, and have You seen Abraham?"

58 Jesus said to them, "Truly, truly, I say to you, before Abraham was born, I am."

59 Therefore they picked up stones to throw at Him, but Jesus hid Himself and went out of the temple.

Healing the Man Born Blind

9 As He passed by, He saw a man blind from birth.

2 And His disciples asked Him, "Rabbi, who sinned, this man or his parents, that he would be born blind?"

3 Jesus answered, "*It was* neither *that* this man

NEW CENTURY VERSION

me, and he is the judge. [51]I tell you the truth, whoever obeys my teaching will never die."

[52]The Jews said to Jesus, "Now we know that you have a demon in you! Even Abraham and the prophets died. But you say, 'Whoever obeys my teaching will never die.' [53]Do you think you are greater than our father Abraham, who died? And the prophets died, too. Who do you think you are?"

[54]Jesus answered, "If I give honor to myself, that honor is worth nothing. The One who gives me honor is my Father, and you say he is your God. [55]You don't really know him, but I know him. If I said I did not know him, I would be a liar like you. But I do know him, and I obey what he says. [56]Your father Abraham was very happy that he would see my day. He saw that day and was glad."

[57]The Jews said to him, "You have never seen Abraham! You are not even fifty years old."

[58]Jesus answered, "I tell you the truth, before Abraham was even born, I am!" [59]When Jesus said this, the people picked up stones to throw at him. But Jesus hid himself, and then he left the Temple.

Jesus Heals a Man Born Blind

9 As Jesus was walking along, he saw a man who had been born blind. [2]His followers asked him, "Teacher, whose sin caused this man to be born blind—his own sin or his parents' sin?"

[3]Jesus answered, "It is not this man's sin or his parents'

CONTEMPORARY ENGLISH VERSION

honored, and he is also the one who judges. [51]I tell you for certain that if you obey my words, you will never die."

[52]Then the people said, "Now we are sure that you have a demon. Abraham is dead, and so are the prophets. How can you say that no one who obeys your words will ever die? [53]Are you greater than our father Abraham? He died, and so did the prophets. Who do you think you are?"

[54]Jesus replied, "If I honored myself, it would mean nothing. My Father is the one who honors me. You claim that he is your God, [55]even though you don't really know him. If I said I didn't know him, I would be a liar, just like all of you. But I know him, and I do what he says. [56]Your father Abraham was really glad to see me."

[57]"You are not even fifty years old!" they said. "How could you have seen Abraham?"

[58]Jesus answered, "I tell you for certain that even before Abraham was, I was, and I am."[g] [59]The people picked up stones to kill Jesus, but he hid and left the temple.

Jesus Heals a Man Born Blind

9 As Jesus walked along, he saw a man who had been blind since birth. [2]Jesus' disciples asked, "Teacher, why was this man born blind? Was it because he or his parents sinned?"

[3]"No, it wasn't!" Jesus answered. "But because of his

[g] 8.58 *I am*: See the note at 8.24.

NEW INTERNATIONAL VERSION

the judge. 51I tell you the truth, if anyone keeps my word,
he will never see death."
52At this the Jews exclaimed, "Now we know that you
are demon-possessed! Abraham died and so did the proph-
ets, yet you say that if anyone keeps your word, he will
never taste death. 53Are you greater than our father
Abraham? He died, and so did the prophets. Who do you
think you are?"
54Jesus replied, "If I glorify myself, my glory means
nothing. My Father, whom you claim as your God, is the
one who glorifies me. 55Though you do not know him, I
know him. If I said I did not, I would be a liar like you, but
I do know him and keep his word. 56Your father Abraham
rejoiced at the thought of seeing my day; he saw it and
was glad."
57"You are not yet fifty years old," the Jews said to him,
"and you have seen Abraham!"
58"I tell you the truth," Jesus answered, "before Abra-
ham was born, I am!" 59At this, they picked up stones to
stone him, but Jesus hid himself, slipping away from the
temple grounds.

Jesus Heals a Man Born Blind

9 As he went along, he saw a man blind from birth.
2His disciples asked him, "Rabbi, who sinned, this
man or his parents, that he was born blind?"
3"Neither this man nor his parents sinned," said Jesus,

NEW LIVING TRANSLATION

the judge. 51I assure you, anyone who obeys my teaching
will never die!"
52The people said, "Now we know you are possessed by
a demon. Even Abraham and the prophets died, but you
say that those who obey your teaching will never die!
53Are you greater than our father Abraham, who died? Are
you greater than the prophets, who died? Who do you
think you are?"
54Jesus answered, "If I am merely boasting about myself,
it doesn't count. But it is my Father who says these glori-
ous things about me. You say, 'He is our God,' 55but you
do not even know him. I know him. If I said otherwise, I
would be as great a liar as you! But it is true—I know him
and obey him. 56Your ancestor Abraham rejoiced as he
looked forward to my coming. He saw it and was glad."
57The people said, "You aren't even fifty years old. How
can you say you have seen Abraham?*"
58Jesus answered, "The truth is, I existed before Abraham
was even born!"* 59At that point they picked up stones to kill
him. But Jesus hid himself from them and left the Temple.

Jesus Heals a Man Born Blind

9 As Jesus was walking along, he saw a man who had
been blind from birth. 2"Teacher," his disciples asked
him, "why was this man born blind? Was it a result of his
own sins or those of his parents?"
3"It was not because of his sins or his parents' sins,"

8:57 Some manuscripts read *How can you say Abraham has seen you?*
8:58 Or *"Truly, truly, before Abraham was, I am."*

NEW KING JAMES VERSION

assuredly, I say to you, if anyone keeps My word he shall
never see death."
52Then the Jews said to Him, "Now we know that You have
a demon! Abraham is dead, and the prophets; and You say,
'If anyone keeps My word he shall never taste death.' 53Are
You greater than our father Abraham, who is dead? And the
prophets are dead. Who do You make Yourself out to be?"
54Jesus answered, "If I honor Myself, My honor is nothing.
It is My Father who honors Me, of whom you say that He is
your[m] God. 55Yet you have not known Him, but I know Him.
And if I say, 'I do not know Him,' I shall be a liar like you;
but I do know Him and keep His word. 56Your father Abra-
ham rejoiced to see My day, and he saw *it* and was glad."
57Then the Jews said to Him, "You are not yet fifty years
old, and have You seen Abraham?"
58Jesus said to them, "Most assuredly, I say to you, be-
fore Abraham was, I AM."
59Then they took up stones to throw at Him; but Jesus
hid Himself and went out of the temple,[n] going through
the midst of them, and so passed by.

A Man Born Blind Receives Sight

9 Now as *Jesus* passed by, He saw a man who was blind
from birth. 2And His disciples asked Him, saying,
"Rabbi, who sinned, this man or his parents, that he was
born blind?"
3Jesus answered, "Neither this man nor his parents

8:54 [m] NU-Text and M-Text read *our*. 8:59 [n] NU-Text omits the rest of this verse.

THE MESSAGE

with absolute confidence. If you practice what I'm telling
you, you'll never have to look death in the face."

At this point the Jews said, "Now we *know* you're crazy. Abraham died. The prophets died. And you show up saying, 'If you practice what I'm telling you, you'll never have to face death, not even a taste.' Are you greater than Abraham, who died? And the prophets died! Who do you think you are!"

Jesus said, "If I turned the spotlight on myself, it wouldn't amount to anything. But my Father, the same One you say is your Father, put me here at this time and place of splendor. You haven't recognized him in this. But I have. If I, in false modesty, said I didn't know what was going on, I would be as much of a liar as you are. But I do know, and I am doing what he says. Abraham—your 'father'—with jubilant faith looked down the corridors of history and saw my day coming. He saw it and cheered."

The Jews said, "You're not even fifty years old—and Abraham saw you?"

"Believe me," said Jesus, "*I am who I am* long before Abraham was anything."

That did it—pushed them over the edge. They picked up rocks to throw at him. But Jesus slipped away, getting out of the Temple.

True Blindness

9 Walking down the street, Jesus saw a man blind from birth. His disciples asked, "Rabbi, who sinned: this man or his parents, causing him to be born blind?"

Jesus said, "You're asking the wrong question. You're

KING JAMES VERSION

parents: but that the works of God should be made manifest in him.

4 I must work the works of him that sent me, while it is day: the night cometh, when no man can work.

5 As long as I am in the world, I am the light of the world.

6 When he had thus spoken, he spat on the ground, and made clay of the spittle, and he anointed the eyes of the blind man with the clay,

7 And said unto him, Go, wash in the pool of Siloam, (which is by interpretation, Sent.) He went his way therefore, and washed, and came seeing.

8 ¶ The neighbours therefore, and they which before had seen him that he was blind, said, Is not this he that sat and begged?

9 Some said, This is he: others *said*, He is like him: *but* he said, I am *he*.

10 Therefore said they unto him, How were thine eyes opened?

11 He answered and said, A man that is called Jesus made clay, and anointed mine eyes, and said unto me, Go to the pool of Siloam, and wash: and I went and washed, and I received sight.

12 Then said they unto him, Where is he? He said, I know not.

13 ¶ They brought to the Pharisees him that aforetime was blind.

14 And it was the sabbath day when Jesus made the clay, and opened his eyes.

NEW AMERICAN STANDARD BIBLE

sinned, nor his parents; but *it was* so that the works of God might be displayed in him.

4 "We must work the works of Him who sent Me as long as it is day; night is coming when no one can work.

5 "While I am in the world, I am the Light of the world."

6 When He had said this, He spat on the ground, and made clay of the spittle, and applied the clay to his eyes,

7 and said to him, "Go, wash in the pool of Siloam" (which is translated, Sent). So he went away and washed, and came *back* seeing.

8 Therefore the neighbors, and those who previously saw him as a beggar, were saying, "Is not this the one who used to sit and beg?"

9 Others were saying, "This is he," *still* others were saying, "No, but he is like him." He kept saying, "I am the one."

10 So they were saying to him, "How then were your eyes opened?"

11 He answered, "The man who is called Jesus made clay, and anointed my eyes, and said to me, 'Go to Siloam and wash'; so I went away and washed, and I received sight."

12 They said to him, "Where is He?" He *said, "I do not know."

Controversy over the Man

13 They *brought to the Pharisees the man who was formerly blind.

14 Now it was a Sabbath on the day when Jesus made the clay and opened his eyes.

NEW CENTURY VERSION

sin that made him be blind. This man was born blind so that God's power could be shown in him. 4While it is daytime, we must continue doing the work of the One who sent me. Night is coming, when no one can work. 5While I am in the world, I am the light of the world."

6After Jesus said this, he spit on the ground and made some mud with it and put the mud on the man's eyes. 7Then he told the man, "Go and wash in the Pool of Siloam." (Siloam means Sent.) So the man went, washed, and came back seeing.

8The neighbors and some people who had earlier seen this man begging said, "Isn't this the same man who used to sit and beg?"

9Some said, "He is the one," but others said, "No, he only looks like him."

The man himself said, "I am the man."

10They asked, "How did you get your sight?"

11He answered, "The man named Jesus made some mud and put it on my eyes. Then he told me to go to Siloam and wash. So I went and washed, and then I could see."

12They asked him, "Where is this man?"

"I don't know," he answered.

Pharisees Question the Healing

13Then the people took to the Pharisees the man who had been blind. 14The day Jesus had made mud and healed

CONTEMPORARY ENGLISH VERSION

blindness, you will see God work a miracle for him. 4As long as it is day, we must do what the one who sent me wants me to do. When night comes, no one can work. 5While I am in the world, I am the light for the world."

6After Jesus said this, he spit on the ground. He made some mud and smeared it on the man's eyes. 7Then he said, "Go and wash off the mud in Siloam Pool." The man went and washed in Siloam, which means "One Who Is Sent." When he had washed off the mud, he could see.

8The man's neighbors and the people who had seen him begging wondered if he really could be the same man. 9Some of them said he was the same beggar, while others said he only looked like him. But he told them, "I am that man."

10"Then how can you see?" they asked.

11He answered, "Someone named Jesus made some mud and smeared it on my eyes. He told me to go and wash it off in Siloam Pool. When I did, I could see."

12"Where is he now?" they asked.

"I don't know," he answered.

The Pharisees Try To Find Out What Happened

13-14The day when Jesus made the mud and healed the man was a Sabbath. So the people took the man to the

NEW INTERNATIONAL VERSION

"but this happened so that the work of God might be displayed in his life. 4As long as it is day, we must do the work of him who sent me. Night is coming, when no one can work. 5While I am in the world, I am the light of the world."

6Having said this, he spit on the ground, made some mud with the saliva, and put it on the man's eyes. 7"Go," he told him, "wash in the Pool of Siloam" (this word means Sent). So the man went and washed, and came home seeing.

8His neighbors and those who had formerly seen him begging asked, "Isn't this the same man who used to sit and beg?" 9Some claimed that he was.

Others said, "No, he only looks like him."

But he himself insisted, "I am the man."

10"How then were your eyes opened?" they demanded.

11He replied, "The man they call Jesus made some mud and put it on my eyes. He told me to go to Siloam and wash. So I went and washed, and then I could see."

12"Where is this man?" they asked him.

"I don't know," he said.

The Pharisees Investigate the Healing

13They brought to the Pharisees the man who had been blind. 14Now the day on which Jesus had made the mud and opened the man's eyes was a Sabbath. 15Therefore the

NEW LIVING TRANSLATION

Jesus answered. "He was born blind so the power of God could be seen in him. 4All of us must quickly carry out the tasks assigned us by the one who sent me, because there is little time left before the night falls and all work comes to an end. 5But while I am still here in the world, I am the light of the world."

6Then he spit on the ground, made mud with the saliva, and smoothed the mud over the blind man's eyes. 7He told him, "Go and wash in the pool of Siloam" (Siloam means Sent). So the man went and washed, and came back seeing!

8His neighbors and others who knew him as a blind beggar asked each other, "Is this the same man—that beggar?" 9Some said he was, and others said, "No, but he surely looks like him!"

And the beggar kept saying, "I am the same man!"

10They asked, "Who healed you? What happened?"

11He told them, "The man they call Jesus made mud and smoothed it over my eyes and told me, 'Go to the pool of Siloam and wash off the mud.' I went and washed, and now I can see!"

12"Where is he now?" they asked.

"I don't know," he replied.

13Then they took the man to the Pharisees. 14Now as it happened, Jesus had healed the man on a Sabbath. 15The

NEW KING JAMES VERSION

sinned, but that the works of God should be revealed in him. 4I[a] must work the works of Him who sent Me while it is day; *the* night is coming when no one can work. 5As long as I am in the world, I am the light of the world."

6When He had said these things, He spat on the ground and made clay with the saliva; and He anointed the eyes of the blind man with the clay. 7And He said to him, "Go, wash in the pool of Siloam" (which is translated, Sent). So he went and washed, and came back seeing.

8Therefore the neighbors and those who previously had seen that he was blind[b] said, "Is not this he who sat and begged?"

9Some said, "This is he." Others *said,* "He is like him."[c]

He said, "I am *he.*"

10Therefore they said to him, "How were your eyes opened?"

11He answered and said, "A Man called Jesus made clay and anointed my eyes and said to me, 'Go to the pool of[d] Siloam and wash.' So I went and washed, and I received sight."

12Then they said to him, "Where is He?"

He said, "I do not know."

The Pharisees Excommunicate the Healed Man

13They brought him who formerly was blind to the Pharisees. 14Now it was a Sabbath when Jesus made the

9:4 [a] NU-Text reads *We.* 9:8 [b] NU-Text reads *a beggar.* 9:9 [c] NU-Text reads *"No, but he is like him."* 9:11 [d] NU-Text omits *the pool of.*

THE MESSAGE

looking for someone to blame. There is no such cause-effect here. Look instead for what God can do. We need to be energetically at work for the One who sent me here, working while the sun shines. When night falls, the workday is over. For as long as I am in the world, there is plenty of light. I am the world's Light."

He said this and then spit in the dust, made a clay paste with the saliva, rubbed the paste on the blind man's eyes, and said, "Go, wash at the Pool of Siloam" (Siloam means "Sent"). The man went and washed—and saw.

Soon the town was buzzing. His relatives and those who year after year had seen him as a blind man begging, were saying, "Why, isn't this the man we knew, who sat here and begged?"

Others said, "It's him all right!"

But others objected, "It's not the same man at all. It just looks like him."

He said, "It's me, the very one."

They said, "How did your eyes get opened?"

"A man named Jesus made a paste and rubbed it on my eyes and told me, 'Go to Siloam and wash.' I did what he said. When I washed, I saw."

"So where is he?"

"I don't know."

They marched the man to the Pharisees. This day when Jesus made the paste and healed his blindness was the

KING JAMES VERSION

15 Then again the Pharisees also asked him how he had received his sight. He said unto them, He put clay upon mine eyes, and I washed, and do see.

16 Therefore said some of the Pharisees, This man is not of God, because he keepeth not the sabbath day. Others said, How can a man that is a sinner do such miracles? And there was a division among them.

17 They say unto the blind man again, What sayest thou of him, that he hath opened thine eyes? He said, He is a prophet.

18 But the Jews did not believe concerning him, that he had been blind, and received his sight, until they called the parents of him that had received his sight.

19 And they asked them, saying, Is this your son, who ye say was born blind? how then doth he now see?

20 His parents answered them and said, We know that this is our son, and that he was born blind:

21 But by what means he now seeth, we know not; or who hath opened his eyes, we know not: he is of age; ask him: he shall speak for himself.

22 These *words* spake his parents, because they feared the Jews: for the Jews had agreed already, that if any man did confess that he was Christ, he should be put out of the synagogue.

23 Therefore said his parents, He is of age; ask him.

24 Then again called they the man that was blind, and said unto him, Give God the praise: we know that this man is a sinner.

NEW AMERICAN STANDARD BIBLE

15 Then the Pharisees also were asking him again how he received his sight. And he said to them, "He applied clay to my eyes, and I washed, and I see."

16 Therefore some of the Pharisees were saying, "This man is not from God, because He does not keep the Sabbath." But others were saying, "How can a man who is a sinner perform such signs?" And there was a division among them.

17 So they *said to the blind man again, "What do you say about Him, since He opened your eyes?" And he said, "He is a prophet."

18 The Jews then did not believe *it* of him, that he had been blind and had received sight, until they called the parents of the very one who had received his sight,

19 and questioned them, saying, "Is this your son, who you say was born blind? Then how does he now see?"

20 His parents answered them and said, "We know that this is our son, and that he was born blind;

21 but how he now sees, we do not know; or who opened his eyes, we do not know. Ask him; he is of age, he will speak for himself."

22 His parents said this because they were afraid of the Jews; for the Jews had already agreed that if anyone confessed Him to be Christ, he was to be put out of the synagogue.

23 For this reason his parents said, "He is of age; ask him."

24 So a second time they called the man who had been blind, and said to him, "Give glory to God; we know that this man is a sinner."

NEW CENTURY VERSION

his eyes was a Sabbath day. 15So now the Pharisees asked
the man, "How did you get your sight?"
He answered, "He put mud on my eyes, I washed, and
now I see."
16So some of the Pharisees were saying, "This man does
not keep the Sabbath day, so he is not from God."
But others said, "A man who is a sinner can't do miracles like these." So they could not agree with each other.
17They asked the man again, "What do you say about
him since it was your eyes he opened?"
The man answered, "He is a prophet."
18The Jews did not believe that he had been blind and
could now see again. So they sent for the man's parents
19and asked them, "Is this your son who you say was born
blind? Then how does he now see?"
20His parents answered, "We know that this is our son
and that he was born blind. 21But we don't know how he
can now see. We don't know who opened his eyes. Ask
him. He is old enough to speak for himself." 22His parents
said this because they were afraid of the Jews, who had
already decided that anyone who said Jesus was the Christ
would be put out of the synagogue. 23That is why his parents said, "He is old enough. Ask him."
24So for the second time, they called the man who had
been blind. They said, "You should give God the glory by
telling the truth. We know that this man is a sinner."

CONTEMPORARY ENGLISH VERSION

Pharisees. 15They asked him how he was able to see, and
he answered, "Jesus made some mud and smeared it on
my eyes. Then after I washed it off, I could see."
16Some of the Pharisees said, "This man Jesus doesn't
come from God. If he did, he would not break the law of
the Sabbath."
Others asked, "How could someone who is a sinner work
such a miracle?"[a]
Since the Pharisees could not agree among themselves,
17they asked the man, "What do you say about this one
who healed your eyes?"
"He is a prophet!" the man told them.
18But the Jewish leaders would not believe that the man
had once been blind. They sent for his parents 19and asked
them, "Is this the son that you said was born blind? How
can he now see?"
20The man's parents answered, "We are certain that he
is our son, and we know that he was born blind. 21But we
don't know how he got his sight or who gave it to him.
Ask him! He is old enough to speak for himself."
22-23The man's parents said this because they were
afraid of the Jewish leaders. The leaders had already
agreed that no one was to have anything to do with anyone who said Jesus was the Messiah.
24The leaders called the man back and said, "Swear by
God to tell the truth! We know that Jesus is a sinner."

[a] **9.16** *miracle*: See the note at 2.11.

NEW INTERNATIONAL VERSION

Pharisees also asked him how he had received his sight. "He put mud on my eyes," the man replied, "and I washed, and now I see."

16Some of the Pharisees said, "This man is not from God, for he does not keep the Sabbath."

But others asked, "How can a sinner do such miraculous signs?" So they were divided.

17Finally they turned again to the blind man, "What have you to say about him? It was your eyes he opened."

The man replied, "He is a prophet."

18The Jews still did not believe that he had been blind and had received his sight until they sent for the man's parents. 19"Is this your son?" they asked. "Is this the one you say was born blind? How is it that now he can see?"

20"We know he is our son," the parents answered, "and we know he was born blind. 21But how he can see now, or who opened his eyes, we don't know. Ask him. He is of age; he will speak for himself." 22His parents said this because they were afraid of the Jews, for already the Jews had decided that anyone who acknowledged that Jesus was the Christ[a] would be put out of the synagogue. 23That was why his parents said, "He is of age; ask him."

24A second time they summoned the man who had been blind. "Give glory to God,[b]" they said. "We know this man is a sinner."

[a] *22* Or *Messiah* [b] *24* A solemn charge to tell the truth (see Joshua 7:19)

NEW LIVING TRANSLATION

Pharisees asked the man all about it. So he told them, "He smoothed the mud over my eyes, and when it was washed away, I could see!"

16Some of the Pharisees said, "This man Jesus is not from God, for he is working on the Sabbath." Others said, "But how could an ordinary sinner do such miraculous signs?" So there was a deep division of opinion among them.

17Then the Pharisees once again questioned the man who had been blind and demanded, "This man who opened your eyes—who do you say he is?"

The man replied, "I think he must be a prophet."

18The Jewish leaders wouldn't believe he had been blind, so they called in his parents. 19They asked them, "Is this your son? Was he born blind? If so, how can he see?"

20His parents replied, "We know this is our son and that he was born blind, 21but we don't know how he can see or who healed him. He is old enough to speak for himself. Ask him." 22They said this because they were afraid of the Jewish leaders, who had announced that anyone saying Jesus was the Messiah would be expelled from the synagogue. 23That's why they said, "He is old enough to speak for himself. Ask him."

24So for the second time they called in the man who had been blind and told him, "Give glory to God by telling the truth,* because we know Jesus is a sinner."

9:24 Or *Give glory to God, not to Jesus;* Greek reads *Give glory to God.*

NEW KING JAMES VERSION

clay and opened his eyes. 15Then the Pharisees also asked him again how he had received his sight. He said to them, "He put clay on my eyes, and I washed, and I see."

16Therefore some of the Pharisees said, "This Man is not from God, because He does not keep the Sabbath."

Others said, "How can a man who is a sinner do such signs?" And there was a division among them.

17They said to the blind man again, "What do you say about Him because He opened your eyes?"

He said, "He is a prophet."

18But the Jews did not believe concerning him, that he had been blind and received his sight, until they called the parents of him who had received his sight. 19And they asked them, saying, "Is this your son, who you say was born blind? How then does he now see?"

20His parents answered them and said, "We know that this is our son, and that he was born blind; 21but by what means he now sees we do not know, or who opened his eyes we do not know. He is of age; ask him. He will speak for himself." 22His parents said these *things* because they feared the Jews, for the Jews had agreed already that if anyone confessed *that* He *was* Christ, he would be put out of the synagogue. 23Therefore his parents said, "He is of age; ask him."

24So they again called the man who was blind, and said to him, "Give God the glory! We know that this Man is a sinner."

THE MESSAGE

Sabbath. The Pharisees grilled him again on how he had come to see. He said, "He put a clay paste on my eyes, and I washed, and now I see."

Some of the Pharisees said, "Obviously, this man can't be from God. He doesn't keep the Sabbath."

Others countered, "How can a bad man do miraculous, God-revealing things like this?" There was a split in their ranks.

They came back at the blind man, "You're the expert. He opened *your* eyes. What do you say about him?"

He said, "He is a prophet."

The Jews didn't believe it, didn't believe the man was blind to begin with. So they called the parents of the man now bright-eyed with sight. They asked them, "Is this your son, the one you say was born blind? So how is it that he now sees?"

His parents said, "We know he is our son, and we know he was born blind. But we don't know how he came to see—haven't a clue about who opened his eyes. Why don't you ask him? He's a grown man and can speak for himself." (His parents were talking like this because they were intimidated by the Jewish leaders, who had already decided that anyone who took a stand that this was the Messiah would be kicked out of the meeting place. That's why his parents said, "Ask him. He's a grown man.")

They called the man back a second time—the man who had been blind—and told him, "Give credit to God. We know this man is an impostor."

KING JAMES VERSION

25 He answered and said, Whether he be a sinner *or no*, I know not: one thing I know, that, whereas I was blind, now I see.

26 Then said they to him again, What did he to thee? how opened he thine eyes?

27 He answered them, I have told you already, and ye did not hear: wherefore would ye hear *it* again? will ye also be his disciples?

28 Then they reviled him, and said, Thou art his disciple; but we are Moses' disciples.

29 We know that God spake unto Moses: *as for* this *fellow*, we know not from whence he is.

30 The man answered and said unto them, Why herein is a marvellous thing, that ye know not from whence he is, and *yet* he hath opened mine eyes.

31 Now we know that God heareth not sinners: but if any man be a worshipper of God, and doeth his will, him he heareth.

32 Since the world began was it not heard that any man opened the eyes of one that was born blind.

33 If this man were not of God, he could do nothing.

34 They answered and said unto him, Thou wast altogether born in sins, and dost thou teach us? And they cast him out.

35 ¶ Jesus heard that they had cast him out; and when he had found him, he said unto him, Dost thou believe on the Son of God?

36 He answered and said, Who is he, Lord, that I might believe on him?

NEW AMERICAN STANDARD BIBLE

25 He then answered, "Whether He is a sinner, I do not know; one thing I do know, that though I was blind, now I see."

26 So they said to him, "What did He do to you? How did He open your eyes?"

27 He answered them, "I told you already and you did not listen; why do you want to hear *it* again? You do not want to become His disciples too, do you?"

28 They reviled him and said, "You are His disciple, but we are disciples of Moses.

29 "We know that God has spoken to Moses, but as for this man, we do not know where He is from."

30 The man answered and said to them, "Well, here is an amazing thing, that you do not know where He is from, and *yet* He opened my eyes.

31 "We know that God does not hear sinners; but if anyone is God-fearing and does His will, He hears him.

32 "Since the beginning of time it has never been heard that anyone opened the eyes of a person born blind.

33 "If this man were not from God, He could do nothing."

34 They answered him, "You were born entirely in sins, and are you teaching us?" So they put him out.

Jesus Affirms His Deity

35 Jesus heard that they had put him out, and finding him, He said, "Do you believe in the Son of Man?"

36 He answered, "Who is He, Lord, that I may believe in Him?"

NEW CENTURY VERSION

25 He answered, "I don't know if he is a sinner. One thing I do know: I was blind, and now I see."

26 They asked, "What did he do to you? How did he make you see again?"

27 He answered, "I already told you, and you didn't listen. Why do you want to hear it again? Do you want to become his followers, too?"

28 Then they insulted him and said, "You are his follow-
er, but we are followers of Moses.
29 We know that God spoke to Moses, but we don't even know where this man comes from."

30 The man answered, "This is a very strange thing. You
don't know where he comes from, and yet he opened my
eyes.
31 We all know that God does not listen to sinners,
but he listens to anyone who worships and obeys him.
32 Nobody has ever heard of anyone giving sight to a man
born blind.
33 If this man were not from God, he could do
nothing."

34 They answered, "You were born full of sin! Are you trying to teach us?" And they threw him out.

Spiritual Blindness

35 When Jesus heard that they had thrown him out, Jesus found him and said, "Do you believe in the Son of Man?"

36 He asked, "Who is the Son of Man, sir, so that I can believe in him?"

CONTEMPORARY ENGLISH VERSION

25 The man replied, "I don't know if he is a sinner or not. All I know is that I used to be blind, but now I can see!"

26 "What did he do to you?" the Jewish leaders asked. "How did he heal your eyes?"

27 The man answered, "I have already told you once, and you refused to listen. Why do you want me to tell you again? Do you also want to become his disciples?"

28 The leaders insulted the man and said, "You are his
follower! We are followers of Moses.
29 We are sure that
God spoke to Moses, but we don't even know where Jesus comes from."

30 "How strange!" the man replied. "He healed my eyes,
and yet you don't know where he comes from.
31 We know
that God listens only to people who love and obey him.
God doesn't listen to sinners.
32 And this is the first time in
history that anyone has ever given sight to someone born
blind.
33 Jesus could not do anything unless he came from
God."

34 The leaders told the man, "You have been a sinner since the day you were born! Do you think you can teach us anything?" Then they said, "You can never come back into any of our meeting places!"

35 When Jesus heard what had happened, he went and found the man. Then Jesus asked, "Do you have faith in the Son of Man?"

36 He replied, "Sir, if you will tell me who he is, I will put my faith in him."

NEW INTERNATIONAL VERSION

25He replied, "Whether he is a sinner or not, I don't know. One thing I do know. I was blind but now I see!"

26Then they asked him, "What did he do to you? How did he open your eyes?"

27He answered, "I have told you already and you did not listen. Why do you want to hear it again? Do you want to become his disciples, too?"

28Then they hurled insults at him and said, "You are this fellow's disciple! We are disciples of Moses! 29We know that God spoke to Moses, but as for this fellow, we don't even know where he comes from."

30The man answered, "Now that is remarkable! You don't know where he comes from, yet he opened my eyes. 31We know that God does not listen to sinners. He listens to the godly man who does his will. 32Nobody has ever heard of opening the eyes of a man born blind. 33If this man were not from God, he could do nothing."

34To this they replied, "You were steeped in sin at birth; how dare you lecture us!" And they threw him out.

Spiritual Blindness

35Jesus heard that they had thrown him out, and when he found him, he said, "Do you believe in the Son of Man?"

36"Who is he, sir?" the man asked. "Tell me so that I may believe in him."

NEW LIVING TRANSLATION

25"I don't know whether he is a sinner," the man replied. "But I know this: I was blind, and now I can see!"

26"But what did he do?" they asked. "How did he heal you?"

27"Look!" the man exclaimed. "I told you once. Didn't you listen? Why do you want to hear it again? Do you want to become his disciples, too?"

28Then they cursed him and said, "You are his disciple, but we are disciples of Moses. 29We know God spoke to Moses, but as for this man, we don't know anything about him."

30"Why, that's very strange!" the man replied. "He healed my eyes, and yet you don't know anything about him! 31Well, God doesn't listen to sinners, but he is ready to hear those who worship him and do his will. 32Never since the world began has anyone been able to open the eyes of someone born blind. 33If this man were not from God, he couldn't do it."

34"You were born in sin!" they answered. "Are you trying to teach us?" And they threw him out of the synagogue.

Spiritual Blindness

35When Jesus heard what had happened, he found the man and said, "Do you believe in the Son of Man*?"

36The man answered, "Who is he, sir, because I would like to."

9:35 Some manuscripts read *the Son of God.*

NEW KING JAMES VERSION

25He answered and said, "Whether He is a sinner *or not* I do not know. One thing I know: that though I was blind, now I see."

26Then they said to him again, "What did He do to you? How did He open your eyes?"

27He answered them, "I told you already, and you did not listen. Why do you want to hear *it* again? Do you also want to become His disciples?"

28Then they reviled him and said, "You are His disciple, but we are Moses' disciples. 29We know that God spoke to Moses; *as for* this *fellow,* we do not know where He is from."

30The man answered and said to them, "Why, this is a marvelous thing, that you do not know where He is from; yet He has opened my eyes! 31Now we know that God does not hear sinners; but if anyone is a worshiper of God and does His will, He hears him. 32Since the world began it has been unheard of that anyone opened the eyes of one who was born blind. 33If this Man were not from God, He could do nothing."

34They answered and said to him, "You were completely born in sins, and are you teaching us?" And they cast him out.

True Vision and True Blindness

35Jesus heard that they had cast him out; and when He had found him, He said to him, "Do you believe in the Son of God?"[e]

36He answered and said, "Who is He, Lord, that I may believe in Him?"

9:35 [e] NU-Text reads *Son of Man.*

THE MESSAGE

He replied, "I know nothing about that one way or the other. But I know one thing for sure: I was blind . . . I now see."

They said, "What did he do to you? How did he open your eyes?"

"I've told you over and over and you haven't listened. Why do you want to hear it again? Are you so eager to become his disciples?"

With that they jumped all over him. "*You* might be a disciple of that man, but we're disciples of Moses. We know for sure that God spoke to Moses, but we have no idea where this man even comes from."

The man replied, "This is amazing! You claim to know nothing about him, but the fact is, he opened my eyes! It's well known that God isn't at the beck and call of sinners, but listens carefully to anyone who lives in reverence and does his will. That someone opened the eyes of a man born blind has never been heard of—ever. If this man didn't come from God, he wouldn't be able to do anything."

They said, "You're nothing but dirt! How dare you take that tone with us!" Then they threw him out in the street.

Jesus heard that they had thrown him out, and went and found him. He asked him, "Do you believe in the Son of Man?"

The man said, "Point him out to me, sir, so that I can believe in him."

KING JAMES VERSION

37 And Jesus said unto him, Thou hast both seen him, and it is he that talketh with thee.

38 And he said, Lord, I believe. And he worshipped him.

39 ¶ And Jesus said, For judgment I am come into this world, that they which see not might see; and that they which see might be made blind.

40 And *some* of the Pharisees which were with him heard these words, and said unto him, Are we blind also?

41 Jesus said unto them, If ye were blind, ye should have no sin: but now ye say, We see; therefore your sin remaineth.

10 Verily, verily, I say unto you, He that entereth not by the door into the sheepfold, but climbeth up some other way, the same is a thief and a robber.

2 But he that entereth in by the door is the shepherd of the sheep.

3 To him the porter openeth; and the sheep hear his voice: and he calleth his own sheep by name, and leadeth them out.

4 And when he putteth forth his own sheep, he goeth before them, and the sheep follow him: for they know his voice.

5 And a stranger will they not follow, but will flee from him: for they know not the voice of strangers.

6 This parable spake Jesus unto them: but they understood not what things they were which he spake unto them.

NEW AMERICAN STANDARD BIBLE

37 Jesus said to him, "You have both seen Him, and He is the one who is talking with you."

38 And he said, "Lord, I believe." And he worshiped Him.

39 And Jesus said, "For judgment I came into this world, so that those who do not see may see, and that those who see may become blind."

40 Those of the Pharisees who were with Him heard these things and said to Him, "We are not blind too, are we?"

41 Jesus said to them, "If you were blind, you would have no sin; but since you say, 'We see,' your sin remains.

Parable of the Good Shepherd

10 "Truly, truly, I say to you, he who does not enter by the door into the fold of the sheep, but climbs up some other way, he is a thief and a robber.

2 "But he who enters by the door is a shepherd of the sheep.

3 "To him the doorkeeper opens, and the sheep hear his voice, and he calls his own sheep by name and leads them out.

4 "When he puts forth all his own, he goes ahead of them, and the sheep follow him because they know his voice.

5 "A stranger they simply will not follow, but will flee from him, because they do not know the voice of strangers."

6 This figure of speech Jesus spoke to them, but they did not understand what those things were which He had been saying to them.

NEW CENTURY VERSION

37 Jesus said to him, "You have seen him. The Son of Man is the one talking with you."

38 He said, "Lord, I believe!" Then the man worshiped Jesus.

39 Jesus said, "I came into this world so that the world could be judged. I came so that the blind[a] would see and so that those who see will become blind."

40 Some of the Pharisees who were nearby heard Jesus say this and asked, "Are you saying we are blind, too?"

41 Jesus said, "If you were blind, you would not be guilty of sin. But since you keep saying you see, your guilt remains."

The Shepherd and His Sheep

10 Jesus said, "I tell you the truth, the person who
does not enter the sheepfold by the door, but
climbs in some other way, is a thief and a robber. 2 The one
who enters by the door is the shepherd of the sheep. 3 The
one who guards the door opens it for him. And the sheep
listen to the voice of the shepherd. He calls his own sheep
by name and leads them out. 4 When he brings all his
sheep out, he goes ahead of them, and they follow him
because they know his voice. 5 But they will never follow a
stranger. They will run away from him because they don't
know his voice." 6 Jesus told the people this story, but they
did not understand what it meant.

9:39 [a] **blind** Jesus is talking about people who are spiritually blind, not physically blind.

CONTEMPORARY ENGLISH VERSION

37 "You have already seen him," Jesus answered, "and right now he is talking with you."

38 The man said, "Lord, I put my faith in you!" Then he worshiped Jesus.

39 Jesus told him, "I came to judge the people of this world. I am here to give sight to the blind and to make blind everyone who can see."

40 When the Pharisees heard Jesus say this, they asked, "Are we blind?"

41 Jesus answered, "If you were blind, you would not be guilty. But now that you claim to see, you will keep on being guilty."

A Story about Sheep

10 Jesus said:
I tell you for certain that only thieves and rob-
bers climb over the fence instead of going in through the
gate to the sheep pen. 2-3 But the gatekeeper opens the
gate for the shepherd, and he goes in through it. The
sheep know their shepherd's voice. He calls each of them
by name and leads them out.

4 When he has led out all of his sheep, he walks in
front of them, and they follow, because they know his
voice. 5 The sheep will not follow strangers. They don't
recognize a stranger's voice, and they run away.

6 Jesus told the people this story. But they did not understand what he was talking about.

NEW INTERNATIONAL VERSION

37 Jesus said, "You have now seen him; in fact, he is the one speaking with you."

38 Then the man said, "Lord, I believe," and he worshiped him.

39 Jesus said, "For judgment I have come into this world, so that the blind will see and those who see will become blind."

40 Some Pharisees who were with him heard him say this and asked, "What? Are we blind too?"

41 Jesus said, "If you were blind, you would not be guilty of sin; but now that you claim you can see, your guilt remains.

The Shepherd and His Flock

10 "I tell you the truth, the man who does not enter the sheep pen by the gate, but climbs in by some other way, is a thief and a robber. 2 The man who enters by the gate is the shepherd of his sheep. 3 The watchman opens the gate for him, and the sheep listen to his voice. He calls his own sheep by name and leads them out. 4 When he has brought out all his own, he goes on ahead of them, and his sheep follow him because they know his voice. 5 But they will never follow a stranger; in fact, they will run away from him because they do not recognize a stranger's voice." 6 Jesus used this figure of speech, but they did not understand what he was telling them.

NEW LIVING TRANSLATION

37 "You have seen him," Jesus said, "and he is speaking to you!"

38 "Yes, Lord," the man said, "I believe!" And he worshiped Jesus.

39 Then Jesus told him, "I have come to judge the world. I have come to give sight to the blind and to show those who think they see that they are blind."

40 The Pharisees who were standing there heard him and asked, "Are you saying we are blind?"

41 "If you were blind, you wouldn't be guilty," Jesus replied. "But you remain guilty because you claim you can see.

The Good Shepherd and His Sheep

10 "I assure you, anyone who sneaks over the wall of a sheepfold, rather than going through the gate, must surely be a thief and a robber! 2 For a shepherd enters through the gate. 3 The gatekeeper opens the gate for him, and the sheep hear his voice and come to him. He calls his own sheep by name and leads them out. 4 After he has gathered his own flock, he walks ahead of them, and they follow him because they recognize his voice. 5 They won't follow a stranger; they will run from him because they don't recognize his voice."

6 Those who heard Jesus use this illustration didn't understand what he meant, 7 so he explained it to them.

NEW KING JAMES VERSION

37 And Jesus said to him, "You have both seen Him and it is He who is talking with you."

38 Then he said, "Lord, I believe!" And he worshiped Him.

39 And Jesus said, "For judgment I have come into this world, that those who do not see may see, and that those who see may be made blind."

40 Then *some* of the Pharisees who were with Him heard these words, and said to Him, "Are we blind also?"

41 Jesus said to them, "If you were blind, you would have no sin; but now you say, 'We see.' Therefore your sin remains.

Jesus the True Shepherd

10 "Most assuredly, I say to you, he who does not enter the sheepfold by the door, but climbs up some other way, the same is a thief and a robber. 2 But he who enters by the door is the shepherd of the sheep. 3 To him the doorkeeper opens, and the sheep hear his voice; and he calls his own sheep by name and leads them out. 4 And when he brings out his own sheep, he goes before them; and the sheep follow him, for they know his voice. 5 Yet they will by no means follow a stranger, but will flee from him, for they do not know the voice of strangers." 6 Jesus used this illustration, but they did not understand the things which He spoke to them.

THE MESSAGE

Jesus said, "You're looking right at him. Don't you recognize my voice?"

"Master, I believe," the man said, and worshiped him.

Jesus then said, "I came into the world to bring everything into the clear light of day, making all the distinctions clear, so that those who have never seen will see, and those who have made a great pretense of seeing will be exposed as blind."

Some Pharisees overheard him and said, "Does that mean you're calling us blind?"

Jesus said, "If you were really blind, you would be blameless, but since you claim to see everything so well, you're accountable for every fault and failure.

He Calls His Sheep By Name

10 "Let me set this before you as plainly as I can. If a person climbs over or through the fence of a sheep pen instead of going through the gate, you know he's up to no good—a sheep rustler! The shepherd walks right up to the gate. The gatekeeper opens the gate to him and the sheep recognize his voice. He calls his own sheep by name and leads them out. When he gets them all out, he leads them and they follow because they are familiar with his voice. They won't follow a stranger's voice but will scatter because they aren't used to the sound of it."

Jesus told this simple story, but they had no idea what he was talking about. So he tried again. "I'll be explicit,

KING JAMES VERSION

7 Then said Jesus unto them again, Verily, verily, I say unto you, I am the door of the sheep.

8 All that ever came before me are thieves and robbers: but the sheep did not hear them.

9 I am the door: by me if any man enter in, he shall be saved, and shall go in and out, and find pasture.

10 The thief cometh not, but for to steal, and to kill, and to destroy: I am come that they might have life, and that they might have *it* more abundantly.

11 I am the good shepherd: the good shepherd giveth his life for the sheep.

12 But he that is an hireling, and not the shepherd, whose own the sheep are not, seeth the wolf coming, and leaveth the sheep, and fleeth: and the wolf catcheth them, and scattereth the sheep.

13 The hireling fleeth, because he is an hireling, and careth not for the sheep.

14 I am the good shepherd, and know my *sheep*, and am known of mine.

15 As the Father knoweth me, even so know I the Father: and I lay down my life for the sheep.

16 And other sheep I have, which are not of this fold: them also I must bring, and they shall hear my voice; and there shall be one fold, *and* one shepherd.

17 Therefore doth my Father love me, because I lay down my life, that I might take it again.

18 No man taketh it from me, but I lay it down of myself. I have power to lay it down, and I have power to take it again. This commandment have I received of my Father.

NEW AMERICAN STANDARD BIBLE

7 So Jesus said to them again, "Truly, truly, I say to you, I am the door of the sheep.

8 "All who came before Me are thieves and robbers, but the sheep did not hear them.

9 "I am the door; if anyone enters through Me, he will be saved, and will go in and out and find pasture.

10 "The thief comes only to steal and kill and destroy; I came that they may have life, and have *it* abundantly.

11 "I am the good shepherd; the good shepherd lays down His life for the sheep.

12 "He who is a hired hand, and not a shepherd, who is not the owner of the sheep, sees the wolf coming, and leaves the sheep and flees, and the wolf snatches them and scatters *them.*

13 "*He flees* because he is a hired hand and is not concerned about the sheep.

14 "I am the good shepherd, and I know My own and My own know Me,

15 even as the Father knows Me and I know the Father; and I lay down My life for the sheep.

16 "I have other sheep, which are not of this fold; I must bring them also, and they will hear My voice; and they will become one flock *with* one shepherd.

17 "For this reason the Father loves Me, because I lay down My life so that I may take it again.

18 "No one has taken it away from Me, but I lay it down on My own initiative. I have authority to lay it down, and I have authority to take it up again. This commandment I received from My Father."

NEW CENTURY VERSION

Jesus Is the Good Shepherd

7So Jesus said again, "I tell you the truth, I am the door
for the sheep. 8All the people who came before me were
thieves and robbers. The sheep did not listen to them. 9I
am the door, and the person who enters through me will
be saved and will be able to come in and go out and find
pasture. 10A thief comes to steal and kill and destroy, but I
came to give life—life in all its fullness.

11"I am the good shepherd. The good shepherd gives his
life for the sheep. 12The worker who is paid to keep the
sheep is different from the shepherd who owns them.
When the worker sees a wolf coming, he runs away and
leaves the sheep alone. Then the wolf attacks the sheep
and scatters them. 13The man runs away because he is
only a paid worker and does not really care about the
sheep.

14–15"I am the good shepherd. I know my sheep, as the
Father knows me. And my sheep know me, as I know the
Father. I give my life for the sheep. 16I have other sheep
that are not in this flock, and I must bring them also. They
will listen to my voice, and there will be one flock and one
shepherd. 17The Father loves me because I give my life so
that I can take it back again. 18No one takes it away from
me; I give my own life freely. I have the right to give my
life, and I have the right to take it back. This is what my
Father commanded me to do."

CONTEMPORARY ENGLISH VERSION

Jesus Is the Good Shepherd

7Jesus said:

I tell you for certain that I am the gate for the sheep.
8Everyone who came before me was a thief or a robber,
and the sheep did not listen to any of them. 9I am the
gate. All who come in through me will be saved.
Through me they will come and go and find pasture.

10A thief comes only to rob, kill, and destroy. I came
so that everyone would have life, and have it in its
fullest. 11I am the good shepherd, and the good shep-
herd gives up his life for his sheep. 12Hired workers are
not like the shepherd. They don't own the sheep, and
when they see a wolf coming, they run off and leave the
sheep. Then the wolf attacks and scatters the flock.
13Hired workers run away because they don't care about
the sheep.

14I am the good shepherd. I know my sheep, and they
know me. 15Just as the Father knows me, I know the
Father, and I give up my life for my sheep. 16I have other
sheep that are not in this sheep pen. I must bring them
together too, when they hear my voice. Then there will
be one flock of sheep and one shepherd.

17The Father loves me, because I give up my life, so
that I may receive it back again. 18No one takes my life
from me. I give it up willingly! I have the power to give
it up and the power to receive it back again, just as my
Father commanded me to do.

NEW INTERNATIONAL VERSION

7Therefore Jesus said again, "I tell you the truth, I am
the gate for the sheep. 8All who ever came before me were
thieves and robbers, but the sheep did not listen to them.
9I am the gate; whoever enters through me will be saved.[a]
He will come in and go out, and find pasture. 10The thief
comes only to steal and kill and destroy; I have come that
they may have life, and have it to the full.

11"I am the good shepherd. The good shepherd lays
down his life for the sheep. 12The hired hand is not the
shepherd who owns the sheep. So when he sees the wolf
coming, he abandons the sheep and runs away. Then the
wolf attacks the flock and scatters it. 13The man runs
away because he is a hired hand and cares nothing for the
sheep.

14"I am the good shepherd; I know my sheep and my
sheep know me— 15just as the Father knows me and I
know the Father—and I lay down my life for the sheep. 16I
have other sheep that are not of this sheep pen. I must
bring them also. They too will listen to my voice, and there
shall be one flock and one shepherd. 17The reason my
Father loves me is that I lay down my life—only to take it
up again. 18No one takes it from me, but I lay it down of
my own accord. I have authority to lay it down and author-
ity to take it up again. This command I received from my
Father."

[a] 9 Or *kept safe*

NEW LIVING TRANSLATION

"I assure you, I am the gate for the sheep," he said. 8"All
others who came before me were thieves and robbers. But
the true sheep did not listen to them. 9Yes, I am the gate.
Those who come in through me will be saved. Wherever
they go, they will find green pastures. 10The thief's pur-
pose is to steal and kill and destroy. My purpose is to give
life in all its fullness.

11"I am the good shepherd. The good shepherd lays
down his life for the sheep. 12A hired hand will run when
he sees a wolf coming. He will leave the sheep because
they aren't his and he isn't their shepherd. And so the wolf
attacks them and scatters the flock. 13The hired hand runs
away because he is merely hired and has no real concern
for the sheep.

14"I am the good shepherd; I know my own sheep, and
they know me, 15just as my Father knows me and I know
the Father. And I lay down my life for the sheep. 16I have
other sheep, too, that are not in this sheepfold. I must
bring them also, and they will listen to my voice; and there
will be one flock with one shepherd.

17"The Father loves me because I lay down my life that I
may have it back again. 18No one can take my life from
me. I lay down my life voluntarily. For I have the right to
lay it down when I want to and also the power to take it
again. For my Father has given me this command."

NEW KING JAMES VERSION

Jesus the Good Shepherd

7Then Jesus said to them again, "Most assuredly, I say
to you, I am the door of the sheep. 8All who *ever* came be-
fore Me[a] are thieves and robbers, but the sheep did not
hear them. 9I am the door. If anyone enters by Me, he will
be saved, and will go in and out and find pasture. 10The
thief does not come except to steal, and to kill, and to
destroy. I have come that they may have life, and that they
may have *it* more abundantly.

11"I am the good shepherd. The good shepherd gives His
life for the sheep. 12But a hireling, *he who is* not the shep-
herd, one who does not own the sheep, sees the wolf com-
ing and leaves the sheep and flees; and the wolf catches
the sheep and scatters them. 13The hireling flees because
he is a hireling and does not care about the sheep. 14I am
the good shepherd; and I know My *sheep,* and am known
by My own. 15As the Father knows Me, even so I know the
Father; and I lay down My life for the sheep. 16And other
sheep I have which are not of this fold; them also I must
bring, and they will hear My voice; and there will be one
flock *and* one shepherd.

17"Therefore My Father loves Me, because I lay down My
life that I may take it again. 18No one takes it from Me, but
I lay it down of Myself. I have power to lay it down, and I
have power to take it again. This command I have received
from My Father."

10:8 [a] M-Text omits *before Me.*

THE MESSAGE

then. I am the Gate for the sheep. All those others are up to no good—sheep stealers, every one of them. But the sheep didn't listen to them. I am the Gate. Anyone who goes through me will be cared for—will freely go in and out, and find pasture. A thief is only there to steal and kill and destroy. I came so they can have real and eternal life, more and better life than they ever dreamed of.

"I am the Good Shepherd. The Good Shepherd puts the sheep before himself, sacrifices himself if necessary. A hired man is not a real shepherd. The sheep mean nothing to him. He sees a wolf come and runs for it, leaving the sheep to be ravaged and scattered by the wolf. He's only in it for the money. The sheep don't matter to him.

"I am the Good Shepherd. I know my own sheep and my own sheep know me. In the same way, the Father knows me and I know the Father. I put the sheep before myself, sacrificing myself if necessary. You need to know that I have other sheep in addition to those in this pen. I need to gather and bring them, too. They'll also recognize my voice. Then it will be one flock, one Shepherd. This is why the Father loves me: because I freely lay down my life. And so I am free to take it up again. No one takes it from me. I lay it down of my own free will. I have the right to lay it down; I also have the right to take it up again. I received this authority personally from my Father."

KING JAMES VERSION

19 ¶ There was a division therefore again among the Jews for these sayings.

20 And many of them said, He hath a devil, and is mad; why hear ye him?

21 Others said, These are not the words of him that hath a devil. Can a devil open the eyes of the blind?

22 ¶ And it was at Jerusalem the feast of the dedication, and it was winter.

23 And Jesus walked in the temple in Solomon's porch.

24 Then came the Jews round about him, and said unto him, How long dost thou make us to doubt? If thou be the Christ, tell us plainly.

25 Jesus answered them, I told you, and ye believed not: the works that I do in my Father's name, they bear witness of me.

26 But ye believe not, because ye are not of my sheep, as I said unto you.

27 My sheep hear my voice, and I know them, and they follow me:

28 And I give unto them eternal life; and they shall never perish, neither shall any *man* pluck them out of my hand.

29 My Father, which gave *them* me, is greater than all; and no *man* is able to pluck *them* out of my Father's hand.

30 I and *my* Father are one.

NEW AMERICAN STANDARD BIBLE

19 A division occurred again among the Jews because of these words.

20 Many of them were saying, "He has a demon and is insane. Why do you listen to Him?"

21 Others were saying, "These are not the sayings of one demon-possessed. A demon cannot open the eyes of the blind, can he?"

Jesus Asserts His Deity

22 At that time the Feast of the Dedication took place at Jerusalem;

23 it was winter, and Jesus was walking in the temple in the portico of Solomon.

24 The Jews then gathered around Him, and were saying to Him, "How long will You keep us in suspense? If You are the Christ, tell us plainly."

25 Jesus answered them, "I told you, and you do not believe; the works that I do in My Father's name, these testify of Me.

26 "But you do not believe because you are not of My sheep.

27 "My sheep hear My voice, and I know them, and they follow Me;

28 and I give eternal life to them, and they will never perish; and no one will snatch them out of My hand.

29 "[1]My Father, who has given *them* to Me, is greater than all; and no one is able to snatch *them* out of the Father's hand.

30 "I and the Father are one."

10:29 [1] One early ms reads *What My Father has given Me is greater than all*

NEW CENTURY VERSION

19Again the Jews did not agree with each other because
of these words of Jesus. 20Many of them said, "A demon
has come into him and made him crazy. Why listen to
him?"

21But others said, "A man who is crazy with a demon
does not say things like this. Can a demon open the eyes of
the blind?"

Jesus Is Rejected

22The time came for the Feast of Dedication at
Jerusalem. It was winter, 23and Jesus was walking in the
Temple in Solomon's Porch. 24The Jews gathered around
him and said, "How long will you make us wonder about
you? If you are the Christ, tell us plainly."

25Jesus answered, "I told you already, but you did not
believe. The miracles I do in my Father's name show who I
am. 26But you don't believe, because you are not my
sheep. 27My sheep listen to my voice; I know them, and
they follow me. 28I give them eternal life, and they will
never die, and no one can steal them out of my hand. 29My
Father gave my sheep to me. He is greater than all, and no
person can steal my sheep out of my Father's hand. 30The
Father and I are one."

CONTEMPORARY ENGLISH VERSION

19The people took sides because of what Jesus had told
them. 20Many of them said, "He has a demon in him! He is
crazy! Why listen to him?"

21But others said, "How could anyone with a demon in
him say these things? No one like that could give sight to
a blind person!"

Jesus Is Rejected

22That winter, Jesus was in Jerusalem for the Temple
Festival. 23One day he was walking in that part of the tem-
ple known as Solomon's Porch,[a] 24and the people gathered
all around him. They said, "How long are you going to
keep us guessing? If you are the Messiah, tell us plainly!"

25Jesus answered:

I have told you, and you refused to believe me. The
things I do by my Father's authority show who I am.
26But since you are not my sheep, you don't believe me.
27My sheep know my voice, and I know them. They fol-
low me, 28and I give them eternal life, so that they will
never be lost. No one can snatch them out of my hand.
29My Father gave them to me, and he is greater than all
others.[b] No one can snatch them from his hands, 30and I
am one with the Father.

[a] **10.23** *Solomon's Porch*: A public place with tall columns along the east side of the temple. [b] **10.29** *he is greater than all others*: Some manuscripts have "they are greater than all others."

NEW INTERNATIONAL VERSION

19At these words the Jews were again divided. 20Many of them said, "He is demon-possessed and raving mad. Why listen to him?"

21But others said, "These are not the sayings of a man possessed by a demon. Can a demon open the eyes of the blind?"

The Unbelief of the Jews

22Then came the Feast of Dedication[b] at Jerusalem. It was winter, 23and Jesus was in the temple area walking in Solomon's Colonnade. 24The Jews gathered around him, saying, "How long will you keep us in suspense? If you are the Christ,[c] tell us plainly."

25Jesus answered, "I did tell you, but you do not believe. The miracles I do in my Father's name speak for me, 26but you do not believe because you are not my sheep. 27My sheep listen to my voice; I know them, and they follow me. 28I give them eternal life, and they shall never perish; no one can snatch them out of my hand. 29My Father, who has given them to me, is greater than all[d]; no one can snatch them out of my Father's hand. 30I and the Father are one."

b 22 That is, Hanukkah *c 24* Or *Messiah* *d 29* Many early manuscripts *What my Father has given me is greater than all*

NEW LIVING TRANSLATION

19When he said these things, the people* were again divided in their opinions about him. 20Some of them said, "He has a demon, or he's crazy. Why listen to a man like that?" 21Others said, "This doesn't sound like a man possessed by a demon! Can a demon open the eyes of the blind?"

Jesus Claims to Be the Son of God

22It was now winter, and Jesus was in Jerusalem at the time of Hanukkah.* 23He was at the Temple, walking through the section known as Solomon's Colonnade. 24The Jewish leaders surrounded him and asked, "How long are you going to keep us in suspense? If you are the Messiah, tell us plainly."

25Jesus replied, "I have already told you, and you don't believe me. The proof is what I do in the name of my Father. 26But you don't believe me because you are not part of my flock. 27My sheep recognize my voice; I know them, and they follow me. 28I give them eternal life, and they will never perish. No one will snatch them away from me, 29for my Father has given them to me, and he is more powerful than anyone else. So no one can take them from me. 30The Father and I are one."

10:19 Greek *Jewish people.* **10:22** Or *the Festival of Dedication.*

NEW KING JAMES VERSION

19Therefore there was a division again among the Jews because of these sayings. 20And many of them said, "He has a demon and is mad. Why do you listen to Him?"

21Others said, "These are not the words of one who has a demon. Can a demon open the eyes of the blind?"

The Shepherd Knows His Sheep

22Now it was the Feast of Dedication in Jerusalem, and it was winter. 23And Jesus walked in the temple, in Solomon's porch. 24Then the Jews surrounded Him and said to Him, "How long do You keep us in doubt? If You are the Christ, tell us plainly."

25Jesus answered them, "I told you, and you do not believe. The works that I do in My Father's name, they bear witness of Me. 26But you do not believe, because you are not of My sheep, as I said to you.[b] 27My sheep hear My voice, and I know them, and they follow Me. 28And I give them eternal life, and they shall never perish; neither shall anyone snatch them out of My hand. 29My Father, who has given *them* to Me, is greater than all; and no one is able to snatch *them* out of My Father's hand. 30I and *My* Father are one."

10:26 *b* NU-Text omits *as I said to you.*

THE MESSAGE

This kind of talk caused another split in the Jewish ranks. A lot of them were saying, "He's crazy, a maniac—out of his head completely. Why bother listening to him?" But others weren't so sure: "These aren't the words of a crazy man. Can a 'maniac' open blind eyes?"

They were celebrating Hanukkah just then in Jerusalem. It was winter. Jesus was strolling in the Temple across Solomon's Porch. The Jews, circling him, said, "How long are you going to keep us guessing? If you're the Messiah, tell us straight out."

Jesus answered, "I told you, but you don't believe. Everything I have done has been authorized by my Father, actions that speak louder than words. You don't believe because you're not my sheep. My sheep recognize my voice. I know them, and they follow me. I give them real and eternal life. They are protected from the Destroyer for good. No one can steal them from out of my hand. The Father who put them under my care is so much greater than the Destroyer and Thief. No one could ever get them away from him. I and the Father are one heart and mind."

KING JAMES VERSION

31 Then the Jews took up stones again to stone him.

32 Jesus answered them, Many good works have I shewed you from my Father; for which of those works do ye stone me?

33 The Jews answered him, saying, For a good work we stone thee not; but for blasphemy; and because that thou, being a man, makest thyself God.

34 Jesus answered them, Is it not written in your law, I said, Ye are gods?

35 If he called them gods, unto whom the word of God came, and the scripture cannot be broken;

36 Say ye of him, whom the Father hath sanctified, and sent into the world, Thou blasphemest; because I said, I am the Son of God?

37 If I do not the works of my Father, believe me not.

38 But if I do, though ye believe not me, believe the works: that ye may know, and believe, that the Father *is* in me, and I in him.

39 ¶ Therefore they sought again to take him: but he escaped out of their hand,

40 And went away again beyond Jordan into the place where John at first baptized; and there he abode.

41 And many resorted unto him, and said, John did no miracle: but all things that John spake of this man were true.

42 And many believed on him there.

NEW AMERICAN STANDARD BIBLE

31 The Jews picked up stones again to stone Him.

32 Jesus answered them, "I showed you many good works from the Father; for which of them are you stoning Me?"

33 The Jews answered Him, "For a good work we do not stone You, but for blasphemy; and because You, being a man, make Yourself out *to be* God."

34 Jesus answered them, "Has it not been written in your Law, 'I SAID, YOU ARE GODS'?

35 "If he called them gods, to whom the word of God came (and the Scripture cannot be broken),

36 do you say of Him, whom the Father sanctified and sent into the world, 'You are blaspheming,' because I said, 'I am the Son of God'?

37 "If I do not do the works of My Father, do not believe Me;

38 but if I do them, though you do not believe Me, believe the works, so that you may know and understand that the Father is in Me, and I in the Father."

39 Therefore they were seeking again to seize Him, and He eluded their grasp.

40 And He went away again beyond the Jordan to the place where John was first baptizing, and He was staying there.

41 Many came to Him and were saying, "While John performed no sign, yet everything John said about this man was true."

42 Many believed in Him there.

NEW CENTURY VERSION

31 Again the Jews picked up stones to kill Jesus.
32 But he
said to them, "I have done many good works from the
Father. Which of these good works are you killing me for?"
33 The Jews answered, "We are not killing you because of
any good work you did, but because you speak against
God. You are only a human, but you say you are the same
as God!"
34 Jesus answered, "It is written in your law that God
said, 'I said, you are gods.'[a]
35 This Scripture called those
people gods who received God's message, and Scripture is
always true.
36 So why do you say that I speak against God
because I said, 'I am God's Son'? I am the one God chose
and sent into the world.
37 If I don't do what my Father
does, then don't believe me.
38 But if I do what my Father
does, even though you don't believe in me, believe what I
do. Then you will know and understand that the Father is
in me and I am in the Father."
39 They tried to take Jesus again, but he escaped from
them.
40 Then he went back across the Jordan River to the place
where John had first baptized. Jesus stayed there,
41 and
many people came to him and said, "John never did a miracle, but everything John said about this man is true."
42 And in that place many believed in Jesus.

10:34 [a] **'I...gods.'** Quotation from Psalm 82:6.

CONTEMPORARY ENGLISH VERSION

31 Once again the Jewish leaders picked up stones in
order to kill Jesus.
32 But he said, "I have shown you many
good things that my Father sent me to do. Which one are
you going to stone me for?"
33 They answered, "We are not stoning you because of
any good thing you did. We are stoning you because you
did a terrible thing. You are just a man, and here you are
claiming to be God!"
34 Jesus replied:

In your Scriptures doesn't God say, "You are gods"?
35 You can't argue with the Scriptures, and God spoke to
those people and called them gods.
36 So why do you
accuse me of a terrible sin for saying that I am the Son
of God? After all, it is the Father who prepared me for
this work. He is also the one who sent me into the
world.
37 If I don't do as my Father does, you should not
believe me.
38 But if I do what my Father does, you
should believe because of that, even if you don't have
faith in me. Then you will know for certain that the
Father is one with me, and I am one with the Father.

39 Again they wanted to arrest Jesus. But he escaped
40 and crossed the Jordan to the place where John had earlier been baptizing. While Jesus was there,
41 many people
came to him. They were saying, "John didn't work any miracles, but everything he said about Jesus is true."
42 A lot
of those people also put their faith in Jesus.

NEW INTERNATIONAL VERSION

31 Again the Jews picked up stones to stone him, 32 but Jesus said to them, "I have shown you many great miracles from the Father. For which of these do you stone me?"

33 "We are not stoning you for any of these," replied the Jews, "but for blasphemy, because you, a mere man, claim to be God."

34 Jesus answered them, "Is it not written in your Law, 'I have said you are gods'[e]? 35 If he called them 'gods,' to whom the word of God came—and the Scripture cannot be broken— 36 what about the one whom the Father set apart as his very own and sent into the world? Why then do you accuse me of blasphemy because I said, 'I am God's Son'? 37 Do not believe me unless I do what my Father does. 38 But if I do it, even though you do not believe me, believe the miracles, that you may know and understand that the Father is in me, and I in the Father." 39 Again they tried to seize him, but he escaped their grasp.

40 Then Jesus went back across the Jordan to the place where John had been baptizing in the early days. Here he stayed 41 and many people came to him. They said, "Though John never performed a miraculous sign, all that John said about this man was true." 42 And in that place many believed in Jesus.

[e] *34* Psalm 82:6

NEW LIVING TRANSLATION

31 Once again the Jewish leaders picked up stones to kill him. 32 Jesus said, "At my Father's direction I have done many things to help the people. For which one of these good deeds are you killing me?"

33 They replied, "Not for any good work, but for blasphemy, because you, a mere man, have made yourself God."

34 Jesus replied, "It is written in your own law that God said to certain leaders of the people, 'I say, you are gods!'* 35 And you know that the Scriptures cannot be altered. So if those people, who received God's message, were called 'gods,' 36 why do you call it blasphemy when the Holy One who was sent into the world by the Father says, 'I am the Son of God'? 37 Don't believe me unless I carry out my Father's work. 38 But if I do his work, believe in what I have done, even if you don't believe me. Then you will realize that the Father is in me, and I am in the Father."

39 Once again they tried to arrest him, but he got away and left them. 40 He went beyond the Jordan River to stay near the place where John was first baptizing. 41 And many followed him. "John didn't do miracles," they remarked to one another, "but all his predictions about this man have come true." 42 And many believed in him there.

10:34 Ps 82:6.

NEW KING JAMES VERSION

Renewed Efforts to Stone Jesus

31 Then the Jews took up stones again to stone Him. 32 Jesus answered them, "Many good works I have shown you from My Father. For which of those works do you stone Me?"

33 The Jews answered Him, saying, "For a good work we do not stone You, but for blasphemy, and because You, being a Man, make Yourself God."

34 Jesus answered them, "Is it not written in your law, *'I said, "You are gods"'*?[c] 35 If He called them gods, to whom the word of God came (and the Scripture cannot be broken), 36 do you say of Him whom the Father sanctified and sent into the world, 'You are blaspheming,' because I said, 'I am the Son of God'? 37 If I do not do the works of My Father, do not believe Me; 38 but if I do, though you do not believe Me, believe the works, that you may know and believe[d] that the Father *is* in Me, and I in Him." 39 Therefore they sought again to seize Him, but He escaped out of their hand.

The Believers Beyond Jordan

40 And He went away again beyond the Jordan to the place where John was baptizing at first, and there He stayed. 41 Then many came to Him and said, "John performed no sign, but all the things that John spoke about this Man were true." 42 And many believed in Him there.

10:34 [c] Psalm 82:6 **10:38** [d] NU-Text reads *understand.*

THE MESSAGE

Again the Jews picked up rocks to throw at him. Jesus said, "I have made a present to you from the Father of a great many good actions. For which of these acts do you stone me?"

The Jews said, "We're not stoning you for anything good you did, but for what you said—this blasphemy of calling yourself God."

Jesus said, "I'm only quoting your inspired Scriptures, where God said, 'I tell you—you are gods.' If God called your ancestors 'gods'—and Scripture doesn't lie—why do you yell, 'Blasphemer! Blasphemer!' at the unique One the Father consecrated and sent into the world, just because I said, 'I am the Son of God'? If I don't do the things my Father does, well and good; don't believe me. But if I am doing them, put aside for a moment what you hear me say about myself and just take the evidence of the actions that are right before your eyes. Then perhaps things will come together for you, and you'll see that not only are we doing the same thing; we *are* the same—Father and Son. He is in me; I am in him."

They tried yet again to arrest him, but he slipped through their fingers. He went back across the Jordan to the place where John first baptized, and stayed there. A lot of people followed him over. They were saying, "John did no miracles, but everything he said about this man has come true." Many believed in him then and there.

KING JAMES VERSION

11 Now a certain *man* was sick, *named* Lazarus, of Bethany, the town of Mary and her sister Martha.

2 (It was *that* Mary which anointed the Lord with ointment, and wiped his feet with her hair, whose brother Lazarus was sick.)

3 Therefore his sisters sent unto him, saying, Lord, behold, he whom thou lovest is sick.

4 When Jesus heard *that*, he said, This sickness is not unto death, but for the glory of God, that the Son of God might be glorified thereby.

5 Now Jesus loved Martha, and her sister, and Lazarus.

6 When he had heard therefore that he was sick, he abode two days still in the same place where he was.

7 Then after that saith he to *his* disciples, Let us go into Judaea again.

8 *His* disciples say unto him, Master, the Jews of late sought to stone thee; and goest thou thither again?

9 Jesus answered, Are there not twelve hours in the day? If any man walk in the day, he stumbleth not, because he seeth the light of this world.

10 But if a man walk in the night, he stumbleth, because there is no light in him.

11 These things said he: and after that he saith unto them, Our friend Lazarus sleepeth; but I go, that I may awake him out of sleep.

12 Then said his disciples, Lord, if he sleep, he shall do well.

13 Howbeit Jesus spake of his death: but they thought that he had spoken of taking of rest in sleep.

NEW AMERICAN STANDARD BIBLE

The Death and Resurrection of Lazarus

11 Now a certain man was sick, Lazarus of Bethany, the village of Mary and her sister Martha.

2 It was the Mary who anointed the Lord with ointment, and wiped His feet with her hair, whose brother Lazarus was sick.

3 So the sisters sent *word* to Him, saying, "Lord, behold, he whom You love is sick."

4 But when Jesus heard *this*, He said, "This sickness is not to end in death, but for the glory of God, so that the Son of God may be glorified by it."

5 Now Jesus loved Martha and her sister and Lazarus.

6 So when He heard that he was sick, He then stayed two days *longer* in the place where He was.

7 Then after this He *said to the disciples, "Let us go to Judea again."

8 The disciples *said to Him, "Rabbi, the Jews were just now seeking to stone You, and are You going there again?"

9 Jesus answered, "Are there not twelve hours in the day? If anyone walks in the day, he does not stumble, because he sees the light of this world.

10 "But if anyone walks in the night, he stumbles, because the light is not in him."

11 This He said, and after that He *said to them, "Our friend Lazarus has fallen asleep; but I go, so that I may awaken him out of sleep."

12 The disciples then said to Him, "Lord, if he has fallen asleep, he will recover."

13 Now Jesus had spoken of his death, but they thought that He was speaking of literal sleep.

NEW CENTURY VERSION

The Death of Lazarus

11 A man named Lazarus was sick. He lived in the
town of Bethany, where Mary and her sister
Martha lived. 2Mary was the woman who later put perfume
on the Lord and wiped his feet with her hair. Mary's broth-
er was Lazarus, the man who was now sick. 3So Mary and
Martha sent someone to tell Jesus, "Lord, the one you love
is sick."
4When Jesus heard this, he said, "This sickness will not
end in death. It is for the glory of God, to bring glory to the
Son of God." 5Jesus loved Martha and her sister and
Lazarus. 6But when he heard that Lazarus was sick, he
stayed where he was for two more days. 7Then Jesus said
to his followers, "Let's go back to Judea."
8The followers said, "But Teacher, the Jews there tried to
stone you to death only a short time ago. Now you want to
go back there?"
9Jesus answered, "Are there not twelve hours in the day?
If anyone walks in the daylight, he will not stumble,
because he can see by this world's light. 10But if anyone
walks at night, he stumbles because there is no light to
help him see."
11After Jesus said this, he added, "Our friend Lazarus
has fallen asleep, but I am going there to wake him."
12The followers said, "But Lord, if he is only asleep, he
will be all right."
13Jesus meant that Lazarus was dead, but his followers
thought he meant Lazarus was really sleeping. 14So then

CONTEMPORARY ENGLISH VERSION

The Death of Lazarus

11 1-2A man by the name of Lazarus was sick in the
village of Bethany. He had two sisters, Mary and
Martha. This was the same Mary who later poured perfume
on the Lord's head and wiped his feet with her hair. 3The
sisters sent a message to the Lord and told him that his
good friend Lazarus was sick.
4When Jesus heard this, he said, "His sickness won't
end in death. It will bring glory to God and his Son."
5Jesus loved Martha and her sister and brother. 6But he
stayed where he was for two more days. 7Then he said to
his disciples, "Now we will go back to Judea."
8"Teacher," they said, "the people there want to stone
you to death! Why do you want to go back?"
9Jesus answered, "Aren't there twelve hours in each
day? If you walk during the day, you will have light from
the sun, and you won't stumble. 10But if you walk during
the night, you will stumble, because you don't have any
light." 11Then he told them, "Our friend Lazarus is asleep,
and I am going there to wake him up."
12They replied, "Lord, if he is asleep, he will get better."
13Jesus really meant that Lazarus was dead, but they
thought he was talking only about sleep.

NEW INTERNATIONAL VERSION

The Death of Lazarus

11 Now a man named Lazarus was sick. He was from Bethany, the village of Mary and her sister Martha. 2This Mary, whose brother Lazarus now lay sick, was the same one who poured perfume on the Lord and wiped his feet with her hair. 3So the sisters sent word to Jesus, "Lord, the one you love is sick."

4When he heard this, Jesus said, "This sickness will not end in death. No, it is for God's glory so that God's Son may be glorified through it." 5Jesus loved Martha and her sister and Lazarus. 6Yet when he heard that Lazarus was sick, he stayed where he was two more days.

7Then he said to his disciples, "Let us go back to Judea."

8"But Rabbi," they said, "a short while ago the Jews tried to stone you, and yet you are going back there?"

9Jesus answered, "Are there not twelve hours of daylight? A man who walks by day will not stumble, for he sees by this world's light. 10It is when he walks by night that he stumbles, for he has no light."

11After he had said this, he went on to tell them, "Our friend Lazarus has fallen asleep; but I am going there to wake him up."

12His disciples replied, "Lord, if he sleeps, he will get better." 13Jesus had been speaking of his death, but his disciples thought he meant natural sleep.

NEW LIVING TRANSLATION

The Death of Lazarus

11 A man named Lazarus was sick. He lived in Bethany with his sisters, Mary and Martha. 2This is the Mary who poured the expensive perfume on the Lord's feet and wiped them with her hair.* Her brother, Lazarus, was sick. 3So the two sisters sent a message to Jesus telling him, "Lord, the one you love is very sick."

4But when Jesus heard about it he said, "Lazarus's sickness will not end in death. No, it is for the glory of God. I, the Son of God, will receive glory from this." 5Although Jesus loved Martha, Mary, and Lazarus, 6he stayed where he was for the next two days and did not go to them. 7Finally after two days, he said to his disciples, "Let's go to Judea again."

8But his disciples objected. "Teacher," they said, "only a few days ago the Jewish leaders in Judea were trying to kill you. Are you going there again?"

9Jesus replied, "There are twelve hours of daylight every day. As long as it is light, people can walk safely. They can see because they have the light of this world. 10Only at night is there danger of stumbling because there is no light." 11Then he said, "Our friend Lazarus has fallen asleep, but now I will go and wake him up."

12The disciples said, "Lord, if he is sleeping, that means he is getting better!" 13They thought Jesus meant Lazarus was having a good night's rest, but Jesus meant Lazarus had died.

11:2 This incident is recorded in chapter 12.

NEW KING JAMES VERSION

The Death of Lazarus

11 Now a certain *man* was sick, Lazarus of Bethany, the town of Mary and her sister Martha. 2It was *that* Mary who anointed the Lord with fragrant oil and wiped His feet with her hair, whose brother Lazarus was sick. 3Therefore the sisters sent to Him, saying, "Lord, behold, he whom You love is sick."

4When Jesus heard *that,* He said, "This sickness is not unto death, but for the glory of God, that the Son of God may be glorified through it."

5Now Jesus loved Martha and her sister and Lazarus. 6So, when He heard that he was sick, He stayed two more days in the place where He was. 7Then after this He said to *the* disciples, "Let us go to Judea again."

8*The* disciples said to Him, "Rabbi, lately the Jews sought to stone You, and are You going there again?"

9Jesus answered, "Are there not twelve hours in the day? If anyone walks in the day, he does not stumble, because he sees the light of this world. 10But if one walks in the night, he stumbles, because the light is not in him." 11These things He said, and after that He said to them, "Our friend Lazarus sleeps, but I go that I may wake him up."

12Then His disciples said, "Lord, if he sleeps he will get well." 13However, Jesus spoke of his death, but they thought that He was speaking about taking rest in sleep.

THE MESSAGE

The Death of Lazarus

11 A man was sick, Lazarus of Bethany, the town of Mary and her sister Martha. This was the same Mary who massaged the Lord's feet with aromatic oils and then wiped them with her hair. It was her brother Lazarus who was sick. So the sisters sent word to Jesus, "Master, the one you love so very much is sick."

When Jesus got the message, he said, "This sickness is not fatal. It will become an occasion to show God's glory by glorifying God's Son."

Jesus loved Martha and her sister and Lazarus, but oddly, when he heard that Lazarus was sick, he stayed on where he was for two more days. After the two days, he said to his disciples, "Let's go back to Judea."

They said, "Rabbi, you can't do that. The Jews are out to kill you, and you're going back?"

Jesus replied, "Are there not twelve hours of daylight? Anyone who walks in daylight doesn't stumble because there's plenty of light from the sun. Walking at night, he might very well stumble because he can't see where he's going."

He said these things, and then announced, "Our friend Lazarus has fallen asleep. I'm going to wake him up."

The disciples said, "Master, if he's gone to sleep, he'll get a good rest and wake up feeling fine." Jesus was talking about death, while his disciples thought he was talking about taking a nap.

KING JAMES VERSION

14 Then said Jesus unto them plainly, Lazarus is dead.
15 And I am glad for your sakes that I was not there, to the intent ye may believe; nevertheless let us go unto him.
16 Then said Thomas, which is called Didymus, unto his fellowdisciples, Let us also go, that we may die with him.
17 ¶ Then when Jesus came, he found that he had *lain* in the grave four days already.
18 Now Bethany was nigh unto Jerusalem, about fifteen furlongs off:
19 And many of the Jews came to Martha and Mary, to comfort them concerning their brother.
20 Then Martha, as soon as she heard that Jesus was coming, went and met him: but Mary sat *still* in the house.
21 Then said Martha unto Jesus, Lord, if thou hadst been here, my brother had not died.
22 But I know, that even now, whatsoever thou wilt ask of God, God will give *it* thee.
23 Jesus saith unto her, Thy brother shall rise again.
24 Martha saith unto him, I know that he shall rise again in the resurrection at the last day.
25 Jesus said unto her, I am the resurrection, and the life: he that believeth in me, though he were dead, yet shall he live:
26 And whosoever liveth and believeth in me shall never die. Believest thou this?
27 She saith unto him, Yea, Lord: I believe that thou art the Christ, the Son of God, which should come into the world.

NEW AMERICAN STANDARD BIBLE

14 So Jesus then said to them plainly, "Lazarus is dead,
15 and I am glad for your sakes that I was not there, so that you may believe; but let us go to him."
16 Therefore Thomas, who is called Didymus, said to *his* fellow disciples, "Let us also go, so that we may die with Him."
17 So when Jesus came, He found that he had already been in the tomb four days.
18 Now Bethany was near Jerusalem, about two miles off;
19 and many of the Jews had come to Martha and Mary, to console them concerning *their* brother.
20 Martha therefore, when she heard that Jesus was coming, went to meet Him, but Mary stayed at the house.
21 Martha then said to Jesus, "Lord, if You had been here, my brother would not have died.
22 "Even now I know that whatever You ask of God, God will give You."
23 Jesus *said to her, "Your brother will rise again."
24 Martha *said to Him, "I know that he will rise again in the resurrection on the last day."
25 Jesus said to her, "I am the resurrection and the life; he who believes in Me will live even if he dies,
26 and everyone who lives and believes in Me will never die. Do you believe this?"
27 She *said to Him, "Yes, Lord; I have believed that You are the Christ, the Son of God, *even* He who comes into the world."

NEW CENTURY VERSION

Jesus said plainly, "Lazarus is dead. 15 And I am glad for your sakes I was not there so that you may believe. But let's go to him now."

16 Then Thomas (the one called Didymus) said to the other followers, "Let us also go so that we can die with him."

Jesus in Bethany

17 When Jesus arrived, he learned that Lazarus had already been dead and in the tomb for four days. 18 Bethany was about two miles from Jerusalem. 19 Many of the Jews had come there to comfort Martha and Mary about their brother.

20 When Martha heard that Jesus was coming, she went out to meet him, but Mary stayed home. 21 Martha said to Jesus, "Lord, if you had been here, my brother would not have died. 22 But I know that even now God will give you anything you ask."

23 Jesus said, "Your brother will rise and live again."

24 Martha answered, "I know that he will rise and live again in the resurrection[a] on the last day."

25 Jesus said to her, "I am the resurrection and the life. Those who believe in me will have life even if they die. 26 And everyone who lives and believes in me will never die. Martha, do you believe this?"

27 Martha answered, "Yes, Lord. I believe that you are the Christ, the Son of God, the One coming to the world."

11:24 [a] **resurrection** Being raised from the dead to live again.

CONTEMPORARY ENGLISH VERSION

14 Then Jesus told them plainly, "Lazarus is dead! 15 I am glad that I wasn't there, because now you will have a chance to put your faith in me. Let's go to him."

16 Thomas, whose nickname was "Twin," said to the other disciples, "Come on. Let's go, so we can die with him."

Jesus Brings Lazarus to Life

17 When Jesus got to Bethany, he found that Lazarus had already been in the tomb four days. 18 Bethany was only about two miles from Jerusalem, 19 and many people had come from the city to comfort Martha and Mary because their brother had died.

20 When Martha heard that Jesus had arrived, she went out to meet him, but Mary stayed in the house. 21 Martha said to Jesus, "Lord, if you had been here, my brother would not have died. 22 Yet even now I know that God will do anything you ask."

23 Jesus told her, "Your brother will live again!"

24 Martha answered, "I know that he will be raised to life on the last day,[a] when all the dead are raised."

25 Jesus then said, "I am the one who raises the dead to life! Everyone who has faith in me will live, even if they die. 26 And everyone who lives because of faith in me will never really die. Do you believe this?"

27 "Yes, Lord!" she replied. "I believe that you are Christ, the Son of God. You are the one we hoped would come into the world."

[a] 11.24 *the last day*: When God will judge all people.

NEW INTERNATIONAL VERSION

14So then he told them plainly, "Lazarus is dead, 15and
for your sake I am glad I was not there, so that you may
believe. But let us go to him."
16Then Thomas (called Didymus) said to the rest of the
disciples, "Let us also go, that we may die with him."

Jesus Comforts the Sisters

17On his arrival, Jesus found that Lazarus had already
been in the tomb for four days. 18Bethany was less than
two miles[a] from Jerusalem, 19and many Jews had come to
Martha and Mary to comfort them in the loss of their
brother. 20When Martha heard that Jesus was coming, she
went out to meet him, but Mary stayed at home.
21"Lord," Martha said to Jesus, "if you had been here,
my brother would not have died. 22But I know that even
now God will give you whatever you ask."
23Jesus said to her, "Your brother will rise again."
24Martha answered, "I know he will rise again in the
resurrection at the last day."
25Jesus said to her, "I am the resurrection and the life.
He who believes in me will live, even though he dies;
26and whoever lives and believes in me will never die. Do
you believe this?"
27"Yes, Lord," she told him, "I believe that you are the
Christ,[b] the Son of God, who was to come into the world."

[a] *18* Greek *fifteen stadia* (about 3 kilometers) [b] *27* Or *Messiah*

NEW LIVING TRANSLATION

14Then he told them plainly, "Lazarus is dead. 15And for
your sake, I am glad I wasn't there, because this will give
you another opportunity to believe in me. Come, let's go
see him."
16Thomas, nicknamed the Twin,* said to his fellow disci-
ples, "Let's go, too—and die with Jesus."
17When Jesus arrived at Bethany, he was told that
Lazarus had already been in his grave for four days.
18Bethany was only a few miles* down the road from
Jerusalem, 19and many of the people* had come to pay
their respects and console Martha and Mary on their loss.
20When Martha got word that Jesus was coming, she went
to meet him. But Mary stayed at home. 21Martha said to
Jesus, "Lord, if you had been here, my brother would not
have died. 22But even now I know that God will give you
whatever you ask."
23Jesus told her, "Your brother will rise again."
24"Yes," Martha said, "when everyone else rises, on res-
urrection day."
25Jesus told her, "I am the resurrection and the life.* Those
who believe in me, even though they die like everyone else,
will live again. 26They are given eternal life for believing in
me and will never perish. Do you believe this, Martha?"
27"Yes, Lord," she told him. "I have always believed you
are the Messiah, the Son of God, the one who has come

11:16 Greek *the one who was called Didymus.* **11:18** Greek *was about 15 stadia* [about 2.8 kilometers]. **11:19** Greek *Jewish people;* also 11:31, 33, 36, 45, 54. **11:25** Some manuscripts do not include *and the life.*

NEW KING JAMES VERSION

14Then Jesus said to them plainly, "Lazarus is dead.
15And I am glad for your sakes that I was not there, that
you may believe. Nevertheless let us go to him."
16Then Thomas, who is called the Twin, said to his fel-
low disciples, "Let us also go, that we may die with Him."

I Am the Resurrection and the Life

17So when Jesus came, He found that he had already
been in the tomb four days. 18Now Bethany was near Jeru-
salem, about two miles[a] away. 19And many of the Jews
had joined the women around Martha and Mary, to com-
fort them concerning their brother.
20Now Martha, as soon as she heard that Jesus was
coming, went and met Him, but Mary was sitting in the
house. 21Now Martha said to Jesus, "Lord, if You had been
here, my brother would not have died. 22But even now I
know that whatever You ask of God, God will give You."
23Jesus said to her, "Your brother will rise again."
24Martha said to Him, "I know that he will rise again in
the resurrection at the last day."
25Jesus said to her, "I am the resurrection and the life.
He who believes in Me, though he may die, he shall live.
26And whoever lives and believes in Me shall never die. Do
you believe this?"
27She said to Him, "Yes, Lord, I believe that You are the
Christ, the Son of God, who is to come into the world."

11:18 [a] Literally *fifteen stadia*

THE MESSAGE

Then Jesus became explicit: "Lazarus died. And I am glad for your sakes that I wasn't there. You're about to be given new grounds for believing. Now let's go to him."

That's when Thomas, the one called the Twin, said to his companions, "Come along. We might as well die with him."

When Jesus finally got there, he found Lazarus already four days dead. Bethany was near Jerusalem, only a couple of miles away, and many of the Jews were visiting Martha and Mary, sympathizing with them over their brother. Martha heard Jesus was coming and went out to meet him. Mary remained in the house.

Martha said, "Master, if you'd been here, my brother wouldn't have died. Even now, I know that whatever you ask God he will give you."

Jesus said, "Your brother will be raised up."

Martha replied, "I know that he will be raised up in the resurrection at the end of time."

"You don't have to wait for the End. I am, right now, Resurrection and Life. The one who believes in me, even though he or she dies, will live. And everyone who lives believing in me does not ultimately die at all. Do you believe this?"

"Yes, Master. All along I have believed that you are the Messiah, the Son of God who comes into the world."

KING JAMES VERSION

28 And when she had so said, she went her way, and called Mary her sister secretly, saying, The Master is come, and calleth for thee.

29 As soon as she heard *that*, she arose quickly, and came unto him.

30 Now Jesus was not yet come into the town, but was in that place where Martha met him.

31 The Jews then which were with her in the house, and comforted her, when they saw Mary, that she rose up hastily and went out, followed her, saying, She goeth unto the grave to weep there.

32 Then when Mary was come where Jesus was, and saw him, she fell down at his feet, saying unto him, Lord, if thou hadst been here, my brother had not died.

33 ¶ When Jesus therefore saw her weeping, and the Jews also weeping which came with her, he groaned in the spirit, and was troubled,

34 And said, Where have ye laid him? They said unto him, Lord, come and see.

35 Jesus wept.

36 Then said the Jews, Behold how he loved him!

37 And some of them said, Could not this man, which opened the eyes of the blind, have caused that even this man should not have died?

38 Jesus therefore again groaning in himself cometh to the grave. It was a cave, and a stone lay upon it.

39 Jesus said, Take ye away the stone. Martha, the sister

NEW AMERICAN STANDARD BIBLE

28 When she had said this, she went away and called Mary her sister, saying secretly, "The Teacher is here and is calling for you."

29 And when she heard it, she *got up quickly and was coming to Him.

30 Now Jesus had not yet come into the village, but was still in the place where Martha met Him.

31 Then the Jews who were with her in the house, and consoling her, when they saw that Mary got up quickly and went out, they followed her, supposing that she was going to the tomb to weep there.

32 Therefore, when Mary came where Jesus was, she saw Him, and fell at His feet, saying to Him, "Lord, if You had been here, my brother would not have died."

33 When Jesus therefore saw her weeping, and the Jews who came with her *also* weeping, He was deeply moved in spirit and was troubled,

34 and said, "Where have you laid him?" They *said to Him, "Lord, come and see."

35 Jesus wept.

36 So the Jews were saying, "See how He loved him!"

37 But some of them said, "Could not this man, who opened the eyes of the blind man, have kept this man also from dying?"

38 So Jesus, again being deeply moved within, *came to the tomb. Now it was a cave, and a stone was lying against it.

39 Jesus *said, "Remove the stone." Martha, the sister of

NEW CENTURY VERSION

Jesus Cries

28After Martha said this, she went back and talked to
her sister Mary alone. Martha said, "The Teacher is here
and he is asking for you." 29When Mary heard this, she got
up quickly and went to Jesus. 30Jesus had not yet come
into the town but was still at the place where Martha had
met him. 31The Jews were with Mary in the house, comfort-
ing her. When they saw her stand and leave quickly, they
followed her, thinking she was going to the tomb to cry
there.

32But Mary went to the place where Jesus was. When
she saw him, she fell at his feet and said, "Lord, if you had
been here, my brother would not have died."

33When Jesus saw Mary crying and the Jews who came
with her also crying, he was upset and was deeply trou-
bled. 34He asked, "Where did you bury him?"

"Come and see, Lord," they said.

35Jesus cried.

36So the Jews said, "See how much he loved him."

37But some of them said, "If Jesus opened the eyes of the
blind man, why couldn't he keep Lazarus from dying?"

Jesus Raises Lazarus

38Again feeling very upset, Jesus came to the tomb. It
was a cave with a large stone covering the entrance.
39Jesus said, "Move the stone away."

CONTEMPORARY ENGLISH VERSION

28After Martha said this, she went and privately said to
her sister Mary, "The Teacher is here, and he wants to see
you." 29As soon as Mary heard this, she got up and went
out to Jesus. 30He was still outside the village where
Martha had gone to meet him. 31Many people had come to
comfort Mary, and when they saw her quickly leave the
house, they thought she was going out to the tomb to cry.
So they followed her.

32Mary went to where Jesus was. Then as soon as she
saw him, she knelt at his feet and said, "Lord, if you had
been here, my brother would not have died."

33When Jesus saw that Mary and the people with her
were crying, he was terribly upset 34and asked, "Where
have you put his body?"

They replied, "Lord, come and you will see."

35Jesus started crying, 36and the people said, "See how
much he loved Lazarus."

37Some of them said, "He gives sight to the blind. Why
couldn't he have kept Lazarus from dying?"

38Jesus was still terribly upset. So he went to the tomb,
which was a cave with a stone rolled against the entrance.
39Then he told the people to roll the stone away. But

NEW INTERNATIONAL VERSION

[28]And after she had said this, she went back and called
her sister Mary aside. "The Teacher is here," she said, "and
is asking for you." [29]When Mary heard this, she got up
quickly and went to him. [30]Now Jesus had not yet entered
the village, but was still at the place where Martha had
met him. [31]When the Jews who had been with Mary in the
house, comforting her, noticed how quickly she got up and
went out, they followed her, supposing she was going to
the tomb to mourn there.

[32]When Mary reached the place where Jesus was and
saw him, she fell at his feet and said, "Lord, if you had
been here, my brother would not have died."

[33]When Jesus saw her weeping, and the Jews who had
come along with her also weeping, he was deeply moved in
spirit and troubled. [34]"Where have you laid him?" he
asked.

"Come and see, Lord," they replied.

[35]Jesus wept.

[36]Then the Jews said, "See how he loved him!"

[37]But some of them said, "Could not he who opened the
eyes of the blind man have kept this man from dying?"

Jesus Raises Lazarus From the Dead

[38]Jesus, once more deeply moved, came to the tomb. It
was a cave with a stone laid across the entrance. [39]"Take
away the stone," he said.

NEW LIVING TRANSLATION

into the world from God." [28]Then she left him and returned
to Mary. She called Mary aside from the mourners and told
her, "The Teacher is here and wants to see you." [29]So Mary
immediately went to him.

[30]Now Jesus had stayed outside the village, at the place
where Martha met him. [31]When the people who were at the
house trying to console Mary saw her leave so hastily, they
assumed she was going to Lazarus's grave to weep. So
they followed her there. [32]When Mary arrived and saw
Jesus, she fell down at his feet and said, "Lord, if you had
been here, my brother would not have died."

[33]When Jesus saw her weeping and saw the other people
wailing with her, he was moved with indignation and was
deeply troubled. [34]"Where have you put him?" he asked
them.

They told him, "Lord, come and see." [35]Then Jesus wept.
[36]The people who were standing nearby said, "See how
much he loved him." [37]But some said, "This man healed a
blind man. Why couldn't he keep Lazarus from dying?"

Jesus Raises Lazarus from the Dead

[38]And again Jesus was deeply troubled. Then they came
to the grave. It was a cave with a stone rolled across its
entrance. [39]"Roll the stone aside," Jesus told them.

NEW KING JAMES VERSION

Jesus and Death, the Last Enemy

[28]And when she had said these things, she went her way
and secretly called Mary her sister, saying, "The Teacher
has come and is calling for you." [29]As soon as she heard
that, she arose quickly and came to Him. [30]Now Jesus had
not yet come into the town, but was[b] in the place where
Martha met Him. [31]Then the Jews who were with her in the
house, and comforting her, when they saw that Mary rose
up quickly and went out, followed her, saying, "She is
going to the tomb to weep there."[c]

[32]Then, when Mary came where Jesus was, and saw
Him, she fell down at His feet, saying to Him, "Lord, if You
had been here, my brother would not have died."

[33]Therefore, when Jesus saw her weeping, and the Jews
who came with her weeping, He groaned in the spirit and
was troubled. [34]And He said, "Where have you laid him?"

They said to Him, "Lord, come and see."

[35]Jesus wept. [36]Then the Jews said, "See how He loved
him!"

[37]And some of them said, "Could not this Man, who
opened the eyes of the blind, also have kept this man from
dying?"

Lazarus Raised from the Dead

[38]Then Jesus, again groaning in Himself, came to the
tomb. It was a cave, and a stone lay against it. [39]Jesus
said, "Take away the stone."

11:30 [b] NU-Text adds *still.* 11:31 [c] NU-Text reads *supposing that she was going to the tomb to weep there.*

THE MESSAGE

After saying this, she went to her sister Mary and whispered in her ear, "The Teacher is here and is asking for you."

The moment she heard that, she jumped up and ran out to him. Jesus had not yet entered the town but was still at the place where Martha had met him. When her sympathizing Jewish friends saw Mary run off, they followed her, thinking she was on her way to the tomb to weep there. Mary came to where Jesus was waiting and fell at his feet, saying, "Master, if only you had been here, my brother would not have died."

When Jesus saw her sobbing and the Jews with her sobbing, a deep anger welled up within him. He said, "Where did you put him?"

"Master, come and see," they said. Now Jesus wept.

The Jews said, "Look how deeply he loved him."

Others among them said, "Well, if he loved him so much, why didn't he do something to keep him from dying? After all, he opened the eyes of a blind man."

Then Jesus, the anger again welling up within him, arrived at the tomb. It was a simple cave in the hillside with a slab of stone laid against it. Jesus said, "Remove the stone."

KING JAMES VERSION

of him that was dead, saith unto him, Lord, by this time he stinketh: for he hath been *dead* four days.

40 Jesus saith unto her, Said I not unto thee, that, if thou wouldest believe, thou shouldest see the glory of God?

41 Then they took away the stone *from the place* where the dead was laid. And Jesus lifted up *his* eyes, and said, Father, I thank thee that thou hast heard me.

42 And I knew that thou hearest me always: but because of the people which stand by I said *it*, that they may believe that thou hast sent me.

43 And when he thus had spoken, he cried with a loud voice, Lazarus, come forth.

44 And he that was dead came forth, bound hand and foot with graveclothes: and his face was bound about with a napkin. Jesus saith unto them, Loose him, and let him go.

45 ¶ Then many of the Jews which came to Mary, and had seen the things which Jesus did, believed on him.

46 But some of them went their ways to the Pharisees, and told them what things Jesus had done.

47 Then gathered the chief priests and the Pharisees a council, and said, What do we? for this man doeth many miracles.

48 If we let him thus alone, all *men* will believe on him: and the Romans shall come and take away both our place and nation.

NEW AMERICAN STANDARD BIBLE

the deceased, *said to Him, "Lord, by this time there will be a stench, for he has been *dead* four days."

40 Jesus *said to her, "Did I not say to you that if you believe, you will see the glory of God?"

41 So they removed the stone. Then Jesus raised His eyes, and said, "Father, I thank You that You have heard Me.

42 "I knew that You always hear Me; but because of the people standing around I said it, so that they may believe that You sent Me."

43 When He had said these things, He cried out with a loud voice, "Lazarus, come forth."

44 The man who had died came forth, bound hand and foot with wrappings, and his face was wrapped around with a cloth. Jesus *said to them, "Unbind him, and let him go."

45 Therefore many of the Jews who came to Mary, and saw what He had done, believed in Him.

46 But some of them went to the Pharisees and told them the things which Jesus had done.

Conspiracy to Kill Jesus

47 Therefore the chief priests and the Pharisees convened a council, and were saying, "What are we doing? For this man is performing many signs.

48 "If we let Him *go on* like this, all men will believe in Him, and the Romans will come and take away both our place and our nation."

NEW CENTURY VERSION

Martha, the sister of the dead man, said, "But, Lord, it has been four days since he died. There will be a bad smell."

40Then Jesus said to her, "Didn't I tell you that if you believed you would see the glory of God?"

41So they moved the stone away from the entrance. Then Jesus looked up and said, "Father, I thank you that you heard me. 42I know that you always hear me, but I said these things because of the people here around me. I want them to believe that you sent me." 43After Jesus said this, he cried out in a loud voice, "Lazarus, come out!" 44The dead man came out, his hands and feet wrapped with pieces of cloth, and a cloth around his face.

Jesus said to them, "Take the cloth off of him and let him go."

The Plan to Kill Jesus

45Many of the Jews, who had come to visit Mary and saw what Jesus did, believed in him. 46But some of them went to the Pharisees and told them what Jesus had done. 47Then the leading priests and Pharisees called a meeting of the Jewish council. They asked, "What should we do? This man is doing many miracles. 48If we let him continue doing these things, everyone will believe in him. Then the Romans will come and take away our Temple and our nation."

CONTEMPORARY ENGLISH VERSION

Martha said, "Lord, you know that Lazarus has been dead four days, and there will be a bad smell."

40Jesus replied, "Didn't I tell you that if you had faith, you would see the glory of God?"

41After the stone had been rolled aside, Jesus looked up toward heaven and prayed, "Father, I thank you for answering my prayer. 42I know that you always answer my prayers. But I said this, so that the people here would believe that you sent me."

43When Jesus had finished praying, he shouted, "Lazarus, come out!" 44The man who had been dead came out. His hands and feet were wrapped with strips of burial cloth, and a cloth covered his face.

Jesus then told the people, "Untie him and let him go."

The Plot To Kill Jesus

(Matthew 26.1-5; Mark 14.1, 2; Luke 22.1, 2)

45Many of the people who had come to visit Mary saw the things that Jesus did, and they put their faith in him. 46Others went to the Pharisees and told what Jesus had done. 47Then the chief priests and the Pharisees called the council together and said, "What should we do? This man is working a lot of miracles.[b] 48If we don't stop him now, everyone will put their faith in him. Then the Romans will come and destroy our temple and our nation."[c]

[b] 11.47 *miracles*: See the note at 2.11. [c] 11.48 *destroy our temple and our nation*: The Jewish leaders were afraid that Jesus would lead his followers to rebel against Rome and that the Roman army would then destroy their nation.

NEW INTERNATIONAL VERSION

"But, Lord," said Martha, the sister of the dead man, "by this time there is a bad odor, for he has been there four days."

40Then Jesus said, "Did I not tell you that if you believed, you would see the glory of God?"

41So they took away the stone. Then Jesus looked up and said, "Father, I thank you that you have heard me. 42I knew that you always hear me, but I said this for the benefit of the people standing here, that they may believe that you sent me."

43When he had said this, Jesus called in a loud voice, "Lazarus, come out!" 44The dead man came out, his hands and feet wrapped with strips of linen, and a cloth around his face.

Jesus said to them, "Take off the grave clothes and let him go."

The Plot to Kill Jesus

45Therefore many of the Jews who had come to visit Mary, and had seen what Jesus did, put their faith in him. 46But some of them went to the Pharisees and told them what Jesus had done. 47Then the chief priests and the Pharisees called a meeting of the Sanhedrin.

"What are we accomplishing?" they asked. "Here is this man performing many miraculous signs. 48If we let him go on like this, everyone will believe in him, and then the Romans will come and take away both our place[c] and our nation."

[c] *48* Or *temple*

NEW LIVING TRANSLATION

But Martha, the dead man's sister, said, "Lord, by now the smell will be terrible because he has been dead for four days."

40Jesus responded, "Didn't I tell you that you will see God's glory if you believe?" 41So they rolled the stone aside. Then Jesus looked up to heaven and said, "Father, thank you for hearing me. 42You always hear me, but I said it out loud for the sake of all these people standing here, so they will believe you sent me." 43Then Jesus shouted, "Lazarus, come out!" 44And Lazarus came out, bound in graveclothes, his face wrapped in a headcloth. Jesus told them, "Unwrap him and let him go!"

The Plot to Kill Jesus

45Many of the people who were with Mary believed in Jesus when they saw this happen. 46But some went to the Pharisees and told them what Jesus had done. 47Then the leading priests and Pharisees called the high council* together to discuss the situation. "What are we going to do?" they asked each other. "This man certainly performs many miraculous signs. 48If we leave him alone, the whole nation will follow him, and then the Roman army will come and destroy both our Temple and our nation."

11:47 Greek *the Sanhedrin.*

NEW KING JAMES VERSION

Martha, the sister of him who was dead, said to Him, "Lord, by this time there is a stench, for he has been *dead* four days."

40Jesus said to her, "Did I not say to you that if you would believe you would see the glory of God?" 41Then they took away the stone *from the place* where the dead man was lying.[d] And Jesus lifted up *His* eyes and said, "Father, I thank You that You have heard Me. 42And I know that You always hear Me, but because of the people who are standing by I said *this,* that they may believe that You sent Me." 43Now when He had said these things, He cried with a loud voice, "Lazarus, come forth!" 44And he who had died came out bound hand and foot with graveclothes, and his face was wrapped with a cloth. Jesus said to them, "Loose him, and let him go."

The Plot to Kill Jesus

45Then many of the Jews who had come to Mary, and had seen the things Jesus did, believed in Him. 46But some of them went away to the Pharisees and told them the things Jesus did. 47Then the chief priests and the Pharisees gathered a council and said, "What shall we do? For this Man works many signs. 48If we let Him alone like this, everyone will believe in Him, and the Romans will come and take away both our place and nation."

11:41 [d] NU-Text omits *from the place where the dead man was lying.*

THE MESSAGE

The sister of the dead man, Martha, said, "Master, by this time there's a stench. He's been dead four days!"

Jesus looked her in the eye. "Didn't I tell you that if you believed, you would see the glory of God?"

Then, to the others, "Go ahead, take away the stone."

They removed the stone. Jesus raised his eyes to heaven and prayed, "Father, I'm grateful that you have listened to me. I know you always do listen, but on account of this crowd standing here I've spoken so that they might believe that you sent me."

Then he shouted, "Lazarus, come out!" And he came out, a cadaver, wrapped from head to toe, and with a kerchief over his face.

Jesus told them, "Unwrap him and let him loose."

The Man Who Creates God-Signs

That was a turnaround for many of the Jews who were with Mary. They saw what Jesus did, and believed in him. But some went back to the Pharisees and told on Jesus. The high priests and Pharisees called a meeting of the Jewish ruling body. "What do we do now?" they asked. "This man keeps on doing things, creating God-signs. If we let him go on, pretty soon everyone will be believing in him and the Romans will come and remove what little power and privilege we still have."

KING JAMES VERSION

49 And one of them, *named* Caiaphas, being the high priest that same year, said unto them, Ye know nothing at all,

50 Nor consider that it is expedient for us, that one man should die for the people, and that the whole nation perish not.

51 And this spake he not of himself: but being high priest that year, he prophesied that Jesus should die for that nation;

52 And not for that nation only, but that also he should gather together in one the children of God that were scattered abroad.

53 Then from that day forth they took counsel together for to put him to death.

54 Jesus therefore walked no more openly among the Jews; but went thence unto a country near to the wilderness, into a city called Ephraim, and there continued with his disciples.

55 And the Jews' passover was nigh at hand: and many went out of the country up to Jerusalem before the passover, to purify themselves.

56 Then sought they for Jesus, and spake among themselves, as they stood in the temple, What think ye, that he will not come to the feast?

57 Now both the chief priests and the Pharisees had given a commandment, that, if any man knew where he were, he should shew *it*, that they might take him.

12 Then Jesus six days before the passover came to Bethany, where Lazarus was which had been dead, whom he raised from the dead.

NEW AMERICAN STANDARD BIBLE

49 But one of them, Caiaphas, who was high priest that year, said to them, "You know nothing at all,

50 nor do you take into account that it is expedient for you that one man die for the people, and that the whole nation not perish."

51 Now he did not say this on his own initiative, but being high priest that year, he prophesied that Jesus was going to die for the nation,

52 and not for the nation only, but in order that He might also gather together into one the children of God who are scattered abroad.

53 So from that day on they planned together to kill Him.

54 Therefore Jesus no longer continued to walk publicly among the Jews, but went away from there to the country near the wilderness, into a city called Ephraim; and there He stayed with the disciples.

55 Now the Passover of the Jews was near, and many went up to Jerusalem out of the country before the Passover to purify themselves.

56 So they were seeking for Jesus, and were saying to one another as they stood in the temple, "What do you think; that He will not come to the feast at all?"

57 Now the chief priests and the Pharisees had given orders that if anyone knew where He was, he was to report it, so that they might seize Him.

Mary Anoints Jesus

12 Jesus, therefore, six days before the Passover, came to Bethany where Lazarus was, whom Jesus had raised from the dead.

NEW CENTURY VERSION

[49]One of the men there was Caiaphas, the high priest that year. He said, "You people know nothing! [50]You don't realize that it is better for one man to die for the people than for the whole nation to be destroyed."

[51]Caiaphas did not think of this himself. As high priest that year, he was really prophesying that Jesus would die for the Jewish nation [52]and for God's scattered children to bring them all together and make them one.

[53]That day they started planning to kill Jesus. [54]So Jesus no longer traveled openly among the Jews. He left there and went to a place near the desert, to a town called Ephraim and stayed there with his followers.

[55]It was almost time for the Jewish Passover Feast. Many from the country went up to Jerusalem before the Passover to do the special things to make themselves pure. [56]The people looked for Jesus and stood in the Temple asking each other, "Is he coming to the Feast? What do you think?" [57]But the leading priests and the Pharisees had given orders that if anyone knew where Jesus was, he must tell them. Then they could arrest him.

Jesus with Friends in Bethany

12 Six days before the Passover Feast, Jesus went to Bethany, where Lazarus lived. (Lazarus is the man Jesus raised from the dead.) [2]There they had a dinner for

CONTEMPORARY ENGLISH VERSION

[49]One of the council members was Caiaphas, who was also high priest that year. He spoke up and said, "You people don't have any sense at all! [50]Don't you know it is better for one person to die for the people than for the whole nation to be destroyed?" [51]Caiaphas did not say this on his own. As high priest that year, he was prophesying that Jesus would die for the nation. [52]Yet Jesus would not die just for the Jewish nation. He would die to bring together all of God's scattered people. [53]From that day on, the council started making plans to put Jesus to death.

[54]Because of this plot against him, Jesus stopped going around in public. He went to the town of Ephraim, which was near the desert, and he stayed there with his disciples.

[55]It was almost time for Passover. Many of the Jewish people who lived out in the country had come to Jerusalem to get themselves ready[d] for the festival. [56]They looked around for Jesus. Then when they were in the temple, they asked each other, "You don't think he will come here for Passover, do you?"

[57]The chief priests and the Pharisees told the people to let them know if any of them saw Jesus. That is how they hoped to arrest him.

At Bethany (Matthew 26.6-13; Mark 14.3-9)

12 Six days before Passover Jesus went back to Bethany, where he had raised Lazarus from death.

[d] 11.55 *get themselves ready*: The Jewish people had to do certain things to prepare themselves to worship God.

NEW INTERNATIONAL VERSION

[49]Then one of them, named Caiaphas, who was high
priest that year, spoke up, "You know nothing at all! [50]You
do not realize that it is better for you that one man die for
the people than that the whole nation perish."
[51]He did not say this on his own, but as high priest that
year he prophesied that Jesus would die for the Jewish
nation, [52]and not only for that nation but also for the scat-
tered children of God, to bring them together and make
them one. [53]So from that day on they plotted to take his
life.
[54]Therefore Jesus no longer moved about publicly among
the Jews. Instead he withdrew to a region near the desert,
to a village called Ephraim, where he stayed with his disci-
ples.
[55]When it was almost time for the Jewish Passover,
many went up from the country to Jerusalem for their cere-
monial cleansing before the Passover. [56]They kept looking
for Jesus, and as they stood in the temple area they asked
one another, "What do you think? Isn't he coming to the
Feast at all?" [57]But the chief priests and Pharisees had
given orders that if anyone found out where Jesus was, he
should report it so that they might arrest him.

Jesus Anointed at Bethany

12 Six days before the Passover, Jesus arrived at
Bethany, where Lazarus lived, whom Jesus had
raised from the dead. [2]Here a dinner was given in Jesus'

NEW LIVING TRANSLATION

[49]And one of them, Caiaphas, who was high priest that
year, said, "How can you be so stupid? [50]Why should the
whole nation be destroyed? Let this one man die for the
people."
[51]This prophecy that Jesus should die for the entire
nation came from Caiaphas in his position as high priest.
He didn't think of it himself; he was inspired to say it. [52]It
was a prediction that Jesus' death would be not for Israel
only, but for the gathering together of all the children of
God scattered around the world.
[53]So from that time on the Jewish leaders began to plot
Jesus' death. [54]As a result, Jesus stopped his public minis-
try among the people and left Jerusalem. He went to a
place near the wilderness, to the village of Ephraim, and
stayed there with his disciples.
[55]It was now almost time for the celebration of Passover,
and many people from the country arrived in Jerusalem
several days early so they could go through the cleansing
ceremony before the Passover began. [56]They wanted to see
Jesus, and as they talked in the Temple, they asked each
other, "What do you think? Will he come for the
Passover?" [57]Meanwhile, the leading priests and Pharisees
had publicly announced that anyone seeing Jesus must
report him immediately so they could arrest him.

Jesus Anointed at Bethany

12 Six days before the Passover ceremonies began,
Jesus arrived in Bethany, the home of Lazarus—
the man he had raised from the dead. [2]A dinner was

NEW KING JAMES VERSION

[49]And one of them, Caiaphas, being high priest that
year, said to them, "You know nothing at all, [50]nor do you
consider that it is expedient for us[e] that one man should
die for the people, and not that the whole nation should
perish." [51]Now this he did not say on his own *authority;*
but being high priest that year he prophesied that Jesus
would die for the nation, [52]and not for that nation only,
but also that He would gather together in one the children
of God who were scattered abroad.
[53]Then, from that day on, they plotted to put Him to
death. [54]Therefore Jesus no longer walked openly among
the Jews, but went from there into the country near the
wilderness, to a city called Ephraim, and there remained
with His disciples.
[55]And the Passover of the Jews was near, and many
went from the country up to Jerusalem before the Passover,
to purify themselves. [56]Then they sought Jesus, and spoke
among themselves as they stood in the temple, "What do
you think—that He will not come to the feast?" [57]Now
both the chief priests and the Pharisees had given a com-
mand, that if anyone knew where He was, he should report
it, that they might seize Him.

The Anointing at Bethany

12 Then, six days before the Passover, Jesus came to
Bethany, where Lazarus was who had been dead,[a]
whom He had raised from the dead. [2]There they made Him

11:50 [e] NU-Text reads *you.* 12:1 [a] NU-Text omits *who had been dead.*

THE MESSAGE

Then one of them—it was Caiaphas, the designated
Chief Priest that year—spoke up, "Don't you know any-
thing? Can't you see that it's to our advantage that one
man dies for the people rather than the whole nation be
destroyed?" He didn't say this of his own accord, but as
Chief Priest that year he unwittingly prophesied that Jesus
was about to die sacrificially for the nation, and not only
for the nation but so that all God's exile-scattered children
might be gathered together into one people.

From that day on, they plotted to kill him. So Jesus no
longer went out in public among the Jews. He withdrew
into the country bordering the desert to a town called
Ephraim and secluded himself there with his disciples.

The Jewish Passover was coming up. Crowds of people
were making their way from the country up to Jerusalem to
get themselves ready for the Feast. They were curious
about Jesus. There was a lot of talk of him among those
standing around in the Temple: "What do you think? Do
you think he'll show up at the Feast or not?"

Meanwhile, the high priests and Pharisees gave out the
word that anyone getting wind of him should inform them.
They were all set to arrest him.

Anointing His Feet

12 Six days before Passover, Jesus entered Bethany
where Lazarus, so recently raised from the dead,
was living. Lazarus and his sisters invited Jesus to dinner

KING JAMES VERSION

2 There they made him a supper; and Martha served: but Lazarus was one of them that sat at the table with him.

3 Then took Mary a pound of ointment of spikenard, very costly, and anointed the feet of Jesus, and wiped his feet with her hair: and the house was filled with the odour of the ointment.

4 Then saith one of his disciples, Judas Iscariot, Simon's *son*, which should betray him,

5 Why was not this ointment sold for three hundred pence, and given to the poor?

6 This he said, not that he cared for the poor; but because he was a thief, and had the bag, and bare what was put therein.

7 Then said Jesus, Let her alone: against the day of my burying hath she kept this.

8 For the poor always ye have with you; but me ye have not always.

9 Much people of the Jews therefore knew that he was there: and they came not for Jesus' sake only, but that they might see Lazarus also, whom he had raised from the dead.

10 But the chief priests consulted that they might put Lazarus also to death;

11 Because that by reason of him many of the Jews went away, and believed on Jesus.

NEW AMERICAN STANDARD BIBLE

2 So they made Him a supper there, and Martha was serving; but Lazarus was one of those reclining *at the table* with Him.

3 Mary then took a pound of very costly perfume of pure nard, and anointed the feet of Jesus and wiped His feet with her hair; and the house was filled with the fragrance of the perfume.

4 But Judas Iscariot, one of His disciples, who was intending to betray Him, *said,

5 "Why was this perfume not sold for [1]three hundred denarii and given to poor *people?*"

6 Now he said this, not because he was concerned about the poor, but because he was a thief, and as he had the money box, he used to pilfer what was put into it.

7 Therefore Jesus said, "Let her alone, so that she may keep [2]it for the day of My burial.

8 "For you always have the poor with you, but you do not always have Me."

9 The large crowd of the Jews then learned that He was there; and they came, not for Jesus' sake only, but that they might also see Lazarus, whom He raised from the dead.

10 But the chief priests planned to put Lazarus to death also;

11 because on account of him many of the Jews were going away and were believing in Jesus.

12:5 [1] Equivalent to 11 months' wages 12:7 [2] I.e. the custom of preparing the body for burial

NEW CENTURY VERSION

Jesus. Martha served the food, and Lazarus was one of the
people eating with Jesus. [3]Mary brought in a pint of very
expensive perfume made from pure nard. She poured the
perfume on Jesus' feet, and then she wiped his feet with
her hair. And the sweet smell from the perfume filled the
whole house.
[4]Judas Iscariot, one of Jesus' followers who would later
turn against him, was there. Judas said, [5]"This perfume
was worth three hundred coins.[a] Why wasn't it sold and
the money given to the poor?" [6]But Judas did not really
care about the poor; he said this because he was a thief.
He was the one who kept the money box, and he often
stole from it.
[7]Jesus answered, "Leave her alone. It was right for her
to save this perfume for today, the day for me to be prepared for burial. [8]You will always have the poor with you,
but you will not always have me."

The Plot Against Lazarus

[9]A large crowd of Jews heard that Jesus was in Bethany.
So they went there to see not only Jesus but Lazarus,
whom Jesus raised from the dead. [10]So the leading priests
made plans to kill Lazarus, too. [11]Because of Lazarus
many of the Jews were leaving them and believing in
Jesus.

12:5 [a] **coins** One coin, a denarius, was the average pay for one day's work.

CONTEMPORARY ENGLISH VERSION

[2]A meal had been prepared for Jesus. Martha was doing
the serving, and Lazarus himself was there.
[3]Mary took a very expensive bottle of perfume[a] and
poured it on Jesus' feet. She wiped them with her hair, and
the sweet smell of the perfume filled the house.
[4]A disciple named Judas Iscariot[b] was there. He was the
one who was going to betray Jesus, and he asked, [5]"Why
wasn't this perfume sold for three hundred silver coins and
the money given to the poor?" [6]Judas did not really care
about the poor. He asked this because he carried the moneybag and sometimes would steal from it.
[7]Jesus replied, "Leave her alone! She has kept this perfume for the day of my burial. [8]You will always have the
poor with you, but you won't always have me."

A Plot To Kill Lazarus

[9]A lot of people came when they heard that Jesus was
there. They also wanted to see Lazarus, because Jesus had
raised him from death. [10]So the chief priests made plans to
kill Lazarus. [11]He was the reason that many of the Jewish
people were turning from them and putting their faith in
Jesus.

[a] 12.3 *very expensive bottle of perfume*: The Greek text has "expensive perfume made of pure spikenard," a plant used to make perfume.
[b] 12.4 *Iscariot*: See the note at 6.71.

NEW INTERNATIONAL VERSION

honor. Martha served, while Lazarus was among those reclining at the table with him. 3Then Mary took about a pint[a] of pure nard, an expensive perfume; she poured it on Jesus' feet and wiped his feet with her hair. And the house was filled with the fragrance of the perfume.

4But one of his disciples, Judas Iscariot, who was later to betray him, objected, 5"Why wasn't this perfume sold and the money given to the poor? It was worth a year's wages.[b]" 6He did not say this because he cared about the poor but because he was a thief; as keeper of the money bag, he used to help himself to what was put into it.

7"Leave her alone," Jesus replied. "⌞It was intended⌟ that she should save this perfume for the day of my burial. 8You will always have the poor among you, but you will not always have me."

9Meanwhile a large crowd of Jews found out that Jesus was there and came, not only because of him but also to see Lazarus, whom he had raised from the dead. 10So the chief priests made plans to kill Lazarus as well, 11for on account of him many of the Jews were going over to Jesus and putting their faith in him.

[a] *3* Greek *a litra* (probably about 0.5 liter) [b] *5* Greek *three hundred denarii*

NEW LIVING TRANSLATION

prepared in Jesus' honor. Martha served, and Lazarus sat at the table with him. 3Then Mary took a twelve-ounce jar* of expensive perfume made from essence of nard, and she anointed Jesus' feet with it and wiped his feet with her hair. And the house was filled with fragrance.

4But Judas Iscariot, one of his disciples—the one who would betray him—said, 5"That perfume was worth a small fortune.* It should have been sold and the money given to the poor." 6Not that he cared for the poor—he was a thief who was in charge of the disciples' funds, and he often took some for his own use.

7Jesus replied, "Leave her alone. She did it in preparation for my burial. 8You will always have the poor among you, but I will not be here with you much longer."

9When all the people* heard of Jesus' arrival, they flocked to see him and also to see Lazarus, the man Jesus had raised from the dead. 10Then the leading priests decided to kill Lazarus, too, 11for it was because of him that many of the people had deserted them and believed in Jesus.

12:3 Greek *took 1 litra* [327 grams]. 12:5 Greek *300 denarii.* A denarius was equivalent to a full day's wage. 12:9 Greek *Jewish people;* also in 12:11.

NEW KING JAMES VERSION

a supper; and Martha served, but Lazarus was one of those who sat at the table with Him. 3Then Mary took a pound of very costly oil of spikenard, anointed the feet of Jesus, and wiped His feet with her hair. And the house was filled with the fragrance of the oil.

4But one of His disciples, Judas Iscariot, Simon's *son,* who would betray Him, said, 5"Why was this fragrant oil not sold for three hundred denarii[b] and given to the poor?" 6This he said, not that he cared for the poor, but because he was a thief, and had the money box; and he used to take what was put in it.

7But Jesus said, "Let her alone; she has kept[c] this for the day of My burial. 8For the poor you have with you always, but Me you do not have always."

The Plot to Kill Lazarus

9Now a great many of the Jews knew that He was there; and they came, not for Jesus' sake only, but that they might also see Lazarus, whom He had raised from the dead. 10But the chief priests plotted to put Lazarus to death also, 11because on account of him many of the Jews went away and believed in Jesus.

12:5 [b] About one year's wages for a worker 12:7 [c] NU-Text reads *that she may keep.*

THE MESSAGE

at their home. Martha served. Lazarus was one of those sitting at the table with them. Mary came in with a jar of very expensive aromatic oils, anointed and massaged Jesus' feet, and then wiped them with her hair. The fragrance of the oils filled the house.

Judas Iscariot, one of his disciples, even then getting ready to betray him, said, "Why wasn't this oil sold and the money given to the poor? It would have easily brought three hundred silver pieces." He said this not because he cared two cents about the poor but because he was a thief. He was in charge of their common funds, but also embezzled them.

Jesus said, "Let her alone. She's anticipating and honoring the day of my burial. You always have the poor with you. You don't always have me."

Word got out among the Jews that he was back in town. The people came to take a look, not only at Jesus but also at Lazarus, who had been raised from the dead. So the high priests plotted to kill Lazarus because so many of the Jews were going over and believing in Jesus on account of him.

KING JAMES VERSION

12 ¶ On the next day much people that were come to the feast, when they heard that Jesus was coming to Jerusalem,
13 Took branches of palm trees, and went forth to meet him, and cried, Hosanna: Blessed *is* the King of Israel that cometh in the name of the Lord.
14 And Jesus, when he had found a young ass, sat thereon; as it is written,
15 Fear not, daughter of Sion: behold, thy King cometh, sitting on an ass's colt.
16 These things understood not his disciples at the first: but when Jesus was glorified, then remembered they that these things were written of him, and *that* they had done these things unto him.

NEW AMERICAN STANDARD BIBLE

Jesus Enters Jerusalem

12 On the next day the large crowd who had come to the feast, when they heard that Jesus was coming to Jerusalem,
13 took the branches of the palm trees and went out to meet Him, and *began* to shout, "Hosanna! Blessed is He who comes in the name of the Lord, even the King of Israel."
14 Jesus, finding a young donkey, sat on it; as it is written,
15 "Fear not, daughter of Zion; behold, your King is coming, seated on a donkey's colt."
16 These things His disciples did not understand at the first; but when Jesus was glorified, then they remembered that these things were written of Him, and that they had done these things to Him.

NEW CENTURY VERSION

Jesus Enters Jerusalem

12 The next day a great crowd who had come to
Jerusalem for the Passover Feast heard that Jesus was
coming there. 13 So they took branches of palm trees and
went out to meet Jesus, shouting,

"Praise[b] God!
God bless the One who comes in the name of the Lord!
God bless the King of Israel!" *Psalm 118:25–26*

14 Jesus found a colt and sat on it. This was as the
Scripture says,

15 "Don't be afraid, people of Jerusalem!
Your king is coming,
sitting on the colt of a donkey." *Zechariah 9:9*

16 The followers of Jesus did not understand this at first.
But after Jesus was raised to glory, they remembered that
this had been written about him and that they had done
these things to him.

12:13 [b] **Praise** Literally, "Hosanna," a Hebrew word used at first in praying to God for help, but at this time it was probably a shout of joy used in praising God or his Messiah.

CONTEMPORARY ENGLISH VERSION

Jesus Enters Jerusalem

(Matthew 21.1-11; Mark 11.1-11; Luke 19.28-40)

12 The next day a large crowd was in Jerusalem for
Passover. When they heard that Jesus was coming for the
festival, 13 they took palm branches and went out to greet
him.[c] They shouted,

"Hooray![d]
God bless the one who comes
in the name of the Lord!
God bless the King
of Israel!"

14 Jesus found a donkey and rode on it, just as the
Scriptures say,

15 "People of Jerusalem,
don't be afraid!
Your King is now coming,
and he is riding
on a donkey."

16 At first, Jesus' disciples did not understand. But after
he had been given his glory,[e] they remembered all this.
Everything had happened exactly as the Scriptures said it
would.

[c] 12.13 *took palm branches and went out to greet him*: This was one way that the Jewish people welcomed a famous person.
[d] 12.13 *Hooray*: This translates a word that can mean "please save us." But it is most often used as a shout of praise to God. [e] 12.16 *had been given his glory*: See the note at 7.39.

NEW INTERNATIONAL VERSION

The Triumphal Entry

12 The next day the great crowd that had come for the Feast heard that Jesus was on his way to Jerusalem. 13 They took palm branches and went out to meet him, shouting,

"Hosanna![c]"

"Blessed is he who comes in the name of the Lord!"[d]

"Blessed is the King of Israel!"

14 Jesus found a young donkey and sat upon it, as it is written,

15 "Do not be afraid, O Daughter of Zion;
see, your king is coming,
seated on a donkey's colt."[e]

16 At first his disciples did not understand all this. Only after Jesus was glorified did they realize that these things had been written about him and that they had done these things to him.

[c] *13* A Hebrew expression meaning "Save!" which became an exclamation of praise [d] *13* Psalm 118:25,26 [e] *15* Zech. 9:9

NEW LIVING TRANSLATION

The Triumphal Entry

12 The next day, the news that Jesus was on the way to Jerusalem swept through the city. A huge crowd of Passover visitors 13 took palm branches and went down the road to meet him. They shouted,

"Praise God!*
Bless the one who comes in the name of the Lord!
Hail to the King of Israel!"*

14 Jesus found a young donkey and sat on it, fulfilling the prophecy that said:

15 "Don't be afraid, people of Israel.*
Look, your King is coming,
sitting on a donkey's colt."*

16 His disciples didn't realize at the time that this was a fulfillment of prophecy. But after Jesus entered into his glory, they remembered that these Scriptures had come true before their eyes.

12:13a Greek *Hosanna,* an exclamation of praise that literally means "save now." 12:13b Ps 118:25-26; Zeph 3:15. 12:15a Greek *daughter of Zion.* 12:15b Zech 9:9.

NEW KING JAMES VERSION

The Triumphal Entry

12 The next day a great multitude that had come to the feast, when they heard that Jesus was coming to Jerusalem, 13 took branches of palm trees and went out to meet Him, and cried out:

"Hosanna!
'*Blessed is He who comes in the name of the* LORD!'[d]
The King of Israel!"

14 Then Jesus, when He had found a young donkey, sat on it; as it is written:

15 "*Fear not, daughter of Zion;*
Behold, your King is coming,
Sitting on a donkey's colt."[e]

16 His disciples did not understand these things at first; but when Jesus was glorified, then they remembered that these things were written about Him and *that* they had done these things to Him.

12:13 [d] Psalm 118:26 12:15 [e] Zechariah 9:9

THE MESSAGE

See How Your King Comes

The next day the huge crowd that had arrived for the Feast heard that Jesus was entering Jerusalem. They broke off palm branches and went out to meet him. And they cheered:

"Hosanna!"
"Blessed is he who comes in God's name!"
"Yes! The King of Israel!"

Jesus got a young donkey and rode it, just as the Scripture has it:

"No fear, Daughter Zion:
See how your king comes,
riding a donkey's colt."

The disciples didn't notice the fulfillment of many Scriptures at the time, but after Jesus was glorified, they remembered that what was written about him matched what was done to him.

KING JAMES VERSION

17 The people therefore that was with him when he called Lazarus out of his grave, and raised him from the dead, bare record.

18 For this cause the people also met him, for that they heard that he had done this miracle.

19 The Pharisees therefore said among themselves, Perceive ye how ye prevail nothing? behold, the world is gone after him.

20 ¶ And there were certain Greeks among them that came up to worship at the feast:

21 The same came therefore to Philip, which was of Bethsaida of Galilee, and desired him, saying, Sir, we would see Jesus.

22 Philip cometh and telleth Andrew: and again Andrew and Philip tell Jesus.

23 And Jesus answered them, saying, The hour is come, that the Son of man should be glorified.

24 Verily, verily, I say unto you, Except a corn of wheat fall into the ground and die, it abideth alone: but if it die, it bringeth forth much fruit.

25 He that loveth his life shall lose it; and he that hateth his life in this world shall keep it unto life eternal.

26 If any man serve me, let him follow me; and where I am, there shall also my servant be: if any man serve me, him will *my* Father honour.

27 ¶ Now is my soul troubled; and what shall I say?

NEW AMERICAN STANDARD BIBLE

17 So the people, who were with Him when He called Lazarus out of the tomb and raised him from the dead, continued to testify *about Him*.

18 For this reason also the people went and met Him, because they heard that He had performed this sign.

19 So the Pharisees said to one another, "You see that you are not doing any good; look, the world has gone after Him."

Greeks Seek Jesus

20 Now there were some Greeks among those who were going up to worship at the feast;

21 these then came to Philip, who was from Bethsaida of Galilee, and *began to* ask him, saying, "Sir, we wish to see Jesus."

22 Philip *came and *told Andrew; Andrew and Philip *came and *told Jesus.

23 And Jesus *answered them, saying, "The hour has come for the Son of Man to be glorified.

24 "Truly, truly, I say to you, unless a grain of wheat falls into the earth and dies, it remains alone; but if it dies, it bears much fruit.

25 "He who loves his life loses it, and he who hates his life in this world will keep it to life eternal.

26 "If anyone serves Me, he must follow Me; and where I am, there My servant will be also; if anyone serves Me, the Father will honor him.

Jesus Foretells His Death

27 "Now My soul has become troubled; and what shall I

NEW CENTURY VERSION

People Tell About Jesus

17There had been many people with Jesus when he raised Lazarus from the dead and told him to come out of the tomb. Now they were telling others about what Jesus did. 18Many people went out to meet Jesus, because they had heard about this miracle. 19So the Pharisees said to each other, "You can see that nothing is going right for us. Look! The whole world is following him."

Jesus Talks About His Death

20There were some Greek people, too, who came to Jerusalem to worship at the Passover Feast. 21They went to Philip, who was from Bethsaida in Galilee, and said, "Sir, we would like to see Jesus." 22Philip told Andrew, and then Andrew and Philip told Jesus.

23Jesus said to them, "The time has come for the Son of Man to receive his glory. 24I tell you the truth, a grain of wheat must fall to the ground and die to make many seeds. But if it never dies, it remains only a single seed. 25Those who love their lives will lose them, but those who hate their lives in this world will keep true life forever. 26Whoever serves me must follow me. Then my servant will be with me everywhere I am. My Father will honor anyone who serves me.

27"Now I am very troubled. Should I say, 'Father, save

CONTEMPORARY ENGLISH VERSION

17-18A crowd had come to meet Jesus because they had seen him call Lazarus out of the tomb. They kept talking about him and this miracle.[f] 19But the Pharisees said to each other, "There is nothing that can be done! Everyone in the world is following Jesus."

Some Greeks Want To Meet Jesus

20Some Greeks[g] had gone to Jerusalem to worship during Passover. 21Philip from Bethsaida in Galilee was there too. So they went to him and said, "Sir, we would like to meet Jesus." 22Philip told Andrew. Then the two of them went to Jesus and told him.

The Son of Man Must Be Lifted Up

23Jesus said:

The time has come for the Son of Man to be given his glory.[h] 24I tell you for certain that a grain of wheat that falls on the ground will never be more than one grain unless it dies. But if it dies, it will produce lots of wheat. 25If you love your life, you will lose it. If you give it up in this world, you will be given eternal life. 26If you serve me, you must go with me. My servants will be with me wherever I am. If you serve me, my Father will honor you.

27Now I am deeply troubled, and I don't know what to

[f] 12.17,18 *miracle*: See the note at 2.11. [g] 12.20 *Greeks*: Perhaps Gentiles who worshiped with the Jews. See the note at 7.35.
[h] 12.23 *be given his glory*: See the note at 7.39.

NEW INTERNATIONAL VERSION

[17]Now the crowd that was with him when he called Lazarus from the tomb and raised him from the dead continued to spread the word. [18]Many people, because they had heard that he had given this miraculous sign, went out to meet him. [19]So the Pharisees said to one another, "See, this is getting us nowhere. Look how the whole world has gone after him!"

Jesus Predicts His Death

[20]Now there were some Greeks among those who went up to worship at the Feast. [21]They came to Philip, who was from Bethsaida in Galilee, with a request. "Sir," they said, "we would like to see Jesus." [22]Philip went to tell Andrew; Andrew and Philip in turn told Jesus.

[23]Jesus replied, "The hour has come for the Son of Man to be glorified. [24]I tell you the truth, unless a kernel of wheat falls to the ground and dies, it remains only a single seed. But if it dies, it produces many seeds. [25]The man who loves his life will lose it, while the man who hates his life in this world will keep it for eternal life. [26]Whoever serves me must follow me; and where I am, my servant also will be. My Father will honor the one who serves me.

[27]"Now my heart is troubled, and what shall I say?

NEW LIVING TRANSLATION

[17]Those in the crowd who had seen Jesus call Lazarus back to life were telling others all about it. [18]That was the main reason so many went out to meet him—because they had heard about this mighty miracle. [19]Then the Pharisees said to each other, "We've lost. Look, the whole world has gone after him!"

Jesus Predicts His Death

[20]Some Greeks who had come to Jerusalem to attend the Passover [21]paid a visit to Philip, who was from Bethsaida in Galilee. They said, "Sir, we want to meet Jesus." [22]Philip told Andrew about it, and they went together to ask Jesus.

[23]Jesus replied, "The time has come for the Son of Man to enter into his glory. [24]The truth is, a kernel of wheat must be planted in the soil. Unless it dies it will be alone—a single seed. But its death will produce many new kernels—a plentiful harvest of new lives. [25]Those who love their life in this world will lose it. Those who despise their life in this world will keep it for eternal life. [26]All those who want to be my disciples must come and follow me, because my servants must be where I am. And if they follow me, the Father will honor them. [27]Now my soul is

NEW KING JAMES VERSION

[17]Therefore the people, who were with Him when He called Lazarus out of his tomb and raised him from the dead, bore witness. [18]For this reason the people also met Him, because they heard that He had done this sign. [19]The Pharisees therefore said among themselves, "You see that you are accomplishing nothing. Look, the world has gone after Him!"

The Fruitful Grain of Wheat

[20]Now there were certain Greeks among those who came up to worship at the feast. [21]Then they came to Philip, who was from Bethsaida of Galilee, and asked him, saying, "Sir, we wish to see Jesus."

[22]Philip came and told Andrew, and in turn Andrew and Philip told Jesus.

[23]But Jesus answered them, saying, "The hour has come that the Son of Man should be glorified. [24]Most assuredly, I say to you, unless a grain of wheat falls into the ground and dies, it remains alone; but if it dies, it produces much grain. [25]He who loves his life will lose it, and he who hates his life in this world will keep it for eternal life. [26]If anyone serves Me, let him follow Me; and where I am, there My servant will be also. If anyone serves Me, him *My* Father will honor.

Jesus Predicts His Death on the Cross

[27]"Now My soul is troubled, and what shall I say? 'Father,

THE MESSAGE

The crowd that had been with him when he called Lazarus from the tomb, raising him from the dead, was there giving eyewitness accounts. It was because they had spread the word of this latest God-sign that the crowd swelled to a welcoming parade. The Pharisees took one look and threw up their hands: "It's out of control. The world's in a stampede after him."

A Grain of Wheat Must Die

There were some Greeks in town who had come up to worship at the Feast. They approached Philip, who was from Bethsaida in Galilee: "Sir, we want to see Jesus. Can you help us?"

Philip went and told Andrew. Andrew and Philip together told Jesus. Jesus answered, "Time's up. The time has come for the Son of Man to be glorified.

"Listen carefully: Unless a grain of wheat is buried in the ground, dead to the world, it is never any more than a grain of wheat. But if it is buried, it sprouts and reproduces itself many times over. In the same way, anyone who holds on to life just as it is destroys that life. But if you let it go, reckless in your love, you'll have it forever, real and eternal.

"If any of you wants to serve me, then follow me. Then you'll be where I am, ready to serve at a moment's notice. The Father will honor and reward anyone who serves me.

"Right now I am storm-tossed. And what am I going to

KING JAMES VERSION

Father, save me from this hour: but for this cause came I unto this hour.
28 Father, glorify thy name. Then came there a voice from heaven, *saying*, I have both glorified *it*, and will glorify *it* again.
29 The people therefore, that stood by, and heard *it*, said that it thundered: others said, An angel spake to him.
30 Jesus answered and said, This voice came not because of me, but for your sakes.
31 Now is the judgment of this world: now shall the prince of this world be cast out.
32 And I, if I be lifted up from the earth, will draw all *men* unto me.
33 This he said, signifying what death he should die.
34 The people answered him, We have heard out of the law that Christ abideth for ever: and how sayest thou, The Son of man must be lifted up? who is this Son of man?
35 Then Jesus said unto them, Yet a little while is the light with you. Walk while ye have the light, lest darkness come upon you: for he that walketh in darkness knoweth not whither he goeth.
36 While ye have light, believe in the light, that ye may be the children of light. These things spake Jesus, and departed, and did hide himself from them.
37 ¶ But though he had done so many miracles before them, yet they believed not on him:

NEW AMERICAN STANDARD BIBLE

say, 'Father, save Me from this hour'? But for this purpose I came to this hour.
28 "Father, glorify Your name." Then a voice came out of heaven: "I have both glorified it, and will glorify it again."
29 So the crowd *of people* who stood by and heard it were saying that it had thundered; others were saying, "An angel has spoken to Him."
30 Jesus answered and said, "This voice has not come for My sake, but for your sakes.
31 "Now judgment is upon this world; now the ruler of this world will be cast out.
32 "And I, if I am lifted up from the earth, will draw all men to Myself."
33 But He was saying this to indicate the kind of death by which He was to die.
34 The crowd then answered Him, "We have heard out of the Law that the Christ is to remain forever; and how can You say, 'The Son of Man must be lifted up'? Who is this Son of Man?"
35 So Jesus said to them, "For a little while longer the Light is among you. Walk while you have the Light, so that darkness will not overtake you; he who walks in the darkness does not know where he goes.
36 "While you have the Light, believe in the Light, so that you may become sons of Light."

These things Jesus spoke, and He went away and hid Himself from them.
37 But though He had performed so many signs before them, *yet* they were not believing in Him.

NEW CENTURY VERSION

me from this time'? No, I came to this time so I could suf-
fer. 28Father, bring glory to your name!"

Then a voice came from heaven, "I have brought glory to it, and I will do it again."

29The crowd standing there, who heard the voice, said it was thunder.

But others said, "An angel has spoken to him."

30Jesus said, "That voice was for your sake, not mine.
31Now is the time for the world to be judged; now the ruler
of this world will be thrown down. 32If I am lifted up from
the earth, I will draw all people toward me." 33Jesus said
this to show how he would die.

34The crowd said, "We have heard from the law that the Christ will live forever. So why do you say, 'The Son of Man must be lifted up'? Who is this 'Son of Man'?"

35Then Jesus said, "The light will be with you for a little
longer, so walk while you have the light. Then the dark-
ness will not catch you. If you walk in the darkness, you
will not know where you are going. 36Believe in the light
while you still have it so that you will become children of
light." When Jesus had said this, he left and hid himself
from them.

Some People Won't Believe in Jesus

37Though Jesus had done many miracles in front of the
people, they still did not believe in him. 38This was to

CONTEMPORARY ENGLISH VERSION

say. But I must not ask my Father to keep me from this time of suffering. In fact, I came into the world to suffer.
28So Father, bring glory to yourself.

A voice from heaven then said, "I have already brought
glory to myself, and I will do it again!" 29When the crowd
heard the voice, some of them thought it was thunder.
Others thought an angel had spoken to Jesus.

30Then Jesus told the crowd, "That voice spoke to help
you, not me. 31This world's people are now being judged,
and the ruler of this world[i] is already being thrown out!
32If I am lifted up above the earth, I will make everyone
want to come to me." 33Jesus was talking about the way he
would be put to death.

34The crowd said to Jesus, "The Scriptures teach that the Messiah will live forever. How can you say that the Son of Man must be lifted up? Who is this Son of Man?"

35Jesus answered, "The light will be with you for only a
little longer. Walk in the light while you can. Then you
won't be caught walking blindly in the dark. 36Have faith
in the light while it is with you, and you will be children of
the light."

The People Refuse To Have Faith in Jesus

After Jesus had said these things, he left and went into
hiding. 37He had worked a lot of miracles[j] among the peo-
ple, but they were still not willing to have faith in him.

[i] 12.31 *world*: In the Gospel of John "world" sometimes refers to the people who live in this world and to the evil forces that control their lives.
[j] 12.37 *miracles*: See the note at 2.11.

NEW INTERNATIONAL VERSION

'Father, save me from this hour'? No, it was for this very
reason I came to this hour. [28]Father, glorify your name!"
Then a voice came from heaven, "I have glorified it, and
will glorify it again." [29]The crowd that was there and
heard it said it had thundered; others said an angel had
spoken to him.
[30]Jesus said, "This voice was for your benefit, not mine.
[31]Now is the time for judgment on this world; now the
prince of this world will be driven out. [32]But I, when I am
lifted up from the earth, will draw all men to myself." [33]He
said this to show the kind of death he was going to die.
[34]The crowd spoke up, "We have heard from the Law
that the Christ[f] will remain forever, so how can you say,
'The Son of Man must be lifted up'? Who is this 'Son of
Man'?"
[35]Then Jesus told them, "You are going to have the light
just a little while longer. Walk while you have the light,
before darkness overtakes you. The man who walks in the
dark does not know where he is going. [36]Put your trust in
the light while you have it, so that you may become sons
of light." When he had finished speaking, Jesus left and
hid himself from them.

The Jews Continue in Their Unbelief

[37]Even after Jesus had done all these miraculous signs
in their presence, they still would not believe in him.

[f] *34* Or *Messiah*

NEW LIVING TRANSLATION

deeply troubled. Should I pray, 'Father, save me from what
lies ahead'? But that is the very reason why I came!
[28]Father, bring glory to your name."
Then a voice spoke from heaven, saying, "I have already
brought it glory, and I will do it again." [29]When the crowd
heard the voice, some thought it was thunder, while others
declared an angel had spoken to him.
[30]Then Jesus told them, "The voice was for your benefit,
not mine. [31]The time of judgment for the world has come,
when the prince of this world* will be cast out. [32]And when
I am lifted up on the cross,* I will draw everyone to
myself." [33]He said this to indicate how he was going to die.
[34]"Die?" asked the crowd. "We understood from
Scripture that the Messiah would live forever. Why are you
saying the Son of Man will die? Who is this Son of Man
you are talking about?"
[35]Jesus replied, "My light will shine out for you just a lit-
tle while longer. Walk in it while you can, so you will not
stumble when the darkness falls. If you walk in the dark-
ness, you cannot see where you are going. [36]Believe in the
light while there is still time; then you will become chil-
dren of the light." After saying these things, Jesus went
away and was hidden from them.

The Unbelief of the People

[37]But despite all the miraculous signs he had done,
most of the people did not believe in him. [38]This is exactly

12:31 *The prince of this world* is a name for Satan. 12:32 Greek *lifted up from the earth.*

NEW KING JAMES VERSION

save Me from this hour'? But for this purpose I came to this
hour. [28]Father, glorify Your name."
Then a voice came from heaven, *saying,* "I have both
glorified *it* and will glorify *it* again."
[29]Therefore the people who stood by and heard *it* said
that it had thundered. Others said, "An angel has spoken
to Him."
[30]Jesus answered and said, "This voice did not come
because of Me, but for your sake. [31]Now is the judgment of
this world; now the ruler of this world will be cast out.
[32]And I, if I am lifted up from the earth, will draw all *peo-
ples* to Myself." [33]This He said, signifying by what death
He would die.
[34]The people answered Him, "We have heard from the
law that the Christ remains forever; and how *can* You say,
'The Son of Man must be lifted up'? Who is this Son of
Man?"
[35]Then Jesus said to them, "A little while longer the light
is with you. Walk while you have the light, lest darkness
overtake you; he who walks in darkness does not know
where he is going. [36]While you have the light, believe in
the light, that you may become sons of light." These things
Jesus spoke, and departed, and was hidden from them.

Who Has Believed Our Report?

[37]But although He had done so many signs before
them, they did not believe in Him, [38]that the word of

THE MESSAGE

say? 'Father, get me out of this'? No, this is why I came in
the first place. I'll say, 'Father, put your glory on display.'"
A voice came out of the sky: "I have glorified it, and I'll
glorify it again."
The listening crowd said, "Thunder!"
Others said, "An angel spoke to him!"
Jesus said, "The voice didn't come for me but for you. At
this moment the world is in crisis. Now Satan, the ruler of
this world, will be thrown out. And I, as I am lifted up
from the earth, will attract everyone to me and gather
them around me." He put it this way to show how he was
going to be put to death.
Voices from the crowd answered, "We heard from God's
Law that the Messiah lasts forever. How can it be neces-
sary, as you put it, that the Son of Man 'be lifted up'? Who
is this 'Son of Man'?"
Jesus said, "For a brief time still, the light is among you.
Walk by the light you have so darkness doesn't destroy
you. If you walk in darkness, you don't know where you're
going. As you have the light, believe in the light. Then the
light will be within you, and shining through your lives.
You'll be children of light."

Their Eyes Are Blinded

Jesus said all this, and then went into hiding. All these
God-signs he had given them and they still didn't get it,

KING JAMES VERSION

38 That the saying of Esaias the prophet might be fulfilled, which he spake, Lord, who hath believed our report? and to whom hath the arm of the Lord been revealed?

39 Therefore they could not believe, because that Esaias said again,

40 He hath blinded their eyes, and hardened their heart; that they should not see with *their* eyes, nor understand with *their* heart, and be converted, and I should heal them.

41 These things said Esaias, when he saw his glory, and spake of him.

42 ¶ Nevertheless among the chief rulers also many believed on him; but because of the Pharisees they did not confess *him*, lest they should be put out of the synagogue:

NEW AMERICAN STANDARD BIBLE

38 *This was* to fulfill the word of Isaiah the prophet which he spoke: "LORD, WHO HAS BELIEVED OUR REPORT? AND TO WHOM HAS THE ARM OF THE LORD BEEN REVEALED?"

39 For this reason they could not believe, for Isaiah said again,

40 "HE HAS BLINDED THEIR EYES AND HE HARDENED THEIR HEART, SO THAT THEY WOULD NOT SEE WITH THEIR EYES AND PERCEIVE WITH THEIR HEART, AND BE CONVERTED AND I HEAL THEM."

41 These things Isaiah said because he saw His glory, and he spoke of Him.

42 Nevertheless many even of the rulers believed in Him, but because of the Pharisees they were not confessing *Him*, for fear that they would be put out of the synagogue;

NEW CENTURY VERSION

bring about what Isaiah the prophet had said:

"Lord, who believed what we told them?
Who saw the Lord's power in this?" *Isaiah 53:1*

39 This is why the people could not believe: Isaiah also had said,

40 "He has blinded their eyes,
and he has closed their minds.
Otherwise they would see with their eyes
and understand in their minds
and come back to me and be healed." *Isaiah 6:10*

41 Isaiah said this because he saw Jesus' glory and spoke about him.

42 But many believed in Jesus, even many of the leaders. But because of the Pharisees, they did not say they believed in him for fear they would be put out of the synagogue.

CONTEMPORARY ENGLISH VERSION

38 This happened so that what the prophet Isaiah had said would come true,

"Lord, who has believed
our message?
And who has seen
your mighty strength?"

39 The people could not have faith in Jesus, because Isaiah had also said,

40 "The Lord has blinded
the eyes of the people,
and he has made
the people stubborn.
He did this so that they
could not see
or understand,
and so that they
would not turn to the Lord
and be healed."

41 Isaiah said this, because he saw the glory of Jesus and spoke about him.[k] 42 Even then, many of the leaders put their faith in Jesus, but they did not tell anyone about it. The Pharisees had already given orders for the people not to have anything to do with anyone who had faith in Jesus.

[k] 12.41 *he saw the glory of Jesus and spoke about him*: Or "he saw the glory of God and spoke about Jesus."

NEW INTERNATIONAL VERSION

38This was to fulfill the word of Isaiah the prophet:

"Lord, who has believed our message
and to whom has the arm of the Lord been revealed?"[g]

39For this reason they could not believe, because, as Isaiah says elsewhere:

40 "He has blinded their eyes
and deadened their hearts,
so they can neither see with their eyes,
nor understand with their hearts,
nor turn—and I would heal them."[h]

41Isaiah said this because he saw Jesus' glory and spoke about him.

42Yet at the same time many even among the leaders believed in him. But because of the Pharisees they would not confess their faith for fear they would be put out of the

[g] *38* Isaiah 53:1 [h] *40* Isaiah 6:10

NEW LIVING TRANSLATION

what Isaiah the prophet had predicted:

"Lord, who has believed our message?
To whom will the Lord reveal his saving power?"*

39But the people couldn't believe, for as Isaiah also said,

40 "The Lord has blinded their eyes
and hardened their hearts—
so their eyes cannot see,
and their hearts cannot understand,
and they cannot turn to me
and let me heal them."*

41Isaiah was referring to Jesus when he made this prediction, because he was given a vision of the Messiah's glory.
42Many people, including some of the Jewish leaders, believed in him. But they wouldn't admit it to anyone because of their fear that the Pharisees would expel them

12:38 Isa 53:1. **12:40** Isa 6:10.

NEW KING JAMES VERSION

Isaiah the prophet might be fulfilled, which he spoke:

"Lord, who has believed our report?
And to whom has the arm of the Lord *been revealed?"*[f]

39Therefore they could not believe, because Isaiah said again:

40 *"He has blinded their eyes and hardened their hearts,*
Lest they should see with their eyes,
Lest they should understand with their hearts and turn,
So that I should heal them."[g]

41These things Isaiah said when[h] he saw His glory and spoke of Him.

Walk in the Light

42Nevertheless even among the rulers many believed in Him, but because of the Pharisees they did not confess *Him,* lest they should be put out of the synagogue; 43for

12:38 [f] Isaiah 53:1 **12:40** [g] Isaiah 6:10 **12:41** [h] NU-Text reads *because.*

THE MESSAGE

still wouldn't trust him. This proved that the prophet Isaiah was right:

"God, who believed what we preached?
Who recognized God's arm, outstretched and ready to act?"

First they wouldn't believe, then they *couldn't*—again, just as Isaiah said:

"Their eyes are blinded,
their hearts are hardened,
So that they wouldn't see with their eyes
and perceive with their hearts,
And turn to me, God,
so I could heal them."

Isaiah said these things after he got a glimpse of God's cascading brightness that would pour through the Messiah.

On the other hand, a considerable number from the ranks of the leaders did believe. But because of the Pharisees, they didn't come out in the open with it. They were afraid of getting kicked out of the meeting place.

KING JAMES VERSION

43 For they loved the praise of men more than the praise of God.

44 ¶ Jesus cried and said, He that believeth on me, believeth not on me, but on him that sent me.

45 And he that seeth me seeth him that sent me.

46 I am come a light into the world, that whosoever believeth on me should not abide in darkness.

47 And if any man hear my words, and believe not, I judge him not: for I came not to judge the world, but to save the world.

48 He that rejecteth me, and receiveth not my words, hath one that judgeth him: the word that I have spoken, the same shall judge him in the last day.

49 For I have not spoken of myself; but the Father which sent me, he gave me a commandment, what I should say, and what I should speak.

50 And I know that his commandment is life everlasting: whatsoever I speak therefore, even as the Father said unto me, so I speak.

13 Now before the feast of the passover, when Jesus knew that his hour was come that he should depart out of this world unto the Father, having loved his own which were in the world, he loved them unto the end.

2 And supper being ended, the devil having now put into the heart of Judas Iscariot, Simon's *son*, to betray him;

NEW AMERICAN STANDARD BIBLE

43 for they loved the approval of men rather than the approval of God.

44 And Jesus cried out and said, "He who believes in Me, does not believe in Me but in Him who sent Me.

45 "He who sees Me sees the One who sent Me.

46 "I have come *as* Light into the world, so that everyone who believes in Me will not remain in darkness.

47 "If anyone hears My sayings and does not keep them, I do not judge him; for I did not come to judge the world, but to save the world.

48 "He who rejects Me and does not receive My sayings, has one who judges him; the word I spoke is what will judge him at the last day.

49 "For I did not speak on My own initiative, but the Father Himself who sent Me has given Me a commandment *as to* what to say and what to speak.

50 "I know that His commandment is eternal life; therefore the things I speak, I speak just as the Father has told Me."

The Lord's Supper

13 Now before the Feast of the Passover, Jesus knowing that His hour had come that He would depart out of this world to the Father, having loved His own who were in the world, He loved them to the end.

2 During supper, the devil having already put into the heart of Judas Iscariot, *the son* of Simon, to betray Him,

NEW CENTURY VERSION

43They loved praise from people more than praise from God.

44Then Jesus cried out, "Whoever believes in me is really believing in the One who sent me. 45Whoever sees me sees the One who sent me. 46I have come as light into the world so that whoever believes in me would not stay in darkness.

47"Anyone who hears my words and does not obey them, I do not judge, because I did not come to judge the world, but to save the world. 48There is a judge for those who refuse to believe in me and do not accept my words. The word I have taught will be their judge on the last day. 49The things I taught were not from myself. The Father who sent me told me what to say and what to teach. 50And I know that eternal life comes from what the Father commands. So whatever I say is what the Father told me to say."

Jesus Washes His Followers' Feet

13 It was almost time for the Jewish Passover Feast. Jesus knew that it was time for him to leave this world and go back to the Father. He had always loved those who were his own in the world, and he loved them all the way to the end.

2Jesus and his followers were at the evening meal. The devil had already persuaded Judas Iscariot, the son of Simon, to turn against Jesus. 3Jesus knew that the Father

CONTEMPORARY ENGLISH VERSION

43And besides, the leaders liked praise from others more than they liked praise from God.

Jesus Came To Save the World

44In a loud voice Jesus said:

Everyone who has faith in me also has faith in the one who sent me. 45And everyone who has seen me has seen the one who sent me. 46I am the light that has come into the world. No one who has faith in me will stay in the dark.

47I am not the one who will judge those who refuse to obey my teachings. I came to save the people of this world, not to be their judge. 48But everyone who rejects me and my teachings will be judged on the last day[l] by what I have said. 49I don't speak on my own. I say only what the Father who sent me has told me to say. 50I know that his commands will bring eternal life. That is why I tell you exactly what the Father has told me.

Jesus Washes the Feet of His Disciples

13 It was before Passover, and Jesus knew that the time had come for him to leave this world and to return to the Father. He had always loved his followers in this world, and he loved them to the very end.

2Even before the evening meal started, the devil had made Judas, the son of Simon Iscariot,[a] decide to betray Jesus.

[l] 12.48 *the last day*: See the note at 6.39. [a] 13.2 *Iscariot*: See the note at 6.71.

NEW INTERNATIONAL VERSION

synagogue; 43for they loved praise from men more than praise from God.

44Then Jesus cried out, "When a man believes in me, he does not believe in me only, but in the one who sent me. 45When he looks at me, he sees the one who sent me. 46I have come into the world as a light, so that no one who believes in me should stay in darkness.

47"As for the person who hears my words but does not keep them, I do not judge him. For I did not come to judge the world, but to save it. 48There is a judge for the one who rejects me and does not accept my words; that very word which I spoke will condemn him at the last day. 49For I did not speak of my own accord, but the Father who sent me commanded me what to say and how to say it. 50I know that his command leads to eternal life. So whatever I say is just what the Father has told me to say."

Jesus Washes His Disciples' Feet

13 It was just before the Passover Feast. Jesus knew that the time had come for him to leave this world and go to the Father. Having loved his own who were in the world, he now showed them the full extent of his love.[a]

2The evening meal was being served, and the devil had already prompted Judas Iscariot, son of Simon, to betray

[a] 1 Or *he loved them to the last*

NEW LIVING TRANSLATION

from the synagogue. 43For they loved human praise more than the praise of God.

44Jesus shouted to the crowds, "If you trust me, you are really trusting God who sent me. 45For when you see me, you are seeing the one who sent me. 46I have come as a light to shine in this dark world, so that all who put their trust in me will no longer remain in the darkness. 47If anyone hears me and doesn't obey me, I am not his judge—for I have come to save the world and not to judge it. 48But all who reject me and my message will be judged at the day of judgment by the truth I have spoken. 49I don't speak on my own authority. The Father who sent me gave me his own instructions as to what I should say. 50And I know his instructions lead to eternal life; so I say whatever the Father tells me to say!"

Jesus Washes His Disciples' Feet

13 Before the Passover celebration, Jesus knew that his hour had come to leave this world and return to his Father. He now showed the disciples the full extent of his love.* 2It was time for supper, and the Devil had already enticed Judas, son of Simon Iscariot, to carry out his plan to betray Jesus. 3Jesus knew that the Father had

13:1 Or *He loved his disciples to the very end.*

NEW KING JAMES VERSION

they loved the praise of men more than the praise of God.

44Then Jesus cried out and said, "He who believes in Me, believes not in Me but in Him who sent Me. 45And he who sees Me sees Him who sent Me. 46I have come *as* a light into the world, that whoever believes in Me should not abide in darkness. 47And if anyone hears My words and does not believe,[i] I do not judge him; for I did not come to judge the world but to save the world. 48He who rejects Me, and does not receive My words, has that which judges him—the word that I have spoken will judge him in the last day. 49For I have not spoken on My own *authority;* but the Father who sent Me gave Me a command, what I should say and what I should speak. 50And I know that His command is everlasting life. Therefore, whatever I speak, just as the Father has told Me, so I speak."

Jesus Washes the Disciples' Feet

13 Now before the Feast of the Passover, when Jesus knew that His hour had come that He should depart from this world to the Father, having loved His own who were in the world, He loved them to the end.

2And supper being ended,[a] the devil having already put it into the heart of Judas Iscariot, Simon's *son,* to betray

12:47 [i] NU-Text reads *keep them.* 13:2 [a] NU-Text reads *And during supper.*

THE MESSAGE

When push came to shove they cared more for human approval than for God's glory.

Jesus summed it all up when he cried out, "Whoever believes in me, believes not just in me but in the One who sent me. Whoever looks at me is looking, in fact, at the One who sent me. I am Light that has come into the world so that all who believe in me won't have to stay any longer in the dark.

"If anyone hears what I am saying and doesn't take it seriously, I don't reject him. I didn't come to reject the world; I came to save the world. But you need to know that whoever puts me off, refusing to take in what I'm saying, is willfully choosing rejection. The Word, the Word-made-flesh that I have spoken and that I am, *that* Word and no other is the last word. I'm not making any of this up on my own. The Father who sent me gave me orders, told me what to say and how to say it. And I know exactly what his command produces: real and eternal life. That's all I have to say. What the Father told me, I tell you."

Washing His Disciples' Feet

13 Just before the Passover Feast, Jesus knew that the time had come to leave this world to go to the Father. Having loved his dear companions, he continued to love them right to the end. It was suppertime. The Devil by now had Judas, son of Simon the Iscariot, firmly in his grip, all set for the betrayal.

KING JAMES VERSION

3 Jesus knowing that the Father had given all things into his hands, and that he was come from God, and went to God;

4 He riseth from supper, and laid aside his garments; and took a towel, and girded himself.

5 After that he poureth water into a bason, and began to wash the disciples' feet, and to wipe *them* with the towel wherewith he was girded.

6 Then cometh he to Simon Peter: and Peter saith unto him, Lord, dost thou wash my feet?

7 Jesus answered and said unto him, What I do thou knowest not now; but thou shalt know hereafter.

8 Peter saith unto him, Thou shalt never wash my feet. Jesus answered him, If I wash thee not, thou hast no part with me.

9 Simon Peter saith unto him, Lord, not my feet only, but also *my* hands and *my* head.

10 Jesus saith to him, He that is washed needeth not save to wash *his* feet, but is clean every whit: and ye are clean, but not all.

11 For he knew who should betray him; therefore said he, Ye are not all clean.

12 So after he had washed their feet, and had taken his garments, and was set down again, he said unto them, Know ye what I have done to you?

13 Ye call me Master and Lord: and ye say well; for *so* I am.

NEW AMERICAN STANDARD BIBLE

3 *Jesus,* knowing that the Father had given all things into His hands, and that He had come forth from God and was going back to God,

4 *got up from supper, and *laid aside His garments; and taking a towel, He girded Himself.

Jesus Washes the Disciples' Feet

5 Then He *poured water into the basin, and began to wash the disciples' feet and to wipe them with the towel with which He was girded.

6 So He *came to Simon Peter. He *said to Him, "Lord, do You wash my feet?"

7 Jesus answered and said to him, "What I do you do not realize now, but you will understand hereafter."

8 Peter *said to Him, "Never shall You wash my feet!" Jesus answered him, "If I do not wash you, you have no part with Me."

9 Simon Peter *said to Him, "Lord, *then wash* not only my feet, but also my hands and my head."

10 Jesus *said to him, "He who has bathed needs only to wash his feet, but is completely clean; and you are clean, but not all *of you.*"

11 For He knew the one who was betraying Him; for this reason He said, "Not all of you are clean."

12 So when He had washed their feet, and taken His garments and reclined *at the table* again, He said to them, "Do you know what I have done to you?

13 "You call Me Teacher and Lord; and you are right, for *so* I am.

NEW CENTURY VERSION

had given him power over everything and that he had come from God and was going back to God. 4So during the meal Jesus stood up and took off his outer clothing. Taking a towel, he wrapped it around his waist. 5Then he poured water into a bowl and began to wash the followers' feet, drying them with the towel that was wrapped around him.

6Jesus came to Simon Peter, who said to him, "Lord, are you going to wash my feet?"

7Jesus answered, "You don't understand now what I am doing, but you will understand later."

8Peter said, "No, you will never wash my feet."

Jesus answered, "If I don't wash your feet, you are not one of my people."

9Simon Peter answered, "Lord, then wash not only my feet, but wash my hands and my head, too!"

10Jesus said, "After a person has had a bath, his whole body is clean. He needs only to wash his feet. And you men are clean, but not all of you." 11Jesus knew who would turn against him, and that is why he said, "Not all of you are clean."

12When he had finished washing their feet, he put on his clothes and sat down again. He asked, "Do you understand what I have just done for you? 13You call me 'Teacher' and 'Lord,' and you are right, because that is what I am. 14If I,

CONTEMPORARY ENGLISH VERSION

3Jesus knew that he had come from God and would go back to God. He also knew that the Father had given him complete power. 4So during the meal Jesus got up, removed his outer garment, and wrapped a towel around his waist. 5He put some water into a large bowl. Then he began washing his disciples' feet and drying them with the towel he was wearing.

6But when he came to Simon Peter, that disciple asked, "Lord, are you going to wash my feet?"

7Jesus answered, "You don't really know what I am doing, but later you will understand."

8"You will never wash my feet!" Peter replied.

"If I don't wash you," Jesus told him, "you don't really belong to me."

9Peter said, "Lord, don't wash just my feet. Wash my hands and my head."

10Jesus answered, "People who have bathed and are clean all over need to wash just their feet. And you, my disciples, are clean, except for one of you." 11Jesus knew who would betray him. That is why he said, "except for one of you."

12After Jesus had washed his disciples' feet and had put his outer garment back on, he sat down again.[b] Then he said:

Do you understand what I have done? 13You call me
your teacher and Lord, and you should, because that is

[b] 13.12 *sat down again*: On special occasions the Jewish people followed the Greek and Roman custom of lying down on their left side and leaning on their left elbow, while eating with their right hand.

NEW INTERNATIONAL VERSION

Jesus. 3Jesus knew that the Father had put all things under his power, and that he had come from God and was returning to God; 4so he got up from the meal, took off his outer clothing, and wrapped a towel around his waist. 5After that, he poured water into a basin and began to wash his disciples' feet, drying them with the towel that was wrapped around him.

6He came to Simon Peter, who said to him, "Lord, are you going to wash my feet?"

7Jesus replied, "You do not realize now what I am doing, but later you will understand."

8"No," said Peter, "you shall never wash my feet."

Jesus answered, "Unless I wash you, you have no part with me."

9"Then, Lord," Simon Peter replied, "not just my feet but my hands and my head as well!"

10Jesus answered, "A person who has had a bath needs only to wash his feet; his whole body is clean. And you are clean, though not every one of you." 11For he knew who was going to betray him, and that was why he said not every one was clean.

12When he had finished washing their feet, he put on his clothes and returned to his place. "Do you understand what I have done for you?" he asked them. 13"You call me 'Teacher' and 'Lord,' and rightly so, for that is what I am.

NEW LIVING TRANSLATION

given him authority over everything and that he had come from God and would return to God. 4So he got up from the table, took off his robe, wrapped a towel around his waist, 5and poured water into a basin. Then he began to wash the disciples' feet and to wipe them with the towel he had around him.

6When he came to Simon Peter, Peter said to him, "Lord, why are you going to wash my feet?"

7Jesus replied, "You don't understand now why I am doing it; someday you will."

8"No," Peter protested, "you will never wash my feet!"

Jesus replied, "But if I don't wash you, you won't belong to me."

9Simon Peter exclaimed, "Then wash my hands and head as well, Lord, not just my feet!"

10Jesus replied, "A person who has bathed all over does not need to wash, except for the feet,* to be entirely clean. And you are clean, but that isn't true of everyone here." 11For Jesus knew who would betray him. That is what he meant when he said, "Not all of you are clean."

12After washing their feet, he put on his robe again and sat down and asked, "Do you understand what I was doing? 13You call me 'Teacher' and 'Lord,' and you are right,

13:10 Some manuscripts do not include *except for the feet.*

NEW KING JAMES VERSION

Him, 3Jesus, knowing that the Father had given all things into His hands, and that He had come from God and was going to God, 4rose from supper and laid aside His garments, took a towel and girded Himself. 5After that, He poured water into a basin and began to wash the disciples' feet, and to wipe *them* with the towel with which He was girded. 6Then He came to Simon Peter. And *Peter* said to Him, "Lord, are You washing my feet?"

7Jesus answered and said to him, "What I am doing you do not understand now, but you will know after this."

8Peter said to Him, "You shall never wash my feet!"

Jesus answered him, "If I do not wash you, you have no part with Me."

9Simon Peter said to Him, "Lord, not my feet only, but also *my* hands and *my* head!"

10Jesus said to him, "He who is bathed needs only to wash *his* feet, but is completely clean; and you are clean, but not all of you." 11For He knew who would betray Him; therefore He said, "You are not all clean."

12So when He had washed their feet, taken His garments, and sat down again, He said to them, "Do you know what I have done to you? 13You call Me Teacher and Lord, and you say well, for *so* I am. 14If I then, *your* Lord

THE MESSAGE

Jesus knew that the Father had put him in complete charge of everything, that he came from God and was on his way back to God. So he got up from the supper table, set aside his robe, and put on an apron. Then he poured water into a basin and began to wash the feet of the disciples, drying them with his apron. When he got to Simon Peter, Peter said, "Master, *you* wash *my* feet?"

Jesus answered, "You don't understand now what I'm doing, but it will be clear enough to you later."

Peter persisted, "You're not going to wash my feet—ever!"

Jesus said, "If I don't wash you, you can't be part of what I'm doing."

"Master!" said Peter. "Not only my feet, then. Wash my hands! Wash my head!"

Jesus said, "If you've had a bath in the morning, you only need your feet washed now and you're clean from head to toe. My concern, you understand, is holiness, not hygiene. So now you're clean. But not every one of you." (He knew who was betraying him. That's why he said, "Not every one of you.") After he had finished washing their feet, he took his robe, put it back on, and went back to his place at the table.

Then he said, "Do you understand what I have done to you? You address me as 'Teacher' and 'Master,' and rightly

KING JAMES VERSION

14 If I then, *your* Lord and Master, have washed your feet; ye also ought to wash one another's feet.
15 For I have given you an example, that ye should do as I have done to you.
16 Verily, verily, I say unto you, The servant is not greater than his lord; neither he that is sent greater than he that sent him.
17 If ye know these things, happy are ye if ye do them.
18 ¶ I speak not of you all: I know whom I have chosen: but that the scripture may be fulfilled, He that eateth bread with me hath lifted up his heel against me.
19 Now I tell you before it come, that, when it is come to pass, ye may believe that I am *he*.
20 Verily, verily, I say unto you, He that receiveth whomsoever I send receiveth me; and he that receiveth me receiveth him that sent me.
21 When Jesus had thus said, he was troubled in spirit, and testified, and said, Verily, verily, I say unto you, that one of you shall betray me.
22 Then the disciples looked one on another, doubting of whom he spake.
23 Now there was leaning on Jesus' bosom one of his disciples, whom Jesus loved.
24 Simon Peter therefore beckoned to him, that he should ask who it should be of whom he spake.
25 He then lying on Jesus' breast saith unto him, Lord, who is it?

NEW AMERICAN STANDARD BIBLE

14 "If I then, the Lord and the Teacher, washed your feet, you also ought to wash one another's feet.
15 "For I gave you an example that you also should do as I did to you.
16 "Truly, truly, I say to you, a slave is not greater than his master, nor *is* one who is sent greater than the one who sent him.
17 "If you know these things, you are blessed if you do them.
18 "I do not speak of all of you. I know the ones I have chosen; but *it is* that the Scripture may be fulfilled, 'HE WHO EATS MY BREAD HAS LIFTED UP HIS HEEL AGAINST ME.'
19 "From now on I am telling you before *it* comes to pass, so that when it does occur, you may believe that I am *He*.
20 "Truly, truly, I say to you, he who receives whomever I send receives Me; and he who receives Me receives Him who sent Me."

Jesus Predicts His Betrayal

21 When Jesus had said this, He became troubled in spirit, and testified and said, "Truly, truly, I say to you, that one of you will betray Me."
22 The disciples *began* looking at one another, at a loss *to know* of which one He was speaking.
23 There was reclining on Jesus' bosom one of His disciples, whom Jesus loved.
24 So Simon Peter *gestured to him, and *said to him, "Tell *us* who it is of whom He is speaking."
25 He, leaning back thus on Jesus' bosom, *said to Him, "Lord, who is it?"

NEW CENTURY VERSION

your Lord and Teacher, have washed your feet, you also should wash each other's feet. 15I did this as an example so that you should do as I have done for you. 16I tell you the truth, a servant is not greater than his master. A messenger is not greater than the one who sent him. 17If you know these things, you will be happy if you do them.

18"I am not talking about all of you. I know those I have chosen. But this is to bring about what the Scripture said: 'The man who ate at my table has turned against me.'[a] 19I am telling you this now before it happens so that when it happens, you will believe that I am he. 20I tell you the truth, whoever accepts anyone I send also accepts me. And whoever accepts me also accepts the One who sent me."

Jesus Talks About His Death

21After Jesus said this, he was very troubled. He said openly, "I tell you the truth, one of you will turn against me."

22The followers all looked at each other, because they did not know whom Jesus was talking about. 23One of the followers sitting[b] next to Jesus was the follower Jesus loved. 24Simon Peter motioned to him to ask Jesus whom he was talking about.

25That follower leaned closer to Jesus and asked, "Lord, who is it?"

13:18 [a] **'The man…me.'** Quotation from Psalm 41:9. 13:23 [b] **sitting** Literally, "lying." The people of that time ate lying down and leaning on one arm.

CONTEMPORARY ENGLISH VERSION

who I am. 14And if your Lord and teacher has washed
your feet, you should do the same for each other. 15I have
set the example, and you should do for each other exactly
what I have done for you. 16I tell you for certain that ser-
vants are not greater than their master, and messengers
are not greater than the one who sent them. 17You know
these things, and God will bless you, if you do them.
18I am not talking about all of you. I know the ones I
have chosen. But what the Scriptures say must come
true. And they say, "The man who ate with me has
turned against me!" 19I am telling you this before it all
happens. Then when it does happen, you will believe
who I am.[c] 20I tell you for certain that anyone who wel-
comes my messengers also welcomes me, and anyone
who welcomes me welcomes the one who sent me.

Jesus Tells What Will Happen to Him

(Matthew 26.20-25; Mark 14.17-21; Luke 22.21-23)

21After Jesus had said these things, he was deeply troubled and told his disciples, "I tell you for certain that one of you will betray me." 22They were confused about what he meant. And they just stared at each other.

23Jesus' favorite disciple was sitting next to him at the meal, 24and Simon motioned for that disciple to find out which one Jesus meant. 25So the disciple leaned toward Jesus and asked, "Lord, which one of us are you talking about?"

[c] **13.19** *I am*: See the note at 8.24.

NEW INTERNATIONAL VERSION

14 Now that I, your Lord and Teacher, have washed your
feet, you also should wash one another's feet. 15 I have set
you an example that you should do as I have done for you.
16 I tell you the truth, no servant is greater than his master,
nor is a messenger greater than the one who sent him.
17 Now that you know these things, you will be blessed if
you do them.

Jesus Predicts His Betrayal

18 "I am not referring to all of you; I know those I have
chosen. But this is to fulfill the scripture: 'He who shares
my bread has lifted up his heel against me.'[b]
19 "I am telling you now before it happens, so that when
it does happen you will believe that I am He. 20 I tell you
the truth, whoever accepts anyone I send accepts me; and
whoever accepts me accepts the one who sent me."
21 After he had said this, Jesus was troubled in spirit and
testified, "I tell you the truth, one of you is going to
betray me."
22 His disciples stared at one another, at a loss to know
which of them he meant. 23 One of them, the disciple whom
Jesus loved, was reclining next to him. 24 Simon Peter
motioned to this disciple and said, "Ask him which one he
means."
25 Leaning back against Jesus, he asked him, "Lord, who
is it?"

[b] *18* Psalm 41:9

NEW LIVING TRANSLATION

because it is true. 14 And since I, the Lord and Teacher, have
washed your feet, you ought to wash each other's feet. 15 I
have given you an example to follow. Do as I have done to
you. 16 How true it is that a servant is not greater than the
master. Nor are messengers more important than the one
who sends them. 17 You know these things—now do them!
That is the path of blessing.

Jesus Predicts His Betrayal

18 "I am not saying these things to all of you; I know so
well each one of you I chose. The Scriptures declare, 'The
one who shares my food has turned against me,'* and this
will soon come true. 19 I tell you this now, so that when it
happens you will believe I am the Messiah. 20 Truly, any-
one who welcomes my messenger is welcoming me, and
anyone who welcomes me is welcoming the Father who
sent me."
21 Now Jesus was in great anguish of spirit, and he
exclaimed, "The truth is, one of you will betray me!"
22 The disciples looked at each other, wondering whom
he could mean. 23 One of Jesus' disciples, the one Jesus
loved, was sitting next to Jesus at the table.* 24 Simon Peter
motioned to him to ask who would do this terrible thing.
25 Leaning toward Jesus, he asked, "Lord, who is it?"

13:18 Ps 41:9. 13:23 Greek *was reclining on Jesus' bosom.* The "disciple whom Jesus loved" was probably John.

NEW KING JAMES VERSION

and Teacher, have washed your feet, you also ought to
wash one another's feet. 15 For I have given you an exam-
ple, that you should do as I have done to you. 16 Most
assuredly, I say to you, a servant is not greater than his
master; nor is he who is sent greater than he who sent
him. 17 If you know these things, blessed are you if you do
them.

Jesus Identifies His Betrayer

18 "I do not speak concerning all of you. I know whom I
have chosen; but that the Scripture may be fulfilled, *'He
who eats bread with Me*[b] *has lifted up his heel against
Me.'*[c] 19 Now I tell you before it comes, that when it does
come to pass, you may believe that I am *He.* 20 Most
assuredly, I say to you, he who receives whomever I send
receives Me; and he who receives Me receives Him who
sent Me."
21 When Jesus had said these things, He was troubled in
spirit, and testified and said, "Most assuredly, I say to you,
one of you will betray Me." 22 Then the disciples looked at
one another, perplexed about whom He spoke.
23 Now there was leaning on Jesus' bosom one of His dis-
ciples, whom Jesus loved. 24 Simon Peter therefore
motioned to him to ask who it was of whom He spoke.
25 Then, leaning back[d] on Jesus' breast, he said to Him,
"Lord, who is it?"

13:18 [b] NU-Text reads *My bread.* [c] Psalm 41:9 13:25 [d] NU-Text and M-Text add *thus.*

THE MESSAGE

so. That is what I am. So if I, the Master and Teacher, washed your feet, you must now wash each other's feet. I've laid down a pattern for you. What I've done, you do. I'm only pointing out the obvious. A servant is not ranked above his master; an employee doesn't give orders to the employer. If you understand what I'm telling you, act like it—and live a blessed life.

The One Who Ate Bread at My Table

"I'm not including all of you in this. I know precisely whom I've selected, so as not to interfere with the fulfillment of this Scripture:

'The one who ate bread at my table
Turned on his heel against me.'

I'm telling you all this ahead of time so that when it happens you will believe that I am who I say I am. Make sure you get this right: Receiving someone I send is the same as receiving me, just as receiving me is the same as receiving the One who sent me."

After he said these things, Jesus became visibly upset, and then he told them why. "One of you is going to betray me."

The disciples looked around at one another, wondering who on earth he was talking about. One of the disciples, the one Jesus loved dearly, was reclining against him, his head on his shoulder. Peter motioned to him to ask who Jesus might be talking about. So, being the closest, he said, "Master, who?"

KING JAMES VERSION

26 Jesus answered, He it is, to whom I shall give a sop, when I have dipped *it*. And when he had dipped the sop, he gave *it* to Judas Iscariot, *the son* of Simon.

27 And after the sop Satan entered into him. Then said Jesus unto him, That thou doest, do quickly.

28 Now no man at the table knew for what intent he spake this unto him.

29 For some *of them* thought, because Judas had the bag, that Jesus had said unto him, Buy *those things* that we have need of against the feast; or, that he should give something to the poor.

30 He then having received the sop went immediately out: and it was night.

31 ¶ Therefore, when he was gone out, Jesus said, Now is the Son of man glorified, and God is glorified in him.

32 If God be glorified in him, God shall also glorify him in himself, and shall straightway glorify him.

33 Little children, yet a little while I am with you. Ye shall seek me: and as I said unto the Jews, Whither I go, ye cannot come; so now I say to you.

34 A new commandment I give unto you, That ye love one another; as I have loved you, that ye also love one another.

35 By this shall all *men* know that ye are my disciples, if ye have love one to another.

NEW AMERICAN STANDARD BIBLE

26 Jesus then *answered, "That is the one for whom I shall dip the morsel and give it to him." So when He had dipped the morsel, He *took and *gave it to Judas, *the son* of Simon Iscariot.

27 After the morsel, Satan then entered into him. Therefore Jesus *said to him, "What you do, do quickly."

28 Now no one of those reclining *at the table* knew for what purpose He had said this to him.

29 For some were supposing, because Judas had the money box, that Jesus was saying to him, "Buy the things we have need of for the feast"; or else, that he should give something to the poor.

30 So after receiving the morsel he went out immediately; and it was night.

31 Therefore when he had gone out, Jesus *said, "Now is the Son of Man glorified, and God is glorified in Him;

32 if God is glorified in Him, God will also glorify Him in Himself, and will glorify Him immediately.

33 "Little children, I am with you a little while longer. You will seek Me; and as I said to the Jews, now I also say to you, 'Where I am going, you cannot come.'

34 "A new commandment I give to you, that you love one another, even as I have loved you, that you also love one another.

35 "By this all men will know that you are My disciples, if you have love for one another."

NEW CENTURY VERSION

26Jesus answered, "I will dip this bread into the dish.
The man I give it to is the man who will turn against me."
So Jesus took a piece of bread, dipped it, and gave it to
Judas Iscariot, the son of Simon. 27As soon as Judas took
the bread, Satan entered him. Jesus said to him, "The
thing that you will do—do it quickly." 28No one at the
table understood why Jesus said this to Judas. 29Since he
was the one who kept the money box, some of the follow-
ers thought Jesus was telling him to buy what was needed
for the feast or to give something to the poor.
30Judas took the bread Jesus gave him and immediately
went out. It was night.
31When Judas was gone, Jesus said, "Now the Son of
Man receives his glory, and God receives glory through
him. 32If God receives glory through him, then God will
give glory to the Son through himself. And God will give
him glory quickly."
33Jesus said, "My children, I will be with you only a little
longer. You will look for me, and what I told the Jews, I tell
you now: Where I am going you cannot come.
34"I give you a new command: Love each other. You
must love each other as I have loved you. 35All people will
know that you are my followers if you love each other."

CONTEMPORARY ENGLISH VERSION

26Jesus answered, "I will dip this piece of bread in the
sauce and give it to the one I was talking about."
Then Jesus dipped the bread and gave it to Judas, the
son of Simon Iscariot.[d] 27Right then Satan took control of
Judas.
Jesus said, "Judas, go quickly and do what you have to
do." 28No one at the meal understood what Jesus meant.
29But because Judas was in charge of the money, some of
them thought that Jesus had told him to buy something
they needed for the festival. Others thought that Jesus had
told him to give some money to the poor. 30Judas took the
piece of bread and went out.
It was already night.

The New Command

31After Judas had gone, Jesus said:
Now the Son of Man will be given glory, and he will
bring glory to God. 32Then, after God is given glory
because of him, God will bring glory to him, and God
will do it very soon.
33My children, I will be with you for a little while
longer. Then you will look for me, but you won't find
me. I tell you just as I told the people, "You cannot go
where I am going." 34But I am giving you a new com-
mand. You must love each other, just as I have loved
you. 35If you love each other, everyone will know that
you are my disciples.

[d] **13.26** *Iscariot*: See the note at 6.71.

NEW INTERNATIONAL VERSION

26Jesus answered, "It is the one to whom I will give this piece of bread when I have dipped it in the dish." Then, dipping the piece of bread, he gave it to Judas Iscariot, son of Simon. 27As soon as Judas took the bread, Satan entered into him.

"What you are about to do, do quickly," Jesus told him, 28but no one at the meal understood why Jesus said this to him. 29Since Judas had charge of the money, some thought Jesus was telling him to buy what was needed for the Feast, or to give something to the poor. 30As soon as Judas had taken the bread, he went out. And it was night.

Jesus Predicts Peter's Denial

31When he was gone, Jesus said, "Now is the Son of Man glorified and God is glorified in him. 32If God is glorified in him,[c] God will glorify the Son in himself, and will glorify him at once.

33"My children, I will be with you only a little longer. You will look for me, and just as I told the Jews, so I tell you now: Where I am going, you cannot come.

34"A new command I give you: Love one another. As I have loved you, so you must love one another. 35By this all men will know that you are my disciples, if you love one another."

[c] *32* Many early manuscripts do not have *If God is glorified in him.*

NEW LIVING TRANSLATION

26Jesus said, "It is the one to whom I give the bread dipped in the sauce." And when he had dipped it, he gave it to Judas, son of Simon Iscariot. 27As soon as Judas had eaten the bread, Satan entered into him. Then Jesus told him, "Hurry. Do it now." 28None of the others at the table knew what Jesus meant. 29Since Judas was their treasurer, some thought Jesus was telling him to go and pay for the food or to give some money to the poor. 30So Judas left at once, going out into the night.

Jesus Predicts Peter's Denial

31As soon as Judas left the room, Jesus said, "The time has come for me, the Son of Man, to enter into my glory, and God will receive glory because of all that happens to me. 32And God will bring* me into my glory very soon. 33Dear children, how brief are these moments before I must go away and leave you! Then, though you search for me, you cannot come to me—just as I told the Jewish leaders. 34So now I am giving you a new commandment: Love each other. Just as I have loved you, you should love each other. 35Your love for one another will prove to the world that you are my disciples."

13:32 Some manuscripts read *And if God is glorified in him [the Son of Man], God will bring.*

NEW KING JAMES VERSION

26Jesus answered, "It is he to whom I shall give a piece of bread when I have dipped *it.*" And having dipped the bread, He gave *it* to Judas Iscariot, *the son* of Simon. 27Now after the piece of bread, Satan entered him. Then Jesus said to him, "What you do, do quickly." 28But no one at the table knew for what reason He said this to him. 29For some thought, because Judas had the money box, that Jesus had said to him, "Buy *those things* we need for the feast," or that he should give something to the poor.

30Having received the piece of bread, he then went out immediately. And it was night.

The New Commandment

31So, when he had gone out, Jesus said, "Now the Son of Man is glorified, and God is glorified in Him. 32If God is glorified in Him, God will also glorify Him in Himself, and glorify Him immediately. 33Little children, I shall be with you a little while longer. You will seek Me; and as I said to the Jews, 'Where I am going, you cannot come,' so now I say to you. 34A new commandment I give to you, that you love one another; as I have loved you, that you also love one another. 35By this all will know that you are My disciples, if you have love for one another."

THE MESSAGE

Jesus said, "The one to whom I give this crust of bread after I've dipped it." Then he dipped the crust and gave it to Judas, son of Simon the Iscariot. As soon as the bread was in his hand, Satan entered him.

"What you must do," said Jesus, "do. Do it and get it over with."

No one around the supper table knew why he said this to him. Some thought that since Judas was their treasurer, Jesus was telling him to buy what they needed for the Feast, or that he should give something to the poor.

Judas, with the piece of bread, left. It was night.

A New Command

When he had left, Jesus said, "Now the Son of Man is seen for who he is, and God seen for who he is in him. The moment God is seen in him, God's glory will be on display. In glorifying him, he himself is glorified—glory all around!

"Children, I am with you for only a short time longer. You are going to look high and low for me. But just as I told the Jews, I'm telling you: 'Where I go, you are not able to come.'

"Let me give you a new command: Love one another. In the same way I loved you, you love one another. This is how everyone will recognize that you are my disciples—when they see the love you have for each other."

KING JAMES VERSION

36 ¶ Simon Peter said unto him, Lord, whither goest thou? Jesus answered him, Whither I go, thou canst not follow me now; but thou shalt follow me afterwards.

37 Peter said unto him, Lord, why cannot I follow thee now? I will lay down my life for thy sake.

38 Jesus answered him, Wilt thou lay down thy life for my sake? Verily, verily, I say unto thee, The cock shall not crow, till thou hast denied me thrice.

14 Let not your heart be troubled: ye believe in God, believe also in me.

2 In my Father's house are many mansions: if *it were* not *so*, I would have told you. I go to prepare a place for you.

3 And if I go and prepare a place for you, I will come again, and receive you unto myself; that where I am, *there* ye may be also.

4 ¶ And whither I go ye know, and the way ye know.

5 Thomas saith unto him, Lord, we know not whither thou goest; and how can we know the way?

6 Jesus saith unto him, I am the way, the truth, and the life: no man cometh unto the Father, but by me.

7 If ye had known me, ye should have known my Father also: and from henceforth ye know him, and have seen him.

NEW AMERICAN STANDARD BIBLE

36 Simon Peter *said to Him, "Lord, where are You going?" Jesus answered, "Where I go, you cannot follow Me now; but you will follow later."

37 Peter *said to Him, "Lord, why can I not follow You right now? I will lay down my life for You."

38 Jesus *answered, "Will you lay down your life for Me? Truly, truly, I say to you, a rooster will not crow until you deny Me three times.

Jesus Comforts His Disciples

14 "Do not let your heart be troubled; [1]believe in God, believe also in Me.

2 "In My Father's house are many dwelling places; if it were not so, I would have told you; for I go to prepare a place for you.

3 "If I go and prepare a place for you, I will come again and receive you to Myself, that where I am, *there* you may be also.

4 "And you know the way where I am going."

5 Thomas *said to Him, "Lord, we do not know where You are going, how do we know the way?"

6 Jesus *said to him, "I am the way, and the truth, and the life; no one comes to the Father but through Me.

Oneness with the Father

7 "If you had known Me, you would have known My Father also; from now on you know Him, and have seen Him."

14:1 [1] Or *you believe in God*

NEW CENTURY VERSION

Peter Will Say He Doesn't Know Jesus

36 Simon Peter asked Jesus, "Lord, where are you going?" Jesus answered, "Where I am going you cannot follow now, but you will follow later."

37 Peter asked, "Lord, why can't I follow you now? I am ready to die for you!"

38 Jesus answered, "Are you ready to die for me? I tell you the truth, before the rooster crows, you will say three times that you don't know me."

Jesus Comforts His Followers

14 Jesus said, "Don't let your hearts be troubled. Trust in God, and trust in me. 2 There are many rooms in my Father's house; I would not tell you this if it were not true. I am going there to prepare a place for you. 3 After I go and prepare a place for you, I will come back and take you to be with me so that you may be where I am. 4 You know the way to the place where I am going."

5 Thomas said to Jesus, "Lord, we don't know where you are going. So how can we know the way?"

6 Jesus answered, "I am the way, and the truth, and the life. The only way to the Father is through me. 7 If you really knew me, you would know my Father, too. But now you do know him, and you have seen him."

CONTEMPORARY ENGLISH VERSION

Peter's Promise

(Matthew 26.31-35; Mark 14.27-31; Luke 22.31-34)

36 Simon Peter asked, "Lord, where are you going?" Jesus answered, "You can't go with me now, but later on you will."

37 Peter asked, "Lord, why can't I go with you now? I would die for you!"

38 "Would you really die for me?" Jesus asked. "I tell you for certain that before a rooster crows, you will say three times that you don't even know me."

Jesus Is the Way to the Father

14 Jesus said to his disciples, "Don't be worried! Have faith in God and have faith in me.[a] 2 There are many rooms in my Father's house. I wouldn't tell you this, unless it was true. I am going there to prepare a place for each of you. 3 After I have done this, I will come back and take you with me. Then we will be together. 4 You know the way to where I am going."

5 Thomas said, "Lord, we don't even know where you are going! How can we know the way?"

6 "I am the way, the truth, and the life!" Jesus answered. "Without me, no one can go to the Father. 7 If you had known me, you would have known the Father. But from now on, you do know him, and you have seen him."

[a] 14.1 *Have faith in God and have faith in me*: Or "You have faith in God, so have faith in me."

NEW INTERNATIONAL VERSION

36 Simon Peter asked him, "Lord, where are you going?"

Jesus replied, "Where I am going, you cannot follow now, but you will follow later."

37 Peter asked, "Lord, why can't I follow you now? I will lay down my life for you."

38 Then Jesus answered, "Will you really lay down your life for me? I tell you the truth, before the rooster crows, you will disown me three times!

Jesus Comforts His Disciples

14 "Do not let your hearts be troubled. Trust in God[a]; trust also in me. 2 In my Father's house are many rooms; if it were not so, I would have told you. I am going there to prepare a place for you. 3 And if I go and prepare a place for you, I will come back and take you to be with me that you also may be where I am. 4 You know the way to the place where I am going."

Jesus the Way to the Father

5 Thomas said to him, "Lord, we don't know where you are going, so how can we know the way?"

6 Jesus answered, "I am the way and the truth and the life. No one comes to the Father except through me. 7 If you really knew me, you would know[b] my Father as well. From now on, you do know him and have seen him."

[a] *1* Or *You trust in God* [b] *7* Some early manuscripts *If you really have known me, you will know*

NEW LIVING TRANSLATION

36 Simon Peter said, "Lord, where are you going?"

And Jesus replied, "You can't go with me now, but you will follow me later."

37 "But why can't I come now, Lord?" he asked. "I am ready to die for you."

38 Jesus answered, "Die for me? No, before the rooster crows tomorrow morning, you will deny three times that you even know me.

Jesus, the Way to the Father

14 "Don't be troubled. You trust God, now trust in me. 2 There are many rooms in my Father's home, and I am going to prepare a place for you. If this were not so, I would tell you plainly. 3 When everything is ready, I will come and get you, so that you will always be with me where I am. 4 And you know where I am going and how to get there."

5 "No, we don't know, Lord," Thomas said. "We haven't any idea where you are going, so how can we know the way?"

6 Jesus told him, "I am the way, the truth, and the life. No one can come to the Father except through me. 7 If you had known who I am, then you would have known who my Father is.* From now on you know him and have seen him!"

14:7 Some manuscripts read *If you really have known me, you will know who my Father is.*

NEW KING JAMES VERSION

Jesus Predicts Peter's Denial

36 Simon Peter said to Him, "Lord, where are You going?"

Jesus answered him, "Where I am going you cannot follow Me now, but you shall follow Me afterward."

37 Peter said to Him, "Lord, why can I not follow You now? I will lay down my life for Your sake."

38 Jesus answered him, "Will you lay down your life for My sake? Most assuredly, I say to you, the rooster shall not crow till you have denied Me three times.

The Way, the Truth, and the Life

14 "Let not your heart be troubled; you believe in God, believe also in Me. 2 In My Father's house are many mansions;[a] if *it were* not *so,* I would have told you. I go to prepare a place for you.[b] 3 And if I go and prepare a place for you, I will come again and receive you to Myself; that where I am, *there* you may be also. 4 And where I go you know, and the way you know."

5 Thomas said to Him, "Lord, we do not know where You are going, and how can we know the way?"

6 Jesus said to him, "I am the way, the truth, and the life. No one comes to the Father except through Me.

The Father Revealed

7 "If you had known Me, you would have known My Father also; and from now on you know Him and have seen Him."

14:2 [a] Literally *dwellings* [b] NU-Text adds a word which would cause the text to read either *if it were not so, would I have told you that I go to prepare a place for you?* or *if it were not so I would have told you; for I go to prepare a place for you.*

THE MESSAGE

Simon Peter asked, "Master, just where are you going?"

Jesus answered, "You can't now follow me where I'm going. You will follow later."

"Master," said Peter, "why can't I follow now? I'll lay down my life for you!"

"Really? You'll lay down your life for me? The truth is that before the rooster crows, you'll deny me three times."

The Road

14 "Don't let this throw you. You trust God, don't you? Trust me. There is plenty of room for you in my Father's home. If that weren't so, would I have told you that I'm on my way to get a room ready for you? And if I'm on my way to get your room ready, I'll come back and get you so you can live where I live. And you already know the road I'm taking."

Thomas said, "Master, we have no idea where you're going. How do you expect us to know the road?"

Jesus said, "I am the Road, also the Truth, also the Life. No one gets to the Father apart from me. If you really knew me, you would know my Father as well. From now on, you do know him. You've even seen him!"

KING JAMES VERSION

8 Philip saith unto him, Lord, shew us the Father, and it sufficeth us.

9 Jesus saith unto him, Have I been so long time with you, and yet hast thou not known me, Philip? he that hath seen me hath seen the Father; and how sayest thou *then*, Shew us the Father?

10 Believest thou not that I am in the Father, and the Father in me? the words that I speak unto you I speak not of myself: but the Father that dwelleth in me, he doeth the works.

11 Believe me that I *am* in the Father, and the Father in me: or else believe me for the very works' sake.

12 ¶ Verily, verily, I say unto you, He that believeth on me, the works that I do shall he do also; and greater *works* than these shall he do; because I go unto my Father.

13 And whatsoever ye shall ask in my name, that will I do, that the Father may be glorified in the Son.

14 If ye shall ask any thing in my name, I will do *it*.

15 ¶ If ye love me, keep my commandments.

16 And I will pray the Father, and he shall give you another Comforter, that he may abide with you for ever;

17 *Even* the Spirit of truth; whom the world cannot receive, because it seeth him not, neither knoweth him: but ye know him; for he dwelleth with you, and shall be in you.

NEW AMERICAN STANDARD BIBLE

8 Philip *said to Him, "Lord, show us the Father, and it is enough for us."

9 Jesus *said to him, "Have I been so long with you, and *yet* you have not come to know Me, Philip? He who has seen Me has seen the Father; how *can* you say, 'Show us the Father'?

10 "Do you not believe that I am in the Father, and the Father is in Me? The words that I say to you I do not speak on My own initiative, but the Father abiding in Me does His works.

11 "Believe Me that I am in the Father and the Father is in Me; otherwise believe because of the works themselves.

12 "Truly, truly, I say to you, he who believes in Me, the works that I do, he will do also; and greater *works* than these he will do; because I go to the Father.

13 "Whatever you ask in My name, that will I do, so that the Father may be glorified in the Son.

14 "If you ask Me anything in My name, I will do *it*.

15 "If you love Me, you will keep My commandments.

Role of the Spirit

16 "I will ask the Father, and He will give you another Helper, that He may be with you forever;

17 *that is* the Spirit of truth, whom the world cannot receive, because it does not see Him or know Him, *but* you know Him because He abides with you and will be in you.

NEW CENTURY VERSION

8Philip said to him, "Lord, show us the Father. That is all we need."

9Jesus answered, "I have been with you a long time now. Do you still not know me, Philip? Whoever has seen me has seen the Father. So why do you say, 'Show us the Father'? 10Don't you believe that I am in the Father and the Father is in me? The words I say to you don't come from me, but the Father lives in me and does his own work. 11Believe me when I say that I am in the Father and the Father is in me. Or believe because of the miracles I have done. 12I tell you the truth, whoever believes in me will do the same things that I do. Those who believe will do even greater things than these, because I am going to the Father. 13And if you ask for anything in my name, I will do it for you so that the Father's glory will be shown through the Son. 14If you ask me for anything in my name, I will do it.

The Promise of the Holy Spirit

15"If you love me, you will obey my commands. 16I will ask the Father, and he will give you another Helper[a] to be with you forever— 17the Spirit of truth. The world cannot accept him, because it does not see him or know him. But you know him, because he lives with you and he will be in you.

14:16 [a] **Helper** "Counselor" or "Comforter." Jesus is talking about the Holy Spirit.

CONTEMPORARY ENGLISH VERSION

8Philip said, "Lord, show us the Father. That is all we need."

9Jesus replied:

Philip, I have been with you for a long time. Don't you know who I am? If you have seen me, you have seen the Father. How can you ask me to show you the Father? 10Don't you believe that I am one with the Father and that the Father is one with me? What I say isn't said on my own. The Father who lives in me does these things.

11Have faith in me when I say that the Father is one with me and that I am one with the Father. Or else have faith in me simply because of the things I do. 12I tell you for certain that if you have faith in me, you will do the same things that I am doing. You will do even greater things, now that I am going back to the Father. 13Ask me, and I will do whatever you ask. This way the Son will bring honor to the Father. 14I will do whatever you ask me to do.

The Holy Spirit Is Promised

15Jesus said to his disciples:

If you love me, you will do as I command. 16Then I will ask the Father to send you the Holy Spirit who will help[b] you and always be with you. 17The Spirit will show you what is true. The people of this world cannot accept the Spirit, because they don't see or know him. But you know the Spirit, who is with you and will keep on living in you.

[b] 14.16 *help*: The Greek word may mean "comfort," "encourage," or "defend."

NEW INTERNATIONAL VERSION

8 Philip said, "Lord, show us the Father and that will be
enough for us."
9 Jesus answered: "Don't you know me, Philip, even after
I have been among you such a long time? Anyone who has
seen me has seen the Father. How can you say, 'Show us
the Father'? 10 Don't you believe that I am in the Father,
and that the Father is in me? The words I say to you are
not just my own. Rather, it is the Father, living in me, who
is doing his work. 11 Believe me when I say that I am in the
Father and the Father is in me; or at least believe on the
evidence of the miracles themselves. 12 I tell you the truth,
anyone who has faith in me will do what I have been
doing. He will do even greater things than these, because I
am going to the Father. 13 And I will do whatever you ask
in my name, so that the Son may bring glory to the Father.
14 You may ask me for anything in my name, and I will
do it.

Jesus Promises the Holy Spirit

15 "If you love me, you will obey what I command. 16 And I
will ask the Father, and he will give you another Counselor
to be with you forever— 17 the Spirit of truth. The world
cannot accept him, because it neither sees him nor knows
him. But you know him, for he lives with you and will be[c]

[c] *17* Some early manuscripts *and is*

NEW LIVING TRANSLATION

8 Philip said, "Lord, show us the Father and we will be
satisfied."
9 Jesus replied, "Philip, don't you even yet know who I am,
even after all the time I have been with you? Anyone who
has seen me has seen the Father! So why are you asking to
see him? 10 Don't you believe that I am in the Father and the
Father is in me? The words I say are not my own, but my
Father who lives in me does his work through me. 11 Just
believe that I am in the Father and the Father is in me. Or at
least believe because of what you have seen me do.
12 "The truth is, anyone who believes in me will do the
same works I have done, and even greater works, because I
am going to be with the Father. 13 You can ask for anything
in my name, and I will do it, because the work of the Son
brings glory to the Father. 14 Yes, ask anything in my
name, and I will do it!

Jesus Promises the Holy Spirit

15 "If you love me, obey my commandments. 16 And I will
ask the Father, and he will give you another Counselor,*
who will never leave you. 17 He is the Holy Spirit, who leads
into all truth. The world at large cannot receive him,
because it isn't looking for him and doesn't recognize him.
But you do, because he lives with you now and later will be

14:16 Or *Comforter,* or *Encourager,* or *Advocate.* Greek *Paraclete;* also in 14:26.

NEW KING JAMES VERSION

8 Philip said to Him, "Lord, show us the Father, and it is
sufficient for us."
9 Jesus said to him, "Have I been with you so long, and
yet you have not known Me, Philip? He who has seen Me
has seen the Father; so how can you say, 'Show us the
Father'? 10 Do you not believe that I am in the Father, and
the Father in Me? The words that I speak to you I do not
speak on My own *authority;* but the Father who dwells in
Me does the works. 11 Believe Me that I *am* in the Father
and the Father in Me, or else believe Me for the sake of the
works themselves.

The Answered Prayer

12 "Most assuredly, I say to you, he who believes in Me,
the works that I do he will do also; and greater *works* than
these he will do, because I go to My Father. 13 And whatev-
er you ask in My name, that I will do, that the Father may
be glorified in the Son. 14 If you ask[c] anything in My name,
I will do *it.*

Jesus Promises Another Helper

15 "If you love Me, keep[d] My commandments. 16 And I will
pray the Father, and He will give you another Helper, that
He may abide with you forever— 17 the Spirit of truth,
whom the world cannot receive, because it neither sees Him
nor knows Him; but you know Him, for He dwells with you

14:14 [c] NU-Text adds *Me.* 14:15 [d] NU-Text reads *you will keep.*

THE MESSAGE

Philip said, "Master, show us the Father; then we'll be content."

"You've been with me all this time, Philip, and you still don't understand? To see me is to see the Father. So how can you ask, 'Where is the Father?' Don't you believe that I am in the Father and the Father is in me? The words that I speak to you aren't mere words. I don't just make them up on my own. The Father who resides in me crafts each word into a divine act.

"Believe me: I am in my Father and my Father is in me. If you can't believe that, believe what you see—these works. The person who trusts me will not only do what I'm doing but even greater things, because I, on my way to the Father, am giving you the same work to do that I've been doing. You can count on it. From now on, whatever you request along the lines of who I am and what I am doing, I'll do it. That's how the Father will be seen for who he is in the Son. I mean it. Whatever you request in this way, I'll do.

The Spirit of Truth

"If you love me, show it by doing what I've told you. I will talk to the Father, and he'll provide you another Friend so that you will always have someone with you. This Friend is the Spirit of Truth. The godless world can't take him in because it doesn't have eyes to see him, doesn't know what to look for. But you know him already because he has been staying with you, and will even be *in* you!

KING JAMES VERSION

18 ¶ I will not leave you comfortless: I will come to you.
19 Yet a little while, and the world seeth me no more; but ye see me: because I live, ye shall live also.
20 At that day ye shall know that I *am* in my Father, and ye in me, and I in you.
21 He that hath my commandments, and keepeth them, he it is that loveth me: and he that loveth me shall be loved of my Father, and I will love him, and will manifest myself to him.
22 Judas saith unto him, not Iscariot, Lord, how is it that thou wilt manifest thyself unto us, and not unto the world?
23 Jesus answered and said unto him, If a man love me, he will keep my words: and my Father will love him, and we will come unto him, and make our abode with him.
24 He that loveth me not keepeth not my sayings: and the word which ye hear is not mine, but the Father's which sent me.
25 ¶ These things have I spoken unto you, being *yet* present with you.
26 But the Comforter, *which is* the Holy Ghost, whom the Father will send in my name, he shall teach you all things, and bring all things to your remembrance, whatsoever I have said unto you.
27 Peace I leave with you, my peace I give unto you: not as the world giveth, give I unto you. Let not your heart be troubled, neither let it be afraid.
28 ¶ Ye have heard how I said unto you, I go away, and

NEW AMERICAN STANDARD BIBLE

18 "I will not leave you as orphans; I will come to you.
19 "After a little while the world will no longer see Me, but you *will* see Me; because I live, you will live also.
20 "In that day you will know that I am in My Father, and you in Me, and I in you.
21 "He who has My commandments and keeps them is the one who loves Me; and he who loves Me will be loved by My Father, and I will love him and will disclose Myself to him."
22 Judas (not Iscariot) *said to Him, "Lord, what then has happened that You are going to disclose Yourself to us and not to the world?"
23 Jesus answered and said to him, "If anyone loves Me, he will keep My word; and My Father will love him, and We will come to him and make Our abode with him.
24 "He who does not love Me does not keep My words; and the word which you hear is not Mine, but the Father's who sent Me.
25 "These things I have spoken to you while abiding with you.
26 "But the Helper, the Holy Spirit, whom the Father will send in My name, He will teach you all things, and bring to your remembrance all that I said to you.
27 "Peace I leave with you; My peace I give to you; not as the world gives do I give to you. Do not let your heart be troubled, nor let it be fearful.
28 "You heard that I said to you, 'I go away, and I will

NEW CENTURY VERSION

18"I will not leave you all alone like orphans; I will come
back to you. 19In a little while the world will not see me
anymore, but you will see me. Because I live, you will live,
too. 20On that day you will know that I am in my Father,
and that you are in me and I am in you. 21Those who know
my commands and obey them are the ones who love me,
and my Father will love those who love me. I will love
them and will show myself to them."
22Then Judas (not Judas Iscariot) said, "But, Lord, why
do you plan to show yourself to us and not to the rest of
the world?"
23Jesus answered, "If people love me, they will obey my
teaching. My Father will love them, and we will come to
them and make our home with them. 24Those who do not
love me do not obey my teaching. This teaching that you
hear is not really mine; it is from my Father, who sent me.
25"I have told you all these things while I am with you.
26But the Helper will teach you everything and will cause
you to remember all that I told you. This Helper is the Holy
Spirit whom the Father will send in my name.
27"I leave you peace; my peace I give you. I do not give it
to you as the world does. So don't let your hearts be trou-
bled or afraid. 28You heard me say to you, 'I am going, but

CONTEMPORARY ENGLISH VERSION

18I won't leave you like orphans. I will come back to
you. 19In a little while the people of this world won't be
able to see me, but you will see me. And because I live,
you will live. 20Then you will know that I am one with
the Father. You will know that you are one with me, and
I am one with you. 21If you love me, you will do what I
have said, and my Father will love you. I will also love
you and show you what I am like.
22The other Judas, not Judas Iscariot,[c] then spoke up
and asked, "Lord, what do you mean by saying that you
will show us what you are like, but you will not show the
people of this world?"
23Jesus replied:
If anyone loves me, they will obey me. Then my Father
will love them, and we will come to them and live in
them. 24But anyone who doesn't love me, won't obey
me. What they have heard me say doesn't really come
from me, but from the Father who sent me.
25I have told you these things while I am still with
you. 26But the Holy Spirit will come and help[d] you,
because the Father will send the Spirit to take my place.
The Spirit will teach you everything and will remind you
of what I said while I was with you.
27I give you peace, the kind of peace that only I can
give. It isn't like the peace that this world can give. So
don't be worried or afraid.
28You have already heard me say that I am going and

c 14.22 *Iscariot*: See the note at 6.71. d 14.26 *help*: See the note at 14.16.

NEW INTERNATIONAL VERSION

in you. 18I will not leave you as orphans; I will come to you. 19Before long, the world will not see me anymore, but you will see me. Because I live, you also will live. 20On that day you will realize that I am in my Father, and you are in me, and I am in you. 21Whoever has my commands and obeys them, he is the one who loves me. He who loves me will be loved by my Father, and I too will love him and show myself to him."

22Then Judas (not Judas Iscariot) said, "But, Lord, why do you intend to show yourself to us and not to the world?"

23Jesus replied, "If anyone loves me, he will obey my teaching. My Father will love him, and we will come to him and make our home with him. 24He who does not love me will not obey my teaching. These words you hear are not my own; they belong to the Father who sent me.

25"All this I have spoken while still with you. 26But the Counselor, the Holy Spirit, whom the Father will send in my name, will teach you all things and will remind you of everything I have said to you. 27Peace I leave with you; my peace I give you. I do not give to you as the world gives. Do not let your hearts be troubled and do not be afraid.

28"You heard me say, 'I am going away and I am coming

NEW LIVING TRANSLATION

in you. 18No, I will not abandon you as orphans—I will come to you. 19In just a little while the world will not see me again, but you will. For I will live again, and you will, too. 20When I am raised to life again, you will know that I am in my Father, and you are in me, and I am in you. 21Those who obey my commandments are the ones who love me. And because they love me, my Father will love them, and I will love them. And I will reveal myself to each one of them."

22Judas (not Judas Iscariot, but the other disciple with that name) said to him, "Lord, why are you going to reveal yourself only to us and not to the world at large?"

23Jesus replied, "All those who love me will do what I say. My Father will love them, and we will come to them and live with them. 24Anyone who doesn't love me will not do what I say. And remember, my words are not my own. This message is from the Father who sent me. 25I am telling you these things now while I am still with you. 26But when the Father sends the Counselor as my representative—and by the Counselor I mean the Holy Spirit—he will teach you everything and will remind you of everything I myself have told you.

27"I am leaving you with a gift—peace of mind and heart. And the peace I give isn't like the peace the world gives. So don't be troubled or afraid. 28Remember what I told you: I am going away, but I will come back to you

NEW KING JAMES VERSION

and will be in you. 18I will not leave you orphans; I will come to you.

Indwelling of the Father and the Son

19"A little while longer and the world will see Me no more, but you will see Me. Because I live, you will live also. 20At that day you will know that I *am* in My Father, and you in Me, and I in you. 21He who has My commandments and keeps them, it is he who loves Me. And he who loves Me will be loved by My Father, and I will love him and manifest Myself to him."

22Judas (not Iscariot) said to Him, "Lord, how is it that You will manifest Yourself to us, and not to the world?"

23Jesus answered and said to him, "If anyone loves Me, he will keep My word; and My Father will love him, and We will come to him and make Our home with him. 24He who does not love Me does not keep My words; and the word which you hear is not Mine but the Father's who sent Me.

The Gift of His Peace

25"These things I have spoken to you while being present with you. 26But the Helper, the Holy Spirit, whom the Father will send in My name, He will teach you all things, and bring to your remembrance all things that I said to you. 27Peace I leave with you, My peace I give to you; not as the world gives do I give to you. Let not your heart be troubled, neither let it be afraid. 28You have heard Me say to you, 'I am going away and coming *back* to you.'

THE MESSAGE

"I will not leave you orphaned. I'm coming back. In just a little while the world will no longer see me, but you're going to see me because I am alive and you're about to come alive. At that moment you will know absolutely that I'm in my Father, and you're in me, and I'm in you.

"The person who knows my commandments and keeps them, that's who loves me. And the person who loves me will be loved by my Father, and I will love him and make myself plain to him."

Judas (not Iscariot) said, "Master, why is it that you are about to make yourself plain to us but not to the world?"

"Because a loveless world," said Jesus, "is a sightless world. If anyone loves me, he will carefully keep my word and my Father will love him—we'll move right into the neighborhood! Not loving me means not keeping my words. The message you are hearing isn't mine. It's the message of the Father who sent me.

"I'm telling you these things while I'm still living with you. The Friend, the Holy Spirit whom the Father will send at my request, will make everything plain to you. He will remind you of all the things I have told you. I'm leaving you well and whole. That's my parting gift to you. Peace. I don't leave you the way you're used to being left—feeling abandoned, bereft. So don't be upset. Don't be distraught.

"You've heard me tell you, 'I'm going away, and I'm

KING JAMES VERSION

come *again* unto you. If ye loved me, ye would rejoice, because I said, I go unto the Father: for my Father is greater than I.

29 And now I have told you before it come to pass, that, when it is come to pass, ye might believe.

30 Hereafter I will not talk much with you: for the prince of this world cometh, and hath nothing in me.

31 But that the world may know that I love the Father; and as the Father gave me commandment, even so I do. Arise, let us go hence.

15 I am the true vine, and my Father is the husbandman.

2 Every branch in me that beareth not fruit he taketh away: and every *branch* that beareth fruit, he purgeth it, that it may bring forth more fruit.

3 Now ye are clean through the word which I have spoken unto you.

4 Abide in me, and I in you. As the branch cannot bear fruit of itself, except it abide in the vine; no more can ye, except ye abide in me.

5 I am the vine, ye *are* the branches: He that abideth in me, and I in him, the same bringeth forth much fruit: for without me ye can do nothing.

6 If a man abide not in me, he is cast forth as a branch, and is withered; and men gather them, and cast *them* into the fire, and they are burned.

NEW AMERICAN STANDARD BIBLE

come to you.' If you loved Me, you would have rejoiced because I go to the Father, for the Father is greater than I.

29 "Now I have told you before it happens, so that when it happens, you may believe.

30 "I will not speak much more with you, for the ruler of the world is coming, and he has nothing in Me;

31 but so that the world may know that I love the Father, I do exactly as the Father commanded Me. Get up, let us go from here.

Jesus Is the Vine—Followers Are Branches

15 "I am the true vine, and My Father is the vinedresser.

2 "Every branch in Me that does not bear fruit, He takes away; and every *branch* that bears fruit, He [1]prunes it so that it may bear more fruit.

3 "You are already clean because of the word which I have spoken to you.

4 "Abide in Me, and I in you. As the branch cannot bear fruit of itself unless it abides in the vine, so neither *can* you unless you abide in Me.

5 "I am the vine, you are the branches; he who abides in Me and I in him, he bears much fruit, for apart from Me you can do nothing.

6 "If anyone does not abide in Me, he is thrown away as a branch and dries up; and they gather them, and cast them into the fire and they are burned.

15:2 [1] Lit *cleans;* used to describe pruning

NEW CENTURY VERSION

I am coming back to you.' If you loved me, you should be
happy that I am going back to the Father, because he is
greater than I am. 29I have told you this now, before it
happens, so that when it happens, you will believe. 30I will
not talk with you much longer, because the ruler of this
world is coming. He has no power over me, 31but the world
must know that I love the Father, so I do exactly what the
Father told me to do.

"Come now, let us go.

Jesus Is Like a Vine

15 "I am the true vine; my Father is the gardener. 2He
cuts off every branch of mine that does not pro-
duce fruit. And he trims and cleans every branch that pro-
duces fruit so that it will produce even more fruit. 3You are
already clean because of the words I have spoken to you.
4Remain in me, and I will remain in you. A branch cannot
produce fruit alone but must remain in the vine. In the
same way, you cannot produce fruit alone but must remain
in me.

5"I am the vine, and you are the branches. If any remain
in me and I remain in them, they produce much fruit. But
without me they can do nothing. 6If any do not remain in
me, they are like a branch that is thrown away and then
dies. People pick up dead branches, throw them into the

CONTEMPORARY ENGLISH VERSION

that I will also come back to you. If you really love me, you should be glad that I am going back to the Father, because he is greater than I am.

29I am telling you this before I leave, so that when it
does happen, you will have faith in me. 30I cannot speak
with you much longer, because the ruler of this world is
coming. But he has no power over me. 31I obey my
Father, so that everyone in the world might know that I
love him.

It is time for us to go now.

Jesus Is the True Vine

15 Jesus said to his disciples:

I am the true vine, and my Father is the gar-
dener. 2He cuts away every branch of mine that doesn't
produce fruit. But he trims clean every branch that does
produce fruit, so that it will produce even more fruit.
3You are already clean because of what I have said to
you.

4Stay joined to me, and I will stay joined to you. Just
as a branch cannot produce fruit unless it stays joined to
the vine, you cannot produce fruit unless you stay joined
to me. 5I am the vine, and you are the branches. If you
stay joined to me, and I stay joined to you, then you will
produce lots of fruit. But you cannot do anything with-
out me. 6If you don't stay joined to me, you will be
thrown away. You will be like dry branches that are
gathered up and burned in a fire.

NEW INTERNATIONAL VERSION

back to you.' If you loved me, you would be glad that I am
going to the Father, for the Father is greater than I. 29 I
have told you now before it happens, so that when it does
happen you will believe. 30 I will not speak with you much
longer, for the prince of this world is coming. He has no
hold on me, 31 but the world must learn that I love the
Father and that I do exactly what my Father has com-
manded me.

"Come now; let us leave.

The Vine and the Branches

15 "I am the true vine, and my Father is the gardener.
2 He cuts off every branch in me that bears no fruit,
while every branch that does bear fruit he prunes[a] so that
it will be even more fruitful. 3 You are already clean
because of the word I have spoken to you. 4 Remain in me,
and I will remain in you. No branch can bear fruit by itself;
it must remain in the vine. Neither can you bear fruit
unless you remain in me.

5 "I am the vine; you are the branches. If a man remains
in me and I in him, he will bear much fruit; apart from me
you can do nothing. 6 If anyone does not remain in me, he
is like a branch that is thrown away and withers; such
branches are picked up, thrown into the fire and burned.

[a] 2 The Greek for *prunes* also means *cleans*.

NEW LIVING TRANSLATION

again. If you really love me, you will be very happy for me,
because now I can go to the Father, who is greater than I
am. 29 I have told you these things before they happen so
that you will believe when they do happen.

30 "I don't have much more time to talk to you, because
the prince of this world approaches. He has no power over
me, 31 but I will do what the Father requires of me, so that
the world will know that I love the Father. Come, let's be
going.

Jesus, the True Vine

15 "I am the true vine, and my Father is the gardener.
2 He cuts off every branch that doesn't produce
fruit, and he prunes the branches that do bear fruit so they
will produce even more. 3 You have already been pruned for
greater fruitfulness by the message I have given you.
4 Remain in me, and I will remain in you. For a branch can-
not produce fruit if it is severed from the vine, and you
cannot be fruitful apart from me.

5 "Yes, I am the vine; you are the branches. Those who
remain in me, and I in them, will produce much fruit. For
apart from me you can do nothing. 6 Anyone who parts
from me is thrown away like a useless branch and withers.
Such branches are gathered into a pile to be burned. 7 But

NEW KING JAMES VERSION

If you loved Me, you would rejoice because I said,[e] 'I am
going to the Father,' for My Father is greater than I.

29 "And now I have told you before it comes, that when it
does come to pass, you may believe. 30 I will no longer talk
much with you, for the ruler of this world is coming, and
he has nothing in Me. 31 But that the world may know that
I love the Father, and as the Father gave Me command-
ment, so I do. Arise, let us go from here.

The True Vine

15 "I am the true vine, and My Father is the vine-
dresser. 2 Every branch in Me that does not bear
fruit He takes away;[a] and every *branch* that bears fruit He
prunes, that it may bear more fruit. 3 You are already clean
because of the word which I have spoken to you. 4 Abide in
Me, and I in you. As the branch cannot bear fruit of itself,
unless it abides in the vine, neither can you, unless you
abide in Me.

5 "I am the vine, you *are* the branches. He who abides in
Me, and I in him, bears much fruit; for without Me you can
do nothing. 6 If anyone does not abide in Me, he is cast out
as a branch and is withered; and they gather them and
throw *them* into the fire, and they are burned. 7 If you

14:28 [e] NU-Text omits *I said.* 15:2 [a] Or *lifts up*

THE MESSAGE

coming back.' If you loved me, you would be glad that I'm
on my way to the Father because the Father is the goal
and purpose of my life.

"I've told you this ahead of time, before it happens, so
that when it does happen, the confirmation will deepen
your belief in me. I'll not be talking with you much more
like this because the chief of this godless world is about to
attack. But don't worry—he has nothing on me, no claim
on me. But so the world might know how thoroughly I love
the Father, I am carrying out my Father's instructions right
down to the last detail.

"Get up. Let's go. It's time to leave here.

The Vine and the Branches

15 "I am the Real Vine and my Father is the Farmer.
He cuts off every branch of me that doesn't bear
grapes. And every branch that is grape-bearing he prunes
back so it will bear even more. You are already pruned
back by the message I have spoken.

"Live in me. Make your home in me just as I do in you.
In the same way that a branch can't bear grapes by itself
but only by being joined to the vine, you can't bear fruit
unless you are joined with me.

"I am the Vine, you are the branches. When you're
joined with me and I with you, the relation intimate and
organic, the harvest is sure to be abundant. Separated, you
can't produce a thing. Anyone who separates from me is
deadwood, gathered up and thrown on the bonfire. But if

KING JAMES VERSION

7 If ye abide in me, and my words abide in you, ye shall ask what ye will, and it shall be done unto you.

8 Herein is my Father glorified, that ye bear much fruit; so shall ye be my disciples.

9 ¶ As the Father hath loved me, so have I loved you: continue ye in my love.

10 If ye keep my commandments, ye shall abide in my love; even as I have kept my Father's commandments, and abide in his love.

11 These things have I spoken unto you, that my joy might remain in you, and *that* your joy might be full.

12 This is my commandment, That ye love one another, as I have loved you.

13 Greater love hath no man than this, that a man lay down his life for his friends.

14 Ye are my friends, if ye do whatsoever I command you.

15 Henceforth I call you not servants; for the servant knoweth not what his lord doeth: but I have called you friends; for all things that I have heard of my Father I have made known unto you.

16 Ye have not chosen me, but I have chosen you, and ordained you, that ye should go and bring forth fruit, and *that* your fruit should remain: that whatsoever ye shall ask of the Father in my name, he may give it you.

17 These things I command you, that ye love one another.

NEW AMERICAN STANDARD BIBLE

7 "If you abide in Me, and My words abide in you, ask whatever you wish, and it will be done for you.

8 "My Father is glorified by this, that you bear much fruit, and *so* prove to be My disciples.

9 "Just as the Father has loved Me, I have also loved you; abide in My love.

10 "If you keep My commandments, you will abide in My love; just as I have kept My Father's commandments and abide in His love.

11 "These things I have spoken to you so that My joy may be in you, and *that* your joy may be made full.

Disciples' Relation to Each Other

12 "This is My commandment, that you love one another, just as I have loved you.

13 "Greater love has no one than this, that one lay down his life for his friends.

14 "You are My friends if you do what I command you.

15 "No longer do I call you slaves, for the slave does not know what his master is doing; but I have called you friends, for all things that I have heard from My Father I have made known to you.

16 "You did not choose Me but I chose you, and appointed you that you would go and bear fruit, and *that* your fruit would remain, so that whatever you ask of the Father in My name He may give to you.

17 "This I command you, that you love one another.

NEW CENTURY VERSION

fire, and burn them. 7If you remain in me and follow my
teachings, you can ask anything you want, and it will be
given to you. 8You should produce much fruit and show
that you are my followers, which brings glory to my
Father. 9I loved you as the Father loved me. Now remain in
my love. 10I have obeyed my Father's commands, and I
remain in his love. In the same way, if you obey my commands, you will remain in my love. 11I have told you these
things so that you can have the same joy I have and so
that your joy will be the fullest possible joy.

12"This is my command: Love each other as I have loved
you. 13The greatest love a person can show is to die for his
friends. 14You are my friends if you do what I command
you. 15I no longer call you servants, because a servant
does not know what his master is doing. But I call you
friends, because I have made known to you everything I
heard from my Father. 16You did not choose me; I chose
you. And I gave you this work: to go and produce fruit,
fruit that will last. Then the Father will give you anything
you ask for in my name. 17This is my command: Love each
other.

CONTEMPORARY ENGLISH VERSION

7Stay joined to me and let my teachings become part
of you. Then you can pray for whatever you want, and
your prayer will be answered. 8When you become fruitful disciples of mine, my Father will be honored. 9I have
loved you, just as my Father has loved me. So remain
faithful to my love for you. 10If you obey me, I will keep
loving you, just as my Father keeps loving me, because I
have obeyed him.

11I have told you this to make you as completely
happy as I am. 12Now I tell you to love each other, as I
have loved you. 13The greatest way to show love for
friends is to die for them. 14And you are my friends, if
you obey me. 15Servants don't know what their master
is doing, and so I don't speak to you as my servants. I
speak to you as my friends, and I have told you everything that my Father has told me.

16You did not choose me. I chose you and sent you out
to produce fruit, the kind of fruit that will last. Then my
Father will give you whatever you ask for in my name.[a]
17So I command you to love each other.

[a] 15.16 *in my name*: Or "because you are my followers."

NEW INTERNATIONAL VERSION

7If you remain in me and my words remain in you, ask whatever you wish, and it will be given you. 8This is to my Father's glory, that you bear much fruit, showing yourselves to be my disciples.

9"As the Father has loved me, so have I loved you. Now remain in my love. 10If you obey my commands, you will remain in my love, just as I have obeyed my Father's commands and remain in his love. 11I have told you this so that my joy may be in you and that your joy may be complete. 12My command is this: Love each other as I have loved you. 13Greater love has no one than this, that he lay down his life for his friends. 14You are my friends if you do what I command. 15I no longer call you servants, because a servant does not know his master's business. Instead, I have called you friends, for everything that I learned from my Father I have made known to you. 16You did not choose me, but I chose you and appointed you to go and bear fruit—fruit that will last. Then the Father will give you whatever you ask in my name. 17This is my command: Love each other.

NEW LIVING TRANSLATION

if you stay joined to me and my words remain in you, you may ask any request you like, and it will be granted! 8My true disciples produce much fruit. This brings great glory to my Father.

9"I have loved you even as the Father has loved me. Remain in my love. 10When you obey me, you remain in my love, just as I obey my Father and remain in his love. 11I have told you this so that you will be filled with my joy. Yes, your joy will overflow! 12I command you to love each other in the same way that I love you. 13And here is how to measure it—the greatest love is shown when people lay down their lives for their friends. 14You are my friends if you obey me. 15I no longer call you servants, because a master doesn't confide in his servants. Now you are my friends, since I have told you everything the Father told me. 16You didn't choose me. I chose you. I appointed you to go and produce fruit that will last, so that the Father will give you whatever you ask for, using my name. 17I command you to love each other.

NEW KING JAMES VERSION

abide in Me, and My words abide in you, you will[b] ask what you desire, and it shall be done for you. 8By this My Father is glorified, that you bear much fruit; so you will be My disciples.

Love and Joy Perfected

9"As the Father loved Me, I also have loved you; abide in My love. 10If you keep My commandments, you will abide in My love, just as I have kept My Father's commandments and abide in His love.

11"These things I have spoken to you, that My joy may remain in you, and *that* your joy may be full. 12This is My commandment, that you love one another as I have loved you. 13Greater love has no one than this, than to lay down one's life for his friends. 14You are My friends if you do whatever I command you. 15No longer do I call you servants, for a servant does not know what his master is doing; but I have called you friends, for all things that I heard from My Father I have made known to you. 16You did not choose Me, but I chose you and appointed you that you should go and bear fruit, and *that* your fruit should remain, that whatever you ask the Father in My name He may give you. 17These things I command you, that you love one another.

15:7 [b] NU-Text omits *you will.*

THE MESSAGE

you make yourselves at home with me and my words are at home in you, you can be sure that whatever you ask will be listened to and acted upon. This is how my Father shows who he is—when you produce grapes, when you mature as my disciples.

"I've loved you the way my Father has loved me. Make yourselves at home in my love. If you keep my commands, you'll remain intimately at home in my love. That's what I've done—kept my Father's commands and made myself at home in his love.

"I've told you these things for a purpose: that my joy might be your joy, and your joy wholly mature. This is my command: Love one another the way I loved you. This is the very best way to love. Put your life on the line for your friends. You are my friends when you do the things I command you. I'm no longer calling you servants because servants don't understand what their master is thinking and planning. No, I've named you friends because I've let you in on everything I've heard from the Father.

"You didn't choose me, remember; I chose you, and put you in the world to bear fruit, fruit that won't spoil. As fruit bearers, whatever you ask the Father in relation to me, he gives you.

"But remember the root command: Love one another.

KING JAMES VERSION

18 ¶ If the world hate you, ye know that it hated me before *it hated* you.

19 If ye were of the world, the world would love his own: but because ye are not of the world, but I have chosen you out of the world, therefore the world hateth you.

20 Remember the word that I said unto you, The servant is not greater than his lord. If they have persecuted me, they will also persecute you; if they have kept my saying, they will keep yours also.

21 But all these things will they do unto you for my name's sake, because they know not him that sent me.

22 If I had not come and spoken unto them, they had not had sin: but now they have no cloke for their sin.

23 He that hateth me hateth my Father also.

24 If I had not done among them the works which none other man did, they had not had sin: but now have they both seen and hated both me and my Father.

25 But *this cometh to pass*, that the word might be fulfilled that is written in their law, They hated me without a cause.

26 ¶ But when the Comforter is come, whom I will send unto you from the Father, *even* the Spirit of truth, which proceedeth from the Father, he shall testify of me:

27 And ye also shall bear witness, because ye have been with me from the beginning.

16 These things have I spoken unto you, that ye should not be offended.

NEW AMERICAN STANDARD BIBLE

Disciples' Relation to the World

18 "If the world hates you, you know that it has hated Me before *it hated* you.

19 "If you were of the world, the world would love its own; but because you are not of the world, but I chose you out of the world, because of this the world hates you.

20 "Remember the word that I said to you, 'A slave is not greater than his master.' If they persecuted Me, they will also persecute you; if they kept My word, they will keep yours also.

21 "But all these things they will do to you for My name's sake, because they do not know the One who sent Me.

22 "If I had not come and spoken to them, they would not have sin, but now they have no excuse for their sin.

23 "He who hates Me hates My Father also.

24 "If I had not done among them the works which no one else did, they would not have sin; but now they have both seen and hated Me and My Father as well.

25 "But *they have done this* to fulfill the word that is written in their Law, 'THEY HATED ME WITHOUT A CAUSE.'

26 "When the Helper comes, whom I will send to you from the Father, *that is* the Spirit of truth who proceeds from the Father, He will testify about Me,

27 and you *will* testify also, because you have been with Me from the beginning.

Jesus' Warning

16 "These things I have spoken to you so that you may be kept from stumbling.

NEW CENTURY VERSION

Jesus Warns His Followers

18"If the world hates you, remember that it hated me
first. 19If you belonged to the world, it would love you as it
loves its own. But I have chosen you out of the world, so
you don't belong to it. That is why the world hates you.
20Remember what I told you: A servant is not greater than
his master. If people did wrong to me, they will do wrong
to you, too. And if they obeyed my teaching, they will obey
yours, too. 21They will do all this to you on account of me,
because they do not know the One who sent me. 22If I had
not come and spoken to them, they would not be guilty of
sin, but now they have no excuse for their sin. 23Whoever
hates me also hates my Father. 24I did works among them
that no one else has ever done. If I had not done these
works, they would not be guilty of sin. But now they have
seen what I have done, and yet they have hated both me
and my Father. 25But this happened so that what is written in their law would be true: 'They hated me for no reason.'[a]
26"I will send you the Helper[b] from the Father; he is the
Spirit of truth who comes from the Father. When he comes,
he will tell about me, 27and you also must tell people
about me, because you have been with me from the beginning.

16 "I have told you these things to keep you from
giving up. 2People will put you out of their syna-

15:25 [a] 'They...reason.' These words could be from Psalm 35:19 or Psalm 69:4. 15:26 [b] **Helper** "Counselor" or "Comforter." Jesus is talking about the Holy Spirit.

CONTEMPORARY ENGLISH VERSION

The World's Hatred

18If the people of this world[b] hate you, just remember
that they hated me first. 19If you belonged to the world,
its people would love you. But you don't belong to the
world. I have chosen you to leave the world behind, and
that is why its people hate you. 20Remember how I told
you that servants are not greater than their master. So if
people mistreat me, they will mistreat you. If they do
what I say, they will do what you say.
21People will do to you exactly what they did to me.
They will do it because you belong to me, and they don't
know the one who sent me. 22If I had not come and spoken to them, they would not be guilty of sin. But now
they have no excuse for their sin.
23Everyone who hates me also hates my Father. 24I
have done things that no one else has ever done. If they
had not seen me do these things, they would not be
guilty. But they did see me do these things, and they still
hate me and my Father too. 25That is why the Scriptures
are true when they say, "People hated me for no reason."
26I will send you the Spirit who comes from the Father
and shows what is true. The Spirit will help[c] you and
will tell you about me. 27Then you will also tell others
about me, because you have been with me from the
beginning.

16 I am telling you this to keep you from being afraid.
2You will be chased out of the Jewish meeting

[b] 15.18 *world*: See the note at 12.31. [c] 15.26 *help*: See the note at 14.16.

NEW INTERNATIONAL VERSION

The World Hates the Disciples

18“If the world hates you, keep in mind that it hated me
first. 19If you belonged to the world, it would love you as
its own. As it is, you do not belong to the world, but I have
chosen you out of the world. That is why the world hates
you. 20Remember the words I spoke to you: ‘No servant is
greater than his master.’[b] If they persecuted me, they will
persecute you also. If they obeyed my teaching, they will
obey yours also. 21They will treat you this way because of
my name, for they do not know the One who sent me. 22If I
had not come and spoken to them, they would not be
guilty of sin. Now, however, they have no excuse for their
sin. 23He who hates me hates my Father as well. 24If I had
not done among them what no one else did, they would
not be guilty of sin. But now they have seen these mira-
cles, and yet they have hated both me and my Father.
25But this is to fulfill what is written in their Law: ‘They
hated me without reason.’[c]

26“When the Counselor comes, whom I will send to you
from the Father, the Spirit of truth who goes out from the
Father, he will testify about me. 27And you also must testi-
fy, for you have been with me from the beginning.

16 “All this I have told you so that you will not go
astray. 2They will put you out of the synagogue; in

[b] *20* John 13:16 [c] *25* Psalms 35:19; 69:4

NEW LIVING TRANSLATION

The World’s Hatred

18“When the world hates you, remember it hated me
before it hated you. 19The world would love you if you
belonged to it, but you don’t. I chose you to come out of
the world, and so it hates you. 20Do you remember what I
told you? ‘A servant is not greater than the master.’ Since
they persecuted me, naturally they will persecute you. And
if they had listened to me, they would listen to you! 21The
people of the world will hate you because you belong to
me, for they don’t know God who sent me. 22They would
not be guilty if I had not come and spoken to them. But
now they have no excuse for their sin. 23Anyone who hates
me hates my Father, too. 24If I hadn’t done such miracu-
lous signs among them that no one else could do, they
would not be counted guilty. But as it is, they saw all that
I did and yet hated both of us—me and my Father. 25This
has fulfilled what the Scriptures said: ‘They hated me
without cause.’*

26“But I will send you the Counselor*—the Spirit of
truth. He will come to you from the Father and will tell you
all about me. 27And you must also tell others about me
because you have been with me from the beginning.

16 “I have told you these things so that you won’t
fall away. 2For you will be expelled from the

15:25 Pss 35:19; 69:4. **15:26** Or *Comforter,* or *Encourager,* or *Advocate.* Greek *Paraclete.*

NEW KING JAMES VERSION

The World’s Hatred

18“If the world hates you, you know that it hated Me
before *it hated* you. 19If you were of the world, the world
would love its own. Yet because you are not of the world,
but I chose you out of the world, therefore the world hates
you. 20Remember the word that I said to you, ‘A servant is
not greater than his master.’ If they persecuted Me, they
will also persecute you. If they kept My word, they will
keep yours also. 21But all these things they will do to you
for My name’s sake, because they do not know Him who
sent Me. 22If I had not come and spoken to them, they
would have no sin, but now they have no excuse for their
sin. 23He who hates Me hates My Father also. 24If I had
not done among them the works which no one else did,
they would have no sin; but now they have seen and also
hated both Me and My Father. 25But *this happened* that
the word might be fulfilled which is written in their law,
‘They hated Me without a cause.’[c]

The Coming Rejection

26“But when the Helper comes, whom I shall send to you
from the Father, the Spirit of truth who proceeds from the
Father, He will testify of Me. 27And you also will bear wit-
ness, because you have been with Me from the beginning.

16 “These things I have spoken to you, that you
should not be made to stumble. 2They will put you

15:25 [c] Psalm 69:4

THE MESSAGE

Hated by the World

“If you find the godless world is hating you, remember it got its start hating me. If you lived on the world’s terms, the world would love you as one of its own. But since I picked you to live on God’s terms and no longer on the world’s terms, the world is going to hate you.

“When that happens, remember this: Servants don’t get better treatment than their masters. If they beat on me, they will certainly beat on you. If they did what I told them, they will do what you tell them.

“They are going to do all these things to you because of the way they treated me, because they don’t know the One who sent me. If I hadn’t come and told them all this in plain language, it wouldn’t be so bad. As it is, they have no excuse. Hate me, hate my Father—it’s all the same. If I hadn’t done what I have done among them, works no one has *ever* done, they wouldn’t be to blame. But they saw the God-signs and hated anyway, both me and my Father. Interesting—they have verified the truth of their own Scriptures where it is written, ‘They hated me for no good reason.’

“When the Friend I plan to send you from the Father comes—the Spirit of Truth issuing from the Father—he will confirm everything about me. You, too, from your side must give your confirming evidence, since you are in this with me from the start.

16 “I’ve told you these things to prepare you for rough times ahead. They are going to throw you

KING JAMES VERSION

2 They shall put you out of the synagogues: yea, the time cometh, that whosoever killeth you will think that he doeth God service.

3 And these things will they do unto you, because they have not known the Father, nor me.

4 But these things have I told you, that when the time shall come, ye may remember that I told you of them. And these things I said not unto you at the beginning, because I was with you.

5 But now I go my way to him that sent me; and none of you asketh me, Whither goest thou?

6 But because I have said these things unto you, sorrow hath filled your heart.

7 ¶ Nevertheless I tell you the truth; It is expedient for you that I go away: for if I go not away, the Comforter will not come unto you; but if I depart, I will send him unto you.

8 And when he is come, he will reprove the world of sin, and of righteousness, and of judgment:

9 Of sin, because they believe not on me;

10 Of righteousness, because I go to my Father, and ye see me no more;

11 Of judgment, because the prince of this world is judged.

12 I have yet many things to say unto you, but ye cannot bear them now.

13 Howbeit when he, the Spirit of truth, is come, he will guide you into all truth: for he shall not speak of himself;

NEW AMERICAN STANDARD BIBLE

2 "They will make you outcasts from the synagogue, but an hour is coming for everyone who kills you to think that he is offering service to God.

3 "These things they will do because they have not known the Father or Me.

4 "But these things I have spoken to you, so that when their hour comes, you may remember that I told you of them. These things I did not say to you at the beginning, because I was with you.

The Holy Spirit Promised

5 "But now I am going to Him who sent Me; and none of you asks Me, 'Where are You going?'

6 "But because I have said these things to you, sorrow has filled your heart.

7 "But I tell you the truth, it is to your advantage that I go away; for if I do not go away, the Helper will not come to you; but if I go, I will send Him to you.

8 "And He, when He comes, will convict the world concerning sin and righteousness and judgment;

9 concerning sin, because they do not believe in Me;

10 and concerning righteousness, because I go to the Father and you no longer see Me;

11 and concerning judgment, because the ruler of this world has been judged.

12 "I have many more things to say to you, but you cannot bear *them* now.

13 "But when He, the Spirit of truth, comes, He will guide you into all the truth; for He will not speak on His own

NEW CENTURY VERSION

gogues. Yes, the time is coming when those who kill you will think they are offering service to God. 3They will do this because they have not known the Father and they have not known me. 4I have told you these things now so that when the time comes you will remember that I warned you.

The Work of the Holy Spirit

"I did not tell you these things at the beginning, because I was with you then. 5Now I am going back to the One who sent me. But none of you asks me, 'Where are you going?' 6Your hearts are filled with sadness because I have told you these things. 7But I tell you the truth, it is better for you that I go away. When I go away, I will send the Helper[a] to you. If I do not go away, the Helper will not come. 8When the Helper comes, he will prove to the people of the world the truth about sin, about being right with God, and about judgment. 9He will prove to them that sin is not believing in me. 10He will prove to them that being right with God comes from my going to the Father and not being seen anymore. 11And the Helper will prove to them that judgment happened when the ruler of this world was judged.

12"I have many more things to say to you, but they are too much for you now. 13But when the Spirit of truth comes, he will lead you into all truth. He will not speak his

16:7 [a] **Helper** "Counselor" or "Comforter." Jesus is talking about the Holy Spirit.

CONTEMPORARY ENGLISH VERSION

places. And the time will come when people will kill you and think they are doing God a favor. 3They will do these things because they don't know either the Father or me. 4I am saying this to you now, so that when the time comes, you will remember what I have said.

The Work of the Holy Spirit

I was with you at the first, and so I didn't tell you these things. 5But now I am going back to the Father who sent me, and none of you asks me where I am going. 6You are very sad from hearing all of this. 7But I tell you that I am going to do what is best for you. That is why I am going away. The Holy Spirit cannot come to help[a] you until I leave. But after I am gone, I will send the Spirit to you.

8The Spirit will come and show the people of this world the truth about sin and God's justice and the judgment. 9The Spirit will show them that they are wrong about sin, because they didn't have faith in me. 10They are wrong about God's justice, because I am going to the Father, and you won't see me again. 11And they are wrong about the judgment, because God has already judged the ruler of this world.

12I have much more to say to you, but right now it would be more than you could understand. 13The Spirit shows what is true and will come and guide you into the full truth. The Spirit doesn't speak on his own. He will

[a] **16.7** *help*: See the note at 14.16.

NEW INTERNATIONAL VERSION

fact, a time is coming when anyone who kills you will think he is offering a service to God. 3They will do such things because they have not known the Father or me. 4I have told you this, so that when the time comes you will remember that I warned you. I did not tell you this at first because I was with you.

The Work of the Holy Spirit

5"Now I am going to him who sent me, yet none of you asks me, 'Where are you going?' 6Because I have said these things, you are filled with grief. 7But I tell you the truth: It is for your good that I am going away. Unless I go away, the Counselor will not come to you; but if I go, I will send him to you. 8When he comes, he will convict the world of guilt[a] in regard to sin and righteousness and judgment: 9in regard to sin, because men do not believe in me; 10in regard to righteousness, because I am going to the Father, where you can see me no longer; 11and in regard to judgment, because the prince of this world now stands condemned.

12"I have much more to say to you, more than you can now bear. 13But when he, the Spirit of truth, comes, he will guide you into all truth. He will not speak on his own; he

[a] 8 Or *will expose the guilt of the world*

NEW LIVING TRANSLATION

synagogues, and the time is coming when those who kill you will think they are doing God a service. 3This is because they have never known the Father or me. 4Yes, I'm telling you these things now, so that when they happen, you will remember I warned you. I didn't tell you earlier because I was going to be with you for a while longer.

The Work of the Holy Spirit

5"But now I am going away to the one who sent me, and none of you has asked me where I am going. 6Instead, you are very sad. 7But it is actually best for you that I go away, because if I don't, the Counselor* won't come. If I do go away, he will come because I will send him to you. 8And when he comes, he will convince the world of its sin, and of God's righteousness, and of the coming judgment. 9The world's sin is unbelief in me. 10Righteousness is available because I go to the Father, and you will see me no more. 11Judgment will come because the prince of this world has already been judged.

12"Oh, there is so much more I want to tell you, but you can't bear it now. 13When the Spirit of truth comes, he will guide you into all truth. He will not be presenting his own

16:7 Or *Comforter*, or *Encourager*, or *Advocate*. Greek *Paraclete*.

NEW KING JAMES VERSION

out of the synagogues; yes, the time is coming that whoever kills you will think that he offers God service. 3And these things they will do to you[a] because they have not known the Father nor Me. 4But these things I have told you, that when the[b] time comes, you may remember that I told you of them.

"And these things I did not say to you at the beginning, because I was with you.

The Work of the Holy Spirit

5"But now I go away to Him who sent Me, and none of you asks Me, 'Where are You going?' 6But because I have said these things to you, sorrow has filled your heart. 7Nevertheless I tell you the truth. It is to your advantage that I go away; for if I do not go away, the Helper will not come to you; but if I depart, I will send Him to you. 8And when He has come, He will convict the world of sin, and of righteousness, and of judgment: 9of sin, because they do not believe in Me; 10of righteousness, because I go to My Father and you see Me no more; 11of judgment, because the ruler of this world is judged.

12"I still have many things to say to you, but you cannot bear *them* now. 13However, when He, the Spirit of truth, has come, He will guide you into all truth; for He will not speak on His own *authority*, but whatever He hears He

16:3 [a] NU-Text and M-Text omit *to you*. 16:4 [b] NU-Text reads *their*.

THE MESSAGE

out of the meeting places. There will even come a time when anyone who kills you will think he's doing God a favor. They will do these things because they never really understood the Father. I've told you these things so that when the time comes and they start in on you, you'll be well-warned and ready for them.

The Friend Will Come

"I didn't tell you this earlier because I was with you every day. But now I am on my way to the One who sent me. Not one of you has asked, 'Where are you going?' Instead, the longer I've talked, the sadder you've become. So let me say it again, this truth: It's better for you that I leave. If I don't leave, the Friend won't come. But if I go, I'll send him to you.

"When he comes, he'll expose the error of the godless world's view of sin, righteousness, and judgment: He'll show them that their refusal to believe in me is their basic sin; that righteousness comes from above, where I am with the Father, out of their sight and control; that judgment takes place as the ruler of this godless world is brought to trial and convicted.

"I still have many things to tell you, but you can't handle them now. But when the Friend comes, the Spirit of the Truth, he will take you by the hand and guide you into all the truth there is. He won't draw attention to himself, but

KING JAMES VERSION

but whatsoever he shall hear, *that* shall he speak: and he will shew you things to come.

14 He shall glorify me: for he shall receive of mine, and shall shew *it* unto you.

15 All things that the Father hath are mine: therefore said I, that he shall take of mine, and shall shew *it* unto you.

16 ¶ A little while, and ye shall not see me: and again, a little while, and ye shall see me, because I go to the Father.

17 Then said *some* of his disciples among themselves, What is this that he saith unto us, A little while, and ye shall not see me: and again, a little while, and ye shall see me: and, Because I go to the Father?

18 They said therefore, What is this that he saith, A little while? we cannot tell what he saith.

19 Now Jesus knew that they were desirous to ask him, and said unto them, Do ye enquire among yourselves of that I said, A little while, and ye shall not see me: and again, a little while, and ye shall see me?

20 Verily, verily, I say unto you, That ye shall weep and lament, but the world shall rejoice: and ye shall be sorrowful, but your sorrow shall be turned into joy.

21 A woman when she is in travail hath sorrow, because her hour is come: but as soon as she is delivered of the child, she remembereth no more the anguish, for joy that a man is born into the world.

22 And ye now therefore have sorrow: but I will see you again, and your heart shall rejoice, and your joy no man taketh from you.

NEW AMERICAN STANDARD BIBLE

initiative, but whatever He hears, He will speak; and He will disclose to you what is to come.

14 "He will glorify Me, for He will take of Mine and will disclose *it* to you.

15 "All things that the Father has are Mine; therefore I said that He takes of Mine and will disclose *it* to you.

Jesus' Death and Resurrection Foretold

16 "A little while, and you will no longer see Me; and again a little while, and you will see Me."

17 *Some* of His disciples then said to one another, "What is this thing He is telling us, 'A little while, and you will not see Me; and again a little while, and you will see Me'; and, 'because I go to the Father'?"

18 So they were saying, "What is this that He says, 'A little while'? We do not know what He is talking about."

19 Jesus knew that they wished to question Him, and He said to them, "Are you deliberating together about this, that I said, 'A little while, and you will not see Me, and again a little while, and you will see Me'?

20 "Truly, truly, I say to you, that you will weep and lament, but the world will rejoice; you will grieve, but your grief will be turned into joy.

21 "Whenever a woman is in labor she has pain, because her hour has come; but when she gives birth to the child, she no longer remembers the anguish because of the joy that a child has been born into the world.

22 "Therefore you too have grief now; but I will see you again, and your heart will rejoice, and no one *will* take your joy away from you.

NEW CENTURY VERSION

own words, but he will speak only what he hears, and he will tell you what is to come. 14The Spirit of truth will bring glory to me, because he will take what I have to say and tell it to you. 15All that the Father has is mine. That is why I said that the Spirit will take what I have to say and tell it to you.

Sadness Will Become Happiness

16"After a little while you will not see me, and then after a little while you will see me again."

17Some of the followers said to each other, "What does Jesus mean when he says, 'After a little while you will not see me, and then after a little while you will see me again'? And what does he mean when he says, 'Because I am going to the Father'?" 18They also asked, "What does he mean by 'a little while'? We don't understand what he is saying."

19Jesus saw that the followers wanted to ask him about this, so he said to them, "Are you asking each other what I meant when I said, 'After a little while you will not see me, and then after a little while you will see me again'? 20I tell you the truth, you will cry and be sad, but the world will be happy. You will be sad, but your sadness will become joy. 21When a woman gives birth to a baby, she has pain, because her time has come. But when her baby is born, she forgets the pain, because she is so happy that a child has

CONTEMPORARY ENGLISH VERSION

tell you only what he has heard from me, and he will let you know what is going to happen. 14The Spirit will bring glory to me by taking my message and telling it to you. 15Everything that the Father has is mine. That is why I have said that the Spirit takes my message and tells it to you.

Sorrow Will Turn into Joy

16Jesus told his disciples, "For a little while you won't see me, but after a while you will see me."

17They said to each other, "What does Jesus mean by saying that for a little while we won't see him, but after a while we will see him? What does he mean by saying that he is going to the Father? 18What is this 'little while' that he is talking about? We don't know what he means."

19Jesus knew that they had some questions, so he said:

You are wondering what I meant when I said that for a little while you won't see me, but after a while you will see me. 20I tell you for certain that you will cry and be sad, but the world will be happy. You will be sad, but later you will be happy.

21When a woman is about to give birth, she is in great pain. But after it is all over, she forgets the pain and is happy, because she has brought a child into the world. 22You are now very sad. But later I will see you, and you will be so happy that no one will be able to change the

NEW INTERNATIONAL VERSION

will speak only what he hears, and he will tell you what is yet to come. [14]He will bring glory to me by taking from what is mine and making it known to you. [15]All that belongs to the Father is mine. That is why I said the Spirit will take from what is mine and make it known to you.

[16]"In a little while you will see me no more, and then after a little while you will see me."

The Disciples' Grief Will Turn to Joy

[17]Some of his disciples said to one another, "What does he mean by saying, 'In a little while you will see me no more, and then after a little while you will see me,' and 'Because I am going to the Father'?" [18]They kept asking, "What does he mean by 'a little while'? We don't understand what he is saying."

[19]Jesus saw that they wanted to ask him about this, so he said to them, "Are you asking one another what I meant when I said, 'In a little while you will see me no more, and then after a little while you will see me'? [20]I tell you the truth, you will weep and mourn while the world rejoices. You will grieve, but your grief will turn to joy. [21]A woman giving birth to a child has pain because her time has come; but when her baby is born she forgets the anguish because of her joy that a child is born into the world. [22]So with you: Now is your time of grief, but I will see you again and you will rejoice, and no one will take

NEW LIVING TRANSLATION

ideas; he will be telling you what he has heard. He will tell you about the future. [14]He will bring me glory by revealing to you whatever he receives from me. [15]All that the Father has is mine; this is what I mean when I say that the Spirit will reveal to you whatever he receives from me.

Sadness Will Be Turned to Joy

[16]"In just a little while I will be gone, and you won't see me anymore. Then, just a little while after that, you will see me again."

[17]The disciples asked each other, "What does he mean when he says, 'You won't see me, and then you will see me'? And what does he mean when he says, 'I am going to the Father'? [18]And what does he mean by 'a little while'? We don't understand."

[19]Jesus realized they wanted to ask him, so he said, "Are you asking yourselves what I meant? I said in just a little while I will be gone, and you won't see me anymore. Then, just a little while after that, you will see me again. [20]Truly, you will weep and mourn over what is going to happen to me, but the world will rejoice. You will grieve, but your grief will suddenly turn to wonderful joy when you see me again. [21]It will be like a woman experiencing the pains of labor. When her child is born, her anguish gives place to joy because she has brought a new person into the world. [22]You have sorrow now, but I will see you again; then you will rejoice, and no one can rob you of that joy. [23]At that

NEW KING JAMES VERSION

will speak; and He will tell you things to come. [14]He will glorify Me, for He will take of what is Mine and declare *it* to you. [15]All things that the Father has are Mine. Therefore I said that He will take of Mine and declare *it* to you.[c]

Sorrow Will Turn to Joy

[16]"A little while, and you will not see Me; and again a little while, and you will see Me, because I go to the Father."

[17]Then *some* of His disciples said among themselves, "What is this that He says to us, 'A little while, and you will not see Me; and again a little while, and you will see Me'; and, 'because I go to the Father'?" [18]They said therefore, "What is this that He says, 'A little while'? We do not know what He is saying."

[19]Now Jesus knew that they desired to ask Him, and He said to them, "Are you inquiring among yourselves about what I said, 'A little while, and you will not see Me; and again a little while, and you will see Me'? [20]Most assuredly, I say to you that you will weep and lament, but the world will rejoice; and you will be sorrowful, but your sorrow will be turned into joy. [21]A woman, when she is in labor, has sorrow because her hour has come; but as soon as she has given birth to the child, she no longer remembers the anguish, for joy that a human being has been born into the world. [22]Therefore you now have sorrow; but I will see you again and your heart will rejoice, and your joy no one will take from you.

16:15 [c] NU-Text and M-Text read *He takes of Mine and will declare it to you.*

THE MESSAGE

will make sense out of what is about to happen and, indeed, out of all that I have done and said. He will honor me; he will take from me and deliver it to you. Everything the Father has is also mine. That is why I've said, 'He takes from me and delivers to you.'

"In a day or so you're not going to see me, but then in another day or so you will see me."

Joy Like a River Overflowing

That stirred up a hornet's nest of questions among the disciples: "What's he talking about: 'In a day or so you're not going to see me, but then in another day or so you will see me'? And, 'Because I'm on my way to the Father'? What is this 'day or so'? We don't know what he's talking about."

Jesus knew they were dying to ask him what he meant, so he said, "Are you trying to figure out among yourselves what I meant when I said, 'In a day or so you're not going to see me, but then in another day or so you will see me'? Then fix this firmly in your minds: You're going to be in deep mourning while the godless world throws a party. You'll be sad, very sad, but your sadness will develop into gladness.

"When a woman gives birth, she has a hard time, there's no getting around it. But when the baby is born, there is joy in the birth. This new life in the world wipes out memory of the pain. The sadness you have right now is similar to that pain, but the coming joy is also similar. When I see you again, you'll be full of joy, and it will be a

KING JAMES VERSION

23 ¶ And in that day ye shall ask me nothing. Verily, verily, I say unto you, Whatsoever ye shall ask the Father in my name, he will give *it* you.

24 Hitherto have ye asked nothing in my name: ask, and ye shall receive, that your joy may be full.

25 These things have I spoken unto you in proverbs: but the time cometh, when I shall no more speak unto you in proverbs, but I shall shew you plainly of the Father.

26 At that day ye shall ask in my name: and I say not unto you, that I will pray the Father for you:

27 For the Father himself loveth you, because ye have loved me, and have believed that I came out from God.

28 ¶ I came forth from the Father, and am come into the world: again, I leave the world, and go to the Father.

29 His disciples said unto him, Lo, now speakest thou plainly, and speakest no proverb.

30 Now are we sure that thou knowest all things, and needest not that any man should ask thee: by this we believe that thou camest forth from God.

31 Jesus answered them, Do ye now believe?

32 Behold, the hour cometh, yea, is now come, that ye shall be scattered, every man to his own, and shall leave me alone: and yet I am not alone, because the Father is with me.

NEW AMERICAN STANDARD BIBLE

Prayer Promises

23 "In that day you will not question Me about anything. Truly, truly, I say to you, if you ask the Father for anything in My name, He will give it to you.

24 "Until now you have asked for nothing in My name; ask and you will receive, so that your joy may be made full.

25 "These things I have spoken to you in figurative language; an hour is coming when I will no longer speak to you in figurative language, but will tell you plainly of the Father.

26 "In that day you will ask in My name, and I do not say to you that I will request of the Father on your behalf;

27 for the Father Himself loves you, because you have loved Me and have believed that I came forth from the Father.

28 "I came forth from the Father and have come into the world; I am leaving the world again and going to the Father."

29 His disciples *said, "Lo, now You are speaking plainly and are not using a figure of speech.

30 "Now we know that You know all things, and have no need for anyone to question You; by this we believe that You came from God."

31 Jesus answered them, "Do you now believe?

32 "Behold, an hour is coming, and has *already* come, for you to be scattered, each to his own *home*, and to leave Me alone; and *yet* I am not alone, because the Father is with Me.

NEW CENTURY VERSION

been born into the world. 22It is the same with you. Now
you are sad, but I will see you again and you will be
happy, and no one will take away your joy. 23In that day
you will not ask me for anything. I tell you the truth, my
Father will give you anything you ask for in my name.
24Until now you have not asked for anything in my name.
Ask and you will receive, so that your joy will be the
fullest possible joy.

Victory over the World

25"I have told you these things, using stories that hide
the meaning. But the time will come when I will not use
stories like that to tell you things; I will speak to you in
plain words about the Father. 26In that day you will ask
the Father for things in my name. I mean, I will not need
to ask the Father for you. 27The Father himself loves you.
He loves you because you loved me and believed that I
came from God. 28I came from the Father into the world.
Now I am leaving the world and going back to the Father."
29Then the followers of Jesus said, "You are speaking
clearly to us now and are not using stories that are hard to
understand. 30We can see now that you know all things.
You can answer a person's question even before it is
asked. This makes us believe you came from God."
31Jesus answered, "So now you believe? 32Listen to me;
a time is coming when you will be scattered, each to his
own home. That time is now here. You will leave me alone,
but I am never really alone, because the Father is with me.

CONTEMPORARY ENGLISH VERSION

way you feel. 23When that time comes, you won't have
to ask me about anything. I tell you for certain that the
Father will give you whatever you ask for in my name.
24You have not asked for anything in this way before,
but now you must ask in my name.[b] Then it will be
given to you, so that you will be completely happy.
25I have used examples to explain to you what I have
been talking about. But the time will come when I will
speak to you plainly about the Father and will no longer
use examples like these. 26You will ask the Father in my
name,[c] and I won't have to ask him for you. 27God the
Father loves you because you love me, and you believe
that I have come from him. 28I came from the Father into
the world, but I am leaving the world and returning to
the Father.
29The disciples said, "Now you are speaking plainly to
us! You are not using examples. 30At last we know that
you understand everything, and we don't have any more
questions. Now we believe that you truly have come from
God."
31Jesus replied:
Do you really believe me? 32The time will come and is
already here when all of you will be scattered. Each of
you will go back home and leave me by myself. But the
Father will be with me, and I won't be alone. 33I have

[b] 16.23,24 *in my name . . . in my name*: Or "as my disciples . . . as my disciples." [c] 16.26 *in my name*: Or "because you are my followers."

NEW INTERNATIONAL VERSION

away your joy. 23In that day you will no longer ask me anything. I tell you the truth, my Father will give you whatever you ask in my name. 24Until now you have not asked for anything in my name. Ask and you will receive, and your joy will be complete.

25"Though I have been speaking figuratively, a time is coming when I will no longer use this kind of language but will tell you plainly about my Father. 26In that day you will ask in my name. I am not saying that I will ask the Father on your behalf. 27No, the Father himself loves you because you have loved me and have believed that I came from God. 28I came from the Father and entered the world; now I am leaving the world and going back to the Father."

29Then Jesus' disciples said, "Now you are speaking clearly and without figures of speech. 30Now we can see that you know all things and that you do not even need to have anyone ask you questions. This makes us believe that you came from God."

31"You believe at last!"[b] Jesus answered. 32"But a time is coming, and has come, when you will be scattered, each to his own home. You will leave me all alone. Yet I am not alone, for my Father is with me.

[b] *31* Or *"Do you now believe?"*

NEW LIVING TRANSLATION

time you won't need to ask me for anything. The truth is, you can go directly to the Father and ask him, and he will grant your request because you use my name. 24You haven't done this before. Ask, using my name, and you will receive, and you will have abundant joy.

25"I have spoken of these matters in parables, but the time will come when this will not be necessary, and I will tell you plainly all about the Father. 26Then you will ask in my name. I'm not saying I will ask the Father on your behalf, 27for the Father himself loves you dearly because you love me and believe that I came from God. 28Yes, I came from the Father into the world, and I will leave the world and return to the Father."

29Then his disciples said, "At last you are speaking plainly and not in parables. 30Now we understand that you know everything and don't need anyone to tell you anything.* From this we believe that you came from God."

31Jesus asked, "Do you finally believe? 32But the time is coming—in fact, it is already here—when you will be scattered, each one going his own way, leaving me alone. Yet I am not alone because the Father is with me. 33I have told

16:30 Or *don't need that anyone should ask you anything.*

NEW KING JAMES VERSION

23"And in that day you will ask Me nothing. Most assuredly, I say to you, whatever you ask the Father in My name He will give you. 24Until now you have asked nothing in My name. Ask, and you will receive, that your joy may be full.

Jesus Christ Has Overcome the World

25"These things I have spoken to you in figurative language; but the time is coming when I will no longer speak to you in figurative language, but I will tell you plainly about the Father. 26In that day you will ask in My name, and I do not say to you that I shall pray the Father for you; 27for the Father Himself loves you, because you have loved Me, and have believed that I came forth from God. 28I came forth from the Father and have come into the world. Again, I leave the world and go to the Father."

29His disciples said to Him, "See, now You are speaking plainly, and using no figure of speech! 30Now we are sure that You know all things, and have no need that anyone should question You. By this we believe that You came forth from God."

31Jesus answered them, "Do you now believe? 32Indeed the hour is coming, yes, has now come, that you will be scattered, each to his own, and will leave Me alone. And yet I am not alone, because the Father is with Me. 33These

THE MESSAGE

joy no one can rob from you. You'll no longer be so full of questions.

"This is what I want you to do: Ask the Father for whatever is in keeping with the things I've revealed to you. Ask in my name, according to my will, and he'll most certainly give it to you. Your joy will be a river overflowing its banks!

"I've used figures of speech in telling you these things. Soon I'll drop the figures and tell you about the Father in plain language. Then you can make your requests directly to him in relation to this life I've revealed to you. I won't continue making requests of the Father on your behalf. I won't need to. Because you've gone out on a limb, committed yourselves to love and trust in me, believing I came directly from the Father, the Father loves you directly. First, I left the Father and arrived in the world; now I leave the world and travel to the Father."

His disciples said, "Finally! You're giving it to us straight, in plain talk—no more figures of speech. Now we know that you know everything—it all comes together in you. You won't have to put up with our questions anymore. We're convinced you came from God."

Jesus answered them, "Do you finally believe? In fact, you're about to make a run for it—saving your own skins and abandoning me. But I'm not abandoned. The Father is

KING JAMES VERSION

33 These things I have spoken unto you, that in me ye might have peace. In the world ye shall have tribulation: but be of good cheer; I have overcome the world.

17 These words spake Jesus, and lifted up his eyes to heaven, and said, Father, the hour is come; glorify thy Son, that thy Son also may glorify thee:

2 As thou hast given him power over all flesh, that he should give eternal life to as many as thou hast given him.

3 And this is life eternal, that they might know thee the only true God, and Jesus Christ, whom thou hast sent.

4 I have glorified thee on the earth: I have finished the work which thou gavest me to do.

5 And now, O Father, glorify thou me with thine own self with the glory which I had with thee before the world was.

6 ¶ I have manifested thy name unto the men which thou gavest me out of the world: thine they were, and thou

NEW AMERICAN STANDARD BIBLE

33 "These things I have spoken to you, so that in Me you may have peace. In the world you have tribulation, but take courage; I have overcome the world."

The High Priestly Prayer

17 Jesus spoke these things; and lifting up His eyes to heaven, He said, "Father, the hour has come; glorify Your Son, that the Son may glorify You,

2 even as You gave Him authority over all flesh, that to all whom You have given Him, He may give eternal life.

3 "This is eternal life, that they may know You, the only true God, and Jesus Christ whom You have sent.

4 "I glorified You on the earth, having accomplished the work which You have given Me to do.

5 "Now, Father, glorify Me together with Yourself, with the glory which I had with You before the world was.

6 "I have manifested Your name to the men whom You gave Me out of the world; they were Yours and You gave

NEW CENTURY VERSION

33 "I told you these things so that you can have peace in
me. In this world you will have trouble, but be brave! I
have defeated the world."

Jesus Prays for His Followers

17 After Jesus said these things, he looked toward
heaven and prayed, "Father, the time has come.
Give glory to your Son so that the Son can give glory to
you. 2 You gave the Son power over all people so that the
Son could give eternal life to all those you gave him. 3 And
this is eternal life: that people know you, the only true
God, and that they know Jesus Christ, the One you sent.
4 Having finished the work you gave me to do, I brought
you glory on earth. 5 And now, Father, give me glory with
you; give me the glory I had with you before the world was
made.

6 "I showed what you are like to those you gave me from
the world. They belonged to you, and you gave them to me,

CONTEMPORARY ENGLISH VERSION

told you this, so that you might have peace in your
hearts because of me. While you are in the world, you
will have to suffer. But cheer up! I have defeated the
world.[d]

Jesus Prays

17 After Jesus had finished speaking to his disciples,
he looked up toward heaven and prayed:

Father, the time has come for you to bring glory to
your Son, in order that he may bring glory to you. 2 And
you gave him power over all people, so that he would
give eternal life to everyone you give him. 3 Eternal life is
to know you, the only true God, and to know Jesus
Christ, the one you sent. 4 I have brought glory to you
here on earth by doing everything you gave me to do.
5 Now, Father, give me back the glory that I had with you
before the world was created.

6 You have given me some followers from this world,
and I have shown them what you are like. They were

[d] 16.33 *world*: See the note at 12.31.

NEW INTERNATIONAL VERSION

33"I have told you these things, so that in me you may have peace. In this world you will have trouble. But take heart! I have overcome the world."

Jesus Prays for Himself

17 After Jesus said this, he looked toward heaven and prayed:

"Father, the time has come. Glorify your Son, that your Son may glorify you. 2For you granted him authority over all people that he might give eternal life to all those you have given him. 3Now this is eternal life: that they may know you, the only true God, and Jesus Christ, whom you have sent. 4I have brought you glory on earth by completing the work you gave me to do. 5And now, Father, glorify me in your presence with the glory I had with you before the world began.

Jesus Prays for His Disciples

6"I have revealed you[a] to those whom you gave me out of the world. They were yours; you gave them to

[a] *6* Greek *your name*; also in verse 26

NEW LIVING TRANSLATION

you all this so that you may have peace in me. Here on earth you will have many trials and sorrows. But take heart, because I have overcome the world."

The Prayer of Jesus

17 When Jesus had finished saying all these things, he looked up to heaven and said, "Father, the time has come. Glorify your Son so he can give glory back to you. 2For you have given him authority over everyone in all the earth. He gives eternal life to each one you have given him. 3And this is the way to have eternal life—to know you, the only true God, and Jesus Christ, the one you sent to earth. 4I brought glory to you here on earth by doing everything you told me to do. 5And now, Father, bring me into the glory we shared before the world began.

6"I have told these men about you. They were in the world, but then you gave them to me. Actually, they were always yours, and you gave them to me; and they have

NEW KING JAMES VERSION

things I have spoken to you, that in Me you may have peace. In the world you will[d] have tribulation; but be of good cheer, I have overcome the world."

Jesus Prays for Himself

17 Jesus spoke these words, lifted up His eyes to heaven, and said: "Father, the hour has come. Glorify Your Son, that Your Son also may glorify You, 2as You have given Him authority over all flesh, that He should[a] give eternal life to as many as You have given Him. 3And this is eternal life, that they may know You, the only true God, and Jesus Christ whom You have sent. 4I have glorified You on the earth. I have finished the work which You have given Me to do. 5And now, O Father, glorify Me together with Yourself, with the glory which I had with You before the world was.

Jesus Prays for His Disciples

6"I have manifested Your name to the men whom You have given Me out of the world. They were Yours, You gave

16:33 [d] NU-Text and M-Text omit *will*. **17:2** [a] M-Text reads *shall*.

THE MESSAGE

with me. I've told you all this so that trusting me, you will be unshakable and assured, deeply at peace. In this godless world you will continue to experience difficulties. But take heart! I've conquered the world."

Jesus' Prayer for His Followers

17 Jesus said these things. Then, raising his eyes in prayer, he said:

"Father, it's time.
Display the bright splendor of your Son
So the Son in turn may show your bright splendor.
You put him in charge of everything human
So he might give real and eternal life to all in his charge.
And this is the real and eternal life:
That they know you,
The one and only true God,
And Jesus Christ, whom you sent.
I glorified you on earth
By completing down to the last detail
What you assigned me to do.
And now, Father, glorify me with your very own splendor,
The very splendor I had in your presence
Before there was a world.

✠

"I spelled out your character in detail
To the men and women you gave me.
They were yours in the first place;

KING JAMES VERSION

gavest them me; and they have kept thy word.

7 Now they have known that all things whatsoever thou hast given me are of thee.

8 For I have given unto them the words which thou gavest me; and they have received *them*, and have known surely that I came out from thee, and they have believed that thou didst send me.

9 I pray for them: I pray not for the world, but for them which thou hast given me; for they are thine.

10 And all mine are thine, and thine are mine; and I am glorified in them.

11 ¶ And now I am no more in the world, but these are in the world, and I come to thee. Holy Father, keep through thine own name those whom thou hast given me, that they may be one, as we *are*.

12 While I was with them in the world, I kept them in thy name: those that thou gavest me I have kept, and none of them is lost, but the son of perdition; that the scripture might be fulfilled.

NEW AMERICAN STANDARD BIBLE

them to Me, and they have kept Your word.

7 "Now they have come to know that everything You have given Me is from You;

8 for the words which You gave Me I have given to them; and they received *them* and truly understood that I came forth from You, and they believed that You sent Me.

9 "I ask on their behalf; I do not ask on behalf of the world, but of those whom You have given Me; for they are Yours;

10 and all things that are Mine are Yours, and Yours are Mine; and I have been glorified in them.

11 "I am no longer in the world; and *yet* they themselves are in the world, and I come to You. Holy Father, keep them in Your name, *the name* which You have given Me, that they may be one even as We *are*.

12 "While I was with them, I was keeping them in Your name which You have given Me; and I guarded them and not one of them perished but the son of perdition, so that the Scripture would be fulfilled.

NEW CENTURY VERSION

and they have obeyed your teaching. 7 Now they know that
everything you gave me comes from you. 8 I gave them the
teachings you gave me, and they accepted them. They
knew that I truly came from you, and they believed that
you sent me. 9 I am praying for them. I am not praying for
people in the world but for those you gave me, because
they are yours. 10 All I have is yours, and all you have is
mine. And my glory is shown through them. 11 I am coming
to you; I will not stay in the world any longer. But they are
still in the world. Holy Father, keep them safe by the
power of your name, the name you gave me, so that they
will be one, just as you and I are one. 12 While I was with
them, I kept them safe by the power of your name, the
name you gave me. I protected them, and only one of
them, the one worthy of destruction, was lost so that the
Scripture would come true.

CONTEMPORARY ENGLISH VERSION

yours, but you gave them to me, and they have obeyed
you. 7 They know that you gave me everything I have. 8 I
told my followers what you told me, and they accepted
it. They know that I came from you, and they believe
that you are the one who sent me. 9 I am praying for
them, but not for those who belong to this world.[a] My
followers belong to you, and I am praying for them. 10 All
that I have is yours, and all that you have is mine, and
they will bring glory to me.

11 Holy Father, I am no longer in the world. I am com-
ing to you, but my followers are still in the world. So
keep them safe by the power of the name that you have
given me. Then they will be one with each other, just as
you and I are one. 12 While I was with them, I kept them
safe by the power you have given me. I guarded them,
and not one of them was lost, except the one who had to
be lost. This happened so that what the Scriptures say
would come true.

[a] 17.9 *world*: See the note at 12.31.

NEW INTERNATIONAL VERSION

me and they have obeyed your word. [7]Now they know
that everything you have given me comes from you.
[8]For I gave them the words you gave me and they
accepted them. They knew with certainty that I came
from you, and they believed that you sent me. [9]I pray
for them. I am not praying for the world, but for those
you have given me, for they are yours. [10]All I have is
yours, and all you have is mine. And glory has come
to me through them. [11]I will remain in the world no
longer, but they are still in the world, and I am coming to you. Holy Father, protect them by the power of
your name—the name you gave me—so that they may
be one as we are one. [12]While I was with them, I protected them and kept them safe by that name you
gave me. None has been lost except the one doomed to
destruction so that Scripture would be fulfilled.

NEW LIVING TRANSLATION

kept your word. [7]Now they know that everything I have is
a gift from you, [8]for I have passed on to them the words
you gave me; and they accepted them and know that I
came from you, and they believe you sent me.
[9]"My prayer is not for the world, but for those you have
given me, because they belong to you. [10]And all of them,
since they are mine, belong to you; and you have given
them back to me, so they are my glory! [11]Now I am departing the world; I am leaving them behind and coming to
you. Holy Father, keep them and care for them—all those
you have given me—so that they will be united just as we
are. [12]During my time here, I have kept them safe.* I
guarded them so that not one was lost, except the one
headed for destruction, as the Scriptures foretold.

17:12 Greek *I have kept in your name those whom you have given me.*

NEW KING JAMES VERSION

them to Me, and they have kept Your word. [7]Now they
have known that all things which You have given Me are
from You. [8]For I have given to them the words which You
have given Me; and they have received *them,* and have
known surely that I came forth from You; and they have
believed that You sent Me.
[9]"I pray for them. I do not pray for the world but for
those whom You have given Me, for they are Yours. [10]And
all Mine are Yours, and Yours are Mine, and I am glorified
in them. [11]Now I am no longer in the world, but these are
in the world, and I come to You. Holy Father, keep through
Your name those whom You have given Me,[b] that they
may be one as We *are.* [12]While I was with them in the
world,[c] I kept them in Your name. Those whom You gave
Me I have kept;[d] and none of them is lost except the son of
perdition, that the Scripture might be fulfilled. [13]But now I

17:11 [b] NU-Text and M-Text read *keep them through Your name which You have given Me.* 17:12 [c] NU-Text omits *in the world.* [d] NU-Text reads *in Your name which You gave Me. And I guarded them;* (or *it;*).

THE MESSAGE

Then you gave them to me,
And they have now done what you said.
They know now, beyond the shadow of a doubt,
That everything you gave me is firsthand from you,
For the message you gave me, I gave them;
And they took it, and were convinced
That I came from you.
They believed that you sent me.
I pray for them.
I'm not praying for the God-rejecting world
But for those you gave me,
For they are yours by right.
Everything mine is yours, and yours mine,
And my life is on display in them.
For I'm no longer going to be visible in the world;
They'll continue in the world
While I return to you.
Holy Father, guard them as they pursue this life
That you conferred as a gift through me,
So they can be one heart and mind
As we are one heart and mind.
As long as I was with them, I guarded them
In the pursuit of the life you gave through me;
I even posted a night watch.
And not one of them got away,
Except for the rebel bent on destruction
(the exception that proved the rule of Scripture).

KING JAMES VERSION

13 And now come I to thee; and these things I speak in the world, that they might have my joy fulfilled in themselves.

14 I have given them thy word; and the world hath hated them, because they are not of the world, even as I am not of the world.

15 I pray not that thou shouldest take them out of the world, but that thou shouldest keep them from the evil.

16 They are not of the world, even as I am not of the world.

17 ¶ Sanctify them through thy truth: thy word is truth.

18 As thou hast sent me into the world, even so have I also sent them into the world.

19 And for their sakes I sanctify myself, that they also might be sanctified through the truth.

20 ¶ Neither pray I for these alone, but for them also which shall believe on me through their word;

21 That they all may be one; as thou, Father, *art* in me, and I in thee, that they also may be one in us: that the world may believe that thou hast sent me.

22 And the glory which thou gavest me I have given them; that they may be one, even as we are one:

NEW AMERICAN STANDARD BIBLE

The Disciples in the World

13 "But now I come to You; and these things I speak in the world so that they may have My joy made full in themselves.

14 "I have given them Your word; and the world has hated them, because they are not of the world, even as I am not of the world.

15 "I do not ask You to take them out of the world, but to keep them from the evil *one*.

16 "They are not of the world, even as I am not of the world.

17 "Sanctify them in the truth; Your word is truth.

18 "As You sent Me into the world, I also have sent them into the world.

19 "For their sakes I sanctify Myself, that they themselves also may be sanctified in truth.

20 "I do not ask on behalf of these alone, but for those also who believe in Me through their word;

21 that they may all be one; even as You, Father, *are* in Me and I in You, that they also may be in Us, so that the world may believe that You sent Me.

Their Future Glory

22 "The glory which You have given Me I have given to them, that they may be one, just as We are one;

NEW CENTURY VERSION

13"I am coming to you now. But I pray these things while I am still in the world so that these followers can have all of my joy in them. 14I have given them your teaching. And the world has hated them, because they don't belong to the world, just as I don't belong to the world. 15I am not asking you to take them out of the world but to keep them safe from the Evil One. 16They don't belong to the world, just as I don't belong to the world. 17Make them ready for your service through your truth; your teaching is truth. 18I have sent them into the world, just as you sent me into the world. 19For their sake, I am making myself ready to serve so that they can be ready for their service of the truth.

20"I pray for these followers, but I am also praying for all those who will believe in me because of their teaching. 21Father, I pray that they can be one. As you are in me and I am in you, I pray that they can also be one in us. Then the world will believe that you sent me. 22I have given these people the glory that you gave me so that they can be one, just as you and I are one. 23I will be in them and

CONTEMPORARY ENGLISH VERSION

13I am on my way to you. But I say these things while I am still in the world, so that my followers will have the same complete joy that I do. 14I have told them your message. But the people of this world hate them, because they don't belong to this world, just as I don't.

15Father, I don't ask you to take my followers out of the world, but keep them safe from the evil one. 16They don't belong to this world, and neither do I. 17Your word is the truth. So let this truth make them completely yours. 18I am sending them into the world, just as you sent me. 19I have given myself completely for their sake, so that they may belong completely to the truth.

20I am not praying just for these followers. I am also praying for everyone else who will have faith because of what my followers will say about me. 21I want all of them to be one with each other, just as I am one with you and you are one with me. I also want them to be one with us. Then the people of this world will believe that you sent me.

22I have honored my followers in the same way that you honored me, in order that they may be one with each other, just as we are one. 23I am one with them,

NEW INTERNATIONAL VERSION

13“I am coming to you now, but I say these things
while I am still in the world, so that they may have
the full measure of my joy within them. 14I have given
them your word and the world has hated them, for
they are not of the world any more than I am of the
world. 15My prayer is not that you take them out of
the world but that you protect them from the evil one.
16They are not of the world, even as I am not of it.
17Sanctify[b] them by the truth; your word is truth. 18As
you sent me into the world, I have sent them into the
world. 19For them I sanctify myself, that they too may
be truly sanctified.

Jesus Prays for All Believers

20“My prayer is not for them alone. I pray also for
those who will believe in me through their message,
21that all of them may be one, Father, just as you are
in me and I am in you. May they also be in us so that
the world may believe that you have sent me. 22I
have given them the glory that you gave me, that
they may be one as we are one: 23I in them and you

b 17 Greek *hagiazo (set apart for sacred use* or *make holy)*; also in verse 19

NEW LIVING TRANSLATION

13“And now I am coming to you. I have told them many
things while I was with them so they would be filled with
my joy. 14I have given them your word. And the world
hates them because they do not belong to the world, just
as I do not. 15I'm not asking you to take them out of the
world, but to keep them safe from the evil one. 16They are
not part of this world any more than I am. 17Make them
pure and holy by teaching them your words of truth. 18As
you sent me into the world, I am sending them into the
world. 19And I give myself entirely to you so they also
might be entirely yours.

20“I am praying not only for these disciples but also for
all who will ever believe in me because of their testimony.
21My prayer for all of them is that they will be one, just as
you and I are one, Father—that just as you are in me and I
am in you, so they will be in us, and the world will believe
you sent me.

22“I have given them the glory you gave me, so that they
may be one, as we are—23I in them and you in me, all

NEW KING JAMES VERSION

come to You, and these things I speak in the world, that
they may have My joy fulfilled in themselves. 14I have
given them Your word; and the world has hated them
because they are not of the world, just as I am not of the
world. 15I do not pray that You should take them out of the
world, but that You should keep them from the evil one.
16They are not of the world, just as I am not of the world.
17Sanctify them by Your truth. Your word is truth. 18As
You sent Me into the world, I also have sent them into the
world. 19And for their sakes I sanctify Myself, that they
also may be sanctified by the truth.

Jesus Prays for All Believers

20“I do not pray for these alone, but also for those who
will[e] believe in Me through their word; 21that they all may
be one, as You, Father, *are* in Me, and I in You; that they
also may be one in Us, that the world may believe that You
sent Me. 22And the glory which You gave Me I have given
them, that they may be one just as We are one: 23I in

17:20 [e] NU-Text and M-Text omit *will.*

THE MESSAGE

“Now I'm returning to you.
I'm saying these things in the world's hearing
So my people can experience
My joy completed in them.
I gave them your word;
The godless world hated them because of it,
Because they didn't join the world's ways,
Just as I didn't join the world's ways.
I'm not asking that you take them out of the world
But that you guard them from the Evil One.
They are no more defined by the world
Than I am defined by the world.
Make them holy—consecrated—with the truth;
Your word is consecrating truth.
In the same way that you gave me a mission in the world,
I give them a mission in the world.
I'm consecrating myself for their sakes
So they'll be truth-consecrated in their mission.

✣

“I'm praying not only for them
But also for those who will believe in me
Because of them and their witness about me.
The goal is for all of them to become one heart and mind—
Just as you, Father, are in me and I in you,
So they might be one heart and mind with us.
Then the world might believe that you, in fact, sent me.
The same glory you gave me, I gave them,
So they'll be as unified and together as we are—

KING JAMES VERSION

23 I in them, and thou in me, that they may be made
perfect in one; and that the world may know that thou
hast sent me, and hast loved them, as thou hast loved me.
24 ¶ Father, I will that they also, whom thou hast given
me, be with me where I am; that they may behold my
glory, which thou hast given me: for thou lovedst me
before the foundation of the world.
25 O righteous Father, the world hath not known thee:
but I have known thee, and these have known that thou
hast sent me.
26 And I have declared unto them thy name, and will
declare *it*: that the love wherewith thou hast loved me may
be in them, and I in them.
18 When Jesus had spoken these words, he went forth
with his disciples over the brook Cedron, where
was a garden, into the which he entered, and his disciples.
2 And Judas also, which betrayed him, knew the place:
for Jesus ofttimes resorted thither with his disciples.
3 Judas then, having received a band *of men* and officers

NEW AMERICAN STANDARD BIBLE

23 I in them and You in Me, that they may be perfected
in unity, so that the world may know that You sent Me,
and loved them, even as You have loved Me.
24 "Father, I desire that they also, whom You have given
Me, be with Me where I am, so that they may see My glory
which You have given Me, for You loved Me before the
foundation of the world.
25 "O righteous Father, although the world has not
known You, yet I have known You; and these have known
that You sent Me;
26 and I have made Your name known to them, and will
make it known, so that the love with which You loved Me
may be in them, and I in them."

Judas Betrays Jesus

18 When Jesus had spoken these words, He went
forth with His disciples over the ravine of the
Kidron, where there was a garden, in which He entered
with His disciples.
2 Now Judas also, who was betraying Him, knew the
place, for Jesus had often met there with His disciples.
3 Judas then, having received the *Roman* cohort and

NEW CENTURY VERSION

you will be in me so that they will be completely one. Then
the world will know that you sent me and that you loved
them just as much as you loved me.
24 "Father, I want these people that you gave me to be
with me where I am. I want them to see my glory, which
you gave me because you loved me before the world was
made. 25 Father, you are the One who is good. The world
does not know you, but I know you, and these people
know you sent me. 26 I showed them what you are like, and
I will show them again. Then they will have the same love
that you have for me, and I will live in them."

Jesus Is Arrested

18 When Jesus finished praying, he went with his fol-
lowers across the Kidron Valley. On the other side
there was a garden, and Jesus and his followers went into it.
2 Judas knew where this place was, because Jesus met
there often with his followers. Judas was the one who turned
against Jesus. 3 So Judas came there with a group of soldiers

CONTEMPORARY ENGLISH VERSION

and you are one with me, so that they may become com-
pletely one. Then this world's people will know that you
sent me. They will know that you love my followers as
much as you love me.
24 Father, I want everyone you have given me to be
with me, wherever I am. Then they will see the glory
that you have given me, because you loved me before
the world was created. 25 Good Father, the people of this
world don't know you. But I know you, and my followers
know that you sent me. 26 I told them what you are like,
and I will tell them even more. Then the love that you
have for me will become part of them, and I will be one
with them.

Jesus Is Betrayed and Arrested

(Matthew 26.47-56; Mark 14.43-50; Luke 22.47-53)

18 When Jesus had finished praying, he and his disci-
ples crossed the Kidron Valley and went into a gar-
den.[a] 2 Jesus had often met there with his disciples, and
Judas knew where the place was.
3-5 Judas had promised to betray Jesus. So he went to the
garden with some Roman soldiers and temple police, who
had been sent by the chief priests and the Pharisees. They

[a] 18.1 *garden*: The Greek word is usually translated "garden," but probably referred to an olive orchard.

NEW INTERNATIONAL VERSION

in me. May they be brought to complete unity to let the world know that you sent me and have loved them even as you have loved me.

24"Father, I want those you have given me to be with me where I am, and to see my glory, the glory you have given me because you loved me before the creation of the world.

25"Righteous Father, though the world does not know you, I know you, and they know that you have sent me. 26I have made you known to them, and will continue to make you known in order that the love you have for me may be in them and that I myself may be in them."

Jesus Arrested

18 When he had finished praying, Jesus left with his disciples and crossed the Kidron Valley. On the other side there was an olive grove, and he and his disciples went into it.

2Now Judas, who betrayed him, knew the place, because Jesus had often met there with his disciples. 3So Judas came to the grove, guiding a detachment of soldiers and

NEW LIVING TRANSLATION

being perfected into one. Then the world will know that you sent me and will understand that you love them as much as you love me. 24Father, I want these whom you've given me to be with me, so they can see my glory. You gave me the glory because you loved me even before the world began!

25"O righteous Father, the world doesn't know you, but I do; and these disciples know you sent me. 26And I have revealed you to them and will keep on revealing you. I will do this so that your love for me may be in them and I in them."

Jesus Is Betrayed and Arrested

18 After saying these things, Jesus crossed the Kidron Valley with his disciples and entered a grove of olive trees. 2Judas, the betrayer, knew this place, because Jesus had gone there many times with his disciples. 3The leading priests and Pharisees had given Judas a battalion of Roman soldiers and Temple guards to accompany him.

NEW KING JAMES VERSION

them, and You in Me; that they may be made perfect in one, and that the world may know that You have sent Me, and have loved them as You have loved Me.

24"Father, I desire that they also whom You gave Me may be with Me where I am, that they may behold My glory which You have given Me; for You loved Me before the foundation of the world. 25O righteous Father! The world has not known You, but I have known You; and these have known that You sent Me. 26And I have declared to them Your name, and will declare *it,* that the love with which You loved Me may be in them, and I in them."

Betrayal and Arrest in Gethsemane

18 When Jesus had spoken these words, He went out with His disciples over the Brook Kidron, where there was a garden, which He and His disciples entered. 2And Judas, who betrayed Him, also knew the place; for Jesus often met there with His disciples. 3Then Judas, having received a detachment *of troops,* and officers from the

THE MESSAGE

I in them and you in me.
Then they'll be mature in this oneness,
And give the godless world evidence
That you've sent me and loved them
In the same way you've loved me.

✠

"Father, I want those you gave me
To be with me, right where I am,
So they can see my glory, the splendor you gave me,
Having loved me
Long before there ever was a world.
Righteous Father, the world has never known you,
But I have known you, and these disciples know
That you sent me on this mission.
I have made your very being known to them—
Who you are and what you do—
And continue to make it known,
So that your love for me
Might be in them
Exactly as I am in them."

Seized in the Garden at Night

18 Jesus, having prayed this prayer, left with his disciples and crossed over the brook Kidron at a place where there was a garden. He and his disciples entered it.

Judas, his betrayer, knew the place because Jesus and his disciples went there often. So Judas led the way to the garden, and the Roman soldiers and police sent by the

KING JAMES VERSION

from the chief priests and Pharisees, cometh thither with lanterns and torches and weapons.

4 Jesus therefore, knowing all things that should come upon him, went forth, and said unto them, Whom seek ye?

5 They answered him, Jesus of Nazareth. Jesus saith unto them, I am *he*. And Judas also, which betrayed him, stood with them.

6 As soon then as he had said unto them, I am *he*, they went backward, and fell to the ground.

7 Then asked he them again, Whom seek ye? And they said, Jesus of Nazareth.

8 Jesus answered, I have told you that I am *he*: if therefore ye seek me, let these go their way:

9 That the saying might be fulfilled, which he spake, Of them which thou gavest me have I lost none.

10 Then Simon Peter having a sword drew it, and smote the high priest's servant, and cut off his right ear. The servant's name was Malchus.

11 Then said Jesus unto Peter, Put up thy sword into the sheath: the cup which my Father hath given me, shall I not drink it?

12 Then the band and the captain and officers of the Jews took Jesus, and bound him,

13 ¶ And led him away to Annas first; for he was father in law to Caiaphas, which was the high priest that same year.

14 Now Caiaphas was he, which gave counsel to the Jews, that it was expedient that one man should die for the people.

NEW AMERICAN STANDARD BIBLE

officers from the chief priests and the Pharisees, *came there with lanterns and torches and weapons.

4 So Jesus, knowing all the things that were coming upon Him, went forth and *said to them, "Whom do you seek?"

5 They answered Him, "Jesus the Nazarene." He *said to them, "I am *He*." And Judas also, who was betraying Him, was standing with them.

6 So when He said to them, "I am *He*," they drew back and fell to the ground.

7 Therefore He again asked them, "Whom do you seek?" And they said, "Jesus the Nazarene."

8 Jesus answered, "I told you that I am *He;* so if you seek Me, let these go their way,"

9 to fulfill the word which He spoke, "Of those whom You have given Me I lost not one."

10 Simon Peter then, having a sword, drew it and struck the high priest's slave, and cut off his right ear; and the slave's name was Malchus.

11 So Jesus said to Peter, "Put the sword into the sheath; the cup which the Father has given Me, shall I not drink it?"

Jesus before the Priests

12 So the *Roman* cohort and the commander and the officers of the Jews, arrested Jesus and bound Him,

13 and led Him to Annas first; for he was father-in-law of Caiaphas, who was high priest that year.

14 Now Caiaphas was the one who had advised the Jews that it was expedient for one man to die on behalf of the people.

NEW CENTURY VERSION

and some guards from the leading priests and the Pharisees. They were carrying torches, lanterns, and weapons.

4Knowing everything that would happen to him, Jesus went out and asked, "Who is it you are looking for?"

5They answered, "Jesus from Nazareth."

"I am he," Jesus said. (Judas, the one who turned
against Jesus, was standing there with them.) 6When Jesus
said, "I am he," they moved back and fell to the ground.

7Jesus asked them again, "Who is it you are looking for?"

They said, "Jesus of Nazareth."

8"I told you that I am he," Jesus said. "So if you are
looking for me, let the others go." 9This happened so that
the words Jesus said before would come true: "I have not
lost any of the ones you gave me."

10Simon Peter, who had a sword, pulled it out and
struck the servant of the high priest, cutting off his right
ear. (The servant's name was Malchus.) 11Jesus said to
Peter, "Put your sword back. Shouldn't I drink the cup[a] the
Father gave me?"

Jesus Is Brought Before Annas

12Then the soldiers with their commander and the
Jewish guards arrested Jesus. They tied him 13and led him
first to Annas, the father-in-law of Caiaphas, the high
priest that year. 14Caiaphas was the one who told the Jews
that it would be better if one man died for all the people.

18:11 [a] **cup** Jesus is talking about the painful things that will happen to him. Accepting these things will be very hard, like drinking a cup of something bitter.

CONTEMPORARY ENGLISH VERSION

carried torches, lanterns, and weapons. Jesus already knew everything that was going to happen, but he asked, "Who are you looking for?"

They answered, "We are looking for Jesus from Nazareth!"

Jesus told them, "I am Jesus!"[b] 6At once they all backed
away and fell to the ground.

7Jesus again asked, "Who are you looking for?"

"We are looking for Jesus from Nazareth," they answered.

8This time Jesus replied, "I have already told you that I
am Jesus. If I am the one you are looking for, let these oth-
ers go. 9Then everything will happen, just as I said, 'I did
not lose anyone you gave me.' "

10Simon Peter had brought along a sword. He now
pulled it out and struck at the servant of the high priest.
The servant's name was Malchus, and Peter cut off his
right ear. 11Jesus told Peter, "Put your sword away. I must
drink from the cup[c] that the Father has given me."

Jesus Is Brought to Annas

(Matthew 26.57, 58; Mark 14.53, 54; Luke 22.54)

12The Roman officer and his men, together with the tem-
ple police, arrested Jesus and tied him up. 13They took him
first to Annas, who was the father-in-law of Caiaphas, the
high priest that year. 14This was the same Caiaphas who
had told the Jewish leaders, "It is better if one person dies
for the people."

[b] **18.3-5** *I am Jesus*: The Greek text has "I am" (see the note at 8.24).
[c] **18.11** *drink from the cup*: In the Scriptures a cup is sometimes used as a symbol of suffering. To "drink from the cup" is to suffer.

NEW INTERNATIONAL VERSION

some officials from the chief priests and Pharisees. They were carrying torches, lanterns and weapons.

4Jesus, knowing all that was going to happen to him, went out and asked them, "Who is it you want?"

5"Jesus of Nazareth," they replied.

"I am he," Jesus said. (And Judas the traitor was standing there with them.) 6When Jesus said, "I am he," they drew back and fell to the ground.

7Again he asked them, "Who is it you want?"

And they said, "Jesus of Nazareth."

8"I told you that I am he," Jesus answered. "If you are looking for me, then let these men go." 9This happened so that the words he had spoken would be fulfilled: "I have not lost one of those you gave me."[a]

10Then Simon Peter, who had a sword, drew it and struck the high priest's servant, cutting off his right ear. (The servant's name was Malchus.)

11Jesus commanded Peter, "Put your sword away! Shall I not drink the cup the Father has given me?"

Jesus Taken to Annas

12Then the detachment of soldiers with its commander and the Jewish officials arrested Jesus. They bound him 13and brought him first to Annas, who was the father-in-law of Caiaphas, the high priest that year. 14Caiaphas was the one who had advised the Jews that it would be good if one man died for the people.

[a] *9* John 6:39

NEW LIVING TRANSLATION

Now with blazing torches, lanterns, and weapons, they arrived at the olive grove.

4Jesus fully realized all that was going to happen to him. Stepping forward to meet them, he asked, "Whom are you looking for?"

5"Jesus of Nazareth," they replied.

"I am he,"* Jesus said. Judas was standing there with them when Jesus identified himself. 6And as he said, "I am he," they all fell backward to the ground! 7Once more he asked them, "Whom are you searching for?"

And again they replied, "Jesus of Nazareth."

8"I told you that I am he," Jesus said. "And since I am the one you want, let these others go." 9He did this to fulfill his own statement: "I have not lost a single one of those you gave me."*

10Then Simon Peter drew a sword and slashed off the right ear of Malchus, the high priest's servant. 11But Jesus said to Peter, "Put your sword back into its sheath. Shall I not drink from the cup the Father has given me?"

Annas Questions Jesus

12So the soldiers, their commanding officer, and the Temple guards arrested Jesus and tied him up. 13First they took him to Annas, the father-in-law of Caiaphas, the high priest that year. 14Caiaphas was the one who had told the other Jewish leaders, "Better that one should die for all."

18:5 Greek *I am;* also in 18:6, 8. **18:9** See John 6:39 and 17:12.

NEW KING JAMES VERSION

chief priests and Pharisees, came there with lanterns, torches, and weapons. 4Jesus therefore, knowing all things that would come upon Him, went forward and said to them, "Whom are you seeking?"

5They answered Him, "Jesus of Nazareth."

Jesus said to them, "I am *He.*" And Judas, who betrayed Him, also stood with them. 6Now when He said to them, "I am *He,*" they drew back and fell to the ground.

7Then He asked them again, "Whom are you seeking?"

And they said, "Jesus of Nazareth."

8Jesus answered, "I have told you that I am *He.* Therefore, if you seek Me, let these go their way," 9that the saying might be fulfilled which He spoke, "Of those whom You gave Me I have lost none."

10Then Simon Peter, having a sword, drew it and struck the high priest's servant, and cut off his right ear. The servant's name was Malchus.

11So Jesus said to Peter, "Put your sword into the sheath. Shall I not drink the cup which My Father has given Me?"

Before the High Priest

12Then the detachment *of troops* and the captain and the officers of the Jews arrested Jesus and bound Him. 13And they led Him away to Annas first, for he was the father-in-law of Caiaphas who was high priest that year. 14Now it was Caiaphas who advised the Jews that it was expedient that one man should die for the people.

THE MESSAGE

high priests and Pharisees followed. They arrived there with lanterns and torches and swords. Jesus, knowing by now everything that was coming down on him, went out and met them. He said, "Who are you after?"

They answered, "Jesus the Nazarene."

He said, "That's me." The soldiers recoiled, totally taken aback. Judas, his betrayer, stood out like a sore thumb.

Jesus asked again, "Who are you after?"

They answered, "Jesus the Nazarene."

"I told you," said Jesus, "that's me. I'm the one. So if it's me you're after, let these others go." (This validated the words in his prayer, "I didn't lose one of those you gave.")

Just then Simon Peter, who was carrying a sword, pulled it from its sheath and struck the Chief Priest's servant, cutting off his right ear. Malchus was the servant's name.

Jesus ordered Peter, "Put back your sword. Do you think for a minute I'm not going to drink this cup the Father gave me?"

Then the Roman soldiers under their commander, joined by the Jewish police, seized Jesus and tied him up. They took him first to Annas, father-in-law of Caiaphas. Caiaphas was the Chief Priest that year. It was Caiaphas who had advised the Jews that it was to their advantage that one man die for the people.

KING JAMES VERSION

15 And Simon Peter followed Jesus, and *so did* another disciple: that disciple was known unto the high priest, and went in with Jesus into the palace of the high priest.

16 But Peter stood at the door without. Then went out that other disciple, which was known unto the high priest, and spake unto her that kept the door, and brought in Peter.

17 Then saith the damsel that kept the door unto Peter, Art not thou also *one* of this man's disciples? He saith, I am not.

18 And the servants and officers stood there, who had made a fire of coals; for it was cold: and they warmed themselves: and Peter stood with them, and warmed himself.

19 The high priest then asked Jesus of his disciples, and of his doctrine.

20 Jesus answered him, I spake openly to the world; I ever taught in the synagogue, and in the temple, whither the Jews always resort; and in secret have I said nothing.

21 Why askest thou me? ask them which heard me, what I have said unto them: behold, they know what I said.

22 And when he had thus spoken, one of the officers which stood by struck Jesus with the palm of his hand, saying, Answerest thou the high priest so?

23 Jesus answered him, If I have spoken evil, bear witness of the evil: but if well, why smitest thou me?

NEW AMERICAN STANDARD BIBLE

15 Simon Peter was following Jesus, and *so was* another disciple. Now that disciple was known to the high priest, and entered with Jesus into the court of the high priest,

16 but Peter was standing at the door outside. So the other disciple, who was known to the high priest, went out and spoke to the doorkeeper, and brought Peter in.

17 Then the slave-girl who kept the door *said to Peter, "You are not also *one* of this man's disciples, are you?" He *said, "I am not."

18 Now the slaves and the officers were standing *there*, having made a charcoal fire, for it was cold and they were warming themselves; and Peter was also with them, standing and warming himself.

19 The high priest then questioned Jesus about His disciples, and about His teaching.

20 Jesus answered him, "I have spoken openly to the world; I always taught in synagogues and in the temple, where all the Jews come together; and I spoke nothing in secret.

21 "Why do you question Me? Question those who have heard what I spoke to them; they know what I said."

22 When He had said this, one of the officers standing nearby struck Jesus, saying, "Is that the way You answer the high priest?"

23 Jesus answered him, "If I have spoken wrongly, testify of the wrong; but if rightly, why do you strike Me?"

NEW CENTURY VERSION

Peter Says He Doesn't Know Jesus

[15]Simon Peter and another one of Jesus' followers went along after Jesus. This follower knew the high priest, so he went with Jesus into the high priest's courtyard. [16]But Peter waited outside near the door. The follower who knew the high priest came back outside, spoke to the girl at the door, and brought Peter inside. [17]The girl at the door said to Peter, "Aren't you also one of that man's followers?"

Peter answered, "No, I am not!"

[18]It was cold, so the servants and guards had built a fire and were standing around it, warming themselves. Peter also was standing with them, warming himself.

The High Priest Questions Jesus

[19]The high priest asked Jesus questions about his followers and his teaching. [20]Jesus answered, "I have spoken openly to everyone. I have always taught in synagogues and in the Temple, where all the Jews come together. I never said anything in secret. [21]So why do you question me? Ask the people who heard my teaching. They know what I said."

[22]When Jesus said this, one of the guards standing there hit him. The guard said, "Is that the way you answer the high priest?"

[23]Jesus answered him, "If I said something wrong, then show what it was. But if what I said is true, why do you hit me?"

CONTEMPORARY ENGLISH VERSION

Peter Says He Doesn't Know Jesus

(Matthew 26.69, 70; Mark 14.66-68; Luke 22.55-57)

[15]Simon Peter and another disciple followed Jesus. That disciple knew the high priest, and he followed Jesus into the courtyard of the high priest's house. [16]Peter stayed outside near the gate. But the other disciple came back out and spoke to the girl at the gate. She let Peter go in, [17]but asked him, "Aren't you one of that man's followers?"

"No, I am not!" Peter answered.

[18]It was cold, and the servants and temple police had made a charcoal fire. They were warming themselves around it, when Peter went over and stood near the fire to warm himself.

Jesus Is Questioned by the High Priest

(Matthew 26.59-66; Mark 14.55-64; Luke 22.66-71)

[19]The high priest questioned Jesus about his followers and his teaching. [20]But Jesus told him, "I have spoken freely in front of everyone. And I have always taught in our meeting places and in the temple, where all of our people come together. I have not said anything in secret. [21]Why are you questioning me? Why don't you ask the people who heard me? They know what I have said."

[22]As soon as Jesus said this, one of the temple police hit him and said, "That's no way to talk to the high priest!"

[23]Jesus answered, "If I have done something wrong, say so. But if not, why did you hit me?" [24]Jesus was still tied

NEW INTERNATIONAL VERSION

Peter's First Denial

15 Simon Peter and another disciple were following Jesus. Because this disciple was known to the high priest, he went with Jesus into the high priest's courtyard, 16 but Peter had to wait outside at the door. The other disciple, who was known to the high priest, came back, spoke to the girl on duty there and brought Peter in.

17 "You are not one of his disciples, are you?" the girl at the door asked Peter.

He replied, "I am not."

18 It was cold, and the servants and officials stood around a fire they had made to keep warm. Peter also was standing with them, warming himself.

The High Priest Questions Jesus

19 Meanwhile, the high priest questioned Jesus about his disciples and his teaching.

20 "I have spoken openly to the world," Jesus replied. "I always taught in synagogues or at the temple, where all the Jews come together. I said nothing in secret. 21 Why question me? Ask those who heard me. Surely they know what I said."

22 When Jesus said this, one of the officials nearby struck him in the face. "Is this the way you answer the high priest?" he demanded.

23 "If I said something wrong," Jesus replied, "testify as to what is wrong. But if I spoke the truth, why did you strike

NEW LIVING TRANSLATION

Peter's First Denial

15 Simon Peter followed along behind, as did another of the disciples. That other disciple was acquainted with the high priest, so he was allowed to enter the courtyard with Jesus. 16 Peter stood outside the gate. Then the other disciple spoke to the woman watching at the gate, and she let Peter in. 17 The woman asked Peter, "Aren't you one of Jesus' disciples?"

"No," he said, "I am not."

18 The guards and the household servants were standing around a charcoal fire they had made because it was cold. And Peter stood there with them, warming himself.

The High Priest Questions Jesus

19 Inside, the high priest began asking Jesus about his followers and what he had been teaching them. 20 Jesus replied, "What I teach is widely known, because I have preached regularly in the synagogues and the Temple. I have been heard by people* everywhere, and I teach nothing in private that I have not said in public. 21 Why are you asking me this question? Ask those who heard me. They know what I said."

22 One of the Temple guards standing there struck Jesus on the face. "Is that the way to answer the high priest?" he demanded.

23 Jesus replied, "If I said anything wrong, you must give evidence for it. Should you hit a man for telling the truth?"

18:20 Greek *Jewish people;* also in 18:38.

NEW KING JAMES VERSION

Peter Denies Jesus

15 And Simon Peter followed Jesus, and so *did* another[a] disciple. Now that disciple was known to the high priest, and went with Jesus into the courtyard of the high priest. 16 But Peter stood at the door outside. Then the other disciple, who was known to the high priest, went out and spoke to her who kept the door, and brought Peter in. 17 Then the servant girl who kept the door said to Peter, "You are not also *one* of this Man's disciples, are you?"

He said, "I am not."

18 Now the servants and officers who had made a fire of coals stood there, for it was cold, and they warmed themselves. And Peter stood with them and warmed himself.

Jesus Questioned by the High Priest

19 The high priest then asked Jesus about His disciples and His doctrine.

20 Jesus answered him, "I spoke openly to the world. I always taught in synagogues and in the temple, where the Jews always meet,[b] and in secret I have said nothing. 21 Why do you ask Me? Ask those who have heard Me what I said to them. Indeed they know what I said."

22 And when He had said these things, one of the officers who stood by struck Jesus with the palm of his hand, saying, "Do You answer the high priest like that?"

23 Jesus answered him, "If I have spoken evil, bear witness of the evil; but if well, why do you strike Me?"

18:15 [a] M-Text reads *the other.* **18:20** [b] NU-Text reads *where all the Jews meet.*

THE MESSAGE

Simon Peter and another disciple followed Jesus. That other disciple was known to the Chief Priest, and so he went in with Jesus to the Chief Priest's courtyard. Peter had to stay outside. Then the other disciple went out, spoke to the doorkeeper, and got Peter in.

The young woman who was the doorkeeper said to Peter, "Aren't you one of this man's disciples?"

He said, "No, I'm not."

The servants and police had made a fire because of the cold and were huddled there warming themselves. Peter stood with them, trying to get warm.

The Interrogation

Annas interrogated Jesus regarding his disciples and his teaching. Jesus answered, "I've spoken openly in public. I've taught regularly in meeting places and the Temple, where the Jews all come together. Everything has been out in the open. I've said nothing in secret. So why are you treating me like a conspirator? Question those who have been listening to me. They know well what I have said. My teachings have all been aboveboard."

When he said this, one of the policemen standing there slapped Jesus across the face, saying, "How dare you speak to the Chief Priest like that!"

Jesus replied, "If I've said something wrong, prove it. But if I've spoken the plain truth, why this slapping around?"

KING JAMES VERSION

24 Now Annas had sent him bound unto Caiaphas the high priest.

25 And Simon Peter stood and warmed himself. They said therefore unto him, Art not thou also *one* of his disciples? He denied *it*, and said, I am not.

26 One of the servants of the high priest, being *his* kinsman whose ear Peter cut off, saith, Did not I see thee in the garden with him?

27 Peter then denied again: and immediately the cock crew.

28 ¶ Then led they Jesus from Caiaphas unto the hall of judgment: and it was early; and they themselves went not into the judgment hall, lest they should be defiled; but that they might eat the passover.

29 Pilate then went out unto them, and said, What accusation bring ye against this man?

30 They answered and said unto him, If he were not a malefactor, we would not have delivered him up unto thee.

31 Then said Pilate unto them, Take ye him, and judge him according to your law. The Jews therefore said unto

NEW AMERICAN STANDARD BIBLE

24 So Annas sent Him bound to Caiaphas the high priest.

Peter's Denial of Jesus

25 Now Simon Peter was standing and warming himself. So they said to him, "You are not also *one* of His disciples, are you?" He denied *it*, and said, "I am not."

26 One of the slaves of the high priest, being a relative of the one whose ear Peter cut off, *said, "Did I not see you in the garden with Him?"

27 Peter then denied *it* again, and immediately a rooster crowed.

Jesus before Pilate

28 Then they *led Jesus from Caiaphas into the [1]Praetorium, and it was early; and they themselves did not enter into the Praetorium so that they would not be defiled, but might eat the Passover.

29 Therefore Pilate went out to them and *said, "What accusation do you bring against this Man?"

30 They answered and said to him, "If this Man were not an evildoer, we would not have delivered Him to you."

31 So Pilate said to them, "Take Him yourselves, and judge Him according to your law." The Jews said to him,

18:28 [1] I.e. governor's official residence

NEW CENTURY VERSION

24Then Annas sent Jesus, who was still tied, to Caiaphas the high priest.

Peter Says Again He Doesn't Know Jesus

25As Simon Peter was standing and warming himself, they said to him, "Aren't you one of that man's followers?"

Peter said it was not true; he said, "No, I am not."

26One of the servants of the high priest was there. This servant was a relative of the man whose ear Peter had cut off. The servant said, "Didn't I see you with him in the garden?"

27Again Peter said it wasn't true. At once a rooster crowed.

Jesus Is Brought Before Pilate

28Early in the morning they led Jesus from Caiaphas's house to the Roman governor's palace. They would not go inside the palace, because they did not want to make themselves unclean;[b] they wanted to eat the Passover
meal. 29So Pilate went outside to them and asked, "What charges do you bring against this man?"

30They answered, "If he were not a criminal, we wouldn't have brought him to you."

31Pilate said to them, "Take him yourselves and judge him by your own law."

18:28 [b] **unclean** Going into a non-Jewish place would make them unfit to eat the Passover Feast, according to Jewish law.

CONTEMPORARY ENGLISH VERSION

up, and Annas sent him to Caiaphas the high priest.

Peter Again Denies that He Knows Jesus

(Matthew 26.71-75; Mark 14.69-72; Luke 22.58-62)

25While Simon Peter was standing there warming himself, someone asked him, "Aren't you one of Jesus' followers?"

Again Peter denied it and said, "No, I am not!"

26One of the high priest's servants was there. He was a relative of the servant whose ear Peter had cut off, and he asked, "Didn't I see you in the garden with that man?"

27Once more Peter denied it, and right then a rooster crowed.

Jesus Is Tried by Pilate

(Matthew 27.1, 2, 11-14; Mark 15.1-5; Luke 23.1-5)

28It was early in the morning when Jesus was taken from Caiaphas to the building where the Roman governor stayed. But the crowd waited outside. Any of them who had gone inside would have become unclean and would not be allowed to eat the Passover meal.[d]

29Pilate came out and asked, "What charges are you bringing against this man?"

30They answered, "He is a criminal! That's why we brought him to you."

31Pilate told them, "Take him and judge him by your own laws."

[d] **18.28** *would have become unclean and would not be allowed to eat the Passover meal*: Jewish people who came in close contact with foreigners right before Passover were not allowed to eat the Passover meal.

NEW INTERNATIONAL VERSION

me?" 24Then Annas sent him, still bound, to Caiaphas the high priest.[b]

Peter's Second and Third Denials

25As Simon Peter stood warming himself, he was asked, "You are not one of his disciples, are you?"

He denied it, saying, "I am not."

26One of the high priest's servants, a relative of the man whose ear Peter had cut off, challenged him, "Didn't I see you with him in the olive grove?" 27Again Peter denied it, and at that moment a rooster began to crow.

Jesus Before Pilate

28Then the Jews led Jesus from Caiaphas to the palace of the Roman governor. By now it was early morning, and to avoid ceremonial uncleanness the Jews did not enter the palace; they wanted to be able to eat the Passover. 29So Pilate came out to them and asked, "What charges are you bringing against this man?"

30"If he were not a criminal," they replied, "we would not have handed him over to you."

31Pilate said, "Take him yourselves and judge him by your own law."

b 24 Or *(Now Annas had sent him, still bound, to Caiaphas the high priest.)*

NEW LIVING TRANSLATION

24Then Annas bound Jesus and sent him to Caiaphas, the high priest.

Peter's Second and Third Denials

25Meanwhile, as Simon Peter was standing by the fire, they asked him again, "Aren't you one of his disciples?"

"I am not," he said.

26But one of the household servants of the high priest, a relative of the man whose ear Peter had cut off, asked, "Didn't I see you out there in the olive grove with Jesus?" 27Again Peter denied it. And immediately a rooster crowed.

Jesus' Trial before Pilate

28Jesus' trial before Caiaphas ended in the early hours of the morning. Then he was taken to the headquarters of the Roman governor. His accusers didn't go in themselves because it would defile them, and they wouldn't be allowed to celebrate the Passover feast. 29So Pilate, the governor, went out to them and asked, "What is your charge against this man?"

30"We wouldn't have handed him over to you if he weren't a criminal!" they retorted.

31"Then take him away and judge him by your own laws," Pilate told them.

NEW KING JAMES VERSION

24Then Annas sent Him bound to Caiaphas the high priest.

Peter Denies Twice More

25Now Simon Peter stood and warmed himself. Therefore they said to him, "You are not also *one* of His disciples, are you?"

He denied *it* and said, "I am not!"

26One of the servants of the high priest, a relative *of him* whose ear Peter cut off, said, "Did I not see you in the garden with Him?" 27Peter then denied again; and immediately a rooster crowed.

In Pilate's Court

28Then they led Jesus from Caiaphas to the Praetorium, and it was early morning. But they themselves did not go into the Praetorium, lest they should be defiled, but that they might eat the Passover. 29Pilate then went out to them and said, "What accusation do you bring against this Man?"

30They answered and said to him, "If He were not an evildoer, we would not have delivered Him up to you."

31Then Pilate said to them, "You take Him and judge Him according to your law."

THE MESSAGE

Then Annas sent him, still tied up, to the Chief Priest Caiaphas.

Meanwhile, Simon Peter was back at the fire, still trying to get warm. The others there said to him, "Aren't you one of his disciples?"

He denied it, "Not me."

One of the Chief Priest's servants, a relative of the man whose ear Peter had cut off, said, "Didn't I see you in the garden with him?"

Again, Peter denied it. Just then a rooster crowed.

The King of the Jews

They led Jesus then from Caiaphas to the Roman governor's palace. It was early morning. They themselves didn't enter the palace because they didn't want to be disqualified from eating the Passover. So Pilate came out to them and spoke. "What charge do you bring against this man?"

They said, "If he hadn't been doing something evil, do you think we'd be here bothering you?"

Pilate said, "You take him. Judge him by *your* law."

KING JAMES VERSION

him, It is not lawful for us to put any man to death:

32 That the saying of Jesus might be fulfilled, which he spake, signifying what death he should die.

33 Then Pilate entered into the judgment hall again, and called Jesus, and said unto him, Art thou the King of the Jews?

34 Jesus answered him, Sayest thou this thing of thyself, or did others tell it thee of me?

35 Pilate answered, Am I a Jew? Thine own nation and the chief priests have delivered thee unto me: what hast thou done?

36 Jesus answered, My kingdom is not of this world: if my kingdom were of this world, then would my servants fight, that I should not be delivered to the Jews: but now is my kingdom not from hence.

37 Pilate therefore said unto him, Art thou a king then? Jesus answered, Thou sayest that I am a king. To this end was I born, and for this cause came I into the world, that I should bear witness unto the truth. Every one that is of the truth heareth my voice.

38 Pilate saith unto him, What is truth? And when he had said this, he went out again unto the Jews, and saith unto them, I find in him no fault *at all.*

39 But ye have a custom, that I should release unto you one at the passover: will ye therefore that I release unto you the King of the Jews?

NEW AMERICAN STANDARD BIBLE

"We are not permitted to put anyone to death,"

32 to fulfill the word of Jesus which He spoke, signifying by what kind of death He was about to die.

33 Therefore Pilate entered again into the Praetorium, and summoned Jesus and said to Him, "Are You the King of the Jews?"

34 Jesus answered, "Are you saying this on your own initiative, or did others tell you about Me?"

35 Pilate answered, "I am not a Jew, am I? Your own nation and the chief priests delivered You to me; what have You done?"

36 Jesus answered, "My kingdom is not of this world. If My kingdom were of this world, then My servants would be fighting so that I would not be handed over to the Jews; but as it is, My kingdom is not [2]of this realm."

37 Therefore Pilate said to Him, "So You are a king?" Jesus answered, "You say *correctly* that I am a king. For this I have been born, and for this I have come into the world, to testify to the truth. Everyone who is of the truth hears My voice."

38 Pilate *said to Him, "What is truth?"

And when he had said this, he went out again to the Jews and *said to them, "I find no guilt in Him.

39 "But you have a custom that I release someone for you at the Passover; do you wish then that I release for you the King of the Jews?"

18:36 [2] Lit *from here*

NEW CENTURY VERSION

"But we are not allowed to put anyone to death," the Jews answered. 32(This happened so that what Jesus said about how he would die would come true.)

33Then Pilate went back inside the palace and called Jesus to him and asked, "Are you the king of the Jews?"

34Jesus said, "Is that your own question, or did others tell you about me?"

35Pilate answered, "I am not Jewish. It was your own people and their leading priests who handed you over to me. What have you done wrong?"

36Jesus answered, "My kingdom does not belong to this world. If it belonged to this world, my servants would fight so that I would not be given over to the Jews. But my kingdom is from another place."

37Pilate said, "So you are a king!"

Jesus answered, "You are the one saying I am a king. This is why I was born and came into the world: to tell people the truth. And everyone who belongs to the truth listens to me."

38Pilate said, "What is truth?" After he said this, he went out to the Jews again and said to them, "I find nothing against this man. 39But it is your custom that I free one prisoner to you at Passover time. Do you want me to free the 'king of the Jews'?"

CONTEMPORARY ENGLISH VERSION

The crowd replied, "We are not allowed to put anyone to death." 32And so what Jesus said about his death[e] would soon come true.

33Pilate then went back inside. He called Jesus over and asked, "Are you the king of the Jews?"

34Jesus answered, "Are you asking this on your own or did someone tell you about me?"

35"You know I'm not a Jew!" Pilate said. "Your own people and the chief priests brought you to me. What have you done?"

36Jesus answered, "My kingdom doesn't belong to this world. If it did, my followers would have fought to keep me from being handed over to the Jewish leaders. No, my kingdom doesn't belong to this world."

37"So you are a king," Pilate replied.

"You are saying that I am a king," Jesus told him. "I was born into this world to tell about the truth. And everyone who belongs to the truth knows my voice."

38Pilate asked Jesus, "What is truth?"

Jesus Is Sentenced to Death

(Matthew 27.15-31; Mark 15.6-20; Luke 23.13-25)

Pilate went back out and said, "I don't find this man guilty of anything! 39And since I usually set a prisoner free for you at Passover, would you like for me to set free the king of the Jews?"

[e] **18.32** *about his death*: Jesus had said that he would die by being "lifted up," which meant that he would die on a cross. The Romans killed criminals by nailing them on a cross, but they did not let the Jews kill anyone in this way.

NEW INTERNATIONAL VERSION

"But we have no right to execute anyone," the Jews objected. 32This happened so that the words Jesus had spoken indicating the kind of death he was going to die would be fulfilled.

33Pilate then went back inside the palace, summoned Jesus and asked him, "Are you the king of the Jews?"

34"Is that your own idea," Jesus asked, "or did others talk to you about me?"

35"Am I a Jew?" Pilate replied. "It was your people and your chief priests who handed you over to me. What is it you have done?"

36Jesus said, "My kingdom is not of this world. If it were, my servants would fight to prevent my arrest by the Jews. But now my kingdom is from another place."

37"You are a king, then!" said Pilate.

Jesus answered, "You are right in saying I am a king. In fact, for this reason I was born, and for this I came into the world, to testify to the truth. Everyone on the side of truth listens to me."

38"What is truth?" Pilate asked. With this he went out again to the Jews and said, "I find no basis for a charge against him. 39But it is your custom for me to release to you one prisoner at the time of the Passover. Do you want me to release 'the king of the Jews'?"

NEW LIVING TRANSLATION

"Only the Romans are permitted to execute someone," the Jewish leaders replied. 32This fulfilled Jesus' prediction about the way he would die.*

33Then Pilate went back inside and called for Jesus to be brought to him. "Are you the King of the Jews?" he asked him.

34Jesus replied, "Is this your own question, or did others tell you about me?"

35"Am I a Jew?" Pilate asked. "Your own people and their leading priests brought you here. Why? What have you done?"

36Then Jesus answered, "I am not an earthly king. If I were, my followers would have fought when I was arrested by the Jewish leaders. But my Kingdom is not of this world."

37Pilate replied, "You are a king then?"

"You say that I am a king, and you are right," Jesus said. "I was born for that purpose. And I came to bring truth to the world. All who love the truth recognize that what I say is true."

38"What is truth?" Pilate asked. Then he went out again to the people and told them, "He is not guilty of any crime. 39But you have a custom of asking me to release someone from prison each year at Passover. So if you want me to, I'll release the King of the Jews."

18:32 See John 12:32-33.

NEW KING JAMES VERSION

Therefore the Jews said to him, "It is not lawful for us to put anyone to death," 32that the saying of Jesus might be fulfilled which He spoke, signifying by what death He would die.

33Then Pilate entered the Praetorium again, called Jesus, and said to Him, "Are You the King of the Jews?"

34Jesus answered him, "Are you speaking for yourself about this, or did others tell you this concerning Me?"

35Pilate answered, "Am I a Jew? Your own nation and the chief priests have delivered You to me. What have You done?"

36Jesus answered, "My kingdom is not of this world. If My kingdom were of this world, My servants would fight, so that I should not be delivered to the Jews; but now My kingdom is not from here."

37Pilate therefore said to Him, "Are You a king then?"

Jesus answered, "You say *rightly* that I am a king. For this cause I was born, and for this cause I have come into the world, that I should bear witness to the truth. Everyone who is of the truth hears My voice."

38Pilate said to Him, "What is truth?" And when he had said this, he went out again to the Jews, and said to them, "I find no fault in Him at all.

Taking the Place of Barabbas

39"But you have a custom that I should release someone to you at the Passover. Do you therefore want me to release to you the King of the Jews?"

THE MESSAGE

The Jews said, "We're not allowed to kill anyone." (This would confirm Jesus' word indicating the way he would die.)

Pilate went back into the palace and called for Jesus. He said, "Are you the 'King of the Jews'?"

Jesus answered, "Are you saying this on your own, or did others tell you this about me?"

Pilate said, "Do I look like a Jew? Your people and your high priests turned you over to me. What did you do?"

"My kingdom," said Jesus, "doesn't consist of what you see around you. If it did, my followers would fight so that I wouldn't be handed over to the Jews. But I'm not that kind of king, not the world's kind of king."

Then Pilate said, "So, are you a king or not?"

Jesus answered, "You tell me. Because I am King, I was born and entered the world so that I could witness to the truth. Everyone who cares for truth, who has any feeling for the truth, recognizes my voice."

Pilate said, "What is truth?"

Then he went back out to the Jews and told them, "I find nothing wrong in this man. It's your custom that I pardon one prisoner at Passover. Do you want me to pardon the 'King of the Jews'?"

KING JAMES VERSION

40 Then cried they all again, saying, Not this man, but Barabbas. Now Barabbas was a robber.

19 Then Pilate therefore took Jesus, and scourged *him*.

2 And the soldiers platted a crown of thorns, and put *it* on his head, and they put on him a purple robe,

3 And said, Hail, King of the Jews! and they smote him with their hands.

4 Pilate therefore went forth again, and saith unto them, Behold, I bring him forth to you, that ye may know that I find no fault in him.

5 Then came Jesus forth, wearing the crown of thorns, and the purple robe. And *Pilate* saith unto them, Behold the man!

6 When the chief priests therefore and officers saw him, they cried out, saying, Crucify *him*, crucify *him*. Pilate saith unto them, Take ye him, and crucify *him*: for I find no fault in him.

7 The Jews answered him, We have a law, and by our law he ought to die, because he made himself the Son of God.

8 When Pilate therefore heard that saying, he was the more afraid;

9 And went again into the judgment hall, and saith unto Jesus, Whence art thou? But Jesus gave him no answer.

NEW AMERICAN STANDARD BIBLE

40 So they cried out again, saying, "Not this Man, but Barabbas." Now Barabbas was a robber.

The Crown of Thorns

19 Pilate then took Jesus and scourged Him.
2 And the soldiers twisted together a crown of thorns and put it on His head, and put a purple robe on Him;

3 and they *began* to come up to Him and say, "Hail, King of the Jews!" and to give Him slaps *in the face.*

4 Pilate came out again and *said to them, "Behold, I am bringing Him out to you so that you may know that I find no guilt in Him."

5 Jesus then came out, wearing the crown of thorns and the purple robe. *Pilate* *said to them, "Behold, the Man!"

6 So when the chief priests and the officers saw Him, they cried out saying, "Crucify, crucify!" Pilate *said to them, "Take Him yourselves and crucify Him, for I find no guilt in Him."

7 The Jews answered him, "We have a law, and by that law He ought to die because He made Himself out *to be* the Son of God."

8 Therefore when Pilate heard this statement, he was *even* more afraid;

9 and he entered into the [1]Praetorium again and *said to Jesus, "Where are You from?" But Jesus gave him no answer.

19:9 [1] I.e. governor's official residence

NEW CENTURY VERSION

40They shouted back, "No, not him! Let Barabbas go
free!" (Barabbas was a robber.)

19 Then Pilate ordered that Jesus be taken away and
whipped. 2The soldiers made a crown from some
thorny branches and put it on Jesus' head and put a purple
robe around him. 3Then they came to him many times and
said, "Hail, King of the Jews!" and hit him in the face.
4Again Pilate came out and said to them, "Look, I am
bringing Jesus out to you. I want you to know that I find
nothing against him." 5So Jesus came out, wearing the
crown of thorns and the purple robe. Pilate said to them,
"Here is the man!"
6When the leading priests and the guards saw Jesus,
they shouted, "Crucify him! Crucify him!"
But Pilate answered, "Crucify him yourselves, because I
find nothing against him."
7The Jews answered, "We have a law that says he
should die, because he said he is the Son of God."
8When Pilate heard this, he was even more afraid. 9He
went back inside the palace and asked Jesus, "Where do
you come from?" But Jesus did not answer him. 10Pilate

CONTEMPORARY ENGLISH VERSION

40They shouted, "No, not him! We want Barabbas." Now
Barabbas was a terrorist.[f]

19 Pilate gave orders for Jesus to be beaten with a
whip. 2The soldiers made a crown out of thorn
branches and put it on Jesus. Then they put a purple robe
on him. 3They came up to him and said, "Hey, you king of
the Jews!" They also hit him with their fists.
4Once again Pilate went out. This time he said, "I will
have Jesus brought out to you again. Then you can see for
yourselves that I have not found him guilty."
5Jesus came out, wearing the crown of thorns and the
purple robe. Pilate said, "Here is the man!"[a]
6When the chief priests and the temple police saw him,
they yelled, "Nail him to a cross! Nail him to a cross!"
Pilate told them, "You take him and nail him to a cross!
I don't find him guilty of anything."
7The crowd replied, "He claimed to be the Son of God!
Our Jewish Law says that he must be put to death."
8When Pilate heard this, he was terrified. 9He went back
inside and asked Jesus, "Where are you from?" But Jesus
did not answer.

[f] **18.40** *terrorist*: Someone who stirred up trouble against the Romans in the hope of gaining freedom for the Jewish people. [a] **19.5** *"Here is the man!"*: Or "Look at the man!"

NEW INTERNATIONAL VERSION

40They shouted back, "No, not him! Give us Barabbas!" Now Barabbas had taken part in a rebellion.

Jesus Sentenced to Be Crucified

19 Then Pilate took Jesus and had him flogged. 2The soldiers twisted together a crown of thorns and put it on his head. They clothed him in a purple robe 3and went up to him again and again, saying, "Hail, king of the Jews!" And they struck him in the face.

4Once more Pilate came out and said to the Jews, "Look, I am bringing him out to you to let you know that I find no basis for a charge against him." 5When Jesus came out wearing the crown of thorns and the purple robe, Pilate said to them, "Here is the man!"

6As soon as the chief priests and their officials saw him, they shouted, "Crucify! Crucify!"

But Pilate answered, "You take him and crucify him. As for me, I find no basis for a charge against him."

7The Jews insisted, "We have a law, and according to that law he must die, because he claimed to be the Son of God."

8When Pilate heard this, he was even more afraid, 9and he went back inside the palace. "Where do you come from?" he asked Jesus, but Jesus gave him no answer.

NEW LIVING TRANSLATION

40But they shouted back, "No! Not this man, but Barabbas!" (Barabbas was a criminal.)

Jesus Sentenced to Death

19 Then Pilate had Jesus flogged with a lead-tipped whip. 2The soldiers made a crown of long, sharp thorns and put it on his head, and they put a royal purple robe on him. 3"Hail! King of the Jews!" they mocked, and they hit him with their fists.

4Pilate went outside again and said to the people, "I am going to bring him out to you now, but understand clearly that I find him not guilty." 5Then Jesus came out wearing the crown of thorns and the purple robe. And Pilate said, "Here is the man!"

6When they saw him, the leading priests and Temple guards began shouting, "Crucify! Crucify!"

"You crucify him," Pilate said. "I find him not guilty."

7The Jewish leaders replied, "By our laws he ought to die because he called himself the Son of God."

8When Pilate heard this, he was more frightened than ever. 9He took Jesus back into the headquarters again and asked him, "Where are you from?" But Jesus gave no

NEW KING JAMES VERSION

40Then they all cried again, saying, "Not this Man, but Barabbas!" Now Barabbas was a robber.

The Soldiers Mock Jesus

19 So then Pilate took Jesus and scourged *Him.* 2And the soldiers twisted a crown of thorns and put *it* on His head, and they put on Him a purple robe. 3Then they said,[a] "Hail, King of the Jews!" And they struck Him with their hands.

4Pilate then went out again, and said to them, "Behold, I am bringing Him out to you, that you may know that I find no fault in Him."

Pilate's Decision

5Then Jesus came out, wearing the crown of thorns and the purple robe. And *Pilate* said to them, "Behold the Man!"

6Therefore, when the chief priests and officers saw Him, they cried out, saying, "Crucify *Him,* crucify *Him!*"

Pilate said to them, "You take Him and crucify *Him,* for I find no fault in Him."

7The Jews answered him, "We have a law, and according to our[b] law He ought to die, because He made Himself the Son of God."

8Therefore, when Pilate heard that saying, he was the more afraid, 9and went again into the Praetorium, and said to Jesus, "Where are You from?" But Jesus gave him no answer.

19:3 [a] NU-Text reads *And they came up to Him and said.*
19:7 [b] NU-Text reads *the law.*

THE MESSAGE

They shouted back, "Not this one, but Barabbas!" Barabbas was a Jewish freedom fighter.

The Thorn Crown of the King

19 So Pilate took Jesus and had him whipped. The soldiers, having braided a crown from thorns, set it on his head, threw a purple robe over him, and approached him with, "Hail, King of the Jews!" Then they greeted him with slaps in the face.

Pilate went back out again and said to them, "I present him to you, but I want you to know that I do not find him guilty of any crime." Just then Jesus came out wearing the thorn crown and purple robe.

Pilate announced, "Here he is: the Man."

When the high priests and police saw him, they shouted in a frenzy, "Crucify! Crucify!"

Pilate told them, "You take him. You crucify him. I find nothing wrong with him."

The Jews answered, "We have a law, and by that law he must die because he claimed to be the Son of God."

When Pilate heard this, he became even more scared. He went back into the palace and said to Jesus, "Where did you come from?"

Jesus gave no answer.

KING JAMES VERSION

10 Then saith Pilate unto him, Speakest thou not unto me? knowest thou not that I have power to crucify thee, and have power to release thee?

11 Jesus answered, Thou couldest have no power *at all* against me, except it were given thee from above: therefore he that delivered me unto thee hath the greater sin.

12 And from thenceforth Pilate sought to release him: but the Jews cried out, saying, If thou let this man go, thou art not Caesar's friend: whosoever maketh himself a king speaketh against Caesar.

13 When Pilate therefore heard that saying, he brought Jesus forth, and sat down in the judgment seat in a place that is called the Pavement, but in the Hebrew, Gabbatha.

14 And it was the preparation of the passover, and about the sixth hour: and he saith unto the Jews, Behold your King!

15 But they cried out, Away with *him*, away with *him*, crucify him. Pilate saith unto them, Shall I crucify your King? The chief priests answered, We have no king but Caesar.

16 ¶ Then delivered he him therefore unto them to be crucified. And they took Jesus, and led *him* away.

17 And he bearing his cross went forth into a place called *the place* of a skull, which is called in the Hebrew Golgotha:

18 Where they crucified him, and two other with him, on either side one, and Jesus in the midst.

NEW AMERICAN STANDARD BIBLE

10 So Pilate *said to Him, "You do not speak to me? Do You not know that I have authority to release You, and I have authority to crucify You?"

11 Jesus answered, "You would have no authority over Me, unless it had been given you from above; for this reason he who delivered Me to you has *the* greater sin."

12 As a result of this Pilate made efforts to release Him, but the Jews cried out saying, "If you release this Man, you are no friend of Caesar; everyone who makes himself out *to be* a king opposes Caesar."

13 Therefore when Pilate heard these words, he brought Jesus out, and sat down on the judgment seat at a place called The Pavement, but in Hebrew, Gabbatha.

14 Now it was the day of preparation for the Passover; it was about the [2]sixth hour. And he *said to the Jews, "Behold, your King!"

15 So they cried out, "Away with *Him*, away with *Him*, crucify Him!" Pilate *said to them, "Shall I crucify your King?" The chief priests answered, "We have no king but Caesar."

The Crucifixion

16 So he then handed Him over to them to be crucified.

17 They took Jesus, therefore, and He went out, bearing His own cross, to the place called the Place of a Skull, which is called in Hebrew, Golgotha.

18 There they crucified Him, and with Him two other men, one on either side, and Jesus in between.

19:14 [2] Perhaps 6 a.m.

NEW CENTURY VERSION

said, "You refuse to speak to me? Don't you know I have
power to set you free and power to have you crucified?"
11 Jesus answered, "The only power you have over me is
the power given to you by God. The man who turned me in
to you is guilty of a greater sin."
12 After this, Pilate tried to let Jesus go. But the Jews
cried out, "Anyone who makes himself king is against
Caesar. If you let this man go, you are no friend of Caesar."
13 When Pilate heard what they were saying, he brought
Jesus out and sat down on the judge's seat at the place called
The Stone Pavement. (In the Jewish language[a] the name is
Gabbatha.) 14 It was about noon on Preparation Day of Pass-
over week. Pilate said to the Jews, "Here is your king!"
15 They shouted, "Take him away! Take him away!
Crucify him!"
Pilate asked them, "Do you want me to crucify your king?"
The leading priests answered, "The only king we have is
Caesar."
16 So Pilate handed Jesus over to them to be crucified.

Jesus Is Crucified

The soldiers took charge of Jesus. 17 Carrying his own
cross, Jesus went out to a place called The Place of the
Skull, which in the Jewish language[a] is called Golgotha.
18 There they crucified Jesus. They also crucified two other
men, one on each side, with Jesus in the middle. 19 Pilate

19:13, 17 [a] **Jewish language** Hebrew or Aramaic, the languages of the Jewish people in the first century.

CONTEMPORARY ENGLISH VERSION

10 "Why won't you answer my question?" Pilate asked.
"Don't you know that I have the power to let you go free or
to nail you to a cross?"
11 Jesus replied, "If God had not given you the power,
you couldn't do anything at all to me. But the one who
handed me over to you did something even worse."
12 Then Pilate wanted to set Jesus free. But the crowd
again yelled, "If you set this man free, you are no friend of
the Emperor! Anyone who claims to be a king is an enemy
of the Emperor."
13 When Pilate heard this, he brought Jesus out. Then he
sat down on the judge's bench at the place known as "The
Stone Pavement." In Aramaic this pavement is called
"Gabbatha." 14 It was about noon on the day before
Passover, and Pilate said to the crowd, "Look at your king!"
15 "Kill him! Kill him!" they yelled. "Nail him to a cross!"
"So you want me to nail your king to a cross?" Pilate
asked.
The chief priests replied, "The Emperor is our king!"
16 Then Pilate handed Jesus over to be nailed to a cross.

Jesus Is Nailed to a Cross

(Matthew 27.32-44; Mark 15.21-32; Luke 23.26-43)

Jesus was taken away, 17 and he carried his cross to a
place known as "The Skull."[b] In Aramaic this place is
called "Golgotha." 18 There Jesus was nailed to the cross,
and on each side of him a man was also nailed to a cross.

[b] **19.17** *The Skull*: The place was probably given this name because it was near a large rock in the shape of a human skull.

NEW INTERNATIONAL VERSION

10"Do you refuse to speak to me?" Pilate said. "Don't you realize I have power either to free you or to crucify you?"

11Jesus answered, "You would have no power over me if it were not given to you from above. Therefore the one who handed me over to you is guilty of a greater sin."

12From then on, Pilate tried to set Jesus free, but the Jews kept shouting, "If you let this man go, you are no friend of Caesar. Anyone who claims to be a king opposes Caesar."

13When Pilate heard this, he brought Jesus out and sat down on the judge's seat at a place known as the Stone
Pavement (which in Aramaic is Gabbatha). 14It was the
day of Preparation of Passover Week, about the sixth hour.

"Here is your king," Pilate said to the Jews.

15But they shouted, "Take him away! Take him away! Crucify him!"

"Shall I crucify your king?" Pilate asked.

"We have no king but Caesar," the chief priests answered.

16Finally Pilate handed him over to them to be crucified.

The Crucifixion

So the soldiers took charge of Jesus. 17Carrying his own
cross, he went out to the place of the Skull (which in
Aramaic is called Golgotha). 18Here they crucified him, and
with him two others—one on each side and Jesus in the middle.

NEW LIVING TRANSLATION

answer. 10"You won't talk to me?" Pilate demanded. "Don't you realize that I have the power to release you or to crucify you?"

11Then Jesus said, "You would have no power over me at all unless it were given to you from above. So the one who brought me to you has the greater sin."

12Then Pilate tried to release him, but the Jewish leaders told him, "If you release this man, you are not a friend of Caesar. Anyone who declares himself a king is a rebel against Caesar."

13When they said this, Pilate brought Jesus out to them again. Then Pilate sat down on the judgment seat on the platform that is called the Stone Pavement (in Hebrew,
Gabbatha). 14It was now about noon of the day of prepara-
tion for the Passover. And Pilate said to the people,* "Here is your king!"

15"Away with him," they yelled. "Away with him—crucify him!"

"What? Crucify your king?" Pilate asked.

"We have no king but Caesar," the leading priests shouted back.

16Then Pilate gave Jesus to them to be crucified.

The Crucifixion

So they took Jesus and led him away. 17Carrying the
cross by himself, Jesus went to the place called Skull Hill
(in Hebrew, *Golgotha*). 18There they crucified him. There
were two others crucified with him, one on either side, with

19:14 Greek *Jewish people;* also in 19:20.

NEW KING JAMES VERSION

10Then Pilate said to Him, "Are You not speaking to me? Do You not know that I have power to crucify You, and power to release You?"

11Jesus answered, "You could have no power at all against Me unless it had been given you from above. Therefore the one who delivered Me to you has the greater sin."

12From then on Pilate sought to release Him, but the Jews cried out, saying, "If you let this Man go, you are not Caesar's friend. Whoever makes himself a king speaks against Caesar."

13When Pilate therefore heard that saying, he brought Jesus out and sat down in the judgment seat in a place that is called *The* Pavement, but in Hebrew, Gabbatha.
14Now it was the Preparation Day of the Passover, and about the sixth hour. And he said to the Jews, "Behold your King!"

15But they cried out, "Away with *Him,* away with *Him!* Crucify Him!"

Pilate said to them, "Shall I crucify your King?"

The chief priests answered, "We have no king but Caesar!"

16Then he delivered Him to them to be crucified. Then they took Jesus and led *Him* away.[c]

The King on a Cross

17And He, bearing His cross, went out to a place called *the Place* of a Skull, which is called in Hebrew, Golgotha,
18where they crucified Him, and two others with Him, one

19:16 [c] NU-Text omits *and led Him away.*

THE MESSAGE

Pilate said, "You won't talk? Don't you know that I have the authority to pardon you, and the authority to—crucify you?"

Jesus said, "You haven't a shred of authority over me except what has been given you from heaven. That's why the one who betrayed me to you has committed a far greater fault."

At this, Pilate tried his best to pardon him, but the Jews shouted him down: "If you pardon this man, you're no friend of Caesar's. Anyone setting himself up as 'king' defies Caesar."

When Pilate heard those words, he led Jesus outside. He sat down at the judgment seat in the area designated Stone Court (in Hebrew, *Gabbatha*). It was the preparation day for Passover. The hour was noon. Pilate said to the Jews, "Here is your king."

They shouted back, "Kill him! Kill him! Crucify him!"

Pilate said, "I am to crucify your king?"

The high priests answered, "We have no king except Caesar."

Pilate caved in to their demand. He turned him over to be crucified.

The Crucifixion

They took Jesus away. Carrying his cross, Jesus went out to the place called Skull Hill (the name in Hebrew is *Golgotha*), where they crucified him, and with him two

KING JAMES VERSION

19 ¶ And Pilate wrote a title, and put *it* on the cross. And the writing was, JESUS OF NAZARETH THE KING OF THE JEWS.

20 This title then read many of the Jews: for the place where Jesus was crucified was nigh to the city: and it was written in Hebrew, *and* Greek, *and* Latin.

21 Then said the chief priests of the Jews to Pilate, Write not, The King of the Jews; but that he said, I am King of the Jews.

22 Pilate answered, What I have written I have written.

23 Then the soldiers, when they had crucified Jesus, took his garments, and made four parts, to every soldier a part; and also *his* coat: now the coat was without seam, woven from the top throughout.

24 They said therefore among themselves, Let us not rend it, but cast lots for it, whose it shall be: that the scripture might be fulfilled, which saith, They parted my raiment among them, and for my vesture they did cast lots. These things therefore the soldiers did.

25 Now there stood by the cross of Jesus his mother,

NEW AMERICAN STANDARD BIBLE

19 Pilate also wrote an inscription and put it on the cross. It was written, "JESUS THE NAZARENE, THE KING OF THE JEWS."

20 Therefore many of the Jews read this inscription, for the place where Jesus was crucified was near the city; and it was written in Hebrew, Latin *and* in Greek.

21 So the chief priests of the Jews were saying to Pilate, "Do not write, 'The King of the Jews'; but that He said, 'I am King of the Jews.' "

22 Pilate answered, "What I have written I have written."

23 Then the soldiers, when they had crucified Jesus, took His outer garments and made four parts, a part to every soldier and *also* the [3]tunic; now the tunic was seamless, woven in one piece.

24 So they said to one another, "Let us not tear it, but cast lots for it, *to decide* whose it shall be"; *this was* to fulfill the Scripture: "THEY DIVIDED MY OUTER GARMENTS AMONG THEM, AND FOR MY CLOTHING THEY CAST LOTS."

25 Therefore the soldiers did these things.

But standing by the cross of Jesus were His mother, and

19:23 [3] Gr *khiton,* the garment worn next to the skin

NEW CENTURY VERSION

wrote a sign and put it on the cross. It read: JESUS OF NAZARETH, THE KING OF THE JEWS. [20]The sign was written in the Jewish language, in Latin, and in Greek. Many of the Jews read the sign, because the place where Jesus was crucified was near the city. [21]The leading Jewish priests said to Pilate, "Don't write, 'The King of the Jews.' But write, 'This man said, "I am the King of the Jews." ' "

[22]Pilate answered, "What I have written, I have written."

[23]After the soldiers crucified Jesus, they took his clothes and divided them into four parts, with each soldier getting one part. They also took his long shirt, which was all one piece of cloth, woven from top to bottom. [24]So the soldiers said to each other, "We should not tear this into parts. Let's throw lots to see who will get it." This happened so that this Scripture would come true:

"They divided my clothes among them,
and they threw lots for my clothing." *Psalm 22:18*

So the soldiers did this.

[25]Standing near his cross were Jesus' mother, his mother's

CONTEMPORARY ENGLISH VERSION

[19]Pilate ordered the charge against Jesus to be written on a board and put above the cross. It read, "Jesus of Nazareth, King of the Jews." [20]The words were written in Hebrew, Latin, and Greek.

The place where Jesus was taken wasn't far from the city, and many of the Jewish people read the charge against him. [21]So the chief priests went to Pilate and said, "Why did you write that he is King of the Jews? You should have written, 'He claimed to be King of the Jews.' "

[22]But Pilate told them, "What is written will not be changed!"

[23]After the soldiers had nailed Jesus to the cross, they divided up his clothes into four parts, one for each of them. But his outer garment was made from a single piece of cloth, and it did not have any seams. [24]The soldiers said to each other, "Let's not rip it apart. We will gamble to see who gets it." This happened so that the Scriptures would come true, which say,

"They divided up my clothes
and gambled
for my garments."

The soldiers then did what they had decided.

[25]Jesus' mother stood beside his cross with her sister and

NEW INTERNATIONAL VERSION

19Pilate had a notice prepared and fastened to the cross.
It read: JESUS OF NAZARETH, THE KING OF THE JEWS. 20Many of
the Jews read this sign, for the place where Jesus was cru-
cified was near the city, and the sign was written in
Aramaic, Latin and Greek. 21The chief priests of the Jews
protested to Pilate, "Do not write 'The King of the Jews,'
but that this man claimed to be king of the Jews."
22Pilate answered, "What I have written, I have written."
23When the soldiers crucified Jesus, they took his
clothes, dividing them into four shares, one for each of
them, with the undergarment remaining. This garment
was seamless, woven in one piece from top to bottom.
24"Let's not tear it," they said to one another. "Let's
decide by lot who will get it."

This happened that the scripture might be fulfilled which said,

"They divided my garments among them
and cast lots for my clothing."[a]

So this is what the soldiers did.

25Near the cross of Jesus stood his mother, his mother's

[a] *24* Psalm 22:18

NEW LIVING TRANSLATION

Jesus between them. 19And Pilate posted a sign over him
that read, "Jesus of Nazareth, the King of the Jews." 20The
place where Jesus was crucified was near the city; and the
sign was written in Hebrew, Latin, and Greek, so that many
people could read it.
21Then the leading priests said to Pilate, "Change it from
'The King of the Jews' to 'He said, I am King of the Jews.' "
22Pilate replied, "What I have written, I have written. It
stays exactly as it is."
23When the soldiers had crucified Jesus, they divided his
clothes among the four of them. They also took his robe,
but it was seamless, woven in one piece from the top. 24So
they said, "Let's not tear it but throw dice* to see who gets
it." This fulfilled the Scripture that says, "They divided my
clothes among themselves and threw dice for my robe."*
25So that is what they did.

Standing near the cross were Jesus' mother, and his

19:24a Greek *cast lots.* **19:24b** Ps 22:18.

NEW KING JAMES VERSION

on either side, and Jesus in the center. 19Now Pilate wrote
a title and put *it* on the cross. And the writing was:

JESUS OF NAZARETH, THE KING OF THE JEWS.

20Then many of the Jews read this title, for the place where
Jesus was crucified was near the city; and it was written in
Hebrew, Greek, *and* Latin.
21Therefore the chief priests of the Jews said to Pilate,
"Do not write, 'The King of the Jews,' but, 'He said, "I am
the King of the Jews." ' "
22Pilate answered, "What I have written, I have written."
23Then the soldiers, when they had crucified Jesus, took
His garments and made four parts, to each soldier a part,
and also the tunic. Now the tunic was without seam,
woven from the top in one piece. 24They said therefore
among themselves, "Let us not tear it, but cast lots for it,
whose it shall be," that the Scripture might be fulfilled
which says:

"They divided My garments among them,
And for My clothing they cast lots."[d]

Therefore the soldiers did these things.

Behold Your Mother

25Now there stood by the cross of Jesus His mother, and

19:24 [d] Psalm 22:18

THE MESSAGE

others, one on each side, Jesus in the middle. Pilate wrote a sign and had it placed on the cross. It read:

JESUS THE NAZARENE
THE KING OF THE JEWS.

Many of the Jews read the sign because the place where Jesus was crucified was right next to the city. It was written in Hebrew, Latin, and Greek. The Jewish high priests objected. "Don't write," they said to Pilate, " 'The King of the Jews.' Make it, 'This man said, "I am the King of the Jews." ' "

Pilate said, "What I've written, I've written."

When they crucified him, the Roman soldiers took his clothes and divided them up four ways, to each soldier a fourth. But his robe was seamless, a single piece of weaving, so they said to each other, "Let's not tear it up. Let's throw dice to see who gets it." This confirmed the Scripture that said, "They divided up my clothes among them and threw dice for my coat." (The soldiers validated the Scriptures!)

While the soldiers were looking after themselves, Jesus'

KING JAMES VERSION

and his mother's sister, Mary the *wife* of Cleophas, and Mary Magdalene.

26 When Jesus therefore saw his mother, and the disciple standing by, whom he loved, he saith unto his mother, Woman, behold thy son!

27 Then saith he to the disciple, Behold thy mother! And from that hour that disciple took her unto his own *home*.

28 After this, Jesus knowing that all things were now accomplished, that the scripture might be fulfilled, saith, I thirst.

29 Now there was set a vessel full of vinegar: and they filled a spunge with vinegar, and put *it* upon hyssop, and put *it* to his mouth.

30 When Jesus therefore had received the vinegar, he said, It is finished: and he bowed his head, and gave up the ghost.

31 ¶ The Jews therefore, because it was the preparation, that the bodies should not remain upon the cross on the sabbath day, (for that sabbath day was an high day,)

NEW AMERICAN STANDARD BIBLE

His mother's sister, Mary the *wife* of Clopas, and Mary Magdalene.

26 When Jesus then saw His mother, and the disciple whom He loved standing nearby, He *said to His mother, "Woman, behold, your son!"

27 Then He *said to the disciple, "Behold, your mother!" From that hour the disciple took her into his own *household.*

28 After this, Jesus, knowing that all things had already been accomplished, to fulfill the Scripture, *said, "I am thirsty."

29 A jar full of sour wine was standing there; so they put a sponge full of the sour wine upon *a branch of* hyssop and brought it up to His mouth.

30 Therefore when Jesus had received the sour wine, He said, "It is finished!" And He bowed His head and gave up His spirit.

Care of the Body of Jesus

31 Then the Jews, because it was the day of preparation, so that the bodies would not remain on the cross on the Sabbath (for that Sabbath was a high day), asked Pilate

NEW CENTURY VERSION

sister, Mary the wife of Clopas, and Mary Magdalene. 26 When Jesus saw his mother and the follower he loved standing nearby, he said to his mother, "Dear woman, here is your son." 27 Then he said to the follower, "Here is your mother." From that time on, the follower took her to live in his home.

Jesus Dies

28 After this, Jesus knew that everything had been done. So that the Scripture would come true, he said, "I am thirsty."[b] 29 There was a jar full of vinegar there, so the soldiers soaked a sponge in it, put the sponge on a branch of a hyssop plant, and lifted it to Jesus' mouth. 30 When Jesus tasted the vinegar, he said, "It is finished." Then he bowed his head and died.

31 This day was Preparation Day, and the next day was a special Sabbath day. Since the Jews did not want the bodies to stay on the cross on the Sabbath day, they asked

19:28 [b] **"I am thirsty."** Read Psalms 22:15; 69:21.

CONTEMPORARY ENGLISH VERSION

Mary the wife of Clopas. Mary Magdalene was standing there too.[c] 26 When Jesus saw his mother and his favorite disciple with her, he said to his mother, "This man is now your son." 27 Then he said to the disciple, "She is now your mother." From then on, that disciple took her into his own home.

The Death of Jesus

(Matthew 27.45-56; Mark 15.33-41; Luke 23.44-49)

28 Jesus knew that he had now finished his work. And in order to make the Scriptures come true, he said, "I am thirsty!" 29 A jar of cheap wine was there. Someone then soaked a sponge with the wine and held it up to Jesus' mouth on the stem of a hyssop plant. 30 After Jesus drank the wine, he said, "Everything is done!" He bowed his head and died.

A Spear Is Stuck in Jesus' Side

31 The next day would be both a Sabbath and the Passover. It was a special day for the Jewish people,[d] and they did not want the bodies to stay on the crosses during

[c] **19.25** *Jesus' mother stood beside his cross with her sister and Mary the wife of Clopas. Mary Magdalene was standing there too*: The Greek text may also be understood to include only three women ("Jesus' mother stood beside the cross with her sister, Mary the mother of Clopas. Mary Magdalene was standing there too.") or merely two women ("Jesus' mother was standing there with her sister Mary of Clopas, that is, Mary Magdalene."). "Of Clopas" may mean "daughter of" or "mother of."

[d] **19.31** *a special day for the Jewish people*: Passover could be any day of the week. But according to the Gospel of John, Passover was on a Sabbath in the year that Jesus was nailed to a cross.

NEW INTERNATIONAL VERSION

sister, Mary the wife of Clopas, and Mary Magdalene. [26]When Jesus saw his mother there, and the disciple whom he loved standing nearby, he said to his mother, "Dear woman, here is your son," [27]and to the disciple, "Here is your mother." From that time on, this disciple took her into his home.

The Death of Jesus

[28]Later, knowing that all was now completed, and so that the Scripture would be fulfilled, Jesus said, "I am thirsty." [29]A jar of wine vinegar was there, so they soaked a sponge in it, put the sponge on a stalk of the hyssop plant, and lifted it to Jesus' lips. [30]When he had received the drink, Jesus said, "It is finished." With that, he bowed his head and gave up his spirit.

[31]Now it was the day of Preparation, and the next day was to be a special Sabbath. Because the Jews did not want the bodies left on the crosses during the Sabbath,

NEW LIVING TRANSLATION

mother's sister, Mary (the wife of Clopas), and Mary Magdalene. [26]When Jesus saw his mother standing there beside the disciple he loved, he said to her, "Woman, he is your son." [27]And he said to this disciple, "She is your mother." And from then on this disciple took her into his home.

The Death of Jesus

[28]Jesus knew that everything was now finished, and to fulfill the Scriptures he said, "I am thirsty."* [29]A jar of sour wine was sitting there, so they soaked a sponge in it, put it on a hyssop branch, and held it up to his lips. [30]When Jesus had tasted it, he said, "It is finished!" Then he bowed his head and gave up his spirit.

[31]The Jewish leaders didn't want the victims hanging there the next day, which was the Sabbath (and a very special Sabbath at that, because it was the Passover), so they

19:28 See Pss 22:15; 69:21.

NEW KING JAMES VERSION

His mother's sister, Mary the *wife* of Clopas, and Mary Magdalene. [26]When Jesus therefore saw His mother, and the disciple whom He loved standing by, He said to His mother, "Woman, behold your son!" [27]Then He said to the disciple, "Behold your mother!" And from that hour that disciple took her to his own *home.*

It Is Finished

[28]After this, Jesus, knowing[e] that all things were now accomplished, that the Scripture might be fulfilled, said, "I thirst!" [29]Now a vessel full of sour wine was sitting there; and they filled a sponge with sour wine, put *it* on hyssop, and put *it* to His mouth. [30]So when Jesus had received the sour wine, He said, "It is finished!" And bowing His head, He gave up His spirit.

Jesus' Side Is Pierced

[31]Therefore, because it was the Preparation *Day,* that the bodies should not remain on the cross on the Sabbath (for that Sabbath was a high day), the Jews asked Pilate that

19:28 [e] M-Text reads *seeing.*

THE MESSAGE

mother, his aunt, Mary the wife of Clopas, and Mary Magdalene stood at the foot of the cross. Jesus saw his mother and the disciple he loved standing near her. He said to his mother, "Woman, here is your son." Then to the disciple, "Here is your mother." From that moment the disciple accepted her as his own mother.

Jesus, seeing that everything had been completed so that the Scripture record might also be complete, then said, "I'm thirsty."

A jug of sour wine was standing by. Someone put a sponge soaked with the wine on a javelin and lifted it to his mouth. After he took the wine, Jesus said, "It's done . . . complete." Bowing his head, he offered up his spirit.

Then the Jews, since it was the day of Sabbath preparation, and so the bodies wouldn't stay on the crosses over the Sabbath (it was a high holy day that year), petitioned

KING JAMES VERSION

besought Pilate that their legs might be broken, and *that* they might be taken away.

32 Then came the soldiers, and brake the legs of the first, and of the other which was crucified with him.

33 But when they came to Jesus, and saw that he was dead already, they brake not his legs:

34 But one of the soldiers with a spear pierced his side, and forthwith came there out blood and water.

35 And he that saw *it* bare record, and his record is true: and he knoweth that he saith true, that ye might believe.

36 For these things were done, that the scripture should be fulfilled, A bone of him shall not be broken.

37 And again another scripture saith, They shall look on him whom they pierced.

38 ¶ And after this Joseph of Arimathaea, being a disciple of Jesus, but secretly for fear of the Jews, besought Pilate that he might take away the body of Jesus: and Pilate gave *him* leave. He came therefore, and took the body of Jesus.

39 And there came also Nicodemus, which at the first came to Jesus by night, and brought a mixture of myrrh and aloes, about an hundred pound *weight*.

40 Then took they the body of Jesus, and wound it in linen clothes with the spices, as the manner of the Jews is to bury.

NEW AMERICAN STANDARD BIBLE

that their legs might be broken, and *that* they might be taken away.

32 So the soldiers came, and broke the legs of the first man and of the other who was crucified with Him;

33 but coming to Jesus, when they saw that He was already dead, they did not break His legs.

34 But one of the soldiers pierced His side with a spear, and immediately blood and water came out.

35 And he who has seen has testified, and his testimony is true; and he knows that he is telling the truth, so that you also may believe.

36 For these things came to pass to fulfill the Scripture, "NOT A BONE OF HIM SHALL BE BROKEN."

37 And again another Scripture says, "THEY SHALL LOOK ON HIM WHOM THEY PIERCED."

38 After these things Joseph of Arimathea, being a disciple of Jesus, but a secret *one* for fear of the Jews, asked Pilate that he might take away the body of Jesus; and Pilate granted permission. So he came and took away His body.

39 Nicodemus, who had first come to Him by night, also came, bringing a mixture of myrrh and aloes, about a hundred pounds *weight*.

40 So they took the body of Jesus and bound it in linen wrappings with the spices, as is the burial custom of the Jews.

NEW CENTURY VERSION

Pilate to order that the legs of the men be broken[c] and the
bodies be taken away. 32So the soldiers came and broke
the legs of the first man on the cross beside Jesus. Then
they broke the legs of the man on the other cross beside
Jesus. 33But when the soldiers came to Jesus and saw that
he was already dead, they did not break his legs. 34But one
of the soldiers stuck his spear into Jesus' side, and at once
blood and water came out. 35(The one who saw this hap-
pen is the one who told us this, and whatever he says is
true. And he knows that he tells the truth, and he tells it
so that you might believe.) 36These things happened to
make the Scripture come true: "Not one of his bones will
be broken."[d] 37And another Scripture says, "They will look
at the one they stabbed."[e]

Jesus Is Buried

38Later, Joseph from Arimathea asked Pilate if he could
take the body of Jesus. (Joseph was a secret follower of
Jesus, because he was afraid of the Jews.) Pilate gave his
permission, so Joseph came and took Jesus' body away.
39Nicodemus, who earlier had come to Jesus at night, went
with Joseph. He brought about seventy-five pounds of
myrrh and aloes. 40These two men took Jesus' body and
wrapped it with the spices in pieces of linen cloth, which is
how the Jewish people bury the dead. 41In the place where

19:31 [c] **broken** The breaking of their bones would make them die sooner. 19:36 [d] **"Not one...broken."** Quotation from Psalm 34:20. The idea is from Exodus 12:46; Numbers 9:12. 19:37 [e] **"They...stabbed."** Quotation from Zechariah 12:10.

CONTEMPORARY ENGLISH VERSION

that day. So they asked Pilate to break the men's legs[e] and
take their bodies down. 32The soldiers first broke the legs
of the other two men who were nailed there. 33But when
they came to Jesus, they saw that he was already dead,
and they did not break his legs.

34One of the soldiers stuck his spear into Jesus' side,
and blood and water came out. 35We know this is true,
because it was told by someone who saw it happen. Now
you can have faith too. 36All this happened so that the
Scriptures would come true, which say, "No bone of his
body will be broken" 37and, "They will see the one in
whose side they stuck a spear."

Jesus Is Buried

(Matthew 27.57-61; Mark 15.42-47; Luke 23.50-56)

38Joseph from Arimathea was one of Jesus' disciples. He
had kept it secret though, because he was afraid of the
Jewish leaders. But now he asked Pilate to let him have
Jesus' body. Pilate gave him permission, and Joseph took it
down from the cross.

39Nicodemus also came with about seventy-five pounds
of spices made from myrrh and aloes. This was the same
Nicodemus who had visited Jesus one night.[f] 40The two
men wrapped the body in a linen cloth, together with the
spices, which was how the Jewish people buried their dead.

[e] **19.31** *break the men's legs*: This was the way that the Romans sometimes speeded up the death of a person who had been nailed to a cross. [f] **19.39** *Nicodemus who had visited Jesus one night*: See 3.1-21.

NEW INTERNATIONAL VERSION

they asked Pilate to have the legs broken and the bodies taken down. [32]The soldiers therefore came and broke the legs of the first man who had been crucified with Jesus, and then those of the other. [33]But when they came to Jesus and found that he was already dead, they did not break his legs. [34]Instead, one of the soldiers pierced Jesus' side with a spear, bringing a sudden flow of blood and water. [35]The man who saw it has given testimony, and his testimony is true. He knows that he tells the truth, and he testifies so that you also may believe. [36]These things happened so that the scripture would be fulfilled: "Not one of his bones will be broken,"[b] [37]and, as another scripture says, "They will look on the one they have pierced."[c]

The Burial of Jesus

[38]Later, Joseph of Arimathea asked Pilate for the body of Jesus. Now Joseph was a disciple of Jesus, but secretly because he feared the Jews. With Pilate's permission, he came and took the body away. [39]He was accompanied by Nicodemus, the man who earlier had visited Jesus at night. Nicodemus brought a mixture of myrrh and aloes, about seventy-five pounds.[d] [40]Taking Jesus' body, the two of them wrapped it, with the spices, in strips of linen. This was in accordance with Jewish burial customs. [41]At the

[b] *36* Exodus 12:46; Num. 9:12; Psalm 34:20 [c] *37* Zech. 12:10
[d] *39* Greek *a hundred litrai* (about 34 kilograms)

NEW LIVING TRANSLATION

asked Pilate to hasten their deaths by ordering that their legs be broken. Then their bodies could be taken down. [32]So the soldiers came and broke the legs of the two men crucified with Jesus. [33]But when they came to Jesus, they saw that he was dead already, so they didn't break his legs. [34]One of the soldiers, however, pierced his side with a spear, and blood and water flowed out. [35]This report is from an eyewitness giving an accurate account; it is presented so that you also can believe. [36]These things happened in fulfillment of the Scriptures that say, "Not one of his bones will be broken,"* [37]and "They will look on him whom they pierced."*

The Burial of Jesus

[38]Afterward Joseph of Arimathea, who had been a secret disciple of Jesus (because he feared the Jewish leaders), asked Pilate for permission to take Jesus' body down. When Pilate gave him permission, he came and took the body away. [39]Nicodemus, the man who had come to Jesus at night, also came, bringing about seventy-five pounds* of embalming ointment made from myrrh and aloes. [40]Together they wrapped Jesus' body in a long linen cloth with the spices, as is the Jewish custom of burial. [41]The

19:36 Exod 12:46; Num 9:12; Ps 34:20. **19:37** Zech 12:10.
19:39 Greek *100 litras* [32.7 kilograms].

NEW KING JAMES VERSION

their legs might be broken, and *that* they might be taken away. [32]Then the soldiers came and broke the legs of the first and of the other who was crucified with Him. [33]But when they came to Jesus and saw that He was already dead, they did not break His legs. [34]But one of the soldiers pierced His side with a spear, and immediately blood and water came out. [35]And he who has seen has testified, and his testimony is true; and he knows that he is telling the truth, so that you may believe. [36]For these things were done that the Scripture should be fulfilled, *"Not one of His bones shall be broken."*[f] [37]And again another Scripture says, *"They shall look on Him whom they pierced."*[g]

Jesus Buried in Joseph's Tomb

[38]After this, Joseph of Arimathea, being a disciple of Jesus, but secretly, for fear of the Jews, asked Pilate that he might take away the body of Jesus; and Pilate gave *him* permission. So he came and took the body of Jesus. [39]And Nicodemus, who at first came to Jesus by night, also came, bringing a mixture of myrrh and aloes, about a hundred pounds. [40]Then they took the body of Jesus, and bound it in strips of linen with the spices, as the custom of the Jews

19:36 [f] Exodus 12:46; Numbers 9:12; Psalm 34:20
19:37 [g] Zechariah 12:10

THE MESSAGE

Pilate that their legs be broken to speed death, and the bodies taken down. So the soldiers came and broke the legs of the first man crucified with Jesus, and then the other. When they got to Jesus, they saw that he was already dead, so they didn't break his legs. One of the soldiers stabbed him in the side with his spear. Blood and water gushed out.

The eyewitness to these things has presented an accurate report. He saw it himself and is telling the truth so that you, also, will believe.

These things that happened confirmed the Scripture, "Not a bone in his body was broken," and the other Scripture that reads, "They will stare at the one they pierced."

✣

After all this, Joseph of Arimathea (he was a disciple of Jesus, but secretly, because he was intimidated by the Jews) petitioned Pilate to take the body of Jesus. Pilate gave permission. So Joseph came and took the body.

Nicodemus, who had first come to Jesus at night, came now in broad daylight carrying a mixture of myrrh and aloes, about seventy-five pounds. They took Jesus' body and, following the Jewish burial custom, wrapped it in

KING JAMES VERSION

41 Now in the place where he was crucified there was a garden; and in the garden a new sepulchre, wherein was never man yet laid.

42 There laid they Jesus therefore because of the Jews' preparation *day*; for the sepulchre was nigh at hand.

20 The first *day* of the week cometh Mary Magdalene early, when it was yet dark, unto the sepulchre, and seeth the stone taken away from the sepulchre.

2 Then she runneth, and cometh to Simon Peter, and to the other disciple, whom Jesus loved, and saith unto them, They have taken away the Lord out of the sepulchre, and we know not where they have laid him.

3 Peter therefore went forth, and that other disciple, and came to the sepulchre.

4 So they ran both together: and the other disciple did outrun Peter, and came first to the sepulchre.

5 And he stooping down, *and looking in*, saw the linen clothes lying; yet went he not in.

6 Then cometh Simon Peter following him, and went into the sepulchre, and seeth the linen clothes lie,

7 And the napkin, that was about his head, not lying with the linen clothes, but wrapped together in a place by itself.

8 Then went in also that other disciple, which came first to the sepulchre, and he saw, and believed.

NEW AMERICAN STANDARD BIBLE

41 Now in the place where He was crucified there was a garden, and in the garden a new tomb in which no one had yet been laid.

42 Therefore because of the Jewish day of preparation, since the tomb was nearby, they laid Jesus there.

The Empty Tomb

20 Now on the first *day* of the week Mary Magdalene *came early to the tomb, while it *was still dark, and *saw the stone *already* taken away from the tomb.

2 So she *ran and *came to Simon Peter and to the other disciple whom Jesus loved, and *said to them, "They have taken away the Lord out of the tomb, and we do not know where they have laid Him."

3 So Peter and the other disciple went forth, and they were going to the tomb.

4 The two were running together; and the other disciple ran ahead faster than Peter and came to the tomb first;

5 and stooping and looking in, he *saw the linen wrappings lying *there;* but he did not go in.

6 And so Simon Peter also *came, following him, and entered the tomb; and he *saw the linen wrappings lying *there,*

7 and the face-cloth which had been on His head, not lying with the linen wrappings, but rolled up in a place by itself.

8 So the other disciple who had first come to the tomb then also entered, and he saw and believed.

NEW CENTURY VERSION

Jesus was crucified, there was a garden. In the garden was
a new tomb that had never been used before. 42The men
laid Jesus in that tomb because it was nearby, and the
Jews were preparing to start their Sabbath day.

Jesus' Tomb Is Empty

20 Early on the first day of the week, Mary Mag-
dalene went to the tomb while it was still dark.
When she saw that the large stone had been moved away
from the tomb, 2she ran to Simon Peter and the follower
whom Jesus loved. Mary said, "They have taken the Lord
out of the tomb, and we don't know where they have put
him."
3So Peter and the other follower started for the tomb.
4They were both running, but the other follower ran faster
than Peter and reached the tomb first. 5He bent down and
looked in and saw the strips of linen cloth lying there, but
he did not go in. 6Then following him, Simon Peter arrived
and went into the tomb and saw the strips of linen lying
there. 7He also saw the cloth that had been around Jesus'
head, which was folded up and laid in a different place
from the strips of linen. 8Then the other follower, who had
reached the tomb first, also went in. He saw and believed.

CONTEMPORARY ENGLISH VERSION

41In the place where Jesus had been nailed to a cross, there
was a garden with a tomb that had never been used. 42The
tomb was nearby, and since it was the time to prepare for
the Sabbath, they were in a hurry to put Jesus' body there.

Jesus Is Alive (Matthew 28.1-10; Mark 16.1-8; Luke 24.1-12)

20 On Sunday morning while it was still dark, Mary
Magdalene went to the tomb and saw that the
stone had been rolled away from the entrance. 2She ran to
Simon Peter and to Jesus' favorite disciple and said, "They
have taken the Lord from the tomb! We don't know where
they have put him."
3Peter and the other disciple started for the tomb. 4They
ran side by side, until the other disciple ran faster than
Peter and got there first. 5He bent over and saw the strips
of linen cloth lying inside the tomb, but he did not go in.
6When Simon Peter got there, he went into the tomb and
saw the strips of cloth. 7He also saw the piece of cloth that
had been used to cover Jesus' face. It was rolled up and in
a place by itself. 8The disciple who got there first then
went into the tomb, and when he saw it, he believed. 9At

NEW INTERNATIONAL VERSION

place where Jesus was crucified, there was a garden, and in the garden a new tomb, in which no one had ever been laid. 42Because it was the Jewish day of Preparation and since the tomb was nearby, they laid Jesus there.

The Empty Tomb

20 Early on the first day of the week, while it was still dark, Mary Magdalene went to the tomb and saw that the stone had been removed from the entrance. 2So she came running to Simon Peter and the other disciple, the one Jesus loved, and said, "They have taken the Lord out of the tomb, and we don't know where they have put him!"

3So Peter and the other disciple started for the tomb. 4Both were running, but the other disciple outran Peter and reached the tomb first. 5He bent over and looked in at the strips of linen lying there but did not go in. 6Then Simon Peter, who was behind him, arrived and went into the tomb. He saw the strips of linen lying there, 7as well as the burial cloth that had been around Jesus' head. The cloth was folded up by itself, separate from the linen. 8Finally the other disciple, who had reached the tomb first, also went inside. He saw and believed. 9(They still did not

NEW LIVING TRANSLATION

place of crucifixion was near a garden, where there was a new tomb, never used before. 42And so, because it was the day of preparation before the Passover and since the tomb was close at hand, they laid Jesus there.

The Resurrection

20 Early Sunday morning,* while it was still dark, Mary Magdalene came to the tomb and found that the stone had been rolled away from the entrance. 2She ran and found Simon Peter and the other disciple, the one whom Jesus loved. She said, "They have taken the Lord's body out of the tomb, and I don't know where they have put him!"

3Peter and the other disciple ran to the tomb to see. 4The other disciple outran Peter and got there first. 5He stooped and looked in and saw the linen cloth lying there, but he didn't go in. 6Then Simon Peter arrived and went inside. He also noticed the linen wrappings lying there, 7while the cloth that had covered Jesus' head was folded up and lying to the side. 8Then the other disciple also went in, and he

20:1 Greek *On the first day of the week.*

NEW KING JAMES VERSION

is to bury. 41Now in the place where He was crucified there was a garden, and in the garden a new tomb in which no one had yet been laid. 42So there they laid Jesus, because of the Jews' Preparation *Day,* for the tomb was nearby.

The Empty Tomb

20 Now the first *day* of the week Mary Magdalene went to the tomb early, while it was still dark, and saw *that* the stone had been taken away from the tomb. 2Then she ran and came to Simon Peter, and to the other disciple, whom Jesus loved, and said to them, "They have taken away the Lord out of the tomb, and we do not know where they have laid Him."

3Peter therefore went out, and the other disciple, and were going to the tomb. 4So they both ran together, and the other disciple outran Peter and came to the tomb first. 5And he, stooping down and looking in, saw the linen cloths lying *there;* yet he did not go in. 6Then Simon Peter came, following him, and went into the tomb; and he saw the linen cloths lying *there,* 7and the handkerchief that had been around His head, not lying with the linen cloths, but folded together in a place by itself. 8Then the other disciple, who came to the tomb first, went in also; and he saw

THE MESSAGE

linen with the spices. There was a garden near the place he was crucified, and in the garden a new tomb in which no one had yet been placed. So, because it was Sabbath preparation for the Jews and the tomb was convenient, they placed Jesus in it.

Resurrection!

20 Early in the morning on the first day of the week, while it was still dark, Mary Magdalene came to the tomb and saw that the stone was moved away from the entrance. She ran at once to Simon Peter and the other disciple, the one Jesus loved, breathlessly panting, "They took the Master from the tomb. We don't know where they've put him."

Peter and the other disciple left immediately for the tomb. They ran, neck and neck. The other disciple got to the tomb first, outrunning Peter. Stooping to look in, he saw the pieces of linen cloth lying there, but he didn't go in. Simon Peter arrived after him, entered the tomb, observed the linen cloths lying there, and the kerchief used to cover his head not lying with the linen cloths but separate, neatly folded by itself. Then the other disciple, the one who had gotten there first, went into the tomb, took one look at the evidence, and believed. No one yet knew

KING JAMES VERSION

9 For as yet they knew not the scripture, that he must rise again from the dead.

10 Then the disciples went away again unto their own home.

11 ¶ But Mary stood without at the sepulchre weeping: and as she wept, she stooped down, *and looked* into the sepulchre,

12 And seeth two angels in white sitting, the one at the head, and the other at the feet, where the body of Jesus had lain.

13 And they say unto her, Woman, why weepest thou? She saith unto them, Because they have taken away my Lord, and I know not where they have laid him.

14 And when she had thus said, she turned herself back, and saw Jesus standing, and knew not that it was Jesus.

15 Jesus saith unto her, Woman, why weepest thou? whom seekest thou? She, supposing him to be the gardener, saith unto him, Sir, if thou have borne him hence, tell me where thou hast laid him, and I will take him away.

16 Jesus saith unto her, Mary. She turned herself, and saith unto him, Rabboni; which is to say, Master.

17 Jesus saith unto her, Touch me not; for I am not yet ascended to my Father: but go to my brethren, and say unto them, I ascend unto my Father, and your Father; and *to* my God, and your God.

NEW AMERICAN STANDARD BIBLE

9 For as yet they did not understand the Scripture, that He must rise again from the dead.

10 So the disciples went away again to their own homes.

11 But Mary was standing outside the tomb weeping; and so, as she wept, she stooped and looked into the tomb;

12 and she *saw two angels in white sitting, one at the head and one at the feet, where the body of Jesus had been lying.

13 And they *said to her, "Woman, why are you weeping?" She *said to them, "Because they have taken away my Lord, and I do not know where they have laid Him."

14 When she had said this, she turned around and *saw Jesus standing *there,* and did not know that it was Jesus.

15 Jesus *said to her, "Woman, why are you weeping? Whom are you seeking?" Supposing Him to be the gardener, she *said to Him, "Sir, if you have carried Him away, tell me where you have laid Him, and I will take Him away."

16 Jesus *said to her, "Mary!" She turned and *said to Him in Hebrew, "Rabboni!" (which means, Teacher).

17 Jesus *said to her, "Stop clinging to Me, for I have not yet ascended to the Father; but go to My brethren and say to them, 'I ascend to My Father and your Father, and My God and your God.' "

NEW CENTURY VERSION

[9](They did not yet understand from the Scriptures that
Jesus must rise from the dead.)

Jesus Appears to Mary Magdalene

[10]Then the followers went back home. [11]But Mary stood
outside the tomb, crying. As she was crying, she bent
down and looked inside the tomb. [12]She saw two angels
dressed in white, sitting where Jesus' body had been, one
at the head and one at the feet.
[13]They asked her, "Woman, why are you crying?"
She answered, "They have taken away my Lord, and I
don't know where they have put him." [14]When Mary said
this, she turned around and saw Jesus standing there, but
she did not know it was Jesus.
[15]Jesus asked her, "Woman, why are you crying? Whom
are you looking for?"
Thinking he was the gardener, she said to him, "Did you
take him away, sir? Tell me where you put him, and I will
get him."
[16]Jesus said to her, "Mary."
Mary turned toward Jesus and said in the Jewish language,[a] "Rabboni." (This means Teacher.)
[17]Jesus said to her, "Don't hold on to me, because I have
not yet gone up to the Father. But go to my brothers and
tell them, 'I am going back to my Father and your Father,
to my God and your God.' "

20:16 [a] **Jewish language** Hebrew or Aramaic, the languages of the Jewish people in the first century.

CONTEMPORARY ENGLISH VERSION

that time Peter and the other disciple did not know that
the Scriptures said Jesus would rise to life. [10]So the two of
them went back to the other disciples.

Jesus Appears to Mary Magdalene (Mark 16.9-11)

[11]Mary Magdalene stood crying outside the tomb. She
was still weeping, when she stooped down [12]and saw two
angels inside. They were dressed in white and were sitting
where Jesus' body had been. One was at the head and the
other was at the foot. [13]The angels asked Mary, "Why are
you crying?"
She answered, "They have taken away my Lord's body! I
don't know where they have put him."
[14]As soon as Mary said this, she turned around and saw
Jesus standing there. But she did not know who he was.
[15]Jesus asked her, "Why are you crying? Who are you looking for?"
She thought he was the gardener and said, "Sir, if you
have taken his body away, please tell me, so I can go and
get him."
[16]Then Jesus said to her, "Mary!"
She turned and said to him, "Rabboni." The Aramaic
word "Rabboni" means "Teacher."
[17]Jesus told her, "Don't hold on to me! I have not yet
gone to the Father. But tell my disciples that I am going to
the one who is my Father and my God, as well as your
Father and your God." [18]Mary Magdalene then went and

NEW INTERNATIONAL VERSION

understand from Scripture that Jesus had to rise from the dead.)

Jesus Appears to Mary Magdalene

10Then the disciples went back to their homes, 11but Mary stood outside the tomb crying. As she wept, she bent over to look into the tomb 12and saw two angels in white, seated where Jesus' body had been, one at the head and the other at the foot.

13They asked her, "Woman, why are you crying?"

"They have taken my Lord away," she said, "and I don't know where they have put him." 14At this, she turned around and saw Jesus standing there, but she did not realize that it was Jesus.

15"Woman," he said, "why are you crying? Who is it you are looking for?"

Thinking he was the gardener, she said, "Sir, if you have carried him away, tell me where you have put him, and I will get him."

16Jesus said to her, "Mary."

She turned toward him and cried out in Aramaic, "Rabboni!" (which means Teacher).

17Jesus said, "Do not hold on to me, for I have not yet returned to the Father. Go instead to my brothers and tell them, 'I am returning to my Father and your Father, to my God and your God.' "

NEW LIVING TRANSLATION

saw and believed—9for until then they hadn't realized that the Scriptures said he would rise from the dead. 10Then they went home.

Jesus Appears to Mary Magdalene

11Mary was standing outside the tomb crying, and as she wept, she stooped and looked in. 12She saw two white-robed angels sitting at the head and foot of the place where the body of Jesus had been lying. 13"Why are you crying?" the angels asked her.

"Because they have taken away my Lord," she replied, "and I don't know where they have put him."

14She glanced over her shoulder and saw someone standing behind her. It was Jesus, but she didn't recognize him. 15"Why are you crying?" Jesus asked her. "Who are you looking for?"

She thought he was the gardener. "Sir," she said, "if you have taken him away, tell me where you have put him, and I will go and get him."

16"Mary!" Jesus said.

She turned toward him and exclaimed, "Teacher!"*

17"Don't cling to me," Jesus said, "for I haven't yet ascended to the Father. But go find my brothers and tell them that I am ascending to my Father and your Father, my God and your God."

20:16 Greek *and said in Hebrew, "Rabboni," which means "Teacher."*

NEW KING JAMES VERSION

and believed. 9For as yet they did not know the Scripture, that He must rise again from the dead. 10Then the disciples went away again to their own homes.

Mary Magdalene Sees the Risen Lord

11But Mary stood outside by the tomb weeping, and as she wept she stooped down *and looked* into the tomb. 12And she saw two angels in white sitting, one at the head and the other at the feet, where the body of Jesus had lain. 13Then they said to her, "Woman, why are you weeping?"

She said to them, "Because they have taken away my Lord, and I do not know where they have laid Him."

14Now when she had said this, she turned around and saw Jesus standing *there,* and did not know that it was Jesus. 15Jesus said to her, "Woman, why are you weeping? Whom are you seeking?"

She, supposing Him to be the gardener, said to Him, "Sir, if You have carried Him away, tell me where You have laid Him, and I will take Him away."

16Jesus said to her, "Mary!"

She turned and said to Him,[a] "Rabboni!" (which is to say, Teacher).

17Jesus said to her, "Do not cling to Me, for I have not yet ascended to My Father; but go to My brethren and say to them, 'I am ascending to My Father and your Father, and *to* My God and your God.' "

20:16 [a] NU-Text adds *in Hebrew.*

THE MESSAGE

from the Scripture that he had to rise from the dead. The disciples then went back home.

But Mary stood outside the tomb weeping. As she wept, she knelt to look into the tomb and saw two angels sitting there, dressed in white, one at the head, the other at the foot of where Jesus' body had been laid. They said to her, "Woman, why do you weep?"

"They took my Master," she said, "and I don't know where they put him." After she said this, she turned away and saw Jesus standing there. But she didn't recognize him.

Jesus spoke to her, "Woman, why do you weep? Who are you looking for?"

She, thinking that he was the gardener, said, "Mister, if you took him, tell me where you put him so I can care for him."

Jesus said, "Mary."

Turning to face him, she said in Hebrew, "*Rabboni!*" meaning "Teacher!"

Jesus said, "Don't cling to me, for I have not yet ascended to the Father. Go to my brothers and tell them, 'I ascend to my Father and your Father, my God and your God.'"

KING JAMES VERSION

18 Mary Magdalene came and told the disciples that she had seen the Lord, and *that* he had spoken these things unto her.

19 ¶ Then the same day at evening, being the first *day* of the week, when the doors were shut where the disciples were assembled for fear of the Jews, came Jesus and stood in the midst, and saith unto them, Peace *be* unto you.

20 And when he had so said, he shewed unto them *his* hands and his side. Then were the disciples glad, when they saw the Lord.

21 Then said Jesus to them again, Peace *be* unto you: as *my* Father hath sent me, even so send I you.

22 And when he had said this, he breathed on *them*, and saith unto them, Receive ye the Holy Ghost:

23 Whose soever sins ye remit, they are remitted unto them; *and* whose soever *sins* ye retain, they are retained.

24 But Thomas, one of the twelve, called Didymus, was not with them when Jesus came.

25 The other disciples therefore said unto him, We have seen the Lord. But he said unto them, Except I shall see in his hands the print of the nails, and put my finger into the print of the nails, and thrust my hand into his side, I will not believe.

26 ¶ And after eight days again his disciples were within, and Thomas with them: *then* came Jesus, the doors being shut, and stood in the midst, and said, Peace *be* unto you.

NEW AMERICAN STANDARD BIBLE

18 Mary Magdalene *came, announcing to the disciples, "I have seen the Lord," and *that* He had said these things to her.

Jesus among His Disciples

19 So when it was evening on that day, the first *day* of the week, and when the doors were shut where the disciples were, for fear of the Jews, Jesus came and stood in their midst and *said to them, "Peace *be* with you."

20 And when He had said this, He showed them both His hands and His side. The disciples then rejoiced when they saw the Lord.

21 So Jesus said to them again, "Peace *be* with you; as the Father has sent Me, I also send you."

22 And when He had said this, He breathed on them and *said to them, "Receive the Holy Spirit.

23 "If you forgive the sins of any, *their sins* have been forgiven them; if you retain the *sins* of any, they have been retained."

24 But Thomas, one of the twelve, called Didymus, was not with them when Jesus came.

25 So the other disciples were saying to him, "We have seen the Lord!" But he said to them, "Unless I see in His hands the imprint of the nails, and put my finger into the place of the nails, and put my hand into His side, I will not believe."

26 After eight days His disciples were again inside, and Thomas with them. Jesus *came, the doors having been shut, and stood in their midst and said, "Peace *be* with you."

NEW CENTURY VERSION

18Mary Magdalene went and said to the followers, "I saw the Lord!" And she told them what Jesus had said to her.

Jesus Appears to His Followers

19When it was evening on the first day of the week, the followers were together. The doors were locked, because they were afraid of the Jews. Then Jesus came and stood right in the middle of them and said, "Peace be with you." 20After he said this, he showed them his hands and his side. The followers were thrilled when they saw the Lord.

21Then Jesus said again, "Peace be with you. As the Father sent me, I now send you." 22After he said this, he breathed on them and said, "Receive the Holy Spirit. 23If you forgive anyone his sins, they are forgiven. If you don't forgive them, they are not forgiven."

Jesus Appears to Thomas

24Thomas (called Didymus), who was one of the twelve, was not with them when Jesus came. 25The other followers kept telling Thomas, "We saw the Lord."

But Thomas said, "I will not believe it until I see the nail marks in his hands and put my finger where the nails were and put my hand into his side."

26A week later the followers were in the house again, and Thomas was with them. The doors were locked, but Jesus came in and stood right in the middle of them. He said, "Peace be with you." 27Then he said to Thomas, "Put

CONTEMPORARY ENGLISH VERSION

told the disciples that she had seen the Lord. She also told them what he had said to her.

Jesus Appears to His Disciples

(Matthew 28.16-20; Mark 16.14-18; Luke 24.36-49)

19The disciples were afraid of the Jewish leaders, and on the evening of that same Sunday they locked themselves in a room. Suddenly, Jesus appeared in the middle of the group. He greeted them 20and showed them his hands and his side. When the disciples saw the Lord, they became very happy.

21After Jesus had greeted them again, he said, "I am sending you, just as the Father has sent me." 22Then he breathed on them and said, "Receive the Holy Spirit. 23If you forgive anyone's sins, they will be forgiven. But if you don't forgive their sins, they will not be forgiven."

Jesus and Thomas

24Although Thomas the Twin was one of the twelve disciples, he wasn't with the others when Jesus appeared to them. 25So they told him, "We have seen the Lord!"

But Thomas said, "First, I must see the nail scars in his hands and touch them with my finger. I must put my hand where the spear went into his side. I won't believe unless I do this!"

26A week later the disciples were together again. This time, Thomas was with them. Jesus came in while the doors were still locked and stood in the middle of the group. He greeted his disciples 27and said to Thomas, "Put

NEW INTERNATIONAL VERSION

[18]Mary Magdalene went to the disciples with the news: "I have seen the Lord!" And she told them that he had said these things to her.

Jesus Appears to His Disciples

[19]On the evening of that first day of the week, when the disciples were together, with the doors locked for fear of the Jews, Jesus came and stood among them and said, "Peace be with you!" [20]After he said this, he showed them his hands and side. The disciples were overjoyed when they saw the Lord.

[21]Again Jesus said, "Peace be with you! As the Father has sent me, I am sending you." [22]And with that he breathed on them and said, "Receive the Holy Spirit. [23]If you forgive anyone his sins, they are forgiven; if you do not forgive them, they are not forgiven."

Jesus Appears to Thomas

[24]Now Thomas (called Didymus), one of the Twelve, was not with the disciples when Jesus came. [25]So the other disciples told him, "We have seen the Lord!"

But he said to them, "Unless I see the nail marks in his hands and put my finger where the nails were, and put my hand into his side, I will not believe it."

[26]A week later his disciples were in the house again, and Thomas was with them. Though the doors were locked, Jesus came and stood among them and said, "Peace be

NEW LIVING TRANSLATION

[18]Mary Magdalene found the disciples and told them, "I have seen the Lord!" Then she gave them his message.

Jesus Appears to His Disciples

[19]That evening, on the first day of the week, the disciples were meeting behind locked doors because they were afraid of the Jewish leaders. Suddenly, Jesus was standing there among them! "Peace be with you," he said. [20]As he spoke, he held out his hands for them to see, and he showed them his side. They were filled with joy when they saw their Lord! [21]He spoke to them again and said, "Peace be with you. As the Father has sent me, so I send you." [22]Then he breathed on them and said to them, "Receive the Holy Spirit. [23]If you forgive anyone's sins, they are forgiven. If you refuse to forgive them, they are unforgiven."

Jesus Appears to Thomas

[24]One of the disciples, Thomas (nicknamed the Twin*), was not with the others when Jesus came. [25]They told him, "We have seen the Lord!" But he replied, "I won't believe it unless I see the nail wounds in his hands, put my fingers into them, and place my hand into the wound in his side."

[26]Eight days later the disciples were together again, and this time Thomas was with them. The doors were locked; but suddenly, as before, Jesus was standing among them. He said, "Peace be with you." [27]Then he said to Thomas,

20:24 Greek *the one who was called Didymus.*

NEW KING JAMES VERSION

[18]Mary Magdalene came and told the disciples that she had seen the Lord,[b] and *that* He had spoken these things to her.

The Apostles Commissioned

[19]Then, the same day at evening, being the first *day* of the week, when the doors were shut where the disciples were assembled,[c] for fear of the Jews, Jesus came and stood in the midst, and said to them, "Peace *be* with you." [20]When He had said this, He showed them *His* hands and His side. Then the disciples were glad when they saw the Lord.

[21]So Jesus said to them again, "Peace to you! As the Father has sent Me, I also send you." [22]And when He had said this, He breathed on *them,* and said to them, "Receive the Holy Spirit. [23]If you forgive the sins of any, they are forgiven them; if you retain the *sins* of any, they are retained."

Seeing and Believing

[24]Now Thomas, called the Twin, one of the twelve, was not with them when Jesus came. [25]The other disciples therefore said to him, "We have seen the Lord."

So he said to them, "Unless I see in His hands the print of the nails, and put my finger into the print of the nails, and put my hand into His side, I will not believe."

[26]And after eight days His disciples were again inside, and Thomas with them. Jesus came, the doors being shut, and stood in the midst, and said, "Peace to you!" [27]Then

20:18 [b] NU-Text reads *disciples, "I have seen the Lord," . . .*
20:19 [c] NU-Text omits *assembled.*

THE MESSAGE

Mary Magdalene went, telling the news to the disciples: "I saw the Master!" And she told them everything he said to her.

To Believe

Later on that day, the disciples had gathered together, but, fearful of the Jews, had locked all the doors in the house. Jesus entered, stood among them, and said, "Peace to you." Then he showed them his hands and side.

The disciples, seeing the Master with their own eyes, were exuberant. Jesus repeated his greeting: "Peace to you. Just as the Father sent me, I send you."

Then he took a deep breath and breathed into them. "Receive the Holy Spirit," he said. "If you forgive someone's sins, they're gone for good. If you don't forgive sins, what are you going to do with them?"

But Thomas, sometimes called the Twin, one of the Twelve, was not with them when Jesus came. The other disciples told him, "We saw the Master."

But he said, "Unless I see the nail holes in his hands, put my finger in the nail holes, and stick my hand in his side, I won't believe it."

Eight days later, his disciples were again in the room. This time Thomas was with them. Jesus came through the locked doors, stood among them, and said, "Peace to you."

KING JAMES VERSION

27 Then saith he to Thomas, Reach hither thy finger, and behold my hands; and reach hither thy hand, and thrust *it* into my side: and be not faithless, but believing.

28 And Thomas answered and said unto him, My Lord and my God.

29 Jesus saith unto him, Thomas, because thou hast seen me, thou hast believed: blessed *are* they that have not seen, and *yet* have believed.

30 And many other signs truly did Jesus in the presence of his disciples, which are not written in this book:

31 But these are written, that ye might believe that Jesus is the Christ, the Son of God; and that believing ye might have life through his name.

21 After these things Jesus shewed himself again to the disciples at the sea of Tiberias; and on this wise shewed he *himself*.

2 There were together Simon Peter, and Thomas called Didymus, and Nathanael of Cana in Galilee, and the *sons* of Zebedee, and two other of his disciples.

3 Simon Peter saith unto them, I go a fishing. They say unto him, We also go with thee. They went forth, and entered into a ship immediately; and that night they caught nothing.

4 But when the morning was now come, Jesus stood on the shore: but the disciples knew not that it was Jesus.

NEW AMERICAN STANDARD BIBLE

27 Then He *said to Thomas, "Reach here with your finger, and see My hands; and reach here your hand and put it into My side; and do not be unbelieving, but believing."

28 Thomas answered and said to Him, "My Lord and my God!"

29 Jesus *said to him, "Because you have seen Me, have you believed? Blessed *are* they who did not see, and *yet* believed."

Why This Gospel Was Written

30 Therefore many other signs Jesus also performed in the presence of the disciples, which are not written in this book;

31 but these have been written so that you may believe that Jesus is the Christ, the Son of God; and that believing you may have life in His name.

Jesus Appears at the Sea of Galilee

21 After these things Jesus manifested Himself again to the disciples at the Sea of Tiberias, and He manifested *Himself* in this way.

2 Simon Peter, and Thomas called Didymus, and Nathanael of Cana in Galilee, and the *sons* of Zebedee, and two others of His disciples were together.

3 Simon Peter *said to them, "I am going fishing." They *said to him, "We will also come with you." They went out and got into the boat; and that night they caught nothing.

4 But when the day was now breaking, Jesus stood on the beach; yet the disciples did not know that it was Jesus.

NEW CENTURY VERSION

your finger here, and look at my hands. Put your hand here in my side. Stop being an unbeliever and believe."

28Thomas said to him, "My Lord and my God!"

29Then Jesus told him, "You believe because you see me. Those who believe without seeing me will be truly happy."

Why John Wrote This Book

30Jesus did many other miracles in the presence of his followers that are not written in this book. 31But these are written so that you may believe that Jesus is the Christ, the Son of God. Then, by believing, you may have life through his name.

Jesus Appears to Seven Followers

21 Later, Jesus showed himself to his followers again—this time at Lake Galilee.[a] This is how he showed himself: 2Some of the followers were together: Simon Peter, Thomas (called Didymus), Nathanael from Cana in Galilee, the two sons of Zebedee, and two other followers. 3Simon Peter said, "I am going out to fish."

The others said, "We will go with you." So they went out and got into the boat. They fished that night but caught nothing.

4Early the next morning Jesus stood on the shore, but the followers did not know it was Jesus. 5Then he said to

21:1 [a] **Lake Galilee** Literally, "Sea of Tiberias."

CONTEMPORARY ENGLISH VERSION

your finger here and look at my hands! Put your hand into my side. Stop doubting and have faith!"

28Thomas replied, "You are my Lord and my God!"

29Jesus said, "Thomas, do you have faith because you have seen me? The people who have faith in me without seeing me are the ones who are really blessed!"

Why John Wrote His Book

30Jesus worked many other miracles[a] for his disciples, and not all of them are written in this book. 31But these are written so that you will put your faith in Jesus as the Messiah and the Son of God. If you have faith in[b] him, you will have true life.

Jesus Appears to Seven Disciples

21 Jesus later appeared to his disciples along the shore of Lake Tiberias. 2Simon Peter, Thomas the Twin, Nathanael from Cana in Galilee, and the brothers James and John,[a] were there, together with two other disciples. 3Simon Peter said, "I'm going fishing!"

The others said, "We will go with you." They went out in their boat. But they didn't catch a thing that night.

4Early the next morning Jesus stood on the shore, but the disciples did not realize who he was. 5Jesus shouted,

[a] 20.30 *miracles*: See the note at 2.11. [b] 20.31 *put your faith in . . . have faith in*: Some manuscripts have "keep on having faith in . . . keep on having faith in." [a] 21.2 *the brothers James and John*: Greek "the two sons of Zebedee."

NEW INTERNATIONAL VERSION

with you!" [27]Then he said to Thomas, "Put your finger here; see my hands. Reach out your hand and put it into my side. Stop doubting and believe."

[28]Thomas said to him, "My Lord and my God!"

[29]Then Jesus told him, "Because you have seen me, you have believed; blessed are those who have not seen and yet have believed."

[30]Jesus did many other miraculous signs in the presence of his disciples, which are not recorded in this book. [31]But these are written that you may[a] believe that Jesus is the Christ, the Son of God, and that by believing you may have life in his name.

Jesus and the Miraculous Catch of Fish

21 Afterward Jesus appeared again to his disciples, by the Sea of Tiberias.[a] It happened this way: [2]Simon Peter, Thomas (called Didymus), Nathanael from Cana in Galilee, the sons of Zebedee, and two other disciples were together. [3]"I'm going out to fish," Simon Peter told them, and they said, "We'll go with you." So they went out and got into the boat, but that night they caught nothing.

[4]Early in the morning, Jesus stood on the shore, but the disciples did not realize that it was Jesus.

[a] *31* Some manuscripts *may continue to* [a] *1* That is, Sea of Galilee

NEW LIVING TRANSLATION

"Put your finger here and see my hands. Put your hand into the wound in my side. Don't be faithless any longer. Believe!"

[28]"My Lord and my God!" Thomas exclaimed.

[29]Then Jesus told him, "You believe because you have seen me. Blessed are those who haven't seen me and believe anyway."

Purpose of the Book

[30]Jesus' disciples saw him do many other miraculous signs besides the ones recorded in this book. [31]But these are written so that you may believe* that Jesus is the Messiah, the Son of God, and that by believing in him you will have life.

Jesus Appears to Seven Disciples

21 Later Jesus appeared again to the disciples beside the Sea of Galilee.* This is how it happened. [2]Several of the disciples were there—Simon Peter, Thomas (nicknamed the Twin*), Nathanael from Cana in Galilee, the sons of Zebedee, and two other disciples.

[3]Simon Peter said, "I'm going fishing."

"We'll come, too," they all said. So they went out in the boat, but they caught nothing all night.

[4]At dawn the disciples saw Jesus standing on the beach, but they couldn't see who he was. [5]He called out, "Friends,

20:31 Some manuscripts read *may continue to believe.* 21:1 Greek *Sea of Tiberias,* another name for the Sea of Galilee. 21:2 Greek *the one who was called Didymus.*

NEW KING JAMES VERSION

He said to Thomas, "Reach your finger here, and look at My hands; and reach your hand *here,* and put *it* into My side. Do not be unbelieving, but believing."

[28]And Thomas answered and said to Him, "My Lord and my God!"

[29]Jesus said to him, "Thomas,[d] because you have seen Me, you have believed. Blessed *are* those who have not seen and *yet* have believed."

That You May Believe

[30]And truly Jesus did many other signs in the presence of His disciples, which are not written in this book; [31]but these are written that you may believe that Jesus is the Christ, the Son of God, and that believing you may have life in His name.

Breakfast by the Sea

21 After these things Jesus showed Himself again to the disciples at the Sea of Tiberias, and in this way He showed *Himself:* [2]Simon Peter, Thomas called the Twin, Nathanael of Cana in Galilee, the *sons* of Zebedee, and two others of His disciples were together. [3]Simon Peter said to them, "I am going fishing."

They said to him, "We are going with you also." They went out and immediately[a] got into the boat, and that night they caught nothing. [4]But when the morning had now come, Jesus stood on the shore; yet the disciples did

20:29 [d] NU-Text and M-Text omit *Thomas.* 21:3 [a] NU-Text omits *immediately.*

THE MESSAGE

Then he focused his attention on Thomas. "Take your finger and examine my hands. Take your hand and stick it in my side. Don't be unbelieving. Believe."

Thomas said, "My Master! My God!"

Jesus said, "So, you believe because you've seen with your own eyes. Even better blessings are in store for those who believe without seeing."

Jesus provided far more God-revealing signs than are written down in this book. These are written down so you will believe that Jesus is the Messiah, the Son of God, and in the act of believing, have real and eternal life in the way he personally revealed it.

Fishing

21 After this, Jesus appeared again to the disciples, this time at the Tiberias Sea (the Sea of Galilee). This is how he did it: Simon Peter, Thomas (nicknamed "Twin"), Nathanael from Cana in Galilee, the brothers Zebedee, and two other disciples were together. Simon Peter announced, "I'm going fishing."

The rest of them replied, "We're going with you." They went out and got in the boat. They caught nothing that night. When the sun came up, Jesus was standing on the beach, but they didn't recognize him.

KING JAMES VERSION

5 Then Jesus saith unto them, Children, have ye any meat? They answered him, No.

6 And he said unto them, Cast the net on the right side of the ship, and ye shall find. They cast therefore, and now they were not able to draw it for the multitude of fishes.

7 Therefore that disciple whom Jesus loved saith unto Peter, It is the Lord. Now when Simon Peter heard that it was the Lord, he girt *his* fisher's coat *unto him*, (for he was naked,) and did cast himself into the sea.

8 And the other disciples came in a little ship; (for they were not far from land, but as it were two hundred cubits,) dragging the net with fishes.

9 As soon then as they were come to land, they saw a fire of coals there, and fish laid thereon, and bread.

10 Jesus saith unto them, Bring of the fish which ye have now caught.

11 Simon Peter went up, and drew the net to land full of great fishes, an hundred and fifty and three: and for all there were so many, yet was not the net broken.

12 Jesus saith unto them, Come *and* dine. And none of the disciples durst ask him, Who art thou? knowing that it was the Lord.

13 Jesus then cometh, and taketh bread, and giveth them, and fish likewise.

14 This is now the third time that Jesus shewed himself to his disciples, after that he was risen from the dead.

NEW AMERICAN STANDARD BIBLE

5 So Jesus *said to them, "Children, you do not have any fish, do you?" They answered Him, "No."

6 And He said to them, "Cast the net on the right-hand side of the boat and you will find *a catch*." So they cast, and then they were not able to haul it in because of the great number of fish.

7 Therefore that disciple whom Jesus loved *said to Peter, "It is the Lord." So when Simon Peter heard that it was the Lord, he put his outer garment on (for he was stripped *for work*), and threw himself into the sea.

8 But the other disciples came in the little boat, for they were not far from the land, but about one hundred yards away, dragging the net *full* of fish.

9 So when they got out on the land, they *saw a charcoal fire *already* laid and fish placed on it, and bread.

10 Jesus *said to them, "Bring some of the fish which you have now caught."

11 Simon Peter went up and drew the net to land, full of large fish, a hundred and fifty-three; and although there were so many, the net was not torn.

Jesus Provides

12 Jesus *said to them, "Come *and* have breakfast." None of the disciples ventured to question Him, "Who are You?" knowing that it was the Lord.

13 Jesus *came and *took the bread and *gave *it* to them, and the fish likewise.

14 This is now the third time that Jesus was manifested to the disciples, after He was raised from the dead.

NEW CENTURY VERSION

them, "Friends, did you catch any fish?"
They answered, "No."
6 He said, "Throw your net on the right side of the boat,
and you will find some." So they did, and they caught so
many fish they could not pull the net back into the boat.
7 The follower whom Jesus loved said to Peter, "It is the
Lord!" When Peter heard him say this, he wrapped his coat
around himself. (Peter had taken his clothes off.) Then he
jumped into the water. 8 The other followers went to shore
in the boat, dragging the net full of fish. They were not
very far from shore, only about a hundred yards. 9 When
the followers stepped out of the boat and onto the shore,
they saw a fire of hot coals. There were fish on the fire,
and there was bread.
10 Then Jesus said, "Bring some of the fish you just
caught."
11 Simon Peter went into the boat and pulled the net to
the shore. It was full of big fish, one hundred fifty-three in
all, but even though there were so many, the net did not
tear. 12 Jesus said to them, "Come and eat." None of the fol-
lowers dared ask him, "Who are you?" because they knew
it was the Lord. 13 Jesus came and took the bread and gave
it to them, along with the fish.
14 This was now the third time Jesus showed himself to
his followers after he was raised from the dead.

CONTEMPORARY ENGLISH VERSION

"Friends, have you caught anything?"
"No!" they answered.
6 So he told them, "Let your net down on the right side of
your boat, and you will catch some fish."
They did, and the net was so full of fish that they could
not drag it up into the boat.
7 Jesus' favorite disciple told Peter, "It's the Lord!" When
Simon heard that it was the Lord, he put on the clothes
that he had taken off while he was working. Then he
jumped into the water. 8 The boat was only about a hun-
dred yards from shore. So the other disciples stayed in the
boat and dragged in the net full of fish.
9 When the disciples got out of the boat, they saw some
bread and a charcoal fire with fish on it. 10 Jesus told his
disciples, "Bring some of the fish you just caught."
11 Simon Peter got back into the boat and dragged the net
to shore. In it were one hundred fifty-three large fish, but
still the net did not rip.
12 Jesus said, "Come and eat!" But none of the disciples
dared ask who he was. They knew he was the Lord. 13 Jesus
took the bread in his hands and gave some of it to his dis-
ciples. He did the same with the fish. 14 This was the third
time that Jesus appeared to his disciples after he was
raised from death.

NEW INTERNATIONAL VERSION

5He called out to them, "Friends, haven't you any fish?"
"No," they answered.
6He said, "Throw your net on the right side of the boat and you will find some." When they did, they were unable to haul the net in because of the large number of fish.
7Then the disciple whom Jesus loved said to Peter, "It is the Lord!" As soon as Simon Peter heard him say, "It is the Lord," he wrapped his outer garment around him (for he had taken it off) and jumped into the water. 8The other disciples followed in the boat, towing the net full of fish, for they were not far from shore, about a hundred yards.[b]
9When they landed, they saw a fire of burning coals there with fish on it, and some bread.
10Jesus said to them, "Bring some of the fish you have just caught."
11Simon Peter climbed aboard and dragged the net ashore. It was full of large fish, 153, but even with so many the net was not torn. 12Jesus said to them, "Come and have breakfast." None of the disciples dared ask him, "Who are you?" They knew it was the Lord. 13Jesus came, took the bread and gave it to them, and did the same with the fish. 14This was now the third time Jesus appeared to his disciples after he was raised from the dead.

[b] 8 Greek *about two hundred cubits* (about 90 meters)

NEW LIVING TRANSLATION

have you caught any fish?"
"No," they replied.
6Then he said, "Throw out your net on the right-hand side of the boat, and you'll get plenty of fish!" So they did, and they couldn't draw in the net because there were so many fish in it.
7Then the disciple whom Jesus loved said to Peter, "It is the Lord!" When Simon Peter heard that it was the Lord, he put on his tunic (for he had stripped for work), jumped into the water, and swam ashore. 8The others stayed with the boat and pulled the loaded net to the shore, for they were only out about three hundred feet.* 9When they got there, they saw that a charcoal fire was burning and fish were frying over it, and there was bread.
10"Bring some of the fish you've just caught," Jesus said.
11So Simon Peter went aboard and dragged the net to the shore. There were 153 large fish, and yet the net hadn't torn.
12"Now come and have some breakfast!" Jesus said. And no one dared ask him if he really was the Lord because they were sure of it. 13Then Jesus served them the bread and the fish. 14This was the third time Jesus had appeared to his disciples since he had been raised from the dead.

21:8 Greek *200 cubits* [90 meters].

NEW KING JAMES VERSION

not know that it was Jesus. 5Then Jesus said to them, "Children, have you any food?"
They answered Him, "No."
6And He said to them, "Cast the net on the right side of the boat, and you will find *some.*" So they cast, and now they were not able to draw it in because of the multitude of fish.
7Therefore that disciple whom Jesus loved said to Peter, "It is the Lord!" Now when Simon Peter heard that it was the Lord, he put on *his* outer garment (for he had removed it), and plunged into the sea. 8But the other disciples came in the little boat (for they were not far from land, but about two hundred cubits), dragging the net with fish.
9Then, as soon as they had come to land, they saw a fire of coals there, and fish laid on it, and bread. 10Jesus said to them, "Bring some of the fish which you have just caught."
11Simon Peter went up and dragged the net to land, full of large fish, one hundred and fifty-three; and although there were so many, the net was not broken. 12Jesus said to them, "Come *and* eat breakfast." Yet none of the disciples dared ask Him, "Who are You?"—knowing that it was the Lord. 13Jesus then came and took the bread and gave it to them, and likewise the fish.
14This *is* now the third time Jesus showed Himself to His disciples after He was raised from the dead.

THE MESSAGE

Jesus spoke to them: "Good morning! Did you catch anything for breakfast?"

They answered, "No."

He said, "Throw the net off the right side of the boat and see what happens."

They did what he said. All of a sudden there were so many fish in it, they weren't strong enough to pull it in.

Then the disciple Jesus loved said to Peter, "It's the Master!"

When Simon Peter realized that it was the Master, he threw on some clothes, for he was stripped for work, and dove into the sea. The other disciples came in by boat for they weren't far from land, a hundred yards or so, pulling along the net full of fish. When they got out of the boat, they saw a fire laid, with fish and bread cooking on it.

Jesus said, "Bring some of the fish you've just caught." Simon Peter joined them and pulled the net to shore—153 big fish! And even with all those fish, the net didn't rip.

Jesus said, "Breakfast is ready." Not one of the disciples dared ask, "Who are you?" They knew it was the Master.

Jesus then took the bread and gave it to them. He did the same with the fish. This was now the third time Jesus had shown himself alive to the disciples since being raised from the dead.

KING JAMES VERSION

15 ¶ So when they had dined, Jesus saith to Simon Peter, Simon, *son* of Jonas, lovest thou me more than these? He saith unto him, Yea, Lord; thou knowest that I love thee. He saith unto him, Feed my lambs.

16 He saith to him again the second time, Simon, *son* of Jonas, lovest thou me? He saith unto him, Yea, Lord; thou knowest that I love thee. He saith unto him, Feed my sheep.

17 He saith unto him the third time, Simon, *son* of Jonas, lovest thou me? Peter was grieved because he said unto him the third time, Lovest thou me? And he said unto him, Lord, thou knowest all things; thou knowest that I love thee. Jesus saith unto him, Feed my sheep.

18 Verily, verily, I say unto thee, When thou wast young, thou girdedst thyself, and walkedst whither thou wouldest: but when thou shalt be old, thou shalt stretch forth thy hands, and another shall gird thee, and carry *thee* whither thou wouldest not.

19 This spake he, signifying by what death he should glorify God. And when he had spoken this, he saith unto him, Follow me.

20 ¶ Then Peter, turning about, seeth the disciple whom Jesus loved following; which also leaned on his breast at supper, and said, Lord, which is he that betrayeth thee?

NEW AMERICAN STANDARD BIBLE

The Love Motivation

15 So when they had finished breakfast, Jesus *said to Simon Peter, "Simon, *son* of John, do you love Me more than these?" He *said to Him, "Yes, Lord; You know that I love You." He *said to him, "Tend My lambs."

16 He *said to him again a second time, "Simon, *son* of John, do you love Me?" He *said to Him, "Yes, Lord; You know that I love You." He *said to him, "Shepherd My sheep."

17 He *said to him the third time, "Simon, *son* of John, do you love Me?" Peter was grieved because He said to him the third time, "Do you love Me?" And he said to Him, "Lord, You know all things; You know that I love You." Jesus *said to him, "Tend My sheep.

Our Times Are in His Hand

18 "Truly, truly, I say to you, when you were younger, you used to gird yourself and walk wherever you wished; but when you grow old, you will stretch out your hands and someone else will gird you, and bring you where you do not wish to *go*."

19 Now this He said, signifying by what kind of death he would glorify God. And when He had spoken this, He *said to him, "Follow Me!"

20 Peter, turning around, *saw the disciple whom Jesus loved following *them;* the one who also had leaned back on His bosom at the supper and said, "Lord, who is the one who betrays You?"

NEW CENTURY VERSION

Jesus Talks to Peter

15When they finished eating, Jesus said to Simon Peter, "Simon son of John do you love me more than these?"

He answered, "Yes, Lord, you know that I love you."

Jesus said, "Feed my lambs."

16Again Jesus said, "Simon son of John do you love me?"

He answered, "Yes, Lord, you know that I love you."

Jesus said, "Take care of my sheep."

17A third time he said, "Simon son of John do you love me?"

Peter was hurt because Jesus asked him the third time, "Do you love me?" Peter said, "Lord, you know everything; you know that I love you!"

He said to him, "Feed my sheep. 18I tell you the truth,
when you were younger, you tied your own belt and went where you wanted. But when you are old, you will put out your hands and someone else will tie you and take you where you don't want to go." 19(Jesus said this to show
how Peter would die to give glory to God.) Then Jesus said to Peter, "Follow me!"

20Peter turned and saw that the follower Jesus loved was walking behind them. (This was the follower who had leaned against Jesus at the supper and had said, "Lord,

CONTEMPORARY ENGLISH VERSION

Jesus and Peter

15When Jesus and his disciples had finished eating, he asked, "Simon son of John, do you love me more than the others do?"[b]

Simon Peter answered, "Yes, Lord, you know I do!"

"Then feed my lambs," Jesus said.

16Jesus asked a second time, "Simon son of John, do you love me?"

Peter answered, "Yes, Lord, you know I love you!"

"Then take care of my sheep," Jesus told him.

17Jesus asked a third time, "Simon son of John, do you love me?"

Peter was hurt because Jesus had asked him three times if he loved him. So he told Jesus, "Lord, you know everything. You know I love you."

Jesus replied, "Feed my sheep. 18I tell you for certain that
when you were a young man, you dressed yourself and went wherever you wanted to go. But when you are old, you will hold out your hands. Then others will wrap your belt around you and lead you where you don't want to go."

19Jesus said this to tell how Peter would die and bring honor to God. Then he said to Peter, "Follow me!"

Jesus and His Favorite Disciple

20Peter turned and saw Jesus' favorite disciple following them. He was the same one who had sat next to Jesus at the meal and had asked, "Lord, who is going to betray

b 21.15 *more than the others do?*: Or "more than you love these things?"

NEW INTERNATIONAL VERSION

Jesus Reinstates Peter

15When they had finished eating, Jesus said to Simon Peter, "Simon son of John, do you truly love me more than these?"

"Yes, Lord," he said, "you know that I love you."

Jesus said, "Feed my lambs."

16Again Jesus said, "Simon son of John, do you truly love me?"

He answered, "Yes, Lord, you know that I love you."

Jesus said, "Take care of my sheep."

17The third time he said to him, "Simon son of John, do you love me?"

Peter was hurt because Jesus asked him the third time, "Do you love me?" He said, "Lord, you know all things; you know that I love you."

Jesus said, "Feed my sheep. 18I tell you the truth, when you were younger you dressed yourself and went where you wanted; but when you are old you will stretch out your hands, and someone else will dress you and lead you where you do not want to go." 19Jesus said this to indicate the kind of death by which Peter would glorify God. Then he said to him, "Follow me!"

20Peter turned and saw that the disciple whom Jesus loved was following them. (This was the one who had leaned back against Jesus at the supper and had said,

NEW LIVING TRANSLATION

Jesus Challenges Peter

15After breakfast Jesus said to Simon Peter, "Simon son of John, do you love me more than these?"

"Yes, Lord," Peter replied, "you know I love you."

"Then feed my lambs," Jesus told him.

16Jesus repeated the question: "Simon son of John, do you love me?"

"Yes, Lord," Peter said, "you know I love you."

"Then take care of my sheep," Jesus said.

17Once more he asked him, "Simon son of John, do you love me?"

Peter was grieved that Jesus asked the question a third time. He said, "Lord, you know everything. You know I love you."

Jesus said, "Then feed my sheep. 18The truth is, when you were young, you were able to do as you liked and go wherever you wanted to. But when you are old, you will stretch out your hands, and others will direct you and take you where you don't want to go." 19Jesus said this to let him know what kind of death he would die to glorify God. Then Jesus told him, "Follow me."

20Peter turned around and saw the disciple Jesus loved following them—the one who had leaned over to Jesus during supper and asked, "Lord, who among us will betray

NEW KING JAMES VERSION

Jesus Restores Peter

15So when they had eaten breakfast, Jesus said to Simon Peter, "Simon, *son* of Jonah,[b] do you love Me more than these?"

He said to Him, "Yes, Lord; You know that I love You."

He said to him, "Feed My lambs."

16He said to him again a second time, "Simon, *son* of Jonah,[c] do you love Me?"

He said to Him, "Yes, Lord; You know that I love You."

He said to him, "Tend My sheep."

17He said to him the third time, "Simon, *son* of Jonah,[d] do you love Me?" Peter was grieved because He said to him the third time, "Do you love Me?"

And he said to Him, "Lord, You know all things; You know that I love You."

Jesus said to him, "Feed My sheep. 18Most assuredly, I say to you, when you were younger, you girded yourself and walked where you wished; but when you are old, you will stretch out your hands, and another will gird you and carry *you* where you do not wish." 19This He spoke, signifying by what death he would glorify God. And when He had spoken this, He said to him, "Follow Me."

The Beloved Disciple and His Book

20Then Peter, turning around, saw the disciple whom Jesus loved following, who also had leaned on His breast at the supper, and said, "Lord, who is the one who betrays

21:15 [b] NU-Text reads *John.* 21:16 [c] NU-Text reads *John.*
21:17 [d] NU-Text reads *John.*

THE MESSAGE

Do You Love Me?

After breakfast, Jesus said to Simon Peter, "Simon, son of John, do you love me more than these?"

"Yes, Master, you know I love you."

Jesus said, "Feed my lambs."

He then asked a second time, "Simon, son of John, do you love me?"

"Yes, Master, you know I love you."

Jesus said, "Shepherd my sheep."

Then he said it a third time: "Simon, son of John, do you love me?"

Peter was upset that he asked for the third time, "Do you love me?" so he answered, "Master, you know everything there is to know. You've got to know that I love you."

Jesus said, "Feed my sheep. I'm telling you the very truth now: When you were young you dressed yourself and went wherever you wished, but when you get old you'll have to stretch out your hands while someone else dresses you and takes you where you don't want to go." He said this to hint at the kind of death by which Peter would glorify God. And then he commanded, "Follow me."

Turning his head, Peter noticed the disciple Jesus loved

KING JAMES VERSION

21 Peter seeing him saith to Jesus, Lord, and what *shall* this man *do*?

22 Jesus saith unto him, If I will that he tarry till I come, what *is that* to thee? follow thou me.

23 Then went this saying abroad among the brethren, that that disciple should not die: yet Jesus said not unto him, He shall not die; but, If I will that he tarry till I come, what *is that* to thee?

24 This is the disciple which testifieth of these things, and wrote these things: and we know that his testimony is true.

25 And there are also many other things which Jesus did, the which, if they should be written every one, I suppose that even the world itself could not contain the books that should be written. Amen.

NEW AMERICAN STANDARD BIBLE

21 So Peter seeing him *said to Jesus, "Lord, and what about this man?"

22 Jesus *said to him, "If I want him to remain until I come, what *is that* to you? You follow Me!"

23 Therefore this saying went out among the brethren that that disciple would not die; yet Jesus did not say to him that he would not die, but *only,* "If I want him to remain until I come, what *is that* to you?"

24 This is the disciple who is testifying to these things and wrote these things, and we know that his testimony is true.

25 And there are also many other things which Jesus did, which if they *were written in detail, I suppose that even the world itself *would not contain the books that *would be written.

NEW CENTURY VERSION

who will turn against you?")
21 When Peter saw him behind them, he asked Jesus, "Lord, what about him?"

22 Jesus answered, "If I want him to live until I come back, that is not your business. You follow me."

23 So a story spread among the followers that this one would not die. But Jesus did not say he would not die. He only said, "If I want him to live until I come back, that is not your business."

24 That follower is the one who is telling these things and who has now written them down. We know that what he says is true.

25 There are many other things Jesus did. If every one of them were written down, I suppose the whole world would not be big enough for all the books that would be written.

CONTEMPORARY ENGLISH VERSION

you?"
21 When Peter saw that disciple, he asked Jesus, "Lord, what about him?"

22 Jesus answered, "What is it to you, if I want him to live until I return? You must follow me."
23 So the rumor spread among the other disciples that this disciple would not die. But Jesus did not say he would not die. He simply said, "What is it to you, if I want him to live until I return?"

24 This disciple is the one who told all of this. He wrote it, and we know he is telling the truth.

25 Jesus did many other things. If they were all written in books, I don't suppose there would be room enough in the whole world for all the books.

NEW INTERNATIONAL VERSION

"Lord, who is going to betray you?") 21When Peter saw him, he asked, "Lord, what about him?"

22Jesus answered, "If I want him to remain alive until I return, what is that to you? You must follow me." 23Because of this, the rumor spread among the brothers that this disciple would not die. But Jesus did not say that he would not die; he only said, "If I want him to remain alive until I return, what is that to you?"

24This is the disciple who testifies to these things and who wrote them down. We know that his testimony is true.

25Jesus did many other things as well. If every one of them were written down, I suppose that even the whole world would not have room for the books that would be written.

NEW LIVING TRANSLATION

you?" 21Peter asked Jesus, "What about him, Lord?"

22Jesus replied, "If I want him to remain alive until I return, what is that to you? You follow me." 23So the rumor spread among the community of believers* that that disciple wouldn't die. But that isn't what Jesus said at all. He only said, "If I want him to remain alive until I return, what is that to you?"

Conclusion

24This is that disciple who saw these events and recorded them here. And we all know that his account of these things is accurate.

25And I suppose that if all the other things Jesus did were written down, the whole world could not contain the books.

21:23 Greek *the brothers.*

NEW KING JAMES VERSION

You?" 21Peter, seeing him, said to Jesus, "But Lord, what *about* this man?"

22Jesus said to him, "If I will that he remain till I come, what *is that* to you? You follow Me."

23Then this saying went out among the brethren that this disciple would not die. Yet Jesus did not say to him that he would not die, but, "If I will that he remain till I come, what *is that* to you?"

24This is the disciple who testifies of these things, and wrote these things; and we know that his testimony is true.

25And there are also many other things that Jesus did, which if they were written one by one, I suppose that even the world itself could not contain the books that would be written. Amen.

THE MESSAGE

following right behind. When Peter noticed him, he asked Jesus, "Master, what's going to happen to *him*?"

Jesus said, "If I want him to live until I come again, what's that to you? You—follow me." That is how the rumor got out among the brothers that this disciple wouldn't die. But that is not what Jesus said. He simply said, "If I want him to live until I come again, what's that to you?"

This is the same disciple who was eyewitness to all these things and wrote them down. And we all know that his eyewitness account is reliable and accurate.

There are so many other things Jesus did. If they were all written down, each of them, one by one, I can't imagine a world big enough to hold such a library of books.

KING JAMES VERSION

THE ACTS
OF THE APOSTLES

1 The former treatise have I made, O Theophilus, of all that Jesus began both to do and teach,

2 Until the day in which he was taken up, after that he through the Holy Ghost had given commandments unto the apostles whom he had chosen:

3 To whom also he shewed himself alive after his passion by many infallible proofs, being seen of them forty days, and speaking of the things pertaining to the kingdom of God:

4 And, being assembled together with *them*, commanded them that they should not depart from Jerusalem, but wait for the promise of the Father, which, *saith he*, ye have heard of me.

5 For John truly baptized with water; but ye shall be baptized with the Holy Ghost not many days hence.

6 ¶ When they therefore were come together, they asked of him, saying, Lord, wilt thou at this time restore again the kingdom to Israel?

7 And he said unto them, It is not for you to know the times or the seasons, which the Father hath put in his own power.

8 But ye shall receive power, after that the Holy Ghost is come upon you: and ye shall be witnesses unto me both

NEW AMERICAN STANDARD BIBLE

THE ACTS
OF THE APOSTLES

Introduction

1 The first account I composed, Theophilus, about all that Jesus began to do and teach,

2 until the day when He was taken up *to heaven*, after He had by the Holy Spirit given orders to the apostles whom He had chosen.

3 To these He also presented Himself alive after His suffering, by many convincing proofs, appearing to them over *a period of* forty days and speaking of the things concerning the kingdom of God.

4 Gathering them together, He commanded them not to leave Jerusalem, but to wait for what the Father had promised, "Which," *He said,* "you heard of from Me;

5 for John baptized with water, but you will be baptized with the Holy Spirit not many days from now."

6 So when they had come together, they were asking Him, saying, "Lord, is it at this time You are restoring the kingdom to Israel?"

7 He said to them, "It is not for you to know times or epochs which the Father has fixed by His own authority;

8 but you will receive power when the Holy Spirit has come upon you; and you shall be My witnesses both in

NEW CENTURY VERSION

ACTS

Luke Writes Another Book

1 To Theophilus.
The first book I wrote was about everything Jesus
began to do and teach 2until the day he was taken up into
heaven. Before this, with the help of the Holy Spirit, Jesus
told the apostles he had chosen what they should do. 3After
his death, he showed himself to them and proved in many
ways that he was alive. The apostles saw Jesus during the
forty days after he was raised from the dead, and he spoke
to them about the kingdom of God. 4Once when he was eating with them, he told them not to leave Jerusalem. He
said, "Wait here to receive the promise from the Father
which I told you about. 5John baptized people with water,
but in a few days you will be baptized with the Holy Spirit."

Jesus Is Taken Up Into Heaven

6When the apostles were all together, they asked Jesus, "Lord, are you now going to give the kingdom back to Israel?"

7Jesus said to them, "The Father is the only One who
has the authority to decide dates and times. These things
are not for you to know. 8But when the Holy Spirit comes
to you, you will receive power. You will be my witnesses—

CONTEMPORARY ENGLISH VERSION

ACTS

1 Theophilus, I first wrote to you[a] about all that Jesus
did and taught from the very first 2until he was taken
up to heaven. But before he was taken up, he gave orders to
the apostles he had chosen with the help of the Holy Spirit.
3For forty days after Jesus had suffered and died, he
proved in many ways that he had been raised from death.
He appeared to his apostles and spoke to them about God's
kingdom. 4While he was still with them, he said:

> Don't leave Jerusalem yet. Wait here for the Father
> to give you the Holy Spirit, just as I told you he has
> promised to do. 5John baptized with water, but in a few
> days you will be baptized with the Holy Spirit.

Jesus Is Taken to Heaven

6While the apostles were still with Jesus, they asked him, "Lord, are you now going to give Israel its own king again?"[b]

7Jesus said to them, "You don't need to know the time of
those events that only the Father controls. 8But the Holy
Spirit will come upon you and give you power. Then you

[a] 1.1 *I first wrote to you*: The Gospel of Luke. [b] 1.6 *are you now going to give Israel its own king again?*: Or "Are you now going to rule Israel as its king?"

NEW INTERNATIONAL VERSION

ACTS

Jesus Taken Up Into Heaven

1 In my former book, Theophilus, I wrote about all that Jesus began to do and to teach [2]until the day he was taken up to heaven, after giving instructions through the Holy Spirit to the apostles he had chosen. [3]After his suffering, he showed himself to these men and gave many convincing proofs that he was alive. He appeared to them over a period of forty days and spoke about the kingdom of God. [4]On one occasion, while he was eating with them, he gave them this command: "Do not leave Jerusalem, but wait for the gift my Father promised, which you have heard me speak about. [5]For John baptized with[a] water, but in a few days you will be baptized with the Holy Spirit."

[6]So when they met together, they asked him, "Lord, are you at this time going to restore the kingdom to Israel?"

[7]He said to them: "It is not for you to know the times or dates the Father has set by his own authority. [8]But you will receive power when the Holy Spirit comes on you; and

[a] *5* Or *in*

NEW LIVING TRANSLATION

ACTS

The Promise of the Holy Spirit

1 Dear Theophilus:

In my first book* I told you about everything Jesus began to do and teach [2]until the day he ascended to heaven after giving his chosen apostles further instructions from the Holy Spirit. [3]During the forty days after his crucifixion, he appeared to the apostles from time to time and proved to them in many ways that he was actually alive. On these occasions he talked to them about the Kingdom of God.

[4]In one of these meetings as he was eating a meal with them, he told them, "Do not leave Jerusalem until the Father sends you what he promised. Remember, I have told you about this before. [5]John baptized with* water, but in just a few days you will be baptized with the Holy Spirit."

The Ascension of Jesus

[6]When the apostles were with Jesus, they kept asking him, "Lord, are you going to free Israel now and restore our kingdom?"

[7]"The Father sets those dates," he replied, "and they are not for you to know. [8]But when the Holy Spirit has come upon you, you will receive power and will tell people about

1:1 The reference is to the book of Luke. 1:5 Or *in;* also in 1:5b.

NEW KING JAMES VERSION

ACTS

OF THE APOSTLES

Prologue

1 The former account I made, O Theophilus, of all that Jesus began both to do and teach, [2]until the day in which He was taken up, after He through the Holy Spirit had given commandments to the apostles whom He had chosen, [3]to whom He also presented Himself alive after His suffering by many infallible proofs, being seen by them during forty days and speaking of the things pertaining to the kingdom of God.

The Holy Spirit Promised

[4]And being assembled together with *them,* He commanded them not to depart from Jerusalem, but to wait for the Promise of the Father, "which," *He said,* "you have heard from Me; [5]for John truly baptized with water, but you shall be baptized with the Holy Spirit not many days from now." [6]Therefore, when they had come together, they asked Him, saying, "Lord, will You at this time restore the kingdom to Israel?" [7]And He said to them, "It is not for you to know times or seasons which the Father has put in His own authority. [8]But you shall receive power when the Holy Spirit has come upon you; and you shall be witnesses to Me[a] in

1:8 [a] NU-Text reads *My witnesses.*

THE MESSAGE

ACTS

To the Ends of the World

1 Dear Theophilus, in the first volume of this book I wrote on everything that Jesus began to do and teach until the day he said goodbye to the apostles, the ones he had chosen through the Holy Spirit, and was taken up to heaven. After his death, he presented himself alive to them in many different settings over a period of forty days. In face-to-face meetings, he talked to them about things concerning the kingdom of God. As they met and ate meals together, he told them that they were on no account to leave Jerusalem but "must wait for what the Father promised: the promise you heard from me. John baptized in water; you will be baptized in the Holy Spirit. And soon."

When they were together for the last time they asked, "Master, are you going to restore the kingdom to Israel now? Is this the time?"

He told them, "You don't get to know the time. Timing is the Father's business. What you'll get is the Holy Spirit. And when the Holy Spirit comes on you, you will be able to

KING JAMES VERSION

in Jerusalem, and in all Judaea, and in Samaria, and unto the uttermost part of the earth.

9 And when he had spoken these things, while they beheld, he was taken up; and a cloud received him out of their sight.

10 And while they looked stedfastly toward heaven as he went up, behold, two men stood by them in white apparel;

11 Which also said, Ye men of Galilee, why stand ye gazing up into heaven? this same Jesus, which is taken up from you into heaven, shall so come in like manner as ye have seen him go into heaven.

12 ¶ Then returned they unto Jerusalem from the mount called Olivet, which is from Jerusalem a sabbath day's journey.

13 And when they were come in, they went up into an upper room, where abode both Peter, and James, and John, and Andrew, Philip, and Thomas, Bartholomew, and Matthew, James *the son* of Alphaeus, and Simon Zelotes, and Judas *the brother* of James.

NEW AMERICAN STANDARD BIBLE

Jerusalem, and in all Judea and Samaria, and even to the remotest part of the earth."

The Ascension

9 And after He had said these things, He was lifted up while they were looking on, and a cloud received Him out of their sight.

10 And as they were gazing intently into the sky while He was going, behold, two men in white clothing stood beside them.

11 They also said, "Men of Galilee, why do you stand looking into the sky? This Jesus, who has been taken up from you into heaven, will come in just the same way as you have watched Him go into heaven."

The Upper Room

12 Then they returned to Jerusalem from the mount called Olivet, which is near Jerusalem, a Sabbath day's journey away.

13 When they had entered *the city*, they went up to the upper room where they were staying; that is, Peter and John and James and Andrew, Philip and Thomas, Bartholomew and Matthew, James *the son* of Alphaeus, and Simon the Zealot, and Judas *the son* of James.

NEW CENTURY VERSION

in Jerusalem, in all of Judea, in Samaria, and in every part of the world."
9After he said this, as they were watching, he was lifted
up, and a cloud hid him from their sight. 10As he was
going, they were looking into the sky. Suddenly, two men
wearing white clothes stood beside them. 11They said,
"Men of Galilee, why are you standing here looking into the sky? Jesus, whom you saw taken up from you into heaven, will come back in the same way you saw him go."

A New Apostle Is Chosen

12Then they went back to Jerusalem from the Mount of Olives. (This mountain is about half a mile from
Jerusalem.) 13When they entered the city, they went to the upstairs room where they were staying. Peter, John, James, Andrew, Philip, Thomas, Bartholomew, Matthew, James son of Alphaeus, Simon (known as the Zealot), and Judas
son of James were there. 14They all continued praying

CONTEMPORARY ENGLISH VERSION

will tell everyone about me in Jerusalem, in all Judea, in
Samaria, and everywhere in the world." 9After Jesus had
said this and while they were watching, he was taken up
into a cloud. They could not see him, 10but as he went up,
they kept looking up into the sky.

Suddenly two men dressed in white clothes were standing there beside them. 11They said, "Why are you men
from Galilee standing here and looking up into the sky? Jesus has been taken to heaven. But he will come back in the same way that you have seen him go."

Someone To Take the Place of Judas

12-13The Mount of Olives was about half a mile from Jerusalem. The apostles who had gone there were Peter, John, James, Andrew, Philip, Thomas, Bartholomew, Matthew, James the son of Alphaeus, Simon, known as the Eager One,[c] and Judas the son of James.

After the apostles returned to the city, they went upstairs to the room where they had been staying.

[c] 1.12,13 *known as the Eager One*: The Greek text has "Zealot," a name later given to the members of a Jewish group that resisted and fought against the Romans.

NEW INTERNATIONAL VERSION

you will be my witnesses in Jerusalem, and in all Judea and Samaria, and to the ends of the earth."

9After he said this, he was taken up before their very eyes, and a cloud hid him from their sight.
10They were looking intently up into the sky as he was going, when suddenly two men dressed in white stood beside them. 11"Men of Galilee," they said, "why do you stand here looking into the sky? This same Jesus, who has been taken from you into heaven, will come back in the same way you have seen him go into heaven."

Matthias Chosen to Replace Judas

12Then they returned to Jerusalem from the hill called the Mount of Olives, a Sabbath day's walk[b] from the city.
13When they arrived, they went upstairs to the room where they were staying. Those present were Peter, John, James and Andrew; Philip and Thomas, Bartholomew and Matthew; James son of Alphaeus and Simon the Zealot, and Judas son of James. 14They all joined together constantly in

[b] *12* That is, about 3/4 mile (about 1,100 meters)

NEW LIVING TRANSLATION

me everywhere—in Jerusalem, throughout Judea, in Samaria, and to the ends of the earth."

9It was not long after he said this that he was taken up into the sky while they were watching, and he disappeared into a cloud. 10As they were straining their eyes to see him, two white-robed men suddenly stood there among them. 11They said, "Men of Galilee, why are you standing here staring at the sky? Jesus has been taken away from you into heaven. And someday, just as you saw him go, he will return!"

Matthias Replaces Judas

12The apostles were at the Mount of Olives when this happened, so they walked the half mile* back to Jerusalem.
13Then they went to the upstairs room of the house where they were staying. Here is the list of those who were present:

Peter,
John,
James,
Andrew,
Philip,
Thomas,
Bartholomew,
Matthew,
James (son of Alphaeus),
Simon (the Zealot),
and Judas (son of James).

1:12 Greek *a Sabbath day's journey.*

NEW KING JAMES VERSION

Jerusalem, and in all Judea and Samaria, and to the end of the earth."

Jesus Ascends to Heaven

9Now when He had spoken these things, while they watched, He was taken up, and a cloud received Him out of their sight. 10And while they looked steadfastly toward heaven as He went up, behold, two men stood by them in white apparel, 11who also said, "Men of Galilee, why do you stand gazing up into heaven? This *same* Jesus, who was taken up from you into heaven, will so come in like manner as you saw Him go into heaven."

The Upper Room Prayer Meeting

12Then they returned to Jerusalem from the mount called Olivet, which is near Jerusalem, a Sabbath day's journey.
13And when they had entered, they went up into the upper room where they were staying: Peter, James, John, and Andrew; Philip and Thomas; Bartholomew and Matthew; James *the son* of Alphaeus and Simon the Zealot; and Judas *the son* of James. 14These all continued with one accord in

THE MESSAGE

be my witnesses in Jerusalem, all over Judea and Samaria, even to the ends of the world."

These were his last words. As they watched, he was taken up and disappeared in a cloud. They stood there, staring into the empty sky. Suddenly two men appeared—in white robes! They said, "You Galileans!—why do you just stand here looking up at an empty sky? This very Jesus who was taken up from among you to heaven will come as certainly—and mysteriously—as he left."

Returning to Jerusalem

So they left the mountain called Olives and returned to Jerusalem. It was a little over half a mile. They went to the upper room they had been using as a meeting place:

Peter,
John,
James,
Andrew,
Philip,
Thomas,
Bartholomew,
Matthew,
James, son of Alphaeus,
Simon the Zealot,
Judas, son of James.

KING JAMES VERSION

14 These all continued with one accord in prayer and supplication, with the women, and Mary the mother of Jesus, and with his brethren.

15 ¶ And in those days Peter stood up in the midst of the disciples, and said, (the number of names together were about an hundred and twenty,)

16 Men *and* brethren, this scripture must needs have been fulfilled, which the Holy Ghost by the mouth of David spake before concerning Judas, which was guide to them that took Jesus.

17 For he was numbered with us, and had obtained part of this ministry.

18 Now this man purchased a field with the reward of iniquity; and falling headlong, he burst asunder in the midst, and all his bowels gushed out.

19 And it was known unto all the dwellers at Jerusalem; insomuch as that field is called in their proper tongue, Aceldama, that is to say, The field of blood.

20 For it is written in the book of Psalms, Let his habitation be desolate, and let no man dwell therein: and his bishoprick let another take.

NEW AMERICAN STANDARD BIBLE

14 These all with one mind were continually devoting themselves to prayer, along with *the* women, and Mary the mother of Jesus, and with His brothers.

15 At this time Peter stood up in the midst of the brethren (a gathering of about one hundred and twenty persons was there together), and said,

16 "Brethren, the Scripture had to be fulfilled, which the Holy Spirit foretold by the mouth of David concerning Judas, who became a guide to those who arrested Jesus.

17 "For he was counted among us and received his share in this ministry."

18 (Now this man acquired a field with the price of his wickedness, and falling headlong, he burst open in the middle and all his intestines gushed out.

19 And it became known to all who were living in Jerusalem; so that in their own language that field was called Hakeldama, that is, Field of Blood.)

20 "For it is written in the book of Psalms,

'LET HIS HOMESTEAD BE MADE DESOLATE,
AND LET NO ONE DWELL IN IT';
and,
'LET ANOTHER MAN TAKE HIS OFFICE.'

NEW CENTURY VERSION

together with some women, including Mary the mother of
Jesus, and Jesus' brothers.
15 During this time there was a meeting of the believers
(about one hundred twenty of them). Peter stood up and
said, 16–17 "Brothers and sisters,[a] in the Scriptures the Holy
Spirit said through David something that must happen
involving Judas. He was one of our own group and served
together with us. He led those who arrested Jesus."
18 (Judas bought a field with the money he got for his evil
act. But he fell to his death, his body burst open, and all
his intestines poured out. 19 Everyone in Jerusalem learned
about this so they named this place Akeldama. In their
language Akeldama means "Field of Blood.") 20 "In the
Book of Psalms," Peter said, "this is written:

'May his place be empty;
leave no one to live in it.' *Psalm 69:25*

And it is also written:

'Let another man replace him as leader.' *Psalm 109:8*

1:16–17 [a] **Brothers and sisters** Although the Greek text says "Brothers" here and throughout this book, the words of the speakers were meant for the entire church, including men and women.

CONTEMPORARY ENGLISH VERSION

14 The apostles often met together and prayed with a sin-
gle purpose in mind.[d] The women and Mary the mother of
Jesus would meet with them, and so would his brothers.
15 One day there were about one hundred twenty of the
Lord's followers meeting together, and Peter stood up to
speak to them. 16–17 He said:

My friends, long ago by the power of the Holy Spirit,
David said something about Judas, and what he said has
now happened. Judas was one of us and had worked
with us, but he brought the mob to arrest Jesus. 18 Then
Judas bought some land with the money he was given
for doing that evil thing. He fell headfirst into the field.
His body burst open, and all his insides came out.
19 When the people of Jerusalem found out about this,
they called the place Akeldama, which in the local lan-
guage means "Field of Blood."
20 In the book of Psalms it says,

"Leave his house empty,
and don't let anyone
live there."

It also says,

"Let someone else
have his job."

[d] **1.14** *met together and prayed with a single purpose in mind*: Or "met together in a special place for prayer."

NEW INTERNATIONAL VERSION

prayer, along with the women and Mary the mother of
Jesus, and with his brothers.
15 In those days Peter stood up among the believers[c] (a
group numbering about a hundred and twenty) 16 and said,
"Brothers, the Scripture had to be fulfilled which the Holy
Spirit spoke long ago through the mouth of David concern-
ing Judas, who served as guide for those who arrested
Jesus— 17 he was one of our number and shared in this
ministry."
18 (With the reward he got for his wickedness, Judas
bought a field; there he fell headlong, his body burst open
and all his intestines spilled out. 19 Everyone in Jerusalem
heard about this, so they called that field in their language
Akeldama, that is, Field of Blood.)
20 "For," said Peter, "it is written in the book of Psalms,

" 'May his place be deserted;
let there be no one to dwell in it,'[d]

and,

" 'May another take his place of leadership.'[e]

[c] *15* Greek *brothers* [d] *20* Psalm 69:25 [e] *20* Psalm 109:8

NEW LIVING TRANSLATION

14 They all met together continually for prayer, along with
Mary the mother of Jesus, several other women, and the
brothers of Jesus.
15 During this time, on a day when about 120 believers*
were present, Peter stood up and addressed them as fol-
lows:
16 "Brothers, it was necessary for the Scriptures to be ful-
filled concerning Judas, who guided the Temple police to
arrest Jesus. This was predicted long ago by the Holy
Spirit, speaking through King David. 17 Judas was one of
us, chosen to share in the ministry with us."
18 (Judas bought a field with the money he received for
his treachery, and falling there, he burst open, spilling out
his intestines. 19 The news of his death spread rapidly
among all the people of Jerusalem, and they gave the place
the Aramaic name *Akeldama,* which means "Field of
Blood.")
20 Peter continued, "This was predicted in the book of
Psalms, where it says, 'Let his home become desolate, with
no one living in it.' And again, 'Let his position be given to
someone else.'*

1:15 Greek *brothers.* 1:20 Pss 69:25; 109:8.

NEW KING JAMES VERSION

prayer and supplication,[b] with the women and Mary the
mother of Jesus, and with His brothers.

Matthias Chosen

15 And in those days Peter stood up in the midst of the
disciples[c] (altogether the number of names was about a
hundred and twenty), and said, 16 "Men *and* brethren, this
Scripture had to be fulfilled, which the Holy Spirit spoke
before by the mouth of David concerning Judas, who
became a guide to those who arrested Jesus; 17 for he was
numbered with us and obtained a part in this ministry."
18 (Now this man purchased a field with the wages of
iniquity; and falling headlong, he burst open in the middle
and all his entrails gushed out. 19 And it became known to
all those dwelling in Jerusalem; so that field is called in
their own language, Akel Dama, that is, Field of Blood.)
20 "For it is written in the Book of Psalms:

'Let his dwelling place be desolate,
And let no one live in it';[d]

and,

'Let[e] another take his office.'[f]

1:14 [b] NU-Text omits *and supplication.* 1:15 [c] NU-Text reads *brethren.* 1:20 [d] Psalm 69:25 [e] Psalm 109:8 [f] Greek *episkopen,* position of overseer

THE MESSAGE

They agreed they were in this for good, completely together
in prayer, the women included. Also Jesus' mother, Mary,
and his brothers.

Replacing Judas

During this time, Peter stood up in the company—there were about one hundred twenty of them in the room at the time—and said, "Friends, long ago the Holy Spirit spoke through David regarding Judas, who became the guide to those who arrested Jesus. That Scripture had to be fulfilled, and now has been. Judas was one of us and had his assigned place in this ministry.

"As you know, he took the evil bribe money and bought a small farm. There he came to a bad end, rupturing his belly and spilling his guts. Everybody in Jerusalem knows this by now; they call the place Murder Meadow. It's exactly what we find written in the Psalms:

'Let his farm become haunted
So no one can ever live there.'

And also what was written later:

'Let someone else take over his post.'

KING JAMES VERSION

21 Wherefore of these men which have companied with us all the time that the Lord Jesus went in and out among us,

22 Beginning from the baptism of John, unto that same day that he was taken up from us, must one be ordained to be a witness with us of his resurrection.

23 And they appointed two, Joseph called Barsabas, who was surnamed Justus, and Matthias.

24 And they prayed, and said, Thou, Lord, which knowest the hearts of all *men*, shew whether of these two thou hast chosen,

25 That he may take part of this ministry and apostleship, from which Judas by transgression fell, that he might go to his own place.

26 And they gave forth their lots; and the lot fell upon Matthias; and he was numbered with the eleven apostles.

2 And when the day of Pentecost was fully come, they were all with one accord in one place.

2 And suddenly there came a sound from heaven as of a rushing mighty wind, and it filled all the house where they were sitting.

3 And there appeared unto them cloven tongues like as of fire, and it sat upon each of them.

4 And they were all filled with the Holy Ghost, and began to speak with other tongues, as the Spirit gave them utterance.

5 ¶ And there were dwelling at Jerusalem Jews, devout men, out of every nation under heaven.

NEW AMERICAN STANDARD BIBLE

21 "Therefore it is necessary that of the men who have accompanied us all the time that the Lord Jesus went in and out among us—

22 beginning with the baptism of John until the day that He was taken up from us—one of these *must* become a witness with us of His resurrection."

23 So they put forward two men, Joseph called Barsabbas (who was also called Justus), and Matthias.

24 And they prayed and said, "You, Lord, who know the hearts of all men, show which one of these two You have chosen

25 to occupy this ministry and apostleship from which Judas turned aside to go to his own place."

26 And they drew lots for them, and the lot fell to Matthias; and he was added to the eleven apostles.

The Day of Pentecost

2 When the day of Pentecost had come, they were all together in one place.

2 And suddenly there came from heaven a noise like a violent rushing wind, and it filled the whole house where they were sitting.

3 And there appeared to them tongues as of fire distributing themselves, and they rested on each one of them.

4 And they were all filled with the Holy Spirit and began to speak with other tongues, as the Spirit was giving them utterance.

5 Now there were Jews living in Jerusalem, devout men from every nation under heaven.

NEW CENTURY VERSION

21-22"So now a man must become a witness with us of Jesus' being raised from the dead. He must be one of the men who were part of our group during all the time the Lord Jesus was among us—from the time John was baptizing people until the day Jesus was taken up from us to heaven."

23They put the names of two men before the group. One was Joseph Barsabbas, who was also called Justus. The other was Matthias. 24-25The apostles prayed, "Lord, you know the thoughts of everyone. Show us which one of these two you have chosen to do this work. Show us who should be an apostle in place of Judas, who turned away and went where he belongs." 26Then they used lots to choose between them, and the lots showed that Matthias was the one. So he became an apostle with the other eleven.

The Coming of the Holy Spirit

2 When the day of Pentecost came, they were all together in one place. 2Suddenly a noise like a strong, blowing wind came from heaven and filled the whole house where they were sitting. 3They saw something like flames of fire that were separated and stood over each person there. 4They were all filled with the Holy Spirit, and they began to speak different languages[a] by the power the Holy Spirit was giving them.

5There were some religious Jews staying in Jerusalem who were from every country in the world. 6When they

2:4 [a] **languages** This can also be translated "tongues."

CONTEMPORARY ENGLISH VERSION

21-22So we need someone else to help us tell others that Jesus has been raised from death. He must also be one of the men who was with us from the very beginning. He must have been with us from the time the Lord Jesus was baptized by John until the day he was taken to heaven.

23Two men were suggested: One of them was Joseph Barsabbas, known as Justus, and the other was Matthias. 24Then they all prayed, "Lord, you know what everyone is like! Show us the one you have chosen 25to be an apostle and to serve in place of Judas, who got what he deserved." 26They drew names, and Matthias was chosen to join the group of the eleven apostles.

The Coming of the Holy Spirit

2 On the day of Pentecost[a] all the Lord's followers were together in one place. 2Suddenly there was a noise from heaven like the sound of a mighty wind! It filled the house where they were meeting. 3Then they saw what looked like fiery tongues moving in all directions, and a tongue came and settled on each person there. 4The Holy Spirit took control of everyone, and they began speaking whatever languages the Spirit let them speak.

5Many religious Jews from every country in the world were living in Jerusalem. 6And when they heard this noise,

[a] 2.1 *Pentecost*: A Jewish festival that came fifty days after Passover and celebrated the wheat harvest. Jews later celebrated Pentecost as the time when they were given the Law of Moses.

NEW INTERNATIONAL VERSION

21Therefore it is necessary to choose one of the men who
have been with us the whole time the Lord Jesus went in
and out among us, 22beginning from John's baptism to the
time when Jesus was taken up from us. For one of these
must become a witness with us of his resurrection."
23So they proposed two men: Joseph called Barsabbas
(also known as Justus) and Matthias. 24Then they prayed,
"Lord, you know everyone's heart. Show us which of these
two you have chosen 25to take over this apostolic ministry,
which Judas left to go where he belongs." 26Then they cast
lots, and the lot fell to Matthias; so he was added to the
eleven apostles.

The Holy Spirit Comes at Pentecost

2 When the day of Pentecost came, they were all togeth-
er in one place. 2Suddenly a sound like the blowing of
a violent wind came from heaven and filled the whole
house where they were sitting. 3They saw what seemed to
be tongues of fire that separated and came to rest on each
of them. 4All of them were filled with the Holy Spirit and
began to speak in other tongues[a] as the Spirit enabled
them.
5Now there were staying in Jerusalem God-fearing Jews
from every nation under heaven. 6When they heard this

[a] *4* Or *languages*; also in verse 11

NEW LIVING TRANSLATION

21"So now we must choose another man to take Judas's
place. It must be someone who has been with us all the
time that we were with the Lord Jesus—22from the time he
was baptized by John until the day he was taken from us
into heaven. Whoever is chosen will join us as a witness of
Jesus' resurrection."
23So they nominated two men: Joseph called Barsabbas
(also known as Justus) and Matthias. 24Then they all
prayed for the right man to be chosen. "O Lord," they said,
"you know every heart. Show us which of these men you
have chosen 25as an apostle to replace Judas the traitor in
this ministry, for he has deserted us and gone where he
belongs." 26Then they cast lots, and in this way Matthias
was chosen and became an apostle with the other eleven.

The Holy Spirit Comes

2 On the day of Pentecost, seven weeks after Jesus' res-
urrection,* the believers were meeting together in one
place. 2Suddenly, there was a sound from heaven like the
roaring of a mighty windstorm in the skies above them,
and it filled the house where they were meeting. 3Then,
what looked like flames or tongues of fire appeared and
settled on each of them. 4And everyone present was filled
with the Holy Spirit and began speaking in other lan-
guages,* as the Holy Spirit gave them this ability.
5Godly Jews from many nations were living in Jerusalem

2:1 Greek *When the day of Pentecost arrived.* This annual celebration came 50 days after the Passover ceremonies. See Lev 23:16. 2:4 Or *in other tongues.*

NEW KING JAMES VERSION

21"Therefore, of these men who have accompanied us all
the time that the Lord Jesus went in and out among us,
22beginning from the baptism of John to that day when He
was taken up from us, one of these must become a witness
with us of His resurrection."
23And they proposed two: Joseph called Barsabas, who
was surnamed Justus, and Matthias. 24And they prayed
and said, "You, O Lord, who know the hearts of all, show
which of these two You have chosen 25to take part in this
ministry and apostleship from which Judas by transgres-
sion fell, that he might go to his own place." 26And they
cast their lots, and the lot fell on Matthias. And he was
numbered with the eleven apostles.

Coming of the Holy Spirit

2 When the Day of Pentecost had fully come, they were
all with one accord[a] in one place. 2And suddenly there
came a sound from heaven, as of a rushing mighty wind,
and it filled the whole house where they were sitting.
3Then there appeared to them divided tongues, as of fire,
and *one* sat upon each of them. 4And they were all filled
with the Holy Spirit and began to speak with other
tongues, as the Spirit gave them utterance.

The Crowd's Response

5And there were dwelling in Jerusalem Jews, devout
men, from every nation under heaven. 6And when this

2:1 [a] NU-Text reads *together.*

THE MESSAGE

"Judas must now be replaced. The replacement must
come from the company of men who stayed together with
us from the time Jesus was baptized by John up to the day
of his ascension, designated along with us as a witness to
his resurrection."
They nominated two: Joseph Barsabbas, nicknamed
Justus, and Matthias. Then they prayed, "You, oh God,
know every one of us inside and out. Make plain which of
these two men you choose to take the place in this minis-
try and leadership that Judas threw away in order to go his
own way." They then drew straws. Matthias won, and was
counted in with the eleven apostles.

A Sound Like a Strong Wind

2 When the Feast of Pentecost came, they were all
together in one place. Without warning there was a
sound like a strong wind, gale force—no one could tell
where it came from. It filled the whole building. Then, like
a wildfire, the Holy Spirit spread through their ranks, and
they started speaking in a number of different languages
as the Spirit prompted them.
There were many Jews staying in Jerusalem just then,
devout pilgrims from all over the world. When they heard

KING JAMES VERSION

6 Now when this was noised abroad, the multitude came together, and were confounded, because that every man heard them speak in his own language.

7 And they were all amazed and marvelled, saying one to another, Behold, are not all these which speak Galilaeans?

8 And how hear we every man in our own tongue, wherein we were born?

9 Parthians, and Medes, and Elamites, and the dwellers in Mesopotamia, and in Judaea, and Cappadocia, in Pontus, and Asia,

10 Phrygia, and Pamphylia, in Egypt, and in the parts of Libya about Cyrene, and strangers of Rome, Jews and proselytes,

11 Cretes and Arabians, we do hear them speak in our tongues the wonderful works of God.

12 And they were all amazed, and were in doubt, saying one to another, What meaneth this?

13 Others mocking said, These men are full of new wine.

14 ¶ But Peter, standing up with the eleven, lifted up his voice, and said unto them, Ye men of Judaea, and all *ye* that dwell at Jerusalem, be this known unto you, and hearken to my words:

15 For these are not drunken, as ye suppose, seeing it is *but* the third hour of the day.

16 But this is that which was spoken by the prophet Joel;

NEW AMERICAN STANDARD BIBLE

6 And when this sound occurred, the crowd came together, and were bewildered because each one of them was hearing them speak in his own language.

7 They were amazed and astonished, saying, "Why, are not all these who are speaking Galileans?

8 "And how is it that we each hear *them* in our own language to which we were born?

9 "Parthians and Medes and Elamites, and residents of Mesopotamia, Judea and Cappadocia, Pontus and Asia,

10 Phrygia and Pamphylia, Egypt and the districts of Libya around Cyrene, and visitors from Rome, both Jews and [1]proselytes,

11 Cretans and Arabs—we hear them in our *own* tongues speaking of the mighty deeds of God."

12 And they all continued in amazement and great perplexity, saying to one another, "What does this mean?"

13 But others were mocking and saying, "They are full of sweet wine."

Peter's Sermon

14 But Peter, taking his stand with the eleven, raised his voice and declared to them: "Men of Judea and all you who live in Jerusalem, let this be known to you and give heed to my words.

15 "For these men are not drunk, as you suppose, for it is *only* the [2]third hour of the day;

16 but this is what was spoken of through the prophet Joel:

2:10 [1] I.e. Gentile converts to Judaism 2:15 [2] I.e. 9 a.m.

NEW CENTURY VERSION

heard this noise, a crowd came together. They were all surprised, because each one heard them speaking in his own
language. 7 They were completely amazed at this. They
said, "Look! Aren't all these people that we hear speaking
from Galilee? 8 Then how is it possible that we each hear
them in our own languages? We are from different places:
9 Parthia, Media, Elam, Mesopotamia, Judea, Cappadocia,
Pontus, Asia, 10 Phrygia, Pamphylia, Egypt, the areas of
Libya near Cyrene, Rome 11 (both Jews and those who had
become Jews), Crete, and Arabia. But we hear them telling
in our own languages about the great things God has
done!" 12 They were all amazed and confused, asking each
other, "What does this mean?"

13 But others were making fun of them, saying, "They
have had too much wine."

Peter Speaks to the People

14 But Peter stood up with the eleven apostles, and in a
loud voice he spoke to the crowd: "My fellow Jews, and all
of you who are in Jerusalem, listen to me. Pay attention to
what I have to say. 15 These people are not drunk, as you
think; it is only nine o'clock in the morning! 16 But Joel the
prophet wrote about what is happening here today:

CONTEMPORARY ENGLISH VERSION

a crowd gathered. But they were surprised, because they
were hearing everything in their own languages. 7 They
were excited and amazed, and said:

Don't all these who are speaking come from Galilee?
8 Then why do we hear them speaking our very own languages? 9 Some of us are from Parthia, Media, and Elam.
Others are from Mesopotamia, Judea, Cappadocia,
Pontus, Asia, 10 Phrygia, Pamphylia, Egypt, parts of
Libya near Cyrene, Rome, 11 Crete, and Arabia. Some of
us were born Jews, and others of us have chosen to be
Jews. Yet we all hear them using our own languages to
tell the wonderful things God has done.

12 Everyone was excited and confused. Some of them
even kept asking each other, "What does all this mean?"

13 Others made fun of the Lord's followers and said,
"They are drunk."

Peter Speaks to the Crowd

14 Peter stood with the eleven apostles and spoke in a
loud and clear voice to the crowd:

Friends and everyone else living in Jerusalem, listen
carefully to what I have to say! 15 You are wrong to think
that these people are drunk. After all, it is only nine
o'clock in the morning. 16 But this is what God had the
prophet Joel say,

NEW INTERNATIONAL VERSION

sound, a crowd came together in bewilderment, because each one heard them speaking in his own language. 7Utterly amazed, they asked: "Are not all these men who are speaking Galileans? 8Then how is it that each of us hears them in his own native language? 9Parthians, Medes and Elamites; residents of Mesopotamia, Judea and Cappadocia, Pontus and Asia, 10Phrygia and Pamphylia, Egypt and the parts of Libya near Cyrene; visitors from Rome 11(both Jews and converts to Judaism); Cretans and Arabs—we hear them declaring the wonders of God in our own tongues!" 12Amazed and perplexed, they asked one another, "What does this mean?"

13Some, however, made fun of them and said, "They have had too much wine.[b]"

Peter Addresses the Crowd

14Then Peter stood up with the Eleven, raised his voice and addressed the crowd: "Fellow Jews and all of you who live in Jerusalem, let me explain this to you; listen carefully to what I say. 15These men are not drunk, as you suppose. It's only nine in the morning! 16No, this is what was spoken by the prophet Joel:

[b] *13* Or *sweet wine*

NEW LIVING TRANSLATION

at that time. 6When they heard this sound, they came running to see what it was all about, and they were bewildered to hear their own languages being spoken by the believers.

7They were beside themselves with wonder. "How can this be?" they exclaimed. "These people are all from Galilee, 8and yet we hear them speaking the languages of the lands where we were born! 9Here we are—Parthians, Medes, Elamites, people from Mesopotamia, Judea, Cappadocia, Pontus, the province of Asia, 10Phrygia, Pamphylia, Egypt, and the areas of Libya toward Cyrene, visitors from Rome (both Jews and converts to Judaism), 11Cretans, and Arabians. And we all hear these people speaking in our own languages about the wonderful things God has done!" 12They stood there amazed and perplexed. "What can this mean?" they asked each other. 13But others in the crowd were mocking. "They're drunk, that's all!" they said.

Peter Preaches to a Crowd

14Then Peter stepped forward with the eleven other apostles and shouted to the crowd, "Listen carefully, all of you, fellow Jews and residents of Jerusalem! Make no mistake about this. 15Some of you are saying these people are drunk. It isn't true! It's much too early for that. People don't get drunk by nine o'clock in the morning. 16No, what you see this morning was predicted centuries ago by the prophet Joel:

NEW KING JAMES VERSION

sound occurred, the multitude came together, and were confused, because everyone heard them speak in his own language. 7Then they were all amazed and marveled, saying to one another, "Look, are not all these who speak Galileans? 8And how *is it that* we hear, each in our own language in which we were born? 9Parthians and Medes and Elamites, those dwelling in Mesopotamia, Judea and Cappadocia, Pontus and Asia, 10Phrygia and Pamphylia, Egypt and the parts of Libya adjoining Cyrene, visitors from Rome, both Jews and proselytes, 11Cretans and Arabs—we hear them speaking in our own tongues the wonderful works of God." 12So they were all amazed and perplexed, saying to one another, "Whatever could this mean?"

13Others mocking said, "They are full of new wine."

Peter's Sermon

14But Peter, standing up with the eleven, raised his voice and said to them, "Men of Judea and all who dwell in Jerusalem, let this be known to you, and heed my words. 15For these are not drunk, as you suppose, since it is *only* the third hour of the day. 16But this is what was spoken by the prophet Joel:

THE MESSAGE

the sound, they came on the run. Then when they heard, one after another, their own mother tongues being spoken, they were thunderstruck. They couldn't for the life of them figure out what was going on, and kept saying, "Aren't these all Galileans? How come we're hearing them talk in our various mother tongues?

Parthians, Medes, and Elamites;
Visitors from Mesopotamia, Judea, and Cappadocia,
Pontus and Asia, Phrygia and Pamphylia,
Egypt and the parts of Libya belonging to Cyrene;
Immigrants from Rome, both Jews and proselytes;
Even Cretans and Arabs!

They're speaking our languages, describing God's mighty works!"

Their heads were spinning; they couldn't make head or tail of any of it. They talked back and forth, confused: "What's going on here?"

Others joked, "They're drunk on cheap wine."

Peter Speaks Up

That's when Peter stood up and, backed by the other eleven, spoke out with bold urgency: "Fellow Jews, all of you who are visiting Jerusalem, listen carefully and get this story straight. These people aren't drunk as some of you suspect. They haven't had time to get drunk—it's only nine o'clock in the morning. This is what the prophet Joel announced would happen:

KING JAMES VERSION

17 And it shall come to pass in the last days, saith God, I will pour out of my Spirit upon all flesh: and your sons and your daughters shall prophesy, and your young men shall see visions, and your old men shall dream dreams:

18 And on my servants and on my handmaidens I will pour out in those days of my Spirit; and they shall prophesy:

19 And I will shew wonders in heaven above, and signs in the earth beneath; blood, and fire, and vapour of smoke:

20 The sun shall be turned into darkness, and the moon into blood, before that great and notable day of the Lord come:

21 And it shall come to pass, *that* whosoever shall call on the name of the Lord shall be saved.

NEW AMERICAN STANDARD BIBLE

17 'AND IT SHALL BE IN THE LAST DAYS,' God says,
'THAT I WILL POUR FORTH OF MY SPIRIT ON ALL MANKIND;
AND YOUR SONS AND YOUR DAUGHTERS SHALL PROPHESY,
AND YOUR YOUNG MEN SHALL SEE VISIONS,
AND YOUR OLD MEN SHALL DREAM DREAMS;
18 EVEN ON MY BONDSLAVES, BOTH MEN AND WOMEN,
I WILL IN THOSE DAYS POUR FORTH OF MY SPIRIT
And they shall prophesy.
19 'AND I WILL GRANT WONDERS IN THE SKY ABOVE
AND SIGNS ON THE EARTH BELOW,
BLOOD, AND FIRE, AND VAPOR OF SMOKE.
20 'THE SUN WILL BE TURNED INTO DARKNESS
AND THE MOON INTO BLOOD,
BEFORE THE GREAT AND GLORIOUS DAY OF THE LORD SHALL COME.
21 'AND IT SHALL BE THAT EVERYONE WHO CALLS ON THE NAME OF THE LORD WILL BE SAVED.'

NEW CENTURY VERSION

17 'God says: In the last days
I will pour out my Spirit on all kinds of people.
Your sons and daughters will prophesy.
Your young men will see visions,
and your old men will dream dreams.
18 At that time I will pour out my Spirit
also on my male slaves and female slaves,
and they will prophesy.
19 I will show miracles
in the sky and on the earth:
blood, fire, and thick smoke.
20 The sun will become dark,
the moon red as blood,
before the overwhelming and glorious day of the Lord
will come.
21 Then anyone who calls on the Lord
will be saved.' *Joel 2:28–32*

CONTEMPORARY ENGLISH VERSION

17 "When the last days come,
I will give my Spirit
to everyone.
Your sons and daughters
will prophesy.
Your young men
will see visions,
and your old men
will have dreams.
18 In those days I will give
my Spirit to my servants,
both men and women,
and they will prophesy.

19 I will work miracles
in the sky above
and wonders
on the earth below.
There will be blood and fire
and clouds of smoke.
20 The sun will turn dark,
and the moon
will be as red as blood
before the great
and wonderful day
of the Lord appears.
21 Then the Lord
will save everyone
who asks for his help."

NEW INTERNATIONAL VERSION

17 " 'In the last days, God says,
I will pour out my Spirit on all people.
Your sons and daughters will prophesy,
your young men will see visions,
your old men will dream dreams.
18 Even on my servants, both men and women,
I will pour out my Spirit in those days,
and they will prophesy.
19 I will show wonders in the heaven above
and signs on the earth below,
blood and fire and billows of smoke.
20 The sun will be turned to darkness
and the moon to blood
before the coming of the great and glorious day of the Lord.
21 And everyone who calls
on the name of the Lord will be saved.'[c]

[c] *21* Joel 2:28–32

NEW LIVING TRANSLATION

17 'In the last days, God said,
I will pour out my Spirit upon all people.
Your sons and daughters will prophesy,
your young men will see visions,
and your old men will dream dreams.
18 In those days I will pour out my Spirit
upon all my servants, men and women alike,
and they will prophesy.
19 And I will cause wonders in the heavens above
and signs on the earth below—
blood and fire and clouds of smoke.
20 The sun will be turned into darkness,
and the moon will turn bloodred,
before that great and glorious day of the Lord arrives.
21 And anyone who calls on the name of the Lord
will be saved.'*

2:17-21 Joel 2:28-32.

NEW KING JAMES VERSION

17 *'And it shall come to pass in the last days, says God,*
That I will pour out of My Spirit on all flesh;
Your sons and your daughters shall prophesy,
Your young men shall see visions,
Your old men shall dream dreams.
18 *And on My menservants and on My maidservants*
I will pour out My Spirit in those days;
And they shall prophesy.
19 *I will show wonders in heaven above*
And signs in the earth beneath:
Blood and fire and vapor of smoke.
20 *The sun shall be turned into darkness,*
And the moon into blood,
Before the coming of the great and awesome day of the LORD.
21 *And it shall come to pass*
That whoever calls on the name of the LORD
Shall be saved.'[b]

2:21 [b] Joel 2:28–32

THE MESSAGE

'"In the Last Days," God says,
"I will pour out my Spirit
on every kind of people:
Your sons will prophesy,
also your daughters;
Your young men will see visions,
your old men dream dreams.
When the time comes,
I'll pour out my Spirit
On those who serve me, men and women both,
and they'll prophesy.
I'll set wonders in the sky above
and signs on the earth below,
Blood and fire and billowing smoke,
the sun turning black and the moon blood-red,
Before the Day of the Lord arrives,
the Day tremendous and marvelous;
And whoever calls out for help
to me, God, will be saved."'

KING JAMES VERSION

22 Ye men of Israel, hear these words; Jesus of Nazareth, a man approved of God among you by miracles and wonders and signs, which God did by him in the midst of you, as ye yourselves also know:

23 Him, being delivered by the determinate counsel and foreknowledge of God, ye have taken, and by wicked hands have crucified and slain:

24 Whom God hath raised up, having loosed the pains of death: because it was not possible that he should be holden of it.

25 For David speaketh concerning him, I foresaw the Lord always before my face, for he is on my right hand, that I should not be moved:

26 Therefore did my heart rejoice, and my tongue was glad; moreover also my flesh shall rest in hope:

27 Because thou wilt not leave my soul in hell, neither wilt thou suffer thine Holy One to see corruption.

28 Thou hast made known to me the ways of life; thou shalt make me full of joy with thy countenance.

29 Men *and* brethren, let me freely speak unto you of the patriarch David, that he is both dead and buried, and his sepulchre is with us unto this day.

NEW AMERICAN STANDARD BIBLE

22 "Men of Israel, listen to these words: Jesus the Nazarene, a man attested to you by God with miracles and wonders and signs which God performed through Him in your midst, just as you yourselves know—

23 this *Man*, delivered over by the predetermined plan and foreknowledge of God, you nailed to a cross by the hands of godless men and put *Him* to death.

24 "But God raised Him up again, putting an end to the agony of death, since it was impossible for Him to be held in its power.

25 "For David says of Him,

'I SAW THE LORD ALWAYS IN MY PRESENCE;
FOR HE IS AT MY RIGHT HAND, SO THAT I WILL NOT BE SHAKEN.
26 'THEREFORE MY HEART WAS GLAD AND MY TONGUE EXULTED;
MOREOVER MY FLESH ALSO WILL LIVE IN HOPE;
27 BECAUSE YOU WILL NOT ABANDON MY SOUL TO HADES,
NOR ALLOW YOUR HOLY ONE TO UNDERGO DECAY.
28 'YOU HAVE MADE KNOWN TO ME THE WAYS OF LIFE;
YOU WILL MAKE ME FULL OF GLADNESS WITH YOUR PRESENCE.'

29 "Brethren, I may confidently say to you regarding the patriarch David that he both died and was buried, and his tomb is with us to this day.

NEW CENTURY VERSION

22 "People of Israel, listen to these words: Jesus from
Nazareth was a very special man. God clearly showed this
to you by the miracles, wonders, and signs he did through
Jesus. You all know this, because it happened right here
among you. 23 Jesus was given to you, and with the help of
those who don't know the law, you put him to death by
nailing him to a cross. But this was God's plan which he
had made long ago; he knew all this would happen. 24 God
raised Jesus from the dead and set him free from the pain
of death, because death could not hold him. 25 For David
said this about him:

'I keep the Lord before me always.
Because he is close by my side,
I will not be hurt.
26 So I am glad, and I rejoice.
Even my body has hope,
27 because you will not leave me in the grave.
You will not let your Holy One rot.
28 You will teach me how to live a holy life.
Being with you will fill me with joy.' *Psalm 16:8–11*

29 "Brothers and sisters, I can tell you truly that David,
our ancestor, died and was buried. His grave is still here

CONTEMPORARY ENGLISH VERSION

22 Now, listen to what I have to say about Jesus from
Nazareth. God proved that he sent Jesus to you by hav-
ing him work miracles, wonders, and signs. All of you
know this. 23 God had already planned and decided that
Jesus would be handed over to you. So you took him and
had evil men put him to death on a cross. 24 But God set
him free from death and raised him to life. Death could
not hold him in its power. 25 What David said are really
the words of Jesus,

"I always see the Lord
near me,
and I will not be afraid
with him at my right side.
26 Because of this,
my heart will be glad,
my words will be joyful,
and I will live in hope.
27 The Lord won't leave me
in the grave.
I am his holy one,
and he won't let
my body decay.
28 He has shown me
the path to life,
and he makes me glad
by being near me."

29 My friends, it is right for me to speak to you about
our ancestor David. He died and was buried, and his

NEW INTERNATIONAL VERSION

22"Men of Israel, listen to this: Jesus of Nazareth was a
man accredited by God to you by miracles, wonders and
signs, which God did among you through him, as you
yourselves know. 23This man was handed over to you by
God's set purpose and foreknowledge; and you, with the
help of wicked men,[d] put him to death by nailing him to
the cross. 24But God raised him from the dead, freeing him
from the agony of death, because it was impossible for
death to keep its hold on him. 25David said about him:

" 'I saw the Lord always before me.
Because he is at my right hand,
I will not be shaken.
26 Therefore my heart is glad and my tongue rejoices;
my body also will live in hope,
27 because you will not abandon me to the grave,
nor will you let your Holy One see decay.
28 You have made known to me the paths of life;
you will fill me with joy in your presence.'[e]

29"Brothers, I can tell you confidently that the patriarch
David died and was buried, and his tomb is here to this

[d] *23* Or *of those not having the law* (that is, Gentiles)
[e] *28* Psalm 16:8–11

NEW LIVING TRANSLATION

22"People of Israel, listen! God publicly endorsed Jesus of
Nazareth by doing wonderful miracles, wonders, and signs
through him, as you well know. 23But you followed God's
prearranged plan. With the help of lawless Gentiles, you
nailed him to the cross and murdered him. 24However, God
released him from the horrors of death and raised him
back to life again, for death could not keep him in its grip.
25King David said this about him:

'I know the Lord is always with me.
I will not be shaken, for he is right beside me.
26 No wonder my heart is filled with joy,
and my mouth shouts his praises!
My body rests in hope.
27 For you will not leave my soul among the dead*
or allow your Holy One to rot in the grave.
28 You have shown me the way of life,
and you will give me wonderful joy in your
presence.'*

29"Dear brothers, think about this! David wasn't referring
to himself when he spoke these words I have quoted, for he
died and was buried, and his tomb is still here among us.

2:27 Greek *in Hades;* also in 2:31. **2:25-28** Ps 16:8-11.

NEW KING JAMES VERSION

22"Men of Israel, hear these words: Jesus of Nazareth, a
Man attested by God to you by miracles, wonders, and
signs which God did through Him in your midst, as you
yourselves also know— 23Him, being delivered by the
determined purpose and foreknowledge of God, you have
taken[c] by lawless hands, have crucified, and put to death;
24whom God raised up, having loosed the pains of death,
because it was not possible that He should be held by it.
25For David says concerning Him:

'I foresaw the LORD always before my face,
For He is at my right hand, that I may not be shaken.
26 *Therefore my heart rejoiced, and my tongue was*
glad;
Moreover my flesh also will rest in hope.
27 *For You will not leave my soul in Hades,*
Nor will You allow Your Holy One to see corruption.
28 *You have made known to me the ways of life;*
You will make me full of joy in Your presence.'[d]

29"Men *and* brethren, let *me* speak freely to you of the
patriarch David, that he is both dead and buried, and his

2:23 [c] NU-Text omits *have taken.* **2:28** [d] Psalm 16:8–11

THE MESSAGE

"Fellow Israelites, listen carefully to these words: Jesus
the Nazarene, a man thoroughly accredited by God to
you—the miracles and wonders and signs that God did
through him are common knowledge—this Jesus, follow-
ing the deliberate and well-thought-out plan of God, was
betrayed by men who took the law into their own hands,
and was handed over to you. And you pinned him to a
cross and killed him. But God untied the death ropes and
raised him up. Death was no match for him. David said it
all:

'I saw God before me for all time.
Nothing can shake me; he's right by my side.
I'm glad from the inside out, ecstatic;
I've pitched my tent in the land of hope.
I know you'll never dump me in Hades;
I'll never even smell the stench of death.
You've got my feet on the life-path,
with your face shining sun-joy all around.'

"Dear friends, let me be completely frank with you. Our
ancestor David is dead and buried—his tomb is in plain

KING JAMES VERSION

30 Therefore being a prophet, and knowing that God had sworn with an oath to him, that of the fruit of his loins, according to the flesh, he would raise up Christ to sit on his throne;

31 He seeing this before spake of the resurrection of Christ, that his soul was not left in hell, neither his flesh did see corruption.

32 This Jesus hath God raised up, whereof we all are witnesses.

33 Therefore being by the right hand of God exalted, and having received of the Father the promise of the Holy Ghost, he hath shed forth this, which ye now see and hear.

34 For David is not ascended into the heavens: but he saith himself, The LORD said unto my Lord, Sit thou on my right hand,

35 Until I make thy foes thy footstool.

36 Therefore let all the house of Israel know assuredly, that God hath made that same Jesus, whom ye have crucified, both Lord and Christ.

37 ¶ Now when they heard *this*, they were pricked in their heart, and said unto Peter and to the rest of the apostles, Men *and* brethren, what shall we do?

38 Then Peter said unto them, Repent, and be baptized every one of you in the name of Jesus Christ for the remission of sins, and ye shall receive the gift of the Holy Ghost.

NEW AMERICAN STANDARD BIBLE

30 "And so, because he was a prophet and knew that GOD HAD SWORN TO HIM WITH AN OATH TO SEAT *one* OF HIS DESCENDANTS ON HIS THRONE,

31 he looked ahead and spoke of the resurrection of [3]the Christ, that HE WAS NEITHER ABANDONED TO HADES, NOR DID His flesh SUFFER DECAY.

32 "This Jesus God raised up again, to which we are all witnesses.

33 "Therefore having been exalted to the right hand of God, and having received from the Father the promise of the Holy Spirit, He has poured forth this which you both see and hear.

34 "For it was not David who ascended into heaven, but he himself says:

'THE LORD SAID TO MY LORD,
" SIT AT MY RIGHT HAND,
35 UNTIL I MAKE YOUR ENEMIES A FOOTSTOOL FOR YOUR FEET." '

36 "Therefore let all the house of Israel know for certain that God has made Him both Lord and Christ—this Jesus whom you crucified."

The Ingathering

37 Now when they heard *this*, they were pierced to the heart, and said to Peter and the rest of the apostles, "Brethren, what shall we do?"

38 Peter *said* to them, "Repent, and each of you be baptized in the name of Jesus Christ for the forgiveness of your sins; and you will receive the gift of the Holy Spirit.

2:31 [3] I.e. the Messiah

NEW CENTURY VERSION

with us today. [30]He was a prophet and knew God had promised him that he would make a person from David's family a king just as he was.[b] [31]Knowing this before it happened, David talked about the Christ rising from the dead. He said:

'He was not left in the grave.
His body did not rot.'

[32]So Jesus is the One whom God raised from the dead. And we are all witnesses to this. [33]Jesus was lifted up to heaven and is now at God's right side. The Father has given the Holy Spirit to Jesus as he promised. So Jesus has poured out that Spirit, and this is what you now see and hear. [34]David was not the one who was lifted up to heaven, but he said:

'The Lord said to my Lord,
"Sit by me at my right side,
35 until I put your enemies under your control." '[c]

Psalm 110:1

[36]"So, all the people of Israel should know this truly: God has made Jesus—the man you nailed to the cross—both Lord and Christ."

[37]When the people heard this, they felt guilty and asked Peter and the other apostles, "What shall we do?"

[38]Peter said to them, "Change your hearts and lives and be baptized, each one of you, in the name of Jesus Christ for the forgiveness of your sins. And you will receive the gift of

2:30 [b] **God...was** See 2 Samuel 7:13; Psalm 132:11.
2:35 [c] **until...control** Literally, "until I make your enemies a footstool for your feet."

CONTEMPORARY ENGLISH VERSION

tomb is still here. [30]But David was a prophet, and he knew that God had made a promise he would not break. He had told David that someone from his own family would someday be king.

[31]David knew this would happen, and so he told us that Christ would be raised to life. He said that God would not leave him in the grave or let his body decay. [32]All of us can tell you that God has raised Jesus to life!

[33]Jesus was taken up to sit at the right side[b] of God, and he was given the Holy Spirit, just as the Father had promised. Jesus is also the one who has given the Spirit to us, and that is what you are now seeing and hearing.

[34]David didn't go up to heaven. So he wasn't talking about himself when he said, "The Lord told my Lord to sit at his right side, [35]until he made my Lord's enemies into a footstool for him." [36]Everyone in Israel should then know for certain that God has made Jesus both Lord and Christ, even though you put him to death on a cross.

[37]When the people heard this, they were very upset. They asked Peter and the other apostles, "Friends, what shall we do?"

[38]Peter said, "Turn back to God! Be baptized in the name of Jesus Christ, so that your sins will be forgiven. Then you will be given the Holy Spirit. [39]This promise is for you and

[b] 2.33 *right side*: The place of honor and power.

NEW INTERNATIONAL VERSION

day. 30But he was a prophet and knew that God had promised him on oath that he would place one of his descendants on his throne. 31Seeing what was ahead, he spoke of the resurrection of the Christ,[f] that he was not abandoned to the grave, nor did his body see decay. 32God has raised this Jesus to life, and we are all witnesses of the fact. 33Exalted to the right hand of God, he has received from the Father the promised Holy Spirit and has poured out what you now see and hear. 34For David did not ascend to heaven, and yet he said,

" 'The Lord said to my Lord:
"Sit at my right hand
35 until I make your enemies
a footstool for your feet." '[g]

36"Therefore let all Israel be assured of this: God has made this Jesus, whom you crucified, both Lord and Christ."

37When the people heard this, they were cut to the heart and said to Peter and the other apostles, "Brothers, what shall we do?"

38Peter replied, "Repent and be baptized, every one of you, in the name of Jesus Christ for the forgiveness of your sins. And you will receive the gift of the Holy Spirit. 39The

[f] *31* Or *Messiah.* "The Christ" (Greek) and "the Messiah" (Hebrew) both mean "the Anointed One"; also in verse 36. [g] *35* Psalm 110:1

NEW LIVING TRANSLATION

30But he was a prophet, and he knew God had promised with an oath that one of David's own descendants would sit on David's throne as the Messiah. 31David was looking into the future and predicting the Messiah's resurrection. He was saying that the Messiah would not be left among the dead and that his body would not rot in the grave.

32"This prophecy was speaking of Jesus, whom God raised from the dead, and we all are witnesses of this. 33Now he sits on the throne of highest honor in heaven, at God's right hand. And the Father, as he had promised, gave him the Holy Spirit to pour out upon us, just as you see and hear today. 34For David himself never ascended into heaven, yet he said,

'The LORD said to my Lord,
Sit in honor at my right hand
35 until I humble your enemies,
making them a footstool under your feet.'*

36So let it be clearly known by everyone in Israel that God has made this Jesus whom you crucified to be both Lord and Messiah!"

37Peter's words convicted them deeply, and they said to him and to the other apostles, "Brothers, what should we do?"

38Peter replied, "Each of you must turn from your sins and turn to God, and be baptized in the name of Jesus Christ for the forgiveness of your sins. Then you will receive the gift of

2:34-35 Ps 110:1.

NEW KING JAMES VERSION

tomb is with us to this day. 30Therefore, being a prophet, and knowing that God had sworn with an oath to him that of the fruit of his body, according to the flesh, He would raise up the Christ to sit on his throne,[e] 31he, foreseeing this, spoke concerning the resurrection of the Christ, that His soul was not left in Hades, nor did His flesh see corruption. 32This Jesus God has raised up, of which we are all witnesses. 33Therefore being exalted to the right hand of God, and having received from the Father the promise of the Holy Spirit, He poured out this which you now see and hear.

34"For David did not ascend into the heavens, but he says himself:

'The LORD said to my Lord,
" Sit at My right hand,
35 *Till I make Your enemies Your footstool." '*[f]

36"Therefore let all the house of Israel know assuredly that God has made this Jesus, whom you crucified, both Lord and Christ."

37Now when they heard *this,* they were cut to the heart, and said to Peter and the rest of the apostles, "Men *and* brethren, what shall we do?"

38Then Peter said to them, "Repent, and let every one of you be baptized in the name of Jesus Christ for the remission of sins; and you shall receive the gift of the Holy

2:30 [e] NU-Text omits *according to the flesh, He would raise up the Christ* and completes the verse with *He would seat one on his throne.*
2:35 [f] Psalm 110:1

THE MESSAGE

sight today. But being also a prophet and knowing that God had solemnly sworn that a descendant of his would rule his kingdom, seeing far ahead, he talked of the resurrection of the Messiah—'no trip to Hades, no stench of death.' This Jesus, God raised up. And every one of us here is a witness to it. Then, raised to the heights at the right hand of God and receiving the promise of the Holy Spirit from the Father, he poured out the Spirit he had just received. That is what you see and hear. For David himself did not ascend to heaven, but he did say,

'God said to my Master, "Sit at my right hand
Until I make your enemies a stool for resting your
feet." '

All Israel, then, know this: There's no longer room for doubt—God made him Master and Messiah, this Jesus whom you killed on a cross."

Cut to the quick, those who were there listening asked Peter and the other apostles, "Brothers! Brothers! So now what do we do?"

Peter said, "Change your life. Turn to God and be baptized, each of you, in the name of Jesus Christ, so your sins are forgiven. Receive the gift of the Holy Spirit. The

KING JAMES VERSION

39 For the promise is unto you, and to your children, and to all that are afar off, *even* as many as the Lord our God shall call.

40 And with many other words did he testify and exhort, saying, Save yourselves from this untoward generation.

41 Then they that gladly received his word were baptized: and the same day there were added *unto them* about three thousand souls.

42 ¶ And they continued stedfastly in the apostles' doctrine and fellowship, and in breaking of bread, and in prayers.

43 And fear came upon every soul: and many wonders and signs were done by the apostles.

44 And all that believed were together, and had all things common;

45 And sold their possessions and goods, and parted them to all *men*, as every man had need.

46 And they, continuing daily with one accord in the temple, and breaking bread from house to house, did eat their meat with gladness and singleness of heart,

47 Praising God, and having favour with all the people. And the Lord added to the church daily such as should be saved.

NEW AMERICAN STANDARD BIBLE

39 "For the promise is for you and your children and for all who are far off, as many as the Lord our God will call to Himself."

40 And with many other words he solemnly testified and kept on exhorting them, saying, "Be saved from this perverse generation!"

41 So then, those who had received his word were baptized; and that day there were added about three thousand [4]souls.

42 They were continually devoting themselves to the apostles' teaching and to fellowship, to the breaking of bread and to prayer.

43 Everyone kept feeling a sense of awe; and many wonders and signs were taking place through the apostles.

44 And all those who had believed [5]were together and had all things in common;

45 and they *began* selling their property and possessions and were sharing them with all, as anyone might have need.

46 Day by day continuing with one mind in the temple, and breaking bread from house to house, they were taking their meals together with gladness and sincerity of heart,

47 praising God and having favor with all the people. And the Lord was adding to their number day by day those who were being saved.

2:41 [4] I.e. persons 2:44 [5] One early ms does not contain *were* and *and*

NEW CENTURY VERSION

the Holy Spirit. [39]This promise is for you, for your children,
and for all who are far away. It is for everyone the Lord our
God calls to himself."
[40]Peter warned them with many other words. He begged
them, "Save yourselves from the evil of today's people!"
[41]Then those people who accepted what Peter said were
baptized. About three thousand people were added to the
number of believers that day. [42]They spent their time
learning the apostles' teaching, sharing, breaking bread,[d]
and praying together.

The Believers Share

[43]The apostles were doing many miracles and signs, and
everyone felt great respect for God. [44]All the believers were
together and shared everything. [45]They would sell their
land and the things they owned and then divide the money
and give it to anyone who needed it. [46]The believers met
together in the Temple every day. They ate together in
their homes, happy to share their food with joyful hearts.
[47]They praised God and were liked by all the people. Every
day the Lord added those who were being saved to the
group of believers.

2:42 [d] **breaking bread** This may mean a meal as in verse 46, or the Lord's Supper, the special meal Jesus told his followers to eat to remember him (Luke 22:14–20).

CONTEMPORARY ENGLISH VERSION

your children. It is for everyone our Lord God will choose,
no matter where they live."
[40]Peter told them many other things as well. Then he
said, "I beg you to save yourselves from what will happen
to all these evil people." [41]On that day about three thou-
sand believed his message and were baptized. [42]They
spent their time learning from the apostles, and they were
like family to each other. They also broke bread[c] and
prayed together.

Life among the Lord's Followers

[43]Everyone was amazed by the many miracles and won-
ders that the apostles worked. [44]All the Lord's followers
often met together, and they shared everything they had.
[45]They would sell their property and possessions and give
the money to whoever needed it. [46]Day after day they met
together in the temple. They broke bread[c] together in dif-
ferent homes and shared their food happily and freely,
[47]while praising God. Everyone liked them, and each day
the Lord added to their group others who were being
saved.

[c] 2.42,46 *broke bread*: They ate together and celebrated the Lord's Supper.

NEW INTERNATIONAL VERSION

promise is for you and your children and for all who are
far off—for all whom the Lord our God will call."
40With many other words he warned them; and he
pleaded with them, "Save yourselves from this corrupt
generation." 41Those who accepted his message were bap-
tized, and about three thousand were added to their num-
ber that day.

The Fellowship of the Believers

42They devoted themselves to the apostles' teaching and
to the fellowship, to the breaking of bread and to prayer.
43Everyone was filled with awe, and many wonders and
miraculous signs were done by the apostles. 44All the
believers were together and had everything in common.
45Selling their possessions and goods, they gave to anyone
as he had need. 46Every day they continued to meet
together in the temple courts. They broke bread in their
homes and ate together with glad and sincere hearts,
47praising God and enjoying the favor of all the people.
And the Lord added to their number daily those who were
being saved.

NEW LIVING TRANSLATION

the Holy Spirit. 39This promise is to you and to your chil-
dren, and even to the Gentiles*—all who have been called by
the Lord our God." 40Then Peter continued preaching for a
long time, strongly urging all his listeners, "Save yourselves
from this generation that has gone astray!"
41Those who believed what Peter said were baptized and
added to the church—about three thousand in all. 42They
joined with the other believers and devoted themselves to
the apostles' teaching and fellowship, sharing in the
Lord's Supper and in prayer.

The Believers Meet Together

43A deep sense of awe came over them all, and the apos-
tles performed many miraculous signs and wonders. 44And
all the believers met together constantly and shared every-
thing they had. 45They sold their possessions and shared
the proceeds with those in need. 46They worshiped togeth-
er at the Temple each day, met in homes for the Lord's
Supper, and shared their meals with great joy and generos-
ity—47all the while praising God and enjoying the goodwill
of all the people. And each day the Lord added to their
group those who were being saved.

2:39 Greek *to those far away.*

NEW KING JAMES VERSION

Spirit. 39For the promise is to you and to your children,
and to all who are afar off, as many as the Lord our God
will call."

A Vital Church Grows

40And with many other words he testified and exhorted
them, saying, "Be saved from this perverse generation."
41Then those who gladly[g] received his word were baptized;
and that day about three thousand souls were added *to
them.* 42And they continued steadfastly in the apostles'
doctrine and fellowship, in the breaking of bread, and in
prayers. 43Then fear came upon every soul, and many won-
ders and signs were done through the apostles. 44Now all
who believed were together, and had all things in common,
45and sold their possessions and goods, and divided them
among all, as anyone had need.
46So continuing daily with one accord in the temple, and
breaking bread from house to house, they ate their food
with gladness and simplicity of heart, 47praising God and
having favor with all the people. And the Lord added to the
church[h] daily those who were being saved.

2:41 [g] NU-Text omits *gladly.* 2:47 [h] NU-Text omits *to the church.*

THE MESSAGE

promise is targeted to you and your children, but also to all who are far away—whomever, in fact, our Master God invites."

He went on in this vein for a long time, urging them over and over, "Get out while you can; get out of this sick and stupid culture!"

That day about three thousand took him at his word, were baptized and were signed up. They committed themselves to the teaching of the apostles, the life together, the common meal, and the prayers.

✠

Everyone around was in awe—all those wonders and signs done through the apostles! And all the believers lived in a wonderful harmony, holding everything in common. They sold whatever they owned and pooled their resources so that each person's need was met.

They followed a daily discipline of worship in the Temple followed by meals at home, every meal a celebration, exuberant and joyful, as they praised God. People in general liked what they saw. Every day their number grew as God added those who were saved.

KING JAMES VERSION

3 Now Peter and John went up together into the temple at the hour of prayer, *being* the ninth *hour*.
2 And a certain man lame from his mother's womb was carried, whom they laid daily at the gate of the temple which is called Beautiful, to ask alms of them that entered into the temple;
3 Who seeing Peter and John about to go into the temple asked an alms.
4 And Peter, fastening his eyes upon him with John, said, Look on us.
5 And he gave heed unto them, expecting to receive something of them.
6 Then Peter said, Silver and gold have I none; but such as I have give I thee: In the name of Jesus Christ of Nazareth rise up and walk.
7 And he took him by the right hand, and lifted *him* up: and immediately his feet and ankle bones received strength.
8 And he leaping up stood, and walked, and entered with them into the temple, walking, and leaping, and praising God.
9 And all the people saw him walking and praising God:
10 And they knew that it was he which sat for alms at the Beautiful gate of the temple: and they were filled with wonder and amazement at that which had happened unto him.

NEW AMERICAN STANDARD BIBLE

Healing the Lame Beggar

3 Now Peter and John were going up to the temple at the [1]ninth *hour,* the hour of prayer.
2 And a man who had been lame from his mother's womb was being carried along, whom they used to set down every day at the gate of the temple which is called Beautiful, in order to beg [2]alms of those who were entering the temple.
3 When he saw Peter and John about to go into the temple, he *began* asking to receive alms.
4 But Peter, along with John, fixed his gaze on him and said, "Look at us!"
5 And he *began* to give them his attention, expecting to receive something from them.
6 But Peter said, "I do not possess silver and gold, but what I do have I give to you: In the name of Jesus Christ the Nazarene—walk!"
7 And seizing him by the right hand, he raised him up; and immediately his feet and his ankles were strengthened.
8 With a leap he stood upright and *began* to walk; and he entered the temple with them, walking and leaping and praising God.
9 And all the people saw him walking and praising God;
10 and they were taking note of him as being the one who used to sit at the Beautiful Gate of the temple to *beg* alms, and they were filled with wonder and amazement at what had happened to him.

3:1 [1] I.e. 3 p.m. 3:2 [2] Or *a gift of charity*

NEW CENTURY VERSION

Peter Heals a Crippled Man

3 One day Peter and John went to the Temple at three
o'clock, the time set each day for the afternoon prayer
service. 2There, at the Temple gate called Beautiful Gate,
was a man who had been crippled all his life. Every day he
was carried to this gate to beg for money from the people
going into the Temple. 3The man saw Peter and John going
into the Temple and asked them for money. 4Peter and
John looked straight at him and said, "Look at us!" 5The
man looked at them, thinking they were going to give him
some money. 6But Peter said, "I don't have any silver or
gold, but I do have something else I can give you. By the
power of Jesus Christ from Nazareth, stand up and walk!"
7Then Peter took the man's right hand and lifted him up.
Immediately the man's feet and ankles became strong. 8He
jumped up, stood on his feet, and began to walk. He went
into the Temple with them, walking and jumping and
praising God. 9–10All the people recognized him as the crip-
pled man who always sat by the Beautiful Gate begging for
money. Now they saw this same man walking and praising
God, and they were amazed. They wondered how this
could happen.

CONTEMPORARY ENGLISH VERSION

Peter and John Heal a Lame Man

3 The time of prayer[a] was about three o'clock in the
afternoon, and Peter and John were going into the
temple. 2A man who had been born lame was being carried
to the temple door. Each day he was placed beside this
door, known as the Beautiful Gate. He sat there and
begged from the people who were going in.
3The man saw Peter and John entering the temple, and
he asked them for money. 4But they looked straight at him
and said, "Look up at us!"
5The man stared at them and thought he was going to
get something. 6But Peter said, "I don't have any silver or
gold! But I will give you what I do have. In the name of
Jesus Christ from Nazareth, get up and start walking."
7Peter then took him by the right hand and helped him up.
At once the man's feet and ankles became strong, 8and
he jumped up and started walking. He went with Peter and
John into the temple, walking and jumping and praising
God. 9Everyone saw him walking around and praising God.
10They knew that he was the beggar who had been lying
beside the Beautiful Gate, and they were completely sur-
prised. They could not imagine what had happened to the
man.

[a] 3.1 *The time of prayer*: Many of the Jewish people prayed in their homes at regular times each day (see Daniel 6.11), and on special occasions they prayed in the temple.

NEW INTERNATIONAL VERSION

Peter Heals the Crippled Beggar

3 One day Peter and John were going up to the temple at
the time of prayer—at three in the afternoon. 2Now a
man crippled from birth was being carried to the temple
gate called Beautiful, where he was put every day to beg
from those going into the temple courts. 3When he saw
Peter and John about to enter, he asked them for money.
4Peter looked straight at him, as did John. Then Peter said,
"Look at us!" 5So the man gave them his attention, expect-
ing to get something from them.

6Then Peter said, "Silver or gold I do not have, but what
I have I give you. In the name of Jesus Christ of Nazareth,
walk." 7Taking him by the right hand, he helped him up,
and instantly the man's feet and ankles became strong.
8He jumped to his feet and began to walk. Then he went
with them into the temple courts, walking and jumping,
and praising God. 9When all the people saw him walking
and praising God, 10they recognized him as the same man
who used to sit begging at the temple gate called
Beautiful, and they were filled with wonder and amaze-
ment at what had happened to him.

NEW LIVING TRANSLATION

Peter Heals a Crippled Beggar

3 Peter and John went to the Temple one afternoon to
take part in the three o'clock prayer service. 2As they
approached the Temple, a man lame from birth was being
carried in. Each day he was put beside the Temple gate,
the one called the Beautiful Gate, so he could beg from the
people going into the Temple. 3When he saw Peter and
John about to enter, he asked them for some money.

4Peter and John looked at him intently, and Peter said,
"Look at us!" 5The lame man looked at them eagerly,
expecting a gift. 6But Peter said, "I don't have any money
for you. But I'll give you what I have. In the name of Jesus
Christ of Nazareth, get up and walk!"

7Then Peter took the lame man by the right hand and
helped him up. And as he did, the man's feet and ankle-
bones were healed and strengthened. 8He jumped up,
stood on his feet, and began to walk! Then, walking, leap-
ing, and praising God, he went into the Temple with them.

9All the people saw him walking and heard him praising
God. 10When they realized he was the lame beggar they had
seen so often at the Beautiful Gate, they were absolutely

NEW KING JAMES VERSION

A Lame Man Healed

3 Now Peter and John went up together to the temple at
the hour of prayer, the ninth *hour.* 2And a certain
man lame from his mother's womb was carried, whom
they laid daily at the gate of the temple which is called
Beautiful, to ask alms from those who entered the temple;
3who, seeing Peter and John about to go into the temple,
asked for alms. 4And fixing his eyes on him, with John, Pe-
ter said, "Look at us." 5So he gave them his attention,
expecting to receive something from them. 6Then Peter
said, "Silver and gold I do not have, but what I do have I
give you: In the name of Jesus Christ of Nazareth, rise up
and walk." 7And he took him by the right hand and lifted
him up, and immediately his feet and ankle bones received
strength. 8So he, leaping up, stood and walked and entered
the temple with them—walking, leaping, and praising God.
9And all the people saw him walking and praising God.
10Then they knew that it was he who sat begging alms at
the Beautiful Gate of the temple; and they were filled with
wonder and amazement at what had happened to him.

THE MESSAGE

3 One day at three o'clock in the afternoon, Peter and John were on their way into the Temple for prayer meeting. At the same time there was a man crippled from birth being carried up. Every day he was set down at the Temple gate, the one named Beautiful, to beg from those going into the Temple. When he saw Peter and John about to enter the Temple, he asked for a handout. Peter, with John at his side, looked him straight in the eye and said, "Look here." He looked up, expecting to get something from them.

Peter said, "I don't have a nickel to my name, but what I do have, I give you: In the name of Jesus Christ of Nazareth, walk!" He grabbed him by the right hand and pulled him up. In an instant his feet and ankles became firm. He jumped to his feet and walked.

The man went into the Temple with them, walking back and forth, dancing and praising God. Everybody there saw him walking around and praising God. They recognized him as the one who sat begging at the Temple's Gate Beautiful and rubbed their eyes, astonished, scarcely believing what they were seeing.

The man threw his arms around Peter and John, ecstatic. All the people ran up to where they were at Solomon's Porch to see it for themselves.

KING JAMES VERSION

11 And as the lame man which was healed held Peter and John, all the people ran together unto them in the porch that is called Solomon's, greatly wondering.

12 ¶ And when Peter saw *it*, he answered unto the people, Ye men of Israel, why marvel ye at this? or why look ye so earnestly on us, as though by our own power or holiness we had made this man to walk?

13 The God of Abraham, and of Isaac, and of Jacob, the God of our fathers, hath glorified his Son Jesus; whom ye delivered up, and denied him in the presence of Pilate, when he was determined to let *him* go.

14 But ye denied the Holy One and the Just, and desired a murderer to be granted unto you;

15 And killed the Prince of life, whom God hath raised from the dead; whereof we are witnesses.

16 And his name through faith in his name hath made this man strong, whom ye see and know: yea, the faith which is by him hath given him this perfect soundness in the presence of you all.

17 And now, brethren, I wot that through ignorance ye did *it*, as *did* also your rulers.

18 But those things, which God before had shewed by the mouth of all his prophets, that Christ should suffer, he hath so fulfilled.

19 Repent ye therefore, and be converted, that your sins may be blotted out, when the times of refreshing shall come from the presence of the Lord;

20 And he shall send Jesus Christ, which before was preached unto you:

NEW AMERICAN STANDARD BIBLE

Peter's Second Sermon

11 While he was clinging to Peter and John, all the people ran together to them at the so-called portico of Solomon, full of amazement.

12 But when Peter saw *this*, he replied to the people, "Men of Israel, why are you amazed at this, or why do you gaze at us, as if by our own power or piety we had made him walk?

13 "The God of Abraham, Isaac and Jacob, the God of our fathers, has glorified His servant Jesus, *the one* whom you delivered and disowned in the presence of Pilate, when he had decided to release Him.

14 "But you disowned the Holy and Righteous One and asked for a murderer to be granted to you,

15 but put to death the Prince of life, *the one* whom God raised from the dead, *a fact* to which we are witnesses.

16 "And on the basis of faith in His name, *it is* the name of Jesus which has strengthened this man whom you see and know; and the faith which *comes* through Him has given him this perfect health in the presence of you all.

17 "And now, brethren, I know that you acted in ignorance, just as your rulers did also.

18 "But the things which God announced beforehand by the mouth of all the prophets, that His Christ would suffer, He has thus fulfilled.

19 "Therefore repent and return, so that your sins may be wiped away, in order that times of refreshing may come from the presence of the Lord;

20 and that He may send Jesus, the Christ appointed for you,

NEW CENTURY VERSION

Peter Speaks to the People

11 While the man was holding on to Peter and John, all
the people were amazed and ran to them at Solomon's
Porch. 12 When Peter saw this, he said to them, "People of
Israel, why are you surprised? You are looking at us as if it
were our own power or goodness that made this man walk.
13 The God of Abraham, Isaac, and Jacob, the God of our
ancestors, gave glory to Jesus, his servant. But you handed
him over to be killed. Pilate decided to let him go free, but
you told Pilate you did not want Jesus. 14 You did not want
the One who is holy and good but asked Pilate to give you
a murderer[a] instead. 15 And so you killed the One who
gives life, but God raised him from the dead. We are witnesses to this. 16 It was faith in Jesus that made this crippled man well. You can see this man, and you know him.
He was made completely well because of trust in Jesus,
and you all saw it happen!
17 "Brothers and sisters, I know you did those things to
Jesus because neither you nor your leaders understood what
you were doing. 18 God said through the prophets that his
Christ would suffer and die. And now God has made these
things come true in this way. 19 So you must change your
hearts and lives! Come back to God, and he will forgive your
sins. Then the Lord will send the time of rest. 20 And he will
send Jesus, the One he chose to be the Christ. 21 But Jesus

3:14 [a] **murderer** Barabbas, the man the crowd asked Pilate to set free instead of Jesus (Luke 23:18).

CONTEMPORARY ENGLISH VERSION

Peter Speaks in the Temple

11 While the man kept holding on to Peter and John, the
whole crowd ran to them in amazement at the place
known as Solomon's Porch.[b] 12 Peter saw that a crowd had
gathered, and he said:

Friends, why are you surprised at what has happened? Why are you staring at us? Do you think we have some power of our own? Do you think we were able to make this man walk because we are so religious?
13 The God that Abraham, Isaac, Jacob, and our other
ancestors worshiped has brought honor to his Servant[c]
Jesus. He is the one you betrayed. You turned against him when he was being tried by Pilate, even though Pilate wanted to set him free.

14 You rejected Jesus, who was holy and good. You
asked for a murderer to be set free, 15 and you killed the
one who leads people to life. But God raised him from
death, and all of us can tell you what he has done. 16 You
see this man, and you know him. He put his faith in the name of Jesus and was made strong. Faith in Jesus made this man completely well while everyone was watching.

17 My friends, I am sure that you and your leaders didn't
know what you were doing. 18 But God had his prophets
tell that his Messiah would suffer, and now he has kept
that promise. 19 So turn to God! Give up your sins, and you
will be forgiven. 20 Then that time will come when the Lord
will give you fresh strength. He will send you Jesus, his

[b] 3.11 *Solomon's Porch*: A public place with tall columns along the east side of the temple. [c] 3.13 *Servant*: Or "Son."

NEW INTERNATIONAL VERSION

Peter Speaks to the Onlookers

[11]While the beggar held on to Peter and John, all the people were astonished and came running to them in the place called Solomon's Colonnade. [12]When Peter saw this, he said to them: "Men of Israel, why does this surprise you? Why do you stare at us as if by our own power or godliness we had made this man walk? [13]The God of Abraham, Isaac and Jacob, the God of our fathers, has glorified his servant Jesus. You handed him over to be killed, and you disowned him before Pilate, though he had decided to let him go. [14]You disowned the Holy and Righteous One and asked that a murderer be released to you. [15]You killed the author of life, but God raised him from the dead. We are witnesses of this. [16]By faith in the name of Jesus, this man whom you see and know was made strong. It is Jesus' name and the faith that comes through him that has given this complete healing to him, as you can all see.

[17]"Now, brothers, I know that you acted in ignorance, as did your leaders. [18]But this is how God fulfilled what he had foretold through all the prophets, saying that his Christ[a] would suffer. [19]Repent, then, and turn to God, so that your sins may be wiped out, that times of refreshing may come from the Lord, [20]and that he may send the Christ, who has been appointed for you—even Jesus. [21]He

[a] *18* Or *Messiah*; also in verse 20

NEW LIVING TRANSLATION

astounded! [11]They all rushed out to Solomon's Colonnade, where he was holding tightly to Peter and John. Everyone stood there in awe of the wonderful thing that had happened.

Peter Preaches in the Temple

[12]Peter saw his opportunity and addressed the crowd. "People of Israel," he said, "what is so astounding about this? And why look at us as though we had made this man walk by our own power and godliness? [13]For it is the God of Abraham, the God of Isaac, the God of Jacob, the God of all our ancestors who has brought glory to his servant Jesus by doing this. This is the same Jesus whom you handed over and rejected before Pilate, despite Pilate's decision to release him. [14]You rejected this holy, righteous one and instead demanded the release of a murderer. [15]You killed the author of life, but God raised him to life. And we are witnesses of this fact!

[16]"The name of Jesus has healed this man—and you know how lame he was before. Faith in Jesus' name has caused this healing before your very eyes.

[17]"Friends,* I realize that what you did to Jesus was done in ignorance; and the same can be said of your leaders. [18]But God was fulfilling what all the prophets had declared about the Messiah beforehand—that he must suffer all these things. [19]Now turn from your sins and turn to God, so you can be cleansed of your sins. [20]Then wonderful times of refreshment will come from the presence of the Lord, and he will send Jesus your Messiah to you again.

3:17 Greek *Brothers.*

NEW KING JAMES VERSION

Preaching in Solomon's Portico

[11]Now as the lame man who was healed held on to Peter and John, all the people ran together to them in the porch which is called Solomon's, greatly amazed. [12]So when Peter saw *it,* he responded to the people: "Men of Israel, why do you marvel at this? Or why look so intently at us, as though by our own power or godliness we had made this man walk? [13]The God of Abraham, Isaac, and Jacob, the God of our fathers, glorified His Servant Jesus, whom you delivered up and denied in the presence of Pilate, when he was determined to let *Him* go. [14]But you denied the Holy One and the Just, and asked for a murderer to be granted to you, [15]and killed the Prince of life, whom God raised from the dead, of which we are witnesses. [16]And His name, through faith in His name, has made this man strong, whom you see and know. Yes, the faith which *comes* through Him has given him this perfect soundness in the presence of you all.

[17]"Yet now, brethren, I know that you did *it* in ignorance, as *did* also your rulers. [18]But those things which God foretold by the mouth of all His prophets, that the Christ would suffer, He has thus fulfilled. [19]Repent therefore and be converted, that your sins may be blotted out, so that times of refreshing may come from the presence of the Lord, [20]and that He may send Jesus Christ, who was preached to you before,[a] [21]whom heaven must receive until

3:20 [a] NU-Text and M-Text read *Christ Jesus, who was ordained for you before.*

THE MESSAGE

Turn to Face God

When Peter saw he had a congregation, he addressed the people:

"Oh, Israelites, why does this take you by such complete surprise, and why stare at us as if *our* power or piety made him walk? The God of Abraham and Isaac and Jacob, the God of our ancestors, has glorified his Son Jesus. The very One that Pilate called innocent, you repudiated. You repudiated the Holy One, the Just One, and asked for a murderer in his place. You no sooner killed the Author of Life than God raised him from the dead—and we're the witnesses. Faith in Jesus' name put this man, whose condition you know so well, on his feet—yes, faith and nothing but faith put this man healed and whole right before your eyes.

"And now, friends, I know you had no idea what you were doing when you killed Jesus, and neither did your leaders. But God, who through the preaching of all the prophets had said all along that his Messiah would be killed, knew exactly what you were doing and used it to fulfill his plans.

"Now it's time to change your ways! Turn to face God so he can wipe away your sins, pour out showers of blessing to refresh you, and send you the Messiah he prepared for

KING JAMES VERSION

21 Whom the heaven must receive until the times of restitution of all things, which God hath spoken by the mouth of all his holy prophets since the world began.

22 For Moses truly said unto the fathers, A prophet shall the Lord your God raise up unto you of your brethren, like unto me; him shall ye hear in all things whatsoever he shall say unto you.

23 And it shall come to pass, *that* every soul, which will not hear that prophet, shall be destroyed from among the people.

24 Yea, and all the prophets from Samuel and those that follow after, as many as have spoken, have likewise foretold of these days.

25 Ye are the children of the prophets, and of the covenant which God made with our fathers, saying unto Abraham, And in thy seed shall all the kindreds of the earth be blessed.

26 Unto you first God, having raised up his Son Jesus, sent him to bless you, in turning away every one of you from his iniquities.

4 And as they spake unto the people, the priests, and the captain of the temple, and the Sadducees, came upon them,

2 Being grieved that they taught the people, and preached through Jesus the resurrection from the dead.

3 And they laid hands on them, and put *them* in hold unto the next day: for it was now eventide.

4 Howbeit many of them which heard the word believed; and the number of the men was about five thousand.

NEW AMERICAN STANDARD BIBLE

21 whom heaven must receive until *the* period of restoration of all things about which God spoke by the mouth of His holy prophets from ancient time.

22 "Moses said, 'THE LORD GOD WILL RAISE UP FOR YOU A PROPHET LIKE ME FROM YOUR BRETHREN; TO HIM YOU SHALL GIVE HEED to everything He says to you.

23 'And it will be that every soul that does not heed that prophet shall be utterly destroyed from among the people.'

24 "And likewise, all the prophets who have spoken, from Samuel and *his* successors onward, also announced these days.

25 "It is you who are the sons of the prophets and of the covenant which God made with your fathers, saying to Abraham, 'AND IN YOUR SEED ALL THE FAMILIES OF THE EARTH SHALL BE BLESSED.'

26 "For you first, God raised up His Servant and sent Him to bless you by turning every one *of you* from your wicked ways."

Peter and John Arrested

4 As they were speaking to the people, the priests and the captain of the temple *guard* and the Sadducees came up to them,

2 being greatly disturbed because they were teaching the people and proclaiming in Jesus the resurrection from the dead.

3 And they laid hands on them and put them in jail until the next day, for it was already evening.

4 But many of those who had heard the message believed; and the number of the men came to be about five thousand.

NEW CENTURY VERSION

must stay in heaven until the time comes when all things will be made right again. God told about this time long ago when he spoke through his holy prophets. 22Moses said, 'The Lord your God will give you a prophet like me, who is one of your own people. You must listen to everything he tells you. 23Anyone who does not listen to that prophet will die, cut off from God's people.'[b] 24Samuel, and all the other prophets who spoke for God after Samuel, told about this time now. 25You are descendants of the prophets. You have received the agreement God made with your ancestors. He said to your father Abraham, 'Through your descendants all the nations on the earth will be blessed.'[c] 26God has raised up his servant Jesus and sent him to you first to bless you by turning each of you away from doing evil."

Peter and John at the Council

4 While Peter and John were speaking to the people, Jewish priests, the captain of the soldiers that guarded the Temple, and Sadducees came up to them. 2They were upset because the two apostles were teaching the people and were preaching that people will rise from the dead through the power of Jesus. 3The Jewish leaders grabbed Peter and John and put them in jail. Since it was already night, they kept them in jail until the next day. 4But many of those who had heard Peter and John preach believed the things they said. There were now about five thousand in the group of believers.

3:23 [b] **'The Lord...people.'** Quotation from Deuteronomy 18:15, 19.
3:25 [c] **'Through...blessed.'** Quotation from Genesis 22:18; 26:4.

CONTEMPORARY ENGLISH VERSION

chosen Messiah. 21But Jesus must stay in heaven until God makes all things new, just as his holy prophets promised long ago.

22Moses said, "The Lord your God will choose one of your own people to be a prophet, just as he chose me. Listen to everything he tells you. 23No one who disobeys that prophet will be one of God's people any longer."

24Samuel and all the other prophets who came later also spoke about what is now happening. 25You are really the ones God told his prophets to speak to. And you were given the promise that God made to your ancestors. He said to Abraham, "All nations on earth will be blessed because of someone from your family." 26God sent his chosen Son[d] to you first, because God wanted to bless you and make each of you turn away from your sins.

Peter and John Are Brought in Front of the Council

4 The apostles were still talking to the people, when some priests, the captain of the temple guard, and some Sadducees arrived. 2These men were angry because the apostles were teaching the people that the dead would be raised from death, just as Jesus had been raised from death. 3It was already late in the afternoon, and they arrested Peter and John and put them in jail for the night. 4But a lot of people who had heard the message believed it. So by now there were about five thousand followers of the Lord.

[d] 3.26 *Son*: Or "Servant."

NEW INTERNATIONAL VERSION

must remain in heaven until the time comes for God to
restore everything, as he promised long ago through his
holy prophets. 22 For Moses said, 'The Lord your God will
raise up for you a prophet like me from among your own
people; you must listen to everything he tells you.
23 Anyone who does not listen to him will be completely cut
off from among his people.'[b]

24 "Indeed, all the prophets from Samuel on, as many as
have spoken, have foretold these days. 25 And you are heirs
of the prophets and of the covenant God made with your
fathers. He said to Abraham, 'Through your offspring all
peoples on earth will be blessed.'[c] 26 When God raised up
his servant, he sent him first to you to bless you by turn-
ing each of you from your wicked ways."

Peter and John Before the Sanhedrin

4 The priests and the captain of the temple guard and
the Sadducees came up to Peter and John while they
were speaking to the people. 2 They were greatly disturbed
because the apostles were teaching the people and pro-
claiming in Jesus the resurrection of the dead. 3 They seized
Peter and John, and because it was evening, they put them
in jail until the next day. 4 But many who heard the mes-
sage believed, and the number of men grew to about five
thousand.

[b] *23* Deut. 18:15,18,19 [c] *25* Gen. 22:18; 26:4

NEW LIVING TRANSLATION

21 For he must remain in heaven until the time for the final
restoration of all things, as God promised long ago
through his prophets. 22 Moses said, 'The Lord your God
will raise up a Prophet like me from among your own peo-
ple. Listen carefully to everything he tells you.'* 23 Then
Moses said, 'Anyone who will not listen to that Prophet
will be cut off from God's people and utterly destroyed.'*

24 "Starting with Samuel, every prophet spoke about
what is happening today. 25 You are the children of those
prophets, and you are included in the covenant God prom-
ised to your ancestors. For God said to Abraham, 'Through
your descendants all the families on earth will be
blessed.'* 26 When God raised up his servant, he sent him
first to you people of Israel, to bless you by turning each of
you back from your sinful ways."

Peter and John before the Council

4 While Peter and John were speaking to the people, the
leading priests, the captain of the Temple guard, and
some of the Sadducees came over to them. 2 They were very
disturbed that Peter and John were claiming, on the
authority of Jesus, that there is a resurrection of the dead.
3 They arrested them and, since it was already evening,
jailed them until morning. 4 But many of the people who
heard their message believed it, so that the number of
believers totaled about five thousand men, not counting
women and children.*

3:22 Deut 18:15. 3:23 Deut 18:19; Lev 23:29. 3:25 Gen 22:18.
4:4 Greek *5,000 adult males.*

NEW KING JAMES VERSION

the times of restoration of all things, which God has spo-
ken by the mouth of all His holy prophets since the world
began. 22 For Moses truly said to the fathers, *'The* L*ORD*
your God will raise up for you a Prophet like me from your
brethren. Him you shall hear in all things, whatever He
says to you. 23 *And it shall be* that *every soul who will not*
hear that Prophet shall be utterly destroyed from among
the people.'[b] 24 Yes, and all the prophets, from Samuel and
those who follow, as many as have spoken, have also fore-
told[c] these days. 25 You are sons of the prophets, and of the
covenant which God made with our fathers, saying to
Abraham, *'And in your seed all the families of the earth*
shall be blessed.'[d] 26 To you first, God, having raised up
His Servant Jesus, sent Him to bless you, in turning away
every one *of you* from your iniquities."

Peter and John Arrested

4 Now as they spoke to the people, the priests, the cap-
tain of the temple, and the Sadducees came upon
them, 2 being greatly disturbed that they taught the people
and preached in Jesus the resurrection from the dead. 3 And
they laid hands on them, and put *them* in custody until the
next day, for it was already evening. 4 However, many of
those who heard the word believed; and the number of the
men came to be about five thousand.

3:23 [b] Deuteronomy 18:15, 18, 19 3:24 [c] NU-Text and M-Text read
proclaimed. 3:25 [d] Genesis 22:18; 26:4; 28:14

THE MESSAGE

you, namely, Jesus. For the time being he must remain out
of sight in heaven until everything is restored to order
again just the way God, through the preaching of his holy
prophets of old, said it would be. Moses, for instance, said,
'Your God will raise up for you a prophet just like me from
your family. Listen to every word he speaks to you. Every
last living soul who refuses to listen to that prophet will be
wiped out from the people.'

"All the prophets from Samuel on down said the same
thing, said most emphatically that these days would come.
These prophets, along with the covenant God made with
your ancestors, are your family tree. God's covenant-word
to Abraham provides the text: 'By your offspring all the
families of the earth will be blessed.' But you are first in
line: God, having raised up his Son, sent him to bless you
as you turn, one by one, from your evil ways."

Nothing to Hide

4 While Peter and John were addressing the people, the
priests, the chief of the Temple police, and some Sad-
ducees came up, indignant that these upstart apostles
were instructing the people and proclaiming that the resur-
rection from the dead had taken place in Jesus. They
arrested them and threw them in jail until morning, for by
now it was late in the evening. But many of those who lis-
tened had already believed the Message—in round num-
bers about five thousand!

KING JAMES VERSION

5 ¶ And it came to pass on the morrow, that their rulers, and elders, and scribes,

6 And Annas the high priest, and Caiaphas, and John, and Alexander, and as many as were of the kindred of the high priest, were gathered together at Jerusalem.

7 And when they had set them in the midst, they asked, By what power, or by what name, have ye done this?

8 Then Peter, filled with the Holy Ghost, said unto them, Ye rulers of the people, and elders of Israel,

9 If we this day be examined of the good deed done to the impotent man, by what means he is made whole;

10 Be it known unto you all, and to all the people of Israel, that by the name of Jesus Christ of Nazareth, whom ye crucified, whom God raised from the dead, *even* by him doth this man stand here before you whole.

11 This is the stone which was set at nought of you builders, which is become the head of the corner.

12 Neither is there salvation in any other: for there is none other name under heaven given among men, whereby we must be saved.

13 Now when they saw the boldness of Peter and John, and perceived that they were unlearned and ignorant men, they marvelled; and they took knowledge of them, that they had been with Jesus.

14 And beholding the man which was healed standing with them, they could say nothing against it.

15 ¶ But when they had commanded them to go aside out of the council, they conferred among themselves,

16 Saying, What shall we do to these men? for that

NEW AMERICAN STANDARD BIBLE

5 On the next day, their rulers and elders and scribes were gathered together in Jerusalem;

6 and Annas the high priest *was there,* and Caiaphas and John and Alexander, and all who were of high-priestly descent.

7 When they had placed them in the center, they *began to* inquire, "By what power, or in what name, have you done this?"

8 Then Peter, filled with the Holy Spirit, said to them, "Rulers and elders of the people,

9 if we are on trial today for a benefit done to a sick man, as to how this man has been made well,

10 let it be known to all of you and to all the people of Israel, that by the name of Jesus Christ the Nazarene, whom you crucified, whom God raised from the dead—by this *name* this man stands here before you in good health.

11 "He is the STONE WHICH WAS REJECTED by you, THE BUILDERS, *but* WHICH BECAME THE CHIEF CORNER *stone.*

12 "And there is salvation in no one else; for there is no other name under heaven that has been given among men by which we must be saved."

Threat and Release

13 Now as they observed the confidence of Peter and John and understood that they were uneducated and untrained men, they were amazed, and *began* to recognize them as having been with Jesus.

14 And seeing the man who had been healed standing with them, they had nothing to say in reply.

NEW CENTURY VERSION

5 The next day the Jewish rulers, the older Jewish lead-
ers, and the teachers of the law met in Jerusalem. 6 Annas
the high priest, Caiaphas, John, and Alexander were there,
as well as everyone from the high priest's family. 7 They
made Peter and John stand before them and then asked
them, "By what power or authority did you do this?"
8 Then Peter, filled with the Holy Spirit, said to them,
"Rulers of the people and you older leaders, 9 are you ques-
tioning us about a good thing that was done to a crippled
man? Are you asking us who made him well? 10 We want
all of you and all the Jewish people to know that this man
was made well by the power of Jesus Christ from Nazareth.
You crucified him, but God raised him from the dead. This
man was crippled, but he is now well and able to stand
here before you because of the power of Jesus. 11 Jesus is

'the stone[a] that you builders rejected,
which has become the cornerstone.' *Psalm 118:22*

12 Jesus is the only One who can save people. His name is
the only power in the world that has been given to save
people. We must be saved through him."
13 The Jewish leaders saw that Peter and John were not
afraid to speak, and they understood that these men had no
special training or education. So they were amazed. Then
they realized that Peter and John had been with Jesus.
14 Because they saw the healed man standing there beside
the two apostles, they could say nothing against them.

4:11 [a] **stone** A symbol meaning Jesus.

CONTEMPORARY ENGLISH VERSION

5 The next morning the leaders, the elders, and the
teachers of the Law of Moses met in Jerusalem. 6 The high
priest Annas was there, as well as Caiaphas, John,
Alexander, and other members of the high priest's family.
7 They brought in Peter and John and made them stand in
the middle while they questioned them. They asked, "By
what power and in whose name have you done this?"
8 Peter was filled with the Holy Spirit and told the
nation's leaders and the elders:

9 You are questioning us today about a kind deed in
which a crippled man was healed. 10 But there is some-
thing we must tell you and everyone else in Israel. This
man is standing here completely well because of the
power of Jesus Christ from Nazareth. You put Jesus to
death on a cross, but God raised him to life. 11 He is the
stone that you builders thought was worthless, and now
he is the most important stone of all. 12 Only Jesus has
the power to save! His name is the only one in all the
world that can save anyone.

13 The officials were amazed to see how brave Peter and
John were, and they knew that these two apostles were
only ordinary men and not well educated. The officials
were certain that these men had been with Jesus. 14 But
they could not deny what had happened. The man who
had been healed was standing there with the apostles.

NEW INTERNATIONAL VERSION

[5]The next day the rulers, elders and teachers of the law met in Jerusalem. [6]Annas the high priest was there, and so were Caiaphas, John, Alexander and the other men of the high priest's family. [7]They had Peter and John brought before them and began to question them: "By what power or what name did you do this?"

[8]Then Peter, filled with the Holy Spirit, said to them: "Rulers and elders of the people! [9]If we are being called to account today for an act of kindness shown to a cripple and are asked how he was healed, [10]then know this, you and all the people of Israel: It is by the name of Jesus Christ of Nazareth, whom you crucified but whom God raised from the dead, that this man stands before you healed. [11]He is

" 'the stone you builders rejected,
which has become the capstone.[a]'[b]

[12]Salvation is found in no one else, for there is no other name under heaven given to men by which we must be saved."

[13]When they saw the courage of Peter and John and realized that they were unschooled, ordinary men, they were astonished and they took note that these men had been with Jesus. [14]But since they could see the man who had been healed standing there with them, there was nothing

[a] *11* Or *cornerstone* [b] *11* Psalm 118:22

NEW LIVING TRANSLATION

[5]The next day the council of all the rulers and elders and teachers of religious law met in Jerusalem. [6]Annas the high priest was there, along with Caiaphas, John, Alexander, and other relatives of the high priest. [7]They brought in the two disciples and demanded, "By what power, or in whose name, have you done this?"

[8]Then Peter, filled with the Holy Spirit, said to them, "Leaders and elders of our nation, [9]are we being questioned because we've done a good deed for a crippled man? Do you want to know how he was healed? [10]Let me clearly state to you and to all the people of Israel that he was healed in the name and power of Jesus Christ from Nazareth, the man you crucified, but whom God raised from the dead. [11]For Jesus is the one referred to in the Scriptures, where it says,

'The stone that you builders rejected
has now become the cornerstone.'*

[12]There is salvation in no one else! There is no other name in all of heaven for people to call on to save them."

[13]The members of the council were amazed when they saw the boldness of Peter and John, for they could see that they were ordinary men who had had no special training. They also recognized them as men who had been with Jesus. [14]But since the man who had been healed was standing right there among them, the council had nothing to say.

4:11 Ps 118:22.

NEW KING JAMES VERSION

Addressing the Sanhedrin

[5]And it came to pass, on the next day, that their rulers, elders, and scribes, [6]as well as Annas the high priest, Caiaphas, John, and Alexander, and as many as were of the family of the high priest, were gathered together at Jerusalem. [7]And when they had set them in the midst, they asked, "By what power or by what name have you done this?"

[8]Then Peter, filled with the Holy Spirit, said to them, "Rulers of the people and elders of Israel: [9]If we this day are judged for a good deed *done* to a helpless man, by what means he has been made well, [10]let it be known to you all, and to all the people of Israel, that by the name of Jesus Christ of Nazareth, whom you crucified, whom God raised from the dead, by Him this man stands here before you whole. [11]This is the *'stone which was rejected by you builders, which has become the chief cornerstone.'*[a] [12]Nor is there salvation in any other, for there is no other name under heaven given among men by which we must be saved."

The Name of Jesus Forbidden

[13]Now when they saw the boldness of Peter and John, and perceived that they were uneducated and untrained men, they marveled. And they realized that they had been with Jesus. [14]And seeing the man who had been healed standing with them, they could say nothing against it.

4:11 [a] Psalm 118:22

THE MESSAGE

The next day a meeting was called in Jerusalem. The rulers, religious leaders, religion scholars, Annas the Chief Priest, Caiaphas, John, Alexander—everybody who was anybody was there. They stood Peter and John in the middle of the room and grilled them: "Who put you in charge here? What business do you have doing this?"

With that, Peter, full of the Holy Spirit, let loose: "Rulers and leaders of the people, if we have been brought to trial today for helping a sick man, put under investigation regarding this healing, I'll be completely frank with you—we have nothing to hide. By the name of Jesus Christ of Nazareth, the One you killed on a cross, the One God raised from the dead, by means of his name this man stands before you healthy and whole. Jesus is 'the stone you masons threw out, which is now the cornerstone.' Salvation comes no other way; no other name has been or will be given to us by which we can be saved, only this one."

They couldn't take their eyes off them—Peter and John standing there so confident, so sure of themselves! Their fascination deepened when they realized these two were laymen with no training in Scripture or formal education. They recognized them as companions of Jesus, but with the man right before them, seeing him standing there so upright—so healed!—what could they say against that?

KING JAMES VERSION

indeed a notable miracle hath been done by them *is* manifest to all them that dwell in Jerusalem; and we cannot deny *it*.

17 But that it spread no further among the people, let us straitly threaten them, that they speak henceforth to no man in this name.

18 And they called them, and commanded them not to speak at all nor teach in the name of Jesus.

19 But Peter and John answered and said unto them, Whether it be right in the sight of God to hearken unto you more than unto God, judge ye.

20 For we cannot but speak the things which we have seen and heard.

21 So when they had further threatened them, they let them go, finding nothing how they might punish them, because of the people: for all *men* glorified God for that which was done.

22 For the man was above forty years old, on whom this miracle of healing was shewed.

23 ¶ And being let go, they went to their own company, and reported all that the chief priests and elders had said unto them.

24 And when they heard that, they lifted up their voice to God with one accord, and said, Lord, thou *art* God, which hast made heaven, and earth, and the sea, and all that in them is:

NEW AMERICAN STANDARD BIBLE

15 But when they had ordered them to leave the Council, they *began* to confer with one another,

16 saying, "What shall we do with these men? For the fact that a noteworthy miracle has taken place through them is apparent to all who live in Jerusalem, and we cannot deny it.

17 "But so that it will not spread any further among the people, let us warn them to speak no longer to any man in this name."

18 And when they had summoned them, they commanded them not to speak or teach at all in the name of Jesus.

19 But Peter and John answered and said to them, "Whether it is right in the sight of God to give heed to you rather than to God, you be the judge;

20 for we cannot stop speaking about what we have seen and heard."

21 When they had threatened them further, they let them go (finding no basis on which to punish them) on account of the people, because they were all glorifying God for what had happened;

22 for the man was more than forty years old on whom this miracle of healing had been performed.

23 When they had been released, they went to their own *companions* and reported all that the chief priests and the elders had said to them.

24 And when they heard *this,* they lifted their voices to God with one accord and said, "O Lord, it is You who MADE THE HEAVEN AND THE EARTH AND THE SEA, AND ALL THAT IS IN THEM,

NEW CENTURY VERSION

15After the Jewish leaders ordered them to leave the meet-
ing, they began to talk to each other. 16They said, "What
shall we do with these men? Everyone in Jerusalem knows
they have done a great miracle, and we cannot say it is not
true. 17But to keep it from spreading among the people, we
must warn them not to talk to people anymore using that
name."
18So they called Peter and John in again and told them
not to speak or to teach at all in the name of Jesus. 19But
Peter and John answered them, "You decide what God
would want. Should we obey you or God? 20We cannot
keep quiet. We must speak about what we have seen and
heard." 21The Jewish leaders warned the apostles again
and let them go free. They could not find a way to punish
them, because all the people were praising God for what
had been done. 22The man who received the miracle of
healing was more than forty years old.

The Believers Pray

23After Peter and John left the meeting of Jewish lead-
ers, they went to their own group and told them every-
thing the leading priests and the older Jewish leaders had
said to them. 24When the believers heard this, they prayed
to God together, "Lord, you are the One who made the
sky, the earth, the sea, and everything in them. 25By the

CONTEMPORARY ENGLISH VERSION

15The officials commanded them to leave the council
room. Then the officials said to each other, 16"What can
we do with these men? Everyone in Jerusalem knows
about this miracle, and we cannot say it didn't happen.
17But to keep this thing from spreading, we will warn them
never again to speak to anyone about the name of Jesus."
18So they called the two apostles back in and told them
that they must never, for any reason, teach anything about
the name of Jesus.
19Peter and John answered, "Do you think God wants us
to obey you or to obey him? 20We cannot keep quiet about
what we have seen and heard."
21-22The officials could not find any reason to punish
Peter and John. So they threatened them and let them go.
The man who was healed by this miracle was more than
forty years old, and everyone was praising God for what
had happened.

Peter and Others Pray for Courage

23As soon as Peter and John had been set free, they went
back and told the others everything that the chief priests
and the leaders had said to them. 24When the rest of the
Lord's followers heard this, they prayed together and said:

Master, you created heaven and earth, the sea, and

NEW INTERNATIONAL VERSION

they could say. 15So they ordered them to withdraw from the Sanhedrin and then conferred together. 16"What are we going to do with these men?" they asked. "Everybody living in Jerusalem knows they have done an outstanding miracle, and we cannot deny it. 17But to stop this thing from spreading any further among the people, we must warn these men to speak no longer to anyone in this name."

18Then they called them in again and commanded them not to speak or teach at all in the name of Jesus. 19But Peter and John replied, "Judge for yourselves whether it is right in God's sight to obey you rather than God. 20For we cannot help speaking about what we have seen and heard."

21After further threats they let them go. They could not decide how to punish them, because all the people were praising God for what had happened. 22For the man who was miraculously healed was over forty years old.

The Believers' Prayer

23On their release, Peter and John went back to their own people and reported all that the chief priests and elders had said to them. 24When they heard this, they raised their voices together in prayer to God. "Sovereign Lord," they said, "you made the heaven and the earth and the sea, and everything in them. 25You spoke by the Holy

NEW LIVING TRANSLATION

15So they sent Peter and John out of the council chamber* and conferred among themselves.

16"What should we do with these men?" they asked each other. "We can't deny they have done a miraculous sign, and everybody in Jerusalem knows about it. 17But perhaps we can stop them from spreading their propaganda. We'll warn them not to speak to anyone in Jesus' name again." 18So they called the apostles back in and told them never again to speak or teach about Jesus.

19But Peter and John replied, "Do you think God wants us to obey you rather than him? 20We cannot stop telling about the wonderful things we have seen and heard."

21The council then threatened them further, but they finally let them go because they didn't know how to punish them without starting a riot. For everyone was praising God 22for this miraculous sign—the healing of a man who had been lame for more than forty years.

The Believers Pray for Courage

23As soon as they were freed, Peter and John found the other believers and told them what the leading priests and elders had said. 24Then all the believers were united as they lifted their voices in prayer: "O Sovereign Lord, Creator of heaven and earth, the sea, and everything in

4:15 Greek *the Sanhedrin.*

NEW KING JAMES VERSION

15But when they had commanded them to go aside out of the council, they conferred among themselves, 16saying, "What shall we do to these men? For, indeed, that a notable miracle has been done through them *is* evident to all who dwell in Jerusalem, and we cannot deny *it.* 17But so that it spreads no further among the people, let us severely threaten them, that from now on they speak to no man in this name."

18So they called them and commanded them not to speak at all nor teach in the name of Jesus. 19But Peter and John answered and said to them, "Whether it is right in the sight of God to listen to you more than to God, you judge. 20For we cannot but speak the things which we have seen and heard." 21So when they had further threatened them, they let them go, finding no way of punishing them, because of the people, since they all glorified God for what had been done. 22For the man was over forty years old on whom this miracle of healing had been performed.

Prayer for Boldness

23And being let go, they went to their own *companions* and reported all that the chief priests and elders had said to them. 24So when they heard that, they raised their voice to God with one accord and said: "Lord, You *are* God, who made heaven and earth and the sea, and all that is in

THE MESSAGE

They sent them out of the room so they could work out a plan. They talked it over: "What can we do with these men? By now it's known all over town that a miracle has occurred, and that they are behind it. There is no way we can refute that. But so that it doesn't go any further, let's silence them with threats so they won't dare to use Jesus' name ever again with anyone."

They called them back and warned them that they were on no account ever again to speak or teach in the name of Jesus. But Peter and John spoke right back, "Whether it's right in God's eyes to listen to you rather than to God, you decide. As for us, there's no question—we can't keep quiet about what we've seen and heard."

The religious leaders renewed their threats, but then released them. They couldn't come up with a charge that would stick, that would keep them in jail. The people wouldn't have stood for it—they were all praising God over what had happened. The man who had been miraculously healed was over forty years old.

One Heart, One Mind

As soon as Peter and John were let go, they went to their friends and told them what the high priests and religious leaders had said. Hearing the report, they lifted their voices in a wonderful harmony in prayer: "Strong God, you made heaven and earth and sea and everything in them.

KING JAMES VERSION

25 Who by the mouth of thy servant David hast said, Why did the heathen rage, and the people imagine vain things?

26 The kings of the earth stood up, and the rulers were gathered together against the Lord, and against his Christ.

27 For of a truth against thy holy child Jesus, whom thou hast anointed, both Herod, and Pontius Pilate, with the Gentiles, and the people of Israel, were gathered together,

28 For to do whatsoever thy hand and thy counsel determined before to be done.

29 And now, Lord, behold their threatenings: and grant unto thy servants, that with all boldness they may speak thy word,

30 By stretching forth thine hand to heal; and that signs and wonders may be done by the name of thy holy child Jesus.

31 And when they had prayed, the place was shaken where they were assembled together; and they were all filled with the Holy Ghost, and they spake the word of God with boldness.

NEW AMERICAN STANDARD BIBLE

25 who by the Holy Spirit, *through* the mouth of our father David Your servant, said,

'WHY DID THE [1]GENTILES RAGE,
AND THE PEOPLES DEVISE FUTILE THINGS?
26 'THE KINGS OF THE EARTH TOOK THEIR STAND,
AND THE RULERS WERE GATHERED TOGETHER
AGAINST THE LORD AND AGAINST HIS CHRIST.'

27 "For truly in this city there were gathered together against Your holy servant Jesus, whom You anointed, both Herod and Pontius Pilate, along with the Gentiles and the peoples of Israel,

28 to do whatever Your hand and Your purpose predestined to occur.

29 "And now, Lord, take note of their threats, and grant that Your bond-servants may speak Your word with all confidence,

30 while You extend Your hand to heal, and signs and wonders take place through the name of Your holy servant Jesus."

31 And when they had prayed, the place where they had gathered together was shaken, and they were all filled with the Holy Spirit and *began* to speak the word of God with boldness.

4:25 [1] Or *nations*

NEW CENTURY VERSION

Holy Spirit, through our father David your servant, you said:

'Why are the nations so angry?
Why are the people making useless plans?
26 The kings of the earth prepare to fight,
and their leaders make plans together
against the Lord
and his Christ.' *Psalm 2:1–2*

27 These things really happened when Herod, Pontius
Pilate, those who are not Jews, and the Jewish people all
came together against Jesus here in Jerusalem. Jesus is
your holy servant, the One you made to be the Christ.
28 These people made your plan happen because of your
power and your will. 29 And now, Lord, listen to their
threats. Lord, help us, your servants, to speak your word
without fear. 30 Help us to be brave by showing us your
power to heal. Give proofs and make miracles happen by
the power of Jesus, your holy servant."

31 After they had prayed, the place where they were meeting was shaken. They were all filled with the Holy Spirit, and they spoke God's word without fear.

CONTEMPORARY ENGLISH VERSION

everything in them. 25 And by the Holy Spirit you spoke
to our ancestor David. He was your servant, and you
told him to say:

"Why are all the Gentiles
so furious?
Why do people
make foolish plans?
26 The kings of earth
prepare for war,
and the rulers
join together
against the Lord
and his Messiah."

27 Here in Jerusalem, Herod[a] and Pontius Pilate got
together with the Gentiles and the people of Israel. Then
they turned against your holy Servant[b] Jesus, your chosen Messiah.
28 They did what you in your power and
wisdom had already decided would happen.

29 Lord, listen to their threats! We are your servants. So
make us brave enough to speak your message. 30 Show
your mighty power, as we heal people and work miracles
and wonders in the name of your holy Servant[b] Jesus.

31 After they had prayed, the meeting place shook. They were all filled with the Holy Spirit and bravely spoke God's message.

[a] 4.27 *Herod*: Herod Antipas, the son of Herod the Great.
[b] 4.27,30 *Servant*: See the note at 3.13.

NEW INTERNATIONAL VERSION

Spirit through the mouth of your servant, our father David:

" 'Why do the nations rage
and the peoples plot in vain?
26 The kings of the earth take their stand
and the rulers gather together
against the Lord
and against his Anointed One.[c,d]

27 Indeed Herod and Pontius Pilate met together with the
Gentiles and the people[e] of Israel in this city to conspire
against your holy servant Jesus, whom you anointed.
28 They did what your power and will had decided before-
hand should happen. 29 Now, Lord, consider their threats
and enable your servants to speak your word with great
boldness. 30 Stretch out your hand to heal and perform
miraculous signs and wonders through the name of your
holy servant Jesus."
31 After they prayed, the place where they were meeting
was shaken. And they were all filled with the Holy Spirit
and spoke the word of God boldly.

[c] *26* That is, Christ or Messiah [d] *26* Psalm 2:1,2 [e] *27* The Greek is plural.

NEW LIVING TRANSLATION

them—25 you spoke long ago by the Holy Spirit through
our ancestor King David, your servant, saying,

'Why did the nations rage?
Why did the people waste their time with futile plans?
26 The kings of the earth prepared for battle;
the rulers gathered together
against the Lord
and against his Messiah.'*

27 "That is what has happened here in this city! For
Herod Antipas, Pontius Pilate the governor, the Gentiles,
and the people of Israel were all united against Jesus, your
holy servant, whom you anointed. 28 In fact, everything
they did occurred according to your eternal will and plan.
29 And now, O Lord, hear their threats, and give your ser-
vants great boldness in their preaching. 30 Send your heal-
ing power; may miraculous signs and wonders be done
through the name of your holy servant Jesus."
31 After this prayer, the building where they were meet-
ing shook, and they were all filled with the Holy Spirit.
And they preached God's message with boldness.

4:25-26 Ps 2:1-2.

NEW KING JAMES VERSION

them, 25 who by the mouth of Your servant David[b] have
said:

'Why did the nations rage,
And the people plot vain things?
26 *The kings of the earth took their stand,*
And the rulers were gathered together
Against the Lord *and against His Christ.'*[c]

27 "For truly against Your holy Servant Jesus, whom You
anointed, both Herod and Pontius Pilate, with the Gentiles
and the people of Israel, were gathered together 28 to do
whatever Your hand and Your purpose determined before
to be done. 29 Now, Lord, look on their threats, and grant to
Your servants that with all boldness they may speak Your
word, 30 by stretching out Your hand to heal, and that
signs and wonders may be done through the name of Your
holy Servant Jesus."
31 And when they had prayed, the place where they were
assembled together was shaken; and they were all filled
with the Holy Spirit, and they spoke the word of God with
boldness.

4:25 [b] NU-Text reads *who through the Holy Spirit, by the mouth of our father, Your servant David.* **4:26** [c] Psalm 2:1, 2

THE MESSAGE

By the Holy Spirit you spoke through the mouth of your servant and our father, David:

'Why the big noise, nations?
Why the mean plots, peoples?
Earth's leaders push for position,
Potentates meet for summit talks,
The God-deniers, the Messiah-defiers!'

"For in fact they did meet—Herod and Pontius Pilate with nations and peoples, even Israel itself!—met in this very city to plot against your holy Son Jesus, the One you made Messiah, to carry out the plans you long ago set in motion.

"And now they're at it again! Take care of their threats and give your servants fearless confidence in preaching your Message, as you stretch out your hand to us in healings and miracles and wonders done in the name of your holy servant Jesus."

While they were praying, the place where they were meeting trembled and shook. They were all filled with the Holy Spirit and continued to speak God's Word with fearless confidence.

KING JAMES VERSION

32 ¶ And the multitude of them that believed were of one heart and of one soul: neither said any *of them* that ought of the things which he possessed was his own; but they had all things common.

33 And with great power gave the apostles witness of the resurrection of the Lord Jesus: and great grace was upon them all.

34 Neither was there any among them that lacked: for as many as were possessors of lands or houses sold them, and brought the prices of the things that were sold,

35 And laid *them* down at the apostles' feet: and distribution was made unto every man according as he had need.

36 And Joses, who by the apostles was surnamed Barnabas, (which is, being interpreted, The son of consolation,) a Levite, *and* of the country of Cyprus,

37 Having land, sold *it*, and brought the money, and laid *it* at the apostles' feet.

5 But a certain man named Ananias, with Sapphira his wife, sold a possession,

2 And kept back *part* of the price, his wife also being privy *to it*, and brought a certain part, and laid *it* at the apostles' feet.

3 But Peter said, Ananias, why hath Satan filled thine heart to lie to the Holy Ghost, and to keep back *part* of the price of the land?

4 Whiles it remained, was it not thine own? and after it

NEW AMERICAN STANDARD BIBLE

Sharing among Believers

32 And the congregation of those who believed were of one heart and soul; and not one *of them* claimed that anything belonging to him was his own, but all things were common property to them.

33 And with great power the apostles were giving testimony to the resurrection of the Lord Jesus, and abundant grace was upon them all.

34 For there was not a needy person among them, for all who were owners of land or houses would sell them and bring the proceeds of the sales

35 and lay them at the apostles' feet, and they would be distributed to each as any had need.

36 Now Joseph, a Levite of Cyprian birth, who was also called Barnabas by the apostles (which translated means Son of Encouragement),

37 and who owned a tract of land, sold it and brought the money and laid it at the apostles' feet.

Fate of Ananias and Sapphira

5 But a man named Ananias, with his wife Sapphira, sold a piece of property,

2 and kept back *some* of the price for himself, with his wife's full knowledge, and bringing a portion of it, he laid it at the apostles' feet.

3 But Peter said, "Ananias, why has Satan filled your heart to lie to the Holy Spirit and to keep back *some* of the price of the land?

4 "While it remained *unsold,* did it not remain your

NEW CENTURY VERSION

The Believers Share

32 The group of believers were united in their hearts and spirit. All those in the group acted as though their private property belonged to everyone in the group. In fact, they shared everything. 33 With great power the apostles were telling people that the Lord Jesus was truly raised from the dead. And God blessed all the believers very much. 34 No one in the group needed anything. From time to time those who owned fields or houses sold them, brought the money, 35 and gave it to the apostles. Then the money was given to anyone who needed it.

36 One of the believers was named Joseph, a Levite born in Cyprus. The apostles called him Barnabas (which means "one who encourages"). 37 Joseph owned a field, sold it, brought the money, and gave it to the apostles.

Ananias and Sapphira Die

5 But a man named Ananias and his wife Sapphira sold some land. 2 He kept back part of the money for himself; his wife knew about this and agreed to it. But he brought the rest of the money and gave it to the apostles. 3 Peter said, "Ananias, why did you let Satan rule your thoughts to lie to the Holy Spirit and to keep for yourself part of the money you received for the land? 4 Before you sold the land, it belonged to you. And even after you sold

CONTEMPORARY ENGLISH VERSION

Sharing Possessions

32 The group of followers all felt the same way about everything. None of them claimed that their possessions were their own, and they shared everything they had with each other. 33 In a powerful way the apostles told everyone that the Lord Jesus was now alive. God greatly blessed his followers,[c] 34 and no one went in need of anything. Everyone who owned land or houses would sell them and bring the money 35 to the apostles. Then they would give the money to anyone who needed it.

36-37 Joseph was one of the followers who had sold a piece of property and brought the money to the apostles. He was a Levite from Cyprus, and the apostles called him Barnabas, which means "one who encourages others."

Peter Condemns Ananias and Sapphira

5 Ananias and his wife Sapphira also sold a piece of property. 2 But they agreed to cheat and keep some of the money for themselves.

So when Ananias took the rest of the money to the apostles, 3 Peter said, "Why has Satan made you keep back some of the money from the sale of the property? Why have you lied to the Holy Spirit? 4 The property was yours before you

c 4.33 *God greatly blessed his followers*: Or "Everyone highly respected his followers."

NEW INTERNATIONAL VERSION

The Believers Share Their Possessions

32All the believers were one in heart and mind. No one
claimed that any of his possessions was his own, but they
shared everything they had. 33With great power the apos-
tles continued to testify to the resurrection of the Lord
Jesus, and much grace was upon them all. 34There were no
needy persons among them. For from time to time those
who owned lands or houses sold them, brought the money
from the sales 35and put it at the apostles' feet, and it was
distributed to anyone as he had need.

36Joseph, a Levite from Cyprus, whom the apostles called
Barnabas (which means Son of Encouragement), 37sold a
field he owned and brought the money and put it at the
apostles' feet.

Ananias and Sapphira

5 Now a man named Ananias, together with his wife
Sapphira, also sold a piece of property. 2With his
wife's full knowledge he kept back part of the money for
himself, but brought the rest and put it at the apostles'
feet.

3Then Peter said, "Ananias, how is it that Satan has so
filled your heart that you have lied to the Holy Spirit and
have kept for yourself some of the money you received for
the land? 4Didn't it belong to you before it was sold? And

NEW LIVING TRANSLATION

The Believers Share Their Possessions

32All the believers were of one heart and mind, and they
felt that what they owned was not their own; they shared
everything they had. 33And the apostles gave powerful wit-
ness to the resurrection of the Lord Jesus, and God's great
favor was upon them all. 34There was no poverty among
them, because people who owned land or houses sold them
35and brought the money to the apostles to give to others
in need.

36For instance, there was Joseph, the one the apostles
nicknamed Barnabas (which means "Son of Encourage-
ment"). He was from the tribe of Levi and came from the
island of Cyprus. 37He sold a field he owned and brought
the money to the apostles for those in need.

Ananias and Sapphira

5 There was also a man named Ananias who, with his
wife, Sapphira, sold some property. 2He brought part
of the money to the apostles, but he claimed it was the full
amount. His wife had agreed to this deception.

3Then Peter said, "Ananias, why has Satan filled your
heart? You lied to the Holy Spirit, and you kept some of
the money for yourself. 4The property was yours to sell or

NEW KING JAMES VERSION

Sharing in All Things

32Now the multitude of those who believed were of one
heart and one soul; neither did anyone say that any of the
things he possessed was his own, but they had all things
in common. 33And with great power the apostles gave wit-
ness to the resurrection of the Lord Jesus. And great grace
was upon them all. 34Nor was there anyone among them
who lacked; for all who were possessors of lands or houses
sold them, and brought the proceeds of the things that
were sold, 35and laid *them* at the apostles' feet; and they
distributed to each as anyone had need.

36And Joses,[d] who was also named Barnabas by the
apostles (which is translated Son of Encouragement), a
Levite of the country of Cyprus, 37having land, sold *it*, and
brought the money and laid *it* at the apostles' feet.

Lying to the Holy Spirit

5 But a certain man named Ananias, with Sapphira his
wife, sold a possession. 2And he kept back *part* of the
proceeds, his wife also being aware *of it*, and brought a
certain part and laid *it* at the apostles' feet. 3But Peter
said, "Ananias, why has Satan filled your heart to lie to
the Holy Spirit and keep back *part* of the price of the land
for yourself? 4While it remained, was it not your own? And

4:36 [d] NU-Text reads *Joseph.*

THE MESSAGE

The whole congregation of believers was united as one—one heart, one mind! They didn't even claim ownership of their own possessions. No one said, "That's mine; you can't have it." They shared everything. The apostles gave powerful witness to the resurrection of the Master Jesus, and grace was on all of them.

And so it turned out that not a person among them was needy. Those who owned fields or houses sold them and brought the price of the sale to the apostles and made an offering of it. The apostles then distributed it according to each person's need.

Joseph, called by the apostles "Barnabas" (which means "Son of Comfort"), a Levite born in Cyprus, sold a field that he owned, brought the money and made an offering of it to the apostles.

Ananias and Sapphira

5 But a man named Ananias—his wife, Sapphira, conniving in this with him—sold a piece of land, secretly kept part of the price for himself, and then brought the rest to the apostles and made an offering of it.

Peter said, "Ananias, how did Satan get you to lie to the Holy Spirit and secretly keep back part of the price of the field? Before you sold it, it was all yours, and after you

KING JAMES VERSION

was sold, was it not in thine own power? why hast thou conceived this thing in thine heart? thou hast not lied unto men, but unto God.

5 And Ananias hearing these words fell down, and gave up the ghost: and great fear came on all them that heard these things.

6 And the young men arose, wound him up, and carried *him* out, and buried *him*.

7 And it was about the space of three hours after, when his wife, not knowing what was done, came in.

8 And Peter answered unto her, Tell me whether ye sold the land for so much? And she said, Yea, for so much.

9 Then Peter said unto her, How is it that ye have agreed together to tempt the Spirit of the Lord? behold, the feet of them which have buried thy husband *are* at the door, and shall carry thee out.

10 Then fell she down straightway at his feet, and yielded up the ghost: and the young men came in, and found her dead, and, carrying *her* forth, buried *her* by her husband.

11 And great fear came upon all the church, and upon as many as heard these things.

12 ¶ And by the hands of the apostles were many signs and wonders wrought among the people; (and they were all with one accord in Solomon's porch.

13 And of the rest durst no man join himself to them: but the people magnified them.

14 And believers were the more added to the Lord, multitudes both of men and women.)

NEW AMERICAN STANDARD BIBLE

own? And after it was sold, was it not under your control? Why is it that you have conceived this deed in your heart? You have not lied to men but to God."

5 And as he heard these words, Ananias fell down and breathed his last; and great fear came over all who heard of it.

6 The young men got up and covered him up, and after carrying him out, they buried him.

7 Now there elapsed an interval of about three hours, and his wife came in, not knowing what had happened.

8 And Peter responded to her, "Tell me whether you sold the land for such and such a price?" And she said, "Yes, that was the price."

9 Then Peter *said* to her, "Why is it that you have agreed together to put the Spirit of the Lord to the test? Behold, the feet of those who have buried your husband are at the door, and they will carry you out *as well*."

10 And immediately she fell at his feet and breathed her last, and the young men came in and found her dead, and they carried her out and buried her beside her husband.

11 And great fear came over the whole church, and over all who heard of these things.

12 At the hands of the apostles many signs and wonders were taking place among the people; and they were all with one accord in Solomon's portico.

13 But none of the rest dared to associate with them; however, the people held them in high esteem.

14 And all the more believers in the Lord, multitudes of men and women, were constantly added to *their number*,

NEW CENTURY VERSION

it, you could have used the money any way you wanted. Why did you think of doing this? You lied to God, not to us!"
5–6When Ananias heard this, he fell down and died. Some young men came in, wrapped up his body, carried it out, and buried it. And everyone who heard about this was filled with fear.

7About three hours later his wife came in, but she did not know what had happened.
8Peter said to her, "Tell me, was the money you got for your field this much?"

Sapphira answered, "Yes, that was the price."

9Peter said to her, "Why did you and your husband agree to test the Spirit of the Lord? Look! The men who buried your husband are at the door, and they will carry you out."
10At that moment Sapphira fell down by his feet and died. When the young men came in and saw that she was dead, they carried her out and buried her beside her husband.
11The whole church and all the others who heard about these things were filled with fear.

The Apostles Heal Many

12The apostles did many signs and miracles among the people. And they would all meet together on Solomon's Porch.
13None of the others dared to join them, but all the people respected them.
14More and more men and women believed in the Lord and were added to the group of

CONTEMPORARY ENGLISH VERSION

sold it, and even after you sold it, the money was still yours. What made you do such a thing? You didn't lie to people. You lied to God!"

5As soon as Ananias heard this, he dropped dead, and everyone who heard about it was frightened.
6Some young men came in and wrapped up his body. Then they took it out and buried it.

7Three hours later Sapphira came in, but she did not know what had happened to her husband.
8Peter asked her, "Tell me, did you sell the property for this amount?"

"Yes," she answered, "that's the amount."

9Then Peter said, "Why did the two of you agree to test the Lord's Spirit? The men who buried Ananias are by the door, and they will carry you out!"
10At once she fell at Peter's feet and died.

When the young men came back in, they found Sapphira lying there dead. So they carried her out and buried her beside her husband.
11The church members were afraid, and so was everyone else who heard what had happened.

Peter's Unusual Power

12The apostles worked many miracles and wonders among the people. All of the Lord's followers often met in the part of the temple known as Solomon's Porch.[a]
13No one outside their group dared join them, even though everyone liked them very much.

14Many men and women started having faith in the Lord.

[a] 5.12 *Solomon's Porch*: See the note at 3.11.

NEW INTERNATIONAL VERSION

after it was sold, wasn't the money at your disposal? What made you think of doing such a thing? You have not lied to men but to God."

5 When Ananias heard this, he fell down and died. And great fear seized all who heard what had happened. 6 Then the young men came forward, wrapped up his body, and carried him out and buried him.

7 About three hours later his wife came in, not knowing what had happened. 8 Peter asked her, "Tell me, is this the price you and Ananias got for the land?"

"Yes," she said, "that is the price."

9 Peter said to her, "How could you agree to test the Spirit of the Lord? Look! The feet of the men who buried your husband are at the door, and they will carry you out also."

10 At that moment she fell down at his feet and died. Then the young men came in and, finding her dead, carried her out and buried her beside her husband. 11 Great fear seized the whole church and all who heard about these events.

The Apostles Heal Many

12 The apostles performed many miraculous signs and wonders among the people. And all the believers used to meet together in Solomon's Colonnade. 13 No one else dared join them, even though they were highly regarded by the people. 14 Nevertheless, more and more men and women believed in the Lord and were added to their number. 15 As a

NEW LIVING TRANSLATION

not sell, as you wished. And after selling it, the money was yours to give away. How could you do a thing like this? You weren't lying to us but to God."

5 As soon as Ananias heard these words, he fell to the floor and died. Everyone who heard about it was terrified. 6 Then some young men wrapped him in a sheet and took him out and buried him.

7 About three hours later his wife came in, not knowing what had happened. 8 Peter asked her, "Was this the price you and your husband received for your land?"

"Yes," she replied, "that was the price."

9 And Peter said, "How could the two of you even think of doing a thing like this—conspiring together to test the Spirit of the Lord? Just outside that door are the young men who buried your husband, and they will carry you out, too."

10 Instantly, she fell to the floor and died. When the young men came in and saw that she was dead, they carried her out and buried her beside her husband. 11 Great fear gripped the entire church and all others who heard what had happened.

The Apostles Heal Many

12 Meanwhile, the apostles were performing many miraculous signs and wonders among the people. And the believers were meeting regularly at the Temple in the area known as Solomon's Colonnade. 13 No one else dared to join them, though everyone had high regard for them. 14 And more and more people believed and were brought to the Lord—crowds of both men and women. 15 As a result of

NEW KING JAMES VERSION

after it was sold, was it not in your own control? Why have you conceived this thing in your heart? You have not lied to men but to God."

5 Then Ananias, hearing these words, fell down and breathed his last. So great fear came upon all those who heard these things. 6 And the young men arose and wrapped him up, carried *him* out, and buried *him*.

7 Now it was about three hours later when his wife came in, not knowing what had happened. 8 And Peter answered her, "Tell me whether you sold the land for so much?"

She said, "Yes, for so much."

9 Then Peter said to her, "How is it that you have agreed together to test the Spirit of the Lord? Look, the feet of those who have buried your husband *are* at the door, and they will carry you out." 10 Then immediately she fell down at his feet and breathed her last. And the young men came in and found her dead, and carrying *her* out, buried *her* by her husband. 11 So great fear came upon all the church and upon all who heard these things.

Continuing Power in the Church

12 And through the hands of the apostles many signs and wonders were done among the people. And they were all with one accord in Solomon's Porch. 13 Yet none of the rest dared join them, but the people esteemed them highly. 14 And believers were increasingly added to the Lord, multitudes of both men and women, 15 so that they brought the

THE MESSAGE

sold it, the money was yours to do with as you wished. So what got into you to pull a trick like this? You didn't lie to men but to God."

Ananias, when he heard those words, fell down dead. *That* put the fear of God into everyone who heard of it. The younger men went right to work and wrapped him up, then carried him out and buried him.

Not more than three hours later, his wife, knowing nothing of what had happened, came in. Peter said, "Tell me, were you given this price for your field?"

"Yes," she said, "that price."

Peter responded, "What's going on here that you connived to conspire against the Spirit of the Master? The men who buried your husband are at the door, and you're next." No sooner were the words out of his mouth than she also fell down, dead. When the young men returned they found her body. They carried her out and buried her beside her husband. By this time the whole church and, in fact, everyone who heard of these things had a healthy respect for God. They knew God was not to be trifled with.

They All Met Regularly

Through the work of the apostles, many God-signs were set up among the people, many wonderful things done. They all met regularly and in remarkable harmony on the Temple porch named after Solomon. But even though people admired them a lot, outsiders were wary about joining them. On the other hand, those who put their trust in the Master were added right and left, men and women both.

KING JAMES VERSION

15 Insomuch that they brought forth the sick into the streets, and laid *them* on beds and couches, that at the least the shadow of Peter passing by might overshadow some of them.

16 There came also a multitude *out* of the cities round about unto Jerusalem, bringing sick folks, and them which were vexed with unclean spirits: and they were healed every one.

17 ¶ Then the high priest rose up, and all they that were with him, (which is the sect of the Sadducees,) and were filled with indignation,

18 And laid their hands on the apostles, and put them in the common prison.

19 But the angel of the Lord by night opened the prison doors, and brought them forth, and said,

20 Go, stand and speak in the temple to the people all the words of this life.

21 And when they heard *that*, they entered into the temple early in the morning, and taught. But the high priest came, and they that were with him, and called the council together, and all the senate of the children of Israel, and sent to the prison to have them brought.

22 But when the officers came, and found them not in the prison, they returned, and told,

NEW AMERICAN STANDARD BIBLE

15 to such an extent that they even carried the sick out into the streets and laid them on cots and pallets, so that when Peter came by at least his shadow might fall on any one of them.

16 Also the people from the cities in the vicinity of Jerusalem were coming together, bringing people who were sick [1]or afflicted with unclean spirits, and they were all being healed.

Imprisonment and Release

17 But the high priest rose up, along with all his associates (that is the sect of the Sadducees), and they were filled with jealousy.

18 They laid hands on the apostles and put them in a public jail.

19 But during the night an angel of the Lord opened the gates of the prison, and taking them out he said,

20 "Go, stand and speak to the people in the temple the whole message of this Life."

21 Upon hearing *this,* they entered into the temple about daybreak and *began* to teach.

Now when the high priest and his associates came, they called the Council together, even all the Senate of the sons of Israel, and sent *orders* to the prison house for them to be brought.

22 But the officers who came did not find them in the prison; and they returned and reported back,

5:16 [1] Lit *and*

NEW CENTURY VERSION

believers. 15The people placed their sick on beds and mats
in the streets, hoping that when Peter passed by at least
his shadow might fall on them. 16Crowds came from all
the towns around Jerusalem, bringing their sick and those
who were bothered by evil spirits, and all of them were
healed.

Leaders Try to Stop the Apostles

17The high priest and all his friends (a group called the
Sadducees) became very jealous. 18They took the apostles
and put them in jail. 19But during the night, an angel of
the Lord opened the doors of the jail and led the apostles
outside. The angel said, 20"Go stand in the Temple and tell
the people everything about this new life." 21When the
apostles heard this, they obeyed and went into the Temple
early in the morning and continued teaching.

When the high priest and his friends arrived, they called
a meeting of the Jewish leaders and all the important older
Jewish men. They sent some men to the jail to bring the
apostles to them. 22But, upon arriving, the officers could
not find the apostles. So they went back and reported to

CONTEMPORARY ENGLISH VERSION

15Then sick people were brought out to the road and placed
on cots and mats. It was hoped that Peter would walk by,
and his shadow would fall on them and heal them. 16A lot
of people living in the towns near Jerusalem brought those
who were sick or troubled by evil spirits, and they were all
healed.

Trouble for the Apostles

17The high priest and all the other Sadducees who were
with him became jealous. 18They arrested the apostles and
put them in the city jail. 19But that night an angel from the
Lord opened the doors of the jail and led the apostles out.
The angel said, 20"Go to the temple and tell the people
everything about this new life." 21So they went into the
temple before sunrise and started teaching.

The high priest and his men called together their coun-
cil, which included all of Israel's leaders. Then they
ordered the apostles to be brought to them from the jail.
22The temple police who were sent to the jail did not find
the apostles. They returned and said, 23"We found the jail

NEW INTERNATIONAL VERSION

result, people brought the sick into the streets and laid them on beds and mats so that at least Peter's shadow might fall on some of them as he passed by. 16Crowds gathered also from the towns around Jerusalem, bringing their sick and those tormented by evil[a] spirits, and all of them were healed.

The Apostles Persecuted

17Then the high priest and all his associates, who were members of the party of the Sadducees, were filled with jealousy. 18They arrested the apostles and put them in the public jail. 19But during the night an angel of the Lord opened the doors of the jail and brought them out. 20"Go, stand in the temple courts," he said, "and tell the people the full message of this new life."

21At daybreak they entered the temple courts, as they had been told, and began to teach the people.

When the high priest and his associates arrived, they called together the Sanhedrin—the full assembly of the elders of Israel—and sent to the jail for the apostles. 22But on arriving at the jail, the officers did not find them there. So they went back and reported, 23"We found the jail

[a] *16* Greek *unclean*

NEW LIVING TRANSLATION

the apostles' work, sick people were brought out into the streets on beds and mats so that Peter's shadow might fall across some of them as he went by. 16Crowds came in from the villages around Jerusalem, bringing their sick and those possessed by evil spirits, and they were all healed.

The Apostles Meet Opposition

17The high priest and his friends, who were Sadducees, reacted with violent jealousy. 18They arrested the apostles and put them in the jail. 19But an angel of the Lord came at night, opened the gates of the jail, and brought them out. Then he told them, 20"Go to the Temple and give the people this message of life!" 21So the apostles entered the Temple about daybreak and immediately began teaching.

When the high priest and his officials arrived, they convened the high council,* along with all the elders of Israel. Then they sent for the apostles to be brought for trial. 22But when the Temple guards went to the jail, the men were gone. So they returned to the council and reported,

5:21 Greek *Sanhedrin;* also in 5:27, 41.

NEW KING JAMES VERSION

sick out into the streets and laid *them* on beds and couches, that at least the shadow of Peter passing by might fall on some of them. 16Also a multitude gathered from the surrounding cities to Jerusalem, bringing sick people and those who were tormented by unclean spirits, and they were all healed.

Imprisoned Apostles Freed

17Then the high priest rose up, and all those who *were* with him (which is the sect of the Sadducees), and they were filled with indignation, 18and laid their hands on the apostles and put them in the common prison. 19But at night an angel of the Lord opened the prison doors and brought them out, and said, 20"Go, stand in the temple and speak to the people all the words of this life."

21And when they heard *that,* they entered the temple early in the morning and taught. But the high priest and those with him came and called the council together, with all the elders of the children of Israel, and sent to the prison to have them brought.

Apostles on Trial Again

22But when the officers came and did not find them in the prison, they returned and reported, 23saying, "Indeed

THE MESSAGE

They even carried the sick out into the streets and laid them on stretchers and bedrolls, hoping they would be touched by Peter's shadow when he walked by. They came from the villages surrounding Jerusalem, throngs of them, bringing the sick and bedeviled. And they all were healed.

To Obey God Rather Than Men

Provoked mightily by all this, the Chief Priest and those on his side, mainly the sect of Sadducees, went into action, arrested the apostles and put them in the town jail. But during the night an angel of God opened the jailhouse door and led them out. He said, "Go to the Temple and take your stand. Tell the people everything there is to say about this Life."

Promptly obedient, they entered the Temple at daybreak and went on with their teaching.

Meanwhile, the Chief Priest and his cronies convened the High Council, Israel's senate, and sent to the jail to have the prisoners brought in. When the police got there, they couldn't find them anywhere in the jail. They went back

KING JAMES VERSION

23 Saying, The prison truly found we shut with all safety, and the keepers standing without before the doors: but when we had opened, we found no man within.

24 Now when the high priest and the captain of the temple and the chief priests heard these things, they doubted of them whereunto this would grow.

25 Then came one and told them, saying, Behold, the men whom ye put in prison are standing in the temple, and teaching the people.

26 ¶ Then went the captain with the officers, and brought them without violence: for they feared the people, lest they should have been stoned.

27 And when they had brought them, they set *them* before the council: and the high priest asked them,

28 Saying, Did not we straitly command you that ye should not teach in this name? and, behold, ye have filled Jerusalem with your doctrine, and intend to bring this man's blood upon us.

29 Then Peter and the *other* apostles answered and said, We ought to obey God rather than men.

30 The God of our fathers raised up Jesus, whom ye slew and hanged on a tree.

31 Him hath God exalted with his right hand *to be* a Prince and a Saviour, for to give repentance to Israel, and forgiveness of sins.

32 And we are his witnesses of these things; and *so is* also the Holy Ghost, whom God hath given to them that obey him.

NEW AMERICAN STANDARD BIBLE

23 saying, "We found the prison house locked quite securely and the guards standing at the doors; but when we had opened up, we found no one inside."

24 Now when the captain of the temple *guard* and the chief priests heard these words, they were greatly perplexed about them as to what would come of this.

25 But someone came and reported to them, "The men whom you put in prison are standing in the temple and teaching the people!"

26 Then the captain went along with the officers and *proceeded* to bring them *back* without violence (for they were afraid of the people, that they might be stoned).

27 When they had brought them, they stood them before the Council. The high priest questioned them,

28 saying, "We gave you strict orders not to continue teaching in this name, and yet, you have filled Jerusalem with your teaching and intend to bring this man's blood upon us."

29 But Peter and the apostles answered, "We must obey God rather than men.

30 "The God of our fathers raised up Jesus, whom you had put to death by hanging Him on a cross.

31 "He is the one whom God exalted to His right hand as a Prince and a Savior, to grant repentance to Israel, and forgiveness of sins.

32 "And we are witnesses [2]of these things; and *so is* the Holy Spirit, whom God has given to those who obey Him."

5:32 [2] One early ms adds *in Him*

NEW CENTURY VERSION

the Jewish leaders. 23They said, "The jail was closed and locked, and the guards were standing at the doors. But when we opened the doors, the jail was empty!" 24Hearing this, the captain of the Temple guards and the leading priests were confused and wondered what was happening.

25Then someone came and told them, "Listen! The men you put in jail are standing in the Temple teaching the people." 26Then the captain and his men went out and brought the apostles back. But the soldiers did not use force, because they were afraid the people would stone them to death.

27The soldiers brought the apostles to the meeting and made them stand before the Jewish leaders. The high priest questioned them, 28saying, "We gave you strict orders not to continue teaching in that name. But look, you have filled Jerusalem with your teaching and are trying to make us responsible for this man's death."

29Peter and the other apostles answered, "We must obey God, not human authority! 30You killed Jesus by hanging him on a cross. But God, the God of our ancestors, raised Jesus up from the dead! 31Jesus is the One whom God raised to be on his right side, as Leader and Savior. Through him, all Jewish people could change their hearts and lives and have their sins forgiven. 32We saw all these things happen. The Holy Spirit, whom God has given to all who obey him, also proves these things are true."

CONTEMPORARY ENGLISH VERSION

locked tight and the guards standing at the doors. But when we opened the doors and went in, we didn't find anyone there." 24The captain of the temple police and the chief priests listened to their report, but they did not know what to think about it.

25Just then someone came in and said, "Right now those men you put in jail are in the temple, teaching the people!" 26The captain went with some of the temple police and brought the apostles back. But they did not use force. They were afraid that the people might start throwing stones at them.

27When the apostles were brought before the council, the high priest said to them, 28"We told you plainly not to teach in the name of Jesus. But look what you have done! You have been teaching all over Jerusalem, and you are trying to blame us for his death."

29Peter and the apostles replied:

We don't obey people. We obey God. 30You killed Jesus by nailing him to a cross. But the God our ancestors worshiped raised him to life 31and made him our Leader and Savior. Then God gave him a place at his right side,[b] so that the people of Israel would turn back to him and be forgiven. 32We are here to tell you about all this, and so is the Holy Spirit, who is God's gift to everyone who obeys God.

[b] 5.31 *right side*: See the note at 2.33.

NEW INTERNATIONAL VERSION

securely locked, with the guards standing at the doors; but when we opened them, we found no one inside." [24]On hearing this report, the captain of the temple guard and the chief priests were puzzled, wondering what would come of this.

[25]Then someone came and said, "Look! The men you put in jail are standing in the temple courts teaching the people." [26]At that, the captain went with his officers and brought the apostles. They did not use force, because they feared that the people would stone them.

[27]Having brought the apostles, they made them appear before the Sanhedrin to be questioned by the high priest. [28]"We gave you strict orders not to teach in this name," he said. "Yet you have filled Jerusalem with your teaching and are determined to make us guilty of this man's blood."

[29]Peter and the other apostles replied: "We must obey God rather than men! [30]The God of our fathers raised Jesus from the dead—whom you had killed by hanging him on a tree. [31]God exalted him to his own right hand as Prince and Savior that he might give repentance and forgiveness of sins to Israel. [32]We are witnesses of these things, and so is the Holy Spirit, whom God has given to those who obey him."

NEW LIVING TRANSLATION

[23]"The jail was locked, with the guards standing outside, but when we opened the gates, no one was there!"

[24]When the captain of the Temple guard and the leading priests heard this, they were perplexed, wondering where it would all end. [25]Then someone arrived with the news that the men they had jailed were out in the Temple, teaching the people.

[26]The captain went with his Temple guards and arrested them, but without violence, for they were afraid the people would kill them if they treated the apostles roughly. [27]Then they brought the apostles in before the council. [28]"Didn't we tell you never again to teach in this man's name?" the high priest demanded. "Instead, you have filled all Jerusalem with your teaching about Jesus, and you intend to blame us for his death!"

[29]But Peter and the apostles replied, "We must obey God rather than human authority. [30]The God of our ancestors raised Jesus from the dead after you killed him by crucifying him. [31]Then God put him in the place of honor at his right hand as Prince and Savior. He did this to give the people of Israel an opportunity to turn from their sins and turn to God so their sins would be forgiven. [32]We are witnesses of these things and so is the Holy Spirit, who is given by God to those who obey him."

NEW KING JAMES VERSION

we found the prison shut securely, and the guards standing outside[a] before the doors; but when we opened them, we found no one inside!" [24]Now when the high priest,[b] the captain of the temple, and the chief priests heard these things, they wondered what the outcome would be. [25]So one came and told them, saying,[c] "Look, the men whom you put in prison are standing in the temple and teaching the people!"

[26]Then the captain went with the officers and brought them without violence, for they feared the people, lest they should be stoned. [27]And when they had brought them, they set *them* before the council. And the high priest asked them, [28]saying, "Did we not strictly command you not to teach in this name? And look, you have filled Jerusalem with your doctrine, and intend to bring this Man's blood on us!"

[29]But Peter and the *other* apostles answered and said: "We ought to obey God rather than men. [30]The God of our fathers raised up Jesus whom you murdered by hanging on a tree. [31]Him God has exalted to His right hand *to be* Prince and Savior, to give repentance to Israel and forgiveness of sins. [32]And we are His witnesses to these things, and *so* also *is* the Holy Spirit whom God has given to those who obey Him."

5:23 [a] NU-Text and M-Text omit *outside.* 5:24 [b] NU-Text omits *the high priest.* 5:25 [c] NU-Text and M-Text omit *saying.*

THE MESSAGE

and reported, "We found the jail locked tight as a drum and the guards posted at the doors, but when we went inside we didn't find a soul."

The chief of the Temple police and the high priests were puzzled. "What's going on here anyway?"

Just then someone showed up and said, "Did you know that the men you put in jail are back in the Temple teaching the people?" The chief and his police went and got them, but they handled them gently, fearful that the people would riot and turn on them.

Bringing them back, they stood them before the High Council. The Chief Priest said, "Didn't we give you strict orders not to teach in Jesus' name? And here you have filled Jerusalem with your teaching and are trying your best to blame us for the death of this man."

Peter and the apostles answered, "It's necessary to obey God rather than men. The God of our ancestors raised up Jesus, the One you killed by hanging him on a cross. God set him on high at his side, Prince and Savior, to give Israel the gift of a changed life and sins forgiven. And we are witnesses to these things. The Holy Spirit, whom God gives to those who obey him, corroborates every detail."

KING JAMES VERSION

33 When they heard *that*, they were cut *to the heart*, and took counsel to slay them.

34 Then stood there up one in the council, a Pharisee, named Gamaliel, a doctor of the law, had in reputation among all the people, and commanded to put the apostles forth a little space;

35 And said unto them, Ye men of Israel, take heed to yourselves what ye intend to do as touching these men.

36 For before these days rose up Theudas, boasting himself to be somebody; to whom a number of men, about four hundred, joined themselves: who was slain; and all, as many as obeyed him, were scattered, and brought to nought.

37 After this man rose up Judas of Galilee in the days of the taxing, and drew away much people after him: he also perished; and all, *even* as many as obeyed him, were dispersed.

38 And now I say unto you, Refrain from these men, and let them alone: for if this counsel or this work be of men, it will come to nought:

39 But if it be of God, ye cannot overthrow it; lest haply ye be found even to fight against God.

40 And to him they agreed: and when they had called the apostles, and beaten *them*, they commanded that they should not speak in the name of Jesus, and let them go.

41 And they departed from the presence of the council, rejoicing that they were counted worthy to suffer shame for his name.

42 And daily in the temple, and in every house, they ceased not to teach and preach Jesus Christ.

NEW AMERICAN STANDARD BIBLE

Gamaliel's Counsel

33 But when they heard this, they were cut to the quick and intended to kill them.

34 But a Pharisee named Gamaliel, a teacher of the Law, respected by all the people, stood up in the Council and gave orders to put the men outside for a short time.

35 And he said to them, "Men of Israel, take care what you propose to do with these men.

36 "For some time ago Theudas rose up, claiming to be somebody, and a group of about four hundred men joined up with him. But he was killed, and all who followed him were dispersed and came to nothing.

37 "After this man, Judas of Galilee rose up in the days of the census and drew away *some* people after him; he too perished, and all those who followed him were scattered.

38 "So in the present case, I say to you, stay away from these men and let them alone, for if this plan or action is of men, it will be overthrown;

39 but if it is of God, you will not be able to overthrow them; or else you may even be found fighting against God."

40 They took his advice; and after calling the apostles in, they flogged them and ordered them not to speak in the name of Jesus, and *then* released them.

41 So they went on their way from the presence of the Council, rejoicing that they had been considered worthy to suffer shame for *His* name.

42 And every day, in the temple and from house to house, they kept right on teaching and preaching Jesus *as* the Christ.

NEW CENTURY VERSION

33When the Jewish leaders heard this, they became angry and wanted to kill them. 34But a Pharisee named Gamaliel stood up in the meeting. He was a teacher of the law, and all the people respected him. He ordered the apostles to leave the meeting for a little while. 35Then he said, "People of Israel, be careful what you are planning to do to these men. 36Remember when Theudas appeared? He said he was a great man, and about four hundred men joined him. But he was killed, and all his followers were scattered; they were able to do nothing. 37Later, a man named Judas came from Galilee at the time of the registration.[a] He also led a group of followers and was killed, and all his followers were scattered. 38And so now I tell you: Stay away from these men, and leave them alone. If their plan comes from human authority, it will fail. 39But if it is from God, you will not be able to stop them. You might even be fighting against God himself!"

The Jewish leaders agreed with what Gamaliel said. 40They called the apostles in, beat them, and told them not to speak in the name of Jesus again. Then they let them go free. 41The apostles left the meeting full of joy because they were given the honor of suffering disgrace for Jesus. 42Every day in the Temple and in people's homes they continued teaching the people and telling the Good News—that Jesus is the Christ.

5:37 [a] **registration** Census. A counting of all the people and the things they own.

CONTEMPORARY ENGLISH VERSION

33When the council members heard this, they became so angry that they wanted to kill the apostles. 34But one of the members was the Pharisee Gamaliel, a highly respected teacher. He ordered the apostles to be taken out of the room for a little while. 35Then he said to the council:

People of Israel, be careful what you do with these men. 36Not long ago Theudas claimed to be someone important, and about four hundred men joined him. But he was killed. All his followers were scattered, and that was the end of that.

37Later, when the people of our nation were being counted, Judas from Galilee showed up. A lot of people followed him, but he was killed, and all his followers were scattered.

38So I advise you to stay away from these men. Leave them alone. If what they are planning is something of their own doing, it will fail. 39But if God is behind it, you cannot stop it anyway, unless you want to fight against God.

The council members agreed with what he said, 40and they called the apostles back in. They had them beaten with a whip and warned them not to speak in the name of Jesus. Then they let them go.

41The apostles left the council and were happy, because God had considered them worthy to suffer for the sake of Jesus. 42Every day they spent time in the temple and in one home after another. They never stopped teaching and telling the good news that Jesus is the Messiah.

NEW INTERNATIONAL VERSION

[33]When they heard this, they were furious and wanted to put them to death. [34]But a Pharisee named Gamaliel, a teacher of the law, who was honored by all the people, stood up in the Sanhedrin and ordered that the men be put outside for a little while. [35]Then he addressed them: "Men of Israel, consider carefully what you intend to do to these men. [36]Some time ago Theudas appeared, claiming to be somebody, and about four hundred men rallied to him. He was killed, all his followers were dispersed, and it all came to nothing. [37]After him, Judas the Galilean appeared in the days of the census and led a band of people in revolt. He too was killed, and all his followers were scattered. [38]Therefore, in the present case I advise you: Leave these men alone! Let them go! For if their purpose or activity is of human origin, it will fail. [39]But if it is from God, you will not be able to stop these men; you will only find yourselves fighting against God."

[40]His speech persuaded them. They called the apostles in and had them flogged. Then they ordered them not to speak in the name of Jesus, and let them go.

[41]The apostles left the Sanhedrin, rejoicing because they had been counted worthy of suffering disgrace for the Name. [42]Day after day, in the temple courts and from house to house, they never stopped teaching and proclaiming the good news that Jesus is the Christ.[b]

[b] *42* Or *Messiah*

NEW LIVING TRANSLATION

[33]At this, the high council was furious and decided to kill them. [34]But one member had a different perspective. He was a Pharisee named Gamaliel, who was an expert on religious law and was very popular with the people. He stood up and ordered that the apostles be sent outside the council chamber for a while. [35]Then he addressed his colleagues as follows: "Men of Israel, take care what you are planning to do to these men! [36]Some time ago there was that fellow Theudas, who pretended to be someone great. About four hundred others joined him, but he was killed, and his followers went their various ways. The whole movement came to nothing. [37]After him, at the time of the census, there was Judas of Galilee. He got some people to follow him, but he was killed, too, and all his followers were scattered.

[38]"So my advice is, leave these men alone. If they are teaching and doing these things merely on their own, it will soon be overthrown. [39]But if it is of God, you will not be able to stop them. You may even find yourselves fighting against God."

[40]The council accepted his advice. They called in the apostles and had them flogged. Then they ordered them never again to speak in the name of Jesus, and they let them go. [41]The apostles left the high council rejoicing that God had counted them worthy to suffer dishonor for the name of Jesus. [42]And every day, in the Temple and in their homes,* they continued to teach and preach this message: "The Messiah you are looking for is Jesus."

5:42 Greek *from house to house.*

NEW KING JAMES VERSION

Gamaliel's Advice

[33]When they heard *this,* they were furious and plotted to kill them. [34]Then one in the council stood up, a Pharisee named Gamaliel, a teacher of the law held in respect by all the people, and commanded them to put the apostles outside for a little while. [35]And he said to them: "Men of Israel, take heed to yourselves what you intend to do regarding these men. [36]For some time ago Theudas rose up, claiming to be somebody. A number of men, about four hundred, joined him. He was slain, and all who obeyed him were scattered and came to nothing. [37]After this man, Judas of Galilee rose up in the days of the census, and drew away many people after him. He also perished, and all who obeyed him were dispersed. [38]And now I say to you, keep away from these men and let them alone; for if this plan or this work is of men, it will come to nothing; [39]but if it is of God, you cannot overthrow it—lest you even be found to fight against God."

[40]And they agreed with him, and when they had called for the apostles and beaten *them,* they commanded that they should not speak in the name of Jesus, and let them go. [41]So they departed from the presence of the council, rejoicing that they were counted worthy to suffer shame for His[d] name. [42]And daily in the temple, and in every house, they did not cease teaching and preaching Jesus *as* the Christ.

5:41 [d] NU-Text reads *the name;* M-Text reads *the name of Jesus.*

THE MESSAGE

When they heard that, they were furious and wanted to kill them on the spot. But one of the council members stood up, a Pharisee by the name of Gamaliel, a teacher of God's Law who was honored by everyone. He ordered the men taken out of the room for a short time, then said, "Fellow Israelites, be careful what you do to these men. Not long ago Theudas made something of a splash, claiming to be somebody, and got about four hundred men to join him. He was killed, his followers dispersed, and nothing came of it. A little later, at the time of the census, Judas the Galilean appeared and acquired a following. He also fizzled out and the people following him were scattered to the four winds.

"So I am telling you: Hands off these men! Let them alone. If this program or this work is merely human, it will fall apart, but if it is of God, there is nothing you can do about it—and you better not be found fighting against God!"

That convinced them. They called the apostles back in. After giving them a thorough whipping, they warned them not to speak in Jesus' name and sent them off. The apostles went out of the High Council overjoyed because they had been given the honor of being dishonored on account of the Name. Every day they were in the Temple and homes, teaching and preaching Christ Jesus, not letting up for a minute.

KING JAMES VERSION

6 And in those days, when the number of the disciples was multiplied, there arose a murmuring of the Grecians against the Hebrews, because their widows were neglected in the daily ministration.

2 Then the twelve called the multitude of the disciples *unto them*, and said, It is not reason that we should leave the word of God, and serve tables.

3 Wherefore, brethren, look ye out among you seven men of honest report, full of the Holy Ghost and wisdom, whom we may appoint over this business.

4 But we will give ourselves continually to prayer, and to the ministry of the word.

5 And the saying pleased the whole multitude: and they chose Stephen, a man full of faith and of the Holy Ghost, and Philip, and Prochorus, and Nicanor, and Timon, and Parmenas, and Nicolas a proselyte of Antioch:

6 Whom they set before the apostles: and when they had prayed, they laid *their* hands on them.

7 And the word of God increased; and the number of the disciples multiplied in Jerusalem greatly; and a great company of the priests were obedient to the faith.

NEW AMERICAN STANDARD BIBLE

Choosing of the Seven

6 Now at this time while the disciples were increasing *in number*, a complaint arose on the part of the [1]Hellenistic *Jews* against the *native* Hebrews, because their widows were being overlooked in the daily serving *of food*.

2 So the twelve summoned the congregation of the disciples and said, "It is not desirable for us to neglect the word of God in order to serve tables.

3 "Therefore, brethren, select from among you seven men of good reputation, full of the Spirit and of wisdom, whom we may put in charge of this task.

4 "But we will devote ourselves to prayer and to the ministry of the word."

5 The statement found approval with the whole congregation; and they chose Stephen, a man full of faith and of the Holy Spirit, and Philip, Prochorus, Nicanor, Timon, Parmenas and Nicolas, a [2]proselyte from Antioch.

6 And these they brought before the apostles; and after praying, they laid their hands on them.

7 The word of God kept on spreading; and the number of the disciples continued to increase greatly in Jerusalem, and a great many of the priests were becoming obedient to the faith.

6:1 [1] Jews who adopted the Gr language and much of Gr culture throughout acculturation 6:5 [2] I.e. a Gentile convert to Judaism

NEW CENTURY VERSION

Seven Leaders Are Chosen

6 The number of followers was growing. But during this same time, the Greek-speaking followers had an argument with the other Jewish followers. The Greek-speaking widows were not getting their share of the food that was given out every day. 2 The twelve apostles called the whole group of followers together and said, "It is not right for us to stop our work of teaching God's word in order to serve tables. 3 So, brothers and sisters, choose seven of your own men who are good, full of the Spirit and full of wisdom. We will put them in charge of this work. 4 Then we can continue to pray and to teach the word of God."

5 The whole group liked the idea, so they chose these seven men: Stephen (a man with great faith and full of the Holy Spirit), Philip,[a] Procorus, Nicanor, Timon, Parmenas, and Nicolas (a man from Antioch who had become a Jew). 6 Then they put these men before the apostles, who prayed and laid their hands[b] on them.

7 The word of God was continuing to spread. The group of followers in Jerusalem increased, and a great number of the Jewish priests believed and obeyed.

6:5 [a] **Philip** Not the apostle named Philip. 6:6 [b] **laid their hands** The laying on of hands had many purposes, including the giving of a blessing, power, or authority.

CONTEMPORARY ENGLISH VERSION

Seven Leaders for the Church

6 A lot of people were now becoming followers of the Lord. But some of the ones who spoke Greek started complaining about the ones who spoke Aramaic. They complained that the Greek-speaking widows were not given their share when the food supplies were handed out each day.

2 The twelve apostles called the whole group of followers together and said, "We should not give up preaching God's message in order to serve at tables.[a] 3 My friends, choose seven men who are respected and wise and filled with God's Spirit. We will put them in charge of these things. 4 We can spend our time praying and serving God by preaching."

5 This suggestion pleased everyone, and they began by choosing Stephen. He had great faith and was filled with the Holy Spirit. Then they chose Philip, Prochorus, Nicanor, Timon, Parmenas, and also Nicolaus, who worshiped with the Jewish people[b] in Antioch. 6 These men were brought to the apostles. Then the apostles prayed and placed their hands on the men to show that they had been chosen to do this work. 7 God's message spread, and many more people in Jerusalem became followers. Even a large number of priests put their faith in the Lord.

[a] **6.2** *to serve at tables*: This may mean either that they were in charge of handing out food to the widows or that they were in charge of the money, since the Greek word "table" may also mean "bank." [b] **6.5** *worshiped with the Jewish people*: This translates the Greek word "proselyte" that means a Gentile who had accepted the Jewish religion.

NEW INTERNATIONAL VERSION

The Choosing of the Seven

6 In those days when the number of disciples was
increasing, the Grecian Jews among them complained
against the Hebraic Jews because their widows were being
overlooked in the daily distribution of food. 2So the Twelve
gathered all the disciples together and said, "It would not
be right for us to neglect the ministry of the word of God in
order to wait on tables. 3Brothers, choose seven men from
among you who are known to be full of the Spirit and wis-
dom. We will turn this responsibility over to them 4and
will give our attention to prayer and the ministry of the
word."
5This proposal pleased the whole group. They chose
Stephen, a man full of faith and of the Holy Spirit; also
Philip, Procorus, Nicanor, Timon, Parmenas, and Nicolas
from Antioch, a convert to Judaism. 6They presented these
men to the apostles, who prayed and laid their hands on
them.
7So the word of God spread. The number of disciples in
Jerusalem increased rapidly, and a large number of priests
became obedient to the faith.

NEW LIVING TRANSLATION

Seven Men Chosen to Serve

6 But as the believers* rapidly multiplied, there were
rumblings of discontent. Those who spoke Greek com-
plained against those who spoke Hebrew, saying that their
widows were being discriminated against in the daily dis-
tribution of food. 2So the Twelve called a meeting of all the
believers.
"We apostles should spend our time preaching and
teaching the word of God, not administering a food pro-
gram," they said. 3"Now look around among yourselves,
brothers, and select seven men who are well respected and
are full of the Holy Spirit and wisdom. We will put them in
charge of this business. 4Then we can spend our time in
prayer and preaching and teaching the word."
5This idea pleased the whole group, and they chose the
following: Stephen (a man full of faith and the Holy
Spirit), Philip, Procorus, Nicanor, Timon, Parmenas, and
Nicolas of Antioch (a Gentile convert to the Jewish faith,
who had now become a Christian). 6These seven were pre-
sented to the apostles, who prayed for them as they laid
their hands on them.
7God's message was preached in ever-widening circles.
The number of believers greatly increased in Jerusalem,
and many of the Jewish priests were converted, too.

6:1 Greek *disciples;* also in 6:2, 7.

NEW KING JAMES VERSION

Seven Chosen to Serve

6 Now in those days, when *the number of* the disciples
was multiplying, there arose a complaint against the
Hebrews by the Hellenists,[a] because their widows were
neglected in the daily distribution. 2Then the twelve sum-
moned the multitude of the disciples and said, "It is not
desirable that we should leave the word of God and serve
tables. 3Therefore, brethren, seek out from among you
seven men of *good* reputation, full of the Holy Spirit and
wisdom, whom we may appoint over this business; 4but
we will give ourselves continually to prayer and to the
ministry of the word."
5And the saying pleased the whole multitude. And they
chose Stephen, a man full of faith and the Holy Spirit, and
Philip, Prochorus, Nicanor, Timon, Parmenas, and Nicolas,
a proselyte from Antioch, 6whom they set before the apos-
tles; and when they had prayed, they laid hands on them.
7Then the word of God spread, and the number of the
disciples multiplied greatly in Jerusalem, and a great many
of the priests were obedient to the faith.

6:1 [a] That is, Greek-speaking Jews

THE MESSAGE

The Word of God Prospered

6 During this time, as the disciples were increasing in numbers by leaps and bounds, hard feelings developed among the Greek-speaking believers—"Hellenists"—toward the Hebrew-speaking believers because their widows were being discriminated against in the daily food lines. So the Twelve called a meeting of the disciples. They said, "It wouldn't be right for us to abandon our responsibilities for preaching and teaching the Word of God to help with the care of the poor. So, friends, choose seven men from among you whom everyone trusts, men full of the Holy Spirit and good sense, and we'll assign them this task. Meanwhile, we'll stick to our assigned tasks of prayer and speaking God's Word."

The congregation thought this was a great idea. They went ahead and chose—

Stephen, a man full of faith and the Holy Spirit,
Philip,
Procorus,
Nicanor,
Timon,
Parmenas,
Nicolas, a convert from Antioch.

Then they presented them to the apostles. Praying, the apostles laid on hands and commissioned them for their task.

The Word of God prospered. The number of disciples in Jerusalem increased dramatically. Not least, a great many priests submitted themselves to the faith.

KING JAMES VERSION

8 ¶ And Stephen, full of faith and power, did great wonders and miracles among the people.

9 Then there arose certain of the synagogue, which is called *the synagogue* of the Libertines, and Cyrenians, and Alexandrians, and of them of Cilicia and of Asia, disputing with Stephen.

10 And they were not able to resist the wisdom and the spirit by which he spake.

11 Then they suborned men, which said, We have heard him speak blasphemous words against Moses, and *against* God.

12 And they stirred up the people, and the elders, and the scribes, and came upon *him*, and caught him, and brought *him* to the council,

13 And set up false witnesses, which said, This man ceaseth not to speak blasphemous words against this holy place, and the law:

14 For we have heard him say, that this Jesus of Nazareth shall destroy this place, and shall change the customs which Moses delivered us.

15 And all that sat in the council, looking stedfastly on him, saw his face as it had been the face of an angel.

7 Then said the high priest, Are these things so?

2 And he said, Men, brethren, and fathers, hearken; The God of glory appeared unto our father Abraham, when he was in Mesopotamia, before he dwelt in Charran,

NEW AMERICAN STANDARD BIBLE

8 And Stephen, full of grace and power, was performing great wonders and signs among the people.

9 But some men from what was called the Synagogue of the Freedmen, *including* both Cyrenians and Alexandrians, and some from Cilicia and Asia, rose up and argued with Stephen.

10 But they were unable to cope with the wisdom and the Spirit with which he was speaking.

11 Then they secretly induced men to say, "We have heard him speak blasphemous words against Moses and *against* God."

12 And they stirred up the people, the elders and the scribes, and they came up to him and dragged him away and brought him before the Council.

13 They put forward false witnesses who said, "This man incessantly speaks against this holy place and the Law;

14 for we have heard him say that this Nazarene, Jesus, will destroy this place and alter the customs which Moses handed down to us."

15 And fixing their gaze on him, all who were sitting in the Council saw his face like the face of an angel.

Stephen's Defense

7 The high priest said, "Are these things so?"

2 And he said, "Hear me, brethren and fathers! The God of glory appeared to our father Abraham when he was in Mesopotamia, before he lived in Haran,

NEW CENTURY VERSION

Stephen Is Accused

8Stephen was richly blessed by God who gave him the
power to do great miracles and signs among the people.
9But some Jewish people were against him. They belonged
to the synagogue of Free Men[c] (as it was called), which
included Jewish people from Cyrene, Alexandria, Cilicia,
and Asia. They all came and argued with Stephen.
10But the Spirit was helping him to speak with wisdom,
and his words were so strong that they could not argue
with him. 11So they secretly urged some men to say, "We
heard Stephen speak against Moses and against God."
12This upset the people, the older Jewish leaders, and
the teachers of the law. They came and grabbed Stephen
and brought him to a meeting of the Jewish leaders. 13They
brought in some people to tell lies about Stephen, saying,
"This man is always speaking against this holy place and
the law of Moses. 14We heard him say that Jesus from
Nazareth will destroy this place and that Jesus will change
the customs Moses gave us." 15All the people in the meet-
ing were watching Stephen closely and saw that his face
looked like the face of an angel.

Stephen's Speech

7 The high priest said to Stephen, "Are these things true?"
2Stephen answered, "Brothers and fathers, listen to
me. Our glorious God appeared to Abraham, our ancestor,
in Mesopotamia before he lived in Haran. 3God said to

6:9 [c] **Free Men** Jewish people who had been slaves or whose fathers had been slaves, but were now free.

CONTEMPORARY ENGLISH VERSION

Stephen Is Arrested

8God gave Stephen the power to work great miracles and
wonders among the people. 9But some Jews from Cyrene
and Alexandria were members of a group who called them-
selves "Free Men."[c] They started arguing with Stephen.
Some others from Cilicia and Asia also argued with him.
10But they were no match for Stephen, who spoke with the
great wisdom that the Spirit gave him. 11So they talked
some men into saying, "We heard Stephen say terrible
things against Moses and God!"
12They turned the people and their leaders and the teach-
ers of the Law of Moses against Stephen. Then they all
grabbed Stephen and dragged him in front of the council.
13Some men agreed to tell lies about Stephen, and they
said, "This man keeps on saying terrible things about this
holy temple and the Law of Moses. 14We have heard him
claim that Jesus from Nazareth will destroy this place and
change the customs that Moses gave us." 15Then all the
council members stared at Stephen. They saw that his face
looked like the face of an angel.

Stephen's Speech

7 The high priest asked Stephen, "Are they telling the truth about you?"
2Stephen answered:

Friends, listen to me. Our glorious God appeared to our ancestor Abraham while he was still in Mesopotamia,

[c] 6.9 *Free Men*: A group of Jewish men who had once been slaves, but had been freed.

NEW INTERNATIONAL VERSION

Stephen Seized

[8]Now Stephen, a man full of God's grace and power, did great wonders and miraculous signs among the people. [9]Opposition arose, however, from members of the Synagogue of the Freedmen (as it was called)—Jews of Cyrene and Alexandria as well as the provinces of Cilicia and Asia. These men began to argue with Stephen, [10]but they could not stand up against his wisdom or the Spirit by whom he spoke.

[11]Then they secretly persuaded some men to say, "We have heard Stephen speak words of blasphemy against Moses and against God."

[12]So they stirred up the people and the elders and the teachers of the law. They seized Stephen and brought him before the Sanhedrin. [13]They produced false witnesses, who testified, "This fellow never stops speaking against this holy place and against the law. [14]For we have heard him say that this Jesus of Nazareth will destroy this place and change the customs Moses handed down to us."

[15]All who were sitting in the Sanhedrin looked intently at Stephen, and they saw that his face was like the face of an angel.

Stephen's Speech to the Sanhedrin

7 Then the high priest asked him, "Are these charges true?"

[2]To this he replied: "Brothers and fathers, listen to me! The God of glory appeared to our father Abraham while he was still in Mesopotamia, before he lived in Haran. [3]'Leave

NEW LIVING TRANSLATION

Stephen Is Arrested

[8]Stephen, a man full of God's grace and power, performed amazing miracles and signs among the people. [9]But one day some men from the Synagogue of Freed Slaves, as it was called, started to debate with him. They were Jews from Cyrene, Alexandria, Cilicia, and the province of Asia. [10]None of them was able to stand against the wisdom and Spirit by which Stephen spoke.

[11]So they persuaded some men to lie about Stephen, saying, "We heard him blaspheme Moses, and even God." [12]Naturally, this roused the crowds, the elders, and the teachers of religious law. So they arrested Stephen and brought him before the high council.* [13]The lying witnesses said, "This man is always speaking against the Temple and against the law of Moses. [14]We have heard him say that this Jesus of Nazareth will destroy the Temple and change the customs Moses handed down to us." [15]At this point everyone in the council stared at Stephen because his face became as bright as an angel's.

Stephen Addresses the Council

7 Then the high priest asked Stephen, "Are these accusations true?"

[2]This was Stephen's reply: "Brothers and honorable fathers, listen to me. Our glorious God appeared to our ancestor Abraham in Mesopotamia before he moved to

6:12 Greek *Sanhedrin;* also in 6:15.

NEW KING JAMES VERSION

Stephen Accused of Blasphemy

[8]And Stephen, full of faith[b] and power, did great wonders and signs among the people. [9]Then there arose some from what is called the Synagogue of the Freedmen (Cyrenians, Alexandrians, and those from Cilicia and Asia), disputing with Stephen. [10]And they were not able to resist the wisdom and the Spirit by which he spoke. [11]Then they secretly induced men to say, "We have heard him speak blasphemous words against Moses and God." [12]And they stirred up the people, the elders, and the scribes; and they came upon *him,* seized him, and brought *him* to the council. [13]They also set up false witnesses who said, "This man does not cease to speak blasphemous[c] words against this holy place and the law; [14]for we have heard him say that this Jesus of Nazareth will destroy this place and change the customs which Moses delivered to us." [15]And all who sat in the council, looking steadfastly at him, saw his face as the face of an angel.

Stephen's Address: The Call of Abraham

7 Then the high priest said, "Are these things so?"

[2]And he said, "Brethren and fathers, listen: The God of glory appeared to our father Abraham when he was in Mesopotamia, before he dwelt in Haran, [3]and said to him,

6:8 [b] NU-Text reads *grace.* 6:13 [c] NU-Text omits *blasphemous.*

THE MESSAGE

✠

Stephen, brimming with God's grace and energy, was doing wonderful things among the people, unmistakable signs that God was among them. But then some men from the meeting place whose membership was made up of freed slaves, Cyrenians, Alexandrians, and some others from Cilicia and Asia, went up against him trying to argue him down. But they were no match for his wisdom and spirit when he spoke.

So in secret they bribed men to lie: "We heard him cursing Moses and God."

That stirred up the people, the religious leaders, and religion scholars. They grabbed Stephen and took him before the High Council. They put forward their bribed witnesses to testify: "This man talks nonstop against this Holy Place and God's Law. We even heard him say that Jesus of Nazareth would tear this place down and throw out all the customs Moses gave us."

As all those who sat on the High Council looked at Stephen, they found they couldn't take their eyes off him—his face was like the face of an angel!

Stephen, Full of the Holy Spirit

7 Then the Chief Priest said, "What do you have to say for yourself?"

Stephen replied, "Friends, fathers, and brothers, the God of glory appeared to our father Abraham when he was still in Mesopotamia, before the move to Haran, and told him,

KING JAMES VERSION

3 And said unto him, Get thee out of thy country, and from thy kindred, and come into the land which I shall shew thee.

4 Then came he out of the land of the Chaldaeans, and dwelt in Charran: and from thence, when his father was dead, he removed him into this land, wherein ye now dwell.

5 And he gave him none inheritance in it, no, not *so much as* to set his foot on: yet he promised that he would give it to him for a possession, and to his seed after him, when *as yet* he had no child.

6 And God spake on this wise, That his seed should sojourn in a strange land; and that they should bring them into bondage, and entreat *them* evil four hundred years.

7 And the nation to whom they shall be in bondage will I judge, said God: and after that shall they come forth, and serve me in this place.

8 And he gave him the covenant of circumcision: and so *Abraham* begat Isaac, and circumcised him the eighth day; and Isaac *begat* Jacob; and Jacob *begat* the twelve patriarchs.

9 And the patriarchs, moved with envy, sold Joseph into Egypt: but God was with him,

10 And delivered him out of all his afflictions, and gave him favour and wisdom in the sight of Pharaoh king of Egypt; and he made him governor over Egypt and all his house.

NEW AMERICAN STANDARD BIBLE

3 and said to him, 'LEAVE YOUR COUNTRY AND YOUR RELATIVES, AND COME INTO THE LAND THAT I WILL SHOW YOU.'

4 "Then he left the land of the Chaldeans and settled in Haran. From there, after his father died, *God* had him move to this country in which you are now living.

5 "But He gave him no inheritance in it, not even a foot of ground, and *yet,* even when he had no child, He promised that HE WOULD GIVE IT TO HIM AS A POSSESSION, AND TO HIS DESCENDANTS AFTER HIM.

6 "But God spoke to this effect, that his DESCENDANTS WOULD BE ALIENS IN A FOREIGN LAND, AND THAT THEY WOULD BE ENSLAVED AND MISTREATED FOR FOUR HUNDRED YEARS.

7 " 'AND WHATEVER NATION TO WHICH THEY WILL BE IN BONDAGE I MYSELF WILL JUDGE,' said God, 'AND AFTER THAT THEY WILL COME OUT AND [1]SERVE ME IN THIS PLACE.'

8 "And He gave him the covenant of circumcision; and so *Abraham* became the father of Isaac, and circumcised him on the eighth day; and Isaac *became the father of* Jacob, and Jacob *of* the twelve patriarchs.

9 "The patriarchs became jealous of Joseph and sold him into Egypt. *Yet* God was with him,

10 and rescued him from all his afflictions, and granted him favor and wisdom in the sight of Pharaoh, king of Egypt, and he made him governor over Egypt and all his household.

7:7 [1] Or *worship*

NEW CENTURY VERSION

Abraham, 'Leave your country and your relatives, and go
to the land I will show you.'[a] 4So Abraham left the country
of Chaldea and went to live in Haran. After Abraham's
father died, God sent him to this place where you now live.
5God did not give Abraham any of this land, not even a
foot of it. But God promised that he would give this land to
him and his descendants, even before Abraham had a
child. 6This is what God said to him: 'Your descendants
will be strangers in a land they don't own. The people
there will make them slaves and will mistreat them for
four hundred years. 7But I will punish the nation where
they are slaves. Then your descendants will leave that land
and will worship me in this place.'[b] 8God made an agree-
ment with Abraham, the sign of which was circumcision.
And so when Abraham had his son Isaac, Abraham cir-
cumcised him when he was eight days old. Isaac also cir-
cumcised his son Jacob, and Jacob did the same for his
sons, the twelve ancestors[c] of our people.
9"Jacob's sons became jealous of Joseph and sold him to
be a slave in Egypt. But God was with him 10and saved
him from all his troubles. The king of Egypt liked Joseph
and respected him because of the wisdom God gave him.
The king made him governor of Egypt and put him in
charge of all the people in his palace.

7:3 [a] **'Leave...you.'** Quotation from Genesis 12:1. 7:7 [b] **'Your descendants...place.'** Quotation from Genesis 15:13–14 and Exodus 3:12. 7:8 [c] **twelve ancestors** Important ancestors of the Jewish people; the leaders of the twelve Jewish tribes.

CONTEMPORARY ENGLISH VERSION

before he had moved to Haran. 3God told him, "Leave
your country and your relatives and go to a land that I
will show you." 4Then Abraham left the land of the
Chaldeans and settled in Haran.

After his father died, Abraham came and settled in
this land where you now live. 5God didn't give him any
part of it, not even a square foot. But God did promise to
give it to him and his family forever, even though
Abraham didn't have any children. 6God said that
Abraham's descendants would live for a while in a for-
eign land. There they would be slaves and would be mis-
treated four hundred years. 7But he also said, "I will
punish the nation that makes them slaves. Then later
they will come and worship me in this place."

8God said to Abraham, "Every son in each family
must be circumcised to show that you have kept your
agreement with me." So when Isaac was eight days old,
Abraham circumcised him. Later, Isaac circumcised his
son Jacob, and Jacob circumcised his twelve sons. 9These
men were our ancestors.

Joseph was also one of our famous ancestors. His
brothers were jealous of him and sold him as a slave to
be taken to Egypt. But God was with him 10and rescued
him from all his troubles. God made him so wise that
the Egyptian king Pharaoh[a] thought highly of him. The
king even made Joseph governor over Egypt and put him
in charge of everything he owned.

[a] **7.10** *Pharaoh*: A Hebrew word sometimes used for the title of the King of Egypt.

NEW INTERNATIONAL VERSION

your country and your people,' God said, 'and go to the land I will show you.'[a]

[4]"So he left the land of the Chaldeans and settled in Haran. After the death of his father, God sent him to this land where you are now living. [5]He gave him no inheritance here, not even a foot of ground. But God promised him that he and his descendants after him would possess the land, even though at that time Abraham had no child. [6]God spoke to him in this way: 'Your descendants will be strangers in a country not their own, and they will be enslaved and mistreated four hundred years. [7]But I will punish the nation they serve as slaves,' God said, 'and afterward they will come out of that country and worship me in this place.'[b] [8]Then he gave Abraham the covenant of circumcision. And Abraham became the father of Isaac and circumcised him eight days after his birth. Later Isaac became the father of Jacob, and Jacob became the father of the twelve patriarchs.

[9]"Because the patriarchs were jealous of Joseph, they sold him as a slave into Egypt. But God was with him [10]and rescued him from all his troubles. He gave Joseph wisdom and enabled him to gain the goodwill of Pharaoh king of Egypt; so he made him ruler over Egypt and all his palace.

[a] *3* Gen. 12:1 [b] *7* Gen. 15:13,14

NEW LIVING TRANSLATION

Haran.* [3]God told him, 'Leave your native land and your relatives, and come to the land that I will show you.'* [4]So Abraham left the land of the Chaldeans and lived in Haran until his father died. Then God brought him here to the land where you now live. [5]But God gave him no inheritance here, not even one square foot of land. God did promise, however, that eventually the whole country would belong to Abraham and his descendants—though he had no children yet. [6]But God also told him that his descendants would live in a foreign country where they would be mistreated as slaves for four hundred years. [7]'But I will punish the nation that enslaves them,' God told him, 'and in the end they will come out and worship me in this place.'* [8]God also gave Abraham the covenant of circumcision at that time. And so Isaac, Abraham's son, was circumcised when he was eight days old. Isaac became the father of Jacob, and Jacob was the father of the twelve patriarchs of the Jewish nation.

[9]"These sons of Jacob were very jealous of their brother Joseph, and they sold him to be a slave in Egypt. But God was with him [10]and delivered him from his anguish. And God gave him favor before Pharaoh, king of Egypt. God also gave Joseph unusual wisdom, so that Pharaoh appointed him governor over all of Egypt and put him in charge of all the affairs of the palace.

7:2 *Mesopotamia* was the region now called Iraq. *Haran* was a city in what is now called Syria. 7:3 Gen 12:1. 7:5-7 Gen 12:7; 15:13-14; Exod 3:12.

NEW KING JAMES VERSION

'Get out of your country and from your relatives, and come to a land that I will show you.'[a] [4]Then he came out of the land of the Chaldeans and dwelt in Haran. And from there, when his father was dead, He moved him to this land in which you now dwell. [5]And *God* gave him no inheritance in it, not even *enough* to set his foot on. But even when *Abraham* had no child, He promised to give it to him for a possession, and to his descendants after him. [6]But God spoke in this way: that his descendants would dwell in a foreign land, and that they would bring them into bondage and oppress *them* four hundred years. [7]*'And the nation to whom they will be in bondage I will judge,'*[b] said God, *'and after that they shall come out and serve Me in this place.'*[c] [8]Then He gave him the covenant of circumcision; and so *Abraham* begot Isaac and circumcised him on the eighth day; and Isaac *begot* Jacob, and Jacob *begot* the twelve patriarchs.

The Patriarchs in Egypt

[9]"And the patriarchs, becoming envious, sold Joseph into Egypt. But God was with him [10]and delivered him out of all his troubles, and gave him favor and wisdom in the presence of Pharaoh, king of Egypt; and he made him governor over Egypt and all his house. [11]Now a famine and

7:3 [a] Genesis 12:1 7:7 [b] Genesis 15:14 [c] Exodus 3:12

THE MESSAGE

'Leave your country and family and go to the land I'll show you.'

"So he left the country of the Chaldees and moved to Haran. After the death of his father, he immigrated to this country where you now live, but God gave him nothing, not so much as a foothold. He did promise to give the country to him and his son later on, even though Abraham had no son at the time. God let him know that his offspring would move to an alien country where they would be enslaved and brutalized for four hundred years. 'But,' God said, 'I will step in and take care of those slaveholders and bring my people out so they can worship me in this place.'

"Then he made a covenant with him and signed it in Abraham's flesh by circumcision. When Abraham had his son Isaac, within eight days he reproduced the sign of circumcision in him. Isaac became father of Jacob, and Jacob father of twelve 'fathers,' each faithfully passing on the covenant sign.

"But then those 'fathers,' burning up with jealousy, sent Joseph off to Egypt as a slave. God was right there with him, though—he not only rescued him from all his troubles but brought him to the attention of Pharaoh, king of Egypt. He was so impressed with Joseph that he put him in charge of the whole country, including his own personal affairs.

KING JAMES VERSION

11 Now there came a dearth over all the land of Egypt and Chanaan, and great affliction: and our fathers found no sustenance.

12 But when Jacob heard that there was corn in Egypt, he sent out our fathers first.

13 And at the second *time* Joseph was made known to his brethren; and Joseph's kindred was made known unto Pharaoh.

14 Then sent Joseph, and called his father Jacob to *him*, and all his kindred, threescore and fifteen souls.

15 So Jacob went down into Egypt, and died, he, and our fathers,

16 And were carried over into Sychem, and laid in the sepulchre that Abraham bought for a sum of money of the sons of Emmor *the father* of Sychem.

17 ¶ But when the time of the promise drew nigh, which God had sworn to Abraham, the people grew and multiplied in Egypt,

18 Till another king arose, which knew not Joseph.

19 The same dealt subtilly with our kindred, and evil entreated our fathers, so that they cast out their young children, to the end they might not live.

20 In which time Moses was born, and was exceeding fair, and nourished up in his father's house three months:

21 And when he was cast out, Pharaoh's daughter took him up, and nourished him for her own son.

22 And Moses was learned in all the wisdom of the Egyptians, and was mighty in words and in deeds.

NEW AMERICAN STANDARD BIBLE

11 "Now a famine came over all Egypt and Canaan, and great affliction *with it,* and our fathers could find no food.

12 "But when Jacob heard that there was grain in Egypt, he sent our fathers *there* the first time.

13 "On the second *visit* Joseph made himself known to his brothers, and Joseph's family was disclosed to Pharaoh.

14 "Then Joseph sent *word* and invited Jacob his father and all his relatives to come to him, seventy-five persons *in all.*

15 "And Jacob went down to Egypt and *there* he and our fathers died.

16 "*From there* they were removed to Shechem and laid in the tomb which Abraham had purchased for a sum of money from the sons of Hamor in Shechem.

17 "But as the time of the promise was approaching which God had assured to Abraham, the people increased and multiplied in Egypt,

18 until THERE AROSE ANOTHER KING OVER EGYPT WHO KNEW NOTHING ABOUT JOSEPH.

19 "It was he who took shrewd advantage of our race and mistreated our fathers so that they would expose their infants and they would not survive.

20 "It was at this time that Moses was born; and he was lovely in the sight of God, and he was nurtured three months in his father's home.

21 "And after he had been set outside, Pharaoh's daughter took him away and nurtured him as her own son.

22 "Moses was educated in all the learning of the Egyptians, and he was a man of power in words and deeds.

NEW CENTURY VERSION

11 "Then all the land of Egypt and Canaan became so dry that nothing would grow, and the people suffered very much. Jacob's sons, our ancestors, could not find anything to eat. 12 But when Jacob heard there was grain in Egypt, he sent his sons there. This was their first trip to Egypt. 13 When they went there a second time, Joseph told his brothers who he was, and the king learned about Joseph's family. 14 Then Joseph sent messengers to invite Jacob, his father, to come to Egypt along with all his relatives (seventy-five persons altogether). 15 So Jacob went down to Egypt, where he and his sons died. 16 Later their bodies were moved to Shechem and put in a grave there. (It was the same grave Abraham had bought for a sum of money from the sons of Hamor in Shechem.)

17 "The promise God made to Abraham was soon to come true, and the number of people in Egypt grew large. 18 Then a new king, who did not know who Joseph was, began to rule Egypt. 19 This king tricked our people and was cruel to our ancestors, forcing them to leave their babies outside to die. 20 At this time Moses was born, and he was very beautiful. For three months Moses was cared for in his father's house. 21 When they put Moses outside, the king's daughter adopted him and raised him as if he were her own son. 22 The Egyptians taught Moses everything they knew, and he was a powerful man in what he said and did.

CONTEMPORARY ENGLISH VERSION

11 Everywhere in Egypt and Canaan the grain crops failed. There was terrible suffering, and our ancestors could not find enough to eat. 12 But when Jacob heard that there was grain in Egypt, he sent our ancestors there for the first time. 13 It was on their second trip that Joseph told his brothers who he was, and Pharaoh learned about Joseph's family.

14 Joseph sent for his father and his relatives. In all, there were seventy-five of them. 15 His father went to Egypt and died there, just as our ancestors did. 16 Later their bodies were taken back to Shechem and placed in the tomb that Abraham had bought from the sons of Hamor.

17 Finally, the time came for God to do what he had promised Abraham. By then the number of our people in Egypt had greatly increased. 18 Another king was ruling Egypt, and he didn't know anything about Joseph. 19 He tricked our ancestors and was cruel to them. He even made them leave their babies outside, so they would die.

20 During this time Moses was born. He was a very beautiful child, and for three months his parents took care of him in their home. 21 Then when they were forced to leave him outside, the king's daughter found him and raised him as her own son. 22 Moses was given the best education in Egypt. He was a strong man and a powerful speaker.

NEW INTERNATIONAL VERSION

[11]"Then a famine struck all Egypt and Canaan, bringing great suffering, and our fathers could not find food. [12]When Jacob heard that there was grain in Egypt, he sent our fathers on their first visit. [13]On their second visit, Joseph told his brothers who he was, and Pharaoh learned about Joseph's family. [14]After this, Joseph sent for his father Jacob and his whole family, seventy-five in all. [15]Then Jacob went down to Egypt, where he and our fathers died. [16]Their bodies were brought back to Shechem and placed in the tomb that Abraham had bought from the sons of Hamor at Shechem for a certain sum of money.

[17]"As the time drew near for God to fulfill his promise to Abraham, the number of our people in Egypt greatly increased. [18]Then another king, who knew nothing about Joseph, became ruler of Egypt. [19]He dealt treacherously with our people and oppressed our forefathers by forcing them to throw out their newborn babies so that they would die.

[20]"At that time Moses was born, and he was no ordinary child.[c] For three months he was cared for in his father's house. [21]When he was placed outside, Pharaoh's daughter took him and brought him up as her own son. [22]Moses was educated in all the wisdom of the Egyptians and was powerful in speech and action.

[c] *20* Or *was fair in the sight of God*

NEW LIVING TRANSLATION

[11]"But a famine came upon Egypt and Canaan. There was great misery for our ancestors, as they ran out of food. [12]Jacob heard that there was still grain in Egypt, so he sent his sons* to buy some. [13]The second time they went, Joseph revealed his identity to his brothers, and they were introduced to Pharaoh. [14]Then Joseph sent for his father, Jacob, and all his relatives to come to Egypt, seventy-five persons in all. [15]So Jacob went to Egypt. He died there, as did all his sons. [16]All of them were taken to Shechem and buried in the tomb Abraham had bought from the sons of Hamor in Shechem.

[17]"As the time drew near when God would fulfill his promise to Abraham, the number of our people in Egypt greatly increased. [18]But then a new king came to the throne of Egypt who knew nothing about Joseph. [19]This king plotted against our people and forced parents to abandon their newborn babies so they would die.

[20]"At that time Moses was born—a beautiful child in God's eyes. His parents cared for him at home for three months. [21]When at last they had to abandon him, Pharaoh's daughter found him and raised him as her own son. [22]Moses was taught all the wisdom of the Egyptians, and he became mighty in both speech and action.

7:12 Greek *our fathers;* also in 7:15.

NEW KING JAMES VERSION

great trouble came over all the land of Egypt and Canaan, and our fathers found no sustenance. [12]But when Jacob heard that there was grain in Egypt, he sent out our fathers first. [13]And the second *time* Joseph was made known to his brothers, and Joseph's family became known to the Pharaoh. [14]Then Joseph sent and called his father Jacob and all his relatives to *him,* seventy-five[d] people. [15]So Jacob went down to Egypt; and he died, he and our fathers. [16]And they were carried back to Shechem and laid in the tomb that Abraham bought for a sum of money from the sons of Hamor, *the father* of Shechem.

God Delivers Israel by Moses

[17]"But when the time of the promise drew near which God had sworn to Abraham, the people grew and multiplied in Egypt [18]till another king arose who did not know Joseph. [19]This man dealt treacherously with our people, and oppressed our forefathers, making them expose their babies, so that they might not live. [20]At this time Moses was born, and was well pleasing to God; and he was brought up in his father's house for three months. [21]But when he was set out, Pharaoh's daughter took him away and brought him up as her own son. [22]And Moses was learned in all the wisdom of the Egyptians, and was mighty in words and deeds.

7:14 [d] Or *seventy* (compare Exodus 1:5)

THE MESSAGE

"Later a famine descended on that entire region, stretching from Egypt to Canaan, bringing terrific hardship. Our hungry fathers looked high and low for food, but the cupboard was bare. Jacob heard there was food in Egypt and sent our fathers to scout it out. Having confirmed the report, they went back to Egypt a second time to get food. On that visit, Joseph revealed his true identity to his brothers and introduced the Jacob family to Pharaoh. Then Joseph sent for his father, Jacob, and everyone else in the family, seventy-five in all. That's how the Jacob family got to Egypt.

"Jacob died, and our fathers after him. They were taken to Shechem and buried in the tomb for which Abraham paid a good price to the sons of Hamor.

"When the four hundred years were nearly up, the time God promised Abraham for deliverance, the population of our people in Egypt had become very large. And there was now a king over Egypt who had never heard of Joseph. He exploited our race mercilessly. He went so far as forcing us to abandon our newborn infants, exposing them to the elements to die a cruel death.

"In just such a time Moses was born, a most beautiful baby. He was hidden at home for three months. When he could be hidden no longer, he was put outside—and immediately rescued by Pharaoh's daughter, who mothered him as her own son. Moses was educated in the best schools in Egypt. He was equally impressive as a thinker and an athlete.

KING JAMES VERSION

23 And when he was full forty years old, it came into his heart to visit his brethren the children of Israel.
24 And seeing one *of them* suffer wrong, he defended *him*, and avenged him that was oppressed, and smote the Egyptian:
25 For he supposed his brethren would have understood how that God by his hand would deliver them: but they understood not.
26 And the next day he shewed himself unto them as they strove, and would have set them at one again, saying, Sirs, ye are brethren; why do ye wrong one to another?
27 But he that did his neighbour wrong thrust him away, saying, Who made thee a ruler and a judge over us?
28 Wilt thou kill me, as thou diddest the Egyptian yesterday?
29 Then fled Moses at this saying, and was a stranger in the land of Madian, where he begat two sons.
30 ¶ And when forty years were expired, there appeared to him in the wilderness of mount Sina an angel of the Lord in a flame of fire in a bush.
31 When Moses saw *it*, he wondered at the sight: and as he drew near to behold *it*, the voice of the Lord came unto him,
32 *Saying*, I *am* the God of thy fathers, the God of Abraham, and the God of Isaac, and the God of Jacob. Then Moses trembled, and durst not behold.
33 Then said the Lord to him, Put off thy shoes from thy feet: for the place where thou standest is holy ground.

NEW AMERICAN STANDARD BIBLE

23 "But when he was approaching the age of forty, it entered his mind to visit his brethren, the sons of Israel.
24 "And when he saw one *of them* being treated unjustly, he defended him and took vengeance for the oppressed by striking down the Egyptian.
25 "And he supposed that his brethren understood that God was granting them deliverance through him, but they did not understand.
26 "On the following day he appeared to them as they were fighting together, and he tried to reconcile them in peace, saying, 'Men, you are brethren, why do you injure one another?'
27 "But the one who was injuring his neighbor pushed him away, saying, 'WHO MADE YOU A RULER AND JUDGE OVER US?
28 'YOU DO NOT MEAN TO KILL ME AS YOU KILLED THE EGYPTIAN YESTERDAY, DO YOU?'
29 "At this remark, MOSES FLED AND BECAME AN ALIEN IN THE LAND OF MIDIAN, where he became the father of two sons.
30 "After forty years had passed, AN ANGEL APPEARED TO HIM IN THE WILDERNESS OF MOUNT Sinai, IN THE FLAME OF A BURNING THORN BUSH.
31 "When Moses saw it, he marveled at the sight; and as he approached to look *more* closely, there came the voice of the Lord:
32 'I AM THE GOD OF YOUR FATHERS, THE GOD OF ABRAHAM AND ISAAC AND JACOB.' Moses shook with fear and would not venture to look.
33 "BUT THE LORD SAID TO HIM, 'TAKE OFF THE SANDALS FROM YOUR FEET, FOR THE PLACE ON WHICH YOU ARE STANDING IS HOLY GROUND.

NEW CENTURY VERSION

23"When Moses was about forty years old, he thought it would be good to visit his own people, the people of Israel.
24Moses saw an Egyptian mistreating an Israelite, so he defended the Israelite and punished the Egyptian by killing him.
25Moses thought his own people would understand that God was using him to save them, but they did not.
26The next day when Moses saw two men of Israel fighting, he tried to make peace between them. He said, 'Men, you are brothers. Why are you hurting each other?'
27The man who was hurting the other pushed Moses away and said, 'Who made you our ruler and judge?
28Are you going to kill me as you killed the Egyptian yesterday?'[d]
29When Moses heard him say this, he left Egypt and went to live in the land of Midian where he was a stranger. While Moses lived in Midian, he had two sons.
30"Forty years later an angel appeared to Moses in the flames of a burning bush as he was in the desert near Mount Sinai.
31When Moses saw this, he was amazed and went near to look closer. Moses heard the Lord's voice say,
32'I am the God of your ancestors, the God of Abraham, Isaac, and Jacob.'[e] Moses began to shake with fear and was afraid to look.
33The Lord said to him, 'Take off your sandals, because you are standing on holy ground.
34I have

7:28 [d] **'Who...yesterday?'** Quotation from Exodus 2:14.
7:32 [e] **'I am...Jacob.'** Quotation from Exodus 3:6.

CONTEMPORARY ENGLISH VERSION

23When Moses was forty years old, he wanted to help the Israelites because they were his own people.
24One day he saw an Egyptian mistreating one of them. So he rescued the man and killed the Egyptian.
25Moses thought the rest of his people would realize that God was going to use him to set them free. But they didn't understand.
26The next day Moses saw two of his own people fighting, and he tried to make them stop. He said, "Men, you are both Israelites. Why are you so cruel to each other?"
27But the man who had started the fight pushed Moses aside and asked, "Who made you our ruler and judge?
28Are you going to kill me, just as you killed that Egyptian yesterday?"
29When Moses heard this, he ran away to live in the country of Midian. His two sons were born there.
30Forty years later, an angel appeared to Moses from a burning bush in the desert near Mount Sinai.
31Moses was surprised by what he saw. He went closer to get a better look, and the Lord said,
32"I am the God who was worshiped by your ancestors, Abraham, Isaac, and Jacob." Moses started shaking all over and didn't dare to look at the bush.
33The Lord said to him, "Take off your sandals. The place where you are standing is holy.
34With my own

NEW INTERNATIONAL VERSION

23 "When Moses was forty years old, he decided to visit his fellow Israelites. 24 He saw one of them being mistreated by an Egyptian, so he went to his defense and avenged him by killing the Egyptian. 25 Moses thought that his own people would realize that God was using him to rescue them, but they did not. 26 The next day Moses came upon two Israelites who were fighting. He tried to reconcile them by saying, 'Men, you are brothers; why do you want to hurt each other?'

27 "But the man who was mistreating the other pushed Moses aside and said, 'Who made you ruler and judge over us? 28 Do you want to kill me as you killed the Egyptian yesterday?'[d] 29 When Moses heard this, he fled to Midian, where he settled as a foreigner and had two sons.

30 "After forty years had passed, an angel appeared to Moses in the flames of a burning bush in the desert near Mount Sinai. 31 When he saw this, he was amazed at the sight. As he went over to look more closely, he heard the Lord's voice: 32 'I am the God of your fathers, the God of Abraham, Isaac and Jacob.'[e] Moses trembled with fear and did not dare to look.

33 "Then the Lord said to him, 'Take off your sandals; the place where you are standing is holy ground. 34 I have

[d] *28* Exodus 2:14 [e] *32* Exodus 3:6

NEW LIVING TRANSLATION

23 "One day when he was forty years old, he decided to visit his relatives, the people of Israel. 24 During this visit, he saw an Egyptian mistreating a man of Israel. So Moses came to his defense and avenged him, killing the Egyptian. 25 Moses assumed his brothers would realize that God had sent him to rescue them, but they didn't.

26 "The next day he visited them again and saw two men of Israel fighting. He tried to be a peacemaker. 'Men,' he said, 'you are brothers. Why are you hurting each other?'

27 "But the man in the wrong pushed Moses aside and told him to mind his own business. 'Who made you a ruler and judge over us?' he asked. 28 'Are you going to kill me as you killed that Egyptian yesterday?' 29 When Moses heard that, he fled the country and lived as a foreigner in the land of Midian, where his two sons were born.

30 "Forty years later, in the desert near Mount Sinai, an angel appeared to Moses in the flame of a burning bush. 31 Moses saw it and wondered what it was. As he went to see, the voice of the Lord called out to him, 32 'I am the God of your ancestors—the God of Abraham, Isaac, and Jacob.' Moses shook with terror and dared not look.

33 "And the Lord said to him, 'Take off your sandals, for you are standing on holy ground. 34 You can be sure that I

NEW KING JAMES VERSION

23 "Now when he was forty years old, it came into his heart to visit his brethren, the children of Israel. 24 And seeing one of *them* suffer wrong, he defended and avenged him who was oppressed, and struck down the Egyptian. 25 For he supposed that his brethren would have understood that God would deliver them by his hand, but they did not understand. 26 And the next day he appeared to two of them as they were fighting, and *tried to* reconcile them, saying, 'Men, you are brethren; why do you wrong one another?' 27 But he who did his neighbor wrong pushed him away, saying, *'Who made you a ruler and a judge over us? 28 Do you want to kill me as you did the Egyptian yesterday?'*[e] 29 Then, at this saying, Moses fled and became a dweller in the land of Midian, where he had two sons.

30 "And when forty years had passed, an Angel of the Lord[f] appeared to him in a flame of fire in a bush, in the wilderness of Mount Sinai. 31 When Moses saw *it,* he marveled at the sight; and as he drew near to observe, the voice of the Lord came to him, 32 *saying, 'I am the God of your fathers—the God of Abraham, the God of Isaac, and the God of Jacob.'*[g] And Moses trembled and dared not look. 33 *'Then the* LORD *said to him, "Take your sandals off your feet, for the place where you stand is holy ground.* 34 *I have*

7:28 [e] Exodus 2:14 7:30 [f] NU-Text omits *of the Lord.*
7:32 [g] Exodus 3:6, 15

THE MESSAGE

"When he was forty years old, he wondered how everything was going with his Hebrew kin and went out to look things over. He saw an Egyptian abusing one of them and stepped in, avenging his underdog brother by knocking the Egyptian flat. He thought his brothers would be glad that he was on their side, and even see him as an instrument of God to deliver them. But they didn't see it that way. The next day two of them were fighting and he tried to break it up, told them to shake hands and get along with each other: 'Friends, you are brothers, why are you beating up on each other?'

"The one who had started the fight said, 'Who put you in charge of us? Are you going to kill me like you killed that Egyptian yesterday?' When Moses heard that, realizing that the word was out, he ran for his life and lived in exile over in Midian. During the years of exile, two sons were born to him.

"Forty years later, in the wilderness of Mount Sinai, an angel appeared to him in the guise of flames of a burning bush. Moses, not believing his eyes, went up to take a closer look. He heard God's voice: 'I am the God of your fathers, the God of Abraham, Isaac, and Jacob.' Frightened nearly out of his skin, Moses shut his eyes and turned away.

"God said, 'Kneel and pray. You are in a holy place, on

KING JAMES VERSION

34 I have seen, I have seen the affliction of my people which is in Egypt, and I have heard their groaning, and am come down to deliver them. And now come, I will send thee into Egypt.

35 This Moses whom they refused, saying, Who made thee a ruler and a judge? the same did God send *to be* a ruler and a deliverer by the hand of the angel which appeared to him in the bush.

36 He brought them out, after that he had shewed wonders and signs in the land of Egypt, and in the Red sea, and in the wilderness forty years.

37 This is that Moses, which said unto the children of Israel, A prophet shall the Lord your God raise up unto you of your brethren, like unto me; him shall ye hear.

38 This is he, that was in the church in the wilderness with the angel which spake to him in the mount Sina, and *with* our fathers: who received the lively oracles to give unto us:

39 To whom our fathers would not obey, but thrust *him* from them, and in their hearts turned back again into Egypt,

40 Saying unto Aaron, Make us gods to go before us: for *as for* this Moses, which brought us out of the land of Egypt, we wot not what is become of him.

41 And they made a calf in those days, and offered sacrifice unto the idol, and rejoiced in the works of their own hands.

42 ¶ Then God turned, and gave them up to worship the host of heaven; as it is written in the book of the prophets,

NEW AMERICAN STANDARD BIBLE

34 'I HAVE CERTAINLY SEEN THE OPPRESSION OF MY PEOPLE IN EGYPT AND HAVE HEARD THEIR GROANS, AND I HAVE COME DOWN TO RESCUE THEM; COME NOW, AND I WILL SEND YOU TO EGYPT.'

35 "This Moses whom they disowned, saying, 'WHO MADE YOU A RULER AND A JUDGE?' is the one whom God sent *to be* both a ruler and a deliverer with the help of the angel who appeared to him in the thorn bush.

36 "This man led them out, performing wonders and signs in the land of Egypt and in the Red Sea and in the wilderness for forty years.

37 "This is the Moses who said to the sons of Israel, 'GOD WILL RAISE UP FOR YOU A PROPHET LIKE ME FROM YOUR BRETHREN.'

38 "This is the one who was in the congregation in the wilderness together with the angel who was speaking to him on Mount Sinai, and *who was* with our fathers; and he received living oracles to pass on to you.

39 "Our fathers were unwilling to be obedient to him, but repudiated him and in their hearts turned back to Egypt,

40 SAYING TO AARON, 'MAKE FOR US GODS WHO WILL GO BEFORE US; FOR THIS MOSES WHO LED US OUT OF THE LAND OF EGYPT—WE DO NOT KNOW WHAT HAPPENED TO HIM.'

41 "At that time they made a calf and brought a sacrifice to the idol, and were rejoicing in the works of their hands.

42 "But God turned away and delivered them up to serve the host of heaven; as it is written in the book of the

NEW CENTURY VERSION

seen the troubles my people have suffered in Egypt. I have heard their cries and have come down to save them. And now, Moses, I am sending you back to Egypt.'[f]

35"This Moses was the same man the two men of Israel rejected, saying, 'Who made you a ruler and judge?'[g] Moses is the same man God sent to be a ruler and savior, with the help of the angel that Moses saw in the burning bush. 36So Moses led the people out of Egypt. He worked miracles and signs in Egypt, at the Red Sea, and then in the desert for forty years. 37This is the same Moses that said to the people of Israel, 'God will give you a prophet like me, who is one of your own people.'[h] 38This is the Moses who was with the gathering of the Israelites in the desert. He was with the angel that spoke to him at Mount Sinai, and he was with our ancestors. He received commands from God that give life, and he gave those commands to us.

39"But our ancestors did not want to obey Moses. They rejected him and wanted to go back to Egypt. 40They said to Aaron, 'Make us gods who will lead us. Moses led us out of Egypt, but we don't know what has happened to him.'[i] 41So the people made an idol that looked like a calf. Then they brought sacrifices to it and were proud of what they had made with their own hands. 42But God turned against them and did not try to stop them from worshiping the sun, moon, and stars. This is what is written in the book of the prophets: God says,

7:34 [f] **'Take...Egypt.'** Quotation from Exodus 3:5–10.
7:35 [g] **'Who...judge?'** Quotation from Exodus 2:14.
7:37 [h] **'God...people.'** Quotation from Deuteronomy 18:15.
7:40 [i] **'Make...him.'** Quotation from Exodus 32:1.

CONTEMPORARY ENGLISH VERSION

eyes I have seen the suffering of my people in Egypt. I have heard their groans and have come down to rescue them. Now I am sending you back to Egypt."

35This was the same Moses that the people rejected by saying, "Who made you our leader and judge?" God's angel had spoken to Moses from the bush. And God had even sent the angel to help Moses rescue the people and be their leader.

36In Egypt and at the Red Sea[b] and in the desert, Moses rescued the people by working miracles and wonders for forty years. 37Moses is the one who told the people of Israel, "God will choose one of your people to be a prophet, just as he chose me." 38Moses brought our people together in the desert, and the angel spoke to him on Mount Sinai. There he was given these life-giving words to pass on to us. 39But our ancestors refused to obey Moses. They rejected him and wanted to go back to Egypt.

40The people said to Aaron, "Make some gods to lead us! Moses led us out of Egypt, but we don't know what's happened to him now." 41Then they made an idol in the shape of a calf. They offered sacrifices to the idol and were pleased with what they had done.

42God turned his back on his people and left them. Then they worshiped the stars in the sky, just as it says in the

[b] 7.36 *Red Sea*: This name comes from the Bible of the early Christians, a translation made into Greek about 200 B.C. It refers to the body of water that the Israelites crossed and was one of the marshes or fresh water lakes near the eastern part of the Nile Delta, where they lived and where the towns of Exodus 13.17—14.9 were located.

NEW INTERNATIONAL VERSION

indeed seen the oppression of my people in Egypt. I have heard their groaning and have come down to set them free. Now come, I will send you back to Egypt.'[f]

35"This is the same Moses whom they had rejected with the words, 'Who made you ruler and judge?' He was sent to be their ruler and deliverer by God himself, through the angel who appeared to him in the bush. 36He led them out of Egypt and did wonders and miraculous signs in Egypt, at the Red Sea[g] and for forty years in the desert.

37"This is that Moses who told the Israelites, 'God will send you a prophet like me from your own people.'[h] 38He was in the assembly in the desert, with the angel who spoke to him on Mount Sinai, and with our fathers; and he received living words to pass on to us.

39"But our fathers refused to obey him. Instead, they rejected him and in their hearts turned back to Egypt. 40They told Aaron, 'Make us gods who will go before us. As for this fellow Moses who led us out of Egypt—we don't know what has happened to him!'[i] 41That was the time they made an idol in the form of a calf. They brought sacrifices to it and held a celebration in honor of what their hands had made. 42But God turned away and gave them over to the worship of the heavenly bodies. This agrees with what is written in the book of the prophets:

[f] *34* Exodus 3:5,7,8,10 [g] *36* That is, Sea of Reeds
[h] *37* Deut. 18:15 [i] *40* Exodus 32:1

NEW LIVING TRANSLATION

have seen the misery of my people in Egypt. I have heard their cries. So I have come to rescue them. Now go, for I will send you to Egypt.'* 35And so God sent back the same man his people had previously rejected by demanding, 'Who made you a ruler and judge over us?' Through the angel who appeared to him in the burning bush, Moses was sent to be their ruler and savior. 36And by means of many miraculous signs and wonders, he led them out of Egypt, through the Red Sea, and back and forth through the wilderness for forty years.

37"Moses himself told the people of Israel, 'God will raise up a Prophet like me from among your own people.'* 38Moses was with the assembly of God's people in the wilderness. He was the mediator between the people of Israel and the angel who gave him life-giving words on Mount Sinai to pass on to us.

39"But our ancestors rejected Moses and wanted to return to Egypt. 40They told Aaron, 'Make us some gods who can lead us, for we don't know what has become of this Moses, who brought us out of Egypt.' 41So they made an idol shaped like a calf, and they sacrificed to it and rejoiced in this thing they had made. 42Then God turned away from them and gave them up to serve the sun, moon, and stars as their gods! In the book of the prophets it is written,

7:31-34 Exod 3:5-10. 7:37 Deut 18:15.

NEW KING JAMES VERSION

surely seen the oppression of My people who are in Egypt; I have heard their groaning and have come down to deliver them. And now come, I will send you to Egypt." '[h]

35"This Moses whom they rejected, saying, *'Who made you a ruler and a judge?'*[i] is the one God sent *to be* a ruler and a deliverer by the hand of the Angel who appeared to him in the bush. 36He brought them out, after he had shown wonders and signs in the land of Egypt, and in the Red Sea, and in the wilderness forty years.

Israel Rebels Against God

37"This is that Moses who said to the children of Israel,[j] *'The LORD your God will raise up for you a Prophet like me from your brethren. Him you shall hear.'*[k]

38"This is he who was in the congregation in the wilderness with the Angel who spoke to him on Mount Sinai, and *with* our fathers, the one who received the living oracles to give to us, 39whom our fathers would not obey, but rejected. And in their hearts they turned back to Egypt, 40saying to Aaron, *'Make us gods to go before us; as for this Moses who brought us out of the land of Egypt, we do not know what has become of him.'*[l] 41And they made a calf in those days, offered sacrifices to the idol, and rejoiced in the works of their own hands. 42Then God turned and gave them up to worship the host of heaven, as it is written in the book of the Prophets:

7:34 [h] Exodus 3:5, 7, 8, 10 7:35 [i] Exodus 2:14
7:37 [j] Deuteronomy 18:15 [k] NU-Text and M-Text omit *Him you shall hear.* 7:40 [l] Exodus 32:1, 23

THE MESSAGE

holy ground. I've seen the agony of my people in Egypt. I've heard their groans. I've come to help them. So get yourself ready; I'm sending you back to Egypt.'

"This is the same Moses whom they earlier rejected, saying, 'Who put you in charge of us?' This is the Moses that God, using the angel flaming in the burning bush, sent back as ruler and redeemer. He led them out of their slavery. He did wonderful things, setting up God-signs all through Egypt, down at the Red Sea, and out in the wilderness for forty years. This is the Moses who said to his congregation, 'God will raise up a prophet just like me from your descendants.' This is the Moses who stood between the angel speaking at Sinai and your fathers assembled in the wilderness and took the life-giving words given to him and handed them over to us, words our fathers would have nothing to do with.

"They craved the old Egyptian ways, whining to Aaron, 'Make us gods we can see and follow. This Moses who got us out here miles from nowhere—who knows what's happened to him!' That was the time when they made a calf-idol, brought sacrifices to it, and congratulated each other on the wonderful religious program they had put together.

"God wasn't at all pleased; but he let them do it their way, worship every new god that came down the pike—and live with the consequences, consequences described by the prophet Amos:

KING JAMES VERSION

O ye house of Israel, have ye offered to me slain beasts and sacrifices *by the space of* forty years in the wilderness?

43 Yea, ye took up the tabernacle of Moloch, and the star of your god Remphan, figures which ye made to worship them: and I will carry you away beyond Babylon.

44 Our fathers had the tabernacle of witness in the wilderness, as he had appointed, speaking unto Moses, that he should make it according to the fashion that he had seen.

45 Which also our fathers that came after brought in with Jesus into the possession of the Gentiles, whom God drave out before the face of our fathers, unto the days of David;

46 Who found favour before God, and desired to find a tabernacle for the God of Jacob.

47 But Solomon built him an house.

48 Howbeit the most High dwelleth not in temples made with hands; as saith the prophet,

49 Heaven *is* my throne, and earth *is* my footstool: what house will ye build me? saith the Lord: or what *is* the place of my rest?

NEW AMERICAN STANDARD BIBLE

prophets, 'IT WAS NOT TO ME THAT YOU OFFERED VICTIMS AND SACRIFICES FORTY YEARS IN THE WILDERNESS, WAS IT, O HOUSE OF ISRAEL?

43 'YOU ALSO TOOK ALONG THE TABERNACLE OF MOLOCH AND THE STAR OF THE GOD ROMPHA, THE IMAGES WHICH YOU MADE TO WORSHIP. I ALSO WILL REMOVE YOU BEYOND BABYLON.'

44 "Our fathers had the tabernacle of testimony in the wilderness, just as He who spoke to Moses directed *him* to make it according to the pattern which he had seen.

45 "And having received it in their turn, our fathers brought it in with Joshua upon dispossessing the nations whom God drove out before our fathers, until the time of David.

46 "*David* found favor in God's sight, and asked that he might find a dwelling place for the [2]God of Jacob.

47 "But it was Solomon who built a house for Him.

48 "However, the Most High does not dwell in *houses* made by *human* hands; as the prophet says:

49 'HEAVEN IS MY THRONE,
AND EARTH IS THE FOOTSTOOL OF MY FEET;
WHAT KIND OF HOUSE WILL YOU BUILD FOR ME?' says the Lord,
'OR WHAT PLACE IS THERE FOR MY REPOSE?

7:46 [2] The earliest mss read *house* instead of *God;* the Septuagint reads *God*

NEW CENTURY VERSION

'People of Israel, you did not bring me sacrifices and offerings
while you traveled in the desert for forty years.
43 You have carried with you
the tent to worship Molech
and the idols of the star god Rephan that you made to worship.
So I will send you away beyond Babylon.' *Amos 5:25–27*

44 "The Holy Tent where God spoke to our ancestors was with them in the desert. God told Moses how to make this Tent, and he made it like the plan God showed him.
45 Later, Joshua led our ancestors to capture the lands of the other nations. Our people went in, and God forced the other people out. When our people went into this new land, they took with them this same Tent they had received from their ancestors. They kept it until the time of
David, 46 who pleased God and asked God to let him build a house for him, the God of Jacob. 47 But Solomon was the one who built the Temple.

48 "But the Most High does not live in houses that people build with their hands. As the prophet says:

49 'Heaven is my throne,
and the earth is my footstool.
So do you think you can build a house for me? says the Lord.
Do I need a place to rest?

CONTEMPORARY ENGLISH VERSION

Book of the Prophets, "People of Israel, you didn't offer sacrifices and offerings to me during those forty years in
the desert. 43 Instead, you carried the tent where the god Molech is worshiped, and you took along the star of your god Rephan. You made those idols and worshiped them. So now I will have you carried off beyond Babylonia."

44 The tent where our ancestors worshiped God was with them in the desert. This was the same tent that God had commanded Moses to make. And it was made like the
model that Moses had seen. 45 Later it was given to our ancestors, and they took it with them when they went with Joshua. They carried the tent along as they took over the land from those people that God had chased out for them. Our ancestors used this tent until the time of King
David. 46 He pleased God and asked him if he could build
a house of worship for the people[c] of Israel. 47 And it was
finally King Solomon who built a house for God.[d]

48 But the Most High God doesn't live in houses made by humans. It is just as the prophet said, when he spoke for the Lord,

49 "Heaven is my throne,
and the earth
is my footstool.
What kind of house
will you build for me?
In what place will I rest?

[c] **7.46** *the people*: Some manuscripts have "God." [d] **7.47** *God*: Or "the people."

NEW INTERNATIONAL VERSION

" 'Did you bring me sacrifices and offerings
forty years in the desert, O house of Israel?
43 You have lifted up the shrine of Molech
and the star of your god Rephan,
the idols you made to worship.
Therefore I will send you into exile'[j] beyond Babylon.

44 "Our forefathers had the tabernacle of the Testimony with them in the desert. It had been made as God directed Moses, according to the pattern he had seen. 45 Having received the tabernacle, our fathers under Joshua brought it with them when they took the land from the nations God drove out before them. It remained in the land until the time of David, 46 who enjoyed God's favor and asked that he might provide a dwelling place for the God of Jacob.[k] 47 But it was Solomon who built the house for him.

48 "However, the Most High does not live in houses made by men. As the prophet says:

49 " 'Heaven is my throne,
and the earth is my footstool.
What kind of house will you build for me?
says the Lord.
Or where will my resting place be?

[j] *43* Amos 5:25–27 [k] *46* Some early manuscripts *the house of Jacob*

NEW LIVING TRANSLATION

'Was it to me you were bringing sacrifices
during those forty years in the wilderness, Israel?
43 No, your real interest was in your pagan gods—
the shrine of Molech,
the star god Rephan,
and the images you made to worship them.
So I will send you into captivity
far away in Babylon.'*

44 "Our ancestors carried the Tabernacle* with them through the wilderness. It was constructed in exact accordance with the plan shown to Moses by God. 45 Years later, when Joshua led the battles against the Gentile nations that God drove out of this land, the Tabernacle was taken with them into their new territory. And it was used there until the time of King David.

46 "David found favor with God and asked for the privilege of building a permanent Temple for the God of Jacob.* 47 But it was Solomon who actually built it. 48 However, the Most High doesn't live in temples made by human hands. As the prophet says,

49 'Heaven is my throne,
and the earth is my footstool.
Could you ever build me a temple as good as that?'
asks the Lord.
'Could you build a dwelling place for me?

7:42-43 Amos 5:25-27. **7:44** Greek *the tent of witness.* **7:46** Some manuscripts read *the house of Jacob.*

NEW KING JAMES VERSION

'Did you offer Me slaughtered animals and sacrifices
during forty years in the wilderness,
O house of Israel?
43 *You also took up the tabernacle of Moloch,*
And the star of your god Remphan,
Images which you made to worship;
And I will carry you away beyond Babylon.'[m]

God's True Tabernacle

44 "Our fathers had the tabernacle of witness in the wilderness, as He appointed, instructing Moses to make it according to the pattern that he had seen, 45 which our fathers, having received it in turn, also brought with Joshua into the land possessed by the Gentiles, whom God drove out before the face of our fathers until the days of David, 46 who found favor before God and asked to find a dwelling for the God of Jacob. 47 But Solomon built Him a house.

48 "However, the Most High does not dwell in temples made with hands, as the prophet says:

49 *'Heaven is My throne,*
And earth is My footstool.
What house will you build for Me? says the LORD,
Or what is the place of My rest?

7:43 [m] Amos 5:25–27

THE MESSAGE

'Did you bring me offerings of animals and grains
those forty wilderness years, oh Israel?
Hardly. You were too busy building shrines
to war gods, to sex goddesses,
Worshiping them with all your might.
That's why I put you in exile in Babylon.'

"And all this time our ancestors had a tent shrine for true worship, made to the exact specifications God provided Moses. They had it with them as they followed Joshua, when God cleared the land of pagans, and still had it right down to the time of David. David asked God for a permanent place for worship. But Solomon built it.

"Yet that doesn't mean that Most High God lives in a building made by carpenters and masons. The prophet Isaiah put it well when he wrote,

' "Heaven is my throne room;
I rest my feet on earth.
So what kind of house
will you build me?" says God.
"Where I can get away and relax?

KING JAMES VERSION

50 Hath not my hand made all these things?
51 ¶ Ye stiffnecked and uncircumcised in heart and
ears, ye do always resist the Holy Ghost: as your fathers
did, so *do* ye.
52 Which of the prophets have not your fathers perse-
cuted? and they have slain them which shewed before of
the coming of the Just One; of whom ye have been now the
betrayers and murderers:
53 Who have received the law by the disposition of
angels, and have not kept *it*.
54 ¶ When they heard these things, they were cut to the
heart, and they gnashed on him with *their* teeth.
55 But he, being full of the Holy Ghost, looked up sted-
fastly into heaven, and saw the glory of God, and Jesus
standing on the right hand of God,
56 And said, Behold, I see the heavens opened, and the
Son of man standing on the right hand of God.
57 Then they cried out with a loud voice, and stopped
their ears, and ran upon him with one accord,
58 And cast *him* out of the city, and stoned *him*: and
the witnesses laid down their clothes at a young man's
feet, whose name was Saul.
59 And they stoned Stephen, calling upon *God*, and say-
ing, Lord Jesus, receive my spirit.
60 And he kneeled down, and cried with a loud voice,
Lord, lay not this sin to their charge. And when he had
said this, he fell asleep.

NEW AMERICAN STANDARD BIBLE

50 'WAS IT NOT MY HAND WHICH MADE ALL THESE THINGS?'
51 "You men who are stiff-necked and uncircumcised in
heart and ears are always resisting the Holy Spirit; you are
doing just as your fathers did.
52 "Which one of the prophets did your fathers not perse-
cute? They killed those who had previously announced the
coming of the Righteous One, whose betrayers and mur-
derers you have now become;
53 you who received the law as ordained by angels, and
yet did not keep it."

Stephen Put to Death

54 Now when they heard this, they were cut to the
quick, and they *began* gnashing their teeth at him.
55 But being full of the Holy Spirit, he gazed intently
into heaven and saw the glory of God, and Jesus standing
at the right hand of God;
56 and he said, "Behold, I see the heavens opened up
and the Son of Man standing at the right hand of God."
57 But they cried out with a loud voice, and covered
their ears and rushed at him with one impulse.
58 When they had driven him out of the city, they *began*
stoning *him;* and the witnesses laid aside their robes at
the feet of a young man named Saul.
59 They went on stoning Stephen as he called on *the
Lord* and said, "Lord Jesus, receive my spirit!"
60 Then falling on his knees, he cried out with a loud
voice, "Lord, do not hold this sin against them!" Having
said this, he fell asleep.

NEW CENTURY VERSION

50 Remember, my hand made all these things!' "

Isaiah 66:1–2

51 Stephen continued speaking: "You stubborn people!
You have not given your hearts to God, nor will you listen
to him! You are always against what the Holy Spirit is try-
ing to tell you, just as your ancestors were. 52 Your ances-
tors tried to hurt every prophet who ever lived. Those
prophets said long ago that the One who is good would
come, but your ancestors killed them. And now you have
turned against and killed the One who is good. 53 You
received the law of Moses, which God gave you through
his angels, but you haven't obeyed it."

Stephen Is Killed

54 When the leaders heard this, they became furious.
They were so mad they were grinding their teeth at
Stephen. 55 But Stephen was full of the Holy Spirit. He
looked up to heaven and saw the glory of God and Jesus
standing at God's right side. 56 He said, "Look! I see heav-
en open and the Son of Man standing at God's right side."
57 Then they shouted loudly and covered their ears and
all ran at Stephen. 58 They took him out of the city and
began to throw stones at him to kill him. And those who
told lies against Stephen left their coats with a young man
named Saul. 59 While they were throwing stones, Stephen
prayed, "Lord Jesus, receive my spirit." 60 He fell on his
knees and cried in a loud voice, "Lord, do not hold this sin
against them." After Stephen said this, he died.

CONTEMPORARY ENGLISH VERSION

50 I have made everything."

51 You stubborn and hardheaded people! You are
always fighting against the Holy Spirit, just as your
ancestors did. 52 Is there one prophet that your ancestors
didn't mistreat? They killed the prophets who told about
the coming of the One Who Obeys God.[e] And now you
have turned against him and killed him. 53 Angels gave
you God's Law, but you still don't obey it.

Stephen Is Stoned to Death

54 When the council members heard Stephen's speech,
they were angry and furious. 55 But Stephen was filled with
the Holy Spirit. He looked toward heaven, where he saw
our glorious God and Jesus standing at his right side.[f]
56 Then Stephen said, "I see heaven open and the Son of
Man standing at the right side of God!"
57 The council members shouted and covered their ears.
At once they all attacked Stephen 58 and dragged him out
of the city. Then they started throwing stones at him. The
men who had brought charges against him put their coats
at the feet of a young man named Saul.[g]
59 As Stephen was being stoned to death, he called out,
"Lord Jesus, please welcome me!" 60 He knelt down and
shouted, "Lord, don't blame them for what they have
done." Then he died.

[e] 7.52 *One Who Obeys God*: That is, Jesus. [f] 7.55 *standing at his right side*: The "right side" is the place of honor and power. "Standing" may mean that Jesus is welcoming Stephen (see verse 59). [g] 7.58 *Saul*: Better known as Paul, who became a famous follower of Jesus.

NEW INTERNATIONAL VERSION

50 Has not my hand made all these things?'[l]

51 "You stiff-necked people, with uncircumcised hearts and ears! You are just like your fathers: You always resist the Holy Spirit! 52 Was there ever a prophet your fathers did not persecute? They even killed those who predicted the coming of the Righteous One. And now you have betrayed and murdered him— 53 you who have received the law that was put into effect through angels but have not obeyed it."

The Stoning of Stephen

54 When they heard this, they were furious and gnashed their teeth at him. 55 But Stephen, full of the Holy Spirit, looked up to heaven and saw the glory of God, and Jesus standing at the right hand of God. 56 "Look," he said, "I see heaven open and the Son of Man standing at the right hand of God."

57 At this they covered their ears and, yelling at the top of their voices, they all rushed at him, 58 dragged him out of the city and began to stone him. Meanwhile, the witnesses laid their clothes at the feet of a young man named Saul.

59 While they were stoning him, Stephen prayed, "Lord Jesus, receive my spirit." 60 Then he fell on his knees and cried out, "Lord, do not hold this sin against them." When he had said this, he fell asleep.

l *50* Isaiah 66:1,2

NEW LIVING TRANSLATION

50 Didn't I make everything in heaven and earth?'*

51 "You stubborn people! You are heathen at heart and deaf to the truth. Must you forever resist the Holy Spirit? But your ancestors did, and so do you! 52 Name one prophet your ancestors didn't persecute! They even killed the ones who predicted the coming of the Righteous One—the Messiah whom you betrayed and murdered. 53 You deliberately disobeyed God's law, though you received it from the hands of angels.*"

54 The Jewish leaders were infuriated by Stephen's accusation, and they shook their fists in rage.* 55 But Stephen, full of the Holy Spirit, gazed steadily upward into heaven and saw the glory of God, and he saw Jesus standing in the place of honor at God's right hand. 56 And he told them, "Look, I see the heavens opened and the Son of Man standing in the place of honor at God's right hand!"

57 Then they put their hands over their ears, and drowning out his voice with their shouts, they rushed at him. 58 They dragged him out of the city and began to stone him. The official witnesses took off their coats and laid them at the feet of a young man named Saul.*

59 And as they stoned him, Stephen prayed, "Lord Jesus, receive my spirit." 60 And he fell to his knees, shouting, "Lord, don't charge them with this sin!" And with that, he died.

7:49-50 Isa 66:1-2. **7:53** Greek *received the Law as it was ordained by angels.* **7:54** Greek *they were grinding their teeth against him.* **7:58** *Saul* is later called Paul; see 13:9.

NEW KING JAMES VERSION

50 *Has My hand not made all these things?'*[n]

Israel Resists the Holy Spirit

51 "*You* stiff-necked and uncircumcised in heart and ears! You always resist the Holy Spirit; as your fathers *did,* so *do* you. 52 Which of the prophets did your fathers not persecute? And they killed those who foretold the coming of the Just One, of whom you now have become the betrayers and murderers, 53 who have received the law by the direction of angels and have not kept *it.*"

Stephen the Martyr

54 When they heard these things they were cut to the heart, and they gnashed at him with *their* teeth. 55 But he, being full of the Holy Spirit, gazed into heaven and saw the glory of God, and Jesus standing at the right hand of God, 56 and said, "Look! I see the heavens opened and the Son of Man standing at the right hand of God!"

57 Then they cried out with a loud voice, stopped their ears, and ran at him with one accord; 58 and they cast *him* out of the city and stoned *him.* And the witnesses laid down their clothes at the feet of a young man named Saul. 59 And they stoned Stephen as he was calling on *God* and saying, "Lord Jesus, receive my spirit." 60 Then he knelt down and cried out with a loud voice, "Lord, do not charge them with this sin." And when he had said this, he fell asleep.

7:50 *n* Isaiah 66:1, 2

THE MESSAGE

It's already built, and I built it."'

"And you continue, so bullheaded! Calluses on your hearts, flaps on your ears! Deliberately ignoring the Holy Spirit, you're just like your ancestors. Was there ever a prophet who didn't get the same treatment? Your ancestors killed anyone who dared talk about the coming of the Just One. And you've kept up the family tradition—traitors and murderers, all of you. You had God's Law handed to you by angels—gift-wrapped!—and you squandered it!"

At that point they went wild, a rioting mob of catcalls and whistles and invective. But Stephen, full of the Holy Spirit, hardly noticed—he only had eyes for God, whom he saw in all his glory with Jesus standing at his side. He said, "Oh! I see heaven wide open and the Son of Man standing at God's side!"

Yelling and hissing, the mob drowned him out. Now in full stampede, they dragged him out of town and pelted him with rocks. The ringleaders took off their coats and asked a young man named Saul to watch them.

As the rocks rained down, Stephen prayed, "Master Jesus, take my life." Then he knelt down, praying loud enough for everyone to hear, "Master, don't blame them for this sin"—his last words. Then he died.

KING JAMES VERSION

8 And Saul was consenting unto his death. And at that time there was a great persecution against the church which was at Jerusalem; and they were all scattered abroad throughout the regions of Judaea and Samaria, except the apostles.

2 And devout men carried Stephen *to his burial*, and made great lamentation over him.

3 As for Saul, he made havock of the church, entering into every house, and haling men and women committed *them* to prison.

4 ¶ Therefore they that were scattered abroad went every where preaching the word.

5 Then Philip went down to the city of Samaria, and preached Christ unto them.

6 And the people with one accord gave heed unto those things which Philip spake, hearing and seeing the miracles which he did.

7 For unclean spirits, crying with loud voice, came out of many that were possessed *with them*: and many taken with palsies, and that were lame, were healed.

8 And there was great joy in that city.

9 But there was a certain man, called Simon, which beforetime in the same city used sorcery, and bewitched the people of Samaria, giving out that himself was some great one:

10 To whom they all gave heed, from the least to the greatest, saying, This man is the great power of God.

NEW AMERICAN STANDARD BIBLE

Saul Persecutes the Church

8 Saul was in hearty agreement with putting him to death.

And on that day a great persecution began against the church in Jerusalem, and they were all scattered throughout the regions of Judea and Samaria, except the apostles.

2 *Some* devout men buried Stephen, and made loud lamentation over him.

3 But Saul *began* ravaging the church, entering house after house, and dragging off men and women, he would put them in prison.

Philip in Samaria

4 Therefore, those who had been scattered went about preaching the word.

5 Philip went down to the city of Samaria and *began* proclaiming Christ to them.

6 The crowds with one accord were giving attention to what was said by Philip, as they heard and saw the signs which he was performing.

7 For *in the case of* many who had unclean spirits, they were coming out *of them* shouting with a loud voice; and many who had been paralyzed and lame were healed.

8 So there was much rejoicing in that city.

9 Now there was a man named Simon, who formerly was practicing magic in the city and astonishing the people of Samaria, claiming to be someone great;

10 and they all, from smallest to greatest, were giving attention to him, saying, "This man is what is called the Great Power of God."

NEW CENTURY VERSION

8 Saul agreed that the killing of Stephen was good.

Troubles for the Believers

On that day the church of Jerusalem began to be persecuted, and all the believers, except the apostles, were scattered throughout Judea and Samaria.

2 And some religious people buried Stephen and cried
loudly for him. 3 Saul was also trying to destroy the
church, going from house to house, dragging out men and
women and putting them in jail. 4 And wherever they were
scattered, they told people the Good News.

Philip Preaches in Samaria

5 Philip[a] went to the city of Samaria and preached about
the Christ. 6 When the people there heard Philip and saw
the miracles he was doing, they all listened carefully to
what he said. 7 Many of these people had evil spirits in
them, but Philip made the evil spirits leave. The spirits
made a loud noise when they came out. Philip also healed
many weak and crippled people there. 8 So the people in
that city were very happy.

9 But there was a man named Simon in that city. Before
Philip came there, Simon had practiced magic and amazed
all the people of Samaria. He bragged and called himself a
great man. 10 All the people—the least important and the
most important—paid attention to Simon, saying, "This
man has the power of God, called 'the Great Power'!"

8:5 [a] **Philip** Not the apostle named Philip.

CONTEMPORARY ENGLISH VERSION

8 1-2 Saul approved the stoning of Stephen. Some faithful followers of the Lord buried Stephen and mourned very much for him.

Saul Makes Trouble for the Church

At that time the church in Jerusalem suffered terribly.
All of the Lord's followers, except the apostles, were scattered everywhere in Judea and Samaria. 3 Saul started mak-
ing a lot of trouble for the church. He went from house to
house, arresting men and women and putting them in jail.

The Good News Is Preached in Samaria

4 The Lord's followers who had been scattered went from
place to place, telling the good news. 5 Philip went to the
city of Samaria and told the people about Christ. 6 They
crowded around Philip because they were eager to hear
what he was saying and to see him work miracles. 7 Many
people with evil spirits were healed, and the spirits went
out of them with a shout. A lot of crippled and lame people
were also healed. 8 Everyone in that city was very glad
because of what was happening.

9 For some time a man named Simon had lived in the city
of Samaria and had amazed the people. He practiced
witchcraft and claimed to be somebody great. 10 Everyone,
rich and poor, crowded around him. They said, "This man
is the power of God called 'The Great Power.' "

NEW INTERNATIONAL VERSION

8 And Saul was there, giving approval to his death.

The Church Persecuted and Scattered

On that day a great persecution broke out against the church at Jerusalem, and all except the apostles were scattered throughout Judea and Samaria. 2Godly men buried Stephen and mourned deeply for him. 3But Saul began to destroy the church. Going from house to house, he dragged off men and women and put them in prison.

Philip in Samaria

4Those who had been scattered preached the word wherever they went. 5Philip went down to a city in Samaria and proclaimed the Christ[a] there. 6When the crowds heard Philip and saw the miraculous signs he did, they all paid close attention to what he said. 7With shrieks, evil[b] spirits came out of many, and many paralytics and cripples were healed. 8So there was great joy in that city.

Simon the Sorcerer

9Now for some time a man named Simon had practiced sorcery in the city and amazed all the people of Samaria. He boasted that he was someone great, 10and all the people, both high and low, gave him their attention and exclaimed, "This man is the divine power known as the Great Power."

[a] 5 Or *Messiah* [b] 7 Greek *unclean*

NEW LIVING TRANSLATION

8 Saul was one of the official witnesses at the killing of Stephen.

Persecution Scatters the Believers

A great wave of persecution began that day, sweeping over the church in Jerusalem, and all the believers except the apostles fled into Judea and Samaria. 2(Some godly men came and buried Stephen with loud weeping.) 3Saul was going everywhere to devastate the church. He went from house to house, dragging out both men and women to throw them into jail.

Philip Preaches in Samaria

4But the believers who had fled Jerusalem went everywhere preaching the Good News about Jesus. 5Philip, for example, went to the city of Samaria and told the people there about the Messiah. 6Crowds listened intently to what he had to say because of the miracles he did. 7Many evil spirits were cast out, screaming as they left their victims. And many who had been paralyzed or lame were healed. 8So there was great joy in that city.

9A man named Simon had been a sorcerer there for many years, claiming to be someone great. 10The Samaritan people, from the least to the greatest, often spoke of him as "the Great One—the Power of God." 11He

NEW KING JAMES VERSION

Saul Persecutes the Church

8 Now Saul was consenting to his death.

At that time a great persecution arose against the church which was at Jerusalem; and they were all scattered throughout the regions of Judea and Samaria, except the apostles. 2And devout men carried Stephen *to his burial,* and made great lamentation over him.

3As for Saul, he made havoc of the church, entering every house, and dragging off men and women, committing *them* to prison.

Christ Is Preached in Samaria

4Therefore those who were scattered went everywhere preaching the word. 5Then Philip went down to the[a] city of Samaria and preached Christ to them. 6And the multitudes with one accord heeded the things spoken by Philip, hearing and seeing the miracles which he did. 7For unclean spirits, crying with a loud voice, came out of many who were possessed; and many who were paralyzed and lame were healed. 8And there was great joy in that city.

The Sorcerer's Profession of Faith

9But there was a certain man called Simon, who previously practiced sorcery in the city and astonished the people of Samaria, claiming that he was someone great, 10to whom they all gave heed, from the least to the greatest, saying, "This man is the great power of God." 11And they

8:5 [a] Or *a*

THE MESSAGE

Saul was right there, congratulating the killers.

Simon the Wizard

8 That set off a terrific persecution of the church in Jerusalem. The believers were all scattered throughout Judea and Samaria. All, that is, but the apostles. Good and brave men buried Stephen, giving him a solemn funeral—not many dry eyes that day!

And Saul just went wild, devastating the church, entering house after house, dragging men and women off to jail. Forced to leave home base, the Christians all became missionaries. Wherever they were scattered, they preached the Message about Jesus. Going down to a Samaritan city, Philip proclaimed the Message of the Messiah. When the people heard what he had to say and saw the miracles, the clear signs of God's action, they hung on his every word. Many who could neither stand nor walk were healed that day. The evil spirits protested loudly as they were sent on their way. And what joy in the city!

Previous to Philip's arrival, a certain Simon had practiced magic in the city, posing as a famous man and dazzling all the Samaritans with his wizardry. He had them all, from little children to old men, eating out of his hand. They all thought he had supernatural powers, and called

KING JAMES VERSION

11 And to him they had regard, because that of long time he had bewitched them with sorceries.

12 But when they believed Philip preaching the things concerning the kingdom of God, and the name of Jesus Christ, they were baptized, both men and women.

13 Then Simon himself believed also: and when he was baptized, he continued with Philip, and wondered, beholding the miracles and signs which were done.

14 ¶ Now when the apostles which were at Jerusalem heard that Samaria had received the word of God, they sent unto them Peter and John:

15 Who, when they were come down, prayed for them, that they might receive the Holy Ghost:

16 (For as yet he was fallen upon none of them: only they were baptized in the name of the Lord Jesus.)

17 Then laid they *their* hands on them, and they received the Holy Ghost.

18 And when Simon saw that through laying on of the apostles' hands the Holy Ghost was given, he offered them money,

19 Saying, Give me also this power, that on whomsoever I lay hands, he may receive the Holy Ghost.

20 But Peter said unto him, Thy money perish with thee, because thou hast thought that the gift of God may be purchased with money.

21 Thou hast neither part nor lot in this matter: for thy heart is not right in the sight of God.

NEW AMERICAN STANDARD BIBLE

11 And they were giving him attention because he had for a long time astonished them with his magic arts.

12 But when they believed Philip preaching the good news about the kingdom of God and the name of Jesus Christ, they were being baptized, men and women alike.

13 Even Simon himself believed; and after being baptized, he continued on with Philip, and as he observed signs and great miracles taking place, he was constantly amazed.

14 Now when the apostles in Jerusalem heard that Samaria had received the word of God, they sent them Peter and John,

15 who came down and prayed for them that they might receive the Holy Spirit.

16 For He had not yet fallen upon any of them; they had simply been baptized in the name of the Lord Jesus.

17 Then they *began* laying their hands on them, and they were receiving the Holy Spirit.

18 Now when Simon saw that the Spirit was bestowed through the laying on of the apostles' hands, he offered them money,

19 saying, "Give this authority to me as well, so that everyone on whom I lay my hands may receive the Holy Spirit."

20 But Peter said to him, "May your silver perish with you, because you thought you could obtain the gift of God with money!

21 "You have no part or portion in this matter, for your heart is not right before God.

NEW CENTURY VERSION

11 Simon had amazed them with his magic so long that the
people became his followers. 12 But when Philip told them
the Good News about the kingdom of God and the power of
Jesus Christ, men and women believed Philip and were
baptized. 13 Simon himself believed, and after he was bap-
tized, he stayed very close to Philip. When he saw the mir-
acles and the powerful things Philip did, Simon was
amazed.
14 When the apostles who were still in Jerusalem heard
that the people of Samaria had accepted the word of God,
they sent Peter and John to them. 15 When Peter and John
arrived, they prayed that the Samaritan believers might
receive the Holy Spirit. 16 These people had been baptized
in the name of the Lord Jesus, but the Holy Spirit had not
yet come upon any of them. 17 Then, when the two apostles
began laying their hands on the people, they received the
Holy Spirit.
18 Simon saw that the Spirit was given to people when
the apostles laid their hands on them. So he offered the
apostles money, 19 saying, "Give me also this power so that
anyone on whom I lay my hands will receive the Holy
Spirit."
20 Peter said to him, "You and your money should both be
destroyed, because you thought you could buy God's gift
with money. 21 You cannot share with us in this work since
your heart is not right before God. 22 Change your heart!

CONTEMPORARY ENGLISH VERSION

11 For a long time, Simon had used witchcraft to amaze
the people, and they kept crowding around him. 12 But
when they believed what Philip was saying about God's
kingdom and about the name of Jesus Christ, they were all
baptized. 13 Even Simon believed and was baptized. He
stayed close to Philip, because he marveled at all the mira-
cles and wonders.
14 The apostles in Jerusalem heard that some people in
Samaria had accepted God's message, and they sent Peter
and John. 15 When the two apostles arrived, they prayed
that the people would be given the Holy Spirit. 16 Before
this, the Holy Spirit had not been given to anyone in
Samaria, though some of them had been baptized in the
name of the Lord Jesus. 17 Peter and John then placed their
hands on everyone who had faith in the Lord, and they
were given the Holy Spirit.
18 Simon noticed that the Spirit was given only when the
apostles placed their hands on the people. So he brought
money 19 and said to Peter and John, "Let me have this
power too! Then anyone I place my hands on will also be
given the Holy Spirit."
20 Peter said to him, "You and your money will both end
up in hell if you think you can buy God's gift! 21 You don't
have any part in this, and God sees that your heart isn't

NEW INTERNATIONAL VERSION

11They followed him because he had amazed them for a
long time with his magic. 12But when they believed Philip as
he preached the good news of the kingdom of God and the
name of Jesus Christ, they were baptized, both men and
women. 13Simon himself believed and was baptized. And he
followed Philip everywhere, astonished by the great signs
and miracles he saw.

14When the apostles in Jerusalem heard that Samaria
had accepted the word of God, they sent Peter and John to
them. 15When they arrived, they prayed for them that they
might receive the Holy Spirit, 16because the Holy Spirit had
not yet come upon any of them; they had simply been bap-
tized into[c] the name of the Lord Jesus. 17Then Peter and
John placed their hands on them, and they received the
Holy Spirit.

18When Simon saw that the Spirit was given at the lay-
ing on of the apostles' hands, he offered them money
19and said, "Give me also this ability so that everyone on
whom I lay my hands may receive the Holy Spirit."

20Peter answered: "May your money perish with you,
because you thought you could buy the gift of God with
money! 21You have no part or share in this ministry,
because your heart is not right before God. 22Repent of this

[c] *16* Or *in*

NEW LIVING TRANSLATION

was very influential because of the magic he performed.
12But now the people believed Philip's message of Good
News concerning the Kingdom of God and the name of
Jesus Christ. As a result, many men and women were bap-
tized. 13Then Simon himself believed and was baptized. He
began following Philip wherever he went, and he was
amazed by the great miracles and signs Philip performed.

14When the apostles back in Jerusalem heard that the
people of Samaria had accepted God's message, they sent
Peter and John there. 15As soon as they arrived, they
prayed for these new Christians to receive the Holy Spirit.
16The Holy Spirit had not yet come upon any of them, for
they had only been baptized in the name of the Lord Jesus.
17Then Peter and John laid their hands upon these believ-
ers, and they received the Holy Spirit.

18When Simon saw that the Holy Spirit was given when
the apostles placed their hands upon people's heads, he
offered money to buy this power. 19"Let me have this
power, too," he exclaimed, "so that when I lay my hands
on people, they will receive the Holy Spirit!"

20But Peter replied, "May your money perish with you
for thinking God's gift can be bought! 21You can have no
part in this, for your heart is not right before God. 22Turn

NEW KING JAMES VERSION

heeded him because he had astonished them with his sor-
ceries for a long time. 12But when they believed Philip as
he preached the things concerning the kingdom of God and
the name of Jesus Christ, both men and women were bap-
tized. 13Then Simon himself also believed; and when he
was baptized he continued with Philip, and was amazed,
seeing the miracles and signs which were done.

The Sorcerer's Sin

14Now when the apostles who were at Jerusalem heard
that Samaria had received the word of God, they sent Peter
and John to them, 15who, when they had come down,
prayed for them that they might receive the Holy Spirit.
16For as yet He had fallen upon none of them. They had
only been baptized in the name of the Lord Jesus. 17Then
they laid hands on them, and they received the Holy Spirit.

18And when Simon saw that through the laying on of
the apostles' hands the Holy Spirit was given, he offered
them money, 19saying, "Give me this power also, that any-
one on whom I lay hands may receive the Holy Spirit."

20But Peter said to him, "Your money perish with you,
because you thought that the gift of God could be pur-
chased with money! 21You have neither part nor portion in
this matter, for your heart is not right in the sight of God.

THE MESSAGE

him "the Great Wizard." He had been around a long time and everyone was more or less in awe of him.

But when Philip came to town announcing the news of God's kingdom and proclaiming the name of Jesus Christ, they forgot Simon and were baptized, becoming believers right and left! Even Simon himself believed and was baptized. From that moment he was like Philip's shadow, so fascinated with all the God-signs and miracles that he wouldn't leave Philip's side.

When the apostles in Jerusalem received the report that Samaria had accepted God's Message, they sent Peter and John down to pray for them to receive the Holy Spirit. Up to this point they had only been baptized in the name of the Master Jesus; the Holy Spirit hadn't yet fallen on them. Then the apostles laid their hands on them and they did receive the Holy Spirit.

When Simon saw that the apostles by merely laying on hands conferred the Spirit, he pulled out his money, excited, and said, "Sell me your secret! Show me how you did that! How much do you want? Name your price!"

Peter said, "To hell with your money! And you along with it. Why, that's unthinkable—trying to buy God's gift! You'll never be part of what God is doing by striking bargains and offering bribes. Change your ways—and now!

KING JAMES VERSION

22 Repent therefore of this thy wickedness, and pray
God, if perhaps the thought of thine heart may be forgiven
thee.
23 For I perceive that thou art in the gall of bitterness,
and *in* the bond of iniquity.
24 Then answered Simon, and said, Pray ye to the Lord
for me, that none of these things which ye have spoken
come upon me.
25 And they, when they had testified and preached the
word of the Lord, returned to Jerusalem, and preached the
gospel in many villages of the Samaritans.
26 ¶ And the angel of the Lord spake unto Philip, say-
ing, Arise, and go toward the south unto the way that
goeth down from Jerusalem unto Gaza, which is desert.
27 And he arose and went: and, behold, a man of
Ethiopia, an eunuch of great authority under Candace
queen of the Ethiopians, who had the charge of all her
treasure, and had come to Jerusalem for to worship,
28 Was returning, and sitting in his chariot read Esaias
the prophet.
29 Then the Spirit said unto Philip, Go near, and join
thyself to this chariot.
30 And Philip ran thither to *him*, and heard him read
the prophet Esaias, and said, Understandest thou what
thou readest?
31 And he said, How can I, except some man should
guide me? And he desired Philip that he would come up
and sit with him.

NEW AMERICAN STANDARD BIBLE

22 "Therefore repent of this wickedness of yours, and
pray the Lord that, if possible, the intention of your heart
may be forgiven you.
23 "For I see that you are in the gall of bitterness and in
the bondage of iniquity."
24 But Simon answered and said, "Pray to the Lord for
me yourselves, so that nothing of what you have said may
come upon me."

An Ethiopian Receives Christ

25 So, when they had solemnly testified and spoken the
word of the Lord, they started back to Jerusalem, and were
preaching the gospel to many villages of the Samaritans.
26 But an angel of the Lord spoke to Philip saying, "Get
up and go south to the road that descends from Jerusalem
to Gaza." (This is a desert *road*.)
27 So he got up and went; and there was an Ethiopian
eunuch, a court official of Candace, queen of the Ethio-
pians, who was in charge of all her treasure; and he had
come to Jerusalem to worship,
28 and he was returning and sitting in his chariot, and
was reading the prophet Isaiah.
29 Then the Spirit said to Philip, "Go up and join this
chariot."
30 Philip ran up and heard him reading Isaiah the proph-
et, and said, "Do you understand what you are reading?"
31 And he said, "Well, how could I, unless someone
guides me?" And he invited Philip to come up and sit with
him.

NEW CENTURY VERSION

Turn away from this evil thing you have done, and pray to
the Lord. Maybe he will forgive you for thinking this. [23]I
see that you are full of bitter jealousy and ruled by sin."
[24]Simon answered, "Both of you pray for me to the Lord
so the things you have said will not happen to me."
[25]After Peter and John told the people what they had
seen Jesus do and after they had spoken the message of
the Lord, they went back to Jerusalem. On the way, they
went through many Samaritan towns and preached the
Good News to the people.

Philip Teaches an Ethiopian

[26]An angel of the Lord said to Philip,[b] "Get ready and go
south to the road that leads down to Gaza from
Jerusalem—the desert road." [27]So Philip got ready and
went. On the road he saw a man from Ethiopia, a eunuch.
He was an important officer in the service of Candace, the
queen of the Ethiopians; he was responsible for taking care
of all her money. He had gone to Jerusalem to worship.
[28]Now, as he was on his way home, he was sitting in his
chariot reading from the Book of Isaiah, the prophet. [29]The
Spirit said to Philip, "Go to that chariot and stay near it."
[30]So when Philip ran toward the chariot, he heard the
man reading from Isaiah the prophet. Philip asked, "Do
you understand what you are reading?"
[31]He answered, "How can I understand unless someone
explains it to me?" Then he invited Philip to climb in and

8:26 [b] **Philip** Not the apostle named Philip.

CONTEMPORARY ENGLISH VERSION

right. [22]Get rid of these evil thoughts and ask God to for-
give you. [23]I can see that you are jealous and bound by
your evil ways."
[24]Simon said, "Please pray to the Lord, so that what you
said won't happen to me."
[25]After Peter and John had preached about the Lord,
they returned to Jerusalem. On their way they told the
good news in many villages of Samaria.

Philip and an Ethiopian Official

[26]The Lord's angel said to Philip, "Go south[a] along the
desert road that leads from Jerusalem to Gaza."[b] [27]So
Philip left.
An important Ethiopian official happened to be going
along that road in his chariot. He was the chief treasurer
for Candace, the Queen of Ethiopia. The official had gone
to Jerusalem to worship [28]and was now on his way home.
He was sitting in his chariot, reading the book of the
prophet Isaiah.
[29]The Spirit told Philip to catch up with the chariot.
[30]Philip ran up close and heard the man reading aloud
from the book of Isaiah. Philip asked him, "Do you under-
stand what you are reading?"
[31]The official answered, "How can I understand unless
someone helps me?" He then invited Philip to come up and
sit beside him.

[a] **8.26** *Go south*: Or "About noon go." [b] **8.26** *the desert road that leads from Jerusalem to Gaza*: Or "the road that leads from Jerusalem to Gaza in the desert."

NEW INTERNATIONAL VERSION

wickedness and pray to the Lord. Perhaps he will forgive you for having such a thought in your heart. 23For I see that you are full of bitterness and captive to sin."

24Then Simon answered, "Pray to the Lord for me so that nothing you have said may happen to me."

25When they had testified and proclaimed the word of the Lord, Peter and John returned to Jerusalem, preaching the gospel in many Samaritan villages.

Philip and the Ethiopian

26Now an angel of the Lord said to Philip, "Go south to the road—the desert road—that goes down from Jerusalem to Gaza." 27So he started out, and on his way he met an Ethiopian[d] eunuch, an important official in charge of all the treasury of Candace, queen of the Ethiopians. This man had gone to Jerusalem to worship, 28and on his way home was sitting in his chariot reading the book of Isaiah the prophet. 29The Spirit told Philip, "Go to that chariot and stay near it."

30Then Philip ran up to the chariot and heard the man reading Isaiah the prophet. "Do you understand what you are reading?" Philip asked.

31"How can I," he said, "unless someone explains it to me?" So he invited Philip to come up and sit with him.

[d] *27* That is, from the upper Nile region

NEW LIVING TRANSLATION

from your wickedness and pray to the Lord. Perhaps he will forgive your evil thoughts, 23for I can see that you are full of bitterness and held captive by sin."

24"Pray to the Lord for me," Simon exclaimed, "that these terrible things won't happen to me!"

25After testifying and preaching the word of the Lord in Samaria, Peter and John returned to Jerusalem. And they stopped in many Samaritan villages along the way to preach the Good News to them, too.

Philip and the Ethiopian Eunuch

26As for Philip, an angel of the Lord said to him, "Go south* down the desert road that runs from Jerusalem to Gaza." 27So he did, and he met the treasurer of Ethiopia, a eunuch of great authority under the queen of Ethiopia.* The eunuch had gone to Jerusalem to worship, 28and he was now returning. Seated in his carriage, he was reading aloud from the book of the prophet Isaiah.

29The Holy Spirit said to Philip, "Go over and walk along beside the carriage."

30Philip ran over and heard the man reading from the prophet Isaiah; so he asked, "Do you understand what you are reading?"

31The man replied, "How can I, when there is no one to instruct me?" And he begged Philip to come up into the

8:26 Or *Go at noon.* **8:27** Greek *under the Candace, the queen of Ethiopia.*

NEW KING JAMES VERSION

22Repent therefore of this your wickedness, and pray God if perhaps the thought of your heart may be forgiven you. 23For I see that you are poisoned by bitterness and bound by iniquity."

24Then Simon answered and said, "Pray to the Lord for me, that none of the things which you have spoken may come upon me."

25So when they had testified and preached the word of the Lord, they returned to Jerusalem, preaching the gospel in many villages of the Samaritans.

Christ Is Preached to an Ethiopian

26Now an angel of the Lord spoke to Philip, saying, "Arise and go toward the south along the road which goes down from Jerusalem to Gaza." This is desert. 27So he arose and went. And behold, a man of Ethiopia, a eunuch of great authority under Candace the queen of the Ethiopians, who had charge of all her treasury, and had come to Jerusalem to worship, 28was returning. And sitting in his chariot, he was reading Isaiah the prophet. 29Then the Spirit said to Philip, "Go near and overtake this chariot."

30So Philip ran to him, and heard him reading the prophet Isaiah, and said, "Do you understand what you are reading?"

31And he said, "How can I, unless someone guides me?" And he asked Philip to come up and sit with him.

THE MESSAGE

Ask the Master to forgive you for trying to use God to make money. I can see this is an old habit with you; you reek with money-lust."

"Oh!" said Simon, "pray for me! Pray to the Master that nothing like that will ever happen to me!"

And with that, the apostles were on their way, continuing to witness and spread the Message of God's salvation, preaching in every Samaritan town they passed through on their return to Jerusalem.

The Ethiopian Eunuch

Later God's angel spoke to Philip: "At noon today I want you to walk over to that desolate road that goes from Jerusalem down to Gaza." He got up and went. He met an Ethiopian eunuch coming down the road. The eunuch had been on a pilgrimage to Jerusalem and was returning to Ethiopia, where he was minister in charge of all the finances of Candace, queen of the Ethiopians. He was riding in a chariot and reading the prophet Isaiah.

The Spirit told Philip, "Climb into the chariot." Running up alongside, Philip heard the eunuch reading Isaiah and asked, "Do you understand what you're reading?"

He answered, "How can I without some help?" and invited

KING JAMES VERSION

32 The place of the scripture which he read was this, He
was led as a sheep to the slaughter; and like a lamb dumb
before his shearer, so opened he not his mouth:
33 In his humiliation his judgment was taken away:
and who shall declare his generation? for his life is taken
from the earth.
34 And the eunuch answered Philip, and said, I pray
thee, of whom speaketh the prophet this? of himself, or of
some other man?
35 Then Philip opened his mouth, and began at the
same scripture, and preached unto him Jesus.
36 And as they went on *their* way, they came unto a
certain water: and the eunuch said, See, *here is* water;
what doth hinder me to be baptized?
37 And Philip said, If thou believest with all thine
heart, thou mayest. And he answered and said, I believe
that Jesus Christ is the Son of God.
38 And he commanded the chariot to stand still: and
they went down both into the water, both Philip and the
eunuch; and he baptized him.
39 And when they were come up out of the water, the

NEW AMERICAN STANDARD BIBLE

32 Now the passage of Scripture which he was reading
was this:

"HE WAS LED AS A SHEEP TO SLAUGHTER;
AND AS A LAMB BEFORE ITS SHEARER IS SILENT,
SO HE DOES NOT OPEN HIS MOUTH.
33 "IN HUMILIATION HIS JUDGMENT WAS TAKEN AWAY;
WHO WILL RELATE HIS GENERATION?
FOR HIS LIFE IS REMOVED FROM THE EARTH."

34 The eunuch answered Philip and said, "Please *tell*
me, of whom does the prophet say this? Of himself or of
someone else?"
35 Then Philip opened his mouth, and beginning from
this Scripture he preached Jesus to him.
36 As they went along the road they came to some
water; and the eunuch *said, "Look! Water! What prevents
me from being baptized?"
37 [[1]And Philip said, "If you believe with all your heart,
you may." And he answered and said, "I believe that Jesus
Christ is the Son of God."]
38 And he ordered the chariot to stop; and they both
went down into the water, Philip as well as the eunuch,
and he baptized him.
39 When they came up out of the water, the Spirit of the

8:37 [1] Early mss do not contain this v

NEW CENTURY VERSION

sit with him. 32The portion of Scripture he was reading
was this:

"He was like a sheep being led to be killed.
He was quiet, as a lamb is quiet while its wool is
being cut;
he never opened his mouth.
33 He was shamed and was treated unfairly.
He died without children to continue his family.
His life on earth has ended." *Isaiah 53:7–8*

34The officer said to Philip, "Please tell me, who is the
prophet talking about—himself or someone else?" 35Philip
began to speak, and starting with this same Scripture, he
told the man the Good News about Jesus.
36While they were traveling down the road, they came to
some water. The officer said, "Look, here is water. What is
stopping me from being baptized?" 37[c] 38Then the officer
commanded the chariot to stop. Both Philip and the officer
went down into the water, and Philip baptized him.
39When they came up out of the water, the Spirit of the

8:37 [c] **Verse 37** Some late copies of Acts add verse 37: "Philip answered, 'If you believe with all your heart, you can.' The officer said, 'I believe that Jesus Christ is the Son of God.' "

CONTEMPORARY ENGLISH VERSION

32The man was reading the passage that said,

"He was led like a sheep
on its way to be killed.
He was silent as a lamb
whose wool
is being cut off,
and he did not say
a word.
33 He was treated like a nobody
and did not receive
a fair trial.
How can he have children,
if his life
is snatched away?"

34The official said to Philip, "Tell me, was the prophet
talking about himself or about someone else?" 35So Philip
began at this place in the Scriptures and explained the
good news about Jesus.
36-37As they were going along the road, they came to a
place where there was some water. The official said,
"Look! Here is some water. Why can't I be baptized?"[c]
38He ordered the chariot to stop. Then they both went
down into the water, and Philip baptized him.
39After they had come out of the water, the Lord's Spirit

[c] **8.36,37** *Why can't I be baptized*: Some manuscripts add, "Philip replied, 'You can, if you believe with all your heart.' "The official answered, 'I believe that Jesus Christ is the Son of God.' "

NEW INTERNATIONAL VERSION

32The eunuch was reading this passage of Scripture:

"He was led like a sheep to the slaughter,
and as a lamb before the shearer is silent,
so he did not open his mouth.
33 In his humiliation he was deprived of justice.
Who can speak of his descendants?
For his life was taken from the earth."[e]

34The eunuch asked Philip, "Tell me, please, who is the
prophet talking about, himself or someone else?" 35Then
Philip began with that very passage of Scripture and told
him the good news about Jesus.
36As they traveled along the road, they came to some
water and the eunuch said, "Look, here is water. Why
shouldn't I be baptized?"[f] 38And he gave orders to stop the
chariot. Then both Philip and the eunuch went down into
the water and Philip baptized him. 39When they came up
out of the water, the Spirit of the Lord suddenly took Philip

[e] *33* Isaiah 53:7,8 [f] *36* Some late manuscripts *baptized?" 37Philip said, "If you believe with all your heart, you may." The eunuch answered, "I believe that Jesus Christ is the Son of God."*

NEW LIVING TRANSLATION

carriage and sit with him. 32The passage of Scripture he
had been reading was this:

"He was led as a sheep to the slaughter.
And as a lamb is silent before the shearers,
he did not open his mouth.
33 He was humiliated and received no justice.
Who can speak of his descendants?
For his life was taken from the earth."*

34The eunuch asked Philip, "Was Isaiah talking about
himself or someone else?" 35So Philip began with this
same Scripture and then used many others to tell him the
Good News about Jesus.
36As they rode along, they came to some water, and the
eunuch said, "Look! There's some water! Why can't I be
baptized?"* 38He ordered the carriage to stop, and they
went down into the water, and Philip baptized him.
39When they came up out of the water, the Spirit of the

8:32-33 Isa 53:7-8. 8:36 Some manuscripts add verse 37, *"You can," Philip answered, "if you believe with all your heart." And the eunuch replied, "I believe that Jesus Christ is the Son of God."*

NEW KING JAMES VERSION

32The place in the Scripture which he read was this:

"He was led as a sheep to the slaughter;
And as a lamb before its shearer is silent,
So He opened not His mouth.
33 *In His humiliation His justice was taken away,*
And who will declare His generation?
For His life is taken from the earth."[b]

34So the eunuch answered Philip and said, "I ask you, of
whom does the prophet say this, of himself or of some
other man?" 35Then Philip opened his mouth, and begin-
ning at this Scripture, preached Jesus to him. 36Now as
they went down the road, they came to some water. And
the eunuch said, "See, *here is* water. What hinders me
from being baptized?"
37Then Philip said, "If you believe with all your heart,
you may."
And he answered and said, "I believe that Jesus Christ is
the Son of God."[c]
38So he commanded the chariot to stand still. And both
Philip and the eunuch went down into the water, and he
baptized him. 39Now when they came up out of the water,
the Spirit of the Lord caught Philip away, so that the eunuch

8:33 [b] Isaiah 53:7, 8 8:37 [c] NU-Text and M-Text omit this verse. It is found in Western texts, including the Latin tradition.

THE MESSAGE

Philip into the chariot with him. The passage he was reading was this:

"As a sheep led to slaughter,
and quiet as a lamb being sheared,
He was silent, saying nothing.
He was mocked and put down, never got a fair trial.
But who now can count his kin
since he's been taken from the earth?"

The eunuch said, "Tell me, who is the prophet talking about: himself or some other?" Philip grabbed his chance. Using this passage as his text, he preached Jesus to him. As they continued down the road, they came to a stream of water. The eunuch said, "Here's water. Why can't I be baptized?" He ordered the chariot to stop. They both went down to the water, and Philip baptized him on the spot. When they came up out of the water, the Spirit of God

KING JAMES VERSION

Spirit of the Lord caught away Philip, that the eunuch saw him no more: and he went on his way rejoicing.

40 But Philip was found at Azotus: and passing through he preached in all the cities, till he came to Caesarea.

9 And Saul, yet breathing out threatenings and slaughter against the disciples of the Lord, went unto the high priest,

2 And desired of him letters to Damascus to the synagogues, that if he found any of this way, whether they were men or women, he might bring them bound unto Jerusalem.

3 And as he journeyed, he came near Damascus: and suddenly there shined round about him a light from heaven:

4 And he fell to the earth, and heard a voice saying unto him, Saul, Saul, why persecutest thou me?

5 And he said, Who art thou, Lord? And the Lord said, I am Jesus whom thou persecutest: *it is* hard for thee to kick against the pricks.

6 And he trembling and astonished said, Lord, what wilt thou have me to do? And the Lord *said* unto him, Arise, and go into the city, and it shall be told thee what thou must do.

7 And the men which journeyed with him stood speechless, hearing a voice, but seeing no man.

8 And Saul arose from the earth; and when his eyes were opened, he saw no man: but they led him by the hand, and brought *him* into Damascus.

9 And he was three days without sight, and neither did eat nor drink.

NEW AMERICAN STANDARD BIBLE

Lord snatched Philip away; and the eunuch no longer saw him, but went on his way rejoicing.

40 But Philip found himself at Azotus, and as he passed through he kept preaching the gospel to all the cities until he came to Caesarea.

The Conversion of Saul

9 Now Saul, still breathing threats and murder against the disciples of the Lord, went to the high priest,

2 and asked for letters from him to the synagogues at Damascus, so that if he found any belonging to the Way, both men and women, he might bring them bound to Jerusalem.

3 As he was traveling, it happened that he was approaching Damascus, and suddenly a light from heaven flashed around him;

4 and he fell to the ground and heard a voice saying to him, "Saul, Saul, why are you persecuting Me?"

5 And he said, "Who are You, Lord?" And He *said*, "I am Jesus whom you are persecuting,

6 but get up and enter the city, and it will be told you what you must do."

7 The men who traveled with him stood speechless, hearing the voice but seeing no one.

8 Saul got up from the ground, and though his eyes were open, he could see nothing; and leading him by the hand, they brought him into Damascus.

9 And he was three days without sight, and neither ate nor drank.

NEW CENTURY VERSION

Lord took Philip away; the officer never saw him again.
And the officer continued on his way home, full of joy.
40But Philip appeared in a city called Azotus and preached
the Good News in all the towns on the way from Azotus to
Caesarea.

Saul Is Converted

9 In Jerusalem Saul was still threatening the followers
of the Lord by saying he would kill them. So he went
to the high priest 2and asked him to write letters to the
synagogues in the city of Damascus. Then if Saul found
any followers of Christ's Way, men or women, he would
arrest them and bring them back to Jerusalem.
3So Saul headed toward Damascus. As he came near the
city, a bright light from heaven suddenly flashed around
him. 4Saul fell to the ground and heard a voice saying to
him, "Saul, Saul! Why are you persecuting me?"
5Saul said, "Who are you, Lord?"
The voice answered, "I am Jesus, whom you are persecuting. 6Get up now and go into the city. Someone there
will tell you what you must do."
7The people traveling with Saul stood there but said
nothing. They heard the voice, but they saw no one. 8Saul
got up from the ground and opened his eyes, but he could
not see. So those with Saul took his hand and led him into
Damascus. 9For three days Saul could not see and did not
eat or drink.

CONTEMPORARY ENGLISH VERSION

took Philip away. The official never saw him again, but he
was very happy as he went on his way.
40Philip later appeared in Azotus. He went from town to
town, all the way to Caesarea, telling people about Jesus.

Saul Becomes a Follower of the Lord
(Acts 22.6-16; 26.12-18)

9 Saul kept on threatening to kill the Lord's followers.
He even went to the high priest 2and asked for letters
to the Jewish leaders in Damascus. He did this because he
wanted to arrest and take to Jerusalem any man or woman
who had accepted the Lord's Way.[a] 3When Saul had
almost reached Damascus, a bright light from heaven suddenly flashed around him. 4He fell to the ground and
heard a voice that said, "Saul! Saul! Why are you so cruel
to me?"
5"Who are you?" Saul asked.
"I am Jesus," the Lord answered. "I am the one you are
so cruel to. 6Now get up and go into the city, where you
will be told what to do."
7The men with Saul stood there speechless. They had
heard the voice, but they had not seen anyone. 8Saul got
up from the ground, and when he opened his eyes, he
could not see a thing. Someone then led him by the hand
to Damascus, 9and for three days he was blind and did not
eat or drink.

[a] **9.2** *accepted the Lord's Way*: In the book of Acts, this means to become a follower of the Lord Jesus.

NEW INTERNATIONAL VERSION

away, and the eunuch did not see him again, but went on
his way rejoicing. [40]Philip, however, appeared at Azotus
and traveled about, preaching the gospel in all the towns
until he reached Caesarea.

Saul's Conversion

9 Meanwhile, Saul was still breathing out murderous
threats against the Lord's disciples. He went to the
high priest [2]and asked him for letters to the synagogues in
Damascus, so that if he found any there who belonged to
the Way, whether men or women, he might take them as
prisoners to Jerusalem. [3]As he neared Damascus on his
journey, suddenly a light from heaven flashed around him.
[4]He fell to the ground and heard a voice say to him, "Saul,
Saul, why do you persecute me?"
[5]"Who are you, Lord?" Saul asked.
"I am Jesus, whom you are persecuting," he replied.
[6]"Now get up and go into the city, and you will be told
what you must do."
[7]The men traveling with Saul stood there speechless;
they heard the sound but did not see anyone. [8]Saul got up
from the ground, but when he opened his eyes he could see
nothing. So they led him by the hand into Damascus. [9]For
three days he was blind, and did not eat or drink anything.

NEW LIVING TRANSLATION

Lord caught Philip away. The eunuch never saw him again
but went on his way rejoicing. [40]Meanwhile, Philip found
himself farther north at the city of Azotus! He preached
the Good News there and in every city along the way until
he came to Caesarea.

Saul's Conversion

9 Meanwhile, Saul was uttering threats with every
breath. He was eager to destroy the Lord's followers,*
so he went to the high priest. [2]He requested letters
addressed to the synagogues in Damascus, asking their
cooperation in the arrest of any followers of the Way he
found there. He wanted to bring them—both men and
women—back to Jerusalem in chains.
[3]As he was nearing Damascus on this mission, a bril-
liant light from heaven suddenly beamed down upon him!
[4]He fell to the ground and heard a voice saying to him,
"Saul! Saul! Why are you persecuting me?"
[5]"Who are you, sir?" Saul asked.
And the voice replied, "I am Jesus, the one you are perse-
cuting! [6]Now get up and go into the city, and you will be
told what you are to do."
[7]The men with Saul stood speechless with surprise, for
they heard the sound of someone's voice, but they saw no
one! [8]As Saul picked himself up off the ground, he found
that he was blind. [9]So his companions led him by the hand
to Damascus. He remained there blind for three days. And
all that time he went without food and water.

9:1 Greek *disciples.*

NEW KING JAMES VERSION

saw him no more; and he went on his way rejoicing. [40]But
Philip was found at Azotus. And passing through, he
preached in all the cities till he came to Caesarea.

The Damascus Road: Saul Converted

9 Then Saul, still breathing threats and murder against
the disciples of the Lord, went to the high priest [2]and
asked letters from him to the synagogues of Damascus, so
that if he found any who were of the Way, whether men or
women, he might bring them bound to Jerusalem.
[3]As he journeyed he came near Damascus, and suddenly
a light shone around him from heaven. [4]Then he fell to the
ground, and heard a voice saying to him, "Saul, Saul, why
are you persecuting Me?"
[5]And he said, "Who are You, Lord?"
Then the Lord said, "I am Jesus, whom you are persecut-
ing.[a] It *is* hard for you to kick against the goads."
[6]So he, trembling and astonished, said, "Lord, what do
You want me to do?"
Then the Lord *said* to him, "Arise and go into the city,
and you will be told what you must do."
[7]And the men who journeyed with him stood speechless,
hearing a voice but seeing no one. [8]Then Saul arose from
the ground, and when his eyes were opened he saw no
one. But they led him by the hand and brought *him* into
Damascus. [9]And he was three days without sight, and nei-
ther ate nor drank.

9:5 [a] NU-Text and M-Text omit the last sentence of verse 5 and begin verse 6 with *But arise and go.*

THE MESSAGE

suddenly took Philip off, and that was the last the eunuch
saw of him. But he didn't mind. He had what he'd come
for and went on down the road as happy as he could be.

Philip showed up in Azotus and continued north, preaching the Message in all the villages along that route until he arrived at Caesarea.

The Blinding of Saul

9 All this time Saul was breathing down the necks of the Master's disciples, out for the kill. He went to the Chief Priest and got arrest warrants to take to the meeting places in Damascus so that if he found anyone there belonging to the Way, whether men or women, he could arrest them and bring them to Jerusalem.

He set off. When he got to the outskirts of Damascus, he was suddenly dazed by a blinding flash of light. As he fell to the ground, he heard a voice: "Saul, Saul, why are you out to get me?"

He said, "Who are you, Master?"

"I am Jesus, the One you're hunting down. I want you to get up and enter the city. In the city you'll be told what to do next."

His companions stood there dumbstruck—they could hear the sound, but couldn't see anyone—while Saul, picking himself up off the ground, found himself stone blind. They had to take him by the hand and lead him into Damascus. He continued blind for three days. He ate nothing, drank nothing.

KING JAMES VERSION

10 ¶ And there was a certain disciple at Damascus, named Ananias; and to him said the Lord in a vision, Ananias. And he said, Behold, I *am here*, Lord.

11 And the Lord *said* unto him, Arise, and go into the street which is called Straight, and enquire in the house of Judas for *one* called Saul, of Tarsus: for, behold, he prayeth,

12 And hath seen in a vision a man named Ananias coming in, and putting *his* hand on him, that he might receive his sight.

13 Then Ananias answered, Lord, I have heard by many of this man, how much evil he hath done to thy saints at Jerusalem:

14 And here he hath authority from the chief priests to bind all that call on thy name.

15 But the Lord said unto him, Go thy way: for he is a chosen vessel unto me, to bear my name before the Gentiles, and kings, and the children of Israel:

16 For I will shew him how great things he must suffer for my name's sake.

17 And Ananias went his way, and entered into the house; and putting his hands on him said, Brother Saul, the Lord, *even* Jesus, that appeared unto thee in the way as thou camest, hath sent me, that thou mightest receive thy sight, and be filled with the Holy Ghost.

18 And immediately there fell from his eyes as it had been scales: and he received sight forthwith, and arose, and was baptized.

19 And when he had received meat, he was strengthened.

NEW AMERICAN STANDARD BIBLE

10 Now there was a disciple at Damascus named Ananias; and the Lord said to him in a vision, "Ananias." And he said, "Here I am, Lord."

11 And the Lord *said* to him, "Get up and go to the street called Straight, and inquire at the house of Judas for a man from Tarsus named Saul, for he is praying,

12 and he has seen [1]in a vision a man named Ananias come in and lay his hands on him, so that he might regain his sight."

13 But Ananias answered, "Lord, I have heard from many about this man, how much harm he did to Your saints at Jerusalem;

14 and here he has authority from the chief priests to bind all who call on Your name."

15 But the Lord said to him, "Go, for he is a chosen [2]instrument of Mine, to bear My name before the Gentiles and kings and the sons of Israel;

16 for I will show him how much he must suffer for My name's sake."

17 So Ananias departed and entered the house, and after laying his hands on him said, "Brother Saul, the Lord Jesus, who appeared to you on the road by which you were coming, has sent me so that you may regain your sight and be filled with the Holy Spirit."

18 And immediately there fell from his eyes something like scales, and he regained his sight, and he got up and was baptized;

19 and he took food and was strengthened.

9:12 [1] A few early mss do not contain *in a vision* 9:15 [2] Or *vessel*

NEW CENTURY VERSION

10 There was a follower of Jesus in Damascus named Ananias. The Lord spoke to Ananias in a vision, "Ananias!"

Ananias answered, "Here I am, Lord."

11 The Lord said to him, "Get up and go to Straight Street. Find the house of Judas,[a] and ask for a man named Saul from the city of Tarsus. He is there now, praying. 12 Saul has seen a vision in which a man named Ananias comes to him and lays his hands on him. Then he is able to see again."

13 But Ananias answered, "Lord, many people have told me about this man and the terrible things he did to your holy people in Jerusalem. 14 Now he has come here to Damascus, and the leading priests have given him the power to arrest everyone who worships you."

15 But the Lord said to Ananias, "Go! I have chosen Saul for an important work. He must tell about me to those who are not Jews, to kings, and to the people of Israel. 16 I will show him how much he must suffer for my name."

17 So Ananias went to the house of Judas. He laid his hands on Saul and said, "Brother Saul, the Lord Jesus sent me. He is the one you saw on the road on your way here. He sent me so that you can see again and be filled with the Holy Spirit." 18 Immediately, something that looked like fish scales fell from Saul's eyes, and he was able to see again! Then Saul got up and was baptized. 19 After he ate some food, his strength returned.

9:11 [a] **Judas** This is not either of the apostles named Judas.

CONTEMPORARY ENGLISH VERSION

10 A follower named Ananias lived in Damascus, and the Lord spoke to him in a vision. Ananias answered, "Lord, here I am."

11 The Lord said to him, "Get up and go to the house of Judas on Straight Street. When you get there, you will find a man named Saul from the city of Tarsus. Saul is praying, 12 and he has seen a vision. He saw a man named Ananias coming to him and putting his hands on him, so that he could see again."

13 Ananias replied, "Lord, a lot of people have told me about the terrible things this man has done to your followers in Jerusalem. 14 Now the chief priests have given him the power to come here and arrest anyone who worships in your name."

15 The Lord said to Ananias, "Go! I have chosen him to tell foreigners, kings, and the people of Israel about me. 16 I will show him how much he must suffer for worshiping in my name."

17 Ananias left and went into the house where Saul was staying. Ananias placed his hands on him and said, "Saul, the Lord Jesus has sent me. He is the same one who appeared to you along the road. He wants you to be able to see and to be filled with the Holy Spirit."

18 Suddenly something like fish scales fell from Saul's eyes, and he could see. He got up and was baptized. 19 Then he ate and felt much better.

NEW INTERNATIONAL VERSION

10In Damascus there was a disciple named Ananias. The Lord called to him in a vision, "Ananias!"

"Yes, Lord," he answered.

11The Lord told him, "Go to the house of Judas on Straight Street and ask for a man from Tarsus named Saul, for he is praying. 12In a vision he has seen a man named Ananias come and place his hands on him to restore his sight."

13"Lord," Ananias answered, "I have heard many reports about this man and all the harm he has done to your saints in Jerusalem. 14And he has come here with authority from the chief priests to arrest all who call on your name."

15But the Lord said to Ananias, "Go! This man is my chosen instrument to carry my name before the Gentiles and their kings and before the people of Israel. 16I will show him how much he must suffer for my name."

17Then Ananias went to the house and entered it. Placing his hands on Saul, he said, "Brother Saul, the Lord—Jesus, who appeared to you on the road as you were coming here—has sent me so that you may see again and be filled with the Holy Spirit." 18Immediately, something like scales fell from Saul's eyes, and he could see again. He got up and was baptized, 19and after taking some food, he regained his strength.

NEW LIVING TRANSLATION

10Now there was a believer* in Damascus named Ananias. The Lord spoke to him in a vision, calling, "Ananias!"

"Yes, Lord!" he replied.

11The Lord said, "Go over to Straight Street, to the house of Judas. When you arrive, ask for Saul of Tarsus. He is praying to me right now. 12I have shown him a vision of a man named Ananias coming in and laying his hands on him so that he can see again."

13"But Lord," exclaimed Ananias, "I've heard about the terrible things this man has done to the believers in Jerusalem! 14And we hear that he is authorized by the leading priests to arrest every believer in Damascus."

15But the Lord said, "Go and do what I say. For Saul is my chosen instrument to take my message to the Gentiles and to kings, as well as to the people of Israel. 16And I will show him how much he must suffer for me."

17So Ananias went and found Saul. He laid his hands on him and said, "Brother Saul, the Lord Jesus, who appeared to you on the road, has sent me so that you may get your sight back and be filled with the Holy Spirit." 18Instantly something like scales fell from Saul's eyes, and he regained his sight. Then he got up and was baptized. 19Afterward he ate some food and was strengthened.

9:10 Greek *disciple;* also in 9:36.

NEW KING JAMES VERSION

Ananias Baptizes Saul

10Now there was a certain disciple at Damascus named Ananias; and to him the Lord said in a vision, "Ananias."

And he said, "Here I am, Lord."

11So the Lord *said* to him, "Arise and go to the street called Straight, and inquire at the house of Judas for *one* called Saul of Tarsus, for behold, he is praying. 12And in a vision he has seen a man named Ananias coming in and putting *his* hand on him, so that he might receive his sight."

13Then Ananias answered, "Lord, I have heard from many about this man, how much harm he has done to Your saints in Jerusalem. 14And here he has authority from the chief priests to bind all who call on Your name."

15But the Lord said to him, "Go, for he is a chosen vessel of Mine to bear My name before Gentiles, kings, and the children of Israel. 16For I will show him how many things he must suffer for My name's sake."

17And Ananias went his way and entered the house; and laying his hands on him he said, "Brother Saul, the Lord Jesus,[b] who appeared to you on the road as you came, has sent me that you may receive your sight and be filled with the Holy Spirit." 18Immediately there fell from his eyes *something* like scales, and he received his sight at once; and he arose and was baptized.

19So when he had received food, he was strengthened.

9:17 [b] M-Text omits *Jesus.*

THE MESSAGE

There was a disciple in Damascus by the name of Ananias. The Master spoke to him in a vision: "Ananias."

"Yes, Master?" he answered.

"Get up and go over to Straight Avenue. Ask at the house of Judas for a man from Tarsus. His name is Saul. He's there praying. He has just had a dream in which he saw a man named Ananias enter the house and lay hands on him so he could see again."

Ananias protested, "Master, you can't be serious. Everybody's talking about this man and the terrible things he's been doing, his reign of terror against your people in Jerusalem! And now he's shown up here with papers from the Chief Priest that give him license to do the same to us."

But the Master said, "Don't argue. Go! I have picked him as my personal representative to Gentiles and kings and Jews. And now I'm about to show him what he's in for—the hard suffering that goes with this job."

So Ananias went and found the house, placed his hands on blind Saul, and said, "Brother Saul, the Master sent me, the same Jesus you saw on your way here. He sent me so you could see again and be filled with the Holy Spirit." No sooner were the words out of his mouth than something like scales fell from Saul's eyes—he could see again! He got to his feet, was baptized, and sat down with them to a hearty meal.

KING JAMES VERSION

Then was Saul certain days with the disciples which were at Damascus.

20 And straightway he preached Christ in the synagogues, that he is the Son of God.

21 But all that heard *him* were amazed, and said; Is not this he that destroyed them which called on this name in Jerusalem, and came hither for that intent, that he might bring them bound unto the chief priests?

22 But Saul increased the more in strength, and confounded the Jews which dwelt at Damascus, proving that this is very Christ.

23 ¶ And after that many days were fulfilled, the Jews took counsel to kill him:

24 But their laying await was known of Saul. And they watched the gates day and night to kill him.

25 Then the disciples took him by night, and let *him* down by the wall in a basket.

26 And when Saul was come to Jerusalem, he assayed to join himself to the disciples: but they were all afraid of him, and believed not that he was a disciple.

27 But Barnabas took him, and brought *him* to the apostles, and declared unto them how he had seen the Lord in the way, and that he had spoken to him, and how he had preached boldly at Damascus in the name of Jesus.

NEW AMERICAN STANDARD BIBLE

Saul Begins to Preach Christ

Now for several days he was with the disciples who were at Damascus,

20 and immediately he *began* to proclaim Jesus in the synagogues, saying, "He is the Son of God."

21 All those hearing him continued to be amazed, and were saying, "Is this not he who in Jerusalem destroyed those who called on this name, and *who* had come here for the purpose of bringing them bound before the chief priests?"

22 But Saul kept increasing in strength and confounding the Jews who lived at Damascus by proving that this *Jesus* is the Christ.

23 When many days had elapsed, the Jews plotted together to do away with him,

24 but their plot became known to Saul. They were also watching the gates day and night so that they might put him to death;

25 but his disciples took him by night and let him down through *an opening in* the wall, lowering him in a large basket.

26 When he came to Jerusalem, he was trying to associate with the disciples; but they were all afraid of him, not believing that he was a disciple.

27 But Barnabas took hold of him and brought him to the apostles and described to them how he had seen the Lord on the road, and that He had talked to him, and how at Damascus he had spoken out boldly in the name of Jesus.

NEW CENTURY VERSION

Saul Preaches in Damascus

Saul stayed with the followers of Jesus in Damascus for
a few days. [20]Soon he began to preach about Jesus in the
synagogues, saying, "Jesus is the Son of God."
[21]All the people who heard him were amazed. They said,
"This is the man who was in Jerusalem trying to destroy
those who trust in this name! He came here to arrest the
followers of Jesus and take them back to the leading
priests."
[22]But Saul grew more powerful. His proofs that Jesus is
the Christ were so strong that the Jewish people in
Damascus could not argue with him.
[23]After many days, some Jewish people made plans to
kill Saul. [24]They were watching the city gates day and
night, but Saul learned about their plan. [25]One night some
followers of Saul helped him leave the city by lowering
him in a basket through an opening in the city wall.

Saul Preaches in Jerusalem

[26]When Saul went to Jerusalem, he tried to join the
group of followers, but they were all afraid of him. They
did not believe he was really a follower. [27]But Barnabas
accepted Saul and took him to the apostles. Barnabas
explained to them that Saul had seen the Lord on the road
and the Lord had spoken to Saul. Then he told them how
boldly Saul had preached in the name of Jesus in
Damascus.

CONTEMPORARY ENGLISH VERSION

Saul Preaches in Damascus

For several days Saul stayed with the Lord's followers in
Damascus. [20]Soon he went to the Jewish meeting places
and started telling people that Jesus is the Son of God.
[21]Everyone who heard Saul was amazed and said, "Isn't
this the man who caused so much trouble for those people
in Jerusalem who worship in the name of Jesus? Didn't he
come here to arrest them and take them to the chief
priests?"
[22]Saul preached with such power that he completely
confused the Jewish people in Damascus, as he tried to
show them that Jesus is the Messiah.
[23]Later some of them made plans to kill Saul, [24]but he
found out about it. He learned that they were guarding the
gates of the city day and night in order to kill him. [25]Then
one night his followers let him down over the city wall in a
large basket.

Saul in Jerusalem

[26]When Saul arrived in Jerusalem, he tried to join the
followers. But they were all afraid of him, because they did
not believe he was a true follower. [27]Then Barnabas helped
him by taking him to the apostles. He explained how Saul
had seen the Lord and how the Lord had spoken to him.
Barnabas also said that when Saul was in Damascus, he
had spoken bravely in the name of Jesus.

NEW INTERNATIONAL VERSION

Saul in Damascus and Jerusalem

Saul spent several days with the disciples in Damascus. 20 At once he began to preach in the synagogues that Jesus is the Son of God. 21 All those who heard him were astonished and asked, "Isn't he the man who raised havoc in Jerusalem among those who call on this name? And hasn't he come here to take them as prisoners to the chief priests?" 22 Yet Saul grew more and more powerful and baffled the Jews living in Damascus by proving that Jesus is the Christ.[a]

23 After many days had gone by, the Jews conspired to kill him, 24 but Saul learned of their plan. Day and night they kept close watch on the city gates in order to kill him. 25 But his followers took him by night and lowered him in a basket through an opening in the wall.

26 When he came to Jerusalem, he tried to join the disciples, but they were all afraid of him, not believing that he really was a disciple. 27 But Barnabas took him and brought him to the apostles. He told them how Saul on his journey had seen the Lord and that the Lord had spoken to him, and how in Damascus he had preached fearlessly in the name of

[a] *22* Or *Messiah*

NEW LIVING TRANSLATION

Saul in Damascus and Jerusalem

Saul stayed with the believers* in Damascus for a few days. 20 And immediately he began preaching about Jesus in the synagogues, saying, "He is indeed the Son of God!"

21 All who heard him were amazed. "Isn't this the same man who persecuted Jesus' followers with such devastation in Jerusalem?" they asked. "And we understand that he came here to arrest them and take them in chains to the leading priests."

22 Saul's preaching became more and more powerful, and the Jews in Damascus couldn't refute his proofs that Jesus was indeed the Messiah. 23 After a while the Jewish leaders decided to kill him. 24 But Saul was told about their plot, and that they were watching for him day and night at the city gate so they could murder him. 25 So during the night, some of the other believers* let him down in a large basket through an opening in the city wall.

26 When Saul arrived in Jerusalem, he tried to meet with the believers, but they were all afraid of him. They thought he was only pretending to be a believer! 27 Then Barnabas brought him to the apostles and told them how Saul had seen the Lord on the way to Damascus. Barnabas also told them what the Lord had said to Saul and how he boldly preached in the name of Jesus in Damascus. 28 Then the

9:19 Greek *disciples;* also in 9:26. **9:25** Greek *his disciples.*

NEW KING JAMES VERSION

Then Saul spent some days with the disciples at Damascus.

Saul Preaches Christ

20 Immediately he preached the Christ[c] in the synagogues, that He is the Son of God.

21 Then all who heard were amazed, and said, "Is this not he who destroyed those who called on this name in Jerusalem, and has come here for that purpose, so that he might bring them bound to the chief priests?"

22 But Saul increased all the more in strength, and confounded the Jews who dwelt in Damascus, proving that this *Jesus* is the Christ.

Saul Escapes Death

23 Now after many days were past, the Jews plotted to kill him. 24 But their plot became known to Saul. And they watched the gates day and night, to kill him. 25 Then the disciples took him by night and let *him* down through the wall in a large basket.

Saul at Jerusalem

26 And when Saul had come to Jerusalem, he tried to join the disciples; but they were all afraid of him, and did not believe that he was a disciple. 27 But Barnabas took him and brought *him* to the apostles. And he declared to them how he had seen the Lord on the road, and that He had spoken to him, and how he had preached boldly at Damascus in the

9:20 [c] NU-Text reads *Jesus.*

THE MESSAGE

Plots Against Saul

Saul spent a few days getting acquainted with the Damascus disciples, but then went right to work, wasting no time, preaching in the meeting places that this Jesus was the Son of God. They were caught off guard by this and, not at all sure they could trust him, they kept saying, "Isn't this the man who wreaked havoc in Jerusalem among the believers? And didn't he come here to do the same thing—arrest us and drag us off to jail in Jerusalem for sentencing by the high priests?"

But their suspicions didn't slow Saul down for even a minute. His momentum was up now and he plowed straight into the opposition, disarming the Damascus Jews and trying to show them that this Jesus was the Messiah.

After this had gone on quite a long time, some Jews conspired to kill him, but Saul got wind of it. They were watching the city gates around the clock so they could kill him. Then one night the disciples engineered his escape by lowering him over the wall in a basket.

Back in Jerusalem he tried to join the disciples, but they were all afraid of him. They didn't trust him one bit. Then Barnabas took him under his wing. He introduced him to the apostles and stood up for him, told them how Saul had seen and spoken to the Master on the Damascus Road and how in Damascus itself he had laid his life on the line with his bold preaching in Jesus' name.

KING JAMES VERSION

28 And he was with them coming in and going out at Jerusalem.

29 And he spake boldly in the name of the Lord Jesus, and disputed against the Grecians: but they went about to slay him.

30 *Which* when the brethren knew, they brought him down to Caesarea, and sent him forth to Tarsus.

31 Then had the churches rest throughout all Judaea and Galilee and Samaria, and were edified; and walking in the fear of the Lord, and in the comfort of the Holy Ghost, were multiplied.

32 ¶ And it came to pass, as Peter passed throughout all *quarters*, he came down also to the saints which dwelt at Lydda.

33 And there he found a certain man named Aeneas, which had kept his bed eight years, and was sick of the palsy.

34 And Peter said unto him, Aeneas, Jesus Christ maketh thee whole: arise, and make thy bed. And he arose immediately.

35 And all that dwelt at Lydda and Saron saw him, and turned to the Lord.

36 ¶ Now there was at Joppa a certain disciple named Tabitha, which by interpretation is called Dorcas: this woman was full of good works and almsdeeds which she did.

37 And it came to pass in those days, that she was sick, and died: whom when they had washed, they laid *her* in an upper chamber.

NEW AMERICAN STANDARD BIBLE

28 And he was with them, moving about freely in Jerusalem, speaking out boldly in the name of the Lord.

29 And he was talking and arguing with the Hellenistic *Jews;* but they were attempting to put him to death.

30 But when the brethren learned *of it,* they brought him down to Caesarea and sent him away to Tarsus.

31 So the church throughout all Judea and Galilee and Samaria enjoyed peace, being built up; and going on in the fear of the Lord and in the comfort of the Holy Spirit, it continued to increase.

Peter's Ministry

32 Now as Peter was traveling through all *those regions,* he came down also to the saints who lived at Lydda.

33 There he found a man named Aeneas, who had been bedridden eight years, for he was paralyzed.

34 Peter said to him, "Aeneas, Jesus Christ heals you; get up and make your bed." Immediately he got up.

35 And all who lived at Lydda and Sharon saw him, and they turned to the Lord.

36 Now in Joppa there was a disciple named Tabitha (which translated *in Greek* is called Dorcas); this woman was abounding with deeds of kindness and charity which she continually did.

37 And it happened at that time that she fell sick and died; and when they had washed her body, they laid it in an upper room.

NEW CENTURY VERSION

28And so Saul stayed with the followers, going every-
where in Jerusalem, preaching boldly in the name of the
Lord. 29He would often talk and argue with the Jewish peo-
ple who spoke Greek, but they were trying to kill him.
30When the followers learned about this, they took Saul to
Caesarea and from there sent him to Tarsus.

31The church everywhere in Judea, Galilee, and Samaria
had a time of peace and became stronger. Respecting the
Lord by the way they lived, and being encouraged by the
Holy Spirit, the group of believers continued to grow.

Peter Heals Aeneas

32As Peter was traveling through all the area, he visited
God's people who lived in Lydda. 33There he met a man
named Aeneas, who was paralyzed and had not been able
to leave his bed for the past eight years. 34Peter said to
him, "Aeneas, Jesus Christ heals you. Stand up and make
your bed." Aeneas stood up immediately. 35All the people
living in Lydda and on the Plain of Sharon saw him and
turned to the Lord.

Peter Heals Tabitha

36In the city of Joppa there was a follower named
Tabitha (whose Greek name was Dorcas). She was always
doing good deeds and kind acts. 37While Peter was in
Lydda, Tabitha became sick and died. Her body was
washed and put in a room upstairs. 38Since Lydda is near

CONTEMPORARY ENGLISH VERSION

28Saul moved about freely with the followers in
Jerusalem and told everyone about the Lord. 29He was
always arguing with the Jews who spoke Greek, and so
they tried to kill him. 30But the followers found out about
this and took Saul to Caesarea. From there they sent him
to the city of Tarsus.

31The church in Judea, Galilee, and Samaria now had a
time of peace and kept on worshiping the Lord. The church
became stronger, as the Holy Spirit encouraged it and
helped it grow.

Peter Heals Aeneas

32While Peter was traveling from place to place, he visit-
ed the Lord's followers who lived in the town of Lydda.
33There he met a man named Aeneas, who for eight years
had been sick in bed and could not move. 34Peter said to
Aeneas, "Jesus Christ has healed you! Get up and make up
your bed."[b] Right away he stood up.

35Many people in the towns of Lydda and Sharon saw
Aeneas and became followers of the Lord.

Peter Brings Dorcas Back to Life

36In Joppa there was a follower named Tabitha. Her
Greek name was Dorcas, which means "deer." She was
always doing good things for people and had given much
to the poor. 37But she got sick and died, and her body was
washed and placed in an upstairs room. 38Joppa wasn't far

[b] 9.34 *and make up your bed*: Or "and fix something to eat."

NEW INTERNATIONAL VERSION

Jesus. [28]So Saul stayed with them and moved about freely in Jerusalem, speaking boldly in the name of the Lord. [29]He talked and debated with the Grecian Jews, but they tried to kill him. [30]When the brothers learned of this, they took him down to Caesarea and sent him off to Tarsus.

[31]Then the church throughout Judea, Galilee and Samaria enjoyed a time of peace. It was strengthened; and encouraged by the Holy Spirit, it grew in numbers, living in the fear of the Lord.

Aeneas and Dorcas

[32]As Peter traveled about the country, he went to visit the saints in Lydda. [33]There he found a man named Aeneas, a paralytic who had been bedridden for eight years. [34]"Aeneas," Peter said to him, "Jesus Christ heals you. Get up and take care of your mat." Immediately Aeneas got up. [35]All those who lived in Lydda and Sharon saw him and turned to the Lord.

[36]In Joppa there was a disciple named Tabitha (which, when translated, is Dorcas[b]), who was always doing good and helping the poor. [37]About that time she became sick and died, and her body was washed and placed in an

[b] *36* Both *Tabitha* (Aramaic) and *Dorcas* (Greek) mean *gazelle*.

NEW LIVING TRANSLATION

apostles accepted Saul, and after that he was constantly with them in Jerusalem, preaching boldly in the name of the Lord. [29]He debated with some Greek-speaking Jews, but they plotted to murder him. [30]When the believers* heard about it, however, they took him to Caesarea and sent him on to his hometown of Tarsus.

[31]The church then had peace throughout Judea, Galilee, and Samaria, and it grew in strength and numbers. The believers were walking in the fear of the Lord and in the comfort of the Holy Spirit.

Peter Heals Aeneas and Raises Dorcas

[32]Peter traveled from place to place to visit the believers, and in his travels he came to the Lord's people in the town of Lydda. [33]There he met a man named Aeneas, who had been paralyzed and bedridden for eight years. [34]Peter said to him, "Aeneas, Jesus Christ heals you! Get up and make your bed!" And he was healed instantly. [35]Then the whole population of Lydda and Sharon turned to the Lord when they saw Aeneas walking around.

[36]There was a believer in Joppa named Tabitha (which in Greek is Dorcas*). She was always doing kind things for others and helping the poor. [37]About this time she became ill and died. Her friends prepared her for burial and laid her

9:30 Greek *brothers*. **9:36** The names *Tabitha* in Aramaic and *Dorcas* in Greek both mean "gazelle."

NEW KING JAMES VERSION

name of Jesus. [28]So he was with them at Jerusalem, coming in and going out. [29]And he spoke boldly in the name of the Lord Jesus and disputed against the Hellenists, but they attempted to kill him. [30]When the brethren found out, they brought him down to Caesarea and sent him out to Tarsus.

The Church Prospers

[31]Then the churches[d] throughout all Judea, Galilee, and Samaria had peace and were edified. And walking in the fear of the Lord and in the comfort of the Holy Spirit, they were multiplied.

Aeneas Healed

[32]Now it came to pass, as Peter went through all *parts of the country,* that he also came down to the saints who dwelt in Lydda. [33]There he found a certain man named Aeneas, who had been bedridden eight years and was paralyzed. [34]And Peter said to him, "Aeneas, Jesus the Christ heals you. Arise and make your bed." Then he arose immediately. [35]So all who dwelt at Lydda and Sharon saw him and turned to the Lord.

Dorcas Restored to Life

[36]At Joppa there was a certain disciple named Tabitha, which is translated Dorcas. This woman was full of good works and charitable deeds which she did. [37]But it happened in those days that she became sick and died. When they had washed her, they laid *her* in an upper room.

9:31 [d] NU-Text reads *church . . . was edified.*

THE MESSAGE

After that he was accepted as one of them, going in and out of Jerusalem with no questions asked, uninhibited as he preached in the Master's name. But then he ran afoul of a group called Hellenists—he had been engaged in a running argument with them—who plotted his murder. When his friends learned of the plot, they got him out of town, took him to Caesarea, and then shipped him off to Tarsus.

Things calmed down after that and the church had smooth sailing for a while. All over the country—Judea, Samaria, Galilee—the church grew. They were permeated with a deep sense of reverence for God. The Holy Spirit was with them, strengthening them. They prospered wonderfully.

Tabitha

Peter went off on a mission to visit all the churches. In the course of his travels he arrived in Lydda and met with the believers there. He came across a man—his name was Aeneas—who had been in bed eight years paralyzed. Peter said, "Aeneas, Jesus Christ heals you. Get up and make your bed!" And he did it—jumped right out of bed. Everybody who lived in Lydda and Sharon saw him walking around and woke up to the fact that God was alive and active among them.

Down the road a way in Joppa there was a disciple named Tabitha, "Gazelle" in our language. She was well-known for doing good and helping out. During the time Peter was in the area she became sick and died. Her friends prepared her body for burial and put her in a cool room.

KING JAMES VERSION

38 And forasmuch as Lydda was nigh to Joppa, and the disciples had heard that Peter was there, they sent unto him two men, desiring *him* that he would not delay to come to them.

39 Then Peter arose and went with them. When he was come, they brought him into the upper chamber: and all the widows stood by him weeping, and shewing the coats and garments which Dorcas made, while she was with them.

40 But Peter put them all forth, and kneeled down, and prayed; and turning *him* to the body said, Tabitha, arise. And she opened her eyes: and when she saw Peter, she sat up.

41 And he gave her *his* hand, and lifted her up, and when he had called the saints and widows, presented her alive.

42 And it was known throughout all Joppa; and many believed in the Lord.

43 And it came to pass, that he tarried many days in Joppa with one Simon a tanner.

10 There was a certain man in Caesarea called Cornelius, a centurion of the band called the Italian *band*,

2 *A* devout *man*, and one that feared God with all his house, which gave much alms to the people, and prayed to God alway.

3 He saw in a vision evidently about the ninth hour of the day an angel of God coming in to him, and saying unto him, Cornelius.

NEW AMERICAN STANDARD BIBLE

38 Since Lydda was near Joppa, the disciples, having heard that Peter was there, sent two men to him, imploring him, "Do not delay in coming to us."

39 So Peter arose and went with them. When he arrived, they brought him into the upper room; and all the widows stood beside him, weeping and showing all the [3]tunics and garments that Dorcas used to make while she was with them.

40 But Peter sent them all out and knelt down and prayed, and turning to the body, he said, "Tabitha, arise." And she opened her eyes, and when she saw Peter, she sat up.

41 And he gave her his hand and raised her up; and calling the saints and widows, he presented her alive.

42 It became known all over Joppa, and many believed in the Lord.

43 And Peter stayed many days in Joppa with a tanner *named* Simon.

Cornelius' Vision

10 Now *there was* a man at Caesarea named Cornelius, a centurion of what was called the Italian [1]cohort,

2 a devout man and one who feared God with all his household, and gave many [2]alms to the *Jewish* people and prayed to God continually.

3 About the [3]ninth hour of the day he clearly saw in a vision an angel of God who had *just* come in and said to him, "Cornelius!"

9:39 [3] Or *inner garments* **10:1** [1] Or *battalion* **10:2** [2] Or *gifts of charity* **10:3** [3] I.e. 3 p.m.

NEW CENTURY VERSION

Joppa and the followers in Joppa heard that Peter was in Lydda, they sent two messengers to Peter. They begged him, "Hurry, please come to us!" [39]So Peter got ready and went with them. When he arrived, they took him to the upstairs room where all the widows stood around Peter, crying. They showed him the shirts and coats Tabitha had made when she was still alive. [40]Peter sent everyone out of the room and kneeled and prayed. Then he turned to the body and said, "Tabitha, stand up." She opened her eyes, and when she saw Peter, she sat up. [41]He gave her his hand and helped her up. Then he called the saints and the widows into the room and showed them that Tabitha was alive. [42]People everywhere in Joppa learned about this, and many believed in the Lord. [43]Peter stayed in Joppa for many days with a man named Simon who was a tanner.

Peter Teaches Cornelius

10 At Caesarea there was a man named Cornelius, an officer in the Italian group of the Roman army. [2]Cornelius was a religious man. He and all the other people who lived in his house worshiped the true God. He gave much of his money to the poor and prayed to God often. [3]One afternoon about three o'clock, Cornelius clearly saw a vision. An angel of God came to him and said, "Cornelius!"

CONTEMPORARY ENGLISH VERSION

from Lydda, and the followers heard that Peter was there. They sent two men to say to him, "Please come with us as quickly as you can!" [39]Right away, Peter went with them.

The men took Peter upstairs into the room. Many widows were there crying. They showed him the coats and clothes that Dorcas had made while she was still alive.

[40]After Peter had sent everyone out of the room, he knelt down and prayed. Then he turned to the body of Dorcas and said, "Tabitha, get up!" The woman opened her eyes, and when she saw Peter, she sat up. [41]He took her by the hand and helped her to her feet.

Peter called in the widows and the other followers and showed them that Dorcas had been raised from death. [42]Everyone in Joppa heard what had happened, and many of them put their faith in the Lord. [43]Peter stayed on for a while in Joppa in the house of a man named Simon, who made leather.

Peter and Cornelius

10 In Caesarea there was a man named Cornelius, who was the captain of a group of soldiers called "The Italian Unit." [2]Cornelius was a very religious man. He worshiped God, and so did everyone else who lived in his house. He had given a lot of money to the poor and was always praying to God.

[3]One afternoon at about three o'clock,[a] Cornelius had a vision. He saw an angel from God coming to him and calling

[a] **10.3** *at about three o'clock*: Probably while he was praying (see 3.1 and the note there).

NEW INTERNATIONAL VERSION

upstairs room. 38Lydda was near Joppa; so when the disciples heard that Peter was in Lydda, they sent two men to him and urged him, "Please come at once!"

39Peter went with them, and when he arrived he was taken upstairs to the room. All the widows stood around him, crying and showing him the robes and other clothing that Dorcas had made while she was still with them.

40Peter sent them all out of the room; then he got down on his knees and prayed. Turning toward the dead woman, he said, "Tabitha, get up." She opened her eyes, and seeing Peter she sat up. 41He took her by the hand and helped her to her feet. Then he called the believers and the widows and presented her to them alive. 42This became known all over Joppa, and many people believed in the Lord. 43Peter stayed in Joppa for some time with a tanner named Simon.

Cornelius Calls for Peter

10 At Caesarea there was a man named Cornelius, a centurion in what was known as the Italian Regiment. 2He and all his family were devout and God-fearing; he gave generously to those in need and prayed to God regularly. 3One day at about three in the afternoon he had a vision. He distinctly saw an angel of God, who came to him and said, "Cornelius!"

NEW LIVING TRANSLATION

in an upstairs room. 38But they had heard that Peter was nearby at Lydda, so they sent two men to beg him, "Please come as soon as possible!"

39So Peter returned with them; and as soon as he arrived, they took him to the upstairs room. The room was filled with widows who were weeping and showing him the coats and other garments Dorcas had made for them. 40But Peter asked them all to leave the room; then he knelt and prayed. Turning to the body he said, "Get up, Tabitha." And she opened her eyes! When she saw Peter, she sat up! 41He gave her his hand and helped her up. Then he called in the widows and all the believers, and he showed them that she was alive.

42The news raced through the whole town, and many believed in the Lord. 43And Peter stayed a long time in Joppa, living with Simon, a leatherworker.

Cornelius Calls for Peter

10 In Caesarea there lived a Roman army officer named Cornelius, who was a captain of the Italian Regiment. 2He was a devout man who feared the God of Israel, as did his entire household. He gave generously to charity and was a man who regularly prayed to God. 3One afternoon about three o'clock, he had a vision in which he saw an angel of God coming toward him. "Cornelius!" the angel said.

NEW KING JAMES VERSION

38And since Lydda was near Joppa, and the disciples had heard that Peter was there, they sent two men to him, imploring *him* not to delay in coming to them. 39Then Peter arose and went with them. When he had come, they brought *him* to the upper room. And all the widows stood by him weeping, showing the tunics and garments which Dorcas had made while she was with them. 40But Peter put them all out, and knelt down and prayed. And turning to the body he said, "Tabitha, arise." And she opened her eyes, and when she saw Peter she sat up. 41Then he gave her *his* hand and lifted her up; and when he had called the saints and widows, he presented her alive. 42And it became known throughout all Joppa, and many believed on the Lord. 43So it was that he stayed many days in Joppa with Simon, a tanner.

Cornelius Sends a Delegation

10 There was a certain man in Caesarea called Cornelius, a centurion of what was called the Italian Regiment, 2a devout *man* and one who feared God with all his household, who gave alms generously to the people, and prayed to God always. 3About the ninth hour of the day he saw clearly in a vision an angel of God coming in and saying to him, "Cornelius!"

THE MESSAGE

Some of the disciples had heard that Peter was visiting in nearby Lydda and sent two men to ask if he would be so kind as to come over. Peter got right up and went with them. They took him into the room where Tabitha's body was laid out. Her old friends, most of them widows, were in the room mourning. They showed Peter pieces of clothing the Gazelle had made while she was with them. Peter put the widows all out of the room. He knelt and prayed. Then he spoke directly to the body: "Tabitha, get up."

She opened her eyes. When she saw Peter, she sat up. He took her hand and helped her up. Then he called in the believers and widows, and presented her to them alive.

When this became known all over Joppa, many put their trust in the Master. Peter stayed on a long time in Joppa as a guest of Simon the Tanner.

Peter's Vision

10 There was a man named Cornelius who lived in Caesarea, captain of the Italian Guard stationed there. He was a thoroughly good man. He had led everyone in his house to live worshipfully before God, was always helping people in need, and had the habit of prayer. One day about three o'clock in the afternoon he had a vision. An angel of God, as real as his next-door neighbor, came in and said, "Cornelius."

KING JAMES VERSION

4 And when he looked on him, he was afraid, and said, What is it, Lord? And he said unto him, Thy prayers and thine alms are come up for a memorial before God.

5 And now send men to Joppa, and call for *one* Simon, whose surname is Peter:

6 He lodgeth with one Simon a tanner, whose house is by the sea side: he shall tell thee what thou oughtest to do.

7 And when the angel which spake unto Cornelius was departed, he called two of his household servants, and a devout soldier of them that waited on him continually;

8 And when he had declared all *these* things unto them, he sent them to Joppa.

9 ¶ On the morrow, as they went on their journey, and drew nigh unto the city, Peter went up upon the housetop to pray about the sixth hour:

10 And he became very hungry, and would have eaten: but while they made ready, he fell into a trance,

11 And saw heaven opened, and a certain vessel descending unto him, as it had been a great sheet knit at the four corners, and let down to the earth:

12 Wherein were all manner of fourfooted beasts of the earth, and wild beasts, and creeping things, and fowls of the air.

13 And there came a voice to him, Rise, Peter; kill, and eat.

14 But Peter said, Not so, Lord; for I have never eaten any thing that is common or unclean.

15 And the voice *spake* unto him again the second time, What God hath cleansed, *that* call not thou common.

NEW AMERICAN STANDARD BIBLE

4 And fixing his gaze on him and being much alarmed, he said, "What is it, Lord?" And he said to him, "Your prayers and [4]alms have ascended as a memorial before God.

5 "Now dispatch *some* men to Joppa and send for a man *named* Simon, who is also called Peter;

6 he is staying with a tanner *named* Simon, whose house is by the sea."

7 When the angel who was speaking to him had left, he summoned two of his servants and a devout soldier of those who were his personal attendants,

8 and after he had explained everything to them, he sent them to Joppa.

9 On the next day, as they were on their way and approaching the city, Peter went up on the housetop about the [5]sixth hour to pray.

10 But he became hungry and was desiring to eat; but while they were making preparations, he fell into a trance;

11 and he *saw the sky opened up, and an [6]object like a great sheet coming down, lowered by four corners to the ground,

12 and there were in it all *kinds of* four-footed animals and [7]crawling creatures of the earth and birds of the air.

13 A voice came to him, "Get up, Peter, kill and eat!"

14 But Peter said, "By no means, Lord, for I have never eaten anything unholy and unclean."

15 Again a voice *came* to him a second time, "What God has cleansed, no *longer* consider unholy."

10:4 [4] Or *deeds of charity* 10:9 [5] I.e. noon 10:11 [6] Or *vessel*
10:12 [7] Or *reptiles*

NEW CENTURY VERSION

4Cornelius stared at the angel. He became afraid and said, "What do you want, Lord?"

The angel said, "God has heard your prayers. He has seen that you give to the poor, and he remembers you. 5Send some men now to Joppa to bring back a man named Simon who is also called Peter. 6He is staying with a man, also named Simon, who is a tanner and has a house beside the sea." 7When the angel who spoke to Cornelius left, Cornelius called two of his servants and a soldier, a religious man who worked for him. 8Cornelius explained everything to them and sent them to Joppa.

9About noon the next day as they came near Joppa, Peter was going up to the roof[a] to pray. 10He was hungry and wanted to eat, but while the food was being prepared, he had a vision. 11He saw heaven opened and something coming down that looked like a big sheet being lowered to earth by its four corners. 12In it were all kinds of animals, reptiles, and birds. 13Then a voice said to Peter, "Get up, Peter; kill and eat."

14But Peter said, "No, Lord! I have never eaten food that is unholy or unclean."

15But the voice said to him again, "God has made these things clean so don't call them 'unholy'!" 16This happened

10:9 [a] **roof** In Bible times houses were built with flat roofs. The roof was used for drying things such as flax and fruit. And it was used as an extra room, as a place for worship, and as a place to sleep in the summer.

CONTEMPORARY ENGLISH VERSION

him by name. 4Cornelius was surprised and stared at the angel. Then he asked, "What is this all about?"

The angel answered, "God has heard your prayers and knows about your gifts to the poor. 5Now send some men to Joppa for a man named Simon Peter. 6He is visiting with Simon the leather maker, who lives in a house near the sea." 7After saying this, the angel left.

Cornelius called in two of his servants and one of his soldiers who worshiped God. 8He explained everything to them and sent them off to Joppa.

9The next day about noon these men were coming near Joppa. Peter went up on the roof[b] of the house to pray 10and became very hungry. While the food was being prepared, he fell sound asleep and had a vision. 11He saw heaven open, and something came down like a huge sheet held up by its four corners. 12In it were all kinds of animals, snakes, and birds. 13A voice said to him, "Peter, get up! Kill these and eat them."

14But Peter said, "Lord, I can't do that! I've never eaten anything that is unclean and not fit to eat."[c]

15The voice spoke to him again, "When God says that something can be used for food, don't say it isn't fit to eat."

[b] **10.9** *roof*: In Palestine the houses usually had a flat roof. Stairs on the outside led up to the roof, which was made of beams and boards covered with packed earth. [c] **10.14** *unclean and not fit to eat*: The Law of Moses taught that some foods were not fit to eat.

NEW INTERNATIONAL VERSION

[4]Cornelius stared at him in fear. "What is it, Lord?" he asked.

The angel answered, "Your prayers and gifts to the poor have come up as a memorial offering before God. [5]Now send men to Joppa to bring back a man named Simon who is called Peter. [6]He is staying with Simon the tanner, whose house is by the sea."

[7]When the angel who spoke to him had gone, Cornelius called two of his servants and a devout soldier who was one of his attendants. [8]He told them everything that had happened and sent them to Joppa.

Peter's Vision

[9]About noon the following day as they were on their journey and approaching the city, Peter went up on the roof to pray. [10]He became hungry and wanted something to eat, and while the meal was being prepared, he fell into a trance. [11]He saw heaven opened and something like a large sheet being let down to earth by its four corners. [12]It contained all kinds of four-footed animals, as well as reptiles of the earth and birds of the air. [13]Then a voice told him, "Get up, Peter. Kill and eat."

[14]"Surely not, Lord!" Peter replied. "I have never eaten anything impure or unclean."

[15]The voice spoke to him a second time, "Do not call anything impure that God has made clean."

NEW LIVING TRANSLATION

[4]Cornelius stared at him in terror. "What is it, sir?" he asked the angel.

And the angel replied, "Your prayers and gifts to the poor have not gone unnoticed by God! [5]Now send some men down to Joppa to find a man named Simon Peter. [6]He is staying with Simon, a leatherworker who lives near the shore. Ask him to come and visit you."

[7]As soon as the angel was gone, Cornelius called two of his household servants and a devout soldier, one of his personal attendants. [8]He told them what had happened and sent them off to Joppa.

Peter Visits Cornelius

[9]The next day as Cornelius's messengers were nearing the city, Peter went up to the flat roof to pray. It was about noon, [10]and he was hungry. But while lunch was being prepared, he fell into a trance. [11]He saw the sky open, and something like a large sheet was let down by its four corners. [12]In the sheet were all sorts of animals, reptiles, and birds. [13]Then a voice said to him, "Get up, Peter; kill and eat them."

[14]"Never, Lord," Peter declared. "I have never in all my life eaten anything forbidden by our Jewish laws.*"

[15]The voice spoke again, "If God says something is acceptable, don't say it isn't."* [16]The same vision was

10:14 Greek *anything common and unclean.* 10:15 Greek *"What God calls clean you must not call unclean."*

NEW KING JAMES VERSION

[4]And when he observed him, he was afraid, and said, "What is it, lord?"

So he said to him, "Your prayers and your alms have come up for a memorial before God. [5]Now send men to Joppa, and send for Simon whose surname is Peter. [6]He is lodging with Simon, a tanner, whose house is by the sea.[a] He will tell you what you must do." [7]And when the angel who spoke to him had departed, Cornelius called two of his household servants and a devout soldier from among those who waited on him continually. [8]So when he had explained all *these* things to them, he sent them to Joppa.

Peter's Vision

[9]The next day, as they went on their journey and drew near the city, Peter went up on the housetop to pray, about the sixth hour. [10]Then he became very hungry and wanted to eat; but while they made ready, he fell into a trance [11]and saw heaven opened and an object like a great sheet bound at the four corners, descending to him and let down to the earth. [12]In it were all kinds of four-footed animals of the earth, wild beasts, creeping things, and birds of the air. [13]And a voice came to him, "Rise, Peter; kill and eat."

[14]But Peter said, "Not so, Lord! For I have never eaten anything common or unclean."

[15]And a voice *spoke* to him again the second time, "What God has cleansed you must not call common."

10:6 [a] NU-Text and M-Text omit the last sentence of this verse.

THE MESSAGE

Cornelius stared hard, wondering if he was seeing things. Then he said, "What do you want, sir?"

The angel said, "Your prayers and neighborly acts have brought you to God's attention. Here's what you are to do. Send men to Joppa to get Simon, the one everyone calls Peter. He is staying with Simon the Tanner, whose house is down by the sea."

As soon as the angel was gone, Cornelius called two servants and one particularly devout soldier from the guard. He went over with them in great detail everything that had just happened, and then sent them off to Joppa.

The next day as the three travelers were approaching the town, Peter went out on the balcony to pray. It was about noon. Peter got hungry and started thinking about lunch. While lunch was being prepared, he fell into a trance. He saw the skies open up. Something that looked like a huge blanket lowered by ropes at its four corners settled on the ground. Every kind of animal and reptile and bird you could think of was on it. Then a voice came: "Go to it, Peter—kill and eat."

Peter said, "Oh, no, Lord. I've never so much as tasted food that was not kosher."

The voice came a second time: "If God says it's okay, it's okay."

KING JAMES VERSION

16 This was done thrice: and the vessel was received up again into heaven.

17 Now while Peter doubted in himself what this vision which he had seen should mean, behold, the men which were sent from Cornelius had made enquiry for Simon's house, and stood before the gate,

18 And called, and asked whether Simon, which was surnamed Peter, were lodged there.

19 ¶ While Peter thought on the vision, the Spirit said unto him, Behold, three men seek thee.

20 Arise therefore, and get thee down, and go with them, doubting nothing: for I have sent them.

21 Then Peter went down to the men which were sent unto him from Cornelius; and said, Behold, I am he whom ye seek: what *is* the cause wherefore ye are come?

22 And they said, Cornelius the centurion, a just man, and one that feareth God, and of good report among all the nation of the Jews, was warned from God by an holy angel to send for thee into his house, and to hear words of thee.

23 Then called he them in, and lodged *them*. And on the morrow Peter went away with them, and certain brethren from Joppa accompanied him.

24 And the morrow after they entered into Caesarea. And Cornelius waited for them, and had called together his kinsmen and near friends.

NEW AMERICAN STANDARD BIBLE

16 This happened three times, and immediately the object was taken up into the sky.

17 Now while Peter was greatly perplexed in mind as to what the vision which he had seen might be, behold, the men who had been sent by Cornelius, having asked directions for Simon's house, appeared at the gate;

18 and calling out, they were asking whether Simon, who was also called Peter, was staying there.

19 While Peter was reflecting on the vision, the Spirit said to him, "Behold, three men are looking for you.

20 "But get up, go downstairs and accompany them without misgivings, for I have sent them Myself."

21 Peter went down to the men and said, "Behold, I am the one you are looking for; what is the reason for which you have come?"

22 They said, "Cornelius, a centurion, a righteous and God-fearing man well spoken of by the entire nation of the Jews, was *divinely* directed by a holy angel to send for you *to come* to his house and hear a message from you."

23 So he invited them in and gave them lodging.

Peter at Caesarea

And on the next day he got up and went away with them, and some of the brethren from Joppa accompanied him.

24 On the following day he entered Caesarea. Now Cornelius was waiting for them and had called together his relatives and close friends.

NEW CENTURY VERSION

three times, and at once the sheet was taken back to heaven.
17While Peter was wondering what this vision meant, the men Cornelius sent had found Simon's house and were standing at the gate.
18They asked, "Is Simon Peter staying here?"
19While Peter was still thinking about the vision, the Spirit said to him, "Listen, three men are looking for you.
20Get up and go downstairs. Go with them without doubting, because I have sent them to you."
21So Peter went down to the men and said, "I am the one you are looking for. Why did you come here?"
22They said, "A holy angel spoke to Cornelius, an army officer and a good man; he worships God. All the Jewish people respect him. The angel told Cornelius to ask you to come to his house so that he can hear what you have to say."
23So Peter asked the men to come in and spend the night.
The next day Peter got ready and went with them, and some of the followers from Joppa joined him.
24On the following day they came to Caesarea. Cornelius was waiting for them and had called together his relatives and close

CONTEMPORARY ENGLISH VERSION

16This happened three times before the sheet was suddenly taken back to heaven.
17Peter was still wondering what all of this meant, when the men sent by Cornelius came and stood at the gate. They had found their way to Simon's house
18and were asking if Simon Peter was staying there.
19While Peter was still thinking about the vision, the Holy Spirit said to him, "Three[d] men are here looking for you.
20Hurry down and go with them. Don't worry, I sent them."
21Peter went down and said to the men, "I am the one you are looking for. Why have you come?"
22They answered, "Captain Cornelius sent us. He is a good man who worships God and is liked by the Jewish people. One of God's holy angels told Cornelius to send for you, so he could hear what you have to say."
23Peter invited them to spend the night.
The next morning, Peter and some of the Lord's followers in Joppa left with the men who had come from Cornelius.
24The next day they arrived in Caesarea where Cornelius was waiting for them. He had also invited his relatives and close friends.

[d] 10.19 *Three*: One manuscript has "two;" some manuscripts have "some."

NEW INTERNATIONAL VERSION

16This happened three times, and immediately the sheet was taken back to heaven.

17While Peter was wondering about the meaning of the vision, the men sent by Cornelius found out where Simon's house was and stopped at the gate. 18They called out, asking if Simon who was known as Peter was staying there.

19While Peter was still thinking about the vision, the Spirit said to him, "Simon, three[a] men are looking for you. 20So get up and go downstairs. Do not hesitate to go with them, for I have sent them."

21Peter went down and said to the men, "I'm the one you're looking for. Why have you come?"

22The men replied, "We have come from Cornelius the centurion. He is a righteous and God-fearing man, who is respected by all the Jewish people. A holy angel told him to have you come to his house so that he could hear what you have to say." 23Then Peter invited the men into the house to be his guests.

Peter at Cornelius' House

The next day Peter started out with them, and some of the brothers from Joppa went along. 24The following day he arrived in Caesarea. Cornelius was expecting them and had called together his relatives and close friends. 25As Peter

[a] *19* One early manuscript *two*; other manuscripts do not have the number.

NEW LIVING TRANSLATION

repeated three times. Then the sheet was pulled up again to heaven.

17Peter was very perplexed. What could the vision mean? Just then the men sent by Cornelius found the house and stood outside at the gate. 18They asked if this was the place where Simon Peter was staying. 19Meanwhile, as Peter was puzzling over the vision, the Holy Spirit said to him, "Three men have come looking for you. 20Go down and go with them without hesitation. All is well, for I have sent them."

21So Peter went down and said, "I'm the man you are looking for. Why have you come?"

22They said, "We were sent by Cornelius, a Roman officer. He is a devout man who fears the God of Israel and is well respected by all the Jews. A holy angel instructed him to send for you so you can go to his house and give him a message." 23So Peter invited the men to be his guests for the night. The next day he went with them, accompanied by some other believers* from Joppa.

24They arrived in Caesarea the following day. Cornelius was waiting for him and had called together his relatives and close friends to meet Peter. 25As Peter entered his

10:23 Greek *brothers.*

NEW KING JAMES VERSION

16This was done three times. And the object was taken up into heaven again.

Summoned to Caesarea

17Now while Peter wondered within himself what this vision which he had seen meant, behold, the men who had been sent from Cornelius had made inquiry for Simon's house, and stood before the gate. 18And they called and asked whether Simon, whose surname was Peter, was lodging there.

19While Peter thought about the vision, the Spirit said to him, "Behold, three men are seeking you. 20Arise therefore, go down and go with them, doubting nothing; for I have sent them."

21Then Peter went down to the men who had been sent to him from Cornelius,[b] and said, "Yes, I am he whom you seek. For what reason have you come?"

22And they said, "Cornelius *the* centurion, a just man, one who fears God and has a good reputation among all the nation of the Jews, was divinely instructed by a holy angel to summon you to his house, and to hear words from you." 23Then he invited them in and lodged *them.*

On the next day Peter went away with them, and some brethren from Joppa accompanied him.

Peter Meets Cornelius

24And the following day they entered Caesarea. Now Cornelius was waiting for them, and had called together

10:21 [b] NU-Text and M-Text omit *who had been sent to him from Cornelius.*

THE MESSAGE

This happened three times, and then the blanket was pulled back up into the skies.

As Peter, puzzled, sat there trying to figure out what it all meant, the men sent by Cornelius showed up at Simon's front door. They called in, asking if there was a Simon, also called Peter, staying there. Peter, lost in thought, didn't hear them, so the Spirit whispered to him, "Three men are knocking at the door looking for you. Get down there and go with them. Don't ask any questions. I sent them to get you."

Peter went down and said to the men, "I think I'm the man you're looking for. What's up?"

They said, "Captain Cornelius, a God-fearing man well-known for his fair play—ask any Jew in this part of the country—was commanded by a holy angel to get you and bring you to his house so he could hear what you had to say." Peter invited them in and made them feel at home.

God Plays No Favorites

The next morning he got up and went with them. Some of his friends from Joppa went along. A day later they entered Caesarea. Cornelius was expecting them and had his relatives and close friends waiting with him. The

KING JAMES VERSION

25 And as Peter was coming in, Cornelius met him, and fell down at his feet, and worshipped *him*.

26 But Peter took him up, saying, Stand up; I myself also am a man.

27 And as he talked with him, he went in, and found many that were come together.

28 And he said unto them, Ye know how that it is an unlawful thing for a man that is a Jew to keep company, or come unto one of another nation; but God hath shewed me that I should not call any man common or unclean.

29 Therefore came I *unto you* without gainsaying, as soon as I was sent for: I ask therefore for what intent ye have sent for me?

30 And Cornelius said, Four days ago I was fasting until this hour; and at the ninth hour I prayed in my house, and, behold, a man stood before me in bright clothing,

31 And said, Cornelius, thy prayer is heard, and thine alms are had in remembrance in the sight of God.

32 Send therefore to Joppa, and call hither Simon, whose surname is Peter; he is lodged in the house of *one* Simon a tanner by the sea side: who, when he cometh, shall speak unto thee.

33 Immediately therefore I sent to thee; and thou hast well done that thou art come. Now therefore are we all here present before God, to hear all things that are commanded thee of God.

34 ¶ Then Peter opened *his* mouth, and said, Of a truth I perceive that God is no respecter of persons:

NEW AMERICAN STANDARD BIBLE

25 When Peter entered, Cornelius met him, and fell at his feet and worshiped *him*.

26 But Peter raised him up, saying, "Stand up; I too am *just* a man."

27 As he talked with him, he entered and *found many people assembled.

28 And he said to them, "You yourselves know how unlawful it is for a man who is a Jew to associate with a foreigner or to visit him; and *yet* God has shown me that I should not call any man unholy or unclean.

29 "That is why I came without even raising any objection when I was sent for. So I ask for what reason you have sent for me."

30 Cornelius said, "Four days ago to this hour, I was praying in my house during the [8]ninth hour; and behold, a man stood before me in shining garments,

31 and he *said, 'Cornelius, your prayer has been heard and your alms have been remembered before God.

32 'Therefore send to Joppa and invite Simon, who is also called Peter, to come to you; he is staying at the house of Simon *the* tanner by the sea.'

33 "So I sent for you immediately, and you have been kind enough to come. Now then, we are all here present before God to hear all that you have been commanded by the Lord."

Gentiles Hear Good News

34 Opening his mouth, Peter said:

"I most certainly understand *now* that God is not one to show partiality,

10:30 [8] I.e. 3 to 4 p.m.

NEW CENTURY VERSION

friends. [25]When Peter entered, Cornelius met him, fell at his feet, and worshiped him. [26]But Peter helped him up, saying, "Stand up. I too am only a human." [27]As he talked with Cornelius, Peter went inside where he saw many people gathered. [28]He said, "You people understand that it is against our Jewish law for Jewish people to associate with or visit anyone who is not Jewish. But God has shown me that I should not call any person 'unholy' or 'unclean.' [29]That is why I did not argue when I was asked to come here. Now, please tell me why you sent for me."

[30]Cornelius said, "Four days ago, I was praying in my house at this same time—three o'clock in the afternoon. Suddenly, there was a man standing before me wearing shining clothes. [31]He said, 'Cornelius, God has heard your prayer and has seen that you give to the poor and remembers you. [32]So send some men to Joppa and ask Simon Peter to come. Peter is staying in the house of a man, also named Simon, who is a tanner and has a house beside the sea.' [33]So I sent for you immediately, and it was very good of you to come. Now we are all here before God to hear everything the Lord has commanded you to tell us."

[34]Peter began to speak: "I really understand now that to God every person is the same. [35]In every country God

CONTEMPORARY ENGLISH VERSION

[25]When Peter arrived, Cornelius greeted him. Then he knelt at Peter's feet and started worshiping him. [26]But Peter took hold of him and said, "Stand up! I am nothing more than a human."

[27]As Peter entered the house, he was still talking with Cornelius. Many people were there, [28]and Peter said to them, "You know that we Jews are not allowed to have anything to do with other people. But God has shown me that he doesn't think anyone is unclean or unfit. [29]I agreed to come here, but I want to know why you sent for me."

[30]Cornelius answered:

Four days ago at about three o'clock in the afternoon I was praying at home. Suddenly a man in bright clothes stood in front of me. [31]He said, "Cornelius, God has heard your prayers, and he knows about your gifts to the poor. [32]Now send to Joppa for Simon Peter. He is visiting in the home of Simon the leather maker, who lives near the sea."

[33]I sent for you right away, and you have been good enough to come. All of us are here in the presence of the Lord God, so that we can hear what he has to say.

[34]Peter then said:

Now I am certain that God treats all people alike.

NEW INTERNATIONAL VERSION

entered the house, Cornelius met him and fell at his feet in reverence. 26But Peter made him get up. "Stand up," he said, "I am only a man myself."

27Talking with him, Peter went inside and found a large gathering of people. 28He said to them: "You are well aware that it is against our law for a Jew to associate with a Gentile or visit him. But God has shown me that I should not call any man impure or unclean. 29So when I was sent for, I came without raising any objection. May I ask why you sent for me?"

30Cornelius answered: "Four days ago I was in my house praying at this hour, at three in the afternoon. Suddenly a man in shining clothes stood before me 31and said, 'Cornelius, God has heard your prayer and remembered your gifts to the poor. 32Send to Joppa for Simon who is called Peter. He is a guest in the home of Simon the tanner, who lives by the sea.' 33So I sent for you immediately, and it was good of you to come. Now we are all here in the presence of God to listen to everything the Lord has commanded you to tell us."

34Then Peter began to speak: "I now realize how true it is that God does not show favoritism 35but accepts men

NEW LIVING TRANSLATION

home, Cornelius fell to the floor before him in worship. 26But Peter pulled him up and said, "Stand up! I'm a human being like you!" 27So Cornelius got up, and they talked together and went inside where the others were assembled.

28Peter told them, "You know it is against the Jewish laws for me to come into a Gentile home like this. But God has shown me that I should never think of anyone as impure. 29So I came as soon as I was sent for. Now tell me why you sent for me."

30Cornelius replied, "Four days ago I was praying in my house at three o'clock in the afternoon. Suddenly, a man in dazzling clothes was standing in front of me. 31He told me, 'Cornelius, your prayers have been heard, and your gifts to the poor have been noticed by God! 32Now send some men to Joppa and summon Simon Peter. He is staying in the home of Simon, a leatherworker who lives near the shore.' 33So I sent for you at once, and it was good of you to come. Now here we are, waiting before God to hear the message the Lord has given you."

The Gentiles Hear the Good News

34Then Peter replied, "I see very clearly that God doesn't show partiality. 35In every nation he accepts those who

NEW KING JAMES VERSION

his relatives and close friends. 25As Peter was coming in, Cornelius met him and fell down at his feet and worshiped *him.* 26But Peter lifted him up, saying, "Stand up; I myself am also a man." 27And as he talked with him, he went in and found many who had come together. 28Then he said to them, "You know how unlawful it is for a Jewish man to keep company with or go to one of another nation. But God has shown me that I should not call any man common or unclean. 29Therefore I came without objection as soon as I was sent for. I ask, then, for what reason have you sent for me?"

30So Cornelius said, "Four days ago I was fasting until this hour; and at the ninth hour[c] I prayed in my house, and behold, a man stood before me in bright clothing, 31and said, 'Cornelius, your prayer has been heard, and your alms are remembered in the sight of God. 32Send therefore to Joppa and call Simon here, whose surname is Peter. He is lodging in the house of Simon, a tanner, by the sea.[d] When he comes, he will speak to you.' 33So I sent to you immediately, and you have done well to come. Now therefore, we are all present before God, to hear all the things commanded you by God."

Preaching to Cornelius' Household

34Then Peter opened *his* mouth and said: "In truth I perceive that God shows no partiality. 35But in every nation

10:30 [c] NU-Text reads *Four days ago to this hour, at the ninth hour.*
10:32 [d] NU-Text omits the last sentence of this verse.

THE MESSAGE

minute Peter came through the door, Cornelius was up on his feet greeting him—and then down on his face worshiping him! Peter pulled him up and said, "None of that—I'm a man and only a man, no different from you."

Talking things over, they went on into the house, where Cornelius introduced Peter to everyone who had come. Peter addressed them, "You know, I'm sure that this is highly irregular. Jews just don't do this—visit and relax with people of another race. But God has just shown me that no race is better than any other. So the minute I was sent for, I came, no questions asked. But now I'd like to know why you sent for me."

Cornelius said, "Four days ago at about this time, midafternoon, I was home praying. Suddenly there was a man right in front of me, flooding the room with light. He said, 'Cornelius, your daily prayers and neighborly acts have brought you to God's attention. I want you to send to Joppa to get Simon, the one they call Peter. He's staying with Simon the Tanner down by the sea.'

"So I did it—I sent for you. And you've been good enough to come. And now we're all here in God's presence, ready to listen to whatever the Master put in your heart to tell us."

Peter fairly exploded with his good news: "It's God's own truth, nothing could be plainer: God plays no favorites! It makes no difference who you are or where

KING JAMES VERSION

35 But in every nation he that feareth him, and worketh righteousness, is accepted with him.

36 The word which *God* sent unto the children of Israel, preaching peace by Jesus Christ: (he is Lord of all:)

37 That word, *I say*, ye know, which was published throughout all Judaea, and began from Galilee, after the baptism which John preached;

38 How God anointed Jesus of Nazareth with the Holy Ghost and with power: who went about doing good, and healing all that were oppressed of the devil; for God was with him.

39 And we are witnesses of all things which he did both in the land of the Jews, and in Jerusalem; whom they slew and hanged on a tree:

40 Him God raised up the third day, and shewed him openly;

41 Not to all the people, but unto witnesses chosen before of God, *even* to us, who did eat and drink with him after he rose from the dead.

42 And he commanded us to preach unto the people, and to testify that it is he which was ordained of God *to be* the Judge of quick and dead.

43 To him give all the prophets witness, that through his name whosoever believeth in him shall receive remission of sins.

44 ¶ While Peter yet spake these words, the Holy Ghost fell on all them which heard the word.

45 And they of the circumcision which believed were astonished, as many as came with Peter, because that on the Gentiles also was poured out the gift of the Holy Ghost.

NEW AMERICAN STANDARD BIBLE

35 but in every nation the man who fears Him and does what is right is welcome to Him.

36 "The word which He sent to the sons of Israel, preaching peace through Jesus Christ (He is Lord of all)—

37 you yourselves know the thing which took place throughout all Judea, starting from Galilee, after the baptism which John proclaimed.

38 "*You know of* Jesus of Nazareth, how God anointed Him with the Holy Spirit and with power, and *how* He went about doing good and healing all who were oppressed by the devil, for God was with Him.

39 "We are witnesses of all the things He did both in the land of the Jews and in Jerusalem. They also put Him to death by hanging Him on a cross.

40 "God raised Him up on the third day and granted that He become visible,

41 not to all the people, but to witnesses who were chosen beforehand by God, *that is,* to us who ate and drank with Him after He arose from the dead.

42 "And He ordered us to preach to the people, and solemnly to testify that this is the One who has been appointed by God as Judge of the living and the dead.

43 "Of Him all the prophets bear witness that through His name everyone who believes in Him receives forgiveness of sins."

44 While Peter was still speaking these words, the Holy Spirit fell upon all those who were listening to the message.

45 All the circumcised believers who came with Peter were amazed, because the gift of the Holy Spirit had been poured out on the Gentiles also.

NEW CENTURY VERSION

accepts anyone who worships him and does what is right.
36You know the message that God has sent to the people of
Israel is the Good News that peace has come through Jesus
Christ. Jesus is the Lord of all people! 37You know what
has happened all over Judea, beginning in Galilee after
John[b] preached to the people about baptism. 38You know
about Jesus from Nazareth, that God gave him the Holy
Spirit and power. You know how Jesus went everywhere
doing good and healing those who were ruled by the devil,
because God was with him. 39We saw what Jesus did in
Judea and in Jerusalem, but the Jews in Jerusalem killed
him by hanging him on a cross. 40Yet, on the third day,
God raised Jesus to life and caused him to be seen, 41not
by all the people, but only by the witnesses God had
already chosen. And we are those witnesses who ate and
drank with him after he was raised from the dead. 42He
told us to preach to the people and to tell them that he is
the one whom God chose to be the judge of the living and
the dead. 43All the prophets say it is true that all who
believe in Jesus will be forgiven of their sins through Jesus'
name."

44While Peter was still saying this, the Holy Spirit came
down on all those who were listening. 45The Jewish believ-
ers who came with Peter were amazed that the gift of the
Holy Spirit had been given even to those who were not

10:37 [b] **John** John the Baptist, who preached to people about Christ's coming (Luke 3).

CONTEMPORARY ENGLISH VERSION

35God is pleased with everyone who worships him and
does right, no matter what nation they come from.
36This is the same message that God gave to the people
of Israel, when he sent Jesus Christ, the Lord of all, to
offer peace to them.

37You surely know what happened[e] everywhere in
Judea. It all began in Galilee after John had told every-
one to be baptized. 38God gave the Holy Spirit and power
to Jesus from Nazareth. He was with Jesus, as he went
around doing good and healing everyone who was under
the power of the devil. 39We all saw what Jesus did both
in Israel and in the city of Jerusalem.

Jesus was put to death on a cross. 40But three days
later, God raised him to life and let him be seen. 41Not
everyone saw him. He was seen only by us, who ate and
drank with him after he was raised from death. We were
the ones God chose to tell others about him.

42God told us to announce clearly to the people that
Jesus is the one he has chosen to judge the living and
the dead. 43Every one of the prophets has said that all
who have faith in Jesus will have their sins forgiven in
his name.

44While Peter was still speaking, the Holy Spirit took
control of everyone who was listening. 45Some Jewish fol-
lowers of the Lord had come with Peter, and they were sur-
prised that the Holy Spirit had been given to Gentiles.

[e] **10.37** *what happened*: Or "the message that went."

NEW INTERNATIONAL VERSION

from every nation who fear him and do what is right. 36You know the message God sent to the people of Israel, telling the good news of peace through Jesus Christ, who is Lord of all. 37You know what has happened throughout Judea, beginning in Galilee after the baptism that John preached— 38how God anointed Jesus of Nazareth with the Holy Spirit and power, and how he went around doing good and healing all who were under the power of the devil, because God was with him.

39"We are witnesses of everything he did in the country of the Jews and in Jerusalem. They killed him by hanging him on a tree, 40but God raised him from the dead on the third day and caused him to be seen. 41He was not seen by all the people, but by witnesses whom God had already chosen—by us who ate and drank with him after he rose from the dead. 42He commanded us to preach to the people and to testify that he is the one whom God appointed as judge of the living and the dead. 43All the prophets testify about him that everyone who believes in him receives forgiveness of sins through his name."

44While Peter was still speaking these words, the Holy Spirit came on all who heard the message. 45The circumcised believers who had come with Peter were astonished that the gift of the Holy Spirit had been poured out even on

NEW LIVING TRANSLATION

fear him and do what is right. 36I'm sure you have heard about the Good News for the people of Israel—that there is peace with God through Jesus Christ, who is Lord of all. 37You know what happened all through Judea, beginning in Galilee after John the Baptist began preaching. 38And no doubt you know that God anointed Jesus of Nazareth with the Holy Spirit and with power. Then Jesus went around doing good and healing all who were oppressed by the Devil, for God was with him.

39"And we apostles are witnesses of all he did throughout Israel and in Jerusalem. They put him to death by crucifying him, 40but God raised him to life three days later. Then God allowed him to appear, 41not to the general public,* but to us whom God had chosen beforehand to be his witnesses. We were those who ate and drank with him after he rose from the dead. 42And he ordered us to preach everywhere and to testify that Jesus is ordained of God to be the judge of all—the living and the dead. 43He is the one all the prophets testified about, saying that everyone who believes in him will have their sins forgiven through his name."

The Gentiles Receive the Holy Spirit

44Even as Peter was saying these things, the Holy Spirit fell upon all who had heard the message. 45The Jewish believers who came with Peter were amazed that the gift of the Holy Spirit had been poured out upon the Gentiles, too.

10:41 Greek *the people.*

NEW KING JAMES VERSION

whoever fears Him and works righteousness is accepted by Him. 36The word which *God* sent to the children of Israel, preaching peace through Jesus Christ—He is Lord of all— 37that word you know, which was proclaimed throughout all Judea, and began from Galilee after the baptism which John preached: 38how God anointed Jesus of Nazareth with the Holy Spirit and with power, who went about doing good and healing all who were oppressed by the devil, for God was with Him. 39And we are witnesses of all things which He did both in the land of the Jews and in Jerusalem, whom they[e] killed by hanging on a tree. 40Him God raised up on the third day, and showed Him openly, 41not to all the people, but to witnesses chosen before by God, *even* to us who ate and drank with Him after He arose from the dead. 42And He commanded us to preach to the people, and to testify that it is He who was ordained by God *to be* Judge of the living and the dead. 43To Him all the prophets witness that, through His name, whoever believes in Him will receive remission of sins."

The Holy Spirit Falls on the Gentiles

44While Peter was still speaking these words, the Holy Spirit fell upon all those who heard the word. 45And those of the circumcision who believed were astonished, as many as came with Peter, because the gift of the Holy Spirit had

10:39 [e] NU-Text and M-Text add *also.*

THE MESSAGE

you're from—if you want God and are ready to do as he says, the door is open. The Message he sent to the children of Israel—that through Jesus Christ everything is being put together again—well, he's doing it everywhere, among everyone.

"You know the story of what happened in Judea. It began in Galilee after John preached a total life-change. Then Jesus arrived from Nazareth, anointed by God with the Holy Spirit, ready for action. He went through the country helping people and healing everyone who was beaten down by the Devil. He was able to do all this because God was with him.

"And we saw it, saw it all, everything he did in the land of the Jews and in Jerusalem where they killed him, hung him from a cross. But in three days God had him up, alive, and out where he could be seen. Not everyone saw him—he wasn't put on public display. Witnesses had been carefully handpicked by God beforehand—us! We were the ones, there to eat and drink with him after he came back from the dead. He commissioned us to announce this in public, to bear solemn witness that he is in fact the One whom God destined as Judge of the living and dead. But we're not alone in this. Our witness that he is the means to forgiveness of sins is backed up by the witness of all the prophets."

No sooner were these words out of Peter's mouth than the Holy Spirit came on the listeners. The believing Jews who had come with Peter couldn't believe it, couldn't believe that the gift of the Holy Spirit was poured out on "outsider"

KING JAMES VERSION

46 For they heard them speak with tongues, and magnify God. Then answered Peter,

47 Can any man forbid water, that these should not be baptized, which have received the Holy Ghost as well as we?

48 And he commanded them to be baptized in the name of the Lord. Then prayed they him to tarry certain days.

11 And the apostles and brethren that were in Judaea heard that the Gentiles had also received the word of God.

2 And when Peter was come up to Jerusalem, they that were of the circumcision contended with him,

3 Saying, Thou wentest in to men uncircumcised, and didst eat with them.

4 But Peter rehearsed *the matter* from the beginning, and expounded *it* by order unto them, saying,

5 I was in the city of Joppa praying: and in a trance I saw a vision, A certain vessel descend, as it had been a great sheet, let down from heaven by four corners; and it came even to me:

6 Upon the which when I had fastened mine eyes, I considered, and saw fourfooted beasts of the earth, and wild beasts, and creeping things, and fowls of the air.

7 And I heard a voice saying unto me, Arise, Peter; slay and eat.

NEW AMERICAN STANDARD BIBLE

46 For they were hearing them speaking with tongues and exalting God. Then Peter answered,

47 "Surely no one can refuse the water for these to be baptized who have received the Holy Spirit just as we *did,* can he?"

48 And he ordered them to be baptized in the name of Jesus Christ. Then they asked him to stay on for a few days.

Peter Reports at Jerusalem

11 Now the apostles and the brethren who were throughout Judea heard that the Gentiles also had received the word of God.

2 And when Peter came up to Jerusalem, those who were circumcised took issue with him,

3 saying, "You went to uncircumcised men and ate with them."

4 But Peter began *speaking* and *proceeded* to explain to them in orderly sequence, saying,

5 "I was in the city of Joppa praying; and in a trance I saw a vision, an object coming down like a great sheet lowered by four corners from the sky; and it came right down to me,

6 and when I had fixed my gaze on it and was observing it I saw the four-footed animals of the earth and the wild beasts and the [1]crawling creatures and the birds of the air.

7 "I also heard a voice saying to me, 'Get up, Peter; kill and eat.'

11:6 [1] Or *reptiles*

NEW CENTURY VERSION

Jews. 46These Jewish believers heard them speaking in different languages[c] and praising God. Then Peter said, 47"Can anyone keep these people from being baptized with water? They have received the Holy Spirit just as we did!" 48So Peter ordered that they be baptized in the name of Jesus Christ. Then they asked Peter to stay with them for a few days.

Peter Returns to Jerusalem

11 The apostles and the believers in Judea heard that some who were not Jewish had accepted God's teaching too. 2But when Peter came to Jerusalem, some Jewish believers argued with him. 3They said, "You went into the homes of people who are not circumcised and ate with them!"

4So Peter explained the whole story to them. 5He said, "I was in the city of Joppa, and while I was praying, I had a vision. I saw something that looked like a big sheet being lowered from heaven by its four corners. It came very close to me. 6I looked inside it and saw animals, wild beasts, reptiles, and birds. 7I heard a voice say to me, 'Get up, Peter.

10:46 [c] **languages** This can also be translated "tongues."

CONTEMPORARY ENGLISH VERSION

46Now they were hearing Gentiles speaking unknown languages and praising God.

Peter said, 47"These Gentiles have been given the Holy Spirit, just as we have! I am certain that no one would dare stop us from baptizing them." 48Peter ordered them to be baptized in the name of Jesus Christ, and they asked him to stay on for a few days.

Peter Reports to the Church in Jerusalem

11 The apostles and the followers in Judea heard that Gentiles had accepted God's message. 2So when Peter came to Jerusalem, some of the Jewish followers started arguing with him. They wanted Gentile followers to be circumcised, and 3they said, "You stayed in the homes of Gentiles, and you even ate with them!"

4Then Peter told them exactly what had happened:

5I was in the town of Joppa and was praying when I fell sound asleep and had a vision. I saw heaven open, and something like a huge sheet held by its four corners came down to me. 6When I looked in it, I saw animals, wild beasts, snakes, and birds. 7I heard a voice saying to me, "Peter, get up! Kill these and eat them."

NEW INTERNATIONAL VERSION

the Gentiles. [46]For they heard them speaking in tongues[b] and praising God.

Then Peter said, [47]"Can anyone keep these people from being baptized with water? They have received the Holy Spirit just as we have." [48]So he ordered that they be baptized in the name of Jesus Christ. Then they asked Peter to stay with them for a few days.

Peter Explains His Actions

11 The apostles and the brothers throughout Judea heard that the Gentiles also had received the word of God. [2]So when Peter went up to Jerusalem, the circumcised believers criticized him [3]and said, "You went into the house of uncircumcised men and ate with them."

[4]Peter began and explained everything to them precisely as it had happened: [5]"I was in the city of Joppa praying, and in a trance I saw a vision. I saw something like a large sheet being let down from heaven by its four corners, and it came down to where I was. [6]I looked into it and saw four-footed animals of the earth, wild beasts, reptiles, and birds of the air. [7]Then I heard a voice telling me, 'Get up, Peter. Kill and eat.'

[b] *46* Or *other languages*

NEW LIVING TRANSLATION

[46]And there could be no doubt about it, for they heard them speaking in tongues and praising God.

Then Peter asked, [47]"Can anyone object to their being baptized, now that they have received the Holy Spirit just as we did?" [48]So he gave orders for them to be baptized in the name of Jesus Christ. Afterward Cornelius asked him to stay with them for several days.

Peter Explains His Actions

11 Soon the news reached the apostles and other believers* in Judea that the Gentiles had received the word of God. [2]But when Peter arrived back in Jerusalem, some of the Jewish believers* criticized him. [3]"You entered the home of Gentiles* and even ate with them!" they said.

[4]Then Peter told them exactly what had happened. [5]"One day in Joppa," he said, "while I was praying, I went into a trance and saw a vision. Something like a large sheet was let down by its four corners from the sky. And it came right down to me. [6]When I looked inside the sheet, I saw all sorts of small animals, wild animals, reptiles, and birds that we are not allowed to eat. [7]And I heard a voice say, 'Get up, Peter; kill and eat them.'

11:1 Greek *brothers.* 11:2 Greek *those of the circumcision.* 11:3 Greek *of uncircumcised men.*

NEW KING JAMES VERSION

been poured out on the Gentiles also. [46]For they heard them speak with tongues and magnify God.

Then Peter answered, [47]"Can anyone forbid water, that these should not be baptized who have received the Holy Spirit just as we *have?*" [48]And he commanded them to be baptized in the name of the Lord. Then they asked him to stay a few days.

Peter Defends God's Grace

11 Now the apostles and brethren who were in Judea heard that the Gentiles had also received the word of God. [2]And when Peter came up to Jerusalem, those of the circumcision contended with him, [3]saying, "You went in to uncircumcised men and ate with them!"

[4]But Peter explained *it* to them in order from the beginning, saying: [5]"I was in the city of Joppa praying; and in a trance I saw a vision, an object descending like a great sheet, let down from heaven by four corners; and it came to me. [6]When I observed it intently and considered, I saw four-footed animals of the earth, wild beasts, creeping things, and birds of the air. [7]And I heard a voice saying to me, 'Rise, Peter; kill and eat.' [8]But I said, 'Not so, Lord!

THE MESSAGE

Gentiles, but there it was—they heard them speaking in tongues, heard them praising God.

Then Peter said, "Do I hear any objections to baptizing these friends with water? They've received the Holy Spirit exactly as we did." Hearing no objections, he ordered that they be baptized in the name of Jesus Christ.

Then they asked Peter to stay on for a few days.

God Has Broken Through

11 The news traveled fast and in no time the leaders and friends back in Jerusalem heard about it—heard that the non-Jewish "outsiders" were now "in." When Peter got back to Jerusalem, some of his old associates, concerned about circumcision, called him on the carpet: "What do you think you're doing rubbing shoulders with that crowd, eating what is prohibited and ruining our good name?"

So Peter, starting from the beginning, laid it out for them step by step: "Recently I was in the town of Joppa praying. I fell into a trance and saw a vision: Something like a huge blanket, lowered by ropes at its four corners, came down out of heaven and settled on the ground in front of me. Milling around on the blanket were farm animals, wild animals, reptiles, birds—you name it, it was there. Fascinated, I took it all in.

"Then I heard a voice: 'Go to it, Peter—kill and eat.' I

KING JAMES VERSION

8 But I said, Not so, Lord: for nothing common or unclean hath at any time entered into my mouth.

9 But the voice answered me again from heaven, What God hath cleansed, *that* call not thou common.

10 And this was done three times: and all were drawn up again into heaven.

11 And, behold, immediately there were three men already come unto the house where I was, sent from Caesarea unto me.

12 And the Spirit bade me go with them, nothing doubting. Moreover these six brethren accompanied me, and we entered into the man's house:

13 And he shewed us how he had seen an angel in his house, which stood and said unto him, Send men to Joppa, and call for Simon, whose surname is Peter;

14 Who shall tell thee words, whereby thou and all thy house shall be saved.

15 And as I began to speak, the Holy Ghost fell on them, as on us at the beginning.

16 Then remembered I the word of the Lord, how that he said, John indeed baptized with water; but ye shall be baptized with the Holy Ghost.

17 Forasmuch then as God gave them the like gift as *he did* unto us, who believed on the Lord Jesus Christ; what was I, that I could withstand God?

18 When they heard these things, they held their peace, and glorified God, saying, Then hath God also to the Gentiles granted repentance unto life.

NEW AMERICAN STANDARD BIBLE

8 "But I said, 'By no means, Lord, for nothing unholy or unclean has ever entered my mouth.'

9 "But a voice from heaven answered a second time, 'What God has cleansed, no longer consider unholy.'

10 "This happened three times, and everything was drawn back up into the sky.

11 "And behold, at that moment three men appeared at the house in which we were *staying,* having been sent to me from Caesarea.

12 "The Spirit told me to go with them without misgivings. These six brethren also went with me and we entered the man's house.

13 "And he reported to us how he had seen the angel standing in his house, and saying, 'Send to Joppa and have Simon, who is also called Peter, brought here;

14 and he will speak words to you by which you will be saved, you and all your household.'

15 "And as I began to speak, the Holy Spirit fell upon them just as *He did* upon us at the beginning.

16 "And I remembered the word of the Lord, how He used to say, 'John baptized with water, but you will be baptized with the Holy Spirit.'

17 "Therefore if God gave to them the same gift as *He gave* to us also after believing in the Lord Jesus Christ, who was I that I could stand in God's way?"

18 When they heard this, they quieted down and glorified God, saying, "Well then, God has granted to the Gentiles also the repentance *that leads* to life."

NEW CENTURY VERSION

Kill and eat.' 8But I said, 'No, Lord! I have never eaten anything that is unholy or unclean.' 9But the voice from heaven spoke again, 'God has made these things clean, so don't call them unholy.' 10This happened three times. Then the whole thing was taken back to heaven. 11Right then three men who were sent to me from Caesarea came to the house where I was staying. 12The Spirit told me to go with them without doubting. These six believers here also went with me, and we entered the house of Cornelius. 13He told us about the angel he saw standing in his house. The angel said to him, 'Send some men to Joppa and invite Simon Peter to come. 14By the words he will say to you, you and all your family will be saved.' 15When I began my speech, the Holy Spirit came on them just as he came on us at the beginning. 16Then I remembered the words of the Lord. He said, 'John baptized with water, but you will be baptized with the Holy Spirit.' 17Since God gave them the same gift he gave us who believed in the Lord Jesus Christ, how could I stop the work of God?"

18When the Jewish believers heard this, they stopped arguing. They praised God and said, "So God is allowing even those who are not Jewish to turn to him and live."

CONTEMPORARY ENGLISH VERSION

8But I said, "Lord, I can't do that! I've never taken a
bite of anything that is unclean and not fit to eat."[a]
9The voice from heaven spoke to me again, "When
God says that something can be used for food, don't say
it isn't fit to eat." 10This happened three times before it
was all taken back into heaven.

11Suddenly three men from Caesarea stood in front of
the house where I was staying. 12The Holy Spirit told me
to go with them and not to worry. Then six of the Lord's
followers went with me to the home of a man 13who told
us that an angel had appeared to him. The angel had
ordered him to send to Joppa for someone named Simon
Peter. 14Then Peter would tell him how he and everyone
in his house could be saved.

15After I started speaking, the Holy Spirit was given to
them, just as the Spirit had been given to us at the
beginning. 16I remembered that the Lord had said, "John
baptized with water, but you will be baptized with the
Holy Spirit." 17God gave those Gentiles the same gift
that he gave us when we put our faith in the Lord Jesus
Christ. So how could I have gone against God?

18When they heard Peter say this, they stopped arguing and started praising God. They said, "God has now let Gentiles turn to him, and he has given life to them!"

[a] **11.8** *unclean and not fit to eat*: See the note at 10.14.

NEW INTERNATIONAL VERSION

8“I replied, ‘Surely not, Lord! Nothing impure or unclean has ever entered my mouth.’

9“The voice spoke from heaven a second time, ‘Do not call anything impure that God has made clean.’ 10This happened three times, and then it was all pulled up to heaven again.

11“Right then three men who had been sent to me from Caesarea stopped at the house where I was staying. 12The Spirit told me to have no hesitation about going with them. These six brothers also went with me, and we entered the man’s house. 13He told us how he had seen an angel appear in his house and say, ‘Send to Joppa for Simon who is called Peter. 14He will bring you a message through which you and all your household will be saved.’

15“As I began to speak, the Holy Spirit came on them as he had come on us at the beginning. 16Then I remembered what the Lord had said: ‘John baptized with[a] water, but you will be baptized with the Holy Spirit.’ 17So if God gave them the same gift as he gave us, who believed in the Lord Jesus Christ, who was I to think that I could oppose God?”

18When they heard this, they had no further objections and praised God, saying, “So then, God has granted even the Gentiles repentance unto life.”

[a] *16* Or *in*

NEW LIVING TRANSLATION

8“ ‘Never, Lord,’ I replied. ‘I have never eaten anything forbidden by our Jewish laws.*’

9“But the voice from heaven came again, ‘If God says something is acceptable, don’t say it isn’t.’*

10“This happened three times before the sheet and all it contained was pulled back up to heaven. 11Just then three men who had been sent from Caesarea arrived at the house where I was staying. 12The Holy Spirit told me to go with them and not to worry about their being Gentiles. These six brothers here accompanied me, and we soon arrived at the home of the man who had sent for us. 13He told us how an angel had appeared to him in his home and had told him, ‘Send messengers to Joppa to find Simon Peter. 14He will tell you how you and all your household will be saved!’

15“Well, I began telling them the Good News, but just as I was getting started, the Holy Spirit fell on them, just as he fell on us at the beginning. 16Then I thought of the Lord’s words when he said, ‘John baptized with* water, but you will be baptized with the Holy Spirit.’ 17And since God gave these Gentiles the same gift he gave us when we believed in the Lord Jesus Christ, who was I to argue?”

18When the others heard this, all their objections were answered and they began praising God. They said, “God has also given the Gentiles the privilege of turning from sin and receiving eternal life.”

11:8 Greek *anything common or unclean.* **11:9** Greek *‘What God calls clean you must not call unclean.’* **11:16** Or *in;* also in 11:16b.

NEW KING JAMES VERSION

For nothing common or unclean has at any time entered my mouth.’ 9But the voice answered me again from heaven, ‘What God has cleansed you must not call common.’ 10Now this was done three times, and all were drawn up again into heaven. 11At that very moment, three men stood before the house where I was, having been sent to me from Caesarea. 12Then the Spirit told me to go with them, doubting nothing. Moreover these six brethren accompanied me, and we entered the man’s house. 13And he told us how he had seen an angel standing in his house, who said to him, ‘Send men to Joppa, and call for Simon whose surname is Peter, 14who will tell you words by which you and all your household will be saved.’ 15And as I began to speak, the Holy Spirit fell upon them, as upon us at the beginning. 16Then I remembered the word of the Lord, how He said, ‘John indeed baptized with water, but you shall be baptized with the Holy Spirit.’ 17If therefore God gave them the same gift as *He gave* us when we believed on the Lord Jesus Christ, who was I that I could withstand God?”

18When they heard these things they became silent; and they glorified God, saying, “Then God has also granted to the Gentiles repentance to life.”

THE MESSAGE

said, ‘Oh, no, Master. I’ve never so much as tasted food that wasn’t kosher.’ The voice spoke again: ‘If God says it’s okay, it’s okay.’ This happened three times, and then the blanket was pulled back up into the sky.

“Just then three men showed up at the house where I was staying, sent from Caesarea to get me. The Spirit told me to go with them, no questions asked. So I went with them, I and six friends, to the man who had sent for me. He told us how he had seen an angel right in his own house, real as his next-door neighbor, saying, ‘Send to Joppa and get Simon, the one they call Peter. He’ll tell you something that will save your life—in fact, you and everyone you care for.’

“So I started in, talking. Before I’d spoken half a dozen sentences, the Holy Spirit fell on them just as he did on us the first time. I remembered Jesus’ words: ‘John baptized with water; you will be baptized with the Holy Spirit.’ So I ask you: If God gave the same exact gift to them as to us when we believed in the Master Jesus Christ, how could I object to God?”

Hearing it all laid out like that, they quieted down. And then, as it sank in, they started praising God. “It’s really happened! God has broken through to the other nations, opened them up to Life!”

KING JAMES VERSION

19 ¶ Now they which were scattered abroad upon the persecution that arose about Stephen travelled as far as Phenice, and Cyprus, and Antioch, preaching the word to none but unto the Jews only.

20 And some of them were men of Cyprus and Cyrene, which, when they were come to Antioch, spake unto the Grecians, preaching the Lord Jesus.

21 And the hand of the Lord was with them: and a great number believed, and turned unto the Lord.

22 Then tidings of these things came unto the ears of the church which was in Jerusalem: and they sent forth Barnabas, that he should go as far as Antioch.

23 Who, when he came, and had seen the grace of God, was glad, and exhorted them all, that with purpose of heart they would cleave unto the Lord.

24 For he was a good man, and full of the Holy Ghost and of faith: and much people was added unto the Lord.

25 Then departed Barnabas to Tarsus, for to seek Saul:

26 And when he had found him, he brought him unto Antioch. And it came to pass, that a whole year they assembled themselves with the church, and taught much people. And the disciples were called Christians first in Antioch.

27 ¶ And in these days came prophets from Jerusalem unto Antioch.

28 And there stood up one of them named Agabus, and signified by the Spirit that there should be great dearth

NEW AMERICAN STANDARD BIBLE

The Church at Antioch

19 So then those who were scattered because of the persecution that occurred in connection with Stephen made their way to Phoenicia and Cyprus and Antioch, speaking the word to no one except to Jews alone.

20 But there were some of them, men of Cyprus and Cyrene, who came to Antioch and *began* speaking to the [2]Greeks also, preaching the Lord Jesus.

21 And the hand of the Lord was with them, and a large number who believed turned to the Lord.

22 The news about them reached the ears of the church at Jerusalem, and they sent Barnabas off to Antioch.

23 Then when he arrived and witnessed the grace of God, he rejoiced and *began* to encourage them all with resolute heart to remain *true* to the Lord;

24 for he was a good man, and full of the Holy Spirit and of faith. And considerable numbers were brought to the Lord.

25 And he left for Tarsus to look for Saul;

26 and when he had found him, he brought him to Antioch. And for an entire year they met with the church and taught considerable numbers; and the disciples were first called Christians in Antioch.

27 Now at this time some prophets came down from Jerusalem to Antioch.

28 One of them named Agabus stood up and *began* to indicate by the Spirit that there would certainly be a great

11:20 [2] Lit *Hellenists;* people who lived by Greek customs and culture

NEW CENTURY VERSION

The Good News Comes to Antioch

19 Many of the believers were scattered when they were
persecuted after Stephen was killed. Some of them went as
far as Phoenicia, Cyprus, and Antioch telling the message
to others, but only to Jews. 20 Some of these believers were
people from Cyprus and Cyrene. When they came to
Antioch, they spoke also to Greeks, telling them the Good
News about the Lord Jesus. 21 The Lord was helping the
believers, and a large group of people believed and turned
to the Lord.
22 The church in Jerusalem heard about all of this, so
they sent Barnabas to Antioch. 23–24 Barnabas was a good
man, full of the Holy Spirit and full of faith. When he
reached Antioch and saw how God had blessed the people,
he was glad. He encouraged all the believers in Antioch
always to obey the Lord with all their hearts, and many
people became followers of the Lord.
25 Then Barnabas went to the city of Tarsus to look for
Saul, 26 and when he found Saul, he brought him to
Antioch. For a whole year Saul and Barnabas met with the
church and taught many people there. In Antioch the followers were called Christians for the first time.
27 About that time some prophets came from Jerusalem
to Antioch. 28 One of them, named Agabus, stood up and
spoke with the help of the Holy Spirit. He said, "A very
hard time is coming to the whole world. There will be no

CONTEMPORARY ENGLISH VERSION

The Church in Antioch

19 Some of the Lord's followers had been scattered
because of the terrible trouble that started when Stephen
was killed. They went as far as Phoenicia, Cyprus, and
Antioch, but they told the message only to the Jews.
20 Some of the followers from Cyprus and Cyrene went to
Antioch and started telling Gentiles[b] the good news about
the Lord Jesus. 21 The Lord's power was with them, and
many people turned to the Lord and put their faith in him.
22 News of what was happening reached the church in
Jerusalem. Then they sent Barnabas to Antioch.
23 When Barnabas got there and saw what God had been
kind enough to do for them, he was very glad. So he
begged them to remain faithful to the Lord with all their
hearts. 24 Barnabas was a good man of great faith, and he
was filled with the Holy Spirit. Many more people turned
to the Lord.
25 Barnabas went to Tarsus to look for Saul. 26 He found
Saul and brought him to Antioch, where they met with the
church for a whole year and taught many of its people.
There in Antioch the Lord's followers were first called
Christians.
27 During this time some prophets from Jerusalem came
to Antioch. 28 One of them was Agabus. Then with the help
of the Spirit, he told that there would be a terrible famine

[b] 11.20 *Gentiles*: This translates a Greek word that may mean "people who speak Greek" or "people who live as Greeks do." Here the word seems to mean "people who are not Jews." Some manuscripts have "Greeks," which also seems to mean "people who are not Jews."

NEW INTERNATIONAL VERSION

The Church in Antioch

19Now those who had been scattered by the persecution in connection with Stephen traveled as far as Phoenicia, Cyprus and Antioch, telling the message only to Jews. 20Some of them, however, men from Cyprus and Cyrene, went to Antioch and began to speak to Greeks also, telling them the good news about the Lord Jesus. 21The Lord's hand was with them, and a great number of people believed and turned to the Lord.

22News of this reached the ears of the church at Jerusalem, and they sent Barnabas to Antioch. 23When he arrived and saw the evidence of the grace of God, he was glad and encouraged them all to remain true to the Lord with all their hearts. 24He was a good man, full of the Holy Spirit and faith, and a great number of people were brought to the Lord.

25Then Barnabas went to Tarsus to look for Saul, 26and when he found him, he brought him to Antioch. So for a whole year Barnabas and Saul met with the church and taught great numbers of people. The disciples were called Christians first at Antioch.

27During this time some prophets came down from Jerusalem to Antioch. 28One of them, named Agabus, stood up and through the Spirit predicted that a severe famine

NEW LIVING TRANSLATION

The Church in Antioch of Syria

19Meanwhile, the believers who had fled from Jerusalem during the persecution after Stephen's death traveled as far as Phoenicia, Cyprus, and Antioch of Syria. They preached the Good News, but only to Jews. 20However, some of the believers who went to Antioch from Cyprus and Cyrene began preaching to Gentiles* about the Lord Jesus. 21The power of the Lord was upon them, and large numbers of these Gentiles believed and turned to the Lord.

22When the church at Jerusalem heard what had happened, they sent Barnabas to Antioch. 23When he arrived and saw this proof of God's favor, he was filled with joy, and he encouraged the believers to stay true to the Lord. 24Barnabas was a good man, full of the Holy Spirit and strong in faith. And large numbers of people were brought to the Lord.

25Then Barnabas went on to Tarsus to find Saul. 26When he found him, he brought him back to Antioch. Both of them stayed there with the church for a full year, teaching great numbers of people. (It was there at Antioch that the believers* were first called Christians.)

27During this time, some prophets traveled from Jerusalem to Antioch. 28One of them named Agabus stood up in one of the meetings to predict by the Spirit that a

11:20 Greek *the Greeks;* other manuscripts read *the Hellenists.*
11:26 Greek *disciples;* also in 11:29.

NEW KING JAMES VERSION

Barnabas and Saul at Antioch

19Now those who were scattered after the persecution that arose over Stephen traveled as far as Phoenicia, Cyprus, and Antioch, preaching the word to no one but the Jews only. 20But some of them were men from Cyprus and Cyrene, who, when they had come to Antioch, spoke to the Hellenists, preaching the Lord Jesus. 21And the hand of the Lord was with them, and a great number believed and turned to the Lord.

22Then news of these things came to the ears of the church in Jerusalem, and they sent out Barnabas to go as far as Antioch. 23When he came and had seen the grace of God, he was glad, and encouraged them all that with purpose of heart they should continue with the Lord. 24For he was a good man, full of the Holy Spirit and of faith. And a great many people were added to the Lord.

25Then Barnabas departed for Tarsus to seek Saul. 26And when he had found him, he brought him to Antioch. So it was that for a whole year they assembled with the church and taught a great many people. And the disciples were first called Christians in Antioch.

Relief to Judea

27And in these days prophets came from Jerusalem to Antioch. 28Then one of them, named Agabus, stood up and showed by the Spirit that there was going to be a great

THE MESSAGE

Those who had been scattered by the persecution triggered by Stephen's death traveled as far as Phoenicia, Cyprus, and Antioch, but they were still only speaking and dealing with their fellow Jews. Then some of the men from Cyprus and Cyrene who had come to Antioch started talking to Greeks, giving them the Message of the Master Jesus. God was pleased with what they were doing and put his stamp of approval on it—quite a number of the Greeks believed and turned to the Master.

When the church in Jerusalem got wind of this, they sent Barnabas to Antioch to check on things. As soon as he arrived, he saw that God was behind and in it all. He threw himself in with them, got behind them, urging them to stay with it the rest of their lives. He was a good man that way, enthusiastic and confident in the Holy Spirit's ways. The community grew large and strong in the Master.

Then Barnabas went on to Tarsus to look for Saul. He found him and brought him back to Antioch. They were there a whole year, meeting with the church and teaching a lot of people. It was in Antioch that the disciples were for the first time called Christians.

It was about this same time that some prophets came to Antioch from Jerusalem. One of them named Agabus stood up one day and, prompted by the Spirit, warned that a

KING JAMES VERSION

throughout all the world: which came to pass in the days of Claudius Caesar.

29 Then the disciples, every man according to his ability, determined to send relief unto the brethren which dwelt in Judaea:

30 Which also they did, and sent it to the elders by the hands of Barnabas and Saul.

12 Now about that time Herod the king stretched forth *his* hands to vex certain of the church.

2 And he killed James the brother of John with the sword.

3 And because he saw it pleased the Jews, he proceeded further to take Peter also. (Then were the days of unleavened bread.)

4 And when he had apprehended him, he put *him* in prison, and delivered *him* to four quaternions of soldiers to keep him; intending after Easter to bring him forth to the people.

5 ¶ Peter therefore was kept in prison: but prayer was made without ceasing of the church unto God for him.

6 And when Herod would have brought him forth, the same night Peter was sleeping between two soldiers, bound with two chains: and the keepers before the door kept the prison.

7 And, behold, the angel of the Lord came upon *him*, and a light shined in the prison: and he smote Peter on the side, and raised him up, saying, Arise up quickly. And his chains fell off from *his* hands.

NEW AMERICAN STANDARD BIBLE

famine all over the world. And this took place in the *reign* of Claudius.

29 And in the proportion that any of the disciples had means, each of them determined to send *a contribution* for the relief of the brethren living in Judea.

30 And this they did, sending it in charge of Barnabas and Saul to the elders.

Peter's Arrest and Deliverance

12 Now about that time Herod the king laid hands on some who belonged to the church in order to mistreat them.

2 And he had James the brother of John put to death with a sword.

3 When he saw that it pleased the Jews, he proceeded to arrest Peter also. Now it was during the days of Unleavened Bread.

4 When he had seized him, he put him in prison, delivering him to four squads of soldiers to guard him, intending after the Passover to bring him out before the people.

5 So Peter was kept in the prison, but prayer for him was being made fervently by the church to God.

6 On the very night when Herod was about to bring him forward, Peter was sleeping between two soldiers, bound with two chains, and guards in front of the door were watching over the prison.

7 And behold, an angel of the Lord suddenly appeared and a light shone in the cell; and he struck Peter's side and woke him up, saying, "Get up quickly." And his chains fell off his hands.

NEW CENTURY VERSION

food to eat." (This happened when Claudius ruled.) 29The
believers all decided to help the followers who lived in
Judea, as much as each one could. 30They gathered the
money and gave it to Barnabas and Saul, who brought it
to the elders in Judea.

Herod Agrippa Hurts the Church

12 During that same time King Herod began to mistreat some who belonged to the church. 2He
ordered James, the brother of John, to be killed by the
sword. 3Herod saw that the Jewish people liked this, so he
decided to arrest Peter, too. (This happened during the
time of the Feast of Unleavened Bread.)

4After Herod arrested Peter, he put him in jail and handed him over to be guarded by sixteen soldiers. Herod
planned to bring Peter before the people for trial after the
Passover Feast. 5So Peter was kept in jail, but the church
prayed earnestly to God for him.

Peter Leaves the Jail

6The night before Herod was to bring him to trial, Peter
was sleeping between two soldiers, bound with two chains.
Other soldiers were guarding the door of the jail.
7Suddenly, an angel of the Lord stood there, and a light
shined in the cell. The angel struck Peter on the side and
woke him up. "Hurry! Get up!" the angel said. And the
chains fell off Peter's hands. 8Then the angel told him,

CONTEMPORARY ENGLISH VERSION

everywhere in the world. And it happened when Claudius
was Emperor.[c] 29The followers in Antioch decided to send
whatever help they could to the followers in Judea. 30So
they had Barnabas and Saul take their gifts to the church
leaders in Jerusalem.

Herod Causes Trouble for the Church

12 At that time King Herod[a] caused terrible suffering for some members of the church. 2He ordered soldiers to cut off the head of James, the brother of John.
3When Herod saw that this pleased the Jewish people, he
had Peter arrested during the Festival of Thin Bread. 4He
put Peter in jail and ordered four squads of soldiers to
guard him. Herod planned to put him on trial in public
after the festival.

5While Peter was being kept in jail, the church never
stopped praying to God for him.

Peter Is Rescued

6The night before Peter was to be put on trial, he was
asleep and bound by two chains. A soldier was guarding
him on each side, and two other soldiers were guarding
the entrance to the jail. 7Suddenly an angel from the Lord
appeared, and light flashed around in the cell. The angel
poked Peter in the side and woke him up. Then he said,
"Quick! Get up!"

The chains fell off his hands, 8and the angel said, "Get

[c] 11.28 *when Claudius was Emperor*: A.D. 41-54. [a] 12.1 *Herod*: Herod Agrippa I, the grandson of Herod the Great.

NEW INTERNATIONAL VERSION

would spread over the entire Roman world. (This happened during the reign of Claudius.) [29]The disciples, each according to his ability, decided to provide help for the brothers living in Judea. [30]This they did, sending their gift to the elders by Barnabas and Saul.

Peter's Miraculous Escape From Prison

12 It was about this time that King Herod arrested some who belonged to the church, intending to persecute them. [2]He had James, the brother of John, put to death with the sword. [3]When he saw that this pleased the Jews, he proceeded to seize Peter also. This happened during the Feast of Unleavened Bread. [4]After arresting him, he put him in prison, handing him over to be guarded by four squads of four soldiers each. Herod intended to bring him out for public trial after the Passover.

[5]So Peter was kept in prison, but the church was earnestly praying to God for him.

[6]The night before Herod was to bring him to trial, Peter was sleeping between two soldiers, bound with two chains, and sentries stood guard at the entrance. [7]Suddenly an angel of the Lord appeared and a light shone in the cell. He struck Peter on the side and woke him up. "Quick, get up!" he said, and the chains fell off Peter's wrists.

NEW LIVING TRANSLATION

great famine was coming upon the entire Roman world. (This was fulfilled during the reign of Claudius.) [29]So the believers in Antioch decided to send relief to the brothers and sisters* in Judea, everyone giving as much as they could. [30]This they did, entrusting their gifts to Barnabas and Saul to take to the elders of the church in Jerusalem.

James Is Killed and Peter Is Imprisoned

12 About that time King Herod Agrippa* began to persecute some believers in the church. [2]He had the apostle James (John's brother) killed with a sword. [3]When Herod saw how much this pleased the Jewish leaders, he arrested Peter during the Passover celebration* [4]and imprisoned him, placing him under the guard of four squads of four soldiers each. Herod's intention was to bring Peter out for public trial after the Passover. [5]But while Peter was in prison, the church prayed very earnestly for him.

Peter's Miraculous Escape from Prison

[6]The night before Peter was to be placed on trial, he was asleep, chained between two soldiers, with others standing guard at the prison gate. [7]Suddenly, there was a bright light in the cell, and an angel of the Lord stood before Peter. The angel tapped him on the side to awaken him and said, "Quick! Get up!" And the chains fell off his

11:29 Greek *the brothers.* 12:1 Greek *Herod the king.* He was the nephew of Herod Antipas and a grandson of Herod the Great.
12:3 Greek *the days of unleavened bread.*

NEW KING JAMES VERSION

famine throughout all the world, which also happened in the days of Claudius Caesar. [29]Then the disciples, each according to his ability, determined to send relief to the brethren dwelling in Judea. [30]This they also did, and sent it to the elders by the hands of Barnabas and Saul.

Herod's Violence to the Church

12 Now about that time Herod the king stretched out *his* hand to harass some from the church. [2]Then he killed James the brother of John with the sword. [3]And because he saw that it pleased the Jews, he proceeded further to seize Peter also. Now it was *during* the Days of Unleavened Bread. [4]So when he had arrested him, he put *him* in prison, and delivered *him* to four squads of soldiers to keep him, intending to bring him before the people after Passover.

Peter Freed from Prison

[5]Peter was therefore kept in prison, but constant[a] prayer was offered to God for him by the church. [6]And when Herod was about to bring him out, that night Peter was sleeping, bound with two chains between two soldiers; and the guards before the door were keeping the prison. [7]Now behold, an angel of the Lord stood by *him,* and a light shone in the prison; and he struck Peter on the side and raised him up, saying, "Arise quickly!" And his chains fell

12:5 [a] NU-Text reads *constantly* (or *earnestly*).

THE MESSAGE

severe famine was about to devastate the country. (The famine eventually came during the rule of Claudius.) So the disciples decided that each of them would send whatever they could to their fellow Christians in Judea to help out. They sent Barnabas and Saul to deliver the collection to the leaders in Jerusalem.

Peter Under Heavy Guard

12 That's when King Herod got it into his head to go after some of the church members. He murdered James, John's brother. When he saw how much it raised his popularity ratings with the Jews, he arrested Peter—all this during Passover Week, mind you—and had him thrown in jail, putting four squads of four soldiers each to guard him. He was planning a public lynching after Passover.

All the time that Peter was under heavy guard in the jailhouse, the church prayed for him most strenuously.

Then the time came for Herod to bring him out for the kill. That night, even though shackled to two soldiers, one on either side, Peter slept like a baby. And there were guards at the door keeping their eyes on the place. Herod was taking no chances!

Suddenly there was an angel at his side and light flooding the room. The angel shook Peter and got him up: "Hurry!" The handcuffs fell off his wrists. The angel said,

KING JAMES VERSION

8 And the angel said unto him, Gird thyself, and bind on thy sandals. And so he did. And he saith unto him, Cast thy garment about thee, and follow me.

9 And he went out, and followed him; and wist not that it was true which was done by the angel; but thought he saw a vision.

10 When they were past the first and the second ward, they came unto the iron gate that leadeth unto the city; which opened to them of his own accord: and they went out, and passed on through one street; and forthwith the angel departed from him.

11 And when Peter was come to himself, he said, Now I know of a surety, that the Lord hath sent his angel, and hath delivered me out of the hand of Herod, and *from* all the expectation of the people of the Jews.

12 And when he had considered *the thing*, he came to the house of Mary the mother of John, whose surname was Mark; where many were gathered together praying.

13 And as Peter knocked at the door of the gate, a damsel came to hearken, named Rhoda.

14 And when she knew Peter's voice, she opened not the gate for gladness, but ran in, and told how Peter stood before the gate.

15 And they said unto her, Thou art mad. But she constantly affirmed that it was even so. Then said they, It is his angel.

16 But Peter continued knocking: and when they had opened *the door*, and saw him, they were astonished.

17 But he, beckoning unto them with the hand to hold

NEW AMERICAN STANDARD BIBLE

8 And the angel said to him, "Gird yourself and put on your sandals." And he did so. And he *said to him, "Wrap your cloak around you and follow me."

9 And he went out and continued to follow, and he did not know that what was being done by the angel was real, but thought he was seeing a vision.

10 When they had passed the first and second guard, they came to the iron gate that leads into the city, which opened for them by itself; and they went out and went along one street, and immediately the angel departed from him.

11 When Peter came to himself, he said, "Now I know for sure that the Lord has sent forth His angel and rescued me from the hand of Herod and from all that the Jewish people were expecting."

12 And when he realized *this,* he went to the house of Mary, the mother of John who was also called Mark, where many were gathered together and were praying.

13 When he knocked at the door of the gate, a servant-girl named Rhoda came to answer.

14 When she recognized Peter's voice, because of her joy she did not open the gate, but ran in and announced that Peter was standing in front of the gate.

15 They said to her, "You are out of your mind!" But she kept insisting that it was so. They kept saying, "It is his angel."

16 But Peter continued knocking; and when they had opened *the door*, they saw him and were amazed.

17 But motioning to them with his hand to be silent, he

NEW CENTURY VERSION

"Get dressed and put on your sandals." And Peter did.
Then the angel said, "Put on your coat and follow me." 9So
Peter followed him out, but he did not know if what the
angel was doing was real; he thought he might be seeing a
vision. 10They went past the first and second guards and
came to the iron gate that separated them from the city.
The gate opened by itself for them, and they went through
it. When they had walked down one street, the angel suddenly left him.
11Then Peter realized what had happened. He thought,
"Now I know that the Lord really sent his angel to me. He
rescued me from Herod and from all the things the Jewish
people thought would happen."
12When he considered this, he went to the home of
Mary, the mother of John Mark. Many people were gathered there, praying. 13Peter knocked on the outside door,
and a servant girl named Rhoda came to answer it.
14When she recognized Peter's voice, she was so happy she
forgot to open the door. Instead, she ran inside and told
the group, "Peter is at the door!"
15They said to her, "You are crazy!" But she kept on saying it was true, so they said, "It must be Peter's angel."
16Peter continued to knock, and when they opened the
door, they saw him and were amazed. 17Peter made a sign
with his hand to tell them to be quiet. He explained how

CONTEMPORARY ENGLISH VERSION

dressed and put on your sandals." Peter did what he was
told. Then the angel said, "Now put on your coat and follow me." 9Peter left with the angel, but he thought everything was only a dream. 10They went past the two groups
of soldiers, and when they came to the iron gate to the
city, it opened by itself. They went out and were going
along the street, when all at once the angel disappeared.
11Peter now realized what had happened, and he said, "I
am certain that the Lord sent his angel to rescue me from
Herod and from everything the Jewish leaders planned to
do to me." 12Then Peter went to the house of Mary the
mother of John whose other name was Mark. Many of the
Lord's followers had come together there and were praying.
13Peter knocked on the gate, and a servant named
Rhoda came to answer. 14When she heard Peter's voice,
she was too excited to open the gate. She ran back into the
house and said that Peter was standing there.
15"You are crazy!" everyone told her. But she kept saying that it was Peter. Then they said, "It must be his
angel."[b] 16But Peter kept on knocking, until finally they
opened the gate. They saw him and were completely
amazed.
17Peter motioned for them to keep quiet. Then he told

[b] 12.15 *his angel*: Probably meaning "his guardian angel."

NEW INTERNATIONAL VERSION

[8]Then the angel said to him, "Put on your clothes and sandals." And Peter did so. "Wrap your cloak around you and follow me," the angel told him. [9]Peter followed him out of the prison, but he had no idea that what the angel was doing was really happening; he thought he was seeing a vision. [10]They passed the first and second guards and came to the iron gate leading to the city. It opened for them by itself, and they went through it. When they had walked the length of one street, suddenly the angel left him.

[11]Then Peter came to himself and said, "Now I know without a doubt that the Lord sent his angel and rescued me from Herod's clutches and from everything the Jewish people were anticipating."

[12]When this had dawned on him, he went to the house of Mary the mother of John, also called Mark, where many people had gathered and were praying. [13]Peter knocked at the outer entrance, and a servant girl named Rhoda came to answer the door. [14]When she recognized Peter's voice, she was so overjoyed she ran back without opening it and exclaimed, "Peter is at the door!"

[15]"You're out of your mind," they told her. When she kept insisting that it was so, they said, "It must be his angel."

[16]But Peter kept on knocking, and when they opened the door and saw him, they were astonished. [17]Peter motioned with his hand for them to be quiet and described how the

NEW LIVING TRANSLATION

wrists. [8]Then the angel told him, "Get dressed and put on your sandals." And he did. "Now put on your coat and follow me," the angel ordered.

[9]So Peter left the cell, following the angel. But all the time he thought it was a vision. He didn't realize it was really happening. [10]They passed the first and second guard posts and came to the iron gate to the street, and this opened to them all by itself. So they passed through and started walking down the street, and then the angel suddenly left him.

[11]Peter finally realized what had happened. "It's really true!" he said to himself. "The Lord has sent his angel and saved me from Herod and from what the Jews were hoping to do to me!"

[12]After a little thought, he went to the home of Mary, the mother of John Mark, where many were gathered for prayer. [13]He knocked at the door in the gate, and a servant girl named Rhoda came to open it. [14]When she recognized Peter's voice, she was so overjoyed that, instead of opening the door, she ran back inside and told everyone, "Peter is standing at the door!"

[15]"You're out of your mind," they said. When she insisted, they decided, "It must be his angel."

[16]Meanwhile, Peter continued knocking. When they finally went out and opened the door, they were amazed. [17]He motioned for them to quiet down and told them what

NEW KING JAMES VERSION

off *his* hands. [8]Then the angel said to him, "Gird yourself and tie on your sandals"; and so he did. And he said to him, "Put on your garment and follow me." [9]So he went out and followed him, and did not know that what was done by the angel was real, but thought he was seeing a vision. [10]When they were past the first and the second guard posts, they came to the iron gate that leads to the city, which opened to them of its own accord; and they went out and went down one street, and immediately the angel departed from him.

[11]And when Peter had come to himself, he said, "Now I know for certain that the Lord has sent His angel, and has delivered me from the hand of Herod and *from* all the expectation of the Jewish people."

[12]So, when he had considered *this,* he came to the house of Mary, the mother of John whose surname was Mark, where many were gathered together praying. [13]And as Peter knocked at the door of the gate, a girl named Rhoda came to answer. [14]When she recognized Peter's voice, because of *her* gladness she did not open the gate, but ran in and announced that Peter stood before the gate. [15]But they said to her, "You are beside yourself!" Yet she kept insisting that it was so. So they said, "It is his angel."

[16]Now Peter continued knocking; and when they opened *the door* and saw him, they were astonished. [17]But motioning to them with his hand to keep silent, he declared to

THE MESSAGE

"Get dressed. Put on your shoes." Peter did it. Then, "Grab your coat and let's get out of here." Peter followed him, but didn't believe it was really an angel—he thought he was dreaming.

Past the first guard and then the second, they came to the iron gate that led into the city. It swung open before them on its own, and they were out on the street, free as the breeze. At the first intersection the angel left him, going his own way. That's when Peter realized it was no dream. "I can't believe it—this really happened! The Master sent his angel and rescued me from Herod's vicious little production and the spectacle the Jewish mob was looking forward to."

Still shaking his head, amazed, he went to Mary's house, the Mary who was John Mark's mother. The house was packed with praying friends. When he knocked on the door to the courtyard, a young woman named Rhoda came to see who it was. But when she recognized his voice—Peter's voice!—she was so excited and eager to tell everyone Peter was there that she forgot to open the door and left him standing in the street.

But they wouldn't believe her, dismissing her, dismissing her report. "You're crazy," they said. She stuck by her story, insisting. They still wouldn't believe her and said, "It must be his angel." All this time poor Peter was standing out in the street, knocking away.

Finally they opened up and saw him—and went wild! Peter put his hands up and calmed them down. He

KING JAMES VERSION

their peace, declared unto them how the Lord had brought him out of the prison. And he said, Go shew these things unto James, and to the brethren. And he departed, and went into another place.

18 Now as soon as it was day, there was no small stir among the soldiers, what was become of Peter.

19 And when Herod had sought for him, and found him not, he examined the keepers, and commanded that *they* should be put to death. And he went down from Judaea to Caesarea, and *there* abode.

20 ¶ And Herod was highly displeased with them of Tyre and Sidon: but they came with one accord to him, and, having made Blastus the king's chamberlain their friend, desired peace; because their country was nourished by the king's *country*.

21 And upon a set day Herod, arrayed in royal apparel, sat upon his throne, and made an oration unto them.

22 And the people gave a shout, *saying, It is* the voice of a god, and not of a man.

23 And immediately the angel of the Lord smote him, because he gave not God the glory: and he was eaten of worms, and gave up the ghost.

24 But the word of God grew and multiplied.

25 And Barnabas and Saul returned from Jerusalem, when they had fulfilled *their* ministry, and took with them John, whose surname was Mark.

NEW AMERICAN STANDARD BIBLE

described to them how the Lord had led him out of the prison. And he said, "Report these things to James and the brethren." Then he left and went to another place.

18 Now when day came, there was no small disturbance among the soldiers *as to* what could have become of Peter.

19 When Herod had searched for him and had not found him, he examined the guards and ordered that they be led away *to execution*. Then he went down from Judea to Caesarea and was spending time there.

Death of Herod

20 Now he was very angry with the people of Tyre and Sidon; and with one accord they came to him, and having won over Blastus the king's chamberlain, they were asking for peace, because their country was fed by the king's country.

21 On an appointed day Herod, having put on his royal apparel, took his seat on the rostrum and *began* delivering an address to them.

22 The people kept crying out, "The voice of a god and not of a man!"

23 And immediately an angel of the Lord struck him because he did not give God the glory, and he was eaten by worms and died.

24 But the word of the Lord continued to grow and to be multiplied.

25 And Barnabas and Saul returned from Jerusalem when they had fulfilled their mission, taking along with *them* John, who was also called Mark.

NEW CENTURY VERSION

the Lord led him out of the jail, and he said, "Tell James and the other believers what happened." Then he left to go to another place.

18The next day the soldiers were very upset and wondered what had happened to Peter. 19Herod looked everywhere for him but could not find him. So he questioned the guards and ordered that they be killed.

The Death of Herod Agrippa

Later Herod moved from Judea and went to the city of Caesarea, where he stayed. 20Herod was very angry with the people of Tyre and Sidon, but the people of those cities all came in a group to him. After convincing Blastus, the king's personal servant, to be on their side, they asked Herod for peace, because their country got its food from his country.

21On a chosen day Herod put on his royal robes, sat on his throne, and made a speech to the people. 22They shouted, "This is the voice of a god, not a human!" 23Because Herod did not give the glory to God, an angel of the Lord immediately caused him to become sick, and he was eaten by worms and died.

24God's message continued to spread and reach people.

25After Barnabas and Saul finished their task in Jerusalem, they returned to Antioch, taking John Mark with them.

CONTEMPORARY ENGLISH VERSION

how the Lord had led him out of jail. He also said, "Tell James[c] and the others what has happened." After that, he left and went somewhere else.

18The next morning the soldiers who had been on guard were terribly worried and wondered what had happened to Peter. 19Herod ordered his own soldiers to search for him, but they could not find him. Then he questioned the guards and had them put to death. After this, Herod left Judea to stay in Caesarea for a while.

Herod Dies

20Herod and the people of Tyre and Sidon were very angry with each other. But their country got its food supply from the region that he ruled. So a group of them went to see Blastus, who was one of Herod's high officials. They convinced Blastus that they wanted to make peace between their cities and Herod, 21and a day was set for them to meet with him.

Herod came dressed in his royal robes. He sat down on his throne and made a speech. 22The people shouted, "You speak more like a god than a man!" 23At once an angel from the Lord struck him down because he took the honor that belonged to God. Later, Herod was eaten by worms and died.

24God's message kept spreading. 25And after Barnabas and Saul had done the work they were sent to do, they went back to Jerusalem[d] with John, whose other name was Mark.

[c] 12.17 *James*: The brother of the Lord. [d] 12.25 *went back to Jerusalem*: Some manuscripts have "left Jerusalem," and others have "went to Antioch."

NEW INTERNATIONAL VERSION

Lord had brought him out of prison. "Tell James and the
brothers about this," he said, and then he left for another
place.
18In the morning, there was no small commotion among
the soldiers as to what had become of Peter. 19After Herod
had a thorough search made for him and did not find him,
he cross-examined the guards and ordered that they be
executed.

Herod's Death

Then Herod went from Judea to Caesarea and stayed
there a while. 20He had been quarreling with the people of
Tyre and Sidon; they now joined together and sought an
audience with him. Having secured the support of Blastus,
a trusted personal servant of the king, they asked for
peace, because they depended on the king's country for
their food supply.
21On the appointed day Herod, wearing his royal robes,
sat on his throne and delivered a public address to the peo-
ple. 22They shouted, "This is the voice of a god, not of a
man." 23Immediately, because Herod did not give praise to
God, an angel of the Lord struck him down, and he was
eaten by worms and died.
24But the word of God continued to increase and spread.
25When Barnabas and Saul had finished their mission,
they returned from[a] Jerusalem, taking with them John, also
called Mark.

[a] *25* Some manuscripts *to*

NEW LIVING TRANSLATION

had happened and how the Lord had led him out of jail.
"Tell James and the other brothers what happened," he
said. And then he went to another place.
18At dawn, there was a great commotion among the sol-
diers about what had happened to Peter. 19Herod Agrippa
ordered a thorough search for him. When he couldn't be
found, Herod interrogated the guards and sentenced them
to death. Afterward Herod left Judea to stay in Caesarea for
a while.

The Death of Herod Agrippa

20Now Herod was very angry with the people of Tyre and
Sidon. So they sent a delegation to make peace with him
because their cities were dependent upon Herod's country
for their food. They made friends with Blastus, Herod's
personal assistant, 21and an appointment with Herod was
granted. When the day arrived, Herod put on his royal
robes, sat on his throne, and made a speech to them. 22The
people gave him a great ovation, shouting, "It is the voice
of a god, not of a man!"
23Instantly, an angel of the Lord struck Herod with a
sickness, because he accepted the people's worship instead
of giving the glory to God. So he was consumed with
worms and died.
24But God's Good News was spreading rapidly, and there
were many new believers.
25When Barnabas and Saul had finished their mission in
Jerusalem, they returned to Antioch, taking John Mark
with them.

NEW KING JAMES VERSION

them how the Lord had brought him out of the prison. And
he said, "Go, tell these things to James and to the
brethren." And he departed and went to another place.
18Then, as soon as it was day, there was no small stir
among the soldiers about what had become of Peter. 19But
when Herod had searched for him and not found him, he
examined the guards and commanded that *they* should be
put to death.
And he went down from Judea to Caesarea, and stayed
there.

Herod's Violent Death

20Now Herod had been very angry with the people of
Tyre and Sidon; but they came to him with one accord, and
having made Blastus the king's personal aide their friend,
they asked for peace, because their country was supplied
with food by the king's *country.*
21So on a set day Herod, arrayed in royal apparel, sat on
his throne and gave an oration to them. 22And the people
kept shouting, "The voice of a god and not of a man!" 23Then
immediately an angel of the Lord struck him, because he did
not give glory to God. And he was eaten by worms and died.
24But the word of God grew and multiplied.

Barnabas and Saul Appointed

25And Barnabas and Saul returned from[b] Jerusalem
when they had fulfilled *their* ministry, and they also took
with them John whose surname was Mark.

12:25 [b] NU-Text and M-Text read *to.*

THE MESSAGE

described how the Master had gotten him out of jail, then
said, "Tell James and the brothers what's happened." He
left them and went off to another place.

At daybreak the jail was in an uproar. "Where is Peter?
What's happened to Peter?" When Herod sent for him and
they could neither produce him nor explain why not, he
ordered their execution: "Off with their heads!" Fed up
with Judea and Jews, he went for a vacation to Caesarea.

The Death of Herod

But things went from bad to worse for Herod. Now peo-
ple from Tyre and Sidon put him on the warpath. But they
got Blastus, King Herod's right-hand man, to put in a good
word for them and got a delegation together to iron things
out. Because they were dependent on Judea for food sup-
plies, they couldn't afford to let this go on too long. On the
day set for their meeting, Herod, robed in pomposity, took
his place on the throne and regaled them with a lot of hot
air. The people played their part to the hilt and shouted
flatteries: "The voice of God! The voice of God!"

That was the last straw. God had had enough of Herod's
arrogance and sent an angel to strike him down. Herod had
given God no credit for anything. Down he went. Rotten to
the core, a maggoty old man if there ever was one, he died.

Meanwhile, the ministry of God's Word grew by leaps
and bounds.

Barnabas and Saul, once they had delivered the relief offer-
ing to the church in Jerusalem, went back to Antioch. This
time they took John with them, the one they called Mark.

KING JAMES VERSION

13 Now there were in the church that was at Antioch certain prophets and teachers; as Barnabas, and Simeon that was called Niger, and Lucius of Cyrene, and Manaen, which had been brought up with Herod the tetrarch, and Saul.

2 As they ministered to the Lord, and fasted, the Holy Ghost said, Separate me Barnabas and Saul for the work whereunto I have called them.

3 And when they had fasted and prayed, and laid *their* hands on them, they sent *them* away.

4 ¶ So they, being sent forth by the Holy Ghost, departed unto Seleucia; and from thence they sailed to Cyprus.

5 And when they were at Salamis, they preached the word of God in the synagogues of the Jews: and they had also John to *their* minister.

6 And when they had gone through the isle unto Paphos, they found a certain sorcerer, a false prophet, a Jew, whose name *was* Bar-jesus:

7 Which was with the deputy of the country, Sergius Paulus, a prudent man; who called for Barnabas and Saul, and desired to hear the word of God.

8 But Elymas the sorcerer (for so is his name by inter-

NEW AMERICAN STANDARD BIBLE

First Missionary Journey

13 Now there were at Antioch, in the church that was *there*, prophets and teachers: Barnabas, and Simeon who was called Niger, and Lucius of Cyrene, and Manaen who had been brought up with Herod the tetrarch, and Saul.

2 While they were ministering to the Lord and fasting, the Holy Spirit said, "Set apart for Me Barnabas and Saul for the work to which I have called them."

3 Then, when they had fasted and prayed and laid their hands on them, they sent them away.

4 So, being sent out by the Holy Spirit, they went down to Seleucia and from there they sailed to Cyprus.

5 When they reached Salamis, they *began* to proclaim the word of God in the synagogues of the Jews; and they also had John as their helper.

6 When they had gone through the whole island as far as Paphos, they found a magician, a Jewish false prophet whose name was Bar-Jesus,

7 who was with the proconsul, Sergius Paulus, a man of intelligence. This man summoned Barnabas and Saul and sought to hear the word of God.

8 But Elymas the magician (for so his name is translated)

NEW CENTURY VERSION

Barnabas and Saul Are Chosen

13 In the church at Antioch there were these prophets and teachers: Barnabas, Simeon (also called Niger), Lucius (from the city of Cyrene), Manaen (who had grown up with Herod, the ruler), and Saul. 2They were all worshiping the Lord and giving up eating for a certain time.[a] During this time the Holy Spirit said to them, "Set apart for me Barnabas and Saul to do a special work for which I have chosen them."

3So after they gave up eating and prayed, they laid their hands on[b] Barnabas and Saul and sent them out.

Barnabas and Saul in Cyprus

4Barnabas and Saul, sent out by the Holy Spirit, went to the city of Seleucia. From there they sailed to the island of Cyprus. 5When they came to Salamis, they preached the Good News of God in the Jewish synagogues. John Mark was with them to help.

6They went across the whole island to Paphos where they met a Jewish magician named Bar-Jesus. He was a false prophet 7who always stayed close to Sergius Paulus, the governor and a smart man. He asked Barnabas and Saul to come to him, because he wanted to hear the message of God. 8But Elymas, the magician, was against them.

13:2 [a] **giving up...time** This is called "fasting." The people would give up eating for a special time of prayer and worship to God. It was also done to show sadness and disappointment. 13:3 [b] **laid their hands on** The laying on of hands had many purposes, including the giving of a blessing, power, or authority.

CONTEMPORARY ENGLISH VERSION

Barnabas and Saul Are Chosen and Sent

13 The church at Antioch had several prophets and teachers. They were Barnabas, Simeon, also called Niger, Lucius from Cyrene, Manaen, who was Herod's[a] close friend, and Saul. 2While they were worshiping the Lord and going without eating,[b] the Holy Spirit told them, "Appoint Barnabas and Saul to do the work for which I have chosen them." 3Everyone prayed and went without eating for a while longer. Next, they placed their hands on Barnabas and Saul to show that they had been appointed to do this work. Then everyone sent them on their way.

Barnabas and Saul in Cyprus

4After Barnabas and Saul had been sent by the Holy Spirit, they went to Seleucia. From there they sailed to the island of Cyprus. 5They arrived at Salamis and began to preach God's message in the Jewish meeting places. They also had John[c] as a helper.

6Barnabas and Saul went all the way to the city of Paphos on the other end of the island, where they met a Jewish man named Bar-Jesus. He practiced witchcraft and was a false prophet. 7He also worked for Sergius Paulus, who was very smart and was the governor of the island. Sergius Paulus wanted to hear God's message, and he sent for Barnabas and Saul. 8But Bar-Jesus, whose other name

[a] 13.1 *Herod's*: Herod Antipas, the son of Herod the Great.
[b] 13.2 *going without eating*: The Jews often went without eating as a way of showing how much they loved God. This is also called "fasting."
[c] 13.5 *John*: Whose other name was Mark (see 12.12, 25).

NEW INTERNATIONAL VERSION

Barnabas and Saul Sent Off

13 In the church at Antioch there were prophets and
teachers: Barnabas, Simeon called Niger, Lucius of
Cyrene, Manaen (who had been brought up with Herod the
tetrarch) and Saul. 2While they were worshiping the Lord
and fasting, the Holy Spirit said, "Set apart for me
Barnabas and Saul for the work to which I have called
them." 3So after they had fasted and prayed, they placed
their hands on them and sent them off.

On Cyprus

4The two of them, sent on their way by the Holy Spirit,
went down to Seleucia and sailed from there to Cyprus.
5When they arrived at Salamis, they proclaimed the word
of God in the Jewish synagogues. John was with them as
their helper.

6They traveled through the whole island until they came
to Paphos. There they met a Jewish sorcerer and false
prophet named Bar-Jesus, 7who was an attendant of the
proconsul, Sergius Paulus. The proconsul, an intelligent
man, sent for Barnabas and Saul because he wanted to
hear the word of God. 8But Elymas the sorcerer (for that is

NEW LIVING TRANSLATION

Barnabas and Saul Are Sent Out

13 Among the prophets and teachers of the church at
Antioch of Syria were Barnabas, Simeon (called
"the black man"*), Lucius (from Cyrene), Manaen (the
childhood companion of King Herod Antipas*), and Saul.
2One day as these men were worshiping the Lord and fast-
ing, the Holy Spirit said, "Dedicate Barnabas and Saul for
the special work I have for them." 3So after more fasting
and prayer, the men laid their hands on them and sent
them on their way.

Paul's First Missionary Journey

4Sent out by the Holy Spirit, Saul and Barnabas went
down to the seaport of Seleucia and then sailed for the
island of Cyprus. 5There, in the town of Salamis, they went
to the Jewish synagogues and preached the word of God.
(John Mark went with them as their assistant.)

6Afterward they preached from town to town across the
entire island until finally they reached Paphos, where they
met a Jewish sorcerer, a false prophet named Bar-Jesus. 7He
had attached himself to the governor, Sergius Paulus, a
man of considerable insight and understanding. The gover-
nor invited Barnabas and Saul to visit him, for he wanted
to hear the word of God. 8But Elymas, the sorcerer (as his

13:1a Greek *who was called Niger.* 13:1b Greek *Herod the tetrarch.*

NEW KING JAMES VERSION

13 Now in the church that was at Antioch there were
certain prophets and teachers: Barnabas, Simeon
who was called Niger, Lucius of Cyrene, Manaen who had
been brought up with Herod the tetrarch, and Saul. 2As
they ministered to the Lord and fasted, the Holy Spirit
said, "Now separate to Me Barnabas and Saul for the work
to which I have called them." 3Then, having fasted and
prayed, and laid hands on them, they sent *them* away.

Preaching in Cyprus

4So, being sent out by the Holy Spirit, they went down
to Seleucia, and from there they sailed to Cyprus. 5And
when they arrived in Salamis, they preached the word of
God in the synagogues of the Jews. They also had John as
their assistant.

6Now when they had gone through the island[a] to Paphos,
they found a certain sorcerer, a false prophet, a Jew whose
name *was* Bar-Jesus, 7who was with the proconsul, Sergius
Paulus, an intelligent man. This man called for Barnabas
and Saul and sought to hear the word of God. 8But Elymas
the sorcerer (for so his name is translated) withstood them,

13:6 [a] NU-Text reads *the whole island.*

THE MESSAGE

Barnabas, Saul, and Doctor Know-It-All

13 The congregation in Antioch was blessed with a
number of prophet-preachers and teachers:

Barnabas,
Simeon, nicknamed Niger,
Lucius the Cyrenian,
Manaen, an advisor to the ruler Herod,
Saul.

One day as they were worshiping God—they were also
fasting as they waited for guidance—the Holy Spirit spoke:
"Take Barnabas and Saul and commission them for the
work I have called them to do."

So they commissioned them. In that circle of intensity
and obedience, of fasting and praying, they laid hands on
their heads and sent them off.

Sent off on their new assignment by the Holy Spirit,
Barnabas and Saul went down to Seleucia and caught a
ship for Cyprus. The first thing they did when they put in
at Salamis was preach God's Word in the Jewish meeting
places. They had John along to help out as needed.

They traveled the length of the island, and at Paphos
came upon a Jewish wizard who had worked himself into
the confidence of the governor, Sergius Paulus, an intelli-
gent man not easily taken in by charlatans. The wizard's
name was Bar-Jesus. He was as crooked as a corkscrew.

The governor invited Barnabas and Saul in, wanting to
hear God's Word firsthand from them. But Dr. Know-It-All

KING JAMES VERSION

pretation) withstood them, seeking to turn away the deputy from the faith.

9 Then Saul, (who also *is called* Paul,) filled with the Holy Ghost, set his eyes on him,

10 And said, O full of all subtilty and all mischief, *thou* child of the devil, *thou* enemy of all righteousness, wilt thou not cease to pervert the right ways of the Lord?

11 And now, behold, the hand of the Lord *is* upon thee, and thou shalt be blind, not seeing the sun for a season. And immediately there fell on him a mist and a darkness; and he went about seeking some to lead him by the hand.

12 Then the deputy, when he saw what was done, believed, being astonished at the doctrine of the Lord.

13 Now when Paul and his company loosed from Paphos, they came to Perga in Pamphylia: and John departing from them returned to Jerusalem.

14 ¶ But when they departed from Perga, they came to Antioch in Pisidia, and went into the synagogue on the sabbath day, and sat down.

15 And after the reading of the law and the prophets the rulers of the synagogue sent unto them, saying, *Ye* men *and* brethren, if ye have any word of exhortation for the people, say on.

16 Then Paul stood up, and beckoning with *his* hand said, Men of Israel, and ye that fear God, give audience.

NEW AMERICAN STANDARD BIBLE

was opposing them, seeking to turn the proconsul away from the faith.

9 But Saul, who was also *known as* Paul, filled with the Holy Spirit, fixed his gaze on him,

10 and said, "You who are full of all deceit and fraud, you son of the devil, you enemy of all righteousness, will you not cease to make crooked the straight ways of the Lord?

11 "Now, behold, the hand of the Lord is upon you, and you will be blind and not see the sun for a time." And immediately a mist and a darkness fell upon him, and he went about seeking those who would lead him by the hand.

12 Then the proconsul believed when he saw what had happened, being amazed at the teaching of the Lord.

13 Now Paul and his companions put out to sea from Paphos and came to Perga in Pamphylia; but John left them and returned to Jerusalem.

14 But going on from Perga, they arrived at Pisidian Antioch, and on the Sabbath day they went into the synagogue and sat down.

15 After the reading of the Law and the Prophets the synagogue officials sent to them, saying, "Brethren, if you have any word of exhortation for the people, say it."

16 Paul stood up, and motioning with his hand said,

"Men of Israel, and you who fear God, listen:

NEW CENTURY VERSION

(Elymas is the name for Bar-Jesus in the Greek language.)
He tried to stop the governor from believing in Jesus. 9But
Saul, who was also called Paul, was filled with the Holy
Spirit. He looked straight at Elymas 10and said, "You son
of the devil! You are an enemy of everything that is right!
You are full of evil tricks and lies, always trying to change
the Lord's truths into lies. 11Now the Lord will touch you,
and you will be blind. For a time you will not be able to see
anything—not even the light from the sun."

Then everything became dark for Elymas, and he walked
around, trying to find someone to lead him by the hand.
12When the governor saw this, he believed because he was
amazed at the teaching about the Lord.

Paul and Barnabas Leave Cyprus

13Paul and those with him sailed from Paphos and came
to Perga, in Pamphylia. There John Mark left them to
return to Jerusalem. 14They continued their trip from Perga
and went to Antioch, a city in Pisidia. On the Sabbath day
they went into the synagogue and sat down. 15After the
law of Moses and the writings of the prophets were read,
the leaders of the synagogue sent a message to Paul and
Barnabas: "Brothers, if you have any message that will
encourage the people, please speak."

16Paul stood up, raised his hand, and said, "You Israel-
ites and you who worship God, please listen! 17The God of

CONTEMPORARY ENGLISH VERSION

was Elymas, was against them. He even tried to keep the
governor from having faith in the Lord.

9Then Saul, better known as Paul, was filled with the
Holy Spirit. He looked straight at Elymas 10and said, "You
son of the devil! You are a liar, a crook, and an enemy of
everything that is right. When will you stop speaking
against the true ways of the Lord? 11The Lord is going to
punish you by making you completely blind for a while."

Suddenly the man's eyes were covered by a dark mist,
and he went around trying to get someone to lead him by
the hand. 12When the governor saw what had happened,
he was amazed at this teaching about the Lord. So he put
his faith in the Lord.

Paul and Barnabas in Antioch of Pisidia

13Paul and the others left Paphos and sailed to Perga in
Pamphylia. But John[c] left them and went back to Jerusalem.
14The rest of them went on from Perga to Antioch in
Pisidia. Then on the Sabbath they went to the Jewish meet-
ing place and sat down.

15After the reading of the Law and the Prophets,[d] the
leaders sent someone over to tell Paul and Barnabas,
"Friends, if you have anything to say that will help the
people, please say it."

16Paul got up. He motioned with his hand and said:

People of Israel, and everyone else who worships God,

c 13.13 *John*: Whose other name was Mark (see 12.12, 25).

d 13.15 *the Law and the Prophets*: The Jewish Scriptures, that is, the Old Testament.

NEW INTERNATIONAL VERSION

what his name means) opposed them and tried to turn the proconsul from the faith. [9]Then Saul, who was also called Paul, filled with the Holy Spirit, looked straight at Elymas and said, [10]"You are a child of the devil and an enemy of everything that is right! You are full of all kinds of deceit and trickery. Will you never stop perverting the right ways of the Lord? [11]Now the hand of the Lord is against you. You are going to be blind, and for a time you will be unable to see the light of the sun."

Immediately mist and darkness came over him, and he groped about, seeking someone to lead him by the hand. [12]When the proconsul saw what had happened, he believed, for he was amazed at the teaching about the Lord.

In Pisidian Antioch

[13]From Paphos, Paul and his companions sailed to Perga in Pamphylia, where John left them to return to Jerusalem. [14]From Perga they went on to Pisidian Antioch. On the Sabbath they entered the synagogue and sat down. [15]After the reading from the Law and the Prophets, the synagogue rulers sent word to them, saying, "Brothers, if you have a message of encouragement for the people, please speak."

[16]Standing up, Paul motioned with his hand and said: "Men of Israel and you Gentiles who worship God, listen to

NEW LIVING TRANSLATION

name means in Greek), interfered and urged the governor to pay no attention to what Saul and Barnabas said. He was trying to turn the governor away from the Christian faith.

[9]Then Saul, also known as Paul, filled with the Holy Spirit, looked the sorcerer in the eye and said, [10]"You son of the Devil, full of every sort of trickery and villainy, enemy of all that is good, will you never stop perverting the true ways of the Lord? [11]And now the Lord has laid his hand of punishment upon you, and you will be stricken awhile with blindness." Instantly mist and darkness fell upon him, and he began wandering around begging for someone to take his hand and lead him. [12]When the governor saw what had happened, he believed and was astonished at what he learned about the Lord.

Paul Preaches in Antioch of Pisidia

[13]Now Paul and those with him left Paphos by ship for Pamphylia,* landing at the port town of Perga. There John Mark left them and returned to Jerusalem. [14]But Barnabas and Paul traveled inland to Antioch of Pisidia.*

On the Sabbath they went to the synagogue for the services. [15]After the usual readings from the books of Moses and from the Prophets, those in charge of the service sent them this message: "Brothers, if you have any word of encouragement for us, come and give it!"

[16]So Paul stood, lifted his hand to quiet them, and started speaking. "People of Israel," he said, "and you devout Gentiles who fear the God of Israel, listen to me.

13:13-14 *Pamphylia* and *Pisidia* were districts in the land now called Turkey.

NEW KING JAMES VERSION

seeking to turn the proconsul away from the faith. [9]Then Saul, who also *is called* Paul, filled with the Holy Spirit, looked intently at him [10]and said, "O full of all deceit and all fraud, *you* son of the devil, *you* enemy of all righteousness, will you not cease perverting the straight ways of the Lord? [11]And now, indeed, the hand of the Lord *is* upon you, and you shall be blind, not seeing the sun for a time."

And immediately a dark mist fell on him, and he went around seeking someone to lead him by the hand. [12]Then the proconsul believed, when he saw what had been done, being astonished at the teaching of the Lord.

At Antioch in Pisidia

[13]Now when Paul and his party set sail from Paphos, they came to Perga in Pamphylia; and John, departing from them, returned to Jerusalem. [14]But when they departed from Perga, they came to Antioch in Pisidia, and went into the synagogue on the Sabbath day and sat down. [15]And after the reading of the Law and the Prophets, the rulers of the synagogue sent to them, saying, "Men *and* brethren, if you have any word of exhortation for the people, say on."

[16]Then Paul stood up, and motioning with *his* hand said, "Men of Israel, and you who fear God, listen: [17]The

THE MESSAGE

(that's the wizard's name in plain English) stirred up a ruckus, trying to divert the governor from becoming a believer. But Saul (or Paul), full of the Holy Spirit and looking him straight in the eye, said, "You bag of wind, you parody of a devil—why, you stay up nights inventing schemes to cheat people out of God. But now you've come up against God himself, and your game is up. You're about to go blind—no sunlight for you for a good long stretch." He was plunged immediately into a shadowy mist and stumbled around, begging people to take his hand and show him the way.

When the governor saw what happened, he became a believer, full of enthusiasm over what they were saying about the Master.

Don't Take This Lightly

From Paphos, Paul and company put out to sea, sailing on to Perga in Pamphylia. That's where John called it quits and went back to Jerusalem. From Perga the rest of them traveled on to Antioch in Pisidia.

On the Sabbath they went to the meeting place and took their places. After the reading of the Scriptures—God's Law and the Prophets—the president of the meeting asked them, "Friends, do you have anything you want to say? A word of encouragement, perhaps?"

Paul stood up, paused and took a deep breath, then said, "Fellow Israelites and friends of God, listen. God took a

KING JAMES VERSION

17 The God of this people of Israel chose our fathers, and exalted the people when they dwelt as strangers in the land of Egypt, and with an high arm brought he them out of it.

18 And about the time of forty years suffered he their manners in the wilderness.

19 And when he had destroyed seven nations in the land of Chanaan, he divided their land to them by lot.

20 And after that he gave *unto them* judges about the space of four hundred and fifty years, until Samuel the prophet.

21 And afterward they desired a king: and God gave unto them Saul the son of Cis, a man of the tribe of Benjamin, by the space of forty years.

22 And when he had removed him, he raised up unto them David to be their king; to whom also he gave testimony, and said, I have found David the *son* of Jesse, a man after mine own heart, which shall fulfil all my will.

23 Of this man's seed hath God according to *his* promise raised unto Israel a Saviour, Jesus:

24 When John had first preached before his coming the baptism of repentance to all the people of Israel.

25 And as John fulfilled his course, he said, Whom think ye that I am? I am not *he*. But, behold, there cometh one after me, whose shoes of *his* feet I am not worthy to loose.

26 Men *and* brethren, children of the stock of Abraham, and whosoever among you feareth God, to you is the word of this salvation sent.

27 For they that dwell at Jerusalem, and their rulers, because they knew him not, nor yet the voices of the

NEW AMERICAN STANDARD BIBLE

17 "The God of this people Israel chose our fathers and made the people great during their stay in the land of Egypt, and with an uplifted arm He led them out from it.

18 "For a period of about forty years He put up with them in the wilderness.

19 "When He had destroyed seven nations in the land of Canaan, He distributed their land as an inheritance—*all of which took* about four hundred and fifty years.

20 "After these things He gave *them* judges until Samuel the prophet.

21 "Then they asked for a king, and God gave them Saul the son of Kish, a man of the tribe of Benjamin, for forty years.

22 "After He had removed him, He raised up David to be their king, concerning whom He also testified and said, 'I HAVE FOUND DAVID the son of Jesse, A MAN AFTER MY HEART, who will do all My will.'

23 "From the descendants of this man, according to promise, God has brought to Israel a Savior, Jesus,

24 after John had proclaimed before His coming a baptism of repentance to all the people of Israel.

25 "And while John was completing his course, he kept saying, 'What do you suppose that I am? I am not *He*. But behold, one is coming after me the sandals of whose feet I am not worthy to untie.'

26 "Brethren, sons of Abraham's family, and those among you who fear God, to us the message of this salvation has been sent.

27 "For those who live in Jerusalem, and their rulers, recognizing neither Him nor the utterances of the prophets

NEW CENTURY VERSION

the Israelites chose our ancestors. He made the people
great during the time they lived in Egypt, and he brought
them out of that country with great power. 18And he was
patient with them for forty years in the desert. 19God
destroyed seven nations in the land of Canaan and gave
the land to his people. 20All this happened in about four
hundred fifty years.

"After this, God gave them judges until the time of
Samuel the prophet. 21Then the people asked for a king, so
God gave them Saul son of Kish. Saul was from the tribe of
Benjamin and was king for forty years. 22After God took
him away, God made David their king. God said about
him: 'I have found in David son of Jesse the kind of man I
want. He will do all I want him to do.' 23So God has
brought Jesus, one of David's descendants, to Israel to be
its Savior, as he promised. 24Before Jesus came, John[c]
preached to all the people of Israel about a baptism of
changed hearts and lives. 25When he was finishing his
work, he said, 'Who do you think I am? I am not the
Christ. He is coming later, and I am not worthy to untie his
sandals.'

26"Brothers, sons of the family of Abraham, and those of
you who are not Jews who worship God, listen! The news
about this salvation has been sent to us. 27Those who live
in Jerusalem and their leaders did not realize that Jesus
was the Savior. They did not understand the words that

13:24 [c] **John** John the Baptist, who preached to people about Christ's coming (Luke 3).

CONTEMPORARY ENGLISH VERSION

listen! 17The God of Israel chose our ancestors, and he
let our people prosper while they were living in Egypt.
Then with his mighty power he led them out, 18and for
about forty years he took care of[e] them in the desert.
19He destroyed seven nations in the land of Canaan and
gave their land to our people. 20All this happened in
about 450 years.

Then God gave our people judges until the time of the
prophet Samuel, 21but the people demanded a king. So
for forty years God gave them King Saul, the son of Kish
from the tribe of Benjamin. 22Later, God removed Saul
and let David rule in his place. God said about him,
"David the son of Jesse is the kind of person who pleases
me most! He does everything I want him to do."

23God promised that someone from David's family
would come to save the people of Israel, and that one is
Jesus. 24But before Jesus came, John was telling everyone in Israel to turn back to God and be baptized.
25Then, when John's work was almost done, he said,
"Who do you people think I am? Do you think I am the
Promised One? He will come later, and I am not good
enough to untie his sandals."

26Now listen, you descendants of Abraham! Pay
attention, all of you Gentiles who are here to worship
God! Listen to this message about how to be saved,
because it is for everyone. 27The people of Jerusalem
and their leaders didn't realize who Jesus was. And they

[e] **13.18** *took care of*: Some manuscripts have "put up with."

NEW INTERNATIONAL VERSION

me! 17The God of the people of Israel chose our fathers; he
made the people prosper during their stay in Egypt, with
mighty power he led them out of that country, 18he
endured their conduct[a] for about forty years in the desert,
19he overthrew seven nations in Canaan and gave their
land to his people as their inheritance. 20All this took
about 450 years.

"After this, God gave them judges until the time of
Samuel the prophet. 21Then the people asked for a king,
and he gave them Saul son of Kish, of the tribe of
Benjamin, who ruled forty years. 22After removing Saul, he
made David their king. He testified concerning him: 'I have
found David son of Jesse a man after my own heart; he
will do everything I want him to do.'

23"From this man's descendants God has brought to
Israel the Savior Jesus, as he promised. 24Before the com-
ing of Jesus, John preached repentance and baptism to all
the people of Israel. 25As John was completing his work, he
said: 'Who do you think I am? I am not that one. No, but
he is coming after me, whose sandals I am not worthy to
untie.'

26"Brothers, children of Abraham, and you God-fearing
Gentiles, it is to us that this message of salvation has been
sent. 27The people of Jerusalem and their rulers did not
recognize Jesus, yet in condemning him they fulfilled the

[a] *18* Some manuscripts *and cared for them*

NEW LIVING TRANSLATION

17"The God of this nation of Israel chose our ancestors
and made them prosper in Egypt. Then he powerfully led
them out of their slavery. 18He put up with them* through
forty years of wandering around in the wilderness. 19Then
he destroyed seven nations in Canaan and gave their land
to Israel as an inheritance. 20All this took about 450 years.
After that, judges ruled until the time of Samuel the proph-
et. 21Then the people begged for a king, and God gave
them Saul son of Kish, a man of the tribe of Benjamin,
who reigned for forty years. 22But God removed him from
the kingship and replaced him with David, a man about
whom God said, 'David son of Jesse is a man after my own
heart, for he will do everything I want him to.'*

23"And it is one of King David's descendants, Jesus, who
is God's promised Savior of Israel! 24But before he came,
John the Baptist preached the need for everyone in Israel to
turn from sin and turn to God and be baptized. 25As John
was finishing his ministry he asked, 'Do you think I am
the Messiah? No! But he is coming soon—and I am not
even worthy to be his slave.'*

26"Brothers—you sons of Abraham, and also all of you
devout Gentiles who fear the God of Israel—this salvation
is for us! 27The people in Jerusalem and their leaders ful-
filled prophecy by condemning Jesus to death. They didn't
recognize him or realize that he is the one the prophets

13:18 Other manuscripts read *He cared for them;* compare Deut 1:31.
13:22 1 Sam 13:14. 13:25 Greek *to untie his sandals.*

NEW KING JAMES VERSION

God of this people Israel[b] chose our fathers, and exalted
the people when they dwelt as strangers in the land of
Egypt, and with an uplifted arm He brought them out of it.
18Now for a time of about forty years He put up with their
ways in the wilderness. 19And when He had destroyed
seven nations in the land of Canaan, He distributed their
land to them by allotment.

20"After that He gave *them* judges for about four hun-
dred and fifty years, until Samuel the prophet. 21And after-
ward they asked for a king; so God gave them Saul the son
of Kish, a man of the tribe of Benjamin, for forty years.
22And when He had removed him, He raised up for them
David as king, to whom also He gave testimony and said,
'I have found David[c] the *son* of Jesse, *a man after My own
heart,* who will do all My will.'[d] 23From this man's seed,
according to *the* promise, God raised up for Israel a Sav-
ior—Jesus[e]— 24after John had first preached, before His
coming, the baptism of repentance to all the people of Is-
rael. 25And as John was finishing his course, he said, 'Who
do you think I am? I am not *He.* But behold, there comes
One after me, the sandals of whose feet I am not worthy to
loose.'

26"Men *and* brethren, sons of the family of Abraham,
and those among you who fear God, to you the word of
this salvation has been sent. 27For those who dwell in Je-
rusalem, and their rulers, because they did not know Him,

13:17 [b] M-Text omits *Israel.* 13:22 [c] Psalm 89:20 [d] 1 Samuel
13:14 13:23 [e] M-Text reads *for Israel salvation.*

THE MESSAGE

special interest in our ancestors, pulled our people who
were beaten down in Egyptian exile to their feet, and led
them out of there in grand style. He took good care of
them for nearly forty years in that godforsaken wilderness
and then, having wiped out seven enemies who stood in
the way, gave them the land of Canaan for their very
own—a span in all of about four hundred fifty years.

"Up to the time of Samuel the prophet, God provided
judges to lead them. But then they asked for a king, and
God gave them Saul, son of Kish, out of the tribe of
Benjamin. After Saul had ruled forty years, God removed
him from office and put King David in his place, with this
commendation: 'I've searched the land and found this
David, son of Jesse. He's a man whose heart beats to my
heart, a man who will do what I tell him.'

"From out of David's descendants God produced a Savior
for Israel, Jesus, exactly as he promised—but only after
John had thoroughly alerted the people to his arrival by
preparing them for a total life-change. As John was finish-
ing up his work, he said, 'Did you think I was the One? No,
I'm not the One. But the One you've been waiting for all
these years is just around the corner, about to appear. And
I'm about to disappear.'

"Dear brothers and sisters, children of Abraham, and
friends of God, this message of salvation has been precise-
ly targeted to you. The citizens and rulers in Jerusalem
didn't recognize who he was and condemned him to death.
They couldn't find a good reason, but demanded that

KING JAMES VERSION

prophets which are read every sabbath day, they have fulfilled *them* in condemning *him*.
28 And though they found no cause of death *in him*, yet desired they Pilate that he should be slain.
29 And when they had fulfilled all that was written of him, they took *him* down from the tree, and laid *him* in a sepulchre.
30 But God raised him from the dead:
31 And he was seen many days of them which came up with him from Galilee to Jerusalem, who are his witnesses unto the people.
32 And we declare unto you glad tidings, how that the promise which was made unto the fathers,
33 God hath fulfilled the same unto us their children, in that he hath raised up Jesus again; as it is also written in the second psalm, Thou art my Son, this day have I begotten thee.
34 And as concerning that he raised him up from the dead, *now* no more to return to corruption, he said on this wise, I will give you the sure mercies of David.
35 Wherefore he saith also in another *psalm*, Thou shalt not suffer thine Holy One to see corruption.

NEW AMERICAN STANDARD BIBLE

which are read every Sabbath, fulfilled *these* by condemning *Him*.
28 "And though they found no ground for *putting Him to* death, they asked Pilate that He be executed.
29 "When they had carried out all that was written concerning Him, they took Him down from the cross and laid Him in a tomb.
30 "But God raised Him from the dead;
31 and for many days He appeared to those who came up with Him from Galilee to Jerusalem, the very ones who are now His witnesses to the people.
32 "And we preach to you the good news of the promise made to the fathers,
33 that God has fulfilled this *promise* to our children in that He raised up Jesus, as it is also written in the second Psalm, 'YOU ARE MY SON; TODAY I HAVE BEGOTTEN YOU.'
34 "*As for the fact* that He raised Him up from the dead, no longer to return to decay, He has spoken in this way: 'I WILL GIVE YOU THE HOLY *and* SURE *blessings* OF DAVID.'
35 "Therefore He also says in another *Psalm*, 'YOU WILL NOT ALLOW YOUR HOLY ONE TO UNDERGO DECAY.'

NEW CENTURY VERSION

the prophets wrote, which are read every Sabbath day. But
they made them come true when they said Jesus was
guilty. 28They could not find any real reason for Jesus to be
put to death, but they asked Pilate to have him killed.
29When they had done to him all that the Scriptures had
said, they took him down from the cross and laid him in a
tomb. 30But God raised him up from the dead! 31After this,
for many days, those who had gone with Jesus from
Galilee to Jerusalem saw him. They are now his witnesses
to the people. 32We tell you the Good News about the
promise God made to our ancestors. 33God has made this
promise come true for us, his children, by raising Jesus
from the dead. We read about this also in Psalm 2:

'You are my Son.
Today I have become your Father.' *Psalm 2:7*

34God raised Jesus from the dead, and he will never go
back to the grave and become dust. So God said:

'I will give you the holy and sure blessings
that I promised to David.' *Isaiah 55:3*

35But in another place God says:

'You will not let your Holy One rot.' *Psalm 16:10*

CONTEMPORARY ENGLISH VERSION

didn't understand the words of the prophets that they
read each Sabbath. So they condemned Jesus just as the
prophets had said.
28-29They did exactly what the Scriptures said they
would. Even though they couldn't find any reason to put
Jesus to death, they still asked Pilate to have him killed.
After Jesus had been put to death, he was taken down
from the cross[f] and placed in a tomb. 30But God raised
him from death! 31Then for many days Jesus appeared to
his followers who had gone with him from Galilee to
Jerusalem. Now they are telling our people about him.
32God made a promise to our ancestors. And we are here
to tell you the good news 33that he has kept this promise
to us. It is just as the second Psalm says about Jesus,

"You are my son because today
I have become your Father."

34God raised Jesus from death and will never let his
body decay. It is just as God said,

"I will make to you
the same holy promise
that I made to David."

35And in another psalm it says, "God will never let the
body of his Holy One decay."

[f] 13.28,29 *cross*: This translates a Greek word that means "wood," "pole," or "tree."

NEW INTERNATIONAL VERSION

words of the prophets that are read every Sabbath.
28Though they found no proper ground for a death sen-
tence, they asked Pilate to have him executed. 29When
they had carried out all that was written about him, they
took him down from the tree and laid him in a tomb. 30But
God raised him from the dead, 31and for many days he was
seen by those who had traveled with him from Galilee to
Jerusalem. They are now his witnesses to our people.
32"We tell you the good news: What God promised our
fathers 33he has fulfilled for us, their children, by raising
up Jesus. As it is written in the second Psalm:

" 'You are my Son;
today I have become your Father.'[b][c]

34The fact that God raised him from the dead, never to
decay, is stated in these words:

" 'I will give you the holy and sure blessings promised
to David.'[d]

35So it is stated elsewhere:

" 'You will not let your Holy One see decay.'[e]

[b] 33 Or *have begotten you* [c] 33 Psalm 2:7 [d] 34 Isaiah 55:3
[e] 35 Psalm 16:10

NEW LIVING TRANSLATION

had written about, though they hear the prophets' words
read every Sabbath. 28They found no just cause to execute
him, but they asked Pilate to have him killed anyway.
29"When they had fulfilled all the prophecies concerning
his death, they took him down from the cross and placed
him in a tomb. 30But God raised him from the dead! 31And
he appeared over a period of many days to those who had
gone with him from Galilee to Jerusalem—these are his
witnesses to the people of Israel.
32"And now Barnabas and I are here to bring you this
Good News. God's promise to our ancestors has come true
in our own time, 33in that God raised Jesus. This is what
the second psalm is talking about when it says concerning
Jesus,

'You are my Son.
Today I have become your Father.*'

34For God had promised to raise him from the dead, never
again to die. This is stated in the Scripture that says, 'I will
give you the sacred blessings I promised to David.'*
35Another psalm explains more fully, saying, 'You will not
allow your Holy One to rot in the grave.'* 36Now this is not a

13:33 Or *Today I reveal you as my Son.* Ps 2:7. 13:34 Isa 55:3.
13:35 Ps 16:10.

NEW KING JAMES VERSION

nor even the voices of the Prophets which are read every
Sabbath, have fulfilled *them* in condemning *Him.* 28And
though they found no cause for death *in Him,* they asked
Pilate that He should be put to death. 29Now when they
had fulfilled all that was written concerning Him, they
took *Him* down from the tree and laid *Him* in a tomb.
30But God raised Him from the dead. 31He was seen for
many days by those who came up with Him from Galilee to
Jerusalem, who are His witnesses to the people. 32And we
declare to you glad tidings—that promise which was made
to the fathers. 33God has fulfilled this for us their children,
in that He has raised up Jesus. As it is also written in the
second Psalm:

'You are My Son,
Today I have begotten You.'[f]

34And that He raised Him from the dead, no more to return
to corruption, He has spoken thus:

'I will give you the sure mercies of David.'[g]

35Therefore He also says in another *Psalm:*

'You will not allow Your Holy One to see corruption.'[h]

13:33 [f] Psalm 2:7 13:34 [g] Isaiah 55:3 13:35 [h] Psalm 16:10

THE MESSAGE

Pilate execute him anyway. They did just what the proph-
ets said they would do, but had no idea they were follow-
ing to the letter the script of the prophets, even though
those same prophets are read every Sabbath in their meet-
ing places.

"After they had done everything the prophets said they
would do, they took him down from the cross and buried
him. And then God raised him from death. There is no dis-
puting that—he appeared over and over again many times
and places to those who had known him well in the
Galilean years, and these same people continue to give
witness that he is alive.

"And we're here today bringing you good news: the
Message that what God promised the fathers has come
true for the children—for us! He raised Jesus, exactly as
described in the second Psalm:

'My Son! My very own Son!
Today I celebrate you!'

When he raised him from the dead, he did it for good—no
going back to that rot and decay for him. That's why
Isaiah said, 'I'll give to all of you David's guaranteed
blessings.' So also the psalmist's prayer: 'You'll never let
your Holy One see death's rot and decay.'

KING JAMES VERSION

36 For David, after he had served his own generation by the will of God, fell on sleep, and was laid unto his fathers, and saw corruption:

37 But he, whom God raised again, saw no corruption.

38 Be it known unto you therefore, men *and* brethren, that through this man is preached unto you the forgiveness of sins:

39 And by him all that believe are justified from all things, from which ye could not be justified by the law of Moses.

40 Beware therefore, lest that come upon you, which is spoken of in the prophets;

41 Behold, ye despisers, and wonder, and perish: for I work a work in your days, a work which ye shall in no wise believe, though a man declare it unto you.

42 ¶ And when the Jews were gone out of the synagogue, the Gentiles besought that these words might be preached to them the next sabbath.

43 Now when the congregation was broken up, many of the Jews and religious proselytes followed Paul and Barnabas: who, speaking to them, persuaded them to continue in the grace of God.

44 And the next sabbath day came almost the whole city together to hear the word of God.

45 But when the Jews saw the multitudes, they were filled with envy, and spake against those things which were spoken by Paul, contradicting and blaspheming.

NEW AMERICAN STANDARD BIBLE

36 "For David, after he had served the purpose of God in his own generation, fell asleep, and was laid among his fathers and underwent decay;

37 but He whom God raised did not undergo decay.

38 "Therefore let it be known to you, brethren, that through Him forgiveness of sins is proclaimed to you,

39 and through Him everyone who believes is freed from all things, from which you could not be freed through the Law of Moses.

40 "Therefore take heed, so that the thing spoken of in the Prophets may not come upon *you:*

41 'BEHOLD, YOU SCOFFERS, AND MARVEL, AND PERISH;
FOR I AM ACCOMPLISHING A WORK IN YOUR DAYS,
A WORK WHICH YOU WILL NEVER BELIEVE, THOUGH
SOMEONE SHOULD DESCRIBE IT TO YOU.'"

42 As Paul and Barnabas were going out, the people kept begging that these things might be spoken to them the next Sabbath.

43 Now when *the meeting of* the synagogue had broken up, many of the Jews and of the God-fearing proselytes followed Paul and Barnabas, who, speaking to them, were urging them to continue in the grace of God.

Paul Turns to the Gentiles

44 The next Sabbath nearly the whole city assembled to hear the word of the Lord.

45 But when the Jews saw the crowds, they were filled with jealousy and *began* contradicting the things spoken by Paul, and were blaspheming.

NEW CENTURY VERSION

36 David did God's will during his lifetime. Then he died
and was buried beside his ancestors, and his body did rot
in the grave. 37 But the One God raised from the dead did
not rot in the grave. 38–39 Brothers, understand what we are
telling you: You can have forgiveness of your sins through
Jesus. The law of Moses could not free you from your sins.
But through Jesus everyone who believes is free from all
sins. 40 Be careful! Don't let what the prophets said happen
to you:

41 'Listen, you people who doubt!
You can wonder, and then die.
I will do something in your lifetime
that you won't believe even when you are told about
it!'" *Habakkuk 1:5*

42 While Paul and Barnabas were leaving the synagogue,
the people asked them to tell them more about these
things on the next Sabbath. 43 When the meeting was over,
many Jews and those who had changed to the Jewish religion
and who worshiped God followed Paul and Barnabas
from that place. Paul and Barnabas were persuading them
to continue trusting in God's grace.

44 On the next Sabbath day, almost everyone in the city
came to hear the word of the Lord. 45 Seeing the crowd, the
Jewish people became very jealous and said insulting
things and argued against what Paul said. 46 But Paul and

CONTEMPORARY ENGLISH VERSION

36 When David was alive, he obeyed God. Then after he
died, he was buried in the family grave, and his body
decayed. 37 But God raised Jesus from death, and his
body did not decay.
38 My friends, the message is that Jesus can forgive
your sins! The Law of Moses could not set you free from
all your sins. 39 But everyone who has faith in Jesus is
set free. 40 Make sure that what the prophets have said
doesn't happen to you. They said,

41 "Look, you people
who make fun of God!
Be amazed
and disappear.
I will do something today
that you won't believe,
even if someone
tells you about it!"

42 As Paul and Barnabas were leaving the meeting, the
people begged them to say more about these same things
on the next Sabbath. 43 After the service, many Jews and a
lot of Gentiles who worshiped God went with them. Paul
and Barnabas begged them all to remain faithful to God,
who had been so kind to them.

44 The next Sabbath almost everyone in town came to
hear the message about the Lord.[g] 45 When the Jewish people
saw the crowds, they were very jealous. They insulted
Paul and spoke against everything he said.

[g] 13.44 *the Lord*: Some manuscripts have "God."

NEW INTERNATIONAL VERSION

36"For when David had served God's purpose in his own generation, he fell asleep; he was buried with his fathers and his body decayed. 37But the one whom God raised from the dead did not see decay.

38"Therefore, my brothers, I want you to know that through Jesus the forgiveness of sins is proclaimed to you. 39Through him everyone who believes is justified from everything you could not be justified from by the law of Moses. 40Take care that what the prophets have said does not happen to you:

41" 'Look, you scoffers,
wonder and perish,
for I am going to do something in your days
that you would never believe,
even if someone told you.'[f]"

42As Paul and Barnabas were leaving the synagogue, the people invited them to speak further about these things on the next Sabbath. 43When the congregation was dismissed, many of the Jews and devout converts to Judaism followed Paul and Barnabas, who talked with them and urged them to continue in the grace of God.

44On the next Sabbath almost the whole city gathered to hear the word of the Lord. 45When the Jews saw the crowds, they were filled with jealousy and talked abusively against what Paul was saying.

[f] *41* Hab. 1:5

NEW LIVING TRANSLATION

reference to David, for after David had served his generation according to the will of God, he died and was buried, and his body decayed. 37No, it was a reference to someone else—someone whom God raised and whose body did not decay.

38"Brothers, listen! In this man Jesus there is forgiveness for your sins. 39Everyone who believes in him is freed from all guilt and declared right with God—something the Jewish law could never do. 40Be careful! Don't let the prophets' words apply to you. For they said,

41 'Look, you mockers,
be amazed and die!
For I am doing something in your own day,
something you wouldn't believe
even if someone told you about it.'* "

42As Paul and Barnabas left the synagogue that day, the people asked them to return again and speak about these things the next week. 43Many Jews and godly converts to Judaism who worshiped at the synagogue followed Paul and Barnabas, and the two men urged them, "By God's grace, remain faithful."

Paul Turns to the Gentiles

44The following week almost the entire city turned out to hear them preach the word of the Lord. 45But when the Jewish leaders saw the crowds, they were jealous; so they slandered Paul and argued against whatever he said.

13:41 Hab 1:5.

NEW KING JAMES VERSION

36"For David, after he had served his own generation by the will of God, fell asleep, was buried with his fathers, and saw corruption; 37but He whom God raised up saw no corruption. 38Therefore let it be known to you, brethren, that through this Man is preached to you the forgiveness of sins; 39and by Him everyone who believes is justified from all things from which you could not be justified by the law of Moses. 40Beware therefore, lest what has been spoken in the prophets come upon you:

41 *'Behold, you despisers,*
Marvel and perish!
For I work a work in your days,
A work which you will by no means believe,
Though one were to declare it to you.' "[i]

Blessing and Conflict at Antioch

42So when the Jews went out of the synagogue,[j] the Gentiles begged that these words might be preached to them the next Sabbath. 43Now when the congregation had broken up, many of the Jews and devout proselytes followed Paul and Barnabas, who, speaking to them, persuaded them to continue in the grace of God.

44On the next Sabbath almost the whole city came together to hear the word of God. 45But when the Jews saw the multitudes, they were filled with envy; and contradicting and blaspheming, they opposed the things spoken by Paul.

13:41 [i] Habakkuk 1:5 13:42 [j] Or *And when they went out of the synagogue of the Jews;* NU-Text reads *And when they went out of the synagogue, they begged.*

THE MESSAGE

"David, of course, having completed the work God set out for him, has been in the grave, dust and ashes, a long time now. But the One God raised up—no dust and ashes for him! I want you to know, my very dear friends, that it is on account of this resurrected Jesus that the forgiveness of your sins can be promised. He accomplishes, in those who believe, everything that the Law of Moses could never make good on. But everyone who believes in this raised-up Jesus is declared good and right and whole before God.

"Don't take this lightly. You don't want the prophet's sermon to describe you:

'Watch out, cynics;
Look hard—watch your world fall to pieces.
I'm doing something right before your eyes
That you won't believe, though it's staring you in the face.'"

When the service was over, Paul and Barnabas were invited back to preach again the next Sabbath. As the meeting broke up, a good many Jews and converts to Judaism went along with Paul and Barnabas, who urged them in long conversations to stick with what they'd started, this living in and by God's grace.

When the next Sabbath came around, practically the whole city showed up to hear the Word of God. Some of the Jews, seeing the crowds, went wild with jealousy and tore into Paul, contradicting everything he was saying, making an ugly scene.

KING JAMES VERSION

46 Then Paul and Barnabas waxed bold, and said, It was necessary that the word of God should first have been spoken to you: but seeing ye put it from you, and judge yourselves unworthy of everlasting life, lo, we turn to the Gentiles.

47 For so hath the Lord commanded us, *saying*, I have set thee to be a light of the Gentiles, that thou shouldest be for salvation unto the ends of the earth.

48 And when the Gentiles heard this, they were glad, and glorified the word of the Lord: and as many as were ordained to eternal life believed.

49 And the word of the Lord was published throughout all the region.

50 But the Jews stirred up the devout and honourable women, and the chief men of the city, and raised persecution against Paul and Barnabas, and expelled them out of their coasts.

51 But they shook off the dust of their feet against them, and came unto Iconium.

52 And the disciples were filled with joy, and with the Holy Ghost.

NEW AMERICAN STANDARD BIBLE

46 Paul and Barnabas spoke out boldly and said, "It was necessary that the word of God be spoken to you first; since you repudiate it and judge yourselves unworthy of eternal life, behold, we are turning to the Gentiles.

47 "For so the Lord has commanded us,

'I HAVE PLACED YOU AS A LIGHT FOR THE GENTILES,
THAT YOU MAY BRING SALVATION TO THE END OF THE EARTH.' "

48 When the Gentiles heard this, they *began* rejoicing and glorifying the word of the Lord; and as many as had been appointed to eternal life believed.

49 And the word of the Lord was being spread through the whole region.

50 But the Jews incited the devout women of prominence and the leading men of the city, and instigated a persecution against Paul and Barnabas, and drove them out of their district.

51 But they shook off the dust of their feet *in protest* against them and went to Iconium.

52 And the disciples were continually filled with joy and with the Holy Spirit.

NEW CENTURY VERSION

Barnabas spoke very boldly, saying, "We must speak the message of God to you first. But you refuse to listen. You are judging yourselves not worthy of having eternal life! So we will now go to the people of other nations. 47This is what the Lord told us to do, saying:

'I have made you a light for the nations;
you will show people all over the world the way to be saved.' " *Isaiah 49:6*

48When those who were not Jewish heard Paul say this, they were happy and gave honor to the message of the Lord. And the people who were chosen to have life forever believed the message.

49So the message of the Lord was spreading through the whole country. 50But the Jewish people stirred up some of the important religious women and the leaders of the city. They started trouble against Paul and Barnabas and forced them out of their area. 51So Paul and Barnabas shook the dust off their feet[d] and went to Iconium. 52But the followers were filled with joy and the Holy Spirit.

13:51 [d] shook...feet A warning. It showed that they had rejected these people.

CONTEMPORARY ENGLISH VERSION

46But Paul and Barnabas bravely said:
We had to tell God's message to you before we told it to anyone else. But you rejected the message! This proves that you don't deserve eternal life. Now we are going to the Gentiles. 47The Lord has given us this command,

"I have placed you here
as a light
for the Gentiles.
You are to take
the saving power of God
to people everywhere on earth."

48This message made the Gentiles glad, and they praised what they had heard about the Lord.[g] Everyone who had been chosen for eternal life then put their faith in the Lord.

49The message about the Lord spread all over that region. 50But the Jewish leaders went to some of the important men in the town and to some respected women who were religious. They turned them against Paul and Barnabas and started making trouble for them. They even chased them out of that part of the country.

51Paul and Barnabas shook the dust from that place off their feet[h] and went on to the city of Iconium.

52But the Lord's followers in Antioch were very happy and were filled with the Holy Spirit.

[g] 13.48 *the Lord*: Some manuscripts have "God." [h] 13.51 *shook the dust from that place off their feet*: This was a way of showing rejection.

NEW INTERNATIONAL VERSION

46Then Paul and Barnabas answered them boldly: "We had to speak the word of God to you first. Since you reject it and do not consider yourselves worthy of eternal life, we now turn to the Gentiles. 47For this is what the Lord has commanded us:

" 'I have made you[g] a light for the Gentiles,
that you[g] may bring salvation to the ends of the earth.'[h]"

48When the Gentiles heard this, they were glad and honored the word of the Lord; and all who were appointed for eternal life believed.

49The word of the Lord spread through the whole region. 50But the Jews incited the God-fearing women of high standing and the leading men of the city. They stirred up persecution against Paul and Barnabas, and expelled them from their region. 51So they shook the dust from their feet in protest against them and went to Iconium. 52And the disciples were filled with joy and with the Holy Spirit.

[g] *47* The Greek is singular. [h] *47* Isaiah 49:6

NEW LIVING TRANSLATION

46Then Paul and Barnabas spoke out boldly and declared, "It was necessary that this Good News from God be given first to you Jews. But since you have rejected it and judged yourselves unworthy of eternal life—well, we will offer it to Gentiles. 47For this is as the Lord commanded us when he said,

'I have made you a light to the Gentiles,
to bring salvation to the farthest corners of the earth.'* "

48When the Gentiles heard this, they were very glad and thanked the Lord for his message; and all who were appointed to eternal life became believers. 49So the Lord's message spread throughout that region.

50Then the Jewish leaders stirred up both the influential religious women and the leaders of the city, and they incited a mob against Paul and Barnabas and ran them out of town. 51But they shook off the dust of their feet against them and went to the city of Iconium. 52And the believers* were filled with joy and with the Holy Spirit.

13:47 Isa 49:6. 13:52 Greek *the disciples.*

NEW KING JAMES VERSION

46Then Paul and Barnabas grew bold and said, "It was necessary that the word of God should be spoken to you first; but since you reject it, and judge yourselves unworthy of everlasting life, behold, we turn to the Gentiles. 47For so the Lord has commanded us:

'I have set you as a light to the Gentiles,
That you should be for salvation to the ends of the earth.' "[k]

48Now when the Gentiles heard this, they were glad and glorified the word of the Lord. And as many as had been appointed to eternal life believed.

49And the word of the Lord was being spread throughout all the region. 50But the Jews stirred up the devout and prominent women and the chief men of the city, raised up persecution against Paul and Barnabas, and expelled them from their region. 51But they shook off the dust from their feet against them, and came to Iconium. 52And the disciples were filled with joy and with the Holy Spirit.

13:47 [k] Isaiah 49:6

THE MESSAGE

But Paul and Barnabas didn't back down. Standing their ground they said, "It was required that God's Word be spoken first of all to you, the Jews. But seeing that you want no part of it—you've made it quite clear that you have no taste or inclination for eternal life—the door is open to all the outsiders. And we're on our way through it, following orders, doing what God commanded when he said,

'I've set you up
as light to all nations.
You'll proclaim salvation
to the four winds and seven seas!'"

When the non-Jewish outsiders heard this, they could hardly believe their good fortune. All who were marked out for *real life* put their trust in God—they honored God's Word by receiving that life. And this Message of salvation spread like wildfire all through the region.

Some of the Jews convinced the most respected women and leading men of the town that their precious way of life was about to be destroyed. Alarmed, they turned on Paul and Barnabas and forced them to leave. Paul and Barnabas shrugged their shoulders and went on to the next town, Iconium, brimming with joy and the Holy Spirit, two happy disciples.

KING JAMES VERSION

14 And it came to pass in Iconium, that they went both together into the synagogue of the Jews, and so spake, that a great multitude both of the Jews and also of the Greeks believed.

2 But the unbelieving Jews stirred up the Gentiles, and made their minds evil affected against the brethren.

3 Long time therefore abode they speaking boldly in the Lord, which gave testimony unto the word of his grace, and granted signs and wonders to be done by their hands.

4 But the multitude of the city was divided: and part held with the Jews, and part with the apostles.

5 And when there was an assault made both of the Gentiles, and also of the Jews with their rulers, to use *them* despitefully, and to stone them,

6 They were ware of *it*, and fled unto Lystra and Derbe, cities of Lycaonia, and unto the region that lieth round about:

7 And there they preached the gospel.

8 ¶ And there sat a certain man at Lystra, impotent in his feet, being a cripple from his mother's womb, who never had walked:

9 The same heard Paul speak: who stedfastly beholding him, and perceiving that he had faith to be healed,

NEW AMERICAN STANDARD BIBLE

Acceptance and Opposition

14 In Iconium they entered the synagogue of the Jews together, and spoke in such a manner that a large number of people believed, both of Jews and of Greeks.

2 But the Jews who disbelieved stirred up the minds of the Gentiles and embittered them against the brethren.

3 Therefore they spent a long time *there* speaking boldly *with reliance* upon the Lord, who was testifying to the word of His grace, granting that signs and wonders be done by their hands.

4 But the people of the city were divided; and some sided with the Jews, and some with the apostles.

5 And when an attempt was made by both the Gentiles and the Jews with their rulers, to mistreat and to stone them,

6 they became aware of it and fled to the cities of Lycaonia, Lystra and Derbe, and the surrounding region;

7 and there they continued to preach the gospel.

8 At Lystra a man was sitting who had no strength in his feet, lame from his mother's womb, who had never walked.

9 This man was listening to Paul as he spoke, who, when he had fixed his gaze on him and had seen that he had faith to be made well,

NEW CENTURY VERSION

Paul and Barnabas in Iconium

14 In Iconium, Paul and Barnabas went as usual to the Jewish synagogue. They spoke so well that a great many Jews and Greeks believed. 2But some of the Jews who did not believe excited the non-Jewish people and turned them against the believers. 3Paul and Barnabas stayed in Iconium a long time and spoke bravely for the Lord. He showed that their message about his grace was true by giving them the power to work miracles and signs. 4But the city was divided. Some of the people agreed with the Jews, and others believed the apostles.

5Some who were not Jews, some Jews, and some of their rulers wanted to mistreat Paul and Barnabas and to stone them to death. 6When Paul and Barnabas learned about this, they ran away to Lystra and Derbe, cities in Lycaonia, and to the areas around those cities. 7They announced the Good News there, too.

Paul in Lystra and Derbe

8In Lystra there sat a man who had been born crippled; he had never walked. 9As this man was listening to Paul speak, Paul looked straight at him and saw that he believed God could heal him. 10So he cried out, "Stand up

CONTEMPORARY ENGLISH VERSION

Paul and Barnabas in Iconium

14 Paul and Barnabas spoke in the Jewish meeting place in Iconium, just as they had done at Antioch, and many Jews and Gentiles[a] put their faith in the Lord. 2But the Jews who did not have faith in him made the other Gentiles angry and turned them against the Lord's followers.

3Paul and Barnabas stayed there for a while, having faith in the Lord and bravely speaking his message. The Lord gave them the power to work miracles and wonders, and he showed that their message about his great kindness was true.

4The people of Iconium did not know what to think. Some of them believed the Jewish group, and others believed the apostles. 5Finally, some Gentiles and Jews, together with their leaders, decided to make trouble for Paul and Barnabas and to stone them to death.

6-7But when the two apostles found out what was happening, they escaped to the region of Lycaonia. They preached the good news there in the towns of Lystra and Derbe and in the nearby countryside.

Paul and Barnabas in Lystra

8In Lystra there was a man who had been born with crippled feet and had never been able to walk. 9The man was listening to Paul speak, when Paul saw that he had faith in Jesus and could be healed. So he looked straight at

[a] 14.1 *Gentiles*: The Greek text has "Greeks," which probably means people who were not Jews. But it may mean Gentiles who worshiped with the Jews.

NEW INTERNATIONAL VERSION

In Iconium

14 At Iconium Paul and Barnabas went as usual into the Jewish synagogue. There they spoke so effectively that a great number of Jews and Gentiles believed. 2But the Jews who refused to believe stirred up the Gentiles and poisoned their minds against the brothers. 3So Paul and Barnabas spent considerable time there, speaking boldly for the Lord, who confirmed the message of his grace by enabling them to do miraculous signs and wonders. 4The people of the city were divided; some sided with the Jews, others with the apostles. 5There was a plot afoot among the Gentiles and Jews, together with their leaders, to mistreat them and stone them. 6But they found out about it and fled to the Lycaonian cities of Lystra and Derbe and to the surrounding country, 7where they continued to preach the good news.

In Lystra and Derbe

8In Lystra there sat a man crippled in his feet, who was lame from birth and had never walked. 9He listened to Paul as he was speaking. Paul looked directly at him, saw that he had faith to be healed 10and called out, "Stand up

NEW LIVING TRANSLATION

Paul and Barnabas in Iconium

14 In Iconium,* Paul and Barnabas went together to the synagogue and preached with such power that a great number of both Jews and Gentiles believed. 2But the Jews who spurned God's message stirred up distrust among the Gentiles against Paul and Barnabas, saying all sorts of evil things about them. 3The apostles stayed there a long time, preaching boldly about the grace of the Lord. The Lord proved their message was true by giving them power to do miraculous signs and wonders. 4But the people of the city were divided in their opinion about them. Some sided with the Jews, and some with the apostles.

5A mob of Gentiles and Jews, along with their leaders, decided to attack and stone them. 6When the apostles learned of it, they fled for their lives. They went to the region of Lycaonia, to the cities of Lystra and Derbe and the surrounding area, 7and they preached the Good News there.

Paul and Barnabas in Lystra and Derbe

8While they were at Lystra, Paul and Barnabas came upon a man with crippled feet. He had been that way from birth, so he had never walked. 9He was listening as Paul preached, and Paul noticed him and realized he had faith to be healed. 10So Paul called to him in a loud voice,

14:1 *Iconium,* as well as *Lystra* and *Derbe* (14:6), were cities in the land now called Turkey.

NEW KING JAMES VERSION

At Iconium

14 Now it happened in Iconium that they went together to the synagogue of the Jews, and so spoke that a great multitude both of the Jews and of the Greeks believed. 2But the unbelieving Jews stirred up the Gentiles and poisoned their minds against the brethren. 3Therefore they stayed there a long time, speaking boldly in the Lord, who was bearing witness to the word of His grace, granting signs and wonders to be done by their hands.

4But the multitude of the city was divided: part sided with the Jews, and part with the apostles. 5And when a violent attempt was made by both the Gentiles and Jews, with their rulers, to abuse and stone them, 6they became aware of it and fled to Lystra and Derbe, cities of Lycaonia, and to the surrounding region. 7And they were preaching the gospel there.

Idolatry at Lystra

8And in Lystra a certain man without strength in his feet was sitting, a cripple from his mother's womb, who had never walked. 9*This* man heard Paul speaking. Paul, observing him intently and seeing that he had faith to be healed,

THE MESSAGE

14 When they got to Iconium they went, as they always did, to the meeting place of the Jews and gave their message. The Message convinced both Jews and non-Jews—and not just a few, either. But the unbelieving Jews worked up a whispering campaign against Paul and Barnabas, sowing mistrust and suspicion in the minds of the people in the street. The two apostles were there a long time, speaking freely, openly, and confidently as they presented the clear evidence of God's gifts, God corroborating their work with miracles and wonders.

But then there was a split in public opinion, some siding with the Jews, some with the apostles. One day, learning that both the Jews and non-Jews had been organized by their leaders to beat them up, they escaped as best they could to the next towns—Lyconia, Lystra, Derbe, and that neighborhood—but then were right back at it again, getting out the Message.

Gods or Men?

There was a man in Lystra who couldn't walk. He sat there, crippled since the day of his birth. He heard Paul talking, and Paul, looking him in the eye, saw that he was ripe for God's work, ready to believe. So he said, loud

KING JAMES VERSION

10 Said with a loud voice, Stand upright on thy feet. And he leaped and walked.

11 And when the people saw what Paul had done, they lifted up their voices, saying in the speech of Lycaonia, The gods are come down to us in the likeness of men.

12 And they called Barnabas, Jupiter; and Paul, Mercurius, because he was the chief speaker.

13 Then the priest of Jupiter, which was before their city, brought oxen and garlands unto the gates, and would have done sacrifice with the people.

14 *Which* when the apostles, Barnabas and Paul, heard *of*, they rent their clothes, and ran in among the people, crying out,

15 And saying, Sirs, why do ye these things? We also are men of like passions with you, and preach unto you that ye should turn from these vanities unto the living God, which made heaven, and earth, and the sea, and all things that are therein:

16 Who in times past suffered all nations to walk in their own ways.

17 Nevertheless he left not himself without witness, in that he did good, and gave us rain from heaven, and fruitful seasons, filling our hearts with food and gladness.

18 And with these sayings scarce restrained they the people, that they had not done sacrifice unto them.

19 ¶ And there came thither *certain* Jews from Antioch and Iconium, who persuaded the people, and, having stoned Paul, drew *him* out of the city, supposing he had been dead.

NEW AMERICAN STANDARD BIBLE

10 said with a loud voice, "Stand upright on your feet." And he leaped up and *began* to walk.

11 When the crowds saw what Paul had done, they raised their voice, saying in the Lycaonian language, "The gods have become like men and have come down to us."

12 And they *began* calling Barnabas, Zeus, and Paul, Hermes, because he was the chief speaker.

13 The priest of Zeus, whose *temple* was just outside the city, brought oxen and garlands to the gates, and wanted to offer sacrifice with the crowds.

14 But when the apostles Barnabas and Paul heard of it, they tore their robes and rushed out into the crowd, crying out

15 and saying, "Men, why are you doing these things? We are also men of the same nature as you, and preach the gospel to you that you should turn from these [1]vain things to a living God, WHO MADE THE HEAVEN AND THE EARTH AND THE SEA AND ALL THAT IS IN THEM.

16 "In the generations gone by He permitted all the nations to go their own ways;

17 and yet He did not leave Himself without witness, in that He did good and gave you rains from heaven and fruitful seasons, satisfying your hearts with food and gladness."

18 *Even* saying these things, with difficulty they restrained the crowds from offering sacrifice to them.

19 But Jews came from Antioch and Iconium, and having won over the crowds, they stoned Paul and dragged him out of the city, supposing him to be dead.

14:15 [1] I.e. idols

NEW CENTURY VERSION

on your feet!" The man jumped up and began walking around.
11When the crowds saw what Paul did, they shouted in the Lycaonian language, "The gods have become like humans and have come down to us!"
12Then the people began to call Barnabas "Zeus"[a] and Paul "Hermes,"[b] because he was the main speaker.
13The priest in the temple of Zeus, which was near the city, brought some bulls and flowers to the city gates. He and the people wanted to offer a sacrifice to Paul and Barnabas.
14But when the apostles, Barnabas and Paul, heard about it, they tore their clothes. They ran in among the people, shouting,
15"Friends, why are you doing these things? We are only human beings like you. We are bringing you the Good News and are telling you to turn away from these worthless things and turn to the living God. He is the One who made the sky, the earth, the sea, and everything in them.
16In the past, God let all the nations do what they wanted.
17Yet he proved he is real by showing kindness, by giving you rain from heaven and crops at the right times, by giving you food and filling your hearts with joy."
18Even with these words, they were barely able to keep the crowd from offering sacrifices to them.

19Then some Jewish people came from Antioch and Iconium and persuaded the people to turn against Paul. So they threw stones at him and dragged him out of town,

14:12 [a] **"Zeus"** The Greeks believed in many gods, of whom Zeus was most important. **14:12** [b] **"Hermes"** The Greeks believed he was a messenger for the other gods.

CONTEMPORARY ENGLISH VERSION

the man
10and shouted, "Stand up!" The man jumped up and started walking around.

11When the crowd saw what Paul had done, they yelled out in the language of Lycaonia, "The gods have turned into humans and have come down to us!"
12The people then gave Barnabas the name Zeus, and they gave Paul the name Hermes,[b] because he did the talking.

13The temple of Zeus was near the entrance to the city. Its priest and the crowds wanted to offer a sacrifice to Barnabas and Paul. So the priest brought some bulls and flowers to the city gates.
14When the two apostles found out about this, they tore their clothes in horror and ran to the crowd, shouting:

15Why are you doing this? We are humans just like you. Please give up all this foolishness. Turn to the living God, who made the sky, the earth, the sea, and everything in them.
16In times past, God let each nation go its own way.
17But he showed that he was there by the good things he did. God sends rain from heaven and makes your crops grow. He gives food to you and makes your hearts glad.

18Even after Paul and Barnabas had said all this, they could hardly keep the people from offering a sacrifice to them.

19Some Jewish leaders from Antioch and Iconium came and turned the crowds against Paul. They hit him with stones and dragged him out of the city, thinking he was

[b] **14.12** *Hermes*: The Greeks thought of Hermes as the messenger of the other gods, especially of Zeus, their chief god.

NEW INTERNATIONAL VERSION

on your feet!" At that, the man jumped up and began to walk.

[11]When the crowd saw what Paul had done, they shouted in the Lycaonian language, "The gods have come down to us in human form!" [12]Barnabas they called Zeus, and Paul they called Hermes because he was the chief speaker. [13]The priest of Zeus, whose temple was just outside the city, brought bulls and wreaths to the city gates because he and the crowd wanted to offer sacrifices to them.

[14]But when the apostles Barnabas and Paul heard of this, they tore their clothes and rushed out into the crowd, shouting: [15]"Men, why are you doing this? We too are only men, human like you. We are bringing you good news, telling you to turn from these worthless things to the living God, who made heaven and earth and sea and everything in them. [16]In the past, he let all nations go their own way. [17]Yet he has not left himself without testimony: He has shown kindness by giving you rain from heaven and crops in their seasons; he provides you with plenty of food and fills your hearts with joy." [18]Even with these words, they had difficulty keeping the crowd from sacrificing to them.

[19]Then some Jews came from Antioch and Iconium and won the crowd over. They stoned Paul and dragged him outside the city, thinking he was dead. [20]But after the dis-

NEW LIVING TRANSLATION

"Stand up!" And the man jumped to his feet and started walking.

[11]When the listening crowd saw what Paul had done, they shouted in their local dialect, "These men are gods in human bodies!" [12]They decided that Barnabas was the Greek god Zeus and that Paul, because he was the chief speaker, was Hermes. [13]The temple of Zeus was located on the outskirts of the city. The priest of the temple and the crowd brought oxen and wreaths of flowers, and they prepared to sacrifice to the apostles at the city gates.

[14]But when Barnabas and Paul heard what was happening, they tore their clothing in dismay and ran out among the people, shouting, [15]"Friends,* why are you doing this? We are merely human beings like yourselves! We have come to bring you the Good News that you should turn from these worthless things to the living God, who made heaven and earth, the sea, and everything in them. [16]In earlier days he permitted all the nations to go their own ways, [17]but he never left himself without a witness. There were always his reminders, such as sending you rain and good crops and giving you food and joyful hearts." [18]But even so, Paul and Barnabas could scarcely restrain the people from sacrificing to them.

[19]Now some Jews arrived from Antioch and Iconium and turned the crowds into a murderous mob. They stoned Paul and dragged him out of the city, apparently dead.

14:15 Greek *Men.*

NEW KING JAMES VERSION

[10]said with a loud voice, "Stand up straight on your feet!" And he leaped and walked. [11]Now when the people saw what Paul had done, they raised their voices, saying in the Lycaonian *language,* "The gods have come down to us in the likeness of men!" [12]And Barnabas they called Zeus, and Paul, Hermes, because he was the chief speaker. [13]Then the priest of Zeus, whose temple was in front of their city, brought oxen and garlands to the gates, intending to sacrifice with the multitudes.

[14]But when the apostles Barnabas and Paul heard this, they tore their clothes and ran in among the multitude, crying out [15]and saying, "Men, why are you doing these things? We also are men with the same nature as you, and preach to you that you should turn from these useless things to the living God, who made the heaven, the earth, the sea, and all things that are in them, [16]who in bygone generations allowed all nations to walk in their own ways. [17]Nevertheless He did not leave Himself without witness, in that He did good, gave us rain from heaven and fruitful seasons, filling our hearts with food and gladness." [18]And with these sayings they could scarcely restrain the multitudes from sacrificing to them.

Stoning, Escape to Derbe

[19]Then Jews from Antioch and Iconium came there; and having persuaded the multitudes, they stoned Paul *and* dragged *him* out of the city, supposing him to be dead.

THE MESSAGE

enough for everyone to hear, "Up on your feet!" The man was up in a flash—jumped up and walked around as if he'd been walking all his life.

When the crowd saw what Paul had done, they went wild, calling out in their Lyconian dialect, "The gods have come down! These men are gods!" They called Barnabas "Zeus" and Paul "Hermes" (since Paul did most of the speaking). The priest of the local Zeus shrine got up a parade—bulls and banners and people lined right up to the gates, ready for the ritual of sacrifice.

When Barnabas and Paul finally realized what was going on, they stopped them. Waving their arms, they interrupted the parade, calling out, "What do you think you're doing! We're not gods! We are men just like you, and we're here to bring you the Message, to persuade you to abandon these silly god-superstitions and embrace God himself, the living God. We don't make God; he makes us, and all of this—sky, earth, sea, and everything in them.

"In the generations before us, God let all the different nations go their own way. But even then he didn't leave them without a clue, for he made a good creation, poured down rain and gave bumper crops. When your bellies were full and your hearts happy, there was evidence of good beyond your doing." Talking fast and hard like this, they prevented them from carrying out the sacrifice that would have honored them as gods—but just barely.

Then some Jews from Antioch and Iconium caught up with them and turned the fickle crowd against them. They beat Paul unconscious, dragged him outside the town and

KING JAMES VERSION

20 Howbeit, as the disciples stood round about him, he rose up, and came into the city: and the next day he departed with Barnabas to Derbe.

21 And when they had preached the gospel to that city, and had taught many, they returned again to Lystra, and *to* Iconium, and Antioch,

22 Confirming the souls of the disciples, *and* exhorting them to continue in the faith, and that we must through much tribulation enter into the kingdom of God.

23 And when they had ordained them elders in every church, and had prayed with fasting, they commended them to the Lord, on whom they believed.

24 And after they had passed throughout Pisidia, they came to Pamphylia.

25 And when they had preached the word in Perga, they went down into Attalia:

26 And thence sailed to Antioch, from whence they had been recommended to the grace of God for the work which they fulfilled.

27 And when they were come, and had gathered the church together, they rehearsed all that God had done with them, and how he had opened the door of faith unto the Gentiles.

28 And there they abode long time with the disciples.

NEW AMERICAN STANDARD BIBLE

20 But while the disciples stood around him, he got up and entered the city. The next day he went away with Barnabas to Derbe.

21 After they had preached the gospel to that city and had made many disciples, they returned to Lystra and to Iconium and to Antioch,

22 strengthening the souls of the disciples, encouraging them to continue in the faith, and *saying,* "Through many tribulations we must enter the kingdom of God."

23 When they had appointed elders for them in every church, having prayed with fasting, they commended them to the Lord in whom they had believed.

24 They passed through Pisidia and came into Pamphylia.

25 When they had spoken the word in Perga, they went down to Attalia.

26 From there they sailed to Antioch, from which they had been commended to the grace of God for the work that they had accomplished.

27 When they had arrived and gathered the church together, they *began* to report all things that God had done with them and how He had opened a door of faith to the Gentiles.

28 And they spent a long time with the disciples.

NEW CENTURY VERSION

thinking they had killed him. 20But the followers gathered around him, and he got up and went back into the town. The next day he and Barnabas left and went to the city of Derbe.

The Return to Antioch in Syria

21Paul and Barnabas told the Good News in Derbe, and many became followers. Paul and Barnabas returned to Lystra, Iconium, and Antioch, 22making the followers of Jesus stronger and helping them stay in the faith. They said, "We must suffer many things to enter God's kingdom." 23They chose elders for each church, by praying and giving up eating for a certain time.[c] These elders had trusted the Lord, so Paul and Barnabas put them in the Lord's care.

24Then they went through Pisidia and came to Pamphylia. 25When they had preached the message in Perga, they went down to Attalia. 26And from there they sailed away to Antioch where the believers had put them into God's care and had sent them out to do this work. Now they had finished.

27When they arrived in Antioch, Paul and Barnabas gathered the church together. They told the church all about what God had done with them and how God had made it possible for those who were not Jewish to believe. 28And they stayed there a long time with the followers.

14:23 [c] **giving...time** This is called "fasting." The people would give up eating for a special time of prayer and worship to God. It was also done to show sadness and disappointment.

CONTEMPORARY ENGLISH VERSION

dead. 20But when the Lord's followers gathered around Paul, he stood up and went back into the city. The next day he and Barnabas went to Derbe.

Paul and Barnabas Return to Antioch in Syria

21Paul and Barnabas preached the good news in Derbe and won some people to the Lord. Then they went back to Lystra, Iconium, and Antioch in Pisidia. 22They encouraged the followers and begged them to remain faithful. They told them, "We have to suffer a lot before we can get into God's kingdom." 23Paul and Barnabas chose some leaders for each of the churches. Then they went without eating[c] and prayed that the Lord would take good care of these leaders.

24Paul and Barnabas went on through Pisidia to Pamphylia, 25where they preached in the town of Perga. Then they went down to Attalia 26and sailed to Antioch in Syria. It was there that they had been placed in God's care for the work they had now completed.[d]

27After arriving in Antioch, they called the church together. They told the people what God had helped them do and how he had made it possible for the Gentiles to believe. 28Then they stayed there with the followers for a long time.

[c] 14.23 *went without eating*: See the note at 13.2. [d] 14.26 *the work they had now completed*: See 13.1-3.

NEW INTERNATIONAL VERSION

ciples had gathered around him, he got up and went back into the city. The next day he and Barnabas left for Derbe.

The Return to Antioch in Syria

21They preached the good news in that city and won a large number of disciples. Then they returned to Lystra, Iconium and Antioch, 22strengthening the disciples and encouraging them to remain true to the faith. "We must go through many hardships to enter the kingdom of God," they said. 23Paul and Barnabas appointed elders[a] for them in each church and, with prayer and fasting, committed them to the Lord, in whom they had put their trust. 24After going through Pisidia, they came into Pamphylia, 25and when they had preached the word in Perga, they went down to Attalia.

26From Attalia they sailed back to Antioch, where they had been committed to the grace of God for the work they had now completed. 27On arriving there, they gathered the church together and reported all that God had done through them and how he had opened the door of faith to the Gentiles. 28And they stayed there a long time with the disciples.

a *23* Or *Barnabas ordained elders*; or *Barnabas had elders elected*

NEW LIVING TRANSLATION

20But as the believers* stood around him, he got up and went back into the city. The next day he left with Barnabas for Derbe.

Paul and Barnabas Return to Antioch of Syria

21After preaching the Good News in Derbe and making many disciples, Paul and Barnabas returned again to Lystra, Iconium, and Antioch of Pisidia, 22where they strengthened the believers. They encouraged them to continue in the faith, reminding them that they must enter into the Kingdom of God through many tribulations. 23Paul and Barnabas also appointed elders in every church and prayed for them with fasting, turning them over to the care of the Lord, in whom they had come to trust. 24Then they traveled back through Pisidia to Pamphylia. 25They preached again in Perga, then went on to Attalia.

26Finally, they returned by ship to Antioch of Syria, where their journey had begun and where they had been committed to the grace of God for the work they had now completed. 27Upon arriving in Antioch, they called the church together and reported about their trip, telling all that God had done and how he had opened the door of faith to the Gentiles, too. 28And they stayed there with the believers in Antioch for a long time.

14:20 Greek *disciples;* also in 14:22, 28.

NEW KING JAMES VERSION

20However, when the disciples gathered around him, he rose up and went into the city. And the next day he departed with Barnabas to Derbe.

Strengthening the Converts

21And when they had preached the gospel to that city and made many disciples, they returned to Lystra, Iconium, and Antioch, 22strengthening the souls of the disciples, exhorting *them* to continue in the faith, and *saying,* "We must through many tribulations enter the kingdom of God." 23So when they had appointed elders in every church, and prayed with fasting, they commended them to the Lord in whom they had believed. 24And after they had passed through Pisidia, they came to Pamphylia. 25Now when they had preached the word in Perga, they went down to Attalia. 26From there they sailed to Antioch, where they had been commended to the grace of God for the work which they had completed.

27Now when they had come and gathered the church together, they reported all that God had done with them, and that He had opened the door of faith to the Gentiles. 28So they stayed there a long time with the disciples.

THE MESSAGE

left him for dead. But as the disciples gathered around him, he came to and got up. He went back into town and the next day left with Barnabas for Derbe.

Plenty of Hard Times

After proclaiming the Message in Derbe and establishing a strong core of disciples, they retraced their steps to Lystra, then Iconium, and then Antioch, putting muscle and sinew in the lives of the disciples, urging them to stick with what they had begun to believe and not quit, making it clear to them that it wouldn't be easy: "Anyone signing up for the kingdom of God has to go through plenty of hard times."

Paul and Barnabas handpicked leaders in each church. After praying—their prayers intensified by fasting—they presented these new leaders to the Master to whom they had entrusted their lives. Working their way back through Pisidia, they came to Pamphylia and preached in Perga. Finally, they made it to Attalia and caught a ship back to Antioch, where it had all started—launched by God's grace and now safely home by God's grace. A good piece of work.

On arrival, they got the church together and reported on their trip, telling in detail how God had used them to throw the door of faith wide open so people of all nations could come streaming in. Then they settled down for a long, leisurely visit with the disciples.

KING JAMES VERSION

15 And certain men which came down from Judaea taught the brethren, *and said*, Except ye be circumcised after the manner of Moses, ye cannot be saved.

2 When therefore Paul and Barnabas had no small dissension and disputation with them, they determined that Paul and Barnabas, and certain other of them, should go up to Jerusalem unto the apostles and elders about this question.

3 And being brought on their way by the church, they passed through Phenice and Samaria, declaring the conversion of the Gentiles: and they caused great joy unto all the brethren.

4 And when they were come to Jerusalem, they were received of the church, and *of* the apostles and elders, and they declared all things that God had done with them.

5 But there rose up certain of the sect of the Pharisees which believed, saying, That it was needful to circumcise them, and to command *them* to keep the law of Moses.

6 ¶ And the apostles and elders came together for to consider of this matter.

7 And when there had been much disputing, Peter rose up, and said unto them, Men *and* brethren, ye know how that a good while ago God made choice among us, that the Gentiles by my mouth should hear the word of the gospel, and believe.

NEW AMERICAN STANDARD BIBLE

The Council at Jerusalem

15 Some men came down from Judea and *began* teaching the brethren, "Unless you are circumcised according to the custom of Moses, you cannot be saved."

2 And when Paul and Barnabas had great dissension and debate with them, *the brethren* determined that Paul and Barnabas and some others of them should go up to Jerusalem to the apostles and elders concerning this issue.

3 Therefore, being sent on their way by the church, they were passing through both Phoenicia and Samaria, describing in detail the conversion of the Gentiles, and were bringing great joy to all the brethren.

4 When they arrived at Jerusalem, they were received by the church and the apostles and the elders, and they reported all that God had done with them.

5 But some of the sect of the Pharisees who had believed stood up, saying, "It is necessary to circumcise them and to direct them to observe the Law of Moses."

6 The apostles and the elders came together to look into this matter.

7 After there had been much debate, Peter stood up and said to them, "Brethren, you know that in the early days God made a choice among you, that by my mouth the Gentiles would hear the word of the gospel and believe.

NEW CENTURY VERSION

The Meeting at Jerusalem

15 Then some people came to Antioch from Judea and
began teaching the non-Jewish believers: "You
cannot be saved if you are not circumcised as Moses
taught us." 2Paul and Barnabas were against this teaching
and argued with them about it. So the church decided to
send Paul, Barnabas, and some others to Jerusalem where
they could talk more about this with the apostles and
elders.
3The church helped them leave on the trip, and they
went through the countries of Phoenicia and Samaria,
telling all about how those who were not Jewish had
turned to God. This made all the believers very happy.
4When they arrived in Jerusalem, they were welcomed by
the apostles, the elders, and the church. Paul, Barnabas,
and the others told about everything God had done with
them. 5But some of the believers who belonged to the
Pharisee group came forward and said, "The non-Jewish
believers must be circumcised. They must be told to obey
the law of Moses."
6The apostles and the elders gathered to consider this
problem. 7After a long debate, Peter stood up and said to
them, "Brothers, you know that in the early days God chose
me from among you to preach the Good News to those who
are not Jewish. They heard the Good News from me, and

CONTEMPORARY ENGLISH VERSION

15 Some people came from Judea and started teaching
the Lord's followers that they could not be saved,
unless they were circumcised as Moses had taught. 2This
caused trouble, and Paul and Barnabas argued with them
about this teaching. So it was decided to send Paul and
Barnabas and a few others to Jerusalem to discuss this
problem with the apostles and the church leaders.

The Church Leaders Meet in Jerusalem

3The men who were sent by the church went through
Phoenicia and Samaria, telling how the Gentiles had
turned to God. This news made the Lord's followers very
happy. 4When the men arrived in Jerusalem, they were
welcomed by the church, including the apostles and the
leaders. They told them everything God had helped them
do. 5But some Pharisees had become followers of the Lord.
They stood up and said, "Gentiles who have faith in the
Lord must be circumcised and told to obey the Law of
Moses."
6The apostles and church leaders met to discuss this
problem about Gentiles. 7They had talked it over for a long
time, when Peter got up and said:

> My friends, you know that God decided long ago to let me be the one from your group to preach the good news to the Gentiles. God did this so that they would hear and

NEW INTERNATIONAL VERSION

The Council at Jerusalem

15 Some men came down from Judea to Antioch and were teaching the brothers: "Unless you are circumcised, according to the custom taught by Moses, you cannot be saved." 2This brought Paul and Barnabas into sharp dispute and debate with them. So Paul and Barnabas were appointed, along with some other believers, to go up to Jerusalem to see the apostles and elders about this question. 3The church sent them on their way, and as they traveled through Phoenicia and Samaria, they told how the Gentiles had been converted. This news made all the brothers very glad. 4When they came to Jerusalem, they were welcomed by the church and the apostles and elders, to whom they reported everything God had done through them.

5Then some of the believers who belonged to the party of the Pharisees stood up and said, "The Gentiles must be circumcised and required to obey the law of Moses."

6The apostles and elders met to consider this question. 7After much discussion, Peter got up and addressed them: "Brothers, you know that some time ago God made a choice among you that the Gentiles might hear from my lips the message of the gospel and believe. 8God, who

NEW LIVING TRANSLATION

The Council at Jerusalem

15 While Paul and Barnabas were at Antioch of Syria, some men from Judea arrived and began to teach the Christians*: "Unless you keep the ancient Jewish custom of circumcision taught by Moses, you cannot be saved." 2Paul and Barnabas, disagreeing with them, argued forcefully and at length. Finally, Paul and Barnabas were sent to Jerusalem, accompanied by some local believers, to talk to the apostles and elders about this question. 3The church sent the delegates to Jerusalem, and they stopped along the way in Phoenicia and Samaria to visit the believers.* They told them—much to everyone's joy—that the Gentiles, too, were being converted.

4When they arrived in Jerusalem, Paul and Barnabas were welcomed by the whole church, including the apostles and elders. They reported on what God had been doing through their ministry. 5But then some of the men who had been Pharisees before their conversion stood up and declared that all Gentile converts must be circumcised and be required to follow the law of Moses.

6So the apostles and church elders got together to decide this question. 7At the meeting, after a long discussion, Peter stood and addressed them as follows: "Brothers, you all know that God chose me from among you some time ago to preach to the Gentiles so that they could hear the

15:1 Greek *brothers;* also in 15:32, 33. **15:3** Greek *brothers;* also in 15:23, 36, 40.

NEW KING JAMES VERSION

Conflict over Circumcision

15 And certain *men* came down from Judea and taught the brethren, "Unless you are circumcised according to the custom of Moses, you cannot be saved." 2Therefore, when Paul and Barnabas had no small dissension and dispute with them, they determined that Paul and Barnabas and certain others of them should go up to Jerusalem, to the apostles and elders, about this question.

3So, being sent on their way by the church, they passed through Phoenicia and Samaria, describing the conversion of the Gentiles; and they caused great joy to all the brethren. 4And when they had come to Jerusalem, they were received by the church and the apostles and the elders; and they reported all things that God had done with them. 5But some of the sect of the Pharisees who believed rose up, saying, "It is necessary to circumcise them, and to command *them* to keep the law of Moses."

The Jerusalem Council

6Now the apostles and elders came together to consider this matter. 7And when there had been much dispute, Peter rose up and said to them: "Men and brethren, you know that a good while ago God chose among us, that by my mouth the Gentiles should hear the word of the gospel and

THE MESSAGE

To Let Outsiders Inside

15 It wasn't long before some Jews showed up from Judea insisting that everyone be circumcised: "If you're not circumcised in the Mosaic fashion, you can't be saved." Paul and Barnabas were up on their feet at once in fierce protest. The church decided to resolve the matter by sending Paul, Barnabas, and a few others to put it before the apostles and leaders in Jerusalem.

After they were sent off and on their way, they told everyone they met as they traveled through Phoenicia and Samaria about the breakthrough to the Gentile outsiders. Everyone who heard the news cheered—it was terrific news!

When they got to Jerusalem, Paul and Barnabas were graciously received by the whole church, including the apostles and leaders. They reported on their recent journey and how God had used them to open things up to the outsiders. Some Pharisees stood up to say their piece. They had become believers, but continued to hold to the hard party line of the Pharisees. "You have to circumcise the pagan converts," they said. "You must make them keep the Law of Moses."

The apostles and leaders called a special meeting to consider the matter. The arguments went on and on, back and forth, getting more and more heated. Then Peter took the floor: "Friends, you well know that from early on God made it quite plain that he wanted the pagans to hear the Message of this good news and embrace it—and not in any secondhand or roundabout way, but firsthand, straight from my mouth. And God, who can't be fooled by any pretense on

KING JAMES VERSION

8 And God, which knoweth the hearts, bare them witness, giving them the Holy Ghost, even as *he did* unto us;
9 And put no difference between us and them, purifying their hearts by faith.
10 Now therefore why tempt ye God, to put a yoke upon the neck of the disciples, which neither our fathers nor we were able to bear?
11 But we believe that through the grace of the Lord Jesus Christ we shall be saved, even as they.
12 Then all the multitude kept silence, and gave audience to Barnabas and Paul, declaring what miracles and wonders God had wrought among the Gentiles by them.
13 And after they had held their peace, James answered, saying, Men *and* brethren, hearken unto me:
14 Simeon hath declared how God at the first did visit the Gentiles, to take out of them a people for his name.
15 And to this agree the words of the prophets; as it is written,
16 After this I will return, and will build again the tabernacle of David, which is fallen down; and I will build again the ruins thereof, and I will set it up:
17 That the residue of men might seek after the Lord, and all the Gentiles, upon whom my name is called,

NEW AMERICAN STANDARD BIBLE

8 "And God, who knows the heart, testified to them giving them the Holy Spirit, just as He also did to us;
9 and He made no distinction between us and them, cleansing their hearts by faith.
10 "Now therefore why do you put God to the test by placing upon the neck of the disciples a yoke which neither our fathers nor we have been able to bear?
11 "But we believe that we are saved through the grace of the Lord Jesus, in the same way as they also are."
12 All the people kept silent, and they were listening to Barnabas and Paul as they were relating what signs and wonders God had done through them among the Gentiles.

James' Judgment

13 After they had stopped speaking, James answered, saying, "Brethren, listen to me.
14 "Simeon has related how God first concerned Himself about taking from among the Gentiles a people for His name.
15 "With this the words of the Prophets agree, just as it is written,
16 'After these things I will return,
And I will rebuild the tabernacle of David which has fallen,
And I will rebuild its ruins,
And I will restore it,
17 So that the rest of mankind may seek the Lord,
And all the Gentiles who are called by My name,'

NEW CENTURY VERSION

they believed. 8God, who knows the thoughts of everyone, accepted them. He showed this to us by giving them the Holy Spirit, just as he did to us. 9To God, those people are not different from us. When they believed, he made their hearts pure. 10So now why are you testing God by putting a heavy load around the necks of the non-Jewish believers? It is a load that neither we nor our ancestors were able to carry. 11But we believe that we and they too will be saved by the grace of the Lord Jesus."

12Then the whole group became quiet. They listened to Paul and Barnabas tell about all the miracles and signs that God did through them among the non-Jewish people. 13After they finished speaking, James said, "Brothers, listen to me. 14Simon has told us how God showed his love for the non-Jewish people. For the first time he is accepting from among them a people to be his own. 15The words of the prophets agree with this too:

16 'After these things I will return.
The kingdom of David is like a fallen tent.
But I will rebuild its ruins,
and I will set it up.
17 Then those people who are left alive may ask the Lord for help,
and the other nations that belong to me,

CONTEMPORARY ENGLISH VERSION

obey him. 8He knows what is in everyone's heart. And he showed that he had chosen the Gentiles, when he gave them the Holy Spirit, just as he had given his Spirit to us. 9God treated them in the same way that he treated us. They put their faith in him, and he made their hearts pure.

10Now why are you trying to make God angry by placing a heavy burden on these followers? This burden was too heavy for us or our ancestors. 11But our Lord Jesus was kind to us, and we are saved by faith in him, just as the Gentiles are.

12Everyone kept quiet and listened as Barnabas and Paul told how God had given them the power to work a lot of miracles and wonders for the Gentiles.

13After they had finished speaking, James[a] said:

My friends, listen to me! 14Simon Peter[b] has told how God first came to the Gentiles and made some of them his own people. 15This agrees with what the prophets wrote,

16 "I, the Lord, will return
and rebuild
David's fallen house.
I will build it from its ruins
and set it up again.
17 Then other nations
will turn to me
and be my chosen ones.

[a] 15.13 *James*: The Lord's brother. [b] 15.14 *Simon Peter*: The Greek text has "Simeon," which is another form of the name "Simon." The apostle Peter is meant.

NEW INTERNATIONAL VERSION

knows the heart, showed that he accepted them by giving
the Holy Spirit to them, just as he did to us. 9He made no
distinction between us and them, for he purified their
hearts by faith. 10Now then, why do you try to test God by
putting on the necks of the disciples a yoke that neither we
nor our fathers have been able to bear? 11No! We believe it
is through the grace of our Lord Jesus that we are saved,
just as they are."
12The whole assembly became silent as they listened to
Barnabas and Paul telling about the miraculous signs and
wonders God had done among the Gentiles through them.
13When they finished, James spoke up: "Brothers, listen to
me. 14Simon[a] has described to us how God at first showed
his concern by taking from the Gentiles a people for him-
self. 15The words of the prophets are in agreement with
this, as it is written:

16" 'After this I will return
and rebuild David's fallen tent.
Its ruins I will rebuild,
and I will restore it,
17 that the remnant of men may seek the Lord,
and all the Gentiles who bear my name,

[a] *14* Greek *Simeon*, a variant of *Simon*; that is, Peter

NEW LIVING TRANSLATION

Good News and believe. 8God, who knows people's hearts,
confirmed that he accepts Gentiles by giving them the Holy
Spirit, just as he gave him to us. 9He made no distinction
between us and them, for he also cleansed their hearts
through faith. 10Why are you now questioning God's way
by burdening the Gentile believers* with a yoke that nei-
ther we nor our ancestors were able to bear? 11We believe
that we are all saved the same way, by the special favor of
the Lord Jesus."
12There was no further discussion, and everyone lis-
tened as Barnabas and Paul told about the miraculous
signs and wonders God had done through them among the
Gentiles.
13When they had finished, James stood and said,
"Brothers, listen to me. 14Peter* has told you about the time
God first visited the Gentiles to take from them a people for
himself. 15And this conversion of Gentiles agrees with what
the prophets predicted. For instance, it is written:

16 'Afterward I will return,
and I will restore the fallen kingdom of David.
From the ruins I will rebuild it,
and I will restore it,
17 so that the rest of humanity might find the Lord,
including the Gentiles—
all those I have called to be mine.

15:10 Greek *disciples.* **15:14** Greek *Simon.*

NEW KING JAMES VERSION

believe. 8So God, who knows the heart, acknowledged
them by giving them the Holy Spirit, just as *He did* to us,
9and made no distinction between us and them, purifying
their hearts by faith. 10Now therefore, why do you test God
by putting a yoke on the neck of the disciples which nei-
ther our fathers nor we were able to bear? 11But we believe
that through the grace of the Lord Jesus Christ[a] we shall be
saved in the same manner as they."
12Then all the multitude kept silent and listened to
Barnabas and Paul declaring how many miracles and won-
ders God had worked through them among the Gentiles.
13And after they had become silent, James answered, say-
ing, "Men *and* brethren, listen to me: 14Simon has declared
how God at the first visited the Gentiles to take out of
them a people for His name. 15And with this the words of
the prophets agree, just as it is written:

16 *'After this I will return*
And will rebuild the tabernacle of David, which has
fallen down;
I will rebuild its ruins,
And I will set it up;
17 *So that the rest of mankind may seek the* LORD,
Even all the Gentiles who are called by My name,

15:11 [a] NU-Text and M-Text omit *Christ.*

THE MESSAGE

our part but always knows a person's thoughts, gave them
the Holy Spirit exactly as he gave him to us. He treated the
outsiders exactly as he treated us, beginning at the very cen-
ter of who they were and working from that center outward,
cleaning up their lives as they trusted and believed him.

"So why are you now trying to out-god God, loading
these new believers down with rules that crushed our
ancestors and crushed us, too? Don't we believe that we
are saved because the Master Jesus amazingly and out of
sheer generosity moved to save us just as he did those
from beyond our nation? So what are we arguing about?"

There was dead silence. No one said a word. With the
room quiet, Barnabas and Paul reported matter-of-factly
on the miracles and wonders God had done among the
other nations through their ministry. The silence deep-
ened; you could hear a pin drop.

James broke the silence. "Friends, listen. Simeon has
told us the story of how God at the very outset made sure
that racial outsiders were included. This is in perfect
agreement with the words of the prophets:

'After this, I'm coming back;
I'll rebuild David's ruined house;
I'll put all the pieces together again;
I'll make it look like new
So outsiders who seek will find,
so they'll have a place to come to,
All the pagan peoples
included in what I'm doing.'

KING JAMES VERSION

saith the Lord, who doeth all these things.
18 Known unto God are all his works from the beginning of the world.
19 Wherefore my sentence is, that we trouble not them, which from among the Gentiles are turned to God:
20 But that we write unto them, that they abstain from pollutions of idols, and *from* fornication, and *from* things strangled, and *from* blood.
21 For Moses of old time hath in every city them that preach him, being read in the synagogues every sabbath day.
22 ¶ Then pleased it the apostles and elders, with the whole church, to send chosen men of their own company to Antioch with Paul and Barnabas; *namely*, Judas surnamed Barsabas, and Silas, chief men among the brethren:
23 And they wrote *letters* by them after this manner; The apostles and elders and brethren *send* greeting unto the brethren which are of the Gentiles in Antioch and Syria and Cilicia:
24 Forasmuch as we have heard, that certain which went out from us have troubled you with words, subverting your souls, saying, *Ye must* be circumcised, and keep the law: to whom we gave no *such* commandment:

NEW AMERICAN STANDARD BIBLE

18 SAYS THE LORD, WHO MAKES THESE THINGS KNOWN FROM LONG AGO.
19 "Therefore it is my judgment that we do not trouble those who are turning to God from among the Gentiles,
20 but that we write to them that they abstain from things contaminated by idols and from fornication and from what is strangled and from blood.
21 "For Moses from ancient generations has in every city those who preach him, since he is read in the synagogues every Sabbath."
22 Then it seemed good to the apostles and the elders, with the whole church, to choose men from among them to send to Antioch with Paul and Barnabas—Judas called Barsabbas, and Silas, leading men among the brethren,
23 and they sent this letter by them,
"The apostles and the brethren who are elders, to the brethren in Antioch and Syria and Cilicia who are from the Gentiles, greetings.
24 "Since we have heard that some of our number to whom we gave no instruction have disturbed you with *their* words, unsettling your souls,

NEW CENTURY VERSION

says the Lord,
who will make it happen.
18 And these things have been known for a long time.'
Amos 9:11–12
19 "So I think we should not bother the non-Jewish people who are turning to God. 20 Instead, we should write a letter to them telling them these things: Stay away from food that has been offered to idols (which makes it unclean), any kind of sexual sin, eating animals that have been strangled, and blood. 21 They should do these things, because for a long time in every city the law of Moses has been taught. And it is still read in the synagogue every Sabbath day."

Letter to Non-Jewish Believers

22 The apostles, the elders, and the whole church decided to send some of their men with Paul and Barnabas to Antioch. They chose Judas Barsabbas and Silas, who were respected by the believers. 23 They sent the following letter with them:

From the apostles and elders, your brothers.
To all the non-Jewish believers in Antioch, Syria, and Cilicia:
Greetings!
24 We have heard that some of our group have come to you and said things that trouble and upset you. But we did not tell them to do this. 25 We have all agreed

CONTEMPORARY ENGLISH VERSION

I, the Lord, say this.
18 I promised it long ago."

19 And so, my friends, I don't think we should place burdens on the Gentiles who are turning to God. 20 We should simply write and tell them not to eat anything that has been offered to idols. They should be told not to eat the meat of any animal that has been strangled or that still has blood in it. They must also not commit any terrible sexual sins.[c]
21 We must remember that the Law of Moses has been preached in city after city for many years, and every Sabbath it is read when we Jews meet.

A Letter to Gentiles Who Had Faith in the Lord

22 The apostles, the leaders, and all the church members decided to send some men to Antioch along with Paul and Barnabas. They chose Silas and Judas Barsabbas,[d] who were two leaders of the Lord's followers. 23 They wrote a letter that said:

We apostles and leaders send friendly greetings to all of you Gentiles who are followers of the Lord in Antioch, Syria, and Cilicia.

24 We have heard that some people from here have terribly upset you by what they said. But we did not send

[c] 15.20 *not commit any terrible sexual sins*: This probably refers to the laws about the wrong kind of marriages that are forbidden in Leviticus 18.6-18 or to some serious sexual sin. [d] 15.22 *Judas Barsabbas*: He may have been a brother of Joseph Barsabbas (see 1.23), but the name "Barsabbas" was often used by the Jewish people.

NEW INTERNATIONAL VERSION

says the Lord, who does these things'[b]
18 that have been known for ages.[c]

19"It is my judgment, therefore, that we should not make
it difficult for the Gentiles who are turning to God.
20Instead we should write to them, telling them to abstain
from food polluted by idols, from sexual immorality, from
the meat of strangled animals and from blood. 21For Moses
has been preached in every city from the earliest times and
is read in the synagogues on every Sabbath."

The Council's Letter to Gentile Believers

22Then the apostles and elders, with the whole church,
decided to choose some of their own men and send them to
Antioch with Paul and Barnabas. They chose Judas (called
Barsabbas) and Silas, two men who were leaders among
the brothers. 23With them they sent the following letter:

The apostles and elders, your brothers,

To the Gentile believers in Antioch, Syria and Cilicia:

Greetings.

24We have heard that some went out from us with-
out our authorization and disturbed you, troubling
your minds by what they said. 25So we all agreed to

[b] *17* Amos 9:11,12 [c] *17,18* Some manuscripts *things'— / 18known to the Lord for ages is his work*

NEW LIVING TRANSLATION

This is what the Lord says,
18 he who made these things known long ago.'*

19And so my judgment is that we should stop troubling the
Gentiles who turn to God, 20except that we should write to
them and tell them to abstain from eating meat sacrificed
to idols, from sexual immorality, and from consuming
blood or eating the meat of strangled animals. 21For these
laws of Moses have been preached in Jewish synagogues in
every city on every Sabbath for many generations."

The Letter for Gentile Believers

22Then the apostles and elders and the whole church in
Jerusalem chose delegates, and they sent them to Antioch
of Syria with Paul and Barnabas to report on this decision.
The men chosen were two of the church leaders*—Judas
(also called Barsabbas) and Silas. 23This is the letter they
took along with them:

"This letter is from the apostles and elders, your broth-
ers in Jerusalem. It is written to the Gentile believers in
Antioch, Syria, and Cilicia. Greetings!

24"We understand that some men from here have
troubled you and upset you with their teaching, but they
had no such instructions from us. 25So it seemed good

15:16-18 Amos 9:11-12; Isa 45:21. **15:22** Greek *were leaders among the brothers.*

NEW KING JAMES VERSION

Says the LORD *who does all these things.'*[b]

18"Known to God from eternity are all His works.[c]
19Therefore I judge that we should not trouble those from
among the Gentiles who are turning to God, 20but that we
write to them to abstain from things polluted by idols,
from sexual immorality,[d] *from* things strangled, and *from*
blood. 21For Moses has had throughout many generations
those who preach him in every city, being read in the syna-
gogues every Sabbath."

The Jerusalem Decree

22Then it pleased the apostles and elders, with the whole
church, to send chosen men of their own company to Antioch
with Paul and Barnabas, *namely,* Judas who was also named
Barsabas,[e] and Silas, leading men among the brethren.
23They wrote this *letter* by them:

The apostles, the elders, and the brethren,

To the brethren who are of the Gentiles in Antioch,
Syria, and Cilicia:

Greetings.

24 Since we have heard that some who went out from us
have troubled you with words, unsettling your souls,
saying, "*You must* be circumcised and keep the
law"[f]—to whom we gave no *such* commandment—

15:17 [b] Amos 9:11, 12 **15:18** [c] NU-Text (combining with verse 17) reads *Says the Lord, who makes these things known from eternity (of old).*
15:20 [d] Or *fornication* **15:22** [e] NU-Text and M-Text read *Barsabbas.*
15:24 [f] NU-Text omits *saying, "You must be circumcised and keep the law."*

THE MESSAGE

God said it and now he's doing it. It's no afterthought;
he's always known he would do this.

"So here is my decision: We're not going to unnecessari-
ly burden non-Jewish people who turn to the Master. We'll
write them a letter and tell them, 'Be careful to not get
involved in activities connected with idols, to guard the
morality of sex and marriage, to not serve food offensive
to Jewish Christians—blood, for instance.' This is basic
wisdom from Moses, preached and honored for centuries
now in city after city as we have met and kept the
Sabbath."

Everyone agreed: apostles, leaders, all the people. They
picked Judas (nicknamed Barsabbas) and Silas—they both
carried considerable weight in the church—and sent them
to Antioch with Paul and Barnabas with this letter:

From the apostles and leaders, your friends, to our
friends in Antioch, Syria, and Cilicia:

Hello!

We heard that some men from our church went to you
and said things that confused and upset you. Mind you,
they had no authority from us; we didn't send them. We

KING JAMES VERSION

25 It seemed good unto us, being assembled with one accord, to send chosen men unto you with our beloved Barnabas and Paul,

26 Men that have hazarded their lives for the name of our Lord Jesus Christ.

27 We have sent therefore Judas and Silas, who shall also tell *you* the same things by mouth.

28 For it seemed good to the Holy Ghost, and to us, to lay upon you no greater burden than these necessary things;

29 That ye abstain from meats offered to idols, and from blood, and from things strangled, and from fornication: from which if ye keep yourselves, ye shall do well. Fare ye well.

30 So when they were dismissed, they came to Antioch: and when they had gathered the multitude together, they delivered the epistle:

31 *Which* when they had read, they rejoiced for the consolation.

32 And Judas and Silas, being prophets also themselves, exhorted the brethren with many words, and confirmed *them*.

33 And after they had tarried *there* a space, they were let go in peace from the brethren unto the apostles.

34 Notwithstanding it pleased Silas to abide there still.

35 Paul also and Barnabas continued in Antioch, teaching and preaching the word of the Lord, with many others also.

NEW AMERICAN STANDARD BIBLE

25 it seemed good to us, having become of one mind, to select men to send to you with our beloved Barnabas and Paul,

26 men who have risked their lives for the name of our Lord Jesus Christ.

27 "Therefore we have sent Judas and Silas, who themselves will also report the same things by word *of mouth*.

28 "For it seemed good to the Holy Spirit and to us to lay upon you no greater burden than these essentials:

29 that you abstain from things sacrificed to idols and from blood and from things strangled and from fornication; if you keep yourselves free from such things, you will do well. Farewell."

30 So when they were sent away, they went down to Antioch; and having gathered the congregation together, they delivered the letter.

31 When they had read it, they rejoiced because of its encouragement.

32 Judas and Silas, also being prophets themselves, encouraged and strengthened the brethren with a lengthy message.

33 After they had spent time *there*, they were sent away from the brethren in peace to those who had sent them out.

34 [[l]But it seemed good to Silas to remain there.]

35 But Paul and Barnabas stayed in Antioch, teaching and preaching with many others also, the word of the Lord.

15:34 [l] Early mss do not contain this v

NEW CENTURY VERSION

to choose some messengers and send them to you with our dear friends Barnabas and Paul— 26people who have given their lives to serve our Lord Jesus Christ. 27So we are sending Judas and Silas, who will tell you the same things. 28It has pleased the Holy Spirit that you should not have a heavy load to carry, and we agree. You need to do only these things: 29Stay away from any food that has been offered to idols, eating any animals that have been strangled, and blood, and any kind of sexual sin. If you stay away from these things, you will do well.

Good-bye.

30So they left Jerusalem and went to Antioch where they gathered the church and gave them the letter. 31When they read it, they were very happy because of the encouraging message. 32Judas and Silas, who were also prophets, said many things to encourage the believers and make them stronger. 33After some time Judas and Silas were sent off in peace by the believers, and they went back to those who had sent them. 34[a]

35But Paul and Barnabas stayed in Antioch and, along with many others, preached the Good News and taught the people the message of the Lord.

15:34 [a] Verse 34 Some Greek copies add verse 34: ". . . but Silas decided to remain there."

CONTEMPORARY ENGLISH VERSION

them! 25So we met together and decided to choose some men and to send them to you along with our good friends Barnabas and Paul. 26These men have risked their lives for our Lord Jesus Christ. 27We are also sending Judas and Silas, who will tell you in person the same things that we are writing.

28The Holy Spirit has shown us that we should not place any extra burden on you. 29But you should not eat anything offered to idols. You should not eat any meat that still has the blood in it or any meat of any animal that has been strangled. You must also not commit any terrible sexual sins. If you follow these instructions, you will do well.

We send our best wishes.

30The four men left Jerusalem and went to Antioch. Then they called the church members together and gave them the letter. 31When the letter was read, everyone was pleased and greatly encouraged. 32Judas and Silas were prophets, and they spoke a long time, encouraging and helping the Lord's followers.

33The men from Jerusalem stayed on in Antioch for a while. And when they left to return to the ones who had sent them, the followers wished them well. 34-35But Paul and Barnabas stayed on in Antioch, where they and many others taught and preached about the Lord.[e]

[e] 15.34,35 Verse 34, which says that Silas decided to stay on in Antioch, is not in some manuscripts.

NEW INTERNATIONAL VERSION

choose some men and send them to you with our dear friends Barnabas and Paul— [26]men who have risked their lives for the name of our Lord Jesus Christ. [27]Therefore we are sending Judas and Silas to confirm by word of mouth what we are writing. [28]It seemed good to the Holy Spirit and to us not to burden you with anything beyond the following requirements: [29]You are to abstain from food sacrificed to idols, from blood, from the meat of strangled animals and from sexual immorality. You will do well to avoid these things.

Farewell.

[30]The men were sent off and went down to Antioch, where they gathered the church together and delivered the letter. [31]The people read it and were glad for its encouraging message. [32]Judas and Silas, who themselves were prophets, said much to encourage and strengthen the brothers. [33]After spending some time there, they were sent off by the brothers with the blessing of peace to return to those who had sent them.[d] [35]But Paul and Barnabas remained in Antioch, where they and many others taught and preached the word of the Lord.

[d] 33 Some manuscripts *them,* [34]*but Silas decided to remain there*

NEW LIVING TRANSLATION

to us, having unanimously agreed on our decision, to send you these official representatives, along with our beloved Barnabas and Paul, [26]who have risked their lives for the sake of our Lord Jesus Christ. [27]So we are sending Judas and Silas to tell you what we have decided concerning your question.

[28]"For it seemed good to the Holy Spirit and to us to lay no greater burden on you than these requirements: [29]You must abstain from eating food offered to idols, from consuming blood or eating the meat of strangled animals, and from sexual immorality. If you do this, you will do well. Farewell."

[30]The four messengers went at once to Antioch, where they called a general meeting of the Christians and delivered the letter. [31]And there was great joy throughout the church that day as they read this encouraging message. [32]Then Judas and Silas, both being prophets, spoke extensively to the Christians, encouraging and strengthening their faith. [33]They stayed for a while, and then Judas and Silas were sent back to Jerusalem, with the blessings of the Christians, to those who had sent them.* [35]Paul and Barnabas stayed in Antioch to assist many others who were teaching and preaching the word of the Lord there.

15:33 Some manuscripts add verse 34, *But Silas decided to stay there.*

NEW KING JAMES VERSION

[25]it seemed good to us, being assembled with one accord, to send chosen men to you with our beloved Barnabas and Paul, [26]men who have risked their lives for the name of our Lord Jesus Christ. [27]We have therefore sent Judas and Silas, who will also report the same things by word of mouth. [28]For it seemed good to the Holy Spirit, and to us, to lay upon you no greater burden than these necessary things: [29]that you abstain from things offered to idols, from blood, from things strangled, and from sexual immorality.[g] If you keep yourselves from these, you will do well.

Farewell.

Continuing Ministry in Syria

[30]So when they were sent off, they came to Antioch; and when they had gathered the multitude together, they delivered the letter. [31]When they had read it, they rejoiced over its encouragement. [32]Now Judas and Silas, themselves being prophets also, exhorted and strengthened the brethren with many words. [33]And after they had stayed *there* for a time, they were sent back with greetings from the brethren to the apostles.[h]

[34]However, it seemed good to Silas to remain there.[i] [35]Paul and Barnabas also remained in Antioch, teaching and preaching the word of the Lord, with many others also.

15:29 [g] Or *fornication* 15:33 [h] NU-Text reads *to those who had sent them.* 15:34 [i] NU-Text and M-Text omit this verse.

THE MESSAGE

have agreed unanimously to pick representatives and send them to you with our good friends Barnabas and Paul. We picked men we knew you could trust, Judas and Silas—they've looked death in the face time and again for the sake of our Master Jesus Christ. We've sent them to confirm in a face-to-face meeting with you what we've written.

It seemed to the Holy Spirit and to us that you should not be saddled with any crushing burden, but be responsible only for these bare necessities: Be careful not to get involved in activities connected with idols; avoid serving food offensive to Jewish Christians (blood, for instance); and guard the morality of sex and marriage.

These guidelines are sufficient to keep relations congenial between us. And God be with you!

Barnabas and Paul Go Their Separate Ways

And so off they went to Antioch. On arrival, they gathered the church and read the letter. The people were greatly relieved and pleased. Judas and Silas, good preachers both of them, strengthened their new friends with many words of courage and hope. Then it was time to go home. They were sent off by their new friends with laughter and embraces all around to report back to those who had sent them.

Paul and Barnabas stayed on in Antioch, teaching and preaching the Word of God. But they weren't alone. There were a number of teachers and preachers at that time in Antioch.

KING JAMES VERSION

36 ¶ And some days after Paul said unto Barnabas, Let us go again and visit our brethren in every city where we have preached the word of the Lord, *and see* how they do.

37 And Barnabas determined to take with them John, whose surname was Mark.

38 But Paul thought not good to take him with them, who departed from them from Pamphylia, and went not with them to the work.

39 And the contention was so sharp between them, that they departed asunder one from the other: and so Barnabas took Mark, and sailed unto Cyprus;

40 And Paul chose Silas, and departed, being recommended by the brethren unto the grace of God.

41 And he went through Syria and Cilicia, confirming the churches.

16 Then came he to Derbe and Lystra: and, behold, a certain disciple was there, named Timotheus, the son of a certain woman, which was a Jewess, and believed; but his father *was* a Greek:

2 Which was well reported of by the brethren that were at Lystra and Iconium.

3 Him would Paul have to go forth with him; and took and circumcised him because of the Jews which were in those quarters: for they knew all that his father was a Greek.

4 And as they went through the cities, they delivered them the decrees for to keep, that were ordained of the

NEW AMERICAN STANDARD BIBLE

Second Missionary Journey

36 After some days Paul said to Barnabas, "Let us return and visit the brethren in every city in which we proclaimed the word of the Lord, *and see* how they are."

37 Barnabas wanted to take John, called Mark, along with them also.

38 But Paul kept insisting that they should not take him along who had deserted them in Pamphylia and had not gone with them to the work.

39 And there occurred such a sharp disagreement that they separated from one another, and Barnabas took Mark with him and sailed away to Cyprus.

40 But Paul chose Silas and left, being committed by the brethren to the grace of the Lord.

41 And he was traveling through Syria and Cilicia, strengthening the churches.

The Macedonian Vision

16 Paul came also to Derbe and to Lystra. And a disciple was there, named Timothy, the son of a Jewish woman who was a believer, but his father was a Greek,

2 and he was well spoken of by the brethren who were in Lystra and Iconium.

3 Paul wanted this man to go with him; and he took him and circumcised him because of the Jews who were in those parts, for they all knew that his father was a Greek.

4 Now while they were passing through the cities, they were delivering the decrees which had been decided upon

NEW CENTURY VERSION

Paul and Barnabas Separate

36 After some time, Paul said to Barnabas, "We should go
back to all those towns where we preached the message of
the Lord. Let's visit the believers and see how they are
doing."
37 Barnabas wanted to take John Mark with them, 38 but
he had left them at Pamphylia; he did not continue with
them in the work. So Paul did not think it was a good idea
to take him. 39 Paul and Barnabas had such a serious argument about this that they separated and went different
ways. Barnabas took Mark and sailed to Cyprus, 40 but Paul
chose Silas and left. The believers in Antioch put Paul into
the Lord's care, 41 and he went through Syria and Cilicia,
giving strength to the churches.

Timothy Goes with Paul

16 Paul came to Derbe and Lystra, where a follower named Timothy lived. Timothy's mother was Jewish and a believer, but his father was a Greek.
2 The believers in Lystra and Iconium respected Timothy
and said good things about him. 3 Paul wanted Timothy to
travel with him, but all the Jews living in that area knew
that Timothy's father was Greek. So Paul circumcised
Timothy to please the Jews. 4 Paul and those with him traveled from town to town and gave the decisions made by
the apostles and elders in Jerusalem for the people to obey.

CONTEMPORARY ENGLISH VERSION

Paul and Barnabas Go Their Separate Ways

36 Sometime later Paul said to Barnabas, "Let's go back
and visit the Lord's followers in the cities where we
preached his message. Then we will know how they are
doing." 37 Barnabas wanted to take along John, whose
other name was Mark. 38 But Paul did not want to, because
Mark had left them in Pamphylia and had stopped working
with them.
39 Paul and Barnabas argued, then each of them went his
own way. Barnabas took Mark and sailed to Cyprus, 40 but
Paul took Silas and left after the followers had placed
them in God's care. 41 They traveled through Syria and
Cilicia, encouraging the churches.

Timothy Works with Paul and Silas

16 Paul and Silas went back to Derbe and Lystra, where there was a follower named Timothy. His
mother was also a follower. She was Jewish, and his father
was Greek. 2 The Lord's followers in Lystra and Iconium
said good things about Timothy, 3 and Paul wanted him to
go with them. But Paul first had him circumcised, because
all the Jewish people around there knew that Timothy's
father was Greek.[a]
4 As Paul and the others went from city to city, they told
the followers what the apostles and leaders in Jerusalem had
decided, and they urged them to follow these instructions.

[a] 16.3 *had him circumcised . . . Timothy's father was Greek*: Timothy would not have been acceptable to the Jews unless he had been circumcised, and Greeks did not circumcise their sons.

NEW INTERNATIONAL VERSION

Disagreement Between Paul and Barnabas

36 Some time later Paul said to Barnabas, "Let us go back
and visit the brothers in all the towns where we preached
the word of the Lord and see how they are doing."
37 Barnabas wanted to take John, also called Mark, with
them, 38 but Paul did not think it wise to take him, because
he had deserted them in Pamphylia and had not continued
with them in the work. 39 They had such a sharp disagree-
ment that they parted company. Barnabas took Mark and
sailed for Cyprus, 40 but Paul chose Silas and left, com-
mended by the brothers to the grace of the Lord. 41 He went
through Syria and Cilicia, strengthening the churches.

Timothy Joins Paul and Silas

16 He came to Derbe and then to Lystra, where a dis-
ciple named Timothy lived, whose mother was a
Jewess and a believer, but whose father was a Greek. 2 The
brothers at Lystra and Iconium spoke well of him. 3 Paul
wanted to take him along on the journey, so he circum-
cised him because of the Jews who lived in that area, for
they all knew that his father was a Greek. 4 As they trav-
eled from town to town, they delivered the decisions
reached by the apostles and elders in Jerusalem for the

NEW LIVING TRANSLATION

Paul and Barnabas Separate

36 After some time Paul said to Barnabas, "Let's return to
each city where we previously preached the word of the
Lord, to see how the new believers are getting along."
37 Barnabas agreed and wanted to take along John Mark.
38 But Paul disagreed strongly, since John Mark had desert-
ed them in Pamphylia and had not shared in their work.
39 Their disagreement over this was so sharp that they sep-
arated. Barnabas took John Mark with him and sailed for
Cyprus. 40 Paul chose Silas, and the believers sent them off,
entrusting them to the Lord's grace. 41 So they traveled
throughout Syria and Cilicia to strengthen the churches
there.

Paul's Second Missionary Journey

16 Paul and Silas went first to Derbe and then on to
Lystra. There they met Timothy, a young disciple
whose mother was a Jewish believer, but whose father was
a Greek. 2 Timothy was well thought of by the believers* in
Lystra and Iconium, 3 so Paul wanted him to join them on
their journey. In deference to the Jews of the area, he
arranged for Timothy to be circumcised before they left, for
everyone knew that his father was a Greek. 4 Then they
went from town to town, explaining the decision regarding
the commandments that were to be obeyed, as decided by

16:2 Greek *brothers;* also in 16:40.

NEW KING JAMES VERSION

Division over John Mark

36 Then after some days Paul said to Barnabas, "Let us
now go back and visit our brethren in every city where we
have preached the word of the Lord, *and see* how they are
doing." 37 Now Barnabas was determined to take with them
John called Mark. 38 But Paul insisted that they should not
take with them the one who had departed from them in
Pamphylia, and had not gone with them to the work.
39 Then the contention became so sharp that they parted
from one another. And so Barnabas took Mark and sailed
to Cyprus; 40 but Paul chose Silas and departed, being com-
mended by the brethren to the grace of God. 41 And he went
through Syria and Cilicia, strengthening the churches.

Timothy Joins Paul and Silas

16 Then he came to Derbe and Lystra. And behold, a
certain disciple was there, named Timothy, *the* son
of a certain Jewish woman who believed, but his father
was Greek. 2 He was well spoken of by the brethren who
were at Lystra and Iconium. 3 Paul wanted to have him go
on with him. And he took *him* and circumcised him
because of the Jews who were in that region, for they all
knew that his father was Greek. 4 And as they went
through the cities, they delivered to them the decrees to
keep, which were determined by the apostles and elders at

THE MESSAGE

After a few days of this, Paul said to Barnabas, "Let's go back and visit all our friends in each of the towns where we preached the Word of God. Let's see how they're doing."

Barnabas wanted to take John along, the John nicknamed Mark. But Paul wouldn't have him; he wasn't about to take along a quitter who, as soon as the going got tough, had jumped ship on them in Pamphylia. Tempers flared, and they ended up going their separate ways: Barnabas took Mark and sailed for Cyprus; Paul chose Silas and, offered up by their friends to the grace of the Master, went to Syria and Cilicia to build up muscle and sinew in those congregations.

A Dream Gave Paul His Map

16 Paul came first to Derbe, then Lystra. He found a
disciple there by the name of Timothy, son of a devout Jewish mother and Greek father. Friends in Lystra and Iconium all said what a fine young man he was. Paul wanted to recruit him for their mission, but first took him aside and circumcised him so he wouldn't offend the Jews who lived in those parts. They all knew that his father was Greek.

As they traveled from town to town, they presented the simple guidelines the Jerusalem apostles and leaders had

KING JAMES VERSION

apostles and elders which were at Jerusalem.

5 And so were the churches established in the faith, and increased in number daily.

6 ¶ Now when they had gone throughout Phrygia and the region of Galatia, and were forbidden of the Holy Ghost to preach the word in Asia,

7 After they were come to Mysia, they assayed to go into Bithynia: but the Spirit suffered them not.

8 And they passing by Mysia came down to Troas.

9 And a vision appeared to Paul in the night; There stood a man of Macedonia, and prayed him, saying, Come over into Macedonia, and help us.

10 And after he had seen the vision, immediately we endeavoured to go into Macedonia, assuredly gathering that the Lord had called us for to preach the gospel unto them.

11 Therefore loosing from Troas, we came with a straight course to Samothracia, and the next *day* to Neapolis;

12 And from thence to Philippi, which is the chief city of that part of Macedonia, *and* a colony: and we were in that city abiding certain days.

13 And on the sabbath we went out of the city by a river side, where prayer was wont to be made; and we sat down, and spake unto the women which resorted *thither*.

14 And a certain woman named Lydia, a seller of purple, of the city of Thyatira, which worshipped God, heard

NEW AMERICAN STANDARD BIBLE

by the apostles and elders who were in Jerusalem, for them to observe.

5 So the churches were being strengthened in the faith, and were increasing in number daily.

6 They passed through the Phrygian and Galatian region, having been forbidden by the Holy Spirit to speak the word in Asia;

7 and after they came to Mysia, they were trying to go into Bithynia, and the Spirit of Jesus did not permit them;

8 and passing by Mysia, they came down to Troas.

9 A vision appeared to Paul in the night: a man of Macedonia was standing and appealing to him, and saying, "Come over to Macedonia and help us."

10 When he had seen the vision, immediately we sought to go into Macedonia, concluding that God had called us to preach the gospel to them.

11 So putting out to sea from Troas, we ran a straight course to Samothrace, and on the day following to Neapolis;

12 and from there to Philippi, which is a leading city of the district of Macedonia, a *Roman* colony; and we were staying in this city for some days.

13 And on the Sabbath day we went outside the gate to a riverside, where we were supposing that there would be a place of prayer; and we sat down and began speaking to the women who had assembled.

First Convert in Europe

14 A woman named Lydia, from the city of Thyatira, a seller of purple fabrics, a worshiper of God, was listening;

NEW CENTURY VERSION

5 So the churches became stronger in the faith and grew larger every day.

Paul Is Called Out of Asia

6 Paul and those with him went through the areas of Phrygia and Galatia since the Holy Spirit did not let them preach the Good News in the country of Asia. 7 When they came near the country of Mysia, they tried to go into Bithynia, but the Spirit of Jesus did not let them. 8 So they passed by Mysia and went to Troas. 9 That night Paul saw in a vision a man from Macedonia. The man stood and begged, "Come over to Macedonia and help us." 10 After Paul had seen the vision, we immediately prepared to leave for Macedonia, understanding that God had called us to tell the Good News to those people.

Lydia Becomes a Christian

11 We left Troas and sailed straight to the island of Samothrace. The next day we sailed to Neapolis.[a] 12 Then we went by land to Philippi, a Roman colony[b] and the leading city in that part of Macedonia. We stayed there for several days.

13 On the Sabbath day we went outside the city gate to the river where we thought we would find a special place for prayer. Some women had gathered there, so we sat down and talked with them. 14 One of the listeners was a woman named Lydia from the city of Thyatira whose job

16:11 [a] **Neapolis** City in Macedonia. It was the first city Paul visited on the continent of Europe. 16:12 [b] **Roman colony** A town begun by Romans with Roman laws, customs, and privileges.

CONTEMPORARY ENGLISH VERSION

5 The churches became stronger in their faith, and each day more people put their faith in the Lord.

Paul's Vision in Troas

6 Paul and his friends went through Phrygia and Galatia, but the Holy Spirit would not let them preach in Asia. 7 After they arrived in Mysia, they tried to go into Bithynia, but the Spirit of Jesus would not let them. 8 So they went on through[b] Mysia until they came to Troas.

9 During the night, Paul had a vision of someone from Macedonia who was standing there and begging him, "Come over to Macedonia and help us!" 10 After Paul had seen the vision, we began looking for a way to go to Macedonia. We were sure that God had called us to preach the good news there.

Lydia Becomes a Follower of the Lord

11 We sailed straight from Troas to Samothrace, and the next day we arrived in Neapolis. 12 From there we went to Philippi, which is a Roman colony in the first district of Macedonia.[c]

We spent several days in Philippi. 13 Then on the Sabbath we went outside the city gate to a place by the river, where we thought there would be a Jewish meeting place for prayer. We sat down and talked with the women who came. 14 One of them was Lydia, who was from the city of Thyatira

[b] 16.8 *went on through*: Or *"passed by."* [c] 16.12 *in the first district of Macedonia*: Some manuscripts have "and the leading city of Macedonia."

NEW INTERNATIONAL VERSION

people to obey. 5So the churches were strengthened in the faith and grew daily in numbers.

Paul's Vision of the Man of Macedonia

6Paul and his companions traveled throughout the region of Phrygia and Galatia, having been kept by the Holy Spirit from preaching the word in the province of Asia. 7When they came to the border of Mysia, they tried to enter Bithynia, but the Spirit of Jesus would not allow them to. 8So they passed by Mysia and went down to Troas. 9During the night Paul had a vision of a man of Macedonia standing and begging him, "Come over to Macedonia and help us." 10After Paul had seen the vision, we got ready at once to leave for Macedonia, concluding that God had called us to preach the gospel to them.

Lydia's Conversion in Philippi

11From Troas we put out to sea and sailed straight for Samothrace, and the next day on to Neapolis. 12From there we traveled to Philippi, a Roman colony and the leading city of that district of Macedonia. And we stayed there several days.

13On the Sabbath we went outside the city gate to the river, where we expected to find a place of prayer. We sat down and began to speak to the women who had gathered there. 14One of those listening was a woman named Lydia, a dealer in purple cloth from the city of Thyatira, who was a worshiper of God. The Lord opened her heart to respond

NEW LIVING TRANSLATION

the apostles and elders in Jerusalem. 5So the churches were strengthened in their faith and grew daily in numbers.

A Call from Macedonia

6Next Paul and Silas traveled through the area of Phrygia and Galatia, because the Holy Spirit had told them not to go into the province of Asia at that time. 7Then coming to the borders of Mysia, they headed for the province of Bithynia,* but again the Spirit of Jesus did not let them go. 8So instead, they went on through Mysia to the city of Troas.

9That night Paul had a vision. He saw a man from Macedonia in northern Greece, pleading with him, "Come over here and help us." 10So we* decided to leave for Macedonia at once, for we could only conclude that God was calling us to preach the Good News there.

Lydia of Philippi Believes in Jesus

11We boarded a boat at Troas and sailed straight across to the island of Samothrace, and the next day we landed at Neapolis. 12From there we reached Philippi, a major city of the district of Macedonia and a Roman colony; we stayed there several days.

13On the Sabbath we went a little way outside the city to a riverbank, where we supposed that some people met for prayer, and we sat down to speak with some women who had come together. 14One of them was Lydia from Thyatira, a merchant of expensive purple cloth. She was a worshiper

16:6-7 *Phrygia, Galatia, Asia, Mysia,* and *Bithynia* were all districts in the land now called Turkey. **16:10** Luke, the writer of this book, here joined Paul and accompanied him on his journey.

NEW KING JAMES VERSION

Jerusalem. 5So the churches were strengthened in the faith, and increased in number daily.

The Macedonian Call

6Now when they had gone through Phrygia and the region of Galatia, they were forbidden by the Holy Spirit to preach the word in Asia. 7After they had come to Mysia, they tried to go into Bithynia, but the Spirit[a] did not permit them. 8So passing by Mysia, they came down to Troas. 9And a vision appeared to Paul in the night. A man of Macedonia stood and pleaded with him, saying, "Come over to Macedonia and help us." 10Now after he had seen the vision, immediately we sought to go to Macedonia, concluding that the Lord had called us to preach the gospel to them.

Lydia Baptized at Philippi

11Therefore, sailing from Troas, we ran a straight course to Samothrace, and the next *day* came to Neapolis, 12and from there to Philippi, which is the foremost city of that part of Macedonia, a colony. And we were staying in that city for some days. 13And on the Sabbath day we went out of the city to the riverside, where prayer was customarily made; and we sat down and spoke to the women who met *there.* 14Now a certain woman named Lydia heard *us.* She was a seller of purple from the city of Thyatira, who worshiped God. The Lord opened her heart to heed the things

16:7 [a] NU-Text adds *of Jesus.*

THE MESSAGE

come up with. That turned out to be most helpful. Day after day the congregations became stronger in faith and larger in size.

They went to Phrygia, and then on through the region of Galatia. Their plan was to turn west into Asia province, but the Holy Spirit blocked that route. So they went to Mysia and tried to go north to Bithynia, but the Spirit of Jesus wouldn't let them go there either. Proceeding on through Mysia, they went down to the seaport Troas.

That night Paul had a dream: A Macedonian stood on the far shore and called across the sea, "Come over to Macedonia and help us!" The dream gave Paul his map. We went to work at once getting things ready to cross over to Macedonia. All the pieces had come together. We knew now for sure that God had called us to preach the good news to the Europeans.

Putting out from the harbor at Troas, we made a straight run for Samothrace. The next day we tied up at New City and walked from there to Philippi, the main city in that part of Macedonia and, even more importantly, a Roman colony. We lingered there several days.

On the Sabbath, we left the city and went down along the river where we had heard there was to be a prayer meeting. We took our place with the women who had gathered there and talked with them. One woman, Lydia, was from Thyatira and a dealer in expensive textiles, known to be a God-fearing woman. As she listened with intensity to

KING JAMES VERSION

us: whose heart the Lord opened, that she attended unto the things which were spoken of Paul.

15 And when she was baptized, and her household, she besought *us*, saying, If ye have judged me to be faithful to the Lord, come into my house, and abide *there*. And she constrained us.

16 ¶ And it came to pass, as we went to prayer, a certain damsel possessed with a spirit of divination met us, which brought her masters much gain by soothsaying:

17 The same followed Paul and us, and cried, saying, These men are the servants of the most high God, which shew unto us the way of salvation.

18 And this did she many days. But Paul, being grieved, turned and said to the spirit, I command thee in the name of Jesus Christ to come out of her. And he came out the same hour.

19 And when her masters saw that the hope of their gains was gone, they caught Paul and Silas, and drew *them* into the marketplace unto the rulers,

20 And brought them to the magistrates, saying, These men, being Jews, do exceedingly trouble our city,

21 And teach customs, which are not lawful for us to receive, neither to observe, being Romans.

22 And the multitude rose up together against them: and the magistrates rent off their clothes, and commanded to beat *them*.

NEW AMERICAN STANDARD BIBLE

and the Lord opened her heart to respond to the things spoken by Paul.

15 And when she and her household had been baptized, she urged us, saying, "If you have judged me to be faithful to the Lord, come into my house and stay." And she prevailed upon us.

16 It happened that as we were going to the place of prayer, a slave-girl having a spirit of divination met us, who was bringing her masters much profit by fortune-telling.

17 Following after Paul and us, she kept crying out, saying, "These men are bond-servants of the Most High God, who are proclaiming to you the way of salvation."

18 She continued doing this for many days. But Paul was greatly annoyed, and turned and said to the spirit, "I command you in the name of Jesus Christ to come out of her!" And it came out at that very moment.

19 But when her masters saw that their hope of profit was gone, they seized Paul and Silas and dragged them into the market place before the authorities,

20 and when they had brought them to the chief magistrates, they said, "These men are throwing our city into confusion, being Jews,

21 and are proclaiming customs which it is not lawful for us to accept or to observe, being Romans."

Paul and Silas Imprisoned

22 The crowd rose up together against them, and the chief magistrates tore their robes off them and proceeded to order *them* to be beaten with rods.

NEW CENTURY VERSION

was selling purple cloth. She worshiped God, and he opened her mind to pay attention to what Paul was saying.
15She and all the people in her house were baptized. Then she invited us to her home, saying, "If you think I am truly a believer in the Lord, then come stay in my house." And she persuaded us to stay with her.

Paul and Silas in Jail

16Once, while we were going to the place for prayer, a servant girl met us. She had a special spirit[c] in her, and she earned a lot of money for her owners by telling fortunes.
17This girl followed Paul and us, shouting, "These men are servants of the Most High God. They are telling you how you can be saved."

18She kept this up for many days. This bothered Paul, so he turned and said to the spirit, "By the power of Jesus Christ, I command you to come out of her!" Immediately, the spirit came out.

19When the owners of the servant girl saw this, they knew that now they could not use her to make money. So they grabbed Paul and Silas and dragged them before the city rulers in the marketplace.
20They brought Paul and Silas to the Roman rulers and said, "These men are Jews and are making trouble in our city.
21They are teaching things that are not right for us as Romans to do."

22The crowd joined the attack against them. The Roman officers tore the clothes of Paul and Silas and had them

16:16 [c] **spirit** This was a spirit from the devil, which caused her to say she had special knowledge.

CONTEMPORARY ENGLISH VERSION

and sold expensive purple cloth. She was a worshiper of the Lord God, and he made her willing to accept what Paul was saying.
15Then after she and her family were baptized, she kept on begging us, "If you think I really do have faith in the Lord, come stay in my home." Finally, we accepted her invitation.

Paul and Silas Are Put in Jail

16One day on our way to the place of prayer, we were met by a slave girl. She had a spirit in her that gave her the power to tell the future. By doing this she made a lot of money for her owners.
17The girl followed Paul and the rest of us and kept yelling, "These men are servants of the Most High God! They are telling you how to be saved."

18This went on for several days. Finally, Paul got so upset that he turned and said to the spirit, "In the name of Jesus Christ, I order you to leave this girl alone!" At once the evil spirit left her.

19When the girl's owners realized that they had lost all chances for making more money, they grabbed Paul and Silas and dragged them into court.
20They told the officials, "These Jews are upsetting our city!
21They are telling us to do things we Romans are not allowed to do."

22The crowd joined in the attack on Paul and Silas. Then the officials tore the clothes off the two men and ordered them to be beaten with a whip.
23After they had been badly

NEW INTERNATIONAL VERSION

to Paul's message. 15When she and the members of her household were baptized, she invited us to her home. "If you consider me a believer in the Lord," she said, "come and stay at my house." And she persuaded us.

Paul and Silas in Prison

16Once when we were going to the place of prayer, we were met by a slave girl who had a spirit by which she predicted the future. She earned a great deal of money for her owners by fortune-telling. 17This girl followed Paul and the rest of us, shouting, "These men are servants of the Most High God, who are telling you the way to be saved." 18She kept this up for many days. Finally Paul became so troubled that he turned around and said to the spirit, "In the name of Jesus Christ I command you to come out of her!" At that moment the spirit left her.

19When the owners of the slave girl realized that their hope of making money was gone, they seized Paul and Silas and dragged them into the marketplace to face the authorities. 20They brought them before the magistrates and said, "These men are Jews, and are throwing our city into an uproar 21by advocating customs unlawful for us Romans to accept or practice."

22The crowd joined in the attack against Paul and Silas, and the magistrates ordered them to be stripped and beaten.

NEW LIVING TRANSLATION

of God. As she listened to us, the Lord opened her heart, and she accepted what Paul was saying. 15She was baptized along with other members of her household, and she asked us to be her guests. "If you agree that I am faithful to the Lord," she said, "come and stay at my home." And she urged us until we did.

Paul and Silas in Prison

16One day as we were going down to the place of prayer, we met a demon-possessed slave girl. She was a fortune-teller who earned a lot of money for her masters. 17She followed along behind us shouting, "These men are servants of the Most High God, and they have come to tell you how to be saved."

18This went on day after day until Paul got so exasperated that he turned and spoke to the demon within her. "I command you in the name of Jesus Christ to come out of her," he said. And instantly it left her.

19Her masters' hopes of wealth were now shattered, so they grabbed Paul and Silas and dragged them before the authorities at the marketplace. 20"The whole city is in an uproar because of these Jews!" they shouted. 21"They are teaching the people to do things that are against Roman customs."

22A mob quickly formed against Paul and Silas, and the city officials ordered them stripped and beaten with wooden

NEW KING JAMES VERSION

spoken by Paul. 15And when she and her household were baptized, she begged *us,* saying, "If you have judged me to be faithful to the Lord, come to my house and stay." So she persuaded us.

Paul and Silas Imprisoned

16Now it happened, as we went to prayer, that a certain slave girl possessed with a spirit of divination met us, who brought her masters much profit by fortune-telling. 17This girl followed Paul and us, and cried out, saying, "These men are the servants of the Most High God, who proclaim to us the way of salvation." 18And this she did for many days.

But Paul, greatly annoyed, turned and said to the spirit, "I command you in the name of Jesus Christ to come out of her." And he came out that very hour. 19But when her masters saw that their hope of profit was gone, they seized Paul and Silas and dragged *them* into the marketplace to the authorities.

20And they brought them to the magistrates, and said, "These men, being Jews, exceedingly trouble our city; 21and they teach customs which are not lawful for us, being Romans, to receive or observe." 22Then the multitude rose up together against them; and the magistrates tore off their clothes and commanded *them* to be beaten

THE MESSAGE

what was being said, the Master gave her a trusting heart—and she believed!

After she was baptized, along with everyone in her household, she said in a surge of hospitality, "If you're confident that I'm in this with you and believe in the Master truly, come home with me and be my guests." We hesitated, but she wouldn't take no for an answer.

Beat Up and Thrown in Jail

One day, on our way to the place of prayer, a slave girl ran into us. She was a psychic and, with her fortune-telling, made a lot of money for the people who owned her. She started following Paul around, calling everyone's attention to us by yelling out, "These men are working for the Most High God. They're laying out the road of salvation for you!" She did this for a number of days until Paul, finally fed up with her, turned and commanded the spirit that possessed her, "Out! In the name of Jesus Christ, get out of her!" And it was gone, just like that.

When her owners saw that their lucrative little business was suddenly bankrupt, they went after Paul and Silas, roughed them up and dragged them into the market square. Then the police arrested them and pulled them into a court with the accusation, "These men are disturbing the peace—dangerous Jewish agitators subverting our Roman law and order." By this time the crowd had turned into a restless mob out for blood.

The judges went along with the mob, had Paul and Silas's clothes ripped off and ordered a public beating.

KING JAMES VERSION

23 And when they had laid many stripes upon them, they cast *them* into prison, charging the jailor to keep them safely:

24 Who, having received such a charge, thrust them into the inner prison, and made their feet fast in the stocks.

25 ¶ And at midnight Paul and Silas prayed, and sang praises unto God: and the prisoners heard them.

26 And suddenly there was a great earthquake, so that the foundations of the prison were shaken: and immediately all the doors were opened, and every one's bands were loosed.

27 And the keeper of the prison awaking out of his sleep, and seeing the prison doors open, he drew out his sword, and would have killed himself, supposing that the prisoners had been fled.

28 But Paul cried with a loud voice, saying, Do thyself no harm: for we are all here.

29 Then he called for a light, and sprang in, and came trembling, and fell down before Paul and Silas,

30 And brought them out, and said, Sirs, what must I do to be saved?

31 And they said, Believe on the Lord Jesus Christ, and thou shalt be saved, and thy house.

32 And they spake unto him the word of the Lord, and to all that were in his house.

33 And he took them the same hour of the night, and washed *their* stripes; and was baptized, he and all his, straightway.

NEW AMERICAN STANDARD BIBLE

23 When they had struck them with many blows, they threw them into prison, commanding the jailer to guard them securely;

24 and he, having received such a command, threw them into the inner prison and fastened their feet in the stocks.

25 But about midnight Paul and Silas were praying and singing hymns of praise to God, and the prisoners were listening to them;

26 and suddenly there came a great earthquake, so that the foundations of the prison house were shaken; and immediately all the doors were opened and everyone's chains were unfastened.

27 When the jailer awoke and saw the prison doors opened, he drew his sword and was about to kill himself, supposing that the prisoners had escaped.

28 But Paul cried out with a loud voice, saying, "Do not harm yourself, for we are all here!"

29 And he called for lights and rushed in, and trembling with fear he fell down before Paul and Silas,

30 and after he brought them out, he said, "Sirs, what must I do to be saved?"

The Jailer Converted

31 They said, "Believe in the Lord Jesus, and you will be saved, you and your household."

32 And they spoke the word of the Lord to him together with all who were in his house.

33 And he took them that *very* hour of the night and washed their wounds, and immediately he was baptized, he and all his *household.*

NEW CENTURY VERSION

beaten with rods. 23Then Paul and Silas were thrown into
jail, and the jailer was ordered to guard them carefully.
24When he heard this order, he put them far inside the jail
and pinned their feet down between large blocks of wood.
25About midnight Paul and Silas were praying and
singing songs to God as the other prisoners listened.
26Suddenly, there was a strong earthquake that shook the
foundation of the jail. Then all the doors of the jail broke
open, and all the prisoners were freed from their chains.
27The jailer woke up and saw that the jail doors were open.
Thinking that the prisoners had already escaped, he got
his sword and was about to kill himself.[d] 28But Paul
shouted, "Don't hurt yourself! We are all here."
29The jailer told someone to bring a light. Then he ran
inside and, shaking with fear, fell down before Paul and
Silas. 30He brought them outside and said, "Men, what
must I do to be saved?"
31They said to him, "Believe in the Lord Jesus and you
will be saved—you and all the people in your house." 32So
Paul and Silas told the message of the Lord to the jailer
and all the people in his house. 33At that hour of the night
the jailer took Paul and Silas and washed their wounds.
Then he and all his people were baptized immediately.

16:27 [d] **kill himself** He thought the leaders would kill him for letting the prisoners escape.

CONTEMPORARY ENGLISH VERSION

beaten, they were put in jail, and the jailer was told to
guard them carefully. 24The jailer did as he was told. He
put them deep inside the jail and chained their feet to
heavy blocks of wood.
25About midnight Paul and Silas were praying and
singing praises to God, while the other prisoners listened.
26Suddenly a strong earthquake shook the jail to its foundations. The doors opened, and the chains fell from all the
prisoners.
27When the jailer woke up and saw that the doors were
open, he thought that the prisoners had escaped. He pulled
out his sword and was about to kill himself. 28But Paul
shouted, "Don't harm yourself! No one has escaped."
29The jailer asked for a torch and went into the jail. He
was shaking all over as he knelt down in front of Paul and
Silas. 30After he had led them out of the jail, he asked,
"What must I do to be saved?"
31They replied, "Have faith in the Lord Jesus and you
will be saved! This is also true for everyone who lives in
your home."
32Then Paul and Silas told him and everyone else in his
house about the Lord. 33While it was still night, the jailer
took them to a place where he could wash their cuts and
bruises. Then he and everyone in his home were baptized.

NEW INTERNATIONAL VERSION

[23]After they had been severely flogged, they were thrown into prison, and the jailer was commanded to guard them carefully. [24]Upon receiving such orders, he put them in the inner cell and fastened their feet in the stocks.

[25]About midnight Paul and Silas were praying and singing hymns to God, and the other prisoners were listening to them. [26]Suddenly there was such a violent earthquake that the foundations of the prison were shaken. At once all the prison doors flew open, and everybody's chains came loose. [27]The jailer woke up, and when he saw the prison doors open, he drew his sword and was about to kill himself because he thought the prisoners had escaped. [28]But Paul shouted, "Don't harm yourself! We are all here!"

[29]The jailer called for lights, rushed in and fell trembling before Paul and Silas. [30]He then brought them out and asked, "Sirs, what must I do to be saved?"

[31]They replied, "Believe in the Lord Jesus, and you will be saved—you and your household." [32]Then they spoke the word of the Lord to him and to all the others in his house. [33]At that hour of the night the jailer took them and washed their wounds; then immediately he and all his family were baptized. [34]The jailer brought them into his

NEW LIVING TRANSLATION

rods. [23]They were severely beaten, and then they were thrown into prison. The jailer was ordered to make sure they didn't escape. [24]So he took no chances but put them into the inner dungeon and clamped their feet in the stocks.

[25]Around midnight, Paul and Silas were praying and singing hymns to God, and the other prisoners were listening. [26]Suddenly, there was a great earthquake, and the prison was shaken to its foundations. All the doors flew open, and the chains of every prisoner fell off! [27]The jailer woke up to see the prison doors wide open. He assumed the prisoners had escaped, so he drew his sword to kill himself. [28]But Paul shouted to him, "Don't do it! We are all here!"

[29]Trembling with fear, the jailer called for lights and ran to the dungeon and fell down before Paul and Silas. [30]He brought them out and asked, "Sirs, what must I do to be saved?"

[31]They replied, "Believe on the Lord Jesus and you will be saved, along with your entire household." [32]Then they shared the word of the Lord with him and all who lived in his household. [33]That same hour the jailer washed their wounds, and he and everyone in his household were immediately baptized. [34]Then he brought them into his

NEW KING JAMES VERSION

with rods. [23]And when they had laid many stripes on them, they threw *them* into prison, commanding the jailer to keep them securely. [24]Having received such a charge, he put them into the inner prison and fastened their feet in the stocks.

The Philippian Jailer Saved

[25]But at midnight Paul and Silas were praying and singing hymns to God, and the prisoners were listening to them. [26]Suddenly there was a great earthquake, so that the foundations of the prison were shaken; and immediately all the doors were opened and everyone's chains were loosed. [27]And the keeper of the prison, awaking from sleep and seeing the prison doors open, supposing the prisoners had fled, drew his sword and was about to kill himself. [28]But Paul called with a loud voice, saying, "Do yourself no harm, for we are all here."

[29]Then he called for a light, ran in, and fell down trembling before Paul and Silas. [30]And he brought them out and said, "Sirs, what must I do to be saved?"

[31]So they said, "Believe on the Lord Jesus Christ, and you will be saved, you and your household." [32]Then they spoke the word of the Lord to him and to all who were in his house. [33]And he took them the same hour of the night and washed *their* stripes. And immediately he and all his family were baptized. [34]Now when he had brought them

THE MESSAGE

After beating them black-and-blue, they threw them into jail, telling the jailkeeper to put them under heavy guard so there would be no chance of escape. He did just that—threw them into the maximum security cell in the jail and clamped leg irons on them.

Along about midnight, Paul and Silas were at prayer and singing a robust hymn to God. The other prisoners couldn't believe their ears. Then, without warning, a huge earthquake! The jailhouse tottered, every door flew open, all the prisoners were loose.

Startled from sleep, the jailer saw all the doors swinging loose on their hinges. Assuming that all the prisoners had escaped, he pulled out his sword and was about to do himself in, figuring he was as good as dead anyway, when Paul stopped him: "Don't do that! We're all still here! Nobody's run away!"

The jailer got a torch and ran inside. Badly shaken, he collapsed in front of Paul and Silas. He led them out of the jail and asked, "Sirs, what do I have to do to be saved, to really live?" They said, "Put your entire trust in the Master Jesus. Then you'll live as you were meant to live—and everyone in your house included!"

They went on to spell out in detail the story of the Master—the entire family got in on this part. They never did get to bed that night. The jailer made them feel at home, dressed their wounds, and then—he couldn't wait till morning!—was baptized, he and everyone in his family.

KING JAMES VERSION

34 And when he had brought them into his house, he set meat before them, and rejoiced, believing in God with all his house.

35 ¶ And when it was day, the magistrates sent the serjeants, saying, Let those men go.

36 And the keeper of the prison told this saying to Paul, The magistrates have sent to let you go: now therefore depart, and go in peace.

37 But Paul said unto them, They have beaten us openly uncondemned, being Romans, and have cast *us* into prison; and now do they thrust us out privily? nay verily; but let them come themselves and fetch us out.

38 And the serjeants told these words unto the magistrates: and they feared, when they heard that they were Romans.

39 And they came and besought them, and brought *them* out, and desired *them* to depart out of the city.

40 And they went out of the prison, and entered into *the house of* Lydia: and when they had seen the brethren, they comforted them, and departed.

17 Now when they had passed through Amphipolis and Apollonia, they came to Thessalonica, where was a synagogue of the Jews:

2 And Paul, as his manner was, went in unto them, and three sabbath days reasoned with them out of the scriptures,

NEW AMERICAN STANDARD BIBLE

34 And he brought them into his house and set food before them, and rejoiced greatly, having believed in God with his whole household.

35 Now when day came, the chief magistrates sent their policemen, saying, "Release those men."

36 And the jailer reported these words to Paul, *saying,* "The chief magistrates have sent to release you. Therefore come out now and go in peace."

37 But Paul said to them, "They have beaten us in public without trial, men who are Romans, and have thrown us into prison; and now are they sending us away secretly? No indeed! But let them come themselves and bring us out."

38 The policemen reported these words to the chief magistrates. They were afraid when they heard that they were Romans,

39 and they came and appealed to them, and when they had brought them out, they kept begging them to leave the city.

40 They went out of the prison and entered *the house of* Lydia, and when they saw the brethren, they encouraged them and departed.

Paul at Thessalonica

17 Now when they had traveled through Amphipolis and Apollonia, they came to Thessalonica, where there was a synagogue of the Jews.

2 And according to Paul's custom, he went to them, and for three Sabbaths reasoned with them from the Scriptures,

NEW CENTURY VERSION

34 After this the jailer took Paul and Silas home and gave them food. He and his family were very happy because they now believed in God.

35 The next morning, the Roman officers sent the police to tell the jailer, "Let these men go free."

36 The jailer said to Paul, "The officers have sent an order to let you go free. You can leave now. Go in peace."

37 But Paul said to the police, "They beat us in public without a trial, even though we are Roman citizens.[e] And they threw us in jail. Now they want to make us go away quietly. No! Let them come themselves and bring us out."

38 The police told the Roman officers what Paul said.
When the officers heard that Paul and Silas were Roman
citizens, they were afraid. 39 So they came and told Paul
and Silas they were sorry and took them out of jail and
asked them to leave the city. 40 So when they came out of
the jail, they went to Lydia's house where they saw some
of the believers and encouraged them. Then they left.

Paul and Silas in Thessalonica

17 Paul and Silas traveled through Amphipolis and
Apollonia and came to Thessalonica where there
was a Jewish synagogue. 2 Paul went into the synagogue as
he always did, and on each Sabbath day for three weeks,
he talked with the Jews about the Scriptures. 3 He

16:37 [e] **Roman citizens** Roman law said that Roman citizens must not be beaten before they had a trial.

CONTEMPORARY ENGLISH VERSION

34 They were very glad that they had put their faith in God. After this, the jailer took Paul and Silas to his home and gave them something to eat.

35 The next morning the officials sent some police with
orders for the jailer to let Paul and Silas go. 36 The jailer
told Paul, "The officials have ordered me to set you free.
Now you can leave in peace."

37 But Paul told the police, "We are Roman citizens,[d] and the Roman officials had us beaten in public without giving us a trial. They threw us into jail. Now do they think they can secretly send us away? No, they cannot! They will have to come here themselves and let us out."

38 When the police told the officials that Paul and Silas
were Roman citizens, the officials were afraid. 39 So they
came and apologized. They led them out of the jail and
asked them to please leave town. 40 But Paul and Silas
went straight to the home of Lydia, where they saw the
Lord's followers and encouraged them. Then they left.

Trouble in Thessalonica

17 After Paul and his friends had traveled through
Amphipolis and Apollonia, they went on to
Thessalonica. A Jewish meeting place was in that city. 2 So
as usual, Paul went there to worship, and on three
Sabbaths he spoke to the people. He used the Scriptures

[d] 16.37 *Roman citizens*: Only a small number of the people living in the Roman Empire were citizens, and they had special rights and privileges.

NEW INTERNATIONAL VERSION

house and set a meal before them; he was filled with joy
because he had come to believe in God—he and his whole
family.
35When it was daylight, the magistrates sent their offi-
cers to the jailer with the order: "Release those men." 36The
jailer told Paul, "The magistrates have ordered that you and
Silas be released. Now you can leave. Go in peace."
37But Paul said to the officers: "They beat us publicly
without a trial, even though we are Roman citizens, and
threw us into prison. And now do they want to get rid of
us quietly? No! Let them come themselves and escort us
out."
38The officers reported this to the magistrates, and when
they heard that Paul and Silas were Roman citizens, they
were alarmed. 39They came to appease them and escorted
them from the prison, requesting them to leave the city.
40After Paul and Silas came out of the prison, they went to
Lydia's house, where they met with the brothers and
encouraged them. Then they left.

In Thessalonica

17 When they had passed through Amphipolis and
Apollonia, they came to Thessalonica, where there
was a Jewish synagogue. 2As his custom was, Paul went
into the synagogue, and on three Sabbath days he rea-
soned with them from the Scriptures, 3explaining and

NEW LIVING TRANSLATION

house and set a meal before them. He and his entire
household rejoiced because they all believed in God.
35The next morning the city officials sent the police to
tell the jailer, "Let those men go!" 36So the jailer told Paul,
"You and Silas are free to leave. Go in peace."
37But Paul replied, "They have publicly beaten us with-
out trial and jailed us—and we are Roman citizens. So
now they want us to leave secretly? Certainly not! Let
them come themselves to release us!"
38When the police made their report, the city officials
were alarmed to learn that Paul and Silas were Roman citi-
zens. 39They came to the jail and apologized to them. Then
they brought them out and begged them to leave the city.
40Paul and Silas then returned to the home of Lydia, where
they met with the believers and encouraged them once
more before leaving town.

Paul Preaches in Thessalonica

17 Now Paul and Silas traveled through the towns of
Amphipolis and Apollonia and came to Thes-
salonica, where there was a Jewish synagogue. 2As was
Paul's custom, he went to the synagogue service, and for
three Sabbaths in a row he interpreted the Scriptures to

NEW KING JAMES VERSION

into his house, he set food before them; and he rejoiced,
having believed in God with all his household.

Paul Refuses to Depart Secretly

35And when it was day, the magistrates sent the officers,
saying, "Let those men go."
36So the keeper of the prison reported these words to
Paul, saying, "The magistrates have sent to let you go.
Now therefore depart, and go in peace."
37But Paul said to them, "They have beaten us openly,
uncondemned Romans, *and* have thrown *us* into prison.
And now do they put us out secretly? No indeed! Let them
come themselves and get us out."
38And the officers told these words to the magistrates,
and they were afraid when they heard that they were Ro-
mans. 39Then they came and pleaded with them and
brought *them* out, and asked *them* to depart from the city.
40So they went out of the prison and entered *the house of*
Lydia; and when they had seen the brethren, they encour-
aged them and departed.

Preaching Christ at Thessalonica

17 Now when they had passed through Amphipolis
and Apollonia, they came to Thessalonica, where
there was a synagogue of the Jews. 2Then Paul, as his
custom was, went in to them, and for three Sabbaths rea-
soned with them from the Scriptures, 3explaining and

THE MESSAGE

There in his home, he had food set out for a festive meal. It
was a night to remember: He and his entire family had put
their trust in God; everyone in the house was in on the cele-
bration.

At daybreak, the court judges sent officers with the
instructions, "Release these men." The jailer gave Paul the
message, "The judges sent word that you're free to go on
your way. Congratulations! Go in peace!"

But Paul wouldn't budge. He told the officers, "They
beat us up in public and threw us in jail, Roman citizens in
good standing! And now they want to get us out of the
way on the sly without anyone knowing? Nothing doing! If
they want us out of here, let them come themselves and
lead us out in broad daylight."

When the officers reported this, the judges panicked.
They had no idea that Paul and Silas were Roman citizens.
They hurried over and apologized, personally escorted
them from the jail, and then asked them if they wouldn't
please leave the city. Walking out of the jail, Paul and
Silas went straight to Lydia's house, saw their friends
again, encouraged them in the faith, and only then went
on their way.

Thessalonica

17 They took the road south through Amphipolis and
Apollonia to Thessalonica, where there was a com-
munity of Jews. Paul went to their meeting place, as he usu-
ally did when he came to a town, and for three Sabbaths run-
ning he preached to them from the Scriptures. He opened up

KING JAMES VERSION

3 Opening and alleging, that Christ must needs have suffered, and risen again from the dead; and that this Jesus, whom I preach unto you, is Christ.

4 And some of them believed, and consorted with Paul and Silas; and of the devout Greeks a great multitude, and of the chief women not a few.

5 But the Jews which believed not, moved with envy, took unto them certain lewd fellows of the baser sort, and gathered a company, and set all the city on an uproar, and assaulted the house of Jason, and sought to bring them out to the people.

6 And when they found them not, they drew Jason and certain brethren unto the rulers of the city, crying, These that have turned the world upside down are come hither also;

7 Whom Jason hath received: and these all do contrary to the decrees of Caesar, saying that there is another king, *one* Jesus.

8 And they troubled the people and the rulers of the city, when they heard these things.

9 And when they had taken security of Jason, and of the other, they let them go.

10 ¶ And the brethren immediately sent away Paul and Silas by night unto Berea: who coming *thither* went into the synagogue of the Jews.

11 These were more noble than those in Thessalonica,

NEW AMERICAN STANDARD BIBLE

3 explaining and giving evidence that the Christ had to suffer and rise again from the dead, and *saying*, "This Jesus whom I am proclaiming to you is the Christ."

4 And some of them were persuaded and joined Paul and Silas, along with a large number of the God-fearing Greeks and a number of the leading women.

5 But the Jews, becoming jealous and taking along some wicked men from the market place, formed a mob and set the city in an uproar; and attacking the house of Jason, they were seeking to bring them out to the people.

6 When they did not find them, they *began* dragging Jason and some brethren before the city authorities, shouting, "These men who have upset [1]the world have come here also;

7 and Jason has welcomed them, and they all act contrary to the decrees of Caesar, saying that there is another king, Jesus."

8 They stirred up the crowd and the city authorities who heard these things.

9 And when they had received a pledge from Jason and the others, they released them.

Paul at Berea

10 The brethren immediately sent Paul and Silas away by night to Berea, and when they arrived, they went into the synagogue of the Jews.

11 Now these were more noble-minded than those in

17:6 [1] Lit *the inhabited earth*

NEW CENTURY VERSION

explained and proved that the Christ must die and then rise from the dead. He said, "This Jesus I am telling you about is the Christ." [4]Some of the Jews were convinced and joined Paul and Silas, along with many of the Greeks who worshiped God and many of the important women.

[5]But the Jews became jealous. So they got some evil men from the marketplace, formed a mob, and started a riot. They ran to Jason's house, looking for Paul and Silas, wanting to bring them out to the people. [6]But when they did not find them, they dragged Jason and some other believers to the leaders of the city. The people were yelling, "These people have made trouble everywhere in the world, and now they have come here too! [7]Jason is keeping them in his house. All of them do things against the laws of Caesar, saying there is another king, called Jesus."

[8]When the people and the leaders of the city heard these things, they became very upset. [9]They made Jason and the others put up a sum of money. Then they let the believers go free.

Paul and Silas Go to Berea

[10]That same night the believers sent Paul and Silas to Berea where they went to the Jewish synagogue. [11]These Jews were more willing to listen than the Jews in Thessalonica. The Bereans were eager to hear what Paul

CONTEMPORARY ENGLISH VERSION

[3]to show them that the Messiah had to suffer, but that he would rise from death. Paul also told them that Jesus is the Messiah he was preaching about. [4]Some of them believed what Paul had said, and they became followers with Paul and Silas. Some Gentiles[a] and many important women also believed the message.

[5]The Jewish leaders were jealous and got some worthless bums who hung around the marketplace to start a riot in the city. They wanted to drag Paul and Silas out to the mob, and so they went straight to Jason's home. [6]But when they did not find them there, they dragged out Jason and some of the Lord's followers. They took them to the city authorities and shouted, "Paul and Silas have been upsetting things everywhere. Now they have come here, [7]and Jason has welcomed them into his home. All of them break the laws of the Roman Emperor by claiming that someone named Jesus is king."

[8]The officials and the people were upset when they heard this. [9]So they made Jason and the other followers pay bail before letting them go.

People in Berea Welcome the Message

[10]That same night the Lord's followers sent Paul and Silas on to Berea, and after they arrived, they went to the Jewish meeting place. [11]The people in Berea were much nicer than those in Thessalonica, and they gladly accepted

[a] 17.4 *Gentiles*: See the note at 14.1.

NEW INTERNATIONAL VERSION

proving that the Christ[a] had to suffer and rise from the dead. "This Jesus I am proclaiming to you is the Christ,[a]" he said. [4]Some of the Jews were persuaded and joined Paul and Silas, as did a large number of God-fearing Greeks and not a few prominent women.

[5]But the Jews were jealous; so they rounded up some bad characters from the marketplace, formed a mob and started a riot in the city. They rushed to Jason's house in search of Paul and Silas in order to bring them out to the crowd.[b] [6]But when they did not find them, they dragged Jason and some other brothers before the city officials, shouting: "These men who have caused trouble all over the world have now come here, [7]and Jason has welcomed them into his house. They are all defying Caesar's decrees, saying that there is another king, one called Jesus." [8]When they heard this, the crowd and the city officials were thrown into turmoil. [9]Then they made Jason and the others post bond and let them go.

In Berea

[10]As soon as it was night, the brothers sent Paul and Silas away to Berea. On arriving there, they went to the Jewish synagogue. [11]Now the Bereans were of more noble character than the Thessalonians, for they received the

[a] *3* Or *Messiah* [b] *5* Or *the assembly of the people*

NEW LIVING TRANSLATION

the people. [3]He was explaining and proving the prophecies about the sufferings of the Messiah and his rising from the dead. He said, "This Jesus I'm telling you about is the Messiah." [4]Some who listened were persuaded and became converts, including a large number of godly Greek men and also many important women of the city.*

[5]But the Jewish leaders were jealous, so they gathered some worthless fellows from the streets to form a mob and start a riot. They attacked the home of Jason, searching for Paul and Silas so they could drag them out to the crowd.* [6]Not finding them there, they dragged out Jason and some of the other believers* instead and took them before the city council. "Paul and Silas have turned the rest of the world upside down, and now they are here disturbing our city," they shouted. [7]"And Jason has let them into his home. They are all guilty of treason against Caesar, for they profess allegiance to another king, Jesus."

[8]The people of the city, as well as the city officials, were thrown into turmoil by these reports. [9]But the officials released Jason and the other believers after they had posted bail.

Paul and Silas in Berea

[10]That very night the believers sent Paul and Silas to Berea. When they arrived there, they went to the synagogue. [11]And the people of Berea were more open-minded than those in Thessalonica, and they listened eagerly to

17:4 Some manuscripts read *many of the wives of the leading men.* 17:5 Or *the city council.* 17:6 Greek *brothers;* also in 17:10, 14.

NEW KING JAMES VERSION

demonstrating that the Christ had to suffer and rise again from the dead, and *saying,* "This Jesus whom I preach to you is the Christ." [4]And some of them were persuaded; and a great multitude of the devout Greeks, and not a few of the leading women, joined Paul and Silas.

Assault on Jason's House

[5]But the Jews who were not persuaded, becoming envious,[a] took some of the evil men from the marketplace, and gathering a mob, set all the city in an uproar and attacked the house of Jason, and sought to bring them out to the people. [6]But when they did not find them, they dragged Jason and some brethren to the rulers of the city, crying out, "These who have turned the world upside down have come here too. [7]Jason has harbored them, and these are all acting contrary to the decrees of Caesar, saying there is another king—Jesus." [8]And they troubled the crowd and the rulers of the city when they heard these things. [9]So when they had taken security from Jason and the rest, they let them go.

Ministering at Berea

[10]Then the brethren immediately sent Paul and Silas away by night to Berea. When they arrived, they went into the synagogue of the Jews. [11]These were more fair-minded than those in Thessalonica, in that they received the word

17:5 [a] NU-Text omits *who were not persuaded;* M-Text omits *becoming envious.*

THE MESSAGE

the texts so they understood what they'd been reading all their lives: that the Messiah absolutely *had* to be put to death and raised from the dead—there were no other options—and that "this Jesus I'm introducing you to is that Messiah."

Some of them were won over and joined ranks with Paul and Silas, among them a great many God-fearing Greeks and a considerable number of women from the aristocracy. But the hard-line Jews became furious over the conversions. Mad with jealousy, they rounded up a bunch of brawlers off the streets and soon had an ugly mob terrorizing the city as they hunted down Paul and Silas.

They broke into Jason's house, thinking that Paul and Silas were there. When they couldn't find them, they collared Jason and his friends instead and dragged them before the city fathers, yelling hysterically, "These people are out to destroy the world, and now they've shown up on our doorstep, attacking everything we hold dear! And Jason is hiding them, these traitors and turncoats who say Jesus is king and Caesar is nothing!"

The city fathers and the crowd of people were totally alarmed by what they heard. They made Jason and his friends post heavy bail and let them go while they investigated the charges.

Berea

That night, under cover of darkness, their friends got Paul and Silas out of town as fast as they could. They sent them to Berea, where they again met with the Jewish community. They were treated a lot better there than in

KING JAMES VERSION

in that they received the word with all readiness of mind, and searched the scriptures daily, whether those things were so.

12 Therefore many of them believed; also of honourable women which were Greeks, and of men, not a few.

13 But when the Jews of Thessalonica had knowledge that the word of God was preached of Paul at Berea, they came thither also, and stirred up the people.

14 And then immediately the brethren sent away Paul to go as it were to the sea: but Silas and Timotheus abode there still.

15 And they that conducted Paul brought him unto Athens: and receiving a commandment unto Silas and Timotheus for to come to him with all speed, they departed.

16 ¶ Now while Paul waited for them at Athens, his spirit was stirred in him, when he saw the city wholly given to idolatry.

17 Therefore disputed he in the synagogue with the Jews, and with the devout persons, and in the market daily with them that met with him.

18 Then certain philosophers of the Epicureans, and of the Stoicks, encountered him. And some said, What will this babbler say? other some, He seemeth to be a setter forth of strange gods: because he preached unto them Jesus, and the resurrection.

NEW AMERICAN STANDARD BIBLE

Thessalonica, for they received the word with great eagerness, examining the Scriptures daily *to see* whether these things were so.

12 Therefore many of them believed, along with a number of prominent Greek women and men.

13 But when the Jews of Thessalonica found out that the word of God had been proclaimed by Paul in Berea also, they came there as well, agitating and stirring up the crowds.

14 Then immediately the brethren sent Paul out to go as far as the sea; and Silas and Timothy remained there.

15 Now those who escorted Paul brought him as far as Athens; and receiving a command for Silas and Timothy to come to him as soon as possible, they left.

Paul at Athens

16 Now while Paul was waiting for them at Athens, his spirit was being provoked within him as he was observing the city full of idols.

17 So he was reasoning in the synagogue with the Jews and the God-fearing *Gentiles,* and in the market place every day with those who happened to be present.

18 And also some of the Epicurean and Stoic philosophers were conversing with him. Some were saying, "What would this idle babbler wish to say?" Others, "He seems to be a proclaimer of strange deities,"—because he was preaching Jesus and the resurrection.

NEW CENTURY VERSION

and Silas said and studied the Scriptures every day to find out if these things were true. 12So, many of them believed, as well as many important Greek women and men. 13But the Jews in Thessalonica learned that Paul was preaching the word of God in Berea, too. So they came there, upsetting the people and making trouble. 14The believers quickly sent Paul away to the coast, but Silas and Timothy stayed in Berea. 15The people leading Paul went with him to Athens. Then they carried a message from Paul back to Silas and Timothy for them to come to him as soon as they could.

Paul Preaches in Athens

16While Paul was waiting for Silas and Timothy in Athens, he was troubled because he saw that the city was full of idols. 17In the synagogue, he talked with the Jews and the Greeks who worshiped God. He also talked every day with people in the marketplace.

18Some of the Epicurean and Stoic philosophers[a] argued with him, saying, "This man doesn't know what he is talking about. What is he trying to say?" Others said, "He seems to be telling us about some other gods," because Paul was telling them about Jesus and his rising from the

17:18 [a] **Epicurean and Stoic philosophers** Philosophers were those who searched for truth. Epicureans believed that pleasures, especially pleasures of the mind, were the goal of life. Stoics believed that life should be without feelings of joy or grief.

CONTEMPORARY ENGLISH VERSION

the message. Day after day they studied the Scriptures to see if these things were true. 12Many of them put their faith in the Lord, including some important Greek women and several men.

13When the Jewish leaders in Thessalonica heard that Paul had been preaching God's message in Berea, they went there and caused trouble by turning the crowds against Paul.

14Right away the followers sent Paul down to the coast, but Silas and Timothy stayed in Berea. 15Some men went with Paul as far as Athens, and then returned with instructions for Silas and Timothy to join him as soon as possible.

Paul in Athens

16While Paul was waiting in Athens, he was upset to see all the idols in the city. 17He went to the Jewish meeting place to speak to the Jews and to anyone who worshiped with them. Day after day he also spoke to everyone he met in the market. 18Some of them were Epicureans[b] and some were Stoics,[c] and they started arguing with him.

People were asking, "What is this know-it-all trying to say?"

Some even said, "Paul must be preaching about foreign gods! That's what he means when he talks about Jesus and about people rising from death."[d]

[b] **17.18** *Epicureans*: People who followed the teaching of a man named Epicurus, who taught that happiness should be the main goal in life.

[c] **17.18** *Stoics*: Followers of a man named Zeno, who taught that people should learn self-control and be guided by their consciences.

[d] **17.18** *people rising from death*: Or "a goddess named 'Rising from Death.'"

NEW INTERNATIONAL VERSION

message with great eagerness and examined the Scriptures every day to see if what Paul said was true. 12Many of the Jews believed, as did also a number of prominent Greek women and many Greek men.

13When the Jews in Thessalonica learned that Paul was preaching the word of God at Berea, they went there too, agitating the crowds and stirring them up. 14The brothers immediately sent Paul to the coast, but Silas and Timothy stayed at Berea. 15The men who escorted Paul brought him to Athens and then left with instructions for Silas and Timothy to join him as soon as possible.

In Athens

16While Paul was waiting for them in Athens, he was greatly distressed to see that the city was full of idols. 17So he reasoned in the synagogue with the Jews and the God-fearing Greeks, as well as in the marketplace day by day with those who happened to be there. 18A group of Epicurean and Stoic philosophers began to dispute with him. Some of them asked, "What is this babbler trying to say?" Others remarked, "He seems to be advocating foreign gods." They said this because Paul was preaching the good news about Jesus and the resurrection. 19Then they

NEW LIVING TRANSLATION

Paul's message. They searched the Scriptures day after day to check up on Paul and Silas, to see if they were really teaching the truth. 12As a result, many Jews believed, as did some of the prominent Greek women and many men.

13But when some Jews in Thessalonica learned that Paul was preaching the word of God in Berea, they went there and stirred up trouble. 14The believers acted at once, sending Paul on to the coast, while Silas and Timothy remained behind. 15Those escorting Paul went with him to Athens; then they returned to Berea with a message for Silas and Timothy to hurry and join him.

Paul Preaches in Athens

16While Paul was waiting for them in Athens, he was deeply troubled by all the idols he saw everywhere in the city. 17He went to the synagogue to debate with the Jews and the God-fearing Gentiles, and he spoke daily in the public square to all who happened to be there.

18He also had a debate with some of the Epicurean and Stoic philosophers. When he told them about Jesus and his resurrection, they said, "This babbler has picked up some strange ideas." Others said, "He's pushing some foreign religion."

NEW KING JAMES VERSION

with all readiness, and searched the Scriptures daily *to find out* whether these things were so. 12Therefore many of them believed, and also not a few of the Greeks, prominent women as well as men. 13But when the Jews from Thessalonica learned that the word of God was preached by Paul at Berea, they came there also and stirred up the crowds. 14Then immediately the brethren sent Paul away, to go to the sea; but both Silas and Timothy remained there. 15So those who conducted Paul brought him to Athens; and receiving a command for Silas and Timothy to come to him with all speed, they departed.

The Philosophers at Athens

16Now while Paul waited for them at Athens, his spirit was provoked within him when he saw that the city was given over to idols. 17Therefore he reasoned in the synagogue with the Jews and with the *Gentile* worshipers, and in the marketplace daily with those who happened to be there. 18Then[b] certain Epicurean and Stoic philosophers encountered him. And some said, "What does this babbler want to say?"

Others said, "He seems to be a proclaimer of foreign gods," because he preached to them Jesus and the resurrection.

17:18 [b] NU-Text and M-Text add *also.*

THE MESSAGE

Thessalonica. The Jews received Paul's message with enthusiasm and met with him daily, examining the Scriptures to see if they supported what he said. A lot of them became believers, including many Greeks who were prominent in the community, women and men of influence.

But it wasn't long before reports got back to the Thessalonian hard-line Jews that Paul was at it again, preaching the Word of God, this time in Berea. They lost no time responding, and created a mob scene there, too. With the help of his friends, Paul gave them the slip—caught a boat and put out to sea. Silas and Timothy stayed behind. The men who helped Paul escape got him as far as Athens and left him there. Paul sent word back with them to Silas and Timothy: "Come as quickly as you can!"

Athens

The longer Paul waited in Athens for Silas and Timothy, the angrier he got—all those idols! The city was a junkyard of idols.

He discussed it with the Jews and other likeminded people at their meeting place. And every day he went out on the streets and talked with anyone who happened along. He got to know some of the Epicurean and Stoic intellectuals pretty well through these conversations. Some of them dismissed him with sarcasm: "What an airhead!" But others, listening to him go on about Jesus and the resurrection, were intrigued: "That's a new slant on the gods. Tell us more."

KING JAMES VERSION

19 And they took him, and brought him unto Areopagus, saying, May we know what this new doctrine, whereof thou speakest, *is?*

20 For thou bringest certain strange things to our ears: we would know therefore what these things mean.

21 (For all the Athenians and strangers which were there spent their time in nothing else, but either to tell, or to hear some new thing.)

22 ¶ Then Paul stood in the midst of Mars' hill, and said, *Ye* men of Athens, I perceive that in all things ye are too superstitious.

23 For as I passed by, and beheld your devotions, I found an altar with this inscription, TO THE UNKNOWN GOD. Whom therefore ye ignorantly worship, him declare I unto you.

24 God that made the world and all things therein, seeing that he is Lord of heaven and earth, dwelleth not in temples made with hands;

25 Neither is worshipped with men's hands, as though he needed any thing, seeing he giveth to all life, and breath, and all things;

26 And hath made of one blood all nations of men for to dwell on all the face of the earth, and hath determined the times before appointed, and the bounds of their habitation;

27 That they should seek the Lord, if haply they might feel after him, and find him, though he be not far from every one of us:

NEW AMERICAN STANDARD BIBLE

19 And they took him and brought him to the Areopagus, saying, "May we know what this new teaching is which you are proclaiming?

20 "For you are bringing some strange things to our ears; so we want to know what these things mean."

21 (Now all the Athenians and the strangers visiting there used to spend their time in nothing other than telling or hearing something new.)

Sermon on Mars Hill

22 So Paul stood in the midst of the Areopagus and said, "Men of Athens, I observe that you are very religious in all respects.

23 "For while I was passing through and examining the objects of your worship, I also found an altar with this inscription, 'TO AN UNKNOWN GOD.' Therefore what you worship in ignorance, this I proclaim to you.

24 "The God who made the world and all things in it, since He is Lord of heaven and earth, does not dwell in temples made with hands;

25 nor is He served by human hands, as though He needed anything, since He Himself gives to all *people* life and breath and all things;

26 and He made from one *man* every nation of mankind to live on all the face of the earth, having determined *their* appointed times and the boundaries of their habitation,

27 that they would seek God, if perhaps they might grope for Him and find Him, though He is not far from each one of us;

NEW CENTURY VERSION

dead. 19They got Paul and took him to a meeting of the Areopagus,[b] where they said, "Please explain to us this new idea you have been teaching. 20The things you are saying are new to us, and we want to know what this teaching means." 21(All the people of Athens and those from other countries who lived there always used their time to talk about the newest ideas.)

22Then Paul stood before the meeting of the Areopagus and said, "People of Athens, I can see you are very religious in all things. 23As I was going through your city, I saw the objects you worship. I found an altar that had these words written on it: TO A GOD WHO IS NOT KNOWN. You worship a god that you don't know, and this is the God I am telling you about! 24The God who made the whole world and everything in it is the Lord of the land and the sky. He does not live in temples built by human hands. 25This God is the One who gives life, breath, and everything else to people. He does not need any help from them; he has everything he needs. 26God began by making one person, and from him came all the different people who live everywhere in the world. God decided exactly when and where they must live. 27God wanted them to look for him and perhaps search all around for him and find him, though he is not far from any of us: 28'We live in him. We

17:19 [b] **Areopagus** A council or group of important leaders in Athens. They were like judges.

CONTEMPORARY ENGLISH VERSION

19They brought Paul before a council called the Areopagus, and said, "Tell us what your new teaching is all about. 20We have heard you say some strange things, and we want to know what you mean."

21More than anything else the people of Athens and the foreigners living there loved to hear and to talk about anything new. 22So Paul stood up in front of the council and said:

People of Athens, I see that you are very religious.
23As I was going through your city and looking at the things you worship, I found an altar with the words, "To an Unknown God." You worship this God, but you don't really know him. So I want to tell you about him. 24This God made the world and everything in it. He is Lord of heaven and earth, and he doesn't live in temples built by human hands. 25He doesn't need help from anyone. He gives life, breath, and everything else to all people.
26From one person God made all nations who live on earth, and he decided when and where every nation would be.

27God has done all this, so that we will look for him and reach out and find him. He isn't far from any of us,

NEW INTERNATIONAL VERSION

took him and brought him to a meeting of the Areopagus, where they said to him, "May we know what this new teaching is that you are presenting? 20You are bringing some strange ideas to our ears, and we want to know what they mean." 21(All the Athenians and the foreigners who lived there spent their time doing nothing but talking about and listening to the latest ideas.)

22Paul then stood up in the meeting of the Areopagus and said: "Men of Athens! I see that in every way you are very religious. 23For as I walked around and looked carefully at your objects of worship, I even found an altar with this inscription: TO AN UNKNOWN GOD. Now what you worship as something unknown I am going to proclaim to you.

24"The God who made the world and everything in it is the Lord of heaven and earth and does not live in temples built by hands. 25And he is not served by human hands, as if he needed anything, because he himself gives all men life and breath and everything else. 26From one man he made every nation of men, that they should inhabit the whole earth; and he determined the times set for them and the exact places where they should live. 27God did this so that men would seek him and perhaps reach out for him and find him, though he is not far from each one of us.

NEW LIVING TRANSLATION

19Then they took him to the Council of Philosophers.* "Come and tell us more about this new religion," they said. 20"You are saying some rather startling things, and we want to know what it's all about." 21(It should be explained that all the Athenians as well as the foreigners in Athens seemed to spend all their time discussing the latest ideas.)

22So Paul, standing before the Council,* addressed them as follows: "Men of Athens, I notice that you are very religious, 23for as I was walking along I saw your many altars. And one of them had this inscription on it—'To an Unknown God.' You have been worshiping him without knowing who he is, and now I wish to tell you about him.

24"He is the God who made the world and everything in it. Since he is Lord of heaven and earth, he doesn't live in man-made temples, 25and human hands can't serve his needs—for he has no needs. He himself gives life and breath to everything, and he satisfies every need there is. 26From one man he created all the nations throughout the whole earth. He decided beforehand which should rise and fall, and he determined their boundaries.

27"His purpose in all of this was that the nations should seek after God and perhaps feel their way toward him and find him—though he is not far from any one of us. 28For in

17:19 Greek *the Areopagus.* 17:22 Or *in the middle of Mars Hill;* Greek reads *in the middle of the Areopagus.*

NEW KING JAMES VERSION

19And they took him and brought him to the Areopagus, saying, "May we know what this new doctrine *is* of which you speak? 20For you are bringing some strange things to our ears. Therefore we want to know what these things mean." 21For all the Athenians and the foreigners who were there spent their time in nothing else but either to tell or to hear some new thing.

Addressing the Areopagus

22Then Paul stood in the midst of the Areopagus and said, "Men of Athens, I perceive that in all things you are very religious; 23for as I was passing through and considering the objects of your worship, I even found an altar with this inscription:

TO THE UNKNOWN GOD.

Therefore, the One whom you worship without knowing, Him I proclaim to you: 24God, who made the world and everything in it, since He is Lord of heaven and earth, does not dwell in temples made with hands. 25Nor is He worshiped with men's hands, as though He needed anything, since He gives to all life, breath, and all things. 26And He has made from one blood[c] every nation of men to dwell on all the face of the earth, and has determined their preappointed times and the boundaries of their dwellings, 27so that they should seek the Lord, in the hope that they might grope for Him and find Him, though He is not far from

17:26 [c] NU-Text omits *blood.*

THE MESSAGE

These people got together and asked him to make a public presentation over at the Areopagus, where things were a little quieter. They said, "This is a new one on us. We've never heard anything quite like it. Where did you come up with this anyway? Explain it so we can understand." Downtown Athens was a great place for gossip. There were always people hanging around, natives and tourists alike, waiting for the latest tidbit on most anything.

So Paul took his stand in the open space at the Areopagus and laid it out for them. "It is plain to see that you Athenians take your religion seriously. When I arrived here the other day, I was fascinated with all the shrines I came across. And then I found one inscribed, TO THE GOD NOBODY KNOWS. I'm here to introduce you to this God so you can worship intelligently, know who you're dealing with.

"The God who made the world and everything in it, this Master of sky and land, doesn't live in custom-made shrines or need the human race to run errands for him, as if he couldn't take care of himself. He makes the creatures; the creatures don't make him. Starting from scratch, he made the entire human race and made the earth hospitable, with plenty of time and space for living so we could seek after God, and not just grope around in the dark but actually *find* him. He doesn't play hide-and-seek with us. He's not remote; he's *near.* We live and move in him,

KING JAMES VERSION

28 For in him we live, and move, and have our being; as certain also of your own poets have said, For we are also his offspring.

29 Forasmuch then as we are the offspring of God, we ought not to think that the Godhead is like unto gold, or silver, or stone, graven by art and man's device.

30 And the times of this ignorance God winked at; but now commandeth all men every where to repent:

31 Because he hath appointed a day, in the which he will judge the world in righteousness by *that* man whom he hath ordained; *whereof* he hath given assurance unto all *men*, in that he hath raised him from the dead.

32 ¶ And when they heard of the resurrection of the dead, some mocked: and others said, We will hear thee again of this *matter*.

33 So Paul departed from among them.

34 Howbeit certain men clave unto him, and believed: among the which *was* Dionysius the Areopagite, and a woman named Damaris, and others with them.

18 After these things Paul departed from Athens, and came to Corinth;

2 And found a certain Jew named Aquila, born in Pontus, lately come from Italy, with his wife Priscilla; (because that Claudius had commanded all Jews to depart from Rome:) and came unto them.

NEW AMERICAN STANDARD BIBLE

28 for in Him we live and move and exist, as even some of your own poets have said, 'For we also are His children.'

29 "Being then the children of God, we ought not to think that the Divine Nature is like gold or silver or stone, an image formed by the art and thought of man.

30 "Therefore having overlooked the times of ignorance, God is now declaring to men that all *people* everywhere should repent,

31 because He has fixed a day in which He will judge the world in righteousness through a Man whom He has appointed, having furnished proof to all men by raising Him from the dead."

32 Now when they heard of the resurrection of the dead, some *began* to sneer, but others said, "We shall hear you again concerning this."

33 So Paul went out of their midst.

34 But some men joined him and believed, among whom also were Dionysius the Areopagite and a woman named Damaris and others with them.

Paul at Corinth

18 After these things he left Athens and went to Corinth.

2 And he found a Jew named Aquila, a native of Pontus, having recently come from Italy with his wife Priscilla, because Claudius had commanded all the Jews to leave Rome. He came to them,

NEW CENTURY VERSION

walk in him. We are in him.' Some of your own poets have said: 'For we are his children.' 29Since we are God's children, you must not think that God is like something that people imagine or make from gold, silver, or rock. 30In the past, people did not understand God, and he ignored this. But now, God tells all people in the world to change their hearts and lives. 31God has set a day that he will judge all the world with fairness, by the man he chose long ago. And God has proved this to everyone by raising that man from the dead!"

32When the people heard about Jesus being raised from the dead, some of them laughed. But others said, "We will hear more about this from you later." 33So Paul went away from them. 34But some of the people believed Paul and joined him. Among those who believed was Dionysius, a member of the Areopagus, a woman named Damaris, and some others.

Paul in Corinth

18 Later Paul left Athens and went to Corinth. 2Here he met a Jew named Aquila who had been born in the country of Pontus. But Aquila and his wife, Priscilla, had recently moved to Corinth from Italy, because Claudius[a] commanded that all Jews must leave Rome. Paul went to visit Aquila and Priscilla. 3Because they were tentmakers,

18:2 [a] **Claudius** The emperor (ruler) of Rome, A.D. 41–54.

CONTEMPORARY ENGLISH VERSION

28and he gives us the power to live, to move, and to be who we are. "We are his children," just as some of your poets have said.

29Since we are God's children, we must not think that he is like an idol made out of gold or silver or stone. He isn't like anything that humans have thought up and made. 30In the past, God forgave all this because people did not know what they were doing. But now he says that everyone everywhere must turn to him. 31He has set a day when he will judge the world's people with fairness. And he has chosen the man Jesus to do the judging for him. God has given proof of this to all of us by raising Jesus from death.

32As soon as the people heard Paul say that a man had been raised from death, some of them started laughing. Others said, "We will hear you talk about this some other time." 33When Paul left the council meeting, 34some of the men put their faith in the Lord and went with Paul. One of them was a council member named Dionysius. A woman named Damaris and several others also put their faith in the Lord.

Paul in Corinth

18 Paul left Athens and went to Corinth, 2where he met Aquila, a Jewish man from Pontus. Not long before this, Aquila had come from Italy with his wife Priscilla, because Emperor Claudius had ordered the Jewish people to leave Rome.[a] Paul went to see Aquila and

[a] 18.2 *Emperor Claudius had ordered the Jewish people to leave Rome*: Probably A.D. 49, though it may have been A.D. 41.

NEW INTERNATIONAL VERSION

[28]'For in him we live and move and have our being.' As some of your own poets have said, 'We are his offspring.'

[29]"Therefore since we are God's offspring, we should not think that the divine being is like gold or silver or stone—an image made by man's design and skill. [30]In the past God overlooked such ignorance, but now he commands all people everywhere to repent. [31]For he has set a day when he will judge the world with justice by the man he has appointed. He has given proof of this to all men by raising him from the dead."

[32]When they heard about the resurrection of the dead, some of them sneered, but others said, "We want to hear you again on this subject." [33]At that, Paul left the Council. [34]A few men became followers of Paul and believed. Among them was Dionysius, a member of the Areopagus, also a woman named Damaris, and a number of others.

In Corinth

18 After this, Paul left Athens and went to Corinth. [2]There he met a Jew named Aquila, a native of Pontus, who had recently come from Italy with his wife Priscilla, because Claudius had ordered all the Jews to leave Rome. Paul went to see them, [3]and because he was a

NEW LIVING TRANSLATION

him we live and move and exist. As one of your own poets says, 'We are his offspring.' [29]And since this is true, we shouldn't think of God as an idol designed by craftsmen from gold or silver or stone. [30]God overlooked people's former ignorance about these things, but now he commands everyone everywhere to turn away from idols and turn to him.* [31]For he has set a day for judging the world with justice by the man he has appointed, and he proved to everyone who this is by raising him from the dead."

[32]When they heard Paul speak of the resurrection of a person who had been dead, some laughed, but others said, "We want to hear more about this later." [33]That ended Paul's discussion with them, [34]but some joined him and became believers. Among them were Dionysius, a member of the Council,* a woman named Damaris, and others.

Paul Meets Priscilla and Aquila in Corinth

18 Then Paul left Athens and went to Corinth.* [2]There he became acquainted with a Jew named Aquila, born in Pontus, who had recently arrived from Italy with his wife, Priscilla. They had been expelled from Italy as a result of Claudius Caesar's order to deport all Jews from

17:30 Greek *everywhere to repent.* **17:34** Greek *an Areopagite.*
18:1 *Athens* and *Corinth* were major cities in Achaia, the region on the southern end of the Greek peninsula.

NEW KING JAMES VERSION

each one of us; [28]for in Him we live and move and have our being, as also some of your own poets have said, 'For we are also His offspring.' [29]Therefore, since we are the offspring of God, we ought not to think that the Divine Nature is like gold or silver or stone, something shaped by art and man's devising. [30]Truly, these times of ignorance God overlooked, but now commands all men everywhere to repent, [31]because He has appointed a day on which He will judge the world in righteousness by the Man whom He has ordained. He has given assurance of this to all by raising Him from the dead."

[32]And when they heard of the resurrection of the dead, some mocked, while others said, "We will hear you again on this *matter.*" [33]So Paul departed from among them. [34]However, some men joined him and believed, among them Dionysius the Areopagite, a woman named Damaris, and others with them.

Ministering at Corinth

18 After these things Paul departed from Athens and went to Corinth. [2]And he found a certain Jew named Aquila, born in Pontus, who had recently come from Italy with his wife Priscilla (because Claudius had commanded all the Jews to depart from Rome); and he

THE MESSAGE

can't get away from him! One of your poets said it well: 'We're the God-created.' Well, if we are the God-created, it doesn't make a lot of sense to think we could hire a sculptor to chisel a god out of stone for *us*, does it?

"God overlooks it as long as you don't know any better—but that time is past. The unknown is now known, and he's calling for a radical life-change. He has set a day when the entire human race will be judged and everything set right. And he has already appointed the judge, confirming him before everyone by raising him from the dead."

At the phrase "raising him from the dead," the listeners split: Some laughed at him and walked off making jokes; others said, "Let's do this again. We want to hear more." But that was it for the day, and Paul left. There were still others, it turned out, who were convinced then and there, and stuck with Paul—among them Dionysius the Areopagite and a woman named Damaris.

Corinth

18 After Athens, Paul went to Corinth. That is where he discovered Aquila, a Jew born in Pontus, and his wife, Priscilla. They had just arrived from Italy, part of the general expulsion of Jews from Rome ordered by

KING JAMES VERSION

3 And because he was of the same craft, he abode with them, and wrought: for by their occupation they were tent-makers.

4 And he reasoned in the synagogue every sabbath, and persuaded the Jews and the Greeks.

5 And when Silas and Timotheus were come from Macedonia, Paul was pressed in the spirit, and testified to the Jews *that* Jesus *was* Christ.

6 And when they opposed themselves, and blasphemed, he shook *his* raiment, and said unto them, Your blood *be* upon your own heads; I *am* clean: from henceforth I will go unto the Gentiles.

7 ¶ And he departed thence, and entered into a certain *man's* house, named Justus, *one* that worshipped God, whose house joined hard to the synagogue.

8 And Crispus, the chief ruler of the synagogue, believed on the Lord with all his house; and many of the Corinthians hearing believed, and were baptized.

9 Then spake the Lord to Paul in the night by a vision, Be not afraid, but speak, and hold not thy peace:

10 For I am with thee, and no man shall set on thee to hurt thee: for I have much people in this city.

11 And he continued *there* a year and six months, teaching the word of God among them.

12 ¶ And when Gallio was the deputy of Achaia, the Jews made insurrection with one accord against Paul, and brought him to the judgment seat,

NEW AMERICAN STANDARD BIBLE

3 and because he was of the same trade, he stayed with them and they were working, for by trade they were tent-makers.

4 And he was reasoning in the synagogue every Sabbath and trying to persuade Jews and Greeks.

5 But when Silas and Timothy came down from Macedonia, Paul *began* devoting himself completely to the word, solemnly testifying to the Jews that Jesus was the Christ.

6 But when they resisted and blasphemed, he shook out his garments and said to them, "Your blood *be* on your own heads! I am clean. From now on I will go to the Gentiles."

7 Then he left there and went to the house of a man named Titius Justus, a worshiper of God, whose house was next to the synagogue.

8 Crispus, the leader of the synagogue, believed in the Lord with all his household, and many of the Corinthians when they heard were believing and being baptized.

9 And the Lord said to Paul in the night by a vision, "Do not be afraid *any longer*, but go on speaking and do not be silent;

10 for I am with you, and no man will attack you in order to harm you, for I have many people in this city."

11 And he settled *there* a year and six months, teaching the word of God among them.

12 But while Gallio was proconsul of Achaia, the Jews with one accord rose up against Paul and brought him before the judgment seat,

NEW CENTURY VERSION

just as he was, he stayed with them and worked with them.
4Every Sabbath day he talked with the Jews and Greeks in
the synagogue, trying to persuade them to believe in Jesus.
5Silas and Timothy came from Macedonia and joined
Paul in Corinth. After this, Paul spent all his time telling
people the Good News, showing the Jews that Jesus is the
Christ. 6But they would not accept Paul's teaching and
said some evil things. So he shook off the dust from his
clothes[b] and said to them, "If you are not saved, it will be
your own fault! I have done all I can do! After this, I will
go only to those who are not Jewish." 7Paul left the syna-
gogue and moved into the home of Titius Justus, next to
the synagogue. This man worshiped God. 8Crispus was the
leader of that synagogue, and he and all the people living
in his house believed in the Lord. Many others in Corinth
also listened to Paul and believed and were baptized.
9During the night, the Lord told Paul in a vision: "Don't
be afraid. Continue talking to people and don't be quiet. 10I
am with you, and no one will hurt you because many of
my people are in this city." 11Paul stayed there for a year
and a half, teaching God's word to the people.

Paul Is Brought Before Gallio

12When Gallio was the governor of the country of
Southern Greece, some of the Jews came together against
Paul and took him to the court. 13They said, "This man is

18:6 [b] **shook...clothes** This was a warning to show that Paul was finished talking to the Jews in that city.

CONTEMPORARY ENGLISH VERSION

Priscilla 3and found out that they were tent makers. Paul
was a tent maker too. So he stayed with them, and they
worked together.
4Every Sabbath, Paul went to the Jewish meeting place.
He spoke to Jews and Gentiles[b] and tried to win them over.
5But after Silas and Timothy came from Macedonia, he
spent all his time preaching to the Jews about Jesus the
Messiah. 6Finally, they turned against him and insulted
him. So he shook the dust from his clothes[c] and told them,
"Whatever happens to you will be your own fault! I am not
to blame. From now on I am going to preach to the
Gentiles."
7Paul then moved into the house of a man named Titius
Justus, who worshiped God and lived next door to the
Jewish meeting place. 8Crispus was the leader of the meet-
ing place. He and everyone in his family put their faith in
the Lord. Many others in Corinth also heard the message,
and all the people who had faith in the Lord were baptized.
9One night, Paul had a vision, and in it the Lord said,
"Don't be afraid to keep on preaching. Don't stop! 10I am
with you, and you won't be harmed. Many people in this
city belong to me." 11Paul stayed on in Corinth for a year
and a half, teaching God's message to the people.
12While Gallio was governor of Achaia, some of the
Jewish leaders got together and grabbed Paul. They
brought him into court 13and said, "This man is trying to

[b] **18.4** *Gentiles*: Here the word is "Greeks." But see the note at 14.1.
[c] **18.6** *shook the dust from his clothes*: This means the same as shaking dust from the feet (see the note at 13.51).

NEW INTERNATIONAL VERSION

tentmaker as they were, he stayed and worked with them.
4Every Sabbath he reasoned in the synagogue, trying to
persuade Jews and Greeks.
5When Silas and Timothy came from Macedonia, Paul
devoted himself exclusively to preaching, testifying to the
Jews that Jesus was the Christ.[a] 6But when the Jews
opposed Paul and became abusive, he shook out his
clothes in protest and said to them, "Your blood be on your
own heads! I am clear of my responsibility. From now on I
will go to the Gentiles."
7Then Paul left the synagogue and went next door to the
house of Titius Justus, a worshiper of God. 8Crispus, the
synagogue ruler, and his entire household believed in the
Lord; and many of the Corinthians who heard him believed
and were baptized.
9One night the Lord spoke to Paul in a vision: "Do not be
afraid; keep on speaking, do not be silent. 10For I am with
you, and no one is going to attack and harm you, because I
have many people in this city." 11So Paul stayed for a year
and a half, teaching them the word of God.
12While Gallio was proconsul of Achaia, the Jews made a
united attack on Paul and brought him into court. 13"This

[a] 5 Or *Messiah;* also in verse 28

NEW LIVING TRANSLATION

Rome. 3Paul lived and worked with them, for they were
tentmakers* just as he was.
4Each Sabbath found Paul at the synagogue, trying to
convince the Jews and Greeks alike. 5And after Silas and
Timothy came down from Macedonia, Paul spent his full
time preaching and testifying to the Jews, telling them,
"The Messiah you are looking for is Jesus." 6But when the
Jews opposed him and insulted him, Paul shook the dust
from his robe and said, "Your blood be upon your own
heads—I am innocent. From now on I will go to the
Gentiles."
7After that he stayed with Titius Justus, a Gentile who
worshiped God and lived next door to the synagogue.
8Crispus, the leader of the synagogue, and all his house-
hold believed in the Lord. Many others in Corinth also
became believers and were baptized.
9One night the Lord spoke to Paul in a vision and told
him, "Don't be afraid! Speak out! Don't be silent! 10For I
am with you, and no one will harm you because many peo-
ple here in this city belong to me." 11So Paul stayed there
for the next year and a half, teaching the word of God.
12But when Gallio became governor of Achaia, some
Jews rose in concerted action against Paul and brought
him before the governor for judgment. 13They accused Paul

18:3 Or *leatherworkers.*

NEW KING JAMES VERSION

came to them. 3So, because he was of the same trade, he
stayed with them and worked; for by occupation they were
tentmakers. 4And he reasoned in the synagogue every
Sabbath, and persuaded both Jews and Greeks.
5When Silas and Timothy had come from Macedonia,
Paul was compelled by the Spirit, and testified to the Jews
that Jesus *is* the Christ. 6But when they opposed him and
blasphemed, he shook *his* garments and said to them,
"Your blood *be* upon your *own* heads; I *am* clean. From
now on I will go to the Gentiles." 7And he departed from
there and entered the house of a certain *man* named
Justus,[a] *one* who worshiped God, whose house was next
door to the synagogue. 8Then Crispus, the ruler of the syn-
agogue, believed on the Lord with all his household. And
many of the Corinthians, hearing, believed and were bap-
tized.
9Now the Lord spoke to Paul in the night by a vision,
"Do not be afraid, but speak, and do not keep silent; 10for I
am with you, and no one will attack you to hurt you; for I
have many people in this city." 11And he continued *there* a
year and six months, teaching the word of God among
them.
12When Gallio was proconsul of Achaia, the Jews with
one accord rose up against Paul and brought him to the

18:7 [a] NU-Text reads *Titius Justus.*

THE MESSAGE

Claudius. Paul moved in with them, and they worked together at their common trade of tentmaking. But every Sabbath he was at the meeting place, doing his best to convince both Jews and Greeks about Jesus.

When Silas and Timothy arrived from Macedonia, Paul was able to give all his time to preaching and teaching, doing everything he could to persuade the Jews that Jesus was in fact God's Messiah. But no such luck. All they did was argue contentiously and contradict him at every turn. Totally exasperated, Paul had finally had it with them and gave it up as a bad job. "Have it your way, then," he said. "You've made your bed; now lie in it. From now on I'm spending my time with the other nations."

He walked out and went to the home of Titius Justus, a God-fearing man who lived right next to the Jews' meeting place. But Paul's efforts with the Jews weren't a total loss, for Crispus, the meeting-place president, put his trust in the Master. His entire family believed with him.

In the course of listening to Paul, a great many Corinthians believed and were baptized. One night the Master spoke to Paul in a dream: "Keep it up, and don't let anyone intimidate or silence you. No matter what happens, I'm with you and no one is going to be able to hurt you. You have no idea how many people I have on my side in this city." That was all he needed to stick it out. He stayed another year and a half, faithfully teaching the Word of God to the Corinthians.

But when Gallio was governor of Achaia province, the Jews got up a campaign against Paul, hauled him into court,

KING JAMES VERSION

13 Saying, This *fellow* persuadeth men to worship God contrary to the law.

14 And when Paul was now about to open *his* mouth, Gallio said unto the Jews, If it were a matter of wrong or wicked lewdness, O *ye* Jews, reason would that I should bear with you:

15 But if it be a question of words and names, and *of* your law, look ye *to it*; for I will be no judge of such *matters*.

16 And he drave them from the judgment seat.

17 Then all the Greeks took Sosthenes, the chief ruler of the synagogue, and beat *him* before the judgment seat. And Gallio cared for none of those things.

18 ¶ And Paul *after this* tarried *there* yet a good while, and then took his leave of the brethren, and sailed thence into Syria, and with him Priscilla and Aquila; having shorn *his* head in Cenchrea: for he had a vow.

19 And he came to Ephesus, and left them there: but he himself entered into the synagogue, and reasoned with the Jews.

20 When they desired *him* to tarry longer time with them, he consented not;

21 But bade them farewell, saying, I must by all means keep this feast that cometh in Jerusalem: but I will return again unto you, if God will. And he sailed from Ephesus.

22 And when he had landed at Caesarea, and gone up, and saluted the church, he went down to Antioch.

23 And after he had spent some time *there*, he departed,

NEW AMERICAN STANDARD BIBLE

13 saying, "This man persuades men to worship God contrary to the law."

14 But when Paul was about to open his mouth, Gallio said to the Jews, "If it were a matter of wrong or of vicious crime, O Jews, it would be reasonable for me to put up with you;

15 but if there are questions about words and names and your own law, look after it yourselves; I am unwilling to be a judge of these matters."

16 And he drove them away from the judgment seat.

17 And they all took hold of Sosthenes, the leader of the synagogue, and *began* beating him in front of the judgment seat. But Gallio was not concerned about any of these things.

18 Paul, having remained many days longer, took leave of the brethren and put out to sea for Syria, and with him were Priscilla and Aquila. In Cenchrea he had his hair cut, for he was keeping a vow.

19 They came to Ephesus, and he left them there. Now he himself entered the synagogue and reasoned with the Jews.

20 When they asked him to stay for a longer time, he did not consent,

21 but taking leave of them and saying, "I will return to you again if God wills," he set sail from Ephesus.

22 When he had landed at Caesarea, he went up and greeted the church, and went down to Antioch.

Third Missionary Journey

23 And having spent some time *there,* he left and passed

NEW CENTURY VERSION

teaching people to worship God in a way that is against our law."
14Paul was about to say something, but Gallio spoke to
the Jews, saying, "I would listen to you Jews if you were
complaining about a crime or some wrong. 15But the
things you are saying are only questions about words and
names—arguments about your own law. So you must
solve this problem yourselves. I don't want to be a judge of
these things." 16And Gallio made them leave the court.
17Then they all grabbed Sosthenes, the leader of the synagogue, and beat him there before the court. But this did not bother Gallio.

Paul Returns to Antioch

18Paul stayed with the believers for many more days.
Then he left and sailed for Syria, with Priscilla and Aquila.
At Cenchrea Paul cut off his hair,[c] because he had made a
promise to God. 19Then they went to Ephesus, where Paul
left Priscilla and Aquila. While Paul was there, he went
into the synagogue and talked with the Jews. 20When they
asked him to stay with them longer, he refused. 21But as
he left, he said, "I will come back to you again if God
wants me to." And so he sailed away from Ephesus.
22When Paul landed at Caesarea, he went and gave
greetings to the church in Jerusalem. After that, Paul went
to Antioch. 23He stayed there for a while and then left and

18:18 [c] **cut...hair** Jews did this to show that the time of a special promise to God was finished.

CONTEMPORARY ENGLISH VERSION

make our people worship God in a way that is against our Law!"
14Even before Paul could speak, Gallio said, "If you were
charging this man with a crime or some other wrong, I
would have to listen to you. 15But since this concerns only
words, names, and your own law, you will have to take
care of it. I refuse to judge such matters." 16Then he sent
them out of the court. 17The crowd grabbed Sosthenes, the
Jewish leader, and beat him up in front of the court. But none of this mattered to Gallio.

Paul Returns to Antioch in Syria

18After Paul had stayed for a while with the Lord's followers in Corinth, he told them good-by and sailed on to Syria with Aquila and Priscilla. But before he left, he had his head shaved[d] at Cenchreae because he had made a promise to God.
19The three of them arrived in Ephesus, where Paul left
Priscilla and Aquila. He then went into the Jewish meeting
place to talk with the people there. 20They asked him to
stay longer, but he refused. 21He told them good-by and
said, "If God lets me, I will come back."
22Paul sailed to Caesarea, where he greeted the church.
Then he went on to Antioch. 23After staying there for a
while, he left and visited several places in Galatia and

[d] **18.18** *he had his head shaved*: Paul had promised to be a "Nazirite" for a while. This meant that for the time of the promise, he could not cut his hair or drink wine. When the time was over, he would have to cut his hair and offer a sacrifice to God.

NEW INTERNATIONAL VERSION

man," they charged, "is persuading the people to worship
God in ways contrary to the law."
[14]Just as Paul was about to speak, Gallio said to the
Jews, "If you Jews were making a complaint about some
misdemeanor or serious crime, it would be reasonable for
me to listen to you. [15]But since it involves questions about
words and names and your own law—settle the matter
yourselves. I will not be a judge of such things." [16]So he
had them ejected from the court. [17]Then they all turned on
Sosthenes the synagogue ruler and beat him in front of the
court. But Gallio showed no concern whatever.

Priscilla, Aquila and Apollos

[18]Paul stayed on in Corinth for some time. Then he left
the brothers and sailed for Syria, accompanied by Priscilla
and Aquila. Before he sailed, he had his hair cut off at
Cenchrea because of a vow he had taken. [19]They arrived at
Ephesus, where Paul left Priscilla and Aquila. He himself
went into the synagogue and reasoned with the Jews.
[20]When they asked him to spend more time with them, he
declined. [21]But as he left, he promised, "I will come back if
it is God's will." Then he set sail from Ephesus. [22]When he
landed at Caesarea, he went up and greeted the church and
then went down to Antioch.
[23]After spending some time in Antioch, Paul set out from

NEW LIVING TRANSLATION

of "persuading people to worship God in ways that are
contrary to the law." [14]But just as Paul started to make his
defense, Gallio turned to Paul's accusers and said, "Listen,
you Jews, if this were a case involving some wrongdoing or
a serious crime, I would be obliged to listen to you. [15]But
since it is merely a question of words and names and your
Jewish laws, you take care of it. I refuse to judge such mat-
ters." [16]And he drove them out of the courtroom. [17]The
mob had grabbed Sosthenes, the leader of the synagogue,
and had beaten him right there in the courtroom. But
Gallio paid no attention.

Paul Returns to Antioch of Syria

[18]Paul stayed in Corinth for some time after that and then
said good-bye to the brothers and sisters* and sailed for the
coast of Syria, taking Priscilla and Aquila with him. (Earlier,
at Cenchrea, Paul had shaved his head according to Jewish
custom, for he had taken a vow.) [19]When they arrived at the
port of Ephesus, Paul left the others behind. But while he
was there, he went to the synagogue to debate with the
Jews. [20]They asked him to stay longer, but he declined. [21]So
he left, saying, "I will come back later,* God willing." Then
he set sail from Ephesus. [22]The next stop was at the port of
Caesarea. From there he went up and visited the church at
Jerusalem* and then went back to Antioch.
[23]After spending some time in Antioch, Paul went back

18:18 Greek *brothers;* also in 18:27. **18:21** Some manuscripts read *"I must by all means be at Jerusalem for the upcoming festival, but I will come back later."* **18:22** Greek *the church.*

NEW KING JAMES VERSION

judgment seat, [13]saying, "This *fellow* persuades men to
worship God contrary to the law."
[14]And when Paul was about to open *his* mouth, Gallio
said to the Jews, "If it were a matter of wrongdoing or
wicked crimes, O Jews, there would be reason why I should
bear with you. [15]But if it is a question of words and names
and your own law, look *to it* yourselves; for I do not want
to be a judge of such *matters.*" [16]And he drove them from
the judgment seat. [17]Then all the Greeks[b] took Sosthenes,
the ruler of the synagogue, and beat *him* before the judg-
ment seat. But Gallio took no notice of these things.

Paul Returns to Antioch

[18]So Paul still remained a good while. Then he took
leave of the brethren and sailed for Syria, and Priscilla and
Aquila *were* with him. He had *his* hair cut off at Cenchrea,
for he had taken a vow. [19]And he came to Ephesus, and
left them there; but he himself entered the synagogue and
reasoned with the Jews. [20]When they asked *him* to stay a
longer time with them, he did not consent, [21]but took leave
of them, saying, "I must by all means keep this coming
feast in Jerusalem;[c] but I will return again to you, God
willing." And he sailed from Ephesus.
[22]And when he had landed at Caesarea, and gone up and
greeted the church, he went down to Antioch. [23]After he
had spent some time *there,* he departed and went over the

18:17 [b] NU-Text reads *they all.* **18:21** [c] NU-Text omits *I must* through *Jerusalem.*

THE MESSAGE

and filed charges: "This man is seducing people into acts of
worship that are illegal."

Just as Paul was about to defend himself, Gallio inter-
rupted and said to the Jews, "If this was a matter of crimi-
nal conduct, I would gladly hear you out. But it sounds to
me like one more Jewish squabble, another of your endless
hairsplitting quarrels over religion. Take care of it on your
own time. I can't be bothered with this nonsense," and he
cleared them out of the courtroom.

Now the street rabble turned on Sosthenes, the new
meeting-place president, and beat him up in plain sight of
the court. Gallio didn't raise a finger. He could not have
cared less.

Ephesus

Paul stayed a while longer in Corinth, but then it was
time to take leave of his friends. Saying his goodbyes, he
sailed for Syria, Priscilla and Aquila with him. Before
boarding the ship in the harbor town of Cenchrea, he had
his head shaved as part of a vow he had taken.

They landed in Ephesus, where Priscilla and Aquila got
off and stayed. Paul left the ship briefly to go to the meet-
ing place and preach to the Jews. They wanted him to stay
longer, but he said he couldn't. But after saying goodbye,
he promised, "I'll be back, God willing."

From Ephesus he sailed to Caesarea. He greeted the
assembly of Christians there, and then went on to Antioch,
completing the journey.

After spending a considerable time with the Antioch

KING JAMES VERSION

and went over *all* the country of Galatia and Phrygia in order, strengthening all the disciples.

24 ¶ And a certain Jew named Apollos, born at Alexandria, an eloquent man, *and* mighty in the scriptures, came to Ephesus.

25 This man was instructed in the way of the Lord; and being fervent in the spirit, he spake and taught diligently the things of the Lord, knowing only the baptism of John.

26 And he began to speak boldly in the synagogue: whom when Aquila and Priscilla had heard, they took him unto *them*, and expounded unto him the way of God more perfectly.

27 And when he was disposed to pass into Achaia, the brethren wrote, exhorting the disciples to receive him: who, when he was come, helped them much which had believed through grace:

28 For he mightily convinced the Jews, *and that* publickly, shewing by the scriptures that Jesus was Christ.

19 And it came to pass, that, while Apollos was at Corinth, Paul having passed through the upper coasts came to Ephesus: and finding certain disciples,

2 He said unto them, Have ye received the Holy Ghost

NEW AMERICAN STANDARD BIBLE

successively through the Galatian region and Phrygia, strengthening all the disciples.

24 Now a Jew named Apollos, an Alexandrian by birth, an eloquent man, came to Ephesus; and he was mighty in the Scriptures.

25 This man had been instructed in the way of the Lord; and being fervent in spirit, he was speaking and teaching accurately the things concerning Jesus, being acquainted only with the baptism of John;

26 and he began to speak out boldly in the synagogue. But when Priscilla and Aquila heard him, they took him aside and explained to him the way of God more accurately.

27 And when he wanted to go across to Achaia, the brethren encouraged him and wrote to the disciples to welcome him; and when he had arrived, he greatly helped those who had believed through grace,

28 for he powerfully refuted the Jews in public, demonstrating by the Scriptures that Jesus was the Christ.

Paul at Ephesus

19 It happened that while Apollos was at Corinth, Paul passed through the upper country and came to Ephesus, and found some disciples.

2 He said to them, "Did you receive the Holy Spirit

NEW CENTURY VERSION

went through the regions of Galatia and Phrygia. He traveled from town to town in these regions, giving strength to all the followers.

Apollos in Ephesus and Corinth

24A Jew named Apollos came to Ephesus. He was born in the city of Alexandria and was a good speaker who knew the Scriptures well. 25He had been taught about the way of the Lord and was always very excited when he spoke and taught the truth about Jesus. But the only baptism Apollos knew about was the baptism that John[d] taught. 26Apollos began to speak very boldly in the synagogue, and when Priscilla and Aquila heard him, they took him to their home and helped him better understand the way of God. 27Now Apollos wanted to go to the country of Southern Greece. So the believers helped him and wrote a letter to the followers there, asking them to accept him. These followers had believed in Jesus because of God's grace, and when Apollos arrived, he helped them very much. 28He argued very strongly with the Jews before all the people, clearly proving with the Scriptures that Jesus is the Christ.

Paul in Ephesus

19 While Apollos was in Corinth, Paul was visiting some places on the way to Ephesus. There he found some followers 2and asked them, "Did you receive the Holy Spirit when you believed?"

18:25 [d] **John** John the Baptist, who preached to people about Christ's coming (Luke 3).

CONTEMPORARY ENGLISH VERSION

Phrygia. He helped the followers there to become stronger in their faith.

Apollos in Ephesus

24A Jewish man named Apollos came to Ephesus. Apollos had been born in the city of Alexandria. He was a very good speaker and knew a lot about the Scriptures. 25He also knew much about the Lord's Way,[e] and he spoke about it with great excitement. What he taught about Jesus was right, but all he knew was John's message about baptism.

26Apollos started speaking bravely in the Jewish meeting place. But when Priscilla and Aquila heard him, they took him to their home and helped him understand God's Way even better.

27Apollos decided to travel through Achaia. So the Lord's followers wrote letters, encouraging the followers there to welcome him. After Apollos arrived in Achaia, he was a great help to everyone who had put their faith in the Lord Jesus because of God's kindness. 28He got into fierce arguments with the Jewish people, and in public he used the Scriptures to prove that Jesus is the Messiah.

Paul in Ephesus

19 While Apollos was in Corinth, Paul traveled across the hill country to Ephesus, where he met some of the Lord's followers. 2He asked them, "When you put your faith in Jesus, were you given the Holy Spirit?"

[e] 18.25 *the Lord's Way*: See the note at 9.2.

NEW INTERNATIONAL VERSION

there and traveled from place to place throughout the region of Galatia and Phrygia, strengthening all the disciples.

24Meanwhile a Jew named Apollos, a native of Alexandria, came to Ephesus. He was a learned man, with a thorough knowledge of the Scriptures. 25He had been instructed in the way of the Lord, and he spoke with great fervor[b] and taught about Jesus accurately, though he knew only the baptism of John. 26He began to speak boldly in the synagogue. When Priscilla and Aquila heard him, they invited him to their home and explained to him the way of God more adequately.

27When Apollos wanted to go to Achaia, the brothers encouraged him and wrote to the disciples there to welcome him. On arriving, he was a great help to those who by grace had believed. 28For he vigorously refuted the Jews in public debate, proving from the Scriptures that Jesus was the Christ.

Paul in Ephesus

19 While Apollos was at Corinth, Paul took the road through the interior and arrived at Ephesus. There he found some disciples 2and asked them, "Did you receive the Holy Spirit when[a] you believed?"

[b] 25 Or *with fervor in the Spirit* [a] 2 Or *after*

NEW LIVING TRANSLATION

to Galatia and Phrygia, visiting all the believers,* encouraging them and helping them to grow in the Lord.

Apollos Instructed at Ephesus

24Meanwhile, a Jew named Apollos, an eloquent speaker who knew the Scriptures well, had just arrived in Ephesus from Alexandria in Egypt. 25He had been taught the way of the Lord and talked to others with great enthusiasm and accuracy about Jesus. However, he knew only about John's baptism. 26When Priscilla and Aquila heard him preaching boldly in the synagogue, they took him aside and explained the way of God more accurately.

27Apollos had been thinking about going to Achaia, and the brothers and sisters in Ephesus encouraged him in this. They wrote to the believers in Achaia, asking them to welcome him. When he arrived there, he proved to be of great benefit to those who, by God's grace, had believed. 28He refuted all the Jews with powerful arguments in public debate. Using the Scriptures, he explained to them, "The Messiah you are looking for is Jesus."

Paul's Third Missionary Journey

19 While Apollos was in Corinth, Paul traveled through the interior provinces. Finally, he came to Ephesus, where he found several believers.* 2"Did you receive the Holy Spirit when you believed?" he asked them.

18:23 Greek *disciples;* also in 18:27. 19:1 Greek *disciples;* also in 19:9, 30.

NEW KING JAMES VERSION

region of Galatia and Phrygia in order, strengthening all the disciples.

Ministry of Apollos

24Now a certain Jew named Apollos, born at Alexandria, an eloquent man *and* mighty in the Scriptures, came to Ephesus. 25This man had been instructed in the way of the Lord; and being fervent in spirit, he spoke and taught accurately the things of the Lord, though he knew only the baptism of John. 26So he began to speak boldly in the synagogue. When Aquila and Priscilla heard him, they took him aside and explained to him the way of God more accurately. 27And when he desired to cross to Achaia, the brethren wrote, exhorting the disciples to receive him; and when he arrived, he greatly helped those who had believed through grace; 28for he vigorously refuted the Jews publicly, showing from the Scriptures that Jesus is the Christ.

Paul at Ephesus

19 And it happened, while Apollos was at Corinth, that Paul, having passed through the upper regions, came to Ephesus. And finding some disciples 2he said to them, "Did you receive the Holy Spirit when you believed?"

THE MESSAGE

Christians, Paul set off again for Galatia and Phrygia, retracing his old tracks, one town after another, putting fresh heart into the disciples.

A man named Apollos came to Ephesus. He was a Jew, born in Alexandria, Egypt, and a terrific speaker, eloquent and powerful in his preaching of the Scriptures. He was well-educated in the way of the Master and fiery in his enthusiasm. Apollos was accurate in everything he taught about Jesus up to a point, but he only went as far as the baptism of John. He preached with power in the meeting place. When Priscilla and Aquila heard him, they took him aside and told him the rest of the story.

When Apollos decided to go on to Achaia province, his Ephesian friends gave their blessing and wrote a letter of recommendation for him, urging the disciples there to welcome him with open arms. The welcome paid off: Apollos turned out to be a great help to those who had become believers through God's immense generosity. He was particularly effective in public debate with the Jews as he brought out proof after convincing proof from the Scriptures that Jesus was in fact God's Messiah.

19 Now, it happened that while Apollos was away in Corinth, Paul made his way down through the mountains, came to Ephesus, and happened on some disciples there. The first thing he said was, "Did you receive the Holy Spirit when you believed? Did you take God into your mind only, or did you also embrace him with your heart? Did he get inside you?"

KING JAMES VERSION

since ye believed? And they said unto him, We have not so
much as heard whether there be any Holy Ghost.
3 And he said unto them, Unto what then were ye baptized? And they said, Unto John's baptism.
4 Then said Paul, John verily baptized with the baptism of repentance, saying unto the people, that they should believe on him which should come after him, that is, on Christ Jesus.
5 When they heard *this*, they were baptized in the name of the Lord Jesus.
6 And when Paul had laid *his* hands upon them, the Holy Ghost came on them; and they spake with tongues, and prophesied.
7 And all the men were about twelve.
8 ¶ And he went into the synagogue, and spake boldly for the space of three months, disputing and persuading the things concerning the kingdom of God.
9 But when divers were hardened, and believed not, but spake evil of that way before the multitude, he departed from them, and separated the disciples, disputing daily in the school of one Tyrannus.
10 And this continued by the space of two years; so that all they which dwelt in Asia heard the word of the Lord Jesus, both Jews and Greeks.
11 And God wrought special miracles by the hands of Paul:

NEW AMERICAN STANDARD BIBLE

when you believed?" And they *said* to him, "No, we have not even heard whether there is a Holy Spirit."
3 And he said, "Into what then were you baptized?" And they said, "Into John's baptism."
4 Paul said, "John baptized with the baptism of repentance, telling the people to believe in Him who was coming after him, that is, in Jesus."
5 When they heard this, they were baptized in the name of the Lord Jesus.
6 And when Paul had laid his hands upon them, the Holy Spirit came on them, and they *began* speaking with tongues and prophesying.
7 There were in all about twelve men.
8 And he entered the synagogue and continued speaking out boldly for three months, reasoning and persuading *them* about the kingdom of God.
9 But when some were becoming hardened and disobedient, speaking evil of the Way before the people, he withdrew from them and took away the disciples, reasoning daily in the school of Tyrannus.
10 This took place for two years, so that all who lived in Asia heard the word of the Lord, both Jews and Greeks.

Miracles at Ephesus

11 God was performing extraordinary miracles by the hands of Paul,

NEW CENTURY VERSION

They said, "We have never even heard of a Holy Spirit."
3So he asked, "What kind of baptism did you have?"
They said, "It was the baptism that John[a] taught."
4Paul said, "John's baptism was a baptism of changed hearts and lives. He told people to believe in the one who would come after him, and that one is Jesus."
5When they heard this, they were baptized in the name
of the Lord Jesus. 6Then Paul laid his hands on them,[b] and the Holy Spirit came upon them. They began speaking different languages[c] and prophesying. 7There were about twelve people in this group.
8Paul went into the synagogue and spoke out boldly for three months. He talked with the Jews and persuaded them to accept the things he said about the kingdom of God.
9But some of the Jews became stubborn. They refused to believe and said evil things about the Way of Jesus before all the people. So Paul left them, and taking the followers with him, he went to the school of a man named Tyrannus.
There Paul talked with people every day 10for two years. Because of his work, every Jew and Greek in the country of Asia heard the word of the Lord.

The Sons of Sceva

11God used Paul to do some very special miracles.

19:3 [a] **John** John the Baptist, who preached to people about Christ's coming (Luke 3). 19:6 [b] **laid his hands on them** The laying on of hands had many purposes, including the giving of a blessing, power, or authority. 19:6 [c] **languages** This can also be translated "tongues."

CONTEMPORARY ENGLISH VERSION

"No!" they answered. "We have never even heard of the Holy Spirit."
3"Then why were you baptized?" Paul asked.
They answered, "Because of what John taught."[a]
4Paul replied, "John baptized people so that they would turn to God. But he also told them that someone else was coming, and that they should put their faith in him. Jesus
is the one that John was talking about." 5After the people
heard Paul say this, they were baptized in the name of the
Lord Jesus. 6Then Paul placed his hands on them. The Holy Spirit was given to them, and they spoke unknown languages and prophesied. 7There were about twelve men in this group.
8For three months Paul went to the Jewish meeting place and talked bravely with the people about God's kingdom.
He tried to win them over, 9but some of them were stubborn and refused to believe. In front of everyone they said terrible things about God's Way. Paul left and took the followers with him to the lecture hall of Tyrannus. He spoke
there every day 10for two years, until every Jew and Gentile[b] in Asia had heard the Lord's message.

The Sons of Sceva

11God gave Paul the power to work great miracles.

[a] **19.3** *Then why were you baptized? . . . Because of what John taught*: Or "In whose name were you baptized? . . . We were baptized in John's name." [b] **19.10** *Gentile(s)*: The text has "Greek(s)" (see the note at 14.1).

NEW INTERNATIONAL VERSION

They answered, "No, we have not even heard that there is a Holy Spirit."

3So Paul asked, "Then what baptism did you receive?"

"John's baptism," they replied.

4Paul said, "John's baptism was a baptism of repentance. He told the people to believe in the one coming after him, that is, in Jesus."
5On hearing this, they were baptized into[b] the name of the Lord Jesus.
6When Paul placed his hands on them, the Holy Spirit came on them, and they spoke in tongues[c] and prophesied.
7There were about twelve men in all.

8Paul entered the synagogue and spoke boldly there for three months, arguing persuasively about the kingdom of God.
9But some of them became obstinate; they refused to believe and publicly maligned the Way. So Paul left them. He took the disciples with him and had discussions daily in the lecture hall of Tyrannus.
10This went on for two years, so that all the Jews and Greeks who lived in the province of Asia heard the word of the Lord.

11God did extraordinary miracles through Paul,
12so that

[b] 5 Or *in* [c] 6 Or *other languages*

NEW LIVING TRANSLATION

"No," they replied, "we don't know what you mean. We haven't even heard that there is a Holy Spirit."

3"Then what baptism did you experience?" he asked.

And they replied, "The baptism of John."

4Paul said, "John's baptism was to demonstrate a desire to turn from sin and turn to God. John himself told the people to believe in Jesus, the one John said would come later."

5As soon as they heard this, they were baptized in the name of the Lord Jesus.
6Then when Paul laid his hands on them, the Holy Spirit came on them, and they spoke in other tongues and prophesied.
7There were about twelve men in all.

Paul Ministers in Ephesus

8Then Paul went to the synagogue and preached boldly for the next three months, arguing persuasively about the Kingdom of God.
9But some rejected his message and publicly spoke against the Way, so Paul left the synagogue and took the believers with him. Then he began preaching daily at the lecture hall of Tyrannus.
10This went on for the next two years, so that people throughout the province of Asia—both Jews and Greeks—heard the Lord's message.

11God gave Paul the power to do unusual miracles,
12so

NEW KING JAMES VERSION

So they said to him, "We have not so much as heard whether there is a Holy Spirit."

3And he said to them, "Into what then were you baptized?"

So they said, "Into John's baptism."

4Then Paul said, "John indeed baptized with a baptism of repentance, saying to the people that they should believe on Him who would come after him, that is, on Christ Jesus."

5When they heard *this,* they were baptized in the name of the Lord Jesus.
6And when Paul had laid hands on them, the Holy Spirit came upon them, and they spoke with tongues and prophesied.
7Now the men were about twelve in all.

8And he went into the synagogue and spoke boldly for three months, reasoning and persuading concerning the things of the kingdom of God.
9But when some were hardened and did not believe, but spoke evil of the Way before the multitude, he departed from them and withdrew the disciples, reasoning daily in the school of Tyrannus.
10And this continued for two years, so that all who dwelt in Asia heard the word of the Lord Jesus, both Jews and Greeks.

Miracles Glorify Christ

11Now God worked unusual miracles by the hands of

THE MESSAGE

"We've never even heard of that—a Holy Spirit? God within us?"

"How were you baptized, then?" asked Paul.

"In John's baptism."

"That explains it," said Paul. "John preached a baptism of radical life-change so that people would be ready to receive the One coming after him, who turned out to be Jesus. If you've been baptized in John's baptism, you're ready now for the real thing, for Jesus."

And they were. As soon as they heard of it, they were baptized in the name of the Master Jesus. Paul put his hands on their heads and the Holy Spirit entered them. From that moment on, they were praising God in tongues and talking about God's actions. Altogether there were about twelve people there that day.

Paul then went straight to the meeting place. He had the run of the place for three months, doing his best to make the things of the kingdom of God real and convincing to them. But then resistance began to form as some of them began spreading evil rumors through the congregation about the Christian way of life. So Paul left, taking the disciples with him, and set up shop in the school of Tyrannus, holding class there daily. He did this for two years, giving everyone in the province of Asia, Jews as well as Greeks, ample opportunity to hear the Message of the Master.

Witches Came Out of the Woodwork

God did powerful things through Paul, things quite out of the ordinary. The word got around and people started taking

KING JAMES VERSION

12 So that from his body were brought unto the sick handkerchiefs or aprons, and the diseases departed from them, and the evil spirits went out of them.

13 ¶ Then certain of the vagabond Jews, exorcists, took upon them to call over them which had evil spirits the name of the Lord Jesus, saying, We adjure you by Jesus whom Paul preacheth.

14 And there were seven sons of *one* Sceva, a Jew, *and* chief of the priests, which did so.

15 And the evil spirit answered and said, Jesus I know, and Paul I know; but who are ye?

16 And the man in whom the evil spirit was leaped on them, and overcame them, and prevailed against them, so that they fled out of that house naked and wounded.

17 And this was known to all the Jews and Greeks also dwelling at Ephesus; and fear fell on them all, and the name of the Lord Jesus was magnified.

18 And many that believed came, and confessed, and shewed their deeds.

19 Many of them also which used curious arts brought their books together, and burned them before all *men*: and they counted the price of them, and found *it* fifty thousand *pieces* of silver.

20 So mightily grew the word of God and prevailed.

21 ¶ After these things were ended, Paul purposed in the spirit, when he had passed through Macedonia and Achaia, to go to Jerusalem, saying, After I have been there, I must also see Rome.

NEW AMERICAN STANDARD BIBLE

12 so that handkerchiefs or aprons were even carried from his body to the sick, and the diseases left them and the evil spirits went out.

13 But also some of the Jewish exorcists, who went from place to place, attempted to name over those who had the evil spirits the name of the Lord Jesus, saying, "I adjure you by Jesus whom Paul preaches."

14 Seven sons of one Sceva, a Jewish chief priest, were doing this.

15 And the evil spirit answered and said to them, "I recognize Jesus, and I know about Paul, but who are you?"

16 And the man, in whom was the evil spirit, leaped on them and subdued all of them and overpowered them, so that they fled out of that house naked and wounded.

17 This became known to all, both Jews and Greeks, who lived in Ephesus; and fear fell upon them all and the name of the Lord Jesus was being magnified.

18 Many also of those who had believed kept coming, confessing and disclosing their practices.

19 And many of those who practiced magic brought their books together and *began* burning them in the sight of everyone; and they counted up the price of them and found it fifty thousand pieces of silver.

20 So the word of the Lord was growing mightily and prevailing.

21 Now after these things were finished, Paul purposed in the spirit to go to Jerusalem after he had passed through Macedonia and Achaia, saying, "After I have been there, I must also see Rome."

NEW CENTURY VERSION

12Some people took handkerchiefs and clothes that Paul had used and put them on the sick. When they did this, the sick were healed and evil spirits left them.

13But some Jews also were traveling around and making evil spirits go out of people. They tried to use the name of the Lord Jesus to force the evil spirits out. They would say, "By the same Jesus that Paul talks about, I order you to come out!" 14Seven sons of Sceva, a leading Jewish priest, were doing this.

15But one time an evil spirit said to them, "I know Jesus, and I know about Paul, but who are you?"

16Then the man who had the evil spirit jumped on them. Because he was so much stronger than all of them, they ran away from the house naked and hurt. 17All the people in Ephesus—Jews and Greeks—learned about this and were filled with fear and gave great honor to the Lord Jesus. 18Many of the believers began to confess openly and tell all the evil things they had done. 19Some of them who had used magic brought their magic books and burned them before everyone. Those books were worth about fifty thousand silver coins.[d]

20So in a powerful way the word of the Lord kept spreading and growing.

21After these things, Paul decided to go to Jerusalem, planning to go through the countries of Macedonia and Southern Greece and then on to Jerusalem. He said, "After I have been to Jerusalem, I must also visit Rome." 22Paul

19:19 [d] **fifty thousand silver coins** Probably drachmas. One coin was enough to pay a worker for one day's labor.

CONTEMPORARY ENGLISH VERSION

12People even took handkerchiefs and aprons that had touched Paul's body, and they carried them to everyone who was sick. All of the sick people were healed, and the evil spirits went out.

13Some Jewish men started going around trying to force out evil spirits by using the name of the Lord Jesus. They said to the spirits, "Come out in the name of that same Jesus that Paul preaches about!"

14Seven sons of a Jewish high priest named Sceva were doing this, 15when an evil spirit said to them, "I know Jesus! And I have heard about Paul. But who are you?" 16Then the man with the evil spirit jumped on them and beat them up. They ran out of the house, naked and bruised.

17When the Jews and Gentiles[b] in Ephesus heard about this, they were so frightened that they praised the name of the Lord Jesus. 18Many who were followers now started telling everyone about the evil things they had been doing. 19Some who had been practicing witchcraft even brought their books and burned them in public. These books were worth about fifty thousand silver coins. 20So the Lord's message spread and became even more powerful.

The Riot in Ephesus

21After all of this had happened, Paul decided[c] to visit Macedonia and Achaia on his way to Jerusalem. Paul had said, "From there I will go on to Rome." 22So he sent his

[b] **19.17** *Gentile(s)*: The text has "Greek(s)" (see the note at 14.1).
[c] **19.21** *Paul decided*: Or "Paul was led by the Holy Spirit."

NEW INTERNATIONAL VERSION

even handkerchiefs and aprons that had touched him were taken to the sick, and their illnesses were cured and the evil spirits left them.

[13]Some Jews who went around driving out evil spirits tried to invoke the name of the Lord Jesus over those who were demon-possessed. They would say, "In the name of Jesus, whom Paul preaches, I command you to come out." [14]Seven sons of Sceva, a Jewish chief priest, were doing this. [15]⌊One day⌋ the evil spirit answered them, "Jesus I know, and I know about Paul, but who are you?" [16]Then the man who had the evil spirit jumped on them and overpowered them all. He gave them such a beating that they ran out of the house naked and bleeding.

[17]When this became known to the Jews and Greeks living in Ephesus, they were all seized with fear, and the name of the Lord Jesus was held in high honor. [18]Many of those who believed now came and openly confessed their evil deeds. [19]A number who had practiced sorcery brought their scrolls together and burned them publicly. When they calculated the value of the scrolls, the total came to fifty thousand drachmas.[d] [20]In this way the word of the Lord spread widely and grew in power.

[21]After all this had happened, Paul decided to go to Jerusalem, passing through Macedonia and Achaia. "After I have been there," he said, "I must visit Rome also." [22]He

[d] *19* A drachma was a silver coin worth about a day's wages.

NEW LIVING TRANSLATION

that even when handkerchiefs or cloths that had touched his skin were placed on sick people, they were healed of their diseases, and any evil spirits within them came out.

[13]A team of Jews who were traveling from town to town casting out evil spirits tried to use the name of the Lord Jesus. The incantation they used was this: "I command you by Jesus, whom Paul preaches, to come out!" [14]Seven sons of Sceva, a leading priest, were doing this. [15]But when they tried it on a man possessed by an evil spirit, the spirit replied, "I know Jesus, and I know Paul. But who are you?" [16]And he leaped on them and attacked them with such violence that they fled from the house, naked and badly injured.

[17]The story of what happened spread quickly all through Ephesus, to Jews and Greeks alike. A solemn fear descended on the city, and the name of the Lord Jesus was greatly honored. [18]Many who became believers confessed their sinful practices. [19]A number of them who had been practicing magic brought their incantation books and burned them at a public bonfire. The value of the books was several million dollars.* [20]So the message about the Lord spread widely and had a powerful effect.

The Riot in Ephesus

[21]Afterward Paul felt impelled by the Holy Spirit* to go over to Macedonia and Achaia before returning to Jerusalem. "And after that," he said, "I must go on to Rome!"

19:19 Greek *50,000 pieces of silver,* each of which was the equivalent of a day's wage. **19:21** Or *purposed in his spirit.*

NEW KING JAMES VERSION

Paul, [12]so that even handkerchiefs or aprons were brought from his body to the sick, and the diseases left them and the evil spirits went out of them. [13]Then some of the itinerant Jewish exorcists took it upon themselves to call the name of the Lord Jesus over those who had evil spirits, saying, "We[a] exorcise you by the Jesus whom Paul preaches." [14]Also there were seven sons of Sceva, a Jewish chief priest, who did so.

[15]And the evil spirit answered and said, "Jesus I know, and Paul I know; but who are you?"

[16]Then the man in whom the evil spirit was leaped on them, overpowered[b] them, and prevailed against them,[c] so that they fled out of that house naked and wounded. [17]This became known both to all Jews and Greeks dwelling in Ephesus; and fear fell on them all, and the name of the Lord Jesus was magnified. [18]And many who had believed came confessing and telling their deeds. [19]Also, many of those who had practiced magic brought their books together and burned *them* in the sight of all. And they counted up the value of them, and *it* totaled fifty thousand *pieces* of silver. [20]So the word of the Lord grew mightily and prevailed.

The Riot at Ephesus

[21]When these things were accomplished, Paul purposed in the Spirit, when he had passed through Macedonia and Achaia, to go to Jerusalem, saying, "After I have been there, I must also see Rome." [22]So he sent into Macedonia

19:13 [a] NU-Text reads *I.* **19:16** [b] M-Text reads *and they overpowered.* [c] NU-Text reads *both of them.*

THE MESSAGE

pieces of clothing—handkerchiefs and scarves and the like—that had touched Paul's skin and then touching the sick with them. The touch did it—they were healed and whole.

Some itinerant Jewish exorcists who happened to be in town at the time tried their hand at what they assumed to be Paul's "game." They pronounced the name of the Master Jesus over victims of evil spirits, saying, "I command you by the Jesus preached by Paul!" The seven sons of a certain Sceva, a Jewish high priest, were trying to do this on a man when the evil spirit talked back: "I know Jesus and I've heard of Paul, but who are you?" Then the possessed man went berserk—jumped the exorcists, beat them up, and tore off their clothes. Naked and bloody, they got away as best they could.

It was soon news all over Ephesus among both Jews and Greeks. The realization spread that God was in and behind this. Curiosity about Paul developed into reverence for the Master Jesus. Many of those who thus believed came out of the closet and made a clean break with their secret sorceries. All kinds of witches and warlocks came out of the woodwork with their books of spells and incantations and made a huge bonfire of them. Someone estimated their worth at fifty thousand silver coins. In such ways it became evident that the Word of the Master was now sovereign and prevailed in Ephesus.

The Goddess Artemis

After all this had come to a head, Paul decided it was time to move on to Macedonia and Achaia provinces, and

KING JAMES VERSION

22 So he sent into Macedonia two of them that ministered unto him, Timotheus and Erastus; but he himself stayed in Asia for a season.

23 And the same time there arose no small stir about that way.

24 For a certain *man* named Demetrius, a silversmith, which made silver shrines for Diana, brought no small gain unto the craftsmen;

25 Whom he called together with the workmen of like occupation, and said, Sirs, ye know that by this craft we have our wealth.

26 Moreover ye see and hear, that not alone at Ephesus, but almost throughout all Asia, this Paul hath persuaded and turned away much people, saying that they be no gods, which are made with hands:

27 So that not only this our craft is in danger to be set at nought; but also that the temple of the great goddess Diana should be despised, and her magnificence should be destroyed, whom all Asia and the world worshippeth.

28 And when they heard *these sayings*, they were full of wrath, and cried out, saying, Great *is* Diana of the Ephesians.

29 And the whole city was filled with confusion: and having caught Gaius and Aristarchus, men of Macedonia, Paul's companions in travel, they rushed with one accord into the theatre.

30 And when Paul would have entered in unto the people, the disciples suffered him not.

NEW AMERICAN STANDARD BIBLE

22 And having sent into Macedonia two of those who ministered to him, Timothy and Erastus, he himself stayed in Asia for a while.

23 About that time there occurred no small disturbance concerning the Way.

24 For a man named Demetrius, a silversmith, who made silver shrines of Artemis, was bringing no little business to the craftsmen;

25 these he gathered together with the workmen of similar *trades,* and said, "Men, you know that our prosperity depends upon this business.

26 "You see and hear that not only in Ephesus, but in almost all of Asia, this Paul has persuaded and turned away a considerable number of people, saying that gods made with hands are no gods *at all.*

27 "Not only is there danger that this trade of ours fall into disrepute, but also that the temple of the great goddess Artemis be regarded as worthless and that she whom all of Asia and the world worship will even be dethroned from her magnificence."

28 When they heard *this* and were filled with rage, they *began* crying out, saying, "Great is Artemis of the Ephesians!"

29 The city was filled with the confusion, and they rushed with one accord into the theater, dragging along Gaius and Aristarchus, Paul's traveling companions from Macedonia.

30 And when Paul wanted to go into the assembly, the disciples would not let him.

NEW CENTURY VERSION

sent Timothy and Erastus, two of his helpers, ahead to Macedonia, but he himself stayed in Asia for a while.

Trouble in Ephesus

23 And during that time, there was some serious trouble
in Ephesus about the Way of Jesus. 24 A man named
Demetrius, who worked with silver, made little silver mod-
els that looked like the temple of the goddess Artemis.[e]
Those who did this work made much money. 25 Demetrius
had a meeting with them and some others who did the
same kind of work. He told them, "Men, you know that we
make a lot of money from our business. 26 But look at what
this man Paul is doing. He has convinced and turned away
many people in Ephesus and in almost all of Asia! He says
the gods made by human hands are not real. 27 There is a
danger that our business will lose its good name, but there
is also another danger: People will begin to think that the
temple of the great goddess Artemis is not important. Her
greatness will be destroyed, and Artemis is the goddess
that everyone in Asia and the whole world worships."
28 When the others heard this, they became very angry
and shouted, "Artemis, the goddess of Ephesus, is great!"
29 The whole city became confused. The people grabbed
Gaius and Aristarchus, who were from Macedonia and
were traveling with Paul, and ran to the theater. 30 Paul
wanted to go in and talk to the crowd, but the followers

19:24 [e] **Artemis** A Greek goddess that the people of Asia Minor worshiped.

CONTEMPORARY ENGLISH VERSION

two helpers, Timothy and Erastus, to Macedonia. But he stayed on in Asia for a while.

23 At that time there was serious trouble because of the
Lord's Way.[d] 24 A silversmith named Demetrius had a busi-
ness that made silver models of the temple of the goddess
Artemis. Those who worked for him earned a lot of money.
25 Demetrius brought together everyone who was in the
same business and said:

Friends, you know that we make a good living at this.
26 But you have surely seen and heard how this man
Paul is upsetting a lot of people, not only in Ephesus,
but almost everywhere in Asia. He claims that the gods
we humans make are not really gods at all. 27 Everyone
will start saying terrible things about our business. They
will stop respecting the temple of the goddess Artemis,
who is worshiped in Asia and all over the world. Our
great goddess will be forgotten!

28 When the workers heard this, they got angry and
started shouting, "Great is Artemis, the goddess of the
Ephesians!" 29 Soon the whole city was in a riot, and some
men grabbed Gaius and Aristarchus, who had come from
Macedonia with Paul. Then everyone in the crowd rushed
to the place where the town meetings were held.
30 Paul wanted to go out and speak to the people, but the
Lord's followers would not let him. 31 A few of the local

[d] **19.23** *the Lord's Way*: See the note at 9.2.

NEW INTERNATIONAL VERSION

sent two of his helpers, Timothy and Erastus, to Macedonia, while he stayed in the province of Asia a little longer.

The Riot in Ephesus

23About that time there arose a great disturbance about the Way. 24A silversmith named Demetrius, who made silver shrines of Artemis, brought in no little business for the craftsmen. 25He called them together, along with the workmen in related trades, and said: "Men, you know we receive a good income from this business. 26And you see and hear how this fellow Paul has convinced and led astray large numbers of people here in Ephesus and in practically the whole province of Asia. He says that man-made gods are no gods at all. 27There is danger not only that our trade will lose its good name, but also that the temple of the great goddess Artemis will be discredited, and the goddess herself, who is worshiped throughout the province of Asia and the world, will be robbed of her divine majesty."

28When they heard this, they were furious and began shouting: "Great is Artemis of the Ephesians!" 29Soon the whole city was in an uproar. The people seized Gaius and Aristarchus, Paul's traveling companions from Macedonia, and rushed as one man into the theater. 30Paul wanted to appear before the crowd, but the disciples would not let

NEW LIVING TRANSLATION

22He sent his two assistants, Timothy and Erastus, on ahead to Macedonia while he stayed awhile longer in the province of Asia.

23But about that time, serious trouble developed in Ephesus concerning the Way. 24It began with Demetrius, a silversmith who had a large business manufacturing silver shrines of the Greek goddess Artemis.* He kept many craftsmen busy. 25He called the craftsmen together, along with others employed in related trades, and addressed them as follows:

"Gentlemen, you know that our wealth comes from this business. 26As you have seen and heard, this man Paul has persuaded many people that handmade gods aren't gods at all. And this is happening not only here in Ephesus but throughout the entire province! 27Of course, I'm not just talking about the loss of public respect for our business. I'm also concerned that the temple of the great goddess Artemis will lose its influence and that Artemis—this magnificent goddess worshiped throughout the province of Asia and all around the world—will be robbed of her prestige!"

28At this their anger boiled, and they began shouting, "Great is Artemis of the Ephesians!" 29A crowd began to gather, and soon the city was filled with confusion. Everyone rushed to the amphitheater, dragging along Gaius and Aristarchus, who were Paul's traveling companions from Macedonia. 30Paul wanted to go in, but the believers wouldn't let him. 31Some of the officials of the

19:24 *Artemis* is otherwise known as Diana.

NEW KING JAMES VERSION

two of those who ministered to him, Timothy and Erastus, but he himself stayed in Asia for a time.

23And about that time there arose a great commotion about the Way. 24For a certain man named Demetrius, a silversmith, who made silver shrines of Diana,[d] brought no small profit to the craftsmen. 25He called them together with the workers of similar occupation, and said: "Men, you know that we have our prosperity by this trade. 26Moreover you see and hear that not only at Ephesus, but throughout almost all Asia, this Paul has persuaded and turned away many people, saying that they are not gods which are made with hands. 27So not only is this trade of ours in danger of falling into disrepute, but also the temple of the great goddess Diana may be despised and her magnificence destroyed,[e] whom all Asia and the world worship."

28Now when they heard *this,* they were full of wrath and cried out, saying, "Great *is* Diana of the Ephesians!" 29So the whole city was filled with confusion, and rushed into the theater with one accord, having seized Gaius and Aristarchus, Macedonians, Paul's travel companions. 30And when Paul wanted to go in to the people, the disciples

19:24 [d] Greek *Artemis* **19:27** [e] NU-Text reads *she be deposed from her magnificence.*

THE MESSAGE

from there to Jerusalem. "Then," he said, "I'm off to Rome. I've got to see Rome!" He sent two of his assistants, Timothy and Erastus, on to Macedonia while he stayed for a while and wrapped things up in Asia.

But before he got away, a huge ruckus occurred over what was now being referred to as "the Way." A certain silversmith, Demetrius, conducted a brisk trade in the manufacture of shrines to the goddess Artemis, employing a number of artisans in his business. He rounded up his workers and others similarly employed and said, "Men, you well know that we have a good thing going here—and you've seen how Paul has barged in and discredited what we're doing by telling people that there's no such thing as a god made with hands. A lot of people are going along with him, not only here in Ephesus but all through Asia province.

"Not only is our little business in danger of falling apart, but the temple of our famous goddess Artemis will certainly end up a pile of rubble as her glorious reputation fades to nothing. And this is no mere local matter—the whole world worships our Artemis!"

That set them off in a frenzy. They ran into the street yelling, "Great Artemis of the Ephesians! Great Artemis of the Ephesians!" They put the whole city in an uproar, stampeding into the stadium, and grabbing two of Paul's associates on the way, the Macedonians Gaius and Aristarchus. Paul wanted to go in, too, but the disciples wouldn't let him. Prominent religious leaders in the city who had become friendly to Paul concurred: "By no means go near that mob!"

KING JAMES VERSION

31 And certain of the chief of Asia, which were his friends, sent unto him, desiring *him* that he would not adventure himself into the theatre.

32 Some therefore cried one thing, and some another: for the assembly was confused; and the more part knew not wherefore they were come together.

33 And they drew Alexander out of the multitude, the Jews putting him forward. And Alexander beckoned with the hand, and would have made his defence unto the people.

34 But when they knew that he was a Jew, all with one voice about the space of two hours cried out, Great *is* Diana of the Ephesians.

35 And when the townclerk had appeased the people, he said, *Ye* men of Ephesus, what man is there that knoweth not how that the city of the Ephesians is a worshipper of the great goddess Diana, and of the *image* which fell down from Jupiter?

36 Seeing then that these things cannot be spoken against, ye ought to be quiet, and to do nothing rashly.

37 For ye have brought hither these men, which are neither robbers of churches, nor yet blasphemers of your goddess.

38 Wherefore if Demetrius, and the craftsmen which are with him, have a matter against any man, the law is open, and there are deputies: let them implead one another.

39 But if ye enquire any thing concerning other matters, it shall be determined in a lawful assembly.

NEW AMERICAN STANDARD BIBLE

31 Also some of the [l]Asiarchs who were friends of his sent to him and repeatedly urged him not to venture into the theater.

32 So then, some were shouting one thing and some another, for the assembly was in confusion and the majority did not know for what reason they had come together.

33 Some of the crowd concluded *it was* Alexander, since the Jews had put him forward; and having motioned with his hand, Alexander was intending to make a defense to the assembly.

34 But when they recognized that he was a Jew, a *single* outcry arose from them all as they shouted for about two hours, "Great is Artemis of the Ephesians!"

35 After quieting the crowd, the town clerk *said, "Men of Ephesus, what man is there after all who does not know that the city of the Ephesians is guardian of the temple of the great Artemis and of the *image* which fell down from heaven?

36 "So, since these are undeniable facts, you ought to keep calm and to do nothing rash.

37 "For you have brought these men *here* who are neither robbers of temples nor blasphemers of our goddess.

38 "So then, if Demetrius and the craftsmen who are with him have a complaint against any man, the courts are in session and proconsuls are *available;* let them bring charges against one another.

39 "But if you want anything beyond this, it shall be settled in the lawful assembly.

19:31 [l] I.e. political or religious officials of the province of Asia

NEW CENTURY VERSION

did not let him. 31Also, some leaders of Asia who were
friends of Paul sent him a message, begging him not to go
into the theater. 32Some people were shouting one thing,
and some were shouting another. The meeting was completely confused; most of them did not know why they had
come together. 33The Jews put a man named Alexander in
front of the people, and some of them told him what to do.
Alexander waved his hand so he could explain things to
the people. 34But when they saw that Alexander was a Jew,
they all shouted the same thing for two hours: "Great is
Artemis of Ephesus!"

35Then the city clerk made the crowd be quiet. He said,
"People of Ephesus, everyone knows that Ephesus is the
city that keeps the temple of the great goddess Artemis
and her holy stone[f] that fell from heaven. 36Since no one
can say this is not true, you should be quiet. Stop and
think before you do anything. 37You brought these men
here, but they have not said anything evil against our goddess or stolen anything from her temple. 38If Demetrius
and those who work with him have a charge against anyone they should go to the courts and judges where they
can argue with each other. 39If there is something else you
want to talk about, it can be decided at the regular town
meeting of the people. 40I say this because some people

19:35 [f] **holy stone** Probably a meteorite or stone that the people thought looked like Artemis.

CONTEMPORARY ENGLISH VERSION

officials were friendly to Paul, and they sent someone to warn him not to go.

32Some of the people in the meeting were shouting one thing, and others were shouting something else. Everyone was completely confused, and most of them did not even know why they were there.

33Several of the Jewish leaders pushed a man named
Alexander to the front of the crowd and started telling him
what to say. He motioned with his hand and tried to
explain what was going on. 34But when the crowd saw
that he was Jewish, they all shouted for two hours, "Great
is Artemis, the goddess of the Ephesians!"

35Finally, a town official made the crowd be quiet. Then he said:

People of Ephesus, who in the world doesn't know
that our city is the center for worshiping the great goddess Artemis? Who doesn't know that her image which
fell from heaven is right here? 36No one can deny this,
and so you should calm down and not do anything foolish. 37You have brought men in here who have not
robbed temples or spoken against our goddess.

38If Demetrius and his workers have a case against
these men, we have courts and judges. Let them take
their complaints there. 39But if you want to do more
than that, the matter will have to be brought before the
city council. 40We could easily be accused of starting a

NEW INTERNATIONAL VERSION

him. 31 Even some of the officials of the province, friends of Paul, sent him a message begging him not to venture into the theater.

32 The assembly was in confusion: Some were shouting one thing, some another. Most of the people did not even know why they were there. 33 The Jews pushed Alexander to the front, and some of the crowd shouted instructions to him. He motioned for silence in order to make a defense before the people. 34 But when they realized he was a Jew, they all shouted in unison for about two hours: "Great is Artemis of the Ephesians!"

35 The city clerk quieted the crowd and said: "Men of Ephesus, doesn't all the world know that the city of Ephesus is the guardian of the temple of the great Artemis and of her image, which fell from heaven? 36 Therefore, since these facts are undeniable, you ought to be quiet and not do anything rash. 37 You have brought these men here, though they have neither robbed temples nor blasphemed our goddess. 38 If, then, Demetrius and his fellow craftsmen have a grievance against anybody, the courts are open and there are proconsuls. They can press charges. 39 If there is anything further you want to bring up, it must be settled in a legal assembly. 40 As it is, we are in danger of being

NEW LIVING TRANSLATION

province, friends of Paul, also sent a message to him, begging him not to risk his life by entering the amphitheater.

32 Inside, the people were all shouting, some one thing and some another. Everything was in confusion. In fact, most of them didn't even know why they were there. 33 Alexander was thrust forward by some of the Jews, who encouraged him to explain the situation. He motioned for silence and tried to speak in defense. 34 But when the crowd realized he was a Jew, they started shouting again and kept it up for two hours: "Great is Artemis of the Ephesians! Great is Artemis of the Ephesians!"

35 At last the mayor was able to quiet them down enough to speak. "Citizens of Ephesus," he said. "Everyone knows that Ephesus is the official guardian of the temple of the great Artemis, whose image fell down to us from heaven. 36 Since this is an indisputable fact, you shouldn't be disturbed, no matter what is said. Don't do anything rash. 37 You have brought these men here, but they have stolen nothing from the temple and have not spoken against our goddess. 38 If Demetrius and the craftsmen have a case against them, the courts are in session and the judges can take the case at once. Let them go through legal channels. 39 And if there are complaints about other matters, they can be settled in a legal assembly. 40 I am afraid we are in

NEW KING JAMES VERSION

would not allow him. 31 Then some of the officials of Asia, who were his friends, sent to him pleading that he would not venture into the theater. 32 Some therefore cried one thing and some another, for the assembly was confused, and most of them did not know why they had come together. 33 And they drew Alexander out of the multitude, the Jews putting him forward. And Alexander motioned with his hand, and wanted to make his defense to the people. 34 But when they found out that he was a Jew, all with one voice cried out for about two hours, "Great *is* Diana of the Ephesians!"

35 And when the city clerk had quieted the crowd, he said: "Men of Ephesus, what man is there who does not know that the city of the Ephesians is temple guardian of the great goddess Diana, and of the *image* which fell down from Zeus? 36 Therefore, since these things cannot be denied, you ought to be quiet and do nothing rashly. 37 For you have brought these men here who are neither robbers of temples nor blasphemers of your[f] goddess. 38 Therefore, if Demetrius and his fellow craftsmen have a case against anyone, the courts are open and there are proconsuls. Let them bring charges against one another. 39 But if you have any other inquiry to make, it shall be determined in the lawful assembly. 40 For we are in danger of being called in

19:37 [f] NU-Text reads *our*.

THE MESSAGE

Some were yelling one thing, some another. Most of them had no idea what was going on or why they were there. As the Jews pushed Alexander to the front to try to gain control, different factions clamored to get him on their side. But he brushed them off and quieted the mob with an impressive sweep of his arms. But the moment he opened his mouth and they knew he was a Jew, they shouted him down: "Great Artemis of the Ephesians! Great Artemis of the Ephesians!"—on and on and on, for over two hours.

Finally, the town clerk got the mob quieted down and said, "Fellow citizens, is there anyone anywhere who doesn't know that our dear city Ephesus is protector of glorious Artemis and her sacred stone image that fell straight out of heaven? Since this is beyond contradiction, you had better get hold of yourselves. This is conduct unworthy of Artemis. These men you've dragged in here have done nothing to harm either our temple or our goddess.

"So if Demetrius and his guild of artisans have a complaint, they can take it to court and make all the accusations they want. If anything else is bothering you, bring it to the regularly scheduled town meeting and let it be settled there. There is no excuse for what's happened today.

KING JAMES VERSION

40 For we are in danger to be called in question for this day's uproar, there being no cause whereby we may give an account of this concourse.

41 And when he had thus spoken, he dismissed the assembly.

20 And after the uproar was ceased, Paul called unto *him* the disciples, and embraced *them*, and departed for to go into Macedonia.

2 And when he had gone over those parts, and had given them much exhortation, he came into Greece,

3 And *there* abode three months. And when the Jews laid wait for him, as he was about to sail into Syria, he purposed to return through Macedonia.

4 And there accompanied him into Asia Sopater of Berea; and of the Thessalonians, Aristarchus and Secundus; and Gaius of Derbe, and Timotheus; and of Asia, Tychicus and Trophimus.

5 These going before tarried for us at Troas.

6 And we sailed away from Philippi after the days of unleavened bread, and came unto them to Troas in five days; where we abode seven days.

7 ¶ And upon the first *day* of the week, when the disciples came together to break bread, Paul preached unto them, ready to depart on the morrow; and continued his speech until midnight.

NEW AMERICAN STANDARD BIBLE

40 "For indeed we are in danger of being accused of a riot in connection with today's events, since there is no *real* cause *for it*, and in this connection we will be unable to account for this disorderly gathering."

41 After saying this he dismissed the assembly.

Paul in Macedonia and Greece

20 After the uproar had ceased, Paul sent for the disciples, and when he had exhorted them and taken his leave of them, he left to go to Macedonia.

2 When he had gone through those districts and had given them much exhortation, he came to Greece.

3 And *there* he spent three months, and when a plot was formed against him by the Jews as he was about to set sail for Syria, he decided to return through Macedonia.

4 And he was accompanied by Sopater of Berea, *the son* of Pyrrhus, and by Aristarchus and Secundus of the Thessalonians, and Gaius of Derbe, and Timothy, and Tychicus and Trophimus of Asia.

5 But these had gone on ahead and were waiting for us at Troas.

6 We sailed from Philippi after the days of Unleavened Bread, and came to them at Troas within five days; and there we stayed seven days.

7 On the first day of the week, when we were gathered together to break bread, Paul *began* talking to them, intending to leave the next day, and he prolonged his message until midnight.

NEW CENTURY VERSION

might see this trouble today and say that we are rioting. We could not explain this, because there is no real reason for this meeting."
41After the city clerk said these things,
he told the people to go home.

Paul In Macedonia and Greece

20 When the trouble stopped, Paul sent for the followers to come to him. After he encouraged them and then told them good-bye, he left and went to the country of
Macedonia. 2He said many things to strengthen the follow-
ers in the different places on his way through Macedonia.
Then he went to Greece, 3where he stayed for three months.
He was ready to sail for Syria, but some Jews were planning something against him. So Paul decided to go back through
Macedonia to Syria. 4The men who went with him were
Sopater son of Pyrrhus, from the city of Berea; Aristarchus and Secundus, from the city of Thessalonica; Gaius, from Derbe; Timothy; and Tychicus and Trophimus, two men
from the country of Asia. 5These men went on ahead and
waited for us at Troas. 6We sailed from Philippi after the
Feast of Unleavened Bread. Five days later we met them in Troas, where we stayed for seven days.

Paul's Last Visit to Troas

7On the first day of the week,[a] we all met together to break bread,[b] and Paul spoke to the group. Because he was

20:7 [a] **first day of the week** Sunday, which for the Jews began at sunset on our Saturday. But if in this part of Asia a different system of time was used, then the meeting was on our Sunday night. 20:7 [b] **break bread** Probably the Lord's Supper, the special meal that Jesus told his followers to eat to remember him (Luke 22:14–20).

CONTEMPORARY ENGLISH VERSION

riot today. There is no excuse for it! We cannot even give a reason for this uproar.

41After saying this, he told the people to leave.

Paul Goes through Macedonia and Greece

20 When the riot was over, Paul sent for the followers and encouraged them. He then told them good-by
and left for Macedonia. 2As he traveled from place to place,
he encouraged the followers with many messages. Finally,
he went to Greece[a] 3and stayed there for three months.

Paul was about to sail to Syria. But some of the Jewish leaders plotted against him, so he decided to return by way
of Macedonia. 4With him were Sopater, son of Pyrrhus
from Berea, and Aristarchus and Secundus from Thessalonica. Gaius from Derbe was also with him, and so were Timothy and the two Asians, Tychicus and Trophimus.
5They went on ahead to Troas and waited for us there.
6After the Festival of Thin Bread, we sailed from Philippi.
Five days later we met them in Troas and stayed there for a week.

Paul's Last Visit to Troas

7On the first day of the week[b] we met to break bread together.[c] Paul spoke to the people until midnight because

[a] 20.2 *Greece*: Probably Corinth. [b] 20.7 *On the first day of the week*: Since the Jewish day began at sunset, the meeting would have begun in the evening. [c] 20.7 *break bread together*: See the note at 2.46.

NEW INTERNATIONAL VERSION

charged with rioting because of today's events. In that case we would not be able to account for this commotion, since there is no reason for it." 41After he had said this, he dismissed the assembly.

Through Macedonia and Greece

20 When the uproar had ended, Paul sent for the disciples and, after encouraging them, said good-by and set out for Macedonia. 2He traveled through that area, speaking many words of encouragement to the people, and finally arrived in Greece, 3where he stayed three months. Because the Jews made a plot against him just as he was about to sail for Syria, he decided to go back through Macedonia. 4He was accompanied by Sopater son of Pyrrhus from Berea, Aristarchus and Secundus from Thessalonica, Gaius from Derbe, Timothy also, and Tychicus and Trophimus from the province of Asia. 5These men went on ahead and waited for us at Troas. 6But we sailed from Philippi after the Feast of Unleavened Bread, and five days later joined the others at Troas, where we stayed seven days.

Eutychus Raised From the Dead at Troas

7On the first day of the week we came together to break bread. Paul spoke to the people and, because he intended to leave the next day, kept on talking until midnight.

NEW LIVING TRANSLATION

danger of being charged with rioting by the Roman government, since there is no cause for all this commotion. And if Rome demands an explanation, we won't know what to say." 41Then he dismissed them, and they dispersed.

Paul Goes to Macedonia and Greece

20 When it was all over, Paul sent for the believers* and encouraged them. Then he said good-bye and left for Macedonia. 2Along the way, he encouraged the believers in all the towns he passed through. Then he traveled down to Greece, 3where he stayed for three months. He was preparing to sail back to Syria when he discovered a plot by some Jews against his life, so he decided to return through Macedonia.

4Several men were traveling with him. They were Sopater of Berea, the son of Pyrrhus; Aristarchus and Secundus, from Thessalonica; Gaius, from Derbe; Timothy; and Tychicus and Trophimus, who were from the province of Asia. 5They went ahead and waited for us at Troas. 6As soon as the Passover season* ended, we boarded a ship at Philippi in Macedonia and five days later arrived in Troas, where we stayed a week.

Paul's Final Visit to Troas

7On the first day of the week, we gathered to observe the Lord's Supper.* Paul was preaching; and since he was

20:1 Greek *disciples.* 20:6 Greek *the days of unleavened bread.*
20:7 Greek *to break bread.*

NEW KING JAMES VERSION

question for today's uproar, there being no reason which we may give to account for this disorderly gathering." 41And when he had said these things, he dismissed the assembly.

Journeys in Greece

20 After the uproar had ceased, Paul called the disciples to *himself,* embraced *them,* and departed to go to Macedonia. 2Now when he had gone over that region and encouraged them with many words, he came to Greece 3and stayed three months. And when the Jews plotted against him as he was about to sail to Syria, he decided to return through Macedonia. 4And Sopater of Berea accompanied him to Asia—also Aristarchus and Secundus of the Thessalonians, and Gaius of Derbe, and Timothy, and Tychicus and Trophimus of Asia. 5These men, going ahead, waited for us at Troas. 6But we sailed away from Philippi after the Days of Unleavened Bread, and in five days joined them at Troas, where we stayed seven days.

Ministering at Troas

7Now on the first *day* of the week, when the disciples came together to break bread, Paul, ready to depart the next day, spoke to them and continued his message until

THE MESSAGE

We're putting our city in serious danger. Rome, remember, does not look kindly on rioters." With that, he sent them home.

Macedonia and Greece

20 With things back to normal, Paul called the disciples together and encouraged them to keep up the good work in Ephesus. Then, saying his goodbyes, he left for Macedonia. Traveling through the country, passing from one gathering to another, he gave constant encouragement, lifting their spirits and charging them with fresh hope.

Then he came to Greece and stayed on for three months. Just as he was about to sail for Syria, the Jews cooked up a plot against him. So he went the other way, by land back through Macedonia, and gave them the slip. His companions for the journey were Sopater, son of Pyrrhus, from Berea; Aristarchus and Secundus, both Thessalonians; Gaius from Derbe; Timothy; and the two from western Asia, Tychicus and Trophimus.

They went on ahead and waited for us in Troas. Meanwhile, we stayed in Philippi for Passover Week, and then set sail. Within five days we were again in Troas and stayed a week.

We met on Sunday to worship and celebrate the Master's Supper. Paul addressed the congregation. Our plan was to leave first thing in the morning, but Paul talked on, way

KING JAMES VERSION

8 And there were many lights in the upper chamber, where they were gathered together.

9 And there sat in a window a certain young man named Eutychus, being fallen into a deep sleep: and as Paul was long preaching, he sunk down with sleep, and fell down from the third loft, and was taken up dead.

10 And Paul went down, and fell on him, and embracing *him* said, Trouble not yourselves; for his life is in him.

11 When he therefore was come up again, and had broken bread, and eaten, and talked a long while, even till break of day, so he departed.

12 And they brought the young man alive, and were not a little comforted.

13 ¶ And we went before to ship, and sailed unto Assos, there intending to take in Paul: for so had he appointed, minding himself to go afoot.

14 And when he met with us at Assos, we took him in, and came to Mitylene.

15 And we sailed thence, and came the next *day* over against Chios; and the next *day* we arrived at Samos, and tarried at Trogyllium; and the next *day* we came to Miletus.

16 For Paul had determined to sail by Ephesus, because he would not spend the time in Asia: for he hasted, if it were possible for him, to be at Jerusalem the day of Pentecost.

NEW AMERICAN STANDARD BIBLE

8 There were many lamps in the upper room where we were gathered together.

9 And there was a young man named Eutychus sitting on the window sill, sinking into a deep sleep; and as Paul kept on talking, he was overcome by sleep and fell down from the third floor and was picked up dead.

10 But Paul went down and fell upon him, and after embracing him, he said, "Do not be troubled, for his life is in him."

11 When he had gone *back* up and had broken the bread and eaten, he talked with them a long while until daybreak, and then left.

12 They took away the boy alive, and were greatly comforted.

Troas to Miletus

13 But we, going ahead to the ship, set sail for Assos, intending from there to take Paul on board; for so he had arranged it, intending himself to go by land.

14 And when he met us at Assos, we took him on board and came to Mitylene.

15 Sailing from there, we arrived the following day opposite Chios; and the next day we crossed over to Samos; and the day following we came to Miletus.

16 For Paul had decided to sail past Ephesus so that he would not have to spend time in Asia; for he was hurrying to be in Jerusalem, if possible, on the day of Pentecost.

NEW CENTURY VERSION

planning to leave the next day, he kept on talking until
midnight. 8 We were all together in a room upstairs, and
there were many lamps in the room. 9 A young man named
Eutychus was sitting in the window. As Paul continued
talking, Eutychus was falling into a deep sleep. Finally, he
went sound asleep and fell to the ground from the third
floor. When they picked him up, he was dead. 10 Paul went
down to Eutychus, knelt down, and put his arms around
him. He said, "Don't worry. He is alive now." 11 Then Paul
went upstairs again, broke bread, and ate. He spoke to
them a long time, until it was early morning, and then he
left. 12 They took the young man home alive and were
greatly comforted.

The Trip from Troas to Miletus

13 We went on ahead of Paul and sailed for the city of
Assos, where he wanted to join us on the ship. Paul
planned it this way because he wanted to go to Assos by
land. 14 When he met us there, we took him aboard and
went to Mitylene. 15 We sailed from Mitylene and the next
day came to a place near Chios. The following day we
sailed to Samos, and the next day we reached Miletus.
16 Paul had already decided not to stop at Ephesus, because
he did not want to stay too long in the country of Asia. He
was hurrying to be in Jerusalem on the day of Pentecost, if
that were possible.

CONTEMPORARY ENGLISH VERSION

he was leaving the next morning. 8 In the upstairs room
where we were meeting, there were a lot of lamps. 9 A
young man by the name of Eutychus was sitting on a window sill. While Paul was speaking, the young man got very
sleepy. Finally, he went to sleep and fell three floors all the
way down to the ground. When they picked him up, he
was dead.

10 Paul went down and bent over Eutychus. He took him
in his arms and said, "Don't worry! He's alive." 11 After
Paul had gone back upstairs, he broke bread, and ate with
us. He then spoke until dawn and left. 12 Then the followers took the young man home alive and were very happy.

The Voyage from Troas to Miletus

13 Paul decided to travel by land to Assos. The rest of us
went on ahead by ship, and we were to take him aboard
there. 14 When he met us in Assos, he came aboard, and we
sailed on to Mitylene. 15 The next day we came to a place
near Chios, and the following day we reached Samos. The
day after that we sailed to Miletus. 16 Paul had decided to
sail on past Ephesus, because he did not want to spend too
much time in Asia. He was in a hurry and wanted to be in
Jerusalem in time for Pentecost.[d]

[d] 20.16 *in time for Pentecost*: The Jewish people liked to be in Jerusalem for this festival (see the note at 2.1).

NEW INTERNATIONAL VERSION

[8]There were many lamps in the upstairs room where we were meeting. [9]Seated in a window was a young man named Eutychus, who was sinking into a deep sleep as Paul talked on and on. When he was sound asleep, he fell to the ground from the third story and was picked up dead. [10]Paul went down, threw himself on the young man and put his arms around him. "Don't be alarmed," he said. "He's alive!" [11]Then he went upstairs again and broke bread and ate. After talking until daylight, he left. [12]The people took the young man home alive and were greatly comforted.

Paul's Farewell to the Ephesian Elders

[13]We went on ahead to the ship and sailed for Assos, where we were going to take Paul aboard. He had made this arrangement because he was going there on foot. [14]When he met us at Assos, we took him aboard and went on to Mitylene. [15]The next day we set sail from there and arrived off Kios. The day after that we crossed over to Samos, and on the following day arrived at Miletus. [16]Paul had decided to sail past Ephesus to avoid spending time in the province of Asia, for he was in a hurry to reach Jerusalem, if possible, by the day of Pentecost.

NEW LIVING TRANSLATION

leaving the next day, he talked until midnight. [8]The upstairs room where we met was lighted with many flickering lamps. [9]As Paul spoke on and on, a young man named Eutychus, sitting on the windowsill, became very drowsy. Finally, he sank into a deep sleep and fell three stories to his death below. [10]Paul went down, bent over him, and took him into his arms. "Don't worry," he said, "he's alive!" [11]Then they all went back upstairs and ate the Lord's Supper together.* And Paul continued talking to them until dawn; then he left. [12]Meanwhile, the young man was taken home unhurt, and everyone was greatly relieved.

Paul Meets the Ephesian Elders

[13]Paul went by land to Assos, where he had arranged for us to join him, and we went on ahead by ship. [14]He joined us there and we sailed together to Mitylene. [15]The next day we passed the island of Kios. The following day, we crossed to the island of Samos. And a day later we arrived at Miletus.

[16]Paul had decided against stopping at Ephesus this time because he didn't want to spend further time in the province of Asia. He was hurrying to get to Jerusalem, if possible, for the Festival of Pentecost. [17]But when we landed at

20:11 Greek *broke the bread.*

NEW KING JAMES VERSION

midnight. [8]There were many lamps in the upper room where they[a] were gathered together. [9]And in a window sat a certain young man named Eutychus, who was sinking into a deep sleep. He was overcome by sleep; and as Paul continued speaking, he fell down from the third story and was taken up dead. [10]But Paul went down, fell on him, and embracing *him* said, "Do not trouble yourselves, for his life is in him." [11]Now when he had come up, had broken bread and eaten, and talked a long while, even till daybreak, he departed. [12]And they brought the young man in alive, and they were not a little comforted.

From Troas to Miletus

[13]Then we went ahead to the ship and sailed to Assos, there intending to take Paul on board; for so he had given orders, intending himself to go on foot. [14]And when he met us at Assos, we took him on board and came to Mitylene. [15]We sailed from there, and the next *day* came opposite Chios. The following *day* we arrived at Samos and stayed at Trogyllium. The next *day* we came to Miletus. [16]For Paul had decided to sail past Ephesus, so that he would not have to spend time in Asia; for he was hurrying to be at Jerusalem, if possible, on the Day of Pentecost.

20:8 [a] NU-Text and M-Text read *we.*

THE MESSAGE

past midnight. We were meeting in a well-lighted upper room. A young man named Eutychus was sitting in an open window. As Paul went on and on, Eutychus fell sound asleep and toppled out the third-story window. When they picked him up, he was dead.

Paul went down, stretched himself on him, and hugged him hard. "No more crying," he said. "There's life in him yet." Then Paul got up and served the Master's Supper. And went on telling stories of the faith until dawn! On that note, they left—Paul going one way, the congregation another, leading the boy off alive, and full of life themselves.

In the meantime, the rest of us had gone on ahead to the ship and sailed for Assos, where we planned to pick up Paul. Paul wanted to walk there, and so had made these arrangements earlier. Things went according to plan: We met him in Assos, took him on board, and sailed to Mitylene. The next day we put in opposite Chios, Samos a day later, and then Miletus. Paul had decided to bypass Ephesus so that he wouldn't be held up in Asia province. He was in a hurry to get to Jerusalem in time for the Feast of Pentecost, if at all possible.

KING JAMES VERSION

17 ¶ And from Miletus he sent to Ephesus, and called the elders of the church.
18 And when they were come to him, he said unto them, Ye know, from the first day that I came into Asia, after what manner I have been with you at all seasons,
19 Serving the Lord with all humility of mind, and with many tears, and temptations, which befell me by the lying in wait of the Jews:
20 *And* how I kept back nothing that was profitable *unto you*, but have shewed you, and have taught you publickly, and from house to house,
21 Testifying both to the Jews, and also to the Greeks, repentance toward God, and faith toward our Lord Jesus Christ.
22 And now, behold, I go bound in the spirit unto Jerusalem, not knowing the things that shall befall me there:
23 Save that the Holy Ghost witnesseth in every city, saying that bonds and afflictions abide me.
24 But none of these things move me, neither count I my life dear unto myself, so that I might finish my course with joy, and the ministry, which I have received of the Lord Jesus, to testify the gospel of the grace of God.
25 And now, behold, I know that ye all, among whom I have gone preaching the kingdom of God, shall see my face no more.
26 Wherefore I take you to record this day, that I *am* pure from the blood of all *men*.
27 For I have not shunned to declare unto you all the counsel of God.

NEW AMERICAN STANDARD BIBLE

Farewell to Ephesus

17 From Miletus he sent to Ephesus and called to him the elders of the church.
18 And when they had come to him, he said to them,
"You yourselves know, from the first day that I set foot in Asia, how I was with you the whole time,
19 serving the Lord with all humility and with tears and with trials which came upon me through the plots of the Jews;
20 how I did not shrink from declaring to you anything that was profitable, and teaching you publicly and from house to house,
21 solemnly testifying to both Jews and Greeks of repentance toward God and faith in our Lord Jesus Christ.
22 "And now, behold, bound in spirit, I am on my way to Jerusalem, not knowing what will happen to me there,
23 except that the Holy Spirit solemnly testifies to me in every city, saying that bonds and afflictions await me.
24 "But I do not consider my life of any account as dear to myself, so that I may finish my course and the ministry which I received from the Lord Jesus, to testify solemnly of the gospel of the grace of God.
25 "And now, behold, I know that all of you, among whom I went about preaching the kingdom, will no longer see my face.
26 "Therefore, I testify to you this day that I am innocent of the blood of all men.
27 "For I did not shrink from declaring to you the whole purpose of God.

NEW CENTURY VERSION

The Elders from Ephesus

17Now from Miletus Paul sent to Ephesus and called for
the elders of the church. 18When they came to him, he
said, "You know about my life from the first day I came to
Asia. You know the way I lived all the time I was with you.
19The Jews made plans against me, which troubled me very
much. But you know I always served the Lord unselfishly,
and I often cried. 20You know I preached to you and did
not hold back anything that would help you. You know
that I taught you in public and in your homes. 21I warned
both Jews and Greeks to change their lives and turn to God
and believe in our Lord Jesus. 22But now I must obey the
Holy Spirit and go to Jerusalem. I don't know what will
happen to me there. 23I know only that in every city the
Holy Spirit tells me that troubles and even jail wait for me.
24I don't care about my own life. The most important thing
is that I complete my mission, the work that the Lord Jesus
gave me—to tell people the Good News about God's grace.
25"And now, I know that none of you among whom I
was preaching the kingdom of God will ever see me again.
26So today I tell you that if any of you should be lost, I am
not responsible, 27because I have told you everything God
wants you to know. 28Be careful for yourselves and for all

CONTEMPORARY ENGLISH VERSION

Paul Says Good-By to the Church Leaders of Ephesus

17From Miletus, Paul sent a message for the church
leaders at Ephesus to come and meet with him. 18When
they got there, he said:
You know everything I did during the time I was with
you when I first came to Asia. 19Some of the Jews plot-
ted against me and caused me a lot of sorrow and trou-
ble. But I served the Lord and was humble. 20When I
preached in public or taught in your homes, I didn't hold
back from telling anything that would help you. 21I told
Jews and Gentiles to turn to God and have faith in our
Lord Jesus.
22I don't know what will happen to me in Jerusalem,
but I must obey God's Spirit and go there. 23In every city
I visit, I am told by the Holy Spirit that I will be put in
jail and will be in trouble in Jerusalem. 24But I don't care
what happens to me, as long as I finish the work that
the Lord Jesus gave me to do. And that work is to tell the
good news about God's great kindness.
25I have gone from place to place, preaching to you
about God's kingdom, but now I know that none of you
will ever see me again. 26I tell you today that I am no
longer responsible for any of you! 27I have told you every-
thing God wants you to know. 28Look after yourselves

NEW INTERNATIONAL VERSION

17From Miletus, Paul sent to Ephesus for the elders of
the church. 18When they arrived, he said to them: "You
know how I lived the whole time I was with you, from the
first day I came into the province of Asia. 19I served the
Lord with great humility and with tears, although I was
severely tested by the plots of the Jews. 20You know that I
have not hesitated to preach anything that would be help-
ful to you but have taught you publicly and from house to
house. 21I have declared to both Jews and Greeks that they
must turn to God in repentance and have faith in our Lord
Jesus.

22"And now, compelled by the Spirit, I am going to Jeru-
salem, not knowing what will happen to me there. 23I only
know that in every city the Holy Spirit warns me that
prison and hardships are facing me. 24However, I consider
my life worth nothing to me, if only I may finish the race
and complete the task the Lord Jesus has given me—the
task of testifying to the gospel of God's grace.

25"Now I know that none of you among whom I have
gone about preaching the kingdom will ever see me again.
26Therefore, I declare to you today that I am innocent of
the blood of all men. 27For I have not hesitated to proclaim
to you the whole will of God. 28Keep watch over yourselves

NEW LIVING TRANSLATION

Miletus, he sent a message to the elders of the church at
Ephesus, asking them to come down to meet him.

18When they arrived he declared, "You know that from
the day I set foot in the province of Asia until now 19I have
done the Lord's work humbly—yes, and with tears. I have
endured the trials that came to me from the plots of the
Jews. 20Yet I never shrank from telling you the truth, either
publicly or in your homes. 21I have had one message for
Jews and Gentiles alike—the necessity of turning from sin
and turning to God, and of faith in our Lord Jesus.

22"And now I am going to Jerusalem, drawn there irre-
sistibly by the Holy Spirit,* not knowing what awaits me,
23except that the Holy Spirit has told me in city after city
that jail and suffering lie ahead. 24But my life is worth
nothing unless I use it for doing the work assigned me by
the Lord Jesus—the work of telling others the Good News
about God's wonderful kindness and love.

25"And now I know that none of you to whom I have
preached the Kingdom will ever see me again. 26Let me say
plainly that I have been faithful. No one's damnation can
be blamed on me,* 27for I didn't shrink from declaring all
that God wants for you.

20:22 Or *by my spirit,* or *by an inner compulsion.* Greek reads *by the spirit.* **20:26** Greek *I am innocent of the blood of all.*

NEW KING JAMES VERSION

The Ephesian Elders Exhorted

17From Miletus he sent to Ephesus and called for the
elders of the church. 18And when they had come to him, he
said to them: "You know, from the first day that I came to
Asia, in what manner I always lived among you, 19serving
the Lord with all humility, with many tears and trials
which happened to me by the plotting of the Jews; 20how I
kept back nothing that was helpful, but proclaimed it to
you, and taught you publicly and from house to house,
21testifying to Jews, and also to Greeks, repentance toward
God and faith toward our Lord Jesus Christ. 22And see,
now I go bound in the spirit to Jerusalem, not knowing the
things that will happen to me there, 23except that the Holy
Spirit testifies in every city, saying that chains and tribula-
tions await me. 24But none of these things move me; nor
do I count my life dear to myself,[b] so that I may finish my
race with joy, and the ministry which I received from the
Lord Jesus, to testify to the gospel of the grace of God.

25"And indeed, now I know that you all, among whom I
have gone preaching the kingdom of God, will see my face
no more. 26Therefore I testify to you this day that I *am* in-
nocent of the blood of all *men.* 27For I have not shunned to
declare to you the whole counsel of God. 28Therefore take

20:24 [b] NU-Text reads *But I do not count my life of any value or dear to myself.*

THE MESSAGE

On to Jerusalem

From Miletus he sent to Ephesus for the leaders of the congregation. When they arrived, he said, "You know that from day one of my arrival in Asia I was with you totally—laying my life on the line, serving the Master no matter what, putting up with no end of scheming by Jews who wanted to do me in. I didn't skimp or trim in any way. Every truth and encouragement that could have made a difference to you, you got. I taught you out in public and I taught you in your homes, urging Jews and Greeks alike to a radical life-change before God and an equally radical trust in our Master Jesus.

"But there is another urgency before me now. I feel compelled to go to Jerusalem. I'm completely in the dark about what will happen when I get there. I do know that it won't be any picnic, for the Holy Spirit has let me know repeatedly and clearly that there are hard times and imprisonment ahead. But that matters little. What matters most to me is to finish what God started: the job the Master Jesus gave me of letting everyone I meet know all about this incredibly extravagant generosity of God.

"And so this is goodbye. You're not going to see me again, nor I you, you whom I have gone among for so long proclaiming the news of God's inaugurated kingdom. I've done my best for you, given you my all, held back nothing of God's will for you.

KING JAMES VERSION

28 Take heed therefore unto yourselves, and to all the flock, over the which the Holy Ghost hath made you overseers, to feed the church of God, which he hath purchased with his own blood.

29 For I know this, that after my departing shall grievous wolves enter in among you, not sparing the flock.

30 Also of your own selves shall men arise, speaking perverse things, to draw away disciples after them.

31 Therefore watch, and remember, that by the space of three years I ceased not to warn every one night and day with tears.

32 And now, brethren, I commend you to God, and to the word of his grace, which is able to build you up, and to give you an inheritance among all them which are sanctified.

33 I have coveted no man's silver, or gold, or apparel.

34 Yea, ye yourselves know, that these hands have ministered unto my necessities, and to them that were with me.

35 I have shewed you all things, how that so labouring ye ought to support the weak, and to remember the words of the Lord Jesus, how he said, It is more blessed to give than to receive.

36 ¶ And when he had thus spoken, he kneeled down, and prayed with them all.

37 And they all wept sore, and fell on Paul's neck, and kissed him,

38 Sorrowing most of all for the words which he spake, that they should see his face no more. And they accompanied him unto the ship.

NEW AMERICAN STANDARD BIBLE

28 "Be on guard for yourselves and for all the flock, among which the Holy Spirit has made you overseers, to shepherd the church of God which He purchased with His own blood.

29 "I know that after my departure savage wolves will come in among you, not sparing the flock;

30 and from among your own selves men will arise, speaking perverse things, to draw away the disciples after them.

31 "Therefore be on the alert, remembering that night and day for a period of three years I did not cease to admonish each one with tears.

32 "And now I commend you to God and to the word of His grace, which is able to build *you* up and to give *you* the inheritance among all those who are sanctified.

33 "I have coveted no one's silver or gold or clothes.

34 "You yourselves know that these hands ministered to my *own* needs and to the men who were with me.

35 "In everything I showed you that by working hard in this manner you must help the weak and remember the words of the Lord Jesus, that He Himself said, 'It is more blessed to give than to receive.'"

36 When he had said these things, he knelt down and prayed with them all.

37 And they *began* to weep aloud and embraced Paul, and repeatedly kissed him,

38 grieving especially over the word which he had spoken, that they would not see his face again. And they were accompanying him to the ship.

NEW CENTURY VERSION

the people the Holy Spirit has given to you to care for. You must be like shepherds to the church of God,[c] which he bought with the death of his own son. 29I know that after I leave, some people will come like wild wolves and try to destroy the flock. 30Also, some from your own group will rise up and twist the truth and will lead away followers after them. 31So be careful! Always remember that for three years, day and night, I never stopped warning each of you, and I often cried over you.

32"Now I am putting you in the care of God and the message about his grace. It is able to give you strength, and it will give you the blessings God has for all his holy people. 33When I was with you, I never wanted anyone's money or fine clothes. 34You know I always worked to take care of my own needs and the needs of those who were with me. 35I showed you in all things that you should work as I did and help the weak. I taught you to remember the words Jesus said: 'It is more blessed to give than to receive.'"

36When Paul had said this, he knelt down with all of them and prayed. 37–38And they all cried because Paul had said they would never see him again. They put their arms around him and kissed him. Then they went with him to the ship.

20:28 [c] of God Some Greek copies say, "of the Lord."

CONTEMPORARY ENGLISH VERSION

and everyone the Holy Spirit has placed in your care. Be like shepherds to God's church. It is the flock that he bought with the blood of his own Son.[e]

29I know that after I am gone, others will come like fierce wolves to attack you. 30Some of your own people will tell lies to win over the Lord's followers. 31Be on your guard! Remember how day and night for three years I kept warning you with tears in my eyes.

32I now place you in God's care. Remember the message about his great kindness! This message can help you and give you what belongs to you as God's people. 33I have never wanted anyone's money or clothes. 34You know how I have worked with my own hands to make a living for myself and my friends. 35By everything I did, I showed how you should work to help everyone who is weak. Remember that our Lord Jesus said, "More blessings come from giving than from receiving."

36After Paul had finished speaking, he knelt down with all of them and prayed. 37Everyone cried and hugged and kissed him. 38They were especially sad because Paul had told them, "You will never see me again."

Then they went with him to the ship.

[e] 20.28 *the blood of his own Son*: Or "his own blood."

NEW INTERNATIONAL VERSION

and all the flock of which the Holy Spirit has made you overseers.[a] Be shepherds of the church of God,[b] which he bought with his own blood. 29 I know that after I leave, savage wolves will come in among you and will not spare the flock. 30 Even from your own number men will arise and distort the truth in order to draw away disciples after them. 31 So be on your guard! Remember that for three years I never stopped warning each of you night and day with tears.

32 "Now I commit you to God and to the word of his grace, which can build you up and give you an inheritance among all those who are sanctified. 33 I have not coveted anyone's silver or gold or clothing. 34 You yourselves know that these hands of mine have supplied my own needs and the needs of my companions. 35 In everything I did, I showed you that by this kind of hard work we must help the weak, remembering the words the Lord Jesus himself said: 'It is more blessed to give than to receive.' "

36 When he had said this, he knelt down with all of them and prayed. 37 They all wept as they embraced him and kissed him. 38 What grieved them most was his statement that they would never see his face again. Then they accompanied him to the ship.

[a] *28* Traditionally *bishops* [b] *28* Many manuscripts *of the Lord*

NEW LIVING TRANSLATION

28 "And now beware! Be sure that you feed and shepherd God's flock—his church, purchased with his blood—over whom the Holy Spirit has appointed you as elders.* 29 I know full well that false teachers, like vicious wolves, will come in among you after I leave, not sparing the flock. 30 Even some of you will distort the truth in order to draw a following. 31 Watch out! Remember the three years I was with you—my constant watch and care over you night and day, and my many tears for you.

32 "And now I entrust you to God and the word of his grace—his message that is able to build you up and give you an inheritance with all those he has set apart for himself.

33 "I have never coveted anyone's money or fine clothing. 34 You know that these hands of mine have worked to pay my own way, and I have even supplied the needs of those who were with me. 35 And I have been a constant example of how you can help the poor by working hard. You should remember the words of the Lord Jesus: 'It is more blessed to give than to receive.' "

36 When he had finished speaking, he knelt and prayed with them. 37 They wept aloud as they embraced him in farewell, 38 sad most of all because he had said that they would never see him again. Then they accompanied him down to the ship.

20:28 Greek *overseers.*

NEW KING JAMES VERSION

heed to yourselves and to all the flock, among which the Holy Spirit has made you overseers, to shepherd the church of God[c] which He purchased with His own blood. 29 For I know this, that after my departure savage wolves will come in among you, not sparing the flock. 30 Also from among yourselves men will rise up, speaking perverse things, to draw away the disciples after themselves. 31 Therefore watch, and remember that for three years I did not cease to warn everyone night and day with tears.

32 "So now, brethren, I commend you to God and to the word of His grace, which is able to build you up and give you an inheritance among all those who are sanctified. 33 I have coveted no one's silver or gold or apparel. 34 Yes,[d] you yourselves know that these hands have provided for my necessities, and for those who were with me. 35 I have shown you in every way, by laboring like this, that you must support the weak. And remember the words of the Lord Jesus, that He said, 'It is more blessed to give than to receive.' "

36 And when he had said these things, he knelt down and prayed with them all. 37 Then they all wept freely, and fell on Paul's neck and kissed him, 38 sorrowing most of all for the words which he spoke, that they would see his face no more. And they accompanied him to the ship.

20:28 [c] M-Text reads *of the Lord and God.* **20:34** [d] NU-Text and M-Text omit *Yes.*

THE MESSAGE

"Now it's up to you. Be on your toes—both for yourselves and your congregation of sheep. The Holy Spirit has put you in charge of these people—God's people they are—to guard and protect them. God himself thought they were worth dying for.

"I know that as soon as I'm gone, vicious wolves are going to show up and rip into this flock, men from your very own ranks twisting words so as to seduce disciples into following them instead of Jesus. So stay awake and keep up your guard. Remember those three years I kept at it with you, never letting up, pouring my heart out with you, one after another.

"Now I'm turning you over to God, our marvelous God whose gracious Word can make you into what he wants you to be and give you everything you could possibly need in this community of holy friends.

"I've never, as you so well know, had any taste for wealth or fashion. With these bare hands I took care of my own basic needs and those who worked with me. In everything I've done, I have demonstrated to you how necessary it is to work on behalf of the weak and not exploit them. You'll not likely go wrong here if you keep remembering that our Master said, 'You're far happier giving than getting.' "

Then Paul went down on his knees, all of them kneeling with him, and prayed. And then a river of tears. Much clinging to Paul, not wanting to let him go. They knew they would never see him again—he had told them quite plainly. The pain cut deep. Then, bravely, they walked him down to the ship.

KING JAMES VERSION

21 And it came to pass, that after we were gotten from them, and had launched, we came with a straight course unto Coos, and the *day* following unto Rhodes, and from thence unto Patara:

2 And finding a ship sailing over unto Phenicia, we went aboard, and set forth.

3 Now when we had discovered Cyprus, we left it on the left hand, and sailed into Syria, and landed at Tyre: for there the ship was to unlade her burden.

4 And finding disciples, we tarried there seven days: who said to Paul through the Spirit, that he should not go up to Jerusalem.

5 And when we had accomplished those days, we departed and went our way; and they all brought us on our way, with wives and children, till *we were* out of the city: and we kneeled down on the shore, and prayed.

6 And when we had taken our leave one of another, we took ship; and they returned home again.

7 And when we had finished *our* course from Tyre, we came to Ptolemais, and saluted the brethren, and abode with them one day.

8 ¶ And the next *day* we that were of Paul's company departed, and came unto Caesarea: and we entered into the house of Philip the evangelist, which was *one* of the seven; and abode with him.

9 And the same man had four daughters, virgins, which did prophesy.

10 And as we tarried *there* many days, there came down from Judaea a certain prophet, named Agabus.

NEW AMERICAN STANDARD BIBLE

Paul Sails from Miletus

21 When we had parted from them and had set sail, we ran a straight course to Cos and the next day to Rhodes and from there to Patara;

2 and having found a ship crossing over to Phoenicia, we went aboard and set sail.

3 When we came in sight of Cyprus, leaving it on the left, we kept sailing to Syria and landed at Tyre; for there the ship was to unload its cargo.

4 After looking up the disciples, we stayed there seven days; and they kept telling Paul through the Spirit not to set foot in Jerusalem.

5 When our days there were ended, we left and started on our journey, while they all, with wives and children, escorted us until *we were* out of the city. After kneeling down on the beach and praying, we said farewell to one another.

6 Then we went on board the ship, and they returned home again.

7 When we had finished the voyage from Tyre, we arrived at Ptolemais, and after greeting the brethren, we stayed with them for a day.

8 On the next day we left and came to Caesarea, and entering the house of Philip the evangelist, who was one of the seven, we stayed with him.

9 Now this man had four virgin daughters who were prophetesses.

10 As we were staying there for some days, a prophet named Agabus came down from Judea.

NEW CENTURY VERSION

Paul Goes to Jerusalem

21 After we all said good-bye to them, we sailed
straight to the island of Cos. The next day we
reached Rhodes, and from there we went to Patara. 2There
we found a ship going to Phoenicia, so we went aboard
and sailed away. 3We sailed near the island of Cyprus, see-
ing it to the north, but we sailed on to Syria. We stopped
at Tyre because the ship needed to unload its cargo there.
4We found some followers in Tyre and stayed with them
for seven days. Through the Holy Spirit they warned Paul
not to go to Jerusalem. 5When we finished our visit, we left
and continued our trip. All the followers, even the women
and children, came outside the city with us. After we all
knelt on the beach and prayed, 6we said good-bye and got
on the ship, and the followers went back home.
7We continued our trip from Tyre and arrived at
Ptolemais, where we greeted the believers and stayed with
them for a day. 8The next day we left Ptolemais and went
to the city of Caesarea. There we went into the home of
Philip the preacher, one of the seven helpers,[a] and stayed
with him. 9He had four unmarried daughters who had the
gift of prophesying. 10After we had been there for some
time, a prophet named Agabus arrived from Judea. 11He

21:8 [a] **helpers** The seven men chosen for a special work described in Acts 6:1–6.

CONTEMPORARY ENGLISH VERSION

Paul Goes to Jerusalem

21 After saying good-by, we sailed straight to Cos.
The next day we reached Rhodes and from there
sailed on to Patara. 2We found a ship going to Phoenicia,
so we got on board and sailed off.
3We came within sight of Cyprus and then sailed south
of it on to the port of Tyre in Syria, where the ship was
going to unload its cargo. 4We looked up the Lord's follow-
ers and stayed with them for a week. The Holy Spirit had
told them to warn Paul not to go on to Jerusalem. 5But
when the week was over, we started on our way again. All
the men, together with their wives and children, walked
with us from the town to the seashore. We knelt on the
beach and prayed. 6Then after saying good-by to each
other, we got into the ship, and they went back home.
7We sailed from Tyre to Ptolemais, where we greeted the
followers and stayed with them for a day. 8The next day
we went to Caesarea and stayed with Philip, the preacher.
He was one of the seven men who helped the apostles,
9and he had four unmarried[a] daughters who prophesied.
10We had been in Caesarea for several days, when the
prophet Agabus came to us from Judea. 11He took Paul's

[a] 21.9 *unmarried:* Or "virgin."

NEW INTERNATIONAL VERSION

On to Jerusalem

21 After we had torn ourselves away from them, we put out to sea and sailed straight to Cos. The next day we went to Rhodes and from there to Patara. 2We found a ship crossing over to Phoenicia, went on board and set sail. 3After sighting Cyprus and passing to the south of it, we sailed on to Syria. We landed at Tyre, where our ship was to unload its cargo. 4Finding the disciples there, we stayed with them seven days. Through the Spirit they urged Paul not to go on to Jerusalem. 5But when our time was up, we left and continued on our way. All the disciples and their wives and children accompanied us out of the city, and there on the beach we knelt to pray. 6After saying good-by to each other, we went aboard the ship, and they returned home.

7We continued our voyage from Tyre and landed at Ptolemais, where we greeted the brothers and stayed with them for a day. 8Leaving the next day, we reached Caesarea and stayed at the house of Philip the evangelist, one of the Seven. 9He had four unmarried daughters who prophesied.

10After we had been there a number of days, a prophet named Agabus came down from Judea. 11Coming over to

NEW LIVING TRANSLATION

Paul's Journey to Jerusalem

21 After saying farewell to the Ephesian elders, we sailed straight to the island of Cos. The next day we reached Rhodes and then went to Patara. 2There we boarded a ship sailing for the Syrian province of Phoenicia. 3We sighted the island of Cyprus, passed it on our left, and landed at the harbor of Tyre, in Syria, where the ship was to unload. 4We went ashore, found the local believers,* and stayed with them a week. These disciples prophesied through the Holy Spirit that Paul should not go on to Jerusalem. 5When we returned to the ship at the end of the week, the entire congregation, including wives and children, came down to the shore with us. There we knelt, prayed, 6and said our farewells. Then we went aboard, and they returned home.

7The next stop after leaving Tyre was Ptolemais, where we greeted the brothers and sisters* but stayed only one day. 8Then we went on to Caesarea and stayed at the home of Philip the Evangelist, one of the seven men who had been chosen to distribute food. 9He had four unmarried daughters who had the gift of prophecy.

10During our stay of several days, a man named Agabus, who also had the gift of prophecy, arrived from Judea.

21:4 Greek *disciples;* also in 21:16. 21:7 Greek *brothers;* also in 21:17.

NEW KING JAMES VERSION

Warnings on the Journey to Jerusalem

21 Now it came to pass, that when we had departed from them and set sail, running a straight course we came to Cos, the following *day* to Rhodes, and from there to Patara. 2And finding a ship sailing over to Phoenicia, we went aboard and set sail. 3When we had sighted Cyprus, we passed it on the left, sailed to Syria, and landed at Tyre; for there the ship was to unload her cargo. 4And finding disciples,[a] we stayed there seven days. They told Paul through the Spirit not to go up to Jerusalem. 5When we had come to the end of those days, we departed and went on our way; and they all accompanied us, with wives and children, till *we were* out of the city. And we knelt down on the shore and prayed. 6When we had taken our leave of one another, we boarded the ship, and they returned home.

7And when we had finished *our* voyage from Tyre, we came to Ptolemais, greeted the brethren, and stayed with them one day. 8On the next *day* we who were Paul's companions[b] departed and came to Caesarea, and entered the house of Philip the evangelist, who was *one* of the seven, and stayed with him. 9Now this man had four virgin daughters who prophesied. 10And as we stayed many days, a certain prophet named Agabus came down from Judea.

21:4 [a] NU-Text reads *the disciples.* 21:8 [b] NU-Text omits *who were Paul's companions.*

THE MESSAGE

Tyre and Caesarea

21 And so, with the tearful goodbyes behind us, we were on our way. We made a straight run to Cos, the next day reached Rhodes, and then Patara. There we found a ship going direct to Phoenicia, got on board, and set sail. Cyprus came into view on our left, but was soon out of sight as we kept on course for Syria, and eventually docked in the port of Tyre. While the cargo was being unloaded, we looked up the local disciples and stayed with them seven days. Their message to Paul, from insight given by the Spirit, was "Don't go to Jerusalem."

When our time was up, they escorted us out of the city to the docks. Everyone came along—men, women, children. They made a farewell party of the occasion! We all kneeled together on the beach and prayed. Then, after another round of saying goodbye, we climbed on board the ship while they drifted back to their homes.

A short run from Tyre to Ptolemais completed the voyage. We greeted our Christian friends there and stayed with them a day. In the morning we went on to Caesarea and stayed with Philip the Evangelist, one of "the Seven." Philip had four virgin daughters who prophesied.

After several days of visiting, a prophet from Judea by the name of Agabus came down to see us. He went right

KING JAMES VERSION

11 And when he was come unto us, he took Paul's girdle, and bound his own hands and feet, and said, Thus saith the Holy Ghost, So shall the Jews at Jerusalem bind the man that owneth this girdle, and shall deliver *him* into the hands of the Gentiles.

12 And when we heard these things, both we, and they of that place, besought him not to go up to Jerusalem.

13 Then Paul answered, What mean ye to weep and to break mine heart? for I am ready not to be bound only, but also to die at Jerusalem for the name of the Lord Jesus.

14 And when he would not be persuaded, we ceased, saying, The will of the Lord be done.

15 ¶ And after those days we took up our carriages, and went up to Jerusalem.

16 There went with us also *certain* of the disciples of Caesarea, and brought with them one Mnason of Cyprus, an old disciple, with whom we should lodge.

17 And when we were come to Jerusalem, the brethren received us gladly.

18 And the *day* following Paul went in with us unto James; and all the elders were present.

19 And when he had saluted them, he declared particularly what things God had wrought among the Gentiles by his ministry.

20 And when they heard *it*, they glorified the Lord, and

NEW AMERICAN STANDARD BIBLE

11 And coming to us, he took Paul's belt and bound his own feet and hands, and said, "This is what the Holy Spirit says: 'In this way the Jews at Jerusalem will bind the man who owns this belt and deliver him into the hands of the Gentiles.' "

12 When we had heard this, we as well as the local residents *began* begging him not to go up to Jerusalem.

13 Then Paul answered, "What are you doing, weeping and breaking my heart? For I am ready not only to be bound, but even to die at Jerusalem for the name of the Lord Jesus."

14 And since he would not be persuaded, we fell silent, remarking, "The will of the Lord be done!"

Paul at Jerusalem

15 After these days we got ready and started on our way up to Jerusalem.

16 *Some* of the disciples from Caesarea also came with us, taking us to Mnason of Cyprus, a disciple of long standing with whom we were to lodge.

17 After we arrived in Jerusalem, the brethren received us gladly.

18 And the following day Paul went in with us to James, and all the elders were present.

19 After he had greeted them, he *began* to relate one by one the things which God had done among the Gentiles through his ministry.

20 And when they heard it they *began* glorifying God; and

NEW CENTURY VERSION

came to us and borrowed Paul's belt and used it to tie his
own hands and feet. He said, "The Holy Spirit says, 'This
is how the Jews in Jerusalem will tie up the man who
wears this belt. Then they will give him to those who are
not Jews.' "

12When we all heard this, we and the people there
begged Paul not to go to Jerusalem. 13But he said, "Why
are you crying and making me so sad? I am not only ready
to be tied up in Jerusalem, I am ready to die for the Lord
Jesus!"

14We could not persuade him to stay away from
Jerusalem. So we stopped begging him and said, "We pray
that what the Lord wants will be done."

15After this, we got ready and started on our way to
Jerusalem. 16Some of the followers from Caesarea went
with us and took us to the home of Mnason, where we
would stay. He was from Cyprus and was one of the first
followers.

Paul Visits James

17In Jerusalem the believers were glad to see us. 18The
next day Paul went with us to visit James, and all the
elders were there. 19Paul greeted them and told them
everything God had done among the non-Jewish people
through him. 20When they heard this, they praised God.

CONTEMPORARY ENGLISH VERSION

belt, and with it he tied up his own hands and feet. Then
he told us, "The Holy Spirit says that some of the Jewish
leaders in Jerusalem will tie up the man who owns this
belt. They will also hand him over to the Gentiles." 12After
Agabus said this, we and the followers living there begged
Paul not to go to Jerusalem.

13But Paul answered, "Why are you crying and breaking
my heart? I am not only willing to be put in jail for the
Lord Jesus. I am even willing to die for him in Jerusalem!"

14Since we could not get Paul to change his mind, we
gave up and prayed, "Lord, please make us willing to do
what you want."

15Then we got ready to go to Jerusalem. 16Some of the
followers from Caesarea went with us and took us to stay
in the home of Mnason. He was from Cyprus and had been
a follower from the beginning.

Paul Visits James

17When we arrived in Jerusalem, the Lord's followers
gladly welcomed us. 18Paul went with us to see James[b] the
next day, and all the church leaders were present. 19Paul
greeted them and told how God had used him to help the
Gentiles. 20Everyone who heard this praised God and said
to Paul:

[b] 21.18 *James*: The Lord's brother.

NEW INTERNATIONAL VERSION

us, he took Paul's belt, tied his own hands and feet with it
and said, "The Holy Spirit says, 'In this way the Jews of
Jerusalem will bind the owner of this belt and will hand
him over to the Gentiles.' "

12When we heard this, we and the people there pleaded
with Paul not to go up to Jerusalem. 13Then Paul
answered, "Why are you weeping and breaking my heart? I
am ready not only to be bound, but also to die in Jeru-
salem for the name of the Lord Jesus." 14When he would
not be dissuaded, we gave up and said, "The Lord's will be
done."

15After this, we got ready and went up to Jerusalem.
16Some of the disciples from Caesarea accompanied us and
brought us to the home of Mnason, where we were to stay.
He was a man from Cyprus and one of the early disciples.

Paul's Arrival at Jerusalem

17When we arrived at Jerusalem, the brothers received us
warmly. 18The next day Paul and the rest of us went to see
James, and all the elders were present. 19Paul greeted them
and reported in detail what God had done among the
Gentiles through his ministry.

20When they heard this, they praised God. Then they

NEW LIVING TRANSLATION

11When he visited us, he took Paul's belt and bound his
own feet and hands with it. Then he said, "The Holy Spirit
declares, 'So shall the owner of this belt be bound by the
Jewish leaders in Jerusalem and turned over to the
Romans.' " 12When we heard this, we who were traveling
with him, as well as the local believers, begged Paul not to
go on to Jerusalem.

13But he said, "Why all this weeping? You are breaking
my heart! For I am ready not only to be jailed at Jerusalem
but also to die for the sake of the Lord Jesus." 14When it
was clear that we couldn't persuade him, we gave up and
said, "The will of the Lord be done."

Paul Arrives at Jerusalem

15Shortly afterward we packed our things and left for
Jerusalem. 16Some believers from Caesarea accompanied
us, and they took us to the home of Mnason, a man origi-
nally from Cyprus and one of the early disciples. 17All the
brothers and sisters in Jerusalem welcomed us cordially.

18The next day Paul went in with us to meet with James,
and all the elders of the Jerusalem church were present.
19After greetings were exchanged, Paul gave a detailed
account of the things God had accomplished among the
Gentiles through his ministry.

20After hearing this, they praised God. But then they

NEW KING JAMES VERSION

11When he had come to us, he took Paul's belt, bound his
own hands and feet, and said, "Thus says the Holy Spirit,
'So shall the Jews at Jerusalem bind the man who owns
this belt, and deliver *him* into the hands of the Gentiles.' "

12Now when we heard these things, both we and those
from that place pleaded with him not to go up to Jerusa-
lem. 13Then Paul answered, "What do you mean by weep-
ing and breaking my heart? For I am ready not only to be
bound, but also to die at Jerusalem for the name of the
Lord Jesus."

14So when he would not be persuaded, we ceased, say-
ing, "The will of the Lord be done."

Paul Urged to Make Peace

15And after those days we packed and went up to Jerusa-
lem. 16Also some of the disciples from Caesarea went with
us and brought with them a certain Mnason of Cyprus, an
early disciple, with whom we were to lodge.

17And when we had come to Jerusalem, the brethren
received us gladly. 18On the following *day* Paul went in
with us to James, and all the elders were present. 19When
he had greeted them, he told in detail those things which
God had done among the Gentiles through his ministry.
20And when they heard *it,* they glorified the Lord. And they

THE MESSAGE

up to Paul, took Paul's belt, and, in a dramatic gesture, tied himself up, hands and feet. He said, "This is what the Holy Spirit says: The Jews in Jerusalem are going to tie up the man who owns this belt just like this and hand him over to godless unbelievers."

When we heard that, we and everyone there that day begged Paul not to be stubborn and persist in going to Jerusalem. But Paul wouldn't budge: "Why all this hysteria? Why do you insist on making a scene and making it even harder for me? You're looking at this backwards. The issue in Jerusalem is not what they do to me, whether arrest or murder, but what the Master Jesus does through my obedience. Can't you see that?"

We saw that we weren't making even a dent in his resolve, and gave up. "It's in God's hands now," we said. "Master, you handle it."

It wasn't long before we had our luggage together and were on our way to Jerusalem. Some of the disciples from Caesarea went with us and took us to the home of Mnason, who received us warmly as his guests. A native of Cyprus, he had been among the earliest disciples.

Jerusalem

In Jerusalem, our friends, glad to see us, received us with open arms. The first thing next morning, we took Paul to see James. All the church leaders were there. After a time of greeting and small talk, Paul told the story, detail by detail, of what God had done among the Gentiles through his ministry. They listened with delight and gave God the glory.

KING JAMES VERSION

said unto him, Thou seest, brother, how many thousands of Jews there are which believe; and they are all zealous of the law:

21 And they are informed of thee, that thou teachest all the Jews which are among the Gentiles to forsake Moses, saying that they ought not to circumcise *their* children, neither to walk after the customs.

22 What is it therefore? the multitude must needs come together: for they will hear that thou art come.

23 Do therefore this that we say to thee: We have four men which have a vow on them;

24 Them take, and purify thyself with them, and be at charges with them, that they may shave *their* heads: and all may know that those things, whereof they were informed concerning thee, are nothing; but *that* thou thyself also walkest orderly, and keepest the law.

25 As touching the Gentiles which believe, we have written *and* concluded that they observe no such thing, save only that they keep themselves from *things* offered to idols, and from blood, and from strangled, and from fornication.

26 Then Paul took the men, and the next day purifying himself with them entered into the temple, to signify the accomplishment of the days of purification, until that an offering should be offered for every one of them.

NEW AMERICAN STANDARD BIBLE

they said to him, "You see, brother, how many thousands there are among the Jews of those who have believed, and they are all zealous for the Law;

21 and they have been told about you, that you are teaching all the Jews who are among the Gentiles to forsake Moses, telling them not to circumcise their children nor to walk according to the customs.

22 "What, then, is *to be done?* They will certainly hear that you have come.

23 "Therefore do this that we tell you. We have four men who are under a vow;

24 take them and purify yourself along with them, and pay their expenses so that they may shave their heads; and all will know that there is nothing to the things which they have been told about you, but that you yourself also walk orderly, keeping the Law.

25 "But concerning the Gentiles who have believed, we wrote, having decided that they should abstain from meat sacrificed to idols and from blood and from what is strangled and from fornication."

26 Then Paul took the men, and the next day, purifying himself along with them, went into the temple giving notice of the completion of the days of purification, until the sacrifice was offered for each one of them.

NEW CENTURY VERSION

Then they said to Paul, "Brother, you can see that many
thousands of Jews have become believers. And they think
it is very important to obey the law of Moses. 21They have
heard about your teaching, that you tell the Jews who live
among those who are not Jews to leave the law of Moses.
They have heard that you tell them not to circumcise their
children and not to obey Jewish customs. 22What should
we do? They will learn that you have come. 23So we will
tell you what to do: Four of our men have made a promise
to God. 24Take these men with you and share in their
cleansing ceremony.[b] Pay their expenses so they can shave
their heads.[c] Then it will prove to everyone that what they
have heard about you is not true and that you follow the
law of Moses in your own life. 25We have already sent a
letter to the non-Jewish believers. The letter said: 'Do not
eat food that has been offered to idols, or blood, or animals that have been strangled. Do not take part in sexual
sin.' "

26The next day Paul took the four men and shared in the
cleansing ceremony with them. Then he went to the
Temple and announced the time when the days of the
cleansing ceremony would be finished. On the last day an
offering would be given for each of the men.

21:24 [b] **cleansing ceremony** The special things Jews did to end the Nazirite promise. 21:24 [c] **shave their heads** The Jews did this to show that their promise was finished.

CONTEMPORARY ENGLISH VERSION

My friend, you can see how many tens of thousands
of the Jewish people have become followers! And all of
them are eager to obey the Law of Moses. 21But they
have been told that you are teaching those who live
among the Gentiles to disobey this Law. They claim that
you are telling them not to circumcise their sons or to
follow Jewish customs.

22What should we do now that our people have heard
that you are here? 23Please do what we ask, because
four of our men have made special promises to God.
24Join with them and prepare yourself for the ceremony
that goes with the promises. Pay the cost for their heads
to be shaved. Then everyone will learn that the reports
about you are not true. They will know that you do obey
the Law of Moses.

25Some while ago we told the Gentile followers what
we think they should do. We instructed them not to eat
anything offered to idols. They were told not to eat any
meat with blood still in it or the meat of an animal that
has been strangled. They were also told not to commit
any terrible sexual sins.[c]

26The next day Paul took the four men with him and got
himself ready at the same time they did. Then he went into
the temple and told when the final ceremony would take
place and when an offering would be made for each of
them.

[c] 21.25 *not to commit any terrible sexual sins*: See the note at 15.20.

NEW INTERNATIONAL VERSION

said to Paul: "You see, brother, how many thousands of Jews have believed, and all of them are zealous for the law. 21 They have been informed that you teach all the Jews who live among the Gentiles to turn away from Moses, telling them not to circumcise their children or live according to our customs. 22 What shall we do? They will certainly hear that you have come, 23 so do what we tell you. There are four men with us who have made a vow. 24 Take these men, join in their purification rites and pay their expenses, so that they can have their heads shaved. Then everybody will know there is no truth in these reports about you, but that you yourself are living in obedience to the law. 25 As for the Gentile believers, we have written to them our decision that they should abstain from food sacrificed to idols, from blood, from the meat of strangled animals and from sexual immorality."

26 The next day Paul took the men and purified himself along with them. Then he went to the temple to give notice of the date when the days of purification would end and the offering would be made for each of them.

NEW LIVING TRANSLATION

said, "You know, dear brother, how many thousands of Jews have also believed, and they all take the law of Moses very seriously. 21 Our Jewish Christians here at Jerusalem have been told that you are teaching all the Jews living in the Gentile world to turn their backs on the laws of Moses. They say that you teach people not to circumcise their children or follow other Jewish customs. 22 Now what can be done? For they will certainly hear that you have come.

23 "Here's our suggestion. We have four men here who have taken a vow and are preparing to shave their heads. 24 Go with them to the Temple and join them in the purification ceremony, and pay for them to have their heads shaved. Then everyone will know that the rumors are all false and that you yourself observe the Jewish laws.

25 "As for the Gentile Christians, all we ask of them is what we already told them in a letter: They should not eat food offered to idols, nor consume blood, nor eat meat from strangled animals, and they should stay away from all sexual immorality."

Paul Is Arrested

26 So Paul agreed to their request, and the next day he went through the purification ritual with the men and went to the Temple. Then he publicly announced the date when their vows would end and sacrifices would be offered for each of them.

NEW KING JAMES VERSION

said to him, "You see, brother, how many myriads of Jews there are who have believed, and they are all zealous for the law; 21 but they have been informed about you that you teach all the Jews who are among the Gentiles to forsake Moses, saying that they ought not to circumcise *their* children nor to walk according to the customs. 22 What then? The assembly must certainly meet, for they will[c] hear that you have come. 23 Therefore do what we tell you: We have four men who have taken a vow. 24 Take them and be purified with them, and pay their expenses so that they may shave *their* heads, and that all may know that those things of which they were informed concerning you are nothing, but *that* you yourself also walk orderly and keep the law. 25 But concerning the Gentiles who believe, we have written *and* decided that they should observe no such thing,[d] except that they should keep themselves from *things* offered to idols, from blood, from things strangled, and from sexual immorality."

Arrested in the Temple

26 Then Paul took the men, and the next day, having been purified with them, entered the temple to announce the expiration of the days of purification, at which time an offering should be made for each one of them.

21:22 [c] NU-Text reads *What then is to be done? They will certainly.*
21:25 [d] NU-Text omits *that they should observe no such thing, except.*

THE MESSAGE

They had a story to tell, too: "And just look at what's been happening here—thousands upon thousands of God-fearing Jews have become believers in Jesus! But there's also a problem because they are more zealous than ever in observing the laws of Moses. They've been told that you advise believing Jews who live surrounded by Gentiles to go light on Moses, telling them that they don't need to circumcise their children or keep up the old traditions. This isn't sitting at all well with them.

"We're worried about what will happen when they discover you're in town. There's bound to be trouble. So here is what we want you to do: There are four men from our company who have taken a vow involving ritual purification, but have no money to pay the expenses. Join these men in their vows and pay their expenses. Then it will become obvious to everyone that there is nothing to the rumors going around about you and that you are in fact scrupulous in your reverence for the laws of Moses.

"In asking you to do this, we're not going back on our agreement regarding Gentiles who have become believers. We continue to hold fast to what we wrote in that letter, namely, to be careful not to get involved in activities connected with idols; to avoid serving food offensive to Jewish Christians; to guard the morality of sex and marriage."

So Paul did it—took the men, joined them in their vows, and paid their way. The next day he went to the Temple to make it official and stay there until the proper sacrifices had been offered and completed for each of them.

KING JAMES VERSION

27 ¶ And when the seven days were almost ended, the Jews which were of Asia, when they saw him in the temple, stirred up all the people, and laid hands on him,

28 Crying out, Men of Israel, help: This is the man, that teacheth all *men* every where against the people, and the law, and this place: and further brought Greeks also into the temple, and hath polluted this holy place.

29 (For they had seen before with him in the city Trophimus an Ephesian, whom they supposed that Paul had brought into the temple.)

30 And all the city was moved, and the people ran together: and they took Paul, and drew him out of the temple: and forthwith the doors were shut.

31 And as they went about to kill him, tidings came unto the chief captain of the band, that all Jerusalem was in an uproar.

32 Who immediately took soldiers and centurions, and ran down unto them: and when they saw the chief captain and the soldiers, they left beating of Paul.

33 Then the chief captain came near, and took him, and commanded *him* to be bound with two chains; and demanded who he was, and what he had done.

34 And some cried one thing, some another, among the multitude: and when he could not know the certainty for the tumult, he commanded him to be carried into the castle.

NEW AMERICAN STANDARD BIBLE

Paul Seized in the Temple

27 When the seven days were almost over, the Jews from Asia, upon seeing him in the temple, *began* to stir up all the crowd and laid hands on him,

28 crying out, "Men of Israel, come to our aid! This is the man who preaches to all men everywhere against our people and the Law and this place; and besides he has even brought Greeks into the temple and has defiled this holy place."

29 For they had previously seen Trophimus the Ephesian in the city with him, and they supposed that Paul had brought him into the temple.

30 Then all the city was provoked, and the people rushed together, and taking hold of Paul they dragged him out of the temple, and immediately the doors were shut.

31 While they were seeking to kill him, a report came up to the [l]commander of the *Roman* cohort that all Jerusalem was in confusion.

32 At once he took along *some* soldiers and centurions and ran down to them; and when they saw the commander and the soldiers, they stopped beating Paul.

33 Then the commander came up and took hold of him, and ordered him to be bound with two chains; and he *began* asking who he was and what he had done.

34 But among the crowd some were shouting one thing *and* some another, and when he could not find out the facts because of the uproar, he ordered him to be brought into the barracks.

21:31 *l* I.e. chiliarch, in command of one thousand troops

NEW CENTURY VERSION

27When the seven days were almost over, some Jews
from Asia saw Paul at the Temple. They caused all the peo-
ple to be upset and grabbed Paul. 28They shouted, "People
of Israel, help us! This is the man who goes everywhere
teaching against the law of Moses, against our people, and
against this Temple. Now he has brought some Greeks into
the Temple and has made this holy place unclean!" 29(The
Jews said this because they had seen Trophimus, a man
from Ephesus, with Paul in Jerusalem. The Jews thought
that Paul had brought him into the Temple.)
30All the people in Jerusalem became upset. Together
they ran, took Paul, and dragged him out of the Temple.
The Temple doors were closed immediately. 31While they
were trying to kill Paul, the commander of the Roman
army in Jerusalem learned that there was trouble in the
whole city. 32Immediately he took some officers and sol-
diers and ran to the place where the crowd was gathered.
When the people saw them, they stopped beating Paul.
33The commander went to Paul and arrested him. He told
his soldiers to tie Paul with two chains. Then he asked
who he was and what he had done wrong. 34Some in the
crowd were yelling one thing, and some were yelling
another. Because of all this confusion and shouting, the
commander could not learn what had happened. So he
ordered the soldiers to take Paul to the army building.

CONTEMPORARY ENGLISH VERSION

Paul Is Arrested

27When the period of seven days for the ceremony was
almost over, some of the Jewish people from Asia saw Paul
in the temple. They got a large crowd together and started
attacking him. 28They were shouting, "Friends, help us!
This man goes around everywhere, saying bad things
about our nation and about the Law of Moses and about
this temple. He has even brought shame to this holy tem-
ple by bringing in Gentiles." 29Some of them thought that
Paul had brought Trophimus from Ephesus into the tem-
ple, because they had seen them together in the city.
30The whole city was in an uproar, and the people
turned into a mob. They grabbed Paul and dragged him out
of the temple. Then suddenly the doors were shut. 31The
people were about to kill Paul when the Roman army com-
mander heard that all Jerusalem was starting to riot. 32So
he quickly took some soldiers and officers and ran to
where the crowd had gathered.

As soon as the mob saw the commander and soldiers,
they stopped beating Paul. 33The army commander went
over and arrested him and had him bound with two
chains. Then he tried to find out who Paul was and what
he had done. 34Part of the crowd shouted one thing, and
part of them shouted something else. But they were mak-
ing so much noise that the commander could not find out
a thing. Then he ordered Paul to be taken into the fortress.

NEW INTERNATIONAL VERSION

Paul Arrested

[27]When the seven days were nearly over, some Jews from the province of Asia saw Paul at the temple. They stirred up the whole crowd and seized him, [28]shouting, "Men of Israel, help us! This is the man who teaches all men everywhere against our people and our law and this place. And besides, he has brought Greeks into the temple area and defiled this holy place." [29](They had previously seen Trophimus the Ephesian in the city with Paul and assumed that Paul had brought him into the temple area.)

[30]The whole city was aroused, and the people came running from all directions. Seizing Paul, they dragged him from the temple, and immediately the gates were shut. [31]While they were trying to kill him, news reached the commander of the Roman troops that the whole city of Jerusalem was in an uproar. [32]He at once took some officers and soldiers and ran down to the crowd. When the rioters saw the commander and his soldiers, they stopped beating Paul.

[33]The commander came up and arrested him and ordered him to be bound with two chains. Then he asked who he was and what he had done. [34]Some in the crowd shouted one thing and some another, and since the commander could not get at the truth because of the uproar, he ordered that Paul be taken into the barracks. [35]When Paul

NEW LIVING TRANSLATION

[27]The seven days were almost ended when some Jews from the province of Asia saw Paul in the Temple and roused a mob against him. They grabbed him, [28]yelling, "Men of Israel! Help! This is the man who teaches against our people and tells everybody to disobey the Jewish laws. He speaks against the Temple—and he even defiles it by bringing Gentiles in!" [29](For earlier that day they had seen him in the city with Trophimus, a Gentile from Ephesus,* and they assumed Paul had taken him into the Temple.)

[30]The whole population of the city was rocked by these accusations, and a great riot followed. Paul was dragged out of the Temple, and immediately the gates were closed behind him. [31]As they were trying to kill him, word reached the commander of the Roman regiment that all Jerusalem was in an uproar. [32]He immediately called out his soldiers and officers and ran down among the crowd. When the mob saw the commander and the troops coming, they stopped beating Paul. [33]The commander arrested him and ordered him bound with two chains. Then he asked the crowd who he was and what he had done. [34]Some shouted one thing and some another. He couldn't find out the truth in all the uproar and confusion, so he ordered Paul to be taken to the fortress. [35]As they reached the

21:29 Greek *Trophimus, the Ephesian.*

NEW KING JAMES VERSION

[27]Now when the seven days were almost ended, the Jews from Asia, seeing him in the temple, stirred up the whole crowd and laid hands on him, [28]crying out, "Men of Israel, help! This is the man who teaches all *men* everywhere against the people, the law, and this place; and furthermore he also brought Greeks into the temple and has defiled this holy place." [29](For they had previously[e] seen Trophimus the Ephesian with him in the city, whom they supposed that Paul had brought into the temple.)

[30]And all the city was disturbed; and the people ran together, seized Paul, and dragged him out of the temple; and immediately the doors were shut. [31]Now as they were seeking to kill him, news came to the commander of the garrison that all Jerusalem was in an uproar. [32]He immediately took soldiers and centurions, and ran down to them. And when they saw the commander and the soldiers, they stopped beating Paul. [33]Then the commander came near and took him, and commanded *him* to be bound with two chains; and he asked who he was and what he had done. [34]And some among the multitude cried one thing and some another.

So when he could not ascertain the truth because of the tumult, he commanded him to be taken into the barracks.

21:29 [e] M-Text omits *previously.*

THE MESSAGE

Paul Under Arrest

When the seven days of their purification were nearly up, some Jews from around Ephesus spotted him in the Temple. At once they turned the place upside-down. They grabbed Paul and started yelling at the top of their lungs, "Help! You Israelites, help! This is the man who is going all over the world telling lies against us and our religion and this place. He's even brought Greeks in here and defiled this holy place." (What had happened was that they had seen Paul and Trophimus, the Ephesian Greek, walking together in the city and had just assumed that he had also taken him to the Temple and shown him around.)

Soon the whole city was in an uproar, people running from everywhere to the Temple to get in on the action. They grabbed Paul, dragged him outside, and locked the Temple gates so he couldn't get back in and gain sanctuary.

As they were trying to kill him, word came to the captain of the guard, "A riot! The whole city's boiling over!" He acted swiftly. His soldiers and centurions ran to the scene at once. As soon as the mob saw the captain and his soldiers, they quit beating Paul.

The captain came up and put Paul under arrest. He first ordered him handcuffed, and then asked who he was and what he had done. All he got from the crowd were shouts, one yelling this, another that. It was impossible to tell one word from another in the mob hysteria, so the captain ordered Paul taken to the military barracks. But when they

KING JAMES VERSION

35 And when he came upon the stairs, so it was, that he was borne of the soldiers for the violence of the people.

36 For the multitude of the people followed after, crying, Away with him.

37 And as Paul was to be led into the castle, he said unto the chief captain, May I speak unto thee? Who said, Canst thou speak Greek?

38 Art not thou that Egyptian, which before these days madest an uproar, and leddest out into the wilderness four thousand men that were murderers?

39 But Paul said, I am a man *which am* a Jew of Tarsus, *a city* in Cilicia, a citizen of no mean city: and, I beseech thee, suffer me to speak unto the people.

40 And when he had given him licence, Paul stood on the stairs, and beckoned with the hand unto the people. And when there was made a great silence, he spake unto *them* in the Hebrew tongue, saying,

22 Men, brethren, and fathers, hear ye my defence *which I make* now unto you.

2 (And when they heard that he spake in the Hebrew tongue to them, they kept the more silence: and he saith,)

3 ¶ I am verily a man *which am* a Jew, born in Tarsus, *a city* in Cilicia, yet brought up in this city at the feet of Gamaliel, *and* taught according to the perfect manner of the law of the fathers, and was zealous toward God, as ye all are this day.

NEW AMERICAN STANDARD BIBLE

35 When he got to the stairs, he was carried by the soldiers because of the violence of the mob;

36 for the multitude of the people kept following them, shouting, "Away with him!"

37 As Paul was about to be brought into the barracks, he said to the commander, "May I say something to you?" And he *said, "Do you know Greek?

38 "Then you are not the Egyptian who some time ago stirred up a revolt and led the four thousand men of the Assassins out into the wilderness?"

39 But Paul said, "I am a Jew of Tarsus in Cilicia, a citizen of no insignificant city; and I beg you, allow me to speak to the people."

40 When he had given him permission, Paul, standing on the stairs, motioned to the people with his hand; and when there was a great hush, he spoke to them in the Hebrew dialect, saying,

Paul's Defense before the Jews

22 "Brethren and fathers, hear my defense which I now *offer* to you."

2 And when they heard that he was addressing them in the Hebrew dialect, they became even more quiet; and he *said,

3 "I am a Jew, born in Tarsus of Cilicia, but brought up in this city, educated under Gamaliel, strictly according to the law of our fathers, being zealous for God just as you all are today.

NEW CENTURY VERSION

35 When Paul came to the steps, the soldiers had to carry him because the people were ready to hurt him.
36 The whole mob was following them, shouting, "Kill him!"

37 As the soldiers were about to take Paul into the army building, he spoke to the commander, "May I say something to you?"

The commander said, "Do you speak Greek?
38 I thought you were the Egyptian who started some trouble against the government not long ago and led four thousand killers out to the desert."

39 Paul said, "No, I am a Jew from Tarsus in the country of Cilicia. I am a citizen of that important city. Please, let me speak to the people."

40 The commander gave permission, so Paul stood on the steps and waved his hand to quiet the people. When there was silence, he spoke to them in the Jewish language.[d]

Paul Speaks to the People

22 Paul said, "Friends, fellow Jews, listen to my defense to you."
2 When the Jews heard him speaking the Jewish language,[d] they became very quiet. Paul said,
3 "I am a Jew, born in Tarsus in the country of Cilicia, but I grew up in this city. I was a student of Gamaliel,[a] who carefully taught me everything about the law of our ancestors. I was very serious about serving God, just as are all of

21:40; 22:2 [d] **Jewish language** Hebrew or Aramaic, the languages of the Jews in the first century. 22:3 [a] **Gamaliel** A very important teacher of the Pharisees, a Jewish religious group (Acts 5:34).

CONTEMPORARY ENGLISH VERSION

35 As they reached the steps, the crowd became so wild that the soldiers had to lift Paul up and carry him.
36 The crowd followed and kept shouting, "Kill him! Kill him!"

Paul Speaks to the Crowd

37 When Paul was about to be taken into the fortress, he asked the commander, "Can I say something to you?"

"How do you know Greek?" the commander asked.
38 "Aren't you that Egyptian who started a riot not long ago and led four thousand terrorists into the desert?"

39 "No!" Paul replied. "I am a Jew from Tarsus, an important city in Cilicia. Please let me speak to the crowd."

40 The commander told him he could speak, so Paul stood on the steps and motioned to the people. When they were quiet, he spoke to them in Aramaic:

22 "My friends and leaders of our nation, listen as I explain what happened!"
2 When the crowd heard Paul speak to them in Aramaic, they became even quieter. Then Paul said:

3 I am a Jew, born and raised in the city of Tarsus in Cilicia. I was a student of Gamaliel and was taught to follow every single law of our ancestors. In fact, I was just as eager to obey God as any of you are today.

NEW INTERNATIONAL VERSION

reached the steps, the violence of the mob was so great he had to be carried by the soldiers. 36 The crowd that followed kept shouting, "Away with him!"

Paul Speaks to the Crowd

37 As the soldiers were about to take Paul into the barracks, he asked the commander, "May I say something to you?"

"Do you speak Greek?" he replied. 38 "Aren't you the Egyptian who started a revolt and led four thousand terrorists out into the desert some time ago?"

39 Paul answered, "I am a Jew, from Tarsus in Cilicia, a citizen of no ordinary city. Please let me speak to the people."

40 Having received the commander's permission, Paul stood on the steps and motioned to the crowd. When they were all silent, he said to them in Aramaic[a]:

22 1 "Brothers and fathers, listen now to my defense."

2 When they heard him speak to them in Aramaic, they became very quiet.

Then Paul said: 3 "I am a Jew, born in Tarsus of Cilicia, but brought up in this city. Under Gamaliel I was thoroughly trained in the law of our fathers and was just as zealous for God as any of you are today. 4 I persecuted the

[a] *40* Or possibly *Hebrew*; also in 22:2

NEW LIVING TRANSLATION

stairs, the mob grew so violent the soldiers had to lift Paul to their shoulders to protect him. 36 And the crowd followed behind shouting, "Kill him, kill him!"

Paul Speaks to the Crowd

37 As Paul was about to be taken inside, he said to the commander, "May I have a word with you?"

"Do you know Greek?" the commander asked, surprised. 38 "Aren't you the Egyptian who led a rebellion some time ago and took four thousand members of the Assassins out into the desert?"

39 "No," Paul replied, "I am a Jew from Tarsus in Cilicia, which is an important city. Please, let me talk to these people." 40 The commander agreed, so Paul stood on the stairs and motioned to the people to be quiet. Soon a deep silence enveloped the crowd, and he addressed them in their own language, Aramaic.*

22 "Brothers and esteemed fathers," Paul said, "listen to me as I offer my defense." 2 When they heard him speaking in their own language,* the silence was even greater. 3 "I am a Jew, born in Tarsus, a city in Cilicia, and I was brought up and educated here in Jerusalem under Gamaliel. At his feet I learned to follow our Jewish laws and customs very carefully. I became very zealous to honor God in everything I did, just as all of you are today. 4 And I

21:40 Or *Hebrew*. 22:2 Greek *in Aramaic*.

NEW KING JAMES VERSION

35 When he reached the stairs, he had to be carried by the soldiers because of the violence of the mob. 36 For the multitude of the people followed after, crying out, "Away with him!"

Addressing the Jerusalem Mob

37 Then as Paul was about to be led into the barracks, he said to the commander, "May I speak to you?"

He replied, "Can you speak Greek? 38 Are you not the Egyptian who some time ago stirred up a rebellion and led the four thousand assassins out into the wilderness?"

39 But Paul said, "I am a Jew from Tarsus, in Cilicia, a citizen of no mean city; and I implore you, permit me to speak to the people."

40 So when he had given him permission, Paul stood on the stairs and motioned with his hand to the people. And when there was a great silence, he spoke to *them* in the Hebrew language, saying,

22 "Brethren and fathers, hear my defense before you now." 2 And when they heard that he spoke to them in the Hebrew language, they kept all the more silent.

Then he said: 3 "I am indeed a Jew, born in Tarsus of Cilicia, but brought up in this city at the feet of Gamaliel, taught according to the strictness of our fathers' law, and was zealous toward God as you all are today. 4 I persecuted

THE MESSAGE

got to the Temple steps, the mob became so violent that the soldiers had to carry Paul. As they carried him away, the crowd followed, shouting, "Kill him! Kill him!"

When they got to the barracks and were about to go in, Paul said to the captain, "Can I say something to you?"

He answered, "Oh, I didn't know you spoke Greek. I thought you were the Egyptian who not long ago started a riot here, and then hid out in the desert with his four thousand thugs."

Paul said, "No, I'm a Jew, born in Tarsus. And I'm a citizen still of that influential city. I have a simple request: Let me speak to the crowd."

Paul Tells His Story

Standing on the barracks steps, Paul turned and held his arms up. A hush fell over the crowd as Paul began to speak. He spoke in Hebrew.

22 "My dear brothers and fathers, listen carefully to what I have to say before you jump to conclusions about me." When they heard him speaking Hebrew, they grew even quieter. No one wanted to miss a word of this.

He continued, "I am a good Jew, born in Tarsus in the province of Cilicia, but educated here in Jerusalem under the exacting eye of Rabbi Gamaliel, thoroughly instructed in our religious traditions. And I've always been passionately on God's side, just as you are right now.

KING JAMES VERSION

4 And I persecuted this way unto the death, binding and delivering into prisons both men and women.

5 As also the high priest doth bear me witness, and all the estate of the elders: from whom also I received letters unto the brethren, and went to Damascus, to bring them which were there bound unto Jerusalem, for to be punished.

6 And it came to pass, that, as I made my journey, and was come nigh unto Damascus about noon, suddenly there shone from heaven a great light round about me.

7 And I fell unto the ground, and heard a voice saying unto me, Saul, Saul, why persecutest thou me?

8 And I answered, Who art thou, Lord? And he said unto me, I am Jesus of Nazareth, whom thou persecutest.

9 And they that were with me saw indeed the light, and were afraid; but they heard not the voice of him that spake to me.

10 And I said, What shall I do, Lord? And the Lord said unto me, Arise, and go into Damascus; and there it shall be told thee of all things which are appointed for thee to do.

11 And when I could not see for the glory of that light, being led by the hand of them that were with me, I came into Damascus.

12 And one Ananias, a devout man according to the law, having a good report of all the Jews which dwelt *there*,

13 Came unto me, and stood, and said unto me, Brother Saul, receive thy sight. And the same hour I looked up upon him.

NEW AMERICAN STANDARD BIBLE

4 "I persecuted this Way to the death, binding and putting both men and women into prisons,

5 as also the high priest and all the Council of the elders can testify. From them I also received letters to the brethren, and started off for Damascus in order to bring even those who were there to Jerusalem as prisoners to be punished.

6 "But it happened that as I was on my way, approaching Damascus about noontime, a very bright light suddenly flashed from heaven all around me,

7 and I fell to the ground and heard a voice saying to me, 'Saul, Saul, why are you persecuting Me?'

8 "And I answered, 'Who are You, Lord?' And He said to me, 'I am Jesus the Nazarene, whom you are persecuting.'

9 "And those who were with me saw the light, to be sure, but did not understand the voice of the One who was speaking to me.

10 "And I said, 'What shall I do, Lord?' And the Lord said to me, 'Get up and go on into Damascus, and there you will be told of all that has been appointed for you to do.'

11 "But since I could not see because of the brightness of that light, I was led by the hand by those who were with me and came into Damascus.

12 "A certain Ananias, a man who was devout by the standard of the Law, *and* well spoken of by all the Jews who lived there,

13 came to me, and standing near said to me, 'Brother Saul, receive your sight!' And at that very time I looked up at him.

NEW CENTURY VERSION

you here today. 4 I persecuted the people who followed the Way of Jesus, and some of them were even killed. I arrested men and women and put them in jail. 5 The high priest and the whole council of older Jewish leaders can tell you this is true. They gave me letters to the Jewish brothers in Damascus. So I was going there to arrest these people and bring them back to Jerusalem to be punished.

6 "About noon when I came near Damascus, a bright light from heaven suddenly flashed all around me. 7 I fell to the ground and heard a voice saying, 'Saul, Saul, why are you persecuting me?' 8 I asked, 'Who are you, Lord?' The voice said, 'I am Jesus from Nazareth whom you are persecuting.' 9 Those who were with me did not hear the voice, but they saw the light. 10 I said, 'What shall I do, Lord?' The Lord answered, 'Get up and go to Damascus. There you will be told about all the things I have planned for you to do.' 11 I could not see, because the bright light had made me blind. So my companions led me into Damascus.

12 "There a man named Ananias came to me. He was a religious man; he obeyed the law of Moses, and all the Jews who lived there respected him. 13 He stood by me and said, 'Brother Saul, see again!' Immediately I was able to

CONTEMPORARY ENGLISH VERSION

4 I made trouble for everyone who followed the Lord's Way,[a] and I even had some of them killed. I had others arrested and put in jail. I didn't care if they were men or women. 5 The high priest and all the council members can tell you that this is true. They even gave me letters to the Jewish leaders in Damascus, so that I could arrest people there and bring them to Jerusalem to be punished.

6 One day about noon I was getting close to Damascus, when a bright light from heaven suddenly flashed around me. 7 I fell to the ground and heard a voice asking, "Saul, Saul, why are you so cruel to me?"

8 "Who are you?" I answered.

The Lord replied, "I am Jesus from Nazareth! I am the one you are so cruel to." 9 The men who were traveling with me saw the light, but did not hear the voice.

10 I asked, "Lord, what do you want me to do?"

Then he told me, "Get up and go to Damascus. When you get there, you will be told what to do." 11 The light had been so bright that I couldn't see. And the other men had to lead me by the hand to Damascus.

12 In that city there was a man named Ananias, who faithfully obeyed the Law of Moses and was well liked by all the Jewish people living there. 13 He came to me and said, "Saul, my friend, you can now see again!"

[a] 22.4 *followed the Lord's Way*: See the note at 9.2.

NEW INTERNATIONAL VERSION

followers of this Way to their death, arresting both men
and women and throwing them into prison, 5as also the
high priest and all the Council can testify. I even obtained
letters from them to their brothers in Damascus, and went
there to bring these people as prisoners to Jerusalem to be
punished.
6"About noon as I came near Damascus, suddenly a
bright light from heaven flashed around me. 7I fell to the
ground and heard a voice say to me, 'Saul! Saul! Why do
you persecute me?'
8" 'Who are you, Lord?' I asked.
" 'I am Jesus of Nazareth, whom you are persecuting,' he
replied. 9My companions saw the light, but they did not
understand the voice of him who was speaking to me.
10" 'What shall I do, Lord?' I asked.
" 'Get up,' the Lord said, 'and go into Damascus. There
you will be told all that you have been assigned to do.'
11My companions led me by the hand into Damascus,
because the brilliance of the light had blinded me.
12"A man named Ananias came to see me. He was a
devout observer of the law and highly respected by all the
Jews living there. 13He stood beside me and said, 'Brother
Saul, receive your sight!' And at that very moment I was
able to see him.

NEW LIVING TRANSLATION

persecuted the followers of the Way, hounding some to
death, binding and delivering both men and women to
prison. 5The high priest and the whole council of leaders
can testify that this is so. For I received letters from them
to our Jewish brothers in Damascus, authorizing me to
bring the Christians from there to Jerusalem, in chains, to
be punished.
6"As I was on the road, nearing Damascus, about noon a
very bright light from heaven suddenly shone around me.
7I fell to the ground and heard a voice saying to me, 'Saul,
Saul, why are you persecuting me?'
8" 'Who are you, sir?' I asked. And he replied, 'I am
Jesus of Nazareth, the one you are persecuting.' 9The peo-
ple with me saw the light but didn't hear the voice.
10"I said, 'What shall I do, Lord?' And the Lord told me,
'Get up and go into Damascus, and there you will be told
all that you are to do.'
11"I was blinded by the intense light and had to be led
into Damascus by my companions. 12A man named
Ananias lived there. He was a godly man in his devotion to
the law, and he was well thought of by all the Jews of
Damascus. 13He came to me and stood beside me and said,
'Brother Saul, receive your sight.' And that very hour I
could see him!

NEW KING JAMES VERSION

this Way to the death, binding and delivering into prisons
both men and women, 5as also the high priest bears me
witness, and all the council of the elders, from whom I also
received letters to the brethren, and went to Damascus to
bring in chains even those who were there to Jerusalem to
be punished.
6"Now it happened, as I journeyed and came near Da-
mascus at about noon, suddenly a great light from heaven
shone around me. 7And I fell to the ground and heard a
voice saying to me, 'Saul, Saul, why are you persecuting
Me?' 8So I answered, 'Who are You, Lord?' And He said to
me, 'I am Jesus of Nazareth, whom you are persecuting.'
9"And those who were with me indeed saw the light and
were afraid,[a] but they did not hear the voice of Him who
spoke to me. 10So I said, 'What shall I do, Lord?' And the
Lord said to me, 'Arise and go into Damascus, and there
you will be told all things which are appointed for you to
do.' 11And since I could not see for the glory of that light,
being led by the hand of those who were with me, I came
into Damascus.
12"Then a certain Ananias, a devout man according to
the law, having a good testimony with all the Jews who
dwelt *there,* 13came to me; and he stood and said to me,
'Brother Saul, receive your sight.' And at that same hour I

22:9 [a] NU-Text omits *and were afraid.*

THE MESSAGE

"I went after anyone connected with this 'Way,' went at them hammer and tongs, ready to kill for God. I rounded up men and women right and left and had them thrown in prison. You can ask the Chief Priest or anyone in the High Council to verify this; they all knew me well. Then I went off to our brothers in Damascus, armed with official documents authorizing me to hunt down the Christians there, arrest them, and bring them back to Jerusalem for sentencing.

"As I arrived on the outskirts of Damascus about noon, a blinding light blazed out of the skies and I fell to the ground, dazed. I heard a voice: 'Saul, Saul, why are you out to get me?'

"'Who are you, Master?' I asked.

"He said, 'I am Jesus the Nazarene, the One you're hunting down.' My companions saw the light, but they didn't hear the conversation.

"Then I said, 'What do I do now, Master?'

"He said, 'Get to your feet and enter Damascus. There you'll be told everything that's been set out for you to do.' And so we entered Damascus, but nothing like the entrance I had planned—I was blind as a bat and my companions had to lead me in by the hand.

"And that's when I met Ananias, a man with a sterling reputation in observing our laws—the Jewish community in Damascus is unanimous on that score. He came and put his arm on my shoulder. 'Look up,' he said. I looked, and found myself looking right into his eyes—I could see again!

KING JAMES VERSION

14 And he said, The God of our fathers hath chosen thee, that thou shouldest know his will, and see that Just One, and shouldest hear the voice of his mouth.

15 For thou shalt be his witness unto all men of what thou hast seen and heard.

16 And now why tarriest thou? arise, and be baptized, and wash away thy sins, calling on the name of the Lord.

17 And it came to pass, that, when I was come again to Jerusalem, even while I prayed in the temple, I was in a trance;

18 And saw him saying unto me, Make haste, and get thee quickly out of Jerusalem: for they will not receive thy testimony concerning me.

19 And I said, Lord, they know that I imprisoned and beat in every synagogue them that believed on thee:

20 And when the blood of thy martyr Stephen was shed, I also was standing by, and consenting unto his death, and kept the raiment of them that slew him.

21 And he said unto me, Depart: for I will send thee far hence unto the Gentiles.

22 ¶ And they gave him audience unto this word, and *then* lifted up their voices, and said, Away with such a *fellow* from the earth: for it is not fit that he should live.

23 And as they cried out, and cast off *their* clothes, and threw dust into the air,

24 The chief captain commanded him to be brought into the castle, and bade that he should be examined by

NEW AMERICAN STANDARD BIBLE

14 "And he said, 'The God of our fathers has appointed you to know His will and to see the Righteous One and to hear an utterance from His mouth.

15 'For you will be a witness for Him to all men of what you have seen and heard.

16 'Now why do you delay? Get up and be baptized, and wash away your sins, calling on His name.'

17 "It happened when I returned to Jerusalem and was praying in the temple, that I fell into a trance,

18 and I saw Him saying to me, 'Make haste, and get out of Jerusalem quickly, because they will not accept your testimony about Me.'

19 "And I said, 'Lord, they themselves understand that in one synagogue after another I used to imprison and beat those who believed in You.

20 'And when the blood of Your witness Stephen was being shed, I also was standing by approving, and watching out for the coats of those who were slaying him.'

21 "And He said to me, 'Go! For I will send you far away to the Gentiles.' "

22 They listened to him up to this statement, and *then* they raised their voices and said, "Away with such a fellow from the earth, for he should not be allowed to live!"

23 And as they were crying out and throwing off their cloaks and tossing dust into the air,

24 the [1]commander ordered him to be brought into the barracks, stating that he should be examined by scourging

22:24 [1] I.e. chiliarch, in command of one thousand troops

NEW CENTURY VERSION

see him. 14He said, 'The God of our ancestors chose you
long ago to know his plan, to see the Righteous One, and
to hear words from him. 15You will be his witness to all
people, telling them about what you have seen and heard.
16Now, why wait any longer? Get up, be baptized, and
wash your sins away, trusting in him to save you.'

17"Later, when I returned to Jerusalem, I was praying in
the Temple, and I saw a vision. 18I saw the Lord saying to
me, 'Hurry! Leave Jerusalem now! The people here will not
accept the truth about me.' 19But I said, 'Lord, they know
that in every synagogue I put the believers in jail and beat
them. 20They also know I was there when Stephen, your
witness, was killed. I stood there agreeing and holding the
coats of those who were killing him!' 21But the Lord said
to me, 'Leave now. I will send you far away to the non-
Jewish people.' "

22The crowd listened to Paul until he said this. Then
they began shouting, "Kill him! Get him out of the world!
He should not be allowed to live!" 23They shouted, threw
off their coats,[b] and threw dust into the air.[c]

24Then the commander ordered the soldiers to take Paul

22:23 [b] **threw off their coats** This showed that the Jews were very angry with Paul. 22:23 [c] **threw dust into the air** This showed even greater anger.

CONTEMPORARY ENGLISH VERSION

At once I could see. 14Then Ananias told me, "The God
that our ancestors worshiped has chosen you to know
what he wants done. He has chosen you to see the One
Who Obeys God[b] and to hear his voice. 15You must tell
everyone what you have seen and heard. 16What are you
waiting for? Get up! Be baptized, and wash away your
sins by praying to the Lord."

17After this I returned to Jerusalem and went to the
temple to pray. There I had a vision 18of the Lord who
said to me, "Hurry and leave Jerusalem! The people
won't listen to what you say about me."

19I replied, "Lord, they know that in many of our
meeting places I arrested and beat people who had faith
in you. 20Stephen was killed because he spoke for you,
and I stood there and cheered them on. I even guarded
the clothes of the men who murdered him."

21But the Lord told me to go, and he promised to send
me far away to the Gentiles.

22The crowd listened until Paul said this. Then they
started shouting, "Get rid of this man! He doesn't deserve
to live." 23They kept shouting. They waved their clothes
around and threw dust into the air.

Paul and the Roman Army Commander

24The Roman commander ordered Paul to be taken into

[b] **22.14** *One Who Obeys God*: See the note at 7.52.

NEW INTERNATIONAL VERSION

[14]"Then he said: 'The God of our fathers has chosen you to know his will and to see the Righteous One and to hear words from his mouth. [15]You will be his witness to all men of what you have seen and heard. [16]And now what are you waiting for? Get up, be baptized and wash your sins away, calling on his name.'

[17]"When I returned to Jerusalem and was praying at the temple, I fell into a trance [18]and saw the Lord speaking. 'Quick!' he said to me. 'Leave Jerusalem immediately, because they will not accept your testimony about me.'

[19]" 'Lord,' I replied, 'these men know that I went from one synagogue to another to imprison and beat those who believe in you. [20]And when the blood of your martyr[a] Stephen was shed, I stood there giving my approval and guarding the clothes of those who were killing him.'

[21]"Then the Lord said to me, 'Go; I will send you far away to the Gentiles.' "

Paul the Roman Citizen

[22]The crowd listened to Paul until he said this. Then they raised their voices and shouted, "Rid the earth of him! He's not fit to live!"

[23]As they were shouting and throwing off their cloaks and flinging dust into the air, [24]the commander ordered Paul to be taken into the barracks. He directed that he be

[a] *20* Or *witness*

NEW LIVING TRANSLATION

[14]"Then he told me, 'The God of our ancestors has chosen you to know his will and to see the Righteous One and hear him speak. [15]You are to take his message everywhere, telling the whole world what you have seen and heard. [16]And now, why delay? Get up and be baptized, and have your sins washed away, calling on the name of the Lord.'

[17]"One day after I returned to Jerusalem, I was praying in the Temple, and I fell into a trance. [18]I saw a vision of Jesus saying to me, 'Hurry! Leave Jerusalem, for the people here won't believe you when you give them your testimony about me.'

[19]" 'But Lord,' I argued, 'they certainly know that I imprisoned and beat those in every synagogue who believed on you. [20]And when your witness Stephen was killed, I was standing there agreeing. I kept the coats they laid aside as they stoned him.'

[21]"But the Lord said to me, 'Leave Jerusalem, for I will send you far away to the Gentiles!' "

[22]The crowd listened until Paul came to that word; then with one voice they shouted, "Away with such a fellow! Kill him! He isn't fit to live!" [23]They yelled, threw off their coats, and tossed handfuls of dust into the air.

Paul Reveals His Roman Citizenship

[24]The commander brought Paul inside and ordered him

NEW KING JAMES VERSION

looked up at him. [14]Then he said, 'The God of our fathers has chosen you that you should know His will, and see the Just One, and hear the voice of His mouth. [15]For you will be His witness to all men of what you have seen and heard. [16]And now why are you waiting? Arise and be baptized, and wash away your sins, calling on the name of the Lord.'

[17]"Now it happened, when I returned to Jerusalem and was praying in the temple, that I was in a trance [18]and saw Him saying to me, 'Make haste and get out of Jerusalem quickly, for they will not receive your testimony concerning Me.' [19]So I said, 'Lord, they know that in every synagogue I imprisoned and beat those who believe on You. [20]And when the blood of Your martyr Stephen was shed, I also was standing by consenting to his death,[b] and guarding the clothes of those who were killing him.' [21]Then He said to me, 'Depart, for I will send you far from here to the Gentiles.' "

Paul's Roman Citizenship

[22]And they listened to him until this word, and *then* they raised their voices and said, "Away with such a *fellow* from the earth, for he is not fit to live!" [23]Then, as they cried out and tore off *their* clothes and threw dust into the air, [24]the commander ordered him to be brought into the

22:20 [b] NU-Text omits *to his death.*

THE MESSAGE

"Then he said, 'The God of our ancestors has handpicked you to be briefed on his plan of action. You've actually seen the Righteous Innocent and heard him speak. You are to be a key witness to everyone you meet of what you've seen and heard. So what are you waiting for? Get up and get yourself baptized, scrubbed clean of those sins and personally acquainted with God.'

"Well, it happened just as Ananias said. After I was back in Jerusalem and praying one day in the Temple, lost in the presence of God, I saw him, saw God's Righteous Innocent, and heard him say to me, 'Hurry up! Get out of here as quickly as you can. None of the Jews here in Jerusalem are going to accept what you say about me.'

"At first I objected: 'Who has better credentials? They all know how obsessed I was with hunting out those who believed in you, beating them up in the meeting places and throwing them in jail. And when your witness Stephen was murdered, I was right there, holding the coats of the murderers and cheering them on. And now they see me totally converted. What better qualification could I have?'

"But he said, 'Don't argue. Go. I'm sending you on a long journey to outsider Gentiles.' "

A Roman Citizen

The people in the crowd had listened attentively up to this point, but now they broke loose, shouting out, "Kill him! He's an insect! Stomp on him!" They shook their fists. They filled the air with curses. That's when the captain intervened and ordered Paul taken into the barracks.

KING JAMES VERSION

scourging; that he might know wherefore they cried so against him.

25 And as they bound him with thongs, Paul said unto the centurion that stood by, Is it lawful for you to scourge a man that is a Roman, and uncondemned?

26 When the centurion heard *that*, he went and told the chief captain, saying, Take heed what thou doest: for this man is a Roman.

27 Then the chief captain came, and said unto him, Tell me, art thou a Roman? He said, Yea.

28 And the chief captain answered, With a great sum obtained I this freedom. And Paul said, But I was *free* born.

29 Then straightway they departed from him which should have examined him: and the chief captain also was afraid, after he knew that he was a Roman, and because he had bound him.

30 On the morrow, because he would have known the certainty wherefore he was accused of the Jews, he loosed him from *his* bands, and commanded the chief priests and all their council to appear, and brought Paul down, and set him before them.

NEW AMERICAN STANDARD BIBLE

so that he might find out the reason why they were shouting against him that way.

25 But when they stretched him out with thongs, Paul said to the centurion who was standing by, "Is it lawful for you to scourge a man who is a Roman and uncondemned?"

26 When the centurion heard *this,* he went to the commander and told him, saying, "What are you about to do? For this man is a Roman."

27 The commander came and said to him, "Tell me, are you a Roman?" And he said, "Yes."

28 The commander answered, "I acquired this citizenship with a large sum of money." And Paul said, "But I was actually born *a citizen.*"

29 Therefore those who were about to examine him immediately let go of him; and the commander also was afraid when he found out that he was a Roman, and because he had put him in chains.

30 But on the next day, wishing to know for certain why he had been accused by the Jews, he released him and ordered the chief priests and all the Council to assemble, and brought Paul down and set him before them.

NEW CENTURY VERSION

into the army building and beat him. He wanted to make Paul tell why the people were shouting against him like this. 25 But as the soldiers were tying him up, preparing to beat him, Paul said to an officer nearby, "Do you have the right to beat a Roman citizen[d] who has not been proven guilty?"

26 When the officer heard this, he went to the commander and reported it. The officer said, "Do you know what you are doing? This man is a Roman citizen."

27 The commander came to Paul and said, "Tell me, are you really a Roman citizen?"

He answered, "Yes."

28 The commander said, "I paid a lot of money to become a Roman citizen."

But Paul said, "I was born a citizen."

29 The men who were preparing to question Paul moved away from him immediately. The commander was frightened because he had already tied Paul, and Paul was a Roman citizen.

Paul Speaks to Jewish Leaders

30 The next day the commander decided to learn why the Jews were accusing Paul. So he ordered the leading priests and the Jewish council to meet. The commander took Paul's chains off. Then he brought Paul out and stood him before their meeting.

22:25 [d] **Roman citizen** Roman law said that Roman citizens must not be beaten before they had a trial.

CONTEMPORARY ENGLISH VERSION

the fortress and beaten with a whip. He did this to find out why the people were screaming at Paul.

25 While the soldiers were tying Paul up to be beaten, he asked the officer standing there, "Is it legal to beat a Roman citizen before he has been tried in court?"

26 When the officer heard this, he went to the commander and said, "What are you doing? This man is a Roman citizen!"

27 The commander went to Paul and asked, "Tell me, are you a Roman citizen?"

"Yes," Paul answered.

28 The commander then said, "I paid a lot of money to become a Roman citizen."[c]

But Paul replied, "I was born a Roman citizen."

29 The men who were about to beat and question Paul quickly backed off. And the commander himself was frightened when he realized that he had put a Roman citizen in chains.

Paul Is Tried by the Council

30 The next day the commander wanted to know the real reason why the Jewish leaders had brought charges against Paul. So he had Paul's chains removed, and he ordered the chief priests and the whole council to meet. Then he had Paul led in and made him stand in front of them.

[c] 22.28 *Roman citizen*: See the note at 16.37.

NEW INTERNATIONAL VERSION

flogged and questioned in order to find out why the people were shouting at him like this. 25As they stretched him out to flog him, Paul said to the centurion standing there, "Is it legal for you to flog a Roman citizen who hasn't even been found guilty?"

26When the centurion heard this, he went to the commander and reported it. "What are you going to do?" he asked. "This man is a Roman citizen."

27The commander went to Paul and asked, "Tell me, are you a Roman citizen?"

"Yes, I am," he answered.

28Then the commander said, "I had to pay a big price for my citizenship."

"But I was born a citizen," Paul replied.

29Those who were about to question him withdrew immediately. The commander himself was alarmed when he realized that he had put Paul, a Roman citizen, in chains.

Before the Sanhedrin

30The next day, since the commander wanted to find out exactly why Paul was being accused by the Jews, he released him and ordered the chief priests and all the Sanhedrin to assemble. Then he brought Paul and had him stand before them.

NEW LIVING TRANSLATION

lashed with whips to make him confess his crime. He wanted to find out why the crowd had become so furious. 25As they tied Paul down to lash him, Paul said to the officer standing there, "Is it legal for you to whip a Roman citizen who hasn't even been tried?"

26The officer went to the commander and asked, "What are you doing? This man is a Roman citizen!"

27So the commander went over and asked Paul, "Tell me, are you a Roman citizen?"

"Yes, I certainly am," Paul replied.

28"I am, too," the commander muttered, "and it cost me plenty!"

"But I am a citizen by birth!"

29The soldiers who were about to interrogate Paul quickly withdrew when they heard he was a Roman citizen, and the commander was frightened because he had ordered him bound and whipped.

Paul before the High Council

30The next day the commander freed Paul from his chains and ordered the leading priests into session with the Jewish high council.* He had Paul brought in before them to try to find out what the trouble was all about.

22:30 Greek *Sanhedrin.*

NEW KING JAMES VERSION

barracks, and said that he should be examined under scourging, so that he might know why they shouted so against him. 25And as they bound him with thongs, Paul said to the centurion who stood by, "Is it lawful for you to scourge a man who is a Roman, and uncondemned?"

26When the centurion heard *that,* he went and told the commander, saying, "Take care what you do, for this man is a Roman."

27Then the commander came and said to him, "Tell me, are you a Roman?"

He said, "Yes."

28The commander answered, "With a large sum I obtained this citizenship."

And Paul said, "But I was born *a citizen.*"

29Then immediately those who were about to examine him withdrew from him; and the commander was also afraid after he found out that he was a Roman, and because he had bound him.

The Sanhedrin Divided

30The next day, because he wanted to know for certain why he was accused by the Jews, he released him from *his* bonds, and commanded the chief priests and all their council to appear, and brought Paul down and set him before them.

THE MESSAGE

By now the captain was thoroughly exasperated. He decided to interrogate Paul under torture in order to get to the bottom of this, to find out what he had done that provoked this outraged violence. As they spread-eagled him with thongs, getting him ready for the whip, Paul said to the centurion standing there, "Is this legal: torturing a Roman citizen without a fair trial?"

When the centurion heard that, he went directly to the captain. "Do you realize what you've done? This man is a Roman citizen!"

The captain came back and took charge. "Is what I hear right? You're a Roman citizen?"

Paul said, "I certainly am."

The captain was impressed. "I paid a huge sum for my citizenship. How much did it cost you?"

"Nothing," said Paul. "It cost me nothing. I was free from the day of my birth."

That put a stop to the interrogation. And it put the fear of God into the captain. He had put a Roman citizen in chains and come within a whisker of putting him under torture!

The next day, determined to get to the root of the trouble and know for sure what was behind the Jewish accusation, the captain released Paul and ordered a meeting of the high priests and the High Council to see what they could make of it. Paul was led in and took his place before them.

KING JAMES VERSION

23 And Paul, earnestly beholding the council, said, Men *and* brethren, I have lived in all good conscience before God until this day.

2 And the high priest Ananias commanded them that stood by him to smite him on the mouth.

3 Then said Paul unto him, God shall smite thee, *thou* whited wall: for sittest thou to judge me after the law, and commandest me to be smitten contrary to the law?

4 And they that stood by said, Revilest thou God's high priest?

5 Then said Paul, I wist not, brethren, that he was the high priest: for it is written, Thou shalt not speak evil of the ruler of thy people.

6 ¶ But when Paul perceived that the one part were Sadducees, and the other Pharisees, he cried out in the council, Men *and* brethren, I am a Pharisee, the son of a Pharisee: of the hope and resurrection of the dead I am called in question.

7 And when he had so said, there arose a dissension between the Pharisees and the Sadducees: and the multitude was divided.

8 For the Sadducees say that there is no resurrection, neither angel, nor spirit: but the Pharisees confess both.

9 And there arose a great cry: and the scribes *that were* of the Pharisees' part arose, and strove, saying, We find no

NEW AMERICAN STANDARD BIBLE

Paul before the Council

23 Paul, looking intently at the Council, said, "Brethren, I have lived my life with a perfectly good conscience before God up to this day."

2 The high priest Ananias commanded those standing beside him to strike him on the mouth.

3 Then Paul said to him, "God is going to strike you, you whitewashed wall! Do you sit to try me according to the Law, and in violation of the Law order me to be struck?"

4 But the bystanders said, "Do you revile God's high priest?"

5 And Paul said, "I was not aware, brethren, that he was high priest; for it is written, 'YOU SHALL NOT SPEAK EVIL OF A RULER OF YOUR PEOPLE.' "

6 But perceiving that one group were Sadducees and the other Pharisees, Paul *began* crying out in the Council, "Brethren, I am a Pharisee, a son of Pharisees; I am on trial for the hope and resurrection of the dead!"

7 As he said this, there occurred a dissension between the Pharisees and Sadducees, and the assembly was divided.

8 For the Sadducees say that there is no resurrection, nor an angel, nor a spirit, but the Pharisees acknowledge them all.

9 And there occurred a great uproar; and some of the scribes of the Pharisaic party stood up and *began* to argue heatedly, saying, "We find nothing wrong with this man;

NEW CENTURY VERSION

23 Paul looked at the Jewish council and said,
"Brothers, I have lived my life without guilt feel-
ings before God up to this day." 2 Ananias,[a] the high priest,
heard this and told the men who were standing near Paul
to hit him on the mouth. 3 Paul said to Ananias, "God will
hit you, too! You are like a wall that has been painted
white. You sit there and judge me, using the law of Moses,
but you are telling them to hit me, and that is against the
law."

4 The men standing near Paul said to him, "You cannot
insult God's high priest like that!"

5 Paul said, "Brothers, I did not know this man was the
high priest. It is written in the Scriptures, 'You must not
curse a leader of your people.' "[b]

6 Some of the men in the meeting were Sadducees, and
others were Pharisees. Knowing this, Paul shouted to
them, "My brothers, I am a Pharisee, and my father was a
Pharisee. I am on trial here because I believe that people
will rise from the dead."

7 When Paul said this, there was an argument between
the Pharisees and the Sadducees, and the group was divid-
ed. 8 (The Sadducees do not believe in angels or spirits or
that people will rise from the dead. But the Pharisees
believe in them all.) 9 So there was a great uproar. Some of
the teachers of the law, who were Pharisees, stood up and

23:2 [a] **Ananias** This is not the same man named Ananias in Acts 22:12.
23:5 [b] **'You...people.'** Quotation from Exodus 22:28.

CONTEMPORARY ENGLISH VERSION

23 Paul looked straight at the council members and
said, "My friends, to this day I have served God
with a clear conscience!"

2 Then Ananias the high priest ordered the men standing
beside Paul to hit him on the mouth. 3 Paul turned to the high
priest and said, "You whitewashed wall![a] God will hit you.
You sit there to judge me by the Law of Moses. But at the
same time you order men to break the Law by hitting me."

4 The men standing beside Paul asked, "Don't you know
you are insulting God's high priest?"

5 Paul replied, "Oh! I didn't know he was the high priest.
The Scriptures do tell us not to speak evil about a leader of
our people."

6 When Paul saw that some of the council members were
Sadducees and others were Pharisees, he shouted, "My
friends, I am a Pharisee and the son of a Pharisee. I am on
trial simply because I believe that the dead will be raised
to life."

7 As soon as Paul said this, the Pharisees and the
Sadducees got into a big argument, and the council mem-
bers started taking sides. 8 The Sadducees do not believe in
angels or spirits or that the dead will rise to life. But the
Pharisees believe in all of these, 9 and so there was a lot of
shouting. Some of the teachers of the Law of Moses were
Pharisees. Finally, they became angry and said, "We don't

[a] 23.3 *whitewashed wall*: Someone who pretends to be good, but really isn't.

NEW INTERNATIONAL VERSION

23 Paul looked straight at the Sanhedrin and said, "My brothers, I have fulfilled my duty to God in all good conscience to this day." 2At this the high priest Ananias ordered those standing near Paul to strike him on the mouth. 3Then Paul said to him, "God will strike you, you whitewashed wall! You sit there to judge me according to the law, yet you yourself violate the law by commanding that I be struck!"

4Those who were standing near Paul said, "You dare to insult God's high priest?"

5Paul replied, "Brothers, I did not realize that he was the high priest; for it is written: 'Do not speak evil about the ruler of your people.'[a]"

6Then Paul, knowing that some of them were Sadducees and the others Pharisees, called out in the Sanhedrin, "My brothers, I am a Pharisee, the son of a Pharisee. I stand on trial because of my hope in the resurrection of the dead." 7When he said this, a dispute broke out between the Pharisees and the Sadducees, and the assembly was divided. 8(The Sadducees say that there is no resurrection, and that there are neither angels nor spirits, but the Pharisees acknowledge them all.)

9There was a great uproar, and some of the teachers of the law who were Pharisees stood up and argued vigorously. "We find nothing wrong with this man," they said.

[a] *5* Exodus 22:28

NEW LIVING TRANSLATION

23 Gazing intently at the high council,* Paul began: "Brothers, I have always lived before God in all good conscience!"

2Instantly Ananias the high priest commanded those close to Paul to slap him on the mouth. 3But Paul said to him, "God will slap you, you whitewashed wall! What kind of judge are you to break the law yourself by ordering me struck like that?"

4Those standing near Paul said to him, "Is that the way to talk to God's high priest?"

5"I'm sorry, brothers. I didn't realize he was the high priest," Paul replied, "for the Scriptures say, 'Do not speak evil of anyone who rules over you.'* "

6Paul realized that some members of the high council were Sadducees and some were Pharisees, so he shouted, "Brothers, I am a Pharisee, as were all my ancestors! And I am on trial because my hope is in the resurrection of the dead!"

7This divided the council—the Pharisees against the Sadducees—8for the Sadducees say there is no resurrection or angels or spirits, but the Pharisees believe in all of these. 9So a great clamor arose. Some of the teachers of religious law who were Pharisees jumped up to argue that Paul was all right. "We see nothing wrong with him," they

23:1 Greek *Sanhedrin;* also in 23:6, 15, 20, 28. 23:5 Exod 22:28.

NEW KING JAMES VERSION

23 Then Paul, looking earnestly at the council, said, "Men *and* brethren, I have lived in all good conscience before God until this day." 2And the high priest Ananias commanded those who stood by him to strike him on the mouth. 3Then Paul said to him, "God will strike you, *you* whitewashed wall! For you sit to judge me according to the law, and do you command me to be struck contrary to the law?"

4And those who stood by said, "Do you revile God's high priest?"

5Then Paul said, "I did not know, brethren, that he was the high priest; for it is written, *'You shall not speak evil of a ruler of your people.'* "[a]

6But when Paul perceived that one part were Sadducees and the other Pharisees, he cried out in the council, "Men *and* brethren, I am a Pharisee, the son of a Pharisee; concerning the hope and resurrection of the dead I am being judged!"

7And when he had said this, a dissension arose between the Pharisees and the Sadducees; and the assembly was divided. 8For Sadducees say that there is no resurrection—and no angel or spirit; but the Pharisees confess both. 9Then there arose a loud outcry. And the scribes of the Pharisees' party arose and protested, saying, "We find no

23:5 [a] Exodus 22:28

THE MESSAGE

Before the High Council

23 Paul surveyed the members of the council with a steady gaze, and then said his piece: "Friends, I've lived with a clear conscience before God all my life, up to this very moment." That set the Chief Priest Ananias off. He ordered his aides to slap Paul in the face. Paul shot back, "God will slap you down! What a fake you are! You sit there and judge me by the Law and then break the Law by ordering me slapped around!"

The aides were scandalized: "How dare you talk to God's Chief Priest like that!"

Paul acted surprised. "How was I to know he was Chief Priest? He doesn't act like a Chief Priest. You're right, the Scripture does say, 'Don't speak abusively to a ruler of the people.' Sorry."

Paul, knowing some of the council was made up of Sadducees and others of Pharisees and how they hated each other, decided to exploit their antagonism: "Friends, I am a stalwart Pharisee from a long line of Pharisees. It's because of my Pharisee convictions—the hope and resurrection of the dead—that I've been hauled into this court."

The moment he said this, the council split right down the middle, Pharisees and Sadducees going at each other in heated argument. Sadducees have nothing to do with a resurrection or angels or even a spirit. If they can't see it, they don't believe it. Pharisees believe it all. And so a huge and noisy quarrel broke out. Then some of the religion scholars on the Pharisee side shouted down the others: "We don't find anything wrong with this man! And what if

KING JAMES VERSION

evil in this man: but if a spirit or an angel hath spoken to him, let us not fight against God.

10 And when there arose a great dissension, the chief captain, fearing lest Paul should have been pulled in pieces of them, commanded the soldiers to go down, and to take him by force from among them, and to bring *him* into the castle.

11 And the night following the Lord stood by him, and said, Be of good cheer, Paul: for as thou hast testified of me in Jerusalem, so must thou bear witness also at Rome.

12 ¶ And when it was day, certain of the Jews banded together, and bound themselves under a curse, saying that they would neither eat nor drink till they had killed Paul.

13 And they were more than forty which had made this conspiracy.

14 And they came to the chief priests and elders, and said, We have bound ourselves under a great curse, that we will eat nothing until we have slain Paul.

15 Now therefore ye with the council signify to the chief captain that he bring him down unto you to morrow, as though ye would enquire something more perfectly concerning him: and we, or ever he come near, are ready to kill him.

16 And when Paul's sister's son heard of their lying in wait, he went and entered into the castle, and told Paul.

17 Then Paul called one of the centurions unto *him*, and said, Bring this young man unto the chief captain: for he hath a certain thing to tell him.

NEW AMERICAN STANDARD BIBLE

suppose a spirit or an angel has spoken to him?"

10 And as a great dissension was developing, the [l]commander was afraid Paul would be torn to pieces by them and ordered the troops to go down and take him away from them by force, and bring him into the barracks.

11 But on the night *immediately* following, the Lord stood at his side and said, "Take courage; for as you have solemnly witnessed to My cause at Jerusalem, so you must witness at Rome also."

A Conspiracy to Kill Paul

12 When it was day, the Jews formed a conspiracy and bound themselves under an oath, saying that they would neither eat nor drink until they had killed Paul.

13 There were more than forty who formed this plot.

14 They came to the chief priests and the elders and said, "We have bound ourselves under a solemn oath to taste nothing until we have killed Paul.

15 "Now therefore, you and the Council notify the commander to bring him down to you, as though you were going to determine his case by a more thorough investigation; and we for our part are ready to slay him before he comes near *the place.*"

16 But the son of Paul's sister heard of their ambush, and he came and entered the barracks and told Paul.

17 Paul called one of the centurions to him and said, "Lead this young man to the commander, for he has something to report to him."

23:10 [l] I.e. chiliarch, in command of one thousand troops

NEW CENTURY VERSION

argued, "We find nothing wrong with this man. Maybe an angel or a spirit did speak to him."

10The argument was beginning to turn into such a fight that the commander was afraid the Jews would tear Paul to pieces. So he told the soldiers to go down and take Paul away and put him in the army building.

11The next night the Lord came and stood by Paul. He said, "Be brave! You have told people in Jerusalem about me. You must do the same in Rome."

12In the morning some of the Jews made a plan to kill Paul, and they took an oath not to eat or drink anything until they had killed him. 13There were more than forty Jews who made this plan. 14They went to the leading priests and the older Jewish leaders and said, "We have taken an oath not to eat or drink until we have killed Paul. 15So this is what we want you to do: Send a message to the commander to bring Paul out to you as though you want to ask him more questions. We will be waiting to kill him while he is on the way here."

16But Paul's nephew heard about this plan and went to the army building and told Paul. 17Then Paul called one of the officers and said, "Take this young man to the commander. He has a message for him."

CONTEMPORARY ENGLISH VERSION

find anything wrong with this man. Maybe a spirit or an angel really did speak to him."

10The argument became fierce, and the commander was afraid that Paul would be pulled apart. So he ordered the soldiers to go in and rescue Paul. Then they took him back into the fortress.

11That night the Lord stood beside Paul and said, "Don't worry! Just as you have told others about me in Jerusalem, you must also tell about me in Rome."

A Plot To Kill Paul

12-13The next morning more than forty Jewish men got together and vowed that they would not eat or drink anything until they had killed Paul. 14Then some of them went to the chief priests and the nation's leaders and said, "We have promised God that we would not eat a thing until we have killed Paul. 15You and everyone in the council must go to the commander and pretend that you want to find out more about the charges against Paul. Ask for him to be brought before your court. Meanwhile, we will be waiting to kill him before he gets there."

16When Paul's nephew heard about the plot, he went to the fortress and told Paul about it. 17So Paul said to one of the army officers, "Take this young man to the commander. He has something to tell him."

NEW INTERNATIONAL VERSION

"What if a spirit or an angel has spoken to him?" 10The dispute became so violent that the commander was afraid Paul would be torn to pieces by them. He ordered the troops to go down and take him away from them by force and bring him into the barracks.

11The following night the Lord stood near Paul and said, "Take courage! As you have testified about me in Jerusalem, so you must also testify in Rome."

The Plot to Kill Paul

12The next morning the Jews formed a conspiracy and bound themselves with an oath not to eat or drink until they had killed Paul. 13More than forty men were involved in this plot. 14They went to the chief priests and elders and said, "We have taken a solemn oath not to eat anything until we have killed Paul. 15Now then, you and the Sanhedrin petition the commander to bring him before you on the pretext of wanting more accurate information about his case. We are ready to kill him before he gets here."

16But when the son of Paul's sister heard of this plot, he went into the barracks and told Paul.

17Then Paul called one of the centurions and said, "Take this young man to the commander; he has something to tell him." 18So he took him to the commander.

NEW LIVING TRANSLATION

shouted. "Perhaps a spirit or an angel spoke to him." 10The shouting grew louder and louder, and the men were tugging at Paul from both sides, pulling him this way and that. Finally, the commander, fearing they would tear him apart, ordered his soldiers to take him away from them and bring him back to the fortress.

11That night the Lord appeared to Paul and said, "Be encouraged, Paul. Just as you have told the people about me here in Jerusalem, you must preach the Good News in Rome."

The Plan to Kill Paul

12The next morning a group of Jews got together and bound themselves with an oath to neither eat nor drink until they had killed Paul. 13There were more than forty of them. 14They went to the leading priests and other leaders and told them what they had done. "We have bound ourselves under oath to neither eat nor drink until we have killed Paul. 15You and the high council should tell the commander to bring Paul back to the council again," they requested. "Pretend you want to examine his case more fully. We will kill him on the way."

16But Paul's nephew heard of their plan and went to the fortress and told Paul. 17Paul called one of the officers and said, "Take this young man to the commander. He has something important to tell him."

NEW KING JAMES VERSION

evil in this man; but if a spirit or an angel has spoken to him, let us not fight against God."[b]

10Now when there arose a great dissension, the commander, fearing lest Paul might be pulled to pieces by them, commanded the soldiers to go down and take him by force from among them, and bring *him* into the barracks.

The Plot Against Paul

11But the following night the Lord stood by him and said, "Be of good cheer, Paul; for as you have testified for Me in Jerusalem, so you must also bear witness at Rome."

12And when it was day, some of the Jews banded together and bound themselves under an oath, saying that they would neither eat nor drink till they had killed Paul. 13Now there were more than forty who had formed this conspiracy. 14They came to the chief priests and elders, and said, "We have bound ourselves under a great oath that we will eat nothing until we have killed Paul. 15Now you, therefore, together with the council, suggest to the commander that he be brought down to you tomorrow,[c] as though you were going to make further inquiries concerning him; but we are ready to kill him before he comes near."

16So when Paul's sister's son heard of their ambush, he went and entered the barracks and told Paul. 17Then Paul called one of the centurions to *him* and said, "Take this young man to the commander, for he has something to tell

23:9 [b] NU-Text omits last clause and reads *what if a spirit or an angel has spoken to him?* 23:15 [c] NU-Text omits *tomorrow.*

THE MESSAGE

a spirit has spoken to him? Or maybe an angel? What if it turns out we're fighting against God?"

That was fuel on the fire. The quarrel flamed up and became so violent the captain was afraid they would tear Paul apart, limb from limb. He ordered the soldiers to get him out of there and escort him back to the safety of the barracks.

A Plot Against Paul

That night the Master appeared to Paul: "It's going to be all right. Everything is going to turn out for the best. You've been a good witness for me here in Jerusalem. Now you're going to be my witness in Rome!"

Next day the Jews worked up a plot against Paul. They took a solemn oath that they would neither eat nor drink until they had killed him. Over forty of them ritually bound themselves to this murder pact and presented themselves to the high priests and religious leaders. "We've bound ourselves by a solemn oath to eat nothing until we have killed Paul. But we need your help. Send a request from the council to the captain to bring Paul back so that you can investigate the charges in more detail. We'll do the rest. Before he gets anywhere near you, we'll have killed him. You won't be involved."

Paul's nephew, his sister's son, overheard them plotting the ambush. He went immediately to the barracks and told Paul. Paul called over one of the centurions and said, "Take this young man to the captain. He has something important to tell him."

KING JAMES VERSION

18 So he took him, and brought *him* to the chief captain, and said, Paul the prisoner called me unto *him*, and prayed me to bring this young man unto thee, who hath something to say unto thee.

19 Then the chief captain took him by the hand, and went *with him* aside privately, and asked *him*, What is that thou hast to tell me?

20 And he said, The Jews have agreed to desire thee that thou wouldest bring down Paul to morrow into the council, as though they would enquire somewhat of him more perfectly.

21 But do not thou yield unto them: for there lie in wait for him of them more than forty men, which have bound themselves with an oath, that they will neither eat nor drink till they have killed him: and now are they ready, looking for a promise from thee.

22 So the chief captain *then* let the young man depart, and charged *him, See thou* tell no man that thou hast shewed these things to me.

23 And he called unto *him* two centurions, saying, Make ready two hundred soldiers to go to Caesarea, and horsemen threescore and ten, and spearmen two hundred, at the third hour of the night;

24 And provide *them* beasts, that they may set Paul on, and bring *him* safe unto Felix the governor.

25 And he wrote a letter after this manner:

26 Claudius Lysias unto the most excellent governor Felix *sendeth* greeting.

NEW AMERICAN STANDARD BIBLE

18 So he took him and led him to the commander and *said, "Paul the prisoner called me to him and asked me to lead this young man to you since he has something to tell you."

19 The commander took him by the hand and stepping aside, *began* to inquire of him privately, "What is it that you have to report to me?"

20 And he said, "The Jews have agreed to ask you to bring Paul down tomorrow to the Council, as though they were going to inquire somewhat more thoroughly about him.

21 "So do not listen to them, for more than forty of them are lying in wait for him who have bound themselves under a curse not to eat or drink until they slay him; and now they are ready and waiting for the promise from you."

22 So the commander let the young man go, instructing him, "Tell no one that you have notified me of these things."

Paul Moved to Caesarea

23 And he called to him two of the centurions and said, "Get two hundred soldiers ready by [2]the third hour of the night to proceed to Caesarea, with seventy horsemen and two hundred spearmen."

24 *They were* also to provide mounts to put Paul on and bring him safely to Felix the governor.

25 And he wrote a letter having this form:

26 "Claudius Lysias, to the most excellent governor Felix, greetings.

23:23 [2] I.e. 9 p.m.

NEW CENTURY VERSION

18So the officer brought Paul's nephew to the command-
er and said, "The prisoner, Paul, asked me to bring this
young man to you. He wants to tell you something."
19The commander took the young man's hand and led
him to a place where they could be alone. He asked, "What
do you want to tell me?"
20The young man said, "The Jews have decided to ask
you to bring Paul down to their council meeting tomorrow.
They want you to think they are going to ask him more
questions. 21But don't believe them! More than forty men
are hiding and waiting to kill Paul. They have all taken an
oath not to eat or drink until they have killed him. Now
they are waiting for you to agree."
22The commander sent the young man away, ordering
him, "Don't tell anyone that you have told me about their
plan."

Paul Is Sent to Caesarea

23Then the commander called two officers and said, "I
need some men to go to Caesarea. Get two hundred sol-
diers, seventy horsemen, and two hundred men with
spears ready to leave at nine o'clock tonight. 24Get some
horses for Paul to ride so he can be taken to Governor Felix
safely." 25And he wrote a letter that said:
26From Claudius Lysias.
To the Most Excellent Governor Felix:
Greetings.

CONTEMPORARY ENGLISH VERSION

18The officer took him to the commander and said, "The
prisoner named Paul asked me to bring this young man to
you, because he has something to tell you."
19The commander took the young man aside and asked
him in private, "What do you want to tell me?"
20He answered, "Some men are planning to ask you to
bring Paul down to the Jewish council tomorrow. They will
claim that they want to find out more about him. 21But
please don't do what they say. More than forty men are
going to attack Paul. They have made a vow not to eat or
drink anything until they have killed him. Even now they
are waiting to hear what you decide."
22The commander sent the young man away after saying
to him, "Don't let anyone know that you told me this."

Paul Is Sent to Felix the Governor

23The commander called in two of his officers and told
them, "By nine o'clock tonight have two hundred soldiers
ready to go to Caesarea. Take along seventy men on horse-
back and two hundred foot soldiers with spears. 24Get a
horse ready for Paul and make sure that he gets safely
through to Felix the governor."
25The commander wrote a letter that said:
26Greetings from Claudius Lysias to the Honorable
Governor Felix:

NEW INTERNATIONAL VERSION

The centurion said, "Paul, the prisoner, sent for me and asked me to bring this young man to you because he has something to tell you."

19The commander took the young man by the hand, drew him aside and asked, "What is it you want to tell me?"

20He said: "The Jews have agreed to ask you to bring Paul before the Sanhedrin tomorrow on the pretext of wanting more accurate information about him. 21Don't give in to them, because more than forty of them are waiting in ambush for him. They have taken an oath not to eat or drink until they have killed him. They are ready now, waiting for your consent to their request."

22The commander dismissed the young man and cautioned him, "Don't tell anyone that you have reported this to me."

Paul Transferred to Caesarea

23Then he called two of his centurions and ordered them, "Get ready a detachment of two hundred soldiers, seventy horsemen and two hundred spearmen[b] to go to Caesarea at nine tonight. 24Provide mounts for Paul so that he may be taken safely to Governor Felix."

25He wrote a letter as follows:

26Claudius Lysias,

To His Excellency, Governor Felix:

Greetings.

[b] *23* The meaning of the Greek for this word is uncertain.

NEW LIVING TRANSLATION

18So the officer did, explaining, "Paul, the prisoner, called me over and asked me to bring this young man to you because he has something to tell you."

19The commander took him by the arm, led him aside, and asked, "What is it you want to tell me?"

20Paul's nephew told him, "Some Jews are going to ask you to bring Paul before the Jewish high council tomorrow, pretending they want to get some more information. 21But don't do it! There are more than forty men hiding along the way ready to jump him and kill him. They have vowed not to eat or drink until they kill him. They are ready, expecting you to agree to their request."

22"Don't let a soul know you told me this," the commander warned the young man as he sent him away.

Paul Is Sent to Caesarea

23Then the commander called two of his officers and ordered, "Get two hundred soldiers ready to leave for Caesarea at nine o'clock tonight. Also take two hundred spearmen and seventy horsemen. 24Provide horses for Paul to ride, and get him safely to Governor Felix." 25Then he wrote this letter to the governor:

26"From Claudius Lysias, to his Excellency, Governor Felix.

NEW KING JAMES VERSION

him." 18So he took him and brought *him* to the commander and said, "Paul the prisoner called me to *him* and asked *me* to bring this young man to you. He has something to say to you."

19Then the commander took him by the hand, went aside, and asked privately, "What is it that you have to tell me?"

20And he said, "The Jews have agreed to ask that you bring Paul down to the council tomorrow, as though they were going to inquire more fully about him. 21But do not yield to them, for more than forty of them lie in wait for him, men who have bound themselves by an oath that they will neither eat nor drink till they have killed him; and now they are ready, waiting for the promise from you."

22So the commander let the young man depart, and commanded *him,* "Tell no one that you have revealed these things to me."

Sent to Felix

23And he called for two centurions, saying, "Prepare two hundred soldiers, seventy horsemen, and two hundred spearmen to go to Caesarea at the third hour of the night; 24and provide mounts to set Paul on, and bring *him* safely to Felix the governor." 25He wrote a letter in the following manner:

26 Claudius Lysias,

To the most excellent governor Felix:

Greetings.

THE MESSAGE

The centurion brought him to the captain and said, "The prisoner Paul asked me to bring this young man to you. He said he has something urgent to tell you."

The captain took him by the arm and led him aside privately. "What is it? What do you have to tell me?"

Paul's nephew said, "The Jews have worked up a plot against Paul. They're going to ask you to bring Paul to the council first thing in the morning on the pretext that they want to investigate the charges against him in more detail. But it's a trick to get him out of your safekeeping so they can murder him. Right now there are more than forty men lying in ambush for him. They've all taken a vow to neither eat nor drink until they've killed him. The ambush is set—all they're waiting for is for you to send him over."

The captain dismissed the nephew with a warning: "Don't breathe a word of this to a soul."

The captain called up two centurions. "Get two hundred soldiers ready to go immediately to Caesarea. Also seventy cavalry and two hundred light infantry. I want them ready to march by nine o'clock tonight. And you'll need a couple of mules for Paul and his gear. We're going to present this man safe and sound to Governor Felix."

Then he wrote this letter:

From Claudius Lysias, to the Most Honorable Governor Felix:

Greetings!

KING JAMES VERSION

27 This man was taken of the Jews, and should have been killed of them: then came I with an army, and rescued him, having understood that he was a Roman.

28 And when I would have known the cause wherefore they accused him, I brought him forth into their council:

29 Whom I perceived to be accused of questions of their law, but to have nothing laid to his charge worthy of death or of bonds.

30 And when it was told me how that the Jews laid wait for the man, I sent straightway to thee, and gave commandment to his accusers also to say before thee what *they had* against him. Farewell.

31 Then the soldiers, as it was commanded them, took Paul, and brought *him* by night to Antipatris.

32 On the morrow they left the horsemen to go with him, and returned to the castle:

33 Who, when they came to Caesarea, and delivered the epistle to the governor, presented Paul also before him.

34 And when the governor had read *the letter*, he asked of what province he was. And when he understood that *he was* of Cilicia;

35 I will hear thee, said he, when thine accusers are also come. And he commanded him to be kept in Herod's judgment hall.

NEW AMERICAN STANDARD BIBLE

27 "When this man was arrested by the Jews and was about to be slain by them, I came up to them with the troops and rescued him, having learned that he was a Roman.

28 "And wanting to ascertain the charge for which they were accusing him, I brought him down to their Council;

29 and I found him to be accused over questions about their Law, but under no accusation deserving death or imprisonment.

30 "When I was informed that there would be a plot against the man, I sent him to you at once, also instructing his accusers to bring charges against him before you."

31 So the soldiers, in accordance with their orders, took Paul and brought him by night to Antipatris.

32 But the next day, leaving the horsemen to go on with him, they returned to the barracks.

33 When these had come to Caesarea and delivered the letter to the governor, they also presented Paul to him.

34 When he had read it, he asked from what province he was, and when he learned that he was from Cilicia,

35 he said, "I will give you a hearing after your accusers arrive also," giving orders for him to be kept in Herod's [3]Praetorium.

23:35 [3] I.e. governor's official residence

NEW CENTURY VERSION

27The Jews had taken this man and planned to kill
him. But I learned that he is a Roman citizen, so I
went with my soldiers and saved him. 28I wanted to
know why they were accusing him, so I brought him
before their council meeting. 29I learned that the Jews
said Paul did some things that were wrong by their
own laws, but no charge was worthy of jail or death.
30When I was told that some of the Jews were plan-
ning to kill Paul, I sent him to you at once. I also told
those Jews to tell you what they have against him.

31So the soldiers did what they were told and took Paul
and brought him to the city of Antipatris that night. 32The
next day the horsemen went with Paul to Caesarea, but the
other soldiers went back to the army building in Jerusalem.
33When the horsemen came to Caesarea and gave the letter
to the governor, they turned Paul over to him. 34The gover-
nor read the letter and asked Paul, "What area are you
from?" When he learned that Paul was from Cilicia, 35he
said, "I will hear your case when those who are against
you come here, too." Then the governor gave orders for
Paul to be kept under guard in Herod's palace.

CONTEMPORARY ENGLISH VERSION

27Some Jews grabbed this man and were about to kill
him. But when I found out that he was a Roman citizen,
I took some soldiers and rescued him.

28I wanted to find out what they had against him. So I
brought him before their council 29and learned that the
charges concern only their religious laws. This man isn't
guilty of anything for which he should die or even be put
in jail.

30As soon as I learned that there was a plot against
him, I sent him to you and told their leaders to bring
charges against him in your court.

31The soldiers obeyed the commander's orders, and that
same night they took Paul to the city of Antipatris. 32The
next day the foot soldiers returned to the fortress and let
the soldiers on horseback take him the rest of the way.
33When they came to Caesarea, they gave the letter to the
governor and handed Paul over to him.

34The governor read the letter. Then he asked Paul and
found out that he was from Cilicia. 35The governor said, "I
will listen to your case as soon as the people come to bring
their charges against you." After saying this, he gave
orders for Paul to be kept as a prisoner in Herod's palace.[b]

[b] **23.35** *Herod's palace*: The palace built by Herod the Great and used by the Roman governors of Palestine.

NEW INTERNATIONAL VERSION

27This man was seized by the Jews and they were
about to kill him, but I came with my troops and res-
cued him, for I had learned that he is a Roman citizen.
28I wanted to know why they were accusing him, so I
brought him to their Sanhedrin. 29I found that the
accusation had to do with questions about their law,
but there was no charge against him that deserved
death or imprisonment. 30When I was informed of a
plot to be carried out against the man, I sent him to
you at once. I also ordered his accusers to present to
you their case against him.

31So the soldiers, carrying out their orders, took Paul
with them during the night and brought him as far as
Antipatris. 32The next day they let the cavalry go on with
him, while they returned to the barracks. 33When the cav-
alry arrived in Caesarea, they delivered the letter to the
governor and handed Paul over to him. 34The governor
read the letter and asked what province he was from.
Learning that he was from Cilicia, 35he said, "I will hear
your case when your accusers get here." Then he ordered
that Paul be kept under guard in Herod's palace.

NEW LIVING TRANSLATION

Greetings! 27This man was seized by some Jews, and they
were about to kill him when I arrived with the troops.
When I learned that he was a Roman citizen, I removed
him to safety. 28Then I took him to their high council to
try to find out what he had done. 29I soon discovered it
was something regarding their religious law—certainly
nothing worthy of imprisonment or death. 30But when I
was informed of a plot to kill him, I immediately sent him
on to you. I have told his accusers to bring their charges
before you."

31So that night, as ordered, the soldiers took Paul as far
as Antipatris. 32They returned to the fortress the next
morning, while the horsemen took him on to Caesarea.
33When they arrived in Caesarea, they presented Paul and
the letter to Governor Felix. 34He read it and then asked
Paul what province he was from. "Cilicia," Paul answered.
35"I will hear your case myself when your accusers
arrive," the governor told him. Then the governor ordered
him kept in the prison at Herod's headquarters.

NEW KING JAMES VERSION

27 This man was seized by the Jews and was about to be
killed by them. Coming with the troops I rescued him,
having learned that he was a Roman. 28And when I
wanted to know the reason they accused him, I
brought him before their council. 29I found out that
he was accused concerning questions of their law,
but had nothing charged against him deserving of
death or chains. 30And when it was told me that the
Jews lay in wait for the man,[d] I sent him immediately
to you, and also commanded his accusers to state
before you the charges against him.

Farewell.

31Then the soldiers, as they were commanded, took Paul
and brought *him* by night to Antipatris. 32The next day
they left the horsemen to go on with him, and returned to
the barracks. 33When they came to Caesarea and had deliv-
ered the letter to the governor, they also presented Paul to
him. 34And when the governor had read *it*, he asked what
province he was from. And when he understood that *he
was* from Cilicia, 35he said, "I will hear you when your
accusers also have come." And he commanded him to be
kept in Herod's Praetorium.

23:30 [d] NU-Text reads *there would be a plot against the man.*

THE MESSAGE

I rescued this man from a Jewish mob. They had seized him and were about to kill him when I learned that he was a Roman citizen. So I sent in my soldiers. Wanting to know what he had done wrong, I had him brought before their council. It turned out to be a squabble turned vicious over some of their religious differences, but nothing remotely criminal.

The next thing I knew, they had cooked up a plot to murder him. I decided that for his own safety I'd better get him out of here in a hurry. So I'm sending him to you. I'm informing his accusers that he's now under your jurisdiction.

The soldiers, following orders, took Paul that same night to safety in Antipatris. In the morning the soldiers returned to their barracks in Jerusalem, sending Paul on to Caesarea under guard of the cavalry. The cavalry entered Caesarea and handed Paul and the letter over to the governor.

After reading the letter, the governor asked Paul what province he came from and was told "Cilicia." Then he said, "I'll take up your case when your accusers show up." He ordered him locked up for the meantime in King Herod's official quarters.

KING JAMES VERSION

24 And after five days Ananias the high priest descended with the elders, and *with* a certain orator *named* Tertullus, who informed the governor against Paul.

2 And when he was called forth, Tertullus began to accuse *him*, saying, Seeing that by thee we enjoy great quietness, and that very worthy deeds are done unto this nation by thy providence,

3 We accept *it* always, and in all places, most noble Felix, with all thankfulness.

4 Notwithstanding, that I be not further tedious unto thee, I pray thee that thou wouldest hear us of thy clemency a few words.

5 For we have found this man *a* pestilent *fellow*, and a mover of sedition among all the Jews throughout the world, and a ringleader of the sect of the Nazarenes:

6 Who also hath gone about to profane the temple: whom we took, and would have judged according to our law.

7 But the chief captain Lysias came *upon us*, and with great violence took *him* away out of our hands,

8 Commanding his accusers to come unto thee: by examining of whom thyself mayest take knowledge of all these things, whereof we accuse him.

9 And the Jews also assented, saying that these things were so.

NEW AMERICAN STANDARD BIBLE

Paul before Felix

24 After five days the high priest Ananias came down with some elders, with an attorney *named* Tertullus, and they brought charges to the governor against Paul.

2 After *Paul* had been summoned, Tertullus began to accuse him, saying *to the governor*,

"Since we have through you attained much peace, and since by your providence reforms are being carried out for this nation,

3 we acknowledge *this* in every way and everywhere, most excellent Felix, with all thankfulness.

4 "But, that I may not weary you any further, I beg you to grant us, by your kindness, a brief hearing.

5 "For we have found this man a real pest and a fellow who stirs up dissension among all the Jews throughout [1]the world, and a ringleader of the sect of the Nazarenes.

6 "And he even tried to desecrate the temple; and then we arrested him. [[2]We wanted to judge him according to our own Law.

7 "But Lysias the commander came along, and with much violence took him out of our hands,

8 ordering his accusers to come before you.] By examining him yourself concerning all these matters you will be able to ascertain the things of which we accuse him."

9 The Jews also joined in the attack, asserting that these things were so.

24:5 [1] Lit *the inhabited earth* 24:6 [2] The early mss do not contain the remainder of v 6, v 7, nor the first part of v 8

NEW CENTURY VERSION

Paul Is Accused

24 Five days later Ananias, the high priest, went to
the city of Caesarea with some of the older Jewish
leaders and a lawyer named Tertullus. They had come to
make charges against Paul before the governor. 2Paul was
called into the meeting, and Tertullus began to accuse him,
saying, "Most Excellent Felix! Our people enjoy much
peace because of you, and many wrong things in our coun-
try are being made right through your wise help. 3We
accept these things always and in every place, and we are
thankful for them. 4But not wanting to take any more of
your time, I beg you to be kind and listen to our few
words. 5We have found this man to be a troublemaker,
stirring up the Jews everywhere in the world. He is a leader
of the Nazarene group. 6Also, he was trying to make the
Temple unclean, but we stopped him.[a] 8By asking him
questions yourself, you can decide if all these things are
true." 9The other Jews agreed and said that all of this was
true.

24:6 [a] **Verse 6** Some Greek copies add 6b–8a: "And we wanted to judge him by our own law. 7But the officer Lysias came and used much force to take him from us. 8And Lysias commanded those who wanted to accuse Paul to come to you."

CONTEMPORARY ENGLISH VERSION

Paul Is Accused in the Court of Felix

24 Five days later Ananias the high priest, together
with some of their leaders and a lawyer named
Tertullus, went to the governor to present their case
against Paul. 2So Paul was called in, and Tertullus stated
the case against him:[a]

Honorable Felix, you have brought our people a long
period of peace, and because of your concern our nation
is much better off. 3All of us are always grateful for
what you have done. 4I don't want to bother you, but
please be patient with us and listen to me for just a few
minutes.

5This man has been found to be a real pest and trou-
blemaker for Jews all over the world. He is also a leader
of a group called Nazarenes. 6-8When he tried to disgrace
the temple, we arrested him.[b] If you question him, you
will find out for yourself that our charges are true.

9The Jewish crowd spoke up and agreed with what
Tertullus had said.

[a] **24.2** *Paul was called in, and Tertullus stated the case against him*: Or "Tertullus was called in and stated the case against Paul."
[b] **24.6-8** *we arrested him*: Some manuscripts add, "We wanted to judge him by our own laws. But Lysias the commander took him away from us by force. Then Lysias ordered us to bring our charges against this man in your court."

NEW INTERNATIONAL VERSION

The Trial Before Felix

24 Five days later the high priest Ananias went down to Caesarea with some of the elders and a lawyer named Tertullus, and they brought their charges against Paul before the governor. [2]When Paul was called in, Tertullus presented his case before Felix: "We have enjoyed a long period of peace under you, and your foresight has brought about reforms in this nation. [3]Everywhere and in every way, most excellent Felix, we acknowledge this with profound gratitude. [4]But in order not to weary you further, I would request that you be kind enough to hear us briefly.

[5]"We have found this man to be a troublemaker, stirring up riots among the Jews all over the world. He is a ringleader of the Nazarene sect [6]and even tried to desecrate the temple; so we seized him. [8]By[a] examining him yourself you will be able to learn the truth about all these charges we are bringing against him."

[9]The Jews joined in the accusation, asserting that these things were true.

[a] 6–8 Some manuscripts *him and wanted to judge him according to our law. [7]But the commander, Lysias, came and with the use of much force snatched him from our hands [8]and ordered his accusers to come before you. By*

NEW LIVING TRANSLATION

Paul Appears before Felix

24 Five days later Ananias, the high priest, arrived with some of the Jewish leaders and the lawyer* Tertullus, to press charges against Paul. [2]When Paul was called in, Tertullus laid charges against Paul in the following address to the governor:

"Your Excellency, you have given peace to us Jews and have enacted reforms for us. [3]And for all of this we are very grateful to you. [4]But lest I bore you, kindly give me your attention for only a moment as I briefly outline our case against this man. [5]For we have found him to be a troublemaker, a man who is constantly inciting the Jews throughout the world to riots and rebellions against the Roman government. He is a ringleader of the sect known as the Nazarenes. [6]Moreover he was trying to defile the Temple when we arrested him.* [8]You can find out the truth of our accusations by examining him yourself." [9]Then the other Jews chimed in, declaring that everything Tertullus said was true.

24:1 Greek *some elders and an orator.* 24:6 Some manuscripts add *We would have judged him by our law, [7]but Lysias, the commander of the garrison, came and took him violently away from us, [8]commanding his accusers to come before you.*

NEW KING JAMES VERSION

Accused of Sedition

24 Now after five days Ananias the high priest came down with the elders and a certain orator *named* Tertullus. These gave evidence to the governor against Paul.

[2]And when he was called upon, Tertullus began his accusation, saying: "Seeing that through you we enjoy great peace, and prosperity is being brought to this nation by your foresight, [3]we accept *it* always and in all places, most noble Felix, with all thankfulness. [4]Nevertheless, not to be tedious to you any further, I beg you to hear, by your courtesy, a few words from us. [5]For we have found this man a plague, a creator of dissension among all the Jews throughout the world, and a ringleader of the sect of the Nazarenes. [6]He even tried to profane the temple, and we seized him,[a] and wanted to judge him according to our law. [7]But the commander Lysias came by and with great violence took *him* out of our hands, [8]commanding his accusers to come to you. By examining him yourself you may ascertain all these things of which we accuse him." [9]And the Jews also assented,[b] maintaining that these things were so.

24:6 [a] NU-Text ends the sentence here and omits the rest of verse 6, all of verse 7, and the first clause of verse 8. 24:9 [b] NU-Text and M-Text read *joined the attack.*

THE MESSAGE

Paul States His Defense

24 Within five days, the Chief Priest Ananias arrived with a contingent of leaders, along with Tertullus, a trial lawyer. They presented the governor with their case against Paul. When Paul was called before the court, Tertullus spoke for the prosecution: "Most Honorable Felix, we are most grateful in all times and places for your wise and gentle rule. We are much aware that it is because of you and you alone that we enjoy all this peace and gain daily profit from your reforms. I'm not going to tire you out with a long speech. I beg your kind indulgence in listening to me. I'll be quite brief.

"We've found this man time and again disturbing the peace, stirring up riots against Jews all over the world, the ringleader of a seditious sect called Nazarenes. He's a real bad apple, I must say. We caught him trying to defile our holy Temple and arrested him. You'll be able to verify all these accusations when you examine him yourself."

The Jews joined in: "Hear, hear! That's right!"

KING JAMES VERSION

10 ¶ Then Paul, after that the governor had beckoned unto him to speak, answered, Forasmuch as I know that thou hast been of many years a judge unto this nation, I do the more cheerfully answer for myself:

11 Because that thou mayest understand, that there are yet but twelve days since I went up to Jerusalem for to worship.

12 And they neither found me in the temple disputing with any man, neither raising up the people, neither in the synagogues, nor in the city:

13 Neither can they prove the things whereof they now accuse me.

14 But this I confess unto thee, that after the way which they call heresy, so worship I the God of my fathers, believing all things which are written in the law and in the prophets:

15 And have hope toward God, which they themselves also allow, that there shall be a resurrection of the dead, both of the just and unjust.

16 And herein do I exercise myself, to have always a conscience void of offence toward God, and *toward* men.

17 Now after many years I came to bring alms to my nation, and offerings.

18 Whereupon certain Jews from Asia found me purified in the temple, neither with multitude, nor with tumult.

19 Who ought to have been here before thee, and object, if they had ought against me.

NEW AMERICAN STANDARD BIBLE

10 When the governor had nodded for him to speak, Paul responded:

"Knowing that for many years you have been a judge to this nation, I cheerfully make my defense,

11 since you can take note of the fact that no more than twelve days ago I went up to Jerusalem to worship.

12 "Neither in the temple, nor in the synagogues, nor in the city *itself* did they find me carrying on a discussion with anyone or causing a riot.

13 "Nor can they prove to you *the charges* of which they now accuse me.

14 "But this I admit to you, that according to the Way which they call a sect I do serve the God of our fathers, believing everything that is in accordance with the Law and that is written in the Prophets;

15 having a hope in God, which these men cherish themselves, that there shall certainly be a resurrection of both the righteous and the wicked.

16 "In view of this, I also do my best to maintain always a blameless conscience *both* before God and before men.

17 "Now after several years I came to bring [3]alms to my nation and to present offerings;

18 in which they found me *occupied* in the temple, having been purified, without *any* crowd or uproar. But *there were* some Jews from Asia—

19 who ought to have been present before you and to make accusation, if they should have anything against me.

24:17 [3] Or *gifts to charity*

NEW CENTURY VERSION

10When the governor made a sign for Paul to speak, Paul
said, "Governor Felix, I know you have been a judge over
this nation for a long time. So I am happy to defend myself
before you. 11You can learn for yourself that I went to wor-
ship in Jerusalem only twelve days ago. 12Those who are
accusing me did not find me arguing with anyone in the
Temple or stirring up the people in the synagogues or in
the city. 13They cannot prove the things they are saying
against me now. 14But I will tell you this: I worship the
God of our ancestors as a follower of the Way of Jesus. The
Jews say that the Way of Jesus is not the right way. But I
believe everything that is taught in the law of Moses and
that is written in the books of the Prophets. 15I have the
same hope in God that they have—the hope that all peo-
ple, good and bad, will surely be raised from the dead.
16This is why I always try to do what I believe is right
before God and people.

17"After being away from Jerusalem for several years, I
went back to bring money to my people and to offer sacri-
fices. 18I was doing this when they found me in the
Temple. I had finished the cleansing ceremony and had not
made any trouble; no people were gathering around me.
19But there were some Jews from the country of Asia who
should be here, standing before you. If I have really done
anything wrong, they are the ones who should accuse me.

CONTEMPORARY ENGLISH VERSION

Paul Defends Himself

10The governor motioned for Paul to speak, and he
began:

I know that you have judged the people of our nation for
many years, and I am glad to defend myself in your court.
11It was no more than twelve days ago that I went to
worship in Jerusalem. You can find this out easily
enough. 12Never once did the Jews find me arguing with
anyone in the temple. I didn't cause trouble in the
Jewish meeting places or in the city itself. 13There is no
way that they can prove these charges that they are now
bringing against me.

14I admit that their leaders think that the Lord's Way[c]
which I follow is based on wrong beliefs. But I still wor-
ship the same God that my ancestors worshiped. And I
believe everything written in the Law of Moses and in
the Prophets.[d] 15I am just as sure as these people are
that God will raise from death everyone who is good or
evil. 16And because I am sure, I try my best to have a
clear conscience in whatever I do for God or for people.

17After being away for several years, I returned here
to bring gifts for the poor people of my nation and to
offer sacrifices. 18This is what I was doing when I was
found going through a ceremony in the temple. I wasn't
with a crowd, and there was no uproar.

19Some Jews from Asia were there at that time, and if
they have anything to say against me, they should be

[c] **24.14** *the Lord's Way*: See the note at 9.2. [d] **24.14** *Law of Moses . . . the Prophets*: The Jewish Scriptures, that is, the Old Testament.

NEW INTERNATIONAL VERSION

10When the governor motioned for him to speak, Paul replied: "I know that for a number of years you have been a judge over this nation; so I gladly make my defense. 11You can easily verify that no more than twelve days ago I went up to Jerusalem to worship. 12My accusers did not find me arguing with anyone at the temple, or stirring up a crowd in the synagogues or anywhere else in the city. 13And they cannot prove to you the charges they are now making against me. 14However, I admit that I worship the God of our fathers as a follower of the Way, which they call a sect. I believe everything that agrees with the Law and that is written in the Prophets, 15and I have the same hope in God as these men, that there will be a resurrection of both the righteous and the wicked. 16So I strive always to keep my conscience clear before God and man.

17"After an absence of several years, I came to Jerusalem to bring my people gifts for the poor and to present offerings. 18I was ceremonially clean when they found me in the temple courts doing this. There was no crowd with me, nor was I involved in any disturbance. 19But there are some Jews from the province of Asia, who ought to be here before you and bring charges if they have anything against

NEW LIVING TRANSLATION

10Now it was Paul's turn. The governor motioned for him to rise and speak. Paul said, "I know, sir, that you have been a judge of Jewish affairs for many years, and this gives me confidence as I make my defense. 11You can quickly discover that it was no more than twelve days ago that I arrived in Jerusalem to worship at the Temple. 12I didn't argue with anyone in the Temple, nor did I incite a riot in any synagogue or on the streets of the city. 13These men certainly cannot prove the things they accuse me of doing.

14"But I admit that I follow the Way, which they call a sect. I worship the God of our ancestors, and I firmly believe the Jewish law and everything written in the books of prophecy. 15I have hope in God, just as these men do, that he will raise both the righteous and the ungodly. 16Because of this, I always try to maintain a clear conscience before God and everyone else.

17"After several years away, I returned to Jerusalem with money to aid my people and to offer sacrifices to God. 18My accusers saw me in the Temple as I was completing a purification ritual. There was no crowd around me and no rioting. 19But some Jews from the province of Asia were there—and they ought to be here to bring charges if they

NEW KING JAMES VERSION

The Defense Before Felix

10Then Paul, after the governor had nodded to him to speak, answered: "Inasmuch as I know that you have been for many years a judge of this nation, I do the more cheerfully answer for myself, 11because you may ascertain that it is no more than twelve days since I went up to Jerusalem to worship. 12And they neither found me in the temple disputing with anyone nor inciting the crowd, either in the synagogues or in the city. 13Nor can they prove the things of which they now accuse me. 14But this I confess to you, that according to the Way which they call a sect, so I worship the God of my fathers, believing all things which are written in the Law and in the Prophets. 15I have hope in God, which they themselves also accept, that there will be a resurrection of *the* dead,[c] both of *the* just and *the* unjust. 16This *being* so, I myself always strive to have a conscience without offense toward God and men.

17"Now after many years I came to bring alms and offerings to my nation, 18in the midst of which some Jews from Asia found me purified in the temple, neither with a mob nor with tumult. 19They ought to have been here before you to object if they had anything against me. 20Or else let

24:15 [c] NU-Text omits *of the dead.*

THE MESSAGE

The governor motioned to Paul that it was now his turn. Paul said, "I count myself fortunate to be defending myself before you, Governor, knowing how fair-minded you've been in judging us all these years. I've been back in the country only twelve days—you can check out these dates easily enough. I came with the express purpose of worshiping in Jerusalem on Pentecost, and I've been minding my own business the whole time. Nobody can say they saw me arguing in the Temple or working up a crowd in the streets. Not one of their charges can be backed up with evidence or witnesses.

"But I do freely admit this: In regard to the Way, which they malign as a dead-end street, I serve and worship the very same God served and worshiped by all our ancestors and embrace everything written in all our Scriptures. And I admit to living in hopeful anticipation that God will raise the dead, both the good and the bad. If that's my crime, my accusers are just as guilty as I am.

"Believe me, I do my level best to keep a clear conscience before God and my neighbors in everything I do. I've been out of the country for a number of years and now I'm back. While I was away, I took up a collection for the poor and brought that with me, along with offerings for the Temple. It was while making those offerings that they found me quietly at my prayers in the Temple. There was no crowd, there was no disturbance. It was some Jews from around Ephesus who started all this trouble. And you'll notice they're not here today. They're cowards, too cowardly to accuse me in front of you.

KING JAMES VERSION

20 Or else let these same *here* say, if they have found any evil doing in me, while I stood before the council,

21 Except it be for this one voice, that I cried standing among them, Touching the resurrection of the dead I am called in question by you this day.

22 ¶ And when Felix heard these things, having more perfect knowledge of *that* way, he deferred them, and said, When Lysias the chief captain shall come down, I will know the uttermost of your matter.

23 And he commanded a centurion to keep Paul, and to let *him* have liberty, and that he should forbid none of his acquaintance to minister or come unto him.

24 And after certain days, when Felix came with his wife Drusilla, which was a Jewess, he sent for Paul, and heard him concerning the faith in Christ.

25 And as he reasoned of righteousness, temperance, and judgment to come, Felix trembled, and answered, Go thy way for this time; when I have a convenient season, I will call for thee.

26 He hoped also that money should have been given him of Paul, that he might loose him: wherefore he sent for him the oftener, and communed with him.

27 But after two years Porcius Festus came into Felix' room: and Felix, willing to shew the Jews a pleasure, left Paul bound.

NEW AMERICAN STANDARD BIBLE

20 "Or else let these men themselves tell what misdeed they found when I stood before the Council,

21 other than for this one statement which I shouted out while standing among them, 'For the resurrection of the dead I am on trial before you today.' "

22 But Felix, having a more exact knowledge about the Way, put them off, saying, "When Lysias the [4]commander comes down, I will decide your case."

23 Then he gave orders to the centurion for him to be kept in custody and *yet* have *some* freedom, and not to prevent any of his friends from ministering to him.

24 But some days later Felix arrived with Drusilla, his wife who was a Jewess, and sent for Paul and heard him *speak* about faith in Christ Jesus.

25 But as he was discussing righteousness, self-control and the judgment to come, Felix became frightened and said, "Go away for the present, and when I find time I will summon you."

26 At the same time too, he was hoping that money would be given him by Paul; therefore he also used to send for him quite often and converse with him.

27 But after two years had passed, Felix was succeeded by Porcius Festus, and wishing to do the Jews a favor, Felix left Paul imprisoned.

24:22 [4] I.e. chiliarch, in command of one thousand troops

NEW CENTURY VERSION

20 Or ask these Jews here if they found any wrong in me when I stood before the Jewish council in Jerusalem. 21 But I did shout one thing when I stood before them: 'You are judging me today because I believe that people will rise from the dead!' "

22 Felix already understood much about the Way of Jesus. He stopped the trial and said, "When commander Lysias comes here, I will decide your case." 23 Felix told the officer to keep Paul guarded but to give him some freedom and to let his friends bring what he needed.

Paul Speaks to Felix and His Wife

24 After some days Felix came with his wife, Drusilla, who was Jewish, and asked for Paul to be brought to him. He listened to Paul talk about believing in Christ Jesus. 25 But Felix became afraid when Paul spoke about living right, self-control, and the time when God will judge the world. He said, "Go away now. When I have more time, I will call for you." 26 At the same time Felix hoped that Paul would give him some money, so he often sent for Paul and talked with him.

27 But after two years, Felix was replaced by Porcius Festus as governor. But Felix had left Paul in prison to please the Jews.

CONTEMPORARY ENGLISH VERSION

here now. 20 Or ask the ones who are here. They can tell you that they didn't find me guilty of anything when I was tried by their own council. 21 The only charge they can bring against me is what I shouted out in court, when I said, "I am on trial today because I believe that the dead will be raised to life!"

22 Felix knew a lot about the Lord's Way.[e] But he brought the trial to an end and said, "I will make my decision after Lysias the commander arrives." 23 He then ordered the army officer to keep Paul under guard, but not to lock him up or to stop his friends from helping him.

Paul Is Kept under Guard

24 Several days later Felix and his wife Drusilla, who was Jewish, went to the place where Paul was kept under guard. They sent for Paul and listened while he spoke to them about having faith in Christ Jesus. 25 But Felix was frightened when Paul started talking to them about doing right, about self-control, and about the coming judgment. So he said to Paul, "That's enough for now. You may go. But when I have time I will send for you." 26 After this, Felix often sent for Paul and talked with him, because he hoped that Paul would offer him a bribe.

27 Two years later Porcius Festus became governor in place of Felix. But since Felix wanted to do the Jewish leaders a favor, he kept Paul in jail.

[e] 24.22 *the Lord's Way*: See the note at 9.2.

NEW INTERNATIONAL VERSION

me. [20]Or these who are here should state what crime they found in me when I stood before the Sanhedrin— [21]unless it was this one thing I shouted as I stood in their presence: 'It is concerning the resurrection of the dead that I am on trial before you today.' "

[22]Then Felix, who was well acquainted with the Way, adjourned the proceedings. "When Lysias the commander comes," he said, "I will decide your case." [23]He ordered the centurion to keep Paul under guard but to give him some freedom and permit his friends to take care of his needs.

[24]Several days later Felix came with his wife Drusilla, who was a Jewess. He sent for Paul and listened to him as he spoke about faith in Christ Jesus. [25]As Paul discoursed on righteousness, self-control and the judgment to come, Felix was afraid and said, "That's enough for now! You may leave. When I find it convenient, I will send for you." [26]At the same time he was hoping that Paul would offer him a bribe, so he sent for him frequently and talked with him.

[27]When two years had passed, Felix was succeeded by Porcius Festus, but because Felix wanted to grant a favor to the Jews, he left Paul in prison.

NEW LIVING TRANSLATION

have anything against me! [20]Ask these men here what wrongdoing the Jewish high council* found in me, [21]except for one thing I said when I shouted out, 'I am on trial before you today because I believe in the resurrection of the dead!' "

[22]Felix, who was quite familiar with the Way, adjourned the hearing and said, "Wait until Lysias, the garrison commander, arrives. Then I will decide the case." [23]He ordered an officer to keep Paul in custody but to give him some freedom and allow his friends to visit him and take care of his needs.

[24]A few days later Felix came with his wife, Drusilla, who was Jewish. Sending for Paul, they listened as he told them about faith in Christ Jesus. [25]As he reasoned with them about righteousness and self-control and the judgment to come, Felix was terrified. "Go away for now," he replied. "When it is more convenient, I'll call for you again." [26]He also hoped that Paul would bribe him, so he sent for him quite often and talked with him.

[27]Two years went by in this way; then Felix was succeeded by Porcius Festus. And because Felix wanted to gain favor with the Jewish leaders, he left Paul in prison.

24:20 Greek *Sanhedrin.*

NEW KING JAMES VERSION

those who are *here* themselves say if they found any wrongdoing[d] in me while I stood before the council, [21]unless *it is* for this one statement which I cried out, standing among them, 'Concerning the resurrection of the dead I am being judged by you this day.' "

Felix Procrastinates

[22]But when Felix heard these things, having more accurate knowledge of *the* Way, he adjourned the proceedings and said, "When Lysias the commander comes down, I will make a decision on your case." [23]So he commanded the centurion to keep Paul and to let *him* have liberty, and told him not to forbid any of his friends to provide for or visit him.

[24]And after some days, when Felix came with his wife Drusilla, who was Jewish, he sent for Paul and heard him concerning the faith in Christ. [25]Now as he reasoned about righteousness, self-control, and the judgment to come, Felix was afraid and answered, "Go away for now; when I have a convenient time I will call for you." [26]Meanwhile he also hoped that money would be given him by Paul, that he might release him.[e] Therefore he sent for him more often and conversed with him.

[27]But after two years Porcius Festus succeeded Felix; and Felix, wanting to do the Jews a favor, left Paul bound.

24:20 [d] NU-Text and M-Text read *say what wrongdoing they found.*
24:26 [e] NU-Text omits *that he might release him.*

THE MESSAGE

"So ask these others what crime they've caught me in. Don't let them hide behind this smooth-talking Tertullus. The only thing they have on me is that one sentence I shouted out in the council: 'It's because I believe in the resurrection that I've been hauled into this court!' Does that sound to you like grounds for a criminal case?"

Felix shilly-shallied. He knew far more about the Way than he let on, and could have settled the case then and there. But uncertain of his best move politically, he played for time. "When Captain Lysias comes down, I'll decide your case." He gave orders to the centurion to keep Paul in custody, but to more or less give him the run of the place and not prevent his friends from helping him.

A few days later Felix and his wife, Drusilla, who was Jewish, sent for Paul and listened to him talk about a life of believing in Jesus Christ. As Paul continued to insist on right relations with God and his people, about a life of moral discipline and the coming Judgment, Felix felt things getting a little too close for comfort and dismissed him. "That's enough for today. I'll call you back when it's convenient." At the same time he was secretly hoping that Paul would offer him a substantial bribe. These conversations were repeated frequently.

After two years of this, Felix was replaced by Porcius Festus. Still playing up to the Jews and ignoring justice, Felix left Paul in prison.

KING JAMES VERSION

25 Now when Festus was come into the province, after three days he ascended from Caesarea to Jerusalem.

2 Then the high priest and the chief of the Jews informed him against Paul, and besought him,

3 And desired favour against him, that he would send for him to Jerusalem, laying wait in the way to kill him.

4 But Festus answered, that Paul should be kept at Caesarea, and that he himself would depart shortly *thither.*

5 Let them therefore, said he, which among you are able, go down with *me,* and accuse this man, if there be any wickedness in him.

6 And when he had tarried among them more than ten days, he went down unto Caesarea; and the next day sitting on the judgment seat commanded Paul to be brought.

7 And when he was come, the Jews which came down from Jerusalem stood round about, and laid many and grievous complaints against Paul, which they could not prove.

8 While he answered for himself, Neither against the law of the Jews, neither against the temple, nor yet against Caesar, have I offended any thing at all.

9 But Festus, willing to do the Jews a pleasure, answered Paul, and said, Wilt thou go up to Jerusalem, and there be judged of these things before me?

10 Then said Paul, I stand at Caesar's judgment seat, where I ought to be judged: to the Jews have I done no wrong, as thou very well knowest.

NEW AMERICAN STANDARD BIBLE

Paul before Festus

25 Festus then, having arrived in the province, three days later went up to Jerusalem from Caesarea.

2 And the chief priests and the leading men of the Jews brought charges against Paul, and they were urging him,

3 requesting a concession against Paul, that he might have him brought to Jerusalem (*at the same time,* setting an ambush to kill him on the way).

4 Festus then answered that Paul was being kept in custody at Caesarea and that he himself was about to leave shortly.

5 "Therefore," he *said, "let the influential men among you go there with me, and if there is anything wrong about the man, let them prosecute him."

6 After he had spent not more than eight or ten days among them, he went down to Caesarea, and on the next day he took his seat on the tribunal and ordered Paul to be brought.

7 After Paul arrived, the Jews who had come down from Jerusalem stood around him, bringing many and serious charges against him which they could not prove,

8 while Paul said in his own defense, "I have committed no offense either against the Law of the Jews or against the temple or against Caesar."

9 But Festus, wishing to do the Jews a favor, answered Paul and said, "Are you willing to go up to Jerusalem and stand trial before me on these *charges?*"

10 But Paul said, "I am standing before Caesar's tribunal, where I ought to be tried. I have done no wrong to *the* Jews, as you also very well know.

NEW CENTURY VERSION

Paul Asks to See Caesar

25 Three days after Festus became governor, he went
from Caesarea to Jerusalem. 2There the leading
priests and the important Jewish leaders made charges
against Paul before Festus. 3They asked Festus to do them
a favor. They wanted him to send Paul back to Jerusalem,
because they had a plan to kill him on the way. 4But
Festus answered that Paul would be kept in Caesarea and
that he himself was returning there soon. 5He said, "Some
of your leaders should go with me. They can accuse the
man there in Caesarea, if he has really done something
wrong."

6Festus stayed in Jerusalem another eight or ten days
and then went back to Caesarea. The next day he told the
soldiers to bring Paul before him. Festus was seated on the
judge's seat 7when Paul came into the room. The Jewish
people who had come from Jerusalem stood around him,
making serious charges against him, which they could not
prove. 8This is what Paul said to defend himself: "I have
done nothing wrong against the Jewish law, against the
Temple, or against Caesar."

9But Festus wanted to please the Jews. So he asked
Paul, "Do you want to go to Jerusalem for me to judge you
there on these charges?"

10Paul said, "I am standing at Caesar's judgment seat
now, where I should be judged. I have done nothing
wrong to the Jews; you know this is true. 11If I have done

CONTEMPORARY ENGLISH VERSION

Paul Asks To Be Tried by the Roman Emperor

25 Three days after Festus had become governor, he
went from Caesarea to Jerusalem. 2There the chief
priests and some Jewish leaders told him about their
charges against Paul. They also asked Festus 3if he would
be willing to bring Paul to Jerusalem. They begged him to
do this because they were planning to attack and kill Paul
on the way. 4But Festus told them, "Paul will be kept in
Caesarea, and I am soon going there myself. 5If he has
done anything wrong, let your leaders go with me and
bring charges against him there."

6Festus stayed in Jerusalem for eight or ten more days
before going to Caesarea. Then the next day he took his
place as judge and had Paul brought into court. 7As soon
as Paul came in, the Jewish leaders from Jerusalem crowd-
ed around him and said he was guilty of many serious
crimes. But they could not prove anything. 8Then Paul
spoke in his own defense, "I have not broken the Law of
my people. And I have not done anything against either
the temple or the Emperor."

9Festus wanted to please the leaders. So he asked Paul,
"Are you willing to go to Jerusalem and be tried by me on
these charges?"

10Paul replied, "I am on trial in the Emperor's court, and
that's where I should be tried. You know very well that I
have not done anything to harm the Jewish nation. 11If I

NEW INTERNATIONAL VERSION

The Trial Before Festus

25 Three days after arriving in the province, Festus went up from Caesarea to Jerusalem, 2where the chief priests and Jewish leaders appeared before him and presented the charges against Paul. 3They urgently requested Festus, as a favor to them, to have Paul transferred to Jerusalem, for they were preparing an ambush to kill him along the way. 4Festus answered, "Paul is being held at Caesarea, and I myself am going there soon. 5Let some of your leaders come with me and press charges against the man there, if he has done anything wrong."

6After spending eight or ten days with them, he went down to Caesarea, and the next day he convened the court and ordered that Paul be brought before him. 7When Paul appeared, the Jews who had come down from Jerusalem stood around him, bringing many serious charges against him, which they could not prove.

8Then Paul made his defense: "I have done nothing wrong against the law of the Jews or against the temple or against Caesar."

9Festus, wishing to do the Jews a favor, said to Paul, "Are you willing to go up to Jerusalem and stand trial before me there on these charges?"

10Paul answered: "I am now standing before Caesar's court, where I ought to be tried. I have not done any wrong to the Jews, as you yourself know very well. 11If, however,

NEW LIVING TRANSLATION

Paul Appears before Festus

25 Three days after Festus arrived in Caesarea to take over his new responsibilities, he left for Jerusalem, 2where the leading priests and other Jewish leaders met with him and made their accusations against Paul. 3They asked Festus as a favor to transfer Paul to Jerusalem. (Their plan was to waylay and kill him.) 4But Festus replied that Paul was at Caesarea and he himself would be returning there soon. 5So he said, "Those of you in authority can return with me. If Paul has done anything wrong, you can make your accusations."

6Eight or ten days later he returned to Caesarea, and on the following day Paul's trial began. 7On Paul's arrival in court, the Jewish leaders from Jerusalem gathered around and made many serious accusations they couldn't prove. 8Paul denied the charges. "I am not guilty," he said. "I have committed no crime against the Jewish laws or the Temple or the Roman government."

9Then Festus, wanting to please the Jews, asked him, "Are you willing to go to Jerusalem and stand trial before me there?"

10But Paul replied, "No! This is the official Roman court, so I ought to be tried right here. You know very well I am

NEW KING JAMES VERSION

Paul Appeals to Caesar

25 Now when Festus had come to the province, after three days he went up from Caesarea to Jerusalem. 2Then the high priest[a] and the chief men of the Jews informed him against Paul; and they petitioned him, 3asking a favor against him, that he would summon him to Jerusalem—while *they* lay in ambush along the road to kill him. 4But Festus answered that Paul should be kept at Caesarea, and that he himself was going *there* shortly. 5"Therefore," he said, "let those who have authority among you go down with *me* and accuse this man, to see if there is any fault in him."

6And when he had remained among them more than ten days, he went down to Caesarea. And the next day, sitting on the judgment seat, he commanded Paul to be brought. 7When he had come, the Jews who had come down from Jerusalem stood about and laid many serious complaints against Paul, which they could not prove, 8while he answered for himself, "Neither against the law of the Jews, nor against the temple, nor against Caesar have I offended in anything at all."

9But Festus, wanting to do the Jews a favor, answered Paul and said, "Are you willing to go up to Jerusalem and there be judged before me concerning these things?"

10So Paul said, "I stand at Caesar's judgment seat, where I ought to be judged. To the Jews I have done no wrong, as you very well know. 11For if I am an offender, or

25:2 [a] NU-Text reads *chief priests.*

THE MESSAGE

An Appeal to Caesar

25 Three days after Festus arrived in Caesarea to take up his duties as governor, he went up to Jerusalem. The high priests and top leaders renewed their vendetta against Paul. They asked Festus if he wouldn't please do them a favor by sending Paul to Jerusalem to respond to their charges. A lie, of course—they had revived their old plot to set an ambush and kill him along the way.

Festus answered that Caesarea was the proper jurisdiction for Paul, and that he himself was going back there in a few days. "You're perfectly welcome," he said, "to go back with me then and accuse him of whatever you think he's done wrong."

About eight or ten days later, Festus returned to Caesarea. The next morning he took his place in the courtroom and had Paul brought in. The minute he walked in, the Jews who had come down from Jerusalem were all over him, hurling the most extreme accusations, none of which they could prove.

Then Paul took the stand and said simply, "I've done nothing wrong against the Jewish religion, or the Temple, or Caesar. Period."

Festus, though, wanted to get on the good side of the Jews and so said, "How would you like to go up to Jerusalem, and let me conduct your trial there?"

Paul answered, "I'm standing at this moment before Caesar's bar of justice, where I have a perfect right to stand. And I'm going to keep standing here. I've done nothing wrong to the Jews, and you know it as well as I

KING JAMES VERSION

11 For if I be an offender, or have committed any thing worthy of death, I refuse not to die: but if there be none of these things whereof these accuse me, no man may deliver me unto them. I appeal unto Caesar.

12 Then Festus, when he had conferred with the council, answered, Hast thou appealed unto Caesar? unto Caesar shalt thou go.

13 ¶ And after certain days king Agrippa and Bernice came unto Caesarea to salute Festus.

14 And when they had been there many days, Festus declared Paul's cause unto the king, saying, There is a certain man left in bonds by Felix:

15 About whom, when I was at Jerusalem, the chief priests and the elders of the Jews informed *me*, desiring *to have* judgment against him.

16 To whom I answered, It is not the manner of the Romans to deliver any man to die, before that he which is accused have the accusers face to face, and have licence to answer for himself concerning the crime laid against him.

17 Therefore, when they were come hither, without any delay on the morrow I sat on the judgment seat, and commanded the man to be brought forth.

18 Against whom when the accusers stood up, they brought none accusation of such things as I supposed:

19 But had certain questions against him of their own superstition, and of one Jesus, which was dead, whom Paul affirmed to be alive.

NEW AMERICAN STANDARD BIBLE

11 "If, then, I am a wrongdoer and have committed anything worthy of death, I do not refuse to die; but if none of those things is *true* of which these men accuse me, no one can hand me over to them. I appeal to Caesar."

12 Then when Festus had conferred with his council, he answered, "You have appealed to Caesar, to Caesar you shall go."

13 Now when several days had elapsed, King Agrippa and Bernice arrived at Caesarea and paid their respects to Festus.

14 While they were spending many days there, Festus laid Paul's case before the king, saying, "There is a man who was left as a prisoner by Felix;

15 and when I was at Jerusalem, the chief priests and the elders of the Jews brought charges against him, asking for a sentence of condemnation against him.

16 "I answered them that it is not the custom of the Romans to hand over any man before the accused meets his accusers face to face and has an opportunity to make his defense against the charges.

17 "So after they had assembled here, I did not delay, but on the next day took my seat on the tribunal and ordered the man to be brought before me.

18 "When the accusers stood up, they *began* bringing charges against him not of such crimes as I was expecting,

19 but they *simply* had some points of disagreement with him about their own religion and about a dead man, Jesus, whom Paul asserted to be alive.

NEW CENTURY VERSION

something wrong and the law says I must die, I do not ask to be saved from death. But if these charges are not true, then no one can give me to them. I want Caesar to hear my case!"
12 Festus talked about this with his advisors. Then he
said, "You have asked to see Caesar, so you will go to
Caesar!"

Paul Before King Agrippa

13 A few days later King Agrippa and Bernice came to
Caesarea to visit Festus. 14 They stayed there for some
time, and Festus told the king about Paul's case. Festus
said, "There is a man that Felix left in prison. 15 When I
went to Jerusalem, the leading priests and the older Jewish
leaders there made charges against him, asking me to sen-
tence him to death. 16 But I answered, 'When a man is
accused of a crime, Romans do not hand him over until he
has been allowed to face his accusers and defend himself
against their charges.' 17 So when these Jews came here to
Caesarea for the trial, I did not waste time. The next day I
sat on the judge's seat and commanded that the man be
brought in. 18 The Jews stood up and accused him, but not
of any serious crime as I thought they would. 19 The things
they said were about their own religion and about a man
named Jesus who died. But Paul said that he is still alive.

CONTEMPORARY ENGLISH VERSION

had done something deserving death, I would not ask to escape the death penalty. But I am not guilty of any of these crimes, and no one has the right to hand me over to these people. I now ask to be tried by the Emperor himself."
12 After Festus had talked this over with members of his
council, he told Paul, "You have asked to be tried by the
Emperor, and to the Emperor you will go!"

Paul Speaks to Agrippa and Bernice

13 A few days later King Agrippa and Bernice came to
Caesarea to visit Festus. 14 They had been there for several
days, when Festus told the king about the charges against
Paul. He said:

> Felix left a man here in jail, 15 and when I went to
> Jerusalem, the chief priests and the Jewish leaders came
> and asked me to find him guilty. 16 I told them that it
> isn't the Roman custom to hand a man over to people
> who are bringing charges against him. He must first
> have the chance to meet them face to face and to defend
> himself against their charges.
>
> 17 So when they came here with me, I wasted no time.
> On the very next day I took my place on the judge's
> bench and ordered him to be brought in. 18 But when the
> men stood up to make their charges against him, they
> did not accuse him of any of the crimes that I thought
> they would. 19 Instead, they argued with him about some
> of their beliefs and about a dead man named Jesus, who
> Paul said was alive.

NEW INTERNATIONAL VERSION

I am guilty of doing anything deserving death, I do not refuse to die. But if the charges brought against me by these Jews are not true, no one has the right to hand me over to them. I appeal to Caesar!"

12After Festus had conferred with his council, he declared: "You have appealed to Caesar. To Caesar you will go!"

Festus Consults King Agrippa

13A few days later King Agrippa and Bernice arrived at Caesarea to pay their respects to Festus. 14Since they were spending many days there, Festus discussed Paul's case with the king. He said: "There is a man here whom Felix left as a prisoner. 15When I went to Jerusalem, the chief priests and elders of the Jews brought charges against him and asked that he be condemned.

16"I told them that it is not the Roman custom to hand over any man before he has faced his accusers and has had an opportunity to defend himself against their charges. 17When they came here with me, I did not delay the case, but convened the court the next day and ordered the man to be brought in. 18When his accusers got up to speak, they did not charge him with any of the crimes I had expected. 19Instead, they had some points of dispute with him about their own religion and about a dead man named Jesus who Paul claimed was alive. 20I was at a loss

NEW LIVING TRANSLATION

not guilty. 11If I have done something worthy of death, I don't refuse to die. But if I am innocent, neither you nor anyone else has a right to turn me over to these men to kill me. I appeal to Caesar!"

12Festus conferred with his advisers and then replied, "Very well! You have appealed to Caesar, and to Caesar you shall go!"

13A few days later King Agrippa arrived with his sister, Bernice,* to pay their respects to Festus. 14During their stay of several days, Festus discussed Paul's case with the king. "There is a prisoner here," he told him, "whose case was left for me by Felix. 15When I was in Jerusalem, the leading priests and other Jewish leaders pressed charges against him and asked me to sentence him. 16Of course, I quickly pointed out to them that Roman law does not convict people without a trial. They are given an opportunity to defend themselves face to face with their accusers.

17"When they came here for the trial, I called the case the very next day and ordered Paul brought in. 18But the accusations made against him weren't at all what I expected. 19It was something about their religion and about someone called Jesus who died, but whom Paul insists is alive. 20I

25:13 Greek *Agrippa the king and Bernice arrived.*

NEW KING JAMES VERSION

have committed anything deserving of death, I do not object to dying; but if there is nothing in these things of which these men accuse me, no one can deliver me to them. I appeal to Caesar."

12Then Festus, when he had conferred with the council, answered, "You have appealed to Caesar? To Caesar you shall go!"

Paul Before Agrippa

13And after some days King Agrippa and Bernice came to Caesarea to greet Festus. 14When they had been there many days, Festus laid Paul's case before the king, saying: "There is a certain man left a prisoner by Felix, 15about whom the chief priests and the elders of the Jews informed *me,* when I was in Jerusalem, asking for a judgment against him. 16To them I answered, 'It is not the custom of the Romans to deliver any man to destruction[b] before the accused meets the accusers face to face, and has opportunity to answer for himself concerning the charge against him.' 17Therefore when they had come together, without any delay, the next day I sat on the judgment seat and commanded the man to be brought in. 18When the accusers stood up, they brought no accusation against him of such things as I supposed, 19but had some questions against him about their own religion and about a certain Jesus, who had died, whom Paul affirmed to be alive.

25:16 [b] NU-Text omits *to destruction,* although it is implied.

THE MESSAGE

do. If I've committed a crime and deserve death, name the day. I can face it. But if there's nothing to their accusations—and you know there isn't—nobody can force me to go along with their nonsense. We've fooled around here long enough. I appeal to Caesar."

Festus huddled with his advisors briefly and then gave his verdict: "You've appealed to Caesar; you'll go to Caesar!"

✠

A few days later King Agrippa and his wife, Bernice, visited Caesarea to welcome Festus to his new post. After several days, Festus brought up Paul's case to the king. "I have a man on my hands here, a prisoner left by Felix. When I was in Jerusalem, the high priests and Jewish leaders brought a bunch of accusations against him and wanted me to sentence him to death. I told them that wasn't the way we Romans did things. Just because a man is accused, we don't throw him out to the dogs. We make sure the accused has a chance to face his accusers and defend himself of the charges. So when they came down here I got right on the case. I took my place in the courtroom and put the man on the stand.

"The accusers came at him from all sides, but their accusations turned out to be nothing more than arguments about their religion and a dead man named Jesus, who the prisoner claimed was alive. Since I'm a newcomer here and

KING JAMES VERSION

20 And because I doubted of such manner of questions, I asked *him* whether he would go to Jerusalem, and there be judged of these matters.

21 But when Paul had appealed to be reserved unto the hearing of Augustus, I commanded him to be kept till I might send him to Caesar.

22 Then Agrippa said unto Festus, I would also hear the man myself. To morrow, said he, thou shalt hear him.

23 And on the morrow, when Agrippa was come, and Bernice, with great pomp, and was entered into the place of hearing, with the chief captains, and principal men of the city, at Festus' commandment Paul was brought forth.

24 And Festus said, King Agrippa, and all men which are here present with us, ye see this man, about whom all the multitude of the Jews have dealt with me, both at Jerusalem, and *also* here, crying that he ought not to live any longer.

25 But when I found that he had committed nothing worthy of death, and that he himself hath appealed to Augustus, I have determined to send him.

26 Of whom I have no certain thing to write unto my lord. Wherefore I have brought him forth before you, and specially before thee, O king Agrippa, that, after examination had, I might have somewhat to write.

27 For it seemeth to me unreasonable to send a prisoner, and not withal to signify the crimes *laid* against him.

NEW AMERICAN STANDARD BIBLE

20 "Being at a loss how to investigate such matters, I asked whether he was willing to go to Jerusalem and there stand trial on these matters.

21 "But when Paul appealed to be held in custody for [1]the Emperor's decision, I ordered him to be kept in custody until I send him to Caesar."

22 Then Agrippa *said* to Festus, "I also would like to hear the man myself." "Tomorrow," he *said, "you shall hear him."

Paul before Agrippa

23 So, on the next day when Agrippa came together with Bernice amid great pomp, and entered the auditorium [2]accompanied by the commanders and the prominent men of the city, at the command of Festus, Paul was brought in.

24 Festus *said, "King Agrippa, and all you gentlemen here present with us, you see this man about whom all the people of the Jews appealed to me, both at Jerusalem and here, loudly declaring that he ought not to live any longer.

25 "But I found that he had committed nothing worthy of death; and since he himself appealed to the Emperor, I decided to send him.

26 "Yet I have nothing definite about him to write to my lord. Therefore I have brought him before you *all* and especially before you, King Agrippa, so that after the investigation has taken place, I may have something to write.

27 "For it seems absurd to me in sending a prisoner, not to indicate also the charges against him."

25:21 [1] Lit *the Augustus'* (in this case Nero) 25:23 [2] Lit *and with*

NEW CENTURY VERSION

20 Not knowing how to find out about these questions, I asked Paul, 'Do you want to go to Jerusalem and be judged there?' 21 But he asked to be kept in Caesarea. He wants a decision from the emperor.[a] So I ordered that he be held until I could send him to Caesar."

22 Agrippa said to Festus, "I would also like to hear this man myself."

Festus said, "Tomorrow you will hear him."

23 The next day Agrippa and Bernice appeared with great show, acting like very important people. They went into the judgment room with the army leaders and the important men of Caesarea. Then Festus ordered the soldiers to bring Paul in. 24 Festus said, "King Agrippa and all who are gathered here with us, you see this man. All the Jewish people, here and in Jerusalem, have complained to me about him, shouting that he should not live any longer. 25 When I judged him, I found no reason to order his death. But since he asked to be judged by Caesar, I decided to send him. 26 But I have nothing definite to write the emperor about him. So I have brought him before all of you—especially you, King Agrippa. I hope you can question him and give me something to write. 27 I think it is foolish to send a prisoner to Caesar without telling what charges are against him."

25:21 [a] **emperor** The ruler of the Roman Empire, which was almost all the known world.

CONTEMPORARY ENGLISH VERSION

20 Since I did not know how to find out the truth about all this, I asked Paul if he would be willing to go to Jerusalem and be put on trial there. 21 But Paul asked to be kept in jail until the Emperor could decide his case. So I ordered him to be kept here until I could send him to the Emperor.

22 Then Agrippa said to Festus, "I would also like to hear what this man has to say."

Festus answered, "You can hear him tomorrow."

23 The next day Agrippa and Bernice made a big show as they came into the meeting room. High ranking army officers and leading citizens of the town were also there. Festus then ordered Paul to be brought in 24 and said:

King Agrippa and other guests, look at this man! Every Jew from Jerusalem and Caesarea has come to me, demanding for him to be put to death. 25 I have not found him guilty of any crime deserving death. But because he has asked to be judged by the Emperor, I have decided to send him to Rome.

26 I have to write some facts about this man to the Emperor. So I have brought him before all of you, but especially before you, King Agrippa. After we have talked about his case, I will then have something to write. 27 It makes no sense to send a prisoner to the Emperor without stating the charges against him.

NEW INTERNATIONAL VERSION

how to investigate such matters; so I asked if he would be willing to go to Jerusalem and stand trial there on these charges. 21When Paul made his appeal to be held over for the Emperor's decision, I ordered him held until I could send him to Caesar."

22Then Agrippa said to Festus, "I would like to hear this man myself."

He replied, "Tomorrow you will hear him."

Paul Before Agrippa

23The next day Agrippa and Bernice came with great pomp and entered the audience room with the high ranking officers and the leading men of the city. At the command of Festus, Paul was brought in. 24Festus said: "King Agrippa, and all who are present with us, you see this man! The whole Jewish community has petitioned me about him in Jerusalem and here in Caesarea, shouting that he ought not to live any longer. 25I found he had done nothing deserving of death, but because he made his appeal to the Emperor I decided to send him to Rome. 26But I have nothing definite to write to His Majesty about him. Therefore I have brought him before all of you, and especially before you, King Agrippa, so that as a result of this investigation I may have something to write. 27For I think it is unreasonable to send on a prisoner without specifying the charges against him."

NEW LIVING TRANSLATION

was perplexed as to how to conduct an investigation of this kind, and I asked him whether he would be willing to stand trial on these charges in Jerusalem. 21But Paul appealed to the emperor. So I ordered him back to jail until I could arrange to send him to Caesar."

22"I'd like to hear the man myself," Agrippa said.

And Festus replied, "You shall—tomorrow!"

Paul Speaks to Agrippa

23So the next day Agrippa and Bernice arrived at the auditorium with great pomp, accompanied by military officers and prominent men of the city. Festus ordered that Paul be brought in. 24Then Festus said, "King Agrippa and all present, this is the man whose death is demanded both by the local Jews and by those in Jerusalem. 25But in my opinion he has done nothing worthy of death. However, he appealed his case to the emperor, and I decided to send him. 26But what shall I write the emperor? For there is no real charge against him. So I have brought him before all of you, and especially you, King Agrippa, so that after we examine him, I might have something to write. 27For it doesn't seem reasonable to send a prisoner to the emperor without specifying the charges against him!"

NEW KING JAMES VERSION

20And because I was uncertain of such questions, I asked whether he was willing to go to Jerusalem and there be judged concerning these matters. 21But when Paul appealed to be reserved for the decision of Augustus, I commanded him to be kept till I could send him to Caesar."

22Then Agrippa said to Festus, "I also would like to hear the man myself."

"Tomorrow," he said, "you shall hear him."

23So the next day, when Agrippa and Bernice had come with great pomp, and had entered the auditorium with the commanders and the prominent men of the city, at Festus' command Paul was brought in. 24And Festus said: "King Agrippa and all the men who are here present with us, you see this man about whom the whole assembly of the Jews petitioned me, both at Jerusalem and here, crying out that he was not fit to live any longer. 25But when I found that he had committed nothing deserving of death, and that he himself had appealed to Augustus, I decided to send him. 26I have nothing certain to write to my lord concerning him. Therefore I have brought him out before you, and especially before you, King Agrippa, so that after the examination has taken place I may have something to write. 27For it seems to me unreasonable to send a prisoner and not to specify the charges against him."

THE MESSAGE

don't understand everything involved in cases like this, I asked if he'd be willing to go to Jerusalem and be tried there. Paul refused and demanded a hearing before His Majesty in our highest court. So I ordered him returned to custody until I could send him to Caesar in Rome."

Agrippa said, "I'd like to see this man and hear his story."

"Good," said Festus. "We'll bring him in first thing in the morning and you'll hear it for yourself."

The next day everybody who was anybody in Caesarea found his way to the Great Hall, along with the top military brass. Agrippa and Bernice made a flourishing grand entrance and took their places. Festus then ordered Paul brought in.

Festus said, "King Agrippa and distinguished guests, take a good look at this man. A bunch of Jews petitioned me first in Jerusalem, and later here, to do away with him. They have been most vehement in demanding his execution. I looked into it and decided that he had committed no crime. He requested a trial before Caesar and I agreed to send him to Rome. But what am I going to write to my master, Caesar? All the charges made by the Jews were fabrications, and I've uncovered nothing else.

"That's why I've brought him before this company, and especially you, King Agrippa: so we can come up with something in the nature of a charge that will hold water. For it seems to me silly to send a prisoner all that way for a trial and not be able to document what he did wrong."

KING JAMES VERSION

26 Then Agrippa said unto Paul, Thou art permitted to speak for thyself. Then Paul stretched forth the hand, and answered for himself:

2 I think myself happy, king Agrippa, because I shall answer for myself this day before thee touching all the things whereof I am accused of the Jews:

3 Especially *because I know* thee to be expert in all customs and questions which are among the Jews: wherefore I beseech thee to hear me patiently.

4 My manner of life from my youth, which was at the first among mine own nation at Jerusalem, know all the Jews;

5 Which knew me from the beginning, if they would testify, that after the most straitest sect of our religion I lived a Pharisee.

6 And now I stand and am judged for the hope of the promise made of God unto our fathers:

7 Unto which *promise* our twelve tribes, instantly serving *God* day and night, hope to come. For which hope's sake, king Agrippa, I am accused of the Jews.

8 Why should it be thought a thing incredible with you, that God should raise the dead?

9 I verily thought with myself, that I ought to do many things contrary to the name of Jesus of Nazareth.

10 Which thing I also did in Jerusalem: and many of the saints did I shut up in prison, having received authority from the chief priests; and when they were put to death, I gave my voice against *them*.

NEW AMERICAN STANDARD BIBLE

Paul's Defense before Agrippa

26 Agrippa said to Paul, "You are permitted to speak for yourself." Then Paul stretched out his hand and *proceeded* to make his defense:

2 "In regard to all the things of which I am accused by the Jews, I consider myself fortunate, King Agrippa, that I am about to make my defense before you today;

3 especially because you are an expert in all customs and questions among *the* Jews; therefore I beg you to listen to me patiently.

4 "So then, all Jews know my manner of life from my youth up, which from the beginning was spent among my *own* nation and at Jerusalem;

5 since they have known about me for a long time, if they are willing to testify, that I lived *as* a Pharisee according to the strictest sect of our religion.

6 "And now I am standing trial for the hope of the promise made by God to our fathers;

7 *the promise* to which our twelve tribes hope to attain, as they earnestly serve *God* night and day. And for this hope, O King, I am being accused by Jews.

8 "Why is it considered incredible among you *people* if God does raise the dead?

9 "So then, I thought to myself that I had to do many things hostile to the name of Jesus of Nazareth.

10 "And this is just what I did in Jerusalem; not only did I lock up many of the saints in prisons, having received authority from the chief priests, but also when they were being put to death I cast my vote against them.

NEW CENTURY VERSION

Paul Defends Himself

26 Agrippa said to Paul, "You may now speak to defend yourself."
Then Paul raised his hand and began to speak. 2He said,
"King Agrippa, I am very happy to stand before you and
will answer all the charges the Jewish people make against
me. 3You know so much about all the Jewish customs and
the things the Jews argue about, so please listen to me
patiently.
4"All the Jewish people know about my whole life, how I
lived from the beginning in my own country and later in
Jerusalem. 5They have known me for a long time. If they
want to, they can tell you that I was a good Pharisee. And
the Pharisees obey the laws of the Jewish religion more
carefully than any other group. 6Now I am on trial because
I hope for the promise that God made to our ancestors.
7This is the promise that the twelve tribes of our people
hope to receive as they serve God day and night. My king,
the Jews have accused me because I hope for this same
promise! 8Why do any of you people think it is impossible
for God to raise people from the dead?
9"I, too, thought I ought to do many things against Jesus
from Nazareth. 10And that is what I did in Jerusalem. The
leading priests gave me the power to put many of God's
people in jail, and when they were being killed, I agreed it

CONTEMPORARY ENGLISH VERSION

Paul's Defense before Agrippa

26 Agrippa told Paul, "You may now speak for yourself."
Paul stretched out his hand and said:
2King Agrippa, I am glad for this chance to defend
myself before you today on all these charges that my
own people have brought against me. 3You know a lot
about our religious customs and the beliefs that divide
us. So I ask you to listen patiently to me.
4-5All the Jews have known me since I was a child.
They know what kind of life I have lived in my own
country and in Jerusalem. And if they were willing, they
could tell you that I was a Pharisee, a member of a
group that is stricter than any other. 6Now I am on trial
because I believe the promise God made to our people
long ago.
7Day and night our twelve tribes have earnestly
served God, waiting for his promised blessings. King
Agrippa, because of this hope, the Jewish leaders have
brought charges against me. 8Why should any of you
doubt that God raises the dead to life?
9I once thought that I should do everything I could to
oppose Jesus from Nazareth. 10I did this first in Jerusalem,
and with the authority of the chief priests I put many of
God's people in jail. I even voted for them to be killed.

NEW INTERNATIONAL VERSION

26 Then Agrippa said to Paul, "You have permission
to speak for yourself."
So Paul motioned with his hand and began his defense:
2"King Agrippa, I consider myself fortunate to stand before
you today as I make my defense against all the accusa-
tions of the Jews, 3and especially so because you are well
acquainted with all the Jewish customs and controversies.
Therefore, I beg you to listen to me patiently.
4"The Jews all know the way I have lived ever since I
was a child, from the beginning of my life in my own coun-
try, and also in Jerusalem. 5They have known me for a
long time and can testify, if they are willing, that accord-
ing to the strictest sect of our religion, I lived as a
Pharisee. 6And now it is because of my hope in what God
has promised our fathers that I am on trial today. 7This is
the promise our twelve tribes are hoping to see fulfilled as
they earnestly serve God day and night. O king, it is
because of this hope that the Jews are accusing me. 8Why
should any of you consider it incredible that God raises the
dead?
9"I too was convinced that I ought to do all that was
possible to oppose the name of Jesus of Nazareth. 10And
that is just what I did in Jerusalem. On the authority of the
chief priests I put many of the saints in prison, and when
they were put to death, I cast my vote against them.

NEW LIVING TRANSLATION

26 Then Agrippa said to Paul, "You may speak in your
defense."
So Paul, with a gesture of his hand, started his defense:
2"I am fortunate, King Agrippa, that you are the one hear-
ing my defense against all these accusations made by the
Jewish leaders, 3for I know you are an expert on Jewish
customs and controversies. Now please listen to me
patiently!
4"As the Jewish leaders are well aware, I was given a
thorough Jewish training from my earliest childhood
among my own people and in Jerusalem. 5If they would
admit it, they know that I have been a member of the
Pharisees, the strictest sect of our religion. 6Now I am on
trial because I am looking forward to the fulfillment of
God's promise made to our ancestors. 7In fact, that is why
the twelve tribes of Israel worship God night and day, and
they share the same hope I have. Yet, O king, they say it is
wrong for me to have this hope! 8Why does it seem incred-
ible to any of you that God can raise the dead?
9"I used to believe that I ought to do everything I could
to oppose the followers of Jesus of Nazareth.* 10Authorized
by the leading priests, I caused many of the believers in
Jerusalem to be sent to prison. And I cast my vote against
them when they were condemned to death. 11Many times I

26:9 Greek *oppose the name of Jesus the Nazarene.*

NEW KING JAMES VERSION

Paul's Early Life

26 Then Agrippa said to Paul, "You are permitted to
speak for yourself."
So Paul stretched out his hand and answered for him-
self: 2"I think myself happy, King Agrippa, because today I
shall answer for myself before you concerning all the
things of which I am accused by the Jews, 3especially
because you are expert in all customs and questions which
have to do with the Jews. Therefore I beg you to hear me
patiently.
4"My manner of life from my youth, which was spent
from the beginning among my own nation at Jerusalem, all
the Jews know. 5They knew me from the first, if they were
willing to testify, that according to the strictest sect of our
religion I lived a Pharisee. 6And now I stand and am
judged for the hope of the promise made by God to our
fathers. 7To this *promise* our twelve tribes, earnestly serv-
ing *God* night and day, hope to attain. For this hope's
sake, King Agrippa, I am accused by the Jews. 8Why
should it be thought incredible by you that God raises the
dead?
9"Indeed, I myself thought I must do many things con-
trary to the name of Jesus of Nazareth. 10This I also did in
Jerusalem, and many of the saints I shut up in prison, hav-
ing received authority from the chief priests; and when
they were put to death, I cast my vote against *them.* 11And

THE MESSAGE

"I Couldn't Just Walk Away"

26 Agrippa spoke directly to Paul: "Go ahead—tell us about yourself."

Paul took the stand and told his story. "I can't think of anyone, King Agrippa, before whom I'd rather be answering all these Jewish accusations than you, knowing how well you are acquainted with Jewish ways and all our family quarrels.

"From the time of my youth, my life has been lived among my own people in Jerusalem. Practically every Jew in town who watched me grow up—and if they were willing to stick their necks out they'd tell you in person—knows that I lived as a strict Pharisee, the most demanding branch of our religion. It's because I believed it and took it seriously, committed myself heart and soul to what God promised my ancestors—the identical hope, mind you, that the twelve tribes have lived for night and day all these centuries—it's because I have held on to this tested and tried hope that I'm being called on the carpet by the Jews. They should be the ones standing trial here, not me! For the life of me, I can't see why it's a criminal offense to believe that God raises the dead.

"I admit that I didn't always hold to this position. For a time I thought it was my duty to oppose this Jesus of Nazareth with all my might. Backed with the full authority of the high priests, I threw these believers—I had no idea they were God's people!—into the Jerusalem jail right and left, and whenever it came to a vote, I voted for their execution.

KING JAMES VERSION

11 And I punished them oft in every synagogue, and
compelled *them* to blaspheme; and being exceedingly mad
against them, I persecuted *them* even unto strange cities.
12 ¶ Whereupon as I went to Damascus with authority
and commission from the chief priests,
13 At midday, O king, I saw in the way a light from
heaven, above the brightness of the sun, shining round
about me and them which journeyed with me.
14 And when we were all fallen to the earth, I heard a
voice speaking unto me, and saying in the Hebrew tongue,
Saul, Saul, why persecutest thou me? *it is* hard for thee to
kick against the pricks.
15 And I said, Who art thou, Lord? And he said, I am
Jesus whom thou persecutest.
16 But rise, and stand upon thy feet: for I have
appeared unto thee for this purpose, to make thee a minis-
ter and a witness both of these things which thou hast
seen, and of those things in the which I will appear unto
thee;
17 Delivering thee from the people, and *from* the
Gentiles, unto whom now I send thee,
18 To open their eyes, *and* to turn *them* from darkness
to light, and *from* the power of Satan unto God, that they
may receive forgiveness of sins, and inheritance among
them which are sanctified by faith that is in me.
19 Whereupon, O king Agrippa, I was not disobedient
unto the heavenly vision:
20 But shewed first unto them of Damascus, and at
Jerusalem, and throughout all the coasts of Judaea, and

NEW AMERICAN STANDARD BIBLE

11 "And as I punished them often in all the synagogues, I
tried to force them to blaspheme; and being furiously
enraged at them, I kept pursuing them even to foreign cit-
ies.
12 "While so engaged as I was journeying to Damascus
with the authority and commission of the chief priests,
13 at midday, O King, I saw on the way a light from
heaven, brighter than the sun, shining all around me and
those who were journeying with me.
14 "And when we had all fallen to the ground, I heard a
voice saying to me in the Hebrew dialect, 'Saul, Saul, why
are you persecuting Me? It is hard for you to kick against
the goads.'
15 "And I said, 'Who are You, Lord?' And the Lord said, 'I
am Jesus whom you are persecuting.
16 'But get up and stand on your feet; for this purpose I
have appeared to you, to appoint you a minister and a wit-
ness not only to the things which you have seen, but also
to the things in which I will appear to you;
17 rescuing you from the *Jewish* people and from the
Gentiles, to whom I am sending you,
18 to open their eyes so that they may turn from dark-
ness to light and from the dominion of Satan to God, that
they may receive forgiveness of sins and an inheritance
among those who have been sanctified by faith in Me.'
19 "So, King Agrippa, I did not prove disobedient to the
heavenly vision,
20 but *kept* declaring both to those of Damascus first,
and *also* at Jerusalem and *then* throughout all the region of

NEW CENTURY VERSION

was a good thing. 11In every synagogue, I often punished
them and tried to make them speak against Jesus. I was so
angry against them I even went to other cities to find them
and punish them.
12"One time the leading priests gave me permission and
the power to go to Damascus. 13On the way there, at noon, I
saw a light from heaven. It was brighter than the sun and
flashed all around me and those who were traveling with
me. 14We all fell to the ground. Then I heard a voice speak-
ing to me in the Jewish language,[a] saying, 'Saul, Saul, why
are you persecuting me? You are only hurting yourself by
fighting me.' 15I said, 'Who are you, Lord?' The Lord said, 'I
am Jesus, the one you are persecuting. 16Stand up! I have
chosen you to be my servant and my witness—you will tell
people the things that you have seen and the things that I
will show you. This is why I have come to you today. 17I
will keep you safe from your own people and also from
those who are not Jewish. I am sending you to them 18to
open their eyes so that they may turn away from darkness
to the light, away from the power of Satan and to God. Then
their sins can be forgiven, and they can have a place with
those people who have been made holy by believing in me.'
19"King Agrippa, after I had this vision from heaven, I
obeyed it. 20I began telling people that they should change
their hearts and lives and turn to God and do things to
show they really had changed. I told this first to those in
Damascus, then in Jerusalem, and in every part of Judea,

26:14 [a] **Jewish language** Hebrew or Aramaic, the languages of the Jews in the first century.

CONTEMPORARY ENGLISH VERSION

11I often had them punished in our meeting places, and I
tried to make them give up their faith. In fact, I was so
angry with them, that I went looking for them in foreign
cities.
12King Agrippa, one day I was on my way to
Damascus with the authority and permission of the chief
priests. 13About noon I saw a light brighter than the
sun. It flashed from heaven on me and on everyone trav-
eling with me. 14We all fell to the ground. Then I heard a
voice say to me in Aramaic, "Saul, Saul, why are you so
cruel to me? It's foolish to fight against me!"
15"Who are you?" I asked.
Then the Lord answered, "I am Jesus! I am the one
you are so cruel to. 16Now stand up. I have appeared to
you, because I have chosen you to be my servant. You
are to tell others what you have learned about me and
what I will show you later."
17The Lord also said, "I will protect you from the Jews
and from the Gentiles that I am sending you to. 18I want
you to open their eyes, so that they will turn from dark-
ness to light and from the power of Satan to God. Then
their sins will be forgiven, and by faith in me they will
become part of God's holy people."
19King Agrippa, I obeyed this vision from heaven.
20First I preached to the people in Damascus, and then I
went to Jerusalem and all over Judea. Finally, I went to

NEW INTERNATIONAL VERSION

11 Many a time I went from one synagogue to another to have them punished, and I tried to force them to blaspheme. In my obsession against them, I even went to foreign cities to persecute them.

12 "On one of these journeys I was going to Damascus with the authority and commission of the chief priests. 13 About noon, O king, as I was on the road, I saw a light from heaven, brighter than the sun, blazing around me and my companions. 14 We all fell to the ground, and I heard a voice saying to me in Aramaic,[a] 'Saul, Saul, why do you persecute me? It is hard for you to kick against the goads.'

15 "Then I asked, 'Who are you, Lord?'

"'I am Jesus, whom you are persecuting,' the Lord replied. 16 'Now get up and stand on your feet. I have appeared to you to appoint you as a servant and as a witness of what you have seen of me and what I will show you. 17 I will rescue you from your own people and from the Gentiles. I am sending you to them 18 to open their eyes and turn them from darkness to light, and from the power of Satan to God, so that they may receive forgiveness of sins and a place among those who are sanctified by faith in me.'

19 "So then, King Agrippa, I was not disobedient to the vision from heaven. 20 First to those in Damascus, then to those in Jerusalem and in all Judea, and to the Gentiles

[a] *14* Or *Hebrew*

NEW LIVING TRANSLATION

had them whipped in the synagogues to try to get them to curse Christ. I was so violently opposed to them that I even hounded them in distant cities of foreign lands.

12 "One day I was on such a mission to Damascus, armed with the authority and commission of the leading priests. 13 About noon, Your Majesty, a light from heaven brighter than the sun shone down on me and my companions. 14 We all fell down, and I heard a voice saying to me in Aramaic,* 'Saul, Saul, why are you persecuting me? It is hard for you to fight against my will.*'

15 "'Who are you, sir?' I asked.

"And the Lord replied, 'I am Jesus, the one you are persecuting. 16 Now stand up! For I have appeared to you to appoint you as my servant and my witness. You are to tell the world about this experience and about other times I will appear to you. 17 And I will protect you from both your own people and the Gentiles. Yes, I am going to send you to the Gentiles, 18 to open their eyes so they may turn from darkness to light, and from the power of Satan to God. Then they will receive forgiveness for their sins and be given a place among God's people, who are set apart by faith in me.'

19 "And so, O King Agrippa, I was not disobedient to that vision from heaven. 20 I preached first to those in Damascus, then in Jerusalem and throughout all Judea,

26:14a Or *Hebrew.* **26:14b** Greek *It is hard for you to kick against the oxgoads.*

NEW KING JAMES VERSION

I punished them often in every synagogue and compelled *them* to blaspheme; and being exceedingly enraged against them, I persecuted *them* even to foreign cities.

Paul Recounts His Conversion

12 "While thus occupied, as I journeyed to Damascus with authority and commission from the chief priests, 13 at midday, O king, along the road I saw a light from heaven, brighter than the sun, shining around me and those who journeyed with me. 14 And when we all had fallen to the ground, I heard a voice speaking to me and saying in the Hebrew language, 'Saul, Saul, why are you persecuting Me? *It is* hard for you to kick against the goads.' 15 So I said, 'Who are You, Lord?' And He said, 'I am Jesus, whom you are persecuting. 16 But rise and stand on your feet; for I have appeared to you for this purpose, to make you a minister and a witness both of the things which you have seen and of the things which I will yet reveal to you. 17 I will deliver you from the *Jewish* people, as well as *from* the Gentiles, to whom I now[a] send you, 18 to open their eyes, *in order* to turn *them* from darkness to light, and *from* the power of Satan to God, that they may receive forgiveness of sins and an inheritance among those who are sanctified by faith in Me.'

Paul's Post-Conversion Life

19 "Therefore, King Agrippa, I was not disobedient to the heavenly vision, 20 but declared first to those in Damascus and in Jerusalem, and throughout all the region of Judea,

26:17 [a] NU-Text and M-Text omit *now.*

THE MESSAGE

I stormed through their meeting places, bullying them into cursing Jesus, a one-man terror obsessed with obliterating these people. And then I started on the towns outside Jerusalem.

"One day on my way to Damascus, armed as always with papers from the high priests authorizing my action, right in the middle of the day a blaze of light, light outshining the sun, poured out of the sky on me and my companions. Oh, King, it was so bright! We fell flat on our faces. Then I heard a voice in Hebrew: 'Saul, Saul, why are you out to get me? Why do you insist on going against the grain?'

"I said, 'Who are you, Master?'

"The voice answered, 'I am Jesus, the One you're hunting down like an animal. But now, up on your feet—I have a job for you. I've handpicked you to be a servant and witness to what's happened today, and to what I am going to show you.

"'I'm sending you off to open the eyes of the outsiders so they can see the difference between dark and light, and choose light, see the difference between Satan and God, and choose God. I'm sending you off to present my offer of sins forgiven, and a place in the family, inviting them into the company of those who begin real living by believing in me.'

"What could I do, King Agrippa? I couldn't just walk away from a vision like that! I became an obedient believer on the spot. I started preaching this life-change—this radical turn to God and everything it meant in everyday life—right there in Damascus, went on to Jerusalem and the surrounding countryside, and from there to the whole world.

KING JAMES VERSION

then to the Gentiles, that they should repent and turn to God, and do works meet for repentance.

21 For these causes the Jews caught me in the temple, and went about to kill *me*.

22 Having therefore obtained help of God, I continue unto this day, witnessing both to small and great, saying none other things than those which the prophets and Moses did say should come:

23 That Christ should suffer, *and* that he should be the first that should rise from the dead, and should shew light unto the people, and to the Gentiles.

24 ¶ And as he thus spake for himself, Festus said with a loud voice, Paul, thou art beside thyself; much learning doth make thee mad.

25 But he said, I am not mad, most noble Festus; but speak forth the words of truth and soberness.

26 For the king knoweth of these things, before whom also I speak freely: for I am persuaded that none of these things are hidden from him; for this thing was not done in a corner.

27 King Agrippa, believest thou the prophets? I know that thou believest.

28 Then Agrippa said unto Paul, Almost thou persuadest me to be a Christian.

29 And Paul said, I would to God, that not only thou, but also all that hear me this day, were both almost, and altogether such as I am, except these bonds.

30 And when he had thus spoken, the king rose up, and the governor, and Bernice, and they that sat with them:

NEW AMERICAN STANDARD BIBLE

Judea, and *even* to the Gentiles, that they should repent and turn to God, performing deeds appropriate to repentance.

21 "For this reason *some* Jews seized me in the temple and tried to put me to death.

22 "So, having obtained help from God, I stand to this day testifying both to small and great, stating nothing but what the Prophets and Moses said was going to take place;

23 that the Christ was to suffer, *and* that by reason of *His* resurrection from the dead He would be the first to proclaim light both to the *Jewish* people and to the Gentiles."

24 While *Paul* was saying this in his defense, Festus *said in a loud voice, "Paul, you are out of your mind! *Your* great learning is driving you mad."

25 But Paul *said, "I am not out of my mind, most excellent Festus, but I utter words of sober truth.

26 "For the king knows about these matters, and I speak to him also with confidence, since I am persuaded that none of these things escape his notice; for this has not been done in a corner.

27 "King Agrippa, do you believe the Prophets? I know that you do."

28 Agrippa *replied* to Paul, "In a short time you will persuade me to become a Christian."

29 And Paul *said,* "I would wish to God, that whether in a short or long time, not only you, but also all who hear me this day, might become such as I am, except for these chains."

30 The king stood up and the governor and Bernice, and those who were sitting with them,

NEW CENTURY VERSION

and also to those who are not Jewish. 21This is why the
Jews took me and were trying to kill me in the Temple.
22But God has helped me, and so I stand here today, telling
all people, small and great, what I have seen. But I am
saying only what Moses and the prophets said would hap-
pen— 23that the Christ would die, and as the first to rise
from the dead, he would bring light to the Jewish and non-Jewish people."

Paul Tries to Persuade Agrippa

24While Paul was saying these things to defend himself, Festus said loudly, "Paul, you are out of your mind! Too much study has driven you crazy!"

25Paul said, "Most excellent Festus, I am not crazy. My
words are true and sensible. 26King Agrippa knows about
these things, and I can speak freely to him. I know he has
heard about all of these things, because they did not hap-
pen off in a corner. 27King Agrippa, do you believe what
the prophets wrote? I know you believe."

28King Agrippa said to Paul, "Do you think you can persuade me to become a Christian in such a short time?"

29Paul said, "Whether it is a short or a long time, I pray to God that not only you but every person listening to me today would be saved and be like me—except for these chains I have."

30Then King Agrippa, Governor Festus, Bernice, and all
the people sitting with them stood up 31and left the room.

CONTEMPORARY ENGLISH VERSION

the Gentiles and said, "Stop sinning and turn to God!
Then prove what you have done by the way you live."

21That is why some men grabbed me in the temple
and tried to kill me. 22But all this time God has helped
me, and I have preached both to the rich and to the poor.
I have told them only what the prophets and Moses said
would happen. 23I told them how the Messiah would
suffer and be the first to be raised from death, so that he
could bring light to his own people and to the Gentiles.

24Before Paul finished defending himself, Festus shouted, "Paul, you're crazy! Too much learning has driven you out of your mind."

25But Paul replied, "Honorable Festus, I am not crazy.
What I am saying is true, and it makes sense. 26None of
these things happened off in a corner somewhere. I am
sure that King Agrippa knows what I am talking about.
That's why I can speak so plainly to him."

27Then Paul said to Agrippa, "Do you believe what the prophets said? I know you do."

28Agrippa asked Paul, "In such a short time do you think you can talk me into being a Christian?"

29Paul answered, "Whether it takes a short time or a long time, I wish you and everyone else who hears me today would become just like me! Except, of course, for these chains."

30Then King Agrippa, Governor Festus, Bernice, and
everyone who was with them got up. 31But before they left,

NEW INTERNATIONAL VERSION

also, I preached that they should repent and turn to God and prove their repentance by their deeds. 21That is why the Jews seized me in the temple courts and tried to kill me. 22But I have had God's help to this very day, and so I stand here and testify to small and great alike. I am saying nothing beyond what the prophets and Moses said would happen— 23that the Christ[b] would suffer and, as the first to rise from the dead, would proclaim light to his own people and to the Gentiles."

24At this point Festus interrupted Paul's defense. "You are out of your mind, Paul!" he shouted. "Your great learning is driving you insane."

25"I am not insane, most excellent Festus," Paul replied. "What I am saying is true and reasonable. 26The king is familiar with these things, and I can speak freely to him. I am convinced that none of this has escaped his notice, because it was not done in a corner. 27King Agrippa, do you believe the prophets? I know you do."

28Then Agrippa said to Paul, "Do you think that in such a short time you can persuade me to be a Christian?"

29Paul replied, "Short time or long—I pray God that not only you but all who are listening to me today may become what I am, except for these chains."

30The king rose, and with him the governor and Bernice and those sitting with them. 31They left the room, and

b 23 Or *Messiah*

NEW LIVING TRANSLATION

and also to the Gentiles, that all must turn from their sins and turn to God—and prove they have changed by the good things they do. 21Some Jews arrested me in the Temple for preaching this, and they tried to kill me. 22But God protected me so that I am still alive today to tell these facts to everyone, from the least to the greatest. I teach nothing except what the prophets and Moses said would happen—23that the Messiah would suffer and be the first to rise from the dead as a light to Jews and Gentiles alike."

24Suddenly, Festus shouted, "Paul, you are insane. Too much study has made you crazy!"

25But Paul replied, "I am not insane, Most Excellent Festus. I am speaking the sober truth. 26And King Agrippa knows about these things. I speak frankly, for I am sure these events are all familiar to him, for they were not done in a corner! 27King Agrippa, do you believe the prophets? I know you do—"

28Agrippa interrupted him. "Do you think you can make me a Christian so quickly?"*

29Paul replied, "Whether quickly or not, I pray to God that both you and everyone here in this audience might become the same as I am, except for these chains."

30Then the king, the governor, Bernice, and all the others stood and left. 31As they talked it over they agreed,

26:28 Or *"A little more, and your arguments would make me a Christian."*

NEW KING JAMES VERSION

and *then* to the Gentiles, that they should repent, turn to God, and do works befitting repentance. 21For these reasons the Jews seized me in the temple and tried to kill *me.* 22Therefore, having obtained help from God, to this day I stand, witnessing both to small and great, saying no other things than those which the prophets and Moses said would come— 23that the Christ would suffer, that He would be the first to rise from the dead, and would proclaim light to the *Jewish* people and to the Gentiles."

Agrippa Parries Paul's Challenge

24Now as he thus made his defense, Festus said with a loud voice, "Paul, you are beside yourself! Much learning is driving you mad!"

25But he said, "I am not mad, most noble Festus, but speak the words of truth and reason. 26For the king, before whom I also speak freely, knows these things; for I am convinced that none of these things escapes his attention, since this thing was not done in a corner. 27King Agrippa, do you believe the prophets? I know that you do believe."

28Then Agrippa said to Paul, "You almost persuade me to become a Christian."

29And Paul said, "I would to God that not only you, but also all who hear me today, might become both almost and altogether such as I am, except for these chains."

30When he had said these things, the king stood up, as well as the governor and Bernice and those who sat with

THE MESSAGE

"It's because of this 'whole world' dimension that the Jews grabbed me in the Temple that day and tried to kill me. They want to keep God for themselves. But God has stood by me, just as he promised, and I'm standing here saying what I've been saying to anyone, whether king or child, who will listen. And everything I'm saying is completely in line with what the prophets and Moses said would happen: One, the Messiah must die; two, raised from the dead, he would be the first rays of God's daylight shining on people far and near, people both godless and God-fearing."

That was too much for Festus. He interrupted with a shout: "Paul, you're crazy! You've read too many books, spent too much time staring off into space! Get a grip on yourself, get back in the real world!"

But Paul stood his ground. "With all respect, Festus, Your Honor, I'm not crazy. I'm both accurate and sane in what I'm saying. The King knows what I'm talking about. I'm sure that nothing of what I've said sounds crazy to him. He's known all about it for a long time. You must realize that this wasn't done behind the scenes. You believe the prophets, don't you, King Agrippa? Don't answer that—I know you believe."

But Agrippa did answer: "Keep this up much longer and you'll make a Christian out of me!"

Paul, still in chains, said, "That's what I'm praying for, whether now or later, and not only you but everyone listening today, to become like me—except, of course, for this prison jewelry!"

The king and the governor, along with Bernice and their

KING JAMES VERSION

31 And when they were gone aside, they talked between themselves, saying, This man doeth nothing worthy of death or of bonds.

32 Then said Agrippa unto Festus, This man might have been set at liberty, if he had not appealed unto Caesar.

27 And when it was determined that we should sail into Italy, they delivered Paul and certain other prisoners unto *one* named Julius, a centurion of Augustus' band.

2 And entering into a ship of Adramyttium, we launched, meaning to sail by the coasts of Asia; *one* Aristarchus, a Macedonian of Thessalonica, being with us.

3 And the next *day* we touched at Sidon. And Julius courteously entreated Paul, and gave *him* liberty to go unto his friends to refresh himself.

4 And when we had launched from thence, we sailed under Cyprus, because the winds were contrary.

5 And when we had sailed over the sea of Cilicia and Pamphylia, we came to Myra, *a city* of Lycia.

6 And there the centurion found a ship of Alexandria sailing into Italy; and he put us therein.

7 And when we had sailed slowly many days, and scarce were come over against Cnidus, the wind not suffering us, we sailed under Crete, over against Salmone;

NEW AMERICAN STANDARD BIBLE

31 and when they had gone aside, they *began* talking to one another, saying, "This man is not doing anything worthy of death or imprisonment."

32 And Agrippa said to Festus, "This man might have been set free if he had not appealed to Caesar."

Paul Is Sent to Rome

27 When it was decided that we would sail for Italy, they proceeded to deliver Paul and some other prisoners to a centurion of the Augustan [1]cohort named Julius.

2 And embarking in an Adramyttian ship, which was about to sail to the regions along the coast of Asia, we put out to sea accompanied by Aristarchus, a Macedonian of Thessalonica.

3 The next day we put in at Sidon; and Julius treated Paul with consideration and allowed him to go to his friends and receive care.

4 From there we put out to sea and sailed under the shelter of Cyprus because the winds were contrary.

5 When we had sailed through the sea along the coast of Cilicia and Pamphylia, we landed at Myra in Lycia.

6 There the centurion found an Alexandrian ship sailing for Italy, and he put us aboard it.

7 When we had sailed slowly for a good many days, and with difficulty had arrived off Cnidus, since the wind did not permit us *to go* farther, we sailed under the shelter of Crete, off Salmone;

27:1 [1] Or *battalion*

NEW CENTURY VERSION

Talking to each other, they said, "There is no reason why
this man should die or be put in jail." 32And Agrippa said
to Festus, "We could let this man go free, but he has asked
Caesar to hear his case."

Paul Sails for Rome

27 It was decided that we would sail for Italy. An officer named Julius, who served in the emperor's[a]
army, guarded Paul and some other prisoners. 2We got on
a ship that was from the city of Adramyttium and was
about to sail to different ports in the country of Asia.
Aristarchus, a man from the city of Thessalonica in
Macedonia, went with us. 3The next day we came to Sidon.
Julius was very good to Paul and gave him freedom to go
visit his friends, who took care of his needs. 4We left Sidon
and sailed close to the island of Cyprus, because the wind
was blowing against us. 5We went across the sea by Cilicia
and Pamphylia and landed at the city of Myra, in Lycia.
6There the officer found a ship from Alexandria that was
going to Italy, so he put us on it.

7We sailed slowly for many days. We had a hard time
reaching Cnidus because the wind was blowing against us,
and we could not go any farther. So we sailed by the south
side of the island of Crete near Salmone. 8Sailing past it

27:1 [a] **emperor** The ruler of the Roman Empire, which was almost all the known world.

CONTEMPORARY ENGLISH VERSION

they said, "This man isn't guilty of anything. He doesn't
deserve to die or to be put in jail."

32Agrippa told Festus, "Paul could have been set free, if
he had not asked to be tried by the Roman Emperor."

Paul Is Taken to Rome

27 When it was time for us to sail to Rome, Captain Julius from the Emperor's special troops was put
in charge of Paul and the other prisoners. 2We went
aboard a ship from Adramyttium that was about to sail to
some ports along the coast of Asia. Aristarchus from
Thessalonica in Macedonia sailed on the ship with us.

3The next day we came to shore at Sidon. Captain Julius
was very kind to Paul. He even let him visit his friends, so
they could give him whatever he needed. 4When we left
Sidon, the winds were blowing against us, and we sailed
close to the island of Cyprus to be safe from the wind.
5Then we sailed south of Cilicia and Pamphylia until we
came to the port of Myra in Lycia. 6There the army captain
found a ship from Alexandria that was going to Italy. So
he ordered us to board that ship.

7We sailed along slowly for several days and had a hard
time reaching Cnidus. The wind would not let us go any
farther in that direction, so we sailed past Cape Salmone,
where the island of Crete would protect us from the wind.

NEW INTERNATIONAL VERSION

while talking with one another, they said, "This man is not doing anything that deserves death or imprisonment."

[32]Agrippa said to Festus, "This man could have been set free if he had not appealed to Caesar."

Paul Sails for Rome

27 When it was decided that we would sail for Italy, Paul and some other prisoners were handed over to a centurion named Julius, who belonged to the Imperial Regiment. [2]We boarded a ship from Adramyttium about to sail for ports along the coast of the province of Asia, and we put out to sea. Aristarchus, a Macedonian from Thessalonica, was with us.

[3]The next day we landed at Sidon; and Julius, in kindness to Paul, allowed him to go to his friends so they might provide for his needs. [4]From there we put out to sea again and passed to the lee of Cyprus because the winds were against us. [5]When we had sailed across the open sea off the coast of Cilicia and Pamphylia, we landed at Myra in Lycia. [6]There the centurion found an Alexandrian ship sailing for Italy and put us on board. [7]We made slow headway for many days and had difficulty arriving off Cnidus. When the wind did not allow us to hold our course, we sailed to the lee of Crete, opposite Salmone. [8]We moved

NEW LIVING TRANSLATION

"This man hasn't done anything worthy of death or imprisonment." [32]And Agrippa said to Festus, "He could be set free if he hadn't appealed to Caesar!"

Paul Sails for Rome

27 When the time came, we set sail for Italy. Paul and several other prisoners were placed in the custody of an army officer named Julius, a captain of the Imperial Regiment. [2]And Aristarchus, a Macedonian from Thessalonica, was also with us. We left on a boat whose home port was Adramyttium; it was scheduled to make several stops at ports along the coast of the province of Asia.

[3]The next day when we docked at Sidon, Julius was very kind to Paul and let him go ashore to visit with friends so they could provide for his needs. [4]Putting out to sea from there, we encountered headwinds that made it difficult to keep the ship on course, so we sailed north of Cyprus between the island and the mainland. [5]We passed along the coast of the provinces of Cilicia and Pamphylia, landing at Myra, in the province of Lycia. [6]There the officer found an Egyptian ship from Alexandria that was bound for Italy, and he put us on board.

[7]We had several days of rough sailing, and after great difficulty we finally neared Cnidus. But the wind was against us, so we sailed down to the leeward side of Crete,

NEW KING JAMES VERSION

them; [31]and when they had gone aside, they talked among themselves, saying, "This man is doing nothing deserving of death or chains."

[32]Then Agrippa said to Festus, "This man might have been set free if he had not appealed to Caesar."

The Voyage to Rome Begins

27 And when it was decided that we should sail to Italy, they delivered Paul and some other prisoners to *one* named Julius, a centurion of the Augustan Regiment. [2]So, entering a ship of Adramyttium, we put to sea, meaning to sail along the coasts of Asia. Aristarchus, a Macedonian of Thessalonica, was with us. [3]And the next *day* we landed at Sidon. And Julius treated Paul kindly and gave *him* liberty to go to his friends and receive care. [4]When we had put to sea from there, we sailed under *the shelter of* Cyprus, because the winds were contrary. [5]And when we had sailed over the sea which is off Cilicia and Pamphylia, we came to Myra, *a city* of Lycia. [6]There the centurion found an Alexandrian ship sailing to Italy, and he put us on board.

[7]When we had sailed slowly many days, and arrived with difficulty off Cnidus, the wind not permitting us to proceed, we sailed under *the shelter of* Crete off Salmone.

THE MESSAGE

advisors, got up and went into the next room to talk over what they had heard. They quickly agreed on Paul's innocence, saying, "There's nothing in this man deserving prison, let alone death."

Agrippa told Festus, "He could be set free right now if he hadn't requested the hearing before Caesar."

A Storm at Sea

27 As soon as arrangements were complete for our sailing to Italy, Paul and a few other prisoners were placed under the supervision of a centurion named Julius, a member of an elite guard. We boarded a ship from Adramyttium that was bound for Ephesus and ports west. Aristarchus, a Macedonian from Thessalonica, went with us.

The next day we put in at Sidon. Julius treated Paul most decently—let him get off the ship and enjoy the hospitality of his friends there.

Out to sea again, we sailed north under the protection of the northeast shore of Cyprus because winds out of the west were against us, and then along the coast westward to the port of Myra. There the centurion found an Egyptian ship headed for Italy and transferred us on board. We ran into bad weather and found it impossible to stay on

KING JAMES VERSION

8 And, hardly passing it, came unto a place which is called The fair havens; nigh whereunto was the city *of* Lasea.

9 Now when much time was spent, and when sailing was now dangerous, because the fast was now already past, Paul admonished *them*,

10 And said unto them, Sirs, I perceive that this voyage will be with hurt and much damage, not only of the lading and ship, but also of our lives.

11 Nevertheless the centurion believed the master and the owner of the ship, more than those things which were spoken by Paul.

12 ¶ And because the haven was not commodious to winter in, the more part advised to depart thence also, if by any means they might attain to Phenice, *and there* to winter; *which is* an haven of Crete, and lieth toward the south west and north west.

13 And when the south wind blew softly, supposing that they had obtained *their* purpose, loosing *thence*, they sailed close by Crete.

14 But not long after there arose against it a tempestuous wind, called Euroclydon.

15 And when the ship was caught, and could not bear up into the wind, we let *her* drive.

16 And running under a certain island which is called Clauda, we had much work to come by the boat:

NEW AMERICAN STANDARD BIBLE

8 and with difficulty sailing past it we came to a place called Fair Havens, near which was the city of Lasea.

9 When considerable time had passed and the voyage was now dangerous, since even the [2]fast was already over, Paul *began* to admonish them,

10 and said to them, "Men, I perceive that the voyage will certainly be with damage and great loss, not only of the cargo and the ship, but also of our lives."

11 But the centurion was more persuaded by the pilot and the captain of the ship than by what was being said by Paul.

12 Because the harbor was not suitable for wintering, the majority reached a decision to put out to sea from there, if somehow they could reach Phoenix, a harbor of Crete, facing southwest and northwest, and spend the winter *there*.

13 When a moderate south wind came up, supposing that they had attained their purpose, they weighed anchor and *began* sailing along Crete, close *inshore*.

Shipwreck

14 But before very long there rushed down from the land a violent wind, called [3]Euraquilo;

15 and when the ship was caught *in it* and could not face the wind, we gave way *to it* and let ourselves be driven along.

16 Running under the shelter of a small island called Clauda, we were scarcely able to get the *ship's* boat under control.

27:9 [2] I.e. Day of Atonement in September or October, which was a dangerous time of year for navigation 27:14 [3] I.e. a northeaster

NEW CENTURY VERSION

was hard. Then we came to a place called Fair Havens, near the city of Lasea.

9We had lost much time, and it was now dangerous to sail, because it was already after the Day of Cleansing.[b] So Paul warned them, 10"Men, I can see there will be a lot of trouble on this trip. The ship, the cargo, and even our lives may be lost." 11But the captain and the owner of the ship did not agree with Paul, and the officer believed what the captain and owner of the ship said. 12Since that harbor was not a good place for the ship to stay for the winter, most of the men decided that the ship should leave. They hoped we could go to Phoenix and stay there for the winter. Phoenix, a city on the island of Crete, had a harbor which faced southwest and northwest.

The Storm

13When a good wind began to blow from the south, the men on the ship thought, "This is the wind we wanted, and now we have it." So they pulled up the anchor, and we sailed very close to the island of Crete. 14But then a very strong wind named the "northeaster" came from the island. 15The ship was caught in it and could not sail against it. So we stopped trying and let the wind carry us. 16When we went below a small island named Cauda, we were barely able to bring in the lifeboat. 17After the men

27:9 [b] **Day of Cleansing** An important Jewish holy day in the fall of the year. This was the time of year that bad storms arose on the sea.

CONTEMPORARY ENGLISH VERSION

8We went slowly along the coast and finally reached a place called Fair Havens, not far from the town of Lasea.

9By now we had already lost a lot of time, and sailing was no longer safe. In fact, even the Great Day of Forgiveness[a] was past. 10Then Paul spoke to the crew of the ship, "Men, listen to me! If we sail now, our ship and its cargo will be badly damaged, and many lives will be lost." 11But Julius listened to the captain of the ship and its owner, rather than to Paul.

12The harbor at Fair Havens wasn't a good place to spend the winter. Because of this, almost everyone agreed that we should at least try to sail along the coast of Crete as far as Phoenix. It had a harbor that opened toward the southwest and northwest,[b] and we could spend the winter there.

The Storm at Sea

13When a gentle wind from the south started blowing, the men thought it was a good time to do what they had planned. So they pulled up the anchor, and we sailed along the coast of Crete. 14But soon a strong wind called "The Northeaster" blew against us from the island. 15The wind struck the ship, and we could not sail against it. So we let the wind carry the ship.

16We went along the island of Cauda on the side that was protected from the wind. We had a hard time holding the

[a] 27.9 *Great Day of Forgiveness*: This Jewish festival took place near the end of September. The sailing season was dangerous after the middle of September, and it was stopped completely between the middle of November and the middle of March. [b] 27.12 *southwest and northwest*: Or "northeast and southeast."

NEW INTERNATIONAL VERSION

along the coast with difficulty and came to a place called Fair Havens, near the town of Lasea.

9 Much time had been lost, and sailing had already become dangerous because by now it was after the Fast.[a] So Paul warned them, 10 "Men, I can see that our voyage is going to be disastrous and bring great loss to ship and cargo, and to our own lives also." 11 But the centurion, instead of listening to what Paul said, followed the advice of the pilot and of the owner of the ship. 12 Since the harbor was unsuitable to winter in, the majority decided that we should sail on, hoping to reach Phoenix and winter there. This was a harbor in Crete, facing both southwest and northwest.

The Storm

13 When a gentle south wind began to blow, they thought they had obtained what they wanted; so they weighed anchor and sailed along the shore of Crete. 14 Before very long, a wind of hurricane force, called the "northeaster," swept down from the island. 15 The ship was caught by the storm and could not head into the wind; so we gave way to it and were driven along. 16 As we passed to the lee of a small island called Cauda, we were hardly able to make the

[a] *9* That is, the Day of Atonement (Yom Kippur)

NEW LIVING TRANSLATION

past the cape of Salmone. 8 We struggled along the coast with great difficulty and finally arrived at Fair Havens, near the city of Lasea. 9 We had lost a lot of time. The weather was becoming dangerous for long voyages by then because it was so late in the fall,* and Paul spoke to the ship's officers about it.

10 "Sirs," he said, "I believe there is trouble ahead if we go on—shipwreck, loss of cargo, injuries, and danger to our lives." 11 But the officer in charge of the prisoners listened more to the ship's captain and the owner than to Paul. 12 And since Fair Havens was an exposed harbor—a poor place to spend the winter—most of the crew wanted to go to Phoenix, farther up the coast of Crete, and spend the winter there. Phoenix was a good harbor with only a southwest and northwest exposure.

The Storm at Sea

13 When a light wind began blowing from the south, the sailors thought they could make it. So they pulled up anchor and sailed along close to shore. 14 But the weather changed abruptly, and a wind of typhoon strength (a "northeaster," they called it) caught the ship and blew it out to sea. 15 They couldn't turn the ship into the wind, so they gave up and let it run before the gale.

16 We sailed behind a small island named Cauda,* where with great difficulty we hoisted aboard the lifeboat that

27:9 Greek *because the fast was now already gone by.* This fast happened on the Day of Atonement (*Yom Kippur*), which occurred in late September or early October. **27:16** Some manuscripts read *Clauda.*

NEW KING JAMES VERSION

8 Passing it with difficulty, we came to a place called Fair Havens, near the city *of* Lasea.

Paul's Warning Ignored

9 Now when much time had been spent, and sailing was now dangerous because the Fast was already over, Paul advised them, 10 saying, "Men, I perceive that this voyage will end with disaster and much loss, not only of the cargo and ship, but also our lives." 11 Nevertheless the centurion was more persuaded by the helmsman and the owner of the ship than by the things spoken by Paul. 12 And because the harbor was not suitable to winter in, the majority advised to set sail from there also, if by any means they could reach Phoenix, a harbor of Crete opening toward the southwest and northwest, *and* winter *there.*

In the Tempest

13 When the south wind blew softly, supposing that they had obtained *their* desire, putting out to sea, they sailed close by Crete. 14 But not long after, a tempestuous head wind arose, called Euroclydon.[a] 15 So when the ship was caught, and could not head into the wind, we let *her* drive. 16 And running under *the shelter of* an island called Clauda,[b] we secured the skiff with difficulty. 17 When they

27:14 [a] NU-Text reads *Euraquilon.* **27:16** [b] NU-Text reads *Cauda.*

THE MESSAGE

course. After much difficulty, we finally made it to the southern coast of the island of Crete and docked at Good Harbor (appropriate name!).

By this time we had lost a lot of time. We had passed the autumn equinox, so it would be stormy weather from now on through the winter, too dangerous for sailing. Paul warned, "I see only disaster ahead for cargo and ship—to say nothing of our lives!—if we put out to sea now."

But it was not the best harbor for staying the winter. Phoenix, a few miles further on, was more suitable. The centurion set Paul's warning aside and let the ship captain and the shipowner talk him into trying for the next harbor.

When a gentle southerly breeze came up, they weighed anchor, thinking it would be smooth sailing. But they were no sooner out to sea than a gale-force wind, the infamous nor'easter, struck. They lost all control of the ship. It was a cork in the storm.

We came under the lee of the small island named Clauda, and managed to get a lifeboat ready and reef the

KING JAMES VERSION

17 Which when they had taken up, they used helps, undergirding the ship; and, fearing lest they should fall into the quicksands, strake sail, and so were driven.

18 And we being exceedingly tossed with a tempest, the next *day* they lightened the ship;

19 And the third *day* we cast out with our own hands the tackling of the ship.

20 And when neither sun nor stars in many days appeared, and no small tempest lay on *us*, all hope that we should be saved was then taken away.

21 ¶ But after long abstinence Paul stood forth in the midst of them, and said, Sirs, ye should have hearkened unto me, and not have loosed from Crete, and to have gained this harm and loss.

22 And now I exhort you to be of good cheer: for there shall be no loss of *any man's* life among you, but of the ship.

23 For there stood by me this night the angel of God, whose I am, and whom I serve,

24 Saying, Fear not, Paul; thou must be brought before Caesar: and, lo, God hath given thee all them that sail with thee.

25 Wherefore, sirs, be of good cheer: for I believe God, that it shall be even as it was told me.

26 Howbeit we must be cast upon a certain island.

27 But when the fourteenth night was come, as we were driven up and down in Adria, about midnight the shipmen deemed that they drew near to some country;

NEW AMERICAN STANDARD BIBLE

17 After they had hoisted it up, they used supporting cables in undergirding the ship; and fearing that they might run aground on *the shallows* of Syrtis, they let down the sea anchor and in this way let themselves be driven along.

18 The next day as we were being violently storm-tossed, they began to jettison the cargo;

19 and on the third day they threw the ship's tackle overboard with their own hands.

20 Since neither sun nor stars appeared for many days, and no small storm was assailing *us*, from then on all hope of our being saved was gradually abandoned.

21 When they had gone a long time without food, then Paul stood up in their midst and said, "Men, you ought to have followed my advice and not to have set sail from Crete and incurred this damage and loss.

22 "*Yet* now I urge you to keep up your courage, for there will be no loss of life among you, but *only* of the ship.

23 "For this very night an angel of the God to whom I belong and whom I serve stood before me,

24 saying, 'Do not be afraid, Paul; you must stand before Caesar; and behold, God has granted you all those who are sailing with you.'

25 "Therefore, keep up your courage, men, for I believe God that it will turn out exactly as I have been told.

26 "But we must run aground on a certain island."

27 But when the fourteenth night came, as we were being driven about in the Adriatic Sea, about midnight the sailors *began* to surmise that they were approaching some land.

NEW CENTURY VERSION

took the lifeboat in, they tied ropes around the ship to hold it together. The men were afraid that the ship would hit the sandbanks of Syrtis,[c] so they lowered the sail and let the wind carry the ship. 18The next day the storm was blowing us so hard that the men threw out some of the cargo. 19A day later with their own hands they threw out the ship's equipment. 20When we could not see the sun or the stars for many days, and the storm was very bad, we lost all hope of being saved.

21After the men had gone without food for a long time, Paul stood up before them and said, "Men, you should have listened to me. You should not have sailed from Crete. Then you would not have all this trouble and loss. 22But now I tell you to cheer up because none of you will die. Only the ship will be lost. 23Last night an angel came to me from the God I belong to and worship. 24The angel said, 'Paul, do not be afraid. You must stand before Caesar. And God has promised you that he will save the lives of everyone sailing with you.' 25So men, have courage. I trust in God that everything will happen as his angel told me. 26But we will crash on an island."

27On the fourteenth night we were still being carried around in the Adriatic Sea.[d] About midnight the sailors thought we were close to land, 28so they lowered a rope

27:17 [c] **Syrtis** Shallow area in the sea near the Libyan coast.
27:27 [d] **Adriatic Sea** The sea between Greece and Italy, including the central Mediterranean.

CONTEMPORARY ENGLISH VERSION

lifeboat in place, 17but finally we got it where it belonged. Then the sailors wrapped ropes around the ship to hold it together. They lowered the sail and let the ship drift along, because they were afraid it might hit the sandbanks in the gulf of Syrtis.

18The storm was so fierce that the next day they threw some of the ship's cargo overboard. 19Then on the third day, with their bare hands they threw overboard some of the ship's gear. 20For several days we could not see either the sun or the stars. A strong wind kept blowing, and we finally gave up all hope of being saved.

21Since none of us had eaten anything for a long time, Paul stood up and told the men:

You should have listened to me! If you had stayed on in Crete, you would not have had this damage and loss.
22But now I beg you to cheer up, because you will be safe. Only the ship will be lost.

23I belong to God, and I worship him. Last night he sent an angel 24to tell me, "Paul, don't be afraid! You will stand trial before the Emperor. And because of you, God will save the lives of everyone on the ship." 25Cheer up! I am sure that God will do exactly what he promised. 26But we will first be shipwrecked on some island.

27For fourteen days and nights we had been blown around over the Mediterranean Sea. But about midnight the sailors realized that we were getting near land. 28They

NEW INTERNATIONAL VERSION

lifeboat secure. [17]When the men had hoisted it aboard, they passed ropes under the ship itself to hold it together. Fearing that they would run aground on the sandbars of Syrtis, they lowered the sea anchor and let the ship be driven along. [18]We took such a violent battering from the storm that the next day they began to throw the cargo overboard. [19]On the third day, they threw the ship's tackle overboard with their own hands. [20]When neither sun nor stars appeared for many days and the storm continued raging, we finally gave up all hope of being saved.

[21]After the men had gone a long time without food, Paul stood up before them and said: "Men, you should have taken my advice not to sail from Crete; then you would have spared yourselves this damage and loss. [22]But now I urge you to keep up your courage, because not one of you will be lost; only the ship will be destroyed. [23]Last night an angel of the God whose I am and whom I serve stood beside me [24]and said, 'Do not be afraid, Paul. You must stand trial before Caesar; and God has graciously given you the lives of all who sail with you.' [25]So keep up your courage, men, for I have faith in God that it will happen just as he told me. [26]Nevertheless, we must run aground on some island."

The Shipwreck

[27]On the fourteenth night we were still being driven across the Adriatic[b] Sea, when about midnight the sailors

[b] *27* In ancient times the name referred to an area extending well south of Italy.

NEW LIVING TRANSLATION

was being towed behind us. [17]Then we banded the ship with ropes to strengthen the hull. The sailors were afraid of being driven across to the sandbars of Syrtis off the African coast, so they lowered the sea anchor and were thus driven before the wind.

[18]The next day, as gale-force winds continued to batter the ship, the crew began throwing the cargo overboard. [19]The following day they even threw out the ship's equipment and anything else they could lay their hands on. [20]The terrible storm raged unabated for many days, blotting out the sun and the stars, until at last all hope was gone.

[21]No one had eaten for a long time. Finally, Paul called the crew together and said, "Men, you should have listened to me in the first place and not left Fair Havens. You would have avoided all this injury and loss. [22]But take courage! None of you will lose your lives, even though the ship will go down. [23]For last night an angel of the God to whom I belong and whom I serve stood beside me, [24]and he said, 'Don't be afraid, Paul, for you will surely stand trial before Caesar! What's more, God in his goodness has granted safety to everyone sailing with you.' [25]So take courage! For I believe God. It will be just as he said. [26]But we will be shipwrecked on an island."

The Shipwreck

[27]About midnight on the fourteenth night of the storm, as we were being driven across the Sea of Adria,* the

27:27 The *Sea of Adria* is in the central Mediterranean; it is not to be confused with the Adriatic Sea.

NEW KING JAMES VERSION

had taken it on board, they used cables to undergird the ship; and fearing lest they should run aground on the Syrtis[c] *Sands,* they struck sail and so were driven. [18]And because we were exceedingly tempest-tossed, the next *day* they lightened the ship. [19]On the third *day* we threw the ship's tackle overboard with our own hands. [20]Now when neither sun nor stars appeared for many days, and no small tempest beat on *us,* all hope that we would be saved was finally given up.

[21]But after long abstinence from food, then Paul stood in the midst of them and said, "Men, you should have listened to me, and not have sailed from Crete and incurred this disaster and loss. [22]And now I urge you to take heart, for there will be no loss of life among you, but only of the ship. [23]For there stood by me this night an angel of the God to whom I belong and whom I serve, [24]saying, 'Do not be afraid, Paul; you must be brought before Caesar; and indeed God has granted you all those who sail with you.' [25]Therefore take heart, men, for I believe God that it will be just as it was told me. [26]However, we must run aground on a certain island."

[27]Now when the fourteenth night had come, as we were driven up and down in the Adriatic *Sea,* about midnight the sailors sensed that they were drawing near some land.

27:17 [c] M-Text reads *Syrtes.*

THE MESSAGE

sails. But rocky shoals prevented us from getting close. We only managed to avoid them by throwing out drift anchors.

Next day, out on the high seas again and badly damaged now by the storm, we dumped the cargo overboard. The third day the sailors lightened the ship further by throwing off all the tackle and provisions. It had been many days since we had seen either sun or stars. Wind and waves were battering us unmercifully, and we lost all hope of rescue.

With our appetite for both food and life long gone, Paul took his place in our midst and said, "Friends, you really should have listened to me back in Crete. We could have avoided all this trouble and trial. But there's no need to dwell on that now. From now on, things are looking up! I can assure you that there'll not be a single drowning among us, although I can't say as much for the ship—the ship itself is doomed.

"Last night God's angel stood at my side, an angel of this God I serve, saying to me, 'Don't give up, Paul. You're going to stand before Caesar yet—and everyone sailing with you is also going to make it.' So, dear friends, take heart. I believe God will do exactly what he told me. But we're going to shipwreck on some island or other."

On the fourteenth night, adrift somewhere on the Adriatic Sea, at about midnight the sailors sensed that we

KING JAMES VERSION

28 And sounded, and found *it* twenty fathoms: and when they had gone a little further, they sounded again, and found *it* fifteen fathoms.

29 Then fearing lest we should have fallen upon rocks, they cast four anchors out of the stern, and wished for the day.

30 And as the shipmen were about to flee out of the ship, when they had let down the boat into the sea, under colour as though they would have cast anchors out of the foreship,

31 Paul said to the centurion and to the soldiers, Except these abide in the ship, ye cannot be saved.

32 Then the soldiers cut off the ropes of the boat, and let her fall off.

33 And while the day was coming on, Paul besought *them* all to take meat, saying, This day is the fourteenth day that ye have tarried and continued fasting, having taken nothing.

34 Wherefore I pray you to take *some* meat: for this is for your health: for there shall not an hair fall from the head of any of you.

35 And when he had thus spoken, he took bread, and gave thanks to God in presence of them all: and when he had broken *it*, he began to eat.

36 Then were they all of good cheer, and they also took *some* meat.

37 And we were in all in the ship two hundred threescore and sixteen souls.

38 And when they had eaten enough, they lightened the ship, and cast out the wheat into the sea.

NEW AMERICAN STANDARD BIBLE

28 They took soundings and found *it to be* twenty fathoms; and a little farther on they took another sounding and found *it to be* fifteen fathoms.

29 Fearing that we might run aground somewhere on the rocks, they cast four anchors from the stern and wished for daybreak.

30 But as the sailors were trying to escape from the ship and had let down the *ship's* boat into the sea, on the pretense of intending to lay out anchors from the bow,

31 Paul said to the centurion and to the soldiers, "Unless these men remain in the ship, you yourselves cannot be saved."

32 Then the soldiers cut away the ropes of the *ship's* boat and let it fall away.

33 Until the day was about to dawn, Paul was encouraging them all to take some food, saying, "Today is the fourteenth day that you have been constantly watching and going without eating, having taken nothing.

34 "Therefore I encourage you to take some food, for this is for your preservation, for not a hair from the head of any of you will perish."

35 Having said this, he took bread and gave thanks to God in the presence of all, and he broke it and began to eat.

36 All of them were encouraged and they themselves also took food.

37 All of us in the ship were two hundred and seventy-six persons.

38 When they had eaten enough, they *began* to lighten the ship by throwing out the wheat into the sea.

NEW CENTURY VERSION

with a weight on the end of it into the water. They found
that the water was one hundred twenty feet deep. They
went a little farther and lowered the rope again. It was
ninety feet deep. 29The sailors were afraid that we would
hit the rocks, so they threw four anchors into the water
and prayed for daylight to come. 30Some of the sailors
wanted to leave the ship, and they lowered the lifeboat,
pretending they were throwing more anchors from the
front of the ship. 31But Paul told the officer and the other
soldiers, "If these men do not stay in the ship, your lives
cannot be saved." 32So the soldiers cut the ropes and let
the lifeboat fall into the water.

33Just before dawn Paul began persuading all the people
to eat something. He said, "For the past fourteen days you
have been waiting and watching and not eating. 34Now I
beg you to eat something. You need it to stay alive. None
of you will lose even one hair off your heads." 35After he
said this, Paul took some bread and thanked God for it
before all of them. He broke off a piece and began eating.
36They all felt better and started eating, too. 37There were
two hundred seventy-six people on the ship. 38When they
had eaten all they wanted, they began making the ship
lighter by throwing the grain into the sea.

CONTEMPORARY ENGLISH VERSION

measured and found that the water was about one hundred twenty feet deep. A little later they measured again
and found it was only about ninety feet. 29The sailors were
afraid that we might hit some rocks, and they let down
four anchors from the back of the ship. Then they prayed
for daylight.

30The sailors wanted to escape from the ship. So they
lowered the lifeboat into the water, pretending that they
were letting down an anchor from the front of the ship.
31But Paul said to Captain Julius and the soldiers, "If the
sailors don't stay on the ship, you won't have any chance
to save your lives." 32The soldiers then cut the ropes that
held the lifeboat and let it fall into the sea.

33Just before daylight Paul begged the people to eat
something. He told them, "For fourteen days you have
been so worried that you haven't eaten a thing. 34I beg you
to eat something. Your lives depend on it. Do this and not
one of you will be hurt."

35After Paul had said this, he took a piece of bread and
gave thanks to God. Then in front of everyone, he broke
the bread and ate some. 36They all felt encouraged, and
each of them ate something. 37There were 276 people on
the ship, 38and after everyone had eaten, they threw the
cargo of wheat into the sea to make the ship lighter.

NEW INTERNATIONAL VERSION

sensed they were approaching land. 28They took soundings and found that the water was a hundred and twenty feet[c] deep. A short time later they took soundings again and found it was ninety feet[d] deep. 29Fearing that we would be dashed against the rocks, they dropped four anchors from the stern and prayed for daylight. 30In an attempt to escape from the ship, the sailors let the lifeboat down into the sea, pretending they were going to lower some anchors from the bow. 31Then Paul said to the centurion and the soldiers, "Unless these men stay with the ship, you cannot be saved." 32So the soldiers cut the ropes that held the lifeboat and let it fall away.

33Just before dawn Paul urged them all to eat. "For the last fourteen days," he said, "you have been in constant suspense and have gone without food—you haven't eaten anything. 34Now I urge you to take some food. You need it to survive. Not one of you will lose a single hair from his head." 35After he said this, he took some bread and gave thanks to God in front of them all. Then he broke it and began to eat. 36They were all encouraged and ate some food themselves. 37Altogether there were 276 of us on board. 38When they had eaten as much as they wanted, they lightened the ship by throwing the grain into the sea.

[c] *28* Greek *twenty orguias* (about 37 meters) [d] *28* Greek *fifteen orguias* (about 27 meters)

NEW LIVING TRANSLATION

sailors sensed land was near. 28They took soundings and found the water was only 120 feet deep. A little later they sounded again and found only 90 feet.* 29At this rate they were afraid we would soon be driven against the rocks along the shore, so they threw out four anchors from the stern and prayed for daylight. 30Then the sailors tried to abandon the ship; they lowered the lifeboat as though they were going to put out anchors from the prow. 31But Paul said to the commanding officer and the soldiers, "You will all die unless the sailors stay aboard." 32So the soldiers cut the ropes and let the boat fall off.

33As the darkness gave way to the early morning light, Paul begged everyone to eat. "You haven't touched food for two weeks," he said. 34"Please eat something now for your own good. For not a hair of your heads will perish." 35Then he took some bread, gave thanks to God before them all, and broke off a piece and ate it. 36Then everyone was encouraged, 37and all 276 of us began eating—for that is the number we had aboard. 38After eating, the crew lightened the ship further by throwing the cargo of wheat overboard.

27:28 Greek *20 fathoms . . . 15 fathoms* [37 meters . . . 27 meters].

NEW KING JAMES VERSION

28And they took soundings and found *it* to be twenty fathoms; and when they had gone a little farther, they took soundings again and found *it* to be fifteen fathoms. 29Then, fearing lest we should run aground on the rocks, they dropped four anchors from the stern, and prayed for day to come. 30And as the sailors were seeking to escape from the ship, when they had let down the skiff into the sea, under pretense of putting out anchors from the prow, 31Paul said to the centurion and the soldiers, "Unless these men stay in the ship, you cannot be saved." 32Then the soldiers cut away the ropes of the skiff and let it fall off.

33And as day was about to dawn, Paul implored *them* all to take food, saying, "Today is the fourteenth day you have waited and continued without food, and eaten nothing. 34Therefore I urge you to take nourishment, for this is for your survival, since not a hair will fall from the head of any of you." 35And when he had said these things, he took bread and gave thanks to God in the presence of them all; and when he had broken *it* he began to eat. 36Then they were all encouraged, and also took food themselves. 37And in all we were two hundred and seventy-six persons on the ship. 38So when they had eaten enough, they lightened the ship and threw out the wheat into the sea.

THE MESSAGE

were approaching land. Sounding, they measured a depth of one hundred twenty feet, and shortly after that ninety feet. Afraid that we were about to run aground, they threw out four anchors and prayed for daylight.

Some of the sailors tried to jump ship. They let down the lifeboat, pretending they were going to set out more anchors from the bow. Paul saw through their guise and told the centurion and his soldiers, "If these sailors don't stay with the ship, we're all going down." So the soldiers cut the lines to the lifeboat and let it drift off.

With dawn about to break, Paul called everyone together and proposed breakfast: "This is the fourteenth day we've gone without food. None of us has felt like eating! But I urge you to eat something now. You'll need strength for the rescue ahead. You're going to come out of this without even a scratch!"

He broke the bread, gave thanks to God, passed it around, and they all ate heartily—two hundred seventy-six of us, all told! With the meal finished and everyone full, the ship was further lightened by dumping the grain overboard.

KING JAMES VERSION

39 And when it was day, they knew not the land: but they discovered a certain creek with a shore, into the which they were minded, if it were possible, to thrust in the ship.

40 And when they had taken up the anchors, they committed *themselves* unto the sea, and loosed the rudder bands, and hoised up the mainsail to the wind, and made toward shore.

41 And falling into a place where two seas met, they ran the ship aground; and the forepart stuck fast, and remained unmoveable, but the hinder part was broken with the violence of the waves.

42 And the soldiers' counsel was to kill the prisoners, lest any of them should swim out, and escape.

43 But the centurion, willing to save Paul, kept them from *their* purpose; and commanded that they which could swim should cast *themselves* first *into the sea*, and get to land:

44 And the rest, some on boards, and some on *broken pieces* of the ship. And so it came to pass, that they escaped all safe to land.

28 And when they were escaped, then they knew that the island was called Melita.

2 And the barbarous people shewed us no little kindness: for they kindled a fire, and received us every one, because of the present rain, and because of the cold.

3 And when Paul had gathered a bundle of sticks, and laid *them* on the fire, there came a viper out of the heat, and fastened on his hand.

NEW AMERICAN STANDARD BIBLE

39 When day came, they could not recognize the land; but they did observe a bay with a beach, and they resolved to drive the ship onto it if they could.

40 And casting off the anchors, they left them in the sea while at the same time they were loosening the ropes of the rudders; and hoisting the foresail to the wind, they were heading for the beach.

41 But striking a reef where two seas met, they ran the vessel aground; and the prow stuck fast and remained immovable, but the stern *began* to be broken up by the force *of the waves.*

42 The soldiers' plan was to kill the prisoners, so that none *of them* would swim away and escape;

43 but the centurion, wanting to bring Paul safely through, kept them from their intention, and commanded that those who could swim should jump overboard first and get to land,

44 and the rest *should follow*, some on planks, and others on various things from the ship. And so it happened that they all were brought safely to land.

Safe at Malta

28 When they had been brought safely through, then we found out that the island was called Malta.

2 The natives showed us extraordinary kindness; for because of the rain that had set in and because of the cold, they kindled a fire and received us all.

3 But when Paul had gathered a bundle of sticks and laid them on the fire, a viper came out because of the heat and fastened itself on his hand.

NEW CENTURY VERSION

The Ship Is Destroyed

39When daylight came, the sailors saw land. They did
not know what land it was, but they saw a bay with a
beach and wanted to sail the ship to the beach if they
could. 40So they cut the ropes to the anchors and left the
anchors in the sea. At the same time, they untied the ropes
that were holding the rudders. Then they raised the front
sail into the wind and sailed toward the beach. 41But the
ship hit a sandbank. The front of the ship stuck there and
could not move, but the back of the ship began to break up
from the big waves.

42The soldiers decided to kill the prisoners so none of
them could swim away and escape. 43But Julius, the offi-
cer, wanted to let Paul live and did not allow the soldiers
to kill the prisoners. Instead he ordered everyone who
could swim to jump into the water first and swim to land.
44The rest were to follow using wooden boards or pieces of
the ship. And this is how all the people made it safely to
land.

Paul on the Island of Malta

28 When we were safe on land, we learned that the
island was called Malta. 2The people who lived
there were very good to us. Because it was raining and
very cold, they made a fire and welcomed all of us. 3Paul
gathered a pile of sticks and was putting them on the fire
when a poisonous snake came out because of the heat and
bit him on the hand. 4The people living on the island saw

CONTEMPORARY ENGLISH VERSION

The Shipwreck

39Morning came, and the ship's crew saw a coast that
they did not recognize. But they did see a cove with a
beach. So they decided to try to run the ship aground on
the beach. 40They cut the anchors loose and let them sink
into the sea. At the same time they untied the ropes that
were holding the rudders. Next, they raised the sail at the
front of the ship and let the wind carry the ship toward the
beach. 41But it ran aground on a sandbank. The front of
the ship stuck firmly in the sand, and the rear was being
smashed by the force of the waves.

42The soldiers decided to kill the prisoners to keep them
from swimming away and escaping. 43But Captain Julius
wanted to save Paul's life, and he did not let the soldiers
do what they had planned. Instead, he ordered everyone
who could swim to dive into the water and head for shore.
44Then he told the others to hold on to planks of wood or
parts of the ship. At last, everyone safely reached shore.

On the Island of Malta

28 When we came ashore, we learned that the island
was called Malta. 2The local people were very
friendly, and they welcomed us by building a fire, because
it was rainy and cold.

3After Paul had gathered some wood and had put it on
the fire, the heat caused a snake to crawl out, and it bit
him on the hand. 4When the local people saw the snake

NEW INTERNATIONAL VERSION

[39]When daylight came, they did not recognize the land,
but they saw a bay with a sandy beach, where they decid-
ed to run the ship aground if they could. [40]Cutting loose
the anchors, they left them in the sea and at the same time
untied the ropes that held the rudders. Then they hoisted
the foresail to the wind and made for the beach. [41]But the
ship struck a sandbar and ran aground. The bow stuck fast
and would not move, and the stern was broken to pieces
by the pounding of the surf.

[42]The soldiers planned to kill the prisoners to prevent
any of them from swimming away and escaping. [43]But the
centurion wanted to spare Paul's life and kept them from
carrying out their plan. He ordered those who could swim
to jump overboard first and get to land. [44]The rest were to
get there on planks or on pieces of the ship. In this way
everyone reached land in safety.

Ashore on Malta

28 Once safely on shore, we found out that the island
was called Malta. [2]The islanders showed us
unusual kindness. They built a fire and welcomed us all
because it was raining and cold. [3]Paul gathered a pile of
brushwood and, as he put it on the fire, a viper, driven out
by the heat, fastened itself on his hand. [4]When the

NEW LIVING TRANSLATION

[39]When morning dawned, they didn't recognize the
coastline, but they saw a bay with a beach and wondered
if they could get between the rocks and get the ship safely
to shore. [40]So they cut off the anchors and left them in the
sea. Then they lowered the rudders, raised the foresail,
and headed toward shore. [41]But the ship hit a shoal and
ran aground. The bow of the ship stuck fast, while the
stern was repeatedly smashed by the force of the waves
and began to break apart.

[42]The soldiers wanted to kill the prisoners to make sure
they didn't swim ashore and escape. [43]But the command-
ing officer wanted to spare Paul, so he didn't let them
carry out their plan. Then he ordered all who could swim
to jump overboard first and make for land, [44]and he told
the others to try for it on planks and debris from the bro-
ken ship. So everyone escaped safely ashore!

Paul on the Island of Malta

28 Once we were safe on shore, we learned that we
were on the island of Malta. [2]The people of the
island were very kind to us. It was cold and rainy, so they
built a fire on the shore to welcome us and warm us.

[3]As Paul gathered an armful of sticks and was laying
them on the fire, a poisonous snake, driven out by the
heat, fastened itself onto his hand. [4]The people of the

NEW KING JAMES VERSION

Shipwrecked on Malta

[39]When it was day, they did not recognize the land; but
they observed a bay with a beach, onto which they planned
to run the ship if possible. [40]And they let go the anchors
and left *them* in the sea, meanwhile loosing the rudder
ropes; and they hoisted the mainsail to the wind and made
for shore. [41]But striking a place where two seas met, they
ran the ship aground; and the prow stuck fast and
remained immovable, but the stern was being broken up
by the violence of the waves.

[42]And the soldiers' plan was to kill the prisoners, lest
any of them should swim away and escape. [43]But the cen-
turion, wanting to save Paul, kept them from *their* pur-
pose, and commanded that those who could swim should
jump *overboard* first and get to land, [44]and the rest, some
on boards and some on *parts* of the ship. And so it was
that they all escaped safely to land.

Paul's Ministry on Malta

28 Now when they had escaped, they then found out
that the island was called Malta. [2]And the natives
showed us unusual kindness; for they kindled a fire and
made us all welcome, because of the rain that was falling
and because of the cold. [3]But when Paul had gathered a
bundle of sticks and laid *them* on the fire, a viper came out
because of the heat, and fastened on his hand. [4]So when

THE MESSAGE

At daybreak, no one recognized the land—but then they did notice a bay with a nice beach. They decided to try to run the ship up on the beach. They cut the anchors, loosed the tiller, raised the sail, and ran before the wind toward the beach. But we didn't make it. Still far from shore, we hit a reef and the ship began to break up.

The soldiers decided to kill the prisoners so none could escape by swimming, but the centurion, determined to save Paul, stopped them. He gave orders for anyone who could swim to dive in and go for it, and for the rest to grab a plank. Everyone made it to shore safely.

28 Once everyone was accounted for and we realized we had all made it, we learned that we were on the island of Malta. The natives went out of their way to be friendly to us. The day was rainy and cold and we were already soaked to the bone, but they built a huge bonfire and gathered us around it.

Paul pitched in and helped. He had gathered up a bundle of sticks, but when he put it on the fire, a venomous snake, roused from its torpor by the heat, struck his hand and held on. Seeing the snake hanging from Paul's hand

KING JAMES VERSION

4 And when the barbarians saw the *venomous* beast hang on his hand, they said among themselves, No doubt this man is a murderer, whom, though he hath escaped the sea, yet vengeance suffereth not to live.

5 And he shook off the beast into the fire, and felt no harm.

6 Howbeit they looked when he should have swollen, or fallen down dead suddenly: but after they had looked a great while, and saw no harm come to him, they changed their minds, and said that he was a god.

7 In the same quarters were possessions of the chief man of the island, whose name was Publius; who received us, and lodged us three days courteously.

8 And it came to pass, that the father of Publius lay sick of a fever and of a bloody flux: to whom Paul entered in, and prayed, and laid his hands on him, and healed him.

9 So when this was done, others also, which had diseases in the island, came, and were healed:

10 Who also honoured us with many honours; and when we departed, they laded *us* with such things as were necessary.

11 ¶ And after three months we departed in a ship of Alexandria, which had wintered in the isle, whose sign was Castor and Pollux.

NEW AMERICAN STANDARD BIBLE

4 When the natives saw the creature hanging from his hand, they *began* saying to one another, "Undoubtedly this man is a murderer, and though he has been saved from the sea, justice has not allowed him to live."

5 However he shook the creature off into the fire and suffered no harm.

6 But they were expecting that he was about to swell up or suddenly fall down dead. But after they had waited a long time and had seen nothing unusual happen to him, they changed their minds and *began* to say that he was a god.

7 Now in the neighborhood of that place were lands belonging to the leading man of the island, named Publius, who welcomed us and entertained us courteously three days.

8 And it happened that the father of Publius was lying *in bed* afflicted with *recurrent* fever and dysentery; and Paul went in *to see* him and after he had prayed, he laid his hands on him and healed him.

9 After this had happened, the rest of the people on the island who had diseases were coming to him and getting cured.

10 They also honored us with many marks of respect; and when we were setting sail, they supplied *us* with all we needed.

Paul Arrives at Rome

11 At the end of three months we set sail on an Alexandrian ship which had wintered at the island, and which had the Twin Brothers for its figurehead.

NEW CENTURY VERSION

the snake hanging from Paul's hand and said to each
other, "This man must be a murderer! He did not die in the
sea, but Justice[a] does not want him to live." 5But Paul
shook the snake off into the fire and was not hurt. 6The
people thought that Paul would swell up or fall down dead.
They waited and watched him for a long time, but nothing
bad happened to him. So they changed their minds and
said, "He is a god!"

7There were some fields around there owned by Publius,
an important man on the island. He welcomed us into his
home and was very good to us for three days. 8Publius'
father was sick with a fever and dysentery.[b] Paul went to
him, prayed, and put his hands on the man and healed
him. 9After this, all the other sick people on the island
came to Paul, and he healed them, too. 10–11The people on
the island gave us many honors. When we were ready to
leave, three months later, they gave us the things we
needed.

Paul Goes to Rome

We got on a ship from Alexandria that had stayed on the
island during the winter. On the front of the ship was the
sign of the twin gods.[c] 12We stopped at Syracuse for three

28:4 [a] **Justice** The people thought there was a god named Justice who would punish bad people. 28:8 [b] **dysentery** A sickness like diarrhea. 28:10-11 [c] **twin gods** Statues of Castor and Pollux, gods in old Greek tales.

CONTEMPORARY ENGLISH VERSION

hanging from Paul's hand, they said to each other, "This
man must be a murderer! He didn't drown in the sea, but
the goddess of justice will kill him anyway."

5Paul shook the snake off into the fire and wasn't
harmed. 6The people kept thinking that Paul would either
swell up or suddenly drop dead. They watched him for a
long time, and when nothing happened to him, they
changed their minds and said, "This man is a god."

7The governor of the island was named Publius, and he
owned some of the land around there. Publius was very
friendly and welcomed us into his home for three days.
8His father was in bed, sick with fever and stomach trou-
ble, and Paul went to visit him. Paul healed the man by
praying and placing his hands on him.

9After this happened, everyone on the island brought
their sick people to Paul, and they were all healed. 10The
people were very respectful to us, and when we sailed,
they gave us everything we needed.

From Malta to Rome

11Three months later we sailed in a ship that had been
docked at Malta for the winter. The ship was from
Alexandria in Egypt and was known as "The Twin Gods."[a]

[a] **28.11** *known as "The Twin Gods"*: Or "carried on its bow a wooden carving of the Twin Gods." These gods were Castor and Pollux, two of the favorite gods among sailors.

NEW INTERNATIONAL VERSION

islanders saw the snake hanging from his hand, they said
to each other, "This man must be a murderer; for though
he escaped from the sea, Justice has not allowed him to
live." 5But Paul shook the snake off into the fire and suf-
fered no ill effects. 6The people expected him to swell up or
suddenly fall dead, but after waiting a long time and see-
ing nothing unusual happen to him, they changed their
minds and said he was a god.

7There was an estate nearby that belonged to Publius,
the chief official of the island. He welcomed us to his home
and for three days entertained us hospitably. 8His father
was sick in bed, suffering from fever and dysentery. Paul
went in to see him and, after prayer, placed his hands on
him and healed him. 9When this had happened, the rest of
the sick on the island came and were cured. 10They hon-
ored us in many ways and when we were ready to sail,
they furnished us with the supplies we needed.

Arrival at Rome

11After three months we put out to sea in a ship that
had wintered in the island. It was an Alexandrian ship
with the figurehead of the twin gods Castor and Pollux.

NEW LIVING TRANSLATION

island saw it hanging there and said to each other, "A
murderer, no doubt! Though he escaped the sea, justice
will not permit him to live." 5But Paul shook off the snake
into the fire and was unharmed. 6The people waited for
him to swell up or suddenly drop dead. But when they had
waited a long time and saw no harm come to him, they
changed their minds and decided he was a god.

7Near the shore where we landed was an estate belong-
ing to Publius, the chief official of the island. He welcomed
us courteously and fed us for three days. 8As it happened,
Publius's father was ill with fever and dysentery. Paul
went in and prayed for him, and laying his hands on him,
he healed him. 9Then all the other sick people on the
island came and were cured. 10As a result we were show-
ered with honors, and when the time came to sail, people
put on board all sorts of things we would need for the trip.

Paul Arrives at Rome

11It was three months after the shipwreck that we set
sail on another ship that had wintered at the island—an
Alexandrian ship with the twin gods* as its figurehead.

28:11 The *twin gods* were the Roman gods Castor and Pollux.

NEW KING JAMES VERSION

the natives saw the creature hanging from his hand, they
said to one another, "No doubt this man is a murderer,
whom, though he has escaped the sea, yet justice does not
allow to live." 5But he shook off the creature into the fire
and suffered no harm. 6However, they were expecting that
he would swell up or suddenly fall down dead. But after
they had looked for a long time and saw no harm come to
him, they changed their minds and said that he was a god.

7In that region there was an estate of the leading citizen
of the island, whose name was Publius, who received us
and entertained us courteously for three days. 8And it hap-
pened that the father of Publius lay sick of a fever and
dysentery. Paul went in to him and prayed, and he laid his
hands on him and healed him. 9So when this was done,
the rest of those on the island who had diseases also came
and were healed. 10They also honored us in many ways;
and when we departed, they provided such things as were
necessary.

Arrival at Rome

11After three months we sailed in an Alexandrian ship
whose figurehead was the Twin Brothers, which had win-
tered at the island. 12And landing at Syracuse, we stayed

THE MESSAGE

like that, the natives jumped to the conclusion that he was a murderer getting his just deserts. Paul shook the snake off into the fire, none the worse for wear. They kept expecting him to drop dead, but when it was obvious he wasn't going to, they jumped to the conclusion that he was a god!

The head man in that part of the island was Publius. He took us into his home as his guests, drying us out and putting us up in fine style for the next three days. Publius's father was sick at the time, down with a high fever and dysentery. Paul went to the old man's room, and when he laid hands on him and prayed, the man was healed. Word of the healing got around fast, and soon everyone on the island who was sick came and got healed.

Rome

We spent a wonderful three months on Malta. They treated us royally, took care of all our needs and outfitted us for the rest of the journey. When an Egyptian ship that had wintered there in the harbor prepared to leave for Italy, we got on board. The ship had a carved Gemini for its figurehead: "the Heavenly Twins."

KING JAMES VERSION

12 And landing at Syracuse, we tarried *there* three days.

13 And from thence we fetched a compass, and came to Rhegium: and after one day the south wind blew, and we came the next day to Puteoli:

14 Where we found brethren, and were desired to tarry with them seven days: and so we went toward Rome.

15 And from thence, when the brethren heard of us, they came to meet us as far as Appii forum, and The three taverns: whom when Paul saw, he thanked God, and took courage.

16 And when we came to Rome, the centurion delivered the prisoners to the captain of the guard: but Paul was suffered to dwell by himself with a soldier that kept him.

17 ¶ And it came to pass, that after three days Paul called the chief of the Jews together: and when they were come together, he said unto them, Men *and* brethren, though I have committed nothing against the people, or customs of our fathers, yet was I delivered prisoner from Jerusalem into the hands of the Romans.

18 Who, when they had examined me, would have let *me* go, because there was no cause of death in me.

19 But when the Jews spake against *it*, I was constrained to appeal unto Caesar; not that I had ought to accuse my nation of.

20 For this cause therefore have I called for you, to see

NEW AMERICAN STANDARD BIBLE

12 After we put in at Syracuse, we stayed there for three days.

13 From there we sailed around and arrived at Rhegium, and a day later a south wind sprang up, and on the second day we came to Puteoli.

14 There we found *some* brethren, and were invited to stay with them for seven days; and thus we came to Rome.

15 And the brethren, when they heard about us, came from there as far as the Market of Appius and Three Inns to meet us; and when Paul saw them, he thanked God and took courage.

16 When we entered Rome, Paul was allowed to stay by himself, with the soldier who was guarding him.

17 After three days Paul called together those who were the leading men of the Jews, and when they came together, he *began* saying to them, "Brethren, though I had done nothing against our people or the customs of our fathers, yet I was delivered as a prisoner from Jerusalem into the hands of the Romans.

18 "And when they had examined me, they were willing to release me because there was no ground for putting me to death.

19 "But when the Jews objected, I was forced to appeal to Caesar, not that I had any accusation against my nation.

20 "For this reason, therefore, I requested to see you and

NEW CENTURY VERSION

days. [13]From there we sailed to Rhegium. The next day a
wind began to blow from the south, and a day later we
came to Puteoli. [14]We found some believers there who
asked us to stay with them for a week. Finally, we came to
Rome. [15]The believers in Rome heard that we were there
and came out as far as the Market of Appius[d] and the
Three Inns[e] to meet us. When Paul saw them, he was
encouraged and thanked God.

Paul in Rome

[16]When we arrived at Rome, Paul was allowed to live
alone, with the soldier who guarded him.

[17]Three days later Paul sent for the Jewish leaders there.
When they came together, he said, "Brothers, I have done
nothing against our people or the customs of our ancestors. But I was arrested in Jerusalem and given to the
Romans. [18]After they asked me many questions, they
could find no reason why I should be killed. They wanted
to let me go free, [19]but the Jewish people there argued
against that. So I had to ask to come to Rome to have my
trial before Caesar. But I have no charge to bring against
my own people. [20]That is why I wanted to see you and talk

28:15 [d] **Market of Appius** A town about twenty-seven miles from Rome.
28:15 [e] **Three Inns** A town about thirty miles from Rome.

CONTEMPORARY ENGLISH VERSION

[12]We arrived in Syracuse and stayed for three days. [13]From
there we sailed to Rhegium. The next day a south wind
began to blow, and two days later we arrived in Puteoli.
[14]There we found some of the Lord's followers, who
begged us to stay with them. A week later we left for the
city of Rome.

[15]Some of the followers in Rome heard about us and
came to meet us at the Market of Appius and at the Three
Inns. When Paul saw them, he thanked God and was
encouraged.

Paul in Rome

[16]We arrived in Rome, and Paul was allowed to live in a
house by himself with a soldier to guard him.

[17]Three days after we got there, Paul called together
some of the Jewish leaders and said:

My friends, I have never done anything to hurt our
people, and I have never gone against the customs of
our ancestors. But in Jerusalem I was handed over as a
prisoner to the Romans. [18]They looked into the charges
against me and wanted to release me. They found that I
had not done anything deserving death. [19]The Jewish
leaders disagreed, so I asked to be tried by the Emperor.

But I don't have anything to say against my own
nation. [20]I am bound by these chains because of what

NEW INTERNATIONAL VERSION

12 We put in at Syracuse and stayed there three days. 13 From there we set sail and arrived at Rhegium. The next day the south wind came up, and on the following day we reached Puteoli. 14 There we found some brothers who invited us to spend a week with them. And so we came to Rome. 15 The brothers there had heard that we were coming, and they traveled as far as the Forum of Appius and the Three Taverns to meet us. At the sight of these men Paul thanked God and was encouraged. 16 When we got to Rome, Paul was allowed to live by himself, with a soldier to guard him.

Paul Preaches at Rome Under Guard

17 Three days later he called together the leaders of the Jews. When they had assembled, Paul said to them: "My brothers, although I have done nothing against our people or against the customs of our ancestors, I was arrested in Jerusalem and handed over to the Romans. 18 They examined me and wanted to release me, because I was not guilty of any crime deserving death. 19 But when the Jews objected, I was compelled to appeal to Caesar—not that I had any charge to bring against my own people. 20 For this reason I have asked to see you and talk with you. It is

NEW LIVING TRANSLATION

12 Our first stop was Syracuse,* where we stayed three days. 13 From there we sailed across to Rhegium.* A day later a south wind began blowing, so the following day we sailed up the coast to Puteoli. 14 There we found some believers,* who invited us to stay with them seven days. And so we came to Rome.

15 The brothers and sisters* in Rome had heard we were coming, and they came to meet us at the Forum* on the Appian Way. Others joined us at The Three Taverns.* When Paul saw them, he thanked God and took courage.

16 When we arrived in Rome, Paul was permitted to have his own private lodging, though he was guarded by a soldier.

Paul Preaches at Rome under Guard

17 Three days after Paul's arrival, he called together the local Jewish leaders. He said to them, "Brothers, I was arrested in Jerusalem and handed over to the Roman government, even though I had done nothing against our people or the customs of our ancestors. 18 The Romans tried me and wanted to release me, for they found no cause for the death sentence. 19 But when the Jewish leaders protested the decision, I felt it necessary to appeal to Caesar, even though I had no desire to press charges against my own people. 20 I asked you to come here today so we could get acquainted and so I could tell you that I am bound with

28:12 *Syracuse* was on the island of Sicily. **28:13** *Rhegium* was on the southern tip of Italy. **28:14** Greek *brothers.* **28:15a** Greek *brothers.* **28:15b** *The Forum* was about 43 miles (70 kilometers) from Rome. **28:15c** *The Three Taverns* was about 35 miles (57 kilometers) from Rome.

NEW KING JAMES VERSION

three days. 13 From there we circled round and reached Rhegium. And after one day the south wind blew; and the next day we came to Puteoli, 14 where we found brethren, and were invited to stay with them seven days. And so we went toward Rome. 15 And from there, when the brethren heard about us, they came to meet us as far as Appii Forum and Three Inns. When Paul saw them, he thanked God and took courage.

16 Now when we came to Rome, the centurion delivered the prisoners to the captain of the guard; but Paul was permitted to dwell by himself with the soldier who guarded him.

Paul's Ministry at Rome

17 And it came to pass after three days that Paul called the leaders of the Jews together. So when they had come together, he said to them: "Men *and* brethren, though I have done nothing against our people or the customs of our fathers, yet I was delivered as a prisoner from Jerusalem into the hands of the Romans, 18 who, when they had examined me, wanted to let *me* go, because there was no cause for putting me to death. 19 But when the Jews[a] spoke against *it,* I was compelled to appeal to Caesar, not that I had anything of which to accuse my nation. 20 For this reason therefore I have called for you, to see *you* and speak

28:19 [a] That is, the ruling authorities

THE MESSAGE

We put in at Syracuse for three days and then went up the coast to Rhegium. Two days later, with the wind out of the south, we sailed into the Bay of Naples. We found Christian friends there and stayed with them for a week.

And then we came to Rome. Friends in Rome heard we were on the way and came out to meet us. One group got as far as Appian Court; another group met us at Three Taverns—emotion-packed meetings, as you can well imagine. Paul, brimming over with praise, led us in prayers of thanksgiving. When we actually entered Rome, they let Paul live in his own private quarters with a soldier who had been assigned to guard him.

Three days later, Paul called the Jewish leaders together for a meeting at his house. He said, "The Jews in Jerusalem arrested me on trumped-up charges, and I was taken into custody by the Romans. I assure you that I did absolutely nothing against Jewish laws or Jewish customs. After the Romans investigated the charges and found there was nothing to them, they wanted to set me free, but the Jews objected so fiercely that I was forced to appeal to Caesar. I did this not to accuse them of any wrongdoing or to get our people in trouble with Rome. We've had enough trouble through the years that way. I did it *for* Israel. I asked you to come and listen to me today to make it clear that

KING JAMES VERSION

you, and to speak with *you*: because that for the hope of
Israel I am bound with this chain.

21 And they said unto him, We neither received letters
out of Judaea concerning thee, neither any of the brethren
that came shewed or spake any harm of thee.

22 But we desire to hear of thee what thou thinkest: for
as concerning this sect, we know that every where it is
spoken against.

23 ¶ And when they had appointed him a day, there
came many to him into *his* lodging; to whom he expound-
ed and testified the kingdom of God, persuading them con-
cerning Jesus, both out of the law of Moses, and *out of* the
prophets, from morning till evening.

24 And some believed the things which were spoken,
and some believed not.

25 And when they agreed not among themselves, they
departed, after that Paul had spoken one word, Well spake
the Holy Ghost by Esaias the prophet unto our fathers,

26 Saying, Go unto this people, and say, Hearing ye
shall hear, and shall not understand; and seeing ye shall
see, and not perceive:

27 For the heart of this people is waxed gross, and their

NEW AMERICAN STANDARD BIBLE

to speak with you, for I am wearing this chain for the sake
of the hope of Israel."

21 They said to him, "We have neither received letters
from Judea concerning you, nor have any of the brethren
come here and reported or spoken anything bad about you.

22 "But we desire to hear from you what your views are;
for concerning this sect, it is known to us that it is spoken
against everywhere."

23 When they had set a day for Paul, they came to him
at his lodging in large numbers; and he was explaining to
them by solemnly testifying about the kingdom of God and
trying to persuade them concerning Jesus, from both the
Law of Moses and from the Prophets, from morning until
evening.

24 Some were being persuaded by the things spoken,
but others would not believe.

25 And when they did not agree with one another, they
began leaving after Paul had spoken one *parting* word,
"The Holy Spirit rightly spoke through Isaiah the prophet
to your fathers,

26 saying,

'GO TO THIS PEOPLE AND SAY,
"YOU WILL KEEP ON HEARING, BUT WILL NOT UNDERSTAND;
AND YOU WILL KEEP ON SEEING, BUT WILL NOT PERCEIVE;

27 FOR THE HEART OF THIS PEOPLE HAS BECOME DULL,

NEW CENTURY VERSION

with you. I am bound with this chain because I believe in
the hope of Israel."

21 They answered Paul, "We have received no letters from
Judea about you. None of our Jewish brothers who have
come from there brought news or told us anything bad
about you. 22 But we want to hear your ideas, because we
know that people everywhere are speaking against this
religious group."

23 Paul and the Jewish people chose a day for a meeting
and on that day many more of the Jews met with Paul at
the place he was staying. He spoke to them all day long.
Using the law of Moses and the prophets' writings, he
explained the kingdom of God, and he tried to persuade
them to believe these things about Jesus. 24 Some believed
what Paul said, but others did not. 25 So they argued and
began leaving after Paul said one more thing to them: "The
Holy Spirit spoke the truth to your ancestors through
Isaiah the prophet, saying,

26 'Go to this people and say:
You will listen and listen, but you will not understand.
You will look and look, but you will not learn,
27 because these people have become stubborn.

CONTEMPORARY ENGLISH VERSION

we people of Israel hope for. That's why I have called
you here to talk about this hope of ours.

21 The leaders replied, "No one from Judea has written us
a letter about you. And not one of them has come here to
report on you or to say anything against you. 22 But we
would like to hear what you have to say. We understand
that people everywhere are against this new group."

23 They agreed on a time to meet with Paul, and many of
them came to his house. From early morning until late in
the afternoon, Paul talked to them about God's kingdom.
He used the Law of Moses and the Books of the Prophets[b]
to try to win them over to Jesus.

24 Some of the leaders agreed with what Paul said, but
others did not. 25 Since they could not agree among them-
selves, they started leaving. But Paul said, "The Holy Spirit
said the right thing when he sent Isaiah the prophet 26 to
tell our ancestors,

'Go to these people
and tell them:
You will listen and listen,
but never understand.
You will look and look,
but never see.
27 All of you
have stubborn hearts.

[b] 28.23 *Law of Moses and the Books of the Prophets*: The Jewish Bible, that is, the Old Testament.

NEW INTERNATIONAL VERSION

because of the hope of Israel that I am bound with this
chain."
21They replied, "We have not received any letters from
Judea concerning you, and none of the brothers who have
come from there has reported or said anything bad about
you. 22But we want to hear what your views are, for we
know that people everywhere are talking against this
sect."
23They arranged to meet Paul on a certain day, and
came in even larger numbers to the place where he was
staying. From morning till evening he explained and
declared to them the kingdom of God and tried to convince
them about Jesus from the Law of Moses and from the
Prophets. 24Some were convinced by what he said, but oth-
ers would not believe. 25They disagreed among themselves
and began to leave after Paul had made this final state-
ment: "The Holy Spirit spoke the truth to your forefathers
when he said through Isaiah the prophet:

26" 'Go to this people and say,
"You will be ever hearing but never understanding;
you will be ever seeing but never perceiving."
27For this people's heart has become calloused;

NEW LIVING TRANSLATION

this chain because I believe that the hope of Israel—the
Messiah—has already come."
21They replied, "We have heard nothing against you. We
have had no letters from Judea or reports from anyone who
has arrived here. 22But we want to hear what you believe,
for the only thing we know about these Christians* is that
they are denounced everywhere."
23So a time was set, and on that day a large number of
people came to Paul's house. He told them about the
Kingdom of God and taught them about Jesus from the
Scriptures—from the five books of Moses and the books of
the prophets. He began lecturing in the morning and went
on into the evening. 24Some believed and some didn't.
25But after they had argued back and forth among them-
selves, they left with this final word from Paul: "The Holy
Spirit was right when he said to our ancestors through
Isaiah the prophet,

26 'Go and say to my people,
You will hear my words,
but you will not understand;
you will see what I do,
but you will not perceive its meaning.
27 For the hearts of these people are hardened,

28:22 Greek *this sect.*

NEW KING JAMES VERSION

with *you,* because for the hope of Israel I am bound with
this chain."
21Then they said to him, "We neither received letters
from Judea concerning you, nor have any of the brethren
who came reported or spoken any evil of you. 22But we
desire to hear from you what you think; for concerning
this sect, we know that it is spoken against everywhere."
23So when they had appointed him a day, many came to
him at *his* lodging, to whom he explained and solemnly
testified of the kingdom of God, persuading them concern-
ing Jesus from both the Law of Moses and the Prophets,
from morning till evening. 24And some were persuaded by
the things which were spoken, and some disbelieved. 25So
when they did not agree among themselves, they departed
after Paul had said one word: "The Holy Spirit spoke right-
ly through Isaiah the prophet to our[b] fathers, 26saying,

'Go to this people and say:
"Hearing you will hear, and shall not understand;
And seeing you will see, and not perceive;
27 *For the hearts of this people have grown dull.*

28:25 [b] NU-Text reads *your.*

THE MESSAGE

I'm on Israel's side, not against her. I'm a hostage here for
hope, not doom."

They said, "Nobody wrote warning us about you. And no
one has shown up saying anything bad about you. But we
would like very much to hear more. The only thing we
know about this Christian sect is that nobody seems to
have anything good to say about it."

They agreed on a time. When the day arrived, they came
back to his home with a number of their friends. Paul
talked to them all day, from morning to evening, explain-
ing everything involved in the kingdom of God, and trying
to persuade them all about Jesus by pointing out what
Moses and the prophets had written about him.

Some of them were persuaded by what he said, but oth-
ers refused to believe a word of it. When the unbelievers
got cantankerous and started bickering with each other,
Paul interrupted: "I have just one more thing to say to you.
The Holy Spirit sure knew what he was talking about
when he addressed our ancestors through Isaiah the
prophet:

'Go to this people and tell them this:
"You're going to listen with your ears,
but you won't hear a word;
You're going to stare with your eyes,
but you won't see a thing.
These people are blockheads!

KING JAMES VERSION

ears are dull of hearing, and their eyes have they closed; lest they should see with *their* eyes, and hear with *their* ears, and understand with *their* heart, and should be converted, and I should heal them.

28 Be it known therefore unto you, that the salvation of God is sent unto the Gentiles, and *that* they will hear it.

29 And when he had said these words, the Jews departed, and had great reasoning among themselves.

30 ¶ And Paul dwelt two whole years in his own hired house, and received all that came in unto him,

31 Preaching the kingdom of God, and teaching those things which concern the Lord Jesus Christ, with all confidence, no man forbidding him.

NEW AMERICAN STANDARD BIBLE

AND WITH THEIR EARS THEY SCARCELY HEAR,
AND THEY HAVE CLOSED THEIR EYES;
OTHERWISE THEY MIGHT SEE WITH THEIR EYES,
AND HEAR WITH THEIR EARS,
AND UNDERSTAND WITH THEIR HEART AND RETURN,
AND I WOULD HEAL THEM." '

28 "Therefore let it be known to you that this salvation of God has been sent to the Gentiles; they will also listen."

29 [[1]When he had spoken these words, the Jews departed, having a great dispute among themselves.]

30 And he stayed two full years in his own rented quarters and was welcoming all who came to him,

31 preaching the kingdom of God and teaching concerning the Lord Jesus Christ with all openness, unhindered.

28:29 [1] Early mss do not contain this v

NEW CENTURY VERSION

They don't hear with their ears,
and they have closed their eyes.
Otherwise, they might really understand
what they see with their eyes
and hear with their ears.
They might really understand in their minds
and come back to me and be healed.' *Isaiah 6:9–10*

28"I want you to know that God has also sent his salvation to those who are not Jewish, and they will listen!" 29[f]

30Paul stayed two full years in his own rented house and welcomed all people who came to visit him. 31He boldly preached about the kingdom of God and taught about the Lord Jesus Christ, and no one tried to stop him.

28:29 [f] **Verse 29** Some late Greek copies add verse 29: "After Paul said this, the Jews left. They were arguing very much with each other."

CONTEMPORARY ENGLISH VERSION

Your ears are stopped up,
and your eyes are covered.
You cannot see or hear
or understand.
If you could,
you would turn to me,
and I would heal you.' "

28-29Paul said, "You may be sure that God wants to save the Gentiles! And they will listen."[c]

30For two years Paul stayed in a rented house and welcomed everyone who came to see him. 31He bravely preached about God's kingdom and taught about the Lord Jesus Christ, and no one tried to stop him.

[c] **28.28,29** *And they will listen*: Some manuscripts add, "After Paul said this, the people left, but they got into a fierce argument among themselves."

NEW INTERNATIONAL VERSION

they hardly hear with their ears,
and they have closed their eyes.
Otherwise they might see with their eyes,
hear with their ears,
understand with their hearts
and turn, and I would heal them.'[a]

28 "Therefore I want you to know that God's salvation has been sent to the Gentiles, and they will listen!"[b]

30 For two whole years Paul stayed there in his own rented house and welcomed all who came to see him. 31 Boldly and without hindrance he preached the kingdom of God and taught about the Lord Jesus Christ.

[a] *27* Isaiah 6:9,10 [b] *28* Some manuscripts *listen!" 29After he said this, the Jews left, arguing vigorously among themselves.*

NEW LIVING TRANSLATION

and their ears cannot hear,
and they have closed their eyes—
so their eyes cannot see,
and their ears cannot hear,
and their hearts cannot understand,
and they cannot turn to me
and let me heal them.'*

28 So I want you to realize that this salvation from God is also available to the Gentiles, and they will accept it."*

30 For the next two years, Paul lived in his own rented house.* He welcomed all who visited him, 31 proclaiming the Kingdom of God with all boldness and teaching about the Lord Jesus Christ. And no one tried to stop him.

28:26-27 Isa 6:9-10. **28:28** Some manuscripts add verse 29, *And when he had said these words, the Jews departed, greatly disagreeing with each other.* **28:30** Or *at his own expense.*

NEW KING JAMES VERSION

Their ears are hard of hearing,
And their eyes they have closed,
Lest they should see with their *eyes and hear with their ears,*
Lest they should understand with their *hearts and turn,*
So that I should heal them." '[c]

28 "Therefore let it be known to you that the salvation of God has been sent to the Gentiles, and they will hear it!" 29 And when he had said these words, the Jews departed and had a great dispute among themselves.[d]

30 Then Paul dwelt two whole years in his own rented house, and received all who came to him, 31 preaching the kingdom of God and teaching the things which concern the Lord Jesus Christ with all confidence, no one forbidding him.

28:27 [c] Isaiah 6:9, 10 **28:29** [d] NU-Text omits this verse.

THE MESSAGE

They stick their fingers in their ears
so they won't have to listen;
They screw their eyes shut
so they won't have to look,
so they won't have to deal with me face-to-face
and let me heal them." '

"You've had your chance. The non-Jewish outsiders are next on the list. And believe me, they're going to receive it with open arms!"

Paul lived for two years in his rented house. He welcomed everyone who came to visit. He urgently presented all matters of the kingdom of God. He explained everything about Jesus Christ. His door was always open.

KING JAMES VERSION

THE EPISTLE OF ST. PAUL TO THE ROMANS

1 Paul, a servant of Jesus Christ, called *to be* an apostle, separated unto the gospel of God,

2 (Which he had promised afore by his prophets in the holy scriptures,)

3 Concerning his Son Jesus Christ our Lord, which was made of the seed of David according to the flesh;

4 And declared *to be* the Son of God with power, according to the spirit of holiness, by the resurrection from the dead:

5 By whom we have received grace and apostleship, for obedience to the faith among all nations, for his name:

6 Among whom are ye also the called of Jesus Christ:

7 To all that be in Rome, beloved of God, called *to be* saints: Grace to you and peace from God our Father, and the Lord Jesus Christ.

8 ¶ First, I thank my God through Jesus Christ for you all, that your faith is spoken of throughout the whole world.

9 For God is my witness, whom I serve with my spirit in

NEW AMERICAN STANDARD BIBLE

THE LETTER OF PAUL TO THE ROMANS

The Gospel Exalted

1 Paul, a bond-servant of Christ Jesus, called *as* an apostle, set apart for the gospel of God,

2 which He promised beforehand through His prophets in the holy Scriptures,

3 concerning His Son, who was born of a descendant of David according to the flesh,

4 who was declared the Son of God with power [1]by the resurrection from the dead, according to the Spirit of holiness, Jesus Christ our Lord,

5 through whom we have received grace and apostleship to bring about *the* obedience of faith among all the Gentiles for His name's sake,

6 among whom you also are the called of Jesus Christ;

7 to all who are beloved of God in Rome, called *as* saints: Grace to you and peace from God our Father and the Lord Jesus Christ.

8 First, I thank my God through Jesus Christ for you all, because your faith is being proclaimed throughout the whole world.

9 For God, whom I serve in my spirit in the *preaching*

1:4 [1] Or *as a result of*

NEW CENTURY VERSION

ROMANS

1 From Paul, a servant of Christ Jesus. God called me to be an apostle and chose me to tell the Good News.
2God promised this Good News long ago through his
prophets, as it is written in the Holy Scriptures. 3-4The
Good News is about God's Son, Jesus Christ our Lord. As a
man, he was born from the family of David. But through
the Spirit of holiness he was appointed to be God's Son
with great power by rising from the dead. 5Through Christ,
God gave me the special work of an apostle, which was to
lead people of all nations to believe and obey. I do this
work for him. 6And you who are in Rome are also called to
belong to Jesus Christ.

7To all of you in Rome whom God loves and has called
to be his holy people:

Grace and peace to you from God our Father and the Lord Jesus Christ.

A Prayer of Thanks

8First I want to say that I thank my God through Jesus
Christ for all of you, because people everywhere in the
world are talking about your faith. 9God, whom I serve
with my whole heart by telling the Good News about his

CONTEMPORARY ENGLISH VERSION

ROMANS

1 From Paul, a servant of Christ Jesus.

God chose me to be an apostle, and he appointed
me to preach the good news 2that he promised long ago by
what his prophets said in the holy Scriptures. 3-4This good
news is about his Son, our Lord Jesus Christ! As a human,
he was from the family of David. But the Holy Spirit[a]
proved that Jesus is the powerful Son of God,[b] because he
was raised from death.

5Jesus was kind to me and chose me to be an apostle,[c]
so that people of all nations would obey and have faith.
6You are some of those people chosen by Jesus Christ.

7This letter is to all of you in Rome. God loves you and
has chosen you to be his very own people.

I pray that God our Father and our Lord Jesus Christ will be kind to you and will bless you with peace!

A Prayer of Thanks

8First, I thank God in the name of Jesus Christ for all of
you. I do this because people everywhere in the world are
talking about your faith. 9God has seen how I never stop

[a] 1.4 *the Holy Spirit*: Or "his own spirit of holiness." [b] 1.4 *proved that Jesus is the powerful Son of God*: Or "proved in a powerful way that Jesus is the Son of God." [c] 1.5 *Jesus was kind to me and chose me to be an apostle*: Or "Jesus was kind to us and chose us to be his apostles."

NEW INTERNATIONAL VERSION

ROMANS

1 Paul, a servant of Christ Jesus, called to be an apostle
and set apart for the gospel of God— 2the gospel he
promised beforehand through his prophets in the Holy
Scriptures 3regarding his Son, who as to his human nature
was a descendant of David, 4and who through the Spirit[a]
of holiness was declared with power to be the Son of God[b]
by his resurrection from the dead: Jesus Christ our Lord.
5Through him and for his name's sake, we received grace
and apostleship to call people from among all the Gentiles
to the obedience that comes from faith. 6And you also are
among those who are called to belong to Jesus Christ.

7To all in Rome who are loved by God and called to be
saints:

Grace and peace to you from God our Father and from the Lord Jesus Christ.

Paul's Longing to Visit Rome

8First, I thank my God through Jesus Christ for all of you,
because your faith is being reported all over the world.
9God, whom I serve with my whole heart in preaching the

[a] 4 Or *who as to his spirit* [b] 4 Or *was appointed to be the Son of God with power*

NEW LIVING TRANSLATION

ROMANS

Greetings from Paul

1 This letter is from Paul, Jesus Christ's slave, chosen by God to be an apostle and sent out to preach his Good
News. 2This Good News was promised long ago by God
through his prophets in the holy Scriptures. 3It is the Good
News about his Son, Jesus, who came as a man, born into
King David's royal family line. 4And Jesus Christ our Lord
was shown to be the Son of God when God powerfully
raised him from the dead by means of the Holy Spirit.*
5Through Christ, God has given us the privilege and
authority to tell Gentiles everywhere what God has done
for them, so that they will believe and obey him, bringing
glory to his name.
6You are among those who have been called to belong to
Jesus Christ, 7dear friends in Rome. God loves you dearly,
and he has called you to be his very own people.

May grace and peace be yours from God our Father and the Lord Jesus Christ.

God's Good News

8Let me say first of all that your faith in God is becom-
ing known throughout the world. How I thank God
through Jesus Christ for each one of you. 9God knows how

1:4 Or *the Spirit of holiness.*

NEW KING JAMES VERSION

THE EPISTLE OF PAUL TO THE

ROMANS

Greeting

1 Paul, a bondservant of Jesus Christ, called *to be* an
apostle, separated to the gospel of God 2which He
promised before through His prophets in the Holy
Scriptures, 3concerning His Son Jesus Christ our Lord, who
was born of the seed of David according to the flesh, 4*and*
declared *to be* the Son of God with power according to the
Spirit of holiness, by the resurrection from the dead.
5Through Him we have received grace and apostleship for
obedience to the faith among all nations for His name,
6among whom you also are the called of Jesus Christ;

7To all who are in Rome, beloved of God, called *to be*
saints:

Grace to you and peace from God our Father and the Lord Jesus Christ.

Desire to Visit Rome

8First, I thank my God through Jesus Christ for you all,
that your faith is spoken of throughout the whole world.
9For God is my witness, whom I serve with my spirit in the

THE MESSAGE

ROMANS

1 I, Paul, am a devoted slave of Jesus Christ on assignment, authorized as an apostle to proclaim God's words and acts. I write this letter to all the Christians in Rome, God's friends.

The sacred writings contain preliminary reports by the prophets on God's Son. His descent from David roots him in history; his unique identity as Son of God was shown by the Spirit when Jesus was raised from the dead, setting him apart as the Messiah, our Master. Through him we received both the generous gift of his life and the urgent task of passing it on to others who receive it by entering into obedient trust in Jesus. You are who you are through this gift and call of Jesus Christ! And I greet you now with all the generosity of God our Father and our Master Jesus, the Messiah.

I thank God through Jesus for every one of you. That's first. People everywhere keep telling me about your lives of faith, and every time I hear them, I thank him. And God, whom I so love to worship and serve by spreading the good

KING JAMES VERSION

the gospel of his Son, that without ceasing I make mention of you always in my prayers;

10 Making request, if by any means now at length I might have a prosperous journey by the will of God to come unto you.

11 For I long to see you, that I may impart unto you some spiritual gift, to the end ye may be established;

12 That is, that I may be comforted together with you by the mutual faith both of you and me.

13 Now I would not have you ignorant, brethren, that oftentimes I purposed to come unto you, (but was let hitherto,) that I might have some fruit among you also, even as among other Gentiles.

14 I am debtor both to the Greeks, and to the Barbarians; both to the wise, and to the unwise.

15 So, as much as in me is, I am ready to preach the gospel to you that are at Rome also.

16 ¶ For I am not ashamed of the gospel of Christ: for it is the power of God unto salvation to every one that believeth; to the Jew first, and also to the Greek.

17 For therein is the righteousness of God revealed from faith to faith: as it is written, The just shall live by faith.

18 For the wrath of God is revealed from heaven against all ungodliness and unrighteousness of men, who hold the truth in unrighteousness;

NEW AMERICAN STANDARD BIBLE

of the gospel of His Son, is my witness *as to* how unceasingly I make mention of you,

10 always in my prayers making request, if perhaps now at last by the will of God I may succeed in coming to you.

11 For I long to see you so that I may impart some spiritual gift to you, that you may be established;

12 that is, that I may be encouraged together with you *while* among you, each of us by the other's faith, both yours and mine.

13 I do not want you to be unaware, brethren, that often I have planned to come to you (and have been prevented so far) so that I may obtain some fruit among you also, even as among the rest of the Gentiles.

14 I am [2]under obligation both to Greeks and to barbarians, both to the wise and to the foolish.

15 So, for my part, I am eager to preach the gospel to you also who are in Rome.

16 For I am not ashamed of the gospel, for it is the power of God for salvation to everyone who believes, to the Jew first and also to the Greek.

17 For in it *the* righteousness of God is revealed from faith to faith; as it is written, "BUT THE RIGHTEOUS *man* SHALL LIVE BY FAITH."

Unbelief and Its Consequences

18 For the wrath of God is revealed from heaven against all ungodliness and unrighteousness of men who suppress the truth in unrighteousness,

1:14 [2] Lit *debtor*

NEW CENTURY VERSION

Son, knows that I always mention you [10]every time I pray. I pray that I will be allowed to come to you, and this will happen if God wants it. [11]I want very much to see you, to give you some spiritual gift to make you strong. [12]I mean that I want us to help each other with the faith we have. Your faith will help me, and my faith will help you. [13]Brothers and sisters,[a] I want you to know that I planned many times to come to you, but this has not been possible. I wanted to come so that I could help you grow spiritually as I have helped the other non-Jewish people.

[14]I have a duty to all people—Greeks and those who are not Greeks, the wise and the foolish. [15]That is why I want so much to preach the Good News to you in Rome.

[16]I am proud of the Good News, because it is the power God uses to save everyone who believes—to save the Jews first, and also to save those who are not Jews. [17]The Good News shows how God makes people right with himself—that it begins and ends with faith. As the Scripture says, "But those who are right with God will live by trusting in him."[b]

All People Have Done Wrong

[18]God's anger is shown from heaven against all the evil and wrong things people do. By their own evil lives they

1:13 [a] **Brothers and sisters** Although the Greek text says "Brothers" here and throughout this book, Paul's words were meant for the entire church, including men and women. 1:17 [b] **"But those...him."** Quotation from Habakkuk 2:4.

CONTEMPORARY ENGLISH VERSION

praying for you, while I serve him with all my heart and tell the good news about his Son.

[10]In all my prayers, I ask God to make it possible for me to visit you. [11]I want to see you and share with you the same blessings that God's Spirit has given me. Then you will grow stronger in your faith. [12]What I am saying is that we can encourage each other by the faith that is ours.

[13]My friends, I want you to know that I have often planned to come for a visit. But something has always kept me from doing it. I want to win followers to Christ in Rome, as I have done in many other places. [14-15]It doesn't matter if people are civilized and educated, or if they are uncivilized and uneducated. I must tell the good news to everyone. That's why I am eager to visit all of you in Rome.

The Power of the Good News

[16]I am proud of the good news! It is God's powerful way of saving all people who have faith, whether they are Jews or Gentiles. [17]The good news tells how God accepts everyone who has faith, but only those who have faith.[d] It is just as the Scriptures say, "The people God accepts because of their faith will live."[e]

Everyone Is Guilty

[18]From heaven God shows how angry he is with all the wicked and evil things that sinful people do to crush the

[d] 1.17 *but only those who have faith*: Or "and faith is all that matters."
[e] 1.17 *The people God accepts because of their faith will live*: Or "The people God accepts will live because of their faith."

NEW INTERNATIONAL VERSION

gospel of his Son, is my witness how constantly I remember
you 10in my prayers at all times; and I pray that now at last
by God's will the way may be opened for me to come to
you.
11I long to see you so that I may impart to you some
spiritual gift to make you strong— 12that is, that you and I
may be mutually encouraged by each other's faith. 13I do
not want you to be unaware, brothers, that I planned
many times to come to you (but have been prevented from
doing so until now) in order that I might have a harvest
among you, just as I have had among the other Gentiles.
14I am obligated both to Greeks and non-Greeks, both to
the wise and the foolish. 15That is why I am so eager to
preach the gospel also to you who are at Rome.
16I am not ashamed of the gospel, because it is the
power of God for the salvation of everyone who believes:
first for the Jew, then for the Gentile. 17For in the gospel a
righteousness from God is revealed, a righteousness that is
by faith from first to last,[c] just as it is written: "The righ-
teous will live by faith."[d]

God's Wrath Against Mankind

18The wrath of God is being revealed from heaven
against all the godlessness and wickedness of men who
suppress the truth by their wickedness, 19since what may

[c] *17* Or *is from faith to faith* [d] *17* Hab. 2:4

NEW LIVING TRANSLATION

often I pray for you. Day and night I bring you and your
needs in prayer to God, whom I serve with all my heart* by
telling others the Good News about his Son.
10One of the things I always pray for is the opportunity,
God willing, to come at last to see you. 11For I long to visit
you so I can share a spiritual blessing with you that will
help you grow strong in the Lord. 12I'm eager to encourage
you in your faith, but I also want to be encouraged by yours.
In this way, each of us will be a blessing to the other.
13I want you to know, dear brothers and sisters,* that I
planned many times to visit you, but I was prevented until
now. I want to work among you and see good results, just
as I have done among other Gentiles. 14For I have a great
sense of obligation to people in our culture and to people
in other cultures,* to the educated and uneducated alike.
15So I am eager to come to you in Rome, too, to preach
God's Good News.
16For I am not ashamed of this Good News about Christ.
It is the power of God at work, saving everyone who
believes—Jews first and also Gentiles. 17This Good News
tells us how God makes us right in his sight. This is accom-
plished from start to finish by faith. As the Scriptures say,
"It is through faith that a righteous person has life."*

God's Anger at Sin

18But God shows his anger from heaven against all sinful,
wicked people who push the truth away from themselves.*

1:9 Or *in my spirit.* **1:13** Greek *brothers.* **1:14** Greek *to Greeks and to barbarians.* **1:17** Hab 2:4. **1:18** Or *who prevent the truth from being known.*

NEW KING JAMES VERSION

gospel of His Son, that without ceasing I make mention of
you always in my prayers, 10making request if, by some
means, now at last I may find a way in the will of God to
come to you. 11For I long to see you, that I may impart to
you some spiritual gift, so that you may be established—
12that is, that I may be encouraged together with you by
the mutual faith both of you and me.
13Now I do not want you to be unaware, brethren, that I
often planned to come to you (but was hindered until
now), that I might have some fruit among you also, just as
among the other Gentiles. 14I am a debtor both to Greeks
and to barbarians, both to wise and to unwise. 15So, as
much as is in me, *I am* ready to preach the gospel to you
who are in Rome also.

The Just Live by Faith

16For I am not ashamed of the gospel of Christ,[a] for it is
the power of God to salvation for everyone who believes,
for the Jew first and also for the Greek. 17For in it the righ-
teousness of God is revealed from faith to faith; as it is
written, *"The just shall live by faith."*[b]

God's Wrath on Unrighteousness

18For the wrath of God is revealed from heaven against
all ungodliness and unrighteousness of men, who sup-
press the truth in unrighteousness, 19because what may be

1:16 [a] NU-Text omits *of Christ.* **1:17** [b] Habakkuk 2:4

THE MESSAGE

news of his Son—the Message!—knows that every time I
think of you in my prayers, which is practically all the
time, I ask him to clear the way for me to come and see
you. The longer this waiting goes on, the deeper the ache. I
so want to be there to deliver God's gift in person and
watch you grow stronger right before my eyes! But don't
think I'm not expecting to get something out of this, too!
You have as much to give me as I do to you.

Please don't misinterpret my failure to visit you, friends.
You have no idea how many times I've made plans for
Rome. I've been determined to get some personal enjoy-
ment out of God's work among you, as I have in so many
other non-Jewish towns and communities. But something
has always come up and prevented it. Everyone I meet—it
matters little whether they're mannered or rude, smart or
simple—deepens my sense of interdependence and obliga-
tion. And that's why I can't wait to get to you in Rome,
preaching this wonderful good news of God.

It's news I'm most proud to proclaim, this extraordinary
Message of God's powerful plan to rescue everyone who
trusts him, starting with Jews and then right on to every-
one else! God's way of putting people right shows up in
the acts of faith, confirming what Scripture has said all
along: "The person in right standing before God by trust-
ing him really lives."

Ignoring God Leads to a Downward Spiral

But God's angry displeasure erupts as acts of human
mistrust and wrongdoing and lying accumulate, as people

KING JAMES VERSION

19 ¶ Because that which may be known of God is manifest in them; for God hath shewed *it* unto them.

20 For the invisible things of him from the creation of the world are clearly seen, being understood by the things that are made, *even* his eternal power and Godhead; so that they are without excuse:

21 Because that, when they knew God, they glorified *him* not as God, neither were thankful; but became vain in their imaginations, and their foolish heart was darkened.

22 Professing themselves to be wise, they became fools,

23 And changed the glory of the uncorruptible God into an image made like to corruptible man, and to birds, and fourfooted beasts, and creeping things.

24 Wherefore God also gave them up to uncleanness through the lusts of their own hearts, to dishonour their own bodies between themselves:

25 Who changed the truth of God into a lie, and worshipped and served the creature more than the Creator, who is blessed for ever. Amen.

26 For this cause God gave them up unto vile affections: for even their women did change the natural use into that which is against nature:

27 And likewise also the men, leaving the natural use of the woman, burned in their lust one toward another; men with men working that which is unseemly, and receiving in themselves that recompence of their error which was meet.

NEW AMERICAN STANDARD BIBLE

19 because that which is known about God is evident within them; for God made it evident to them.

20 For since the creation of the world His invisible attributes, His eternal power and divine nature, have been clearly seen, being understood through what has been made, so that they are without excuse.

21 For even though they knew God, they did not [3]honor Him as God or give thanks, but they became futile in their speculations, and their foolish heart was darkened.

22 Professing to be wise, they became fools,

23 and exchanged the glory of the incorruptible God for an image in the form of corruptible man and of birds and four-footed animals and [4]crawling creatures.

24 Therefore God gave them over in the lusts of their hearts to impurity, so that their bodies would be dishonored among them.

25 For they exchanged the truth of God for a lie, and worshiped and served the creature rather than the Creator, who is blessed forever. Amen.

26 For this reason God gave them over to degrading passions; for their women exchanged the natural function for that which is unnatural,

27 and in the same way also the men abandoned the natural function of the woman and burned in their desire toward one another, men with men committing indecent acts and receiving in their own persons the due penalty of their error.

1:21 [3] Lit *glorify* 1:23 [4] Or *reptiles*

NEW CENTURY VERSION

hide the truth. [19]God shows his anger because some knowledge of him has been made clear to them. Yes, God has shown himself to them. [20]There are things about him that people cannot see—his eternal power and all the things that make him God. But since the beginning of the world those things have been easy to understand by what God has made. So people have no excuse for the bad things they do. [21]They knew God, but they did not give glory to God or thank him. Their thinking became useless. Their foolish minds were filled with darkness. [22]They said they were wise, but they became fools. [23]They traded the glory of God who lives forever for the worship of idols made to look like earthly people, birds, animals, and snakes.

[24]Because they did these things, God left them and let them go their sinful way, wanting only to do evil. As a result, they became full of sexual sin, using their bodies wrongly with each other. [25]They traded the truth of God for a lie. They worshiped and served what had been created instead of the God who created those things, who should be praised forever. Amen.

[26]Because people did those things, God left them and let them do the shameful things they wanted to do. Women stopped having natural sex and started having sex with other women. [27]In the same way, men stopped having natural sex and began wanting each other. Men did shameful things with other men, and in their bodies they received the punishment for those wrongs.

CONTEMPORARY ENGLISH VERSION

truth. [19]They know everything that can be known about God, because God has shown it all to them. [20]God's eternal power and character cannot be seen. But from the beginning of creation, God has shown what these are like by all he has made. That's why those people don't have any excuse. [21]They know about God, but they don't honor him or even thank him. Their thoughts are useless, and their stupid minds are in the dark. [22]They claim to be wise, but they are fools. [23]They don't worship the glorious and eternal God. Instead, they worship idols that are made to look like humans who cannot live forever, and like birds, animals, and reptiles.

[24]So God let these people go their own way. They did what they wanted to do, and their filthy thoughts made them do shameful things with their bodies. [25]They gave up the truth about God for a lie, and they worshiped God's creation instead of God, who will be praised forever. Amen.

[26]God let them follow their own evil desires. Women no longer wanted to have sex in a natural way, and they did things with each other that were not natural. [27]Men behaved in the same way. They stopped wanting to have sex with women and had strong desires for sex with other men. They did shameful things with each other, and what has happened to them is punishment for their foolish deeds.

NEW INTERNATIONAL VERSION

be known about God is plain to them, because God has made it plain to them. 20For since the creation of the world God's invisible qualities—his eternal power and divine nature—have been clearly seen, being understood from what has been made, so that men are without excuse.

21For although they knew God, they neither glorified him as God nor gave thanks to him, but their thinking became futile and their foolish hearts were darkened. 22Although they claimed to be wise, they became fools 23and exchanged the glory of the immortal God for images made to look like mortal man and birds and animals and reptiles.

24Therefore God gave them over in the sinful desires of their hearts to sexual impurity for the degrading of their bodies with one another. 25They exchanged the truth of God for a lie, and worshiped and served created things rather than the Creator—who is forever praised. Amen.

26Because of this, God gave them over to shameful lusts. Even their women exchanged natural relations for unnatural ones. 27In the same way the men also abandoned natural relations with women and were inflamed with lust for one another. Men committed indecent acts with other men, and received in themselves the due penalty for their perversion.

NEW LIVING TRANSLATION

19For the truth about God is known to them instinctively.* God has put this knowledge in their hearts. 20From the time the world was created, people have seen the earth and sky and all that God made. They can clearly see his invisible qualities—his eternal power and divine nature. So they have no excuse whatsoever for not knowing God.

21Yes, they knew God, but they wouldn't worship him as God or even give him thanks. And they began to think up foolish ideas of what God was like. The result was that their minds became dark and confused. 22Claiming to be wise, they became utter fools instead. 23And instead of worshiping the glorious, ever-living God, they worshiped idols made to look like mere people, or birds and animals and snakes.

24So God let them go ahead and do whatever shameful things their hearts desired. As a result, they did vile and degrading things with each other's bodies. 25Instead of believing what they knew was the truth about God, they deliberately chose to believe lies. So they worshiped the things God made but not the Creator himself, who is to be praised forever. Amen.

26That is why God abandoned them to their shameful desires. Even the women turned against the natural way to have sex and instead indulged in sex with each other. 27And the men, instead of having normal sexual relationships with women, burned with lust for each other. Men did shameful things with other men and, as a result, suffered within themselves the penalty they so richly deserved.

1:19 Greek *is manifest in them.*

NEW KING JAMES VERSION

known of God is manifest in them, for God has shown *it* to them. 20For since the creation of the world His invisible *attributes* are clearly seen, being understood by the things that are made, *even* His eternal power and Godhead, so that they are without excuse, 21because, although they knew God, they did not glorify *Him* as God, nor were thankful, but became futile in their thoughts, and their foolish hearts were darkened. 22Professing to be wise, they became fools, 23and changed the glory of the incorruptible God into an image made like corruptible man—and birds and four-footed animals and creeping things.

24Therefore God also gave them up to uncleanness, in the lusts of their hearts, to dishonor their bodies among themselves, 25who exchanged the truth of God for the lie, and worshiped and served the creature rather than the Creator, who is blessed forever. Amen.

26For this reason God gave them up to vile passions. For even their women exchanged the natural use for what is against nature. 27Likewise also the men, leaving the natural use of the woman, burned in their lust for one another, men with men committing what is shameful, and receiving in themselves the penalty of their error which was due.

THE MESSAGE

try to put a shroud over truth. But the basic reality of God is plain enough. Open your eyes and there it is! By taking a long and thoughtful look at what God has created, people have always been able to see what their eyes as such can't see: eternal power, for instance, and the mystery of his divine being. So nobody has a good excuse. What happened was this: People knew God perfectly well, but when they didn't treat him like God, refusing to worship him, they trivialized themselves into silliness and confusion so that there was neither sense nor direction left in their lives. They pretended to know it all, but were illiterate regarding life. They traded the glory of God who holds the whole world in his hands for cheap figurines you can buy at any roadside stand.

So God said, in effect, "If that's what you want, that's what you get." It wasn't long before they were living in a pigpen, smeared with filth, filthy inside and out. And all this because they traded the true God for a fake god, and worshiped the god they made instead of the God who made them—the God we bless, the God who blesses *us*. Oh, yes!

Worse followed. Refusing to know God, they soon didn't know how to be human either—women didn't know how to be women, men didn't know how to be men. Sexually confused, they abused and defiled one another, women with women, men with men—all lust, no love. And then they paid for it, oh, how they paid for it—emptied of God and love, godless and loveless wretches.

KING JAMES VERSION

28 And even as they did not like to retain God in *their* knowledge, God gave them over to a reprobate mind, to do those things which are not convenient;

29 Being filled with all unrighteousness, fornication, wickedness, covetousness, maliciousness; full of envy, murder, debate, deceit, malignity; whisperers,

30 Backbiters, haters of God, despiteful, proud, boasters, inventors of evil things, disobedient to parents,

31 Without understanding, covenantbreakers, without natural affection, implacable, unmerciful:

32 Who knowing the judgment of God, that they which commit such things are worthy of death, not only do the same, but have pleasure in them that do them.

2 Therefore thou art inexcusable, O man, whosoever thou art that judgest: for wherein thou judgest another, thou condemnest thyself; for thou that judgest doest the same things.

2 But we are sure that the judgment of God is according to truth against them which commit such things.

3 And thinkest thou this, O man, that judgest them which do such things, and doest the same, that thou shalt escape the judgment of God?

4 Or despisest thou the riches of his goodness and forbearance and longsuffering; not knowing that the goodness of God leadeth thee to repentance?

NEW AMERICAN STANDARD BIBLE

28 And just as they did not see fit to acknowledge God any longer, God gave them over to a depraved mind, to do those things which are not proper,

29 being filled with all unrighteousness, wickedness, greed, evil; full of envy, murder, strife, deceit, malice; *they are* gossips,

30 slanderers, haters of God, insolent, arrogant, boastful, inventors of evil, disobedient to parents,

31 without understanding, untrustworthy, unloving, unmerciful;

32 and although they know the ordinance of God, that those who practice such things are worthy of death, they not only do the same, but also give hearty approval to those who practice them.

The Impartiality of God

2 Therefore you have no excuse, everyone of you who passes judgment, for in that which you judge another, you condemn yourself; for you who judge practice the same things.

2 And we know that the judgment of God rightly falls upon those who practice such things.

3 But do you suppose this, O man, when you pass judgment on those who practice such things and do the same *yourself,* that you will escape the judgment of God?

4 Or do you think lightly of the riches of His kindness and tolerance and patience, not knowing that the kindness of God leads you to repentance?

NEW CENTURY VERSION

28People did not think it was important to have a true knowledge of God. So God left them and allowed them to have their own worthless thinking and to do things they should not do. 29They are filled with every kind of sin, evil, selfishness, and hatred. They are full of jealousy, murder, fighting, lying, and thinking the worst about each other. They gossip 30and say evil things about each other. They hate God. They are rude and conceited and brag about themselves. They invent ways of doing evil. They do not obey their parents. 31They are foolish, they do not keep their promises, and they show no kindness or mercy to others. 32They know God's law says that those who live like this should die. But they themselves not only continue to do these evil things, they applaud others who do them.

You People Also Are Sinful

2 If you think you can judge others, you are wrong. When you judge them, you are really judging yourself guilty, because you do the same things they do. 2God judges those who do wrong things, and we know that his judging is right. 3You judge those who do wrong, but you do wrong yourselves. Do you think you will be able to escape the judgment of God? 4He has been very kind and patient, waiting for you to change, but you think nothing of his kindness. Perhaps you do not understand that God is kind to you so you will change your hearts and lives.

CONTEMPORARY ENGLISH VERSION

28Since these people refused even to think about God, he let their useless minds rule over them. That's why they do all sorts of indecent things. 29They are evil, wicked, and greedy, as well as mean in every possible way. They want what others have, and they murder, argue, cheat, and are hard to get along with. They gossip, 30say cruel things about others, and hate God. They are proud, conceited, and boastful, always thinking up new ways to do evil.

These people don't respect their parents. 31They are stupid, unreliable, and don't have any love or pity for others. 32They know God has said that anyone who acts this way deserves to die. But they keep on doing evil things, and they even encourage others to do them.

God's Judgment Is Fair

2 Some of you accuse others of doing wrong. But there is no excuse for what you do. When you judge others, you condemn yourselves, because you are guilty of doing the very same things. 2We know that God is right to judge everyone who behaves in this way. 3Do you really think God won't punish you, when you behave exactly like the people you accuse? 4You surely don't think much of God's wonderful goodness or of his patience and willingness to put up with you. Don't you know that the reason God is good to you is because he wants you to turn to him?

NEW INTERNATIONAL VERSION

[28]Furthermore, since they did not think it worthwhile to retain the knowledge of God, he gave them over to a depraved mind, to do what ought not to be done. [29]They have become filled with every kind of wickedness, evil, greed and depravity. They are full of envy, murder, strife, deceit and malice. They are gossips, [30]slanderers, God-haters, insolent, arrogant and boastful; they invent ways of doing evil; they disobey their parents; [31]they are senseless, faithless, heartless, ruthless. [32]Although they know God's righteous decree that those who do such things deserve death, they not only continue to do these very things but also approve of those who practice them.

God's Righteous Judgment

2 You, therefore, have no excuse, you who pass judgment on someone else, for at whatever point you judge the other, you are condemning yourself, because you who pass judgment do the same things. [2]Now we know that God's judgment against those who do such things is based on truth. [3]So when you, a mere man, pass judgment on them and yet do the same things, do you think you will escape God's judgment? [4]Or do you show contempt for the riches of his kindness, tolerance and patience, not realizing that God's kindness leads you toward repentance?

NEW LIVING TRANSLATION

[28]When they refused to acknowledge God, he abandoned them to their evil minds and let them do things that should never be done. [29]Their lives became full of every kind of wickedness, sin, greed, hate, envy, murder, fighting, deception, malicious behavior, and gossip. [30]They are backstabbers, haters of God, insolent, proud, and boastful. They are forever inventing new ways of sinning and are disobedient to their parents. [31]They refuse to understand, break their promises, and are heartless and unforgiving. [32]They are fully aware of God's death penalty for those who do these things, yet they go right ahead and do them anyway. And, worse yet, they encourage others to do them, too.

God's Judgment of Sin

2 You may be saying, "What terrible people you have been talking about!" But you are just as bad, and you have no excuse! When you say they are wicked and should be punished, you are condemning yourself, for you do these very same things. [2]And we know that God, in his justice, will punish anyone who does such things. [3]Do you think that God will judge and condemn others for doing them and not judge you when you do them, too? [4]Don't you realize how kind, tolerant, and patient God is with you? Or don't you care? Can't you see how kind he has been in giving you time to turn from your sin?

NEW KING JAMES VERSION

[28]And even as they did not like to retain God in *their* knowledge, God gave them over to a debased mind, to do those things which are not fitting; [29]being filled with all unrighteousness, sexual immorality,[c] wickedness, covetousness, maliciousness; full of envy, murder, strife, deceit, evil-mindedness; *they are* whisperers, [30]backbiters, haters of God, violent, proud, boasters, inventors of evil things, disobedient to parents, [31]undiscerning, untrustworthy, unloving, unforgiving,[d] unmerciful; [32]who, knowing the righteous judgment of God, that those who practice such things are deserving of death, not only do the same but also approve of those who practice them.

God's Righteous Judgment

2 Therefore you are inexcusable, O man, whoever you are who judge, for in whatever you judge another you condemn yourself; for you who judge practice the same things. [2]But we know that the judgment of God is according to truth against those who practice such things. [3]And do you think this, O man, you who judge those practicing such things, and doing the same, that you will escape the judgment of God? [4]Or do you despise the riches of His goodness, forbearance, and longsuffering, not knowing that the goodness of God leads you to repentance? [5]But in

1:29 [c] NU-Text omits *sexual immorality.* 1:31 [d] NU-Text omits *unforgiving.*

THE MESSAGE

Since they didn't bother to acknowledge God, God quit bothering them and let them run loose. And then all hell broke loose: rampant evil, grabbing and grasping, vicious backstabbing. They made life hell on earth with their envy, wanton killing, bickering, and cheating. Look at them: mean-spirited, venomous, fork-tongued God-bashers. Bullies, swaggerers, insufferable windbags! They keep inventing new ways of wrecking lives. They ditch their parents when they get in the way. Stupid, slimy, cruel, coldblooded. And it's not as if they don't know better. They know perfectly well they're spitting in God's face. And they don't care—worse, they hand out prizes to those who do the worst things best!

God Is Kind, But Not Soft

2 Those people are on a dark spiral downward. But if you think that leaves you on the high ground where you can point your finger at others, think again. Every time you criticize someone, you condemn yourself. It takes one to know one. Judgmental criticism of others is a well-known way of escaping detection in your own crimes and misdemeanors. But God isn't so easily diverted. He sees right through all such smoke screens and holds you to what *you've* done.

You didn't think, did you, that just by pointing your finger at others you would distract God from seeing all your misdoings and from coming down on you hard? Or did you think that because he's such a nice God, he'd let you off the hook? Better think this one through from the beginning. God is kind, but he's not soft. In kindness he takes us firmly by the hand and leads us into a radical life change.

KING JAMES VERSION

5 But after thy hardness and impenitent heart treasurest up unto thyself wrath against the day of wrath and revelation of the righteous judgment of God;

6 Who will render to every man according to his deeds:

7 To them who by patient continuance in well doing seek for glory and honour and immortality, eternal life:

8 But unto them that are contentious, and do not obey the truth, but obey unrighteousness, indignation and wrath,

9 Tribulation and anguish, upon every soul of man that doeth evil, of the Jew first, and also of the Gentile;

10 But glory, honour, and peace, to every man that worketh good, to the Jew first, and also to the Gentile:

11 For there is no respect of persons with God.

12 For as many as have sinned without law shall also perish without law: and as many as have sinned in the law shall be judged by the law;

13 (For not the hearers of the law *are* just before God, but the doers of the law shall be justified.

14 For when the Gentiles, which have not the law, do by nature the things contained in the law, these, having not the law, are a law unto themselves:

15 Which shew the work of the law written in their hearts, their conscience also bearing witness, and *their* thoughts the mean while accusing or else excusing one another;)

NEW AMERICAN STANDARD BIBLE

5 But because of your stubbornness and unrepentant heart you are storing up wrath for yourself in the day of wrath and revelation of the righteous judgment of God,

6 WHO WILL RENDER TO EACH PERSON ACCORDING TO HIS DEEDS:

7 to those who by perseverance in doing good seek for glory and honor and immortality, eternal life;

8 but to those who are selfishly ambitious and do not obey the truth, but obey unrighteousness, wrath and indignation.

9 *There will be* tribulation and distress for every soul of man who does evil, of the Jew first and also of the Greek,

10 but glory and honor and peace to everyone who does good, to the Jew first and also to the Greek.

11 For there is no partiality with God.

12 For all who have sinned without the Law will also perish without the Law, and all who have sinned under the Law will be judged by the Law;

13 for *it is* not the hearers of the Law *who* are just before God, but the doers of the Law will be justified.

14 For when Gentiles who do not have the Law do instinctively the things of the Law, these, not having the Law, are a law to themselves,

15 in that they show the work of the Law written in their hearts, their conscience bearing witness and their thoughts alternately accusing or else defending them,

NEW CENTURY VERSION

5But you are stubborn and refuse to change, so you are
making your own punishment even greater on the day he
shows his anger. On that day everyone will see God's right
judgments. 6God will reward or punish every person for
what that person has done. 7Some people, by always con-
tinuing to do good, live for God's glory, for honor, and for
life that has no end. God will give them life forever. 8But
other people are selfish. They refuse to follow truth and,
instead, follow evil. God will give them his punishment
and anger. 9He will give trouble and suffering to everyone
who does evil—to the Jews first and also to those who are
not Jews. 10But he will give glory, honor, and peace to
everyone who does good—to the Jews first and also to
those who are not Jews. 11For God judges all people in the
same way.

12People who do not have the law and who are sinners
will be lost, although they do not have the law. And, in the
same way, those who have the law and are sinners will be
judged by the law. 13Hearing the law does not make people
right with God. It is those who obey the law who will be
right with him. 14(Those who are not Jews do not have the
law, but when they freely do what the law commands, they
are the law for themselves. This is true even though they
do not have the law. 15They show that in their hearts they
know what is right and wrong, just as the law commands.
And they show this by their consciences. Sometimes their
thoughts tell them they did wrong, and sometimes their
thoughts tell them they did right.) 16All these things will

CONTEMPORARY ENGLISH VERSION

5But you are stubborn and refuse to turn to God. So you
are making things even worse for yourselves on that day
when he will show how angry he is and will judge the
world with fairness. 6God will reward each of us for what
we have done. 7He will give eternal life to everyone who
has patiently done what is good in the hope of receiving
glory, honor, and life that lasts forever. 8But he will show
how angry and furious he can be with every selfish person
who rejects the truth and wants to do evil. 9All who are
wicked will be punished with trouble and suffering. It
doesn't matter if they are Jews or Gentiles. 10But all who
do right will be rewarded with glory, honor, and peace,
whether they are Jews or Gentiles. 11God doesn't have any
favorites!

12Those people who don't know about God's Law will
still be punished for what they do wrong. And the Law will
be used to judge everyone who knows what it says. 13God
accepts those who obey his Law, but not those who simply
hear it.

14Some people naturally obey the Law's commands,
even though they don't have the Law. 15This proves that
the conscience is like a law written in the human heart.
And it will show whether we are forgiven or condemned,

NEW INTERNATIONAL VERSION

5 But because of your stubbornness and your unrepentant heart, you are storing up wrath against yourself for the day of God's wrath, when his righteous judgment will be revealed. 6 God "will give to each person according to what he has done."[a] 7 To those who by persistence in doing good seek glory, honor and immortality, he will give eternal life. 8 But for those who are self-seeking and who reject the truth and follow evil, there will be wrath and anger. 9 There will be trouble and distress for every human being who does evil: first for the Jew, then for the Gentile; 10 but glory, honor and peace for everyone who does good: first for the Jew, then for the Gentile. 11 For God does not show favoritism.

12 All who sin apart from the law will also perish apart from the law, and all who sin under the law will be judged by the law. 13 For it is not those who hear the law who are righteous in God's sight, but it is those who obey the law who will be declared righteous. 14 (Indeed, when Gentiles, who do not have the law, do by nature things required by the law, they are a law for themselves, even though they do not have the law, 15 since they show that the requirements of the law are written on their hearts, their consciences also bearing witness, and their thoughts now accusing, now even defending them.) 16 This will take place

a 6 Psalm 62:12; Prov. 24:12

NEW LIVING TRANSLATION

5 But no, you won't listen. So you are storing up terrible punishment for yourself because of your stubbornness in refusing to turn from your sin. For there is going to come a day of judgment when God, the just judge of all the world, 6 will judge all people according to what they have done. 7 He will give eternal life to those who persist in doing what is good, seeking after the glory and honor and immortality that God offers. 8 But he will pour out his anger and wrath on those who live for themselves, who refuse to obey the truth and practice evil deeds. 9 There will be trouble and calamity for everyone who keeps on sinning—for the Jew first and also for the Gentile. 10 But there will be glory and honor and peace from God for all who do good—for the Jew first and also for the Gentile. 11 For God does not show favoritism.

12 God will punish the Gentiles when they sin, even though they never had God's written law. And he will punish the Jews when they sin, for they do have the law. 13 For it is not merely knowing the law that brings God's approval. Those who obey the law will be declared right in God's sight. 14 Even when Gentiles, who do not have God's written law, instinctively follow what the law says, they show that in their hearts they know right from wrong. 15 They demonstrate that God's law is written within them, for their own consciences either accuse them or tell them they are doing what is right. 16 The day will surely come

NEW KING JAMES VERSION

accordance with your hardness and your impenitent heart you are treasuring up for yourself wrath in the day of wrath and revelation of the righteous judgment of God, 6 who *"will render to each one according to his deeds"*:[a] 7 eternal life to those who by patient continuance in doing good seek for glory, honor, and immortality; 8 but to those who are self-seeking and do not obey the truth, but obey unrighteousness—indignation and wrath, 9 tribulation and anguish, on every soul of man who does evil, of the Jew first and also of the Greek; 10 but glory, honor, and peace to everyone who works what is good, to the Jew first and also to the Greek. 11 For there is no partiality with God.

12 For as many as have sinned without law will also perish without law, and as many as have sinned in the law will be judged by the law 13 (for not the hearers of the law *are* just in the sight of God, but the doers of the law will be justified; 14 for when Gentiles, who do not have the law, by nature do the things in the law, these, although not having the law, are a law to themselves, 15 who show the work of the law written in their hearts, their conscience also bearing witness, and between themselves *their* thoughts accusing or else excusing *them*) 16 in the day when God will

2:6 [a] Psalm 62:12; Proverbs 24:12

THE MESSAGE

You're not getting by with anything. Every refusal and avoidance of God adds fuel to the fire. The day is coming when it's going to blaze hot and high, God's fiery and righteous judgment. Make no mistake: In the end you get what's coming to you—*Real Life* for those who work on God's side, but to those who insist on getting their own way and take the path of least resistance, *Fire!*

If you go against the grain, you get splinters, regardless of which neighborhood you're from, what your parents taught you, what schools you attended. But if you embrace the way God does things, there are wonderful payoffs, again without regard to where you are from or how you were brought up. Being a Jew won't give you an automatic stamp of approval. God pays no attention to what others say (or what you think) about you. He makes up his own mind.

If you sin without knowing what you're doing, God takes that into account. But if you sin knowing full well what you're doing, that's a different story entirely. Merely hearing God's law is a waste of your time if you don't do what he commands. Doing, not hearing, is what makes the difference with God.

When outsiders who have never heard of God's law follow it more or less by instinct, they confirm its truth by their obedience. They show that God's law is not something alien, imposed on us from without, but woven into the very fabric of our creation. There is something deep within them that echoes God's yes and no, right and wrong. Their response to God's yes and no will become public knowledge on the day God makes his final decision about every man

KING JAMES VERSION

16 In the day when God shall judge the secrets of men by Jesus Christ according to my gospel.

17 ¶ Behold, thou art called a Jew, and restest in the law, and makest thy boast of God,

18 And knowest *his* will, and approvest the things that are more excellent, being instructed out of the law;

19 And art confident that thou thyself art a guide of the blind, a light of them which are in darkness,

20 An instructor of the foolish, a teacher of babes, which hast the form of knowledge and of the truth in the law.

21 Thou therefore which teachest another, teachest thou not thyself? thou that preachest a man should not steal, dost thou steal?

22 Thou that sayest a man should not commit adultery, dost thou commit adultery? thou that abhorrest idols, dost thou commit sacrilege?

23 Thou that makest thy boast of the law, through breaking the law dishonourest thou God?

24 For the name of God is blasphemed among the Gentiles through you, as it is written.

25 For circumcision verily profiteth, if thou keep the law: but if thou be a breaker of the law, thy circumcision is made uncircumcision.

26 Therefore if the uncircumcision keep the righteousness of the law, shall not his uncircumcision be counted for circumcision?

NEW AMERICAN STANDARD BIBLE

16 on the day when, according to my gospel, God will judge the secrets of men through Christ Jesus.

The Jew Is Condemned by the Law

17 But if you bear the name "Jew" and rely upon the Law and boast in God,

18 and know *His* will and approve the things that are essential, being instructed out of the Law,

19 and are confident that you yourself are a guide to the blind, a light to those who are in darkness,

20 a corrector of the foolish, a teacher of the immature, having in the Law the embodiment of knowledge and of the truth,

21 you, therefore, who teach another, do you not teach yourself? You who preach that one shall not steal, do you steal?

22 You who say that one should not commit adultery, do you commit adultery? You who abhor idols, do you rob temples?

23 You who boast in the Law, through your breaking the Law, do you dishonor God?

24 For "THE NAME OF GOD IS BLASPHEMED AMONG THE GENTILES BECAUSE OF YOU," just as it is written.

25 For indeed circumcision is of value if you practice the Law; but if you are a transgressor of the Law, your circumcision has become uncircumcision.

26 So if the uncircumcised man keeps the requirements of the Law, will not his uncircumcision be regarded as circumcision?

NEW CENTURY VERSION

happen on the day when God, through Christ Jesus, will
judge people's secret thoughts. The Good News that I
preach says this.

The Jews and the Law

17What about you? You call yourself a Jew. You trust in
the law of Moses and brag that you are close to God. 18You
know what he wants you to do and what is important,
because you have learned the law. 19You think you are a
guide for the blind and a light for those who are in dark-
ness. 20You think you can show foolish people what is
right and teach those who know nothing. You have the
law; so you think you know everything and have all truth.
21You teach others, so why don't you teach yourself? You
tell others not to steal, but you steal. 22You say that others
must not take part in adultery, but you are guilty of that
sin. You hate idols, but you steal from temples. 23You brag
about having God's law, but you bring shame to God by
breaking his law, 24just as the Scriptures say: "Those who
are not Jews speak against God's name because of you."[a]
25If you follow the law, your circumcision has meaning.
But if you break the law, it is as if you were never circum-
cised. 26People who are not Jews are not circumcised, but if
they do what the law says, it is as if they were circumcised.

2:24 [a] **"Those...you."** Quotation from Isaiah 52:5; Ezekiel 36:20.

CONTEMPORARY ENGLISH VERSION

16when God has Jesus Christ judge everyone's secret
thoughts, just as my message says.

The Jews and the Law

17Some of you call yourselves Jews. You trust in the Law
and take pride in God. 18By reading the Scriptures you
learn how God wants you to behave, and you discover
what is right. 19You are sure that you are a guide for the
blind and a light for all who are in the dark. 20And since
there is knowledge and truth in God's Law, you think you
can instruct fools and teach young people.
21But how can you teach others when you refuse to
learn? You preach that it is wrong to steal. But do you
steal? 22You say people should be faithful in marriage. But
are you faithful? You hate idols, yet you rob their temples.
23You take pride in the Law, but you disobey the Law and
bring shame to God. 24It is just as the Scriptures tell us,
"You have made foreigners say insulting things about
God."
25Being circumcised is worthwhile, if you obey the Law.
But if you don't obey the Law, you are no better off than
people who are not circumcised. 26In fact, if they obey the
Law, they are as good as anyone who is circumcised. 27So

NEW INTERNATIONAL VERSION

on the day when God will judge men's secrets through
Jesus Christ, as my gospel declares.

The Jews and the Law

17Now you, if you call yourself a Jew; if you rely on the
law and brag about your relationship to God; 18if you
know his will and approve of what is superior because you
are instructed by the law; 19if you are convinced that you
are a guide for the blind, a light for those who are in the
dark, 20an instructor of the foolish, a teacher of infants,
because you have in the law the embodiment of knowledge
and truth— 21you, then, who teach others, do you not
teach yourself? You who preach against stealing, do you
steal? 22You who say that people should not commit adul-
tery, do you commit adultery? You who abhor idols, do you
rob temples? 23You who brag about the law, do you dis-
honor God by breaking the law? 24As it is written: "God's
name is blasphemed among the Gentiles because of you."[b]
25Circumcision has value if you observe the law, but if
you break the law, you have become as though you had not
been circumcised. 26If those who are not circumcised keep
the law's requirements, will they not be regarded as though
they were circumcised? 27The one who is not circumcised

[b] *24* Isaiah 52:5; Ezek. 36:22

NEW LIVING TRANSLATION

when God, by Jesus Christ, will judge everyone's secret life.
This is my message.

The Jews and the Law

17If you are a Jew, you are relying on God's law for your
special relationship with him. You boast that all is well
between yourself and God. 18Yes, you know what he
wants; you know right from wrong because you have been
taught his law. 19You are convinced that you are a guide
for the blind and a beacon light for people who are lost in
darkness without God. 20You think you can instruct the
ignorant and teach children the ways of God. For you are
certain that in God's law you have complete knowledge
and truth.
21Well then, if you teach others, why don't you teach
yourself? You tell others not to steal, but do you steal?
22You say it is wrong to commit adultery, but do you do it?
You condemn idolatry, but do you steal from pagan tem-
ples? 23You are so proud of knowing the law, but you dis-
honor God by breaking it. 24No wonder the Scriptures say,
"The world blasphemes the name of God because of you."*
25The Jewish ceremony of circumcision is worth some-
thing only if you obey God's law. But if you don't obey
God's law, you are no better off than an uncircumcised
Gentile. 26And if the Gentiles obey God's law, won't God give
them all the rights and honors of being his own people? 27In

2:24 Isa 52:5.

NEW KING JAMES VERSION

judge the secrets of men by Jesus Christ, according to my
gospel.

The Jews Guilty as the Gentiles

17Indeed[b] you are called a Jew, and rest on the law, and
make your boast in God, 18and know *His* will, and approve
the things that are excellent, being instructed out of the
law, 19and are confident that you yourself are a guide to
the blind, a light to those who are in darkness, 20an
instructor of the foolish, a teacher of babes, having the
form of knowledge and truth in the law. 21You, therefore,
who teach another, do you not teach yourself? You who
preach that a man should not steal, do you steal? 22You
who say, "Do not commit adultery," do you commit adul-
tery? You who abhor idols, do you rob temples? 23You who
make your boast in the law, do you dishonor God through
breaking the law? 24For *"the name of God is blasphemed
among the Gentiles because of you,"*[c] as it is written.

Circumcision of No Avail

25For circumcision is indeed profitable if you keep the
law; but if you are a breaker of the law, your circumcision
has become uncircumcision. 26Therefore, if an uncircum-
cised man keeps the righteous requirements of the law,
will not his uncircumcision be counted as circumcision?

2:17 [b] NU-Text reads *But if.* 2:24 [c] Isaiah 52:5; Ezekiel 36:22

THE MESSAGE

and woman. The Message from God that I proclaim through Jesus Christ takes into account all these differences.

Religion Can't Save You

If you're brought up Jewish, don't assume that you can lean back in the arms of your religion and take it easy, feeling smug because you're an insider to God's revelation, a connoisseur of the best things of God, informed on the latest doctrines! I have a special word of caution for you who are sure that you have it all together yourselves and, because you know God's revealed Word inside and out, feel qualified to guide others through their blind alleys and dark nights and confused emotions to God. While you are guiding others, who is going to guide you? I'm quite serious. While preaching "Don't steal!" are you going to rob people blind? Who would suspect you? The same with adultery. The same with idolatry. You can get by with almost anything if you front it with eloquent talk about God and his law. The line from Scripture, "It's because of you Jews that the outsiders are down on God," shows it's an old problem that isn't going to go away.

Circumcision, the surgical ritual that marks you as a Jew, is great if you live in accord with God's law. But if you don't, it's worse than not being circumcised. The reverse is also true: The uncircumcised who keep God's ways are as good as the circumcised—in fact, better. Better to keep

KING JAMES VERSION

27 And shall not uncircumcision which is by nature, if
it fulfil the law, judge thee, who by the letter and circumci-
sion dost transgress the law?
28 For he is not a Jew, which is one outwardly; neither
is that circumcision, which is outward in the flesh:
29 But he *is* a Jew, which is one inwardly; and circumci-
sion *is that* of the heart, in the spirit, *and* not in the letter;
whose praise *is* not of men, but of God.
3 What advantage then hath the Jew? or what profit *is*
there of circumcision?
2 Much every way: chiefly, because that unto them were
committed the oracles of God.
3 For what if some did not believe? shall their unbelief
make the faith of God without effect?
4 God forbid: yea, let God be true, but every man a liar;
as it is written, That thou mightest be justified in thy say-
ings, and mightest overcome when thou art judged.
5 But if our unrighteousness commend the righteous-
ness of God, what shall we say? *Is* God unrighteous who
taketh vengeance? (I speak as a man)
6 God forbid: for then how shall God judge the world?

NEW AMERICAN STANDARD BIBLE

27 And he who is physically uncircumcised, if he keeps
the Law, will he not judge you who though having the let-
ter *of the Law* and circumcision are a transgressor of the
Law?
28 For he is not a Jew who is one outwardly, nor is cir-
cumcision that which is outward in the flesh.
29 But he is a Jew who is one inwardly; and circumci-
sion is that which is of the heart, by the Spirit, not by the
letter; and his praise is not from men, but from God.

All the World Guilty

3 Then what advantage has the Jew? Or what is the
benefit of circumcision?
2 Great in every respect. First of all, that they were
entrusted with the oracles of God.
3 What then? If some did not believe, their unbelief
will not nullify the faithfulness of God, will it?
4 May it never be! Rather, let God be found true,
though every man *be found* a liar, as it is written,
"THAT YOU MAY BE JUSTIFIED IN YOUR WORDS,
AND PREVAIL WHEN YOU ARE JUDGED."
5 But if our unrighteousness demonstrates the righ-
teousness of God, what shall we say? The God who inflicts
wrath is not unrighteous, is He? (I am speaking in human
terms.)
6 May it never be! For otherwise, how will God judge
the world?

NEW CENTURY VERSION

27 You Jews have the written law and circumcision, but you
break the law. So those who are not circumcised in their
bodies, but still obey the law, will show that you are guilty.
28 They can do this because a person is not a true Jew if he
is only a Jew in his physical body; true circumcision is not
only on the outside of the body. 29 A person is a Jew only if
he is a Jew inside; true circumcision is done in the heart by
the Spirit, not by the written law. Such a person gets praise
from God rather than from people.
3 So, do Jews have anything that other people do not
have? Is there anything special about being circum-
cised? 2 Yes, of course, there is in every way. The most
important thing is this: God trusted the Jews with his
teachings. 3 If some Jews were not faithful to him, will that
stop God from doing what he promised? 4 No! God will con-
tinue to be true even when every person is false. As the
Scriptures say:
"So you will be shown to be right when you speak,
and you will win your case." *Psalm 51:4*
5 When we do wrong, that shows more clearly that God is
right. So can we say that God is wrong to punish us? (I am
talking as people might talk.) 6 No! If God could not punish
us, he could not judge the world.

CONTEMPORARY ENGLISH VERSION

everyone who obeys the Law, but has never been circum-
cised, will condemn you. Even though you are circumcised
and have the Law, you still don't obey its teachings.
28 Just because you live like a Jew and are circumcised
doesn't make you a real Jew. 29 To be a real Jew you must
obey the Law. True circumcision is something that hap-
pens deep in your heart, not something done to your body.
And besides, you should want praise from God and not
from humans.
3 What good is it to be a Jew? What good is it to be cir-
cumcised? 2 It is good in a lot of ways! First of all,
God's messages were spoken to the Jews. 3 It is true that
some of them did not believe the message. But does this
mean that God cannot be trusted, just because they did not
have faith? 4 No, indeed! God tells the truth, even if every-
one else is a liar. The Scriptures say about God,
"Your words
will be proven true,
and in court
you will win your case."
5 If our evil deeds show how right God is, then what can
we say? Is it wrong for God to become angry and punish us?
What a foolish thing to ask. 6 But the answer is, "No."
Otherwise, how could God judge the world? 7 Since your lies

NEW INTERNATIONAL VERSION

physically and yet obeys the law will condemn you who, even though you have the[c] written code and circumcision, are a lawbreaker.

28A man is not a Jew if he is only one outwardly, nor is circumcision merely outward and physical. 29No, a man is a Jew if he is one inwardly; and circumcision is circumcision of the heart, by the Spirit, not by the written code. Such a man's praise is not from men, but from God.

God's Faithfulness

3 What advantage, then, is there in being a Jew, or what value is there in circumcision? 2Much in every way! First of all, they have been entrusted with the very words of God.

3What if some did not have faith? Will their lack of faith nullify God's faithfulness? 4Not at all! Let God be true, and every man a liar. As it is written:

"So that you may be proved right when you speak
and prevail when you judge."[a]

5But if our unrighteousness brings out God's righteousness more clearly, what shall we say? That God is unjust in bringing his wrath on us? (I am using a human argument.) 6Certainly not! If that were so, how could God judge the

c *27* Or *who, by means of a* a *4* Psalm 51:4

NEW LIVING TRANSLATION

fact, uncircumcised Gentiles who keep God's law will be much better off than you Jews who are circumcised and know so much about God's law but don't obey it.

28For you are not a true Jew just because you were born of Jewish parents or because you have gone through the Jewish ceremony of circumcision. 29No, a true Jew is one whose heart is right with God. And true circumcision is not a cutting of the body but a change of heart produced by God's Spirit. Whoever has that kind of change seeks praise from God, not from people.

God Remains Faithful

3 Then what's the advantage of being a Jew? Is there any value in the Jewish ceremony of circumcision? 2Yes, being a Jew has many advantages. First of all, the Jews were entrusted with the whole revelation of God.*

3True, some of them were unfaithful; but just because they broke their promises, does that mean God will break his promises? 4Of course not! Though everyone else in the world is a liar, God is true. As the Scriptures say, "He will be proved right in what he says, and he will win his case in court."*

5"But," some say, "our sins serve a good purpose, for people will see God's goodness when he declares us sinners to be innocent. Isn't it unfair, then, for God to punish us?" (That is actually the way some people talk.) 6Of course not! If God is not just, how is he qualified to judge the world?

3:2 Greek *the oracles of God.* 3:4 Ps 51:4.

NEW KING JAMES VERSION

27And will not the physically uncircumcised, if he fulfills the law, judge you who, *even* with *your* written *code* and circumcision, *are* a transgressor of the law? 28For he is not a Jew who *is one* outwardly, nor *is* circumcision that which *is* outward in the flesh; 29but *he is* a Jew who *is one* inwardly; and circumcision *is that* of the heart, in the Spirit, not in the letter; whose praise *is* not from men but from God.

God's Judgment Defended

3 What advantage then has the Jew, or what *is* the profit of circumcision? 2Much in every way! Chiefly because to them were committed the oracles of God. 3For what if some did not believe? Will their unbelief make the faithfulness of God without effect? 4Certainly not! Indeed, let God be true but every man a liar. As it is written:

"That You may be justified in Your words,
And may overcome when You are judged."[a]

5But if our unrighteousness demonstrates the righteousness of God, what shall we say? *Is* God unjust who inflicts wrath? (I speak as a man.) 6Certainly not! For then how will God judge the world?

3:4 a Psalm 51:4

THE MESSAGE

God's law uncircumcised than break it circumcised. Don't you see: It's not the cut of a knife that makes a Jew. You become a Jew by who you *are*. It's the mark of God on your heart, not of a knife on your skin, that makes a Jew. And recognition comes from God, not legalistic critics.

✢

3 So what difference does it make who's a Jew and who isn't, who has been trained in God's ways and who hasn't? As it turns out, it makes a lot of difference—but not the difference so many have assumed.

First, there's the matter of being put in charge of writing down and caring for God's revelation, these Holy Scriptures. So, what if, in the course of doing that, some of those Jews abandoned their post? God didn't abandon them. Do you think their faithlessness cancels out his faithfulness? Not on your life! Depend on it: God keeps his word even when the whole world is lying through its teeth. Scripture says the same:

"Your words stand fast and true;
Rejection doesn't faze you."

But if our wrongdoing only underlines and confirms God's rightdoing, shouldn't we be commended for helping out? Since our bad words don't even make a dent in his good words, isn't it wrong of God to back us to the wall and hold us to our word? These questions come up. The answer to such questions is *no*, a most emphatic *No!* How else would things ever get straightened out if *God* didn't do the straightening?

KING JAMES VERSION

7 For if the truth of God hath more abounded through my lie unto his glory; why yet am I also judged as a sinner?

8 And not *rather*, (as we be slanderously reported, and as some affirm that we say,) Let us do evil, that good may come? whose damnation is just.

9 What then? are we better *than they*? No, in no wise: for we have before proved both Jews and Gentiles, that they are all under sin;

10 As it is written, There is none righteous, no, not one:

11 There is none that understandeth, there is none that seeketh after God.

12 They are all gone out of the way, they are together become unprofitable; there is none that doeth good, no, not one.

13 Their throat *is* an open sepulchre; with their tongues they have used deceit; the poison of asps *is* under their lips:

14 Whose mouth *is* full of cursing and bitterness:

NEW AMERICAN STANDARD BIBLE

7 But if through my lie the truth of God abounded to His glory, why am I also still being judged as a sinner?

8 And why not *say* (as we are slanderously reported and as some claim that we say), "Let us do evil that good may come"? Their condemnation is just.

9 What then? Are we better than they? Not at all; for we have already charged that both Jews and Greeks are all under sin;

10 as it is written,

"THERE IS NONE RIGHTEOUS, NOT EVEN ONE;
11 THERE IS NONE WHO UNDERSTANDS,
THERE IS NONE WHO SEEKS FOR GOD;
12 ALL HAVE TURNED ASIDE, TOGETHER THEY HAVE BECOME USELESS;
THERE IS NONE WHO DOES GOOD,
THERE IS NOT EVEN ONE."
13 "THEIR THROAT IS AN OPEN GRAVE,
WITH THEIR TONGUES THEY KEEP DECEIVING,"
"THE POISON OF ASPS IS UNDER THEIR LIPS";
14 "WHOSE MOUTH IS FULL OF CURSING AND BITTERNESS";

NEW CENTURY VERSION

7A person might say, "When I lie, it really gives him glory, because my lie shows God's truth. So why am I judged a sinner?" 8It would be the same to say, "We should do evil so that good will come." Some people find fault with us and say we teach this, but they are wrong and deserve the punishment they will receive.

All People Are Guilty

9So are we Jews better than others? No! We have already said that Jews and those who are not Jews are all guilty of sin. 10As the Scriptures say:

"There is no one who always does what is right,
not even one.
11 There is no one who understands.
There is no one who looks to God for help.
12 All have turned away.
Together, everyone has become useless.
There is no one who does anything good;
there is not even one." *Psalm 14:1–3*
13 "Their throats are like open graves;
they use their tongues for telling lies." *Psalm 5:9*
"Their words are like snake poison." *Psalm 140:3*
14 "Their mouths are full of cursing and hate."
Psalm 10:7

CONTEMPORARY ENGLISH VERSION

bring great honor to God by showing how truthful he is, you may ask why God still says you are a sinner. 8You might as well say, "Let's do something evil, so that something good will come of it!" Some people even claim that we are saying this. But God is fair and will judge them as well.

No One Is Good

9What does all this mean? Does it mean that we Jews are better off[a] than the Gentiles? No, it doesn't! Jews, as well as Gentiles, are ruled by sin, just as I have said. 10The Scriptures tell us,

"No one is acceptable to God!
11 Not one of them understands
or even searches for God.
12 They have all turned away
and are worthless.
There isn't one person
who does right.
13 Their words are like
an open pit,
and their tongues are good
only for telling lies.
Each word is as deadly
as the fangs of a snake,
14 and they say nothing
but bitter curses.

[a] **3.9** *better off*: Or "worse off."

NEW INTERNATIONAL VERSION

world? 7Someone might argue, "If my falsehood enhances
God's truthfulness and so increases his glory, why am I still
condemned as a sinner?" 8Why not say—as we are being
slanderously reported as saying and as some claim that we
say—"Let us do evil that good may result"? Their condem-
nation is deserved.

No One Is Righteous

9What shall we conclude then? Are we any better[b]? Not
at all! We have already made the charge that Jews and
Gentiles alike are all under sin. 10As it is written:

"There is no one righteous, not even one;
11 there is no one who understands,
no one who seeks God.
12 All have turned away,
they have together become worthless;
there is no one who does good,
not even one."[c]
13 "Their throats are open graves;
their tongues practice deceit."[d]
"The poison of vipers is on their lips."[e]
14 "Their mouths are full of cursing and bitterness."[f]

[b] *9* Or *worse* [c] *12* Psalms 14:1–3; 53:1–3; Eccles. 7:20
[d] *13* Psalm 5:9 [e] *13* Psalm 140:3 [f] *14* Psalm 10:7

NEW LIVING TRANSLATION

7"But," some might still argue, "how can God judge and
condemn me as a sinner if my dishonesty highlights his
truthfulness and brings him more glory?" 8If you follow
that kind of thinking, however, you might as well say that
the more we sin the better it is! Those who say such things
deserve to be condemned, yet some slander me by saying
this is what I preach!

All People Are Sinners

9Well then, are we Jews better than others?* No, not at
all, for we have already shown that all people, whether
Jews or Gentiles, are under the power of sin. 10As the
Scriptures say,

"No one is good—
not even one.
11 No one has real understanding;
no one is seeking God.
12 All have turned away from God;
all have gone wrong.
No one does good,
not even one."*
13 "Their talk is foul, like the stench from an open grave.
Their speech is filled with lies."
"The poison of a deadly snake drips from their lips."*
14 "Their mouths are full of cursing and bitterness."*

3:9 Greek *Are we better?* **3:10-12** Pss 14:1-3; 53:1-3.
3:13 Pss 5:9; 140:3. **3:14** Ps 10:7.

NEW KING JAMES VERSION

7For if the truth of God has increased through my lie to
His glory, why am I also still judged as a sinner? 8And *why*
not *say,* "Let us do evil that good may come"?—as we are
slanderously reported and as some affirm that we say.
Their condemnation is just.

All Have Sinned

9What then? Are we better *than they?* Not at all. For we
have previously charged both Jews and Greeks that they
are all under sin.

10As it is written:

"There is none righteous, no, not one;
11 *There is none who understands;*
There is none who seeks after God.
12 *They have all turned aside;*
They have together become unprofitable;
There is none who does good, no, not one."[b]
13 *"Their throat is an open tomb;*
With their tongues they have practiced deceit";[c]
"The poison of asps is under their lips";[d]
14 *"Whose mouth is full of cursing and bitterness."*[e]

3:12 [b] Psalms 14:1–3; 53:1–3; Ecclesiastes 7:20 **3:13** [c] Psalm 5:9
[d] Psalm 140:3 **3:14** [e] Psalm 10:7

THE MESSAGE

It's simply perverse to say, "If my lies serve to show off God's truth all the more gloriously, why blame me? I'm doing God a favor." Some people are actually trying to put such words in our mouths, claiming that we go around saying, "The more evil we do, the more good God does, so let's just do it!" That's pure slander, as I'm sure you'll agree.

We're All in the Same Sinking Boat

So where does that put us? Do we Jews get a better break than the others? Not really. Basically, all of us, whether insiders or outsiders, start out in identical conditions, which is to say that we all start out as sinners. Scripture leaves no doubt about it:

"There's nobody living right, not even one,
nobody who knows the score, nobody alert for God.
They've all taken the wrong turn;
they've all wandered down blind alleys.
No one's living right;
I can't find a single one.
Their throats are gaping graves,
their tongues slick as mud slides.
Every word they speak is tinged with poison.
They open their mouths and pollute the air.

KING JAMES VERSION

15 Their feet *are* swift to shed blood:
16 Destruction and misery *are* in their ways:
17 And the way of peace have they not known:
18 There is no fear of God before their eyes.
19 ¶ Now we know that what things soever the law
saith, it saith to them who are under the law: that every
mouth may be stopped, and all the world may become
guilty before God.
20 Therefore by the deeds of the law there shall no flesh
be justified in his sight: for by the law *is* the knowledge of
sin.
21 But now the righteousness of God without the law is
manifested, being witnessed by the law and the prophets;
22 Even the righteousness of God *which is* by faith of
Jesus Christ unto all and upon all them that believe: for
there is no difference:
23 For all have sinned, and come short of the glory of
God;
24 Being justified freely by his grace through the
redemption that is in Christ Jesus:

NEW AMERICAN STANDARD BIBLE

15 "THEIR FEET ARE SWIFT TO SHED BLOOD,
16 DESTRUCTION AND MISERY ARE IN THEIR PATHS,
17 AND THE PATH OF PEACE THEY HAVE NOT KNOWN."
18 "THERE IS NO FEAR OF GOD BEFORE THEIR EYES."
19 Now we know that whatever the Law says, it speaks
to those who are under the Law, so that every mouth may
be closed and all the world may become accountable to
God;
20 because by the works of the Law no flesh will be jus-
tified in His sight; for through the Law *comes* the knowl-
edge of sin.

Justification by Faith

21 But now apart from the Law *the* righteousness of God
has been manifested, being witnessed by the Law and the
Prophets,
22 even *the* righteousness of God through faith in Jesus
Christ for all those who believe; for there is no distinction;
23 for all have sinned and fall short of the glory of God,
24 being justified as a gift by His grace through the
redemption which is in Christ Jesus;

NEW CENTURY VERSION

15 "They are always ready to kill people.
16 Everywhere they go they cause ruin and misery.
17 They don't know how to live in peace." *Isaiah 59:7–8*
18 "They have no fear of God." *Psalm 36:1*
19 We know that the law's commands are for those who
have the law. This stops all excuses and brings the whole
world under God's judgment, 20 because no one can be
made right with God by following the law. The law only
shows us our sin.

How God Makes People Right

21 But God has a way to make people right with him with-
out the law, and he has now shown us that way which the
law and the prophets told us about. 22 God makes people
right with himself through their faith in Jesus Christ. This
is true for all who believe in Christ, because all people are
the same: 23 All have sinned and are not good enough for
God's glory, 24 and all need to be made right with God by
his grace, which is a free gift. They need to be made free
from sin through Jesus Christ. 25 God gave him as a way to

CONTEMPORARY ENGLISH VERSION

15 These people quickly
become violent.
16 Wherever they go,
they leave ruin
and destruction.
17 They don't know how
to live in peace.
18 They don't even fear God."

19 We know that everything in the Law was written for
those who are under its power. The Law says these things
to stop anyone from making excuses and to let God show
that the whole world is guilty. 20 God doesn't accept people
simply because they obey the Law. No, indeed! All the Law
does is to point out our sin.

God's Way of Accepting People

21 Now we see how God does make us acceptable to him.
The Law and the Prophets[b] tell how we become acceptable,
and it isn't by obeying the Law of Moses. 22 God treats
everyone alike. He accepts people only because they have
faith in Jesus Christ. 23 All of us have sinned and fallen
short of God's glory. 24 But God treats us much better than
we deserve,[c] and because of Christ Jesus, he freely accepts
us and sets us free from our sins. 25-26 God sent Christ to be

[b] **3.21** *The Law and the Prophets*: The Jewish Scriptures, that is, the Old Testament. [c] **3.24** *treats us much better than we deserve*: The Greek word *charis*, traditionally rendered "grace," is translated here and other places in the CEV to express the overwhelming kindness of God.

NEW INTERNATIONAL VERSION

15 "Their feet are swift to shed blood;
16 ruin and misery mark their ways,
17 and the way of peace they do not know."[g]
18 "There is no fear of God before their eyes."[h]

19 Now we know that whatever the law says, it says to
those who are under the law, so that every mouth may be
silenced and the whole world held accountable to God.
20 Therefore no one will be declared righteous in his sight
by observing the law; rather, through the law we become
conscious of sin.

Righteousness Through Faith

21 But now a righteousness from God, apart from law,
has been made known, to which the Law and the Prophets
testify. 22 This righteousness from God comes through faith
in Jesus Christ to all who believe. There is no difference,
23 for all have sinned and fall short of the glory of God,
24 and are justified freely by his grace through the redemp-
tion that came by Christ Jesus. 25 God presented him as a

[g] *17* Isaiah 59:7,8 [h] *18* Psalm 36:1

NEW LIVING TRANSLATION

15 "They are quick to commit murder.
16 Wherever they go, destruction and misery follow
them.
17 They do not know what true peace is."*
18 "They have no fear of God to restrain them."*

19 Obviously, the law applies to those to whom it was
given, for its purpose is to keep people from having
excuses and to bring the entire world into judgment before
God. 20 For no one can ever be made right in God's sight by
doing what his law commands. For the more we know
God's law, the clearer it becomes that we aren't obeying it.

Christ Took Our Punishment

21 But now God has shown us a different way of being
right in his sight—not by obeying the law but by the way
promised in the Scriptures long ago. 22 We are made right
in God's sight when we trust in Jesus Christ to take away
our sins. And we all can be saved in this same way, no
matter who we are or what we have done.

23 For all have sinned; all fall short of God's glorious
standard. 24 Yet now God in his gracious kindness declares
us not guilty. He has done this through Christ Jesus, who
has freed us by taking away our sins. 25 For God sent Jesus

3:15-17 Isa 59:7-8. **3:18** Ps 36:1.

NEW KING JAMES VERSION

15 *"Their feet are swift to shed blood;*
16 *Destruction and misery are in their ways;*
17 *And the way of peace they have not known."*[f]
18 *"There is no fear of God before their eyes."*[g]

19 Now we know that whatever the law says, it says to
those who are under the law, that every mouth may be
stopped, and all the world may become guilty before God.
20 Therefore by the deeds of the law no flesh will be justi-
fied in His sight, for by the law *is* the knowledge of sin.

God's Righteousness Through Faith

21 But now the righteousness of God apart from the law
is revealed, being witnessed by the Law and the Prophets,
22 even the righteousness of God, through faith in Jesus
Christ, to all and on all[h] who believe. For there is no differ-
ence; 23 for all have sinned and fall short of the glory of
God, 24 being justified freely by His grace through the
redemption that is in Christ Jesus, 25 whom God set forth *as*

3:17 [f] Isaiah 59:7, 8 **3:18** [g] Psalm 36:1 **3:22** [h] NU-Text omits *and on all.*

THE MESSAGE

They race for the honor of sinner-of-the-year,
litter the land with heartbreak and ruin,
Don't know the first thing about living with others.
They never give God the time of day."

This makes it clear, doesn't it, that whatever is written in these Scriptures is not what God says *about others* but *to us* to whom these Scriptures were addressed in the first place! And it's clear enough, isn't it, that we're sinners, every one of us, in the same sinking boat with everybody else? Our involvement with God's revelation doesn't put us right with God. What it does is force us to face our complicity in everyone else's sin.

God Has Set Things Right

But in our time something new has been added. What Moses and the prophets witnessed to all those years has happened. The God-setting-things-right that we read about has become Jesus-setting-things-right for us. And not only for us, but for everyone who believes in him. For there is no difference between us and them in this. Since we've compiled this long and sorry record as sinners (both us and them) and proved that we are utterly incapable of living the glorious lives God wills for us, God did it for us. Out of sheer generosity he put us in right standing with himself. A pure gift. He got us out of the mess we're in and restored us to where he always wanted us to be. And he did it by means of Jesus Christ.

KING JAMES VERSION

25 Whom God hath set forth *to be* a propitiation through faith in his blood, to declare his righteousness for the remission of sins that are past, through the forbearance of God;

26 To declare, *I say*, at this time his righteousness: that he might be just, and the justifier of him which believeth in Jesus.

27 Where *is* boasting then? It is excluded. By what law? of works? Nay: but by the law of faith.

28 Therefore we conclude that a man is justified by faith without the deeds of the law.

29 *Is he* the God of the Jews only? *is he* not also of the Gentiles? Yes, of the Gentiles also:

30 Seeing *it is* one God, which shall justify the circumcision by faith, and uncircumcision through faith.

31 Do we then make void the law through faith? God forbid: yea, we establish the law.

NEW AMERICAN STANDARD BIBLE

25 whom God displayed publicly as a propitiation in His blood through faith. *This was* to demonstrate His righteousness, because in the forbearance of God He passed over the sins previously committed;

26 for the demonstration, *I say*, of His righteousness at the present time, so that He would be just and the justifier of the one who has faith in Jesus.

27 Where then is boasting? It is excluded. By what kind of law? Of works? No, but by a law of faith.

28 For we maintain that a man is justified by faith apart from works of the Law.

29 Or is God *the God* of Jews only? Is He not *the God* of Gentiles also? Yes, of Gentiles also,

30 since indeed God who will justify the circumcised by faith and the uncircumcised through faith is one.

31 Do we then nullify the Law through faith? May it never be! On the contrary, we establish the Law.

NEW CENTURY VERSION

forgive sin through faith in the blood of Jesus' death. This
showed that God always does what is right and fair, as in
the past when he was patient and did not punish people for
their sins. [26]And God gave Jesus to show today that he does
what is right. God did this so he could judge rightly and so
he could make right any person who has faith in Jesus.
[27]So do we have a reason to brag about ourselves? No!
And why not? It is the way of faith that stops all bragging,
not the way of trying to obey the law. [28]A person is made
right with God through faith, not through obeying the law.
[29]Is God only the God of the Jews? Is he not also the God of
those who are not Jews? [30]Of course he is, because there is
only one God. He will make Jews right with him by their
faith, and he will also make those who are not Jews right
with him through their faith. [31]So do we destroy the law
by following the way of faith? No! Faith causes us to be
what the law truly wants.

CONTEMPORARY ENGLISH VERSION

our sacrifice. Christ offered his life's blood, so that by faith
in him we could come to God. And God did this to show
that in the past he was right to be patient and forgive sinners. This also shows that God is right when he accepts
people who have faith in Jesus.
[27]What is left for us to brag about? Not a thing! Is it
because we obeyed some law? No! It is because of faith.
[28]We see that people are acceptable to God because they
have faith, and not because they obey the Law. [29]Does God
belong only to the Jews? Isn't he also the God of the
Gentiles? Yes, he is! [30]There is only one God, and he
accepts Gentiles as well as Jews, simply because of their
faith. [31]Do we destroy the Law by our faith? Not at all! We
make it even more powerful.

NEW INTERNATIONAL VERSION

sacrifice of atonement,[i] through faith in his blood. He did this to demonstrate his justice, because in his forbearance he had left the sins committed beforehand unpunished—[26]he did it to demonstrate his justice at the present time, so as to be just and the one who justifies those who have faith in Jesus.

[27]Where, then, is boasting? It is excluded. On what principle? On that of observing the law? No, but on that of faith. [28]For we maintain that a man is justified by faith apart from observing the law. [29]Is God the God of Jews only? Is he not the God of Gentiles too? Yes, of Gentiles too, [30]since there is only one God, who will justify the circumcised by faith and the uncircumcised through that same faith. [31]Do we, then, nullify the law by this faith? Not at all! Rather, we uphold the law.

[i] *25* Or *as the one who would turn aside his wrath, taking away sin*

NEW LIVING TRANSLATION

to take the punishment for our sins and to satisfy God's anger against us. We are made right with God when we believe that Jesus shed his blood, sacrificing his life for us. God was being entirely fair and just when he did not punish those who sinned in former times. [26]And he is entirely fair and just in this present time when he declares sinners to be right in his sight because they believe in Jesus.

[27]Can we boast, then, that we have done anything to be accepted by God? No, because our acquittal is not based on our good deeds. It is based on our faith. [28]So we are made right with God through faith and not by obeying the law.

[29]After all, God is not the God of the Jews only, is he? Isn't he also the God of the Gentiles? Of course he is. [30]There is only one God, and there is only one way of being accepted by him. He makes people right with himself only by faith, whether they are Jews or Gentiles. [31]Well then, if we emphasize faith, does this mean that we can forget about the law? Of course not! In fact, only when we have faith do we truly fulfill the law.

NEW KING JAMES VERSION

a propitiation by His blood, through faith, to demonstrate His righteousness, because in His forbearance God had passed over the sins that were previously committed, [26]to demonstrate at the present time His righteousness, that He might be just and the justifier of the one who has faith in Jesus.

Boasting Excluded

[27]Where *is* boasting then? It is excluded. By what law? Of works? No, but by the law of faith. [28]Therefore we conclude that a man is justified by faith apart from the deeds of the law. [29]Or *is He* the God of the Jews only? *Is He* not also the God of the Gentiles? Yes, of the Gentiles also, [30]since *there is* one God who will justify the circumcised by faith and the uncircumcised through faith. [31]Do we then make void the law through faith? Certainly not! On the contrary, we establish the law.

THE MESSAGE

God sacrificed Jesus on the altar of the world to clear that world of sin. Having faith in him sets us in the clear. God decided on this course of action in full view of the public—to set the world in the clear with himself through the sacrifice of Jesus, finally taking care of the sins he had so patiently endured. This is not only clear, but it's *now*—this is current history! God sets things right. He also makes it possible for us to live in his rightness.

So where does that leave our proud Jewish insider claims and counterclaims? Canceled? Yes, canceled. What we've learned is this: God does not respond to what *we* do; we respond to what *God* does. We've finally figured it out. Our lives get in step with God and all others by letting him set the pace, not by proudly or anxiously trying to run the parade.

And where does that leave our proud Jewish claim of having a corner on God? Also canceled. God is the God of outsider non-Jews as well as insider Jews. How could it be otherwise since there is only one God? God sets right all who welcome his action and enter into it, both those who follow our religious system and those who have never heard of our religion.

But by shifting our focus from what *we* do to what *God* does, don't we cancel out all our careful keeping of the rules and ways God commanded? Not at all. What happens, in fact, is that by putting that entire way of life in its proper place, we confirm it.

KING JAMES VERSION

4 What shall we say then that Abraham our father, as pertaining to the flesh, hath found?
2 For if Abraham were justified by works, he hath *whereof* to glory; but not before God.
3 For what saith the scripture? Abraham believed God, and it was counted unto him for righteousness.
4 Now to him that worketh is the reward not reckoned of grace, but of debt.
5 But to him that worketh not, but believeth on him that justifieth the ungodly, his faith is counted for righteousness.
6 Even as David also describeth the blessedness of the man, unto whom God imputeth righteousness without works,
7 *Saying*, Blessed *are* they whose iniquities are forgiven, and whose sins are covered.
8 Blessed *is* the man to whom the Lord will not impute sin.
9 ¶ *Cometh* this blessedness then upon the circumcision

NEW AMERICAN STANDARD BIBLE

Justification by Faith Evidenced in Old Testament

4 What then shall we say that Abraham, our forefather according to the flesh, has found?
2 For if Abraham was justified by works, he has something to boast about, but not before God.
3 For what does the Scripture say? "ABRAHAM BELIEVED GOD, AND IT WAS CREDITED TO HIM AS RIGHTEOUSNESS."
4 Now to the one who works, his wage is not credited as a favor, but as what is due.
5 But to the one who does not work, but believes in Him who justifies the ungodly, his faith is credited as righteousness,
6 just as David also speaks of the blessing on the man to whom God credits righteousness apart from works:
7 "BLESSED ARE THOSE WHOSE LAWLESS DEEDS HAVE BEEN
FORGIVEN,
AND WHOSE SINS HAVE BEEN COVERED.
8 "BLESSED IS THE MAN WHOSE SIN THE LORD WILL NOT TAKE
INTO ACCOUNT."
9 Is this blessing then on the circumcised, or on the

NEW CENTURY VERSION

The Example of Abraham

4 So what can we say that Abraham,[a] the father of our people, learned about faith? [2]If Abraham was made right by the things he did, he had a reason to brag. But this is not God's view, [3]because the Scripture says, "Abraham believed God, and God accepted Abraham's faith, and that faith made him right with God."[b]

[4]When people work, their pay is not given as a gift, but as something earned. [5]But people cannot do any work that will make them right with God. So they must trust in him, who makes even evil people right in his sight. Then God accepts their faith, and that makes them right with him. [6]David said the same thing. He said that people are truly blessed when God, without paying attention to good deeds, makes people right with himself.

[7]"Happy are they
whose sins are forgiven,
whose wrongs are pardoned.
[8]Happy is the person
whom the Lord does not consider guilty." *Psalm 32:1–2*

[9]Is this blessing only for those who are circumcised or also for those who are not circumcised? We have already said

4:1 [a] **Abraham** Most respected ancestor of the Jews. Every Jew hoped to see Abraham. 4:3 [b] **"Abraham...God."** Quotation from Genesis 15:6.

CONTEMPORARY ENGLISH VERSION

The Example of Abraham

4 Well then, what can we say about our ancestor Abraham? [2]If he became acceptable to God because of what he did, then he would have something to brag about. But he would never be able to brag about it to God. [3]The Scriptures say, "God accepted Abraham because Abraham had faith in him."

[4]Money paid to workers isn't a gift. It is something they earn by working. [5]But you cannot make God accept you because of something you do. God accepts sinners only because they have faith in him. [6]In the Scriptures David talks about the blessings that come to people who are acceptable to God, even though they don't do anything to deserve these blessings. David says,

[7]"God blesses people
whose sins are forgiven
and whose evil deeds
are forgotten.
[8]The Lord blesses people
whose sins are erased
from his book."

[9]Are these blessings meant for circumcised people or for those who are not circumcised? Well, the Scriptures say

NEW INTERNATIONAL VERSION

Abraham Justified by Faith

4 What then shall we say that Abraham, our forefather,
discovered in this matter? [2]If, in fact, Abraham was
justified by works, he had something to boast about—but
not before God. [3]What does the Scripture say? "Abraham
believed God, and it was credited to him as righteous-
ness."[a]

[4]Now when a man works, his wages are not credited to
him as a gift, but as an obligation. [5]However, to the man
who does not work but trusts God who justifies the
wicked, his faith is credited as righteousness. [6]David says
the same thing when he speaks of the blessedness of the
man to whom God credits righteousness apart from works:

[7]"Blessed are they
whose transgressions are forgiven,
whose sins are covered.
[8]Blessed is the man
whose sin the Lord will never count against him."[b]

[9]Is this blessedness only for the circumcised, or also for

[a] *3* Gen. 15:6; also in verse 22 [b] *8* Psalm 32:1,2

NEW LIVING TRANSLATION

The Faith of Abraham

4 Abraham was, humanly speaking, the founder of our
Jewish nation. What were his experiences concerning
this question of being saved by faith? [2]Was it because of
his good deeds that God accepted him? If so, he would
have had something to boast about. But from God's point
of view Abraham had no basis at all for pride. [3]For the
Scriptures tell us, "Abraham believed God, so God declared
him to be righteous."*

[4]When people work, their wages are not a gift. Workers
earn what they receive. [5]But people are declared righteous
because of their faith, not because of their work.

[6]King David spoke of this, describing the happiness of
an undeserving sinner who is declared to be righteous:

7 "Oh, what joy for those whose disobedience is forgiven,
whose sins are put out of sight.
8 Yes, what joy for those
whose sin is no longer counted against them by the
Lord."*

[9]Now then, is this blessing only for the Jews, or is it for

4:3 Gen 15:6. **4:7-8** Ps 32:1-2.

NEW KING JAMES VERSION

Abraham Justified by Faith

4 What then shall we say that Abraham our father has
found according to the flesh?[a] [2]For if Abraham was jus-
tified by works, he has *something* to boast about, but not
before God. [3]For what does the Scripture say? *"Abraham
believed God, and it was accounted to him for righteous-
ness."*[b] [4]Now to him who works, the wages are not counted
as grace but as debt.

David Celebrates the Same Truth

[5]But to him who does not work but believes on Him who
justifies the ungodly, his faith is accounted for righteous-
ness, [6]just as David also describes the blessedness of the
man to whom God imputes righteousness apart from
works:

7 *"Blessed are those whose lawless deeds are forgiven,
And whose sins are covered;*
8 *Blessed is the man to whom the* L*ORD shall not
impute sin."*[c]

Abraham Justified Before Circumcision

[9]*Does* this blessedness then *come* upon the circumcised
only, or upon the uncircumcised also? For we say that

4:1 [a] Or *Abraham our (fore)father according to the flesh has found?*
4:3 [b] Genesis 15:6 **4:8** [c] Psalm 32:1, 2

THE MESSAGE

Trusting God

4 So how do we fit what we know of Abraham, our first
father in the faith, into this new way of looking at
things? If Abraham, by what he *did* for God, got God to
approve him, he could certainly have taken credit for it.
But the story we're given is a God-story, not an Abraham-
story. What we read in Scripture is, "Abraham entered into
what God was doing for him, and *that* was the turning
point. He trusted God to set him right instead of trying to
be right on his own."

If you're a hard worker and do a good job, you deserve
your pay; we don't call your wages a gift. But if you see
that the job is too big for you, that it's something only *God*
can do, and you trust him to do it—you could never do it
for yourself no matter how hard and long you worked—
well, that trusting-him-to-do-it is what gets you set right
with God, *by* God. Sheer gift.

David confirms this way of looking at it, saying that the
one who trusts God to do the putting-everything-right with-
out insisting on having a say in it is one fortunate man:

"Fortunate those whose crimes are carted off,
whose sins are wiped clean from the slate.
Fortunate the person against
whom the Lord does not keep score."

Do you think for a minute that this blessing is only pro-
nounced over those of us who keep our religious ways and
are circumcised? Or do you think it possible that the blessing

KING JAMES VERSION

only, or upon the uncircumcision also? for we say that faith was reckoned to Abraham for righteousness.

10 How was it then reckoned? when he was in circumcision, or in uncircumcision? Not in circumcision, but in uncircumcision.

11 And he received the sign of circumcision, a seal of the righteousness of the faith which *he had yet* being uncircumcised: that he might be the father of all them that believe, though they be not circumcised; that righteousness might be imputed unto them also:

12 And the father of circumcision to them who are not of the circumcision only, but who also walk in the steps of that faith of our father Abraham, which *he had* being *yet* uncircumcised.

13 For the promise, that he should be the heir of the world, *was* not to Abraham, or to his seed, through the law, but through the righteousness of faith.

14 For if they which are of the law *be* heirs, faith is made void, and the promise made of none effect:

NEW AMERICAN STANDARD BIBLE

uncircumcised also? For we say, "FAITH WAS CREDITED TO ABRAHAM AS RIGHTEOUSNESS."

10 How then was it credited? While he was circumcised, or uncircumcised? Not while circumcised, but while uncircumcised;

11 and he received the sign of circumcision, a seal of the righteousness of the faith which he had while uncircumcised, so that he might be the father of all who believe without being circumcised, that righteousness might be credited to them,

12 and the father of circumcision to those who not only are of the circumcision, but who also follow in the steps of the faith of our father Abraham which he had while uncircumcised.

13 For the promise to Abraham or to his descendants that he would be heir of the world was not through the Law, but through the righteousness of faith.

14 For if those who are of the Law are heirs, faith is made void and the promise is nullified;

NEW CENTURY VERSION

that God accepted Abraham's faith and that faith made
him right with God. 10So how did this happen? Did God
accept Abraham before or after he was circumcised? It was
before his circumcision. 11Abraham was circumcised to
show that he was right with God through faith before he
was circumcised. So Abraham is the father of all those
who believe but are not circumcised; he is the father of all
believers who are accepted as being right with God. 12And
Abraham is also the father of those who have been circumcised and who live following the faith that our father
Abraham had before he was circumcised.

God Keeps His Promise

13Abraham[c] and his descendants received the promise
that they would get the whole world. He did not receive
that promise through the law, but through being right with
God by his faith. 14If people could receive what God promised by following the law, then faith is worthless. And
God's promise to Abraham is worthless, 15because the law

4:13 [c] **Abraham** Most respected ancestor of the Jews. Every Jew hoped to see Abraham.

CONTEMPORARY ENGLISH VERSION

that God accepted Abraham because Abraham had faith in
him. 10But when did this happen? Was it before or after
Abraham was circumcised? Of course, it was before.

11Abraham let himself be circumcised to show that he
had been accepted because of his faith even before he was
circumcised. This makes Abraham the father of all who are
acceptable to God because of their faith, even though they
are not circumcised. 12This also makes Abraham the father
of everyone who is circumcised and has faith in God, as
Abraham did before he was circumcised.

The Promise Is for All Who Have Faith

13God promised Abraham and his descendants that he
would give them the world. This promise wasn't made
because Abraham had obeyed a law, but because his faith
in God made him acceptable. 14If Abraham and his descendants were given this promise because they had obeyed a
law, then faith would mean nothing, and the promise
would be worthless.

NEW INTERNATIONAL VERSION

the uncircumcised? We have been saying that Abraham's
faith was credited to him as righteousness. 10Under what
circumstances was it credited? Was it after he was circum-
cised, or before? It was not after, but before! 11And he
received the sign of circumcision, a seal of the righteous-
ness that he had by faith while he was still uncircumcised.
So then, he is the father of all who believe but have not
been circumcised, in order that righteousness might be
credited to them. 12And he is also the father of the circum-
cised who not only are circumcised but who also walk in
the footsteps of the faith that our father Abraham had
before he was circumcised.
13It was not through law that Abraham and his offspring
received the promise that he would be heir of the world,
but through the righteousness that comes by faith. 14For if
those who live by law are heirs, faith has no value and the

NEW LIVING TRANSLATION

Gentiles, too? Well, what about Abraham? We have been
saying he was declared righteous by God because of his
faith. 10But how did his faith help him? Was he declared
righteous only after he had been circumcised, or was it
before he was circumcised? The answer is that God accept-
ed him first, and then he was circumcised later!
11The circumcision ceremony was a sign that Abraham
already had faith and that God had already accepted him
and declared him to be righteous—even before he was cir-
cumcised. So Abraham is the spiritual father of those who
have faith but have not been circumcised. They are made
right with God by faith. 12And Abraham is also the spiritu-
al father of those who have been circumcised, but only if
they have the same kind of faith Abraham had before he
was circumcised.
13It is clear, then, that God's promise to give the whole
earth to Abraham and his descendants was not based on
obedience to God's law, but on the new relationship with
God that comes by faith. 14So if you claim that God's
promise is for those who obey God's law and think they
are "good enough" in God's sight, then you are saying that
faith is useless. And in that case, the promise is also

NEW KING JAMES VERSION

faith was accounted to Abraham for righteousness. 10How
then was it accounted? While he was circumcised, or
uncircumcised? Not while circumcised, but while uncir-
cumcised. 11And he received the sign of circumcision, a
seal of the righteousness of the faith which *he had while
still* uncircumcised, that he might be the father of all those
who believe, though they are uncircumcised, that righ-
teousness might be imputed to them also, 12and the father
of circumcision to those who not only *are* of the circumci-
sion, but who also walk in the steps of the faith which our
father Abraham *had while still* uncircumcised.

The Promise Granted Through Faith

13For the promise that he would be the heir of the world
was not to Abraham or to his seed through the law, but
through the righteousness of faith. 14For if those who are
of the law *are* heirs, faith is made void and the promise

THE MESSAGE

could be given to those who never even heard of our ways, who were never brought up in the disciplines of God? We all agree, don't we, that it was by embracing what God did for him that Abraham was declared fit before God?

Now *think*: Was that declaration made before or after he was marked by the covenant rite of circumcision? That's right, *before* he was marked. That means that he underwent circumcision as evidence and confirmation of what God had done long before to bring him into this acceptable standing with himself, an act of God he had embraced with his whole life.

And it means further that Abraham is father of *all* people who embrace what God does for them while they are still on the "outs" with God, as yet unidentified as God's, in an "uncircumcised" condition. It is precisely these people in this condition who are called "set right by God and with God"! Abraham is also, of course, father of those who have undergone the religious rite of circumcision *not* just because of the ritual but because they were willing to live in the risky faith-embrace of God's action for them, the way Abraham lived long before he was marked by circumcision.

That famous promise God gave Abraham—that he and his children would possess the earth—was not given because of something Abraham did or would do. It was based on God's decision to put everything together for him, which Abraham then entered when he believed. If those who get what God gives them only get it by doing everything they are told to do and filling out all the right forms properly signed, that eliminates personal trust completely

KING JAMES VERSION

15 Because the law worketh wrath: for where no law is, *there is* no transgression.

16 Therefore *it is* of faith, that *it might be* by grace; to the end the promise might be sure to all the seed; not to that only which is of the law, but to that also which is of the faith of Abraham; who is the father of us all,

17 ¶ (As it is written, I have made thee a father of many nations,) before him whom he believed, *even* God, who quickeneth the dead, and calleth those things which be not as though they were.

18 Who against hope believed in hope, that he might become the father of many nations; according to that which was spoken, So shall thy seed be.

19 And being not weak in faith, he considered not his own body now dead, when he was about an hundred years old, neither yet the deadness of Sara's womb:

NEW AMERICAN STANDARD BIBLE

15 for the Law brings about wrath, but where there is no law, there also is no violation.

16 For this reason *it is* by faith, in order that *it may be* in accordance with grace, so that the promise will be guaranteed to all the descendants, not only to those who are of the Law, but also to those who are of the faith of Abraham, who is the father of us all,

17 (as it is written, "A FATHER OF MANY NATIONS HAVE I MADE YOU") in the presence of Him whom he believed, *even* God, who gives life to the dead and calls into being that which does not exist.

18 In hope against hope he believed, so that he might become a father of many nations according to that which had been spoken, "SO SHALL YOUR DESCENDANTS BE."

19 Without becoming weak in faith he contemplated his own body, now as good as dead since he was about a hundred years old, and the deadness of Sarah's womb;

NEW CENTURY VERSION

can only bring God's anger. But if there is no law, there is nothing to disobey.

16So people receive God's promise by having faith. This happens so the promise can be a free gift. Then all of Abraham's children can have that promise. It is not only for those who live under the law of Moses but for anyone who lives with faith like that of Abraham, who is the father of us all. 17As it is written in the Scriptures: "I am making you a father of many nations."[d] This is true before God, the God Abraham believed, the God who gives life to the dead and who creates something out of nothing.

18There was no hope that Abraham would have children. But Abraham believed God and continued hoping, and so he became the father of many nations. As God told him, "Your descendants also will be too many to count."[e] 19Abraham was almost a hundred years old, much past the age for having children, and Sarah could not have children. Abraham thought about all this, but his faith in God

4:17 [d] **"I...nations."** Quotation from Genesis 17:5.
4:18 [e] **"Your...count."** Quotation from Genesis 15:5.

CONTEMPORARY ENGLISH VERSION

15God becomes angry when his Law is broken. But where there isn't a law, it cannot be broken. 16Everything depends on having faith in God, so that God's promise is assured by his great kindness. This promise isn't only for Abraham's descendants who have the Law. It is for all who are Abraham's descendants because they have faith, just as he did. Abraham is the ancestor of us all. 17The Scriptures say that Abraham would become the ancestor of many nations. This promise was made to Abraham because he had faith in God, who raises the dead to life and creates new things.

18God promised Abraham a lot of descendants. And when it all seemed hopeless, Abraham still had faith in God and became the ancestor of many nations. 19Abraham's faith never became weak, not even when he was nearly a hundred years old. He knew that he was almost dead and that his wife Sarah could not have children.

NEW INTERNATIONAL VERSION

promise is worthless, 15because law brings wrath. And where there is no law there is no transgression.

16Therefore, the promise comes by faith, so that it may be by grace and may be guaranteed to all Abraham's offspring—not only to those who are of the law but also to those who are of the faith of Abraham. He is the father of us all. 17As it is written: "I have made you a father of many nations."[c] He is our father in the sight of God, in whom he believed—the God who gives life to the dead and calls things that are not as though they were.

18Against all hope, Abraham in hope believed and so became the father of many nations, just as it had been said to him, "So shall your offspring be."[d] 19Without weakening in his faith, he faced the fact that his body was as good as dead—since he was about a hundred years old—and that Sarah's womb was also dead. 20Yet he did

[c] *17* Gen. 17:5 [d] *18* Gen. 15:5

NEW LIVING TRANSLATION

meaningless. 15But the law brings punishment on those who try to obey it. (The only way to avoid breaking the law is to have no law to break!)

16So that's why faith is the key! God's promise is given to us as a free gift. And we are certain to receive it, whether or not we follow Jewish customs, if we have faith like Abraham's. For Abraham is the father of all who believe. 17That is what the Scriptures mean when God told him, "I have made you the father of many nations."* This happened because Abraham believed in the God who brings the dead back to life and who brings into existence what didn't exist before.

18When God promised Abraham that he would become the father of many nations, Abraham believed him. God had also said, "Your descendants will be as numerous as the stars,"* even though such a promise seemed utterly impossible! 19And Abraham's faith did not weaken, even though he knew that he was too old to be a father at the age of one hundred and that Sarah, his wife, had never been able to have children.

4:17 Gen 17:5. **4:18** Gen 15:5.

NEW KING JAMES VERSION

made of no effect, 15because the law brings about wrath; for where there is no law *there is* no transgression.

16Therefore *it is* of faith that *it might be* according to grace, so that the promise might be sure to all the seed, not only to those who are of the law, but also to those who are of the faith of Abraham, who is the father of us all 17(as it is written, *"I have made you a father of many nations"*[d]) in the presence of Him whom he believed—God, who gives life to the dead and calls those things which do not exist as though they did; 18who, contrary to hope, in hope believed, so that he became the father of many nations, according to what was spoken, *"So shall your descendants be."*[e] 19And not being weak in faith, he did not consider his own body, already dead (since he was about a hundred years old), and the deadness of Sarah's

4:17 [d] Genesis 17:5 **4:18** [e] Genesis 15:5

THE MESSAGE

and turns the promise into an ironclad *contract*! That's not a holy promise; that's a business deal. A contract drawn up by a hard-nosed lawyer and with plenty of fine print only makes sure that you will never be able to collect. But if there is no contract in the first place, simply a *promise*—and God's promise at that—you can't break it.

This is why the fulfillment of God's promise depends entirely on trusting God and his way, and then simply embracing him and what he does. God's promise arrives as pure gift. That's the only way everyone can be sure to get in on it, those who keep the religious traditions *and* those who have never heard of them. For Abraham is father of us all. He is not our racial father—that's reading the story backwards. He is our *faith* father.

We call Abraham "father" not because he got God's attention by living like a saint, but because God made something out of Abraham when he was a nobody. Isn't that what we've always read in Scripture, God saying to Abraham, "I set you up as father of many peoples"? Abraham was first named "father" and then *became* a father because he dared to trust God to do what only God could do: raise the dead to life, with a word make something out of nothing. When everything was hopeless, Abraham believed anyway, deciding to live not on the basis of what he saw he *couldn't* do but on what God said he *would* do. And so he was made father of a multitude of peoples. God himself said to him, "You're going to have a big family, Abraham!"

Abraham didn't focus on his own impotence and say, "It's hopeless. This hundred-year-old body could never

KING JAMES VERSION

20 He staggered not at the promise of God through unbelief; but was strong in faith, giving glory to God;

21 And being fully persuaded that, what he had promised, he was able also to perform.

22 And therefore it was imputed to him for righteousness.

23 ¶ Now it was not written for his sake alone, that it was imputed to him;

24 But for us also, to whom it shall be imputed, if we believe on him that raised up Jesus our Lord from the dead;

25 Who was delivered for our offences, and was raised again for our justification.

5 Therefore being justified by faith, we have peace with God through our Lord Jesus Christ:

2 By whom also we have access by faith into this grace wherein we stand, and rejoice in hope of the glory of God.

3 And not only *so*, but we glory in tribulations also: knowing that tribulation worketh patience;

4 And patience, experience; and experience, hope:

NEW AMERICAN STANDARD BIBLE

20 yet, with respect to the promise of God, he did not waver in unbelief but grew strong in faith, giving glory to God,

21 and being fully assured that what God had promised, He was able also to perform.

22 Therefore IT WAS ALSO CREDITED TO HIM AS RIGHTEOUSNESS.

23 Now not for his sake only was it written that it was credited to him,

24 but for our sake also, to whom it will be credited, as those who believe in Him who raised Jesus our Lord from the dead,

25 *He* who was delivered over because of our transgressions, and was raised because of our justification.

Results of Justification

5 Therefore, having been justified by faith, we have peace with God through our Lord Jesus Christ,

2 through whom also we have obtained our introduction by faith into this grace in which we stand; and we exult in hope of the glory of God.

3 And not only this, but we also exult in our tribulations, knowing that tribulation brings about perseverance;

4 and perseverance, proven character; and proven character, hope;

NEW CENTURY VERSION

did not become weak. 20He never doubted that God would
keep his promise, and he never stopped believing. He grew
stronger in his faith and gave praise to God. 21Abraham
felt sure that God was able to do what he had promised.
22So, "God accepted Abraham's faith, and that faith made
him right with God."[f] 23Those words ("God accepted
Abraham's faith") were written not only for Abraham 24but
also for us. God will accept us also because we believe in
the One who raised Jesus our Lord from the dead. 25Jesus
was given to die for our sins, and he was raised from the
dead to make us right with God.

Right with God

5 Since we have been made right with God by our faith,
we have peace with God. This happened through our
Lord Jesus Christ, 2who has brought us into that blessing
of God's grace that we now enjoy. And we are happy
because of the hope we have of sharing God's glory. 3We
also have joy with our troubles, because we know that
these troubles produce patience. 4And patience produces
character, and character produces hope. 5And this hope

4:22 [f] "God…God." Quotation from Genesis 15:6.

CONTEMPORARY ENGLISH VERSION

20But Abraham never doubted or questioned God's promise. His faith made him strong, and he gave all the credit
to God.
21Abraham was certain that God could do what he had
promised. 22So God accepted him, 23just as we read in the
Scriptures. But these words were not written only for
Abraham. 24They were written for us, since we will also be
accepted because of our faith in God, who raised our Lord
Jesus to life. 25God gave Jesus to die for our sins, and he
raised him to life, so that we would be made acceptable to
God.

What It Means To Be Acceptable to God

5 By faith we have been made acceptable to God. And
now, because of our Lord Jesus Christ, we live at
peace[a] with God. 2Christ has also introduced us[b] to God's
undeserved kindness on which we take our stand. So we
are happy, as we look forward to sharing in the glory of
God. 3But that's not all! We gladly suffer,[c] because we
know that suffering helps us to endure. 4And endurance
builds character, which gives us a hope 5that will never

[a] 5.1 *we live at peace*: Some manuscripts have "let us live at peace."
[b] 5.2 *introduced us*: Some manuscripts add "by faith." [c] 5.3 *We gladly suffer*: Or "Let us gladly suffer."

NEW INTERNATIONAL VERSION

not waver through unbelief regarding the promise of God,
but was strengthened in his faith and gave glory to God,
[21]being fully persuaded that God had power to do what he
had promised. [22]This is why "it was credited to him as
righteousness." [23]The words "it was credited to him" were
written not for him alone, [24]but also for us, to whom God
will credit righteousness—for us who believe in him who
raised Jesus our Lord from the dead. [25]He was delivered
over to death for our sins and was raised to life for our jus-
tification.

Peace and Joy

5 Therefore, since we have been justified through faith,
we[a] have peace with God through our Lord Jesus
Christ, [2]through whom we have gained access by faith into
this grace in which we now stand. And we[a] rejoice in the
hope of the glory of God. [3]Not only so, but we[a] also rejoice
in our sufferings, because we know that suffering produces
perseverance; [4]perseverance, character; and character,

[a] *1,2,3* Or *let us*

NEW LIVING TRANSLATION

[20]Abraham never wavered in believing God's promise. In
fact, his faith grew stronger, and in this he brought glory
to God. [21]He was absolutely convinced that God was able
to do anything he promised. [22]And because of Abraham's
faith, God declared him to be righteous.

[23]Now this wonderful truth—that God declared him to
be righteous—wasn't just for Abraham's benefit. [24]It was
for us, too, assuring us that God will also declare us to be
righteous if we believe in God, who brought Jesus our Lord
back from the dead. [25]He was handed over to die because
of our sins, and he was raised from the dead to make us
right with God.

Faith Brings Joy

5 Therefore, since we have been made right in God's
sight by faith, we have peace with God because of
what Jesus Christ our Lord has done for us. [2]Because of
our faith, Christ has brought us into this place of highest
privilege where we now stand, and we confidently and joy-
fully look forward to sharing God's glory.

[3]We can rejoice, too, when we run into problems and
trials, for we know that they are good for us—they help
us learn to endure. [4]And endurance develops strength of
character in us, and character strengthens our confident
expectation of salvation. [5]And this expectation will not

NEW KING JAMES VERSION

womb. [20]He did not waver at the promise of God through
unbelief, but was strengthened in faith, giving glory to
God, [21]and being fully convinced that what He had prom-
ised He was also able to perform. [22]And therefore *"it was
accounted to him for righteousness."*[f]

[23]Now it was not written for his sake alone that it was
imputed to him, [24]but also for us. It shall be imputed to us
who believe in Him who raised up Jesus our Lord from the
dead, [25]who was delivered up because of our offenses, and
was raised because of our justification.

Faith Triumphs in Trouble

5 Therefore, having been justified by faith, we have[a]
peace with God through our Lord Jesus Christ,
[2]through whom also we have access by faith into this
grace in which we stand, and rejoice in hope of the glory of
God. [3]And not only *that,* but we also glory in tribulations,
knowing that tribulation produces perseverance; [4]and per-
severance, character; and character, hope. [5]Now hope does

4:22 [f] Genesis 15:6   5:1 [a] Another ancient reading is, *let us have
peace.*

THE MESSAGE

father a child." Nor did he survey Sarah's decades of infer-
tility and give up. He didn't tiptoe around God's promise
asking cautiously skeptical questions. He plunged into the
promise and came up strong, ready for God, sure that God
would make good on what he had said. That's why it is
said, "Abraham was declared fit before God by trusting
God to set him right." But it's not just Abraham; it's also
us! The same thing gets said about us when we embrace
and believe the One who brought Jesus to life when the
conditions were equally hopeless. The sacrificed Jesus
made us fit for God, set us *right with God.*

Developing Patience

5 By entering through faith into what God has always
wanted to do for us—set us right with him, make us
fit for him—we have it all together with God because of
our Master Jesus. And that's not all: We throw open our
doors to God and discover at the same moment that he has
already thrown open his door to us. We find ourselves
standing where we always hoped we might stand—out in
the wide open spaces of God's grace and glory, standing
tall and shouting our praise.

There's more to come: We continue to shout our praise
even when we're hemmed in with troubles, because we
know how troubles can develop passionate patience in us,
and how that patience in turn forges the tempered steel of
virtue, keeping us alert for whatever God will do next. In
alert expectancy such as this, we're never left feeling short-
changed. Quite the contrary—we can't round up enough

KING JAMES VERSION

5 And hope maketh not ashamed; because the love of God is shed abroad in our hearts by the Holy Ghost which is given unto us.

6 ¶ For when we were yet without strength, in due time Christ died for the ungodly.

7 For scarcely for a righteous man will one die: yet peradventure for a good man some would even dare to die.

8 But God commendeth his love toward us, in that, while we were yet sinners, Christ died for us.

9 Much more then, being now justified by his blood, we shall be saved from wrath through him.

10 For if, when we were enemies, we were reconciled to God by the death of his Son, much more, being reconciled, we shall be saved by his life.

11 And not only *so*, but we also joy in God through our Lord Jesus Christ, by whom we have now received the atonement.

12 Wherefore, as by one man sin entered into the world, and death by sin; and so death passed upon all men, for that all have sinned:

13 (For until the law sin was in the world: but sin is not imputed when there is no law.

NEW AMERICAN STANDARD BIBLE

5 and hope does not disappoint, because the love of God has been poured out within our hearts through the Holy Spirit who was given to us.

6 For while we were still helpless, at the right time Christ died for the ungodly.

7 For one will hardly die for a righteous man; though perhaps for the good man someone would dare even to die.

8 But God demonstrates His own love toward us, in that while we were yet sinners, Christ died for us.

9 Much more then, having now been justified by His blood, we shall be saved from the wrath *of God* through Him.

10 For if while we were enemies we were reconciled to God through the death of His Son, much more, having been reconciled, we shall be saved by His life.

11 And not only this, but we also exult in God through our Lord Jesus Christ, through whom we have now received the reconciliation.

12 Therefore, just as through one man sin entered into the world, and death through sin, and so death spread to all men, because all sinned—

13 for until the Law sin was in the world, but sin is not imputed when there is no law.

NEW CENTURY VERSION

will never disappoint us, because God has poured out his love to fill our hearts. He gave us his love through the Holy Spirit, whom God has given to us.

6When we were unable to help ourselves, at the moment of our need, Christ died for us, although we were living against God. 7Very few people will die to save the life of someone else. Although perhaps for a good person someone might possibly die. 8But God shows his great love for us in this way: Christ died for us while we were still sinners.

9So through Christ we will surely be saved from God's anger, because we have been made right with God by the blood of Christ's death. 10While we were God's enemies, he made friends with us through the death of his Son. Surely, now that we are his friends, he will save us through his Son's life. 11And not only that, but now we are also very happy in God through our Lord Jesus Christ. Through him we are now God's friends again.

Adam and Christ Compared

12Sin came into the world because of what one man did, and with sin came death. This is why everyone must die—because everyone sinned. 13Sin was in the world before the law of Moses, but sin is not counted against us as breaking a command when there is no law. 14But from the time

CONTEMPORARY ENGLISH VERSION

disappoint us. All of this happens because God has given us the Holy Spirit, who fills our hearts with his love.

6Christ died for us at a time when we were helpless and sinful. 7No one is really willing to die for an honest person, though someone might be willing to die for a truly good person. 8But God showed how much he loved us by having Christ die for us, even though we were sinful.

9But there is more! Now that God has accepted us because Christ sacrificed his life's blood, we will also be kept safe from God's anger. 10Even when we were God's enemies, he made peace with us, because his Son died for us. Yet something even greater than friendship is ours. Now that we are at peace with God, we will be saved by his Son's life. 11And in addition to everything else, we are happy because God sent our Lord Jesus Christ to make peace with us.

Adam and Christ

12Adam sinned, and that sin brought death into the world. Now everyone has sinned, and so everyone must die. 13Sin was in the world before the Law came. But no record of sin was kept, because there was no Law. 14Yet

NEW INTERNATIONAL VERSION

hope. 5And hope does not disappoint us, because God has poured out his love into our hearts by the Holy Spirit, whom he has given us.

6You see, at just the right time, when we were still powerless, Christ died for the ungodly. 7Very rarely will anyone die for a righteous man, though for a good man someone might possibly dare to die. 8But God demonstrates his own love for us in this: While we were still sinners, Christ died for us.

9Since we have now been justified by his blood, how much more shall we be saved from God's wrath through him! 10For if, when we were God's enemies, we were reconciled to him through the death of his Son, how much more, having been reconciled, shall we be saved through his life! 11Not only is this so, but we also rejoice in God through our Lord Jesus Christ, through whom we have now received reconciliation.

Death Through Adam, Life Through Christ

12Therefore, just as sin entered the world through one man, and death through sin, and in this way death came to all men, because all sinned— 13for before the law was given, sin was in the world. But sin is not taken into account when there is no law. 14Nevertheless, death

NEW LIVING TRANSLATION

disappoint us. For we know how dearly God loves us, because he has given us the Holy Spirit to fill our hearts with his love.

6When we were utterly helpless, Christ came at just the right time and died for us sinners. 7Now, no one is likely to die for a good person, though someone might be willing to die for a person who is especially good. 8But God showed his great love for us by sending Christ to die for us while we were still sinners. 9And since we have been made right in God's sight by the blood of Christ, he will certainly save us from God's judgment. 10For since we were restored to friendship with God by the death of his Son while we were still his enemies, we will certainly be delivered from eternal punishment by his life. 11So now we can rejoice in our wonderful new relationship with God—all because of what our Lord Jesus Christ has done for us in making us friends of God.

Adam and Christ Contrasted

12When Adam sinned, sin entered the entire human race. Adam's sin brought death, so death spread to everyone, for everyone sinned. 13Yes, people sinned even before the law was given. And though there was no law to break, since it had not yet been given, 14they all died anyway—

NEW KING JAMES VERSION

not disappoint, because the love of God has been poured out in our hearts by the Holy Spirit who was given to us.

Christ in Our Place

6For when we were still without strength, in due time Christ died for the ungodly. 7For scarcely for a righteous man will one die; yet perhaps for a good man someone would even dare to die. 8But God demonstrates His own love toward us, in that while we were still sinners, Christ died for us. 9Much more then, having now been justified by His blood, we shall be saved from wrath through Him. 10For if when we were enemies we were reconciled to God through the death of His Son, much more, having been reconciled, we shall be saved by His life. 11And not only *that,* but we also rejoice in God through our Lord Jesus Christ, through whom we have now received the reconciliation.

Death in Adam, Life in Christ

12Therefore, just as through one man sin entered the world, and death through sin, and thus death spread to all men, because all sinned— 13(For until the law sin was in the world, but sin is not imputed when there is no law.

THE MESSAGE

containers to hold everything God generously pours into our lives through the Holy Spirit!

Christ arrives right on time to make this happen. He didn't, and doesn't, wait for us to get ready. He presented himself for this sacrificial death when we were far too weak and rebellious to do anything to get ourselves ready. And even if we hadn't been so weak, we wouldn't have known what to do anyway. We can understand someone dying for a person worth dying for, and we can understand how someone good and noble could inspire us to selfless sacrifice. But God put his love on the line for us by offering his Son in sacrificial death while we were of no use whatever to him.

Now that we are set right with God by means of this sacrificial death, the consummate blood sacrifice, there is no longer a question of being at odds with God in any way. If, when we were at our worst, we were put on friendly terms with God by the sacrificial death of his Son, now that we're at our best, just think of how our lives will expand and deepen by means of his resurrection life! Now that we have actually received this amazing friendship with God, we are no longer content to simply say it in plodding prose. We sing and shout our praises to God through Jesus, the Messiah!

The Death-Dealing Sin, The Life-Giving Gift

You know the story of how Adam landed us in the dilemma we're in—first sin, then death, and no one exempt from either sin or death. That sin disturbed relations with God in everything and everyone, but the extent of the disturbance was not clear until God spelled it out in detail to Moses. So

KING JAMES VERSION

14 Nevertheless death reigned from Adam to Moses, even over them that had not sinned after the similitude of Adam's transgression, who is the figure of him that was to come.

15 But not as the offence, so also *is* the free gift. For if through the offence of one many be dead, much more the grace of God, and the gift by grace, *which is* by one man, Jesus Christ, hath abounded unto many.

16 And not as *it was* by one that sinned, *so is* the gift: for the judgment *was* by one to condemnation, but the free gift *is* of many offences unto justification.

17 For if by one man's offence death reigned by one; much more they which receive abundance of grace and of the gift of righteousness shall reign in life by one, Jesus Christ.)

18 Therefore as by the offence of one *judgment came* upon all men to condemnation; even so by the righteousness of one *the free gift came* upon all men unto justification of life.

19 For as by one man's disobedience many were made sinners, so by the obedience of one shall many be made righteous.

20 Moreover the law entered, that the offence might abound. But where sin abounded, grace did much more abound:

NEW AMERICAN STANDARD BIBLE

14 Nevertheless death reigned from Adam until Moses, even over those who had not sinned in the likeness of the offense of Adam, who is a [1]type of Him who was to come.

15 But the free gift is not like the transgression. For if by the transgression of the one the many died, much more did the grace of God and the gift by the grace of the one Man, Jesus Christ, abound to the many.

16 The gift is not like *that which came* through the one who sinned; for on the one hand the judgment *arose* from one *transgression* resulting in condemnation, but on the other hand the free gift *arose* from many transgressions resulting in justification.

17 For if by the transgression of the one, death reigned through the one, much more those who receive the abundance of grace and of the gift of righteousness will reign in life through the One, Jesus Christ.

18 So then as through one transgression there resulted condemnation to all men, even so through one act of righteousness there resulted justification of life to all men.

19 For as through the one man's disobedience the many were made sinners, even so through the obedience of the One the many will be made righteous.

20 The Law came in so that the transgression would increase; but where sin increased, grace abounded all the more,

5:14 [1] Or *foreshadowing*

NEW CENTURY VERSION

of Adam to the time of Moses, everyone had to die, even
those who had not sinned by breaking a command, as
Adam had.
Adam was like the One who was coming in the future.
15 But God's free gift is not like Adam's sin. Many people
died because of the sin of that one man. But the grace
from God was much greater; many people received God's
gift of life by the grace of the one man, Jesus Christ.
16 After Adam sinned once, he was judged guilty. But the
gift of God is different. God's free gift came after many
sins, and it makes people right with God. 17 One man
sinned, and so death ruled all people because of that one
man. But now those people who accept God's full grace
and the great gift of being made right with him will surely
have true life and rule through the one man, Jesus Christ.
18 So as one sin of Adam brought the punishment of
death to all people, one good act that Christ did makes all
people right with God. And that brings true life for all.
19 One man disobeyed God, and many became sinners. In
the same way, one man obeyed God, and many will be
made right. 20 The law came to make sin worse. But when
sin grew worse, God's grace increased. 21 Sin once used

CONTEMPORARY ENGLISH VERSION

death still had power over all who lived from the time of
Adam to the time of Moses. This happened, though not
everyone disobeyed a direct command from God, as Adam
did.
In some ways Adam is like Christ who came later. 15 But
the gift that God was kind enough to give was very different from Adam's sin. That one sin brought death to many
others. Yet in an even greater way, Jesus Christ alone
brought God's gift of kindness to many people.
16 There is a lot of difference between Adam's sin and
God's gift. That one sin led to punishment. But God's gift
made it possible for us to be acceptable to him, even
though we have sinned many times. 17 Death ruled like a
king because Adam had sinned. But that cannot compare
with what Jesus Christ has done. God has been so kind to
us, and he has accepted us because of Jesus. And so we
will live and rule like kings.
18 Everyone was going to be punished because Adam
sinned. But because of the good thing that Christ has
done, God accepts us and gives us the gift of life. 19 Adam
disobeyed God and caused many others to be sinners. But
Jesus obeyed him and will make many people acceptable to
God.
20 The Law came, so that the full power of sin could be
seen. Yet where sin was powerful, God's kindness was even

NEW INTERNATIONAL VERSION

reigned from the time of Adam to the time of Moses, even
over those who did not sin by breaking a command, as did
Adam, who was a pattern of the one to come.
15 But the gift is not like the trespass. For if the many
died by the trespass of the one man, how much more did
God's grace and the gift that came by the grace of the one
man, Jesus Christ, overflow to the many! 16 Again, the gift
of God is not like the result of the one man's sin: The judg-
ment followed one sin and brought condemnation, but the
gift followed many trespasses and brought justification.
17 For if, by the trespass of the one man, death reigned
through that one man, how much more will those who
receive God's abundant provision of grace and of the gift of
righteousness reign in life through the one man, Jesus
Christ.
18 Consequently, just as the result of one trespass was
condemnation for all men, so also the result of one act of
righteousness was justification that brings life for all men.
19 For just as through the disobedience of the one man the
many were made sinners, so also through the obedience of
the one man the many will be made righteous.
20 The law was added so that the trespass might
increase. But where sin increased, grace increased all the

NEW LIVING TRANSLATION

even though they did not disobey an explicit command-
ment of God, as Adam did. What a contrast between Adam
and Christ, who was yet to come! 15 And what a difference
between our sin and God's generous gift of forgiveness.
For this one man, Adam, brought death to many through
his sin. But this other man, Jesus Christ, brought forgive-
ness to many through God's bountiful gift. 16 And the
result of God's gracious gift is very different from the
result of that one man's sin. For Adam's sin led to con-
demnation, but we have the free gift of being accepted by
God, even though we are guilty of many sins. 17 The sin of
this one man, Adam, caused death to rule over us, but all
who receive God's wonderful, gracious gift of righteous-
ness will live in triumph over sin and death through this
one man, Jesus Christ.
18 Yes, Adam's one sin brought condemnation upon
everyone, but Christ's one act of righteousness makes all
people right in God's sight and gives them life. 19 Because
one person disobeyed God, many people became sinners.
But because one other person obeyed God, many people
will be made right in God's sight.
20 God's law was given so that all people could see how
sinful they were. But as people sinned more and more,
God's wonderful kindness became more abundant. 21 So

NEW KING JAMES VERSION

14 Nevertheless death reigned from Adam to Moses, even
over those who had not sinned according to the likeness of
the transgression of Adam, who is a type of Him who was
to come. 15 But the free gift *is* not like the offense. For if by
the one man's offense many died, much more the grace of
God and the gift by the grace of the one Man, Jesus Christ,
abounded to many. 16 And the gift *is* not like *that which*
came through the one who sinned. For the judgment *which*
came from one *offense resulted* in condemnation, but the
free gift *which came* from many offenses *resulted* in justifi-
cation. 17 For if by the one man's offense death reigned
through the one, much more those who receive abundance
of grace and of the gift of righteousness will reign in life
through the One, Jesus Christ.)
18 Therefore, as through one man's offense *judgment*
came to all men, resulting in condemnation, even so
through one Man's righteous act *the free gift came* to all
men, resulting in justification of life. 19 For as by one
man's disobedience many were made sinners, so also by
one Man's obedience many will be made righteous.
20 Moreover the law entered that the offense might
abound. But where sin abounded, grace abounded much

THE MESSAGE

death, this huge abyss separating us from God, dominated the landscape from Adam to Moses. Even those who didn't sin precisely as Adam did by disobeying a specific command of God still had to experience this termination of life, this separation from God. But Adam, who got us into this, also points ahead to the One who will get us out of it.

Yet the rescuing gift is not exactly parallel to the death-dealing sin. If one man's sin put crowds of people at the dead-end abyss of separation from God, just think what God's gift poured through one man, Jesus Christ, will do! There's no comparison between that death-dealing sin and this generous, life-giving gift. The verdict on that one sin was the death sentence; the verdict on the many sins that followed was this wonderful life sentence. If death got the upper hand through one man's wrongdoing, can you imagine the breathtaking recovery life makes, sovereign life, in those who grasp with both hands this wildly extravagant life-gift, this grand setting-everything-right, that the one man Jesus Christ provides?

Here it is in a nutshell: Just as one person did it wrong and got us in all this trouble with sin and death, another person did it right and got us out of it. But more than just getting us out of trouble, he got us into life! One man said no to God and put many people in the wrong; one man said yes to God and put many in the right.

All that passing laws against sin did was produce more lawbreakers. But sin didn't, and doesn't, have a chance in competition with the aggressive forgiveness we call *grace*. When it's sin versus grace, grace wins hands down. All sin

KING JAMES VERSION

21 That as sin hath reigned unto death, even so might grace reign through righteousness unto eternal life by Jesus Christ our Lord.

6 What shall we say then? Shall we continue in sin, that grace may abound?

2 God forbid. How shall we, that are dead to sin, live any longer therein?

3 Know ye not, that so many of us as were baptized into Jesus Christ were baptized into his death?

4 Therefore we are buried with him by baptism into death: that like as Christ was raised up from the dead by the glory of the Father, even so we also should walk in newness of life.

5 For if we have been planted together in the likeness of his death, we shall be also *in the likeness* of *his* resurrection:

6 Knowing this, that our old man is crucified with *him*, that the body of sin might be destroyed, that henceforth we should not serve sin.

7 For he that is dead is freed from sin.

8 Now if we be dead with Christ, we believe that we shall also live with him:

9 Knowing that Christ being raised from the dead dieth no more; death hath no more dominion over him.

10 For in that he died, he died unto sin once: but in that he liveth, he liveth unto God.

NEW AMERICAN STANDARD BIBLE

21 so that, as sin reigned in death, even so grace would reign through righteousness to eternal life through Jesus Christ our Lord.

Believers Are Dead to Sin, Alive to God

6 What shall we say then? Are we to continue in sin so that grace may increase?

2 May it never be! How shall we who died to sin still live in it?

3 Or do you not know that all of us who have been baptized into Christ Jesus have been baptized into His death?

4 Therefore we have been buried with Him through baptism into death, so that as Christ was raised from the dead through the glory of the Father, so we too might walk in newness of life.

5 For if we have become united with *Him* in the likeness of His death, certainly we shall also be *in the likeness* of His resurrection,

6 knowing this, that our old self was crucified with *Him,* in order that our body of sin might be done away with, so that we would no longer be slaves to sin;

7 for he who has died is freed from sin.

8 Now if we have died with Christ, we believe that we shall also live with Him,

9 knowing that Christ, having been raised from the dead, is never to die again; death no longer is master over Him.

10 For the death that He died, He died to sin once for all; but the life that He lives, He lives to God.

NEW CENTURY VERSION

death to rule us, but God gave people more of his grace so that grace could rule by making people right with him. And this brings life forever through Jesus Christ our Lord.

Dead to Sin but Alive in Christ

6 So do you think we should continue sinning so that
God will give us even more grace? 2No! We died to our
old sinful lives, so how can we continue living with sin?
3Did you forget that all of us became part of Christ when
we were baptized? We shared his death in our baptism.
4When we were baptized, we were buried with Christ and
shared his death. So, just as Christ was raised from the
dead by the wonderful power of the Father, we also can
live a new life.
5Christ died, and we have been joined with him by dying
too. So we will also be joined with him by rising from the
dead as he did. 6We know that our old life died with Christ
on the cross so that our sinful selves would have no power
over us and we would not be slaves to sin. 7Anyone who
has died is made free from sin's control.
8If we died with Christ, we know we will also live with
him. 9Christ was raised from the dead, and we know that
he cannot die again. Death has no power over him now.
10Yes, when Christ died, he died to defeat the power of sin
one time—enough for all time. He now has a new life, and
his new life is with God. 11In the same way, you should

CONTEMPORARY ENGLISH VERSION

more powerful. 21Sin ruled by means of death. But God's
kindness now rules, and God has accepted us because of
Jesus Christ our Lord. This means that we will have eternal
life.

Dead to Sin but Alive because of Christ

6 What should we say? Should we keep on sinning, so
that God's wonderful kindness will show up even bet-
ter? 2No, we should not! If we are dead to sin, how can we
go on sinning? 3Don't you know that all who share in
Christ Jesus by being baptized also share in his death?
4When we were baptized, we died and were buried with
Christ. We were baptized, so that we would live a new life,
as Christ was raised to life by the glory of God the Father.
5If we shared in Jesus' death by being baptized, we will
be raised to life with him. 6We know that the persons we
used to be were nailed to the cross with Jesus. This was
done, so that our sinful bodies would no longer be the
slaves of sin. 7We know that sin doesn't have power over
dead people.
8As surely as we died with Christ, we believe we will
also live with him. 9We know that death no longer has any
power over Christ. He died and was raised to life, never
again to die. 10When Christ died, he died for sin once and
for all. But now he is alive, and he lives only for God. 11In

NEW INTERNATIONAL VERSION

more, [21]so that, just as sin reigned in death, so also grace might reign through righteousness to bring eternal life through Jesus Christ our Lord.

Dead to Sin, Alive in Christ

6 What shall we say, then? Shall we go on sinning so that grace may increase? [2]By no means! We died to sin; how can we live in it any longer? [3]Or don't you know that all of us who were baptized into Christ Jesus were baptized into his death? [4]We were therefore buried with him through baptism into death in order that, just as Christ was raised from the dead through the glory of the Father, we too may live a new life.

[5]If we have been united with him like this in his death, we will certainly also be united with him in his resurrection. [6]For we know that our old self was crucified with him so that the body of sin might be done away with,[a] that we should no longer be slaves to sin— [7]because anyone who has died has been freed from sin.

[8]Now if we died with Christ, we believe that we will also live with him. [9]For we know that since Christ was raised from the dead, he cannot die again; death no longer has mastery over him. [10]The death he died, he died to sin once for all; but the life he lives, he lives to God.

[a] 6 Or *be rendered powerless*

NEW LIVING TRANSLATION

just as sin ruled over all people and brought them to death, now God's wonderful kindness rules instead, giving us right standing with God and resulting in eternal life through Jesus Christ our Lord.

Sin's Power Is Broken

6 Well then, should we keep on sinning so that God can show us more and more kindness and forgiveness? [2]Of course not! Since we have died to sin, how can we continue to live in it? [3]Or have you forgotten that when we became Christians and were baptized to become one with Christ Jesus, we died with him? [4]For we died and were buried with Christ by baptism. And just as Christ was raised from the dead by the glorious power of the Father, now we also may live new lives.

[5]Since we have been united with him in his death, we will also be raised as he was. [6]Our old sinful selves were crucified with Christ so that sin might lose its power in our lives. We are no longer slaves to sin. [7]For when we died with Christ we were set free from the power of sin. [8]And since we died with Christ, we know we will also share his new life. [9]We are sure of this because Christ rose from the dead, and he will never die again. Death no longer has any power over him. [10]He died once to defeat sin, and now he lives for the glory of God. [11]So you should consider your-

NEW KING JAMES VERSION

more, [21]so that as sin reigned in death, even so grace might reign through righteousness to eternal life through Jesus Christ our Lord.

Dead to Sin, Alive to God

6 What shall we say then? Shall we continue in sin that grace may abound? [2]Certainly not! How shall we who died to sin live any longer in it? [3]Or do you not know that as many of us as were baptized into Christ Jesus were baptized into His death? [4]Therefore we were buried with Him through baptism into death, that just as Christ was raised from the dead by the glory of the Father, even so we also should walk in newness of life.

[5]For if we have been united together in the likeness of His death, certainly we also shall be *in the likeness* of *His* resurrection, [6]knowing this, that our old man was crucified with *Him,* that the body of sin might be done away with, that we should no longer be slaves of sin. [7]For he who has died has been freed from sin. [8]Now if we died with Christ, we believe that we shall also live with Him, [9]knowing that Christ, having been raised from the dead, dies no more. Death no longer has dominion over Him. [10]For *the death* that He died, He died to sin once for all; but *the life* that He lives, He lives to God. [11]Likewise you

THE MESSAGE

can do is threaten us with death, and that's the end of it. Grace, because God is putting everything together again through the Messiah, invites us into life—a life that goes on and on and on, world without end.

When Death Becomes Life

6 So what do we do? Keep on sinning so God can keep on forgiving? I should hope not! If we've left the country where sin is sovereign, how can we still live in our old house there? Or didn't you realize we packed up and left there for good? That is what happened in baptism. When we went under the water, we left the old country of sin behind; when we came up out of the water, we entered into the new country of grace—a new life in a new land!

That's what baptism into the life of Jesus means. When we are lowered into the water, it is like the burial of Jesus; when we are raised up out of the water, it is like the resurrection of Jesus. Each of us is raised into a light-filled world by our Father so that we can see where we're going in our new grace-sovereign country.

Could it be any clearer? Our old way of life was nailed to the Cross with Christ, a decisive end to that sin-miserable life—no longer at sin's every beck and call! What we believe is this: If we get included in Christ's sin-conquering death, we also get included in his life-saving resurrection. We know that when Jesus was raised from the dead it was a signal of the end of death-as-the-end. Never again will death have the last word. When Jesus died, he took sin down with him, but alive he brings God down to us. From

KING JAMES VERSION

11 Likewise reckon ye also yourselves to be dead indeed unto sin, but alive unto God through Jesus Christ our Lord.

12 Let not sin therefore reign in your mortal body, that ye should obey it in the lusts thereof.

13 Neither yield ye your members *as* instruments of unrighteousness unto sin: but yield yourselves unto God, as those that are alive from the dead, and your members *as* instruments of righteousness unto God.

14 For sin shall not have dominion over you: for ye are not under the law, but under grace.

15 What then? shall we sin, because we are not under the law, but under grace? God forbid.

16 Know ye not, that to whom ye yield yourselves servants to obey, his servants ye are to whom ye obey; whether of sin unto death, or of obedience unto righteousness?

17 But God be thanked, that ye were the servants of sin, but ye have obeyed from the heart that form of doctrine which was delivered you.

18 Being then made free from sin, ye became the servants of righteousness.

19 I speak after the manner of men because of the infirmity of your flesh: for as ye have yielded your members servants to uncleanness and to iniquity unto iniquity; even so now yield your members servants to righteousness unto holiness.

NEW AMERICAN STANDARD BIBLE

11 Even so consider yourselves to be dead to sin, but alive to God in Christ Jesus.

12 Therefore do not let sin reign in your mortal body so that you obey its lusts,

13 and do not go on presenting the members of your body to sin *as* instruments of unrighteousness; but present yourselves to God as those alive from the dead, and your members *as* instruments of righteousness to God.

14 For sin shall not be master over you, for you are not under law but under grace.

15 What then? Shall we sin because we are not under law but under grace? May it never be!

16 Do you not know that when you present yourselves to someone *as* slaves for obedience, you are slaves of the one whom you obey, either of sin resulting in death, or of obedience resulting in righteousness?

17 But thanks be to God that though you were slaves of sin, you became obedient from the heart to that form of teaching to which you were committed,

18 and having been freed from sin, you became slaves of righteousness.

19 I am speaking in human terms because of the weakness of your flesh. For just as you presented your members as slaves to impurity and to lawlessness, resulting in *further* lawlessness, so now present your members as slaves to righteousness, resulting in sanctification.

NEW CENTURY VERSION

see yourselves as being dead to the power of sin and alive with God through Christ Jesus.

12So, do not let sin control your life here on earth so that you do what your sinful self wants to do. 13Do not offer the parts of your body to serve sin, as things to be used in doing evil. Instead, offer yourselves to God as people who have died and now live. Offer the parts of your body to God to be used in doing good. 14Sin will not be your master, because you are not under law but under God's grace.

Be Slaves of Righteousness

15So what should we do? Should we sin because we are under grace and not under law? No! 16Surely you know that when you give yourselves like slaves to obey someone, then you are really slaves of that person. The person you obey is your master. You can follow sin, which brings spiritual death, or you can obey God, which makes you right with him. 17In the past you were slaves to sin—sin controlled you. But thank God, you fully obeyed the things that you were taught. 18You were made free from sin, and now you are slaves to goodness. 19I use this example because this is hard for you to understand. In the past you offered the parts of your body to be slaves to sin and evil; you lived only for evil. In the same way now you must give yourselves to be slaves of goodness. Then you will live only for God.

CONTEMPORARY ENGLISH VERSION

the same way, you must think of yourselves as dead to the power of sin. But Christ Jesus has given life to you, and you live for God.

12Don't let sin rule your body. After all, your body is bound to die, so don't obey its desires 13or let any part of it become a slave of evil. Give yourselves to God, as people who have been raised from death to life. Make every part of your body a slave that pleases God. 14Don't let sin keep ruling your lives. You are ruled by God's kindness and not by the Law.

Slaves Who Do What Pleases God

15What does all this mean? Does it mean we are free to sin, because we are ruled by God's wonderful kindness and not by the Law? Certainly not! 16Don't you know that you are slaves of anyone you obey? You can be slaves of sin and die, or you can be obedient slaves of God and be acceptable to him. 17You used to be slaves of sin. But I thank God that with all your heart you obeyed the teaching you received from me. 18Now you are set free from sin and are slaves who please God.

19I am using these everyday examples, because in some ways you are still weak. You used to let the different parts of your body be slaves of your evil thoughts. But now you must make every part of your body serve God, so that you will belong completely to him.

NEW INTERNATIONAL VERSION

11 In the same way, count yourselves dead to sin but
alive to God in Christ Jesus. 12 Therefore do not let sin reign
in your mortal body so that you obey its evil desires. 13 Do
not offer the parts of your body to sin, as instruments of
wickedness, but rather offer yourselves to God, as those
who have been brought from death to life; and offer the
parts of your body to him as instruments of righteousness.
14 For sin shall not be your master, because you are not
under law, but under grace.

Slaves to Righteousness

15 What then? Shall we sin because we are not under law
but under grace? By no means! 16 Don't you know that
when you offer yourselves to someone to obey him as
slaves, you are slaves to the one whom you obey—whether
you are slaves to sin, which leads to death, or to obedi-
ence, which leads to righteousness? 17 But thanks be to
God that, though you used to be slaves to sin, you whole-
heartedly obeyed the form of teaching to which you were
entrusted. 18 You have been set free from sin and have
become slaves to righteousness.

19 I put this in human terms because you are weak in
your natural selves. Just as you used to offer the parts of
your body in slavery to impurity and to ever-increasing
wickedness, so now offer them in slavery to righteousness

NEW LIVING TRANSLATION

selves dead to sin and able to live for the glory of God
through Christ Jesus.

12 Do not let sin control the way you live;* do not give in
to its lustful desires. 13 Do not let any part of your body
become a tool of wickedness, to be used for sinning.
Instead, give yourselves completely to God since you have
been given new life. And use your whole body as a tool to
do what is right for the glory of God. 14 Sin is no longer your
master, for you are no longer subject to the law, which
enslaves you to sin. Instead, you are free by God's grace.

Freedom to Obey God

15 So since God's grace has set us free from the law, does
this mean we can go on sinning? Of course not! 16 Don't
you realize that whatever you choose to obey becomes
your master? You can choose sin, which leads to death, or
you can choose to obey God and receive his approval.
17 Thank God! Once you were slaves of sin, but now you
have obeyed with all your heart the new teaching God has
given you. 18 Now you are free from sin, your old master,
and you have become slaves to your new master, righ-
teousness.

19 I speak this way, using the illustration of slaves and
masters, because it is easy to understand. Before, you let
yourselves be slaves of impurity and lawlessness. Now you
must choose to be slaves of righteousness so that you will
become holy.

6:12 Or *Do not let sin reign in your body, which is subject to death.*

NEW KING JAMES VERSION

also, reckon yourselves to be dead indeed to sin, but alive
to God in Christ Jesus our Lord.

12 Therefore do not let sin reign in your mortal body, that
you should obey it in its lusts. 13 And do not present your
members *as* instruments of unrighteousness to sin, but
present yourselves to God as being alive from the dead,
and your members *as* instruments of righteousness to God.
14 For sin shall not have dominion over you, for you are not
under law but under grace.

From Slaves of Sin to Slaves of God

15 What then? Shall we sin because we are not under law
but under grace? Certainly not! 16 Do you not know that to
whom you present yourselves slaves to obey, you are that
one's slaves whom you obey, whether of sin *leading* to
death, or of obedience *leading* to righteousness? 17 But God
be thanked that *though* you were slaves of sin, yet you
obeyed from the heart that form of doctrine to which you
were delivered. 18 And having been set free from sin, you
became slaves of righteousness. 19 I speak in human *terms*
because of the weakness of your flesh. For just as you pre-
sented your members *as* slaves of uncleanness, and of
lawlessness *leading* to *more* lawlessness, so now present
your members *as* slaves *of* righteousness for holiness.

THE MESSAGE

now on, think of it this way: Sin speaks a dead language that means nothing to you; God speaks your mother tongue, and you hang on every word. You are dead to sin and alive to God. That's what Jesus did.

That means you must not give sin a vote in the way you conduct your lives. Don't give it the time of day. Don't even run little errands that are connected with that old way of life. Throw yourselves wholeheartedly and full-time—remember, you've been raised from the dead!—into God's way of doing things. Sin can't tell you how to live. After all, you're not living under that old tyranny any longer. You're living in the freedom of God.

What Is True Freedom?

So, since we're out from under the old tyranny, does that mean we can live any old way we want? Since we're free in the freedom of God, can we do anything that comes to mind? Hardly. You know well enough from your own experience that there are some acts of so-called freedom that destroy freedom. Offer yourselves to sin, for instance, and it's your last free act. But offer yourselves to the ways of God and the freedom never quits. All your lives you've let sin tell you what to do. But thank God you've started listening to a new master, one whose commands set you free to live openly in *his* freedom!

I'm using this freedom language because it's easy to picture. You can readily recall, can't you, how at one time the more you did just what you felt like doing—not caring about others, not caring about God—the worse your life became

KING JAMES VERSION

20 For when ye were the servants of sin, ye were free from righteousness.

21 What fruit had ye then in those things whereof ye are now ashamed? for the end of those things *is* death.

22 But now being made free from sin, and become servants to God, ye have your fruit unto holiness, and the end everlasting life.

23 For the wages of sin *is* death; but the gift of God *is* eternal life through Jesus Christ our Lord.

7 Know ye not, brethren, (for I speak to them that know the law,) how that the law hath dominion over a man as long as he liveth?

2 For the woman which hath an husband is bound by the law to *her* husband so long as he liveth; but if the husband be dead, she is loosed from the law of *her* husband.

3 So then if, while *her* husband liveth, she be married to another man, she shall be called an adulteress: but if her husband be dead, she is free from that law; so that she is no adulteress, though she be married to another man.

4 Wherefore, my brethren, ye also are become dead to the law by the body of Christ; that ye should be married to another, *even* to him who is raised from the dead, that we should bring forth fruit unto God.

NEW AMERICAN STANDARD BIBLE

20 For when you were slaves of sin, you were free in regard to righteousness.

21 Therefore what benefit were you then deriving from the things of which you are now ashamed? For the outcome of those things is death.

22 But now having been freed from sin and enslaved to God, you derive your benefit, resulting in sanctification, and the outcome, eternal life.

23 For the wages of sin is death, but the free gift of God is eternal life in Christ Jesus our Lord.

Believers United to Christ

7 Or do you not know, brethren (for I am speaking to those who know the law), that the law has jurisdiction over a person as long as he lives?

2 For the married woman is bound by law to her husband while he is living; but if her husband dies, she is released from the law concerning the husband.

3 So then, if while her husband is living she is joined to another man, she shall be called an adulteress; but if her husband dies, she is free from the law, so that she is not an adulteress though she is joined to another man.

4 Therefore, my brethren, you also were made to die to the Law through the body of Christ, so that you might be joined to another, to Him who was raised from the dead, in order that we might bear fruit for God.

NEW CENTURY VERSION

[20]In the past you were slaves to sin, and goodness did
not control you. [21]You did evil things, and now you are
ashamed of them. Those things only bring death. [22]But
now you are free from sin and have become slaves of God.
This brings you a life that is only for God, and this gives
you life forever. [23]When people sin, they earn what sin
pays—death. But God gives us a free gift—life forever in
Christ Jesus our Lord.

An Example from Marriage

7 Brothers and sisters, all of you understand the law of
Moses. So surely you know that the law rules over
people only while they are alive. [2]For example, a woman
must stay married to her husband as long as he is alive.
But if her husband dies, she is free from the law of mar-
riage. [3]But if she marries another man while her husband
is still alive, the law says she is guilty of adultery. But if
her husband dies, she is free from the law of marriage.
Then if she marries another man, she is not guilty of adul-
tery.
[4]In the same way, my brothers and sisters, your old
selves died, and you became free from the law through the
body of Christ. This happened so that you might belong to
someone else—the One who was raised from the dead—

CONTEMPORARY ENGLISH VERSION

[20]When you were slaves of sin, you didn't have to please
God. [21]But what good did you receive from the things you
did? All you have to show for them is your shame, and
they lead to death. [22]Now you have been set free from sin,
and you are God's slaves. This will make you holy and will
lead you to eternal life. [23]Sin pays off with death. But
God's gift is eternal life given by Jesus Christ our Lord.

An Example from Marriage

7 My friends, you surely understand enough about law
to know that laws only have power over people who
are alive. [2]For example, the Law says that a man's wife
must remain his wife as long as he lives. But once her hus-
band is dead, she is free [3]to marry someone else. However,
if she goes off with another man while her husband is still
alive, she is said to be unfaithful.
[4]That is how it is with you, my friends. You are now
part of the body of Christ and are dead to the power of the
Law. You are free to belong to Christ, who was raised to

NEW INTERNATIONAL VERSION

leading to holiness. [20]When you were slaves to sin, you
were free from the control of righteousness. [21]What benefit
did you reap at that time from the things you are now
ashamed of? Those things result in death! [22]But now that
you have been set free from sin and have become slaves to
God, the benefit you reap leads to holiness, and the result
is eternal life. [23]For the wages of sin is death, but the gift
of God is eternal life in[b] Christ Jesus our Lord.

An Illustration From Marriage

7 Do you not know, brothers—for I am speaking to men
who know the law—that the law has authority over a
man only as long as he lives? [2]For example, by law a mar-
ried woman is bound to her husband as long as he is alive,
but if her husband dies, she is released from the law of
marriage. [3]So then, if she marries another man while her
husband is still alive, she is called an adulteress. But if her
husband dies, she is released from that law and is not an
adulteress, even though she marries another man.
[4]So, my brothers, you also died to the law through the
body of Christ, that you might belong to another, to him
who was raised from the dead, in order that we might bear

[b] 23 Or *through*

NEW LIVING TRANSLATION

[20]In those days, when you were slaves of sin, you
weren't concerned with doing what was right. [21]And what
was the result? It was not good, since now you are
ashamed of the things you used to do, things that end in
eternal doom. [22]But now you are free from the power of sin
and have become slaves of God. Now you do those things
that lead to holiness and result in eternal life. [23]For the
wages of sin is death, but the free gift of God is eternal life
through Christ Jesus our Lord.

No Longer Bound to the Law

7 Now, dear brothers and sisters*—you who are famil-
iar with the law—don't you know that the law applies
only to a person who is still living? [2]Let me illustrate.
When a woman marries, the law binds her to her husband
as long as he is alive. But if he dies, the laws of marriage
no longer apply to her. [3]So while her husband is alive, she
would be committing adultery if she married another man.
But if her husband dies, she is free from that law and does
not commit adultery when she remarries.
[4]So this is the point: The law no longer holds you in its
power, because you died to its power when you died with
Christ on the cross. And now you are united with the one
who was raised from the dead. As a result, you can produce

7:1 Greek *brothers.*

NEW KING JAMES VERSION

[20]For when you were slaves of sin, you were free in
regard to righteousness. [21]What fruit did you have then in
the things of which you are now ashamed? For the end of
those things *is* death. [22]But now having been set free from
sin, and having become slaves of God, you have your fruit
to holiness, and the end, everlasting life. [23]For the wages
of sin *is* death, but the gift of God *is* eternal life in Christ
Jesus our Lord.

Freed from the Law

7 Or do you not know, brethren (for I speak to those
who know the law), that the law has dominion over a
man as long as he lives? [2]For the woman who has a hus-
band is bound by the law to *her* husband as long as he
lives. But if the husband dies, she is released from the law
of *her* husband. [3]So then if, while *her* husband lives, she
marries another man, she will be called an adulteress; but
if her husband dies, she is free from that law, so that she
is no adulteress, though she has married another man.
[4]Therefore, my brethren, you also have become dead to the
law through the body of Christ, that you may be married to
another—to Him who was raised from the dead, that we

THE MESSAGE

and the less freedom you had? And how much different is it now as you live in God's freedom, your lives healed and expansive in holiness?

As long as you did what you felt like doing, ignoring God, you didn't have to bother with right thinking or right living, or right *anything* for that matter. But do you call that a free life? What did you get out of it? Nothing you're proud of now. Where did it get you? A dead end.

But now that you've found you don't have to listen to sin tell you what to do, and have discovered the delight of listening to God telling you, what a surprise! A whole, healed, put-together life right now, with more and more of life on the way! Work hard for sin your whole life and your pension is death. But God's gift is *real life*, eternal life, delivered by Jesus, our Master.

Torn Between One Way and Another

7 You shouldn't have any trouble understanding this, friends, for you know all the ins and outs of the law—how it works and how its power touches only the living. For instance, a wife is legally tied to her husband while he lives, but if he dies, she's free. If she lives with another man while her husband is living, she's obviously an adulteress. But if he dies, she is quite free to marry another man in good conscience, with no one's disapproval.

So, my friends, this is something like what has taken place with you. When Christ died he took that entire rule-dominated way of life down with him and left it in the tomb, leaving you free to "marry" a resurrection life and

KING JAMES VERSION

5 For when we were in the flesh, the motions of sins, which were by the law, did work in our members to bring forth fruit unto death.

6 But now we are delivered from the law, that being dead wherein we were held; that we should serve in newness of spirit, and not *in* the oldness of the letter.

7 ¶ What shall we say then? *Is* the law sin? God forbid. Nay, I had not known sin, but by the law: for I had not known lust, except the law had said, Thou shalt not covet.

8 But sin, taking occasion by the commandment, wrought in me all manner of concupiscence. For without the law sin *was* dead.

9 For I was alive without the law once: but when the commandment came, sin revived, and I died.

10 And the commandment, which *was ordained* to life, I found *to be* unto death.

11 For sin, taking occasion by the commandment, deceived me, and by it slew *me*.

NEW AMERICAN STANDARD BIBLE

5 For while we were in the flesh, the sinful passions, which were *aroused* by the Law, were at work in the members of our body to bear fruit for death.

6 But now we have been released from the Law, having died to that by which we were bound, so that we serve in newness of the [1]Spirit and not in oldness of the letter.

7 What shall we say then? Is the Law sin? May it never be! On the contrary, I would not have come to know sin except through the Law; for I would not have known about coveting if the Law had not said, "YOU SHALL NOT COVET."

8 But sin, taking opportunity through the commandment, produced in me coveting of every kind; for apart from the Law sin *is* dead.

9 I was once alive apart from the Law; but when the commandment came, sin became alive and I died;

10 and this commandment, which was to result in life, proved to result in death for me;

11 for sin, taking an opportunity through the commandment, deceived me and through it killed me.

7:6 [1] Or *spirit*

NEW CENTURY VERSION

and so that we might be used in service to God. 5 In the
past, we were ruled by our sinful selves. The law made us
want to do sinful things that controlled our bodies, so the
things we did were bringing us death. 6 In the past, the law
held us like prisoners, but our old selves died, and we were
made free from the law. So now we serve God in a new
way with the Spirit, and not in the old way with written
rules.

Our Fight Against Sin

7 You might think I am saying that sin and the law are
the same thing. That is not true. But the law was the only
way I could learn what sin meant. I would never have
known what it means to want to take something belonging
to someone else if the law had not said, "You must not
want to take your neighbor's things."[a] 8 And sin found a
way to use that command and cause me to want all kinds
of things I should not want. But without the law, sin has
no power. 9 I was alive before I knew the law. But when the
law's command came to me, then sin began to live, 10 and I
died. The command was meant to bring life, but for me it
brought death. 11 Sin found a way to fool me by using the
command to make me die.

7:7 [a] **"You...things."** Quotation from Exodus 20:17.

CONTEMPORARY ENGLISH VERSION

life so that we could serve God. 5 When we thought only of
ourselves, the Law made us have sinful desires. It made
every part of our bodies into slaves who are doomed to die.
6 But the Law no longer rules over us. We are like dead
people, and it cannot have any power over us. Now we can
serve God in a new way by obeying his Spirit, and not in
the old way by obeying the written Law.

The Battle with Sin

7 Does this mean that the Law is sinful? Certainly not!
But if it had not been for the Law, I would not have known
what sin is really like. For example, I would not have
known what it means to want something that belongs to
someone else, unless the Law had told me not to do that.
8 It was sin that used this command as a way of making
me have all kinds of desires. But without the Law, sin is
dead.

9 Before I knew about the Law, I was alive. But as soon as
I heard that command, sin came to life, 10 and I died. The
very command that was supposed to bring life to me,
instead brought death. 11 Sin used this command to trick me,

NEW INTERNATIONAL VERSION

fruit to God. 5For when we were controlled by the sinful
nature,[a] the sinful passions aroused by the law were at
work in our bodies, so that we bore fruit for death. 6But
now, by dying to what once bound us, we have been
released from the law so that we serve in the new way of
the Spirit, and not in the old way of the written code.

Struggling With Sin

7What shall we say, then? Is the law sin? Certainly not!
Indeed I would not have known what sin was except
through the law. For I would not have known what covet-
ing really was if the law had not said, "Do not covet."[b]
8But sin, seizing the opportunity afforded by the com-
mandment, produced in me every kind of covetous desire.
For apart from law, sin is dead. 9Once I was alive apart
from law; but when the commandment came, sin sprang to
life and I died. 10I found that the very commandment that
was intended to bring life actually brought death. 11For
sin, seizing the opportunity afforded by the command-
ment, deceived me, and through the commandment put me

[a] *5* Or *the flesh*; also in verse 25 [b] *7* Exodus 20:17; Deut. 5:21

NEW LIVING TRANSLATION

good fruit, that is, good deeds for God. 5When we were con-
trolled by our old nature, sinful desires were at work within
us, and the law aroused these evil desires that produced
sinful deeds, resulting in death. 6But now we have been
released from the law, for we died with Christ, and we are
no longer captive to its power. Now we can really serve
God, not in the old way by obeying the letter of the law, but
in the new way, by the Spirit.

God's Law Reveals Our Sin

7Well then, am I suggesting that the law of God is evil?
Of course not! The law is not sinful, but it was the law
that showed me my sin. I would never have known that
coveting is wrong if the law had not said, "Do not covet."*
8But sin took advantage of this law and aroused all kinds
of forbidden desires within me! If there were no law, sin
would not have that power.

9I felt fine when I did not understand what the law
demanded. But when I learned the truth, I realized I had
broken the law and was a sinner, doomed to die. 10So the
good law, which was supposed to show me the way of life,
instead gave me the death penalty. 11Sin took advantage
of the law and fooled me; it took the good law and used it

7:7 Exod 20:17; Deut 5:21.

NEW KING JAMES VERSION

should bear fruit to God. 5For when we were in the flesh,
the sinful passions which were aroused by the law were at
work in our members to bear fruit to death. 6But now we
have been delivered from the law, having died to what we
were held by, so that we should serve in the newness of
the Spirit and not *in* the oldness of the letter.

Sin's Advantage in the Law

7What shall we say then? *Is* the law sin? Certainly not!
On the contrary, I would not have known sin except through
the law. For I would not have known covetousness unless
the law had said, *"You shall not covet."*[a] 8But sin, taking
opportunity by the commandment, produced in me all *man-
ner of evil* desire. For apart from the law sin *was* dead. 9I
was alive once without the law, but when the command-
ment came, sin revived and I died. 10And the command-
ment, which *was* to *bring* life, I found to *bring* death. 11For
sin, taking occasion by the commandment, deceived me, and

7:7 [a] Exodus 20:17; Deuteronomy 5:21

THE MESSAGE

bear "offspring" of faith for God. For as long as we lived
that old way of life, doing whatever we felt we could get
away with, sin was calling most of the shots as the old law
code hemmed us in. And this made us all the more rebel-
lious. In the end, all we had to show for it was miscar-
riages and stillbirths. But now that we're no longer shack-
led to that domineering mate of sin, and out from under all
those oppressive regulations and fine print, we're free to
live a new life in the freedom of God.

But I can hear you say, "If the law code was as bad as
all that, it's no better than sin itself." That's certainly not
true. The law code had a perfectly legitimate function.
Without its clear guidelines for right and wrong, moral
behavior would be mostly guesswork. Apart from the suc-
cinct, surgical command, "You shall not covet," I could
have dressed covetousness up to look like a virtue and
ruined my life with it.

Don't you remember how it was? I do, perfectly well. The
law code started out as an excellent piece of work. What
happened, though, was that sin found a way to pervert the
command into a temptation, making a piece of "forbidden
fruit" out of it. The law code, instead of being used to guide
me, was used to seduce me. Without all the paraphernalia of
the law code, sin looked pretty dull and lifeless, and I went
along without paying much attention to it. But once sin got
its hands on the law code and decked itself out in all that
finery, I was fooled, and fell for it. The very command that
was supposed to guide me into life was cleverly used to trip
me up, throwing me headlong. So sin was plenty alive, and I

KING JAMES VERSION

12 Wherefore the law *is* holy, and the commandment holy, and just, and good.

13 Was then that which is good made death unto me? God forbid. But sin, that it might appear sin, working death in me by that which is good; that sin by the commandment might become exceeding sinful.

14 ¶ For we know that the law is spiritual: but I am carnal, sold under sin.

15 For that which I do I allow not: for what I would, that do I not; but what I hate, that do I.

16 If then I do that which I would not, I consent unto the law that *it is* good.

17 Now then it is no more I that do it, but sin that dwelleth in me.

18 For I know that in me (that is, in my flesh,) dwelleth no good thing: for to will is present with me; but *how* to perform that which is good I find not.

19 For the good that I would I do not: but the evil which I would not, that I do.

20 Now if I do that I would not, it is no more I that do it, but sin that dwelleth in me.

21 I find then a law, that, when I would do good, evil is present with me.

22 For I delight in the law of God after the inward man:

NEW AMERICAN STANDARD BIBLE

12 So then, the Law is holy, and the commandment is holy and righteous and good.

13 Therefore did that which is good become *a cause of* death for me? May it never be! Rather it was sin, in order that it might be shown to be sin by effecting my death through that which is good, so that through the commandment sin would become utterly sinful.

The Conflict of Two Natures

14 For we know that the Law is spiritual, but I am of flesh, sold into bondage to sin.

15 For what I am doing, I do not understand; for I am not practicing what I *would* like to *do,* but I am doing the very thing I hate.

16 But if I do the very thing I do not want *to do,* I agree with the Law, *confessing* that the Law is good.

17 So now, no longer am I the one doing it, but sin which dwells in me.

18 For I know that nothing good dwells in me, that is, in my flesh; for the willing is present in me, but the doing of the good *is* not.

19 For the good that I want, I do not do, but I practice the very evil that I do not want.

20 But if I am doing the very thing I do not want, I am no longer the one doing it, but sin which dwells in me.

21 I find then the principle that evil is present in me, the one who wants to do good.

22 For I joyfully concur with the law of God in the inner man,

NEW CENTURY VERSION

12So the law is holy, and the command is holy and right
and good. 13Does this mean that something that is good
brought death to me? No! Sin used something that is good
to bring death to me. This happened so that I could see
what sin is really like; the command was used to show
that sin is very evil.

The War Within Us

14We know that the law is spiritual, but I am not spiritu-
al since sin rules me as if I were its slave. 15I do not under-
stand the things I do. I do not do what I want to do, and I
do the things I hate. 16And if I do not want to do the hated
things I do, that means I agree that the law is good. 17But I
am not really the one who is doing these hated things; it is
sin living in me that does them. 18Yes, I know that nothing
good lives in me—I mean nothing good lives in the part of
me that is earthly and sinful. I want to do the things that
are good, but I do not do them. 19I do not do the good
things I want to do, but I do the bad things I do not want
to do. 20So if I do things I do not want to do, then I am not
the one doing them. It is sin living in me that does those
things.

21So I have learned this rule: When I want to do good,
evil is there with me. 22In my mind, I am happy with God's

CONTEMPORARY ENGLISH VERSION

and because of it I died. 12Still, the Law and its commands
are holy and correct and good.

13Am I saying that something good caused my death?
Certainly not! It was sin that killed me by using something
good. Now we can see how terrible and evil sin really is.
14We know that the Law is spiritual. But I am merely a
human, and I have been sold as a slave to sin. 15In fact, I
don't understand why I act the way I do. I don't do what I
know is right. I do the things I hate. 16Although I don't do
what I know is right, I agree that the Law is good. 17So I
am not the one doing these evil things. The sin that lives
in me is what does them.

18I know that my selfish desires won't let me do any-
thing that is good. Even when I want to do right, I cannot.
19Instead of doing what I know is right, I do wrong. 20And
so, if I don't do what I know is right, I am no longer the
one doing these evil things. The sin that lives in me is
what does them.

21The Law has shown me that something in me keeps
me from doing what I know is right. 22With my whole
heart I agree with the Law of God. 23But in every part of

NEW INTERNATIONAL VERSION

to death. 12So then, the law is holy, and the commandment is holy, righteous and good.

13Did that which is good, then, become death to me? By no means! But in order that sin might be recognized as sin, it produced death in me through what was good, so that through the commandment sin might become utterly sinful.

14We know that the law is spiritual; but I am unspiritual, sold as a slave to sin. 15I do not understand what I do. For what I want to do I do not do, but what I hate I do. 16And if I do what I do not want to do, I agree that the law is good. 17As it is, it is no longer I myself who do it, but it is sin living in me. 18I know that nothing good lives in me, that is, in my sinful nature.[c] For I have the desire to do what is good, but I cannot carry it out. 19For what I do is not the good I want to do; no, the evil I do not want to do—this I keep on doing. 20Now if I do what I do not want to do, it is no longer I who do it, but it is sin living in me that does it.

21So I find this law at work: When I want to do good, evil is right there with me. 22For in my inner being I delight in God's law; 23but I see another law at work in the

c *18* Or *my flesh*

NEW LIVING TRANSLATION

to make me guilty of death. 12But still, the law itself is holy and right and good.

13But how can that be? Did the law, which is good, cause my doom? Of course not! Sin used what was good to bring about my condemnation. So we can see how terrible sin really is. It uses God's good commandment for its own evil purposes.

Struggling with Sin

14The law is good, then. The trouble is not with the law but with me, because I am sold into slavery, with sin as my master. 15I don't understand myself at all, for I really want to do what is right, but I don't do it. Instead, I do the very thing I hate. 16I know perfectly well that what I am doing is wrong, and my bad conscience shows that I agree that the law is good. 17But I can't help myself, because it is sin inside me that makes me do these evil things.

18I know I am rotten through and through so far as my old sinful nature is concerned. No matter which way I turn, I can't make myself do right. I want to, but I can't. 19When I want to do good, I don't. And when I try not to do wrong, I do it anyway. 20But if I am doing what I don't want to do, I am not really the one doing it; the sin within me is doing it.

21It seems to be a fact of life that when I want to do what is right, I inevitably do what is wrong. 22I love God's law with all my heart. 23But there is another law at work

NEW KING JAMES VERSION

by it killed *me.* 12Therefore the law *is* holy, and the commandment holy and just and good.

Law Cannot Save from Sin

13Has then what is good become death to me? Certainly not! But sin, that it might appear sin, was producing death in me through what is good, so that sin through the commandment might become exceedingly sinful. 14For we know that the law is spiritual, but I am carnal, sold under sin. 15For what I am doing, I do not understand. For what I will to do, that I do not practice; but what I hate, that I do. 16If, then, I do what I will not to do, I agree with the law that *it is* good. 17But now, *it is* no longer I who do it, but sin that dwells in me. 18For I know that in me (that is, in my flesh) nothing good dwells; for to will is present with me, but *how* to perform what is good I do not find. 19For the good that I will *to do,* I do not do; but the evil I will not *to do,* that I practice. 20Now if I do what I will not *to do,* it is no longer I who do it, but sin that dwells in me.

21I find then a law, that evil is present with me, the one who wills to do good. 22For I delight in the law of God according to the inward man. 23But I see another law in my

THE MESSAGE

was stone dead. But the law code itself is God's good and common sense, each command sane and holy counsel.

I can already hear your next question: "Does that mean I can't even trust what is good [that is, the law]? Is good just as dangerous as evil?" No again! Sin simply did what sin is so famous for doing: using the good as a cover to tempt me to do what would finally destroy me. By hiding within God's good commandment, sin did far more mischief than it could ever have accomplished on its own.

I can anticipate the response that is coming: "I know that all God's commands are spiritual, but I'm not. Isn't this also your experience?" Yes. I'm full of myself—after all, I've spent a long time in sin's prison. What I don't understand about myself is that I decide one way, but then I act another, doing things I absolutely despise. So if I can't be trusted to figure out what is best for myself and then do it, it becomes obvious that God's command is necessary.

But I need something *more*! For if I know the law but still can't keep it, and if the power of sin within me keeps sabotaging my best intentions, I obviously need help! I realize that I don't have what it takes. I can will it, but I can't *do* it. I decide to do good, but I don't *really* do it; I decide not to do bad, but then I do it anyway. My decisions, such as they are, don't result in actions. Something has gone wrong deep within me and gets the better of me every time.

It happens so regularly that it's predictable. The moment I decide to do good, sin is there to trip me up. I truly delight in God's commands, but it's pretty obvious that not

KING JAMES VERSION

23 But I see another law in my members, warring against the law of my mind, and bringing me into captivity to the law of sin which is in my members.
24 O wretched man that I am! who shall deliver me from the body of this death?
25 I thank God through Jesus Christ our Lord. So then with the mind I myself serve the law of God; but with the flesh the law of sin.

8 *There is* therefore now no condemnation to them which are in Christ Jesus, who walk not after the flesh, but after the Spirit.
2 For the law of the Spirit of life in Christ Jesus hath made me free from the law of sin and death.
3 For what the law could not do, in that it was weak through the flesh, God sending his own Son in the likeness of sinful flesh, and for sin, condemned sin in the flesh:
4 That the righteousness of the law might be fulfilled in

NEW AMERICAN STANDARD BIBLE

23 but I see a different law in the members of my body, waging war against the law of my mind and making me a prisoner of the law of sin which is in my members.
24 Wretched man that I am! Who will set me free from the body of this death?
25 Thanks be to God through Jesus Christ our Lord! So then, on the one hand I myself with my mind am serving the law of God, but on the other, with my flesh the law of sin.

Deliverance from Bondage

8 Therefore there is now no condemnation for those who are in Christ Jesus.
2 For the law of the Spirit of life in Christ Jesus has set you free from the law of sin and of death.
3 For what the Law could not do, weak as it was through the flesh, God *did:* sending His own Son in the likeness of sinful flesh and *as an offering* for sin, He condemned sin in the flesh,
4 so that the requirement of the Law might be fulfilled

NEW CENTURY VERSION

law. [23]But I see another law working in my body, which
makes war against the law that my mind accepts. That
other law working in my body is the law of sin, and it
makes me its prisoner. [24]What a miserable man I am! Who
will save me from this body that brings me death? [25]I
thank God for saving me through Jesus Christ our Lord!
So in my mind I am a slave to God's law, but in my sinful self I am a slave to the law of sin.

Be Ruled by the Spirit

8 So now, those who are in Christ Jesus are not judged
guilty. [2]Through Christ Jesus the law of the Spirit that
brings life made me free from the law that brings sin and
death. [3]The law was without power, because the law was
made weak by our sinful selves. But God did what the law
could not do. He sent his own Son to earth with the same
human life that others use for sin. By sending his Son to
be an offering to pay for sin, God used a human life to
destroy sin. [4]He did this so that we could be the kind of

CONTEMPORARY ENGLISH VERSION

me I discover something fighting against my mind, and it
makes me a prisoner of sin that controls everything I do.
[24]What a miserable person I am. Who will rescue me from
this body that is doomed to die? [25]Thank God! Jesus Christ
will rescue me.
So with my mind I serve the Law of God, although my selfish desires make me serve the law of sin.

Living by the Power of God's Spirit

8 If you belong to Christ Jesus, you won't be punished.
[2]The Holy Spirit will give you life that comes from
Christ Jesus and will set you[a] free from sin and death. [3]The
Law of Moses cannot do this, because our selfish desires
make the Law weak. But God set you free when he sent his
own Son to be like us sinners and to be a sacrifice for our
sin. God used Christ's body to condemn sin. [4]He did this,

[a] 8.2 *you*: Some manuscripts have "me."

NEW INTERNATIONAL VERSION

members of my body, waging war against the law of my mind and making me a prisoner of the law of sin at work within my members. [24]What a wretched man I am! Who will rescue me from this body of death? [25]Thanks be to God—through Jesus Christ our Lord!

So then, I myself in my mind am a slave to God's law, but in the sinful nature a slave to the law of sin.

Life Through the Spirit

8 Therefore, there is now no condemnation for those who are in Christ Jesus,[a] [2]because through Christ Jesus the law of the Spirit of life set me free from the law of sin and death. [3]For what the law was powerless to do in that it was weakened by the sinful nature,[b] God did by sending his own Son in the likeness of sinful man to be a sin offering.[c] And so he condemned sin in sinful man,[d] [4]in order that the righteous requirements of the law might be

[a] *1* Some later manuscripts *Jesus, who do not live according to the sinful nature but according to the Spirit,* [b] *3* Or *the flesh*; also in verses 4, 5, 8, 9, 12 and 13 [c] *3* Or *man, for sin* [d] *3* Or *in the flesh*

NEW LIVING TRANSLATION

within me that is at war with my mind. This law wins the fight and makes me a slave to the sin that is still within me. [24]Oh, what a miserable person I am! Who will free me from this life that is dominated by sin?* [25]Thank God! The answer is in Jesus Christ our Lord. So you see how it is: In my mind I really want to obey God's law, but because of my sinful nature I am a slave to sin.

Life in the Spirit

8 So now there is no condemnation for those who belong to Christ Jesus. [2]For the power* of the life-giving Spirit has freed you* through Christ Jesus from the power of sin that leads to death. [3]The law of Moses could not save us, because of our sinful nature. But God put into effect a different plan to save us. He sent his own Son in a human body like ours, except that ours are sinful. God destroyed sin's control over us by giving his Son as a sacrifice for our sins. [4]He did this so that the requirement of

7:24 Greek *from this body of death?* **8:2a** Greek *the law;* also in 8:2b. **8:2b** Some manuscripts read *me.*

NEW KING JAMES VERSION

members, warring against the law of my mind, and bringing me into captivity to the law of sin which is in my members. [24]O wretched man that I am! Who will deliver me from this body of death? [25]I thank God—through Jesus Christ our Lord!

So then, with the mind I myself serve the law of God, but with the flesh the law of sin.

Free from Indwelling Sin

8 *There is* therefore now no condemnation to those who are in Christ Jesus,[a] who do not walk according to the flesh, but according to the Spirit. [2]For the law of the Spirit of life in Christ Jesus has made me free from the law of sin and death. [3]For what the law could not do in that it was weak through the flesh, God *did* by sending His own Son in the likeness of sinful flesh, on account of sin: He condemned sin in the flesh, [4]that the righteous requirement of

8:1 [a] NU-Text omits the rest of this verse.

THE MESSAGE

all of me joins in that delight. Parts of me covertly rebel, and just when I least expect it, they take charge.

I've tried everything and nothing helps. I'm at the end of my rope. Is there no one who can do anything for me? Isn't that the real question?

The answer, thank God, is that Jesus Christ can and does. He acted to set things right in this life of contradictions where I want to serve God with all my heart and mind, but am pulled by the influence of sin to do something totally different.

The Solution Is Life on God's Terms

8 With the arrival of Jesus, the Messiah, that fateful dilemma is resolved. Those who enter into Christ's being-here-for-us no longer have to live under a continuous, low-lying black cloud. A new power is in operation. The Spirit of life in Christ, like a strong wind, has magnificently cleared the air, freeing you from a fated lifetime of brutal tyranny at the hands of sin and death.

God went for the jugular when he sent his own Son. He didn't deal with the problem as something remote and unimportant. In his Son, Jesus, he personally took on the human condition, entered the disordered mess of struggling humanity in order to set it right once and for all. The law code, weakened as it always was by fractured human nature, could never have done that.

The law always ended up being used as a band-aid on sin instead of a deep healing of it. And now what the law code asked for but we couldn't deliver is accomplished as

KING JAMES VERSION

us, who walk not after the flesh, but after the Spirit.
5 For they that are after the flesh do mind the things of the flesh; but they that are after the Spirit the things of the Spirit.
6 For to be carnally minded *is* death; but to be spiritually minded *is* life and peace.
7 Because the carnal mind *is* enmity against God: for it is not subject to the law of God, neither indeed can be.
8 So then they that are in the flesh cannot please God.
9 But ye are not in the flesh, but in the Spirit, if so be that the Spirit of God dwell in you. Now if any man have not the Spirit of Christ, he is none of his.
10 ¶ And if Christ *be* in you, the body *is* dead because of sin; but the Spirit *is* life because of righteousness.
11 But if the Spirit of him that raised up Jesus from the dead dwell in you, he that raised up Christ from the dead shall also quicken your mortal bodies by his Spirit that dwelleth in you.
12 Therefore, brethren, we are debtors, not to the flesh, to live after the flesh.

NEW AMERICAN STANDARD BIBLE

in us, who do not walk according to the flesh but according to the Spirit.
5 For those who are according to the flesh set their minds on the things of the flesh, but those who are according to the Spirit, the things of the Spirit.
6 For the mind set on the flesh is death, but the mind set on the Spirit is life and peace,
7 because the mind set on the flesh is hostile toward God; for it does not subject itself to the law of God, for it is not even able *to do so,*
8 and those who are in the flesh cannot please God.
9 However, you are not in the flesh but in the Spirit, if indeed the Spirit of God dwells in you. But if anyone does not have the Spirit of Christ, he does not belong to Him.
10 If Christ is in you, though the body is dead because of sin, yet the spirit is alive because of righteousness.
11 But if the Spirit of Him who raised Jesus from the dead dwells in you, He who raised Christ Jesus from the dead will also give life to your mortal bodies [1]through His Spirit who dwells in you.
12 So then, brethren, we are under obligation, not to the flesh, to live according to the flesh—

8:11 [1] One early ms reads *because of*

NEW CENTURY VERSION

people the law correctly wants us to be. Now we do not live
following our sinful selves, but we live following the Spirit.
5Those who live following their sinful selves think only
about things that their sinful selves want. But those who
live following the Spirit are thinking about the things the
Spirit wants them to do. 6If people's thinking is controlled
by the sinful self, there is death. But if their thinking is
controlled by the Spirit, there is life and peace. 7When peo-
ple's thinking is controlled by the sinful self, they are
against God, because they refuse to obey God's law and
really are not even able to obey God's law. 8Those people
who are ruled by their sinful selves cannot please God.
9But you are not ruled by your sinful selves. You are
ruled by the Spirit, if that Spirit of God really lives in you.
But the person who does not have the Spirit of Christ does
not belong to Christ. 10Your body will always be dead
because of sin. But if Christ is in you, then the Spirit gives
you life, because Christ made you right with God. 11God
raised Jesus from the dead, and if God's Spirit is living in
you, he will also give life to your bodies that die. God is
the One who raised Christ from the dead, and he will give
life through his Spirit that lives in you.
12So, my brothers and sisters, we must not be ruled by
our sinful selves or live the way our sinful selves want. 13If

CONTEMPORARY ENGLISH VERSION

so that we would do what the Law commands by obeying
the Spirit instead of our own desires.
5People who are ruled by their desires think only of
themselves. Everyone who is ruled by the Holy Spirit
thinks about spiritual things. 6If our minds are ruled by
our desires, we will die. But if our minds are ruled by the
Spirit, we will have life and peace. 7Our desires fight
against God, because they do not and cannot obey God's
laws. 8If we follow our desires, we cannot please God.
9You are no longer ruled by your desires, but by God's
Spirit, who lives in you. People who don't have the Spirit
of Christ in them don't belong to him. 10But Christ lives in
you. So you are alive because God has accepted you, even
though your bodies must die because of your sins. 11Yet
God raised Jesus to life! God's Spirit now lives in you, and
he will raise you to life by his Spirit.
12My dear friends, we must not live to satisfy our desires.

NEW INTERNATIONAL VERSION

fully met in us, who do not live according to the sinful
nature but according to the Spirit.
5Those who live according to the sinful nature have
their minds set on what that nature desires; but those who
live in accordance with the Spirit have their minds set on
what the Spirit desires. 6The mind of sinful man[e] is death,
but the mind controlled by the Spirit is life and peace; 7the
sinful mind[f] is hostile to God. It does not submit to God's
law, nor can it do so. 8Those controlled by the sinful
nature cannot please God.
9You, however, are controlled not by the sinful nature
but by the Spirit, if the Spirit of God lives in you. And if
anyone does not have the Spirit of Christ, he does not
belong to Christ. 10But if Christ is in you, your body is
dead because of sin, yet your spirit is alive because of righ-
teousness. 11And if the Spirit of him who raised Jesus from
the dead is living in you, he who raised Christ from the
dead will also give life to your mortal bodies through his
Spirit, who lives in you.
12Therefore, brothers, we have an obligation—but it is
not to the sinful nature, to live according to it. 13For if you

[e] 6 Or *mind set on the flesh* [f] 7 Or *the mind set on the flesh*

NEW LIVING TRANSLATION

the law would be fully accomplished for us* who no longer
follow our sinful nature but instead follow the Spirit.
5Those who are dominated by the sinful nature think
about sinful things, but those who are controlled by the
Holy Spirit think about things that please the Spirit. 6If
your sinful nature controls your mind, there is death. But
if the Holy Spirit controls your mind, there is life and
peace. 7For the sinful nature is always hostile to God. It
never did obey God's laws, and it never will. 8That's why
those who are still under the control of their sinful nature
can never please God.
9But you are not controlled by your sinful nature. You
are controlled by the Spirit if you have the Spirit of God
living in you. (And remember that those who do not have
the Spirit of Christ living in them are not Christians at all.)
10Since Christ lives within you, even though your body will
die because of sin, your spirit is alive* because you have
been made right with God. 11The Spirit of God, who raised
Jesus from the dead, lives in you. And just as he raised
Christ from the dead, he will give life to your mortal body
by this same Spirit living within you.
12So, dear brothers and sisters,* you have no obligation
whatsoever to do what your sinful nature urges you to do.

8:4 Or *accomplished by us.* 8:10 Or *the Spirit will bring you eternal life.* 8:12 Greek *brothers;* also in 8:29.

NEW KING JAMES VERSION

the law might be fulfilled in us who do not walk according
to the flesh but according to the Spirit. 5For those who live
according to the flesh set their minds on the things of the
flesh, but those *who live* according to the Spirit, the things
of the Spirit. 6For to be carnally minded *is* death, but to be
spiritually minded *is* life and peace. 7Because the carnal
mind *is* enmity against God; for it is not subject to the law
of God, nor indeed can be. 8So then, those who are in the
flesh cannot please God.
9But you are not in the flesh but in the Spirit, if indeed
the Spirit of God dwells in you. Now if anyone does not
have the Spirit of Christ, he is not His. 10And if Christ *is* in
you, the body *is* dead because of sin, but the Spirit *is* life
because of righteousness. 11But if the Spirit of Him who
raised Jesus from the dead dwells in you, He who raised
Christ from the dead will also give life to your mortal bod-
ies through His Spirit who dwells in you.

Sonship Through the Spirit

12Therefore, brethren, we are debtors—not to the flesh,
to live according to the flesh. 13For if you live according to

THE MESSAGE

we, instead of redoubling our own efforts, simply embrace
what the Spirit is doing in us.

Those who think they can do it on their own end up obsessed with measuring their own moral muscle but never get around to exercising it in real life. Those who trust God's action in them find that God's Spirit is in them—living and breathing God! Obsession with self in these matters is a dead end; attention to God leads us out into the open, into a spacious, free life. Focusing on the self is the opposite of focusing on God. Anyone completely absorbed in self ignores God, ends up thinking more about self than God. That person ignores who God is and what he is doing. And God isn't pleased at being ignored.

But if God himself has taken up residence in your life, you can hardly be thinking more of yourself than of him. Anyone, of course, who has not welcomed this invisible but clearly present God, the Spirit of Christ, won't know what we're talking about. But for you who welcome him, in whom he dwells—even though you still experience all the limitations of sin—you yourself experience life on God's terms. It stands to reason, doesn't it, that if the alive-and-present God who raised Jesus from the dead moves into your life, he'll do the same thing in you that he did in Jesus, bringing you alive to himself? When God lives and breathes in you (and he does, as surely as he did in Jesus), you are delivered from that dead life. With his Spirit living in you, your body will be as alive as Christ's!

So don't you see that we don't owe this old do-it-yourself life one red cent. There's nothing in it for us, nothing

KING JAMES VERSION

13 For if ye live after the flesh, ye shall die: but if ye through the Spirit do mortify the deeds of the body, ye shall live.

14 For as many as are led by the Spirit of God, they are the sons of God.

15 For ye have not received the spirit of bondage again to fear; but ye have received the Spirit of adoption, whereby we cry, Abba, Father.

16 The Spirit itself beareth witness with our spirit, that we are the children of God:

17 ¶ And if children, then heirs; heirs of God, and joint-heirs with Christ; if so be that we suffer with *him*, that we may be also glorified together.

18 For I reckon that the sufferings of this present time *are* not worthy *to be compared* with the glory which shall be revealed in us.

19 For the earnest expectation of the creature waiteth for the manifestation of the sons of God.

20 For the creature was made subject to vanity, not willingly, but by reason of him who hath subjected *the same* in hope,

21 Because the creature itself also shall be delivered from the bondage of corruption into the glorious liberty of the children of God.

22 For we know that the whole creation groaneth and travaileth in pain together until now.

23 And not only *they*, but ourselves also, which have the firstfruits of the Spirit, even we ourselves groan within

NEW AMERICAN STANDARD BIBLE

13 for if you are living according to the flesh, you must die; but if by the Spirit you are putting to death the deeds of the body, you will live.

14 For all who are being led by the Spirit of God, these are sons of God.

15 For you have not received a spirit of slavery leading to fear again, but you have received a spirit of adoption as sons by which we cry out, "Abba! Father!"

16 The Spirit Himself testifies with our spirit that we are children of God,

17 and if children, heirs also, heirs of God and fellow heirs with Christ, if indeed we suffer with *Him* so that we may also be glorified with *Him*.

18 For I consider that the sufferings of this present time are not worthy to be compared with the glory that is to be revealed to us.

19 For the anxious longing of the creation waits eagerly for the revealing of the sons of God.

20 For the creation was subjected to futility, not willingly, but because of Him who subjected it, [2]in hope

21 that the creation itself also will be set free from its slavery to corruption into the freedom of the glory of the children of God.

22 For we know that the whole creation groans and suffers the pains of childbirth together until now.

23 And not only this, but also we ourselves, having the first fruits of the Spirit, even we ourselves groan within

8:20 [2] Or *in hope; because the creation*

NEW CENTURY VERSION

you use your lives to do the wrong things your sinful selves want, you will die spiritually. But if you use the Spirit's help to stop doing the wrong things you do with your body, you will have true life.

[14]The true children of God are those who let God's Spirit lead them. [15]The Spirit we received does not make us slaves again to fear; it makes us children of God. With that Spirit we cry out, "Father."[a] [16]And the Spirit himself joins with our spirits to say we are God's children. [17]If we are God's children, we will receive blessings from God together with Christ. But we must suffer as Christ suffered so that we will have glory as Christ has glory.

Our Future Glory

[18]The sufferings we have now are nothing compared to the great glory that will be shown to us. [19]Everything God made is waiting with excitement for God to show his children's glory completely. [20]Everything God made was changed to become useless, not by its own wish but because God wanted it and because all along there was this hope: [21]that everything God made would be set free from ruin to have the freedom and glory that belong to God's children.

[22]We know that everything God made has been waiting until now in pain, like a woman ready to give birth. [23]Not only the world, but we also have been waiting with pain inside us. We have the Spirit as the first part of God's promise. So we are waiting for God to finish making us his

8:15 [a] **"Father"** Literally, "Abba, Father." Jewish children called their fathers "Abba."

CONTEMPORARY ENGLISH VERSION

[13]If you do, you will die. But you will live, if by the help of God's Spirit you say "No" to your desires. [14]Only those people who are led by God's Spirit are his children. [15]God's Spirit doesn't make us slaves who are afraid of him. Instead, we become his children and call him our Father.[b] [16]God's Spirit makes us sure that we are his children. [17]His Spirit lets us know that together with Christ we will be given what God has promised. We will also share in the glory of Christ, because we have suffered with him.

A Wonderful Future for God's People

[18]I am sure that what we are suffering now cannot compare with the glory that will be shown to us. [19]In fact, all creation is eagerly waiting for God to show who his children are. [20]Meanwhile, creation is confused, but not because it wants to be confused. God made it this way in the hope [21]that creation would be set free from decay and would share in the glorious freedom of his children. [22]We know that all creation is still groaning and is in pain, like a woman about to give birth.

[23]The Spirit makes us sure about what we will be in the future. But now we groan silently, while we wait for God to show that we are his children.[c] This means that our

[b] **8.15** *our Father*: The Greek text uses the Aramaic word "Abba" (meaning "father"), which shows the close relation between the children and their father. [c] **8.23** *to show that we are his children*: These words are not in some manuscripts. The translation of the remainder of the verse would then read, "while we wait for God to set our bodies free."

NEW INTERNATIONAL VERSION

live according to the sinful nature, you will die; but if by the Spirit you put to death the misdeeds of the body, you will live, 14because those who are led by the Spirit of God are sons of God. 15For you did not receive a spirit that makes you a slave again to fear, but you received the Spirit of sonship.[g] And by him we cry, *"Abba,*[h] Father." 16The Spirit himself testifies with our spirit that we are God's children. 17Now if we are children, then we are heirs—heirs of God and co-heirs with Christ, if indeed we share in his sufferings in order that we may also share in his glory.

Future Glory

18I consider that our present sufferings are not worth comparing with the glory that will be revealed in us. 19The creation waits in eager expectation for the sons of God to be revealed. 20For the creation was subjected to frustration, not by its own choice, but by the will of the one who subjected it, in hope 21that[i] the creation itself will be liberated from its bondage to decay and brought into the glorious freedom of the children of God.

22We know that the whole creation has been groaning as in the pains of childbirth right up to the present time. 23Not only so, but we ourselves, who have the firstfruits of the Spirit, groan inwardly as we wait eagerly for our adoption

g 15 Or *adoption* *h 15* Aramaic for *Father* *i 20,21* Or *subjected it in hope. 21For*

NEW LIVING TRANSLATION

13For if you keep on following it, you will perish. But if through the power of the Holy Spirit you turn from it* and its evil deeds, you will live. 14For all who are led by the Spirit of God are children* of God.

15So you should not be like cowering, fearful slaves. You should behave instead like God's very own children, adopted into his family*—calling him "Father, dear Father."* 16For his Holy Spirit speaks to us deep in our hearts and tells us that we are God's children. 17And since we are his children, we will share his treasures—for everything God gives to his Son, Christ, is ours, too. But if we are to share his glory, we must also share his suffering.

The Future Glory

18Yet what we suffer now is nothing compared to the glory he will give us later. 19For all creation is waiting eagerly for that future day when God will reveal who his children really are. 20Against its will, everything on earth was subjected to God's curse. 21All creation anticipates the day when it will join God's children in glorious freedom from death and decay. 22For we know that all creation has been groaning as in the pains of childbirth right up to the present time. 23And even we Christians, although we have the Holy Spirit within us as a foretaste of future glory, also groan to be released from pain and suffering. We, too, wait anxiously for that day when God will give us our full rights

8:13 Greek *put it to death.* **8:14** Greek *sons;* also in 8:19. **8:15a** Greek *You received a spirit of sonship.* **8:15b** Greek *"Abba, Father." Abba* is an Aramaic term for "father."

NEW KING JAMES VERSION

the flesh you will die; but if by the Spirit you put to death the deeds of the body, you will live. 14For as many as are led by the Spirit of God, these are sons of God. 15For you did not receive the spirit of bondage again to fear, but you received the Spirit of adoption by whom we cry out, "Abba, Father." 16The Spirit Himself bears witness with our spirit that we are children of God, 17and if children, then heirs—heirs of God and joint heirs with Christ, if indeed we suffer with *Him,* that we may also be glorified together.

From Suffering to Glory

18For I consider that the sufferings of this present time are not worthy *to be compared* with the glory which shall be revealed in us. 19For the earnest expectation of the creation eagerly waits for the revealing of the sons of God. 20For the creation was subjected to futility, not willingly, but because of Him who subjected *it* in hope; 21because the creation itself also will be delivered from the bondage of corruption into the glorious liberty of the children of God. 22For we know that the whole creation groans and labors with birth pangs together until now. 23Not only *that,* but we also who have the firstfruits of the Spirit, even we ourselves groan within ourselves, eagerly waiting for the

THE MESSAGE

at all. The best thing to do is give it a decent burial and get on with your new life. God's Spirit beckons. There are things to do and places to go!

This resurrection life you received from God is not a timid, grave-tending life. It's adventurously expectant, greeting God with a childlike "What's next, Papa?" God's Spirit touches our spirits and confirms who we really are. We know who he is, and we know who we are: Father and children. And we know we are going to get what's coming to us—an unbelievable inheritance! We go through exactly what Christ goes through. If we go through the hard times with him, then we're certainly going to go through the good times with him!

✠

That's why I don't think there's any comparison between the present hard times and the coming good times. The created world itself can hardly wait for what's coming next. Everything in creation is being more or less held back. God reins it in until both creation and all the creatures are ready and can be released at the same moment into the glorious times ahead. Meanwhile, the joyful anticipation deepens.

All around us we observe a pregnant creation. The difficult times of pain throughout the world are simply birth pangs. But it's not only around us; it's *within* us. The Spirit of God is arousing us within. We're also feeling the birth pangs. These sterile and barren bodies of ours are yearning for full deliverance. That is why waiting does not

KING JAMES VERSION

ourselves, waiting for the adoption, *to wit*, the redemption of our body.
24 For we are saved by hope: but hope that is seen is not hope: for what a man seeth, why doth he yet hope for?
25 But if we hope for that we see not, *then* do we with patience wait for *it*.
26 ¶ Likewise the Spirit also helpeth our infirmities: for we know not what we should pray for as we ought: but the Spirit itself maketh intercession for us with groanings which cannot be uttered.
27 And he that searcheth the hearts knoweth what *is* the mind of the Spirit, because he maketh intercession for the saints according to *the will of* God.
28 And we know that all things work together for good to them that love God, to them who are the called according to *his* purpose.
29 ¶ For whom he did foreknow, he also did predestinate *to be* conformed to the image of his Son, that he might be the firstborn among many brethren.
30 Moreover whom he did predestinate, them he also called: and whom he called, them he also justified: and whom he justified, them he also glorified.
31 ¶ What shall we then say to these things? If God *be* for us, who *can be* against us?
32 He that spared not his own Son, but delivered him up for us all, how shall he not with him also freely give us all things?

NEW AMERICAN STANDARD BIBLE

ourselves, waiting eagerly for *our* adoption as sons, the redemption of our body.
24 For in hope we have been saved, but hope that is seen is not hope; for who hopes for what he *already* sees?
25 But if we hope for what we do not see, with perseverance we wait eagerly for it.

Our Victory in Christ

26 In the same way the Spirit also helps our weakness; for we do not know how to pray as we should, but the Spirit Himself intercedes for *us* with groanings too deep for words;
27 and He who searches the hearts knows what the mind of the Spirit is, because He intercedes for the saints according to *the will of* God.
28 And we know that [3]God causes all things to work together for good to those who love God, to those who are called according to *His* purpose.
29 For those whom He foreknew, He also predestined *to become* conformed to the image of His Son, so that He would be the firstborn among many brethren;
30 and these whom He predestined, He also called; and these whom He called, He also justified; and these whom He justified, He also glorified.
31 What then shall we say to these things? If God *is* for us, who *is* against us?
32 He who did not spare His own Son, but delivered Him over for us all, how will He not also with Him freely give us all things?

8:28 [3] One early ms reads *all things work together for good*

NEW CENTURY VERSION

own children, which means our bodies will be made free.
24 We were saved, and we have this hope. If we see what
we are waiting for, that is not really hope. People do not
hope for something they already have. 25 But we are hoping
for something we do not have yet, and we are waiting for
it patiently.
26 Also, the Spirit helps us with our weakness. We do not
know how to pray as we should. But the Spirit himself
speaks to God for us, even begs God for us with deep feel-
ings that words cannot explain. 27 God can see what is in
people's hearts. And he knows what is in the mind of the
Spirit, because the Spirit speaks to God for his people in
the way God wants.
28 We know that in everything God works for the good of
those who love him. They are the people he called, because
that was his plan. 29 God knew them before he made the
world, and he decided that they would be like his Son so
that Jesus would be the firstborn[b] of many brothers. 30 God
planned for them to be like his Son; and those he planned
to be like his Son, he also called; and those he called, he
also made right with him; and those he made right, he
also glorified.

God's Love in Christ Jesus

31 So what should we say about this? If God is with us, no
one can defeat us. 32 He did not spare his own Son but gave
him for us all. So with Jesus, God will surely give us all

8:29 [b] **firstborn** Here this probably means that Christ was the first in God's family to share God's glory.

CONTEMPORARY ENGLISH VERSION

bodies will also be set free. 24 And this hope is what saves
us. But if we already have what we hope for, there is no
need to keep on hoping. 25 However, we hope for something
we have not yet seen, and we patiently wait for it.
26 In certain ways we are weak, but the Spirit is here to
help us. For example, when we don't know what to pray
for, the Spirit prays for us in ways that cannot be put into
words. 27 All of our thoughts are known to God. He can
understand what is in the mind of the Spirit, as the Spirit
prays for God's people. 28 We know that God is always at
work for the good of everyone who loves him.[d] They are
the ones God has chosen for his purpose, 29 and he has
always known who his chosen ones would be. He had
decided to let them become like his own Son, so that his
Son would be the first of many children. 30 God then
accepted the people he had already decided to choose, and
he has shared his glory with them.

God's Love

31 What can we say about all this? If God is on our side,
can anyone be against us? 32 God did not keep back his
own Son, but he gave him for us. If God did this, won't he
freely give us everything else? 33 If God says his chosen

[d] **8.28** *God is always at work for the good of everyone who loves him*: Or "All things work for the good of everyone who loves God" or "God's Spirit always works for the good of everyone who loves God."

NEW INTERNATIONAL VERSION

as sons, the redemption of our bodies. 24For in this hope we
were saved. But hope that is seen is no hope at all. Who
hopes for what he already has? 25But if we hope for what
we do not yet have, we wait for it patiently.

26In the same way, the Spirit helps us in our weakness.
We do not know what we ought to pray for, but the Spirit
himself intercedes for us with groans that words cannot
express. 27And he who searches our hearts knows the
mind of the Spirit, because the Spirit intercedes for the
saints in accordance with God's will.

More Than Conquerors

28And we know that in all things God works for the good
of those who love him,[j] who[k] have been called according to
his purpose. 29For those God foreknew he also predestined
to be conformed to the likeness of his Son, that he might
be the firstborn among many brothers. 30And those he pre-
destined, he also called; those he called, he also justified;
those he justified, he also glorified.

31What, then, shall we say in response to this? If God is
for us, who can be against us? 32He who did not spare his
own Son, but gave him up for us all—how will he not also,
along with him, graciously give us all things? 33Who will

j 28 Some manuscripts *And we know that all things work together for good to those who love God* *k 28* Or *works together with those who love him to bring about what is good—with those who*

NEW LIVING TRANSLATION

as his children,* including the new bodies he has promised
us. 24Now that we are saved, we eagerly look forward to
this freedom. For if you already have something, you don't
need to hope for it. 25But if we look forward to something
we don't have yet, we must wait patiently and confidently.

26And the Holy Spirit helps us in our distress. For we
don't even know what we should pray for, nor how we
should pray. But the Holy Spirit prays for us with groan-
ings that cannot be expressed in words. 27And the Father
who knows all hearts knows what the Spirit is saying, for
the Spirit pleads for us believers in harmony with God's
own will. 28And we know that God causes everything to
work together* for the good of those who love God and are
called according to his purpose for them. 29For God knew
his people in advance, and he chose them to become like
his Son, so that his Son would be the firstborn, with many
brothers and sisters. 30And having chosen them, he called
them to come to him. And he gave them right standing
with himself, and he promised them his glory.

Nothing Can Separate Us from God's Love

31What can we say about such wonderful things as
these? If God is for us, who can ever be against us? 32Since
God did not spare even his own Son but gave him up for us
all, won't God, who gave us Christ, also give us everything
else?

8:23 Greek *wait anxiously for sonship.* 8:28 Some manuscripts read *And we know that everything works together.*

NEW KING JAMES VERSION

adoption, the redemption of our body. 24For we were saved
in this hope, but hope that is seen is not hope; for why
does one still hope for what he sees? 25But if we hope for
what we do not see, we eagerly wait for *it* with persever-
ance.

26Likewise the Spirit also helps in our weaknesses. For
we do not know what we should pray for as we ought, but
the Spirit Himself makes intercession for us[b] with groan-
ings which cannot be uttered. 27Now He who searches the
hearts knows what the mind of the Spirit *is,* because He
makes intercession for the saints according to *the will of*
God.

28And we know that all things work together for good to
those who love God, to those who are the called according
to *His* purpose. 29For whom He foreknew, He also predes-
tined *to be* conformed to the image of His Son, that He
might be the firstborn among many brethren. 30Moreover
whom He predestined, these He also called; whom He
called, these He also justified; and whom He justified,
these He also glorified.

God's Everlasting Love

31What then shall we say to these things? If God *is* for
us, who *can be* against us? 32He who did not spare His
own Son, but delivered Him up for us all, how shall He not
with Him also freely give us all things? 33Who shall bring

8:26 *b* NU-Text omits *for us.*

THE MESSAGE

diminish us, any more than waiting diminishes a pregnant mother. We are enlarged in the waiting. We, of course, don't see what is enlarging us. But the longer we wait, the larger we become, and the more joyful our expectancy.

Meanwhile, the moment we get tired in the waiting, God's Spirit is right alongside helping us along. If we don't know how or what to pray, it doesn't matter. He does our praying in and for us, making prayer out of our wordless sighs, our aching groans. He knows us far better than we know ourselves, knows our pregnant condition, and keeps us present before God. That's why we can be so sure that every detail in our lives of love for God is worked into something good.

God knew what he was doing from the very beginning. He decided from the outset to shape the lives of those who love him along the same lines as the life of his Son. The Son stands first in the line of humanity he restored. We see the original and intended shape of our lives there in him. After God made that decision of what his children should be like, he followed it up by calling people by name. After he called them by name, he set them on a solid basis with himself. And then, after getting them established, he stayed with them to the end, gloriously completing what he had begun.

So, what do you think? With God on our side like this, how can we lose? If God didn't hesitate to put everything on the line for us, embracing our condition and exposing himself to the worst by sending his own Son, is there anything else he wouldn't gladly and freely do for us? And

KING JAMES VERSION

33 Who shall lay any thing to the charge of God's elect? *It is* God that justifieth.

34 Who *is* he that condemneth? *It is* Christ that died, yea rather, that is risen again, who is even at the right hand of God, who also maketh intercession for us.

35 Who shall separate us from the love of Christ? *shall* tribulation, or distress, or persecution, or famine, or nakedness, or peril, or sword?

36 As it is written, For thy sake we are killed all the day long; we are accounted as sheep for the slaughter.

37 Nay, in all these things we are more than conquerors through him that loved us.

38 For I am persuaded, that neither death, nor life, nor angels, nor principalities, nor powers, nor things present, nor things to come,

39 Nor height, nor depth, nor any other creature, shall be able to separate us from the love of God, which is in Christ Jesus our Lord.

9 I say the truth in Christ, I lie not, my conscience also bearing me witness in the Holy Ghost,

2 That I have great heaviness and continual sorrow in my heart.

3 For I could wish that myself were accursed from

NEW AMERICAN STANDARD BIBLE

33 Who will bring a charge against God's elect? God is the one who justifies;

34 who is the one who condemns? Christ Jesus is He who died, yes, rather who was [4]raised, who is at the right hand of God, who also intercedes for us.

35 Who will separate us from the love of [5]Christ? Will tribulation, or distress, or persecution, or famine, or nakedness, or peril, or sword?

36 Just as it is written,

"FOR YOUR SAKE WE ARE BEING PUT TO DEATH ALL DAY
LONG;
WE WERE CONSIDERED AS SHEEP TO BE SLAUGHTERED."

37 But in all these things we overwhelmingly conquer through Him who loved us.

38 For I am convinced that neither death, nor life, nor angels, nor principalities, nor things present, nor things to come, nor powers,

39 nor height, nor depth, nor any other created thing, will be able to separate us from the love of God, which is in Christ Jesus our Lord.

Solicitude for Israel

9 I am telling the truth in Christ, I am not lying, my conscience testifies with me in the Holy Spirit,

2 that I have great sorrow and unceasing grief in my heart.

3 For I could wish that I myself were accursed, *separated*

8:34 [4] One early ms reads *raised from the dead* 8:35 [5] Two early mss read *God*

NEW CENTURY VERSION

things. 33 Who can accuse the people God has chosen? No
one, because God is the One who makes them right. 34 Who
can say God's people are guilty? No one, because Christ
Jesus died, but he was also raised from the dead, and now
he is on God's right side, begging God for us. 35 Can any-
thing separate us from the love Christ has for us? Can trou-
bles or problems or sufferings or hunger or nakedness or
danger or violent death? 36 As it is written in the Scriptures:

"For you we are in danger of death all the time.
People think we are worth no more than sheep to be
killed." *Psalm 44:22*

37 But in all these things we have full victory through
God who showed his love for us. 38 Yes, I am sure that nei-
ther death, nor life, nor angels, nor ruling spirits, nothing
now, nothing in the future, no powers, 39 nothing above us,
nothing below us, nor anything else in the whole world
will ever be able to separate us from the love of God that is
in Christ Jesus our Lord.

God and the Jewish People

9 I am in Christ, and I am telling you the truth; I do not
lie. My conscience is ruled by the Holy Spirit, and it
tells me I am not lying. 2 I have great sorrow and always
feel much sadness. 3 I wish I could help my Jewish brothers
and sisters, my people. I would even wish that I were
cursed and cut off from Christ if that would help them.

CONTEMPORARY ENGLISH VERSION

ones are acceptable to him, can anyone bring charges
against them? 34 Or can anyone condemn them? No indeed!
Christ died and was raised to life, and now he is at God's
right side,[e] speaking to him for us. 35 Can anything sepa-
rate us from the love of Christ? Can trouble, suffering, and
hard times, or hunger and nakedness, or danger and
death? 36 It is exactly as the Scriptures say,

"For you we face death
all day long.
We are like sheep
on their way
to be butchered."

37 In everything we have won more than a victory because
of Christ who loves us. 38 I am sure that nothing can sepa-
rate us from God's love—not life or death, not angels or
spirits, not the present or the future, 39 and not powers
above or powers below. Nothing in all creation can sepa-
rate us from God's love for us in Christ Jesus our Lord!

God's Choice of Israel

9 I am a follower of Christ, and the Holy Spirit is a wit-
ness to my conscience. So I tell the truth and I am not
lying when I say 2 my heart is broken and I am in great sor-
row. 3 I would gladly be placed under God's curse and be

[e] 8.34 *right side*: The place of power and honor.

NEW INTERNATIONAL VERSION

bring any charge against those whom God has chosen? It is God who justifies. 34Who is he that condemns? Christ Jesus, who died—more than that, who was raised to life—is at the right hand of God and is also interceding for us. 35Who shall separate us from the love of Christ? Shall trouble or hardship or persecution or famine or nakedness or danger or sword? 36As it is written:

"For your sake we face death all day long;
we are considered as sheep to be slaughtered."[l]

37No, in all these things we are more than conquerors through him who loved us. 38For I am convinced that neither death nor life, neither angels nor demons,[m] neither the present nor the future, nor any powers, 39neither height nor depth, nor anything else in all creation, will be able to separate us from the love of God that is in Christ Jesus our Lord.

God's Sovereign Choice

9 I speak the truth in Christ—I am not lying, my conscience confirms it in the Holy Spirit— 2I have great sorrow and unceasing anguish in my heart. 3For I could wish that I myself were cursed and cut off from Christ for

[l] *36* Psalm 44:22 [m] *38* Or *nor heavenly rulers*

NEW LIVING TRANSLATION

33Who dares accuse us whom God has chosen for his own? Will God? No! He is the one who has given us right standing with himself. 34Who then will condemn us? Will Christ Jesus? No, for he is the one who died for us and was raised to life for us and is sitting at the place of highest honor next to God, pleading for us.

35Can anything ever separate us from Christ's love? Does it mean he no longer loves us if we have trouble or calamity, or are persecuted, or are hungry or cold or in danger or threatened with death? 36(Even the Scriptures say, "For your sake we are killed every day; we are being slaughtered like sheep."*) 37No, despite all these things, overwhelming victory is ours through Christ, who loved us.

38And I am convinced that nothing can ever separate us from his love. Death can't, and life can't. The angels can't, and the demons can't. Our fears for today, our worries about tomorrow, and even the powers of hell can't keep God's love away. 39Whether we are high above the sky or in the deepest ocean, nothing in all creation will ever be able to separate us from the love of God that is revealed in Christ Jesus our Lord.

God's Selection of Israel

9 In the presence of Christ, I speak with utter truthfulness—I do not lie—and my conscience and the Holy Spirit confirm that what I am saying is true. 2My heart is filled with bitter sorrow and unending grief 3for my people, my Jewish brothers and sisters.* I would be willing to be forever cursed—cut off from Christ!—if that would save

8:36 Ps 44:22. **9:3** Greek *my brothers.*

NEW KING JAMES VERSION

a charge against God's elect? *It is* God who justifies. 34Who *is* he who condemns? *It is* Christ who died, and furthermore is also risen, who is even at the right hand of God, who also makes intercession for us. 35Who shall separate us from the love of Christ? *Shall* tribulation, or distress, or persecution, or famine, or nakedness, or peril, or sword? 36As it is written:

"For Your sake we are killed all day long;
We are accounted as sheep for the slaughter."[c]

37Yet in all these things we are more than conquerors through Him who loved us. 38For I am persuaded that neither death nor life, nor angels nor principalities nor powers, nor things present nor things to come, 39nor height nor depth, nor any other created thing, shall be able to separate us from the love of God which is in Christ Jesus our Lord.

Israel's Rejection of Christ

9 I tell the truth in Christ, I am not lying, my conscience also bearing me witness in the Holy Spirit, 2that I have great sorrow and continual grief in my heart. 3For I could wish that I myself were accursed from Christ for my

8:36 [c] Psalm 44:22

THE MESSAGE

who would dare tangle with God by messing with one of God's chosen? Who would dare even to point a finger? The One who died for us—who was raised to life for us!—is in the presence of God at this very moment sticking up for us. Do you think anyone is going to be able to drive a wedge between us and Christ's love for us? There is no way! Not trouble, not hard times, not hatred, not hunger, not homelessness, not bullying threats, not backstabbing, not even the worst sins listed in Scripture:

"They kill us in cold blood because they hate you.
We're sitting ducks; they pick us off one by one."

None of this fazes us because Jesus loves us. I'm absolutely convinced that nothing—nothing living or dead, angelic or demonic, today or tomorrow, high or low, thinkable or unthinkable—absolutely *nothing* can get between us and God's love because of the way that Jesus our Master has embraced us.

God Is Calling His People

9 At the same time, you need to know that I carry with me at all times a huge sorrow. It's an enormous pain deep within me, and I'm never free of it. I'm not exaggerating—Christ and the Holy Spirit are my witnesses. It's the Israelites . . . If there were any way I could be cursed by the Messiah so they could be blessed by him, I'd do it in a

KING JAMES VERSION

Christ for my brethren, my kinsmen according to the flesh:

4 Who are Israelites; to whom *pertaineth* the adoption, and the glory, and the covenants, and the giving of the law, and the service *of God*, and the promises;

5 Whose *are* the fathers, and of whom as concerning the flesh Christ *came*, who is over all, God blessed for ever. Amen.

6 ¶ Not as though the word of God hath taken none effect. For they *are* not all Israel, which are of Israel:

7 Neither, because they are the seed of Abraham, *are they* all children: but, In Isaac shall thy seed be called.

8 That is, They which are the children of the flesh, these *are* not the children of God: but the children of the promise are counted for the seed.

9 For this *is* the word of promise, At this time will I come, and Sara shall have a son.

10 And not only *this*; but when Rebecca also had conceived by one, *even* by our father Isaac;

11 (For *the children* being not yet born, neither having done any good or evil, that the purpose of God according to election might stand, not of works, but of him that calleth;)

12 It was said unto her, The elder shall serve the younger.

NEW AMERICAN STANDARD BIBLE

from Christ for the sake of my brethren, my kinsmen according to the flesh,

4 who are Israelites, to whom belongs the adoption as sons, and the glory and the covenants and the giving of the Law and the *temple* service and the promises,

5 whose are the fathers, and from whom is the Christ according to the flesh, who is over all, God blessed forever. Amen.

6 But *it is* not as though the word of God has failed. For they are not all Israel who are *descended* from Israel;

7 nor are they all children because they are Abraham's descendants, but: "THROUGH ISAAC YOUR DESCENDANTS WILL BE NAMED."

8 That is, it is not the children of the flesh who are children of God, but the children of the promise are regarded as descendants.

9 For this is the word of promise: "AT THIS TIME I WILL COME, AND SARAH SHALL HAVE A SON."

10 And not only this, but there was Rebekah also, when she had conceived *twins* by one man, our father Isaac;

11 for though *the twins* were not yet born and had not done anything good or bad, so that God's purpose according to *His* choice would stand, not because of works but because of Him who calls,

12 it was said to her, "THE OLDER WILL SERVE THE YOUNGER."

NEW CENTURY VERSION

4They are the people of Israel, God's chosen children. They have seen the glory of God, and they have the agreements that God made between himself and his people. God gave them the law of Moses and the right way of worship and his promises. 5They are the descendants of our great ancestors, and they are the earthly family into which Christ was born, who is God over all. Praise him forever![a] Amen.

6It is not that God failed to keep his promise to them. But only some of the people of Israel are truly God's people,[b] 7and only some of Abraham's[c] descendants are true children of Abraham. But God said to Abraham: "The descendants I promised you will be from Isaac."[d] 8This means that not all of Abraham's descendants are God's true children. Abraham's true children are those who become God's children because of the promise God made to Abraham. 9God's promise to Abraham was this: "At the right time I will return, and Sarah will have a son."[e] 10And that is not all. Rebekah's sons had the same father, our father Isaac. 11-12But before the two boys were born, God told Rebekah, "The older will serve the younger."[f] This was before the boys had done anything good or bad. God said this so that the one chosen would be chosen because of God's own plan. He was chosen because he was the one God wanted to call, not because of

9:5 [a] **born...forever!** This can also mean, "born. May God, who rules over all things, be praised forever!" 9:6 [b] **God's people** Literally, "Israel," the people God chose to bring his blessings to the world.
9:7 [c] **Abraham** Most respected ancestor of the Jews. Every Jew hoped to see Abraham. 9:7 [d] **"The descendants...Isaac."** Quotation from Genesis 21:12. 9:9 [e] **"At...son."** Quotation from Genesis 18:10, 14.
9:11-12 [f] **"The older...younger."** Quotation from Genesis 25:23.

CONTEMPORARY ENGLISH VERSION

separated from Christ for the good of my own people. 4They are the descendants of Israel, and they are also God's chosen people. God showed them his glory. He made agreements with them and gave them his Law. The temple is theirs and so are the promises that God made to them. 5They have those famous ancestors, who were also the ancestors of Jesus Christ. I pray that God, who rules over all, will be praised forever![a] Amen.

6It cannot be said that God broke his promise. After all, not all of the people of Israel are the true people of God. 7-8In fact, when God made the promise to Abraham, he meant only Abraham's descendants by his son Isaac. God was talking only about Isaac when he promised 9Sarah, "At this time next year I will return, and you will already have a son."

10Don't forget what happened to the twin sons of Isaac and Rebekah. 11-12Even before they were born or had done anything good or bad, the Lord told Rebekah that her older son would serve the younger one. The Lord said this to show that he makes his own choices and that it wasn't because of anything either of them had done. 13That's why

[a] **9.5** *Christ. I pray that God, who rules over all, will be praised forever*: Or "Christ, who rules over all. I pray that God will be praised forever" or "Christ. And I pray that Christ, who is God and rules over all, will be praised forever."

NEW INTERNATIONAL VERSION

the sake of my brothers, those of my own race, [4]the people of Israel. Theirs is the adoption as sons; theirs the divine glory, the covenants, the receiving of the law, the temple worship and the promises. [5]Theirs are the patriarchs, and from them is traced the human ancestry of Christ, who is God over all, forever praised![a] Amen.

[6]It is not as though God's word had failed. For not all who are descended from Israel are Israel. [7]Nor because they are his descendants are they all Abraham's children. On the contrary, "It is through Isaac that your offspring will be reckoned."[b] [8]In other words, it is not the natural children who are God's children, but it is the children of the promise who are regarded as Abraham's offspring. [9]For this was how the promise was stated: "At the appointed time I will return, and Sarah will have a son."[c]

[10]Not only that, but Rebekah's children had one and the same father, our father Isaac. [11]Yet, before the twins were born or had done anything good or bad—in order that God's purpose in election might stand: [12]not by works but by him who calls—she was told, "The older will serve the younger."[d]

[a] *5* Or *Christ, who is over all. God be forever praised!* Or *Christ. God who is over all be forever praised!* [b] *7* Gen. 21:12 [c] *9* Gen. 18:10,14
[d] *12* Gen. 25:23

NEW LIVING TRANSLATION

them. [4]They are the people of Israel, chosen to be God's special children.* God revealed his glory to them. He made covenants with them and gave his law to them. They have the privilege of worshiping him and receiving his wonderful promises. [5]Their ancestors were great people of God, and Christ himself was a Jew as far as his human nature is concerned. And he is God, who rules over everything and is worthy of eternal praise! Amen.*

[6]Well then, has God failed to fulfill his promise to the Jews? No, for not everyone born into a Jewish family is truly a Jew! [7]Just the fact that they are descendants of Abraham doesn't make them truly Abraham's children. For the Scriptures say, "Isaac is the son through whom your descendants will be counted,"* though Abraham had other children, too. [8]This means that Abraham's physical descendants are not necessarily children of God. It is the children of the promise who are considered to be Abraham's children. [9]For God had promised, "Next year I will return, and Sarah will have a son."*

[10]This son was our ancestor Isaac. When he grew up, he married Rebekah, who gave birth to twins. [11]But before they were born, before they had done anything good or bad, she received a message from God. (This message proves that God chooses according to his own plan, [12]not according to our good or bad works.) She was told, "The descendants of your older son will serve the descendants of your younger son."*

9:4 Greek *chosen for sonship.* **9:5** Or *May God, who rules over everything, be praised forever. Amen.* **9:7** Gen 21:12. **9:9** Gen 18:10, 14. **9:12** Gen 25:23.

NEW KING JAMES VERSION

brethren, my countrymen[a] according to the flesh, [4]who are Israelites, to whom *pertain* the adoption, the glory, the covenants, the giving of the law, the service *of God,* and the promises; [5]of whom *are* the fathers and from whom, according to the flesh, Christ *came,* who is over all, *the* eternally blessed God. Amen.

Israel's Rejection and God's Purpose

[6]But it is not that the word of God has taken no effect. For they *are* not all Israel who *are* of Israel, [7]nor *are they* all children because they are the seed of Abraham; but, *"In Isaac your seed shall be called."*[b] [8]That is, those who *are* the children of the flesh, these *are* not the children of God; but the children of the promise are counted as the seed. [9]For this *is* the word of promise: *"At this time I will come and Sarah shall have a son."*[c]

[10]And not only *this,* but when Rebecca also had conceived by one man, *even* by our father Isaac [11](for *the children* not yet being born, nor having done any good or evil, that the purpose of God according to election might stand, not of works but of Him who calls), [12]it was said to her, *"The older shall serve the younger."*[d] [13]As it is written,

9:3 [a] Or *relatives* **9:7** [b] Genesis 21:12 **9:9** [c] Genesis 18:10, 14
9:12 [d] Genesis 25:23

THE MESSAGE

minute. They're my family. I grew up with them. They had everything going for them—family, glory, covenants, revelation, worship, promises, to say nothing of being the race that produced the Messiah, the Christ, who is God over everything, always. Oh, yes!

Don't suppose for a moment, though, that God's Word has malfunctioned in some way or other. The problem goes back a long way. From the outset, not all Israelites of the flesh were Israelites of the spirit. It wasn't Abraham's sperm that gave identity here, but God's *promise.* Remember how it was put: "Your family will be defined by Isaac"? That means that Israelite identity was never racially determined by sexual transmission, but it was *God*-determined by promise. Remember that promise, "When I come back next year at this time, Sarah will have a son"?

And that's not the only time. To Rebecca, also, a promise was made that took priority over genetics. When she became pregnant by our one-of-a-kind ancestor, Isaac, and her babies were still innocent in the womb—incapable of good or bad—she received a special assurance from God. What God did in this case made it perfectly plain that his purpose is not a hit-or-miss thing dependent on what we do or don't do, but a sure thing determined by his decision, flowing steadily from his initiative. God told Rebecca, "The firstborn of your twins will take second place." Later that

KING JAMES VERSION

13 As it is written, Jacob have I loved, but Esau have I hated.

14 ¶ What shall we say then? *Is there* unrighteousness with God? God forbid.

15 For he saith to Moses, I will have mercy on whom I will have mercy, and I will have compassion on whom I will have compassion.

16 So then *it is* not of him that willeth, nor of him that runneth, but of God that sheweth mercy.

17 For the scripture saith unto Pharaoh, Even for this same purpose have I raised thee up, that I might shew my power in thee, and that my name might be declared throughout all the earth.

18 Therefore hath he mercy on whom he will *have mercy*, and whom he will he hardeneth.

19 Thou wilt say then unto me, Why doth he yet find fault? For who hath resisted his will?

20 Nay but, O man, who art thou that repliest against God? Shall the thing formed say to him that formed *it*, Why hast thou made me thus?

21 Hath not the potter power over the clay, of the same lump to make one vessel unto honour, and another unto dishonour?

22 *What* if God, willing to shew *his* wrath, and to make his power known, endured with much longsuffering the vessels of wrath fitted to destruction:

NEW AMERICAN STANDARD BIBLE

13 Just as it is written, "JACOB I LOVED, BUT ESAU I HATED."

14 What shall we say then? There is no injustice with God, is there? May it never be!

15 For He says to Moses, "I WILL HAVE MERCY ON WHOM I HAVE MERCY, AND I WILL HAVE COMPASSION ON WHOM I HAVE COMPASSION."

16 So then it *does* not *depend* on the man who wills or the man who runs, but on God who has mercy.

17 For the Scripture says to Pharaoh, "FOR THIS VERY PURPOSE I RAISED YOU UP, TO DEMONSTRATE MY POWER IN YOU, AND THAT MY NAME MIGHT BE PROCLAIMED THROUGHOUT THE WHOLE EARTH."

18 So then He has mercy on whom He desires, and He hardens whom He desires.

19 You will say to me then, "Why does He still find fault? For who resists His will?"

20 On the contrary, who are you, O man, who answers back to God? The thing molded will not say to the molder, "Why did you make me like this," will it?

21 Or does not the potter have a right over the clay, to make from the same lump one vessel for honorable use and another for common use?

22 What if God, although willing to demonstrate His wrath and to make His power known, endured with much patience vessels of wrath prepared for destruction?

NEW CENTURY VERSION

anything he did. 13As the Scripture says, "I loved Jacob, but
I hated Esau."[g]
14So what should we say about this? Is God unfair? In
no way. 15God said to Moses, "I will show kindness to any-
one to whom I want to show kindness, and I will show
mercy to anyone to whom I want to show mercy."[h] 16So
God will choose the one to whom he decides to show
mercy; his choice does not depend on what people want or
try to do. 17The Scripture says to the king of Egypt: "I
made you king for this reason: to show my power in you
so that my name will be talked about in all the earth."[i]
18So God shows mercy where he wants to show mercy, and
he makes stubborn the people he wants to make stubborn.
19So one of you will ask me: "Then why does God blame
us for our sins? Who can fight his will?" 20You are only
human, and human beings have no right to question God.
An object should not ask the person who made it, "Why
did you make me like this?" 21The potter can make any-
thing he wants to make. He can use the same clay to make
one thing for special use and another thing for daily use.
22It is the same way with God. He wanted to show his
anger and to let people see his power. But he patiently
stayed with those people he was angry with—people who

9:13 [g] **"I...Esau."** Quotation from Malachi 1:2–3. **9:15** [h] **"I...mercy."** Quotation from Exodus 33:19. **9:17** [i] **"I...earth."** Quotation from Exodus 9:16.

CONTEMPORARY ENGLISH VERSION

the Scriptures say that the Lord liked Jacob more than
Esau.
14Are we saying that God is unfair? Certainly not! 15The
Lord told Moses that he has pity and mercy on anyone he
wants to. 16Everything then depends on God's mercy and
not on what people want or do. 17In the Scriptures the Lord
says to Pharaoh of Egypt, "I let you become king, so that I
could show you my power and be praised by all people on
earth." 18Everything depends on what God decides to do,
and he can either have pity on people or make them stub-
born.

God's Anger and Mercy

19Someone may ask, "How can God blame us, if he
makes us behave in the way he wants us to?" 20But, my
friend, I ask, "Who do you think you are to question God?
Does the clay have the right to ask the potter why he
shaped it the way he did? 21Doesn't a potter have the right
to make a fancy bowl and a plain bowl out of the same
lump of clay?"
22God wanted to show his anger and reveal his power
against everyone who deserved to be destroyed. But instead,

NEW INTERNATIONAL VERSION

13Just as it is written: "Jacob I loved, but Esau I hated."[e]
14What then shall we say? Is God unjust? Not at all!
15For he says to Moses,

"I will have mercy on whom I have mercy,
and I will have compassion on whom I have
compassion."[f]

16It does not, therefore, depend on man's desire or effort,
but on God's mercy. 17For the Scripture says to Pharaoh: "I
raised you up for this very purpose, that I might display
my power in you and that my name might be proclaimed in
all the earth."[g] 18Therefore God has mercy on whom he
wants to have mercy, and he hardens whom he wants to
harden.
19One of you will say to me: "Then why does God still
blame us? For who resists his will?" 20But who are you,
O man, to talk back to God? "Shall what is formed say to
him who formed it, 'Why did you make me like this?' "[h]
21Does not the potter have the right to make out of the
same lump of clay some pottery for noble purposes and
some for common use?
22What if God, choosing to show his wrath and make his
power known, bore with great patience the objects of his

[e] *13* Mal. 1:2,3 [f] *15* Exodus 33:19 [g] *17* Exodus 9:16
[h] *20* Isaiah 29:16; 45:9

NEW LIVING TRANSLATION

13In the words of the Scriptures, "I loved Jacob, but I rejected
Esau."*
14What can we say? Was God being unfair? Of course
not! 15For God said to Moses,

"I will show mercy to anyone I choose,
and I will show compassion to anyone I choose."*

16So receiving God's promise is not up to us. We can't get
it by choosing it or working hard for it. God will show
mercy to anyone he chooses.
17For the Scriptures say that God told Pharaoh, "I have
appointed you for the very purpose of displaying my power
in you, and so that my fame might spread throughout the
earth."* 18So you see, God shows mercy to some just
because he wants to, and he chooses to make some people
refuse to listen.
19Well then, you might say, "Why does God blame peo-
ple for not listening? Haven't they simply done what he
made them do?"
20No, don't say that. Who are you, a mere human being,
to criticize God? Should the thing that was created say to
the one who made it, "Why have you made me like this?"
21When a potter makes jars out of clay, doesn't he have a
right to use the same lump of clay to make one jar for dec-
oration and another to throw garbage into? 22God has
every right to exercise his judgment and his power, but he
also has the right to be very patient with those who are the

9:13 Mal 1:2-3. **9:15** Exod 33:19. **9:17** Exod 9:16.

NEW KING JAMES VERSION

"Jacob I have loved, but Esau I have hated."[e]

Israel's Rejection and God's Justice

14What shall we say then? *Is there* unrighteousness with
God? Certainly not! 15For He says to Moses, *"I will have
mercy on whomever I will have mercy, and I will have
compassion on whomever I will have compassion."*[f] 16So
then *it is* not of him who wills, nor of him who runs, but of
God who shows mercy. 17For the Scripture says to the
Pharaoh, *"For this very purpose I have raised you up, that
I may show My power in you, and that My name may be
declared in all the earth."*[g] 18Therefore He has mercy on
whom He wills, and whom He wills He hardens.
19You will say to me then, "Why does He still find fault?
For who has resisted His will?" 20But indeed, O man, who
are you to reply against God? Will the thing formed say to
him who formed *it*, "Why have you made me like this?"
21Does not the potter have power over the clay, from the
same lump to make one vessel for honor and another for
dishonor?
22*What* if God, wanting to show *His* wrath and to make
His power known, endured with much longsuffering the

9:13 [e] Malachi 1:2, 3 **9:15** [f] Exodus 33:19 **9:17** [g] Exodus 9:16

THE MESSAGE

was turned into a stark epigram: "I loved Jacob; I hated
Esau."

Is that grounds for complaining that God is unfair? Not
so fast, please. God told Moses, "*I'm* in charge of mercy.
I'm in charge of compassion." Compassion doesn't origi-
nate in our bleeding hearts or moral sweat, but in God's
mercy. The same point was made when God said to
Pharaoh, "I picked you as a bit player in this drama of my
salvation power." All we're saying is that God has the first
word, initiating the action in which we play our part for
good or ill.

Are you going to object, "So how can God blame us for
anything since he's in charge of everything? If the big deci-
sions are already made, what say do we have in it?"

Who in the world do you think you are to second-guess
God? Do you for one moment suppose any of us knows
enough to call God into question? Clay doesn't talk back
to the fingers that mold it, saying, "Why did you shape
me like this?" Isn't it obvious that a potter has a perfect
right to shape one lump of clay into a vase for holding
flowers and another into a pot for cooking beans? If God
needs one style of pottery especially designed to show his

KING JAMES VERSION

23 And that he might make known the riches of his glory on the vessels of mercy, which he had afore prepared unto glory,

24 Even us, whom he hath called, not of the Jews only, but also of the Gentiles?

25 ¶ As he saith also in Osee, I will call them my people, which were not my people; and her beloved, which was not beloved.

26 And it shall come to pass, *that* in the place where it was said unto them, Ye *are* not my people; there shall they be called the children of the living God.

27 Esaias also crieth concerning Israel, Though the number of the children of Israel be as the sand of the sea, a remnant shall be saved:

28 For he will finish the work, and cut *it* short in righteousness: because a short work will the Lord make upon the earth.

NEW AMERICAN STANDARD BIBLE

23 And *He did so* to make known the riches of His glory upon vessels of mercy, which He prepared beforehand for glory,

24 *even* us, whom He also called, not from among Jews only, but also from among Gentiles.

25 As He says also in Hosea,

"I WILL CALL THOSE WHO WERE NOT MY PEOPLE, 'MY PEOPLE,'
AND HER WHO WAS NOT BELOVED, 'BELOVED.' "

26 "AND IT SHALL BE THAT IN THE PLACE WHERE IT WAS SAID TO THEM, 'YOU ARE NOT MY PEOPLE,'
THERE THEY SHALL BE CALLED SONS OF THE LIVING GOD."

27 Isaiah cries out concerning Israel, "THOUGH THE NUMBER OF THE SONS OF ISRAEL BE LIKE THE SAND OF THE SEA, IT IS THE REMNANT THAT WILL BE SAVED;

28 FOR THE LORD WILL EXECUTE HIS WORD ON THE EARTH, THOROUGHLY AND QUICKLY."

NEW CENTURY VERSION

were made ready to be destroyed. 23He waited with
patience so that he could make known his rich glory to the
people who receive his mercy. He has prepared these peo-
ple to have his glory, 24and we are those people whom God
called. He called us not from the Jews only but also from
those who are not Jews. 25As the Scripture says in Hosea:

"I will say, 'You are my people'
to those I had called 'not my people.'
And I will show my love
to those people I did not love." *Hosea 2:1,23*

26 "They were called,
'You are not my people,'
but later they will be called
'children of the living God.' " *Hosea 1:10*

27And Isaiah cries out about Israel:
"The people of Israel are many,
like the grains of sand by the sea.
But only a few of them will be saved,
28 because the Lord will quickly and completely punish
the people on the earth." *Isaiah 10:22–23*

CONTEMPORARY ENGLISH VERSION

he patiently put up with them. 23He did this by showing
how glorious he is when he has pity on the people he has
chosen to share in his glory. 24Whether Jews or Gentiles, we
are those chosen ones, 25just as the Lord says in the book of
Hosea,

"Although they are not
my people,
I will make them my people.
I will treat with love
those nations
that have never been loved.

26 "Once they were told,
'You are not my people.'
But in that very place
they will be called
children of the living God."

27And this is what the prophet Isaiah said about the
people of Israel,

"The people of Israel
are as many
as the grains of sand
along the beach.
But only a few who are left
will be saved.
28 The Lord will be quick
and sure to do on earth

NEW INTERNATIONAL VERSION

wrath—prepared for destruction? 23What if he did this to
make the riches of his glory known to the objects of his
mercy, whom he prepared in advance for glory— 24even
us, whom he also called, not only from the Jews but also
from the Gentiles? 25As he says in Hosea:

"I will call them 'my people' who are not my people;
and I will call her 'my loved one' who is not my loved
one,"[i]

26and,

"It will happen that in the very place where it was said
to them,
'You are not my people,'
they will be called 'sons of the living God.' "[j]

27Isaiah cries out concerning Israel:

"Though the number of the Israelites be like the sand by
the sea,
only the remnant will be saved.
28For the Lord will carry out
his sentence on earth with speed and finality."[k]

[i] *25* Hosea 2:23 [j] *26* Hosea 1:10 [k] *28* Isaiah 10:22,23

NEW LIVING TRANSLATION

objects of his judgment and are fit only for destruction.
23He also has the right to pour out the riches of his glory
upon those he prepared to be the objects of his mercy—
24even upon us, whom he selected, both from the Jews and
from the Gentiles.
25Concerning the Gentiles, God says in the prophecy of
Hosea,

"Those who were not my people,
I will now call my people.
And I will love those
whom I did not love before."*

26And,

"Once they were told,
'You are not my people.'
But now he will say,
'You are children of the living God.'* "

27Concerning Israel, Isaiah the prophet cried out,

"Though the people of Israel are as numerous as the
sand on the seashore,
only a small number will be saved.
28 For the Lord will carry out his sentence upon the earth
quickly and with finality."*

9:25 Hos 2:23. **9:26** Greek *You are sons of the living God.* Hos 1:10.
9:27-28 Isa 10:22-23.

NEW KING JAMES VERSION

vessels of wrath prepared for destruction, 23and that He
might make known the riches of His glory on the vessels of
mercy, which He had prepared beforehand for glory, 24*even*
us whom He called, not of the Jews only, but also of the
Gentiles?
25As He says also in Hosea:

"I will call them My people, who were not My people,
And her beloved, who was not beloved."[h]
26 *"And it shall come to pass in the place where it was*
said to them,
'You are not My people,'
There they shall be called sons of the living God."[i]

27Isaiah also cries out concerning Israel:[j]

"Though the number of the children of Israel be as the
sand of the sea,
The remnant will be saved.
28 *For He will finish the work and cut it short in*
righteousness,
Because the LORD *will make a short work upon the*
earth."[k]

9:25 [h] Hosea 2:23 **9:26** [i] Hosea 1:10 **9:27** [j] Isaiah 10:22, 23
9:28 [k] NU-Text reads *For the LORD will finish the work and cut it short upon the earth.*

THE MESSAGE

angry displeasure and another style carefully crafted to
show his glorious goodness, isn't that all right? Either or
both happens to Jews, but it also happens to the other
people. Hosea put it well:

"I'll call nobodies and make them somebodies;
I'll call the unloved and make them beloved.
In the place where they yelled out, 'You're nobody!'
they're calling you 'God's living children.'"

Isaiah maintained this same emphasis:
"If each grain of sand on the seashore were numbered
and the sum labeled 'chosen of God,'
They'd be numbers still, not names;
salvation comes by personal selection.
God doesn't count us; he calls us by name.
Arithmetic is not his focus."

KING JAMES VERSION

29 And as Esaias said before, Except the Lord of
Sabaoth had left us a seed, we had been as Sodoma, and
been made like unto Gomorrha.

30 ¶ What shall we say then? That the Gentiles, which
followed not after righteousness, have attained to righ-
teousness, even the righteousness which is of faith.

31 But Israel, which followed after the law of righteous-
ness, hath not attained to the law of righteousness.

32 Wherefore? Because *they sought it* not by faith, but
as it were by the works of the law. For they stumbled at
that stumblingstone;

33 As it is written, Behold, I lay in Sion a stumblingstone

NEW AMERICAN STANDARD BIBLE

29 And just as Isaiah foretold,
"UNLESS THE LORD OF SABAOTH HAD LEFT TO US A
POSTERITY,
WE WOULD HAVE BECOME LIKE SODOM, AND WOULD HAVE
RESEMBLED GOMORRAH."

30 What shall we say then? That Gentiles, who did not
pursue righteousness, attained righteousness, even the
righteousness which is by faith;

31 but Israel, pursuing a law of righteousness, did not
arrive at *that* law.

32 Why? Because *they did* not *pursue it* by faith, but as
though *it were* by works. They stumbled over the stum-
bling stone,

33 just as it is written,
"BEHOLD, I LAY IN ZION A STONE OF STUMBLING AND A ROCK
OF OFFENSE,

NEW CENTURY VERSION

29 It is as Isaiah said:
"The Lord All-Powerful
allowed a few of our descendants to live.
Otherwise we would have been completely destroyed
like the cities of Sodom and Gomorrah."[j] *Isaiah 1:9*

30 So what does all this mean? Those who are not Jews
were not trying to make themselves right with God, but
they were made right with God because of their faith.
31 The people of Israel tried to follow a law to make them-
selves right with God. But they did not succeed, 32 because
they tried to make themselves right by the things they did
instead of trusting in God to make them right. They stum-
bled over the stone that causes people to stumble. 33 As it
is written in the Scripture:
"I will put in Jerusalem a stone that causes people to
stumble,
a rock that makes them fall.

9:29 [j] **Sodom and Gomorrah** Two cities that God destroyed because the people were so evil.

CONTEMPORARY ENGLISH VERSION

what he has warned
he will do."

29 Isaiah also said,

"If the Lord All-Powerful
had not spared some
of our descendants,
we would have been destroyed
like the cities of Sodom
and Gomorrah."[b]

Israel and the Good News

30 What does all of this mean? It means that the Gentiles
were not trying to be acceptable to God, but they found
that he would accept them if they had faith. 31-32 It also
means that the people of Israel were not acceptable to God.
And why not? It was because they were trying[c] to be
acceptable by obeying the Law instead of by having faith
in God. The people of Israel fell over the stone that makes
people stumble, 33 just as God says in the Scriptures,

"Look! I am placing in Zion
a stone to make people
stumble and fall.

[b] 9.29 *Sodom and Gomorrah*: During the time of Abraham the Lord destroyed these two cities because their people were so sinful.
[c] 9.31 *because they were trying*: Or "while they were trying" or "even though they were trying."

NEW INTERNATIONAL VERSION

29It is just as Isaiah said previously:

"Unless the Lord Almighty
had left us descendants,
we would have become like Sodom,
we would have been like Gomorrah."[l]

Israel's Unbelief

30What then shall we say? That the Gentiles, who did not pursue righteousness, have obtained it, a righteousness that is by faith; 31but Israel, who pursued a law of righteousness, has not attained it. 32Why not? Because they pursued it not by faith but as if it were by works. They stumbled over the "stumbling stone." 33As it is written:

"See, I lay in Zion a stone that causes men to stumble
and a rock that makes them fall,

l 29 Isaiah 1:9

NEW LIVING TRANSLATION

29And Isaiah said in another place,

"If the Lord Almighty
had not spared a few of us,
we would have been wiped out
as completely as Sodom and Gomorrah."*

Israel's Unbelief

30Well then, what shall we say about these things? Just this: The Gentiles have been made right with God by faith, even though they were not seeking him. 31But the Jews, who tried so hard to get right with God by keeping the law, never succeeded. 32Why not? Because they were trying to get right with God by keeping the law and being good instead of by depending on faith. They stumbled over the great rock in their path. 33God warned them of this in the Scriptures when he said,

"I am placing a stone in Jerusalem* that causes people
to stumble,
and a rock that makes them fall.*

9:29 Isa 1:9. **9:33a** Greek *in Zion.* **9:33b** Isa 8:14.

NEW KING JAMES VERSION

29And as Isaiah said before:

"Unless the LORD of Sabaoth[l] *had left us a seed,*
We would have become like Sodom,
And we would have been made like Gomorrah."[m]

Present Condition of Israel

30What shall we say then? That Gentiles, who did not pursue righteousness, have attained to righteousness, even the righteousness of faith; 31but Israel, pursuing the law of righteousness, has not attained to the law of righteousness.[n] 32Why? Because *they did* not *seek it* by faith, but as it were, by the works of the law.[o] For they stumbled at that stumbling stone. 33As it is written:

"Behold, I lay in Zion a stumbling stone and rock of
offense,

9:29 [l] Literally, in Hebrew, *Hosts* [m] Isaiah 1:9 **9:31** [n] NU-Text omits *of righteousness.* **9:32** [o] NU-Text reads *by works.*

THE MESSAGE

Isaiah had looked ahead and spoken the truth:

"If our powerful God
had not provided us a legacy of living children,
We would have ended up like ghost towns,
like Sodom and Gomorrah."

How can we sum this up? All those people who didn't seem interested in what God was doing actually *embraced* what God was doing as he straightened out their lives. And Israel, who seemed so interested in reading and talking about what God was doing, missed it. How could they miss it? Because instead of trusting God, *they* took over. They were absorbed in what they themselves were doing. They were so absorbed in their "God projects" that they didn't notice God right in front of them, like a huge rock in the middle of the road. And so they stumbled into him and went sprawling. Isaiah (again!) gives us the metaphor for pulling this together:

"Careful! I've put a huge stone on the road
to Mount Zion,
a stone you can't get around.

KING JAMES VERSION

and rock of offence: and whosoever believeth on him shall not be ashamed.

10 Brethren, my heart's desire and prayer to God for Israel is, that they might be saved.

2 For I bear them record that they have a zeal of God, but not according to knowledge.

3 For they being ignorant of God's righteousness, and going about to establish their own righteousness, have not submitted themselves unto the righteousness of God.

4 For Christ *is* the end of the law for righteousness to every one that believeth.

5 For Moses describeth the righteousness which is of the law, That the man which doeth those things shall live by them.

6 But the righteousness which is of faith speaketh on this wise, Say not in thine heart, Who shall ascend into heaven? (that is, to bring Christ down *from above*:)

7 Or, Who shall descend into the deep? (that is, to bring up Christ again from the dead.)

8 But what saith it? The word is nigh thee, *even* in thy mouth, and in thy heart: that is, the word of faith, which we preach;

NEW AMERICAN STANDARD BIBLE

AND HE WHO BELIEVES IN HIM WILL NOT BE
DISAPPOINTED."

The Word of Faith Brings Salvation

10 Brethren, my heart's desire and my prayer to God for them is for *their* salvation.

2 For I testify about them that they have a zeal for God, but not in accordance with knowledge.

3 For not knowing about God's righteousness and seeking to establish their own, they did not subject themselves to the righteousness of God.

4 For Christ is the end of the law for righteousness to everyone who believes.

5 For Moses writes that the man who practices the righteousness which is based on law shall live by that righteousness.

6 But the righteousness based on faith speaks as follows: "DO NOT SAY IN YOUR HEART, 'WHO WILL ASCEND INTO HEAVEN?' (that is, to bring Christ down),

7 or 'WHO WILL DESCEND INTO THE ABYSS?' (that is, to bring Christ up from the dead)."

8 But what does it say? "THE WORD IS NEAR YOU, in your mouth and in your heart"—that is, the word of faith which we are preaching,

NEW CENTURY VERSION

Anyone who trusts in him will never be disappointed."

Isaiah 8:14; 28:16

10 Brothers and sisters, the thing I want most is for all the Jews to be saved. That is my prayer to God.
2I can say this about them: They really try to follow God,
but they do not know the right way. 3Because they did not
know the way that God makes people right with him, they tried to make themselves right in their own way. So they did not accept God's way of making people right. 4Christ
ended the law so that everyone who believes in him may be right with God.

5Moses writes about being made right by following the law. He says, "A person who obeys these things will live because of them."[a] 6But this is what the Scripture says
about being made right through faith: "Don't say to yourself, 'Who will go up into heaven?' " (That means, "Who will go up to heaven and bring Christ down to earth?")
7"And do not say, 'Who will go down into the world below?' " (That means, "Who will go down and bring Christ up from the dead?") 8This is what the Scripture says: "The
word is near you; it is in your mouth and in your heart."[b]

10:5 [a] **"A person...them."** Quotation from Leviticus 18:5.
10:8 [b] **Verses 6–8** Quotations from Deuteronomy 9:4; 30:12–14; Psalm 107:26.

CONTEMPORARY ENGLISH VERSION

But those who have faith
in that one will never
be disappointed."

10 Dear friends, my greatest wish and my prayer to God is for the people of Israel to be saved. 2I know
they love God, but they don't understand 3what makes
people acceptable to him. So they refuse to trust God, and they try to be acceptable by obeying the Law. 4But Christ
makes the Law no longer necessary[a] for those who become acceptable to God by faith.

Anyone Can Be Saved

5Moses said that a person could become acceptable to God by obeying the Law. He did this when he wrote, "If you want to live, you must do all that the Law commands."

6But people whose faith makes them acceptable to God will never ask, "Who will go up to heaven to bring Christ
down?" 7Neither will they ask, "Who will go down into the world of the dead to raise him to life?"

8All who are acceptable because of their faith simply say, "The message is as near as your mouth or your heart." And

[a] **10.4** *But Christ makes the Law no longer necessary*: Or "But Christ gives the full meaning to the Law."

NEW INTERNATIONAL VERSION

and the one who trusts in him will never be put to
shame."[m]

10 Brothers, my heart's desire and prayer to God for
the Israelites is that they may be saved. 2For I can
testify about them that they are zealous for God, but their
zeal is not based on knowledge. 3Since they did not know
the righteousness that comes from God and sought to
establish their own, they did not submit to God's righ-
teousness. 4Christ is the end of the law so that there may
be righteousness for everyone who believes.
5Moses describes in this way the righteousness that is
by the law: "The man who does these things will live by
them."[a] 6But the righteousness that is by faith says: "Do
not say in your heart, 'Who will ascend into heaven?'[b]"
(that is, to bring Christ down) 7"or 'Who will descend into
the deep?'[c]" (that is, to bring Christ up from the dead).
8But what does it say? "The word is near you; it is in your
mouth and in your heart,"[d] that is, the word of faith we

[m] *33* Isaiah 8:14; 28:16 [a] *5* Lev. 18:5 [b] *6* Deut. 30:12
[c] *7* Deut. 30:13 [d] *8* Deut. 30:14

NEW LIVING TRANSLATION

But anyone who believes in him
will not be disappointed.*"

10 Dear brothers and sisters,* the longing of my heart
and my prayer to God is that the Jewish people
might be saved. 2I know what enthusiasm they have for
God, but it is misdirected zeal. 3For they don't understand
God's way of making people right with himself. Instead,
they are clinging to their own way of getting right with
God by trying to keep the law. They won't go along with
God's way. 4For Christ has accomplished the whole pur-
pose* of the law. All who believe in him are made right
with God.

Salvation Is for Everyone

5For Moses wrote that the law's way of making a person
right with God requires obedience to all of its commands.*
6But the way of getting right with God through faith says,
"You don't need to go to heaven" (to find Christ and bring
him down to help you). 7And it says, "You don't need to go
to the place of the dead" (to bring Christ back to life
again). 8Salvation that comes from trusting Christ—which
is the message we preach—is already within easy reach. In
fact, the Scriptures say, "The message is close at hand; it
is on your lips and in your heart."*

9:33c Or *will not be put to shame.* Isa 28:16. **10:1** Greek *Brothers.*
10:4 Or *the end.* **10:5** Lev 18:5. **10:6-8** Deut 30:12-14.

NEW KING JAMES VERSION

*And whoever believes on Him will not be put to
shame."*[p]

Israel Needs the Gospel

10 Brethren, my heart's desire and prayer to God for
Israel[a] is that they may be saved. 2For I bear them
witness that they have a zeal for God, but not according to
knowledge. 3For they being ignorant of God's righteous-
ness, and seeking to establish their own righteousness,
have not submitted to the righteousness of God. 4For
Christ *is* the end of the law for righteousness to everyone
who believes.
5For Moses writes about the righteousness which is of
the law, *"The man who does those things shall live by
them."*[b] 6But the righteousness of faith speaks in this way,
*"Do not say in your heart, 'Who will ascend into
heaven?'* "[c] (that is, to bring Christ down *from above*) 7or,
" *'Who will descend into the abyss?'* "[d] (that is, to bring
Christ up from the dead). 8But what does it say? *"The word
is near you, in your mouth and in your heart"*[e] (that is, the

9:33 [p] Isaiah 8:14; 28:16 **10:1** [a] NU-Text reads *them.*
10:5 [b] Leviticus 18:5 **10:6** [c] Deuteronomy 30:12
10:7 [d] Deuteronomy 30:13 **10:8** [e] Deuteronomy 30:14

THE MESSAGE

But the stone is me! If you're looking for me,
you'll find me on the way, not in the way."

Israel Reduced to Religion

10 Believe me, friends, all I want for Israel is what's
best for Israel: salvation, nothing less. I want it
with all my heart and pray to God for it all the time. I read-
ily admit that the Jews are impressively energetic regard-
ing God—but they are doing everything exactly backwards.
They don't seem to realize that this comprehensive setting-
things-right that is salvation is *God's* business, and a most
flourishing business it is. Right across the street they set
up their own salvation shops and noisily hawk their
wares. After all these years of refusing to really deal with
God on his terms, insisting instead on making their own
deals, they have nothing to show for it.
The earlier revelation was intended simply to get us
ready for the Messiah, who then puts everything right for
those who trust him to do it. Moses wrote that anyone who
insists on using the law code to live right before God soon
discovers it's not so easy—every detail of life regulated by
fine print! But trusting God to shape the right living in us
is a different story—no precarious climb up to heaven to
recruit the Messiah, no dangerous descent into hell to res-
cue the Messiah. So what exactly was Moses saying?

"The word that saves is right here,
as near as the tongue in your mouth,
as close as the heart in your chest."

KING JAMES VERSION

9 That if thou shalt confess with thy mouth the Lord Jesus, and shalt believe in thine heart that God hath raised him from the dead, thou shalt be saved.

10 For with the heart man believeth unto righteousness; and with the mouth confession is made unto salvation.

11 For the scripture saith, Whosoever believeth on him shall not be ashamed.

12 ¶ For there is no difference between the Jew and the Greek: for the same Lord over all is rich unto all that call upon him.

13 For whosoever shall call upon the name of the Lord shall be saved.

14 How then shall they call on him in whom they have not believed? and how shall they believe in him of whom they have not heard? and how shall they hear without a preacher?

15 And how shall they preach, except they be sent? as it is written, How beautiful are the feet of them that preach the gospel of peace, and bring glad tidings of good things!

16 But they have not all obeyed the gospel. For Esaias

NEW AMERICAN STANDARD BIBLE

9 that if you confess with your mouth Jesus *as* Lord, and believe in your heart that God raised Him from the dead, you will be saved;

10 for with the heart a person believes, resulting in righteousness, and with the mouth he confesses, resulting in salvation.

11 For the Scripture says, "WHOEVER BELIEVES IN HIM WILL NOT BE DISAPPOINTED."

12 For there is no distinction between Jew and Greek; for the same *Lord* is Lord of all, abounding in riches for all who call on Him;

13 for "WHOEVER WILL CALL ON THE NAME OF THE LORD WILL BE SAVED."

14 How then will they call on Him in whom they have not believed? How will they believe in Him whom they have not heard? And how will they hear without a preacher?

15 How will they preach unless they are sent? Just as it is written, "HOW BEAUTIFUL ARE THE FEET OF THOSE WHO BRING GOOD NEWS OF GOOD THINGS!"

16 However, they did not all heed the good news; for

NEW CENTURY VERSION

That is the teaching of faith that we are telling. 9If you use
your mouth to say, "Jesus is Lord," and if you believe in
your heart that God raised Jesus from the dead, you will be
saved. 10We believe with our hearts, and so we are made
right with God. And we use our mouths to say that we
believe, and so we are saved. 11As the Scripture says,
"Anyone who trusts in him will never be disappointed."[c]
12That Scripture says "anyone" because there is no difference between those who are Jews and those who are not.
The same Lord is the Lord of all and gives many blessings
to all who trust in him, 13as the Scripture says, "Anyone
who calls on the Lord will be saved."[d]

14But before people can ask the Lord for help, they must
believe in him; and before they can believe in him, they
must hear about him; and for them to hear about the Lord,
someone must tell them; 15and before someone can go and
tell them, that person must be sent. It is written, "How
beautiful is the person who comes to bring good news."[e]
16But not all the Jews accepted the good news. Isaiah said,

10:11 [c] "Anyone...disappointed." Quotation from Isaiah 28:16.
10:13 [d] "Anyone...saved." Quotation from Joel 2:32.
10:15 [e] "How...news." Quotation from Isaiah 52:7.

CONTEMPORARY ENGLISH VERSION

this is the same message we preach about faith. 9So you
will be saved, if you honestly say, "Jesus is Lord," and if
you believe with all your heart that God raised him from
death. 10God will accept you and save you, if you truly
believe this and tell it to others.

11The Scriptures say that no one who has faith will be
disappointed, 12no matter if that person is a Jew or a
Gentile. There is only one Lord, and he is generous to
everyone who asks for his help. 13All who call out to the
Lord will be saved.

14How can people have faith in the Lord and ask him to
save them, if they have never heard about him? And how
can they hear, unless someone tells them? 15And how can
anyone tell them without being sent by the Lord? The
Scriptures say it is a beautiful sight to see even the feet of
someone coming to preach the good news. 16Yet not everyone has believed the message. For example, the prophet

NEW INTERNATIONAL VERSION

are proclaiming: [9]That if you confess with your mouth, "Jesus is Lord," and believe in your heart that God raised him from the dead, you will be saved. [10]For it is with your heart that you believe and are justified, and it is with your mouth that you confess and are saved. [11]As the Scripture says, "Anyone who trusts in him will never be put to shame."[e] [12]For there is no difference between Jew and Gentile—the same Lord is Lord of all and richly blesses all who call on him, [13]for, "Everyone who calls on the name of the Lord will be saved."[f]

[14]How, then, can they call on the one they have not believed in? And how can they believe in the one of whom they have not heard? And how can they hear without someone preaching to them? [15]And how can they preach unless they are sent? As it is written, "How beautiful are the feet of those who bring good news!"[g]

[16]But not all the Israelites accepted the good news. For

[e] *11* Isaiah 28:16 [f] *13* Joel 2:32 [g] *15* Isaiah 52:7

NEW LIVING TRANSLATION

[9]For if you confess with your mouth that Jesus is Lord and believe in your heart that God raised him from the dead, you will be saved. [10]For it is by believing in your heart that you are made right with God, and it is by confessing with your mouth that you are saved. [11]As the Scriptures tell us, "Anyone who believes in him will not be disappointed.*" [12]Jew and Gentile are the same in this respect. They all have the same Lord, who generously gives his riches to all who ask for them. [13]For "Anyone who calls on the name of the Lord will be saved."*

[14]But how can they call on him to save them unless they believe in him? And how can they believe in him if they have never heard about him? And how can they hear about him unless someone tells them? [15]And how will anyone go and tell them without being sent? That is what the Scriptures mean when they say, "How beautiful are the feet of those who bring good news!"*

[16]But not everyone welcomes the Good News, for Isaiah

10:11 Or *will not be put to shame.* Isa 28:16. **10:13** Joel 2:32. **10:15** Isa 52:7.

NEW KING JAMES VERSION

word of faith which we preach): [9]that if you confess with your mouth the Lord Jesus and believe in your heart that God has raised Him from the dead, you will be saved. [10]For with the heart one believes unto righteousness, and with the mouth confession is made unto salvation. [11]For the Scripture says, *"Whoever believes on Him will not be put to shame."*[f] [12]For there is no distinction between Jew and Greek, for the same Lord over all is rich to all who call upon Him. [13]For *"whoever calls on the name of the* L*ORD* *shall be saved."*[g]

Israel Rejects the Gospel

[14]How then shall they call on Him in whom they have not believed? And how shall they believe in Him of whom they have not heard? And how shall they hear without a preacher? [15]And how shall they preach unless they are sent? As it is written:

"How beautiful are the feet of those who preach the
gospel of peace,[h]
Who bring glad tidings of good things!"[i]

[16]But they have not all obeyed the gospel. For Isaiah says,

10:11 [f]Isaiah 28:16 **10:13** [g]Joel 2:32 **10:15** [h]NU-Text omits *preach the gospel of peace, Who.* [i]Isaiah 52:7; Nahum 1:15

THE MESSAGE

It's the word of faith that welcomes God to go to work and set things right for us. This is the core of our preaching. Say the welcoming word to God—"Jesus is my Master"—embracing, body and soul, God's work of doing in us what he did in raising Jesus from the dead. That's it. You're not "doing" anything; you're simply calling out to God, trusting him to do it for you. That's salvation. With your whole being you embrace God setting things right, and then you say it, right out loud: "God has set everything right between him and me!"

Scripture reassures us, "No one who trusts God like this—heart and soul—will ever regret it." It's exactly the same no matter what a person's religious background may be: the same God for all of us, acting the same incredibly generous way to everyone who calls out for help. "Everyone who calls, 'Help, God!' gets help."

But how can people call for help if they don't know who to trust? And how can they know who to trust if they haven't heard of the One who can be trusted? And how can they hear if nobody tells them? And how is anyone going to tell them, unless someone is sent to do it? That's why Scripture exclaims,

"A sight to take your breath away!
Grand processions of people
telling all the good things of God!"

But not everybody is ready for this, ready to see and hear and act. Isaiah asked what we all ask at one time or

KING JAMES VERSION

saith, Lord, who hath believed our report?

17 So then faith *cometh* by hearing, and hearing by the word of God.

18 But I say, Have they not heard? Yes verily, their sound went into all the earth, and their words unto the ends of the world.

19 But I say, Did not Israel know? First Moses saith, I will provoke you to jealousy by *them that are* no people, *and* by a foolish nation I will anger you.

20 But Esaias is very bold, and saith, I was found of

NEW AMERICAN STANDARD BIBLE

Isaiah says, "LORD, WHO HAS BELIEVED OUR REPORT?"

17 So faith *comes* from hearing, and hearing by the word of Christ.

18 But I say, surely they have never heard, have they? Indeed they have;

"THEIR VOICE HAS GONE OUT INTO ALL THE EARTH,
AND THEIR WORDS TO THE ENDS OF THE WORLD."

19 But I say, surely Israel did not know, did they? First Moses says,

"I WILL MAKE YOU JEALOUS BY THAT WHICH IS NOT A
NATION,
BY A NATION WITHOUT UNDERSTANDING WILL I ANGER
YOU."

20 And Isaiah is very bold and says,

"I WAS FOUND BY THOSE WHO DID NOT SEEK ME,

NEW CENTURY VERSION

"Lord, who believed what we told them?"[f] 17So faith comes from hearing the Good News, and people hear the Good News when someone tells them about Christ.

18But I ask: Didn't people hear the Good News? Yes, they heard—as the Scripture says:

"Their message went out through all the world;
their words go everywhere on earth." *Psalm 19:4*

19Again I ask: Didn't the people of Israel understand? Yes, they did understand. First, Moses says:

"I will use those who are not a nation to make you
jealous.
I will use a nation that does not understand to make
you angry." *Deuteronomy 32:21*

20Then Isaiah is bold enough to say:

"I was found by those who were not asking me for help.

10:16 [f] "Lord,...them?" Quotation from Isaiah 53:1.

CONTEMPORARY ENGLISH VERSION

Isaiah asked, "Lord, has anyone believed what we said?"

17No one can have faith without hearing the message about Christ. 18But am I saying that the people of Israel did not hear? No, I am not! The Scriptures say,

"The message was told
everywhere on earth.
It was announced
all over the world."

19Did the people of Israel understand or not? Moses answered this question when he told that the Lord had said,

"I will make Israel jealous
of people
who are a nation
of nobodies.
I will make them angry
at people
who don't understand
a thing."

20Isaiah was fearless enough to tell that the Lord had said,

"I was found by people
who were not looking
for me.

NEW INTERNATIONAL VERSION

Isaiah says, "Lord, who has believed our message?"[h]
17Consequently, faith comes from hearing the message,
and the message is heard through the word of Christ. 18But
I ask: Did they not hear? Of course they did:

"Their voice has gone out into all the earth,
their words to the ends of the world."[i]

19Again I ask: Did Israel not understand? First, Moses
says,

"I will make you envious by those who are not a nation;
I will make you angry by a nation that has no
understanding."[j]

20And Isaiah boldly says,

"I was found by those who did not seek me;

[h] *16* Isaiah 53:1 [i] *18* Psalm 19:4 [j] *19* Deut. 32:21

NEW LIVING TRANSLATION

the prophet said, "Lord, who has believed our message?"*
17Yet faith comes from listening to this message of good
news—the Good News about Christ.

18But what about the Jews? Have they actually heard the
message? Yes, they have:

"The message of God's creation has gone out to
everyone,
and its words to all the world."*

19But did the people of Israel really understand? Yes, they
did, for even in the time of Moses, God had said,

"I will rouse your jealousy by blessing other nations.
I will make you angry by blessing the foolish
Gentiles."*

20And later Isaiah spoke boldly for God:

"I was found by people
who were not looking for me.

10:16 Isa 53:1. **10:18** Ps 19:4. **10:19** Deut 32:21.

NEW KING JAMES VERSION

"LORD, who has believed our report?"[j] 17So then faith
comes by hearing, and hearing by the word of God.
18But I say, have they not heard? Yes indeed:

"Their sound has gone out to all the earth,
And their words to the ends of the world."[k]

19But I say, did Israel not know? First Moses says:

"I will provoke you to jealousy by those who are not a
nation,
I will move you to anger by a foolish nation."[l]

20But Isaiah is very bold and says:

"I was found by those who did not seek Me;

10:16 [j] Isaiah 53:1 **10:18** [k] Psalm 19:4
10:19 [l] Deuteronomy 32:21

THE MESSAGE

another: "Does anyone care, God? Is anyone listening and
believing a word of it?" The point is, Before you trust, you
have to listen. But unless Christ's Word is preached,
there's nothing to listen to.

But haven't there been plenty of opportunities for Israel
to listen and understand what's going on? *Plenty*, I'd say.

"Preachers' voices have gone 'round the world,
Their message to earth's seven seas."

So the big question is, Why didn't Israel understand that
she had no corner on this message? Moses had it right
when he predicted,

"When you see God reach out to those
you consider your inferiors—outsiders!—
you'll become insanely jealous.
When you see God reach out to people
you think are religiously stupid,
you'll throw temper tantrums."

Isaiah dared to speak out these words of God:
"People found and welcomed me
who never so much as looked for me.

KING JAMES VERSION

them that sought me not; I was made manifest unto them
that asked not after me.
21 But to Israel he saith, All day long I have stretched
forth my hands unto a disobedient and gainsaying people.
11 I say then, Hath God cast away his people? God
forbid. For I also am an Israelite, of the seed of
Abraham, *of* the tribe of Benjamin.
2 God hath not cast away his people which he
foreknew. Wot ye not what the scripture saith of Elias?
how he maketh intercession to God against Israel, saying,
3 Lord, they have killed thy prophets, and digged down
thine altars; and I am left alone, and they seek my life.
4 But what saith the answer of God unto him? I have
reserved to myself seven thousand men, who have not
bowed the knee to *the image of* Baal.

NEW AMERICAN STANDARD BIBLE

I BECAME MANIFEST TO THOSE WHO DID NOT ASK FOR ME."
21 But as for Israel He says, "ALL THE DAY LONG I HAVE
STRETCHED OUT MY HANDS TO A DISOBEDIENT AND OBSTINATE
PEOPLE."

Israel Is Not Cast Away

11 I say then, God has not rejected His people, has
He? May it never be! For I too am an Israelite, a
descendant of Abraham, of the tribe of Benjamin.
2 God has not rejected His people whom He foreknew.
Or do you not know what the Scripture says in *the passage
about* Elijah, how he pleads with God against Israel?
3 "Lord, THEY HAVE KILLED YOUR PROPHETS, THEY HAVE TORN
DOWN YOUR ALTARS, AND I ALONE AM LEFT, AND THEY ARE SEEK-
ING MY LIFE."
4 But what is the divine response to him? "I HAVE KEPT
for Myself SEVEN THOUSAND MEN WHO HAVE NOT BOWED THE
KNEE TO BAAL."

NEW CENTURY VERSION

I made myself known to people who were not looking
for me." *Isaiah 65:1*

21 But about Israel God says,
"All day long I stood ready to accept
people who disobey and are stubborn." *Isaiah 65:2*

God Shows Mercy to All People

11 So I ask: Did God throw out his people? No! I
myself am an Israelite from the family of
Abraham, from the tribe of Benjamin. 2 God chose the
Israelites to be his people before they were born, and he
has not thrown his people out. Surely you know what the
Scripture says about Elijah, how he prayed to God against
the people of Israel. 3 "Lord," he said, "they have killed
your prophets, and they have destroyed your altars. I am
the only prophet left, and now they are trying to kill me,
too."[a] 4 But what answer did God give Elijah? He said, "But
I have left seven thousand people in Israel who have never
bowed down before Baal."[b] 5 It is the same now. There are

11:3 [a] **"They...too."** Quotation from 1 Kings 19:10, 14.
11:4 [b] **"But...Baal."** Quotation from 1 Kings 19:18.

CONTEMPORARY ENGLISH VERSION

I appeared to the ones
who were not asking
about me."

21 And Isaiah said about the people of Israel,

"All day long the Lord
has reached out
to people who are stubborn
and refuse to obey."

God Has Not Rejected His People

11 Am I saying that God has turned his back on his
people? Certainly not! I am one of the people of
Israel, and I myself am a descendant of Abraham from the
tribe of Benjamin. 2 God did not turn his back on his cho-
sen people. Don't you remember reading in the Scriptures
how Elijah complained to God about the people of Israel?
3 He said, "Lord, they killed your prophets and destroyed
your altars. I am the only one left, and now they want to
kill me."
4 But the Lord told Elijah, "I still have seven thousand fol-
lowers who have not worshiped Baal." 5 It is the same way

NEW INTERNATIONAL VERSION

I revealed myself to those who did not ask for me."[k]

21But concerning Israel he says,

"All day long I have held out my hands
to a disobedient and obstinate people."[l]

The Remnant of Israel

11 I ask then: Did God reject his people? By no
means! I am an Israelite myself, a descendant of
Abraham, from the tribe of Benjamin. 2God did not reject
his people, whom he foreknew. Don't you know what the
Scripture says in the passage about Elijah—how he
appealed to God against Israel: 3"Lord, they have killed
your prophets and torn down your altars; I am the only
one left, and they are trying to kill me"[a]? 4And what was
God's answer to him? "I have reserved for myself seven
thousand who have not bowed the knee to Baal."[b] 5So too,

[k] *20* Isaiah 65:1 [l] *21* Isaiah 65:2 [a] *3* 1 Kings 19:10,14
[b] *4* 1 Kings 19:18

NEW LIVING TRANSLATION

I showed myself to those
who were not asking for me."*

21But regarding Israel, God said,

"All day long I opened my arms to them,
but they kept disobeying me and arguing with me."*

God's Mercy on Israel

11 I ask, then, has God rejected his people, the Jews?
Of course not! Remember that I myself am a Jew, a
descendant of Abraham and a member of the tribe of
Benjamin.

2No, God has not rejected his own people, whom he
chose from the very beginning. Do you remember what the
Scriptures say about this? Elijah the prophet complained to
God about the people of Israel and said, 3"Lord, they have
killed your prophets and torn down your altars. I alone am
left, and now they are trying to kill me, too."*

4And do you remember God's reply? He said, "You are
not the only one left. I have seven thousand others who
have never bowed down to Baal!"*

10:20 Isa 65:1. 10:21 Isa 65:2. 11:3 1 Kgs 19:10, 14.
11:4 1 Kgs 19:18.

NEW KING JAMES VERSION

*I was made manifest to those who did not ask
for Me."*[m]

21But to Israel he says:

*"All day long I have stretched out My hands
To a disobedient and contrary people."*[n]

Israel's Rejection Not Total

11 I say then, has God cast away His people? Cer-
tainly not! For I also am an Israelite, of the seed of
Abraham, *of* the tribe of Benjamin. 2God has not cast away
His people whom He foreknew. Or do you not know what
the Scripture says of Elijah, how he pleads with God
against Israel, saying, 3*"LORD, they have killed Your proph-
ets and torn down Your altars, and I alone am left, and
they seek my life"*? [a] 4But what does the divine response
say to him? *"I have reserved for Myself seven thousand
men who have not bowed the knee to Baal."*[b] 5Even so

10:20 [m] Isaiah 65:1 10:21 [n] Isaiah 65:2 11:3 [a] 1 Kings 19:10, 14
11:4 [b] 1 Kings 19:18

THE MESSAGE

And I found and welcomed people
who had never even asked about me."

Then he capped it with a damning indictment:

"Day after day after day,
I beckoned Israel with open arms,
And got nothing for my trouble
but cold shoulders and icy stares."

The Loyal Minority

11 Does this mean, then, that God is so fed up with
Israel that he'll have nothing more to do with
them? Hardly. Remember that I, the one writing these
things, am an Israelite, a descendant of Abraham out of
the tribe of Benjamin. You can't get much more Semitic
than that! So we're not talking about repudiation. God has
been too long involved with Israel, has too much invested,
to simply wash his hands of them.

Do you remember that time Elijah was agonizing over
this same Israel and cried out in prayer?

"God, they murdered your prophets,
They trashed your altars;
I'm the only one left and now they're after me!"

And do you remember God's answer?
"I still have seven thousand who haven't quit,
Seven thousand who are loyal to the finish."

KING JAMES VERSION

5 Even so then at this present time also there is a remnant according to the election of grace.

6 And if by grace, then *is it* no more of works: otherwise grace is no more grace. But if *it be* of works, then is it no more grace: otherwise work is no more work.

7 What then? Israel hath not obtained that which he seeketh for; but the election hath obtained it, and the rest were blinded

8 (According as it is written, God hath given them the spirit of slumber, eyes that they should not see, and ears that they should not hear;) unto this day.

9 And David saith, Let their table be made a snare, and a trap, and a stumblingblock, and a recompence unto them:

10 Let their eyes be darkened, that they may not see, and bow down their back alway.

11 I say then, Have they stumbled that they should fall? God forbid: but *rather* through their fall salvation *is come* unto the Gentiles, for to provoke them to jealousy.

NEW AMERICAN STANDARD BIBLE

5 In the same way then, there has also come to be at the present time a remnant according to *God's* gracious choice.

6 But if it is by grace, it is no longer on the basis of works, otherwise grace is no longer grace.

7 What then? What Israel is seeking, it has not obtained, but those who were chosen obtained it, and the rest were hardened;

8 just as it is written,
"God gave them a spirit of stupor,
Eyes to see not and ears to hear not,
Down to this very day."

9 And David says,
"Let their table become a snare and a trap,
And a stumbling block and a retribution to them.

10 "Let their eyes be darkened to see not,
And bend their backs forever."

11 I say then, they did not stumble so as to fall, did they? May it never be! But by their transgression salvation *has come* to the Gentiles, to make them jealous.

NEW CENTURY VERSION

a few people that God has chosen by his grace. 6And if he
chose them by grace, it is not for the things they have
done. If they could be made God's people by what they did,
God's gift of grace would not really be a gift.

7So this is what has happened: Although the Israelites
tried to be right with God, they did not succeed, but the
ones God chose did become right with him. The others
were made stubborn and refused to listen to God. 8As it is
written in the Scriptures:

"God gave the people a dull mind so they could not
understand." *Isaiah 29:10*

"He closed their eyes so they could not see
and their ears so they could not hear.
This continues until today." *Deuteronomy 29:4*

9And David says:

"Let their own feasts trap them and cause their ruin;
let their feasts cause them to stumble and be paid
back.

10Let their eyes be closed so they cannot see
and their backs be forever weak from troubles."
Psalm 69:22–23

11So I ask: When the Jews fell, did that fall destroy
them? No! But their mistake brought salvation to those
who are not Jews, in order to make the Jews jealous. 12The

CONTEMPORARY ENGLISH VERSION

now. God was kind to the people of Israel, and so a few of
them are still his followers. 6This happened because of God's
undeserved kindness and not because of anything they have
done. It could not have happened except for God's kindness.

7This means that only a chosen few of the people of
Israel found what all of them were searching for. And the
rest of them were stubborn, 8just as the Scriptures say,

"God made them so stupid
that their eyes are blind,
and their ears
are still deaf."

9Then David said,

"Turn their meals
into bait for a trap,
so that they will stumble
and be given
what they deserve.

10Blindfold their eyes!
Don't let them see.
Bend their backs
beneath a burden
that will never be lifted."

Gentiles Will Be Saved

11Do I mean that the people of Israel fell, never to get up
again? Certainly not! Their failure made it possible for the

NEW INTERNATIONAL VERSION

at the present time there is a remnant chosen by grace.
6And if by grace, then it is no longer by works; if it were,
grace would no longer be grace.[c]
7What then? What Israel sought so earnestly it did not
obtain, but the elect did. The others were hardened, 8as it
is written:

"God gave them a spirit of stupor,
eyes so that they could not see
and ears so that they could not hear,
to this very day."[d]

9And David says:

"May their table become a snare and a trap,
a stumbling block and a retribution for them.
10May their eyes be darkened so they cannot see,
and their backs be bent forever."[e]

Ingrafted Branches

11Again I ask: Did they stumble so as to fall beyond
recovery? Not at all! Rather, because of their transgres-
sion, salvation has come to the Gentiles to make Israel

[c] *6* Some manuscripts *by grace. But if by works, then it is no longer grace; if it were, work would no longer be work.* [d] *8* Deut. 29:4; Isaiah 29:10 [e] *10* Psalm 69:22,23

NEW LIVING TRANSLATION

5It is the same today, for not all the Jews have turned
away from God. A few* are being saved as a result of God's
kindness in choosing them. 6And if they are saved by
God's kindness, then it is not by their good works. For in
that case, God's wonderful kindness would not be what it
really is—free and undeserved.
7So this is the situation: Most of the Jews have not
found the favor of God they are looking for so earnestly. A
few have—the ones God has chosen—but the rest were
made unresponsive. 8As the Scriptures say,

"God has put them into a deep sleep.
To this very day he has shut their eyes so they do not
see,
and closed their ears so they do not hear."*

9David spoke of this same thing when he said,

"Let their bountiful table become a snare,
a trap that makes them think all is well.
Let their blessings cause them to stumble.
10 Let their eyes go blind so they cannot see,
and let their backs grow weaker and weaker."*

11Did God's people stumble and fall beyond recovery? Of
course not! His purpose was to make his salvation avail-
able to the Gentiles, and then the Jews would be jealous

11:5 Greek *A remnant.* 11:8 Deut 29:4; Isa 29:10.
11:9-10 Ps 69:22-23.

NEW KING JAMES VERSION

then, at this present time there is a remnant according to
the election of grace. 6And if by grace, then *it is* no longer
of works; otherwise grace is no longer grace.[c] But if *it is* of
works, it is no longer grace; otherwise work is no longer
work.
7What then? Israel has not obtained what it seeks; but
the elect have obtained it, and the rest were blinded. 8Just
as it is written:

"God has given them a spirit of stupor,
Eyes that they should not see
And ears that they should not hear,
To this very day."[d]

9And David says:

"Let their table become a snare and a trap,
A stumbling block and a recompense to them.
10 *Let their eyes be darkened, so that they do not see,*
And bow down their back always."[e]

Israel's Rejection Not Final

11I say then, have they stumbled that they should fall?
Certainly not! But through their fall, to provoke them to
jealousy, salvation *has come* to the Gentiles. 12Now if their

11:6 [c] NU-Text omits the rest of this verse. 11:8 [d] Deuteronomy 29:4; Isaiah 29:10 11:10 [e] Psalm 69:22, 23

THE MESSAGE

It's the same today. There's a fiercely loyal minority still—
not many, perhaps, but probably more than you think.
They're holding on, not because of what they think they're
going to get out of it, but because they're convinced of
God's grace and purpose in choosing them. If they were
only thinking of their own immediate self-interest, they
would have left long ago.
And then what happened? Well, when Israel tried to be
right with God on her own, pursuing her own self-interest,
she didn't succeed. The chosen ones of God were those
who let God pursue his interest in them, and as a result
received his stamp of legitimacy. The "self-interest Israel"
became thick-skinned toward God. Moses and Isaiah both
commented on this:

"Fed up with their quarrelsome, self-centered ways,
God blurred their eyes and dulled their ears,
Shut them in on themselves in a hall of mirrors,
and they're there to this day."

David was upset about the same thing:
"I hope they get sick eating self-serving meals,
break a leg walking their self-serving ways.
I hope they go blind staring in their mirrors,
get ulcers from playing at god."

Pruning and Grafting Branches

The next question is, "Are they down for the count? Are
they out of this for good?" And the answer is a clear-cut

KING JAMES VERSION

12 Now if the fall of them *be* the riches of the world, and the diminishing of them the riches of the Gentiles; how much more their fulness?

13 For I speak to you Gentiles, inasmuch as I am the apostle of the Gentiles, I magnify mine office:

14 If by any means I may provoke to emulation *them which are* my flesh, and might save some of them.

15 For if the casting away of them *be* the reconciling of the world, what *shall* the receiving *of them be*, but life from the dead?

16 For if the firstfruit *be* holy, the lump *is* also *holy*: and if the root *be* holy, so *are* the branches.

17 And if some of the branches be broken off, and thou, being a wild olive tree, wert graffed in among them, and with them partakest of the root and fatness of the olive tree;

18 Boast not against the branches. But if thou boast, thou bearest not the root, but the root thee.

19 Thou wilt say then, The branches were broken off, that I might be graffed in.

20 Well; because of unbelief they were broken off, and thou standest by faith. Be not highminded, but fear:

NEW AMERICAN STANDARD BIBLE

12 Now if their transgression is riches for the world and their failure is riches for the Gentiles, how much more will their fulfillment be!

13 But I am speaking to you who are Gentiles. Inasmuch then as I am an apostle of Gentiles, I magnify my ministry,

14 if somehow I might move to jealousy my fellow countrymen and save some of them.

15 For if their rejection is the reconciliation of the world, what will *their* acceptance be but life from the dead?

16 If the first piece *of dough* is holy, the lump is also; and if the root is holy, the branches are too.

17 But if some of the branches were broken off, and you, being a wild olive, were grafted in among them and became partaker with them of the rich root of the olive tree,

18 do not be arrogant toward the branches; but if you are arrogant, *remember that* it is not you who supports the root, but the root *supports* you.

19 You will say then, "Branches were broken off so that I might be grafted in."

20 Quite right, they were broken off for their unbelief, but you stand by your faith. Do not be conceited, but fear;

NEW CENTURY VERSION

Jews' mistake brought rich blessings for the world, and the Jews' loss brought rich blessings for the non-Jewish people. So surely the world will receive much richer blessings when enough Jews become the kind of people God wants.

13 Now I am speaking to you who are not Jews. I am an apostle to those who are not Jews, and since I have that work, I will make the most of it. 14 I hope I can make my own people jealous and, in that way, help some of them to be saved. 15 When God turned away from the Jews, he became friends with other people in the world. So when God accepts the Jews, surely that will bring them life after death.

16 If the first piece of bread is offered to God, then the whole loaf is made holy. If the roots of a tree are holy, then the tree's branches are holy too.

17 It is as if some of the branches from an olive tree have been broken off. You non-Jewish people are like the branch of a wild olive tree that has been joined to that first tree. You now share the strength and life of the first tree, the Jews. 18 So do not brag about those branches that were broken off. If you brag, remember that you do not support the root, but the root supports you. 19 You will say, "Branches were broken off so that I could be joined to their tree." 20 That is true. But those branches were broken off because they did not believe, and you continue to be part of the tree only because you believe. Do not be proud, but be

CONTEMPORARY ENGLISH VERSION

Gentiles to be saved, and this will make the people of Israel jealous. 12 But if the rest of the world's people were helped so much by Israel's sin and loss, they will be helped even more by their full return.

13 I am now speaking to you Gentiles, and as long as I am an apostle to you, I will take pride in my work. 14 I hope in this way to make some of my own people jealous enough to be saved. 15 When Israel rejected God,[a] the rest of the people in the world were able to turn to him. So when God makes friends with Israel, it will be like bringing the dead back to life. 16 If part of a batch of dough is made holy by being offered to God, then all of the dough is holy. If the roots of a tree are holy, the rest of the tree is holy too.

17 You Gentiles are like branches of a wild olive tree that were made to be part of a cultivated olive tree. You have taken the place of some branches that were cut away from it. And because of this, you enjoy the blessings that come from being part of that cultivated tree. 18 But don't think you are better than the branches that were cut away. Just remember that you are not supporting the roots of that tree. Its roots are supporting you.

19 Maybe you think those branches were cut away, so that you could be put in their place. 20 That's true enough. But they were cut away because they did not have faith, and you are where you are because you do have faith. So

[a] 11.15 *When Israel rejected God*: Or "When Israel was rejected."

NEW INTERNATIONAL VERSION

envious. 12But if their transgression means riches for the world, and their loss means riches for the Gentiles, how much greater riches will their fullness bring!

13I am talking to you Gentiles. Inasmuch as I am the apostle to the Gentiles, I make much of my ministry 14in the hope that I may somehow arouse my own people to envy and save some of them. 15For if their rejection is the reconciliation of the world, what will their acceptance be but life from the dead? 16If the part of the dough offered as firstfruits is holy, then the whole batch is holy; if the root is holy, so are the branches.

17If some of the branches have been broken off, and you, though a wild olive shoot, have been grafted in among the others and now share in the nourishing sap from the olive root, 18do not boast over those branches. If you do, consider this: You do not support the root, but the root supports you. 19You will say then, "Branches were broken off so that I could be grafted in." 20Granted. But they were broken off because of unbelief, and you stand by faith. Do not

NEW LIVING TRANSLATION

and want it for themselves. 12Now if the Gentiles were enriched because the Jews turned down God's offer of salvation, think how much greater a blessing the world will share when the Jews finally accept it.

13I am saying all of this especially for you Gentiles. God has appointed me as the apostle to the Gentiles. I lay great stress on this, 14for I want to find a way to make the Jews want what you Gentiles have, and in that way I might save some of them. 15For since the Jews' rejection meant that God offered salvation to the rest of the world, how much more wonderful their acceptance will be. It will be life for those who were dead! 16And since Abraham and the other patriarchs were holy, their children will also be holy.* For if the roots of the tree are holy, the branches will be, too.

17But some of these branches from Abraham's tree, some of the Jews, have been broken off. And you Gentiles, who were branches from a wild olive tree, were grafted in. So now you also receive the blessing God has promised Abraham and his children, sharing in God's rich nourishment of his special olive tree. 18But you must be careful not to brag about being grafted in to replace the branches that were broken off. Remember, you are just a branch, not the root.

19"Well," you may say, "those branches were broken off to make room for me." 20Yes, but remember—those branches, the Jews, were broken off because they didn't believe God, and you are there because you do believe. Don't think highly of yourself, but fear what could happen.

11:16 Greek *If the dough offered as firstfruits is holy, so is the whole lump.*

NEW KING JAMES VERSION

fall *is* riches for the world, and their failure riches for the Gentiles, how much more their fullness!

13For I speak to you Gentiles; inasmuch as I am an apostle to the Gentiles, I magnify my ministry, 14if by any means I may provoke to jealousy *those who are* my flesh and save some of them. 15For if their being cast away *is* the reconciling of the world, what *will* their acceptance *be* but life from the dead?

16For if the firstfruit *is* holy, the lump *is* also *holy;* and if the root *is* holy, so *are* the branches. 17And if some of the branches were broken off, and you, being a wild olive tree, were grafted in among them, and with them became a partaker of the root and fatness of the olive tree, 18do not boast against the branches. But if you do boast, *remember that* you do not support the root, but the root supports you.

19You will say then, "Branches were broken off that I might be grafted in." 20Well *said.* Because of unbelief they were broken off, and you stand by faith. Do not be

THE MESSAGE

no. Ironically when they walked out, they left the door open and the outsiders walked in. But the next thing you know, the Jews were starting to wonder if perhaps they had walked out on a good thing. Now, if their leaving triggered this worldwide coming of non-Jewish outsiders to God's kingdom, just imagine the effect of their coming back! What a homecoming!

But I don't want to go on about them. It's you, the outsiders, that I'm concerned with now. Because my personal assignment is focused on the so-called outsiders, I make as much of this as I can when I'm among my Israelite kin, the so-called insiders, hoping they'll realize what they're missing and want to get in on what God is doing. If their falling out initiated this worldwide coming together, their recovery is going to set off something even better: mass homecoming! If the first thing the Jews did, even though it was wrong for them, turned out for your good, just think what's going to happen when they get it right!

Behind and underneath all this there is a holy, God-planted, God-tended root. If the primary root of the tree is holy, there's bound to be some holy fruit. Some of the tree's branches were pruned and you wild olive shoots were grafted in. Yet the fact that you are now fed by that rich and holy root gives you no cause to crow over the pruned branches. Remember, you aren't feeding the root; the root is feeding you.

It's certainly possible to say, "Other branches were pruned so that *I* could be grafted in!" Well and good. But they were pruned because they were deadwood, no longer connected

KING JAMES VERSION

21 For if God spared not the natural branches, *take heed* lest he also spare not thee.

22 Behold therefore the goodness and severity of God: on them which fell, severity; but toward thee, goodness, if thou continue in *his* goodness: otherwise thou also shalt be cut off.

23 And they also, if they abide not still in unbelief, shall be graffed in: for God is able to graff them in again.

24 For if thou wert cut out of the olive tree which is wild by nature, and wert graffed contrary to nature into a good olive tree: how much more shall these, which be the natural *branches*, be graffed into their own olive tree?

25 For I would not, brethren, that ye should be ignorant of this mystery, lest ye should be wise in your own conceits; that blindness in part is happened to Israel, until

NEW AMERICAN STANDARD BIBLE

21 for if God did not spare the natural branches, He will not spare you, either.

22 Behold then the kindness and severity of God; to those who fell, severity, but to you, God's kindness, if you continue in His kindness; otherwise you also will be cut off.

23 And they also, if they do not continue in their unbelief, will be grafted in, for God is able to graft them in again.

24 For if you were cut off from what is by nature a wild olive tree, and were grafted contrary to nature into a cultivated olive tree, how much more will these who are the natural *branches* be grafted into their own olive tree?

25 For I do not want you, brethren, to be uninformed of this mystery—so that you will not be wise in your own estimation—that a partial hardening has happened to

NEW CENTURY VERSION

afraid. 21If God did not let the natural branches of that tree
stay, then he will not let you stay if you don't believe.
22So you see that God is kind and also very strict. He
punishes those who stop following him. But God is kind to
you, if you continue following in his kindness. If you do
not, you will be cut off from the tree. 23And if the Jews will
believe in God again, he will accept them back. God is able
to put them back where they were. 24It is not natural for a
wild branch to be part of a good tree. And you who are not
Jews are like a branch cut from a wild olive tree and joined
to a good olive tree. But since those Jews are like a branch
that grew from the good tree, surely they can be joined to
their own tree again.
25I want you to understand this secret, brothers and sisters, so you will understand that you do not know everything: Part of Israel has been made stubborn, but that will

CONTEMPORARY ENGLISH VERSION

don't be proud, but be afraid. 21If God cut away those natural branches, couldn't he do the same to you?
22Now you see both how kind and how hard God can be.
He was hard on those who fell, but he was kind to you.
And he will keep on being kind to you, if you keep on
trusting in his kindness. Otherwise, you will be cut away
too.
23If those other branches will start having faith, they
will be made a part of that tree again. God has the power
to put them back. 24After all, it wasn't natural for branches
to be cut from a wild olive tree and to be made part of a
cultivated olive tree. So it is much more likely that God
will join the natural branches back to the cultivated olive
tree.

The People of Israel Will Be Brought Back

25My friends, I don't want you Gentiles to be too proud of yourselves. So I will explain the mystery of what has happened to the people of Israel. Some of them have become stubborn, and they will stay like that until the

NEW INTERNATIONAL VERSION

be arrogant, but be afraid. 21For if God did not spare the natural branches, he will not spare you either.

22Consider therefore the kindness and sternness of God: sternness to those who fell, but kindness to you, provided that you continue in his kindness. Otherwise, you also will be cut off. 23And if they do not persist in unbelief, they will be grafted in, for God is able to graft them in again. 24After all, if you were cut out of an olive tree that is wild by nature, and contrary to nature were grafted into a cultivated olive tree, how much more readily will these, the natural branches, be grafted into their own olive tree!

All Israel Will Be Saved

25I do not want you to be ignorant of this mystery, brothers, so that you may not be conceited: Israel has experienced a hardening in part until the full number of

NEW LIVING TRANSLATION

21For if God did not spare the branches he put there in the first place, he won't spare you either.

22Notice how God is both kind and severe. He is severe to those who disobeyed, but kind to you as you continue to trust in his kindness. But if you stop trusting, you also will be cut off. 23And if the Jews turn from their unbelief, God will graft them back into the tree again. He has the power to do it.

24For if God was willing to take you who were, by nature, branches from a wild olive tree and graft you into his own good tree—a very unusual thing to do—he will be far more eager to graft the Jews back into the tree where they belong.

God's Mercy Is for Everyone

25I want you to understand this mystery, dear brothers and sisters,* so that you will not feel proud and start bragging. Some of the Jews have hard hearts, but this will last

11:25 Greek *brothers.*

NEW KING JAMES VERSION

haughty, but fear. 21For if God did not spare the natural branches, He may not spare you either. 22Therefore consider the goodness and severity of God: on those who fell, severity; but toward you, goodness,[f] if you continue in *His* goodness. Otherwise you also will be cut off. 23And they also, if they do not continue in unbelief, will be grafted in, for God is able to graft them in again. 24For if you were cut out of the olive tree which is wild by nature, and were grafted contrary to nature into a cultivated olive tree, how much more will these, who *are* natural *branches,* be grafted into their own olive tree?

25For I do not desire, brethren, that you should be ignorant of this mystery, lest you should be wise in your own opinion, that blindness in part has happened to Israel until

11:22 [f] NU-Text adds *of God.*

THE MESSAGE

by belief and commitment to the root. The only reason you're on the tree is because your graft "took" when you believed, and because you're connected to that belief-nurturing root. So don't get cocky and strut your branch. Be humbly mindful of the root that keeps you lithe and green.

If God didn't think twice about taking pruning shears to the natural branches, why would he hesitate over you? He wouldn't give it a second thought. Make sure you stay alert to these qualities of gentle kindness and ruthless severity that exist side by side in God—ruthless with the deadwood, gentle with the grafted shoot. But don't presume on this gentleness. The moment you become deadwood, you're out of there.

And don't get to feeling superior to those pruned branches down on the ground. If they don't persist in remaining deadwood, they could very well get grafted back in. God can do that. He can perform miracle grafts. Why, if he could graft *you*—branches cut from a tree out in the wild—into an orchard tree, he certainly isn't going to have any trouble grafting branches back into the tree they grew from in the first place. Just be glad you're in the tree, and hope for the best for the others.

A Complete Israel

I want to lay all this out on the table as clearly as I can, friends. This is complicated. It would be easy to misinterpret what's going on and arrogantly assume that you're royalty and they're just rabble, out on their ears for good. But that's not it at all. This hardness on the part of insider Israel

KING JAMES VERSION

the fulness of the Gentiles be come in.

26 And so all Israel shall be saved: as it is written, There shall come out of Sion the Deliverer, and shall turn away ungodliness from Jacob:

27 For this *is* my covenant unto them, when I shall take away their sins.

28 As concerning the gospel, *they are* enemies for your sakes: but as touching the election, *they are* beloved for the fathers' sakes.

29 For the gifts and calling of God *are* without repentance.

30 For as ye in times past have not believed God, yet have now obtained mercy through their unbelief:

31 Even so have these also now not believed, that through your mercy they also may obtain mercy.

32 For God hath concluded them all in unbelief, that he might have mercy upon all.

33 ¶ O the depth of the riches both of the wisdom and knowledge of God! how unsearchable *are* his judgments, and his ways past finding out!

34 For who hath known the mind of the Lord? or who hath been his counsellor?

NEW AMERICAN STANDARD BIBLE

Israel until the fullness of the Gentiles has come in;

26 and so all Israel will be saved; just as it is written,

"The Deliverer will come from Zion,
He will remove ungodliness from Jacob."

27 "This is My covenant with them,
When I take away their sins."

28 From the standpoint of the gospel they are enemies for your sake, but from the standpoint of *God's* choice they are beloved for the sake of the fathers;

29 for the gifts and the calling of God are irrevocable.

30 For just as you once were disobedient to God, but now have been shown mercy because of their disobedience,

31 so these also now have been disobedient, that because of the mercy shown to you they also may now be shown mercy.

32 For God has shut up all in disobedience so that He may show mercy to all.

33 Oh, the depth of the riches both of the wisdom and knowledge of God! How unsearchable are His judgments and unfathomable His ways!

34 For who has known the mind of the Lord, or who became His counselor?

NEW CENTURY VERSION

change when many who are not Jews have come to God.
26 And that is how all Israel will be saved. It is written in the Scriptures:

"The Savior will come from Jerusalem;
he will take away all evil from the family of Jacob.[c]
27 And I will make this agreement with those people
when I take away their sins." *Isaiah 59:20–21; 27:9*

28 The Jews refuse to accept the Good News, so they are
God's enemies. This has happened to help you who are not
Jews. But the Jews are still God's chosen people, and he
loves them very much because of the promises he made to
their ancestors. 29 God never changes his mind about the
people he calls and the things he gives them. 30 At one time
you refused to obey God. But now you have received
mercy, because those people refused to obey. 31 And now
the Jews refuse to obey, because God showed mercy to you.
But this happened so that they also can receive mercy from
him. 32 God has given all people over to their stubborn
ways so that he can show mercy to all.

Praise to God

33 Yes, God's riches are very great, and his wisdom and
knowledge have no end! No one can explain the things
God decides or understand his ways. 34 As the Scripture
says,

"Who has known the mind of the Lord,
or who has been able to give him advice?" *Isaiah 40:13*

11:26 [c] **Jacob** Father of the twelve family groups of Israel, the people God chose to be his people.

CONTEMPORARY ENGLISH VERSION

complete number of you Gentiles has come in. 26 In this
way all of Israel will be saved, as the Scriptures say,

"From Zion someone will come
to rescue us.
Then Jacob's descendants
will stop being evil.
27 This is what the Lord
has promised to do
when he forgives their sins."

28 The people of Israel are treated as God's enemies, so
that the good news can come to you Gentiles. But they are
still the chosen ones, and God loves them because of their
famous ancestors. 29 God doesn't take back the gifts he has
given or forget about the people he has chosen.

30 At one time you Gentiles rejected God. But now Israel
has rejected God, and you have been shown mercy. 31 And
because of the mercy shown to you, they will also be
shown mercy. 32 All people have disobeyed God, and that's
why he treats them as prisoners. But he does this, so that
he can have mercy on all of them.

33 Who can measure the wealth and wisdom and knowl-
edge of God? Who can understand his decisions or explain
what he does?

34 "Has anyone known
the thoughts of the Lord
or given him advice?

NEW INTERNATIONAL VERSION

the Gentiles has come in. 26And so all Israel will be saved,
as it is written:

"The deliverer will come from Zion;
he will turn godlessness away from Jacob.
27 And this is[f] my covenant with them
when I take away their sins."[g]

28As far as the gospel is concerned, they are enemies on
your account; but as far as election is concerned, they are
loved on account of the patriarchs, 29for God's gifts and
his call are irrevocable. 30Just as you who were at one time
disobedient to God have now received mercy as a result of
their disobedience, 31so they too have now become disobe-
dient in order that they too may now[h] receive mercy as a
result of God's mercy to you. 32For God has bound all men
over to disobedience so that he may have mercy on them
all.

Doxology

33 Oh, the depth of the riches of the wisdom and[i]
knowledge of God!
How unsearchable his judgments,
and his paths beyond tracing out!
34 "Who has known the mind of the Lord?
Or who has been his counselor?"[j]

[f] *27* Or *will be* [g] *27* Isaiah 59:20,21; 27:9; Jer. 31:33,34 [h] *31* Some manuscripts do not have *now*. [i] *33* Or *riches and the wisdom and the* [j] *34* Isaiah 40:13

NEW LIVING TRANSLATION

only until the complete number of Gentiles comes to Christ.
26And so all Israel will be saved. Do you remember what
the prophets said about this?

"A Deliverer will come from Jerusalem,*
and he will turn Israel* from all ungodliness.
27 And then I will keep my covenant with them
and take away their sins."*

28Many of the Jews are now enemies of the Good News.
But this has been to your benefit, for God has given his
gifts to you Gentiles. Yet the Jews are still his chosen peo-
ple because of his promises to Abraham, Isaac, and Jacob.
29For God's gifts and his call can never be withdrawn.
30Once, you Gentiles were rebels against God, but when
the Jews refused his mercy, God was merciful to you
instead. 31And now, in the same way, the Jews are the
rebels, and God's mercy has come to you. But someday
they,* too, will share in God's mercy. 32For God has impris-
oned all people in their own disobedience so he could have
mercy on everyone.
33Oh, what a wonderful God we have! How great are his
riches and wisdom and knowledge! How impossible it is
for us to understand his decisions and his methods! 34For
who can know what the Lord is thinking? Who knows
enough to be his counselor?* 35And who could ever give

11:26a Greek *from Zion.* **11:26b** Greek *Jacob.* **11:26-27** Isa 59:20-21. **11:31** Some manuscripts read *But now they;* other manuscripts read *But they.* **11:34** See Isa 40:13.

NEW KING JAMES VERSION

the fullness of the Gentiles has come in. 26And so all Israel
will be saved,[g] as it is written:

"The Deliverer will come out of Zion,
And He will turn away ungodliness from Jacob;
27 *For this is My covenant with them,*
When I take away their sins."[h]

28Concerning the gospel *they are* enemies for your sake,
but concerning the election *they are* beloved for the sake of
the fathers. 29For the gifts and the calling of God *are* irrev-
ocable. 30For as you were once disobedient to God, yet
have now obtained mercy through their disobedience,
31even so these also have now been disobedient, that
through the mercy shown you they also may obtain mercy.
32For God has committed them all to disobedience, that He
might have mercy on all.
33Oh, the depth of the riches both of the wisdom and
knowledge of God! How unsearchable *are* His judgments
and His ways past finding out!

34 *"For who has known the mind of the* LORD?
Or who has become His counselor?"[i]

11:26 [g] Or *delivered* **11:27** [h] Isaiah 59:20, 21
11:34 [i] Isaiah 40:13; Jeremiah 23:18

THE MESSAGE

toward God is temporary. Its effect is to open things up to all the outsiders so that we end up with a full house. Before it's all over, there will be a complete Israel. As it is written,

"A champion will stride down from the mountain of
Zion;
he'll clean house in Jacob.
And this is my commitment to my people:
removal of their sins."

From your point of view as you hear and embrace the good news of the Message, it looks like the Jews are God's enemies. But looked at from the long-range perspective of God's overall purpose, they remain God's oldest friends. God's gifts and God's call are under full warranty—never canceled, never rescinded.

There was a time not so long ago when you were on the outs with God. But then the Jews slammed the door on him and things opened up for you. Now *they* are on the outs. But with the door held wide open for you, they have a way back in. In one way or another, God makes sure that we all experience what it means to be outside so that he can personally open the door and welcome us back in.

Have you ever come on anything quite like this extravagant generosity of God, this deep, deep wisdom? It's way over our heads. We'll never figure it out.

"Is there anyone around who can explain God?
Anyone smart enough to tell him what to do?

KING JAMES VERSION

35 Or who hath first given to him, and it shall be rec-
ompensed unto him again?

36 For of him, and through him, and to him, *are* all
things: to whom *be* glory for ever. Amen.

12 I beseech you therefore, brethren, by the mercies of
God, that ye present your bodies a living sacrifice,
holy, acceptable unto God, *which is* your reasonable ser-
vice.

2 And be not conformed to this world: but be ye trans-
formed by the renewing of your mind, that ye may prove
what *is* that good, and acceptable, and perfect, will of God.

3 For I say, through the grace given unto me, to every
man that is among you, not to think *of himself* more high-
ly than he ought to think; but to think soberly, according
as God hath dealt to every man the measure of faith.

NEW AMERICAN STANDARD BIBLE

35 OR WHO HAS FIRST GIVEN TO HIM THAT IT MIGHT BE PAID
BACK TO HIM AGAIN?

36 For from Him and through Him and to Him are all
things. To Him *be* the glory forever. Amen.

Dedicated Service

12 Therefore I urge you, brethren, by the mercies of
God, to present your bodies a living and holy sacri-
fice, acceptable to God, *which is* your spiritual service of
worship.

2 And do not be conformed to this world, but be trans-
formed by the renewing of your mind, so that you may
prove what the will of God is, that which is good and
acceptable and perfect.

3 For through the grace given to me I say to everyone
among you not to think more highly of himself than he
ought to think; but to think so as to have sound judgment,
as God has allotted to each a measure of faith.

NEW CENTURY VERSION

35 "No one has ever given God anything
that he must pay back." *Job 41:11*

36 Yes, God made all things, and everything continues
through him and for him. To him be the glory forever!
Amen.

Give Your Lives to God

12 So brothers and sisters, since God has shown us
great mercy, I beg you to offer your lives as a liv-
ing sacrifice to him. Your offering must be only for God
and pleasing to him, which is the spiritual way for you to
worship. 2 Do not change yourselves to be like the people of
this world, but be changed within by a new way of think-
ing. Then you will be able to decide what God wants for
you; you will know what is good and pleasing to him and
what is perfect. 3 Because God has given me a special gift, I
have something to say to everyone among you. Do not
think you are better than you are. You must decide what
you really are by the amount of faith God has given you.

CONTEMPORARY ENGLISH VERSION

35 Has anyone loaned
something to the Lord
that must be repaid?"

36 Everything comes from the Lord. All things were made
because of him and will return to him. Praise the Lord for-
ever! Amen.

Christ Brings New Life

12 Dear friends, God is good. So I beg you to offer
your bodies to him as a living sacrifice, pure and
pleasing. That's the most sensible way to serve God.
2 Don't be like the people of this world, but let God change
the way you think. Then you will know how to do every-
thing that is good and pleasing to him.

3 I realize how kind God has been to me, and so I tell each
of you not to think you are better than you really are. Use
good sense and measure yourself by the amount of faith

NEW INTERNATIONAL VERSION

35 "Who has ever given to God,
that God should repay him?"[k]
36 For from him and through him and to him are all
things.
To him be the glory forever! Amen.

Living Sacrifices

12 Therefore, I urge you, brothers, in view of God's mercy, to offer your bodies as living sacrifices, holy and pleasing to God—this is your spiritual[a] act of worship. 2 Do not conform any longer to the pattern of this world, but be transformed by the renewing of your mind. Then you will be able to test and approve what God's will is—his good, pleasing and perfect will.

3 For by the grace given me I say to every one of you: Do not think of yourself more highly than you ought, but rather think of yourself with sober judgment, in accordance with the measure of faith God has given you. 4 Just

[k] *35* Job 41:11 [a] *1* Or *reasonable*

NEW LIVING TRANSLATION

him so much that he would have to pay it back? 36 For everything comes from him; everything exists by his power and is intended for his glory. To him be glory evermore. Amen.

A Living Sacrifice to God

12 And so, dear brothers and sisters,* I plead with you to give your bodies to God. Let them be a living and holy sacrifice—the kind he will accept. When you think of what he has done for you, is this too much to ask? 2 Don't copy the behavior and customs of this world, but let God transform you into a new person by changing the way you think. Then you will know what God wants you to do, and you will know how good and pleasing and perfect his will really is.

3 As God's messenger, I give each of you this warning: Be honest in your estimate of yourselves, measuring your value by how much faith God has given you. 4 Just as our

12:1 Greek *brothers.*

NEW KING JAMES VERSION

35 "*Or who has first given to Him*
And it shall be repaid to him?"[j]

36 For of Him and through Him and to Him *are* all things, to whom *be* glory forever. Amen.

Living Sacrifices to God

12 I beseech you therefore, brethren, by the mercies of God, that you present your bodies a living sacrifice, holy, acceptable to God, *which is* your reasonable service. 2 And do not be conformed to this world, but be transformed by the renewing of your mind, that you may prove what *is* that good and acceptable and perfect will of God.

Serve God with Spiritual Gifts

3 For I say, through the grace given to me, to everyone who is among you, not to think *of himself* more highly than he ought to think, but to think soberly, as God has dealt to each one a measure of faith. 4 For as we have

11:35 [j] Job 41:11

THE MESSAGE

Anyone who has done him such a huge favor
that God has to ask his advice?"

Everything comes from him;
Everything happens through him;
Everything ends up in him.
Always glory! Always praise!
Yes. Yes. Yes.

Place Your Life Before God

12 So here's what I want you to do, God helping you: Take your everyday, ordinary life—your sleeping, eating, going-to-work, and walking-around life—and place it before God as an offering. Embracing what God does for you is the best thing you can do for him. Don't become so well-adjusted to your culture that you fit into it without even thinking. Instead, fix your attention on God. You'll be changed from the inside out. Readily recognize what he wants from you, and quickly respond to it. Unlike the culture around you, always dragging you down to its level of immaturity, God brings the best out of you, develops well-formed maturity in you.

I'm speaking to you out of deep gratitude for all that God has given me, and especially as I have responsibilities in relation to you. Living then, as every one of you does, in pure grace, it's important that you not misinterpret yourselves as people who are bringing this goodness to God. No, God brings it all to you. The only accurate way to understand ourselves is by what God is and by what he does for us, not by what we are and what we do for him.

KING JAMES VERSION

4 For as we have many members in one body, and all members have not the same office:

5 So we, *being* many, are one body in Christ, and every one members one of another.

6 Having then gifts differing according to the grace that is given to us, whether prophecy, *let us prophesy* according to the proportion of faith;

7 Or ministry, *let us wait* on *our* ministering: or he that teacheth, on teaching;

8 Or he that exhorteth, on exhortation: he that giveth, *let him do it* with simplicity; he that ruleth, with diligence; he that sheweth mercy, with cheerfulness.

9 *Let* love be without dissimulation. Abhor that which is evil; cleave to that which is good.

10 *Be* kindly affectioned one to another with brotherly love; in honour preferring one another;

11 Not slothful in business; fervent in spirit; serving the Lord;

12 Rejoicing in hope; patient in tribulation; continuing instant in prayer;

13 Distributing to the necessity of saints; given to hospitality.

14 Bless them which persecute you: bless, and curse not.

NEW AMERICAN STANDARD BIBLE

4 For just as we have many members in one body and all the members do not have the same function,

5 so we, who are many, are one body in Christ, and individually members one of another.

6 Since we have gifts that differ according to the grace given to us, *each of us is to exercise them accordingly:* if prophecy, according to the proportion of his faith;

7 if service, in his serving; or he who teaches, in his teaching;

8 or he who exhorts, in his exhortation; he who gives, with [1]liberality; he who leads, with diligence; he who shows mercy, with cheerfulness.

9 *Let* love *be* without hypocrisy. Abhor what is evil; cling to what is good.

10 *Be* devoted to one another in brotherly love; give preference to one another in honor;

11 not lagging behind in diligence, fervent in spirit, serving the Lord;

12 rejoicing in hope, persevering in tribulation, devoted to prayer,

13 contributing to the needs of the saints, practicing hospitality.

14 Bless those who persecute [2]you; bless and do not curse.

12:8 [1] Or *simplicity* 12:14 [2] Two early mss do not contain *you*

NEW CENTURY VERSION

4Each one of us has a body with many parts, and these
parts all have different uses. 5In the same way, we are
many, but in Christ we are all one body. Each one is a part
of that body, and each part belongs to all the other parts.
6We all have different gifts, each of which came because of
the grace God gave us. The person who has the gift of
prophecy should use that gift in agreement with the faith.
7Anyone who has the gift of serving should serve. Anyone
who has the gift of teaching should teach. 8Whoever has
the gift of encouraging others should encourage. Whoever
has the gift of giving to others should give freely. Anyone
who has the gift of being a leader should try hard when he
leads. Whoever has the gift of showing mercy to others
should do so with joy.

9Your love must be real. Hate what is evil, and hold on
to what is good. 10Love each other like brothers and sis-
ters. Give each other more honor than you want for your-
selves. 11Do not be lazy but work hard, serving the Lord
with all your heart. 12Be joyful because you have hope. Be
patient when trouble comes, and pray at all times. 13Share
with God's people who need help. Bring strangers in need
into your homes.

14Wish good for those who harm you; wish them well
and do not curse them. 15Be happy with those who are

CONTEMPORARY ENGLISH VERSION

that God has given you. 4A body is made up of many parts,
and each of them has its own use. 5That's how it is with
us. There are many of us, but we each are part of the body
of Christ, as well as part of one another.

6God has also given each of us different gifts to use. If
we can prophesy, we should do it according to the amount
of faith we have. 7If we can serve others, we should serve.
If we can teach, we should teach. 8If we can encourage
others, we should encourage them. If we can give, we
should be generous. If we are leaders, we should do our
best. If we are good to others, we should do it cheerfully.

Rules for Christian Living

9Be sincere in your love for others. Hate everything that
is evil and hold tight to everything that is good. 10Love
each other as brothers and sisters and honor others more
than you do yourself. 11Never give up. Eagerly follow the
Holy Spirit and serve the Lord. 12Let your hope make you
glad. Be patient in time of trouble and never stop praying.
13Take care of God's needy people and welcome strangers
into your home.

14Ask God to bless everyone who mistreats you. Ask him
to bless them and not to curse them. 15When others are

NEW INTERNATIONAL VERSION

as each of us has one body with many members, and these members do not all have the same function, 5so in Christ we who are many form one body, and each member belongs to all the others. 6We have different gifts, according to the grace given us. If a man's gift is prophesying, let him use it in proportion to his[b] faith. 7If it is serving, let him serve; if it is teaching, let him teach; 8if it is encouraging, let him encourage; if it is contributing to the needs of others, let him give generously; if it is leadership, let him govern diligently; if it is showing mercy, let him do it cheerfully.

Love

9Love must be sincere. Hate what is evil; cling to what is good. 10Be devoted to one another in brotherly love. Honor one another above yourselves. 11Never be lacking in zeal, but keep your spiritual fervor, serving the Lord. 12Be joyful in hope, patient in affliction, faithful in prayer. 13Share with God's people who are in need. Practice hospitality.

14Bless those who persecute you; bless and do not curse.

[b] 6 Or *in agreement with the*

NEW LIVING TRANSLATION

bodies have many parts and each part has a special function, 5so it is with Christ's body. We are all parts of his one body, and each of us has different work to do. And since we are all one body in Christ, we belong to each other, and each of us needs all the others.

6God has given each of us the ability to do certain things well. So if God has given you the ability to prophesy, speak out when you have faith that God is speaking through you. 7If your gift is that of serving others, serve them well. If you are a teacher, do a good job of teaching. 8If your gift is to encourage others, do it! If you have money, share it generously. If God has given you leadership ability, take the responsibility seriously. And if you have a gift for showing kindness to others, do it gladly.

9Don't just pretend that you love others. Really love them. Hate what is wrong. Stand on the side of the good. 10Love each other with genuine affection,* and take delight in honoring each other. 11Never be lazy in your work, but serve the Lord enthusiastically.

12Be glad for all God is planning for you. Be patient in trouble, and always be prayerful. 13When God's children are in need, be the one to help them out. And get into the habit of inviting guests home for dinner or, if they need lodging, for the night.

14If people persecute you because you are a Christian, don't curse them; pray that God will bless them. 15When

12:10 Greek *with brotherly love.*

NEW KING JAMES VERSION

many members in one body, but all the members do not have the same function, 5so we, *being* many, are one body in Christ, and individually members of one another. 6Having then gifts differing according to the grace that is given to us, *let us use them:* if prophecy, *let us prophesy* in proportion to our faith; 7or ministry, *let us use it* in *our* ministering; he who teaches, in teaching; 8he who exhorts, in exhortation; he who gives, with liberality; he who leads, with diligence; he who shows mercy, with cheerfulness.

Behave Like a Christian

9*Let* love *be* without hypocrisy. Abhor what is evil. Cling to what is good. 10*Be* kindly affectionate to one another with brotherly love, in honor giving preference to one another; 11not lagging in diligence, fervent in spirit, serving the Lord; 12rejoicing in hope, patient in tribulation, continuing steadfastly in prayer; 13distributing to the needs of the saints, given to hospitality.

14Bless those who persecute you; bless and do not curse.

THE MESSAGE

In this way we are like the various parts of a human body. Each part gets its meaning from the body as a whole, not the other way around. The body we're talking about is Christ's body of chosen people. Each of us finds our meaning and function as a part of his body. But as a chopped-off finger or cut-off toe we wouldn't amount to much, would we? So since we find ourselves fashioned into all these excellently formed and marvelously functioning parts in Christ's body, let's just go ahead and be what we were made to be, without enviously or pridefully comparing ourselves with each other, or trying to be something we aren't.

If you preach, just preach God's Message, nothing else; if you help, just help, don't take over; if you teach, stick to your teaching; if you give encouraging guidance, be careful that you don't get bossy; if you're put in charge, don't manipulate; if you're called to give aid to people in distress, keep your eyes open and be quick to respond; if you work with the disadvantaged, don't let yourself get irritated with them or depressed by them. Keep a smile on your face.

✠

Love from the center of who you are; don't fake it. Run for dear life from evil; hold on for dear life to good. Be good friends who love deeply; practice playing second fiddle.

Don't burn out; keep yourselves fueled and aflame. Be alert servants of the Master, cheerfully expectant. Don't quit in hard times; pray all the harder. Help needy Christians; be inventive in hospitality.

Bless your enemies; no cursing under your breath.

KING JAMES VERSION

15 Rejoice with them that do rejoice, and weep with them that weep.
16 *Be* of the same mind one toward another. Mind not high things, but condescend to men of low estate. Be not wise in your own conceits.
17 Recompense to no man evil for evil. Provide things honest in the sight of all men.
18 If it be possible, as much as lieth in you, live peaceably with all men.
19 Dearly beloved, avenge not yourselves, but *rather* give place unto wrath: for it is written, Vengeance *is* mine; I will repay, saith the Lord.
20 Therefore if thine enemy hunger, feed him; if he thirst, give him drink: for in so doing thou shalt heap coals of fire on his head.
21 Be not overcome of evil, but overcome evil with good.

13 Let every soul be subject unto the higher powers. For there is no power but of God: the powers that be are ordained of God.

NEW AMERICAN STANDARD BIBLE

15 Rejoice with those who rejoice, and weep with those who weep.
16 Be of the same mind toward one another; do not be haughty in mind, but associate with the lowly. Do not be wise in your own estimation.
17 Never pay back evil for evil to anyone. Respect what is right in the sight of all men.
18 If possible, so far as it depends on you, be at peace with all men.
19 Never take your own revenge, beloved, but leave room for the wrath *of God,* for it is written, "VENGEANCE IS MINE, I WILL REPAY," says the Lord.
20 "BUT IF YOUR ENEMY IS HUNGRY, FEED HIM, AND IF HE IS THIRSTY, GIVE HIM A DRINK; FOR IN SO DOING YOU WILL HEAP BURNING COALS ON HIS HEAD."
21 Do not be overcome by evil, but overcome evil with good.

Be Subject to Government

13 Every person is to be in subjection to the governing authorities. For there is no authority except from God, and those which exist are established by God.

NEW CENTURY VERSION

happy, and be sad with those who are sad. 16Live in peace
with each other. Do not be proud, but make friends with those who seem unimportant. Do not think how smart you are.
17If someone does wrong to you, do not pay him back by doing wrong to him. Try to do what everyone thinks is
right. 18Do your best to live in peace with everyone. 19My
friends, do not try to punish others when they wrong you, but wait for God to punish them with his anger. It is written: "I will punish those who do wrong; I will repay
them,"[a] says the Lord. 20But you should do this:

"If your enemy is hungry, feed him;
if he is thirsty, give him a drink.
Doing this will be like pouring burning coals on his
head." *Proverbs 25:21–22*

21Do not let evil defeat you, but defeat evil by doing good.

Christians Should Obey the Law

13 All of you must yield to the government rulers. No one rules unless God has given him the power to rule, and no one rules now without that power from God.

12:19 [a] **"I...them"** Quotation from Deuteronomy 32:35.

CONTEMPORARY ENGLISH VERSION

happy, be happy with them, and when they are sad, be
sad. 16Be friendly with everyone. Don't be proud and feel that you are smarter than others. Make friends with ordinary people.[a] 17Don't mistreat someone who has mistreated you. But try to earn the respect of others, 18and do your
best to live at peace with everyone.
19Dear friends, don't try to get even. Let God take revenge. In the Scriptures the Lord says,

"I am the one to take revenge
and pay them back."

20The Scriptures also say,

"If your enemies are hungry,
give them something to eat.
And if they are thirsty,
give them something
to drink.
This will be the same
as piling burning coals
on their heads."

21Don't let evil defeat you, but defeat evil with good.

Obey Rulers

13 Obey the rulers who have authority over you. Only God can give authority to anyone, and he puts

[a] 12.16 *Make friends with ordinary people*: Or "Do ordinary jobs."

NEW INTERNATIONAL VERSION

15Rejoice with those who rejoice; mourn with those who
mourn. 16Live in harmony with one another. Do not be
proud, but be willing to associate with people of low posi-
tion.[c] Do not be conceited.
17Do not repay anyone evil for evil. Be careful to do what
is right in the eyes of everybody. 18If it is possible, as far
as it depends on you, live at peace with everyone. 19Do not
take revenge, my friends, but leave room for God's wrath,
for it is written: "It is mine to avenge; I will repay,"[d] says
the Lord. 20On the contrary:

"If your enemy is hungry, feed him;
if he is thirsty, give him something to drink.
In doing this, you will heap burning coals on his
head."[e]

21Do not be overcome by evil, but overcome evil with good.

Submission to the Authorities

13 Everyone must submit himself to the governing
authorities, for there is no authority except that
which God has established. The authorities that exist have

[c] *16* Or *willing to do menial work* [d] *19* Deut. 32:35
[e] *20* Prov. 25:21,22

NEW LIVING TRANSLATION

others are happy, be happy with them. If they are sad,
share their sorrow. 16Live in harmony with each other.
Don't try to act important, but enjoy the company of ordi-
nary people. And don't think you know it all!
17Never pay back evil for evil to anyone. Do things in such
a way that everyone can see you are honorable. 18Do your
part to live in peace with everyone, as much as possible.
19Dear friends, never avenge yourselves. Leave that to
God. For it is written,

"I will take vengeance;
I will repay those who deserve it,"*
says the Lord.

20Instead, do what the Scriptures say:

"If your enemies are hungry, feed them.
If they are thirsty, give them something to drink,
and they will be ashamed of what they have done to
you."*

21Don't let evil get the best of you, but conquer evil by
doing good.

Respect for Authority

13 Obey the government, for God is the one who put it
there. All governments have been placed in power

12:19 Deut 32:35. 12:20 Greek *and you will heap burning coals on their heads.* Prov 25:21-22.

NEW KING JAMES VERSION

15Rejoice with those who rejoice, and weep with those who
weep. 16Be of the same mind toward one another. Do not
set your mind on high things, but associate with the hum-
ble. Do not be wise in your own opinion.
17Repay no one evil for evil. Have regard for good things
in the sight of all men. 18If it is possible, as much as
depends on you, live peaceably with all men. 19Beloved, do
not avenge yourselves, but *rather* give place to wrath; for
it is written, *"Vengeance is Mine, I will repay,"*[a] says the
Lord. 20Therefore

"If your enemy is hungry, feed him;
If he is thirsty, give him a drink;
For in so doing you will heap coals of fire on his
head."[b]

21Do not be overcome by evil, but overcome evil with good.

Submit to Government

13 Let every soul be subject to the governing authori-
ties. For there is no authority except from God, and
the authorities that exist are appointed by God. 2Therefore

12:19 [a] Deuteronomy 32:35 12:20 [b] Proverbs 25:21, 22

THE MESSAGE

Laugh with your happy friends when they're happy; share
tears when they're down. Get along with each other; don't
be stuck-up. Make friends with nobodies; don't be the
great somebody.
Don't hit back; discover beauty in everyone. If you've got
it in you, get along with everybody. Don't insist on getting
even; that's not for you to do. "I'll do the judging," says
God. "I'll take care of it."
Our Scriptures tell us that if you see your enemy hungry,
go buy that person lunch, or if he's thirsty, get him a
drink. Your generosity will surprise him with goodness.
Don't let evil get the best of you; get the best of evil by
doing good.

To Be a Responsible Citizen

13 Be a good citizen. All governments are under God.
Insofar as there is peace and order, it's God's order.

KING JAMES VERSION

2 Whosoever therefore resisteth the power, resisteth the ordinance of God: and they that resist shall receive to themselves damnation.

3 For rulers are not a terror to good works, but to the evil. Wilt thou then not be afraid of the power? do that which is good, and thou shalt have praise of the same:

4 For he is the minister of God to thee for good. But if thou do that which is evil, be afraid; for he beareth not the sword in vain: for he is the minister of God, a revenger to *execute* wrath upon him that doeth evil.

5 Wherefore *ye* must needs be subject, not only for wrath, but also for conscience sake.

6 For for this cause pay ye tribute also: for they are God's ministers, attending continually upon this very thing.

7 ¶ Render therefore to all their dues: tribute to whom tribute *is due*; custom to whom custom; fear to whom fear; honour to whom honour.

8 Owe no man any thing, but to love one another: for he that loveth another hath fulfilled the law.

9 For this, Thou shalt not commit adultery, Thou shalt not kill, Thou shalt not steal, Thou shalt not bear false witness, Thou shalt not covet; and if *there be* any other commandment, it is briefly comprehended in this saying, namely, Thou shalt love thy neighbour as thyself.

10 Love worketh no ill to his neighbour: therefore love *is* the fulfilling of the law.

NEW AMERICAN STANDARD BIBLE

2 Therefore whoever resists authority has opposed the ordinance of God; and they who have opposed will receive condemnation upon themselves.

3 For rulers are not a cause of fear for good behavior, but for evil. Do you want to have no fear of authority? Do what is good and you will have praise from the same;

4 for it is a minister of God to you for good. But if you do what is evil, be afraid; for it does not bear the sword for nothing; for it is a minister of God, an avenger who brings wrath on the one who practices evil.

5 Therefore it is necessary to be in subjection, not only because of wrath, but also for conscience' sake.

6 For because of this you also pay taxes, for *rulers* are servants of God, devoting themselves to this very thing.

7 Render to all what is due them: tax to whom tax *is due;* custom to whom custom; fear to whom fear; honor to whom honor.

8 Owe nothing to anyone except to love one another; for he who loves his neighbor has fulfilled *the* law.

9 For this, "YOU SHALL NOT COMMIT ADULTERY, YOU SHALL NOT MURDER, YOU SHALL NOT STEAL, YOU SHALL NOT COVET," and if there is any other commandment, it is summed up in this saying, "YOU SHALL LOVE YOUR NEIGHBOR AS YOURSELF."

10 Love does no wrong to a neighbor; therefore love is the fulfillment of *the* law.

NEW CENTURY VERSION

2So those who are against the government are really against what God has commanded. And they will bring punishment on themselves. 3Those who do right do not have to fear the rulers; only those who do wrong fear them. Do you want to be unafraid of the rulers? Then do what is right, and they will praise you. 4The ruler is God's servant to help you. But if you do wrong, then be afraid. He has the power to punish; he is God's servant to punish those who do wrong. 5So you must yield to the government, not only because you might be punished, but because you know it is right.

6This is also why you pay taxes. Rulers are working for God and give their time to their work. 7Pay everyone, then, what you owe. If you owe any kind of tax, pay it. Show respect and honor to them all.

Loving Others

8Do not owe people anything, except always owe love to each other, because the person who loves others has obeyed all the law. 9The law says, "You must not be guilty of adultery. You must not murder anyone. You must not steal. You must not want to take your neighbor's things."[a] All these commands and all others are really only one rule: "Love your neighbor as you love yourself."[b] 10Love never hurts a neighbor, so loving is obeying all the law.

13:9 [a] "You...things." Quotation from Exodus 20:13–15, 17.
13:9 [b] "Love...yourself." Quotation from Leviticus 19:18.

CONTEMPORARY ENGLISH VERSION

these rulers in their places of power. 2People who oppose the authorities are opposing what God has done, and they will be punished. 3Rulers are a threat to evil people, not to good people. There is no need to be afraid of the authorities. Just do right, and they will praise you for it. 4After all, they are God's servants, and it is their duty to help you.

If you do something wrong, you ought to be afraid, because these rulers have the right to punish you. They are God's servants who punish criminals to show how angry God is. 5But you should obey the rulers because you know it is the right thing to do, and not just because of God's anger.

6You must also pay your taxes. The authorities are God's servants, and it is their duty to take care of these matters. 7Pay all that you owe, whether it is taxes and fees or respect and honor.

Love

8Let love be your only debt! If you love others, you have done all that the Law demands. 9In the Law there are many commands, such as, "Be faithful in marriage. Do not murder. Do not steal. Do not want what belongs to others." But all of these are summed up in the command that says, "Love others as much as you love yourself." 10No one who loves others will harm them. So love is all that the Law demands.

NEW INTERNATIONAL VERSION

been established by God. [2]Consequently, he who rebels against the authority is rebelling against what God has instituted, and those who do so will bring judgment on themselves. [3]For rulers hold no terror for those who do right, but for those who do wrong. Do you want to be free from fear of the one in authority? Then do what is right and he will commend you. [4]For he is God's servant to do you good. But if you do wrong, be afraid, for he does not bear the sword for nothing. He is God's servant, an agent of wrath to bring punishment on the wrongdoer. [5]Therefore, it is necessary to submit to the authorities, not only because of possible punishment but also because of conscience.

[6]This is also why you pay taxes, for the authorities are God's servants, who give their full time to governing. [7]Give everyone what you owe him: If you owe taxes, pay taxes; if revenue, then revenue; if respect, then respect; if honor, then honor.

Love, for the Day Is Near

[8]Let no debt remain outstanding, except the continuing debt to love one another, for he who loves his fellowman has fulfilled the law. [9]The commandments, "Do not commit adultery," "Do not murder," "Do not steal," "Do not covet,"[a] and whatever other commandment there may be, are summed up in this one rule: "Love your neighbor as yourself."[b] [10]Love does no harm to its neighbor. Therefore love is the fulfillment of the law.

[a] *9* Exodus 20:13–15,17; Deut. 5:17–19,21 [b] *9* Lev. 19:18

NEW LIVING TRANSLATION

by God. [2]So those who refuse to obey the laws of the land are refusing to obey God, and punishment will follow. [3]For the authorities do not frighten people who are doing right, but they frighten those who do wrong. So do what they say, and you will get along well. [4]The authorities are sent by God to help you. But if you are doing something wrong, of course you should be afraid, for you will be punished. The authorities are established by God for that very purpose, to punish those who do wrong. [5]So you must obey the government for two reasons: to keep from being punished and to keep a clear conscience.

[6]Pay your taxes, too, for these same reasons. For government workers need to be paid so they can keep on doing the work God intended them to do. [7]Give to everyone what you owe them: Pay your taxes and import duties, and give respect and honor to all to whom it is due.

Love Fulfills God's Requirements

[8]Pay all your debts, except the debt of love for others. You can never finish paying that! If you love your neighbor, you will fulfill all the requirements of God's law. [9]For the commandments against adultery and murder and stealing and coveting—and any other commandment—are all summed up in this one commandment: "Love your neighbor as yourself."* [10]Love does no wrong to anyone, so love satisfies all of God's requirements.

13:9 Lev 19:18.

NEW KING JAMES VERSION

whoever resists the authority resists the ordinance of God, and those who resist will bring judgment on themselves. [3]For rulers are not a terror to good works, but to evil. Do you want to be unafraid of the authority? Do what is good, and you will have praise from the same. [4]For he is God's minister to you for good. But if you do evil, be afraid; for he does not bear the sword in vain; for he is God's minister, an avenger to *execute* wrath on him who practices evil. [5]Therefore *you* must be subject, not only because of wrath but also for conscience' sake. [6]For because of this you also pay taxes, for they are God's ministers attending continually to this very thing. [7]Render therefore to all their due: taxes to whom taxes *are due,* customs to whom customs, fear to whom fear, honor to whom honor.

Love Your Neighbor

[8]Owe no one anything except to love one another, for he who loves another has fulfilled the law. [9]For the commandments, *"You shall not commit adultery," "You shall not murder," "You shall not steal," "You shall not bear false witness,"*[a] *"You shall not covet,"*[b] and if *there is* any other commandment, are *all* summed up in this saying, namely, *"You shall love your neighbor as yourself."*[c] [10]Love does no harm to a neighbor; therefore love *is* the fulfillment of the law.

13:9 [a] NU-Text omits *"You shall not bear false witness."* [b] Exodus 20:13–15, 17; Deuteronomy 5:17–19, 21 [c] Leviticus 19:18

THE MESSAGE

So live responsibly as a citizen. If you're irresponsible to the state, then you're irresponsible with God, and God will hold you responsible. Duly constituted authorities are only a threat if you're trying to get by with something. Decent citizens should have nothing to fear.

Do you want to be on good terms with the government? Be a responsible citizen and you'll get on just fine, the government working to your advantage. But if you're breaking the rules right and left, watch out. The police aren't there just to be admired in their uniforms. God also has an interest in keeping order, and he uses them to do it. That's why you must live responsibly—not just to avoid punishment but also because it's the right way to live.

That's also why you pay taxes—so that an orderly way of life can be maintained. Fulfill your obligations as a citizen. Pay your taxes, pay your bills, respect your leaders.

✠

Don't run up debts, except for the huge debt of love you owe each other. When you love others, you complete what the law has been after all along. The law code—don't sleep with another person's spouse, don't take someone's life, don't take what isn't yours, don't always be wanting what you don't have, and any other "don't" you can think of—finally adds up to this: Love other people as well as you do yourself. You can't go wrong when you love others. When you add up everything in the law code, the sum total is *love.*

KING JAMES VERSION

11 ¶ And that, knowing the time, that now *it is* high time to awake out of sleep: for now *is* our salvation nearer than when we believed.

12 The night is far spent, the day is at hand: let us therefore cast off the works of darkness, and let us put on the armour of light.

13 Let us walk honestly, as in the day; not in rioting and drunkenness, not in chambering and wantonness, not in strife and envying.

14 But put ye on the Lord Jesus Christ, and make not provision for the flesh, to *fulfil* the lusts *thereof*.

14 Him that is weak in the faith receive ye, *but* not to doubtful disputations.

2 For one believeth that he may eat all things: another, who is weak, eateth herbs.

3 Let not him that eateth despise him that eateth not; and let not him which eateth not judge him that eateth: for God hath received him.

4 Who art thou that judgest another man's servant? to

NEW AMERICAN STANDARD BIBLE

11 *Do* this, knowing the time, that it is already the hour for you to awaken from sleep; for now [l]salvation is nearer to us than when we believed.

12 The night is almost gone, and the day is near. Therefore let us lay aside the deeds of darkness and put on the armor of light.

13 Let us behave properly as in the day, not in carousing and drunkenness, not in sexual promiscuity and sensuality, not in strife and jealousy.

14 But put on the Lord Jesus Christ, and make no provision for the flesh in regard to *its* lusts.

Principles of Conscience

14 Now accept the one who is weak in faith, *but* not for *the purpose of* passing judgment on his opinions.

2 One person has faith that he may eat all things, but he who is weak eats vegetables *only*.

3 The one who eats is not to regard with contempt the one who does not eat, and the one who does not eat is not to judge the one who eats, for God has accepted him.

4 Who are you to judge the servant of another? To his

13:11 [l] Or *our salvation is nearer than when*

NEW CENTURY VERSION

11Do this because we live in an important time. It is now time for you to wake up from your sleep, because our sal-
vation is nearer now than when we first believed. 12The
"night"[c] is almost finished, and the "day"[d] is almost here. So we should stop doing things that belong to darkness and take up the weapons used for fighting in the light.
13Let us live in a right way, like people who belong to the day. We should not have wild parties or get drunk. There should be no sexual sins of any kind, no fighting or jeal-
ousy. 14But clothe yourselves with the Lord Jesus Christ and forget about satisfying your sinful self.

Do Not Criticize Other People

14 Accept into your group someone who is weak in faith, and do not argue about opinions. 2One per-
son believes it is right to eat all kinds of food.[a] But anoth-
er, who is weak, believes it is right to eat only vegetables.
3The one who knows that it is right to eat any kind of food must not reject the one who eats only vegetables. And the person who eats only vegetables must not think that the one who eats all foods is wrong, because God has accepted that person. 4You cannot judge another person's servant.

13:12 [c] **"night"** This is used as a symbol of the sinful world we live in. This world will soon end. 13:12 [d] **"day"** This is used as a symbol of the good time that is coming, when we will be with God.
14:2 [a] **all...food** The Jewish law said there were some foods Jews should not eat. When Jews became Christians, some of them did not understand they could now eat all foods.

CONTEMPORARY ENGLISH VERSION

The Day When Christ Returns

11You know what sort of times we live in, and so you should live properly. It is time to wake up. You know that the day when we will be saved is nearer now than when we first put our faith in the Lord. 12Night is almost over, and day will soon appear. We must stop behaving as peo-
ple do in the dark and be ready to live in the light. 13So behave properly, as people do in the day. Don't go to wild parties or get drunk or be vulgar or indecent. Don't quarrel or be jealous. 14Let the Lord Jesus Christ be as near to you as the clothes you wear. Then you won't try to satisfy your selfish desires.

Don't Criticize Others

14 Welcome all the Lord's followers, even those whose faith is weak. Don't criticize them for hav-
ing beliefs that are different from yours. 2Some think it is all right to eat anything, while those whose faith is weak will eat only vegetables. 3But you should not criticize oth-
ers for eating or for not eating. After all, God welcomes everyone. 4What right do you have to criticize someone

NEW INTERNATIONAL VERSION

11And do this, understanding the present time. The hour
has come for you to wake up from your slumber, because
our salvation is nearer now than when we first believed.
12The night is nearly over; the day is almost here. So let us
put aside the deeds of darkness and put on the armor of
light. 13Let us behave decently, as in the daytime, not in
orgies and drunkenness, not in sexual immorality and
debauchery, not in dissension and jealousy. 14Rather,
clothe yourselves with the Lord Jesus Christ, and do not
think about how to gratify the desires of the sinful
nature.[c]

The Weak and the Strong

14 Accept him whose faith is weak, without passing
judgment on disputable matters. 2One man's faith
allows him to eat everything, but another man, whose
faith is weak, eats only vegetables. 3The man who eats
everything must not look down on him who does not, and
the man who does not eat everything must not condemn
the man who does, for God has accepted him. 4Who are
you to judge someone else's servant? To his own master he

[c] *14* Or *the flesh*

NEW LIVING TRANSLATION

11Another reason for right living is that you know how
late it is; time is running out. Wake up, for the coming of
our salvation is nearer now than when we first believed.
12The night is almost gone; the day of salvation will soon
be here. So don't live in darkness. Get rid of your evil
deeds. Shed them like dirty clothes. Clothe yourselves with
the armor of right living, as those who live in the light.
13We should be decent and true in everything we do, so
that everyone can approve of our behavior. Don't partici-
pate in wild parties and getting drunk, or in adultery and
immoral living, or in fighting and jealousy. 14But let the
Lord Jesus Christ take control of you, and don't think of
ways to indulge your evil desires.

The Danger of Criticism

14 Accept Christians who are weak in faith, and don't
argue with them about what they think is right or
wrong. 2For instance, one person believes it is all right to
eat anything. But another believer who has a sensitive
conscience will eat only vegetables. 3Those who think it is
all right to eat anything must not look down on those who
won't. And those who won't eat certain foods must not
condemn those who do, for God has accepted them. 4Who
are you to condemn God's servants? They are responsible

NEW KING JAMES VERSION

Put on Christ

11And *do* this, knowing the time, that now *it is* high
time to awake out of sleep; for now our salvation *is* nearer
than when we *first* believed. 12The night is far spent, the
day is at hand. Therefore let us cast off the works of dark-
ness, and let us put on the armor of light. 13Let us walk
properly, as in the day, not in revelry and drunkenness,
not in lewdness and lust, not in strife and envy. 14But put
on the Lord Jesus Christ, and make no provision for the
flesh, to *fulfill its* lusts.

The Law of Liberty

14 Receive one who is weak in the faith, *but* not to
disputes over doubtful things. 2For one believes he
may eat all things, but he who is weak eats *only* vegeta-
bles. 3Let not him who eats despise him who does not eat,
and let not him who does not eat judge him who eats; for
God has received him. 4Who are you to judge another's

THE MESSAGE

But make sure that you don't get so absorbed and exhausted in taking care of all your day-by-day obligations that you lose track of the time and doze off, oblivious to God. The night is about over, dawn is about to break. Be up and awake to what God is doing! God is putting the finishing touches on the salvation work he began when we first believed. We can't afford to waste a minute, must not squander these precious daylight hours in frivolity and indulgence, in sleeping around and dissipation, in bickering and grabbing everything in sight. Get out of bed and get dressed! Don't loiter and linger, waiting until the very last minute. Dress yourselves in Christ, and be up and about!

Cultivating Good Relationships

14 Welcome with open arms fellow believers who don't see things the way you do. And don't jump all over them every time they do or say something you don't agree with—even when it seems that they are strong on opinions but weak in the faith department. Remember, they have their own history to deal with. Treat them gently.

For instance, a person who has been around for a while might well be convinced that he can eat anything on the table, while another, with a different background, might assume all Christians should be vegetarians and eat accordingly. But since both are guests at Christ's table, wouldn't it be terribly rude if they fell to criticizing what the other ate or didn't eat? God, after all, invited them both to the table. Do you have any business crossing people off the guest list or interfering with God's welcome? If

KING JAMES VERSION

his own master he standeth or falleth. Yea, he shall be holden up: for God is able to make him stand.

5 One man esteemeth one day above another: another esteemeth every day *alike*. Let every man be fully persuaded in his own mind.

6 He that regardeth the day, regardeth *it* unto the Lord; and he that regardeth not the day, to the Lord he doth not regard *it*. He that eateth, eateth to the Lord, for he giveth God thanks; and he that eateth not, to the Lord he eateth not, and giveth God thanks.

7 For none of us liveth to himself, and no man dieth to himself.

8 For whether we live, we live unto the Lord; and whether we die, we die unto the Lord: whether we live therefore, or die, we are the Lord's.

9 For to this end Christ both died, and rose, and revived, that he might be Lord both of the dead and living.

10 But why dost thou judge thy brother? or why dost thou set at nought thy brother? for we shall all stand before the judgment seat of Christ.

11 For it is written, *As* I live, saith the Lord, every knee shall bow to me, and every tongue shall confess to God.

NEW AMERICAN STANDARD BIBLE

own master he stands or falls; and he will stand, for the Lord is able to make him stand.

5 One person regards one day above another, another regards every day *alike*. Each person must be fully convinced in his own mind.

6 He who observes the day, observes it for the Lord, and he who eats, does so for the Lord, for he gives thanks to God; and he who eats not, for the Lord he does not eat, and gives thanks to God.

7 For not one of us lives for himself, and not one dies for himself;

8 for if we live, we live for the Lord, or if we die, we die for the Lord; therefore whether we live or die, we are the Lord's.

9 For to this end Christ died and lived again, that He might be Lord both of the dead and of the living.

10 But you, why do you judge your brother? Or you again, why do you regard your brother with contempt? For we will all stand before the judgment seat of God.

11 For it is written,

"As I live, says the Lord, every knee shall bow to Me,
And every tongue shall give praise to God."

NEW CENTURY VERSION

The master decides if the servant is doing well or not. And
the Lord's servant will do well because the Lord helps him
do well.
[5]Some think that one day is more important than anoth-
er, and others think that every day is the same. Let all be
sure in their own mind. [6]Those who think one day is more
important than other days are doing that for the Lord. And
those who eat all kinds of food are doing that for the Lord,
and they give thanks to God. Others who refuse to eat
some foods do that for the Lord, and they give thanks to
God. [7]We do not live or die for ourselves. [8]If we live, we
are living for the Lord, and if we die, we are dying for the
Lord. So living or dying, we belong to the Lord.

[9]The reason Christ died and rose from the dead to live
again was so he would be Lord over both the dead and the
living. [10]So why do you judge your brothers or sisters in
Christ? And why do you think you are better than they
are? We will all stand before God to be judged, [11]because it
is written in the Scriptures:

" 'As surely as I live,' says the Lord,
'Everyone will bow before me;
everyone will say that I am God.' " *Isaiah 45:23*

CONTEMPORARY ENGLISH VERSION

else's servants? Only their Lord can decide if they are
doing right, and the Lord will make sure that they do right.
[5]Some of the Lord's followers think one day is more
important than another. Others think all days are the
same. But each of you should make up your own mind.
[6]Any followers who count one day more important than
another day do it to honor their Lord. And any followers
who eat meat give thanks to God, just like the ones who
don't eat meat.

[7]Whether we live or die, it must be for God, rather than
for ourselves. [8]Whether we live or die, it must be for the
Lord. Alive or dead, we still belong to the Lord. [9]This is
because Christ died and rose to life, so that he would be
the Lord of the dead and of the living. [10]Why do you criti-
cize other followers of the Lord? Why do you look down on
them? The day is coming when God will judge all of us.
[11]In the Scriptures God says,

"I swear by my very life
that everyone will kneel down
and praise my name!"

NEW INTERNATIONAL VERSION

stands or falls. And he will stand, for the Lord is able to make him stand.

[5]One man considers one day more sacred than another; another man considers every day alike. Each one should be fully convinced in his own mind. [6]He who regards one day as special, does so to the Lord. He who eats meat, eats to the Lord, for he gives thanks to God; and he who abstains, does so to the Lord and gives thanks to God. [7]For none of us lives to himself alone and none of us dies to himself alone. [8]If we live, we live to the Lord; and if we die, we die to the Lord. So, whether we live or die, we belong to the Lord.

[9]For this very reason, Christ died and returned to life so that he might be the Lord of both the dead and the living. [10]You, then, why do you judge your brother? Or why do you look down on your brother? For we will all stand before God's judgment seat. [11]It is written:

"'As surely as I live,' says the Lord,
'every knee will bow before me;
every tongue will confess to God.'"[a]

[a] *11* Isaiah 45:23

NEW LIVING TRANSLATION

to the Lord, so let him tell them whether they are right or wrong. The Lord's power will help them do as they should.

[5]In the same way, some think one day is more holy than another day, while others think every day is alike. Each person should have a personal conviction about this matter. [6]Those who have a special day for worshiping the Lord are trying to honor him. Those who eat all kinds of food do so to honor the Lord, since they give thanks to God before eating. And those who won't eat everything also want to please the Lord and give thanks to God. [7]For we are not our own masters when we live or when we die. [8]While we live, we live to please the Lord. And when we die, we go to be with the Lord. So in life and in death, we belong to the Lord. [9]Christ died and rose again for this very purpose, so that he might be Lord of those who are alive and of those who have died.

[10]So why do you condemn another Christian*? Why do you look down on another Christian? Remember, each of us will stand personally before the judgment seat of God. [11]For the Scriptures say,

"'As surely as I live,' says the Lord,
'every knee will bow to me
and every tongue will confess allegiance to God.'"*

14:10 Greek *your brother;* also in 14:10b, 13, 15, 21. **14:11** Isa 45:23.

NEW KING JAMES VERSION

servant? To his own master he stands or falls. Indeed, he will be made to stand, for God is able to make him stand.

[5]One person esteems *one* day above another; another esteems every day *alike.* Let each be fully convinced in his own mind. [6]He who observes the day, observes *it* to the Lord;[a] and he who does not observe the day, to the Lord he does not observe *it.* He who eats, eats to the Lord, for he gives God thanks; and he who does not eat, to the Lord he does not eat, and gives God thanks. [7]For none of us lives to himself, and no one dies to himself. [8]For if we live, we live to the Lord; and if we die, we die to the Lord. Therefore, whether we live or die, we are the Lord's. [9]For to this end Christ died and rose[b] and lived again, that He might be Lord of both the dead and the living. [10]But why do you judge your brother? Or why do you show contempt for your brother? For we shall all stand before the judgment seat of Christ.[c] [11]For it is written:

"As I live, says the LORD,
Every knee shall bow to Me,
And every tongue shall confess to God."[d]

14:6 [a] NU-Text omits the rest of this sentence. **14:9** [b] NU-Text omits *and rose.* **14:10** [c] NU-Text reads *of God.* **14:11** [d] Isaiah 45:23

THE MESSAGE

there are corrections to be made or manners to be learned, God can handle that without your help.

Or, say, one person thinks that some days should be set aside as holy and another thinks that each day is pretty much like any other. There are good reasons either way. So, each person is free to follow the convictions of conscience.

What's important in all this is that if you keep a holy day, keep it for *God's* sake; if you eat meat, eat it to the glory of God and thank God for prime rib; if you're a vegetarian, eat vegetables to the glory of God and thank God for broccoli. None of us are permitted to insist on our own way in these matters. It's *God* we are answerable to—all the way from life to death and everything in between—not each other. That's why Jesus lived and died and then lived again: so that he could be our Master across the entire range of life and death, and free us from the petty tyrannies of each other.

So where does that leave you when you criticize a brother? And where does that leave you when you condescend to a sister? I'd say it leaves you looking pretty silly—or worse. Eventually, we're all going to end up kneeling side by side in the place of judgment, facing God. Your critical and condescending ways aren't going to improve your position there one bit. Read it for yourself in Scripture:

"'As I live and breathe,' God says,
'every knee will bow before me;
Every tongue will tell the honest truth
that I and only I am God.'"

KING JAMES VERSION

12 So then every one of us shall give account of himself to God.

13 Let us not therefore judge one another any more: but judge this rather, that no man put a stumblingblock or an occasion to fall in *his* brother's way.

14 I know, and am persuaded by the Lord Jesus, that *there is* nothing unclean of itself: but to him that esteemeth any thing to be unclean, to him *it is* unclean.

15 But if thy brother be grieved with *thy* meat, now walkest thou not charitably. Destroy not him with thy meat, for whom Christ died.

16 Let not then your good be evil spoken of:

17 For the kingdom of God is not meat and drink; but righteousness, and peace, and joy in the Holy Ghost.

18 For he that in these things serveth Christ *is* acceptable to God, and approved of men.

19 Let us therefore follow after the things which make for peace, and things wherewith one may edify another.

20 For meat destroy not the work of God. All things indeed *are* pure; but *it is* evil for that man who eateth with offence.

21 *It is* good neither to eat flesh, nor to drink wine, nor *any thing* whereby thy brother stumbleth, or is offended, or is made weak.

NEW AMERICAN STANDARD BIBLE

12 So then each one of us will give an account of himself to God.

13 Therefore let us not judge one another anymore, but rather determine this—not to put an obstacle or a stumbling block in a brother's way.

14 I know and am convinced in the Lord Jesus that nothing is unclean in itself; but to him who thinks anything to be unclean, to him it is unclean.

15 For if because of food your brother is hurt, you are no longer walking according to love. Do not destroy with your food him for whom Christ died.

16 Therefore do not let what is for you a good thing be spoken of as evil;

17 for the kingdom of God is not eating and drinking, but righteousness and peace and joy in the Holy Spirit.

18 For he who in this *way* serves Christ is acceptable to God and approved by men.

19 So then [l]we pursue the things which make for peace and the building up of one another.

20 Do not tear down the work of God for the sake of food. All things indeed are clean, but they are evil for the man who eats and gives offense.

21 It is good not to eat meat or to drink wine, or *to do anything* by which your brother stumbles.

14:19 [l] Later mss read *let us pursue*

NEW CENTURY VERSION

12So each of us will have to answer to God.

Do Not Cause Others to Sin

13For that reason we should stop judging each other. We must make up our minds not to do anything that will make another Christian sin. 14I am in the Lord Jesus, and I know that there is no food that is wrong to eat. But if a person believes something is wrong, that thing is wrong for him. 15If you hurt your brother's or sister's faith because of something you eat, you are not really following the way of love. Do not destroy someone's faith by eating food he thinks is wrong, because Christ died for him. 16Do not allow what you think is good to become what others say is evil. 17In the kingdom of God, eating and drinking are not important. The important things are living right with God, peace, and joy in the Holy Spirit. 18Anyone who serves Christ by living this way is pleasing God and will be accepted by other people.

19So let us try to do what makes peace and helps one another. 20Do not let the eating of food destroy the work of God. All foods are all right to eat, but it is wrong to eat food that causes someone else to sin. 21It is better not to eat meat or drink wine or do anything that will cause your brother or sister to sin.

CONTEMPORARY ENGLISH VERSION

12And so, each of us must give an account to God for what we do.

Don't Cause Problems for Others

13We must stop judging others. We must also make up our minds not to upset anyone's faith. 14The Lord Jesus has made it clear to me that God considers all foods fit to eat. But if you think some foods are unfit to eat, then for you they are not fit.

15If you are hurting others by the foods you eat, you are not guided by love. Don't let your appetite destroy someone Christ died for. 16Don't let your right to eat bring shame to Christ. 17God's kingdom isn't about eating and drinking. It is about pleasing God, about living in peace, and about true happiness. All this comes from the Holy Spirit. 18If you serve Christ in this way, you will please God and be respected by people. 19We should try[a] to live at peace and help each other have a strong faith.

20Don't let your appetite destroy what God has done. All foods are fit to eat, but it is wrong to cause problems for others by what you eat. 21It is best not to eat meat or drink wine or do anything else that causes problems for other

[a] **14.19** *We should try*: Some manuscripts have "We try."

NEW INTERNATIONAL VERSION

12So then, each of us will give an account of himself to God.

13Therefore let us stop passing judgment on one another. Instead, make up your mind not to put any stumbling block or obstacle in your brother's way. 14As one who is in the Lord Jesus, I am fully convinced that no food[b] is unclean in itself. But if anyone regards something as unclean, then for him it is unclean. 15If your brother is distressed because of what you eat, you are no longer acting in love. Do not by your eating destroy your brother for whom Christ died. 16Do not allow what you consider good to be spoken of as evil. 17For the kingdom of God is not a matter of eating and drinking, but of righteousness, peace and joy in the Holy Spirit, 18because anyone who serves Christ in this way is pleasing to God and approved by men.

19Let us therefore make every effort to do what leads to peace and to mutual edification. 20Do not destroy the work of God for the sake of food. All food is clean, but it is wrong for a man to eat anything that causes someone else to stumble. 21It is better not to eat meat or drink wine or to do anything else that will cause your brother to fall.

[b] *14* Or *that nothing*

NEW LIVING TRANSLATION

12Yes, each of us will have to give a personal account to God. 13So don't condemn each other anymore. Decide instead to live in such a way that you will not put an obstacle in another Christian's path.

14I know and am perfectly sure on the authority of the Lord Jesus that no food, in and of itself, is wrong to eat. But if someone believes it is wrong, then for that person it is wrong. 15And if another Christian is distressed by what you eat, you are not acting in love if you eat it. Don't let your eating ruin someone for whom Christ died. 16Then you will not be condemned for doing something you know is all right.

17For the Kingdom of God is not a matter of what we eat or drink, but of living a life of goodness and peace and joy in the Holy Spirit. 18If you serve Christ with this attitude, you will please God. And other people will approve of you, too. 19So then, let us aim for harmony in the church and try to build each other up.

20Don't tear apart the work of God over what you eat. Remember, there is nothing wrong with these things in themselves. But it is wrong to eat anything if it makes another person stumble. 21Don't eat meat or drink wine or do anything else if it might cause another Christian to

NEW KING JAMES VERSION

12So then each of us shall give account of himself to God. 13Therefore let us not judge one another anymore, but rather resolve this, not to put a stumbling block or a cause to fall in *our* brother's way.

The Law of Love

14I know and am convinced by the Lord Jesus that *there is* nothing unclean of itself; but to him who considers anything to be unclean, to him *it is* unclean. 15Yet if your brother is grieved because of *your* food, you are no longer walking in love. Do not destroy with your food the one for whom Christ died. 16Therefore do not let your good be spoken of as evil; 17for the kingdom of God is not eating and drinking, but righteousness and peace and joy in the Holy Spirit. 18For he who serves Christ in these things[e] *is* acceptable to God and approved by men.

19Therefore let us pursue the things *which make* for peace and the things by which one may edify another. 20Do not destroy the work of God for the sake of food. All things indeed *are* pure, but *it is* evil for the man who eats with offense. 21*It is* good neither to eat meat nor drink wine nor *do anything* by which your brother stumbles or is offended

14:18 [e] NU-Text reads *this.*

THE MESSAGE

So tend to your knitting. You've got your hands full just taking care of your own life before God.

Forget about deciding what's right for each other. Here's what you need to be concerned about: that you don't get in the way of someone else, making life more difficult than it already is. I'm convinced—Jesus convinced me!—that everything as it is in itself is holy. We, of course, by the way we treat it or talk about it, can contaminate it.

If you confuse others by making a big issue over what they eat or don't eat, you're no longer a companion with them in love, are you? These, remember, are persons for whom Christ died. Would you risk sending them to hell over an item in their diet? Don't you dare let a piece of God-blessed food become an occasion of soul-poisoning!

God's kingdom isn't a matter of what you put in your stomach, for goodness' sake. It's what God does with your life as he sets it right, puts it together, and completes it with joy. Your task is to single-mindedly serve Christ. Do that and you'll kill two birds with one stone: pleasing the God above you and proving your worth to the people around you.

So let's agree to use all our energy in getting along with each other. Help others with encouraging words; don't drag them down by finding fault. You're certainly not going to permit an argument over what is served or not served at supper to wreck God's work among you, are you? I said it before and I'll say it again: All food is good, but it can turn bad if you use it badly, if you use it to trip others up and send them sprawling. When you sit down to a meal, your primary concern should not be to feed your own

KING JAMES VERSION

22 Hast thou faith? have *it* to thyself before God. Happy *is* he that condemneth not himself in that thing which he alloweth.

23 And he that doubteth is damned if he eat, because *he eateth* not of faith: for whatsoever *is* not of faith is sin.

15 We then that are strong ought to bear the infirmities of the weak, and not to please ourselves.

2 Let every one of us please *his* neighbour for *his* good to edification.

3 For even Christ pleased not himself; but, as it is written, The reproaches of them that reproached thee fell on me.

4 For whatsoever things were written aforetime were written for our learning, that we through patience and comfort of the scriptures might have hope.

5 ¶ Now the God of patience and consolation grant you to be likeminded one toward another according to Christ Jesus:

NEW AMERICAN STANDARD BIBLE

22 The faith which you have, have as your own conviction before God. Happy is he who does not condemn himself in what he approves.

23 But he who doubts is condemned if he eats, because *his eating is* not from faith; and whatever is not from faith is sin.

Self-denial on Behalf of Others

15 Now we who are strong ought to bear the weaknesses of those without strength and not *just* please ourselves.

2 Each of us is to please his neighbor for his good, to his edification.

3 For even Christ did not please Himself; but as it is written, "THE REPROACHES OF THOSE WHO REPROACHED YOU FELL ON ME."

4 For whatever was written in earlier times was written for our instruction, so that through perseverance and the encouragement of the Scriptures we might have hope.

5 Now may the God who gives perseverance and encouragement grant you to be of the same mind with one another according to Christ Jesus,

NEW CENTURY VERSION

22Your beliefs about these things should be kept secret
between you and God. People are happy if they can do
what they think is right without feeling guilty. 23But those
who eat something without being sure it is right are wrong
because they did not believe it was right. Anything that is
done without believing it is right is a sin.

15 We who are strong in faith should help the weak
with their weaknesses, and not please only our-
selves. 2Let each of us please our neighbors for their good,
to help them be stronger in faith. 3Even Christ did not live
to please himself. It was as the Scriptures said: "When
people insult you, it hurts me."[a] 4Everything that was
written in the past was written to teach us. The Scriptures
give us patience and encouragement so that we can have
hope. 5Patience and encouragement come from God. And I
pray that God will help you all agree with each other the

15:3 [a] "When…me." Quotation from Psalm 69:9.

CONTEMPORARY ENGLISH VERSION

followers of the Lord. 22What you believe about these
things should be kept between you and God. You are fortu-
nate, if your actions don't make you have doubts. 23But if
you do have doubts about what you eat, you are going
against your beliefs. And you know that is wrong, because
anything you do against your beliefs is sin.

Please Others and Not Yourself

15 If our faith is strong, we should be patient with
the Lord's followers whose faith is weak. We
should try to please them instead of ourselves. 2We should
think of their good and try to help them by doing what
pleases them. 3Even Christ did not try to please himself.
But as the Scriptures say, "The people who insulted you
also insulted me." 4And the Scriptures were written to
teach and encourage us by giving us hope. 5God is the one
who makes us patient and cheerful. I pray that he will help
you live at peace with each other, as you follow Christ.

NEW INTERNATIONAL VERSION

22So whatever you believe about these things keep between yourself and God. Blessed is the man who does not condemn himself by what he approves. 23But the man who has doubts is condemned if he eats, because his eating is not from faith; and everything that does not come from faith is sin.

15 We who are strong ought to bear with the failings of the weak and not to please ourselves. 2Each of us should please his neighbor for his good, to build him up. 3For even Christ did not please himself but, as it is written: "The insults of those who insult you have fallen on me."[a] 4For everything that was written in the past was written to teach us, so that through endurance and the encouragement of the Scriptures we might have hope.

5May the God who gives endurance and encouragement give you a spirit of unity among yourselves as you follow

[a] *3* Psalm 69:9

NEW LIVING TRANSLATION

stumble. 22You may have the faith to believe that there is nothing wrong with what you are doing, but keep it between yourself and God. Blessed are those who do not condemn themselves by doing something they know is all right. 23But if people have doubts about whether they should eat something, they shouldn't eat it. They would be condemned for not acting in faith before God. If you do anything you believe is not right, you are sinning.

Living to Please Others

15 We may know that these things make no difference, but we cannot just go ahead and do them to please ourselves. We must be considerate of the doubts and fears of those who think these things are wrong. 2We should please others. If we do what helps them, we will build them up in the Lord. 3For even Christ didn't please himself. As the Scriptures say, "Those who insult you are also insulting me."* 4Such things were written in the Scriptures long ago to teach us. They give us hope and encouragement as we wait patiently for God's promises.

5May God, who gives this patience and encouragement, help you live in complete harmony with each other—each with the attitude of Christ Jesus toward the other. 6Then

15:3 Ps 69:9.

NEW KING JAMES VERSION

or is made weak.[f] 22Do you have faith?[g] Have *it* to yourself before God. Happy *is* he who does not condemn himself in what he approves. 23But he who doubts is condemned if he eats, because *he does* not *eat* from faith; for whatever *is* not from faith is sin.[h]

Bearing Others' Burdens

15 We then who are strong ought to bear with the scruples of the weak, and not to please ourselves. 2Let each of us please *his* neighbor for *his* good, leading to edification. 3For even Christ did not please Himself; but as it is written, *"The reproaches of those who reproached You fell on Me."*[a] 4For whatever things were written before were written for our learning, that we through the patience and comfort of the Scriptures might have hope. 5Now may the God of patience and comfort grant you to be like-minded toward one another, according to Christ Jesus, 6that you

14:21 [f] NU-Text omits *or is offended or is made weak.* 14:22 [g] NU-Text reads *The faith which you have—have.* 14:23 [h] M-Text puts Romans 16:25–27 here. 15:3 [a] Psalm 69:9

THE MESSAGE

face but to share the life of Jesus. So be sensitive and courteous to the others who are eating. Don't eat or say or do things that might interfere with the free exchange of love.

Cultivate your own relationship with God, but don't impose it on others. You're fortunate if your behavior and your belief are coherent. But if you're not sure, if you notice that you are acting in ways inconsistent with what you believe—some days trying to impose your opinions on others, other days just trying to please them—then you know that you're out of line. If the way you live isn't consistent with what you believe, then it's wrong.

15 Those of us who are strong and able in the faith need to step in and lend a hand to those who falter, and not just do what is most convenient for us. Strength is for service, not status. Each one of us needs to look after the good of the people around us, asking ourselves, "How can I help?"

That's exactly what Jesus did. He didn't make it easy for himself by avoiding people's troubles, but waded right in and helped out. "I took on the troubles of the troubled," is the way Scripture puts it. Even if it was written in Scripture long ago, you can be sure it's written for *us*. God wants the combination of his steady, constant calling and warm, personal counsel in Scripture to come to characterize *us*, keeping us alert for whatever he will do next. May our dependably steady and warmly personal God develop maturity in you so that you get along with each other as well as Jesus gets along with us all. Then we'll be a choir—not our voices only, but our very lives singing in

KING JAMES VERSION

6 That ye may with one mind *and* one mouth glorify
God, even the Father of our Lord Jesus Christ.
7 ¶ Wherefore receive ye one another, as Christ also
received us to the glory of God.
8 Now I say that Jesus Christ was a minister of the cir-
cumcision for the truth of God, to confirm the promises
made unto the fathers:
9 And that the Gentiles might glorify God for *his* mercy;
as it is written, For this cause I will confess to thee among
the Gentiles, and sing unto thy name.
10 And again he saith, Rejoice, ye Gentiles, with his
people.
11 And again, Praise the Lord, all ye Gentiles; and laud
him, all ye people.
12 And again, Esaias saith, There shall be a root of Jesse,

NEW AMERICAN STANDARD BIBLE

6 so that with one accord you may with one voice glori-
fy the God and Father of our Lord Jesus Christ.
7 Therefore, accept one another, just as Christ also
accepted us to the glory of God.
8 For I say that Christ has become a servant to the cir-
cumcision on behalf of the truth of God to confirm the
promises *given* to the fathers,
9 and for the Gentiles to glorify God for His mercy; as it
is written,

"THEREFORE I WILL GIVE PRAISE TO YOU AMONG THE
GENTILES,
AND I WILL SING TO YOUR NAME."

10 Again he says,

"REJOICE, O GENTILES, WITH HIS PEOPLE."

11 And again,

"PRAISE THE LORD ALL YOU GENTILES,
AND LET ALL THE PEOPLES PRAISE HIM."

12 Again Isaiah says,

"THERE SHALL COME THE ROOT OF JESSE,

NEW CENTURY VERSION

way Christ Jesus wants. [6]Then you will all be joined
together, and you will give glory to God the Father of our
Lord Jesus Christ. [7]Christ accepted you, so you should
accept each other, which will bring glory to God. [8]I tell you
that Christ became a servant of the Jews to show that
God's promises to the Jewish ancestors are true. [9]And he
also did this so that those who are not Jews could give
glory to God for the mercy he gives to them. It is written in
the Scriptures:

"So I will praise you among the non-Jewish people.
I will sing praises to your name." *Psalm 18:49*

[10]The Scripture also says,

"Be happy, you who are not Jews, together with his
people." *Deuteronomy 32:43*

[11]Again the Scripture says,

"All you who are not Jews, praise the Lord.
All you people, sing praises to him." *Psalm 117:1*

[12]And Isaiah says,

"A new king will come from the family of Jesse.[b]

15:12 [b] **Jesse** Jesse was the father of David, king of Israel. Jesus was from their family.

CONTEMPORARY ENGLISH VERSION

[6]Then all of you together will praise God, the Father of our
Lord Jesus Christ.

The Good News Is for Jews and Gentiles

[7]Honor God by accepting each other, as Christ has
accepted you. [8]I tell you that Christ came as a servant of
the Jews to show that God has kept the promises he made
to their famous ancestors. Christ also came, [9]so that the
Gentiles would praise God for being kind to them. It is just
as the Scriptures say,

"I will tell the nations
about you,
and I will sing praises
to your name."

[10]The Scriptures also say to the Gentiles, "Come and cel-
ebrate with God's people."
[11]Again the Scriptures say,

"Praise the Lord,
all you Gentiles.
All you nations, come
and worship him."

[12]Isaiah says,

"Someone from David's family
will come to power.

NEW INTERNATIONAL VERSION

Christ Jesus, 6so that with one heart and mouth you may
glorify the God and Father of our Lord Jesus Christ.
7Accept one another, then, just as Christ accepted you,
in order to bring praise to God. 8For I tell you that Christ
has become a servant of the Jews[b] on behalf of God's
truth, to confirm the promises made to the patriarchs 9so
that the Gentiles may glorify God for his mercy, as it is
written:

"Therefore I will praise you among the Gentiles;
I will sing hymns to your name."[c]

10Again, it says,

"Rejoice, O Gentiles, with his people."[d]

11And again,

"Praise the Lord, all you Gentiles,
and sing praises to him, all you peoples."[e]

12And again, Isaiah says,

"The Root of Jesse will spring up,

[b] *8* Greek *circumcision* [c] *9* 2 Samuel 22:50; Psalm 18:49
[d] *10* Deut. 32:43 [e] *11* Psalm 117:1

NEW LIVING TRANSLATION

all of you can join together with one voice, giving praise
and glory to God, the Father of our Lord Jesus Christ.
7So accept each other just as Christ has accepted you;
then God will be glorified. 8Remember that Christ came as
a servant to the Jews to show that God is true to the prom-
ises he made to their ancestors. 9And he came so the
Gentiles might also give glory to God for his mercies to
them. That is what the psalmist meant when he wrote:

"I will praise you among the Gentiles;
I will sing praises to your name."*

10And in another place it is written,

"Rejoice, O you Gentiles,
along with his people, the Jews."*

11And yet again,

"Praise the Lord, all you Gentiles;
praise him, all you people of the earth."*

12And the prophet Isaiah said,

"The heir to David's throne* will come,

15:9 Ps 18:49. **15:10** Deut 32:43. **15:11** Ps 117:1.
15:12a Greek *The root of Jesse.*

NEW KING JAMES VERSION

may with one mind *and* one mouth glorify the God and
Father of our Lord Jesus Christ.

Glorify God Together

7Therefore receive one another, just as Christ also
received us,[b] to the glory of God. 8Now I say that Jesus
Christ has become a servant to the circumcision for the
truth of God, to confirm the promises *made* to the fathers,
9and that the Gentiles might glorify God for *His* mercy, as
it is written:

"For this reason I will confess to You among the
Gentiles,
And sing to Your name."[c]

10And again he says:

"Rejoice, O Gentiles, with His people!"[d]

11And again:

"Praise the LORD, all you Gentiles!
Laud Him, all you peoples!"[e]

12And again, Isaiah says:

"There shall be a root of Jesse;

15:7 [b] NU-Text and M-Text read *you.* 15:9 [c] 2 Samuel 22:50; Psalm
18:49 15:10 [d] Deuteronomy 32:43 15:11 [e] Psalm 117:1

THE MESSAGE

harmony in a stunning anthem to the God and Father of
our Master Jesus!

So reach out and welcome one another to God's glory.
Jesus did it; now *you* do it! Jesus, staying true to God's
purposes, reached out in a special way to the Jewish insid-
ers so that the old ancestral promises would come true for
them. As a result, the non-Jewish outsiders have been able
to experience mercy and to show appreciation to God. Just
think of all the Scriptures that will come true in what we
do! For instance:

"Then I'll join outsiders in a hymn-sing;
I'll sing to your name!"

And this one:

"Outsiders and insiders, rejoice together!"

And again:

"People of all nations, celebrate God!
All colors and races, give hearty praise!"

And Isaiah's word:

"There's the root of our ancestor Jesse,
breaking through the earth and growing tree tall,

KING JAMES VERSION

and he that shall rise to reign over the Gentiles; in him shall the Gentiles trust.

13 ¶ Now the God of hope fill you with all joy and peace in believing, that ye may abound in hope, through the power of the Holy Ghost.

14 ¶ And I myself also am persuaded of you, my brethren, that ye also are full of goodness, filled with all knowledge, able also to admonish one another.

15 Nevertheless, brethren, I have written the more boldly unto you in some sort, as putting you in mind, because of the grace that is given to me of God,

16 That I should be the minister of Jesus Christ to the Gentiles, ministering the gospel of God, that the offering up of the Gentiles might be acceptable, being sanctified by the Holy Ghost.

17 ¶ I have therefore whereof I may glory through Jesus Christ in those things which pertain to God.

18 For I will not dare to speak of any of those things which Christ hath not wrought by me, to make the Gentiles obedient, by word and deed,

19 Through mighty signs and wonders, by the power of the Spirit of God; so that from Jerusalem, and round about unto Illyricum, I have fully preached the gospel of Christ.

NEW AMERICAN STANDARD BIBLE

AND HE WHO ARISES TO RULE OVER THE GENTILES,
IN HIM SHALL THE GENTILES HOPE."

13 Now may the God of hope fill you with all joy and peace in believing, so that you will abound in hope by the power of the Holy Spirit.

14 And concerning you, my brethren, I myself also am convinced that you yourselves are full of goodness, filled with all knowledge and able also to admonish one another.

15 But I have written very boldly to you on some points so as to remind you again, because of the grace that was given me from God,

16 to be a minister of Christ Jesus to the Gentiles, ministering as a priest the gospel of God, so that *my* offering of the Gentiles may become acceptable, sanctified by the Holy Spirit.

17 Therefore in Christ Jesus I have found reason for boasting in things pertaining to God.

18 For I will not presume to speak of anything except what Christ has accomplished through me, resulting in the obedience of the Gentiles by word and deed,

19 in the power of signs and wonders, in the power of the Spirit; so that from Jerusalem and round about as far as Illyricum I have fully preached the gospel of Christ.

NEW CENTURY VERSION

He will come to rule over the non-Jewish people,
and they will have hope because of him." *Isaiah 11:10*

13 I pray that the God who gives hope will fill you with much joy and peace while you trust in him. Then your hope will overflow by the power of the Holy Spirit.

Paul Talks About His Work

14 My brothers and sisters, I am sure that you are full of
goodness. I know that you have all the knowledge you
need and that you are able to teach each other. 15 But I
have written to you very openly about some things I want-
ed you to remember. I did this because God gave me this
special gift: 16 to be a minister of Christ Jesus to those who
are not Jews. I served God by teaching his Good News, so
that the non-Jewish people could be an offering that God
would accept—an offering made holy by the Holy Spirit.

17 So I am proud of what I have done for God in Christ
Jesus. 18 I will not talk about anything except what Christ
has done through me in leading those who are not Jews to
obey God. They have obeyed God because of what I have
said and done, 19 because of the power of miracles and the
great things they saw, and because of the power of the Holy
Spirit. I preached the Good News from Jerusalem all the
way around to Illyricum, and so I have finished that part of

CONTEMPORARY ENGLISH VERSION

He will rule the nations,
and they will put their hope
in him."

13 I pray that God, who gives hope, will bless you with complete happiness and peace because of your faith. And may the power of the Holy Spirit fill you with hope.

Paul's Work as a Missionary

14 My friends, I am sure that you are very good and that
you have all the knowledge you need to teach each other.
15 But I have spoken to you plainly and have tried to
remind you of some things. God was so kind to me! 16 He
chose me to be a servant of Christ Jesus for the Gentiles
and to do the work of a priest in the service of his good
news. God did this so that the Holy Spirit could make the
Gentiles into a holy offering, pleasing to him.

17 Because of Christ Jesus, I can take pride in my service
for God. 18 In fact, all I will talk about is how Christ let me
speak and work, so that the Gentiles would obey him.
19 Indeed, I will tell how Christ worked miracles and wonders
by the power of the Holy Spirit. I have preached the good
news about him all the way from Jerusalem to Illyricum.

NEW INTERNATIONAL VERSION

one who will arise to rule over the nations;
the Gentiles will hope in him."[f]

13May the God of hope fill you with all joy and peace as
you trust in him, so that you may overflow with hope by
the power of the Holy Spirit.

Paul the Minister to the Gentiles

14I myself am convinced, my brothers, that you your-
selves are full of goodness, complete in knowledge and
competent to instruct one another. 15I have written you
quite boldly on some points, as if to remind you of them
again, because of the grace God gave me 16to be a minister
of Christ Jesus to the Gentiles with the priestly duty of pro-
claiming the gospel of God, so that the Gentiles might
become an offering acceptable to God, sanctified by the
Holy Spirit.
17Therefore I glory in Christ Jesus in my service to God.
18I will not venture to speak of anything except what
Christ has accomplished through me in leading the
Gentiles to obey God by what I have said and done— 19by
the power of signs and miracles, through the power of the
Spirit. So from Jerusalem all the way around to Illyricum, I
have fully proclaimed the gospel of Christ. 20It has always

[f] *12* Isaiah 11:10

NEW LIVING TRANSLATION

and he will rule over the Gentiles.
They will place their hopes on him."*

13So I pray that God, who gives you hope, will keep you
happy and full of peace as you believe in him. May you
overflow with hope through the power of the Holy Spirit.

Paul's Reason for Writing

14I am fully convinced, dear brothers and sisters,* that
you are full of goodness. You know these things so well
that you are able to teach others all about them. 15Even so,
I have been bold enough to emphasize some of these
points, knowing that all you need is this reminder from
me. For I am, by God's grace, 16a special messenger from
Christ Jesus to you Gentiles. I bring you the Good News
and offer you up as a fragrant sacrifice to God so that you
might be pure and pleasing to him by the Holy Spirit. 17So
it is right for me to be enthusiastic about all Christ Jesus
has done through me in my service to God. 18I dare not
boast of anything else. I have brought the Gentiles to God
by my message and by the way I lived before them. 19I
have won them over by the miracles done through me as
signs from God—all by the power of God's Spirit. In this
way, I have fully presented the Good News of Christ all the
way from Jerusalem clear over into Illyricum.*

15:12b Isa 11:10. **15:14** Greek *brothers;* also in 15:30.
15:19 *Illyricum* was a region northeast of Italy.

NEW KING JAMES VERSION

And He who shall rise to reign over the Gentiles,
In Him the Gentiles shall hope."[f]

13Now may the God of hope fill you with all joy and
peace in believing, that you may abound in hope by the
power of the Holy Spirit.

From Jerusalem to Illyricum

14Now I myself am confident concerning you, my
brethren, that you also are full of goodness, filled with all
knowledge, able also to admonish one another.[g] 15Never-
theless, brethren, I have written more boldly to you on
some points, as reminding you, because of the grace given
to me by God, 16that I might be a minister of Jesus Christ
to the Gentiles, ministering the gospel of God, that the of-
fering of the Gentiles might be acceptable, sanctified by the
Holy Spirit. 17Therefore I have reason to glory in Christ
Jesus in the things *which pertain* to God. 18For I will not
dare to speak of any of those things which Christ has not
accomplished through me, in word and deed, to make the
Gentiles obedient— 19in mighty signs and wonders, by the
power of the Spirit of God, so that from Jerusalem and
round about to Illyricum I have fully preached the gospel

15:12 [f] Isaiah 11:10 **15:14** [g] M-Text reads *others.*

THE MESSAGE

Tall enough for everyone everywhere to see and take
hope!"

Oh! May the God of green hope fill you up with joy, fill you
up with peace, so that your believing lives, filled with the
life-giving energy of the Holy Spirit, will brim over with hope!

✠

Personally, I've been completely satisfied with who you are and what you are doing. You seem to me to be well-motivated and well-instructed, quite capable of guiding and advising one another. So, my dear friends, don't take my rather bold and blunt language as criticism. It's not criticism. I'm simply underlining how very much I need your help in carrying out this highly focused assignment God gave me, this priestly and gospel work of serving the spiritual needs of the non-Jewish outsiders so they can be presented as an acceptable offering to God, made whole and holy by God's Holy Spirit.

Looking back over what has been accomplished and what I have observed, I must say I am most pleased—in the context of Jesus, I'd even say *proud*, but only in that context. I have no interest in giving you a chatty account of my adventures, only the wondrously powerful and transformingly present words and deeds of Christ in me that triggered a believing response among the outsiders. In such ways I have trailblazed a preaching of the Message of Jesus all the way from Jerusalem far into northwestern Greece. This has all been pioneer work, bringing the

KING JAMES VERSION

20 Yea, so have I strived to preach the gospel, not where Christ was named, lest I should build upon another man's foundation:

21 But as it is written, To whom he was not spoken of, they shall see: and they that have not heard shall understand.

22 ¶ For which cause also I have been much hindered from coming to you.

23 But now having no more place in these parts, and having a great desire these many years to come unto you;

24 Whensoever I take my journey into Spain, I will come to you: for I trust to see you in my journey, and to be brought on my way thitherward by you, if first I be somewhat filled with your *company*.

25 But now I go unto Jerusalem to minister unto the saints.

26 For it hath pleased them of Macedonia and Achaia to make a certain contribution for the poor saints which are at Jerusalem.

27 It hath pleased them verily; and their debtors they are. For if the Gentiles have been made partakers of their spiritual things, their duty is also to minister unto them in carnal things.

NEW AMERICAN STANDARD BIBLE

20 And thus I aspired to preach the gospel, not where Christ was *already* named, so that I would not build on another man's foundation;

21 but as it is written,

"THEY WHO HAD NO NEWS OF HIM SHALL SEE,
AND THEY WHO HAVE NOT HEARD SHALL UNDERSTAND."

22 For this reason I have often been prevented from coming to you;

23 but now, with no further place for me in these regions, and since I have had for many years a longing to come to you

24 whenever I go to Spain—for I hope to see you in passing, and to be helped on my way there by you, when I have first enjoyed your company for a while—

25 but now, I am going to Jerusalem serving the saints.

26 For Macedonia and Achaia have been pleased to make a contribution for the poor among the saints in Jerusalem.

27 Yes, they were pleased *to do so,* and they are indebted to them. For if the Gentiles have shared in their spiritual things, they are indebted to minister to them also in material things.

NEW CENTURY VERSION

my work. 20I always want to preach the Good News in places where people have never heard of Christ, because I do not want to build on the work someone else has already started. 21But it is written in the Scriptures:

"Those who were not told about him will see,
and those who have not heard about him will
understand." *Isaiah 52:15*

Paul's Plan to Visit Rome

22This is the reason I was stopped many times from coming to you. 23Now I have finished my work here. Since for many years I have wanted to come to you, 24I hope to visit you on my way to Spain. After I enjoy being with you for a while, I hope you can help me on my trip. 25Now I am going to Jerusalem to help God's people. 26The believers in Macedonia and Southern Greece were happy to give their money to help the poor among God's people at Jerusalem. 27They were happy to do this, and really they owe it to them. These who are not Jews have shared in the Jews' spiritual blessings, so they should use their material possessions to help the Jews. 28After I am sure the poor in

CONTEMPORARY ENGLISH VERSION

20But I have always tried to preach where people have never heard about Christ. I am like a builder who doesn't build on anyone else's foundation. 21It is just as the Scriptures say,

"All who haven't been told
about him
will see him,
and those who haven't heard
about him
will understand."

Paul's Plan To Visit Rome

22My work has always kept me from coming to see you. 23Now there is nothing left for me to do in this part of the world, and for years I have wanted to visit you. 24So I plan to stop off on my way to Spain. Then after a short, but refreshing, visit with you, I hope you will quickly send me on.

25-26I am now on my way to Jerusalem to deliver the money that the Lord's followers in Macedonia and Achaia collected for God's needy people. 27This is something they really wanted to do. But sharing their money with the Jews was also like paying back a debt, because the Jews had already shared their spiritual blessings with the Gentiles.

NEW INTERNATIONAL VERSION

been my ambition to preach the gospel where Christ was not known, so that I would not be building on someone else's foundation. 21Rather, as it is written:

"Those who were not told about him will see,
and those who have not heard will understand."[g]

22This is why I have often been hindered from coming to you.

Paul's Plan to Visit Rome

23But now that there is no more place for me to work in these regions, and since I have been longing for many years to see you, 24I plan to do so when I go to Spain. I hope to visit you while passing through and to have you assist me on my journey there, after I have enjoyed your company for a while. 25Now, however, I am on my way to Jerusalem in the service of the saints there. 26For Macedonia and Achaia were pleased to make a contribution for the poor among the saints in Jerusalem. 27They were pleased to do it, and indeed they owe it to them. For if the Gentiles have shared in the Jews' spiritual blessings, they owe it to the Jews to share with them their material

[g] *21* Isaiah 52:15

NEW LIVING TRANSLATION

20My ambition has always been to preach the Good News where the name of Christ has never been heard, rather than where a church has already been started by someone else. 21I have been following the plan spoken of in the Scriptures, where it says,

"Those who have never been told about him will see,
and those who have never heard of him will
understand."*

22In fact, my visit to you has been delayed so long because I have been preaching in these places.

Paul's Travel Plans

23But now I have finished my work in these regions, and after all these long years of waiting, I am eager to visit you. 24I am planning to go to Spain, and when I do, I will stop off in Rome. And after I have enjoyed your fellowship for a little while, you can send me on my way again.

25But before I come, I must go down to Jerusalem to take a gift to the Christians there. 26For you see, the believers in Greece* have eagerly taken up an offering for the Christians in Jerusalem, who are going through such hard times. 27They were very glad to do this because they feel they owe a real debt to them. Since the Gentiles received the wonderful spiritual blessings of the Good News from the Jewish Christians, they feel the least they can do in return is help

15:21 Isa 52:15. **15:26** Greek *Macedonia and Achaia,* the northern and southern regions of Greece.

NEW KING JAMES VERSION

of Christ. 20And so I have made it my aim to preach the gospel, not where Christ was named, lest I should build on another man's foundation, 21but as it is written:

"To whom He was not announced, they shall see;
And those who have not heard shall understand."[h]

Plan to Visit Rome

22For this reason I also have been much hindered from coming to you. 23But now no longer having a place in these parts, and having a great desire these many years to come to you, 24whenever I journey to Spain, I shall come to you.[i] For I hope to see you on my journey, and to be helped on my way there by you, if first I may enjoy your *company* for a while. 25But now I am going to Jerusalem to minister to the saints. 26For it pleased those from Macedonia and Achaia to make a certain contribution for the poor among the saints who are in Jerusalem. 27It pleased them indeed, and they are their debtors. For if the Gentiles have been partakers of their spiritual things, their duty is also to minister to them in material things. 28Therefore, when I

15:21 [h] Isaiah 52:15 **15:24** [i] NU-Text omits *I shall come to you* (and joins *Spain* with the next sentence).

THE MESSAGE

Message only into those places where Jesus was not yet known and worshiped. My text has been,

"Those who were never told of him—
they'll see him!
Those who've never heard of him—
they'll get the message!"

✠

And that's why it has taken me so long to finally get around to coming to you. But now that there is no more pioneering work to be done in these parts, and since I have looked forward to seeing you for many years, I'm planning my visit. I'm headed for Spain, and expect to stop off on the way to enjoy a good visit with you, and eventually have you send me off with God's blessing.

First, though, I'm going to Jerusalem to deliver a relief offering to the Christians there. The Greeks—all the way from the Macedonians in the north to the Achaians in the south—decided they wanted to take up a collection for the poor among the believers in Jerusalem. They were happy to do this, but it was also their duty. Seeing that they got in on all the spiritual gifts that flowed out of the Jerusalem community so generously, it is only right that they do what they can to relieve their poverty. As soon as I have

KING JAMES VERSION

28 When therefore I have performed this, and have sealed to them this fruit, I will come by you into Spain.

29 And I am sure that, when I come unto you, I shall come in the fulness of the blessing of the gospel of Christ.

30 ¶ Now I beseech you, brethren, for the Lord Jesus Christ's sake, and for the love of the Spirit, that ye strive together with me in *your* prayers to God for me;

31 That I may be delivered from them that do not believe in Judaea; and that my service which *I have* for Jerusalem may be accepted of the saints;

32 That I may come unto you with joy by the will of God, and may with you be refreshed.

33 Now the God of peace *be* with you all. Amen.

16 I commend unto you Phebe our sister, which is a servant of the church which is at Cenchrea:

2 That ye receive her in the Lord, as becometh saints, and that ye assist her in whatsoever business she hath need of you: for she hath been a succourer of many, and of myself also.

3 Greet Priscilla and Aquila my helpers in Christ Jesus:

4 Who have for my life laid down their own necks: unto whom not only I give thanks, but also all the churches of the Gentiles.

5 Likewise *greet* the church that is in their house. Salute my wellbeloved Epaenetus, who is the firstfruits of Achaia unto Christ.

NEW AMERICAN STANDARD BIBLE

28 Therefore, when I have finished this, and have put my seal on this fruit of theirs, I will go on by way of you to Spain.

29 I know that when I come to you, I will come in the fullness of the blessing of Christ.

30 Now I urge you, brethren, by our Lord Jesus Christ and by the love of the Spirit, to strive together with me in your prayers to God for me,

31 that I may be rescued from those who are disobedient in Judea, and *that* my service for Jerusalem may prove acceptable to the saints;

32 so that I may come to you in joy by the will of God and find *refreshing* rest in your company.

33 Now the God of peace be with you all. Amen.

Greetings and Love Expressed

16 I commend to you our sister Phoebe, who is a servant of the church which is at Cenchrea;

2 that you receive her in the Lord in a manner worthy of the saints, and that you help her in whatever matter she may have need of you; for she herself has also been a helper of many, and of myself as well.

3 Greet Prisca and Aquila, my fellow workers in Christ Jesus,

4 who for my life risked their own necks, to whom not only do I give thanks, but also all the churches of the Gentiles;

5 also *greet* the church that is in their house. Greet Epaenetus, my beloved, who is the first convert to Christ from Asia.

NEW CENTURY VERSION

Jerusalem get the money that has been given for them, I
will leave for Spain and stop and visit you. 29 I know that
when I come to you I will bring Christ's full blessing.

30 Brothers and sisters, I beg you to help me in my work
by praying to God for me. Do this because of our Lord
Jesus and the love that the Holy Spirit gives us. 31 Pray that
I will be saved from the non-believers in Judea and that
this help I bring to Jerusalem will please God's people
there. 32 Then, if God wants me to, I will come to you with
joy, and together you and I will have a time of rest. 33 The
God who gives peace be with you all. Amen.

Greetings to the Christians

16 I recommend to you our sister Phoebe, who is a
helper[a] in the church in Cenchrea. 2 I ask you to
accept her in the Lord in the way God's people should.
Help her with anything she needs, because she has helped
me and many other people also.

3 Give my greetings to Priscilla and Aquila, who work
together with me in Christ Jesus 4 and who risked their own
lives to save my life. I am thankful to them, and all the
non-Jewish churches are thankful as well. 5 Also, greet for
me the church that meets at their house.

Greetings to my dear friend Epenetus, who was the first
person in the country of Asia to follow Christ. 6 Greetings

16:1 [a] **helper** Literally, "deaconess." This might mean the same as one of the special women helpers in 1 Timothy 3:11.

CONTEMPORARY ENGLISH VERSION

28 After I have safely delivered this money, I will visit you
and then go on to Spain. 29 And when I do arrive in Rome, I
know it will be with the full blessings of Christ.

30 My friends, by the power of the Lord Jesus Christ and
by the love that comes from the Holy Spirit, I beg you to
pray sincerely with me and for me. 31 Pray that God will
protect me from the unbelievers in Judea, and that his peo-
ple in Jerusalem will be pleased with what I am doing.
32 Ask God to let me come to you and have a pleasant and
refreshing visit. 33 I pray that God, who gives peace, will be
with all of you. Amen.

Personal Greetings

16 I have good things to say about Phoebe, who is a
leader in the church at Cenchreae. 2 Welcome her in
a way that is proper for someone who has faith in the Lord
and is one of God's own people. Help her in any way you
can. After all, she has proved to be a respected leader for
many others, including me.

3 Give my greetings to Priscilla and Aquila. They have
not only served Christ Jesus together with me, 4 but they
have even risked their lives for me. I am grateful for them
and so are all the Gentile churches. 5 Greet the church that
meets in their home.

Greet my dear friend Epaenetus, who was the first per-
son in Asia to have faith in Christ.

NEW INTERNATIONAL VERSION

blessings. 28So after I have completed this task and have made sure that they have received this fruit, I will go to Spain and visit you on the way. 29I know that when I come to you, I will come in the full measure of the blessing of Christ.

30I urge you, brothers, by our Lord Jesus Christ and by the love of the Spirit, to join me in my struggle by praying to God for me. 31Pray that I may be rescued from the unbelievers in Judea and that my service in Jerusalem may be acceptable to the saints there, 32so that by God's will I may come to you with joy and together with you be refreshed. 33The God of peace be with you all. Amen.

Personal Greetings

16 I commend to you our sister Phoebe, a servant[a] of the church in Cenchrea. 2I ask you to receive her in the Lord in a way worthy of the saints and to give her any help she may need from you, for she has been a great help to many people, including me.

3Greet Priscilla[b] and Aquila, my fellow workers in Christ Jesus. 4They risked their lives for me. Not only I but all the churches of the Gentiles are grateful to them. 5Greet also the church that meets at their house.

Greet my dear friend Epenetus, who was the first convert to Christ in the province of Asia.

[a] *1* Or *deaconess* [b] *3* Greek *Prisca*, a variant of *Priscilla*

NEW LIVING TRANSLATION

them financially. 28As soon as I have delivered this money and completed this good deed of theirs, I will come to see you on my way to Spain. 29And I am sure that when I come, Christ will give me a great blessing for you.

30Dear brothers and sisters, I urge you in the name of our Lord Jesus Christ to join me in my struggle by praying to God for me. Do this because of your love for me, given to you by the Holy Spirit. 31Pray that I will be rescued from those in Judea who refuse to obey God. Pray also that the Christians there will be willing to accept the donation I am bringing them. 32Then, by the will of God, I will be able to come to you with a happy heart, and we will be an encouragement to each other.

33And now may God, who gives us his peace, be with you all. Amen.

Paul Greets His Friends

16 Our sister Phoebe, a deacon in the church in Cenchrea, will be coming to see you soon. 2Receive her in the Lord, as one who is worthy of high honor. Help her in every way you can, for she has helped many in their needs, including me.

3Greet Priscilla and Aquila. They have been co-workers in my ministry for Christ Jesus. 4In fact, they risked their lives for me. I am not the only one who is thankful to them; so are all the Gentile churches. 5Please give my greetings to the church that meets in their home.

Greet my dear friend Epenetus. He was the very first person to become a Christian in the province of Asia. 6Give my

NEW KING JAMES VERSION

have performed this and have sealed to them this fruit, I shall go by way of you to Spain. 29But I know that when I come to you, I shall come in the fullness of the blessing of the gospel[i] of Christ.

30Now I beg you, brethren, through the Lord Jesus Christ, and through the love of the Spirit, that you strive together with me in prayers to God for me, 31that I may be delivered from those in Judea who do not believe, and that my service for Jerusalem may be acceptable to the saints, 32that I may come to you with joy by the will of God, and may be refreshed together with you. 33Now the God of peace *be* with you all. Amen.

Sister Phoebe Commended

16 I commend to you Phoebe our sister, who is a servant of the church in Cenchrea, 2that you may receive her in the Lord in a manner worthy of the saints, and assist her in whatever business she has need of you; for indeed she has been a helper of many and of myself also.

Greeting Roman Saints

3Greet Priscilla and Aquila, my fellow workers in Christ Jesus, 4who risked their own necks for my life, to whom not only I give thanks, but also all the churches of the Gentiles. 5Likewise *greet* the church that is in their house.

Greet my beloved Epaenetus, who is the firstfruits of Achaia[a] to Christ. 6Greet Mary, who labored much for us.

15:29 [i] NU-Text omits *of the gospel*. 16:5 [a] NU-Text reads *Asia*.

THE MESSAGE

done this—personally handed over this "fruit basket"—I'm off to Spain, with a stopover with you in Rome. My hope is that my visit with you is going to be one of Christ's more extravagant blessings.

I have one request, dear friends: Pray for me. Pray strenuously with and for me—to God the Father, through the power of our Master Jesus, through the love of the Spirit—that I will be delivered from the lions' den of unbelievers in Judea. Pray also that my relief offering to the Jerusalem Christians will be accepted in the spirit in which it is given. Then, God willing, I'll be on my way to you with a light and eager heart, looking forward to being refreshed by your company. God's peace be with all of you. Oh, yes!

✠

16 Be sure to welcome our friend Phoebe in the way of the Master, with all the generous hospitality we Christians are famous for. I heartily endorse both her and her work. She's a key representative of the church at Cenchrea. Help her out in whatever she asks. She deserves anything you can do for her. She's helped many a person, including me.

Say hello to Priscilla and Aquila, who have worked hand in hand with me in serving Jesus. They once put their lives on the line for me. And I'm not the only one grateful to them. All the non-Jewish gatherings of believers also owe them plenty, to say nothing of the church that meets in their house.

Hello to my dear friend Epenetus. He was the very first Christian in the province of Asia.

KING JAMES VERSION

6 Greet Mary, who bestowed much labour on us.

7 Salute Andronicus and Junia, my kinsmen, and my fellowprisoners, who are of note among the apostles, who also were in Christ before me.

8 Greet Amplias my beloved in the Lord.

9 Salute Urbane, our helper in Christ, and Stachys my beloved.

10 Salute Apelles approved in Christ. Salute them which are of Aristobulus' *household*.

11 Salute Herodion my kinsman. Greet them that be of the *household* of Narcissus, which are in the Lord.

12 Salute Tryphena and Tryphosa, who labour in the Lord. Salute the beloved Persis, which laboured much in the Lord.

13 Salute Rufus chosen in the Lord, and his mother and mine.

14 Salute Asyncritus, Phlegon, Hermas, Patrobas, Hermes, and the brethren which are with them.

15 Salute Philologus, and Julia, Nereus, and his sister, and Olympas, and all the saints which are with them.

16 Salute one another with an holy kiss. The churches of Christ salute you.

17 ¶ Now I beseech you, brethren, mark them which cause divisions and offences contrary to the doctrine which ye have learned; and avoid them.

NEW AMERICAN STANDARD BIBLE

6 Greet Mary, who has worked hard for you.

7 Greet Andronicus and Junias, my kinsmen and my fellow prisoners, who are outstanding among the apostles, who also were in Christ before me.

8 Greet Ampliatus, my beloved in the Lord.

9 Greet Urbanus, our fellow worker in Christ, and Stachys my beloved.

10 Greet Apelles, the approved in Christ. Greet those who are of the *household* of Aristobulus.

11 Greet Herodion, my kinsman. Greet those of the *household* of Narcissus, who are in the Lord.

12 Greet Tryphaena and Tryphosa, workers in the Lord. Greet Persis the beloved, who has worked hard in the Lord.

13 Greet Rufus, a choice man in the Lord, also his mother and mine.

14 Greet Asyncritus, Phlegon, Hermes, Patrobas, Hermas and the brethren with them.

15 Greet Philologus and Julia, Nereus and his sister, and Olympas, and all the saints who are with them.

16 Greet one another with a holy kiss. All the churches of Christ greet you.

17 Now I urge you, brethren, keep your eye on those who cause dissensions and hindrances contrary to the teaching which you learned, and turn away from them.

NEW CENTURY VERSION

to Mary, who worked very hard for you. 7 Greetings to
Andronicus and Junia, my relatives, who were in prison
with me. They are very important apostles. They were
believers in Christ before I was. 8 Greetings to Ampliatus,
my dear friend in the Lord. 9 Greetings to Urbanus, a work-
er together with me for Christ. And greetings to my dear
friend Stachys. 10 Greetings to Apelles, who was tested and
proved that he truly loves Christ. Greetings to all those
who are in the family of Aristobulus. 11 Greetings to
Herodion, my fellow citizen. Greetings to all those in the
family of Narcissus who belong to the Lord. 12 Greetings to
Tryphena and Tryphosa, women who work very hard for
the Lord. Greetings to my dear friend Persis, who also has
worked very hard for the Lord. 13 Greetings to Rufus, who
is a special person in the Lord, and to his mother, who has
been like a mother to me also. 14 Greetings to Asyncritus,
Phlegon, Hermes, Patrobas, Hermas, and all the brothers
who are with them. 15 Greetings to Philologus and Julia,
Nereus and his sister, and Olympas, and to all God's peo-
ple with them. 16 Greet each other with a holy kiss. All of
Christ's churches send greetings to you.

17 Brothers and sisters, I ask you to look out for those
who cause people to be against each other and who upset
other people's faith. They are against the true teaching you
learned, so stay away from them. 18 Such people are not

CONTEMPORARY ENGLISH VERSION

6 Greet Mary, who has worked so hard for you.

7 Greet my relatives[a] Andronicus and Junias,[b] who were in jail with me. They are highly respected by the apostles and were followers of Christ before I was.

8 Greet Ampliatus, my dear friend whose faith is in the Lord.

9 Greet Urbanus, who serves Christ along with us.
Greet my dear friend Stachys.

10 Greet Apelles, a faithful servant of Christ.
Greet Aristobulus and his family.

11 Greet Herodion, who is a relative[c] of mine.
Greet Narcissus and the others in his family, who have faith in the Lord.

12 Greet Tryphaena and Tryphosa, who work hard for the Lord.
Greet my dear friend Persis. She also works hard for the Lord.

13 Greet Rufus, that special servant of the Lord, and greet his mother, who has been like a mother to me.

14 Greet Asyncritus, Phlegon, Hermes, Patrobas, and Hermas, as well as our friends who are with them.

15 Greet Philologus, Julia, Nereus and his sister, and Olympas, and all of God's people who are with them.

16 Be sure to give each other a warm greeting.
All of Christ's churches greet you.

17 My friends, I beg you to watch out for anyone who causes trouble and divides the church by refusing to do what all of you were taught. Stay away from them! 18 They

[a] 16.7 *relatives*: Or "Jewish friends." [b] 16.7 *Junias*: Or "Junia." Some manuscripts have Julia. [c] 16.11 *relative(s)*: See the note at verse 7.

NEW INTERNATIONAL VERSION

6 Greet Mary, who worked very hard for you.

7 Greet Andronicus and Junias, my relatives who have been in prison with me. They are outstanding among the apostles, and they were in Christ before I was.

8 Greet Ampliatus, whom I love in the Lord.

9 Greet Urbanus, our fellow worker in Christ, and my dear friend Stachys.

10 Greet Apelles, tested and approved in Christ.

Greet those who belong to the household of Aristobulus.

11 Greet Herodion, my relative.

Greet those in the household of Narcissus who are in the Lord.

12 Greet Tryphena and Tryphosa, those women who work hard in the Lord.

Greet my dear friend Persis, another woman who has worked very hard in the Lord.

13 Greet Rufus, chosen in the Lord, and his mother, who has been a mother to me, too.

14 Greet Asyncritus, Phlegon, Hermes, Patrobas, Hermas and the brothers with them.

15 Greet Philologus, Julia, Nereus and his sister, and Olympas and all the saints with them.

16 Greet one another with a holy kiss.

All the churches of Christ send greetings.

17 I urge you, brothers, to watch out for those who cause divisions and put obstacles in your way that are contrary to the teaching you have learned. Keep away from them.

NEW LIVING TRANSLATION

greetings to Mary, who has worked so hard for your bene-
fit. 7 Then there are Andronicus and Junia,* my relatives,*
who were in prison with me. They are respected among the
apostles and became Christians before I did. Please give
them my greetings. 8 Say hello to Ampliatus, whom I love
as one of the Lord's own children, 9 and Urbanus, our co-
worker in Christ, and beloved Stachys.
10 Give my greetings to Apelles, a good man whom Christ
approves. And give my best regards to the members of the
household of Aristobulus. 11 Greet Herodion, my relative.*
Greet the Christians in the household of Narcissus. 12 Say
hello to Tryphena and Tryphosa, the Lord's workers, and to
dear Persis, who has worked so hard for the Lord. 13 Greet
Rufus, whom the Lord picked out to be his very own; and
also his dear mother, who has been a mother to me.
14 And please give my greetings to Asyncritus, Phlegon,
Hermes, Patrobas, Hermas, and the brothers and sisters*
who are with them. 15 Give my greetings to Philologus, Julia,
Nereus and his sister, and to Olympas and all the other
believers who are with them. 16 Greet each other in Christian
love.* All the churches of Christ send you their greetings.

Paul's Final Instructions

17 And now I make one more appeal, my dear brothers
and sisters. Watch out for people who cause divisions and
upset people's faith by teaching things that are contrary to

16:7a Or *Junias;* some manuscripts read *Julia.* **16:7b** Or *compatriots;* also in 16:21. **16:11** Or *compatriot.* **16:14** Greek *brothers;* also in 16:17. **16:16** Greek *with a sacred kiss.*

NEW KING JAMES VERSION

7 Greet Andronicus and Junia, my countrymen and my fel-
low prisoners, who are of note among the apostles, who
also were in Christ before me.
8 Greet Amplias, my beloved in the Lord. 9 Greet Urbanus,
our fellow worker in Christ, and Stachys, my beloved.
10 Greet Apelles, approved in Christ. Greet those who are of
the *household* of Aristobulus. 11 Greet Herodion, my coun-
tryman.[b] Greet those who are of the *household* of Nar-
cissus who are in the Lord.
12 Greet Tryphena and Tryphosa, who have labored in the
Lord. Greet the beloved Persis, who labored much in the
Lord. 13 Greet Rufus, chosen in the Lord, and his mother
and mine. 14 Greet Asyncritus, Phlegon, Hermas, Patrobas,
Hermes, and the brethren who are with them. 15 Greet Phi-
lologus and Julia, Nereus and his sister, and Olympas, and
all the saints who are with them.
16 Greet one another with a holy kiss. The[c] churches of
Christ greet you.

Avoid Divisive Persons

17 Now I urge you, brethren, note those who cause divi-
sions and offenses, contrary to the doctrine which you

16:11 [b] Or *relative* 16:16 [c] NU-Text reads *All the churches.*

THE MESSAGE

Hello to Mary. What a worker she has turned out to be!

Hello to my cousins Andronicus and Junias. We once shared a jail cell. They were believers in Christ before I was. Both of them are outstanding leaders.

Hello to Ampliatus, my good friend in the family of God.

Hello to Urbanus, our companion in Christ's work, and my good friend Stachys.

Hello to Apelles, a tried-and-true veteran in following Christ.

Hello to the family of Aristobulus.

Hello to my cousin Herodion.

Hello to those Christians from the family of Narcissus.

Hello to Tryphena and Tryphosa—such diligent women in serving the Master.

Hello to Persis, a dear friend and hard worker in Christ.

Hello to Rufus—a good choice by the Master!—and his mother. She has also been a dear mother to me.

Hello to Asyncritus, Phlegon, Hermes, Patrobas, Hermas, and also to all of their families.

Hello to Philologus, Julia, Nereus and his sister, and Olympas— and all the Christians who live with them.

Holy embraces all around! All the churches of Christ send their warmest greetings!

One final word of counsel, friends. Keep a sharp eye out for those who take bits and pieces of the teaching that you learned and then use them to make trouble. Give these

KING JAMES VERSION

18 For they that are such serve not our Lord Jesus Christ, but their own belly; and by good words and fair speeches deceive the hearts of the simple.

19 For your obedience is come abroad unto all *men*. I am glad therefore on your behalf: but yet I would have you wise unto that which is good, and simple concerning evil.

20 And the God of peace shall bruise Satan under your feet shortly. The grace of our Lord Jesus Christ *be* with you. Amen.

21 ¶ Timotheus my workfellow, and Lucius, and Jason, and Sosipater, my kinsmen, salute you.

22 I Tertius, who wrote *this* epistle, salute you in the Lord.

23 Gaius mine host, and of the whole church, saluteth you. Erastus the chamberlain of the city saluteth you, and Quartus a brother.

24 The grace of our Lord Jesus Christ *be* with you all. Amen.

25 ¶ Now to him that is of power to stablish you according to my gospel, and the preaching of Jesus Christ, according to the revelation of the mystery, which was kept secret since the world began,

26 But now is made manifest, and by the scriptures of the prophets, according to the commandment of the everlasting God, made known to all nations for the obedience of faith:

27 To God only wise, *be* glory through Jesus Christ for ever. Amen.

NEW AMERICAN STANDARD BIBLE

18 For such men are slaves, not of our Lord Christ but of their own appetites; and by their smooth and flattering speech they deceive the hearts of the unsuspecting.

19 For the report of your obedience has reached to all; therefore I am rejoicing over you, but I want you to be wise in what is good and innocent in what is evil.

20 The God of peace will soon crush Satan under your feet.

The grace of our Lord Jesus be with you.

21 Timothy my fellow worker greets you, and *so do* Lucius and Jason and Sosipater, my kinsmen.

22 I, Tertius, who write this letter, greet you in the Lord.

23 Gaius, host to me and to the whole church, greets you. Erastus, the city treasurer greets you, and Quartus, the brother.

24 [[l]The grace of our Lord Jesus Christ be with you all. Amen.]

25 Now to Him who is able to establish you according to my gospel and the preaching of Jesus Christ, according to the revelation of the mystery which has been kept secret for long ages past,

26 but now is manifested, and by the Scriptures of the prophets, according to the commandment of the eternal God, has been made known to all the nations, *leading* to obedience of faith;

27 to the only wise God, through Jesus Christ, be the glory forever. Amen.

16:24 [l] Early mss do not contain this v

NEW CENTURY VERSION

serving our Lord Christ but are only doing what pleases
themselves. They use fancy talk and fine words to fool the
minds of those who do not know about evil. 19All the
believers have heard that you obey, so I am very happy
because of you. But I want you to be wise in what is good
and innocent in what is evil.

20The God who brings peace will soon defeat Satan and
give you power over him.

The grace of our Lord Jesus be with you.

21Timothy, a worker together with me, sends greetings,
as well as Lucius, Jason, and Sosipater, my relatives.

22I am Tertius, and I am writing this letter from Paul. I
send greetings to you in the Lord.

23Gaius is letting me and the whole church here use his
home. He also sends greetings to you, as do Erastus, the
city treasurer, and our brother Quartus. 24[b]

25Glory to God who can make you strong in faith by the
Good News that I tell people and by the message about
Jesus Christ. The message about Christ is the secret that
was hidden for long ages past but is now made known. 26It
has been made clear through the writings of the prophets.
And by the command of the eternal God it is made known
to all nations that they might believe and obey.

27To the only wise God be glory forever through Jesus
Christ! Amen.

16:24 [b] **Verse 24** Some Greek copies add verse 24: "The grace of our Lord Jesus Christ be with all of you. Amen."

CONTEMPORARY ENGLISH VERSION

want to serve themselves and not Christ the Lord. Their
flattery and fancy talk fool people who don't know any
better. 19I am glad that everyone knows how well you obey
the Lord. But still, I want you to understand what is good
and not have anything to do with evil. 20Then God, who
gives peace, will soon crush Satan under your feet. I pray
that our Lord Jesus will be kind to you.

21Timothy, who works with me, sends his greetings, and
so do my relatives,[c] Lucius, Jason, and Sosipater.

22I, Tertius, also send my greetings. I am a follower of
the Lord, and I wrote this letter.[d]

23-24Gaius welcomes me and the whole church into his
home, and he sends his greetings.

Erastus, the city treasurer, and our dear friend Quartus
send their greetings too.[e]

Paul's Closing Prayer

25Praise God! He can make you strong by means of my
good news, which is the message about[f] Jesus Christ. For
ages and ages this message was kept secret, 26but now at
last it has been told. The eternal God commanded his
prophets to write about the good news, so that all nations
would obey and have faith. 27And now, because of Jesus
Christ, we can praise the only wise God forever! Amen.[g]

[c] 16.21 *relative(s)*: See the note at verse 7. [d] 16.22 *I wrote this letter*: Paul probably dictated this letter to Tertius. [e] 16.23,24 *send their greetings too*: Some manuscripts add, "I pray that our Lord Jesus Christ will always be kind to you. Amen." [f] 16.25 *about*: Or "from."
[g] 16.27 *Amen*: Some manuscripts have verses 25-27 after 14.23. Others have the verses here and after 14.23, and one manuscript has them after 15.33.

NEW INTERNATIONAL VERSION

[18]For such people are not serving our Lord Christ, but their own appetites. By smooth talk and flattery they deceive the minds of naive people. [19]Everyone has heard about your obedience, so I am full of joy over you; but I want you to be wise about what is good, and innocent about what is evil.

[20]The God of peace will soon crush Satan under your feet.

The grace of our Lord Jesus be with you.

[21]Timothy, my fellow worker, sends his greetings to you, as do Lucius, Jason and Sosipater, my relatives.

[22]I, Tertius, who wrote down this letter, greet you in the Lord.

[23]Gaius, whose hospitality I and the whole church here enjoy, sends you his greetings.

Erastus, who is the city's director of public works, and our brother Quartus send you their greetings.[c]

[25]Now to him who is able to establish you by my gospel and the proclamation of Jesus Christ, according to the revelation of the mystery hidden for long ages past, [26]but now revealed and made known through the prophetic writings by the command of the eternal God, so that all nations might believe and obey him— [27]to the only wise God be glory forever through Jesus Christ! Amen.

[c] 23 Some manuscripts *their greetings.* [24]*May the grace of our Lord Jesus Christ be with all of you. Amen.*

NEW LIVING TRANSLATION

what you have been taught. Stay away from them. [18]Such people are not serving Christ our Lord; they are serving their own personal interests. By smooth talk and glowing words they deceive innocent people. [19]But everyone knows that you are obedient to the Lord. This makes me very happy. I want you to see clearly what is right and to stay innocent of any wrong. [20]The God of peace will soon crush Satan under your feet. May the grace of our Lord Jesus Christ be with you.

[21]Timothy, my fellow worker, and Lucius, Jason, and Sosipater, my relatives, send you their good wishes.

[22]I, Tertius, the one who is writing this letter for Paul, send my greetings, too, as a Christian brother.

[23]Gaius says hello to you. I am his guest, and the church meets here in his home. Erastus, the city treasurer, sends you his greetings, and so does Quartus, a Christian brother.*

[25]God is able to make you strong, just as the Good News says. It is the message about Jesus Christ and his plan for you Gentiles, a plan kept secret from the beginning of time. [26]But now as the prophets* foretold and as the eternal God has commanded, this message is made known to all Gentiles everywhere, so that they might believe and obey Christ. [27]To God, who alone is wise, be the glory forever through Jesus Christ. Amen.

16:23 Some manuscripts add verse 24, *May the grace of our Lord Jesus Christ be with you all. Amen.* **16:26** Greek *the prophetic writings.*

NEW KING JAMES VERSION

learned, and avoid them. [18]For those who are such do not serve our Lord Jesus[d] Christ, but their own belly, and by smooth words and flattering speech deceive the hearts of the simple. [19]For your obedience has become known to all. Therefore I am glad on your behalf; but I want you to be wise in what is good, and simple concerning evil. [20]And the God of peace will crush Satan under your feet shortly.

The grace of our Lord Jesus Christ *be* with you. Amen.

Greetings from Paul's Friends

[21]Timothy, my fellow worker, and Lucius, Jason, and Sosipater, my countrymen, greet you.

[22]I, Tertius, who wrote *this* epistle, greet you in the Lord.

[23]Gaius, my host and *the host* of the whole church, greets you. Erastus, the treasurer of the city, greets you, and Quartus, a brother. [24]The grace of our Lord Jesus Christ *be* with you all. Amen.[e]

Benediction

[25]Now to Him who is able to establish you according to my gospel and the preaching of Jesus Christ, according to the revelation of the mystery kept secret since the world began [26]but now made manifest, and by the prophetic Scriptures made known to all nations, according to the commandment of the everlasting God, for obedience to the faith— [27]to God, alone wise, *be* glory through Jesus Christ forever. Amen.[f]

16:18 [d] NU-Text and M-Text omit *Jesus.* **16:24** [e] NU-Text omits this verse. **16:27** [f] M-Text puts Romans 16:25–27 after Romans 14:23.

THE MESSAGE

people a wide berth. They have no intention of living for our Master Christ. They're only in this for what they can get out of it, and aren't above using pious sweet-talk to dupe unsuspecting innocents.

And so while there has never been any question about your honesty in these matters—I couldn't be more proud of you!—I want you also to be smart, making sure every "good" thing is the *real* thing. Don't be gullible in regard to smooth-talking evil. Stay alert like this, and before you know it the God of peace will come down on Satan with both feet, stomping him into the dirt. Enjoy the best of Jesus!

And here are some more greetings from our end. Timothy, my partner in this work, Lucius, and my cousins Jason and Sosipater all said to tell you hello.

I, Tertius, who wrote this letter at Paul's dictation, send you my personal greetings.

Gaius, who is host here to both me and the whole church, wants to be remembered to you.

Erastus, the city treasurer, and our good friend Quartus send their greetings.

All of our praise rises to the One who is strong enough to make *you* strong, exactly as preached in Jesus Christ, precisely as revealed in the mystery kept secret for so long but now an open book through the prophetic Scriptures. All the nations of the world can now know the truth and be brought into obedient belief, carrying out the orders of God, who got all this started, down to the very last letter.

All our praise is focused through Jesus on this incomparably wise God! Yes!

KING JAMES VERSION

THE FIRST EPISTLE OF ST. PAUL TO THE CORINTHIANS

1 Paul, called *to be* an apostle of Jesus Christ through the will of God, and Sosthenes *our* brother,

2 Unto the church of God which is at Corinth, to them that are sanctified in Christ Jesus, called *to be* saints, with all that in every place call upon the name of Jesus Christ our Lord, both theirs and ours:

3 Grace *be* unto you, and peace, from God our Father, and *from* the Lord Jesus Christ.

4 I thank my God always on your behalf, for the grace of God which is given you by Jesus Christ;

5 That in every thing ye are enriched by him, in all utterance, and *in* all knowledge;

6 Even as the testimony of Christ was confirmed in you:

7 So that ye come behind in no gift; waiting for the coming of our Lord Jesus Christ:

8 Who shall also confirm you unto the end, *that ye may be* blameless in the day of our Lord Jesus Christ.

9 God *is* faithful, by whom ye were called unto the fellowship of his Son Jesus Christ our Lord.

NEW AMERICAN STANDARD BIBLE

THE FIRST LETTER OF PAUL TO THE CORINTHIANS

Appeal to Unity

1 Paul, called *as* an apostle of Jesus Christ by the will of God, and Sosthenes our brother,

2 To the church of God which is at Corinth, to those who have been sanctified in Christ Jesus, saints by calling, with all who in every place call on the name of our Lord Jesus Christ, their *Lord* and ours:

3 Grace to you and peace from God our Father and the Lord Jesus Christ.

4 I thank [1]my God always concerning you for the grace of God which was given you in Christ Jesus,

5 that in everything you were enriched in Him, in all speech and all knowledge,

6 even as the testimony concerning Christ was confirmed in you,

7 so that you are not lacking in any gift, awaiting eagerly the revelation of our Lord Jesus Christ,

8 who will also confirm you to the end, blameless in the day of our Lord Jesus Christ.

9 God is faithful, through whom you were called into fellowship with His Son, Jesus Christ our Lord.

1:4 [1] Two early mss do not contain *my*

NEW CENTURY VERSION

1 CORINTHIANS

1 From Paul. God called me to be an apostle of Christ
Jesus because that is what God wanted. Also from
Sosthenes, our brother in Christ.
2To the church of God in Corinth, to you who have been
made holy in Christ Jesus. You were called to be God's holy
people with all people everywhere who pray in the name of
the Lord Jesus Christ—their Lord and ours:
3Grace and peace to you from God our Father and the
Lord Jesus Christ.

Paul Gives Thanks to God

4I always thank my God for you because of the grace
God has given you in Christ Jesus.
5I thank God because in
Christ you have been made rich in every way, in all your
speaking and in all your knowledge.
6Just as our witness
about Christ has been guaranteed to you,
7so you have
every gift from God while you wait for our Lord Jesus
Christ to come again.
8Jesus will keep you strong until the
end so that there will be no wrong in you on the day our
Lord Jesus Christ comes again.
9God, who has called you to
share everything with his Son, Jesus Christ our Lord, is
faithful.

CONTEMPORARY ENGLISH VERSION

1 CORINTHIANS

1 From Paul, chosen by God to be an apostle of Christ
Jesus, and from Sosthenes, who is also a follower.
2To God's church in Corinth. Christ Jesus chose you to be
his very own people, and you worship in his name, as we
and all others do who call him Lord.
3My prayer is that God our Father and the Lord Jesus
Christ will be kind to you and will bless you with peace!
4I never stop thanking my God for being kind enough to
give you Christ Jesus,
5who helps you speak and under-
stand so well.
6Now you are certain that everything we
told you about our Lord Christ Jesus is true.
7You are not
missing out on any blessings, as you wait for him to
return.
8And until the day Christ does return, he will keep
you completely innocent.
9God can be trusted, and he
chose you to be partners with his Son, our Lord Jesus
Christ.

NEW INTERNATIONAL VERSION

1 CORINTHIANS

1 Paul, called to be an apostle of Christ Jesus by the will of God, and our brother Sosthenes,

2To the church of God in Corinth, to those sanctified in Christ Jesus and called to be holy, together with all those everywhere who call on the name of our Lord Jesus Christ—their Lord and ours:

3Grace and peace to you from God our Father and the Lord Jesus Christ.

Thanksgiving

4I always thank God for you because of his grace given you in Christ Jesus. 5For in him you have been enriched in every way—in all your speaking and in all your knowledge— 6because our testimony about Christ was confirmed in you. 7Therefore you do not lack any spiritual gift as you eagerly wait for our Lord Jesus Christ to be revealed. 8He will keep you strong to the end, so that you will be blameless on the day of our Lord Jesus Christ. 9God, who has called you into fellowship with his Son Jesus Christ our Lord, is faithful.

NEW LIVING TRANSLATION

1 CORINTHIANS

Greetings from Paul

1 This letter is from Paul, chosen by the will of God to be an apostle of Christ Jesus, and from our brother Sosthenes.

2We are writing to the church of God in Corinth, you who have been called by God to be his own holy people. He made you holy by means of Christ Jesus, just as he did all Christians everywhere—whoever calls upon the name of Jesus Christ, our Lord and theirs.

3May God our Father and the Lord Jesus Christ give you his grace and peace.

Paul Gives Thanks to God

4I can never stop thanking God for all the generous gifts he has given you, now that you belong to Christ Jesus. 5He has enriched your church with the gifts of eloquence and every kind of knowledge. 6This shows that what I told you about Christ is true. 7Now you have every spiritual gift you need as you eagerly wait for the return of our Lord Jesus Christ. 8He will keep you strong right up to the end, and he will keep you free from all blame on the great day when our Lord Jesus Christ returns. 9God will surely do this for you, for he always does just what he says, and he is the one who invited you into this wonderful friendship with his Son, Jesus Christ our Lord.

NEW KING JAMES VERSION

THE FIRST EPISTLE OF PAUL TO THE CORINTHIANS

Greeting

1 Paul, called *to be* an apostle of Jesus Christ through the will of God, and Sosthenes *our* brother,

2To the church of God which is at Corinth, to those who are sanctified in Christ Jesus, called *to be* saints, with all who in every place call on the name of Jesus Christ our Lord, both theirs and ours:

3Grace to you and peace from God our Father and the Lord Jesus Christ.

Spiritual Gifts at Corinth

4I thank my God always concerning you for the grace of God which was given to you by Christ Jesus, 5that you were enriched in everything by Him in all utterance and all knowledge, 6even as the testimony of Christ was confirmed in you, 7so that you come short in no gift, eagerly waiting for the revelation of our Lord Jesus Christ, 8who will also confirm you to the end, *that you may be* blameless in the day of our Lord Jesus Christ. 9God *is* faithful, by whom you were called into the fellowship of His Son, Jesus Christ our Lord.

THE MESSAGE

1 CORINTHIANS

1 I, Paul, have been called and sent by Jesus, the Messiah, according to God's plan, along with my friend Sosthenes. I send this letter to you in God's church at Corinth, Christians cleaned up by Jesus and set apart for a God-filled life. I include in my greeting all who call out to Jesus, wherever they live. He's their Master as well as ours!

May all the gifts and benefits that come from God our Father, and the Master, Jesus Christ, be yours.

Every time I think of you—and I think of you often!—I thank God for your lives of free and open access to God, given by Jesus. There's no end to what has happened in you—it's beyond speech, beyond knowledge. The evidence of Christ has been clearly verified in your lives.

Just think—you don't need a thing, you've got it all! All God's gifts are right in front of you as you wait expectantly for our Master Jesus to arrive on the scene for the Finale. And not only that, but God himself is right alongside to keep you steady and on track until things are all wrapped up by Jesus. God, who got you started in this spiritual adventure, shares with us the life of his Son and our Master Jesus. He will never give up on you. Never forget that.

KING JAMES VERSION

10 ¶ Now I beseech you, brethren, by the name of our Lord Jesus Christ, that ye all speak the same thing, and *that* there be no divisions among you; but *that* ye be perfectly joined together in the same mind and in the same judgment.

11 For it hath been declared unto me of you, my brethren, by them *which are of the house* of Chloe, that there are contentions among you.

12 Now this I say, that every one of you saith, I am of Paul; and I of Apollos; and I of Cephas; and I of Christ.

13 Is Christ divided? was Paul crucified for you? or were ye baptized in the name of Paul?

14 ¶ I thank God that I baptized none of you, but Crispus and Gaius;

15 Lest any should say that I had baptized in mine own name.

16 And I baptized also the household of Stephanas: besides, I know not whether I baptized any other.

17 ¶ For Christ sent me not to baptize, but to preach the gospel: not with wisdom of words, lest the cross of Christ should be made of none effect.

18 For the preaching of the cross is to them that perish foolishness; but unto us which are saved it is the power of God.

NEW AMERICAN STANDARD BIBLE

10 Now I exhort you, brethren, by the name of our Lord Jesus Christ, that you all agree and that there be no divisions among you, but that you be made complete in the same mind and in the same judgment.

11 For I have been informed concerning you, my brethren, by Chloe's *people,* that there are quarrels among you.

12 Now I mean this, that each one of you is saying, "I am of Paul," and "I of Apollos," and "I of Cephas," and "I of Christ."

13 Has Christ been divided? Paul was not crucified for you, was he? Or were you baptized in the name of Paul?

14 [2]I thank God that I baptized none of you except Crispus and Gaius,

15 so that no one would say you were baptized in my name.

16 Now I did baptize also the household of Stephanas; beyond that, I do not know whether I baptized any other.

17 For Christ did not send me to baptize, but to preach the gospel, not in cleverness of speech, so that the cross of Christ would not be made void.

The Wisdom of God

18 For the word of the cross is foolishness to those who are perishing, but to us who are being saved it is the power of God.

19 For it is written,

1:14 [2] Two early mss read *I give thanks that*

NEW CENTURY VERSION

Problems in the Church

10 I beg you, brothers and sisters,[a] by the name of our Lord Jesus Christ that all of you agree with each other and not be split into groups. I beg that you be completely joined together by having the same kind of thinking and the same purpose. 11 My brothers and sisters, some people from Chloe's family have told me quite plainly that there are quarrels among you. 12 This is what I mean: One of you says, "I follow Paul"; another says, "I follow Apollos"; another says, "I follow Peter"; and another says, "I follow Christ." 13 Christ has been divided up into different groups! Did Paul die on the cross for you? No! Were you baptized in the name of Paul? No! 14 I thank God I did not baptize any of you except Crispus and Gaius 15 so that now no one can say you were baptized in my name. 16 (I also baptized the family of Stephanas, but I do not remember that I baptized anyone else.) 17 Christ did not send me to baptize people but to preach the Good News. And he sent me to preach the Good News without using words of human wisdom so that the cross[b] of Christ would not lose its power.

Christ Is God's Power and Wisdom

18 The teaching about the cross is foolishness to those who are being lost, but to us who are being saved it is the power of God. 19 It is written in the Scriptures:

1:10 [a] **brothers and sisters** Although the Greek text says "brothers" here and throughout this book, Paul's words were meant for the entire church, including men and women. 1:17 [b] **cross** Paul uses the cross as a picture of the gospel, the story of Christ's death and rising from the dead to pay for people's sins. The cross, or Christ's death, was God's way to save people.

CONTEMPORARY ENGLISH VERSION

Taking Sides

10 My dear friends, as a follower of our Lord Jesus Christ, I beg you to get along with each other. Don't take sides. Always try to agree in what you think. 11 Several people from Chloe's family[a] have already reported to me that you keep arguing with each other. 12 They have said that some of you claim to follow me, while others claim to follow Apollos or Peter[b] or Christ.

13 Has Christ been divided up? Was I nailed to a cross for you? Were you baptized in my name? 14 I thank God[c] that I didn't baptize any of you except Crispus and Gaius. 15 Not one of you can say that you were baptized in my name. 16 I did baptize the family[d] of Stephanas, but I don't remember if I baptized anyone else. 17 Christ did not send me to baptize. He sent me to tell the good news without using big words that would make the cross of Christ lose its power.

Christ Is God's Power and Wisdom

18 The message about the cross doesn't make any sense to lost people. But for those of us who are being saved, it is God's power at work. 19 As God says in the Scriptures,

[a] 1.11 *family*: Family members and possibly slaves and others who may have lived in the house. [b] 1.12 *Peter*: The Greek text has "Cephas," which is an Aramaic name meaning "rock." Peter is the Greek name with the same meaning. [c] 1.14 *I thank God*: Some manuscripts have "I thank my God." [d] 1.16 *family*: See the note at 1.11.

NEW INTERNATIONAL VERSION

Divisions in the Church

10 I appeal to you, brothers, in the name of our Lord
Jesus Christ, that all of you agree with one another so that
there may be no divisions among you and that you may be
perfectly united in mind and thought. 11 My brothers, some
from Chloe's household have informed me that there are
quarrels among you. 12 What I mean is this: One of you
says, "I follow Paul"; another, "I follow Apollos"; another,
"I follow Cephas[a]"; still another, "I follow Christ."
13 Is Christ divided? Was Paul crucified for you? Were
you baptized into[b] the name of Paul? 14 I am thankful that
I did not baptize any of you except Crispus and Gaius, 15 so
no one can say that you were baptized into my name.
16 (Yes, I also baptized the household of Stephanas; beyond
that, I don't remember if I baptized anyone else.) 17 For
Christ did not send me to baptize, but to preach the
gospel—not with words of human wisdom, lest the cross
of Christ be emptied of its power.

Christ the Wisdom and Power of God

18 For the message of the cross is foolishness to those
who are perishing, but to us who are being saved it is the
power of God. 19 For it is written:

[a] *12* That is, Peter [b] *13* Or *in*; also in verse 15

NEW LIVING TRANSLATION

Divisions in the Church

10 Now, dear brothers and sisters,* I appeal to you by the
authority of the Lord Jesus Christ to stop arguing among
yourselves. Let there be real harmony so there won't be
divisions in the church. I plead with you to be of one mind,
united in thought and purpose. 11 For some members of
Chloe's household have told me about your arguments,
dear brothers and sisters. 12 Some of you are saying, "I am
a follower of Paul." Others are saying, "I follow Apollos,"
or "I follow Peter,*" or "I follow only Christ." 13 Can Christ
be divided into pieces?

Was I, Paul, crucified for you? Were any of you baptized
in the name of Paul? 14 I thank God that I did not baptize
any of you except Crispus and Gaius, 15 for now no one can
say they were baptized in my name. 16 (Oh yes, I also bap-
tized the household of Stephanas. I don't remember baptiz-
ing anyone else.) 17 For Christ didn't send me to baptize,
but to preach the Good News—and not with clever
speeches and high-sounding ideas, for fear that the cross
of Christ would lose its power.

The Wisdom of God

18 I know very well how foolish the message of the cross
sounds to those who are on the road to destruction. But we
who are being saved recognize this message as the very
power of God. 19 As the Scriptures say,

1:10 Greek *brothers;* also in 1:11, 26. 1:12 Greek *Cephas.*

NEW KING JAMES VERSION

Sectarianism Is Sin

10 Now I plead with you, brethren, by the name of our
Lord Jesus Christ, that you all speak the same thing, and
that there be no divisions among you, but *that* you be per-
fectly joined together in the same mind and in the same
judgment. 11 For it has been declared to me concerning you,
my brethren, by those of Chloe's *household,* that there are
contentions among you. 12 Now I say this, that each of you
says, "I am of Paul," or "I am of Apollos," or "I am of
Cephas," or "I am of Christ." 13 Is Christ divided? Was Paul
crucified for you? Or were you baptized in the name of
Paul?

14 I thank God that I baptized none of you except Crispus
and Gaius, 15 lest anyone should say that I had baptized in
my own name. 16 Yes, I also baptized the household of
Stephanas. Besides, I do not know whether I baptized any
other. 17 For Christ did not send me to baptize, but to
preach the gospel, not with wisdom of words, lest the cross
of Christ should be made of no effect.

Christ the Power and Wisdom of God

18 For the message of the cross is foolishness to those
who are perishing, but to us who are being saved it is the
power of God. 19 For it is written:

THE MESSAGE

The Cross: The Irony of God's Wisdom

I have a serious concern to bring up with you, my friends, using the authority of Jesus, our Master. I'll put it as urgently as I can: You *must* get along with each other. You must learn to be considerate of one another, cultivating a life in common.

I bring this up because some from Chloe's family brought a most disturbing report to my attention—that you're fighting among yourselves! I'll tell you exactly what I was told: You're all picking sides, going around saying, "I'm on Paul's side," or "I'm for Apollos," or "Peter is my man," or "I'm in the Messiah group."

I ask you, "Has the Messiah been chopped up in little pieces so we can each have a relic all our own? Was Paul crucified for you? Was a single one of you baptized in Paul's name?" I was not involved with any of your baptisms—except for Crispus and Gaius—and on getting this report, I'm sure glad I wasn't. At least no one can go around saying he was baptized in my name. (Come to think of it, I also baptized Stephanas's family, but as far as I can recall, that's it.)

God didn't send me out to collect a following for myself, but to preach the Message of what he has done, collecting a following for him. And he didn't send me to do it with a lot of fancy rhetoric of my own, lest the powerful action at the center—Christ on the Cross—be trivialized into mere words.

The Message that points to Christ on the Cross seems like sheer silliness to those hellbent on destruction, but for those on the way of salvation it makes perfect sense. This is the way God works, and most powerfully as it turns out. It's written,

KING JAMES VERSION

19 For it is written, I will destroy the wisdom of the wise, and will bring to nothing the understanding of the prudent.

20 Where *is* the wise? where *is* the scribe? where *is* the disputer of this world? hath not God made foolish the wisdom of this world?

21 For after that in the wisdom of God the world by wisdom knew not God, it pleased God by the foolishness of preaching to save them that believe.

22 For the Jews require a sign, and the Greeks seek after wisdom:

23 But we preach Christ crucified, unto the Jews a stumblingblock, and unto the Greeks foolishness;

24 But unto them which are called, both Jews and Greeks, Christ the power of God, and the wisdom of God.

25 Because the foolishness of God is wiser than men; and the weakness of God is stronger than men.

26 For ye see your calling, brethren, how that not many wise men after the flesh, not many mighty, not many noble, *are called*:

27 But God hath chosen the foolish things of the world to confound the wise; and God hath chosen the weak things of the world to confound the things which are mighty;

NEW AMERICAN STANDARD BIBLE

"I WILL DESTROY THE WISDOM OF THE WISE,
AND THE CLEVERNESS OF THE CLEVER I WILL SET ASIDE."

20 Where is the wise man? Where is the scribe? Where is the debater of this age? Has not God made foolish the wisdom of the world?

21 For since in the wisdom of God the world through its wisdom did not *come to* know God, God was well-pleased through the foolishness of the message preached to save those who believe.

22 For indeed Jews ask for signs and Greeks search for wisdom;

23 but we preach [3]Christ crucified, to Jews a stumbling block and to Gentiles foolishness,

24 but to those who are the called, both Jews and Greeks, Christ the power of God and the wisdom of God.

25 Because the foolishness of God is wiser than men, and the weakness of God is stronger than men.

26 For consider your calling, brethren, that there were not many wise according to the flesh, not many mighty, not many noble;

27 but God has chosen the foolish things of the world to shame the wise, and God has chosen the weak things of the world to shame the things which are strong,

1:23 [3] I.e. Messiah

NEW CENTURY VERSION

"I will cause the wise men to lose their wisdom;
I will make the wise men unable to understand."
Isaiah 29:14

[20]Where is the wise person? Where is the educated per-
son? Where is the skilled talker of this world? God has
made the wisdom of the world foolish. [21]In the wisdom of
God the world did not know God through its own wisdom.
So God chose to use the message that sounds foolish to
save those who believe. [22]The Jews ask for miracles, and
the Greeks want wisdom. [23]But we preach a crucified
Christ. This is a big problem to the Jews, and it is foolish-
ness to those who are not Jews. [24]But Christ is the power
of God and the wisdom of God to those people God has
called—Jews and Greeks. [25]Even the foolishness of God is
wiser than human wisdom, and the weakness of God is
stronger than human strength.

[26]Brothers and sisters, look at what you were when God
called you. Not many of you were wise in the way the
world judges wisdom. Not many of you had great influ-
ence. Not many of you came from important families.
[27]But God chose the foolish things of the world to shame
the wise, and he chose the weak things of the world to

CONTEMPORARY ENGLISH VERSION

"I will destroy the wisdom
of all who claim
to be wise.
I will confuse those
who think they know
so much."

[20]What happened to those wise people? What happened
to those experts in the Scriptures? What happened to the
ones who think they have all the answers? Didn't God
show that the wisdom of this world is foolish? [21]God was
wise and decided not to let the people of this world use
their wisdom to learn about him.

Instead, God chose to save only those who believe the
foolish message we preach. [22]Jews ask for miracles, and
Greeks want something that sounds wise. [23]But we preach
that Christ was nailed to a cross. Most Jews have problems
with this, and most Gentiles think it is foolish. [24]Our mes-
sage is God's power and wisdom for the Jews and the
Greeks that he has chosen. [25]Even when God is foolish, he
is wiser than everyone else, and even when God is weak,
he is stronger than everyone else.

[26]My dear friends, remember what you were when God
chose you. The people of this world didn't think that many
of you were wise. Only a few of you were in places of
power, and not many of you came from important families.
[27]But God chose the foolish things of this world to put the
wise to shame. He chose the weak things of this world to
put the powerful to shame.

NEW INTERNATIONAL VERSION

"I will destroy the wisdom of the wise;
the intelligence of the intelligent I will frustrate."[c]

[20]Where is the wise man? Where is the scholar? Where is the philosopher of this age? Has not God made foolish the wisdom of the world? [21]For since in the wisdom of God the world through its wisdom did not know him, God was pleased through the foolishness of what was preached to save those who believe. [22]Jews demand miraculous signs and Greeks look for wisdom, [23]but we preach Christ crucified: a stumbling block to Jews and foolishness to Gentiles, [24]but to those whom God has called, both Jews and Greeks, Christ the power of God and the wisdom of God. [25]For the foolishness of God is wiser than man's wisdom, and the weakness of God is stronger than man's strength.

[26]Brothers, think of what you were when you were called. Not many of you were wise by human standards; not many were influential; not many were of noble birth. [27]But God chose the foolish things of the world to shame the wise; God chose the weak things of the world to shame

c 19 Isaiah 29:14

NEW LIVING TRANSLATION

"I will destroy human wisdom
and discard their most brilliant ideas."*

[20]So where does this leave the philosophers, the scholars, and the world's brilliant debaters? God has made them all look foolish and has shown their wisdom to be useless nonsense. [21]Since God in his wisdom saw to it that the world would never find him through human wisdom, he has used our foolish preaching to save all who believe. [22]God's way seems foolish to the Jews because they want a sign from heaven to prove it is true. And it is foolish to the Greeks because they believe only what agrees with their own wisdom. [23]So when we preach that Christ was crucified, the Jews are offended, and the Gentiles say it's all nonsense. [24]But to those called by God to salvation, both Jews and Gentiles,* Christ is the mighty power of God and the wonderful wisdom of God. [25]This "foolish" plan of God is far wiser than the wisest of human plans, and God's weakness is far stronger than the greatest of human strength.

[26]Remember, dear brothers and sisters, that few of you were wise in the world's eyes, or powerful, or wealthy when God called you. [27]Instead, God deliberately chose things the world considers foolish in order to shame those who think they are wise. And he chose those who are powerless to shame those who are powerful. [28]God chose

1:19 Isa 29:14. **1:24** Greek *Greeks.*

NEW KING JAMES VERSION

"I will destroy the wisdom of the wise,
And bring to nothing the understanding of the prudent."[a]

[20]Where *is* the wise? Where *is* the scribe? Where *is* the disputer of this age? Has not God made foolish the wisdom of this world? [21]For since, in the wisdom of God, the world through wisdom did not know God, it pleased God through the foolishness of the message preached to save those who believe. [22]For Jews request a sign, and Greeks seek after wisdom; [23]but we preach Christ crucified, to the Jews a stumbling block and to the Greeks[b] foolishness, [24]but to those who are called, both Jews and Greeks, Christ the power of God and the wisdom of God. [25]Because the foolishness of God is wiser than men, and the weakness of God is stronger than men.

Glory Only in the Lord

[26]For you see your calling, brethren, that not many wise according to the flesh, not many mighty, not many noble, *are called.* [27]But God has chosen the foolish things of the world to put to shame the wise, and God has chosen the weak things of the world to put to shame the things which

1:19 [a] Isaiah 29:14 **1:23** [b] NU-Text reads *Gentiles.*

THE MESSAGE

"I'll turn conventional wisdom on its head,
I'll expose so-called experts as crackpots."

So where can you find someone truly wise, truly educated, truly intelligent in this day and age? Hasn't God exposed it all as pretentious nonsense? Since the world in all its fancy wisdom never had a clue when it came to knowing God, God in his wisdom took delight in using what the world considered dumb—*preaching*, of all things!—to bring those who trust him into the way of salvation.

While Jews clamor for miraculous demonstrations and Greeks go in for philosophical wisdom, we go right on proclaiming Christ, the Crucified. Jews treat this like an *anti*-miracle—and Greeks pass it off as absurd. But to us who are personally called by God himself—both Jews and Greeks—Christ is God's ultimate miracle and wisdom all wrapped up in one. Human wisdom is so tinny, so impotent, next to the seeming absurdity of God. Human strength can't begin to compete with God's "weakness."

Take a good look, friends, at who you were when you got called into this life. I don't see many of "the brightest and the best" among you, not many influential, not many from high-society families. Isn't it obvious that God deliberately chose men and women that the culture overlooks and exploits and abuses, chose these "nobodies" to expose the hollow pretensions of the "somebodies"? That makes it

KING JAMES VERSION

28 And base things of the world, and things which are despised, hath God chosen, *yea*, and things which are not, to bring to nought things that are:

29 That no flesh should glory in his presence.

30 But of him are ye in Christ Jesus, who of God is made unto us wisdom, and righteousness, and sanctification, and redemption:

31 That, according as it is written, He that glorieth, let him glory in the Lord.

2 And I, brethren, when I came to you, came not with excellency of speech or of wisdom, declaring unto you the testimony of God.

2 For I determined not to know any thing among you, save Jesus Christ, and him crucified.

3 And I was with you in weakness, and in fear, and in much trembling.

4 And my speech and my preaching *was* not with enticing words of man's wisdom, but in demonstration of the Spirit and of power:

5 That your faith should not stand in the wisdom of men, but in the power of God.

6 ¶ Howbeit we speak wisdom among them that are perfect: yet not the wisdom of this world, nor of the princes of this world, that come to nought:

NEW AMERICAN STANDARD BIBLE

28 and the base things of the world and the despised God has chosen, the things that are not, so that He may nullify the things that are,

29 so that no man may boast before God.

30 But by His doing you are in Christ Jesus, who became to us wisdom from God, and righteousness and sanctification, and redemption,

31 so that, just as it is written, "LET HIM WHO BOASTS, BOAST IN THE LORD."

Paul's Reliance upon the Spirit

2 And when I came to you, brethren, I did not come with superiority of speech or of wisdom, proclaiming to you the [1]testimony of God.

2 For I determined to know nothing among you except Jesus Christ, and Him crucified.

3 I was with you in weakness and in fear and in much trembling,

4 and my message and my preaching were not in persuasive words of wisdom, but in demonstration of the Spirit and of power,

5 so that your faith would not rest on the wisdom of men, but on the power of God.

6 Yet we do speak wisdom among those who are mature; a wisdom, however, not of this age nor of the rulers of this age, who are passing away;

2:1 [1] One early ms reads *mystery*

NEW CENTURY VERSION

shame the strong. 28He chose what the world thinks is
unimportant and what the world looks down on and
thinks is nothing in order to destroy what the world thinks
is important. 29God did this so that no one can brag in his
presence. 30Because of God you are in Christ Jesus, who
has become for us wisdom from God. In Christ we are put
right with God, and have been made holy, and have been
set free from sin. 31So, as the Scripture says, "If someone
wants to brag, he should brag only about the Lord."[c]

The Message of Christ's Death

2 Dear brothers and sisters, when I came to you, I did
not come preaching God's secret with fancy words or
a show of human wisdom. 2I decided that while I was with
you I would forget about everything except Jesus Christ
and his death on the cross. 3So when I came to you, I was
weak and fearful and trembling. 4My teaching and preaching were not with words of human wisdom that persuade
people but with proof of the power that the Spirit gives.
5This was so that your faith would be in God's power and
not in human wisdom.

God's Wisdom

6However, I speak a wisdom to those who are mature.
But this wisdom is not from this world or from the rulers
of this world, who are losing their power. 7I speak God's

1:31 [c] "If...Lord." Quotation from Jeremiah 9:24.

CONTEMPORARY ENGLISH VERSION

28What the world thinks is worthless, useless, and nothing at all is what God has used to destroy what the world
considers important. 29God did all this to keep anyone
from bragging to him. 30You are God's children. He sent
Christ Jesus to save us and to make us wise, acceptable,
and holy. 31So if you want to brag, do what the Scriptures
say and brag about the Lord.

Telling about Christ and the Cross

2 Friends, when I came and told you the mystery[a] that
God had shared with us, I didn't use big words or try
to sound wise. 2In fact, while I was with you, I made up
my mind to speak only about Jesus Christ, who had been
nailed to a cross.

3At first, I was weak and trembling with fear. 4When I
talked with you or preached, I didn't try to prove anything
by sounding wise. I simply let God's Spirit show his power.
5That way you would have faith because of God's power
and not because of human wisdom.

6We do use wisdom when speaking to people who are
mature in their faith. But it isn't the wisdom of this world or
of its rulers, who will soon disappear. 7We speak of God's

[a] 2.1 *mystery*: Some manuscripts have "testimony."

NEW INTERNATIONAL VERSION

the strong. 28He chose the lowly things of this world and
the despised things—and the things that are not—to nulli-
fy the things that are, 29so that no one may boast before
him. 30It is because of him that you are in Christ Jesus,
who has become for us wisdom from God—that is, our
righteousness, holiness and redemption. 31Therefore, as it
is written: "Let him who boasts boast in the Lord."[d]

2 When I came to you, brothers, I did not come with elo-
quence or superior wisdom as I proclaimed to you the
testimony about God.[a] 2For I resolved to know nothing
while I was with you except Jesus Christ and him crucified.
3I came to you in weakness and fear, and with much trem-
bling. 4My message and my preaching were not with wise
and persuasive words, but with a demonstration of the
Spirit's power, 5so that your faith might not rest on men's
wisdom, but on God's power.

Wisdom From the Spirit

6We do, however, speak a message of wisdom among
the mature, but not the wisdom of this age or of the rulers
of this age, who are coming to nothing. 7No, we speak of

[d] *31* Jer. 9:24 [a] *1* Some manuscripts *as I proclaimed to you God's mystery*

NEW LIVING TRANSLATION

things despised by the world, things counted as nothing at
all, and used them to bring to nothing what the world con-
siders important, 29so that no one can ever boast in the
presence of God.

30God alone made it possible for you to be in Christ
Jesus. For our benefit God made Christ to be wisdom itself.
He is the one who made us acceptable to God. He made us
pure and holy, and he gave himself to purchase our free-
dom. 31As the Scriptures say,

"The person who wishes to boast
should boast only of what the Lord has done."*

Paul Preaches Wisdom

2 Dear brothers and sisters,* when I first came to you I
didn't use lofty words and brilliant ideas to tell you
God's message.* 2For I decided to concentrate only on
Jesus Christ and his death on the cross. 3I came to you in
weakness—timid and trembling. 4And my message and my
preaching were very plain. I did not use wise and persua-
sive speeches, but the Holy Spirit was powerful among
you. 5I did this so that you might trust the power of God
rather than human wisdom.

6Yet when I am among mature Christians, I do speak
with words of wisdom, but not the kind of wisdom that
belongs to this world, and not the kind that appeals to the
rulers of this world, who are being brought to nothing.

1:31 Jer 9:24. 2:1a Greek *Brothers.* 2:1b Greek *mystery;* other manuscripts read *testimony.*

NEW KING JAMES VERSION

are mighty; 28and the base things of the world and the
things which are despised God has chosen, and the things
which are not, to bring to nothing the things that are,
29that no flesh should glory in His presence. 30But of Him
you are in Christ Jesus, who became for us wisdom from
God—and righteousness and sanctification and redemp-
tion— 31that, as it is written, *"He who glories, let him
glory in the* L*ORD*."[c]

Christ Crucified

2 And I, brethren, when I came to you, did not come
with excellence of speech or of wisdom declaring to
you the testimony[a] of God. 2For I determined not to know
anything among you except Jesus Christ and Him crucified.
3I was with you in weakness, in fear, and in much trem-
bling. 4And my speech and my preaching *were* not with
persuasive words of human[b] wisdom, but in demonstra-
tion of the Spirit and of power, 5that your faith should not
be in the wisdom of men but in the power of God.

Spiritual Wisdom

6However, we speak wisdom among those who are
mature, yet not the wisdom of this age, nor of the rulers of
this age, who are coming to nothing. 7But we speak the

1:31 [c] Jeremiah 9:24 2:1 [a] NU-Text reads *mystery.* 2:4 [b] NU-Text omits *human.*

THE MESSAGE

quite clear that none of you can get by with blowing your
own horn before God. Everything that we have—right
thinking and right living, a clean slate and a fresh start—
comes from God by way of Jesus Christ. That's why we
have the saying, "If you're going to blow a horn, blow a
trumpet for God."

2 You'll remember, friends, that when I first came to
you to let you in on God's master stroke, I didn't try
to impress you with polished speeches and the latest phi-
losophy. I deliberately kept it plain and simple: first Jesus
and who he is; then Jesus and what he did—Jesus cruci-
fied.

I was unsure of how to go about this, and felt totally
inadequate—I was scared to death, if you want the truth
of it—and so nothing I said could have impressed you or
anyone else. But the Message came through anyway. God's
Spirit and God's power did it, which made it clear that
your life of faith is a response to God's power, not to some
fancy mental or emotional footwork by me or anyone else.

We, of course, have plenty of wisdom to pass on to you
once you get your feet on firm spiritual ground, but it's not
popular wisdom, the fashionable wisdom of high-priced
experts that will be out-of-date in a year or so. God's wisdom

KING JAMES VERSION

7 But we speak the wisdom of God in a mystery, *even* the hidden *wisdom*, which God ordained before the world unto our glory:

8 Which none of the princes of this world knew: for had they known *it*, they would not have crucified the Lord of glory.

9 But as it is written, Eye hath not seen, nor ear heard, neither have entered into the heart of man, the things which God hath prepared for them that love him.

10 But God hath revealed *them* unto us by his Spirit: for the Spirit searcheth all things, yea, the deep things of God.

11 For what man knoweth the things of a man, save the spirit of man which is in him? even so the things of God knoweth no man, but the Spirit of God.

12 Now we have received, not the spirit of the world, but the spirit which is of God; that we might know the things that are freely given to us of God.

13 Which things also we speak, not in the words which man's wisdom teacheth, but which the Holy Ghost teacheth; comparing spiritual things with spiritual.

14 But the natural man receiveth not the things of the Spirit of God: for they are foolishness unto him: neither can he know *them*, because they are spiritually discerned.

NEW AMERICAN STANDARD BIBLE

7 but we speak God's wisdom in a mystery, the hidden *wisdom* which God predestined before the ages to our glory;

8 *the wisdom* which none of the rulers of this age has understood; for if they had understood it they would not have crucified the Lord of glory;

9 but just as it is written,

"THINGS WHICH EYE HAS NOT SEEN AND EAR HAS NOT HEARD,
AND *WHICH* HAVE NOT ENTERED THE HEART OF MAN,
ALL THAT GOD HAS PREPARED FOR THOSE WHO LOVE HIM."

10 [2]For to us God revealed *them* through the Spirit; for the Spirit searches all things, even the depths of God.

11 For who among men knows the *thoughts* of a man except the spirit of the man which is in him? Even so the *thoughts* of God no one knows except the Spirit of God.

12 Now we have received, not the spirit of the world, but the Spirit who is from God, so that we may know the things freely given to us by God,

13 which things we also speak, not in words taught by human wisdom, but in those taught by the Spirit, combining spiritual *thoughts* with spiritual *words*.

14 But a natural man does not accept the things of the Spirit of God, for they are foolishness to him; and he cannot understand them, because they are spiritually appraised.

2:10 [2] One early ms reads *But*

NEW CENTURY VERSION

secret wisdom, which he has kept hidden. Before the world began, God planned this wisdom for our glory. 8None of the rulers of this world understood it. If they had, they would not have crucified the Lord of glory. 9But as it is written in the Scriptures:

"No one has ever seen this,
and no one has ever heard about it.
No one has ever imagined
what God has prepared for those
who love him." *Isaiah 64:4*

10But God has shown us these things through the Spirit.

The Spirit searches out all things, even the deep secrets of God. 11Who knows the thoughts that another person has? Only a person's spirit that lives within him knows his thoughts. It is the same with God. No one knows the thoughts of God except the Spirit of God. 12Now we did not receive the spirit of the world, but we received the Spirit that is from God so that we can know all that God has given us. 13And we speak about these things, not with words taught us by human wisdom but with words taught us by the Spirit. And so we explain spiritual truths to spiritual people. 14A person who does not have the Spirit does not accept the truths that come from the Spirit of God. That person thinks they are foolish and cannot understand them, because they can only be judged to be true by the

CONTEMPORARY ENGLISH VERSION

hidden and mysterious wisdom that God decided to use for our glory long before the world began. 8The rulers of this world didn't know anything about this wisdom. If they had known about it, they would not have nailed the glorious Lord to a cross. 9But it is just as the Scriptures say,

"What God has planned
for people who love him
is more than eyes have seen
or ears have heard.
It has never even
entered our minds!"

10God's Spirit has shown you everything. His Spirit finds out everything, even what is deep in the mind of God. 11You are the only one who knows what is in your own mind, and God's Spirit is the only one who knows what is in God's mind. 12But God has given us his Spirit. That's why we don't think the same way that the people of this world think. That's also why we can recognize the blessings that God has given us.

13Every word we speak was taught to us by God's Spirit, not by human wisdom. And this same Spirit helps us teach spiritual things to spiritual people.[b] 14That's why only someone who has God's Spirit can understand spiritual blessings. Anyone who doesn't have God's Spirit thinks these blessings are foolish. 15People who are guided by the

[b] 2.13 *teach spiritual things to spiritual people*: Or "compare spiritual things with spiritual things."

NEW INTERNATIONAL VERSION

God's secret wisdom, a wisdom that has been hidden and
that God destined for our glory before time began. 8None
of the rulers of this age understood it, for if they had, they
would not have crucified the Lord of glory. 9However, as it
is written:

"No eye has seen,
  no ear has heard,
no mind has conceived
  what God has prepared for those who love him"[b]—

10but God has revealed it to us by his Spirit.
The Spirit searches all things, even the deep things of
God. 11For who among men knows the thoughts of a man
except the man's spirit within him? In the same way no
one knows the thoughts of God except the Spirit of God.
12We have not received the spirit of the world but the
Spirit who is from God, that we may understand what God
has freely given us. 13This is what we speak, not in words
taught us by human wisdom but in words taught by the
Spirit, expressing spiritual truths in spiritual words.[c] 14The
man without the Spirit does not accept the things that
come from the Spirit of God, for they are foolishness to
him, and he cannot understand them, because they are

[b] *9* Isaiah 64:4 [c] *13* Or *Spirit, interpreting spiritual truths to spiritual men*

NEW LIVING TRANSLATION

7No, the wisdom we speak of is the secret wisdom of God,*
which was hidden in former times, though he made it for
our benefit before the world began. 8But the rulers of this
world have not understood it; if they had, they would
never have crucified our glorious Lord. 9That is what the
Scriptures mean when they say,

"No eye has seen, no ear has heard,
  and no mind has imagined
what God has prepared
  for those who love him."*

10But we know these things because God has revealed
them to us by his Spirit, and his Spirit searches out every-
thing and shows us even God's deep secrets. 11No one can
know what anyone else is really thinking except that per-
son alone, and no one can know God's thoughts except
God's own Spirit. 12And God has actually given us his
Spirit (not the world's spirit) so we can know the wonder-
ful things God has freely given us. 13When we tell you this,
we do not use words of human wisdom. We speak words
given to us by the Spirit, using the Spirit's words to
explain spiritual truths.* 14But people who aren't Chris-
tians can't understand these truths from God's Spirit. It all
sounds foolish to them because only those who have the
Spirit can understand what the Spirit means. 15We who

2:7 Greek *we speak God's wisdom in a mystery.* 2:9 Isa 64:4.
2:13 Or *explaining spiritual truths in spiritual language,* or *explaining spiritual truths to spiritual people.*

NEW KING JAMES VERSION

wisdom of God in a mystery, the hidden *wisdom* which
God ordained before the ages for our glory, 8which none of
the rulers of this age knew; for had they known, they
would not have crucified the Lord of glory.
9But as it is written:

"Eye has not seen, nor ear heard,
Nor have entered into the heart of man
The things which God has prepared for those who
love Him."[c]

10But God has revealed *them* to us through His Spirit. For
the Spirit searches all things, yes, the deep things of God.
11For what man knows the things of a man except the spir-
it of the man which is in him? Even so no one knows the
things of God except the Spirit of God. 12Now we have
received, not the spirit of the world, but the Spirit who is
from God, that we might know the things that have been
freely given to us by God.
13These things we also speak, not in words which man's
wisdom teaches but which the Holy[d] Spirit teaches, com-
paring spiritual things with spiritual. 14But the natural
man does not receive the things of the Spirit of God, for
they are foolishness to him; nor can he know *them,*
because they are spiritually discerned. 15But he who is

2:9 [c] Isaiah 64:4 2:13 [d] NU-Text omits *Holy.*

THE MESSAGE

is something mysterious that goes deep into the interior of
his purposes. You don't find it lying around on the surface.
It's not the latest message, but more like the oldest—what
God determined as the way to bring out his best in us, long
before we ever arrived on the scene. The experts of our day
haven't a clue about what this eternal plan is. If they had,
they wouldn't have killed the Master of the God-designed life
on a cross. That's why we have this Scripture text:

"No one's ever seen or heard anything like this,
Never so much as imagined anything quite like it—
What God has arranged for those who love him."

But *you've* seen and heard it because God by his Spirit has
brought it all out into the open before you.

The Spirit, not content to flit around on the surface, dives
into the depths of God, and brings out what God planned
all along. Who ever knows what you're thinking and plan-
ning except you yourself? The same with God—except that
he not only knows what he's thinking, but he lets *us* in on
it. God offers a full report on the gifts of life and salvation
that he is giving us. We don't have to rely on the world's
guesses and opinions. We didn't learn this by reading
books or going to school; we learned it from God, who
taught us person-to-person through Jesus, and we're pass-
ing it on to you in the same firsthand, personal way.

The unspiritual self, just as it is by nature, can't receive
the gifts of God's Spirit. There's no capacity for them. They
seem like so much silliness. Spirit can be known only by

KING JAMES VERSION

15 But he that is spiritual judgeth all things, yet he himself is judged of no man.

16 For who hath known the mind of the Lord, that he may instruct him? But we have the mind of Christ.

3 And I, brethren, could not speak unto you as unto spiritual, but as unto carnal, *even* as unto babes in Christ.

2 I have fed you with milk, and not with meat: for hitherto ye were not able *to bear it*, neither yet now are ye able.

3 For ye are yet carnal: for whereas *there is* among you envying, and strife, and divisions, are ye not carnal, and walk as men?

4 For while one saith, I am of Paul; and another, I *am* of Apollos; are ye not carnal?

5 ¶ Who then is Paul, and who *is* Apollos, but ministers by whom ye believed, even as the Lord gave to every man?

6 I have planted, Apollos watered; but God gave the increase.

NEW AMERICAN STANDARD BIBLE

15 But he who is spiritual appraises all things, yet he himself is appraised by no one.

16 For WHO HAS KNOWN THE MIND OF THE LORD, THAT HE WILL INSTRUCT HIM? But we have the mind of Christ.

Foundations for Living

3 And I, brethren, could not speak to you as to spiritual men, but as to men of flesh, as to infants in Christ.

2 I gave you milk to drink, not solid food; for you were not yet able *to receive it*. Indeed, even now you are not yet able,

3 for you are still fleshly. For since there is jealousy and strife among you, are you not fleshly, and are you not walking like mere men?

4 For when one says, "I am of Paul," and another, "I am of Apollos," are you not *mere* men?

5 What then is Apollos? And what is Paul? Servants through whom you believed, even as the Lord gave *opportunity* to each one.

6 I planted, Apollos watered, but God was causing the growth.

NEW CENTURY VERSION

Spirit. [15]The spiritual person is able to judge all things, but
no one can judge him. The Scripture says:
[16]"Who has known the mind of the Lord?
Who has been able to teach him?" *Isaiah 40:13*
But we have the mind of Christ.

Following People Is Wrong

3 Brothers and sisters, in the past I could not talk to
you as I talk to spiritual people. I had to talk to you as
I would to people without the Spirit—babies in Christ. [2]The
teaching I gave you was like milk, not solid food, because
you were not able to take solid food. And even now you are
not ready. [3]You are still not spiritual, because there is jeal-
ousy and quarreling among you, and this shows that you
are not spiritual. You are acting like people of the world.
[4]One of you says, "I belong to Paul," and another says, "I
belong to Apollos." When you say things like this, you are
acting like people of the world.

[5]Is Apollos important? No! Is Paul important? No! We are
only servants of God who helped you believe. Each one of
us did the work God gave us to do. [6]I planted the seed, and
Apollos watered it. But God is the One who made it grow.

CONTEMPORARY ENGLISH VERSION

Spirit can make all kinds of judgments, but they cannot be
judged by others. [16]The Scriptures ask,

"Has anyone ever known
the thoughts of the Lord
or given him advice?"

But we understand what Christ is thinking.[c]

Working Together for God

3 My friends, you are acting like the people of this
world. That's why I could not speak to you as spiritu-
al people. You are like babies as far as your faith in Christ
is concerned. [2]So I had to treat you like babies and feed
you milk. You could not take solid food, and you still can-
not, [3]because you are not yet spiritual. You are jealous and
argue with each other. This proves that you are not spiritu-
al and that you are acting like the people of this world.

[4]Some of you say that you follow me, and others claim
to follow Apollos. Isn't that how ordinary people behave?
[5]Apollos and I are merely servants who helped you to have
faith. It was the Lord who made it all happen. [6]I planted
the seeds, Apollos watered them, but God made them

[c] 2.16 *we understand what Christ is thinking*: Or "we think as Christ does."

NEW INTERNATIONAL VERSION

spiritually discerned. 15The spiritual man makes judgments about all things, but he himself is not subject to any man's judgment:

16"For who has known the mind of the Lord
that he may instruct him?"[d]

But we have the mind of Christ.

On Divisions in the Church

3 Brothers, I could not address you as spiritual but as worldly—mere infants in Christ. 2I gave you milk, not solid food, for you were not yet ready for it. Indeed, you are still not ready. 3You are still worldly. For since there is jealousy and quarreling among you, are you not worldly? Are you not acting like mere men? 4For when one says, "I follow Paul," and another, "I follow Apollos," are you not mere men?

5What, after all, is Apollos? And what is Paul? Only servants, through whom you came to believe—as the Lord has assigned to each his task. 6I planted the seed, Apollos watered it, but God made it grow. 7So neither he who

[d] *16* Isaiah 40:13

NEW LIVING TRANSLATION

have the Spirit understand these things, but others can't understand us at all. 16How could they? For,

"Who can know what the Lord is thinking?
Who can give him counsel?"*

But we can understand these things, for we have the mind of Christ.

Paul and Apollos, Servants of Christ

3 Dear brothers and sisters,* when I was with you I couldn't talk to you as I would to mature Christians. I had to talk as though you belonged to this world or as though you were infants in the Christian life.* 2I had to feed you with milk and not with solid food, because you couldn't handle anything stronger. And you still aren't ready, 3for you are still controlled by your own sinful desires. You are jealous of one another and quarrel with each other. Doesn't that prove you are controlled by your own desires? You are acting like people who don't belong to the Lord. 4When one of you says, "I am a follower of Paul," and another says, "I prefer Apollos," aren't you acting like those who are not Christians?*

5Who is Apollos, and who is Paul, that we should be the cause of such quarrels? Why, we're only servants. Through us God caused you to believe. Each of us did the work the Lord gave us. 6My job was to plant the seed in your hearts,

2:16 Isa 40:13. 3:1a Greek *Brothers.* 3:1b Greek *in Christ.*
3:4 Greek *aren't you merely human?*

NEW KING JAMES VERSION

spiritual judges all things, yet he himself is *rightly* judged by no one. 16For *"who has known the mind of the LORD that he may instruct Him?"*[e] But we have the mind of Christ.

Sectarianism Is Carnal

3 And I, brethren, could not speak to you as to spiritual *people* but as to carnal, as to babes in Christ. 2I fed you with milk and not with solid food; for until now you were not able *to receive it,* and even now you are still not able; 3for you are still carnal. For where *there are* envy, strife, and divisions among you, are you not carnal and behaving like *mere* men? 4For when one says, "I am of Paul," and another, "I *am* of Apollos," are you not carnal?

Watering, Working, Warning

5Who then is Paul, and who *is* Apollos, but ministers through whom you believed, as the Lord gave to each one? 6I planted, Apollos watered, but God gave the increase. 7So

2:16 [e] Isaiah 40:13

THE MESSAGE

spirit—God's Spirit and our spirits in open communion. Spiritually alive, we have access to everything God's Spirit is doing, and can't be judged by unspiritual critics. Isaiah's question, "Is there anyone around who knows God's Spirit, anyone who knows what he is doing?" has been answered: Christ knows, and we have Christ's Spirit.

✢

3 But for right now, friends, I'm completely frustrated by your unspiritual dealings with each other and with God. You're acting like infants in relation to Christ, capable of nothing much more than nursing at the breast. Well, then, I'll nurse you since you don't seem capable of anything more. As long as you grab for what makes you feel good or makes you look important, are you really much different than a babe at the breast, content only when everything's going your way? When one of you says, "I'm on Paul's side," and another says, "I'm for Apollos," aren't you being totally infantile?

Who do you think Paul is, anyway? Or Apollos, for that matter? Servants, both of us—servants who waited on you as you gradually learned to entrust your lives to our mutual Master. We each carried out our servant assignment. I planted the seed, Apollos watered the plants, but *God*

KING JAMES VERSION

7 So then neither is he that planteth any thing, neither he that watereth; but God that giveth the increase.

8 Now he that planteth and he that watereth are one: and every man shall receive his own reward according to his own labour.

9 For we are labourers together with God: ye are God's husbandry, *ye are* God's building.

10 According to the grace of God which is given unto me, as a wise masterbuilder, I have laid the foundation, and another buildeth thereon. But let every man take heed how he buildeth thereupon.

11 ¶ For other foundation can no man lay than that is laid, which is Jesus Christ.

12 Now if any man build upon this foundation gold, silver, precious stones, wood, hay, stubble;

13 Every man's work shall be made manifest: for the day shall declare it, because it shall be revealed by fire; and the fire shall try every man's work of what sort it is.

14 If any man's work abide which he hath built thereupon, he shall receive a reward.

15 If any man's work shall be burned, he shall suffer loss: but he himself shall be saved; yet so as by fire.

16 ¶ Know ye not that ye are the temple of God, and *that* the Spirit of God dwelleth in you?

17 If any man defile the temple of God, him shall God destroy; for the temple of God is holy, which *temple* ye are.

18 ¶ Let no man deceive himself. If any man among you seemeth to be wise in this world, let him become a fool, that he may be wise.

NEW AMERICAN STANDARD BIBLE

7 So then neither the one who plants nor the one who waters is anything, but God who causes the growth.

8 Now he who plants and he who waters are one; but each will receive his own reward according to his own labor.

9 For we are God's fellow workers; you are God's field, God's building.

10 According to the grace of God which was given to me, like a wise master builder I laid a foundation, and another is building on it. But each man must be careful how he builds on it.

11 For no man can lay a foundation other than the one which is laid, which is Jesus Christ.

12 Now if any man builds on the foundation with gold, silver, precious stones, wood, hay, straw,

13 each man's work will become evident; for the day will show it because it is *to be* revealed with fire, and the fire itself will test the quality of each man's work.

14 If any man's work which he has built on it remains, he will receive a reward.

15 If any man's work is burned up, he will suffer loss; but he himself will be saved, yet so as through fire.

16 Do you not know that you are a temple of God and *that* the Spirit of God dwells in you?

17 If any man destroys the temple of God, God will destroy him, for the temple of God is holy, and that is what you are.

18 Let no man deceive himself. If any man among you thinks that he is wise in this age, he must become foolish, so that he may become wise.

NEW CENTURY VERSION

7 So the one who plants is not important, and the one who
waters is not important. Only God, who makes things grow,
is important. 8 The one who plants and the one who waters
have the same purpose, and each will be rewarded for his
own work. 9 We are God's workers, working together; you
are like God's farm, God's house.

10 Using the gift God gave me, I laid the foundation of
that house like an expert builder. Others are building on
that foundation, but all people should be careful how they
build on it. 11 The foundation that has already been laid is
Jesus Christ, and no one can lay down any other founda-
tion. 12 But if people build on that foundation, using gold,
silver, jewels, wood, grass, or straw, 13 their work will be
clearly seen, because the Day of Judgment[a] will make it
visible. That Day will appear with fire, and the fire will test
everyone's work to show what sort of work it was. 14 If the
building that has been put on the foundation still stands,
the builder will get a reward. 15 But if the building is
burned up, the builder will suffer loss. The builder will be
saved, but it will be as one who escaped from a fire.

16 Don't you know that you are God's temple and that
God's Spirit lives in you? 17 If anyone destroys God's tem-
ple, God will destroy that person, because God's temple is
holy and you are that temple.

18 Do not fool yourselves. If you think you are wise in
this world, you should become a fool so that you can

3:13 [a] **Day of Judgment** The day Christ will come to judge all people and take his people home to live with him.

CONTEMPORARY ENGLISH VERSION

sprout and grow. 7 What matters isn't those who planted or
watered, but God who made the plants grow. 8 The one who
plants is just as important as the one who waters. And
each one will be paid for what they do. 9 Apollos and I work
together for God, and you are God's garden and God's
building.

Only One Foundation

10 God was kind and let me become an expert builder. I
laid a foundation on which others have built. But we must
each be careful how we build, 11 because Christ is the only
foundation. 12-13 Whatever we build on that foundation will
be tested by fire on the day of judgment. Then everyone
will find out if we have used gold, silver, and precious
stones, or wood, hay, and straw. 14 We will be rewarded if
our building is left standing. 15 But if it is destroyed by the
fire, we will lose everything. Yet we ourselves will be
saved, like someone escaping from flames.

16 All of you surely know that you are God's temple and
that his Spirit lives in you. 17 Together you are God's holy
temple, and God will destroy anyone who destroys his
temple.

18 Don't fool yourselves! If any of you think you are wise
in the things of this world, you will have to become foolish

NEW INTERNATIONAL VERSION

plants nor he who waters is anything, but only God, who
makes things grow. 8The man who plants and the man
who waters have one purpose, and each will be rewarded
according to his own labor. 9For we are God's fellow work-
ers; you are God's field, God's building.
10By the grace God has given me, I laid a foundation as
an expert builder, and someone else is building on it. But
each one should be careful how he builds. 11For no one
can lay any foundation other than the one already laid,
which is Jesus Christ. 12If any man builds on this founda-
tion using gold, silver, costly stones, wood, hay or straw,
13his work will be shown for what it is, because the Day
will bring it to light. It will be revealed with fire, and the
fire will test the quality of each man's work. 14If what he
has built survives, he will receive his reward. 15If it is
burned up, he will suffer loss; he himself will be saved, but
only as one escaping through the flames.
16Don't you know that you yourselves are God's temple
and that God's Spirit lives in you? 17If anyone destroys
God's temple, God will destroy him; for God's temple is
sacred, and you are that temple.
18Do not deceive yourselves. If any one of you thinks he
is wise by the standards of this age, he should become a
"fool" so that he may become wise. 19For the wisdom of

NEW LIVING TRANSLATION

and Apollos watered it, but it was God, not we, who made
it grow. 7The ones who do the planting or watering aren't
important, but God is important because he is the one who
makes the seed grow. 8The one who plants and the one
who waters work as a team with the same purpose. Yet
they will be rewarded individually, according to their own
hard work. 9We work together as partners who belong to
God. You are God's field, God's building—not ours.
10Because of God's special favor to me, I have laid the
foundation like an expert builder. Now others are building
on it. But whoever is building on this foundation must be
very careful. 11For no one can lay any other foundation
than the one we already have—Jesus Christ. 12Now anyone
who builds on that foundation may use gold, silver, jewels,
wood, hay, or straw. 13But there is going to come a time of
testing at the judgment day to see what kind of work each
builder has done. Everyone's work will be put through the
fire to see whether or not it keeps its value. 14If the work
survives the fire, that builder will receive a reward. 15But if
the work is burned up, the builder will suffer great loss.
The builders themselves will be saved, but like someone
escaping through a wall of flames.
16Don't you realize that all of you together are the tem-
ple of God and that the Spirit of God lives in* you? 17God
will bring ruin upon anyone who ruins this temple. For
God's temple is holy, and you Christians are that temple.
18Stop fooling yourselves. If you think you are wise by
this world's standards, you will have to become a fool so

3:16 Or *among.*

NEW KING JAMES VERSION

then neither he who plants is anything, nor he who
waters, but God who gives the increase. 8Now he who
plants and he who waters are one, and each one will
receive his own reward according to his own labor.
9For we are God's fellow workers; you are God's field,
you are God's building. 10According to the grace of God
which was given to me, as a wise master builder I have
laid the foundation, and another builds on it. But let each
one take heed how he builds on it. 11For no other founda-
tion can anyone lay than that which is laid, which is Jesus
Christ. 12Now if anyone builds on this foundation *with*
gold, silver, precious stones, wood, hay, straw, 13each
one's work will become clear; for the Day will declare it,
because it will be revealed by fire; and the fire will test
each one's work, of what sort it is. 14If anyone's work
which he has built on *it* endures, he will receive a reward.
15If anyone's work is burned, he will suffer loss; but he
himself will be saved, yet so as through fire.
16Do you not know that you are the temple of God and
that the Spirit of God dwells in you? 17If anyone defiles the
temple of God, God will destroy him. For the temple of God
is holy, which *temple* you are.

Avoid Worldly Wisdom

18Let no one deceive himself. If anyone among you
seems to be wise in this age, let him become a fool that he

THE MESSAGE

made you grow. It's not the one who plants or the one who
waters who is at the center of this process but God, who
makes things grow. Planting and watering are menial ser-
vant jobs at minimum wages. What makes them worth
doing is the God we are serving. You happen to be God's
field in which we are working.

Or, to put it another way, you are God's house. Using
the gift God gave me as a good architect, I designed blue-
prints; Apollos is putting up the walls. Let each carpenter
who comes on the job take care to build on the foundation!
Remember, there is only one foundation, the one already
laid: Jesus Christ. Take particular care in picking out your
building materials. Eventually there is going to be an
inspection. If you use cheap or inferior materials, you'll be
found out. The inspection will be thorough and rigorous.
You won't get by with a thing. If your work passes inspec-
tion, fine; if it doesn't, your part of the building will be
torn out and started over. But *you* won't be torn out; you'll
survive—but just barely.

You realize, don't you, that you are the temple of God,
and God himself is present in you? No one will get by with
vandalizing God's temple, you can be sure of that. God's
temple is sacred—and you, remember, *are* the temple.

Don't fool yourself. Don't think that you can be wise
merely by being up-to-date with the times. Be God's fool—

KING JAMES VERSION

19 For the wisdom of this world is foolishness with God. For it is written, He taketh the wise in their own craftiness.

20 And again, The Lord knoweth the thoughts of the wise, that they are vain.

21 ¶ Therefore let no man glory in men. For all things are yours;

22 Whether Paul, or Apollos, or Cephas, or the world, or life, or death, or things present, or things to come; all are yours;

23 And ye are Christ's; and Christ *is* God's.

4 Let a man so account of us, as of the ministers of Christ, and stewards of the mysteries of God.

2 Moreover it is required in stewards, that a man be found faithful.

3 But with me it is a very small thing that I should be judged of you, or of man's judgment: yea, I judge not mine own self.

4 For I know nothing by myself; yet am I not hereby justified: but he that judgeth me is the Lord.

5 Therefore judge nothing before the time, until the Lord

NEW AMERICAN STANDARD BIBLE

19 For the wisdom of this world is foolishness before God. For it is written, "*He is* THE ONE WHO CATCHES THE WISE IN THEIR CRAFTINESS";

20 and again, "THE LORD KNOWS THE REASONINGS of the wise, THAT THEY ARE USELESS."

21 So then let no one boast in men. For all things belong to you,

22 whether Paul or Apollos or Cephas or the world or life or death or things present or things to come; all things belong to you,

23 and you belong to Christ; and Christ belongs to God.

Servants of Christ

4 Let a man regard us in this manner, as servants of Christ and stewards of the mysteries of God.

2 In this case, moreover, it is required of stewards that one be found trustworthy.

3 But to me it is a very small thing that I may be examined by you, or by *any* human court; in fact, I do not even examine myself.

4 For I am conscious of nothing against myself, yet I am not by this acquitted; but the one who examines me is the Lord.

5 Therefore do not go on passing judgment before [1]the time, *but wait* until the Lord comes who will both bring to

4:5 [1] I.e. the appointed time of judgment

NEW CENTURY VERSION

become truly wise, 19because the wisdom of this world is
foolishness with God. It is written in the Scriptures, "He
catches those who are wise in their own clever traps."[b] 20It
is also written in the Scriptures, "The Lord knows what
wise people think. He knows their thoughts are just a puff
of wind."[c] 21So you should not brag about human leaders.
All things belong to you: 22Paul, Apollos, and Peter; the
world, life, death, the present, and the future—all these
belong to you. 23And you belong to Christ, and Christ
belongs to God.

Apostles Are Servants of Christ

4 People should think of us as servants of Christ, the
ones God has trusted with his secrets. 2Now in this way
those who are trusted with something valuable must show
they are worthy of that trust. 3As for myself, I do not care if
I am judged by you or by any human court. I do not even
judge myself. 4I know of no wrong I have done, but this
does not make me right before the Lord. The Lord is the One
who judges me. 5So do not judge before the right time; wait

3:19 [b] "He...traps." Quotation from Job 5:13. 3:20 [c] "The Lord...wind." Quotation from Psalm 94:11.

CONTEMPORARY ENGLISH VERSION

before you can be truly wise. 19This is because God consid-
ers the wisdom of this world to be foolish. It is just as the
Scriptures say, "God catches the wise when they try to out-
smart him." 20The Scriptures also say, "The Lord knows
that the plans made by wise people are useless." 21-22So
stop bragging about what anyone has done. Paul and
Apollos and Peter[a] all belong to you. In fact, everything is
yours, including the world, life, death, the present, and the
future. Everything belongs to you, 23and you belong to
Christ, and Christ belongs to God.

The Work of the Apostles

4 Think of us as servants of Christ who have been given
the work of explaining God's mysterious ways. 2And
since our first duty is to be faithful to the one we work for,
3it doesn't matter to me if I am judged by you or even by a
court of law. In fact, I don't judge myself. 4I don't know of
anything against me, but that doesn't prove that I am
right. The Lord is my judge. 5So don't judge anyone until

[a] 3.21,22 *Peter*: See the note at 1.12.

NEW INTERNATIONAL VERSION

this world is foolishness in God's sight. As it is written: "He catches the wise in their craftiness"[a]; 20and again, "The Lord knows that the thoughts of the wise are futile."[b] 21So then, no more boasting about men! All things are yours, 22whether Paul or Apollos or Cephas[c] or the world or life or death or the present or the future—all are yours, 23and you are of Christ, and Christ is of God.

Apostles of Christ

4 So then, men ought to regard us as servants of Christ and as those entrusted with the secret things of God. 2Now it is required that those who have been given a trust must prove faithful. 3I care very little if I am judged by you or by any human court; indeed, I do not even judge myself. 4My conscience is clear, but that does not make me innocent. It is the Lord who judges me. 5Therefore judge nothing before the appointed time; wait till the Lord comes. He

[a] *19* Job 5:13 [b] *20* Psalm 94:11 [c] *22* That is, Peter

NEW LIVING TRANSLATION

you can become wise by God's standards. 19For the wisdom of this world is foolishness to God. As the Scriptures say,

"God catches those who think they are wise
in their own cleverness."*

20And again,

"The Lord knows the thoughts of the wise,
that they are worthless."*

21So don't take pride in following a particular leader. Everything belongs to you: 22Paul and Apollos and Peter*; the whole world and life and death; the present and the future. Everything belongs to you, 23and you belong to Christ, and Christ belongs to God.

Paul and the Corinthians

4 So look at Apollos and me as mere servants of Christ who have been put in charge of explaining God's secrets. 2Now, a person who is put in charge as a manager must be faithful. 3What about me? Have I been faithful? Well, it matters very little what you or anyone else thinks. I don't even trust my own judgment on this point. 4My conscience is clear, but that isn't what matters. It is the Lord himself who will examine me and decide.

5So be careful not to jump to conclusions before the Lord

3:19 Job 5:13. 3:20 Ps 94:11. 3:22 Greek *Cephas.*

NEW KING JAMES VERSION

may become wise. 19For the wisdom of this world is foolishness with God. For it is written, *"He catches the wise in their own craftiness"*;[a] 20and again, *"The LORD knows the thoughts of the wise, that they are futile."*[b] 21Therefore let no one boast in men. For all things are yours: 22whether Paul or Apollos or Cephas, or the world or life or death, or things present or things to come—all are yours. 23And you *are* Christ's, and Christ *is* God's.

Stewards of the Mysteries of God

4 Let a man so consider us, as servants of Christ and stewards of the mysteries of God. 2Moreover it is required in stewards that one be found faithful. 3But with me it is a very small thing that I should be judged by you or by a human court.[a] In fact, I do not even judge myself. 4For I know of nothing against myself, yet I am not justified by this; but He who judges me is the Lord. 5Therefore judge nothing before the time, until the Lord comes, who

3:19 [a] Job 5:13 3:20 [b] Psalm 94:11 4:3 [a] Literally *day*

THE MESSAGE

that's the path to true wisdom. What the world calls smart, God calls stupid. It's written in Scripture,

"He exposes the chicanery of the chic.
The Master sees through the smoke screens of the
know-it-alls."

I don't want to hear any of you bragging about yourself or anyone else. Everything is already yours as a gift—Paul, Apollos, Peter, the world, life, death, the present, the future—all of it is yours, and you are privileged to be in union with Christ, who is in union with God.

✠

4 Don't imagine us leaders to be something we aren't. We are servants of Christ, not his masters. We are guides into God's most sublime secrets, not security guards posted to protect them. The requirements for a good guide are reliability and accurate knowledge. It matters very little to me what you think of me, even less where I rank in popular opinion. I don't even rank myself. Comparisons in these matters are pointless. I'm not aware of anything that would disqualify me from being a good guide for you, but that doesn't mean much. The *Master* makes that judgment.

So don't get ahead of the Master and jump to conclusions with your judgments before all the evidence is in. When he comes, he will bring out in the open and place in

KING JAMES VERSION

come, who both will bring to light the hidden things of darkness, and will make manifest the counsels of the hearts: and then shall every man have praise of God.

6 And these things, brethren, I have in a figure transferred to myself and *to* Apollos for your sakes; that ye might learn in us not to think *of men* above that which is written, that no one of you be puffed up for one against another.

7 ¶ For who maketh thee to differ *from another?* and what hast thou that thou didst not receive? now if thou didst receive *it*, why dost thou glory, as if thou hadst not received *it?*

8 Now ye are full, now ye are rich, ye have reigned as kings without us: and I would to God ye did reign, that we also might reign with you.

9 For I think that God hath set forth us the apostles last, as it were appointed to death: for we are made a spectacle unto the world, and to angels, and to men.

10 We *are* fools for Christ's sake, but ye *are* wise in Christ; we *are* weak, but ye *are* strong; ye *are* honourable, but we *are* despised.

11 Even unto this present hour we both hunger, and thirst, and are naked, and are buffeted, and have no certain dwellingplace;

12 And labour, working with our own hands: being reviled, we bless; being persecuted, we suffer it:

NEW AMERICAN STANDARD BIBLE

light the things hidden in the darkness and disclose the motives of *men's* hearts; and then each man's praise will come to him from God.

6 Now these things, brethren, I have figuratively applied to myself and Apollos for your sakes, so that in us you may learn not to exceed what is written, so that no one of you will become arrogant in behalf of one against the other.

7 For who regards you as superior? What do you have that you did not receive? And if you did receive it, why do you boast as if you had not received it?

8 You are already filled, you have already become rich, you have become kings without us; and indeed, *I* wish that you had become kings so that we also might reign with you.

9 For, I think, God has exhibited us apostles last of all, as men condemned to death; because we have become a spectacle to the world, both to angels and to men.

10 We are fools for Christ's sake, but you are prudent in Christ; we are weak, but you are strong; you are distinguished, but we are without honor.

11 To this present hour we are both hungry and thirsty, and are poorly clothed, and are roughly treated, and are homeless;

12 and we toil, working with our own hands; when we are reviled, we bless; when we are persecuted, we endure;

NEW CENTURY VERSION

until the Lord comes. He will bring to light things that are now hidden in darkness, and will make known the secret purposes of people's hearts. Then God will praise each one of them.

6Brothers and sisters, I have used Apollos and myself as
examples so you could learn through us the meaning of
the saying, "Follow only what is written in the Scriptures."
Then you will not be more proud of one person than anoth-
er. 7Who says you are better than others? What do you
have that was not given to you? And if it was given to you,
why do you brag as if you did not receive it as a gift?
8You think you already have everything you need. You
think you are rich. You think you have become kings with-
out us. I wish you really were kings so we could be kings
together with you. 9But it seems to me that God has put us
apostles in last place, like those sentenced to die. We are
like a show for the whole world to see—angels and people.
10We are fools for Christ's sake, but you are very wise in
Christ. We are weak, but you are strong. You receive
honor, but we are shamed. 11Even to this very hour we do
not have enough to eat or drink or to wear. We are often
beaten, and we have no homes in which to live. 12We work
hard with our own hands for our food. When people curse
us, we bless them. When they hurt us, we put up with it.

CONTEMPORARY ENGLISH VERSION

the Lord returns. He will show what is hidden in the dark and what is in everyone's heart. Then God will be the one who praises each of us.

6Friends, I have used Apollos and myself as examples to
teach you the meaning of the saying, "Follow the rules." I
want you to stop saying that one of us is better than the
other. 7What is so special about you? What do you have
that you were not given? And if it was given to you, how
can you brag? 8Are you already satisfied? Are you now
rich? Have you become kings while we are still nobodies? I
wish you were kings. Then we could have a share in your
kingdom.
9It seems to me that God has put us apostles in the
worst possible place. We are like prisoners on their way to
death. Angels and the people of this world just laugh at us.
10Because of Christ we are thought of as fools, but Christ
has made you wise. We are weak and hated, but you are
powerful and respected. 11Even today we go hungry and
thirsty and don't have anything to wear except rags. We
are mistreated and don't have a place to live. 12We work
hard with our own hands, and when people abuse us, we
wish them well. When we suffer, we are patient. 13When

NEW INTERNATIONAL VERSION

will bring to light what is hidden in darkness and will expose the motives of men's hearts. At that time each will receive his praise from God.

[6]Now, brothers, I have applied these things to myself and Apollos for your benefit, so that you may learn from us the meaning of the saying, "Do not go beyond what is written." Then you will not take pride in one man over against another. [7]For who makes you different from anyone else? What do you have that you did not receive? And if you did receive it, why do you boast as though you did not?

[8]Already you have all you want! Already you have become rich! You have become kings—and that without us! How I wish that you really had become kings so that we might be kings with you! [9]For it seems to me that God has put us apostles on display at the end of the procession, like men condemned to die in the arena. We have been made a spectacle to the whole universe, to angels as well as to men. [10]We are fools for Christ, but you are so wise in Christ! We are weak, but you are strong! You are honored, we are dishonored! [11]To this very hour we go hungry and thirsty, we are in rags, we are brutally treated, we are homeless. [12]We work hard with our own hands. When we are cursed, we bless; when we are persecuted, we

NEW LIVING TRANSLATION

returns as to whether or not someone is faithful. When the Lord comes, he will bring our deepest secrets to light and will reveal our private motives. And then God will give to everyone whatever praise is due.

[6]Dear brothers and sisters,* I have used Apollos and myself to illustrate what I've been saying. If you pay attention to the Scriptures,* you won't brag about one of your leaders at the expense of another. [7]What makes you better than anyone else? What do you have that God hasn't given you? And if all you have is from God, why boast as though you have accomplished something on your own?

[8]You think you already have everything you need! You are already rich! Without us you have become kings! I wish you really were on your thrones already, for then we would be reigning with you! [9]But sometimes I think God has put us apostles on display, like prisoners of war at the end of a victor's parade, condemned to die. We have become a spectacle to the entire world—to people and angels alike.

[10]Our dedication to Christ makes us look like fools, but you are so wise! We are weak, but you are so powerful! You are well thought of, but we are laughed at. [11]To this very hour we go hungry and thirsty, without enough clothes to keep us warm. We have endured many beatings, and we have no homes of our own. [12]We have worked wearily with our own hands to earn our living. We bless those who curse us. We are patient with those who abuse

4:6a Greek *Brothers.* **4:6b** Or *You must learn not to go beyond "what is written," so that.*

NEW KING JAMES VERSION

will both bring to light the hidden things of darkness and reveal the counsels of the hearts. Then each one's praise will come from God.

Fools for Christ's Sake

[6]Now these things, brethren, I have figuratively transferred to myself and Apollos for your sakes, that you may learn in us not to think beyond what is written, that none of you may be puffed up on behalf of one against the other. [7]For who makes you differ *from another?* And what do you have that you did not receive? Now if you did indeed receive *it,* why do you boast as if you had not received *it?*

[8]You are already full! You are already rich! You have reigned as kings without us—and indeed I could wish you did reign, that we also might reign with you! [9]For I think that God has displayed us, the apostles, last, as men condemned to death; for we have been made a spectacle to the world, both to angels and to men. [10]We *are* fools for Christ's sake, but you *are* wise in Christ! We *are* weak, but you *are* strong! You *are* distinguished, but we *are* dishonored! [11]To the present hour we both hunger and thirst, and we are poorly clothed, and beaten, and homeless. [12]And we labor, working with our own hands. Being reviled, we bless; being persecuted, we endure; [13]being defamed, we

THE MESSAGE

evidence all kinds of things we never even dreamed of—inner motives and purposes and prayers. Only then will any one of us get to hear the "Well done!" of God.

All I'm doing right now, friends, is showing how these things pertain to Apollos and me so that you will learn restraint and not rush into making judgments without knowing all the facts. It's important to look at things from God's point of view. I would rather not see you inflating or deflating reputations based on mere hearsay.

For who do you know that really knows *you*, knows your heart? And even if they did, is there anything they would discover in you that you could take credit for? Isn't everything you *have* and everything you *are* sheer gifts from God? So what's the point of all this comparing and competing? You already have all you need. You already have more access to God than you can handle. Without bringing either Apollos or me into it, you're sitting on top of the world—at least God's world—and we're right there, sitting alongside you!

It seems to me that God has put us who bear his Message on stage in a theater in which no one wants to buy a ticket. We're something everyone stands around and stares at, like an accident in the street. We're the Messiah's misfits. You might be sure of yourselves, but we live in the midst of frailties and uncertainties. You might be well-thought-of by others, but we're mostly kicked around. Much of the time we don't have enough to eat, we wear patched and threadbare clothes, we get doors slammed in our faces, and we pick up odd jobs anywhere we can to eke out a living. When they call us names, we say, "God bless you." When they

KING JAMES VERSION

13 Being defamed, we intreat: we are made as the filth of the world, *and are* the offscouring of all things unto this day.

14 ¶ I write not these things to shame you, but as my beloved sons I warn *you*.

15 For though ye have ten thousand instructors in Christ, yet *have ye* not many fathers: for in Christ Jesus I have begotten you through the gospel.

16 Wherefore I beseech you, be ye followers of me.

17 ¶ For this cause have I sent unto you Timotheus, who is my beloved son, and faithful in the Lord, who shall bring you into remembrance of my ways which be in Christ, as I teach every where in every church.

18 Now some are puffed up, as though I would not come to you.

19 But I will come to you shortly, if the Lord will, and will know, not the speech of them which are puffed up, but the power.

20 For the kingdom of God *is* not in word, but in power.

21 What will ye? shall I come unto you with a rod, or in love, and *in* the spirit of meekness?

5 It is reported commonly *that there is* fornication among you, and such fornication as is not so much as

NEW AMERICAN STANDARD BIBLE

13 when we are slandered, we try to conciliate; we have become as the scum of the world, the dregs of all things, *even* until now.

14 I do not write these things to shame you, but to admonish you as my beloved children.

15 For if you were to have countless tutors in Christ, yet *you would* not *have* many fathers, for in Christ Jesus I became your father through the gospel.

16 Therefore I exhort you, be imitators of me.

17 For this reason I have sent to you Timothy, who is my beloved and faithful child in the Lord, and he will remind you of my ways which are in Christ, just as I teach everywhere in every church.

18 Now some have become arrogant, as though I were not coming to you.

19 But I will come to you soon, if the Lord wills, and I shall find out, not the words of those who are arrogant but their power.

20 For the kingdom of God does not consist in words but in power.

21 What do you desire? Shall I come to you with a rod, or with love and a spirit of gentleness?

Immorality Rebuked

5 It is actually reported that there is immorality among you, and immorality of such a kind as does not exist

NEW CENTURY VERSION

13 When they tell evil lies about us, we speak nice words
about them. Even today, we are treated as though we were
the garbage of the world—the filth of the earth.
14 I am not trying to make you feel ashamed. I am writ-
ing this to give you a warning as my own dear children.
15 For though you may have ten thousand teachers in
Christ, you do not have many fathers. Through the Good
News I became your father in Christ Jesus, 16 so I beg you,
please follow my example. 17 That is why I am sending to
you Timothy, my son in the Lord. I love Timothy, and he is
faithful. He will help you remember my way of life in
Christ Jesus, just as I teach it in all the churches every-
where.
18 Some of you have become proud, thinking that I will
not come to you again. 19 But I will come to you very soon
if the Lord wishes. Then I will know what the proud ones
do, not what they say, 20 because the kingdom of God is
present not in talk but in power. 21 Which do you want:
that I come to you with punishment or with love and gen-
tleness?

Wickedness in the Church

5 It is actually being said that there is sexual sin among
you. And it is a kind that does not happen even among

CONTEMPORARY ENGLISH VERSION

someone curses us, we answer with kind words. Until now
we are thought of as nothing more than the trash and
garbage of this world.
14 I am not writing to embarrass you. I want to help you,
just as parents help their own dear children. 15 Ten thou-
sand people may teach you about Christ, but I am your
only father. You became my children when I told you about
Christ Jesus, 16 and I want you to be like me. 17 That's why I
sent Timothy to you. I love him like a son, and he is a
faithful servant of the Lord. Timothy will tell you what I do
to follow Christ and how it agrees with what I always
teach about Christ in every church.
18 Some of you think I am not coming for a visit, and so
you are bragging. 19 But if the Lord lets me come, I will
soon be there. Then I will find out if the ones who are
doing all this bragging really have any power. 20 God's
kingdom isn't just a lot of words. It is power. 21 What do
you want me to do when I arrive? Do you want me to be
hard on you or to be kind and gentle?

Immoral Followers

5 I have heard terrible things about some of you. In
fact, you are behaving worse than the Gentiles. A man

NEW INTERNATIONAL VERSION

endure it; 13when we are slandered, we answer kindly. Up
to this moment we have become the scum of the earth, the
refuse of the world.
14I am not writing this to shame you, but to warn you,
as my dear children. 15Even though you have ten thousand
guardians in Christ, you do not have many fathers, for in
Christ Jesus I became your father through the gospel.
16Therefore I urge you to imitate me. 17For this reason I
am sending to you Timothy, my son whom I love, who is
faithful in the Lord. He will remind you of my way of life
in Christ Jesus, which agrees with what I teach everywhere
in every church.
18Some of you have become arrogant, as if I were not
coming to you. 19But I will come to you very soon, if the
Lord is willing, and then I will find out not only how these
arrogant people are talking, but what power they have.
20For the kingdom of God is not a matter of talk but of
power. 21What do you prefer? Shall I come to you with a
whip, or in love and with a gentle spirit?

Expel the Immoral Brother!

5 It is actually reported that there is sexual immorality
among you, and of a kind that does not occur even

NEW LIVING TRANSLATION

us. 13We respond gently when evil things are said about
us. Yet we are treated like the world's garbage, like every-
body's trash—right up to the present moment.
14I am not writing these things to shame you, but to
warn you as my beloved children. 15For even if you had ten
thousand others to teach you about Christ, you have only
one spiritual father. For I became your father in Christ
Jesus when I preached the Good News to you. 16So I ask
you to follow my example and do as I do.
17That is the very reason I am sending Timothy—to help
you do this. For he is my beloved and trustworthy child in
the Lord. He will remind you of what I teach about Christ
Jesus in all the churches wherever I go.
18I know that some of you have become arrogant, think-
ing I will never visit you again. 19But I will come—and
soon—if the Lord will let me, and then I'll find out
whether these arrogant people are just big talkers or
whether they really have God's power. 20For the Kingdom
of God is not just fancy talk; it is living by God's power.
21Which do you choose? Should I come with punishment
and scolding, or should I come with quiet love and gentle-
ness?

Paul Condemns Spiritual Pride

5 I can hardly believe the report about the sexual
immorality going on among you, something so evil

NEW KING JAMES VERSION

entreat. We have been made as the filth of the world, the
offscouring of all things until now.

Paul's Paternal Care

14I do not write these things to shame you, but as my
beloved children I warn *you.* 15For though you might have
ten thousand instructors in Christ, yet *you do* not *have*
many fathers; for in Christ Jesus I have begotten you
through the gospel. 16Therefore I urge you, imitate me.
17For this reason I have sent Timothy to you, who is my
beloved and faithful son in the Lord, who will remind you
of my ways in Christ, as I teach everywhere in every
church.
18Now some are puffed up, as though I were not coming
to you. 19But I will come to you shortly, if the Lord wills,
and I will know, not the word of those who are puffed up,
but the power. 20For the kingdom of God *is* not in word but
in power. 21What do you want? Shall I come to you with a
rod, or in love and a spirit of gentleness?

Immorality Defiles the Church

5 It is actually reported *that there is* sexual immorality
among you, and such sexual immorality as is not

THE MESSAGE

spread rumors about *us*, we put in a good word for *them*.
We're treated like garbage, potato peelings from the cul-
ture's kitchen. And it's not getting any better.

I'm not writing all this as a neighborhood scold just to
make you feel rotten. I'm writing as a father to you, my
children. I love you and want you to grow up well, not
spoiled. There are a lot of people around who can't wait to
tell you what you've done wrong, but there aren't many
fathers willing to take the time and effort to help you grow
up. It was as Jesus helped me proclaim God's Message to
you that I became your father. I'm not, you know, asking
you to do anything I'm not already doing myself.

This is why I sent Timothy to you earlier. He is also my
dear son, and true to the Master. He will refresh your
memory on the instructions I regularly give all the
churches on the way of Christ.

I know there are some among you who are so full of
themselves they never listen to anyone, let alone me. They
don't think I'll ever show up in person. But I'll be there
sooner than you think, God willing, and then we'll see if
they're full of anything but hot air. God's Way is not a
matter of mere talk; it's an empowered life.

So how should I prepare to come to you? As a severe dis-
ciplinarian who makes you toe the mark? Or as a good
friend and counselor who wants to share heart-to-heart
with you? You decide.

The Mystery of Sex

5 I also received a report of scandalous sex within your
church family, a kind that wouldn't be tolerated even

KING JAMES VERSION

named among the Gentiles, that one should have his father's wife.

2 And ye are puffed up, and have not rather mourned, that he that hath done this deed might be taken away from among you.

3 For I verily, as absent in body, but present in spirit, have judged already, as though I were present, *concerning* him that hath so done this deed,

4 In the name of our Lord Jesus Christ, when ye are gathered together, and my spirit, with the power of our Lord Jesus Christ,

5 To deliver such an one unto Satan for the destruction of the flesh, that the spirit may be saved in the day of the Lord Jesus.

6 Your glorying *is* not good. Know ye not that a little leaven leaveneth the whole lump?

7 ¶ Purge out therefore the old leaven, that ye may be a new lump, as ye are unleavened. For even Christ our passover is sacrificed for us:

8 Therefore let us keep the feast, not with old leaven, neither with the leaven of malice and wickedness; but with the unleavened *bread* of sincerity and truth.

NEW AMERICAN STANDARD BIBLE

even among the Gentiles, that someone has his father's wife.

2 You have become arrogant and have not mourned instead, so that the one who had done this deed would be removed from your midst.

3 For I, on my part, though absent in body but present in spirit, have already judged him who has so committed this, as though I were present.

4 In the name of our Lord Jesus, when you are assembled, and I with you in spirit, with the power of our Lord Jesus,

5 *I have decided* to deliver such a one to Satan for the destruction of his flesh, so that his spirit may be saved in the day of the Lord [1]Jesus.

6 Your boasting is not good. Do you not know that a little leaven leavens the whole lump *of dough?*

7 Clean out the old leaven so that you may be a new lump, just as you are *in fact* unleavened. For Christ our Passover also has been sacrificed.

8 Therefore let us celebrate the feast, not with old leaven, nor with the leaven of malice and wickedness, but with the unleavened bread of sincerity and truth.

5:5 [1] Two early mss do not contain *Jesus*

NEW CENTURY VERSION

people who do not know God. A man there has his father's
wife. 2And you are proud! You should have been filled with
sadness so that the man who did this should be put out of
your group. 3I am not there with you in person, but I am
with you in spirit. And I have already judged the man who
did that sin as if I were really there. 4When you meet
together in the name of our Lord Jesus, and I meet with you
in spirit with the power of our Lord Jesus, 5then hand this
man over to Satan. So his sinful self[a] will be destroyed, and
his spirit will be saved on the day of the Lord.
6Your bragging is not good. You know the saying, "Just
a little yeast makes the whole batch of dough rise." 7Take
out all the old yeast so that you will be a new batch of
dough without yeast, which you really are. For Christ, our
Passover lamb, has been sacrificed. 8So let us celebrate
this feast, but not with the bread that has the old yeast—
the yeast of sin and wickedness. Let us celebrate this feast
with the bread that has no yeast—the bread of goodness
and truth.

5:5 [a] **sinful self** Literally, "flesh." This could also mean his body.

CONTEMPORARY ENGLISH VERSION

is even sleeping with his own stepmother.[a] 2You are proud,
when you ought to feel bad enough to chase away anyone
who acts like that.
3-4I am with you only in my thoughts. But in the name
of our Lord Jesus I have already judged this man, as
though I were with you in person. So when you meet
together and the power of the Lord Jesus is with you, I will
be there too. 5You must then hand that man over to Satan.
His body will be destroyed, but his spirit will be saved
when the Lord Jesus returns.
6Stop being proud! Don't you know how a little yeast
can spread through the whole batch of dough? 7Get rid of
the old yeast! Then you will be like fresh bread made without yeast, and that is what you are. Our Passover lamb is
Christ, who has already been sacrificed. 8So don't celebrate
the festival by being evil and sinful, which is like serving
bread made with yeast. Be pure and truthful and celebrate
by using bread made without yeast.

[a] 5.1 *is even sleeping with his own stepmother*: Or "has even married his own stepmother."

NEW INTERNATIONAL VERSION

among pagans: A man has his father's wife. [2]And you are
proud! Shouldn't you rather have been filled with grief and
have put out of your fellowship the man who did this?
[3]Even though I am not physically present, I am with you in
spirit. And I have already passed judgment on the one who
did this, just as if I were present. [4]When you are assem-
bled in the name of our Lord Jesus and I am with you in
spirit, and the power of our Lord Jesus is present, [5]hand
this man over to Satan, so that the sinful nature[a] may be
destroyed and his spirit saved on the day of the Lord.
[6]Your boasting is not good. Don't you know that a little
yeast works through the whole batch of dough? [7]Get rid of
the old yeast that you may be a new batch without yeast—
as you really are. For Christ, our Passover lamb, has been
sacrificed. [8]Therefore let us keep the Festival, not with the
old yeast, the yeast of malice and wickedness, but with
bread without yeast, the bread of sincerity and truth.

[a] 5 Or *that his body*; or *that the flesh*

NEW LIVING TRANSLATION

that even the pagans don't do it. I am told that you have a
man in your church who is living in sin with his father's
wife. [2]And you are so proud of yourselves! Why aren't you
mourning in sorrow and shame? And why haven't you
removed this man from your fellowship?
[3]Even though I am not there with you in person, I am
with you in the Spirit.* Concerning the one who has done
this, I have already passed judgment [4]in the name of the
Lord Jesus. You are to call a meeting of the church,* and I
will be there in spirit, and the power of the Lord Jesus will
be with you as you meet. [5]Then you must cast this man
out of the church and into Satan's hands, so that his sin-
ful nature will be destroyed* and he himself* will be saved
when the Lord returns.
[6]How terrible that you should boast about your spiritu-
ality, and yet you let this sort of thing go on. Don't you
realize that if even one person is allowed to go on sinning,
soon all will be affected? [7]Remove this wicked person from
among you so that you can stay pure.* Christ, our Passover
Lamb, has been sacrificed for us. [8]So let us celebrate the
festival, not by eating the old bread* of wickedness and
evil, but by eating the new bread* of purity and truth.

5:3 Or *in spirit.* **5:4** Or *In the name of the Lord Jesus, you are to call a meeting of the church.* **5:5a** Or *so that he will die;* Greek reads *for the destruction of the flesh.* **5:5b** Greek *and the spirit.* **5:6-7** Greek *Don't you realize that even a little leaven spreads quickly through the whole batch of dough? [7]Purge out the old leaven so that you can be a new batch of dough, just as you are already unleavened.* **5:8a** Greek *not with old leaven.* **5:8b** Greek *but with unleavened [bread].*

NEW KING JAMES VERSION

even named[a] among the Gentiles—that a man has his
father's wife! [2]And you are puffed up, and have not rather
mourned, that he who has done this deed might be taken
away from among you. [3]For I indeed, as absent in body
but present in spirit, have already judged (as though I were
present) him who has so done this deed. [4]In the name of
our Lord Jesus Christ, when you are gathered together,
along with my spirit, with the power of our Lord Jesus
Christ, [5]deliver such a one to Satan for the destruction of
the flesh, that his spirit may be saved in the day of the
Lord Jesus.[b]
[6]Your glorying *is* not good. Do you not know that a little
leaven leavens the whole lump? [7]Therefore purge out the
old leaven, that you may be a new lump, since you truly
are unleavened. For indeed Christ, our Passover, was sacri-
ficed for us.[c] [8]Therefore let us keep the feast, not with old
leaven, nor with the leaven of malice and wickedness, but
with the unleavened *bread* of sincerity and truth.

5:1 [a] NU-Text omits *named.* **5:5** [b] NU-Text omits *Jesus.*
5:7 [c] NU-Text omits *for us.*

THE MESSAGE

outside the church: One of your men is sleeping with his
stepmother. And you're so above it all that it doesn't even
faze you! Shouldn't this break your hearts? Shouldn't it
bring you to your knees in tears? Shouldn't this person
and his conduct be confronted and dealt with?

I'll tell you what I would do. Even though I'm not there
in person, consider me right there with you, because I can
fully see what's going on. I'm telling you that this is wrong.
You must not simply look the other way and hope it goes
away on its own. Bring it out in the open and deal with it
in the authority of Jesus our Master. Assemble the commu-
nity—I'll be present in spirit with you and our Master Jesus
will be present in power. Hold this man's conduct up to
public scrutiny. Let him defend it if he can! But if he can't,
then out with him! It will be totally devastating to him, of
course, and embarrassing to you. But better devastation
and embarrassment than damnation. You want him on his
feet and forgiven before the Master on the Day of Judgment.

Your flip and callous arrogance in these things bothers
me. You pass it off as a small thing, but it's anything but
that. Yeast, too, is a "small thing," but it works its way
through a whole batch of bread dough pretty fast. So get
rid of this "yeast." Our true identity is flat and plain, not
puffed up with the wrong kind of ingredient. The Messiah,
our Passover Lamb, has already been sacrificed for the
Passover meal, and we are the Unraised Bread part of the
Feast. So let's live out our part in the Feast, not as raised
bread swollen with the yeast of evil, but as flat bread—
simple, genuine, unpretentious.

KING JAMES VERSION

9 ¶ I wrote unto you in an epistle not to company with fornicators:

10 Yet not altogether with the fornicators of this world, or with the covetous, or extortioners, or with idolaters; for then must ye needs go out of the world.

11 But now I have written unto you not to keep company, if any man that is called a brother be a fornicator, or covetous, or an idolater, or a railer, or a drunkard, or an extortioner; with such an one no not to eat.

12 For what have I to do to judge them also that are without? do not ye judge them that are within?

13 But them that are without God judgeth. Therefore put away from among yourselves that wicked person.

6 Dare any of you, having a matter against another, go to law before the unjust, and not before the saints?

2 Do ye not know that the saints shall judge the world? and if the world shall be judged by you, are ye unworthy to judge the smallest matters?

3 Know ye not that we shall judge angels? how much more things that pertain to this life?

4 If then ye have judgments of things pertaining to this life, set them to judge who are least esteemed in the church.

NEW AMERICAN STANDARD BIBLE

9 I wrote you in my letter not to associate with immoral people;

10 I *did* not at all *mean* with the immoral people of this world, or with the covetous and swindlers, or with idolaters, for then you would have to go out of the world.

11 But actually, I wrote to you not to associate with any so-called brother if he is an immoral person, or covetous, or an idolater, or a reviler, or a drunkard, or a swindler—not even to eat with such a one.

12 For what have I to do with judging outsiders? Do you not judge those who are within *the church?*

13 But those who are outside, God judges. REMOVE THE WICKED MAN FROM AMONG YOURSELVES.

Lawsuits Discouraged

6 Does any one of you, when he has a case against his neighbor, dare to go to law before the unrighteous and not before the saints?

2 Or do you not know that the saints will judge the world? If the world is judged by you, are you not competent *to constitute* the smallest law courts?

3 Do you not know that we will judge angels? How much more matters of this life?

4 So if you have law courts dealing with matters of this life, do you appoint them as judges who are of no account in the church?

NEW CENTURY VERSION

9I wrote you in my earlier letter not to associate with
those who sin sexually. 10But I did not mean you should
not associate with those of this world who sin sexually, or
with the greedy, or robbers, or those who worship idols. To
get away from them you would have to leave this world.
11I am writing to tell you that you must not associate with
those who call themselves believers in Christ but who sin
sexually, or are greedy, or worship idols, or abuse others
with words, or get drunk, or cheat people. Do not even eat
with people like that.
12–13It is not my business to judge those who are not
part of the church. God will judge them. But you must
judge the people who are part of the church. The Scripture
says, "You must get rid of the evil person among you."[b]

Judging Problems Among Christians

6 When you have something against another Christian,
how can you bring yourself to go before judges who
are not right with God? Why do you not let God's people
decide who is right? 2Surely you know that God's people
will judge the world. So if you are to judge the world, are
you not able to judge small cases as well? 3You know that
in the future we will judge angels, so surely we can judge
the ordinary things of this life. 4If you have ordinary cases
that must be judged, are you going to appoint people as
judges who mean nothing to the church? 5I say this to

5:12-13 [b] "You...you." Quotation from Deuteronomy 17:7; 19:19; 22:21, 24; 24:7.

CONTEMPORARY ENGLISH VERSION

9In my other letter[b] I told you not to have anything to do
with immoral people. 10But I wasn't talking about the peo-
ple of this world. You would have to leave this world to get
away from everyone who is immoral or greedy or who
cheats or worships idols. 11I was talking about your own
people who are immoral or greedy or worship idols or
curse others or get drunk or cheat. Don't even eat with
them! 12Why should I judge outsiders? Aren't we supposed
to judge only church members? 13God judges everyone
else. The Scriptures say, "Chase away any of your own
people who are evil."

Taking Each Other to Court

6 When one of you has a complaint against another, do
you take your complaint to a court of sinners? Or do
you take it to God's people? 2Don't you know that God's
people will judge the world? And if you are going to judge
the world, can't you settle small problems? 3Don't you
know that we will judge angels? And if that is so, we can
surely judge everyday matters. 4Why do you take everyday
complaints to judges who are not respected by the church?

[b] 5.9 *other letter*: An unknown letter that Paul wrote to the Christians at Corinth before he wrote this one.

NEW INTERNATIONAL VERSION

9I have written you in my letter not to associate with sexually immoral people— 10not at all meaning the people of this world who are immoral, or the greedy and swindlers, or idolaters. In that case you would have to leave this world. 11But now I am writing you that you must not associate with anyone who calls himself a brother but is sexually immoral or greedy, an idolater or a slanderer, a drunkard or a swindler. With such a man do not even eat.

12What business is it of mine to judge those outside the church? Are you not to judge those inside? 13God will judge those outside. "Expel the wicked man from among you."[b]

Lawsuits Among Believers

6 If any of you has a dispute with another, dare he take it before the ungodly for judgment instead of before the saints? 2Do you not know that the saints will judge the world? And if you are to judge the world, are you not competent to judge trivial cases? 3Do you not know that we will judge angels? How much more the things of this life! 4Therefore, if you have disputes about such matters, appoint as judges even men of little account in the church![a]

[b] *13* Deut. 17:7; 19:19; 21:21; 22:21,24; 24:7 [a] *4* Or *matters, do you appoint as judges men of little account in the church?*

NEW LIVING TRANSLATION

9When I wrote to you before, I told you not to associate with people who indulge in sexual sin. 10But I wasn't talking about unbelievers who indulge in sexual sin, or who are greedy or are swindlers or idol worshipers. You would have to leave this world to avoid people like that. 11What I meant was that you are not to associate with anyone who claims to be a Christian* yet indulges in sexual sin, or is greedy, or worships idols, or is abusive, or a drunkard, or a swindler. Don't even eat with such people.

12It isn't my responsibility to judge outsiders, but it certainly is your job to judge those inside the church who are sinning in these ways. 13God will judge those on the outside; but as the Scriptures say, "You must remove the evil person from among you."*

Avoiding Lawsuits with Christians

6 When you have something against another Christian, why do you file a lawsuit and ask a secular court to decide the matter, instead of taking it to other Christians to decide who is right? 2Don't you know that someday we Christians are going to judge the world? And since you are going to judge the world, can't you decide these little things among yourselves? 3Don't you realize that we Christians will judge angels? So you should surely be able to resolve ordinary disagreements here on earth. 4If you have legal disputes about such matters, why do you go to outside judges who are not respected by the church? 5I am saying

5:11 Greek *a brother.* 5:13 Deut 17:7.

NEW KING JAMES VERSION

Immorality Must Be Judged

9I wrote to you in my epistle not to keep company with sexually immoral people. 10Yet *I* certainly *did* not *mean* with the sexually immoral people of this world, or with the covetous, or extortioners, or idolaters, since then you would need to go out of the world. 11But now I have written to you not to keep company with anyone named a brother, who is sexually immoral, or covetous, or an idolater, or a reviler, or a drunkard, or an extortioner—not even to eat with such a person.

12For what *have* I *to do* with judging those also who are outside? Do you not judge those who are inside? 13But those who are outside God judges. Therefore *"put away from yourselves the evil person."*[d]

Do Not Sue the Brethren

6 Dare any of you, having a matter against another, go to law before the unrighteous, and not before the saints? 2Do you not know that the saints will judge the world? And if the world will be judged by you, are you unworthy to judge the smallest matters? 3Do you not know that we shall judge angels? How much more, things that pertain to this life? 4If then you have judgments concerning things pertaining to this life, do you appoint those who are least esteemed by the church to judge? 5I say this to

5:13 [d] Deuteronomy 17:7; 19:19; 22:21, 24; 24:7

THE MESSAGE

I wrote you in my earlier letter that you shouldn't make yourselves at home among the sexually promiscuous. I didn't mean that you should have nothing at all to do with outsiders of that sort. Or with crooks, whether blue- or white-collar. Or with spiritual phonies, for that matter. You'd have to leave the world entirely to do that! But I *am* saying that you shouldn't act as if everything is just fine when one of your Christian companions is promiscuous or crooked, is flip with God or rude to friends, gets drunk or becomes greedy and predatory. You can't just go along with this, treating it as acceptable behavior. I'm not responsible for what the *outsiders* do, but don't we have some responsibility for those within our community of believers? God decides on the outsiders, but we need to decide when our brothers and sisters are out of line and, if necessary, clean house.

6 And how dare you take each other to court! When you think you have been wronged, does it make any sense to go before a court that knows nothing of God's ways instead of a family of Christians? The day is coming when the world is going to stand before a jury made up of Christians. If someday you are going to rule on the world's fate, wouldn't it be a good idea to practice on some of these smaller cases? Why, we're even going to judge angels! So why not these everyday affairs? As these disagreements and wrongs surface, why would you ever entrust them to the judgment of people you don't trust in any other way?

KING JAMES VERSION

5 I speak to your shame. Is it so, that there is not a wise man among you? no, not one that shall be able to judge between his brethren?

6 But brother goeth to law with brother, and that before the unbelievers.

7 Now therefore there is utterly a fault among you, because ye go to law one with another. Why do ye not rather take wrong? why do ye not rather *suffer yourselves to* be defrauded?

8 Nay, ye do wrong, and defraud, and that *your* brethren.

9 ¶ Know ye not that the unrighteous shall not inherit the kingdom of God? Be not deceived: neither fornicators, nor idolaters, nor adulterers, nor effeminate, nor abusers of themselves with mankind,

10 Nor thieves, nor covetous, nor drunkards, nor revilers, nor extortioners, shall inherit the kingdom of God.

11 And such were some of you: but ye are washed, but ye are sanctified, but ye are justified in the name of the Lord Jesus, and by the Spirit of our God.

12 ¶ All things are lawful unto me, but all things are not expedient: all things are lawful for me, but I will not be brought under the power of any.

13 Meats for the belly, and the belly for meats: but God shall destroy both it and them. Now the body *is* not for fornication, but for the Lord; and the Lord for the body.

NEW AMERICAN STANDARD BIBLE

5 I say *this* to your shame. *Is it* so, *that* there is not among you one wise man who will be able to decide between his brethren,

6 but brother goes to law with brother, and that before unbelievers?

7 Actually, then, it is already a defeat for you, that you have lawsuits with one another. Why not rather be wronged? Why not rather be defrauded?

8 On the contrary, you yourselves wrong and defraud. *You do* this even to *your* brethren.

9 Or do you not know that the unrighteous will not inherit the kingdom of God? Do not be deceived; neither fornicators, nor idolaters, nor adulterers, nor [1]effeminate, nor homosexuals,

10 nor thieves, nor *the* covetous, nor drunkards, nor revilers, nor swindlers, will inherit the kingdom of God.

11 Such were some of you; but you were washed, but you were sanctified, but you were justified in the name of the Lord Jesus Christ and in the Spirit of our God.

The Body Is the Lord's

12 All things are lawful for me, but not all things are profitable. All things are lawful for me, but I will not be mastered by anything.

13 Food is for the stomach and the stomach is for food, but God will do away with both of them. Yet the body is not for immorality, but for the Lord, and the Lord is for the body.

6:9 [1] I.e. effeminate by perversion

NEW CENTURY VERSION

shame you. Surely there is someone among you wise enough to judge a complaint between believers. 6But now one believer goes to court against another believer—and you do this in front of unbelievers!

7The fact that you have lawsuits against each other shows that you are already defeated. Why not let yourselves be wronged? Why not let yourselves be cheated? 8But you yourselves do wrong and cheat, and you do this to other believers!

9–10Surely you know that the people who do wrong will not inherit God's kingdom. Do not be fooled. Those who sin sexually, worship idols, take part in adultery, those who are male prostitutes, or men who have sexual relations with other men, those who steal, are greedy, get drunk, lie about others, or rob—these people will not inherit God's kingdom. 11In the past, some of you were like that, but you were washed clean. You were made holy, and you were made right with God in the name of the Lord Jesus Christ and in the Spirit of our God.

Use Your Bodies for God's Glory

12"I am allowed to do all things," but all things are not good for me to do. "I am allowed to do all things," but I will not let anything make me its slave. 13"Food is for the stomach, and the stomach for food," but God will destroy them both. The body is not for sexual sin but for the Lord, and

CONTEMPORARY ENGLISH VERSION

5I say this to your shame. Aren't any of you wise enough to act as a judge between one follower and another? 6Why should one of you take another to be tried by unbelievers? 7When one of you takes another to court, all of you lose. It would be better to let yourselves be cheated and robbed. 8But instead, you cheat and rob other followers.

9Don't you know that evil people won't have a share in the blessings of God's kingdom? Don't fool yourselves! No one who is immoral or worships idols or is unfaithful in marriage or is a pervert or behaves like a homosexual 10will share in God's kingdom. Neither will any thief or greedy person or drunkard or anyone who curses and cheats others. 11Some of you used to be like that. But now the name of our Lord Jesus Christ and the power of God's Spirit have washed you and made you holy and acceptable to God.

Honor God with Your Body

12Some of you say, "We can do anything we want to." But I tell you that not everything is good for us. So I refuse to let anything have power over me. 13You also say, "Food is meant for our bodies, and our bodies are meant for food." But I tell you that God will destroy them both. We are not supposed to do indecent things with our bodies. We are to use them for the Lord who is in charge of our

NEW INTERNATIONAL VERSION

5I say this to shame you. Is it possible that there is nobody among you wise enough to judge a dispute between believers? 6But instead, one brother goes to law against another—and this in front of unbelievers!

7The very fact that you have lawsuits among you means you have been completely defeated already. Why not rather be wronged? Why not rather be cheated? 8Instead, you yourselves cheat and do wrong, and you do this to your brothers.

9Do you not know that the wicked will not inherit the kingdom of God? Do not be deceived: Neither the sexually immoral nor idolaters nor adulterers nor male prostitutes nor homosexual offenders 10nor thieves nor the greedy nor drunkards nor slanderers nor swindlers will inherit the kingdom of God. 11And that is what some of you were. But you were washed, you were sanctified, you were justified in the name of the Lord Jesus Christ and by the Spirit of our God.

Sexual Immorality

12“Everything is permissible for me”—but not everything is beneficial. “Everything is permissible for me”—but I will not be mastered by anything. 13“Food for the stomach and the stomach for food”—but God will destroy them both. The body is not meant for sexual immorality, but for the Lord, and the Lord for the body. 14By his power God

NEW LIVING TRANSLATION

this to shame you. Isn't there anyone in all the church who is wise enough to decide these arguments? 6But instead, one Christian* sues another—right in front of unbelievers!

7To have such lawsuits at all is a real defeat for you. Why not just accept the injustice and leave it at that? Why not let yourselves be cheated? 8But instead, you yourselves are the ones who do wrong and cheat even your own Christian brothers and sisters.*

Avoiding Sexual Sin

9Don't you know that those who do wrong will have no share in the Kingdom of God? Don't fool yourselves. Those who indulge in sexual sin, who are idol worshipers, adulterers, male prostitutes, homosexuals, 10thieves, greedy people, drunkards, abusers, and swindlers—none of these will have a share in the Kingdom of God. 11There was a time when some of you were just like that, but now your sins have been washed away,* and you have been set apart for God. You have been made right with God because of what the Lord Jesus Christ and the Spirit of our God have done for you.

12You may say, “I am allowed to do anything.” But I reply, “Not everything is good for you.” And even though “I am allowed to do anything,” I must not become a slave to anything. 13You say, “Food is for the stomach, and the stomach is for food.” This is true, though someday God will do away with both of them. But our bodies were not made for sexual immorality. They were made for the Lord,

6:6 Greek *one brother.* **6:8** Greek *brothers.* **6:11** Or *you have been cleansed.*

NEW KING JAMES VERSION

your shame. Is it so, that there is not a wise man among you, not even one, who will be able to judge between his brethren? 6But brother goes to law against brother, and that before unbelievers!

7Now therefore, it is already an utter failure for you that you go to law against one another. Why do you not rather accept wrong? Why do you not rather *let yourselves* be cheated? 8No, you yourselves do wrong and cheat, and *you do* these things *to your* brethren! 9Do you not know that the unrighteous will not inherit the kingdom of God? Do not be deceived. Neither fornicators, nor idolaters, nor adulterers, nor homosexuals,[a] nor sodomites, 10nor thieves, nor covetous, nor drunkards, nor revilers, nor extortioners will inherit the kingdom of God. 11And such were some of you. But you were washed, but you were sanctified, but you were justified in the name of the Lord Jesus and by the Spirit of our God.

Glorify God in Body and Spirit

12All things are lawful for me, but all things are not helpful. All things are lawful for me, but I will not be brought under the power of any. 13Foods for the stomach and the stomach for foods, but God will destroy both it and them. Now the body *is* not for sexual immorality but for the Lord,

6:9 [a] That is, catamites

THE MESSAGE

I say this as bluntly as I can to wake you up to the stupidity of what you're doing. Is it possible that there isn't one levelheaded person among you who can make fair decisions when disagreements and disputes come up? I don't believe it. And here you are taking each other to court before people who don't even believe in God! How can they render justice if they don't believe in the *God* of justice?

These court cases are an ugly blot on your community. Wouldn't it be far better to just take it, to let yourselves be wronged and forget it? All you're doing is providing fuel for more wrong, more injustice, bringing more hurt to the people of your own spiritual family.

Don't you realize that this is not the way to live? Unjust people who don't care about God will not be joining in his kingdom. Those who use and abuse each other, use and abuse sex, use and abuse the earth and everything in it, don't qualify as citizens in God's kingdom. A number of you know from experience what I'm talking about, for not so long ago you were on that list. Since then, you've been cleaned up and given a fresh start by Jesus, our Master, our Messiah, and by our God present in us, the Spirit.

Just because something is technically legal doesn't mean that it's spiritually appropriate. If I went around doing whatever I thought I could get by with, I'd be a slave to my whims.

You know the old saying, “First you eat to live, and then you live to eat”? Well, it may be true that the body is only a temporary thing, but that's no excuse for stuffing your body with food, or indulging it with sex. Since the Master honors you with a body, honor him with your body!

KING JAMES VERSION

14 And God hath both raised up the Lord, and will also raise up us by his own power.

15 Know ye not that your bodies are the members of Christ? shall I then take the members of Christ, and make *them* the members of an harlot? God forbid.

16 What? know ye not that he which is joined to an harlot is one body? for two, saith he, shall be one flesh.

17 But he that is joined unto the Lord is one spirit.

18 Flee fornication. Every sin that a man doeth is without the body; but he that committeth fornication sinneth against his own body.

19 What? know ye not that your body is the temple of the Holy Ghost *which is* in you, which ye have of God, and ye are not your own?

20 For ye are bought with a price: therefore glorify God in your body, and in your spirit, which are God's.

7 Now concerning the things whereof ye wrote unto me: *It is* good for a man not to touch a woman.

2 Nevertheless, *to avoid* fornication, let every man have his own wife, and let every woman have her own husband.

NEW AMERICAN STANDARD BIBLE

14 Now God has not only raised the Lord, but will also raise us up through His power.

15 Do you not know that your bodies are members of Christ? Shall I then take away the members of Christ and make them members of a prostitute? May it never be!

16 Or do you not know that the one who joins himself to a prostitute is one body *with her?* For He says, "THE TWO SHALL BECOME ONE FLESH."

17 But the one who joins himself to the Lord is one spirit *with Him.*

18 Flee immorality. Every *other* sin that a man commits is outside the body, but the immoral man sins against his own body.

19 Or do you not know that your body is a temple of the Holy Spirit who is in you, whom you have from God, and that you are not your own?

20 For you have been bought with a price: therefore glorify God in your body.

Teaching on Marriage

7 Now concerning the things about which you wrote, it is good for a man not to touch a woman.

2 But because of immoralities, each man is to have his own wife, and each woman is to have her own husband.

NEW CENTURY VERSION

the Lord is for the body. 14By his power God has raised the
Lord from the dead and will also raise us from the dead.
15Surely you know that your bodies are parts of Christ him-
self. So I must never take the parts of Christ and join them
to a prostitute! 16It is written in the Scriptures, "The two
will become one body."[a] So you should know that anyone
who joins with a prostitute becomes one body with the
prostitute. 17But the one who joins with the Lord is one
spirit with the Lord.
18So run away from sexual sin. Every other sin people
do is outside their bodies, but those who sin sexually sin
against their own bodies. 19You should know that your
body is a temple for the Holy Spirit who is in you. You
have received the Holy Spirit from God. So you do not
belong to yourselves, 20because you were bought by God
for a price. So honor God with your bodies.

About Marriage

7 Now I will discuss the things you wrote me about. It
is good for a man not to have sexual relations with a
woman. 2But because sexual sin is a danger, each man
should have his own wife, and each woman should have
her own husband. 3The husband should give his wife all

6:16 [a] "The two...body." Quotation from Genesis 2:24.

CONTEMPORARY ENGLISH VERSION

bodies. 14God will raise us from death by the same power
that he used when he raised our Lord to life.
15Don't you know that your bodies are part of the body
of Christ? Is it right for me to join part of the body of Christ
to a prostitute? No, it isn't! 16Don't you know that a man
who does that becomes part of her body? The Scriptures
say, "The two of them will be like one person." 17But any-
one who is joined to the Lord is one in spirit with him.
18Don't be immoral in matters of sex. That is a sin
against your own body in a way that no other sin is. 19You
surely know that your body is a temple where the Holy
Spirit lives. The Spirit is in you and is a gift from God. You
are no longer your own. 20God paid a great price for you.
So use your body to honor God.

Questions about Marriage

7 Now I will answer the questions that you asked in
your letter. You asked, "Is it best for people not to
marry?"[a] 2Well, having your own husband or wife should
keep you from doing something immoral. 3Husbands and

[a] 7.1 *people not to marry*: Or "married couples not to have sex."

NEW INTERNATIONAL VERSION

raised the Lord from the dead, and he will raise us also. [15]Do you not know that your bodies are members of Christ himself? Shall I then take the members of Christ and unite them with a prostitute? Never! [16]Do you not know that he who unites himself with a prostitute is one with her in body? For it is said, "The two will become one flesh."[b] [17]But he who unites himself with the Lord is one with him in spirit.

[18]Flee from sexual immorality. All other sins a man commits are outside his body, but he who sins sexually sins against his own body. [19]Do you not know that your body is a temple of the Holy Spirit, who is in you, whom you have received from God? You are not your own; [20]you were bought at a price. Therefore honor God with your body.

Marriage

7 Now for the matters you wrote about: It is good for a man not to marry.[a] [2]But since there is so much immorality, each man should have his own wife, and each woman her own husband. [3]The husband should fulfill his

b 16 Gen. 2:24 *a 1* Or "*It is good for a man not to have sexual relations with a woman.*"

NEW LIVING TRANSLATION

and the Lord cares about our bodies. [14]And God will raise our bodies from the dead by his marvelous power, just as he raised our Lord from the dead. [15]Don't you realize that your bodies are actually parts of Christ? Should a man take his body, which belongs to Christ, and join it to a prostitute? Never! [16]And don't you know that if a man joins himself to a prostitute, he becomes one body with her? For the Scriptures say, "The two are united into one."* [17]But the person who is joined to the Lord becomes one spirit with him.

[18]Run away from sexual sin! No other sin so clearly affects the body as this one does. For sexual immorality is a sin against your own body. [19]Or don't you know that your body is the temple of the Holy Spirit, who lives in you and was given to you by God? You do not belong to yourself, [20]for God bought you with a high price. So you must honor God with your body.

Instruction on Marriage

7 Now about the questions you asked in your letter. Yes, it is good to live a celibate life. [2]But because there is so much sexual immorality, each man should have his own wife, and each woman should have her own husband.

6:16 Gen 2:24.

NEW KING JAMES VERSION

and the Lord for the body. [14]And God both raised up the Lord and will also raise us up by His power.

[15]Do you not know that your bodies are members of Christ? Shall I then take the members of Christ and make *them* members of a harlot? Certainly not! [16]Or do you not know that he who is joined to a harlot is one body *with her?* For *"the two,"* He says, *"shall become one flesh."*[b] [17]But he who is joined to the Lord is one spirit *with Him.*

[18]Flee sexual immorality. Every sin that a man does is outside the body, but he who commits sexual immorality sins against his own body. [19]Or do you not know that your body is the temple of the Holy Spirit *who is* in you, whom you have from God, and you are not your own? [20]For you were bought at a price; therefore glorify God in your body[c] and in your spirit, which are God's.

Principles of Marriage

7 Now concerning the things of which you wrote to me: *It is* good for a man not to touch a woman. [2]Nevertheless, because of sexual immorality, let each man have his own wife, and let each woman have her own husband. [3]Let

6:16 *b* Genesis 2:24 **6:20** *c* NU-Text ends the verse at *body.*

THE MESSAGE

God honored the Master's body by raising it from the grave. He'll treat yours with the same resurrection power. Until that time, remember that your bodies are created with the same dignity as the Master's body. You wouldn't take the Master's body off to a whorehouse, would you? I should hope not.

There's more to sex than mere skin on skin. Sex is as much spiritual mystery as physical fact. As written in Scripture, "The two become one." Since we want to become spiritually one with the Master, we must not pursue the kind of sex that avoids commitment and intimacy, leaving us more lonely than ever—the kind of sex that can never "become one." There is a sense in which sexual sins are different from all others. In sexual sin we violate the sacredness of our own bodies, these bodies that were made for God-given and God-modeled love, for "becoming one" with another. Or didn't you realize that your body is a sacred place, the place of the Holy Spirit? Don't you see that you can't live however you please, squandering what God paid such a high price for? The physical part of you is not some piece of property belonging to the spiritual part of you. God owns the whole works. So let people see God in and through your body.

To Be Married, To Be Single . . .

7 Now, getting down to the questions you asked in your letter to me. First, Is it a good thing to have sexual relations?

Certainly—but only within a certain context. It's good for a man to have a wife, and for a woman to have a husband.

KING JAMES VERSION

3 Let the husband render unto the wife due benevolence: and likewise also the wife unto the husband.

4 The wife hath not power of her own body, but the husband: and likewise also the husband hath not power of his own body, but the wife.

5 Defraud ye not one the other, except *it be* with consent for a time, that ye may give yourselves to fasting and prayer; and come together again, that Satan tempt you not for your incontinency.

6 But I speak this by permission, *and* not of commandment.

7 For I would that all men were even as I myself. But every man hath his proper gift of God, one after this manner, and another after that.

8 I say therefore to the unmarried and widows, It is good for them if they abide even as I.

9 But if they cannot contain, let them marry: for it is better to marry than to burn.

10 ¶ And unto the married I command, *yet* not I, but the Lord, Let not the wife depart from *her* husband:

11 But and if she depart, let her remain unmarried, or be reconciled to *her* husband: and let not the husband put away *his* wife.

NEW AMERICAN STANDARD BIBLE

3 The husband must fulfill his duty to his wife, and likewise also the wife to her husband.

4 The wife does not have authority over her own body, but the husband *does;* and likewise also the husband does not have authority over his own body, but the wife *does.*

5 Stop depriving one another, except by agreement for a time, so that you may devote yourselves to prayer, and come together again so that Satan will not tempt you because of your lack of self-control.

6 But this I say by way of concession, not of command.

7 [1]Yet I wish that all men were even as I myself am. However, each man has his own gift from God, one in this manner, and another in that.

8 But I say to the unmarried and to widows that it is good for them if they remain even as I.

9 But if they do not have self-control, let them marry; for it is better to marry than to burn *with passion*.

10 But to the married I give instructions, not I, but the Lord, that the wife should not leave her husband

11 (but if she does leave, she must remain unmarried, or else be reconciled to her husband), and that the husband should not divorce his wife.

7:7 [1] One early ms reads *For*

NEW CENTURY VERSION

that he owes her as his wife. And the wife should give her husband all that she owes him as her husband. 4The wife does not have full rights over her own body; her husband shares them. And the husband does not have full rights over his own body; his wife shares them. 5Do not refuse to give your bodies to each other, unless you both agree to stay away from sexual relations for a time so you can give your time to prayer. Then come together again so Satan cannot tempt you because of a lack of self-control. 6I say this to give you permission to stay away from sexual relations for a time. It is not a command to do so. 7I wish that everyone were like me, but each person has his own gift from God. One has one gift, another has another gift.

8Now for those who are not married and for the widows I say this: It is good for them to stay unmarried as I am. 9But if they cannot control themselves, they should marry. It is better to marry than to burn with sexual desire.

10Now I give this command for the married people. (The command is not from me; it is from the Lord.) A wife should not leave her husband. 11But if she does leave, she must not marry again, or she should make up with her husband. Also the husband should not divorce his wife.

CONTEMPORARY ENGLISH VERSION

wives should be fair with each other about having sex. 4A wife belongs to her husband instead of to herself, and a husband belongs to his wife instead of to himself. 5So don't refuse sex to each other, unless you agree not to have sex for a little while, in order to spend time in prayer. Then Satan won't be able to tempt you because of your lack of self-control. 6In my opinion that is what should be done, though I don't know of anything the Lord said about this matter. 7I wish that all of you were like me, but God has given different gifts to each of us.

8Here is my advice for people who have never been married and for widows. You should stay single, just as I am. 9But if you don't have enough self-control, then go ahead and get married. After all, it is better to marry than to burn with desire.[b]

10I instruct married couples to stay together, and this is exactly what the Lord himself taught. A wife who leaves her husband 11should either stay single or go back to her husband. And a husband should not leave his wife.

[b] **7.9** *with desire*: Or "in the flames of hell."

NEW INTERNATIONAL VERSION

marital duty to his wife, and likewise the wife to her hus-
band. 4The wife's body does not belong to her alone but
also to her husband. In the same way, the husband's body
does not belong to him alone but also to his wife. 5Do not
deprive each other except by mutual consent and for a
time, so that you may devote yourselves to prayer. Then
come together again so that Satan will not tempt you
because of your lack of self-control. 6I say this as a conces-
sion, not as a command. 7I wish that all men were as I am.
But each man has his own gift from God; one has this gift,
another has that.

8Now to the unmarried and the widows I say: It is good
for them to stay unmarried, as I am. 9But if they cannot
control themselves, they should marry, for it is better to
marry than to burn with passion.

10To the married I give this command (not I, but the
Lord): A wife must not separate from her husband. 11But if
she does, she must remain unmarried or else be reconciled
to her husband. And a husband must not divorce his wife.

NEW LIVING TRANSLATION

3The husband should not deprive his wife of sexual inti-
macy, which is her right as a married woman, nor should
the wife deprive her husband. 4The wife gives authority
over her body to her husband, and the husband also gives
authority over his body to his wife. 5So do not deprive
each other of sexual relations. The only exception to this
rule would be the agreement of both husband and wife to
refrain from sexual intimacy for a limited time, so they can
give themselves more completely to prayer. Afterward they
should come together again so that Satan won't be able to
tempt them because of their lack of self-control. 6This is
only my suggestion. It's not meant to be an absolute rule.
7I wish everyone could get along without marrying, just as
I do. But we are not all the same. God gives some the gift
of marriage, and to others he gives the gift of singleness.

8Now I say to those who aren't married and to widows—
it's better to stay unmarried, just as I am. 9But if they
can't control themselves, they should go ahead and marry.
It's better to marry than to burn with lust.

10Now, for those who are married I have a command
that comes not from me, but from the Lord.* A wife must
not leave her husband. 11But if she does leave him, let her
remain single or else go back to him. And the husband
must not leave his wife.

7:10 See Matt 5:32; 19:9; Mark 10:11-12; Luke 16:18.

NEW KING JAMES VERSION

the husband render to his wife the affection due her, and
likewise also the wife to her husband. 4The wife does not
have authority over her own body, but the husband *does.*
And likewise the husband does not have authority over his
own body, but the wife *does.* 5Do not deprive one another
except with consent for a time, that you may give your-
selves to fasting and prayer; and come together again so
that Satan does not tempt you because of your lack of self-
control. 6But I say this as a concession, not as a command-
ment. 7For I wish that all men were even as I myself. But
each one has his own gift from God, one in this manner
and another in that.

8But I say to the unmarried and to the widows: It is
good for them if they remain even as I am; 9but if they
cannot exercise self-control, let them marry. For it is better
to marry than to burn *with passion.*

Keep Your Marriage Vows

10Now to the married I command, *yet* not I but the Lord:
A wife is not to depart from *her* husband. 11But even if she
does depart, let her remain unmarried or be reconciled to
her husband. And a husband is not to divorce *his* wife.

THE MESSAGE

Sexual drives are strong, but marriage is strong enough to contain them and provide for a balanced and fulfilling sexual life in a world of sexual disorder. The marriage bed must be a place of mutuality—the husband seeking to satisfy his wife, the wife seeking to satisfy her husband. Marriage is not a place to "stand up for your rights." Marriage is a decision to serve the other, whether in bed or out. Abstaining from sex is permissible for a period of time if you both agree to it, and if it's for the purposes of prayer and fasting—but only for such times. Then come back together again. Satan has an ingenious way of tempting us when we least expect it. I'm not, understand, commanding these periods of abstinence—only providing my best counsel if you should choose them.

Sometimes I wish everyone were single like me—a simpler life in many ways! But celibacy is not for everyone any more than marriage is. God gives the gift of the single life to some, the gift of the married life to others.

I do, though, tell the unmarried and widows that singleness might well be the best thing for them, as it has been for me. But if they can't manage their desires and emotions, they should by all means go ahead and get married. The difficulties of marriage are preferable by far to a sexually tortured life as a single.

And if you are married, stay married. This is the Master's command, not mine. If a wife should leave her husband, she must either remain single or else come back and make things right with him. And a husband has no right to get rid of his wife.

KING JAMES VERSION

12 But to the rest speak I, not the Lord: If any brother hath a wife that believeth not, and she be pleased to dwell with him, let him not put her away.

13 And the woman which hath an husband that believeth not, and if he be pleased to dwell with her, let her not leave him.

14 For the unbelieving husband is sanctified by the wife, and the unbelieving wife is sanctified by the husband: else were your children unclean; but now are they holy.

15 But if the unbelieving depart, let him depart. A brother or a sister is not under bondage in such *cases*: but God hath called us to peace.

16 For what knowest thou, O wife, whether thou shalt save *thy* husband? or how knowest thou, O man, whether thou shalt save *thy* wife?

17 ¶ But as God hath distributed to every man, as the Lord hath called every one, so let him walk. And so ordain I in all churches.

18 Is any man called being circumcised? let him not become uncircumcised. Is any called in uncircumcision? let him not be circumcised.

19 Circumcision is nothing, and uncircumcision is nothing, but the keeping of the commandments of God.

NEW AMERICAN STANDARD BIBLE

12 But to the rest I say, not the Lord, that if any brother has a wife who is an unbeliever, and she consents to live with him, he must not divorce her.

13 And a woman who has an unbelieving husband, and he consents to live with her, she must not send her husband away.

14 For the unbelieving husband is sanctified through his wife, and the unbelieving wife is sanctified through her believing husband; for otherwise your children are unclean, but now they are holy.

15 Yet if the unbelieving one leaves, let him leave; the brother or the sister is not under bondage in such *cases,* but God has called [2]us to peace.

16 For how do you know, O wife, whether you will save your husband? Or how do you know, O husband, whether you will save your wife?

17 Only, as the Lord has assigned to each one, as God has called each, in this manner let him walk. And so I direct in all the churches.

18 Was any man called *when he was already* circumcised? He is not to become uncircumcised. Has anyone been called in uncircumcision? He is not to be circumcised.

19 Circumcision is nothing, and uncircumcision is nothing, but *what matters is* the keeping of the commandments of God.

7:15 [2] One early ms reads *you*

NEW CENTURY VERSION

12For all the others I say this (I am saying this, not the
Lord): If a Christian man has a wife who is not a believer,
and she is happy to live with him, he must not divorce her.
13And if a Christian woman has a husband who is not a
believer, and he is happy to live with her, she must not
divorce him. 14The husband who is not a believer is made
holy through his believing wife. And the wife who is not a
believer is made holy through her believing husband. If
this were not true, your children would not be clean, but
now your children are holy.
15But if those who are not believers decide to leave, let
them leave. When this happens, the Christian man or
woman is free. But God called us to live in peace. 16Wife,
you don't know; maybe you will save your husband. And
husband, you don't know; maybe you will save your wife.

Live as God Called You

17But in any case each one of you should continue to
live the way God has given you to live—the way you were
when God called you. This is a rule I make in all the
churches. 18If a man was already circumcised when he was
called, he should not undo his circumcision. If a man was
without circumcision when he was called, he should not be
circumcised. 19It is not important if a man is circumcised
or not. The important thing is obeying God's commands.

CONTEMPORARY ENGLISH VERSION

12I don't know of anything else the Lord said about marriage. All I can do is to give you my own advice. If your
wife isn't a follower of the Lord, but is willing to stay with
you, don't divorce her. 13If your husband isn't a follower,
but is willing to stay with you, don't divorce him. 14Your
husband or wife who isn't a follower is made holy by having you as a mate. This also makes your children holy and
keeps them from being unclean in God's sight.
15If your husband or wife isn't a follower of the Lord
and decides to divorce you, then you should agree to it.
You are no longer bound to that person. After all, God
chose you and wants you to live at peace. 16And besides,
how do you know if you will be able to save your husband
or wife who isn't a follower?

Obeying the Lord at All Times

17In every church I tell the people to stay as they were
when the Lord Jesus chose them and God called them to be
his own. Now I say the same thing to you. 18If you are
already circumcised, don't try to change it. If you are not
circumcised, don't get circumcised. 19Being circumcised or
uncircumcised isn't really what matters. The important
thing is to obey God's commands. 20So don't try to change

NEW INTERNATIONAL VERSION

12To the rest I say this (I, not the Lord): If any brother has a wife who is not a believer and she is willing to live with him, he must not divorce her. 13And if a woman has a husband who is not a believer and he is willing to live with her, she must not divorce him. 14For the unbelieving husband has been sanctified through his wife, and the unbelieving wife has been sanctified through her believing husband. Otherwise your children would be unclean, but as it is, they are holy.

15But if the unbeliever leaves, let him do so. A believing man or woman is not bound in such circumstances; God has called us to live in peace. 16How do you know, wife, whether you will save your husband? Or, how do you know, husband, whether you will save your wife?

17Nevertheless, each one should retain the place in life that the Lord assigned to him and to which God has called him. This is the rule I lay down in all the churches. 18Was a man already circumcised when he was called? He should not become uncircumcised. Was a man uncircumcised when he was called? He should not be circumcised. 19Circumcision is nothing and uncircumcision is nothing. Keeping God's commands is what counts. 20Each one

NEW LIVING TRANSLATION

12Now, I will speak to the rest of you, though I do not have a direct command from the Lord. If a Christian man* has a wife who is an unbeliever and she is willing to continue living with him, he must not leave her. 13And if a Christian woman has a husband who is an unbeliever, and he is willing to continue living with her, she must not leave him. 14For the Christian wife brings holiness to her marriage, and the Christian husband brings holiness to his marriage. Otherwise, your children would not have a godly influence, but now they are set apart for him. 15(But if the husband or wife who isn't a Christian insists on leaving, let them go. In such cases the Christian husband or wife is not required to stay with them, for God wants his children to live in peace.) 16You wives must remember that your husbands might be converted because of you. And you husbands must remember that your wives might be converted because of you.

17You must accept whatever situation the Lord has put you in, and continue on as you were when God first called you. This is my rule for all the churches. 18For instance, a man who was circumcised before he became a believer should not try to reverse it. And the man who was uncircumcised when he became a believer should not be circumcised now. 19For it makes no difference whether or not a man has been circumcised. The important thing is to keep God's commandments.

7:12 Greek *a brother.*

NEW KING JAMES VERSION

12But to the rest I, not the Lord, say: If any brother has a wife who does not believe, and she is willing to live with him, let him not divorce her. 13And a woman who has a husband who does not believe, if he is willing to live with her, let her not divorce him. 14For the unbelieving husband is sanctified by the wife, and the unbelieving wife is sanctified by the husband; otherwise your children would be unclean, but now they are holy. 15But if the unbeliever departs, let him depart; a brother or a sister is not under bondage in such *cases.* But God has called us to peace. 16For how do you know, O wife, whether you will save *your* husband? Or how do you know, O husband, whether you will save *your* wife?

Live as You Are Called

17But as God has distributed to each one, as the Lord has called each one, so let him walk. And so I ordain in all the churches. 18Was anyone called while circumcised? Let him not become uncircumcised. Was anyone called while uncircumcised? Let him not be circumcised. 19Circumcision is nothing and uncircumcision is nothing, but keeping the commandments of God *is what matters.* 20Let each one

THE MESSAGE

For the rest of you who are in mixed marriages—Christian married to nonChristian—we have no explicit command from the Master. So this is what you must do. If you are a man with a wife who is not a believer but who still wants to live with you, hold on to her. If you are a woman with a husband who is not a believer but he wants to live with you, hold on to him. The unbelieving husband shares to an extent in the holiness of his wife, and the unbelieving wife is likewise touched by the holiness of her husband. Otherwise, your children would be left out; as it is, they also are included in the spiritual purposes of God.

On the other hand, if the unbelieving spouse walks out, you've got to let him or her go. You don't have to hold on desperately. God has called us to make the best of it, as peacefully as we can. You never know, wife: The way you handle this might bring your husband not only back to you but to God. You never know, husband: The way you handle this might bring your wife not only back to you but to God.

And don't be wishing you were someplace else or with someone else. Where you are right now is God's place for you. Live and obey and love and believe right there. God, not your marital status, defines your life. Don't think I'm being harder on you than on the others. I give this same counsel in all the churches.

Were you Jewish at the time God called you? Don't try to remove the evidence. Were you non-Jewish at the time of your call? Don't become a Jew. Being Jewish isn't the point. The really important thing is obeying God's call, following his commands.

KING JAMES VERSION

20 Let every man abide in the same calling wherein he was called.

21 Art thou called *being* a servant? care not for it: but if thou mayest be made free, use *it* rather.

22 For he that is called in the Lord, *being* a servant, is the Lord's freeman: likewise also he that is called, *being* free, is Christ's servant.

23 Ye are bought with a price; be not ye the servants of men.

24 Brethren, let every man, wherein he is called, therein abide with God.

25 ¶ Now concerning virgins I have no commandment of the Lord: yet I give my judgment, as one that hath obtained mercy of the Lord to be faithful.

26 I suppose therefore that this is good for the present distress, *I say*, that *it is* good for a man so to be.

27 Art thou bound unto a wife? seek not to be loosed. Art thou loosed from a wife? seek not a wife.

28 But and if thou marry, thou hast not sinned; and if a virgin marry, she hath not sinned. Nevertheless such shall have trouble in the flesh: but I spare you.

29 But this I say, brethren, the time *is* short: it remaineth, that both they that have wives be as though they had none;

30 And they that weep, as though they wept not; and they that rejoice, as though they rejoiced not; and they that buy, as though they possessed not;

NEW AMERICAN STANDARD BIBLE

20 Each man must remain in that condition in which he was called.

21 Were you called while a slave? Do not worry about it; but if you are able also to become free, rather do that.

22 For he who was called in the Lord while a slave, is the Lord's freedman; likewise he who was called while free, is Christ's slave.

23 You were bought with a price; do not become slaves of men.

24 Brethren, each one is to remain with God in that *condition* in which he was called.

25 Now concerning virgins I have no command of the Lord, but I give an opinion as one who by the mercy of the Lord is trustworthy.

26 I think then that this is good in view of the present distress, that it is good for a man to remain as he is.

27 Are you bound to a wife? Do not seek to be released. Are you released from a wife? Do not seek a wife.

28 But if you marry, you have not sinned; and if a virgin marries, she has not sinned. Yet such will have trouble in this life, and I am trying to spare you.

29 But this I say, brethren, the time has been shortened, so that from now on those who have wives should be as though they had none;

30 and those who weep, as though they did not weep; and those who rejoice, as though they did not rejoice; and those who buy, as though they did not possess;

NEW CENTURY VERSION

[20]Each one of you should stay the way you were when God called you. [21]If you were a slave when God called you, do not let that bother you. But if you can be free, then make good use of your freedom. [22]Those who were slaves when the Lord called them are free persons who belong to the Lord. In the same way, those who were free when they were called are now Christ's slaves. [23]You all were bought at a great price, so do not become slaves of people. [24]Brothers and sisters, each of you should stay as you were when you were called, and stay there with God.

Questions About Getting Married

[25]Now I write about people who are not married. I have no command from the Lord about this; I give my opinion. But I can be trusted, because the Lord has shown me mercy. [26]The present time is a time of trouble, so I think it is good for you to stay the way you are. [27]If you have a wife, do not try to become free from her. If you are not married, do not try to find a wife. [28]But if you decide to marry, you have not sinned. And if a girl who has never married decides to marry, she has not sinned. But those who marry will have trouble in this life, and I want you to be free from trouble.

[29]Brothers and sisters, this is what I mean: We do not have much time left. So starting now, those who have wives should live as if they had no wives. [30]Those who are crying should live as if they were not crying. Those who are happy should live as if they were not happy. Those who buy things should live as if they own nothing.

CONTEMPORARY ENGLISH VERSION

what you were when God chose you. [21]Are you a slave? Don't let that bother you. But if you can win your freedom, you should. [22]When the Lord chooses slaves, they become his free people. And when he chooses free people, they become slaves of Christ. [23]God paid a great price for you. So don't become slaves of anyone else. [24]Stay what you were when God chose you.

Unmarried People

[25]I don't know of anything that the Lord said about people who have never been married.[c] But I will tell you what I think. And you can trust me, because the Lord has treated me with kindness. [26]We are now going through hard times, and I think it is best for you to stay as you are. [27]If you are married, stay married. If you are not married, don't try to get married. [28]It isn't wrong to marry, even if you have never been married before. But those who marry will have a lot of trouble, and I want to protect you from that.

[29]My friends, what I mean is that the Lord will soon come,[d] and it won't matter if you are married or not. [30]It will be all the same if you are crying or laughing, or if you are buying or are completely broke. [31]It won't make any

[c] **7.25** *people who have never been married*: Or "virgins." [d] **7.29** *the Lord will soon come*: Or "there's not much time left" or "the time for decision comes quickly."

NEW INTERNATIONAL VERSION

should remain in the situation which he was in when God called him. 21Were you a slave when you were called? Don't let it trouble you—although if you can gain your freedom, do so. 22For he who was a slave when he was called by the Lord is the Lord's freedman; similarly, he who was a free man when he was called is Christ's slave. 23You were bought at a price; do not become slaves of men. 24Brothers, each man, as responsible to God, should remain in the situation God called him to.

25Now about virgins: I have no command from the Lord, but I give a judgment as one who by the Lord's mercy is trustworthy. 26Because of the present crisis, I think that it is good for you to remain as you are. 27Are you married? Do not seek a divorce. Are you unmarried? Do not look for a wife. 28But if you do marry, you have not sinned; and if a virgin marries, she has not sinned. But those who marry will face many troubles in this life, and I want to spare you this.

29What I mean, brothers, is that the time is short. From now on those who have wives should live as if they had none; 30those who mourn, as if they did not; those who are happy, as if they were not; those who buy something, as if it were not theirs to keep; 31those who use the things

NEW LIVING TRANSLATION

20You should continue on as you were when God called you. 21Are you a slave? Don't let that worry you—but if you get a chance to be free, take it. 22And remember, if you were a slave when the Lord called you, the Lord has now set you free from the awful power of sin. And if you were free when the Lord called you, you are now a slave of Christ. 23God purchased you at a high price. Don't be enslaved by the world.* 24So, dear brothers and sisters,* whatever situation you were in when you became a believer, stay there in your new relationship with God.

25Now, about the young women who are not yet married. I do not have a command from the Lord for them. But the Lord in his kindness has given me wisdom that can be trusted, and I will share it with you. 26Because of the present crisis,* I think it is best to remain just as you are. 27If you have a wife, do not end the marriage. If you do not have a wife, do not get married. 28But if you do get married, it is not a sin. And if a young woman gets married, it is not a sin. However, I am trying to spare you the extra problems that come with marriage.

29Now let me say this, dear brothers and sisters: The time that remains is very short, so husbands should not let marriage be their major concern. 30Happiness or sadness or wealth should not keep anyone from doing God's work.

7:23 Greek *don't become slaves of people.* 7:24 Greek *brothers;* also in 7:29. 7:26 Or *pressures of life.*

NEW KING JAMES VERSION

remain in the same calling in which he was called. 21Were you called *while* a slave? Do not be concerned about it; but if you can be made free, rather use *it.* 22For he who is called in the Lord *while* a slave is the Lord's freedman. Likewise he who is called *while* free is Christ's slave. 23You were bought at a price; do not become slaves of men. 24Brethren, let each one remain with God in that *state* in which he was called.

To the Unmarried and Widows

25Now concerning virgins: I have no commandment from the Lord; yet I give judgment as one whom the Lord in His mercy *has made* trustworthy. 26I suppose therefore that this is good because of the present distress—that *it is* good for a man to remain as he is: 27Are you bound to a wife? Do not seek to be loosed. Are you loosed from a wife? Do not seek a wife. 28But even if you do marry, you have not sinned; and if a virgin marries, she has not sinned. Nevertheless such will have trouble in the flesh, but I would spare you.

29But this I say, brethren, the time *is* short, so that from now on even those who have wives should be as though they had none, 30those who weep as though they did not weep, those who rejoice as though they did not rejoice, those who buy as though they did not possess, 31and those

THE MESSAGE

Stay where you were when God called your name. Were you a slave? Slavery is no roadblock to obeying and believing. I don't mean you're stuck and can't leave. If you have a chance at freedom, go ahead and take it. I'm simply trying to point out that under your new Master you're going to experience a marvelous freedom you would never have dreamed of. On the other hand, if you were free when Christ called you, you'll experience a delightful "enslavement to God" you would never have dreamed of.

All of you, slave and free both, were once held hostage in a sinful society. Then a huge sum was paid out for your ransom. So please don't, out of old habit, slip back into being or doing what everyone else tells you. Friends, stay where you were called to be. God is there. Hold the high ground with him at your side.

The Master did not give explicit direction regarding virgins, but as one much experienced in the mercy of the Master and loyal to him all the way, you can trust my counsel. Because of the current pressures on us from all sides, I think it would probably be best to stay just as you are. Are you married? Stay married. Are you unmarried? Don't get married. But there's certainly no sin in getting married, whether you're a virgin or not. All I am saying is that when you marry, you take on additional stress in an already stressful time, and I want to spare you if possible.

I do want to point out, friends, that time is of the essence. There is no time to waste, so don't complicate your lives unnecessarily. Keep it simple—in marriage, grief, joy, whatever. Even in ordinary things—your daily routines of

KING JAMES VERSION

31 And they that use this world, as not abusing *it*: for the fashion of this world passeth away.

32 But I would have you without carefulness. He that is unmarried careth for the things that belong to the Lord, how he may please the Lord:

33 But he that is married careth for the things that are of the world, how he may please *his* wife.

34 There is difference *also* between a wife and a virgin. The unmarried woman careth for the things of the Lord, that she may be holy both in body and in spirit: but she that is married careth for the things of the world, how she may please *her* husband.

35 And this I speak for your own profit; not that I may cast a snare upon you, but for that which is comely, and that ye may attend upon the Lord without distraction.

36 ¶ But if any man think that he behaveth himself uncomely toward his virgin, if she pass the flower of *her* age, and need so require, let him do what he will, he sinneth not: let them marry.

37 Nevertheless he that standeth stedfast in his heart, having no necessity, but hath power over his own will, and hath so decreed in his heart that he will keep his virgin, doeth well.

38 So then he that giveth *her* in marriage doeth well; but he that giveth *her* not in marriage doeth better.

NEW AMERICAN STANDARD BIBLE

31 and those who use the world, as though they did not make full use of it; for the form of this world is passing away.

32 But I want you to be free from concern. One who is unmarried is concerned about the things of the Lord, how he may please the Lord;

33 but one who is married is concerned about the things of the world, how he may please his wife,

34 and *his interests* are divided. The woman who is unmarried, and the virgin, is concerned about the things of the Lord, that she may be holy both in body and spirit; but one who is married is concerned about the things of the world, how she may please her husband.

35 This I say for your own benefit; not to put a restraint upon you, but to promote what is appropriate and *to secure* undistracted devotion to the Lord.

36 But if any man thinks that he is acting unbecomingly toward his virgin *daughter,* if she is past her youth, and if it must be so, let him do what he wishes, he does not sin; let her marry.

37 But he who stands firm in his heart, being under no constraint, but has authority over his own will, and has decided this in his own heart, to keep his own virgin *daughter,* he will do well.

38 So then both he who gives his own virgin *daughter* in marriage does well, and he who does not give her in marriage will do better.

NEW CENTURY VERSION

31 Those who use the things of the world should live as if they were not using them, because this world in its present form will soon be gone.

32 I want you to be free from worry. A man who is not married is busy with the Lord's work, trying to please the Lord. 33 But a man who is married is busy with things of the world, trying to please his wife. 34 He must think about two things—pleasing his wife and pleasing the Lord. A woman who is not married or a girl who has never married is busy with the Lord's work. She wants to be holy in body and spirit. But a married woman is busy with things of the world, as to how she can please her husband. 35 I am saying this to help you, not to limit you. But I want you to live in the right way, to give yourselves fully to the Lord without concern for other things.

36 If a man thinks he is not doing the right thing with the girl he is engaged to, if she is almost past the best age to marry and he feels he should marry her, he should do what he wants. They should get married. It is no sin. 37 But if a man is sure in his mind that there is no need for marriage, and has his own desires under control, and has decided not to marry the one to whom he is engaged, he is doing the right thing. 38 So the man who marries his girl does right, but the man who does not marry will do better.

CONTEMPORARY ENGLISH VERSION

difference how much good you are getting from this world or how much you like it. This world as we know it is now passing away.

32 I want all of you to be free from worry. An unmarried man worries about how to please the Lord. 33 But a married man has more worries. He must worry about the things of this world, because he wants to please his wife. 34 So he is pulled in two directions. Unmarried women and women who have never been married[e] worry only about pleasing the Lord, and they keep their bodies and minds pure. But a married woman worries about the things of this world, because she wants to please her husband. 35 What I am saying is for your own good—it isn't to limit your freedom. I want to help you to live right and to love the Lord above all else.

36 But suppose you are engaged to someone old enough to be married, and you want her so much that all you can think about is getting married. Then go ahead and marry.[f] There is nothing wrong with that. 37 But it is better to have self-control and to make up your mind not to marry. 38 It is perfectly all right to marry, but it is better not to get married at all.

[e] **7.34** *women who have never been married*: Or "virgins." [f] **7.36** *But suppose you are engaged . . . go ahead and marry*: Verses 36-38 may also be translated: 36 "If you feel that you are not treating your grown daughter right by keeping her from getting married, then let her marry. You won't be doing anything wrong. 37 But it is better to have self-control and make up your mind not to let your daughter get married. 38 It is all right for you to let her marry. But it is better if you don't let her marry at all."

NEW INTERNATIONAL VERSION

of the world, as if not engrossed in them. For this world in
its present form is passing away.
[32]I would like you to be free from concern. An unmarried
man is concerned about the Lord's affairs—how he can
please the Lord. [33]But a married man is concerned about
the affairs of this world—how he can please his wife—
[34]and his interests are divided. An unmarried woman or
virgin is concerned about the Lord's affairs: Her aim is to
be devoted to the Lord in both body and spirit. But a mar-
ried woman is concerned about the affairs of this world—
how she can please her husband. [35]I am saying this for
your own good, not to restrict you, but that you may live
in a right way in undivided devotion to the Lord.
[36]If anyone thinks he is acting improperly toward the vir-
gin he is engaged to, and if she is getting along in years and
he feels he ought to marry, he should do as he wants. He is
not sinning. They should get married. [37]But the man who
has settled the matter in his own mind, who is under no
compulsion but has control over his own will, and who has
made up his mind not to marry the virgin—this man also
does the right thing. [38]So then, he who marries the virgin
does right, but he who does not marry her does even better.[b]

[b] *36–38* Or *[36]If anyone thinks he is not treating his daughter properly, and if she is getting along in years, and he feels she ought to marry, he should do as he wants. He is not sinning. He should let her get married. [37]But the man who has settled the matter in his own mind, who is under no compulsion but has control over his own will, and who has made up his mind to keep the virgin unmarried—this man also does the right thing. [38]So then, he who gives his virgin in marriage does right, but he who does not give her in marriage does even better.*

NEW LIVING TRANSLATION

[31]Those in frequent contact with the things of the world
should make good use of them without becoming attached
to them, for this world and all it contains will pass away.
[32]In everything you do, I want you to be free from the con-
cerns of this life. An unmarried man can spend his time
doing the Lord's work and thinking how to please him.
[33]But a married man can't do that so well. He has to think
about his earthly responsibilities and how to please his
wife. [34]His interests are divided. In the same way, a
woman who is no longer married or has never been mar-
ried can be more devoted to the Lord in body and in spirit,
while the married woman must be concerned about her
earthly responsibilities and how to please her husband.
[35]I am saying this for your benefit, not to place restric-
tions on you. I want you to do whatever will help you
serve the Lord best, with as few distractions as possible.
[36]But if a man thinks he ought to marry his fiancée
because he has trouble controlling his passions and time is
passing, it is all right; it is not a sin. Let them marry.
[37]But if he has decided firmly not to marry and there is no
urgency and he can control his passion, he does well not to
marry. [38]So the person who marries does well, and the per-
son who doesn't marry does even better.

NEW KING JAMES VERSION

who use this world as not misusing *it.* For the form of this
world is passing away.
[32]But I want you to be without care. He who is unmar-
ried cares for the things of the Lord—how he may please
the Lord. [33]But he who is married cares about the things of
the world—how he may please *his* wife. [34]There is[a] a dif-
ference between a wife and a virgin. The unmarried
woman cares about the things of the Lord, that she may be
holy both in body and in spirit. But she who is married
cares about the things of the world—how she may please
her husband. [35]And this I say for your own profit, not that
I may put a leash on you, but for what is proper, and that
you may serve the Lord without distraction.
[36]But if any man thinks he is behaving improperly
toward his virgin, if she is past the flower of youth, and
thus it must be, let him do what he wishes. He does not
sin; let them marry. [37]Nevertheless he who stands stead-
fast in his heart, having no necessity, but has power over
his own will, and has so determined in his heart that he
will keep his virgin,[b] does well. [38]So then he who gives
her[c] in marriage does well, but he who does not give *her* in
marriage does better.

7:34 [a] M-Text adds *also.* 7:37 [b] Or *virgin daughter*
7:38 [c] NU-Text reads *his own virgin.*

THE MESSAGE

shopping, and so on. Deal as sparingly as possible with the things the world thrusts on you. This world as you see it is on its way out.

I want you to live as free of complications as possible. When you're unmarried, you're free to concentrate on simply pleasing the Master. Marriage involves you in all the nuts and bolts of domestic life and in wanting to please your spouse, leading to so many more demands on your attention. The time and energy that married people spend on caring for and nurturing each other, the unmarried can spend in becoming whole and holy instruments of God. I'm trying to be helpful and make it as easy as possible for you, not make things harder. All I want is for you to be able to develop a way of life in which you can spend plenty of time together with the Master without a lot of distractions.

If a man has a woman friend to whom he is loyal but never intended to marry, having decided to serve God as a "single," and then changes his mind, deciding he should marry her, he should go ahead and marry. It's no sin; it's not even a "step down" from celibacy, as some say. On the other hand, if a man is comfortable in his decision for a single life in service to God and it's entirely his own conviction and not imposed on him by others, he ought to stick with it. Marriage is spiritually and morally right and not inferior to singleness in any way, although as I indicated earlier, because of the times we live in, I do have pastoral reasons for encouraging singleness.

KING JAMES VERSION

39 ¶ The wife is bound by the law as long as her husband liveth; but if her husband be dead, she is at liberty to be married to whom she will; only in the Lord.

40 But she is happier if she so abide, after my judgment: and I think also that I have the Spirit of God.

8 Now as touching things offered unto idols, we know that we all have knowledge. Knowledge puffeth up, but charity edifieth.

2 And if any man think that he knoweth any thing, he knoweth nothing yet as he ought to know.

3 But if any man love God, the same is known of him.

4 ¶ As concerning therefore the eating of those things that are offered in sacrifice unto idols, we know that an idol *is* nothing in the world, and that *there is* none other God but one.

5 For though there be that are called gods, whether in heaven or in earth, (as there be gods many, and lords many,)

6 But to us *there is but* one God, the Father, of whom *are* all things, and we in him; and one Lord Jesus Christ, by whom *are* all things, and we by him.

7 ¶ Howbeit *there is* not in every man that knowledge:

NEW AMERICAN STANDARD BIBLE

39 A wife is bound as long as her husband lives; but if her husband is dead, she is free to be married to whom she wishes, only in the Lord.

40 But in my opinion she is happier if she remains as she is; and I think that I also have the Spirit of God.

Take Care with Your Liberty

8 Now concerning things sacrificed to idols, we know that we all have knowledge. Knowledge makes arrogant, but love edifies.

2 If anyone supposes that he knows anything, he has not yet known as he ought to know;

3 but if anyone loves God, he is known by Him.

4 Therefore concerning the eating of things sacrificed to idols, we know that [l]there is no such thing as an idol in the world, and that there is no God but one.

5 For even if there are so-called gods whether in heaven or on earth, as indeed there are many gods and many lords,

6 yet for us there is *but* one God, the Father, from whom are all things and we *exist* for Him; and one Lord, Jesus Christ, by whom are all things, and we *exist* through Him.

7 However not all men have this knowledge; but some,

8:4 [l] Lit *nothing is an idol in the world;* i.e. an idol has no real existence

NEW CENTURY VERSION

[39]A woman must stay with her husband as long as he lives. But if her husband dies, she is free to marry any man she wants, but she must marry in the Lord. [40]The woman is happier if she does not marry again. This is my opinion, but I believe I also have God's Spirit.

About Food Offered to Idols

8 Now I will write about meat that is sacrificed to idols. We know that "we all have knowledge." Knowledge puffs you up with pride, but love builds up. [2]If you think you know something, you do not yet know anything as you should. [3]But if any person loves God, that person is known by God.

[4]So this is what I say about eating meat sacrificed to idols: We know that an idol is really nothing in the world, and we know there is only one God. [5]Even though there are things called gods, in heaven or on earth (and there are many "gods" and "lords"), [6]for us there is only one God—our Father. All things came from him, and we live for him. And there is only one Lord—Jesus Christ. All things were made through him, and we also were made through him.

[7]But not all people know this. Some people are still so

CONTEMPORARY ENGLISH VERSION

[39]A wife should stay married to her husband until he dies. Then she is free to marry again, but only to a man who is a follower of the Lord. [40]However, I think I am obeying God's Spirit when I say she would be happier to stay single.

Food Offered to Idols

8 In your letter you asked me about food offered to idols. All of us know something about this subject. But knowledge makes us proud of ourselves, while love makes us helpful to others. [2]In fact, people who think they know so much don't know anything at all. [3]But God has no doubts about who loves him.

[4]Even though food is offered to idols, we know that none of the idols in this world are alive. After all, there is only one God. [5]Many things in heaven and on earth are called gods and lords, but none of them really are gods or lords. [6]We have only one God, and he is the Father. He created everything, and we live for him. Jesus Christ is our only Lord. Everything was made by him, and by him life was given to us.

[7]Not everyone knows these things. In fact, many people

NEW INTERNATIONAL VERSION

[39]A woman is bound to her husband as long as he lives. But if her husband dies, she is free to marry anyone she wishes, but he must belong to the Lord. [40]In my judgment, she is happier if she stays as she is—and I think that I too have the Spirit of God.

Food Sacrificed to Idols

8 Now about food sacrificed to idols: We know that we all possess knowledge.[a] Knowledge puffs up, but love builds up. [2]The man who thinks he knows something does not yet know as he ought to know. [3]But the man who loves God is known by God.

[4]So then, about eating food sacrificed to idols: We know that an idol is nothing at all in the world and that there is no God but one. [5]For even if there are so-called gods, whether in heaven or on earth (as indeed there are many "gods" and many "lords"), [6]yet for us there is but one God, the Father, from whom all things came and for whom we live; and there is but one Lord, Jesus Christ, through whom all things came and through whom we live.

[7]But not everyone knows this. Some people are still so

[a] *1* Or *"We all possess knowledge," as you say*

NEW LIVING TRANSLATION

[39]A wife is married to her husband as long as he lives. If her husband dies, she is free to marry whomever she wishes, but this must be a marriage acceptable to the Lord.* [40]But in my opinion it will be better for her if she doesn't marry again, and I think I am giving you counsel from God's Spirit when I say this.

Food Sacrificed to Idols

8 Now let's talk about food that has been sacrificed to idols. You think that everyone should agree with your perfect knowledge. While knowledge may make us feel important, it is love that really builds up the church. [2]Anyone who claims to know all the answers doesn't really know very much. [3]But the person who loves God is the one God knows and cares for.

[4]So now, what about it? Should we eat meat that has been sacrificed to idols? Well, we all know that an idol is not really a god and that there is only one God and no other. [5]According to some people, there are many so-called gods and many lords, both in heaven and on earth. [6]But we know that there is only one God, the Father, who created everything, and we exist for him. And there is only one Lord, Jesus Christ, through whom God made everything and through whom we have been given life.

[7]However, not all Christians realize this. Some are

7:39 Or *but only to a Christian;* Greek reads *but only in the Lord.*

NEW KING JAMES VERSION

[39]A wife is bound by law as long as her husband lives; but if her husband dies, she is at liberty to be married to whom she wishes, only in the Lord. [40]But she is happier if she remains as she is, according to my judgment—and I think I also have the Spirit of God.

Be Sensitive to Conscience

8 Now concerning things offered to idols: We know that we all have knowledge. Knowledge puffs up, but love edifies. [2]And if anyone thinks that he knows anything, he knows nothing yet as he ought to know. [3]But if anyone loves God, this one is known by Him.

[4]Therefore concerning the eating of things offered to idols, we know that an idol *is* nothing in the world, and that *there is* no other God but one. [5]For even if there are so-called gods, whether in heaven or on earth (as there are many gods and many lords), [6]yet for us *there is* one God, the Father, of whom *are* all things, and we for Him; and one Lord Jesus Christ, through whom *are* all things, and through whom we *live.*

[7]However, *there is* not in everyone that knowledge; for

THE MESSAGE

A wife must stay with her husband as long as he lives. If he dies, she is free to marry anyone she chooses. She will, of course, want to marry a believer and have the blessing of the Master. By now you know that I think she'll be better off staying single. The Master, in my opinion, thinks so, too.

Freedom With Responsibility

8 The question keeps coming up regarding meat that has been offered up to an idol: Should you attend meals where such meat is served, or not? We sometimes tend to think we know all we need to know to answer these kinds of questions—*but* sometimes our humble hearts can help us more than our proud minds. We never really know enough until we recognize that God alone knows it all.

Some people say, quite rightly, that idols have no actual existence, that there's nothing to them, that there is no God other than our one God, that no matter how many of these so-called gods are named and worshiped they still don't add up to anything but a tall story. They say—again, quite rightly—that there is only one God the Father, that everything comes from him, and that he wants us to live for him. Also, they say that there is only one Master—Jesus the Messiah—and that everything is for his sake, including us. Yes. It's true.

In strict logic, then, nothing happened to the meat when it was offered up to an idol. It's just like any other meat. I know that, and you know that. But knowing isn't everything. If it becomes everything, some people end up as know-it-alls who treat others as know-nothings. Real knowledge isn't that insensitive.

KING JAMES VERSION

for some with conscience of the idol unto this hour eat *it* as a thing offered unto an idol; and their conscience being weak is defiled.

8 But meat commendeth us not to God: for neither, if we eat, are we the better; neither, if we eat not, are we the worse.

9 But take heed lest by any means this liberty of yours become a stumblingblock to them that are weak.

10 For if any man see thee which hast knowledge sit at meat in the idol's temple, shall not the conscience of him which is weak be emboldened to eat those things which are offered to idols;

11 And through thy knowledge shall the weak brother perish, for whom Christ died?

12 But when ye sin so against the brethren, and wound their weak conscience, ye sin against Christ.

13 Wherefore, if meat make my brother to offend, I will eat no flesh while the world standeth, lest I make my brother to offend.

NEW AMERICAN STANDARD BIBLE

being accustomed to the idol until now, eat *food* as if it were sacrificed to an idol; and their conscience being weak is defiled.

8 But food will not commend us to God; we are neither the worse if we do not eat, nor the better if we do eat.

9 But take care that this liberty of yours does not somehow become a stumbling block to the weak.

10 For if someone sees you, who have knowledge, dining in an idol's temple, will not his conscience, if he is weak, be strengthened to eat things sacrificed to idols?

11 For through your knowledge he who is weak is ruined, the brother for whose sake Christ died.

12 And so, by sinning against the brethren and wounding their conscience when it is weak, you sin against Christ.

13 Therefore, if food causes my brother to stumble, I will never eat meat again, so that I will not cause my brother to stumble.

NEW CENTURY VERSION

used to idols that when they eat meat, they still think of it
as being sacrificed to an idol. Because their conscience is
weak, when they eat it, they feel guilty. [8]But food will not
bring us closer to God. Refusing to eat does not make us
less pleasing to God, and eating does not make us better in
God's sight.

[9]But be careful that your freedom does not cause those
who are weak in faith to fall into sin. [10]You have "knowl-
edge," so you eat in an idol's temple.[a] But someone who is
weak in faith might see you eating there and be encour-
aged to eat meat sacrificed to idols while thinking it is
wrong to do so. [11]This weak believer for whom Christ died
is ruined because of your "knowledge." [12]When you sin
against your brothers and sisters in Christ like this and
cause them to do what they feel is wrong, you are also sin-
ning against Christ. [13]So if the food I eat causes them to
fall into sin, I will never eat meat again so that I will not
cause any of them to sin.

8:10 [a] **idol's temple** Building where a god is worshiped.

CONTEMPORARY ENGLISH VERSION

have grown up with the belief that idols have life in them.
So when they eat meat offered to idols, they are bothered
by a weak conscience. [8]But food doesn't bring us any clos-
er to God. We are no worse off if we don't eat, and we are
no better off if we do.

[9]Don't cause problems for someone with a weak con-
science, just because you have the right to eat anything.
[10]You know all this, and so it doesn't bother you to eat in
the temple of an idol. But suppose a person with a weak
conscience sees you and decides to eat food that has been
offered to idols. [11]Then what you know has destroyed
someone Christ died for. [12]When you sin by hurting a fol-
lower with a weak conscience, you sin against Christ. [13]So
if I hurt one of the Lord's followers by what I eat, I will
never eat meat as long as I live.

NEW INTERNATIONAL VERSION

accustomed to idols that when they eat such food they think of it as having been sacrificed to an idol, and since their conscience is weak, it is defiled. 8But food does not bring us near to God; we are no worse if we do not eat, and no better if we do.

9Be careful, however, that the exercise of your freedom does not become a stumbling block to the weak. 10For if anyone with a weak conscience sees you who have this knowledge eating in an idol's temple, won't he be emboldened to eat what has been sacrificed to idols? 11So this weak brother, for whom Christ died, is destroyed by your knowledge. 12When you sin against your brothers in this way and wound their weak conscience, you sin against Christ. 13Therefore, if what I eat causes my brother to fall into sin, I will never eat meat again, so that I will not cause him to fall.

NEW LIVING TRANSLATION

accustomed to thinking of idols as being real, so when they eat food that has been offered to idols, they think of it as the worship of real gods, and their weak consciences are violated. 8It's true that we can't win God's approval by what we eat. We don't miss out on anything if we don't eat it, and we don't gain anything if we do. 9But you must be careful with this freedom of yours. Do not cause a brother or sister with a weaker conscience to stumble.

10You see, this is what can happen: Weak Christians who think it is wrong to eat this food will see you eating in the temple of an idol. You know there's nothing wrong with it, but they will be encouraged to violate their conscience by eating food that has been dedicated to the idol. 11So because of your superior knowledge, a weak Christian,* for whom Christ died, will be destroyed. 12And you are sinning against Christ when you sin against other Christians* by encouraging them to do something they believe is wrong. 13If what I eat is going to make another Christian sin, I will never eat meat again as long as I live—for I don't want to make another Christian stumble.

8:11 Greek *brother;* also in 8:13. 8:12 Greek *brothers.*

NEW KING JAMES VERSION

some, with consciousness of the idol, until now eat *it* as a thing offered to an idol; and their conscience, being weak, is defiled. 8But food does not commend us to God; for neither if we eat are we the better, nor if we do not eat are we the worse.

9But beware lest somehow this liberty of yours become a stumbling block to those who are weak. 10For if anyone sees you who have knowledge eating in an idol's temple, will not the conscience of him who is weak be emboldened to eat those things offered to idols? 11And because of your knowledge shall the weak brother perish, for whom Christ died? 12But when you thus sin against the brethren, and wound their weak conscience, you sin against Christ. 13Therefore, if food makes my brother stumble, I will never again eat meat, lest I make my brother stumble.

THE MESSAGE

We need to be sensitive to the fact that we're not all at the same level of understanding in this. Some of you have spent your entire lives eating "idol meat," and are sure that there's something bad in the meat that then becomes something bad inside of you. An imagination and conscience shaped under those conditions isn't going to change overnight.

But fortunately God doesn't grade us on our diet. We're neither commended when we clean our plate nor reprimanded when we just can't stomach it. But God *does* care when you use your freedom carelessly in a way that leads a Christian still vulnerable to those old associations to be thrown off track.

For instance, say you flaunt your freedom by going to a banquet thrown in honor of idols, where the main course is meat sacrificed to idols. Isn't there great danger if someone still struggling over this issue, someone who looks up to you as knowledgeable and mature, sees you go into that banquet? The danger is that he will become terribly confused—maybe even to the point of getting mixed up himself in what his conscience tells him is wrong.

Christ gave up his life for that person. Wouldn't you at least be willing to give up going to dinner for him—because, as you say, it doesn't really make any difference? But it *does* make a difference if you hurt your friend terribly, risking his eternal ruin! When you hurt your friend, you hurt Christ. A free meal here and there isn't worth it at the cost of even one of these "weak ones." So, never go to these idol-tainted meals if there's any chance it will trip up one of your brothers or sisters.

KING JAMES VERSION

9 Am I not an apostle? am I not free? have I not seen Jesus Christ our Lord? are not ye my work in the Lord?

2 If I be not an apostle unto others, yet doubtless I am to you: for the seal of mine apostleship are ye in the Lord.

3 ¶ Mine answer to them that do examine me is this,

4 Have we not power to eat and to drink?

5 Have we not power to lead about a sister, a wife, as well as other apostles, and *as* the brethren of the Lord, and Cephas?

6 Or I only and Barnabas, have not we power to forbear working?

7 Who goeth a warfare any time at his own charges? who planteth a vineyard, and eateth not of the fruit thereof? or who feedeth a flock, and eateth not of the milk of the flock?

8 Say I these things as a man? or saith not the law the same also?

9 For it is written in the law of Moses, Thou shalt not muzzle the mouth of the ox that treadeth out the corn. Doth God take care for oxen?

10 Or saith he *it* altogether for our sakes? For our sakes, no doubt, *this* is written: that he that ploweth should plow in hope; and that he that thresheth in hope should be partaker of his hope.

11 If we have sown unto you spiritual things, *is it* a great thing if we shall reap your carnal things?

NEW AMERICAN STANDARD BIBLE

Paul's Use of Liberty

9 Am I not free? Am I not an apostle? Have I not seen Jesus our Lord? Are you not my work in the Lord?

2 If to others I am not an apostle, at least I am to you; for you are the seal of my apostleship in the Lord.

3 My defense to those who examine me is this:

4 Do we not have a right to eat and drink?

5 Do we not have a right to take along a believing wife, even as the rest of the apostles and the brothers of the Lord and Cephas?

6 Or do only Barnabas and I not have a right to refrain from working?

7 Who at any time serves as a soldier at his own expense? Who plants a vineyard and does not eat the fruit of it? Or who tends a flock and does not use the milk of the flock?

8 I am not speaking these things according to human judgment, am I? Or does not the Law also say these things?

9 For it is written in the Law of Moses, "YOU SHALL NOT MUZZLE THE OX WHILE HE IS THRESHING." God is not concerned about oxen, is He?

10 Or is He speaking altogether for our sake? Yes, for our sake it was written, because the plowman ought to plow in hope, and the thresher *to thresh* in hope of sharing *the crops.*

11 If we sowed spiritual things in you, is it too much if we reap material things from you?

NEW CENTURY VERSION

Paul Is like the Other Apostles

9 I am a free man. I am an apostle. I have seen Jesus our Lord. You people are all an example of my work in the Lord. 2If others do not accept me as an apostle, surely you do, because you are proof that I am an apostle in the Lord.

3This is the answer I give people who want to judge me: 4Do we not have the right to eat and drink? 5Do we not have the right to bring a believing wife with us when we travel as do the other apostles and the Lord's brothers and Peter? 6Are Barnabas and I the only ones who must work to earn our living? 7No soldier ever serves in the army and pays his own salary. No one ever plants a vineyard without eating some of the grapes. No person takes care of a flock without drinking some of the milk.

8I do not say this by human authority; God's law also says the same thing. 9It is written in the law of Moses: "When an ox is working in the grain, do not cover its mouth to keep it from eating."[a] When God said this, was he thinking only about oxen? No. 10He was really talking about us. Yes, that Scripture was written for us, because it goes on to say: "The one who plows and the one who works in the grain should hope to get some of the grain for their work." 11Since we planted spiritual seed among you, is it too much if we should harvest from you some things

9:9 [a] **"When an ox…eating."** Quotation from Deuteronomy 25:4.

CONTEMPORARY ENGLISH VERSION

The Rights of an Apostle

9 I am free. I am an apostle. I have seen the Lord Jesus and have led you to have faith in him. 2Others may think that I am not an apostle, but you are proof that I am an apostle to you.

3When people question me, I tell them 4that Barnabas and I have the right to our food and drink. 5We each have the right to marry one of the Lord's followers and to take her along with us, just as the other apostles and the Lord's brothers and Peter[a] do. 6Are we the only ones who have to support ourselves by working at another job? 7Do soldiers pay their own salaries? Don't people who raise grapes eat some of what they grow? Don't shepherds get milk from their own goats?

8-9I am not saying this on my own authority. The Law of Moses tells us not to muzzle an ox when it is grinding grain. But was God concerned only about an ox? 10No, he wasn't! He was talking about us. This was written in the Scriptures so that all who plow and all who grind the grain will look forward to sharing in the harvest.

11When we told the message to you, it was like planting spiritual seed. So we have the right to accept material things as our harvest from you. 12If others have the right

[a] **9.5** *Peter*: See the note at 1.12.

NEW INTERNATIONAL VERSION

The Rights of an Apostle

9 Am I not free? Am I not an apostle? Have I not seen Jesus our Lord? Are you not the result of my work in the Lord? 2 Even though I may not be an apostle to others, surely I am to you! For you are the seal of my apostleship in the Lord.

3 This is my defense to those who sit in judgment on me. 4 Don't we have the right to food and drink? 5 Don't we have the right to take a believing wife along with us, as do the other apostles and the Lord's brothers and Cephas[a]? 6 Or is it only I and Barnabas who must work for a living?

7 Who serves as a soldier at his own expense? Who plants a vineyard and does not eat of its grapes? Who tends a flock and does not drink of the milk? 8 Do I say this merely from a human point of view? Doesn't the Law say the same thing? 9 For it is written in the Law of Moses: "Do not muzzle an ox while it is treading out the grain."[b] Is it about oxen that God is concerned? 10 Surely he says this for us, doesn't he? Yes, this was written for us, because when the plowman plows and the thresher threshes, they ought to do so in the hope of sharing in the harvest. 11 If we have sown spiritual seed among you, is it too much if we reap a material harvest from you? 12 If others have this

[a] *5* That is, Peter [b] *9* Deut. 25:4

NEW LIVING TRANSLATION

Paul Gives Up His Rights

9 Do I not have as much freedom as anyone else?* Am I not an apostle? Haven't I seen Jesus our Lord with my own eyes? Isn't it because of my hard work that you are in the Lord? 2 Even if others think I am not an apostle, I certainly am to you, for you are living proof that I am the Lord's apostle.

3 This is my answer to those who question my authority as an apostle.* 4 Don't we have the right to live in your homes and share your meals? 5 Don't we have the right to bring a Christian wife* along with us as the other disciples and the Lord's brothers and Peter* do? 6 Or is it only Barnabas and I who have to work to support ourselves? 7 What soldier has to pay his own expenses? And have you ever heard of a farmer who harvests his crop and doesn't have the right to eat some of it? What shepherd takes care of a flock of sheep and isn't allowed to drink some of the milk? 8 And this isn't merely human opinion. Doesn't God's law say the same thing? 9 For the law of Moses says, "Do not keep an ox from eating as it treads out the grain."* Do you suppose God was thinking only about oxen when he said this? 10 Wasn't he also speaking to us? Of course he was. Just as farm workers who plow fields and thresh the grain expect a share of the harvest, Christian workers should be paid by those they serve.

11 We have planted good spiritual seed among you. Is it too much to ask, in return, for mere food and clothing? 12 If

9:1 Greek *Am I not free?* **9:3** Greek *those who examine me.* **9:5a** Greek *a sister, a wife.* **9:5b** Greek *Cephas.* **9:9** Deut 25:4.

NEW KING JAMES VERSION

A Pattern of Self-Denial

9 Am I not an apostle? Am I not free? Have I not seen Jesus Christ our Lord? Are you not my work in the Lord? 2 If I am not an apostle to others, yet doubtless I am to you. For you are the seal of my apostleship in the Lord.

3 My defense to those who examine me is this: 4 Do we have no right to eat and drink? 5 Do we have no right to take along a believing wife, as *do* also the other apostles, the brothers of the Lord, and Cephas? 6 Or *is it* only Barnabas and I *who* have no right to refrain from working? 7 Who ever goes to war at his own expense? Who plants a vineyard and does not eat of its fruit? Or who tends a flock and does not drink of the milk of the flock?

8 Do I say these things as a *mere* man? Or does not the law say the same also? 9 For it is written in the law of Moses, *"You shall not muzzle an ox while it treads out the grain."*[a] Is it oxen God is concerned about? 10 Or does He say *it* altogether for our sakes? For our sakes, no doubt, *this* is written, that he who plows should plow in hope, and he who threshes in hope should be partaker of his hope. 11 If we have sown spiritual things for you, *is it* a great thing if we reap your material things? 12 If others

9:9 [a] Deuteronomy 25:4

THE MESSAGE

✢

9 And don't tell me that I have no authority to write like this. I'm perfectly free to do this—isn't that obvious? Haven't I been given a job to do? Wasn't I commissioned to this work in a face-to-face meeting with Jesus, our Master? Aren't you yourselves proof of the good work that I've done for the Master? Even if no one else admits the authority of my commission, *you* can't deny it. Why, my work with you is living proof of my authority!

I'm not shy in standing up to my critics. We who are on missionary assignments for God have a right to decent accommodations, and we have a right to support for us and our families. You don't seem to have raised questions with the other apostles and our Master's brothers and Peter in these matters. So, why me? Is it just Barnabas and I who have to go it alone and pay our own way? Are soldiers self-employed? Are gardeners forbidden to eat vegetables from their own gardens? Don't milkmaids get to drink their fill from the pail?

I'm not just sounding off because I'm irritated. This is all written in the scriptural law. Moses wrote, "Don't muzzle an ox to keep it from eating the grain when it's threshing." Do you think Moses' primary concern was the care of farm animals? Don't you think his concern extends to us? Of course. Farmers plow and thresh expecting something when the crop comes in. So if we have planted spiritual seed among you, is it out of line to expect a meal or two

KING JAMES VERSION

12 If others be partakers of *this* power over you, *are* not we rather? Nevertheless we have not used this power; but suffer all things, lest we should hinder the gospel of Christ.

13 Do ye not know that they which minister about holy things live *of the things* of the temple? and they which wait at the altar are partakers with the altar?

14 Even so hath the Lord ordained that they which preach the gospel should live of the gospel.

15 ¶ But I have used none of these things: neither have I written these things, that it should be so done unto me: for *it were* better for me to die, than that any man should make my glorying void.

16 For though I preach the gospel, I have nothing to glory of: for necessity is laid upon me; yea, woe is unto me, if I preach not the gospel!

17 For if I do this thing willingly, I have a reward: but if against my will, a dispensation *of the gospel* is committed unto me.

18 What is my reward then? *Verily* that, when I preach the gospel, I may make the gospel of Christ without charge, that I abuse not my power in the gospel.

19 ¶ For though I be free from all *men*, yet have I made myself servant unto all, that I might gain the more.

NEW AMERICAN STANDARD BIBLE

12 If others share the right over you, do we not more? Nevertheless, we did not use this right, but we endure all things so that we will cause no hindrance to the gospel of Christ.

13 Do you not know that those who perform sacred services eat the *food* of the temple, *and* those who attend regularly to the altar have their share from the altar?

14 So also the Lord directed those who proclaim the gospel to get their living from the gospel.

15 But I have used none of these things. And I am not writing these things so that it will be done so in my case; for it would be better for me to die than have any man make my boast an empty one.

16 For if I preach the gospel, I have nothing to boast of, for I am under compulsion; for woe is me if I do not preach the gospel.

17 For if I do this voluntarily, I have a reward; but if against my will, I have a stewardship entrusted to me.

18 What then is my reward? That, when I preach the gospel, I may offer the gospel without charge, so as not to make full use of my right in the gospel.

19 For though I am free from all *men,* I have made myself a slave to all, so that I may win more.

NEW CENTURY VERSION

for this life? [12]If others have the right to get something
from you, surely we have this right, too. But we do not use
it. No, we put up with everything ourselves so that we will
not keep anyone from believing the Good News of Christ.
[13]Surely you know that those who work at the Temple get
their food from the Temple, and those who serve at the
altar get part of what is offered at the altar. [14]In the same
way, the Lord has commanded that those who tell the
Good News should get their living from this work.
[15]But I have not used any of these rights. And I am not
writing this now to get anything from you. I would rather
die than to have my reason for bragging taken away.
[16]Telling the Good News does not give me any reason for
bragging. Telling the Good News is my duty—something I
must do. And how terrible it will be for me if I do not tell
the Good News. [17]If I preach because it is my own choice, I
have a reward. But if I preach and it is not my choice to do
so, I am only doing the duty that was given to me. [18]So
what reward do I get? This is my reward: that when I tell
the Good News I can offer it freely. I do not use my full
rights in my work of preaching the Good News.
[19]I am free and belong to no one. But I make myself a
slave to all people to win as many as I can. [20]To the Jews I

CONTEMPORARY ENGLISH VERSION

to do this, we have an even greater right. But we haven't
used this right of ours. We are willing to put up with anything to keep from causing trouble for the message about
Christ.
[13]Don't you know that people who work in the temple
make their living from what is brought to the temple?
Don't you know that a person who serves at the altar is
given part of what is offered? [14]In the same way, the Lord
wants everyone who preaches the good news to make a
living from preaching this message.
[15]But I have never used these privileges of mine, and I
am not writing this because I want to start now. I would
rather die than have someone rob me of the right to take
pride in this. [16]I don't have any reason to brag about
preaching the good news. Preaching is something God told
me to do, and if I don't do it, I am doomed. [17]If I preach
because I want to, I will be paid. But even if I don't want
to, it is still something God has sent me to do. [18]What pay
am I given? It is the chance to preach the good news free
of charge and not to use the privileges that are mine
because I am a preacher.
[19]I am not anyone's slave. But I have become a slave to
everyone, so that I can win as many people as possible.

NEW INTERNATIONAL VERSION

right of support from you, shouldn't we have it all the more?

But we did not use this right. On the contrary, we put up with anything rather than hinder the gospel of Christ. [13]Don't you know that those who work in the temple get their food from the temple, and those who serve at the altar share in what is offered on the altar? [14]In the same way, the Lord has commanded that those who preach the gospel should receive their living from the gospel.

[15]But I have not used any of these rights. And I am not writing this in the hope that you will do such things for me. I would rather die than have anyone deprive me of this boast. [16]Yet when I preach the gospel, I cannot boast, for I am compelled to preach. Woe to me if I do not preach the gospel! [17]If I preach voluntarily, I have a reward; if not voluntarily, I am simply discharging the trust committed to me. [18]What then is my reward? Just this: that in preaching the gospel I may offer it free of charge, and so not make use of my rights in preaching it.

[19]Though I am free and belong to no man, I make myself a slave to everyone, to win as many as possible. [20]To the

NEW LIVING TRANSLATION

you support others who preach to you, shouldn't we have an even greater right to be supported? Yet we have never used this right. We would rather put up with anything than put an obstacle in the way of the Good News about Christ.

[13]Don't you know that those who work in the Temple get their meals from the food brought to the Temple as offerings? And those who serve at the altar get a share of the sacrificial offerings. [14]In the same way, the Lord gave orders that those who preach the Good News should be supported by those who benefit from it. [15]Yet I have never used any of these rights. And I am not writing this to suggest that I would like to start now. In fact, I would rather die than lose my distinction of preaching without charge. [16]For preaching the Good News is not something I can boast about. I am compelled by God to do it. How terrible for me if I didn't do it!

[17]If I were doing this of my own free will, then I would deserve payment. But God has chosen me and given me this sacred trust, and I have no choice. [18]What then is my pay? It is the satisfaction I get from preaching the Good News without expense to anyone, never demanding my rights as a preacher.

[19]This means I am not bound to obey people just because they pay me, yet I have become a servant of everyone so that I can bring them to Christ. [20]When I am with the Jews, I

NEW KING JAMES VERSION

are partakers of *this* right over you, *are* we not even more?

Nevertheless we have not used this right, but endure all things lest we hinder the gospel of Christ. [13]Do you not know that those who minister the holy things eat *of the things* of the temple, and those who serve at the altar partake of *the offerings of* the altar? [14]Even so the Lord has commanded that those who preach the gospel should live from the gospel.

[15]But I have used none of these things, nor have I written these things that it should be done so to me; for it *would be* better for me to die than that anyone should make my boasting void. [16]For if I preach the gospel, I have nothing to boast of, for necessity is laid upon me; yes, woe is me if I do not preach the gospel! [17]For if I do this willingly, I have a reward; but if against my will, I have been entrusted with a stewardship. [18]What is my reward then? That when I preach the gospel, I may present the gospel of Christ[b] without charge, that I may not abuse my authority in the gospel.

Serving All Men

[19]For though I am free from all *men,* I have made myself a servant to all, that I might win the more; [20]and to the

9:18 [b] NU-Text omits *of Christ.*

THE MESSAGE

from you? Others demand plenty from you in these ways. Don't we who have never demanded deserve even more?

But we're not going to start demanding now what we've always had a perfect right to. Our decision all along has been to put up with anything rather than to get in the way or detract from the Message of Christ. All I'm concerned with right now is that you not use our decision to take advantage of others, depriving them of what is rightly theirs. You know, don't you, that it's always been taken for granted that those who work in the Temple live off the proceeds of the Temple, and that those who offer sacrifices at the altar eat their meals from what has been sacrificed? Along the same lines, the Master directed that those who spread the Message be supported by those who believe the Message.

Still, I want it made clear that I've never gotten anything out of this for myself, and that I'm not writing now to get something. I'd rather die than give anyone ammunition to discredit me or impugn my motives. If I proclaim the Message, it's not to get something out of it for myself. I'm *compelled* to do it, and doomed if I don't! If this was my own idea of just another way to make a living, I'd expect some pay. But since it's *not* my idea but something solemnly entrusted to me, why would I expect to get paid? So am I getting anything out of it? Yes, as a matter of fact: the pleasure of proclaiming the Message at no cost to you. You don't even have to pay my expenses!

Even though I am free of the demands and expectations of everyone, I have voluntarily become a servant to any and all in order to reach a wide range of people: religious,

KING JAMES VERSION

20 And unto the Jews I became as a Jew, that I might gain the Jews; to them that are under the law, as under the law, that I might gain them that are under the law;

21 To them that are without law, as without law, (being not without law to God, but under the law to Christ,) that I might gain them that are without law.

22 To the weak became I as weak, that I might gain the weak: I am made all things to all *men*, that I might by all means save some.

23 And this I do for the gospel's sake, that I might be partaker thereof with *you*.

24 ¶ Know ye not that they which run in a race run all, but one receiveth the prize? So run, that ye may obtain.

25 And every man that striveth for the mastery is temperate in all things. Now they *do it* to obtain a corruptible crown; but we an incorruptible.

26 I therefore so run, not as uncertainly; so fight I, not as one that beateth the air:

27 But I keep under my body, and bring *it* into subjection: lest that by any means, when I have preached to others, I myself should be a castaway.

10 Moreover, brethren, I would not that ye should be ignorant, how that all our fathers were under the cloud, and all passed through the sea;

NEW AMERICAN STANDARD BIBLE

20 To the Jews I became as a Jew, so that I might win Jews; to those who are under the Law, as under the Law though not being myself under the Law, so that I might win those who are under the Law;

21 to those who are without law, as without law, though not being without the law of God but under the law of Christ, so that I might win those who are without law.

22 To the weak I became weak, that I might win the weak; I have become all things to all men, so that I may by all means save some.

23 I do all things for the sake of the gospel, so that I may become a fellow partaker of it.

24 Do you not know that those who run in a race all run, but *only* one receives the prize? Run in such a way that you may win.

25 Everyone who competes in the games exercises self-control in all things. They then *do it* to receive a perishable wreath, but we an imperishable.

26 Therefore I run in such a way, as not without aim; I box in such a way, as not beating the air;

27 but I discipline my body and make it my slave, so that, after I have preached to others, I myself will not be disqualified.

Avoid Israel's Mistakes

10 For I do not want you to be unaware, brethren, that our fathers were all under the cloud and all passed through the sea;

NEW CENTURY VERSION

became like a Jew to win the Jews. I myself am not ruled by the law. But to those who are ruled by the law I became like a person who is ruled by the law. I did this to win those who are ruled by the law. 21To those who are without the law I became like a person who is without the law. I did this to win those people who are without the law. (But really, I am not without God's law—I am ruled by Christ's law.) 22To those who are weak, I became weak so I could win the weak. I have become all things to all people so I could save some of them in any way possible. 23I do all this because of the Good News and so I can share in its blessings.

24You know that in a race all the runners run, but only one gets the prize. So run to win! 25All those who compete in the games use self-control so they can win a crown. That crown is an earthly thing that lasts only a short time, but our crown will never be destroyed. 26So I do not run without a goal. I fight like a boxer who is hitting something—not just the air. 27I treat my body hard and make it my slave so that I myself will not be disqualified after I have preached to others.

Warnings from Israel's Past

10 Brothers and sisters, I want you to know what happened to our ancestors who followed Moses. They were all under the cloud and all went through the

CONTEMPORARY ENGLISH VERSION

20When I am with the Jews, I live like a Jew to win Jews. They are ruled by the Law of Moses, and I am not. But I live by the Law to win them. 21And when I am with people who are not ruled by the Law, I forget about the Law to win them. Of course, I never really forget about the law of God. In fact, I am ruled by the law of Christ. 22When I am with people whose faith is weak, I live as they do to win them. I do everything I can to win everyone I possibly can. 23I do all this for the good news, because I want to share in its blessings.

A Race and a Fight

24You know that many runners enter a race, and only one of them wins the prize. So run to win! 25Athletes work hard to win a crown that cannot last, but we do it for a crown that will last forever. 26I don't run without a goal. And I don't box by beating my fists in the air. 27I keep my body under control and make it my slave, so I won't lose out after telling the good news to others.

Don't Worship Idols

10 Friends, I want to remind you that all of our ancestors walked under the cloud and went through

NEW INTERNATIONAL VERSION

Jews I became like a Jew, to win the Jews. To those under the law I became like one under the law (though I myself am not under the law), so as to win those under the law. [21]To those not having the law I became like one not having the law (though I am not free from God's law but am under Christ's law), so as to win those not having the law. [22]To the weak I became weak, to win the weak. I have become all things to all men so that by all possible means I might save some. [23]I do all this for the sake of the gospel, that I may share in its blessings.

[24]Do you not know that in a race all the runners run, but only one gets the prize? Run in such a way as to get the prize. [25]Everyone who competes in the games goes into strict training. They do it to get a crown that will not last; but we do it to get a crown that will last forever. [26]Therefore I do not run like a man running aimlessly; I do not fight like a man beating the air. [27]No, I beat my body and make it my slave so that after I have preached to others, I myself will not be disqualified for the prize.

Warnings From Israel's History

10 For I do not want you to be ignorant of the fact, brothers, that our forefathers were all under the cloud and that they all passed through the sea. [2]They were

NEW LIVING TRANSLATION

become one of them so that I can bring them to Christ. When I am with those who follow the Jewish laws, I do the same, even though I am not subject to the law, so that I can bring them to Christ. [21]When I am with the Gentiles who do not have the Jewish law,* I fit in with them as much as I can. In this way, I gain their confidence and bring them to Christ. But I do not discard the law of God; I obey the law of Christ.

[22]When I am with those who are oppressed, I share their oppression so that I might bring them to Christ. Yes, I try to find common ground with everyone so that I might bring them to Christ. [23]I do all this to spread the Good News, and in doing so I enjoy its blessings.

[24]Remember that in a race everyone runs, but only one person gets the prize. You also must run in such a way that you will win. [25]All athletes practice strict self-control. They do it to win a prize that will fade away, but we do it for an eternal prize. [26]So I run straight to the goal with purpose in every step. I am not like a boxer who misses his punches.* [27]I discipline my body like an athlete, training it to do what it should. Otherwise, I fear that after preaching to others I myself might be disqualified.

Warnings against Idolatry

10 I don't want you to forget, dear brothers and sisters,* what happened to our ancestors in the wilderness long ago. God guided all of them by sending a cloud that moved along ahead of them, and he brought them all safely

9:21 Greek *those without the law.* **9:26** Or *I am not just shadowboxing.* **10:1** Greek *brothers.*

NEW KING JAMES VERSION

Jews I became as a Jew, that I might win Jews; to those *who are* under the law, as under the law,[c] that I might win those *who are* under the law; [21]to those *who are* without law, as without law (not being without law toward God,[d] but under law toward Christ[e]), that I might win those *who are* without law; [22]to the weak I became as[f] weak, that I might win the weak. I have become all things to all *men,* that I might by all means save some. [23]Now this I do for the gospel's sake, that I may be partaker of it with *you.*

Striving for a Crown

[24]Do you not know that those who run in a race all run, but one receives the prize? Run in such a way that you may obtain *it.* [25]And everyone who competes *for the prize* is temperate in all things. Now they *do it* to obtain a perishable crown, but we *for* an imperishable *crown.* [26]Therefore I run thus: not with uncertainty. Thus I fight: not as *one who* beats the air. [27]But I discipline my body and bring *it* into subjection, lest, when I have preached to others, I myself should become disqualified.

Old Testament Examples

10 Moreover, brethren, I do not want you to be unaware that all our fathers were under the cloud,

9:20 [c] NU-Text adds *though not being myself under the law.*
9:21 [d] NU-Text reads *God's law.* [e] NU-Text reads *Christ's law.*
9:22 [f] NU-Text omits *as.*

THE MESSAGE

nonreligious, meticulous moralists, loose-living immoralists, the defeated, the demoralized—whoever. I didn't take on their way of life. I kept my bearings in Christ—but I entered their world and tried to experience things from their point of view. I've become just about every sort of servant there is in my attempts to lead those I meet into a God-saved life. I did all this because of the Message. I didn't just want to talk about it; I wanted to be *in* on it!

You've all been to the stadium and seen the athletes race. Everyone runs; one wins. Run to win. All good athletes train hard. They do it for a gold medal that tarnishes and fades. You're after one that's gold eternally.

I don't know about you, but I'm running hard for the finish line. I'm giving it everything I've got. No sloppy living for me! I'm staying alert and in top condition. I'm not going to get caught napping, telling everyone else all about it and then missing out myself.

10 Remember our history, friends, and be warned. All our ancestors were led by the providential Cloud and taken miraculously through the Sea. They went

KING JAMES VERSION

2 And were all baptized unto Moses in the cloud and in the sea;

3 And did all eat the same spiritual meat;

4 And did all drink the same spiritual drink: for they drank of that spiritual Rock that followed them: and that Rock was Christ.

5 But with many of them God was not well pleased: for they were overthrown in the wilderness.

6 ¶ Now these things were our examples, to the intent we should not lust after evil things, as they also lusted.

7 Neither be ye idolaters, as *were* some of them; as it is written, The people sat down to eat and drink, and rose up to play.

8 Neither let us commit fornication, as some of them committed, and fell in one day three and twenty thousand.

9 Neither let us tempt Christ, as some of them also tempted, and were destroyed of serpents.

10 Neither murmur ye, as some of them also murmured, and were destroyed of the destroyer.

11 Now all these things happened unto them for ensamples: and they are written for our admonition, upon whom the ends of the world are come.

12 Wherefore let him that thinketh he standeth take heed lest he fall.

13 There hath no temptation taken you but such as is

NEW AMERICAN STANDARD BIBLE

2 and all were baptized into Moses in the cloud and in the sea;

3 and all ate the same spiritual food;

4 and all drank the same spiritual drink, for they were drinking from a spiritual rock which followed them; and the rock was Christ.

5 Nevertheless, with most of them God was not well-pleased; for they were laid low in the wilderness.

6 Now these things happened as examples for us, so that we would not crave evil things as they also craved.

7 Do not be idolaters, as some of them were; as it is written, "THE PEOPLE SAT DOWN TO EAT AND DRINK, AND STOOD UP TO PLAY."

8 Nor let us act immorally, as some of them did, and twenty-three thousand fell in one day.

9 Nor let us try the Lord, as some of them did, and were destroyed by the serpents.

10 Nor grumble, as some of them did, and were destroyed by the destroyer.

11 Now these things happened to them as an example, and they were written for our instruction, upon whom the ends of the ages have come.

12 Therefore let him who thinks he stands take heed that he does not fall.

13 No temptation has overtaken you but such as is

NEW CENTURY VERSION

sea. 2They were all baptized as followers of Moses in the
cloud and in the sea. 3They all ate the same spiritual food,
4and all drank the same spiritual drink. They drank from
that spiritual rock that followed them, and that rock was
Christ. 5But God was not pleased with most of them, so
they died in the desert.
6And these things happened as examples for us, to stop
us from wanting evil things as those people did. 7Do not
worship idols, as some of them did. Just as it is written in
the Scriptures: "They sat down to eat and drink, and then
they got up and sinned sexually."[a] 8We must not take part
in sexual sins, as some of them did. In one day twenty-
three thousand of them died because of their sins. 9We
must not test Christ as some of them did; they were killed
by snakes. 10Do not complain as some of them did; they
were killed by the angel that destroys.
11The things that happened to those people are exam-
ples. They were written down to teach us, because we live
in a time when all these things of the past have reached
their goal. 12If you think you are strong, you should be
careful not to fall. 13The only temptation that has come to

10:7 [a] **"They...sexually."** Quotation from Exodus 32:6.

CONTEMPORARY ENGLISH VERSION

the sea. 2This was like being baptized and becoming fol-
lowers of Moses. 3All of them also ate the same spiritual
food 4and drank the same spiritual drink, which flowed
from the spiritual rock that followed them. That rock was
Christ. 5But most of them did not please God. So they died,
and their bodies were scattered all over the desert.
6What happened to them is a warning to keep us from
wanting to do the same evil things. 7They worshiped idols,
just as the Scriptures say, "The people sat down to eat and
drink. Then they got up to dance around." So don't wor-
ship idols. 8Some of those people did shameful things, and
in a single day about twenty-three thousand of them died.
Don't do shameful things as they did. 9And don't try to
test Christ,[a] as some of them did and were later bitten by
poisonous snakes. 10Don't even grumble, as some of them
did and were killed by the destroying angel. 11These things
happened to them as a warning to us. All this was written
in the Scriptures to teach us who live in these last days.
12Even if you think you can stand up to temptation, be
careful not to fall. 13You are tempted in the same way that

[a] **10.9** *Christ*: Some manuscripts have "the Lord."

NEW INTERNATIONAL VERSION

all baptized into Moses in the cloud and in the sea. 3 They all ate the same spiritual food 4 and drank the same spiritual drink; for they drank from the spiritual rock that accompanied them, and that rock was Christ. 5 Nevertheless, God was not pleased with most of them; their bodies were scattered over the desert.

6 Now these things occurred as examples[a] to keep us from setting our hearts on evil things as they did. 7 Do not be idolaters, as some of them were; as it is written: "The people sat down to eat and drink and got up to indulge in pagan revelry."[b] 8 We should not commit sexual immorality, as some of them did—and in one day twenty-three thousand of them died. 9 We should not test the Lord, as some of them did—and were killed by snakes. 10 And do not grumble, as some of them did—and were killed by the destroying angel.

11 These things happened to them as examples and were written down as warnings for us, on whom the fulfillment of the ages has come. 12 So, if you think you are standing firm, be careful that you don't fall! 13 No temptation has

[a] *6* Or *types*; also in verse 11 [b] *7* Exodus 32:6

NEW LIVING TRANSLATION

through the waters of the sea on dry ground. 2 As followers of Moses, they were all baptized in the cloud and the sea. 3 And all of them ate the same miraculous* food, 4 and all of them drank the same miraculous water. For they all drank from the miraculous rock that traveled with them, and that rock was Christ. 5 Yet after all this, God was not pleased with most of them, and he destroyed them in the wilderness.

6 These events happened as a warning to us, so that we would not crave evil things as they did 7 or worship idols as some of them did. For the Scriptures say, "The people celebrated with feasting and drinking, and they indulged themselves in pagan revelry."* 8 And we must not engage in sexual immorality as some of them did, causing 23,000 of them to die in one day. 9 Nor should we put Christ* to the test, as some of them did and then died from snakebites. 10 And don't grumble as some of them did, for that is why God sent his angel of death to destroy them. 11 All these events happened to them as examples for us. They were written down to warn us, who live at the time when this age is drawing to a close.

12 If you think you are standing strong, be careful, for you, too, may fall into the same sin. 13 But remember that the temptations that come into your life are no different

10:3 Greek *spiritual;* also in 10:4. **10:7** Exod 32:6. **10:9** Some manuscripts read *the Lord.*

NEW KING JAMES VERSION

all passed through the sea, 2 all were baptized into Moses in the cloud and in the sea, 3 all ate the same spiritual food, 4 and all drank the same spiritual drink. For they drank of that spiritual Rock that followed them, and that Rock was Christ. 5 But with most of them God was not well pleased, for *their bodies* were scattered in the wilderness.

6 Now these things became our examples, to the intent that we should not lust after evil things as they also lusted. 7 And do not become idolaters as *were* some of them. As it is written, *"The people sat down to eat and drink, and rose up to play."*[a] 8 Nor let us commit sexual immorality, as some of them did, and in one day twenty-three thousand fell; 9 nor let us tempt Christ, as some of them also tempted, and were destroyed by serpents; 10 nor complain, as some of them also complained, and were destroyed by the destroyer. 11 Now all[b] these things happened to them as examples, and they were written for our admonition, upon whom the ends of the ages have come.

12 Therefore let him who thinks he stands take heed lest he fall. 13 No temptation has overtaken you except such as

10:7 [a] Exodus 32:6 **10:11** [b] NU-Text omits *all.*

THE MESSAGE

through the waters, in a baptism like ours, as Moses led them from enslaving death to salvation life. They all ate and drank identical food and drink, meals provided daily by God. They drank from the Rock, God's fountain for them that stayed with them wherever they were. And the Rock was Christ. But just experiencing God's wonder and grace didn't seem to mean much—most of them were defeated by temptation during the hard times in the desert, and God was not pleased.

The same thing could happen to us. We must be on guard so that we never get caught up in wanting our own way as they did. And we must not turn our religion into a circus as they did—"First the people partied, then they threw a dance." We must not be sexually promiscuous—they paid for that, remember, with twenty-three thousand deaths in one day! We must never try to get Christ to serve us instead of us serving him; they tried it, and God launched an epidemic of poisonous snakes. We must be careful not to stir up discontent; discontent destroyed them.

These are all warning markers—DANGER!—in our history books, written down so that we don't repeat their mistakes. Our positions in the story are parallel—they at the beginning, we at the end—and we are just as capable of messing it up as they were. Don't be so naive and self-confident. You're not exempt. You could fall flat on your face as easily as anyone else. Forget about self-confidence; it's useless. Cultivate God-confidence.

No test or temptation that comes your way is beyond the course of what others have had to face. All you need to

KING JAMES VERSION

common to man: but God *is* faithful, who will not suffer you to be tempted above that ye are able; but will with the temptation also make a way to escape, that ye may be able to bear *it*.

14 Wherefore, my dearly beloved, flee from idolatry.

15 ¶ I speak as to wise men; judge ye what I say.

16 The cup of blessing which we bless, is it not the communion of the blood of Christ? The bread which we break, is it not the communion of the body of Christ?

17 For we *being* many are one bread, *and* one body: for we are all partakers of that one bread.

18 Behold Israel after the flesh: are not they which eat of the sacrifices partakers of the altar?

19 What say I then? that the idol is any thing, or that which is offered in sacrifice to idols is any thing?

20 But I *say*, that the things which the Gentiles sacrifice, they sacrifice to devils, and not to God: and I would not that ye should have fellowship with devils.

21 Ye cannot drink the cup of the Lord, and the cup of devils: ye cannot be partakers of the Lord's table, and of the table of devils.

22 Do we provoke the Lord to jealousy? are we stronger than he?

23 ¶ All things are lawful for me, but all things are not expedient: all things are lawful for me, but all things edify not.

NEW AMERICAN STANDARD BIBLE

common to man; and God is faithful, who will not allow you to be tempted beyond what you are able, but with the temptation will provide the way of escape also, so that you will be able to endure it.

14 Therefore, my beloved, flee from idolatry.

15 I speak as to wise men; you judge what I say.

16 Is not the cup of blessing which we bless a sharing in the blood of Christ? Is not the bread which we break a sharing in the body of Christ?

17 Since there is one bread, we who are many are one body; for we all partake of the one bread.

18 Look at the nation Israel; are not those who eat the sacrifices sharers in the altar?

19 What do I mean then? That a thing sacrificed to idols is anything, or that an idol is anything?

20 *No,* but *I say* that the things which the Gentiles sacrifice, they sacrifice to demons and not to God; and I do not want you to become sharers in demons.

21 You cannot drink the cup of the Lord and the cup of demons; you cannot partake of the table of the Lord and the table of demons.

22 Or do we provoke the Lord to jealousy? We are not stronger than He, are we?

23 All things are lawful, but not all things are profitable. All things are lawful, but not all things edify.

NEW CENTURY VERSION

you is that which everyone has. But you can trust God, who will not permit you to be tempted more than you can stand. But when you are tempted, he will also give you a way to escape so that you will be able to stand it.

[14]So, my dear friends, run away from the worship of
idols. [15]I am speaking to you as to intelligent people; judge
for yourselves what I say. [16]We give thanks for the cup of
blessing,[b] which is a sharing in the blood of Christ. And
the bread that we break is a sharing in the body of Christ.
[17]Because there is one loaf of bread, we who are many are
one body, because we all share that one loaf.

[18]Think about the Israelites: Do not those who eat the
sacrifices share in the altar? [19]I do not mean that the food
sacrificed to an idol is important. I do not mean that an
idol is anything at all. [20]But I say that what is sacrificed to
idols is offered to demons, not to God. And I do not want
you to share anything with demons. [21]You cannot drink
the cup of the Lord and the cup of demons also. You cannot share in the Lord's table and the table of demons.
[22]Are we trying to make the Lord jealous? We are not
stronger than he is, are we?

How to Use Christian Freedom

[23]"We are allowed to do all things," but all things are
not good for us to do. "We are allowed to do all things,"
but not all things help others grow stronger. [24]Do not look

10:16 [b] **cup of blessing** The cup of the fruit of the vine that Christians thank God for and drink at the Lord's Supper.

CONTEMPORARY ENGLISH VERSION

everyone else is tempted. But God can be trusted not to let you be tempted too much, and he will show you how to escape from your temptations.

[14]My friends, you must keep away from idols. [15]I am
speaking to you as people who have enough sense to know
what I am talking about. [16]When we drink from the cup
that we ask God to bless, isn't that sharing in the blood of
Christ? When we eat the bread that we break, isn't that
sharing in the body of Christ? [17]By sharing in the same
loaf of bread, we become one body, even though there are
many of us.

[18]Aren't the people of Israel sharing in the worship
when they gather around the altar and eat the sacrifices
offered there? [19]Am I saying that either the idols or the
food sacrificed to them is anything at all? [20]No, I am not!
That food is really sacrificed to demons and not to God. I
don't want you to have anything to do with demons. [21]You
cannot drink from the cup of demons and still drink from
the Lord's cup. You cannot eat at the table of demons and
still eat at the Lord's table. [22]We would make the Lord
jealous if we did that. And we are not stronger than the
Lord.

Always Honor God

[23]Some of you say, "We can do whatever we want to!"
But I tell you that not everything may be good or helpful.

NEW INTERNATIONAL VERSION

seized you except what is common to man. And God is
faithful; he will not let you be tempted beyond what you
can bear. But when you are tempted, he will also provide a
way out so that you can stand up under it.

Idol Feasts and the Lord's Supper

14 Therefore, my dear friends, flee from idolatry. 15 I
speak to sensible people; judge for yourselves what I say.
16 Is not the cup of thanksgiving for which we give thanks
a participation in the blood of Christ? And is not the bread
that we break a participation in the body of Christ?
17 Because there is one loaf, we, who are many, are one
body, for we all partake of the one loaf.

18 Consider the people of Israel: Do not those who eat the
sacrifices participate in the altar? 19 Do I mean then that a
sacrifice offered to an idol is anything, or that an idol is
anything? 20 No, but the sacrifices of pagans are offered to
demons, not to God, and I do not want you to be partici-
pants with demons. 21 You cannot drink the cup of the Lord
and the cup of demons too; you cannot have a part in both
the Lord's table and the table of demons. 22 Are we trying
to arouse the Lord's jealousy? Are we stronger than he?

The Believer's Freedom

23 "Everything is permissible"—but not everything is
beneficial. "Everything is permissible"—but not everything

NEW LIVING TRANSLATION

from what others experience. And God is faithful. He will
keep the temptation from becoming so strong that you
can't stand up against it. When you are tempted, he will
show you a way out so that you will not give in to it.

14 So, my dear friends, flee from the worship of idols.
15 You are reasonable people. Decide for yourselves if what
I am about to say is true. 16 When we bless the cup at the
Lord's Table, aren't we sharing in the benefits of the blood
of Christ? And when we break the loaf of bread, aren't we
sharing in the benefits of the body of Christ? 17 And we all
eat from one loaf, showing that we are one body. 18 And
think about the nation of Israel; all who eat the sacrifices
are united by that act.

19 What am I trying to say? Am I saying that the idols to
whom the pagans bring sacrifices are real gods and that
these sacrifices are of some value? 20 No, not at all. What I
am saying is that these sacrifices are offered to demons,
not to God. And I don't want any of you to be partners
with demons. 21 You cannot drink from the cup of the Lord
and from the cup of demons, too. You cannot eat at the
Lord's Table and at the table of demons, too. 22 What? Do
you dare to rouse the Lord's jealousy as Israel did? Do you
think we are stronger than he is?

23 You say, "I am allowed to do anything"—but not
everything is helpful. You say, "I am allowed to do any-
thing"—but not everything is beneficial. 24 Don't think only

NEW KING JAMES VERSION

is common to man; but God *is* faithful, who will not allow
you to be tempted beyond what you are able, but with the
temptation will also make the way of escape, that you may
be able to bear *it.*

Flee from Idolatry

14 Therefore, my beloved, flee from idolatry. 15 I speak as
to wise men; judge for yourselves what I say. 16 The cup of
blessing which we bless, is it not the communion of the
blood of Christ? The bread which we break, is it not the
communion of the body of Christ? 17 For we, *though* many,
are one bread *and* one body; for we all partake of that one
bread.

18 Observe Israel after the flesh: Are not those who eat of
the sacrifices partakers of the altar? 19 What am I saying
then? That an idol is anything, or what is offered to idols
is anything? 20 Rather, that the things which the Gentiles
sacrifice they sacrifice to demons and not to God, and I do
not want you to have fellowship with demons. 21 You can-
not drink the cup of the Lord and the cup of demons; you
cannot partake of the Lord's table and of the table of
demons. 22 Or do we provoke the Lord to jealousy? Are we
stronger than He?

All to the Glory of God

23 All things are lawful for me,[c] but not all things are
helpful; all things are lawful for me,[d] but not all things

10:23 [c] NU-Text omits *for me.* [d] NU-Text omits *for me.*

THE MESSAGE

remember is that God will never let you down; he'll never
let you be pushed past your limit; he'll always be there to
help you come through it.

So, my very dear friends, when you see people reducing
God to something they can use or control, get out of their
company as fast as you can.

I assume I'm addressing believers now who are mature.
Draw your own conclusions: When we drink the cup of
blessing, aren't we taking into ourselves the blood, the
very life, of Christ? And isn't it the same with the loaf of
bread we break and eat? Don't we take into ourselves the
body, the very life, of Christ? Because there is one loaf, our
many-ness becomes one-ness—Christ doesn't become frag-
mented in us. Rather, we become unified in him. We don't
reduce Christ to what we are; he raises us to what he is.
That's basically what happened even in old Israel—those
who ate the sacrifices offered on God's altar entered into
God's action at the altar.

Do you see the difference? Sacrifices offered to idols are
offered to nothing, for what's the idol but a nothing? Or
worse than nothing, a minus, a demon! I don't want you to
become part of something that reduces you to less than
yourself. And you can't have it both ways, banqueting with
the Master one day and slumming with demons the next.
Besides, the Master won't put up with it. He wants *us*—all
or nothing. Do you think you can get off with anything less?

Looking at it one way, you could say, "Anything goes.
Because of God's immense generosity and grace, we don't
have to dissect and scrutinize every action to see if it will

KING JAMES VERSION

24 Let no man seek his own, but every man another's
wealth.
25 Whatsoever is sold in the shambles, *that* eat, asking
no question for conscience sake:
26 For the earth *is* the Lord's, and the fulness thereof.
27 If any of them that believe not bid you *to a feast*,
and ye be disposed to go; whatsoever is set before you, eat,
asking no question for conscience sake.
28 But if any man say unto you, This is offered in sacri-
fice unto idols, eat not for his sake that shewed it, and for
conscience sake: for the earth *is* the Lord's, and the ful-
ness thereof:
29 Conscience, I say, not thine own, but of the other: for
why is my liberty judged of another *man's* conscience?
30 For if I by grace be a partaker, why am I evil spoken
of for that for which I give thanks?
31 Whether therefore ye eat, or drink, or whatsoever ye
do, do all to the glory of God.

NEW AMERICAN STANDARD BIBLE

24 Let no one seek his own *good,* but that of his neigh-
bor.
25 Eat anything that is sold in the meat market without
asking questions for conscience' sake;
26 FOR THE EARTH IS THE LORD'S, AND ALL IT CONTAINS.
27 If one of the unbelievers invites you and you want to
go, eat anything that is set before you without asking
questions for conscience' sake.
28 But if anyone says to you, "This is meat sacrificed to
idols," do not eat *it,* for the sake of the one who informed
you, and for conscience' sake;
29 I mean not your own conscience, but the other
man's; for why is my freedom judged by another's con-
science?
30 If I partake with thankfulness, why am I slandered
concerning that for which I give thanks?
31 Whether, then, you eat or drink or whatever you do,
do all to the glory of God.

NEW CENTURY VERSION

out only for yourselves. Look out for the good of others
also.
25Eat any meat that is sold in the meat market. Do not
ask questions to see if it is meat you think is wrong to eat.
26You may eat it, "because the earth belongs to the Lord,
and everything in it."[c]
27Those who are not believers may invite you to eat with
them. If you want to go, eat anything that is put before
you. Do not ask questions to see if you think it might be
wrong to eat. 28But if anyone says to you, "That food was
offered to idols," do not eat it. Do not eat it because of that
person who told you and because eating it might be
thought to be wrong. 29I don't mean you think it is wrong,
but the other person might. But why, you ask, should my
freedom be judged by someone else's conscience? 30If I eat
the meal with thankfulness, why am I criticized because of
something for which I thank God?
31The answer is, if you eat or drink, or if you do any-
thing, do it all for the glory of God. 32Never do anything

10:26 [c] **"because…it"** Quotation from Psalms 24:1; 50:12; 89:11.

CONTEMPORARY ENGLISH VERSION

24We should think about others and not about ourselves.
25However, when you buy meat in the market, go ahead
and eat it. Keep your conscience clear by not asking where
the meat came from. 26The Scriptures say, "The earth and
everything in it belong to the Lord."
27If an unbeliever invites you to dinner, and you want to
go, then go. Eat whatever you are served. Don't cause a
problem for someone's conscience by asking where the
food came from. 28-29But if you are told that it has been
sacrificed to idols, don't cause a problem by eating it. I
don't mean a problem for yourself, but for the one who
told you. Why should my freedom be limited by someone
else's conscience? 30If I give thanks for what I eat, why
should anyone accuse me of doing wrong?
31When you eat or drink or do anything else, always do it
to honor God. 32Don't cause problems for Jews or Greeks or

NEW INTERNATIONAL VERSION

is constructive. [24]Nobody should seek his own good, but
the good of others.
[25]Eat anything sold in the meat market without raising
questions of conscience, [26]for, "The earth is the Lord's,
and everything in it."[c]
[27]If some unbeliever invites you to a meal and you want
to go, eat whatever is put before you without raising ques-
tions of conscience. [28]But if anyone says to you, "This has
been offered in sacrifice," then do not eat it, both for the
sake of the man who told you and for conscience' sake[d]—
[29]the other man's conscience, I mean, not yours. For why
should my freedom be judged by another's conscience? [30]If
I take part in the meal with thankfulness, why am I
denounced because of something I thank God for?
[31]So whether you eat or drink or whatever you do, do it
all for the glory of God. [32]Do not cause anyone to stumble,

[c] *26* Psalm 24:1 [d] *28* Some manuscripts *conscience' sake, for "the earth is the Lord's and everything in it"*

NEW LIVING TRANSLATION

of your own good. Think of other Christians and what is
best for them.
[25]Here's what you should do. You may eat any meat
that is sold in the marketplace. Don't ask whether or not it
was offered to idols, and then your conscience won't be
bothered. [26]For "the earth is the Lord's, and everything in
it."*
[27]If someone who isn't a Christian asks you home for
dinner, go ahead; accept the invitation if you want to. Eat
whatever is offered to you and don't ask any questions
about it. Your conscience should not be bothered by this.
[28]But suppose someone warns you that this meat has been
offered to an idol. Don't eat it, out of consideration for the
conscience of the one who told you. [29]It might not be a
matter of conscience for you, but it is for the other person.
Now, why should my freedom be limited by what some-
one else thinks? [30]If I can thank God for the food and
enjoy it, why should I be condemned for eating it? [31]What-
ever you eat or drink or whatever you do, you must do all
for the glory of God. [32]Don't give offense to Jews or

10:26 Ps 24:1.

NEW KING JAMES VERSION

edify. [24]Let no one seek his own, but each one the other's
well-being.
[25]Eat whatever is sold in the meat market, asking no
questions for conscience' sake; [26]for *"the earth is the
LORD's, and all its fullness."*[e]
[27]If any of those who do not believe invites you *to din-
ner,* and you desire to go, eat whatever is set before you,
asking no question for conscience' sake. [28]But if anyone
says to you, "This was offered to idols," do not eat it for
the sake of the one who told you, and for conscience'
sake;[f] for *"the earth is the LORD's, and all its fullness."*[g]
[29]"Conscience," I say, not your own, but that of the other.
For why is my liberty judged by another *man's* conscience?
[30]But if I partake with thanks, why am I evil spoken of for
the food over which I give thanks?
[31]Therefore, whether you eat or drink, or whatever you
do, do all to the glory of God. [32]Give no offense, either to

10:26 [e] Psalm 24:1 **10:28** [f] NU-Text omits the rest of this verse. [g] Psalm 24:1

THE MESSAGE

pass muster." But the point is not to just get by. We want to live well, but our foremost efforts should be to help *others* live well.

With that as a base to work from, common sense can take you the rest of the way. Eat anything sold at the butcher shop, for instance; you don't have to run an "idolatry test" on every item. "The earth," after all, "is God's, and everything in it." That "everything" certainly includes the leg of lamb in the butcher shop. If a nonbeliever invites you to dinner and you feel like going, go ahead and enjoy yourself; eat everything placed before you. It would be both bad manners and bad spirituality to cross-examine your host on the ethical purity of each course as it is served. On the other hand, if he goes out of his way to tell you that this or that was sacrificed to god or goddess so-and-so, you should pass. Even though you may be indifferent as to where it came from, he isn't, and you don't want to send mixed messages to him about who *you* are worshiping.

But, except for these special cases, I'm not going to walk around on eggshells worrying about what small-minded people might say; I'm going to stride free and easy, knowing what our large-minded Master has already said. If I eat what is served to me, grateful to God for what is on the table, how can I worry about what someone will say? I thanked God for it and he blessed it!

So eat your meals heartily, not worrying about what others say about you—you're eating to God's glory, after all, not to please them. As a matter of fact, do everything that way, heartily and freely to God's glory. At the same

KING JAMES VERSION

32 Give none offence, neither to the Jews, nor to the Gentiles, nor to the church of God:

33 Even as I please all *men* in all *things*, not seeking mine own profit, but the *profit* of many, that they may be saved.

11 Be ye followers of me, even as I also *am* of Christ.

2 Now I praise you, brethren, that ye remember me in all things, and keep the ordinances, as I delivered *them* to you.

3 But I would have you know, that the head of every man is Christ; and the head of the woman *is* the man; and the head of Christ *is* God.

4 Every man praying or prophesying, having *his* head covered, dishonoureth his head.

5 But every woman that prayeth or prophesieth with *her* head uncovered dishonoureth her head: for that is even all one as if she were shaven.

6 For if the woman be not covered, let her also be shorn: but if it be a shame for a woman to be shorn or shaven, let her be covered.

7 For a man indeed ought not to cover *his* head, forasmuch as he is the image and glory of God: but the woman is the glory of the man.

8 For the man is not of the woman; but the woman of the man.

9 Neither was the man created for the woman; but the woman for the man.

NEW AMERICAN STANDARD BIBLE

32 Give no offense either to Jews or to Greeks or to the church of God;

33 just as I also please all men in all things, not seeking my own profit but the *profit* of the many, so that they may be saved.

Christian Order

11 Be imitators of me, just as I also am of Christ.

2 Now I praise you because you remember me in everything and hold firmly to the traditions, just as I delivered them to you.

3 But I want you to understand that Christ is the head of every man, and the man is the head of a woman, and God is the head of Christ.

4 Every man who has *something* on his head while praying or prophesying disgraces his head.

5 But every woman who has her head uncovered while praying or prophesying disgraces her head, for she is one and the same as the woman whose head is shaved.

6 For if a woman does not cover her head, let her also have her hair cut off; but if it is disgraceful for a woman to have her hair cut off or her head shaved, let her cover her head.

7 For a man ought not to have his head covered, since he is the image and glory of God; but the woman is the glory of man.

8 For man does not originate from woman, but woman from man;

9 for indeed man was not created for the woman's sake, but woman for the man's sake.

NEW CENTURY VERSION

that might hurt others—Jews, Greeks, or God's church—
33just as I, also, try to please everybody in every way. I am
not trying to do what is good for me but what is good for
most people so they can be saved.

11 Follow my example, as I follow the example of Christ.

Being Under Authority

2I praise you because you remember me in everything,
and you follow closely the teachings just as I gave them to
you. 3But I want you to understand this: The head of every
man is Christ, the head of a woman is the man,[a] and the
head of Christ is God. 4Every man who prays or prophesies
with his head covered brings shame to his head. 5But
every woman who prays or prophesies with her head
uncovered brings shame to her head. She is the same as a
woman who has her head shaved. 6If a woman does not
cover her head, she should have her hair cut off. But since
it is shameful for a woman to cut off her hair or to shave
her head, she should cover her head. 7But a man should
not cover his head, because he is the likeness and glory of
God. But woman is man's glory. 8Man did not come from
woman, but woman came from man. 9And man was not
made for woman, but woman was made for man. 10So that

11:3 [a] **the man** This could also mean "her husband."

CONTEMPORARY ENGLISH VERSION

anyone else who belongs to God's church. 33I always try to
please others instead of myself, in the hope that many of
them will be saved. 1You must follow my example,
as I follow the example of Christ.

Rules for Worship

2I am proud of you, because you always remember me
and obey the teachings I gave you. 3Now I want you to
know that Christ is the head over all men, and a man is
the head over a woman. But God is the head over Christ.
4This means that any man who prays or prophesies with
something on his head brings shame to his head.
5But any woman who prays or prophesies without something on her head brings shame to her head. In fact, she
may as well shave her head.[a] 6A woman should wear
something on her head. It is a disgrace for a woman to
shave her head or cut her hair. But if she refuses to wear
something on her head, let her cut off her hair.
7Men were created to be like God and to bring honor to
God. This means that a man should not wear anything on
his head. Women were created to bring honor to men. 8It
was the woman who was made from a man, and not the
man who was made from a woman. 9He wasn't created for
her. She was created for him. 10And so, because of this,

[a] 11.5 *she may as well shave her head*: A woman's hair was a mark of beauty, and it was shameful for a woman to cut her hair short or to shave her head, so that she looked like a man.

NEW INTERNATIONAL VERSION

whether Jews, Greeks or the church of God— [33]even as I try to please everybody in every way. For I am not seeking my own good but the good of many, so that they may be saved.

11 [1]Follow my example, as I follow the example of Christ.

Propriety in Worship

[2]I praise you for remembering me in everything and for holding to the teachings,[a] just as I passed them on to you.

[3]Now I want you to realize that the head of every man is Christ, and the head of the woman is man, and the head of Christ is God. [4]Every man who prays or prophesies with his head covered dishonors his head. [5]And every woman who prays or prophesies with her head uncovered dishonors her head—it is just as though her head were shaved. [6]If a woman does not cover her head, she should have her hair cut off; and if it is a disgrace for a woman to have her hair cut or shaved off, she should cover her head. [7]A man ought not to cover his head,[b] since he is the image and glory of God; but the woman is the glory of man. [8]For man did not come from woman, but woman from man; [9]neither was man created for woman, but woman for man. [10]For

[a] 2 Or *traditions* [b] 4–7 Or *[4]Every man who prays or prophesies with long hair dishonors his head. [5]And every woman who prays or prophesies with no covering ˛of hair˛ on her head dishonors her head—she is just like one of the "shorn women." [6]If a woman has no covering, let her be for now with short hair, but since it is a disgrace for a woman to have her hair shorn or shaved, she should grow it again. [7]A man ought not to have long hair*

NEW LIVING TRANSLATION

Gentiles or the church of God. [33]That is the plan I follow, too. I try to please everyone in everything I do. I don't just do what I like or what is best for me, but what is best for them so they may be saved.

11 And you should follow my example, just as I follow Christ's.

Instructions for Public Worship

[2]I am so glad, dear friends, that you always keep me in your thoughts and you are following the Christian teaching I passed on to you. [3]But there is one thing I want you to know: A man is responsible to Christ, a woman is responsible to her husband, and Christ is responsible to God. [4]A man dishonors Christ* if he covers his head while praying or prophesying. [5]But a woman dishonors her husband* if she prays or prophesies without a covering on her head, for this is the same as shaving her head. [6]Yes, if she refuses to wear a head covering, she should cut off all her hair. And since it is shameful for a woman to have her hair cut or her head shaved, then she should wear a covering.* [7]A man should not wear anything on his head when worshiping, for man is God's glory, made in God's own image, but woman is the glory of man. [8]For the first man didn't come from woman, but the first woman came from man. [9]And man was not made for woman's benefit, but woman was made for man.

11:4 Greek *his head.* 11:5 Greek *her head.* 11:6 Or *then she should have long hair.*

NEW KING JAMES VERSION

the Jews or to the Greeks or to the church of God, [33]just as I also please all *men* in all *things,* not seeking my own profit, but the *profit* of many, that they may be saved.

11 Imitate me, just as I also *imitate* Christ.

Head Coverings

[2]Now I praise you, brethren, that you remember me in all things and keep the traditions just as I delivered *them* to you. [3]But I want you to know that the head of every man is Christ, the head of woman *is* man, and the head of Christ *is* God. [4]Every man praying or prophesying, having *his* head covered, dishonors his head. [5]But every woman who prays or prophesies with *her* head uncovered dishonors her head, for that is one and the same as if her head were shaved. [6]For if a woman is not covered, let her also be shorn. But if it is shameful for a woman to be shorn or shaved, let her be covered. [7]For a man indeed ought not to cover *his* head, since he is the image and glory of God; but woman is the glory of man. [8]For man is not from woman, but woman from man. [9]Nor was man created for the woman, but woman for the man. [10]For this reason the

THE MESSAGE

time, don't be callous in your exercise of freedom, thoughtlessly stepping on the toes of those who aren't as free as you are. I try my best to be considerate of everyone's feelings in all these matters; I hope you will be, too.

To Honor God

11 It pleases me that you continue to remember and honor me by keeping up the traditions of the faith I taught you. All actual authority stems from Christ.

In a marriage relationship, there is authority from Christ to husband, and from husband to wife. The authority of Christ is the authority of God. Any man who speaks with God or about God in a way that shows a lack of respect for the authority of Christ, dishonors Christ. In the same way, a wife who speaks with God in a way that shows a lack of respect for the authority of her husband, dishonors her husband. Worse, she dishonors herself—an ugly sight, like a woman with her head shaved. This is basically the origin of these customs we have of women wearing head coverings in worship, while men take their hats off. By these symbolic acts, men and women, who far too often butt heads with each other, submit their "heads" to the Head: God.

Don't, by the way, read too much into the differences here between men and women. Neither man nor woman can go it alone or claim priority. Man was created first, as a beautiful shining reflection of God—that is true. But the head on a woman's body clearly outshines in beauty the head of her "head," her husband. The first woman came

KING JAMES VERSION

10 For this cause ought the woman to have power on *her* head because of the angels.

11 Nevertheless neither is the man without the woman, neither the woman without the man, in the Lord.

12 For as the woman *is* of the man, even so *is* the man also by the woman; but all things of God.

13 Judge in yourselves: is it comely that a woman pray unto God uncovered?

14 Doth not even nature itself teach you, that, if a man have long hair, it is a shame unto him?

15 But if a woman have long hair, it is a glory to her: for *her* hair is given her for a covering.

16 But if any man seem to be contentious, we have no such custom, neither the churches of God.

17 ¶ Now in this that I declare *unto you* I praise *you* not, that ye come together not for the better, but for the worse.

18 For first of all, when ye come together in the church, I hear that there be divisions among you; and I partly believe it.

19 For there must be also heresies among you, that they which are approved may be made manifest among you.

20 When ye come together therefore into one place, *this* is not to eat the Lord's supper.

21 For in eating every one taketh before *other* his own supper: and one is hungry, and another is drunken.

22 What? have ye not houses to eat and to drink in? or

NEW AMERICAN STANDARD BIBLE

10 Therefore the woman ought to have *a symbol of* authority on her head, because of the angels.

11 However, in the Lord, neither is woman independent of man, nor is man independent of woman.

12 For as the woman originates from the man, so also the man *has his birth* through the woman; and all things originate from God.

13 Judge for yourselves: is it proper for a woman to pray to God *with her head* uncovered?

14 Does not even nature itself teach you that if a man has long hair, it is a dishonor to him,

15 but if a woman has long hair, it is a glory to her? For her hair is given to her for a covering.

16 But if one is inclined to be contentious, we have no other practice, nor have the churches of God.

17 But in giving this instruction, I do not praise you, because you come together not for the better but for the worse.

18 For, in the first place, when you come together as a church, I hear that divisions exist among you; and in part I believe it.

19 For there must also be factions among you, so that those who are approved may become evident among you.

20 Therefore when you meet together, it is not to eat the Lord's Supper,

21 for in your eating each one takes his own supper first; and one is hungry and another is drunk.

22 What! Do you not have houses in which to eat and

NEW CENTURY VERSION

is why a woman should have a symbol of authority on her
head, because of the angels.
11But in the Lord women are not independent of men,
and men are not independent of women. 12This is true
because woman came from man, but also man is born
from woman. But everything comes from God. 13Decide
this for yourselves: Is it right for a woman to pray to God
with her head uncovered? 14Even nature itself teaches you
that wearing long hair is shameful for a man. 15But long
hair is a woman's glory. Long hair is given to her as a cov-
ering. 16Some people may still want to argue about this,
but I would add that neither we nor the churches of God
have any other practice.

The Lord's Supper

17In the things I tell you now I do not praise you,
because when you come together you do more harm than
good. 18First, I hear that when you meet together as a
church you are divided, and I believe some of this. 19(It is
necessary to have differences among you so that it may be
clear which of you really have God's approval.) 20When
you come together, you are not really eating the Lord's
Supper.[b] 21This is because when you eat, each person eats
without waiting for the others. Some people do not get
enough to eat, while others have too much to drink. 22You
can eat and drink in your own homes! You seem to think

11:20 [b] **Lord's Supper** The meal Jesus told his followers to eat to remember him (Luke 22:14–20).

CONTEMPORARY ENGLISH VERSION

and also because of the angels, a woman ought to wear
something on her head, as a sign of her authority.[b]
11As far as the Lord is concerned, men and women need
each other. 12It is true that the first woman came from a
man, but all other men have been given birth by women.
Yet God is the one who created everything. 13Ask your-
selves if it is proper for a woman to pray without some-
thing on her head. 14Isn't it unnatural and disgraceful for
men to have long hair? 15But long hair is a beautiful way
for a woman to cover her head. 16This is how things are
done in all of God's churches,[c] and that's why none of you
should argue about what I have said.

Rules for the Lord's Supper

17Your worship services do you more harm than good. I
am certainly not going to praise you for this. 18I am told
that you can't get along with each other when you wor-
ship, and I am sure that some of what I have heard is true.
19You are bound to argue with each other, but it is easy to
see which of you have God's approval.
20When you meet together, you don't really celebrate the
Lord's Supper. 21You even start eating before everyone
gets to the meeting, and some of you go hungry, while oth-
ers get drunk. 22Don't you have homes where you can eat

[b] 11.10 *as a sign of her authority*: Or "as a sign that she is under someone's authority." [c] 11.16 *This is how things are done in all of God's churches*: Or "There is no set rule for this in any of God's churches."

NEW INTERNATIONAL VERSION

this reason, and because of the angels, the woman ought
to have a sign of authority on her head.
[11]In the Lord, however, woman is not independent of
man, nor is man independent of woman. [12]For as woman
came from man, so also man is born of woman. But every-
thing comes from God. [13]Judge for yourselves: Is it proper
for a woman to pray to God with her head uncovered?
[14]Does not the very nature of things teach you that if a
man has long hair, it is a disgrace to him, [15]but that if a
woman has long hair, it is her glory? For long hair is given
to her as a covering. [16]If anyone wants to be contentious
about this, we have no other practice—nor do the churches
of God.

The Lord's Supper

[17]In the following directives I have no praise for you, for
your meetings do more harm than good. [18]In the first
place, I hear that when you come together as a church,
there are divisions among you, and to some extent I
believe it. [19]No doubt there have to be differences among
you to show which of you have God's approval. [20]When
you come together, it is not the Lord's Supper you eat,
[21]for as you eat, each of you goes ahead without waiting
for anybody else. One remains hungry, another gets drunk.
[22]Don't you have homes to eat and drink in? Or do you

NEW LIVING TRANSLATION

[10]So a woman should wear a covering on her head as a sign
of authority because the angels are watching.
[11]But in relationships among the Lord's people, women
are not independent of men, and men are not independent
of women. [12]For although the first woman came from man,
all men have been born from women ever since, and every-
thing comes from God.
[13]What do you think about this? Is it right for a woman
to pray to God in public without covering her head? [14]Isn't
it obvious that it's disgraceful for a man to have long hair?
[15]And isn't it obvious that long hair is a woman's pride
and joy? For it has been given to her as a covering. [16]But if
anyone wants to argue about this, all I can say is that we
have no other custom than this, and all the churches of
God feel the same way about it.

Order at the Lord's Supper

[17]But now when I mention this next issue, I cannot
praise you. For it sounds as if more harm than good is
done when you meet together. [18]First of all, I hear that
there are divisions among you when you meet as a church,
and to some extent I believe it. [19]But, of course, there must
be divisions among you so that those of you who are right
will be recognized!
[20]It's not the Lord's Supper you are concerned about
when you come together. [21]For I am told that some of you
hurry to eat your own meal without sharing with others. As
a result, some go hungry while others get drunk. [22]What? Is
this really true? Don't you have your own homes for eating

NEW KING JAMES VERSION

woman ought to have *a symbol of* authority on *her* head,
because of the angels. [11]Nevertheless, neither *is* man inde-
pendent of woman, nor woman independent of man, in the
Lord. [12]For as woman *came* from man, even so man also
comes through woman; but all things are from God.
[13]Judge among yourselves. Is it proper for a woman to
pray to God with her head uncovered? [14]Does not even
nature itself teach you that if a man has long hair, it is a
dishonor to him? [15]But if a woman has long hair, it is a
glory to her; for *her* hair is given to her[a] for a covering.
[16]But if anyone seems to be contentious, we have no such
custom, nor *do* the churches of God.

Conduct at the Lord's Supper

[17]Now in giving these instructions I do not praise *you,*
since you come together not for the better but for the
worse. [18]For first of all, when you come together as a
church, I hear that there are divisions among you, and in
part I believe it. [19]For there must also be factions among
you, that those who are approved may be recognized
among you. [20]Therefore when you come together in one
place, it is not to eat the Lord's Supper. [21]For in eating,
each one takes his own supper ahead of *others;* and one is
hungry and another is drunk. [22]What! Do you not have
houses to eat and drink in? Or do you despise the church

11:15 [a] M-Text omits *to her.*

THE MESSAGE

from man, true—but ever since then, every man comes
from a woman! And since virtually everything comes from
God anyway, let's quit going through these "who's first"
routines.

Don't you agree there is something naturally powerful in
the symbolism—a woman, her beautiful hair reminiscent
of angels, praying in adoration; a man, his head bared in
reverence, praying in submission? I hope you're not going
to be argumentative about this. All God's churches see it
this way; I don't want you standing out as an exception.

Regarding this next item, I'm not at all pleased. I am
getting the picture that when you meet together it brings
out your worst side instead of your best! First, I get this
report on your divisiveness, competing with and criticizing
each other. I'm reluctant to believe it, but there it is. The
best that can be said for it is that the testing process will
bring truth into the open and confirm it.

And then I find that you bring your divisions to wor-
ship—you come together, and instead of eating the Lord's
Supper, you bring in a lot of food from the outside and
make pigs of yourselves. Some are left out, and go home
hungry. Others have to be carried out, too drunk to walk. I
can't believe it! Don't you have your own homes to eat and

KING JAMES VERSION

despise ye the church of God, and shame them that have
not? What shall I say to you? shall I praise you in this? I
praise *you* not.
23 ¶ For I have received of the Lord that which also I
delivered unto you, That the Lord Jesus the *same* night in
which he was betrayed took bread:
24 And when he had given thanks, he brake *it*, and
said, Take, eat: this is my body, which is broken for you:
this do in remembrance of me.
25 After the same manner also *he took* the cup, when
he had supped, saying, This cup is the new testament in
my blood: this do ye, as oft as ye drink *it*, in remembrance
of me.
26 For as often as ye eat this bread, and drink this cup,
ye do shew the Lord's death till he come.
27 Wherefore whosoever shall eat this bread, and drink
this cup of the Lord, unworthily, shall be guilty of the body
and blood of the Lord.
28 But let a man examine himself, and so let him eat of
that bread, and drink of *that* cup.

NEW AMERICAN STANDARD BIBLE

drink? Or do you despise the church of God and shame
those who have nothing? What shall I say to you? Shall I
praise you? In this I will not praise you.

The Lord's Supper

23 For I received from the Lord that which I also deliv-
ered to you, that the Lord Jesus in the night in which He
was betrayed took bread;
24 and when He had given thanks, He broke it and said,
"This is My body, which is for you; do this in remembrance
of Me."
25 In the same way *He took* the cup also after supper,
saying, "This cup is the new covenant in My blood; do this,
as often as you drink *it*, in remembrance of Me."
26 For as often as you eat this bread and drink the cup,
you proclaim the Lord's death until He comes.
27 Therefore whoever eats the bread or drinks the cup of
the Lord in an unworthy manner, shall be guilty of the
body and the blood of the Lord.
28 But a man must examine himself, and in so doing he
is to eat of the bread and drink of the cup.

NEW CENTURY VERSION

God's church is not important, and you embarrass those
who are poor. What should I tell you? Should I praise you?
I do not praise you for doing this.
23 The teaching I gave you is the same teaching I
received from the Lord: On the night when the Lord Jesus
was handed over to be killed, he took bread 24 and gave
thanks for it. Then he broke the bread and said, "This is
my body; it is for you. Do this to remember me." 25 In the
same way, after they ate, Jesus took the cup. He said,
"This cup is the new agreement that is sealed with the
blood of my death. When you drink this, do it to remember
me." 26 Every time you eat this bread and drink this cup
you are telling others about the Lord's death until he
comes.
27 So a person who eats the bread or drinks the cup of
the Lord in a way that is not worthy of it will be guilty of
sinning against the body and the blood of the Lord. 28 Look
into your own hearts before you eat the bread and drink

CONTEMPORARY ENGLISH VERSION

and drink? Do you hate God's church? Do you want to
embarrass people who don't have anything? What can I
say to you? I certainly cannot praise you.

The Lord's Supper

(Matthew 26.26-29; Mark 14.22-25; Luke 22.14-20)

23 I have already told you what the Lord Jesus did on the
night he was betrayed. And it came from the Lord himself.
He took some bread in his hands. 24 Then after he had
given thanks, he broke it and said, "This is my body,
which is given for you. Eat this and remember me."
25 After the meal, Jesus took a cup of wine in his
hands and said, "This is my blood, and with it God
makes his new agreement with you. Drink this and
remember me."
26 The Lord meant that when you eat this bread and
drink from this cup, you tell about his death until he
comes.
27 But if you eat the bread and drink the wine in a way
that isn't worthy of the Lord, you sin against his body and
blood. 28 That's why you must examine the way you eat

NEW INTERNATIONAL VERSION

despise the church of God and humiliate those who have
nothing? What shall I say to you? Shall I praise you for
this? Certainly not!
23 For I received from the Lord what I also passed on to
you: The Lord Jesus, on the night he was betrayed, took
bread, 24 and when he had given thanks, he broke it and
said, "This is my body, which is for you; do this in remem-
brance of me." 25 In the same way, after supper he took the
cup, saying, "This cup is the new covenant in my blood; do
this, whenever you drink it, in remembrance of me." 26 For
whenever you eat this bread and drink this cup, you pro-
claim the Lord's death until he comes.
27 Therefore, whoever eats the bread or drinks the cup of
the Lord in an unworthy manner will be guilty of sinning
against the body and blood of the Lord. 28 A man ought to
examine himself before he eats of the bread and drinks of

NEW LIVING TRANSLATION

and drinking? Or do you really want to disgrace the church
of God and shame the poor? What am I supposed to say
about these things? Do you want me to praise you? Well, I
certainly do not!
23 For this is what the Lord himself said, and I pass it on
to you just as I received it. On the night when he was
betrayed, the Lord Jesus took a loaf of bread, 24 and when
he had given thanks, he broke it and said, "This is my
body, which is given* for you. Do this in remembrance of
me." 25 In the same way, he took the cup of wine after sup-
per, saying, "This cup is the new covenant between God
and you, sealed by the shedding of my blood. Do this in
remembrance of me as often as you drink it." 26 For every
time you eat this bread and drink this cup, you are
announcing the Lord's death until he comes again.
27 So if anyone eats this bread or drinks this cup of the
Lord unworthily, that person is guilty of sinning against the
body and the blood of the Lord. 28 That is why you should
examine yourself before eating the bread and drinking from

11:24 Some manuscripts read *broken.*

NEW KING JAMES VERSION

of God and shame those who have nothing? What shall I
say to you? Shall I praise you in this? I do not praise *you.*

Institution of the Lord's Supper

23 For I received from the Lord that which I also delivered
to you: that the Lord Jesus on the *same* night in which He
was betrayed took bread; 24 and when He had given
thanks, He broke *it* and said, "Take, eat;[b] this is My body
which is broken[c] for you; do this in remembrance of Me."
25 In the same manner *He* also *took* the cup after supper,
saying, "This cup is the new covenant in My blood. This
do, as often as you drink *it,* in remembrance of Me."
26 For as often as you eat this bread and drink this cup,
you proclaim the Lord's death till He comes.

Examine Yourself

27 Therefore whoever eats this bread or drinks *this* cup of
the Lord in an unworthy manner will be guilty of the body
and blood[d] of the Lord. 28 But let a man examine himself,
and so let him eat of the bread and drink of the cup. 29 For

11:24 [b] NU-Text omits *Take, eat.* [c] NU-Text omits *broken.*
11:27 [d] NU-Text and M-Text read *the blood.*

THE MESSAGE

drink in? Why would you stoop to desecrating God's
church? Why would you actually shame God's poor? I
never would have believed you would stoop to this. And
I'm not going to stand by and say nothing.

Let me go over with you again exactly what goes on in
the Lord's Supper and why it is so centrally important. I
received my instructions from the Master himself and
passed them on to you. The Master, Jesus, on the night of
his betrayal, took bread. Having given thanks, he broke it
and said,

"This is my body, broken for you.
Do this to remember me."

After supper, he did the same thing with the cup:

"This cup is my blood, my new covenant with you.
Each time you drink this cup, remember me."

What you must solemnly realize is that every time you eat
this bread and every time you drink this cup, you reenact in
your words and actions the death of the Master. You will be
drawn back to this meal again and again until the Master
returns. You must never let familiarity breed contempt.

Anyone who eats the bread or drinks the cup of the
Master irreverently is like part of the crowd that jeered and
spit on him at his death. Is that the kind of "remem-
brance" you want to be part of? Examine your motives,
test your heart, come to this meal in holy awe.

KING JAMES VERSION

29 For he that eateth and drinketh unworthily, eateth and drinketh damnation to himself, not discerning the Lord's body.

30 For this cause many *are* weak and sickly among you, and many sleep.

31 For if we would judge ourselves, we should not be judged.

32 But when we are judged, we are chastened of the Lord, that we should not be condemned with the world.

33 Wherefore, my brethren, when ye come together to eat, tarry one for another.

34 And if any man hunger, let him eat at home; that ye come not together unto condemnation. And the rest will I set in order when I come.

12 Now concerning spiritual *gifts*, brethren, I would not have you ignorant.

2 Ye know that ye were Gentiles, carried away unto these dumb idols, even as ye were led.

3 Wherefore I give you to understand, that no man speaking by the Spirit of God calleth Jesus accursed: and *that* no man can say that Jesus is the Lord, but by the Holy Ghost.

NEW AMERICAN STANDARD BIBLE

29 For he who eats and drinks, eats and drinks judgment to himself if he does not judge the body rightly.

30 For this reason many among you are weak and sick, and a number sleep.

31 But if we judged ourselves rightly, we would not be judged.

32 But when we are judged, we are disciplined by the Lord so that we will not be condemned along with the world.

33 So then, my brethren, when you come together to eat, wait for one another.

34 If anyone is hungry, let him eat at home, so that you will not come together for judgment. The remaining matters I will arrange when I come.

The Use of Spiritual Gifts

12 Now concerning spiritual *gifts,* brethren, I do not want you to be unaware.

2 You know that when you were pagans, *you were* led astray to the mute idols, however you were led.

3 Therefore I make known to you that no one speaking by the Spirit of God says, "Jesus is accursed"; and no one can say, "Jesus is Lord," except by the Holy Spirit.

NEW CENTURY VERSION

the cup, 29because all who eat the bread and drink the cup without recognizing the body eat and drink judgment against themselves. 30That is why many in your group are sick and weak, and many have died. 31But if we judged ourselves in the right way, God would not judge us. 32But when the Lord judges us, he punishes us so that we will not be destroyed along with the world.

33So my brothers and sisters, when you come together to eat, wait for each other. 34Anyone who is too hungry should eat at home so that in meeting together you will not bring God's judgment on yourselves. I will tell you what to do about the other things when I come.

Gifts from the Holy Spirit

12 Now, brothers and sisters, I want you to understand about spiritual gifts. 2You know the way you lived before you were believers. You let yourselves be influenced and led away to worship idols—things that could not speak. 3So I want you to understand that no one who is speaking with the help of God's Spirit says, "Jesus be cursed." And no one can say, "Jesus is Lord," without the help of the Holy Spirit.

CONTEMPORARY ENGLISH VERSION

and drink. 29If you fail to understand that you are the body of the Lord, you will condemn yourselves by the way you eat and drink. 30That's why many of you are sick and weak and why a lot of others have died. 31If we carefully judge ourselves, we won't be punished. 32But when the Lord judges and punishes us, he does it to keep us from being condemned with the rest of the world.

33My dear friends, you should wait until everyone gets there before you start eating. 34If you really are hungry, you can eat at home. Then you won't condemn yourselves when you meet together.

After I arrive, I will instruct you about the other matters.

Spiritual Gifts

12 My friends, you asked me about spiritual gifts. 2I want you to remember that before you became followers of the Lord, you were led in all the wrong ways by idols that cannot even talk. 3Now I want you to know that if you are led by God's Spirit, you will say that Jesus is Lord, and you will never curse Jesus.

NEW INTERNATIONAL VERSION

the cup. 29 For anyone who eats and drinks without recognizing the body of the Lord eats and drinks judgment on himself. 30 That is why many among you are weak and sick, and a number of you have fallen asleep. 31 But if we judged ourselves, we would not come under judgment. 32 When we are judged by the Lord, we are being disciplined so that we will not be condemned with the world.

33 So then, my brothers, when you come together to eat, wait for each other. 34 If anyone is hungry, he should eat at home, so that when you meet together it may not result in judgment.

And when I come I will give further directions.

Spiritual Gifts

12 Now about spiritual gifts, brothers, I do not want you to be ignorant. 2 You know that when you were pagans, somehow or other you were influenced and led astray to mute idols. 3 Therefore I tell you that no one who is speaking by the Spirit of God says, "Jesus be cursed," and no one can say, "Jesus is Lord," except by the Holy Spirit.

NEW LIVING TRANSLATION

the cup. 29 For if you eat the bread or drink the cup unworthily, not honoring the body of Christ,* you are eating and drinking God's judgment upon yourself. 30 That is why many of you are weak and sick and some have even died.

31 But if we examine ourselves, we will not be examined by God and judged in this way. 32 But when we are judged and disciplined by the Lord, we will not be condemned with the world. 33 So, dear brothers and sisters,* when you gather for the Lord's Supper, wait for each other. 34 If you are really hungry, eat at home so you won't bring judgment upon yourselves when you meet together.

I'll give you instructions about the other matters after I arrive.

Spiritual Gifts

12 And now, dear brothers and sisters,* I will write about the special abilities the Holy Spirit gives to each of us, for I must correct your misunderstandings about them. 2 You know that when you were still pagans you were led astray and swept along in worshiping speechless idols. 3 So I want you to know how to discern what is truly from God: No one speaking by the Spirit of God can curse Jesus, and no one is able to say, "Jesus is Lord," except by the Holy Spirit.

11:29 Greek *the body;* some manuscripts read *the Lord's body.*
11:33 Greek *brothers.* 12:1 Greek *brothers.*

NEW KING JAMES VERSION

he who eats and drinks in an unworthy manner[e] eats and drinks judgment to himself, not discerning the Lord's[f] body. 30 For this reason many *are* weak and sick among you, and many sleep. 31 For if we would judge ourselves, we would not be judged. 32 But when we are judged, we are chastened by the Lord, that we may not be condemned with the world.

33 Therefore, my brethren, when you come together to eat, wait for one another. 34 But if anyone is hungry, let him eat at home, lest you come together for judgment. And the rest I will set in order when I come.

Spiritual Gifts: Unity in Diversity

12 Now concerning spiritual *gifts,* brethren, I do not want you to be ignorant: 2 You know that[a] you were Gentiles, carried away to these dumb idols, however you were led. 3 Therefore I make known to you that no one speaking by the Spirit of God calls Jesus accursed, and no one can say that Jesus is Lord except by the Holy Spirit.

11:29 [e] NU-Text omits *in an unworthy manner.* [f] NU-Text omits *Lord's.* 12:2 [a] NU-Text and M-Text add *when.*

THE MESSAGE

If you give no thought (or worse, don't care) about the broken body of the Master when you eat and drink, you're running the risk of serious consequences. That's why so many of you even now are listless and sick, and others have gone to an early grave. If we get this straight now, we won't have to be straightened out later on. Better to be confronted by the Master now than to face a fiery confrontation later.

So, my friends, when you come together to the Lord's Table, be reverent and courteous with one another. If you're so hungry that you can't wait to be served, go home and get a sandwich. But by no means risk turning this Meal into an eating and drinking binge or a family squabble. It is a spiritual meal—a love feast.

The other things you asked about, I'll respond to in person when I make my next visit.

Spiritual Gifts

12 What I want to talk about now is the various ways God's Spirit gets worked into our lives. This is complex and often misunderstood, but I want you to be informed and knowledgeable. Remember how you were when you didn't know God, led from one phony god to another, never knowing what you were doing, just doing it because everybody else did it? It's different in this life. God wants us to use our intelligence, to seek to understand as well as we can. For instance, by using your heads, you know perfectly well that the Spirit of God would never prompt anyone to say "Jesus be damned!" Nor would anyone be inclined to say "Jesus is Master!" without the insight of the Holy Spirit.

KING JAMES VERSION

4 Now there are diversities of gifts, but the same Spirit.
5 And there are differences of administrations, but the same Lord.
6 And there are diversities of operations, but it is the same God which worketh all in all.
7 But the manifestation of the Spirit is given to every man to profit withal.
8 For to one is given by the Spirit the word of wisdom; to another the word of knowledge by the same Spirit;
9 To another faith by the same Spirit; to another the gifts of healing by the same Spirit;
10 To another the working of miracles; to another prophecy; to another discerning of spirits; to another *divers* kinds of tongues; to another the interpretation of tongues:
11 But all these worketh that one and the selfsame Spirit, dividing to every man severally as he will.
12 ¶ For as the body is one, and hath many members, and all the members of that one body, being many, are one body: so also *is* Christ.

NEW AMERICAN STANDARD BIBLE

4 Now there are varieties of gifts, but the same Spirit.
5 And there are varieties of ministries, and the same Lord.
6 There are varieties of effects, but the same God who works all things in all *persons.*
7 But to each one is given the manifestation of the Spirit for the common good.
8 For to one is given the word of wisdom through the Spirit, and to another the word of knowledge according to the same Spirit;
9 to another faith by the same Spirit, and to another gifts of healing by the one Spirit,
10 and to another the effecting of miracles, and to another prophecy, and to another the distinguishing of spirits, to another *various* kinds of tongues, and to another the interpretation of tongues.
11 But one and the same Spirit works all these things, distributing to each one individually just as He wills.
12 For even as the body is one and *yet* has many members, and all the members of the body, though they are many, are one body, so also is Christ.

NEW CENTURY VERSION

[4]There are different kinds of gifts, but they are all from the same Spirit. [5]There are different ways to serve but the same Lord to serve. [6]And there are different ways that God works through people but the same God. God works in all of us in everything we do. [7]Something from the Spirit can be seen in each person, for the common good. [8]The Spirit gives one person the ability to speak with wisdom, and the same Spirit gives another the ability to speak with knowledge. [9]The same Spirit gives faith to one person. And, to another, that one Spirit gives gifts of healing. [10]The Spirit gives to another person the power to do miracles, to another the ability to prophesy. And he gives to another the ability to know the difference between good and evil spirits. The Spirit gives one person the ability to speak in different kinds of languages[a] and to another the ability to interpret those languages. [11]One Spirit, the same Spirit, does all these things, and the Spirit decides what to give each person.

The Body of Christ Works Together

[12]A person's body is only one thing, but it has many parts. Though there are many parts to a body, all those parts make only one body. Christ is like that also. [13]Some

12:10 [a] **languages** This can also be translated "tongues."

CONTEMPORARY ENGLISH VERSION

[4]There are different kinds of spiritual gifts, but they all come from the same Spirit. [5]There are different ways to serve the same Lord, [6]and we can each do different things. Yet the same God works in all of us and helps us in everything we do.

[7]The Spirit has given each of us a special way of serving others. [8]Some of us can speak with wisdom, while others can speak with knowledge, but these gifts come from the same Spirit. [9]To others the Spirit has given great faith or the power to heal the sick [10]or the power to work mighty miracles. Some of us are prophets, and some of us recognize when God's Spirit is present.[a] Others can speak different kinds of languages, and still others can tell what these languages mean. [11]But it is the Spirit who does all this and decides which gifts to give to each of us.

One Body with Many Parts

[12]The body of Christ has many different parts, just as any other body does. [13]Some of us are Jews, and others are

[a] **12.10** *and some of us . . . present*: Or "and some of us recognize the difference between God's Spirit and other spirits."

NEW INTERNATIONAL VERSION

4There are different kinds of gifts, but the same Spirit.
5There are different kinds of service, but the same Lord.
6There are different kinds of working, but the same God
works all of them in all men.

7Now to each one the manifestation of the Spirit is given
for the common good. 8To one there is given through the
Spirit the message of wisdom, to another the message of
knowledge by means of the same Spirit, 9to another faith
by the same Spirit, to another gifts of healing by that one
Spirit, 10to another miraculous powers, to another prophe-
cy, to another distinguishing between spirits, to another
speaking in different kinds of tongues,[a] and to still anoth-
er the interpretation of tongues.[a] 11All these are the work
of one and the same Spirit, and he gives them to each one,
just as he determines.

One Body, Many Parts

12The body is a unit, though it is made up of many parts;
and though all its parts are many, they form one body. So it

[a] *10* Or *languages*; also in verse 28

NEW LIVING TRANSLATION

4Now there are different kinds of spiritual gifts, but it is
the same Holy Spirit who is the source of them all. 5There
are different kinds of service in the church, but it is the
same Lord we are serving. 6There are different ways God
works in our lives, but it is the same God who does the
work through all of us. 7A spiritual gift is given to each of
us as a means of helping the entire church.

8To one person the Spirit gives the ability to give wise
advice; to another he gives the gift of special knowledge.
9The Spirit gives special faith to another, and to someone
else he gives the power to heal the sick. 10He gives one
person the power to perform miracles, and to another the
ability to prophesy. He gives someone else the ability to
know whether it is really the Spirit of God or another spirit
that is speaking. Still another person is given the ability to
speak in unknown languages,* and another is given the
ability to interpret what is being said. 11It is the one and
only Holy Spirit who distributes these gifts. He alone
decides which gift each person should have.

One Body with Many Parts

12The human body has many parts, but the many parts
make up only one body. So it is with the body of Christ.

12:10 Or *in tongues;* also in 12:28, 30.

NEW KING JAMES VERSION

4There are diversities of gifts, but the same Spirit.
5There are differences of ministries, but the same Lord.
6And there are diversities of activities, but it is the same
God who works all in all. 7But the manifestation of the
Spirit is given to each one for the profit *of all:* 8for to one
is given the word of wisdom through the Spirit, to another
the word of knowledge through the same Spirit, 9to anoth-
er faith by the same Spirit, to another gifts of healings by
the same[b] Spirit, 10to another the working of miracles, to
another prophecy, to another discerning of spirits, to
another *different* kinds of tongues, to another the interpre-
tation of tongues. 11But one and the same Spirit works all
these things, distributing to each one individually as He
wills.

Unity and Diversity in One Body

12For as the body is one and has many members, but all
the members of that one body, being many, are one body,

12:9 [b] NU-Text reads *one.*

THE MESSAGE

God's various gifts are handed out everywhere; but they all originate in God's Spirit. God's various ministries are carried out everywhere; but they all originate in God's Spirit. God's various expressions of power are in action everywhere; but God himself is behind it all. Each person is given something to do that shows who God is: Everyone gets in on it, everyone benefits. All kinds of things are handed out by the Spirit, and to all kinds of people! The variety is wonderful:

wise counsel
clear understanding
simple trust
healing the sick
miraculous acts
proclamation
distinguishing between spirits
tongues
interpretation of tongues.

All these gifts have a common origin, but are handed out one by one by the one Spirit of God. He decides who gets what, and when.

You can easily enough see how this kind of thing works by looking no further than your own body. Your body has many parts—limbs, organs, cells—but no matter how many parts you can name, you're still one body. It's exactly the same with Christ. By means of his one Spirit, we all said goodbye to our partial and piecemeal lives. We each

KING JAMES VERSION

13 For by one Spirit are we all baptized into one body, whether *we be* Jews or Gentiles, whether *we be* bond or free; and have been all made to drink into one Spirit.

14 For the body is not one member, but many.

15 If the foot shall say, Because I am not the hand, I am not of the body; is it therefore not of the body?

16 And if the ear shall say, Because I am not the eye, I am not of the body; is it therefore not of the body?

17 If the whole body *were* an eye, where *were* the hearing? If the whole *were* hearing, where *were* the smelling?

18 But now hath God set the members every one of them in the body, as it hath pleased him.

19 And if they were all one member, where *were* the body?

20 But now *are they* many members, yet but one body.

21 And the eye cannot say unto the hand, I have no need of thee: nor again the head to the feet, I have no need of you.

NEW AMERICAN STANDARD BIBLE

13 For by one Spirit we were all baptized into one body, whether Jews or Greeks, whether slaves or free, and we were all made to drink of one Spirit.

14 For the body is not one member, but many.

15 If the foot says, "Because I am not a hand, I am not *a part* of the body," it is not for this reason any the less *a part* of the body.

16 And if the ear says, "Because I am not an eye, I am not *a part* of the body," it is not for this reason any the less *a part* of the body.

17 If the whole body were an eye, where would the hearing be? If the whole were hearing, where would the sense of smell be?

18 But now God has placed the members, each one of them, in the body, just as He desired.

19 If they were all one member, where would the body be?

20 But now there are many members, but one body.

21 And the eye cannot say to the hand, "I have no need of you"; or again the head to the feet, "I have no need of you."

NEW CENTURY VERSION

of us are Jews, and some are Greeks. Some of us are
slaves, and some are free. But we were all baptized into
one body through one Spirit. And we were all made to
share in the one Spirit.
14The human body has many parts. 15The foot might
say, "Because I am not a hand, I am not part of the body."
But saying this would not stop the foot from being a part
of the body. 16The ear might say, "Because I am not an
eye, I am not part of the body." But saying this would not
stop the ear from being a part of the body. 17If the whole
body were an eye, it would not be able to hear. If the whole
body were an ear, it would not be able to smell. 18–19If each
part of the body were the same part, there would be no
body. But truly God put all the parts, each one of them, in
the body as he wanted them. 20So then there are many
parts, but only one body.
21The eye cannot say to the hand, "I don't need you!"
And the head cannot say to the foot, "I don't need you!"

CONTEMPORARY ENGLISH VERSION

Gentiles. Some of us are slaves, and others are free. But
God's Spirit baptized each of us and made us part of the
body of Christ. Now we each drink from that same Spirit.[b]
14Our bodies don't have just one part. They have many
parts. 15Suppose a foot says, "I'm not a hand, and so I'm
not part of the body." Wouldn't the foot still belong to the
body? 16Or suppose an ear says, "I'm not an eye, and so
I'm not part of the body." Wouldn't the ear still belong to
the body? 17If our bodies were only an eye, we couldn't
hear a thing. And if they were only an ear, we couldn't
smell a thing. 18But God has put all parts of our body
together in the way that he decided is best.
19A body isn't really a body, unless there is more than
one part. 20It takes many parts to make a single body.
21That's why the eyes cannot say they don't need the
hands. That's also why the head cannot say it doesn't

[b] 12.13 *Some of us are Jews . . . that same Spirit*: Verse 13 may also be translated, "God's Spirit is inside each of us, and all around us as well. So it doesn't matter that some of us are Jews and others are Gentiles and that some are slaves and others are free. Together we are one body."

NEW INTERNATIONAL VERSION

is with Christ. 13For we were all baptized by[b] one Spirit into
one body—whether Jews or Greeks, slave or free—and we
were all given the one Spirit to drink.
14Now the body is not made up of one part but of many.
15If the foot should say, "Because I am not a hand, I do not
belong to the body," it would not for that reason cease to
be part of the body. 16And if the ear should say, "Because I
am not an eye, I do not belong to the body," it would not
for that reason cease to be part of the body. 17If the whole
body were an eye, where would the sense of hearing be? If
the whole body were an ear, where would the sense of
smell be? 18But in fact God has arranged the parts in the
body, every one of them, just as he wanted them to be. 19If
they were all one part, where would the body be? 20As it is,
there are many parts, but one body.
21The eye cannot say to the hand, "I don't need you!"
And the head cannot say to the feet, "I don't need you!"

b 13 Or *with*; or *in*

NEW LIVING TRANSLATION

13Some of us are Jews, some are Gentiles, some are slaves,
and some are free. But we have all been baptized into
Christ's body by one Spirit, and we have all received the
same Spirit.*
14Yes, the body has many different parts, not just one
part. 15If the foot says, "I am not a part of the body
because I am not a hand," that does not make it any less a
part of the body. 16And if the ear says, "I am not part of
the body because I am only an ear and not an eye," would
that make it any less a part of the body? 17Suppose the
whole body were an eye—then how would you hear? Or if
your whole body were just one big ear, how could you
smell anything?
18But God made our bodies with many parts, and he has
put each part just where he wants it. 19What a strange
thing a body would be if it had only one part! 20Yes, there
are many parts, but only one body. 21The eye can never
say to the hand, "I don't need you." The head can't say to
the feet, "I don't need you."

12:13 Greek *we were all given one Spirit to drink.*

NEW KING JAMES VERSION

so also *is* Christ. 13For by one Spirit we were all baptized
into one body—whether Jews or Greeks, whether slaves or
free—and have all been made to drink into[c] one Spirit.
14For in fact the body is not one member but many.
15If the foot should say, "Because I am not a hand, I am
not of the body," is it therefore not of the body? 16And if
the ear should say, "Because I am not an eye, I am not of
the body," is it therefore not of the body? 17If the whole
body *were* an eye, where *would be* the hearing? If the
whole *were* hearing, where *would be* the smelling? 18But
now God has set the members, each one of them, in the
body just as He pleased. 19And if they *were* all one mem-
ber, where *would* the body *be?*
20But now indeed *there are* many members, yet one body.
21And the eye cannot say to the hand, "I have no need of
you"; nor again the head to the feet, "I have no need of

12:13 [c] NU-Text omits *into.*

THE MESSAGE

used to independently call our own shots, but then we entered into a large and integrated life in which *he* has the final say in everything. (This is what we proclaimed in word and action when we were baptized.) Each of us is now a part of his resurrection body, refreshed and sustained at one fountain—his Spirit—where we all come to drink. The old labels we once used to identify ourselves—labels like Jew or Greek, slave or free—are no longer useful. We need something larger, more comprehensive.

I want you to think about how all this makes you more significant, not less. A body isn't just a single part blown up into something huge. It's all the different-but-similar parts arranged and functioning together. If Foot said, "I'm not elegant like Hand, embellished with rings; I guess I don't belong to this body," would that make it so? If Ear said, "I'm not beautiful like Eye, limpid and expressive; I don't deserve a place on the head," would you want to remove it from the body? If the body was all eye, how could it hear? If all ear, how could it smell? As it is, we see that God has carefully placed each part of the body right where he wanted it.

But I also want you to think about how this keeps your significance from getting blown up into self-importance. For no matter how significant you are, it is only because of what you are a *part* of. An enormous eye or a gigantic hand wouldn't be a body, but a monster. What we have is one body with many parts, each its proper size and in its proper place. No part is important on its own. Can you imagine Eye telling Hand, "Get lost; I don't need you"? Or, Head telling Foot, "You're fired; your job has been phased out"? As a mat-

KING JAMES VERSION

22 Nay, much more those members of the body, which seem to be more feeble, are necessary:

23 And those *members* of the body, which we think to be less honourable, upon these we bestow more abundant honour; and our uncomely *parts* have more abundant comeliness.

24 For our comely *parts* have no need: but God hath tempered the body together, having given more abundant honour to that *part* which lacked:

25 That there should be no schism in the body; but *that* the members should have the same care one for another.

26 And whether one member suffer, all the members suffer with it; or one member be honoured, all the members rejoice with it.

27 ¶ Now ye are the body of Christ, and members in particular.

28 And God hath set some in the church, first apostles, secondarily prophets, thirdly teachers, after that miracles, then gifts of healings, helps, governments, diversities of tongues.

NEW AMERICAN STANDARD BIBLE

22 On the contrary, it is much truer that the members of the body which seem to be weaker are necessary;

23 and those *members* of the body which we deem less honorable, on these we bestow more abundant honor, and our less presentable members become much more presentable,

24 whereas our more presentable members have no need *of it*. But God has *so* composed the body, giving more abundant honor to that *member* which lacked,

25 so that there may be no division in the body, but *that* the members may have the same care for one another.

26 And if one member suffers, all the members suffer with it; if *one* member is honored, all the members rejoice with it.

27 Now you are Christ's body, and individually members of it.

28 And God has appointed in the church, first apostles, second prophets, third teachers, then miracles, then gifts of healings, helps, administrations, *various* kinds of tongues.

NEW CENTURY VERSION

22 No! Those parts of the body that seem to be the weaker
are really necessary. 23 And the parts of the body we think
are less deserving are the parts to which we give the most
honor. We give special respect to the parts we want to
hide. 24 The more respectable parts of our body need no
special care. But God put the body together and gave more
honor to the parts that need it 25 so our body would not be
divided. God wanted the different parts to care the same
for each other. 26 If one part of the body suffers, all the
other parts suffer with it. Or if one part of our body is honored, all the other parts share its honor.

27 Together you are the body of Christ, and each one of
you is a part of that body. 28 In the church God has given a
place first to apostles, second to prophets, and third to teachers. Then God has given a place to those who do miracles, those who have gifts of healing, those who can help others, those who are able to govern, and those who can

CONTEMPORARY ENGLISH VERSION

need the feet. 22 In fact, we cannot get along without the
parts of the body that seem to be the weakest. 23 We take
special care to dress up some parts of our bodies. We are
modest about our personal parts, 24 but we don't have to be
modest about other parts.

God put our bodies together in such a way that even the
parts that seem the least important are valuable. 25 He did
this to make all parts of the body work together smoothly,
with each part caring about the others. 26 If one part of our
body hurts, we hurt all over. If one part of our body is honored, the whole body will be happy.

27 Together you are the body of Christ. Each one of you is
part of his body. 28 First, God chose some people to be
apostles and prophets and teachers for the church. But he also chose some to work miracles or heal the sick or help others or be leaders or speak different kinds of languages.

NEW INTERNATIONAL VERSION

[22]On the contrary, those parts of the body that seem to be weaker are indispensable, [23]and the parts that we think are less honorable we treat with special honor. And the parts that are unpresentable are treated with special modesty, [24]while our presentable parts need no special treatment. But God has combined the members of the body and has given greater honor to the parts that lacked it, [25]so that there should be no division in the body, but that its parts should have equal concern for each other. [26]If one part suffers, every part suffers with it; if one part is honored, every part rejoices with it.

[27]Now you are the body of Christ, and each one of you is a part of it. [28]And in the church God has appointed first of all apostles, second prophets, third teachers, then workers of miracles, also those having gifts of healing, those able to help others, those with gifts of administration, and those speaking in different kinds of tongues. [29]Are all

NEW LIVING TRANSLATION

[22]In fact, some of the parts that seem weakest and least important are really the most necessary. [23]And the parts we regard as less honorable are those we clothe with the greatest care. So we carefully protect from the eyes of others those parts that should not be seen, [24]while other parts do not require this special care. So God has put the body together in such a way that extra honor and care are given to those parts that have less dignity. [25]This makes for harmony among the members, so that all the members care for each other equally. [26]If one part suffers, all the parts suffer with it, and if one part is honored, all the parts are glad.

[27]Now all of you together are Christ's body, and each one of you is a separate and necessary part of it. [28]Here is a list of some of the members that God has placed in the body of Christ:

first are apostles,
second are prophets,
third are teachers,
then those who do miracles,
those who have the gift of healing,
those who can help others,
those who can get others to work together,
those who speak in unknown languages.

NEW KING JAMES VERSION

you." [22]No, much rather, those members of the body which seem to be weaker are necessary. [23]And those *members* of the body which we think to be less honorable, on these we bestow greater honor; and our unpresentable *parts* have greater modesty, [24]but our presentable *parts* have no need. But God composed the body, having given greater honor to that *part* which lacks it, [25]that there should be no schism in the body, but *that* the members should have the same care for one another. [26]And if one member suffers, all the members suffer with *it;* or if one member is honored, all the members rejoice with *it.*

[27]Now you are the body of Christ, and members individually. [28]And God has appointed these in the church: first apostles, second prophets, third teachers, after that miracles, then gifts of healings, helps, administrations, varieties

THE MESSAGE

ter of fact, in practice it works the other way—the "lower" the part, the more basic, and therefore necessary. You can live without an eye, for instance, but not without a stomach. When it's a part of your own body you are concerned with, it makes *no* difference whether the part is visible or clothed, higher or lower. You give it dignity and honor just as it is, without comparisons. If anything, you have more concern for the lower parts than the higher. If you had to choose, wouldn't you prefer good digestion to full-bodied hair?

The way God designed our bodies is a model for understanding our lives together as a church: every part dependent on every other part, the parts we mention and the parts we don't, the parts we see and the parts we don't. If one part hurts, every other part is involved in the hurt, and in the healing. If one part flourishes, every other part enters into the exuberance.

You are Christ's body—that's who you are! You must never forget this. Only as you accept your part of that body does your "part" mean anything. You're familiar with some of the parts that God has formed in his church, which is his "body":

apostles
prophets
teachers
miracle workers
healers
helpers
organizers
those who pray in tongues.

KING JAMES VERSION

29 *Are* all apostles? *are* all prophets? *are* all teachers? *are* all workers of miracles?
30 Have all the gifts of healing? do all speak with tongues? do all interpret?
31 But covet earnestly the best gifts: and yet shew I unto you a more excellent way.
13 Though I speak with the tongues of men and of angels, and have not charity, I am become *as* sounding brass, or a tinkling cymbal.
2 And though I have *the gift of* prophecy, and understand all mysteries, and all knowledge; and though I have all faith, so that I could remove mountains, and have not charity, I am nothing.
3 And though I bestow all my goods to feed *the poor*, and though I give my body to be burned, and have not charity, it profiteth me nothing.

NEW AMERICAN STANDARD BIBLE

29 All are not apostles, are they? All are not prophets, are they? All are not teachers, are they? All are not *workers of* miracles, are they?
30 All do not have gifts of healings, do they? All do not speak with tongues, do they? All do not interpret, do they?
31 But earnestly desire the greater gifts.
And I show you a still more excellent way.

The Excellence of Love

13 If I speak with the tongues of men and of angels, but do not have love, I have become a noisy gong or a clanging cymbal.
2 If I have *the gift of* prophecy, and know all mysteries and all knowledge; and if I have all faith, so as to remove mountains, but do not have love, I am nothing.
3 And if I give all my possessions to feed *the poor,* and if I surrender my body [1]to be burned, but do not have love, it profits me nothing.

13:3 [1] Early mss read *that I may boast*

NEW CENTURY VERSION

speak in different languages.[b] 29Not all are apostles. Not
all are prophets. Not all are teachers. Not all do miracles.
30Not all have gifts of healing. Not all speak in different
languages. Not all interpret those languages. 31But you
should truly want to have the greater gifts.

Love Is the Greatest Gift

And now I will show you the best way of all.

13 I may speak in different languages[b] of people or
even angels. But if I do not have love, I am only a
noisy bell or a crashing cymbal. 2I may have the gift of
prophecy. I may understand all the secret things of God
and have all knowledge, and I may have faith so great I
can move mountains. But even with all these things, if I do
not have love, then I am nothing. 3I may give away everything I have, and I may even give my body as an offering
to be burned.[a] But I gain nothing if I do not have love.

12:28; 13:1 [b] **languages** This can also be translated "tongues."
13:3 [a] **Verse 3** Other Greek copies read: "hand over my body in order that I may brag."

CONTEMPORARY ENGLISH VERSION

29Not everyone is an apostle. Not everyone is a prophet.
Not everyone is a teacher. Not everyone can work miracles.
30Not everyone can heal the sick. Not everyone can speak
different kinds of languages. Not everyone can tell what
these languages mean. 31I want you to desire the best
gifts.[c] So I will show you a much better way.

Love

13 What if I could speak
all languages of humans
and of angels?
If I did not love others,
I would be nothing more
than a noisy gong
or a clanging cymbal.
2 What if I could prophesy
and understand all secrets
and all knowledge?
And what if I had faith
that moved mountains?
I would be nothing,
unless I loved others.
3 What if I gave away all
that I owned
and let myself
be burned alive?[a]

[c] **12.31** *I want you to desire the best gifts*: Or "You desire the best gifts."
[a] **13.3** *and let myself be burned alive*: Some manuscripts have "so that I could brag."

NEW INTERNATIONAL VERSION

apostles? Are all prophets? Are all teachers? Do all work
miracles? 30 Do all have gifts of healing? Do all speak in
tongues[c]? Do all interpret? 31 But eagerly desire[d] the
greater gifts.

Love

And now I will show you the most excellent way.

13 If I speak in the tongues[a] of men and of angels,
but have not love, I am only a resounding gong or
a clanging cymbal. 2 If I have the gift of prophecy and can
fathom all mysteries and all knowledge, and if I have a
faith that can move mountains, but have not love, I am
nothing. 3 If I give all I possess to the poor and surrender
my body to the flames,[b] but have not love, I gain nothing.

[c] *30* Or *other languages* [d] *31* Or *But you are eagerly desiring*
[a] *1* Or *languages* [b] *3* Some early manuscripts *body that I may boast*

NEW LIVING TRANSLATION

29 Is everyone an apostle? Of course not. Is everyone a
prophet? No. Are all teachers? Does everyone have the
power to do miracles? 30 Does everyone have the gift of
healing? Of course not. Does God give all of us the ability
to speak in unknown languages? Can everyone interpret
unknown languages? No! 31 And in any event, you should
desire the most helpful gifts.

Love Is the Greatest

First, however, let me tell you about something else that
is better than any of them!

13 If I could speak in any language in heaven or on
earth* but didn't love others, I would only be mak-
ing meaningless noise like a loud gong or a clanging cym-
bal. 2 If I had the gift of prophecy, and if I knew all the
mysteries of the future and knew everything about every-
thing, but didn't love others, what good would I be? And if
I had the gift of faith so that I could speak to a mountain
and make it move, without love I would be no good to any-
body. 3 If I gave everything I have to the poor and even sac-
rificed my body, I could boast about it;* but if I didn't love
others, I would be of no value whatsoever.

13:1 Greek *in tongues of people and angels.* 13:3 Some manuscripts read *and even gave my body to be burned.*

NEW KING JAMES VERSION

of tongues. 29 *Are* all apostles? *Are* all prophets? *Are* all
teachers? *Are* all workers of miracles? 30 Do all have gifts of
healings? Do all speak with tongues? Do all interpret?
31 But earnestly desire the best[d] gifts. And yet I show you a
more excellent way.

The Greatest Gift

13 Though I speak with the tongues of men and of
angels, but have not love, I have become sounding
brass or a clanging cymbal. 2 And though I have *the gift of*
prophecy, and understand all mysteries and all knowledge,
and though I have all faith, so that I could remove moun-
tains, but have not love, I am nothing. 3 And though I
bestow all my goods to feed *the poor,* and though I give my
body to be burned,[a] but have not love, it profits me noth-
ing.

12:31 [d] NU-Text reads *greater.* 13:3 [a] NU-Text reads *so I may boast.*

THE MESSAGE

But it's obvious by now, isn't it, that Christ's church is a complete Body and not a gigantic, unidimensional Part? It's not all Apostle, not all Prophet, not all Miracle Worker, not all Healer, not all Prayer in Tongues, not all Interpreter of Tongues. And yet some of you keep competing for so-called "important" parts.

But now I want to lay out a far better way for you.

The Way of Love

13 If I speak with human eloquence and angelic ecstasy but don't love, I'm nothing but the creaking of a rusty gate.

If I speak God's Word with power, revealing all his mysteries and making everything plain as day, and if I have faith that says to a mountain, "Jump," and it jumps, but I don't love, I'm nothing.

If I give everything I own to the poor and even go to the stake to be burned as a martyr, but I don't love, I've gotten nowhere. So, no matter what I say, what I believe, and what I do, I'm bankrupt without love.

KING JAMES VERSION

4 ¶ Charity suffereth long, *and* is kind; charity envieth
not; charity vaunteth not itself, is not puffed up,
5 Doth not behave itself unseemly, seeketh not her own,
is not easily provoked, thinketh no evil;
6 Rejoiceth not in iniquity, but rejoiceth in the truth;
7 Beareth all things, believeth all things, hopeth all
things, endureth all things.
8 ¶ Charity never faileth: but whether *there be* prophe-
cies, they shall fail; whether *there be* tongues, they shall
cease; whether *there be* knowledge, it shall vanish away.
9 For we know in part, and we prophesy in part.
10 But when that which is perfect is come, then that
which is in part shall be done away.

NEW AMERICAN STANDARD BIBLE

4 Love is patient, love is kind *and* is not jealous; love
does not brag *and* is not arrogant,
5 does not act unbecomingly; it does not seek its own,
is not provoked, does not take into account a wrong *suf-
fered,*
6 does not rejoice in unrighteousness, but rejoices with
the truth;
7 bears all things, believes all things, hopes all things,
endures all things.
8 Love never fails; but if *there are gifts of* prophecy,
they will be done away; if *there are* tongues, they will
cease; if *there is* knowledge, it will be done away.
9 For we know in part and we prophesy in part;
10 but when the perfect comes, the partial will be done
away.

NEW CENTURY VERSION

[4]Love is patient and kind. Love is not jealous, it does
not brag, and it is not proud. [5]Love is not rude, is not self-
ish, and does not get upset with others. Love does not
count up wrongs that have been done. [6]Love is not happy
with evil but is happy with the truth. [7]Love patiently
accepts all things. It always trusts, always hopes, and
always remains strong.

[8]Love never ends. There are gifts of prophecy, but they
will be ended. There are gifts of speaking in different lan-
guages, but those gifts will stop. There is the gift of knowl-
edge, but it will come to an end. [9]The reason is that our
knowledge and our ability to prophesy are not perfect. [10]But
when perfection comes, the things that are not perfect will

CONTEMPORARY ENGLISH VERSION

I would gain nothing,
  unless I loved others.
[4]Love is kind and patient,
never jealous, boastful,
  proud, or [5]rude.
Love isn't selfish
  or quick tempered.
It doesn't keep a record
  of wrongs that others do.
[6]Love rejoices in the truth,
  but not in evil.
[7]Love is always supportive,
loyal, hopeful,
  and trusting.
[8]Love never fails!

Everyone who prophesies
  will stop,
and unknown languages
will no longer
  be spoken.
All that we know
  will be forgotten.
[9]We don't know everything,
and our prophecies
  are not complete.
[10]But what is perfect
  will someday appear,
and what isn't perfect
  will then disappear.

NEW INTERNATIONAL VERSION

[4]Love is patient, love is kind. It does not envy, it does
not boast, it is not proud. [5]It is not rude, it is not self-seek-
ing, it is not easily angered, it keeps no record of wrongs.
[6]Love does not delight in evil but rejoices with the truth.
[7]It always protects, always trusts, always hopes, always
perseveres.

[8]Love never fails. But where there are prophecies, they
will cease; where there are tongues, they will be stilled;
where there is knowledge, it will pass away. [9]For we know
in part and we prophesy in part, [10]but when perfection
comes, the imperfect disappears. [11]When I was a child, I

NEW LIVING TRANSLATION

[4]Love is patient and kind. Love is not jealous or boastful
or proud [5]or rude. Love does not demand its own way.
Love is not irritable, and it keeps no record of when it has
been wronged. [6]It is never glad about injustice but rejoices
whenever the truth wins out. [7]Love never gives up, never
loses faith, is always hopeful, and endures through every
circumstance.

[8]Love will last forever, but prophecy and speaking in
unknown languages* and special knowledge will all disap-
pear. [9]Now we know only a little, and even the gift of
prophecy reveals little! [10]But when the end comes, these
special gifts will all disappear.

13:8 Or *in tongues.*

NEW KING JAMES VERSION

[4]Love suffers long *and* is kind; love does not envy; love
does not parade itself, is not puffed up; [5]does not behave
rudely, does not seek its own, is not provoked, thinks no
evil; [6]does not rejoice in iniquity, but rejoices in the truth;
[7]bears all things, believes all things, hopes all things,
endures all things.

[8]Love never fails. But whether *there are* prophecies, they
will fail; whether *there are* tongues, they will cease;
whether *there is* knowledge, it will vanish away. [9]For we
know in part and we prophesy in part. [10]But when that
which is perfect has come, then that which is in part will
be done away.

THE MESSAGE

Love never gives up.
Love cares more for others than for self.
Love doesn't want what it doesn't have.
Love doesn't strut,
Doesn't have a swelled head,
Doesn't force itself on others,
Isn't always "me first,"
Doesn't fly off the handle,
Doesn't keep score of the sins of others,
Doesn't revel when others grovel,
Takes pleasure in the flowering of truth,
Puts up with anything,
Trusts God always,
Always looks for the best,
Never looks back,
But keeps going to the end.

Love never dies. Inspired speech will be over some day; praying in tongues will end; understanding will reach its limit. We know only a portion of the truth, and what we say about God is always incomplete. But when the Complete arrives, our incompletes will be canceled.

KING JAMES VERSION

11 When I was a child, I spake as a child, I understood as a child, I thought as a child: but when I became a man, I put away childish things.

12 For now we see through a glass, darkly; but then face to face: now I know in part; but then shall I know even as also I am known.

13 And now abideth faith, hope, charity, these three; but the greatest of these *is* charity.

14 Follow after charity, and desire spiritual *gifts*, but rather that ye may prophesy.

2 For he that speaketh in an *unknown* tongue speaketh not unto men, but unto God: for no man understandeth *him*; howbeit in the spirit he speaketh mysteries.

3 But he that prophesieth speaketh unto men *to* edification, and exhortation, and comfort.

NEW AMERICAN STANDARD BIBLE

11 When I was a child, I used to speak like a child, think like a child, reason like a child; when I became a man, I did away with childish things.

12 For now we see in a mirror dimly, but then face to face; now I know in part, but then I will know fully just as I also have been fully known.

13 But now faith, hope, love, abide these three; but the greatest of these is love.

Prophecy a Superior Gift

14 Pursue love, yet desire earnestly spiritual *gifts*, but especially that you may prophesy.

2 For one who speaks in a tongue does not speak to men but to God; for no one understands, but in *his* spirit he speaks mysteries.

3 But one who prophesies speaks to men for edification and exhortation and consolation.

NEW CENTURY VERSION

end. 11When I was a child, I talked like a child, I thought
like a child, I reasoned like a child. When I became a man, I
stopped those childish ways. 12It is the same with us. Now
we see a dim reflection, as if we were looking into a mirror,
but then we shall see clearly. Now I know only a part, but
then I will know fully, as God has known me. 13So these
three things continue forever: faith, hope, and love. And the
greatest of these is love.

Desire Spiritual Gifts

14 You should seek after love, and you should truly
want to have the spiritual gifts, especially the gift
of prophecy. 2I will explain why. Those who have the gift
of speaking in different languages[a] are not speaking to
people; they are speaking to God. No one understands
them; they are speaking secret things through the Spirit.
3But those who prophesy are speaking to people to give
them strength, encouragement, and comfort. 4The ones

14:2 [a] **languages** This can also be translated "tongues."

CONTEMPORARY ENGLISH VERSION

11 When we were children,
we thought and reasoned
as children do.
But when we grew up,
we quit our childish ways.
12 Now all we can see of God
is like a cloudy picture
in a mirror.
Later we will see him
face to face.
We don't know everything,
but then we will,
just as God completely
understands us.
13 For now there are faith,
hope, and love.
But of these three,
the greatest is love.

Speaking Unknown Languages and Prophesying

14 Love should be your guide. Be eager to have the
gifts that come from the Holy Spirit, especially the
gift of prophecy. 2If you speak languages that others don't
know, God will understand what you are saying, though
no one else will know what you mean. You will be talking
about mysteries that only the Spirit understands. 3But
when you prophesy, you will be understood, and others
will be helped. They will be encouraged and made to feel
better.

NEW INTERNATIONAL VERSION

talked like a child, I thought like a child, I reasoned like a child. When I became a man, I put childish ways behind me. 12 Now we see but a poor reflection as in a mirror; then we shall see face to face. Now I know in part; then I shall know fully, even as I am fully known.

13 And now these three remain: faith, hope and love. But the greatest of these is love.

Gifts of Prophecy and Tongues

14 Follow the way of love and eagerly desire spiritual gifts, especially the gift of prophecy. 2 For anyone who speaks in a tongue[a] does not speak to men but to God. Indeed, no one understands him; he utters mysteries with his spirit.[b] 3 But everyone who prophesies speaks to men for their strengthening, encouragement and comfort.

[a] 2 Or *another language*; also in verses 4, 13, 14, 19, 26 and 27
[b] 2 Or *by the Spirit*

NEW LIVING TRANSLATION

11 It's like this: When I was a child, I spoke and thought and reasoned as a child does. But when I grew up, I put away childish things. 12 Now we see things imperfectly as in a poor mirror, but then we will see everything with perfect clarity.* All that I know now is partial and incomplete, but then I will know everything completely, just as God knows me now.

13 There are three things that will endure—faith, hope, and love—and the greatest of these is love.

The Gifts of Tongues and Prophecy

14 Let love be your highest goal, but also desire the special abilities the Spirit gives, especially the gift of prophecy. 2 For if your gift is the ability to speak in tongues,* you will be talking to God but not to people, since they won't be able to understand you. You will be speaking by the power of the Spirit, but it will all be mysterious. 3 But one who prophesies is helping others grow in the Lord, encouraging and comforting them. 4 A person who speaks in

13:12 Greek *see face to face.* 14:2 Or *in unknown languages;* also in 14:4, 5, 13, 14, 18, 22, 28, 39.

NEW KING JAMES VERSION

11 When I was a child, I spoke as a child, I understood as a child, I thought as a child; but when I became a man, I put away childish things. 12 For now we see in a mirror, dimly, but then face to face. Now I know in part, but then I shall know just as I also am known.

13 And now abide faith, hope, love, these three; but the greatest of these *is* love.

Prophecy and Tongues

14 Pursue love, and desire spiritual *gifts,* but especially that you may prophesy. 2 For he who speaks in a tongue does not speak to men but to God, for no one understands *him;* however, in the spirit he speaks mysteries. 3 But he who prophesies speaks edification and exhortation and

THE MESSAGE

When I was an infant at my mother's breast, I gurgled and cooed like any infant. When I grew up, I left those infant ways for good.

We don't yet see things clearly. We're squinting in a fog, peering through a mist. But it won't be long before the weather clears and the sun shines bright! We'll see it all then, see it all as clearly as God sees us, knowing him directly just as he knows us!

But for right now, until that completeness, we have three things to do to lead us toward that consummation: Trust steadily in God, hope unswervingly, love extravagantly. And the best of the three is love.

Prayer Language

14 Go after a life of love as if your life depended on it—because it does. Give yourselves to the gifts God gives you. Most of all, try to proclaim his truth. If you praise him in the private language of tongues, God understands you but no one else does, for you are sharing intimacies just between you and him. But when you proclaim his truth in everyday speech, you're letting *others* in on the truth so that they can grow and be strong and experience his presence with you.

KING JAMES VERSION

4 He that speaketh in an *unknown* tongue edifieth himself; but he that prophesieth edifieth the church.

5 I would that ye all spake with tongues, but rather that ye prophesied: for greater *is* he that prophesieth than he that speaketh with tongues, except he interpret, that the church may receive edifying.

6 ¶ Now, brethren, if I come unto you speaking with tongues, what shall I profit you, except I shall speak to you either by revelation, or by knowledge, or by prophesying, or by doctrine?

7 And even things without life giving sound, whether pipe or harp, except they give a distinction in the sounds, how shall it be known what is piped or harped?

8 For if the trumpet give an uncertain sound, who shall prepare himself to the battle?

9 So likewise ye, except ye utter by the tongue words easy to be understood, how shall it be known what is spoken? for ye shall speak into the air.

10 There are, it may be, so many kinds of voices in the world, and none of them *is* without signification.

11 Therefore if I know not the meaning of the voice, I shall be unto him that speaketh a barbarian, and he that speaketh *shall be* a barbarian unto me.

12 Even so ye, forasmuch as ye are zealous of spiritual *gifts*, seek that ye may excel to the edifying of the church.

13 Wherefore let him that speaketh in an *unknown* tongue pray that he may interpret.

NEW AMERICAN STANDARD BIBLE

4 One who speaks in a tongue edifies himself; but one who prophesies edifies the church.

5 Now I wish that you all spoke in tongues, but *even* more that you would prophesy; and greater is one who prophesies than one who speaks in tongues, unless he interprets, so that the church may receive edifying.

6 But now, brethren, if I come to you speaking in tongues, what will I profit you unless I speak to you either by way of revelation or of knowledge or of prophecy or of teaching?

7 Yet *even* lifeless things, either flute or harp, in producing a sound, if they do not produce a distinction in the tones, how will it be known what is played on the flute or on the harp?

8 For if the bugle produces an indistinct sound, who will prepare himself for battle?

9 So also you, unless you utter by the tongue speech that is clear, how will it be known what is spoken? For you will be speaking into the air.

10 There are, perhaps, a great many kinds of languages in the world, and no *kind* is without meaning.

11 If then I do not know the meaning of the language, I will be to the one who speaks a barbarian, and the one who speaks will be a barbarian to me.

12 So also you, since you are zealous of spiritual *gifts*, seek to abound for the edification of the church.

13 Therefore let one who speaks in a tongue pray that he may interpret.

NEW CENTURY VERSION

who speak in different languages are helping only them-
selves, but those who prophesy are helping the whole
church. 5 I wish all of you had the gift of speaking in differ-
ent kinds of languages, but more, I wish you would proph-
esy. Those who prophesy are greater than those who can
only speak in different languages—unless someone is
there who can explain what is said so that the whole
church can be helped.
6 Brothers and sisters, will it help you if I come to you
speaking in different languages? No! It will help you only
if I bring you a new truth or some new knowledge, or
prophecy, or teaching. 7 It is the same as with lifeless
things that make sounds—like a flute or a harp. If they do
not make clear musical notes, you will not know what is
being played. 8 And in a war, if the trumpet does not give a
clear sound, who will prepare for battle? 9 It is the same
with you. Unless you speak clearly with your tongue, no
one can understand what you are saying. You will be talk-
ing into the air! 10 It may be true that there are all kinds of
sounds in the world, and none is without meaning. 11 But
unless I understand the meaning of what someone says to
me, I will be a foreigner to him, and he will be a foreigner
to me. 12 It is the same with you. Since you want spiritual
gifts very much, seek most of all to have the gifts that help
the church grow stronger.
13 The one who has the gift of speaking in a different lan-
guage should pray for the gift to interpret what is spoken.

CONTEMPORARY ENGLISH VERSION

4 By speaking languages that others don't know, you
help only yourself. But by prophesying you help everyone
in the church. 5 I am glad for you to speak unknown lan-
guages, although I had rather for you to prophesy. In fact,
prophesying does much more good than speaking
unknown languages, unless someone can help the church
by explaining what you mean.
6 My friends, what good would it do, if I came and spoke
unknown languages to you and didn't explain what I
meant? How would I help you, unless I told you what God
had shown me or gave you some knowledge or prophecy or
teaching? 7 If all musical instruments sounded alike, how
would you know the difference between a flute and a
harp? 8 If a bugle call isn't clear, how would you know to
get ready for battle?
9 That's how it is when you speak unknown languages.
If no one can understand what you are talking about, you
will only be talking to the wind. 10 There are many different
languages in this world, and all of them make sense. 11 But
if I don't understand the language that someone is using,
we will be like foreigners to each other. 12 If you really
want spiritual gifts, choose the ones that will be most
helpful to the church.
13 When we speak languages that others don't know, we
should pray for the power to explain what we mean. 14 For

NEW INTERNATIONAL VERSION

4He who speaks in a tongue edifies himself, but he who
prophesies edifies the church. 5I would like every one of
you to speak in tongues,[c] but I would rather have you
prophesy. He who prophesies is greater than one who
speaks in tongues,[c] unless he interprets, so that the
church may be edified.

6Now, brothers, if I come to you and speak in tongues,
what good will I be to you, unless I bring you some revela-
tion or knowledge or prophecy or word of instruction?
7Even in the case of lifeless things that make sounds, such
as the flute or harp, how will anyone know what tune is
being played unless there is a distinction in the notes?
8Again, if the trumpet does not sound a clear call, who will
get ready for battle? 9So it is with you. Unless you speak
intelligible words with your tongue, how will anyone know
what you are saying? You will just be speaking into the
air. 10Undoubtedly there are all sorts of languages in the
world, yet none of them is without meaning. 11If then I do
not grasp the meaning of what someone is saying, I am a
foreigner to the speaker, and he is a foreigner to me. 12So
it is with you. Since you are eager to have spiritual gifts,
try to excel in gifts that build up the church.

13For this reason anyone who speaks in a tongue should

[c] *5* Or *other languages*; also in verses 6, 18, 22, 23 and 39

NEW LIVING TRANSLATION

tongues is strengthened personally in the Lord, but one who
speaks a word of prophecy strengthens the entire church.

5I wish you all had the gift of speaking in tongues, but
even more I wish you were all able to prophesy. For proph-
ecy is a greater and more useful gift than speaking in
tongues, unless someone interprets what you are saying so
that the whole church can get some good out of it.

6Dear brothers and sisters,* if I should come to you talk-
ing in an unknown language,* how would that help you?
But if I bring you some revelation or some special knowl-
edge or some prophecy or some teaching—that is what will
help you. 7Even musical instruments like the flute or the
harp, though they are lifeless, are examples of the need for
speaking in plain language. For no one will recognize the
melody unless the notes are played clearly. 8And if the
bugler doesn't sound a clear call, how will the soldiers
know they are being called to battle? 9And it's the same
for you. If you talk to people in a language they don't
understand, how will they know what you mean? You
might as well be talking to an empty room.

10There are so many different languages in the world,
and all are excellent for those who understand them, 11but
to me they mean nothing. I will not understand people
who speak those languages, and they will not understand
me. 12Since you are so eager to have spiritual gifts, ask
God for those that will be of real help to the whole church.

13So anyone who has the gift of speaking in tongues

14:6a Greek *brothers;* also in 14:20, 26, 39. **14:6b** Or *in tongues;* also in 14:19, 23, 26, 27.

NEW KING JAMES VERSION

comfort to men. 4He who speaks in a tongue edifies himself,
but he who prophesies edifies the church. 5I wish you all
spoke with tongues, but even more that you prophesied; for[a]
he who prophesies *is* greater than he who speaks with
tongues, unless indeed he interprets, that the church may
receive edification.

Tongues Must Be Interpreted

6But now, brethren, if I come to you speaking with
tongues, what shall I profit you unless I speak to you
either by revelation, by knowledge, by prophesying, or by
teaching? 7Even things without life, whether flute or harp,
when they make a sound, unless they make a distinction
in the sounds, how will it be known what is piped or
played? 8For if the trumpet makes an uncertain sound,
who will prepare for battle? 9So likewise you, unless you
utter by the tongue words easy to understand, how will it
be known what is spoken? For you will be speaking into
the air. 10There are, it may be, so many kinds of languages
in the world, and none of them *is* without significance.
11Therefore, if I do not know the meaning of the language,
I shall be a foreigner to him who speaks, and he who
speaks *will be* a foreigner to me. 12Even so you, since you
are zealous for spiritual *gifts, let it be* for the edification of
the church *that* you seek to excel.

13Therefore let him who speaks in a tongue pray that he

14:5 [a] NU-Text reads *and.*

THE MESSAGE

The one who prays using a private "prayer language" cer-
tainly gets a lot out of it, but proclaiming God's truth to the
church in its common language brings the whole church
into growth and strength. I want all of you to develop inti-
macies with God in prayer, but please don't stop with that.
Go on and proclaim his clear truth to others. It's more
important that everyone have access to the knowledge and
love of God in language everyone understands than that
you go off and cultivate God's presence in a mysterious
prayer language—unless, of course, there is someone who
can interpret what you are saying for the benefit of all.

Think, friends: If I come to you and all I do is pray pri-
vately to God in a way only he can understand, what are
you going to get out of that? If I don't address you plainly
with some insight or truth or proclamation or teaching,
what help am I to you? If musical instruments—flutes,
say, or harps—aren't played so that each note is distinct
and in tune, how will anyone be able to catch the melody
and enjoy the music? If the trumpet call can't be distin-
guished, will anyone show up for the battle?

So if you speak in a way no one can understand, what's
the point of opening your mouth? There are many lan-
guages in the world and they all mean something to some-
one. But if *I* don't understand the language, it's not going
to do me much good. It's no different with you. Since you're
so eager to participate in what God is doing, why don't you
concentrate on doing what helps everyone in the church?

So, when you pray in your private prayer language, don't
hoard the experience for yourself. Pray for the insight and

KING JAMES VERSION

14 For if I pray in an *unknown* tongue, my spirit prayeth, but my understanding is unfruitful.

15 ¶ What is it then? I will pray with the spirit, and I will pray with the understanding also: I will sing with the spirit, and I will sing with the understanding also.

16 Else when thou shalt bless with the spirit, how shall he that occupieth the room of the unlearned say Amen at thy giving of thanks, seeing he understandeth not what thou sayest?

17 For thou verily givest thanks well, but the other is not edified.

18 I thank my God, I speak with tongues more than ye all:

19 Yet in the church I had rather speak five words with my understanding, that *by my voice* I might teach others also, than ten thousand words in an *unknown* tongue.

20 Brethren, be not children in understanding: howbeit in malice be ye children, but in understanding be men.

21 ¶ In the law it is written, With *men of* other tongues and other lips will I speak unto this people; and yet for all that will they not hear me, saith the Lord.

NEW AMERICAN STANDARD BIBLE

14 For if I pray in a tongue, my spirit prays, but my mind is unfruitful.

15 What is *the outcome* then? I will pray with the spirit and I will pray with the mind also; I will sing with the spirit and I will sing with the mind also.

16 Otherwise if you bless in the spirit *only,* how will the one who fills the place of the ungifted say the "Amen" at your giving of thanks, since he does not know what you are saying?

17 For you are giving thanks well enough, but the other person is not edified.

18 I thank God, I speak in tongues more than you all;

19 however, in the church I desire to speak five words with my mind so that I may instruct others also, rather than ten thousand words in a tongue.

Instruction for the Church

20 Brethren, do not be children in your thinking; yet in evil be infants, but in your thinking be mature.

21 In the Law it is written, "BY MEN OF STRANGE TONGUES AND BY THE LIPS OF STRANGERS I WILL SPEAK TO THIS PEOPLE, AND EVEN SO THEY WILL NOT LISTEN TO ME," says the Lord.

NEW CENTURY VERSION

14If I pray in a different language, my spirit is praying, but
my mind does nothing. 15So what should I do? I will pray
with my spirit, but I will also pray with my mind. I will sing
with my spirit, but I will also sing with my mind. 16If you
praise God with your spirit, those persons there without
understanding cannot say amen[b] to your prayer of thanks,
because they do not know what you are saying. 17You may
be thanking God in a good way, but the other person is not
helped.

18I thank God that I speak in different kinds of languages more than all of you. 19But in the church meetings
I would rather speak five words I understand in order to teach others than thousands of words in a different language.

20Brothers and sisters, do not think like children. In evil
things be like babies, but in your thinking you should be
like adults. 21It is written in the Scriptures:

"With people who use strange words and foreign languages
I will speak to these people.
But even then they will not listen to me," *Isaiah 28:11–12*
says the Lord.

14:16 [b] amen To say amen means to agree with the things that were said.

CONTEMPORARY ENGLISH VERSION

example, if I use an unknown language in my prayers, my
spirit prays but my mind is useless. 15Then what should I
do? There are times when I should pray with my spirit, and times when I should pray with my mind. Sometimes I should sing with my spirit, and at other times I should sing with my mind.

16Suppose some strangers are in your worship service,
when you are praising God with your spirit. If they don't
understand you, how will they know to say, "Amen"?
17You may be worshiping God in a wonderful way, but no
one else will be helped. 18I thank God that I speak
unknown languages more than any of you. 19But words
that make sense can help the church. That's why in church I had rather speak five words that make sense than to speak ten thousand words in a language that others don't know.

20My friends, stop thinking like children. Think like
mature people and be as innocent as tiny babies. 21In the
Scriptures the Lord says,

"I will use strangers
who speak unknown languages
to talk to my people.
They will speak to them
in foreign languages,
but still my people
won't listen to me."

NEW INTERNATIONAL VERSION

pray that he may interpret what he says. 14For if I pray in
a tongue, my spirit prays, but my mind is unfruitful. 15So
what shall I do? I will pray with my spirit, but I will also
pray with my mind; I will sing with my spirit, but I will
also sing with my mind. 16If you are praising God with
your spirit, how can one who finds himself among those
who do not understand[d] say "Amen" to your thanksgiving,
since he does not know what you are saying? 17You may
be giving thanks well enough, but the other man is not
edified.

18I thank God that I speak in tongues more than all of
you. 19But in the church I would rather speak five intelligi-
ble words to instruct others than ten thousand words in a
tongue.

20Brothers, stop thinking like children. In regard to evil
be infants, but in your thinking be adults. 21In the Law it
is written:

"Through men of strange tongues
and through the lips of foreigners
I will speak to this people,
but even then they will not listen to me,"[e]
says the Lord.

[d] *16* Or *among the inquirers* [e] *21* Isaiah 28:11,12

NEW LIVING TRANSLATION

should pray also for the gift of interpretation in order to
tell people plainly what has been said. 14For if I pray in
tongues, my spirit is praying, but I don't understand what
I am saying.

15Well then, what shall I do? I will do both. I will pray in
the spirit,* and I will pray in words I understand. I will
sing in the spirit, and I will sing in words I understand.
16For if you praise God only in the spirit, how can those
who don't understand you praise God along with you?
How can they join you in giving thanks when they don't
understand what you are saying? 17You will be giving
thanks very nicely, no doubt, but it doesn't help the other
people present.

18I thank God that I speak in tongues more than all of
you. 19But in a church meeting I would much rather speak
five understandable words that will help others than ten
thousand words in an unknown language.

20Dear brothers and sisters, don't be childish in your
understanding of these things. Be innocent as babies when
it comes to evil, but be mature and wise in understanding
matters of this kind. 21It is written in the Scriptures,*

"I will speak to my own people
through unknown languages
and through the lips of foreigners.
But even then, they will not listen to me,"*
says the Lord.

14:15 Or *in the Spirit;* also in 14:15b, 16. **14:21a** Greek *in the law.*
14:21b Isa 28:11-12.

NEW KING JAMES VERSION

may interpret. 14For if I pray in a tongue, my spirit prays,
but my understanding is unfruitful. 15What is *the conclu-
sion* then? I will pray with the spirit, and I will also pray
with the understanding. I will sing with the spirit, and I
will also sing with the understanding. 16Otherwise, if you
bless with the spirit, how will he who occupies the place of
the uninformed say "Amen" at your giving of thanks, since
he does not understand what you say? 17For you indeed
give thanks well, but the other is not edified.

18I thank my God I speak with tongues more than you
all; 19yet in the church I would rather speak five words
with my understanding, that I may teach others also, than
ten thousand words in a tongue.

Tongues a Sign to Unbelievers

20Brethren, do not be children in understanding; howev-
er, in malice be babes, but in understanding be mature.
21In the law it is written:

*"With men of other tongues and other lips
I will speak to this people;
And yet, for all that, they will not hear Me,"*[b]

says the Lord.

14:21 [b] Isaiah 28:11, 12

THE MESSAGE

ability to bring others into that intimacy. If I pray in tongues,
my spirit prays but my mind lies fallow, and all that intelli-
gence is wasted. So what's the solution? The answer is sim-
ple enough. Do both. I should be spiritually free and expres-
sive as I pray, but I should also be thoughtful and mindful
as I pray. I should sing with my spirit, and sing with my
mind. If you give a blessing using your private prayer lan-
guage, which no one else understands, how can some out-
sider who has just shown up and has no idea what's going
on know when to say "Amen"? Your blessing might be beau-
tiful, but you have very effectively cut that person out of it.

I'm grateful to God for the gift of praying in tongues that
he gives us for praising him, which leads to wonderful
intimacies we enjoy with him. I enter into this as much or
more than any of you. But when I'm in a church assembled
for worship, I'd rather say five words that everyone can
understand and learn from than say ten thousand that
sound to others like gibberish.

To be perfectly frank, I'm getting exasperated with your
infantile thinking. How long before you grow up and use
your head—your *adult* head? It's all right to have a childlike
unfamiliarity with evil; a simple *no* is all that's needed
there. But there's far more to saying *yes* to something. Only
mature and well-exercised intelligence can save you from
falling into gullibility. It's written in Scripture that God said,

"In strange tongues
and from the mouths of strangers
I will preach to this people,
but they'll neither listen nor believe."

KING JAMES VERSION

22 Wherefore tongues are for a sign, not to them that believe, but to them that believe not: but prophesying *serveth* not for them that believe not, but for them which believe.

23 If therefore the whole church be come together into one place, and all speak with tongues, and there come in *those that are* unlearned, or unbelievers, will they not say that ye are mad?

24 But if all prophesy, and there come in one that believeth not, or *one* unlearned, he is convinced of all, he is judged of all:

25 And thus are the secrets of his heart made manifest; and so falling down on *his* face he will worship God, and report that God is in you of a truth.

26 ¶ How is it then, brethren? when ye come together, every one of you hath a psalm, hath a doctrine, hath a tongue, hath a revelation, hath an interpretation. Let all things be done unto edifying.

27 If any man speak in an *unknown* tongue, *let it be* by two, or at the most *by* three, and *that* by course; and let one interpret.

28 But if there be no interpreter, let him keep silence in the church; and let him speak to himself, and to God.

29 Let the prophets speak two or three, and let the other judge.

NEW AMERICAN STANDARD BIBLE

22 So then tongues are for a sign, not to those who believe but to unbelievers; but prophecy *is for a sign*, not to unbelievers but to those who believe.

23 Therefore if the whole church assembles together and all speak in tongues, and ungifted men or unbelievers enter, will they not say that you are mad?

24 But if all prophesy, and an unbeliever or an ungifted man enters, he is convicted by all, he is called to account by all;

25 the secrets of his heart are disclosed; and so he will fall on his face and worship God, declaring that God is certainly among you.

26 What is *the outcome* then, brethren? When you assemble, each one has a psalm, has a teaching, has a revelation, has a tongue, has an interpretation. Let all things be done for edification.

27 If anyone speaks in a tongue, *it should be* by two or at the most three, and *each* in turn, and one must interpret;

28 but if there is no interpreter, he must keep silent in the church; and let him speak to himself and to God.

29 Let two or three prophets speak, and let the others pass judgment.

NEW CENTURY VERSION

22 So the gift of speaking in different kinds of languages
is a proof for those who do not believe, not for those who
do believe. And prophecy is for people who believe, not for
those who do not believe. 23 Suppose the whole church
meets together and everyone speaks in different languages. If some people come in who do not understand or
do not believe, they will say you are crazy. 24 But suppose
everyone is prophesying and some people come in who do
not believe or do not understand. If everyone is prophesying, their sin will be shown to them, and they will be
judged by all that they hear. 25 The secret things in their
hearts will be made known. So they will bow down and
worship God saying, "Truly, God is with you."

Meetings Should Help the Church

26 So, brothers and sisters, what should you do? When
you meet together, one person has a song, and another has
a teaching. Another has a new truth from God. Another
speaks in a different language,[c] and another person interprets that language. The purpose of all these things should
be to help the church grow strong. 27 When you meet
together, if anyone speaks in a different language, it should
be only two, or not more than three, who speak. They
should speak one after the other, and someone else should
interpret. 28 But if there is no interpreter, then those who
speak in a different language should be quiet in the church
meeting. They should speak only to themselves and to God.
29 Only two or three prophets should speak, and the others

14:26 [c] **language** This can also be translated "tongue."

CONTEMPORARY ENGLISH VERSION

22 Languages that others don't know may mean something to unbelievers, but not to the Lord's followers.
Prophecy, on the other hand, is for followers, not for unbelievers. 23 Suppose everyone in your worship service started
speaking unknown languages, and some outsiders or some
unbelievers come in. Won't they think you are crazy? 24 But
suppose all of you are prophesying when those unbelievers
and outsiders come in. They will realize that they are sinners, and they will want to change their ways because of
what you are saying. 25 They will tell what is hidden in
their hearts. Then they will kneel down and say to God,
"We are certain that you are with these people."

Worship Must Be Orderly

26 My friends, when you meet to worship, you must do
everything for the good of everyone there. That's how it
should be when someone sings or teaches or tells what
God has said or speaks an unknown language or explains
what the language means. 27 No more than two or three of
you should speak unknown languages during the meeting.
You must take turns, and someone should always be there
to explain what you mean. 28 If no one can explain, you
must keep silent in church and speak only to yourself and
to God.

29 Two or three persons may prophesy, and everyone else

NEW INTERNATIONAL VERSION

22 Tongues, then, are a sign, not for believers but for
unbelievers; prophecy, however, is for believers, not for
unbelievers. 23 So if the whole church comes together and
everyone speaks in tongues, and some who do not under-
stand[f] or some unbelievers come in, will they not say that
you are out of your mind? 24 But if an unbeliever or some-
one who does not understand[g] comes in while everybody is
prophesying, he will be convinced by all that he is a sinner
and will be judged by all, 25 and the secrets of his heart will
be laid bare. So he will fall down and worship God,
exclaiming, "God is really among you!"

Orderly Worship

26 What then shall we say, brothers? When you come
together, everyone has a hymn, or a word of instruction, a
revelation, a tongue or an interpretation. All of these must
be done for the strengthening of the church. 27 If anyone
speaks in a tongue, two—or at the most three—should
speak, one at a time, and someone must interpret. 28 If
there is no interpreter, the speaker should keep quiet in the
church and speak to himself and God.
29 Two or three prophets should speak, and the others

[f] *23* Or *some inquirers* [g] *24* Or *or some inquirer*

NEW LIVING TRANSLATION

22 So you see that speaking in tongues is a sign, not for
believers, but for unbelievers; prophecy, however, is for the
benefit of believers, not unbelievers. 23 Even so, if unbeliev-
ers or people who don't understand these things come into
your meeting and hear everyone talking in an unknown
language, they will think you are crazy. 24 But if all of you
are prophesying, and unbelievers or people who don't
understand these things come into your meeting, they will
be convicted of sin, and they will be condemned by what
you say. 25 As they listen, their secret thoughts will be laid
bare, and they will fall down on their knees and worship
God, declaring, "God is really here among you."

A Call to Orderly Worship

26 Well, my brothers and sisters, let's summarize what I
am saying. When you meet, one will sing, another will
teach, another will tell some special revelation God has
given, one will speak in an unknown language, while
another will interpret what is said. But everything that is
done must be useful to all and build them up in the Lord.
27 No more than two or three should speak in an unknown
language. They must speak one at a time, and someone
must be ready to interpret what they are saying. 28 But if no
one is present who can interpret, they must be silent in
your church meeting and speak in tongues to God privately.
29 Let two or three prophesy, and let the others evaluate

NEW KING JAMES VERSION

22 Therefore tongues are for a sign, not to those who
believe but to unbelievers; but prophesying is not for unbe-
lievers but for those who believe. 23 Therefore if the whole
church comes together in one place, and all speak with
tongues, and there come in *those who are* uninformed or
unbelievers, will they not say that you are out of your
mind? 24 But if all prophesy, and an unbeliever or an unin-
formed person comes in, he is convinced by all, he is con-
victed by all. 25 And thus[c] the secrets of his heart are
revealed; and so, falling down on *his* face, he will worship
God and report that God is truly among you.

Order in Church Meetings

26 How is it then, brethren? Whenever you come togeth-
er, each of you has a psalm, has a teaching, has a tongue,
has a revelation, has an interpretation. Let all things be
done for edification. 27 If anyone speaks in a tongue, *let
there be* two or at the most three, *each* in turn, and let one
interpret. 28 But if there is no interpreter, let him keep
silent in church, and let him speak to himself and to God.
29 Let two or three prophets speak, and let the others judge.

14:25 [c] NU-Text omits *And thus.*

THE MESSAGE

So where does it get you, all this speaking in tongues no one understands? It doesn't help believers, and it only gives unbelievers something to gawk at. Plain truth-speaking, on the other hand, goes straight to the heart of believers and doesn't get in the way of unbelievers. If you come together as a congregation and some unbelieving outsiders walk in on you as you're all praying in tongues, unintelligible to each other and to them, won't they assume you've taken leave of your senses and get out of there as fast as they can? But if some unbelieving outsiders walk in on a service where people are speaking out God's truth, the plain words will bring them up against the truth and probe their hearts. Before you know it, they're going to be on their faces before God, recognizing that God is among you.

So here's what I want you to do. When you gather for worship, each one of you be prepared with something that will be useful for all: Sing a hymn, teach a lesson, tell a story, lead a prayer, provide an insight. If prayers are offered in tongues, two or three's the limit, and then only if someone is present who can interpret what you're saying.

KING JAMES VERSION

30 If *any thing* be revealed to another that sitteth by, let the first hold his peace.

31 For ye may all prophesy one by one, that all may learn, and all may be comforted.

32 And the spirits of the prophets are subject to the prophets.

33 For God is not *the author* of confusion, but of peace, as in all churches of the saints.

34 ¶ Let your women keep silence in the churches: for it is not permitted unto them to speak; but *they are commanded* to be under obedience, as also saith the law.

35 And if they will learn any thing, let them ask their husbands at home: for it is a shame for women to speak in the church.

36 ¶ What? came the word of God out from you? or came it unto you only?

37 If any man think himself to be a prophet, or spiritual, let him acknowledge that the things that I write unto you are the commandments of the Lord.

38 But if any man be ignorant, let him be ignorant.

39 Wherefore, brethren, covet to prophesy, and forbid not to speak with tongues.

40 Let all things be done decently and in order.

NEW AMERICAN STANDARD BIBLE

30 But if a revelation is made to another who is seated, the first one must keep silent.

31 For you can all prophesy one by one, so that all may learn and all may be exhorted;

32 and the spirits of prophets are subject to prophets;

33 for God is not *a God* of confusion but of peace, as in all the churches of the saints.

34 The women are to keep silent in the churches; for they are not permitted to speak, but are to subject themselves, just as the Law also says.

35 If they desire to learn anything, let them ask their own husbands at home; for it is improper for a woman to speak in church.

36 Was it from you that the word of God *first* went forth? Or has it come to you only?

37 If anyone thinks he is a prophet or spiritual, let him recognize that the things which I write to you are the Lord's commandment.

38 But if anyone does not recognize *this*, he [1]is not recognized.

39 Therefore, my brethren, desire earnestly to prophesy, and do not forbid to speak in tongues.

40 But all things must be done properly and in an orderly manner.

14:38 [1] Two early mss read *is not to be recognized*

NEW CENTURY VERSION

should judge what they say. [30]If a message from God comes
to another person who is sitting, the first speaker should
stop. [31]You can all prophesy one after the other. In this way
all the people can be taught and encouraged. [32]The spirits of
prophets are under the control of the prophets themselves.
[33]God is not a God of confusion but a God of peace.

As is true in all the churches of God's people, [34]women
should keep quiet in the church meetings. They are not
allowed to speak, but they must yield to this rule as the
law says. [35]If they want to learn something, they should
ask their own husbands at home. It is shameful for a
woman to speak in the church meeting. [36]Did God's teaching come from you? Or are you the only ones to whom it
has come?

[37]Those who think they are prophets or spiritual persons
should understand that what I am writing to you is the
Lord's command. [38]Those who ignore this will be ignored
by God.

[39]So my brothers and sisters, you should truly want to
prophesy. But do not stop people from using the gift of
speaking in different kinds of languages. [40]But let everything be done in a right and orderly way.

CONTEMPORARY ENGLISH VERSION

must listen carefully. [30]If someone sitting there receives a
message from God, the speaker must stop and let the other
person speak. [31]Let only one person speak at a time, then
all of you will learn something and be encouraged. [32]A
prophet should be willing to stop and let someone else
speak. [33]God wants everything to be done peacefully and
in order.

When God's people meet in church, [34]the women must
not be allowed to speak. They must keep quiet and listen,
as the Law of Moses teaches. [35]If there is something they
want to know, they can ask their husbands when they get
home. It is disgraceful for women to speak in church.
[36]God's message did not start with you people, and you are
not the only ones it has reached.

[37]If you think of yourself as a prophet or a spiritual person, you will know that I am writing only what the Lord
has commanded. [38]So don't pay attention to anyone who
ignores what I am writing. [39]My friends, be eager to prophesy and don't stop anyone from speaking languages that
others don't know. [40]But do everything properly and in
order.

NEW INTERNATIONAL VERSION

should weigh carefully what is said. 30And if a revelation comes to someone who is sitting down, the first speaker should stop. 31For you can all prophesy in turn so that everyone may be instructed and encouraged. 32The spirits of prophets are subject to the control of prophets. 33For God is not a God of disorder but of peace.

As in all the congregations of the saints, 34women should remain silent in the churches. They are not allowed to speak, but must be in submission, as the Law says. 35If they want to inquire about something, they should ask their own husbands at home; for it is disgraceful for a woman to speak in the church.

36Did the word of God originate with you? Or are you the only people it has reached? 37If anybody thinks he is a prophet or spiritually gifted, let him acknowledge that what I am writing to you is the Lord's command. 38If he ignores this, he himself will be ignored.[h]

39Therefore, my brothers, be eager to prophesy, and do not forbid speaking in tongues. 40But everything should be done in a fitting and orderly way.

[h] *38* Some manuscripts *If he is ignorant of this, let him be ignorant*

NEW LIVING TRANSLATION

what is said. 30But if someone is prophesying and another person receives a revelation from the Lord, the one who is speaking must stop. 31In this way, all who prophesy will have a turn to speak, one after the other, so that everyone will learn and be encouraged. 32Remember that people who prophesy are in control of their spirit and can wait their turn. 33For God is not a God of disorder but of peace, as in all the other churches.*

34Women should be silent during the church meetings. It is not proper for them to speak. They should be submissive, just as the law says. 35If they have any questions to ask, let them ask their husbands at home, for it is improper for women to speak in church meetings.*

36Do you think that the knowledge of God's word begins and ends with you Corinthians? Well, you are mistaken! 37If you claim to be a prophet or think you are very spiritual, you should recognize that what I am saying is a command from the Lord himself. 38But if you do not recognize this, you will not be recognized.*

39So, dear brothers and sisters, be eager to prophesy, and don't forbid speaking in tongues. 40But be sure that everything is done properly and in order.

14:33 The phrase *as in all the other churches* could be joined to the beginning of 14:34. **14:35** Some manuscripts place verses 34-35 after 14:40. **14:38** Some manuscripts read *If you are ignorant of this, stay in your ignorance.*

NEW KING JAMES VERSION

30But if *anything* is revealed to another who sits by, let the first keep silent. 31For you can all prophesy one by one, that all may learn and all may be encouraged. 32And the spirits of the prophets are subject to the prophets. 33For God is not *the author* of confusion but of peace, as in all the churches of the saints.

34Let your[d] women keep silent in the churches, for they are not permitted to speak; but *they are* to be submissive, as the law also says. 35And if they want to learn something, let them ask their own husbands at home; for it is shameful for women to speak in church.

36Or did the word of God come *originally* from you? Or *was it* you only that it reached? 37If anyone thinks himself to be a prophet or spiritual, let him acknowledge that the things which I write to you are the commandments of the Lord. 38But if anyone is ignorant, let him be ignorant.[e]

39Therefore, brethren, desire earnestly to prophesy, and do not forbid to speak with tongues. 40Let all things be done decently and in order.

14:34 [d] NU-Text omits *your.* **14:38** [e] NU-Text reads *if anyone does not recognize this, he is not recognized.*

THE MESSAGE

Otherwise, keep it between God and yourself. And no more than two or three speakers at a meeting, with the rest of you listening and taking it to heart. Take your turn, no one person taking over. Then each speaker gets a chance to say something special from God, and you all learn from each other. If you choose to speak, you're also responsible for how and when you speak. When we worship the right way, God doesn't stir us up into confusion; he brings us into harmony. This goes for all the churches—no exceptions.

Wives must not disrupt worship, talking when they should be listening, asking questions that could more appropriately be asked of their husbands at home. God's Book of the law guides our manners and customs here. Wives have no license to use the time of worship for unwarranted speaking. Do you—both women *and* men—imagine that you're a sacred oracle determining what's right and wrong? Do you think everything revolves around you?

If any one of you thinks God has something for you to say or has inspired you to do something, pay close attention to what I have written. This is the way the Master wants it. If you won't play by these rules, God can't use you. Sorry.

Three things, then, to sum this up: When you speak forth God's truth, speak your heart out. Don't tell people how they should or shouldn't pray when they're praying in tongues that you don't understand. Be courteous and considerate in everything.

KING JAMES VERSION

15 Moreover, brethren, I declare unto you the gospel which I preached unto you, which also ye have received, and wherein ye stand;

2 By which also ye are saved, if ye keep in memory what I preached unto you, unless ye have believed in vain.

3 For I delivered unto you first of all that which I also received, how that Christ died for our sins according to the scriptures;

4 And that he was buried, and that he rose again the third day according to the scriptures:

5 And that he was seen of Cephas, then of the twelve:

6 After that, he was seen of above five hundred brethren at once; of whom the greater part remain unto this present, but some are fallen asleep.

7 After that, he was seen of James; then of all the apostles.

8 And last of all he was seen of me also, as of one born out of due time.

NEW AMERICAN STANDARD BIBLE

The Fact of Christ's Resurrection

15 Now I make known to you, brethren, the gospel which I preached to you, which also you received, in which also you stand,

2 by which also you are saved, if you hold fast the word which I preached to you, unless you believed in vain.

3 For I delivered to you as of first importance what I also received, that Christ died for our sins according to the Scriptures,

4 and that He was buried, and that He was raised on the third day according to the Scriptures,

5 and that He appeared to Cephas, then to the twelve.

6 After that He appeared to more than five hundred brethren at one time, most of whom remain until now, but some have fallen asleep;

7 then He appeared to James, then to all the apostles;

8 and last of all, as to one untimely born, He appeared to me also.

NEW CENTURY VERSION

The Good News About Christ

15 Now, brothers and sisters, I want you to remember
the Good News I brought to you. You received this
Good News and continue strong in it. 2And you are being
saved by it if you continue believing what I told you. If you
do not, then you believed for nothing.
3I passed on to you what I received, of which this was
most important: that Christ died for our sins, as the
Scriptures say; 4that he was buried and was raised to life
on the third day as the Scriptures say; 5and that he was
seen by Peter and then by the twelve apostles. 6After that,
Jesus was seen by more than five hundred of the believers
at the same time. Most of them are still living today, but
some have died. 7Then he was seen by James and later by
all the apostles. 8Last of all he was seen by me—as by a
person not born at the normal time. 9All the other apostles

CONTEMPORARY ENGLISH VERSION

Christ Was Raised to Life

15 My friends, I want you to remember the message
that I preached and that you believed and trusted.
2You will be saved by this message, if you hold firmly to it.
But if you don't, your faith was all for nothing.
3I told you the most important part of the message
exactly as it was told to me. That part is:

Christ died for our sins,
as the Scriptures say.
4He was buried,
and three days later
he was raised to life,
as the Scriptures say.
5Christ appeared to Peter,[a]
then to the twelve.
6After this, he appeared
to more than five hundred
other followers.
Most of them are still alive,
but some have died.
7He also appeared to James,
and then to all
of the apostles.

8Finally, he appeared to me, even though I am like
someone who was born at the wrong time.[b]

[a] 15.5 *Peter*: See the note at 1.12. [b] 15.8 *who was born at the wrong time*: The meaning of these words in Greek is not clear.

NEW INTERNATIONAL VERSION

The Resurrection of Christ

15 Now, brothers, I want to remind you of the gospel I preached to you, which you received and on which you have taken your stand. [2]By this gospel you are saved, if you hold firmly to the word I preached to you. Otherwise, you have believed in vain.

[3]For what I received I passed on to you as of first importance[a]: that Christ died for our sins according to the Scriptures, [4]that he was buried, that he was raised on the third day according to the Scriptures, [5]and that he appeared to Peter,[b] and then to the Twelve. [6]After that, he appeared to more than five hundred of the brothers at the same time, most of whom are still living, though some have fallen asleep. [7]Then he appeared to James, then to all the apostles, [8]and last of all he appeared to me also, as to one abnormally born.

[a] 3 Or *you at the first* [b] 5 Greek *Cephas*

NEW LIVING TRANSLATION

The Resurrection of Christ

15 Now let me remind you, dear brothers and sisters,* of the Good News I preached to you before. You welcomed it then and still do now, for your faith is built on this wonderful message. [2]And it is this Good News that saves you if you firmly believe it—unless, of course, you believed something that was never true in the first place.

[3]I passed on to you what was most important and what had also been passed on to me—that Christ died for our sins, just as the Scriptures said. [4]He was buried, and he was raised from the dead on the third day, as the Scriptures said. [5]He was seen by Peter* and then by the twelve apostles. [6]After that, he was seen by more than five hundred of his followers* at one time, most of whom are still alive, though some have died by now. [7]Then he was seen by James and later by all the apostles. [8]Last of all, I saw him, too, long after the others, as though I had been born at the wrong time. [9]For I am the least of all the

15:1 Greek *brothers;* also in 15:31, 50, 58. 15:5 Greek *Cephas.* 15:6 Greek *the brothers.*

NEW KING JAMES VERSION

The Risen Christ, Faith's Reality

15 Moreover, brethren, I declare to you the gospel which I preached to you, which also you received and in which you stand, [2]by which also you are saved, if you hold fast that word which I preached to you—unless you believed in vain.

[3]For I delivered to you first of all that which I also received: that Christ died for our sins according to the Scriptures, [4]and that He was buried, and that He rose again the third day according to the Scriptures, [5]and that He was seen by Cephas, then by the twelve. [6]After that He was seen by over five hundred brethren at once, of whom the greater part remain to the present, but some have fallen asleep. [7]After that He was seen by James, then by all the apostles. [8]Then last of all He was seen by me also, as by one born out of due time.

THE MESSAGE

Resurrection

15 Friends, let me go over the Message with you one final time—this Message that I proclaimed and that you made your own; this Message on which you took your stand and by which your life has been saved. (I'm assuming, now, that your belief was the real thing and not a passing fancy, that you're in this for good and holding fast.)

The first thing I did was place before you what was placed so emphatically before me: that the Messiah died for our sins, exactly as Scripture tells it; that he was buried; that he was raised from death on the third day, again exactly as Scripture says; that he presented himself alive to Peter, then to his closest followers, and later to more than five hundred of his followers all at the same time, most of them still around (although a few have since died); that he then spent time with James and the rest of those he commissioned to represent him; and that he finally presented himself alive to *me*. It was fitting that I bring up the rear. I

KING JAMES VERSION

9 For I am the least of the apostles, that am not meet to be called an apostle, because I persecuted the church of God.

10 But by the grace of God I am what I am: and his grace which *was bestowed* upon me was not in vain; but I laboured more abundantly than they all: yet not I, but the grace of God which was with me.

11 Therefore whether *it were* I or they, so we preach, and so ye believed.

12 ¶ Now if Christ be preached that he rose from the dead, how say some among you that there is no resurrection of the dead?

13 But if there be no resurrection of the dead, then is Christ not risen:

14 And if Christ be not risen, then *is* our preaching vain, and your faith *is* also vain.

15 Yea, and we are found false witnesses of God; because we have testified of God that he raised up Christ: whom he raised not up, if so be that the dead rise not.

16 For if the dead rise not, then is not Christ raised:

17 And if Christ be not raised, your faith *is* vain; ye are yet in your sins.

18 Then they also which are fallen asleep in Christ are perished.

19 If in this life only we have hope in Christ, we are of all men most miserable.

NEW AMERICAN STANDARD BIBLE

9 For I am the least of the apostles, and not fit to be called an apostle, because I persecuted the church of God.

10 But by the grace of God I am what I am, and His grace toward me did not prove vain; but I labored even more than all of them, yet not I, but the grace of God with me.

11 Whether then *it was* I or they, so we preach and so you believed.

12 Now if Christ is preached, that He has been raised from the dead, how do some among you say that there is no resurrection of the dead?

13 But if there is no resurrection of the dead, not even Christ has been raised;

14 and if Christ has not been raised, then our preaching is vain, your faith also is vain.

15 Moreover we are even found *to be* false witnesses of God, because we testified against God that He raised [7]Christ, whom He did not raise, if in fact the dead are not raised.

16 For if the dead are not raised, not even Christ has been raised;

17 and if Christ has not been raised, your faith is worthless; you are still in your sins.

18 Then those also who have fallen asleep in Christ have perished.

19 If we have hoped in Christ in this life only, we are of all men most to be pitied.

15:15 [7] I.e. the Messiah

NEW CENTURY VERSION

are greater than I am. I am not even good enough to be
called an apostle, because I persecuted the church of God.
10But God's grace has made me what I am, and his grace
to me was not wasted. I worked harder than all the other
apostles. (But it was not I really; it was God's grace that
was with me.) 11So if I preached to you or the other apos-
tles preached to you, we all preach the same thing, and
this is what you believed.

We Will Be Raised from the Dead

12Now since we preached that Christ was raised from the
dead, why do some of you say that people will not be
raised from the dead? 13If no one is ever raised from the
dead, then Christ has not been raised. 14And if Christ has
not been raised, then our preaching is worth nothing, and
your faith is worth nothing. 15And also, we are guilty of
lying about God, because we testified of him that he raised
Christ from the dead. But if people are not raised from the
dead, then God never raised Christ. 16If the dead are not
raised, Christ has not been raised either. 17And if Christ
has not been raised, then your faith has nothing to it; you
are still guilty of your sins. 18And those in Christ who have
already died are lost. 19If our hope in Christ is for this life
only, we should be pitied more than anyone else in the
world.

CONTEMPORARY ENGLISH VERSION

9I am the least important of all the apostles. In fact, I
caused so much trouble for God's church that I don't even
deserve to be called an apostle. 10But God was kind! He
made me what I am, and his wonderful kindness wasn't
wasted. I worked much harder than any of the other apos-
tles, although it was really God's kindness at work and not
me. 11But it doesn't matter if I preached or if they
preached. All of you believed the message just the same.

God's People Will Be Raised to Life

12If we preach that Christ was raised from death, how
can some of you say that the dead will not be raised to
life? 13If they won't be raised to life, Christ himself wasn't
raised to life. 14And if Christ wasn't raised to life, our mes-
sage is worthless, and so is your faith. 15If the dead won't
be raised to life, we have told lies about God by saying
that he raised Christ to life, when he really did not.

16So if the dead won't be raised to life, Christ wasn't
raised to life. 17Unless Christ was raised to life, your faith
is useless, and you are still living in your sins. 18And those
people who died after putting their faith in him are com-
pletely lost. 19If our hope in Christ is good only for this life,
we are worse off than anyone else.

NEW INTERNATIONAL VERSION

9For I am the least of the apostles and do not even
deserve to be called an apostle, because I persecuted the
church of God. 10But by the grace of God I am what I am,
and his grace to me was not without effect. No, I worked
harder than all of them—yet not I, but the grace of God
that was with me. 11Whether, then, it was I or they, this is
what we preach, and this is what you believed.

The Resurrection of the Dead

12But if it is preached that Christ has been raised from
the dead, how can some of you say that there is no resur-
rection of the dead? 13If there is no resurrection of the
dead, then not even Christ has been raised. 14And if Christ
has not been raised, our preaching is useless and so is
your faith. 15More than that, we are then found to be false
witnesses about God, for we have testified about God that
he raised Christ from the dead. But he did not raise him if
in fact the dead are not raised. 16For if the dead are not
raised, then Christ has not been raised either. 17And if
Christ has not been raised, your faith is futile; you are still
in your sins. 18Then those also who have fallen asleep in
Christ are lost. 19If only for this life we have hope in Christ,
we are to be pitied more than all men.

NEW LIVING TRANSLATION

apostles, and I am not worthy to be called an apostle after
the way I persecuted the church of God.

10But whatever I am now, it is all because God poured
out his special favor on me—and not without results. For I
have worked harder than all the other apostles, yet it was
not I but God who was working through me by his grace.
11So it makes no difference whether I preach or they
preach. The important thing is that you believed what we
preached to you.

The Resurrection of the Dead

12But tell me this—since we preach that Christ rose from
the dead, why are some of you saying there will be no res-
urrection of the dead? 13For if there is no resurrection of
the dead, then Christ has not been raised either. 14And if
Christ was not raised, then all our preaching is useless,
and your trust in God is useless. 15And we apostles would
all be lying about God, for we have said that God raised
Christ from the grave, but that can't be true if there is no
resurrection of the dead. 16If there is no resurrection of the
dead, then Christ has not been raised. 17And if Christ has
not been raised, then your faith is useless, and you are
still under condemnation for your sins. 18In that case, all
who have died believing in Christ have perished! 19And if
we have hope in Christ only for this life, we are the most
miserable people in the world.

NEW KING JAMES VERSION

9For I am the least of the apostles, who am not worthy
to be called an apostle, because I persecuted the church of
God. 10But by the grace of God I am what I am, and His
grace toward me was not in vain; but I labored more abun-
dantly than they all, yet not I, but the grace of God *which
was* with me. 11Therefore, whether *it was* I or they, so we
preach and so you believed.

The Risen Christ, Our Hope

12Now if Christ is preached that He has been raised from
the dead, how do some among you say that there is no res-
urrection of the dead? 13But if there is no resurrection of
the dead, then Christ is not risen. 14And if Christ is not
risen, then our preaching *is* empty and your faith *is* also
empty. 15Yes, and we are found false witnesses of God,
because we have testified of God that He raised up Christ,
whom He did not raise up—if in fact the dead do not rise.
16For if *the* dead do not rise, then Christ is not risen. 17And
if Christ is not risen, your faith *is* futile; you are still in
your sins! 18Then also those who have fallen asleep in
Christ have perished. 19If in this life only we have hope
in Christ, we are of all men the most pitiable.

THE MESSAGE

don't deserve to be included in that inner circle, as you well
know, having spent all those early years trying my best to
stamp God's church right out of existence.

But because God was so gracious, so very generous, here
I am. And I'm not about to let his grace go to waste.
Haven't I worked hard trying to do more than any of the
others? Even then, my work didn't amount to all that
much. It was God giving me the work to do, God giving me
the energy to do it. So whether you heard it from me or
from those others, it's all the same: We spoke God's truth
and you entrusted your lives.

Now, let me ask you something profound yet troubling. If
you became believers because you trusted the proclamation
that Christ is alive, risen from the dead, how can you let peo-
ple say that there is no such thing as a resurrection? If
there's no resurrection, there's no living Christ. And face it—
if there's no resurrection for Christ, everything we've told
you is smoke and mirrors, and everything you've staked your
life on is smoke and mirrors. Not only that, but we would be
guilty of telling a string of barefaced lies about God, all these
affidavits we passed on to you verifying that God raised up
Christ—sheer fabrications, if there's no resurrection.

If corpses can't be raised, then Christ wasn't, because he
was indeed dead. And if Christ wasn't raised, then all
you're doing is wandering about in the dark, as lost as
ever. It's even worse for those who died hoping in Christ
and resurrection, because they're already in their graves. If
all we get out of Christ is a little inspiration for a few short
years, we're a pretty sorry lot. But the truth is that Christ

KING JAMES VERSION

20 ¶ But now is Christ risen from the dead, *and* become the firstfruits of them that slept.

21 For since by man *came* death, by man *came* also the resurrection of the dead.

22 For as in Adam all die, even so in Christ shall all be made alive.

23 But every man in his own order: Christ the firstfruits; afterward they that are Christ's at his coming.

24 Then *cometh* the end, when he shall have delivered up the kingdom to God, even the Father; when he shall have put down all rule and all authority and power.

25 For he must reign, till he hath put all enemies under his feet.

26 The last enemy *that* shall be destroyed *is* death.

27 For he hath put all things under his feet. But when he saith all things are put under *him, it is* manifest that he is excepted, which did put all things under him.

28 And when all things shall be subdued unto him, then shall the Son also himself be subject unto him that put all things under him, that God may be all in all.

29 Else what shall they do which are baptized for the dead, if the dead rise not at all? why are they then baptized for the dead?

30 And why stand we in jeopardy every hour?

31 I protest by your rejoicing which I have in Christ Jesus our Lord, I die daily.

NEW AMERICAN STANDARD BIBLE

The Order of Resurrection

20 But now Christ has been raised from the dead, the first fruits of those who are asleep.

21 For since by a man *came* death, by a man also *came* the resurrection of the dead.

22 For as in Adam all die, so also in Christ all will be made alive.

23 But each in his own order: Christ the first fruits, after that those who are Christ's at His coming,

24 then *comes* the end, when He hands over the kingdom to the God and Father, when He has abolished all rule and all authority and power.

25 For He must reign until He has put all His enemies under His feet.

26 The last enemy that will be abolished is death.

27 For HE HAS PUT ALL THINGS IN SUBJECTION UNDER HIS FEET. But when He says, "All things are put in subjection," it is evident that He is excepted who put all things in subjection to Him.

28 When all things are subjected to Him, then the Son Himself also will be subjected to the One who subjected all things to Him, so that God may be all in all.

29 Otherwise, what will those do who are baptized for the dead? If the dead are not raised at all, why then are they baptized for them?

30 Why are we also in danger every hour?

31 I affirm, brethren, by the boasting in you which I have in Christ Jesus our Lord, I die daily.

NEW CENTURY VERSION

20But Christ has truly been raised from the dead—the
first one and proof that those who sleep in death will also
be raised. 21Death has come because of what one man did,
but the rising from death also comes because of one man.
22In Adam all of us die. In the same way, in Christ all of us
will be made alive again. 23But everyone will be raised to
life in the right order. Christ was first to be raised. When
Christ comes again, those who belong to him will be raised
to life, 24and then the end will come. At that time Christ
will destroy all rulers, authorities, and powers, and he will
hand over the kingdom to God the Father. 25Christ must
rule until he puts all enemies under his control. 26The last
enemy to be destroyed will be death. 27The Scripture says
that God put all things under his control.[a] When it says
"all things" are under him, it is clear this does not include
God himself. God is the One who put everything under his
control. 28After everything has been put under the Son,
then he will put himself under God, who had put all things
under him. Then God will be the complete ruler over everything.

29If the dead are never raised, what will people do who
are being baptized for the dead? If the dead are not raised
at all, why are people being baptized for them?

30And what about us? Why do we put ourselves in dan-
ger every hour? 31I die every day. That is true, brothers
and sisters, just as it is true that I brag about you in Christ

15:27 [a] **God put...control.** From Psalm 8:6.

CONTEMPORARY ENGLISH VERSION

20But Christ has been raised to life! And he makes us
certain that others will also be raised to life. 21Just as we
will die because of Adam, we will be raised to life because
of Christ. 22Adam brought death to all of us, and Christ
will bring life to all of us. 23But we must each wait our
turn. Christ was the first to be raised to life, and his people
will be raised to life when he returns. 24Then after Christ
has destroyed all powers and forces, the end will come,
and he will give the kingdom to God the Father.

25Christ will rule until he puts all his enemies under his
power, 26and the last enemy he destroys will be death.
27When the Scriptures say that he will put everything
under his power, they don't include God. It was God who
put everything under the power of Christ. 28After every-
thing is under the power of God's Son, he will put himself
under the power of God, who put everything under his
Son's power. Then God will mean everything to everyone.

29If the dead are not going to be raised to life, what will
people do who are being baptized for them? Why are they
being baptized for those dead people? 30And why do we
always risk our lives 31and face death every day? The pride
that I have in you because of Christ Jesus our Lord is what

NEW INTERNATIONAL VERSION

[20]But Christ has indeed been raised from the dead, the firstfruits of those who have fallen asleep. [21]For since death came through a man, the resurrection of the dead comes also through a man. [22]For as in Adam all die, so in Christ all will be made alive. [23]But each in his own turn: Christ, the firstfruits; then, when he comes, those who belong to him. [24]Then the end will come, when he hands over the kingdom to God the Father after he has destroyed all dominion, authority and power. [25]For he must reign until he has put all his enemies under his feet. [26]The last enemy to be destroyed is death. [27]For he "has put everything under his feet."[c] Now when it says that "everything" has been put under him, it is clear that this does not include God himself, who put everything under Christ. [28]When he has done this, then the Son himself will be made subject to him who put everything under him, so that God may be all in all.

[29]Now if there is no resurrection, what will those do who are baptized for the dead? If the dead are not raised at all, why are people baptized for them? [30]And as for us, why do we endanger ourselves every hour? [31]I die every day—I mean that, brothers—just as surely as I glory over you in

[c] *27* Psalm 8:6

NEW LIVING TRANSLATION

[20]But the fact is that Christ has been raised from the dead. He has become the first of a great harvest of those who will be raised to life again.

[21]So you see, just as death came into the world through a man, Adam, now the resurrection from the dead has begun through another man, Christ. [22]Everyone dies because all of us are related to Adam, the first man. But all who are related to Christ, the other man, will be given new life. [23]But there is an order to this resurrection: Christ was raised first; then when Christ comes back, all his people will be raised.

[24]After that the end will come, when he will turn the Kingdom over to God the Father, having put down all enemies of every kind.* [25]For Christ must reign until he humbles all his enemies beneath his feet. [26]And the last enemy to be destroyed is death. [27]For the Scriptures say, "God has given him authority over all things."* (Of course, when it says "authority over all things," it does not include God himself, who gave Christ his authority.) [28]Then, when he has conquered all things, the Son will present himself to God, so that God, who gave his Son authority over all things, will be utterly supreme over everything everywhere.

[29]If the dead will not be raised, then what point is there in people being baptized for those who are dead? Why do it unless the dead will someday rise again?

[30]And why should we ourselves be continually risking our lives, facing death hour by hour? [31]For I swear, dear brothers and sisters, I face death daily. This is as certain as my pride in what the Lord Jesus Christ has done in you.

15:24 Greek *every ruler and every authority and power.* **15:27** Ps 8:6.

NEW KING JAMES VERSION

The Last Enemy Destroyed

[20]But now Christ is risen from the dead, *and* has become the firstfruits of those who have fallen asleep. [21]For since by man *came* death, by Man also *came* the resurrection of the dead. [22]For as in Adam all die, even so in Christ all shall be made alive. [23]But each one in his own order: Christ the firstfruits, afterward those *who are* Christ's at His coming. [24]Then *comes* the end, when He delivers the kingdom to God the Father, when He puts an end to all rule and all authority and power. [25]For He must reign till He has put all enemies under His feet. [26]The last enemy *that* will be destroyed *is* death. [27]For *"He has put all things under His feet."*[a] But when He says "all things are put under *Him,*" *it is* evident that He who put all things under Him is excepted. [28]Now when all things are made subject to Him, then the Son Himself will also be subject to Him who put all things under Him, that God may be all in all.

Effects of Denying the Resurrection

[29]Otherwise, what will they do who are baptized for the dead, if the dead do not rise at all? Why then are they baptized for the dead? [30]And why do we stand in jeopardy every hour? [31]I affirm, by the boasting in you which I have in Christ Jesus our Lord, I die daily. [32]If, in the manner of

15:27 [a] Psalm 8:6

THE MESSAGE

has been raised up, the first in a long legacy of those who are going to leave the cemeteries.

There is a nice symmetry in this: Death initially came by a man, and resurrection from death came by a man. Everybody dies in Adam; everybody comes alive in Christ. But we have to wait our turn: Christ is first, then those with him at his Coming, the grand consummation when, after crushing the opposition, he hands over his kingdom to God the Father. He won't let up until the last enemy is down—and the very last enemy is death! As the psalmist said, "He laid them low, one and all; he walked all over them." When Scripture says that "he walked all over them," it's obvious that he couldn't at the same time be walked on. When everything and everyone is finally under God's rule, the Son will step down, taking his place with everyone else, showing that God's rule is absolutely comprehensive—a perfect ending!

Why do you think people offer themselves to be baptized for those already in the grave? If there's no chance of resurrection for a corpse, if God's power stops at the cemetery gates, why do we keep doing things that suggest he's going to clean the place out someday, pulling everyone up on their feet alive?

And why do you think I keep risking my neck in this dangerous work? I look death in the face practically every day I live. Do you think I'd do this if I wasn't convinced of your resurrection and mine as guaranteed by the resurrected

KING JAMES VERSION

32 If after the manner of men I have fought with beasts at Ephesus, what advantageth it me, if the dead rise not? let us eat and drink; for to morrow we die.

33 Be not deceived: evil communications corrupt good manners.

34 Awake to righteousness, and sin not; for some have not the knowledge of God: I speak *this* to your shame.

35 ¶ But some *man* will say, How are the dead raised up? and with what body do they come?

36 *Thou* fool, that which thou sowest is not quickened, except it die:

37 And that which thou sowest, thou sowest not that body that shall be, but bare grain, it may chance of wheat, or of some other *grain*:

38 But God giveth it a body as it hath pleased him, and to every seed his own body.

39 All flesh *is* not the same flesh: but *there is* one *kind of* flesh of men, another flesh of beasts, another of fishes, *and* another of birds.

NEW AMERICAN STANDARD BIBLE

32 If from human motives I fought with wild beasts at Ephesus, what does it profit me? If the dead are not raised, LET US EAT AND DRINK, FOR TOMORROW WE DIE.

33 Do not be deceived: "Bad company corrupts good morals."

34 Become sober-minded as you ought, and stop sinning; for some have no knowledge of God. I speak *this* to your shame.

35 But someone will say, "How are the dead raised? And with what kind of body do they come?"

36 You fool! That which you sow does not come to life unless it dies;

37 and that which you sow, you do not sow the body which is to be, but a bare grain, perhaps of wheat or of something else.

38 But God gives it a body just as He wished, and to each of the seeds a body of its own.

39 All flesh is not the same flesh, but there is one *flesh* of men, and another flesh of beasts, and another flesh of birds, and another of fish.

NEW CENTURY VERSION

Jesus our Lord. 32If I fought wild animals in Ephesus only
with human hopes, I have gained nothing. If the dead are
not raised, "Let us eat and drink, because tomorrow we
will die."[b]

33Do not be fooled: "Bad friends will ruin good habits."
34Come back to your right way of thinking and stop sin-
ning. Some of you do not know God—I say this to shame
you.

What Kind of Body Will We Have?

35But someone may ask, "How are the dead raised?
What kind of body will they have?" 36Foolish person!
When you sow a seed, it must die in the ground before it
can live and grow. 37And when you sow it, it does not have
the same "body" it will have later. What you sow is only a
bare seed, maybe wheat or something else. 38But God gives
it a body that he has planned for it, and God gives each
kind of seed its own body. 39All things made of flesh are
not the same: People have one kind of flesh, animals have
another, birds have another, and fish have another. 40Also

15:32 [b] "Let us...die." Quotation from Isaiah 22:13; 56:12.

CONTEMPORARY ENGLISH VERSION

makes me say this. 32What do you think I gained by fight-
ing wild animals in Ephesus? If the dead are not raised to
life,

"Let's eat and drink.
Tomorrow we die."

33Don't fool yourselves. Bad friends will destroy you. 34Be
sensible and stop sinning. You should be embarrassed that
some people still don't know about God.

What Our Bodies Will Be Like

35Some of you have asked, "How will the dead be raised
to life? What kind of bodies will they have?" 36Don't be
foolish. A seed must die before it can sprout from the
ground. 37Wheat seeds and all other seeds look different
from the sprouts that come up. 38This is because God gives
everything the kind of body he wants it to have. 39People,
animals, birds, and fish are each made of flesh, but none

NEW INTERNATIONAL VERSION

Christ Jesus our Lord. 32 If I fought wild beasts in Ephesus for merely human reasons, what have I gained? If the dead are not raised,

"Let us eat and drink,
for tomorrow we die."[d]

33 Do not be misled: "Bad company corrupts good character." 34 Come back to your senses as you ought, and stop sinning; for there are some who are ignorant of God—I say this to your shame.

The Resurrection Body

35 But someone may ask, "How are the dead raised? With what kind of body will they come?" 36 How foolish! What you sow does not come to life unless it dies. 37 When you sow, you do not plant the body that will be, but just a seed, perhaps of wheat or of something else. 38 But God gives it a body as he has determined, and to each kind of seed he gives its own body. 39 All flesh is not the same: Men have one kind of flesh, animals have another, birds another and

d 32 Isaiah 22:13

NEW LIVING TRANSLATION

32 And what value was there in fighting wild beasts—those men of Ephesus*—if there will be no resurrection from the dead? If there is no resurrection,

"Let's feast and get drunk,
for tomorrow we die!"*

33 Don't be fooled by those who say such things, for "bad company corrupts good character." 34 Come to your senses and stop sinning. For to your shame I say that some of you don't even know God.

The Resurrection Body

35 But someone may ask, "How will the dead be raised? What kind of bodies will they have?" 36 What a foolish question! When you put a seed into the ground, it doesn't grow into a plant unless it dies first. 37 And what you put in the ground is not the plant that will grow, but only a dry little seed of wheat or whatever it is you are planting. 38 Then God gives it a new body—just the kind he wants it to have. A different kind of plant grows from each kind of seed. 39 And just as there are different kinds of seeds and plants, so also there are different kinds of flesh—whether of humans, animals, birds, or fish.

15:32a Greek *fighting wild beasts in Ephesus.* **15:32b** Isa 22:13.

NEW KING JAMES VERSION

men, I have fought with beasts at Ephesus, what advantage *is it* to me? If *the* dead do not rise, *"Let us eat and drink, for tomorrow we die!"*[b]

33 Do not be deceived: "Evil company corrupts good habits." 34 Awake to righteousness, and do not sin; for some do not have the knowledge of God. I speak *this* to your shame.

A Glorious Body

35 But someone will say, "How are the dead raised up? And with what body do they come?" 36 Foolish one, what you sow is not made alive unless it dies. 37 And what you sow, you do not sow that body that shall be, but mere grain—perhaps wheat or some other *grain.* 38 But God gives it a body as He pleases, and to each seed its own body.

39 All flesh *is* not the same flesh, but *there is* one *kind of* flesh[c] of men, another flesh of animals, another of fish, *and* another of birds.

15:32 *b* Isaiah 22:13 **15:39** *c* NU-Text and M-Text omit *of flesh.*

THE MESSAGE

Messiah Jesus? Do you think I was just trying to act heroic when I fought the wild beasts at Ephesus, hoping it wouldn't be the end of me? Not on your life! It's resurrection, resurrection, always resurrection, that undergirds what I do and say, the way I live. If there's no resurrection, "We eat, we drink, the next day we die," and that's all there is to it. But don't fool yourselves. Don't let yourselves be poisoned by this anti-resurrection loose talk. "Bad company ruins good manners."

Think straight. Awaken to the holiness of life. No more playing fast and loose with resurrection facts. Ignorance of God is a luxury you can't afford in times like these. Aren't you embarrassed that you've let this kind of thing go on as long as you have?

Some skeptic is sure to ask, "Show me how resurrection works. Give me a diagram; draw me a picture. What does this 'resurrection body' look like?" If you look at this question closely, you realize how absurd it is. There are no diagrams for this kind of thing. We do have a parallel experience in gardening. You plant a "dead" seed; soon there is a flourishing plant. There is no visual likeness between seed and plant. You could never guess what a tomato would look like by looking at a tomato seed. What we plant in the soil and what grows out of it don't look anything alike. The dead body that we bury in the ground and the resurrection body that comes from it will be dramatically different.

You will notice that the variety of bodies is stunning. Just as there are different kinds of seeds, there are different kinds of bodies—humans, animals, birds, fish—each

KING JAMES VERSION

40 *There are* also celestial bodies, and bodies terrestrial: but the glory of the celestial *is* one, and the *glory* of the terrestrial *is* another.

41 *There is* one glory of the sun, and another glory of the moon, and another glory of the stars: for *one* star differeth from *another* star in glory.

42 So also *is* the resurrection of the dead. It is sown in corruption; it is raised in incorruption:

43 It is sown in dishonour; it is raised in glory: it is sown in weakness; it is raised in power:

44 It is sown a natural body; it is raised a spiritual body. There is a natural body, and there is a spiritual body.

45 And so it is written, The first man Adam was made a living soul; the last Adam *was made* a quickening spirit.

46 Howbeit that *was* not first which is spiritual, but that which is natural; and afterward that which is spiritual.

47 The first man *is* of the earth, earthy: the second man *is* the Lord from heaven.

48 As *is* the earthy, such *are* they also that are earthy: and as *is* the heavenly, such *are* they also that are heavenly.

49 And as we have borne the image of the earthy, we shall also bear the image of the heavenly.

50 Now this I say, brethren, that flesh and blood cannot inherit the kingdom of God; neither doth corruption inherit incorruption.

NEW AMERICAN STANDARD BIBLE

40 There are also heavenly bodies and earthly bodies, but the glory of the heavenly is one, and the *glory* of the earthly is another.

41 There is one glory of the sun, and another glory of the moon, and another glory of the stars; for star differs from star in glory.

42 So also is the resurrection of the dead. It is sown a perishable *body*, it is raised an imperishable *body;*

43 it is sown in dishonor, it is raised in glory; it is sown in weakness, it is raised in power;

44 it is sown a natural body, it is raised a spiritual body. If there is a natural body, there is also a spiritual *body.*

45 So also it is written, "The first MAN, Adam, BECAME A LIVING SOUL." The last Adam *became* a life-giving spirit.

46 However, the spiritual is not first, but the natural; then the spiritual.

47 The first man is from the earth, earthy; the second man is from heaven.

48 As is the earthy, so also are those who are earthy; and as is the heavenly, so also are those who are heavenly.

49 Just as we have borne the image of the earthy, [2]we will also bear the image of the heavenly.

The Mystery of Resurrection

50 Now I say this, brethren, that flesh and blood cannot inherit the kingdom of God; nor does the perishable inherit the imperishable.

15:49 [2] Two early mss read *let us also*

NEW CENTURY VERSION

there are heavenly bodies and earthly bodies. But the beauty of the heavenly bodies is one kind, and the beauty of the earthly bodies is another. [41]The sun has one kind of beauty, the moon has another beauty, and the stars have another. And each star is different in its beauty.

[42]It is the same with the dead who are raised to life. The body that is "planted" will ruin and decay, but it is raised to a life that cannot be destroyed. [43]When the body is "planted," it is without honor, but it is raised in glory. When the body is "planted," it is weak, but when it is raised, it is powerful. [44]The body that is "planted" is a physical body. When it is raised, it is a spiritual body.

There is a physical body, and there is also a spiritual body. [45]It is written in the Scriptures: "The first man, Adam, became a living person."[c] But the last Adam became a spirit that gives life. [46]The spiritual did not come first, but the physical and then the spiritual. [47]The first man came from the dust of the earth. The second man came from heaven. [48]People who belong to the earth are like the first man of earth. But those people who belong to heaven are like the man of heaven. [49]Just as we were made like the man of earth, so we will also be made like the man of heaven.

[50]I tell you this, brothers and sisters: Flesh and blood cannot have a part in the kingdom of God. Something that will ruin cannot have a part in something that never ruins.

15:45 [c] **"The first...person."** Quotation from Genesis 2:7.

CONTEMPORARY ENGLISH VERSION

of them are alike. [40]Everything in the heavens has a body, and so does everything on earth. But each one is very different from all the others. [41]The sun isn't like the moon, the moon isn't like the stars, and each star is different.

[42]That's how it will be when our bodies are raised to life. These bodies will die, but the bodies that are raised will live forever. [43]These ugly and weak bodies will become beautiful and strong. [44]As surely as there are physical bodies, there are spiritual bodies. And our physical bodies will be changed into spiritual bodies.

[45]The first man was named Adam, and the Scriptures tell us that he was a living person. But Jesus, who may be called the last Adam, is a life-giving spirit. [46]We see that the one with a spiritual body did not come first. He came after the one who had a physical body. [47]The first man was made from the dust of the earth, but the second man came from heaven. [48]Everyone on earth has a body like the body of the one who was made from the dust of the earth. And everyone in heaven has a body like the body of the one who came from heaven. [49]Just as we are like the one who was made out of earth, we will be like the one who came from heaven.

[50]My friends, I want you to know that our bodies of flesh and blood will decay. This means that they cannot share in God's kingdom, which lasts forever. [51]I will

NEW INTERNATIONAL VERSION

fish another. 40There are also heavenly bodies and there are earthly bodies; but the splendor of the heavenly bodies is one kind, and the splendor of the earthly bodies is another. 41The sun has one kind of splendor, the moon another and the stars another; and star differs from star in splendor.

42So will it be with the resurrection of the dead. The body that is sown is perishable, it is raised imperishable; 43it is sown in dishonor, it is raised in glory; it is sown in weakness, it is raised in power; 44it is sown a natural body, it is raised a spiritual body.

If there is a natural body, there is also a spiritual body. 45So it is written: "The first man Adam became a living being"[e]; the last Adam, a life-giving spirit. 46The spiritual did not come first, but the natural, and after that the spiritual. 47The first man was of the dust of the earth, the second man from heaven. 48As was the earthly man, so are those who are of the earth; and as is the man from heaven, so also are those who are of heaven. 49And just as we have borne the likeness of the earthly man, so shall we[f] bear the likeness of the man from heaven.

50I declare to you, brothers, that flesh and blood cannot inherit the kingdom of God, nor does the perishable inherit

[e] *45* Gen. 2:7 [f] *49* Some early manuscripts *so let us*

NEW LIVING TRANSLATION

40There are bodies in the heavens, and there are bodies on earth. The glory of the heavenly bodies is different from the beauty of the earthly bodies. 41The sun has one kind of glory, while the moon and stars each have another kind. And even the stars differ from each other in their beauty and brightness.

42It is the same way for the resurrection of the dead. Our earthly bodies, which die and decay, will be different when they are resurrected, for they will never die. 43Our bodies now disappoint us, but when they are raised, they will be full of glory. They are weak now, but when they are raised, they will be full of power. 44They are natural human bodies now, but when they are raised, they will be spiritual bodies. For just as there are natural bodies, so also there are spiritual bodies.

45The Scriptures tell us, "The first man, Adam, became a living person."* But the last Adam—that is, Christ—is a life-giving Spirit. 46What came first was the natural body, then the spiritual body comes later. 47Adam, the first man, was made from the dust of the earth, while Christ, the second man, came from heaven. 48Every human being has an earthly body just like Adam's, but our heavenly bodies will be just like Christ's. 49Just as we are now like Adam, the man of the earth, so we will someday be like Christ, the man from heaven.

50What I am saying, dear brothers and sisters, is that flesh and blood cannot inherit the Kingdom of God. These perishable bodies of ours are not able to live forever.

15:45 Gen 2:7.

NEW KING JAMES VERSION

40*There are* also celestial bodies and terrestrial bodies; but the glory of the celestial *is* one, and the *glory* of the terrestrial *is* another. 41*There is* one glory of the sun, another glory of the moon, and another glory of the stars; for *one* star differs from *another* star in glory.

42So also *is* the resurrection of the dead. *The body* is sown in corruption, it is raised in incorruption. 43It is sown in dishonor, it is raised in glory. It is sown in weakness, it is raised in power. 44It is sown a natural body, it is raised a spiritual body. There is a natural body, and there is a spiritual body. 45And so it is written, *"The first man Adam became a living being."*[d] The last Adam *became* a life-giving spirit.

46However, the spiritual is not first, but the natural, and afterward the spiritual. 47The first man *was* of the earth, *made* of dust; the second Man *is* the Lord[e] from heaven. 48As *was* the *man* of dust, so also *are* those *who are made* of dust; and as *is* the heavenly *Man,* so also *are* those *who are* heavenly. 49And as we have borne the image of the *man* of dust, we shall also bear[f] the image of the heavenly *Man.*

Our Final Victory

50Now this I say, brethren, that flesh and blood cannot inherit the kingdom of God; nor does corruption inherit

15:45 [d] Genesis 2:7 **15:47** [e] NU-Text omits *the Lord.*
15:49 [f] M-Text reads *let us also bear.*

THE MESSAGE

unprecedented in its form. You get a hint at the diversity of resurrection glory by looking at the diversity of bodies not only on earth but in the skies—sun, moon, stars—all these varieties of beauty and brightness. And we're only looking at pre-resurrection "seeds"—who can imagine what the resurrection "plants" will be like!

This image of planting a dead seed and raising a live plant is a mere sketch at best, but perhaps it will help in approaching the mystery of the resurrection body—but only if you keep in mind that when we're raised, we're raised for *good*, alive forever! The corpse that's planted is no beauty, but when it's raised, it's glorious. Put in the ground weak, it comes up powerful. The seed sown is natural; the seed grown is supernatural—same seed, same body, but what a difference from when it goes down in physical mortality to when it is raised up in spiritual immortality!

We follow this sequence in Scripture: The First Adam received life, the Last Adam is a life-giving Spirit. Physical life comes first, then spiritual—a firm base shaped from the earth, a final completion coming out of heaven. The First Man was made out of earth, and people since then are earthy; the Second Man was made out of heaven, and people now can be heavenly. In the same way that we've worked from our earthy origins, let's embrace our heavenly ends.

I need to emphasize, friends, that our natural, earthy lives don't in themselves lead us by their very nature into the kingdom of God. Their very "nature" is to die, so how could they "naturally" end up in the Life kingdom?

KING JAMES VERSION

51 ¶ Behold, I shew you a mystery; We shall not all sleep, but we shall all be changed,

52 In a moment, in the twinkling of an eye, at the last trump: for the trumpet shall sound, and the dead shall be raised incorruptible, and we shall be changed.

53 For this corruptible must put on incorruption, and this mortal *must* put on immortality.

54 So when this corruptible shall have put on incorruption, and this mortal shall have put on immortality, then shall be brought to pass the saying that is written, Death is swallowed up in victory.

55 O death, where *is* thy sting? O grave, where *is* thy victory?

56 The sting of death *is* sin; and the strength of sin *is* the law.

57 But thanks *be* to God, which giveth us the victory through our Lord Jesus Christ.

58 ¶ Therefore, my beloved brethren, be ye stedfast, unmoveable, always abounding in the work of the Lord, forasmuch as ye know that your labour is not in vain in the Lord.

16 Now concerning the collection for the saints, as I have given order to the churches of Galatia, even so do ye.

NEW AMERICAN STANDARD BIBLE

51 Behold, I tell you a mystery; we will not all sleep, but we will all be changed,

52 in a moment, in the twinkling of an eye, at the last trumpet; for the trumpet will sound, and the dead will be raised imperishable, and we will be changed.

53 For this perishable must put on the imperishable, and this mortal must put on immortality.

54 But when this perishable will have put on the imperishable, and this mortal will have put on immortality, then will come about the saying that is written, "DEATH IS SWALLOWED UP in victory.

55 "O DEATH, WHERE IS YOUR VICTORY? O DEATH, WHERE IS YOUR STING?"

56 The sting of death is sin, and the power of sin is the law;

57 but thanks be to God, who gives us the victory through our Lord Jesus Christ.

58 Therefore, my beloved brethren, be steadfast, immovable, always abounding in the work of the Lord, knowing that your toil is not *in* vain in the Lord.

Instructions and Greetings

16 Now concerning the collection for the saints, as I directed the churches of Galatia, so do you also.

NEW CENTURY VERSION

51 But look! I tell you this secret: We will not all sleep in
death, but we will all be changed. 52 It will take only a sec-
ond—as quickly as an eye blinks—when the last trumpet
sounds. The trumpet will sound, and those who have died
will be raised to live forever, and we will all be changed.
53 This body that can be destroyed must clothe itself with
something that can never be destroyed. And this body that
dies must clothe itself with something that can never die.
54 So this body that can be destroyed will clothe itself with
that which can never be destroyed, and this body that dies
will clothe itself with that which can never die. When this
happens, this Scripture will be made true:

"Death is destroyed forever in victory." *Isaiah 25:8*

55 "Death, where is your victory?
Death, where is your pain?" *Hosea 13:14*

56 Death's power to hurt is sin, and the power of sin is the
law. 57 But we thank God! He gives us the victory through
our Lord Jesus Christ.

58 So my dear brothers and sisters, stand strong. Do not
let anything change you. Always give yourselves fully to
the work of the Lord, because you know that your work in
the Lord is never wasted.

The Gift for Other Believers

16 Now I will write about the collection of money for God's people. Do the same thing I told the Galatian

CONTEMPORARY ENGLISH VERSION

explain a mystery to you. Not every one of us will die, but
we will all be changed. 52 It will happen suddenly, quicker
than the blink of an eye. At the sound of the last trumpet
the dead will be raised. We will all be changed, so that we
will never die again. 53 Our dead and decaying bodies will
be changed into bodies that won't die or decay. 54 The bod-
ies we now have are weak and can die. But they will be
changed into bodies that are eternal. Then the Scriptures
will come true,

"Death has lost the battle!
55 Where is its victory?
Where is its sting?"

56 Sin is what gives death its sting, and the Law is the
power behind sin. 57 But thank God for letting our Lord
Jesus Christ give us the victory!

58 My dear friends, stand firm and don't be shaken.
Always keep busy working for the Lord. You know that
everything you do for him is worthwhile.

A Collection for God's People

16 When you collect money for God's people, I want you to do exactly what I told the churches in

NEW INTERNATIONAL VERSION

the imperishable. 51 Listen, I tell you a mystery: We will not all sleep, but we will all be changed— 52 in a flash, in the twinkling of an eye, at the last trumpet. For the trumpet will sound, the dead will be raised imperishable, and we will be changed. 53 For the perishable must clothe itself with the imperishable, and the mortal with immortality. 54 When the perishable has been clothed with the imperishable, and the mortal with immortality, then the saying that is written will come true: "Death has been swallowed up in victory."[g]

55 "Where, O death, is your victory?
Where, O death, is your sting?"[h]

56 The sting of death is sin, and the power of sin is the law. 57 But thanks be to God! He gives us the victory through our Lord Jesus Christ.

58 Therefore, my dear brothers, stand firm. Let nothing move you. Always give yourselves fully to the work of the Lord, because you know that your labor in the Lord is not in vain.

The Collection for God's People

16 Now about the collection for God's people: Do what I told the Galatian churches to do. 2 On the

[g] *54* Isaiah 25:8 [h] *55* Hosea 13:14

NEW LIVING TRANSLATION

51 But let me tell you a wonderful secret God has revealed to us. Not all of us will die, but we will all be transformed. 52 It will happen in a moment, in the blinking of an eye, when the last trumpet is blown. For when the trumpet sounds, the Christians who have died* will be raised with transformed bodies. And then we who are living will be transformed so that we will never die. 53 For our perishable earthly bodies must be transformed into heavenly bodies that will never die.

54 When this happens—when our perishable earthly bodies have been transformed into heavenly bodies that will never die—then at last the Scriptures will come true:

"Death is swallowed up in victory.*
55 O death, where is your victory?
O death, where is your sting?"*

56 For sin is the sting that results in death, and the law gives sin its power. 57 How we thank God, who gives us victory over sin and death through Jesus Christ our Lord!

58 So, my dear brothers and sisters, be strong and steady, always enthusiastic about the Lord's work, for you know that nothing you do for the Lord is ever useless.

The Collection for Jerusalem

16 Now about the money being collected for the Christians in Jerusalem: You should follow the same procedures I gave to the churches in Galatia. 2 On

15:52 Greek *the dead.* 15:54 Isa 25:8. 15:55 Hos 13:14.

NEW KING JAMES VERSION

incorruption. 51 Behold, I tell you a mystery: We shall not all sleep, but we shall all be changed— 52 in a moment, in the twinkling of an eye, at the last trumpet. For the trumpet will sound, and the dead will be raised incorruptible, and we shall be changed. 53 For this corruptible must put on incorruption, and this mortal *must* put on immortality. 54 So when this corruptible has put on incorruption, and this mortal has put on immortality, then shall be brought to pass the saying that is written: *"Death is swallowed up in victory."*[g]

55 *"O Death, where is your sting?*[h]
O Hades, where is your victory?"[i]

56 The sting of death *is* sin, and the strength of sin *is* the law. 57 But thanks *be* to God, who gives us the victory through our Lord Jesus Christ.

58 Therefore, my beloved brethren, be steadfast, immovable, always abounding in the work of the Lord, knowing that your labor is not in vain in the Lord.

Collection for the Saints

16 Now concerning the collection for the saints, as I have given orders to the churches of Galatia, so

15:54 [g] Isaiah 25:8 15:55 [h] Hosea 13:14 [i] NU-Text reads *O Death, where is your victory? O Death, where is your sting?*

THE MESSAGE

But let me tell you something wonderful, a mystery I'll probably never fully understand. We're not all going to die—*but* we are all going to be changed. You hear a blast to end all blasts from a trumpet, and in the time that you look up and blink your eyes—it's over. On signal from that trumpet from heaven, the dead will be up and out of their graves, beyond the reach of death, never to die again. At the same moment and in the same way, we'll all be changed. In the resurrection scheme of things, this has to happen: everything perishable taken off the shelves and replaced by the imperishable, this mortal replaced by the immortal. Then the saying will come true:

"Death swallowed by triumphant Life!
Who got the last word, oh, Death?
Oh, Death, who's afraid of you now?"

It was sin that made death so frightening and law-code guilt that gave sin its leverage, its destructive power. But now in a single victorious stroke of Life, all three—sin, guilt, death—are gone, the gift of our Master, Jesus Christ. Thank God!

With all this going for us, my dear, dear friends, stand your ground. And don't hold back. Throw yourselves into the work of the Master, confident that nothing you do for him is a waste of time or effort.

Coming to See You

16 Regarding the relief offering for poor Christians that is being collected, you get the same instructions I

KING JAMES VERSION

2 Upon the first *day* of the week let every one of you lay by him in store, as *God* hath prospered him, that there be no gatherings when I come.

3 And when I come, whomsoever ye shall approve by *your* letters, them will I send to bring your liberality unto Jerusalem.

4 And if it be meet that I go also, they shall go with me.

5 ¶ Now I will come unto you, when I shall pass through Macedonia: for I do pass through Macedonia.

6 And it may be that I will abide, yea, and winter with you, that ye may bring me on my journey whithersoever I go.

7 For I will not see you now by the way; but I trust to tarry a while with you, if the Lord permit.

8 But I will tarry at Ephesus until Pentecost.

9 For a great door and effectual is opened unto me, and *there are* many adversaries.

10 ¶ Now if Timotheus come, see that he may be with you without fear: for he worketh the work of the Lord, as I also *do*.

11 Let no man therefore despise him: but conduct him forth in peace, that he may come unto me: for I look for him with the brethren.

12 As touching *our* brother Apollos, I greatly desired him to come unto you with the brethren: but his will was not at all to come at this time; but he will come when he shall have convenient time.

NEW AMERICAN STANDARD BIBLE

2 On the first day of every week each one of you is to put aside and save, as he may prosper, so that no collections be made when I come.

3 When I arrive, whomever you may approve, I will send them with letters to carry your gift to Jerusalem;

4 and if it is fitting for me to go also, they will go with me.

5 But I will come to you after I go through Macedonia, for I am going through Macedonia;

6 and perhaps I will stay with you, or even spend the winter, so that you may send me on my way wherever I may go.

7 For I do not wish to see you now *just* in passing; for I hope to remain with you for some time, if the Lord permits.

8 But I will remain in Ephesus until Pentecost;

9 for a wide door for effective *service* has opened to me, and there are many adversaries.

10 Now if Timothy comes, see that he is with you without cause to be afraid, for he is doing the Lord's work, as I also am.

11 So let no one despise him. But send him on his way in peace, so that he may come to me; for I expect him with the brethren.

12 But concerning Apollos our brother, I encouraged him greatly to come to you with the brethren; and it was not at all *his* desire to come now, but he will come when he has opportunity.

NEW CENTURY VERSION

churches to do: 2On the first day of every week, each one
of you should put aside money as you have been blessed.
Save it up so you will not have to collect money after I
come. 3When I arrive, I will send whomever you approve to
take your gift to Jerusalem. I will send them with letters of
introduction, 4and if it seems good for me to go also, they
will go along with me.

Paul's Plans

5I plan to go through Macedonia, so I will come to you
after I go through there. 6Perhaps I will stay with you for a
time or even all winter. Then you can help me on my trip,
wherever I go. 7I do not want to see you now just in passing. I hope to stay a longer time with you if the Lord
allows it. 8But I will stay at Ephesus until Pentecost,
9because a good opportunity for a great and growing work
has been given to me now. And there are many people
working against me.

10If Timothy comes to you, see to it that he has nothing
to fear with you, because he is working for the Lord just as
I am. 11So none of you should treat Timothy as unimportant, but help him on his trip in peace so that he can come
back to me. I am expecting him to come with the brothers.

12Now about our brother Apollos: I strongly encouraged
him to visit you with the other brothers. He did not at all
want to come now; he will come when he has the opportunity.

CONTEMPORARY ENGLISH VERSION

Galatia to do. 2That is, each Sunday each of you must put
aside part of what you have earned. If you do this, you
won't have to take up a collection when I come. 3Choose
some followers to take the money to Jerusalem. I will send
them on with the money and with letters which show that
you approve of them. 4If you think I should go along, they
can go with me.

Paul's Travel Plans

5After I have gone through Macedonia, I hope to see you
6and visit with you for a while. I may even stay all winter,
so that you can help me on my way to wherever I will be
going next. 7If the Lord lets me, I would rather come later
for a longer visit than to stop off now for only a short visit.
8I will stay in Ephesus until Pentecost, 9because there is a
wonderful opportunity for me to do some work here. But
there are also many people who are against me.

10When Timothy arrives, give him a friendly welcome.
He is doing the Lord's work, just as I am. 11Don't let anyone mistreat him. I am looking for him to return to me
together with the other followers. So when he leaves, send
him off with your blessings.

12I have tried hard to get our friend Apollos to visit you
with the other followers. He doesn't want to come just
now, but he will come when he can.

NEW INTERNATIONAL VERSION

first day of every week, each one of you should set aside a
sum of money in keeping with his income, saving it up, so
that when I come no collections will have to be made.
3Then, when I arrive, I will give letters of introduction to
the men you approve and send them with your gift to Jeru-
salem. 4If it seems advisable for me to go also, they will
accompany me.

Personal Requests

5After I go through Macedonia, I will come to you—for I
will be going through Macedonia. 6Perhaps I will stay with
you awhile, or even spend the winter, so that you can help
me on my journey, wherever I go. 7I do not want to see you
now and make only a passing visit; I hope to spend some
time with you, if the Lord permits. 8But I will stay on at
Ephesus until Pentecost, 9because a great door for effective
work has opened to me, and there are many who op-
pose me.

10If Timothy comes, see to it that he has nothing to fear
while he is with you, for he is carrying on the work of the
Lord, just as I am. 11No one, then, should refuse to accept
him. Send him on his way in peace so that he may return
to me. I am expecting him along with the brothers.

12Now about our brother Apollos: I strongly urged him
to go to you with the brothers. He was quite unwilling to
go now, but he will go when he has the opportunity.

NEW LIVING TRANSLATION

every Lord's Day,* each of you should put aside some
amount of money in relation to what you have earned and
save it for this offering. Don't wait until I get there and
then try to collect it all at once. 3When I come I will write
letters of recommendation for the messengers you choose
to deliver your gift to Jerusalem. 4And if it seems appropri-
ate for me also to go along, then we can travel together.

Paul's Final Instructions

5I am coming to visit you after I have been to
Macedonia, for I am planning to travel through Macedonia.
6It could be that I will stay awhile with you, perhaps all
winter, and then you can send me on my way to the next
destination. 7This time I don't want to make just a short
visit and then go right on. I want to come and stay awhile,
if the Lord will let me. 8In the meantime, I will be staying
here at Ephesus until the Festival of Pentecost, 9for there
is a wide-open door for a great work here, and many peo-
ple are responding. But there are many who oppose me.

10When Timothy comes, treat him with respect. He is
doing the Lord's work, just as I am. 11Don't let anyone
despise him. Send him on his way with your blessings
when he returns to me. I am looking forward to seeing him
soon, along with the other brothers.

12Now about our brother Apollos—I urged him to join
the other brothers when they visit you, but he was not
willing to come right now. He will be seeing you later,
when the time is right.

16:2 Greek *every first day of the week.*

NEW KING JAMES VERSION

you must do also: 2On the first *day* of the week let each
one of you lay something aside, storing up as he may pros-
per, that there be no collections when I come. 3And when I
come, whomever you approve by *your* letters I will send to
bear your gift to Jerusalem. 4But if it is fitting that I go
also, they will go with me.

Personal Plans

5Now I will come to you when I pass through Macedonia
(for I am passing through Macedonia). 6And it may be that
I will remain, or even spend the winter with you, that you
may send me on my journey, wherever I go. 7For I do not
wish to see you now on the way; but I hope to stay a while
with you, if the Lord permits.

8But I will tarry in Ephesus until Pentecost. 9For a great
and effective door has opened to me, and *there are* many
adversaries.

10And if Timothy comes, see that he may be with you
without fear; for he does the work of the Lord, as I also *do*.
11Therefore let no one despise him. But send him on his
journey in peace, that he may come to me; for I am waiting
for him with the brethren.

12Now concerning *our* brother Apollos, I strongly urged
him to come to you with the brethren, but he was quite
unwilling to come at this time; however, he will come
when he has a convenient time.

THE MESSAGE

gave the churches in Galatia. Every Sunday each of you make an offering and put it in safekeeping. Be as generous as you can. When I get there you'll have it ready, and I won't have to make a special appeal. Then after I arrive, I'll write letters authorizing whomever you delegate, and send them off to Jerusalem to deliver your gift. If you think it best that I go along, I'll be glad to travel with them.

I plan to visit you after passing through northern Greece. I won't be staying long there, but maybe I can stay awhile with you—maybe even spend the winter? Then you could give me a good send-off, wherever I may be headed next. I don't want to just drop by in between other "primary" destinations. I want a good, long, leisurely visit. If the Master agrees, we'll have it! For the present, I'm staying right here in Ephesus. A huge door of opportunity for good work has opened up here. (There is also mushrooming opposition.)

If Timothy shows up, take good care of him. Make him feel completely at home among you. He works so hard for the Master, just as I do. Don't let anyone disparage him. After a while, send him on to me with your blessing. Tell him I'm expecting him, and any friends he has with him.

About our friend Apollos, I've done my best to get him to pay you a visit, but haven't talked him into it yet. He doesn't think this is the right time. But there will be a "right time."

KING JAMES VERSION

13 ¶ Watch ye, stand fast in the faith, quit you like men, be strong.

14 Let all your things be done with charity.

15 I beseech you, brethren, (ye know the house of Stephanas, that it is the firstfruits of Achaia, and *that* they have addicted themselves to the ministry of the saints,)

16 That ye submit yourselves unto such, and to every one that helpeth with *us*, and laboureth.

17 I am glad of the coming of Stephanas and Fortunatus and Achaicus: for that which was lacking on your part they have supplied.

18 For they have refreshed my spirit and yours: therefore acknowledge ye them that are such.

19 ¶ The churches of Asia salute you. Aquila and Priscilla salute you much in the Lord, with the church that is in their house.

20 All the brethren greet you. Greet ye one another with an holy kiss.

21 The salutation of *me* Paul with mine own hand.

22 If any man love not the Lord Jesus Christ, let him be Anathema Maranatha.

23 The grace of our Lord Jesus Christ *be* with you.

24 My love *be* with you all in Christ Jesus. Amen.

NEW AMERICAN STANDARD BIBLE

13 Be on the alert, stand firm in the faith, act like men, be strong.

14 Let all that you do be done in love.

15 Now I urge you, brethren (you know the household of Stephanas, that they were the first fruits of Achaia, and that they have devoted themselves for ministry to the saints),

16 that you also be in subjection to such men and to everyone who helps in the work and labors.

17 I rejoice over the coming of Stephanas and Fortunatus and Achaicus, because they have supplied what was lacking on your part.

18 For they have refreshed my spirit and yours. Therefore acknowledge such men.

19 The churches of Asia greet you. Aquila and Prisca greet you heartily in the Lord, with the church that is in their house.

20 All the brethren greet you. Greet one another with a holy kiss.

21 The greeting is in my own hand—Paul.

22 If anyone does not love the Lord, he is to be accursed. Maranatha.

23 The grace of the Lord Jesus be with you.

24 My love be with you all in Christ Jesus. Amen.

NEW CENTURY VERSION

Paul Ends His Letter

13Be alert. Continue strong in the faith. Have courage,
and be strong. 14Do everything in love.

15You know that the family of Stephanas were the first
believers in Southern Greece and that they have given
themselves to the service of God's people. I ask you, brothers and sisters, 16to follow the leading of people like these
and anyone else who works and serves with them.

17I am happy that Stephanas, Fortunatus, and Achaicus
have come. You are not here, but they have filled your
place. 18They have refreshed my spirit and yours. You
should recognize the value of people like these.

19The churches in the country of Asia send greetings to
you. Aquila and Priscilla greet you in the Lord, as does the
church that meets in their house. 20All the brothers and
sisters here send greetings. Give each other a holy kiss
when you meet.

21I, Paul, am writing this greeting with my own hand.

22If anyone does not love the Lord, let him be separated
from God—lost forever!

Come, O Lord!

23The grace of the Lord Jesus be with you.

24My love be with all of you in Christ Jesus.

CONTEMPORARY ENGLISH VERSION

Personal Concerns and Greetings

13Keep alert. Be firm in your faith. Stay brave and
strong. 14Show love in everything you do.

15You know that Stephanas and his family were the first
in Achaia to have faith in the Lord. They have done all
they can for God's people. My friends, I ask you 16to obey
leaders like them and to do the same for all others who
work hard with you.

17I was glad to see Stephanas and Fortunatus and
Achaicus. Having them here was like having you. 18They
made me feel much better, just as they made you feel better. You should appreciate people like them.

19Greetings from the churches in Asia.

Aquila and Priscilla, together with the church that meets in their house, send greetings in the name of the Lord.

20All of the Lord's followers send their greetings.

Give each other a warm greeting.

21I am signing this letter myself: PAUL.

22I pray that God will put a curse on everyone who
doesn't love the Lord. And may the Lord come soon.

23I pray that the Lord Jesus will be kind to you.

24I love everyone who belongs to Christ Jesus.

NEW INTERNATIONAL VERSION

13 Be on your guard; stand firm in the faith; be men of courage; be strong. 14 Do everything in love.

15 You know that the household of Stephanas were the first converts in Achaia, and they have devoted themselves to the service of the saints. I urge you, brothers, 16 to submit to such as these and to everyone who joins in the work, and labors at it. 17 I was glad when Stephanas, Fortunatus and Achaicus arrived, because they have supplied what was lacking from you. 18 For they refreshed my spirit and yours also. Such men deserve recognition.

Final Greetings

19 The churches in the province of Asia send you greetings. Aquila and Priscilla[a] greet you warmly in the Lord, and so does the church that meets at their house. 20 All the brothers here send you greetings. Greet one another with a holy kiss.

21 I, Paul, write this greeting in my own hand.

22 If anyone does not love the Lord—a curse be on him. Come, O Lord[b]!

23 The grace of the Lord Jesus be with you.

24 My love to all of you in Christ Jesus. Amen.[c]

[a] *19* Greek *Prisca*, a variant of *Priscilla* [b] *22* In Aramaic the expression *Come, O Lord* is *Marana tha.* [c] *24* Some manuscripts do not have *Amen*.

NEW LIVING TRANSLATION

13 Be on guard. Stand true to what you believe. Be courageous. Be strong. 14 And everything you do must be done with love.

15 You know that Stephanas and his household were the first to become Christians in Greece,* and they are spending their lives in service to other Christians. I urge you, dear brothers and sisters,* 16 to respect them fully and others like them who serve with such real devotion. 17 I am so glad that Stephanas, Fortunatus, and Achaicus have come here. They have been making up for the help you weren't here to give me. 18 They have been a wonderful encouragement to me, as they have been to you, too. You must give proper honor to all who serve so well.

Paul's Final Greetings

19 The churches here in the province of Asia* greet you heartily in the Lord, along with Aquila and Priscilla and all the others who gather in their home for church meetings. 20 All the brothers and sisters here have asked me to greet you for them. Greet each other in Christian love.*

21 Here is my greeting, which I write with my own hand—PAUL.

22 If anyone does not love the Lord, that person is cursed. Our Lord, come!*

23 May the grace of the Lord Jesus be with you.

24 My love to all of you in Christ Jesus.*

16:15a Greek *were the firstfruits in Achaia,* the southern region of the Greek peninsula. **16:15b** Greek *brothers;* also in 16:20. **16:19** *Asia* was a Roman province in what is now western Turkey. **16:20** Greek *with a sacred kiss.* **16:22** From Aramaic, *Marana tha.* **16:24** Some manuscripts add *Amen.*

NEW KING JAMES VERSION

Final Exhortations

13 Watch, stand fast in the faith, be brave, be strong. 14 Let all *that* you *do* be done with love.

15 I urge you, brethren—you know the household of Stephanas, that it is the firstfruits of Achaia, and *that* they have devoted themselves to the ministry of the saints— 16 that you also submit to such, and to everyone who works and labors with *us.*

17 I am glad about the coming of Stephanas, Fortunatus, and Achaicus, for what was lacking on your part they supplied. 18 For they refreshed my spirit and yours. Therefore acknowledge such men.

Greetings and a Solemn Farewell

19 The churches of Asia greet you. Aquila and Priscilla greet you heartily in the Lord, with the church that is in their house. 20 All the brethren greet you.

Greet one another with a holy kiss.

21 The salutation with my own hand—Paul's.

22 If anyone does not love the Lord Jesus Christ, let him be accursed.[a] O Lord, come![b]

23 The grace of our Lord Jesus Christ *be* with you. 24 My love *be* with you all in Christ Jesus. Amen.

16:22 [a] Greek *anathema* [b] Aramaic *Maranatha*

THE MESSAGE

Keep your eyes open, hold tight to your convictions, give it all you've got, be resolute, and love without stopping.

Would you do me a favor, friends, and give special recognition to the family of Stephanas? You know, they were among the first converts in Greece, and they've put themselves out, serving Christians ever since then. I want you to honor and look up to people like that: companions and workers who show us how to do it, giving us something to aspire to.

I want you to know how delighted I am to have Stephanas, Fortunatus, and Achaicus here with me. They partially make up for your absence! They've refreshed me by keeping me in touch with you. Be proud that you have people like this among you.

The churches here in western Asia send greetings.

Aquila, Priscilla, and the church that meets in their house say hello.

All the friends here say hello.

Pass the greetings around with holy embraces!

And I, Paul—in my own handwriting!—send you my regards.

If anyone won't love the Master, throw him out. Make room for the Master!

Our Master Jesus has his arms wide open for you.

And I love all of you in the Messiah, in Jesus.

KING JAMES VERSION

THE SECOND EPISTLE OF ST. PAUL TO THE CORINTHIANS

1 Paul, an apostle of Jesus Christ by the will of God, and Timothy *our* brother, unto the church of God which is at Corinth, with all the saints which are in all Achaia:

2 Grace *be* to you and peace from God our Father, and *from* the Lord Jesus Christ.

3 ¶ Blessed *be* God, even the Father of our Lord Jesus Christ, the Father of mercies, and the God of all comfort;

4 Who comforteth us in all our tribulation, that we may be able to comfort them which are in any trouble, by the comfort wherewith we ourselves are comforted of God.

5 For as the sufferings of Christ abound in us, so our consolation also aboundeth by Christ.

6 And whether we be afflicted, *it is* for your consolation and salvation, which is effectual in the enduring of the same sufferings which we also suffer: or whether we be comforted, *it is* for your consolation and salvation.

NEW AMERICAN STANDARD BIBLE

THE SECOND LETTER OF PAUL TO THE CORINTHIANS

Introduction

1 Paul, an apostle of Christ Jesus by the will of God, and Timothy *our* brother,

To the church of God which is at Corinth with all the saints who are throughout Achaia:

2 Grace to you and peace from God our Father and the Lord Jesus Christ.

3 Blessed *be* the God and Father of our Lord Jesus Christ, the Father of mercies and God of all comfort,

4 who comforts us in all our affliction so that we will be able to comfort those who are in any affliction with the comfort with which we ourselves are comforted by God.

5 For just as the sufferings of Christ are ours in abundance, so also our comfort is abundant through Christ.

6 But if we are afflicted, it is for your comfort and salvation; or if we are comforted, it is for your comfort, which is effective in the patient enduring of the same sufferings which we also suffer;

NEW CENTURY VERSION

2 CORINTHIANS

1 From Paul, an apostle of Christ Jesus. I am an apostle because that is what God wanted. Also from Timothy our brother in Christ.

To the church of God in Corinth, and to all of God's people everywhere in Southern Greece:

2Grace and peace to you from God our Father and the Lord Jesus Christ.

Paul Gives Thanks to God

3Praise be to the God and Father of our Lord Jesus Christ. God is the Father who is full of mercy and all comfort. 4He comforts us every time we have trouble, so when others have trouble, we can comfort them with the same comfort God gives us. 5We share in the many sufferings of Christ. In the same way, much comfort comes to us through Christ. 6If we have troubles, it is for your comfort and salvation, and if we have comfort, you also have comfort. This helps you to accept patiently the same sufferings

CONTEMPORARY ENGLISH VERSION

2 CORINTHIANS

1 From Paul, chosen by God to be an apostle of Jesus Christ, and from Timothy, who is also a follower.

To God's church in Corinth and to all of God's people in Achaia.

2I pray that God our Father and the Lord Jesus Christ will be kind to you and will bless you with peace!

Paul Gives Thanks

3Praise God, the Father of our Lord Jesus Christ! The Father is a merciful God, who always gives us comfort. 4He comforts us when we are in trouble, so that we can share that same comfort with others in trouble. 5We share in the terrible sufferings of Christ, but also in the wonderful comfort he gives. 6We suffer in the hope that you will be comforted and saved. And because we are comforted, you will also be comforted, as you patiently endure suffering like

NEW INTERNATIONAL VERSION

2 CORINTHIANS

1 Paul, an apostle of Christ Jesus by the will of God, and
Timothy our brother,

To the church of God in Corinth, together with all the
saints throughout Achaia:

2Grace and peace to you from God our Father and the
Lord Jesus Christ.

The God of All Comfort

3Praise be to the God and Father of our Lord Jesus Christ,
the Father of compassion and the God of all comfort, 4who
comforts us in all our troubles, so that we can comfort
those in any trouble with the comfort we ourselves have
received from God. 5For just as the sufferings of Christ flow
over into our lives, so also through Christ our comfort over-
flows. 6If we are distressed, it is for your comfort and salva-
tion; if we are comforted, it is for your comfort, which pro-
duces in you patient endurance of the same sufferings we

NEW LIVING TRANSLATION

2 CORINTHIANS

Greetings from Paul

1 This letter is from Paul, appointed by God to be an
apostle of Christ Jesus, and from our dear brother
Timothy.

We are writing to God's church in Corinth and to all the
Christians throughout Greece.*

2May God our Father and the Lord Jesus Christ give you
his grace and peace.

God Offers Comfort to All

3All praise to the God and Father of our Lord Jesus
Christ. He is the source* of every mercy and the God who
comforts us. 4He comforts us in all our troubles so that we
can comfort others. When others are troubled, we will be
able to give them the same comfort God has given us. 5You
can be sure that the more we suffer for Christ, the more
God will shower us with his comfort through Christ. 6So
when we are weighed down with troubles, it is for your
benefit and salvation! For when God comforts us, it is so
that we, in turn, can be an encouragement to you. Then
you can patiently endure the same things we suffer. 7We

1:1 Greek *Achaia,* the southern region of the Greek peninsula.
1:3 Greek *the Father.*

NEW KING JAMES VERSION

THE SECOND EPISTLE OF PAUL TO THE

CORINTHIANS

Greeting

1 Paul, an apostle of Jesus Christ by the will of God, and
Timothy *our* brother,

To the church of God which is at Corinth, with all the
saints who are in all Achaia:

2Grace to you and peace from God our Father and the
Lord Jesus Christ.

Comfort in Suffering

3Blessed *be* the God and Father of our Lord Jesus Christ,
the Father of mercies and God of all comfort, 4who com-
forts us in all our tribulation, that we may be able to com-
fort those who are in any trouble, with the comfort with
which we ourselves are comforted by God. 5For as the suf-
ferings of Christ abound in us, so our consolation also
abounds through Christ. 6Now if we are afflicted, *it is* for
your consolation and salvation, which is effective for
enduring the same sufferings which we also suffer. Or if
we are comforted, *it is* for your consolation and salvation.

THE MESSAGE

2 CORINTHIANS

1 I, Paul, have been sent on a special mission by the
Messiah, Jesus, planned by God himself. I write this to
God's congregation in Corinth, and to believers all over
Achaia province. May all the gifts and benefits that come
from God our Father and the Master, Jesus Christ, be
yours! Timothy, someone you know and trust, joins me in
this greeting.

The Rescue

All praise to the God and Father of our Master, Jesus the Messiah! Father of all mercy! God of all healing counsel! He comes alongside us when we go through hard times, and before you know it, he brings us alongside someone else who is going through hard times so that we can be there for that person just as God was there for us. We have plenty of hard times that come from following the Messiah, but no more so than the good times of his healing comfort—we get a full measure of that, too.

When we suffer for Jesus, it works out for your healing and salvation. If we are treated well, given a helping hand and encouraging word, that also works to your benefit, spurring you on, face forward, unflinching. Your hard times are also our hard times. When we see that you're just as

KING JAMES VERSION

7 ¶ And our hope of you *is* stedfast, knowing, that as ye are partakers of the sufferings, so *shall ye be* also of the consolation.

8 For we would not, brethren, have you ignorant of our trouble which came to us in Asia, that we were pressed out of measure, above strength, insomuch that we despaired even of life:

9 But we had the sentence of death in ourselves, that we should not trust in ourselves, but in God which raiseth the dead:

10 Who delivered us from so great a death, and doth deliver: in whom we trust that he will yet deliver *us*;

11 Ye also helping together by prayer for us, that for the gift *bestowed* upon us by the means of many persons thanks may be given by many on our behalf.

12 ¶ For our rejoicing is this, the testimony of our conscience, that in simplicity and godly sincerity, not with fleshly wisdom, but by the grace of God, we have had our conversation in the world, and more abundantly to you-ward.

13 For we write none other things unto you, than what ye read or acknowledge; and I trust ye shall acknowledge even to the end;

14 As also ye have acknowledged us in part, that we are your rejoicing, even as ye also *are* ours in the day of the Lord Jesus.

NEW AMERICAN STANDARD BIBLE

7 and our hope for you is firmly grounded, knowing that as you are sharers of our sufferings, so also you are *sharers* of our comfort.

8 For we do not want you to be unaware, brethren, of our affliction which came *to us* in Asia, that we were burdened excessively, beyond our strength, so that we despaired even of life;

9 indeed, we had the sentence of death within ourselves so that we would not trust in ourselves, but in God who raises the dead;

10 who delivered us from so great a *peril of* death, and will deliver *us*, He on whom we have set our hope. And He will yet deliver us,

11 you also joining in helping us through your prayers, so that thanks may be given by many persons on our behalf for the favor bestowed on us through *the prayers of* many.

Paul's Integrity

12 For our proud confidence is this: the testimony of our conscience, that in holiness and godly sincerity, not in fleshly wisdom but in the grace of God, we have conducted ourselves in the world, and especially toward you.

13 For we write nothing else to you than what you read and understand, and I hope you will understand until the end;

14 just as you also partially did understand us, that we are your reason to be proud as you also are ours, in the day of our Lord Jesus.

NEW CENTURY VERSION

we have. 7Our hope for you is strong, knowing that you
share in our sufferings and also in the comfort we receive.
8Brothers and sisters,[a] we want you to know about the
trouble we suffered in Asia. We had great burdens there
that were beyond our own strength. We even gave up hope
of living. 9Truly, in our own hearts we believed we would
die. But this happened so we would not trust in ourselves
but in God, who raises people from the dead. 10God saved
us from these great dangers of death, and he will continue
to save us. We have put our hope in him, and he will save
us again. 11And you can help us with your prayers. Then
many people will give thanks for us—that God blessed us
because of their many prayers.

The Change in Paul's Plans

12This is what we are proud of, and I can say it with a
clear conscience: In everything we have done in the world,
and especially with you, we have had an honest and sin-
cere heart from God. We did this by God's grace, not by the
kind of wisdom the world has. 13–14We write to you only
what you can read and understand. And I hope that as you
have understood some things about us, you may come to
know everything about us. Then you can be proud of us, as
we will be proud of you on the day our Lord Jesus Christ
comes again.

1:8 [a] **Brothers and sisters** Although the Greek text says "Brothers" here and throughout this book, Paul's words were meant for the entire church, including men and women.

CONTEMPORARY ENGLISH VERSION

ours. 7You never disappoint us. You suffered as much as
we did, and we know that you will be comforted as we
were.
8My friends, I want you to know what a hard time we
had in Asia. Our sufferings were so horrible and so
unbearable that death seemed certain. 9In fact, we felt sure
that we were going to die. But this made us stop trusting
in ourselves and start trusting God, who raises the dead to
life. 10God saved us from the threat of death,[a] and we are
sure that he will do it again and again. 11Please help us by
praying for us. Then many people will give thanks for the
blessings we receive in answer to all these prayers.

Paul's Change of Plans

12We can be proud of our clear conscience. We have
always lived honestly and sincerely, especially when we
were with you. And we were guided by God's wonderful
kindness instead of by the wisdom of this world. 13I am
not writing anything you cannot read and understand. I
hope you will understand it completely, 14just as you
already partly understand us. Then when our Lord Jesus
returns, you can be as proud of us as we are of you.

[a] 1.10 *the threat of death*: Some manuscripts have "many threats of death."

NEW INTERNATIONAL VERSION

suffer. 7And our hope for you is firm, because we know that
just as you share in our sufferings, so also you share in our
comfort.
8We do not want you to be uninformed, brothers, about
the hardships we suffered in the province of Asia. We were
under great pressure, far beyond our ability to endure, so
that we despaired even of life. 9Indeed, in our hearts we
felt the sentence of death. But this happened that we
might not rely on ourselves but on God, who raises the
dead. 10He has delivered us from such a deadly peril, and
he will deliver us. On him we have set our hope that he
will continue to deliver us, 11as you help us by your
prayers. Then many will give thanks on our[a] behalf for the
gracious favor granted us in answer to the prayers of
many.

Paul's Change of Plans

12Now this is our boast: Our conscience testifies that we
have conducted ourselves in the world, and especially in
our relations with you, in the holiness and sincerity that
are from God. We have done so not according to worldly
wisdom but according to God's grace. 13For we do not
write you anything you cannot read or understand. And I
hope that, 14as you have understood us in part, you will
come to understand fully that you can boast of us just as
we will boast of you in the day of the Lord Jesus.

[a] *11* Many manuscripts *your*

NEW LIVING TRANSLATION

are confident that as you share in suffering, you will also
share God's comfort.
8I think you ought to know, dear brothers and sisters,*
about the trouble we went through in the province of Asia.
We were crushed and completely overwhelmed, and we
thought we would never live through it. 9In fact, we
expected to die. But as a result, we learned not to rely on
ourselves, but on God who can raise the dead. 10And he
did deliver us from mortal danger. And we are confident
that he will continue to deliver us. 11He will rescue us
because you are helping by praying for us. As a result,
many will give thanks to God because so many people's
prayers for our safety have been answered.

Paul's Change of Plans

12We can say with confidence and a clear conscience
that we have been honest* and sincere in all our dealings.
We have depended on God's grace, not on our own earthly
wisdom. That is how we have acted toward everyone, and
especially toward you. 13My letters have been straightfor-
ward, and there is nothing written between the lines and
nothing you can't understand. I hope someday you will
fully understand us, 14even if you don't fully understand
us now. Then on the day when our Lord Jesus comes back
again, you will be proud of us in the same way we are
proud of you.

1:8 Greek *brothers.* 1:12 Some manuscripts read *holy.*

NEW KING JAMES VERSION

7And our hope for you *is* steadfast, because we know that
as you are partakers of the sufferings, so also *you will par-
take* of the consolation.

Delivered from Suffering

8For we do not want you to be ignorant, brethren, of our
trouble which came to us in Asia: that we were burdened
beyond measure, above strength, so that we despaired
even of life. 9Yes, we had the sentence of death in our-
selves, that we should not trust in ourselves but in God
who raises the dead, 10who delivered us from so great a
death, and does[a] deliver us; in whom we trust that He will
still deliver *us,* 11you also helping together in prayer for
us, that thanks may be given by many persons on our[b]
behalf for the gift *granted* to us through many.

Paul's Sincerity

12For our boasting is this: the testimony of our con-
science that we conducted ourselves in the world in sim-
plicity and godly sincerity, not with fleshly wisdom but by
the grace of God, and more abundantly toward you. 13For
we are not writing any other things to you than what you
read or understand. Now I trust you will understand, even
to the end 14(as also you have understood us in part), that
we are your boast as you also *are* ours, in the day of the
Lord Jesus.

1:10 [a] NU-Text reads *shall.* 1:11 [b] M-Text reads *your behalf.*

THE MESSAGE

willing to endure the hard times as to enjoy the good times,
we know you're going to make it, no doubt about it.

We don't want you in the dark, friends, about how hard it was when all this came down on us in Asia province. It was so bad we didn't think we were going to make it. We felt like we'd been sent to death row, that it was all over for us. As it turned out, it was the best thing that could have happened. Instead of trusting in our own strength or wits to get out of it, we were forced to trust God totally—not a bad idea since he's the God who raises the dead! And he did it, rescued us from certain doom. *And* he'll do it again, rescuing us as many times as we need rescuing. You and your prayers are part of the rescue operation—I don't want you in the dark about that either. I can see your faces even now, lifted in praise for God's deliverance of us, a rescue in which your prayers played such a crucial part.

Now that the worst is over, we're pleased we can report that we've come out of this with conscience and faith intact, and can face the world—and even more importantly, face you with our heads held high. But it wasn't by any fancy footwork on our part. It was *God* who kept us focused on him, uncompromised. Don't try to read between the lines or look for hidden meanings in this letter. We're writing plain, unembellished truth, hoping that you'll now see the whole picture as well as you've seen some of the details. We want you to be as proud of us as we are of you when we stand together before our Master Jesus.

KING JAMES VERSION

15 ¶ And in this confidence I was minded to come unto you before, that ye might have a second benefit;

16 And to pass by you into Macedonia, and to come again out of Macedonia unto you, and of you to be brought on my way toward Judaea.

17 When I therefore was thus minded, did I use lightness? or the things that I purpose, do I purpose according to the flesh, that with me there should be yea yea, and nay nay?

18 But *as* God *is* true, our word toward you was not yea and nay.

19 For the Son of God, Jesus Christ, who was preached among you by us, *even* by me and Silvanus and Timotheus, was not yea and nay, but in him was yea.

20 For all the promises of God in him *are* yea, and in him Amen, unto the glory of God by us.

21 Now he which stablisheth us with you in Christ, and hath anointed us, *is* God;

22 Who hath also sealed us, and given the earnest of the Spirit in our hearts.

23 Moreover I call God for a record upon my soul, that to spare you I came not as yet unto Corinth.

24 Not for that we have dominion over your faith, but are helpers of your joy: for by faith ye stand.

NEW AMERICAN STANDARD BIBLE

15 In this confidence I intended at first to come to you, so that you might twice receive a blessing;

16 that is, to pass your way into Macedonia, and again from Macedonia to come to you, and by you to be helped on my journey to Judea.

17 Therefore, I was not vacillating when I intended to do this, was I? Or what I purpose, do I purpose according to the flesh, so that with me there will be yes, yes and no, no *at the same time?*

18 But as God is faithful, our word to you is not yes and no.

19 For the Son of God, Christ Jesus, who was preached among you by us—by me and Silvanus and Timothy—was not yes and no, but is yes in Him.

20 For as many as are the promises of God, in Him they are yes; therefore also through Him is our Amen to the glory of God through us.

21 Now He who establishes us with you in Christ and anointed us is God,

22 who also sealed us and gave *us* the Spirit in our hearts as a pledge.

23 But I call God as witness to my soul, that to spare you I did not come again to Corinth.

24 Not that we lord it over your faith, but are workers with you for your joy; for in your faith you are standing firm.

NEW CENTURY VERSION

15 I was so sure of all this that I made plans to visit you
first so you could be blessed twice. 16 I planned to visit you
on my way to Macedonia and again on my way back. I
wanted to get help from you for my trip to Judea. 17 Do you
think that I made these plans without really meaning it?
Or maybe you think I make plans as the world does, so
that I say yes, yes and at the same time no, no.
18 But if you can believe God, you can believe that what
we tell you is never both yes and no. 19 The Son of God,
Jesus Christ, that Silas and Timothy and I preached to you,
was not yes and no. In Christ it has always been yes. 20 The
yes to all of God's promises is in Christ, and through Christ
we say yes to the glory of God. 21 Remember, God is the
One who makes you and us strong in Christ. God made us
his chosen people. 22 He put his mark on us to show that
we are his, and he put his Spirit in our hearts to be a guarantee for all he has promised.
23 I tell you this, and I ask God to be my witness that this
is true: The reason I did not come back to Corinth was to
keep you from being punished or hurt. 24 We are not trying
to control your faith. You are strong in faith. But we are
workers with you for your own joy.

CONTEMPORARY ENGLISH VERSION

15 I was so sure of your pride in us that I had planned to
visit you first of all. In this way you would have the blessing of two visits from me. 16 Once on my way to Macedonia
and again on my return from there. Then you could send
me on to Judea. 17 Do you think I couldn't make up my
mind about what to do? Or do I seem like someone who
says "Yes" or "No" simply to please others? 18 God can be
trusted, and so can I, when I say that our answer to you
has always been "Yes" and never "No." 19 This is because
Jesus Christ the Son of God is always "Yes" and never
"No." And he is the one that Silas,[b] Timothy, and I told
you about.
20 Christ says "Yes" to all of God's promises. That's why
we have Christ to say "Amen"[c] for us to the glory of God.
21 And so God makes it possible for you and us to stand
firmly together with Christ. God is also the one who chose
us 22 and put his Spirit in our hearts to show that we
belong only to him.
23 God is my witness that I stayed away from Corinth,
just to keep from being hard on you. 24 We are not bosses
who tell you what to believe. We are working with you to
make you glad, because your faith is strong.

[b] 1.19 *Silas*: The Greek text has "Silvanus," which is another form of the name Silas. [c] 1.20 *Amen*: The word "amen" is used here with the meaning of "yes."

NEW INTERNATIONAL VERSION

15Because I was confident of this, I planned to visit you
first so that you might benefit twice. 16I planned to visit
you on my way to Macedonia and to come back to you
from Macedonia, and then to have you send me on my way
to Judea. 17When I planned this, did I do it lightly? Or do I
make my plans in a worldly manner so that in the same
breath I say, "Yes, yes" and "No, no"?

18But as surely as God is faithful, our message to you is
not "Yes" and "No." 19For the Son of God, Jesus Christ,
who was preached among you by me and Silas[b] and
Timothy, was not "Yes" and "No," but in him it has always
been "Yes." 20For no matter how many promises God has
made, they are "Yes" in Christ. And so through him the
"Amen" is spoken by us to the glory of God. 21Now it is
God who makes both us and you stand firm in Christ. He
anointed us, 22set his seal of ownership on us, and put his
Spirit in our hearts as a deposit, guaranteeing what is to
come.

23I call God as my witness that it was in order to spare
you that I did not return to Corinth. 24Not that we lord it
over your faith, but we work with you for your joy, because

b 19 Greek *Silvanus*, a variant of *Silas*

NEW LIVING TRANSLATION

15Since I was so sure of your understanding and trust, I
wanted to give you a double blessing. 16I wanted to stop
and see you on my way to Macedonia and again on my
return trip. Then you could send me on my way to Judea.

17You may be asking why I changed my plan. Hadn't I
made up my mind yet? Or am I like people of the world
who say yes when they really mean no? 18As surely as God
is true, I am not that sort of person. My yes means yes
19because Jesus Christ, the Son of God, never wavers
between yes and no. He is the one whom Timothy, Silas,*
and I preached to you, and he is the divine Yes—God's
affirmation. 20For all of God's promises have been fulfilled
in him. That is why we say "Amen" when we give glory to
God through Christ. 21It is God who gives us, along with
you, the ability to stand firm for Christ.* He has commis-
sioned us, 22and he has identified us as his own by placing
the Holy Spirit in our hearts as the first installment of
everything he will give us.

23Now I call upon God as my witness that I am telling
the truth. The reason I didn't return to Corinth was to
spare you from a severe rebuke. 24But that does not mean
we want to tell you exactly how to put your faith into prac-
tice.* We want to work together with you so you will be
full of joy as you stand firm in your faith.

1:19 Greek *Silvanus.* 1:21 Or *who has identified us and you as genuine Christians.* 1:24 Greek *want to lord it over your faith.*

NEW KING JAMES VERSION

Sparing the Church

15And in this confidence I intended to come to you
before, that you might have a second benefit— 16to pass
by way of you to Macedonia, to come again from Mace-
donia to you, and be helped by you on my way to Judea.
17Therefore, when I was planning this, did I do it lightly?
Or the things I plan, do I plan according to the flesh, that
with me there should be Yes, Yes, and No, No? 18But *as*
God *is* faithful, our word to you was not Yes and No. 19For
the Son of God, Jesus Christ, who was preached among you
by us—by me, Silvanus, and Timothy—was not Yes and
No, but in Him was Yes. 20For all the promises of God in
Him *are* Yes, and in Him Amen, to the glory of God
through us. 21Now He who establishes us with you in
Christ and has anointed us *is* God, 22who also has sealed
us and given us the Spirit in our hearts as a guarantee.

23Moreover I call God as witness against my soul, that to
spare you I came no more to Corinth. 24Not that we have
dominion over your faith, but are fellow workers for your
joy; for by faith you stand.

THE MESSAGE

Confident of your welcome, I had originally planned two great visits with you—coming by on my way to Macedonia province, and then again on my return trip. Then we could have had a bon-voyage party as you sent me off to Judea. That was the plan.

Are you now going to accuse me of being flip with my promises because it didn't work out? Do you think I talk out of both sides of my mouth—a glib *yes* one moment, a glib *no* the next? Well, you're wrong. I try to be as true to my word as God is to his. Our word to you wasn't a careless yes canceled by an indifferent no. How could it be? When Silas and Timothy and I proclaimed the Son of God among you, did you pick up on any yes-and-no, on-again, off-again waffling? Wasn't it a clean, strong Yes?

Whatever God has promised gets stamped with the Yes of Jesus. In him, this is what we preach and pray, the great Amen, God's Yes and our Yes together, gloriously evident. God affirms us, making us a sure thing in Christ, putting his Yes within us. By his Spirit he has stamped us with his eternal pledge—a sure beginning of what he is destined to complete.

Now, are you ready for the real reason I didn't visit you in Corinth? As God is my witness, the only reason I didn't come was to spare you pain. I was being *considerate* of you, not indifferent, not manipulative.

We're not in charge of how you live out the faith, looking over your shoulders, suspiciously critical. We're partners, working alongside you, joyfully expectant. I know that you stand by your own faith, not by ours.

KING JAMES VERSION

2 But I determined this with myself, that I would not
come again to you in heaviness.
2 For if I make you sorry, who is he then that maketh
me glad, but the same which is made sorry by me?
3 And I wrote this same unto you, lest, when I came, I
should have sorrow from them of whom I ought to rejoice;
having confidence in you all, that my joy is *the joy* of you
all.
4 For out of much affliction and anguish of heart I
wrote unto you with many tears; not that ye should be
grieved, but that ye might know the love which I have
more abundantly unto you.
5 ¶ But if any have caused grief, he hath not grieved
me, but in part: that I may not overcharge you all.
6 Sufficient to such a man *is* this punishment, which
was inflicted of many.
7 So that contrariwise ye *ought* rather to forgive *him*,
and comfort *him*, lest perhaps such a one should be swallowed up with overmuch sorrow.
8 Wherefore I beseech you that ye would confirm *your*
love toward him.
9 For to this end also did I write, that I might know the
proof of you, whether ye be obedient in all things.
10 To whom ye forgive any thing, I *forgive* also: for if I
forgave any thing, to whom I forgave *it*, for your sakes *forgave I it* in the person of Christ;
11 Lest Satan should get an advantage of us: for we are
not ignorant of his devices.

NEW AMERICAN STANDARD BIBLE

Reaffirm Your Love

2 But I determined this for my own sake, that I would
not come to you in sorrow again.
2 For if I cause you sorrow, who then makes me glad
but the one whom I made sorrowful?
3 This is the very thing I wrote you, so that when I
came, I would not have sorrow from those who ought to
make me rejoice; having confidence in you all that my joy
would be *the joy* of you all.
4 For out of much affliction and anguish of heart I
wrote to you with many tears; not so that you would be
made sorrowful, but that you might know the love which I
have especially for you.
5 But if any has caused sorrow, he has caused sorrow
not to me, but in some degree—in order not to say too
much—to all of you.
6 Sufficient for such a one is this punishment which
was inflicted by the majority,
7 so that on the contrary you should rather forgive and
comfort *him*, otherwise such a one might be overwhelmed
by excessive sorrow.
8 Wherefore I urge you to reaffirm *your* love for him.
9 For to this end also I wrote, so that I might put you
to the test, whether you are obedient in all things.
10 But one whom you forgive anything, I *forgive* also;
for indeed what I have forgiven, if I have forgiven anything, *I did it* for your sakes in the presence of Christ,
11 so that no advantage would be taken of us by Satan,
for we are not ignorant of his schemes.

NEW CENTURY VERSION

2 So I decided that my next visit to you would not be
another one to make you sad. 2If I make you sad, who
will make me glad? Only you can make me glad—particularly the person whom I made sad. 3I wrote you a letter for
this reason: that when I came to you I would not be made
sad by the people who should make me happy. I felt sure
of all of you, that you would share my joy. 4When I wrote
to you before, I was very troubled and unhappy in my
heart, and I wrote with many tears. I did not write to make
you sad, but to let you know how much I love you.

Forgive the Sinner

5Someone there among you has caused sadness, not to
me, but to all of you. I mean he caused sadness to all in
some way. (I do not want to make it sound worse than it
really is.) 6The punishment that most of you gave him is
enough for him. 7But now you should forgive him and
comfort him to keep him from having too much sadness
and giving up completely. 8So I beg you to show that you
love him. 9I wrote you to test you and to see if you obey in
everything. 10If you forgive someone, I also forgive him.
And what I have forgiven—if I had anything to forgive—I
forgave it for you, as if Christ were with me. 11I did this so
that Satan would not win anything from us, because we
know very well what Satan's plans are.

CONTEMPORARY ENGLISH VERSION

2 I have decided not to make my next visit with you so
painful. 2If I make you feel bad, who would be left to
cheer me up, except the people I had made to feel bad?
3The reason I want to be happy is to make you happy. I
wrote as I did because I didn't want to visit you and be
made to feel bad, when you should make me feel happy.
4At the time I wrote, I was suffering terribly. My eyes were
full of tears, and my heart was broken. But I didn't want to
make you feel bad. I only wanted to let you know how
much I cared for you.

Forgiveness

5I don't want to be hard on you. But if one of you has
made someone feel bad, I am not really the one who has
been made to feel bad. Some of you are the ones. 6Most of
you have already pointed out the wrong that person did,
and that is punishment enough for what was done.

7When people sin, you should forgive and comfort them,
so they won't give up in despair. 8You should make them
sure of your love for them.

9I also wrote because I wanted to test you and find out if
you would follow my instructions. 10I will forgive anyone
you forgive. Yes, for your sake and with Christ as my witness, I have forgiven whatever needed to be forgiven. 11I
have done this to keep Satan from getting the better of us.
We all know what goes on in his mind.

NEW INTERNATIONAL VERSION

2 it is by faith you stand firm. 1So I made up my mind
that I would not make another painful visit to you.
2For if I grieve you, who is left to make me glad but you
whom I have grieved? 3I wrote as I did so that when I
came I should not be distressed by those who ought to
make me rejoice. I had confidence in all of you, that you
would all share my joy. 4For I wrote you out of great dis-
tress and anguish of heart and with many tears, not to
grieve you but to let you know the depth of my love for
you.

Forgiveness for the Sinner

5If anyone has caused grief, he has not so much grieved
me as he has grieved all of you, to some extent—not to put
it too severely. 6The punishment inflicted on him by the
majority is sufficient for him. 7Now instead, you ought to
forgive and comfort him, so that he will not be over-
whelmed by excessive sorrow. 8I urge you, therefore, to
reaffirm your love for him. 9The reason I wrote you was to
see if you would stand the test and be obedient in every-
thing. 10If you forgive anyone, I also forgive him. And
what I have forgiven—if there was anything to forgive—I
have forgiven in the sight of Christ for your sake, 11in
order that Satan might not outwit us. For we are not
unaware of his schemes.

NEW LIVING TRANSLATION

2 So I said to myself, "No, I won't do it. I won't make
them unhappy with another painful visit." 2For if I
cause you pain and make you sad, who is going to make
me glad? 3That is why I wrote as I did in my last letter, so
that when I do come, I will not be made sad by the very
ones who ought to give me the greatest joy. Surely you
know that my happiness depends on your happiness.
4How painful it was to write that letter! Heartbroken, I
cried over it. I didn't want to hurt you, but I wanted you to
know how very much I love you.

Forgiveness for the Sinner

5I am not overstating it when I say that the man who
caused all the trouble hurt your entire church more than
he hurt me. 6He was punished enough when most of you
were united in your judgment against him. 7Now it is time
to forgive him and comfort him. Otherwise he may become
so discouraged that he won't be able to recover. 8Now
show him that you still love him.

9I wrote to you as I did to find out how far you would go
in obeying me. 10When you forgive this man, I forgive him,
too. And when I forgive him (for whatever is to be forgiv-
en), I do so with Christ's authority for your benefit, 11so
that Satan will not outsmart us. For we are very familiar
with his evil schemes.

NEW KING JAMES VERSION

2 But I determined this within myself, that I would not
come again to you in sorrow. 2For if I make you sor-
rowful, then who is he who makes me glad but the one
who is made sorrowful by me?

Forgive the Offender

3And I wrote this very thing to you, lest, when I came, I
should have sorrow over those from whom I ought to have
joy, having confidence in you all that my joy is *the joy* of
you all. 4For out of much affliction and anguish of heart I
wrote to you, with many tears, not that you should be
grieved, but that you might know the love which I have so
abundantly for you.

5But if anyone has caused grief, he has not grieved me,
but all of you to some extent—not to be too severe. 6This
punishment which *was inflicted* by the majority *is* suffi-
cient for such a man, 7so that, on the contrary, you *ought*
rather to forgive and comfort *him,* lest perhaps such a one
be swallowed up with too much sorrow. 8Therefore I urge
you to reaffirm *your* love to him. 9For to this end I also
wrote, that I might put you to the test, whether you are
obedient in all things. 10Now whom you forgive anything, I
also *forgive.* For if indeed I have forgiven anything, I have
forgiven that one[a] for your sakes in the presence of Christ,
11lest Satan should take advantage of us; for we are not
ignorant of his devices.

2:10 [a] NU-Text reads *For indeed, what I have forgiven, if I have forgiven anything, I did it.*

THE MESSAGE

2 That's why I decided not to make another visit that could only be painful to both of us. If by merely showing up I would put you in an embarrassingly painful position, how would you then be free to cheer and refresh me?

That was my reason for writing a letter instead of coming—so I wouldn't have to spend a miserable time disappointing the very friends I had looked forward to cheering me up. I was convinced at the time I wrote it that what was best for me was also best for you. As it turned out, there was pain enough just in writing that letter, more tears than ink on the parchment. But I didn't write it to cause pain; I wrote it so you would know how much I care—oh, more than care—*love* you!

Now, regarding the one who started all this—the person in question who caused all this pain—I want you to know that I am not the one injured in this as much as, with a few exceptions, all of you. So I don't want to come down too hard. What the majority of you agreed to as punishment is punishment enough. Now is the time to forgive this man and help him back on his feet. If all you do is pour on the guilt, you could very well drown him in it. My counsel now is to pour on the love.

The focus of my letter wasn't on punishing the offender but on getting you to take responsibility for the health of the church. So if you forgive him, I forgive him. Don't think I'm carrying around a list of personal grudges. The fact is that I'm joining in with *your* forgiveness, as Christ is with us, guiding us. After all, we don't want to unwittingly give Satan an opening for yet more mischief—we're not oblivious to his sly ways!

KING JAMES VERSION

12 ¶ Furthermore, when I came to Troas to *preach* Christ's gospel, and a door was opened unto me of the Lord,

13 I had no rest in my spirit, because I found not Titus my brother: but taking my leave of them, I went from thence into Macedonia.

14 Now thanks *be* unto God, which always causeth us to triumph in Christ, and maketh manifest the savour of his knowledge by us in every place.

15 For we are unto God a sweet savour of Christ, in them that are saved, and in them that perish:

16 To the one *we are* the savour of death unto death; and to the other the savour of life unto life. And who *is* sufficient for these things?

17 For we are not as many, which corrupt the word of God: but as of sincerity, but as of God, in the sight of God speak we in Christ.

3 Do we begin again to commend ourselves? or need we, as some *others*, epistles of commendation to you, or *letters* of commendation from you?

2 Ye are our epistle written in our hearts, known and read of all men:

NEW AMERICAN STANDARD BIBLE

12 Now when I came to Troas for the gospel of Christ and when a door was opened for me in the Lord,

13 I had no rest for my spirit, not finding Titus my brother; but taking my leave of them, I went on to Macedonia.

14 But thanks be to God, who always leads us in triumph in Christ, and manifests through us the sweet aroma of the knowledge of Him in every place.

15 For we are a fragrance of Christ to God among those who are being saved and among those who are perishing;

16 to the one an aroma from death to death, to the other an aroma from life to life. And who is adequate for these things?

17 For we are not like many, [1]peddling the word of God, but as from sincerity, but as from God, we speak in Christ in the sight of God.

Ministers of a New Covenant

3 Are we beginning to commend ourselves again? Or do we need, as some, letters of commendation to you or from you?

2 You are our letter, written in our hearts, known and read by all men;

2:17 [1] Or *corrupting*

NEW CENTURY VERSION

Paul's Concern in Troas

12When I came to Troas to preach the Good News of Christ, the Lord gave me a good opportunity there. 13But I had no peace, because I did not find my brother Titus. So I said good-bye to them at Troas and went to Macedonia.

Victory Through Christ

14But thanks be to God, who always leads us in victory through Christ. God uses us to spread his knowledge everywhere like a sweet-smelling perfume. 15Our offering to God is this: We are the sweet smell of Christ among those who are being saved and among those who are being lost. 16To those who are lost, we are the smell of death that brings death, but to those who are being saved, we are the smell of life that brings life. So who is able to do this work? 17We do not sell the word of God for a profit as many other people do. But in Christ we speak the truth before God, as messengers of God.

Servants of the New Agreement

3 Are we starting to brag about ourselves again? Do we need letters of introduction to you or from you, like some other people? 2You yourselves are our letter, written on our hearts, known and read by everyone. 3You show

CONTEMPORARY ENGLISH VERSION

12When I went to Troas to preach the good news about Christ, I found that the Lord had already prepared the way. 13But I was worried when I didn't find my friend Titus there. So I left the other followers and went on to Macedonia.

14I am grateful that God always makes it possible for Christ to lead us to victory. God also helps us spread the knowledge about Christ everywhere, and this knowledge is like the smell of perfume. 15-16In fact, God thinks of us as a perfume that brings Christ to everyone. For people who are being saved, this perfume has a sweet smell and leads them to a better life. But for people who are lost, it has a bad smell and leads them to a horrible death.

No one really has what it takes to do this work. 17A lot of people try to get rich from preaching God's message. But we are God's sincere messengers, and by the power of Christ we speak our message with God as our witness.

God's New Agreement

3 Are we once again bragging about ourselves? Do we need letters to you or from you to tell others about us? Some people do need letters that tell about them. 2But you are our letter, and you are in our[a] hearts for everyone to read and understand. 3You are like a letter written by

[a] 3.2 *our*: Some manuscripts have "your."

NEW INTERNATIONAL VERSION

Ministers of the New Covenant

12 Now when I went to Troas to preach the gospel of
Christ and found that the Lord had opened a door for me,
13 I still had no peace of mind, because I did not find my
brother Titus there. So I said good-by to them and went on
to Macedonia.
14 But thanks be to God, who always leads us in tri-
umphal procession in Christ and through us spreads every-
where the fragrance of the knowledge of him. 15 For we are
to God the aroma of Christ among those who are being
saved and those who are perishing. 16 To the one we are
the smell of death; to the other, the fragrance of life. And
who is equal to such a task? 17 Unlike so many, we do not
peddle the word of God for profit. On the contrary, in Christ
we speak before God with sincerity, like men sent from
God.
3 Are we beginning to commend ourselves again? Or do
we need, like some people, letters of recommendation
to you or from you? 2 You yourselves are our letter, written
on our hearts, known and read by everybody. 3 You show

NEW LIVING TRANSLATION

Ministers of the New Covenant

12 Well, when I came to the city of Troas to preach the
Good News of Christ, the Lord gave me tremendous oppor-
tunities. 13 But I couldn't rest because my dear brother
Titus hadn't yet arrived with a report from you. So I said
good-bye and went on to Macedonia to find him.
14 But thanks be to God, who made us his captives and
leads us along in Christ's triumphal procession. Now wher-
ever we go he uses us to tell others about the Lord and to
spread the Good News like a sweet perfume. 15 Our lives are
a fragrance presented by Christ to God. But this fragrance
is perceived differently by those being saved and by those
perishing. 16 To those who are perishing we are a fearful
smell of death and doom. But to those who are being
saved we are a life-giving perfume. And who is adequate
for such a task as this? 17 You see, we are not like those
hucksters—and there are many of them—who preach just
to make money. We preach God's message with sincerity
and with Christ's authority. And we know that the God
who sent us is watching us.
3 Are we beginning again to tell you how good we are?
Some people need to bring letters of recommendation
with them or ask you to write letters of recommendation
for them. 2 But the only letter of recommendation we need
is you yourselves! Your lives are a letter written in our*
hearts, and everyone can read it and recognize our good
work among you. 3 Clearly, you are a letter from Christ

3:2 Some manuscripts read *your.*

NEW KING JAMES VERSION

Triumph in Christ

12 Furthermore, when I came to Troas to *preach* Christ's
gospel, and a door was opened to me by the Lord, 13 I had
no rest in my spirit, because I did not find Titus my broth-
er; but taking my leave of them, I departed for Macedonia.
14 Now thanks *be* to God who always leads us in triumph
in Christ, and through us diffuses the fragrance of His
knowledge in every place. 15 For we are to God the fra-
grance of Christ among those who are being saved and
among those who are perishing. 16 To the one *we are* the
aroma of death *leading* to death, and to the other the
aroma of life *leading* to life. And who *is* sufficient for these
things? 17 For we are not, as so many,[b] peddling the word
of God; but as of sincerity, but as from God, we speak in
the sight of God in Christ.

Christ's Epistle

3 Do we begin again to commend ourselves? Or do we
need, as some *others,* epistles of commendation to you
or *letters* of commendation from you? 2 You are our epistle
written in our hearts, known and read by all men; 3 clearly

2:17 [b] M-Text reads *the rest.*

THE MESSAGE

An Open Door

When I arrived in Troas to proclaim the Message of the
Messiah, I found the place wide open: God had opened the
door; all I had to do was walk through it. But when I didn't
find Titus waiting for me with news of your condition, I
couldn't relax. Worried about you, I left and came on to
Macedonia province looking for Titus and a reassuring
word on you. And I got it, thank God!

In the Messiah, in Christ, God leads us from place to
place in one perpetual victory parade. Through us, he
brings knowledge of Christ. Everywhere we go, people
breathe in the exquisite fragrance. Because of Christ, we
give off a sweet scent rising to God, which is recognized by
those on the way of salvation—an aroma redolent with
life. But those on the way to destruction treat us more like
the stench from a rotting corpse.

This is a terrific responsibility. Is anyone competent to
take it on? No—but at least we don't take God's Word,
water it down, and then take it to the streets to sell it
cheap. We stand in Christ's presence when we speak; God
looks us in the face. We get what we say straight from God
and say it as honestly as we can.

3 Does it sound like we're patting ourselves on the back,
insisting on our credentials, asserting our authority?
Well, we're not. Neither do we need letters of endorsement,
either to you or from you. You yourselves are all the
endorsement we need. Your very lives are a letter that any-

KING JAMES VERSION

3 *Forasmuch as ye are* manifestly declared to be the epistle of Christ ministered by us, written not with ink, but with the Spirit of the living God; not in tables of stone, but in fleshy tables of the heart.

4 And such trust have we through Christ to God-ward:

5 Not that we are sufficient of ourselves to think any thing as of ourselves; but our sufficiency *is* of God;

6 ¶ Who also hath made us able ministers of the new testament; not of the letter, but of the spirit: for the letter killeth, but the spirit giveth life.

7 But if the ministration of death, written *and* engraven in stones, was glorious, so that the children of Israel could not stedfastly behold the face of Moses for the glory of his countenance; which *glory* was to be done away:

8 How shall not the ministration of the spirit be rather glorious?

9 For if the ministration of condemnation *be* glory, much more doth the ministration of righteousness exceed in glory.

10 For even that which was made glorious had no glory in this respect, by reason of the glory that excelleth.

11 For if that which is done away *was* glorious, much more that which remaineth *is* glorious.

12 ¶ Seeing then that we have such hope, we use great plainness of speech:

13 And not as Moses, *which* put a vail over his face, that the children of Israel could not stedfastly look to the end of that which is abolished:

NEW AMERICAN STANDARD BIBLE

3 being manifested that you are a letter of Christ, cared for by us, written not with ink but with the Spirit of the living God, not on tablets of stone but on tablets of human hearts.

4 Such confidence we have through Christ toward God.

5 Not that we are adequate in ourselves to consider anything as *coming* from ourselves, but our adequacy is from God,

6 who also made us adequate *as* servants of a new covenant, not of the letter but of the Spirit; for the letter kills, but the Spirit gives life.

7 But if the ministry of death, in letters engraved on stones, came with glory, so that the sons of Israel could not look intently at the face of Moses because of the glory of his face, fading *as* it was,

8 how will the ministry of the Spirit fail to be even more with glory?

9 For if the ministry of condemnation has glory, much more does the ministry of righteousness abound in glory.

10 For indeed what had glory, in this case has no glory because of the glory that surpasses *it.*

11 For if that which fades away *was* with glory, much more that which remains *is* in glory.

12 Therefore having such a hope, we use great boldness in *our* speech,

13 and *are* not like Moses, *who* used to put a veil over his face so that the sons of Israel would not look intently at the end of what was fading away.

NEW CENTURY VERSION

that you are a letter from Christ sent through us. This let-
ter is not written with ink but with the Spirit of the living
God. It is not written on stone tablets[a] but on human
hearts.
4We can say this, because through Christ we feel certain
before God. 5We are not saying that we can do this work
ourselves. It is God who makes us able to do all that we
do. 6He made us able to be servants of a new agreement
from himself to his people. This new agreement is not a
written law, but it is of the Spirit. The written law brings
death, but the Spirit gives life.
7The law that brought death was written in words on
stone. It came with God's glory, which made Moses' face
so bright that the Israelites could not continue to look at
it. But that glory later disappeared. 8So surely the new way
that brings the Spirit has even more glory. 9If the law that
judged people guilty of sin had glory, surely the new way
that makes people right with God has much greater glory.
10That old law had glory, but it really loses its glory when
it is compared to the much greater glory of this new way.
11If that law which disappeared came with glory, then this
new way which continues forever has much greater glory.
12We have this hope, so we are very bold. 13We are not
like Moses, who put a covering over his face so the
Israelites would not see it. The glory was disappearing,
and Moses did not want them to see it end. 14But their

3:3 [a] **stone tablets** Meaning the law of Moses that was written on stone tablets (Exodus 24:12; 25:16).

CONTEMPORARY ENGLISH VERSION

Christ and delivered by us. But you are not written with
pen and ink or on tablets made of stone. You are written in
our hearts by the Spirit of the living God.
4We are sure about all this. Christ makes us sure in the
very presence of God. 5We don't have the right to claim
that we have done anything on our own. God gives us
what it takes to do all that we do. 6He makes us worthy to
be the servants of his new agreement that comes from the
Holy Spirit and not from a written Law. After all, the Law
brings death, but the Spirit brings life.
7The Law of Moses brought only the promise of death,
even though it was carved on stones and given in a won-
derful way. Still the Law made Moses' face shine so bright-
ly that the people of Israel could not look at it, even
though it was a fading glory. 8So won't the agreement that
the Spirit brings to us be even more wonderful? 9If some-
thing that brings the death sentence is glorious, won't
something that makes us acceptable to God be even more
glorious? 10In fact, the new agreement is so wonderful that
the Law is no longer glorious at all. 11The Law was given
with a glory that faded away. But the glory of the new
agreement is much greater, because it will never fade
away.
12This wonderful hope makes us feel like speaking
freely. 13We are not like Moses. His face was shining, but
he covered it to keep the people of Israel from seeing the
brightness fade away. 14The people were stubborn, and

NEW INTERNATIONAL VERSION

that you are a letter from Christ, the result of our ministry, written not with ink but with the Spirit of the living God, not on tablets of stone but on tablets of human hearts.

[4]Such confidence as this is ours through Christ before God. [5]Not that we are competent in ourselves to claim anything for ourselves, but our competence comes from God. [6]He has made us competent as ministers of a new covenant—not of the letter but of the Spirit; for the letter kills, but the Spirit gives life.

The Glory of the New Covenant

[7]Now if the ministry that brought death, which was engraved in letters on stone, came with glory, so that the Israelites could not look steadily at the face of Moses because of its glory, fading though it was, [8]will not the ministry of the Spirit be even more glorious? [9]If the ministry that condemns men is glorious, how much more glorious is the ministry that brings righteousness! [10]For what was glorious has no glory now in comparison with the surpassing glory. [11]And if what was fading away came with glory, how much greater is the glory of that which lasts!

[12]Therefore, since we have such a hope, we are very bold. [13]We are not like Moses, who would put a veil over his face to keep the Israelites from gazing at it while the radiance was fading away. [14]But their minds were made

NEW LIVING TRANSLATION

prepared by us. It is written not with pen and ink, but with the Spirit of the living God. It is carved not on stone, but on human hearts.

[4]We are confident of all this because of our great trust in God through Christ. [5]It is not that we think we can do anything of lasting value by ourselves. Our only power and success come from God. [6]He is the one who has enabled us to represent his new covenant. This is a covenant, not of written laws, but of the Spirit. The old way ends in death; in the new way, the Holy Spirit gives life.

The Glory of the New Covenant

[7]That old system of law etched in stone led to death, yet it began with such glory that the people of Israel could not bear to look at Moses' face. For his face shone with the glory of God, even though the brightness was already fading away. [8]Shouldn't we expect far greater glory when the Holy Spirit is giving life? [9]If the old covenant, which brings condemnation, was glorious, how much more glorious is the new covenant, which makes us right with God! [10]In fact, that first glory was not glorious at all compared with the overwhelming glory of the new covenant. [11]So if the old covenant, which has been set aside, was full of glory, then the new covenant, which remains forever, has far greater glory.

[12]Since this new covenant gives us such confidence, we can be very bold. [13]We are not like Moses, who put a veil over his face so the people of Israel would not see the glory fading away. [14]But the people's minds were hardened, and

NEW KING JAMES VERSION

you are an epistle of Christ, ministered by us, written not with ink but by the Spirit of the living God, not on tablets of stone but on tablets of flesh, *that is,* of the heart.

The Spirit, Not the Letter

[4]And we have such trust through Christ toward God. [5]Not that we are sufficient of ourselves to think of anything as *being* from ourselves, but our sufficiency *is* from God, [6]who also made us sufficient as ministers of the new covenant, not of the letter but of the Spirit;[a] for the letter kills, but the Spirit gives life.

Glory of the New Covenant

[7]But if the ministry of death, written *and* engraved on stones, was glorious, so that the children of Israel could not look steadily at the face of Moses because of the glory of his countenance, which *glory* was passing away, [8]how will the ministry of the Spirit not be more glorious? [9]For if the ministry of condemnation *had* glory, the ministry of righteousness exceeds much more in glory. [10]For even what was made glorious had no glory in this respect, because of the glory that excels. [11]For if what is passing away *was* glorious, what remains *is* much more glorious.

[12]Therefore, since we have such hope, we use great boldness of speech— [13]unlike Moses, *who* put a veil over his face so that the children of Israel could not look steadily at the end of what was passing away. [14]But their minds were

3:6 [a] Or *spirit*

THE MESSAGE

one can read by just looking at you. Christ himself wrote it—not with ink, but with God's living Spirit; not chiseled into stone, but carved into human lives—and we publish it.

We couldn't be more sure of ourselves in this—that *you*, written by Christ himself for God, are our letter of recommendation. We wouldn't think of writing this kind of letter about ourselves. Only God can write such a letter. His letter authorizes us to help carry out this new plan of action. The plan wasn't written out with ink on paper, with pages and pages of legal footnotes, killing your spirit. It's written with Spirit on spirit, his life on our lives!

Lifting the Veil

The Government of Death, its constitution chiseled on stone tablets, had a dazzling inaugural. Moses' face as he delivered the tablets was so bright that day (even though it would fade soon enough) that the people of Israel could no more look right at him than stare into the sun. How much more dazzling, then, the Government of Living Spirit?

If the Government of Condemnation was impressive, how about this Government of Affirmation? Bright as that old government was, it would look downright dull alongside this new one. If that makeshift arrangement impressed us, how much more this brightly shining government installed for eternity?

With that kind of hope to excite us, nothing holds us back. Unlike Moses, we have nothing to hide. Everything is out in the open with us. He wore a veil so the children of Israel wouldn't notice that the glory was fading away—

KING JAMES VERSION

14 But their minds were blinded: for until this day remaineth the same vail untaken away in the reading of the old testament; which *vail* is done away in Christ.

15 But even unto this day, when Moses is read, the vail is upon their heart.

16 Nevertheless when it shall turn to the Lord, the vail shall be taken away.

17 Now the Lord is that Spirit: and where the Spirit of the Lord *is*, there *is* liberty.

18 But we all, with open face beholding as in a glass the glory of the Lord, are changed into the same image from glory to glory, *even* as by the Spirit of the Lord.

4 Therefore seeing we have this ministry, as we have received mercy, we faint not;

2 But have renounced the hidden things of dishonesty, not walking in craftiness, nor handling the word of God deceitfully; but by manifestation of the truth commending ourselves to every man's conscience in the sight of God.

3 But if our gospel be hid, it is hid to them that are lost:

NEW AMERICAN STANDARD BIBLE

14 But their minds were hardened; for until this very day at the reading of the old covenant the same veil remains unlifted, because it is removed in Christ.

15 But to this day whenever Moses is read, a veil lies over their heart;

16 but whenever a person turns to the Lord, the veil is taken away.

17 Now the Lord is the Spirit, and where the Spirit of the Lord is, *there* is liberty.

18 But we all, with unveiled face, beholding as in a mirror the glory of the Lord, are being transformed into the same image from glory to glory, just as from the Lord, the Spirit.

Paul's Apostolic Ministry

4 Therefore, since we have this ministry, as we received mercy, we do not lose heart,

2 but we have renounced the things hidden because of shame, not walking in craftiness or adulterating the word of God, but by the manifestation of truth commending ourselves to every man's conscience in the sight of God.

3 And even if our gospel is veiled, it is veiled to those who are perishing,

NEW CENTURY VERSION

minds were closed, and even today that same covering
hides the meaning when they read the old agreement. That
covering is taken away only through Christ. 15Even today,
when they read the law of Moses, there is a covering over
their minds. 16But when a person changes and follows the
Lord, that covering is taken away. 17The Lord is the Spirit,
and where the Spirit of the Lord is, there is freedom. 18Our
faces, then, are not covered. We all show the Lord's glory,
and we are being changed to be like him. This change in
us brings ever greater glory, which comes from the Lord,
who is the Spirit.

Preaching the Good News

4 God, with his mercy, gave us this work to do, so we
don't give up. 2But we have turned away from secret
and shameful ways. We use no trickery, and we do not
change the teaching of God. We teach the truth plainly,
showing everyone who we are. Then they can know in
their hearts what kind of people we are in God's sight. 3If
the Good News that we preach is hidden, it is hidden only
to those who are lost. 4The devil who rules this world has

CONTEMPORARY ENGLISH VERSION

something still keeps them from seeing the truth when the
Law is read. Only Christ can take away the covering that
keeps them from seeing.

15When the Law of Moses is read, they have their minds
covered over 16with a covering that is removed only for
those who turn to the Lord. 17The Lord and the Spirit are
one and the same, and the Lord's Spirit sets us free. 18So
our faces are not covered. They show the bright glory of
the Lord, as the Lord's Spirit makes us more and more like
our glorious Lord.

Treasure in Clay Jars

4 God has been kind enough to trust us with this work.
That's why we never give up. 2We don't do shameful
things that must be kept secret. And we don't try to fool
anyone or twist God's message around. God is our witness
that we speak only the truth, so others will be sure that we
can be trusted. 3If there is anything hidden about our mes-
sage, it is hidden only to someone who is lost.

NEW INTERNATIONAL VERSION

dull, for to this day the same veil remains when the old covenant is read. It has not been removed, because only in Christ is it taken away. [15]Even to this day when Moses is read, a veil covers their hearts. [16]But whenever anyone turns to the Lord, the veil is taken away. [17]Now the Lord is the Spirit, and where the Spirit of the Lord is, there is freedom. [18]And we, who with unveiled faces all reflect[a] the Lord's glory, are being transformed into his likeness with ever-increasing glory, which comes from the Lord, who is the Spirit.

Treasures in Jars of Clay

4 Therefore, since through God's mercy we have this ministry, we do not lose heart. [2]Rather, we have renounced secret and shameful ways; we do not use deception, nor do we distort the word of God. On the contrary, by setting forth the truth plainly we commend ourselves to every man's conscience in the sight of God. [3]And even if our gospel is veiled, it is veiled to those who are perishing.

[a] *18* Or *contemplate*

NEW LIVING TRANSLATION

even to this day whenever the old covenant is being read, a veil covers their minds so they cannot understand the truth. And this veil can be removed only by believing in Christ. [15]Yes, even today when they read Moses' writings, their hearts are covered with that veil, and they do not understand.

[16]But whenever anyone turns to the Lord, then the veil is taken away. [17]Now, the Lord is the Spirit, and wherever the Spirit of the Lord is, he gives freedom. [18]And all of us have had that veil removed so that we can be mirrors that brightly reflect* the glory of the Lord. And as the Spirit of the Lord works within us, we become more and more like him and reflect his glory even more.

Treasure in Perishable Containers

4 And so, since God in his mercy has given us this wonderful ministry, we never give up. [2]We reject all shameful and underhanded methods. We do not try to trick anyone, and we do not distort the word of God. We tell the truth before God, and all who are honest know that.

[3]If the Good News we preach is veiled from anyone, it is a sign that they are perishing. [4]Satan, the god of this evil

3:18 Or *so that we can see in a mirror.*

NEW KING JAMES VERSION

blinded. For until this day the same veil remains unlifted in the reading of the Old Testament, because the *veil* is taken away in Christ. [15]But even to this day, when Moses is read, a veil lies on their heart. [16]Nevertheless when one turns to the Lord, the veil is taken away. [17]Now the Lord is the Spirit; and where the Spirit of the Lord *is,* there *is* liberty. [18]But we all, with unveiled face, beholding as in a mirror the glory of the Lord, are being transformed into the same image from glory to glory, just as by the Spirit of the Lord.

The Light of Christ's Gospel

4 Therefore, since we have this ministry, as we have received mercy, we do not lose heart. [2]But we have renounced the hidden things of shame, not walking in craftiness nor handling the word of God deceitfully, but by manifestation of the truth commending ourselves to every man's conscience in the sight of God. [3]But even if our gospel is veiled, it is veiled to those who are perishing,

THE MESSAGE

and they *didn't* notice. They didn't notice it then and they don't notice it now, don't notice that there's nothing left behind that veil. Even today when the proclamations of that old, bankrupt government are read out, they can't see through it. Only Christ can get rid of the veil so they can see for themselves that there's nothing there.

Whenever, though, they turn to face God as Moses did, God removes the veil and there they are—face to face! They suddenly recognize that God is a living, personal presence, not a piece of chiseled stone. And when God is personally present, a living Spirit, that old, constricting legislation is recognized as obsolete. We're free of it! All of us! Nothing between us and God, our faces shining with the brightness of his face. And so we are transfigured much like the Messiah, our lives gradually becoming brighter and more beautiful as God enters our lives and we become like him.

Trial and Torture

4 Since God has so generously let us in on what he is doing, we're not about to throw up our hands and walk off the job just because we run into occasional hard times. We refuse to wear masks and play games. We don't maneuver and manipulate behind the scenes. And we don't twist God's Word to suit ourselves. Rather, we keep everything we do and say out in the open, the whole truth on display, so that those who want to can see and judge for themselves in the presence of God.

If our Message is obscure to anyone, it's not because we're holding back in any way. No, it's because these other

KING JAMES VERSION

4 In whom the god of this world hath blinded the minds
of them which believe not, lest the light of the glorious
gospel of Christ, who is the image of God, should shine
unto them.
5 For we preach not ourselves, but Christ Jesus the
Lord; and ourselves your servants for Jesus' sake.
6 For God, who commanded the light to shine out of
darkness, hath shined in our hearts, to *give* the light of the
knowledge of the glory of God in the face of Jesus Christ.
7 But we have this treasure in earthen vessels, that the
excellency of the power may be of God, and not of us.
8 ¶ *We are* troubled on every side, yet not distressed; *we
are* perplexed, but not in despair;
9 Persecuted, but not forsaken; cast down, but not
destroyed;
10 Always bearing about in the body the dying of the
Lord Jesus, that the life also of Jesus might be made mani-
fest in our body.
11 For we which live are alway delivered unto death for
Jesus' sake, that the life also of Jesus might be made mani-
fest in our mortal flesh.
12 So then death worketh in us, but life in you.

NEW AMERICAN STANDARD BIBLE

4 in whose case the god of this world has blinded the
minds of the unbelieving so that they might not see the
light of the gospel of the glory of Christ, who is the image
of God.
5 For we do not preach ourselves but Christ Jesus as
Lord, and ourselves as your bond-servants for Jesus' sake.
6 For God, who said, "Light shall shine out of dark-
ness," is the One who has shone in our hearts to give the
Light of the knowledge of the glory of God in the face of
Christ.
7 But we have this treasure in earthen vessels, so that
the surpassing greatness of the power will be of God and
not from ourselves;
8 *we are* afflicted in every way, but not crushed; per-
plexed, but not despairing;
9 persecuted, but not forsaken; struck down, but not
destroyed;
10 always carrying about in the body the dying of Jesus,
so that the life of Jesus also may be manifested in our
body.
11 For we who live are constantly being delivered over
to death for Jesus' sake, so that the life of Jesus also may
be manifested in our mortal flesh.
12 So death works in us, but life in you.

NEW CENTURY VERSION

blinded the minds of those who do not believe. They can-
not see the light of the Good News—the Good News about
the glory of Christ, who is exactly like God. [5]We do not
preach about ourselves, but we preach that Jesus Christ is
Lord and that we are your servants for Jesus. [6]God once
said, "Let the light shine out of the darkness!" This is the
same God who made his light shine in our hearts by let-
ting us know the glory of God that is in the face of Christ.

Spiritual Treasure in Clay Jars

[7]We have this treasure from God, but we are like clay
jars that hold the treasure. This shows that the great
power is from God, not from us. [8]We have troubles all
around us, but we are not defeated. We do not know what
to do, but we do not give up the hope of living. [9]We are
persecuted, but God does not leave us. We are hurt some-
times, but we are not destroyed. [10]We carry the death of
Jesus in our own bodies so that the life of Jesus can also be
seen in our bodies. [11]We are alive, but for Jesus we are
always in danger of death so that the life of Jesus can be
seen in our bodies that die. [12]So death is working in us,
but life is working in you.

CONTEMPORARY ENGLISH VERSION

[4]The god who rules this world has blinded the minds of
unbelievers. They cannot see the light, which is the good
news about our glorious Christ, who shows what God is
like. [5]We are not preaching about ourselves. Our message
is that Jesus Christ is Lord. He also sent us to be your ser-
vants. [6]The Scriptures say, "God commanded light to shine
in the dark." Now God is shining in our hearts to let you
know that his glory is seen in Jesus Christ.
[7]We are like clay jars in which this treasure is stored.
The real power comes from God and not from us. [8]We
often suffer, but we are never crushed. Even when we
don't know what to do, we never give up. [9]In times of trou-
ble, God is with us, and when we are knocked down, we
get up again. [10-11]We face death every day because of
Jesus. Our bodies show what his death was like, so that
his life can also be seen in us. [12]This means that death is
working in us, but life is working in you.

NEW INTERNATIONAL VERSION

4 The god of this age has blinded the minds of unbelievers,
so that they cannot see the light of the gospel of the glory
of Christ, who is the image of God. 5 For we do not preach
ourselves, but Jesus Christ as Lord, and ourselves as your
servants for Jesus' sake. 6 For God, who said, "Let light
shine out of darkness,"[a] made his light shine in our hearts
to give us the light of the knowledge of the glory of God in
the face of Christ.
7 But we have this treasure in jars of clay to show that
this all-surpassing power is from God and not from us.
8 We are hard pressed on every side, but not crushed; perplexed, but not in despair; 9 persecuted, but not abandoned; struck down, but not destroyed. 10 We always carry
around in our body the death of Jesus, so that the life of
Jesus may also be revealed in our body. 11 For we who are
alive are always being given over to death for Jesus' sake,
so that his life may be revealed in our mortal body. 12 So
then, death is at work in us, but life is at work in you.

[a] *6* Gen. 1:3

NEW LIVING TRANSLATION

world, has blinded the minds of those who don't believe,
so they are unable to see the glorious light of the Good
News that is shining upon them. They don't understand
the message we preach about the glory of Christ, who is
the exact likeness of God.
5 We don't go around preaching about ourselves; we
preach Christ Jesus, the Lord. All we say about ourselves is
that we are your servants because of what Jesus has done
for us. 6 For God, who said, "Let there be light in the darkness," has made us understand that this light is the
brightness of the glory of God that is seen in the face of
Jesus Christ.
7 But this precious treasure—this light and power that
now shine within us—is held in perishable containers,
that is, in our weak bodies.* So everyone can see that our
glorious power is from God and is not our own.
8 We are pressed on every side by troubles, but we are
not crushed and broken. We are perplexed, but we don't
give up and quit. 9 We are hunted down, but God never
abandons us. We get knocked down, but we get up again
and keep going. 10 Through suffering, these bodies of ours
constantly share in the death of Jesus so that the life of
Jesus may also be seen in our bodies.
11 Yes, we live under constant danger of death because
we serve Jesus, so that the life of Jesus will be obvious in
our dying bodies. 12 So we live in the face of death, but it
has resulted in eternal life for you.

4:7 Greek *But we have this treasure in earthen vessels.*

NEW KING JAMES VERSION

4 whose minds the god of this age has blinded, who do not
believe, lest the light of the gospel of the glory of Christ,
who is the image of God, should shine on them. 5 For we do
not preach ourselves, but Christ Jesus the Lord, and ourselves your bondservants for Jesus' sake. 6 For it is the God
who commanded light to shine out of darkness, who has
shone in our hearts to *give* the light of the knowledge of
the glory of God in the face of Jesus Christ.

Cast Down but Unconquered

7 But we have this treasure in earthen vessels, that the
excellence of the power may be of God and not of us. 8 *We
are* hard-pressed on every side, yet not crushed; *we are*
perplexed, but not in despair; 9 persecuted, but not forsaken; struck down, but not destroyed— 10 always carrying
about in the body the dying of the Lord Jesus, that the life
of Jesus also may be manifested in our body. 11 For we who
live are always delivered to death for Jesus' sake, that the
life of Jesus also may be manifested in our mortal flesh.
12 So then death is working in us, but life in you.

THE MESSAGE

people are looking or going the wrong way and refuse to give it serious attention. All they have eyes for is the fashionable god of darkness. They think he can give them what they want, and that they won't have to bother believing a Truth they can't see. They're stone-blind to the dayspring brightness of the Message that shines with Christ, who gives us the best picture of God we'll ever get.

Remember, our Message is not about ourselves; we're proclaiming Jesus Christ, the Master. All we are is messengers, errand runners from Jesus for you. It started when God said, "Light up the darkness!" and our lives filled up with light as we saw and understood God in the face of Christ, all bright and beautiful.

If you only look at *us*, you might well miss the brightness. We carry this precious Message around in the unadorned clay pots of our ordinary lives. That's to prevent anyone from confusing God's incomparable power with us. As it is, there's not much chance of that. You know for yourselves that we're not much to look at. We've been surrounded and battered by troubles, but we're not demoralized; we're not sure what to do, but we know that God knows what to do; we've been spiritually terrorized, but God hasn't left our side; we've been thrown down, but we haven't broken. What they did to Jesus, they do to us—trial and torture, mockery and murder; what Jesus did among them, he does in us—he lives! Our lives are at constant risk for Jesus' sake, which makes Jesus' life all the more evident in us. While we're going through the worst, you're getting in on the best!

KING JAMES VERSION

13 We having the same spirit of faith, according as it is written, I believed, and therefore have I spoken; we also believe, and therefore speak;

14 Knowing that he which raised up the Lord Jesus shall raise up us also by Jesus, and shall present *us* with you.

15 For all things *are* for your sakes, that the abundant grace might through the thanksgiving of many redound to the glory of God.

16 For which cause we faint not; but though our outward man perish, yet the inward *man* is renewed day by day.

17 For our light affliction, which is but for a moment, worketh for us a far more exceeding *and* eternal weight of glory;

18 While we look not at the things which are seen, but at the things which are not seen: for the things which are seen *are* temporal; but the things which are not seen *are* eternal.

5 For we know that if our earthly house of *this* tabernacle were dissolved, we have a building of God, an house not made with hands, eternal in the heavens.

2 For in this we groan, earnestly desiring to be clothed upon with our house which is from heaven:

3 If so be that being clothed we shall not be found naked.

4 For we that are in *this* tabernacle do groan, being burdened: not for that we would be unclothed, but clothed upon, that mortality might be swallowed up of life.

NEW AMERICAN STANDARD BIBLE

13 But having the same spirit of faith, according to what is written, "I BELIEVED, THEREFORE I SPOKE," we also believe, therefore we also speak,

14 knowing that He who raised the Lord Jesus will raise us also with Jesus and will present us with you.

15 For all things *are* for your sakes, so that the grace which is spreading to more and more people may cause the giving of thanks to abound to the glory of God.

16 Therefore we do not lose heart, but though our outer man is decaying, yet our inner man is being renewed day by day.

17 For momentary, light affliction is producing for us an eternal weight of glory far beyond all comparison,

18 while we look not at the things which are seen, but at the things which are not seen; for the things which are seen are temporal, but the things which are not seen are eternal.

The Temporal and Eternal

5 For we know that if the earthly tent which is our house is torn down, we have a building from God, a house not made with hands, eternal in the heavens.

2 For indeed in this *house* we groan, longing to be clothed with our dwelling from heaven,

3 inasmuch as we, having put it on, will not be found naked.

4 For indeed while we are in this tent, we groan, being burdened, because we do not want to be unclothed but to be clothed, so that what is mortal will be swallowed up by life.

NEW CENTURY VERSION

13 It is written in the Scriptures, "I believed, so I spoke."[a]
Our faith is like this, too. We believe, and so we speak.
14 God raised the Lord Jesus from the dead, and we know
that God will also raise us with Jesus. God will bring us
together with you, and we will stand before him. 15 All
these things are for you. And so the grace of God that is
being given to more and more people will bring increasing
thanks to God for his glory.

Living by Faith

16 So we do not give up. Our physical body is becoming
older and weaker, but our spirit inside us is made new
every day. 17 We have small troubles for a while now, but
they are helping us gain an eternal glory that is much
greater than the troubles. 18 We set our eyes not on what
we see but on what we cannot see. What we see will last
only a short time, but what we cannot see will last forever.
5 We know that our body—the tent we live in here on
earth—will be destroyed. But when that happens, God
will have a house for us. It will not be a house made by
human hands; instead, it will be a home in heaven that
will last forever. 2 But now we groan in this tent. We want
God to give us our heavenly home, 3 because it will clothe
us so we will not be naked. 4 While we live in this body, we
have burdens, and we groan. We do not want to be naked,
but we want to be clothed with our heavenly home. Then

4:13 [a] **"I...spoke."** Quotation from Psalm 116:10.

CONTEMPORARY ENGLISH VERSION

13 In the Scriptures it says, "I spoke because I had faith."
We have that same kind of faith. So we speak 14 because
we know that God raised the Lord Jesus to life. And just as
God raised Jesus, he will also raise us to life. Then he will
bring us into his presence together with you. 15 All of this
has been done for you, so that more and more people will
know how kind God is and will praise and honor him.

Faith in the Lord

16 We never give up. Our bodies are gradually dying, but
we ourselves are being made stronger each day. 17 These
little troubles are getting us ready for an eternal glory that
will make all our troubles seem like nothing. 18 Things that
are seen don't last forever, but things that are not seen are
eternal. That's why we keep our minds on the things that
cannot be seen.

5 Our bodies are like tents that we live in here on earth.
But when these tents are destroyed, we know that
God will give each of us a place to live. These homes will
not be buildings that someone has made, but they are in
heaven and will last forever. 2 While we are here on earth,
we sigh because we want to live in that heavenly home.
3 We want to put it on like clothes and not be naked.

4 These tents we now live in are like a heavy burden, and
we groan. But we don't do this just because we want to
leave these bodies that will die. It is because we want to

NEW INTERNATIONAL VERSION

[13]It is written: "I believed; therefore I have spoken."[b] With that same spirit of faith we also believe and therefore speak, [14]because we know that the one who raised the Lord Jesus from the dead will also raise us with Jesus and present us with you in his presence. [15]All this is for your benefit, so that the grace that is reaching more and more people may cause thanksgiving to overflow to the glory of God.

[16]Therefore we do not lose heart. Though outwardly we are wasting away, yet inwardly we are being renewed day by day. [17]For our light and momentary troubles are achieving for us an eternal glory that far outweighs them all. [18]So we fix our eyes not on what is seen, but on what is unseen. For what is seen is temporary, but what is unseen is eternal.

Our Heavenly Dwelling

5 Now we know that if the earthly tent we live in is destroyed, we have a building from God, an eternal house in heaven, not built by human hands. [2]Meanwhile we groan, longing to be clothed with our heavenly dwelling, [3]because when we are clothed, we will not be found naked. [4]For while we are in this tent, we groan and are burdened, because we do not wish to be unclothed but to be clothed with our heavenly dwelling, so that what is

[b] *13* Psalm 116:10

NEW LIVING TRANSLATION

[13]But we continue to preach because we have the same kind of faith the psalmist had when he said, "I believed in God, and so I speak."* [14]We know that the same God who raised our Lord Jesus will also raise us with Jesus and present us to himself along with you. [15]All of these things are for your benefit. And as God's grace brings more and more people to Christ, there will be great thanksgiving, and God will receive more and more glory.

[16]That is why we never give up. Though our bodies are dying, our spirits are* being renewed every day. [17]For our present troubles are quite small and won't last very long. Yet they produce for us an immeasurably great glory that will last forever! [18]So we don't look at the troubles we can see right now; rather, we look forward to what we have not yet seen. For the troubles we see will soon be over, but the joys to come will last forever.

New Bodies

5 For we know that when this earthly tent we live in is taken down—when we die and leave these bodies—we will have a home in heaven, an eternal body made for us by God himself and not by human hands. [2]We grow weary in our present bodies, and we long for the day when we will put on our heavenly bodies like new clothing. [3]For we will not be spirits without bodies, but we will put on new heavenly bodies. [4]Our dying bodies make us groan and sigh, but it's not that we want to die and have no bodies at all. We want to slip into our new bodies so that

4:13 Ps 116:10. **4:16** Greek *our inner being is.*

NEW KING JAMES VERSION

[13]And since we have the same spirit of faith, according to what is written, *"I believed and therefore I spoke,"*[a] we also believe and therefore speak, [14]knowing that He who raised up the Lord Jesus will also raise us up with Jesus, and will present *us* with you. [15]For all things *are* for your sakes, that grace, having spread through the many, may cause thanksgiving to abound to the glory of God.

Seeing the Invisible

[16]Therefore we do not lose heart. Even though our outward man is perishing, yet the inward *man* is being renewed day by day. [17]For our light affliction, which is but for a moment, is working for us a far more exceeding *and* eternal weight of glory, [18]while we do not look at the things which are seen, but at the things which are not seen. For the things which are seen *are* temporary, but the things which are not seen *are* eternal.

Assurance of the Resurrection

5 For we know that if our earthly house, *this* tent, is destroyed, we have a building from God, a house not made with hands, eternal in the heavens. [2]For in this we groan, earnestly desiring to be clothed with our habitation which is from heaven, [3]if indeed, having been clothed, we shall not be found naked. [4]For we who are in *this* tent groan, being burdened, not because we want to be unclothed, but further clothed, that mortality may be swallowed up by life.

4:13 [a] Psalm 116:10

THE MESSAGE

We're not keeping this quiet, not on your life. Just like the psalmist who wrote, "I believed it, so I said it," we say what we believe. And what we believe is that the One who raised up the Master Jesus will just as certainly raise us up with you, alive. Every detail works to your advantage and to God's glory: more and more grace, more and more people, more and more praise!

So we're not giving up. How could we! Even though on the outside it often looks like things are falling apart on us, on the inside, where God is making new life, not a day goes by without his unfolding grace. These hard times are small potatoes compared to the coming good times, the lavish celebration prepared for us. There's far more here than meets the eye. The things we see now are here today, gone tomorrow. But the things we can't see now will last forever.

5 For instance, we know that when these bodies of ours are taken down like tents and folded away, they will be replaced by resurrection bodies in heaven—God-made, not handmade—and we'll never have to relocate our "tents" again. Sometimes we can hardly wait to move—and so we cry out in frustration. Compared to what's coming, living conditions around here seem like a stopover in an unfurnished shack, and we're tired of it! We've been given a glimpse of the real thing, our true home, our resurrection bodies! The Spirit of God whets our appetite by giving us a

KING JAMES VERSION

5 Now he that hath wrought us for the selfsame thing *is* God, who also hath given unto us the earnest of the Spirit.

6 Therefore *we are* always confident, knowing that, whilst we are at home in the body, we are absent from the Lord:

7 (For we walk by faith, not by sight:)

8 We are confident, *I say*, and willing rather to be absent from the body, and to be present with the Lord.

9 Wherefore we labour, that, whether present or absent, we may be accepted of him.

10 For we must all appear before the judgment seat of Christ; that every one may receive the things *done* in *his* body, according to that he hath done, whether *it be* good or bad.

11 Knowing therefore the terror of the Lord, we persuade men; but we are made manifest unto God; and I trust also are made manifest in your consciences.

12 ¶ For we commend not ourselves again unto you, but give you occasion to glory on our behalf, that ye may have somewhat to *answer* them which glory in appearance, and not in heart.

13 For whether we be beside ourselves, *it is* to God: or whether we be sober, *it is* for your cause.

14 For the love of Christ constraineth us; because we thus judge, that if one died for all, then were all dead:

NEW AMERICAN STANDARD BIBLE

5 Now He who prepared us for this very purpose is God, who gave to us the Spirit as a pledge.

6 Therefore, being always of good courage, and knowing that while we are at home in the body we are absent from the Lord—

7 for we walk by faith, not by sight—

8 we are of good courage, I say, and prefer rather to be absent from the body and to be at home with the Lord.

9 Therefore we also have as our ambition, whether at home or absent, to be pleasing to Him.

10 For we must all appear before the judgment seat of Christ, so that each one may be recompensed for his deeds in the body, according to what he has done, whether good or bad.

11 Therefore, knowing the fear of the Lord, we persuade men, but we are made manifest to God; and I hope that we are made manifest also in your consciences.

12 We are not again commending ourselves to you but *are* giving you an occasion to be proud of us, so that you will have *an answer* for those who take pride in appearance and not in heart.

13 For if we are beside ourselves, it is for God; if we are of sound mind, it is for you.

14 For the love of Christ controls us, having concluded this, that one died for all, therefore all died;

NEW CENTURY VERSION

this body that dies will be fully covered with life. 5This is
what God made us for, and he has given us the Spirit to be
a guarantee for this new life.
6So we always have courage. We know that while we
live in this body, we are away from the Lord. 7We live by
what we believe, not by what we can see. 8So I say that we
have courage. We really want to be away from this body
and be at home with the Lord. 9Our only goal is to please
God whether we live here or there, 10because we must all
stand before Christ to be judged. Each of us will receive
what we should get—good or bad—for the things we did
in the earthly body.

Becoming Friends with God

11Since we know what it means to fear the Lord, we try
to help people accept the truth about us. God knows what
we really are, and I hope that in your hearts you know, too.
12We are not trying to prove ourselves to you again, but we
are telling you about ourselves so you will be proud of us.
Then you will have an answer for those who are proud
about things that can be seen rather than what is in the
heart. 13If we are out of our minds, it is for God. If we have
our right minds, it is for you. 14The love of Christ controls
us, because we know that One died for all, so all have died.

CONTEMPORARY ENGLISH VERSION

change them for bodies that will never die. 5God is the one
who makes all of this possible. He has given us his Spirit to
make us certain that he will do it. 6So always be cheerful!
As long as we are in these bodies, we are away from the
Lord. 7But we live by faith, not by what we see. 8We
should be cheerful, because we would rather leave these
bodies and be at home with the Lord. 9But whether we are
at home with the Lord or away from him, we still try our
best to please him. 10After all, Christ will judge each of us
for the good or the bad that we do while living in these
bodies.

Bringing People to God

11We know what it means to respect the Lord, and we
encourage everyone to turn to him. God himself knows
what we are like, and I hope you also know what kind of
people we are. 12We are not trying once more to brag about
ourselves. But we want you to be proud of us, when you
are with those who are not sincere and brag about what
others think of them.
13If we seem out of our minds, it is between God and us.
But if we are in our right minds, it is for your good. 14We
are ruled by Christ's love for us. We are certain that if one
person died for everyone else, then all of us have died.

NEW INTERNATIONAL VERSION

mortal may be swallowed up by life. 5Now it is God who has made us for this very purpose and has given us the Spirit as a deposit, guaranteeing what is to come.

6Therefore we are always confident and know that as long as we are at home in the body we are away from the Lord. 7We live by faith, not by sight. 8We are confident, I say, and would prefer to be away from the body and at home with the Lord. 9So we make it our goal to please him, whether we are at home in the body or away from it. 10For we must all appear before the judgment seat of Christ, that each one may receive what is due him for the things done while in the body, whether good or bad.

The Ministry of Reconciliation

11Since, then, we know what it is to fear the Lord, we try to persuade men. What we are is plain to God, and I hope it is also plain to your conscience. 12We are not trying to commend ourselves to you again, but are giving you an opportunity to take pride in us, so that you can answer those who take pride in what is seen rather than in what is in the heart. 13If we are out of our mind, it is for the sake of God; if we are in our right mind, it is for you. 14For Christ's love compels us, because we are convinced that one died for all, and therefore all died. 15And

NEW LIVING TRANSLATION

these dying bodies will be swallowed up by everlasting life. 5God himself has prepared us for this, and as a guarantee he has given us his Holy Spirit.

6So we are always confident, even though we know that as long as we live in these bodies we are not at home with the Lord. 7That is why we live by believing and not by seeing. 8Yes, we are fully confident, and we would rather be away from these bodies, for then we will be at home with the Lord. 9So our aim is to please him always, whether we are here in this body or away from this body. 10For we must all stand before Christ to be judged. We will each receive whatever we deserve for the good or evil we have done in our bodies.

We Are God's Ambassadors

11It is because we know this solemn fear of the Lord that we work so hard to persuade others. God knows we are sincere, and I hope you know this, too. 12Are we trying to pat ourselves on the back again? No, we are giving you a reason to be proud of us, so you can answer those who brag about having a spectacular ministry rather than having a sincere heart before God. 13If it seems that we are crazy, it is to bring glory to God. And if we are in our right minds, it is for your benefit. 14Whatever we do, it is because Christ's love controls us.* Since we believe that Christ died for everyone, we also believe that we have all died to the old life we used to live.* 15He died for

5:14a Or *urges us on.* **5:14b** Greek *Since one died on behalf of all, then all died.*

NEW KING JAMES VERSION

5Now He who has prepared us for this very thing *is* God, who also has given us the Spirit as a guarantee.

6So *we are* always confident, knowing that while we are at home in the body we are absent from the Lord. 7For we walk by faith, not by sight. 8We are confident, yes, well pleased rather to be absent from the body and to be present with the Lord.

The Judgment Seat of Christ

9Therefore we make it our aim, whether present or absent, to be well pleasing to Him. 10For we must all appear before the judgment seat of Christ, that each one may receive the things *done* in the body, according to what he has done, whether good or bad. 11Knowing, therefore, the terror of the Lord, we persuade men; but we are well known to God, and I also trust are well known in your consciences.

Be Reconciled to God

12For we do not commend ourselves again to you, but give you opportunity to boast on our behalf, that you may have *an answer* for those who boast in appearance and not in heart. 13For if we are beside ourselves, *it is* for God; or if we are of sound mind, *it is* for you. 14For the love of Christ compels us, because we judge thus: that if One died for all,

THE MESSAGE

taste of what's ahead. He puts a little of heaven in our hearts so that we'll never settle for less.

That's why we live with such good cheer. You won't see us drooping our heads or dragging our feet! Cramped conditions here don't get us down. They only remind us of the spacious living conditions ahead. It's what we trust in but don't yet see that keeps us going. Do you suppose a few ruts in the road or rocks in the path are going to stop us? When the time comes, we'll be plenty ready to exchange exile for homecoming.

But neither exile nor homecoming is the main thing. Cheerfully pleasing God is the main thing, and that's what we aim to do, regardless of our conditions. Sooner or later we'll all have to face God, regardless of our conditions. We will appear before Christ and take what's coming to us as a result of our actions, either good or bad.

That keeps us vigilant, you can be sure. It's no light thing to know that we'll all one day stand in that place of Judgment. That's why we work urgently with everyone we meet to get them ready to face God. God alone knows how well we do this, but I hope you realize how much and deeply we care. We're not saying this to make ourselves look good to you. We just thought it would make you feel good, proud even, that we're on your side and not just nice to your face as so many people are. If I acted crazy, I did it for God; if I acted overly serious, I did it for you. Christ's love has moved me to such extremes. His love has the first and last word in everything we do.

KING JAMES VERSION

15 And *that* he died for all, that they which live should not henceforth live unto themselves, but unto him which died for them, and rose again.

16 ¶ Wherefore henceforth know we no man after the flesh: yea, though we have known Christ after the flesh, yet now henceforth know we *him* no more.

17 Therefore if any man *be* in Christ, *he is* a new creature: old things are passed away; behold, all things are become new.

18 And all things *are* of God, who hath reconciled us to himself by Jesus Christ, and hath given to us the ministry of reconciliation;

19 To wit, that God was in Christ, reconciling the world unto himself, not imputing their trespasses unto them; and hath committed unto us the word of reconciliation.

20 Now then we are ambassadors for Christ, as though God did beseech *you* by us: we pray *you* in Christ's stead, be ye reconciled to God.

21 For he hath made him *to be* sin for us, who knew no sin; that we might be made the righteousness of God in him.

6 We then, *as* workers together *with him*, beseech *you* also that ye receive not the grace of God in vain.

NEW AMERICAN STANDARD BIBLE

15 and He died for all, so that they who live might no longer live for themselves, but for Him who died and rose again on their behalf.

16 Therefore from now on we recognize no one according to the flesh; even though we have known Christ according to the flesh, yet now we know *Him in this way* no longer.

17 Therefore if anyone is in Christ, *he is* a new creature; the old things passed away; behold, new things have come.

18 Now all *these* things are from God, who reconciled us to Himself through Christ and gave us the ministry of reconciliation,

19 namely, that God was in Christ reconciling the world to Himself, not counting their trespasses against them, and He has committed to us the word of reconciliation.

20 Therefore, we are ambassadors for Christ, as though God were making an appeal through us; we beg you on behalf of Christ, be reconciled to God.

21 He made Him who knew no sin *to be* sin on our behalf, so that we might become the righteousness of God in Him.

Their Ministry Commended

6 And working together *with Him,* we also urge you not to receive the grace of God in vain—

NEW CENTURY VERSION

[15]Christ died for all so that those who live would not con-
tinue to live for themselves. He died for them and was
raised from the dead so that they would live for him.
[16]From this time on we do not think of anyone as the
world does. In the past we thought of Christ as the world
thinks, but we no longer think of him in that way. [17]If
anyone belongs to Christ, there is a new creation. The old
things have gone; everything is made new! [18]All this is
from God. Through Christ, God made peace between us and
himself, and God gave us the work of telling everyone
about the peace we can have with him. [19]God was in
Christ, making peace between the world and himself. In
Christ, God did not hold the world guilty of its sins. And he
gave us this message of peace. [20]So we have been sent to
speak for Christ. It is as if God is calling to you through us.
We speak for Christ when we beg you to be at peace with
God. [21]Christ had no sin, but God made him become sin so
that in Christ we could become right with God.

6 We are workers together with God, so we beg you: Do
not let the grace that you received from God be for
nothing. [2]God says,

CONTEMPORARY ENGLISH VERSION

[15]And Christ did die for all of us. He died so we would no
longer live for ourselves, but for the one who died and was
raised to life for us.
[16]We are careful not to judge people by what they seem
to be, though we once judged Christ in that way. [17]Anyone
who belongs to Christ is a new person. The past is forgot-
ten, and everything is new. [18]God has done it all! He sent
Christ to make peace between himself and us, and he has
given us the work of making peace between himself and
others.
[19]What we mean is that God was in Christ, offering
peace and forgiveness to the people of this world. And he
has given us the work of sharing his message about peace.
[20]We were sent to speak for Christ, and God is begging you
to listen to our message. We speak for Christ and sincerely
ask you to make peace with God. [21]Christ never sinned!
But God treated him as a sinner, so that Christ could make
us acceptable to God.

6 We work together with God, and we beg you to make
good use of God's kindness to you. [2]In the Scriptures
God says,

NEW INTERNATIONAL VERSION

he died for all, that those who live should no longer live
for themselves but for him who died for them and was
raised again.
16 So from now on we regard no one from a worldly point
of view. Though we once regarded Christ in this way, we
do so no longer. 17 Therefore, if anyone is in Christ, he is a
new creation; the old has gone, the new has come! 18 All
this is from God, who reconciled us to himself through
Christ and gave us the ministry of reconciliation: 19 that
God was reconciling the world to himself in Christ, not
counting men's sins against them. And he has committed
to us the message of reconciliation. 20 We are therefore
Christ's ambassadors, as though God were making his
appeal through us. We implore you on Christ's behalf: Be
reconciled to God. 21 God made him who had no sin to be
sin[a] for us, so that in him we might become the righteous-
ness of God.

6 As God's fellow workers we urge you not to receive
God's grace in vain. 2 For he says,

[a] 21 Or *be a sin offering*

NEW LIVING TRANSLATION

everyone so that those who receive his new life will no
longer live to please themselves. Instead, they will live to
please Christ, who died and was raised for them.
16 So we have stopped evaluating others by what the
world thinks about them. Once I mistakenly thought of
Christ that way, as though he were merely a human being.
How differently I think about him now! 17 What this means
is that those who become Christians become new persons.
They are not the same anymore, for the old life is gone. A
new life has begun!
18 All this newness of life is from God, who brought us
back to himself through what Christ did. And God has
given us the task of reconciling people to him. 19 For God
was in Christ, reconciling the world to himself, no longer
counting people's sins against them. This is the wonderful
message he has given us to tell others. 20 We are Christ's
ambassadors, and God is using us to speak to you. We
urge you, as though Christ himself were here pleading with
you, "Be reconciled to God!" 21 For God made Christ, who
never sinned, to be the offering for our sin, so that we
could be made right with God through Christ.

6 As God's partners,* we beg you not to reject this mar-
velous message of God's great kindness. 2 For God
says,

6:1 Or *As we work together.*

NEW KING JAMES VERSION

then all died; 15 and He died for all, that those who live
should live no longer for themselves, but for Him who died
for them and rose again.
16 Therefore, from now on, we regard no one according to
the flesh. Even though we have known Christ according to
the flesh, yet now we know *Him thus* no longer. 17 There-
fore, if anyone *is* in Christ, *he is* a new creation; old things
have passed away; behold, all things have become new.
18 Now all things *are* of God, who has reconciled us to
Himself through Jesus Christ, and has given us the minis-
try of reconciliation, 19 that is, that God was in Christ rec-
onciling the world to Himself, not imputing their tres-
passes to them, and has committed to us the word of
reconciliation.
20 Now then, we are ambassadors for Christ, as though
God were pleading through us: we implore *you* on Christ's
behalf, be reconciled to God. 21 For He made Him who knew
no sin *to be* sin for us, that we might become the righ-
teousness of God in Him.

Marks of the Ministry

6 We then, *as* workers together *with Him* also plead
with *you* not to receive the grace of God in vain. 2 For
He says:

THE MESSAGE

A New Life

Our firm decision is to work from this focused center: One man died for everyone. That puts everyone in the same boat. He included everyone in his death so that everyone could also be included in his life, a resurrection life, a far better life than people ever lived on their own.

Because of this decision we don't evaluate people by what they have or how they look. We looked at the Messiah that way once and got it all wrong, as you know. We certainly don't look at him that way anymore. Now we look inside, and what we see is that anyone united with the Messiah gets a fresh start, is created new. The old life is gone; a new life burgeons! Look at it! All this comes from the God who settled the relationship between us and him, and then called us to settle our relationships with each other. God put the world square with himself through the Messiah, giving the world a fresh start by offering forgiveness of sins. God has given us the task of telling everyone what he is doing. We're Christ's representatives. God uses us to persuade men and women to drop their differences and enter into God's work of making things right between them. We're speaking for Christ himself now: Become friends with God; he's already a friend with you.

How? you say. In Christ. God put on him the wrong who never did anything wrong, so we could be put right with God.

Staying at Our Post

6 Companions as we are in this work with you, we beg you, please don't squander one bit of this marvelous life God has given us. God reminds us,

KING JAMES VERSION

2 (For he saith, I have heard thee in a time accepted, and in the day of salvation have I succoured thee: behold, now *is* the accepted time; behold, now *is* the day of salvation.)

3 Giving no offence in any thing, that the ministry be not blamed:

4 But in all *things* approving ourselves as the ministers of God, in much patience, in afflictions, in necessities, in distresses,

5 In stripes, in imprisonments, in tumults, in labours, in watchings, in fastings;

6 By pureness, by knowledge, by longsuffering, by kindness, by the Holy Ghost, by love unfeigned,

7 By the word of truth, by the power of God, by the armour of righteousness on the right hand and on the left,

8 By honour and dishonour, by evil report and good report: as deceivers, and *yet* true;

9 As unknown, and *yet* well known; as dying, and, behold, we live; as chastened, and not killed;

10 As sorrowful, yet alway rejoicing; as poor, yet making many rich; as having nothing, and *yet* possessing all things.

NEW AMERICAN STANDARD BIBLE

2 for He says,

"AT THE ACCEPTABLE TIME I LISTENED TO YOU,

AND ON THE DAY OF SALVATION I HELPED YOU."

Behold, now is "THE ACCEPTABLE TIME," behold, now is "THE DAY OF SALVATION"—

3 giving no cause for offense in anything, so that the ministry will not be discredited,

4 but in everything commending ourselves as servants of God, in much endurance, in afflictions, in hardships, in distresses,

5 in beatings, in imprisonments, in tumults, in labors, in sleeplessness, in hunger,

6 in purity, in knowledge, in patience, in kindness, in the Holy Spirit, in genuine love,

7 in the word of truth, in the power of God; by the weapons of righteousness for the right hand and the left,

8 by glory and dishonor, by evil report and good report; *regarded* as deceivers and yet true;

9 as unknown yet well-known, as dying yet behold, we live; as punished yet not put to death,

10 as sorrowful yet always rejoicing, as poor yet making many rich, as having nothing yet possessing all things.

NEW CENTURY VERSION

"At the right time I heard your prayers.
On the day of salvation I helped you." *Isaiah 49:8*

I tell you that the "right time" is now, and the "day of salvation" is now.

3 We do not want anyone to find fault with our work, so nothing we do will be a problem for anyone. 4 But in every way we show we are servants of God: in accepting many hard things, in troubles, in difficulties, and in great problems. 5 We are beaten and thrown into prison. We meet those who become upset with us and start riots. We work hard, and sometimes we get no sleep or food. 6 We show we are servants of God by our pure lives, our understanding, patience, and kindness, by the Holy Spirit, by true love, 7 by speaking the truth, and by God's power. We use our right living to defend ourselves against everything. 8 Some people honor us, but others blame us. Some people say evil things about us, but others say good things. Some people say we are liars, but we speak the truth. 9 We are not known, but we are well known. We seem to be dying, but we continue to live. We are punished, but we are not killed. 10 We have much sadness, but we are always rejoicing. We are poor, but we are making many people rich in faith. We have nothing, but really we have everything.

CONTEMPORARY ENGLISH VERSION

"When the time came,
I listened to you,
and when you needed help,
I came to save you."

That time has come. This is the day for you to be saved.

3 We don't want anyone to find fault with our work, and so we try hard not to cause problems. 4 But in everything and in every way we show that we truly are God's servants. We have always been patient, though we have had a lot of trouble, suffering, and hard times. 5 We have been beaten, put in jail, and hurt in riots. We have worked hard and have gone without sleep or food. 6 But we have kept ourselves pure and have been understanding, patient, and kind. The Holy Spirit has been with us, and our love has been real. 7 We have spoken the truth, and God's power has worked in us. In all our struggles we have said and done only what is right.

8 Whether we were honored or dishonored or praised or cursed, we always told the truth about ourselves. But some people said we did not. 9 We are unknown to others, but well known to you. We seem to be dying, and yet we are still alive. We have been punished, but never killed, 10 and we are always happy, even in times of suffering. Although we are poor, we have made many people rich. And though we own nothing, everything is ours.

NEW INTERNATIONAL VERSION

"In the time of my favor I heard you,
and in the day of salvation I helped you."[a]

I tell you, now is the time of God's favor, now is the day of salvation.

Paul's Hardships

[3]We put no stumbling block in anyone's path, so that our ministry will not be discredited. [4]Rather, as servants of God we commend ourselves in every way: in great endurance; in troubles, hardships and distresses; [5]in beatings, imprisonments and riots; in hard work, sleepless nights and hunger; [6]in purity, understanding, patience and kindness; in the Holy Spirit and in sincere love; [7]in truthful speech and in the power of God; with weapons of righteousness in the right hand and in the left; [8]through glory and dishonor, bad report and good report; genuine, yet regarded as impostors; [9]known, yet regarded as unknown; dying, and yet we live on; beaten, and yet not killed; [10]sorrowful, yet always rejoicing; poor, yet making many rich; having nothing, and yet possessing everything.

[a] *2* Isaiah 49:8

NEW LIVING TRANSLATION

"At just the right time, I heard you.
On the day of salvation, I helped you."*

Indeed, God is ready to help you right now. Today is the day of salvation.

Paul's Hardships

[3]We try to live in such a way that no one will be hindered from finding the Lord by the way we act, and so no one can find fault with our ministry. [4]In everything we do we try to show that we are true ministers of God. We patiently endure troubles and hardships and calamities of every kind. [5]We have been beaten, been put in jail, faced angry mobs, worked to exhaustion, endured sleepless nights, and gone without food. [6]We have proved ourselves by our purity, our understanding, our patience, our kindness, our sincere love, and the power of the Holy Spirit.* [7]We have faithfully preached the truth. God's power has been working in us. We have righteousness as our weapon, both to attack and to defend ourselves. [8]We serve God whether people honor us or despise us, whether they slander us or praise us. We are honest, but they call us impostors. [9]We are well known, but we are treated as unknown. We live close to death, but here we are, still alive. We have been beaten within an inch of our lives. [10]Our hearts ache, but we always have joy. We are poor, but we give spiritual riches to others. We own nothing, and yet we have everything.

6:2 Isa 49:8. 6:6 Or *the holiness of spirit.*

NEW KING JAMES VERSION

"In an acceptable time I have heard you,
And in the day of salvation I have helped you."[a]

Behold, now *is* the accepted time; behold, now *is* the day of salvation.

[3]We give no offense in anything, that our ministry may not be blamed. [4]But in all *things* we commend ourselves as ministers of God: in much patience, in tribulations, in needs, in distresses, [5]in stripes, in imprisonments, in tumults, in labors, in sleeplessness, in fastings; [6]by purity, by knowledge, by longsuffering, by kindness, by the Holy Spirit, by sincere love, [7]by the word of truth, by the power of God, by the armor of righteousness on the right hand and on the left, [8]by honor and dishonor, by evil report and good report; as deceivers, and *yet* true; [9]as unknown, and *yet* well known; as dying, and behold we live; as chastened, and *yet* not killed; [10]as sorrowful, yet always rejoicing; as poor, yet making many rich; as having nothing, and *yet* possessing all things.

6:2 [a] Isaiah 49:8

THE MESSAGE

"I heard your call in the nick of time;
The day you needed me, I was there to help."

Well, now is the right time to listen, the day to be helped. Don't put it off; don't frustrate God's work by showing up late, throwing a question mark over everything we're doing. Our work as God's servants gets validated—or not—in the details. People are watching us as we stay at our post, alertly, unswervingly . . . in hard times, tough times, bad times; when we're beaten up, jailed, and mobbed; working hard, working late, working without eating; with pure heart, clear head, steady hand; in gentleness, holiness, and honest love; when we're telling the truth, and when God's showing his power; when we're doing our best setting things right; when we're praised, and when we're blamed; slandered, and honored; true to our word, though distrusted; ignored by the world, but recognized by God; terrifically alive, though rumored to be dead; beaten within an inch of our lives, but refusing to die; immersed in tears, yet always filled with deep joy; living on handouts, yet enriching many; having nothing, having it all.

KING JAMES VERSION

11 ¶ O *ye* Corinthians, our mouth is open unto you, our heart is enlarged.

12 Ye are not straitened in us, but ye are straitened in your own bowels.

13 Now for a recompence in the same, (I speak as unto *my* children,) be ye also enlarged.

14 Be ye not unequally yoked together with unbelievers: for what fellowship hath righteousness with unrighteousness? and what communion hath light with darkness?

15 And what concord hath Christ with Belial? or what part hath he that believeth with an infidel?

16 And what agreement hath the temple of God with idols? for ye are the temple of the living God; as God hath said, I will dwell in them, and walk in *them*; and I will be their God, and they shall be my people.

17 Wherefore come out from among them, and be ye separate, saith the Lord, and touch not the unclean *thing*; and I will receive you,

NEW AMERICAN STANDARD BIBLE

11 Our mouth has spoken freely to you, O Corinthians, our heart is opened wide.

12 You are not restrained by us, but you are restrained in your own affections.

13 Now in a like exchange—I speak as to children—open wide *to us* also.

14 Do not be bound together with unbelievers; for what partnership have righteousness and lawlessness, or what fellowship has light with darkness?

15 Or what harmony has Christ with Belial, or what has a believer in common with an unbeliever?

16 Or what agreement has the temple of God with idols? For we are the temple of the living God; just as God said,

"I WILL DWELL IN THEM AND WALK AMONG THEM;
AND I WILL BE THEIR GOD, AND THEY SHALL BE MY PEOPLE.

17 "Therefore, COME OUT FROM THEIR MIDST AND BE SEPARATE," says the Lord.
"AND DO NOT TOUCH WHAT IS UNCLEAN;
And I will welcome you.

NEW CENTURY VERSION

11We have spoken freely to you in Corinth and have opened our hearts to you. 12Our feelings of love for you have not stopped, but you have stopped your feelings of love for us. 13I speak to you as if you were my children. Do to us as we have done—open your hearts to us.

Warning About Non-Christians

14You are not the same as those who do not believe. So do not join yourselves to them. Good and bad do not belong together. Light and darkness cannot share together. 15How can Christ and Belial, the devil, have any agreement? What can a believer have together with a nonbeliever? 16The temple of God cannot have any agreement with idols, and we are the temple of the living God. As God said: "I will live with them and walk with them. And I will be their God, and they will be my people."[a]

17"Leave those people,
 and be separate, says the Lord.
Touch nothing that is unclean,
 and I will accept you." *Isaiah 52:11; Ezekiel 20:34, 41*

6:16 [a] "I...people." Quotation from Leviticus 26:11–12; Jeremiah 32:38; Ezekiel 37:27.

CONTEMPORARY ENGLISH VERSION

11Friends in Corinth, we are telling the truth when we say that there is room in our hearts for you. 12We are not holding back on our love for you, but you are holding back on your love for us. 13I speak to you as I would speak to my own children. Please make room in your hearts for us.

The Temple of the Living God

14Stay away from people who are not followers of the Lord! Can someone who is good get along with someone who is evil? Are light and darkness the same? 15Is Christ a friend of Satan?[a] Can people who follow the Lord have anything in common with those who don't? 16Do idols belong in the temple of God? We are the temple of the living God, as God himself says,

"I will live with these people
 and walk among them.
I will be their God,
 and they will be
 my people."

17The Lord also says,

"Leave them and stay away!
Don't touch anything
 that isn't clean.
Then I will welcome you

[a] 6.15 *Satan*: The Greek text has "Beliar," which is another form of the Hebrew word "Belial," meaning "wicked" or "useless." The Jewish people sometimes used this as a name for Satan.

NEW INTERNATIONAL VERSION

11We have spoken freely to you, Corinthians, and opened
wide our hearts to you. 12We are not withholding our
affection from you, but you are withholding yours from us.
13As a fair exchange—I speak as to my children—open
wide your hearts also.

Do Not Be Yoked With Unbelievers

14Do not be yoked together with unbelievers. For what
do righteousness and wickedness have in common? Or
what fellowship can light have with darkness? 15What
harmony is there between Christ and Belial[b]? What does a
believer have in common with an unbeliever? 16What
agreement is there between the temple of God and idols?
For we are the temple of the living God. As God has said: "I
will live with them and walk among them, and I will be
their God, and they will be my people."[c]

17"Therefore come out from them
and be separate,
says the Lord.
Touch no unclean thing,
and I will receive you."[d]

[b] *15* Greek *Beliar,* a variant of *Belial* [c] *16* Lev. 26:12; Jer. 32:38; Ezek. 37:27 [d] *17* Isaiah 52:11; Ezek. 20:34,41

NEW LIVING TRANSLATION

11Oh, dear Corinthian friends! We have spoken honestly
with you. Our hearts are open to you. 12If there is a prob-
lem between us, it is not because of a lack of love on our
part, but because you have withheld your love from us. 13I
am talking now as I would to my own children. Open your
hearts to us!

The Temple of the Living God

14Don't team up with those who are unbelievers. How
can goodness be a partner with wickedness? How can light
live with darkness? 15What harmony can there be between
Christ and the Devil*? How can a believer be a partner with
an unbeliever? 16And what union can there be between
God's temple and idols? For we are the temple of the living
God. As God said:

"I will live in them
and walk among them.
I will be their God,
and they will be my people.*
17 Therefore, come out from them
and separate yourselves from them, says the Lord.
Don't touch their filthy things,
and I will welcome you.*

6:15 Greek *and Beliar.* **6:16** Lev 26:12; Ezek 37:27. **6:17** Isa 52:11; Ezek 20:34.

NEW KING JAMES VERSION

Be Holy

11O Corinthians! We have spoken openly to you, our
heart is wide open. 12You are not restricted by us, but you
are restricted by your *own* affections. 13Now in return for
the same (I speak as to children), you also be open.

14Do not be unequally yoked together with unbelievers.
For what fellowship has righteousness with lawlessness?
And what communion has light with darkness? 15And
what accord has Christ with Belial? Or what part has a
believer with an unbeliever? 16And what agreement has
the temple of God with idols? For you[b] are the temple of
the living God. As God has said:

"I will dwell in them
And walk among them.
I will be their God,
And they shall be My people."[c]

17Therefore

"Come out from among them
And be separate, says the Lord.
Do not touch what is unclean,
And I will receive you."[d]

6:16 [b] NU-Text reads *we.* [c] Leviticus 26:12; Jeremiah 32:38; Ezekiel 37:27 **6:17** [d] Isaiah 52:11; Ezekiel 20:34, 41

THE MESSAGE

Dear, dear Corinthians, I can't tell you how much I long for you to enter this wide-open, spacious life. We didn't fence you in. The smallness you feel comes from within you. Your lives aren't small, but you're living them in a small way. I'm speaking as plainly as I can and with great affection. Open up your lives. Live openly and expansively!

✢

Don't become partners with those who reject God. How can you make a partnership out of right and wrong? That's not partnership; that's war. Is light best friends with dark? Does Christ go strolling with the Devil? Do trust and mistrust hold hands? Who would think of setting up pagan idols in God's holy Temple? But that is exactly what we are, each of us a temple in whom God lives. God himself put it this way:

"'I'll live in them, move into them;
I'll be their God and they'll be my people.
So leave the corruption and compromise;
leave it for good,' says God.
'Don't link up with those who will pollute you.
I want you all for myself.

KING JAMES VERSION

18 And will be a Father unto you, and ye shall be my sons and daughters, saith the Lord Almighty.

7 Having therefore these promises, dearly beloved, let us cleanse ourselves from all filthiness of the flesh and spirit, perfecting holiness in the fear of God.

2 Receive us; we have wronged no man, we have corrupted no man, we have defrauded no man.

3 I speak not *this* to condemn *you*: for I have said before, that ye are in our hearts to die and live with *you*.

4 Great *is* my boldness of speech toward you, great *is* my glorying of you: I am filled with comfort, I am exceeding joyful in all our tribulation.

5 ¶ For, when we were come into Macedonia, our flesh had no rest, but we were troubled on every side; without *were* fightings, within *were* fears.

6 Nevertheless God, that comforteth those that are cast down, comforted us by the coming of Titus;

7 And not by his coming only, but by the consolation wherewith he was comforted in you, when he told us your earnest desire, your mourning, your fervent mind toward me; so that I rejoiced the more.

NEW AMERICAN STANDARD BIBLE

18 "And I will be a father to you,
And you shall be sons and daughters to Me,"
Says the Lord Almighty.

Paul Reveals His Heart

7 Therefore, having these promises, beloved, let us cleanse ourselves from all defilement of flesh and spirit, perfecting holiness in the fear of God.

2 Make room for us *in your hearts;* we wronged no one, we corrupted no one, we took advantage of no one.

3 I do not speak to condemn you, for I have said before that you are in our hearts to die together and to live together.

4 Great is my confidence in you; great is my boasting on your behalf. I am filled with comfort; I am overflowing with joy in all our affliction.

5 For even when we came into Macedonia our flesh had no rest, but we were afflicted on every side: conflicts without, fears within.

6 But God, who comforts the depressed, comforted us by the coming of Titus;

7 and not only by his coming, but also by the comfort with which he was comforted in you, as he reported to us your longing, your mourning, your zeal for me; so that I rejoiced even more.

NEW CENTURY VERSION

18 "I will be your father,
and you will be my sons and daughters,
says the Lord Almighty." *2 Samuel 7:14; 7:8*

7 Dear friends, we have these promises from God, so we should make ourselves pure—free from anything that makes body or soul unclean. We should try to become holy in the way we live, because we respect God.

Paul's Joy

2 Open your hearts to us. We have not done wrong to anyone, we have not ruined the faith of anyone, and we
have not cheated anyone. 3 I do not say this to blame you. I
told you before that we love you so much we would live or
die with you. 4 I feel very sure of you and am very proud of you. You give me much comfort, and in all of our troubles I have great joy.

5 When we came into Macedonia, we had no rest. We found trouble all around us. We had fighting on the out-
side and fear on the inside. 6 But God, who comforts those
who are troubled, comforted us when Titus came. 7 We
were comforted, not only by his coming but also by the comfort you gave him. Titus told us about your wish to see me and that you are very sorry for what you did. He also told me about your great care for me, and when I heard this, I was much happier.

CONTEMPORARY ENGLISH VERSION

18 and be your Father.
You will be my sons
and my daughters,
as surely as I am God,
the All-Powerful."

7 My friends, God has made us these promises. So we should stay away from everything that keeps our bodies and spirits from being clean. We should honor God and try to be completely like him.

The Church Makes Paul Happy

2 Make a place for us in your hearts! We haven't mistreat-
ed or hurt anyone. We haven't cheated anyone. 3 I am not
saying this to be hard on you. But, as I have said before, you will always be in our thoughts, whether we live or die.
4 I trust you completely.[a] I am always proud of you, and I am greatly encouraged. In all my trouble I am still very happy.

5 After we came to Macedonia, we didn't have any chance to rest. We were faced with all kinds of problems.
We were troubled by enemies and troubled by fears. 6 But
God cheers up people in need, and that is what he did
when he sent Titus to us. 7 Of course, we were glad to see
Titus, but what really made us glad is the way you cheered him up. He told how sorry you were and how concerned you were about me. And this made me even happier.

[a] 7.4 *I trust you completely*: Or "I have always spoken the truth to you" or "I can speak freely to you."

NEW INTERNATIONAL VERSION

18 "I will be a Father to you,
and you will be my sons and daughters,
says the Lord Almighty."[e]

7 Since we have these promises, dear friends, let us purify ourselves from everything that contaminates body and spirit, perfecting holiness out of reverence for God.

Paul's Joy

2 Make room for us in your hearts. We have wronged no one, we have corrupted no one, we have exploited no one. 3 I do not say this to condemn you; I have said before that you have such a place in our hearts that we would live or die with you. 4 I have great confidence in you; I take great pride in you. I am greatly encouraged; in all our troubles my joy knows no bounds.

5 For when we came into Macedonia, this body of ours had no rest, but we were harassed at every turn—conflicts on the outside, fears within. 6 But God, who comforts the downcast, comforted us by the coming of Titus, 7 and not only by his coming but also by the comfort you had given him. He told us about your longing for me, your deep sorrow, your ardent concern for me, so that my joy was greater than ever.

[e] *18* 2 Samuel 7:14; 7:8

NEW LIVING TRANSLATION

18 And I will be your Father,
and you will be my sons and daughters,
says the Lord Almighty.*"

7 Because we have these promises, dear friends, let us cleanse ourselves from everything that can defile our body or spirit. And let us work toward complete purity because we fear God.

Paul's Joy at the Church's Repentance

2 Please open your hearts to us. We have not done wrong to anyone. We have not led anyone astray. We have not taken advantage of anyone. 3 I'm not saying this to condemn you, for I said before that you are in our hearts forever. We live or die together with you. 4 I have the highest confidence in you, and my pride in you is great. You have greatly encouraged me; you have made me happy despite all our troubles.

5 When we arrived in Macedonia there was no rest for us. Outside there was conflict from every direction, and inside there was fear. 6 But God, who encourages those who are discouraged, encouraged us by the arrival of Titus. 7 His presence was a joy, but so was the news he brought of the encouragement he received from you. When he told me how much you were looking forward to my visit, and how sorry you were about what had happened, and how loyal your love is for me, I was filled with joy!

6:18 2 Sam 7:14.

NEW KING JAMES VERSION

18 *"I will be a Father to you,*
And you shall be My sons and daughters,
Says the LORD *Almighty."*[e]

7 Therefore, having these promises, beloved, let us cleanse ourselves from all filthiness of the flesh and spirit, perfecting holiness in the fear of God.

The Corinthians' Repentance

2 Open *your hearts* to us. We have wronged no one, we have corrupted no one, we have cheated no one. 3 I do not say *this* to condemn; for I have said before that you are in our hearts, to die together and to live together. 4 Great *is* my boldness of speech toward you, great *is* my boasting on your behalf. I am filled with comfort. I am exceedingly joyful in all our tribulation.

5 For indeed, when we came to Macedonia, our bodies had no rest, but we were troubled on every side. Outside *were* conflicts, inside *were* fears. 6 Nevertheless God, who comforts the downcast, comforted us by the coming of Titus, 7 and not only by his coming, but also by the consolation with which he was comforted in you, when he told us of your earnest desire, your mourning, your zeal for me, so that I rejoiced even more.

6:18 [e] 2 Samuel 7:14

THE MESSAGE

I'll be a Father to you;
you'll be sons and daughters to me.'
The Word of the Master, God."

7 With promises like this to pull us on, dear friends, let's make a clean break with everything that defiles or distracts us, both within and without. Let's make our entire lives fit and holy temples for the worship of God.

More Passionate, More Responsible

Trust us. We've never hurt a soul, never exploited or taken advantage of anyone. Don't think I'm finding fault with you. I told you earlier that I'm with you all the way, no matter what. I have, in fact, the greatest confidence in you. If only you knew how proud I am of you! I am overwhelmed with joy despite all our troubles.

When we arrived in Macedonia province, we couldn't settle down. The fights in the church and the fears in our hearts kept us on pins and needles. We couldn't relax because we didn't know how it would turn out. Then the God who lifts up the downcast lifted our heads and our hearts with the arrival of Titus. We were glad just to see him, but the true reassurance came in what he told us about you: how much you cared, how much you grieved, how concerned you were for me. I went from worry to tranquility in no time!

KING JAMES VERSION

8 For though I made you sorry with a letter, I do not repent, though I did repent: for I perceive that the same epistle hath made you sorry, though *it were* but for a season.

9 Now I rejoice, not that ye were made sorry, but that ye sorrowed to repentance: for ye were made sorry after a godly manner, that ye might receive damage by us in nothing.

10 For godly sorrow worketh repentance to salvation not to be repented of: but the sorrow of the world worketh death.

11 For behold this selfsame thing, that ye sorrowed after a godly sort, what carefulness it wrought in you, yea, *what* clearing of yourselves, yea, *what* indignation, yea, *what* fear, yea, *what* vehement desire, yea, *what* zeal, yea, *what* revenge! In all *things* ye have approved yourselves to be clear in this matter.

12 ¶ Wherefore, though I wrote unto you, *I did it* not for his cause that had done the wrong, nor for his cause that suffered wrong, but that our care for you in the sight of God might appear unto you.

13 Therefore we were comforted in your comfort: yea, and exceedingly the more joyed we for the joy of Titus, because his spirit was refreshed by you all.

14 For if I have boasted any thing to him of you, I am not ashamed; but as we spake all things to you in truth, even so our boasting, which *I made* before Titus, is found a truth.

NEW AMERICAN STANDARD BIBLE

8 For though I caused you sorrow by my letter, I do not regret it; though I did regret it—*for* I see that that letter caused you sorrow, though only for a while—

9 I now rejoice, not that you were made sorrowful, but that you were made sorrowful to *the point of* repentance; for you were made sorrowful according to *the will of* God, so that you might not suffer loss in anything through us.

10 For the sorrow that is according to *the will of* God produces a repentance without regret, *leading* to salvation, but the sorrow of the world produces death.

11 For behold what earnestness this very thing, this godly sorrow, has produced in you: what vindication of yourselves, what indignation, what fear, what longing, what zeal, what avenging of wrong! In everything you demonstrated yourselves to be innocent in the matter.

12 So although I wrote to you, *it was* not for the sake of the offender nor for the sake of the one offended, but that your earnestness on our behalf might be made known to you in the sight of God.

13 For this reason we have been comforted.

And besides our comfort, we rejoiced even much more for the joy of Titus, because his spirit has been refreshed by you all.

14 For if in anything I have boasted to him about you, I was not put to shame; but as we spoke all things to you in truth, so also our boasting before Titus proved to be *the* truth.

NEW CENTURY VERSION

8Even if my letter made you sad, I am not sorry I wrote it.
At first I was sorry, because it made you sad, but you were
sad only for a short time. 9Now I am happy, not because
you were made sad, but because your sorrow made you
change your lives. You became sad in the way God wanted
you to, so you were not hurt by us in any way. 10The kind
of sorrow God wants makes people change their hearts and
lives. This leads to salvation, and you cannot be sorry for
that. But the kind of sorrow the world has brings death.
11See what this sorrow—the sorrow God wanted you to
have—has done to you: It has made you very serious. It
made you want to prove you were not wrong. It made you
angry and afraid. It made you want to see me. It made you
care. It made you want the right thing to be done. You
proved you were innocent in the problem. 12I wrote that let-
ter, not because of the one who did the wrong or because of
the person who was hurt. I wrote the letter so you could
see, before God, the great care you have for us. 13That is
why we were comforted.

Not only were we very comforted, we were even happier to
see that Titus was so happy. All of you made him feel much
better. 14I bragged to Titus about you, and you showed that
I was right. Everything we said to you was true, and you
have proved that what we bragged about to Titus is true.

CONTEMPORARY ENGLISH VERSION

8I don't feel bad anymore, even though my letter[b] hurt
your feelings. I did feel bad at first, but I don't now. I
know that the letter hurt you for a while. 9Now I am
happy, but not because I hurt your feelings. It is because
God used your hurt feelings to make you turn back to him,
and none of you were harmed by us. 10When God makes
you feel sorry enough to turn to him and be saved, you
don't have anything to feel bad about. But when this world
makes you feel sorry, it can cause your death.

11Just look what God has done by making you feel sorry!
You sincerely want to prove that you are innocent. You are
angry. You are shocked. You are eager to see that justice is
done. You have proved that you were completely right in
this matter. 12When I wrote you, it wasn't to accuse the
one who was wrong or to take up for the one who was
hurt. I wrote, so that God would show you how much you
do care for us. 13And we were greatly encouraged.

Although we were encouraged, we felt even better when
we saw how happy Titus was, because you had shown that
he had nothing to worry about. 14We had told him how
much we thought of you, and you did not disappoint us.
Just as we have always told you the truth, so everything
we told him about you has also proved to be true. 15Titus

[b] 7.8 *my letter*: There is no copy of this letter that Paul wrote to the church at Corinth.

NEW INTERNATIONAL VERSION

8Even if I caused you sorrow by my letter, I do not regret it. Though I did regret it—I see that my letter hurt you, but only for a little while— 9yet now I am happy, not because you were made sorry, but because your sorrow led you to repentance. For you became sorrowful as God intended and so were not harmed in any way by us. 10Godly sorrow brings repentance that leads to salvation and leaves no regret, but worldly sorrow brings death. 11See what this godly sorrow has produced in you: what earnestness, what eagerness to clear yourselves, what indignation, what alarm, what longing, what concern, what readiness to see justice done. At every point you have proved yourselves to be innocent in this matter. 12So even though I wrote to you, it was not on account of the one who did the wrong or of the injured party, but rather that before God you could see for yourselves how devoted to us you are. 13By all this we are encouraged.

In addition to our own encouragement, we were especially delighted to see how happy Titus was, because his spirit has been refreshed by all of you. 14I had boasted to him about you, and you have not embarrassed me. But just as everything we said to you was true, so our boasting about you to Titus has proved to be true as well. 15And his

NEW LIVING TRANSLATION

8I am no longer sorry that I sent that letter to you, though I was sorry for a time, for I know that it was painful to you for a little while. 9Now I am glad I sent it, not because it hurt you, but because the pain caused you to have remorse and change your ways. It was the kind of sorrow God wants his people to have, so you were not harmed by us in any way. 10For God can use sorrow in our lives to help us turn away from sin and seek salvation. We will never regret that kind of sorrow. But sorrow without repentance is the kind that results in death.

11Just see what this godly sorrow produced in you! Such earnestness, such concern to clear yourselves, such indignation, such alarm, such longing to see me, such zeal, and such a readiness to punish the wrongdoer. You showed that you have done everything you could to make things right. 12My purpose was not to write about who did the wrong or who was wronged. I wrote to you so that in the sight of God you could show how much you really do care for us. 13We have been encouraged by this.

In addition to our own encouragement, we were especially delighted to see how happy Titus was at the way you welcomed him and set his mind at ease. 14I had told him how proud I was of you—and you didn't disappoint me. I have always told you the truth, and now my boasting to Titus has also proved true! 15Now he cares for you more

NEW KING JAMES VERSION

8For even if I made you sorry with my letter, I do not regret it; though I did regret it. For I perceive that the same epistle made you sorry, though only for a while. 9Now I rejoice, not that you were made sorry, but that your sorrow led to repentance. For you were made sorry in a godly manner, that you might suffer loss from us in nothing. 10For godly sorrow produces repentance *leading* to salvation, not to be regretted; but the sorrow of the world produces death. 11For observe this very thing, that you sorrowed in a godly manner: What diligence it produced in you, *what* clearing *of yourselves, what* indignation, *what* fear, *what* vehement desire, *what* zeal, *what* vindication! In all *things* you proved yourselves to be clear in this matter. 12Therefore, although I wrote to you, *I did* not *do it* for the sake of him who had done the wrong, nor for the sake of him who suffered wrong, but that our care for you in the sight of God might appear to you.

The Joy of Titus

13Therefore we have been comforted in your comfort. And we rejoiced exceedingly more for the joy of Titus, because his spirit has been refreshed by you all. 14For if in anything I have boasted to him about you, I am not ashamed. But as we spoke all things to you in truth, even so our boasting to Titus was found true. 15And his affec-

THE MESSAGE

I know I distressed you greatly with my letter. Although I felt awful at the time, I don't feel at all bad now that I see how it turned out. The letter upset you, but only for a while. Now I'm glad—not that you were upset, but that you were jarred into turning things around. You let the distress bring you to God, not drive you from him. The result was all gain, no loss.

Distress that drives us to God does that. It turns us around. It gets us back in the way of salvation. We never regret that kind of pain. But those who let distress drive them away from God are full of regrets, end up on a deathbed of regrets.

And now, isn't it wonderful all the ways in which this distress has goaded you closer to God? You're more alive, more concerned, more sensitive, more reverent, more human, more passionate, more responsible. Looked at from any angle, you've come out of this with purity of heart. And that is what I was hoping for in the first place when I wrote the letter. My primary concern was not for the one who did the wrong or even the one wronged, but for you—that you would realize and act upon the deep, deep ties between us before God. That's what happened—and we felt just great.

And then, when we saw how Titus felt—his exuberance over your response—our joy doubled. It was wonderful to see how revived and refreshed he was by everything you did. If I went out on a limb in telling Titus how great I thought you were, you didn't cut off that limb. As it turned out, I hadn't exaggerated one bit. Titus saw for himself that everything I had said about you was true. He can't quit talking about it,

KING JAMES VERSION

15 And his inward affection is more abundant toward you, whilst he remembereth the obedience of you all, how with fear and trembling ye received him.

16 I rejoice therefore that I have confidence in you in all *things*.

8 Moreover, brethren, we do you to wit of the grace of God bestowed on the churches of Macedonia;

2 How that in a great trial of affliction the abundance of their joy and their deep poverty abounded unto the riches of their liberality.

3 For to *their* power, I bear record, yea, and beyond *their* power *they were* willing of themselves;

4 Praying us with much intreaty that we would receive the gift, and *take upon us* the fellowship of the ministering to the saints.

5 And *this they did*, not as we hoped, but first gave their own selves to the Lord, and unto us by the will of God.

6 Insomuch that we desired Titus, that as he had begun, so he would also finish in you the same grace also.

7 ¶ Therefore, as ye abound in every *thing, in* faith, and utterance, and knowledge, and *in* all diligence, and *in* your love to us, *see* that ye abound in this grace also.

8 I speak not by commandment, but by occasion of the forwardness of others, and to prove the sincerity of your love.

NEW AMERICAN STANDARD BIBLE

15 His affection abounds all the more toward you, as he remembers the obedience of you all, how you received him with fear and trembling.

16 I rejoice that in everything I have confidence in you.

Great Generosity

8 Now, brethren, we *wish to* make known to you the grace of God which has been given in the churches of Macedonia,

2 that in a great ordeal of affliction their abundance of joy and their deep poverty overflowed in the wealth of their liberality.

3 For I testify that according to their ability, and beyond their ability, *they gave* of their own accord,

4 begging us with much urging for the favor of participation in the support of the saints,

5 and *this,* not as we had expected, but they first gave themselves to the Lord and to us by the will of God.

6 So we urged Titus that as he had previously made a beginning, so he would also complete in you this gracious work as well.

7 But just as you abound in everything, in faith and utterance and knowledge and in all earnestness and in the [1]love we inspired in you, *see* that you abound in this gracious work also.

8 I am not speaking *this* as a command, but as proving through the earnestness of others the sincerity of your love also.

8:7 [1] Lit *love from us in you;* one early ms reads *your love for us*

NEW CENTURY VERSION

15And his love for you is stronger when he remembers that
you were all ready to obey. You welcomed him with respect
and fear. 16I am very happy that I can trust you fully.

Christian Giving

8 And now, brothers and sisters, we want you to know
about the grace God gave the churches in Macedonia.
2They have been tested by great troubles, and they are
very poor. But they gave much because of their great joy. 3I
can tell you that they gave as much as they were able and
even more than they could afford. No one told them to do
it. 4But they begged and pleaded with us to let them share
in this service for God's people. 5And they gave in a way
we did not expect: They first gave themselves to the Lord
and to us. This is what God wants. 6So we asked Titus to
help you finish this special work of grace since he is the
one who started it. 7You are rich in everything—in faith, in
speaking, in knowledge, in truly wanting to help, and in
the love you learned from us. In the same way, be strong
also in the grace of giving.

8I am not commanding you to give. But I want to see if
your love is true by comparing you with others that really

CONTEMPORARY ENGLISH VERSION

loves all of you very much, especially when he remembers
how you obeyed him and how you trembled with fear
when you welcomed him. 16It makes me really glad to
know that I can depend on you.

Generous Giving

8 My friends, we want you to know that the churches in
Macedonia[a] have shown others how kind God is.
2Although they were going through hard times and were
very poor, they were glad to give generously. 3They gave
as much as they could afford and even more, simply
because they wanted to. 4They even asked and begged us
to let them have the joy of giving their money for God's
people. 5And they did more than we had hoped. They gave
themselves first to the Lord and then to us, just as God
wanted them to do.

6Titus was the one who got you started doing this good
thing, so we begged him to have you finish what you had
begun. 7You do everything better than anyone else. You
have stronger faith. You speak better and know more. You
are eager to give, and you love us better.[b] Now you must
give more generously than anyone else.

8I am not ordering you to do this. I am simply testing
how real your love is by comparing it with the concern that

[a] 8.1 *churches in Macedonia*: The churches that Paul had started in Philippi and Thessalonica. The church in Berea is probably also meant.
[b] 8.7 *you love us better*: Some manuscripts have "we love you better."

NEW INTERNATIONAL VERSION

affection for you is all the greater when he remembers that you were all obedient, receiving him with fear and trembling. [16]I am glad I can have complete confidence in you.

Generosity Encouraged

8 And now, brothers, we want you to know about the grace that God has given the Macedonian churches. [2]Out of the most severe trial, their overflowing joy and their extreme poverty welled up in rich generosity. [3]For I testify that they gave as much as they were able, and even beyond their ability. Entirely on their own, [4]they urgently pleaded with us for the privilege of sharing in this service to the saints. [5]And they did not do as we expected, but they gave themselves first to the Lord and then to us in keeping with God's will. [6]So we urged Titus, since he had earlier made a beginning, to bring also to completion this act of grace on your part. [7]But just as you excel in everything—in faith, in speech, in knowledge, in complete earnestness and in your love for us[a]—see that you also excel in this grace of giving.

[8]I am not commanding you, but I want to test the sincerity of your love by comparing it with the earnestness of

[a] 7 Some manuscripts *in our love for you*

NEW LIVING TRANSLATION

than ever when he remembers the way you listened to him and welcomed him with such respect and deep concern. [16]I am very happy now because I have complete confidence in you.

A Call to Generous Giving

8 Now I want to tell you, dear brothers and sisters,* what God in his kindness has done for the churches in Macedonia. [2]Though they have been going through much trouble and hard times, their wonderful joy and deep poverty have overflowed in rich generosity. [3]For I can testify that they gave not only what they could afford but far more. And they did it of their own free will. [4]They begged us again and again for the gracious privilege of sharing in the gift for the Christians in Jerusalem. [5]Best of all, they went beyond our highest hopes, for their first action was to dedicate themselves to the Lord and to us for whatever directions God might give them.

[6]So we have urged Titus, who encouraged your giving in the first place, to return to you and encourage you to complete your share in this ministry of giving. [7]Since you excel in so many ways—you have so much faith, such gifted speakers, such knowledge, such enthusiasm, and such love for us*—now I want you to excel also in this gracious ministry of giving. [8]I am not saying you must do it, even though the other churches are eager to do it. This is one way to prove your love is real.

8:1 Greek *brothers.* 8:7 Some manuscripts read *love from us to you.*

NEW KING JAMES VERSION

tions are greater for you as he remembers the obedience of you all, how with fear and trembling you received him. [16]Therefore I rejoice that I have confidence in you in everything.

Excel in Giving

8 Moreover, brethren, we make known to you the grace of God bestowed on the churches of Macedonia: [2]that in a great trial of affliction the abundance of their joy and their deep poverty abounded in the riches of their liberality. [3]For I bear witness that according to *their* ability, yes, and beyond *their* ability, *they were* freely willing, [4]imploring us with much urgency that we would receive[a] the gift and the fellowship of the ministering to the saints. [5]And not *only* as we had hoped, but they first gave themselves to the Lord, and *then* to us by the will of God. [6]So we urged Titus, that as he had begun, so he would also complete this grace in you as well. [7]But as you abound in everything—in faith, in speech, in knowledge, in all diligence, and in your love for us—*see* that you abound in this grace also.

Christ Our Pattern

[8]I speak not by commandment, but I am testing the sincerity of your love by the diligence of others. [9]For you

8:4 [a] NU-Text and M-Text omit *that we would receive,* thus changing text to *urgency for the favor and fellowship . . . .*

THE MESSAGE

going over again and again the story of your prompt obedience, and the dignity and sensitivity of your hospitality. He was quite overwhelmed by it all! And I couldn't be more pleased—I'm so confident and proud of you.

The Offering

8 Now, friends, I want to report on the surprising and generous ways in which God is working in the churches in Macedonia province. Fierce troubles came down on the people of those churches, pushing them to the very limit. The trial exposed their true colors: They were incredibly happy, though desperately poor. The pressure triggered something totally unexpected: an outpouring of pure and generous gifts. I was there and saw it for myself. They gave offerings of whatever they could—far more than they could afford!—pleading for the privilege of helping out in the relief of poor Christians.

This was totally spontaneous, entirely their own idea, and caught us completely off guard. What explains it was that they had first given themselves unreservedly to God and to us. The other giving simply flowed out of the purposes of God working in their lives. That's what prompted us to ask Titus to bring the relief offering to your attention, so that what was so well begun could be finished up. You do so well in so many things—you trust God, you're articulate, you're insightful, you're passionate, you love us—now, do your best in this, too.

I'm not trying to order you around against your will. But by bringing in the Macedonians' enthusiasm as a stimulus

KING JAMES VERSION

9 For ye know the grace of our Lord Jesus Christ, that, though he was rich, yet for your sakes he became poor, that ye through his poverty might be rich.

10 And herein I give *my* advice: for this is expedient for you, who have begun before, not only to do, but also to be forward a year ago.

11 Now therefore perform the doing *of it*; that as *there was* a readiness to will, so *there may be* a performance also out of that which ye have.

12 For if there be first a willing mind, *it is* accepted according to that a man hath, *and* not according to that he hath not.

13 For *I mean* not that other men be eased, and ye burdened:

14 But by an equality, *that* now at this time your abundance *may be a supply* for their want, that their abundance also may be *a supply* for your want: that there may be equality:

15 As it is written, He that *had gathered* much had nothing over; and he that *had gathered* little had no lack.

16 ¶ But thanks *be* to God, which put the same earnest care into the heart of Titus for you.

17 For indeed he accepted the exhortation; but being more forward, of his own accord he went unto you.

18 And we have sent with him the brother, whose

NEW AMERICAN STANDARD BIBLE

9 For you know the grace of our Lord Jesus Christ, that though He was rich, yet for your sake He became poor, so that you through His poverty might become rich.

10 I give *my* opinion in this matter, for this is to your advantage, who were the first to begin a year ago not only to do *this,* but also to desire *to do it.*

11 But now finish doing it also, so that just as *there was* the readiness to desire it, so *there may be* also the completion of it by your ability.

12 For if the readiness is present, it is acceptable according to what *a person* has, not according to what he does not have.

13 For *this* is not for the ease of others *and* for your affliction, but by way of equality—

14 at this present time your abundance *being a supply* for their need, so that their abundance also may become *a supply* for your need, that there may be equality;

15 as it is written, "HE WHO *gathered* MUCH DID NOT HAVE TOO MUCH, AND HE WHO *gathered* LITTLE HAD NO LACK."

16 But thanks be to God who puts the same earnestness on your behalf in the heart of Titus.

17 For he not only accepted our appeal, but being himself very earnest, he has gone to you of his own accord.

18 We have sent along with him the brother whose fame

NEW CENTURY VERSION

want to help. [9]You know the grace of our Lord Jesus Christ.
You know that Christ was rich, but for you he became poor
so that by his becoming poor you might become rich.
[10]This is what I think you should do: Last year you were
the first to want to give, and you were the first who gave.
[11]So now finish the work you started. Then your "doing"
will be equal to your "wanting to do." Give from what you
have. [12]If you want to give, your gift will be accepted. It
will be judged by what you have, not by what you do not
have. [13]We do not want you to have troubles while other
people are at ease, but we want everything to be equal.
[14]At this time you have plenty. What you have can help
others who are in need. Then later, when they have plenty,
they can help you when you are in need, and all will be
equal. [15]As it is written in the Scriptures, "The person who
gathered more did not have too much, nor did the person
who gathered less have too little."[a]

Titus and His Companions Help

[16]I thank God because he gave Titus the same love for
you that I have. [17]Titus accepted what we asked him to do.
He wanted very much to go to you, and this was his own
idea. [18]We are sending with him the brother who is praised

8:15 [a] **"The person...little."** Quotation from Exodus 16:18.

CONTEMPORARY ENGLISH VERSION

others have shown. [9]You know that our Lord Jesus Christ
was kind enough to give up all his riches and become poor,
so that you could become rich.
[10]A year ago you were the first ones to give, and you
gave because you wanted to. So listen to my advice. [11]I
think you should finish what you started. If you give
according to what you have, you will prove that you are as
eager to give as you were to think about giving. [12]It doesn't
matter how much you have. What matters is how much you
are willing to give from what you have.
[13]I am not trying to make life easier for others by making life harder for you. But it is only fair [14]for you to share
with them when you have so much, and they have so little.
Later, when they have more than enough, and you are in
need, they can share with you. Then everyone will have a
fair share, [15]just as the Scriptures say,

"Those who gathered
too much
had nothing left.
Those who gathered
only a little
had all they needed."

Titus and His Friends

[16]I am grateful that God made Titus care as much about
you as we do. [17]When we begged Titus to visit you, he said
he would. He wanted to because he cared so much for you.
[18]With Titus we are also sending one of the Lord's followers

NEW INTERNATIONAL VERSION

others. 9For you know the grace of our Lord Jesus Christ,
that though he was rich, yet for your sakes he became
poor, so that you through his poverty might become rich.
10And here is my advice about what is best for you in
this matter: Last year you were the first not only to give
but also to have the desire to do so. 11Now finish the work,
so that your eager willingness to do it may be matched by
your completion of it, according to your means. 12For if the
willingness is there, the gift is acceptable according to
what one has, not according to what he does not have.
13Our desire is not that others might be relieved while
you are hard pressed, but that there might be equality.
14At the present time your plenty will supply what they
need, so that in turn their plenty will supply what you
need. Then there will be equality, 15as it is written: "He
who gathered much did not have too much, and he who
gathered little did not have too little."[b]

Titus Sent to Corinth

16I thank God, who put into the heart of Titus the same
concern I have for you. 17For Titus not only welcomed our
appeal, but he is coming to you with much enthusiasm
and on his own initiative. 18And we are sending along

[b] *15* Exodus 16:18

NEW LIVING TRANSLATION

9You know how full of love and kindness our Lord Jesus
Christ was. Though he was very rich, yet for your sakes he
became poor, so that by his poverty he could make you
rich.
10I suggest that you finish what you started a year ago,
for you were the first to propose this idea, and you were
the first to begin doing something about it. 11Now you
should carry this project through to completion just as
enthusiastically as you began it. Give whatever you can
according to what you have. 12If you are really eager to
give, it isn't important how much you are able to give. God
wants you to give what you have, not what you don't
have. 13Of course, I don't mean you should give so much
that you suffer from having too little. I only mean that
there should be some equality. 14Right now you have plen-
ty and can help them. Then at some other time they can
share with you when you need it. In this way, everyone's
needs will be met. 15Do you remember what the Scriptures
say about this? "Those who gathered a lot had nothing left
over, and those who gathered only a little had enough."*

Titus and His Companions

16I am thankful to God that he has given Titus the same
enthusiasm for you that I have. 17He welcomed our request
that he visit you again. In fact, he himself was eager to go
and see you. 18We are also sending another brother with

8:15 Exod 16:18.

NEW KING JAMES VERSION

know the grace of our Lord Jesus Christ, that though He
was rich, yet for your sakes He became poor, that you
through His poverty might become rich.
10And in this I give advice: It is to your advantage not
only to be doing what you began and were desiring to do a
year ago; 11but now you also must complete the doing *of
it;* that as *there was* a readiness to desire *it,* so *there* also
may be a completion out of what *you* have. 12For if there is
first a willing mind, *it is* accepted according to what one
has, *and* not according to what he does not have.
13For *I do* not *mean* that others should be eased and you
burdened; 14but by an equality, *that* now at this time your
abundance *may supply* their lack, that their abundance
also may supply your lack—that there may be equality.
15As it is written, *"He who gathered much had nothing left
over, and he who gathered little had no lack."*[b]

Collection for the Judean Saints

16But thanks *be* to God who puts[c] the same earnest care
for you into the heart of Titus. 17For he not only accepted
the exhortation, but being more diligent, he went to you of
his own accord. 18And we have sent with him the brother

8:15 [b] Exodus 16:18 8:16 [c] NU-Text reads *has put.*

THE MESSAGE

to your love, I am hoping to bring the best out of you. You are familiar with the generosity of our Master, Jesus Christ. Rich as he was, he gave it all away for us—in one stroke he became poor and we became rich.

So here's what I think: The best thing you can do right now is to finish what you started last year and not let those good intentions grow stale. Your heart's been in the right place all along. You've got what it takes to finish it up, so go to it. Once the commitment is clear, you do what you can, not what you can't. The heart regulates the hands. This isn't so others can take it easy while you sweat it out. No, you're shoulder to shoulder with them all the way, your surplus matching their deficit, their surplus matching your deficit. In the end you come out even. As it is written,

"Nothing left over to the one with the most,
Nothing lacking to the one with the least."

I thank God for giving Titus the same devoted concern for you that I have. He was most considerate of how we felt, but his eagerness to go to you and help out with this relief offering is his own idea. We're sending a companion along

KING JAMES VERSION

praise *is* in the gospel throughout all the churches;
19 And not *that* only, but who was also chosen of the churches to travel with us with this grace, which is administered by us to the glory of the same Lord, and *declaration of* your ready mind:
20 Avoiding this, that no man should blame us in this abundance which is administered by us:
21 Providing for honest things, not only in the sight of the Lord, but also in the sight of men.
22 And we have sent with them our brother, whom we have oftentimes proved diligent in many things, but now much more diligent, upon the great confidence which *I have* in you.
23 Whether *any do enquire* of Titus, *he is* my partner and fellowhelper concerning you: or our brethren *be enquired of, they are* the messengers of the churches, *and* the glory of Christ.
24 Wherefore shew ye to them, and before the churches, the proof of your love, and of our boasting on your behalf.

9 For as touching the ministering to the saints, it is superfluous for me to write to you:
2 For I know the forwardness of your mind, for which I boast of you to them of Macedonia, that Achaia was ready a year ago; and your zeal hath provoked very many.

NEW AMERICAN STANDARD BIBLE

in *the things of* the gospel *has spread* through all the churches;
19 and not only *this,* but he has also been appointed by the churches to travel with us in this gracious work, which is being administered by us for the glory of the Lord Himself, and *to show* our readiness,
20 taking precaution so that no one will discredit us in our administration of this generous gift;
21 for we have regard for what is honorable, not only in the sight of the Lord, but also in the sight of men.
22 We have sent with them our brother, whom we have often tested and found diligent in many things, but now even more diligent because of *his* great confidence in you.
23 As for Titus, *he is* my partner and fellow worker among you; as for our brethren, *they are* messengers of the churches, a glory to Christ.
24 Therefore openly before the churches, show them the proof of your love and of our reason for boasting about you.

God Gives Most

9 For it is superfluous for me to write to you about this ministry to the saints;
2 for I know your readiness, of which I boast about you to the Macedonians, *namely,* that Achaia has been prepared since last year, and your zeal has stirred up most of them.

NEW CENTURY VERSION

by all the churches because of his service in preaching the
Good News. 19 Also, this brother was chosen by the
churches to go with us when we deliver this gift of money.
We are doing this service to bring glory to the Lord and to
show that we really want to help.
20 We are being careful so that no one will criticize us for
the way we are handling this large gift. 21 We are trying
hard to do what the Lord accepts as right and also what
people think is right.
22 Also, we are sending with them our brother, who is
always ready to help. He has proved this to us in many
ways, and he wants to help even more now, because he
has much faith in you.
23 Now about Titus—he is my partner who is working
with me to help you. And about the other brothers—they
are sent from the churches, and they bring glory to Christ.
24 So show these men the proof of your love and the reason
we are proud of you. Then all the churches can see it.

Help for Fellow Christians

9 I really do not need to write you about this help for
God's people. 2 I know you want to help. I have been
bragging about this to the people in Macedonia, telling
them that you in Southern Greece have been ready to give
since last year. And your desire to give has made most of

CONTEMPORARY ENGLISH VERSION

who is well known in every church for spreading the good
news. 19 The churches chose this follower to travel with us
while we carry this gift that will bring praise to the Lord and
show how much we hope to help. 20 We don't want anyone
to find fault with the way we handle your generous gift.
21 But we want to do what pleases the Lord and what people
think is right.
22 We are also sending someone else with Titus and the
other follower. We approve of this man. In fact, he has
already shown us many times that he wants to help. And
now he wants to help even more than ever, because he
trusts you so much. 23 Titus is my partner, who works with
me to serve you. The other two followers are sent by the
churches, and they bring honor to Christ. 24 Treat them in
such a way that the churches will see your love and will
know why we bragged about you.

The Money for God's People

9 I don't need to write you about the money you plan to
give for God's people. 2 I know how eager you are to
give. And I have proudly told the Lord's followers in
Macedonia that you people in Achaia have been ready for a
whole year. Now your desire to give has made them want

NEW INTERNATIONAL VERSION

with him the brother who is praised by all the churches for
his service to the gospel. 19What is more, he was chosen
by the churches to accompany us as we carry the offering,
which we administer in order to honor the Lord himself
and to show our eagerness to help. 20We want to avoid
any criticism of the way we administer this liberal gift.
21For we are taking pains to do what is right, not only in
the eyes of the Lord but also in the eyes of men.

22In addition, we are sending with them our brother who
has often proved to us in many ways that he is zealous,
and now even more so because of his great confidence in
you. 23As for Titus, he is my partner and fellow worker
among you; as for our brothers, they are representatives of
the churches and an honor to Christ. 24Therefore show
these men the proof of your love and the reason for our
pride in you, so that the churches can see it.

9 There is no need for me to write to you about this ser-
vice to the saints. 2For I know your eagerness to help,
and I have been boasting about it to the Macedonians,
telling them that since last year you in Achaia were ready
to give; and your enthusiasm has stirred most of them to

NEW LIVING TRANSLATION

Titus. He is highly praised in all the churches as a preach-
er of the Good News. 19He was appointed by the churches
to accompany us as we take the offering to Jerusalem*—a
service that glorifies the Lord and shows our eagerness to
help. 20By traveling together we will guard against any
suspicion, for we are anxious that no one should find fault
with the way we are handling this generous gift. 21We are
careful to be honorable before the Lord, but we also want
everyone else to know we are honorable.

22And we are also sending with them another brother
who has been thoroughly tested and has shown how
earnest he is on many occasions. He is now even more
enthusiastic because of his increased confidence in you.
23If anyone asks about Titus, say that he is my partner
who works with me to help you. And these brothers are
representatives* of the churches. They are splendid exam-
ples of those who bring glory to Christ. 24So show them
your love, and prove to all the churches that our boasting
about you is justified.

The Collection for Christians in Jerusalem

9 I really don't need to write to you about this gift for
the Christians in Jerusalem.* 2For I know how eager
you are to help, and I have been boasting to our friends in
Macedonia that you Christians in Greece* were ready to
send an offering a year ago. In fact, it was your enthusiasm

8:19 See 1 Cor 16:3-4. 8:23 Greek *apostles.* 9:1 Greek *about the offering for the saints.* 9:2 Greek *Achaia,* the southern region of the Greek peninsula.

NEW KING JAMES VERSION

whose praise *is* in the gospel throughout all the churches,
19and not only *that,* but who was also chosen by the
churches to travel with us with this gift, which is adminis-
tered by us to the glory of the Lord Himself and *to show*
your ready mind, 20avoiding this: that anyone should
blame us in this lavish gift which is administered by us—
21providing honorable things, not only in the sight of the
Lord, but also in the sight of men.

22And we have sent with them our brother whom we
have often proved diligent in many things, but now much
more diligent, because of the great confidence which *we
have* in you. 23If *anyone inquires* about Titus, *he is* my
partner and fellow worker concerning you. Or if our
brethren *are inquired about, they are* messengers of the
churches, the glory of Christ. 24Therefore show to them,
and[d] before the churches the proof of your love and of our
boasting on your behalf.

Administering the Gift

9 Now concerning the ministering to the saints, it is
superfluous for me to write to you; 2for I know your
willingness, about which I boast of you to the Macedoni-
ans, that Achaia was ready a year ago; and your zeal has

8:24 *d* NU-Text and M-Text omit *and.*

THE MESSAGE

with him, someone very popular in the churches for his
preaching of the Message. But there's far more to him than
popularity. He's rock-solid trustworthy. The churches
handpicked him to go with us as we travel about doing
this work of sharing God's gifts to honor God as well as we
can, taking every precaution against scandal.

We don't want anyone suspecting us of taking one
penny of this money for ourselves. We're being as careful
in our reputation with the public as in our reputation with
God. That's why we're sending another trusted friend
along. He's proved his dependability many times over, and
carries on as energetically as the day he started. He's
heard much about you, and liked what he's heard—so
much so that he can't wait to get there.

I don't need to say anything further about Titus. We've
been close associates in this work of serving you for a long
time. The brothers who travel with him are delegates from
churches, a real credit to Christ. Show them what you're
made of, the love I've been talking up in the churches. Let
them see it for themselves!

9 If I wrote any more on this relief offering for the poor
Christians, I'd be repeating myself. I know you're on
board and ready to go. I've been bragging about you all
through Macedonia province, telling them, "Achaia prov-
ince has been ready to go on this since last year." Your
enthusiasm by now has spread to most of them.

KING JAMES VERSION

3 Yet have I sent the brethren, lest our boasting of you
should be in vain in this behalf; that, as I said, ye may be
ready:
4 Lest haply if they of Macedonia come with me, and
find you unprepared, we (that we say not, ye) should be
ashamed in this same confident boasting.
5 Therefore I thought it necessary to exhort the
brethren, that they would go before unto you, and make up
beforehand your bounty, whereof ye had notice before,
that the same might be ready, as *a matter of* bounty, and
not as *of* covetousness.
6 ¶ But this *I say*, He which soweth sparingly shall reap
also sparingly; and he which soweth bountifully shall reap
also bountifully.
7 Every man according as he purposeth in his heart, *so
let him give*; not grudgingly, or of necessity: for God loveth
a cheerful giver.
8 And God *is* able to make all grace abound toward you;
that ye, always having all sufficiency in all *things*, may
abound to every good work:
9 (As it is written, He hath dispersed abroad; he hath
given to the poor: his righteousness remaineth for ever.

NEW AMERICAN STANDARD BIBLE

3 But I have sent the brethren, in order that our boast-
ing about you may not be made empty in this case, so
that, as I was saying, you may be prepared;
4 otherwise if any Macedonians come with me and find
you unprepared, we—not to speak of you—will be put to
shame by this confidence.
5 So I thought it necessary to urge the brethren that
they would go on ahead to you and arrange beforehand
your previously promised bountiful gift, so that the same
would be ready as a bountiful gift and not affected by cov-
etousness.
6 Now this *I say*, he who sows sparingly will also reap
sparingly, and he who sows bountifully will also reap
bountifully.
7 Each one *must do* just as he has purposed in his
heart, not grudgingly or under compulsion, for God loves a
cheerful giver.
8 And God is able to make all grace abound to you, so
that always having all sufficiency in everything, you may
have an abundance for every good deed;
9 as it is written,

"HE SCATTERED ABROAD, HE GAVE TO THE POOR,
HIS RIGHTEOUSNESS ENDURES FOREVER."

NEW CENTURY VERSION

them ready to give also. [3]But I am sending the brothers to
you so that our bragging about you in this will not be
empty words. I want you to be ready, as I said you would
be. [4]If any of the people from Macedonia come with me
and find that you are not ready, we will be ashamed that
we were so sure of you. (And you will be ashamed, too!)
[5]So I thought I should ask these brothers to go to you
before we do. They will finish getting in order the generous
gift you promised so it will be ready when we come. And it
will be a generous gift—not one that you did not want to
give.

[6]Remember this: The person who plants a little will have
a small harvest, but the person who plants a lot will have
a big harvest. [7]Each one should give as you have decided
in your heart to give. You should not be sad when you
give, and you should not give because you feel forced to
give. God loves the person who gives happily. [8]And God
can give you more blessings than you need. Then you will
always have plenty of everything—enough to give to every
good work. [9]It is written in the Scriptures:

"He gives freely to the poor.
The things he does are right and will continue
forever." *Psalm 112:9*

CONTEMPORARY ENGLISH VERSION

to give. [3]That's why I am sending Titus and the two others
to you. I want you to be ready, just as I promised. This will
prove that we were not wrong to brag about you.
[4]Some followers from Macedonia may come with me,
and I want them to find that you have the money ready. If
you don't, I would be embarrassed for trusting you to do
this. But you would be embarrassed even more. [5]So I have
decided to ask Titus and the others to spend some time
with you before I arrive. This way they can arrange to col-
lect the money you have promised. Then you will have the
chance to give because you want to, and not because you
feel forced to.
[6]Remember this saying,

"A few seeds make
a small harvest,
but a lot of seeds make
a big harvest."

[7]Each of you must make up your own mind about how
much to give. But don't feel sorry that you must give and
don't feel that you are forced to give. God loves people who
love to give. [8]God can bless you with everything you need,
and you will always have more than enough to do all
kinds of good things for others. [9]The Scriptures say,

"God freely gives his gifts
to the poor,
and always does right."

NEW INTERNATIONAL VERSION

action. [3]But I am sending the brothers in order that our boasting about you in this matter should not prove hollow, but that you may be ready, as I said you would be. [4]For if any Macedonians come with me and find you unprepared, we—not to say anything about you—would be ashamed of having been so confident. [5]So I thought it necessary to urge the brothers to visit you in advance and finish the arrangements for the generous gift you had promised. Then it will be ready as a generous gift, not as one grudgingly given.

Sowing Generously

[6]Remember this: Whoever sows sparingly will also reap sparingly, and whoever sows generously will also reap generously. [7]Each man should give what he has decided in his heart to give, not reluctantly or under compulsion, for God loves a cheerful giver. [8]And God is able to make all grace abound to you, so that in all things at all times, having all that you need, you will abound in every good work. [9]As it is written:

> "He has scattered abroad his gifts to the poor;
> his righteousness endures forever."[a]

[a] *9* Psalm 112:9

NEW LIVING TRANSLATION

that stirred up many of them to begin helping. [3]But I am sending these brothers just to be sure that you really are ready, as I told them you would be, with your money all collected. I don't want it to turn out that I was wrong in my boasting about you. [4]I would be humiliated—and so would you—if some Macedonian Christians came with me, only to find that you still weren't ready after all I had told them! [5]So I thought I should send these brothers ahead of me to make sure the gift you promised is ready. But I want it to be a willing gift, not one given under pressure.

[6]Remember this—a farmer who plants only a few seeds will get a small crop. But the one who plants generously will get a generous crop. [7]You must each make up your own mind as to how much you should give. Don't give reluctantly or in response to pressure. For God loves the person who gives cheerfully. [8]And God will generously provide all you need. Then you will always have everything you need and plenty left over to share with others. [9]As the Scriptures say,

> "Godly people give generously to the poor.
> Their good deeds will never be forgotten."*

9:9 Ps 112:9.

NEW KING JAMES VERSION

stirred up the majority. [3]Yet I have sent the brethren, lest our boasting of you should be in vain in this respect, that, as I said, you may be ready; [4]lest if *some* Macedonians come with me and find you unprepared, we (not to mention you!) should be ashamed of this confident boasting.[a] [5]Therefore I thought it necessary to exhort the brethren to go to you ahead of time, and prepare your generous gift beforehand, which *you had* previously promised, that it may be ready as *a matter of* generosity and not as a grudging obligation.

The Cheerful Giver

[6]But this *I say:* He who sows sparingly will also reap sparingly, and he who sows bountifully will also reap bountifully. [7]*So let* each one *give* as he purposes in his heart, not grudgingly or of necessity; for God loves a cheerful giver. [8]And God *is* able to make all grace abound toward you, that you, always having all sufficiency in all *things,* may have an abundance for every good work. [9]As it is written:

> *"He has dispersed abroad,*
> *He has given to the poor;*
> *His righteousness endures forever."*[b]

9:4 [a] NU-Text reads *this confidence.* **9:9** [b] Psalm 112:9

THE MESSAGE

Now I'm sending the brothers to make sure you're ready, as I said you would be, so my bragging won't turn out to be just so much hot air. If some Macedonians and I happened to drop in on you and found you weren't prepared, we'd all be pretty red-faced—you and us—for acting so sure of ourselves. So to make sure there will be no slip-up, I've recruited these brothers as an advance team to get you and your promised offering all ready before I get there. I want you to have all the time you need to make this offering in your own way. I don't want anything forced or hurried at the last minute.

Remember: A stingy planter gets a stingy crop; a lavish planter gets a lavish crop. I want each of you to take plenty of time to think it over, and make up your own mind what you will give. That will protect you against sob stories and arm-twisting. God loves it when the giver delights in the giving.

God can pour on the blessings in astonishing ways so that you're ready for anything and everything, more than just ready to do what needs to be done. As one psalmist puts it,

> "He throws caution to the winds,
> giving to the needy in reckless abandon.
> His right-living, right-giving ways
> never run out, never wear out."

KING JAMES VERSION

10 Now he that ministereth seed to the sower both minister bread for *your* food, and multiply your seed sown, and increase the fruits of your righteousness;)

11 Being enriched in every thing to all bountifulness, which causeth through us thanksgiving to God.

12 For the administration of this service not only supplieth the want of the saints, but is abundant also by many thanksgivings unto God;

13 Whiles by the experiment of this ministration they glorify God for your professed subjection unto the gospel of Christ, and for *your* liberal distribution unto them, and unto all *men*;

14 And by their prayer for you, which long after you for the exceeding grace of God in you.

15 Thanks *be* unto God for his unspeakable gift.

10 Now I Paul myself beseech you by the meekness and gentleness of Christ, who in presence *am* base among you, but being absent am bold toward you:

2 But I beseech *you*, that I may not be bold when I am present with that confidence, wherewith I think to be bold against some, which think of us as if we walked according to the flesh.

NEW AMERICAN STANDARD BIBLE

10 Now He who supplies seed to the sower and bread for food will supply and multiply your seed for sowing and increase the harvest of your righteousness;

11 you will be enriched in everything for all liberality, which through us is producing thanksgiving to God.

12 For the ministry of this service is not only fully supplying the needs of the saints, but is also overflowing through many thanksgivings to God.

13 Because of the proof given by this ministry, they will glorify God for *your* obedience to your confession of the gospel of Christ and for the liberality of your contribution to them and to all,

14 while they also, by prayer on your behalf, yearn for you because of the surpassing grace of God in you.

15 Thanks be to God for His indescribable gift!

Paul Describes Himself

10 Now I, Paul, myself urge you by the meekness and gentleness of Christ—I who am meek when face to face with you, but bold toward you when absent!

2 I ask that when I am present I *need* not be bold with the confidence with which I propose to be courageous against some, who regard us as if we walked according to the flesh.

NEW CENTURY VERSION

10God is the One who gives seed to the farmer and bread for food. He will give you all the seed you need and make it grow so there will be a great harvest from your goodness. 11He will make you rich in every way so that you can always give freely. And your giving through us will cause many to give thanks to God. 12This service you do not only helps the needs of God's people, it also brings many more thanks to God. 13It is a proof of your faith. Many people will praise God because you obey the Good News of Christ—the gospel you say you believe—and because you freely share with them and with all others. 14And when they pray, they will wish they could be with you because of the great grace that God has given you. 15Thanks be to God for his gift that is too wonderful for words.

Paul Defends His Ministry

10 I, Paul, am begging you with the gentleness and the kindness of Christ. Some people say that I am easy on you when I am with you and bold when I am away. 2They think we live in a worldly way, and I plan to be very bold with them when I come. I beg you that when I come I will not need to use that same boldness with you.

CONTEMPORARY ENGLISH VERSION

10God gives seed to farmers and provides everyone with food. He will increase what you have, so that you can give even more to those in need. 11You will be blessed in every way, and you will be able to keep on being generous. Then many people will thank God when we deliver your gift. 12What you are doing is much more than a service that supplies God's people with what they need. It is something that will make many others thank God. 13The way in which you have proved yourselves by this service will bring honor and praise to God. You believed the message about Christ, and you obeyed it by sharing generously with God's people and with everyone else. 14Now they are praying for you and want to see you, because God used you to bless them so very much. 15Thank God for his gift that is too wonderful for words!

Paul Defends His Work for Christ

10 Do you think I am a coward when I am with you and brave when I am far away? Well, I ask you to listen, because Christ himself was humble and gentle. 2Some people have said that we act like the people of this world. So when I arrive, I expect I will have to be firm and forceful in what I say to them. Please don't make me treat

NEW INTERNATIONAL VERSION

10Now he who supplies seed to the sower and bread for
food will also supply and increase your store of seed and
will enlarge the harvest of your righteousness. 11You will
be made rich in every way so that you can be generous on
every occasion, and through us your generosity will result
in thanksgiving to God.

12This service that you perform is not only supplying the
needs of God's people but is also overflowing in many
expressions of thanks to God. 13Because of the service by
which you have proved yourselves, men will praise God for
the obedience that accompanies your confession of the
gospel of Christ, and for your generosity in sharing with
them and with everyone else. 14And in their prayers for
you their hearts will go out to you, because of the surpass-
ing grace God has given you. 15Thanks be to God for his
indescribable gift!

Paul's Defense of His Ministry

10 By the meekness and gentleness of Christ, I appeal
to you—I, Paul, who am "timid" when face to face
with you, but "bold" when away! 2I beg you that when I
come I may not have to be as bold as I expect to be toward
some people who think that we live by the standards of this

NEW LIVING TRANSLATION

10For God is the one who gives seed to the farmer and then
bread to eat. In the same way, he will give you many
opportunities to do good, and he will produce a great har-
vest of generosity* in you.

11Yes, you will be enriched so that you can give even
more generously. And when we take your gifts to those
who need them, they will break out in thanksgiving to
God. 12So two good things will happen—the needs of the
Christians in Jerusalem will be met, and they will joyfully
express their thanksgiving to God. 13You will be glorifying
God through your generous gifts. For your generosity to
them will prove that you are obedient to the Good News of
Christ. 14And they will pray for you with deep affection
because of the wonderful grace of God shown through you.

15Thank God for his Son—a gift too wonderful for
words!*

Paul Defends His Authority

10 Now I, Paul, plead with you. I plead with the gen-
tleness and kindness that Christ himself would
use, even though some of you say I am bold in my letters
but timid in person. 2I hope it won't be necessary, but
when I come I may have to be very bold with those who
think we act from purely human motives. 3We are human,

9:10 Greek *righteousness.* 9:15 Greek *Thank God for his indescribable gift.*

NEW KING JAMES VERSION

10Now may[c] He who supplies seed to the sower, and
bread for food, supply and multiply the seed you have
sown and increase the fruits of your righteousness, 11while
you are enriched in everything for all liberality, which
causes thanksgiving through us to God. 12For the adminis-
tration of this service not only supplies the needs of the
saints, but also is abounding through many thanksgivings
to God, 13while, through the proof of this ministry, they
glorify God for the obedience of your confession to the
gospel of Christ, and for *your* liberal sharing with them
and all *men,* 14and by their prayer for you, who long for
you because of the exceeding grace of God in you.
15Thanks *be* to God for His indescribable gift!

The Spiritual War

10 Now I, Paul, myself am pleading with you by the
meekness and gentleness of Christ—who in pres-
ence *am* lowly among you, but being absent am bold toward
you. 2But I beg *you* that when I am present I may not be
bold with that confidence by which I intend to be bold
against some, who think of us as if we walked according to

9:10 [c] NU-Text reads *Now He who supplies . . . will supply . . . .*

THE MESSAGE

This most generous God who gives seed to the farmer that
becomes bread for your meals is more than extravagant
with you. He gives you something you can then give away,
which grows into full-formed lives, robust in God, wealthy
in every way, so that you can be generous in every way,
producing with us great praise to God.

Carrying out this social relief work involves far more
than helping meet the bare needs of poor Christians. It also
produces abundant and bountiful thanksgivings to God.
This relief offering is a prod to live at your very best,
showing your gratitude to God by being openly obedient to
the plain meaning of the Message of Christ. You show your
gratitude through your generous offerings to your needy
brothers and sisters, and really toward everyone. Mean-
while, moved by the extravagance of God in your lives,
they'll respond by praying for you in passionate interces-
sion for whatever you need. Thank God for this gift, his
gift. No language can praise it enough!

Tearing Down Barriers

10 And now a personal but most urgent matter; I
write in the gentle but firm spirit of Christ. I hear
that I'm being painted as cringing and wishy-washy when
I'm with you, but harsh and demanding when at a safe
distance writing letters. Please don't force me to take a
hard line when I'm present with you. Don't think that I'll
hesitate a single minute to stand up to those who say I'm
an unprincipled opportunist. Then they'll have to eat their
words.

KING JAMES VERSION

3 For though we walk in the flesh, we do not war after the flesh:

4 (For the weapons of our warfare *are* not carnal, but mighty through God to the pulling down of strong holds;)

5 Casting down imaginations, and every high thing that exalteth itself against the knowledge of God, and bringing into captivity every thought to the obedience of Christ;

6 And having in a readiness to revenge all disobedience, when your obedience is fulfilled.

7 ¶ Do ye look on things after the outward appearance? If any man trust to himself that he is Christ's, let him of himself think this again, that, as he *is* Christ's, even so *are* we Christ's.

8 For though I should boast somewhat more of our authority, which the Lord hath given us for edification, and not for your destruction, I should not be ashamed:

9 That I may not seem as if I would terrify you by letters.

10 For *his* letters, say they, *are* weighty and powerful; but *his* bodily presence *is* weak, and *his* speech contemptible.

11 Let such an one think this, that, such as we are in word by letters when we are absent, such *will we be* also in deed when we are present.

12 ¶ For we dare not make ourselves of the number, or compare ourselves with some that commend themselves: but they measuring themselves by themselves, and comparing themselves among themselves, are not wise.

NEW AMERICAN STANDARD BIBLE

3 For though we walk in the flesh, we do not war according to the flesh,

4 for the weapons of our warfare are not of the flesh, but divinely powerful for the destruction of fortresses.

5 *We are* destroying speculations and every lofty thing raised up against the knowledge of God, and *we are* taking every thought captive to the obedience of Christ,

6 and we are ready to punish all disobedience, whenever your obedience is complete.

7 You are looking at things as they are outwardly. If anyone is confident in himself that he is Christ's, let him consider this again within himself, that just as he is Christ's, so also are we.

8 For even if I boast somewhat further about our authority, which the Lord gave for building you up and not for destroying you, I will not be put to shame,

9 for I do not wish to seem as if I would terrify you by my letters.

10 For they say, "His letters are weighty and strong, but his personal presence is unimpressive and his speech contemptible."

11 Let such a person consider this, that what we are in word by letters when absent, such persons *we are* also in deed when present.

12 For we are not bold to class or compare ourselves with some of those who commend themselves; but when they measure themselves by themselves and compare themselves with themselves, they are without understanding.

NEW CENTURY VERSION

3We do live in the world, but we do not fight in the same
way the world fights. 4We fight with weapons that are dif-
ferent from those the world uses. Our weapons have power
from God that can destroy the enemy's strong places. We
destroy people's arguments 5and every proud thing that
raises itself against the knowledge of God. We capture
every thought and make it give up and obey Christ. 6We
are ready to punish anyone there who does not obey, but
first we want you to obey fully.

7You must look at the facts before you. If you feel sure
that you belong to Christ, you must remember that we
belong to Christ just as you do. 8It is true that we brag
freely about the authority the Lord gave us. But this
authority is to build you up, not to tear you down. So I will
not be ashamed. 9I do not want you to think I am trying to
scare you with my letters. 10Some people say, "Paul's let-
ters are powerful and sound important, but when he is
with us, he is weak. And his speaking is nothing." 11They
should know this: We are not there with you now, so we
say these things in letters. But when we are there with
you, we will show the same authority that we show in our
letters.

12We do not dare to compare ourselves with those who
think they are very important. They use themselves to
measure themselves, and they judge themselves by what
they themselves are. This shows that they know nothing.

CONTEMPORARY ENGLISH VERSION

you that way. 3We live in this world, but we don't act like
its people 4or fight our battles with the weapons of this
world. Instead, we use God's power that can destroy
fortresses. We destroy arguments 5and every bit of pride
that keeps anyone from knowing God. We capture people's
thoughts and make them obey Christ. 6And when you com-
pletely obey him, we will punish anyone who refuses to
obey.

7You judge by appearances.[a] If any of you think you are
the only ones who belong to Christ, then think again. We
belong to Christ as much as you do. 8Maybe I brag a little
too much about the authority that the Lord gave me to
help you and not to hurt you. Yet I am not embarrassed to
brag. 9And I am not trying to scare you with my letters.
10Some of you are saying, "Paul's letters are harsh and
powerful. But in person, he is a weakling and has nothing
worth saying." 11Those people had better understand that
when I am with you, I will do exactly what I say in my
letters.

12We won't dare compare ourselves with those who
think so much of themselves. But they are foolish to com-
pare themselves with themselves. 13We won't brag about

[a] 10.7 *You judge by appearances*: Or "Take a close look at yourselves."

NEW INTERNATIONAL VERSION

world. 3For though we live in the world, we do not wage war as the world does. 4The weapons we fight with are not the weapons of the world. On the contrary, they have divine power to demolish strongholds. 5We demolish arguments and every pretension that sets itself up against the knowledge of God, and we take captive every thought to make it obedient to Christ. 6And we will be ready to punish every act of disobedience, once your obedience is complete.

7You are looking only on the surface of things.[a] If anyone is confident that he belongs to Christ, he should consider again that we belong to Christ just as much as he. 8For even if I boast somewhat freely about the authority the Lord gave us for building you up rather than pulling you down, I will not be ashamed of it. 9I do not want to seem to be trying to frighten you with my letters. 10For some say, "His letters are weighty and forceful, but in person he is unimpressive and his speaking amounts to nothing." 11Such people should realize that what we are in our letters when we are absent, we will be in our actions when we are present.

12We do not dare to classify or compare ourselves with some who commend themselves. When they measure themselves by themselves and compare themselves with themselves, they are not wise. 13We, however, will not

[a] 7 Or *Look at the obvious facts*

NEW LIVING TRANSLATION

but we don't wage war with human plans and methods. 4We use God's mighty weapons, not mere worldly weapons, to knock down the Devil's strongholds. 5With these weapons we break down every proud argument that keeps people from knowing God. With these weapons we conquer their rebellious ideas, and we teach them to obey Christ. 6And we will punish those who remained disobedient after the rest of you became loyal and obedient.

7The trouble with you is that you make your decisions on the basis of appearance.* You must recognize that we belong to Christ just as much as those who proudly declare that they belong to Christ. 8I may seem to be boasting too much about the authority given to us by the Lord. But this authority is to build you up, not to tear you down. And I will not be put to shame by having my work among you destroyed.

9Now this is not just an attempt to frighten you by my letters. 10For some say, "Don't worry about Paul. His letters are demanding and forceful, but in person he is weak, and his speeches are really bad!" 11The ones who say this must realize that we will be just as demanding and forceful in person as we are in our letters.

12Oh, don't worry; I wouldn't dare say that I am as wonderful as these other men who tell you how important they are! But they are only comparing themselves with each other, and measuring themselves by themselves. What foolishness!

10:7 Or *Look at the obvious facts.*

NEW KING JAMES VERSION

the flesh. 3For though we walk in the flesh, we do not war according to the flesh. 4For the weapons of our warfare *are* not carnal but mighty in God for pulling down strongholds, 5casting down arguments and every high thing that exalts itself against the knowledge of God, bringing every thought into captivity to the obedience of Christ, 6and being ready to punish all disobedience when your obedience is fulfilled.

Reality of Paul's Authority

7Do you look at things according to the outward appearance? If anyone is convinced in himself that he is Christ's, let him again consider this in himself, that just as he *is* Christ's, even so we *are* Christ's.[a] 8For even if I should boast somewhat more about our authority, which the Lord gave us[b] for edification and not for your destruction, I shall not be ashamed— 9lest I seem to terrify you by letters. 10"For *his* letters," they say, "*are* weighty and powerful, but *his* bodily presence *is* weak, and *his* speech contemptible." 11Let such a person consider this, that what we are in word by letters when we are absent, such *we will* also *be* in deed when we are present.

Limits of Paul's Authority

12For we dare not class ourselves or compare ourselves with those who commend themselves. But they, measuring themselves by themselves, and comparing themselves among themselves, are not wise. 13We, however, will not

10:7 [a] NU-Text reads *even as we are.* 10:8 [b] NU-Text omits *us.*

THE MESSAGE

The world is unprincipled. It's dog-eat-dog out there! The world doesn't fight fair. But we don't live or fight our battles that way—never have and never will. The tools of our trade aren't for marketing or manipulation, but they are for demolishing that entire massively corrupt culture. We use our powerful God-tools for smashing warped philosophies, tearing down barriers erected against the truth of God, fitting every loose thought and emotion and impulse into the structure of life shaped by Christ. Our tools are ready at hand for clearing the ground of every obstruction and building lives of obedience into maturity.

You stare and stare at the obvious, but you can't see the forest for the trees. If you're looking for a clear example of someone on Christ's side, why do you so quickly cut me out? Believe me, I am quite sure of my standing with Christ. You may think I overstate the authority he gave me, but I'm not backing off. Every bit of my commitment is for the purpose of building you up, after all, not tearing you down.

And what's this talk about me bullying you with my letters? "His letters are brawny and potent, but in person he's a weakling and mumbles when he talks." Such talk won't survive scrutiny. What we write when away, we do when present. We're the exact same people, absent or present, in letter or in person.

We're not, understand, putting ourselves in a league with those who boast that they're our superiors. We wouldn't dare do that. But in all this comparing and grading and competing, they quite miss the point.

KING JAMES VERSION

13 But we will not boast of things without *our* measure, but according to the measure of the rule which God hath distributed to us, a measure to reach even unto you.

14 For we stretch not ourselves beyond *our measure*, as though we reached not unto you: for we are come as far as to you also in *preaching* the gospel of Christ:

15 Not boasting of things without *our* measure, *that is*, of other men's labours; but having hope, when your faith is increased, that we shall be enlarged by you according to our rule abundantly,

16 To preach the gospel in the *regions* beyond you, *and* not to boast in another man's line of things made ready to our hand.

17 But he that glorieth, let him glory in the Lord.

18 For not he that commendeth himself is approved, but whom the Lord commendeth.

11 Would to God ye could bear with me a little in *my* folly: and indeed bear with me.

2 For I am jealous over you with godly jealousy: for I have espoused you to one husband, that I may present *you as* a chaste virgin to Christ.

3 But I fear, lest by any means, as the serpent beguiled Eve through his subtilty, so your minds should be corrupted from the simplicity that is in Christ.

NEW AMERICAN STANDARD BIBLE

13 But we will not boast beyond *our* measure, but within the measure of the sphere which God apportioned to us as a measure, to reach even as far as you.

14 For we are not overextending ourselves, as if we did not reach to you, for we were the first to come even as far as you in the gospel of Christ;

15 not boasting beyond *our* measure, *that is,* in other men's labors, but with the hope that as your faith grows, we will be, within our sphere, enlarged even more by you,

16 so as to preach the gospel even to the regions beyond you, *and* not to boast in what has been accomplished in the sphere of another.

17 But HE WHO BOASTS IS TO BOAST IN THE LORD.

18 For it is not he who commends himself that is approved, but he whom the Lord commends.

Paul Defends His Apostleship

11 I wish that you would bear with me in a little foolishness; but indeed you are bearing with me.

2 For I am jealous for you with a godly jealousy; for I betrothed you to one husband, so that to Christ I might present you *as* a pure virgin.

3 But I am afraid that, as the serpent deceived Eve by his craftiness, your minds will be led astray from the simplicity and purity *of devotion* to Christ.

NEW CENTURY VERSION

13But we will not brag about things outside the work that
was given us to do. We will limit our bragging to the work
that God gave us, and this includes our work with you.
14We are not bragging too much, as we would be if we had
not already come to you. But we have come to you with
the Good News of Christ. 15We limit our bragging to the
work that is ours, not what others have done. We hope
that as your faith continues to grow, you will help our
work to grow much larger. 16We want to tell the Good
News in the areas beyond your city. We do not want to
brag about work that has already been done in another
person's area. 17But, "If someone wants to brag, he should
brag only about the Lord."[a] 18It is not those who say they
are good who are accepted but those who the Lord thinks
are good.

Paul and the False Apostles

11 I wish you would be patient with me even when I
am a little foolish, but you are already doing that.
2I am jealous over you with a jealousy that comes from
God. I promised to give you to Christ, as your only husband. I want to give you as his pure bride. 3But I am afraid
that your minds will be led away from your true and pure
following of Christ just as Eve was tricked by the snake

10:17 [a] "If...Lord." Quotation from Jeremiah 9:24.

CONTEMPORARY ENGLISH VERSION

something we don't have a right to brag about. We will
only brag about the work that God has sent us to do, and
you are part of that work. 14We are not bragging more
than we should. After all, we did bring the message about
Christ to you.

15We don't brag about what others have done, as if we
had done those things ourselves. But I hope that as you
become stronger in your faith, we will be able to reach
many more of the people around you.[b] That has always
been our goal. 16Then we will be able to preach the good
news in other lands where we cannot take credit for work
someone else has already done. 17The Scriptures say, "If
you want to brag, then brag about the Lord." 18You may
brag about yourself, but the only approval that counts is
the Lord's approval.

Paul and the False Apostles

11 Please put up with a little of my foolishness. 2I am
as concerned about you as God is. You were like a
virgin bride I had chosen only for Christ. 3But now I fear
that you will be tricked, just as Eve was tricked by that
lying snake. I am afraid that you might stop thinking
about Christ in an honest and sincere way. 4We told you

[b] 10.15 *we will be able to reach many more of the people around you*: Or "you will praise us even more because of our work among you."

NEW INTERNATIONAL VERSION

boast beyond proper limits, but will confine our boasting to the field God has assigned to us, a field that reaches even to you. [14]We are not going too far in our boasting, as would be the case if we had not come to you, for we did get as far as you with the gospel of Christ. [15]Neither do we go beyond our limits by boasting of work done by others.[b] Our hope is that, as your faith continues to grow, our area of activity among you will greatly expand, [16]so that we can preach the gospel in the regions beyond you. For we do not want to boast about work already done in another man's territory. [17]But, "Let him who boasts boast in the Lord."[c] [18]For it is not the one who commends himself who is approved, but the one whom the Lord commends.

Paul and the False Apostles

11 I hope you will put up with a little of my foolishness; but you are already doing that. [2]I am jealous for you with a godly jealousy. I promised you to one husband, to Christ, so that I might present you as a pure virgin to him. [3]But I am afraid that just as Eve was deceived by the serpent's cunning, your minds may somehow be led astray from your sincere and pure devotion to Christ. [4]For

[b] *13–15* Or *[13]We, however, will not boast about things that cannot be measured, but we will boast according to the standard of measurement that the God of measure has assigned us—a measurement that relates even to you. [14] . . . . [15]Neither do we boast about things that cannot be measured in regard to the work done by others.* [c] *17* Jer. 9:24

NEW LIVING TRANSLATION

[13]But we will not boast of authority we do not have. Our goal is to stay within the boundaries of God's plan for us, and this plan includes our working there with you. [14]We are not going too far when we claim authority over you, for we were the first to travel all the way to you with the Good News of Christ. [15]Nor do we claim credit for the work someone else has done. Instead, we hope that your faith will grow and that our work among you will be greatly enlarged. [16]Then we will be able to go and preach the Good News in other places that are far beyond you, where no one else is working. Then there will be no question about being in someone else's territory. [17]As the Scriptures say,

"The person who wishes to boast
should boast only of what the Lord has done."*

[18]When people boast about themselves, it doesn't count for much. But when the Lord commends someone, that's different!

Paul and the False Apostles

11 I hope you will be patient with me as I keep on talking like a fool. Please bear with me. [2]I am jealous for you with the jealousy of God himself. For I promised you as a pure bride* to one husband, Christ. [3]But I fear that somehow you will be led away from your pure and simple devotion to Christ, just as Eve was deceived by the serpent.

10:17 Jer 9:24. 11:2 Greek *a virgin.*

NEW KING JAMES VERSION

boast beyond measure, but within the limits of the sphere which God appointed us—a sphere which especially includes you. [14]For we are not overextending ourselves (as though *our authority* did not extend to you), for it was to you that we came with the gospel of Christ; [15]not boasting of things beyond measure, *that is,* in other men's labors, but having hope, *that* as your faith is increased, we shall be greatly enlarged by you in our sphere, [16]to preach the gospel in the *regions* beyond you, *and* not to boast in another man's sphere of accomplishment.

[17]But *"he who glories, let him glory in the* L*ORD*."[c] [18]For not he who commends himself is approved, but whom the Lord commends.

Concern for Their Faithfulness

11 Oh, that you would bear with me in a little folly—and indeed you do bear with me. [2]For I am jealous for you with godly jealousy. For I have betrothed you to one husband, that I may present *you as* a chaste virgin to Christ. [3]But I fear, lest somehow, as the serpent deceived Eve by his craftiness, so your minds may be corrupted from the simplicity[a] that is in Christ. [4]For if he who comes

10:17 [c] Jeremiah 9:24 11:3 [a] NU-Text adds *and purity.*

THE MESSAGE

We aren't making outrageous claims here. We're sticking to the limits of what God has set for us. But there can be no question that those limits reach to and include you. We're not moving into someone else's "territory." We were already there with you, weren't we? We were the first ones to get there with the Message of Christ, right? So how can there be any question of overstepping our bounds by writing or visiting you?

We're not barging in on the rightful work of others, interfering with their ministries, demanding a place in the sun with them. What we're hoping for is that as your lives grow in faith, you'll play a part within our expanding work. And we'll all still be within the limits God sets as we proclaim the Message in countries beyond Corinth. But we have no intention of moving in on what others have done and taking credit for it. "If you want to claim credit, claim it for God." What you say about yourself means nothing in God's work. It's what God says about you that makes the difference.

Pseudo-Servants of God

11 Will you put up with a little foolish aside from me? Please, just for a moment. The thing that has me so upset is that I care about you so much—this is the passion of God burning inside me! I promised your hand in marriage to Christ, presented you as a pure virgin to her husband. And now I'm afraid that exactly as the Snake seduced Eve with his smooth patter, you are being lured away from the simple purity of your love for Christ.

KING JAMES VERSION

4 For if he that cometh preacheth another Jesus, whom we have not preached, or *if* ye receive another spirit, which ye have not received, or another gospel, which ye have not accepted, ye might well bear with *him*.

5 ¶ For I suppose I was not a whit behind the very chiefest apostles.

6 But though *I be* rude in speech, yet not in knowledge; but we have been throughly made manifest among you in all things.

7 Have I committed an offence in abasing myself that ye might be exalted, because I have preached to you the gospel of God freely?

8 I robbed other churches, taking wages *of them*, to do you service.

9 And when I was present with you, and wanted, I was chargeable to no man: for that which was lacking to me the brethren which came from Macedonia supplied: and in all *things* I have kept myself from being burdensome unto you, and *so* will I keep *myself*.

10 As the truth of Christ is in me, no man shall stop me of this boasting in the regions of Achaia.

11 Wherefore? because I love you not? God knoweth.

12 But what I do, that I will do, that I may cut off occasion from them which desire occasion; that wherein they glory, they may be found even as we.

13 For such *are* false apostles, deceitful workers, transforming themselves into the apostles of Christ.

NEW AMERICAN STANDARD BIBLE

4 For if one comes and preaches another Jesus whom we have not preached, or you receive a different spirit which you have not received, or a different gospel which you have not accepted, you bear *this* beautifully.

5 For I consider myself not in the least inferior to the most eminent apostles.

6 But even if I am unskilled in speech, yet I am not *so* in knowledge; in fact, in every way we have made *this* evident to you in all things.

7 Or did I commit a sin in humbling myself so that you might be exalted, because I preached the gospel of God to you without charge?

8 I robbed other churches by taking wages *from them* to serve you;

9 and when I was present with you and was in need, I was not a burden to anyone; for when the brethren came from Macedonia they fully supplied my need, and in everything I kept myself from being a burden to you, and will continue to do so.

10 As the truth of Christ is in me, this boasting of mine will not be stopped in the regions of Achaia.

11 Why? Because I do not love you? God knows *I do!*

12 But what I am doing I will continue to do, so that I may cut off opportunity from those who desire an opportunity to be regarded just as we are in the matter about which they are boasting.

13 For such men are false apostles, deceitful workers, disguising themselves as apostles of Christ.

NEW CENTURY VERSION

with his evil ways. [4]You are very patient with anyone who
comes to you and preaches a different Jesus from the one
we preached. You are very willing to accept a spirit or
gospel that is different from the Spirit and Good News you
received from us.

[5]I do not think that those "great apostles" are any better
than I am. [6]I may not be a trained speaker, but I do have
knowledge. We have shown this to you clearly in every
way.

[7]I preached God's Good News to you without pay. I made
myself unimportant to make you important. Do you think
that was wrong? [8]I accepted pay from other churches, tak-
ing their money so I could serve you. [9]If I needed some-
thing when I was with you, I did not trouble any of you.
The brothers who came from Macedonia gave me all that I
needed. I did not allow myself to depend on you in any
way, and I will never depend on you. [10]No one in Southern
Greece will stop me from bragging about that. I say this
with the truth of Christ in me. [11]And why do I not depend
on you? Do you think it is because I do not love you? God
knows that I love you.

[12]And I will continue doing what I am doing now,
because I want to stop those people from having a reason
to brag. They would like to say that the work they brag
about is the same as ours. [13]Such men are not true apos-
tles but are workers who lie. They change themselves to
look like apostles of Christ. [14]This does not surprise us.

CONTEMPORARY ENGLISH VERSION

about Jesus, and you received the Holy Spirit and accepted
our message. But you let some people tell you about
another Jesus. Now you are ready to receive another spirit
and accept a different message. [5]I think I am as good as
any of those super apostles. [6]I may not speak as well as
they do, but I know as much. And this has already been
made perfectly clear to you.

[7]Was it wrong for me to lower myself and honor you by
preaching God's message free of charge? [8]I robbed other
churches by taking money from them to serve you. [9]Even
when I was in need, I still didn't bother you. In fact, some
of the Lord's followers from Macedonia brought me what I
needed. I have not been a burden to you in the past, and I
will never be a burden. [10]As surely as I speak the truth
about Christ, no one in Achaia can stop me from bragging
about this. [11]And it isn't because I don't love you. God
himself knows how much I do love you.

[12]I plan to go on doing just what I have always done.
Then those people won't be able to brag about doing the
same things we are doing. [13]Anyway, they are no more
than false apostles and dishonest workers. They only pre-
tend to be apostles of Christ. [14]And it is no wonder. Even

NEW INTERNATIONAL VERSION

if someone comes to you and preaches a Jesus other than the Jesus we preached, or if you receive a different spirit from the one you received, or a different gospel from the one you accepted, you put up with it easily enough. 5But I do not think I am in the least inferior to those "super-apostles." 6I may not be a trained speaker, but I do have knowledge. We have made this perfectly clear to you in every way.

7Was it a sin for me to lower myself in order to elevate you by preaching the gospel of God to you free of charge? 8I robbed other churches by receiving support from them so as to serve you. 9And when I was with you and needed something, I was not a burden to anyone, for the brothers who came from Macedonia supplied what I needed. I have kept myself from being a burden to you in any way, and will continue to do so. 10As surely as the truth of Christ is in me, nobody in the regions of Achaia will stop this boasting of mine. 11Why? Because I do not love you? God knows I do! 12And I will keep on doing what I am doing in order to cut the ground from under those who want an opportunity to be considered equal with us in the things they boast about.

13For such men are false apostles, deceitful workmen, masquerading as apostles of Christ. 14And no wonder, for

NEW LIVING TRANSLATION

4You seem to believe whatever anyone tells you, even if they preach about a different Jesus than the one we preach, or a different Spirit than the one you received, or a different kind of gospel than the one you believed. 5But I don't think I am inferior to these "super apostles." 6I may not be a trained speaker, but I know what I am talking about. I think you realize this by now, for we have proved it again and again.

7Did I do wrong when I humbled myself and honored you by preaching God's Good News to you without expecting anything in return? 8I "robbed" other churches by accepting their contributions so I could serve you at no cost. 9And when I was with you and didn't have enough to live on, I did not ask you to help me. For the brothers who came from Macedonia brought me another gift. I have never yet asked you for any support, and I never will. 10As surely as the truth of Christ is in me, I will never stop boasting about this all over Greece.* 11Why? Because I don't love you? God knows I do.

12But I will continue doing this to cut the ground out from under the feet of those who boast that their work is just like ours. 13These people are false apostles. They have fooled you by disguising themselves as apostles of Christ.

11:10 Greek *Achaia.*

NEW KING JAMES VERSION

preaches another Jesus whom we have not preached, or *if* you receive a different spirit which you have not received, or a different gospel which you have not accepted—you may well put up with it!

Paul and False Apostles

5For I consider that I am not at all inferior to the most eminent apostles. 6Even though *I am* untrained in speech, yet *I am* not in knowledge. But we have been thoroughly manifested[b] among you in all things.

7Did I commit sin in humbling myself that you might be exalted, because I preached the gospel of God to you free of charge? 8I robbed other churches, taking wages *from them* to minister to you. 9And when I was present with you, and in need, I was a burden to no one, for what I lacked the brethren who came from Macedonia supplied. And in everything I kept myself from being burdensome to you, and so I will keep *myself.* 10As the truth of Christ is in me, no one shall stop me from this boasting in the regions of Achaia. 11Why? Because I do not love you? God knows!

12But what I do, I will also continue to do, that I may cut off the opportunity from those who desire an opportunity to be regarded just as we are in the things of which they boast. 13For such *are* false apostles, deceitful workers, transforming themselves into apostles of Christ. 14And no

11:6 [b] NU-Text omits *been.*

THE MESSAGE

It seems that if someone shows up preaching quite another Jesus than we preached—different spirit, different message—you put up with him quite nicely. But if you put up with these big-shot "apostles," why can't you put up with simple me? I'm as good as they are. It's true that I don't have their voice, haven't mastered that smooth eloquence that impresses you so much. But when I do open my mouth, I at least know what I'm talking about. We haven't kept anything back. We let you in on everything.

I wonder, did I make a bad mistake in proclaiming God's Message to you without asking for something in return, serving you free of charge so that you wouldn't be inconvenienced by me? It turns out that the other churches paid my way so that you could have a free ride. Not once during the time I lived among you did anyone have to lift a finger to help me out. My needs were always supplied by the Christians from Macedonia province. I was careful never to be a burden to you, and I never will be, you can count on it. With Christ as my witness, it's a point of honor with me, and I'm not going to keep it quiet just to protect you from what the neighbors will think. It's not that I don't love you; God knows I do. I'm just trying to keep things open and honest between us.

And I'm not changing my position on this. I'd die before taking your money. I'm giving nobody grounds for lumping me in with those money-grubbing "preachers," vaunting themselves as something special. They're a sorry bunch—pseudo-apostles, lying preachers, crooked workers—posing as Christ's agents but sham to the core. And

KING JAMES VERSION

14 And no marvel; for Satan himself is transformed into an angel of light.

15 Therefore *it is* no great thing if his ministers also be transformed as the ministers of righteousness; whose end shall be according to their works.

16 ¶ I say again, Let no man think me a fool; if otherwise, yet as a fool receive me, that I may boast myself a little.

17 That which I speak, I speak *it* not after the Lord, but as it were foolishly, in this confidence of boasting.

18 Seeing that many glory after the flesh, I will glory also.

19 For ye suffer fools gladly, seeing ye *yourselves* are wise.

20 For ye suffer, if a man bring you into bondage, if a man devour *you*, if a man take *of you*, if a man exalt himself, if a man smite you on the face.

21 I speak as concerning reproach, as though we had been weak. Howbeit whereinsoever any is bold, (I speak foolishly,) I am bold also.

22 ¶ Are they Hebrews? so *am* I. Are they Israelites? so *am* I. Are they the seed of Abraham? so *am* I.

23 Are they ministers of Christ? (I speak as a fool) I *am* more; in labours more abundant, in stripes above measure, in prisons more frequent, in deaths oft.

24 Of the Jews five times received I forty *stripes* save one.

25 Thrice was I beaten with rods, once was I stoned,

NEW AMERICAN STANDARD BIBLE

14 No wonder, for even Satan disguises himself as an angel of light.

15 Therefore it is not surprising if his servants also disguise themselves as servants of righteousness, whose end will be according to their deeds.

16 Again I say, let no one think me foolish; but if *you do,* receive me even as foolish, so that I also may boast a little.

17 What I am saying, I am not saying as the Lord would, but as in foolishness, in this confidence of boasting.

18 Since many boast according to the flesh, I will boast also.

19 For you, being *so* wise, tolerate the foolish gladly.

20 For you tolerate it if anyone enslaves you, anyone devours you, anyone takes advantage of you, anyone exalts himself, anyone hits you in the face.

21 To *my* shame I *must* say that we have been weak *by comparison.*

But in whatever respect anyone *else* is bold—I speak in foolishness—I am just as bold myself.

22 Are they Hebrews? So am I. Are they Israelites? So am I. Are they descendants of Abraham? So am I.

23 Are they servants of Christ?—I speak as if insane—I more so; in far more labors, in far more imprisonments, beaten times without number, often in danger of death.

24 Five times I received from the Jews thirty-nine *lashes.*

25 Three times I was beaten with rods, once I was

NEW CENTURY VERSION

Even Satan changes himself to look like an angel of light.[a]
15So it does not surprise us if Satan's servants also make
themselves look like servants who work for what is right.
But in the end they will be punished for what they do.

Paul Tells About His Sufferings

16I tell you again: No one should think I am a fool. But if
you think so, accept me as you would accept a fool. Then I
can brag a little, too. 17When I brag because I feel sure of
myself, I am not talking as the Lord would talk but as a fool.
18Many people are bragging about their lives in the world. So
I will brag too. 19You are wise, so you will gladly be patient
with fools! 20You are even patient with those who order you
around, or use you, or trick you, or think they are better
than you, or hit you in the face. 21It is shameful to me to say
this, but we were too "weak" to do those things to you!

But if anyone else is brave enough to brag, then I also
will be brave and brag. (I am talking as a fool.) 22Are they
Hebrews?[b] So am I. Are they Israelites? So am I. Are they
from Abraham's family? So am I. 23Are they serving Christ?
I am serving him more. (I am crazy to talk like this.) I have
worked much harder than they. I have been in prison more
often. I have been hurt more in beatings. I have been near
death many times. 24Five times the Jews have given me
their punishment of thirty-nine lashes with a whip. 25Three
different times I was beaten with rods. One time I was

11:14 [a] **angel of light** Messenger from God. The devil fools people so that they think he is from God. 11:22 [b] **Hebrews** A name for the Jews that some Jews were very proud of.

CONTEMPORARY ENGLISH VERSION

Satan tries to make himself look like an angel of light.
15So why does it seem strange for Satan's servants to pre-
tend to do what is right? Someday they will get exactly
what they deserve.

Paul's Sufferings for Christ

16I don't want any of you to think that I am a fool. But if
you do, then let me be a fool and brag a little. 17When I do
all this bragging, I do it as a fool and not for the Lord.
18Yet if others want to brag about what they have done, so
will I. 19And since you are so smart, you will gladly put up
with a fool. 20In fact, you let people make slaves of you
and cheat you and steal from you. Why, you even let them
strut around and slap you in the face. 21I am ashamed to
say that we are too weak to behave in such a way.

If they can brag, so can I, but it is a foolish thing to do.
22Are they Hebrews? So am I. Are they Jews? So am I. Are
they from the family of Abraham? Well, so am I. 23Are they
servants of Christ? I am a fool to talk this way, but I serve
him better than they do. I have worked harder and have
been put in jail more times. I have been beaten with whips
more and have been in danger of death more often.

24Five times the Jews gave me thirty-nine lashes with a
whip. 25Three times the Romans beat me with a big stick,

NEW INTERNATIONAL VERSION

Satan himself masquerades as an angel of light. 15 It is not
surprising, then, if his servants masquerade as servants of
righteousness. Their end will be what their actions
deserve.

Paul Boasts About His Sufferings

16 I repeat: Let no one take me for a fool. But if you do,
then receive me just as you would a fool, so that I may do
a little boasting. 17 In this self-confident boasting I am not
talking as the Lord would, but as a fool. 18 Since many are
boasting in the way the world does, I too will boast. 19 You
gladly put up with fools since you are so wise! 20 In fact,
you even put up with anyone who enslaves you or exploits
you or takes advantage of you or pushes himself forward
or slaps you in the face. 21 To my shame I admit that we
were too weak for that!

What anyone else dares to boast about—I am speaking
as a fool—I also dare to boast about. 22 Are they Hebrews?
So am I. Are they Israelites? So am I. Are they Abraham's
descendants? So am I. 23 Are they servants of Christ? (I am
out of my mind to talk like this.) I am more. I have worked
much harder, been in prison more frequently, been flogged
more severely, and been exposed to death again and again.
24 Five times I received from the Jews the forty lashes
minus one. 25 Three times I was beaten with rods, once I

NEW LIVING TRANSLATION

14 But I am not surprised! Even Satan can disguise himself
as an angel of light. 15 So it is no wonder his servants can
also do it by pretending to be godly ministers. In the end
they will get every bit of punishment their wicked deeds
deserve.

Paul's Many Trials

16 Once again, don't think that I have lost my wits to talk
like this. But even if you do, listen to me, as you would to
a foolish person, while I also boast a little. 17 Such brag-
ging is not something the Lord wants, but I am acting like
a fool. 18 And since others boast about their human
achievements, I will, too. 19 After all, you, who think you
are so wise, enjoy listening to fools! 20 You put up with it
when they make you their slaves, take everything you
have, take advantage of you, put on airs, and slap you in
the face. 21 I'm ashamed to say that we were not strong
enough to do that!

But whatever they dare to boast about—I'm talking like
a fool again—I can boast about it, too. 22 They say they are
Hebrews, do they? So am I. And they say they are
Israelites? So am I. And they are descendants of Abraham?
So am I. 23 They say they serve Christ? I know I sound like
a madman, but I have served him far more! I have worked
harder, been put in jail more often, been whipped times
without number, and faced death again and again. 24 Five
different times the Jews gave me thirty-nine lashes.
25 Three times I was beaten with rods. Once I was stoned.

NEW KING JAMES VERSION

wonder! For Satan himself transforms himself into an
angel of light. 15 Therefore *it is* no great thing if his minis-
ters also transform themselves into ministers of righteous-
ness, whose end will be according to their works.

Reluctant Boasting

16 I say again, let no one think me a fool. If otherwise, at
least receive me as a fool, that I also may boast a little.
17 What I speak, I speak not according to the Lord, but as it
were, foolishly, in this confidence of boasting. 18 Seeing
that many boast according to the flesh, I also will boast.
19 For you put up with fools gladly, since you *yourselves*
are wise! 20 For you put up with it if one brings you into
bondage, if one devours *you,* if one takes *from you,* if one
exalts himself, if one strikes you on the face. 21 To *our*
shame I say that we were too weak for that! But in what-
ever anyone is bold—I speak foolishly—I am bold also.

Suffering for Christ

22 Are they Hebrews? So *am* I. Are they Israelites? So *am* I.
Are they the seed of Abraham? So *am* I. 23 Are they ministers
of Christ?—I speak as a fool—I *am* more: in labors more
abundant, in stripes above measure, in prisons more fre-
quently, in deaths often. 24 From the Jews five times I
received forty *stripes* minus one. 25 Three times I was beaten

THE MESSAGE

no wonder! Satan does it all the time, dressing up as a beautiful angel of light. So it shouldn't surprise us when his servants masquerade as servants of God. But they're not getting by with anything. They'll pay for it in the end.

Many a Long and Lonely Night

Let me come back to where I started—and don't hold it against me if I continue to sound a little foolish. Or if you'd rather, just accept that I am a fool and let me rant on a little. I didn't learn this kind of talk from Christ. Oh, no, it's a bad habit I picked up from the three-ring preachers that are so popular these days. Since you sit there in the judgment seat observing all these shenanigans, you can afford to humor an occasional fool who happens along. You have such admirable tolerance for impostors who rob your freedom, rip you off, steal you blind, put you down—even slap your face! I shouldn't admit it to you, but our stomachs aren't strong enough to tolerate that kind of stuff.

Since you admire the egomaniacs of the pulpit so much (remember, this is your old friend, the fool, talking), let me try my hand at it. Do they brag of being Hebrews, Israelites, the pure race of Abraham? I'm their match. Are they servants of Christ? I can go them one better. (I can't believe I'm saying these things. It's crazy to talk this way! But I started, and I'm going to finish.)

I've worked much harder, been jailed more often, beaten up more times than I can count, and at death's door time after time. I've been flogged five times with the Jews' thirty-nine lashes, beaten by Roman rods three times, pummeled

KING JAMES VERSION

thrice I suffered shipwreck, a night and a day I have been in the deep;

26 *In* journeyings often, *in* perils of waters, *in* perils of robbers, *in* perils by *mine own* countrymen, *in* perils by the heathen, *in* perils in the city, *in* perils in the wilderness, *in* perils in the sea, *in* perils among false brethren;

27 In weariness and painfulness, in watchings often, in hunger and thirst, in fastings often, in cold and nakedness.

28 Beside those things that are without, that which cometh upon me daily, the care of all the churches.

29 Who is weak, and I am not weak? who is offended, and I burn not?

30 If I must needs glory, I will glory of the things which concern mine infirmities.

31 The God and Father of our Lord Jesus Christ, which is blessed for evermore, knoweth that I lie not.

32 In Damascus the governor under Aretas the king kept the city of the Damascenes with a garrison, desirous to apprehend me:

33 And through a window in a basket was I let down by the wall, and escaped his hands.

12 It is not expedient for me doubtless to glory. I will come to visions and revelations of the Lord.

2 I knew a man in Christ above fourteen years ago, (whether in the body, I cannot tell; or whether out of the body, I cannot tell: God knoweth;) such an one caught up to the third heaven.

NEW AMERICAN STANDARD BIBLE

stoned, three times I was shipwrecked, a night and a day I have spent in the deep.

26 *I have been* on frequent journeys, in dangers from rivers, dangers from robbers, dangers from *my* countrymen, dangers from the Gentiles, dangers in the city, dangers in the wilderness, dangers on the sea, dangers among false brethren;

27 *I have been* in labor and hardship, through many sleepless nights, in hunger and thirst, often without food, in cold and exposure.

28 Apart from *such* external things, there is the daily pressure on me *of* concern for all the churches.

29 Who is weak without my being weak? Who is led into sin without my intense concern?

30 If I have to boast, I will boast of what pertains to my weakness.

31 The God and Father of the Lord Jesus, He who is blessed forever, knows that I am not lying.

32 In Damascus the ethnarch under Aretas the king was guarding the city of the Damascenes in order to seize me,

33 and I was let down in a basket through a window in the wall, and *so* escaped his hands.

Paul's Vision

12 Boasting is necessary, though it is not profitable; but I will go on to visions and revelations of the Lord.

2 I know a man in Christ who fourteen years ago—whether in the body I do not know, or out of the body I do not know, God knows—such a man was caught up to the third heaven.

NEW CENTURY VERSION

almost stoned to death. Three times I was in ships that
wrecked, and one of those times I spent a night and a day
in the sea. 26I have gone on many travels and have been in
danger from rivers, thieves, my own people, the Jews, and
those who are not Jews. I have been in danger in cities, in
places where no one lives, and on the sea. And I have been
in danger with false Christians. 27I have done hard and tir-
ing work, and many times I did not sleep. I have been hun-
gry and thirsty, and many times I have been without food. I
have been cold and without clothes. 28Besides all this, there
is on me every day the load of my concern for all the
churches. 29I feel weak every time someone is weak, and I
feel upset every time someone is led into sin.
30If I must brag, I will brag about the things that show I
am weak. 31God knows I am not lying. He is the God and
Father of the Lord Jesus Christ, and he is to be praised for-
ever. 32When I was in Damascus, the governor under King
Aretas wanted to arrest me, so he put guards around the
city. 33But my friends lowered me in a basket through a
hole in the city wall. So I escaped from the governor.

A Special Blessing in Paul's Life

12 I must continue to brag. It will do no good, but I
will talk now about visions and revelations[a] from
the Lord. 2I know a man in Christ who was taken up to the
third heaven fourteen years ago. I do not know whether the
man was in his body or out of his body, but God knows.

12:1 [a] **revelations** Revelation is making known a truth that was hidden.

CONTEMPORARY ENGLISH VERSION

and once my enemies stoned me. I have been shipwrecked
three times, and I even had to spend a night and a day in
the sea. 26During my many travels, I have been in danger
from rivers, robbers, my own people, and foreigners. My
life has been in danger in cities, in deserts, at sea, and
with people who only pretended to be the Lord's followers.
27I have worked and struggled and spent many sleepless
nights. I have gone hungry and thirsty and often had noth-
ing to eat. I have been cold from not having enough
clothes to keep me warm. 28Besides everything else, each
day I am burdened down, worrying about all the churches.
29When others are weak, I am weak too. When others are
tricked into sin, I get angry.[a]
30If I have to brag, I will brag about how weak I am.
31God, the Father of our Lord Jesus, knows I am not lying.
And God is to be praised forever! 32The governor of Damas-
cus at the time of King Aretas had the city gates guarded,
so that he could capture me. 33But I escaped by being let
down in a basket through a window in the city wall.

Visions from the Lord

12 I have to brag. There is nothing to be gained by it,
but I must brag about the visions and other things
that the Lord has shown me. 2I know about one of Christ's
followers who was taken up into the third heaven fourteen
years ago. I don't know if the man was still in his body
when it happened, but God certainly knows.

[a] 11.29 *When others are tricked into sin, I get angry*: Or "When others stumble into sin, I hurt for them."

NEW INTERNATIONAL VERSION

was stoned, three times I was shipwrecked, I spent a night
and a day in the open sea, [26]I have been constantly on the
move. I have been in danger from rivers, in danger from
bandits, in danger from my own countrymen, in danger
from Gentiles; in danger in the city, in danger in the coun-
try, in danger at sea; and in danger from false brothers. [27]I
have labored and toiled and have often gone without
sleep; I have known hunger and thirst and have often gone
without food; I have been cold and naked. [28]Besides every-
thing else, I face daily the pressure of my concern for all
the churches. [29]Who is weak, and I do not feel weak? Who
is led into sin, and I do not inwardly burn?

[30]If I must boast, I will boast of the things that show my
weakness. [31]The God and Father of the Lord Jesus, who is
to be praised forever, knows that I am not lying. [32]In
Damascus the governor under King Aretas had the city of
the Damascenes guarded in order to arrest me. [33]But I was
lowered in a basket from a window in the wall and slipped
through his hands.

Paul's Vision and His Thorn

12 I must go on boasting. Although there is nothing
to be gained, I will go on to visions and revela-
tions from the Lord. [2]I know a man in Christ who fourteen
years ago was caught up to the third heaven. Whether it
was in the body or out of the body I do not know—God

NEW LIVING TRANSLATION

Three times I was shipwrecked. Once I spent a whole night
and a day adrift at sea. [26]I have traveled many weary
miles. I have faced danger from flooded rivers and from
robbers. I have faced danger from my own people, the
Jews, as well as from the Gentiles. I have faced danger in
the cities, in the deserts, and on the stormy seas. And I
have faced danger from men who claim to be Christians
but are not.* [27]I have lived with weariness and pain and
sleepless nights. Often I have been hungry and thirsty and
have gone without food. Often I have shivered with cold,
without enough clothing to keep me warm.

[28]Then, besides all this, I have the daily burden of how
the churches are getting along. [29]Who is weak without my
feeling that weakness? Who is led astray, and I do not
burn with anger?

[30]If I must boast, I would rather boast about the things
that show how weak I am. [31]God, the Father of our Lord
Jesus, who is to be praised forever, knows I tell the truth.
[32]When I was in Damascus, the governor under King
Aretas kept guards at the city gates to catch me. [33]But I
was lowered in a basket through a window in the city wall,
and that's how I got away!

Paul's Vision and His Thorn in the Flesh

12 This boasting is all so foolish, but let me go on. Let
me tell about the visions and revelations I received
from the Lord. [2]I* was caught up into the third heaven

11:26 Greek *from false brothers.* 12:2 Greek *I know a man in Christ who.*

NEW KING JAMES VERSION

with rods; once I was stoned; three times I was ship-
wrecked; a night and a day I have been in the deep; [26]*in*
journeys often, *in* perils of waters, *in* perils of robbers, *in*
perils of *my own* countrymen, *in* perils of the Gentiles, *in*
perils in the city, *in* perils in the wilderness, *in* perils in the
sea, *in* perils among false brethren; [27]in weariness and toil,
in sleeplessness often, in hunger and thirst, in fastings
often, in cold and nakedness— [28]besides the other things,
what comes upon me daily: my deep concern for all the
churches. [29]Who is weak, and I am not weak? Who is made
to stumble, and I do not burn *with indignation?*

[30]If I must boast, I will boast in the things which con-
cern my infirmity. [31]The God and Father of our Lord Jesus
Christ, who is blessed forever, knows that I am not lying.
[32]In Damascus the governor, under Aretas the king, was
guarding the city of the Damascenes with a garrison, desir-
ing to arrest me; [33]but I was let down in a basket through
a window in the wall, and escaped from his hands.

The Vision of Paradise

12 It is doubtless[a] not profitable for me to boast. I will
come to visions and revelations of the Lord: [2]I
know a man in Christ who fourteen years ago—whether in
the body I do not know, or whether out of the body I do not
know, God knows—such a one was caught up to the third

12:1 [a] NU-Text reads *necessary, though not profitable, to boast.*

THE MESSAGE

with rocks once. I've been shipwrecked three times, and
immersed in the open sea for a night and a day. In hard
traveling year in and year out, I've had to ford rivers, fend
off robbers, struggle with friends, struggle with foes. I've
been at risk in the city, at risk in the country, endangered
by desert sun and sea storm, and betrayed by those I
thought were my brothers. I've known drudgery and hard
labor, many a long and lonely night without sleep, many a
missed meal, blasted by the cold, naked to the weather.

And that's not the half of it, when you throw in the daily
pressures and anxieties of all the churches. When someone
gets to the end of his rope, I feel the desperation in my
bones. When someone is duped into sin, an angry fire
burns in my gut.

If I have to "brag" about myself, I'll brag about the
humiliations that make me like Jesus. The eternal and
blessed God and Father of our Master Jesus knows I'm not
lying. Remember the time I was in Damascus and the gov-
ernor of King Aretas posted guards at the city gates to
arrest me? I crawled through a window in the wall, was let
down in a basket, and had to run for my life.

Strength From Weakness

12 You've forced me to talk this way, and I do it against
my better judgment. But now that we're at it, I may
as well bring up the matter of visions and revelations that
God gave me. For instance, I know a man who, fourteen
years ago, was seized by Christ and swept in ecstasy to the
heights of heaven. I really don't know if this took place in the

KING JAMES VERSION

3 And I knew such a man, (whether in the body, or out of the body, I cannot tell: God knoweth;)

4 How that he was caught up into paradise, and heard unspeakable words, which it is not lawful for a man to utter.

5 Of such an one will I glory: yet of myself I will not glory, but in mine infirmities.

6 For though I would desire to glory, I shall not be a fool; for I will say the truth: but *now* I forbear, lest any man should think of me above that which he seeth me *to be*, or *that* he heareth of me.

7 And lest I should be exalted above measure through the abundance of the revelations, there was given to me a thorn in the flesh, the messenger of Satan to buffet me, lest I should be exalted above measure.

8 For this thing I besought the Lord thrice, that it might depart from me.

9 And he said unto me, My grace is sufficient for thee: for my strength is made perfect in weakness. Most gladly therefore will I rather glory in my infirmities, that the power of Christ may rest upon me.

10 Therefore I take pleasure in infirmities, in reproaches, in necessities, in persecutions, in distresses for Christ's sake: for when I am weak, then am I strong.

NEW AMERICAN STANDARD BIBLE

3 And I know how such a man—whether in the body or apart from the body I do not know, God knows—

4 was caught up into Paradise and heard inexpressible words, which a man is not permitted to speak.

5 On behalf of such a man I will boast; but on my own behalf I will not boast, except in regard to *my* weaknesses.

6 For if I do wish to boast I will not be foolish, for I will be speaking the truth; but I refrain *from this,* so that no one will credit me with more than he sees *in* me or hears from me.

A Thorn in the Flesh

7 Because of the surpassing greatness of the revelations, for this reason, to keep me from exalting myself, there was given me a thorn in the flesh, a messenger of Satan to torment me—to keep me from exalting myself!

8 Concerning this I implored the Lord three times that it might leave me.

9 And He has said to me, "My grace is sufficient for you, for power is perfected in weakness." Most gladly, therefore, I will rather boast about my weaknesses, so that the power of Christ may dwell in me.

10 Therefore I am well content with weaknesses, with insults, with distresses, with persecutions, with difficulties, for Christ's sake; for when I am weak, then I am strong.

NEW CENTURY VERSION

3–4And I know that this man was taken up to paradise.[b] I
don't know if he was in his body or away from his body,
but God knows. He heard things he is not able to explain,
things that no human is allowed to tell. 5I will brag about a
man like that, but I will not brag about myself, except
about my weaknesses. 6But if I wanted to brag about
myself, I would not be a fool, because I would be telling the
truth. But I will not brag about myself. I do not want people
to think more of me than what they see me do or hear me
say.
7So that I would not become too proud of the wonderful
things that were shown to me, a painful physical problem[c]
was given to me. This problem was a messenger from
Satan, sent to beat me and keep me from being too proud.
8I begged the Lord three times to take this problem away
from me. 9But he said to me, "My grace is enough for you.
When you are weak, my power is made perfect in you." So
I am very happy to brag about my weaknesses. Then
Christ's power can live in me. 10For this reason I am happy
when I have weaknesses, insults, hard times, sufferings,
and all kinds of troubles for Christ. Because when I am
weak, then I am truly strong.

12:3–4 [b] **paradise** A place where good people go when they die.
12:7 [c] **painful physical problem** Literally, "thorn in the flesh."

CONTEMPORARY ENGLISH VERSION

3As I said, only God really knows if this man was in his
body at the time. 4But he was taken up into paradise,[a]
where he heard things that are too wonderful to tell. 5I will
brag about that man, but not about myself, except to say
how weak I am.
6Yet even if I did brag, I would not be foolish. I would
simply be speaking the truth. But I will try not to say too
much. That way, none of you will think more highly of me
than you should because of what you have seen me do and
say. 7Of course, I am now referring to the wonderful things
I saw. One of Satan's angels was sent to make me suffer
terribly, so that I would not feel too proud.[b]
8Three times I begged the Lord to make this suffering go
away. 9But he replied, "My kindness is all you need. My
power is strongest when you are weak." So if Christ keeps
giving me his power, I will gladly brag about how weak I
am. 10Yes, I am glad to be weak or insulted or mistreated
or to have troubles and sufferings, if it is for Christ.
Because when I am weak, I am strong.

[a] 12.4 *paradise*: In the Greek translation of the Old Testament, this word is used for the Garden of Eden. In New Testament times it was sometimes used for the place where God's people are happy and at rest, as they wait for the final judgment. [b] 12.7 *Of course . . . too proud*: Or "Because of the wonderful things that I saw, one of Satan's angels was sent to make me suffer terribly, so that I would not feel too proud."

NEW INTERNATIONAL VERSION

knows. 3And I know that this man—whether in the body
or apart from the body I do not know, but God knows—
4was caught up to paradise. He heard inexpressible things,
things that man is not permitted to tell. 5I will boast about
a man like that, but I will not boast about myself, except
about my weaknesses. 6Even if I should choose to boast, I
would not be a fool, because I would be speaking the truth.
But I refrain, so no one will think more of me than is war-
ranted by what I do or say.

7To keep me from becoming conceited because of these
surpassingly great revelations, there was given me a thorn
in my flesh, a messenger of Satan, to torment me. 8Three
times I pleaded with the Lord to take it away from me. 9But
he said to me, "My grace is sufficient for you, for my power
is made perfect in weakness." Therefore I will boast all the
more gladly about my weaknesses, so that Christ's power
may rest on me. 10That is why, for Christ's sake, I delight in
weaknesses, in insults, in hardships, in persecutions, in
difficulties. For when I am weak, then I am strong.

NEW LIVING TRANSLATION

fourteen years ago. 3Whether my body was there or just my
spirit, I don't know; only God knows. 4But I do know that I*
was caught up into paradise and heard things so astound-
ing that they cannot be told. 5That experience is something
worth boasting about, but I am not going to do it. I am
going to boast only about my weaknesses. 6I have plenty to
boast about and would be no fool in doing it, because I
would be telling the truth. But I won't do it. I don't want
anyone to think more highly of me than what they can
actually see in my life and my message, 7even though I
have received wonderful revelations from God. But to keep
me from getting puffed up, I was given a thorn in my flesh,
a messenger from Satan to torment me and keep me from
getting proud.

8Three different times I begged the Lord to take it away.
9Each time he said, "My gracious favor is all you need. My
power works best in your weakness." So now I am glad to
boast about my weaknesses, so that the power of Christ
may work through me. 10Since I know it is all for Christ's
good, I am quite content with my weaknesses and with
insults, hardships, persecutions, and calamities. For when
I am weak, then I am strong.

12:4 Greek *he.*

NEW KING JAMES VERSION

heaven. 3And I know such a man—whether in the body or
out of the body I do not know, God knows— 4how he was
caught up into Paradise and heard inexpressible words,
which it is not lawful for a man to utter. 5Of such a one I
will boast; yet of myself I will not boast, except in my infir-
mities. 6For though I might desire to boast, I will not be a
fool; for I will speak the truth. But I refrain, lest anyone
should think of me above what he sees me *to be* or hears
from me.

The Thorn in the Flesh

7And lest I should be exalted above measure by the
abundance of the revelations, a thorn in the flesh was
given to me, a messenger of Satan to buffet me, lest I be
exalted above measure. 8Concerning this thing I pleaded
with the Lord three times that it might depart from me.
9And He said to me, "My grace is sufficient for you, for My
strength is made perfect in weakness." Therefore most
gladly I will rather boast in my infirmities, that the power
of Christ may rest upon me. 10Therefore I take pleasure in
infirmities, in reproaches, in needs, in persecutions, in dis-
tresses, for Christ's sake. For when I am weak, then I am
strong.

THE MESSAGE

body or out of it; only God knows. I also know that this man was hijacked into paradise—again, whether in or out of the body, I don't know; God knows. There he heard the unspeakable spoken, but was forbidden to tell what he heard. This is the man I want to talk about. But about myself, I'm not saying another word apart from the humiliations.

If I had a mind to brag a little, I could probably do it without looking ridiculous, and I'd still be speaking plain truth all the way. But I'll spare you. I don't want anyone imagining me as anything other than the fool you'd encounter if you saw me on the street or heard me talk.

Because of the extravagance of those revelations, and so I wouldn't get a big head, I was given the gift of a handicap to keep me in constant touch with my limitations. Satan's angel did his best to get me down; what he in fact did was push me to my knees. No danger then of walking around high and mighty! At first I didn't think of it as a gift, and begged God to remove it. Three times I did that, and then he told me,

"My grace is enough; it's all you need.
My strength comes into its own in your weakness."

Once I heard that, I was glad to let it happen. I quit focusing on the handicap and began appreciating the gift. It was a case of Christ's strength moving in on my weakness. Now I take limitations in stride, and with good cheer, these limitations that cut me down to size—abuse, accidents, opposition, bad breaks. I just let Christ take over! And so the weaker I get, the stronger I become.

KING JAMES VERSION

11 ¶ I am become a fool in glorying; ye have compelled me: for I ought to have been commended of you: for in nothing am I behind the very chiefest apostles, though I be nothing.

12 Truly the signs of an apostle were wrought among you in all patience, in signs, and wonders, and mighty deeds.

13 For what is it wherein ye were inferior to other churches, except *it be* that I myself was not burdensome to you? forgive me this wrong.

14 Behold, the third time I am ready to come to you; and I will not be burdensome to you: for I seek not yours, but you: for the children ought not to lay up for the parents, but the parents for the children.

15 And I will very gladly spend and be spent for you; though the more abundantly I love you, the less I be loved.

16 But be it so, I did not burden you: nevertheless, being crafty, I caught you with guile.

17 Did I make a gain of you by any of them whom I sent unto you?

18 I desired Titus, and with *him* I sent a brother. Did Titus make a gain of you? walked we not in the same spirit? *walked we* not in the same steps?

NEW AMERICAN STANDARD BIBLE

11 I have become foolish; you yourselves compelled me. Actually I should have been commended by you, for in no respect was I inferior to the most eminent apostles, even though I am a nobody.

12 The signs of a true apostle were performed among you with all perseverance, by signs and wonders and miracles.

13 For in what respect were you treated as inferior to the rest of the churches, except that I myself did not become a burden to you? Forgive me this wrong!

14 Here for this third time I am ready to come to you, and I will not be a burden to you; for I do not seek what is yours, but you; for children are not responsible to save up for *their* parents, but parents for *their* children.

15 I will most gladly spend and be expended for your souls. If I love you more, am I to be loved less?

16 But be that as it may, I did not burden you myself; nevertheless, crafty fellow that I am, I took you in by deceit.

17 *Certainly* I have not taken advantage of you through any of those whom I have sent to you, have I?

18 I urged Titus *to go,* and I sent the brother with him. Titus did not take any advantage of you, did he? Did we not conduct ourselves in the same spirit *and walk* in the same steps?

NEW CENTURY VERSION

Paul's Love for the Christians

[11]I have been talking like a fool, but you made me do it. You are the ones who should say good things about me. I am worth nothing, but those "great apostles" are not worth any more than I am!

[12]When I was with you, I patiently did the things that prove I am an apostle—signs, wonders, and miracles. [13]So you received everything that the other churches have received. Only one thing was different: I was not a burden to you. Forgive me for this!

[14]I am now ready to visit you the third time, and I will not be a burden to you. I want nothing from you, except you. Children should not have to save up to give to their parents. Parents should save to give to their children. [15]So I am happy to give everything I have for you, even myself. If I love you more, will you love me less?

[16]It is clear I was not a burden to you, but you think I was tricky and lied to catch you. [17]Did I cheat you by using any of the messengers I sent to you? No, you know I did not. [18]I asked Titus to go to you, and I sent our brother with him. Titus did not cheat you, did he? No, you know that Titus and I did the same thing and with the same spirit.

CONTEMPORARY ENGLISH VERSION

Paul's Concern for the Lord's Followers at Corinth

[11]I have been making a fool of myself. But you forced me to do it, when you should have been speaking up for me. I may be nothing at all, but I am as good as those super apostles. [12]When I was with you, I was patient and worked all the powerful miracles and signs and wonders of a true apostle. [13]You missed out on only one blessing that the other churches received. That is, you didn't have to support me. Forgive me for doing you wrong.

[14]I am planning to visit you for the third time. But I still won't make a burden of myself. What I really want is you, and not what you have. Children are not supposed to save up for their parents, but parents are supposed to take care of their children. [15]So I will gladly give all that I have and all that I am. Will you love me less for loving you too much? [16]You agree that I wasn't a burden to you. Maybe that's because I was trying to catch you off guard and trick you. [17]Were you cheated by any of those I sent to you? [18]I urged Titus to visit you, and I sent another follower with him. But Titus didn't cheat you, and we felt and behaved the same way he did.

NEW INTERNATIONAL VERSION

Paul's Concern for the Corinthians

11I have made a fool of myself, but you drove me to it. I ought to have been commended by you, for I am not in the least inferior to the "super-apostles," even though I am nothing. 12The things that mark an apostle—signs, wonders and miracles—were done among you with great perseverance. 13How were you inferior to the other churches, except that I was never a burden to you? Forgive me this wrong!

14Now I am ready to visit you for the third time, and I will not be a burden to you, because what I want is not your possessions but you. After all, children should not have to save up for their parents, but parents for their children. 15So I will very gladly spend for you everything I have and expend myself as well. If I love you more, will you love me less? 16Be that as it may, I have not been a burden to you. Yet, crafty fellow that I am, I caught you by trickery! 17Did I exploit you through any of the men I sent you? 18I urged Titus to go to you and I sent our brother with him. Titus did not exploit you, did he? Did we not act in the same spirit and follow the same course?

NEW LIVING TRANSLATION

Paul's Concern for the Corinthians

11You have made me act like a fool—boasting like this. You ought to be writing commendations for me, for I am not at all inferior to these "super apostles," even though I am nothing at all. 12When I was with you, I certainly gave you every proof that I am truly an apostle, sent to you by God himself. For I patiently did many signs and wonders and miracles among you. 13The only thing I didn't do, which I do in the other churches, was to become a burden to you. Please forgive me for this wrong!

14Now I am coming to you for the third time, and I will not be a burden to you. I don't want what you have; I want you. And anyway, little children don't pay for their parents' food. It's the other way around; parents supply food for their children. 15I will gladly spend myself and all I have for your spiritual good, even though it seems that the more I love you, the less you love me.

16Some of you admit I was not a burden to you. But they still think I was sneaky and took advantage of you by trickery. 17But how? Did any of the men I sent to you take advantage of you? 18When I urged Titus to visit you and sent our other brother with him, did Titus take advantage of you? No, of course not! For we both have the same Spirit and walk in each other's steps, doing things the same way.

NEW KING JAMES VERSION

Signs of an Apostle

11I have become a fool in boasting;[b] you have compelled me. For I ought to have been commended by you; for in nothing was I behind the most eminent apostles, though I am nothing. 12Truly the signs of an apostle were accomplished among you with all perseverance, in signs and wonders and mighty deeds. 13For what is it in which you were inferior to other churches, except that I myself was not burdensome to you? Forgive me this wrong!

Love for the Church

14Now *for* the third time I am ready to come to you. And I will not be burdensome to you; for I do not seek yours, but you. For the children ought not to lay up for the parents, but the parents for the children. 15And I will very gladly spend and be spent for your souls; though the more abundantly I love you, the less I am loved.

16But be that *as it may,* I did not burden you. Nevertheless, being crafty, I caught you by cunning! 17Did I take advantage of you by any of those whom I sent to you? 18I urged Titus, and sent our brother with *him.* Did Titus take advantage of you? Did we not walk in the same spirit? Did *we* not *walk* in the same steps?

12:11 [b] NU-Text omits *in boasting.*

THE MESSAGE

Well, now I've done it! I've made a complete fool of myself by going on like this. But it's not all my fault; you put me up to it. You should have been doing this for me, sticking up for me and commending me instead of making me do it for myself. You know from personal experience that even if I'm a nobody, a nothing, I wasn't second-rate compared to those big-shot apostles you're so taken with. All the signs that mark a true apostle were in evidence while I was with you through both good times and bad: signs of portent, signs of wonder, signs of power. Did you get less of me or of God than any of the other churches? The only thing you got less of was less responsibility for my upkeep. Well, I'm sorry. Forgive me for depriving you.

Everything is in readiness now for this, my third visit to you. But don't worry about it; you won't have to put yourselves out. I'll be no more of a bother to you this time than on the other visits. I have no interest in what you have—only in you. Children shouldn't have to look out for their parents; parents look out for the children. I'd be most happy to empty my pockets, even mortgage my life, for your good. So how does it happen that the more I love you, the less I'm loved?

And why is it that I keep coming across these whiffs of gossip about how my self-support was a front behind which I worked an elaborate scam? Where's the evidence? Did I cheat or trick you through anyone I sent? I asked Titus to visit, and sent some brothers along. Did they swindle you out of anything? And haven't we always been just as aboveboard, just as honest?

KING JAMES VERSION

19 Again, think ye that we excuse ourselves unto you? we speak before God in Christ: but *we do* all things, dearly beloved, for your edifying.

20 For I fear, lest, when I come, I shall not find you such as I would, and *that* I shall be found unto you such as ye would not: lest *there be* debates, envyings, wraths, strifes, backbitings, whisperings, swellings, tumults:

21 *And* lest, when I come again, my God will humble me among you, and *that* I shall bewail many which have sinned already, and have not repented of the uncleanness and fornication and lasciviousness which they have committed.

13 This *is* the third *time* I am coming to you. In the mouth of two or three witnesses shall every word be established.

2 I told you before, and foretell you, as if I were present, the second time; and being absent now I write to them which heretofore have sinned, and to all other, that, if I come again, I will not spare:

3 Since ye seek a proof of Christ speaking in me, which to you-ward is not weak, but is mighty in you.

NEW AMERICAN STANDARD BIBLE

19 All this time you have been thinking that we are defending ourselves to you. *Actually,* it is in the sight of God that we have been speaking in Christ; and all for your upbuilding, beloved.

20 For I am afraid that perhaps when I come I may find you to be not what I wish and may be found by you to be not what you wish; that perhaps *there will be* strife, jealousy, angry tempers, disputes, slanders, gossip, arrogance, disturbances;

21 I am afraid that when I come again my God may humiliate me before you, and I may mourn over many of those who have sinned in the past and not repented of the impurity, immorality and sensuality which they have practiced.

Examine Yourselves

13 This is the third time I am coming to you. EVERY FACT IS TO BE CONFIRMED BY THE TESTIMONY OF TWO OR THREE WITNESSES.

2 I have previously said when present the second time, and though now absent I say in advance to those who have sinned in the past and to all the rest *as well,* that if I come again I will not spare *anyone,*

3 since you are seeking for proof of the Christ who speaks in me, and who is not weak toward you, but mighty in you.

NEW CENTURY VERSION

[19]Do you think we have been defending ourselves to you
all this time? We have been speaking in Christ and before
God. You are our dear friends, and everything we do is to
make you stronger. [20]I am afraid that when I come, you
will not be what I want you to be, and I will not be what
you want me to be. I am afraid that among you there may
be arguing, jealousy, anger, selfish fighting, evil talk, gos-
sip, pride, and confusion. [21]I am afraid that when I come
to you again, my God will make me ashamed before you. I
may be saddened by many of those who have sinned
because they have not changed their hearts or turned from
their sexual sins and the shameful things they have done.

Final Warnings and Greetings

13 I will come to you for the third time. "Every case
must be proved by two or three witnesses."[a]
[2]When I was with you the second time, I gave a warning to
those who had sinned. Now I am away from you, and I
give a warning to all the others. When I come to you
again, I will not be easy with them. [3]You want proof that
Christ is speaking through me. My proof is that he is not
weak among you, but he is powerful. [4]It is true that he

13:1 [a] **"Every...witnesses."** Quotation from Deuteronomy 19:15.

CONTEMPORARY ENGLISH VERSION

[19]Have you been thinking all along that we have been
defending ourselves to you? Actually, we have been speak-
ing to God as followers of Christ. But, my friends, we did it
all for your good.

[20]I am afraid that when I come, we won't be pleased
with each other. I fear that some of you may be arguing or
jealous or angry or selfish or gossiping or insulting each
other. I even fear that you may be proud and acting like a
mob. [21]I am afraid God will make me ashamed when I visit
you again. I will feel like crying because many of you have
never given up your old sins. You are still doing things
that are immoral, indecent, and shameful.

Final Warnings and Greetings

13 I am on my way to visit you for the third time. And
as the Scriptures say, "Any charges must be
proved true by at least two or three witnesses." [2]During
my second visit I warned you that I would punish you
and anyone else who doesn't stop sinning. I am far away
from you now, but I give you the same warning. [3]This
should prove to you that I am speaking for Christ. When he
corrects you, he won't be weak. He will be powerful!

NEW INTERNATIONAL VERSION

19 Have you been thinking all along that we have been defending ourselves to you? We have been speaking in the sight of God as those in Christ; and everything we do, dear friends, is for your strengthening. 20 For I am afraid that when I come I may not find you as I want you to be, and you may not find me as you want me to be. I fear that there may be quarreling, jealousy, outbursts of anger, factions, slander, gossip, arrogance and disorder. 21 I am afraid that when I come again my God will humble me before you, and I will be grieved over many who have sinned earlier and have not repented of the impurity, sexual sin and debauchery in which they have indulged.

Final Warnings

13 This will be my third visit to you. "Every matter must be established by the testimony of two or three witnesses."[a] 2 I already gave you a warning when I was with you the second time. I now repeat it while absent: On my return I will not spare those who sinned earlier or any of the others, 3 since you are demanding proof that Christ is speaking through me. He is not weak in dealing with you, but is powerful among you. 4 For to be

[a] *1* Deut. 19:15

NEW LIVING TRANSLATION

19 Perhaps you think we are saying all this just to defend ourselves. That isn't it at all. We tell you this as Christ's servants, and we know that God is listening. Everything we do, dear friends, is for your benefit. 20 For I am afraid that when I come to visit you I won't like what I find, and then you won't like my response. I am afraid that I will find quarreling, jealousy, outbursts of anger, selfishness, backstabbing, gossip, conceit, and disorderly behavior. 21 Yes, I am afraid that when I come, God will humble me again because of you. And I will have to grieve because many of you who sinned earlier have not repented of your impurity, sexual immorality, and eagerness for lustful pleasure.

Paul's Final Advice

13 This is the third time I am coming to visit you. As the Scriptures say, "The facts of every case must be established by the testimony of two or three witnesses."* 2 I have already warned those who had been sinning when I was there on my second visit. Now I again warn them and all others, just as I did before, that this next time I will not spare them.

3 I will give you all the proof you want that Christ speaks through me. Christ is not weak in his dealings with you; he is a mighty power among you. 4 Although he died on the

13:1 Deut 19:15.

NEW KING JAMES VERSION

19 Again, do you think[c] that we excuse ourselves to you? We speak before God in Christ. But *we do* all things, beloved, for your edification. 20 For I fear lest, when I come, I shall not find you such as I wish, and *that* I shall be found by you such as you do not wish; lest *there be* contentions, jealousies, outbursts of wrath, selfish ambitions, backbitings, whisperings, conceits, tumults; 21 lest, when I come again, my God will humble me among you, and I shall mourn for many who have sinned before and have not repented of the uncleanness, fornication, and lewdness which they have practiced.

Coming with Authority

13 This *will be* the third *time* I am coming to you. *"By the mouth of two or three witnesses every word shall be established."*[a] 2 I have told you before, and foretell as if I were present the second time, and now being absent I write[b] to those who have sinned before, and to all the rest, that if I come again I will not spare— 3 since you seek a proof of Christ speaking in me, who is not weak toward you, but mighty in you. 4 For though He

12:19 [c] NU-Text reads *You have been thinking for a long time. . . .*
13:1 [a] Deuteronomy 19:15 13:2 [b] NU-Text omits *I write.*

THE MESSAGE

I hope you don't think that all along we've been making our defense before you, the jury. You're not the jury; God is the jury—God revealed in Christ—and we make our case before him. And we've gone to all the trouble of supporting ourselves so that we won't be in the way or get in the way of your growing up.

I do admit that I have fears that when I come you'll disappoint me and I'll disappoint you, and in frustration with each other everything will fall to pieces—quarrels, jealousy, flaring tempers, taking sides, angry words, vicious rumors, swelled heads, and general bedlam. I don't look forward to a second humiliation by God among you, compounded by hot tears over that crowd that keeps sinning over and over in the same old ways, who refuse to turn away from the pigsty of evil, sexual disorder, and indecency in which they wallow.

He's Alive Now!

13 Well, this is my third visit coming up. Remember the Scripture that says, "A matter becomes clear after two or three witnesses give evidence"? On my second visit I warned that bunch that keeps sinning over and over in the same old ways that when I came back I wouldn't go easy on them. Now, preparing for the third, I'm saying it again from a distance. If you haven't changed your ways by the time I get there, look out. You who have been demanding proof that Christ speaks through me will get more than you bargained for. You'll get the full force of Christ, don't think you won't. He was sheer weakness and

KING JAMES VERSION

4 For though he was crucified through weakness, yet he
liveth by the power of God. For we also are weak in him,
but we shall live with him by the power of God toward
you.
5 Examine yourselves, whether ye be in the faith; prove
your own selves. Know ye not your own selves, how that
Jesus Christ is in you, except ye be reprobates?
6 But I trust that ye shall know that we are not repro-
bates.
7 ¶ Now I pray to God that ye do no evil; not that we
should appear approved, but that ye should do that which
is honest, though we be as reprobates.
8 For we can do nothing against the truth, but for the
truth.
9 For we are glad, when we are weak, and ye are
strong: and this also we wish, *even* your perfection.
10 Therefore I write these things being absent, lest
being present I should use sharpness, according to the
power which the Lord hath given me to edification, and
not to destruction.
11 ¶ Finally, brethren, farewell. Be perfect, be of good
comfort, be of one mind, live in peace; and the God of love
and peace shall be with you.

NEW AMERICAN STANDARD BIBLE

4 For indeed He was crucified because of weakness, yet
He lives because of the power of God. For we also are weak
[1]in Him, yet we will live with Him because of the power of
God *directed* toward you.
5 Test yourselves *to see* if you are in the faith; examine
yourselves! Or do you not recognize this about yourselves,
that Jesus Christ is in you—unless indeed you fail the test?
6 But I trust that you will realize that we ourselves do
not fail the test.
7 Now we pray to God that you do no wrong; not that
we ourselves may appear approved, but that you may do
what is right, even though we may appear unapproved.
8 For we can do nothing against the truth, but *only* for
the truth.
9 For we rejoice when we ourselves are weak but you
are strong; this we also pray for, that you be made com-
plete.
10 For this reason I am writing these things while
absent, so that when present I *need* not use severity, in
accordance with the authority which the Lord gave me for
building up and not for tearing down.
11 Finally, brethren, rejoice, be made complete, be com-
forted, be like-minded, live in peace; and the God of love
and peace will be with you.

13:4 [1] One early ms reads *with Him*

NEW CENTURY VERSION

was weak when he was killed on the cross, but he lives
now by God's power. It is true that we are weak in Christ,
but for you we will be alive in Christ by God's power.
5 Look closely at yourselves. Test yourselves to see if you
are living in the faith. You know that Jesus Christ is in
you—unless you fail the test. 6 But I hope you will see that
we ourselves have not failed the test. 7 We pray to God that
you will not do anything wrong. It is not important to see
that we have passed the test, but it is important that you
do what is right, even if it seems we have failed. 8 We can-
not do anything against the truth, but only for the truth.
9 We are happy to be weak, if you are strong, and we pray
that you will become complete. 10 I am writing this while I
am away from you so that when I come I will not have to
be harsh in my use of authority. The Lord gave me this
authority to build you up, not to tear you down.
11 Now, brothers and sisters, I say good-bye. Try to be
complete. Do what I have asked you to do. Agree with each
other, and live in peace. Then the God of love and peace
will be with you.

CONTEMPORARY ENGLISH VERSION

4 Although he was weak when he was nailed to the cross,
he now lives by the power of God. We are weak, just as
Christ was. But you will see that we will live by the power
of God, just as Christ does.
5 Test yourselves and find out if you really are true to
your faith. If you pass the test, you will discover that
Christ is living in you. But if Christ isn't living in you, you
have failed. 6 I hope you will discover that we have not
failed. 7 We pray that you will stop doing evil things. We
don't pray like this to make ourselves look good, but to get
you to do right, even if we are failures.
8 All we can do is to follow the truth and not fight
against it. 9 Even though we are weak, we are glad that
you are strong, and we pray that you will do even better.
10 I am writing these things to you before I arrive. This way
I won't have to be hard on you when I use the authority
that the Lord has given me. I was given this authority, so
that I could help you and not destroy you.
11 Good-by, my friends. Do better and pay attention to
what I have said. Try to get along and live peacefully with
each other.
Now I pray that God, who gives love and peace, will be

NEW INTERNATIONAL VERSION

sure, he was crucified in weakness, yet he lives by God's power. Likewise, we are weak in him, yet by God's power we will live with him to serve you.

5Examine yourselves to see whether you are in the faith; test yourselves. Do you not realize that Christ Jesus is in you—unless, of course, you fail the test? 6And I trust that you will discover that we have not failed the test. 7Now we pray to God that you will not do anything wrong. Not that people will see that we have stood the test but that you will do what is right even though we may seem to have failed. 8For we cannot do anything against the truth, but only for the truth. 9We are glad whenever we are weak but you are strong; and our prayer is for your perfection. 10This is why I write these things when I am absent, that when I come I may not have to be harsh in my use of authority—the authority the Lord gave me for building you up, not for tearing you down.

Final Greetings

11Finally, brothers, good-by. Aim for perfection, listen to my appeal, be of one mind, live in peace. And the God of love and peace will be with you.

NEW LIVING TRANSLATION

cross in weakness, he now lives by the mighty power of God. We, too, are weak, but we live in him and have God's power—the power we use in dealing with you.

5Examine yourselves to see if your faith is really genuine. Test yourselves. If you cannot tell that Jesus Christ is among you,* it means you have failed the test. 6I hope you recognize that we have passed the test and are approved by God.

7We pray to God that you will not do anything wrong. We pray this, not to show that our ministry to you has been successful, but because we want you to do right even if we ourselves seem to have failed. 8Our responsibility is never to oppose the truth, but to stand for the truth at all times. 9We are glad to be weak, if you are really strong. What we pray for is your restoration to maturity.

10I am writing this to you before I come, hoping that I won't need to deal harshly with you when I do come. For I want to use the authority the Lord has given me to build you up, not to tear you down.

Paul's Final Greetings

11Dear brothers and sisters,* I close my letter with these last words: Rejoice. Change your ways. Encourage each other. Live in harmony and peace. Then the God of love and peace will be with you.

13:5 Or *in you.* 13:11 Greek *Brothers.*

NEW KING JAMES VERSION

was crucified in weakness, yet He lives by the power of God. For we also are weak in Him, but we shall live with Him by the power of God toward you.

5Examine yourselves *as to* whether you are in the faith. Test yourselves. Do you not know yourselves, that Jesus Christ is in you?—unless indeed you are disqualified. 6But I trust that you will know that we are not disqualified.

Paul Prefers Gentleness

7Now I[c] pray to God that you do no evil, not that we should appear approved, but that you should do what is honorable, though we may seem disqualified. 8For we can do nothing against the truth, but for the truth. 9For we are glad when we are weak and you are strong. And this also we pray, that you may be made complete. 10Therefore I write these things being absent, lest being present I should use sharpness, according to the authority which the Lord has given me for edification and not for destruction.

Greetings and Benediction

11Finally, brethren, farewell. Become complete. Be of good comfort, be of one mind, live in peace; and the God of love and peace will be with you.

13:7 [c] NU-Text reads *we.*

THE MESSAGE

humiliation when he was killed on the Cross, but oh, he's alive now—in the mighty power of God! We weren't much to look at, either, when we were humiliated among you, but when we deal with you this next time, we'll be alive in Christ, strengthened by God.

Test yourselves to make sure you are solid in the faith. Don't drift along taking everything for granted. Give yourselves regular checkups. You need firsthand evidence, not mere hearsay, that Jesus Christ is in you. Test it out. If you fail the test, do something about it. I hope the test won't show that we have failed. But if it comes to that, we'd rather the test showed our failure than yours. We're rooting for the truth to win out in you. We couldn't possibly do otherwise.

We don't just put up with our limitations; we celebrate them, and then go on to celebrate every strength, every triumph of the truth in you. We pray hard that it will all come together in your lives.

I'm writing this to you now so that when I come I won't have to say another word on the subject. The authority the Master gave me is for putting people together, not taking them apart. I want to get on with it, and not have to spend time on reprimands.

✢

And that's about it, friends. Be cheerful. Keep things in good repair. Keep your spirits up. Think in harmony. Be agreeable. Do all that, and the God of love and peace will

KING JAMES VERSION

12 Greet one another with an holy kiss.
13 All the saints salute you.
14 The grace of the Lord Jesus Christ, and the love of God, and the communion of the Holy Ghost, *be* with you all. Amen.

NEW AMERICAN STANDARD BIBLE

12 Greet one another with a holy kiss.
13 All the saints greet you.
14 The grace of the Lord Jesus Christ, and the love of God, and the fellowship of the Holy Spirit, be with you all.

NEW CENTURY VERSION

12Greet each other with a holy kiss. 13All of God's holy
people send greetings to you.
14The grace of the Lord Jesus Christ, the love of God, and the fellowship of the Holy Spirit be with you all.

CONTEMPORARY ENGLISH VERSION

with you. 12Give each other a warm greeting. All of God's people send their greetings.
13I pray that the Lord Jesus Christ will bless you and be kind to you! May God bless you with his love, and may the Holy Spirit join all your hearts together.

NEW INTERNATIONAL VERSION

12Greet one another with a holy kiss. 13All the saints send their greetings.

14May the grace of the Lord Jesus Christ, and the love of God, and the fellowship of the Holy Spirit be with you all.

NEW LIVING TRANSLATION

12Greet each other in Christian love.* All the Christians here send you their greetings.

13May the grace of our Lord Jesus Christ, the love of God, and the fellowship of the Holy Spirit be with you all.*

13:12 Greek *with a sacred kiss.* 13:12-13 Some English versions divide verse 12 into verses 12 and 13, and then verse 13 becomes verse 14.

NEW KING JAMES VERSION

12Greet one another with a holy kiss.

13All the saints greet you.

14The grace of the Lord Jesus Christ, and the love of God, and the communion of the Holy Spirit *be* with you all. Amen.

THE MESSAGE

be with you for sure. Greet one another with a holy embrace. All the brothers and sisters here say hello.

The amazing grace of the Master, Jesus Christ, the extravagant love of God, the intimate friendship of the Holy Spirit, be with all of you.

KING JAMES VERSION

THE EPISTLE OF ST. PAUL TO THE

GALATIANS

1 Paul, an apostle, (not of men, neither by man, but by Jesus Christ, and God the Father, who raised him from the dead;)

2 And all the brethren which are with me, unto the churches of Galatia:

3 Grace *be* to you and peace from God the Father, and *from* our Lord Jesus Christ,

4 Who gave himself for our sins, that he might deliver us from this present evil world, according to the will of God and our Father:

5 To whom *be* glory for ever and ever. Amen.

6 ¶ I marvel that ye are so soon removed from him that called you into the grace of Christ unto another gospel:

7 Which is not another; but there be some that trouble you, and would pervert the gospel of Christ.

8 But though we, or an angel from heaven, preach any other gospel unto you than that which we have preached unto you, let him be accursed.

NEW AMERICAN STANDARD BIBLE

THE LETTER OF PAUL TO THE

GALATIANS

Introduction

1 Paul, an apostle (not *sent* from men nor through the agency of man, but through Jesus Christ and God the Father, who raised Him from the dead),

2 and all the brethren who are with me,

To the churches of Galatia:

3 Grace to you and peace from God our Father and the Lord Jesus Christ,

4 who gave Himself for our sins so that He might rescue us from this present evil age, according to the will of our God and Father,

5 to whom *be* the glory forevermore. Amen.

Perversion of the Gospel

6 I am amazed that you are so quickly deserting Him who called you by the grace of Christ, for a different gospel;

7 which is *really* not another; only there are some who are disturbing you and want to distort the gospel of Christ.

8 But even if we, or an angel from heaven, should preach to you a gospel contrary to what we have preached to you, he is to be accursed!

NEW CENTURY VERSION

GALATIANS

1 From Paul, an apostle. I was not chosen to be an apostle by human beings, nor was I sent from human beings. I was made an apostle through Jesus Christ and God the Father who raised Jesus from the dead. 2This letter is also from all those of God's family[a] who are with me.

To the churches in Galatia:[b]

3Grace and peace to you from God our Father and the Lord Jesus Christ. 4Jesus gave himself for our sins to free us from this evil world we live in, as God the Father planned. 5The glory belongs to God forever and ever. Amen.

The Only Good News

6God, by his grace through Christ, called you to become his people. So I am amazed that you are turning away so quickly and believing something different than the Good News. 7Really, there is no other Good News. But some people are confusing you; they want to change the Good News of Christ. 8We preached to you the Good News. So if we ourselves, or even an angel from heaven, should preach to you something different, we should be judged guilty! 9I

1:2 [a] **those...family** The Greek text says "brothers." 1:2 [b] **Galatia** Probably the same country where Paul preached and began churches on his first missionary trip. Read the book of Acts, chapters 13 and 14.

CONTEMPORARY ENGLISH VERSION

GALATIANS

1 1-2From the apostle Paul and from all the Lord's followers with me.

I was chosen to be an apostle by Jesus Christ and by God the Father, who raised him from death. No mere human chose or appointed me to this work.

To the churches in Galatia.

3I pray that God the Father and our Lord Jesus Christ will be kind to you and will bless you with peace! 4Christ obeyed God our Father and gave himself as a sacrifice for our sins to rescue us from this evil world. 5God will be given glory forever and ever. Amen.

The Only True Message

6I am shocked that you have so quickly turned from God, who chose you because of his wonderful kindness.[a] You have believed another message, 7when there is really only one true message. But some people are causing you trouble and want to make you turn away from the good news about Christ. 8I pray that God will punish anyone who preaches anything different from our message to you! It doesn't matter if that person is one of us or an angel

[a] **1.6** *his wonderful kindness*: Some manuscripts have "the wonderful kindness of Christ."

NEW INTERNATIONAL VERSION

GALATIANS

1 Paul, an apostle—sent not from men nor by man, but by Jesus Christ and God the Father, who raised him from the dead— 2and all the brothers with me,

To the churches in Galatia:

3Grace and peace to you from God our Father and the Lord Jesus Christ, 4who gave himself for our sins to rescue us from the present evil age, according to the will of our God and Father, 5to whom be glory for ever and ever. Amen.

No Other Gospel

6I am astonished that you are so quickly deserting the one who called you by the grace of Christ and are turning to a different gospel— 7which is really no gospel at all. Evidently some people are throwing you into confusion and are trying to pervert the gospel of Christ. 8But even if we or an angel from heaven should preach a gospel other than the one we preached to you, let him be eternally condemned!

NEW LIVING TRANSLATION

GALATIANS

Greetings from Paul

1 This letter is from Paul, an apostle. I was not appointed by any group or by human authority. My call is from Jesus Christ himself and from God the Father, who raised Jesus from the dead.

2All the brothers and sisters* here join me in sending greetings to the churches of Galatia.

3May grace and peace be yours from God our Father and from the Lord Jesus Christ. 4He died for our sins, just as God our Father planned, in order to rescue us from this evil world in which we live. 5That is why all glory belongs to God through all the ages of eternity. Amen.

There Is Only One Good News

6I am shocked that you are turning away so soon from God, who in his love and mercy called you to share the eternal life he gives through Christ. You are already following a different way 7that pretends to be the Good News but is not the Good News at all. You are being fooled by those who twist and change the truth concerning Christ.

8Let God's curse fall on anyone, including myself, who preaches any other message than the one we told you about. Even if an angel comes from heaven and preaches

1:2 Greek *brothers;* also in 1:11.

NEW KING JAMES VERSION

THE EPISTLE OF PAUL TO THE

GALATIANS

Greeting

1 Paul, an apostle (not from men nor through man, but through Jesus Christ and God the Father who raised Him from the dead), 2and all the brethren who are with me,

To the churches of Galatia:

3Grace to you and peace from God the Father and our Lord Jesus Christ, 4who gave Himself for our sins, that He might deliver us from this present evil age, according to the will of our God and Father, 5to whom *be* glory forever and ever. Amen.

Only One Gospel

6I marvel that you are turning away so soon from Him who called you in the grace of Christ, to a different gospel, 7which is not another; but there are some who trouble you and want to pervert the gospel of Christ. 8But even if we, or an angel from heaven, preach any other gospel to you than what we have preached to you, let him be accursed.

THE MESSAGE

GALATIANS

1 I, Paul, and my companions in faith here, send greetings to the Galatian churches. My authority for writing to you does not come from any popular vote of the people, nor does it come through the appointment of some human higher-up. It comes directly from Jesus the Messiah and God the Father, who raised him from the dead. I'm God-commissioned. So I greet you with the great words, grace and peace! We know the meaning of those words because Jesus Christ rescued us from this evil world we're in by offering himself as a sacrifice for our sins. God's plan is that we all experience that rescue. Glory to God forever! Oh, yes!

The Message

I can't believe your fickleness—how easily you have turned traitor to him who called you by the grace of Christ by embracing a variant message! It is not a minor variation, you know; it is completely other, an alien message, a no-message, a lie about God. Those who are provoking this agitation among you are turning the Message of Christ on its head. Let me be blunt: If one of us—even if an angel from heaven!—were to preach something other than what we preached originally, let him be cursed. I said it once; I'll

KING JAMES VERSION

9 As we said before, so say I now again, If any *man* preach any other gospel unto you than that ye have received, let him be accursed.

10 ¶ For do I now persuade men, or God? or do I seek to please men? for if I yet pleased men, I should not be the servant of Christ.

11 But I certify you, brethren, that the gospel which was preached of me is not after man.

12 For I neither received it of man, neither was I taught *it*, but by the revelation of Jesus Christ.

13 For ye have heard of my conversation in time past in the Jews' religion, how that beyond measure I persecuted the church of God, and wasted it:

14 And profited in the Jews' religion above many my equals in mine own nation, being more exceedingly zealous of the traditions of my fathers.

15 But when it pleased God, who separated me from my mother's womb, and called *me* by his grace,

16 To reveal his Son in me, that I might preach him among the heathen; immediately I conferred not with flesh and blood:

17 Neither went I up to Jerusalem to them which were apostles before me; but I went into Arabia, and returned again unto Damascus.

NEW AMERICAN STANDARD BIBLE

9 As we have said before, so I say again now, if any man is preaching to you a gospel contrary to what you received, he is to be accursed!

10 For am I now seeking the favor of men, or of God? Or am I striving to please men? If I were still trying to please men, I would not be a bond-servant of Christ.

Paul Defends His Ministry

11 For I would have you know, brethren, that the gospel which was preached by me is not according to man.

12 For I neither received it from man, nor was I taught it, but *I received it* through a revelation of Jesus Christ.

13 For you have heard of my former manner of life in Judaism, how I used to persecute the church of God beyond measure and tried to destroy it;

14 and I was advancing in Judaism beyond many of my contemporaries among my countrymen, being more extremely zealous for my ancestral traditions.

15 But when God, who had set me apart *even* from my mother's womb and called me through His grace, was pleased

16 to reveal His Son in me so that I might preach Him among the Gentiles, I did not immediately consult with flesh and blood,

17 nor did I go up to Jerusalem to those who were apostles before me; but I went away to Arabia, and returned once more to Damascus.

NEW CENTURY VERSION

said this before, and now I say it again: You have already accepted the Good News. If anyone is preaching something different to you, he should be judged guilty!

[10]Do you think I am trying to make people accept me? No, God is the One I am trying to please. Am I trying to please people? If I still wanted to please people, I would not be a servant of Christ.

Paul's Authority Is from God

[11]Brothers and sisters,[c] I want you to know that the Good News I preached to you was not made up by human beings. [12]I did not get it from humans, nor did anyone teach it to me, but Jesus Christ showed it to me.

[13]You have heard about my past life in the Jewish religion. I attacked the church of God and tried to destroy it. [14]I was becoming a leader in the Jewish religion, doing better than most other Jews of my age. I tried harder than anyone else to follow the teachings handed down by our ancestors.

[15]But God had special plans for me and set me apart for his work even before I was born. He called me through his grace [16]and showed his son to me so that I might tell the Good News about him to those who are not Jewish. When God called me, I did not get advice or help from any person. [17]I did not go to Jerusalem to see those who were apostles before I was. But, without waiting, I went away to Arabia and later went back to Damascus.

1:11 [c] **Brothers and sisters** Although the Greek text says "Brothers" here and throughout this book, Paul's words were meant for the entire church, including men and women.

CONTEMPORARY ENGLISH VERSION

from heaven. [9]I have said it before, and I will say it again. I hope God will punish anyone who preaches anything different from what you have already believed.

[10]I am not trying to please people. I want to please God. Do you think I am trying to please people? If I were doing that, I would not be a servant of Christ.

How Paul Became an Apostle

[11]My friends, I want you to know that no one made up the message I preach. [12]It wasn't given or taught to me by some mere human. My message came directly from Jesus Christ when he appeared to me.

[13]You know how I used to live as a Jew. I was cruel to God's church and even tried to destroy it. [14]I was a much better Jew than anyone else my own age, and I obeyed every law that our ancestors had given us. [15]But even before I was born, God had chosen me. He was kind and had decided [16]to show me his Son, so that I would announce his message to the Gentiles. I didn't talk this over with anyone. [17]I didn't say a word, not even to the men in Jerusalem who were apostles before I was. Instead, I went at once to Arabia, and afterwards I returned to Damascus.

NEW INTERNATIONAL VERSION

9 As we have already said, so now I say again: If anybody is
preaching to you a gospel other than what you accepted, let
him be eternally condemned!
10 Am I now trying to win the approval of men, or of
God? Or am I trying to please men? If I were still trying to
please men, I would not be a servant of Christ.

Paul Called by God

11 I want you to know, brothers, that the gospel I
preached is not something that man made up. 12 I did not
receive it from any man, nor was I taught it; rather, I
received it by revelation from Jesus Christ.
13 For you have heard of my previous way of life in
Judaism, how intensely I persecuted the church of God and
tried to destroy it. 14 I was advancing in Judaism beyond
many Jews of my own age and was extremely zealous for
the traditions of my fathers. 15 But when God, who set me
apart from birth[a] and called me by his grace, was pleased
16 to reveal his Son in me so that I might preach him
among the Gentiles, I did not consult any man, 17 nor did I
go up to Jerusalem to see those who were apostles before I
was, but I went immediately into Arabia and later returned
to Damascus.

[a] *15* Or *from my mother's womb*

NEW LIVING TRANSLATION

any other message, let him be forever cursed. 9 I will say it
again: If anyone preaches any other gospel than the one
you welcomed, let God's curse fall upon that person.
10 Obviously, I'm not trying to be a people pleaser! No, I
am trying to please God. If I were still trying to please peo-
ple, I would not be Christ's servant.

Paul's Message Comes from Christ

11 Dear brothers and sisters, I solemnly assure you that
the Good News of salvation which I preach is not based on
mere human reasoning or logic. 12 For my message came by
a direct revelation from Jesus Christ himself. No one else
taught me.
13 You know what I was like when I followed the Jewish
religion—how I violently persecuted the Christians.* I did
my best to get rid of them. 14 I was one of the most reli-
gious Jews of my own age, and I tried as hard as possible
to follow all the old traditions of my religion.
15 But then something happened! For it pleased God in
his kindness to choose me and call me, even before I was
born! What undeserved mercy! 16 Then he revealed his Son
to me* so that I could proclaim the Good News about Jesus
to the Gentiles. When all this happened to me, I did not
rush out to consult with anyone else; 17 nor did I go up to
Jerusalem to consult with those who were apostles before I
was. No, I went away into Arabia and later returned to the

1:13 Greek *the church of God.* 1:16 Or *in me.*

NEW KING JAMES VERSION

9 As we have said before, so now I say again, if anyone
preaches any other gospel to you than what you have
received, let him be accursed.
10 For do I now persuade men, or God? Or do I seek to
please men? For if I still pleased men, I would not be a
bondservant of Christ.

Call to Apostleship

11 But I make known to you, brethren, that the gospel
which was preached by me is not according to man. 12 For I
neither received it from man, nor was I taught *it,* but *it
came* through the revelation of Jesus Christ.
13 For you have heard of my former conduct in Judaism,
how I persecuted the church of God beyond measure and
tried to destroy it. 14 And I advanced in Judaism beyond
many of my contemporaries in my own nation, being more
exceedingly zealous for the traditions of my fathers.
15 But when it pleased God, who separated me from my
mother's womb and called *me* through His grace, 16 to
reveal His Son in me, that I might preach Him among the
Gentiles, I did not immediately confer with flesh and
blood, 17 nor did I go up to Jerusalem to those *who were*
apostles before me; but I went to Arabia, and returned
again to Damascus.

THE MESSAGE

say it again: If anyone, regardless of reputation or creden-
tials, preaches something other than what you received
originally, let him be cursed.

Do you think I speak this strongly in order to manipu-
late crowds? Or curry favor with God? Or get popular
applause? If my goal was popularity, I wouldn't bother
being Christ's slave. Know this—I am most emphatic here,
friends—this great Message I delivered to you is not mere
human optimism. I didn't receive it through the traditions,
and I wasn't taught it in some school. I got it straight from
God, received the Message directly from Jesus Christ.

I'm sure that you've heard the story of my earlier life
when I lived in the Jewish way. In those days I went all out
in persecuting God's church. I was systematically destroy-
ing it. I was so enthusiastic about the traditions of my
ancestors that I advanced head and shoulders above my
peers in my career. Even then God had designs on me.
Why, when I was still in my mother's womb he chose and
called me out of sheer generosity! Now he has intervened
and revealed his Son to me so that I might joyfully tell
non-Jews about him.

Immediately after my calling—without consulting any-
one around me and without going up to Jerusalem to con-
fer with those who were apostles long before I was—I got
away to Arabia. Later I returned to Damascus, but it was

KING JAMES VERSION

18 Then after three years I went up to Jerusalem to see Peter, and abode with him fifteen days.

19 But other of the apostles saw I none, save James the Lord's brother.

20 Now the things which I write unto you, behold, before God, I lie not.

21 Afterwards I came into the regions of Syria and Cilicia;

22 And was unknown by face unto the churches of Judaea which were in Christ:

23 But they had heard only, That he which persecuted us in times past now preacheth the faith which once he destroyed.

24 And they glorified God in me.

2 Then fourteen years after I went up again to Jerusalem with Barnabas, and took Titus with *me* also.

2 And I went up by revelation, and communicated unto them that gospel which I preach among the Gentiles, but privately to them which were of reputation, lest by any means I should run, or had run, in vain.

3 But neither Titus, who was with me, being a Greek, was compelled to be circumcised:

4 And that because of false brethren unawares brought in, who came in privily to spy out our liberty which we have in Christ Jesus, that they might bring us into bondage:

NEW AMERICAN STANDARD BIBLE

18 Then three years later I went up to Jerusalem to become acquainted with Cephas, and stayed with him fifteen days.

19 But I did not see any other of the apostles except James, the Lord's brother.

20 (Now in what I am writing to you, I assure you before God that I am not lying.)

21 Then I went into the regions of Syria and Cilicia.

22 I was *still* unknown by sight to the churches of Judea which were in Christ;

23 but only, they kept hearing, "He who once persecuted us is now preaching the faith which he once tried to destroy."

24 And they were glorifying God because of me.

The Council at Jerusalem

2 Then after an interval of fourteen years I went up again to Jerusalem with Barnabas, taking Titus along also.

2 It was because of a revelation that I went up; and I submitted to them the gospel which I preach among the Gentiles, but *I did so* in private to those who were of reputation, for fear that I might be running, or had run, in vain.

3 But not even Titus, who was with me, though he was a Greek, was compelled to be circumcised.

4 But *it was* because of the false brethren secretly brought in, who had sneaked in to spy out our liberty which we have in Christ Jesus, in order to bring us into bondage.

NEW CENTURY VERSION

18After three years I went to Jerusalem to meet Peter and
stayed with him for fifteen days. 19I met no other apostles,
except James, the brother of the Lord. 20God knows that
these things I write are not lies. 21Later, I went to the
areas of Syria and Cilicia.
22In Judea the churches in Christ had never met me.
23They had only heard it said, "This man who was attack-
ing us is now preaching the same faith that he once tried to
destroy." 24And these believers praised God because of me.

Other Apostles Accepted Paul

2 After fourteen years I went to Jerusalem again, this
time with Barnabas. I also took Titus with me. 2I went
because God showed me I should go. I met with the believ-
ers there, and in private I told their leaders the Good News
that I preach to the non-Jewish people. I did not want my
past work and the work I am now doing to be wasted. 3Titus
was with me, but he was not forced to be circumcised, even
though he was a Greek. 4We talked about this problem
because some false believers had come into our group
secretly. They came in like spies to overturn the freedom we
have in Christ Jesus. They wanted to make us slaves. 5But

CONTEMPORARY ENGLISH VERSION

18Three years later I went to visit Peter[b] in Jerusalem
and stayed with him for fifteen days. 19The only other
apostle I saw was James, the Lord's brother. 20And in the
presence of God I swear I am telling the truth.
21Later, I went to the regions of Syria and Cilicia. 22But
no one who belonged to Christ's churches in Judea had
ever seen me in person. 23They had only heard that the one
who had been cruel to them was now preaching the mes-
sage that he had once tried to destroy. 24And because of
me, they praised God.

2 Fourteen years later I went to Jerusalem with
Barnabas. I also took along Titus. 2But I went there
because God had told me to go, and I explained the good
news that I had been preaching to the Gentiles. Then I met
privately with the ones who seemed to be the most impor-
tant leaders. I wanted to make sure that my work in the
past and my future work would not be for nothing.
3Titus went to Jerusalem with me. He was a Greek, but
still he wasn't forced to be circumcised. 4We went there
because of those who pretended to be followers and had
sneaked in among us as spies. They had come to take
away the freedom that Christ Jesus had given us, and they
were trying to make us their slaves. 5But we wanted you to

[b] 1.18 *Peter*: The Greek text has "Cephas," which is an Aramaic name meaning "rock." Peter is the Greek name with the same meaning.

NEW INTERNATIONAL VERSION

18Then after three years, I went up to Jerusalem to get acquainted with Peter[b] and stayed with him fifteen days. 19I saw none of the other apostles—only James, the Lord's brother. 20I assure you before God that what I am writing you is no lie. 21Later I went to Syria and Cilicia. 22I was personally unknown to the churches of Judea that are in Christ. 23They only heard the report: "The man who formerly persecuted us is now preaching the faith he once tried to destroy." 24And they praised God because of me.

Paul Accepted by the Apostles

2 Fourteen years later I went up again to Jerusalem, this time with Barnabas. I took Titus along also. 2I went in response to a revelation and set before them the gospel that I preach among the Gentiles. But I did this privately to those who seemed to be leaders, for fear that I was running or had run my race in vain. 3Yet not even Titus, who was with me, was compelled to be circumcised, even though he was a Greek. 4⌊This matter arose⌋ because some false brothers had infiltrated our ranks to spy on the freedom we have in Christ Jesus and to make us slaves. 5We

b 18 Greek *Cephas*

NEW LIVING TRANSLATION

city of Damascus. 18It was not until three years later that I finally went to Jerusalem for a visit with Peter* and stayed there with him for fifteen days. 19And the only other apostle I met at that time was James, our Lord's brother. 20You must believe what I am saying, for I declare before God that I am not lying. 21Then after this visit, I went north into the provinces of Syria and Cilicia. 22And still the Christians in the churches in Judea didn't know me personally. 23All they knew was that people were saying, "The one who used to persecute us now preaches the very faith he tried to destroy!" 24And they gave glory to God because of me.

The Apostles Accept Paul

2 Then fourteen years later I went back to Jerusalem again, this time with Barnabas; and Titus came along, too. 2I went there because God revealed to me that I should go. While I was there I talked privately with the leaders of the church. I wanted them to understand what I had been preaching to the Gentiles. I wanted to make sure they did not disagree, or my ministry would have been useless. 3And they did agree. They did not even demand that my companion Titus be circumcised, though he was a Gentile.*

4Even that question wouldn't have come up except for some so-called Christians there—false ones, really*—who came to spy on us and see our freedom in Christ Jesus. They wanted to force us, like slaves, to follow their Jewish

1:18 Greek *Cephas.* 2:3 Greek *a Greek.* 2:4 Greek *some false brothers.*

NEW KING JAMES VERSION

Contacts at Jerusalem

18Then after three years I went up to Jerusalem to see Peter,[a] and remained with him fifteen days. 19But I saw none of the other apostles except James, the Lord's brother. 20(Now *concerning* the things which I write to you, indeed, before God, I do not lie.)

21Afterward I went into the regions of Syria and Cilicia. 22And I was unknown by face to the churches of Judea which *were* in Christ. 23But they were hearing only, "He who formerly persecuted us now preaches the faith which he once *tried to* destroy." 24And they glorified God in me.

Defending the Gospel

2 Then after fourteen years I went up again to Jerusalem with Barnabas, and also took Titus with *me.* 2And I went up by revelation, and communicated to them that gospel which I preach among the Gentiles, but privately to those who were of reputation, lest by any means I might run, or had run, in vain. 3Yet not even Titus who *was* with me, being a Greek, was compelled to be circumcised. 4And *this occurred* because of false brethren secretly brought in (who came in by stealth to spy out our liberty which we have in Christ Jesus, that they might bring us into bondage),

1:18 [a] NU-Text reads *Cephas.*

THE MESSAGE

three years before I went up to Jerusalem to compare stories with Peter. I was there only fifteen days—but what days they were! Except for our Master's brother James, I saw no other apostles. (I'm telling you the absolute truth in this.)

Then I began my ministry in the regions of Syria and Cilicia. After all that time and activity I was still unknown by face among the Christian churches in Judea. There was only this report: "That man who once persecuted us is now preaching the very message he used to try to destroy." Their response was to recognize and worship *God* because of *me*!

What Is Central?

2 Fourteen years after that first visit, Barnabas and I went up to Jerusalem and took Titus with us. I went to clarify with them what had been revealed to me. At that time I placed before them exactly what I was preaching to the non-Jews. I did this in private with the leaders, those held in esteem by the church, so that our concern would not become a controversial public issue, marred by ethnic tensions, exposing my years of work to denigration and endangering my present ministry. Significantly, Titus, non-Jewish though he was, was not required to be circumcised. While we were in conference we were infiltrated by spies pretending to be Christians, who slipped in to find out just how free true Christians are. Their ulterior motive was to reduce us to their brand of servitude. We didn't give

KING JAMES VERSION

5 To whom we gave place by subjection, no, not for an hour; that the truth of the gospel might continue with you.

6 But of these who seemed to be somewhat, (whatsoever they were, it maketh no matter to me: God accepteth no man's person:) for they who seemed *to be somewhat* in conference added nothing to me:

7 But contrariwise, when they saw that the gospel of the uncircumcision was committed unto me, as *the gospel* of the circumcision *was* unto Peter;

8 (For he that wrought effectually in Peter to the apostleship of the circumcision, the same was mighty in me toward the Gentiles:)

9 And when James, Cephas, and John, who seemed to be pillars, perceived the grace that was given unto me, they gave to me and Barnabas the right hands of fellowship; that we *should go* unto the heathen, and they unto the circumcision.

10 Only *they would* that we should remember the poor; the same which I also was forward to do.

11 ¶ But when Peter was come to Antioch, I withstood him to the face, because he was to be blamed.

12 For before that certain came from James, he did eat with the Gentiles: but when they were come, he withdrew and separated himself, fearing them which were of the circumcision.

NEW AMERICAN STANDARD BIBLE

5 But we did not yield in subjection to them for even an hour, so that the truth of the gospel would remain with you.

6 But from those who were of high reputation (what they were makes no difference to me; God shows no partiality)—well, those who were of reputation contributed nothing to me.

7 But on the contrary, seeing that I had been entrusted with the gospel to the uncircumcised, just as Peter *had been* to the circumcised

8 (for He who effectually worked for Peter in *his* apostleship to the circumcised effectually worked for me also to the Gentiles),

9 and recognizing the grace that had been given to me, James and Cephas and John, who were reputed to be pillars, gave to me and Barnabas the right hand of fellowship, so that we *might go* to the Gentiles and they to the circumcised.

10 *They* only *asked* us to remember the poor—the very thing I also was eager to do.

Peter (Cephas) Opposed by Paul

11 But when Cephas came to Antioch, I opposed him to his face, because he stood condemned.

12 For prior to the coming of certain men from James, he used to eat with the Gentiles; but when they came, he *began* to withdraw and hold himself aloof, fearing the party of the circumcision.

NEW CENTURY VERSION

we did not give in to those false believers for a minute. We wanted the truth of the Good News to continue for you.

6 Those leaders who seemed to be important did not
change the Good News that I preach. (It doesn't matter to
me if they were "important" or not. To God everyone is the
same.) 7 But these leaders saw that I had been given the
work of telling the Good News to those who are not Jewish,
just as Peter had the work of telling the Jews. 8 God gave
Peter the power to work as an apostle for the Jewish people. But he also gave me the power to work as an apostle
for those who are not Jews. 9 James, Peter, and John, who
seemed to be the leaders, understood that God had given me this special grace, so they accepted Barnabas and me. They agreed that they would go to the Jewish people and
that we should go to those who are not Jewish. 10 The only
thing they asked us was to remember to help the poor—something I really wanted to do.

Paul Shows that Peter Was Wrong

11 When Peter came to Antioch, I challenged him to his
face, because he was wrong. 12 Peter ate with the non-Jewish people until some Jewish people sent from James came to Antioch. When they arrived, Peter stopped eating with those who weren't Jewish, and he separated himself
from them. He was afraid of the Jews. 13 So Peter was a

CONTEMPORARY ENGLISH VERSION

have the true message. That's why we didn't give in to them, not even for a second.

6 Some of them were supposed to be important leaders,
but I didn't care who they were. God doesn't have any favorites! None of these so-called special leaders added any-
thing to my message. 7 They realized that God had sent me
with the good news for Gentiles, and that he had sent Peter
with the same message for Jews. 8 God, who had sent Peter
on a mission to the Jews, was now using me to preach to the Gentiles.

9 James, Peter,[a] and John realized that God had given me
the message about his undeserved kindness. And these men are supposed to be the backbone of the church. They even gave Barnabas and me a friendly handshake. This was to show that we would work with Gentiles and that
they would work with Jews. 10 They only asked us to
remember the poor, and that was something I had always been eager to do.

Paul Corrects Peter at Antioch

11 When Peter came to Antioch, I told him face to face
that he was wrong. 12 He used to eat with Gentile followers
of the Lord, until James sent some Jewish followers. Peter was afraid of the Jews and soon stopped eating with

[a] 2.9 *Peter*: The Greek text has "Cephas," which is an Aramaic name meaning "rock." Peter is the Greek name with the same meaning.

NEW INTERNATIONAL VERSION

did not give in to them for a moment, so that the truth of the gospel might remain with you.

6As for those who seemed to be important—whatever they were makes no difference to me; God does not judge by external appearance—those men added nothing to my message. 7On the contrary, they saw that I had been entrusted with the task of preaching the gospel to the Gentiles,[a] just as Peter had been to the Jews.[b] 8For God, who was at work in the ministry of Peter as an apostle to the Jews, was also at work in my ministry as an apostle to the Gentiles. 9James, Peter[c] and John, those reputed to be pillars, gave me and Barnabas the right hand of fellowship when they recognized the grace given to me. They agreed that we should go to the Gentiles, and they to the Jews. 10All they asked was that we should continue to remember the poor, the very thing I was eager to do.

Paul Opposes Peter

11When Peter came to Antioch, I opposed him to his face, because he was clearly in the wrong. 12Before certain men came from James, he used to eat with the Gentiles. But when they arrived, he began to draw back and separate himself from the Gentiles because he was afraid of those who belonged to the circumcision group. 13The other Jews

[a] *7* Greek *uncircumcised* [b] *7* Greek *circumcised*; also in verses 8 and 9
[c] *9* Greek *Cephas*; also in verses 11 and 14

NEW LIVING TRANSLATION

regulations. 5But we refused to listen to them for a single moment. We wanted to preserve the truth of the Good News for you.

6And the leaders of the church who were there had nothing to add to what I was preaching. (By the way, their reputation as great leaders made no difference to me, for God has no favorites.) 7They saw that God had given me the responsibility of preaching the Good News to the Gentiles, just as he had given Peter the responsibility of preaching to the Jews. 8For the same God who worked through Peter for the benefit of the Jews worked through me for the benefit of the Gentiles. 9In fact, James, Peter,* and John, who were known as pillars of the church, recognized the gift God had given me, and they accepted Barnabas and me as their co-workers. They encouraged us to keep preaching to the Gentiles, while they continued their work with the Jews. 10The only thing they suggested was that we remember to help the poor, and I have certainly been eager to do that.

Paul Confronts Peter

11But when Peter came to Antioch, I had to oppose him publicly, speaking strongly against what he was doing, for it was very wrong. 12When he first arrived, he ate with the Gentile Christians, who don't bother with circumcision. But afterward, when some Jewish friends of James came, Peter wouldn't eat with the Gentiles anymore because he was afraid of what these legalists would say. 13Then the other

2:9 Greek *Cephas;* also in 2:11, 14.

NEW KING JAMES VERSION

5to whom we did not yield submission even for an hour, that the truth of the gospel might continue with you.

6But from those who seemed to be something—whatever they were, it makes no difference to me; God shows personal favoritism to no man—for those who seemed *to be something* added nothing to me. 7But on the contrary, when they saw that the gospel for the uncircumcised had been committed to me, as *the gospel* for the circumcised *was* to Peter 8(for He who worked effectively in Peter for the apostleship to the circumcised also worked effectively in me toward the Gentiles), 9and when James, Cephas, and John, who seemed to be pillars, perceived the grace that had been given to me, they gave me and Barnabas the right hand of fellowship, that we *should go* to the Gentiles and they to the circumcised. 10*They desired* only that we should remember the poor, the very thing which I also was eager to do.

No Return to the Law

11Now when Peter[a] had come to Antioch, I withstood him to his face, because he was to be blamed; 12for before certain men came from James, he would eat with the Gentiles; but when they came, he withdrew and separated himself, fearing those who were of the circumcision. 13And

2:11 [a] NU-Text reads *Cephas.*

THE MESSAGE

them the time of day. We were determined to preserve the truth of the Message for you.

As for those who were considered important in the church, their reputation doesn't concern me. God isn't impressed with mere appearances, and neither am I. And of course these leaders were able to add nothing to the message I had been preaching. It was soon evident that God had entrusted me with the same message to the non-Jews as Peter had been preaching to the Jews. Recognizing that my calling had been given by God, James, Peter, and John—the pillars of the church—shook hands with me and Barnabas, assigning us to a ministry to the non-Jews, while they continued to be responsible for reaching out to the Jews. The only additional thing they asked was that we remember the poor, and I was already eager to do that.

Later, when Peter came to Antioch, I had a face-to-face confrontation with him because he was clearly out of line. Here's the situation. Earlier, before certain persons had come from James, Peter regularly ate with the non-Jews. But when that conservative group came from Jerusalem, he cautiously pulled back and put as much distance as he could manage between himself and his non-Jewish friends. That's how fearful he was of the conservative Jewish clique that's been pushing the old system of circumcision.

KING JAMES VERSION

13 And the other Jews dissembled likewise with him; insomuch that Barnabas also was carried away with their dissimulation.

14 But when I saw that they walked not uprightly according to the truth of the gospel, I said unto Peter before *them* all, If thou, being a Jew, livest after the manner of Gentiles, and not as do the Jews, why compellest thou the Gentiles to live as do the Jews?

15 We *who are* Jews by nature, and not sinners of the Gentiles,

16 Knowing that a man is not justified by the works of the law, but by the faith of Jesus Christ, even we have believed in Jesus Christ, that we might be justified by the faith of Christ, and not by the works of the law: for by the works of the law shall no flesh be justified.

17 But if, while we seek to be justified by Christ, we ourselves also are found sinners, *is* therefore Christ the minister of sin? God forbid.

18 For if I build again the things which I destroyed, I make myself a transgressor.

NEW AMERICAN STANDARD BIBLE

13 The rest of the Jews joined him in hypocrisy, with the result that even Barnabas was carried away by their hypocrisy.

14 But when I saw that they were not straightforward about the truth of the gospel, I said to Cephas in the presence of all, "If you, being a Jew, live like the Gentiles and not like the Jews, how *is it that* you compel the Gentiles to live like Jews?

15 "We *are* Jews by nature and not sinners from among the Gentiles;

16 nevertheless knowing that a man is not justified by the works of the Law but through faith in Christ Jesus, even we have believed in Christ Jesus, so that we may be justified by faith in Christ and not by the works of the Law; since by the works of the Law no flesh will be justified.

17 "But if, while seeking to be justified in Christ, we ourselves have also been found sinners, is Christ then a minister of sin? May it never be!

18 "For if I rebuild what I have *once* destroyed, I prove myself to be a transgressor.

NEW CENTURY VERSION

hypocrite, as were the other Jewish believers who joined
with him. Even Barnabas was influenced by what these
Jewish believers did. 14When I saw they were not following
the truth of the Good News, I spoke to Peter in front of
them all. I said, "Peter, you are a Jew, but you are not living like a Jew. You are living like those who are not
Jewish. So why do you now try to force those who are not
Jewish to live like Jews?"

15We were not born as non-Jewish "sinners," but as
Jews. 16Yet we know that a person is made right with God
not by following the law, but by trusting in Jesus Christ. So
we, too, have put our faith in Christ Jesus, that we might
be made right with God because we trusted in Christ. It is
not because we followed the law, because no one can be
made right with God by following the law.

17We Jews came to Christ, trying to be made right with
God, and it became clear that we are sinners, too. Does
this mean that Christ encourages sin? No! 18But I would
really be wrong to begin teaching again those things that I

CONTEMPORARY ENGLISH VERSION

Gentiles. 13He and the other Jews hid their true feelings so
well that even Barnabas was fooled. 14But when I saw that
they were not really obeying the truth that is in the good
news, I corrected Peter in front of everyone and said:

Peter, you are a Jew, but you live like a Gentile. So
how can you force Gentiles to live like Jews?

15We are Jews by birth and are not sinners like
Gentiles. 16But we know that God accepts only those
who have faith in Jesus Christ. No one can please God by
simply obeying the Law. So we put our faith in Christ
Jesus, and God accepted us because of our faith.

17When we Jews started looking for a way to please
God, we discovered that we are sinners too. Does this
mean that Christ is the one who makes us sinners? No,
it doesn't! 18But if I tear down something and then build
it again, I prove that I was wrong at first. 19It was the

NEW INTERNATIONAL VERSION

joined him in his hypocrisy, so that by their hypocrisy even Barnabas was led astray.

14 When I saw that they were not acting in line with the truth of the gospel, I said to Peter in front of them all, "You are a Jew, yet you live like a Gentile and not like a Jew. How is it, then, that you force Gentiles to follow Jewish customs?

15 "We who are Jews by birth and not 'Gentile sinners' 16 know that a man is not justified by observing the law, but by faith in Jesus Christ. So we, too, have put our faith in Christ Jesus that we may be justified by faith in Christ and not by observing the law, because by observing the law no one will be justified.

17 "If, while we seek to be justified in Christ, it becomes evident that we ourselves are sinners, does that mean that Christ promotes sin? Absolutely not! 18 If I rebuild what I destroyed, I prove that I am a lawbreaker. 19 For through

NEW LIVING TRANSLATION

Jewish Christians followed Peter's hypocrisy, and even Barnabas was influenced to join them in their hypocrisy.

14 When I saw that they were not following the truth of the Good News, I said to Peter in front of all the others, "Since you, a Jew by birth, have discarded the Jewish laws and are living like a Gentile, why are you trying to make these Gentiles obey the Jewish laws you abandoned? 15 You and I are Jews by birth, not 'sinners' like the Gentiles. 16 And yet we Jewish Christians know that we become right with God, not by doing what the law commands, but by faith in Jesus Christ. So we have believed in Christ Jesus, that we might be accepted by God because of our faith in Christ—and not because we have obeyed the law. For no one will ever be saved by obeying the law."*

17 But what if we seek to be made right with God through faith in Christ and then find out that we are still sinners? Has Christ led us into sin? Of course not! 18 Rather, I make myself guilty if I rebuild the old system I already tore down.

2:16 Some translators hold that the quotation extends through verse 14; others through verse 16; and still others through verse 21.

NEW KING JAMES VERSION

the rest of the Jews also played the hypocrite with him, so that even Barnabas was carried away with their hypocrisy.

14 But when I saw that they were not straightforward about the truth of the gospel, I said to Peter before *them* all, "If you, being a Jew, live in the manner of Gentiles and not as the Jews, why do you[b] compel Gentiles to live as Jews?[c] 15 We *who are* Jews by nature, and not sinners of the Gentiles, 16 knowing that a man is not justified by the works of the law but by faith in Jesus Christ, even we have believed in Christ Jesus, that we might be justified by faith in Christ and not by the works of the law; for by the works of the law no flesh shall be justified.

17 "But if, while we seek to be justified by Christ, we ourselves also are found sinners, *is* Christ therefore a minister of sin? Certainly not! 18 For if I build again those things which I destroyed, I make myself a transgressor. 19 For I

2:14 [b] NU-Text reads *how can you.* [c] Some interpreters stop the quotation here.

THE MESSAGE

Unfortunately, the rest of the Jews in the Antioch church joined in that hypocrisy so that even Barnabas was swept along in the charade.

But when I saw that they were not maintaining a steady, straight course according to the Message, I spoke up to Peter in front of them all: "If you, a Jew, live like a non-Jew when you're not being observed by the watchdogs from Jerusalem, what right do you have to require non-Jews to conform to Jewish customs just to make a favorable impression on your old Jerusalem cronies?"

We Jews know that we have no advantage of birth over "non-Jewish sinners." We know very well that we are not set right with God by rule keeping but only through personal faith in Jesus Christ. How do we know? We tried it—and we had the best system of rules the world has ever seen! Convinced that no human being can please God by self-improvement, we believed in Jesus as the Messiah so that we might be set right before God by trusting in the Messiah, not by trying to be good.

Have some of you noticed that we are not yet perfect? (No great surprise, right?) And are you ready to make the accusation that since people like me, who go through Christ in order to get things right with God, aren't perfectly virtuous, Christ must therefore be an accessory to sin? The accusation is frivolous. If I was "trying to be good," I would be rebuilding the same old barn that I tore down. I would be acting as a charlatan.

What actually took place is this: I tried keeping rules and working my head off to please God, and it didn't work.

KING JAMES VERSION

19 For I through the law am dead to the law, that I might live unto God.

20 I am crucified with Christ: nevertheless I live; yet not I, but Christ liveth in me: and the life which I now live in the flesh I live by the faith of the Son of God, who loved me, and gave himself for me.

21 I do not frustrate the grace of God: for if righteousness *come* by the law, then Christ is dead in vain.

3 O foolish Galatians, who hath bewitched you, that ye should not obey the truth, before whose eyes Jesus Christ hath been evidently set forth, crucified among you?

2 This only would I learn of you, Received ye the Spirit by the works of the law, or by the hearing of faith?

3 Are ye so foolish? having begun in the Spirit, are ye now made perfect by the flesh?

NEW AMERICAN STANDARD BIBLE

19 "For through the Law I died to the Law, so that I might live to God.

20 "I have been crucified with Christ; and it is no longer I who live, but Christ lives in me; and the *life* which I now live in the flesh I live by faith in the Son of God, who loved me and gave Himself up for me.

21 "I do not nullify the grace of God, for if righteousness *comes* through the Law, then Christ died needlessly."

Faith Brings Righteousness

3 You foolish Galatians, who has bewitched you, before whose eyes Jesus Christ was publicly portrayed *as* crucified?

2 This is the only thing I want to find out from you: did you receive the Spirit by the works of the Law, or by hearing with faith?

3 Are you so foolish? Having begun by the Spirit, are you now being perfected by the flesh?

NEW CENTURY VERSION

gave up. 19It was the law that put me to death, and I died
to the law so that I can now live for God. 20I was put to
death on the cross with Christ, and I do not live anymore—
it is Christ who lives in me. I still live in my body, but I live
by faith in the Son of God who loved me and gave himself
to save me. 21By saying these things I am not going
against God's grace. Just the opposite, if the law could
make us right with God, then Christ's death would be useless.

Blessing Comes Through Faith

3 You people in Galatia were told very clearly about the
death of Jesus Christ on the cross. But you were foolish; you let someone trick you. 2Tell me this one thing:
How did you receive the Holy Spirit? Did you receive the
Spirit by following the law? No, you received the Spirit
because you heard the Good News and believed it. 3You
began your life in Christ by the Spirit. Now are you trying
to make it complete by your own power? That is foolish.

CONTEMPORARY ENGLISH VERSION

Law itself that killed me and freed me from its power, so
that I could live for God.

I have been nailed to the cross with Christ. 20I have
died, but Christ lives in me. And I now live by faith in
the Son of God, who loved me and gave his life for me.
21I don't turn my back on God's undeserved kindness. If
we can be acceptable to God by obeying the Law, it was
useless for Christ to die.

Faith Is the Only Way

3 You stupid Galatians! I told you exactly how Jesus
Christ was nailed to a cross. Has someone now put an
evil spell on you? 2I want to know only one thing. How
were you given God's Spirit? Was it by obeying the Law of
Moses or by hearing about Christ and having faith in him?
3How can you be so stupid? Do you think that by yourself
you can complete what God's Spirit started in you? 4Have

NEW INTERNATIONAL VERSION

the law I died to the law so that I might live for God. 20I have been crucified with Christ and I no longer live, but Christ lives in me. The life I live in the body, I live by faith in the Son of God, who loved me and gave himself for me. 21I do not set aside the grace of God, for if righteousness could be gained through the law, Christ died for nothing!"[d]

Faith or Observance of the Law

3 You foolish Galatians! Who has bewitched you? Before your very eyes Jesus Christ was clearly portrayed as crucified. 2I would like to learn just one thing from you: Did you receive the Spirit by observing the law, or by believing what you heard? 3Are you so foolish? After beginning with the Spirit, are you now trying to attain your goal by human effort? 4Have you suffered so much

[d] *21* Some interpreters end the quotation after verse 14.

NEW LIVING TRANSLATION

19For when I tried to keep the law, I realized I could never earn God's approval. So I died to the law so that I might live for God. I have been crucified with Christ. 20I myself no longer live, but Christ lives in me. So I live my life in this earthly body by trusting in the Son of God, who loved me and gave himself for me. 21I am not one of those who treats the grace of God as meaningless. For if we could be saved by keeping the law, then there was no need for Christ to die.

The Law and Faith in Christ

3 Oh, foolish Galatians! What magician has cast an evil spell on you? For you used to see the meaning of Jesus Christ's death as clearly as though I had shown you a signboard with a picture of Christ dying on the cross. 2Let me ask you this one question: Did you receive the Holy Spirit by keeping the law? Of course not, for the Holy Spirit came upon you only after you believed the message you heard about Christ. 3Have you lost your senses? After starting your Christian lives in the Spirit, why are you now trying to become perfect by your own human effort? 4You

NEW KING JAMES VERSION

through the law died to the law that I might live to God. 20I have been crucified with Christ; it is no longer I who live, but Christ lives in me; and the *life* which I now live in the flesh I live by faith in the Son of God, who loved me and gave Himself for me. 21I do not set aside the grace of God; for if righteousness *comes* through the law, then Christ died in vain."

Justification by Faith

3 O foolish Galatians! Who has bewitched you that you should not obey the truth,[a] before whose eyes Jesus Christ was clearly portrayed among you[b] as crucified? 2This only I want to learn from you: Did you receive the Spirit by the works of the law, or by the hearing of faith? 3Are you so foolish? Having begun in the Spirit, are you

3:1 [a] NU-Text omits *that you should not obey the truth.* [b] NU-Text omits *among you.*

THE MESSAGE

So I quit being a "law man" so that I could be *God's* man. Christ's life showed me how, and enabled me to do it. I identified myself completely with him. Indeed, I have been crucified with Christ. My ego is no longer central. It is no longer important that I appear righteous before you or have your good opinion, and I am no longer driven to impress God. Christ lives in me. The life you see me living is not "mine," but it is lived by faith in the Son of God, who loved me and gave himself for me. I am not going to go back on that.

Is it not clear to you that to go back to that old rule-keeping, peer-pleasing religion would be an abandonment of everything personal and free in my relationship with God? I refuse to do that, to repudiate God's grace. If a living relationship with God could come by rule keeping, then Christ died unnecessarily.

Trust in Christ, Not the Law

3 You crazy Galatians! Did someone put a hex on you? Have you taken leave of your senses? Something crazy has happened, for it's obvious that you no longer have the crucified Jesus in clear focus in your lives. His sacrifice on the Cross was certainly set before you clearly enough.

Let me put this question to you: How did your new life begin? Was it by working your heads off to please God? Or was it by responding to God's Message to you? Are you going to continue this craziness? For only crazy people would think they could complete by their own efforts what was begun by God. If you weren't smart enough or strong

KING JAMES VERSION

4 Have ye suffered so many things in vain? if *it be* yet in vain.

5 He therefore that ministereth to you the Spirit, and worketh miracles among you, *doeth he it* by the works of the law, or by the hearing of faith?

6 ¶ Even as Abraham believed God, and it was accounted to him for righteousness.

7 Know ye therefore that they which are of faith, the same are the children of Abraham.

8 And the scripture, foreseeing that God would justify the heathen through faith, preached before the gospel unto Abraham, *saying*, In thee shall all nations be blessed.

9 So then they which be of faith are blessed with faithful Abraham.

10 For as many as are of the works of the law are under the curse: for it is written, Cursed *is* every one that continueth not in all things which are written in the book of the law to do them.

11 But that no man is justified by the law in the sight

NEW AMERICAN STANDARD BIBLE

4 Did you suffer so many things in vain—if indeed it was in vain?

5 So then, does He who provides you with the Spirit and works miracles among you, do it by the works of the Law, or by hearing with faith?

6 Even so Abraham BELIEVED GOD, AND IT WAS RECKONED TO HIM AS RIGHTEOUSNESS.

7 Therefore, be sure that it is those who are of faith who are sons of Abraham.

8 The Scripture, foreseeing that God would justify the Gentiles by faith, preached the gospel beforehand to Abraham, *saying*, "ALL THE NATIONS WILL BE BLESSED IN YOU."

9 So then those who are of faith are blessed with Abraham, the believer.

10 For as many as are of the works of the Law are under a curse; for it is written, "CURSED IS EVERYONE WHO DOES NOT ABIDE BY ALL THINGS WRITTEN IN THE BOOK OF THE LAW, TO PERFORM THEM."

11 Now that no one is justified by the Law before God is

NEW CENTURY VERSION

[4]Were all your experiences wasted? I hope not! [5]Does God give you the Spirit and work miracles among you because you follow the law? No, he does these things because you heard the Good News and believed it.

[6]The Scriptures say the same thing about Abraham: "Abraham believed God, and God accepted Abraham's faith, and that faith made him right with God."[a] [7]So you should know that the true children of Abraham are those who have faith. [8]The Scriptures, telling what would happen in the future, said that God would make the non-Jewish people right through their faith. This Good News was told to Abraham beforehand, as the Scripture says: "All nations will be blessed through you."[b] [9]So all who believe as Abraham believed are blessed just as Abraham was. [10]But those who depend on following the law to make them right are under a curse, because the Scriptures say, "Anyone will be cursed who does not always obey what is written in the Book of the Law."[c] [11]Now it is clear that no one can be made right with God by the law, because the

3:6 [a] **"Abraham...God."** Quotation from Genesis 15:6.
3:8 [b] **"All...you."** Quotation from Genesis 12:3 and 18:18.
3:10 [c] **"Anyone...Law."** Quotation from Deuteronomy 27:26.

CONTEMPORARY ENGLISH VERSION

you gone through all of this for nothing? Is it all really for nothing? [5]God gives you his Spirit and works miracles in you. But does he do this because you obey the Law of Moses or because you have heard about Christ and have faith in him?

[6]The Scriptures say that God accepted Abraham because Abraham had faith. [7]And so, you should understand that everyone who has faith is a child of Abraham.[a] [8]Long ago the Scriptures said that God would accept the Gentiles because of their faith. That's why God told Abraham the good news that all nations would be blessed because of him. [9]This means that everyone who has faith will share in the blessings that were given to Abraham because of his faith.

[10]Anyone who tries to please God by obeying the Law is under a curse. The Scriptures say, "Everyone who doesn't obey everything in the Law is under a curse." [11]No one can please God by obeying the Law. The Scriptures also say,

[a] 3.7 *a child of Abraham*: God chose Abraham, and so it was believed that anyone who was a child of Abraham was also a child of God (see the note at 3.29).

NEW INTERNATIONAL VERSION

for nothing—if it really was for nothing? 5 Does God give
you his Spirit and work miracles among you because you
observe the law, or because you believe what you heard?
6 Consider Abraham: "He believed God, and it was credit-
ed to him as righteousness."[a] 7 Understand, then, that
those who believe are children of Abraham. 8 The Scripture
foresaw that God would justify the Gentiles by faith, and
announced the gospel in advance to Abraham: "All nations
will be blessed through you."[b] 9 So those who have faith
are blessed along with Abraham, the man of faith.
10 All who rely on observing the law are under a curse,
for it is written: "Cursed is everyone who does not continue
to do everything written in the Book of the Law."[c] 11 Clearly
no one is justified before God by the law, because, "The

[a] *6* Gen. 15:6 [b] *8* Gen. 12:3; 18:18; 22:18 [c] *10* Deut. 27:26

NEW LIVING TRANSLATION

have suffered so much for the Good News. Surely it was
not in vain, was it? Are you now going to just throw it all
away?
5 I ask you again, does God give you the Holy Spirit and
work miracles among you because you obey the law of
Moses? Of course not! It is because you believe the mes-
sage you heard about Christ.
6 In the same way, "Abraham believed God, so God
declared him righteous because of his faith."* 7 The real
children of Abraham, then, are all those who put their
faith in God.
8 What's more, the Scriptures looked forward to this time
when God would accept the Gentiles, too, on the basis of
their faith. God promised this good news to Abraham long
ago when he said, "All nations will be blessed through
you."* 9 And so it is: All who put their faith in Christ share
the same blessing Abraham received because of his faith.
10 But those who depend on the law to make them right
with God are under his curse, for the Scriptures say,
"Cursed is everyone who does not observe and obey all
these commands that are written in God's Book of the
Law."* 11 Consequently, it is clear that no one can ever be
right with God by trying to keep the law. For the Scriptures

3:6 Gen 15:6. **3:8** Gen 12:3; 18:18; 22:18. **3:10** Deut 27:26.

NEW KING JAMES VERSION

now being made perfect by the flesh? 4 Have you suffered
so many things in vain—if indeed *it was* in vain?
5 Therefore He who supplies the Spirit to you and works
miracles among you, *does He do it* by the works of the law,
or by the hearing of faith?— 6 just as Abraham *"believed
God, and it was accounted to him for righteousness."*[c]
7 Therefore know that *only* those who are of faith are sons
of Abraham. 8 And the Scripture, foreseeing that God would
justify the Gentiles by faith, preached the gospel to Abra-
ham beforehand, *saying, "In you all the nations shall be
blessed."*[d] 9 So then those who *are* of faith are blessed with
believing Abraham.

The Law Brings a Curse

10 For as many as are of the works of the law are under
the curse; for it is written, *"Cursed is everyone who does
not continue in all things which are written in the book of
the law, to do them."*[e] 11 But that no one is justified by the

3:6 [c] Genesis 15:6 **3:8** [d] Genesis 12:3; 18:18; 22:18; 26:4; 28:14
3:10 [e] Deuteronomy 27:26

THE MESSAGE

enough to begin it, how do you suppose you could perfect it? Did you go through this whole painful learning process for nothing? It is not yet a total loss, but it certainly will be if you keep this up!

Answer this question: Does the God who lavishly provides you with his own presence, his Holy Spirit, working things in your lives you could never do for yourselves, does he do these things because of your strenuous moral striving *or* because you trust him to do them in you? Don't these things happen among you just as they happened with Abraham? He believed God, and that act of belief was turned into a life that was right with God.

Is it not obvious to you that persons who put their trust in Christ (not persons who put their trust in the law!) are like Abraham: children of faith? It was all laid out beforehand in Scripture that God would set things right with non-Jews by *faith*. Scripture anticipated this in the promise to Abraham: "All nations will be blessed in you."

So those now who live by faith are blessed along with Abraham, who lived by faith—this is no new doctrine! And that means that anyone who tries to live by his own effort, independent of God, is doomed to failure. Scripture backs this up: "Utterly cursed is every person who fails to carry out every detail written in the Book of the law."

The obvious impossibility of carrying out such a moral program should make it plain that no one can sustain a relationship with God that way. The person who lives in right relationship with God does it by embracing what God arranges for him. Doing things for God is the opposite of

KING JAMES VERSION

of God, *it is* evident: for, The just shall live by faith.

12 And the law is not of faith: but, The man that doeth them shall live in them.

13 Christ hath redeemed us from the curse of the law, being made a curse for us: for it is written, Cursed *is* every one that hangeth on a tree:

14 That the blessing of Abraham might come on the Gentiles through Jesus Christ; that we might receive the promise of the Spirit through faith.

15 Brethren, I speak after the manner of men; Though *it be* but a man's covenant, yet *if it be* confirmed, no man disannulleth, or addeth thereto.

16 Now to Abraham and his seed were the promises made. He saith not, And to seeds, as of many; but as of one, And to thy seed, which is Christ.

17 And this I say, *that* the covenant, that was confirmed before of God in Christ, the law, which was four hundred and thirty years after, cannot disannul, that it should make the promise of none effect.

NEW AMERICAN STANDARD BIBLE

evident; for, "THE RIGHTEOUS MAN SHALL LIVE BY FAITH."

12 However, the Law is not of faith; on the contrary, "HE WHO PRACTICES THEM SHALL LIVE BY THEM."

13 Christ redeemed us from the curse of the Law, having become a curse for us—for it is written, "CURSED IS EVERYONE WHO HANGS ON A TREE"—

14 in order that in Christ Jesus the blessing of Abraham might come to the Gentiles, so that we would receive the promise of the Spirit through faith.

Intent of the Law

15 Brethren, I speak in terms of human relations: even though it is *only* a man's covenant, yet when it has been ratified, no one sets it aside or adds conditions to it.

16 Now the promises were spoken to Abraham and to his seed. He does not say, "And to seeds," as *referring* to many, but *rather* to one, "And to your seed," that is, Christ.

17 What I am saying is this: the Law, which came four hundred and thirty years later, does not invalidate a covenant previously ratified by God, so as to nullify the promise.

NEW CENTURY VERSION

Scriptures say, "Those who are right with God will live by
trusting in him."[d] [12]The law is not based on faith. It says,
"A person who obeys these things will live because of
them."[e] [13]Christ took away the curse the law put on us. He
changed places with us and put himself under that curse.
It is written in the Scriptures, "Anyone whose body is dis-
played on a tree[f] is cursed." [14]Christ did this so that God's
blessing promised to Abraham might come through Jesus
Christ to those who are not Jews. Jesus died so that by our
believing we could receive the Spirit that God promised.

The Law and the Promise

[15]Brothers and sisters, let us think in human terms:
Even an agreement made between two persons is firm.
After that agreement is accepted by both people, no one
can stop it or add anything to it. [16]God made promises
both to Abraham and to his descendant. God did not say,
"and to your descendants." That would mean many people.
But God said, "and to your descendant." That means only
one person; that person is Christ. [17]This is what I mean:
God had an agreement with Abraham and promised to
keep it. The law, which came four hundred thirty years
later, cannot change that agreement and so destroy God's

3:11 [d] **"Those...him."** Quotation from Habakkuk 2:4. 3:12 [e] **"A person...them."** Quotation from Leviticus 18:5. 3:13 [f] **displayed on a tree** Deuteronomy 21:22–23 says that when a person was killed for doing wrong, the body was hung on a tree to show shame. Paul means that the cross of Jesus was like that.

CONTEMPORARY ENGLISH VERSION

"The people God accepts because of their faith will live."[b]
[12]The Law isn't based on faith. It promises life only to
people who obey its commands. [13]But Christ rescued us
from the Law's curse, when he became a curse in our
place. This is because the Scriptures say that anyone who
is nailed to a tree is under a curse. [14]And because of what
Jesus Christ has done, the blessing that was promised to
Abraham was taken to the Gentiles. This happened so that
by faith we would be given the promised Holy Spirit.

The Law and the Promise

[15]My friends, I will use an everyday example to explain
what I mean. Once someone agrees to something, no one
else can change or cancel the agreement.[c] [16]That is how it
is with the promises God made to Abraham and his
descendant.[d] The promises were not made to many descen-
dants, but only to one, and that one is Christ. [17]What I am
saying is that the Law cannot change or cancel God's
promise that was made 430 years before the Law was

[b] **3.11** *The people God accepts because of their faith will live*: Or "The people God accepts will live because of their faith." [c] **3.15** *Once someone . . . cancel the agreement*: Or "Once a person makes out a will, no one can change or cancel it." [d] **3.16** *descendant*: The Greek text has "seed," which may mean one or many descendants. In this verse Paul says it means Christ.

NEW INTERNATIONAL VERSION

righteous will live by faith."[d] 12The law is not based on
faith; on the contrary, "The man who does these things
will live by them."[e] 13Christ redeemed us from the curse of
the law by becoming a curse for us, for it is written:
"Cursed is everyone who is hung on a tree."[f] 14He
redeemed us in order that the blessing given to Abraham
might come to the Gentiles through Christ Jesus, so that by
faith we might receive the promise of the Spirit.

The Law and the Promise

15Brothers, let me take an example from everyday life.
Just as no one can set aside or add to a human covenant
that has been duly established, so it is in this case. 16The
promises were spoken to Abraham and to his seed. The
Scripture does not say "and to seeds," meaning many people,
but "and to your seed,"[g] meaning one person, who is
Christ. 17What I mean is this: The law, introduced 430
years later, does not set aside the covenant previously
established by God and thus do away with the promise.

[d] *11* Hab. 2:4 [e] *12* Lev. 18:5 [f] *13* Deut. 21:23 [g] *16* Gen. 12:7; 13:15; 24:7

NEW LIVING TRANSLATION

say, "It is through faith that a righteous person has life."*
12How different from this way of faith is the way of law,
which says, "If you wish to find life by obeying the law,
you must obey all of its commands."* 13But Christ has rescued
us from the curse pronounced by the law. When he
was hung on the cross, he took upon himself the curse for
our wrongdoing. For it is written in the Scriptures, "Cursed
is everyone who is hung on a tree."* 14Through the work
of Christ Jesus, God has blessed the Gentiles with the same
blessing he promised to Abraham, and we Christians
receive the promised Holy Spirit through faith.

The Law and God's Promises

15Dear brothers and sisters,* here's an example from
everyday life. Just as no one can set aside or amend an
irrevocable agreement, so it is in this case. 16God gave the
promise to Abraham and his child.* And notice that it
doesn't say the promise was to his children,* as if it meant
many descendants. But the promise was to his child—and
that, of course, means Christ. 17This is what I am trying to
say: The agreement God made with Abraham could not be
canceled 430 years later when God gave the law to Moses.
God would be breaking his promise. 18For if the inheritance

3:11 Hab 2:4. **3:12** Lev 18:5. **3:13** Deut 21:23. **3:15** Greek *Brothers.* **3:16a** Greek *seed;* also in 3:16c, 19. See Gen 12:7. **3:16b** Greek *seeds.*

NEW KING JAMES VERSION

law in the sight of God *is* evident, for *"the just shall live by
faith."*[f] 12Yet the law is not of faith, but *"the man who
does them shall live by them."*[g]

13Christ has redeemed us from the curse of the law, having
become a curse for us (for it is written, *"Cursed is
everyone who hangs on a tree"*[h]), 14that the blessing of
Abraham might come upon the Gentiles in Christ Jesus,
that we might receive the promise of the Spirit through
faith.

The Changeless Promise

15Brethren, I speak in the manner of men: Though *it is*
only a man's covenant, yet *if it is* confirmed, no one
annuls or adds to it. 16Now to Abraham and his Seed were
the promises made. He does not say, "And to seeds," as of
many, but as of one, *"And to your Seed,"*[i] who is Christ.
17And this I say, *that* the law, which was four hundred and
thirty years later, cannot annul the covenant that was confirmed
before by God in Christ,[j] that it should make the

3:11 [f] Habakkuk 2:4 **3:12** [g] Leviticus 18:5
3:13 [h] Deuteronomy 21:23 **3:16** [i] Genesis 12:7; 13:15; 24:7
3:17 [j] NU-Text omits *in Christ.*

THE MESSAGE

entering into what God does for you. Habakkuk had it
right: "The person who believes God, is set right by God—
and that's the real life." Rule keeping does not naturally
evolve into living by faith, but only perpetuates itself in
more and more rule keeping, a fact observed in Scripture:
"The one who does these things [rule keeping] continues
to live by them."

Christ redeemed us from that self-defeating, cursed life
by absorbing it completely into himself. Do you remember
the Scripture that says, "Cursed is everyone who hangs on
a tree"? That is what happened when Jesus was nailed to
the Cross: He became a curse, and at the same time dissolved
the curse. And now, because of that, the air is
cleared and we can see that Abraham's blessing is present
and available for non-Jews, too. We are *all* able to receive
God's life, his Spirit, in and with us by believing—just the
way Abraham received it.

✠

Friends, let me give you an example from everyday affairs
of the free life I am talking about. Once a person's will has
been ratified, no one else can annul it or add to it. Now, the
promises were made to Abraham and to his descendant. You
will observe that Scripture, in the careful language of a legal
document, does not say "to descendants," referring to everybody
in general, but "to your descendant" (the noun, note,
is singular), referring to Christ. This is the way I interpret
this: A will, earlier ratified by God, is not annulled by an
addendum attached 430 years later, thereby negating the

KING JAMES VERSION

18 For if the inheritance *be* of the law, *it is* no more of promise: but God gave *it* to Abraham by promise.

19 ¶ Wherefore then *serveth* the law? It was added because of transgressions, till the seed should come to whom the promise was made; *and it was* ordained by angels in the hand of a mediator.

20 Now a mediator is not *a mediator* of one, but God is one.

21 *Is* the law then against the promises of God? God forbid: for if there had been a law given which could have given life, verily righteousness should have been by the law.

22 But the scripture hath concluded all under sin, that the promise by faith of Jesus Christ might be given to them that believe.

23 But before faith came, we were kept under the law, shut up unto the faith which should afterwards be revealed.

24 Wherefore the law was our schoolmaster *to bring us* unto Christ, that we might be justified by faith.

25 But after that faith is come, we are no longer under a schoolmaster.

NEW AMERICAN STANDARD BIBLE

18 For if the inheritance is based on law, it is no longer based on a promise; but God has granted it to Abraham by means of a promise.

19 Why the Law then? It was added because of transgressions, having been ordained through angels by the agency of a mediator, until the seed would come to whom the promise had been made.

20 Now a mediator is not for one *party only;* whereas God is *only* one.

21 Is the Law then contrary to the promises of God? May it never be! For if a law had been given which was able to impart life, then righteousness would indeed have been based on law.

22 But the Scripture has shut up everyone under sin, so that the promise by faith in Jesus Christ might be given to those who believe.

23 But before faith came, we were kept in custody under the law, being shut up to the faith which was later to be revealed.

24 Therefore the Law has become our tutor *to lead us* to Christ, so that we may be justified by faith.

25 But now that faith has come, we are no longer under a tutor.

NEW CENTURY VERSION

promise to Abraham. 18If the law could give us Abraham's
blessing, then the promise would not be necessary. But
that is not possible, because God freely gave his blessings
to Abraham through the promise he had made.
19So what was the law for? It was given to show that
the wrong things people do are against God's will. And it
continued until the special descendant, who had been
promised, came. The law was given through angels who
used Moses for a mediator[g] to give the law to people. 20But
a mediator is not needed when there is only one side, and
God is only one.

The Purpose of the Law of Moses

21Does this mean that the law is against God's prom-
ises? Never! That would be true only if the law could make
us right. But God did not give a law that can bring life.
22Instead, the Scriptures showed that the whole world is
bound by sin. This was so the promise would be given
through faith to people who believe in Jesus Christ.
23Before this faith came, we were all held prisoners by
the law. We had no freedom until God showed us the way
of faith that was coming. 24In other words, the law was
our guardian leading us to Christ so that we could be made
right with God through faith. 25Now the way of faith has
come, and we no longer live under a guardian.

3:19 [g] **mediator** A person who helps one person talk to or give something to another person.

CONTEMPORARY ENGLISH VERSION

given. 18If we have to obey the Law in order to receive
God's blessings, those blessings don't really come to us
because of God's promise. But God was kind to Abraham
and made him a promise.
19What is the use of the Law? It was given later to show
that we sin. But it was only supposed to last until the com-
ing of that descendant[e] who was given the promise. In
fact, angels gave the Law to Moses, and he gave it to the
people. 20There is only one God, and the Law did not come
directly from him.

Slaves and Children

21Does the Law disagree with God's promises? No, it
doesn't! If any law could give life to us, we could become
acceptable to God by obeying that law. 22But the Scriptures
say that sin controls everyone, so that God's promises will
be for anyone who has faith in Jesus Christ.
23The Law controlled us and kept us under its power
until the time came when we would have faith. 24In fact,
the Law was our teacher. It was supposed to teach us until
we had faith and were acceptable to God. 25But once a per-
son has learned to have faith, there is no more need to
have the Law as a teacher.

[e] **3.19** *that descendant*: Jesus.

NEW INTERNATIONAL VERSION

18For if the inheritance depends on the law, then it no
longer depends on a promise; but God in his grace gave it
to Abraham through a promise.
19What, then, was the purpose of the law? It was added
because of transgressions until the Seed to whom the
promise referred had come. The law was put into effect
through angels by a mediator. 20A mediator, however, does
not represent just one party; but God is one.
21Is the law, therefore, opposed to the promises of God?
Absolutely not! For if a law had been given that could
impart life, then righteousness would certainly have come
by the law. 22But the Scripture declares that the whole
world is a prisoner of sin, so that what was promised,
being given through faith in Jesus Christ, might be given to
those who believe.
23Before this faith came, we were held prisoners by the
law, locked up until faith should be revealed. 24So the law
was put in charge to lead us to Christ[h] that we might be
justified by faith. 25Now that faith has come, we are no
longer under the supervision of the law.

[h] *24* Or *charge until Christ came*

NEW LIVING TRANSLATION

could be received only by keeping the law, then it would
not be the result of accepting God's promise. But God gave
it to Abraham as a promise.
19Well then, why was the law given? It was given to
show people how guilty they are. But this system of law
was to last only until the coming of the child to whom
God's promise was made. And there is this further differ-
ence. God gave his laws to angels to give to Moses, who
was the mediator between God and the people. 20Now a
mediator is needed if two people enter into an agreement,
but God acted on his own when he made his promise to
Abraham.
21Well then, is there a conflict between God's law and
God's promises? Absolutely not! If the law could have
given us new life, we could have been made right with God
by obeying it. 22But the Scriptures have declared that we
are all prisoners of sin, so the only way to receive God's
promise is to believe in Jesus Christ.
23Until faith in Christ was shown to us as the way of
becoming right with God, we were guarded by the law. We
were kept in protective custody, so to speak, until we could
put our faith in the coming Savior.

God's Children through Faith

24Let me put it another way. The law was our guardian
and teacher to lead us until Christ came. So now, through
faith in Christ, we are made right with God. 25But now that
faith in Christ has come, we no longer need the law as our

NEW KING JAMES VERSION

promise of no effect. 18For if the inheritance *is* of the law,
it is no longer of promise; but God gave *it* to Abraham by
promise.

Purpose of the Law

19What purpose then *does* the law *serve?* It was added
because of transgressions, till the Seed should come to
whom the promise was made; *and it was* appointed
through angels by the hand of a mediator. 20Now a media-
tor does not *mediate* for one *only,* but God is one.
21*Is* the law then against the promises of God? Certainly
not! For if there had been a law given which could have
given life, truly righteousness would have been by the law.
22But the Scripture has confined all under sin, that the
promise by faith in Jesus Christ might be given to those
who believe. 23But before faith came, we were kept under
guard by the law, kept for the faith which would afterward
be revealed. 24Therefore the law was our tutor *to bring us*
to Christ, that we might be justified by faith. 25But after
faith has come, we are no longer under a tutor.

THE MESSAGE

promise of the will. No, this addendum, with its instructions and regulations, has nothing to do with the promised inheritance in the will.

What is the point, then, of the law, the attached addendum? It was a thoughtful addition to the original covenant promises made to Abraham. The purpose of the law was to keep a sinful people in the way of salvation until Christ (the descendant) came, inheriting the promises and distributing them to us. Obviously this law was not a firsthand encounter with God. It was arranged by angelic messengers through a middleman, Moses. But if there is a middleman as there was at Sinai, then the people are not dealing directly with God, are they? But the original promise is the *direct* blessing of God, received by faith.

If such is the case, is the law, then, an anti-promise, a negation of God's will for us? Not at all. Its purpose was to make obvious to everyone that we are, in ourselves, out of right relationship with God, and therefore to show us the futility of devising some religious system for getting by our own efforts what we can only get by waiting in faith for God to complete his promise. For if any kind of rule keeping had power to create life in us, we would certainly have gotten it by this time.

Until the time when we were mature enough to respond freely in faith to the living God, we were carefully surrounded and protected by the Mosaic law. The law was like those Greek tutors, with which you are familiar, who escort children to school and protect them from danger or distraction, making sure the children will really get to the place they set out for.

KING JAMES VERSION

26 For ye are all the children of God by faith in Christ Jesus.

27 For as many of you as have been baptized into Christ have put on Christ.

28 There is neither Jew nor Greek, there is neither bond nor free, there is neither male nor female: for ye are all one in Christ Jesus.

29 And if ye *be* Christ's, then are ye Abraham's seed, and heirs according to the promise.

4 Now I say, *That* the heir, as long as he is a child, differeth nothing from a servant, though he be lord of all;

2 But is under tutors and governors until the time appointed of the father.

3 Even so we, when we were children, were in bondage under the elements of the world:

4 But when the fulness of the time was come, God sent forth his Son, made of a woman, made under the law,

5 To redeem them that were under the law, that we might receive the adoption of sons.

NEW AMERICAN STANDARD BIBLE

26 For you are all sons of God through faith in Christ Jesus.

27 For all of you who were baptized into Christ have clothed yourselves with Christ.

28 There is neither Jew nor Greek, there is neither slave nor free man, there is neither male nor female; for you are all one in Christ Jesus.

29 And if you belong to Christ, then you are Abraham's descendants, heirs according to promise.

Sonship in Christ

4 Now I say, as long as the heir is a child, he does not differ at all from a slave although he is owner of everything,

2 but he is under guardians and managers until the date set by the father.

3 So also we, while we were children, were held in bondage under the elemental things of the world.

4 But when the fullness of the time came, God sent forth His Son, born of a woman, born under the Law,

5 so that He might redeem those who were under the Law, that we might receive the adoption as sons.

NEW CENTURY VERSION

[26–27]You were all baptized into Christ, and so you were all clothed with Christ. This means that you are all children of God through faith in Christ Jesus. [28]In Christ, there is no difference between Jew and Greek, slave and free person, male and female. You are all the same in Christ Jesus. [29]You belong to Christ, so you are Abraham's descendants. You will inherit all of God's blessings because of the promise God made to Abraham.

4 I want to tell you this: While those who will inherit their fathers' property are still children, they are no different from slaves. It does not matter that the children own everything. [2]While they are children, they must obey those who are chosen to care for them. But when the children reach the age set by their fathers, they are free. [3]It is the same for us. We were once like children, slaves to the useless rules of this world. [4]But when the right time came, God sent his Son who was born of a woman and lived under the law. [5]God did this so he could buy freedom for those who were under the law and so we could become his children.

CONTEMPORARY ENGLISH VERSION

[26]All of you are God's children because of your faith in Christ Jesus. [27]And when you were baptized, it was as though you had put on Christ in the same way you put on new clothes. [28]Faith in Christ Jesus is what makes each of you equal with each other, whether you are a Jew or a Greek, a slave or a free person, a man or a woman. [29]So if you belong to Christ, you are now part of Abraham's family,[f] and you will be given what God has promised.

4 [1]Children who are under age are no better off than slaves, even though everything their parents own will someday be theirs. [2]This is because children are placed in the care of guardians and teachers until the time their parents have set. [3]That is how it was with us. We were like children ruled by the powers of this world.

[4]But when the time was right, God sent his Son, and a woman gave birth to him. His Son obeyed the Law, [5]so he could set us free from the Law, and we could become God's

[f] 3.29 *you are now part of Abraham's family*: Paul tells the Galatians that faith in Jesus Christ is what makes someone a true child of Abraham and of God (see the note at 3.7).

NEW INTERNATIONAL VERSION

Sons of God

[26]You are all sons of God through faith in Christ Jesus, [27]for all of you who were baptized into Christ have clothed yourselves with Christ. [28]There is neither Jew nor Greek, slave nor free, male nor female, for you are all one in Christ Jesus. [29]If you belong to Christ, then you are Abraham's seed, and heirs according to the promise.

4 What I am saying is that as long as the heir is a child, he is no different from a slave, although he owns the whole estate. [2]He is subject to guardians and trustees until the time set by his father. [3]So also, when we were children, we were in slavery under the basic principles of the world. [4]But when the time had fully come, God sent his Son, born of a woman, born under law, [5]to redeem those under law, that we might receive the full rights of sons.

NEW LIVING TRANSLATION

guardian. [26]So you are all children* of God through faith in Christ Jesus. [27]And all who have been united with Christ in baptism have been made like him. [28]There is no longer Jew or Gentile,* slave or free, male or female. For you are all Christians—you are one in Christ Jesus. [29]And now that you belong to Christ, you are the true children of Abraham. You are his heirs, and now all the promises God gave to him belong to you.

4 Think of it this way. If a father dies and leaves great wealth for his young children, those children are not much better off than slaves until they grow up, even though they actually own everything their father had. [2]They have to obey their guardians until they reach whatever age their father set.

[3]And that's the way it was with us before Christ came. We were slaves to the spiritual powers of this world. [4]But when the right time came, God sent his Son, born of a woman, subject to the law. [5]God sent him to buy freedom for us who were slaves to the law, so that he could adopt us as his very own children.* [6]And because you Gentiles

3:26 Greek *sons.* 3:28 Greek *Jew or Greek.* 4:5 Greek *sons;* also in 4:6.

NEW KING JAMES VERSION

Sons and Heirs

[26]For you are all sons of God through faith in Christ Jesus. [27]For as many of you as were baptized into Christ have put on Christ. [28]There is neither Jew nor Greek, there is neither slave nor free, there is neither male nor female; for you are all one in Christ Jesus. [29]And if you *are* Christ's, then you are Abraham's seed, and heirs according to the promise.

4 Now I say *that* the heir, as long as he is a child, does not differ at all from a slave, though he is master of all, [2]but is under guardians and stewards until the time appointed by the father. [3]Even so we, when we were children, were in bondage under the elements of the world. [4]But when the fullness of the time had come, God sent forth His Son, born[a] of a woman, born under the law, [5]to redeem those who were under the law, that we might receive the adoption as sons.

4:4 [a] Or *made*

THE MESSAGE

But now you have arrived at your destination: By faith in Christ you are in direct relationship with God. Your baptism in Christ was not just washing you up for a fresh start. It also involved dressing you in an adult faith wardrobe—Christ's life, the fulfillment of God's original promise.

In Christ's Family

In Christ's family there can be no division into Jew and non-Jew, slave and free, male and female. Among us you are all equal. That is, we are all in a common relationship with Jesus Christ. Also, since you are Christ's family, then you are Abraham's famous "descendant," heirs according to the covenant promises.

4 Let me show you the implications of this. As long as the heir is a minor, he has no advantage over the slave. Though legally he owns the entire inheritance, he is subject to tutors and administrators until whatever date the father has set for emancipation. That is the way it is with us: When we were minors, we were just like slaves ordered around by simple instructions (the tutors and administrators of this world), with no say in the conduct of our own lives.

But when the time arrived that was set by God the Father, God sent his Son, born among us of a woman, born under the conditions of the law so that he might redeem those of us who have been kidnapped by the law. Thus we have been set free to experience our rightful heritage. You can tell for sure that you are now fully adopted as his own

KING JAMES VERSION

6 And because ye are sons, God hath sent forth the Spirit of his Son into your hearts, crying, Abba, Father.

7 Wherefore thou art no more a servant, but a son; and if a son, then an heir of God through Christ.

8 ¶ Howbeit then, when ye knew not God, ye did service unto them which by nature are no gods.

9 But now, after that ye have known God, or rather are known of God, how turn ye again to the weak and beggarly elements, whereunto ye desire again to be in bondage?

10 Ye observe days, and months, and times, and years.

11 I am afraid of you, lest I have bestowed upon you labour in vain.

12 ¶ Brethren, I beseech you, be as I *am*; for I *am* as ye *are*: ye have not injured me at all.

13 Ye know how through infirmity of the flesh I preached the gospel unto you at the first.

14 And my temptation which was in my flesh ye despised not, nor rejected; but received me as an angel of God, *even* as Christ Jesus.

15 Where is then the blessedness ye spake of? for I bear

NEW AMERICAN STANDARD BIBLE

6 Because you are sons, God has sent forth the Spirit of His Son into our hearts, crying, "Abba! Father!"

7 Therefore you are no longer a slave, but a son; and if a son, then an heir through God.

8 However at that time, when you did not know God, you were slaves to those which by nature are no gods.

9 But now that you have come to know God, or rather to be known by God, how is it that you turn back again to the weak and worthless elemental things, to which you desire to be enslaved all over again?

10 You observe days and months and seasons and years.

11 I fear for you, that perhaps I have labored over you in vain.

12 I beg of you, brethren, become as I *am*, for I also *have become* as you *are*. You have done me no wrong;

13 but you know that it was because of a bodily illness that I preached the gospel to you the first time;

14 and that which was a trial to you in my bodily condition you did not despise or loathe, but you received me as an angel of God, as Christ Jesus *Himself*.

15 Where then is that sense of blessing you had? For I

NEW CENTURY VERSION

[6]Since you are God's children, God sent the Spirit of his
Son into your hearts, and the Spirit cries out, "Father."[a]
[7]So now you are not a slave; you are God's child, and God
will give you the blessing he promised, because you are his
child.

Paul's Love for the Christians

[8]In the past you did not know God. You were slaves to
gods that were not real. [9]But now you know the true God.
Really, it is God who knows you. So why do you turn back
to those weak and useless rules you followed before? Do
you want to be slaves to those things again? [10]You still
follow teachings about special days, months, seasons, and
years. [11]I am afraid for you, that my work for you has been
wasted.

[12]Brothers and sisters, I became like you, so I beg you
to become like me. You were very good to me before.
[13]You remember that it was because of an illness that I
came to you the first time, preaching the Good News.
[14]Though my sickness was a trouble for you, you did not
hate me or make me leave. But you welcomed me as an
angel from God, as if I were Jesus Christ himself! [15]You
were very happy then, but where is that joy now? I am

4:6 [a] **"Father"** Literally, "Abba, Father." Jewish children called their fathers "Abba."

CONTEMPORARY ENGLISH VERSION

children. [6]Now that we are his children, God has sent the
Spirit of his Son into our hearts. And his Spirit tells us that
God is our Father. [7]You are no longer slaves. You are God's
children, and you will be given what he has promised.

Paul's Concern for the Galatians

[8]Before you knew God, you were slaves of gods that are
not real. [9]But now you know God, or better still, God
knows you. How can you turn back and become the slaves
of those weak and pitiful powers?[a] [10]You even celebrate
certain days, months, seasons, and years. [11]I am afraid I
have wasted my time working with you.

[12]My friends, I beg you to be like me, just as I once tried
to be like you. Did you mistreat me [13]when I first preached
to you? No you didn't, even though you knew I had come
there because I was sick. [14]My illness must have caused
you some trouble, but you didn't hate me or turn me away
because of it. You welcomed me as though I were one of
God's angels or even Christ Jesus himself. [15]Where is that
good feeling now? I am sure that if it had been possible,

[a] **4.9** *powers*: Spirits were thought to control human lives and were believed to be connected with the movements of the stars.

NEW INTERNATIONAL VERSION

6Because you are sons, God sent the Spirit of his Son into
our hearts, the Spirit who calls out, *"Abba,*[a] Father." 7So
you are no longer a slave, but a son; and since you are a
son, God has made you also an heir.

Paul's Concern for the Galatians

8Formerly, when you did not know God, you were slaves
to those who by nature are not gods. 9But now that you
know God—or rather are known by God—how is it that
you are turning back to those weak and miserable princi-
ples? Do you wish to be enslaved by them all over again?
10You are observing special days and months and seasons
and years! 11I fear for you, that somehow I have wasted
my efforts on you.

12I plead with you, brothers, become like me, for I
became like you. You have done me no wrong. 13As you
know, it was because of an illness that I first preached the
gospel to you. 14Even though my illness was a trial to you,
you did not treat me with contempt or scorn. Instead, you
welcomed me as if I were an angel of God, as if I were
Christ Jesus himself. 15What has happened to all your joy?

[a] 6 Aramaic for *Father*

NEW LIVING TRANSLATION

have become his children, God has sent the Spirit of his
Son into your hearts, and now you can call God your dear
Father.* 7Now you are no longer a slave but God's own
child.* And since you are his child, everything he has
belongs to you.

Paul's Concern for the Galatians

8Before you Gentiles knew God, you were slaves to so-
called gods that do not even exist. 9And now that you have
found God (or should I say, now that God has found you),
why do you want to go back again and become slaves once
more to the weak and useless spiritual powers of this
world? 10You are trying to find favor with God by what you
do or don't do on certain days or months or seasons or
years. 11I fear for you. I am afraid that all my hard work
for you was worth nothing. 12Dear brothers and sisters,*
I plead with you to live as I do in freedom from these
things, for I have become like you Gentiles were—free from
the law.

You did not mistreat me when I first preached to you.
13Surely you remember that I was sick when I first brought
you the Good News of Christ. 14But even though my sick-
ness was revolting to you, you did not reject me and turn
me away. No, you took me in and cared for me as though I
were an angel from God or even Christ Jesus himself.
15Where is that joyful spirit we felt together then? In those

4:6 Greek *into your hearts, crying, "Abba, Father." Abba* is an Aramaic term for "father." **4:7** Greek *son;* also in 4:7b. **4:12** Greek *brothers;* also in 4:28, 31.

NEW KING JAMES VERSION

6And because you are sons, God has sent forth the Spirit
of His Son into your hearts, crying out, "Abba, Father!"
7Therefore you are no longer a slave but a son, and if a
son, then an heir of[b] God through Christ.

Fears for the Church

8But then, indeed, when you did not know God, you
served those which by nature are not gods. 9But now after
you have known God, or rather are known by God, how *is
it that* you turn again to the weak and beggarly elements,
to which you desire again to be in bondage? 10You observe
days and months and seasons and years. 11I am afraid for
you, lest I have labored for you in vain.

12Brethren, I urge you to become like me, for I *became*
like you. You have not injured me at all. 13You know that
because of physical infirmity I preached the gospel to you
at the first. 14And my trial which was in my flesh you did
not despise or reject, but you received me as an angel of
God, *even* as Christ Jesus. 15What[c] then was the blessing

4:7 [b] NU-Text reads *through God* and omits *through Christ.*
4:15 [c] NU-Text reads *Where.*

THE MESSAGE

children because God sent the Spirit of his Son into our lives crying out, "Papa! Father!" Doesn't that privilege of intimate conversation with God make it plain that you are not a slave, but a child? And if you are a child, you're also an heir, with complete access to the inheritance.

Earlier, before you knew God personally, you were enslaved to so-called gods that had nothing of the divine about them. But now that you know the real God—or rather since God knows you—how can you possibly subject yourselves again to those paper tigers? For that is exactly what you do when you are intimidated into scrupulously observing all the traditions, taboos, and superstitions associated with special days and seasons and years. I am afraid that all my hard work among you has gone up in a puff of smoke!

My dear friends, what I would really like you to do is try to put yourselves in my shoes to the same extent that I, when I was with you, put myself in yours. You were very sensitive and kind then. You did not come down on me personally. You were well aware that the reason I ended up preaching to you was that I was physically broken, and so, prevented from continuing my journey, I was forced to stop with you. That is how I came to preach to you.

And don't you remember that even though taking in a sick guest was most troublesome for you, you chose to treat me as well as you would have treated an angel of God—as well as you would have treated Jesus himself if he had visited you? What has happened to the satisfaction you felt at that time? There were some of you then who, if possible,

KING JAMES VERSION

you record, that, if *it had been* possible, ye would have plucked out your own eyes, and have given them to me.
16 Am I therefore become your enemy, because I tell you the truth?
17 ¶ They zealously affect you, *but* not well; yea, they would exclude you, that ye might affect them.
18 But *it is* good to be zealously affected always in *a* good *thing*, and not only when I am present with you.
19 ¶ My little children, of whom I travail in birth again until Christ be formed in you,
20 I desire to be present with you now, and to change my voice; for I stand in doubt of you.
21 ¶ Tell me, ye that desire to be under the law, do ye not hear the law?
22 For it is written, that Abraham had two sons, the one by a bondmaid, the other by a freewoman.
23 But he *who was* of the bondwoman was born after the flesh; but he of the freewoman *was* by promise.
24 Which things are an allegory: for these are the two covenants; the one from the mount Sinai, which gendereth to bondage, which is Agar.

NEW AMERICAN STANDARD BIBLE

bear you witness that, if possible, you would have plucked out your eyes and given them to me.
16 So have I become your enemy by telling you the truth?
17 They eagerly seek you, not commendably, but they wish to shut you out so that you will seek them.
18 But it is good always to be eagerly sought in a commendable manner, and not only when I am present with you.
19 My children, with whom I am again in labor until Christ is formed in you—
20 but I could wish to be present with you now and to change my tone, for I am perplexed about you.

Bond and Free

21 Tell me, you who want to be under law, do you not listen to the law?
22 For it is written that Abraham had two sons, one by the bondwoman and one by the free woman.
23 But the son by the bondwoman was born according to the flesh, and the son by the free woman through the promise.
24 This is allegorically speaking, for these *women* are two covenants: one *proceeding* from Mount Sinai bearing children who are to be slaves; she is Hagar.

NEW CENTURY VERSION

ready to testify that you would have taken out your eyes
and given them to me if that were possible. 16Now am I
your enemy because I tell you the truth?
17Those people[b] are working hard to persuade you, but
this is not good for you. They want to persuade you to turn
against us and follow only them. 18It is good for people to
show interest in you, but only if their purpose is good.
This is always true, not just when I am with you. 19My lit-
tle children, again I feel the pain of childbirth for you until
you truly become like Christ. 20I wish I could be with you
now and could change the way I am talking to you,
because I do not know what to think about you.

The Example of Hagar and Sarah

21Some of you still want to be under the law. Tell me, do
you know what the law says? 22The Scriptures say that
Abraham had two sons. The mother of one son was a slave
woman, and the mother of the other son was a free
woman. 23Abraham's son from the slave woman was born
in the normal human way. But the son from the free
woman was born because of the promise God made to
Abraham.
24This story teaches something else: The two women are
like the two agreements between God and his people. One
agreement is the law that God made on Mount Sinai,[c] and
the people who are under this agreement are like slaves.

4:17 [b] **Those people** They are the false teachers who were bothering the believers in Galatia (Galatians 1:7). 4:24 [c] **Mount Sinai** Mountain in Arabia where God gave his laws to Moses (Exodus 19 and 20).

CONTEMPORARY ENGLISH VERSION

you would have taken out your own eyes and given them
to me. 16Am I now your enemy, just because I told you the
truth?
17Those people may be paying you a lot of attention, but
it isn't for your good. They only want to keep you away
from me, so you will pay them a lot of attention. 18It is
always good to give your attention to something worth-
while, even when I am not with you. 19My children, I am in
terrible pain until Christ may be seen living in you. 20I
wish I were with you now. Then I would not have to talk
this way. You really have me puzzled.

Hagar and Sarah

21Some of you would like to be under the rule of the Law
of Moses. But do you know what the Law says? 22In the
Scriptures we learn that Abraham had two sons. The moth-
er of one of them was a slave, while the mother of the
other one had always been free. 23The son of the slave
woman was born in the usual way. But the son of the free
woman was born because of God's promise.
24All of this has another meaning as well. Each of the
two women stands for one of the agreements God made
with his people. Hagar, the slave woman, stands for the
agreement that was made at Mount Sinai. Everyone born

NEW INTERNATIONAL VERSION

I can testify that, if you could have done so, you would
have torn out your eyes and given them to me. [16]Have I
now become your enemy by telling you the truth?
[17]Those people are zealous to win you over, but for no
good. What they want is to alienate you ⌊from us⌋, so that
you may be zealous for them. [18]It is fine to be zealous,
provided the purpose is good, and to be so always and not
just when I am with you. [19]My dear children, for whom I
am again in the pains of childbirth until Christ is formed
in you, [20]how I wish I could be with you now and change
my tone, because I am perplexed about you!

Hagar and Sarah

[21]Tell me, you who want to be under the law, are you
not aware of what the law says? [22]For it is written that
Abraham had two sons, one by the slave woman and the
other by the free woman. [23]His son by the slave woman
was born in the ordinary way; but his son by the free
woman was born as the result of a promise.
[24]These things may be taken figuratively, for the women
represent two covenants. One covenant is from Mount Sinai
and bears children who are to be slaves: This is Hagar.

NEW LIVING TRANSLATION

days, I know you would gladly have taken out your own
eyes and given them to me if it had been possible. [16]Have I
now become your enemy because I am telling you the
truth?
[17]Those false teachers who are so anxious to win your
favor are not doing it for your good. They are trying to
shut you off from me so that you will pay more attention
to them. [18]Now it's wonderful if you are eager to do good,
and especially when I am not with you. [19]But oh, my dear
children! I feel as if I am going through labor pains for you
again, and they will continue until Christ is fully developed
in your lives. [20]How I wish I were there with you right
now, so that I could be more gentle with you. But at this
distance I frankly don't know what else to do.

Abraham's Two Children

[21]Listen to me, you who want to live under the law. Do
you know what the law really says? [22]The Scriptures say
that Abraham had two sons, one from his slave-wife and
one from his freeborn wife.* [23]The son of the slave-wife
was born in a human attempt to bring about the fulfill-
ment of God's promise. But the son of the freeborn wife
was born as God's own fulfillment of his promise.
[24]Now these two women serve as an illustration of God's
two covenants. Hagar, the slave-wife, represents Mount
Sinai where people first became enslaved to the law. [25]And

4:22 See Gen 16:15; 21:2-3.

NEW KING JAMES VERSION

you *enjoyed?* For I bear you witness that, if possible, you
would have plucked out your own eyes and given them to
me. [16]Have I therefore become your enemy because I tell
you the truth?
[17]They zealously court you, *but* for no good; yes, they
want to exclude you, that you may be zealous for them.
[18]But it is good to be zealous in a good thing always, and
not only when I am present with you. [19]My little children,
for whom I labor in birth again until Christ is formed in
you, [20]I would like to be present with you now and to
change my tone; for I have doubts about you.

Two Covenants

[21]Tell me, you who desire to be under the law, do you not
hear the law? [22]For it is written that Abraham had two sons:
the one by a bondwoman, the other by a freewoman. [23]But
he *who was* of the bondwoman was born according to the
flesh, and he of the freewoman through promise, [24]which
things are symbolic. For these are the[d] two covenants: the
one from Mount Sinai which gives birth to bondage, which is

4:24 [d] NU-Text and M-Text omit *the*.

THE MESSAGE

would have given your very eyes to me—that is how deeply
you cared! And now have I suddenly become your enemy
simply by telling you the truth? I can't believe it.

Those heretical teachers go to great lengths to flatter
you, but their motives are rotten. They want to shut you
out of the free world of God's grace so that you will always
depend on them for approval and direction, making them
feel important.

✛

It is a good thing to be ardent in doing good, but not just
when I am in your presence. Can't you continue the same
concern for both my person and my message when I am
away from you that you had when I was with you? Do you
know how I feel right now, and will feel until Christ's life
becomes visible in your lives? Like a mother in the pain of
childbirth. Oh, I keep wishing that I was with you. Then I
wouldn't be reduced to this blunt, letter-writing language
out of sheer frustration.

Tell me now, you who have become so enamored with the
law: Have you paid close attention to that law? Abraham,
remember, had *two* sons: one by the slave woman and one
by the free woman. The son of the slave woman was born by
human connivance; the son of the free woman was born by
God's promise. This illustrates the very thing we are dealing
with now. The two births represent two ways of being in
relationship with God. One is from Mount Sinai in Arabia. It
corresponds with what is now going on in Jerusalem—a
slave life, producing slaves as offspring. This is the way of

KING JAMES VERSION

25 For this Agar is mount Sinai in Arabia, and answereth to Jerusalem which now is, and is in bondage with her children.

26 But Jerusalem which is above is free, which is the mother of us all.

27 For it is written, Rejoice, *thou* barren that bearest not; break forth and cry, thou that travailest not: for the desolate hath many more children than she which hath an husband.

28 Now we, brethren, as Isaac was, are the children of promise.

29 But as then he that was born after the flesh persecuted him *that was born* after the Spirit, even so *it is* now.

30 Nevertheless what saith the scripture? Cast out the bondwoman and her son: for the son of the bondwoman shall not be heir with the son of the freewoman.

31 So then, brethren, we are not children of the bondwoman, but of the free.

NEW AMERICAN STANDARD BIBLE

25 Now this Hagar is Mount Sinai in Arabia and corresponds to the present Jerusalem, for she is in slavery with her children.

26 But the Jerusalem above is free; she is our mother.

27 For it is written,

"REJOICE, BARREN WOMAN WHO DOES NOT BEAR;
BREAK FORTH AND SHOUT, YOU WHO ARE NOT IN LABOR;
FOR MORE NUMEROUS ARE THE CHILDREN OF THE DESOLATE
THAN OF THE ONE WHO HAS A HUSBAND."

28 And you brethren, like Isaac, are children of promise.

29 But as at that time he who was born according to the flesh persecuted him *who was born* according to the Spirit, so it is now also.

30 But what does the Scripture say?
"CAST OUT THE BONDWOMAN AND HER SON,
FOR THE SON OF THE BONDWOMAN SHALL NOT BE AN HEIR
WITH THE SON OF THE FREE WOMAN."

31 So then, brethren, we are not children of a bondwoman, but of the free woman.

NEW CENTURY VERSION

The mother named Hagar is like that agreement.
25She is like Mount Sinai in Arabia and is a picture of the earthly Jewish city of Jerusalem. This city and its people, the Jews, are slaves to the law.
26But the heavenly Jerusalem, which is above, is like the free woman. She is our mother.
27It is written in the Scriptures:

"Be happy, Jerusalem.
You are like a woman who never gave birth to children.
Start singing and shout for joy.
You never felt the pain of giving birth,
but you will have more children
than the woman who has a husband." *Isaiah 54:1*

28My brothers and sisters, you are God's children because of his promise, as Isaac was then.
29The son who was born in the normal way treated the other son badly. It is the same today.
30But what does the Scripture say? "Throw out the slave woman and her son. The son of the slave woman should not inherit anything. The son of the free woman should receive it all."[d]
31So, my brothers and sisters, we are not children of the slave woman, but of the free woman.

4:30 [d] "Throw...all." Quotation from Genesis 21:10.

CONTEMPORARY ENGLISH VERSION

into her family is a slave.
25Hagar also stands for Mount Sinai in Arabia[b] and for the present city of Jerusalem. She[c] and her children are slaves.

26But our mother is the city of Jerusalem in heaven above, and she isn't a slave.
27The Scriptures say about her,

"You have never had children,
but now you can be glad.
You have never given birth,
but now you can shout.
Once you had no children,
but now you will have
more children than a woman
who has been married
for a long time."

28My friends, you were born because of this promise, just as Isaac was.
29But the child who was born in the natural way made trouble for the child who was born because of the Spirit. The same thing is happening today.
30The Scriptures say, "Get rid of the slave woman and her son! He won't be given anything. The son of the free woman will receive everything."
31My friends, we are children of the free woman and not of the slave.

[b] 4.25 *Hagar also stands for Mount Sinai in Arabia*: Some manuscripts have "Sinai is a mountain in Arabia." This sentence would then be translated: "Sinai is a mountain in Arabia, and Hagar stands for the present city of Jerusalem." [c] 4.25 *She*: "Hagar" or "Jerusalem."

NEW INTERNATIONAL VERSION

25 Now Hagar stands for Mount Sinai in Arabia and corresponds to the present city of Jerusalem, because she is in slavery with her children. 26 But the Jerusalem that is above is free, and she is our mother. 27 For it is written:

"Be glad, O barren woman,
 who bears no children;
break forth and cry aloud,
 you who have no labor pains;
because more are the children of the desolate woman
 than of her who has a husband."[b]

28 Now you, brothers, like Isaac, are children of promise. 29 At that time the son born in the ordinary way persecuted the son born by the power of the Spirit. It is the same now. 30 But what does the Scripture say? "Get rid of the slave woman and her son, for the slave woman's son will never share in the inheritance with the free woman's son."[c] 31 Therefore, brothers, we are not children of the slave woman, but of the free woman.

[b] *27* Isaiah 54:1 [c] *30* Gen. 21:10

NEW LIVING TRANSLATION

now Jerusalem is just like Mount Sinai in Arabia, because she and her children live in slavery. 26 But Sarah, the free woman, represents the heavenly Jerusalem. And she is our mother. 27 That is what Isaiah meant when he prophesied,

"Rejoice, O childless woman!
Break forth into loud and joyful song,
 even though you never gave birth to a child.
For the woman who could bear no children
 now has more than all the other women!"*

28 And you, dear brothers and sisters, are children of the promise, just like Isaac. 29 And we who are born of the Holy Spirit are persecuted by those who want us to keep the law, just as Isaac, the child of promise, was persecuted by Ishmael, the son of the slave-wife.

30 But what do the Scriptures say about that? "Get rid of the slave and her son, for the son of the slave woman will not share the family inheritance with the free woman's son."* 31 So, dear brothers and sisters, we are not children of the slave woman, obligated to the law. We are children of the free woman, acceptable to God because of our faith.

4:27 Isa 54:1. **4:30** Gen 21:10.

NEW KING JAMES VERSION

Hagar— 25 for this Hagar is Mount Sinai in Arabia, and corresponds to Jerusalem which now is, and is in bondage with her children— 26 but the Jerusalem above is free, which is the mother of us all. 27 For it is written:

"Rejoice, O barren,
You who do not bear!
Break forth and shout,
You who are not in labor!
For the desolate has many more children
Than she who has a husband."[e]

28 Now we, brethren, as Isaac *was,* are children of promise. 29 But, as he who was born according to the flesh then persecuted him *who was born* according to the Spirit, even so *it is* now. 30 Nevertheless what does the Scripture say? *"Cast out the bondwoman and her son, for the son of the bondwoman shall not be heir with the son of the freewoman."*[f] 31 So then, brethren, we are not children of the bondwoman but of the free.

4:27 [e] Isaiah 54:1 **4:30** [f] Genesis 21:10

THE MESSAGE

Hagar. In contrast to that, there is an invisible Jerusalem, a free Jerusalem, and she is our mother—this is the way of Sarah. Remember what Isaiah wrote:

"Rejoice, barren woman who bears no children,
 shout and cry out, woman who has no birth pangs,
Because the children of the barren woman
 now surpass the children of the chosen woman."

Isn't it clear, friends, that you, like Isaac, are children of promise? In the days of Hagar and Sarah, the child who came from faithless connivance (Ishmael) harassed the child who came—empowered by the Spirit—from the faithful promise (Isaac). Isn't it clear that the harassment you are now experiencing from the Jerusalem heretics follows that old pattern? There is a Scripture that tells us what to do: "Expel the slave mother with her son, for the slave son will not inherit with the free son." Isn't that conclusive? We are not children of the slave woman, but of the free woman.

KING JAMES VERSION

5 Stand fast therefore in the liberty wherewith Christ hath made us free, and be not entangled again with the yoke of bondage.

2 Behold, I Paul say unto you, that if ye be circumcised, Christ shall profit you nothing.

3 For I testify again to every man that is circumcised, that he is a debtor to do the whole law.

4 Christ is become of no effect unto you, whosoever of you are justified by the law; ye are fallen from grace.

5 For we through the Spirit wait for the hope of righteousness by faith.

6 For in Jesus Christ neither circumcision availeth any thing, nor uncircumcision; but faith which worketh by love.

7 Ye did run well; who did hinder you that ye should not obey the truth?

8 This persuasion *cometh* not of him that calleth you.

9 A little leaven leaveneth the whole lump.

10 I have confidence in you through the Lord, that ye will be none otherwise minded: but he that troubleth you shall bear his judgment, whosoever he be.

NEW AMERICAN STANDARD BIBLE

Walk by the Spirit

5 It was for freedom that Christ set us free; therefore keep standing firm and do not be subject again to a yoke of slavery.

2 Behold I, Paul, say to you that if you receive circumcision, Christ will be of no benefit to you.

3 And I testify again to every man who receives circumcision, that he is under obligation to keep the whole Law.

4 You have been severed from Christ, you who are seeking to be justified by law; you have fallen from grace.

5 For we through the Spirit, by faith, are waiting for the hope of righteousness.

6 For in Christ Jesus neither circumcision nor uncircumcision means anything, but faith working through love.

7 You were running well; who hindered you from obeying the truth?

8 This persuasion *did* not *come* from Him who calls you.

9 A little leaven leavens the whole lump *of dough.*

10 I have confidence in you in the Lord that you will adopt no other view; but the one who is disturbing you will bear his judgment, whoever he is.

NEW CENTURY VERSION

Keep Your Freedom

5 We have freedom now, because Christ made us free.
So stand strong. Do not change and go back into the
slavery of the law. 2Listen, I Paul tell you that if you go
back to the law by being circumcised, Christ does you no
good. 3Again, I warn every man: If you allow yourselves to
be circumcised, you must follow all the law. 4If you try to
be made right with God through the law, your life with
Christ is over—you have left God's grace. 5But we have the
true hope that comes from being made right with God, and
by the Spirit we wait eagerly for this hope. 6When we are
in Christ Jesus, it is not important if we are circumcised or
not. The important thing is faith—the kind of faith that
works through love.

7You were running a good race. Who stopped you from
following the true way? 8This change did not come from
the One who chose you. 9Be careful! "Just a little yeast
makes the whole batch of dough rise." 10But I trust in the
Lord that you will not believe those different ideas. Whoever is confusing you with such ideas will be punished.

CONTEMPORARY ENGLISH VERSION

Christ Gives Freedom

5 Christ has set us free! This means we are really free.
Now hold on to your freedom and don't ever become
slaves of the Law again.

2I, Paul, promise you that Christ won't do you any good
if you get circumcised. 3If you do, you must obey the whole
Law. 4And if you try to please God by obeying the Law,
you have cut yourself off from Christ and his wonderful
kindness. 5But the Spirit makes us sure that God will
accept us because of our faith in Christ. 6If you are a follower of Christ Jesus, it makes no difference whether you
are circumcised or not. All that matters is your faith that
makes you love others.

7You were doing so well until someone made you turn
from the truth. 8And that person was certainly not sent by
the one who chose you. 9A little yeast can change a whole
batch of dough, 10but you belong to the Lord. That makes
me certain that you will do what I say, instead of what
someone else tells you to do. Whoever is causing trouble
for you will be punished.

NEW INTERNATIONAL VERSION

Freedom in Christ

5 It is for freedom that Christ has set us free. Stand firm, then, and do not let yourselves be burdened again by a yoke of slavery.

2Mark my words! I, Paul, tell you that if you let yourselves be circumcised, Christ will be of no value to you at all. 3Again I declare to every man who lets himself be circumcised that he is obligated to obey the whole law. 4You who are trying to be justified by law have been alienated from Christ; you have fallen away from grace. 5But by faith we eagerly await through the Spirit the righteousness for which we hope. 6For in Christ Jesus neither circumcision nor uncircumcision has any value. The only thing that counts is faith expressing itself through love.

7You were running a good race. Who cut in on you and kept you from obeying the truth? 8That kind of persuasion does not come from the one who calls you. 9"A little yeast works through the whole batch of dough." 10I am confident in the Lord that you will take no other view. The one who is throwing you into confusion will pay the penalty,

NEW LIVING TRANSLATION

Freedom in Christ

5 So Christ has really set us free. Now make sure that you stay free, and don't get tied up again in slavery to the law.

2Listen! I, Paul, tell you this: If you are counting on circumcision to make you right with God, then Christ cannot help you. 3I'll say it again. If you are trying to find favor with God by being circumcised, you must obey all of the regulations in the whole law of Moses. 4For if you are trying to make yourselves right with God by keeping the law, you have been cut off from Christ! You have fallen away from God's grace.

5But we who live by the Spirit eagerly wait to receive everything promised to us who are right with God through faith. 6For when we place our faith in Christ Jesus, it makes no difference to God whether we are circumcised or not circumcised. What is important is faith expressing itself in love.

7You were getting along so well. Who has interfered with you to hold you back from following the truth? 8It certainly isn't God, for he is the one who called you to freedom. 9But it takes only one wrong person among you to infect all the others—a little yeast spreads quickly through the whole batch of dough! 10I am trusting the Lord to bring you back to believing as I do about these things. God will judge that person, whoever it is, who has been troubling and confusing you.

NEW KING JAMES VERSION

Christian Liberty

5 Stand fast therefore in the liberty by which Christ has made us free,[a] and do not be entangled again with a yoke of bondage. 2Indeed I, Paul, say to you that if you become circumcised, Christ will profit you nothing. 3And I testify again to every man who becomes circumcised that he is a debtor to keep the whole law. 4You have become estranged from Christ, you who *attempt to* be justified by law; you have fallen from grace. 5For we through the Spirit eagerly wait for the hope of righteousness by faith. 6For in Christ Jesus neither circumcision nor uncircumcision avails anything, but faith working through love.

Love Fulfills the Law

7You ran well. Who hindered you from obeying the truth? 8This persuasion does not *come* from Him who calls you. 9A little leaven leavens the whole lump. 10I have confidence in you, in the Lord, that you will have no other mind; but he who troubles you shall bear his judgment, whoever he is.

5:1 [a] NU-Text reads *For freedom Christ has made us free; stand fast therefore.*

THE MESSAGE

The Life of Freedom

5 Christ has set us free to live a free life. So take your stand! Never again let anyone put a harness of slavery on you.

I am emphatic about this. The moment any one of you submits to circumcision or any other rule-keeping system, at that same moment Christ's hard-won gift of freedom is squandered. I repeat my warning: The person who accepts the ways of circumcision trades all the advantages of the free life in Christ for the obligations of the slave life of the law.

I suspect you would never intend this, but this is what happens. When you attempt to live by your own religious plans and projects, you are cut off from Christ, you fall out of grace. Meanwhile we expectantly wait for a satisfying relationship with the Spirit. For in Christ, neither our most conscientious religion nor disregard of religion amounts to anything. What matters is something far more interior: faith expressed in love.

You were running superbly! Who cut in on you, deflecting you from the true course of obedience? This detour doesn't come from the One who called you into the race in the first place. And please don't toss this off as insignificant. It only takes a minute amount of yeast, you know, to permeate an entire loaf of bread. Deep down, the Master has given me confidence that you will not defect. But the one who is upsetting you, whoever he is, will bear the divine judgment.

KING JAMES VERSION

11 And I, brethren, if I yet preach circumcision, why do I yet suffer persecution? then is the offence of the cross ceased.

12 I would they were even cut off which trouble you.

13 ¶ For, brethren, ye have been called unto liberty; only *use* not liberty for an occasion to the flesh, but by love serve one another.

14 For all the law is fulfilled in one word, *even* in this; Thou shalt love thy neighbour as thyself.

15 But if ye bite and devour one another, take heed that ye be not consumed one of another.

16 *This* I say then, Walk in the Spirit, and ye shall not fulfil the lust of the flesh.

17 For the flesh lusteth against the Spirit, and the Spirit against the flesh: and these are contrary the one to the other: so that ye cannot do the things that ye would.

18 But if ye be led of the Spirit, ye are not under the law.

NEW AMERICAN STANDARD BIBLE

11 But I, brethren, if I still preach circumcision, why am I still persecuted? Then the stumbling block of the cross has been abolished.

12 I wish that those who are troubling you would even mutilate themselves.

13 For you were called to freedom, brethren; only *do* not *turn* your freedom into an opportunity for the flesh, but through love serve one another.

14 For the whole Law is fulfilled in one word, in the *statement*, "YOU SHALL LOVE YOUR NEIGHBOR AS YOURSELF."

15 But if you bite and devour one another, take care that you are not consumed by one another.

16 But I say, walk by the Spirit, and you will not carry out the desire of the flesh.

17 For the flesh sets its desire against the Spirit, and the Spirit against the flesh; for these are in opposition to one another, so that you may not do the things that you please.

18 But if you are led by the Spirit, you are not under the Law.

NEW CENTURY VERSION

11My brothers and sisters, I do not teach that a man must be circumcised. If I teach circumcision, why am I still being attacked? If I still taught circumcision, my preaching about the cross would not be a problem. 12I wish the people who are bothering you would castrate[a] themselves!

13My brothers and sisters, God called you to be free, but do not use your freedom as an excuse to do what pleases your sinful self. Serve each other with love. 14The whole law is made complete in this one command: "Love your neighbor as you love yourself."[b] 15If you go on hurting each other and tearing each other apart, be careful, or you will completely destroy each other.

The Spirit and Human Nature

16So I tell you: Live by following the Spirit. Then you will not do what your sinful selves want. 17Our sinful selves want what is against the Spirit, and the Spirit wants what is against our sinful selves. The two are against each other, so you cannot do just what you please. 18But if the Spirit is leading you, you are not under the law.

5:12 [a] **castrate** To cut off part of the male sex organ. Paul uses this word because it is similar to "circumcision." Paul wanted to show that he is very upset with the false teachers. 5:14 [b] **"Love...yourself."** Quotation from Leviticus 19:18.

CONTEMPORARY ENGLISH VERSION

11My friends, if I still preach that people need to be circumcised, why am I in so much trouble? The message about the cross would no longer be a problem, if I told people to be circumcised. 12I wish that everyone who is upsetting you would not only get circumcised, but would cut off much more!

13My friends, you were chosen to be free. So don't use your freedom as an excuse to do anything you want. Use it as an opportunity to serve each other with love. 14All that the Law says can be summed up in the command to love others as much as you love yourself. 15But if you keep attacking each other like wild animals, you had better watch out or you will destroy yourselves.

God's Spirit and Our Own Desires

16If you are guided by the Spirit, you won't obey your selfish desires. 17The Spirit and your desires are enemies of each other. They are always fighting each other and keeping you from doing what you feel you should. 18But if you obey the Spirit, the Law of Moses has no control over you.

NEW INTERNATIONAL VERSION

whoever he may be. [11]Brothers, if I am still preaching circumcision, why am I still being persecuted? In that case the offense of the cross has been abolished. [12]As for those agitators, I wish they would go the whole way and emasculate themselves!

[13]You, my brothers, were called to be free. But do not use your freedom to indulge the sinful nature[a]; rather, serve one another in love. [14]The entire law is summed up in a single command: "Love your neighbor as yourself."[b] [15]If you keep on biting and devouring each other, watch out or you will be destroyed by each other.

Life by the Spirit

[16]So I say, live by the Spirit, and you will not gratify the desires of the sinful nature. [17]For the sinful nature desires what is contrary to the Spirit, and the Spirit what is contrary to the sinful nature. They are in conflict with each other, so that you do not do what you want. [18]But if you are led by the Spirit, you are not under law.

[a] *13* Or *the flesh*; also in verses 16, 17, 19 and 24 [b] *14* Lev. 19:18

NEW LIVING TRANSLATION

[11]Dear brothers and sisters,* if I were still preaching that you must be circumcised—as some say I do—why would the Jews persecute me? The fact that I am still being persecuted proves that I am still preaching salvation through the cross of Christ alone. [12]I only wish that those troublemakers who want to mutilate you by circumcision would mutilate themselves.*

[13]For you have been called to live in freedom—not freedom to satisfy your sinful nature, but freedom to serve one another in love. [14]For the whole law can be summed up in this one command: "Love your neighbor as yourself."* [15]But if instead of showing love among yourselves you are always biting and devouring one another, watch out! Beware of destroying one another.

Living by the Spirit's Power

[16]So I advise you to live according to your new life in the Holy Spirit. Then you won't be doing what your sinful nature craves. [17]The old sinful nature loves to do evil, which is just opposite from what the Holy Spirit wants. And the Spirit gives us desires that are opposite from what the sinful nature desires. These two forces are constantly fighting each other, and your choices are never free from this conflict. [18]But when you are directed by the Holy Spirit, you are no longer subject to the law.

5:11 Greek *Brothers.* 5:12 Or *castrate themselves;* Greek reads *cut themselves off.* 5:14 Lev 19:18.

NEW KING JAMES VERSION

[11]And I, brethren, if I still preach circumcision, why do I still suffer persecution? Then the offense of the cross has ceased. [12]I could wish that those who trouble you would even cut themselves off!

[13]For you, brethren, have been called to liberty; only do not *use* liberty as an opportunity for the flesh, but through love serve one another. [14]For all the law is fulfilled in one word, *even* in this: *"You shall love your neighbor as yourself."*[b] [15]But if you bite and devour one another, beware lest you be consumed by one another!

Walking in the Spirit

[16]I say then: Walk in the Spirit, and you shall not fulfill the lust of the flesh. [17]For the flesh lusts against the Spirit, and the Spirit against the flesh; and these are contrary to one another, so that you do not do the things that you wish. [18]But if you are led by the Spirit, you are not under the law.

5:14 [b] Leviticus 19:18

THE MESSAGE

As for the rumor that I continue to preach the ways of circumcision (as I did in those pre-Damascus Road days), that is absurd. Why would I still be persecuted, then? If I were preaching that old message, no one would be offended if I mentioned the Cross now and then—it would be so watered-down it wouldn't matter one way or the other. Why don't these agitators, obsessive as they are about circumcision, go all the way and castrate themselves!

It is absolutely clear that God has called you to a free life. Just make sure that you don't use this freedom as an excuse to do whatever you want to do and destroy your freedom. Rather, use your freedom to serve one another in love; that's how freedom grows. For everything we know about God's Word is summed up in a single sentence: Love others as you love yourself. That's an act of true freedom. If you bite and ravage each other, watch out—in no time at all you will be annihilating each other, and where will your precious freedom be then?

My counsel is this: Live freely, animated and motivated by God's Spirit. Then you won't feed the compulsions of selfishness. For there is a root of sinful self-interest in us that is at odds with a free spirit, just as the free spirit is incompatible with selfishness. These two ways of life are antithetical, so that you cannot live at times one way and at times another way according to how you feel on any given day. Why don't you choose to be led by the Spirit and so escape the erratic compulsions of a law-dominated existence?

KING JAMES VERSION

19 Now the works of the flesh are manifest, which are *these*; Adultery, fornication, uncleanness, lasciviousness,
20 Idolatry, witchcraft, hatred, variance, emulations, wrath, strife, seditions, heresies,
21 Envyings, murders, drunkenness, revellings, and such like: of the which I tell you before, as I have also told *you* in time past, that they which do such things shall not inherit the kingdom of God.
22 But the fruit of the Spirit is love, joy, peace, longsuffering, gentleness, goodness, faith,
23 Meekness, temperance: against such there is no law.
24 And they that are Christ's have crucified the flesh with the affections and lusts.

NEW AMERICAN STANDARD BIBLE

19 Now the deeds of the flesh are evident, which are: immorality, impurity, sensuality,
20 idolatry, sorcery, enmities, strife, jealousy, outbursts of anger, disputes, dissensions, factions,
21 envying, drunkenness, carousing, and things like these, of which I forewarn you, just as I have forewarned you, that those who practice such things will not inherit the kingdom of God.
22 But the fruit of the Spirit is love, joy, peace, patience, kindness, goodness, faithfulness,
23 gentleness, self-control; against such things there is no law.
24 Now those who belong to Christ Jesus have crucified the flesh with its passions and desires.

NEW CENTURY VERSION

19The wrong things the sinful self does are clear: being
sexually unfaithful, not being pure, taking part in sexual
sins, 20worshiping gods, doing witchcraft, hating, making
trouble, being jealous, being angry, being selfish, making
people angry with each other, causing divisions among
people, 21feeling envy, being drunk, having wild and
wasteful parties, and doing other things like these. I warn
you now as I warned you before: Those who do these
things will not inherit God's kingdom. 22But the Spirit pro-
duces the fruit of love, joy, peace, patience, kindness,
goodness, faithfulness, 23gentleness, self-control. There is
no law that says these things are wrong. 24Those who
belong to Christ Jesus have crucified their own sinful
selves. They have given up their old selfish feelings and
the evil things they wanted to do. 25We get our new life

CONTEMPORARY ENGLISH VERSION

19People's desires make them give in to immoral ways,
filthy thoughts, and shameful deeds. 20They worship idols,
practice witchcraft, hate others, and are hard to get along
with. People become jealous, angry, and selfish. They not
only argue and cause trouble, but they are 21envious. They
get drunk, carry on at wild parties, and do other evil things
as well. I told you before, and I am telling you again: No
one who does these things will share in the blessings of
God's kingdom.
22God's Spirit makes us loving, happy, peaceful, patient,
kind, good, faithful, 23gentle, and self-controlled. There is
no law against behaving in any of these ways. 24And
because we belong to Christ Jesus, we have killed our selfish

NEW INTERNATIONAL VERSION

19The acts of the sinful nature are obvious: sexual immorality, impurity and debauchery; 20idolatry and witchcraft; hatred, discord, jealousy, fits of rage, selfish ambition, dissensions, factions 21and envy; drunkenness, orgies, and the like. I warn you, as I did before, that those who live like this will not inherit the kingdom of God.

22But the fruit of the Spirit is love, joy, peace, patience, kindness, goodness, faithfulness, 23gentleness and self-control. Against such things there is no law. 24Those who belong to Christ Jesus have crucified the sinful nature with

NEW LIVING TRANSLATION

19When you follow the desires of your sinful nature, your lives will produce these evil results: sexual immorality, impure thoughts, eagerness for lustful pleasure, 20idolatry, participation in demonic activities, hostility, quarreling, jealousy, outbursts of anger, selfish ambition, divisions, the feeling that everyone is wrong except those in your own little group, 21envy, drunkenness, wild parties, and other kinds of sin. Let me tell you again, as I have before, that anyone living that sort of life will not inherit the Kingdom of God.

22But when the Holy Spirit controls our lives, he will produce this kind of fruit in us: love, joy, peace, patience, kindness, goodness, faithfulness, 23gentleness, and self-control. Here there is no conflict with the law.

24Those who belong to Christ Jesus have nailed the passions and desires of their sinful nature to his cross and

NEW KING JAMES VERSION

19Now the works of the flesh are evident, which are: adultery,[c] fornication, uncleanness, lewdness, 20idolatry, sorcery, hatred, contentions, jealousies, outbursts of wrath, selfish ambitions, dissensions, heresies, 21envy, murders,[d] drunkenness, revelries, and the like; of which I tell you beforehand, just as I also told *you* in time past, that those who practice such things will not inherit the kingdom of God.

22But the fruit of the Spirit is love, joy, peace, longsuffering, kindness, goodness, faithfulness, 23gentleness, self-control. Against such there is no law. 24And those *who are* Christ's have crucified the flesh with its passions and

5:19 [c] NU-Text omits *adultery.* 5:21 [d] NU-Text omits *murders.*

THE MESSAGE

✝

It is obvious what kind of life develops out of trying to get your own way all the time: repetitive, loveless, cheap sex; a stinking accumulation of mental and emotional garbage; frenzied and joyless grabs for happiness; trinket gods; magic-show religion; paranoid loneliness; cutthroat competition; all-consuming-yet-never-satisfied wants; a brutal temper; an impotence to love or be loved; divided homes and divided lives; small-minded and lopsided pursuits; the vicious habit of depersonalizing everyone into a rival; uncontrolled and uncontrollable addictions; ugly parodies of community. I could go on.

This isn't the first time I have warned you, you know. If you use your freedom this way, you will not inherit God's kingdom.

But what happens when we live God's way? He brings gifts into our lives, much the same way that fruit appears in an orchard—things like affection for others, exuberance about life, serenity. We develop a willingness to stick with things, a sense of compassion in the heart, and a conviction that a basic holiness permeates things and people. We find ourselves involved in loyal commitments, not needing to force our way in life, able to marshal and direct our energies wisely.

Legalism is helpless in bringing this about; it only gets in the way. Among those who belong to Christ, everything connected with getting our own way and mindlessly responding to what everyone else calls necessities is killed off for good—crucified.

KING JAMES VERSION

25 If we live in the Spirit, let us also walk in the Spirit.

26 Let us not be desirous of vain glory, provoking one another, envying one another.

6 Brethren, if a man be overtaken in a fault, ye which are spiritual, restore such an one in the spirit of meekness; considering thyself, lest thou also be tempted.

2 Bear ye one another's burdens, and so fulfil the law of Christ.

3 For if a man think himself to be something, when he is nothing, he deceiveth himself.

4 But let every man prove his own work, and then shall he have rejoicing in himself alone, and not in another.

5 For every man shall bear his own burden.

6 Let him that is taught in the word communicate unto him that teacheth in all good things.

7 Be not deceived; God is not mocked: for whatsoever a man soweth, that shall he also reap.

8 For he that soweth to his flesh shall of the flesh reap

NEW AMERICAN STANDARD BIBLE

25 If we live by the Spirit, let us also walk by the Spirit.

26 Let us not become boastful, challenging one another, envying one another.

Bear One Another's Burdens

6 Brethren, even if anyone is caught in any trespass, you who are spiritual, restore such a one in a spirit of gentleness; *each one* looking to yourself, so that you too will not be tempted.

2 Bear one another's burdens, and thereby fulfill the law of Christ.

3 For if anyone thinks he is something when he is nothing, he deceives himself.

4 But each one must examine his own work, and then he will have *reason for* boasting in regard to himself alone, and not in regard to another.

5 For each one will bear his own load.

6 The one who is taught the word is to share all good things with the one who teaches *him*.

7 Do not be deceived, God is not mocked; for whatever a man sows, this he will also reap.

8 For the one who sows to his own flesh will from the

NEW CENTURY VERSION

from the Spirit, so we should follow the Spirit. 26We must
not be proud or make trouble with each other or be jealous
of each other.

Help Each Other

6 Brothers and sisters, if someone in your group does
something wrong, you who are spiritual should go to
that person and gently help make him right again. But be
careful, because you might be tempted to sin, too. 2By
helping each other with your troubles, you truly obey the
law of Christ. 3If anyone thinks he is important when he
really is not, he is only fooling himself. 4Each person
should judge his own actions and not compare himself
with others. Then he can be proud for what he himself has
done. 5Each person must be responsible for himself.

6Anyone who is learning the teaching of God should
share all the good things he has with his teacher.

Life Is like Planting a Field

7Do not be fooled: You cannot cheat God. People harvest
only what they plant. 8If they plant to satisfy their sinful
selves, their sinful selves will bring them ruin. But if they

CONTEMPORARY ENGLISH VERSION

feelings and desires. 25God's Spirit has given us life, and so
we should follow the Spirit. 26But don't be conceited or
make others jealous by claiming to be better than they are.

Help Each Other

6 My friends, you are spiritual. So if someone is trapped
in sin, you should gently lead that person back to the
right path. But watch out, and don't be tempted yourself.
2You obey the law of Christ when you offer each other a
helping hand.

3If you think you are better than others, when you really
aren't, you are wrong. 4Do your own work well, and then
you will have something to be proud of. But don't compare
yourself with others. 5We each must carry our own load.

6Share every good thing you have with anyone who
teaches you what God has said.

7You cannot fool God, so don't make a fool of yourself!
You will harvest what you plant. 8If you follow your self-
ish desires, you will harvest destruction, but if you follow

NEW INTERNATIONAL VERSION

its passions and desires. 25Since we live by the Spirit, let
us keep in step with the Spirit. 26Let us not become con-
ceited, provoking and envying each other.

Doing Good to All

6 Brothers, if someone is caught in a sin, you who are
spiritual should restore him gently. But watch your-
self, or you also may be tempted. 2Carry each other's bur-
dens, and in this way you will fulfill the law of Christ. 3If
anyone thinks he is something when he is nothing, he
deceives himself. 4Each one should test his own actions.
Then he can take pride in himself, without comparing him-
self to somebody else, 5for each one should carry his own
load.

6Anyone who receives instruction in the word must
share all good things with his instructor.
7Do not be deceived: God cannot be mocked. A man
reaps what he sows. 8The one who sows to please his sin-
ful nature, from that nature[a] will reap destruction; the one

[a] 8 Or *his flesh, from the flesh*

NEW LIVING TRANSLATION

crucified them there. 25If we are living now by the Holy
Spirit, let us follow the Holy Spirit's leading in every part
of our lives. 26Let us not become conceited, or irritate one
another, or be jealous of one another.

We Reap What We Sow

6 Dear brothers and sisters, if another Christian* is
overcome by some sin, you who are godly should gen-
tly and humbly help that person back onto the right path.
And be careful not to fall into the same temptation your-
self. 2Share each other's troubles and problems, and in
this way obey the law of Christ. 3If you think you are too
important to help someone in need, you are only fooling
yourself. You are really a nobody.

4Be sure to do what you should, for then you will enjoy
the personal satisfaction of having done your work well,
and you won't need to compare yourself to anyone else.
5For we are each responsible for our own conduct.

6Those who are taught the word of God should help
their teachers by paying them.

7Don't be misled. Remember that you can't ignore God
and get away with it. You will always reap what you sow!
8Those who live only to satisfy their own sinful desires
will harvest the consequences of decay and death. But

6:1 Greek *Brothers, if a man.*

NEW KING JAMES VERSION

desires. 25If we live in the Spirit, let us also walk in the
Spirit. 26Let us not become conceited, provoking one
another, envying one another.

Bear and Share the Burdens

6 Brethren, if a man is overtaken in any trespass, you
who *are* spiritual restore such a one in a spirit of gen-
tleness, considering yourself lest you also be tempted.
2Bear one another's burdens, and so fulfill the law of
Christ. 3For if anyone thinks himself to be something,
when he is nothing, he deceives himself. 4But let each one
examine his own work, and then he will have rejoicing in
himself alone, and not in another. 5For each one shall bear
his own load.

Be Generous and Do Good

6Let him who is taught the word share in all good things
with him who teaches.

7Do not be deceived, God is not mocked; for whatever a
man sows, that he will also reap. 8For he who sows to his
flesh will of the flesh reap corruption, but he who sows to

THE MESSAGE

Since this is the kind of life we have chosen, the life of the Spirit, let us make sure that we do not just hold it as an idea in our heads or a sentiment in our hearts, but work out its implications in every detail of our lives. That means we will not compare ourselves with each other as if one of us were better and another worse. We have far more interesting things to do with our lives. Each of us is an original.

Nothing But the Cross

6 Live creatively, friends. If someone falls into sin, forgivingly restore him, saving your critical comments for yourself. *You* might be needing forgiveness before the day's out. Stoop down and reach out to those who are oppressed. Share their burdens, and so complete Christ's law. If you think you are too good for that, you are badly deceived.

Make a careful exploration of who you are and the work you have been given, and then sink yourself into that. Don't be impressed with yourself. Don't compare yourself with others. Each of you must take responsibility for doing the creative best you can with your own life.

Be very sure now, you who have been trained to a self-sufficient maturity, that you enter into a generous common life with those who have trained you, sharing all the good things that you have and experience.

Don't be misled: No one makes a fool of God. What a person plants, he will harvest. The person who plants selfishness, ignoring the needs of others—ignoring God!—harvests a crop of weeds. All he'll have to show for his life is

KING JAMES VERSION

corruption; but he that soweth to the Spirit shall of the Spirit reap life everlasting.

9 And let us not be weary in well doing: for in due season we shall reap, if we faint not.

10 As we have therefore opportunity, let us do good unto all *men*, especially unto them who are of the household of faith.

11 ¶ Ye see how large a letter I have written unto you with mine own hand.

12 As many as desire to make a fair shew in the flesh, they constrain you to be circumcised; only lest they should suffer persecution for the cross of Christ.

13 For neither they themselves who are circumcised keep the law; but desire to have you circumcised, that they may glory in your flesh.

14 But God forbid that I should glory, save in the cross of our Lord Jesus Christ, by whom the world is crucified unto me, and I unto the world.

15 For in Christ Jesus neither circumcision availeth any thing, nor uncircumcision, but a new creature.

NEW AMERICAN STANDARD BIBLE

flesh reap corruption, but the one who sows to the Spirit will from the Spirit reap eternal life.

9 Let us not lose heart in doing good, for in due time we will reap if we do not grow weary.

10 So then, while we have opportunity, let us do good to all people, and especially to those who are of the household of the faith.

11 See with what large letters I am writing to you with my own hand.

12 Those who desire to make a good showing in the flesh try to compel you to be circumcised, simply so that they will not be persecuted for the cross of Christ.

13 For those who [l]are circumcised do not even keep the Law themselves, but they desire to have you circumcised so that they may boast in your flesh.

14 But may it never be that I would boast, except in the cross of our Lord Jesus Christ, through which the world has been crucified to me, and I to the world.

15 For neither is circumcision anything, nor uncircumcision, but a new creation.

6:13 [l] Two early mss read *have been*

NEW CENTURY VERSION

plant to please the Spirit, they will receive eternal life from
the Spirit. 9We must not become tired of doing good. We
will receive our harvest of eternal life at the right time if
we do not give up. 10When we have the opportunity to help
anyone, we should do it. But we should give special attention to those who are in the family of believers.

Paul Ends His Letter

11See what large letters I use to write this myself.
12Some people are trying to force you to be circumcised so
the Jews will accept them. They are afraid they will be
attacked if they follow only the cross of Christ.[a] 13Those
who are circumcised do not obey the law themselves, but
they want you to be circumcised so they can brag about
what they forced you to do. 14I hope I will never brag
about things like that. The cross of our Lord Jesus Christ is
my only reason for bragging. Through the cross of Jesus
my world was crucified, and I died to the world. 15It is not
important if a man is circumcised or uncircumcised. The
important thing is being the new people God has made.

6:12 [a] **cross of Christ** Paul uses the cross as a picture of the gospel, the story of Christ's death and rising from the dead to pay for our sins. The cross, or Christ's death, was God's way to save us.

CONTEMPORARY ENGLISH VERSION

the Spirit, you will harvest eternal life. 9Don't get tired of
helping others. You will be rewarded when the time is
right, if you don't give up. 10We should help people whenever we can, especially if they are followers of the Lord.

Final Warnings

11You can see what big letters I make when I write with
my own hand.

12Those people who are telling you to get circumcised
are only trying to show how important they are. And they
don't want to get into trouble for preaching about the cross
of Christ. 13They are circumcised, but they don't obey the
Law of Moses. All they want is to brag about having you
circumcised. 14But I will never brag about anything except
the cross of our Lord Jesus Christ. Because of his cross, the
world is dead as far as I am concerned, and I am dead as
far as the world is concerned.

15It doesn't matter if you are circumcised or not. All that
matters is that you are a new person.

NEW INTERNATIONAL VERSION

who sows to please the Spirit, from the Spirit will reap eternal life. 9Let us not become weary in doing good, for at the proper time we will reap a harvest if we do not give up. 10Therefore, as we have opportunity, let us do good to all people, especially to those who belong to the family of believers.

Not Circumcision but a New Creation

11See what large letters I use as I write to you with my own hand!

12Those who want to make a good impression outwardly are trying to compel you to be circumcised. The only reason they do this is to avoid being persecuted for the cross of Christ. 13Not even those who are circumcised obey the law, yet they want you to be circumcised that they may boast about your flesh. 14May I never boast except in the cross of our Lord Jesus Christ, through which[b] the world has been crucified to me, and I to the world. 15Neither circumcision nor uncircumcision means anything; what counts is a new

[b] *14* Or *whom*

NEW LIVING TRANSLATION

those who live to please the Spirit will harvest everlasting life from the Spirit. 9So don't get tired of doing what is good. Don't get discouraged and give up, for we will reap a harvest of blessing at the appropriate time. 10Whenever we have the opportunity, we should do good to everyone, especially to our Christian brothers and sisters.

Paul's Final Advice

11Notice what large letters I use as I write these closing words in my own handwriting. 12Those who are trying to force you to be circumcised are doing it for just one reason. They don't want to be persecuted for teaching that the cross of Christ alone can save. 13And even those who advocate circumcision don't really keep the whole law. They only want you to be circumcised so they can brag about it and claim you as their disciples.

14As for me, God forbid that I should boast about anything except the cross of our Lord Jesus Christ. Because of that cross,* my interest in this world died long ago, and the world's interest in me is also long dead. 15It doesn't make any difference now whether we have been circumcised or not. What counts is whether we really have been changed into new and different people. 16May God's mercy

6:14 Or *Because of him.*

NEW KING JAMES VERSION

the Spirit will of the Spirit reap everlasting life. 9And let us not grow weary while doing good, for in due season we shall reap if we do not lose heart. 10Therefore, as we have opportunity, let us do good to all, especially to those who are of the household of faith.

Glory Only in the Cross

11See with what large letters I have written to you with my own hand! 12As many as desire to make a good showing in the flesh, these *would* compel you to be circumcised, only that they may not suffer persecution for the cross of Christ. 13For not even those who are circumcised keep the law, but they desire to have you circumcised that they may boast in your flesh. 14But God forbid that I should boast except in the cross of our Lord Jesus Christ, by whom[a] the world has been crucified to me, and I to the world. 15For in Christ Jesus neither circumcision nor uncircumcision avails anything, but a new creation.

6:14 [a] Or *by which* (the cross)

THE MESSAGE

weeds! But the one who plants in response to God, letting God's Spirit do the growth work in him, harvests a crop of real life, eternal life.

So let's not allow ourselves to get fatigued doing good. At the right time we will harvest a good crop if we don't give up, or quit. Right now, therefore, every time we get the chance, let us work for the benefit of all, starting with the people closest to us in the community of faith.

Now, in these last sentences, I want to emphasize in the bold scrawls of my personal handwriting the immense importance of what I have written to you. These people who are attempting to force the ways of circumcision on you have only one motive: They want an easy way to look good before others, lacking the courage to live by a faith that shares Christ's suffering and death. All their talk about the law is gas. They *themselves* don't keep the law! And they are highly selective in the laws they *do* observe. They only want you to be circumcised so they can boast of their success in recruiting you to their side. That is contemptible!

For my part, I am going to boast about nothing but the Cross of our Master, Jesus Christ. Because of that Cross, I have been crucified in relation to the world, set free from the stifling atmosphere of pleasing others and fitting into the little patterns that they dictate. Can't you see the central issue in all this? It is not what you and I do—submit to circumcision, reject circumcision. It is what *God* is doing, and he is creating something totally new, a free life!

KING JAMES VERSION

16 And as many as walk according to this rule, peace *be* on them, and mercy, and upon the Israel of God.

17 From henceforth let no man trouble me: for I bear in my body the marks of the Lord Jesus.

18 Brethren, the grace of our Lord Jesus Christ *be* with your spirit. Amen.

NEW AMERICAN STANDARD BIBLE

16 And those who will walk by this rule, peace and mercy *be* upon them, and upon the Israel of God.

17 From now on let no one cause trouble for me, for I bear on my body the brand-marks of Jesus.

18 The grace of our Lord Jesus Christ be with your spirit, brethren. Amen.

NEW CENTURY VERSION

16Peace and mercy to those who follow this rule—and to all of God's people.

17So do not give me any more trouble. I have scars on my body that show[b] I belong to Christ Jesus.

18My brothers and sisters, the grace of our Lord Jesus Christ be with your spirit. Amen.

6:17 [b] **that show** Many times Paul was beaten and whipped by people who were against him because he was teaching about Christ. The scars were from these beatings.

CONTEMPORARY ENGLISH VERSION

16If you follow this rule, you will belong to God's true people. God will treat you with undeserved kindness and will bless you with peace.

17On my own body are scars that prove I belong to Christ Jesus. So I don't want anyone to bother me anymore.

18My friends, I pray that the Lord Jesus Christ will be kind to you! Amen.

NEW INTERNATIONAL VERSION

creation. 16Peace and mercy to all who follow this rule, even to the Israel of God.

17Finally, let no one cause me trouble, for I bear on my body the marks of Jesus.

18The grace of our Lord Jesus Christ be with your spirit, brothers. Amen.

NEW LIVING TRANSLATION

and peace be upon all those who live by this principle. They are the new people of God.*

17From now on, don't let anyone trouble me with these things. For I bear on my body the scars that show I belong to Jesus.

18My dear brothers and sisters,* may the grace of our Lord Jesus Christ be with you all. Amen.

6:16 Greek *the Israel of God.* **6:18** Greek *Brothers.*

NEW KING JAMES VERSION

Blessing and a Plea

16And as many as walk according to this rule, peace and mercy *be* upon them, and upon the Israel of God.

17From now on let no one trouble me, for I bear in my body the marks of the Lord Jesus.

18Brethren, the grace of our Lord Jesus Christ *be* with your spirit. Amen.

THE MESSAGE

All who walk by this standard are the true Israel of God—his chosen people. Peace and mercy on them!

Quite frankly, I don't want to be bothered anymore by these disputes. I have far more important things to do—the serious living of this faith. I bear in my body scars from my service to Jesus.

May what our Master Jesus Christ gives freely be deeply and personally yours, my friends. Oh, yes!

KING JAMES VERSION

THE EPISTLE OF ST. PAUL TO THE

EPHESIANS

1 Paul, an apostle of Jesus Christ by the will of God, to the saints which are at Ephesus, and to the faithful in Christ Jesus:

2 Grace *be* to you, and peace, from God our Father, and *from* the Lord Jesus Christ.

3 ¶ Blessed *be* the God and Father of our Lord Jesus Christ, who hath blessed us with all spiritual blessings in heavenly *places* in Christ:

4 According as he hath chosen us in him before the foundation of the world, that we should be holy and without blame before him in love:

5 Having predestinated us unto the adoption of children by Jesus Christ to himself, according to the good pleasure of his will,

6 To the praise of the glory of his grace, wherein he hath made us accepted in the beloved.

7 In whom we have redemption through his blood, the forgiveness of sins, according to the riches of his grace;

NEW AMERICAN STANDARD BIBLE

THE LETTER OF PAUL TO THE

EPHESIANS

The Blessings of Redemption

1 Paul, an apostle of Christ Jesus by the will of God,
To the saints who are [1]at Ephesus and *who are* faithful in Christ Jesus:

2 Grace to you and peace from God our Father and the Lord Jesus Christ.

3 Blessed *be* the God and Father of our Lord Jesus Christ, who has blessed us with every spiritual blessing in the heavenly *places* in Christ,

4 just as He chose us in Him before the foundation of the world, that we would be holy and blameless before [2]Him. In love

5 He predestined us to adoption as sons through Jesus Christ to Himself, according to the kind intention of His will,

6 to the praise of the glory of His grace, which He freely bestowed on us in the Beloved.

7 In Him we have redemption through His blood, the forgiveness of our trespasses, according to the riches of His grace

1:1 [1] Three early mss do not contain *at Ephesus* 1:4 [2] Or *Him, in love*

NEW CENTURY VERSION

EPHESIANS

1 From Paul, an apostle of Christ Jesus. I am an apostle because that is what God wanted.

To God's holy people living in Ephesus, believers in Christ Jesus:

2Grace and peace to you from God our Father and the Lord Jesus Christ.

Spiritual Blessings in Christ

3Praise be to the God and Father of our Lord Jesus Christ. In Christ, God has given us every spiritual blessing in the heavenly world. 4That is, in Christ, he chose us before the world was made so that we would be his holy people—people without blame before him. 5Because of his love, God had already decided to make us his own children through Jesus Christ. That was what he wanted and what pleased him, 6and it brings praise to God because of his wonderful grace. God gave that grace to us freely, in Christ, the One he loves. 7In Christ we are set free by the blood of his death, and so we have forgiveness of sins.

CONTEMPORARY ENGLISH VERSION

EPHESIANS

1 From Paul, chosen by God to be an apostle of Christ Jesus.

To God's people who live in Ephesus and[a] are faithful followers of Christ Jesus.

2I pray that God our Father and our Lord Jesus Christ will be kind to you and will bless you with peace!

Christ Brings Spiritual Blessings

3Praise the God and Father of our Lord Jesus Christ for the spiritual blessings that Christ has brought us from heaven! 4Before the world was created, God had Christ choose us to live with him and to be his holy and innocent and loving people. 5God was kind[b] and decided that Christ would choose us to be God's own adopted children. 6God was very kind to us because of the Son he dearly loves, and so we should praise God.

7-8Christ sacrificed his life's blood to set us free, which means that our sins are now forgiven. Christ did this

[a] 1.1 *live in Ephesus and*: Some manuscripts do not have these words.
[b] 1.4,5 *holy and innocent and loving people. 5God was kind*: Or "holy and innocent people. God was loving 5and kind."

NEW INTERNATIONAL VERSION

EPHESIANS

1 Paul, an apostle of Christ Jesus by the will of God,

To the saints in Ephesus,[a] the faithful[b] in Christ Jesus:

[2]Grace and peace to you from God our Father and the
Lord Jesus Christ.

Spiritual Blessings in Christ

[3]Praise be to the God and Father of our Lord Jesus
Christ, who has blessed us in the heavenly realms with
every spiritual blessing in Christ. [4]For he chose us in him
before the creation of the world to be holy and blameless
in his sight. In love [5]he[c] predestined us to be adopted as
his sons through Jesus Christ, in accordance with his plea-
sure and will— [6]to the praise of his glorious grace, which
he has freely given us in the One he loves. [7]In him we have
redemption through his blood, the forgiveness of sins, in
accordance with the riches of God's grace [8]that he lavished

[a] *1* Some early manuscripts do not have *in Ephesus.* [b] *1* Or *believers who are* [c] *4,5* Or *sight in love.* [5]*He*

NEW LIVING TRANSLATION

EPHESIANS

Greetings from Paul

1 This letter is from Paul, chosen by God to be an apos-
tle of Christ Jesus.

It is written to God's holy people in Ephesus,* who are
faithful followers of Christ Jesus.

[2]May grace and peace be yours, sent to you from God
our Father and Jesus Christ our Lord.

Spiritual Blessings

[3]How we praise God, the Father of our Lord Jesus Christ,
who has blessed us with every spiritual blessing in the
heavenly realms because we belong to Christ. [4]Long ago,
even before he made the world, God loved us and chose us
in Christ to be holy and without fault in his eyes. [5]His
unchanging plan has always been to adopt us into his own
family by bringing us to himself through Jesus Christ. And
this gave him great pleasure.

[6]So we praise God for the wonderful kindness he has
poured out on us because we belong to his dearly loved Son.
[7]He is so rich in kindness that he purchased our freedom
through the blood of his Son, and our sins are forgiven. [8]He

1:1 Some manuscripts do not include *in Ephesus.*

NEW KING JAMES VERSION

THE EPISTLE OF PAUL TO THE

EPHESIANS

Greeting

1 Paul, an apostle of Jesus Christ by the will of God,

To the saints who are in Ephesus, and faithful in Christ
Jesus:

[2]Grace to you and peace from God our Father and the
Lord Jesus Christ.

Redemption in Christ

[3]Blessed *be* the God and Father of our Lord Jesus Christ,
who has blessed us with every spiritual blessing in the
heavenly *places* in Christ, [4]just as He chose us in Him be-
fore the foundation of the world, that we should be holy
and without blame before Him in love, [5]having predestined
us to adoption as sons by Jesus Christ to Himself, accord-
ing to the good pleasure of His will, [6]to the praise of the
glory of His grace, by which He made us accepted in the
Beloved.

[7]In Him we have redemption through His blood, the for-
giveness of sins, according to the riches of His grace

THE MESSAGE

EPHESIANS

1 I, Paul, am under God's plan as an apostle, a special
agent of Christ Jesus, writing to you faithful
Christians in Ephesus. I greet you with the grace and peace
poured into our lives by God our Father and our Master,
Jesus Christ.

The God of Glory

How blessed is God! And what a blessing he is! He's the
Father of our Master, Jesus Christ, and takes us to the high
places of blessing in him. Long before he laid down earth's
foundations, he had us in mind, had settled on us as the
focus of his love, to be made whole and holy by his love.
Long, long ago he decided to adopt us into his family
through Jesus Christ. (What pleasure he took in planning
this!) He wanted us to enter into the celebration of his lav-
ish gift-giving by the hand of his beloved Son.

Because of the sacrifice of the Messiah, his blood poured
out on the altar of the Cross, we're a free people—free of
penalties and punishments chalked up by all our mis-
deeds. And not just barely free, either. *Abundantly* free! He

KING JAMES VERSION

8 Wherein he hath abounded toward us in all wisdom and prudence;

9 Having made known unto us the mystery of his will, according to his good pleasure which he hath purposed in himself:

10 That in the dispensation of the fulness of times he might gather together in one all things in Christ, both which are in heaven, and which are on earth; *even* in him:

11 In whom also we have obtained an inheritance, being predestinated according to the purpose of him who worketh all things after the counsel of his own will:

12 That we should be to the praise of his glory, who first trusted in Christ.

13 In whom ye also *trusted*, after that ye heard the word of truth, the gospel of your salvation: in whom also after that ye believed, ye were sealed with that holy Spirit of promise,

14 Which is the earnest of our inheritance until the redemption of the purchased possession, unto the praise of his glory.

15 ¶ Wherefore I also, after I heard of your faith in the Lord Jesus, and love unto all the saints,

16 Cease not to give thanks for you, making mention of you in my prayers;

17 That the God of our Lord Jesus Christ, the Father of glory, may give unto you the spirit of wisdom and revelation in the knowledge of him:

18 The eyes of your understanding being enlightened;

NEW AMERICAN STANDARD BIBLE

8 which He lavished on us. In all wisdom and insight

9 He made known to us the mystery of His will, according to His kind intention which He purposed in Him

10 with a view to an administration suitable to the fullness of the times, *that is*, the summing up of all things in Christ, things in the heavens and things on the earth. In Him

11 also we have obtained an inheritance, having been predestined according to His purpose who works all things after the counsel of His will,

12 to the end that we who were the first to hope in [3]Christ would be to the praise of His glory.

13 In Him, you also, after listening to the message of truth, the gospel of your salvation—having also believed, you were sealed in Him with the Holy Spirit of promise,

14 who is given as a pledge of our inheritance, with a view to the redemption of *God's own* possession, to the praise of His glory.

15 For this reason I too, having heard of the faith in the Lord Jesus which *exists* among you and [4]your love for all the saints,

16 do not cease giving thanks for you, while making mention *of you* in my prayers;

17 that the God of our Lord Jesus Christ, the Father of glory, may give to you a spirit of wisdom and of revelation in the knowledge of Him.

18 *I pray that* the eyes of your heart may be enlightened,

1:12 [3] I.e. the Messiah 1:15 [4] Three early mss do not contain *your love*

NEW CENTURY VERSION

How rich is God's grace, [8]which he has given to us so fully
and freely. God, with full wisdom and understanding, [9]let
us know his secret purpose. This was what God wanted,
and he planned to do it through Christ. [10]His goal was to
carry out his plan, when the right time came, that all
things in heaven and on earth would be joined together in
Christ as the head.
[11]In Christ we were chosen to be God's people, because
from the very beginning God had decided this in keeping
with his plan. And he is the One who makes everything
agree with what he decides and wants. [12]We are the first
people who hoped in Christ, and we were chosen so that
we would bring praise to God's glory. [13]So it is with you.
When you heard the true teaching—the Good News about
your salvation—you believed in Christ. And in Christ, God
put his special mark of ownership on you by giving you
the Holy Spirit that he had promised. [14]That Holy Spirit is
the guarantee that we will receive what God promised for
his people until God gives full freedom to those who are
his—to bring praise to God's glory.

Paul's Prayer

[15]That is why since I heard about your faith in the Lord
Jesus and your love for all God's people, [16]I have not
stopped giving thanks to God for you. I always remember
you in my prayers, [17]asking the God of our Lord Jesus
Christ, the glorious Father, to give you a spirit of wisdom
and revelation so that you will know him better. [18]I pray
also that you will have greater understanding in your

CONTEMPORARY ENGLISH VERSION

because God was so kind to us. God has great wisdom and
understanding, [9]and by what Christ has done, God has
shown us his own mysterious ways. [10]Then when the time
is right, God will do all that he has planned, and Christ
will bring together everything in heaven and on earth.
[11]God always does what he plans, and that's why he
appointed Christ to choose us. [12]He did this so that we
Jews would bring honor to him and be the first ones to
have hope because of him. [13]Christ also brought you the
truth, which is the good news about how you can be
saved. You put your faith in Christ and were given the
promised Holy Spirit to show that you belong to God.
[14]The Spirit also makes us sure that we will be given what
God has stored up for his people. Then we will be set free,
and God will be honored and praised.

Paul's Prayer

[15]I have heard about your faith in the Lord Jesus and
your love for all of God's people. [16]So I never stop being
grateful for you, as I mention you in my prayers. [17]I ask the
glorious Father and God of our Lord Jesus Christ to give you
his Spirit. The Spirit will make you wise and let you under-
stand what it means to know God. [18]My prayer is that light
will flood your hearts and that you will understand the

NEW INTERNATIONAL VERSION

on us with all wisdom and understanding. 9And he[d] made known to us the mystery of his will according to his good pleasure, which he purposed in Christ, 10to be put into effect when the times will have reached their fulfillment—to bring all things in heaven and on earth together under one head, even Christ.

11In him we were also chosen,[e] having been predestined according to the plan of him who works out everything in conformity with the purpose of his will, 12in order that we, who were the first to hope in Christ, might be for the praise of his glory. 13And you also were included in Christ when you heard the word of truth, the gospel of your salvation. Having believed, you were marked in him with a seal, the promised Holy Spirit, 14who is a deposit guaranteeing our inheritance until the redemption of those who are God's possession—to the praise of his glory.

Thanksgiving and Prayer

15For this reason, ever since I heard about your faith in the Lord Jesus and your love for all the saints, 16I have not stopped giving thanks for you, remembering you in my prayers. 17I keep asking that the God of our Lord Jesus Christ, the glorious Father, may give you the Spirit[f] of wisdom and revelation, so that you may know him better. 18I pray also that the eyes of your heart may be enlightened in

[d] *8,9* Or *us. With all wisdom and understanding,* 9*he*   [e] *11* Or *were made heirs*   [f] *17* Or *a spirit*

NEW LIVING TRANSLATION

has showered his kindness on us, along with all wisdom and understanding.

9God's secret plan has now been revealed to us; it is a plan centered on Christ, designed long ago according to his good pleasure. 10And this is his plan: At the right time he will bring everything together under the authority of Christ—everything in heaven and on earth. 11Furthermore, because of Christ, we have received an inheritance from God,* for he chose us from the beginning, and all things happen just as he decided long ago. 12God's purpose was that we who were the first to trust in Christ should praise our glorious God. 13And now you also have heard the truth, the Good News that God saves you. And when you believed in Christ, he identified you as his own by giving you the Holy Spirit, whom he promised long ago. 14The Spirit is God's guarantee that he will give us everything he promised and that he has purchased us to be his own people. This is just one more reason for us to praise our glorious God.

Paul's Prayer for Spiritual Wisdom

15Ever since I first heard of your strong faith in the Lord Jesus and your love for Christians everywhere, 16I have never stopped thanking God for you. I pray for you constantly, 17asking God, the glorious Father of our Lord Jesus Christ, to give you spiritual wisdom and understanding, so that you might grow in your knowledge of God. 18I pray that your hearts will be flooded with light so that you can

1:11 Or *we have become God's inheritance.*

NEW KING JAMES VERSION

8which He made to abound toward us in all wisdom and prudence, 9having made known to us the mystery of His will, according to His good pleasure which He purposed in Himself, 10that in the dispensation of the fullness of the times He might gather together in one all things in Christ, both[a] which are in heaven and which are on earth—in Him. 11In Him also we have obtained an inheritance, being predestined according to the purpose of Him who works all things according to the counsel of His will, 12that we who first trusted in Christ should be to the praise of His glory.

13In Him you also *trusted,* after you heard the word of truth, the gospel of your salvation; in whom also, having believed, you were sealed with the Holy Spirit of promise, 14who[b] is the guarantee of our inheritance until the redemption of the purchased possession, to the praise of His glory.

Prayer for Spiritual Wisdom

15Therefore I also, after I heard of your faith in the Lord Jesus and your love for all the saints, 16do not cease to give thanks for you, making mention of you in my prayers: 17that the God of our Lord Jesus Christ, the Father of glory, may give to you the spirit of wisdom and revelation in the knowledge of Him, 18the eyes of your understanding[c] being enlightened; that you may know what is the hope of

1:10 [a] NU-Text and M-Text omit *both.*   **1:14** [b] NU-Text reads *which.*
1:18 [c] NU-Text and M-Text read *hearts.*

THE MESSAGE

thought of everything, provided for everything we could possibly need, letting us in on the plans he took such delight in making. He set it all out before us in Christ, a long-range plan in which everything would be brought together and summed up in him, everything in deepest heaven, everything on planet earth.

It's in Christ that we find out who we are and what we are living for. Long before we first heard of Christ and got our hopes up, he had his eye on us, had designs on us for glorious living, part of the overall purpose he is working out in everything and everyone.

It's in Christ that you, once you heard the truth and believed it (this Message of your salvation), found yourselves home free—signed, sealed, and delivered by the Holy Spirit. This signet from God is the first installment on what's coming, a reminder that we'll get everything God has planned for us, a praising and glorious life.

That's why, when I heard of the solid trust you have in the Master Jesus and your outpouring of love to all the Christians, I couldn't stop thanking God for you—every time I prayed, I'd think of you and give thanks. But I do more than thank. I ask—ask the God of our Master, Jesus Christ, the God of glory—to make you intelligent and discerning in knowing him personally, your eyes focused and clear, so that you can see exactly what it is he is calling

KING JAMES VERSION

that ye may know what is the hope of his calling, and what
the riches of the glory of his inheritance in the saints,
19 And what *is* the exceeding greatness of his power to
us-ward who believe, according to the working of his
mighty power,
20 Which he wrought in Christ, when he raised him
from the dead, and set *him* at his own right hand in the
heavenly *places*,
21 Far above all principality, and power, and might,
and dominion, and every name that is named, not only in
this world, but also in that which is to come:
22 And hath put all *things* under his feet, and gave him
to be the head over all *things* to the church,
23 Which is his body, the fulness of him that filleth all
in all.

2 And you *hath he quickened*, who were dead in tres-
passes and sins;
2 Wherein in time past ye walked according to the
course of this world, according to the prince of the power
of the air, the spirit that now worketh in the children of
disobedience:
3 Among whom also we all had our conversation in
times past in the lusts of our flesh, fulfilling the desires of
the flesh and of the mind; and were by nature the children
of wrath, even as others.
4 ¶ But God, who is rich in mercy, for his great love
wherewith he loved us,
5 Even when we were dead in sins, hath quickened us
together with Christ, (by grace ye are saved;)

NEW AMERICAN STANDARD BIBLE

so that you will know what is the hope of His calling, what
are the riches of the glory of His inheritance in the saints,
19 and what is the surpassing greatness of His power
toward us who believe. *These are* in accordance with the
working of the strength of His might
20 which He brought about in Christ, when He raised
Him from the dead and seated Him at His right hand in the
heavenly *places*,
21 far above all rule and authority and power and
dominion, and every name that is named, not only in this
age but also in the one to come.
22 And He put all things in subjection under His feet,
and gave Him as head over all things to the church,
23 which is His body, the fullness of Him who fills all in
all.

Made Alive in Christ

2 And you were dead in your trespasses and sins,
2 in which you formerly walked according to the course
of this world, according to the prince of the power of the air,
of the spirit that is now working in the sons of disobedience.
3 Among them we too all formerly lived in the lusts of
our flesh, indulging the desires of the flesh and of the mind,
and were by nature children of wrath, even as the rest.
4 But God, being rich in mercy, because of His great
love with which He loved us,
5 even when we were dead in our transgressions, made
us alive together [l] with Christ (by grace you have been saved),

2:5 [l] Two early mss reads *in Christ*

NEW CENTURY VERSION

heart so you will know the hope to which he has called us
and that you will know how rich and glorious are the
blessings God has promised his holy people. 19And you
will know that God's power is very great for us who
believe. That power is the same as the great strength
20God used to raise Christ from the dead and put him at
his right side in the heavenly world. 21God has put Christ
over all rulers, authorities, powers, and kings, not only in
this world but also in the next. 22God put everything under
his power and made him the head over everything for the
church, 23which is Christ's body. The church is filled with
Christ, and Christ fills everything in every way.

We Now Have Life

2 In the past you were spiritually dead because of your
sins and the things you did against God. 2Yes, in the
past you lived the way the world lives, following the ruler
of the evil powers that are above the earth. That same spir-
it is now working in those who refuse to obey God. 3In the
past all of us lived like them, trying to please our sinful
selves and doing all the things our bodies and minds
wanted. We should have suffered God's anger because of
the way we were. We were the same as all other people.
4But God's mercy is great, and he loved us very much.
5Though we were spiritually dead because of the things we
did against God, he gave us new life with Christ. You have
been saved by God's grace. 6And he raised us up with Christ

CONTEMPORARY ENGLISH VERSION

hope that was given to you when God chose you. Then you
will discover the glorious blessings that will be yours
together with all of God's people.
19I want you to know about the great and mighty power
that God has for us followers. It is the same wonderful
power he used 20when he raised Christ from death and let
him sit at his right side[c] in heaven. 21There Christ rules
over all forces, authorities, powers, and rulers. He rules
over all beings in this world and will rule in the future
world as well. 22God has put all things under the power of
Christ, and for the good of the church he has made him the
head of everything. 23The church is Christ's body and is
filled with Christ who completely fills everything.[d]

From Death to Life

2 In the past you were dead because you sinned and
fought against God. 2You followed the ways of this
world and obeyed the devil. He rules the world, and his
spirit has power over everyone who doesn't obey God.
3Once we were also ruled by the selfish desires of our bod-
ies and minds. We had made God angry, and we were
going to be punished like everyone else.
4-5But God was merciful! We were dead because of our
sins, but God loved us so much that he made us alive with
Christ, and God's wonderful kindness is what saves you.

[c] 1.20 *right side*: The place of power and honor. [d] 1.23 *and is filled with Christ who completely fills everything*: Or "which completely fills Christ and fully completes his work."

NEW INTERNATIONAL VERSION

order that you may know the hope to which he has called
you, the riches of his glorious inheritance in the saints,
19and his incomparably great power for us who believe.
That power is like the working of his mighty strength,
20which he exerted in Christ when he raised him from the
dead and seated him at his right hand in the heavenly
realms, 21far above all rule and authority, power and
dominion, and every title that can be given, not only in the
present age but also in the one to come. 22And God placed
all things under his feet and appointed him to be head
over everything for the church, 23which is his body, the
fullness of him who fills everything in every way.

Made Alive in Christ

2 As for you, you were dead in your transgressions and
sins, 2in which you used to live when you followed the
ways of this world and of the ruler of the kingdom of the air,
the spirit who is now at work in those who are disobedient.
3All of us also lived among them at one time, gratifying the
cravings of our sinful nature[a] and following its desires and
thoughts. Like the rest, we were by nature objects of wrath.
4But because of his great love for us, God, who is rich in
mercy, 5made us alive with Christ even when we were dead
in transgressions—it is by grace you have been saved. 6And

[a] *3* Or *our flesh*

NEW LIVING TRANSLATION

understand the wonderful future he has promised to those
he called. I want you to realize what a rich and glorious
inheritance he has given to his people.*

19I pray that you will begin to understand the incredible
greatness of his power for us who believe him. This is the
same mighty power 20that raised Christ from the dead and
seated him in the place of honor at God's right hand in the
heavenly realms. 21Now he is far above any ruler or
authority or power or leader or anything else in this world
or in the world to come. 22And God has put all things
under the authority of Christ, and he gave him this author-
ity for the benefit of the church. 23And the church is his
body; it is filled by Christ, who fills everything everywhere
with his presence.

Made Alive with Christ

2 Once you were dead, doomed forever because of your
many sins. 2You used to live just like the rest of the
world, full of sin, obeying Satan, the mighty prince of the
power of the air. He is the spirit at work in the hearts of
those who refuse to obey God. 3All of us used to live that
way, following the passions and desires of our evil nature.
We were born with an evil nature, and we were under
God's anger just like everyone else.

4But God is so rich in mercy, and he loved us so very
much, 5that even while we were dead because of our sins,
he gave us life when he raised Christ from the dead. (It is
only by God's special favor that you have been saved!)

1:18 Or *realize how much God has been honored by acquiring his people.*

NEW KING JAMES VERSION

His calling, what are the riches of the glory of His inheri-
tance in the saints, 19and what *is* the exceeding greatness
of His power toward us who believe, according to the
working of His mighty power 20which He worked in Christ
when He raised Him from the dead and seated *Him* at His
right hand in the heavenly *places,* 21far above all principal-
ity and power and might and dominion, and every name
that is named, not only in this age but also in that which
is to come.

22And He put all *things* under His feet, and gave Him *to
be* head over all *things* to the church, 23which is His body,
the fullness of Him who fills all in all.

By Grace Through Faith

2 And you *He made alive,* who were dead in trespasses
and sins, 2in which you once walked according to the
course of this world, according to the prince of the power
of the air, the spirit who now works in the sons of disobe-
dience, 3among whom also we all once conducted our-
selves in the lusts of our flesh, fulfilling the desires of the
flesh and of the mind, and were by nature children of
wrath, just as the others.

4But God, who is rich in mercy, because of His great love
with which He loved us, 5even when we were dead in tres-
passes, made us alive together with Christ (by grace you

THE MESSAGE

you to do, grasp the immensity of this glorious way of life
he has for Christians, oh, the utter extravagance of his
work in us who trust him—endless energy, boundless
strength!

All this energy issues from Christ: God raised him from
death and set him on a throne in deep heaven, in charge of
running the universe, everything from galaxies to govern-
ments, no name and no power exempt from his rule. And
not just for the time being, but *forever.* He is in charge of it
all, has the final word on everything. At the center of all
this, Christ rules the church. The church, you see, is not
peripheral to the world; the world is peripheral to the
church. The church is Christ's body, in which he speaks
and acts, by which he fills everything with his presence.

He Tore Down the Wall

2 It wasn't so long ago that you were mired in that old
stagnant life of sin. You let the world, which doesn't
know the first thing about living, tell you how to live. You
filled your lungs with polluted unbelief, and then exhaled
disobedience. We all did it, all of us doing what we felt like
doing, when we felt like doing it, all of us in the same
boat. It's a wonder God didn't lose his temper and do away
with the whole lot of us. Instead, immense in mercy and
with an incredible love, he embraced us. He took our sin-
dead lives and made us alive in Christ. He did all this on
his own, with no help from us! Then he picked us up and

KING JAMES VERSION

6 And hath raised *us* up together, and made *us* sit together in heavenly *places* in Christ Jesus:

7 That in the ages to come he might shew the exceeding riches of his grace in *his* kindness toward us through Christ Jesus.

8 For by grace are ye saved through faith; and that not of yourselves: *it is* the gift of God:

9 Not of works, lest any man should boast.

10 For we are his workmanship, created in Christ Jesus unto good works, which God hath before ordained that we should walk in them.

11 ¶ Wherefore remember, that ye *being* in time past Gentiles in the flesh, who are called Uncircumcision by that which is called the Circumcision in the flesh made by hands;

12 That at that time ye were without Christ, being aliens from the commonwealth of Israel, and strangers from the covenants of promise, having no hope, and without God in the world:

13 But now in Christ Jesus ye who sometimes were far off are made nigh by the blood of Christ.

14 ¶ For he is our peace, who hath made both one, and hath broken down the middle wall of partition *between us;*

15 Having abolished in his flesh the enmity, *even* the law of commandments *contained* in ordinances; for to

NEW AMERICAN STANDARD BIBLE

6 and raised us up with Him, and seated us with Him in the heavenly *places* in Christ Jesus,

7 so that in the ages to come He might show the surpassing riches of His grace in kindness toward us in Christ Jesus.

8 For by grace you have been saved through faith; and that not of yourselves, *it is* the gift of God;

9 not as a result of works, so that no one may boast.

10 For we are His workmanship, created in Christ Jesus for good works, which God prepared beforehand so that we would walk in them.

11 Therefore remember that formerly you, the Gentiles in the flesh, who are called "Uncircumcision" by the so-called "Circumcision," *which is* performed in the flesh by human hands—

12 *remember* that you were at that time separate from Christ, excluded from the commonwealth of Israel, and strangers to the covenants of promise, having no hope and without God in the world.

13 But now in Christ Jesus you who formerly were far off have been brought near by the blood of Christ.

14 For He Himself is our peace, who made both *groups into* one and broke down the barrier of the dividing wall,

15 by abolishing in His flesh the enmity, *which is* the Law of commandments *contained* in ordinances, so that in

NEW CENTURY VERSION

and gave us a seat with him in the heavens. He did this for those in Christ Jesus 7so that for all future time he could show the very great riches of his grace by being kind to us in Christ Jesus. 8I mean that you have been saved by grace through believing. You did not save yourselves; it was a gift from God. 9It was not the result of your own efforts, so you cannot brag about it. 10God has made us what we are. In Christ Jesus, God made us to do good works, which God planned in advance for us to live our lives doing.

One in Christ

11You were not born Jewish. You are the people the Jews call "uncircumcised."[a] Those who call you "uncircumcised" call themselves "circumcised." (Their circumcision is only something they themselves do on their bodies.) 12Remember that in the past you were without Christ. You were not citizens of Israel, and you had no part in the agreements[b] with the promise that God made to his people. You had no hope, and you did not know God. 13But now in Christ Jesus, you who were far away from God are brought near through the blood of Christ's death. 14Christ himself is our peace. He made both Jewish people and those who are not Jews one people. They were separated as if there were a wall between them, but Christ broke down that wall of hate by giving his own body. 15The Jewish law had many commands and rules, but Christ ended that law.

2:11 [a] **uncircumcised** People not having the mark of circumcision as the Jews had. 2:12 [b] **agreements** The agreements that God gave to his people in the Old Testament.

CONTEMPORARY ENGLISH VERSION

6God raised us from death to life with Christ Jesus, and he has given us a place beside Christ in heaven. 7God did this so that in the future world he could show how truly good and kind he is to us because of what Christ Jesus has done. 8You were saved by faith in God, who treats us much better than we deserve.[a] This is God's gift to you, and not anything you have done on your own. 9It isn't something you have earned, so there is nothing you can brag about. 10God planned for us to do good things and to live as he has always wanted us to live. That's why he sent Christ to make us what we are.

United by Christ

11Don't forget that you are Gentiles. In fact, you used to be called "uncircumcised" by those who take pride in being circumcised. 12At that time you did not know about Christ. You were foreigners to the people of Israel, and you had no part in the promises that God had made to them. You were living in this world without hope and without God, 13and you were far from God. But Christ offered his life's blood as a sacrifice and brought you near God.

14Christ has made peace between Jews and Gentiles, and he has united us by breaking down the wall of hatred that separated us. Christ gave his own body 15to destroy the Law of Moses with all its rules and commands. He even

[a] 2.8 *treats us much better than we deserve*: The Greek word *charis*, traditionally rendered "grace," is translated here and other places in the CEV to express the overwhelming kindness of God.

NEW INTERNATIONAL VERSION

God raised us up with Christ and seated us with him in the heavenly realms in Christ Jesus, 7in order that in the coming ages he might show the incomparable riches of his grace, expressed in his kindness to us in Christ Jesus. 8For it is by grace you have been saved, through faith—and this not from yourselves, it is the gift of God— 9not by works, so that no one can boast. 10For we are God's workmanship, created in Christ Jesus to do good works, which God prepared in advance for us to do.

One in Christ

11Therefore, remember that formerly you who are Gentiles by birth and called "uncircumcised" by those who call themselves "the circumcision" (that done in the body by the hands of men)— 12remember that at that time you were separate from Christ, excluded from citizenship in Israel and foreigners to the covenants of the promise, without hope and without God in the world. 13But now in Christ Jesus you who once were far away have been brought near through the blood of Christ.

14For he himself is our peace, who has made the two one and has destroyed the barrier, the dividing wall of hostility, 15by abolishing in his flesh the law with its commandments and regulations. His purpose was to create in himself one

NEW LIVING TRANSLATION

6For he raised us from the dead along with Christ, and we are seated with him in the heavenly realms—all because we are one with Christ Jesus. 7And so God can always point to us as examples of the incredible wealth of his favor and kindness toward us, as shown in all he has done for us through Christ Jesus.

8God saved you by his special favor when you believed. And you can't take credit for this; it is a gift from God. 9Salvation is not a reward for the good things we have done, so none of us can boast about it. 10For we are God's masterpiece. He has created us anew in Christ Jesus, so that we can do the good things he planned for us long ago.

Oneness and Peace in Christ

11Don't forget that you Gentiles used to be outsiders by birth. You were called "the uncircumcised ones" by the Jews, who were proud of their circumcision, even though it affected only their bodies and not their hearts. 12In those days you were living apart from Christ. You were excluded from God's people, Israel, and you did not know the promises God had made to them. You lived in this world without God and without hope. 13But now you belong to Christ Jesus. Though you once were far away from God, now you have been brought near to him because of the blood of Christ.

14For Christ himself has made peace between us Jews and you Gentiles by making us all one people. He has broken down the wall of hostility that used to separate us. 15By his death he ended the whole system of Jewish law that excluded the Gentiles. His purpose was to make peace

NEW KING JAMES VERSION

have been saved), 6and raised *us* up together, and made *us* sit together in the heavenly *places* in Christ Jesus, 7that in the ages to come He might show the exceeding riches of His grace in *His* kindness toward us in Christ Jesus. 8For by grace you have been saved through faith, and that not of yourselves; *it is* the gift of God, 9not of works, lest anyone should boast. 10For we are His workmanship, created in Christ Jesus for good works, which God prepared beforehand that we should walk in them.

Brought Near by His Blood

11Therefore remember that you, once Gentiles in the flesh—who are called Uncircumcision by what is called the Circumcision made in the flesh by hands— 12that at that time you were without Christ, being aliens from the commonwealth of Israel and strangers from the covenants of promise, having no hope and without God in the world. 13But now in Christ Jesus you who once were far off have been brought near by the blood of Christ.

Christ Our Peace

14For He Himself is our peace, who has made both one, and has broken down the middle wall of separation, 15having abolished in His flesh the enmity, *that is,* the law of commandments *contained* in ordinances, so as to create in

THE MESSAGE

set us down in highest heaven in company with Jesus, our Messiah.

Now God has us where he wants us, with all the time in this world and the next to shower grace and kindness upon us in Christ Jesus. Saving is all his idea, and all his work. All we do is trust him enough to let him do it. It's God's gift from start to finish! We don't play the major role. If we did, we'd probably go around bragging that we'd done the whole thing! No, we neither make nor save ourselves. God does both the making and saving. He creates each of us by Christ Jesus to join him in the work he does, the good work he has gotten ready for us to do, work we had better be doing.

But don't take any of this for granted. It was only yesterday that you outsiders to God's ways had no idea of any of this, didn't know the first thing about the way God works, hadn't the faintest idea of Christ. You knew nothing of that rich history of God's covenants and promises in Israel, hadn't a clue about what God was doing in the world at large. Now because of Christ—dying that death, shedding that blood—you who were once out of it altogether are in on everything.

The Messiah has made things up between us so that we're now together on this, both non-Jewish outsiders and Jewish insiders. He tore down the wall we used to keep each other at a distance. He repealed the law code that had become so clogged with fine print and footnotes that it hindered more than it helped. Then he started over. Instead of continuing with two groups of people separated

KING JAMES VERSION

make in himself of twain one new man, *so* making peace;

16 And that he might reconcile both unto God in one body by the cross, having slain the enmity thereby:

17 And came and preached peace to you which were afar off, and to them that were nigh.

18 For through him we both have access by one Spirit unto the Father.

19 Now therefore ye are no more strangers and foreigners, but fellowcitizens with the saints, and of the household of God;

20 And are built upon the foundation of the apostles and prophets, Jesus Christ himself being the chief corner *stone;*

21 In whom all the building fitly framed together groweth unto an holy temple in the Lord:

22 In whom ye also are builded together for an habitation of God through the Spirit.

3 For this cause I Paul, the prisoner of Jesus Christ for you Gentiles,

2 If ye have heard of the dispensation of the grace of God which is given me to you-ward:

3 How that by revelation he made known unto me the mystery; (as I wrote afore in few words,

4 Whereby, when ye read, ye may understand my knowledge in the mystery of Christ)

NEW AMERICAN STANDARD BIBLE

Himself He might make the two into one new man, *thus* establishing peace,

16 and might reconcile them both in one body to God through the cross, by it having put to death the enmity.

17 AND HE CAME AND PREACHED PEACE TO YOU WHO WERE FAR AWAY, AND PEACE TO THOSE WHO WERE NEAR;

18 for through Him we both have our access in one Spirit to the Father.

19 So then you are no longer strangers and aliens, but you are fellow citizens with the saints, and are of God's household,

20 having been built on the foundation of the apostles and prophets, Christ Jesus Himself being the corner *stone,*

21 in whom the whole building, being fitted together, is growing into a holy temple in the Lord,

22 in whom you also are being built together into a dwelling of God in the Spirit.

Paul's Stewardship

3 For this reason I, Paul, the prisoner of Christ Jesus for the sake of you Gentiles—

2 if indeed you have heard of the stewardship of God's grace which was given to me for you;

3 that by revelation there was made known to me the mystery, as I wrote before in brief.

4 By referring to this, when you read you can understand my insight into the mystery of Christ,

NEW CENTURY VERSION

His purpose was to make the two groups of people become
one new people in him and in this way make peace. 16It
was also Christ's purpose to end the hatred between the
two groups, to make them into one body, and to bring
them back to God. Christ did all this with his death on the
cross. 17Christ came and preached peace to you who were
far away from God, and to those who were near to God.
18Yes, it is through Christ we all have the right to come to
the Father in one Spirit.

19Now you who are not Jewish are not foreigners or
strangers any longer, but are citizens together with God's
holy people. You belong to God's family. 20You are like a
building that was built on the foundation of the apostles
and prophets. Christ Jesus himself is the most important
stone[c] in that building, 21and that whole building is joined
together in Christ. He makes it grow and become a holy
temple in the Lord. 22And in Christ you, too, are being built
together with the Jews into a place where God lives
through the Spirit.

Paul's Work in Telling the Good News

3 So I, Paul, am a prisoner of Christ Jesus for you who
are not Jews. 2Surely you have heard that God gave
me this work through his grace to help you. 3He let me
know his secret by showing it to me. I have already written
a little about this. 4If you read what I wrote then, you can
see that I truly understand the secret about the Christ.

2:20 [c] **most important stone** Literally, "cornerstone." The first and most important stone in a building.

CONTEMPORARY ENGLISH VERSION

brought Jews and Gentiles together as though we were
only one person, when he united us in peace. 16On the
cross Christ did away with our hatred for each other. He
also made peace[b] between us and God by uniting Jews and
Gentiles in one body. 17Christ came and preached peace to
you Gentiles, who were far from God, and peace to us Jews,
who were near God. 18And because of Christ, all of us can
come to the Father by the same Spirit.

19You Gentiles are no longer strangers and foreigners.
You are citizens with everyone else who belongs to the
family of God. 20You are like a building with the apostles
and prophets as the foundation and with Christ as the
most important stone. 21Christ is the one who holds the
building together and makes it grow into a holy temple for
the Lord. 22And you are part of that building Christ has
built as a place for God's own Spirit to live.

Paul's Mission to the Gentiles

3 Christ Jesus made me his prisoner, so that I could help
you Gentiles. 2You have surely heard about God's
kindness in choosing me to help you. 3In fact, this letter
tells you a little about how God has shown me his mysterious ways. 4As you read the letter, you will also find out
how well I really do understand the mystery about Christ.

[b] 2.16 *He also made peace*: Or "The cross also made peace."

NEW INTERNATIONAL VERSION

new man out of the two, thus making peace, 16and in this
one body to reconcile both of them to God through the
cross, by which he put to death their hostility. 17He came
and preached peace to you who were far away and peace to
those who were near. 18For through him we both have
access to the Father by one Spirit.
19Consequently, you are no longer foreigners and aliens,
but fellow citizens with God's people and members of
God's household, 20built on the foundation of the apostles
and prophets, with Christ Jesus himself as the chief corner-
stone. 21In him the whole building is joined together and
rises to become a holy temple in the Lord. 22And in him
you too are being built together to become a dwelling in
which God lives by his Spirit.

Paul the Preacher to the Gentiles

3 For this reason I, Paul, the prisoner of Christ Jesus for
the sake of you Gentiles—
2Surely you have heard about the administration of
God's grace that was given to me for you, 3that is, the
mystery made known to me by revelation, as I have
already written briefly. 4In reading this, then, you will be
able to understand my insight into the mystery of Christ,

NEW LIVING TRANSLATION

between Jews and Gentiles by creating in himself one new
person from the two groups. 16Together as one body, Christ
reconciled both groups to God by means of his death, and
our hostility toward each other was put to death. 17He has
brought this Good News of peace to you Gentiles who were
far away from him, and to us Jews who were near. 18Now
all of us, both Jews and Gentiles, may come to the Father
through the same Holy Spirit because of what Christ has
done for us.

A Temple for the Lord

19So now you Gentiles are no longer strangers and for-
eigners. You are citizens along with all of God's holy peo-
ple. You are members of God's family. 20We are his house,
built on the foundation of the apostles and the prophets.
And the cornerstone is Christ Jesus himself. 21We who
believe are carefully joined together, becoming a holy tem-
ple for the Lord. 22Through him you Gentiles are also
joined together as part of this dwelling where God lives by
his Spirit.

God's Secret Plan Revealed

3 I, Paul, am a prisoner of Christ Jesus because of my
preaching to you Gentiles. 2As you already know, God
has given me this special ministry of announcing his favor
to you Gentiles. 3As I briefly mentioned earlier in this let-
ter, God himself revealed his secret plan to me. 4As you
read what I have written, you will understand what I know
about this plan regarding Christ. 5God did not reveal it to

NEW KING JAMES VERSION

Himself one new man *from* the two, *thus* making peace,
16and that He might reconcile them both to God in one
body through the cross, thereby putting to death the enmi-
ty. 17And He came and preached peace to you who were
afar off and to those who were near. 18For through Him we
both have access by one Spirit to the Father.

Christ Our Cornerstone

19Now, therefore, you are no longer strangers and for-
eigners, but fellow citizens with the saints and members of
the household of God, 20having been built on the founda-
tion of the apostles and prophets, Jesus Christ Himself
being the chief corner*stone,* 21in whom the whole building,
being fitted together, grows into a holy temple in the Lord,
22in whom you also are being built together for a dwelling
place of God in the Spirit.

The Mystery Revealed

3 For this reason I, Paul, the prisoner of Christ Jesus for
you Gentiles— 2if indeed you have heard of the dispen-
sation of the grace of God which was given to me for you,
3how that by revelation He made known to me the mystery
(as I have briefly written already, 4by which, when you read,
you may understand my knowledge in the mystery of

THE MESSAGE

by centuries of animosity and suspicion, he created a new
kind of human being, a fresh start for everybody.

Christ brought us together through his death on the
Cross. The Cross got us to embrace, and that was the end
of the hostility. Christ came and preached peace to you
outsiders and peace to us insiders. He treated us as equals,
and so made us equals. Through him we both share the
same Spirit and have equal access to the Father.

That's plain enough, isn't it? You're no longer wander-
ing exiles. This kingdom of faith is now your home coun-
try. You're no longer strangers or outsiders. You *belong*
here, with as much right to the name Christian as anyone.
God is building a home. He's using us all—irrespective of
how we got here—in what he is building. He used the
apostles and prophets for the foundation. Now he's using
you, fitting you in brick by brick, stone by stone, with
Christ Jesus as the cornerstone that holds all the parts
together. We see it taking shape day after day—a holy
temple built by God, all of us built into it, a temple in
which God is quite at home.

The Secret Plan of God

3 This is why I, Paul, am in jail for Christ, having taken
up the cause of you outsiders, so-called. I take it that
you're familiar with the part I was given in God's plan for
including everybody. I got the inside story on this from
God himself, as I just wrote you in brief.

As you read over what I have written to you, you'll be
able to see for yourselves into the mystery of Christ. None

KING JAMES VERSION

5 Which in other ages was not made known unto the sons of men, as it is now revealed unto his holy apostles and prophets by the Spirit;

6 That the Gentiles should be fellowheirs, and of the same body, and partakers of his promise in Christ by the gospel:

7 Whereof I was made a minister, according to the gift of the grace of God given unto me by the effectual working of his power.

8 Unto me, who am less than the least of all saints, is this grace given, that I should preach among the Gentiles the unsearchable riches of Christ;

9 And to make all *men* see what *is* the fellowship of the mystery, which from the beginning of the world hath been hid in God, who created all things by Jesus Christ:

10 To the intent that now unto the principalities and powers in heavenly *places* might be known by the church the manifold wisdom of God,

11 According to the eternal purpose which he purposed in Christ Jesus our Lord:

12 In whom we have boldness and access with confidence by the faith of him.

13 Wherefore I desire that ye faint not at my tribulations for you, which is your glory.

NEW AMERICAN STANDARD BIBLE

5 which in other generations was not made known to the sons of men, as it has now been revealed to His holy apostles and prophets in the Spirit;

6 *to be specific*, that the Gentiles are fellow heirs and fellow members of the body, and fellow partakers of the promise in Christ Jesus through the gospel,

7 of which I was made a minister, according to the gift of God's grace which was given to me according to the working of His power.

8 To me, the very least of all saints, this grace was given, to preach to the Gentiles the unfathomable riches of Christ,

9 and to bring to light what is the administration of the mystery which for ages has been hidden in God who created all things;

10 so that the manifold wisdom of God might now be made known through the church to the rulers and the authorities in the heavenly *places.*

11 *This was* in accordance with the eternal purpose which He carried out in Christ Jesus our Lord,

12 in whom we have boldness and confident access through faith in Him.

13 Therefore I ask you not to lose heart at my tribulations on your behalf, for they are your glory.

NEW CENTURY VERSION

5People who lived in other times were not told that secret.
But now, through the Spirit, God has shown that secret to
his holy apostles and prophets. 6This is that secret: that
through the Good News those who are not Jews will share
with the Jews in God's blessing. They belong to the same
body, and they share together in the promise that God
made in Christ Jesus.

7By God's special gift of grace given to me through his
power, I became a servant to tell that Good News. 8I am
the least important of all God's people, but God gave me
this gift—to tell those who are not Jews the Good News
about the riches of Christ, which are too great to under-
stand fully. 9And God gave me the work of telling all peo-
ple about the plan for his secret, which has been hidden in
him since the beginning of time. He is the One who created
everything. 10His purpose was that through the church all
the rulers and powers in the heavenly world will now
know God's wisdom, which has so many forms. 11This
agrees with the purpose God had since the beginning of
time, and he carried out his plan through Christ Jesus our
Lord. 12In Christ we can come before God with freedom and
without fear. We can do this through faith in Christ. 13So I
ask you not to become discouraged because of the suffer-
ings I am having for you. My sufferings are for your glory.

CONTEMPORARY ENGLISH VERSION

5No one knew about this mystery until God's Spirit told it
to his holy apostles and prophets. 6And the mystery is
this: Because of Christ Jesus, the good news has given the
Gentiles a share in the promises that God gave to the Jews.
God has also let the Gentiles be part of the same body.

7God treated me with kindness. His power worked in me,
and it became my job to spread the good news. 8I am the
least important of all God's people. But God was kind and
chose me to tell the Gentiles that because of Christ there
are blessings that cannot be measured. 9God, who created
everything, wanted me to help everyone understand the
mysterious plan that had always been hidden in his mind.
10Then God would use the church to show the powers and
authorities in the spiritual world that he has many differ-
ent kinds of wisdom.

11God did this according to his eternal plan. And he was
able to do what he had planned because of all that Christ
Jesus our Lord had done. 12Christ now gives us courage
and confidence, so that we can come to God by faith.
13That's why you should not be discouraged when I suffer
for you. After all, it will bring honor to you.

NEW INTERNATIONAL VERSION

5which was not made known to men in other generations as it has now been revealed by the Spirit to God's holy apostles and prophets. 6This mystery is that through the gospel the Gentiles are heirs together with Israel, members together of one body, and sharers together in the promise in Christ Jesus.

7I became a servant of this gospel by the gift of God's grace given me through the working of his power. 8Although I am less than the least of all God's people, this grace was given me: to preach to the Gentiles the unsearchable riches of Christ, 9and to make plain to everyone the administration of this mystery, which for ages past was kept hidden in God, who created all things. 10His intent was that now, through the church, the manifold wisdom of God should be made known to the rulers and authorities in the heavenly realms, 11according to his eternal purpose which he accomplished in Christ Jesus our Lord. 12In him and through faith in him we may approach God with freedom and confidence. 13I ask you, therefore, not to be discouraged because of my sufferings for you, which are your glory.

NEW LIVING TRANSLATION

previous generations, but now he has revealed it by the Holy Spirit to his holy apostles and prophets.

6And this is the secret plan: The Gentiles have an equal share with the Jews in all the riches inherited by God's children. Both groups have believed the Good News, and both are part of the same body and enjoy together the promise of blessings through Christ Jesus. 7By God's special favor and mighty power, I have been given the wonderful privilege of serving him by spreading this Good News.

8Just think! Though I did nothing to deserve it, and though I am the least deserving Christian there is, I was chosen for this special joy of telling the Gentiles about the endless treasures available to them in Christ. 9I was chosen to explain to everyone this plan that God, the Creator of all things, had kept secret from the beginning.

10God's purpose was to show his wisdom in all its rich variety to all the rulers and authorities in the heavenly realms. They will see this when Jews and Gentiles are joined together in his church. 11This was his plan from all eternity, and it has now been carried out through Christ Jesus our Lord.

12Because of Christ and our faith in him, we can now come fearlessly into God's presence, assured of his glad welcome. 13So please don't despair because of what they are doing to me here. It is for you that I am suffering, so you should feel honored and encouraged.

NEW KING JAMES VERSION

Christ), 5which in other ages was not made known to the sons of men, as it has now been revealed by the Spirit to His holy apostles and prophets: 6that the Gentiles should be fellow heirs, of the same body, and partakers of His promise in Christ through the gospel, 7of which I became a minister according to the gift of the grace of God given to me by the effective working of His power.

Purpose of the Mystery

8To me, who am less than the least of all the saints, this grace was given, that I should preach among the Gentiles the unsearchable riches of Christ, 9and to make all see what *is* the fellowship[a] of the mystery, which from the beginning of the ages has been hidden in God who created all things through Jesus Christ;[b] 10to the intent that now the manifold wisdom of God might be made known by the church to the principalities and powers in the heavenly *places,* 11according to the eternal purpose which He accomplished in Christ Jesus our Lord, 12in whom we have boldness and access with confidence through faith in Him. 13Therefore I ask that you do not lose heart at my tribulations for you, which is your glory.

3:9 [a] NU-Text and M-Text read *stewardship* (dispensation). [b] NU-Text omits *through Jesus Christ.*

THE MESSAGE

of our ancestors understood this. Only in our time has it been made clear by God's Spirit through his holy apostles and prophets of this new order. The mystery is that people who have never heard of God and those who have heard of him all their lives (what I've been calling outsiders and insiders) stand on the same ground before God. They get the same offer, same help, same promises in Christ Jesus. The Message is accessible and welcoming to everyone, across the board.

This is my life work: helping people understand and respond to this Message. It came as a sheer gift to me, a real surprise, God handling all the details. When it came to presenting the Message to people who had no background in God's way, I was the least qualified of any of the available Christians. God saw to it that I was equipped, but you can be sure that it had nothing to do with my natural abilities.

And so here I am, preaching and writing about things that are way over my head, the inexhaustible riches and generosity of Christ. My task is to bring out in the open and make plain what God, who created all this in the first place, has been doing in secret and behind the scenes all along. Through Christians like yourselves gathered in churches, this extraordinary plan of God is becoming known and talked about even among the angels!

All this is proceeding along lines planned all along by God and then executed in Christ Jesus. When we trust in him, we're free to say whatever needs to be said, bold to go wherever we need to go. So don't let my present trouble on your behalf get you down. Be proud!

KING JAMES VERSION

14 ¶ For this cause I bow my knees unto the Father of our Lord Jesus Christ,

15 Of whom the whole family in heaven and earth is named,

16 That he would grant you, according to the riches of his glory, to be strengthened with might by his Spirit in the inner man;

17 That Christ may dwell in your hearts by faith; that ye, being rooted and grounded in love,

18 May be able to comprehend with all saints what *is* the breadth, and length, and depth, and height;

19 And to know the love of Christ, which passeth knowledge, that ye might be filled with all the fulness of God.

20 Now unto him that is able to do exceeding abundantly above all that we ask or think, according to the power that worketh in us,

21 Unto him *be* glory in the church by Christ Jesus throughout all ages, world without end. Amen.

4 I therefore, the prisoner of the Lord, beseech you that ye walk worthy of the vocation wherewith ye are called,

2 ¶ With all lowliness and meekness, with longsuffering, forbearing one another in love;

NEW AMERICAN STANDARD BIBLE

14 For this reason I bow my knees before the Father,

15 from whom every family in heaven and on earth derives its name,

16 that He would grant you, according to the riches of His glory, to be strengthened with power through His Spirit in the inner man,

17 so that Christ may dwell in your hearts through faith; *and* that you, being rooted and grounded in love,

18 may be able to comprehend with all the saints what is the breadth and length and height and depth,

19 and to know the love of Christ which surpasses knowledge, that you may be filled up to all the fullness of God.

20 Now to Him who is able to do far more abundantly beyond all that we ask or think, according to the power that works within us,

21 to Him *be* the glory in the church and in Christ Jesus to all generations forever and ever. Amen.

Unity of the Spirit

4 Therefore I, the prisoner of the Lord, implore you to walk in a manner worthy of the calling with which you have been called,

2 with all humility and gentleness, with patience, showing tolerance for one another in love,

NEW CENTURY VERSION

The Love of Christ

14So I bow in prayer before the Father 15from whom
every family in heaven and on earth gets its true name. 16I
ask the Father in his great glory to give you the power to
be strong inwardly through his Spirit. 17I pray that Christ
will live in your hearts by faith and that your life will be
strong in love and be built on love. 18And I pray that you
and all God's holy people will have the power to understand the greatness of Christ's love—how wide and how
long and how high and how deep that love is. 19Christ's
love is greater than anyone can ever know, but I pray that
you will be able to know that love. Then you can be filled
with the fullness of God.
20With God's power working in us, God can do much,
much more than anything we can ask or imagine. 21To him
be glory in the church and in Christ Jesus for all time, forever and ever. Amen.

The Unity of the Body

4 I am in prison because I belong to the Lord. God chose you to be his people, so I urge you now to live the life to which God called you.
2Always be humble, gentle, and
patient, accepting each other in love. 3You are joined

CONTEMPORARY ENGLISH VERSION

Christ's Love for Us

14I kneel in prayer to the Father. 15All beings in heaven
and on earth receive their life from him.[a] 16God is wonderful and glorious. I pray that his Spirit will make you
become strong followers 17and that Christ will live in your
hearts because of your faith. Stand firm and be deeply
rooted in his love. 18I pray that you and all of God's people
will understand what is called wide or long or high or
deep.[b] 19I want you to know all about Christ's love,
although it is too wonderful to be measured. Then your
lives will be filled with all that God is.
20-21I pray that Christ Jesus and the church will forever
bring praise to God. His power at work in us can do far
more than we dare ask or imagine. Amen.

Unity with Christ

4 As a prisoner of the Lord, I beg you to live in a way that is worthy of the people God has chosen to be his
own. 2Always be humble and gentle. Patiently put up with
each other and love each other. 3Try your best to let God's

[a] 3.15 *receive their life from him*: Or "know who they really are because of him." [b] 3.18 *what is called wide or long or high or deep*: This may refer to the heavenly Jerusalem or to God's love or wisdom or to the meaning of the cross.

NEW INTERNATIONAL VERSION

A Prayer for the Ephesians

14For this reason I kneel before the Father, 15from whom his whole family[a] in heaven and on earth derives its name. 16I pray that out of his glorious riches he may strengthen you with power through his Spirit in your inner being, 17so that Christ may dwell in your hearts through faith. And I pray that you, being rooted and established in love, 18may have power, together with all the saints, to grasp how wide and long and high and deep is the love of Christ, 19and to know this love that surpasses knowledge—that you may be filled to the measure of all the fullness of God.

20Now to him who is able to do immeasurably more than all we ask or imagine, according to his power that is at work within us, 21to him be glory in the church and in Christ Jesus throughout all generations, for ever and ever! Amen.

Unity in the Body of Christ

4 As a prisoner for the Lord, then, I urge you to live a life worthy of the calling you have received. 2Be completely humble and gentle; be patient, bearing with one

[a] *15* Or *whom all fatherhood*

NEW LIVING TRANSLATION

Paul's Prayer for Spiritual Empowering

14When I think of the wisdom and scope of God's plan, I fall to my knees and pray to the Father,* 15the Creator of everything in heaven and on earth. 16I pray that from his glorious, unlimited resources he will give you mighty inner strength through his Holy Spirit. 17And I pray that Christ will be more and more at home in your hearts as you trust in him. May your roots go down deep into the soil of God's marvelous love. 18And may you have the power to understand, as all God's people should, how wide, how long, how high, and how deep his love really is. 19May you experience the love of Christ, though it is so great you will never fully understand it. Then you will be filled with the fullness of life and power that comes from God.

20Now glory be to God! By his mighty power at work within us, he is able to accomplish infinitely more than we would ever dare to ask or hope. 21May he be given glory in the church and in Christ Jesus forever and ever through endless ages. Amen.

Unity in the Body

4 Therefore I, a prisoner for serving the Lord, beg you to lead a life worthy of your calling, for you have been called by God. 2Be humble and gentle. Be patient with each other, making allowance for each other's faults because of

3:14 Some manuscripts read *the Father of our Lord Jesus Christ.*

NEW KING JAMES VERSION

Appreciation of the Mystery

14For this reason I bow my knees to the Father of our Lord Jesus Christ,[c] 15from whom the whole family in heaven and earth is named, 16that He would grant you, according to the riches of His glory, to be strengthened with might through His Spirit in the inner man, 17that Christ may dwell in your hearts through faith; that you, being rooted and grounded in love, 18may be able to comprehend with all the saints what *is* the width and length and depth and height— 19to know the love of Christ which passes knowledge; that you may be filled with all the fullness of God.

20Now to Him who is able to do exceedingly abundantly above all that we ask or think, according to the power that works in us, 21to Him *be* glory in the church by Christ Jesus to all generations, forever and ever. Amen.

Walk in Unity

4 I, therefore, the prisoner of the Lord, beseech you to walk worthy of the calling with which you were called, 2with all lowliness and gentleness, with longsuffering, bearing with one another in love, 3endeavoring to

3:14 [c] NU-Text omits *of our Lord Jesus Christ.*

THE MESSAGE

✢

My response is to get down on my knees before the Father, this magnificent Father who parcels out all heaven and earth. I ask him to strengthen you by his Spirit—not a brute strength but a glorious inner strength—that Christ will live in you as you open the door and invite him in. And I ask him that with both feet planted firmly on love, you'll be able to take in with all Christians the extravagant dimensions of Christ's love. Reach out and experience the breadth! Test its length! Plumb the depths! Rise to the heights! Live full lives, full in the fullness of God.

God can do anything, you know—far more than you could ever imagine or guess or request in your wildest dreams! He does it not by pushing us around but by working within us, his Spirit deeply and gently within us.

Glory to God in the church!
Glory to God in the Messiah, in Jesus!
Glory down all the generations!
Glory through all millennia! Oh, yes!

To Be Mature

4 In light of all this, here's what I want you to do. While I'm locked up here, a prisoner for the Master, I want you to get out there and walk—better yet, run!—on the road God called you to travel. I don't want any of you sitting around on your hands. I don't want anyone strolling off, down some path that goes nowhere. And mark that you do this with humility and discipline—not in fits and

KING JAMES VERSION

3 Endeavouring to keep the unity of the Spirit in the bond of peace.

4 *There is* one body, and one Spirit, even as ye are called in one hope of your calling;

5 One Lord, one faith, one baptism,

6 One God and Father of all, who *is* above all, and through all, and in you all.

7 But unto every one of us is given grace according to the measure of the gift of Christ.

8 Wherefore he saith, When he ascended up on high, he led captivity captive, and gave gifts unto men.

9 (Now that he ascended, what is it but that he also descended first into the lower parts of the earth?

10 He that descended is the same also that ascended up far above all heavens, that he might fill all things.)

11 And he gave some, apostles; and some, prophets; and some, evangelists; and some, pastors and teachers;

12 For the perfecting of the saints, for the work of the ministry, for the edifying of the body of Christ:

13 Till we all come in the unity of the faith, and of the knowledge of the Son of God, unto a perfect man, unto the measure of the stature of the fulness of Christ:

NEW AMERICAN STANDARD BIBLE

3 being diligent to preserve the unity of the Spirit in the bond of peace.

4 *There is* one body and one Spirit, just as also you were called in one hope of your calling;

5 one Lord, one faith, one baptism,

6 one God and Father of all who is over all and through all and in all.

7 But to each one of us grace was given according to the measure of Christ's gift.

8 Therefore it says,

"WHEN HE ASCENDED ON HIGH,
HE LED CAPTIVE A HOST OF CAPTIVES,
AND HE GAVE GIFTS TO MEN."

9 (Now this *expression,* "He ascended," what does it mean except that He also had descended into the lower parts of the earth?

10 He who descended is Himself also He who ascended far above all the heavens, so that He might fill all things.)

11 And He gave some *as* apostles, and some *as* prophets, and some *as* evangelists, and some *as* pastors and teachers,

12 for the equipping of the saints for the work of service, to the building up of the body of Christ;

13 until we all attain to the unity of the faith, and of the knowledge of the Son of God, to a mature man, to the measure of the stature which belongs to the fullness of Christ.

NEW CENTURY VERSION

together with peace through the Spirit, so make every effort to continue together in this way. 4There is one body and one Spirit, and God called you to have one hope. 5There is one Lord, one faith, and one baptism. 6There is one God and Father of everything. He rules everything and is everywhere and is in everything.

7Christ gave each one of us the special gift of grace, showing how generous he is. 8That is why it says in the Scriptures,

"When he went up to the heights,
he led a parade of captives,
and he gave gifts to people." *Psalm 68:18*

9When it says, "He went up," what does it mean? It means that he first came down to the earth. 10So Jesus came down, and he is the same One who went up above all the sky. Christ did that to fill everything with his presence. 11And Christ gave gifts to people—he made some to be apostles, some to be prophets, some to go and tell the Good News, and some to have the work of caring for and teaching God's people. 12Christ gave those gifts to prepare God's holy people for the work of serving, to make the body of Christ stronger. 13This work must continue until we are all joined together in the same faith and in the same knowledge of the Son of God. We must become like a mature person, growing until we become like Christ and have his perfection.

CONTEMPORARY ENGLISH VERSION

Spirit keep your hearts united. Do this by living at peace. 4All of you are part of the same body. There is only one Spirit of God, just as you were given one hope when you were chosen to be God's people. 5We have only one Lord, one faith, and one baptism. 6There is one God who is the Father of all people. Not only is God above all others, but he works by using all of us, and he lives in all of us.

7Christ has generously divided out his gifts to us. 8As the Scriptures say,

"When he went up
to the highest place,
he led away many prisoners
and gave gifts to people."

9When it says, "he went up," it means that Christ had been deep in the earth. 10This also means that the one who went deep into the earth is the same one who went into the highest heaven, so that he would fill the whole universe.

11Christ chose some of us to be apostles, prophets, missionaries, pastors, and teachers, 12so that his people would learn to serve and his body would grow strong. 13This will continue until we are united by our faith and by our understanding of the Son of God. Then we will be mature, just as Christ is, and we will be completely like him.[a]

[a] **4.13** *and we will be completely like him*: Or "and he is completely perfect."

NEW INTERNATIONAL VERSION

another in love. 3Make every effort to keep the unity of the
Spirit through the bond of peace. 4There is one body and
one Spirit— just as you were called to one hope when you
were called— 5one Lord, one faith, one baptism; 6one God
and Father of all, who is over all and through all and in
all.
7But to each one of us grace has been given as Christ
apportioned it. 8This is why it[a] says:

"When he ascended on high,
he led captives in his train
and gave gifts to men."[b]

9(What does "he ascended" mean except that he also de-
scended to the lower, earthly regions[c]? 10He who descend-
ed is the very one who ascended higher than all the heav-
ens, in order to fill the whole universe.) 11It was he who
gave some to be apostles, some to be prophets, some to be
evangelists, and some to be pastors and teachers, 12to pre-
pare God's people for works of service, so that the body of
Christ may be built up 13until we all reach unity in the
faith and in the knowledge of the Son of God and become
mature, attaining to the whole measure of the fullness of
Christ.

[a] *8* Or *God* [b] *8* Psalm 68:18 [c] *9* Or *the depths of the earth*

NEW LIVING TRANSLATION

your love. 3Always keep yourselves united in the Holy
Spirit, and bind yourselves together with peace.
4We are all one body, we have the same Spirit, and we
have all been called to the same glorious future. 5There is
only one Lord, one faith, one baptism, 6and there is only
one God and Father, who is over us all and in us all and
living through us all. 7However, he has given each one of
us a special gift according to the generosity of Christ.
8That is why the Scriptures say,

"When he ascended to the heights,
he led a crowd of captives
and gave gifts to his people."*

9Notice that it says "he ascended." This means that Christ
first came down to the lowly world in which we live.*
10The same one who came down is the one who ascended
higher than all the heavens, so that his rule might fill the
entire universe.
11He is the one who gave these gifts to the church: the
apostles, the prophets, the evangelists, and the pastors
and teachers. 12Their responsibility is to equip God's peo-
ple to do his work and build up the church, the body of
Christ, 13until we come to such unity in our faith and
knowledge of God's Son that we will be mature and full
grown in the Lord, measuring up to the full stature of
Christ.

4:8 Ps 68:18. **4:9** Or *to the lowest parts of the earth.*

NEW KING JAMES VERSION

keep the unity of the Spirit in the bond of peace. 4*There is*
one body and one Spirit, just as you were called in one
hope of your calling; 5one Lord, one faith, one baptism;
6one God and Father of all, who *is* above all, and through
all, and in you[a] all.

Spiritual Gifts

7But to each one of us grace was given according to the
measure of Christ's gift. 8Therefore He says:

"*When He ascended on high,*
He led captivity captive,
And gave gifts to men."[b]

9(Now this, *"He ascended"*—what does it mean but that
He also first[c] descended into the lower parts of the earth?
10He who descended is also the One who ascended far
above all the heavens, that He might fill all things.)
11And He Himself gave some *to be* apostles, some proph-
ets, some evangelists, and some pastors and teachers, 12for
the equipping of the saints for the work of ministry, for the
edifying of the body of Christ, 13till we all come to the unity
of the faith and of the knowledge of the Son of God, to a
perfect man, to the measure of the stature of the fullness of

4:6 [a] NU-Text omits *you;* M-Text reads *us.* **4:8** [b] Psalm 68:18
4:9 [c] NU-Text omits *first.*

THE MESSAGE

starts, but steadily, pouring yourselves out for each other
in acts of love, alert at noticing differences and quick at
mending fences.

You were all called to travel on the same road and in the
same direction, so stay together, both outwardly and
inwardly. You have one Master, one faith, one baptism,
one God and Father of all, who rules over all, works
through all, and is present in all. Everything you are and
think and do is permeated with Oneness.

But that doesn't mean you should all look and speak
and act the same. Out of the generosity of Christ, each of
us is given his own gift. The text for this is,

"He climbed the high mountain,
He captured the enemy and seized the booty,
He handed it all out in gifts to the people."

It's true, is it not, that the One who climbed up also
climbed down, down to the valley of earth? And the One
who climbed down is the One who climbed back up, up to
highest heaven. He handed out gifts above and below,
filled heaven with his gifts, filled earth with his gifts. He
handed out gifts of apostle, prophet, evangelist, and pas-
tor-teacher to train Christians in skilled servant work,
working within Christ's body, the church, until we're all
moving rhythmically and easily with each other, efficient
and graceful in response to God's Son, fully mature adults,
fully developed within and without, fully alive like Christ.

KING JAMES VERSION

14 That we *henceforth* be no more children, tossed to and fro, and carried about with every wind of doctrine, by the sleight of men, *and* cunning craftiness, whereby they lie in wait to deceive;

15 But speaking the truth in love, may grow up into him in all things, which is the head, *even* Christ:

16 From whom the whole body fitly joined together and compacted by that which every joint supplieth, according to the effectual working in the measure of every part, maketh increase of the body unto the edifying of itself in love.

17 ¶ This I say therefore, and testify in the Lord, that ye henceforth walk not as other Gentiles walk, in the vanity of their mind,

18 Having the understanding darkened, being alienated from the life of God through the ignorance that is in them, because of the blindness of their heart:

19 Who being past feeling have given themselves over unto lasciviousness, to work all uncleanness with greediness.

20 But ye have not so learned Christ;

21 If so be that ye have heard him, and have been taught by him, as the truth is in Jesus:

22 That ye put off concerning the former conversation the old man, which is corrupt according to the deceitful lusts;

23 And be renewed in the spirit of your mind;

24 And that ye put on the new man, which after God is created in righteousness and true holiness.

NEW AMERICAN STANDARD BIBLE

14 As a result, we are no longer to be children, tossed here and there by waves and carried about by every wind of doctrine, by the trickery of men, by craftiness in deceitful scheming;

15 but speaking the truth in love, we are to grow up in all *aspects* into Him who is the head, *even* Christ,

16 from whom the whole body, being fitted and held together by what every joint supplies, according to the proper working of each individual part, causes the growth of the body for the building up of itself in love.

The Christian's Walk

17 So this I say, and affirm together with the Lord, that you walk no longer just as the Gentiles also walk, in the futility of their mind,

18 being darkened in their understanding, excluded from the life of God because of the ignorance that is in them, because of the hardness of their heart;

19 and they, having become callous, have given themselves over to sensuality for the practice of every kind of impurity with greediness.

20 But you did not learn Christ in this way,

21 if indeed you have heard Him and have been taught in Him, just as truth is in Jesus,

22 that, in reference to your former manner of life, you lay aside the old self, which is being corrupted in accordance with the lusts of deceit,

23 and that you be renewed in the spirit of your mind,

24 and put on the new self, which in *the likeness of* God has been created in righteousness and holiness of the truth.

NEW CENTURY VERSION

[14]Then we will no longer be babies. We will not be tossed about like a ship that the waves carry one way and then another. We will not be influenced by every new teaching we hear from people who are trying to fool us. They make plans and try any kind of trick to fool people into following the wrong path. [15]No! Speaking the truth with love, we will grow up in every way into Christ, who is the head. [16]The whole body depends on Christ, and all the parts of the body are joined and held together. Each part does its own work to make the whole body grow and be strong with love.

The Way You Should Live

[17]In the Lord's name, I tell you this. Do not continue living like those who do not believe. Their thoughts are worth nothing. [18]They do not understand, and they know nothing, because they refuse to listen. So they cannot have the life that God gives. [19]They have lost all feeling of shame, and they use their lives for doing evil. They continually want to do all kinds of evil. [20]But what you learned in Christ was not like this. [21]I know that you heard about him, and you are in him, so you were taught the truth that is in Jesus. [22]You were taught to leave your old self—to stop living the evil way you lived before. That old self becomes worse, because people are fooled by the evil things they want to do. [23]But you were taught to be made new in your hearts, [24]to become a new person. That new person is made to be like God—made to be truly good and holy.

CONTEMPORARY ENGLISH VERSION

[14]We must stop acting like children. We must not let deceitful people trick us by their false teachings, which are like winds that toss us around from place to place. [15]Love should always make us tell the truth. Then we will grow in every way and be more like Christ, the head [16]of the body. Christ holds it together and makes all of its parts work perfectly, as it grows and becomes strong because of love.

The Old Life and the New Life

[17]As a follower of the Lord, I order you to stop living like stupid, godless people. [18]Their minds are in the dark, and they are stubborn and ignorant and have missed out on the life that comes from God. They no longer have any feelings about what is right, [19]and they are so greedy that they do all kinds of indecent things.

[20-21]But that isn't what you were taught about Jesus Christ. He is the truth, and you heard about him and learned about him. [22]You were told that your foolish desires will destroy you and that you must give up your old way of life with all its bad habits. [23]Let the Spirit change your way of thinking [24]and make you into a new person. You were created to be like God, and so you must please him and be truly holy.

NEW INTERNATIONAL VERSION

14 Then we will no longer be infants, tossed back and forth by the waves, and blown here and there by every wind of teaching and by the cunning and craftiness of men in their deceitful scheming. 15 Instead, speaking the truth in love, we will in all things grow up into him who is the Head, that is, Christ. 16 From him the whole body, joined and held together by every supporting ligament, grows and builds itself up in love, as each part does its work.

Living as Children of Light

17 So I tell you this, and insist on it in the Lord, that you must no longer live as the Gentiles do, in the futility of their thinking. 18 They are darkened in their understanding and separated from the life of God because of the ignorance that is in them due to the hardening of their hearts. 19 Having lost all sensitivity, they have given themselves over to sensuality so as to indulge in every kind of impurity, with a continual lust for more.

20 You, however, did not come to know Christ that way. 21 Surely you heard of him and were taught in him in accordance with the truth that is in Jesus. 22 You were taught, with regard to your former way of life, to put off your old self, which is being corrupted by its deceitful desires; 23 to be made new in the attitude of your minds; 24 and to put on the new self, created to be like God in true righteousness and holiness.

NEW LIVING TRANSLATION

14 Then we will no longer be like children, forever changing our minds about what we believe because someone has told us something different or because someone has cleverly lied to us and made the lie sound like the truth. 15 Instead, we will hold to the truth in love, becoming more and more in every way like Christ, who is the head of his body, the church. 16 Under his direction, the whole body is fitted together perfectly. As each part does its own special work, it helps the other parts grow, so that the whole body is healthy and growing and full of love.

Living as Children of Light

17 With the Lord's authority let me say this: Live no longer as the ungodly* do, for they are hopelessly confused. 18 Their closed minds are full of darkness; they are far away from the life of God because they have shut their minds and hardened their hearts against him. 19 They don't care anymore about right and wrong, and they have given themselves over to immoral ways. Their lives are filled with all kinds of impurity and greed.

20 But that isn't what you were taught when you learned about Christ. 21 Since you have heard all about him and have learned the truth that is in Jesus, 22 throw off your old evil nature and your former way of life, which is rotten through and through, full of lust and deception. 23 Instead, there must be a spiritual renewal of your thoughts and attitudes. 24 You must display a new nature because you are a new person, created in God's likeness—righteous, holy, and true.

4:17 Greek *Gentiles.*

NEW KING JAMES VERSION

Christ; 14 that we should no longer be children, tossed to and fro and carried about with every wind of doctrine, by the trickery of men, in the cunning craftiness of deceitful plotting, 15 but, speaking the truth in love, may grow up in all things into Him who is the head—Christ— 16 from whom the whole body, joined and knit together by what every joint supplies, according to the effective working by which every part does its share, causes growth of the body for the edifying of itself in love.

The New Man

17 This I say, therefore, and testify in the Lord, that you should no longer walk as the rest of[d] the Gentiles walk, in the futility of their mind, 18 having their understanding darkened, being alienated from the life of God, because of the ignorance that is in them, because of the blindness of their heart; 19 who, being past feeling, have given themselves over to lewdness, to work all uncleanness with greediness.

20 But you have not so learned Christ, 21 if indeed you have heard Him and have been taught by Him, as the truth is in Jesus: 22 that you put off, concerning your former conduct, the old man which grows corrupt according to the deceitful lusts, 23 and be renewed in the spirit of your mind, 24 and that you put on the new man which was created according to God, in true righteousness and holiness.

4:17 [d] NU-Text omits *the rest of.*

THE MESSAGE

No prolonged infancies among us, please. We'll not tolerate babes in the woods, small children who are an easy mark for impostors. God wants us to grow up, to know the whole truth and tell it in love—like Christ in everything. We take our lead from Christ, who is the source of everything we do. He keeps us in step with each other. His very breath and blood flow through us, nourishing us so that we will grow up healthy in God, robust in love.

The Old Way Has to Go

And so I insist—and God backs me up on this—that there be no going along with the crowd, the empty-headed, mindless crowd. They've refused for so long to deal with God that they've lost touch not only with God but with reality itself. They can't think straight anymore. Feeling no pain, they let themselves go in sexual obsession, addicted to every sort of perversion.

But that's no life for you. You learned Christ! My assumption is that you have paid careful attention to him, been well instructed in the truth precisely as we have it in Jesus. Since, then, we do not have the excuse of ignorance, everything—and I do mean everything—connected with that old way of life has to go. It's rotten through and through. Get rid of it! And then take on an entirely new way of life—a God-fashioned life, a life renewed from the inside and working itself into your conduct as God accurately reproduces his character in you.

KING JAMES VERSION

25 Wherefore putting away lying, speak every man truth with his neighbour: for we are members one of another.

26 Be ye angry, and sin not: let not the sun go down upon your wrath:

27 Neither give place to the devil.

28 Let him that stole steal no more: but rather let him labour, working with *his* hands the thing which is good, that he may have to give to him that needeth.

29 Let no corrupt communication proceed out of your mouth, but that which is good to the use of edifying, that it may minister grace unto the hearers.

30 And grieve not the holy Spirit of God, whereby ye are sealed unto the day of redemption.

31 Let all bitterness, and wrath, and anger, and clamour, and evil speaking, be put away from you, with all malice:

32 And be ye kind one to another, tenderhearted, forgiving one another, even as God for Christ's sake hath forgiven you.

5 Be ye therefore followers of God, as dear children;

2 And walk in love, as Christ also hath loved us, and hath given himself for us an offering and a sacrifice to God for a sweetsmelling savour.

NEW AMERICAN STANDARD BIBLE

25 Therefore, laying aside falsehood, SPEAK TRUTH EACH ONE *OF* YOU WITH HIS NEIGHBOR, for we are members of one another.

26 BE ANGRY, AND *YET* DO NOT SIN; do not let the sun go down on your anger,

27 and do not give the devil an opportunity.

28 He who steals must steal no longer; but rather he must labor, performing with his own hands what is good, so that he will have *something* to share with one who has need.

29 Let no unwholesome word proceed from your mouth, but only such *a word* as is good for edification according to the need *of the moment,* so that it will give grace to those who hear.

30 Do not grieve the Holy Spirit of God, by whom you were sealed for the day of redemption.

31 Let all bitterness and wrath and anger and clamor and slander be put away from you, along with all malice.

32 Be kind to one another, tender-hearted, forgiving each other, just as God in Christ also has forgiven [1]you.

Be Imitators of God

5 Therefore be imitators of God, as beloved children;

2 and walk in love, just as Christ also loved [1]you and gave Himself up for us, an offering and a sacrifice to God as a fragrant aroma.

4:32 [1] Two early mss read *us* 5:2 [1] One early ms reads *us*

NEW CENTURY VERSION

[25]So you must stop telling lies. Tell each other the truth, because we all belong to each other in the same body.[a] [26]When you are angry, do not sin, and be sure to stop being angry before the end of the day. [27]Do not give the devil a way to defeat you. [28]Those who are stealing must stop stealing and start working. They should earn an honest living for themselves. Then they will have something to share with those who are poor.

[29]When you talk, do not say harmful things, but say what people need—words that will help others become stronger. Then what you say will do good to those who listen to you. [30]And do not make the Holy Spirit sad. The Spirit is God's proof that you belong to him. God gave you the Spirit to show that God will make you free when the final day comes. [31]Do not be bitter or angry or mad. Never shout angrily or say things to hurt others. Never do anything evil. [32]Be kind and loving to each other, and forgive each other just as God forgave you in Christ.

Living in the Light

5 You are God's children whom he loves, so try to be like him. [2]Live a life of love just as Christ loved us and gave himself for us as a sweet-smelling offering and sacrifice to God.

4:25 [a] **Tell...body.** Quotation from Zechariah 8:16.

CONTEMPORARY ENGLISH VERSION

Rules for the New Life

[25]We are part of the same body. Stop lying and start telling each other the truth. [26]Don't get so angry that you sin. Don't go to bed angry [27]and don't give the devil a chance.

[28]If you are a thief, quit stealing. Be honest and work hard, so you will have something to give to people in need.

[29]Stop all your dirty talk. Say the right thing at the right time and help others by what you say.

[30]Don't make God's Spirit sad. The Spirit makes you sure that someday you will be free from your sins.

[31]Stop being bitter and angry and mad at others. Don't yell at one another or curse each other or ever be rude. [32]Instead, be kind and merciful, and forgive others, just as God forgave you because of Christ.

5 Do as God does. After all, you are his dear children. [2]Let love be your guide. Christ loved us[a] and offered his life for us as a sacrifice that pleases God.

[a] 5.2 *us:* Some manuscripts have "you."

NEW INTERNATIONAL VERSION

[25]Therefore each of you must put off falsehood and speak truthfully to his neighbor, for we are all members of one body. [26]"In your anger do not sin"[d]: Do not let the sun go down while you are still angry, [27]and do not give the devil a foothold. [28]He who has been stealing must steal no longer, but must work, doing something useful with his own hands, that he may have something to share with those in need.

[29]Do not let any unwholesome talk come out of your mouths, but only what is helpful for building others up according to their needs, that it may benefit those who listen. [30]And do not grieve the Holy Spirit of God, with whom you were sealed for the day of redemption. [31]Get rid of all bitterness, rage and anger, brawling and slander, along with every form of malice. [32]Be kind and compassionate to one another, forgiving each other, just as in Christ God forgave you.

5 Be imitators of God, therefore, as dearly loved children [2]and live a life of love, just as Christ loved us and gave himself up for us as a fragrant offering and sacrifice to God.

[d] *26* Psalm 4:4

NEW LIVING TRANSLATION

[25]So put away all falsehood and "tell your neighbor the truth"* because we belong to each other. [26]And "don't sin by letting anger gain control over you."* Don't let the sun go down while you are still angry, [27]for anger gives a mighty foothold to the Devil.

[28]If you are a thief, stop stealing. Begin using your hands for honest work, and then give generously to others in need. [29]Don't use foul or abusive language. Let everything you say be good and helpful, so that your words will be an encouragement to those who hear them.

[30]And do not bring sorrow to God's Holy Spirit by the way you live. Remember, he is the one who has identified you as his own, guaranteeing that you will be saved on the day of redemption.

[31]Get rid of all bitterness, rage, anger, harsh words, and slander, as well as all types of malicious behavior. [32]Instead, be kind to each other, tenderhearted, forgiving one another, just as God through Christ has forgiven you.

Living in the Light

5 Follow God's example in everything you do, because you are his dear children. [2]Live a life filled with love for others, following the example of Christ, who loved you and gave himself as a sacrifice to take away your sins. And God was pleased, because that sacrifice was like sweet perfume to him.

4:25 Zech 8:16. **4:26** Ps 4:4.

NEW KING JAMES VERSION

Do Not Grieve the Spirit

[25]Therefore, putting away lying, *"Let each one of you speak truth with his neighbor,"*[e] for we are members of one another. [26]*"Be angry, and do not sin"*:[f] do not let the sun go down on your wrath, [27]nor give place to the devil. [28]Let him who stole steal no longer, but rather let him labor, working with *his* hands what is good, that he may have something to give him who has need. [29]Let no corrupt word proceed out of your mouth, but what is good for necessary edification, that it may impart grace to the hearers. [30]And do not grieve the Holy Spirit of God, by whom you were sealed for the day of redemption. [31]Let all bitterness, wrath, anger, clamor, and evil speaking be put away from you, with all malice. [32]And be kind to one another, tenderhearted, forgiving one another, even as God in Christ forgave you.

Walk in Love

5 Therefore be imitators of God as dear children. [2]And walk in love, as Christ also has loved us and given Himself for us, an offering and a sacrifice to God for a sweet-smelling aroma.

4:25 [e] Zechariah 8:16 **4:26** [f] Psalm 4:4

THE MESSAGE

What this adds up to, then, is this: no more lies, no more pretense. Tell your neighbor the truth. In Christ's body we're all connected to each other, after all. When you lie to others, you end up lying to yourself.

Go ahead and be angry. You do well to be angry—but don't use your anger as fuel for revenge. And don't stay angry. Don't go to bed angry. Don't give the Devil that kind of foothold in your life.

Did you used to make ends meet by stealing? Well, no more! Get an honest job so that you can help others who can't work.

Watch the way you talk. Let nothing foul or dirty come out of your mouth. Say only what helps, each word a gift.

Don't grieve God. Don't break his heart. His Holy Spirit, moving and breathing in you, is the most intimate part of your life, making you fit for himself. Don't take such a gift for granted.

Make a clean break with all cutting, backbiting, profane talk. Be gentle with one another, sensitive. Forgive one another as quickly and thoroughly as God in Christ forgave you.

Wake Up From Your Sleep

5 Watch what God does, and then you do it, like children who learn proper behavior from their parents. Mostly what God does is love you. Keep company with him and learn a life of love. Observe how Christ loved us. His love was not cautious but extravagant. He didn't love in order to get something from us but to give everything of himself to us. Love like that.

KING JAMES VERSION

3 ¶ But fornication, and all uncleanness, or covetousness, let it not be once named among you, as becometh saints;

4 Neither filthiness, nor foolish talking, nor jesting, which are not convenient: but rather giving of thanks.

5 For this ye know, that no whoremonger, nor unclean person, nor covetous man, who is an idolater, hath any inheritance in the kingdom of Christ and of God.

6 Let no man deceive you with vain words: for because of these things cometh the wrath of God upon the children of disobedience.

7 Be not ye therefore partakers with them.

8 For ye were sometimes darkness, but now *are ye* light in the Lord: walk as children of light:

9 (For the fruit of the Spirit *is* in all goodness and righteousness and truth;)

10 Proving what is acceptable unto the Lord.

11 And have no fellowship with the unfruitful works of darkness, but rather reprove *them*.

12 For it is a shame even to speak of those things which are done of them in secret.

13 But all things that are reproved are made manifest by the light: for whatsoever doth make manifest is light.

14 Wherefore he saith, Awake thou that sleepest, and arise from the dead, and Christ shall give thee light.

NEW AMERICAN STANDARD BIBLE

3 But immorality or any impurity or greed must not even be named among you, as is proper among saints;

4 and *there must be no* filthiness and silly talk, or coarse jesting, which are not fitting, but rather giving of thanks.

5 For this you know with certainty, that no immoral or impure person or covetous man, who is an idolater, has an inheritance in the kingdom of Christ and God.

6 Let no one deceive you with empty words, for because of these things the wrath of God comes upon the sons of disobedience.

7 Therefore do not be partakers with them;

8 for you were formerly darkness, but now you are Light in the Lord; walk as children of Light

9 (for the fruit of the Light *consists* in all goodness and righteousness and truth),

10 trying to learn what is pleasing to the Lord.

11 Do not participate in the unfruitful deeds of darkness, but instead even expose them;

12 for it is disgraceful even to speak of the things which are done by them in secret.

13 But all things become visible when they are exposed by the light, for everything that becomes visible is light.

14 For this reason it says,

"Awake, sleeper,
And arise from the dead,
And Christ will shine on you."

NEW CENTURY VERSION

3But there must be no sexual sin among you, or any
kind of evil or greed. Those things are not right for God's
holy people. 4Also, there must be no evil talk among you,
and you must not speak foolishly or tell evil jokes. These
things are not right for you. Instead, you should be giving
thanks to God. 5You can be sure of this: No one will have a
place in the kingdom of Christ and of God who sins sexually, or does evil things, or is greedy. Anyone who is greedy
is serving a false god.

6Do not let anyone fool you by telling you things that
are not true, because these things will bring God's anger
on those who do not obey him. 7So have nothing to do
with them. 8In the past you were full of darkness, but now
you are full of light in the Lord. So live like children who
belong to the light. 9Light brings every kind of goodness,
right living, and truth. 10Try to learn what pleases the
Lord. 11Have nothing to do with the things done in darkness, which are not worth anything. But show that they
are wrong. 12It is shameful even to talk about what those
people do in secret. 13But the light makes all things easy to
see, 14and everything that is made easy to see can become
light. This is why it is said:

"Wake up, sleeper!
Rise from death,
and Christ will shine on you."

CONTEMPORARY ENGLISH VERSION

3You are God's people, so don't let it be said that any of
you are immoral or indecent or greedy. 4Don't use dirty or
foolish or filthy words. Instead, say how thankful you are.
5Being greedy, indecent, or immoral is just another way of
worshiping idols. You can be sure that people who behave
in this way will never be part of the kingdom that belongs
to Christ and to God.

Living as People of Light

6Don't let anyone trick you with foolish talk. God punishes everyone who disobeys him and says[b] foolish things.
7So don't have anything to do with anyone like that.
8You used to be like people living in the dark, but now
you are people of the light because you belong to the Lord.
So act like people of the light 9and make your light shine.
Be good and honest and truthful, 10as you try to please the
Lord. 11Don't take part in doing those worthless things
that are done in the dark. Instead, show how wrong they
are. 12It is disgusting even to talk about what is done in
the dark. 13But the light will show what these things are
really like. 14Light shows up everything,[c] just as the
Scriptures say,

"Wake up from your sleep
and rise from death.
Then Christ will shine on you."

[b] 5.6 *says*: Or "does." [c] 5.14 *Light shows up everything*: Or "Everything that is seen in the light becomes light itself."

NEW INTERNATIONAL VERSION

[3]But among you there must not be even a hint of sexual immorality, or of any kind of impurity, or of greed, because these are improper for God's holy people. [4]Nor should there be obscenity, foolish talk or coarse joking, which are out of place, but rather thanksgiving. [5]For of this you can be sure: No immoral, impure or greedy person—such a man is an idolater—has any inheritance in the kingdom of Christ and of God.[a] [6]Let no one deceive you with empty words, for because of such things God's wrath comes on those who are disobedient. [7]Therefore do not be partners with them.

[8]For you were once darkness, but now you are light in the Lord. Live as children of light [9](for the fruit of the light consists in all goodness, righteousness and truth) [10]and find out what pleases the Lord. [11]Have nothing to do with the fruitless deeds of darkness, but rather expose them. [12]For it is shameful even to mention what the disobedient do in secret. [13]But everything exposed by the light becomes visible, [14]for it is light that makes everything visible. This is why it is said:

"Wake up, O sleeper,
rise from the dead,
and Christ will shine on you."

[a] 5 Or *kingdom of the Christ and God*

NEW LIVING TRANSLATION

[3]Let there be no sexual immorality, impurity, or greed among you. Such sins have no place among God's people. [4]Obscene stories, foolish talk, and coarse jokes—these are not for you. Instead, let there be thankfulness to God. [5]You can be sure that no immoral, impure, or greedy person will inherit the Kingdom of Christ and of God. For a greedy person is really an idolater who worships the things of this world. [6]Don't be fooled by those who try to excuse these sins, for the terrible anger of God comes upon all those who disobey him. [7]Don't participate in the things these people do. [8]For though your hearts were once full of darkness, now you are full of light from the Lord, and your behavior should show it! [9]For this light within you produces only what is good and right and true.

[10]Try to find out what is pleasing to the Lord. [11]Take no part in the worthless deeds of evil and darkness; instead, rebuke and expose them. [12]It is shameful even to talk about the things that ungodly people do in secret. [13]But when the light shines on them, it becomes clear how evil these things are. [14]And where your light shines, it will expose their evil deeds. This is why it is said,

"Awake, O sleeper,
rise up from the dead,
and Christ will give you light."

NEW KING JAMES VERSION

[3]But fornication and all uncleanness or covetousness, let it not even be named among you, as is fitting for saints; [4]neither filthiness, nor foolish talking, nor coarse jesting, which are not fitting, but rather giving of thanks. [5]For this you know,[a] that no fornicator, unclean person, nor covetous man, who is an idolater, has any inheritance in the kingdom of Christ and God. [6]Let no one deceive you with empty words, for because of these things the wrath of God comes upon the sons of disobedience. [7]Therefore do not be partakers with them.

Walk in Light

[8]For you were once darkness, but now *you are* light in the Lord. Walk as children of light [9](for the fruit of the Spirit[b] *is* in all goodness, righteousness, and truth), [10]finding out what is acceptable to the Lord. [11]And have no fellowship with the unfruitful works of darkness, but rather expose *them.* [12]For it is shameful even to speak of those things which are done by them in secret. [13]But all things that are exposed are made manifest by the light, for whatever makes manifest is light. [14]Therefore He says:

"Awake, you who sleep,
Arise from the dead,
And Christ will give you light."

5:5 [a] NU-Text reads *For know this.* 5:9 [b] NU-Text reads *light.*

THE MESSAGE

Don't allow love to turn into lust, setting off a downhill slide into sexual promiscuity, filthy practices, or bullying greed. Though some tongues just love the taste of gossip, Christians have better uses for language than that. Don't talk dirty or silly. That kind of talk doesn't fit our style. Thanksgiving is our dialect.

You can be sure that using people or religion or things just for what you can get out of them—the usual variations on idolatry—will get you nowhere, and certainly nowhere near the kingdom of Christ, the kingdom of God.

Don't let yourselves get taken in by religious smooth talk. God gets furious with people who are full of religious sales talk but want nothing to do with him. Don't even hang around people like that.

You groped your way through that murk once, but no longer. You're out in the open now. The bright light of Christ makes your way plain. So no more stumbling around. Get on with it! The good, the right, the true—these are the actions appropriate for daylight hours. Figure out what will please Christ, and then do it.

Don't waste your time on useless work, mere busywork, the barren pursuits of darkness. Expose these things for the sham they are. It's a scandal when people waste their lives on things they must do in the darkness where no one will see. Rip the cover off those frauds and see how attractive they look in the light of Christ.

"Wake up from your sleep,
Climb out of your coffins;
Christ will show you the light!"

KING JAMES VERSION

15 See then that ye walk circumspectly, not as fools, but as wise,

16 Redeeming the time, because the days are evil.

17 Wherefore be ye not unwise, but understanding what the will of the Lord *is*.

18 And be not drunk with wine, wherein is excess; but be filled with the Spirit;

19 Speaking to yourselves in psalms and hymns and spiritual songs, singing and making melody in your heart to the Lord;

20 Giving thanks always for all things unto God and the Father in the name of our Lord Jesus Christ;

21 ¶ Submitting yourselves one to another in the fear of God.

22 Wives, submit yourselves unto your own husbands, as unto the Lord.

23 For the husband is the head of the wife, even as Christ is the head of the church: and he is the saviour of the body.

24 Therefore as the church is subject unto Christ, so *let* the wives *be* to their own husbands in every thing.

25 Husbands, love your wives, even as Christ also loved the church, and gave himself for it;

26 That he might sanctify and cleanse it with the washing of water by the word,

27 That he might present it to himself a glorious church, not having spot, or wrinkle, or any such thing; but that it should be holy and without blemish.

NEW AMERICAN STANDARD BIBLE

15 Therefore be careful how you walk, not as unwise men but as wise,

16 making the most of your time, because the days are evil.

17 So then do not be foolish, but understand what the will of the Lord is.

18 And do not get drunk with wine, for that is dissipation, but be filled with the Spirit,

19 speaking to one another in psalms and hymns and spiritual songs, singing and making melody with your heart to the Lord;

20 always giving thanks for all things in the name of our Lord Jesus Christ to God, even the Father;

21 and be subject to one another in the fear of Christ.

Marriage Like Christ and the Church

22 Wives, *be subject* to your own husbands, as to the Lord.

23 For the husband is the head of the wife, as Christ also is the head of the church, He Himself *being* the Savior of the body.

24 But as the church is subject to Christ, so also the wives *ought to be* to their husbands in everything.

25 Husbands, love your wives, just as Christ also loved the church and gave Himself up for her,

26 so that He might sanctify her, having cleansed her by the washing of water with the word,

27 that He might present to Himself the church in all her glory, having no spot or wrinkle or any such thing; but that she would be holy and blameless.

NEW CENTURY VERSION

15So be very careful how you live. Do not live like those who are not wise, but live wisely. 16Use every chance you have for doing good, because these are evil times. 17So do not be foolish but learn what the Lord wants you to do. 18Do not be drunk with wine, which will ruin you, but be filled with the Spirit. 19Speak to each other with psalms, hymns, and spiritual songs, singing and making music in your hearts to the Lord. 20Always give thanks to God the Father for everything, in the name of our Lord Jesus Christ.

Wives and Husbands

21Yield to obey each other because you respect Christ.

22Wives, yield to your husbands, as you do to the Lord, 23because the husband is the head of the wife, as Christ is the head of the church. And he is the Savior of the body, which is the church. 24As the church yields to Christ, so you wives should yield to your husbands in everything.

25Husbands, love your wives as Christ loved the church and gave himself for it 26to make it belong to God. Christ used the word to make the church clean by washing it with water. 27He died so that he could give the church to himself like a bride in all her beauty. He died so that the church could be pure and without fault, with no evil or sin or any other wrong thing in it. 28In the same way, hus-

CONTEMPORARY ENGLISH VERSION

15Act like people with good sense and not like fools. 16These are evil times, so make every minute count. 17Don't be stupid. Instead, find out what the Lord wants you to do. 18Don't destroy yourself by getting drunk, but let the Spirit fill your life. 19When you meet together, sing psalms, hymns, and spiritual songs, as you praise the Lord with all your heart. 20Always use the name of our Lord Jesus Christ to thank God the Father for everything.

Wives and Husbands

21Honor Christ and put others first. 22A wife should put her husband first, as she does the Lord. 23A husband is the head of his wife, as Christ is the head and the Savior of the church, which is his own body. 24Wives should always put their husbands first, as the church puts Christ first.

25A husband should love his wife as much as Christ loved the church and gave his life for it. 26He made the church holy by the power of his word, and he made it pure by washing it with water. 27Christ did this, so that he would have a glorious and holy church, without faults or spots or wrinkles or any other flaws.

NEW INTERNATIONAL VERSION

[15]Be very careful, then, how you live—not as unwise but as wise, [16]making the most of every opportunity, because the days are evil. [17]Therefore do not be foolish, but understand what the Lord's will is. [18]Do not get drunk on wine, which leads to debauchery. Instead, be filled with the Spirit. [19]Speak to one another with psalms, hymns and spiritual songs. Sing and make music in your heart to the Lord, [20]always giving thanks to God the Father for everything, in the name of our Lord Jesus Christ.

[21]Submit to one another out of reverence for Christ.

Wives and Husbands

[22]Wives, submit to your husbands as to the Lord. [23]For the husband is the head of the wife as Christ is the head of the church, his body, of which he is the Savior. [24]Now as the church submits to Christ, so also wives should submit to their husbands in everything.

[25]Husbands, love your wives, just as Christ loved the church and gave himself up for her [26]to make her holy, cleansing[b] her by the washing with water through the word, [27]and to present her to himself as a radiant church, without stain or wrinkle or any other blemish, but holy

[b] 26 Or *having cleansed*

NEW LIVING TRANSLATION

Living by the Spirit's Power

[15]So be careful how you live, not as fools but as those who are wise. [16]Make the most of every opportunity for doing good in these evil days. [17]Don't act thoughtlessly, but try to understand what the Lord wants you to do. [18]Don't be drunk with wine, because that will ruin your life. Instead, let the Holy Spirit fill and control you. [19]Then you will sing psalms and hymns and spiritual songs among yourselves, making music to the Lord in your hearts. [20]And you will always give thanks for everything to God the Father in the name of our Lord Jesus Christ.

Spirit-Guided Relationships: Wives and Husbands

[21]And further, you will submit to one another out of reverence for Christ. [22]You wives will submit to your husbands as you do to the Lord. [23]For a husband is the head of his wife as Christ is the head of his body, the church; he gave his life to be her Savior. [24]As the church submits to Christ, so you wives must submit to your husbands in everything.

[25]And you husbands must love your wives with the same love Christ showed the church. He gave up his life for her [26]to make her holy and clean, washed by baptism and God's word.* [27]He did this to present her to himself as a glorious church without a spot or wrinkle or any other blemish. Instead, she will be holy and without fault. [28]In

5:26 Greek *having cleansed her by the washing of water with the word.*

NEW KING JAMES VERSION

Walk in Wisdom

[15]See then that you walk circumspectly, not as fools but as wise, [16]redeeming the time, because the days are evil.

[17]Therefore do not be unwise, but understand what the will of the Lord *is.* [18]And do not be drunk with wine, in which is dissipation; but be filled with the Spirit, [19]speaking to one another in psalms and hymns and spiritual songs, singing and making melody in your heart to the Lord, [20]giving thanks always for all things to God the Father in the name of our Lord Jesus Christ, [21]submitting to one another in the fear of God.[c]

Marriage—Christ and the Church

[22]Wives, submit to your own husbands, as to the Lord. [23]For the husband is head of the wife, as also Christ is head of the church; and He is the Savior of the body. [24]Therefore, just as the church is subject to Christ, so *let* the wives *be* to their own husbands in everything.

[25]Husbands, love your wives, just as Christ also loved the church and gave Himself for her, [26]that He might sanctify and cleanse her with the washing of water by the word, [27]that He might present her to Himself a glorious church, not having spot or wrinkle or any such thing, but that she should be holy and without blemish. [28]So husbands ought

5:21 [c] NU-Text reads *Christ.*

THE MESSAGE

So watch your step. Use your head. Make the most of every chance you get. These are desperate times!

Don't live carelessly, unthinkingly. Make sure you understand what the Master wants.

Don't drink too much wine. That cheapens your life. Drink the Spirit of God, huge draughts of him. Sing hymns instead of drinking songs! Sing songs from your heart to Christ. Sing praises over everything, any excuse for a song to God the Father in the name of our Master, Jesus Christ.

Relationships

Out of respect for Christ, be courteously reverent to one another.

Wives, understand and support your husbands in ways that show your support for Christ. The husband provides leadership to his wife the way Christ does to his church, not by domineering but by cherishing. So just as the church submits to Christ as he exercises such leadership, wives should likewise submit to their husbands.

Husbands, go all out in your love for your wives, exactly as Christ did for the church—a love marked by giving, not getting. Christ's love makes the church whole. His words evoke her beauty. Everything he does and says is designed to bring the best out of her, dressing her in dazzling white silk, radiant with holiness. And that is how husbands

KING JAMES VERSION

28 So ought men to love their wives as their own bodies. He that loveth his wife loveth himself.

29 For no man ever yet hated his own flesh; but nourisheth and cherisheth it, even as the Lord the church:

30 For we are members of his body, of his flesh, and of his bones.

31 For this cause shall a man leave his father and mother, and shall be joined unto his wife, and they two shall be one flesh.

32 This is a great mystery: but I speak concerning Christ and the church.

33 Nevertheless let every one of you in particular so love his wife even as himself; and the wife *see* that she reverence *her* husband.

6 Children, obey your parents in the Lord: for this is right.

2 Honour thy father and mother; (which is the first commandment with promise;)

3 That it may be well with thee, and thou mayest live long on the earth.

4 And, ye fathers, provoke not your children to wrath: but bring them up in the nurture and admonition of the Lord.

5 Servants, be obedient to them that are *your* masters according to the flesh, with fear and trembling, in singleness of your heart, as unto Christ;

NEW AMERICAN STANDARD BIBLE

28 So husbands ought also to love their own wives as their own bodies. He who loves his own wife loves himself;

29 for no one ever hated his own flesh, but nourishes and cherishes it, just as Christ also *does* the church,

30 because we are members of His body.

31 FOR THIS REASON A MAN SHALL LEAVE HIS FATHER AND MOTHER AND SHALL BE JOINED TO HIS WIFE, AND THE TWO SHALL BECOME ONE FLESH.

32 This mystery is great; but I am speaking with reference to Christ and the church.

33 Nevertheless, each individual among you also is to love his own wife even as himself, and the wife must *see to it* that she respects her husband.

Family Relationships

6 Children, obey your parents in the Lord, for this is right.

2 HONOR YOUR FATHER AND MOTHER (which is the first commandment with a promise),

3 SO THAT IT MAY BE WELL WITH YOU, AND THAT YOU MAY LIVE LONG ON THE EARTH.

4 Fathers, do not provoke your children to anger, but bring them up in the discipline and instruction of the Lord.

5 Slaves, be obedient to those who are your masters according to the flesh, with fear and trembling, in the sincerity of your heart, as to Christ;

NEW CENTURY VERSION

bands should love their wives as they love their own bod-
ies. The man who loves his wife loves himself. 29No one
ever hates his own body, but feeds and takes care of it.
And that is what Christ does for the church, 30because we
are parts of his body. 31The Scripture says, "So a man will
leave his father and mother and be united with his wife,
and the two will become one body."[a] 32That secret is very
important—I am talking about Christ and the church.
33But each one of you must love his wife as he loves him-
self, and a wife must respect her husband.

Children and Parents

6 Children, obey your parents as the Lord wants,
because this is the right thing to do. 2The command
says, "Honor your father and mother."[a] This is the first
command that has a promise with it— 3"Then everything
will be well with you, and you will have a long life on the
earth."[b]

4Fathers, do not make your children angry, but raise
them with the training and teaching of the Lord.

Slaves and Masters

5Slaves, obey your masters here on earth with fear and
respect and from a sincere heart, just as you obey Christ.

5:31 [a] **"So...body."** Quotation from Genesis 2:24.
6:2 [a] **"Honor...mother."** Quotation from Exodus 20:12; Deuteronomy 5:16. 6:3 [b] **"Then...earth."** Quotation from Exodus 20:12; Deuteronomy 5:16.

CONTEMPORARY ENGLISH VERSION

28In the same way, a husband should love his wife as
much as he loves himself. A husband who loves his wife
shows that he loves himself. 29None of us hate our own
bodies. We provide for them and take good care of them,
just as Christ does for the church, 30because we are each
part of his body. 31As the Scriptures say, "A man leaves
his father and mother to get married, and he becomes like
one person with his wife." 32This is a great mystery, but I
understand it to mean Christ and his church. 33So each
husband should love his wife as much as he loves himself,
and each wife should respect her husband.

Children and Parents

6 Children, you belong to the Lord, and you do the right
thing when you obey your parents. The first com-
mandment with a promise says, 2"Obey your father and
your mother, 3and you will have a long and happy life."

4Parents, don't be hard on your children. Raise them
properly. Teach them and instruct them about the Lord.

Slaves and Masters

5Slaves, you must obey your earthly masters. Show them
great respect and be as loyal to them as you are to Christ.

NEW INTERNATIONAL VERSION

and blameless. [28]In this same way, husbands ought to love their wives as their own bodies. He who loves his wife loves himself. [29]After all, no one ever hated his own body, but he feeds and cares for it, just as Christ does the church— [30]for we are members of his body. [31]"For this reason a man will leave his father and mother and be united to his wife, and the two will become one flesh."[c] [32]This is a profound mystery—but I am talking about Christ and the church. [33]However, each one of you also must love his wife as he loves himself, and the wife must respect her husband.

Children and Parents

6 Children, obey your parents in the Lord, for this is right. [2]"Honor your father and mother"—which is the first commandment with a promise— [3]"that it may go well with you and that you may enjoy long life on the earth."[a]

[4]Fathers, do not exasperate your children; instead, bring them up in the training and instruction of the Lord.

Slaves and Masters

[5]Slaves, obey your earthly masters with respect and fear, and with sincerity of heart, just as you would obey Christ.

[c] *31* Gen. 2:24 [a] *3* Deut. 5:16

NEW LIVING TRANSLATION

the same way, husbands ought to love their wives as they love their own bodies. For a man is actually loving himself when he loves his wife. [29]No one hates his own body but lovingly cares for it, just as Christ cares for his body, which is the church. [30]And we are his body.

[31]As the Scriptures say, "A man leaves his father and mother and is joined to his wife, and the two are united into one."* [32]This is a great mystery, but it is an illustration of the way Christ and the church are one. [33]So again I say, each man must love his wife as he loves himself, and the wife must respect her husband.

Children and Parents

6 Children, obey your parents because you belong to the Lord, for this is the right thing to do. [2]"Honor your father and mother." This is the first of the Ten Commandments that ends with a promise. [3]And this is the promise: If you honor your father and mother, "you will live a long life, full of blessing."*

[4]And now a word to you fathers. Don't make your children angry by the way you treat them. Rather, bring them up with the discipline and instruction approved by the Lord.

Slaves and Masters

[5]Slaves, obey your earthly masters with deep respect and fear. Serve them sincerely as you would serve Christ.

5:31 Gen 2:24. 6:2-3 Exod 20:12; Deut 5:16.

NEW KING JAMES VERSION

to love their own wives as their own bodies; he who loves his wife loves himself. [29]For no one ever hated his own flesh, but nourishes and cherishes it, just as the Lord *does* the church. [30]For we are members of His body,[d] of His flesh and of His bones. [31]*"For this reason a man shall leave his father and mother and be joined to his wife, and the two shall become one flesh."*[e] [32]This is a great mystery, but I speak concerning Christ and the church. [33]Nevertheless let each one of you in particular so love his own wife as himself, and let the wife *see* that she respects *her* husband.

Children and Parents

6 Children, obey your parents in the Lord, for this is right. [2]*"Honor your father and mother,"* which is the first commandment with promise: [3]*"that it may be well with you and you may live long on the earth."*[a]

[4]And you, fathers, do not provoke your children to wrath, but bring them up in the training and admonition of the Lord.

Bondservants and Masters

[5]Bondservants, be obedient to those who are your masters according to the flesh, with fear and trembling, in sincerity of heart, as to Christ; [6]not with eyeservice, as

5:30 [d] NU-Text omits the rest of this verse. **5:31** [e] Genesis 2:24
6:3 [a] Deuteronomy 5:16

THE MESSAGE

ought to love their wives. They're really doing themselves a favor—since they're already "one" in marriage.

No one abuses his own body, does he? No, he feeds and pampers it. That's how Christ treats us, the church, since we are part of his body. And this is why a man leaves father and mother and cherishes his wife. No longer two, they become "one flesh." This is a huge mystery, and I don't pretend to understand it all. What is clearest to me is the way Christ treats the church. And this provides a good picture of how each husband is to treat his wife, loving himself in loving her, and how each wife is to honor her husband.

6 Children, do what your parents tell you. This is only right. "Honor your father and mother" is the first commandment that has a promise attached to it, namely, "so you will live well and have a long life."

Fathers, don't exasperate your children by coming down hard on them. Take them by the hand and lead them in the way of the Master.

Servants, respectfully obey your earthly masters but always with an eye to obeying the *real* master, Christ.

KING JAMES VERSION

6 Not with eyeservice, as menpleasers; but as the servants of Christ, doing the will of God from the heart;

7 With good will doing service, as to the Lord, and not to men:

8 Knowing that whatsoever good thing any man doeth, the same shall he receive of the Lord, whether *he be* bond or free.

9 And, ye masters, do the same things unto them, forbearing threatening: knowing that your Master also is in heaven; neither is there respect of persons with him.

10 ¶ Finally, my brethren, be strong in the Lord, and in the power of his might.

11 Put on the whole armour of God, that ye may be able to stand against the wiles of the devil.

12 For we wrestle not against flesh and blood, but against principalities, against powers, against the rulers of the darkness of this world, against spiritual wickedness in high *places*.

13 Wherefore take unto you the whole armour of God, that ye may be able to withstand in the evil day, and having done all, to stand.

14 Stand therefore, having your loins girt about with truth, and having on the breastplate of righteousness;

15 And your feet shod with the preparation of the gospel of peace;

NEW AMERICAN STANDARD BIBLE

6 not by way of eyeservice, as men-pleasers, but as slaves of Christ, doing the will of God from the heart.

7 With good will render service, as to the Lord, and not to men,

8 knowing that whatever good thing each one does, this he will receive back from the Lord, whether slave or free.

9 And masters, do the same things to them, and give up threatening, knowing that both their Master and yours is in heaven, and there is no partiality with Him.

The Armor of God

10 Finally, be strong in the Lord and in the strength of His might.

11 Put on the full armor of God, so that you will be able to stand firm against the schemes of the devil.

12 For our struggle is not against flesh and blood, but against the rulers, against the powers, against the world forces of this darkness, against the spiritual *forces* of wickedness in the heavenly *places*.

13 Therefore, take up the full armor of God, so that you will be able to resist in the evil day, and having done everything, to stand firm.

14 Stand firm therefore, HAVING GIRDED YOUR LOINS WITH TRUTH, and HAVING PUT ON THE BREASTPLATE OF RIGHTEOUSNESS,

15 and having shod YOUR FEET WITH THE PREPARATION OF THE GOSPEL OF PEACE;

NEW CENTURY VERSION

6You must do this not only while they are watching you, to
please them. With all your heart you must do what God
wants as people who are obeying Christ. 7Do your work
with enthusiasm. Work as if you were serving the Lord,
not as if you were serving only men and women.
8Remember that the Lord will give a reward to everyone,
slave or free, for doing good.
9Masters, in the same way, be good to your slaves. Do
not threaten them. Remember that the One who is your
Master and their Master is in heaven, and he treats everyone alike.

Wear the Full Armor of God

10Finally, be strong in the Lord and in his great power.
11Put on the full armor of God so that you can fight
against the devil's evil tricks. 12Our fight is not against
people on earth but against the rulers and authorities and
the powers of this world's darkness, against the spiritual
powers of evil in the heavenly world. 13That is why you
need to put on God's full armor. Then on the day of evil
you will be able to stand strong. And when you have finished the whole fight, you will still be standing. 14So stand
strong, with the belt of truth tied around your waist and
the protection of right living on your chest. 15On your feet
wear the Good News of peace to help you stand strong.

CONTEMPORARY ENGLISH VERSION

6Try to please them at all times, and not just when you
think they are watching. You are slaves of Christ, so with
your whole heart you must do what God wants you to do.
7Gladly serve your masters, as though they were the Lord
himself, and not simply people. 8You know that you will be
rewarded for any good things you do, whether you are
slaves or free.
9Slave owners, you must treat your slaves with this
same respect. Don't threaten them. They have the same
Master in heaven that you do, and he doesn't have any
favorites.

The Fight against Evil

10Finally, let the mighty strength of the Lord make you
strong. 11Put on all the armor that God gives, so you can
defend yourself against the devil's tricks. 12We are not
fighting against humans. We are fighting against forces
and authorities and against rulers of darkness and powers
in the spiritual world. 13So put on all the armor that God
gives. Then when that evil day[a] comes, you will be able to
defend yourself. And when the battle is over, you will still
be standing firm.
14Be ready! Let the truth be like a belt around your
waist, and let God's justice protect you like armor. 15Your
desire to tell the good news about peace should be like

[a] 6.13 *that evil day*: Either the present (see 5.16) or "the day of death" or "the day of judgment."

NEW INTERNATIONAL VERSION

6Obey them not only to win their favor when their eye is on
you, but like slaves of Christ, doing the will of God from
your heart. 7Serve wholeheartedly, as if you were serving
the Lord, not men, 8because you know that the Lord will
reward everyone for whatever good he does, whether he is
slave or free.

9And masters, treat your slaves in the same way. Do not
threaten them, since you know that he who is both their
Master and yours is in heaven, and there is no favoritism
with him.

The Armor of God

10Finally, be strong in the Lord and in his mighty power.
11Put on the full armor of God so that you can take your
stand against the devil's schemes. 12For our struggle is not
against flesh and blood, but against the rulers, against the
authorities, against the powers of this dark world and
against the spiritual forces of evil in the heavenly realms.
13Therefore put on the full armor of God, so that when the
day of evil comes, you may be able to stand your ground,
and after you have done everything, to stand. 14Stand firm
then, with the belt of truth buckled around your waist,
with the breastplate of righteousness in place, 15and with
your feet fitted with the readiness that comes from the
gospel of peace. 16In addition to all this, take up the shield

NEW LIVING TRANSLATION

6Work hard, but not just to please your masters when they
are watching. As slaves of Christ, do the will of God with
all your heart. 7Work with enthusiasm, as though you
were working for the Lord rather than for people.
8Remember that the Lord will reward each one of us for
the good we do, whether we are slaves or free.

9And in the same way, you masters must treat your
slaves right. Don't threaten them; remember, you both
have the same Master in heaven, and he has no favorites.

The Whole Armor of God

10A final word: Be strong with the Lord's mighty power.
11Put on all of God's armor so that you will be able to
stand firm against all strategies and tricks of the Devil.
12For we are not fighting against people made of flesh and
blood, but against the evil rulers and authorities of the
unseen world, against those mighty powers of darkness
who rule this world, and against wicked spirits in the
heavenly realms.

13Use every piece of God's armor to resist the enemy in
the time of evil, so that after the battle you will still be
standing firm. 14Stand your ground, putting on the sturdy
belt of truth and the body armor of God's righteousness.
15For shoes, put on the peace that comes from the Good
News, so that you will be fully prepared.* 16In every battle

6:15 Or *For shoes, put on the readiness to preach the Good News of peace with God.*

NEW KING JAMES VERSION

men-pleasers, but as bondservants of Christ, doing the
will of God from the heart, 7with goodwill doing service,
as to the Lord, and not to men, 8knowing that whatever
good anyone does, he will receive the same from the Lord,
whether *he is* a slave or free.

9And you, masters, do the same things to them, giving
up threatening, knowing that your own Master also[b] is in
heaven, and there is no partiality with Him.

The Whole Armor of God

10Finally, my brethren, be strong in the Lord and in the
power of His might. 11Put on the whole armor of God, that
you may be able to stand against the wiles of the devil.
12For we do not wrestle against flesh and blood, but
against principalities, against powers, against the rulers of
the darkness of this age,[c] against spiritual *hosts* of
wickedness in the heavenly *places.* 13Therefore take up the
whole armor of God, that you may be able to withstand in
the evil day, and having done all, to stand.

14Stand therefore, having girded your waist with truth,
having put on the breastplate of righteousness, 15and hav-
ing shod your feet with the preparation of the gospel of

6:9 [b] NU-Text reads *He who is both their Master and yours.*
6:12 [c] NU-Text reads *rulers of this darkness.*

THE MESSAGE

Don't just do what you have to do to get by, but work heartily, as Christ's servants doing what God wants you to do. And work with a smile on your face, always keeping in mind that no matter who happens to be giving the orders, you're really serving God. Good work will get you good pay from the Master, regardless of whether you are slave or free.

Masters, it's the same with you. No abuse, please, and no threats. You and your servants are both under the same Master in heaven. He makes no distinction between you and them.

A Fight to the Finish

And that about wraps it up. God is strong, and he wants you strong. So take everything the Master has set out for you, well-made weapons of the best materials. And put them to use so you will be able to stand up to everything the Devil throws your way. This is no afternoon athletic contest that we'll walk away from and forget about in a couple of hours. This is for keeps, a life-or-death fight to the finish against the Devil and all his angels.

Be prepared. You're up against far more than you can handle on your own. Take all the help you can get, every weapon God has issued, so that when it's all over but the shouting you'll still be on your feet. Truth, righteousness,

KING JAMES VERSION

16 Above all, taking the shield of faith, wherewith ye shall be able to quench all the fiery darts of the wicked.

17 And take the helmet of salvation, and the sword of the Spirit, which is the word of God:

18 Praying always with all prayer and supplication in the Spirit, and watching thereunto with all perseverance and supplication for all saints;

19 ¶ And for me, that utterance may be given unto me, that I may open my mouth boldly, to make known the mystery of the gospel,

20 For which I am an ambassador in bonds: that therein I may speak boldly, as I ought to speak.

21 But that ye also may know my affairs, *and* how I do, Tychicus, a beloved brother and faithful minister in the Lord, shall make known to you all things:

22 Whom I have sent unto you for the same purpose, that ye might know our affairs, and *that* he might comfort your hearts.

23 Peace *be* to the brethren, and love with faith, from God the Father and the Lord Jesus Christ.

24 Grace *be* with all them that love our Lord Jesus Christ in sincerity. Amen.

NEW AMERICAN STANDARD BIBLE

16 in addition to all, taking up the shield of faith with which you will be able to extinguish all the flaming arrows of the evil *one.*

17 And take THE HELMET OF SALVATION, and the sword of the Spirit, which is the word of God.

18 With all prayer and petition pray at all times in the Spirit, and with this in view, be on the alert with all perseverance and petition for all the saints,

19 and *pray* on my behalf, that utterance may be given to me in the opening of my mouth, to make known with boldness the mystery of the gospel,

20 for which I am an ambassador in chains; that [j]in *proclaiming* it I may speak boldly, as I ought to speak.

21 But that you also may know about my circumstances, how I am doing, Tychicus, the beloved brother and faithful minister in the Lord, will make everything known to you.

22 I have sent him to you for this very purpose, so that you may know about us, and that he may comfort your hearts.

23 Peace be to the brethren, and love with faith, from God the Father and the Lord Jesus Christ.

24 Grace be with all those who love our Lord Jesus Christ with incorruptible *love.*

6:20 [j] Two early mss read *I may speak it boldly*

NEW CENTURY VERSION

16And also use the shield of faith with which you can stop all the burning arrows of the Evil One. 17Accept God's salvation as your helmet, and take the sword of the Spirit, which is the word of God. 18Pray in the Spirit at all times with all kinds of prayers, asking for everything you need. To do this you must always be ready and never give up. Always pray for all God's people.

19Also pray for me that when I speak, God will give me words so that I can tell the secret of the Good News without fear. 20I have been sent to preach this Good News, and I am doing that now, here in prison. Pray that when I preach the Good News I will speak without fear, as I should.

Final Greetings

21I am sending to you Tychicus, our brother whom we love and a faithful servant of the Lord's work. He will tell you everything that is happening with me. Then you will know how I am and what I am doing. 22I am sending him to you for this reason—so that you will know how we are, and he can encourage you.

23Peace and love with faith to you from God the Father and the Lord Jesus Christ. 24Grace to all of you who love our Lord Jesus Christ with love that never ends.

CONTEMPORARY ENGLISH VERSION

shoes on your feet. 16Let your faith be like a shield, and you will be able to stop all the flaming arrows of the evil one. 17Let God's saving power be like a helmet, and for a sword use God's message that comes from the Spirit.

18Never stop praying, especially for others. Always pray by the power of the Spirit. Stay alert and keep praying for God's people. 19Pray that I will be given the message to speak and that I may fearlessly explain the mystery about the good news. 20I was sent to do this work, and that's the reason I am in jail. So pray that I will be brave and will speak as I should.

Final Greetings

21-22I want you to know how I am getting along and what I am doing. That's why I am sending Tychicus to you. He is a dear friend, as well as a faithful servant of the Lord. He will tell you how I am doing, and he will cheer you up.

23I pray that God the Father and the Lord Jesus Christ will give peace, love, and faith to every follower! 24May God be kind to everyone who keeps on loving our Lord Jesus Christ.

NEW INTERNATIONAL VERSION

of faith, with which you can extinguish all the flaming
arrows of the evil one. 17 Take the helmet of salvation and
the sword of the Spirit, which is the word of God. 18 And
pray in the Spirit on all occasions with all kinds of prayers
and requests. With this in mind, be alert and always keep
on praying for all the saints.

19 Pray also for me, that whenever I open my mouth,
words may be given me so that I will fearlessly make
known the mystery of the gospel, 20 for which I am an
ambassador in chains. Pray that I may declare it fearlessly,
as I should.

Final Greetings

21 Tychicus, the dear brother and faithful servant in the
Lord, will tell you everything, so that you also may know
how I am and what I am doing. 22 I am sending him to you
for this very purpose, that you may know how we are, and
that he may encourage you.

23 Peace to the brothers, and love with faith from God the
Father and the Lord Jesus Christ. 24 Grace to all who love
our Lord Jesus Christ with an undying love.

NEW LIVING TRANSLATION

you will need faith as your shield to stop the fiery arrows
aimed at you by Satan.* 17 Put on salvation as your helmet,
and take the sword of the Spirit, which is the word of God.
18 Pray at all times and on every occasion in the power of
the Holy Spirit. Stay alert and be persistent in your prayers
for all Christians everywhere.

19 And pray for me, too. Ask God to give me the right
words as I boldly explain God's secret plan that the Good
News is for the Gentiles, too.* 20 I am in chains now for
preaching this message as God's ambassador. But pray
that I will keep on speaking boldly for him, as I should.

Final Greetings

21 Tychicus, a much loved brother and faithful helper in
the Lord's work, will tell you all about how I am getting
along. 22 I am sending him to you for just this purpose. He
will let you know how we are, and he will encourage you.

23 May God give you peace, dear brothers and sisters,*
and love with faith, from God the Father and the Lord
Jesus Christ. 24 May God's grace be upon all who love our
Lord Jesus Christ with an undying love.

6:16 Greek *by the evil one.* 6:19 Greek *explain the mystery of the gospel.* 6:23 Greek *brothers.*

NEW KING JAMES VERSION

peace; 16 above all, taking the shield of faith with which
you will be able to quench all the fiery darts of the wicked
one. 17 And take the helmet of salvation, and the sword of
the Spirit, which is the word of God; 18 praying always with
all prayer and supplication in the Spirit, being watchful to
this end with all perseverance and supplication for all the
saints— 19 and for me, that utterance may be given to me,
that I may open my mouth boldly to make known the mys-
tery of the gospel, 20 for which I am an ambassador in
chains; that in it I may speak boldly, as I ought to speak.

A Gracious Greeting

21 But that you also may know my affairs *and* how I am
doing, Tychicus, a beloved brother and faithful minister in
the Lord, will make all things known to you; 22 whom I
have sent to you for this very purpose, that you may know
our affairs, and *that* he may comfort your hearts.

23 Peace to the brethren, and love with faith, from God
the Father and the Lord Jesus Christ. 24 Grace *be* with all
those who love our Lord Jesus Christ in sincerity. Amen.

THE MESSAGE

peace, faith, and salvation are more than words. Learn how to apply them. You'll need them throughout your life. God's Word is an *indispensable* weapon. In the same way, prayer is essential in this ongoing warfare. Pray hard and long. Pray for your brothers and sisters. Keep your eyes open. Keep each other's spirits up so that no one falls behind or drops out.

And don't forget to pray for me. Pray that I'll know what to say and have the courage to say it at the right time, telling the mystery to one and all, the Message that I, jailbird preacher that I am, am responsible for getting out.

Tychicus, my good friend here, will tell you what I'm doing and how things are going with me. He is certainly a dependable servant of the Master! I've sent him not only to tell you about us but to cheer you on in your faith.

Goodbye, friends. Love mixed with faith be yours from God the Father and from the Master, Jesus Christ. Pure grace and nothing but grace be with all who love our Master, Jesus Christ.

KING JAMES VERSION

THE EPISTLE OF ST. PAUL TO THE

PHILIPPIANS

1 Paul and Timotheus, the servants of Jesus Christ, to all the saints in Christ Jesus which are at Philippi, with the bishops and deacons:

2 Grace *be* unto you, and peace, from God our Father, and *from* the Lord Jesus Christ.

3 ¶ I thank my God upon every remembrance of you,

4 Always in every prayer of mine for you all making request with joy,

5 For your fellowship in the gospel from the first day until now;

6 Being confident of this very thing, that he which hath begun a good work in you will perform *it* until the day of Jesus Christ:

7 ¶ Even as it is meet for me to think this of you all, because I have you in my heart; inasmuch as both in my bonds, and in the defence and confirmation of the gospel, ye all are partakers of my grace.

8 For God is my record, how greatly I long after you all in the bowels of Jesus Christ.

NEW AMERICAN STANDARD BIBLE

THE LETTER OF PAUL TO THE

PHILIPPIANS

Thanksgiving

1 Paul and Timothy, bond-servants of Christ Jesus, To all the saints in Christ Jesus who are in Philippi, including the overseers and deacons:

2 Grace to you and peace from God our Father and the Lord Jesus Christ.

3 I thank my God in all my remembrance of you,

4 always offering prayer with joy in my every prayer for you all,

5 in view of your participation in the gospel from the first day until now.

6 *For I am* confident of this very thing, that He who began a good work in you will perfect it until the day of Christ Jesus.

7 For it is only right for me to feel this way about you all, because I have you in my heart, since both in my imprisonment and in the defense and confirmation of the gospel, you all are partakers of grace with me.

8 For God is my witness, how I long for you all with the affection of Christ Jesus.

NEW CENTURY VERSION

PHILIPPIANS

1 From Paul and Timothy, servants of Christ Jesus.
To all of God's holy people in Christ Jesus who live in Philippi, including your elders and deacons:

2 Grace and peace to you from God our Father and the Lord Jesus Christ.

Paul's Prayer

3 I thank my God every time I remember you, 4 always
praying with joy for all of you. 5 I thank God for the help
you gave me while I preached the Good News—help you
gave from the first day you believed until now. 6 God began
doing a good work in you, and I am sure he will continue
it until it is finished when Jesus Christ comes again.

7 And I know that I am right to think like this about all
of you, because I have you in my heart. All of you share in
God's grace with me while I am in prison and while I am
defending and proving the truth of the Good News. 8 God
knows that I want to see you very much, because I love all
of you with the love of Christ Jesus.

CONTEMPORARY ENGLISH VERSION

PHILIPPIANS

1 From Paul and Timothy, servants of Christ Jesus.
To all of God's people who belong to Christ Jesus at Philippi and to all of your church officials and officers.[a]

2 I pray that God our Father and the Lord Jesus Christ will be kind to you and will bless you with peace!

Paul's Prayer for the Church in Philippi

3 Every time I think of you, I thank my God. 4 And when-
ever I mention you in my prayers, it makes me happy.
5 This is because you have taken part with me in spreading
the good news from the first day you heard about it. 6 God
is the one who began this good work in you, and I am cer-
tain that he won't stop before it is complete on the day
that Christ Jesus returns.

7 You have a special place in my heart. So it is only nat-
ural for me to feel the way I do. All of you have helped in
the work that God has given me, as I defend the good news
and tell about it here in jail. 8 God himself knows how
much I want to see you. He knows that I care for you in
the same way that Christ Jesus does.

[a] 1.1 *church officials and officers*: Or "bishops and deacons."

NEW INTERNATIONAL VERSION

PHILIPPIANS

1 Paul and Timothy, servants of Christ Jesus,

To all the saints in Christ Jesus at Philippi, together with
the overseers[a] and deacons:

2 Grace and peace to you from God our Father and the
Lord Jesus Christ.

Thanksgiving and Prayer

3 I thank my God every time I remember you. 4 In all my
prayers for all of you, I always pray with joy 5 because of
your partnership in the gospel from the first day until now,
6 being confident of this, that he who began a good work in
you will carry it on to completion until the day of Christ
Jesus.
7 It is right for me to feel this way about all of you, since
I have you in my heart; for whether I am in chains or
defending and confirming the gospel, all of you share in
God's grace with me. 8 God can testify how I long for all of
you with the affection of Christ Jesus.

[a] *1* Traditionally *bishops*

NEW LIVING TRANSLATION

PHILIPPIANS

Greetings from Paul

1 This letter is from Paul and Timothy, slaves of Christ
Jesus.
It is written to all of God's people in Philippi, who
believe in Christ Jesus, and to the elders* and deacons.
2 May God our Father and the Lord Jesus Christ give you
grace and peace.

Paul's Thanksgiving and Prayer

3 Every time I think of you, I give thanks to my God. 4 I
always pray for you, and I make my requests with a heart
full of joy 5 because you have been my partners in spreading
the Good News about Christ from the time you first heard it
until now. 6 And I am sure that God, who began the good
work within you, will continue his work until it is finally
finished on that day when Christ Jesus comes back again.
7 It is right that I should feel as I do about all of you, for
you have a very special place in my heart. We have shared
together the blessings of God, both when I was in prison
and when I was out, defending the truth and telling others
the Good News. 8 God knows how much I love you and long
for you with the tender compassion of Christ Jesus. 9 I pray

1:1 Greek *overseers.*

NEW KING JAMES VERSION

THE EPISTLE OF PAUL TO THE

PHILIPPIANS

Greeting

1 Paul and Timothy, bondservants of Jesus Christ,

To all the saints in Christ Jesus who are in Philippi, with
the bishops[a] and deacons:

2 Grace to you and peace from God our Father and the
Lord Jesus Christ.

Thankfulness and Prayer

3 I thank my God upon every remembrance of you, 4 al-
ways in every prayer of mine making request for you all
with joy, 5 for your fellowship in the gospel from the first
day until now, 6 being confident of this very thing, that He
who has begun a good work in you will complete *it* until
the day of Jesus Christ; 7 just as it is right for me to think
this of you all, because I have you in my heart, inasmuch
as both in my chains and in the defense and confirmation
of the gospel, you all are partakers with me of grace. 8 For
God is my witness, how greatly I long for you all with the
affection of Jesus Christ.

1:1 [a] Literally *overseers*

THE MESSAGE

PHILIPPIANS

1 Paul and Timothy, both of us committed servants of Christ Jesus, write this letter to all the Christians in Philippi, pastors and ministers included. We greet you with the grace and peace that comes from God our Father and our Master, Jesus Christ.

A Love That Will Grow

Every time you cross my mind, I break out in exclamations of thanks to God. Each exclamation is a trigger to prayer. I find myself praying for you with a glad heart. I am so pleased that you have continued on in this with us, believing and proclaiming God's Message, from the day you heard it right up to the present. There has never been the slightest doubt in my mind that the God who started this great work in you would keep at it and bring it to a flourishing finish on the very day Christ Jesus appears.

It's not at all fanciful for me to think this way about you. My prayers and hopes have deep roots in reality. You have, after all, stuck with me all the way from the time I was thrown in jail, put on trial, and came out of it in one piece. All along you have experienced with me the most generous help from God. He knows how much I love and miss you these days. Sometimes I think I feel as strongly about you as Christ does!

KING JAMES VERSION

9 ¶ And this I pray, that your love may abound yet more and more in knowledge and *in* all judgment;

10 That ye may approve things that are excellent; that ye may be sincere and without offence till the day of Christ;

11 Being filled with the fruits of righteousness, which are by Jesus Christ, unto the glory and praise of God.

12 ¶ But I would ye should understand, brethren, that the things *which happened* unto me have fallen out rather unto the furtherance of the gospel;

13 So that my bonds in Christ are manifest in all the palace, and in all other *places*;

14 And many of the brethren in the Lord, waxing confident by my bonds, are much more bold to speak the word without fear.

15 Some indeed preach Christ even of envy and strife; and some also of good will:

16 The one preach Christ of contention, not sincerely, supposing to add affliction to my bonds:

17 But the other of love, knowing that I am set for the defence of the gospel.

18 What then? notwithstanding, every way, whether in

NEW AMERICAN STANDARD BIBLE

9 And this I pray, that your love may abound still more and more in real knowledge and all discernment,

10 so that you may approve the things that are excellent, in order to be sincere and blameless until the day of Christ;

11 having been filled with the fruit of righteousness which *comes* through Jesus Christ, to the glory and praise of God.

The Gospel Is Preached

12 Now I want you to know, brethren, that my circumstances have turned out for the greater progress of the gospel,

13 so that my imprisonment in *the cause of* Christ has become well known throughout the whole [1]praetorian guard and to everyone else,

14 and that most of the brethren, trusting in the Lord because of my imprisonment, have far more courage to speak the word of God without fear.

15 Some, to be sure, are preaching Christ even from envy and strife, but some also from good will;

16 the latter *do it* out of love, knowing that I am appointed for the defense of the gospel;

17 the former proclaim Christ out of selfish ambition rather than from pure motives, thinking to cause me distress in my imprisonment.

18 What then? Only that in every way, whether in pre-

1:13 [1] Or *governor's palace*

NEW CENTURY VERSION

9This is my prayer for you: that your love will grow more and more; that you will have knowledge and understanding with your love; 10that you will see the difference between good and bad and will choose the good; that you will be pure and without wrong for the coming of Christ; 11that you will do many good things with the help of Christ to bring glory and praise to God.

Paul's Troubles Help the Work

12I want you brothers and sisters[a] to know that what has happened to me has helped to spread the Good News. 13All the palace guards and everyone else knows that I am in prison because I am a believer in Christ. 14Because I am in prison, most of the believers have become more bold in Christ and are not afraid to speak the word of God.

15It is true that some preach about Christ because they are jealous and ambitious, but others preach about Christ because they want to help. 16They preach because they have love, and they know that God gave me the work of defending the Good News. 17But the others preach about Christ for selfish and wrong reasons, wanting to make trouble for me in prison.

18But it doesn't matter. The important thing is that in

1:12 [a] **brothers and sisters** Although the Greek text says "brothers" here and throughout this book, Paul's words were meant for the entire church, including men and women.

CONTEMPORARY ENGLISH VERSION

9I pray that your love will keep on growing and that you will fully know and understand 10how to make the right choices. Then you will still be pure and innocent when Christ returns. And until that day, 11Jesus Christ will keep you busy doing good deeds that bring glory and praise to God.

What Life Means to Paul

12My dear friends, I want you to know that what has happened to me has helped to spread the good news. 13The Roman guards and all the others know that I am here in jail because I serve Christ. 14Now most of the Lord's followers have become brave and are fearlessly telling the message.[b]

15Some are preaching about Christ because they are jealous and envious of us. Others are preaching because they want to help. 16They love Christ and know that I am here to defend the good news about him. 17But the ones who are jealous of us are not sincere. They just want to cause trouble for me while I am in jail. 18But that doesn't matter.

[b] 1.14 *the message*: Some manuscripts have "the Lord's message," and others have "God's message."

NEW INTERNATIONAL VERSION

9And this is my prayer: that your love may abound more and more in knowledge and depth of insight, 10so that you may be able to discern what is best and may be pure and blameless until the day of Christ, 11filled with the fruit of righteousness that comes through Jesus Christ—to the glory and praise of God.

Paul's Chains Advance the Gospel

12Now I want you to know, brothers, that what has happened to me has really served to advance the gospel. 13As a result, it has become clear throughout the whole palace guard[b] and to everyone else that I am in chains for Christ. 14Because of my chains, most of the brothers in the Lord have been encouraged to speak the word of God more courageously and fearlessly.

15It is true that some preach Christ out of envy and rivalry, but others out of goodwill. 16The latter do so in love, knowing that I am put here for the defense of the gospel. 17The former preach Christ out of selfish ambition, not sincerely, supposing that they can stir up trouble for me while I am in chains.[c] 18But what does it matter? The important

[b] *13* Or *whole palace* [c] *16,17* Some late manuscripts have verses 16 and 17 in reverse order.

NEW LIVING TRANSLATION

that your love for each other will overflow more and more, and that you will keep on growing in your knowledge and understanding. 10For I want you to understand what really matters, so that you may live pure and blameless lives until Christ returns. 11May you always be filled with the fruit of your salvation*—those good things that are produced in your life by Jesus Christ—for this will bring much glory and praise to God.

Paul's Joy That Christ Is Preached

12And I want you to know, dear brothers and sisters,* that everything that has happened to me here has helped to spread the Good News. 13For everyone here, including all the soldiers in the palace guard, knows that I am in chains because of Christ. 14And because of my imprisonment, many of the Christians* here have gained confidence and become more bold in telling others about Christ.

15Some are preaching out of jealousy and rivalry. But others preach about Christ with pure motives. 16They preach because they love me, for they know the Lord brought me here to defend the Good News. 17Those others do not have pure motives as they preach about Christ. They preach with selfish ambition, not sincerely, intending to make my chains more painful to me. 18But whether or

1:11 Greek *the fruit of righteousness.* 1:12 Greek *brothers.* 1:14 Greek *brothers in the Lord.*

NEW KING JAMES VERSION

9And this I pray, that your love may abound still more and more in knowledge and all discernment, 10that you may approve the things that are excellent, that you may be sincere and without offense till the day of Christ, 11being filled with the fruits of righteousness which *are* by Jesus Christ, to the glory and praise of God.

Christ Is Preached

12But I want you to know, brethren, that the things *which happened* to me have actually turned out for the furtherance of the gospel, 13so that it has become evident to the whole palace guard, and to all the rest, that my chains are in Christ; 14and most of the brethren in the Lord, having become confident by my chains, are much more bold to speak the word without fear.

15Some indeed preach Christ even from envy and strife, and some also from goodwill: 16The former[b] preach Christ from selfish ambition, not sincerely, supposing to add affliction to my chains; 17but the latter out of love, knowing that I am appointed for the defense of the gospel. 18What then? Only *that* in every way, whether in pretense

1:16 [b] NU-Text reverses the contents of verses 16 and 17.

THE MESSAGE

So this is my prayer: that your love will flourish and that you will not only love much but well. Learn to love appropriately. You need to use your head and test your feelings so that your love is sincere and intelligent, not sentimental gush. Live a lover's life, circumspect and exemplary, a life Jesus will be proud of: bountiful in fruits from the soul, making Jesus Christ attractive to all, getting everyone involved in the glory and praise of God.

They Can't Imprison the Message

I want to report to you, friends, that my imprisonment here has had the opposite of its intended effect. Instead of being squelched, the Message has actually prospered. All the soldiers here, and everyone else too, found out that I'm in jail because of this Messiah. That piqued their curiosity, and now they've learned all about him. Not only that, but most of the Christians here have become far more sure of themselves in the faith than ever, speaking out fearlessly about God, about the Messiah.

It's true that some here preach Christ because with me out of the way, they think they'll step right into the spotlight. But the others do it with the best heart in the world. One group is motivated by pure love, knowing that I am here defending the Message, wanting to help. The others, now that I'm out of the picture, are merely greedy, hoping to get something out of it for themselves. Their motives are bad. They see me as their competition, and so the worse it goes for me, the better—they think—for them.

So how am I to respond? I've decided that I really don't

KING JAMES VERSION

pretence, or in truth, Christ is preached; and I therein do rejoice, yea, and will rejoice.

19 For I know that this shall turn to my salvation through your prayer, and the supply of the Spirit of Jesus Christ,

20 According to my earnest expectation and *my* hope, that in nothing I shall be ashamed, but *that* with all boldness, as always, *so* now also Christ shall be magnified in my body, whether *it be* by life, or by death.

21 ¶ For to me to live *is* Christ, and to die *is* gain.

22 But if I live in the flesh, this *is* the fruit of my labour: yet what I shall choose I wot not.

23 For I am in a strait betwixt two, having a desire to depart, and to be with Christ; which is far better:

24 Nevertheless to abide in the flesh *is* more needful for you.

25 And having this confidence, I know that I shall abide and continue with you all for your furtherance and joy of faith;

26 That your rejoicing may be more abundant in Jesus Christ for me by my coming to you again.

27 ¶ Only let your conversation be as it becometh the gospel of Christ: that whether I come and see you, or else

NEW AMERICAN STANDARD BIBLE

tense or in truth, Christ is proclaimed; and in this I rejoice.

Yes, and I will rejoice,

19 for I know that this will turn out for my deliverance through your prayers and the provision of the Spirit of Jesus Christ,

20 according to my earnest expectation and hope, that I will not be put to shame in anything, but *that* with all boldness, Christ will even now, as always, be exalted in my body, whether by life or by death.

To Live Is Christ

21 For to me, to live is Christ and to die is gain.

22 But if *I am* to live *on* in the flesh, this *will mean* fruitful labor for me; and I do not know which to choose.

23 But I am hard-pressed from both *directions,* having the desire to depart and be with Christ, for *that* is very much better;

24 yet to remain on in the flesh is more necessary for your sake.

25 Convinced of this, I know that I will remain and continue with you all for your progress and joy in the faith,

26 so that your proud confidence in me may abound in Christ Jesus through my coming to you again.

27 Only conduct yourselves in a manner worthy of the gospel of Christ, so that whether I come and see you or

NEW CENTURY VERSION

every way, whether for right or wrong reasons, they are
preaching about Christ. So I am happy, and I will continue
to be happy. [19]Because you are praying for me and the
Spirit of Jesus Christ is helping me, I know this trouble will
bring my freedom. [20]I expect and hope that I will not fail
Christ in anything but that I will have the courage now, as
always, to show the greatness of Christ in my life here on
earth, whether I live or die. [21]To me the only important
thing about living is Christ, and dying would be profit for
me. [22]If I continue living in my body, I will be able to work
for the Lord. I do not know what to choose—living or
dying. [23]It is hard to choose between the two. I want to
leave this life and be with Christ, which is much better,
[24]but you need me here in my body. [25]Since I am sure of
this, I know I will stay with you to help you grow and have
joy in your faith. [26]You will be very happy in Christ Jesus
when I am with you again.

[27]Only one thing concerns me: Be sure that you live in a
way that brings honor to the Good News of Christ. Then
whether I come and visit you or am away from you, I will

CONTEMPORARY ENGLISH VERSION

All that matters is that people are telling about Christ,
whether they are sincere or not. That is what makes me
glad.

I will keep on being glad, [19]because I know that your
prayers and the help that comes from the Spirit of Christ
Jesus will keep me safe. [20]I honestly expect and hope that I
will never do anything to be ashamed of. Whether I live or
die, I always want to be as brave as I am now and bring
honor to Christ.

[21]If I live, it will be for Christ, and if I die, I will gain
even more. [22]I don't know what to choose. I could keep on
living and doing something useful. [23]It is a hard choice to
make. I want to die and be with Christ, because that would
be much better. [24-25]But I know that all of you still need
me. That's why I am sure I will stay on to help you grow
and be happy in your faith. [26]Then, when I visit you again,
you will have good reason to take great pride in Christ
Jesus because of me.[c]

[27]Above all else, you must live in a way that brings
honor to the good news about Christ. Then, whether I visit

[c] 1.26 *take great pride in Christ Jesus because of me*: Or "take great pride in me because of Christ Jesus."

NEW INTERNATIONAL VERSION

thing is that in every way, whether from false motives or true, Christ is preached. And because of this I rejoice.

Yes, and I will continue to rejoice, [19]for I know that through your prayers and the help given by the Spirit of Jesus Christ, what has happened to me will turn out for my deliverance.[d] [20]I eagerly expect and hope that I will in no way be ashamed, but will have sufficient courage so that now as always Christ will be exalted in my body, whether by life or by death. [21]For to me, to live is Christ and to die is gain. [22]If I am to go on living in the body, this will mean fruitful labor for me. Yet what shall I choose? I do not know! [23]I am torn between the two: I desire to depart and be with Christ, which is better by far; [24]but it is more necessary for you that I remain in the body. [25]Convinced of this, I know that I will remain, and I will continue with all of you for your progress and joy in the faith, [26]so that through my being with you again your joy in Christ Jesus will overflow on account of me.

[27]Whatever happens, conduct yourselves in a manner worthy of the gospel of Christ. Then, whether I come and see you or only hear about you in my absence, I will know

[d] *19* Or *salvation*

NEW LIVING TRANSLATION

not their motives are pure, the fact remains that the message about Christ is being preached, so I rejoice. And I will continue to rejoice. [19]For I know that as you pray for me and as the Spirit of Jesus Christ helps me, this will all turn out for my deliverance.

Paul's Life for Christ

[20]For I live in eager expectation and hope that I will never do anything that causes me shame, but that I will always be bold for Christ, as I have been in the past, and that my life will always honor Christ, whether I live or I die. [21]For to me, living is for Christ, and dying is even better. [22]Yet if I live, that means fruitful service for Christ. I really don't know which is better. [23]I'm torn between two desires: Sometimes I want to live, and sometimes I long to go and be with Christ. That would be far better for me, [24]but it is better for you that I live.

[25]I am convinced of this, so I will continue with you so that you will grow and experience the joy of your faith. [26]Then when I return to you, you will have even more reason to boast about what Christ Jesus has done for me.

Live as Citizens of Heaven

[27]But whatever happens to me, you must live in a manner worthy of the Good News about Christ, as citizens of heaven. Then, whether I come and see you again or only

NEW KING JAMES VERSION

or in truth, Christ is preached; and in this I rejoice, yes, and will rejoice.

To Live Is Christ

[19]For I know that this will turn out for my deliverance through your prayer and the supply of the Spirit of Jesus Christ, [20]according to my earnest expectation and hope that in nothing I shall be ashamed, but with all boldness, as always, so now also Christ will be magnified in my body, whether by life or by death. [21]For to me, to live *is* Christ, and to die *is* gain. [22]But if *I* live on in the flesh, this *will mean* fruit from *my* labor; yet what I shall choose I cannot tell. [23]For[c] I am hard-pressed between the two, having a desire to depart and be with Christ, *which is* far better. [24]Nevertheless to remain in the flesh *is* more needful for you. [25]And being confident of this, I know that I shall remain and continue with you all for your progress and joy of faith, [26]that your rejoicing for me may be more abundant in Jesus Christ by my coming to you again.

Striving and Suffering for Christ

[27]Only let your conduct be worthy of the gospel of Christ, so that whether I come and see you or am absent, I may hear of your affairs, that you stand fast in one spirit,

1:23 [c] NU-Text and M-Text read *But.*

THE MESSAGE

care about their motives, whether mixed, bad, or indifferent. Every time one of them opens his mouth, Christ is proclaimed, so I just cheer them on!

And I'm going to keep that celebration going because I know how it's going to turn out. Through your faithful prayers and the generous response of the Spirit of Jesus Christ, everything he wants to do in and through me will be done. I can hardly wait to continue on my course. I don't expect to be embarrassed in the least. On the contrary, everything happening to me in this jail only serves to make Christ more accurately known, regardless of whether I live or die. They didn't shut me up; they gave me a pulpit! Alive, I'm Christ's messenger; dead, I'm his bounty. Life versus even more life! I can't lose.

As long as I'm alive in this body, there is good work for me to do. If I had to choose right now, I hardly know which I'd choose. Hard choice! The desire to break camp here and be with Christ is powerful. Some days I can think of nothing better. But most days, because of what you are going through, I am sure that it's better for me to stick it out here. So I plan to be around awhile, companion to you as your growth and joy in this life of trusting God continues. You can start looking forward to a great reunion when I come visit you again. We'll be praising Christ, enjoying each other.

Meanwhile, live in such a way that you are a credit to the Message of Christ. Let nothing in your conduct hang on whether I come or not. Your conduct must be the same whether I show up to see things for myself or hear of it

KING JAMES VERSION

be absent, I may hear of your affairs, that ye stand fast in one spirit, with one mind striving together for the faith of the gospel;

28 And in nothing terrified by your adversaries: which is to them an evident token of perdition, but to you of salvation, and that of God.

29 For unto you it is given in the behalf of Christ, not only to believe on him, but also to suffer for his sake;

30 Having the same conflict which ye saw in me, and now hear *to be* in me.

2 If *there be* therefore any consolation in Christ, if any comfort of love, if any fellowship of the Spirit, if any bowels and mercies,

2 Fulfil ye my joy, that ye be likeminded, having the same love, *being* of one accord, of one mind.

3 *Let* nothing *be done* through strife or vainglory; but in lowliness of mind let each esteem other better than themselves.

4 Look not every man on his own things, but every man also on the things of others.

5 Let this mind be in you, which was also in Christ Jesus:

6 Who, being in the form of God, thought it not robbery to be equal with God:

NEW AMERICAN STANDARD BIBLE

remain absent, I will hear of you that you are standing firm in one spirit, with one mind striving together for the faith of the gospel;

28 in no way alarmed by *your* opponents—which is a sign of destruction for them, but of salvation for you, and that *too*, from God.

29 For to you it has been granted for Christ's sake, not only to believe in Him, but also to suffer for His sake,

30 experiencing the same conflict which you saw in me, and now hear *to be* in me.

Be Like Christ

2 Therefore if there is any encouragement in Christ, if there is any consolation of love, if there is any fellowship of the Spirit, if any affection and compassion,

2 make my joy complete by being of the same mind, maintaining the same love, united in spirit, intent on one purpose.

3 Do nothing from selfishness or empty conceit, but with humility of mind regard one another as more important than yourselves;

4 do not *merely* look out for your own personal interests, but also for the interests of others.

5 Have this attitude in yourselves which was also in Christ Jesus,

6 who, although He existed in the form of God, did not regard equality with God a thing to be grasped,

NEW CENTURY VERSION

hear that you are standing strong with one purpose, that
you work together as one for the faith of the Good News,
28 and that you are not afraid of those who are against you.
All of this is proof that your enemies will be destroyed but
that you will be saved by God. 29 God gave you the honor
not only of believing in Christ but also of suffering for him,
both of which bring glory to Christ. 30 When I was with
you, you saw the struggles I had, and you hear about the
struggles I am having now. You yourselves are having the
same kind of struggles.

2 Does your life in Christ give you strength? Does his
love comfort you? Do we share together in the spirit?
Do you have mercy and kindness? 2 If so, make me very
happy by having the same thoughts, sharing the same
love, and having one mind and purpose. 3 When you do
things, do not let selfishness or pride be your guide.
Instead, be humble and give more honor to others than to
yourselves. 4 Do not be interested only in your own life, but
be interested in the lives of others.

Be Unselfish like Christ

5 In your lives you must think and act like Christ Jesus.

6 Christ himself was like God in everything.
But he did not think that being equal with God was
something to be used for his own benefit.

CONTEMPORARY ENGLISH VERSION

you or not, I will hear that all of you think alike. I will
know that you are working together and that you are struggling
side by side to get others to believe the good news.

28 Be brave when you face your enemies. Your courage
will show them that they are going to be destroyed, and it
will show you that you will be saved. God will make all of
this happen, 29 and he has blessed you. Not only do you
have faith in Christ, but you suffer for him. 30 You saw me
suffer, and you still hear about my troubles. Now you must
suffer in the same way.

True Humility

2 Christ encourages you, and his love comforts you.
God's Spirit unites you, and you are concerned for
others. 2 Now make me completely happy! Live in harmony
by showing love for each other. Be united in what you
think, as if you were only one person. 3 Don't be jealous or
proud, but be humble and consider others more important
than yourselves. 4 Care about them as much as you care
about yourselves 5 and think the same way that Christ
Jesus thought:[a]

6 Christ was truly God.
But he did not try to remain[b]
equal with God.

[a] 2.5 *think the same way that Christ Jesus thought*: Or "think the way you should because you belong to Christ Jesus." [b] 2.6 *remain*: Or "become."

NEW INTERNATIONAL VERSION

that you stand firm in one spirit, contending as one man
for the faith of the gospel 28without being frightened in
any way by those who oppose you. This is a sign to them
that they will be destroyed, but that you will be saved—
and that by God. 29For it has been granted to you on
behalf of Christ not only to believe on him, but also to suf-
fer for him, 30since you are going through the same strug-
gle you saw I had, and now hear that I still have.

Imitating Christ's Humility

2 If you have any encouragement from being united
with Christ, if any comfort from his love, if any fellow-
ship with the Spirit, if any tenderness and compassion,
2then make my joy complete by being like-minded, having
the same love, being one in spirit and purpose. 3Do noth-
ing out of selfish ambition or vain conceit, but in humility
consider others better than yourselves. 4Each of you
should look not only to your own interests, but also to the
interests of others.

5Your attitude should be the same as that of Christ
Jesus:

6Who, being in very nature[a] God,
did not consider equality with God something to be
grasped,

[a] 6 Or *in the form of*

NEW LIVING TRANSLATION

hear about you, I will know that you are standing side by
side, fighting together for the Good News. 28Don't be
intimidated by your enemies. This will be a sign to them
that they are going to be destroyed, but that you are going
to be saved, even by God himself. 29For you have been
given not only the privilege of trusting in Christ but also
the privilege of suffering for him. 30We are in this fight
together. You have seen me suffer for him in the past, and
you know that I am still in the midst of this great struggle.

Unity through Humility

2 Is there any encouragement from belonging to Christ?
Any comfort from his love? Any fellowship together in
the Spirit? Are your hearts tender and sympathetic? 2Then
make me truly happy by agreeing wholeheartedly with
each other, loving one another, and working together with
one heart and purpose.

3Don't be selfish; don't live to make a good impression
on others. Be humble, thinking of others as better than
yourself. 4Don't think only about your own affairs, but be
interested in others, too, and what they are doing.

Christ's Humility and Exaltation

5Your attitude should be the same that Christ Jesus had.
6Though he was God, he did not demand and cling to his

NEW KING JAMES VERSION

with one mind striving together for the faith of the gospel,
28and not in any way terrified by your adversaries, which
is to them a proof of perdition, but to you of salvation,[d]
and that from God. 29For to you it has been granted on
behalf of Christ, not only to believe in Him, but also to suf-
fer for His sake, 30having the same conflict which you saw
in me and now hear *is* in me.

Unity Through Humility

2 Therefore if *there is* any consolation in Christ, if any
comfort of love, if any fellowship of the Spirit, if any
affection and mercy, 2fulfill my joy by being like-minded,
having the same love, *being* of one accord, of one mind.
3*Let* nothing *be done* through selfish ambition or conceit,
but in lowliness of mind let each esteem others better than
himself. 4Let each of you look out not only for his own
interests, but also for the interests of others.

The Humbled and Exalted Christ

5Let this mind be in you which was also in Christ Jesus,
6who, being in the form of God, did not consider it robbery

1:28 [d] NU-Text reads *of your salvation.*

THE MESSAGE

from a distance. Stand united, singular in vision, contend-
ing for people's trust in the Message, the good news, not
flinching or dodging in the slightest before the opposition.
Your courage and unity will show them what they're up
against: defeat for them, victory for you—and both because
of God. There's far more to this life than trusting in Christ.
There's also suffering for him. And the suffering is as much
a gift as the trusting. You're involved in the same kind of
struggle you saw me go through, on which you are now
getting an updated report in this letter.

He Took On the Status of a Slave

2 If you've gotten anything at all out of following
Christ, if his love has made any difference in your life,
if being in a community of the Spirit means anything to
you, if you have a heart, if you *care*—then do me a favor:
Agree with each other, love each other, be deep-spirited
friends. Don't push your way to the front; don't sweet-talk
your way to the top. Put yourself aside, and help others get
ahead. Don't be obsessed with getting your own advan-
tage. Forget yourselves long enough to lend a helping
hand.

Think of yourselves the way Christ Jesus thought of him-
self. He had equal status with God but didn't think so
much of himself that he had to cling to the advantages of
that status no matter what. Not at all. When the time

KING JAMES VERSION

7 But made himself of no reputation, and took upon him the form of a servant, and was made in the likeness of men:

8 And being found in fashion as a man, he humbled himself, and became obedient unto death, even the death of the cross.

9 Wherefore God also hath highly exalted him, and given him a name which is above every name:

10 That at the name of Jesus every knee should bow, of *things* in heaven, and *things* in earth, and *things* under the earth;

11 And *that* every tongue should confess that Jesus Christ *is* Lord, to the glory of God the Father.

12 ¶ Wherefore, my beloved, as ye have always obeyed, not as in my presence only, but now much more in my absence, work out your own salvation with fear and trembling.

13 For it is God which worketh in you both to will and to do of *his* good pleasure.

NEW AMERICAN STANDARD BIBLE

7 but [1]emptied Himself, taking the form of a bond-servant, *and* being made in the likeness of men.

8 Being found in appearance as a man, He humbled Himself by becoming obedient to the point of death, even death on a cross.

9 For this reason also, God highly exalted Him, and bestowed on Him the name which is above every name,

10 so that at the name of Jesus EVERY KNEE WILL BOW, of those who are in heaven and on earth and under the earth,

11 and that every tongue will confess that Jesus Christ is Lord, to the glory of God the Father.

12 So then, my beloved, just as you have always obeyed, not as in my presence only, but now much more in my absence, work out your salvation with fear and trembling;

13 for it is God who is at work in you, both to will and to work for *His* good pleasure.

2:7 [1] I.e. laid aside His privileges

NEW CENTURY VERSION

7 But he gave up his place with God and made himself
nothing.
He was born to be a man
and became like a servant.
8 And when he was living as a man,
he humbled himself and was fully obedient to God,
even when that caused his death—death on a cross.
9 So God raised him to the highest place.
God made his name greater than every other name
10 so that every knee will bow to the name of Jesus—
everyone in heaven, on earth, and under the earth.
11 And everyone will confess that Jesus Christ is Lord
and bring glory to God the Father.

Be the People God Wants You to Be

12 My dear friends, you have always obeyed God when I was with you. It is even more important that you obey now while I am away from you. Keep on working to complete your salvation with fear and trembling,
13 because God is working in you to help you want to do and be able to do what pleases him.

CONTEMPORARY ENGLISH VERSION

7 Instead he gave up everything[c]
and became a slave,
when he became
like one of us.

8 Christ was humble.
He obeyed God and even died
on a cross.
9 Then God gave Christ
the highest place
and honored his name
above all others.

10 So at the name of Jesus
everyone will bow down,
those in heaven, on earth,
and under the earth.
11 And to the glory
of God the Father
everyone will openly agree,
"Jesus Christ is Lord!"

Lights in the World

12 My dear friends, you always obeyed when I was with you. Now that I am away, you should obey even more. So work with fear and trembling to discover what it really means to be saved.
13 God is working in you to make you willing and able to obey him.

[c] 2.7 *He gave up everything*: Greek, "He emptied himself."

NEW INTERNATIONAL VERSION

7 but made himself nothing,
taking the very nature[b] of a servant,
being made in human likeness.
8 And being found in appearance as a man,
he humbled himself
and became obedient to death—
even death on a cross!
9 Therefore God exalted him to the highest place
and gave him the name that is above every name,
10 that at the name of Jesus every knee should bow,
in heaven and on earth and under the earth,
11 and every tongue confess that Jesus Christ is Lord,
to the glory of God the Father.

Shining as Stars

12Therefore, my dear friends, as you have always
obeyed—not only in my presence, but now much more in
my absence—continue to work out your salvation with
fear and trembling, 13for it is God who works in you to will
and to act according to his good purpose.

[b] 7 Or *the form*

NEW LIVING TRANSLATION

rights as God. 7He made himself nothing;* he took the
humble position of a slave and appeared in human form.*
8And in human form he obediently humbled himself even
further by dying a criminal's death on a cross. 9Because of
this, God raised him up to the heights of heaven and gave
him a name that is above every other name, 10so that at
the name of Jesus every knee will bow, in heaven and on
earth and under the earth, 11and every tongue will confess
that Jesus Christ is Lord, to the glory of God the Father.

Shine Brightly for Christ

12Dearest friends, you were always so careful to follow
my instructions when I was with you. And now that I am
away you must be even more careful to put into action
God's saving work in your lives, obeying God with deep
reverence and fear. 13For God is working in you, giving you
the desire to obey him and the power to do what pleases
him.

2:7a Or *He laid aside his mighty power and glory.* **2:7b** Greek *and was born in the likeness of men and was found in appearance as a man.*

NEW KING JAMES VERSION

to be equal with God, 7but made Himself of no reputation,
taking the form of a bondservant, *and* coming in the like-
ness of men. 8And being found in appearance as a man, He
humbled Himself and became obedient to *the point of*
death, even the death of the cross. 9Therefore God also has
highly exalted Him and given Him the name which is
above every name, 10that at the name of Jesus every knee
should bow, of those in heaven, and of those on earth, and
of those under the earth, 11and *that* every tongue should
confess that Jesus Christ *is* Lord, to the glory of God the
Father.

Light Bearers

12Therefore, my beloved, as you have always obeyed, not
as in my presence only, but now much more in my
absence, work out your own salvation with fear and trem-
bling; 13for it is God who works in you both to will and to
do for *His* good pleasure.

THE MESSAGE

came, he set aside the privileges of deity and took on the status of a slave, became *human*! Having become human, he stayed human. It was an incredibly humbling process. He didn't claim special privileges. Instead, he lived a selfless, obedient life and then died a selfless, obedient death—and the worst kind of death at that: a crucifixion.

Because of that obedience, God lifted him high and honored him far beyond anyone or anything, ever, so that all created beings in heaven and on earth—even those long ago dead and buried—will bow in worship before this Jesus Christ, and call out in praise that he is the Master of all, to the glorious honor of God the Father.

Rejoicing Together

What I'm getting at, friends, is that you should simply keep on doing what you've done from the beginning. When I was living among you, you lived in responsive obedience. Now that I'm separated from you, keep it up. Better yet, redouble your efforts. Be energetic in your life of salvation, reverent and sensitive before God. That energy is *God's* energy, an energy deep within you, God himself willing and working at what will give him the most pleasure.

KING JAMES VERSION

14 ¶ Do all things without murmurings and disputings:

15 That ye may be blameless and harmless, the sons of God, without rebuke, in the midst of a crooked and perverse nation, among whom ye shine as lights in the world;

16 Holding forth the word of life; that I may rejoice in the day of Christ, that I have not run in vain, neither laboured in vain.

17 Yea, and if I be offered upon the sacrifice and service of your faith, I joy, and rejoice with you all.

18 For the same cause also do ye joy, and rejoice with me.

19 But I trust in the Lord Jesus to send Timotheus shortly unto you, that I also may be of good comfort, when I know your state.

20 For I have no man likeminded, who will naturally care for your state.

21 For all seek their own, not the things which are Jesus Christ's.

22 But ye know the proof of him, that, as a son with the father, he hath served with me in the gospel.

23 Him therefore I hope to send presently, so soon as I shall see how it will go with me.

24 But I trust in the Lord that I also myself shall come shortly.

NEW AMERICAN STANDARD BIBLE

14 Do all things without grumbling or disputing;

15 so that you will prove yourselves to be blameless and innocent, children of God above reproach in the midst of a crooked and perverse generation, among whom you appear as lights in the world,

16 holding fast the word of life, so that in the day of Christ I will have reason to glory because I did not run in vain nor toil in vain.

17 But even if I am being poured out as a drink offering upon the sacrifice and service of your faith, I rejoice and share my joy with you all.

18 You too, *I urge you,* rejoice in the same way and share your joy with me.

Timothy and Epaphroditus

19 But I hope in the Lord Jesus to send Timothy to you shortly, so that I also may be encouraged when I learn of your condition.

20 For I have no one *else* of kindred spirit who will genuinely be concerned for your welfare.

21 For they all seek after their own interests, not those of Christ Jesus.

22 But you know of his proven worth, that he served with me in the furtherance of the gospel like a child *serving* his father.

23 Therefore I hope to send him immediately, as soon as I see how things *go* with me;

24 and I trust in the Lord that I myself also will be coming shortly.

NEW CENTURY VERSION

14Do everything without complaining or arguing. 15Then
you will be innocent and without any wrong. You will be God's children without fault. But you are living with crooked and mean people all around you, among whom
you shine like stars in the dark world. 16You offer the
teaching that gives life. So when Christ comes again, I can be happy because my work was not wasted. I ran the race and won.

17Your faith makes you offer your lives as a sacrifice in serving God. If I have to offer my own blood with your sacrifice, I will be happy and full of joy with all of you. 18You
also should be happy and full of joy with me.

Timothy and Epaphroditus

19I hope in the Lord Jesus to send Timothy to you soon. I
will be happy to learn how you are. 20I have no one else
like Timothy, who truly cares for you. 21Other people are
interested only in their own lives, not in the work of Jesus
Christ. 22You know the kind of person Timothy is. You
know he has served with me in telling the Good News, as a
son serves his father. 23I plan to send him to you quickly
when I know what will happen to me. 24I am sure that the
Lord will help me to come to you soon.

CONTEMPORARY ENGLISH VERSION

14Do everything without grumbling or arguing. 15Then
you will be the pure and innocent children of God. You live among people who are crooked and evil, but you must not do anything that they can say is wrong. Try to shine as
lights among the people of this world, 16as you hold firmly
to[d] the message that gives life. Then on the day when Christ returns, I can take pride in you. I can also know that my work and efforts were not useless.

17Your faith in the Lord and your service are like a sacrifice offered to him. And my own blood may have to be poured out with the sacrifice.[e] If this happens, I will be
glad and rejoice with you. 18In the same way, you should
be glad and rejoice with me.

Timothy and Epaphroditus

19I want to be encouraged by news about you. So I hope
the Lord Jesus will soon let me send Timothy to you. 20I
don't have anyone else who cares about you as much as he
does. 21The others think only about what interests them
and not about what concerns Christ Jesus. 22But you know
what kind of person Timothy is. He has worked with me
like a son in spreading the good news. 23I hope to send
him to you, as soon as I find out what is going to happen
to me. 24And I feel sure that the Lord will also let me come
soon.

[d] **2.16** *hold firmly to*: Or "offer them." [e] **2.17** *my own blood may have to be poured out with the sacrifice*: Offerings of water or wine were sometimes poured out when animals were sacrificed on the altar.

NEW INTERNATIONAL VERSION

14Do everything without complaining or arguing, 15so
that you may become blameless and pure, children of God
without fault in a crooked and depraved generation, in
which you shine like stars in the universe 16as you hold
out[c] the word of life—in order that I may boast on the day
of Christ that I did not run or labor for nothing. 17But even
if I am being poured out like a drink offering on the sacri-
fice and service coming from your faith, I am glad and
rejoice with all of you. 18So you too should be glad and
rejoice with me.

Timothy and Epaphroditus

19I hope in the Lord Jesus to send Timothy to you soon,
that I also may be cheered when I receive news about you.
20I have no one else like him, who takes a genuine interest
in your welfare. 21For everyone looks out for his own inter-
ests, not those of Jesus Christ. 22But you know that
Timothy has proved himself, because as a son with his
father he has served with me in the work of the gospel. 23I
hope, therefore, to send him as soon as I see how things
go with me. 24And I am confident in the Lord that I myself
will come soon.

[c] *16* Or *hold on to*

NEW LIVING TRANSLATION

14In everything you do, stay away from complaining and
arguing, 15so that no one can speak a word of blame
against you. You are to live clean, innocent lives as chil-
dren of God in a dark world full of crooked and perverse
people. Let your lives shine brightly before them. 16Hold
tightly to the word of life, so that when Christ returns, I
will be proud that I did not lose the race and that my work
was not useless. 17But even if my life is to be poured out
like a drink offering to complete the sacrifice of your faith-
ful service (that is, if I am to die for you), I will rejoice, and
I want to share my joy with all of you. 18And you should
be happy about this and rejoice with me.

Paul Commends Timothy

19If the Lord Jesus is willing, I hope to send Timothy to
you soon. Then when he comes back, he can cheer me up
by telling me how you are getting along. 20I have no one
else like Timothy, who genuinely cares about your welfare.
21All the others care only for themselves and not for what
matters to Jesus Christ. 22But you know how Timothy has
proved himself. Like a son with his father, he has helped
me in preaching the Good News. 23I hope to send him to
you just as soon as I find out what is going to happen to
me here. 24And I have confidence from the Lord that I
myself will come to see you soon.

NEW KING JAMES VERSION

14Do all things without complaining and disputing,
15that you may become blameless and harmless, children
of God without fault in the midst of a crooked and perverse
generation, among whom you shine as lights in the world,
16holding fast the word of life, so that I may rejoice in the
day of Christ that I have not run in vain or labored in vain.

17Yes, and if I am being poured out *as a drink offering*
on the sacrifice and service of your faith, I am glad and
rejoice with you all. 18For the same reason you also be
glad and rejoice with me.

Timothy Commended

19But I trust in the Lord Jesus to send Timothy to you
shortly, that I also may be encouraged when I know your
state. 20For I have no one like-minded, who will sincerely
care for your state. 21For all seek their own, not the things
which are of Christ Jesus. 22But you know his proven char-
acter, that as a son with *his* father he served with me in
the gospel. 23Therefore I hope to send him at once, as soon
as I see how it goes with me. 24But I trust in the Lord that
I myself shall also come shortly.

THE MESSAGE

Do everything readily and cheerfully—no bickering, no second-guessing allowed! Go out into the world uncorrupted, a breath of fresh air in this squalid and polluted society. Provide people with a glimpse of good living and of the living God. Carry the light-giving Message into the night so I'll have good cause to be proud of you on the day that Christ returns. You'll be living proof that I didn't go to all this work for nothing.

Even if I am executed here and now, I'll rejoice in being an element in the offering of your faith that you make on Christ's altar, a part of your rejoicing. But turnabout's fair play—you must join me in *my* rejoicing. Whatever you do, don't feel sorry for me.

I plan (according to Jesus' plan) to send Timothy to you very soon so he can bring back all the news of you he can gather. Oh, how that will do my heart good! I have no one quite like Timothy. He is loyal, and genuinely concerned for you. Most people around here are looking out for themselves, with little concern for the things of Jesus. But you know yourselves that Timothy's the real thing. He's been a devoted son to me as together we've delivered the Message. As soon as I see how things are going to fall out for me here, I plan to send him off. And then I'm hoping and praying to be right on his heels.

KING JAMES VERSION

25 Yet I supposed it necessary to send to you Epaphroditus, my brother, and companion in labour, and fellowsoldier, but your messenger, and he that ministered to my wants.

26 For he longed after you all, and was full of heaviness, because that ye had heard that he had been sick.

27 For indeed he was sick nigh unto death: but God had mercy on him; and not on him only, but on me also, lest I should have sorrow upon sorrow.

28 I sent him therefore the more carefully, that, when ye see him again, ye may rejoice, and that I may be the less sorrowful.

29 Receive him therefore in the Lord with all gladness; and hold such in reputation:

30 Because for the work of Christ he was nigh unto death, not regarding his life, to supply your lack of service toward me.

3 Finally, my brethren, rejoice in the Lord. To write the same things to you, to me indeed *is* not grievous, but for you *it is* safe.

2 Beware of dogs, beware of evil workers, beware of the concision.

3 For we are the circumcision, which worship God in the spirit, and rejoice in Christ Jesus, and have no confidence in the flesh.

NEW AMERICAN STANDARD BIBLE

25 But I thought it necessary to send to you Epaphroditus, my brother and fellow worker and fellow soldier, who is also your messenger and minister to my need;

26 because he was longing [2]for you all and was distressed because you had heard that he was sick.

27 For indeed he was sick to the point of death, but God had mercy on him, and not on him only but also on me, so that I would not have sorrow upon sorrow.

28 Therefore I have sent him all the more eagerly so that when you see him again you may rejoice and I may be less concerned *about you.*

29 Receive him then in the Lord with all joy, and hold men like him in high regard;

30 because he came close to death for the work of Christ, risking his life to complete what was deficient in your service to me.

The Goal of Life

3 Finally, my brethren, rejoice in the Lord. To write the same things *again* is no trouble to me, and it is a safeguard for you.

2 Beware of the dogs, beware of the evil workers, beware of the false circumcision;

3 for we are the *true* circumcision, who worship in the Spirit of God and glory in Christ Jesus and put no confidence in the flesh,

2:26 [2] One early ms reads *to see you all*

NEW CENTURY VERSION

25 Epaphroditus, my brother in Christ, works and serves with me in the army of Christ. When I needed help, you sent him to me. I think now that I must send him back to you, 26 because he wants very much to see all of you. He is worried because you heard that he was sick. 27 Yes, he was sick, and nearly died, but God had mercy on him and me too so that I would not have more sadness. 28 I want very much to send him to you so that when you see him you can be happy, and I can stop worrying about you. 29 Welcome him in the Lord with much joy. Give honor to people like him, 30 because he almost died for the work of Christ. He risked his life to give me the help you could not give in your service to me.

The Importance of Christ

3 My brothers and sisters, be full of joy in the Lord. It is no trouble for me to write the same things to you again, and it will help you to be more ready. 2 Watch out for those who do evil, who are like dogs, who demand to cut[a] the body. 3 We are the ones who are truly circumcised. We worship God through his Spirit, and our pride is in Christ Jesus. We do not put trust in ourselves or anything we can

3:2 [a] **cut** The word in Greek is like the word "circumcise," but it means "to cut completely off."

CONTEMPORARY ENGLISH VERSION

25 I think I ought to send my dear friend Epaphroditus back to you. He is a follower and a worker and a soldier of the Lord, just as I am. You sent him to look after me, 26 but now he is eager to see you. He is worried, because you heard he was sick. 27 In fact, he was very sick and almost died. But God was kind to him, and also to me, and he kept me from being burdened down with sorrow.

28 Now I am more eager than ever to send Epaphroditus back again. You will be glad to see him, and I won't have to worry any longer. 29 Be sure to give him a cheerful welcome, just as people who serve the Lord deserve. 30 He almost died working for Christ, and he risked his own life to do for me what you could not.

Being Acceptable to God

3 Finally, my dear friends, be glad that you belong to the Lord. It doesn't bother me to write the same things to you that I have written before. In fact, it is for your own good.

2 Watch out for those people who behave like dogs! They are evil and want to do more than just circumcise you. 3 But we are the ones who are truly circumcised, because we worship by the power of God's Spirit[a] and take pride in Christ Jesus. We don't brag about what we have done,

[a] **3.3** *by the power of God's Spirit*: Some manuscripts have "sincerely."

NEW INTERNATIONAL VERSION

25 But I think it is necessary to send back to you Epaphroditus, my brother, fellow worker and fellow soldier, who is also your messenger, whom you sent to take care of my needs. 26 For he longs for all of you and is distressed because you heard he was ill. 27 Indeed he was ill, and almost died. But God had mercy on him, and not on him only but also on me, to spare me sorrow upon sorrow. 28 Therefore I am all the more eager to send him, so that when you see him again you may be glad and I may have less anxiety. 29 Welcome him in the Lord with great joy, and honor men like him, 30 because he almost died for the work of Christ, risking his life to make up for the help you could not give me.

No Confidence in the Flesh

3 Finally, my brothers, rejoice in the Lord! It is no trouble for me to write the same things to you again, and it is a safeguard for you.

2 Watch out for those dogs, those men who do evil, those mutilators of the flesh. 3 For it is we who are the circumcision, we who worship by the Spirit of God, who glory in Christ Jesus, and who put no confidence in the flesh—

NEW LIVING TRANSLATION

Paul Commends Epaphroditus

25 Meanwhile, I thought I should send Epaphroditus back to you. He is a true brother, a faithful worker, and a courageous soldier. And he was your messenger to help me in my need. 26 Now I am sending him home again, for he has been longing to see you, and he was very distressed that you heard he was ill. 27 And he surely was ill; in fact, he almost died. But God had mercy on him—and also on me, so that I would not have such unbearable sorrow.

28 So I am all the more anxious to send him back to you, for I know you will be glad to see him, and that will lighten all my cares. 29 Welcome him with Christian love* and with great joy, and be sure to honor people like him. 30 For he risked his life for the work of Christ, and he was at the point of death while trying to do for me the things you couldn't do because you were far away.

The Priceless Gain of Knowing Christ

3 Whatever happens, dear brothers and sisters,* may the Lord give you joy. I never get tired of telling you this. I am doing this for your own good.

2 Watch out for those dogs, those wicked men and their evil deeds, those mutilators who say you must be circumcised to be saved. 3 For we who worship God in the Spirit* are the only ones who are truly circumcised. We put no confidence in human effort. Instead, we boast about what Christ Jesus has done for us.

2:29 Greek *in the Lord.* 3:1 Greek *brothers;* also in 3:13, 17.
3:3 Or *in spirit;* some manuscripts read *worship by the Spirit of God.*

NEW KING JAMES VERSION

Epaphroditus Praised

25 Yet I considered it necessary to send to you Epaphroditus, my brother, fellow worker, and fellow soldier, but your messenger and the one who ministered to my need; 26 since he was longing for you all, and was distressed because you had heard that he was sick. 27 For indeed he was sick almost unto death; but God had mercy on him, and not only on him but on me also, lest I should have sorrow upon sorrow. 28 Therefore I sent him the more eagerly, that when you see him again you may rejoice, and I may be less sorrowful. 29 Receive him therefore in the Lord with all gladness, and hold such men in esteem; 30 because for the work of Christ he came close to death, not regarding his life, to supply what was lacking in your service toward me.

All for Christ

3 Finally, my brethren, rejoice in the Lord. For me to write the same things to you *is* not tedious, but for you *it is* safe.

2 Beware of dogs, beware of evil workers, beware of the mutilation! 3 For we are the circumcision, who worship God in the Spirit,[a] rejoice in Christ Jesus, and have no confidence

3:3 [a] NU-Text and M-Text read *who worship in the Spirit of God.*

THE MESSAGE

But for right now, I'm dispatching Epaphroditus, my good friend and companion in my work. You sent him to help me out; now I'm sending him to help you out. He has been wanting in the worst way to get back with you. Especially since recovering from the illness you heard about, he's been wanting to get back and reassure you that he is just fine. He nearly died, as you know, but God had mercy on him. And not only on him—he had mercy on me, too. His death would have been one huge grief piled on top of all the others.

So you can see why I'm so delighted to send him on to you. When you see him again, hale and hearty, how you'll rejoice and how relieved I'll be. Give him a grand welcome, a joyful embrace! People like him deserve the best you can give. Remember the ministry to me that you started but weren't able to complete? Well, in the process of finishing up that work, he put his life on the line and nearly died doing it.

To Know Him Personally

3 And that's about it, friends. Be glad in God!

I don't mind repeating what I have written in earlier letters, and I hope you don't mind hearing it again. Better safe than sorry—so here goes.

Steer clear of the barking dogs, those religious busybodies, all bark and no bite. All they're interested in is appearances—knife-happy circumcisers, I call them. The *real* believers are the ones the Spirit of God leads to work away at this ministry, filling the air with Christ's praise as we do it. We couldn't carry this off by our own efforts, and we

KING JAMES VERSION

4 ¶ Though I might also have confidence in the flesh. If any other man thinketh that he hath whereof he might trust in the flesh, I more:

5 Circumcised the eighth day, of the stock of Israel, *of* the tribe of Benjamin, an Hebrew of the Hebrews; as touching the law, a Pharisee;

6 Concerning zeal, persecuting the church; touching the righteousness which is in the law, blameless.

7 But what things were gain to me, those I counted loss for Christ.

8 Yea doubtless, and I count all things *but* loss for the excellency of the knowledge of Christ Jesus my Lord: for whom I have suffered the loss of all things, and do count them *but* dung, that I may win Christ,

9 ¶ And be found in him, not having mine own righteousness, which is of the law, but that which is through the faith of Christ, the righteousness which is of God by faith:

10 That I may know him, and the power of his resurrection, and the fellowship of his sufferings, being made conformable unto his death;

11 If by any means I might attain unto the resurrection of the dead.

12 Not as though I had already attained, either were already perfect: but I follow after, if that I may apprehend

NEW AMERICAN STANDARD BIBLE

4 although I myself might have confidence even in the flesh. If anyone else has a mind to put confidence in the flesh, I far more:

5 circumcised the eighth day, of the nation of Israel, of the tribe of Benjamin, a Hebrew of Hebrews; as to the Law, a Pharisee;

6 as to zeal, a persecutor of the church; as to the righteousness which is in the Law, found blameless.

7 But whatever things were gain to me, those things I have counted as loss for the sake of Christ.

8 More than that, I count all things to be loss in view of the surpassing value of knowing Christ Jesus my Lord, for whom I have suffered the loss of all things, and count them but rubbish so that I may gain Christ,

9 and may be found in Him, not having a righteousness of my own derived from *the* Law, but that which is through faith in Christ, the righteousness which *comes* from God on the basis of faith,

10 that I may know Him and the power of His resurrection and the fellowship of His sufferings, being conformed to His death;

11 in order that I may attain to the resurrection from the dead.

12 Not that I have already obtained *it* or have already become perfect, but I press on so that I may lay hold of

NEW CENTURY VERSION

do, 4although I might be able to put trust in myself. If any-
one thinks he has a reason to trust in himself, he should
know that I have greater reason for trusting in myself. 5I
was circumcised eight days after my birth. I am from the
people of Israel and the tribe of Benjamin. I am a Hebrew,
and my parents were Hebrews. I had a strict view of the
law, which is why I became a Pharisee. 6I was so enthusi-
astic I tried to hurt the church. No one could find fault with
the way I obeyed the law of Moses. 7Those things were
important to me, but now I think they are worth nothing
because of Christ. 8Not only those things, but I think that
all things are worth nothing compared with the greatness
of knowing Christ Jesus my Lord. Because of him, I have
lost all those things, and now I know they are worthless
trash. This allows me to have Christ 9and to belong to him.
Now I am right with God, not because I followed the law,
but because I believed in Christ. God uses my faith to make
me right with him. 10I want to know Christ and the power
that raised him from the dead. I want to share in his suffer-
ings and become like him in his death. 11Then I have hope
that I myself will be raised from the dead.

Continuing Toward Our Goal

12I do not mean that I am already as God wants me to
be. I have not yet reached that goal, but I continue trying

CONTEMPORARY ENGLISH VERSION

4although I could. Others may brag about themselves, but I
have more reason to brag than anyone else. 5I was circum-
cised when I was eight days old,[b] and I am from the nation
of Israel and the tribe of Benjamin. I am a true Hebrew. As
a Pharisee, I strictly obeyed the Law of Moses. 6And I was
so eager that I even made trouble for the church. I did
everything the Law demands in order to please God.

7But Christ has shown me that what I once thought was
valuable is worthless. 8Nothing is as wonderful as know-
ing Christ Jesus my Lord. I have given up everything else
and count it all as garbage. All I want is Christ 9and to
know that I belong to him. I could not make myself accept-
able to God by obeying the Law of Moses. God accepted me
simply because of my faith in Christ. 10All I want is to
know Christ and the power that raised him to life. I want
to suffer and die as he did, 11so that somehow I also may
be raised to life.

Running toward the Goal

12I have not yet reached my goal, and I am not perfect.
But Christ has taken hold of me. So I keep on running and

[b] 3.5 *when I was eight days old*: Jewish boys are circumcised eight days after birth.

NEW INTERNATIONAL VERSION

4though I myself have reasons for such confidence.
If anyone else thinks he has reasons to put confidence in
the flesh, I have more: 5circumcised on the eighth day, of
the people of Israel, of the tribe of Benjamin, a Hebrew of
Hebrews; in regard to the law, a Pharisee; 6as for zeal, per-
secuting the church; as for legalistic righteousness, fault-
less.
7But whatever was to my profit I now consider loss for
the sake of Christ. 8What is more, I consider everything a
loss compared to the surpassing greatness of knowing
Christ Jesus my Lord, for whose sake I have lost all things.
I consider them rubbish, that I may gain Christ 9and be
found in him, not having a righteousness of my own that
comes from the law, but that which is through faith in
Christ—the righteousness that comes from God and is by
faith. 10I want to know Christ and the power of his resur-
rection and the fellowship of sharing in his sufferings,
becoming like him in his death, 11and so, somehow, to
attain to the resurrection from the dead.

Pressing on Toward the Goal

12Not that I have already obtained all this, or have
already been made perfect, but I press on to take hold of

NEW LIVING TRANSLATION

4Yet I could have confidence in myself if anyone could. If
others have reason for confidence in their own efforts, I
have even more! 5For I was circumcised when I was eight
days old, having been born into a pure-blooded Jewish
family that is a branch of the tribe of Benjamin. So I am a
real Jew if there ever was one! What's more, I was a mem-
ber of the Pharisees, who demand the strictest obedience
to the Jewish law. 6And zealous? Yes, in fact, I harshly per-
secuted the church. And I obeyed the Jewish law so care-
fully that I was never accused of any fault.
7I once thought all these things were so very important,
but now I consider them worthless because of what Christ
has done. 8Yes, everything else is worthless when com-
pared with the priceless gain of knowing Christ Jesus my
Lord. I have discarded everything else, counting it all as
garbage, so that I may have Christ 9and become one with
him. I no longer count on my own goodness or my ability
to obey God's law, but I trust Christ to save me. For God's
way of making us right with himself depends on faith.
10As a result, I can really know Christ and experience the
mighty power that raised him from the dead. I can learn
what it means to suffer with him, sharing in his death,
11so that, somehow, I can experience the resurrection from
the dead!

Pressing toward the Goal

12I don't mean to say that I have already achieved these
things or that I have already reached perfection! But I keep
working toward that day when I will finally be all that

NEW KING JAMES VERSION

in the flesh, 4though I also might have confidence in the
flesh. If anyone else thinks he may have confidence in the
flesh, I more so: 5circumcised the eighth day, of the stock of
Israel, *of* the tribe of Benjamin, a Hebrew of the Hebrews;
concerning the law, a Pharisee; 6concerning zeal, persecut-
ing the church; concerning the righteousness which is in the
law, blameless.
7But what things were gain to me, these I have counted
loss for Christ. 8Yet indeed I also count all things loss for
the excellence of the knowledge of Christ Jesus my Lord,
for whom I have suffered the loss of all things, and count
them as rubbish, that I may gain Christ 9and be found in
Him, not having my own righteousness, which *is* from the
law, but that which *is* through faith in Christ, the righ-
teousness which is from God by faith; 10that I may know
Him and the power of His resurrection, and the fellowship
of His sufferings, being conformed to His death, 11if, by
any means, I may attain to the resurrection from the dead.

Pressing Toward the Goal

12Not that I have already attained, or am already per-
fected; but I press on, that I may lay hold of that for which

THE MESSAGE

know it—even though we can list what many might think
are impressive credentials. You know my pedigree: a legiti-
mate birth, circumcised on the eighth day; an Israelite
from the elite tribe of Benjamin; a strict and devout adher-
ent to God's law; a fiery defender of the purity of my reli-
gion, even to the point of persecuting Christians; a meticu-
lous observer of everything set down in God's law Book.

The very credentials these people are waving around as
something special, I'm tearing up and throwing out with
the trash—along with everything else I used to take credit
for. And why? Because of Christ. Yes, all the things I once
thought were so important are gone from my life.
Compared to the high privilege of knowing Christ Jesus as
my Master, firsthand, everything I once thought I had
going for me is insignificant—dog dung. I've dumped it all
in the trash so that I could embrace Christ and be
embraced by him. I didn't want some petty, inferior brand
of righteousness that comes from keeping a list of rules
when I could get the robust kind that comes from trusting
Christ—*God's* righteousness.

I gave up all that inferior stuff so I could know Christ
personally, experience his resurrection power, be a partner
in his suffering, and go all the way with him to death
itself. If there was any way to get in on the resurrection
from the dead, I wanted to do it.

Focused on the Goal

I'm not saying that I have this all together, that I have it
made. But I am well on my way, reaching out for Christ,

KING JAMES VERSION

that for which also I am apprehended of Christ Jesus.

13 Brethren, I count not myself to have apprehended: but *this* one thing *I do*, forgetting those things which are behind, and reaching forth unto those things which are before,

14 I press toward the mark for the prize of the high calling of God in Christ Jesus.

15 ¶ Let us therefore, as many as be perfect, be thus minded: and if in any thing ye be otherwise minded, God shall reveal even this unto you.

16 Nevertheless, whereto we have already attained, let us walk by the same rule, let us mind the same thing.

17 ¶ Brethren, be followers together of me, and mark them which walk so as ye have us for an ensample.

18 (For many walk, of whom I have told you often, and now tell you even weeping, *that they are* the enemies of the cross of Christ:

19 Whose end *is* destruction, whose God *is their* belly, and *whose* glory *is* in their shame, who mind earthly things.)

20 For our conversation is in heaven; from whence also we look for the Saviour, the Lord Jesus Christ:

21 Who shall change our vile body, that it may be fashioned like unto his glorious body, according to the working whereby he is able even to subdue all things unto himself.

4 Therefore, my brethren dearly beloved and longed for, my joy and crown, so stand fast in the Lord, *my* dearly beloved.

NEW AMERICAN STANDARD BIBLE

that for which also I was laid hold of by Christ Jesus.

13 Brethren, I do not regard myself as having laid hold of *it* yet; but one thing *I do:* forgetting what *lies* behind and reaching forward to what *lies* ahead,

14 I press on toward the goal for the prize of the upward call of God in Christ Jesus.

15 Let us therefore, as many as are perfect, have this attitude; and if in anything you have a different attitude, God will reveal that also to you;

16 however, let us keep living by that same *standard* to which we have attained.

17 Brethren, join in following my example, and observe those who walk according to the pattern you have in us.

18 For many walk, of whom I often told you, and now tell you even weeping, *that they are* enemies of the cross of Christ,

19 whose end is destruction, whose god is *their* appetite, and *whose* glory is in their shame, who set their minds on earthly things.

20 For our citizenship is in heaven, from which also we eagerly wait for a Savior, the Lord Jesus Christ;

21 who will transform the body of our humble state into conformity with the body of His glory, by the exertion of the power that He has even to subject all things to Himself.

Think of Excellence

4 Therefore, my beloved brethren whom I long *to see*, my joy and crown, in this way stand firm in the Lord, my beloved.

NEW CENTURY VERSION

to reach it and to make it mine. Christ wants me to do
that, which is the reason he made me his. 13Brothers and
sisters, I know that I have not yet reached that goal, but
there is one thing I always do. Forgetting the past and
straining toward what is ahead, 14I keep trying to reach
the goal and get the prize for which God called me through
Christ to the life above.

15All of us who are spiritually mature should think this
way, too. And if there are things you do not agree with,
God will make them clear to you. 16But we should continue
following the truth we already have.

17Brothers and sisters, all of you should try to follow my
example and to copy those who live the way we showed
you. 18Many people live like enemies of the cross of Christ.
I have often told you about them, and it makes me cry to
tell you about them now. 19In the end, they will be
destroyed. They do whatever their bodies want, they are
proud of their shameful acts, and they think only about
earthly things. 20But our homeland is in heaven, and we
are waiting for our Savior, the Lord Jesus Christ, to come
from heaven. 21By his power to rule all things, he will
change our simple bodies and make them like his own glorious body.

What the Christians Are to Do

4 My dear brothers and sisters, I love you and want to see you. You bring me joy and make me proud of you, so stand strong in the Lord as I have told you.

CONTEMPORARY ENGLISH VERSION

struggling to take hold of the prize. 13My friends, I don't
feel that I have already arrived. But I forget what is
behind, and I struggle for what is ahead. 14I run toward
the goal, so that I can win the prize of being called to
heaven. This is the prize that God offers because of what
Christ Jesus has done. 15All of us who are mature should
think in this same way. And if any of you think differently,
God will make it clear to you. 16But we must keep going in
the direction that we are now headed.

17My friends, I want you to follow my example and learn
from others who closely follow the example we set for you.
18I often warned you that many people are living as enemies of the cross of Christ. And now with tears in my eyes,
I warn you again 19that they are headed for hell! They
worship their stomachs and brag about the disgusting
things they do. All they can think about are the things of
this world.

20But we are citizens of heaven and are eagerly waiting
for our Savior to come from there. Our Lord Jesus Christ
21has power over everything, and he will make these poor
bodies of ours like his own glorious body.

4 Dear friends, I love you and long to see you. Please keep on being faithful to the Lord. You are my pride and joy.

NEW INTERNATIONAL VERSION

that for which Christ Jesus took hold of me. [13]Brothers, I do not consider myself yet to have taken hold of it. But one thing I do: Forgetting what is behind and straining toward what is ahead, [14]I press on toward the goal to win the prize for which God has called me heavenward in Christ Jesus.

[15]All of us who are mature should take such a view of things. And if on some point you think differently, that too God will make clear to you. [16]Only let us live up to what we have already attained.

[17]Join with others in following my example, brothers, and take note of those who live according to the pattern we gave you. [18]For, as I have often told you before and now say again even with tears, many live as enemies of the cross of Christ. [19]Their destiny is destruction, their god is their stomach, and their glory is in their shame. Their mind is on earthly things. [20]But our citizenship is in heaven. And we eagerly await a Savior from there, the Lord Jesus Christ, [21]who, by the power that enables him to bring everything under his control, will transform our lowly bodies so that they will be like his glorious body.

4 Therefore, my brothers, you whom I love and long for, my joy and crown, that is how you should stand firm in the Lord, dear friends!

NEW LIVING TRANSLATION

Christ Jesus saved me for and wants me to be. [13]No, dear brothers and sisters, I am still not all I should be,* but I am focusing all my energies on this one thing: Forgetting the past and looking forward to what lies ahead, [14]I strain to reach the end of the race and receive the prize for which God, through Christ Jesus, is calling us up to heaven.*

[15]I hope all of you who are mature Christians will agree on these things. If you disagree on some point, I believe God will make it plain to you. [16]But we must be sure to obey the truth we have learned already.

[17]Dear brothers and sisters, pattern your lives after mine, and learn from those who follow our example. [18]For I have told you often before, and I say it again with tears in my eyes, that there are many whose conduct shows they are really enemies of the cross of Christ. [19]Their future is eternal destruction. Their god is their appetite, they brag about shameful things, and all they think about is this life here on earth. [20]But we are citizens of heaven, where the Lord Jesus Christ lives. And we are eagerly waiting for him to return as our Savior. [21]He will take these weak mortal bodies of ours and change them into glorious bodies like his own, using the same mighty power that he will use to conquer everything, everywhere.

4 Dear brothers and sisters,* I love you and long to see you, for you are my joy and the reward for my work. So please stay true to the Lord, my dear friends.

3:13 Some manuscripts read *I am not all I should be.* 3:14 Or *from heaven.* 4:1 Greek *brothers;* also in 4:8.

NEW KING JAMES VERSION

Christ Jesus has also laid hold of me. [13]Brethren, I do not count myself to have apprehended; but one thing *I do,* forgetting those things which are behind and reaching forward to those things which are ahead, [14]I press toward the goal for the prize of the upward call of God in Christ Jesus.

[15]Therefore let us, as many as are mature, have this mind; and if in anything you think otherwise, God will reveal even this to you. [16]Nevertheless, to *the degree* that we have already attained, let us walk by the same rule,[b] let us be of the same mind.

Our Citizenship in Heaven

[17]Brethren, join in following my example, and note those who so walk, as you have us for a pattern. [18]For many walk, of whom I have told you often, and now tell you even weeping, *that they are* the enemies of the cross of Christ: [19]whose end *is* destruction, whose god *is their* belly, and *whose* glory *is* in their shame—who set their mind on earthly things. [20]For our citizenship is in heaven, from which we also eagerly wait for the Savior, the Lord Jesus Christ, [21]who will transform our lowly body that it may be conformed to His glorious body, according to the working by which He is able even to subdue all things to Himself.

4 Therefore, my beloved and longed-for brethren, my joy and crown, so stand fast in the Lord, beloved.

3:16 [b] NU-Text omits *rule* and the rest of the verse.

THE MESSAGE

who has so wondrously reached out for me. Friends, don't get me wrong: By no means do I count myself an expert in all of this, but I've got my eye on the goal, where God is beckoning us onward—to Jesus. I'm off and running, and I'm not turning back.

So let's keep focused on that goal, those of us who want everything God has for us. If any of you have something else in mind, something less than total commitment, God will clear your blurred vision—you'll see it yet! Now that we're on the right track, let's stay on it.

Stick with me, friends. Keep track of those you see running this same course, headed for this same goal. There are many out there taking other paths, choosing other goals, and trying to get you to go along with them. I've warned you of them many times; sadly, I'm having to do it again. All they want is easy street. They hate Christ's Cross. But easy street is a dead-end street. Those who live there make their bellies their gods; belches are their praise; all they can think of is their appetites.

But there's far more to life for us. We're citizens of high heaven! We're waiting the arrival of the Savior, the Master, Jesus Christ, who will transform our earthy bodies into glorious bodies like his own. He'll make us beautiful and whole with the same powerful skill by which he is putting everything as it should be, under and around him.

4 My dear, dear friends! I love you so much. I do want the very best for you. You make me feel such joy, fill me with such pride. Don't waver. Stay on track, steady in God.

KING JAMES VERSION

2 I beseech Euodias, and beseech Syntyche, that they be of the same mind in the Lord.

3 And I intreat thee also, true yokefellow, help those women which laboured with me in the gospel, with Clement also, and *with* other my fellowlabourers, whose names *are* in the book of life.

4 Rejoice in the Lord alway: *and* again I say, Rejoice.

5 Let your moderation be known unto all men. The Lord *is* at hand.

6 Be careful for nothing; but in every thing by prayer and supplication with thanksgiving let your requests be made known unto God.

7 And the peace of God, which passeth all understanding, shall keep your hearts and minds through Christ Jesus.

8 Finally, brethren, whatsoever things are true, whatsoever things *are* honest, whatsoever things *are* just, whatsoever things *are* pure, whatsoever things *are* lovely, whatsoever things *are* of good report; if *there be* any virtue, and if *there be* any praise, think on these things.

9 Those things, which ye have both learned, and received, and heard, and seen in me, do: and the God of peace shall be with you.

NEW AMERICAN STANDARD BIBLE

2 I urge Euodia and I urge Syntyche to live in harmony in the Lord.

3 Indeed, true companion, I ask you also to help these women who have shared my struggle in *the cause of* the gospel, together with Clement also and the rest of my fellow workers, whose names are in the book of life.

4 Rejoice in the Lord always; again I will say, rejoice!

5 Let your gentle *spirit* be known to all men. The Lord is near.

6 Be anxious for nothing, but in everything by prayer and supplication with thanksgiving let your requests be made known to God.

7 And the peace of God, which surpasses all comprehension, will guard your hearts and your minds in Christ Jesus.

8 Finally, brethren, whatever is true, whatever is honorable, whatever is right, whatever is pure, whatever is lovely, whatever is of good repute, if there is any excellence and if anything worthy of praise, dwell on these things.

9 The things you have learned and received and heard and seen in me, practice these things, and the God of peace will be with you.

NEW CENTURY VERSION

2 I ask Euodia and Syntyche to agree in the Lord. 3 And I ask you, my faithful friend, to help these women. They served with me in telling the Good News, together with Clement and others who worked with me, whose names are written in the book of life.[a]

4 Be full of joy in the Lord always. I will say again, be full of joy.

5 Let everyone see that you are gentle and kind. The Lord is coming soon. 6 Do not worry about anything, but pray and ask God for everything you need, always giving thanks. 7 And God's peace, which is so great we cannot understand it, will keep your hearts and minds in Christ Jesus.

8 Brothers and sisters, think about the things that are good and worthy of praise. Think about the things that are true and honorable and right and pure and beautiful and respected. 9 Do what you learned and received from me, what I told you, and what you saw me do. And the God who gives peace will be with you.

4:3 [a] **book of life** God's book that has the names of all God's chosen people (Revelation 3:5; 21:27).

CONTEMPORARY ENGLISH VERSION

Paul Encourages the Lord's Followers

2 Euodia and Syntyche, you belong to the Lord, so I beg you to stop arguing with each other. 3 And, my true partner,[a] I ask you to help them. These women have worked together with me and with Clement and with the others in spreading the good news. Their names are now written in the book of life.[b]

4 Always be glad because of the Lord! I will say it again: Be glad. 5 Always be gentle with others. The Lord will soon be here. 6 Don't worry about anything, but pray about everything. With thankful hearts offer up your prayers and requests to God. 7 Then, because you belong to Christ Jesus, God will bless you with peace that no one can completely understand. And this peace will control the way you think and feel.

8 Finally, my friends, keep your minds on whatever is true, pure, right, holy, friendly, and proper. Don't ever stop thinking about what is truly worthwhile and worthy of praise. 9 You know the teachings I gave you, and you know what you heard me say and saw me do. So follow my example. And God, who gives peace, will be with you.

[a] 4.3 *partner*: Or "Syzygus," a person's name. [b] 4.3 *the book of life*: A book in which the names of God's people are written.

NEW INTERNATIONAL VERSION

Exhortations

2 I plead with Euodia and I plead with Syntyche to agree with each other in the Lord. 3 Yes, and I ask you, loyal yokefellow,[a] help these women who have contended at my side in the cause of the gospel, along with Clement and the rest of my fellow workers, whose names are in the book of life.

4 Rejoice in the Lord always. I will say it again: Rejoice! 5 Let your gentleness be evident to all. The Lord is near. 6 Do not be anxious about anything, but in everything, by prayer and petition, with thanksgiving, present your requests to God. 7 And the peace of God, which transcends all understanding, will guard your hearts and your minds in Christ Jesus.

8 Finally, brothers, whatever is true, whatever is noble, whatever is right, whatever is pure, whatever is lovely, whatever is admirable—if anything is excellent or praiseworthy—think about such things. 9 Whatever you have learned or received or heard from me, or seen in me—put it into practice. And the God of peace will be with you.

[a] *3* Or *loyal Syzygus*

NEW LIVING TRANSLATION

Paul's Final Thoughts

2 And now I want to plead with those two women, Euodia and Syntyche. Please, because you belong to the Lord, settle your disagreement. 3 And I ask you, my true teammate,* to help these women, for they worked hard with me in telling others the Good News. And they worked with Clement and the rest of my co-workers, whose names are written in the Book of Life.

4 Always be full of joy in the Lord. I say it again—rejoice! 5 Let everyone see that you are considerate in all you do. Remember, the Lord is coming soon.

6 Don't worry about anything; instead, pray about everything. Tell God what you need, and thank him for all he has done. 7 If you do this, you will experience God's peace, which is far more wonderful than the human mind can understand. His peace will guard your hearts and minds as you live in Christ Jesus.

8 And now, dear brothers and sisters, let me say one more thing as I close this letter. Fix your thoughts on what is true and honorable and right. Think about things that are pure and lovely and admirable. Think about things that are excellent and worthy of praise. 9 Keep putting into practice all you learned from me and heard from me and saw me doing, and the God of peace will be with you.

4:3 Greek *true yokefellow*, or *loyal Syzygus*.

NEW KING JAMES VERSION

Be United, Joyful, and in Prayer

2 I implore Euodia and I implore Syntyche to be of the same mind in the Lord. 3 And[a] I urge you also, true companion, help these women who labored with me in the gospel, with Clement also, and the rest of my fellow workers, whose names *are* in the Book of Life.

4 Rejoice in the Lord always. Again I will say, rejoice!

5 Let your gentleness be known to all men. The Lord *is* at hand.

6 Be anxious for nothing, but in everything by prayer and supplication, with thanksgiving, let your requests be made known to God; 7 and the peace of God, which surpasses all understanding, will guard your hearts and minds through Christ Jesus.

Meditate on These Things

8 Finally, brethren, whatever things are true, whatever things *are* noble, whatever things *are* just, whatever things *are* pure, whatever things *are* lovely, whatever things *are* of good report, if *there is* any virtue and if *there is* anything praiseworthy—meditate on these things. 9 The things which you learned and received and heard and saw in me, these do, and the God of peace will be with you.

4:3 [a] NU-Text and M-Text read *Yes.*

THE MESSAGE

Pray About Everything

I urge Euodia and Syntyche to iron out their differences and make up. God doesn't want his children holding grudges.

And, oh, yes, Syzygus, since you're right there to help them work things out, do your best with them. These women worked for the Message hand in hand with Clement and me, and with the other veterans—worked as hard as any of us. Remember, their names are also in the book of life.

Celebrate God all day, every day. I mean, *revel* in him! Make it as clear as you can to all you meet that you're on their side, working with them and not against them. Help them see that the Master is about to arrive. He could show up any minute!

Don't fret or worry. Instead of worrying, pray. Let petitions and praises shape your worries into prayers, letting God know your concerns. Before you know it, a sense of God's wholeness, everything coming together for good, will come and settle you down. It's wonderful what happens when Christ displaces worry at the center of your life.

Summing it all up, friends, I'd say you'll do best by filling your minds and meditating on things true, noble, reputable, authentic, compelling, gracious—the best, not the worst; the beautiful, not the ugly; things to praise, not things to curse. Put into practice what you learned from me, what you heard and saw and realized. Do that, and God, who makes everything work together, will work you into his most excellent harmonies.

KING JAMES VERSION

10 ¶ But I rejoiced in the Lord greatly, that now at the last your care of me hath flourished again; wherein ye were also careful, but ye lacked opportunity.

11 Not that I speak in respect of want: for I have learned, in whatsoever state I am, *therewith* to be content.

12 I know both how to be abased, and I know how to abound: every where and in all things I am instructed both to be full and to be hungry, both to abound and to suffer need.

13 I can do all things through Christ which strengtheneth me.

14 Notwithstanding ye have well done, that ye did communicate with my affliction.

15 Now ye Philippians know also, that in the beginning of the gospel, when I departed from Macedonia, no church communicated with me as concerning giving and receiving, but ye only.

16 For even in Thessalonica ye sent once and again unto my necessity.

17 Not because I desire a gift: but I desire fruit that may abound to your account.

18 But I have all, and abound: I am full, having received of Epaphroditus the things *which were sent* from you, an odour of a sweet smell, a sacrifice acceptable, wellpleasing to God.

19 But my God shall supply all your need according to his riches in glory by Christ Jesus.

NEW AMERICAN STANDARD BIBLE

God's Provisions

10 But I rejoiced in the Lord greatly, that now at last you have revived your concern for me; indeed, you were concerned *before,* but you lacked opportunity.

11 Not that I speak from want, for I have learned to be content in whatever circumstances I am.

12 I know how to get along with humble means, and I also know how to live in prosperity; in any and every circumstance I have learned the secret of being filled and going hungry, both of having abundance and suffering need.

13 I can do all things through Him who strengthens me.

14 Nevertheless, you have done well to share *with me* in my affliction.

15 You yourselves also know, Philippians, that at the first preaching of the gospel, after I left Macedonia, no church shared with me in the matter of giving and receiving but you alone;

16 for even in Thessalonica you sent *a gift* more than once for my needs.

17 Not that I seek the gift itself, but I seek for the profit which increases to your account.

18 But I have received everything in full and have an abundance; I am amply supplied, having received from Epaphroditus what you have sent, a fragrant aroma, an acceptable sacrifice, well-pleasing to God.

19 And my God will supply all your needs according to His riches in glory in Christ Jesus.

NEW CENTURY VERSION

Paul Thanks the Christians

10I am very happy in the Lord that you have shown your
care for me again. You continued to care about me, but
there was no way for you to show it. 11I am not telling you
this because I need anything. I have learned to be satisfied
with the things I have and with everything that happens.
12I know how to live when I am poor, and I know how to
live when I have plenty. I have learned the secret of being
happy at any time in everything that happens, when I have
enough to eat and when I go hungry, when I have more
than I need and when I do not have enough. 13I can do all
things through Christ, because he gives me strength.
14But it was good that you helped me when I needed it.
15You Philippians remember when I first preached the
Good News there. When I left Macedonia, you were the
only church that gave me help. 16Several times you sent
me things I needed when I was in Thessalonica. 17Really,
it is not that I want to receive gifts from you, but I want
you to have the good that comes from giving. 18And now I
have everything, and more. I have all I need, because
Epaphroditus brought your gift to me. It is like a sweet-
smelling sacrifice offered to God, who accepts that sacrifice
and is pleased with it. 19My God will use his wonderful
riches in Christ Jesus to give you everything you need.

CONTEMPORARY ENGLISH VERSION

Paul Gives Thanks for the Gifts He Was Given

10The Lord has made me very grateful that at last you
have thought about me once again. Actually, you were
thinking about me all along, but you didn't have any
chance to show it. 11I am not complaining about having
too little. I have learned to be satisfied with[c] whatever I
have. 12I know what it is to be poor or to have plenty, and
I have lived under all kinds of conditions. I know what it
means to be full or to be hungry, to have too much or too
little. 13Christ gives me the strength to face anything.
14It was good of you to help me when I was having such
a hard time. 15My friends at Philippi, you remember what
it was like when I started preaching the good news in
Macedonia.[d] After I left there, you were the only church
that became my partner by giving blessings and by receiv-
ing them in return. 16Even when I was in Thessalonica,
you helped me more than once. 17I am not trying to get
something from you, but I want you to receive the bless-
ings that come from giving.
18I have been paid back everything, and with interest. I
am completely satisfied with the gifts that you had
Epaphroditus bring me. They are like a sweet-smelling
offering or like the right kind of sacrifice that pleases God.
19I pray that God will take care of all your needs with the

[c] 4.11 *be satisfied with*: Or "get by on." [d] 4.15 *when I started preaching the good news in Macedonia*: Paul is talking about his first visit to Philippi (see Acts 16.12-40).

NEW INTERNATIONAL VERSION

Thanks for Their Gifts

10I rejoice greatly in the Lord that at last you have renewed your concern for me. Indeed, you have been concerned, but you had no opportunity to show it. 11I am not saying this because I am in need, for I have learned to be content whatever the circumstances. 12I know what it is to be in need, and I know what it is to have plenty. I have learned the secret of being content in any and every situation, whether well fed or hungry, whether living in plenty or in want. 13I can do everything through him who gives me strength.

14Yet it was good of you to share in my troubles. 15Moreover, as you Philippians know, in the early days of your acquaintance with the gospel, when I set out from Macedonia, not one church shared with me in the matter of giving and receiving, except you only; 16for even when I was in Thessalonica, you sent me aid again and again when I was in need. 17Not that I am looking for a gift, but I am looking for what may be credited to your account. 18I have received full payment and even more; I am amply supplied, now that I have received from Epaphroditus the gifts you sent. They are a fragrant offering, an acceptable sacrifice, pleasing to God. 19And my God will meet all your needs according to his glorious riches in Christ Jesus.

NEW LIVING TRANSLATION

Paul's Thanks for Their Gifts

10How grateful I am, and how I praise the Lord that you are concerned about me again. I know you have always been concerned for me, but for a while you didn't have the chance to help me. 11Not that I was ever in need, for I have learned how to get along happily whether I have much or little. 12I know how to live on almost nothing or with everything. I have learned the secret of living in every situation, whether it is with a full stomach or empty, with plenty or little. 13For I can do everything with the help of Christ who gives me the strength I need. 14But even so, you have done well to share with me in my present difficulty.

15As you know, you Philippians were the only ones who gave me financial help when I brought you the Good News and then traveled on from Macedonia. No other church did this. 16Even when I was in Thessalonica you sent help more than once. 17I don't say this because I want a gift from you. What I want is for you to receive a well-earned reward because of your kindness.

18At the moment I have all I need—more than I need! I am generously supplied with the gifts you sent me with Epaphroditus. They are a sweet-smelling sacrifice that is acceptable to God and pleases him. 19And this same God who takes care of me will supply all your needs from his glorious riches, which have been given to us in Christ

NEW KING JAMES VERSION

Philippian Generosity

10But I rejoiced in the Lord greatly that now at last your care for me has flourished again; though you surely did care, but you lacked opportunity. 11Not that I speak in regard to need, for I have learned in whatever state I am, to be content: 12I know how to be abased, and I know how to abound. Everywhere and in all things I have learned both to be full and to be hungry, both to abound and to suffer need. 13I can do all things through Christ[b] who strengthens me.

14Nevertheless you have done well that you shared in my distress. 15Now you Philippians know also that in the beginning of the gospel, when I departed from Macedonia, no church shared with me concerning giving and receiving but you only. 16For even in Thessalonica you sent *aid* once and again for my necessities. 17Not that I seek the gift, but I seek the fruit that abounds to your account. 18Indeed I have all and abound. I am full, having received from Epaphroditus the things *sent* from you, a sweet-smelling aroma, an acceptable sacrifice, well pleasing to God. 19And my God shall supply all your need according to His riches

4:13 [b] NU-Text reads *Him who.*

THE MESSAGE

Content Whatever the Circumstances

I'm glad in God, far happier than you would ever guess—happy that you're again showing such strong concern for me. Not that you ever quit praying and thinking about me. You just had no chance to show it. Actually, I don't have a sense of needing anything personally. I've learned by now to be quite content whatever my circumstances. I'm just as happy with little as with much, with much as with little. I've found the recipe for being happy whether full or hungry, hands full or hands empty. Whatever I have, wherever I am, I can make it through anything in the One who makes me who I am. I don't mean that your help didn't mean a lot to me—it did. It was a beautiful thing that you came alongside me in my troubles.

You Philippians well know, and you can be sure I'll never forget it, that when I first left Macedonia province, venturing out with the Message, not one church helped out in the give-and-take of this work except you. You were the only one. Even while I was in Thessalonica, you helped out—and not only once, but twice. Not that I'm looking for handouts, but I do want you to experience the blessing that issues from generosity.

And now I have it all—and keep getting more! The gifts you sent with Epaphroditus were more than enough, like a sweet-smelling sacrifice roasting on the altar, filling the air with fragrance, pleasing God no end. You can be sure that God will take care of everything you need, his generosity exceeding even yours in the glory that pours from

KING JAMES VERSION

20 ¶ Now unto God and our Father *be* glory for ever and ever. Amen.

21 Salute every saint in Christ Jesus. The brethren which are with me greet you.

22 All the saints salute you, chiefly they that are of Caesar's household.

23 The grace of our Lord Jesus Christ *be* with you all. Amen.

NEW AMERICAN STANDARD BIBLE

20 Now to our God and Father *be* the glory forever and ever. Amen.

21 Greet every saint in Christ Jesus. The brethren who are with me greet you.

22 All the saints greet you, especially those of Caesar's household.

23 The grace of the Lord Jesus Christ be with your spirit.

NEW CENTURY VERSION

20Glory to our God and Father forever and ever! Amen.

21Greet each of God's people in Christ. Those who are with me send greetings to you. 22All of God's people greet you, particularly those from the palace of Caesar.

23The grace of the Lord Jesus Christ be with you all.

CONTEMPORARY ENGLISH VERSION

wonderful blessings that come from Christ Jesus! 20May God our Father be praised forever and ever. Amen.

Final Greetings

21Give my greetings to all who are God's people because of Christ Jesus.

The Lord's followers here with me send you their greetings.

22All of God's people send their greetings, especially those in the service of the Emperor.

23I pray that our Lord Jesus Christ will be kind to you and will bless your life!

NEW INTERNATIONAL VERSION

[20]To our God and Father be glory for ever and ever. Amen.

Final Greetings

[21]Greet all the saints in Christ Jesus. The brothers who are with me send greetings. [22]All the saints send you greetings, especially those who belong to Caesar's household.

[23]The grace of the Lord Jesus Christ be with your spirit. Amen.[b]

[b] 23 Some manuscripts do not have *Amen*.

NEW LIVING TRANSLATION

Jesus. [20]Now glory be to God our Father forever and ever. Amen.

Paul's Final Greetings

[21]Give my greetings to all the Christians there. The brothers who are with me here send you their greetings. [22]And all the other Christians send their greetings, too, especially those who work in Caesar's palace.

[23]May the grace of the Lord Jesus Christ be with your spirit.

NEW KING JAMES VERSION

in glory by Christ Jesus. [20]Now to our God and Father *be* glory forever and ever. Amen.

Greeting and Blessing

[21]Greet every saint in Christ Jesus. The brethren who are with me greet you. [22]All the saints greet you, but especially those who are of Caesar's household.

[23]The grace of our Lord Jesus Christ be with you all.[c] Amen.

4:23 [c] NU-Text reads *your spirit.*

THE MESSAGE

Jesus. Our God and Father abounds in glory that just pours out into eternity. Yes.

Give our regards to every Christian you meet. Our friends here say hello. All the Christians here, especially the believers who work in the palace of Caesar, want to be remembered to you.

Receive and experience the amazing grace of the Master, Jesus Christ, deep, deep within yourselves.

KING JAMES VERSION

THE EPISTLE OF ST. PAUL TO THE COLOSSIANS

1 Paul, an apostle of Jesus Christ by the will of God, and Timotheus *our* brother,

2 To the saints and faithful brethren in Christ which are at Colosse: Grace *be* unto you, and peace, from God our Father and the Lord Jesus Christ.

3 ¶ We give thanks to God and the Father of our Lord Jesus Christ, praying always for you,

4 Since we heard of your faith in Christ Jesus, and of the love *which ye have* to all the saints,

5 For the hope which is laid up for you in heaven, whereof ye heard before in the word of the truth of the gospel;

6 Which is come unto you, as *it is* in all the world; and bringeth forth fruit, as *it doth* also in you, since the day ye heard *of it*, and knew the grace of God in truth:

7 As ye also learned of Epaphras our dear fellowservant, who is for you a faithful minister of Christ;

NEW AMERICAN STANDARD BIBLE

THE LETTER OF PAUL TO THE COLOSSIANS

Thankfulness for Spiritual Attainments

1 Paul, an apostle of Jesus Christ by the will of God, and Timothy our brother,

2 To the saints and faithful brethren in Christ *who are* at Colossae: Grace to you and peace from God our Father.

3 We give thanks to God, the Father of our Lord Jesus Christ, praying always for you,

4 since we heard of your faith in Christ Jesus and the love which you have for all the saints;

5 because of the hope laid up for you in heaven, of which you previously heard in the word of truth, the gospel

6 which has come to you, just as in all the world also it is constantly bearing fruit and increasing, even as *it has been doing* in you also since the day you heard *of it* and understood the grace of God in truth;

7 just as you learned *it* from Epaphras, our beloved fellow bond-servant, who is a faithful servant of Christ on our behalf,

NEW CENTURY VERSION

COLOSSIANS

1 From Paul, an apostle of Christ Jesus. I am an apostle because that is what God wanted. Also from Timothy, our brother.

2To the holy and faithful brothers and sisters[a] in Christ that live in Colosse:

Grace and peace to you from God our Father.

3In our prayers for you we always thank God, the Father
of our Lord Jesus Christ, 4because we have heard about the
faith you have in Christ Jesus and the love you have for all
of God's people. 5You have this faith and love because of
your hope, and what you hope for is kept safe for you in
heaven. You learned about this hope when you heard the
message about the truth, the Good News 6that was told to
you. Everywhere in the world that Good News is bringing
blessings and is growing. This has happened with you,
too, since you heard the Good News and understood the
truth about the grace of God. 7You learned about God's
grace from Epaphras, whom we love. He works together
with us and is a faithful servant of Christ for us. 8He also

1:2 [a] **brothers and sisters** Although the Greek text says "brothers" here and throughout this book, Paul's words were meant for the entire church, including men and women.

CONTEMPORARY ENGLISH VERSION

COLOSSIANS

1 From Paul, chosen by God to be an apostle of Christ Jesus, and from Timothy, who is also a follower.

2To God's people who live in Colossae and are faithful followers of Christ.

I pray that God our Father will be kind to you and will bless you with peace!

A Prayer of Thanks

3Each time we pray for you, we thank God, the Father of
our Lord Jesus Christ. 4We have heard of your faith in
Christ and of your love for all of God's people, 5because
what you hope for is kept safe for you in heaven. You first
heard about this hope when you believed the true message, which is the good news.

6The good news is spreading all over the world with great
success. It has spread in that same way among you, ever
since the first day you learned the truth about God's wonderful kindness 7from our good friend Epaphras. He works
together with us for Christ and is a faithful worker for you.[a]

[a] 1.7 *you*: Some manuscripts have "us."

NEW INTERNATIONAL VERSION

COLOSSIANS

1 Paul, an apostle of Christ Jesus by the will of God, and
Timothy our brother,

2 To the holy and faithful[a] brothers in Christ at Colosse:

Grace and peace to you from God our Father.[b]

Thanksgiving and Prayer

3 We always thank God, the Father of our Lord Jesus
Christ, when we pray for you, 4 because we have heard of
your faith in Christ Jesus and of the love you have for all
the saints— 5 the faith and love that spring from the hope
that is stored up for you in heaven and that you have
already heard about in the word of truth, the gospel 6 that
has come to you. All over the world this gospel is bearing
fruit and growing, just as it has been doing among you
since the day you heard it and understood God's grace in
all its truth. 7 You learned it from Epaphras, our dear fel-
low servant, who is a faithful minister of Christ on our[c]

[a] 2 Or *believing* [b] 2 Some manuscripts *Father and the Lord Jesus Christ* [c] 7 Some manuscripts *your*

NEW LIVING TRANSLATION

COLOSSIANS

Greetings from Paul

1 This letter is from Paul, chosen by God to be an apos-
tle of Christ Jesus, and from our brother Timothy.
2 It is written to God's holy people in the city of Colosse,
who are faithful brothers and sisters* in Christ.
May God our Father give you grace and peace.

Paul's Thanksgiving and Prayer

3 We always pray for you, and we give thanks to God the
Father of our Lord Jesus Christ, 4 for we have heard that
you trust in Christ Jesus and that you love all of God's peo-
ple. 5 You do this because you are looking forward to the
joys of heaven—as you have been ever since you first
heard the truth of the Good News. 6 This same Good News
that came to you is going out all over the world. It is
changing lives everywhere, just as it changed yours that
very first day you heard and understood the truth about
God's great kindness to sinners.
7 Epaphras, our much loved co-worker, was the one who
brought you the Good News. He is Christ's faithful servant,
and he is helping us in your place.* 8 He is the one who

1:2 Greek *faithful brothers.* 1:7 Greek *he is ministering on your behalf;* other manuscripts read *he is ministering on our behalf.*

NEW KING JAMES VERSION

THE EPISTLE OF PAUL TO THE

COLOSSIANS

Greeting

1 Paul, an apostle of Jesus Christ by the will of God, and
Timothy our brother,

2 To the saints and faithful brethren in Christ *who are* in
Colosse:

Grace to you and peace from God our Father and the
Lord Jesus Christ.[a]

Their Faith in Christ

3 We give thanks to the God and Father of our Lord Jesus
Christ, praying always for you, 4 since we heard of your
faith in Christ Jesus and of your love for all the saints; 5 be-
cause of the hope which is laid up for you in heaven, of
which you heard before in the word of the truth of the
gospel, 6 which has come to you, as *it has* also in all the
world, and is bringing forth fruit,[b] as *it is* also among you
since the day you heard and knew the grace of God in
truth; 7 as you also learned from Epaphras, our dear fellow
servant, who is a faithful minister of Christ on your behalf,

1:2 [a] NU-Text omits *and the Lord Jesus Christ.* 1:6 [b] NU-Text and M-Text add *and growing.*

THE MESSAGE

COLOSSIANS

1 I, Paul, have been sent on special assignment by Christ as part of God's master plan. Together with my friend Timothy, I greet the Christians and stalwart followers of Christ who live in Colosse. May everything good from God our Father be yours!

Working in His Orchard

Our prayers for you are always spilling over into thanksgivings. We can't quit thanking God our Father and Jesus our Messiah for you! We keep getting reports on your steady faith in Christ, our Jesus, and the love you continuously extend to all Christians. The lines of purpose in your lives never grow slack, tightly tied as they are to your future in heaven, kept taut by hope.

The Message is as true among you today as when you first heard it. It doesn't diminish or weaken over time. It's the same all over the world. The Message bears fruit and gets larger and stronger, just as it has in you. From the very first day you heard and recognized the truth of what God is doing, you've been hungry for more. It's as vigorous in you now as when you learned it from our friend and close associate Epaphras. He is one reliable worker for Christ! I could always depend on him. He's the one who

KING JAMES VERSION

8 Who also declared unto us your love in the Spirit.

9 ¶ For this cause we also, since the day we heard *it*, do not cease to pray for you, and to desire that ye might be filled with the knowledge of his will in all wisdom and spiritual understanding;

10 That ye might walk worthy of the Lord unto all pleasing, being fruitful in every good work, and increasing in the knowledge of God;

11 Strengthened with all might, according to his glorious power, unto all patience and longsuffering with joyfulness;

12 ¶ Giving thanks unto the Father, which hath made us meet to be partakers of the inheritance of the saints in light:

13 Who hath delivered us from the power of darkness, and hath translated *us* into the kingdom of his dear Son:

14 In whom we have redemption through his blood, *even* the forgiveness of sins:

15 Who is the image of the invisible God, the firstborn of every creature:

16 For by him were all things created, that are in heaven, and that are in earth, visible and invisible, whether

NEW AMERICAN STANDARD BIBLE

8 and he also informed us of your love in the Spirit.

9 For this reason also, since the day we heard *of it*, we have not ceased to pray for you and to ask that you may be filled with the knowledge of His will in all spiritual wisdom and understanding,

10 so that you will walk in a manner worthy of the Lord, to please *Him* in all respects, bearing fruit in every good work and increasing in the knowledge of God;

11 strengthened with all power, according to His glorious might, for the attaining of all steadfastness and patience; joyously

12 giving thanks to the Father, who has qualified us to share in the inheritance of the saints in Light.

The Incomparable Christ

13 For He rescued us from the domain of darkness, and transferred us to the kingdom of His beloved Son,

14 in whom we have redemption, the forgiveness of sins.

15 He is the image of the invisible God, the firstborn of all creation.

16 For by Him all things were created, *both* in the heavens and on earth, visible and invisible, whether thrones or

NEW CENTURY VERSION

told us about the love you have from the Holy Spirit.

9 Because of this, since the day we heard about you, we have continued praying for you, asking God that you will know fully what he wants. We pray that you will also have great wisdom and understanding in spiritual things 10 so that you will live the kind of life that honors and pleases the Lord in every way. You will produce fruit in every good work and grow in the knowledge of God. 11 God will strengthen you with his own great power so that you will not give up when troubles come, but you will be patient. 12 And you will joyfully give thanks to the Father who has made you able to have a share in all that he has prepared for his people in the kingdom of light. 13 God has freed us from the power of darkness, and he brought us into the kingdom of his dear Son. 14 The Son paid for our sins, and in him we have forgiveness.

The Importance of Christ

15 No one can see God, but Jesus Christ is exactly like him. He ranks higher than everything that has been made. 16 Through his power all things were made—things in heaven and on earth, things seen and unseen, all powers,

CONTEMPORARY ENGLISH VERSION

8 He is also the one who told us about the love that God's Spirit has given you.

The Person and Work of Christ

9 We have not stopped praying for you since the first day we heard about you. In fact, we always pray that God will show you everything he wants you to do and that you may have all the wisdom and understanding that his Spirit gives. 10 Then you will live a life that honors the Lord, and you will always please him by doing good deeds. You will come to know God even better. 11 His glorious power will make you patient and strong enough to endure anything, and you will be truly happy.

12 I pray that you will be grateful to God for letting you[a] have part in what he has promised his people in the kingdom of light. 13 God rescued us from the dark power of Satan and brought us into the kingdom of his dear Son, 14 who forgives our sins and sets us free.

15 Christ is exactly like God,
who cannot be seen.
He is the first-born Son,
superior to all creation.
16 Everything was created by him,
everything in heaven
and on earth,
everything seen and unseen,

[a] 1.12 *you*: Some manuscripts have "us."

NEW INTERNATIONAL VERSION

behalf, [8]and who also told us of your love in the Spirit.

[9]For this reason, since the day we heard about you, we have not stopped praying for you and asking God to fill you with the knowledge of his will through all spiritual wisdom and understanding. [10]And we pray this in order that you may live a life worthy of the Lord and may please him in every way: bearing fruit in every good work, growing in the knowledge of God, [11]being strengthened with all power according to his glorious might so that you may have great endurance and patience, and joyfully [12]giving thanks to the Father, who has qualified you[d] to share in the inheritance of the saints in the kingdom of light. [13]For he has rescued us from the dominion of darkness and brought us into the kingdom of the Son he loves, [14]in whom we have redemption,[e] the forgiveness of sins.

The Supremacy of Christ

[15]He is the image of the invisible God, the firstborn over all creation. [16]For by him all things were created: things in heaven and on earth, visible and invisible, whether

[d] *12* Some manuscripts *us* [e] *14* A few late manuscripts *redemption through his blood*

NEW LIVING TRANSLATION

told us about the great love for others that the Holy Spirit has given you.

[9]So we have continued praying for you ever since we first heard about you. We ask God to give you a complete understanding of what he wants to do in your lives, and we ask him to make you wise with spiritual wisdom. [10]Then the way you live will always honor and please the Lord, and you will continually do good, kind things for others. All the while, you will learn to know God better and better.

[11]We also pray that you will be strengthened with his glorious power so that you will have all the patience and endurance you need. May you be filled with joy, [12]always thanking the Father, who has enabled you to share the inheritance that belongs to God's holy people, who live in the light. [13]For he has rescued us from the one who rules in the kingdom of darkness, and he has brought us into the Kingdom of his dear Son. [14]God has purchased our freedom with his blood* and has forgiven all our sins.

Christ Is Supreme

[15]Christ is the visible image of the invisible God. He existed before God made anything at all and is supreme over all creation.* [16]Christ is the one through whom God created everything in heaven and earth. He made the things we can see and the things we can't see—kings,

1:14 Some manuscripts do not include *with his blood.* 1:15 Greek *He is the firstborn of all creation.*

NEW KING JAMES VERSION

[8]who also declared to us your love in the Spirit.

Preeminence of Christ

[9]For this reason we also, since the day we heard it, do not cease to pray for you, and to ask that you may be filled with the knowledge of His will in all wisdom and spiritual understanding; [10]that you may walk worthy of the Lord, fully pleasing *Him,* being fruitful in every good work and increasing in the knowledge of God; [11]strengthened with all might, according to His glorious power, for all patience and longsuffering with joy; [12]giving thanks to the Father who has qualified us to be partakers of the inheritance of the saints in the light. [13]He has delivered us from the power of darkness and conveyed *us* into the kingdom of the Son of His love, [14]in whom we have redemption through His blood,[c] the forgiveness of sins.

[15]He is the image of the invisible God, the firstborn over all creation. [16]For by Him all things were created that are in heaven and that are on earth, visible and invisible,

1:14 [c] NU-Text and M-Text omit *through His blood.*

THE MESSAGE

told us how thoroughly love had been worked into your lives by the Spirit.

Be assured that from the first day we heard of you, we haven't stopped praying for you, asking God to give you wise minds and spirits attuned to his will, and so acquire a thorough understanding of the ways in which God works. We pray that you'll live well for the Master, making him proud of you as you work hard in his orchard. As you learn more and more how God works, you will learn how to do *your* work. We pray that you'll have the strength to stick it out over the long haul—not the grim strength of gritting your teeth but the glory-strength God gives. It is strength that endures the unendurable and spills over into joy, thanking the Father who makes us strong enough to take part in everything bright and beautiful that he has for us.

God rescued us from dead-end alleys and dark dungeons. He's set us up in the kingdom of the Son he loves so much, the Son who got us out of the pit we were in, got rid of the sins we were doomed to keep repeating.

Christ Holds It All Together

We look at this Son and see the God who cannot be seen. We look at this Son and see God's original purpose in everything created. For everything, absolutely everything, above and below, visible and invisible, rank after

KING JAMES VERSION

they be thrones, or dominions, or principalities, or powers:
all things were created by him, and for him:
17 And he is before all things, and by him all things
consist.
18 And he is the head of the body, the church: who is
the beginning, the firstborn from the dead; that in all
things he might have the preeminence.
19 For it pleased *the Father* that in him should all ful-
ness dwell;
20 And, having made peace through the blood of his
cross, by him to reconcile all things unto himself; by him, *I*
say, whether *they be* things in earth, or things in heaven.

NEW AMERICAN STANDARD BIBLE

dominions or rulers or authorities—all things have been
created through Him and for Him.
17 He is before all things, and in Him all things hold
together.
18 He is also head of the body, the church; and He is the
beginning, the firstborn from the dead, so that He Himself
will come to have first place in everything.
19 For it was the *Father's* good pleasure for all the full-
ness to dwell in Him,
20 and through Him to reconcile all things to Himself,
having made peace through the blood of His cross;
through Him, *I say*, whether things on earth or things in
heaven.

NEW CENTURY VERSION

authorities, lords, and rulers. All things were made
through Christ and for Christ. 17He was there before any-
thing was made, and all things continue because of him.
18He is the head of the body, which is the church.
Everything comes from him. He is the first one who was
raised from the dead. So in all things Jesus has first place.
19God was pleased for all of himself to live in Christ. 20And
through Christ, God has brought all things back to himself
again—things on earth and things in heaven. God made
peace through the blood of Christ's death on the cross.

CONTEMPORARY ENGLISH VERSION

including all forces
and powers,
and all rulers
and authorities.
All things were created
by God's Son,
and everything was made
for him.

17God's Son was before all else,
and by him everything
is held together.
18He is the head of his body,
which is the church.
He is the very beginning,
the first to be raised
from death,
so that he would be
above all others.

19God himself was pleased
to live fully in his Son.
20And God was pleased
for him to make peace
by sacrificing his blood
on the cross,
so that all beings in heaven
and on earth
would be brought back to God.

NEW INTERNATIONAL VERSION

thrones or powers or rulers or authorities; all things were
created by him and for him. [17]He is before all things, and
in him all things hold together. [18]And he is the head of the
body, the church; he is the beginning and the firstborn
from among the dead, so that in everything he might have
the supremacy. [19]For God was pleased to have all his full-
ness dwell in him, [20]and through him to reconcile to him-
self all things, whether things on earth or things in heav-
en, by making peace through his blood, shed on the cross.

NEW LIVING TRANSLATION

kingdoms, rulers, and authorities. Everything has been
created through him and for him. [17]He existed before
everything else began, and he holds all creation together.
[18]Christ is the head of the church, which is his body. He
is the first of all who will rise from the dead,* so he is first
in everything. [19]For God in all his fullness was pleased to
live in Christ, [20]and by him God reconciled everything to
himself. He made peace with everything in heaven and on
earth by means of his blood on the cross. [21]This includes

1:18 Greek *He is the beginning, the firstborn from the dead.*

NEW KING JAMES VERSION

whether thrones or dominions or principalities or powers.
All things were created through Him and for Him. [17]And
He is before all things, and in Him all things consist.
[18]And He is the head of the body, the church, who is the
beginning, the firstborn from the dead, that in all things
He may have the preeminence.

Reconciled in Christ

[19]For it pleased *the Father that* in Him all the fullness
should dwell, [20]and by Him to reconcile all things to
Himself, by Him, whether things on earth or things in
heaven, having made peace through the blood of His cross.

THE MESSAGE

rank after rank of angels—*everything* got started in him and finds its purpose in him. He was there before any of it came into existence and holds it all together right up to this moment. And when it comes to the church, he organizes and holds it together, like a head does a body.

He was supreme in the beginning and—leading the resurrection parade—he is supreme in the end. From beginning to end he's there, towering far above everything, everyone. So spacious is he, so roomy, that everything of God finds its proper place in him without crowding. Not only that, but all the broken and dislocated pieces of the universe—people and things, animals and atoms—get properly fixed and fit together in vibrant harmonies, all because of his death, his blood that poured down from the Cross.

KING JAMES VERSION

21 And you, that were sometime alienated and enemies in *your* mind by wicked works, yet now hath he reconciled

22 In the body of his flesh through death, to present you holy and unblameable and unreproveable in his sight:

23 If ye continue in the faith grounded and settled, and *be* not moved away from the hope of the gospel, which ye have heard, *and* which was preached to every creature which is under heaven; whereof I Paul am made a minister;

24 Who now rejoice in my sufferings for you, and fill up that which is behind of the afflictions of Christ in my flesh for his body's sake, which is the church:

25 Whereof I am made a minister, according to the dispensation of God which is given to me for you, to fulfil the word of God;

26 *Even* the mystery which hath been hid from ages and from generations, but now is made manifest to his saints:

27 To whom God would make known what *is* the riches of the glory of this mystery among the Gentiles; which is Christ in you, the hope of glory:

NEW AMERICAN STANDARD BIBLE

21 And although you were formerly alienated and hostile in mind, *engaged* in evil deeds,

22 yet He has now reconciled you in His fleshly body through death, in order to present you before Him holy and blameless and beyond reproach—

23 if indeed you continue in the faith firmly established and steadfast, and not moved away from the hope of the gospel that you have heard, which was proclaimed in all creation under heaven, and of which I, Paul, was made a minister.

24 Now I rejoice in my sufferings for your sake, and in my flesh I do my share on behalf of His body, which is the church, in filling up what is lacking in Christ's afflictions.

25 Of *this church* I was made a minister according to the stewardship from God bestowed on me for your benefit, so that I might fully carry out the *preaching of* the word of God,

26 *that is,* the mystery which has been hidden from the *past* ages and generations, but has now been manifested to His saints,

27 to whom God willed to make known what is the riches of the glory of this mystery among the Gentiles, which is Christ in you, the hope of glory.

NEW CENTURY VERSION

21 At one time you were separated from God. You were
his enemies in your minds, and the evil things you did
were against God. 22 But now God has made you his friends
again. He did this through Christ's death in the body so
that he might bring you into God's presence as people who
are holy, with no wrong, and with nothing of which God
can judge you guilty. 23 This will happen if you continue
strong and sure in your faith. You must not be moved
away from the hope brought to you by the Good News that
you heard. That same Good News has been told to every-
one in the world, and I, Paul, help in preaching that Good
News.

Paul's Work for the Church

24 I am happy in my sufferings for you. There are things
that Christ must still suffer through his body, the church. I
am accepting, in my body, my part of these things that
must be suffered. 25 I became a servant of the church
because God gave me a special work to do that helps you,
and that work is to tell fully the message of God. 26 This
message is the secret that was hidden from everyone since
the beginning of time, but now it is made known to God's
holy people. 27 God decided to let his people know this rich
and glorious secret which he has for all people. This secret
is Christ himself, who is in you. He is our only hope for

CONTEMPORARY ENGLISH VERSION

21 You used to be far from God. Your thoughts made you
his enemies, and you did evil things. 22 But his Son became
a human and died. So God made peace with you, and now
he lets you stand in his presence as people who are holy
and faultless and innocent. 23 But you must stay deeply
rooted and firm in your faith. You must not give up the
hope you received when you heard the good news. It was
preached to everyone on earth, and I myself have become a
servant of this message.

Paul's Service to the Church

24 I am glad that I can suffer for you. I am pleased also
that in my own body I can continue[b] the suffering of Christ
for his body, the church. 25 God's plan was to make me a
servant of his church and to send me to preach his com-
plete message to you. 26 For ages and ages this message
was kept secret from everyone, but now it has been
explained to God's people. 27 God did this because he want-
ed you Gentiles to understand his wonderful and glorious
mystery. And the mystery is that Christ lives in you, and
he is your hope of sharing in God's glory.

[b] **1.24** *continue*: Or "complete."

NEW INTERNATIONAL VERSION

21 Once you were alienated from God and were enemies
in your minds because of[f] your evil behavior. 22 But now he
has reconciled you by Christ's physical body through death
to present you holy in his sight, without blemish and free
from accusation— 23 if you continue in your faith, estab-
lished and firm, not moved from the hope held out in the
gospel. This is the gospel that you heard and that has been
proclaimed to every creature under heaven, and of which I,
Paul, have become a servant.

Paul's Labor for the Church

24 Now I rejoice in what was suffered for you, and I fill
up in my flesh what is still lacking in regard to Christ's
afflictions, for the sake of his body, which is the church.
25 I have become its servant by the commission God gave
me to present to you the word of God in its fullness—
26 the mystery that has been kept hidden for ages and gen-
erations, but is now disclosed to the saints. 27 To them God
has chosen to make known among the Gentiles the glori-
ous riches of this mystery, which is Christ in you, the hope
of glory.

[f] 21 Or *minds, as shown by*

NEW LIVING TRANSLATION

you who were once so far away from God. You were his
enemies, separated from him by your evil thoughts and
actions, 22 yet now he has brought you back as his friends.
He has done this through his death on the cross in his own
human body. As a result, he has brought you into the very
presence of God, and you are holy and blameless as you
stand before him without a single fault. 23 But you must
continue to believe this truth and stand in it firmly. Don't
drift away from the assurance you received when you
heard the Good News. The Good News has been preached
all over the world, and I, Paul, have been appointed by God
to proclaim it.

Paul's Work for the Church

24 I am glad when I suffer for you in my body, for I am
completing what remains of Christ's sufferings for his
body, the church. 25 God has given me the responsibility of
serving his church by proclaiming his message in all its
fullness to you Gentiles. 26 This message was kept secret
for centuries and generations past, but now it has been
revealed to his own holy people. 27 For it has pleased God
to tell his people that the riches and glory of Christ are for
you Gentiles, too. For this is the secret: Christ lives in you,
and this is your assurance that you will share in his glory.

NEW KING JAMES VERSION

21 And you, who once were alienated and enemies in
your mind by wicked works, yet now He has reconciled
22 in the body of His flesh through death, to present you
holy, and blameless, and above reproach in His sight— 23 if
indeed you continue in the faith, grounded and steadfast,
and are not moved away from the hope of the gospel which
you heard, which was preached to every creature under
heaven, of which I, Paul, became a minister.

Sacrificial Service for Christ

24 I now rejoice in my sufferings for you, and fill up in
my flesh what is lacking in the afflictions of Christ, for the
sake of His body, which is the church, 25 of which I became
a minister according to the stewardship from God which
was given to me for you, to fulfill the word of God, 26 the
mystery which has been hidden from ages and from gener-
ations, but now has been revealed to His saints. 27 To them
God willed to make known what are the riches of the glory
of this mystery among the Gentiles: which[d] is Christ in
you, the hope of glory. 28 Him we preach, warning every

1:27 [d] M-Text reads *who.*

THE MESSAGE

You yourselves are a case study of what he does. At one time you all had your backs turned to God, thinking rebellious thoughts of him, giving him trouble every chance you got. But now, by giving himself completely at the Cross, actually *dying* for you, Christ brought you over to God's side and put your lives together, whole and holy in his presence. You don't walk away from a gift like that! You stay grounded and steady in that bond of trust, constantly tuned in to the Message, careful not to be distracted or diverted. There is no other Message—just this one. Every creature under heaven gets this same Message. I, Paul, am a messenger of this Message.

✠

I want you to know how glad I am that it's me sitting here in this jail and not you. There's a lot of suffering to be entered into in this world—the kind of suffering Christ takes on. I welcome the chance to take my share in the church's part of that suffering. When I became a servant in this church, I experienced this suffering as a sheer gift, God's way of helping me serve you, laying out the whole truth.

This mystery has been kept in the dark for a long time, but now it's out in the open. God wanted everyone, not just Jews, to know this rich and glorious secret inside and out, regardless of their background, regardless of their religious standing. The mystery in a nutshell is just this: Christ is in you, therefore you can look forward to sharing in God's glory. It's that simple. That is the substance of

KING JAMES VERSION

28 Whom we preach, warning every man, and teaching every man in all wisdom; that we may present every man perfect in Christ Jesus:

29 Whereunto I also labour, striving according to his working, which worketh in me mightily.

2 For I would that ye knew what great conflict I have for you, and *for* them at Laodicea, and *for* as many as have not seen my face in the flesh;

2 That their hearts might be comforted, being knit together in love, and unto all riches of the full assurance of understanding, to the acknowledgement of the mystery of God, and of the Father, and of Christ;

3 In whom are hid all the treasures of wisdom and knowledge.

4 ¶ And this I say, lest any man should beguile you with enticing words.

5 For though I be absent in the flesh, yet am I with you in the spirit, joying and beholding your order, and the stedfastness of your faith in Christ.

6 As ye have therefore received Christ Jesus the Lord, *so* walk ye in him:

NEW AMERICAN STANDARD BIBLE

28 We proclaim Him, admonishing every man and teaching every man with all wisdom, so that we may present every man complete in Christ.

29 For this purpose also I labor, striving according to His power, which mightily works within me.

You Are Built Up in Christ

2 For I want you to know how great a struggle I have on your behalf and for those who are at Laodicea, and for all those who have not personally seen my face,

2 that their hearts may be encouraged, having been knit together in love, and *attaining* to all the wealth that comes from the full assurance of understanding, *resulting* in a true knowledge of God's mystery, *that is,* Christ *Himself,*

3 in whom are hidden all the treasures of wisdom and knowledge.

4 I say this so that no one will delude you with persuasive argument.

5 For even though I am absent in body, nevertheless I am with you in spirit, rejoicing to see your good discipline and the stability of your faith in Christ.

6 Therefore as you have received Christ Jesus the Lord, *so* walk in Him,

NEW CENTURY VERSION

glory. 28 So we continue to preach Christ to each person,
using all wisdom to warn and to teach everyone, in order
to bring each one into God's presence as a mature person
in Christ. 29 To do this, I work and struggle, using Christ's
great strength that works so powerfully in me.

2 I want you to know how hard I work for you, those in
Laodicea, and others who have never seen me. 2 I want
them to be strengthened and joined together with love so
that they may be rich in their understanding. This leads to
their knowing fully God's secret, that is, Christ himself. 3 In
him all the treasures of wisdom and knowledge are safely
kept.

4 I say this so that no one can fool you by arguments
that seem good, but are false. 5 Though I am absent from
you in my body, my heart is with you, and I am happy to
see your good lives and your strong faith in Christ.

Continue to Live in Christ

6 As you received Christ Jesus the Lord, so continue to
live in him. 7 Keep your roots deep in him and have your

CONTEMPORARY ENGLISH VERSION

28 We announce the message about Christ, and we use
all our wisdom to warn and teach everyone, so that all of
Christ's followers will grow and become mature. 29 That's
why I work so hard and use the mighty power he gives me.

2 I want you to know what a struggle I am going
through for you, for God's people at Laodicea, and for
all of those followers who have never met me. 2 I do it to
encourage them. Then as their hearts are joined together
in love, they will be wonderfully blessed with complete
understanding. And they will truly know Christ. Not only
is he the key to God's mystery, 3 but all wisdom and knowl-
edge are hidden away in him. 4 I tell you these things to
keep you from being fooled by fancy talk. 5 Even though I
am not with you, I keep thinking about you. I am glad to
know that you are living as you should and that your faith
in Christ is strong.

Christ Brings Real Life

6 You have accepted Christ Jesus as your Lord. Now keep
on following him. 7 Plant your roots in Christ and let him

NEW INTERNATIONAL VERSION

[28]We proclaim him, admonishing and teaching everyone
with all wisdom, so that we may present everyone perfect
in Christ. [29]To this end I labor, struggling with all his ener-
gy, which so powerfully works in me.
2 I want you to know how much I am struggling for you
and for those at Laodicea, and for all who have not
met me personally. [2]My purpose is that they may be
encouraged in heart and united in love, so that they may
have the full riches of complete understanding, in order
that they may know the mystery of God, namely, Christ,
[3]in whom are hidden all the treasures of wisdom and
knowledge. [4]I tell you this so that no one may deceive you
by fine-sounding arguments. [5]For though I am absent from
you in body, I am present with you in spirit and delight to
see how orderly you are and how firm your faith in
Christ is.

Freedom From Human Regulations Through Life With Christ

[6]So then, just as you received Christ Jesus as Lord, contin-
ue to live in him, [7]rooted and built up in him, strengthened

NEW LIVING TRANSLATION

[28]So everywhere we go, we tell everyone about Christ.
We warn them and teach them with all the wisdom God
has given us, for we want to present them to God, perfect*
in their relationship to Christ. [29]I work very hard at this, as
I depend on Christ's mighty power that works within me.
2 I want you to know how much I have agonized for
you and for the church at Laodicea, and for many
other friends who have never known me personally. [2]My
goal is that they will be encouraged and knit together by
strong ties of love. I want them to have full confidence
because they have complete understanding of God's secret
plan, which is Christ himself. [3]In him lie hidden all the
treasures of wisdom and knowledge.
[4]I am telling you this so that no one will be able to
deceive you with persuasive arguments. [5]For though I am
far away from you, my heart is with you. And I am very
happy because you are living as you should and because of
your strong faith in Christ.

Freedom from Rules and New Life in Christ

[6]And now, just as you accepted Christ Jesus as your
Lord, you must continue to live in obedience to him. [7]Let

1:28 Or *mature.*

NEW KING JAMES VERSION

man and teaching every man in all wisdom, that we may
present every man perfect in Christ Jesus. [29]To this *end* I
also labor, striving according to His working which works
in me mightily.

Not Philosophy but Christ

2 For I want you to know what a great conflict I have
for you and those in Laodicea, and *for* as many as
have not seen my face in the flesh, [2]that their hearts may
be encouraged, being knit together in love, and *attaining*
to all riches of the full assurance of understanding, to the
knowledge of the mystery of God, both of the Father and[a]
of Christ, [3]in whom are hidden all the treasures of wisdom
and knowledge.
[4]Now this I say lest anyone should deceive you with per-
suasive words. [5]For though I am absent in the flesh, yet I
am with you in spirit, rejoicing to see your *good* order and
the steadfastness of your faith in Christ.
[6]As you therefore have received Christ Jesus the Lord, so
walk in Him, [7]rooted and built up in Him and established

2:2 [a] NU-Text omits *both of the Father and.*

THE MESSAGE

our Message. We preach *Christ,* warning people not to add
to the Message. We teach in a spirit of profound common
sense so that we can bring each person to maturity. To be
mature is to be basic. Christ! No more, no less. That's what
I'm working so hard at day after day, year after year, doing
my best with the energy God so generously gives me.
2 I want you to realize that I continue to work as hard
as I know how for you, and also for the Christians
over at Laodicea. Not many of you have met me face-to-
face, but that doesn't make any difference. Know that I'm
on your side, right alongside you. You're not in this alone.
I want you woven into a tapestry of love, in touch with
everything there is to know of God. Then you will have
minds confident and at rest, focused on Christ, God's great
mystery. All the richest treasures of wisdom and knowl-
edge are embedded in that mystery and nowhere else. And
we've been shown the mystery! I'm telling you this
because I don't want anyone leading you off on some wild-
goose chase, after other so-called mysteries, or "the
Secret."

I'm a long way off, true, and you may never lay eyes on
me, but believe me, I'm on your side, right beside you. I am
delighted to hear of the careful and orderly ways you con-
duct your affairs, and impressed with the solid substance
of your faith in Christ.

From the Shadows to the Substance

My counsel for you is simple and straightforward: Just
go ahead with what you've been given. You received Christ

KING JAMES VERSION

7 Rooted and built up in him, and stablished in the faith, as ye have been taught, abounding therein with thanksgiving.

8 Beware lest any man spoil you through philosophy and vain deceit, after the tradition of men, after the rudiments of the world, and not after Christ.

9 For in him dwelleth all the fulness of the Godhead bodily.

10 And ye are complete in him, which is the head of all principality and power:

11 In whom also ye are circumcised with the circumcision made without hands, in putting off the body of the sins of the flesh by the circumcision of Christ:

12 Buried with him in baptism, wherein also ye are risen with *him* through the faith of the operation of God, who hath raised him from the dead.

13 ¶ And you, being dead in your sins and the uncircumcision of your flesh, hath he quickened together with him, having forgiven you all trespasses;

NEW AMERICAN STANDARD BIBLE

7 having been firmly rooted *and now* being built up in Him and established [1]in your faith, just as you were instructed, *and* overflowing with gratitude.

8 See to it that no one takes you captive through philosophy and empty deception, according to the tradition of men, according to the elementary principles of the world, rather than according to Christ.

9 For in Him all the fullness of Deity dwells in bodily form,

10 and in Him you have been made complete, and He is the head over all rule and authority;

11 and in Him you were also circumcised with a circumcision made without hands, in the removal of the body of the flesh by the circumcision of Christ;

12 having been buried with Him in baptism, in which you were also raised up with Him through faith in the working of God, who raised Him from the dead.

13 When you were dead in your transgressions and the uncircumcision of your flesh, He made you alive together with Him, having forgiven us all our transgressions,

2:7 [1] Or *by*

NEW CENTURY VERSION

lives built on him. Be strong in the faith, just as you were taught, and always be thankful.

8 Be sure that no one leads you away with false and empty teaching that is only human, which comes from the ruling spirits of this world, and not from Christ. 9 All of God lives in Christ fully (even when Christ was on earth), 10 and you have a full and true life in Christ, who is ruler over all rulers and powers.

11 Also in Christ you had a different kind of circumcision, a circumcision not done by hands. It was through Christ's circumcision, that is, his death, that you were made free from the power of your sinful self. 12 When you were baptized, you were buried with Christ, and you were raised up with him through your faith in God's power that was shown when he raised Christ from the dead. 13 When you were spiritually dead because of your sins and because you were not free from the power of your sinful self, God made you alive with Christ, and he forgave all our sins. 14 He

CONTEMPORARY ENGLISH VERSION

be the foundation for your life. Be strong in your faith, just as you were taught. And be grateful.

8 Don't let anyone fool you by using senseless arguments. These arguments may sound wise, but they are only human teachings. They come from the powers of this world[a] and not from Christ.

9 God lives fully in Christ. 10 And you are fully grown because you belong to Christ, who is over every power and authority. 11 Christ has also taken away your selfish desires, just as circumcision removes flesh from the body. 12 And when you were baptized, it was the same as being buried with Christ. Then you were raised to life because you had faith in the power of God, who raised Christ from death. 13 You were dead, because you were sinful and were not God's people. But God let Christ make you[b] alive, when he forgave all our sins.

[a] 2.8 *powers of this world*: Spirits and unseen forces were thought to control human lives and were believed to be connected with the movements of the stars. [b] 2.13 *you*: See the note at 1.7.

NEW INTERNATIONAL VERSION

in the faith as you were taught, and overflowing with thankfulness.

[8]See to it that no one takes you captive through hollow and deceptive philosophy, which depends on human tradition and the basic principles of this world rather than on Christ.

[9]For in Christ all the fullness of the Deity lives in bodily form, [10]and you have been given fullness in Christ, who is the head over every power and authority. [11]In him you were also circumcised, in the putting off of the sinful nature,[a] not with a circumcision done by the hands of men but with the circumcision done by Christ, [12]having been buried with him in baptism and raised with him through your faith in the power of God, who raised him from the dead.

[13]When you were dead in your sins and in the uncircumcision of your sinful nature,[b] God made you[c] alive with Christ. He forgave us all our sins, [14]having canceled the

[a] *11* Or *the flesh* [b] *13* Or *your flesh* [c] *13* Some manuscripts *us*

NEW LIVING TRANSLATION

your roots grow down into him and draw up nourishment from him, so you will grow in faith, strong and vigorous in the truth you were taught. Let your lives overflow with thanksgiving for all he has done.

[8]Don't let anyone lead you astray with empty philosophy and high-sounding nonsense that come from human thinking and from the evil powers of this world,* and not from Christ. [9]For in Christ the fullness of God lives in a human body,* [10]and you are complete through your union with Christ. He is the Lord over every ruler and authority in the universe.

[11]When you came to Christ, you were "circumcised," but not by a physical procedure. It was a spiritual procedure—the cutting away of your sinful nature. [12]For you were buried with Christ when you were baptized. And with him you were raised to a new life because you trusted the mighty power of God, who raised Christ from the dead.

[13]You were dead because of your sins and because your sinful nature was not yet cut away. Then God made you alive with Christ. He forgave all our sins. [14]He canceled the

2:8 Or *from the basic principles of this world;* also in 2:20. 2:9 Greek *in him dwells all the fullness of the Godhead bodily.*

NEW KING JAMES VERSION

in the faith, as you have been taught, abounding in it[b] with thanksgiving.

[8]Beware lest anyone cheat you through philosophy and empty deceit, according to the tradition of men, according to the basic principles of the world, and not according to Christ. [9]For in Him dwells all the fullness of the Godhead bodily; [10]and you are complete in Him, who is the head of all principality and power.

Not Legalism but Christ

[11]In Him you were also circumcised with the circumcision made without hands, by putting off the body of the sins[c] of the flesh, by the circumcision of Christ, [12]buried with Him in baptism, in which you also were raised with *Him* through faith in the working of God, who raised Him from the dead. [13]And you, being dead in your trespasses and the uncircumcision of your flesh, He has made alive together with Him, having forgiven you all trespasses,

2:7 [b] NU-Text omits *in it.* 2:11 [c] NU-Text omits *of the sins.*

THE MESSAGE

Jesus, the Master; now *live* him. You're deeply rooted in him. You're well constructed upon him. You know your way around the faith. Now do what you've been taught. School's out; quit studying the subject and start *living* it! And let your living spill over into thanksgiving.

Watch out for people who try to dazzle you with big words and intellectual double-talk. They want to drag you off into endless arguments that never amount to anything. They spread their ideas through the empty traditions of human beings and the empty superstitions of spirit beings. But that's not the way of Christ. Everything of God gets expressed in him, so you can see and hear him clearly. You don't need a telescope, a microscope, or a horoscope to realize the fullness of Christ, and the emptiness of the universe without him. When you come to him, that fullness comes together for you, too. His power extends over everything.

Entering into this fullness is not something you figure out or achieve. It's not a matter of being circumcised or keeping a long list of laws. No, you're already *in*—insiders—not through some secretive initiation rite but rather through what Christ has already gone through for you, destroying the power of sin. If it's an initiation ritual you're after, you've already been through it by submitting to baptism. Going under the water was a burial of your old life; coming up out of it was a resurrection, God raising you from the dead as he did Christ. When you were stuck in your old sin-dead life, you were incapable of responding to God. God brought you alive—right along with Christ! Think of it! All sins forgiven, the slate wiped clean, that

KING JAMES VERSION

14 Blotting out the handwriting of ordinances that was against us, which was contrary to us, and took it out of the way, nailing it to his cross;

15 *And* having spoiled principalities and powers, he made a shew of them openly, triumphing over them in it.

16 ¶ Let no man therefore judge you in meat, or in drink, or in respect of an holyday, or of the new moon, or of the sabbath *days*:

17 Which are a shadow of things to come; but the body *is* of Christ.

18 Let no man beguile you of your reward in a voluntary humility and worshipping of angels, intruding into those things which he hath not seen, vainly puffed up by his fleshly mind,

19 And not holding the Head, from which all the body by joints and bands having nourishment ministered, and knit together, increaseth with the increase of God.

20 Wherefore if ye be dead with Christ from the rudiments of the world, why, as though living in the world, are ye subject to ordinances,

21 (Touch not; taste not; handle not;

22 Which all are to perish with the using;) after the commandments and doctrines of men?

23 Which things have indeed a shew of wisdom in will worship, and humility, and neglecting of the body; not in any honour to the satisfying of the flesh.

NEW AMERICAN STANDARD BIBLE

14 having canceled out the certificate of debt consisting of decrees against us, which was hostile to us; and He has taken it out of the way, having nailed it to the cross.

15 When He had disarmed the rulers and authorities, He made a public display of them, having triumphed over them through Him.

16 Therefore no one is to act as your judge in regard to food or drink or in respect to a festival or a new moon or a Sabbath day—

17 things which are a *mere* shadow of what is to come; but the substance belongs to Christ.

18 Let no one keep defrauding you of your prize by delighting in self-abasement and the worship of the angels, taking his stand on *visions* he has seen, inflated without cause by his fleshly mind,

19 and not holding fast to the head, from whom the entire body, being supplied and held together by the joints and ligaments, grows with a growth which is from God.

20 If you have died with Christ to the elementary principles of the world, why, as if you were living in the world, do you submit yourself to decrees, such as,

21 "Do not handle, do not taste, do not touch!"

22 (which all *refer to* things destined to perish with use)—in accordance with the commandments and teachings of men?

23 These are matters which have, to be sure, the appearance of wisdom in self-made religion and self-abasement and severe treatment of the body, *but are* of no value against fleshly indulgence.

NEW CENTURY VERSION

canceled the debt, which listed all the rules we failed to
follow. He took away that record with its rules and nailed
it to the cross. 15God stripped the spiritual rulers and pow-
ers of their authority. With the cross, he won the victory
and showed the world that they were powerless.

Don't Follow People's Rules

16So do not let anyone make rules for you about eating
and drinking or about a religious feast, a New Moon
Festival, or a Sabbath day. 17These things were like a
shadow of what was to come. But what is true and real
has come and is found in Christ. 18Do not let anyone dis-
qualify you by making you humiliate yourself and worship
angels. Such people enter into visions, which fill them
with foolish pride because of their human way of thinking.
19They do not hold tightly to Christ, the head. It is from
him that all the parts of the body are cared for and held
together. So it grows in the way God wants it to grow.
20Since you died with Christ and were made free from
the ruling spirits of the world, why do you act as if you
still belong to this world by following rules like these:
21"Don't eat this," "Don't taste that," "Don't even touch
that thing"? 22These rules refer to earthly things that are
gone as soon as they are used. They are only man-made
commands and teachings. 23They seem to be wise, but
they are only part of a man-made religion. They make peo-
ple pretend not to be proud and make them punish their
bodies, but they do not really control the evil desires of the
sinful self.

CONTEMPORARY ENGLISH VERSION

14God wiped out the charges that were against us for
disobeying the Law of Moses. He took them away and
nailed them to the cross. 15There Christ defeated all powers
and forces. He let the whole world see them being led
away as prisoners when he celebrated his victory.
16Don't let anyone tell you what you must eat or drink.
Don't let them say that you must celebrate the New Moon
festival, the Sabbath, or any other festival. 17These things
are only a shadow of what was to come. But Christ is real!
18Don't be cheated by people who make a show of acting
humble and who worship angels.[c] They brag about seeing
visions. But it is all nonsense, because their minds are
filled with selfish desires. 19They are no longer part of
Christ, who is the head of the whole body. Christ gives the
body its strength, and he uses its joints and muscles to
hold it together, as it grows by the power of God.

Christ Brings New Life

20You died with Christ. Now the forces of the universe[d]
don't have any power over you. Why do you live as if you
had to obey such rules as, 21"Don't handle this. Don't taste
that. Don't touch this."? 22After these things are used,
they are no longer good for anything. So why be bothered
with the rules that humans have made up? 23Obeying
these rules may seem to be the smart thing to do. They
appear to make you love God more and to be very humble
and to have control over your body. But they don't really
have any power over our desires.

[c] **2.18** *worship angels*: Or "worship with angels (in visions of heaven)."
[d] **2.20** *forces of the universe*: See the note at 2.8.

NEW INTERNATIONAL VERSION

written code, with its regulations, that was against us and that stood opposed to us; he took it away, nailing it to the cross. 15And having disarmed the powers and authorities, he made a public spectacle of them, triumphing over them by the cross.[d]

16Therefore do not let anyone judge you by what you eat or drink, or with regard to a religious festival, a New Moon celebration or a Sabbath day. 17These are a shadow of the things that were to come; the reality, however, is found in Christ. 18Do not let anyone who delights in false humility and the worship of angels disqualify you for the prize. Such a person goes into great detail about what he has seen, and his unspiritual mind puffs him up with idle notions. 19He has lost connection with the Head, from whom the whole body, supported and held together by its ligaments and sinews, grows as God causes it to grow.

20Since you died with Christ to the basic principles of this world, why, as though you still belonged to it, do you submit to its rules: 21"Do not handle! Do not taste! Do not touch!"? 22These are all destined to perish with use, because they are based on human commands and teachings. 23Such regulations indeed have an appearance of wisdom, with their self-imposed worship, their false humility and their harsh treatment of the body, but they lack any value in restraining sensual indulgence.

[d] *15* Or *them in him*

NEW LIVING TRANSLATION

record that contained the charges against us. He took it and destroyed it by nailing it to Christ's cross. 15In this way, God disarmed the evil rulers and authorities. He shamed them publicly by his victory over them on the cross of Christ.

16So don't let anyone condemn you for what you eat or drink, or for not celebrating certain holy days or new-moon ceremonies or Sabbaths. 17For these rules were only shadows of the real thing, Christ himself. 18Don't let anyone condemn you by insisting on self-denial. And don't let anyone say you must worship angels, even though they say they have had visions about this. These people claim to be so humble, but their sinful minds have made them proud. 19But they are not connected to Christ, the head of the body. For we are joined together in his body by his strong sinews, and we grow only as we get our nourishment and strength from God.

20You have died with Christ, and he has set you free from the evil powers of this world. So why do you keep on following rules of the world, such as, 21"Don't handle, don't eat, don't touch." 22Such rules are mere human teaching about things that are gone as soon as we use them. 23These rules may seem wise because they require strong devotion, humility, and severe bodily discipline. But they have no effect when it comes to conquering a person's evil thoughts and desires.

NEW KING JAMES VERSION

14having wiped out the handwriting of requirements that was against us, which was contrary to us. And He has taken it out of the way, having nailed it to the cross. 15Having disarmed principalities and powers, He made a public spectacle of them, triumphing over them in it.

16So let no one judge you in food or in drink, or regarding a festival or a new moon or sabbaths, 17which are a shadow of things to come, but the substance is of Christ. 18Let no one cheat you of your reward, taking delight in *false* humility and worship of angels, intruding into those things which he has not[d] seen, vainly puffed up by his fleshly mind, 19and not holding fast to the Head, from whom all the body, nourished and knit together by joints and ligaments, grows with the increase *that is* from God.

20Therefore,[e] if you died with Christ from the basic principles of the world, why, as *though* living in the world, do you subject yourselves to regulations—21"Do not touch, do not taste, do not handle," 22which all concern things which perish with the using—according to the commandments and doctrines of men? 23These things indeed have an appearance of wisdom in self-imposed religion, *false* humility, and neglect of the body, *but are* of no value against the indulgence of the flesh.

2:18 [d] NU-Text omits *not.* **2:20** [e] NU-Text and M-Text omit *Therefore.*

THE MESSAGE

old arrest warrant canceled and nailed to Christ's Cross. He stripped all the spiritual tyrants in the universe of their sham authority at the Cross and marched them naked through the streets.

So don't put up with anyone pressuring you in details of diet, worship services, or holy days. All those things are mere shadows cast before what was to come; the substance is Christ.

Don't tolerate people who try to run your life, ordering you to bow and scrape, insisting that you join their obsession with angels and that you seek out visions. They're a lot of hot air, that's all they are. They're completely out of touch with the source of life, Christ, who puts us together in one piece, whose very breath and blood flow through us. He is the Head and we are the body. We can grow up healthy in God only as he nourishes us.

So, then, if with Christ you've put all that pretentious and infantile religion behind you, why do you let yourselves be bullied by it? "Don't touch this! Don't taste that! Don't go near this!" Do you think things that are here today and gone tomorrow are worth that kind of attention? Such things sound impressive if said in a deep enough voice. They even give the illusion of being pious and humble and ascetic. But they're just another way of showing off, making yourselves look important.

KING JAMES VERSION

3 If ye then be risen with Christ, seek those things which are above, where Christ sitteth on the right hand of God.

2 Set your affection on things above, not on things on the earth.

3 For ye are dead, and your life is hid with Christ in God.

4 When Christ, *who is* our life, shall appear, then shall ye also appear with him in glory.

5 ¶ Mortify therefore your members which are upon the earth; fornication, uncleanness, inordinate affection, evil concupiscence, and covetousness, which is idolatry:

6 For which things' sake the wrath of God cometh on the children of disobedience:

7 In the which ye also walked some time, when ye lived in them.

8 ¶ But now ye also put off all these; anger, wrath, malice, blasphemy, filthy communication out of your mouth.

9 Lie not one to another, seeing that ye have put off the old man with his deeds;

10 And have put on the new *man*, which is renewed in knowledge after the image of him that created him:

NEW AMERICAN STANDARD BIBLE

Put On the New Self

3 Therefore if you have been raised up with Christ, keep seeking the things above, where Christ is, seated at the right hand of God.

2 Set your mind on the things above, not on the things that are on earth.

3 For you have died and your life is hidden with Christ in God.

4 When Christ, who is our life, is revealed, then you also will be revealed with Him in glory.

5 Therefore consider the members of your earthly body as dead to immorality, impurity, passion, evil desire, and greed, which amounts to idolatry.

6 For it is because of these things that the wrath of God will come [1]upon the sons of disobedience,

7 and in them you also once walked, when you were living in them.

8 But now you also, put them all aside: anger, wrath, malice, slander, *and* abusive speech from your mouth.

9 Do not lie to one another, since you laid aside the old self with its *evil* practices,

10 and have put on the new self who is being renewed to a true knowledge according to the image of the One who created him—

3:6 [1] Two early mss do not contain *upon the sons of disobedience*

NEW CENTURY VERSION

Your New Life in Christ

3 Since you were raised from the dead with Christ, aim at what is in heaven, where Christ is sitting at the
right hand of God. 2 Think only about the things in heaven,
not the things on earth. 3 Your old sinful self has died, and
your new life is kept with Christ in God. 4 Christ is our life,
and when he comes again, you will share in his glory.

5 So put all evil things out of your life: sexual sinning,
doing evil, letting evil thoughts control you, wanting
things that are evil, and greed. This is really serving a
false god. 6 These things make God angry.[a] 7 In your past,
evil life you also did these things.

8 But now also put these things out of your life: anger,
bad temper, doing or saying things to hurt others, and
using evil words when you talk. 9 Do not lie to each other.
You have left your old sinful life and the things you did
before. 10 You have begun to live the new life, in which you
are being made new and are becoming like the One who
made you. This new life brings you the true knowledge of

3:6 [a] **These...angry** Some Greek copies add: "against the people who do not obey God."

CONTEMPORARY ENGLISH VERSION

3 You have been raised to life with Christ. Now set your heart on what is in heaven, where Christ rules at
God's right side.[a] 2 Think about what is up there, not about
what is here on earth. 3 You died, which means that your
life is hidden with Christ, who sits beside God. 4 Christ
gives meaning to your[b] life, and when he appears, you will
also appear with him in glory.

5 Don't be controlled by your body. Kill every desire for
the wrong kind of sex. Don't be immoral or indecent or
have evil thoughts. Don't be greedy, which is the same as
worshiping idols. 6 God is angry with people who disobey
him by doing[c] these things. 7 And that is exactly what you
did, when you lived among people who behaved in this
way. 8 But now you must stop doing such things. You must
quit being angry, hateful, and evil. You must no longer say
insulting or cruel things about others. 9 And stop lying to
each other. You have given up your old way of life with its
habits.

10 Each of you is now a new person. You are becoming
more and more like your Creator, and you will understand

[a] 3.1 *right side*: The place of power and honor. [b] 3.4 *your*: Some manuscripts have "our." [c] 3.6 *people who disobey him by doing*: Some manuscripts do not have these words.

NEW INTERNATIONAL VERSION

Rules for Holy Living

3 Since, then, you have been raised with Christ, set your
hearts on things above, where Christ is seated at the
right hand of God. 2Set your minds on things above, not
on earthly things. 3For you died, and your life is now hid-
den with Christ in God. 4When Christ, who is your[a] life,
appears, then you also will appear with him in glory.
5Put to death, therefore, whatever belongs to your earth-
ly nature: sexual immorality, impurity, lust, evil desires
and greed, which is idolatry. 6Because of these, the wrath
of God is coming.[b] 7You used to walk in these ways, in the
life you once lived. 8But now you must rid yourselves of all
such things as these: anger, rage, malice, slander, and
filthy language from your lips. 9Do not lie to each other,
since you have taken off your old self with its practices
10and have put on the new self, which is being renewed in
knowledge in the image of its Creator. 11Here there is no

[a] 4 Some manuscripts *our* [b] 6 Some early manuscripts *coming on those who are disobedient*

NEW LIVING TRANSLATION

Living the New Life

3 Since you have been raised to new life with Christ, set
your sights on the realities of heaven, where Christ
sits at God's right hand in the place of honor and power.
2Let heaven fill your thoughts. Do not think only about
things down here on earth. 3For you died when Christ died,
and your real life is hidden with Christ in God. 4And when
Christ, who is your* real life, is revealed to the whole
world, you will share in all his glory.
5So put to death the sinful, earthly things lurking within
you. Have nothing to do with sexual sin, impurity, lust,
and shameful desires. Don't be greedy for the good things
of this life, for that is idolatry. 6God's terrible anger will
come upon those who do such things. 7You used to do
them when your life was still part of this world. 8But now
is the time to get rid of anger, rage, malicious behavior,
slander, and dirty language. 9Don't lie to each other, for
you have stripped off your old evil nature and all its
wicked deeds. 10In its place you have clothed yourselves
with a brand-new nature that is continually being renewed
as you learn more and more about Christ, who created this
new nature within you. 11In this new life, it doesn't matter

3:4 Some manuscripts read *our*.

NEW KING JAMES VERSION

Not Carnality but Christ

3 If then you were raised with Christ, seek those things
which are above, where Christ is, sitting at the right
hand of God. 2Set your mind on things above, not on
things on the earth. 3For you died, and your life is hidden
with Christ in God. 4When Christ *who is* our life appears,
then you also will appear with Him in glory.
5Therefore put to death your members which are on the
earth: fornication, uncleanness, passion, evil desire, and
covetousness, which is idolatry. 6Because of these things
the wrath of God is coming upon the sons of disobedience,
7in which you yourselves once walked when you lived in
them.
8But now you yourselves are to put off all these: anger,
wrath, malice, blasphemy, filthy language out of your
mouth. 9Do not lie to one another, since you have put off
the old man with his deeds, 10and have put on the new
man who is renewed in knowledge according to the image
of Him who created him, 11where there is neither Greek

THE MESSAGE

He Is Your Life

3 So if you're serious about living this new resurrection life with Christ, *act* like it. Pursue the things over which Christ presides. Don't shuffle along, eyes to the ground, absorbed with the things right in front of you. Look up, and be alert to what is going on around Christ—that's where the action is. See things from *his* perspective.

Your old life is dead. Your new life, which is your *real* life—even though invisible to spectators—is with Christ in God. *He* is your life. When Christ (your real life, remember) shows up again on this earth, you'll show up, too—the real you, the glorious you. Meanwhile, be content with obscurity, like Christ.

And that means killing off everything connected with that way of death: sexual promiscuity, impurity, lust, doing whatever you feel like whenever you feel like it, and grabbing whatever attracts your fancy. That's a life shaped by things and feelings instead of by God. It's because of this kind of thing that God is about to explode in anger. It wasn't long ago that you were doing all that stuff and not knowing any better. But you know better now, so make sure it's all gone for good: bad temper, irritability, meanness, profanity, dirty talk.

Don't lie to one another. You're done with that old life. It's like a filthy set of ill-fitting clothes you've stripped off and put in the fire. Now you're dressed in a new wardrobe. Every item of your new way of life is custom-made by the Creator, with his label on it. All the old fashions are now obsolete. Words like Jewish and non-Jewish, religious and

KING JAMES VERSION

11 Where there is neither Greek nor Jew, circumcision nor uncircumcision, Barbarian, Scythian, bond *nor* free: but Christ *is* all, and in all.

12 ¶ Put on therefore, as the elect of God, holy and beloved, bowels of mercies, kindness, humbleness of mind, meekness, longsuffering;

13 Forbearing one another, and forgiving one another, if any man have a quarrel against any: even as Christ forgave you, so also *do* ye.

14 And above all these things *put on* charity, which is the bond of perfectness.

15 And let the peace of God rule in your hearts, to the which also ye are called in one body; and be ye thankful.

16 Let the word of Christ dwell in you richly in all wisdom; teaching and admonishing one another in psalms and hymns and spiritual songs, singing with grace in your hearts to the Lord.

17 And whatsoever ye do in word or deed, *do* all in the name of the Lord Jesus, giving thanks to God and the Father by him.

18 ¶ Wives, submit yourselves unto your own husbands, as it is fit in the Lord.

19 Husbands, love *your* wives, and be not bitter against them.

NEW AMERICAN STANDARD BIBLE

11 *a renewal* in which there is no *distinction between* Greek and Jew, circumcised and uncircumcised, barbarian, Scythian, slave and freeman, but Christ is all, and in all.

12 So, as those who have been chosen of God, holy and beloved, put on a heart of compassion, kindness, humility, gentleness and patience;

13 bearing with one another, and forgiving each other, whoever has a complaint against anyone; just as the Lord forgave you, so also should you.

14 Beyond all these things *put on* love, which is the perfect bond of unity.

15 Let the peace of Christ rule in your hearts, to which indeed you were called in one body; and be thankful.

16 Let the word of [2]Christ richly dwell within you, with all wisdom teaching and admonishing one another with psalms *and* hymns *and* spiritual songs, singing with thankfulness in your hearts to God.

17 Whatever you do in word or deed, *do* all in the name of the Lord Jesus, giving thanks through Him to God the Father.

Family Relations

18 Wives, be subject to your husbands, as is fitting in the Lord.

19 Husbands, love your wives and do not be embittered against them.

3:16 [2] One early ms reads *the Lord*

NEW CENTURY VERSION

God. 11In the new life there is no difference between Greeks
and Jews, those who are circumcised and those who are not
circumcised, or people who are foreigners, or Scythians.[b]
There is no difference between slaves and free people. But
Christ is in all believers, and Christ is all that is important.
12God has chosen you and made you his holy people. He
loves you. So always do these things: Show mercy to others, be kind, humble, gentle, and patient. 13Get along with
each other, and forgive each other. If someone does wrong
to you, forgive that person because the Lord forgave you.
14Do all these things; but most important, love each other.
Love is what holds you all together in perfect unity. 15Let
the peace that Christ gives control your thinking, because
you were all called together in one body[c] to have peace.
Always be thankful. 16Let the teaching of Christ live in you
richly. Use all wisdom to teach and instruct each other by
singing psalms, hymns, and spiritual songs with thankfulness in your hearts to God. 17Everything you do or say
should be done to obey Jesus your Lord. And in all you do,
give thanks to God the Father through Jesus.

Your New Life with Other People

18Wives, yield to the authority of your husbands,
because this is the right thing to do in the Lord.
19Husbands, love your wives and be gentle with them.

3:11 [b] **Scythians** The Scythians were known as very wild and cruel people. 3:15 [c] **body** The spiritual body of Christ, meaning the church or his people.

CONTEMPORARY ENGLISH VERSION

him better. 11It doesn't matter if you are a Greek or a Jew,
or if you are circumcised or not. You may even be a barbarian or a Scythian,[d] and you may be a slave or a free person. Yet Christ is all that matters, and he lives in all of us.
12God loves you and has chosen you as his own special
people. So be gentle, kind, humble, meek, and patient.
13Put up with each other, and forgive anyone who does
you wrong, just as Christ has forgiven you. 14Love is more
important than anything else. It is what ties everything
completely together.
15Each one of you is part of the body of Christ, and you
were chosen to live together in peace. So let the peace that
comes from Christ control your thoughts. And be grateful.
16Let the message about Christ completely fill your lives,
while you use all your wisdom to teach and instruct each
other. With thankful hearts, sing psalms, hymns, and spiritual songs to God. 17Whatever you say or do should be
done in the name of the Lord Jesus, as you give thanks to
God the Father because of him.

Some Rules for Christian Living

18A wife must put her husband first. This is her duty as
a follower of the Lord.
19A husband must love his wife and not abuse her.

[d] 3.11 *a barbarian or a Scythian*: Barbarians were people who could not speak Greek and would be in the lower class of society. Scythians were people who were known for their cruelty.

NEW INTERNATIONAL VERSION

Greek or Jew, circumcised or uncircumcised, barbarian, Scythian, slave or free, but Christ is all, and is in all.

12Therefore, as God's chosen people, holy and dearly loved, clothe yourselves with compassion, kindness, humility, gentleness and patience. 13Bear with each other and forgive whatever grievances you may have against one another. Forgive as the Lord forgave you. 14And over all these virtues put on love, which binds them all together in perfect unity.

15Let the peace of Christ rule in your hearts, since as members of one body you were called to peace. And be thankful. 16Let the word of Christ dwell in you richly as you teach and admonish one another with all wisdom, and as you sing psalms, hymns and spiritual songs with gratitude in your hearts to God. 17And whatever you do, whether in word or deed, do it all in the name of the Lord Jesus, giving thanks to God the Father through him.

Rules for Christian Households

18Wives, submit to your husbands, as is fitting in the Lord.

19Husbands, love your wives and do not be harsh with them.

NEW LIVING TRANSLATION

if you are a Jew or a Gentile,* circumcised or uncircumcised, barbaric, uncivilized,* slave, or free. Christ is all that matters, and he lives in all of us.

12Since God chose you to be the holy people whom he loves, you must clothe yourselves with tenderhearted mercy, kindness, humility, gentleness, and patience. 13You must make allowance for each other's faults and forgive the person who offends you. Remember, the Lord forgave you, so you must forgive others. 14And the most important piece of clothing you must wear is love. Love is what binds us all together in perfect harmony. 15And let the peace that comes from Christ rule in your hearts. For as members of one body you are all called to live in peace. And always be thankful.

16Let the words of Christ, in all their richness, live in your hearts and make you wise. Use his words to teach and counsel each other. Sing psalms and hymns and spiritual songs to God with thankful hearts. 17And whatever you do or say, let it be as a representative of the Lord Jesus, all the while giving thanks through him to God the Father.

Instructions for Christian Households

18You wives must submit to your husbands, as is fitting for those who belong to the Lord. 19And you husbands must love your wives and never treat them harshly.

3:11a Greek *Greek*. **3:11b** Greek *Barbarian, Scythian*.

NEW KING JAMES VERSION

nor Jew, circumcised nor uncircumcised, barbarian, Scythian, slave *nor* free, but Christ *is* all and in all.

Character of the New Man

12Therefore, as *the* elect of God, holy and beloved, put on tender mercies, kindness, humility, meekness, longsuffering; 13bearing with one another, and forgiving one another, if anyone has a complaint against another; even as Christ forgave you, so you also *must do.* 14But above all these things put on love, which is the bond of perfection. 15And let the peace of God rule in your hearts, to which also you were called in one body; and be thankful. 16Let the word of Christ dwell in you richly in all wisdom, teaching and admonishing one another in psalms and hymns and spiritual songs, singing with grace in your hearts to the Lord. 17And *whatever* you do in word or deed, *do* all in the name of the Lord Jesus, giving thanks to God the Father through Him.

The Christian Home

18Wives, submit to your own husbands, as is fitting in the Lord.

19Husbands, love your wives and do not be bitter toward them.

THE MESSAGE

irreligious, insider and outsider, uncivilized and uncouth, slave and free, mean nothing. From now on everyone is defined by Christ, everyone is included in Christ.

So, chosen by God for this new life of love, dress in the wardrobe God picked out for you: compassion, kindness, humility, quiet strength, discipline. Be even-tempered, content with second place, quick to forgive an offense. Forgive as quickly and completely as the Master forgave you. And regardless of what else you put on, wear love. It's your basic, all-purpose garment. Never be without it.

Let the peace of Christ keep you in tune with each other, in step with each other. None of this going off and doing your own thing. And cultivate thankfulness. Let the Word of Christ—the Message—have the run of the house. Give it plenty of room in your lives. Instruct and direct one another using good common sense. And sing, sing your hearts out to God! Let every detail in your lives—words, actions, whatever—be done in the name of the Master, Jesus, thanking God the Father every step of the way.

✠

Wives, understand and support your husbands by submitting to them in ways that honor the Master.

Husbands, go all out in love for your wives. Don't take advantage of them.

KING JAMES VERSION

20 Children, obey *your* parents in all things: for this is well pleasing unto the Lord.

21 Fathers, provoke not your children *to anger*, lest they be discouraged.

22 Servants, obey in all things *your* masters according to the flesh; not with eyeservice, as menpleasers; but in singleness of heart, fearing God:

23 And whatsoever ye do, do *it* heartily, as to the Lord, and not unto men;

24 Knowing that of the Lord ye shall receive the reward of the inheritance: for ye serve the Lord Christ.

25 But he that doeth wrong shall receive for the wrong which he hath done: and there is no respect of persons.

4 Masters, give unto *your* servants that which is just and equal; knowing that ye also have a Master in heaven.

2 ¶ Continue in prayer, and watch in the same with thanksgiving;

3 Withal praying also for us, that God would open unto us a door of utterance, to speak the mystery of Christ, for which I am also in bonds:

4 That I may make it manifest, as I ought to speak.

5 ¶ Walk in wisdom toward them that are without, redeeming the time.

6 Let your speech *be* alway with grace, seasoned with salt, that ye may know how ye ought to answer every man.

NEW AMERICAN STANDARD BIBLE

20 Children, be obedient to your parents in all things, for this is well-pleasing to the Lord.

21 Fathers, do not exasperate your children, so that they will not lose heart.

22 Slaves, in all things obey those who are your masters on earth, not with external service, as those who *merely* please men, but with sincerity of heart, fearing the Lord.

23 Whatever you do, do your work heartily, as for the Lord rather than for men,

24 knowing that from the Lord you will receive the reward of the inheritance. It is the Lord Christ whom you serve.

25 For he who does wrong will receive the consequences of the wrong which he has done, and that without partiality.

Fellow Workers

4 Masters, grant to your slaves justice and fairness, knowing that you too have a Master in heaven.

2 Devote yourselves to prayer, keeping alert in it with *an attitude of* thanksgiving;

3 praying at the same time for us as well, that God will open up to us a door for the word, so that we may speak forth the mystery of Christ, for which I have also been imprisoned;

4 that I may make it clear in the way I ought to speak.

5 Conduct yourselves with wisdom toward outsiders, making the most of the opportunity.

6 Let your speech always be with grace, *as though* seasoned with salt, so that you will know how you should respond to each person.

NEW CENTURY VERSION

20 Children, obey your parents in all things, because this pleases the Lord.

21 Fathers, do not nag your children. If you are too hard to please, they may want to stop trying.

22 Slaves, obey your masters in all things. Do not obey
just when they are watching you, to gain their favor, but
serve them honestly, because you respect the Lord. 23 In all
the work you are doing, work the best you can. Work as if
you were doing it for the Lord, not for people. 24 Remember
that you will receive your reward from the Lord, which he
promised to his people. You are serving the Lord Christ.
25 But remember that anyone who does wrong will be pun-
ished for that wrong, and the Lord treats everyone the
same.

4 Masters, give what is good and fair to your slaves. Remember that you have a Master in heaven.

What the Christians Are to Do

2 Continue praying, keeping alert, and always thanking
God. 3 Also pray for us that God will give us an opportunity
to tell people his message. Pray that we can preach the
secret that God has made known about Christ. This is why
I am in prison. 4 Pray that I can speak in a way that will
make it clear, as I should.

5 Be wise in the way you act with people who are not
believers, making the most of every opportunity. 6 When
you talk, you should always be kind and pleasant so you
will be able to answer everyone in the way you should.

CONTEMPORARY ENGLISH VERSION

20 Children must always obey their parents. This pleases the Lord.

21 Parents, don't be hard on your children. If you are, they might give up.

22 Slaves, you must always obey your earthly masters.
Try to please them at all times, and not just when you
think they are watching. Honor the Lord and serve your
masters with your whole heart. 23 Do your work willingly,
as though you were serving the Lord himself, and not just
your earthly master. 24 In fact, the Lord Christ is the one
you are really serving, and you know that he will reward
you. 25 But Christ has no favorites! He will punish evil peo-
ple, just as they deserve.

4 Slave owners, be fair and honest with your slaves. Don't forget that you have a Master in heaven.

2 Never give up praying. And when you pray, keep alert
and be thankful. 3 Be sure to pray that God will make a
way for us to spread his message and explain the mystery
about Christ, even though I am in jail for doing this.
4 Please pray that I will make the message as clear as pos-
sible.

5 When you are with unbelievers, always make good use
of the time. 6 Be pleasant and hold their interest when you
speak the message. Choose your words carefully and be
ready to give answers to anyone who asks questions.

NEW INTERNATIONAL VERSION

20Children, obey your parents in everything, for this
pleases the Lord.

21Fathers, do not embitter your children, or they will
become discouraged.

22Slaves, obey your earthly masters in everything; and
do it, not only when their eye is on you and to win their
favor, but with sincerity of heart and reverence for the
Lord. 23Whatever you do, work at it with all your heart, as
working for the Lord, not for men, 24since you know that
you will receive an inheritance from the Lord as a reward.
It is the Lord Christ you are serving. 25Anyone who does
wrong will be repaid for his wrong, and there is no
favoritism.

4 Masters, provide your slaves with what is right and
fair, because you know that you also have a Master in
heaven.

Further Instructions

2Devote yourselves to prayer, being watchful and thank-
ful. 3And pray for us, too, that God may open a door for
our message, so that we may proclaim the mystery of
Christ, for which I am in chains. 4Pray that I may proclaim
it clearly, as I should. 5Be wise in the way you act toward
outsiders; make the most of every opportunity. 6Let your
conversation be always full of grace, seasoned with salt,
so that you may know how to answer everyone.

NEW LIVING TRANSLATION

20You children must always obey your parents, for this
is what pleases the Lord. 21Fathers, don't aggravate your
children. If you do, they will become discouraged and quit
trying.

22You slaves must obey your earthly masters in every-
thing you do. Try to please them all the time, not just
when they are watching you. Obey them willingly because
of your reverent fear of the Lord. 23Work hard and cheer-
fully at whatever you do, as though you were working for
the Lord rather than for people. 24Remember that the Lord
will give you an inheritance as your reward, and the
Master you are serving is Christ. 25But if you do what is
wrong, you will be paid back for the wrong you have done.
For God has no favorites who can get away with evil.

4 You slave owners must be just and fair to your slaves.
Remember that you also have a Master—in heaven.

An Encouragement for Prayer

2Devote yourselves to prayer with an alert mind and a
thankful heart. 3Don't forget to pray for us, too, that God
will give us many opportunities to preach about his secret
plan—that Christ is also for you Gentiles. That is why I am
here in chains. 4Pray that I will proclaim this message as
clearly as I should.

5Live wisely among those who are not Christians, and
make the most of every opportunity. 6Let your conversa-
tion be gracious and effective so that you will have the
right answer for everyone.

NEW KING JAMES VERSION

20Children, obey your parents in all things, for this is
well pleasing to the Lord.

21Fathers, do not provoke your children, lest they
become discouraged.

22Bondservants, obey in all things your masters accord-
ing to the flesh, not with eyeservice, as men-pleasers, but
in sincerity of heart, fearing God. 23And whatever you do,
do it heartily, as to the Lord and not to men, 24knowing
that from the Lord you will receive the reward of the inher-
itance; for[a] you serve the Lord Christ. 25But he who does
wrong will be repaid for what he has done, and there is no
partiality.

4 Masters, give your bondservants what is just and fair,
knowing that you also have a Master in heaven.

Christian Graces

2Continue earnestly in prayer, being vigilant in it with
thanksgiving; 3meanwhile praying also for us, that God
would open to us a door for the word, to speak the mystery
of Christ, for which I am also in chains, 4that I may make
it manifest, as I ought to speak.

5Walk in wisdom toward those *who are* outside, redeem-
ing the time. 6*Let* your speech always *be* with grace, sea-
soned with salt, that you may know how you ought to
answer each one.

3:24 [a] NU-Text omits *for*.

THE MESSAGE

Children, do what your parents tell you. This delights the Master no end.

Parents, don't come down too hard on your children or you'll crush their spirits.

Servants, do what you're told by your earthly masters. And don't just do the minimum that will get you by. Do your best. Work from the heart for your real Master, for God, confident that you'll get paid in full when you come into your inheritance. Keep in mind always that the ultimate Master you're serving is Christ. The sullen servant who does shoddy work will be held responsible. Being Christian doesn't cover up bad work.

4 And masters, treat your servants considerately. Be fair with them. Don't forget for a minute that you, too, serve a Master—God in heaven.

Pray for Open Doors

Pray diligently. Stay alert, with your eyes wide open in gratitude. Don't forget to pray for us, that God will open doors for telling the mystery of Christ, even while I'm locked up in this jail. Pray that every time I open my mouth I'll be able to make Christ plain as day to them.

Use your heads as you live and work among outsiders. Don't miss a trick. Make the most of every opportunity. Be gracious in your speech. The goal is to bring out the best in others in a conversation, not put them down, not cut them out.

KING JAMES VERSION

7 ¶ All my state shall Tychicus declare unto you, *who is* a beloved brother, and a faithful minister and fellowservant in the Lord:

8 Whom I have sent unto you for the same purpose, that he might know your estate, and comfort your hearts;

9 With Onesimus, a faithful and beloved brother, who is *one* of you. They shall make known unto you all things which *are done* here.

10 Aristarchus my fellowprisoner saluteth you, and Marcus, sister's son to Barnabas, (touching whom ye received commandments: if he come unto you, receive him;)

11 And Jesus, which is called Justus, who are of the circumcision. These only *are my* fellowworkers unto the kingdom of God, which have been a comfort unto me.

12 Epaphras, who is *one* of you, a servant of Christ, saluteth you, always labouring fervently for you in prayers, that ye may stand perfect and complete in all the will of God.

13 For I bear him record, that he hath a great zeal for you, and them *that are* in Laodicea, and them in Hierapolis.

14 Luke, the beloved physician, and Demas, greet you.

15 Salute the brethren which are in Laodicea, and Nymphas, and the church which is in his house.

NEW AMERICAN STANDARD BIBLE

7 As to all my affairs, Tychicus, *our* beloved brother and faithful servant and fellow bond-servant in the Lord, will bring you information.

8 *For* I have sent him to you for this very purpose, that you may know about our circumstances and that he may encourage your hearts;

9 and with him Onesimus, *our* faithful and beloved brother, who is one of your *number.* They will inform you about the whole situation here.

10 Aristarchus, my fellow prisoner, sends you his greetings; and *also* Barnabas' cousin Mark (about whom you received instructions; if he comes to you, welcome him);

11 and *also* Jesus who is called Justus; these are the only fellow workers for the kingdom of God who are from the circumcision, and they have proved to be an encouragement to me.

12 Epaphras, who is one of your number, a bondslave of Jesus Christ, sends you his greetings, always laboring earnestly for you in his prayers, that you may stand perfect and fully assured in all the will of God.

13 For I testify for him that he has a deep concern for you and for those who are in Laodicea and Hierapolis.

14 Luke, the beloved physician, sends you his greetings, and *also* Demas.

15 Greet the brethren who are in Laodicea and also [1]Nympha and the church that is in her house.

4:15 [1] Or *Nymphas* (masc)

NEW CENTURY VERSION

News About the People with Paul

7Tychicus is my dear brother in Christ and a faithful
minister and servant with me in the Lord. He will tell you
all the things that are happening to me. 8This is why I am
sending him: so you may know how we are and he may
encourage you. 9I send him with Onesimus, a faithful and
dear brother in Christ, and one of your group. They will tell
you all that has happened here.

10Aristarchus, a prisoner with me, and Mark, the cousin
of Barnabas, greet you. (I have already told you what to do
about Mark. If he comes, welcome him.) 11Jesus, who is
called Justus, also greets you. These are the only Jewish
believers who work with me for the kingdom of God, and
they have been a comfort to me.

12Epaphras, a servant of Jesus Christ, from your group,
also greets you. He always prays for you that you will
grow to be spiritually mature and have everything God
wants for you. 13I know he has worked hard for you and
the people in Laodicea and in Hierapolis. 14Demas and our
dear friend Luke, the doctor, greet you.

15Greet the brothers in Laodicea. And greet Nympha and
the church that meets in her house. 16After this letter is

CONTEMPORARY ENGLISH VERSION

Final Greetings

7Tychicus is the dear friend, who faithfully works and
serves the Lord with us, and he will give you the news
about me. 8I am sending him to cheer you up by telling
you how we are getting along. 9Onesimus, that dear and
faithful follower from your own group, is coming with him.
The two of them will tell you everything that has happened
here.

10Aristarchus is in jail with me. He sends greetings to
you, and so does Mark, the cousin of Barnabas. You have
already been told to welcome Mark, if he visits you.
11Jesus, who is known as Justus, sends his greetings.
These three men are the only Jewish followers who have
worked with me for the kingdom of God. They have given
me much comfort.

12Your own Epaphras, who serves Christ Jesus, sends his
greetings. He always prays hard that you may fully know
what the Lord wants you to do and that you may do it
completely. 13I have seen how much trouble he has gone
through for you and for the followers in Laodicea and
Hierapolis.

14Our dear doctor Luke sends you his greetings, and so
does Demas.

15Give my greetings to the followers at Laodicea, especially to Nympha and the church that meets in her home.

NEW INTERNATIONAL VERSION

Final Greetings

[7]Tychicus will tell you all the news about me. He is a dear brother, a faithful minister and fellow servant in the Lord. [8]I am sending him to you for the express purpose that you may know about our[a] circumstances and that he may encourage your hearts. [9]He is coming with Onesimus, our faithful and dear brother, who is one of you. They will tell you everything that is happening here.

[10]My fellow prisoner Aristarchus sends you his greetings, as does Mark, the cousin of Barnabas. (You have received instructions about him; if he comes to you, welcome him.) [11]Jesus, who is called Justus, also sends greetings. These are the only Jews among my fellow workers for the kingdom of God, and they have proved a comfort to me. [12]Epaphras, who is one of you and a servant of Christ Jesus, sends greetings. He is always wrestling in prayer for you, that you may stand firm in all the will of God, mature and fully assured. [13]I vouch for him that he is working hard for you and for those at Laodicea and Hierapolis. [14]Our dear friend Luke, the doctor, and Demas send greetings. [15]Give my greetings to the brothers at Laodicea, and to Nympha and the church in her house.

[a] *8* Some manuscripts *that he may know about your*

NEW LIVING TRANSLATION

Paul's Final Instructions and Greetings

[7]Tychicus, a much loved brother, will tell you how I am getting along. He is a faithful helper who serves the Lord with me. [8]I have sent him on this special trip to let you know how we are doing and to encourage you. [9]I am also sending Onesimus, a faithful and much loved brother, one of your own people. He and Tychicus will give you all the latest news.

[10]Aristarchus, who is in prison with me, sends you his greetings, and so does Mark, Barnabas's cousin. And as you were instructed before, make Mark welcome if he comes your way. [11]Jesus (the one we call Justus) also sends his greetings. These are the only Jewish Christians among my co-workers; they are working with me here for the Kingdom of God. And what a comfort they have been!

[12]Epaphras, from your city, a servant of Christ Jesus, sends you his greetings. He always prays earnestly for you, asking God to make you strong and perfect, fully confident of the whole will of God. [13]I can assure you that he has agonized for you and also for the Christians in Laodicea and Hierapolis.

[14]Dear Doctor Luke sends his greetings, and so does Demas. [15]Please give my greetings to our Christian brothers and sisters* at Laodicea, and to Nympha and those who meet in her house.

4:15 Greek *brothers.*

NEW KING JAMES VERSION

Final Greetings

[7]Tychicus, a beloved brother, faithful minister, and fellow servant in the Lord, will tell you all the news about me. [8]I am sending him to you for this very purpose, that he[a] may know your circumstances and comfort your hearts, [9]with Onesimus, a faithful and beloved brother, who is *one* of you. They will make known to you all things which *are happening* here.

[10]Aristarchus my fellow prisoner greets you, with Mark the cousin of Barnabas (about whom you received instructions: if he comes to you, welcome him), [11]and Jesus who is called Justus. These *are my* only fellow workers for the kingdom of God who are of the circumcision; they have proved to be a comfort to me.

[12]Epaphras, who is *one* of you, a bondservant of Christ, greets you, always laboring fervently for you in prayers, that you may stand perfect and complete[b] in all the will of God. [13]For I bear him witness that he has a great zeal[c] for you, and those who are in Laodicea, and those in Hierapolis. [14]Luke the beloved physician and Demas greet you. [15]Greet the brethren who are in Laodicea, and Nymphas and the church that *is* in his[d] house.

4:8 [a] NU-Text reads *you may know our circumstances and he may.*
4:12 [b] NU-Text reads *fully assured.* **4:13** [c] NU-Text reads *concern.*
4:15 [d] NU-Text reads *Nympha . . . her house.*

THE MESSAGE

My good friend Tychicus will tell you all about me. He's a trusted minister and companion in the service of the Master. I've sent him to you so that you would know how things are with us, and so he could encourage you in your faith. And I've sent Onesimus with him. Onesimus is one of you, and has become such a trusted and dear brother! Together they'll bring you up-to-date on everything that has been going on here.

Aristarchus, who is in jail here with me, sends greetings; also Mark, cousin of Barnabas (you received a letter regarding him; if he shows up, welcome him); and also Jesus, the one they call Justus. These are the only ones left from the old crowd who have stuck with me in working for God's kingdom. Don't think they haven't been a big help!

Epaphras, who is one of you, says hello. What a trooper he has been! He's been tireless in his prayers for you, praying that you'll stand firm, mature and confident in everything God wants you to do. I've watched him closely, and can report on how hard he has worked for you and for those in Laodicea and Hierapolis.

Luke, good friend and physician, and Demas both send greetings.

Say hello to our friends in Laodicea; also to Nympha and the church that meets in her house.

KING JAMES VERSION

16 And when this epistle is read among you, cause that it be read also in the church of the Laodiceans; and that ye likewise read the *epistle* from Laodicea.

17 And say to Archippus, Take heed to the ministry which thou hast received in the Lord, that thou fulfil it.

18 The salutation by the hand of me Paul. Remember my bonds. Grace *be* with you. Amen.

NEW AMERICAN STANDARD BIBLE

16 When this letter is read among you, have it also read in the church of the Laodiceans; and you, for your part read my letter *that is coming* from Laodicea.

17 Say to Archippus, "Take heed to the ministry which you have received in the Lord, that you may fulfill it."

18 I, Paul, write this greeting with my own hand. Remember my imprisonment. Grace be with you.

NEW CENTURY VERSION

read to you, be sure it is also read to the church in Laodicea. And you read the letter that I wrote to Laodicea.
17Tell Archippus, "Be sure to finish the work the Lord gave you."

18I, Paul, greet you and write this with my own hand. Remember me in prison. Grace be with you.

CONTEMPORARY ENGLISH VERSION

16After this letter has been read to your people, be sure to have it read in the church at Laodicea. And you should read the letter that I have sent to them.[a]

17Remind Archippus to do the work that the Lord has given him to do.

18I am signing this letter myself: PAUL.

Don't forget that I am in jail.

I pray that God will be kind to you.

[a] 4.16 *the letter that I have sent to them*: This is the only mention of the letter to the church at Laodicea.

NEW INTERNATIONAL VERSION

16After this letter has been read to you, see that it is also read in the church of the Laodiceans and that you in turn read the letter from Laodicea.

17Tell Archippus: "See to it that you complete the work you have received in the Lord."

18I, Paul, write this greeting in my own hand. Remember my chains. Grace be with you.

NEW LIVING TRANSLATION

16After you have read this letter, pass it on to the church at Laodicea so they can read it, too. And you should read the letter I wrote to them. 17And say to Archippus, "Be sure to carry out the work the Lord gave you."

18Here is my greeting in my own handwriting—PAUL. Remember my chains.

May the grace of God be with you.

NEW KING JAMES VERSION

Closing Exhortations and Blessing

16Now when this epistle is read among you, see that it is read also in the church of the Laodiceans, and that you likewise read the epistle from Laodicea. 17And say to Archippus, "Take heed to the ministry which you have received in the Lord, that you may fulfill it."

18This salutation by my own hand—Paul. Remember my chains. Grace *be* with you. Amen.

THE MESSAGE

After this letter has been read to you, make sure it gets read also in Laodicea. And get the letter that went to Laodicea and have it read to you.

And, oh, yes, tell Archippus, "Do your best in the job you received from the Master. Do your very best."

I'm signing off in my own handwriting—Paul. Remember to pray for me in this jail. Grace be with you.

KING JAMES VERSION

THE FIRST EPISTLE OF ST. PAUL TO THE THESSALONIANS

1 Paul, and Silvanus, and Timotheus, unto the church of the Thessalonians *which is* in God the Father and *in* the Lord Jesus Christ: Grace *be* unto you, and peace, from God our Father, and the Lord Jesus Christ.

2 ¶ We give thanks to God always for you all, making mention of you in our prayers;

3 Remembering without ceasing your work of faith, and labour of love, and patience of hope in our Lord Jesus Christ, in the sight of God and our Father;

4 Knowing, brethren beloved, your election of God.

5 For our gospel came not unto you in word only, but also in power, and in the Holy Ghost, and in much assurance; as ye know what manner of men we were among you for your sake.

6 ¶ And ye became followers of us, and of the Lord, having received the word in much affliction, with joy of the Holy Ghost:

7 So that ye were ensamples to all that believe in Macedonia and Achaia.

NEW AMERICAN STANDARD BIBLE

THE FIRST LETTER OF PAUL TO THE THESSALONIANS

Thanksgiving for These Believers

1 Paul and Silvanus and Timothy,
To the church of the Thessalonians in God the Father and the Lord Jesus Christ: Grace to you and peace.

2 We give thanks to God always for all of you, making mention *of you* in our prayers;

3 constantly bearing in mind your work of faith and labor of love and steadfastness of hope in our Lord Jesus Christ in the presence of our God and Father,

4 knowing, brethren beloved by God, *His* choice of you;

5 for our gospel did not come to you in word only, but also in power and in the Holy Spirit and with full conviction; just as you know what kind of men we proved to be among you for your sake.

6 You also became imitators of us and of the Lord, having received the word in much tribulation with the joy of the Holy Spirit,

7 so that you became an example to all the believers in Macedonia and in Achaia.

NEW CENTURY VERSION

1 THESSALONIANS

1 From Paul, Silas, and Timothy.
To the church in Thessalonica, the church in God the Father and the Lord Jesus Christ:
Grace and peace to you.

The Faith of the Thessalonians

2 We always thank God for all of you and mention you when we pray. 3 We continually recall before God our Father the things you have done because of your faith and the work you have done because of your love. And we thank him that you continue to be strong because of your hope in our Lord Jesus Christ.

4 Brothers and sisters,[a] God loves you, and we know he has chosen you, 5 because the Good News we brought to you came not only with words, but with power, with the Holy Spirit, and with sure knowledge that it is true. Also you know how we lived when we were with you in order to help you. 6 And you became like us and like the Lord. You suffered much, but still you accepted the teaching with the joy that comes from the Holy Spirit. 7 So you became an example to

1:4 [a] **Brothers and sisters** Although the Greek text says "Brothers" here and throughout this book, Paul's words were meant for the entire church, including men and women.

CONTEMPORARY ENGLISH VERSION

1 THESSALONIANS

1 From Paul, Silas,[a] and Timothy.
To the church in Thessalonica, the people of God the Father and of the Lord Jesus Christ.
I pray that God will be kind to you and will bless you with peace!

2 We thank God for you and always mention you in our prayers. Each time we pray, 3 we tell God our Father about your faith and loving work and about your firm hope in our Lord Jesus Christ.

The Thessalonians' Faith and Example

4 My dear friends, God loves you, and we know he has chosen you to be his people. 5 When we told you the good news, it was with the power and assurance that come from the Holy Spirit, and not simply with words. You knew what kind of people we were and how we helped you. 6 So, when you accepted the message, you followed our example and the example of the Lord. You suffered, but the Holy Spirit made you glad.

7 You became an example for all the Lord's followers in Macedonia and Achaia. 8 And because of you, the Lord's

[a] 1.1 *Silas*: The Greek text has "Silvanus," another form of the name Silas.

NEW INTERNATIONAL VERSION

1 THESSALONIANS

1 Paul, Silas[a] and Timothy,

To the church of the Thessalonians in God the Father and the Lord Jesus Christ:

Grace and peace to you.[b]

Thanksgiving for the Thessalonians' Faith

[2]We always thank God for all of you, mentioning you in our prayers. [3]We continually remember before our God and Father your work produced by faith, your labor prompted by love, and your endurance inspired by hope in our Lord Jesus Christ.

[4]For we know, brothers loved by God, that he has chosen you, [5]because our gospel came to you not simply with words, but also with power, with the Holy Spirit and with deep conviction. You know how we lived among you for your sake. [6]You became imitators of us and of the Lord; in spite of severe suffering, you welcomed the message with the joy given by the Holy Spirit. [7]And so you became a model to all the believers in Macedonia and Achaia. [8]The

[a] *1* Greek *Silvanus*, a variant of *Silas* [b] *1* Some early manuscripts *you from God our Father and the Lord Jesus Christ*

NEW LIVING TRANSLATION

1 THESSALONIANS

Greetings from Paul

1 This letter is from Paul, Silas,* and Timothy.

It is written to the church in Thessalonica, you who belong to God the Father and the Lord Jesus Christ.

May his grace and peace be yours.

The Faith of the Thessalonian Believers

[2]We always thank God for all of you and pray for you constantly. [3]As we talk to our God and Father about you, we think of your faithful work, your loving deeds, and your continual anticipation of the return of our Lord Jesus Christ.

[4]We know that God loves you, dear brothers and sisters,* and that he chose you to be his own people. [5]For when we brought you the Good News, it was not only with words but also with power, for the Holy Spirit gave you full assurance that what we said was true. And you know that the way we lived among you was further proof of the truth of our message. [6]So you received the message with joy from the Holy Spirit in spite of the severe suffering it brought you. In this way, you imitated both us and the Lord. [7]As a result, you yourselves became an example to all the Christians in Greece.* [8]And now the word of the Lord is ringing out from

1:1 Greek *Silvanus.* 1:4 Greek *brothers.* 1:7 Greek *Macedonia and Achaia,* the northern and southern regions of Greece; also in 1:8.

NEW KING JAMES VERSION

THE FIRST EPISTLE OF PAUL TO THE THESSALONIANS

Greeting

1 Paul, Silvanus, and Timothy,

To the church of the Thessalonians in God the Father and the Lord Jesus Christ:

Grace to you and peace from God our Father and the Lord Jesus Christ.[a]

Their Good Example

[2]We give thanks to God always for you all, making mention of you in our prayers, [3]remembering without ceasing your work of faith, labor of love, and patience of hope in our Lord Jesus Christ in the sight of our God and Father, [4]knowing, beloved brethren, your election by God. [5]For our gospel did not come to you in word only, but also in power, and in the Holy Spirit and in much assurance, as you know what kind of men we were among you for your sake.

[6]And you became followers of us and of the Lord, having received the word in much affliction, with joy of the Holy Spirit, [7]so that you became examples to all in Macedonia and Achaia who believe. [8]For from you the word of the

1:1 [a] NU-Text omits *from God our Father and the Lord Jesus Christ.*

THE MESSAGE

1 THESSALONIANS

1 I, Paul, together here with Silas and Timothy, send greetings to the church at Thessalonica, Christians assembled by God the Father and by the Master, Jesus Christ. God's amazing grace be with you! God's robust peace!

Convictions of Steel

Every time we think of you, we thank God for you. Day and night you're in our prayers as we call to mind your work of faith, your labor of love, and your patience of hope in following our Master, Jesus Christ, before God our Father. It is clear to us, friends, that God not only loves you very much but also has put his hand on you for something special. When the Message we preached came to you, it wasn't just words. Something happened in you. The Holy Spirit put steel in your convictions.

You paid careful attention to the way we lived among you, and determined to live that way yourselves. In imitating us, you imitated the Master. Although great trouble accompanied the Word, you were able to take great joy from the Holy Spirit!—taking the trouble with the joy, the joy with the trouble.

Do you know that all over the provinces of both Macedonia and Achaia believers look up to you? The word

KING JAMES VERSION

8 For from you sounded out the word of the Lord not only in Macedonia and Achaia, but also in every place your faith to God-ward is spread abroad; so that we need not to speak any thing.

9 For they themselves shew of us what manner of entering in we had unto you, and how ye turned to God from idols to serve the living and true God;

10 And to wait for his Son from heaven, whom he raised from the dead, *even* Jesus, which delivered us from the wrath to come.

2 For yourselves, brethren, know our entrance in unto you, that it was not in vain:

2 But even after that we had suffered before, and were shamefully entreated, as ye know, at Philippi, we were bold in our God to speak unto you the gospel of God with much contention.

3 For our exhortation *was* not of deceit, nor of uncleanness, nor in guile:

4 But as we were allowed of God to be put in trust with the gospel, even so we speak; not as pleasing men, but God, which trieth our hearts.

5 For neither at any time used we flattering words, as ye know, nor a cloke of covetousness; God *is* witness:

6 Nor of men sought we glory, neither of you, nor *yet* of others, when we might have been burdensome, as the apostles of Christ.

NEW AMERICAN STANDARD BIBLE

8 For the word of the Lord has sounded forth from you, not only in Macedonia and Achaia, but also in every place your faith toward God has gone forth, so that we have no need to say anything.

9 For they themselves report about us what kind of a reception we had with you, and how you turned to God from idols to serve a living and true God,

10 and to wait for His Son from heaven, whom He raised from the dead, *that is* Jesus, who rescues us from the wrath to come.

Paul's Ministry

2 For you yourselves know, brethren, that our coming to you was not in vain,

2 but after we had already suffered and been mistreated in Philippi, as you know, we had the boldness in our God to speak to you the gospel of God amid much opposition.

3 For our exhortation does not *come* from error or impurity or by way of deceit;

4 but just as we have been approved by God to be entrusted with the gospel, so we speak, not as pleasing men, but God who examines our hearts.

5 For we never came with flattering speech, as you know, nor with a pretext for greed—God is witness—

6 nor did we seek glory from men, either from you or from others, even though as apostles of Christ we might have asserted our authority.

NEW CENTURY VERSION

all the believers in Macedonia and Southern Greece. [8]And the
Lord's teaching spread from you not only into Macedonia
and Southern Greece, but now your faith in God has become
known everywhere. So we do not need to say anything about
it. [9]People everywhere are telling about the way you accepted
us when we were there with you. They tell how you stopped
worshiping idols and began serving the living and true God.
[10]And you wait for God's Son, whom God raised from the
dead, to come from heaven. He is Jesus, who saves us from
God's angry judgment that is sure to come.

Paul's Work in Thessalonica

2 Brothers and sisters, you know our visit to you was
not a failure. [2]Before we came to you, we suffered in
Philippi. People there insulted us, as you know, and many
people were against us. But our God helped us to be brave
and to tell you his Good News. [3]Our appeal does not come
from lies or wrong reasons, nor were we trying to trick
you. [4]But we speak the Good News because God tested us
and trusted us to do it. When we speak, we are not trying
to please people, but God, who tests our hearts. [5]You know
that we never tried to influence you by saying nice things
about you. We were not trying to get your money; we had
no selfishness to hide from you. God knows that this is
true. [6]We were not looking for human praise, from you or
anyone else, [7]even though as apostles of Christ we could
have used our authority over you.

CONTEMPORARY ENGLISH VERSION

message has spread everywhere in those regions. Now the
news of your faith in God is known all over the world, and
we don't have to say a thing about it. [9]Everyone is talking
about how you welcomed us and how you turned away
from idols to serve the true and living God. [10]They also tell
how you are waiting for his Son Jesus to come from heaven.
God raised him from death, and on the day of judgment
Jesus will save us from God's anger.

Paul's Work in Thessalonica

2 My friends, you know that our time with you wasn't
wasted. [2]As you remember, we had been mistreated
and insulted at Philippi. But God gave us the courage to
tell you the good news about him, even though many people
caused us trouble. [3]We didn't have any hidden motives
when we won you over, and we didn't try to fool or trick
anyone. [4]God was pleased to trust us with his message.
We didn't speak to please people, but to please God who
knows our motives.

[5]You also know that we didn't try to flatter anyone. God
himself knows that what we did wasn't a cover-up for greed.
[6]We were not trying to get you or anyone else to praise us.
[7]But as apostles, we could have demanded help from you.

NEW INTERNATIONAL VERSION

Lord's message rang out from you not only in Macedonia and Achaia—your faith in God has become known everywhere. Therefore we do not need to say anything about it, 9for they themselves report what kind of reception you gave us. They tell how you turned to God from idols to serve the living and true God, 10and to wait for his Son from heaven, whom he raised from the dead—Jesus, who rescues us from the coming wrath.

Paul's Ministry in Thessalonica

2 You know, brothers, that our visit to you was not a failure. 2We had previously suffered and been insulted in Philippi, as you know, but with the help of our God we dared to tell you his gospel in spite of strong opposition. 3For the appeal we make does not spring from error or impure motives, nor are we trying to trick you. 4On the contrary, we speak as men approved by God to be entrusted with the gospel. We are not trying to please men but God, who tests our hearts. 5You know we never used flattery, nor did we put on a mask to cover up greed—God is our witness. 6We were not looking for praise from men, not from you or anyone else.

As apostles of Christ we could have been a burden to you,

NEW LIVING TRANSLATION

you to people everywhere, even beyond Greece, for wherever we go we find people telling us about your faith in God. We don't need to tell them about it, 9for they themselves keep talking about the wonderful welcome you gave us and how you turned away from idols to serve the true and living God. 10And they speak of how you are looking forward to the coming of God's Son from heaven—Jesus, whom God raised from the dead. He is the one who has rescued us from the terrors of the coming judgment.

Paul Remembers His Visit

2 You yourselves know, dear brothers and sisters,* that our visit to you was not a failure. 2You know how badly we had been treated at Philippi just before we came to you and how much we suffered there. Yet our God gave us the courage to declare his Good News to you boldly, even though we were surrounded by many who opposed us. 3So you can see that we were not preaching with any deceit or impure purposes or trickery.

4For we speak as messengers who have been approved by God to be entrusted with the Good News. Our purpose is to please God, not people. He is the one who examines the motives of our hearts. 5Never once did we try to win you with flattery, as you very well know. And God is our witness that we were not just pretending to be your friends so you would give us money! 6As for praise, we have never asked for it from you or anyone else. 7As apostles of Christ

2:1 Greek *brothers;* also in 2:9, 14, 17.

NEW KING JAMES VERSION

Lord has sounded forth, not only in Macedonia and Achaia, but also in every place. Your faith toward God has gone out, so that we do not need to say anything. 9For they themselves declare concerning us what manner of entry we had to you, and how you turned to God from idols to serve the living and true God, 10and to wait for His Son from heaven, whom He raised from the dead, *even* Jesus who delivers us from the wrath to come.

Paul's Conduct

2 For you yourselves know, brethren, that our coming to you was not in vain. 2But even[a] after we had suffered before and were spitefully treated at Philippi, as you know, we were bold in our God to speak to you the gospel of God in much conflict. 3For our exhortation *did* not *come* from error or uncleanness, nor *was it* in deceit.

4But as we have been approved by God to be entrusted with the gospel, even so we speak, not as pleasing men, but God who tests our hearts. 5For neither at any time did we use flattering words, as you know, nor a cloak for covetousness—God *is* witness. 6Nor did we seek glory from men, either from you or from others, when we might have made demands as apostles of Christ. 7But we were gentle

2:2 [a] NU-Text and M-Text omit *even.*

THE MESSAGE

has gotten around. Your lives are echoing the Master's Word, not only in the provinces but all over the place. The news of your faith in God is out. We don't even have to say anything anymore—*you're* the message! People come up and tell us how you received us with open arms, how you deserted the dead idols of your old life so you could embrace and serve God, the true God. They marvel at how expectantly you await the arrival of his Son, whom he raised from the dead—Jesus, who rescued us from certain doom.

2 So, friends, it's obvious that our visit to you was no waste of time. We had just been given rough treatment in Philippi, as you know, but that didn't slow us down. We were sure of ourselves in God, and went right ahead and said our piece, presenting God's Message to you, defiant of the opposition.

No Hidden Agendas

God tested us thoroughly to make sure we were qualified to be trusted with this Message. Be assured that when we speak to you we're not after crowd approval—only God approval. Since we've been put through that battery of tests, you're guaranteed that both we and the Message are free of error, mixed motives, or hidden agendas. We never used words to butter you up. No one knows that better than you. And God knows we never used words as a smoke screen to take advantage of you.

Even though we had some standing as Christ's apostles,

KING JAMES VERSION

7 ¶ But we were gentle among you, even as a nurse cherisheth her children:

8 So being affectionately desirous of you, we were willing to have imparted unto you, not the gospel of God only, but also our own souls, because ye were dear unto us.

9 For ye remember, brethren, our labour and travail: for labouring night and day, because we would not be chargeable unto any of you, we preached unto you the gospel of God.

10 Ye *are* witnesses, and God *also*, how holily and justly and unblameably we behaved ourselves among you that believe:

11 As ye know how we exhorted and comforted and charged every one of you, as a father *doth* his children,

12 That ye would walk worthy of God, who hath called you unto his kingdom and glory.

13 ¶ For this cause also thank we God without ceasing, because, when ye received the word of God which ye heard of us, ye received *it* not *as* the word of men, but as it is in truth, the word of God, which effectually worketh also in you that believe.

14 For ye, brethren, became followers of the churches of God which in Judaea are in Christ Jesus: for ye also have suffered like things of your own countrymen, even as they *have* of the Jews:

15 Who both killed the Lord Jesus, and their own prophets, and have persecuted us; and they please not God, and are contrary to all men:

NEW AMERICAN STANDARD BIBLE

7 But we proved to be [1]gentle among you, as a nursing *mother* tenderly cares for her own children.

8 Having so fond an affection for you, we were well-pleased to impart to you not only the gospel of God but also our own lives, because you had become very dear to us.

9 For you recall, brethren, our labor and hardship, *how* working night and day so as not to be a burden to any of you, we proclaimed to you the gospel of God.

10 You are witnesses, and *so is* God, how devoutly and uprightly and blamelessly we behaved toward you believers;

11 just as you know how we *were* exhorting and encouraging and imploring each one of you as a father *would* his own children,

12 so that you would walk in a manner worthy of the God who calls you into His own kingdom and glory.

13 For this reason we also constantly thank God that when you received the word of God which you heard from us, you accepted *it* not *as* the word of men, but *for* what it really is, the word of God, which also performs its work in you who believe.

14 For you, brethren, became imitators of the churches of God in Christ Jesus that are in Judea, for you also endured the same sufferings at the hands of your own countrymen, even as they *did* from the Jews,

15 who both killed the Lord Jesus and the prophets, and drove us out. They are not pleasing to God, but hostile to all men,

2:7 [1] Three early mss read *babes*

NEW CENTURY VERSION

But we were very gentle with you, like a mother caring
for her little children. [8]Because we loved you, we were
happy to share not only God's Good News with you, but
even our own lives. You had become so dear to us!
[9]Brothers and sisters, I know you remember our hard work
and difficulties. We worked night and day so we would not
burden any of you while we preached God's Good News to
you.
[10]When we were with you, we lived in a holy and honest
way, without fault. You know this is true, and so does
God. [11]You know that we treated each of you as a father
treats his own children. [12]We encouraged you, we urged
you, and we insisted that you live good lives for God, who
calls you to his glorious kingdom.
[13]Also, we always thank God because when you heard
his message from us, you accepted it as the word of God,
not the words of humans. And it really is God's message
which works in you who believe. [14]Brothers and sisters,
your experiences have been like those of God's churches in
Christ that are in Judea.[a] You suffered from the people of
your own country, as they suffered from the Jews, [15]who
killed both the Lord Jesus and the prophets and forced us
to leave that country. They do not please God and are

2:14 [a] **Judea** The Jewish land where Jesus lived and taught and where the church first began.

CONTEMPORARY ENGLISH VERSION

After all, Christ is the one who sent us. We chose to be like
children or like a mother[a] nursing her baby. [8]We cared so
much for you, and you became so dear to us, that we were
willing to give our lives for you when we gave you God's
message.
[9]My dear friends, you surely haven't forgotten our hard
work and hardships. You remember how night and day we
struggled to make a living, so that we could tell you God's
message without being a burden to anyone. [10]Both you
and God are witnesses that we were pure and honest and
innocent in our dealings with you followers of the Lord.
[11]You also know we did everything for you that parents
would do for their own children. [12]We begged, encouraged,
and urged each of you to live in a way that would honor
God. He is the one who chose you to share in his own
kingdom and glory.
[13]We always thank God that you believed the message
we preached. It came from him, and it isn't something
made up by humans. You accepted it as God's message,
and now he is working in you. [14]My friends, you did just
like God's churches in Judea and like the other followers of
Christ Jesus there. And so, you were mistreated by your
own people, in the same way they were mistreated by their
people.
[15]Those Jews killed the Lord Jesus and the prophets, and
they even chased us away. God doesn't like what they do

[a] **2.7** *like children or like a mother*: Some manuscripts have "as gentle as a mother."

NEW INTERNATIONAL VERSION

7but we were gentle among you, like a mother caring for her little children. 8We loved you so much that we were delighted to share with you not only the gospel of God but our lives as well, because you had become so dear to us. 9Surely you remember, brothers, our toil and hardship; we worked night and day in order not to be a burden to anyone while we preached the gospel of God to you.

10You are witnesses, and so is God, of how holy, righteous and blameless we were among you who believed. 11For you know that we dealt with each of you as a father deals with his own children, 12encouraging, comforting and urging you to live lives worthy of God, who calls you into his kingdom and glory.

13And we also thank God continually because, when you received the word of God, which you heard from us, you accepted it not as the word of men, but as it actually is, the word of God, which is at work in you who believe. 14For you, brothers, became imitators of God's churches in Judea, which are in Christ Jesus: You suffered from your own countrymen the same things those churches suffered from the Jews, 15who killed the Lord Jesus and the prophets and also drove us out. They displease God and are hostile to all

NEW LIVING TRANSLATION

we certainly had a right to make some demands of you, but we were as gentle among you as a mother* feeding and caring for her own children. 8We loved you so much that we gave you not only God's Good News but our own lives, too.

9Don't you remember, dear brothers and sisters, how hard we worked among you? Night and day we toiled to earn a living so that our expenses would not be a burden to anyone there as we preached God's Good News among you. 10You yourselves are our witnesses—and so is God—that we were pure and honest and faultless toward all of you believers. 11And you know that we treated each of you as a father treats his own children. 12We pleaded with you, encouraged you, and urged you to live your lives in a way that God would consider worthy. For he called you into his Kingdom to share his glory.

13And we will never stop thanking God that when we preached his message to you, you didn't think of the words we spoke as being just our own. You accepted what we said as the very word of God—which, of course, it was. And this word continues to work in you who believe.

14And then, dear brothers and sisters, you suffered persecution from your own countrymen. In this way, you imitated the believers in God's churches in Judea who, because of their belief in Christ Jesus, suffered from their own people, the Jews.

15For some of the Jews had killed their own prophets, and some even killed the Lord Jesus. Now they have persecuted

2:7 Some manuscripts read *we were as infants among you; we were as a mother.*

NEW KING JAMES VERSION

among you, just as a nursing *mother* cherishes her own children. 8So, affectionately longing for you, we were well pleased to impart to you not only the gospel of God, but also our own lives, because you had become dear to us. 9For you remember, brethren, our labor and toil; for laboring night and day, that we might not be a burden to any of you, we preached to you the gospel of God.

10You *are* witnesses, and God *also,* how devoutly and justly and blamelessly we behaved ourselves among you who believe; 11as you know how we exhorted, and comforted, and charged[b] every one of you, as a father *does* his own children, 12that you would walk worthy of God who calls you into His own kingdom and glory.

Their Conversion

13For this reason we also thank God without ceasing, because when you received the word of God which you heard from us, you welcomed *it* not *as* the word of men, but as it is in truth, the word of God, which also effectively works in you who believe. 14For you, brethren, became imitators of the churches of God which are in Judea in Christ Jesus. For you also suffered the same things from your own countrymen, just as they *did* from the Judeans, 15who killed both the Lord Jesus and their own prophets, and have persecuted us; and they do not please God and are

2:11 [b] NU-Text and M-Text read *implored.*

THE MESSAGE

we never threw our weight around or tried to come across as important, with you or anyone else. We weren't aloof with you. We took you just as you were. We were never patronizing, never condescending, but we cared for you the way a mother cares for her children. We loved you dearly. Not content to just pass on the Message, we wanted to give you our hearts. And we *did.*

You remember us in those days, friends, working our fingers to the bone, up half the night, moonlighting so you wouldn't have the burden of supporting us while we proclaimed God's Message to you. You saw with your own eyes how discreet and courteous we were among you, with keen sensitivity to you as fellow believers. And God knows we weren't freeloaders! You experienced it all firsthand. With each of you we were like a father with his child, holding your hand, whispering encouragement, showing you step by step how to live well before God, who called us into his own kingdom, into this delightful life.

And now we look back on all this and thank God, an artesian well of thanks! When you got the Message of God we preached, you didn't pass it off as just one more human opinion, but you took it to heart as God's true word to you, which it is, God himself at work in you believers!

Friends, do you realize that you followed in the exact footsteps of the churches of God in Judea, those who were the first to follow in the footsteps of Jesus Christ? You got the same bad treatment from your countrymen as they did from theirs, the Jews who killed the Master Jesus (to say nothing of the prophets) and followed it up by running us

KING JAMES VERSION

16 Forbidding us to speak to the Gentiles that they might be saved, to fill up their sins alway: for the wrath is come upon them to the uttermost.

17 ¶ But we, brethren, being taken from you for a short time in presence, not in heart, endeavoured the more abundantly to see your face with great desire.

18 Wherefore we would have come unto you, even I Paul, once and again; but Satan hindered us.

19 For what *is* our hope, or joy, or crown of rejoicing? *Are* not even ye in the presence of our Lord Jesus Christ at his coming?

20 For ye are our glory and joy.

3 Wherefore when we could no longer forbear, we thought it good to be left at Athens alone;

2 And sent Timotheus, our brother, and minister of God, and our fellowlabourer in the gospel of Christ, to establish you, and to comfort you concerning your faith:

3 That no man should be moved by these afflictions: for yourselves know that we are appointed thereunto.

4 For verily, when we were with you, we told you before that we should suffer tribulation; even as it came to pass, and ye know.

5 For this cause, when I could no longer forbear, I sent to know your faith, lest by some means the tempter have tempted you, and our labour be in vain.

NEW AMERICAN STANDARD BIBLE

16 hindering us from speaking to the Gentiles so that they may be saved; with the result that they always fill up the measure of their sins. But wrath has come upon them [2]to the utmost.

17 But we, brethren, having been taken away from you for a short while—in person, not in spirit—were all the more eager with great desire to see your face.

18 For we wanted to come to you—I, Paul, more than once—and *yet* Satan hindered us.

19 For who is our hope or joy or crown of exultation? Is it not even you, in the presence of our Lord Jesus at His coming?

20 For you are our glory and joy.

Encouragement of Timothy's Visit

3 Therefore when we could endure *it* no longer, we thought it best to be left behind at Athens alone,

2 and we sent Timothy, our brother and God's fellow worker in the gospel of Christ, to strengthen and encourage you as to your faith,

3 so that no one would be disturbed by these afflictions; for you yourselves know that we have been destined for this.

4 For indeed when we were with you, we *kept* telling you in advance that we were going to suffer affliction; and so it came to pass, as you know.

5 For this reason, when I could endure *it* no longer, I also sent to find out about your faith, for fear that the tempter might have tempted you, and our labor would be in vain.

2:16 [2] Or *forever* or *altogether;* lit *to the end*

NEW CENTURY VERSION

against all people. [16]They try to stop us from teaching those who are not Jews so they may be saved. By doing this, they are increasing their sins to the limit. The anger of God has come to them at last.

Paul Wants to Visit Them Again

[17]Brothers and sisters, though we were separated from you for a short time, our thoughts were still with you. We wanted very much to see you and tried hard to do so. [18]We wanted to come to you. I, Paul, tried to come more than once, but Satan stopped us. [19]You are our hope, our joy, and the crown we will take pride in when our Lord Jesus Christ comes. [20]Truly you are our glory and our joy.

3 When we could not wait any longer, we decided it was best to stay in Athens alone [2]and send Timothy to you. Timothy, our brother, works with us for God and helps us tell people the Good News about Christ. We sent him to strengthen and encourage you in your faith [3]so none of you would be upset by these troubles. You yourselves know that we must face these troubles. [4]Even when we were with you, we told you we all would have to suffer, and you know it has happened. [5]Because of this, when I could wait no longer, I sent Timothy to you so I could learn about your faith. I was afraid the devil had tempted you, and then our hard work would have been wasted.

CONTEMPORARY ENGLISH VERSION

and neither does anyone else. [16]They keep us from speaking his message to the Gentiles and from leading them to be saved. The Jews have always gone too far with their sins. Now God has finally become angry and will punish them.

Paul Wants To Visit the Church Again

[17]My friends, we were kept from coming to you for a while, but we never stopped thinking about you. We were eager to see you and tried our best to visit you in person. [18]We really wanted to come. I myself tried several times, but Satan always stopped us. [19]After all, when the Lord Jesus appears, who else but you will give us hope and joy and be like a glorious crown for us? [20]You alone are our glory and joy!

3 Finally, we couldn't stand it any longer. We decided to stay in Athens by ourselves [2]and send our friend Timothy to you. He works with us as God's servant and preaches the good news about Christ. We wanted him to make you strong in your faith and to encourage you. [3]We didn't want any of you to be discouraged by all these troubles. You knew we would have to suffer, [4]because when we were with you, we told you this would happen. And we did suffer, as you well know. [5]At last, when I could not wait any longer, I sent Timothy to find out about your faith. I hoped that Satan had not tempted you and made all our work useless.

NEW INTERNATIONAL VERSION

men [16]in their effort to keep us from speaking to the Gentiles so that they may be saved. In this way they always heap up their sins to the limit. The wrath of God has come upon them at last.[a]

Paul's Longing to See the Thessalonians

[17]But, brothers, when we were torn away from you for a short time (in person, not in thought), out of our intense longing we made every effort to see you. [18]For we wanted to come to you—certainly I, Paul, did, again and again—but Satan stopped us. [19]For what is our hope, our joy, or the crown in which we will glory in the presence of our Lord Jesus when he comes? Is it not you? [20]Indeed, you are our glory and joy.

3 So when we could stand it no longer, we thought it best to be left by ourselves in Athens. [2]We sent Timothy, who is our brother and God's fellow worker[a] in spreading the gospel of Christ, to strengthen and encourage you in your faith, [3]so that no one would be unsettled by these trials. You know quite well that we were destined for them. [4]In fact, when we were with you, we kept telling you that we would be persecuted. And it turned out that way, as you well know. [5]For this reason, when I could stand it no longer, I sent to find out about your faith. I was afraid that in some way the tempter might have tempted you and our efforts might have been useless.

[a] *16* Or *them fully* [a] *2* Some manuscripts *brother and fellow worker;* other manuscripts *brother and God's servant*

NEW LIVING TRANSLATION

us and driven us out. They displease God and oppose everyone [16]by trying to keep us from preaching the Good News to the Gentiles, for fear some might be saved. By doing this, they continue to pile up their sins. But the anger of God has caught up with them at last.

Timothy's Good Report about the Church

[17]Dear brothers and sisters, after we were separated from you for a little while (though our hearts never left you), we tried very hard to come back because of our intense longing to see you again. [18]We wanted very much to come, and I, Paul, tried again and again, but Satan prevented us. [19]After all, what gives us hope and joy, and what is our proud reward and crown? It is you! Yes, you will bring us much joy as we stand together before our Lord Jesus when he comes back again. [20]For you are our pride and joy.

3 Finally, when we could stand it no longer, we decided that I should stay alone in Athens, [2]and we sent Timothy to visit you. He is our co-worker for God and our brother in proclaiming the Good News of Christ. We sent him to strengthen you, to encourage you in your faith, [3]and to keep you from becoming disturbed by the troubles you were going through. But, of course, you know that such troubles are going to happen to us Christians. [4]Even while we were with you, we warned you that troubles would soon come—and they did, as you well know.

[5]That is why, when I could bear it no longer, I sent Timothy to find out whether your faith was still strong. I was afraid that the Tempter had gotten the best of you and

NEW KING JAMES VERSION

contrary to all men, [16]forbidding us to speak to the Gentiles that they may be saved, so as always to fill up *the measure of* their sins; but wrath has come upon them to the uttermost.

Longing to See Them

[17]But we, brethren, having been taken away from you for a short time in presence, not in heart, endeavored more eagerly to see your face with great desire. [18]Therefore we wanted to come to you—even I, Paul, time and again—but Satan hindered us. [19]For what *is* our hope, or joy, or crown of rejoicing? *Is it* not even you in the presence of our Lord Jesus Christ at His coming? [20]For you are our glory and joy.

Concern for Their Faith

3 Therefore, when we could no longer endure it, we thought it good to be left in Athens alone, [2]and sent Timothy, our brother and minister of God, and our fellow laborer in the gospel of Christ, to establish you and encourage you concerning your faith, [3]that no one should be shaken by these afflictions; for you yourselves know that we are appointed to this. [4]For, in fact, we told you before when we were with you that we would suffer tribulation, just as it happened, and you know. [5]For this reason, when I could no longer endure it, I sent to know your faith, lest by some means the tempter had tempted you, and our labor might be in vain.

THE MESSAGE

out of town. They make themselves offensive to God and everyone else by trying to keep us from telling people who've never heard of our God how to be saved. They've made a career of opposing God, and have gotten mighty good at it. But God is fed up, ready to put an end to it.

✠

Do you have any idea how very homesick we became for you, dear friends? Even though it hadn't been that long and it was only our bodies that were separated from you, not our hearts, we tried our very best to get back to see you. You can't imagine how much we missed you! I, Paul, tried over and over to get back, but Satan stymied us each time. Who do you think we're going to be proud of when our Master Jesus appears if it's not you? You're our pride and joy!

3 So when we couldn't stand being separated from you any longer and could find no way to visit you ourselves, we stayed in Athens and sent Timothy to get you up and about, cheering you on so you wouldn't be discouraged by these hard times. He's a brother and companion in the faith, God's man in spreading the Message, preaching Christ.

Not that the troubles should come as any surprise to you. You've always known that we're in for this kind of thing. It's part of our calling. When we were with you, we made it quite clear that there was trouble ahead. And now that it's happened, you know what it's like. That's why I couldn't quit worrying; I had to know for myself how you were doing in the faith. I didn't want the Tempter getting to you and tearing down everything we had built up together.

KING JAMES VERSION

6 ¶ But now when Timotheus came from you unto us, and brought us good tidings of your faith and charity, and that ye have good remembrance of us always, desiring greatly to see us, as we also *to see* you:

7 Therefore, brethren, we were comforted over you in all our affliction and distress by your faith:

8 For now we live, if ye stand fast in the Lord.

9 For what thanks can we render to God again for you, for all the joy wherewith we joy for your sakes before our God;

10 Night and day praying exceedingly that we might see your face, and might perfect that which is lacking in your faith?

11 ¶ Now God himself and our Father, and our Lord Jesus Christ, direct our way unto you.

12 And the Lord make you to increase and abound in love one toward another, and toward all *men*, even as we *do* toward you:

13 To the end he may stablish your hearts unblameable in holiness before God, even our Father, at the coming of our Lord Jesus Christ with all his saints.

4 Furthermore then we beseech you, brethren, and exhort *you* by the Lord Jesus, that as ye have received of us how ye ought to walk and to please God, *so* ye would abound more and more.

NEW AMERICAN STANDARD BIBLE

6 But now that Timothy has come to us from you, and has brought us good news of your faith and love, and that you always think kindly of us, longing to see us just as we also long to see you,

7 for this reason, brethren, in all our distress and affliction we were comforted about you through your faith;

8 for now we *really* live, if you stand firm in the Lord.

9 For what thanks can we render to God for you in return for all the joy with which we rejoice before our God on your account,

10 as we night and day keep praying most earnestly that we may see your face, and may complete what is lacking in your faith?

11 Now may our God and Father Himself and Jesus our Lord direct our way to you;

12 and may the Lord cause you to increase and abound in love for one another, and for all people, just as we also *do* for you;

13 so that He may establish your hearts without blame in holiness before our God and Father at the coming of our Lord Jesus with all His saints.

Sanctification and Love

4 Finally then, brethren, we request and exhort you in the Lord Jesus, that as you received from us *instruction* as to how you ought to walk and please God (just as you actually do [1]walk), that you excel still more.

4:1 [1] Or *conduct yourselves*

NEW CENTURY VERSION

[6]But Timothy now has come back to us from you and
has brought us good news about your faith and love. He
told us that you always remember us in a good way and
that you want to see us just as much as we want to see
you. [7]So, brothers and sisters, while we have much trouble
and suffering, we are encouraged about you because of
your faith. [8]Our life is really full if you stand strong in the
Lord. [9]We have so much joy before our God because of
you. We cannot thank him enough for all the joy we feel.
[10]Night and day we continue praying with all our heart
that we can see you again and give you all the things you
need to make your faith strong.

[11]Now may our God and Father himself and our Lord
Jesus prepare the way for us to come to you. [12]May the
Lord make your love grow more and multiply for each
other and for all people so that you will love others as we
love you. [13]May your hearts be made strong so that you
will be holy and without fault before our God and Father
when our Lord Jesus comes with all his holy ones.

A Life that Pleases God

4 Brothers and sisters, we taught you how to live in a
way that will please God, and you are living that way.
Now we ask and encourage you in the Lord Jesus to live

CONTEMPORARY ENGLISH VERSION

[6]Timothy has come back from his visit with you and has
told us about your faith and love. He also said that you
always have happy memories of us and that you want to
see us as much as we want to see you.

[7]My friends, even though we have a lot of trouble and
suffering, your faith makes us feel better about you. [8]Your
strong faith in the Lord is like a breath of new life. [9]How
can we possibly thank God enough for all the happiness
you have brought us? [10]Day and night we sincerely pray
that we will see you again and help you to have an even
stronger faith.

[11]We pray that God our Father and our Lord Jesus will
let us visit you. [12]May the Lord make your love for each
other and for everyone else grow by leaps and bounds.
That's how our love for you has grown. [13]And when our
Lord comes with all of his people, I pray that he will make
your hearts pure and innocent in the sight of God the
Father.

A Life That Pleases God

4 Finally, my dear friends, since you belong to the Lord
Jesus, we beg and urge you to live as we taught you.
Then you will please God. You are already living that way,

NEW INTERNATIONAL VERSION

Timothy's Encouraging Report

6But Timothy has just now come to us from you and has
brought good news about your faith and love. He has told
us that you always have pleasant memories of us and that
you long to see us, just as we also long to see you.
7Therefore, brothers, in all our distress and persecution we
were encouraged about you because of your faith. 8For
now we really live, since you are standing firm in the Lord.
9How can we thank God enough for you in return for all
the joy we have in the presence of our God because of you?
10Night and day we pray most earnestly that we may see
you again and supply what is lacking in your faith.

11Now may our God and Father himself and our Lord
Jesus clear the way for us to come to you. 12May the Lord
make your love increase and overflow for each other and
for everyone else, just as ours does for you. 13May he
strengthen your hearts so that you will be blameless and
holy in the presence of our God and Father when our Lord
Jesus comes with all his holy ones.

Living to Please God

4 Finally, brothers, we instructed you how to live in
order to please God, as in fact you are living. Now we
ask you and urge you in the Lord Jesus to do this more and

NEW LIVING TRANSLATION

that all our work had been useless. 6Now Timothy has just
returned, bringing the good news that your faith and love
are as strong as ever. He reports that you remember our
visit with joy and that you want to see us just as much as
we want to see you. 7So we have been greatly comforted,
dear brothers and sisters,* in all of our own crushing trou-
bles and suffering, because you have remained strong in
your faith. 8It gives us new life, knowing you remain
strong in the Lord.

9How we thank God for you! Because of you we have
great joy in the presence of God. 10Night and day we pray
earnestly for you, asking God to let us see you again to fill
up anything that may still be missing in your faith.

11May God himself, our Father, and our Lord Jesus make
it possible for us to come to you very soon. 12And may the
Lord make your love grow and overflow to each other and
to everyone else, just as our love overflows toward you.
13As a result, Christ will make your hearts strong, blame-
less, and holy when you stand before God our Father on
that day when our Lord Jesus comes with all those who
belong to him.

Live to Please God

4 Finally, dear brothers and sisters,* we urge you in the
name of the Lord Jesus to live in a way that pleases
God, as we have taught you. You are doing this already,
and we encourage you to do so more and more. 2For you

3:7 Greek *brothers.* 4:1 Greek *brothers;* also in 4:10, 13.

NEW KING JAMES VERSION

Encouraged by Timothy

6But now that Timothy has come to us from you, and
brought us good news of your faith and love, and that you
always have good remembrance of us, greatly desiring to
see us, as we also *to see* you— 7therefore, brethren, in all
our affliction and distress we were comforted concerning
you by your faith. 8For now we live, if you stand fast in
the Lord.

9For what thanks can we render to God for you, for all
the joy with which we rejoice for your sake before our God,
10night and day praying exceedingly that we may see your
face and perfect what is lacking in your faith?

Prayer for the Church

11Now may our God and Father Himself, and our Lord
Jesus Christ, direct our way to you. 12And may the Lord
make you increase and abound in love to one another and
to all, just as we *do* to you, 13so that He may establish
your hearts blameless in holiness before our God and
Father at the coming of our Lord Jesus Christ with all His
saints.

Plea for Purity

4 Finally then, brethren, we urge and exhort in the Lord
Jesus that you should abound more and more, just as
you received from us how you ought to walk and to please

THE MESSAGE

But now that Timothy is back, bringing this terrific report on your faith and love, we feel a lot better. It's especially gratifying to know that you continue to think well of us, and that you want to see us as much as we want to see you! In the middle of our trouble and hard times here, just knowing how you're doing keeps us going. Knowing that your faith is alive keeps us alive.

What would be an adequate thanksgiving to offer God for all the joy we experience before him because of you? We do what we can, praying away, night and day, asking for the bonus of seeing your faces again and doing what we can to help when your faith falters.

May God our Father himself and our Master Jesus clear the road to you! And may the Master pour on the love so it fills your lives and splashes over on everyone around you, just as it does from us to you. May you be infused with strength and purity, filled with confidence in the presence of God our Father when our Master Jesus arrives with all his followers.

You're God-Taught

4 One final word, friends. We ask you—*urge* is more like it—that you keep on doing what we told you to do to please God, not in a dogged religious plod, but in a

KING JAMES VERSION

2 For ye know what commandments we gave you by the Lord Jesus.

3 For this is the will of God, *even* your sanctification, that ye should abstain from fornication:

4 That every one of you should know how to possess his vessel in sanctification and honour;

5 Not in the lust of concupiscence, even as the Gentiles which know not God:

6 That no *man* go beyond and defraud his brother in *any* matter: because that the Lord *is* the avenger of all such, as we also have forewarned you and testified.

7 For God hath not called us unto uncleanness, but unto holiness.

8 He therefore that despiseth, despiseth not man, but God, who hath also given unto us his holy Spirit.

9 ¶ But as touching brotherly love ye need not that I write unto you: for ye yourselves are taught of God to love one another.

10 And indeed ye do it toward all the brethren which are in all Macedonia: but we beseech you, brethren, that ye increase more and more;

11 And that ye study to be quiet, and to do your own business, and to work with your own hands, as we commanded you;

12 That ye may walk honestly toward them that are without, and *that* ye may have lack of nothing.

NEW AMERICAN STANDARD BIBLE

2 For you know what commandments we gave you [2]by *the authority of* the Lord Jesus.

3 For this is the will of God, your sanctification; *that is,* that you abstain from sexual immorality;

4 that each of you know how to possess his own [3]vessel in sanctification and honor,

5 not in lustful passion, like the Gentiles who do not know God;

6 *and* that no man transgress and defraud his brother in the matter because the Lord is *the* avenger in all these things, just as we also told you before and solemnly warned *you.*

7 For God has not called us for the purpose of impurity, but in sanctification.

8 So, he who rejects *this* is not rejecting man but the God who gives His Holy Spirit to you.

9 Now as to the love of the brethren, you have no need for *anyone* to write to you, for you yourselves are taught by God to love one another;

10 for indeed you do practice it toward all the brethren who are in all Macedonia. But we urge you, brethren, to excel still more,

11 and to make it your ambition to lead a quiet life and attend to your own business and work with your hands, just as we commanded you,

12 so that you will behave properly toward outsiders and not be in any need.

4:2 [2] Lit *through the Lord* **4:4** [3] I.e. body; or wife

NEW CENTURY VERSION

that way even more. 2You know what we told you to do by
the authority of the Lord Jesus. 3God wants you to be holy
and to stay away from sexual sins. 4He wants each of you
to learn to control your own body[a] in a way that is holy
and honorable. 5Don't use your body for sexual sin like the
people who do not know God. 6Also, do not wrong or cheat
another Christian in this way. The Lord will punish people
who do those things as we have already told you and
warned you. 7God called us to be holy and does not want
us to live in sin. 8So the person who refuses to obey this
teaching is disobeying God, not simply a human teaching.
And God is the One who gives us his Holy Spirit.

9We do not need to write you about having love for your
Christian family, because God has already taught you to
love each other. 10And truly you do love the Christians in
all of Macedonia. Brothers and sisters, now we encourage
you to love them even more.

11Do all you can to live a peaceful life. Take care of your
own business, and do your own work as we have already
told you. 12If you do, then people who are not believers
will respect you, and you will not have to depend on others
for what you need.

4:4 [a] **learn...body** This might also mean "learn to live with your own wife."

CONTEMPORARY ENGLISH VERSION

but try even harder. 2Remember the instructions we gave
you as followers of the Lord Jesus. 3God wants you to be
holy, so don't be immoral in matters of sex. 4Respect and
honor your wife.[a] 5Don't be a slave of your desires or live
like people who don't know God. 6You must not cheat any
of the Lord's followers in matters of sex.[b] Remember, we
warned you that he punishes everyone who does such
things. 7God didn't choose you to be filthy, but to be pure.
8So if you don't obey these rules, you are not really dis-
obeying us. You are disobeying God, who gives you his
Holy Spirit.

9We don't have to write you about the need to love each
other. God has taught you to do this, 10and you already
have shown your love for all of his people in Macedonia.
But, my dear friends, we ask you to do even more. 11Try
your best to live quietly, to mind your own business, and
to work hard, just as we taught you to do. 12Then you will
be respected by people who are not followers of the Lord,
and you won't have to depend on anyone.

[a] **4.4** *your wife*: Or "your body." [b] **4.6** *in matters of sex*: Or "in business."

NEW INTERNATIONAL VERSION

more. 2For you know what instructions we gave you by the authority of the Lord Jesus.

3It is God's will that you should be sanctified: that you should avoid sexual immorality; 4that each of you should learn to control his own body[a] in a way that is holy and honorable, 5not in passionate lust like the heathen, who do not know God; 6and that in this matter no one should wrong his brother or take advantage of him. The Lord will punish men for all such sins, as we have already told you and warned you. 7For God did not call us to be impure, but to live a holy life. 8Therefore, he who rejects this instruction does not reject man but God, who gives you his Holy Spirit.

9Now about brotherly love we do not need to write to you, for you yourselves have been taught by God to love each other. 10And in fact, you do love all the brothers throughout Macedonia. Yet we urge you, brothers, to do so more and more.

11Make it your ambition to lead a quiet life, to mind your own business and to work with your hands, just as we told you, 12so that your daily life may win the respect of outsiders and so that you will not be dependent on anybody.

[a] 4 Or *learn to live with his own wife*; or *learn to acquire a wife*

NEW LIVING TRANSLATION

remember what we taught you in the name of the Lord Jesus. 3God wants you to be holy, so you should keep clear of all sexual sin. 4Then each of you will control your body* and live in holiness and honor—5not in lustful passion as the pagans do, in their ignorance of God and his ways.

6Never cheat a Christian brother in this matter by taking his wife, for the Lord avenges all such sins, as we have solemnly warned you before. 7God has called us to be holy, not to live impure lives. 8Anyone who refuses to live by these rules is not disobeying human rules but is rejecting God, who gives his Holy Spirit to you.

9But I don't need to write to you about the Christian love* that should be shown among God's people. For God himself has taught you to love one another. 10Indeed, your love is already strong toward all the Christians* in all of Macedonia. Even so, dear brothers and sisters, we beg you to love them more and more. 11This should be your ambition: to live a quiet life, minding your own business and working with your hands, just as we commanded you before. 12As a result, people who are not Christians will respect the way you live, and you will not need to depend on others to meet your financial needs.

4:4 Or *will know how to take a wife for himself;* Greek reads *will know how to possess his own vessel.* **4:9** Greek *brotherly love.* **4:10** Greek *the brothers.*

NEW KING JAMES VERSION

God; 2for you know what commandments we gave you through the Lord Jesus.

3For this is the will of God, your sanctification: that you should abstain from sexual immorality; 4that each of you should know how to possess his own vessel in sanctification and honor, 5not in passion of lust, like the Gentiles who do not know God; 6that no one should take advantage of and defraud his brother in this matter, because the Lord *is* the avenger of all such, as we also forewarned you and testified. 7For God did not call us to uncleanness, but in holiness. 8Therefore he who rejects *this* does not reject man, but God, who has also given[a] us His Holy Spirit.

A Brotherly and Orderly Life

9But concerning brotherly love you have no need that I should write to you, for you yourselves are taught by God to love one another; 10and indeed you do so toward all the brethren who are in all Macedonia. But we urge you, brethren, that you increase more and more; 11that you also aspire to lead a quiet life, to mind your own business, and to work with your own hands, as we commanded you, 12that you may walk properly toward those who are outside, and *that* you may lack nothing.

4:8 [a] NU-Text reads *who also gives.*

THE MESSAGE

living, spirited dance. You know the guidelines we laid out for you from the Master Jesus. God wants you to live a pure life.

Keep yourselves from sexual promiscuity.

Learn to appreciate and give dignity to your body, not abusing it, as is so common among those who know nothing of God.

Don't run roughshod over the concerns of your brothers and sisters. Their concerns are God's concerns, and *he* will take care of them. We've warned you about this before. God hasn't invited us into a disorderly, unkempt life but into something holy and beautiful—as beautiful on the inside as the outside.

If you disregard this advice, you're not offending your neighbors; you're rejecting God, who is making you a gift of his Holy Spirit.

Regarding life together and getting along with each other, you don't need me to tell you what to do. You're *God*-taught in these matters. Just love one another! You're already good at it; your friends all over the province of Macedonia are the evidence. Keep it up; get better and better at it.

Stay calm; mind your own business; do your own job. You've heard all this from us before, but a reminder never hurts. We want you living in a way that will command the respect of outsiders, not lying around sponging off your friends.

KING JAMES VERSION

13 ¶ But I would not have you to be ignorant, brethren, concerning them which are asleep, that ye sorrow not, even as others which have no hope.

14 For if we believe that Jesus died and rose again, even so them also which sleep in Jesus will God bring with him.

15 For this we say unto you by the word of the Lord, that we which are alive *and* remain unto the coming of the Lord shall not prevent them which are asleep.

16 For the Lord himself shall descend from heaven with a shout, with the voice of the archangel, and with the trump of God: and the dead in Christ shall rise first:

17 Then we which are alive *and* remain shall be caught up together with them in the clouds, to meet the Lord in the air: and so shall we ever be with the Lord.

18 Wherefore comfort one another with these words.

5 But of the times and the seasons, brethren, ye have no need that I write unto you.

2 For yourselves know perfectly that the day of the Lord so cometh as a thief in the night.

3 For when they shall say, Peace and safety; then sudden destruction cometh upon them, as travail upon a woman with child; and they shall not escape.

NEW AMERICAN STANDARD BIBLE

Those Who Died in Christ

13 But we do not want you to be uninformed, brethren, about those who are asleep, so that you will not grieve as do the rest who have no hope.

14 For if we believe that Jesus died and rose again, even so God will bring with Him those who have fallen asleep in Jesus.

15 For this we say to you by the word of the Lord, that we who are alive and remain until the coming of the Lord, will not precede those who have fallen asleep.

16 For the Lord Himself will descend from heaven with a shout, with the voice of *the* archangel and with the trumpet of God, and the dead in Christ will rise first.

17 Then we who are alive and remain will be caught up together with them in the clouds to meet the Lord in the air, and so we shall always be with the Lord.

18 Therefore comfort one another with these words.

The Day of the Lord

5 Now as to the times and the epochs, brethren, you have no need of anything to be written to you.

2 For you yourselves know full well that the day of the Lord will come just like a thief in the night.

3 While they are saying, "Peace and safety!" then destruction will come upon them suddenly like labor pains upon a woman with child, and they will not escape.

NEW CENTURY VERSION

The Lord's Coming

13 Brothers and sisters, we want you to know about
those Christians who have died so you will not be sad, as
others who have no hope. 14 We believe that Jesus died and
that he rose again. So, because of him, God will raise with
Jesus those who have died. 15 What we tell you now is the
Lord's own message. We who are living when the Lord
comes again will not go before those who have already
died. 16 The Lord himself will come down from heaven with
a loud command, with the voice of the archangel,[b] and
with the trumpet call of God. And those who have died
believing in Christ will rise first. 17 After that, we who are
still alive will be gathered up with them in the clouds to
meet the Lord in the air. And we will be with the Lord forever. 18 So encourage each other with these words.

Be Ready for the Lord's Coming

5 Now, brothers and sisters, we do not need to write
you about times and dates. 2 You know very well that
the day the Lord comes again will be a surprise, like a thief
that comes in the night. 3 While people are saying, "We
have peace and we are safe," they will be destroyed quickly. It is like pains that come quickly to a woman having a
baby. Those people will not escape. 4 But you, brothers and

4:16 [b] **archangel** The leader among God's angels or messengers.

CONTEMPORARY ENGLISH VERSION

The Lord's Coming

13 My friends, we want you to understand how it will be
for those followers who have already died. Then you won't
grieve over them and be like people who don't have any
hope. 14 We believe that Jesus died and was raised to life.
We also believe that when God brings Jesus back again, he
will bring with him all who had faith in Jesus before they
died. 15 Our Lord Jesus told us that when he comes, we
won't go up to meet him ahead of his followers who have
already died.

16 With a loud command and with the shout of the chief
angel and a blast of God's trumpet, the Lord will return
from heaven. Then those who had faith in Christ before
they died will be raised to life. 17 Next, all of us who are
still alive will be taken up into the clouds together with
them to meet the Lord in the sky. From that time on we
will all be with the Lord forever. 18 Encourage each other
with these words.

5 I don't need to write you about the time or date when
all this will happen. 2 You surely know that the Lord's
return[a] will be as a thief coming at night. 3 People will
think they are safe and secure. But destruction will suddenly strike them like the pains of a woman about to give
birth. And they won't escape.

[a] 5.2 *the Lord's return*: The Greek text has "the day of the Lord."

NEW INTERNATIONAL VERSION

The Coming of the Lord

13Brothers, we do not want you to be ignorant about
those who fall asleep, or to grieve like the rest of men, who
have no hope. 14We believe that Jesus died and rose again
and so we believe that God will bring with Jesus those who
have fallen asleep in him. 15According to the Lord's own
word, we tell you that we who are still alive, who are left
till the coming of the Lord, will certainly not precede those
who have fallen asleep. 16For the Lord himself will come
down from heaven, with a loud command, with the voice
of the archangel and with the trumpet call of God, and the
dead in Christ will rise first. 17After that, we who are still
alive and are left will be caught up together with them in
the clouds to meet the Lord in the air. And so we will be
with the Lord forever. 18Therefore encourage each other
with these words.

5 Now, brothers, about times and dates we do not need
to write to you, 2for you know very well that the day
of the Lord will come like a thief in the night. 3While peo-
ple are saying, "Peace and safety," destruction will come
on them suddenly, as labor pains on a pregnant woman,
and they will not escape.

NEW LIVING TRANSLATION

The Hope of the Resurrection

13And now, brothers and sisters, I want you to know
what will happen to the Christians who have died so you
will not be full of sorrow like people who have no hope.
14For since we believe that Jesus died and was raised to
life again, we also believe that when Jesus comes, God will
bring back with Jesus all the Christians who have died.

15I can tell you this directly from the Lord: We who are
still living when the Lord returns will not rise to meet him
ahead of those who are in their graves. 16For the Lord him-
self will come down from heaven with a commanding
shout, with the call of the archangel, and with the trumpet
call of God. First, all the Christians who have died will rise
from their graves. 17Then, together with them, we who are
still alive and remain on the earth will be caught up in the
clouds to meet the Lord in the air and remain with him for-
ever. 18So comfort and encourage each other with these
words.

5 I really don't need to write to you about how and
when all this will happen, dear brothers and sisters.*
2For you know quite well that the day of the Lord will
come unexpectedly, like a thief in the night. 3When people
are saying, "All is well; everything is peaceful and secure,"
then disaster will fall upon them as suddenly as a wom-
an's birth pains begin when her child is about to be born.
And there will be no escape.

5:1 Greek *brothers;* also in 5:4, 12, 14, 25, 26, 27.

NEW KING JAMES VERSION

The Comfort of Christ's Coming

13But I do not want you to be ignorant, brethren, con-
cerning those who have fallen asleep, lest you sorrow as
others who have no hope. 14For if we believe that Jesus
died and rose again, even so God will bring with Him those
who sleep in Jesus.[b]

15For this we say to you by the word of the Lord, that we
who are alive *and* remain until the coming of the Lord will
by no means precede those who are asleep. 16For the Lord
Himself will descend from heaven with a shout, with the
voice of an archangel, and with the trumpet of God. And
the dead in Christ will rise first. 17Then we who are alive
and remain shall be caught up together with them in the
clouds to meet the Lord in the air. And thus we shall
always be with the Lord. 18Therefore comfort one another
with these words.

The Day of the Lord

5 But concerning the times and the seasons, brethren,
you have no need that I should write to you. 2For you
yourselves know perfectly that the day of the Lord so
comes as a thief in the night. 3For when they say, "Peace
and safety!" then sudden destruction comes upon them, as
labor pains upon a pregnant woman. And they shall not

4:14 [b] Or *those who through Jesus sleep*

THE MESSAGE

The Master's Coming

And regarding the question, friends, that has come up about what happens to those already dead and buried, we don't want you in the dark any longer. First off, you must not carry on over them like people who have nothing to look forward to, as if the grave were the last word. Since Jesus died and broke loose from the grave, God will most certainly bring back to life those who died in Jesus.

And then this: We can tell you with complete confidence—we have the Master's word on it—that when the Master comes again to get us, those of us who are still alive will not get a jump on the dead and leave them behind. In actual fact, they'll be ahead of us. The Master himself will give the command. Archangel thunder! God's trumpet blast! He'll come down from heaven and the dead in Christ will rise—they'll go first. Then the rest of us who are still alive at the time will be caught up with them into the clouds to meet the Master. Oh, we'll be walking on air! And then there will be one huge family reunion with the Master. So reassure one another with these words.

5 I don't think, friends, that I need to deal with the question of when all this is going to happen. You know as well as I that the day of the Master's coming can't be posted on our calendars. He won't call ahead and make an appointment any more than a burglar would. About the time everybody's walking around complacently, congratulating each other—"We've sure got it made! Now we can take it easy!"—suddenly everything will fall apart. It's going to come as suddenly and inescapably as birth pangs to a pregnant woman.

KING JAMES VERSION

4 But ye, brethren, are not in darkness, that that day should overtake you as a thief.

5 Ye are all the children of light, and the children of the day: we are not of the night, nor of darkness.

6 ¶ Therefore let us not sleep, as *do* others; but let us watch and be sober.

7 For they that sleep sleep in the night; and they that be drunken are drunken in the night.

8 But let us, who are of the day, be sober, putting on the breastplate of faith and love; and for an helmet, the hope of salvation.

9 For God hath not appointed us to wrath, but to obtain salvation by our Lord Jesus Christ,

10 Who died for us, that, whether we wake or sleep, we should live together with him.

11 ¶ Wherefore comfort yourselves together, and edify one another, even as also ye do.

12 And we beseech you, brethren, to know them which labour among you, and are over you in the Lord, and admonish you;

13 And to esteem them very highly in love for their work's sake. *And* be at peace among yourselves.

14 Now we exhort you, brethren, warn them that are unruly, comfort the feebleminded, support the weak, be patient toward all *men*.

NEW AMERICAN STANDARD BIBLE

4 But you, brethren, are not in darkness, that the day would overtake you like a thief;

5 for you are all sons of light and sons of day. We are not of night nor of darkness;

6 so then let us not sleep as others do, but let us be alert and [1]sober.

7 For those who sleep do their sleeping at night, and those who get drunk get drunk at night.

8 But since we are of *the* day, let us be [1]sober, having put on the breastplate of faith and love, and as a helmet, the hope of salvation.

9 For God has not destined us for wrath, but for obtaining salvation through our Lord Jesus Christ,

10 who died for us, so that whether we are awake or asleep, we will live together with Him.

11 Therefore encourage one another and build up one another, just as you also are doing.

Christian Conduct

12 But we request of you, brethren, that you appreciate those who diligently labor among you, and have charge over you in the Lord and give you instruction,

13 and that you esteem them very highly in love because of their work. Live in peace with one another.

14 We urge you, brethren, admonish the unruly, encourage the fainthearted, help the weak, be patient with everyone.

5:6,8 [1] Or *self-controlled*

NEW CENTURY VERSION

sisters, are not living in darkness, and so that day will not surprise you like a thief. 5You are all people who belong to the light and to the day. We do not belong to the night or to darkness. 6So we should not be like other people who are sleeping, but we should be alert and have self-control. 7Those who sleep, sleep at night. Those who get drunk, get drunk at night. 8But we belong to the day, so we should control ourselves. We should wear faith and love to protect us, and the hope of salvation should be our helmet. 9God did not choose us to suffer his anger but to have salvation through our Lord Jesus Christ. 10Jesus died for us so that we can live together with him, whether we are alive or dead when he comes. 11So encourage each other and give each other strength, just as you are doing now.

Final Instructions and Greetings

12Now, brothers and sisters, we ask you to appreciate those who work hard among you, who lead you in the Lord and teach you. 13Respect them with a very special love because of the work they do.

Live in peace with each other. 14We ask you, brothers and sisters, to warn those who do not work. Encourage the people who are afraid. Help those who are weak. Be patient

CONTEMPORARY ENGLISH VERSION

4My dear friends, you don't live in darkness, and so that day won't surprise you like a thief. 5You belong to the light and live in the day. We don't live in the night or belong to the dark. 6Others may sleep, but we should stay awake and be alert. 7People sleep during the night, and some even get drunk. 8But we belong to the day. So we must stay sober and let our faith and love be like a suit of armor. Our firm hope that we will be saved is our helmet.

9God doesn't intend to punish us, but wants us to be saved by our Lord Jesus Christ. 10Christ died for us, so that we could live with him, whether we are alive or dead when he comes. 11That's why you must encourage and help each other, just as you are already doing.

Final Instructions and Greetings

12My friends, we ask you to be thoughtful of your leaders who work hard and tell you how to live for the Lord. 13Show them great respect and love because of their work. Try to get along with each other. 14My friends, we beg you to warn anyone who isn't living right. Encourage anyone who feels left out, help all who are weak, and be patient

NEW INTERNATIONAL VERSION

4But you, brothers, are not in darkness so that this day
should surprise you like a thief. 5You are all sons of the
light and sons of the day. We do not belong to the night or
to the darkness. 6So then, let us not be like others, who
are asleep, but let us be alert and self-controlled. 7For
those who sleep, sleep at night, and those who get drunk,
get drunk at night. 8But since we belong to the day, let us
be self-controlled, putting on faith and love as a breast-
plate, and the hope of salvation as a helmet. 9For God did
not appoint us to suffer wrath but to receive salvation
through our Lord Jesus Christ. 10He died for us so that,
whether we are awake or asleep, we may live together with
him. 11Therefore encourage one another and build each
other up, just as in fact you are doing.

Final Instructions

12Now we ask you, brothers, to respect those who work
hard among you, who are over you in the Lord and who
admonish you. 13Hold them in the highest regard in love
because of their work. Live in peace with each other. 14And
we urge you, brothers, warn those who are idle, encourage
the timid, help the weak, be patient with everyone. 15Make

NEW LIVING TRANSLATION

4But you aren't in the dark about these things, dear
brothers and sisters, and you won't be surprised when the
day of the Lord comes like a thief. 5For you are all children
of the light and of the day; we don't belong to darkness
and night. 6So be on your guard, not asleep like the others.
Stay alert and be sober. 7Night is the time for sleep and
the time when people get drunk. 8But let us who live in the
light think clearly, protected by the body armor of faith
and love, and wearing as our helmet the confidence of our
salvation. 9For God decided to save us through our Lord
Jesus Christ, not to pour out his anger on us. 10He died for
us so that we can live with him forever, whether we are
dead or alive at the time of his return. 11So encourage each
other and build each other up, just as you are already
doing.

Paul's Final Advice

12Dear brothers and sisters, honor those who are your
leaders in the Lord's work. They work hard among you and
warn you against all that is wrong. 13Think highly of them
and give them your wholehearted love because of their
work. And remember to live peaceably with each other.

14Brothers and sisters, we urge you to warn those who
are lazy. Encourage those who are timid. Take tender care
of those who are weak. Be patient with everyone.

NEW KING JAMES VERSION

escape. 4But you, brethren, are not in darkness, so that
this Day should overtake you as a thief. 5You are all sons
of light and sons of the day. We are not of the night nor of
darkness. 6Therefore let us not sleep, as others *do,* but let
us watch and be sober. 7For those who sleep, sleep at
night, and those who get drunk are drunk at night. 8But
let us who are of the day be sober, putting on the breast-
plate of faith and love, and *as* a helmet the hope of salva-
tion. 9For God did not appoint us to wrath, but to obtain
salvation through our Lord Jesus Christ, 10who died for us,
that whether we wake or sleep, we should live together
with Him.

11Therefore comfort each other and edify one another,
just as you also are doing.

Various Exhortations

12And we urge you, brethren, to recognize those who
labor among you, and are over you in the Lord and admon-
ish you, 13and to esteem them very highly in love for their
work's sake. Be at peace among yourselves.

14Now we exhort you, brethren, warn those who are un-
ruly, comfort the fainthearted, uphold the weak, be patient

THE MESSAGE

But friends, you're not in the dark, so how could you be taken off guard by any of this? You're sons of Light, daughters of Day. We live under wide open skies and know where we stand. So let's not sleepwalk through life like those others. Let's keep our eyes open and be smart. People sleep at night and get drunk at night. But not us! Since we're creatures of Day, let's act like it. Walk out into the daylight sober, dressed up in faith, love, and the hope of salvation.

God didn't set us up for an angry rejection but for salvation by our Master, Jesus Christ. He died for us, a death that triggered life. Whether we're awake with the living or asleep with the dead, we're *alive* with him! So speak encouraging words to one another. Build up hope so you'll all be together in this, no one left out, no one left behind. I know you're already doing this; just keep on doing it.

The Way He Wants You to Live

And now, friends, we ask you to honor those leaders who work so hard for you, who have been given the responsibility of urging and guiding you along in your obedience. Overwhelm them with appreciation and love!

Get along among yourselves, each of you doing your part. Our counsel is that you warn the freeloaders to get a move on. Gently encourage the stragglers, and reach out for the exhausted, pulling them to their feet. Be patient with each person, attentive to individual needs. And be

KING JAMES VERSION

15 See that none render evil for evil unto any *man*; but ever follow that which is good, both among yourselves, and to all *men*.

16 ¶ Rejoice evermore.

17 Pray without ceasing.

18 In every thing give thanks: for this is the will of God in Christ Jesus concerning you.

19 Quench not the Spirit.

20 Despise not prophesyings.

21 Prove all things; hold fast that which is good.

22 Abstain from all appearance of evil.

23 ¶ And the very God of peace sanctify you wholly; and *I pray God* your whole spirit and soul and body be preserved blameless unto the coming of our Lord Jesus Christ.

24 Faithful *is* he that calleth you, who also will do *it*.

25 Brethren, pray for us.

26 Greet all the brethren with an holy kiss.

27 I charge you by the Lord that this epistle be read unto all the holy brethren.

28 The grace of our Lord Jesus Christ *be* with you. Amen.

NEW AMERICAN STANDARD BIBLE

15 See that no one repays another with evil for evil, but always seek after that which is good for one another and for all people.

16 Rejoice always;

17 pray without ceasing;

18 in everything give thanks; for this is God's will for you in Christ Jesus.

19 Do not quench the Spirit;

20 do not despise prophetic [2]utterances.

21 But examine everything *carefully;* hold fast to that which is good;

22 abstain from every [3]form of evil.

23 Now may the God of peace Himself sanctify you entirely; and may your spirit and soul and body be preserved complete, without blame at the coming of our Lord Jesus Christ.

24 Faithful is He who calls you, and He also will bring it to pass.

25 Brethren, pray for us[4].

26 Greet all the brethren with a holy kiss.

27 I adjure you by the Lord to have this letter read to all the brethren.

28 The grace of our Lord Jesus Christ be with you.

5:20 [2] Or *gifts* 5:22 [3] Or *appearance* 5:25 [4] Two early mss add *also*

NEW CENTURY VERSION

with everyone. 15 Be sure that no one pays back wrong for
wrong, but always try to do what is good for each other and
for all people.
16 Always be joyful. 17 Pray continually, 18 and give
thanks whatever happens. That is what God wants for you
in Christ Jesus.
19 Do not hold back the work of the Holy Spirit. 20 Do not
treat prophecy as if it were unimportant. 21 But test every-
thing. Keep what is good, 22 and stay away from everything
that is evil.
23 Now may God himself, the God of peace, make you
pure, belonging only to him. May your whole self—spirit,
soul, and body—be kept safe and without fault when our
Lord Jesus Christ comes. 24 You can trust the One who calls
you to do that for you.
25 Brothers and sisters, pray for us.
26 Give each other a holy kiss when you meet. 27 I tell you
by the authority of the Lord to read this letter to all the
believers.
28 The grace of our Lord Jesus Christ be with you.

CONTEMPORARY ENGLISH VERSION

with everyone. 15 Don't be hateful to people, just because
they are hateful to you. Rather, be good to each other and
to everyone else.
16 Always be joyful 17 and never stop praying. 18 Whatever
happens, keep thanking God because of Jesus Christ. This
is what God wants you to do.
19 Don't turn away God's Spirit 20 or ignore prophecies.
21 Put everything to the test. Accept what is good 22 and
don't have anything to do with evil.
23 I pray that God, who gives peace, will make you com-
pletely holy. And may your spirit, soul, and body be kept
healthy and faultless until our Lord Jesus Christ returns.
24 The one who chose you can be trusted, and he will do
this.
25 Friends, please pray for us.
26 Give the Lord's followers a warm greeting.
27 In the name of the Lord I beg you to read this letter to
all his followers.
28 I pray that our Lord Jesus Christ will be kind to you!

NEW INTERNATIONAL VERSION

sure that nobody pays back wrong for wrong, but always try to be kind to each other and to everyone else.

16Be joyful always; 17pray continually; 18give thanks in all circumstances, for this is God's will for you in Christ Jesus.

19Do not put out the Spirit's fire; 20do not treat prophecies with contempt. 21Test everything. Hold on to the good. 22Avoid every kind of evil.

23May God himself, the God of peace, sanctify you through and through. May your whole spirit, soul and body be kept blameless at the coming of our Lord Jesus Christ. 24The one who calls you is faithful and he will do it.

25Brothers, pray for us. 26Greet all the brothers with a holy kiss. 27I charge you before the Lord to have this letter read to all the brothers.

28The grace of our Lord Jesus Christ be with you.

NEW LIVING TRANSLATION

15See that no one pays back evil for evil, but always try to do good to each other and to everyone else.

16Always be joyful. 17Keep on praying. 18No matter what happens, always be thankful, for this is God's will for you who belong to Christ Jesus.

19Do not stifle the Holy Spirit. 20Do not scoff at prophecies, 21but test everything that is said. Hold on to what is good. 22Keep away from every kind of evil.

Paul's Final Greetings

23Now may the God of peace make you holy in every way, and may your whole spirit and soul and body be kept blameless until that day when our Lord Jesus Christ comes again. 24God, who calls you, is faithful; he will do this.

25Dear brothers and sisters, pray for us.

26Greet all the brothers and sisters in Christian love.*

27I command you in the name of the Lord to read this letter to all the brothers and sisters.

28And may the grace of our Lord Jesus Christ be with all of you.

5:26 Greek *with a holy kiss.*

NEW KING JAMES VERSION

with all. 15See that no one renders evil for evil to anyone, but always pursue what is good both for yourselves and for all.

16Rejoice always, 17pray without ceasing, 18in everything give thanks; for this is the will of God in Christ Jesus for you.

19Do not quench the Spirit. 20Do not despise prophecies. 21Test all things; hold fast what is good. 22Abstain from every form of evil.

Blessing and Admonition

23Now may the God of peace Himself sanctify you completely; and may your whole spirit, soul, and body be preserved blameless at the coming of our Lord Jesus Christ. 24He who calls you *is* faithful, who also will do *it.*

25Brethren, pray for us.

26Greet all the brethren with a holy kiss.

27I charge you by the Lord that this epistle be read to all the holy[a] brethren.

28The grace of our Lord Jesus Christ *be* with you. Amen.

5:27 [a] NU-Text omits *holy.*

THE MESSAGE

careful that when you get on each other's nerves you don't snap at each other. Look for the best in each other, and always do your best to bring it out.

Be cheerful no matter what; pray all the time; thank God no matter what happens. This is the way God wants you who belong to Christ Jesus to live.

Don't suppress the Spirit, and don't stifle those who have a word from the Master. On the other hand, don't be gullible. Check out everything, and keep only what's good. Throw out anything tainted with evil.

May God himself, the God who makes everything holy and whole, make you holy and whole, put you together—spirit, soul, and body—and keep you fit for the coming of our Master, Jesus Christ. The One who called you is completely dependable. If he said it, he'll do it!

Friends, keep up your prayers for us. Greet all the Christians there with a holy embrace. And make sure this letter gets read to all the brothers and sisters. Don't leave anyone out.

The amazing grace of Jesus Christ be with you!

KING JAMES VERSION

THE SECOND EPISTLE OF ST. PAUL TO THE THESSALONIANS

1 Paul, and Silvanus, and Timotheus, unto the church of the Thessalonians in God our Father and the Lord Jesus Christ:

2 Grace unto you, and peace, from God our Father and the Lord Jesus Christ.

3 We are bound to thank God always for you, brethren, as it is meet, because that your faith groweth exceedingly, and the charity of every one of you all toward each other aboundeth;

4 So that we ourselves glory in you in the churches of God for your patience and faith in all your persecutions and tribulations that ye endure:

5 ¶ *Which is* a manifest token of the righteous judgment of God, that ye may be counted worthy of the kingdom of God, for which ye also suffer:

6 Seeing *it is* a righteous thing with God to recompense tribulation to them that trouble you;

7 And to you who are troubled rest with us, when the Lord Jesus shall be revealed from heaven with his mighty angels,

NEW AMERICAN STANDARD BIBLE

THE SECOND LETTER OF PAUL TO THE THESSALONIANS

Thanksgiving for Faith and Perseverance

1 Paul and Silvanus and Timothy,
To the church of the Thessalonians in God our Father and the Lord Jesus Christ:

2 Grace to you and peace from God the Father and the Lord Jesus Christ.

3 We ought always to give thanks to God for you, brethren, as is *only* fitting, because your faith is greatly enlarged, and the love of each one of you toward one another grows *ever* greater;

4 therefore, we ourselves speak proudly of you among the churches of God for your perseverance and faith in the midst of all your persecutions and afflictions which you endure.

5 *This is* a plain indication of God's righteous judgment so that you will be considered worthy of the kingdom of God, for which indeed you are suffering.

6 For after all it is *only* just for God to repay with affliction those who afflict you,

7 and *to give* relief to you who are afflicted and to us as well when the Lord Jesus will be revealed from heaven with His mighty angels in flaming fire,

NEW CENTURY VERSION

2 THESSALONIANS

1 From Paul, Silas, and Timothy.
To the church in Thessalonica in God our Father and
the Lord Jesus Christ:
2Grace and peace to you from God the Father and the
Lord Jesus Christ.

Paul Talks About God's Judgment

3We must always thank God for you, brothers and sis-
ters.[a] This is only right, because your faith is growing
more and more, and the love that every one of you has for
each other is increasing. 4So we brag about you to the
other churches of God. We tell them about the way you
continue to be strong and have faith even though you are
being treated badly and are suffering many troubles.
5This is proof that God is right in his judgment. He wants
you to be counted worthy of his kingdom for which you are
suffering. 6God will do what is right. He will give trouble to
those who trouble you. 7And he will give rest to you who
are troubled and to us also when the Lord Jesus appears
with burning fire from heaven with his powerful angels.

1:3 [a] **brothers and sisters** Although the Greek text says "brothers" here and throughout this book, Paul's words were meant for the entire church, including men and women.

CONTEMPORARY ENGLISH VERSION

2 THESSALONIANS

1 From Paul, Silas,[a] and Timothy.
To the church in Thessalonica, the people of God
our Father and of the Lord Jesus Christ.
2I pray that God our Father and the Lord Jesus Christ
will be kind to you and will bless you with peace!

When Christ Returns

3My dear friends, we always have good reason to thank
God for you, because your faith in God and your love for
each other keep growing all the time. 4That's why we brag
about you to all of God's churches. We tell them how patient
you are and how you keep on having faith, even though you
are going through a lot of trouble and suffering.
5All of this shows that God judges fairly and that he is
making you fit to share in his kingdom for which you are
suffering. 6It is only right for God to punish everyone who
is causing you trouble, 7but he will give you relief from
your troubles. He will do the same for us, when the Lord
Jesus comes from heaven with his powerful angels 8and
with a flaming fire.

[a] 1.1 *Silas*: The Greek text has "Silvanus," which is another form of the name Silas.

NEW INTERNATIONAL VERSION

2 THESSALONIANS

1 Paul, Silas[a] and Timothy,

To the church of the Thessalonians in God our Father
and the Lord Jesus Christ:

2 Grace and peace to you from God the Father and the
Lord Jesus Christ.

Thanksgiving and Prayer

3 We ought always to thank God for you, brothers, and
rightly so, because your faith is growing more and more,
and the love every one of you has for each other is increas-
ing. 4 Therefore, among God's churches we boast about
your perseverance and faith in all the persecutions and tri-
als you are enduring.
5 All this is evidence that God's judgment is right, and as
a result you will be counted worthy of the kingdom of God,
for which you are suffering. 6 God is just: He will pay back
trouble to those who trouble you 7 and give relief to you
who are troubled, and to us as well. This will happen when
the Lord Jesus is revealed from heaven in blazing fire with
his powerful angels. 8 He will punish those who do not

[a] *1* Greek *Silvanus*, a variant of *Silas*

NEW LIVING TRANSLATION

2 THESSALONIANS

Greetings from Paul

1 This letter is from Paul, Silas,* and Timothy.
It is written to the church in Thessalonica, you who
belong to God our Father and the Lord Jesus Christ.
2 May God our Father and the Lord Jesus Christ give you
grace and peace.

Encouragement during Persecution

3 Dear brothers and sisters,* we always thank God for
you, as is right, for we are thankful that your faith is
flourishing and you are all growing in love for each other.
4 We proudly tell God's other churches about your
endurance and faithfulness in all the persecutions and
hardships you are suffering. 5 But God will use this perse-
cution to show his justice. For he will make you worthy of
his Kingdom, for which you are suffering, 6 and in his jus-
tice he will punish those who persecute you. 7 And God will
provide rest for you who are being persecuted and also for
us when the Lord Jesus appears from heaven. He will come
with his mighty angels, 8 in flaming fire, bringing judgment

1:1 Greek *Silvanus*. 1:3 Greek *Brothers*.

NEW KING JAMES VERSION

THE SECOND EPISTLE OF PAUL TO THE

THESSALONIANS

Greeting

1 Paul, Silvanus, and Timothy,

To the church of the Thessalonians in God our Father
and the Lord Jesus Christ:

2 Grace to you and peace from God our Father and the
Lord Jesus Christ.

God's Final Judgment and Glory

3 We are bound to thank God always for you, brethren, as
it is fitting, because your faith grows exceedingly, and the
love of every one of you all abounds toward each other, 4 so
that we ourselves boast of you among the churches of God
for your patience and faith in all your persecutions and
tribulations that you endure, 5 *which is* manifest evidence
of the righteous judgment of God, that you may be counted
worthy of the kingdom of God, for which you also suffer;
6 since *it is* a righteous thing with God to repay with tribu-
lation those who trouble you, 7 and to *give* you who are
troubled rest with us when the Lord Jesus is revealed from
heaven with His mighty angels, 8 in flaming fire taking

THE MESSAGE

2 THESSALONIANS

1 I, Paul, together with Silas and Timothy, greet the
church of the Thessalonian Christians in the name of
God our Father and our Master, Jesus Christ. Our God gives
you everything you need, makes you everything you're to be.

Justice Is On the Way

You need to know, friends, that thanking God over and
over for you is not only a pleasure; it's a must. We *have* to
do it. Your faith is growing phenomenally; your love for
each other is developing wonderfully. Why, it's only right
that we give thanks. We're so proud of you; you're so
steady and determined in your faith despite all the hard
times that have come down on you. We tell everyone we
meet in the churches all about you.

All this trouble is a clear sign that God has decided to
make you fit for the kingdom. You're suffering now, but
justice is on the way. When the Master Jesus appears out
of heaven in a blaze of fire with his strong angels, he'll
even up the score by settling accounts with those who
gave you such a bad time. His coming will be the break

KING JAMES VERSION

8 In flaming fire taking vengeance on them that know not God, and that obey not the gospel of our Lord Jesus Christ:

9 Who shall be punished with everlasting destruction from the presence of the Lord, and from the glory of his power;

10 When he shall come to be glorified in his saints, and to be admired in all them that believe (because our testimony among you was believed) in that day.

11 ¶ Wherefore also we pray always for you, that our God would count you worthy of *this* calling, and fulfil all the good pleasure of *his* goodness, and the work of faith with power:

12 That the name of our Lord Jesus Christ may be glorified in you, and ye in him, according to the grace of our God and the Lord Jesus Christ.

2 Now we beseech you, brethren, by the coming of our Lord Jesus Christ, and *by* our gathering together unto him,

2 That ye be not soon shaken in mind, or be troubled, neither by spirit, nor by word, nor by letter as from us, as that the day of Christ is at hand.

3 ¶ Let no man deceive you by any means: for *that day shall not come*, except there come a falling away first, and that man of sin be revealed, the son of perdition;

NEW AMERICAN STANDARD BIBLE

8 dealing out retribution to those who do not know God and to those who do not obey the gospel of our Lord Jesus.

9 These will pay the penalty of eternal destruction, away from the presence of the Lord and from the glory of His power,

10 when He comes to be glorified in His saints on that day, and to be marveled at among all who have believed—for our testimony to you was believed.

11 To this end also we pray for you always, that our God will count you worthy of your calling, and fulfill every desire for goodness and the work of faith with power,

12 so that the name of our Lord Jesus will be glorified in you, and you in Him, according to the grace of our God and *the* Lord Jesus Christ.

Man of Lawlessness

2 Now we request you, brethren, with regard to the coming of our Lord Jesus Christ and our gathering together to Him,

2 that you not be quickly shaken from your composure or be disturbed either by a spirit or a message or a letter as if from us, to the effect that the day of the Lord has come.

3 Let no one in any way deceive you, for *it will not come* unless the [1]apostasy comes first, and the man of lawlessness is revealed, the son of destruction,

2:3 [1] Or *falling away* from the faith

NEW CENTURY VERSION

8Then he will punish those who do not know God and who do not obey the Good News about our Lord Jesus Christ. 9Those people will be punished with a destruction that continues forever. They will be kept away from the Lord and from his great power. 10This will happen on the day when the Lord Jesus comes to receive glory because of his holy people. And all the people who have believed will be amazed at Jesus. You will be in that group, because you believed what we told you.

11That is why we always pray for you, asking our God to help you live the kind of life he called you to live. We pray that with his power God will help you do the good things you want and perform the works that come from your faith. 12We pray all this so that the name of our Lord Jesus Christ will have glory in you, and you will have glory in him. That glory comes from the grace of our God and the Lord Jesus Christ.

Evil Things Will Happen

2 Brothers and sisters, we have something to say about the coming of our Lord Jesus Christ and the time when we will meet together with him. 2Do not become easily upset in your thinking or afraid if you hear that the day of the Lord has already come. Someone may say this in a prophecy or in a message or in a letter as if it came from us. 3Do not let anyone fool you in any way. That day of the Lord will not come until the turning away[a] from God happens and the Man of Evil, who is on his way to hell,

2:3 [a] **turning away** Or "the rebellion."

CONTEMPORARY ENGLISH VERSION

Our Lord Jesus will punish anyone who doesn't know God and won't obey his message. 9Their punishment will be eternal destruction, and they will be kept far from the presence of our Lord and his glorious strength. 10This will happen on that day when the Lord returns to be praised and honored by all who have faith in him and belong to him. This includes you, because you believed what we said.

11God chose you, and we keep praying that God will make you worthy of being his people. We pray for God's power to help you do all the good things that you hope to do and that your faith makes you want to do. 12Then, because God and our Lord Jesus Christ are so kind, you will bring honor to the name of our Lord Jesus, and he will bring honor to you.

The Lord's Return

2 When our Lord Jesus returns, we will be gathered up to meet him. So I ask you, my friends, 2not to be easily upset or disturbed by people who claim that the Lord[a] has already come. They may say that they heard this directly from the Holy Spirit, or from someone else, or even that they read it in one of our letters. 3But don't be fooled! People will rebel against God. Then before the Lord returns, the wicked[b] one who is doomed to be destroyed will appear.

[a] **2.2** *Lord*: The Greek text has "day of the Lord." [b] **2.3** *wicked*: Some manuscripts have "sinful."

NEW INTERNATIONAL VERSION

know God and do not obey the gospel of our Lord Jesus. [9]They will be punished with everlasting destruction and shut out from the presence of the Lord and from the majesty of his power [10]on the day he comes to be glorified in his holy people and to be marveled at among all those who have believed. This includes you, because you believed our testimony to you.

[11]With this in mind, we constantly pray for you, that our God may count you worthy of his calling, and that by his power he may fulfill every good purpose of yours and every act prompted by your faith. [12]We pray this so that the name of our Lord Jesus may be glorified in you, and you in him, according to the grace of our God and the Lord Jesus Christ.[b]

The Man of Lawlessness

2 Concerning the coming of our Lord Jesus Christ and our being gathered to him, we ask you, brothers, [2]not to become easily unsettled or alarmed by some prophecy, report or letter supposed to have come from us, saying that the day of the Lord has already come. [3]Don't let anyone deceive you in any way, for ⌊that day will not come⌋ until the rebellion occurs and the man of lawlessness[a] is revealed, the man doomed to destruction. [4]He will oppose

[b] *12* Or *God and Lord, Jesus Christ* [a] *3* Some manuscripts *sin*

NEW LIVING TRANSLATION

on those who don't know God and on those who refuse to obey the Good News of our Lord Jesus. [9]They will be punished with everlasting destruction, forever separated from the Lord and from his glorious power [10]when he comes to receive glory and praise from his holy people. And you will be among those praising him on that day, for you believed what we testified about him.

[11]And so we keep on praying for you, that our God will make you worthy of the life to which he called you. And we pray that God, by his power, will fulfill all your good intentions and faithful deeds. [12]Then everyone will give honor to the name of our Lord Jesus because of you, and you will be honored along with him. This is all made possible because of the undeserved favor of our God and Lord, Jesus Christ.*

Events prior to the Lord's Second Coming

2 And now, brothers and sisters,* let us tell you about the coming again of our Lord Jesus Christ and how we will be gathered together to meet him. [2]Please don't be so easily shaken and troubled by those who say that the day of the Lord has already begun. Even if they claim to have had a vision, a revelation, or a letter supposedly from us, don't believe them. [3]Don't be fooled by what they say.

For that day will not come until there is a great rebellion against God and the man of lawlessness is revealed—the one who brings destruction.* [4]He will exalt himself and

1:12 Or *of our God and the Lord Jesus Christ.* 2:1 Greek *brothers;* also in 2:13, 15. 2:3 Greek *the son of destruction.*

NEW KING JAMES VERSION

vengeance on those who do not know God, and on those who do not obey the gospel of our Lord Jesus Christ. [9]These shall be punished with everlasting destruction from the presence of the Lord and from the glory of His power, [10]when He comes, in that Day, to be glorified in His saints and to be admired among all those who believe,[a] because our testimony among you was believed.

[11]Therefore we also pray always for you that our God would count you worthy of *this* calling, and fulfill all the good pleasure of *His* goodness and the work of faith with power, [12]that the name of our Lord Jesus Christ may be glorified in you, and you in Him, according to the grace of our God and the Lord Jesus Christ.

The Great Apostasy

2 Now, brethren, concerning the coming of our Lord Jesus Christ and our gathering together to Him, we ask you, [2]not to be soon shaken in mind or troubled, either by spirit or by word or by letter, as if from us, as though the day of Christ[a] had come. [3]Let no one deceive you by any means; for *that Day will not come* unless the falling away comes first, and the man of sin[b] is revealed, the son of

1:10 [a] NU-Text and M-Text read *have believed.* 2:2 [a] NU-Text reads *the Lord.* 2:3 [b] NU-Text reads *lawlessness.*

THE MESSAGE

we've been waiting for. Those who refuse to know God and refuse to obey the Message will pay for what they've done. Eternal exile from the presence of the Master and his splendid power is their sentence. But on that very same day when he comes, he will be exalted by his followers and celebrated by all who believe—and all because you believed what we told you.

Because we know that this extraordinary day is just ahead, we pray for you all the time—pray that our God will make you fit for what he's called you to be, pray that he'll fill your good ideas and acts of faith with his own energy so that it all amounts to something. If your life honors the name of Jesus, he will honor you. Grace is behind and through all of this, our God giving himself freely, the Master, Jesus Christ, giving himself freely.

The Anarchist

2 Now, friends, read these next words carefully. Slow down and don't go jumping to conclusions regarding the day when our Master, Jesus Christ, will come back and we assemble to welcome him. Don't let anyone shake you up or get you excited over some breathless report or rumored letter from me that the day of the Master's arrival has come and gone. Don't fall for any line like that.

Before that day comes, a couple of things have to happen. First, the Apostasy. Second, the debut of the Anarchist, a real dog of Satan. He'll defy and then take over every

KING JAMES VERSION

4 Who opposeth and exalteth himself above all that is called God, or that is worshipped; so that he as God sitteth in the temple of God, shewing himself that he is God.

5 Remember ye not, that, when I was yet with you, I told you these things?

6 And now ye know what withholdeth that he might be revealed in his time.

7 For the mystery of iniquity doth already work: only he who now letteth *will let*, until he be taken out of the way.

8 And then shall that Wicked be revealed, whom the Lord shall consume with the spirit of his mouth, and shall destroy with the brightness of his coming:

9 *Even him*, whose coming is after the working of Satan with all power and signs and lying wonders,

10 And with all deceivableness of unrighteousness in them that perish; because they received not the love of the truth, that they might be saved.

11 And for this cause God shall send them strong delusion, that they should believe a lie:

12 That they all might be damned who believed not the truth, but had pleasure in unrighteousness.

13 ¶ But we are bound to give thanks alway to God for you, brethren beloved of the Lord, because God hath from the beginning chosen you to salvation through sanctification of the Spirit and belief of the truth:

NEW AMERICAN STANDARD BIBLE

4 who opposes and exalts himself above every so-called god or object of worship, so that he takes his seat in the temple of God, displaying himself as being God.

5 Do you not remember that while I was still with you, I was telling you these things?

6 And you know what restrains him now, so that in his time he will be revealed.

7 For the mystery of lawlessness is already at work; only he who now restrains *will do so* until he is taken out of the way.

8 Then that lawless one will be revealed whom the Lord will slay with the breath of His mouth and bring to an end by the appearance of His coming;

9 *that is,* the one whose coming is in accord with the activity of Satan, with all power and signs and false wonders,

10 and with all the deception of wickedness for those who perish, because they did not receive the love of the truth so as to be saved.

11 For this reason God will send upon them a deluding influence so that they will believe what is false,

12 in order that they all may be judged who did not believe the truth, but took pleasure in wickedness.

13 But we should always give thanks to God for you, brethren beloved by the Lord, because God has chosen you [2]from the beginning for salvation through sanctification by the Spirit and faith in the truth.

2:13 [2] One early ms reads *first fruits*

NEW CENTURY VERSION

appears. 4He will be against and put himself above any-
thing called God or anything that people worship. And that
Man of Evil will even go into God's Temple and sit there
and say that he is God.
5I told you when I was with you that all this would hap-
pen. Do you not remember? 6And now you know what is
stopping that Man of Evil so he will appear at the right
time. 7The secret power of evil is already working in the
world, but there is one who is stopping that power. And he
will continue to stop it until he is taken out of the way.
8Then that Man of Evil will appear, and the Lord Jesus will
kill him with the breath that comes from his mouth and
will destroy him with the glory of his coming. 9The Man of
Evil will come by the power of Satan. He will have great
power, and he will do many different false miracles, signs,
and wonders. 10He will use every kind of evil to trick those
who are lost. They will die, because they refused to love
the truth. (If they loved the truth, they would be saved.)
11For this reason God sends them something powerful that
leads them away from the truth so they will believe a lie.
12So all those will be judged guilty who did not believe the
truth, but enjoyed doing evil.

You Are Chosen for Salvation

13Brothers and sisters, whom the Lord loves, God chose
you from the beginning to be saved. So we must always
thank God for you. You are saved by the Spirit that makes
you holy and by your faith in the truth. 14God used the

CONTEMPORARY ENGLISH VERSION

4He will brag and oppose everything that is holy or sacred.
He will even sit in God's temple and claim to be God. 5Don't
you remember that I told you this while I was still with
you?
6You already know what is holding this wicked one back
until it is time for him to come. 7His mysterious power is
already at work, but someone is holding him back. And the
wicked one won't appear until that someone is out of the
way. 8Then he will appear, but the Lord Jesus will kill him
simply by breathing on him. He will be completely
destroyed by the Lord's glorious return.
9When the wicked one appears, Satan will pretend to
work all kinds of miracles, wonders, and signs. 10Lost peo-
ple will be fooled by his evil deeds. They could be saved,
but they will refuse to love the truth and accept it. 11So
God will make sure that they are fooled into believing a lie.
12All of them will be punished, because they would rather
do evil than believe the truth.

Be Faithful

13My friends, the Lord loves you, and it is only natural for
us to thank God for you. God chose you to be the first ones
to be saved.[c] His Spirit made you holy, and you put your

[c] 2.13 *God chose you to be the first ones to be saved*: Some manuscripts have "From the beginning God chose you to be saved."

NEW INTERNATIONAL VERSION

and will exalt himself over everything that is called God or is worshiped, so that he sets himself up in God's temple, proclaiming himself to be God.

5Don't you remember that when I was with you I used to tell you these things? 6And now you know what is holding him back, so that he may be revealed at the proper time. 7For the secret power of lawlessness is already at work; but the one who now holds it back will continue to do so till he is taken out of the way. 8And then the lawless one will be revealed, whom the Lord Jesus will overthrow with the breath of his mouth and destroy by the splendor of his coming. 9The coming of the lawless one will be in accordance with the work of Satan displayed in all kinds of counterfeit miracles, signs and wonders, 10and in every sort of evil that deceives those who are perishing. They perish because they refused to love the truth and so be saved. 11For this reason God sends them a powerful delusion so that they will believe the lie 12and so that all will be condemned who have not believed the truth but have delighted in wickedness.

Stand Firm

13But we ought always to thank God for you, brothers loved by the Lord, because from the beginning God chose you[b] to be saved through the sanctifying work of the Spirit and through belief in the truth. 14He called you to this

[b] 13 Some manuscripts *because God chose you as his firstfruits*

NEW LIVING TRANSLATION

defy every god there is and tear down every object of adoration and worship. He will position himself in the temple of God, claiming that he himself is God. 5Don't you remember that I told you this when I was with you? 6And you know what is holding him back, for he can be revealed only when his time comes.

7For this lawlessness is already at work secretly, and it will remain secret until the one who is holding it back steps out of the way. 8Then the man of lawlessness will be revealed, whom the Lord Jesus will consume with the breath of his mouth and destroy by the splendor of his coming. 9This evil man will come to do the work of Satan with counterfeit power and signs and miracles. 10He will use every kind of wicked deception to fool those who are on their way to destruction because they refuse to believe the truth that would save them. 11So God will send great deception upon them, and they will believe all these lies. 12Then they will be condemned for not believing the truth and for enjoying the evil they do.

Believers Should Stand Firm

13As for us, we always thank God for you, dear brothers and sisters loved by the Lord. We are thankful that God chose you to be among the first* to experience salvation, a salvation that came through the Spirit who makes you holy and by your belief in the truth. 14He called you to

2:13 Some manuscripts read *God chose you from the very beginning.*

NEW KING JAMES VERSION

perdition, 4who opposes and exalts himself above all that is called God or that is worshiped, so that he sits as God[c] in the temple of God, showing himself that he is God.

5Do you not remember that when I was still with you I told you these things? 6And now you know what is restraining, that he may be revealed in his own time. 7For the mystery of lawlessness is already at work; only He[d] who now restrains *will do so* until He[e] is taken out of the way. 8And then the lawless one will be revealed, whom the Lord will consume with the breath of His mouth and destroy with the brightness of His coming. 9The coming of the *lawless one* is according to the working of Satan, with all power, signs, and lying wonders, 10and with all unrighteous deception among those who perish, because they did not receive the love of the truth, that they might be saved. 11And for this reason God will send them strong delusion, that they should believe the lie, 12that they all may be condemned who did not believe the truth but had pleasure in unrighteousness.

Stand Fast

13But we are bound to give thanks to God always for you, brethren beloved by the Lord, because God from the beginning chose you for salvation through sanctification by the Spirit and belief in the truth, 14to which He called

2:4 [c] NU-Text omits *as God.* 2:7 [d] Or *he* [e] Or *he*

THE MESSAGE

so-called god or altar. Having cleared away the opposition, he'll then set himself up in God's Temple as "God Almighty." Don't you remember me going over all this in detail when I was with you? Are your memories that short?

You'll also remember that I told you the Anarchist is being held back until just the right time. That doesn't mean that the spirit of anarchy is not now at work. It is, secretly and underground. But the time will come when the Anarchist will no longer be held back, but will be let loose. But don't worry. The Master Jesus will be right on his heels and blow him away. The Master appears and—puff!—the Anarchist is out of there.

The Anarchist's coming is all Satan's work. All his power and signs and miracles are fake, evil sleight of hand that plays to the gallery of those who hate the truth that could save them. And since they're so obsessed with evil, God rubs their noses in it—gives them what they want. Since they refuse to trust truth, they're banished to their chosen world of lies and illusions.

Meanwhile, we've got our hands full continually thanking God for you, our good friends—so loved by God! God picked you out as his from the very start. Think of it: included in God's original plan of salvation by the bond of faith in the living truth. This is the life of the Spirit he

KING JAMES VERSION

14 Whereunto he called you by our gospel, to the obtaining of the glory of our Lord Jesus Christ.

15 Therefore, brethren, stand fast, and hold the traditions which ye have been taught, whether by word, or our epistle.

16 ¶ Now our Lord Jesus Christ himself, and God, even our Father, which hath loved us, and hath given *us* everlasting consolation and good hope through grace,

17 Comfort your hearts, and stablish you in every good word and work.

3 Finally, brethren, pray for us, that the word of the Lord may have *free* course, and be glorified, even as *it is* with you:

2 And that we may be delivered from unreasonable and wicked men: for all *men* have not faith.

3 But the Lord is faithful, who shall stablish you, and keep *you* from evil.

4 And we have confidence in the Lord touching you, that ye both do and will do the things which we command you.

5 And the Lord direct your hearts into the love of God, and into the patient waiting for Christ.

6 ¶ Now we command you, brethren, in the name of our Lord Jesus Christ, that ye withdraw yourselves from every brother that walketh disorderly, and not after the tradition which he received of us.

NEW AMERICAN STANDARD BIBLE

14 It was for this He called you through our gospel, that you may gain the glory of our Lord Jesus Christ.

15 So then, brethren, stand firm and hold to the traditions which you were taught, whether by word *of mouth* or by letter from us.

16 Now may our Lord Jesus Christ Himself and God our Father, who has loved us and given us eternal comfort and good hope by grace,

17 comfort and strengthen your hearts in every good work and word.

Exhortation

3 Finally, brethren, pray for us that the word of the Lord will spread rapidly and be glorified, just as *it did* also with you;

2 and that we will be rescued from perverse and evil men; for not all have faith.

3 But the Lord is faithful, and He will strengthen and protect you from the evil *one.*

4 We have confidence in the Lord concerning you, that you are doing and will *continue to* do what we command.

5 May the Lord direct your hearts into the love of God and into the steadfastness of Christ.

6 Now we command you, brethren, in the name of our Lord Jesus Christ, that you keep away from every brother who leads an unruly life and not according to the tradition which you received from us.

NEW CENTURY VERSION

Good News that we preached to call you to be saved so you
can share in the glory of our Lord Jesus Christ. 15 So, broth-
ers and sisters, stand strong and continue to believe the
teachings we gave you in our speaking and in our letter.
16–17 May our Lord Jesus Christ himself and God our
Father encourage you and strengthen you in every good
thing you do and say. God loved us, and through his grace
he gave us a good hope and encouragement that continues
forever.

Pray for Us

3 And now, brothers and sisters, pray for us that the
Lord's teaching will continue to spread quickly and
that people will give honor to that teaching, just as hap-
pened with you. 2 And pray that we will be protected from
stubborn and evil people, because not all people believe.
3 But the Lord is faithful and will give you strength and
will protect you from the Evil One. 4 The Lord makes us feel
sure that you are doing and will continue to do the things
we told you. 5 May the Lord lead your hearts into God's
love and Christ's patience.

The Duty to Work

6 Brothers and sisters, by the authority of our Lord Jesus
Christ we command you to stay away from any believer
who refuses to work and does not follow the teaching we

CONTEMPORARY ENGLISH VERSION

faith in the truth. 14 God used our preaching as his way of
inviting you to share in the glory of our Lord Jesus Christ.
15 My friends, that's why you must remain faithful and fol-
low closely what we taught you in person and by our letters.
16 God our Father loves us. He is kind and has given us
eternal comfort and a wonderful hope. We pray that our
Lord Jesus Christ and God our Father 17 will encourage you
and help you always to do and say the right thing.

Pray for Us

3 Finally, our friends, please pray for us. This will help
the message about the Lord to spread quickly, and
others will respect it, just as you do. 2 Pray that we may be
kept safe from worthless and evil people. After all, not
everyone has faith. 3 But the Lord can be trusted to make
you strong and protect you from harm. 4 He has made us
sure that you are obeying what we taught you and that
you will keep on obeying. 5 I pray that the Lord will guide
you to be as loving as God and as patient as Christ.

Warnings against Laziness

6 My dear friends, in the name of[a] the Lord Jesus, I beg
you not to have anything to do with any of your people
who loaf around and refuse to obey the instructions we

[a] 3.6 *in the name of*: Or "as a follower of."

NEW INTERNATIONAL VERSION

through our gospel, that you might share in the glory of our Lord Jesus Christ. 15So then, brothers, stand firm and hold to the teachings[c] we passed on to you, whether by word of mouth or by letter.

16May our Lord Jesus Christ himself and God our Father, who loved us and by his grace gave us eternal encouragement and good hope, 17encourage your hearts and strengthen you in every good deed and word.

Request for Prayer

3 Finally, brothers, pray for us that the message of the Lord may spread rapidly and be honored, just as it was with you. 2And pray that we may be delivered from wicked and evil men, for not everyone has faith. 3But the Lord is faithful, and he will strengthen and protect you from the evil one. 4We have confidence in the Lord that you are doing and will continue to do the things we command. 5May the Lord direct your hearts into God's love and Christ's perseverance.

Warning Against Idleness

6In the name of the Lord Jesus Christ, we command you, brothers, to keep away from every brother who is idle and does not live according to the teaching[a] you received from

[c] *15* Or *traditions* [a] *6* Or *tradition*

NEW LIVING TRANSLATION

salvation when we told you the Good News; now you can share in the glory of our Lord Jesus Christ.

15With all these things in mind, dear brothers and sisters, stand firm and keep a strong grip on everything we taught you both in person and by letter.

16May our Lord Jesus Christ and God our Father, who loved us and in his special favor gave us everlasting comfort and good hope, 17comfort your hearts and give you strength in every good thing you do and say.

Paul's Request for Prayer

3 Finally, dear brothers and sisters,* I ask you to pray for us. Pray first that the Lord's message will spread rapidly and be honored wherever it goes, just as when it came to you. 2Pray, too, that we will be saved from wicked and evil people, for not everyone believes in the Lord. 3But the Lord is faithful; he will make you strong and guard you from the evil one.* 4And we are confident in the Lord that you are practicing the things we commanded you, and that you always will. 5May the Lord bring you into an ever deeper understanding of the love of God and the endurance that comes from Christ.

An Exhortation to Proper Living

6And now, dear brothers and sisters, we give you this command with the authority of our Lord Jesus Christ: Stay away from any Christian* who lives in idleness and doesn't

3:1 Greek *brothers;* also in 3:6, 13. 3:3 Or *from evil.* 3:6 Greek *brother;* also in 3:15.

NEW KING JAMES VERSION

you by our gospel, for the obtaining of the glory of our Lord Jesus Christ. 15Therefore, brethren, stand fast and hold the traditions which you were taught, whether by word or our epistle.

16Now may our Lord Jesus Christ Himself, and our God and Father, who has loved us and given *us* everlasting consolation and good hope by grace, 17comfort your hearts and establish you in every good word and work.

Pray for Us

3 Finally, brethren, pray for us, that the word of the Lord may run *swiftly* and be glorified, just as *it is* with you, 2and that we may be delivered from unreasonable and wicked men; for not all have faith.

3But the Lord is faithful, who will establish you and guard *you* from the evil one. 4And we have confidence in the Lord concerning you, both that you do and will do the things we command you.

5Now may the Lord direct your hearts into the love of God and into the patience of Christ.

Warning Against Idleness

6But we command you, brethren, in the name of our Lord Jesus Christ, that you withdraw from every brother who walks disorderly and not according to the tradition

THE MESSAGE

invited you to through the Message we delivered, in which you get in on the glory of our Master, Jesus Christ.

So, friends, take a firm stand, feet on the ground and head high. Keep a tight grip on what you were taught, whether in personal conversation or by our letter. May Jesus himself and God our Father, who reached out in love and surprised you with gifts of unending help and confidence, put a fresh heart in you, invigorate your work, enliven your speech.

Those Who Are Lazy

3 One more thing, friends: Pray for us. Pray that the Master's Word will simply take off and race through the country to a groundswell of response, just as it did among you. And pray that we'll be rescued from these scoundrels who are trying to do us in. I'm finding that not all "believers" are believers. But the Master never lets us down. He'll stick by you and protect you from evil.

Because of the *Master*, we have great confidence in *you*. We know you're doing everything we told you and will continue doing it. May the Master take you by the hand and lead you along the path of God's love and Christ's endurance.

Our orders—backed up by the Master, Jesus—are to refuse to have anything to do with those among you who are lazy and refuse to work the way we taught you. Don't permit them to freeload on the rest. We showed you how to pull your weight when we were with you, so get on with it.

KING JAMES VERSION

7 For yourselves know how ye ought to follow us: for we behaved not ourselves disorderly among you;

8 Neither did we eat any man's bread for nought; but wrought with labour and travail night and day, that we might not be chargeable to any of you:

9 Not because we have not power, but to make ourselves an ensample unto you to follow us.

10 For even when we were with you, this we commanded you, that if any would not work, neither should he eat.

11 For we hear that there are some which walk among you disorderly, working not at all, but are busybodies.

12 Now them that are such we command and exhort by our Lord Jesus Christ, that with quietness they work, and eat their own bread.

13 But ye, brethren, be not weary in well doing.

14 And if any man obey not our word by this epistle, note that man, and have no company with him, that he may be ashamed.

15 Yet count *him* not as an enemy, but admonish *him* as a brother.

16 ¶ Now the Lord of peace himself give you peace always by all means. The Lord *be* with you all.

17 The salutation of Paul with mine own hand, which is the token in every epistle: so I write.

18 The grace of our Lord Jesus Christ *be* with you all. Amen.

NEW AMERICAN STANDARD BIBLE

7 For you yourselves know how you ought to follow our example, because we did not act in an undisciplined manner among you,

8 nor did we eat anyone's bread without paying for it, but with labor and hardship we *kept* working night and day so that we would not be a burden to any of you;

9 not because we do not have the right *to this,* but in order to offer ourselves as a model for you, so that you would follow our example.

10 For even when we were with you, we used to give you this order: if anyone is not willing to work, then he is not to eat, either.

11 For we hear that some among you are leading an undisciplined life, doing no work at all, but acting like busybodies.

12 Now such persons we command and exhort in the Lord Jesus Christ to work in quiet fashion and eat their own bread.

13 But as for you, brethren, do not grow weary of doing good.

14 If anyone does not obey our instruction in this letter, take special note of that person and do not associate with him, so that he will be put to shame.

15 *Yet* do not regard him as an enemy, but admonish him as a brother.

16 Now may the Lord of peace Himself continually grant you peace in every circumstance. The Lord be with you all!

17 I, Paul, write this greeting with my own hand, and this is a distinguishing mark in every letter; this is the way I write.

18 The grace of our Lord Jesus Christ be with you all.

NEW CENTURY VERSION

gave you. 7You yourselves know that you should live as
we live. We were not lazy when we were with you. 8And
when we ate another person's food, we always paid for it.
We worked very hard night and day so we would not be an
expense to any of you. 9We had the right to ask you to
help us, but we worked to take care of ourselves so we
would be an example for you to follow. 10When we were
with you, we gave you this rule: "Anyone who refuses to
work should not eat."

11We hear that some people in your group refuse to
work. They do nothing but busy themselves in other people's lives. 12We command those people and beg them in
the Lord Jesus Christ to work quietly and earn their own
food. 13But you, brothers and sisters, never become tired of
doing good.

14If some people do not obey what we tell you in this letter, then take note of them. Have nothing to do with them
so they will feel ashamed. 15But do not treat them as enemies. Warn them as fellow believers.

Final Words

16Now may the Lord of peace give you peace at all times
and in every way. The Lord be with all of you.

17I, Paul, end this letter now in my own handwriting. All
my letters have this to show they are from me. This is the
way I write.

18The grace of our Lord Jesus Christ be with you all.

CONTEMPORARY ENGLISH VERSION

gave you. 7You surely know that you should follow our
example. We didn't waste our time loafing, 8and we didn't
accept food from anyone without paying for it. We didn't
want to be a burden to any of you, so night and day we
worked as hard as we could.

9We had the right not to work, but we wanted to set an
example for you. 10We also gave you the rule that if you
don't work, you don't eat. 11Now we learn that some of
you just loaf around and won't do any work, except the
work of a busybody. 12So, for the sake of our Lord Jesus
Christ, we ask and beg these people to settle down and
start working for a living. 13Dear friends, you must never
become tired of doing right.

14Be on your guard against any followers who refuse to
obey what we have written in this letter. Put them to
shame by not having anything to do with them. 15Don't
consider them your enemies, but speak kindly to them as
you would to any other follower.

Final Prayer

16I pray that the Lord, who gives peace, will always
bless you with peace. May the Lord be with all of you.

17I always sign my letters as I am now doing: PAUL.

18I pray that our Lord Jesus Christ will be kind to all of
you.

NEW INTERNATIONAL VERSION

us. 7For you yourselves know how you ought to follow our example. We were not idle when we were with you, 8nor did we eat anyone's food without paying for it. On the contrary, we worked night and day, laboring and toiling so that we would not be a burden to any of you. 9We did this, not because we do not have the right to such help, but in order to make ourselves a model for you to follow. 10For even when we were with you, we gave you this rule: "If a man will not work, he shall not eat."

11We hear that some among you are idle. They are not busy; they are busybodies. 12Such people we command and urge in the Lord Jesus Christ to settle down and earn the bread they eat. 13And as for you, brothers, never tire of doing what is right.

14If anyone does not obey our instruction in this letter, take special note of him. Do not associate with him, in order that he may feel ashamed. 15Yet do not regard him as an enemy, but warn him as a brother.

Final Greetings

16Now may the Lord of peace himself give you peace at all times and in every way. The Lord be with all of you.

17I, Paul, write this greeting in my own hand, which is the distinguishing mark in all my letters. This is how I write.

18The grace of our Lord Jesus Christ be with you all.

NEW LIVING TRANSLATION

follow the tradition of hard work we gave you. 7For you know that you ought to follow our example. We were never lazy when we were with you. 8We never accepted food from anyone without paying for it. We worked hard day and night so that we would not be a burden to any of you. 9It wasn't that we didn't have the right to ask you to feed us, but we wanted to give you an example to follow. 10Even while we were with you, we gave you this rule: "Whoever does not work should not eat."

11Yet we hear that some of you are living idle lives, refusing to work and wasting time meddling in other people's business. 12In the name of the Lord Jesus Christ, we appeal to such people—no, we command them: Settle down and get to work. Earn your own living. 13And I say to the rest of you, dear brothers and sisters, never get tired of doing good.

14Take note of those who refuse to obey what we say in this letter. Stay away from them so they will be ashamed. 15Don't think of them as enemies, but speak to them as you would to a Christian who needs to be warned.

Paul's Final Greetings

16May the Lord of peace himself always give you his peace no matter what happens. The Lord be with you all.

17Now here is my greeting, which I write with my own hand—PAUL. I do this at the end of all my letters to prove that they really are from me.

18May the grace of our Lord Jesus Christ be with you all.

NEW KING JAMES VERSION

which he[a] received from us. 7For you yourselves know how you ought to follow us, for we were not disorderly among you; 8nor did we eat anyone's bread free of charge, but worked with labor and toil night and day, that we might not be a burden to any of you, 9not because we do not have authority, but to make ourselves an example of how you should follow us.

10For even when we were with you, we commanded you this: If anyone will not work, neither shall he eat. 11For we hear that there are some who walk among you in a disorderly manner, not working at all, but are busybodies. 12Now those who are such we command and exhort through our Lord Jesus Christ that they work in quietness and eat their own bread.

13But *as for* you, brethren, do not grow weary *in* doing good. 14And if anyone does not obey our word in this epistle, note that person and do not keep company with him, that he may be ashamed. 15Yet do not count *him* as an enemy, but admonish *him* as a brother.

Benediction

16Now may the Lord of peace Himself give you peace always in every way. The Lord *be* with you all.

17The salutation of Paul with my own hand, which is a sign in every epistle; so I write.

18The grace of our Lord Jesus Christ *be* with you all. Amen.

3:6 [a] NU-Text and M-Text read *they.*

THE MESSAGE

We didn't sit around on our hands expecting others to take care of us. In fact, we worked our fingers to the bone, up half the night moonlighting so you wouldn't be burdened with taking care of us. And it wasn't because we didn't have a right to your support; we did. We simply wanted to provide an example of diligence, hoping it would prove contagious.

Don't you remember the rule we had when we lived with you? "If you don't work, you don't eat." And now we're getting reports that a bunch of lazy good-for-nothings are taking advantage of you. This must not be tolerated. We command them to get to work immediately—no excuses, no arguments—and earn their own keep. Friends, don't slack off in doing your duty.

If anyone refuses to obey our clear command written in this letter, don't let him get by with it. Point out such a person and refuse to subsidize his freeloading. Maybe then he'll think twice. But don't treat him as an enemy. Sit him down and talk about the problem as someone who cares.

May the Master of Peace himself give you the gift of getting along with each other at all times, in all ways. May the Master be truly among you!

I, Paul, bid you goodbye in my own handwriting. I do this in all my letters, so examine my signature as proof that the letter is genuine.

The incredible grace of our Master, Jesus Christ, be with all of you!

KING JAMES VERSION

THE FIRST EPISTLE OF ST. PAUL TO
TIMOTHY

1 Paul, an apostle of Jesus Christ by the commandment of God our Saviour, and Lord Jesus Christ, *which is* our hope;

2 Unto Timothy, *my* own son in the faith: Grace, mercy, *and* peace, from God our Father and Jesus Christ our Lord.

3 As I besought thee to abide still at Ephesus, when I went into Macedonia, that thou mightest charge some that they teach no other doctrine,

4 Neither give heed to fables and endless genealogies, which minister questions, rather than godly edifying which is in faith: *so do*.

5 ¶ Now the end of the commandment is charity out of a pure heart, and *of* a good conscience, and *of* faith unfeigned:

6 From which some having swerved have turned aside unto vain jangling;

7 Desiring to be teachers of the law; understanding neither what they say, nor whereof they affirm.

NEW AMERICAN STANDARD BIBLE

THE FIRST LETTER OF PAUL TO
TIMOTHY

Misleadings in Doctrine and Living

1 Paul, an apostle of Christ Jesus according to the commandment of God our Savior, and of Christ Jesus, *who is* our hope,

2 To Timothy, *my* true child in *the* faith: Grace, mercy *and* peace from God the Father and Christ Jesus our Lord.

3 As I urged you upon my departure for Macedonia, remain on at Ephesus so that you may instruct certain men not to teach strange doctrines,

4 nor to pay attention to myths and endless genealogies, which give rise to mere speculation rather than *furthering* the administration of God which is by faith.

5 But the goal of our instruction is love from a pure heart and a good conscience and a sincere faith.

6 For some men, straying from these things, have turned aside to fruitless discussion,

7 wanting to be teachers of the Law, even though they do not understand either what they are saying or the matters about which they make confident assertions.

NEW CENTURY VERSION

1 TIMOTHY

1 From Paul, an apostle of Christ Jesus, by the command of God our Savior and Christ Jesus our hope.
2 To Timothy, a true child to me because you believe:
Grace, mercy, and peace from God the Father and Christ Jesus our Lord.

Warning Against False Teaching

3 I asked you to stay longer in Ephesus when I went into
Macedonia so you could command some people there to
stop teaching false things. 4 Tell them not to spend their
time on stories that are not true and on long lists of names
in family histories. These things only bring arguments;
they do not help God's work, which is done in faith. 5 The
purpose of this command is for people to have love, a love
that comes from a pure heart and a good conscience and a
true faith. 6 Some people have missed these things and
turned to useless talk. 7 They want to be teachers of the
law, but they do not understand either what they are talking about or what they are sure about.

CONTEMPORARY ENGLISH VERSION

1 TIMOTHY

1 From Paul.
God our Savior and Christ Jesus commanded me to be an apostle of Christ Jesus, who gives us hope.
2 Timothy, because of our faith, you are like a son to me.
I pray that God our Father and our Lord Jesus Christ will be kind and merciful to you. May they bless you with peace!

Warning against False Teaching

3 When I was leaving for Macedonia, I asked you to stay
on in Ephesus and warn certain people there to stop
spreading their false teachings. 4 You needed to warn them
to stop wasting their time on senseless stories and endless
lists of ancestors. Such things only cause arguments. They
don't help anyone to do God's work that can only be done
by faith.
5 You must teach people to have genuine love, as well as
a good conscience and true faith. 6 There are some who
have given up these for nothing but empty talk. 7 They
want to be teachers of the Law of Moses. But they don't
know what they are talking about, even though they think
they do.

NEW INTERNATIONAL VERSION

1 TIMOTHY

1 Paul, an apostle of Christ Jesus by the command of God our Savior and of Christ Jesus our hope,

2To Timothy my true son in the faith:

Grace, mercy and peace from God the Father and Christ Jesus our Lord.

Warning Against False Teachers of the Law

3As I urged you when I went into Macedonia, stay there in Ephesus so that you may command certain men not to teach false doctrines any longer 4nor to devote themselves to myths and endless genealogies. These promote controversies rather than God's work—which is by faith. 5The goal of this command is love, which comes from a pure heart and a good conscience and a sincere faith. 6Some have wandered away from these and turned to meaningless talk. 7They want to be teachers of the law, but they do not know what they are talking about or what they so confidently affirm.

NEW LIVING TRANSLATION

1 TIMOTHY

Greetings from Paul

1 This letter is from Paul, an apostle of Christ Jesus, appointed by the command of God our Savior and by Christ Jesus our hope.

2It is written to Timothy, my true child in the faith.

May God our Father and Christ Jesus our Lord give you grace, mercy, and peace.

Warnings against False Teachings

3When I left for Macedonia, I urged you to stay there in Ephesus and stop those who are teaching wrong doctrine. 4Don't let people waste time in endless speculation over myths and spiritual pedigrees.* For these things only cause arguments; they don't help people live a life of faith in God.* 5The purpose of my instruction is that all the Christians there would be filled with love that comes from a pure heart, a clear conscience, and sincere faith.

6But some teachers have missed this whole point. They have turned away from these things and spend their time arguing and talking foolishness. 7They want to be known as teachers of the law of Moses, but they don't know what they are talking about, even though they seem so confident.

1:4a Greek *in myths and endless genealogies, which cause speculation.*
1:4b Greek *a stewardship of God in faith.*

NEW KING JAMES VERSION

THE FIRST EPISTLE OF PAUL TO

TIMOTHY

Greeting

1 Paul, an apostle of Jesus Christ, by the commandment of God our Savior and the Lord Jesus Christ, our hope,

2To Timothy, a true son in the faith:

Grace, mercy, *and* peace from God our Father and Jesus Christ our Lord.

No Other Doctrine

3As I urged you when I went into Macedonia—remain in Ephesus that you may charge some that they teach no other doctrine, 4nor give heed to fables and endless genealogies, which cause disputes rather than godly edification which is in faith. 5Now the purpose of the commandment is love from a pure heart, *from* a good conscience, and *from* sincere faith, 6from which some, having strayed, have turned aside to idle talk, 7desiring to be teachers of the law, understanding neither what they say nor the things which they affirm.

THE MESSAGE

1 TIMOTHY

1 I, Paul, am an apostle on special assignment for Christ, our living hope. Under God our Savior's command, I'm writing this to you, Timothy, my son in the faith. All the best from our God and Christ be yours!

Self-Appointed Experts on Life

On my way to the province of Macedonia, I advised you to stay in Ephesus. Well, I haven't changed my mind. Stay right there on top of things so that the teaching stays on track. Apparently some people have been introducing fantasy stories and fanciful family trees that digress into silliness instead of pulling the people back into the center, deepening faith and obedience.

The whole point of what we're urging is simply *love*—love uncontaminated by self-interest and counterfeit faith, a life open to God. Those who fail to keep to this point soon wander off into cul-de-sacs of gossip. They set themselves up as experts on religious issues, but haven't the remotest idea of what they're holding forth with such imposing eloquence.

KING JAMES VERSION

8 But we know that the law *is* good, if a man use it lawfully;

9 Knowing this, that the law is not made for a righteous man, but for the lawless and disobedient, for the ungodly and for sinners, for unholy and profane, for murderers of fathers and murderers of mothers, for manslayers,

10 For whoremongers, for them that defile themselves with mankind, for menstealers, for liars, for perjured persons, and if there be any other thing that is contrary to sound doctrine;

11 According to the glorious gospel of the blessed God, which was committed to my trust.

12 ¶ And I thank Christ Jesus our Lord, who hath enabled me, for that he counted me faithful, putting me into the ministry;

13 Who was before a blasphemer, and a persecutor, and injurious: but I obtained mercy, because I did *it* ignorantly in unbelief.

14 And the grace of our Lord was exceeding abundant with faith and love which is in Christ Jesus.

15 This *is* a faithful saying, and worthy of all acceptation, that Christ Jesus came into the world to save sinners; of whom I am chief.

16 Howbeit for this cause I obtained mercy, that in me first Jesus Christ might shew forth all longsuffering, for a pattern to them which should hereafter believe on him to life everlasting.

17 Now unto the King eternal, immortal, invisible, the only wise God, *be* honour and glory for ever and ever. Amen.

NEW AMERICAN STANDARD BIBLE

8 But we know that the Law is good, if one uses it lawfully,

9 realizing the fact that law is not made for a righteous person, but for those who are lawless and rebellious, for the ungodly and sinners, for the unholy and profane, for those who kill their fathers or mothers, for murderers

10 and immoral men and homosexuals and kidnappers and liars and perjurers, and whatever else is contrary to sound teaching,

11 according to the glorious gospel of the blessed God, with which I have been entrusted.

12 I thank Christ Jesus our Lord, who has strengthened me, because He considered me faithful, putting me into service,

13 even though I was formerly a blasphemer and a persecutor and a violent aggressor. Yet I was shown mercy because I acted ignorantly in unbelief;

14 and the grace of our Lord was more than abundant, with the faith and love which are *found* in Christ Jesus.

15 It is a trustworthy statement, deserving full acceptance, that Christ Jesus came into the world to save sinners, among whom I am foremost *of all*.

16 Yet for this reason I found mercy, so that in me as the foremost, Jesus Christ might demonstrate His perfect patience as an example for those who would believe in Him for eternal life.

17 Now to the King eternal, immortal, invisible, the only God, *be* honor and glory forever and ever. Amen.

NEW CENTURY VERSION

8But we know that the law is good if someone uses it lawfully. 9We also know that the law is not made for good people but for those who are against the law and for those who refuse to follow it. It is for people who are against God and are sinful, who are not holy and have no religion, who kill their fathers and mothers, who murder, 10who take part in sexual sins, who have sexual relations with people of the same sex, who sell slaves, who tell lies, who speak falsely, and who do anything against the true teaching of God. 11That teaching is part of the Good News of the blessed God that he gave me to tell.

Thanks for God's Mercy

12I thank Christ Jesus our Lord, who gave me strength, because he trusted me and gave me this work of serving him. 13In the past I spoke against Christ and persecuted him and did all kinds of things to hurt him. But God showed me mercy, because I did not know what I was doing. I did not believe. 14But the grace of our Lord was fully given to me, and with that grace came the faith and love that are in Christ Jesus.

15What I say is true, and you should fully accept it: Christ Jesus came into the world to save sinners, of whom I am the worst. 16But I was given mercy so that in me, the worst of all sinners, Christ Jesus could show that he has patience without limit. His patience with me made me an example for those who would believe in him and have life forever. 17To the King that rules forever, who will never die, who cannot be seen, the only God, be honor and glory forever and ever. Amen.

CONTEMPORARY ENGLISH VERSION

8We know that the Law is good, if it is used in the right way. 9We also understand that it wasn't given to control people who please God, but to control lawbreakers, criminals, godless people, and sinners. It is for wicked and evil people, and for murderers, who would even kill their own parents. 10The Law was written for people who are sexual perverts or who live as homosexuals or are kidnappers or liars or won't tell the truth in court. It is for anything else that opposes the correct teaching 11of the good news that the glorious and wonderful God has given me.

Being Thankful for God's Kindness

12I thank Christ Jesus our Lord. He has given me the strength for my work because he knew that he could trust me. 13I used to say terrible and insulting things about him, and I was cruel. But he had mercy on me because I didn't know what I was doing, and I had not yet put my faith in him. 14Christ Jesus our Lord was very kind to me. He has greatly blessed my life with faith and love just like his own.

15"Christ Jesus came into the world to save sinners." This saying is true, and it can be trusted. I was the worst sinner of all! 16But since I was worse than anyone else, God had mercy on me and let me be an example of the endless patience of Christ Jesus. He did this so that others would put their faith in Christ and have eternal life. 17I pray that honor and glory will always be given to the only God, who lives forever and is the invisible and eternal King! Amen.

NEW INTERNATIONAL VERSION

8 We know that the law is good if one uses it properly. 9 We also know that law[a] is made not for the righteous but for lawbreakers and rebels, the ungodly and sinful, the unholy and irreligious; for those who kill their fathers or mothers, for murderers, 10 for adulterers and perverts, for slave traders and liars and perjurers—and for whatever else is contrary to the sound doctrine 11 that conforms to the glorious gospel of the blessed God, which he entrusted to me.

The Lord's Grace to Paul

12 I thank Christ Jesus our Lord, who has given me strength, that he considered me faithful, appointing me to his service. 13 Even though I was once a blasphemer and a persecutor and a violent man, I was shown mercy because I acted in ignorance and unbelief. 14 The grace of our Lord was poured out on me abundantly, along with the faith and love that are in Christ Jesus.

15 Here is a trustworthy saying that deserves full acceptance: Christ Jesus came into the world to save sinners—of whom I am the worst. 16 But for that very reason I was shown mercy so that in me, the worst of sinners, Christ Jesus might display his unlimited patience as an example for those who would believe on him and receive eternal life. 17 Now to the King eternal, immortal, invisible, the only God, be honor and glory for ever and ever. Amen.

[a] 9 Or *that the law*

NEW LIVING TRANSLATION

8 We know these laws are good when they are used as God intended. 9 But they were not made for people who do what is right. They are for people who are disobedient and rebellious, who are ungodly and sinful, who consider nothing sacred and defile what is holy, who murder their father or mother or other people. 10 These laws are for people who are sexually immoral, for homosexuals and slave traders, for liars and oath breakers, and for those who do anything else that contradicts the right teaching 11 that comes from the glorious Good News entrusted to me by our blessed God.

Paul's Gratitude for God's Mercy

12 How thankful I am to Christ Jesus our Lord for considering me trustworthy and appointing me to serve him, 13 even though I used to scoff at the name of Christ. I hunted down his people, harming them in every way I could. But God had mercy on me because I did it in ignorance and unbelief. 14 Oh, how kind and gracious the Lord was! He filled me completely with faith and the love of Christ Jesus.

15 This is a true saying, and everyone should believe it: Christ Jesus came into the world to save sinners—and I was the worst of them all. 16 But that is why God had mercy on me, so that Christ Jesus could use me as a prime example of his great patience with even the worst sinners. Then others will realize that they, too, can believe in him and receive eternal life. 17 Glory and honor to God forever and ever. He is the eternal King, the unseen one who never dies; he alone is God. Amen.

NEW KING JAMES VERSION

8 But we know that the law *is* good if one uses it lawfully, 9 knowing this: that the law is not made for a righteous person, but for *the* lawless and insubordinate, for *the* ungodly and for sinners, for *the* unholy and profane, for murderers of fathers and murderers of mothers, for manslayers, 10 for fornicators, for sodomites, for kidnappers, for liars, for perjurers, and if there is any other thing that is contrary to sound doctrine, 11 according to the glorious gospel of the blessed God which was committed to my trust.

Glory to God for His Grace

12 And I thank Christ Jesus our Lord who has enabled me, because He counted me faithful, putting *me* into the ministry, 13 although I was formerly a blasphemer, a persecutor, and an insolent man; but I obtained mercy because I did *it* ignorantly in unbelief. 14 And the grace of our Lord was exceedingly abundant, with faith and love which are in Christ Jesus. 15 This *is* a faithful saying and worthy of all acceptance, that Christ Jesus came into the world to save sinners, of whom I am chief. 16 However, for this reason I obtained mercy, that in me first Jesus Christ might show all longsuffering, as a pattern to those who are going to believe on Him for everlasting life. 17 Now to the King eternal, immortal, invisible, to God who alone is wise,[a] *be* honor and glory forever and ever. Amen.

1:17 [a] NU-Text reads *to the only God.*

THE MESSAGE

It's true that moral guidance and counsel need to be given, but the way you say it and to whom you say it are as important as what you say. It's obvious, isn't it, that the law code isn't primarily for people who live responsibly, but for the irresponsible, who defy all authority, riding roughshod over God, life, sex, truth, whatever! They are contemptuous of this great Message I've been put in charge of by this great God.

✠

I'm so grateful to Christ Jesus for making me adequate to do this work. He went out on a limb, you know, in trusting me with this ministry. The only credentials I brought to it were invective and witch hunts and arrogance. But I was treated mercifully because I didn't know what I was doing—didn't know Who I was doing it against! Grace mixed with faith and love poured over me and into me. And all because of Jesus.

Here's a word you can take to heart and depend on: Jesus Christ came into the world to save sinners. I'm proof—Public Sinner Number One—of someone who could never have made it apart from sheer mercy. And now he shows me off—evidence of his endless patience—to those who are right on the edge of trusting him forever.

Deep honor and bright glory
to the King of All Time—
One God, Immortal, Invisible,
ever and always. Oh, yes!

KING JAMES VERSION

18 ¶ This charge I commit unto thee, son Timothy, according to the prophecies which went before on thee, that thou by them mightest war a good warfare;

19 Holding faith, and a good conscience; which some having put away concerning faith have made shipwreck:

20 Of whom is Hymenaeus and Alexander; whom I have delivered unto Satan, that they may learn not to blaspheme.

2 I exhort therefore, that, first of all, supplications, prayers, intercessions, *and* giving of thanks, be made for all men;

2 For kings, and *for* all that are in authority; that we may lead a quiet and peaceable life in all godliness and honesty.

3 For this *is* good and acceptable in the sight of God our Saviour;

4 Who will have all men to be saved, and to come unto the knowledge of the truth.

5 For *there is* one God, and one mediator between God and men, the man Christ Jesus;

6 Who gave himself a ransom for all, to be testified in due time.

NEW AMERICAN STANDARD BIBLE

18 This command I entrust to you, Timothy, *my* son, in accordance with the prophecies previously made concerning you, that by them you fight the good fight,

19 keeping faith and a good conscience, which some have rejected and suffered shipwreck in regard to their faith.

20 Among these are Hymenaeus and Alexander, whom I have handed over to Satan, so that they will be taught not to blaspheme.

A Call to Prayer

2 First of all, then, I urge that entreaties *and* prayers, petitions *and* thanksgivings, be made on behalf of all men,

2 for kings and all who are in authority, so that we may lead a tranquil and quiet life in all godliness and dignity.

3 This is good and acceptable in the sight of God our Savior,

4 who desires all men to be saved and to come to the knowledge of the truth.

5 For there is one God, *and* one mediator also between God and men, *the* man Christ Jesus,

6 who gave Himself as a ransom for all, the testimony *given* at the proper time.

NEW CENTURY VERSION

18Timothy, my child, I am giving you a command that
agrees with the prophecies that were given about you in
the past. I tell you this so you can follow them and fight
the good fight. 19Continue to have faith and do what you
know is right. Some people have rejected this, and their
faith has been shipwrecked. 20Hymenaeus and Alexander
have done that, and I have given them to Satan so they
will learn not to speak against God.

Some Rules for Men and Women

2 First, I tell you to pray for all people, asking God for
what they need and being thankful to him. 2Pray for
rulers and for all who have authority so that we can have
quiet and peaceful lives full of worship and respect for
God. 3This is good, and it pleases God our Savior, 4who
wants all people to be saved and to know the truth. 5There
is one God and one way human beings can reach God. That
way is through Christ Jesus, who is himself human. 6He
gave himself as a payment to free all people. He is proof
that came at the right time. 7That is why I was chosen to

CONTEMPORARY ENGLISH VERSION

18Timothy, my son, the instructions I am giving you are
based on what some prophets[a] once said about you. If you
follow these instructions, you will fight like a good soldier.
19You will be faithful and have a clear conscience. Some
people have made a mess of their faith because they didn't
listen to their consciences. 20Two of them are Hymenaeus
and Alexander. I have given these men over to the power
of Satan, so they will learn not to oppose God.

How To Pray

2 First of all, I ask you to pray for everyone. Ask God to
help and bless them all, and tell God how thankful
you are for each of them. 2Pray for kings and others in
power, so that we may live quiet and peaceful lives as we
worship and honor God. 3This kind of prayer is good, and
it pleases God our Savior. 4God wants everyone to be saved
and to know the whole truth, which is,

5 There is only one God,
and Christ Jesus
is the only one
who can bring us
to God.
Jesus was truly human,
and he gave himself
to rescue all of us.
6 God showed us this
at the right time.

[a] **1.18** *prophets*: Probably the Christian prophets referred to in 4.14.

NEW INTERNATIONAL VERSION

[18]Timothy, my son, I give you this instruction in keeping with the prophecies once made about you, so that by following them you may fight the good fight, [19]holding on to faith and a good conscience. Some have rejected these and so have shipwrecked their faith. [20]Among them are Hymenaeus and Alexander, whom I have handed over to Satan to be taught not to blaspheme.

Instructions on Worship

2 I urge, then, first of all, that requests, prayers, intercession and thanksgiving be made for everyone— [2]for kings and all those in authority, that we may live peaceful and quiet lives in all godliness and holiness. [3]This is good, and pleases God our Savior, [4]who wants all men to be saved and to come to a knowledge of the truth. [5]For there is one God and one mediator between God and men, the man Christ Jesus, [6]who gave himself as a ransom for all men—the testimony given in its proper time. [7]And for this

NEW LIVING TRANSLATION

Timothy's Responsibility

[18]Timothy, my son, here are my instructions for you, based on the prophetic words spoken about you earlier. May they give you the confidence to fight well in the Lord's battles. [19]Cling tightly to your faith in Christ, and always keep your conscience clear. For some people have deliberately violated their consciences; as a result, their faith has been shipwrecked. [20]Hymenaeus and Alexander are two examples of this. I turned them over to Satan so they would learn not to blaspheme God.

Instructions about Worship

2 I urge you, first of all, to pray for all people. As you make your requests, plead for God's mercy upon them, and give thanks. [2]Pray this way for kings and all others who are in authority, so that we can live in peace and quietness, in godliness and dignity. [3]This is good and pleases God our Savior, [4]for he wants everyone to be saved and to understand the truth. [5]For there is only one God and one Mediator who can reconcile God and people. He is the man Christ Jesus. [6]He gave his life to purchase freedom for everyone. This is the message that God gave to the world at the proper time. [7]And I have been chosen—this is

NEW KING JAMES VERSION

Fight the Good Fight

[18]This charge I commit to you, son Timothy, according to the prophecies previously made concerning you, that by them you may wage the good warfare, [19]having faith and a good conscience, which some having rejected, concerning the faith have suffered shipwreck, [20]of whom are Hymenaeus and Alexander, whom I delivered to Satan that they may learn not to blaspheme.

Pray for All Men

2 Therefore I exhort first of all that supplications, prayers, intercessions, *and* giving of thanks be made for all men, [2]for kings and all who are in authority, that we may lead a quiet and peaceable life in all godliness and reverence. [3]For this *is* good and acceptable in the sight of God our Savior, [4]who desires all men to be saved and to come to the knowledge of the truth. [5]For *there is* one God and one Mediator between God and men, *the* Man Christ Jesus, [6]who gave Himself a ransom for all, to be testified in due time, [7]for which I was appointed a preacher and an

THE MESSAGE

I'm passing this work on to you, my son Timothy. The prophetic word that was directed to you prepared us for this. All those prayers are coming together now so you will do this well, fearless in your struggle, keeping a firm grip on your faith and on yourself. After all, this is a fight we're in.

There are some, you know, who by relaxing their grip and thinking anything goes have made a thorough mess of their faith. Hymenaeus and Alexander are two of them. I let them wander off to Satan to be taught a lesson or two about not blaspheming.

Simple Faith and Plain Truth

2 The first thing I want you to do is pray. Pray every way you know how, for everyone you know. Pray especially for rulers and their governments to rule well so we can be quietly about our business of living simply, in humble contemplation. This is the way our Savior God wants us to live.

He wants not only us but *everyone* saved, you know, everyone to get to know the truth *we've* learned: that there's one God and only one, and one Priest-Mediator between God and us—Jesus, who offered himself in exchange for everyone held captive by sin, to set them all free. Eventually the news is going to get out. This and this

KING JAMES VERSION

7 Whereunto I am ordained a preacher, and an apostle, (I speak the truth in Christ, *and* lie not;) a teacher of the Gentiles in faith and verity.

8 I will therefore that men pray every where, lifting up holy hands, without wrath and doubting.

9 ¶ In like manner also, that women adorn themselves in modest apparel, with shamefacedness and sobriety; not with broided hair, or gold, or pearls, or costly array;

10 But (which becometh women professing godliness) with good works.

11 Let the woman learn in silence with all subjection.

12 But I suffer not a woman to teach, nor to usurp authority over the man, but to be in silence.

13 For Adam was first formed, then Eve.

14 And Adam was not deceived, but the woman being deceived was in the transgression.

15 Notwithstanding she shall be saved in childbearing, if they continue in faith and charity and holiness with sobriety.

3 This *is* a true saying, If a man desire the office of a bishop, he desireth a good work.

2 A bishop then must be blameless, the husband of one wife, vigilant, sober, of good behaviour, given to hospitality, apt to teach;

NEW AMERICAN STANDARD BIBLE

7 For this I was appointed a preacher and an apostle (I am telling the truth, I am not lying) as a teacher of the Gentiles in faith and truth.

8 Therefore I want the men in every place to pray, lifting up holy hands, without wrath and dissension.

Women Instructed

9 Likewise, *I want* women to adorn themselves with proper clothing, modestly and discreetly, not with braided hair and gold or pearls or costly garments,

10 but rather by means of good works, as is proper for women making a claim to godliness.

11 A woman must quietly receive instruction with entire submissiveness.

12 But I do not allow a woman to teach or exercise authority over a man, but to remain quiet.

13 For it was Adam who was first created, *and* then Eve.

14 And *it was* not Adam *who* was deceived, but the woman being deceived, fell into transgression.

15 But *women* will be preserved through the bearing of children if they continue in faith and love and sanctity with self-restraint.

Overseers and Deacons

3 It is a trustworthy statement: if any man aspires to the office of overseer, it is a fine work he desires *to do.*

2 An overseer, then, must be above reproach, the husband of one wife, temperate, prudent, respectable, hospitable, able to teach,

NEW CENTURY VERSION

tell the Good News and to be an apostle. (I am telling the truth; I am not lying.) I was chosen to teach those who are not Jews to believe and to know the truth.

8So, I want the men everywhere to pray, lifting up their hands in a holy manner, without anger and arguments.

9Also, women should wear proper clothes that show respect and self-control, not using braided hair or gold or pearls or expensive clothes. 10Instead, they should do good deeds, which is right for women who say they worship God.

11Let a woman learn by listening quietly and being
ready to cooperate in everything. 12But I do not allow a
woman to teach or to have authority over a man, but to
listen quietly, 13because Adam was formed first and then
Eve. 14And Adam was not tricked, but the woman was
tricked and became a sinner. 15But she will be saved
through having children if they continue in faith, love, and
holiness, with self-control.

Elders in the Church

3 What I say is true: Anyone wanting to become an
elder desires a good work. 2An elder must not give
people a reason to criticize him, and he must have only
one wife. He must be self-controlled, wise, respected by
others, ready to welcome guests, and able to teach. 3He

CONTEMPORARY ENGLISH VERSION

7This is why God chose me to be a preacher and an apostle of the good news. I am telling the truth. I am not lying. God sent me to teach the Gentiles about faith and truth.

8I want everyone everywhere to lift innocent hands toward heaven and pray, without being angry or arguing with each other.

9I would like for women to wear modest and sensible
clothes. They should not have fancy hairdos, or wear
expensive clothes, or put on jewelry made of gold or pearls.
10Women who claim to love God should do helpful things
for others, 11and they should learn by being quiet and pay-
ing attention. 12They should be silent and not be allowed
to teach or to tell men what to do. 13After all, Adam was
created before Eve, 14and the man Adam wasn't the one
who was fooled. It was the woman Eve who was complete-
ly fooled and sinned. 15But women will be saved by having
children,[a] if they stay faithful, loving, holy, and modest.

Church Officials

3 It is true that[a] anyone who desires to be a church offi-
cial[b] wants to be something worthwhile. 2That's why
officials must have a good reputation and be faithful in mar-
riage.[c] They must be self-controlled, sensible, well-behaved,

[a] 2.15 *saved by having children*: Or "brought safely through childbirth" or "saved by the birth of a child" (that is, by the birth of Jesus) or "saved by being good mothers." [a] 3.1 *It is true that*: These words may be taken with 2.15. If so, that verse would be translated: "It is true that women will be saved . . . holy, and modest." And 3.1 would be translated, "Anyone who desires . . . something worthwhile." [b] 3.1 *church official*: Or "bishop." [c] 3.2 *be faithful in marriage*: Or "be the husband of only one wife" or "have never been divorced."

NEW INTERNATIONAL VERSION

purpose I was appointed a herald and an apostle—I am
telling the truth, I am not lying—and a teacher of the true
faith to the Gentiles.
8I want men everywhere to lift up holy hands in prayer,
without anger or disputing.
9I also want women to dress modestly, with decency and
propriety, not with braided hair or gold or pearls or expen-
sive clothes, 10but with good deeds, appropriate for women
who profess to worship God.
11A woman should learn in quietness and full submis-
sion. 12I do not permit a woman to teach or to have
authority over a man; she must be silent. 13For Adam was
formed first, then Eve. 14And Adam was not the one
deceived; it was the woman who was deceived and became
a sinner. 15But women[a] will be saved[b] through childbear-
ing—if they continue in faith, love and holiness with pro-
priety.

Overseers and Deacons

3 Here is a trustworthy saying: If anyone sets his heart
on being an overseer,[a] he desires a noble task. 2Now
the overseer must be above reproach, the husband of but
one wife, temperate, self-controlled, respectable, hospitable,

[a] *15* Greek *she* [b] *15* Or *restored* [a] *1* Traditionally *bishop*; also in verse 2

NEW LIVING TRANSLATION

the absolute truth—as a preacher and apostle to teach the
Gentiles about faith and truth.
8So wherever you assemble, I want men to pray with
holy hands lifted up to God, free from anger and controver-
sy. 9And I want women to be modest in their appearance.
They should wear decent and appropriate clothing and not
draw attention to themselves by the way they fix their hair
or by wearing gold or pearls or expensive clothes. 10For
women who claim to be devoted to God should make them-
selves attractive by the good things they do.
11Women should listen and learn quietly and submis-
sively. 12I do not let women teach men or have authority
over them. Let them listen quietly. 13For God made Adam
first, and afterward he made Eve. 14And it was the woman,
not Adam, who was deceived by Satan, and sin was the
result. 15But women will be saved through childbearing*
and by continuing to live in faith, love, holiness, and mod-
esty.

Leaders in the Church

3 It is a true saying that if someone wants to be an
elder,* he desires an honorable responsibility. 2For an
elder must be a man whose life cannot be spoken against.
He must be faithful to his wife.* He must exhibit self-con-
trol, live wisely, and have a good reputation. He must enjoy
having guests in his home and must be able to teach. 3He

2:15 Or *will be saved by accepting their role as mothers,* or *will be saved by the birth of the Child.* 3:1 Greek *overseer;* also in 3:2. 3:2 Greek *be the husband of one wife;* also in 3:12.

NEW KING JAMES VERSION

apostle—I am speaking the truth in Christ[a] *and* not
lying—a teacher of the Gentiles in faith and truth.

Men and Women in the Church

8I desire therefore that the men pray everywhere, lifting
up holy hands, without wrath and doubting; 9in like man-
ner also, that the women adorn themselves in modest
apparel, with propriety and moderation, not with braided
hair or gold or pearls or costly clothing, 10but, which is
proper for women professing godliness, with good works.
11Let a woman learn in silence with all submission. 12And
I do not permit a woman to teach or to have authority over
a man, but to be in silence. 13For Adam was formed first,
then Eve. 14And Adam was not deceived, but the woman
being deceived, fell into transgression. 15Nevertheless she
will be saved in childbearing if they continue in faith, love,
and holiness, with self-control.

Qualifications of Overseers

3 This *is* a faithful saying: If a man desires the position
of a bishop,[a] he desires a good work. 2A bishop then
must be blameless, the husband of one wife, temperate,
sober-minded, of good behavior, hospitable, able to teach;

2:7 [a] NU-Text omits *in Christ.* 3:1 [a] Literally *overseer*

THE MESSAGE

only has been my appointed work: getting this news to
those who have never heard of God, and explaining how it
works by simple faith and plain truth.
Since prayer is at the bottom of all this, what I want
mostly is for men to pray—not shaking angry fists at ene-
mies but raising holy hands to God. And I want women to
get in there with the men in humility before God, not
primping before a mirror or chasing the latest fashions but
doing something beautiful for God and becoming beautiful
doing it.
I don't let women take over and tell the men what to do.
They should study to be quiet and obedient along with
everyone else. Adam was made first, then Eve; woman was
deceived first—our pioneer in sin!—with Adam right on
her heels. On the other hand, her childbearing brought
about salvation, reversing Eve. But this salvation only
comes to those who continue in faith, love, and holiness,
gathering it all into maturity. You can depend on this.

Leadership in the Church

3 If anyone wants to provide leadership in the church,
good! But there are preconditions: A leader must be
well-thought-of, committed to his wife, cool and collected,
accessible, and hospitable. He must know what he's talking

KING JAMES VERSION

3 Not given to wine, no striker, not greedy of filthy lucre; but patient, not a brawler, not covetous;

4 One that ruleth well his own house, having his children in subjection with all gravity;

5 (For if a man know not how to rule his own house, how shall he take care of the church of God?)

6 Not a novice, lest being lifted up with pride he fall into the condemnation of the devil.

7 Moreover he must have a good report of them which are without; lest he fall into reproach and the snare of the devil.

8 ¶ Likewise *must* the deacons *be* grave, not double-tongued, not given to much wine, not greedy of filthy lucre;

9 Holding the mystery of the faith in a pure conscience.

10 And let these also first be proved; then let them use the office of a deacon, being *found* blameless.

11 Even so *must their* wives *be* grave, not slanderers, sober, faithful in all things.

12 Let the deacons be the husbands of one wife, ruling their children and their own houses well.

NEW AMERICAN STANDARD BIBLE

3 not addicted to wine or pugnacious, but gentle, peaceable, free from the love of money.

4 *He must be* one who manages his own household well, keeping his children under control with all dignity

5 (but if a man does not know how to manage his own household, how will he take care of the church of God?),

6 *and* not a new convert, so that he will not become conceited and fall into the condemnation incurred by the devil.

7 And he must have a good reputation with those outside *the church,* so that he will not fall into reproach and the snare of the devil.

8 Deacons likewise *must be* men of dignity, not double-tongued, or addicted to much wine or fond of sordid gain,

9 *but* holding to the mystery of the faith with a clear conscience.

10 These men must also first be tested; then let them serve as deacons if they are beyond reproach.

11 Women *must* likewise *be* dignified, not malicious gossips, but temperate, faithful in all things.

12 Deacons must be husbands of *only* one wife, *and* good managers of *their* children and their own households.

NEW CENTURY VERSION

must not drink too much wine or like to fight, but rather
be gentle and peaceable, not loving money. 4He must be a
good family leader, having children who cooperate with
full respect. 5(If someone does not know how to lead the
family, how can that person take care of God's church?)
6But an elder must not be a new believer, or he might be
too proud of himself and be judged guilty just as the devil
was. 7An elder must also have the respect of people who
are not in the church so he will not be criticized by others
and caught in the devil's trap.

Deacons in the Church

8In the same way, deacons must be respected by others,
not saying things they do not mean. They must not drink
too much wine or try to get rich by cheating others. 9With
a clear conscience they must follow the secret of the faith
that God made known to us. 10Test them first. Then let
them serve as deacons if you find nothing wrong in them.
11In the same way, women[a] must be respected by others.
They must not speak evil of others. They must be self-con-
trolled and trustworthy in everything. 12Deacons must
have only one wife and be good leaders of their children

3:11 [a] **women** This might mean the wives of the deacons, or it might mean women who serve in the same way as deacons.

CONTEMPORARY ENGLISH VERSION

friendly to strangers, and able to teach. 3They must not be
heavy drinkers or troublemakers. Instead, they must be kind
and gentle and not love money.

4Church officials must be in control of their own fami-
lies, and they must see that their children are obedient and
always respectful. 5If they don't know how to control their
own families, how can they look after God's people?
6They must not be new followers of the Lord. If they are,
they might become proud and be doomed along with the
devil. 7Finally, they must be well-respected by people who
are not followers. Then they won't be trapped and dis-
graced by the devil.

Church Officers

8Church officers[d] should be serious. They must not be
liars, heavy drinkers, or greedy for money. 9And they must
have a clear conscience and hold firmly to what God has
shown us about our faith. 10They must first prove them-
selves. Then if no one has anything against them, they can
serve as officers.

11Women[e] must also be serious. They must not gossip or
be heavy drinkers, and they must be faithful in everything
they do.

12Church officers must be faithful in marriage.[f] They
must be in full control of their children and everyone else

[d] 3.8 *Church officers*: Or "Deacons." [e] 3.11 *Women*: Either church officers or the wives of church officers. [f] 3.12 *be faithful in marriage*: See the note at 3.2.

NEW INTERNATIONAL VERSION

able to teach, [3]not given to drunkenness, not violent but
gentle, not quarrelsome, not a lover of money. [4]He must
manage his own family well and see that his children obey
him with proper respect. [5](If anyone does not know how to
manage his own family, how can he take care of God's
church?) [6]He must not be a recent convert, or he may
become conceited and fall under the same judgment as the
devil. [7]He must also have a good reputation with outsiders,
so that he will not fall into disgrace and into the devil's
trap.

[8]Deacons, likewise, are to be men worthy of respect, sin-
cere, not indulging in much wine, and not pursuing dis-
honest gain. [9]They must keep hold of the deep truths of
the faith with a clear conscience. [10]They must first be test-
ed; and then if there is nothing against them, let them
serve as deacons.

[11]In the same way, their wives[b] are to be women worthy
of respect, not malicious talkers but temperate and trust-
worthy in everything.

[12]A deacon must be the husband of but one wife and
must manage his children and his household well. [13]Those

[b] *11* Or *way, deaconesses*

NEW LIVING TRANSLATION

must not be a heavy drinker or be violent. He must be gen-
tle, peace loving, and not one who loves money. [4]He must
manage his own family well, with children who respect and
obey him. [5]For if a man cannot manage his own household,
how can he take care of God's church?

[6]An elder must not be a new Christian, because he might
be proud of being chosen so soon, and the Devil will use
that pride to make him fall.* [7]Also, people outside the
church must speak well of him so that he will not fall into
the Devil's trap and be disgraced.

[8]In the same way, deacons must be people who are
respected and have integrity. They must not be heavy
drinkers and must not be greedy for money. [9]They must be
committed to the revealed truths of the Christian faith and
must live with a clear conscience. [10]Before they are
appointed as deacons, they should be given other respon-
sibilities in the church as a test of their character and abil-
ity. If they do well, then they may serve as deacons.

[11]In the same way, their wives* must be respected and
must not speak evil of others. They must exercise self-con-
trol and be faithful in everything they do.

[12]A deacon must be faithful to his wife, and he must
manage his children and household well. [13]Those who do

3:6 Or *he might fall into the same judgment as the Devil.* 3:11 Or *the women deacons.* The Greek word can be translated *women* or *wives.*

NEW KING JAMES VERSION

[3]not given to wine, not violent, not greedy for money,[b] but
gentle, not quarrelsome, not covetous; [4]one who rules his
own house well, having *his* children in submission with all
reverence [5](for if a man does not know how to rule his
own house, how will he take care of the church of God?);
[6]not a novice, lest being puffed up with pride he fall into
the *same* condemnation as the devil. [7]Moreover he must
have a good testimony among those who are outside, lest
he fall into reproach and the snare of the devil.

Qualifications of Deacons

[8]Likewise deacons *must be* reverent, not double-
tongued, not given to much wine, not greedy for money,
[9]holding the mystery of the faith with a pure conscience.
[10]But let these also first be tested; then let them serve as
deacons, being *found* blameless. [11]Likewise, *their* wives
must be reverent, not slanderers, temperate, faithful in all
things. [12]Let deacons be the husbands of one wife, ruling
their children and their own houses well. [13]For those who

3:3 [b] NU-Text omits *not greedy for money.*

THE MESSAGE

about, not be overfond of wine, not pushy but gentle, not
thin-skinned, not money-hungry. He must handle his own
affairs well, attentive to his own children and having their
respect. For if someone is unable to handle his own affairs,
how can he take care of God's church? He must not be a
new believer, lest the position go to his head and the Devil
trip him up. Outsiders must think well of him, or else the
Devil will figure out a way to lure him into his trap.

The same goes for those who want to be servants in the
church: serious, not deceitful, not too free with the bottle,
not in it for what they can get out of it. They must be rever-
ent before the mystery of the faith, not using their position
to try to run things. Let them prove themselves first. If they
show they can do it, take them on. No exceptions are to be
made for women—same qualifications: serious, depend-
able, not sharp-tongued, not overfond of wine. Servants in
the church are to be committed to their spouses, attentive
to their own children, and diligent in looking after their

KING JAMES VERSION

13 For they that have used the office of a deacon well purchase to themselves a good degree, and great boldness in the faith which is in Christ Jesus.

14 ¶ These things write I unto thee, hoping to come unto thee shortly:

15 But if I tarry long, that thou mayest know how thou oughtest to behave thyself in the house of God, which is the church of the living God, the pillar and ground of the truth.

16 And without controversy great is the mystery of godliness: God was manifest in the flesh, justified in the Spirit, seen of angels, preached unto the Gentiles, believed on in the world, received up into glory.

4 Now the Spirit speaketh expressly, that in the latter times some shall depart from the faith, giving heed to seducing spirits, and doctrines of devils;

NEW AMERICAN STANDARD BIBLE

13 For those who have served well as deacons obtain for themselves a high standing and great confidence in the faith that is in Christ Jesus.

14 I am writing these things to you, hoping to come to you before long;

15 but in case I am delayed, *I write* so that you will know how one ought to conduct himself in the household of God, which is the church of the living God, the pillar and support of the truth.

16 By common confession, great is the mystery of godliness:

He who was revealed in the flesh,
Was vindicated in the Spirit,
Seen by angels,
Proclaimed among the nations,
Believed on in the world,
Taken up in glory.

Apostasy

4 But the Spirit explicitly says that in later times some will fall away from the faith, paying attention to deceitful spirits and doctrines of demons,

NEW CENTURY VERSION

and their own families. 13Those who serve well as deacons are making an honorable place for themselves, and they will be very bold in their faith in Christ Jesus.

The Secret of Our Life

14Although I hope I can come to you soon, I am writing these things to you now. 15Then, even if I am delayed, you will know how to live in the family of God. That family is the church of the living God, the support and foundation of the truth. 16Without doubt, the secret of our life of worship is great:

He was shown to us in a human body,
proved right in spirit,
and seen by angels.
He was preached to those who are not Jews,
believed in by the world,
and taken up in glory.

A Warning About False Teachers

4 Now the Holy Spirit clearly says that in the later times some people will stop believing the faith. They will follow spirits that lie and teachings of demons. 2Such

CONTEMPORARY ENGLISH VERSION

in their home. 13Those who serve well as officers will earn a good reputation and will be highly respected for their faith in Christ Jesus.

The Mystery of Our Religion

14I hope to visit you soon. But I am writing these instructions, 15so that if I am delayed, you will know how everyone who belongs to God's family ought to behave. After all, the church of the living God is the strong foundation of truth.

16Here is the great mystery of our religion:

Christ[g] came as a human.
The Spirit proved
that he pleased God,
and he was seen by angels.
Christ was preached
to the nations.
People in this world
put their faith in him,
and he was taken up to glory.

People Will Turn from Their Faith

4 God's Spirit clearly says that in the last days many people will turn from their faith. They will be fooled by evil spirits and by teachings that come from demons.

[g] 3.16 *Christ*: The Greek text has "he," probably meaning "Christ." Some manuscripts have "God."

NEW INTERNATIONAL VERSION

who have served well gain an excellent standing and great assurance in their faith in Christ Jesus.

14Although I hope to come to you soon, I am writing you these instructions so that, 15if I am delayed, you will know how people ought to conduct themselves in God's household, which is the church of the living God, the pillar and foundation of the truth. 16Beyond all question, the mystery of godliness is great:

He[c] appeared in a body,[d]
  was vindicated by the Spirit,
was seen by angels,
  was preached among the nations,
was believed on in the world,
  was taken up in glory.

Instructions to Timothy

4 The Spirit clearly says that in later times some will abandon the faith and follow deceiving spirits and things taught by demons. 2Such teachings come through

[c] *16* Some manuscripts *God* [d] *16* Or *in the flesh*

NEW LIVING TRANSLATION

well as deacons will be rewarded with respect from others and will have increased confidence in their faith in Christ Jesus.

The Truths of Our Faith

14I am writing these things to you now, even though I hope to be with you soon, 15so that if I can't come for a while, you will know how people must conduct themselves in the household of God. This is the church of the living God, which is the pillar and support of the truth.

16Without question, this is the great mystery of our faith:

Christ* appeared in the flesh
  and was shown to be righteous by the Spirit.*
He was seen by angels
  and was announced to the nations.
He was believed on in the world
  and was taken up into heaven.*

Warnings against False Teachers

4 Now the Holy Spirit tells us clearly that in the last times some will turn away from what we believe; they will follow lying spirits and teachings that come from

3:16a Greek *Who;* some manuscripts read *God.* **3:16b** Or *in his spirit.*
3:16c Greek *in glory.*

NEW KING JAMES VERSION

have served well as deacons obtain for themselves a good standing and great boldness in the faith which is in Christ Jesus.

The Great Mystery

14These things I write to you, though I hope to come to you shortly; 15but if I am delayed, *I write* so that you may know how you ought to conduct yourself in the house of God, which is the church of the living God, the pillar and ground of the truth. 16And without controversy great is the mystery of godliness:

God[c] was manifested in the flesh,
Justified in the Spirit,
Seen by angels,
Preached among the Gentiles,
Believed on in the world,
Received up in glory.

The Great Apostasy

4 Now the Spirit expressly says that in latter times some will depart from the faith, giving heed to deceiving spirits and doctrines of demons, 2speaking lies in

3:16 [c] NU-Text reads *Who.*

THE MESSAGE

own affairs. Those who do this servant work will come to be highly respected, a real credit to this Jesus-faith.

I hope to visit you soon, but just in case I'm delayed, I'm writing this letter so you'll know how things ought to go in God's household, this God-alive church, bastion of truth. This Christian life is a great mystery, far exceeding our understanding, but some things are clear enough:

He appeared in a human body,
  was proved right by the invisible Spirit,
    was seen by angels.
He was proclaimed among all kinds of peoples,
  believed in all over the world,
    taken up into heavenly glory.

Teach With Your Life

4 The Spirit makes it clear that as time goes on, some are going to give up on the faith and chase after demonic illusions put forth by professional liars. These

KING JAMES VERSION

2 Speaking lies in hypocrisy; having their conscience seared with a hot iron;

3 Forbidding to marry, *and commanding* to abstain from meats, which God hath created to be received with thanksgiving of them which believe and know the truth.

4 For every creature of God *is* good, and nothing to be refused, if it be received with thanksgiving:

5 For it is sanctified by the word of God and prayer.

6 ¶ If thou put the brethren in remembrance of these things, thou shalt be a good minister of Jesus Christ, nourished up in the words of faith and of good doctrine, whereunto thou hast attained.

7 But refuse profane and old wives' fables, and exercise thyself *rather* unto godliness.

8 For bodily exercise profiteth little: but godliness is profitable unto all things, having promise of the life that now is, and of that which is to come.

9 This *is* a faithful saying and worthy of all acceptation.

10 For therefore we both labour and suffer reproach, because we trust in the living God, who is the Saviour of all men, specially of those that believe.

NEW AMERICAN STANDARD BIBLE

2 by means of the hypocrisy of liars seared in their own conscience as with a branding iron,

3 *men* who forbid marriage *and advocate* abstaining from foods which God has created to be gratefully shared in by those who believe and know the truth.

4 For everything created by God is good, and nothing is to be rejected if it is received with gratitude;

5 for it is sanctified by means of the word of God and prayer.

A Good Minister's Discipline

6 In pointing out these things to the brethren, you will be a good servant of Christ Jesus, *constantly* nourished on the words of the faith and of the sound doctrine which you have been following.

7 But have nothing to do with worldly fables fit only for old women. On the other hand, discipline yourself for the purpose of godliness;

8 for bodily discipline is only of little profit, but godliness is profitable for all things, since it holds promise for the present life and *also* for the *life* to come.

9 It is a trustworthy statement deserving full acceptance.

10 For it is for this we labor and strive, because we have fixed our hope on the living God, who is the Savior of all men, especially of believers.

NEW CENTURY VERSION

teachings come from the false words of liars whose con-
sciences are destroyed as if by a hot iron. 3They forbid peo-
ple to marry and tell them not to eat certain foods which
God created to be eaten with thanks by people who believe
and know the truth. 4Everything God made is good, and
nothing should be refused if it is accepted with thanks,
5because it is made holy by what God has said and by
prayer.

Be a Good Servant of Christ

6By telling these things to the brothers and sisters,[a] you
will be a good servant of Christ Jesus. You will be made
strong by the words of the faith and the good teaching
which you have been following. 7But do not follow foolish
stories that disagree with God's truth, but train yourself to
serve God. 8Training your body helps you in some ways,
but serving God helps you in every way by bringing you
blessings in this life and in the future life, too. 9What I say
is true, and you should fully accept it. 10This is why we
work and struggle: We hope in the living God who is the
Savior of all people, especially of those who believe.

4:6 [a] **brothers and sisters** Although the Greek text says "brothers" here and throughout this book, Paul's words refer to the entire church, including men and women.

CONTEMPORARY ENGLISH VERSION

2They will also be fooled by the false claims of liars whose
consciences have lost all feeling. These liars 3will forbid
people to marry or to eat certain foods. But God created
these foods to be eaten with thankful hearts by his follow-
ers who know the truth. 4Everything God created is good.
And if you give thanks, you may eat anything. 5What God
has said and your prayer will make it fit to eat.

Paul's Advice to Timothy

6If you teach these things to other followers, you will be
a good servant of Christ Jesus. You will show that you
have grown up on the teachings about our faith and on the
good instructions you have obeyed. 7Don't have anything
to do with worthless, senseless stories. Work hard to be
truly religious. 8-9As the saying goes,

"Exercise is good
for your body,
but religion helps you
in every way.
It promises life
now and forever."

These words are worthwhile and should not be forgotten.
10We have put our hope in the living God, who is the
Savior of everyone, but especially of those who have faith.
That's why we work and struggle so hard.[a]

[a] **4.10** *struggle so hard*: Some manuscripts have "are treated so badly."

NEW INTERNATIONAL VERSION

hypocritical liars, whose consciences have been seared as
with a hot iron. 3They forbid people to marry and order
them to abstain from certain foods, which God created to
be received with thanksgiving by those who believe and
who know the truth. 4For everything God created is good,
and nothing is to be rejected if it is received with thanks-
giving, 5because it is consecrated by the word of God and
prayer.

6If you point these things out to the brothers, you will
be a good minister of Christ Jesus, brought up in the truths
of the faith and of the good teaching that you have fol-
lowed. 7Have nothing to do with godless myths and old
wives' tales; rather, train yourself to be godly. 8For physi-
cal training is of some value, but godliness has value for
all things, holding promise for both the present life and
the life to come.

9This is a trustworthy saying that deserves full accep-
tance 10(and for this we labor and strive), that we have put
our hope in the living God, who is the Savior of all men,
and especially of those who believe.

NEW LIVING TRANSLATION

demons. 2These teachers are hypocrites and liars. They
pretend to be religious, but their consciences are dead.*

3They will say it is wrong to be married and wrong to
eat certain foods. But God created those foods to be eaten
with thanksgiving by people who know and believe the
truth. 4Since everything God created is good, we should
not reject any of it. We may receive it gladly, with thankful
hearts. 5For we know it is made holy by the word of God
and prayer.

A Good Servant of Christ Jesus

6If you explain this to the brothers and sisters,* you will
be doing your duty as a worthy servant of Christ Jesus, one
who is fed by the message of faith and the true teaching
you have followed. 7Do not waste time arguing over god-
less ideas and old wives' tales. Spend your time and ener-
gy in training yourself for spiritual fitness. 8Physical exer-
cise has some value, but spiritual exercise is much more
important, for it promises a reward in both this life and
the next. 9This is true, and everyone should accept it. 10We
work hard and suffer much* in order that people will
believe the truth, for our hope is in the living God, who is
the Savior of all people, and particularly of those who
believe.

4:2 Greek *are seared.* 4:6 Greek *brothers.* 4:10 Some manuscripts read *and strive.*

NEW KING JAMES VERSION

hypocrisy, having their own conscience seared with a hot
iron, 3forbidding to marry, *and commanding* to abstain
from foods which God created to be received with
thanksgiving by those who believe and know the truth.
4For every creature of God *is* good, and nothing is to be
refused if it is received with thanksgiving; 5for it is sancti-
fied by the word of God and prayer.

A Good Servant of Jesus Christ

6If you instruct the brethren in these things, you will be
a good minister of Jesus Christ, nourished in the words of
faith and of the good doctrine which you have carefully
followed. 7But reject profane and old wives' fables, and
exercise yourself toward godliness. 8For bodily exercise
profits a little, but godliness is profitable for all things,
having promise of the life that now is and of that which is
to come. 9This *is* a faithful saying and worthy of all
acceptance. 10For to this *end* we both labor and suffer
reproach,[a] because we trust in the living God, who is *the*
Savior of all men, especially of those who believe. 11These

4:10 [a] NU-Text reads *we labor and strive.*

THE MESSAGE

liars have lied so well and for so long that they've lost
their capacity for truth. They will tell you not to get mar-
ried. They'll tell you not to eat this or that food—perfectly
good food God created to be eaten heartily and with
thanksgiving by Christians! Everything God created is
good, and to be received with thanks. Nothing is to be
sneered at and thrown out. God's Word and our prayers
make every item in creation holy.

You've been raised on the Message of the faith and have
followed sound teaching. Now pass on this counsel to the
Christians there, and you'll be a good servant of Jesus.
Stay clear of silly stories that get dressed up as religion.
Exercise daily in God—no spiritual flabbiness, please!
Workouts in the gymnasium are useful, but a disciplined
life in God is far more so, making you fit both today and
forever. You can count on this. Take it to heart. This is
why we've thrown ourselves into this venture so totally.
We're banking on the living God, Savior of all men and
women, especially believers.

KING JAMES VERSION

11 These things command and teach.

12 Let no man despise thy youth; but be thou an example of the believers, in word, in conversation, in charity, in spirit, in faith, in purity.

13 Till I come, give attendance to reading, to exhortation, to doctrine.

14 Neglect not the gift that is in thee, which was given thee by prophecy, with the laying on of the hands of the presbytery.

15 Meditate upon these things; give thyself wholly to them; that thy profiting may appear to all.

16 Take heed unto thyself, and unto the doctrine; continue in them: for in doing this thou shalt both save thyself, and them that hear thee.

5 Rebuke not an elder, but intreat *him* as a father; *and* the younger men as brethren;

2 The elder women as mothers; the younger as sisters, with all purity.

3 ¶ Honour widows that are widows indeed.

4 But if any widow have children or nephews, let them learn first to shew piety at home, and to requite their parents: for that is good and acceptable before God.

5 Now she that is a widow indeed, and desolate,

NEW AMERICAN STANDARD BIBLE

11 Prescribe and teach these things.

12 Let no one look down on your youthfulness, but *rather* in speech, conduct, love, faith *and* purity, show yourself an example of those who believe.

13 Until I come, give attention to the *public* reading *of Scripture,* to exhortation and teaching.

14 Do not neglect the spiritual gift within you, which was bestowed on you through prophetic utterance with the laying on of hands by the presbytery.

15 Take pains with these things; be *absorbed* in them, so that your progress will be evident to all.

16 Pay close attention to yourself and to your teaching; persevere in these things, for as you do this you will ensure salvation both for yourself and for those who hear you.

Honor Widows

5 Do not sharply rebuke an older man, but *rather* appeal to *him* as a father, *to* the younger men as brothers,

2 the older women as mothers, *and* the younger women as sisters, in all purity.

3 Honor widows who are widows indeed;

4 but if any widow has children or grandchildren, they must first learn to practice piety in regard to their own family and to make some return to their parents; for this is acceptable in the sight of God.

5 Now she who is a widow indeed and who has been

NEW CENTURY VERSION

11Command and teach these things. 12Do not let anyone
treat you as if you are unimportant because you are
young. Instead, be an example to the believers with your
words, your actions, your love, your faith, and your pure
life. 13Until I come, continue to read the Scriptures to the
people, strengthen them, and teach them. 14Use the gift
you have, which was given to you through prophecy when
the group of elders laid their hands on[b] you. 15Continue to
do those things; give your life to doing them so your
progress may be seen by everyone. 16Be careful in your life
and in your teaching. If you continue to live and teach
rightly, you will save both yourself and those who listen to
you.

Rules for Living with Others

5 Do not speak angrily to an older man, but plead with
him as if he were your father. Treat younger men like
brothers, 2older women like mothers, and younger women
like sisters. Always treat them in a pure way.

3Take care of widows who are truly widows. 4But if a
widow has children or grandchildren, let them first learn
to do their duty to their own family and to repay their parents or grandparents. That pleases God. 5The true widow,
who is all alone, puts her hope in God and continues to

4:14 [b] **laid their hands on** The laying on of hands had many purposes, including the giving of a blessing, power, or authority.

CONTEMPORARY ENGLISH VERSION

11Teach these things and tell everyone to do what you
say. 12Don't let anyone make fun of you, just because you
are young. Set an example for other followers by what
you say and do, as well as by your love, faith, and purity.
13Until I arrive, be sure to keep on reading the Scriptures
in worship, and don't stop preaching and teaching. 14Use
the gift you were given when the prophets spoke and the
group of church leaders[b] blessed you by placing their
hands on you. 15Remember these things and think about
them, so everyone can see how well you are doing. 16Be
careful about the way you live and about what you teach.
Keep on doing this, and you will save not only yourself,
but the people who hear you.

How To Act toward Others

5 Don't correct an older man. Encourage him, as you
would your own father. Treat younger men as
you would your own brother, 2and treat older women as
you would your own mother. Show the same respect to
younger women that you would to your sister.

3Take care of any widow who is really in need. 4But if a
widow has children or grandchildren, they should learn to
serve God by taking care of her, as she once took care of
them. This is what God wants them to do. 5A widow who
is really in need is one who doesn't have any relatives. She

[b] **4.14** *group of church leaders*: Or "group of elders" or "group of presbyters" or "group of priests." This translates one Greek word, and it is related to the one used in 5.17, 19.

NEW INTERNATIONAL VERSION

[11]Command and teach these things. [12]Don't let anyone look down on you because you are young, but set an example for the believers in speech, in life, in love, in faith and in purity. [13]Until I come, devote yourself to the public reading of Scripture, to preaching and to teaching. [14]Do not neglect your gift, which was given you through a prophetic message when the body of elders laid their hands on you.

[15]Be diligent in these matters; give yourself wholly to them, so that everyone may see your progress. [16]Watch your life and doctrine closely. Persevere in them, because if you do, you will save both yourself and your hearers.

Advice About Widows, Elders and Slaves

5 Do not rebuke an older man harshly, but exhort him as if he were your father. Treat younger men as brothers, [2]older women as mothers, and younger women as sisters, with absolute purity.

[3]Give proper recognition to those widows who are really in need. [4]But if a widow has children or grandchildren, these should learn first of all to put their religion into practice by caring for their own family and so repaying their parents and grandparents, for this is pleasing to God. [5]The widow who is really in need and left all alone puts

NEW LIVING TRANSLATION

[11]Teach these things and insist that everyone learn them. [12]Don't let anyone think less of you because you are young. Be an example to all believers in what you teach, in the way you live, in your love, your faith, and your purity. [13]Until I get there, focus on reading the Scriptures to the church, encouraging the believers, and teaching them.

[14]Do not neglect the spiritual gift you received through the prophecies spoken to you when the elders of the church laid their hands on you. [15]Give your complete attention to these matters. Throw yourself into your tasks so that everyone will see your progress. [16]Keep a close watch on yourself and on your teaching. Stay true to what is right, and God will save you and those who hear you.

5 Never speak harshly to an older man,* but appeal to him respectfully as though he were your own father. Talk to the younger men as you would to your own brothers. [2]Treat the older women as you would your mother, and treat the younger women with all purity as your own sisters.

Advice about Widows, Elders, and Slaves

[3]The church should care for any widow who has no one else to care for her. [4]But if she has children or grandchildren, their first responsibility is to show godliness at home and repay their parents by taking care of them. This is something that pleases God very much.

[5]But a woman who is a true widow, one who is truly

5:1 Or *an elder.*

NEW KING JAMES VERSION

things command and teach.

Take Heed to Your Ministry

[12]Let no one despise your youth, but be an example to the believers in word, in conduct, in love, in spirit,[b] in faith, in purity. [13]Till I come, give attention to reading, to exhortation, to doctrine. [14]Do not neglect the gift that is in you, which was given to you by prophecy with the laying on of the hands of the eldership. [15]Meditate on these things; give yourself entirely to them, that your progress may be evident to all. [16]Take heed to yourself and to the doctrine. Continue in them, for in doing this you will save both yourself and those who hear you.

Treatment of Church Members

5 Do not rebuke an older man, but exhort *him* as a father, younger men as brothers, [2]older women as mothers, younger women as sisters, with all purity.

Honor True Widows

[3]Honor widows who are really widows. [4]But if any widow has children or grandchildren, let them first learn to show piety at home and to repay their parents; for this is good and[a] acceptable before God. [5]Now she who is really a widow, and left alone, trusts in God and continues in

4:12 [b] NU-Text omits *in spirit.* 5:4 [a] NU-Text and M-Text omit *good and.*

THE MESSAGE

Get the word out. Teach all these things. And don't let anyone put you down because you're young. Teach believers with your life: by word, by demeanor, by love, by faith, by integrity. Stay at your post reading Scripture, giving counsel, teaching. And that special gift of ministry you were given when the leaders of the church laid hands on you and prayed—keep that dusted off and in use.

Cultivate these things. Immerse yourself in them. The people will all see you mature right before their eyes! Keep a firm grasp on both your character and your teaching. Don't be diverted. Just keep at it. Both you and those who hear you will experience salvation.

The Family of Faith

5 Don't be harsh or impatient with an older man. Talk to him as you would your own father, and to the younger men as your brothers. Reverently honor an older woman as you would your mother, and the younger women as sisters.

Take care of widows who are destitute. If a widow has family members to take care of her, let them learn that religion begins at their own doorstep and that they should pay back with gratitude some of what they have received. This pleases God immensely. You can tell a legitimate widow by the way she has put all her hope in God, praying

KING JAMES VERSION

trusteth in God, and continueth in supplications and prayers night and day.

6 But she that liveth in pleasure is dead while she liveth.

7 And these things give in charge, that they may be blameless.

8 But if any provide not for his own, and specially for those of his own house, he hath denied the faith, and is worse than an infidel.

9 Let not a widow be taken into the number under threescore years old, having been the wife of one man,

10 Well reported of for good works; if she have brought up children, if she have lodged strangers, if she have washed the saints' feet, if she have relieved the afflicted, if she have diligently followed every good work.

11 But the younger widows refuse: for when they have begun to wax wanton against Christ, they will marry;

12 Having damnation, because they have cast off their first faith.

13 And withal they learn *to be* idle, wandering about from house to house; and not only idle, but tattlers also and busybodies, speaking things which they ought not.

14 I will therefore that the younger women marry, bear children, guide the house, give none occasion to the adversary to speak reproachfully.

NEW AMERICAN STANDARD BIBLE

left alone, has fixed her hope on God and continues in entreaties and prayers night and day.

6 But she who gives herself to wanton pleasure is dead even while she lives.

7 Prescribe these things as well, so that they may be above reproach.

8 But if anyone does not provide for his own, and especially for those of his household, he has denied the faith and is worse than an unbeliever.

9 A widow is to be put on the list only if she is not less than sixty years old, *having been* the wife of one man,

10 having a reputation for good works; *and* if she has brought up children, if she has shown hospitality to strangers, if she has washed the saints' feet, if she has assisted those in distress, *and* if she has devoted herself to every good work.

11 But refuse *to put* younger widows *on the list*, for when they feel sensual desires in disregard of Christ, they want to get married,

12 *thus* incurring condemnation, because they have set aside their previous pledge.

13 At the same time they also learn *to be* idle, as they go around from house to house; and not merely idle, but also gossips and busybodies, talking about things not proper *to mention.*

14 Therefore, I want younger *widows* to get married, bear children, keep house, *and* give the enemy no occasion for reproach;

NEW CENTURY VERSION

pray night and day for God's help. 6 But the widow who
uses her life to please herself is really dead while she is
alive. 7 Tell the believers to do these things so that no one
can criticize them. 8 Whoever does not care for his own rel-
atives, especially his own family members, has turned
against the faith and is worse than someone who does not
believe in God.

9 To be on the list of widows, a woman must be at least
sixty years old. She must have been faithful to her hus-
band. 10 She must be known for her good works—works
such as raising her children, welcoming strangers, wash-
ing the feet of God's people, helping those in trouble, and
giving her life to do all kinds of good deeds.

11 But do not put younger widows on that list. After they
give themselves to Christ, they are pulled away from him by
their physical needs, and then they want to marry again.
12 They will be judged for not doing what they first prom-
ised to do. 13 Besides that, they learn to waste their time,
going from house to house. And they not only waste their
time but also begin to gossip and busy themselves with
other people's lives, saying things they should not say. 14 So
I want the younger widows to marry, have children, and
manage their homes. Then no enemy will have any reason

CONTEMPORARY ENGLISH VERSION

has faith in God, and she keeps praying to him night and
day, asking for his help.

6 A widow who thinks only about having a good time is
already dead, even though she is still alive.

7 Tell all of this to everyone, so they will do the right
thing. 8 People who don't take care of their relatives, and
especially their own families, have given up their faith. They
are worse than someone who doesn't have faith in the Lord.

9 For a widow to be put on the list of widows, she must
be at least sixty years old, and she must have been faithful
in marriage.[a] 10 She must also be well-known for doing all
sorts of good things, such as raising children, giving food
to strangers, welcoming God's people into her home,[b] help-
ing people in need, and always making herself useful.

11 Don't put young widows on the list. They may later
have a strong desire to get married. Then they will turn
away from Christ 12 and become guilty of breaking their
promise to him. 13 Besides, they will become lazy and get
into the habit of going from house to house. Next, they
will start gossiping and become busybodies, talking about
things that are none of their business.

14 I would prefer that young widows get married, have
children, and look after their families. Then the enemy
won't have any reason to say insulting things about us.

[a] 5.9 *been faithful in marriage*: Or "been the wife of only one husband" or "never been divorced." [b] 5.10 *welcoming God's people into her home*: The Greek text has "washing the feet of God's people." In New Testament times most people either went barefoot or wore sandals, and a host would often wash the feet of special guests.

NEW INTERNATIONAL VERSION

her hope in God and continues night and day to pray and
to ask God for help. 6But the widow who lives for pleasure
is dead even while she lives. 7Give the people these
instructions, too, so that no one may be open to blame. 8If
anyone does not provide for his relatives, and especially
for his immediate family, he has denied the faith and is
worse than an unbeliever.
9No widow may be put on the list of widows unless she
is over sixty, has been faithful to her husband,[a] 10and is
well known for her good deeds, such as bringing up chil-
dren, showing hospitality, washing the feet of the saints,
helping those in trouble and devoting herself to all kinds
of good deeds.
11As for younger widows, do not put them on such a list.
For when their sensual desires overcome their dedication to
Christ, they want to marry. 12Thus they bring judgment on
themselves, because they have broken their first pledge.
13Besides, they get into the habit of being idle and going
about from house to house. And not only do they become
idlers, but also gossips and busybodies, saying things they
ought not to. 14So I counsel younger widows to marry, to
have children, to manage their homes and to give the enemy

a 9 Or *has had but one husband*

NEW LIVING TRANSLATION

alone in this world, has placed her hope in God. Night and
day she asks God for help and spends much time in prayer.
6But the widow who lives only for pleasure is spiritually
dead. 7Give these instructions to the church so that the
widows you support* will not be criticized.
8But those who won't care for their own relatives, espe-
cially those living in the same household, have denied
what we believe. Such people are worse than unbelievers.
9A widow who is put on the list for support must be a
woman who is at least sixty years old and was faithful to
her husband.* 10She must be well respected by everyone
because of the good she has done. Has she brought up her
children well? Has she been kind to strangers? Has she
served other Christians humbly?* Has she helped those
who are in trouble? Has she always been ready to do
good?
11The younger widows should not be on the list, because
their physical desires will overpower their devotion to
Christ and they will want to remarry. 12Then they would be
guilty of breaking their previous pledge. 13Besides, they are
likely to become lazy and spend their time gossiping from
house to house, getting into other people's business and
saying things they shouldn't. 14So I advise these younger
widows to marry again, have children, and take care of
their own homes. Then the enemy will not be able to say

5:7 Or *so the church;* Greek reads *so they.* 5:9 Greek *was the wife of one man.* 5:10 Greek *Has she washed the feet of saints?*

NEW KING JAMES VERSION

supplications and prayers night and day. 6But she who
lives in pleasure is dead while she lives. 7And these things
command, that they may be blameless. 8But if anyone
does not provide for his own, and especially for those of
his household, he has denied the faith and is worse than
an unbeliever.
9Do not let a widow under sixty years old be taken into
the number, *and not unless* she has been the wife of one
man, 10well reported for good works: if she has brought up
children, if she has lodged strangers, if she has washed
the saints' feet, if she has relieved the afflicted, if she has
diligently followed every good work.
11But refuse *the* younger widows; for when they have
begun to grow wanton against Christ, they desire to marry,
12having condemnation because they have cast off their first
faith. 13And besides they learn *to be* idle, wandering about
from house to house, and not only idle but also gossips and
busybodies, saying things which they ought not. 14Therefore
I desire that *the* younger *widows* marry, bear children, man-
age the house, give no opportunity to the adversary to speak

THE MESSAGE

to him constantly for the needs of others as well as her
own. But a widow who exploits people's emotions and
pocketbooks—well, there's nothing to her. Tell these
things to the people so that they will do the right thing in
their extended family. Anyone who neglects to care for
family members in need repudiates the faith. That's worse
than refusing to believe in the first place.

Sign some widows up for the special ministry of offering
assistance. They will in turn receive support from the
church. They must be over sixty, married only once, and
have a reputation for helping out with children, strangers,
tired Christians, the hurt and troubled.

Don't put young widows on this list. No sooner will they
get on than they'll want to get off, obsessed with wanting
to get a husband rather than serving Christ in this way. By
breaking their word, they're liable to go from bad to worse,
frittering away their days on empty talk, gossip, and trivi-
alities. No, I'd rather the young widows go ahead and get
married in the first place, have children, manage their
homes, and not give critics any foothold for finding fault.

KING JAMES VERSION

15 For some are already turned aside after Satan.

16 If any man or woman that believeth have widows, let them relieve them, and let not the church be charged; that it may relieve them that are widows indeed.

17 ¶ Let the elders that rule well be counted worthy of double honour, especially they who labour in the word and doctrine.

18 For the scripture saith, Thou shalt not muzzle the ox that treadeth out the corn. And, The labourer *is* worthy of his reward.

19 Against an elder receive not an accusation, but before two or three witnesses.

20 Them that sin rebuke before all, that others also may fear.

21 I charge *thee* before God, and the Lord Jesus Christ, and the elect angels, that thou observe these things without preferring one before another, doing nothing by partiality.

22 Lay hands suddenly on no man, neither be partaker of other men's sins: keep thyself pure.

NEW AMERICAN STANDARD BIBLE

15 for some have already turned aside to follow Satan.

16 If any woman who is a believer has *dependent* widows, she must assist them and the church must not be burdened, so that it may assist those who are widows indeed.

Concerning Elders

17 The elders who rule well are to be considered worthy of double honor, especially those who work hard at preaching and teaching.

18 For the Scripture says, "YOU SHALL NOT MUZZLE THE OX WHILE HE IS THRESHING," and "The laborer is worthy of his wages."

19 Do not receive an accusation against an elder except on the basis of two or three witnesses.

20 Those who continue in sin, rebuke in the presence of all, so that the rest also will be fearful *of sinning.*

21 I solemnly charge you in the presence of God and of Christ Jesus and of *His* chosen angels, to maintain these *principles* without bias, doing nothing in a *spirit of* partiality.

22 Do not lay hands upon anyone *too* hastily and thereby share *responsibility for* the sins of others; keep yourself free from sin.

NEW CENTURY VERSION

to criticize them. 15But some have already turned away to follow Satan.

16If any woman who is a believer has widows in her family, she should care for them herself. The church should not have to care for them. Then it will be able to take care of those who are truly widows.

17The elders who lead the church well should receive double honor, especially those who work hard by speaking and teaching, 18because the Scripture says: "When an ox is working in the grain, do not cover its mouth to keep it from eating,"[a] and "A worker should be given his pay."[b]

19Do not listen to someone who accuses an elder, without two or three witnesses. 20Tell those who continue sinning that they are wrong. Do this in front of the whole church so that the others will have a warning.

21Before God and Christ Jesus and the chosen angels, I command you to do these things without showing favor of any kind to anyone.

22Think carefully before you lay your hands on[c] anyone, and don't share in the sins of others. Keep yourself pure.

5:18 [a] **"When...eating,"** Quotation from Deuteronomy 25:4.
5:18 [b] **"A worker...pay."** Quotation from Luke 10:7. 5:22 [c] **lay your hands on** The laying on of hands had many purposes, including the giving of a blessing, power, or authority.

CONTEMPORARY ENGLISH VERSION

15Look what's already happened to some of the young widows! They have turned away to follow Satan.

16If a woman who is a follower has any widows in her family, she[c] should help them. This will keep the church from having that burden, and then the church can help widows who are really in need.

Church Leaders

17Church leaders[d] who do their job well deserve to be paid[e] twice as much, especially if they work hard at preaching and teaching. 18It is just as the Scriptures say, "Don't muzzle an ox when you are using it to grind grain." You also know the saying, "Workers are worth their pay."

19Don't listen to any charge against a church leader, unless at least two or three people bring the same charges. 20But if any of the leaders should keep on sinning, they must be corrected in front of the whole group, as a warning to everyone else.

21In the presence of God and Christ Jesus and their chosen angels, I order you to follow my instructions! Be fair with everyone, and don't have any favorites.

22Don't be too quick to accept people into the service of the Lord[f] by placing your hands on them.

Don't sin because others do, but stay close to God.

[c] **5.16** *woman . . . she*: Some manuscripts have "man or woman . . . that person." [d] **5.17** *leaders*: Or "elders" or "presbyters" or "priests." [e] **5.17** *paid*: Or "honored" or "respected." [f] **5.22** *to accept people into the service of the Lord*: Or "to forgive people."

NEW INTERNATIONAL VERSION

no opportunity for slander. [15]Some have in fact already turned away to follow Satan.

[16]If any woman who is a believer has widows in her family, she should help them and not let the church be burdened with them, so that the church can help those widows who are really in need.

[17]The elders who direct the affairs of the church well are worthy of double honor, especially those whose work is preaching and teaching. [18]For the Scripture says, "Do not muzzle the ox while it is treading out the grain,"[b] and "The worker deserves his wages."[c] [19]Do not entertain an accusation against an elder unless it is brought by two or three witnesses. [20]Those who sin are to be rebuked publicly, so that the others may take warning.

[21]I charge you, in the sight of God and Christ Jesus and the elect angels, to keep these instructions without partiality, and to do nothing out of favoritism.

[22]Do not be hasty in the laying on of hands, and do not share in the sins of others. Keep yourself pure.

[b] *18* Deut. 25:4 [c] *18* Luke 10:7

NEW LIVING TRANSLATION

anything against them. [15]For I am afraid that some of them have already gone astray and now follow Satan.

[16]If a Christian woman has relatives who are widows, she must take care of them and not put the responsibility on the church. Then the church can care for widows who are truly alone.

[17]Elders who do their work well should be paid well,* especially those who work hard at both preaching and teaching. [18]For the Scripture says, "Do not keep an ox from eating as it treads out the grain." And in another place, "Those who work deserve their pay!"*

[19]Do not listen to complaints against an elder unless there are two or three witnesses to accuse him. [20]Anyone who sins should be rebuked in front of the whole church so that others will have a proper fear of God.

[21]I solemnly command you in the presence of God and Christ Jesus and the holy angels to obey these instructions without taking sides or showing special favor to anyone. [22]Never be in a hurry about appointing an elder. Do not participate in the sins of others. Keep yourself pure.

5:17 Greek *should be worthy of double honor.* **5:18** Deut 25:4; Luke 10:7.

NEW KING JAMES VERSION

reproachfully. [15]For some have already turned aside after Satan. [16]If any believing man or[b] woman has widows, let them relieve them, and do not let the church be burdened, that it may relieve those who are really widows.

Honor the Elders

[17]Let the elders who rule well be counted worthy of double honor, especially those who labor in the word and doctrine. [18]For the Scripture says, *"You shall not muzzle an ox while it treads out the grain,"*[c] and, "The laborer *is* worthy of his wages."[d] [19]Do not receive an accusation against an elder except from two or three witnesses. [20]Those who are sinning rebuke in the presence of all, that the rest also may fear.

[21]I charge *you* before God and the Lord Jesus Christ and the elect angels that you observe these things without prejudice, doing nothing with partiality. [22]Do not lay hands on anyone hastily, nor share in other people's sins; keep yourself pure.

5:16 [b] NU-Text omits *man or.* **5:18** [c] Deuteronomy 25:4 [d] Luke 10:7

THE MESSAGE

Some of them have already left and gone after Satan.

Any Christian woman who has widows in her family is responsible for them. They shouldn't be dumped on the church. The church has its hands full already with widows who need help.

✠

Give a bonus to leaders who do a good job, especially the ones who work hard at preaching and teaching. Scripture tells us, "Don't muzzle a working ox," and, "A worker deserves his pay."

Don't listen to a complaint against a leader that isn't backed up by two or three responsible witnesses.

If anyone falls into sin, call that person on the carpet. Those who are inclined that way will know right off they can't get by with it.

God and Jesus and angels all back me up in these instructions. Carry them out without favoritism, without taking sides. Don't appoint people to church leadership positions too hastily. If a person is involved in some serious sins, you don't want to become an unwitting accomplice. In any event, keep a close check on yourself. And don't worry too much about what the critics will say. Go

KING JAMES VERSION

23 Drink no longer water, but use a little wine for thy stomach's sake and thine often infirmities.

24 Some men's sins are open beforehand, going before to judgment; and some *men* they follow after.

25 Likewise also the good works *of some* are manifest beforehand; and they that are otherwise cannot be hid.

6 Let as many servants as are under the yoke count their own masters worthy of all honour, that the name of God and *his* doctrine be not blasphemed.

2 And they that have believing masters, let them not despise *them*, because they are brethren; but rather do *them* service, because they are faithful and beloved, partakers of the benefit. These things teach and exhort.

3 If any man teach otherwise, and consent not to wholesome words, *even* the words of our Lord Jesus Christ, and to the doctrine which is according to godliness;

4 He is proud, knowing nothing, but doting about questions and strifes of words, whereof cometh envy, strife, railings, evil surmisings,

5 Perverse disputings of men of corrupt minds, and destitute of the truth, supposing that gain is godliness: from such withdraw thyself.

6 ¶ But godliness with contentment is great gain.

NEW AMERICAN STANDARD BIBLE

23 No longer drink water *exclusively*, but use a little wine for the sake of your stomach and your frequent ailments.

24 The sins of some men are quite evident, going before them to judgment; for others, their *sins* follow after.

25 Likewise also, deeds that are good are quite evident, and those which are otherwise cannot be concealed.

Instructions to Those Who Minister

6 All who are under the yoke as slaves are to regard their own masters as worthy of all honor so that the name of God and *our* doctrine will not be spoken against.

2 Those who have believers as their masters must not be disrespectful to them because they are brethren, but must serve them all the more, because those who partake of the benefit are believers and beloved. Teach and preach these *principles.*

3 If anyone advocates a different doctrine and does not agree with sound words, those of our Lord Jesus Christ, and with the doctrine conforming to godliness,

4 he is conceited *and* understands nothing; but he has a morbid interest in controversial questions and disputes about words, out of which arise envy, strife, abusive language, evil suspicions,

5 and constant friction between men of depraved mind and deprived of the truth, who suppose that godliness is a means of gain.

6 But godliness *actually* is a means of great gain when accompanied by contentment.

NEW CENTURY VERSION

23 Stop drinking only water, but drink a little wine to
help your stomach and your frequent sicknesses.
24 The sins of some people are easy to see even before
they are judged, but the sins of others are seen only later.
25 So also good deeds are easy to see, but even those that
are not easily seen cannot stay hidden.

6 All who are slaves under a yoke should show full
respect to their masters so no one will speak against
God's name and our teaching. 2 The slaves whose masters
are believers should not show their masters any less
respect because they are believers. They should serve their
masters even better, because they are helping believers
they love.

You must teach and preach these things.

False Teaching and True Riches

3 Anyone who has a different teaching does not agree
with the true teaching of our Lord Jesus Christ and the
teaching that shows the true way to serve God. 4 This person is full of pride and understands nothing, but is sick
with a love for arguing and fighting about words. This
brings jealousy, fighting, speaking against others, evil
mistrust, 5 and constant quarrels from those who have evil
minds and have lost the truth. They think that serving God
is a way to get rich.

6 Serving God does make us very rich, if we are satisfied
with what we have. 7 We brought nothing into the world,

CONTEMPORARY ENGLISH VERSION

23 Stop drinking only water. Take a little wine to help
your stomach trouble and the other illnesses you always
have.

24 Some people get caught in their sins right away, even
before the time of judgment. But other people's sins don't
show up until later. 25 It is the same with good deeds.
Some are easily seen, but none of them can be hidden.

6 If you are a slave, you should respect and honor your
owner. This will keep people from saying bad things
about God and about our teaching. 2 If any of you slaves
have owners who are followers, you should show them
respect. After all, they are also followers of Christ, and he
loves them. So you should serve and help them the best
you can.

False Teaching and True Wealth

These are the things you must teach and tell the people
to do. 3 Anyone who teaches something different disagrees
with the correct and godly teaching of our Lord Jesus
Christ. 4 Those people who disagree are proud of themselves, but they don't really know a thing. Their minds are
sick, and they like to argue over words. They cause jealousy, disagreements, unkind words, evil suspicions, 5 and
nasty quarrels. They have wicked minds and have missed
out on the truth.

These people think religion is supposed to make you
rich. 6 And religion does make your life rich, by making you
content with what you have. 7 We didn't bring anything

NEW INTERNATIONAL VERSION

23 Stop drinking only water, and use a little wine because of your stomach and your frequent illnesses.

24 The sins of some men are obvious, reaching the place of judgment ahead of them; the sins of others trail behind them. 25 In the same way, good deeds are obvious, and even those that are not cannot be hidden.

6 All who are under the yoke of slavery should consider their masters worthy of full respect, so that God's name and our teaching may not be slandered. 2 Those who have believing masters are not to show less respect for them because they are brothers. Instead, they are to serve them even better, because those who benefit from their service are believers, and dear to them. These are the things you are to teach and urge on them.

Love of Money

3 If anyone teaches false doctrines and does not agree to the sound instruction of our Lord Jesus Christ and to godly teaching, 4 he is conceited and understands nothing. He has an unhealthy interest in controversies and quarrels about words that result in envy, strife, malicious talk, evil suspicions 5 and constant friction between men of corrupt mind, who have been robbed of the truth and who think that godliness is a means to financial gain.

6 But godliness with contentment is great gain. 7 For we

NEW LIVING TRANSLATION

23 Don't drink only water. You ought to drink a little wine for the sake of your stomach because you are sick so often.

24 Remember that some people lead sinful lives, and everyone knows they will be judged. But there are others whose sin will not be revealed until later. 25 In the same way, everyone knows how much good some people do, but there are others whose good deeds won't be known until later.

6 Christians who are slaves should give their masters full respect so that the name of God and his teaching will not be shamed. 2 If your master is a Christian, that is no excuse for being disrespectful. You should work all the harder because you are helping another believer* by your efforts.

False Teaching and True Riches

Teach these truths, Timothy, and encourage everyone to obey them. 3 Some false teachers may deny these things, but these are the sound, wholesome teachings of the Lord Jesus Christ, and they are the foundation for a godly life. 4 Anyone who teaches anything different is both conceited and ignorant. Such a person has an unhealthy desire to quibble over the meaning of words. This stirs up arguments ending in jealousy, fighting, slander, and evil suspicions. 5 These people always cause trouble. Their minds are corrupt, and they don't tell the truth. To them religion is just a way to get rich.

6 Yet true religion with contentment is great wealth.

6:2 Greek *a brother.*

NEW KING JAMES VERSION

23 No longer drink only water, but use a little wine for your stomach's sake and your frequent infirmities.

24 Some men's sins are clearly evident, preceding *them* to judgment, but those of some *men* follow later. 25 Likewise, the good works *of some* are clearly evident, and those that are otherwise cannot be hidden.

Honor Masters

6 Let as many bondservants as are under the yoke count their own masters worthy of all honor, so that the name of God and *His* doctrine may not be blasphemed. 2 And those who have believing masters, let them not despise *them* because they are brethren, but rather serve *them* because those who are benefited are believers and beloved. Teach and exhort these things.

Error and Greed

3 If anyone teaches otherwise and does not consent to wholesome words, *even* the words of our Lord Jesus Christ, and to the doctrine which accords with godliness, 4 he is proud, knowing nothing, but is obsessed with disputes and arguments over words, from which come envy, strife, reviling, evil suspicions, 5 useless wranglings[a] of men of corrupt minds and destitute of the truth, who suppose that godliness is a *means of* gain. From such withdraw yourself.[b]

6 Now godliness with contentment is great gain. 7 For we

6:5 [a] NU-Text and M-Text read *constant friction.* [b] NU-Text omits this sentence.

THE MESSAGE

ahead and drink a little wine, for instance; it's good for your digestion, good medicine for what ails you.

The sins of some people are blatant and march them right into court. The sins of others don't show up until much later. The same with good deeds. Some you see right off, but none are hidden forever.

6 Whoever is a slave must make the best of it, giving respect to his master so that outsiders don't blame God and our teaching for his behavior. Slaves with Christian masters all the more so—their masters are really their beloved brothers!

The Lust for Money

These are the things I want you to teach and preach. If you have leaders there who teach otherwise, who refuse the solid words of our Master Jesus and this godly instruction, tag them for what they are: ignorant windbags who infect the air with germs of envy, controversy, badmouthing, suspicious rumors. Eventually there's an epidemic of backstabbing, and truth is but a distant memory. They think religion is a way to make a fast buck.

A devout life does bring wealth, but it's the rich simplicity of being yourself before God. Since we entered the world

KING JAMES VERSION

7 For we brought nothing into *this* world, *and it is* certain we can carry nothing out.

8 And having food and raiment let us be therewith content.

9 But they that will be rich fall into temptation and a snare, and *into* many foolish and hurtful lusts, which drown men in destruction and perdition.

10 For the love of money is the root of all evil: which while some coveted after, they have erred from the faith, and pierced themselves through with many sorrows.

11 But thou, O man of God, flee these things; and follow after righteousness, godliness, faith, love, patience, meekness.

12 Fight the good fight of faith, lay hold on eternal life, whereunto thou art also called, and hast professed a good profession before many witnesses.

13 ¶ I give thee charge in the sight of God, who quickeneth all things, and *before* Christ Jesus, who before Pontius Pilate witnessed a good confession;

14 That thou keep *this* commandment without spot, unrebukeable, until the appearing of our Lord Jesus Christ:

15 Which in his times he shall shew, *who is* the blessed and only Potentate, the King of kings, and Lord of lords;

NEW AMERICAN STANDARD BIBLE

7 For we have brought nothing into the world, so we cannot take anything out of it either.

8 If we have food and covering, with these we shall be content.

9 But those who want to get rich fall into temptation and a snare and many foolish and harmful desires which plunge men into ruin and destruction.

10 For the love of money is a root of all sorts of evil, and some by longing for it have wandered away from the faith and pierced themselves with many griefs.

11 But flee from these things, you man of God, and pursue righteousness, godliness, faith, love, perseverance *and* gentleness.

12 Fight the good fight of faith; take hold of the eternal life to which you were called, and you made the good confession in the presence of many witnesses.

13 I charge you in the presence of God, who gives life to all things, and of Christ Jesus, who testified the good confession before Pontius Pilate,

14 that you keep the commandment without stain or reproach until the appearing of our Lord Jesus Christ,

15 which He will bring about at the proper time—He who is the blessed and only Sovereign, the King of kings and Lord of lords,

NEW CENTURY VERSION

so we can take nothing out. 8But, if we have food and
clothes, we will be satisfied with that. 9Those who want to
become rich bring temptation to themselves and are
caught in a trap. They want many foolish and harmful
things that ruin and destroy people. 10The love of money
causes all kinds of evil. Some people have left the faith,
because they wanted to get more money, but they have
caused themselves much sorrow.

Some Things to Remember

11But you, man of God, run away from all those things.
Instead, live in the right way, serve God, have faith, love,
patience, and gentleness. 12Fight the good fight of faith,
grabbing hold of the life that continues forever. You were
called to have that life when you confessed the good con-
fession before many witnesses. 13In the sight of God, who
gives life to everything, and of Christ Jesus, I give you a
command. Christ Jesus made the good confession when he
stood before Pontius Pilate. 14Do what you were command-
ed to do without wrong or blame until our Lord Jesus
Christ comes again. 15God will make that happen at the
right time. He is the blessed and only Ruler, the King of all
kings and the Lord of all lords. 16He is the only One who

CONTEMPORARY ENGLISH VERSION

into this world, and we won't[a] take anything with us when
we leave. 8So we should be satisfied just to have food and
clothes. 9People who want to be rich fall into all sorts of
temptations and traps. They are caught by foolish and
harmful desires that drag them down and destroy them.
10The love of money causes all kinds of trouble. Some peo-
ple want money so much that they have given up their
faith and caused themselves a lot of pain.

Fighting a Good Fight for the Faith

11Timothy, you belong to God, so keep away from all
these evil things. Try your best to please God and to be like
him. Be faithful, loving, dependable, and gentle. 12Fight a
good fight for the faith and claim eternal life. God offered
it to you when you clearly told about your faith, while so
many people listened. 13Now I ask you to make a promise.
Make it in the presence of God, who gives life to all, and in
the presence of Jesus Christ, who openly told Pontius Pilate
about his faith. 14Promise to obey completely and fully all
that you have been told until our Lord Jesus Christ returns.

15The glorious God
is the only Ruler,
the King of kings
and Lord of lords.
At the time that God
has already decided,

[a] 6.7 *we won't*: Some manuscripts have "we surely won't."

NEW INTERNATIONAL VERSION

brought nothing into the world, and we can take nothing
out of it. [8]But if we have food and clothing, we will be con-
tent with that. [9]People who want to get rich fall into temp-
tation and a trap and into many foolish and harmful
desires that plunge men into ruin and destruction. [10]For
the love of money is a root of all kinds of evil. Some peo-
ple, eager for money, have wandered from the faith and
pierced themselves with many griefs.

Paul's Charge to Timothy

[11]But you, man of God, flee from all this, and pursue
righteousness, godliness, faith, love, endurance and gentle-
ness. [12]Fight the good fight of the faith. Take hold of the
eternal life to which you were called when you made your
good confession in the presence of many witnesses. [13]In the
sight of God, who gives life to everything, and of Christ
Jesus, who while testifying before Pontius Pilate made the
good confession, I charge you [14]to keep this command
without spot or blame until the appearing of our Lord Jesus
Christ, [15]which God will bring about in his own time—God,
the blessed and only Ruler, the King of kings and Lord of

NEW LIVING TRANSLATION

[7]After all, we didn't bring anything with us when we came
into the world, and we certainly cannot carry anything
with us when we die. [8]So if we have enough food and
clothing, let us be content. [9]But people who long to be rich
fall into temptation and are trapped by many foolish and
harmful desires that plunge them into ruin and destruc-
tion. [10]For the love of money is at the root of all kinds of
evil. And some people, craving money, have wandered
from the faith and pierced themselves with many sorrows.

Paul's Final Instructions

[11]But you, Timothy, belong to God; so run from all these
evil things, and follow what is right and good. Pursue a
godly life, along with faith, love, perseverance, and gentle-
ness. [12]Fight the good fight for what we believe. Hold
tightly to the eternal life that God has given you, which
you have confessed so well before many witnesses. [13]And I
command you before God, who gives life to all, and before
Christ Jesus, who gave a good testimony before Pontius
Pilate, [14]that you obey his commands with all purity. Then
no one can find fault with you from now until our Lord
Jesus Christ returns. [15]For at the right time Christ will be
revealed from heaven by the blessed and only almighty
God, the King of kings and Lord of lords. [16]He alone can

NEW KING JAMES VERSION

brought nothing into *this* world, *and it is* certain[c] we can
carry nothing out. [8]And having food and clothing, with
these we shall be content. [9]But those who desire to be rich
fall into temptation and a snare, and *into* many foolish
and harmful lusts which drown men in destruction and
perdition. [10]For the love of money is a root of all *kinds of*
evil, for which some have strayed from the faith in their
greediness, and pierced themselves through with many
sorrows.

The Good Confession

[11]But you, O man of God, flee these things and pursue
righteousness, godliness, faith, love, patience, gentleness.
[12]Fight the good fight of faith, lay hold on eternal life, to
which you were also called and have confessed the good
confession in the presence of many witnesses. [13]I urge you
in the sight of God who gives life to all things, and *before*
Christ Jesus who witnessed the good confession before
Pontius Pilate, [14]that you keep *this* commandment without
spot, blameless until our Lord Jesus Christ's appearing,
[15]which He will manifest in His own time, *He who is* the
blessed and only Potentate, the King of kings and Lord of

6:7 [c] NU-Text omits *and it is certain.*

THE MESSAGE

penniless and will leave it penniless, if we have bread on
the table and shoes on our feet, that's enough.

But if it's only money these leaders are after, they'll self-destruct in no time. Lust for money brings trouble and nothing but trouble. Going down that path, some lose their footing in the faith completely and live to regret it bitterly ever after.

Running Hard

But you, Timothy, man of God: Run for your life from all this. Pursue a righteous life—a life of wonder, faith, love, steadiness, courtesy. Run hard and fast in the faith. Seize the eternal life, the life you were called to, the life you so fervently embraced in the presence of so many witnesses.

I'm charging you before the life-giving God and before Christ, who took his stand before Pontius Pilate and didn't give an inch: Keep this command to the letter, and don't slack off. Our Master, Jesus Christ, is on his way. He'll show up right on time, his arrival guaranteed by the Blessed and Undisputed Ruler, High King, High God. He's

KING JAMES VERSION

16 Who only hath immortality, dwelling in the light which no man can approach unto; whom no man hath seen, nor can see: to whom *be* honour and power everlasting. Amen.
17 Charge them that are rich in this world, that they be not highminded, nor trust in uncertain riches, but in the living God, who giveth us richly all things to enjoy;
18 That they do good, that they be rich in good works, ready to distribute, willing to communicate;
19 Laying up in store for themselves a good foundation against the time to come, that they may lay hold on eternal life.
20 O Timothy, keep that which is committed to thy trust, avoiding profane *and* vain babblings, and oppositions of science falsely so called:
21 Which some professing have erred concerning the faith. Grace *be* with thee. Amen.

NEW AMERICAN STANDARD BIBLE

16 who alone possesses immortality and dwells in unapproachable light, whom no man has seen or can see. To Him *be* honor and eternal dominion! Amen.
17 Instruct those who are rich in this present world not to be conceited or to fix their hope on the uncertainty of riches, but on God, who richly supplies us with all things to enjoy.
18 *Instruct them* to do good, to be rich in good works, to be generous and ready to share,
19 storing up for themselves the treasure of a good foundation for the future, so that they may take hold of that which is life indeed.
20 O Timothy, guard what has been entrusted to you, avoiding worldly *and* empty chatter *and* the opposing arguments of what is falsely called "knowledge"—
21 which some have professed and thus gone astray from the faith.

Grace be with you.

NEW CENTURY VERSION

never dies. He lives in light so bright no one can go near it. No one has ever seen God, or can see him. May honor and power belong to God forever. Amen.

17Command those who are rich with things of this world not to be proud. Tell them to hope in God, not in their uncertain riches. God richly gives us everything to enjoy.
18Tell the rich people to do good, to be rich in doing good deeds, to be generous and ready to share. 19By doing that,
they will be saving a treasure for themselves as a strong foundation for the future. Then they will be able to have the life that is true life.

20Timothy, guard what God has trusted to you. Stay away from foolish, useless talk and from the arguments of what is falsely called "knowledge." 21By saying they have
that "knowledge," some have missed the true faith.

Grace be with you.

CONTEMPORARY ENGLISH VERSION

he will send Jesus Christ
back again.

16Only God lives forever!
And he lives in light
that no one can come near.
No human has ever seen God
or ever can see him.
God will be honored,
and his power
will last forever. Amen.

17Warn the rich people of this world not to be proud or to trust in wealth that is easily lost. Tell them to have faith in God, who is rich and blesses us with everything we need to enjoy life. 18Instruct them to do as many good deeds as they can and to help everyone. Remind the rich to be generous and share what they have. 19This will lay a solid foundation for the future, so that they will know what true life is like.

20Timothy, guard what God has placed in your care! Don't pay any attention to that godless and stupid talk that sounds smart but really isn't. 21Some people have
even lost their faith by believing this talk.

I pray that the Lord will be kind to all of you!

NEW INTERNATIONAL VERSION

lords, 16who alone is immortal and who lives in unapproachable light, whom no one has seen or can see. To him be honor and might forever. Amen.

17Command those who are rich in this present world not to be arrogant nor to put their hope in wealth, which is so uncertain, but to put their hope in God, who richly provides us with everything for our enjoyment. 18Command them to do good, to be rich in good deeds, and to be generous and willing to share. 19In this way they will lay up treasure for themselves as a firm foundation for the coming age, so that they may take hold of the life that is truly life.

20Timothy, guard what has been entrusted to your care. Turn away from godless chatter and the opposing ideas of what is falsely called knowledge, 21which some have professed and in so doing have wandered from the faith.

Grace be with you.

NEW LIVING TRANSLATION

never die, and he lives in light so brilliant that no human can approach him. No one has ever seen him, nor ever will. To him be honor and power forever. Amen.

17Tell those who are rich in this world not to be proud and not to trust in their money, which will soon be gone. But their trust should be in the living God, who richly gives us all we need for our enjoyment. 18Tell them to use their money to do good. They should be rich in good works and should give generously to those in need, always being ready to share with others whatever God has given them. 19By doing this they will be storing up their treasure as a good foundation for the future so that they may take hold of real life.

20Timothy, guard what God has entrusted to you. Avoid godless, foolish discussions with those who oppose you with their so-called knowledge. 21Some people have wandered from the faith by following such foolishness.

May God's grace be with you all.

NEW KING JAMES VERSION

lords, 16who alone has immortality, dwelling in unapproachable light, whom no man has seen or can see, to whom *be* honor and everlasting power. Amen.

Instructions to the Rich

17Command those who are rich in this present age not to be haughty, nor to trust in uncertain riches but in the living God, who gives us richly all things to enjoy. 18*Let them* do good, that they be rich in good works, ready to give, willing to share, 19storing up for themselves a good foundation for the time to come, that they may lay hold on eternal life.

Guard the Faith

20O Timothy! Guard what was committed to your trust, avoiding the profane *and* idle babblings and contradictions of what is falsely called knowledge— 21by professing it some have strayed concerning the faith.

Grace *be* with you. Amen.

THE MESSAGE

the only one death can't touch, his light so bright no one can get close. He's never been seen by human eyes—human eyes can't take him in! Honor to him, and eternal rule! Oh, yes.

Tell those rich in this world's wealth to quit being so full of themselves and so obsessed with money, which is here today and gone tomorrow. Tell them to go after God, who piles on all the riches we could ever manage—to do good, to be rich in helping others, to be extravagantly generous. If they do that, they'll build a treasury that will last, gaining life that is truly life.

And oh, my dear Timothy, guard the treasure you were given! Guard it with your life. Avoid the talk-show religion and the practiced confusion of the so-called experts. People caught up in a lot of talk can miss the whole point of faith.

Overwhelming grace keep you!

KING JAMES VERSION

THE SECOND EPISTLE OF ST. PAUL TO TIMOTHY

1 Paul, an apostle of Jesus Christ by the will of God, according to the promise of life which is in Christ Jesus,

2 To Timothy, *my* dearly beloved son: Grace, mercy, *and* peace, from God the Father and Christ Jesus our Lord.

3 I thank God, whom I serve from *my* forefathers with pure conscience, that without ceasing I have remembrance of thee in my prayers night and day;

4 Greatly desiring to see thee, being mindful of thy tears, that I may be filled with joy;

5 When I call to remembrance the unfeigned faith that is in thee, which dwelt first in thy grandmother Lois, and thy mother Eunice; and I am persuaded that in thee also.

6 ¶ Wherefore I put thee in remembrance that thou stir up the gift of God, which is in thee by the putting on of my hands.

7 For God hath not given us the spirit of fear; but of power, and of love, and of a sound mind.

NEW AMERICAN STANDARD BIBLE

THE SECOND LETTER OF PAUL TO TIMOTHY

Timothy Charged to Guard His Trust

1 Paul, an apostle of Christ Jesus by the will of God, according to the promise of life in Christ Jesus,

2 To Timothy, my beloved son: Grace, mercy *and* peace from God the Father and Christ Jesus our Lord.

3 I thank God, whom I serve with a clear conscience the way my forefathers did, as I constantly remember you in my prayers night and day,

4 longing to see you, even as I recall your tears, so that I may be filled with joy.

5 For I am mindful of the sincere faith within you, which first dwelt in your grandmother Lois and your mother Eunice, and I am sure that *it is* in you as well.

6 For this reason I remind you to kindle afresh the gift of God which is in you through the laying on of my hands.

7 For God has not given us a spirit of timidity, but of power and love and discipline.

NEW CENTURY VERSION

2 TIMOTHY

1 From Paul, an apostle of Christ Jesus by the will of God. God sent me to tell about the promise of life that is in Christ Jesus.

2To Timothy, a dear child to me:

Grace, mercy, and peace to you from God the Father and Christ Jesus our Lord.

Encouragement for Timothy

3I thank God as I always mention you in my prayers,
day and night. I serve him, doing what I know is right as
my ancestors did. 4Remembering that you cried for me, I
want very much to see you so I can be filled with joy. 5I
remember your true faith. That faith first lived in your
grandmother Lois and in your mother Eunice, and I know
you now have that same faith. 6This is why I remind you
to keep using the gift God gave you when I laid my hands
on[a] you. Now let it grow, as a small flame grows into a
fire. 7God did not give us a spirit that makes us afraid but
a spirit of power and love and self-control.

1:6 [a] **laid my hands on** The laying on of hands had many purposes, including the giving of a blessing, power, or authority.

CONTEMPORARY ENGLISH VERSION

2 TIMOTHY

1 From Paul, an apostle of Christ Jesus.

God himself chose me to be an apostle, and he gave me the promised life that Jesus Christ makes possible.

2Timothy, you are like a dear child to me. I pray that God our Father and our Lord Christ Jesus will be kind and merciful to you and will bless you with peace!

Do Not Be Ashamed of the Lord

3Night and day I mention you in my prayers. I am
always grateful for you, as I pray to the God my ancestors
and I have served with a clear conscience. 4I remember
how you cried, and I want to see you, because that will
make me truly happy. 5I also remember the genuine faith
of your mother Eunice. Your grandmother Lois had the
same sort of faith, and I am sure that you have it as well.
6So I ask you to make full use of the gift that God gave
you when I placed my hands on you.[a] Use it well. 7God's
Spirit[b] doesn't make cowards out of us. The Spirit gives us
power, love, and self-control.

[a] 1.6 *when I placed my hands on you*: Church leaders placed their hands on people who were being appointed to preach or teach (see 1 Timothy 4.14). [b] 1.7 *God's Spirit*: Or "God."

NEW INTERNATIONAL VERSION

2 TIMOTHY

1 Paul, an apostle of Christ Jesus by the will of God, according to the promise of life that is in Christ Jesus,

2To Timothy, my dear son:

Grace, mercy and peace from God the Father and Christ Jesus our Lord.

Encouragement to Be Faithful

3I thank God, whom I serve, as my forefathers did, with a clear conscience, as night and day I constantly remember you in my prayers. 4Recalling your tears, I long to see you, so that I may be filled with joy. 5I have been reminded of your sincere faith, which first lived in your grandmother Lois and in your mother Eunice and, I am persuaded, now lives in you also. 6For this reason I remind you to fan into flame the gift of God, which is in you through the laying on of my hands. 7For God did not give us a spirit of timidity, but a spirit of power, of love and of self-discipline.

NEW LIVING TRANSLATION

2 TIMOTHY

Greetings from Paul

1 This letter is from Paul, an apostle of Christ Jesus by God's will, sent out to tell others about the life he has promised through faith in Christ Jesus.

2It is written to Timothy, my dear son.

May God our Father and Christ Jesus our Lord give you grace, mercy, and peace.

Encouragement to Be Faithful

3Timothy, I thank God for you. He is the God I serve with a clear conscience, just as my ancestors did. Night and day I constantly remember you in my prayers. 4I long to see you again, for I remember your tears as we parted. And I will be filled with joy when we are together again.

5I know that you sincerely trust the Lord, for you have the faith of your mother, Eunice, and your grandmother, Lois. 6This is why I remind you to fan into flames the spiritual gift God gave you when I laid my hands on you. 7For God has not given us a spirit of fear and timidity, but of power, love, and self-discipline. 8So you must never be

NEW KING JAMES VERSION

THE SECOND EPISTLE OF PAUL TO

TIMOTHY

Greeting

1 Paul, an apostle of Jesus Christ[a] by the will of God, according to the promise of life which is in Christ Jesus,

2To Timothy, a beloved son:

Grace, mercy, *and* peace from God the Father and Christ Jesus our Lord.

Timothy's Faith and Heritage

3I thank God, whom I serve with a pure conscience, as *my* forefathers *did,* as without ceasing I remember you in my prayers night and day, 4greatly desiring to see you, being mindful of your tears, that I may be filled with joy, 5when I call to remembrance the genuine faith that is in you, which dwelt first in your grandmother Lois and your mother Eunice, and I am persuaded is in you also. 6Therefore I remind you to stir up the gift of God which is in you through the laying on of my hands. 7For God has not given us a spirit of fear, but of power and of love and of a sound mind.

1:1 [a] NU-Text and M-Text read *Christ Jesus.*

THE MESSAGE

2 TIMOTHY

1 I, Paul, am on special assignment for Christ, carrying out God's plan laid out in the Message of Life by Jesus. I write this to you, Timothy, the son I love so much. All the best from our God and Christ be yours!

To Be Bold With God's Gifts

Every time I say your name in prayer—which is practically all the time—I thank God for you, the God I worship with my whole life in the tradition of my ancestors. I miss you a lot, especially when I remember that last tearful goodbye, and I look forward to a joy-packed reunion.

That precious memory triggers another: your honest faith—and what a rich faith it is, handed down from your grandmother Lois to your mother Eunice, and now to you! And the special gift of ministry you received when I laid hands on you and prayed—keep that ablaze! God doesn't want us to be shy with his gifts, but bold and loving and sensible.

KING JAMES VERSION

8 Be not thou therefore ashamed of the testimony of
our Lord, nor of me his prisoner: but be thou partaker of
the afflictions of the gospel according to the power of God;
9 Who hath saved us, and called *us* with an holy call-
ing, not according to our works, but according to his own
purpose and grace, which was given us in Christ Jesus
before the world began,
10 But is now made manifest by the appearing of our
Saviour Jesus Christ, who hath abolished death, and hath
brought life and immortality to light through the gospel:
11 Whereunto I am appointed a preacher, and an apos-
tle, and a teacher of the Gentiles.
12 For the which cause I also suffer these things: never-

NEW AMERICAN STANDARD BIBLE

8 Therefore do not be ashamed of the testimony of our
Lord or of me His prisoner, but join with *me* in suffering
for the gospel according to the power of God,
9 who has saved us and called us with a holy calling,
not according to our works, but according to His own pur-
pose and grace which was granted us in Christ Jesus from
all eternity,
10 but now has been revealed by the appearing of our
Savior Christ Jesus, who abolished death and brought life
and immortality to light through the gospel,
11 for which I was appointed a preacher and an apostle
and a teacher.
12 For this reason I also suffer these things, but I am

NEW CENTURY VERSION

8So do not be ashamed to tell people about our Lord
Jesus, and do not be ashamed of me, in prison for the Lord.
But suffer with me for the Good News. God, who gives us
the strength to do that, 9saved us and made us his holy
people. That was not because of anything we did ourselves
but because of God's purpose and grace. That grace was
given to us through Christ Jesus before time began, 10but it
is now shown to us by the coming of our Savior Christ
Jesus. He destroyed death, and through the Good News he
showed us the way to have life that cannot be destroyed.
11I was chosen to tell that Good News and to be an apostle
and a teacher. 12I am suffering now because I tell the Good

CONTEMPORARY ENGLISH VERSION

8Don't be ashamed to speak for our Lord. And don't be
ashamed of me, just because I am in jail for serving him.
Use the power that comes from God and join with me in
suffering for telling the good news.

9God saved us and chose us
to be his holy people.
We did nothing
to deserve this,
but God planned it
because he is so kind.
Even before time began
God planned for Christ Jesus
to show kindness to us.

10Now Christ Jesus has come
to show us the kindness
of God.
Christ our Savior defeated death
and brought us
the good news.
It shines like a light
and offers life
that never ends.

11My work is to be a preacher, an apostle, and a teacher.[c]
12That's why I am suffering now. But I am not ashamed! I

c 1.11 *teacher*: Some manuscripts add "of the Gentiles."

NEW INTERNATIONAL VERSION

8So do not be ashamed to testify about our Lord, or ashamed of me his prisoner. But join with me in suffering for the gospel, by the power of God, 9who has saved us and called us to a holy life—not because of anything we have done but because of his own purpose and grace. This grace was given us in Christ Jesus before the beginning of time, 10but it has now been revealed through the appearing of our Savior, Christ Jesus, who has destroyed death and has brought life and immortality to light through the gospel. 11And of this gospel I was appointed a herald and an apostle and a teacher. 12That is why I am suffering as I

NEW LIVING TRANSLATION

ashamed to tell others about our Lord. And don't be ashamed of me, either, even though I'm in prison for Christ. With the strength God gives you, be ready to suffer with me for the proclamation of the Good News.

9It is God who saved us and chose us to live a holy life. He did this not because we deserved it, but because that was his plan long before the world began—to show his love and kindness to us through Christ Jesus. 10And now he has made all of this plain to us by the coming of Christ Jesus, our Savior, who broke the power of death and showed us the way to everlasting life through the Good News. 11And God chose me to be a preacher, an apostle, and a teacher of this Good News.

12And that is why I am suffering here in prison. But I am

NEW KING JAMES VERSION

Not Ashamed of the Gospel

8Therefore do not be ashamed of the testimony of our Lord, nor of me His prisoner, but share with me in the sufferings for the gospel according to the power of God, 9who has saved us and called *us* with a holy calling, not according to our works, but according to His own purpose and grace which was given to us in Christ Jesus before time began, 10but has now been revealed by the appearing of our Savior Jesus Christ, *who* has abolished death and brought life and immortality to light through the gospel, 11to which I was appointed a preacher, an apostle, and a teacher of the Gentiles.[b] 12For this reason I also suffer

1:11 [b] NU-Text omits *of the Gentiles.*

THE MESSAGE

So don't be embarrassed to speak up for our Master or for me, his prisoner. Take your share of suffering for the Message along with the rest of us. We can only keep on going, after all, by the power of God, who first saved us and then called us to this holy work. We had nothing to do with it. It was all *his* idea, a gift prepared for us in Jesus long before we knew anything about it. But we know it now. Since the appearance of our Savior, nothing could be plainer: death defeated, life vindicated in a steady blaze of light, all through the work of Jesus.

This is the Message I've been set apart to proclaim as preacher, emissary, and teacher. It's also the cause of all this trouble I'm in. But I have no regrets. I couldn't be

KING JAMES VERSION

theless I am not ashamed: for I know whom I have believed, and am persuaded that he is able to keep that which I have committed unto him against that day.

13 Hold fast the form of sound words, which thou hast heard of me, in faith and love which is in Christ Jesus.

14 That good thing which was committed unto thee keep by the Holy Ghost which dwelleth in us.

15 ¶ This thou knowest, that all they which are in Asia be turned away from me; of whom are Phygellus and Hermogenes.

16 The Lord give mercy unto the house of Onesiphorus; for he oft refreshed me, and was not ashamed of my chain:

17 But, when he was in Rome, he sought me out very diligently, and found *me*.

18 The Lord grant unto him that he may find mercy of the Lord in that day: and in how many things he ministered unto me at Ephesus, thou knowest very well.

2 Thou therefore, my son, be strong in the grace that is in Christ Jesus.

2 And the things that thou hast heard of me among many witnesses, the same commit thou to faithful men, who shall be able to teach others also.

3 Thou therefore endure hardness, as a good soldier of Jesus Christ.

4 No man that warreth entangleth himself with the affairs of *this* life; that he may please him who hath chosen him to be a soldier.

NEW AMERICAN STANDARD BIBLE

not ashamed; for I know whom I have believed and I am convinced that He is able to guard what I have entrusted to Him until that day.

13 Retain the standard of sound words which you have heard from me, in the faith and love which are in Christ Jesus.

14 Guard, through the Holy Spirit who dwells in us, the treasure which has been entrusted to *you*.

15 You are aware of the fact that all who are in Asia turned away from me, among whom are Phygelus and Hermogenes.

16 The Lord grant mercy to the house of Onesiphorus, for he often refreshed me and was not ashamed of my chains;

17 but when he was in Rome, he eagerly searched for me and found me—

18 the Lord grant to him to find mercy from the Lord on that day—and you know very well what services he rendered at Ephesus.

Be Strong

2 You therefore, my son, be strong in the grace that is in Christ Jesus.

2 The things which you have heard from me in the presence of many witnesses, entrust these to faithful men who will be able to teach others also.

3 Suffer hardship with *me,* as a good soldier of Christ Jesus.

4 No soldier in active service entangles himself in the affairs of everyday life, so that he may please the one who enlisted him as a soldier.

NEW CENTURY VERSION

News, but I am not ashamed, because I know Jesus, the
One in whom I have believed. And I am sure he is able to
protect what he has trusted me with until that day.[b]
13Follow the pattern of true teachings that you heard from
me in faith and love, which are in Christ Jesus. 14Protect
the truth that you were given; protect it with the help of
the Holy Spirit who lives in us.
15You know that everyone in the country of Asia has left
me, even Phygelus and Hermogenes. 16May the Lord show
mercy to the family of Onesiphorus, who has often helped
me and was not ashamed that I was in prison. 17When he
came to Rome, he looked eagerly for me until he found me.
18May the Lord allow him to find mercy from the Lord on
that day. You know how many ways he helped me in
Ephesus.

A Loyal Soldier of Christ Jesus

2 You then, Timothy, my child, be strong in the grace
we have in Christ Jesus. 2You should teach people
whom you can trust the things you and many others have
heard me say. Then they will be able to teach others.
3Share in the troubles we have like a good soldier of Christ
Jesus. 4A soldier wants to please the enlisting officer, so
no one serving in the army wastes time with everyday

1:12 [b] day The day Christ will come to judge all people and take his people to live with him.

CONTEMPORARY ENGLISH VERSION

know the one I have faith in, and I am sure that he can
guard until the last day what he has trusted me with.[d]
13Now follow the example of the correct teaching I gave
you, and let the faith and love of Christ Jesus be your
model. 14You have been trusted with a wonderful treasure.
Guard it with the help of the Holy Spirit, who lives within
you.
15You know that everyone in Asia has turned against
me, especially Phygelus and Hermogenes.
16I pray that the Lord will be kind to the family of
Onesiphorus. He often cheered me up and wasn't ashamed
of me when I was put in jail. 17Then after he arrived in
Rome, he searched everywhere until he found me. 18I pray
that the Lord Jesus will ask God to show mercy to
Onesiphorus on the day of judgment. You know how much
he helped me in Ephesus.

A Good Soldier of Christ Jesus

2 Timothy, my child, Christ Jesus is kind, and you must
let him make you strong. 2You have often heard me
teach. Now I want you to tell these same things to followers who can be trusted to tell others.
3As a good soldier of Christ Jesus you must endure your
share of suffering. 4Soldiers on duty don't work at outside
jobs. They try only to please their commanding officer. 5No

[d] 1.12 *what he has trusted me with*: Or "what I have trusted him with."

NEW INTERNATIONAL VERSION

am. Yet I am not ashamed, because I know whom I have believed, and am convinced that he is able to guard what I have entrusted to him for that day.

13 What you heard from me, keep as the pattern of sound teaching, with faith and love in Christ Jesus. 14 Guard the good deposit that was entrusted to you—guard it with the help of the Holy Spirit who lives in us.

15 You know that everyone in the province of Asia has deserted me, including Phygelus and Hermogenes.

16 May the Lord show mercy to the household of Onesiphorus, because he often refreshed me and was not ashamed of my chains. 17 On the contrary, when he was in Rome, he searched hard for me until he found me. 18 May the Lord grant that he will find mercy from the Lord on that day! You know very well in how many ways he helped me in Ephesus.

2 You then, my son, be strong in the grace that is in Christ Jesus. 2 And the things you have heard me say in the presence of many witnesses entrust to reliable men who will also be qualified to teach others. 3 Endure hardship with us like a good soldier of Christ Jesus. 4 No one serving as a soldier gets involved in civilian affairs—he wants to please his commanding officer. 5 Similarly, if

NEW LIVING TRANSLATION

not ashamed of it, for I know the one in whom I trust, and I am sure that he is able to guard what I have entrusted to him* until the day of his return.

13 Hold on to the pattern of right teaching you learned from me. And remember to live in the faith and love that you have in Christ Jesus. 14 With the help of the Holy Spirit who lives within us, carefully guard what has been entrusted to you.

15 As you know, all the Christians who came here from the province of Asia have deserted me; even Phygelus and Hermogenes are gone. 16 May the Lord show special kindness to Onesiphorus and all his family because he often visited and encouraged me. He was never ashamed of me because I was in prison. 17 When he came to Rome, he searched everywhere until he found me. 18 May the Lord show him special kindness on the day of Christ's return. And you know how much he helped me at Ephesus.

A Good Soldier of Christ Jesus

2 Timothy, my dear son, be strong with the special favor God gives you in Christ Jesus. 2 You have heard me teach many things that have been confirmed by many reliable witnesses. Teach these great truths to trustworthy people who are able to pass them on to others.

3 Endure suffering along with me, as a good soldier of Christ Jesus. 4 And as Christ's soldier, do not let yourself become tied up in the affairs of this life, for then you cannot satisfy the one who has enlisted you in his army.

1:12 Or *what has been entrusted to me.*

NEW KING JAMES VERSION

these things; nevertheless I am not ashamed, for I know whom I have believed and am persuaded that He is able to keep what I have committed to Him until that Day.

Be Loyal to the Faith

13 Hold fast the pattern of sound words which you have heard from me, in faith and love which are in Christ Jesus. 14 That good thing which was committed to you, keep by the Holy Spirit who dwells in us.

15 This you know, that all those in Asia have turned away from me, among whom are Phygellus and Hermogenes. 16 The Lord grant mercy to the household of Onesiphorus, for he often refreshed me, and was not ashamed of my chain; 17 but when he arrived in Rome, he sought me out very zealously and found *me.* 18 The Lord grant to him that he may find mercy from the Lord in that Day—and you know very well how many ways he ministered *to me*[c] at Ephesus.

Be Strong in Grace

2 You therefore, my son, be strong in the grace that is in Christ Jesus. 2 And the things that you have heard from me among many witnesses, commit these to faithful men who will be able to teach others also. 3 You therefore must endure[a] hardship as a good soldier of Jesus Christ. 4 No one engaged in warfare entangles himself with the affairs of *this* life, that he may please him who enlisted

1:18 [c] *To me* is from the Vulgate and a few Greek manuscripts.
2:3 [a] NU-Text reads *You must share.*

THE MESSAGE

more sure of my ground—the One I've trusted in can take care of what he's trusted me to do right to the end.

So keep at your work, this faith and love rooted in Christ, exactly as I set it out for you. It's as sound as the day you first heard it from me. Guard this precious thing placed in your custody by the Holy Spirit who works in us.

I'm sure you know by now that everyone in the province of Asia deserted me, even Phygelus and Hermogenes. But God bless Onesiphorus and his family! Many's the time I've been refreshed in that house. And he wasn't embarrassed a bit that I was in jail. The first thing he did when he got to Rome was look me up. May God on the Last Day treat him as well as he treated me. And then there was all the help he provided in Ephesus—but you know that better than I.

Doing Your Best for God

2 So, my son, throw yourself into this work for Christ. Pass on what you heard from me—the whole congregation saying Amen!—to reliable leaders who are competent to teach others. When the going gets rough, take it on the chin with the rest of us, the way Jesus did. A soldier on duty doesn't get caught up in making deals at the marketplace. He concentrates on carrying out orders. An athlete

KING JAMES VERSION

5 And if a man also strive for masteries, *yet* is he not crowned, except he strive lawfully.

6 The husbandman that laboureth must be first partaker of the fruits.

7 Consider what I say; and the Lord give thee understanding in all things.

8 ¶ Remember that Jesus Christ of the seed of David was raised from the dead according to my gospel:

9 Wherein I suffer trouble, as an evil doer, *even* unto bonds; but the word of God is not bound.

10 Therefore I endure all things for the elect's sakes, that they may also obtain the salvation which is in Christ Jesus with eternal glory.

11 *It is* a faithful saying: For if we be dead with *him*, we shall also live with *him*:

12 If we suffer, we shall also reign with *him*: if we deny *him*, he also will deny us:

13 If we believe not, *yet* he abideth faithful: he cannot deny himself.

NEW AMERICAN STANDARD BIBLE

5 Also if anyone competes as an athlete, he does not win the prize unless he competes according to the rules.

6 The hard-working farmer ought to be the first to receive his share of the crops.

7 Consider what I say, for the Lord will give you understanding in everything.

8 Remember Jesus Christ, risen from the dead, descendant of David, according to my gospel,

9 for which I suffer hardship even to imprisonment as a criminal; but the word of God is not imprisoned.

10 For this reason I endure all things for the sake of those who are chosen, so that they also may obtain the salvation which is in Christ Jesus *and* with *it* eternal glory.

11 It is a trustworthy statement:
For if we died with Him, we will also live with Him;
12 If we endure, we will also reign with Him;
If we deny Him, He also will deny us;
13 If we are faithless, He remains faithful, for He cannot
deny Himself.

NEW CENTURY VERSION

matters. 5 Also an athlete who takes part in a contest must
obey all the rules in order to win. 6 The farmer who works
hard should be the first person to get some of the food that
was grown. 7 Think about what I am saying, because the
Lord will give you the ability to understand everything.

8 Remember Jesus Christ, who was raised from the dead,
who is from the family of David. This is the Good News I
preach, 9 and I am suffering because of it to the point of
being bound with chains like a criminal. But God's teaching is not in chains. 10 So I patiently accept all these troubles so that those whom God has chosen can have the salvation that is in Christ Jesus. With that salvation comes
glory that never ends.

11 This teaching is true:
If we died with him, we will also live with him.
12 If we accept suffering, we will also rule with him.
If we refuse to accept him, he will refuse to accept us.
13 If we are not faithful, he will still be faithful,
because he cannot be false to himself.

CONTEMPORARY ENGLISH VERSION

one wins an athletic contest without obeying the rules.
6 And farmers who work hard are the first to eat what
grows in their field. 7 If you keep in mind what I have told
you, the Lord will help you understand completely.

8 Keep your mind on Jesus Christ! He was from the family of David and was raised from death, just as my good
news says. 9 And because of this message, I am locked up
in jail and treated like a criminal. But God's good news
isn't locked in jail, 10 and so I am willing to put up with
anything. Then God's special people will be saved. They
will be given eternal glory because they belong to Christ
Jesus. 11 Here is a true message:

"If we died with Christ,
we will live with him.
12 If we don't give up,
we will rule with him.
If we deny
that we know him,
he will deny
that he knows us.
13 If we are not faithful,
he will still be faithful.
Christ cannot deny
who he is."

NEW INTERNATIONAL VERSION

anyone competes as an athlete, he does not receive the
victor's crown unless he competes according to the rules.
[6]The hardworking farmer should be the first to receive a
share of the crops. [7]Reflect on what I am saying, for the
Lord will give you insight into all this.
[8]Remember Jesus Christ, raised from the dead, descend-
ed from David. This is my gospel, [9]for which I am suffering
even to the point of being chained like a criminal. But
God's word is not chained. [10]Therefore I endure everything
for the sake of the elect, that they too may obtain the sal-
vation that is in Christ Jesus, with eternal glory.
[11]Here is a trustworthy saying:

If we died with him,
we will also live with him;
[12]if we endure,
we will also reign with him.
If we disown him,
he will also disown us;
[13]if we are faithless,
he will remain faithful,
for he cannot disown himself.

NEW LIVING TRANSLATION

[5]Follow the Lord's rules for doing his work, just as an ath-
lete either follows the rules or is disqualified and wins no
prize. [6]Hardworking farmers are the first to enjoy the fruit
of their labor. [7]Think about what I am saying. The Lord
will give you understanding in all these things.
[8]Never forget that Jesus Christ was a man born into King
David's family and that he was raised from the dead. This
is the Good News I preach. [9]And because I preach this
Good News, I am suffering and have been chained like a
criminal. But the word of God cannot be chained. [10]I am
willing to endure anything if it will bring salvation and
eternal glory in Christ Jesus to those God has chosen.
[11]This is a true saying:

If we die with him,
we will also live with him.
[12] If we endure hardship,
we will reign with him.
If we deny him,
he will deny us.
[13] If we are unfaithful,
he remains faithful,
for he cannot deny himself.

NEW KING JAMES VERSION

him as a soldier. [5]And also if anyone competes in athlet-
ics, he is not crowned unless he competes according to the
rules. [6]The hardworking farmer must be first to partake of
the crops. [7]Consider what I say, and may[b] the Lord give
you understanding in all things.
[8]Remember that Jesus Christ, of the seed of David, was
raised from the dead according to my gospel, [9]for which I
suffer trouble as an evildoer, *even* to the point of chains;
but the word of God is not chained. [10]Therefore I endure all
things for the sake of the elect, that they also may obtain
the salvation which is in Christ Jesus with eternal glory.
[11]*This is* a faithful saying:

For if we died with *Him*,
We shall also live with *Him*.
[12] If we endure,
We shall also reign with *Him*.
If we deny *Him*,
He also will deny us.
[13] If we are faithless,
He remains faithful;
He cannot deny Himself.

2:7 [b] NU-Text reads *the Lord will give you.*

THE MESSAGE

who refuses to play by the rules will never get anywhere.
It's the diligent farmer who gets the produce. Think it over.
God will make it all plain.
Fix this picture firmly in your mind: Jesus, descended
from the line of David, raised from the dead. It's what
you've heard from me all along. It's what I'm sitting in jail
for right now—but God's Word isn't in jail! That's why I
stick it out here—so that everyone God calls will get in on
the salvation of Christ in all its glory. This is a sure thing:

If we die with him, we'll live with him;
If we stick it out with him, we'll rule with him;
If we turn our backs on him, he'll turn his back on us;
If we give up on him, he does not give up—
for there's no way he can be false to himself.

KING JAMES VERSION

14 ¶ Of these things put *them* in remembrance, charging *them* before the Lord that they strive not about words to no profit, *but* to the subverting of the hearers.

15 Study to shew thyself approved unto God, a workman that needeth not to be ashamed, rightly dividing the word of truth.

16 But shun profane *and* vain babblings: for they will increase unto more ungodliness.

17 And their word will eat as doth a canker: of whom is Hymenaeus and Philetus;

18 Who concerning the truth have erred, saying that the resurrection is past already; and overthrow the faith of some.

19 ¶ Nevertheless the foundation of God standeth sure, having this seal, The Lord knoweth them that are his. And, Let every one that nameth the name of Christ depart from iniquity.

20 But in a great house there are not only vessels of gold and of silver, but also of wood and of earth; and some to honour, and some to dishonour.

21 If a man therefore purge himself from these, he shall be a vessel unto honour, sanctified, and meet for the master's use, *and* prepared unto every good work.

22 ¶ Flee also youthful lusts: but follow righteousness, faith, charity, peace, with them that call on the Lord out of a pure heart.

NEW AMERICAN STANDARD BIBLE

An Unashamed Workman

14 Remind *them* of these things, and solemnly charge *them* in the presence of God not to wrangle about words, which is useless *and leads* to the ruin of the hearers.

15 Be diligent to present yourself approved to God as a workman who does not need to be ashamed, accurately handling the word of truth.

16 But avoid worldly *and* empty chatter, for it will lead to further ungodliness,

17 and their talk will spread like [7]gangrene. Among them are Hymenaeus and Philetus,

18 *men* who have gone astray from the truth saying that the resurrection has already taken place, and they upset the faith of some.

19 Nevertheless, the firm foundation of God stands, having this seal, "The Lord knows those who are His," and, "Everyone who names the name of the Lord is to abstain from wickedness."

20 Now in a large house there are not only gold and silver vessels, but also vessels of wood and of earthenware, and some to honor and some to dishonor.

21 Therefore, if anyone cleanses himself from these *things*, he will be a vessel for honor, sanctified, useful to the Master, prepared for every good work.

22 Now flee from youthful lusts and pursue righteousness, faith, love *and* peace, with those who call on the Lord from a pure heart.

2:17 [7] Or *cancer*

NEW CENTURY VERSION

A Worker Pleasing to God

14Continue teaching these things, warning people in
God's presence not to argue about words. It does not help
anyone, and it ruins those who listen. 15Make every effort
to give yourself to God as the kind of person he will accept.
Be a worker who is not ashamed and who uses the true
teaching in the right way. 16Stay away from foolish, use-
less talk, because that will lead people further away from
God. 17Their evil teaching will spread like a sickness inside
the body. Hymenaeus and Philetus are like that. 18They
have left the true teaching, saying that the rising from the
dead has already taken place, and so they are destroying
the faith of some people. 19But God's strong foundation
continues to stand. These words are written on the seal:
"The Lord knows those who belong to him,"[a] and
"Everyone who wants to belong to the Lord must stop
doing wrong."

20In a large house there are not only things made of gold
and silver, but also things made of wood and clay. Some
things are used for special purposes, and others are made
for ordinary jobs. 21All who make themselves clean from
evil will be used for special purposes. They will be made
holy, useful to the Master, ready to do any good work.

22But run away from the evil young people like to do.
Try hard to live right and to have faith, love, and peace,
together with those who trust in the Lord from pure hearts.

2:19 [a] **"The Lord...him"** Quotation from Numbers 16:5.

CONTEMPORARY ENGLISH VERSION

An Approved Worker

14Don't let anyone forget these things. And with God[a] as
your witness, you must warn them not to argue about
words. These arguments don't help anyone. In fact, they
ruin everyone who listens to them. 15Do your best to win
God's approval as a worker who doesn't need to be
ashamed and who teaches only the true message.

16Keep away from worthless and useless talk. It only
leads people farther away from God. 17That sort of talk is
like a sore that won't heal. And Hymenaeus and Philetus
have been talking this way 18by teaching that the dead
have already been raised to life. This is far from the truth,
and it is destroying the faith of some people.

19But the foundation that God has laid is solid. On it is
written, "The Lord knows who his people are. So everyone
who worships the Lord must turn away from evil."

20In a large house some dishes are made of gold or sil-
ver, while others are made of wood or clay. Some of these
are special, and others are not. 21That's also how it is with
people. The ones who stop doing evil and make themselves
pure will become special. Their lives will be holy and
pleasing to their Master, and they will be able to do all
kinds of good deeds.

22Run from temptations that capture young people.
Always do the right thing. Be faithful, loving, and easy to
get along with. Worship with people whose hearts are

[a] **2.14** *God*: Some manuscripts have "the Lord," and others have "Christ."

NEW INTERNATIONAL VERSION

A Workman Approved by God

14Keep reminding them of these things. Warn them before God against quarreling about words; it is of no value, and only ruins those who listen. 15Do your best to present yourself to God as one approved, a workman who does not need to be ashamed and who correctly handles the word of truth. 16Avoid godless chatter, because those who indulge in it will become more and more ungodly. 17Their teaching will spread like gangrene. Among them are Hymenaeus and Philetus, 18who have wandered away from the truth. They say that the resurrection has already taken place, and they destroy the faith of some. 19Nevertheless, God's solid foundation stands firm, sealed with this inscription: "The Lord knows those who are his,"[a] and, "Everyone who confesses the name of the Lord must turn away from wickedness."

20In a large house there are articles not only of gold and silver, but also of wood and clay; some are for noble purposes and some for ignoble. 21If a man cleanses himself from the latter, he will be an instrument for noble purposes, made holy, useful to the Master and prepared to do any good work.

22Flee the evil desires of youth, and pursue righteousness, faith, love and peace, along with those who call on the Lord out of a pure heart. 23Don't have anything to do

[a] *19* Num. 16:5 (see Septuagint)

NEW LIVING TRANSLATION

An Approved Worker

14Remind everyone of these things, and command them in God's name to stop fighting over words. Such arguments are useless, and they can ruin those who hear them. 15Work hard so God can approve you. Be a good worker, one who does not need to be ashamed and who correctly explains the word of truth. 16Avoid godless, foolish discussions that lead to more and more ungodliness. 17This kind of talk spreads like cancer. Hymenaeus and Philetus are examples of this. 18They have left the path of truth, preaching the lie that the resurrection of the dead has already occurred; and they have undermined the faith of some.

19But God's truth stands firm like a foundation stone with this inscription: "The Lord knows those who are his,"* and "Those who claim they belong to the Lord must turn away from all wickedness."*

20In a wealthy home some utensils are made of gold and silver, and some are made of wood and clay. The expensive utensils are used for special occasions, and the cheap ones are for everyday use. 21If you keep yourself pure, you will be a utensil God can use for his purpose. Your life will be clean, and you will be ready for the Master to use you for every good work.

22Run from anything that stimulates youthful lust. Follow anything that makes you want to do right. Pursue faith and love and peace, and enjoy the companionship of those who call on the Lord with pure hearts.

2:19a Num 16:5. **2:19b** See Isa 52:11.

NEW KING JAMES VERSION

Approved and Disapproved Workers

14Remind *them* of these things, charging *them* before the Lord not to strive about words to no profit, to the ruin of the hearers. 15Be diligent to present yourself approved to God, a worker who does not need to be ashamed, rightly dividing the word of truth. 16But shun profane *and* idle babblings, for they will increase to more ungodliness. 17And their message will spread like cancer. Hymenaeus and Philetus are of this sort, 18who have strayed concerning the truth, saying that the resurrection is already past; and they overthrow the faith of some. 19Nevertheless the solid foundation of God stands, having this seal: "The Lord knows those who are His," and, "Let everyone who names the name of Christ[c] depart from iniquity."

20But in a great house there are not only vessels of gold and silver, but also of wood and clay, some for honor and some for dishonor. 21Therefore if anyone cleanses himself from the latter, he will be a vessel for honor, sanctified and useful for the Master, prepared for every good work. 22Flee also youthful lusts; but pursue righteousness, faith, love, peace with those who call on the Lord out of a pure

2:19 [c] NU-Text and M-Text read *the Lord*.

THE MESSAGE

Repeat these basic essentials over and over to God's people. Warn them before God against pious nitpicking, which chips away at the faith. It just wears everyone out. Concentrate on doing your best for God, work you won't be ashamed of, laying out the truth plain and simple. Stay clear of pious talk that is only talk. Words are not mere words, you know. If they're not backed by a godly life, they accumulate as poison in the soul. Hymenaeus and Philetus are examples, throwing believers off stride and missing the truth by a mile by saying the resurrection is over and done with.

Meanwhile, God's firm foundation is as firm as ever, these sentences engraved on the stones:

GOD KNOWS WHO BELONGS TO HIM.

SPURN EVIL, ALL YOU WHO NAME GOD AS GOD.

In a well-furnished kitchen there are not only crystal goblets and silver platters, but waste cans and compost buckets—some containers used to serve fine meals, others to take out the garbage. Become the kind of container God can use to present any and every kind of gift to his guests for their blessing.

Run away from infantile indulgence. Run after mature righteousness—faith, love, peace—joining those who are in honest and serious prayer before God. Refuse to get

KING JAMES VERSION

23 But foolish and unlearned questions avoid, knowing that they do gender strifes.

24 And the servant of the Lord must not strive; but be gentle unto all *men*, apt to teach, patient,

25 In meekness instructing those that oppose themselves; if God peradventure will give them repentance to the acknowledging of the truth;

26 And *that* they may recover themselves out of the snare of the devil, who are taken captive by him at his will.

3 This know also, that in the last days perilous times shall come.

2 For men shall be lovers of their own selves, covetous, boasters, proud, blasphemers, disobedient to parents, unthankful, unholy,

3 Without natural affection, trucebreakers, false accusers, incontinent, fierce, despisers of those that are good,

4 Traitors, heady, highminded, lovers of pleasures more than lovers of God;

5 Having a form of godliness, but denying the power thereof: from such turn away.

6 For of this sort are they which creep into houses, and lead captive silly women laden with sins, led away with divers lusts,

7 Ever learning, and never able to come to the knowledge of the truth.

NEW AMERICAN STANDARD BIBLE

23 But refuse foolish and ignorant speculations, knowing that they produce quarrels.

24 The Lord's bond-servant must not be quarrelsome, but be kind to all, able to teach, patient when wronged,

25 with gentleness correcting those who are in opposition, if perhaps God may grant them repentance leading to the knowledge of the truth,

26 and they may come to their senses *and escape* from the snare of the devil, having been held captive by him to do his will.

"Difficult Times Will Come"

3 But realize this, that in the last days difficult times will come.

2 For men will be lovers of self, lovers of money, boastful, arrogant, revilers, disobedient to parents, ungrateful, unholy,

3 unloving, irreconcilable, malicious gossips, without self-control, brutal, haters of good,

4 treacherous, reckless, conceited, lovers of pleasure rather than lovers of God,

5 holding to a form of godliness, although they have denied its power; Avoid such men as these.

6 For among them are those who enter into households and captivate weak women weighed down with sins, led on by various impulses,

7 always learning and never able to come to the knowledge of the truth.

NEW CENTURY VERSION

[23]Stay away from foolish and stupid arguments, because
you know they grow into quarrels. [24]And a servant of the
Lord must not quarrel but must be kind to everyone, a
good teacher, and patient. [25]The Lord's servant must gen-
tly teach those who disagree. Then maybe God will let
them change their minds so they can accept the truth.
[26]And they may wake up and escape from the trap of the
devil, who catches them to do what he wants.

The Last Days

3 Remember this! In the last days there will be many
troubles, [2]because people will love themselves, love
money, brag, and be proud. They will say evil things
against others and will not obey their parents or be thank-
ful or be the kind of people God wants. [3]They will not love
others, will refuse to forgive, will gossip, and will not con-
trol themselves. They will be cruel, will hate what is good,
[4]will turn against their friends, and will do foolish things
without thinking. They will be conceited, will love pleasure
instead of God, [5]and will act as if they serve God but will
not have his power. Stay away from those people. [6]Some
of them go into homes and get control of silly women who
are full of sin and are led by many evil desires. [7]These
women are always learning new teachings, but they are
never able to understand the truth fully. [8]Just as Jannes

CONTEMPORARY ENGLISH VERSION

pure. [23]Stay away from stupid and senseless arguments.
These only lead to trouble, [24]and God's servants must not
be troublemakers. They must be kind to everyone, and they
must be good teachers and very patient.
[25]Be humble when you correct people who oppose you.
Maybe God will lead them to turn to him and learn the
truth. [26]They have been trapped by the devil, and he
makes them obey him, but God may help them escape.

What People Will Be Like in the Last Days

3 You can be certain that in the last days there will be
some very hard times. [2]People will love only them-
selves and money. They will be proud, stuck-up, rude, and
disobedient to their parents. They will also be ungrateful,
godless, [3]heartless, and hateful. Their words will be cruel,
and they will have no self-control or pity. These people will
hate everything that is good. [4]They will be sneaky, reck-
less, and puffed up with pride. Instead of loving God, they
will love pleasure. [5]Even though they will make a show of
being religious, their religion won't be real. Don't have
anything to do with such people.
[6]Some men fool whole families, just to get power over
those women who are slaves of sin and are controlled by
all sorts of desires. [7]These women always want to learn
something new, but they never can discover the truth.

NEW INTERNATIONAL VERSION

with foolish and stupid arguments, because you know they
produce quarrels. 24And the Lord's servant must not quar-
rel; instead, he must be kind to everyone, able to teach,
not resentful. 25Those who oppose him he must gently
instruct, in the hope that God will grant them repentance
leading them to a knowledge of the truth, 26and that they
will come to their senses and escape from the trap of the
devil, who has taken them captive to do his will.

Godlessness in the Last Days

3 But mark this: There will be terrible times in the last
days. 2People will be lovers of themselves, lovers of
money, boastful, proud, abusive, disobedient to their par-
ents, ungrateful, unholy, 3without love, unforgiving, slan-
derous, without self-control, brutal, not lovers of the good,
4treacherous, rash, conceited, lovers of pleasure rather
than lovers of God— 5having a form of godliness but deny-
ing its power. Have nothing to do with them.
6They are the kind who worm their way into homes and
gain control over weak-willed women, who are loaded
down with sins and are swayed by all kinds of evil desires,
7always learning but never able to acknowledge the truth.

NEW LIVING TRANSLATION

23Again I say, don't get involved in foolish, ignorant
arguments that only start fights. 24The Lord's servants
must not quarrel but must be kind to everyone. They must
be able to teach effectively and be patient with difficult
people. 25They should gently teach those who oppose the
truth. Perhaps God will change those people's hearts, and
they will believe the truth. 26Then they will come to their
senses and escape from the Devil's trap. For they have
been held captive by him to do whatever he wants.

The Dangers of the Last Days

3 You should also know this, Timothy, that in the last
days there will be very difficult times. 2For people will
love only themselves and their money. They will be boast-
ful and proud, scoffing at God, disobedient to their par-
ents, and ungrateful. They will consider nothing sacred.
3They will be unloving and unforgiving; they will slander
others and have no self-control; they will be cruel and
have no interest in what is good. 4They will betray their
friends, be reckless, be puffed up with pride, and love plea-
sure rather than God. 5They will act as if they are reli-
gious, but they will reject the power that could make them
godly. You must stay away from people like that.
6They are the kind who work their way into people's
homes and win the confidence of* vulnerable women who
are burdened with the guilt of sin and controlled by many
desires. 7Such women are forever following new teachings,
but they never understand the truth. 8And these teachers

3:6 Greek *and take captive.*

NEW KING JAMES VERSION

heart. 23But avoid foolish and ignorant disputes, knowing
that they generate strife. 24And a servant of the Lord must
not quarrel but be gentle to all, able to teach, patient, 25in
humility correcting those who are in opposition, if God per-
haps will grant them repentance, so that they may know
the truth, 26and *that* they may come to their senses *and es-
cape* the snare of the devil, having been taken captive by
him to *do* his will.

Perilous Times and Perilous Men

3 But know this, that in the last days perilous times will
come: 2For men will be lovers of themselves, lovers of
money, boasters, proud, blasphemers, disobedient to par-
ents, unthankful, unholy, 3unloving, unforgiving, slander-
ers, without self-control, brutal, despisers of good, 4trai-
tors, headstrong, haughty, lovers of pleasure rather than
lovers of God, 5having a form of godliness but denying its
power. And from such people turn away! 6For of this sort
are those who creep into households and make captives of
gullible women loaded down with sins, led away by vari-
ous lusts, 7always learning and never able to come to the
knowledge of the truth. 8Now as Jannes and Jambres

THE MESSAGE

involved in inane discussions; they always end up in
fights. God's servant must not be argumentative, but a
gentle listener and a teacher who keeps cool, working firm-
ly but patiently with those who refuse to obey. You never
know how or when God might sober them up with a
change of heart and a turning to the truth, enabling them
to escape the Devil's trap, where they are caught and held
captive, forced to run his errands.

Difficult Times Ahead

3 Don't be naive. There are difficult times ahead. As the
end approaches, people are going to be self-absorbed,
money-hungry, self-promoting, stuck-up, profane, con-
temptuous of parents, crude, coarse, dog-eat-dog, unbend-
ing, slanderers, impulsively wild, savage, cynical, treacher-
ous, ruthless, bloated windbags, addicted to lust, and
allergic to God. They'll make a show of religion, but behind
the scenes they're animals. Stay clear of these people.

These are the kind of people who smooth-talk themselves
into the homes of unstable and needy women and take
advantage of them, women who, depressed by their sinful-
ness, take up with every new religious fad that calls itself
"truth." They get exploited every time and never really

KING JAMES VERSION

8 Now as Jannes and Jambres withstood Moses, so do these also resist the truth: men of corrupt minds, reprobate concerning the faith.

9 But they shall proceed no further: for their folly shall be manifest unto all *men*, as theirs also was.

10 ¶ But thou hast fully known my doctrine, manner of life, purpose, faith, longsuffering, charity, patience,

11 Persecutions, afflictions, which came unto me at Antioch, at Iconium, at Lystra; what persecutions I endured: but out of *them* all the Lord delivered me.

12 Yea, and all that will live godly in Christ Jesus shall suffer persecution.

13 But evil men and seducers shall wax worse and worse, deceiving, and being deceived.

14 But continue thou in the things which thou hast learned and hast been assured of, knowing of whom thou hast learned *them*;

15 And that from a child thou hast known the holy scriptures, which are able to make thee wise unto salvation through faith which is in Christ Jesus.

16 All scripture *is* given by inspiration of God, and *is* profitable for doctrine, for reproof, for correction, for instruction in righteousness:

17 That the man of God may be perfect, throughly furnished unto all good works.

NEW AMERICAN STANDARD BIBLE

8 Just as Jannes and Jambres opposed Moses, so these *men* also oppose the truth, men of depraved mind, rejected in regard to the faith.

9 But they will not make further progress; for their folly will be obvious to all, just as Jannes' and Jambres' folly was also.

10 Now you followed my teaching, conduct, purpose, faith, patience, love, perseverance,

11 persecutions, *and* sufferings, such as happened to me at Antioch, at Iconium *and* at Lystra; what persecutions I endured, and out of them all the Lord rescued me!

12 Indeed, all who desire to live godly in Christ Jesus will be persecuted.

13 But evil men and impostors will proceed *from bad* to worse, deceiving and being deceived.

14 You, however, continue in the things you have learned and become convinced of, knowing from whom you have learned *them*,

15 and that from childhood you have known the sacred writings which are able to give you the wisdom that leads to salvation through faith which is in Christ Jesus.

16 All Scripture is inspired by God and profitable for teaching, for reproof, for correction, for training in righteousness;

17 so that the man of God may be adequate, equipped for every good work.

NEW CENTURY VERSION

and Jambres were against Moses, these people are against the truth. Their thinking has been ruined, and they have failed in trying to follow the faith. 9But they will not be successful in what they do, because as with Jannes and Jambres, everyone will see that they are foolish.

Obey the Teachings

10But you have followed what I teach, the way I live, my goal, faith, patience, and love. You know I never give up. 11You know how I have been hurt and have suffered, as in Antioch, Iconium, and Lystra. I have suffered, but the Lord saved me from all those troubles. 12Everyone who wants to live as God desires, in Christ Jesus, will be hurt. 13But people who are evil and cheat others will go from bad to worse. They will fool others, but they will also be fooling themselves.

14But you should continue following the teachings you learned. You know they are true, because you trust those who taught you. 15Since you were a child you have known the Holy Scriptures which are able to make you wise. And that wisdom leads to salvation through faith in Christ Jesus. 16All Scripture is given by God and is useful for teaching, for showing people what is wrong in their lives, for correcting faults, and for teaching how to live right. 17Using the Scriptures, the person who serves God will be capable, having all that is needed to do every good work.

CONTEMPORARY ENGLISH VERSION

8Just as Jannes and Jambres[a] opposed Moses, these people are enemies of the truth. Their minds are sick, and their faith isn't real. 9But they won't get very far with their foolishness. Soon everyone will know the truth about them, just as Jannes and Jambres were found out.

Paul's Last Instructions to Timothy

10Timothy, you know what I teach and how I live. You know what I want to do and what I believe. You have seen how patient and loving I am, and how in the past I put up with 11trouble and suffering in the cities of Antioch, Iconium, and Lystra. Yet the Lord rescued me from all those terrible troubles. 12Anyone who belongs to Christ Jesus and wants to live right will have trouble from others. 13But evil people who pretend to be what they are not will become worse than ever, as they fool others and are fooled themselves.

14Keep on being faithful to what you were taught and to what you believed. After all, you know who taught you these things. 15Since childhood, you have known the Holy Scriptures that are able to make you wise enough to have faith in Christ Jesus and be saved. 16Everything in the Scriptures is God's Word. All of it is useful for teaching and helping people and for correcting them and showing them how to live. 17The Scriptures train God's servants to do all kinds of good deeds.

[a] 3.8 *Jannes and Jambres*: These names are not found in the Old Testament. But many believe these were the names of the two Egyptian magicians who opposed Moses when he wanted to lead the people of Israel out of Egypt (see Exodus 7.11, 22).

NEW INTERNATIONAL VERSION

8Just as Jannes and Jambres opposed Moses, so also these
men oppose the truth—men of depraved minds, who, as
far as the faith is concerned, are rejected. 9But they will
not get very far because, as in the case of those men, their
folly will be clear to everyone.

Paul's Charge to Timothy

10You, however, know all about my teaching, my way of
life, my purpose, faith, patience, love, endurance, 11perse-
cutions, sufferings—what kinds of things happened to me
in Antioch, Iconium and Lystra, the persecutions I
endured. Yet the Lord rescued me from all of them. 12In
fact, everyone who wants to live a godly life in Christ Jesus
will be persecuted, 13while evil men and impostors will go
from bad to worse, deceiving and being deceived. 14But as
for you, continue in what you have learned and have
become convinced of, because you know those from whom
you learned it, 15and how from infancy you have known
the holy Scriptures, which are able to make you wise for
salvation through faith in Christ Jesus. 16All Scripture is
God-breathed and is useful for teaching, rebuking, correct-
ing and training in righteousness, 17so that the man of
God may be thoroughly equipped for every good work.

NEW LIVING TRANSLATION

fight the truth just as Jannes and Jambres fought against
Moses. Their minds are depraved, and their faith is coun-
terfeit. 9But they won't get away with this for long.
Someday everyone will recognize what fools they are, just
as happened with Jannes and Jambres.

Paul's Charge to Timothy

10But you know what I teach, Timothy, and how I live,
and what my purpose in life is. You know my faith and
how long I have suffered. You know my love and my
patient endurance. 11You know how much persecution and
suffering I have endured. You know all about how I was
persecuted in Antioch, Iconium, and Lystra—but the Lord
delivered me from all of it. 12Yes, and everyone who wants
to live a godly life in Christ Jesus will suffer persecution.
13But evil people and impostors will flourish. They will go
on deceiving others, and they themselves will be deceived.

14But you must remain faithful to the things you have
been taught. You know they are true, for you know you
can trust those who taught you. 15You have been taught
the holy Scriptures from childhood, and they have given
you the wisdom to receive the salvation that comes by
trusting in Christ Jesus. 16All Scripture is inspired by God
and is useful to teach us what is true and to make us real-
ize what is wrong in our lives. It straightens us out and
teaches us to do what is right. 17It is God's way of prepar-
ing us in every way, fully equipped for every good thing
God wants us to do.

NEW KING JAMES VERSION

resisted Moses, so do these also resist the truth: men of
corrupt minds, disapproved concerning the faith; 9but they
will progress no further, for their folly will be manifest to
all, as theirs also was.

The Man of God and the Word of God

10But you have carefully followed my doctrine, manner
of life, purpose, faith, longsuffering, love, perseverance,
11persecutions, afflictions, which happened to me at Anti-
och, at Iconium, at Lystra—what persecutions I endured.
And out of *them* all the Lord delivered me. 12Yes, and all
who desire to live godly in Christ Jesus will suffer persecu-
tion. 13But evil men and impostors will grow worse and
worse, deceiving and being deceived. 14But you must con-
tinue in the things which you have learned and been
assured of, knowing from whom you have learned *them,*
15and that from childhood you have known the Holy
Scriptures, which are able to make you wise for salvation
through faith which is in Christ Jesus.

16All Scripture *is* given by inspiration of God, and *is*
profitable for doctrine, for reproof, for correction, for in-
struction in righteousness, 17that the man of God may be
complete, thoroughly equipped for every good work.

THE MESSAGE

learn. These men are like those old Egyptian frauds Jannes
and Jambres, who challenged Moses. They were rejects from
the faith, twisted in their thinking, defying truth itself. But
nothing will come of these latest impostors. Everyone will
see through them, just as people saw through that Egyptian
hoax.

Keep the Message Alive

You've been a good apprentice to me, a part of my teach-
ing, my manner of life, direction, faith, steadiness, love,
patience, troubles, sufferings—suffering along with me in
all the grief I had to put up with in Antioch, Iconium, and
Lystra. And you also well know that God rescued me!
Anyone who wants to live all out for Christ is in for a lot of
trouble; there's no getting around it. Unscrupulous con
men will continue to exploit the faith. They're as deceived
as the people they lead astray. As long as they are out
there, things can only get worse.

But don't let it faze you. Stick with what you learned
and believed, sure of the integrity of your teachers—why,
you took in the sacred Scriptures with your mother's milk!
There's nothing like the written Word of God for showing
you the way to salvation through faith in Christ Jesus.
Every part of Scripture is God-breathed and useful one way
or another—showing us truth, exposing our rebellion, cor-
recting our mistakes, training us to live God's way.
Through the Word we are put together and shaped up for
the tasks God has for us.

KING JAMES VERSION

4 I charge *thee* therefore before God, and the Lord Jesus Christ, who shall judge the quick and the dead at his appearing and his kingdom;

2 Preach the word; be instant in season, out of season; reprove, rebuke, exhort with all longsuffering and doctrine.

3 For the time will come when they will not endure sound doctrine; but after their own lusts shall they heap to themselves teachers, having itching ears;

4 And they shall turn away *their* ears from the truth, and shall be turned unto fables.

5 But watch thou in all things, endure afflictions, do the work of an evangelist, make full proof of thy ministry.

6 For I am now ready to be offered, and the time of my departure is at hand.

7 I have fought a good fight, I have finished *my* course, I have kept the faith:

8 Henceforth there is laid up for me a crown of righteousness, which the Lord, the righteous judge, shall give me at that day: and not to me only, but unto all them also that love his appearing.

9 ¶ Do thy diligence to come shortly unto me:

10 For Demas hath forsaken me, having loved this present world, and is departed unto Thessalonica; Crescens to Galatia, Titus unto Dalmatia.

11 Only Luke is with me. Take Mark, and bring him with thee: for he is profitable to me for the ministry.

NEW AMERICAN STANDARD BIBLE

"Preach the Word"

4 I solemnly charge *you* in the presence of God and of Christ Jesus, who is to judge the living and the dead, and by His appearing and His kingdom:

2 preach the word; be ready in season *and* out of season; reprove, rebuke, exhort, with great patience and instruction.

3 For the time will come when they will not endure sound doctrine; but *wanting* to have their ears tickled, they will accumulate for themselves teachers in accordance to their own desires,

4 and will turn away their ears from the truth and will turn aside to myths.

5 But you, be sober in all things, endure hardship, do the work of an evangelist, fulfill your ministry.

6 For I am already being poured out as a drink offering, and the time of my departure has come.

7 I have fought the good fight, I have finished the course, I have kept the faith;

8 in the future there is laid up for me the crown of righteousness, which the Lord, the righteous Judge, will award to me on that day; and not only to me, but also to all who have loved His appearing.

Personal Concerns

9 Make every effort to come to me soon;

10 for Demas, having loved this present world, has deserted me and gone to Thessalonica; Crescens *has gone* to Galatia, Titus to Dalmatia.

11 Only Luke is with me. Pick up Mark and bring him with you, for he is useful to me for service.

NEW CENTURY VERSION

4 I give you a command in the presence of God and
Christ Jesus, the One who will judge the living and the
dead, and by his coming and his kingdom: [2]Preach the
Good News. Be ready at all times, and tell people what
they need to do. Tell them when they are wrong.
Encourage them with great patience and careful teaching,
[3]because the time will come when people will not listen to
the true teaching but will find many more teachers who
please them by saying the things they want to hear. [4]They
will stop listening to the truth and will begin to follow
false stories. [5]But you should control yourself at all times,
accept troubles, do the work of telling the Good News, and
complete all the duties of a servant of God.

[6]My life is being given as an offering to God, and the
time has come for me to leave this life. [7]I have fought the
good fight, I have finished the race, I have kept the faith.
[8]Now, a crown is being held for me—a crown for being
right with God. The Lord, the judge who judges rightly, will
give the crown to me on that day[a]—not only to me but to
all those who have waited with love for him to come again.

Personal Words

[9]Do your best to come to me as soon as you can,
[10]because Demas, who loved this world, left me and went
to Thessalonica. Crescens went to Galatia, and Titus went
to Dalmatia. [11]Luke is the only one still with me. Get Mark
and bring him with you when you come, because he can

4:8 [a] **day** The day Christ will come to judge all people and take his people to live with him.

CONTEMPORARY ENGLISH VERSION

4 When Christ Jesus comes as king, he will be the judge
of everyone, whether they are living or dead. So with
God and Christ as witnesses, I command you [2]to preach
God's message. Do it willingly, even if it isn't the popular
thing to do. You must correct people and point out their
sins. But also cheer them up, and when you instruct them,
always be patient. [3]The time is coming when people won't
listen to good teaching. Instead, they will look for teachers
who will please them by telling them only what they are
itching to hear. [4]They will turn from the truth and eagerly
listen to senseless stories. [5]But you must stay calm and be
willing to suffer. You must work hard to tell the good news
and to do your job well.

[6]Now the time has come for me to die. My life is like a
drink offering[a] being poured out on the altar. [7]I have
fought well. I have finished the race, and I have been faith-
ful. [8]So a crown will be given to me for pleasing the Lord.
He judges fairly, and on the day of judgment he will give a
crown to me and to everyone else who wants him to
appear with power.

Personal Instructions

[9]Come to see me as soon as you can. [10]Demas loves the
things of this world so much that he left me and went to
Thessalonica. Crescens has gone to Galatia, and Titus has
gone to Dalmatia. [11]Only Luke has stayed with me.

Mark can be very helpful to me, so please find him and

[a] **4.6** *drink offering*: Water or wine was sometimes poured out as an offering when an animal sacrifice was made.

NEW INTERNATIONAL VERSION

4 In the presence of God and of Christ Jesus, who will
judge the living and the dead, and in view of his
appearing and his kingdom, I give you this charge: 2Preach
the Word; be prepared in season and out of season; cor-
rect, rebuke and encourage—with great patience and care-
ful instruction. 3For the time will come when men will not
put up with sound doctrine. Instead, to suit their own
desires, they will gather around them a great number of
teachers to say what their itching ears want to hear. 4They
will turn their ears away from the truth and turn aside to
myths. 5But you, keep your head in all situations, endure
hardship, do the work of an evangelist, discharge all the
duties of your ministry.
6For I am already being poured out like a drink offering,
and the time has come for my departure. 7I have fought
the good fight, I have finished the race, I have kept the
faith. 8Now there is in store for me the crown of righteous-
ness, which the Lord, the righteous Judge, will award to
me on that day—and not only to me, but also to all who
have longed for his appearing.

Personal Remarks

9Do your best to come to me quickly, 10for Demas,
because he loved this world, has deserted me and has gone
to Thessalonica. Crescens has gone to Galatia, and Titus to
Dalmatia. 11Only Luke is with me. Get Mark and bring him
with you, because he is helpful to me in my ministry. 12I

NEW LIVING TRANSLATION

4 And so I solemnly urge you before God and before
Christ Jesus—who will someday judge the living and
the dead when he appears to set up his Kingdom: 2Preach
the word of God. Be persistent, whether the time is favor-
able or not. Patiently correct, rebuke, and encourage your
people with good teaching.
3For a time is coming when people will no longer listen
to right teaching. They will follow their own desires and
will look for teachers who will tell them whatever they
want to hear. 4They will reject the truth and follow strange
myths.
5But you should keep a clear mind in every situation.
Don't be afraid of suffering for the Lord. Work at bringing
others to Christ. Complete the ministry God has given you.

Paul's Final Words

6As for me, my life has already been poured out as an
offering to God. The time of my death is near. 7I have
fought a good fight, I have finished the race, and I have
remained faithful. 8And now the prize awaits me—the
crown of righteousness that the Lord, the righteous Judge,
will give me on that great day of his return. And the prize
is not just for me but for all who eagerly look forward to
his glorious return.
9Please come as soon as you can. 10Demas has deserted
me because he loves the things of this life and has gone to
Thessalonica. Crescens has gone to Galatia, and Titus has
gone to Dalmatia. 11Only Luke is with me. Bring Mark with
you when you come, for he will be helpful to me. 12I sent

NEW KING JAMES VERSION

Preach the Word

4 I charge *you* therefore before God and the Lord Jesus
Christ, who will judge the living and the dead at[a] His
appearing and His kingdom: 2Preach the word! Be ready in
season *and* out of season. Convince, rebuke, exhort, with
all longsuffering and teaching. 3For the time will come
when they will not endure sound doctrine, but according to
their own desires, *because* they have itching ears, they will
heap up for themselves teachers; 4and they will turn *their*
ears away from the truth, and be turned aside to fables.
5But you be watchful in all things, endure afflictions, do
the work of an evangelist, fulfill your ministry.

Paul's Valedictory

6For I am already being poured out as a drink offering, and
the time of my departure is at hand. 7I have fought the good
fight, I have finished the race, I have kept the faith. 8Finally,
there is laid up for me the crown of righteousness, which the
Lord, the righteous Judge, will give to me on that Day, and
not to me only but also to all who have loved His appearing.

The Abandoned Apostle

9Be diligent to come to me quickly; 10for Demas has for-
saken me, having loved this present world, and has de-
parted for Thessalonica—Crescens for Galatia, Titus for
Dalmatia. 11Only Luke is with me. Get Mark and bring
him with you, for he is useful to me for ministry. 12And

4:1 [a] NU-Text omits *therefore* and reads *and by* for *at*.

THE MESSAGE

4 I can't impress this on you too strongly. God is look-
ing over your shoulder. Christ himself is the Judge,
with the final say on everyone, living and dead. He is
about to break into the open with his rule, so proclaim the
Message with intensity; keep on your watch. Challenge,
warn, and urge your people. Don't ever quit. Just keep it
simple.

You're going to find that there will be times when people
will have no stomach for solid teaching, but will fill up on
spiritual junk food—catchy opinions that tickle their
fancy. They'll turn their backs on truth and chase mirages.
But *you*—keep your eye on what you're doing; accept the
hard times along with the good; keep the Message alive;
do a thorough job as God's servant.

You take over. I'm about to die, my life an offering on
God's altar. This is the only race worth running. I've run
hard right to the finish, believed all the way. All that's left
now is the shouting—God's applause! Depend on it, he's
an honest judge. He'll do right not only by me, but by
everyone eager for his coming.

✠

Get here as fast as you can. Demas, chasing fads, went
off to Thessalonica and left me here. Crescens is in Galatia
province, Titus in Dalmatia. Luke is the only one here with
me. Bring Mark with you; he'll be my right-hand man

KING JAMES VERSION

12 And Tychicus have I sent to Ephesus.

13 The cloke that I left at Troas with Carpus, when thou comest, bring *with thee*, and the books, *but* especially the parchments.

14 Alexander the coppersmith did me much evil: the Lord reward him according to his works:

15 Of whom be thou ware also; for he hath greatly withstood our words.

16 ¶ At my first answer no man stood with me, but all *men* forsook me: *I pray God* that it may not be laid to their charge.

17 Notwithstanding the Lord stood with me, and strengthened me; that by me the preaching might be fully known, and *that* all the Gentiles might hear: and I was delivered out of the mouth of the lion.

18 And the Lord shall deliver me from every evil work, and will preserve *me* unto his heavenly kingdom: to whom *be* glory for ever and ever. Amen.

19 Salute Prisca and Aquila, and the household of Onesiphorus.

20 Erastus abode at Corinth: but Trophimus have I left at Miletum sick.

21 Do thy diligence to come before winter. Eubulus greeteth thee, and Pudens, and Linus, and Claudia, and all the brethren.

22 The Lord Jesus Christ *be* with thy spirit. Grace *be* with you. Amen.

NEW AMERICAN STANDARD BIBLE

12 But Tychicus I have sent to Ephesus.

13 When you come bring the cloak which I left at Troas with Carpus, and the books, especially the parchments.

14 Alexander the coppersmith did me much harm; the Lord will repay him according to his deeds.

15 Be on guard against him yourself, for he vigorously opposed our teaching.

16 At my first defense no one supported me, but all deserted me; may it not be counted against them.

17 But the Lord stood with me and strengthened me, so that through me the proclamation might be fully accomplished, and that all the Gentiles might hear; and I was rescued out of the lion's mouth.

18 The Lord will rescue me from every evil deed, and will bring me safely to His heavenly kingdom; to Him *be* the glory forever and ever. Amen.

19 Greet Prisca and Aquila, and the household of Onesiphorus.

20 Erastus remained at Corinth, but Trophimus I left sick at Miletus.

21 Make every effort to come before winter. Eubulus greets you, also Pudens and Linus and Claudia and all the brethren.

22 The Lord be with your spirit. Grace be with you.

NEW CENTURY VERSION

help me in my work here. [12]I sent Tychicus to Ephesus.
[13]When I was in Troas, I left my coat there with Carpus. So
when you come, bring it to me, along with my books, particularly the ones written on parchment.[b]

[14]Alexander the metalworker did many harmful things
against me. The Lord will punish him for what he did.
[15]You also should be careful that he does not hurt you,
because he fought strongly against our teaching.

[16]The first time I defended myself, no one helped me;
everyone left me. May they be forgiven. [17]But the Lord
stayed with me and gave me strength so I could fully tell
the Good News to all those who are not Jews. So I was
saved from the lion's mouth. [18]The Lord will save me
when anyone tries to hurt me, and he will bring me safely
to his heavenly kingdom. Glory forever and ever be the
Lord's. Amen.

Final Greetings

[19]Greet Priscilla and Aquila and the family of
Onesiphorus. [20]Erastus stayed in Corinth, and I left
Trophimus sick in Miletus. [21]Try as hard as you can to
come to me before winter.

Eubulus sends greetings to you. Also Pudens, Linus, Claudia, and all the brothers and sisters in Christ greet you.

[22]The Lord be with your spirit. Grace be with you.

4:13 [b] **parchment** A writing paper made from the skins of sheep.

CONTEMPORARY ENGLISH VERSION

bring him with you. [12]I sent Tychicus to Ephesus.

[13]When you come, bring the coat I left at Troas with Carpus. Don't forget to bring the scrolls, especially the ones made of leather.[b]

[14]Alexander, the metalworker, has hurt me in many
ways. But the Lord will pay him back for what he has done.
[15]Alexander opposes what we preach. You had better watch
out for him.

[16]When I was first put on trial, no one helped me. In
fact, everyone deserted me. I hope it won't be held against
them. [17]But the Lord stood beside me. He gave me the
strength to tell his full message, so that all Gentiles would
hear it. And I was kept safe from hungry lions. [18]The Lord
will always keep me from being harmed by evil, and he
will bring me safely into his heavenly kingdom. Praise him
forever and ever! Amen.

Final Greetings

[19]Give my greetings to Priscilla and Aquila and to the family of Onesiphorus.

[20]Erastus stayed at Corinth.

Trophimus was sick when I left him at Miletus.

[21]Do your best to come before winter.

Eubulus, Pudens, Linus, and Claudia send you their greetings, and so do the rest of the Lord's followers.

[22]I pray that the Lord will bless your life and will be kind to you.

[b] 4.13 *the ones made of leather*: A scroll was a kind of rolled up book, and it could be made out of paper (called "papyrus") or leather (that is, animal skin) or even copper.

NEW INTERNATIONAL VERSION

sent Tychicus to Ephesus. 13When you come, bring the cloak that I left with Carpus at Troas, and my scrolls, especially the parchments.

14Alexander the metalworker did me a great deal of harm. The Lord will repay him for what he has done. 15You too should be on your guard against him, because he strongly opposed our message.

16At my first defense, no one came to my support, but everyone deserted me. May it not be held against them. 17But the Lord stood at my side and gave me strength, so that through me the message might be fully proclaimed and all the Gentiles might hear it. And I was delivered from the lion's mouth. 18The Lord will rescue me from every evil attack and will bring me safely to his heavenly kingdom. To him be glory for ever and ever. Amen.

Final Greetings

19Greet Priscilla[a] and Aquila and the household of Onesiphorus. 20Erastus stayed in Corinth, and I left Trophimus sick in Miletus. 21Do your best to get here before winter. Eubulus greets you, and so do Pudens, Linus, Claudia and all the brothers.

22The Lord be with your spirit. Grace be with you.

[a] *19* Greek *Prisca*, a variant of *Priscilla*

NEW LIVING TRANSLATION

Tychicus to Ephesus. 13When you come, be sure to bring the coat I left with Carpus at Troas. Also bring my books, and especially my papers.*

14Alexander the coppersmith has done me much harm, but the Lord will judge him for what he has done. 15Be careful of him, for he fought against everything we said.

16The first time I was brought before the judge, no one was with me. Everyone had abandoned me. I hope it will not be counted against them. 17But the Lord stood with me and gave me strength, that I might preach the Good News in all its fullness for all the Gentiles to hear. And he saved me from certain death.* 18Yes, and the Lord will deliver me from every evil attack and will bring me safely to his heavenly Kingdom. To God be the glory forever and ever. Amen.

Paul's Final Greetings

19Give my greetings to Priscilla and Aquila and those living at the household of Onesiphorus. 20Erastus stayed at Corinth, and I left Trophimus sick at Miletus.

21Hurry so you can get here before winter. Eubulus sends you greetings, and so do Pudens, Linus, Claudia, and all the brothers and sisters.*

22May the Lord be with your spirit. Grace be with you all.

4:13 Greek *especially the parchments.* 4:17 Greek *from the mouth of a lion.* 4:21 Greek *brothers.*

NEW KING JAMES VERSION

Tychicus I have sent to Ephesus. 13Bring the cloak that I left with Carpus at Troas when you come—and the books, especially the parchments.

14Alexander the coppersmith did me much harm. May the Lord repay him according to his works. 15You also must beware of him, for he has greatly resisted our words.

16At my first defense no one stood with me, but all forsook me. May it not be charged against them.

The Lord Is Faithful

17But the Lord stood with me and strengthened me, so that the message might be preached fully through me, and *that* all the Gentiles might hear. Also I was delivered out of the mouth of the lion. 18And the Lord will deliver me from every evil work and preserve *me* for His heavenly kingdom. To Him *be* glory forever and ever. Amen!

Come Before Winter

19Greet Prisca and Aquila, and the household of Onesiphorus. 20Erastus stayed in Corinth, but Trophimus I have left in Miletus sick.

21Do your utmost to come before winter.

Eubulus greets you, as well as Pudens, Linus, Claudia, and all the brethren.

Farewell

22The Lord Jesus Christ[b] be with your spirit. Grace be with you. Amen.

4:22 [b] NU-Text omits *Jesus Christ.*

THE MESSAGE

since I'm sending Tychicus to Ephesus. Bring the winter coat I left in Troas with Carpus; also the books and parchment notebooks.

Watch out for Alexander the coppersmith. Fiercely opposed to our Message, he caused no end of trouble. God will give him what he's got coming.

At my preliminary hearing no one stood by me. They all ran like scared rabbits. But it doesn't matter—the Master stood by me and helped me spread the Message loud and clear to those who had never heard it. I was snatched from the jaws of the lion! God's looking after me, keeping me safe in the kingdom of heaven. All praise to him, praise forever! Oh, yes!

Say hello to Priscilla and Aquila; also, the family of Onesiphorus. Erastus stayed behind in Corinth. I had to leave Trophimus sick in Miletus.

Try hard to get here before winter.

Eubulus, Pudens, Linus, Claudia, and all your friends here send greetings.

God be with you. Grace be with you.

KING JAMES VERSION

THE EPISTLE OF ST. PAUL TO
TITUS

1 Paul, a servant of God, and an apostle of Jesus Christ, according to the faith of God's elect, and the acknowledging of the truth which is after godliness;

2 In hope of eternal life, which God, that cannot lie, promised before the world began;

3 But hath in due times manifested his word through preaching, which is committed unto me according to the commandment of God our Saviour;

4 To Titus, *mine* own son after the common faith: Grace, mercy, *and* peace, from God the Father and the Lord Jesus Christ our Saviour.

5 ¶ For this cause left I thee in Crete, that thou shouldest set in order the things that are wanting, and ordain elders in every city, as I had appointed thee:

6 ¶ If any be blameless, the husband of one wife, having faithful children not accused of riot or unruly.

NEW AMERICAN STANDARD BIBLE

THE LETTER OF PAUL TO
TITUS

Salutation

1 Paul, a bond-servant of God and an apostle of Jesus Christ, for the faith of those chosen of God and the knowledge of the truth which is according to godliness,

2 in the hope of eternal life, which God, who cannot lie, promised long ages ago,

3 but at the proper time manifested, *even* His word, in the proclamation with which I was entrusted according to the commandment of God our Savior,

4 To Titus, my true child in a common faith: Grace and peace from God the Father and Christ Jesus our Savior.

Qualifications of Elders

5 For this reason I left you in Crete, that you would set in order what remains and appoint elders in every city as I directed you,

6 *namely,* if any man is above reproach, the husband of one wife, having children who believe, not accused of dissipation or rebellion.

NEW CENTURY VERSION

TITUS

1 From Paul, a servant of God and an apostle of Jesus Christ. I was sent to help the faith of God's chosen people and to help them know the truth that shows people how to serve God. 2 That faith and that knowledge come from the hope for life forever, which God promised to us before time began. And God cannot lie. 3 At the right time God let the world know about that life through preaching. He trusted me with that work, and I preached by the command of God our Savior.

4 To Titus, my true child in the faith we share:

Grace and peace from God the Father and Christ Jesus our Savior.

Titus' Work in Crete

5 I left you in Crete so you could finish doing the things that still needed to be done and so you could appoint elders in every town, as I directed you. 6 An elder must not be guilty of doing wrong, must have only one wife, and must have believing children. They must not be known as children who are wild and do not cooperate. 7 As God's

CONTEMPORARY ENGLISH VERSION

TITUS

1 From Paul, a servant of God and an apostle of Jesus Christ.

I encourage God's own people to have more faith and to understand the truth about religion. 2 Then they will have the hope of eternal life that God promised long ago. And God never tells a lie! 3 So, at the proper time, God our Savior gave this message and told me to announce what he had said.

4 Titus, because of our faith, you are like a son to me. I pray that God our Father and Christ Jesus our Savior will be kind to you and will bless you with peace!

What Titus Was To Do in Crete

5 I left you in Crete to do what had been left undone and to appoint leaders[a] for the churches in each town. As I told you, 6 they must have a good reputation and be faithful in marriage.[b] Their children must be followers of the Lord and not have a reputation for being wild and disobedient.

[a] 1.5 *leaders*: Or "elders" or "presbyters" or "priests." [b] 1.6 *be faithful in marriage*: Or "be the husband of only one wife" or "have never been divorced."

NEW INTERNATIONAL VERSION

TITUS

1 Paul, a servant of God and an apostle of Jesus Christ for the faith of God's elect and the knowledge of the truth that leads to godliness— 2a faith and knowledge resting on the hope of eternal life, which God, who does not lie, promised before the beginning of time, 3and at his appointed season he brought his word to light through the preaching entrusted to me by the command of God our Savior,

4To Titus, my true son in our common faith:

Grace and peace from God the Father and Christ Jesus our Savior.

Titus's Task on Crete

5The reason I left you in Crete was that you might straighten out what was left unfinished and appoint[a] elders in every town, as I directed you. 6An elder must be blameless, the husband of but one wife, a man whose children believe and are not open to the charge of being wild

[a] 5 Or *ordain*

NEW LIVING TRANSLATION

TITUS

Greetings from Paul

1 This letter is from Paul, a slave of God and an apostle of Jesus Christ. I have been sent to bring faith to those God has chosen and to teach them to know the truth that shows them how to live godly lives. 2This truth gives them the confidence of eternal life, which God promised them before the world began—and he cannot lie. 3And now at the right time he has revealed this Good News, and we announce it to everyone. It is by the command of God our Savior that I have been trusted to do this work for him.

4This letter is written to Titus, my true child in the faith that we share.

May God the Father and Christ Jesus our Savior give you grace and peace.

Titus's Work in Crete

5I left you on the island of Crete so you could complete our work there and appoint elders in each town as I instructed you. 6An elder must be well thought of for his good life. He must be faithful to his wife,* and his children must be believers who are not wild or rebellious. 7An

1:6 Or *have only one wife,* or *be married only once;* Greek reads *be the husband of one wife.*

NEW KING JAMES VERSION

THE EPISTLE OF PAUL TO

TITUS

Greeting

1 Paul, a bondservant of God and an apostle of Jesus Christ, according to the faith of God's elect and the acknowledgment of the truth which accords with godliness, 2in hope of eternal life which God, who cannot lie, promised before time began, 3but has in due time manifested His word through preaching, which was committed to me according to the commandment of God our Savior;

4To Titus, a true son in *our* common faith:

Grace, mercy, *and* peace from God the Father and the Lord Jesus Christ[a] our Savior.

Qualified Elders

5For this reason I left you in Crete, that you should set in order the things that are lacking, and appoint elders in every city as I commanded you— 6if a man is blameless, the husband of one wife, having faithful children not accused of dissipation or insubordination. 7For a bishop[b]

1:4 [a] NU-Text reads *and Christ Jesus.* 1:7 [b] Literally *overseer*

THE MESSAGE

TITUS

1 I, Paul, am God's slave and Christ's agent for promoting the faith among God's chosen people, getting out the accurate word on God and how to respond rightly to it. My aim is to raise hopes by pointing the way to life without end. This is the life God promised long ago—and he doesn't break promises! And then when the time was ripe, he went public with his truth. I've been entrusted to proclaim this Message by order of our Savior, God himself. Dear Titus, legitimate son in the faith: Receive everything God our Father and Jesus our Savior give you!

A Good Grip on the Message

I left you in charge in Crete so you could complete what I left half-done. Appoint leaders in every town according to my instructions. As you select them, ask, "Is this man well-thought-of? Are his children believers? Do they respect him and stay out of trouble?" It's important that a

KING JAMES VERSION

7 For a bishop must be blameless, as the steward of God; not selfwilled, not soon angry, not given to wine, no striker, not given to filthy lucre;

8 But a lover of hospitality, a lover of good men, sober, just, holy, temperate;

9 Holding fast the faithful word as he hath been taught, that he may be able by sound doctrine both to exhort and to convince the gainsayers.

10 For there are many unruly and vain talkers and deceivers, specially they of the circumcision:

11 Whose mouths must be stopped, who subvert whole houses, teaching things which they ought not, for filthy lucre's sake.

12 One of themselves, *even* a prophet of their own, said, The Cretians *are* alway liars, evil beasts, slow bellies.

13 This witness is true. Wherefore rebuke them sharply, that they may be sound in the faith;

14 Not giving heed to Jewish fables, and commandments of men, that turn from the truth.

15 Unto the pure all things *are* pure: but unto them that are defiled and unbelieving *is* nothing pure; but even their mind and conscience is defiled.

NEW AMERICAN STANDARD BIBLE

7 For the overseer must be above reproach as God's steward, not self-willed, not quick-tempered, not addicted to wine, not pugnacious, not fond of sordid gain,

8 but hospitable, loving what is good, sensible, just, devout, self-controlled,

9 holding fast the faithful word which is in accordance with the teaching, so that he will be able both to exhort in sound doctrine and to refute those who contradict.

10 For there are many rebellious men, empty talkers and deceivers, especially those of the circumcision,

11 who must be silenced because they are upsetting whole families, teaching things they should not *teach* for the sake of sordid gain.

12 One of themselves, a prophet of their own, said, "Cretans are always liars, evil beasts, lazy gluttons."

13 This testimony is true. For this reason reprove them severely so that they may be sound in the faith,

14 not paying attention to Jewish myths and commandments of men who turn away from the truth.

15 To the pure, all things are pure; but to those who are defiled and unbelieving, nothing is pure, but both their mind and their conscience are defiled.

NEW CENTURY VERSION

manager, an elder must not be guilty of doing wrong,
being selfish, or becoming angry quickly. He must not
drink too much wine, like to fight, or try to get rich by
cheating others. 8An elder must be ready to welcome
guests, love what is good, be wise, live right, and be holy
and self-controlled. 9By holding on to the trustworthy
word just as we teach it, an elder can help people by using
true teaching, and he can show those who are against the
true teaching that they are wrong.
10There are many people who refuse to cooperate, who
talk about worthless things and lead others into the wrong
way—mainly those who say all who are not Jews must be
circumcised. 11These people must be stopped, because they
are upsetting whole families by teaching things they
should not teach, which they do to get rich by cheating
people. 12Even one of their own prophets said, "Cretans are
always liars, evil animals, and lazy people who do nothing
but eat." 13The words that prophet said are true. So firmly
tell those people they are wrong so they may become
strong in the faith, 14not accepting Jewish false stories and
the commands of people who reject the truth. 15To those
who are pure, all things are pure, but to those who are full
of sin and do not believe, nothing is pure. Both their minds
and their consciences have been ruined. 16They say they

CONTEMPORARY ENGLISH VERSION

7Church officials[c] are in charge of God's work, and so
they must also have a good reputation. They must not be
bossy, quick-tempered, heavy drinkers, bullies, or dishonest
in business. 8Instead, they must be friendly to strangers
and enjoy doing good things. They must also be sensible,
fair, pure, and self-controlled. 9They must stick to the true
message they were taught, so that their good teaching can
help others and correct everyone who opposes it.
10There are many who don't respect authority, and they
fool others by talking nonsense. This is especially true of
some Jewish followers. 11But you must make them be
quiet. They are after money, and they upset whole families
by teaching what they should not. 12It is like one of their
own prophets once said,

"The people of Crete
always tell lies.
They are greedy and lazy
like wild animals."

13That surely is a true saying. And you should be hard
on such people, so you can help them grow stronger in
their faith. 14Don't pay any attention to any of those
senseless Jewish stories and human commands. These are
made up by people who won't obey the truth.
15Everything is pure for someone whose heart is pure.
But nothing is pure for an unbeliever with a dirty mind.
That person's mind and conscience are destroyed. 16Such

[c] 1.7 *Church officials*: Or "Bishops."

NEW INTERNATIONAL VERSION

and disobedient. 7Since an overseer[b] is entrusted with God's work, he must be blameless—not overbearing, not quick-tempered, not given to drunkenness, not violent, not pursuing dishonest gain. 8Rather he must be hospitable, one who loves what is good, who is self-controlled, upright, holy and disciplined. 9He must hold firmly to the trustworthy message as it has been taught, so that he can encourage others by sound doctrine and refute those who oppose it.

10For there are many rebellious people, mere talkers and deceivers, especially those of the circumcision group. 11They must be silenced, because they are ruining whole households by teaching things they ought not to teach—and that for the sake of dishonest gain. 12Even one of their own prophets has said, "Cretans are always liars, evil brutes, lazy gluttons." 13This testimony is true. Therefore, rebuke them sharply, so that they will be sound in the faith 14and will pay no attention to Jewish myths or to the commands of those who reject the truth. 15To the pure, all things are pure, but to those who are corrupted and do not believe, nothing is pure. In fact, both their minds and consciences

b 7 Traditionally *bishop*

NEW LIVING TRANSLATION

elder* must live a blameless life because he is God's minister. He must not be arrogant or quick-tempered; he must not be a heavy drinker, violent, or greedy for money. 8He must enjoy having guests in his home and must love all that is good. He must live wisely and be fair. He must live a devout and disciplined life. 9He must have a strong and steadfast belief in the trustworthy message he was taught; then he will be able to encourage others with right teaching and show those who oppose it where they are wrong.

10For there are many who rebel against right teaching; they engage in useless talk and deceive people. This is especially true of those who insist on circumcision for salvation. 11They must be silenced. By their wrong teaching, they have already turned whole families away from the truth. Such teachers only want your money. 12One of their own men, a prophet from Crete, has said about them, "The people of Crete are all liars; they are cruel animals and lazy gluttons." 13This is true. So rebuke them as sternly as necessary to make them strong in the faith. 14They must stop listening to Jewish myths and the commands of people who have turned their backs on the truth.

15Everything is pure to those whose hearts are pure. But nothing is pure to those who are corrupt and unbelieving, because their minds and consciences are defiled. 16Such

1:7 Greek *overseer.*

NEW KING JAMES VERSION

must be blameless, as a steward of God, not self-willed, not quick-tempered, not given to wine, not violent, not greedy for money, 8but hospitable, a lover of what is good, sober-minded, just, holy, self-controlled, 9holding fast the faithful word as he has been taught, that he may be able, by sound doctrine, both to exhort and convict those who contradict.

The Elders' Task

10For there are many insubordinate, both idle talkers and deceivers, especially those of the circumcision, 11whose mouths must be stopped, who subvert whole households, teaching things which they ought not, for the sake of dishonest gain. 12One of them, a prophet of their own, said, "Cretans *are* always liars, evil beasts, lazy gluttons." 13This testimony is true. Therefore rebuke them sharply, that they may be sound in the faith, 14not giving heed to Jewish fables and commandments of men who turn from the truth. 15To the pure all things are pure, but to those who are defiled and unbelieving nothing is pure; but even their mind and conscience are defiled. 16They profess

THE MESSAGE

church leader, responsible for the affairs in God's house, be looked up to—not pushy, not short-tempered, not a drunk, not a bully, not money-hungry. He must welcome people, be helpful, wise, fair, reverent, have a good grip on himself, and have a good grip on the Message, knowing how to use the truth to either spur people on in knowledge or stop them in their tracks if they oppose it.

For there are a lot of rebels out there, full of loose, confusing, and deceiving talk. Those who were brought up religious and ought to know better are the worst. They've got to be shut up. They're disrupting entire families with their teaching, and all for the sake of a fast buck. One of their own prophets said it best:

"The Cretans are liars from the womb,
barking dogs, lazy bellies."

He certainly spoke the truth. Get on them right away. Stop that diseased talk of Jewish make-believe and made-up rules so they can recover a robust faith. Everything is clean to the clean-minded; nothing is clean to dirty-minded unbelievers. They leave their dirty fingerprints on every

KING JAMES VERSION

16 They profess that they know God; but in works they deny *him*, being abominable, and disobedient, and unto every good work reprobate.

2 But speak thou the things which become sound doctrine:

2 That the aged men be sober, grave, temperate, sound in faith, in charity, in patience.

3 The aged women likewise, that *they be* in behaviour as becometh holiness, not false accusers, not given to much wine, teachers of good things;

4 That they may teach the young women to be sober, to love their husbands, to love their children,

5 *To be* discreet, chaste, keepers at home, good, obedient to their own husbands, that the word of God be not blasphemed.

6 Young men likewise exhort to be sober minded.

7 In all things shewing thyself a pattern of good works: in doctrine *shewing* uncorruptness, gravity, sincerity,

8 Sound speech, that cannot be condemned; that he that is of the contrary part may be ashamed, having no evil thing to say of you.

9 *Exhort* servants to be obedient unto their own masters, *and* to please *them* well in all *things*; not answering again;

NEW AMERICAN STANDARD BIBLE

16 They profess to know God, but by *their* deeds they deny *Him*, being detestable and disobedient and worthless for any good deed.

Duties of the Older and Younger

2 But as for you, speak the things which are fitting for sound doctrine.

2 Older men are to be temperate, dignified, sensible, sound in faith, in love, in perseverance.

3 Older women likewise are to be reverent in their behavior, not malicious gossips nor enslaved to much wine, teaching what is good,

4 so that they may encourage the young women to love their husbands, to love their children,

5 *to be* sensible, pure, workers at home, kind, being subject to their own husbands, so that the word of God will not be dishonored.

6 Likewise urge the young men to be sensible;

7 in all things show yourself to be an example of good deeds, *with* purity in doctrine, dignified,

8 sound *in* speech which is beyond reproach, so that the opponent will be put to shame, having nothing bad to say about us.

9 *Urge* bondslaves to be subject to their own masters in everything, to be well-pleasing, not argumentative,

NEW CENTURY VERSION

know God, but their actions show they do not accept him. They are hateful people, they refuse to obey, and they are useless for doing anything good.

Following the True Teaching

2 But you must tell everyone what to do to follow the
true teaching. [2]Teach older men to be self-controlled,
serious, wise, strong in faith, in love, and in patience.
[3]In the same way, teach older women to be holy in their
behavior, not speaking against others or enslaved to too
much wine, but teaching what is good. [4]Then they can
teach the young women to love their husbands, to love
their children, [5]to be wise and pure, to be good workers at
home, to be kind, and to yield to their husbands. Then no
one will be able to criticize the teaching God gave us.
[6]In the same way, encourage young men to be wise. [7]In
every way be an example of doing good deeds. When you
teach, do it with honesty and seriousness. [8]Speak the truth
so that you cannot be criticized. Then those who are
against you will be ashamed because there is nothing bad
to say about us.
[9]Slaves should yield to their own masters at all times,
trying to please them and not arguing with them. [10]They

CONTEMPORARY ENGLISH VERSION

people claim to know God, but their actions prove that they really don't. They are disgusting. They won't obey God, and they are too worthless to do anything good.

Instructions for Different Groups of People

2 Titus, you must teach only what is correct. [2]Tell the
older men to have self-control and to be serious and
sensible. Their faith, love, and patience must never fail.
[3]Tell the older women to behave as those who love the
Lord should. They must not gossip about others or be
slaves of wine. They must teach what is proper, [4]so the
younger women will be loving wives and mothers. [5]Each of
the younger women must be sensible and kind, as well as
a good homemaker, who puts her own husband first. Then
no one can say insulting things about God's message.
[6]Tell the young men to have self-control in everything.
[7]Always set a good example for others. Be sincere and
serious when you teach. [8]Use clean language that no one
can criticize. Do this, and your enemies will be too
ashamed to say anything against you.
[9]Tell slaves always to please their owners by obeying
them in everything. Slaves must not talk back to their

NEW INTERNATIONAL VERSION

are corrupted. [16]They claim to know God, but by their actions they deny him. They are detestable, disobedient and unfit for doing anything good.

What Must Be Taught to Various Groups

2 You must teach what is in accord with sound doctrine. [2]Teach the older men to be temperate, worthy of respect, self-controlled, and sound in faith, in love and in endurance.

[3]Likewise, teach the older women to be reverent in the way they live, not to be slanderers or addicted to much wine, but to teach what is good. [4]Then they can train the younger women to love their husbands and children, [5]to be self-controlled and pure, to be busy at home, to be kind, and to be subject to their husbands, so that no one will malign the word of God.

[6]Similarly, encourage the young men to be self-controlled. [7]In everything set them an example by doing what is good. In your teaching show integrity, seriousness [8]and soundness of speech that cannot be condemned, so that those who oppose you may be ashamed because they have nothing bad to say about us.

[9]Teach slaves to be subject to their masters in everything, to try to please them, not to talk back to them,

NEW LIVING TRANSLATION

people claim they know God, but they deny him by the way they live. They are despicable and disobedient, worthless for doing anything good.

Promote Right Teaching

2 But as for you, promote the kind of living that reflects right teaching. [2]Teach the older men to exercise self-control, to be worthy of respect, and to live wisely. They must have strong faith and be filled with love and patience.

[3]Similarly, teach the older women to live in a way that is appropriate for someone serving the Lord. They must not go around speaking evil of others and must not be heavy drinkers. Instead, they should teach others what is good. [4]These older women must train the younger women to love their husbands and their children, [5]to live wisely and be pure, to take care of their homes, to do good, and to be submissive to their husbands. Then they will not bring shame on the word of God.

[6]In the same way, encourage the young men to live wisely in all they do. [7]And you yourself must be an example to them by doing good deeds of every kind. Let everything you do reflect the integrity and seriousness of your teaching. [8]Let your teaching be so correct that it can't be criticized. Then those who want to argue will be ashamed because they won't have anything bad to say about us.

[9]Slaves must obey their masters and do their best to please them. They must not talk back [10]or steal, but they

NEW KING JAMES VERSION

to know God, but in works they deny Him, being abominable, disobedient, and disqualified for every good work.

Qualities of a Sound Church

2 But as for you, speak the things which are proper for sound doctrine: [2]that the older men be sober, reverent, temperate, sound in faith, in love, in patience; [3]the older women likewise, that they be reverent in behavior, not slanderers, not given to much wine, teachers of good things— [4]that they admonish the young women to love their husbands, to love their children, [5]to be discreet, chaste, homemakers, good, obedient to their own husbands, that the word of God may not be blasphemed.

[6]Likewise, exhort the young men to be sober-minded, [7]in all things showing yourself *to be* a pattern of good works; in doctrine *showing* integrity, reverence, incorruptibility,[a] [8]sound speech that cannot be condemned, that one who is an opponent may be ashamed, having nothing evil to say of you.[b]

[9]*Exhort* bondservants to be obedient to their own masters, to be well pleasing in all *things,* not answering back,

2:7 [a] NU-Text omits *incorruptibility.* 2:8 [b] NU-Text and M-Text read *us.*

THE MESSAGE

thought and act. They say they know God, but their actions speak louder than their words. They're real creeps, disobedient good-for-nothings.

A God-Filled Life

2 Your job is to speak out on the things that make for solid doctrine. Guide older men into lives of temperance, dignity, and wisdom, into healthy faith, love, and endurance. Guide older women into lives of reverence so they end up as neither gossips nor drunks, but models of goodness. By looking at them, the younger women will know how to love their husbands and children, be virtuous and pure, keep a good house, be good wives. We don't want anyone looking down on God's Message because of their behavior. Also, guide the young men to live disciplined lives.

But mostly, show them all this by doing it yourself, incorruptible in your teaching, your words solid and sane. Then anyone who is dead set against us, when he finds nothing weird or misguided, might eventually come around.

Guide slaves into being loyal workers, a bonus to their

KING JAMES VERSION

10 Not purloining, but shewing all good fidelity; that they may adorn the doctrine of God our Saviour in all things.

11 ¶ For the grace of God that bringeth salvation hath appeared to all men,

12 Teaching us that, denying ungodliness and worldly lusts, we should live soberly, righteously, and godly, in this present world;

13 Looking for that blessed hope, and the glorious appearing of the great God and our Saviour Jesus Christ;

14 Who gave himself for us, that he might redeem us from all iniquity, and purify unto himself a peculiar people, zealous of good works.

15 ¶ These things speak, and exhort, and rebuke with all authority. Let no man despise thee.

3 Put them in mind to be subject to principalities and powers, to obey magistrates, to be ready to every good work,

2 To speak evil of no man, to be no brawlers, *but* gentle, shewing all meekness unto all men.

3 For we ourselves also were sometimes foolish, disobedient, deceived, serving divers lusts and pleasures, living in malice and envy, hateful, *and* hating one another.

NEW AMERICAN STANDARD BIBLE

10 not pilfering, but showing all good faith so that they will adorn the doctrine of God our Savior in every respect.

11 For the grace of God has appeared, bringing salvation to all men,

12 instructing us to deny ungodliness and worldly desires and to live sensibly, righteously and godly in the present age,

13 looking for the blessed hope and the appearing of the glory of our great God and Savior, Christ Jesus,

14 who gave Himself for us to redeem us from every lawless deed, and to purify for Himself a people for His own possession, zealous for good deeds.

15 These things speak and exhort and reprove with all authority. Let no one disregard you.

Godly Living

3 Remind them to be subject to rulers, to authorities, to be obedient, to be ready for every good deed,

2 to malign no one, to be peaceable, gentle, showing every consideration for all men.

3 For we also once were foolish ourselves, disobedient, deceived, enslaved to various lusts and pleasures, spending our life in malice and envy, hateful, hating one another.

NEW CENTURY VERSION

should not steal from them but should show their masters
they can be fully trusted so that in everything they do they
will make the teaching of God our Savior attractive.

[11]That is the way we should live, because God's grace
that can save everyone has come. [12]It teaches us not to
live against God nor to do the evil things the world wants
to do. Instead, that grace teaches us to live now in a wise
and right way and in a way that shows we serve God. [13]We
should live like that while we wait for our great hope and
the coming of the glory of our great God and Savior Jesus
Christ. [14]He gave himself for us so he might pay the price
to free us from all evil and to make us pure people who
belong only to him—people who are always wanting to do
good deeds.

[15]Say these things and encourage the people and tell
them what is wrong in their lives, with all authority. Do
not let anyone treat you as if you were unimportant.

The Right Way to Live

3 Remind the believers to yield to the authority of rulers
and government leaders, to obey them, to be ready to
do good, [2]to speak no evil about anyone, to live in peace,
and to be gentle and polite to all people.

[3]In the past we also were foolish. We did not obey, we
were wrong, and we were slaves to many things our bodies
wanted and enjoyed. We spent our lives doing evil and
being jealous. People hated us, and we hated each other.

CONTEMPORARY ENGLISH VERSION

owners [10]or steal from them. They must be completely
honest and trustworthy. Then everyone will show great
respect for what is taught about God our Savior.

God's Kindness and the New Life

[11]God has shown us how kind he is by coming to save
all people. [12]He taught us to give up our wicked ways and
our worldly desires and to live decent and honest lives in
this world. [13]We are filled with hope, as we wait for the
glorious return of our great God and Savior Jesus Christ.[a]
[14]He gave himself to rescue us from everything that is evil
and to make our hearts pure. He wanted us to be his own
people and to be eager to do right.

[15]Teach these things, as you use your full authority to
encourage and correct people. Make sure you earn everyone's respect.

Doing Helpful Things

3 Remind your people to obey the rulers and authorities
and not to be rebellious. They must always be ready
to do something helpful [2]and not say cruel things or
argue. They should be gentle and kind to everyone. [3]We
used to be stupid, disobedient, and foolish, as well as
slaves of all sorts of desires and pleasures. We were evil
and jealous. Everyone hated us, and we hated everyone.

[a] 2.13 *the glorious return of our great God and Savior Jesus Christ*: Or "the glorious return of our great God and our Savior Jesus Christ" or "the return of Jesus Christ, who is the glory of our great God and Savior."

NEW INTERNATIONAL VERSION

10and not to steal from them, but to show that they can be fully trusted, so that in every way they will make the teaching about God our Savior attractive.

11For the grace of God that brings salvation has appeared to all men. 12It teaches us to say "No" to ungodliness and worldly passions, and to live self-controlled, upright and godly lives in this present age, 13while we wait for the blessed hope—the glorious appearing of our great God and Savior, Jesus Christ, 14who gave himself for us to redeem us from all wickedness and to purify for himself a people that are his very own, eager to do what is good.

15These, then, are the things you should teach. Encourage and rebuke with all authority. Do not let anyone despise you.

Doing What Is Good

3 Remind the people to be subject to rulers and authorities, to be obedient, to be ready to do whatever is good, 2to slander no one, to be peaceable and considerate, and to show true humility toward all men.

3At one time we too were foolish, disobedient, deceived and enslaved by all kinds of passions and pleasures. We lived in malice and envy, being hated and hating one

NEW LIVING TRANSLATION

must show themselves to be entirely trustworthy and good. Then they will make the teaching about God our Savior attractive in every way.

11For the grace of God has been revealed, bringing salvation to all people. 12And we are instructed to turn from godless living and sinful pleasures. We should live in this evil world with self-control, right conduct, and devotion to God, 13while we look forward to that wonderful event when the glory of our great God and Savior, Jesus Christ, will be revealed. 14He gave his life to free us from every kind of sin, to cleanse us, and to make us his very own people, totally committed to doing what is right. 15You must teach these things and encourage your people to do them, correcting them when necessary. You have the authority to do this, so don't let anyone ignore you or disregard what you say.

Do What Is Good

3 Remind your people to submit to the government and its officers. They should be obedient, always ready to do what is good. 2They must not speak evil of anyone, and they must avoid quarreling. Instead, they should be gentle and show true humility to everyone.

3Once we, too, were foolish and disobedient. We were misled by others and became slaves to many wicked desires and evil pleasures. Our lives were full of evil and envy. We hated others, and they hated us.

NEW KING JAMES VERSION

10not pilfering, but showing all good fidelity, that they may adorn the doctrine of God our Savior in all things.

Trained by Saving Grace

11For the grace of God that brings salvation has appeared to all men, 12teaching us that, denying ungodliness and worldly lusts, we should live soberly, righteously, and godly in the present age, 13looking for the blessed hope and glorious appearing of our great God and Savior Jesus Christ, 14who gave Himself for us, that He might redeem us from every lawless deed and purify for Himself *His* own special people, zealous for good works.

15Speak these things, exhort, and rebuke with all authority. Let no one despise you.

Graces of the Heirs of Grace

3 Remind them to be subject to rulers and authorities, to obey, to be ready for every good work, 2to speak evil of no one, to be peaceable, gentle, showing all humility to all men. 3For we ourselves were also once foolish, disobedient, deceived, serving various lusts and pleasures, living in malice and envy, hateful and hating one another.

THE MESSAGE

masters—no back talk, no petty thievery. Then their good character will shine through their actions, adding luster to the teaching of our Savior God.

God's readiness to give and forgive is now public. Salvation's available for everyone! We're being shown how to turn our backs on a godless, indulgent life, and how to take on a God-filled, God-honoring life. This new life is starting right now, and is whetting our appetites for the glorious day when our great God and Savior, Jesus Christ, appears. He offered himself as a sacrifice to free us from a dark, rebellious life into this good, pure life, making us a people he can be proud of, energetic in goodness.

Tell them all this. Build up their courage, and discipline them if they get out of line. You're in charge. Don't let anyone put you down.

He Put Our Lives Together

3 Remind the people to respect the government and be law-abiding, always ready to lend a helping hand. No insults, no fights. God's people should be bighearted and courteous.

It wasn't so long ago that we ourselves were stupid and stubborn, dupes of sin, ordered every which way by our glands, going around with a chip on our shoulder, hated

KING JAMES VERSION

4 But after that the kindness and love of God our
Saviour toward man appeared,
5 Not by works of righteousness which we have done,
but according to his mercy he saved us, by the washing of
regeneration, and renewing of the Holy Ghost;
6 Which he shed on us abundantly through Jesus Christ
our Saviour;
7 That being justified by his grace, we should be made
heirs according to the hope of eternal life.
8 *This is* a faithful saying, and these things I will that
thou affirm constantly, that they which have believed in
God might be careful to maintain good works. These things
are good and profitable unto men.
9 ¶ But avoid foolish questions, and genealogies, and
contentions, and strivings about the law; for they are
unprofitable and vain.

NEW AMERICAN STANDARD BIBLE

4 But when the kindness of God our Savior and *His*
love for mankind appeared,
5 He saved us, not on the basis of deeds which we have
done in righteousness, but according to His mercy, by the
washing of regeneration and renewing by the Holy Spirit,
6 whom He poured out upon us richly through Jesus
Christ our Savior,
7 so that being justified by His grace we would be
made heirs according to *the* hope of eternal life.
8 This is a trustworthy statement; and concerning
these things I want you to speak confidently, so that those
who have believed God will be careful to engage in good
deeds. These things are good and profitable for men.
9 But avoid foolish controversies and genealogies and
strife and disputes about the Law, for they are unprofitable
and worthless.

NEW CENTURY VERSION

4But when the kindness and love of God our Savior was
shown, 5he saved us because of his mercy. It was not
because of good deeds we did to be right with him. He
saved us through the washing that made us new people
through the Holy Spirit. 6God poured out richly upon us
that Holy Spirit through Jesus Christ our Savior. 7Being
made right with God by his grace, we could have the hope
of receiving the life that never ends.
8This teaching is true, and I want you to be sure the
people understand these things. Then those who believe in
God will be careful to use their lives for doing good. These
things are good and will help everyone.
9But stay away from those who have foolish arguments
and talk about useless family histories and argue and quar-
rel about the law. Those things are worth nothing and will

CONTEMPORARY ENGLISH VERSION

4God our Savior showed us
how good and kind he is.
5He saved us because
of his mercy,
and not because
of any good things
that we have done.

God washed us by the power
of the Holy Spirit.
He gave us new birth
and a fresh beginning.
6God sent Jesus Christ
our Savior
to give us his Spirit.

7Jesus treated us much better
than we deserve.
He made us acceptable to God
and gave us the hope
of eternal life.

8This message is certainly true.

These teachings are useful and helpful for everyone. I want
you to insist that the people follow them, so that all who
have faith in God will be sure to do good deeds. 9But don't
have anything to do with stupid arguments about ancestors.
And stay away from disagreements and quarrels about the
Law of Moses. Such arguments are useless and senseless.

NEW INTERNATIONAL VERSION

another. 4But when the kindness and love of God our
Savior appeared, 5he saved us, not because of righteous
things we had done, but because of his mercy. He saved us
through the washing of rebirth and renewal by the Holy
Spirit, 6whom he poured out on us generously through
Jesus Christ our Savior, 7so that, having been justified by
his grace, we might become heirs having the hope of eter-
nal life. 8This is a trustworthy saying. And I want you to
stress these things, so that those who have trusted in God
may be careful to devote themselves to doing what is good.
These things are excellent and profitable for everyone.
9But avoid foolish controversies and genealogies and
arguments and quarrels about the law, because these are

NEW LIVING TRANSLATION

4But then God our Savior showed us his kindness and
love. 5He saved us, not because of the good things we did,
but because of his mercy. He washed away our sins and
gave us a new life through the Holy Spirit.* 6He generous-
ly poured out the Spirit upon us because of what Jesus
Christ our Savior did. 7He declared us not guilty because of
his great kindness. And now we know that we will inherit
eternal life. 8These things I have told you are all true. I
want you to insist on them so that everyone who trusts in
God will be careful to do good deeds all the time. These
things are good and beneficial for everyone.

Paul's Final Remarks and Greetings

9Do not get involved in foolish discussions about spiri-
tual pedigrees* or in quarrels and fights about obedience
to Jewish laws. These kinds of things are useless and a

3:5 Greek *He saved us through the washing of regeneration and renewing of the Holy Spirit.* 3:9 Greek *discussions and genealogies.*

NEW KING JAMES VERSION

4But when the kindness and the love of God our Savior
toward man appeared, 5not by works of righteousness
which we have done, but according to His mercy He saved
us, through the washing of regeneration and renewing of
the Holy Spirit, 6whom He poured out on us abundantly
through Jesus Christ our Savior, 7that having been justified
by His grace we should become heirs according to the hope
of eternal life.
8This is a faithful saying, and these things I want you to
affirm constantly, that those who have believed in God
should be careful to maintain good works. These things
are good and profitable to men.

Avoid Dissension

9But avoid foolish disputes, genealogies, contentions,
and strivings about the law; for they are unprofitable and

THE MESSAGE

and hating back. But when God, our kind and loving Savior God, stepped in, he saved us from all that. It was all his doing; we had nothing to do with it. He gave us a good bath, and we came out of it new people, washed inside and out by the Holy Spirit. Our Savior Jesus poured out new life so generously. God's gift has restored our relationship with him and given us back our lives. And there's more life to come—an eternity of life! You can count on this.

I want you to put your foot down. Take a firm stand on these matters so that those who have put their trust in God will concentrate on the essentials that are good for everyone. Stay away from mindless, pointless quarreling over genealogies and fine print in the law code. That gets

KING JAMES VERSION

10 A man that is an heretick after the first and second admonition reject;

11 Knowing that he that is such is subverted, and sinneth, being condemned of himself.

12 When I shall send Artemas unto thee, or Tychicus, be diligent to come unto me to Nicopolis: for I have determined there to winter.

13 Bring Zenas the lawyer and Apollos on their journey diligently, that nothing be wanting unto them.

14 And let ours also learn to maintain good works for necessary uses, that they be not unfruitful.

15 All that are with me salute thee. Greet them that love us in the faith. Grace *be* with you all. Amen.

NEW AMERICAN STANDARD BIBLE

10 Reject a factious man after a first and second warning,

11 knowing that such a man is perverted and is sinning, being self-condemned.

Personal Concerns

12 When I send Artemas or Tychicus to you, make every effort to come to me at Nicopolis, for I have decided to spend the winter there.

13 Diligently help Zenas the lawyer and Apollos on their way so that nothing is lacking for them.

14 Our people must also learn to engage in good deeds to meet pressing needs, so that they will not be unfruitful.

15 All who are with me greet you. Greet those who love us in *the* faith.

Grace be with you all.

NEW CENTURY VERSION

not help anyone. 10After a first and second warning, avoid
someone who causes arguments. 11You can know that such
people are evil and sinful; their own sins prove them
wrong.

Some Things to Remember

12When I send Artemas or Tychicus to you, make every
effort to come to me at Nicopolis, because I have decided to
stay there this winter. 13Do all you can to help Zenas the
lawyer and Apollos on their journey so that they have
everything they need. 14Our people must learn to use their
lives for doing good deeds to provide what is necessary so
that their lives will not be useless.

15All who are with me greet you. Greet those who love us in the faith.

Grace be with you all.

CONTEMPORARY ENGLISH VERSION

10Warn troublemakers once or twice. Then don't have
anything else to do with them. 11You know that their
minds are twisted, and their own sins show how guilty
they are.

Personal Instructions and Greetings

12I plan to send Artemas or Tychicus to you. After he arrives, please try your best to meet me at Nicopolis. I have decided to spend the winter there.

13When Zenas the lawyer and Apollos get ready to leave, help them as much as you can, so they won't have need of anything.

14Our people should learn to spend their time doing something useful and worthwhile.

15Greetings to you from everyone here. Greet all of our friends who share in our faith.

I pray that the Lord will be kind to all of you!

NEW INTERNATIONAL VERSION

unprofitable and useless. [10]Warn a divisive person once, and then warn him a second time. After that, have nothing to do with him. [11]You may be sure that such a man is warped and sinful; he is self-condemned.

Final Remarks

[12]As soon as I send Artemas or Tychicus to you, do your best to come to me at Nicopolis, because I have decided to winter there. [13]Do everything you can to help Zenas the lawyer and Apollos on their way and see that they have everything they need. [14]Our people must learn to devote themselves to doing what is good, in order that they may provide for daily necessities and not live unproductive lives.

[15]Everyone with me sends you greetings. Greet those who love us in the faith.

Grace be with you all.

NEW LIVING TRANSLATION

waste of time. [10]If anyone is causing divisions among you, give a first and second warning. After that, have nothing more to do with that person. [11]For people like that have turned away from the truth. They are sinning, and they condemn themselves.

[12]I am planning to send either Artemas or Tychicus to you. As soon as one of them arrives, do your best to meet me at Nicopolis as quickly as you can, for I have decided to stay there for the winter. [13]Do everything you can to help Zenas the lawyer and Apollos with their trip. See that they are given everything they need. [14]For our people should not have unproductive lives. They must learn to do good by helping others who have urgent needs.

[15]Everybody here sends greetings. Please give my greetings to all of the believers who love us.

May God's grace be with you all.

NEW KING JAMES VERSION

useless. [10]Reject a divisive man after the first and second admonition, [11]knowing that such a person is warped and sinning, being self-condemned.

Final Messages

[12]When I send Artemas to you, or Tychicus, be diligent to come to me at Nicopolis, for I have decided to spend the winter there. [13]Send Zenas the lawyer and Apollos on their journey with haste, that they may lack nothing. [14]And let our *people* also learn to maintain good works, to *meet* urgent needs, that they may not be unfruitful.

Farewell

[15]All who *are* with me greet you. Greet those who love us in the faith.

Grace *be* with you all. Amen.

THE MESSAGE

you nowhere. Warn a quarrelsome person once or twice, but then be done with him. It's obvious that such a person is out of line, rebellious against God. By persisting in divisiveness he cuts himself off.

As soon as I send either Artemas or Tychicus to you, come immediately and meet me in Nicopolis. I've decided to spend the winter there. Give Zenas the lawyer and Apollos a hearty sendoff. Take good care of them.

Our people have to learn to be diligent in their work so that all necessities are met (especially among the needy) and they don't end up with nothing to show for their lives.

All here want to be remembered to you. Say hello to our friends in the faith. Grace to all of you.

KING JAMES VERSION

THE EPISTLE OF ST. PAUL TO

PHILEMON

1 ¶ Paul, a prisoner of Jesus Christ, and Timothy *our* brother, unto Philemon our dearly beloved, and fellowlabourer,

2 And to *our* beloved Apphia, and Archippus our fellowsoldier, and to the church in thy house:

3 Grace to you, and peace, from God our Father and the Lord Jesus Christ.

4 ¶ I thank my God, making mention of thee always in my prayers,

5 Hearing of thy love and faith, which thou hast toward the Lord Jesus, and toward all saints;

6 That the communication of thy faith may become effectual by the acknowledging of every good thing which is in you in Christ Jesus.

7 For we have great joy and consolation in thy love, because the bowels of the saints are refreshed by thee, brother.

NEW AMERICAN STANDARD BIBLE

THE LETTER OF PAUL TO

PHILEMON

Salutation

1 Paul, a prisoner of Christ Jesus, and Timothy our brother,

To Philemon our beloved *brother* and fellow worker,

2 and to Apphia our sister, and to Archippus our fellow soldier, and to the church in your house:

3 Grace to you and peace from God our Father and the Lord Jesus Christ.

Philemon's Love and Faith

4 I thank my God always, making mention of you in my prayers,

5 because I hear of your love and of the faith which you have toward the Lord Jesus and toward all the saints;

6 *and I pray* that the fellowship of your faith may become effective [1]through the knowledge of every good thing which is in you for Christ's sake.

7 For I have come to have much joy and comfort in your love, because the hearts of the saints have been refreshed through you, brother.

6 [1] Or *in*

NEW CENTURY VERSION

PHILEMON

1From Paul, a prisoner of Christ Jesus, and from
Timothy, our brother.
To Philemon, our dear friend and worker with us; 2to
Apphia, our sister; to Archippus, a worker with us; and to
the church that meets in your home:
3Grace and peace to you from God our Father and the
Lord Jesus Christ.

Philemon's Love and Faith

4I always thank my God when I mention you in my
prayers, 5because I hear about the love you have for all
God's holy people and the faith you have in the Lord Jesus.
6I pray that the faith you share may make you understand
every blessing we have in Christ. 7I have great joy and
comfort, my brother, because the love you have shown to
God's people has refreshed them.

CONTEMPORARY ENGLISH VERSION

PHILEMON

1From Paul, who is in jail for serving Christ Jesus, and
from Timothy, who is like a brother because of our faith.
Philemon, you work with us and are very dear to us.
This letter is to you 2and to the church that meets in your
home. It is also to our dear friend Apphia and to
Archippus, who serves the Lord as we do.
3I pray that God our Father and our Lord Jesus Christ
will be kind to you and will bless you with peace!

Philemon's Love and Faith

4Philemon, each time I mention you in my prayers, I
thank God. 5I hear about your faith in our Lord Jesus and
about your love for all of God's people. 6As you share your
faith with others, I pray that they may come to know all
the blessings Christ has given us. 7My friend, your love
has made me happy and has greatly encouraged me. It has
also cheered the hearts of God's people.

NEW INTERNATIONAL VERSION

PHILEMON

1Paul, a prisoner of Christ Jesus, and Timothy our brother,

To Philemon our dear friend and fellow worker, 2to Apphia our sister, to Archippus our fellow soldier and to the church that meets in your home:

3Grace to you and peace from God our Father and the Lord Jesus Christ.

Thanksgiving and Prayer

4I always thank my God as I remember you in my prayers, 5because I hear about your faith in the Lord Jesus and your love for all the saints. 6I pray that you may be active in sharing your faith, so that you will have a full understanding of every good thing we have in Christ. 7Your love has given me great joy and encouragement, because you, brother, have refreshed the hearts of the saints.

NEW LIVING TRANSLATION

PHILEMON

Greetings from Paul

This letter is from Paul, in prison for preaching the Good News about Christ Jesus, and from our brother Timothy.

It is written to Philemon, our much loved co-worker, 2and to our sister Apphia and to Archippus, a fellow soldier of the cross. I am also writing to the church that meets in your house.

3May God our Father and the Lord Jesus Christ give you grace and peace.

Paul's Thanksgiving and Prayer

4I always thank God when I pray for you, Philemon, 5because I keep hearing of your trust in the Lord Jesus and your love for all of God's people. 6You are generous because of your faith. And I am praying that you will really put your generosity to work, for in so doing you will come to an understanding of all the good things we can do for Christ. 7I myself have gained much joy and comfort from your love, my brother, because your kindness has so often refreshed the hearts of God's people.

NEW KING JAMES VERSION

THE EPISTLE OF PAUL TO

PHILEMON

Greeting

1 Paul, a prisoner of Christ Jesus, and Timothy *our* brother,

To Philemon our beloved *friend* and fellow laborer, 2to the beloved[a] Apphia, Archippus our fellow soldier, and to the church in your house:

3Grace to you and peace from God our Father and the Lord Jesus Christ.

Philemon's Love and Faith

4I thank my God, making mention of you always in my prayers, 5hearing of your love and faith which you have toward the Lord Jesus and toward all the saints, 6that the sharing of your faith may become effective by the acknowledgment of every good thing which is in you[b] in Christ Jesus. 7For we have[c] great joy[d] and consolation in your love, because the hearts of the saints have been refreshed by you, brother.

2 [a] NU-Text reads *to our sister Apphia.* 6 [b] NU-Text and M-Text read *us.* 7 [c] NU-Text reads *had.* [d] M-Text reads *thanksgiving.*

THE MESSAGE

PHILEMON

I, Paul, am a prisoner for the sake of Christ, here with my brother Timothy. I write this letter to you, Philemon, my good friend and companion in this work—also to our sister Apphia, to Archippus, a real trooper, and to the church that meets in your house. God's best to you! Christ's blessings on you!

Every time your name comes up in my prayers, I say, "Oh, thank you, God!" I keep hearing of the love and faith you have for the Master Jesus, which brims over to other Christians. And I keep praying that this faith we hold in common keeps showing up in the good things we do, and that people recognize Christ in all of it. Friend, you have no idea how good your love makes me feel, doubly so when I see your hospitality to fellow believers.

KING JAMES VERSION

8 ¶ Wherefore, though I might be much bold in Christ to enjoin thee that which is convenient,

9 Yet for love's sake I rather beseech *thee*, being such an one as Paul the aged, and now also a prisoner of Jesus Christ.

10 I beseech thee for my son Onesimus, whom I have begotten in my bonds:

11 Which in time past was to thee unprofitable, but now profitable to thee and to me:

12 Whom I have sent again: thou therefore receive him, that is, mine own bowels:

13 Whom I would have retained with me, that in thy stead he might have ministered unto me in the bonds of the gospel:

14 But without thy mind would I do nothing; that thy benefit should not be as it were of necessity, but willingly.

15 For perhaps he therefore departed for a season, that thou shouldest receive him for ever;

16 Not now as a servant, but above a servant, a brother beloved, specially to me, but how much more unto thee, both in the flesh, and in the Lord?

17 If thou count me therefore a partner, receive him as myself.

NEW AMERICAN STANDARD BIBLE

8 Therefore, though I have enough confidence in Christ to order you *to do* what is proper,

9 yet for love's sake I rather appeal *to you*—since I am such a person as Paul, the aged, and now also a prisoner of Christ Jesus—

Plea for Onesimus, a Free Man

10 I appeal to you for my child [2]Onesimus, whom I have begotten in my imprisonment,

11 who formerly was useless to you, but now is useful both to you and to me.

12 I have sent him back to you in person, that is, *sending* my very heart,

13 whom I wished to keep with me, so that on your behalf he might minister to me in my imprisonment for the gospel;

14 but without your consent I did not want to do anything, so that your goodness would not be, in effect, by compulsion but of your own free will.

15 For perhaps he was for this reason separated *from you* for a while, that you would have him back forever,

16 no longer as a slave, but more than a slave, a beloved brother, especially to me, but how much more to you, both in the flesh and in the Lord.

17 If then you regard me a partner, accept him as *you would* me.

10 [2] I.e. useful

NEW CENTURY VERSION

Accept Onesimus as a Brother

8So, in Christ, I could be bold and order you to do what
is right. 9But because I love you, I am pleading with you
instead. I, Paul, an old man now and also a prisoner for
Christ Jesus, 10am pleading with you for my child
Onesimus, who became my child while I was in prison.
11In the past he was useless to you, but now he has
become useful for both you and me.
12I am sending him back to you, and with him I am
sending my own heart. 13I wanted to keep him with me so
that in your place he might help me while I am in prison
for the Good News. 14But I did not want to do anything
without asking you first so that any good you do for me
will be because you want to do it, not because I forced you.
15Maybe Onesimus was separated from you for a short
time so you could have him back forever— 16no longer as
a slave, but better than a slave, as a loved brother. I love
him very much, but you will love him even more, both as a
person and as a believer in the Lord.
17So if you consider me your partner, welcome Onesimus
as you would welcome me. 18If he has done anything

CONTEMPORARY ENGLISH VERSION

Paul Speaks to Philemon about Onesimus

8Christ gives me the courage to tell you what to do. 9But
I would rather ask you to do it simply because of love. Yes,
as someone[a] in jail for Christ, 10I beg you to help Onesi-
mus![b] He is like a son to me because I led him to Christ
here in jail. 11Before this, he was useless to you, but now
he is useful both to you and to me.
12Sending Onesimus back to you makes me very sad. 13I
would like to keep him here with me, where he could take
your place in helping me while I am here in prison for
preaching the good news. 14But I won't do anything unless
you agree to it first. I want your act of kindness to come
from your heart, and not be something you feel forced to
do.
15Perhaps Onesimus was taken from you for a little
while so that you could have him back for good, 16but not
as a slave. Onesimus is much more than a slave. To me he
is a dear friend, but to you he is even more, both as a per-
son and as a follower of the Lord.
17If you consider me a friend because of Christ, then
welcome Onesimus as you would welcome me. 18If he has

[a] **9** *someone*: Greek "a messenger" or "an old man." [b] **10** *Onesimus*: In Greek this name means "useful."

NEW INTERNATIONAL VERSION

Paul's Plea for Onesimus

[8]Therefore, although in Christ I could be bold and order you to do what you ought to do, [9]yet I appeal to you on the basis of love. I then, as Paul—an old man and now also a prisoner of Christ Jesus— [10]I appeal to you for my son Onesimus,[a] who became my son while I was in chains. [11]Formerly he was useless to you, but now he has become useful both to you and to me.

[12]I am sending him—who is my very heart—back to you. [13]I would have liked to keep him with me so that he could take your place in helping me while I am in chains for the gospel. [14]But I did not want to do anything without your consent, so that any favor you do will be spontaneous and not forced. [15]Perhaps the reason he was separated from you for a little while was that you might have him back for good— [16]no longer as a slave, but better than a slave, as a dear brother. He is very dear to me but even dearer to you, both as a man and as a brother in the Lord.

[17]So if you consider me a partner, welcome him as you

[a] *10 Onesimus* means *useful.*

NEW LIVING TRANSLATION

Paul's Appeal for Onesimus

[8]That is why I am boldly asking a favor of you. I could demand it in the name of Christ because it is the right thing for you to do, [9]but because of our love, I prefer just to ask you. So take this as a request from your friend Paul, an old man, now in prison for the sake of Christ Jesus.

[10]My plea is that you show kindness to Onesimus. I think of him as my own son because he became a believer as a result of my ministry here in prison. [11]Onesimus* hasn't been of much use to you in the past, but now he is very useful to both of us. [12]I am sending him back to you, and with him comes my own heart.

[13]I really wanted to keep him here with me while I am in these chains for preaching the Good News, and he would have helped me on your behalf. [14]But I didn't want to do anything without your consent. And I didn't want you to help because you were forced to do it but because you wanted to. [15]Perhaps you could think of it this way: Onesimus ran away for a little while so you could have him back forever. [16]He is no longer just a slave; he is a beloved brother, especially to me. Now he will mean much more to you, both as a slave and as a brother in the Lord.

[17]So if you consider me your partner, give him the same welcome you would give me if I were coming. [18]If he has

11 *Onesimus* means "useful."

NEW KING JAMES VERSION

The Plea for Onesimus

[8]Therefore, though I might be very bold in Christ to command you what is fitting, [9]*yet* for love's sake I rather appeal *to you*—being such a one as Paul, the aged, and now also a prisoner of Jesus Christ— [10]I appeal to you for my son Onesimus, whom I have begotten *while* in my chains, [11]who once was unprofitable to you, but now is profitable to you and to me.

[12]I am sending him back.[e] You therefore receive him, that is, my own heart, [13]whom I wished to keep with me, that on your behalf he might minister to me in my chains for the gospel. [14]But without your consent I wanted to do nothing, that your good deed might not be by compulsion, as it were, but voluntary.

[15]For perhaps he departed for a while for this *purpose,* that you might receive him forever, [16]no longer as a slave but more than a slave—a beloved brother, especially to me but how much more to you, both in the flesh and in the Lord.

Philemon's Obedience Encouraged

[17]If then you count me as a partner, receive him as *you*

12 [e] NU-Text reads *back to you in person, that is, my own heart.*

THE MESSAGE

To Call the Slave Your Friend

In line with all this I have a favor to ask of you. As Christ's ambassador and now a prisoner for him, I wouldn't hesitate to command this if I thought it necessary, but I'd rather make it a personal request.

While here in jail, I've fathered a child, so to speak. And here he is, hand-carrying this letter—Onesimus! He was useless to you before; now he's useful to both of us. I'm sending him back to you, but it feels like I'm cutting off my right arm in doing so. I wanted in the worst way to keep him here as your stand-in to help out while I'm in jail for the Message. But I didn't want to do anything behind your back, make you do a good deed that you hadn't willingly agreed to.

Maybe it's all for the best that you lost him for a while. You're getting him back now for good—and no mere slave this time, but a true Christian brother! That's what he was to me—he'll be even more than that to you.

So if you still consider me a comrade-in-arms, welcome him back as you would me. If he damaged anything or

KING JAMES VERSION

18 If he hath wronged thee, or oweth *thee* ought, put that on mine account;

19 I Paul have written *it* with mine own hand, I will repay *it*: albeit I do not say to thee how thou owest unto me even thine own self besides.

20 Yea, brother, let me have joy of thee in the Lord: refresh my bowels in the Lord.

21 Having confidence in thy obedience I wrote unto thee, knowing that thou wilt also do more than I say.

22 But withal prepare me also a lodging: for I trust that through your prayers I shall be given unto you.

23 There salute thee Epaphras, my fellowprisoner in Christ Jesus;

24 Marcus, Aristarchus, Demas, Lucas, my fellowlabourers.

25 The grace of our Lord Jesus Christ *be* with your spirit. Amen.

NEW AMERICAN STANDARD BIBLE

18 But if he has wronged you in any way or owes you anything, charge that to my account;

19 I, Paul, am writing this with my own hand, I will repay it (not to mention to you that you owe to me even your own self as well).

20 Yes, brother, let me benefit from you in the Lord; refresh my heart in Christ.

21 Having confidence in your obedience, I write to you, since I know that you will do even more than what I say.

22 At the same time also prepare me a lodging, for I hope that through your prayers I will be given to you.

23 Epaphras, my fellow prisoner in Christ Jesus, greets you,

24 *as do* Mark, Aristarchus, Demas, Luke, my fellow workers.

25 The grace of the Lord Jesus Christ be with your spirit.[3]

25 [3] One early ms adds *Amen*

NEW CENTURY VERSION

wrong to you or if he owes you anything, charge that to
me. 19I, Paul, am writing this with my own hand. I will pay
it back, and I will say nothing about what you owe me for
your own life. 20So, my brother, I ask that you do this for
me in the Lord: Refresh my heart in Christ. 21I write this
letter, knowing that you will do what I ask you and even
more.

22One more thing—prepare a room for me in which to
stay, because I hope God will answer your prayers and I
will be able to come to you.

Final Greetings

23Epaphras, a prisoner with me for Christ Jesus, sends
greetings to you. 24And also Mark, Aristarchus, Demas,
and Luke, workers together with me, send greetings.

25The grace of our Lord Jesus Christ be with your spirit.

CONTEMPORARY ENGLISH VERSION

cheated you or owes you anything, charge it to my
account. 19With my own hand I write: I, PAUL, WILL PAY
YOU BACK. But don't forget that you owe me your life.
20My dear friend and follower of Christ our Lord, please
cheer me up by doing this for me.

21I am sure you will do all I have asked, and even more.
22Please get a room ready for me. I hope your prayers will
be answered, and I can visit you.

23Epaphras is also here in jail for being a follower of
Christ Jesus. He sends his greetings, 24and so do Mark,
Aristarchus, Demas, and Luke, who work together with
me.

25I pray that the Lord Jesus Christ will be kind to you!

NEW INTERNATIONAL VERSION

would welcome me. 18If he has done you any wrong or
owes you anything, charge it to me. 19I, Paul, am writing
this with my own hand. I will pay it back—not to mention
that you owe me your very self. 20I do wish, brother, that I
may have some benefit from you in the Lord; refresh my
heart in Christ. 21Confident of your obedience, I write to
you, knowing that you will do even more than I ask.
22And one thing more: Prepare a guest room for me,
because I hope to be restored to you in answer to your
prayers.

23Epaphras, my fellow prisoner in Christ Jesus, sends
you greetings. 24And so do Mark, Aristarchus, Demas and
Luke, my fellow workers.
25The grace of the Lord Jesus Christ be with your spirit.

NEW LIVING TRANSLATION

harmed you in any way or stolen anything from you,
charge me for it. 19I, Paul, write this in my own handwrit-
ing: "I will repay it." And I won't mention that you owe me
your very soul!
20Yes, dear brother, please do me this favor for the
Lord's sake. Give me this encouragement in Christ. 21I am
confident as I write this letter that you will do what I ask
and even more!
22Please keep a guest room ready for me, for I am hop-
ing that God will answer your prayers and let me return to
you soon.

Paul's Final Greetings

23Epaphras, my fellow prisoner in Christ Jesus, sends
you his greetings. 24So do Mark, Aristarchus, Demas, and
Luke, my co-workers.
25The grace of the Lord Jesus Christ be with your spirit.

NEW KING JAMES VERSION

would me. 18But if he has wronged you or owes anything,
put that on my account. 19I, Paul, am writing with my own
hand. I will repay—not to mention to you that you owe me
even your own self besides. 20Yes, brother, let me have joy
from you in the Lord; refresh my heart in the Lord.
21Having confidence in your obedience, I write to you,
knowing that you will do even more than I say. 22But,
meanwhile, also prepare a guest room for me, for I trust
that through your prayers I shall be granted to you.

Farewell

23Epaphras, my fellow prisoner in Christ Jesus, greets
you, 24*as do* Mark, Aristarchus, Demas, Luke, my fellow
laborers.
25The grace of our Lord Jesus Christ *be* with your spirit.
Amen.

THE MESSAGE

owes you anything, chalk it up to my account. This is my personal signature—Paul—and I stand behind it. (I don't need to remind you, do I, that you owe your very life to me?) Do me this big favor, friend. You'll be doing it for Christ, but it will also do my heart good.

I know you well enough to know you will. You'll probably go far beyond what I've written. And by the way, get a room ready for me. Because of your prayers, I fully expect to be your guest again.

Epaphras, my cellmate in the cause of Christ, says hello. Also my coworkers Mark, Aristarchus, Demas, and Luke. All the best to you from the Master, Jesus Christ!

KING JAMES VERSION

THE EPISTLE TO THE
HEBREWS

1 God, who at sundry times and in divers manners spake in time past unto the fathers by the prophets,

2 Hath in these last days spoken unto us by *his* Son, whom he hath appointed heir of all things, by whom also he made the worlds;

3 Who being the brightness of *his* glory, and the express image of his person, and upholding all things by the word of his power, when he had by himself purged our sins, sat down on the right hand of the Majesty on high;

4 ¶ Being made so much better than the angels, as he hath by inheritance obtained a more excellent name than they.

5 For unto which of the angels said he at any time, Thou art my Son, this day have I begotten thee? And again, I will be to him a Father, and he shall be to me a Son?

NEW AMERICAN STANDARD BIBLE

THE LETTER TO THE
HEBREWS

God's Final Word in His Son

1 God, after He spoke long ago to the fathers in the prophets in many portions and in many ways,

2 in these last days has spoken to us in His Son, whom He appointed heir of all things, through whom also He made the world.

3 And He is the radiance of His glory and the exact representation of His nature, and upholds all things by the word of His power. When He had made purification of sins, He sat down at the right hand of the Majesty on high,

4 having become as much better than the angels, as He has inherited a more excellent name than they.

5 For to which of the angels did He ever say,

"You are My Son,
Today I have begotten You"?

And again,

"I will be a Father to Him
And He shall be a Son to Me"?

NEW CENTURY VERSION

HEBREWS

God Spoke Through His Son

1 In the past God spoke to our ancestors through the prophets many times and in many different ways. [2]But now in these last days God has spoken to us through his Son. God has chosen his Son to own all things, and through him he made the world. [3]The Son reflects the glory of God and shows exactly what God is like. He holds everything together with his powerful word. When the Son made people clean from their sins, he sat down at the right side of God, the Great One in heaven. [4]The Son became much greater than the angels, and God gave him a name that is much greater than theirs.

[5]This is because God never said to any of the angels,

"You are my Son.
Today I have become your Father." *Psalm 2:7*

Nor did God say of any angel,

"I will be his Father,
and he will be my Son." *2 Samuel 7:14*

CONTEMPORARY ENGLISH VERSION

HEBREWS

1 Long ago in many ways and at many times God's prophets spoke his message to our ancestors. [2]But now at last, God sent his Son to bring his message to us. God created the universe by his Son, and everything will someday belong to the Son. [3]God's Son has all the brightness of God's own glory and is like him in every way. By his own mighty word, he holds the universe together.

After the Son had washed away our sins, he sat down at the right side[a] of the glorious God in heaven. [4]He had become much greater than the angels, and the name he was given is far greater than any of theirs.

God's Son Is Greater than Angels

[5]God has never said
to any of the angels,
"You are my Son, because today
I have become your Father!"
Neither has God said
to any of them,
"I will be his Father,
and he will be my Son!"

[a] **1.3** *right side*: The place of honor and power.

NEW INTERNATIONAL VERSION

HEBREWS

The Son Superior to Angels

1 In the past God spoke to our forefathers through the
prophets at many times and in various ways, 2but in
these last days he has spoken to us by his Son, whom he
appointed heir of all things, and through whom he made
the universe. 3The Son is the radiance of God's glory and
the exact representation of his being, sustaining all things
by his powerful word. After he had provided purification
for sins, he sat down at the right hand of the Majesty in
heaven. 4So he became as much superior to the angels as
the name he has inherited is superior to theirs.
5For to which of the angels did God ever say,

"You are my Son;
today I have become your Father[a]"[b]?

Or again,

"I will be his Father,
and he will be my Son"[c]?

[a] 5 Or *have begotten you* [b] 5 Psalm 2:7 [c] 5 2 Samuel 7:14; 1 Chron. 17:13

NEW LIVING TRANSLATION

HEBREWS

Jesus Christ Is God's Son

1 Long ago God spoke many times and in many ways to
our ancestors through the prophets. 2But now in these
final days, he has spoken to us through his Son. God
promised everything to the Son as an inheritance, and
through the Son he made the universe and everything in it.
3The Son reflects God's own glory, and everything about
him represents God exactly. He sustains the universe by
the mighty power of his command. After he died to cleanse
us from the stain of sin, he sat down in the place of honor
at the right hand of the majestic God of heaven.

Christ Is Greater Than the Angels

4This shows that God's Son is far greater than the
angels, just as the name God gave him is far greater than
their names. 5For God never said to any angel what he
said to Jesus:

"You are my Son.
Today I have become your Father.*"

1:5a Or *Today I reveal you as my Son.* Ps 2:7.

NEW KING JAMES VERSION

THE EPISTLE TO THE

HEBREWS

God's Supreme Revelation

1 God, who at various times and in various ways spoke
in time past to the fathers by the prophets, 2has in
these last days spoken to us by *His* Son, whom He has
appointed heir of all things, through whom also He made
the worlds; 3who being the brightness of *His* glory and the
express image of His person, and upholding all things by
the word of His power, when He had by Himself[a] purged
our[b] sins, sat down at the right hand of the Majesty on high,
4having become so much better than the angels, as He has
by inheritance obtained a more excellent name than they.

The Son Exalted Above Angels

5For to which of the angels did He ever say:

"You are My Son,
Today I have begotten You"?[c]

And again:

"I will be to Him a Father,
And He shall be to Me a Son"?[d]

1:3 [a] NU-Text omits *by Himself.* [b] NU-Text omits *our.*
1:5 [c] Psalm 2:7 [d] 2 Samuel 7:14

THE MESSAGE

HEBREWS

1 Going through a long line of prophets, God has been
addressing our ancestors in different ways for cen-
turies. Recently he spoke to us directly through his Son. By
his Son, God created the world in the beginning, and it will
all belong to the Son at the end. This Son perfectly mirrors
God, and is stamped with God's nature. He holds every-
thing together by what he says—powerful words!

The Son Is Higher Than Angels

After he finished the sacrifice for sins, the Son took his
honored place high in the heavens right alongside God,
far higher than any angel in rank and rule. Did God ever
say to an angel, "You're my Son; today I celebrate you"?
Or, "I'm his Father, he's my Son"? When he presents his

KING JAMES VERSION

6 And again, when he bringeth in the firstbegotten into the world, he saith, And let all the angels of God worship him.

7 And of the angels he saith, Who maketh his angels spirits, and his ministers a flame of fire.

8 But unto the Son *he saith*, Thy throne, O God, *is* for ever and ever: a sceptre of righteousness *is* the sceptre of thy kingdom.

9 Thou hast loved righteousness, and hated iniquity; therefore God, *even* thy God, hath anointed thee with the oil of gladness above thy fellows.

10 And, Thou, Lord, in the beginning hast laid the foun-

NEW AMERICAN STANDARD BIBLE

6 And when He again brings the firstborn into the world, He says,

"AND LET ALL THE ANGELS OF GOD WORSHIP HIM."

7 And of the angels He says,

"WHO MAKES HIS ANGELS WINDS,
AND HIS MINISTERS A FLAME OF FIRE."

8 But of the Son *He says*,

"YOUR THRONE, O GOD, IS FOREVER AND EVER,
AND THE RIGHTEOUS SCEPTER IS THE SCEPTER OF [1]HIS KINGDOM.

9 "YOU HAVE LOVED RIGHTEOUSNESS AND HATED LAWLESSNESS;
THEREFORE GOD, YOUR GOD, HAS ANOINTED YOU
WITH THE OIL OF GLADNESS ABOVE YOUR COMPANIONS."

10 And,

"YOU, LORD, IN THE BEGINNING LAID THE FOUNDATION OF THE EARTH,

1:8 [1] Late mss read *Your*

NEW CENTURY VERSION

6 And when God brings his firstborn Son into the world, he says,

"Let all God's angels worship him."[a] *Psalm 97:7*

7 This is what God said about the angels:

"God makes his angels become like winds.
He makes his servants become like flames of fire."
Psalm 104:4

8 But God said this about his Son:

"God, your throne will last forever and ever.
You will rule your kingdom with fairness.
9 You love right and hate evil,
so God has chosen you from among your friends;
he has set you apart with much joy." *Psalm 45:6–7*

10 God also says,

"Lord, in the beginning you made the earth,

1:6 [a] "**Let...him.**" These words are found in Deuteronomy 32:43 in the Septuagint, the Greek version of the Old Testament, and in a Hebrew copy among the Dead Sea Scrolls.

CONTEMPORARY ENGLISH VERSION

6 When God brings his first-born Son[b] into the world, he commands all of his angels to worship him.

7 And when God speaks about the angels, he says,

"I change my angels into wind
and my servants
into flaming fire."

8 But God says about his Son,

"You are God,
and you will rule
as King forever!
Your[c] royal power
brings about justice.
9 You loved justice
and hated evil,
and so I, your God,
have chosen you.
I appointed you
and made you happier
than any of your friends."

10 The Scriptures also say,

"In the beginning, Lord,

[b] 1.6 *first-born Son*: The first son born into a family had certain privileges that the other children did not have. In 12.23 "first-born" refers to God's special people. [c] 1.8 *Your*: Some manuscripts have "His."

NEW INTERNATIONAL VERSION

6And again, when God brings his firstborn into the world, he says,

"Let all God's angels worship him."[d]

7In speaking of the angels he says,

"He makes his angels winds,
his servants flames of fire."[e]

8But about the Son he says,

"Your throne, O God, will last for ever and ever,
and righteousness will be the scepter of your kingdom.
9You have loved righteousness and hated wickedness;
therefore God, your God, has set you above your companions
by anointing you with the oil of joy."[f]

10He also says,

"In the beginning, O Lord, you laid the foundations of the earth,

[d] 6 Deut. 32:43 (see Dead Sea Scrolls and Septuagint)
[e] 7 Psalm 104:4 [f] 9 Psalm 45:6,7

NEW LIVING TRANSLATION

And again God said,

"I will be his Father,
and he will be my Son."*

6And then, when he presented his honored* Son to the world, God said, "Let all the angels of God worship him."*
7God calls his angels

"messengers swift as the wind,
and servants made of flaming fire."*

8But to his Son he says,

"Your throne, O God, endures forever and ever.
Your royal power is expressed in righteousness.
9 You love what is right and hate what is wrong.
Therefore God, your God, has anointed you,
pouring out the oil of joy on you more than on anyone else."*

10And,

"Lord, in the beginning you laid the foundation of the earth,

1:5b 2 Sam 7:14. **1:6a** Greek *firstborn.* **1:6b** Deut 32:43.
1:7 Ps 104:4. **1:8-9** Ps 45:6-7.

NEW KING JAMES VERSION

6But when He again brings the firstborn into the world, He says:

"Let all the angels of God worship Him."[e]

7And of the angels He says:

*"Who makes His angels spirits
And His ministers a flame of fire."*[f]

8But to the Son *He says:*

*"Your throne, O God, is forever and ever;
A scepter of righteousness is the scepter of Your kingdom.*
9 *You have loved righteousness and hated lawlessness;
Therefore God, Your God, has anointed You
With the oil of gladness more than Your companions."*[g]

10And:

"You, Lord, in the beginning laid the foundation of the earth,

1:6 [e] Deuteronomy 32:43 (Septuagint, Dead Sea Scrolls); Psalm 97:7
1:7 [f] Psalm 104:4 1:9 [g] Psalm 45:6, 7

THE MESSAGE

honored Son to the world, he says, "All angels must worship him."
Regarding angels he says,

"The messengers are winds,
the servants are tongues of fire."

But he says to the Son,
"You're God, and on the throne for good;
your rule makes everything right.
You love it when things are right;
you hate it when things are wrong.
That is why God, your God,
poured fragrant oil on your head,
Marking you out as king,
far above your dear companions."

And again to the Son,
"You, Master, started it all, laid earth's foundations,

KING JAMES VERSION

dation of the earth; and the heavens are the works of thine hands:

11 They shall perish; but thou remainest; and they all shall wax old as doth a garment;

12 And as a vesture shalt thou fold them up, and they shall be changed: but thou art the same, and thy years shall not fail.

13 But to which of the angels said he at any time, Sit on my right hand, until I make thine enemies thy footstool?

14 Are they not all ministering spirits, sent forth to minister for them who shall be heirs of salvation?

2 Therefore we ought to give the more earnest heed to the things which we have heard, lest at any time we should let *them* slip.

2 For if the word spoken by angels was stedfast, and every transgression and disobedience received a just recompence of reward;

3 How shall we escape, if we neglect so great salvation;

NEW AMERICAN STANDARD BIBLE

AND THE HEAVENS ARE THE WORKS OF YOUR HANDS;
11 THEY WILL PERISH, BUT YOU REMAIN;
AND THEY ALL WILL BECOME OLD LIKE A GARMENT,
12 AND LIKE A MANTLE YOU WILL ROLL THEM UP;
LIKE A GARMENT THEY WILL ALSO BE CHANGED.
BUT YOU ARE THE SAME,
AND YOUR YEARS WILL NOT COME TO AN END."
13 But to which of the angels has He ever said,
"SIT AT MY RIGHT HAND,
UNTIL I MAKE YOUR ENEMIES
A FOOTSTOOL FOR YOUR FEET"?
14 Are they not all ministering spirits, sent out to render service for the sake of those who will inherit salvation?

Give Heed

2 For this reason we must pay much closer attention to what we have heard, so that we do not drift away *from it.*

2 For if the word spoken through angels proved unalterable, and every transgression and disobedience received a just penalty,

3 how will we escape if we neglect so great a salvation?

NEW CENTURY VERSION

and your hands made the skies.
11 They will be destroyed, but you will remain.
They will all wear out like clothes.
12 You will fold them like a coat.
And, like clothes, you will change them.
But you never change,
and your life will never end." *Psalm 102:25–27*
13 And God never said this to an angel:
"Sit by me at my right side
until I put your enemies under your control."[b]
Psalm 110:1

14 All the angels are spirits who serve God and are sent to help those who will receive salvation.

Our Salvation Is Great

2 So we must be more careful to follow what we were taught. Then we will not stray away from the truth.
2 The teaching God spoke through angels was shown to be true, and anyone who did not follow it or obey it received the punishment that was earned. 3 So surely we also will be punished if we ignore this great salvation. The Lord

1:13 [b] **until...control** Literally, "until I make your enemies a footstool for your feet."

CONTEMPORARY ENGLISH VERSION

you were the one
who laid the foundation
of the earth
and created the heavens.
11 They will all disappear
and wear out like clothes,
but you will last forever.
12 You will roll them up
like a robe
and change them
like a garment.
But you are always the same,
and you will live forever."
13 God never said to any
of the angels,
"Sit at my right side
until I make your enemies
into a footstool for you!"

14 Angels are merely spirits sent to serve people who are going to be saved.

This Great Way of Being Saved

2 We must give our full attention to what we were told,
so that we won't drift away. 2 The message spoken by
angels proved to be true, and all who disobeyed or rejected
it were punished as they deserved. 3 So if we refuse this
great way of being saved, how can we hope to escape? The

NEW INTERNATIONAL VERSION

and the heavens are the work of your hands.
11 They will perish, but you remain;
they will all wear out like a garment.
12 You will roll them up like a robe;
like a garment they will be changed.
But you remain the same,
and your years will never end."[g]

13 To which of the angels did God ever say,

"Sit at my right hand
until I make your enemies
a footstool for your feet"[h]?

14 Are not all angels ministering spirits sent to serve those who will inherit salvation?

Warning to Pay Attention

2 We must pay more careful attention, therefore, to what
we have heard, so that we do not drift away. 2 For if
the message spoken by angels was binding, and every vio-
lation and disobedience received its just punishment, 3 how
shall we escape if we ignore such a great salvation? This

[g] *12* Psalm 102:25–27 [h] *13* Psalm 110:1

NEW LIVING TRANSLATION

and the heavens are the work of your hands.
11 Even they will perish, but you remain forever.
They will wear out like old clothing.
12 You will roll them up like an old coat.
They will fade away like old clothing.
But you are always the same;
you will never grow old."*

13 And God never said to an angel, as he did to his Son,

"Sit in honor at my right hand
until I humble your enemies,
making them a footstool under your feet."*

14 But angels are only servants. They are spirits sent from God to care for those who will receive salvation.

A Warning against Drifting Away

2 So we must listen very carefully to the truth we have
heard, or we may drift away from it. 2 The message
God delivered through angels has always proved true, and
the people were punished for every violation of the law
and every act of disobedience. 3 What makes us think that
we can escape if we are indifferent to this great salvation

1:10-12 Ps 102:25-27. 1:13 Ps 110:1.

NEW KING JAMES VERSION

And the heavens are the work of Your hands.
11 *They will perish, but You remain;*
And they will all grow old like a garment;
12 *Like a cloak You will fold them up,*
And they will be changed.
But You are the same,
And Your years will not fail."[h]

13 But to which of the angels has He ever said:

"Sit at My right hand,
Till I make Your enemies Your footstool"?[i]

14 Are they not all ministering spirits sent forth to minister for those who will inherit salvation?

Do Not Neglect Salvation

2 Therefore we must give the more earnest heed to the
things we have heard, lest we drift away. 2 For if the
word spoken through angels proved steadfast, and every
transgression and disobedience received a just reward,
3 how shall we escape if we neglect so great a salvation,

1:12 [h] Psalm 102:25–27 1:13 [i] Psalm 110:1

THE MESSAGE

then crafted the stars in the sky.
Earth and sky will wear out, but not you;
they become threadbare like an old coat;
You'll fold them up like a worn-out cloak,
and lay them away on the shelf.
But you'll stay the same, year after year;
you'll never fade, you'll never wear out."

And did he ever say anything like this to an angel?
"Sit alongside me here on my throne
Until I make your enemies a stool for your feet."

Isn't it obvious that all angels are sent to help out with those lined up to receive salvation?

2 It's crucial that we keep a firm grip on what we've heard so that we don't drift off. If the old message delivered by the angels was valid and nobody got away with anything, do you think we can risk neglecting this latest message, this magnificent salvation? First of all, it

KING JAMES VERSION

which at the first began to be spoken by the Lord, and was confirmed unto us by them that heard *him*;

4 God also bearing *them* witness, both with signs and wonders, and with divers miracles, and gifts of the Holy Ghost, according to his own will?

5 ¶ For unto the angels hath he not put in subjection the world to come, whereof we speak.

6 But one in a certain place testified, saying, What is man, that thou art mindful of him? or the son of man, that thou visitest him?

7 Thou madest him a little lower than the angels; thou crownedst him with glory and honour, and didst set him over the works of thy hands:

8 Thou hast put all things in subjection under his feet. For in that he put all in subjection under him, he left nothing *that is* not put under him. But now we see not yet all things put under him.

9 But we see Jesus, who was made a little lower than the angels for the suffering of death, crowned with glory

NEW AMERICAN STANDARD BIBLE

After it was at the first spoken through the Lord, it was confirmed to us by those who heard,

4 God also testifying with them, both by signs and wonders and by various miracles and by gifts of the Holy Spirit according to His own will.

Earth Subject to Man

5 For He did not subject to angels the world to come, concerning which we are speaking.

6 But one has testified somewhere, saying,

"WHAT IS MAN, THAT YOU REMEMBER HIM?
OR THE SON OF MAN, THAT YOU ARE CONCERNED ABOUT HIM?
7 "YOU HAVE MADE HIM FOR A LITTLE WHILE LOWER THAN THE ANGELS;
YOU HAVE CROWNED HIM WITH GLORY AND HONOR,
[1]AND HAVE APPOINTED HIM OVER THE WORKS OF YOUR HANDS;
8 YOU HAVE PUT ALL THINGS IN SUBJECTION UNDER HIS FEET."

For in subjecting all things to him, He left nothing that is not subject to him. But now we do not yet see all things subjected to him.

Jesus Briefly Humbled

9 But we do see Him who was made for a little while lower than the angels, *namely,* Jesus, because of the suffer-

2:7 [1] Two early mss do not contain *And...hands*

NEW CENTURY VERSION

himself first told about this salvation, and it was proven
true to us by those who heard him. 4God also proved it by
using wonders, great signs, many kinds of miracles, and
by giving people gifts through the Holy Spirit, just as he
wanted.

Christ Became like Humans

5God did not choose angels to be the rulers of the new
world that was coming, which is what we have been talk-
ing about. 6It is written in the Scriptures,

"Why are people important to you?
Why do you take care of human beings?
7You made them a little lower than the angels
and crowned them with glory and honor.
8 You put all things under their control." *Psalm 8:4–6*

When God put everything under their control, there was
nothing left that they did not rule. Still, we do not yet see
them ruling over everything. 9But we see Jesus, who for a
short time was made lower than the angels. And now he is

CONTEMPORARY ENGLISH VERSION

Lord himself was the first to tell about it, and people who
heard the message proved to us that it was true. 4God him-
self showed that his message was true by working all
kinds of powerful miracles and wonders. He also gave his
Holy Spirit to anyone he chose to.

The One Who Leads Us To Be Saved

5We know that God did not put the future world under
the power of angels. 6Somewhere in the Scriptures some-
one says to God,

"What makes you care
about us humans?
Why are you concerned
for weaklings such as we?
7You made us lower
than the angels
for a while.
Yet you have crowned us
with glory and honor.[a]
8And you have put everything
under our power!"

God has put everything under our power and has not left
anything out of our power. But we still don't see it all under
our power. 9What we do see is Jesus, who for a little while
was made lower than the angels. Because of God's wonder-

[a] 2.7 *and honor*: Some manuscripts add "and you have placed us in charge of all you created."

NEW INTERNATIONAL VERSION

salvation, which was first announced by the Lord, was con-
firmed to us by those who heard him. 4God also testified to
it by signs, wonders and various miracles, and gifts of the
Holy Spirit distributed according to his will.

Jesus Made Like His Brothers

5It is not to angels that he has subjected the world to
come, about which we are speaking. 6But there is a place
where someone has testified:

"What is man that you are mindful of him,
the son of man that you care for him?
7 You made him a little[a] lower than the angels;
you crowned him with glory and honor
8 and put everything under his feet."[b]

In putting everything under him, God left nothing that is
not subject to him. Yet at present we do not see everything
subject to him. 9But we see Jesus, who was made a little
lower than the angels, now crowned with glory and honor

[a] 7 Or *him for a little while*; also in verse 9 [b] 8 Psalm 8:4–6

NEW LIVING TRANSLATION

that was announced by the Lord Jesus himself? It was
passed on* to us by those who heard him speak, 4and God
verified the message by signs and wonders and various
miracles and by giving gifts of the Holy Spirit whenever he
chose to do so.

Jesus, the Man

5And furthermore, the future world we are talking about
will not be controlled by angels. 6For somewhere in the
Scriptures it says,

"What is man that you should think of him,
and the son of man* that you should care for him?
7 For a little while you made him lower than the angels,
and you crowned him with glory and honor.*
8 You gave him authority over all things."*

Now when it says "all things," it means nothing is left out.
But we have not yet seen all of this happen. 9What we do
see is Jesus, who "for a little while was made lower than
the angels" and now is "crowned with glory and honor"

2:3 Or *and confirmed.* **2:6** Or *Son of Man.* **2:7** Some manuscripts add *You put him in charge of everything you made.* **2:6-8** Ps 8:4-6.

NEW KING JAMES VERSION

which at the first began to be spoken by the Lord, and was
confirmed to us by those who heard *Him,* 4God also bear-
ing witness both with signs and wonders, with various
miracles, and gifts of the Holy Spirit, according to His own
will?

The Son Made Lower than Angels

5For He has not put the world to come, of which we
speak, in subjection to angels. 6But one testified in a cer-
tain place, saying:

"*What is man that You are mindful of him,*
Or the son of man that You take care of him?
7 *You have made him a little lower than the angels;*
You have crowned him with glory and honor,[a]
And set him over the works of Your hands.
8 *You have put all things in subjection under his*
feet."[b]

For in that He put all in subjection under him, He left
nothing *that is* not put under him. But now we do not yet
see all things put under him. 9But we see Jesus, who was
made a little lower than the angels, for the suffering of

2:7 [a] NU-Text and M-Text omit the rest of verse 7. 2:8 [b] Psalm 8:4–6

THE MESSAGE

was delivered in person by the Master, then accurately
passed on to us by those who heard it from him. All the
while God was validating it with gifts through the Holy
Spirit, all sorts of signs and miracles, as he saw fit.

The Salvation Pioneer

God didn't put angels in charge of this business of sal-
vation that we're dealing with here. It says in Scripture,

"What is man and woman that you bother with them;
why take a second look their way?
You made them not quite as high as angels,
bright with Eden's dawn light;
Then you put them in charge
of your entire handcrafted world."

When God put them in charge of everything, nothing was
excluded. But we don't see it yet, don't see everything under
human jurisdiction. What we do see is Jesus, made "not
quite as high as angels," and then, through the experience

KING JAMES VERSION

and honour; that he by the grace of God should taste death
for every man.
10 ¶ For it became him, for whom *are* all things, and by
whom *are* all things, in bringing many sons unto glory, to
make the captain of their salvation perfect through suffer-
ings.
11 For both he that sanctifieth and they who are sancti-
fied *are* all of one: for which cause he is not ashamed to
call them brethren,
12 Saying, I will declare thy name unto my brethren, in
the midst of the church will I sing praise unto thee.
13 And again, I will put my trust in him. And again,
Behold I and the children which God hath given me.
14 ¶ Forasmuch then as the children are partakers of
flesh and blood, he also himself likewise took part of the
same; that through death he might destroy him that had
the power of death, that is, the devil;
15 And deliver them who through fear of death were all
their lifetime subject to bondage.

NEW AMERICAN STANDARD BIBLE

ing of death crowned with glory and honor, so that by the
grace of God He might taste death for everyone.
10 For it was fitting for Him, for whom are all things,
and through whom are all things, in bringing many sons
to glory, to perfect the author of their salvation through
sufferings.
11 For both He who sanctifies and those who are sancti-
fied are all from one *Father;* for which reason He is not
ashamed to call them brethren,
12 saying,

"I WILL PROCLAIM YOUR NAME TO MY BRETHREN,
IN THE MIDST OF THE CONGREGATION I WILL SING YOUR
PRAISE."

13 And again,

"I WILL PUT MY TRUST IN HIM."

And again,

"BEHOLD, I AND THE CHILDREN WHOM GOD HAS GIVEN ME."

14 Therefore, since the children share in flesh and
blood, He Himself likewise also partook of the same, that
through death He might render powerless him who had the
power of death, that is, the devil,
15 and might free those who through fear of death were
subject to slavery all their lives.

NEW CENTURY VERSION

wearing a crown of glory and honor because he suffered
and died. And by God's grace, he died for everyone.
10God is the One who made all things, and all things are
for his glory. He wanted to have many children share his
glory, so he made the One who leads people to salvation
perfect through suffering.
11Jesus, who makes people holy, and those who are
made holy are from the same family. So he is not ashamed
to call them his brothers and sisters.[a] 12He says,

"Then, I will tell my fellow Israelites about you;
I will praise you in the public meeting." *Psalm 22:22*

13He also says,

"I will trust in God." *Isaiah 8:17*

And he also says,

"I am here, and with me are the children God has given
me." *Isaiah 8:18*

14Since these children are people with physical bodies,
Jesus himself became like them. He did this so that, by
dying, he could destroy the one who has the power of
death—the devil— 15and free those who were like slaves
all their lives because of their fear of death. 16Clearly, it is

2:11 [a] **brothers and sisters** Although the Greek text says "brothers" here and throughout this book, the writer's words were meant for the entire church, including men and women.

CONTEMPORARY ENGLISH VERSION

ful kindness, Jesus died for everyone. And now that Jesus
has suffered and died, he is crowned with glory and honor!
10Everything belongs to God, and all things were created
by his power. So God did the right thing when he made
Jesus perfect by suffering, as Jesus led many of God's chil-
dren to be saved and to share in his glory. 11Jesus and the
people he makes holy all belong to the same family. That
is why he isn't ashamed to call them his brothers and sis-
ters. 12He even said to God,

"I will tell them your name
and sing your praises
when they come together
to worship."

13He also said,

"I will trust God."

Then he said,

"Here I am with the children
God has given me."

14We are people of flesh and blood. That is why Jesus
became one of us. He died to destroy the devil, who had
power over death. 15But he also died to rescue all of us
who live each day in fear of dying. 16Jesus clearly did not

NEW INTERNATIONAL VERSION

because he suffered death, so that by the grace of God he might taste death for everyone.

10 In bringing many sons to glory, it was fitting that God, for whom and through whom everything exists, should make the author of their salvation perfect through suffering. 11 Both the one who makes men holy and those who are made holy are of the same family. So Jesus is not ashamed to call them brothers. 12 He says,

"I will declare your name to my brothers;
in the presence of the congregation I will sing your praises."[c]

13 And again,

"I will put my trust in him."[d]

And again he says,

"Here am I, and the children God has given me."[e]

14 Since the children have flesh and blood, he too shared in their humanity so that by his death he might destroy him who holds the power of death—that is, the devil—15 and free those who all their lives were held in slavery by

[c] *12* Psalm 22:22 [d] *13* Isaiah 8:17 [e] *13* Isaiah 8:18

NEW LIVING TRANSLATION

because he suffered death for us. Yes, by God's grace, Jesus tasted death for everyone in all the world. 10 And it was only right that God—who made everything and for whom everything was made—should bring his many children into glory. Through the suffering of Jesus, God made him a perfect leader, one fit to bring them into their salvation.

11 So now Jesus and the ones he makes holy have the same Father. That is why Jesus is not ashamed to call them his brothers and sisters.* 12 For he said to God,

"I will declare the wonder of your name to my brothers and sisters.*
I will praise you among all your people."

13 He also said, "I will put my trust in him." And in the same context he said, "Here I am—together with the children God has given me."*

14 Because God's children are human beings—made of flesh and blood—Jesus also became flesh and blood by being born in human form. For only as a human being could he die, and only by dying could he break the power of the Devil, who had the power of death. 15 Only in this way could he deliver those who have lived all their lives as slaves to the fear of dying.

2:11 Greek *his brothers;* also in 2:17. 2:12 Greek *my brothers.* Ps 22:22. 2:13 Isa 8:17-18.

NEW KING JAMES VERSION

death crowned with glory and honor, that He, by the grace of God, might taste death for everyone.

Bringing Many Sons to Glory

10 For it was fitting for Him, for whom *are* all things and by whom *are* all things, in bringing many sons to glory, to make the captain of their salvation perfect through sufferings. 11 For both He who sanctifies and those who are being sanctified *are* all of one, for which reason He is not ashamed to call them brethren, 12 saying:

"I will declare Your name to My brethren;
In the midst of the assembly I will sing praise to You."[c]

13 And again:

"I will put My trust in Him."[d]

And again:

"Here am I and the children whom God has given Me."[e]

14 Inasmuch then as the children have partaken of flesh and blood, He Himself likewise shared in the same, that through death He might destroy him who had the power of death, that is, the devil, 15 and release those who through fear of death were all their lifetime subject to bondage.

2:12 [c] Psalm 22:22 2:13 [d] 2 Samuel 22:3; Isaiah 8:17
[e] Isaiah 8:18

THE MESSAGE

of death, crowned so much higher than any angel, with a glory "bright with Eden's dawn light." In that death, by God's grace, he fully experienced death in every person's place.

It makes good sense that the God who got everything started and keeps everything going now completes the work by making the Salvation Pioneer perfect through suffering as he leads all these people to glory. Since the One who saves and those who are saved have a common origin, Jesus doesn't hesitate to treat them as family, saying,

"I'll tell my good friends, my brothers and sisters,
all I know about you;
I'll join them in worship and praise to you."

Again, he puts himself in the same family circle when he says,

"Even *I* live by placing my trust in God."

And yet again,

"I'm here with the children God gave me."

Since the children are made of flesh and blood, it's logical that the Savior took on flesh and blood in order to rescue them by his death. By embracing death, taking it into himself, he destroyed the Devil's hold on death and freed all who cower through life, scared to death of death.

KING JAMES VERSION

16 For verily he took not on *him the nature of* angels; but he took on *him* the seed of Abraham.

17 Wherefore in all things it behoved him to be made like unto *his* brethren, that he might be a merciful and faithful high priest in things *pertaining* to God, to make reconciliation for the sins of the people.

18 For in that he himself hath suffered being tempted, he is able to succour them that are tempted.

3 Wherefore, holy brethren, partakers of the heavenly calling, consider the Apostle and High Priest of our profession, Christ Jesus;

2 Who was faithful to him that appointed him, as also Moses *was faithful* in all his house.

3 For this *man* was counted worthy of more glory than Moses, inasmuch as he who hath builded the house hath more honour than the house.

4 For every house is builded by some *man*; but he that built all things *is* God.

5 And Moses verily *was* faithful in all his house, as a servant, for a testimony of those things which were to be spoken after;

6 But Christ as a son over his own house; whose house are we, if we hold fast the confidence and the rejoicing of the hope firm unto the end.

7 ¶ Wherefore (as the Holy Ghost saith, To day if ye will hear his voice,

NEW AMERICAN STANDARD BIBLE

16 For assuredly He does not give help to angels, but He gives help to the descendant of Abraham.

17 Therefore, He had to be made like His brethren in all things, so that He might become a merciful and faithful high priest in things pertaining to God, to make propitiation for the sins of the people.

18 For since He Himself was tempted in that which He has suffered, He is able to come to the aid of those who are tempted.

Jesus Our High Priest

3 Therefore, holy brethren, partakers of a heavenly calling, consider Jesus, the Apostle and High Priest of our confession;

2 He was faithful to Him who appointed Him, as Moses also was in all His house.

3 For He has been counted worthy of more glory than Moses, by just so much as the builder of the house has more honor than the house.

4 For every house is built by someone, but the builder of all things is God.

5 Now Moses was faithful in all His house as a servant, for a testimony of those things which were to be spoken later;

6 but Christ *was faithful* as a Son over His house—whose house we are, if we hold fast our confidence and the boast of our hope firm until the end.

7 Therefore, just as the Holy Spirit says,

"TODAY IF YOU HEAR HIS VOICE,

NEW CENTURY VERSION

not angels that Jesus helps, but the people who are from
Abraham.[b] 17For this reason Jesus had to be made like his
brothers in every way so he could be their merciful and
faithful high priest in service to God. Then Jesus could
bring forgiveness for their sins. 18And now he can help
those who are tempted, because he himself suffered and
was tempted.

Jesus Is Greater than Moses

3 So all of you holy brothers and sisters, who were
called by God, think about Jesus, who was sent to us
and is the high priest of our faith. 2Jesus was faithful to
God as Moses was in God's family. 3Jesus has more honor
than Moses, just as the builder of a house has more honor
than the house itself. 4Every house is built by someone,
but the builder of everything is God himself. 5Moses was
faithful in God's family as a servant, and he told what God
would say in the future. 6But Christ is faithful as a Son
over God's house. And we are God's house if we keep on
being very sure about our great hope.

We Must Continue to Follow God

7So it is as the Holy Spirit says:

"Today listen to what he says.

2:16 [b] **Abraham** Most respected ancestor of the Jews. Every Jew hoped to see Abraham.

CONTEMPORARY ENGLISH VERSION

come to help angels, but he did come to help Abraham's
descendants. 17He had to be one of us, so that he could
serve God as our merciful and faithful high priest and sac-
rifice himself for the forgiveness of our sins. 18And now
that Jesus has suffered and was tempted, he can help any-
one else who is tempted.

Jesus Is Greater than Moses

3 My friends, God has chosen you to be his holy people.
So think about Jesus, the one we call our apostle and
high priest! 2Jesus was faithful to God, who appointed
him, just as Moses was faithful in serving all of[a] God's
people. 3But Jesus deserves more honor than Moses, just
as the builder of a house deserves more honor than the
house. 4Of course, every house is built by someone, and
God is really the one who built everything.

5Moses was a faithful servant and told God's people
what would be said in the future. 6But Christ is the Son in
charge of God's people. And we are those people, if we
keep on being brave and don't lose hope.

A Rest for God's People

7It is just as the Holy Spirit says,

"If you hear God's voice today,

[a] **3.2** *all of*: Some manuscripts do not have these words.

NEW INTERNATIONAL VERSION

their fear of death. 16For surely it is not angels he helps,
but Abraham's descendants. 17For this reason he had to be
made like his brothers in every way, in order that he might
become a merciful and faithful high priest in service to
God, and that he might make atonement for[f] the sins of
the people. 18Because he himself suffered when he was
tempted, he is able to help those who are being tempted.

Jesus Greater Than Moses

3 Therefore, holy brothers, who share in the heavenly
calling, fix your thoughts on Jesus, the apostle and
high priest whom we confess. 2He was faithful to the one
who appointed him, just as Moses was faithful in all God's
house. 3Jesus has been found worthy of greater honor than
Moses, just as the builder of a house has greater honor
than the house itself. 4For every house is built by some-
one, but God is the builder of everything. 5Moses was
faithful as a servant in all God's house, testifying to what
would be said in the future. 6But Christ is faithful as a son
over God's house. And we are his house, if we hold on to
our courage and the hope of which we boast.

Warning Against Unbelief

7So, as the Holy Spirit says:

"Today, if you hear his voice,

[f] 17 Or *and that he might turn aside God's wrath, taking away*

NEW LIVING TRANSLATION

16We all know that Jesus came to help the descendants
of Abraham, not to help the angels. 17Therefore, it was
necessary for Jesus to be in every respect like us, his broth-
ers and sisters, so that he could be our merciful and faith-
ful High Priest before God. He then could offer a sacrifice
that would take away the sins of the people. 18Since he
himself has gone through suffering and temptation, he is
able to help us when we are being tempted.

Jesus Is Greater Than Moses

3 And so, dear brothers and sisters who belong to God*
and are bound for heaven, think about this Jesus
whom we declare to be God's Messenger and High Priest.
2For he was faithful to God, who appointed him, just as
Moses served faithfully and was entrusted with God's
entire house. 3But Jesus deserves far more glory than
Moses, just as a person who builds a fine house deserves
more praise than the house itself. 4For every house has a
builder, but God is the one who made everything.
5Moses was certainly faithful in God's house, but only
as a servant. His work was an illustration of the truths
God would reveal later. 6But Christ, the faithful Son, was
in charge of the entire household. And we are God's house-
hold, if we keep up our courage and remain confident in
our hope in Christ. 7That is why the Holy Spirit says,

"Today you must listen to his voice.

3:1 Greek *And so, holy brothers.*

NEW KING JAMES VERSION

16For indeed He does not give aid to angels, but He does
give aid to the seed of Abraham. 17Therefore, in all things
He had to be made like *His* brethren, that He might be a
merciful and faithful High Priest in things *pertaining* to
God, to make propitiation for the sins of the people. 18For
in that He Himself has suffered, being tempted, He is able
to aid those who are tempted.

The Son Was Faithful

3 Therefore, holy brethren, partakers of the heavenly
calling, consider the Apostle and High Priest of our
confession, Christ Jesus, 2who was faithful to Him who
appointed Him, as Moses also *was faithful* in all His
house. 3For this One has been counted worthy of more
glory than Moses, inasmuch as He who built the house has
more honor than the house. 4For every house is built by
someone, but He who built all things *is* God. 5And Moses
indeed *was* faithful in all His house as a servant, for a tes-
timony of those things which would be spoken *afterward,*
6but Christ as a Son over His own house, whose house we
are if we hold fast the confidence and the rejoicing of the
hope firm to the end.[a]

Be Faithful

7Therefore, as the Holy Spirit says:

"Today, if you will hear His voice,

3:6 [a] NU-Text omits *firm to the end.*

THE MESSAGE

It's obvious, of course, that he didn't go to all this trou-
ble for angels. It was for people like us, children of
Abraham. That's why he had to enter into every detail of
human life. Then, when he came before God as high priest
to get rid of the people's sins, he would have already expe-
rienced it all himself—all the pain, all the testing—and
would be able to help where help was needed.

The Centerpiece of All We Believe

3 So, my dear Christian friends, companions in follow-
ing this call to the heights, take a good hard look at
Jesus. He's the centerpiece of everything we believe, faith-
ful in everything God gave him to do. Moses was also
faithful, but Jesus gets far more honor. A builder is more
valuable than a building any day. Every house has a
builder, but the Builder behind them all is God. Moses did
a good job in God's house, but it was all servant work, get-
ting things ready for what was to come. Christ as Son is in
charge of the house.

Now, if we can only keep a firm grip on this bold confi-
dence, we're the house! That's why the Holy Spirit says,

"Today, please listen;

KING JAMES VERSION

8 Harden not your hearts, as in the provocation, in the day of temptation in the wilderness:

9 When your fathers tempted me, proved me, and saw my works forty years.

10 Wherefore I was grieved with that generation, and said, They do alway err in *their* heart; and they have not known my ways.

11 So I sware in my wrath, They shall not enter into my rest.)

12 Take heed, brethren, lest there be in any of you an evil heart of unbelief, in departing from the living God.

13 But exhort one another daily, while it is called To day; lest any of you be hardened through the deceitfulness of sin.

14 For we are made partakers of Christ, if we hold the beginning of our confidence stedfast unto the end;

15 While it is said, To day if ye will hear his voice,

NEW AMERICAN STANDARD BIBLE

8 Do not harden your hearts as when they provoked
Me,
As in the day of trial in the wilderness,
9 Where your fathers tried *Me* by testing *Me*,
And saw My works for forty years.
10 "Therefore I was angry with this generation,
And said, 'They always go astray in their heart,
And they did not know My ways';
11 As I swore in My wrath,
'They shall not enter My rest.' "

The Peril of Unbelief

12 Take care, brethren, that there not be in any one of you an evil, unbelieving heart that falls away from the living God.

13 But encourage one another day after day, as long as it is *still* called "Today," so that none of you will be hardened by the deceitfulness of sin.

14 For we have become partakers of Christ, if we hold fast the beginning of our assurance firm until the end,

15 while it is said,
"Today if you hear His voice,

NEW CENTURY VERSION

8 Do not be stubborn as in the past
when you turned against God,
when you tested God in the desert.
9 There your ancestors tried me and tested me
and saw the things I did for forty years.
10 I was angry with them.
I said, 'They are not loyal to me
and have not understood my ways.'
11 I was angry and made a promise,
'They will never enter my rest.' "[a] *Psalm 95:7–11*

12 So brothers and sisters, be careful that none of you
has an evil, unbelieving heart that will turn you away from
the living God.
13 But encourage each other every day while
it is "today."[b] Help each other so none of you will become
hardened because sin has tricked you.
14 We all share in
Christ if we keep till the end the sure faith we had in the
beginning.
15 This is what the Scripture says:
"Today listen to what he says.

3:11 [a] **rest** A place of rest God promised to give his people.
3:13 [b] **"today"** This word is taken from verse 7. It means that it is important to do these things now.

CONTEMPORARY ENGLISH VERSION

8 don't be stubborn!
Don't rebel like those people
who were tested
in the desert.
9 For forty years your ancestors
tested God and saw
the things he did.

10 "Then God got tired of them
and said,
'You people never
show good sense,
and you don't understand
what I want you to do.'
11 God became angry
and told the people,
'You will never enter
my place of rest!' "

12 My friends, watch out! Don't let evil thoughts or
doubts make any of you turn from the living God.
13 You
must encourage one another each day. And you must keep
on while there is still a time that can be called "today." If
you don't, then sin may fool some of you and make you
stubborn.
14 We were sure about Christ when we first
became his people. So let's hold tightly to our faith until
the end.
15 The Scriptures say,

"If you hear his voice today,

NEW INTERNATIONAL VERSION

8 do not harden your hearts
as you did in the rebellion,
during the time of testing in the desert,
9 where your fathers tested and tried me
and for forty years saw what I did.
10 That is why I was angry with that generation,
and I said, 'Their hearts are always going astray,
and they have not known my ways.'
11 So I declared on oath in my anger,
'They shall never enter my rest.' "[a]

12 See to it, brothers, that none of you has a sinful, unbe-
lieving heart that turns away from the living God. 13 But
encourage one another daily, as long as it is called Today,
so that none of you may be hardened by sin's deceitful-
ness. 14 We have come to share in Christ if we hold firmly
till the end the confidence we had at first. 15 As has just
been said:

"Today, if you hear his voice,

[a] *11* Psalm 95:7–11

NEW LIVING TRANSLATION

8 Don't harden your hearts against him
as Israel did when they rebelled,
when they tested God's patience in the wilderness.
9 There your ancestors tried my patience,
even though they saw my miracles for forty years.
10 So I was angry with them, and I said,
'Their hearts always turn away from me.
They refuse to do what I tell them.'
11 So in my anger I made a vow:
'They will never enter my place of rest.' "*

12 Be careful then, dear brothers and sisters.* Make sure
that your own hearts are not evil and unbelieving, turning
you away from the living God. 13 You must warn each other
every day, as long as it is called "today," so that none of
you will be deceived by sin and hardened against God.
14 For if we are faithful to the end, trusting God just as
firmly as when we first believed, we will share in all that
belongs to Christ. 15 But never forget the warning:

"Today you must listen to his voice.

3:7-11 Ps 95:7-11. 3:12 Greek *brothers.*

NEW KING JAMES VERSION

8 *Do not harden your hearts as in the rebellion,*
In the day of trial in the wilderness,
9 *Where your fathers tested Me, tried Me,*
And saw My works forty years.
10 *Therefore I was angry with that generation,*
And said, 'They always go astray in their heart,
And they have not known My ways.'
11 *So I swore in My wrath,*
'They shall not enter My rest.' "[b]

12 Beware, brethren, lest there be in any of you an evil
heart of unbelief in departing from the living God; 13 but
exhort one another daily, while it is called *"Today,"* lest
any of you be hardened through the deceitfulness of sin.
14 For we have become partakers of Christ if we hold the
beginning of our confidence steadfast to the end, 15 while it
is said:

"Today, if you will hear His voice,

3:11 [b] Psalm 95:7–11

THE MESSAGE

don't turn a deaf ear as in 'the bitter uprising,'
that time of wilderness testing!
Even though they watched me at work for forty years,
your ancestors refused to let me do it my way;
over and over they tried my patience.
And I was provoked, oh, so provoked!
I said, 'They'll never keep their minds on God;
they refuse to walk down my road.'
Exasperated, I vowed,
'They'll never get where they're going,
never be able to sit down and rest.' "

So watch your step, friends. Make sure there's no evil unbelief lying around that will trip you up and throw you off course, diverting you from the living God. For as long as it's still God's Today, keep each other on your toes so sin doesn't slow down your reflexes. If we can only keep our grip on the sure thing we started out with, we're in this with Christ for the long haul.

These words keep ringing in our ears:

"Today, please listen;

KING JAMES VERSION

harden not your hearts, as in the provocation.

16 For some, when they had heard, did provoke: howbeit not all that came out of Egypt by Moses.

17 But with whom was he grieved forty years? *was it* not with them that had sinned, whose carcases fell in the wilderness?

18 And to whom sware he that they should not enter into his rest, but to them that believed not?

19 So we see that they could not enter in because of unbelief.

4 Let us therefore fear, lest, a promise being left *us* of entering into his rest, any of you should seem to come short of it.

2 For unto us was the gospel preached, as well as unto them: but the word preached did not profit them, not being mixed with faith in them that heard *it*.

3 For we which have believed do enter into rest, as he said, As I have sworn in my wrath, if they shall enter into my rest: although the works were finished from the foundation of the world.

4 For he spake in a certain place of the seventh *day* on this wise, And God did rest the seventh day from all his works.

NEW AMERICAN STANDARD BIBLE

DO NOT HARDEN YOUR HEARTS, AS WHEN THEY PROVOKED
ME."

16 For who provoked *Him* when they had heard? Indeed, did not all those who came out of Egypt *led* by Moses?

17 And with whom was He angry for forty years? Was it not with those who sinned, whose bodies fell in the wilderness?

18 And to whom did He swear that they would not enter His rest, but to those who were disobedient?

19 *So* we see that they were not able to enter because of unbelief.

The Believer's Rest

4 Therefore, let us fear if, while a promise remains of entering His rest, any one of you may seem to have come short of it.

2 For indeed we have had good news preached to us, just as they also; but the word they heard did not profit them, because it was not united by faith in those who heard.

3 For we who have believed enter that rest, just as He has said,

"AS I SWORE IN MY WRATH,
THEY SHALL NOT ENTER MY REST,"

although His works were finished from the foundation of the world.

4 For He has said somewhere concerning the seventh *day:* "AND GOD RESTED ON THE SEVENTH DAY FROM ALL HIS WORKS";

NEW CENTURY VERSION

Do not be stubborn as in the past
when you turned against God." *Psalm 95:7–8*

16 Who heard God's voice and was against him? It was all
those people Moses led out of Egypt. 17 And with whom
was God angry for forty years? He was angry with those
who sinned, who died in the desert. 18 And to whom was
God talking when he promised that they would never enter
his rest? He was talking to those who did not obey him.
19 So we see they were not allowed to enter and have God's
rest, because they did not believe.

4 Now, since God has left us the promise that we may
enter his rest, let us be very careful so none of you
will fail to enter. 2 The Good News was preached to us just
as it was to them. But the teaching they heard did not help
them, because they heard it but did not accept it with
faith. 3 We who have believed are able to enter and have
God's rest. As God has said,

"I was angry and made a promise,
'They will never enter my rest.' " *Psalm 95:11*

But God's work was finished from the time he made the
world. 4 In the Scriptures he talked about the seventh day
of the week: "And on the seventh day God rested from all

CONTEMPORARY ENGLISH VERSION

don't be stubborn
like those who rebelled."

16 Who were those people that heard God's voice and
rebelled? Weren't they the same ones that came out of
Egypt with Moses? 17 Who were the people that made God
angry for forty years? Weren't they the ones that sinned
and died in the desert? 18 And who did God say would
never enter his place of rest? Weren't they the ones that
disobeyed him? 19 We see that those people did not enter
the place of rest because they did not have faith.

4 The promise to enter the place of rest is still good, and
we must take care that none of you miss out. 2 We
have heard the message, just as they did. But they failed
to believe what they heard, and the message did not do
them any good. 3 Only people who have faith will enter the
place of rest. It is just as the Scriptures say,

"God became angry
and told the people,
'You will never enter
my place of rest!' "

God said this, even though everything has been ready
from the time of creation. 4 In fact, somewhere the
Scriptures say that by the seventh day, God had finished
his work, and so he rested. 5 We also read that he later

NEW INTERNATIONAL VERSION

do not harden your hearts
as you did in the rebellion."[b]

16 Who were they who heard and rebelled? Were they not
all those Moses led out of Egypt? 17 And with whom was he
angry for forty years? Was it not with those who sinned,
whose bodies fell in the desert? 18 And to whom did God
swear that they would never enter his rest if not to those
who disobeyed[c]? 19 So we see that they were not able to
enter, because of their unbelief.

A Sabbath-Rest for the People of God

4 Therefore, since the promise of entering his rest still
stands, let us be careful that none of you be found to
have fallen short of it. 2 For we also have had the gospel
preached to us, just as they did; but the message they
heard was of no value to them, because those who heard
did not combine it with faith.[a] 3 Now we who have believed
enter that rest, just as God has said,

"So I declared on oath in my anger,
'They shall never enter my rest.' "[b]

And yet his work has been finished since the creation of
the world. 4 For somewhere he has spoken about the sev-
enth day in these words: "And on the seventh day God

[b] *15* Psalm 95:7,8 [c] *18* Or *disbelieved* [a] *2* Many manuscripts *because they did not share in the faith of those who obeyed*
[b] *3* Psalm 95:11; also in verse 5

NEW LIVING TRANSLATION

Don't harden your hearts against him
as Israel did when they rebelled."*

16 And who were those people who rebelled against God,
even though they heard his voice? Weren't they the ones
Moses led out of Egypt? 17 And who made God angry for forty
years? Wasn't it the people who sinned, whose bodies fell in
the wilderness? 18 And to whom was God speaking when he
vowed that they would never enter his place of rest? He was
speaking to those who disobeyed him. 19 So we see that they
were not allowed to enter his rest because of their unbelief.

Promised Rest for God's People

4 God's promise of entering his place of rest still stands,
so we ought to tremble with fear that some of you might
fail to get there. 2 For this Good News—that God has prepared
a place of rest—has been announced to us just as it was to
them. But it did them no good because they didn't believe
what God told them.* 3 For only we who believe can enter his
place of rest. As for those who didn't believe, God said,

"In my anger I made a vow:
'They will never enter my place of rest,' "*

even though his place of rest has been ready since he made
the world. 4 We know it is ready because the Scriptures
mention the seventh day, saying, "On the seventh day God

3:15 Ps 95:7-8. 4:2 Some manuscripts read *they didn't share the faith of those who listened [to God].* 4:3 Ps 95:11.

NEW KING JAMES VERSION

Do not harden your hearts as in the rebellion."[c]

Failure of the Wilderness Wanderers

16 For who, having heard, rebelled? Indeed, *was it* not all
who came out of Egypt, *led* by Moses? 17 Now with whom
was He angry forty years? *Was it* not with those who
sinned, whose corpses fell in the wilderness? 18 And to
whom did He swear that they would not enter His rest, but
to those who did not obey? 19 So we see that they could not
enter in because of unbelief.

The Promise of Rest

4 Therefore, since a promise remains of entering His
rest, let us fear lest any of you seem to have come
short of it. 2 For indeed the gospel was preached to us as
well as to them; but the word which they heard did not
profit them,[a] not being mixed with faith in those who
heard *it*. 3 For we who have believed do enter that rest, as
He has said:

"So I swore in My wrath,
'They shall not enter My rest,' "[b]

although the works were finished from the foundation of
the world. 4 For He has spoken in a certain place of the sev-
enth *day* in this way: *"And God rested on the seventh day*

3:15 [c] Psalm 95:7, 8 4:2 [a] NU-Text and M-Text read *profit them, since they were not united by faith with those who heeded it.*
4:3 [b] Psalm 95:11

THE MESSAGE

don't turn a deaf ear as in the bitter uprising."

For who were the people who turned a deaf ear? Weren't they the very ones Moses led out of Egypt? And who was God provoked with for forty years? Wasn't it those who turned a deaf ear and ended up corpses in the wilderness? And when he swore that they'd never get where they were going, wasn't he talking to the ones who turned a deaf ear? They never got there because they never listened, never believed.

When the Promises Are Mixed With Faith

4 For as long, then, as that promise of resting in him pulls us on to God's goal for us, we need to be careful that we're not disqualified. We received the same promises as those people in the wilderness, but the promises didn't do them a bit of good because they didn't receive the promises with faith. If we believe, though, we'll experience that state of resting. But not if we don't have faith. Remember that God said,

"Exasperated, I vowed,
'They'll never get where they're going,
never be able to sit down and rest.'"

God made that vow, even though he'd finished *his* part before the foundation of the world. Somewhere it's written, "God rested the seventh day, having completed his work,"

KING JAMES VERSION

5 And in this *place* again, If they shall enter into my rest.

6 Seeing therefore it remaineth that some must enter therein, and they to whom it was first preached entered not in because of unbelief:

7 Again, he limiteth a certain day, saying in David, To day, after so long a time; as it is said, To day if ye will hear his voice, harden not your hearts.

8 For if Jesus had given them rest, then would he not afterward have spoken of another day.

9 There remaineth therefore a rest to the people of God.

10 For he that is entered into his rest, he also hath ceased from his own works, as God *did* from his.

11 ¶ Let us labour therefore to enter into that rest, lest any man fall after the same example of unbelief.

12 For the word of God *is* quick, and powerful, and sharper than any twoedged sword, piercing even to the dividing asunder of soul and spirit, and of the joints and marrow, and *is* a discerner of the thoughts and intents of the heart.

13 Neither is there any creature that is not manifest in his sight: but all things *are* naked and opened unto the eyes of him with whom we have to do.

NEW AMERICAN STANDARD BIBLE

5 and again in this *passage*, "THEY SHALL NOT ENTER MY REST."

6 Therefore, since it remains for some to enter it, and those who formerly had good news preached to them failed to enter because of disobedience,

7 He again fixes a certain day, "Today," saying through David after so long a time just as has been said before,

"TODAY IF YOU HEAR HIS VOICE,
DO NOT HARDEN YOUR HEARTS."

8 For if Joshua had given them rest, He would not have spoken of another day after that.

9 So there remains a Sabbath rest for the people of God.

10 For the one who has entered His rest has himself also rested from his works, as God did from His.

11 Therefore let us be diligent to enter that rest, so that no one will fall, through *following* the same example of disobedience.

12 For the word of God is living and active and sharper than any two-edged sword, and piercing as far as the division of soul and spirit, of both joints and marrow, and able to judge the thoughts and intentions of the heart.

13 And there is no creature hidden from His sight, but all things are open and laid bare to the eyes of Him with whom we have to do.

NEW CENTURY VERSION

his works."[a] 5And again in the Scripture God said, "They will never enter my rest."

6It is still true that some people will enter God's rest, but those who first heard the way to be saved did not enter, because they did not obey. 7So God planned another day, called "today." He spoke about that day through David a long time later in the same Scripture used before:

"Today listen to what he says.
Do not be stubborn." *Psalm 95:7–8*

8We know that Joshua[b] did not lead the people into that rest, because God spoke later about another day. 9This shows that the rest[c] for God's people is still coming. 10Anyone who enters God's rest will rest from his work as God did. 11Let us try as hard as we can to enter God's rest so that no one will fail by following the example of those who refused to obey.

12God's word is alive and working and is sharper than a double-edged sword. It cuts all the way into us, where the soul and the spirit are joined, to the center of our joints and bones. And it judges the thoughts and feelings in our hearts. 13Nothing in all the world can be hidden from God. Everything is clear and lies open before him, and to him we must explain the way we have lived.

4:4 [a] **"And...works."** Quotation from Genesis 2:2. **4:8** [b] **Joshua** After Moses died, Joshua became leader of the Jewish people and led them into the land that God promised to give them. **4:9** [c] **rest** Literally, "sabbath rest," meaning a sharing in the rest that God began after he created the world.

CONTEMPORARY ENGLISH VERSION

said, "You people will never enter my place of rest!" 6This means that the promise to enter is still good, because those who first heard about it disobeyed and did not enter. 7Much later God told David to make the promise again, just as I have already said,

"If you hear his voice today,
don't be stubborn!"

8If Joshua had really given the people rest, there would not be any need for God to talk about another day of rest. 9But God has promised us a Sabbath when we will rest, even though it has not yet come. 10On that day God's people will rest from their work, just as God rested from his work.

11We should do our best to enter that place of rest, so that none of us will disobey and miss going there, as they did. 12What God has said isn't only alive and active! It is sharper than any double-edged sword. His word can cut through our spirits and souls and through our joints and marrow, until it discovers the desires and thoughts of our hearts. 13Nothing is hidden from God! He sees through everything, and we will have to tell him the truth.

NEW INTERNATIONAL VERSION

rested from all his work."[c] [5]And again in the passage above he says, "They shall never enter my rest."

[6]It still remains that some will enter that rest, and those who formerly had the gospel preached to them did not go in, because of their disobedience. [7]Therefore God again set a certain day, calling it Today, when a long time later he spoke through David, as was said before:

"Today, if you hear his voice,
do not harden your hearts."[d]

[8]For if Joshua had given them rest, God would not have spoken later about another day. [9]There remains, then, a Sabbath-rest for the people of God; [10]for anyone who enters God's rest also rests from his own work, just as God did from his. [11]Let us, therefore, make every effort to enter that rest, so that no one will fall by following their example of disobedience.

[12]For the word of God is living and active. Sharper than any double-edged sword, it penetrates even to dividing soul and spirit, joints and marrow; it judges the thoughts and attitudes of the heart. [13]Nothing in all creation is hidden from God's sight. Everything is uncovered and laid bare before the eyes of him to whom we must give account.

[c] *4* Gen. 2:2 [d] *7* Psalm 95:7,8

NEW LIVING TRANSLATION

rested from all his work."* [5]But in the other passage God said, "They will never enter my place of rest."* [6]So God's rest is there for people to enter. But those who formerly heard the Good News failed to enter because they disobeyed God. [7]So God set another time for entering his place of rest, and that time is today. God announced this through David a long time later in the words already quoted:

"Today you must listen to his voice.
Don't harden your hearts against him."*

[8]This new place of rest was not the land of Canaan, where Joshua led them. If it had been, God would not have spoken later about another day of rest. [9]So there is a special rest* still waiting for the people of God. [10]For all who enter into God's rest will find rest from their labors, just as God rested after creating the world. [11]Let us do our best to enter that place of rest. For anyone who disobeys God, as the people of Israel did, will fall.

[12]For the word of God is full of living power. It is sharper than the sharpest knife, cutting deep into our innermost thoughts and desires. It exposes us for what we really are. [13]Nothing in all creation can hide from him. Everything is naked and exposed before his eyes. This is the God to whom we must explain all that we have done.

4:4 Gen 2:2. **4:5** Ps 95:11. **4:7** Ps 95:7-8. **4:9** Or *Sabbath rest.*

NEW KING JAMES VERSION

from all His works";[c] [5]and again in this *place: "They shall not enter My rest."*[d]

[6]Since therefore it remains that some *must* enter it, and those to whom it was first preached did not enter because of disobedience, [7]again He designates a certain day, saying in David, *"Today,"* after such a long time, as it has been said:

"Today, if you will hear His voice,
Do not harden your hearts."[e]

[8]For if Joshua had given them rest, then He would not afterward have spoken of another day. [9]There remains therefore a rest for the people of God. [10]For he who has entered His rest has himself also ceased from his works as God *did* from His.

The Word Discovers Our Condition

[11]Let us therefore be diligent to enter that rest, lest anyone fall according to the same example of disobedience. [12]For the word of God *is* living and powerful, and sharper than any two-edged sword, piercing even to the division of soul and spirit, and of joints and marrow, and is a discerner of the thoughts and intents of the heart. [13]And there is no creature hidden from His sight, but all things *are* naked and open to the eyes of Him to whom we *must give* account.

4:4 [c] Genesis 2:2 **4:5** [d] Psalm 95:11 **4:7** [e] Psalm 95:7, 8

THE MESSAGE

but in this other text he says, "They'll never be able to sit down and rest." So this promise has not yet been fulfilled. Those earlier ones never did get to the place of rest because they were disobedient. God keeps renewing the promise and setting the date as *today*, just as he did in David's psalm, centuries later than the original invitation:

"Today, please listen,
don't turn a deaf ear . . ."

And so this is still a live promise. It wasn't canceled at the time of Joshua; otherwise, God wouldn't keep renewing the appointment for "today." The promise of "arrival" and "rest" is still there for God's people. God himself is at rest. And at the end of the journey we'll surely rest with God. So let's keep at it and eventually arrive at the place of rest, not drop out through some sort of disobedience.

God means what he says. What he says goes. His powerful Word is sharp as a surgeon's scalpel, cutting through everything, whether doubt or defense, laying us open to listen and obey. Nothing and no one is impervious to God's Word. We can't get away from it—no matter what.

KING JAMES VERSION

14 Seeing then that we have a great high priest, that is passed into the heavens, Jesus the Son of God, let us hold fast *our* profession.

15 For we have not an high priest which cannot be touched with the feeling of our infirmities; but was in all points tempted like as *we are, yet* without sin.

16 Let us therefore come boldly unto the throne of grace, that we may obtain mercy, and find grace to help in time of need.

5 For every high priest taken from among men is ordained for men in things *pertaining* to God, that he may offer both gifts and sacrifices for sins:

2 Who can have compassion on the ignorant, and on them that are out of the way; for that he himself also is compassed with infirmity.

3 And by reason hereof he ought, as for the people, so also for himself, to offer for sins.

4 And no man taketh this honour unto himself, but he that is called of God, as *was* Aaron.

5 So also Christ glorified not himself to be made an high priest; but he that said unto him, Thou art my Son, to day have I begotten thee.

NEW AMERICAN STANDARD BIBLE

14 Therefore, since we have a great high priest who has passed through the heavens, Jesus the Son of God, let us hold fast our confession.

15 For we do not have a high priest who cannot sympathize with our weaknesses, but One who has been tempted in all things as *we are, yet* without sin.

16 Therefore let us draw near with confidence to the throne of grace, so that we may receive mercy and find grace to help in time of need.

The Perfect High Priest

5 For every high priest taken from among men is appointed on behalf of men in things pertaining to God, in order to offer both gifts and sacrifices for sins;

2 he can deal gently with the ignorant and misguided, since he himself also is beset with weakness;

3 and because of it he is obligated to offer *sacrifices* for sins, as for the people, so also for himself.

4 And no one takes the honor to himself, but *receives it* when he is called by God, even as Aaron was.

5 So also Christ did not glorify Himself so as to become a high priest, but He who said to Him,

"YOU ARE MY SON,
TODAY I HAVE BEGOTTEN YOU";

NEW CENTURY VERSION

Jesus Is Our High Priest

14 Since we have a great high priest, Jesus the Son of God, who has gone into heaven, let us hold on to the faith we have. 15 For our high priest is able to understand our weaknesses. When he lived on earth, he was tempted in every way that we are, but he did not sin. 16 Let us, then, feel very sure that we can come before God's throne where there is grace. There we can receive mercy and grace to help us when we need it.

5 Every high priest is chosen from among other people. He is given the work of going before God for them to offer gifts and sacrifices for sins. 2 Since he himself is weak, he is able to be gentle with those who do not understand and who are doing wrong things. 3 Because he is weak, the high priest must offer sacrifices for his own sins and also for the sins of the people.

4 To be a high priest is an honor, but no one chooses himself for this work. He must be called by God as Aaron[a] was. 5 So also Christ did not choose himself to have the honor of being a high priest, but God chose him. God said to him,

"You are my Son.
Today I have become your Father." *Psalm 2:7*

5:4 [a] **Aaron** Aaron was Moses' brother and the first Jewish high priest.

CONTEMPORARY ENGLISH VERSION

Jesus Is the Great High Priest

14 We have a great high priest, who has gone into heaven, and he is Jesus the Son of God. That is why we must hold on to what we have said about him. 15 Jesus understands every weakness of ours, because he was tempted in every way that we are. But he did not sin! 16 So whenever we are in need, we should come bravely before the throne of our merciful God. There we will be treated with undeserved kindness, and we will find help.

5 Every high priest is appointed to help others by offering gifts and sacrifices to God because of their sins. 2 A high priest has weaknesses of his own, and he feels sorry for foolish and sinful people. 3 That is why he must offer sacrifices for his own sins and for the sins of others. 4 But no one can have the honor of being a high priest simply by wanting to be one. Only God can choose a priest, and God is the one who chose Aaron.

5 That is how it was with Christ. He became a high priest, but not just because he wanted the honor of being one. It was God who told him,

"You are my Son, because today
I have become your Father!"

NEW INTERNATIONAL VERSION

Jesus the Great High Priest

14 Therefore, since we have a great high priest who has gone through the heavens,[e] Jesus the Son of God, let us hold firmly to the faith we profess. 15 For we do not have a high priest who is unable to sympathize with our weaknesses, but we have one who has been tempted in every way, just as we are—yet was without sin. 16 Let us then approach the throne of grace with confidence, so that we may receive mercy and find grace to help us in our time of need.

5 Every high priest is selected from among men and is appointed to represent them in matters related to God, to offer gifts and sacrifices for sins. 2 He is able to deal gently with those who are ignorant and are going astray, since he himself is subject to weakness. 3 This is why he has to offer sacrifices for his own sins, as well as for the sins of the people.

4 No one takes this honor upon himself; he must be called by God, just as Aaron was. 5 So Christ also did not take upon himself the glory of becoming a high priest. But God said to him,

"You are my Son;
today I have become your Father."[a][b]

[e] *14* Or *gone into heaven* [a] *5* Or *have begotten you* [b] *5* Psalm 2:7

NEW LIVING TRANSLATION

Christ Is Our High Priest

14 That is why we have a great High Priest who has gone to heaven, Jesus the Son of God. Let us cling to him and never stop trusting him. 15 This High Priest of ours understands our weaknesses, for he faced all of the same temptations we do, yet he did not sin. 16 So let us come boldly to the throne of our gracious God. There we will receive his mercy, and we will find grace to help us when we need it.

5 Now a high priest is a man chosen to represent other human beings in their dealings with God. He presents their gifts to God and offers their sacrifices for sins. 2 And because he is human, he is able to deal gently with the people, though they are ignorant and wayward. For he is subject to the same weaknesses they have. 3 That is why he has to offer sacrifices, both for their sins and for his own sins. 4 And no one can become a high priest simply because he wants such an honor. He has to be called by God for this work, just as Aaron was.

5 That is why Christ did not exalt himself to become High Priest. No, he was chosen by God, who said to him,

"You are my Son.
Today I have become your Father.*"

5:5 Or *Today I reveal you as my Son.* Ps 2:7.

NEW KING JAMES VERSION

Our Compassionate High Priest

14 Seeing then that we have a great High Priest who has passed through the heavens, Jesus the Son of God, let us hold fast *our* confession. 15 For we do not have a High Priest who cannot sympathize with our weaknesses, but was in all *points* tempted as *we are, yet* without sin. 16 Let us therefore come boldly to the throne of grace, that we may obtain mercy and find grace to help in time of need.

Qualifications for High Priesthood

5 For every high priest taken from among men is appointed for men in things *pertaining* to God, that he may offer both gifts and sacrifices for sins. 2 He can have compassion on those who are ignorant and going astray, since he himself is also subject to weakness. 3 Because of this he is required as for the people, so also for himself, to offer *sacrifices* for sins. 4 And no man takes this honor to himself, but he who is called by God, just as Aaron *was.*

A Priest Forever

5 So also Christ did not glorify Himself to become High Priest, *but it* was He who said to Him:

*"You are My Son,
Today I have begotten You."*[a]

5:5 [a] Psalm 2:7

THE MESSAGE

The High Priest Who Cried Out in Pain

Now that we know what we have—Jesus, this great High Priest with ready access to God—let's not let it slip through our fingers. We don't have a priest who is out of touch with our reality. He's been through weakness and testing, experienced it all—all but the sin. So let's walk right up to him and get what he is so ready to give. Take the mercy, accept the help.

5 Every high priest selected to represent men and women before God and offer sacrifices for their sins should be able to deal gently with their failings, since he knows what it's like from his own experience. But that also means that he has to offer sacrifices for his own sins as well as the people's.

No one elects himself to this honored position. He's called to it by God, as Aaron was. Neither did Christ presume to set himself up as high priest, but was set apart by the One who said to him, "You're my Son; today I celebrate

KING JAMES VERSION

6 As he saith also in another *place*, Thou *art* a priest for ever after the order of Melchisedec.

7 Who in the days of his flesh, when he had offered up prayers and supplications with strong crying and tears unto him that was able to save him from death, and was heard in that he feared;

8 Though he were a Son, yet learned he obedience by the things which he suffered;

9 And being made perfect, he became the author of eternal salvation unto all them that obey him;

10 ¶ Called of God an high priest after the order of Melchisedec.

11 Of whom we have many things to say, and hard to be uttered, seeing ye are dull of hearing.

12 For when for the time ye ought to be teachers, ye have need that one teach you again which *be* the first principles of the oracles of God; and are become such as have need of milk, and not of strong meat.

13 For every one that useth milk *is* unskilful in the word of righteousness: for he is a babe.

14 But strong meat belongeth to them that are of full age, *even* those who by reason of use have their senses exercised to discern both good and evil.

NEW AMERICAN STANDARD BIBLE

6 just as He says also in another *passage*,

"You are a priest forever
According to the order of Melchizedek."

7 In the days of His flesh, He offered up both prayers and supplications with loud crying and tears to the One able to save Him from death, and He was heard because of His piety.

8 Although He was a Son, He learned obedience from the things which He suffered.

9 And having been made perfect, He became to all those who obey Him the source of eternal salvation,

10 being designated by God as a high priest according to the order of Melchizedek.

11 Concerning [1]him we have much to say, and *it is* hard to explain, since you have become dull of hearing.

12 For though by this time you ought to be teachers, you have need again for someone to teach you the elementary principles of the oracles of God, and you have come to need milk and not solid food.

13 For everyone who partakes *only* of milk is not accustomed to the word of righteousness, for he is an infant.

14 But solid food is for the mature, who because of practice have their senses trained to discern good and evil.

5:11 [1] Lit *whom* or *which*

NEW CENTURY VERSION

6And in another Scripture God says,

"You are a priest forever,
a priest like Melchizedek."[b] *Psalm 110:4*

7While Jesus lived on earth, he prayed to God and asked
God for help. He prayed with loud cries and tears to the
One who could save him from death, and his prayer was
heard because he trusted God. 8Even though Jesus was the
Son of God, he learned obedience by what he suffered.
9And because his obedience was perfect, he was able to
give eternal salvation to all who obey him. 10In this way
God made Jesus a high priest, a priest like Melchizedek.

Warning Against Falling Away

11We have much to say about this, but it is hard to
explain because you are so slow to understand. 12By now
you should be teachers, but you need someone to teach
you again the first lessons of God's message. You still
need the teaching that is like milk. You are not ready for
solid food. 13Anyone who lives on milk is still a baby and
knows nothing about right teaching. 14But solid food is for
those who are grown up. They have practiced in order to
know the difference between good and evil.

5:6 [b] **Melchizedek** A priest and king who lived in the time of Abraham. (Read Genesis 14:17–24.)

CONTEMPORARY ENGLISH VERSION

6In another place, God says,

"You are a priest forever
just like Melchizedek."[a]

7God had the power to save Jesus from death. And while
Jesus was on earth, he begged God with loud crying and
tears to save him. He truly worshiped God, and God lis-
tened to his prayers. 8Jesus is God's own Son, but still he
had to suffer before he could learn what it really means to
obey God. 9Suffering made Jesus perfect, and now he can
save forever all who obey him. 10This is because God chose
him to be a high priest like Melchizedek.

Warning against Turning Away

11Much more could be said about this subject. But it is
hard to explain, and all of you are slow to understand.
12By now you should have been teachers, but once again
you need to be taught the simplest things about what God
has said. You need milk instead of solid food. 13People
who live on milk are like babies who don't really know
what is right. 14Solid food is for mature people who have
been trained to know right from wrong.

[a] **5.6** *Melchizedek*: When Melchizedek is mentioned in the Old Testament, he is described as a priest who lived before Aaron. Nothing is said about his ancestors or his death (see 7.3 and Genesis 14.17-20).

NEW INTERNATIONAL VERSION

6And he says in another place,

> "You are a priest forever,
> in the order of Melchizedek."[c]

7During the days of Jesus' life on earth, he offered up prayers and petitions with loud cries and tears to the one who could save him from death, and he was heard because of his reverent submission. 8Although he was a son, he learned obedience from what he suffered 9and, once made perfect, he became the source of eternal salvation for all who obey him 10and was designated by God to be high priest in the order of Melchizedek.

Warning Against Falling Away

11We have much to say about this, but it is hard to explain because you are slow to learn. 12In fact, though by this time you ought to be teachers, you need someone to teach you the elementary truths of God's word all over again. You need milk, not solid food! 13Anyone who lives on milk, being still an infant, is not acquainted with the teaching about righteousness. 14But solid food is for the mature, who by constant use have trained themselves to distinguish good from evil.

[c] *6* Psalm 110:4

NEW LIVING TRANSLATION

6And in another passage God said to him,

> "You are a priest forever
> in the line of Melchizedek."*

7While Jesus was here on earth, he offered prayers and pleadings, with a loud cry and tears, to the one who could deliver him out of death. And God heard his prayers because of his reverence for God. 8So even though Jesus was God's Son, he learned obedience from the things he suffered. 9In this way, God qualified him as a perfect High Priest, and he became the source of eternal salvation for all those who obey him. 10And God designated him to be a High Priest in the line of Melchizedek.

A Call to Spiritual Growth

11There is so much more we would like to say about this. But you don't seem to listen, so it's hard to make you understand. 12You have been Christians a long time now, and you ought to be teaching others. Instead, you need someone to teach you again the basic things a beginner must learn about the Scriptures.* You are like babies who drink only milk and cannot eat solid food. 13And a person who is living on milk isn't very far along in the Christian life and doesn't know much about doing what is right. 14Solid food is for those who are mature, who have trained themselves to recognize the difference between right and wrong and then do what is right.

5:6 Ps 110:4. **5:12** Or *about the oracles of God.*

NEW KING JAMES VERSION

6As *He* also *says* in another *place:*

> *"You are a priest forever
> According to the order of Melchizedek"*;[b]

7who, in the days of His flesh, when He had offered up prayers and supplications, with vehement cries and tears to Him who was able to save Him from death, and was heard because of His godly fear, 8though He was a Son, *yet* He learned obedience by the things which He suffered. 9And having been perfected, He became the author of eternal salvation to all who obey Him, 10called by God as High Priest *"according to the order of Melchizedek,"* 11of whom we have much to say, and hard to explain, since you have become dull of hearing.

Spiritual Immaturity

12For though by this time you ought to be teachers, you need *someone* to teach you again the first principles of the oracles of God; and you have come to need milk and not solid food. 13For everyone who partakes *only* of milk *is* unskilled in the word of righteousness, for he is a babe. 14But solid food belongs to those who are of full age, *that is,* those who by reason of use have their senses exercised to discern both good and evil.

5:6 [b] Psalm 110:4

THE MESSAGE

you!" In another place God declares, "You're a priest forever in the royal order of Melchizedek."

While he lived on earth, anticipating death, Jesus cried out in pain and wept in sorrow as he offered up priestly prayers to God. Because he honored God, God answered him. Though he was God's Son, he learned trusting-obedience by what he suffered, just as we do. Then, having arrived at the full stature of his maturity and having been announced by God as high priest in the order of Melchizedek, he became the source of eternal salvation to all who believingly obey him.

Re-crucifying Jesus

I have a lot more to say about this, but it is hard to get it across to you since you've picked up this bad habit of not listening. By this time you ought to be teachers yourselves, yet here I find you need someone to sit down with you and go over the basics on God again, starting from square one—baby's milk, when you should have been on solid food long ago! Milk is for beginners, inexperienced in God's ways; solid food is for the mature, who have some practice in telling right from wrong.

KING JAMES VERSION

6 Therefore leaving the principles of the doctrine of Christ, let us go on unto perfection; not laying again the foundation of repentance from dead works, and of faith toward God,

2 Of the doctrine of baptisms, and of laying on of hands, and of resurrection of the dead, and of eternal judgment.

3 And this will we do, if God permit.

4 For *it is* impossible for those who were once enlightened, and have tasted of the heavenly gift, and were made partakers of the Holy Ghost,

5 And have tasted the good word of God, and the powers of the world to come,

6 If they shall fall away, to renew them again unto repentance; seeing they crucify to themselves the Son of God afresh, and put *him* to an open shame.

7 For the earth which drinketh in the rain that cometh oft upon it, and bringeth forth herbs meet for them by whom it is dressed, receiveth blessing from God:

8 But that which beareth thorns and briers *is* rejected, and *is* nigh unto cursing; whose end *is* to be burned.

9 ¶ But, beloved, we are persuaded better things of you, and things that accompany salvation, though we thus speak.

10 For God *is* not unrighteous to forget your work and labour of love, which ye have shewed toward his name, in that ye have ministered to the saints, and do minister.

NEW AMERICAN STANDARD BIBLE

The Peril of Falling Away

6 Therefore leaving the elementary teaching about the Christ, let us press on to maturity, not laying again a foundation of repentance from dead works and of faith toward God,

2 of instruction about washings and laying on of hands, and the resurrection of the dead and eternal judgment.

3 And this we will do, if God permits.

4 For in the case of those who have once been enlightened and have tasted of the heavenly gift and have been made partakers of the Holy Spirit,

5 and have tasted the good word of God and the powers of the age to come,

6 and *then* have fallen away, it is impossible to renew them again to repentance, since they again crucify to themselves the Son of God and put Him to open shame.

7 For ground that drinks the rain which often falls on it and brings forth vegetation useful to those for whose sake it is also tilled, receives a blessing from God;

8 but if it yields thorns and thistles, it is worthless and close to being cursed, and it ends up being burned.

Better Things for You

9 But, beloved, we are convinced of better things concerning you, and things that accompany salvation, though we are speaking in this way.

10 For God is not unjust so as to forget your work and the love which you have shown toward His name, in having ministered and in still ministering to the saints.

NEW CENTURY VERSION

6 So let us go on to grown-up teaching. Let us not go back over the beginning lessons we learned about Christ. We should not again start teaching about faith in God and about turning away from those acts that lead to death. 2 We should not return to the teaching about baptisms,[a] about laying on of hands,[b] about the raising of the dead and eternal judgment. 3 And we will go on to grown-up teaching if God allows.

4 Some people cannot be brought back again to a changed life. They were once in God's light, and enjoyed heaven's gift, and shared in the Holy Spirit. 5 They found out how good God's word is, and they received the powers of his new world. 6 But they fell away from Christ. It is impossible to bring them back to a changed life again, because they are nailing the Son of God to a cross again and are shaming him in front of others.

7 Some people are like land that gets plenty of rain. The land produces a good crop for those who work it, and it receives God's blessings. 8 Other people are like land that grows thorns and weeds and is worthless. It is in danger of being cursed by God and will be destroyed by fire.

9 Dear friends, we are saying this to you, but we really expect better things from you that will lead to your salvation. 10 God is fair; he will not forget the work you did and the love you showed for him by helping his people. And he

6:2 [a] **baptisms** The word here may refer to Christian baptism, or it may refer to the Jewish ceremonial washings. 6:2 [b] **laying on of hands** The laying on of hands had many purposes, including the giving of a blessing, power, or authority.

CONTEMPORARY ENGLISH VERSION

6 We must try to become mature and start thinking about more than just the basic things we were taught about Christ. We shouldn't need to keep talking about why we ought to turn from deeds that bring death and why we ought to have faith in God. 2 And we shouldn't need to keep teaching about baptisms[a] or about the laying on of hands[b] or about people being raised from death and the future judgment. 3 Let's grow up, if God is willing.

4-6 But what about people who turn away after they have already seen the light and have received the gift from heaven and have shared in the Holy Spirit? What about those who turn away after they have received the good message of God and the powers of the future world? There is no way to bring them back. What they are doing is the same as nailing the Son of God to a cross and insulting him in public!

7 A field is useful to farmers, if there is enough rain to make good crops grow. In fact, God will bless that field. 8 But land that produces only thornbushes is worthless. It is likely to fall under God's curse, and in the end it will be set on fire.

9 My friends, we are talking this way. But we are sure that you are doing those really good things that people do when they are being saved. 10 God is always fair. He will remember how you helped his people in the past and how you are still helping them. You belong to God, and he won't forget the love you have shown his people. 11 We

[a] **6.2** *baptisms*: Or "ceremonies of washing." [b] **6.2** *laying on of hands*: This was a ceremony in which church leaders and others put their hands on people to show that those people were chosen to do some special kind of work.

NEW INTERNATIONAL VERSION

6 Therefore let us leave the elementary teachings about Christ and go on to maturity, not laying again the foundation of repentance from acts that lead to death,[a] and of faith in God, 2instruction about baptisms, the laying on of hands, the resurrection of the dead, and eternal judgment. 3And God permitting, we will do so.

4It is impossible for those who have once been enlightened, who have tasted the heavenly gift, who have shared in the Holy Spirit, 5who have tasted the goodness of the word of God and the powers of the coming age, 6if they fall away, to be brought back to repentance, because[b] to their loss they are crucifying the Son of God all over again and subjecting him to public disgrace.

7Land that drinks in the rain often falling on it and that produces a crop useful to those for whom it is farmed receives the blessing of God. 8But land that produces thorns and thistles is worthless and is in danger of being cursed. In the end it will be burned.

9Even though we speak like this, dear friends, we are confident of better things in your case—things that accompany salvation. 10God is not unjust; he will not forget your work and the love you have shown him as you have helped his people and continue to help them. 11We want each of

[a] *1* Or *from useless rituals* [b] *6* Or *repentance while*

NEW LIVING TRANSLATION

6 So let us stop going over the basics of Christianity* again and again. Let us go on instead and become mature in our understanding. Surely we don't need to start all over again with the importance of turning away from evil deeds and placing our faith in God. 2You don't need further instruction about baptisms, the laying on of hands, the resurrection of the dead, and eternal judgment. 3And so, God willing, we will move forward to further understanding.

4For it is impossible to restore to repentance those who were once enlightened—those who have experienced the good things of heaven and shared in the Holy Spirit, 5who have tasted the goodness of the word of God and the power of the age to come—6and who then turn away from God. It is impossible to bring such people to repentance again because they are nailing the Son of God to the cross again by rejecting him, holding him up to public shame.

7When the ground soaks up the rain that falls on it and bears a good crop for the farmer, it has the blessing of God. 8But if a field bears thistles and thorns, it is useless. The farmer will condemn that field and burn it.

9Dear friends, even though we are talking like this, we really don't believe that it applies to you. We are confident that you are meant for better things, things that come with salvation. 10For God is not unfair. He will not forget how hard you have worked for him and how you have shown your love to him by caring for other Christians, as you still

6:1 Or *the basics about Christ.*

NEW KING JAMES VERSION

The Peril of Not Progressing

6 Therefore, leaving the discussion of the elementary *principles* of Christ, let us go on to perfection, not laying again the foundation of repentance from dead works and of faith toward God, 2of the doctrine of baptisms, of laying on of hands, of resurrection of the dead, and of eternal judgment. 3And this we will[a] do if God permits.

4For *it is* impossible for those who were once enlightened, and have tasted the heavenly gift, and have become partakers of the Holy Spirit, 5and have tasted the good word of God and the powers of the age to come, 6if they fall away,[b] to renew them again to repentance, since they crucify again for themselves the Son of God, and put *Him* to an open shame.

7For the earth which drinks in the rain that often comes upon it, and bears herbs useful for those by whom it is cultivated, receives blessing from God; 8but if it bears thorns and briers, *it is* rejected and near to being cursed, whose end *is* to be burned.

A Better Estimate

9But, beloved, we are confident of better things concerning you, yes, things that accompany salvation, though we speak in this manner. 10For God *is* not unjust to forget your work and labor of[c] love which you have shown toward His name, *in that* you have ministered to the saints, and do

6:3 [a] M-Text reads *let us do.* 6:6 [b] Or *and have fallen away*
6:10 [c] NU-Text omits *labor of.*

THE MESSAGE

6 So come on, let's leave the preschool fingerpainting exercises on Christ and get on with the grand work of art. Grow up in Christ. The basic foundational truths are in place: turning your back on "salvation by self-help" and turning in trust toward God; baptismal instructions; laying on of hands; resurrection of the dead; eternal judgment. God helping us, we'll stay true to all that. But there's so much more. Let's get on with it!

Once people have seen the light, gotten a taste of heaven and been part of the work of the Holy Spirit, once they've personally experienced the sheer goodness of God's Word and the powers breaking in on us—if then they turn their backs on it, washing their hands of the whole thing, well, they can't start over as if nothing happened. That's impossible. Why, they've re-crucified Jesus! They've repudiated him in public! Parched ground that soaks up the rain and then produces an abundance of carrots and corn for its gardener gets God's "Well done!" But if it produces weeds and thistles, it's more likely to get cussed out. Fields like that are burned, not harvested.

I'm sure that won't happen to you, friends. I have better things in mind for you—salvation things! God doesn't miss anything. He knows perfectly well all the love you've shown him by helping needy Christians, and that you keep

KING JAMES VERSION

11 And we desire that every one of you do shew the same diligence to the full assurance of hope unto the end:

12 That ye be not slothful, but followers of them who through faith and patience inherit the promises.

13 For when God made promise to Abraham, because he could swear by no greater, he sware by himself,

14 Saying, Surely blessing I will bless thee, and multiplying I will multiply thee.

15 And so, after he had patiently endured, he obtained the promise.

16 For men verily swear by the greater: and an oath for confirmation *is* to them an end of all strife.

17 Wherein God, willing more abundantly to shew unto the heirs of promise the immutability of his counsel, confirmed *it* by an oath:

18 That by two immutable things, in which *it was* impossible for God to lie, we might have a strong consolation, who have fled for refuge to lay hold upon the hope set before us:

NEW AMERICAN STANDARD BIBLE

11 And we desire that each one of you show the same diligence so as to realize the full assurance of hope until the end,

12 so that you will not be sluggish, but imitators of those who through faith and patience inherit the promises.

13 For when God made the promise to Abraham, since He could swear by no one greater, He swore by Himself,

14 saying, "I WILL SURELY BLESS YOU AND I WILL SURELY MULTIPLY YOU."

15 And so, having patiently waited, he obtained the promise.

16 For men swear by one greater *than themselves*, and with them an oath *given* as confirmation is an end of every dispute.

17 In the same way God, desiring even more to show to the heirs of the promise the unchangeableness of His purpose, interposed with an oath,

18 so that by two unchangeable things in which it is impossible for God to lie, we who have taken refuge would have strong encouragement to take hold of the hope set before us.

NEW CENTURY VERSION

will remember that you are still helping them.
11We want
each of you to go on with the same hard work all your lives so you will surely get what you hope for.
12We do not
want you to become lazy. Be like those who through faith and patience will receive what God has promised.

13God made a promise to Abraham. And as there is no one greater than God, he used himself when he swore to Abraham,
14saying, "I will surely bless you and give you many descendants."[c]
15Abraham waited patiently for this to happen, and he received what God promised.

16People always use the name of someone greater than themselves when they swear. The oath proves that what they say is true, and this ends all arguing.
17God wanted to
prove that his promise was true to those who would get what he promised. And he wanted them to understand clearly that his purposes never change, so he made an oath.
18These two things cannot change: God cannot lie when he makes a promise, and he cannot lie when he makes an oath. These things encourage us who came to God for safety. They give us strength to hold on to the hope we have been given.

6:14 c **"I...descendants."** Quotation from Genesis 22:17.

CONTEMPORARY ENGLISH VERSION

wish that each of you would always be eager to show how strong and lasting your hope really is.
12Then you would
never be lazy. You would be following the example of those who had faith and were patient until God kept his promise to them.

God's Promise Is Sure

13No one is greater than God. So he made a promise in his own name when he said to Abraham,
14"I, the Lord,
will bless you with many descendants!"
15Then after
Abraham had been very patient, he was given what God had promised.
16When anyone wants to settle an argument, they make a vow by using the name of someone or something greater than themselves.
17So when God wanted to prove for certain that his promise to his people could not be broken, he made a vow.
18God cannot tell lies! And
so his promises and vows are two things that can never be changed.

We have run to God for safety. Now his promises should greatly encourage us to take hold of the hope that is right

NEW INTERNATIONAL VERSION

you to show this same diligence to the very end, in order
to make your hope sure. 12We do not want you to become
lazy, but to imitate those who through faith and patience
inherit what has been promised.

The Certainty of God's Promise

13When God made his promise to Abraham, since there
was no one greater for him to swear by, he swore by him-
self, 14saying, "I will surely bless you and give you many
descendants."[c] 15And so after waiting patiently, Abraham
received what was promised.

16Men swear by someone greater than themselves, and
the oath confirms what is said and puts an end to all argu-
ment. 17Because God wanted to make the unchanging
nature of his purpose very clear to the heirs of what was
promised, he confirmed it with an oath. 18God did this so
that, by two unchangeable things in which it is impossible
for God to lie, we who have fled to take hold of the hope
offered to us may be greatly encouraged. 19We have this

c *14* Gen. 22:17

NEW LIVING TRANSLATION

do. 11Our great desire is that you will keep right on loving
others as long as life lasts, in order to make certain that
what you hope for will come true. 12Then you will not
become spiritually dull and indifferent. Instead, you will
follow the example of those who are going to inherit God's
promises because of their faith and patience.

God's Promises Bring Hope

13For example, there was God's promise to Abraham.
Since there was no one greater to swear by, God took an
oath in his own name, saying:

14 "I will certainly bless you richly,
and I will multiply your descendants into countless
millions."*

15Then Abraham waited patiently, and he received what
God had promised.

16When people take an oath, they call on someone
greater than themselves to hold them to it. And without
any question that oath is binding. 17God also bound him-
self with an oath, so that those who received the promise
could be perfectly sure that he would never change his
mind. 18So God has given us both his promise and his
oath. These two things are unchangeable because it is
impossible for God to lie. Therefore, we who have fled to
him for refuge can take new courage, for we can hold on to
his promise with confidence.

6:14 Gen 22:17.

NEW KING JAMES VERSION

minister. 11And we desire that each one of you show the
same diligence to the full assurance of hope until the end,
12that you do not become sluggish, but imitate those who
through faith and patience inherit the promises.

God's Infallible Purpose in Christ

13For when God made a promise to Abraham, because
He could swear by no one greater, He swore by Himself,
14saying, *"Surely blessing I will bless you, and multiplying
I will multiply you."*[d] 15And so, after he had patiently
endured, he obtained the promise. 16For men indeed swear
by the greater, and an oath for confirmation *is* for them an
end of all dispute. 17Thus God, determining to show more
abundantly to the heirs of promise the immutability of His
counsel, confirmed *it* by an oath, 18that by two immutable
things, in which it *is* impossible for God to lie, we might[e]
have strong consolation, who have fled for refuge to lay
hold of the hope set before *us*.

6:14 d Genesis 22:17 6:18 e M-Text omits *might.*

THE MESSAGE

at it. And now I want each of you to extend that same
intensity toward a full-bodied hope, and keep at it till the
finish. Don't drag your feet. Be like those who stay the
course with committed faith and then get everything prom-
ised to them.

God Gave His Word

When God made his promise to Abraham, he backed it to
the hilt, putting his own reputation on the line. He said, "I
promise that I'll bless you with everything I have—bless
and bless and bless!" Abraham stuck it out and got every-
thing that had been promised to him. When people make
promises, they guarantee them by appeal to some authori-
ty above them so that if there is any question that they'll
make good on the promise, the authority will back them
up. When God wanted to guarantee his promises, he gave
his word, a rock-solid guarantee—God *can't* break his
word. And because his word cannot change, the promise is
likewise unchangeable.

KING JAMES VERSION

19 Which *hope* we have as an anchor of the soul, both sure and stedfast, and which entereth into that within the veil;

20 Whither the forerunner is for us entered, *even* Jesus, made an high priest for ever after the order of Melchisedec.

7 For this Melchisedec, king of Salem, priest of the most high God, who met Abraham returning from the slaughter of the kings, and blessed him;

2 To whom also Abraham gave a tenth part of all; first being by interpretation King of righteousness, and after that also King of Salem, which is, King of peace;

3 Without father, without mother, without descent, having neither beginning of days, nor end of life; but made like unto the Son of God; abideth a priest continually.

4 Now consider how great this man *was*, unto whom even the patriarch Abraham gave the tenth of the spoils.

5 And verily they that are of the sons of Levi, who receive the office of the priesthood, have a commandment to take tithes of the people according to the law, that is, of their brethren, though they come out of the loins of Abraham:

6 But he whose descent is not counted from them received tithes of Abraham, and blessed him that had the promises.

NEW AMERICAN STANDARD BIBLE

19 This hope we have as an anchor of the soul, a *hope* both sure and steadfast and one which enters within the veil,

20 where Jesus has entered as a forerunner for us, having become a high priest forever according to the order of Melchizedek.

Melchizedek's Priesthood Like Christ's

7 For this Melchizedek, king of Salem, priest of the Most High God, who met Abraham as he was returning from the slaughter of the kings and blessed him,

2 to whom also Abraham apportioned a tenth part of all *the spoils*, was first of all, by the translation *of his name*, king of righteousness, and then also king of Salem, which is king of peace.

3 Without father, without mother, without genealogy, having neither beginning of days nor end of life, but made like the Son of God, he remains a priest perpetually.

4 Now observe how great this man was to whom Abraham, the patriarch, gave a tenth of the choicest spoils.

5 And those indeed of the sons of Levi who receive the priest's office have commandment in the Law to collect a tenth from the people, that is, from their brethren, although these are descended from Abraham.

6 But the one whose genealogy is not traced from them collected a tenth from Abraham and blessed the one who had the promises.

NEW CENTURY VERSION

[19]We have this hope as an anchor for the soul, sure and
strong. It enters behind the curtain in the Most Holy Place in
heaven, [20]where Jesus has gone ahead of us and for us. He
has become the high priest forever, a priest like Melchize-
dek.[d]

The Priest Melchizedek

7 Melchizedek[d] was the king of Salem and a priest for
God Most High. He met Abraham when Abraham was
coming back after defeating the kings. When they met,
Melchizedek blessed Abraham, [2]and Abraham gave him a
tenth of everything he had brought back from the battle.
First, Melchizedek's name means "king of goodness," and
he is king of Salem, which means "king of peace." [3]No one
knows who Melchizedek's father or mother was,[a] where he
came from, when he was born, or when he died. Melchize-
dek is like the Son of God; he continues being a priest for-
ever.
[4]You can see how great Melchizedek was. Abraham, the
great father, gave him a tenth of everything that he won in
battle. [5]Now the law says that those in the tribe of Levi
who become priests must collect a tenth from the people—
their own people—even though the priests and the people
are from the family of Abraham. [6]Melchizedek was not
from the tribe of Levi, but he collected a tenth from Abra-
ham. And he blessed Abraham, the man who had God's

6:20; 7:1 [d] **Melchizedek** A priest and king who lived in the time of Abraham. (Read Genesis 14:17–24.) **7:3** [a] **No...was** Literally, "Melchizedek was without father, without mother, without genealogy."

CONTEMPORARY ENGLISH VERSION

in front of us. [19]This hope is like a firm and steady anchor
for our souls. In fact, hope reaches behind the curtain[c] and
into the most holy place. [20]Jesus has gone there ahead of
us, and he is our high priest forever, just like Melchizedek.[d]

The Priestly Family of Melchizedek

7 Melchizedek was both king of Salem and priest of God
Most High. He was the one who went out and gave
Abraham his blessing, when Abraham returned from
killing the kings. [2]Then Abraham gave him a tenth of
everything he had.
The meaning of the name Melchizedek is "King of
Justice." But since Salem means "peace," he is also "King
of Peace." [3]We are not told that he had a father or mother
or ancestors or beginning or end. He is like the Son of God
and will be a priest forever.[a]
[4]Notice how great Melchizedek is! Our famous ancestor
Abraham gave him a tenth of what he had taken from his
enemies. [5]The Law teaches that even Abraham's descen-
dants must give a tenth of what they possess. And they are
to give this to their own relatives, who are the descendants
of Levi and are priests. [6]Although Melchizedek wasn't a
descendant of Levi, Abraham gave him a tenth of what he
had. Then Melchizedek blessed Abraham, who had been

[c] **6.19** *behind the curtain*: In the tent that was used for worship, a curtain separated the "holy place" from the "most holy place," which only the high priest could enter. [d] **6.20** *Melchizedek*: See the note at 5.6.
[a] **7.3** *will be a priest forever*: See the note at 5.6.

NEW INTERNATIONAL VERSION

hope as an anchor for the soul, firm and secure. It enters
the inner sanctuary behind the curtain, 20where Jesus, who
went before us, has entered on our behalf. He has become
a high priest forever, in the order of Melchizedek.

Melchizedek the Priest

7 This Melchizedek was king of Salem and priest of God
Most High. He met Abraham returning from the defeat
of the kings and blessed him, 2and Abraham gave him a
tenth of everything. First, his name means "king of righ-
teousness"; then also, "king of Salem" means "king of
peace." 3Without father or mother, without genealogy,
without beginning of days or end of life, like the Son of
God he remains a priest forever.

4Just think how great he was: Even the patriarch Abra-
ham gave him a tenth of the plunder! 5Now the law
requires the descendants of Levi who become priests to col-
lect a tenth from the people—that is, their brothers—even
though their brothers are descended from Abraham. 6This
man, however, did not trace his descent from Levi, yet he
collected a tenth from Abraham and blessed him who had

NEW LIVING TRANSLATION

19This confidence is like a strong and trustworthy
anchor for our souls. It leads us through the curtain of
heaven into God's inner sanctuary. 20Jesus has already
gone in there for us. He has become our eternal High Priest
in the line of Melchizedek.

Melchizedek Is Compared to Abraham

7 This Melchizedek was king of the city of Salem and
also a priest of God Most High. When Abraham was
returning home after winning a great battle against many
kings, Melchizedek met him and blessed him. 2Then
Abraham took a tenth of all he had won in the battle and
gave it to Melchizedek. His name means "king of justice."
He is also "king of peace" because *Salem* means "peace."
3There is no record of his father or mother or any of his
ancestors—no beginning or end to his life. He remains a
priest forever, resembling the Son of God.

4Consider then how great this Melchizedek was. Even
Abraham, the great patriarch of Israel, recognized how great
Melchizedek was by giving him a tenth of what he had
taken in battle. 5Now the priests, who are descendants of
Levi, are commanded in the law of Moses to collect a tithe
from all the people, even though they are their own rela-
tives.* 6But Melchizedek, who was not even related to Levi,
collected a tenth from Abraham. And Melchizedek placed a
blessing upon Abraham, the one who had already received

7:5 Greek *their brothers, who are descendants of Abraham.*

NEW KING JAMES VERSION

19This *hope* we have as an anchor of the soul, both sure
and steadfast, and which enters the Presence *behind* the
veil, 20where the forerunner has entered for us, *even* Jesus,
having become High Priest forever according to the order
of Melchizedek.

The King of Righteousness

7 For this Melchizedek, king of Salem, priest of the Most
High God, who met Abraham returning from the
slaughter of the kings and blessed him, 2to whom also
Abraham gave a tenth part of all, first being translated
"king of righteousness," and then also king of Salem,
meaning "king of peace," 3without father, without mother,
without genealogy, having neither beginning of days nor
end of life, but made like the Son of God, remains a priest
continually.

4Now consider how great this man *was,* to whom even
the patriarch Abraham gave a tenth of the spoils. 5And
indeed those who are of the sons of Levi, who receive the
priesthood, have a commandment to receive tithes from
the people according to the law, that is, from their
brethren, though they have come from the loins of Abra-
ham; 6but he whose genealogy is not derived from them
received tithes from Abraham and blessed him who had

THE MESSAGE

We who have run for our very lives to God have every
reason to grab the promised hope with both hands and
never let go. It's an unbreakable spiritual lifeline, reaching
past all appearances right to the very presence of God
where Jesus, running on ahead of us, has taken up his per-
manent post as high priest for us, in the order of Melchize-
dek.

Melchizedek, Priest of God

7 Melchizedek was king of Salem and priest of the
Highest God. He met Abraham, who was returning
from "the royal massacre," and gave him his blessing.
Abraham in turn gave him a tenth of the spoils.
"Melchizedek" means "King of Righteousness." "Salem"
means "Peace." So, he is also "King of Peace." Melchizedek
towers out of the past—without record of family ties, no
account of beginning or end. In this way he is like the Son
of God, one huge priestly presence dominating the land-
scape always.

You realize just how great Melchizedek is when you see
that Father Abraham gave him a tenth of the captured trea-
sure. Priests descended from Levi are commanded by law to
collect tithes from the people, even though they are all more
or less equals, priests and people, having a common father
in Abraham. But this man, a complete outsider, collected
tithes from Abraham and blessed him, the one to whom the

KING JAMES VERSION

7 And without all contradiction the less is blessed of the better.

8 And here men that die receive tithes; but there he *receiveth them*, of whom it is witnessed that he liveth.

9 And as I may so say, Levi also, who receiveth tithes, payed tithes in Abraham.

10 For he was yet in the loins of his father, when Melchisedec met him.

11 ¶ If therefore perfection were by the Levitical priesthood, (for under it the people received the law,) what further need *was there* that another priest should rise after the order of Melchisedec, and not be called after the order of Aaron?

12 For the priesthood being changed, there is made of necessity a change also of the law.

13 For he of whom these things are spoken pertaineth to another tribe, of which no man gave attendance at the altar.

14 For *it is* evident that our Lord sprang out of Juda; of which tribe Moses spake nothing concerning priesthood.

15 And it is yet far more evident: for that after the similitude of Melchisedec there ariseth another priest,

NEW AMERICAN STANDARD BIBLE

7 But without any dispute the lesser is blessed by the greater.

8 In this case mortal men receive tithes, but in that case one *receives them*, of whom it is witnessed that he lives on.

9 And, so to speak, through Abraham even Levi, who received tithes, paid tithes,

10 for he was still in the loins of his father when Melchizedek met him.

11 Now if perfection was through the Levitical priesthood (for on the basis of it the people received the Law), what further need *was there* for another priest to arise according to the order of Melchizedek, and not be designated according to the order of Aaron?

12 For when the priesthood is changed, of necessity there takes place a change of law also.

13 For the one concerning whom these things are spoken belongs to another tribe, from which no one has officiated at the altar.

14 For it is evident that our Lord was descended from Judah, a tribe with reference to which Moses spoke nothing concerning priests.

15 And this is clearer still, if another priest arises according to the likeness of Melchizedek,

NEW CENTURY VERSION

promises. 7Now everyone knows that the more important
person blesses the less important person. 8Priests receive a
tenth, even though they are only men who live and then
die. But Melchizedek, who received a tenth from Abraham,
continues living, as the Scripture says. 9We might even say
that Levi, who receives a tenth, also paid it when Abraham
paid Melchizedek a tenth. 10Levi was not yet born, but he
was in the body of his ancestor when Melchizedek met
Abraham.

11The people were given the law[b] based on a system of
priests from the tribe of Levi, but they could not be made
perfect through that system. So there was a need for
another priest to come, a priest like Melchizedek, not
Aaron. 12And when a different kind of priest comes, the
law must be changed, too. 13We are saying these things
about Christ, who belonged to a different tribe. No one
from that tribe ever served as a priest at the altar. 14It is
clear that our Lord came from the tribe of Judah, and
Moses said nothing about priests belonging to that tribe.

Jesus Is like Melchizedek

15And this becomes even more clear when we see that
another priest comes who is like Melchizedek.[c] 16He was

7:11 [b] **The...law** This refers to the people of Israel who were given the law of Moses. 7:15 [c] **Melchizedek** A priest and king who lived in the time of Abraham. (Read Genesis 14:17–24.)

CONTEMPORARY ENGLISH VERSION

given God's promise. 7Everyone agrees that a person who
gives a blessing is greater than the one who receives the
blessing.

8Priests are given a tenth of what people earn. But all
priests die, except Melchizedek, and the Scriptures teach
that he is alive. 9Levi's descendants are now the ones who
receive a tenth from people. We could even say that when
Abraham gave Melchizedek a tenth, Levi also gave him a
tenth. 10This is because Levi was born later into the family
of Abraham, who gave a tenth to Melchizedek.

11Even though the Law of Moses says that the priests
must be descendants of Levi, those priests cannot make
anyone perfect. So there needs to be a priest like
Melchizedek, rather than one from the priestly family of
Aaron.[b] 12And when the rules for selecting a priest are
changed, the Law must also be changed.

13The person we are talking about is our Lord, who
came from a tribe that had never had anyone to serve as a
priest at the altar. 14Everyone knows he came from the
tribe of Judah, and Moses never said that priests would
come from that tribe.

15All of this becomes clearer, when someone who is like
Melchizedek is appointed to be a priest. 16That person

[b] 7.11 *descendants of Levi . . . from the priestly family of Aaron*: Levi was the ancestor of the tribe from which priests and their helpers (called "Levites") were chosen. Aaron was the first high priest.

NEW INTERNATIONAL VERSION

the promises. 7And without doubt the lesser person is
blessed by the greater. 8In the one case, the tenth is collect-
ed by men who die; but in the other case, by him who is
declared to be living. 9One might even say that Levi, who
collects the tenth, paid the tenth through Abraham,
10because when Melchizedek met Abraham, Levi was still
in the body of his ancestor.

Jesus Like Melchizedek

11If perfection could have been attained through the
Levitical priesthood (for on the basis of it the law was
given to the people), why was there still need for another
priest to come—one in the order of Melchizedek, not in the
order of Aaron? 12For when there is a change of the priest-
hood, there must also be a change of the law. 13He of
whom these things are said belonged to a different tribe,
and no one from that tribe has ever served at the altar.
14For it is clear that our Lord descended from Judah, and in
regard to that tribe Moses said nothing about priests.
15And what we have said is even more clear if another
priest like Melchizedek appears, 16one who has become a

NEW LIVING TRANSLATION

the promises of God. 7And without question, the person who
has the power to bless is always greater than the person
who is blessed.

8In the case of Jewish priests, tithes are paid to men who
will die. But Melchizedek is greater than they are, because
we are told that he lives on. 9In addition, we might even
say that Levi's descendants, the ones who collect the tithe,
paid a tithe to Melchizedek through their ancestor
Abraham. 10For although Levi wasn't born yet, the seed
from which he came was in Abraham's loins when Mel-
chizedek collected the tithe from him.

11And finally, if the priesthood of Levi could have
achieved God's purposes—and it was that priesthood on
which the law was based—why did God need to send a dif-
ferent priest from the line of Melchizedek, instead of from
the line of Levi and Aaron?*

12And when the priesthood is changed, the law must
also be changed to permit it. 13For the one we are talking
about belongs to a different tribe, whose members do not
serve at the altar. 14What I mean is, our Lord came from
the tribe of Judah, and Moses never mentioned Judah in
connection with the priesthood.

Christ Is like Melchizedek

15The change in God's law is even more evident from the
fact that a different priest, who is like Melchizedek, has

7:11 Greek *according to the order of Aaron.*

NEW KING JAMES VERSION

the promises. 7Now beyond all contradiction the lesser is
blessed by the better. 8Here mortal men receive tithes, but
there he *receives them,* of whom it is witnessed that he
lives. 9Even Levi, who receives tithes, paid tithes through
Abraham, so to speak, 10for he was still in the loins of his
father when Melchizedek met him.

Need for a New Priesthood

11Therefore, if perfection were through the Levitical
priesthood (for under it the people received the law), what
further need *was there* that another priest should rise
according to the order of Melchizedek, and not be called
according to the order of Aaron? 12For the priesthood being
changed, of necessity there is also a change of the law.
13For He of whom these things are spoken belongs to
another tribe, from which no man has officiated at the
altar.

14For *it is* evident that our Lord arose from Judah, of
which tribe Moses spoke nothing concerning priesthood.[a]
15And it is yet far more evident if, in the likeness of Mel-
chizedek, there arises another priest 16who has come, not

7:14 [a] NU-Text reads *priests.*

THE MESSAGE

promises had been given. In acts of blessing, the lesser is
blessed by the greater.

Or look at it this way: We pay our tithes to priests who
die, but Abraham paid tithes to a priest who, the Scripture
says, "lives." Ultimately you could even say that since Levi
descended from Abraham, who paid tithes to Melchizedek,
when we pay tithes to the priestly tribe of Levi they end up
with Melchizedek.

A Permanent Priesthood

If the priesthood of Levi and Aaron, which provided the
framework for the giving of the law, could really make
people perfect, there wouldn't have been need for a new
priesthood like that of Melchizedek. But since it didn't get
the job done, there was a change of priesthood, which
brought with it a radical new kind of law. There is no way
of understanding this in terms of the old Levitical priest-
hood, which is why there is nothing in Jesus' family tree
connecting him with that priestly line.

But the Melchizedek story provides a perfect analogy:
Jesus, a priest like Melchizedek, not by genealogical descent

KING JAMES VERSION

16 Who is made, not after the law of a carnal commandment, but after the power of an endless life.

17 For he testifieth, Thou *art* a priest for ever after the order of Melchisedec.

18 For there is verily a disannulling of the commandment going before for the weakness and unprofitableness thereof.

19 For the law made nothing perfect, but the bringing in of a better hope *did*; by the which we draw nigh unto God.

20 And inasmuch as not without an oath *he was made priest*:

21 (For those priests were made without an oath; but this with an oath by him that said unto him, The Lord sware and will not repent, Thou *art* a priest for ever after the order of Melchisedec:)

22 By so much was Jesus made a surety of a better testament.

23 And they truly were many priests, because they were not suffered to continue by reason of death:

24 But this *man*, because he continueth ever, hath an unchangeable priesthood.

NEW AMERICAN STANDARD BIBLE

16 who has become *such* not on the basis of a law of physical requirement, but according to the power of an indestructible life.

17 For it is attested *of Him*,

"YOU ARE A PRIEST FOREVER
ACCORDING TO THE ORDER OF MELCHIZEDEK."

18 For, on the one hand, there is a setting aside of a former commandment because of its weakness and uselessness

19 (for the Law made nothing perfect), and on the other hand there is a bringing in of a better hope, through which we draw near to God.

20 And inasmuch as *it was* not without an oath

21 (for they indeed became priests without an oath, but He with an oath through the One who said to Him,

"THE LORD HAS SWORN
AND WILL NOT CHANGE HIS MIND,
'YOU ARE A PRIEST FOREVER' ");

22 so much the more also Jesus has become the guarantee of a better covenant.

23 The *former* priests, on the one hand, existed in greater numbers because they were prevented by death from continuing,

24 but Jesus, on the other hand, because He continues forever, holds His priesthood permanently.

NEW CENTURY VERSION

not made a priest by human rules and laws but through
the power of his life, which continues forever. 17It is said
about him,

"You are a priest forever,
a priest like Melchizedek." *Psalm 110:4*

18The old rule is now set aside, because it was weak and
useless. 19The law of Moses could not make anything perfect.
But now a better hope has been given to us, and with
this hope we can come near to God. 20It is important that
God did this with an oath. Others became priests without
an oath, 21but Christ became a priest with God's oath. God
said:

"The Lord has made a promise
and will not change his mind.
'You are a priest forever.' " *Psalm 110:4*

22This means that Jesus is the guarantee of a better agreement[d] from God to his people.

23When one of the other priests died, he could not continue
being a priest. So there were many priests. 24But because
Jesus lives forever, he will never stop serving as priest. 25So

7:22 [d] **agreement** God gives a contract or agreement to his people. For the Jews, this agreement was the law of Moses. But now God has given a better agreement to his people through Christ.

CONTEMPORARY ENGLISH VERSION

wasn't appointed because of his ancestors, but because
his life can never end. 17The Scriptures say about him,

"You are a priest forever,
just like Melchizedek."

18In this way a weak and useless command was put aside,
19because the Law cannot make anything perfect. At the
same time, we are given a much better hope, and it can
bring us close to God.

20-21God himself made a promise when this priest was
appointed. But he did not make a promise like this when
the other priests were appointed. The promise he made is,

"I, the Lord, promise that you
will be a priest forever!
And I will never
change my mind!"

22This means that Jesus guarantees us a better agreement
with God. 23There have been a lot of other priests, and all of
them have died. 24But Jesus will never die, and so he will be

NEW INTERNATIONAL VERSION

priest not on the basis of a regulation as to his ancestry but on the basis of the power of an indestructible life. 17For it is declared:

"You are a priest forever,
in the order of Melchizedek."[a]

18The former regulation is set aside because it was weak and useless 19(for the law made nothing perfect), and a better hope is introduced, by which we draw near to God.

20And it was not without an oath! Others became priests without any oath, 21but he became a priest with an oath when God said to him:

"The Lord has sworn
and will not change his mind:
'You are a priest forever.' "[b]

22Because of this oath, Jesus has become the guarantee of a better covenant.

23Now there have been many of those priests, since death prevented them from continuing in office; 24but because Jesus lives forever, he has a permanent priesthood.

[a] *17* Psalm 110:4 [b] *21* Psalm 110:4

NEW LIVING TRANSLATION

now come. 16He became a priest, not by meeting the old requirement of belonging to the tribe of Levi, but by the power of a life that cannot be destroyed. 17And the psalmist pointed this out when he said of Christ,

"You are a priest forever
in the line of Melchizedek."*

18Yes, the old requirement about the priesthood was set aside because it was weak and useless. 19For the law made nothing perfect, and now a better hope has taken its place. And that is how we draw near to God.

20God took an oath that Christ would always be a priest, but he never did this for any other priest. 21Only to Jesus did he say,

"The Lord has taken an oath
and will not break his vow:
'You are a priest forever.'"*

22Because of God's oath, it is Jesus who guarantees the effectiveness of this better covenant.

23Another difference is that there were many priests under the old system. When one priest died, another had to take his place. 24But Jesus remains a priest forever; his priesthood will never end. 25Therefore he is able, once and

7:17 Ps 110:4. 7:21 Ps 110:4.

NEW KING JAMES VERSION

according to the law of a fleshly commandment, but according to the power of an endless life. 17For He testifies:[b]

"You are a priest forever
According to the order of Melchizedek."[c]

18For on the one hand there is an annulling of the former commandment because of its weakness and unprofitableness, 19for the law made nothing perfect; on the other hand, *there is the* bringing in of a better hope, through which we draw near to God.

Greatness of the New Priest

20And inasmuch as *He was* not *made priest* without an oath 21(for they have become priests without an oath, but He with an oath by Him who said to Him:

"The LORD has sworn
And will not relent,
'You are a priest forever[d]
According to the order of Melchizedek' "),[e]

22by so much more Jesus has become a surety of a better covenant.

23Also there were many priests, because they were prevented by death from continuing. 24But He, because He continues forever, has an unchangeable priesthood. 25Therefore

7:17 [b] NU-Text reads *it is testified.* [c] Psalm 110:4 7:21 [d] NU-Text ends the quotation here. [e] Psalm 110:4

THE MESSAGE

but by the sheer force of resurrection life—he lives!—"priest forever in the royal order of Melchizedek." The former way of doing things, a system of commandments that never worked out the way it was supposed to, was set aside; the law brought nothing to maturity. Another way—Jesus!—a way that *does* work, that brings us right into the presence of God, is put in its place.

The old priesthood of Aaron perpetuated itself automatically, father to son, without explicit confirmation by God. But then God intervened and called this new, permanent priesthood into being with an added promise:

"God gave his word;
he won't take it back:
'You're the permanent priest.'"

This makes Jesus the guarantee of a far better way between us and God—one that really works! A new covenant.

Earlier there were a lot of priests, for they died and had to be replaced. But Jesus' priesthood is permanent. He's

KING JAMES VERSION

25 Wherefore he is able also to save them to the uttermost that come unto God by him, seeing he ever liveth to make intercession for them.

26 For such an high priest became us, *who is* holy, harmless, undefiled, separate from sinners, and made higher than the heavens;

27 Who needeth not daily, as those high priests, to offer up sacrifice, first for his own sins, and then for the people's: for this he did once, when he offered up himself.

28 For the law maketh men high priests which have infirmity; but the word of the oath, which was since the law, *maketh* the Son, who is consecrated for evermore.

8 Now of the things which we have spoken *this is* the sum: We have such an high priest, who is set on the right hand of the throne of the Majesty in the heavens;

2 A minister of the sanctuary, and of the true tabernacle, which the Lord pitched, and not man.

3 For every high priest is ordained to offer gifts and sacrifices: wherefore *it is* of necessity that this man have somewhat also to offer.

4 For if he were on earth, he should not be a priest, seeing that there are priests that offer gifts according to the law:

5 Who serve unto the example and shadow of heavenly things, as Moses was admonished of God when he was about to make the tabernacle: for, See, saith he, *that* thou make all things according to the pattern shewed to thee in the mount.

NEW AMERICAN STANDARD BIBLE

25 Therefore He is able also to save forever those who draw near to God through Him, since He always lives to make intercession for them.

26 For it was fitting for us to have such a high priest, holy, innocent, undefiled, separated from sinners and exalted above the heavens;

27 who does not need daily, like those high priests, to offer up sacrifices, first for His own sins and then for the *sins* of the people, because this He did once for all when He offered up Himself.

28 For the Law appoints men as high priests who are weak, but the word of the oath, which came after the Law, *appoints* a Son, made perfect forever.

A Better Ministry

8 Now the main point in what has been said *is this:* we have such a high priest, who has taken His seat at the right hand of the throne of the Majesty in the heavens,

2 a minister in the sanctuary and in the true tabernacle, which the Lord pitched, not man.

3 For every high priest is appointed to offer both gifts and sacrifices; so it is necessary that this *high priest* also have something to offer.

4 Now if He were on earth, He would not be a priest at all, since there are those who offer the gifts according to the Law;

5 who serve a copy and shadow of the heavenly things, just as Moses was warned *by God* when he was about to erect the tabernacle; for, "SEE," He says, "THAT YOU MAKE all things ACCORDING TO THE PATTERN WHICH WAS SHOWN YOU ON THE MOUNTAIN."

NEW CENTURY VERSION

he is able always to save those who come to God through him because he always lives, asking God to help them.

26Jesus is the kind of high priest we need. He is holy, sinless, pure, not influenced by sinners, and he is raised above the heavens. 27He is not like the other priests who had to offer sacrifices every day, first for their own sins, and then for the sins of the people. Christ offered his sacrifice only once and for all time when he offered himself. 28The law chooses high priests who are people with weaknesses, but the word of God's oath came later than the law. It made God's Son to be the high priest, and that Son has been made perfect forever.

Jesus Is Our High Priest

8 Here is the point of what we are saying: We have a high priest who sits on the right side of God's throne in heaven. 2Our high priest serves in the Most Holy Place, the true place of worship that was made by God, not by humans.

3Every high priest has the work of offering gifts and sacrifices to God. So our high priest must also offer something to God. 4If our high priest were now living on earth, he would not be a priest, because there are already priests here who follow the law by offering gifts to God. 5The work they do as priests is only a copy and a shadow of what is in heaven. This is why God warned Moses when he was ready to build the Holy Tent: "Be very careful to make everything by the plan I showed you on the mountain."[a]

8:5 [a] **"Be...mountain."** Quotation from Exodus 25:40.

CONTEMPORARY ENGLISH VERSION

a priest forever! 25He is forever able to save[c] the people he leads to God, because he always lives to speak to God for them.

26Jesus is the high priest we need. He is holy and innocent and faultless, and not at all like us sinners. Jesus is honored above all beings in heaven, 27and he is better than any other high priest. Jesus doesn't need to offer sacrifices each day for his own sins and then for the sins of the people. He offered a sacrifice once for all, when he gave himself. 28The Law appoints priests who have weaknesses. But God's promise, which came later than the Law, appoints his Son. And he is the perfect high priest forever.

A Better Promise

8 What I mean is that we have a high priest who sits at the right side[a] of God's great throne in heaven. 2He also serves as the priest in the most holy place[b] inside the real tent there in heaven. This tent of worship was set up by the Lord, not by humans.

3Since all priests must offer gifts and sacrifices, Christ also needed to have something to offer. 4If he were here on earth, he would not be a priest at all, because here the Law appoints other priests to offer sacrifices. 5But the tent where they serve is just a copy and a shadow of the real one in heaven. Before Moses made the tent, he was told, "Be sure to make it exactly like the pattern you were shown

[c] **7.25** *forever able to save*: Or "able to save forever." [a] **8.1** *right side*: See the note at 1.3. [b] **8.2** *most holy place*: See the note at 6.19.

NEW INTERNATIONAL VERSION

25 Therefore he is able to save completely[c] those who come to God through him, because he always lives to intercede for them.

26 Such a high priest meets our need—one who is holy, blameless, pure, set apart from sinners, exalted above the heavens. 27 Unlike the other high priests, he does not need to offer sacrifices day after day, first for his own sins, and then for the sins of the people. He sacrificed for their sins once for all when he offered himself. 28 For the law appoints as high priests men who are weak; but the oath, which came after the law, appointed the Son, who has been made perfect forever.

The High Priest of a New Covenant

8 The point of what we are saying is this: We do have such a high priest, who sat down at the right hand of the throne of the Majesty in heaven, 2 and who serves in the sanctuary, the true tabernacle set up by the Lord, not by man.

3 Every high priest is appointed to offer both gifts and sacrifices, and so it was necessary for this one also to have something to offer. 4 If he were on earth, he would not be a priest, for there are already men who offer the gifts prescribed by the law. 5 They serve at a sanctuary that is a copy and shadow of what is in heaven. This is why Moses was warned when he was about to build the tabernacle: "See to it that you make everything according to the pattern shown

[c] *25* Or *forever*

NEW LIVING TRANSLATION

forever, to save* everyone who comes to God through him. He lives forever to plead with God on their behalf.

26 He is the kind of high priest we need because he is holy and blameless, unstained by sin. He has now been set apart from sinners, and he has been given the highest place of honor in heaven. 27 He does not need to offer sacrifices every day like the other high priests. They did this for their own sins first and then for the sins of the people. But Jesus did this once for all when he sacrificed himself on the cross. 28 Those who were high priests under the law of Moses were limited by human weakness. But after the law was given, God appointed his Son with an oath, and his Son has been made perfect forever.

Christ Is Our High Priest

8 Here is the main point: Our High Priest sat down in the place of highest honor in heaven, at God's right hand. 2 There he ministers in the sacred tent, the true place of worship that was built by the Lord and not by human hands.

3 And since every high priest is required to offer gifts and sacrifices, our High Priest must make an offering, too. 4 If he were here on earth, he would not even be a priest, since there already are priests who offer the gifts required by the law of Moses. 5 They serve in a place of worship that is only a copy, a shadow of the real one in heaven. For when Moses was getting ready to build the Tabernacle, God gave him this warning: "Be sure that you make everything according to the design I have shown you here on the mountain."*

7:25 Or *able to save completely.* 8:5 Exod 25:40; 26:30.

NEW KING JAMES VERSION

He is also able to save to the uttermost those who come to God through Him, since He always lives to make intercession for them.

26 For such a High Priest was fitting for us, *who is* holy, harmless, undefiled, separate from sinners, and has become higher than the heavens; 27 who does not need daily, as those high priests, to offer up sacrifices, first for His own sins and then for the people's, for this He did once for all when He offered up Himself. 28 For the law appoints as high priests men who have weakness, but the word of the oath, which came after the law, *appoints* the Son who has been perfected forever.

The New Priestly Service

8 Now *this is* the main point of the things we are saying: We have such a High Priest, who is seated at the right hand of the throne of the Majesty in the heavens, 2 a Minister of the sanctuary and of the true tabernacle which the Lord erected, and not man.

3 For every high priest is appointed to offer both gifts and sacrifices. Therefore *it is* necessary that this One also have something to offer. 4 For if He were on earth, He would not be a priest, since there are priests who offer the gifts according to the law; 5 who serve the copy and shadow of the heavenly things, as Moses was divinely instructed when he was about to make the tabernacle. For He said, *"See that you make all things according to the pattern shown you on the mountain."*[a] 6 But now He has obtained

8:5 [a] Exodus 25:40

THE MESSAGE

there from now to eternity to save everyone who comes to God through him, always on the job to speak up for them.

So now we have a high priest who perfectly fits our needs: completely holy, uncompromised by sin, with authority extending as high as God's presence in heaven itself. Unlike the other high priests, he doesn't have to offer sacrifices for his own sins every day before he can get around to us and our sins. He's done it, once and for all: offered up *himself* as the sacrifice. The law appoints as high priests men who are never able to get the job done right. But this intervening command of God, which came later, appoints the Son, who is absolutely, eternally perfect.

A New Plan With Israel

8 In essence, we have just such a high priest: authoritative right alongside God, conducting worship in the one true sanctuary built by God.

The assigned task of a high priest is to offer both gifts and sacrifices, and it's no different with the priesthood of Jesus. If he were limited to earth, he wouldn't even be a priest. We wouldn't need him since there are plenty of priests who offer the gifts designated in the law. These priests provide only a hint of what goes on in the true sanctuary of heaven, which Moses caught a glimpse of as he was about to set up the tent-shrine. It was then that God said, "Be careful to do it exactly as you saw it on the Mountain."

KING JAMES VERSION

6 ¶ But now hath he obtained a more excellent ministry, by how much also he is the mediator of a better covenant, which was established upon better promises.
7 For if that first *covenant* had been faultless, then should no place have been sought for the second.
8 For finding fault with them, he saith, Behold, the days come, saith the Lord, when I will make a new covenant with the house of Israel and with the house of Judah:
9 Not according to the covenant that I made with their fathers in the day when I took them by the hand to lead them out of the land of Egypt; because they continued not in my covenant, and I regarded them not, saith the Lord.
10 For this *is* the covenant that I will make with the house of Israel after those days, saith the Lord; I will put my laws into their mind, and write them in their hearts:

NEW AMERICAN STANDARD BIBLE

6 But now He has obtained a more excellent ministry, by as much as He is also the mediator of a better covenant, which has been enacted on better promises.

A New Covenant

7 For if that first *covenant* had been faultless, there would have been no occasion sought for a second.
8 For finding fault with them, He says,

"Behold, days are coming, says the Lord,
When I will effect a new covenant
With the house of Israel and with the house of Judah;
9 Not like the covenant which I made with their fathers
On the day when I took them by the hand
To lead them out of the land of Egypt;
For they did not continue in My covenant,
And I did not care for them, says the Lord.
10 "For this is the covenant that I will make with the house of Israel
After those days, says the Lord:
I will put My laws into their minds,
And I will write them on their hearts.

NEW CENTURY VERSION

6 But the priestly work that has been given to Jesus is much
greater than the work that was given to the other priests.
In the same way, the new agreement that Jesus brought
from God to his people is much greater than the old one.
And the new agreement is based on promises of better
things.
7 If there had been nothing wrong with the first agreement,[b] there would have been no need for a second agreement.
8 But God found something wrong with his people.
He says:

"Look, the time is coming, says the Lord,
when I will make a new agreement
with the people of Israel
and the people of Judah.
9 It will not be like the agreement
I made with their ancestors
when I took them by the hand
to bring them out of Egypt.
But they broke that agreement,
and I turned away from them, says the Lord.
10 This is the agreement I will make
with the people of Israel at that time, says the Lord.
I will put my teachings in their minds
and write them on their hearts.

8:7 [b] **first agreement** The contract God gave the Jewish people when he gave them the law of Moses.

CONTEMPORARY ENGLISH VERSION

on the mountain!"
6 Now Christ has been appointed to serve
as a priest in a much better way, and he has given us much
assurance of a better agreement.
7 If the first agreement with God had been all right, there
would not have been any need for another one.
8 But the
Lord found fault with it and said,

"I tell you the time will come,
when I will make
a new agreement
with the people of Israel
and the people of Judah.
9 It won't be like the agreement
that I made
with their ancestors,
when I took them by the hand
and led them out of Egypt.
They broke their agreement
with me,
and I stopped caring
about them!

10 "But now I tell the people
of Israel
this is my new agreement:
'The time will come
when I, the Lord,
will write my laws
on their minds and hearts.

NEW INTERNATIONAL VERSION

you on the mountain."[a] 6But the ministry Jesus has received
is as superior to theirs as the covenant of which he is medi-
ator is superior to the old one, and it is founded on better
promises.

7For if there had been nothing wrong with that first cov-
enant, no place would have been sought for another. 8But
God found fault with the people and said[b]:

"The time is coming, declares the Lord,
when I will make a new covenant
with the house of Israel
and with the house of Judah.
9It will not be like the covenant
I made with their forefathers
when I took them by the hand
to lead them out of Egypt,
because they did not remain faithful to my covenant,
and I turned away from them,
declares the Lord.
10This is the covenant I will make with the house of Israel
after that time, declares the Lord.
I will put my laws in their minds
and write them on their hearts.

[a] *5* Exodus 25:40 [b] *8* Some manuscripts may be translated *fault and said to the people.*

NEW LIVING TRANSLATION

6But our High Priest has been given a ministry that is far
superior to the ministry of those who serve under the old
laws, for he is the one who guarantees for us a better cov-
enant with God, based on better promises.

7If the first covenant had been faultless, there would
have been no need for a second covenant to replace it. 8But
God himself found fault with the old one when he said:

"The day will come, says the Lord,
when I will make a new covenant
with the people of Israel and Judah.
9 This covenant will not be like the one
I made with their ancestors
when I took them by the hand
and led them out of the land of Egypt.
They did not remain faithful to my covenant,
so I turned my back on them, says the Lord.
10 But this is the new covenant I will make
with the people of Israel on that day, says the Lord:
I will put my laws in their minds
so they will understand them,
and I will write them on their hearts
so they will obey them.

NEW KING JAMES VERSION

a more excellent ministry, inasmuch as He is also Mediator
of a better covenant, which was established on better
promises.

A New Covenant

7For if that first *covenant* had been faultless, then no
place would have been sought for a second. 8Because find-
ing fault with them, He says: *"Behold, the days are com-
ing, says the* Lord, *when I will make a new covenant with
the house of Israel and with the house of Judah—* 9*not
according to the covenant that I made with their fathers in
the day when I took them by the hand to lead them out of
the land of Egypt; because they did not continue in My
covenant, and I disregarded them, says the* Lord. 10*For this
is the covenant that I will make with the house of Israel
after those days, says the* Lord: *I will put My laws in their
mind and write them on their hearts; and I will be their*

THE MESSAGE

But Jesus' priestly work far surpasses what these other
priests do, since he's working from a far better plan. If the
first plan—the old covenant—had worked out, a second
wouldn't have been needed. But we know the first was
found wanting, because God said,

"Heads up! The days are coming
when I'll set up a new plan
for dealing with Israel and Judah.
I'll throw out the old plan
I set up with their ancestors
when I led them by the hand out of Egypt.
They didn't keep their part of the bargain,
so I looked away and let it go.
This new plan I'm making with Israel
isn't going to be written on paper,
isn't going to be chiseled in stone;
This time I'm writing out the plan *in* them,
carving it on the lining of their hearts.

KING JAMES VERSION

and I will be to them a God, and they shall be to me a peo-
ple:
11 And they shall not teach every man his neighbour,
and every man his brother, saying, Know the Lord: for all
shall know me, from the least to the greatest.
12 For I will be merciful to their unrighteousness, and
their sins and their iniquities will I remember no more.
13 In that he saith, A new *covenant*, he hath made the
first old. Now that which decayeth and waxeth old *is* ready
to vanish away.

9 Then verily the first *covenant* had also ordinances of
divine service, and a worldly sanctuary.
2 For there was a tabernacle made; the first, wherein
was the candlestick, and the table, and the shewbread;
which is called the sanctuary.
3 And after the second veil, the tabernacle which is
called the Holiest of all;
4 Which had the golden censer, and the ark of the cov-
enant overlaid round about with gold, wherein *was* the

NEW AMERICAN STANDARD BIBLE

AND I WILL BE THEIR GOD,
AND THEY SHALL BE MY PEOPLE.
11 "AND THEY SHALL NOT TEACH EVERYONE HIS FELLOW
CITIZEN,
AND EVERYONE HIS BROTHER, SAYING, 'KNOW THE LORD,'
FOR ALL WILL KNOW ME,
FROM THE LEAST TO THE GREATEST OF THEM.
12 "FOR I WILL BE MERCIFUL TO THEIR INIQUITIES,
AND I WILL REMEMBER THEIR SINS NO MORE."
13 When He said, "A new *covenant*," He has made the
first obsolete. But whatever is becoming obsolete and
growing old is ready to disappear.

The Old and the New

9 Now even the first *covenant* had regulations of divine
worship and the earthly sanctuary.
2 For there was a tabernacle prepared, the outer one, in
which *were* the lampstand and the table and the sacred
bread; this is called the holy place.
3 Behind the second veil there was a tabernacle which
is called the Holy of Holies,
4 having a golden altar of incense and the ark of the
covenant covered on all sides with gold, in which was a

NEW CENTURY VERSION

I will be their God,
and they will be my people.
11 People will no longer have to teach their neighbors and
relatives
to know the Lord,
because all people will know me,
from the least to the most important.
12 I will forgive them for the wicked things they did,
and I will not remember their sins anymore."
Jeremiah 31:31–34

13 God called this a new agreement, so he has made the
first agreement old. And anything that is old and worn out
is ready to disappear.

The Old Agreement

9 The first agreement[a] had rules for worship and a man-
made place for worship. 2 The Holy Tent was set up for
this. The first area in the Tent was called the Holy Place. In
it were the lamp and the table with the bread that was
made holy for God. 3 Behind the second curtain was a room
called the Most Holy Place. 4 In it was a golden altar for
burning incense and the Ark covered with gold that held
the old agreement. Inside this Ark was a golden jar of

9:1 [a] **first agreement** The contract God gave the Jewish people when he gave them the law of Moses.

CONTEMPORARY ENGLISH VERSION

I will be their God,
and they will be
my people.
11 Not one of them
will have to teach another
to know me, their Lord.'
"All of them will know me,
no matter who they are.
12 I will treat them with kindness,
even though they are wicked.
I will forget their sins."
13 When the Lord talks about a new agreement, he
means that the first one is out of date. And anything that
is old and useless will soon disappear.

The Tent in Heaven

9 The first promise that was made included rules for wor-
ship and a tent for worship here on earth. 2 The first
part of the tent was called the holy place, and a lampstand,
a table, and the sacred loaves of bread were kept there.
3 Behind the curtain was the most holy place. 4 The gold
altar that was used for burning incense was in this holy
place. The gold-covered sacred chest was also there, and
inside it were three things. First, there was a gold jar filled

NEW INTERNATIONAL VERSION

I will be their God,
and they will be my people.
11 No longer will a man teach his neighbor,
or a man his brother, saying, 'Know the Lord,'
because they will all know me,
from the least of them to the greatest.
12 For I will forgive their wickedness
and will remember their sins no more."[c]

13 By calling this covenant "new," he has made the first
one obsolete; and what is obsolete and aging will soon dis-
appear.

Worship in the Earthly Tabernacle

9 Now the first covenant had regulations for worship
and also an earthly sanctuary. 2 A tabernacle was set
up. In its first room were the lampstand, the table and the
consecrated bread; this was called the Holy Place. 3 Behind
the second curtain was a room called the Most Holy Place,
4 which had the golden altar of incense and the gold-cov-
ered ark of the covenant. This ark contained the gold jar of

[c] *12* Jer. 31:31–34

NEW LIVING TRANSLATION

I will be their God,
and they will be my people.
11 And they will not need to teach their neighbors,
nor will they need to teach their family,
saying, 'You should know the Lord.'
For everyone, from the least to the greatest,
will already know me.
12 And I will forgive their wrongdoings,
and I will never again remember their sins."*

13 When God speaks of a new covenant, it means he has
made the first one obsolete. It is now out of date and ready
to be put aside.

Old Rules about Worship

9 Now in that first covenant between God and Israel,
there were regulations for worship and a sacred tent
here on earth. 2 There were two rooms in this tent. In the
first room were a lampstand, a table, and loaves of holy
bread on the table. This was called the Holy Place. 3 Then
there was a curtain, and behind the curtain was the second
room called the Most Holy Place. 4 In that room were a gold
incense altar and a wooden chest called the Ark of the
Covenant, which was covered with gold on all sides. Inside

8:8-12 Jer 31:31-34.

NEW KING JAMES VERSION

God, and they shall be My people. 11 *None of them shall
teach his neighbor, and none his brother, saying, 'Know
the LORD,' for all shall know Me, from the least of them to
the greatest of them.* 12 *For I will be merciful to their
unrighteousness, and their sins and their lawless deeds*[b] *I
will remember no more."*[c]
13 In that He says, *"A new covenant,"* He has made the
first obsolete. Now what is becoming obsolete and growing
old is ready to vanish away.

The Earthly Sanctuary

9 Then indeed, even the first *covenant* had ordinances
of divine service and the earthly sanctuary. 2 For a
tabernacle was prepared: the first *part,* in which *was* the
lampstand, the table, and the showbread, which is called
the sanctuary; 3 and behind the second veil, the part of the
tabernacle which is called the Holiest of All, 4 which had
the golden censer and the ark of the covenant overlaid on
all sides with gold, in which *were* the golden pot that had

8:12 [b] NU-Text omits *and their lawless deeds.* [c] Jeremiah 31:31–34

THE MESSAGE

I'll be their God,
they'll be my people.
They won't go to school to learn about me,
or buy a book called *God in Five Easy Lessons*.
They'll all get to know me firsthand,
the little and the big, the small and the great.
They'll get to know me by being kindly forgiven,
with the slate of their sins forever wiped clean."

By coming up with a new plan, a new covenant between
God and his people, God put the old plan on the shelf. And
there it stays, gathering dust.

A Visible Parable

9 That first plan contained directions for worship, and a
specially designed place of worship. A large outer tent
was set up. The lampstand, the table, and "the bread of
presence" were placed in it. This was called "the Holy
Place." Then a curtain was stretched, and behind it a
smaller, inside tent set up. This was called "the Holy of
Holies." In it were placed the gold incense altar and the
gold-covered ark of the covenant containing the gold urn

KING JAMES VERSION

golden pot that had manna, and Aaron's rod that budded, and the tables of the covenant;

5 And over it the cherubims of glory shadowing the mercyseat; of which we cannot now speak particularly.

6 Now when these things were thus ordained, the priests went always into the first tabernacle, accomplishing the service *of God*.

7 But into the second *went* the high priest alone once every year, not without blood, which he offered for himself, and *for* the errors of the people:

8 ¶ The Holy Ghost this signifying, that the way into the holiest of all was not yet made manifest, while as the first tabernacle was yet standing:

9 Which *was* a figure for the time then present, in which were offered both gifts and sacrifices, that could not make him that did the service perfect, as pertaining to the conscience;

10 *Which stood* only in meats and drinks, and divers washings, and carnal ordinances, imposed *on them* until the time of reformation.

NEW AMERICAN STANDARD BIBLE

golden jar holding the manna, and Aaron's rod which budded, and the tables of the covenant;

5 and above it *were* the cherubim of glory overshadowing the mercy seat; but of these things we cannot now speak in detail.

6 Now when these things have been so prepared, the priests are continually entering the outer tabernacle performing the divine worship,

7 but into the second, only the high priest *enters* once a year, not without *taking* blood, which he offers for himself and for the sins of the people committed in ignorance.

8 The Holy Spirit *is* signifying this, that the way into the holy place has not yet been disclosed while the outer tabernacle is still standing,

9 which *is* a symbol for the present time. Accordingly both gifts and sacrifices are offered which cannot make the worshiper perfect in conscience,

10 since they *relate* only to food and drink and various washings, regulations for the body imposed until a time of reformation.

NEW CENTURY VERSION

manna, Aaron's rod that once grew leaves, and the stone
tablets of the old agreement. [5]Above the Ark were the crea-
tures that showed God's glory, whose wings reached over
the lid. But we cannot tell everything about these things
now.
[6]When everything in the Tent was made ready in this
way, the priests went into the first room every day to wor-
ship. [7]But only the high priest could go into the second
room, and he did that only once a year. He could never
enter the inner room without taking blood with him, which
he offered to God for himself and for sins the people did
without knowing they did them. [8]The Holy Spirit uses this
to show that the way into the Most Holy Place was not
open while the system of the old Holy Tent was still being
used. [9]This is an example for the present time. It shows
that the gifts and sacrifices offered cannot make the con-
science of the worshiper perfect. [10]These gifts and sacri-
fices were only about food and drink and special washings.
They were rules for the body, to be followed until the time
of God's new way.

CONTEMPORARY ENGLISH VERSION

with manna.[a] Then there was Aaron's walking stick that
sprouted.[b] Finally, there were the flat stones with the Ten
Commandments written on them. [5]On top of the chest were
the glorious creatures with wings[c] opened out above the
place of mercy.[d]
Now isn't the time to go into detail about these things.
[6]But this is how everything was when the priests went
each day into the first part of the tent to do their duties.
[7]However, only the high priest could go into the second
part of the tent, and he went in only once a year. Each
time he carried blood to offer for his sins and for any sins
that the people had committed without meaning to.
[8]All of this is the Holy Spirit's way of saying that no one
could enter the most holy place while the tent was still the
place of worship. [9]This also has a meaning for today. It
shows that we cannot make our consciences clear by offer-
ing gifts and sacrifices. [10]These rules are merely about
such things as eating and drinking and ceremonies for
washing ourselves. And rules about physical things will
last only until the time comes to change them for some-
thing better.

[a] **9.4** *manna*: When the people of Israel were wandering through the desert, the Lord provided them with food that could be made into thin wafers. This food was called manna, which in Hebrew means "What is it?" [b] **9.4** *Aaron's walking stick that sprouted*: According to Numbers 17.1-11, Aaron's walking stick sprouted and produced almonds to show that the Lord was pleased with him and Moses. [c] **9.5** *glorious creatures with wings*: Two of these creatures (called "cherubim" in Hebrew and Greek) with outspread wings were on top of the sacred chest and were symbols of God's throne. [d] **9.5** *place of mercy*: The lid of the sacred chest, which was thought to be God's throne on earth.

NEW INTERNATIONAL VERSION

manna, Aaron's staff that had budded, and the stone tablets of the covenant. [5]Above the ark were the cherubim of the Glory, overshadowing the atonement cover.[a] But we cannot discuss these things in detail now.

[6]When everything had been arranged like this, the priests entered regularly into the outer room to carry on their ministry. [7]But only the high priest entered the inner room, and that only once a year, and never without blood, which he offered for himself and for the sins the people had committed in ignorance. [8]The Holy Spirit was showing by this that the way into the Most Holy Place had not yet been disclosed as long as the first tabernacle was still standing. [9]This is an illustration for the present time, indicating that the gifts and sacrifices being offered were not able to clear the conscience of the worshiper. [10]They are only a matter of food and drink and various ceremonial washings—external regulations applying until the time of the new order.

[a] *5* Traditionally *the mercy seat*

NEW LIVING TRANSLATION

the Ark were a gold jar containing some manna, Aaron's staff that sprouted leaves, and the stone tablets of the covenant with the Ten Commandments written on them. [5]The glorious cherubim were above the Ark. Their wings were stretched out over the Ark's cover, the place of atonement. But we cannot explain all of these things now.

[6]When these things were all in place, the priests went in and out of the first room* regularly as they performed their religious duties. [7]But only the high priest goes into the Most Holy Place, and only once a year, and always with blood, which he offers to God to cover his own sins and the sins the people have committed in ignorance. [8]By these regulations the Holy Spirit revealed that the Most Holy Place was not open to the people as long as the first room and the entire system it represents were still in use.

[9]This is an illustration pointing to the present time. For the gifts and sacrifices that the priests offer are not able to cleanse the consciences of the people who bring them. [10]For that old system deals only with food and drink and ritual washing—external regulations that are in effect only until their limitations can be corrected.

9:6 Greek *first tent;* also in 9:8.

NEW KING JAMES VERSION

the manna, Aaron's rod that budded, and the tablets of the covenant; [5]and above it were the cherubim of glory overshadowing the mercy seat. Of these things we cannot now speak in detail.

Limitations of the Earthly Service

[6]Now when these things had been thus prepared, the priests always went into the first part of the tabernacle, performing *the services.* [7]But into the second part the high priest *went* alone once a year, not without blood, which he offered for himself and *for* the people's sins *committed* in ignorance; [8]the Holy Spirit indicating this, that the way into the Holiest of All was not yet made manifest while the first tabernacle was still standing. [9]It *was* symbolic for the present time in which both gifts and sacrifices are offered which cannot make him who performed the service perfect in regard to the conscience— [10]*concerned* only with foods and drinks, various washings, and fleshly ordinances imposed until the time of reformation.

THE MESSAGE

of manna, Aaron's rod that budded, the covenant tablets, and the angel-wing-shadowed mercy seat. But we don't have time to comment on these now.

After this was set up, the priests went about their duties in the large tent. Only the high priest entered the smaller, inside tent, and then only once a year, offering a blood sacrifice for his own sins and the people's accumulated sins. This was the Holy Spirit's way of showing with a visible parable that as long as the large tent stands, people can't just walk in on God. Under this system, the gifts and sacrifices can't really get to the heart of the matter, can't assuage the conscience of the people, but are limited to matters of ritual and behavior. It's essentially a temporary arrangement until a complete overhaul could be made.

KING JAMES VERSION

11 But Christ being come an high priest of good things to come, by a greater and more perfect tabernacle, not made with hands, that is to say, not of this building;

12 Neither by the blood of goats and calves, but by his own blood he entered in once into the holy place, having obtained eternal redemption *for us*.

13 For if the blood of bulls and of goats, and the ashes of an heifer sprinkling the unclean, sanctifieth to the purifying of the flesh:

14 How much more shall the blood of Christ, who through the eternal Spirit offered himself without spot to God, purge your conscience from dead works to serve the living God?

15 ¶ And for this cause he is the mediator of the new testament, that by means of death, for the redemption of the transgressions *that were* under the first testament, they which are called might receive the promise of eternal inheritance.

16 For where a testament *is*, there must also of necessity be the death of the testator.

17 For a testament *is* of force after men are dead: otherwise it is of no strength at all while the testator liveth.

NEW AMERICAN STANDARD BIBLE

11 But when Christ appeared *as* a high priest of the good things [1]to come, *He entered* through the greater and more perfect tabernacle, not made with hands, that is to say, not of this creation;

12 and not through the blood of goats and calves, but through His own blood, He entered the holy place once for all, having obtained eternal redemption.

13 For if the blood of goats and bulls and the ashes of a heifer sprinkling those who have been defiled sanctify for the cleansing of the flesh,

14 how much more will the blood of Christ, who through the eternal Spirit offered Himself without blemish to God, cleanse your conscience from dead works to serve the living God?

15 For this reason He is the mediator of a new covenant, so that, since a death has taken place for the redemption of the transgressions that were *committed* under the first covenant, those who have been called may receive the promise of the eternal inheritance.

16 For where a covenant is, there must of necessity be the death of the one who made it.

17 For a covenant is valid *only* when men are dead, [2]for it is never in force while the one who made it lives.

9:11 [1] Two early mss read *that have come* **9:17** [2] Two early mss read *for is it then...lives?*

NEW CENTURY VERSION

The New Agreement

11But when Christ came as the high priest of the good things we now have, he entered the greater and more perfect tent. It is not made by humans and does not belong to this world. 12Christ entered the Most Holy Place only once—and for all time. He did not take with him the blood of goats and calves. His sacrifice was his own blood, and by it he set us free from sin forever. 13The blood of goats and bulls and the ashes of a cow are sprinkled on the people who are unclean, and this makes their bodies clean again. 14How much more is done by the blood of Christ. He offered himself through the eternal Spirit[b] as a perfect sacrifice to God. His blood will make our consciences pure from useless acts so we may serve the living God.

15For this reason Christ brings a new agreement from God to his people. Those who are called by God can now receive the blessings he has promised, blessings that will last forever. They can have those things because Christ died so that the people who lived under the first agreement could be set free from sin.

16When there is a will,[c] it must be proven that the one who wrote that will is dead. 17A will means nothing while the person is alive; it can be used only after the person

9:14 [b] **Spirit** This refers to the Holy Spirit, to Christ's own spirit, or to the spiritual and eternal nature of his sacrifice. **9:16** [c] **will** A legal document that shows how a person's money and property are to be distributed at the time of death. This is the same word in Greek as "agreement" in verse 15.

CONTEMPORARY ENGLISH VERSION

11Christ came as the high priest of the good things that are now here.[e] He also went into a much better tent that wasn't made by humans and that doesn't belong to this world. 12Then Christ went once for all into the most holy place and freed us from sin forever. He did this by offering his own blood instead of the blood of goats and bulls.

13According to the Law of Moses, those people who become unclean are not fit to worship God. Yet they will be considered clean, if they are sprinkled with the blood of goats and bulls and with the ashes of a sacrificed calf. 14But Christ was sinless, and he offered himself as an eternal and spiritual sacrifice to God. That's why his blood is much more powerful and makes our[f] consciences clear. Now we can serve the living God and no longer do things that lead to death.

15Christ died to rescue those who had sinned and broken the old agreement. Now he brings his chosen ones a new agreement with its guarantee of God's eternal blessings! 16In fact, making an agreement of this kind is like writing a will. This is because the one who makes the will must die before it is of any use. 17In other words, a will doesn't go into effect as long as the one who made it is still alive.

[e] **9.11** *that are now here*: Some manuscripts have "that were coming."
[f] **9.14** *our*: Some manuscripts have "your," and others have "their."

NEW INTERNATIONAL VERSION

The Blood of Christ

[11]When Christ came as high priest of the good things that are already here,[b] he went through the greater and more perfect tabernacle that is not man-made, that is to say, not a part of this creation. [12]He did not enter by means of the blood of goats and calves; but he entered the Most Holy Place once for all by his own blood, having obtained eternal redemption. [13]The blood of goats and bulls and the ashes of a heifer sprinkled on those who are ceremonially unclean sanctify them so that they are outwardly clean. [14]How much more, then, will the blood of Christ, who through the eternal Spirit offered himself unblemished to God, cleanse our consciences from acts that lead to death,[c] so that we may serve the living God!

[15]For this reason Christ is the mediator of a new covenant, that those who are called may receive the promised eternal inheritance—now that he has died as a ransom to set them free from the sins committed under the first covenant.

[16]In the case of a will,[d] it is necessary to prove the death of the one who made it, [17]because a will is in force only when somebody has died; it never takes effect while the one who made it is living. [18]This is why even the first

[b] *11* Some early manuscripts *are to come* [c] *14* Or *from useless rituals*
[d] *16* Same Greek word as *covenant*; also in verse 17

NEW LIVING TRANSLATION

Christ Is the Perfect Sacrifice

[11]So Christ has now become the High Priest over all the good things that have come. He has entered that great, perfect sanctuary in heaven, not made by human hands and not part of this created world. [12]Once for all time he took blood into that Most Holy Place, but not the blood of goats and calves. He took his own blood, and with it he secured our salvation forever.

[13]Under the old system, the blood of goats and bulls and the ashes of a young cow could cleanse people's bodies from ritual defilement. [14]Just think how much more the blood of Christ will purify our hearts from deeds that lead to death so that we can worship the living God. For by the power of the eternal Spirit, Christ offered himself to God as a perfect sacrifice for our sins. [15]That is why he is the one who mediates the new covenant between God and people, so that all who are invited can receive the eternal inheritance God has promised them. For Christ died to set them free from the penalty of the sins they had committed under that first covenant.

[16]Now when someone dies and leaves a will, no one gets anything until it is proved that the person who wrote the will* is dead.* [17]The will goes into effect only after the death of the person who wrote it. While the person is still alive, no one can use the will to get any of the things promised to them.

9:16a Or *covenant.* **9:16b** Or *Now when someone makes a covenant, it is necessary to ratify it with the death of a sacrifice.*

NEW KING JAMES VERSION

The Heavenly Sanctuary

[11]But Christ came *as* High Priest of the good things to come,[a] with the greater and more perfect tabernacle not made with hands, that is, not of this creation. [12]Not with the blood of goats and calves, but with His own blood He entered the Most Holy Place once for all, having obtained eternal redemption. [13]For if the blood of bulls and goats and the ashes of a heifer, sprinkling the unclean, sanctifies for the purifying of the flesh, [14]how much more shall the blood of Christ, who through the eternal Spirit offered Himself without spot to God, cleanse your conscience from dead works to serve the living God? [15]And for this reason He is the Mediator of the new covenant, by means of death, for the redemption of the transgressions under the first covenant, that those who are called may receive the promise of the eternal inheritance.

The Mediator's Death Necessary

[16]For where there *is* a testament, there must also of necessity be the death of the testator. [17]For a testament *is* in force after men are dead, since it has no power at all while the testator lives. [18]Therefore not even the first

9:11 [a] NU-Text reads *that have come.*

THE MESSAGE

Pointing to the Realities of Heaven

But when the Messiah arrived, high priest of the superior things of this new covenant, he bypassed the old tent and its trappings in this created world and went straight into heaven's "tent"—the true Holy Place—once and for all. He also bypassed the sacrifices consisting of goat and calf blood, instead using his own blood as the price to set us free once and for all. If that animal blood and the other rituals of purification were effective in cleaning up certain matters of our religion and behavior, think how much more the blood of Christ cleans up our whole lives, inside and out. Through the Spirit, Christ offered himself as an unblemished sacrifice, freeing us from all those dead-end efforts to make ourselves respectable, so that we can live all out for God.

Like a will that takes effect when someone dies, the new covenant was put into action at Jesus' death. His death marked the transition from the old plan to the new one, canceling the old obligations and accompanying sins, and summoning the heirs to receive the eternal inheritance that was promised them. He brought together God and his people in this new way.

KING JAMES VERSION

18 Whereupon neither the first *testament* was dedicated without blood.

19 For when Moses had spoken every precept to all the people according to the law, he took the blood of calves and of goats, with water, and scarlet wool, and hyssop, and sprinkled both the book, and all the people,

20 Saying, This *is* the blood of the testament which God hath enjoined unto you.

21 Moreover he sprinkled with blood both the tabernacle, and all the vessels of the ministry.

22 And almost all things are by the law purged with blood; and without shedding of blood is no remission.

23 ¶ *It was* therefore necessary that the patterns of things in the heavens should be purified with these; but the heavenly things themselves with better sacrifices than these.

24 For Christ is not entered into the holy places made with hands, *which are* the figures of the true; but into heaven itself, now to appear in the presence of God for us:

25 Nor yet that he should offer himself often, as the high priest entereth into the holy place every year with blood of others;

26 For then must he often have suffered since the foundation of the world: but now once in the end of the world hath he appeared to put away sin by the sacrifice of himself.

NEW AMERICAN STANDARD BIBLE

18 Therefore even the first *covenant* was not inaugurated without blood.

19 For when every commandment had been spoken by Moses to all the people according to the Law, he took the blood of the calves and the goats, with water and scarlet wool and hyssop, and sprinkled both the book itself and all the people,

20 saying, "THIS IS THE BLOOD OF THE COVENANT WHICH GOD COMMANDED YOU."

21 And in the same way he sprinkled both the tabernacle and all the vessels of the ministry with the blood.

22 And according to the Law, *one may* almost *say*, all things are cleansed with blood, and without shedding of blood there is no forgiveness.

23 Therefore it was necessary for the copies of the things in the heavens to be cleansed with these, but the heavenly things themselves with better sacrifices than these.

24 For Christ did not enter a holy place made with hands, a *mere* copy of the true one, but into heaven itself, now to appear in the presence of God for us;

25 nor was it that He would offer Himself often, as the high priest enters the holy place year by year with blood that is not his own.

26 Otherwise, He would have needed to suffer often since the foundation of the world; but now once at the consummation of the ages He has been manifested to put away sin by the sacrifice of Himself.

NEW CENTURY VERSION

dies. [18]This is why even the first agreement could not begin without blood to show death. [19]First, Moses told all the people every command in the law. Next he took the blood of calves and mixed it with water. Then he used red wool and a branch of the hyssop plant to sprinkle it on the book of the law and on all the people. [20]He said, "This is the blood that begins the Agreement that God commanded you to obey."[d] [21]In the same way, Moses sprinkled the blood on the Holy Tent and over all the things used in worship. [22]The law says that almost everything must be made clean by blood, and sins cannot be forgiven without blood to show death.

Christ's Death Takes Away Sins

[23]So the copies of the real things in heaven had to be made clean by animal sacrifices. But the real things in heaven need much better sacrifices. [24]Christ did not go into the Most Holy Place made by humans, which is only a copy of the real one. He went into heaven itself and is there now before God to help us. [25]The high priest enters the Most Holy Place once every year with blood that is not his own. But Christ did not offer himself many times. [26]Then he would have had to suffer many times since the world was made. But Christ came only once and for all time at just the right time to take away all sin by sacrificing himself. [27]Just

9:20 [d] **"This...obey."** Quotation from Exodus 24:8.

CONTEMPORARY ENGLISH VERSION

[18]Blood was also used[g] to put the first agreement into effect. [19]Moses told the people all that the Law said they must do. Then he used red wool and a hyssop plant to sprinkle the people and the book of the Law with the blood of bulls and goats[h] and with water. [20]He told the people, "With this blood God makes his agreement with you." [21]Moses also sprinkled blood on the tent and on everything else that was used in worship. [22]The Law says that almost everything must be sprinkled with blood, and no sins can be forgiven unless blood is offered.

Christ's Great Sacrifice

[23]These things are only copies of what is in heaven, and so they had to be made holy by these ceremonies. But the real things in heaven must be made holy by something better. [24]This is why Christ did not go into a tent that had been made by humans and was only a copy of the real one. Instead, he went into heaven and is now there with God to help us.

[25]Christ did not have to offer himself many times. He wasn't like a high priest who goes into the most holy place each year to offer the blood of an animal. [26]If he had offered himself every year, he would have suffered many times since the creation of the world. But instead, near the end of time he offered himself once and for all, so that he could be a sacrifice that does away with sin.

[g] **9.18** *Blood was also used*: Or "There also had to be a death."
[h] **9.19** *blood of bulls and goats*: Some manuscripts do not have "and goats."

NEW INTERNATIONAL VERSION

covenant was not put into effect without blood. 19When Moses had proclaimed every commandment of the law to all the people, he took the blood of calves, together with water, scarlet wool and branches of hyssop, and sprinkled the scroll and all the people. 20He said, "This is the blood of the covenant, which God has commanded you to keep."[e] 21In the same way, he sprinkled with the blood both the tabernacle and everything used in its ceremonies. 22In fact, the law requires that nearly everything be cleansed with blood, and without the shedding of blood there is no forgiveness.

23It was necessary, then, for the copies of the heavenly things to be purified with these sacrifices, but the heavenly things themselves with better sacrifices than these. 24For Christ did not enter a man-made sanctuary that was only a copy of the true one; he entered heaven itself, now to appear for us in God's presence. 25Nor did he enter heaven to offer himself again and again, the way the high priest enters the Most Holy Place every year with blood that is not his own. 26Then Christ would have had to suffer many times since the creation of the world. But now he has appeared once for all at the end of the ages to do away with sin by the sacrifice of himself. 27Just as man is

e 20 Exodus 24:8

NEW LIVING TRANSLATION

18That is why blood was required under the first covenant as a proof of death. 19For after Moses had given the people all of God's laws, he took the blood of calves and goats, along with water, and sprinkled both the book of God's laws and all the people, using branches of hyssop bushes and scarlet wool. 20Then he said, "This blood confirms the covenant God has made with you."* 21And in the same way, he sprinkled blood on the sacred tent and on everything used for worship. 22In fact, we can say that according to the law of Moses, nearly everything was purified by sprinkling with blood. Without the shedding of blood, there is no forgiveness of sins.

23That is why the earthly tent and everything in it—which were copies of things in heaven—had to be purified by the blood of animals. But the real things in heaven had to be purified with far better sacrifices than the blood of animals.

24For Christ has entered into heaven itself to appear now before God as our Advocate.* He did not go into the earthly place of worship, for that was merely a copy of the real Temple in heaven. 25Nor did he enter heaven to offer himself again and again, like the earthly high priest who enters the Most Holy Place year after year to offer the blood of an animal. 26If that had been necessary, he would have had to die again and again, ever since the world began. But no! He came once for all time, at the end of the age, to remove the power of sin forever by his sacrificial death for us.

9:20 Exod 24:8. **9:24** Greek *on our behalf.*

NEW KING JAMES VERSION

covenant was dedicated without blood. 19For when Moses had spoken every precept to all the people according to the law, he took the blood of calves and goats, with water, scarlet wool, and hyssop, and sprinkled both the book itself and all the people, 20saying, *"This is the blood of the covenant which God has commanded you."*[b] 21Then likewise he sprinkled with blood both the tabernacle and all the vessels of the ministry. 22And according to the law almost all things are purified with blood, and without shedding of blood there is no remission.

Greatness of Christ's Sacrifice

23Therefore *it was* necessary that the copies of the things in the heavens should be purified with these, but the heavenly things themselves with better sacrifices than these. 24For Christ has not entered the holy places made with hands, *which are* copies of the true, but into heaven itself, now to appear in the presence of God for us; 25not that He should offer Himself often, as the high priest enters the Most Holy Place every year with blood of another— 26He then would have had to suffer often since the foundation of the world; but now, once at the end of the ages, He has appeared to put away sin by the sacrifice of Himself. 27And

9:20 *b* Exodus 24:8

THE MESSAGE

Even the first plan required a death to set it in motion. After Moses had read out all the terms of the plan of the law—God's "will"—he took the blood of sacrificed animals and, in a solemn ritual, sprinkled the document and the people who were its beneficiaries. And then he attested its validity with the words, "This is the blood of the covenant commanded by God." He did the same thing with the place of worship and its furniture. Moses said to the people, "This is the blood of the covenant God has established with you." Practically everything in a will hinges on a death. That's why blood, the evidence of death, is used so much in our tradition, especially regarding forgiveness of sins.

That accounts for the prominence of blood and death in all these secondary practices that point to the realities of heaven. It also accounts for why, when the real thing takes place, these animal sacrifices aren't needed anymore, having served their purpose. For Christ didn't enter the earthly version of the Holy Place; he entered the Place Itself, and offered himself to God as the sacrifice for our sins. He doesn't do this every year as the high priests did under the old plan with blood that was not their own; if that had been the case, he would have to sacrifice himself repeatedly throughout the course of history. But instead he sacrificed himself once and for all, summing up all the other sacrifices in this sacrifice of himself, the final solution of sin.

KING JAMES VERSION

27 And as it is appointed unto men once to die, but
after this the judgment:
28 So Christ was once offered to bear the sins of many;
and unto them that look for him shall he appear the sec-
ond time without sin unto salvation.

10 For the law having a shadow of good things to
come, *and* not the very image of the things, can
never with those sacrifices which they offered year by year
continually make the comers thereunto perfect.
2 For then would they not have ceased to be offered?
because that the worshippers once purged should have had
no more conscience of sins.
3 But in those *sacrifices there is* a remembrance again
made of sins every year.
4 For *it is* not possible that the blood of bulls and of
goats should take away sins.
5 Wherefore when he cometh into the world, he saith,
Sacrifice and offering thou wouldest not, but a body hast
thou prepared me:
6 In burnt offerings and *sacrifices* for sin thou hast had
no pleasure.
7 ¶ Then said I, Lo, I come (in the volume of the book it
is written of me,) to do thy will, O God.

NEW AMERICAN STANDARD BIBLE

27 And inasmuch as it is appointed for men to die once
and after this *comes* judgment,
28 so Christ also, having been offered once to bear the
sins of many, will appear a second time for salvation with-
out *reference to* sin, to those who eagerly await Him.

One Sacrifice of Christ Is Sufficient

10 For the Law, since it has *only* a shadow of the
good things to come *and* not the very form of
things, [l]can never, by the same sacrifices which they offer
continually year by year, make perfect those who draw
near.
2 Otherwise, would they not have ceased to be offered,
because the worshipers, having once been cleansed, would
no longer have had consciousness of sins?
3 But in those *sacrifices* there is a reminder of sins
year by year.
4 For it is impossible for the blood of bulls and goats to
take away sins.
5 Therefore, when He comes into the world, He says,
"Sacrifice and offering You have not desired,
But a body You have prepared for Me;
6 In whole burnt offerings and *sacrifices* for sin You
have taken no pleasure.
7 "Then I said, 'Behold, I have come
(In the scroll of the book it is written of Me)
To do Your will, O God.' "

10:1 [l] Two early mss read *they can*

NEW CENTURY VERSION

as everyone must die once and be judged, 28So Christ was
offered as a sacrifice one time to take away the sins of
many people. And he will come a second time, not to offer
himself for sin, but to bring salvation to those who are
waiting for him.

10 The law is only an unclear picture of the good
things coming in the future; it is not the real
thing. The people under the law offer the same sacrifices
every year, but these sacrifices can never make perfect
those who come near to worship God. 2If the law could
make them perfect, the sacrifices would have already
stopped. The worshipers would be made clean, and they
would no longer have a sense of sin. 3But these sacrifices
remind them of their sins every year, 4because it is impos-
sible for the blood of bulls and goats to take away sins.
5So when Christ came into the world, he said:
"You do not want sacrifices and offerings,
but you have prepared a body for me.
6You do not ask for burnt offerings
and offerings to take away sins.
7Then I said, 'Look, I have come.
It is written about me in the book.
God, I have come to do what you want.' " *Psalm 40:6–8*

CONTEMPORARY ENGLISH VERSION

27We die only once, and then we are judged. 28So Christ
died only once to take away the sins of many people. But
when he comes again, it will not be to take away sin. He
will come to save everyone who is waiting for him.

10 The Law of Moses is like a shadow of the good
things to come. This shadow isn't the good things
themselves, because it cannot free people from sin by the
sacrifices that are offered year after year. 2If there were
worshipers who already have their sins washed away and
their consciences made clear, there would not be any need
to go on offering sacrifices. 3-4But the blood of bulls and
goats cannot take away sins. It only reminds people of
their sins from one year to the next.
5When Christ came into the world, he said to God,

"Sacrifices and offerings
are not what you want,
but you have given me
my body.
6No, you are not pleased
with animal sacrifices
and offerings for sin."
7Then Christ said,

"And so, my God,
I have come to do
what you want,
as the Scriptures say."

NEW INTERNATIONAL VERSION

destined to die once, and after that to face judgment, [28]so
Christ was sacrificed once to take away the sins of many
people; and he will appear a second time, not to bear sin,
but to bring salvation to those who are waiting for him.

Christ's Sacrifice Once for All

10 The law is only a shadow of the good things that
are coming—not the realities themselves. For this
reason it can never, by the same sacrifices repeated end-
lessly year after year, make perfect those who draw near to
worship. [2]If it could, would they not have stopped being
offered? For the worshipers would have been cleansed
once for all, and would no longer have felt guilty for their
sins. [3]But those sacrifices are an annual reminder of sins,
[4]because it is impossible for the blood of bulls and goats to
take away sins.

[5]Therefore, when Christ came into the world, he said:

"Sacrifice and offering you did not desire,
but a body you prepared for me;
6 with burnt offerings and sin offerings
you were not pleased.
7 Then I said, 'Here I am—it is written about me in the
scroll—
I have come to do your will, O God.' "[a]

[a] *7* Psalm 40:6–8 (see Septuagint)

NEW LIVING TRANSLATION

[27]And just as it is destined that each person dies only
once and after that comes judgment, [28]so also Christ died
only once as a sacrifice to take away the sins of many peo-
ple. He will come again but not to deal with our sins
again. This time he will bring salvation to all those who
are eagerly waiting for him.

Christ's Sacrifice Once for All

10 The old system in the law of Moses was only a
shadow of the things to come, not the reality of the
good things Christ has done for us. The sacrifices under the
old system were repeated again and again, year after year,
but they were never able to provide perfect cleansing for
those who came to worship. [2]If they could have provided
perfect cleansing, the sacrifices would have stopped, for the
worshipers would have been purified once for all time, and
their feelings of guilt would have disappeared.

[3]But just the opposite happened. Those yearly sacrifices
reminded them of their sins year after year. [4]For it is not
possible for the blood of bulls and goats to take away sins.
[5]That is why Christ, when he came into the world, said,

"You did not want animal sacrifices and grain offerings.
But you have given me a body so that I may obey you.
6 No, you were not pleased with animals burned on the altar
or with other offerings for sin.
7 Then I said, 'Look, I have come to do your will, O God—
just as it is written about me in the Scriptures.' "*

10:5-7 Ps 40:6-8.

NEW KING JAMES VERSION

as it is appointed for men to die once, but after this the
judgment, [28]so Christ was offered once to bear the sins of
many. To those who eagerly wait for Him He will appear a
second time, apart from sin, for salvation.

Animal Sacrifices Insufficient

10 For the law, having a shadow of the good things to
come, *and* not the very image of the things, can
never with these same sacrifices, which they offer continu-
ally year by year, make those who approach perfect. [2]For
then would they not have ceased to be offered? For the
worshipers, once purified, would have had no more con-
sciousness of sins. [3]But in those *sacrifices there is* a
reminder of sins every year. [4]For *it is* not possible that the
blood of bulls and goats could take away sins.

Christ's Death Fulfills God's Will

[5]Therefore, when He came into the world, He said:

"*Sacrifice and offering You did not desire,*
But a body You have prepared for Me.
6 *In burnt offerings and sacrifices for sin*
You had no pleasure.
7 *Then I said, 'Behold, I have come—*
In the volume of the book it is written of Me—
To do Your will, O God.' "[a]

10:7 [a] Psalm 40:6–8

THE MESSAGE

Everyone has to die once, then face the consequences.
Christ's death was also a one-time event, but it was a sac-
rifice that took care of sins forever. And so, when he next
appears, the outcome for those eager to greet him is, pre-
cisely, *salvation*.

The Sacrifice of Jesus

10 The old plan was only a hint of the good things in
the new plan. Since that old "law plan" wasn't
complete in itself, it couldn't complete those who followed
it. No matter how many sacrifices were offered year after
year, they never added up to a complete solution. If they
had, the worshipers would have gone merrily on their way,
no longer dragged down by their sins. But instead of
removing awareness of sin, when those animal sacrifices
were repeated over and over they actually heightened
awareness and guilt. The plain fact is that bull and goat
blood can't get rid of sin. That is what is meant by this
prophecy, put in the mouth of Christ:

"You don't want sacrifices and offerings year after year;
you've prepared a body for me for a sacrifice.
It's not fragrance and smoke from the altar
that whet your appetite.
So I said, 'I'm here to do it your way, oh God,
the way it's described in your Book.'"

KING JAMES VERSION

8 Above when he said, Sacrifice and offering and burnt offerings and *offering* for sin thou wouldest not, neither hadst pleasure *therein*; which are offered by the law;

9 Then said he, Lo, I come to do thy will, O God. He taketh away the first, that he may establish the second.

10 By the which will we are sanctified through the offering of the body of Jesus Christ once *for all*.

11 And every priest standeth daily ministering and offering oftentimes the same sacrifices, which can never take away sins:

12 But this man, after he had offered one sacrifice for sins for ever, sat down on the right hand of God;

13 From henceforth expecting till his enemies be made his footstool.

14 For by one offering he hath perfected for ever them that are sanctified.

15 *Whereof* the Holy Ghost also is a witness to us: for after that he had said before,

16 This *is* the covenant that I will make with them after those days, saith the Lord, I will put my laws into their hearts, and in their minds will I write them;

NEW AMERICAN STANDARD BIBLE

8 After saying above, "SACRIFICES AND OFFERINGS AND WHOLE BURNT OFFERINGS AND *sacrifices* FOR SIN YOU HAVE NOT DESIRED, NOR HAVE YOU TAKEN PLEASURE *in them*" (which are offered according to the Law),

9 then He said, "BEHOLD, I HAVE COME TO DO YOUR WILL." He takes away the first in order to establish the second.

10 By this will we have been sanctified through the offering of the body of Jesus Christ once for all.

11 Every priest stands daily ministering and offering time after time the same sacrifices, which can never take away sins;

12 but He, having offered one sacrifice for sins for all time, SAT DOWN AT THE RIGHT HAND OF GOD,

13 waiting from that time onward UNTIL HIS ENEMIES BE MADE A FOOTSTOOL FOR HIS FEET.

14 For by one offering He has perfected for all time those who are sanctified.

15 And the Holy Spirit also testifies to us; for after saying,

16 "THIS IS THE COVENANT THAT I WILL MAKE WITH THEM
AFTER THOSE DAYS, SAYS THE LORD:
I WILL PUT MY LAWS UPON THEIR HEART,
AND ON THEIR MIND I WILL WRITE THEM,"

NEW CENTURY VERSION

8 In this Scripture he first said, "You do not want sacrifices
and offerings. You do not ask for burnt offerings and offer-
ings to take away sins." (These are all sacrifices that the
law commands.) 9 Then he said, "Look, I have come to do
what you want." God ends the first system of sacrifices so
he can set up the new system. 10 And because of this, we
are made holy through the sacrifice Christ made in his
body once and for all time.

11 Every day the priests stand and do their religious ser-
vice, often offering the same sacrifices. Those sacrifices
can never take away sins. 12 But after Christ offered one
sacrifice for sins, forever, he sat down at the right side of
God. 13 And now Christ waits there for his enemies to be
put under his power. 14 With one sacrifice he made perfect
forever those who are being made holy.

15 The Holy Spirit also tells us about this. First he says:

16 "This is the agreement[a] I will make
with them at that time, says the Lord.
I will put my teachings in their hearts
and write them on their minds." *Jeremiah 31:33*

10:16 [a] **agreement** God gives a contract or agreement to his people. For the Jews, this agreement was the law of Moses. But now God has given a better agreement to his people through Christ.

CONTEMPORARY ENGLISH VERSION

8 The Law teaches that offerings and sacrifices must be
made because of sin. But why did Christ mention these
things and say that God did not want them? 9 Well, it was
to do away with offerings and sacrifices and to replace
them. That is what he meant by saying to God, "I have
come to do what you want." 10 So we are made holy
because Christ obeyed God and offered himself once for all.

11 The priests do their work each day, and they keep on
offering sacrifices that can never take away sins. 12 But
Christ offered himself as a sacrifice that is good forever.
Now he is sitting at God's right side,[a] 13 and he will stay
there until his enemies are put under his power. 14 By his
one sacrifice he has forever set free from sin the people he
brings to God.

15 The Holy Spirit also speaks of this by telling us that
the Lord said,

16 "When the time comes,
I will make an agreement
with them.
I will write my laws
on their minds and hearts.

[a] **10.12** *right side*: See the note at 1.3.

NEW INTERNATIONAL VERSION

8First he said, "Sacrifices and offerings, burnt offerings
and sin offerings you did not desire, nor were you pleased
with them" (although the law required them to be made).
9Then he said, "Here I am, I have come to do your will." He
sets aside the first to establish the second. 10And by that
will, we have been made holy through the sacrifice of the
body of Jesus Christ once for all.

11Day after day every priest stands and performs his reli-
gious duties; again and again he offers the same sacri-
fices, which can never take away sins. 12But when this
priest had offered for all time one sacrifice for sins, he sat
down at the right hand of God. 13Since that time he waits
for his enemies to be made his footstool, 14because by one
sacrifice he has made perfect forever those who are being
made holy.

15The Holy Spirit also testifies to us about this. First he
says:

16"This is the covenant I will make with them
after that time, says the Lord.
I will put my laws in their hearts,
and I will write them on their minds."[b]

[b] *16* Jer. 31:33

NEW LIVING TRANSLATION

8Christ said, "You did not want animal sacrifices or grain
offerings or animals burned on the altar or other offerings
for sin, nor were you pleased with them" (though they are
required by the law of Moses). 9Then he added, "Look, I
have come to do your will." He cancels the first covenant
in order to establish the second. 10And what God wants is
for us to be made holy by the sacrifice of the body of Jesus
Christ once for all time.

11Under the old covenant, the priest stands before the
altar day after day, offering sacrifices that can never take
away sins. 12But our High Priest offered himself to God as
one sacrifice for sins, good for all time. Then he sat down
at the place of highest honor at God's right hand. 13There
he waits until his enemies are humbled as a footstool
under his feet. 14For by that one offering he perfected for-
ever all those whom he is making holy.

15And the Holy Spirit also testifies that this is so. First
he says,

16"This is the new covenant I will make
with my people on that day, says the Lord:
I will put my laws in their hearts
so they will understand them,
and I will write them on their minds
so they will obey them."

NEW KING JAMES VERSION

8Previously saying, *"Sacrifice and offering, burnt offerings,
and offerings for sin You did not desire, nor had pleasure
in them"* (which are offered according to the law), 9then He
said, *"Behold, I have come to do Your will, O God."*[b] He
takes away the first that He may establish the second.
10By that will we have been sanctified through the offering
of the body of Jesus Christ once *for all.*

Christ's Death Perfects the Sanctified

11And every priest stands ministering daily and offering
repeatedly the same sacrifices, which can never take away
sins. 12But this Man, after He had offered one sacrifice for
sins forever, sat down at the right hand of God, 13from
that time waiting till His enemies are made His footstool.
14For by one offering He has perfected forever those who
are being sanctified.

15But the Holy Spirit also witnesses to us; for after He
had said before,

16*"This is the covenant that I will make with them after
those days, says the* Lord: *I will put My laws into their
hearts, and in their minds I will write them,"*[c] 17*then He*

10:9 [b] NU-Text and M-Text omit *O God.* 10:16 [c] Jeremiah 31:33

THE MESSAGE

When he said, "You don't want sacrifices and offerings,"
he was referring to practices according to the old plan.
When he added, "I'm here to do it your way," he set aside
the first in order to enact the new plan—*God's* way—by
which we are made fit for God by the once-for-all sacrifice
of Jesus.

Every priest goes to work at the altar each day, offers
the same old sacrifices year in, year out, and never makes
a dent in the sin problem. As a priest, Christ made a single
sacrifice for sins, and that was it! Then he sat down right
beside God and waited for his enemies to cave in. It was a
perfect sacrifice by a perfect person to perfect some very
imperfect people. By that single offering, he did everything
that needed to be done for everyone who takes part in the
purifying process. The Holy Spirit confirms this:

"This new plan I'm making with Israel
isn't going to be written on paper,
isn't going to be chiseled in stone;
This time 'I'm writing out the plan *in* them,
carving it on the lining of their hearts.'"

KING JAMES VERSION

17 And their sins and iniquities will I remember no more.

18 Now where remission of these *is, there is* no more offering for sin.

19 ¶ Having therefore, brethren, boldness to enter into the holiest by the blood of Jesus,

20 By a new and living way, which he hath consecrated for us, through the veil, that is to say, his flesh;

21 And *having* an high priest over the house of God;

22 Let us draw near with a true heart in full assurance of faith, having our hearts sprinkled from an evil conscience, and our bodies washed with pure water.

23 Let us hold fast the profession of *our* faith without wavering; (for he *is* faithful that promised;)

24 And let us consider one another to provoke unto love and to good works:

25 Not forsaking the assembling of ourselves together, as the manner of some *is*; but exhorting *one another*: and so much the more, as ye see the day approaching.

26 For if we sin wilfully after that we have received the knowledge of the truth, there remaineth no more sacrifice for sins,

NEW AMERICAN STANDARD BIBLE

He then says,

17 "AND THEIR SINS AND THEIR LAWLESS DEEDS
I WILL REMEMBER NO MORE."

18 Now where there is forgiveness of these things, there is no longer *any* offering for sin.

A New and Living Way

19 Therefore, brethren, since we have confidence to enter the holy place by the blood of Jesus,

20 by a new and living way which He inaugurated for us through the veil, that is, His flesh,

21 and since *we have* a great priest over the house of God,

22 let us draw near with a sincere heart in full assurance of faith, having our hearts sprinkled *clean* from an evil conscience and our bodies washed with pure water.

23 Let us hold fast the confession of our hope without wavering, for He who promised is faithful;

24 and let us consider how to stimulate one another to love and good deeds,

25 not forsaking our own assembling together, as is the habit of some, but encouraging *one another;* and all the more as you see the day drawing near.

Christ or Judgment

26 For if we go on sinning willfully after receiving the knowledge of the truth, there no longer remains a sacrifice for sins,

NEW CENTURY VERSION

[17]Then he says:

"Their sins and the evil things they do—
I will not remember anymore." *Jeremiah 31:34*

[18]Now when these have been forgiven, there is no more need for a sacrifice for sins.

Continue to Trust God

[19]So, brothers and sisters, we are completely free to enter the Most Holy Place without fear because of the blood of Jesus' death. [20]We can enter through a new and living way that Jesus opened for us. It leads through the curtain—Christ's body. [21]And since we have a great priest over God's house, [22]let us come near to God with a sincere heart and a sure faith, because we have been made free from a guilty conscience, and our bodies have been washed with pure water. [23]Let us hold firmly to the hope that we have confessed, because we can trust God to do what he promised.

[24]Let us think about each other and help each other to show love and do good deeds. [25]You should not stay away from the church meetings, as some are doing, but you should meet together and encourage each other. Do this even more as you see the day[b] coming.

[26]If we decide to go on sinning after we have learned the truth, there is no longer any sacrifice for sins. [27]There is

10:25 *b* **day** The day Christ will come to judge all people and take his people to live with him.

CONTEMPORARY ENGLISH VERSION

[17]Then I will forget
about their sins
and no longer remember
their evil deeds."

[18]When sins are forgiven, there is no more need to offer sacrifices.

Encouragement and Warning

[19]My friends, the blood of Jesus gives us courage to enter the most holy place [20]by a new way that leads to life! And this way takes us through the curtain that is Christ himself.

[21]We have a great high priest who is in charge of God's house. [22]So let's come near God with pure hearts and a confidence that comes from having faith. Let's keep our hearts pure, our consciences free from evil, and our bodies washed with clean water. [23]We must hold tightly to the hope that we say is ours. After all, we can trust the one who made the agreement with us. [24]We should keep on encouraging each other to be thoughtful and to do helpful things. [25]Some people have gotten out of the habit of meeting for worship, but we must not do that. We should keep on encouraging each other, especially since you know that the day of the Lord's coming is getting closer.

[26]No sacrifices can be made for people who decide to sin after they find out about the truth. [27]They are God's

NEW INTERNATIONAL VERSION

17Then he adds:

"Their sins and lawless acts
I will remember no more."[c]

18And where these have been forgiven, there is no longer
any sacrifice for sin.

A Call to Persevere

19Therefore, brothers, since we have confidence to enter
the Most Holy Place by the blood of Jesus, 20by a new and
living way opened for us through the curtain, that is, his
body, 21and since we have a great priest over the house of
God, 22let us draw near to God with a sincere heart in full
assurance of faith, having our hearts sprinkled to cleanse
us from a guilty conscience and having our bodies washed
with pure water. 23Let us hold unswervingly to the hope
we profess, for he who promised is faithful. 24And let us
consider how we may spur one another on toward love and
good deeds. 25Let us not give up meeting together, as some
are in the habit of doing, but let us encourage one anoth-
er—and all the more as you see the Day approaching.

26If we deliberately keep on sinning after we have
received the knowledge of the truth, no sacrifice for sins is

[c] *17* Jer. 31:34

NEW LIVING TRANSLATION

17Then he adds,

"I will never again remember
their sins and lawless deeds."*

18Now when sins have been forgiven, there is no need to
offer any more sacrifices.

A Call to Persevere

19And so, dear brothers and sisters,* we can boldly enter
heaven's Most Holy Place because of the blood of Jesus.
20This is the new, life-giving way that Christ has opened
up for us through the sacred curtain, by means of his
death for us.*

21And since we have a great High Priest who rules over
God's people, 22let us go right into the presence of God,
with true hearts fully trusting him. For our evil consciences
have been sprinkled with Christ's blood to make us clean,
and our bodies have been washed with pure water.

23Without wavering, let us hold tightly to the hope we
say we have, for God can be trusted to keep his promise.
24Think of ways to encourage one another to outbursts of
love and good deeds. 25And let us not neglect our meeting
together, as some people do, but encourage and warn each
other, especially now that the day of his coming back
again is drawing near.

26Dear friends, if we deliberately continue sinning after
we have received a full knowledge of the truth, there is no

10:16-17 Jer 31:33-34. **10:19** Greek *brothers.* **10:20** Greek *his flesh.*

NEW KING JAMES VERSION

*adds, "Their sins and their lawless deeds I will remember
no more."*[d] 18Now where there is remission of these, *there
is* no longer an offering for sin.

Hold Fast Your Confession

19Therefore, brethren, having boldness to enter the
Holiest by the blood of Jesus, 20by a new and living way
which He consecrated for us, through the veil, that is, His
flesh, 21and *having* a High Priest over the house of God,
22let us draw near with a true heart in full assurance of
faith, having our hearts sprinkled from an evil conscience
and our bodies washed with pure water. 23Let us hold fast
the confession of *our* hope without wavering, for He who
promised *is* faithful. 24And let us consider one another in
order to stir up love and good works, 25not forsaking the
assembling of ourselves together, as *is* the manner of
some, but exhorting *one another,* and so much the more as
you see the Day approaching.

The Just Live by Faith

26For if we sin willfully after we have received the
knowledge of the truth, there no longer remains a sacrifice

10:17 [d] Jeremiah 31:34

THE MESSAGE

He concludes,

"I'll forever wipe the slate clean of their sins."

Once sins are taken care of for good, there's no longer any
need to offer sacrifices for them.

Don't Throw It All Away

So, friends, we can now—without hesitation—walk right up to God, into "the Holy Place." Jesus has cleared the way by the blood of his sacrifice, acting as our priest before God. The "curtain" into God's presence is his body.

So let's *do* it—full of belief, confident that we're presentable inside and out. Let's keep a firm grip on the promises that keep us going. He always keeps his word. Let's see how inventive we can be in encouraging love and helping out, not avoiding worshiping together as some do but spurring each other on, especially as we see the big Day approaching.

If we give up and turn our backs on all we've learned, all we've been given, all the truth we now know, we repudiate

KING JAMES VERSION

27 But a certain fearful looking for of judgment and fiery indignation, which shall devour the adversaries.

28 He that despised Moses' law died without mercy under two or three witnesses:

29 Of how much sorer punishment, suppose ye, shall he be thought worthy, who hath trodden under foot the Son of God, and hath counted the blood of the covenant, wherewith he was sanctified, an unholy thing, and hath done despite unto the Spirit of grace?

30 For we know him that hath said, Vengeance *belongeth* unto me, I will recompense, saith the Lord. And again, The Lord shall judge his people.

31 *It is* a fearful thing to fall into the hands of the living God.

32 But call to remembrance the former days, in which, after ye were illuminated, ye endured a great fight of afflictions;

33 Partly, whilst ye were made a gazingstock both by reproaches and afflictions; and partly, whilst ye became companions of them that were so used.

34 For ye had compassion of me in my bonds, and took joyfully the spoiling of your goods, knowing in yourselves

NEW AMERICAN STANDARD BIBLE

27 but a terrifying expectation of judgment and THE FURY OF A FIRE WHICH WILL CONSUME THE ADVERSARIES.

28 Anyone who has set aside the Law of Moses dies without mercy on *the testimony of* two or three witnesses.

29 How much severer punishment do you think he will deserve who has trampled under foot the Son of God, and has regarded as unclean the blood of the covenant by which he was sanctified, and has insulted the Spirit of grace?

30 For we know Him who said, "VENGEANCE IS MINE, I WILL REPAY." And again, "THE LORD WILL JUDGE HIS PEOPLE."

31 It is a terrifying thing to fall into the hands of the living God.

32 But remember the former days, when, after being enlightened, you endured a great conflict of sufferings,

33 partly by being made a public spectacle through reproaches and tribulations, and partly by becoming sharers with those who were so treated.

34 For you showed sympathy to the prisoners and accepted joyfully the seizure of your property, knowing

NEW CENTURY VERSION

nothing but fear in waiting for the judgment and the terrible fire that will destroy all those who live against God. [28]Anyone who refused to obey the law of Moses was found guilty from the proof given by two or three witnesses. He was put to death without mercy. [29]So what do you think should be done to those who do not respect the Son of God, who look at the blood of the agreement that made them holy as no different from others' blood, who insult the Spirit of God's grace? Surely they should have a much worse punishment. [30]We know that God said, "I will punish those who do wrong; I will repay them."[c] And he also said, "The Lord will judge his people."[d] [31]It is a terrible thing to fall into the hands of the living God.

[32]Remember those days in the past when you first learned the truth. You had a hard struggle with many sufferings, but you continued strong. [33]Sometimes you were hurt and attacked before crowds of people, and sometimes you shared with those who were being treated that way. [34]You helped the prisoners. You even had joy when all that

10:30 [c] **"I...them."** Quotation from Deuteronomy 32:35. **10:30** [d] **"The Lord...people."** Quotation from Deuteronomy 32:36; Psalm 135:14.

CONTEMPORARY ENGLISH VERSION

enemies, and all they can look forward to is a terrible judgment and a furious fire. [28]If two or more witnesses accused someone of breaking the Law of Moses, that person could be put to death. [29]But it is much worse to dishonor God's Son and to disgrace the blood of the promise that made us holy. And it is just as bad to insult the Holy Spirit, who shows us mercy. [30]We know that God has said he will punish and take revenge. We also know that the Scriptures say the Lord will judge his people. [31]It is a terrible thing to fall into the hands of the living God!

[32]Don't forget all the hard times you went through when you first received the light. [33]Sometimes you were abused and mistreated in public, and at other times you shared in the sufferings of others. [34]You were kind to people in jail. And you gladly let your possessions be taken away,

NEW INTERNATIONAL VERSION

left, [27]but only a fearful expectation of judgment and of raging fire that will consume the enemies of God. [28]Anyone who rejected the law of Moses died without mercy on the testimony of two or three witnesses. [29]How much more severely do you think a man deserves to be punished who has trampled the Son of God under foot, who has treated as an unholy thing the blood of the covenant that sanctified him, and who has insulted the Spirit of grace? [30]For we know him who said, "It is mine to avenge; I will repay,"[d] and again, "The Lord will judge his people."[e] [31]It is a dreadful thing to fall into the hands of the living God.

[32]Remember those earlier days after you had received the light, when you stood your ground in a great contest in the face of suffering. [33]Sometimes you were publicly exposed to insult and persecution; at other times you stood side by side with those who were so treated. [34]You sympathized with those in prison and joyfully accepted the

[d] *30* Deut. 32:35 [e] *30* Deut. 32:36; Psalm 135:14

NEW LIVING TRANSLATION

other sacrifice that will cover these sins. [27]There will be nothing to look forward to but the terrible expectation of God's judgment and the raging fire that will consume his enemies. [28]Anyone who refused to obey the law of Moses was put to death without mercy on the testimony of two or three witnesses. [29]Think how much more terrible the punishment will be for those who have trampled on the Son of God and have treated the blood of the covenant as if it were common and unholy. Such people have insulted and enraged the Holy Spirit who brings God's mercy to his people.

[30]For we know the one who said,

"I will take vengeance.
I will repay those who deserve it."

He also said,

"The Lord will judge his own people."*

[31]It is a terrible thing to fall into the hands of the living God.

[32]Don't ever forget those early days when you first learned about Christ. Remember how you remained faithful even though it meant terrible suffering. [33]Sometimes you were exposed to public ridicule and were beaten, and sometimes you helped others who were suffering the same things. [34]You suffered along with those who were thrown

10:30 Deut 32:35-36.

NEW KING JAMES VERSION

for sins, [27]but a certain fearful expectation of judgment, and fiery indignation which will devour the adversaries. [28]Anyone who has rejected Moses' law dies without mercy on the testimony of two or three witnesses. [29]Of how much worse punishment, do you suppose, will he be thought worthy who has trampled the Son of God underfoot, counted the blood of the covenant by which he was sanctified a common thing, and insulted the Spirit of grace? [30]For we know Him who said, *"Vengeance is Mine, I will repay,"*[e] says the Lord.[f] And again, *"The* LORD *will judge His people."*[g] [31]It is a fearful thing to fall into the hands of the living God.

[32]But recall the former days in which, after you were illuminated, you endured a great struggle with sufferings: [33]partly while you were made a spectacle both by reproaches and tribulations, and partly while you became companions of those who were so treated; [34]for you had compassion on me[h] in my chains, and joyfully accepted the plundering of

10:30 [e] Deuteronomy 32:35 [f] NU-Text omits *says the Lord.* [g] Deuteronomy 32:36 **10:34** [h] NU-Text reads *the prisoners* instead of *me in my chains.*

THE MESSAGE

Christ's sacrifice and are left on our own to face the Judgment—and a mighty fierce judgment it will be! If the penalty for breaking the law of Moses is physical death, what do you think will happen if you turn on God's Son, spit on the sacrifice that made you whole, and insult this most gracious Spirit? This is no light matter. God has warned us that he'll hold us to account and make us pay. He was quite explicit: "Vengeance is mine, and I won't overlook a thing," and, "God will judge his people." Nobody's getting by with anything, believe me.

Remember those early days after you first saw the light? Those were the hard times! Kicked around in public, targets of every kind of abuse—some days it was you, other days your friends. If some friends went to prison, you stuck by them. If some enemies broke in and seized your goods, you

KING JAMES VERSION

that ye have in heaven a better and an enduring substance.

35 Cast not away therefore your confidence, which hath great recompence of reward.

36 For ye have need of patience, that, after ye have done the will of God, ye might receive the promise.

37 For yet a little while, and he that shall come will come, and will not tarry.

38 Now the just shall live by faith: but if *any man* draw back, my soul shall have no pleasure in him.

39 But we are not of them who draw back unto perdition; but of them that believe to the saving of the soul.

11 Now faith is the substance of things hoped for, the evidence of things not seen.

2 For by it the elders obtained a good report.

3 Through faith we understand that the worlds were framed by the word of God, so that things which are seen were not made of things which do appear.

NEW AMERICAN STANDARD BIBLE

that you have for yourselves a better possession and a lasting one.

35 Therefore, do not throw away your confidence, which has a great reward.

36 For you have need of endurance, so that when you have done the will of God, you may receive what was promised.

37 FOR YET IN A VERY LITTLE WHILE,
HE WHO IS COMING WILL COME, AND WILL NOT DELAY.

38 BUT MY RIGHTEOUS ONE SHALL LIVE BY FAITH;
AND IF HE SHRINKS BACK, MY SOUL HAS NO PLEASURE IN HIM.

39 But we are not of those who shrink back to destruction, but of those who have faith to the preserving of the soul.

The Triumphs of Faith

11 Now faith is the assurance of *things* hoped for, the conviction of things not seen.

2 For by it the men of old gained approval.

3 By faith we understand that the worlds were prepared by the word of God, so that what is seen was not made out of things which are visible.

NEW CENTURY VERSION

you owned was taken from you, because you knew you had something better and more lasting.

35 So do not lose the courage you had in the past, which has a great reward. 36 You must hold on, so you can do what God wants and receive what he has promised. 37 For in a very short time,

"The One who is coming will come
and will not be delayed.
38 The person who is right with me
will live by trusting in me.
But if he turns back with fear,
I will not be pleased with him." *Habakkuk 2:3–4*

39 But we are not those who turn back and are lost. We are people who have faith and are saved.

What Is Faith?

11 Faith means being sure of the things we hope for and knowing that something is real even if we do not see it. 2 Faith is the reason we remember great people who lived in the past.

3 It is by faith we understand that the whole world was made by God's command so what we see was made by something that cannot be seen.

CONTEMPORARY ENGLISH VERSION

because you knew you had something better, something that would last forever.

35 Keep on being brave! It will bring you great rewards. 36 Learn to be patient, so that you will please God and be given what he has promised. 37 As the Scriptures say,

"God is coming soon!
It won't be very long.
38 The people God accepts
will live because
of their faith.[b]
But he isn't pleased
with anyone
who turns back."

39 We are not like those people who turn back and get destroyed. We will keep on having faith until we are saved.

The Great Faith of God's People

11 Faith makes us sure of what we hope for and gives us proof of what we cannot see. 2 It was their faith that made our ancestors pleasing to God.

3 Because of our faith, we know that the world was made at God's command. We also know that what can be seen was made out of what cannot be seen.

[b] **10.38** *The people God accepts will live because of their faith*: Or "The people God accepts because of their faith will live."

NEW INTERNATIONAL VERSION

confiscation of your property, because you knew that you
yourselves had better and lasting possessions.
35So do not throw away your confidence; it will be richly
rewarded. 36You need to persevere so that when you have
done the will of God, you will receive what he has prom-
ised. 37For in just a very little while,

"He who is coming will come and will not delay.
38 But my righteous one[f] will live by faith.
And if he shrinks back,
I will not be pleased with him."[g]

39But we are not of those who shrink back and are
destroyed, but of those who believe and are saved.

By Faith

11 Now faith is being sure of what we hope for and
certain of what we do not see. 2This is what the
ancients were commended for.
3By faith we understand that the universe was formed at
God's command, so that what is seen was not made out of
what was visible.

f 38 One early manuscript *But the righteous* g 38 Hab. 2:3,4

NEW LIVING TRANSLATION

into jail. When all you owned was taken from you, you
accepted it with joy. You knew you had better things wait-
ing for you in eternity.
35Do not throw away this confident trust in the Lord, no
matter what happens. Remember the great reward it brings
you! 36Patient endurance is what you need now, so you
will continue to do God's will. Then you will receive all
that he has promised.

37 "For in just a little while,
the Coming One will come and not delay.
38 And a righteous person will live by faith.
But I will have no pleasure in anyone who turns
away."*

39But we are not like those who turn their backs on God
and seal their fate. We have faith that assures our salva-
tion.

Great Examples of Faith

11 What is faith? It is the confident assurance that
what we hope for is going to happen. It is the evi-
dence of things we cannot yet see. 2God gave his approval
to people in days of old because of their faith.
3By faith we understand that the entire universe was
formed at God's command, that what we now see did not
come from anything that can be seen.

10:37-38 Hab 2:3-4.

NEW KING JAMES VERSION

your goods, knowing that you have a better and an endur-
ing possession for yourselves in heaven.[i] 35Therefore do not
cast away your confidence, which has great reward. 36For
you have need of endurance, so that after you have done the
will of God, you may receive the promise:

37 *"For yet a little while,*
And He[j] who is coming will come and will not tarry.
38 *Now the[k] just shall live by faith;*
But if anyone draws back,
My soul has no pleasure in him."[l]

39But we are not of those who draw back to perdition, but
of those who believe to the saving of the soul.

By Faith We Understand

11 Now faith is the substance of things hoped for, the
evidence of things not seen. 2For by it the elders
obtained a *good* testimony.
3By faith we understand that the worlds were framed by
the word of God, so that the things which are seen were
not made of things which are visible.

10:34 i NU-Text omits *in heaven.* **10:37** j Or *that which*
10:38 k NU-Text reads *My just one.* l Habakkuk 2:3, 4

THE MESSAGE

let them go with a smile, knowing they couldn't touch your
real treasure. Nothing they did bothered you, nothing set
you back. So don't throw it all away now. You were sure of
yourselves then. It's *still* a sure thing! But you need to stick
it out, staying with God's plan so you'll be there for the
promised completion.

"It won't be long now, he's on the way;
he'll show up most any minute.
But anyone who is right with me thrives on loyal trust;
if he cuts and runs, I won't be very happy."

But we're not quitters who lose out. Oh, no! We'll stay
with it and survive, trusting all the way.

Faith in What We Don't See

11 The fundamental fact of existence is that this trust
in God, this faith, is the firm foundation under
everything that makes life worth living. It's our handle on
what we can't see. The act of faith is what distinguished
our ancestors, set them above the crowd.
By faith, we see the world called into existence by God's
word, what we see created by what we don't see.

KING JAMES VERSION

4 ¶ By faith Abel offered unto God a more excellent sacrifice than Cain, by which he obtained witness that he was righteous, God testifying of his gifts: and by it he being dead yet speaketh.

5 By faith Enoch was translated that he should not see death; and was not found, because God had translated him: for before his translation he had this testimony, that he pleased God.

6 But without faith *it is* impossible to please *him*: for he that cometh to God must believe that he is, and *that* he is a rewarder of them that diligently seek him.

7 By faith Noah, being warned of God of things not seen as yet, moved with fear, prepared an ark to the saving of his house; by the which he condemned the world, and became heir of the righteousness which is by faith.

8 By faith Abraham, when he was called to go out into a place which he should after receive for an inheritance, obeyed; and he went out, not knowing whither he went.

9 By faith he sojourned in the land of promise, as *in* a strange country, dwelling in tabernacles with Isaac and Jacob, the heirs with him of the same promise:

10 For he looked for a city which hath foundations, whose builder and maker *is* God.

NEW AMERICAN STANDARD BIBLE

4 By faith Abel offered to God a better sacrifice than Cain, through which he obtained the testimony that he was righteous, God testifying about his gifts, and through faith, though he is dead, he still speaks.

5 By faith Enoch was taken up so that he would not see death; AND HE WAS NOT FOUND BECAUSE GOD TOOK HIM UP; for he obtained the witness that before his being taken up he was pleasing to God.

6 And without faith it is impossible to please *Him*, for he who comes to God must believe that He is and *that* He is a rewarder of those who seek Him.

7 By faith Noah, being warned *by God* about things not yet seen, in reverence prepared an ark for the salvation of his household, by which he condemned the world, and became an heir of the righteousness which is according to faith.

8 By faith Abraham, when he was called, obeyed by going out to a place which he was to receive for an inheritance; and he went out, not knowing where he was going.

9 By faith he lived as an alien in the land of promise, as in a foreign *land*, dwelling in tents with Isaac and Jacob, fellow heirs of the same promise;

10 for he was looking for the city which has foundations, whose architect and builder is God.

NEW CENTURY VERSION

4 It was by faith that Abel offered God a better sacrifice than Cain did. God said he was pleased with the gifts Abel offered and called Abel a good man because of his faith. Abel died, but through his faith he is still speaking.

5 It was by faith that Enoch was taken to heaven so he would not die. He could not be found, because God had taken him away. Before he was taken, the Scripture says
that he was a man who truly pleased God. 6 Without faith
no one can please God. Anyone who comes to God must believe that he is real and that he rewards those who truly want to find him.

7 It was by faith that Noah heard God's warnings about things he could not yet see. He obeyed God and built a large boat to save his family. By his faith, Noah showed that the world was wrong, and he became one of those who are made right with God through faith.

8 It was by faith Abraham obeyed God's call to go to another place God promised to give him. He left his own
country, not knowing where he was to go. 9 It was by faith
that he lived like a foreigner in the country God promised to give him. He lived in tents with Isaac and Jacob, who
had received that same promise from God. 10 Abraham was
waiting for the city[a] that has real foundations—the city planned and built by God.

11:10 [a] **city** The spiritual "city" where God's people live with him. Also called "the heavenly Jerusalem." (See Hebrews 12:22.)

CONTEMPORARY ENGLISH VERSION

4 Because Abel had faith, he offered God a better sacrifice than Cain did. God was pleased with him and his gift, and even though Abel is now dead, his faith still speaks for him.

5 Enoch had faith and did not die. He pleased God, and God took him up to heaven. That's why his body was never
found. 6 But without faith no one can please God. We must
believe that God is real and that he rewards everyone who searches for him.

7 Because Noah had faith, he was warned about something that had not yet happened. He obeyed and built a boat that saved him and his family. In this way the people of the world were judged, and Noah was given the blessings that come to everyone who pleases God.

8 Abraham had faith and obeyed God. He was told to go to the land that God had said would be his, and he left for
a country he had never seen. 9 Because Abraham had faith,
he lived as a stranger in the promised land. He lived there in a tent, and so did Isaac and Jacob, who were later given
the same promise. 10 Abraham did this, because he was
waiting for the eternal city that God had planned and built.

NEW INTERNATIONAL VERSION

4 By faith Abel offered God a better sacrifice than Cain did. By faith he was commended as a righteous man, when God spoke well of his offerings. And by faith he still speaks, even though he is dead.

5 By faith Enoch was taken from this life, so that he did not experience death; he could not be found, because God had taken him away. For before he was taken, he was commended as one who pleased God. 6 And without faith it is impossible to please God, because anyone who comes to him must believe that he exists and that he rewards those who earnestly seek him.

7 By faith Noah, when warned about things not yet seen, in holy fear built an ark to save his family. By his faith he condemned the world and became heir of the righteousness that comes by faith.

8 By faith Abraham, when called to go to a place he would later receive as his inheritance, obeyed and went, even though he did not know where he was going. 9 By faith he made his home in the promised land like a stranger in a foreign country; he lived in tents, as did Isaac and Jacob, who were heirs with him of the same promise. 10 For he was looking forward to the city with foundations, whose architect and builder is God.

NEW LIVING TRANSLATION

4 It was by faith that Abel brought a more acceptable offering to God than Cain did. God accepted Abel's offering to show that he was a righteous man. And although Abel is long dead, he still speaks to us because of his faith.

5 It was by faith that Enoch was taken up to heaven without dying—"suddenly he disappeared because God took him."* But before he was taken up, he was approved as pleasing to God. 6 So, you see, it is impossible to please God without faith. Anyone who wants to come to him must believe that there is a God and that he rewards those who sincerely seek him.

7 It was by faith that Noah built an ark to save his family from the flood. He obeyed God, who warned him about something that had never happened before. By his faith he condemned the rest of the world and was made right in God's sight.

8 It was by faith that Abraham obeyed when God called him to leave home and go to another land that God would give him as his inheritance. He went without knowing where he was going. 9 And even when he reached the land God promised him, he lived there by faith—for he was like a foreigner, living in a tent. And so did Isaac and Jacob, to whom God gave the same promise. 10 Abraham did this because he was confidently looking forward to a city with eternal foundations, a city designed and built by God.

11:5 Gen 5:24.

NEW KING JAMES VERSION

Faith at the Dawn of History

4 By faith Abel offered to God a more excellent sacrifice than Cain, through which he obtained witness that he was righteous, God testifying of his gifts; and through it he being dead still speaks.

5 By faith Enoch was taken away so that he did not see death, *"and was not found, because God had taken him"*;[a] for before he was taken he had this testimony, that he pleased God. 6 But without faith *it is* impossible to please *Him,* for he who comes to God must believe that He is, and *that* He is a rewarder of those who diligently seek Him.

7 By faith Noah, being divinely warned of things not yet seen, moved with godly fear, prepared an ark for the saving of his household, by which he condemned the world and became heir of the righteousness which is according to faith.

Faithful Abraham

8 By faith Abraham obeyed when he was called to go out to the place which he would receive as an inheritance. And he went out, not knowing where he was going. 9 By faith he dwelt in the land of promise as *in* a foreign country, dwelling in tents with Isaac and Jacob, the heirs with him of the same promise; 10 for he waited for the city which has foundations, whose builder and maker *is* God.

11:5 [a] Genesis 5:24

THE MESSAGE

By an act of faith, Abel brought a better sacrifice to God than Cain. It was what he *believed*, not what he *brought*, that made the difference. That's what God noticed and approved as righteous. After all these centuries, that belief continues to catch our notice.

By an act of faith, Enoch skipped death completely. "They looked all over and couldn't find him because God had taken him." We know on the basis of reliable testimony that before he was taken "he pleased God." It's impossible to please God apart from faith. And why? Because anyone who wants to approach God must believe both that he exists *and* that he cares enough to respond to those who seek him.

By faith, Noah built a ship in the middle of dry land. He was warned about something he couldn't see, and acted on what he was told. The result? His family was saved. His act of faith drew a sharp line between the evil of the unbelieving world and the rightness of the believing world. As a result, Noah became intimate with God.

By an act of faith, Abraham said yes to God's call to travel to an unknown place that would become his home. When he left he had no idea where he was going. By an act of faith he lived in the country promised him, lived as a stranger camping in tents. Isaac and Jacob did the same, living under the same promise. Abraham did it by keeping his eye on an unseen city with real, eternal foundations—the City designed and built by God.

KING JAMES VERSION

11 Through faith also Sara herself received strength to conceive seed, and was delivered of a child when she was past age, because she judged him faithful who had promised.

12 Therefore sprang there even of one, and him as good as dead, *so many* as the stars of the sky in multitude, and as the sand which is by the sea shore innumerable.

13 These all died in faith, not having received the promises, but having seen them afar off, and were persuaded of *them*, and embraced *them*, and confessed that they were strangers and pilgrims on the earth.

14 For they that say such things declare plainly that they seek a country.

15 And truly, if they had been mindful of that *country* from whence they came out, they might have had opportunity to have returned.

16 But now they desire a better *country*, that is, an heavenly: wherefore God is not ashamed to be called their God: for he hath prepared for them a city.

17 By faith Abraham, when he was tried, offered up Isaac: and he that had received the promises offered up his only begotten *son*,

18 Of whom it was said, That in Isaac shall thy seed be called:

19 Accounting that God *was* able to raise *him* up, even from the dead; from whence also he received him in a figure.

NEW AMERICAN STANDARD BIBLE

11 By faith even Sarah herself received ability to conceive, even beyond the proper time of life, since she considered Him faithful who had promised.

12 Therefore there was born even of one man, and him as good as dead at that, *as many descendants* AS THE STARS OF HEAVEN IN NUMBER, AND INNUMERABLE AS THE SAND WHICH IS BY THE SEASHORE.

13 All these died in faith, without receiving the promises, but having seen them and having welcomed them from a distance, and having confessed that they were strangers and exiles on the earth.

14 For those who say such things make it clear that they are seeking a country of their own.

15 And indeed if they had been thinking of that *country* from which they went out, they would have had opportunity to return.

16 But as it is, they desire a better *country*, that is, a heavenly one. Therefore God is not ashamed to be called their God; for He has prepared a city for them.

17 By faith Abraham, when he was tested, offered up Isaac, and he who had received the promises was offering up his only begotten *son;*

18 *it was he* to whom it was said, "IN ISAAC YOUR DESCENDANTS SHALL BE CALLED."

19 He considered that God is able to raise *people* even from the dead, from which he also received him back as a type.

NEW CENTURY VERSION

11He was too old to have children, and Sarah could not have children. It was by faith that Abraham was made able to become a father, because he trusted God to do what he
had promised. 12This man was so old he was almost dead, but from him came as many descendants as there are stars in the sky. Like the sand on the seashore, they could not be counted.

13All these great people died in faith. They did not get the things that God promised his people, but they saw them coming far in the future and were glad. They said they were like visitors and strangers on earth. 14When peo-
ple say such things, they show they are looking for a country that will be their own. 15If they had been thinking about the country they had left, they could have gone
back. 16But they were waiting for a better country—a heavenly country. So God is not ashamed to be called their God, because he has prepared a city for them.

17It was by faith that Abraham, when God tested him, offered his son Isaac as a sacrifice. God made the promises to Abraham, but Abraham was ready to offer his own son
as a sacrifice. 18God had said, "The descendants I promised you will be from Isaac."[b] 19Abraham believed that God could raise the dead, and really, it was as if Abraham got Isaac back from death.

11:18 [b] "The descendants...Isaac." Quotation from Genesis 21:12.

CONTEMPORARY ENGLISH VERSION

11Even when Sarah was too old to have children, she had faith that God would do what he had promised, and
she had a son. 12Her husband Abraham was almost dead, but he became the ancestor of many people. In fact, there are as many of them as there are stars in the sky or grains of sand along the beach.

13Every one of those people died. But they still had faith, even though they had not received what they had been promised. They were glad just to see these things from far away, and they agreed that they were only strangers and foreigners on this earth. 14When people talk
this way, it is clear that they are looking for a place to call their own. 15If they had been talking about the land where
they had once lived, they could have gone back at any time. 16But they were looking forward to a better home in heaven. That's why God wasn't ashamed for them to call him their God. He even built a city for them.

17-18Abraham had been promised that Isaac, his only son,[a] would continue his family. But when Abraham was tested, he had faith and was willing to sacrifice Isaac,
19because he was sure that God could raise people to life. This was just like getting Isaac back from death.

[a] 11.17,18 *his only son*: Although Abraham had a son by a slave woman, his son Isaac was considered his only son, because he was born as a result of God's promise to Abraham.

NEW INTERNATIONAL VERSION

[11]By faith Abraham, even though he was past age—and Sarah herself was barren—was enabled to become a father because he[a] considered him faithful who had made the promise. [12]And so from this one man, and he as good as dead, came descendants as numerous as the stars in the sky and as countless as the sand on the seashore.

[13]All these people were still living by faith when they died. They did not receive the things promised; they only saw them and welcomed them from a distance. And they admitted that they were aliens and strangers on earth. [14]People who say such things show that they are looking for a country of their own. [15]If they had been thinking of the country they had left, they would have had opportunity to return. [16]Instead, they were longing for a better country—a heavenly one. Therefore God is not ashamed to be called their God, for he has prepared a city for them.

[17]By faith Abraham, when God tested him, offered Isaac as a sacrifice. He who had received the promises was about to sacrifice his one and only son, [18]even though God had said to him, "It is through Isaac that your offspring[b] will be reckoned."[c] [19]Abraham reasoned that God could raise the dead, and figuratively speaking, he did receive Isaac back from death.

[a] *11* Or *By faith even Sarah, who was past age, was enabled to bear children because she* [b] *18* Greek *seed* [c] *18* Gen. 21:12

NEW LIVING TRANSLATION

[11]It was by faith that Sarah together with Abraham was able to have a child, even though they were too old and Sarah was barren. Abraham believed that God would keep his promise.* [12]And so a whole nation came from this one man, Abraham, who was too old to have any children—a nation with so many people that, like the stars of the sky and the sand on the seashore, there is no way to count them.

[13]All these faithful ones died without receiving what God had promised them, but they saw it all from a distance and welcomed the promises of God. They agreed that they were no more than foreigners and nomads here on earth. [14]And obviously people who talk like that are looking forward to a country they can call their own. [15]If they had meant the country they came from, they would have found a way to go back. [16]But they were looking for a better place, a heavenly homeland. That is why God is not ashamed to be called their God, for he has prepared a heavenly city for them.

[17]It was by faith that Abraham offered Isaac as a sacrifice when God was testing him. Abraham, who had received God's promises, was ready to sacrifice his only son, Isaac, [18]though God had promised him, "Isaac is the son through whom your descendants will be counted."* [19]Abraham assumed that if Isaac died, God was able to bring him back to life again. And in a sense, Abraham did receive his son back from the dead.

11:11 Some manuscripts read *It was by faith that Sarah was able to have a child, even though she was too old and barren. Sarah believed that God would keep his promise.* **11:18** Gen 21:12.

NEW KING JAMES VERSION

[11]By faith Sarah herself also received strength to conceive seed, and she bore a child[b] when she was past the age, because she judged Him faithful who had promised. [12]Therefore from one man, and him as good as dead, were born *as many* as the stars of the sky in multitude—innumerable as the sand which is by the seashore.

The Heavenly Hope

[13]These all died in faith, not having received the promises, but having seen them afar off were assured of them,[c] embraced *them* and confessed that they were strangers and pilgrims on the earth. [14]For those who say such things declare plainly that they seek a homeland. [15]And truly if they had called to mind that *country* from which they had come out, they would have had opportunity to return. [16]But now they desire a better, that is, a heavenly *country.* Therefore God is not ashamed to be called their God, for He has prepared a city for them.

The Faith of the Patriarchs

[17]By faith Abraham, when he was tested, offered up Isaac, and he who had received the promises offered up his only begotten *son,* [18]of whom it was said, *"In Isaac your seed shall be called,"*[d] [19]concluding that God *was* able to raise *him* up, even from the dead, from which he also received him in a figurative sense.

11:11 [b] NU-Text omits *she bore a child.* **11:13** [c] NU-Text and M-Text omit *were assured of them.* **11:18** [d] Genesis 21:12

THE MESSAGE

By faith, barren Sarah was able to become pregnant, old woman as she was at the time, because she believed the One who made a promise would do what he said. That's how it happened that from one man's dead and shriveled loins there are now people numbering into the millions.

Each one of these people of faith died not yet having in hand what was promised, but still believing. How did they do it? They saw it way off in the distance, waved their greeting, and accepted the fact that they were transients in this world. People who live this way make it plain that they are looking for their true home. If they were homesick for the old country, they could have gone back any time they wanted. But they were after a far better country than that—*heaven* country. You can see why God is so proud of them, and has a City waiting for them.

By faith, Abraham, at the time of testing, offered Isaac back to God. Acting in faith, he was as ready to return the promised son, his only son, as he had been to receive him—and this after he had already been told, "Your descendants shall come from Isaac." Abraham figured that if God wanted to, he could raise the dead. In a sense, that's what happened when he received Isaac back, alive from off the altar.

KING JAMES VERSION

20 By faith Isaac blessed Jacob and Esau concerning things to come.

21 By faith Jacob, when he was a dying, blessed both the sons of Joseph; and worshipped, *leaning* upon the top of his staff.

22 By faith Joseph, when he died, made mention of the departing of the children of Israel; and gave commandment concerning his bones.

23 By faith Moses, when he was born, was hid three months of his parents, because they saw *he was* a proper child; and they were not afraid of the king's commandment.

24 By faith Moses, when he was come to years, refused to be called the son of Pharaoh's daughter;

25 Choosing rather to suffer affliction with the people of God, than to enjoy the pleasures of sin for a season;

26 Esteeming the reproach of Christ greater riches than the treasures in Egypt: for he had respect unto the recompence of the reward.

27 By faith he forsook Egypt, not fearing the wrath of the king: for he endured, as seeing him who is invisible.

28 Through faith he kept the passover, and the sprinkling of blood, lest he that destroyed the firstborn should touch them.

NEW AMERICAN STANDARD BIBLE

20 By faith Isaac blessed Jacob and Esau, even regarding things to come.

21 By faith Jacob, as he was dying, blessed each of the sons of Joseph, and worshiped, *leaning* on the top of his staff.

22 By faith Joseph, when he was dying, made mention of the exodus of the sons of Israel, and gave orders concerning his bones.

23 By faith Moses, when he was born, was hidden for three months by his parents, because they saw he was a beautiful child; and they were not afraid of the king's edict.

24 By faith Moses, when he had grown up, refused to be called the son of Pharaoh's daughter,

25 choosing rather to endure ill-treatment with the people of God than to enjoy the passing pleasures of sin,

26 considering the reproach of Christ greater riches than the treasures of Egypt; for he was looking to the reward.

27 By faith he left Egypt, not fearing the wrath of the king; for he endured, as seeing Him who is unseen.

28 By faith he kept the Passover and the sprinkling of the blood, so that he who destroyed the firstborn would not touch them.

NEW CENTURY VERSION

[20]It was by faith that Isaac blessed the future of Jacob and Esau. [21]It was by faith that Jacob, as he was dying, blessed each one of Joseph's sons. Then he worshiped as he leaned on the top of his walking stick.

[22]It was by faith that Joseph, while he was dying, spoke about the Israelites leaving Egypt and gave instructions about what to do with his body.

[23]It was by faith that Moses' parents hid him for three months after he was born. They saw that Moses was a beautiful baby, and they were not afraid to disobey the king's order.

[24]It was by faith that Moses, when he grew up, refused to be called the son of the king of Egypt's daughter. [25]He chose to suffer with God's people instead of enjoying sin for a short time. [26]He thought it was better to suffer for the Christ than to have all the treasures of Egypt, because he was looking for God's reward. [27]It was by faith that Moses left Egypt and was not afraid of the king's anger. Moses continued strong as if he could see the God that no one can see. [28]It was by faith that Moses prepared the Passover and spread the blood on the doors so the one who brings death would not kill the firstborn sons of Israel.

CONTEMPORARY ENGLISH VERSION

[20]Isaac had faith, and he promised blessings to Jacob and Esau. [21]Later, when Jacob was about to die, he leaned on his walking stick and worshiped. Then because of his faith he blessed each of Joseph's sons. [22]And right before Joseph died, he had faith that God would lead the people of Israel out of Egypt. So he told them to take his bones with them.

[23]Because Moses' parents had faith, they kept him hidden until he was three months old. They saw that he was a beautiful child, and they were not afraid to disobey the king's orders.[b] [24]Then after Moses grew up, his faith made him refuse to be called Pharaoh's grandson. [25]He chose to be mistreated with God's people instead of having the good time that sin could bring for a little while. [26]Moses knew that the treasures of Egypt were not as wonderful as what he would receive from suffering for the Messiah,[c] and he looked forward to his reward.

[27]Because of his faith, Moses left Egypt. Moses had seen the invisible God and wasn't afraid of the king's anger. [28]His faith also made him celebrate Passover. He sprinkled the blood of animals on the doorposts, so that the firstborn sons of the people of Israel would not be killed by the destroying angel.

[b] 11.23 *the king's orders*: The king of Egypt ordered all Israelite baby boys to be left outside of their homes, so they would die or be killed.
[c] 11.26 *the Messiah*: Or "Christ."

NEW INTERNATIONAL VERSION

20 By faith Isaac blessed Jacob and Esau in regard to
their future.
21 By faith Jacob, when he was dying, blessed each of
Joseph's sons, and worshiped as he leaned on the top of
his staff.
22 By faith Joseph, when his end was near, spoke about
the exodus of the Israelites from Egypt and gave instruc-
tions about his bones.
23 By faith Moses' parents hid him for three months after
he was born, because they saw he was no ordinary child,
and they were not afraid of the king's edict.
24 By faith Moses, when he had grown up, refused to be
known as the son of Pharaoh's daughter. 25 He chose to be
mistreated along with the people of God rather than to
enjoy the pleasures of sin for a short time. 26 He regarded
disgrace for the sake of Christ as of greater value than the
treasures of Egypt, because he was looking ahead to his
reward. 27 By faith he left Egypt, not fearing the king's
anger; he persevered because he saw him who is invisible.
28 By faith he kept the Passover and the sprinkling of
blood, so that the destroyer of the firstborn would not
touch the firstborn of Israel.

NEW LIVING TRANSLATION

20 It was by faith that Isaac blessed his two sons, Jacob
and Esau. He had confidence in what God was going to do
in the future.
21 It was by faith that Jacob, when he was old and dying,
blessed each of Joseph's sons and bowed in worship as he
leaned on his staff.
22 And it was by faith that Joseph, when he was about to
die, confidently spoke of God's bringing the people of
Israel out of Egypt. He was so sure of it that he command-
ed them to carry his bones with them when they left!
23 It was by faith that Moses' parents hid him for three
months. They saw that God had given them an unusual
child, and they were not afraid of what the king might do.
24 It was by faith that Moses, when he grew up, refused
to be treated as the son of Pharaoh's daughter. 25 He chose
to share the oppression of God's people instead of enjoying
the fleeting pleasures of sin. 26 He thought it was better to
suffer for the sake of the Messiah than to own the trea-
sures of Egypt, for he was looking ahead to the great
reward that God would give him. 27 It was by faith that
Moses left the land of Egypt. He was not afraid of the king.
Moses kept right on going because he kept his eyes on the
one who is invisible. 28 It was by faith that Moses com-
manded the people of Israel to keep the Passover and to
sprinkle blood on the doorposts so that the angel of death
would not kill their firstborn sons.

NEW KING JAMES VERSION

20 By faith Isaac blessed Jacob and Esau concerning
things to come.
21 By faith Jacob, when he was dying, blessed each of the
sons of Joseph, and worshiped, *leaning* on the top of his
staff.
22 By faith Joseph, when he was dying, made mention of
the departure of the children of Israel, and gave instruc-
tions concerning his bones.

The Faith of Moses

23 By faith Moses, when he was born, was hidden three
months by his parents, because they saw *he was* a beauti-
ful child; and they were not afraid of the king's command.
24 By faith Moses, when he became of age, refused to be
called the son of Pharaoh's daughter, 25 choosing rather to
suffer affliction with the people of God than to enjoy the
passing pleasures of sin, 26 esteeming the reproach of
Christ greater riches than the treasures in[e] Egypt; for he
looked to the reward.
27 By faith he forsook Egypt, not fearing the wrath of the
king; for he endured as seeing Him who is invisible. 28 By
faith he kept the Passover and the sprinkling of blood, lest
he who destroyed the firstborn should touch them.

11:26 [e] NU-Text and M-Text read *of.*

THE MESSAGE

By an act of faith, Isaac reached into the future as he blessed Jacob and Esau.

By an act of faith, Jacob on his deathbed blessed each of Joseph's sons in turn, blessing them with God's blessing, not his own—as he bowed worshipfully upon his staff.

By an act of faith, Joseph, while dying, prophesied the exodus of Israel, and made arrangements for his own burial.

By an act of faith, Moses' parents hid him away for three months after his birth. They saw the child's beauty, and they braved the king's decree.

By faith, Moses, when grown, refused the privileges of the Egyptian royal house. He chose a hard life with God's people rather than an opportunistic soft life of sin with the oppressors. He valued suffering in the Messiah's camp far greater than Egyptian wealth because he was looking ahead, anticipating the payoff. By an act of faith, he turned his heel on Egypt, indifferent to the king's blind rage. He had his eye on the One no eye can see, and kept right on going. By an act of faith, he kept the Passover Feast and sprinkled Passover blood on each house so that the destroyer of the firstborn wouldn't touch them.

KING JAMES VERSION

29 By faith they passed through the Red sea as by dry *land*: which the Egyptians assaying to do were drowned.

30 By faith the walls of Jericho fell down, after they were compassed about seven days.

31 By faith the harlot Rahab perished not with them that believed not, when she had received the spies with peace.

32 ¶ And what shall I more say? for the time would fail me to tell of Gedeon, and *of* Barak, and *of* Samson, and *of* Jephthae; *of* David also, and Samuel, and *of* the prophets:

33 Who through faith subdued kingdoms, wrought righteousness, obtained promises, stopped the mouths of lions,

34 Quenched the violence of fire, escaped the edge of the sword, out of weakness were made strong, waxed valiant in fight, turned to flight the armies of the aliens.

35 Women received their dead raised to life again: and others were tortured, not accepting deliverance; that they might obtain a better resurrection:

36 And others had trial of *cruel* mockings and scourgings, yea, moreover of bonds and imprisonment:

37 They were stoned, they were sawn asunder, were tempted, were slain with the sword: they wandered about in sheepskins and goatskins; being destitute, afflicted, tormented;

NEW AMERICAN STANDARD BIBLE

29 By faith they passed through the Red Sea as though *they were passing* through dry land; and the Egyptians, when they attempted it, were drowned.

30 By faith the walls of Jericho fell down after they had been encircled for seven days.

31 By faith Rahab the harlot did not perish along with those who were disobedient, after she had welcomed the spies in peace.

32 And what more shall I say? For time will fail me if I tell of Gideon, Barak, Samson, Jephthah, of David and Samuel and the prophets,

33 who by faith conquered kingdoms, performed *acts of* righteousness, obtained promises, shut the mouths of lions,

34 quenched the power of fire, escaped the edge of the sword, from weakness were made strong, became mighty in war, put foreign armies to flight.

35 Women received *back* their dead by resurrection; and others were tortured, not accepting their release, so that they might obtain a better resurrection;

36 and others experienced mockings and scourgings, yes, also chains and imprisonment.

37 They were stoned, they were sawn in two, [1]they were tempted, they were put to death with the sword; they went about in sheepskins, in goatskins, being destitute, afflicted, ill-treated

11:37 [1] One early ms does not contain *they were tempted*

NEW CENTURY VERSION

29It was by faith that the people crossed the Red Sea as
if it were dry land. But when the Egyptians tried it, they
were drowned.

30It was by faith that the walls of Jericho fell after the
people had marched around them for seven days.

31It was by faith that Rahab, the prostitute, welcomed
the spies and was not killed with those who refused to
obey God.

32Do I need to give more examples? I do not have time to
tell you about Gideon, Barak, Samson, Jephthah, David,
Samuel, and the prophets. 33Through their faith they
defeated kingdoms. They did what was right, received
God's promises, and shut the mouths of lions. 34They
stopped great fires and were saved from being killed with
swords. They were weak, and yet were made strong. They
were powerful in battle and defeated other armies.
35Women received their dead relatives raised back to life.
Others were tortured and refused to accept their freedom
so they could be raised from the dead to a better life.
36Some were laughed at and beaten. Others were put in
chains and thrown into prison. 37They were stoned to
death, they were cut in half, and they were killed with
swords. Some wore the skins of sheep and goats. They
were poor, abused, and treated badly. 38The world was not

CONTEMPORARY ENGLISH VERSION

29Because of their faith, the people walked through the
Red Sea[d] on dry land. But when the Egyptians tried to do
it, they were drowned.

30God's people had faith, and when they had walked
around the city of Jericho for seven days, its walls fell down.

31Rahab had been a prostitute, but she had faith and
welcomed the spies. So she wasn't killed with the people
who disobeyed.

32What else can I say? There isn't enough time to tell
about Gideon, Barak, Samson, Jephthah, David, Samuel,
and the prophets. 33Their faith helped them conquer kingdoms,
and because they did right, God made promises to
them. They closed the jaws of lions 34and put out raging
fires and escaped from the swords of their enemies.
Although they were weak, they were given the strength
and power to chase foreign armies away.

35Some women received their loved ones back from
death. Many of these people were tortured, but they refused
to be released. They were sure that they would get a better
reward when the dead are raised to life. 36Others were
made fun of and beaten with whips, and some were
chained in jail. 37Still others were stoned to death or sawed
in two[e] or killed with swords. Some had nothing but sheep
skins or goat skins to wear. They were poor, mistreated,

[d] **11.29** *Red Sea*: This name comes from the Bible of the early Christians, a translation made into Greek about 200 B.C. It refers to the body of water that the Israelites crossed and was one of the marshes or fresh water lakes near the eastern part of the Nile Delta, where they lived and where the towns of Exodus 13.17—14.9 were located. [e] **11.37** *sawed in two*: Some manuscripts have "tested" or "tempted."

NEW INTERNATIONAL VERSION

29 By faith the people passed through the Red Sea[d] as on dry land; but when the Egyptians tried to do so, they were drowned.

30 By faith the walls of Jericho fell, after the people had marched around them for seven days.

31 By faith the prostitute Rahab, because she welcomed the spies, was not killed with those who were disobedient.[e]

32 And what more shall I say? I do not have time to tell about Gideon, Barak, Samson, Jephthah, David, Samuel and the prophets, 33 who through faith conquered kingdoms, administered justice, and gained what was promised; who shut the mouths of lions, 34 quenched the fury of the flames, and escaped the edge of the sword; whose weakness was turned to strength; and who became powerful in battle and routed foreign armies. 35 Women received back their dead, raised to life again. Others were tortured and refused to be released, so that they might gain a better resurrection. 36 Some faced jeers and flogging, while still others were chained and put in prison. 37 They were stoned[f]; they were sawed in two; they were put to death by the sword. They went about in sheepskins and goatskins, destitute, persecuted and mistreated— 38 the world was not

[d] *29* That is, Sea of Reeds [e] *31* Or *unbelieving* [f] *37* Some early manuscripts *stoned; they were put to the test;*

NEW LIVING TRANSLATION

29 It was by faith that the people of Israel went right through the Red Sea as though they were on dry ground. But when the Egyptians followed, they were all drowned.

30 It was by faith that the people of Israel marched around Jericho seven days, and the walls came crashing down.

31 It was by faith that Rahab the prostitute did not die with all the others in her city who refused to obey God. For she had given a friendly welcome to the spies.

32 Well, how much more do I need to say? It would take too long to recount the stories of the faith of Gideon, Barak, Samson, Jephthah, David, Samuel, and all the prophets. 33 By faith these people overthrew kingdoms, ruled with justice, and received what God had promised them. They shut the mouths of lions, 34 quenched the flames of fire, and escaped death by the edge of the sword. Their weakness was turned to strength. They became strong in battle and put whole armies to flight. 35 Women received their loved ones back again from death.

But others trusted God and were tortured, preferring to die rather than turn from God and be free. They placed their hope in the resurrection to a better life. 36 Some were mocked, and their backs were cut open with whips. Others were chained in dungeons. 37 Some died by stoning, and some were sawed in half; others were killed with the sword. Some went about in skins of sheep and goats, hungry and oppressed and mistreated. 38 They were too good

NEW KING JAMES VERSION

29 By faith they passed through the Red Sea as by dry *land, whereas* the Egyptians, attempting *to do* so, were drowned.

By Faith They Overcame

30 By faith the walls of Jericho fell down after they were encircled for seven days. 31 By faith the harlot Rahab did not perish with those who did not believe, when she had received the spies with peace.

32 And what more shall I say? For the time would fail me to tell of Gideon and Barak and Samson and Jephthah, also *of* David and Samuel and the prophets: 33 who through faith subdued kingdoms, worked righteousness, obtained promises, stopped the mouths of lions, 34 quenched the violence of fire, escaped the edge of the sword, out of weakness were made strong, became valiant in battle, turned to flight the armies of the aliens. 35 Women received their dead raised to life again.

Others were tortured, not accepting deliverance, that they might obtain a better resurrection. 36 Still others had trial of mockings and scourgings, yes, and of chains and imprisonment. 37 They were stoned, they were sawn in two, were tempted,[f] were slain with the sword. They wandered about in sheepskins and goatskins, being destitute, afflicted,

11:37 [f] NU-Text omits *were tempted.*

THE MESSAGE

By an act of faith, Israel walked through the Red Sea on dry ground. The Egyptians tried it and drowned.

By faith, the Israelites marched around the walls of Jericho for seven days, and the walls fell flat.

By an act of faith, Rahab, the Jericho harlot, welcomed the spies and escaped the destruction that came on those who refused to trust God.

✣

I could go on and on, but I've run out of time. There are so many more—Gideon, Barak, Samson, Jephthah, David, Samuel, the prophets. . . . Through acts of faith, they toppled kingdoms, made justice work, took the promises for themselves. They were protected from lions, fires, and sword thrusts, turned disadvantage to advantage, won battles, routed alien armies. Women received their loved ones back from the dead. There were those who, under torture, refused to give in and go free, preferring something better: resurrection. Others braved abuse and whips, and, yes, chains and dungeons. We have stories of those who were stoned, sawed in two, murdered in cold blood; stories of vagrants wandering the earth in animal skins, homeless,

KING JAMES VERSION

38 (Of whom the world was not worthy:) they wandered in deserts, and *in* mountains, and *in* dens and caves of the earth.

39 And these all, having obtained a good report through faith, received not the promise:

40 God having provided some better thing for us, that they without us should not be made perfect.

12 Wherefore seeing we also are compassed about with so great a cloud of witnesses, let us lay aside every weight, and the sin which doth so easily beset *us*, and let us run with patience the race that is set before us,

2 Looking unto Jesus the author and finisher of *our* faith; who for the joy that was set before him endured the cross, despising the shame, and is set down at the right hand of the throne of God.

3 For consider him that endured such contradiction of sinners against himself, lest ye be wearied and faint in your minds.

4 ¶ Ye have not yet resisted unto blood, striving against sin.

5 And ye have forgotten the exhortation which speaketh

NEW AMERICAN STANDARD BIBLE

38 (*men* of whom the world was not worthy), wandering in deserts and mountains and caves and holes in the ground.

39 And all these, having gained approval through their faith, did not receive what was promised,

40 because God had provided something better for us, so that apart from us they would not be made perfect.

Jesus, the Example

12 Therefore, since we have so great a cloud of witnesses surrounding us, let us also lay aside every encumbrance and the sin which so easily entangles us, and let us run with endurance the race that is set before us,

2 fixing our eyes on Jesus, the author and perfecter of faith, who for the joy set before Him endured the cross, despising the shame, and has sat down at the right hand of the throne of God.

3 For consider Him who has endured such hostility by sinners against Himself, so that you will not grow weary and lose heart.

A Father's Discipline

4 You have not yet resisted to the point of shedding blood in your striving against sin;

5 and you have forgotten the exhortation which is addressed to you as sons,

NEW CENTURY VERSION

good enough for them! They wandered in deserts and
mountains, living in caves and holes in the earth.
39 All these people are known for their faith, but none of
them received what God had promised. 40 God planned to
give us something better so that they would be made perfect, but only together with us.

Follow Jesus' Example

12 We have around us many people whose lives tell
us what faith means. So let us run the race that is
before us and never give up. We should remove from our
lives anything that would get in the way and the sin that
so easily holds us back. 2 Let us look only to Jesus, the One
who began our faith and who makes it perfect. He suffered
death on the cross. But he accepted the shame as if it were
nothing because of the joy that God put before him. And
now he is sitting at the right side of God's throne. 3 Think
about Jesus' example. He held on while wicked people were
doing evil things to him. So do not get tired and stop trying.

God Is like a Father

4 You are struggling against sin, but your struggles have
not yet caused you to be killed. 5 You have forgotten the
encouraging words that call you his children:

CONTEMPORARY ENGLISH VERSION

and tortured. 38 The world did not deserve these good peo-
ple, who had to wander in deserts and on mountains and
had to live in caves and holes in the ground.
39 All of them pleased God because of their faith! But
still they died without being given what had been prom-
ised. 40 This was because God had something better in
store for us. And he did not want them to reach the goal of
their faith without us.

A Large Crowd of Witnesses

12 Such a large crowd of witnesses is all around us!
So we must get rid of everything that slows us
down, especially the sin that just won't let go. And we
must be determined to run the race that is ahead of us.
2 We must keep our eyes on Jesus, who leads us and makes
our faith complete. He endured the shame of being nailed
to a cross, because he knew that later on he would be glad
he did. Now he is seated at the right side[a] of God's throne!
3 So keep your mind on Jesus, who put up with many
insults from sinners. Then you won't get discouraged and
give up.
4 None of you have yet been hurt[b] in your battle against
sin. 5 But you have forgotten that the Scriptures say to
God's children,

[a] 12.2 *right side*: See the note at 1.3. [b] 12.4 *hurt*: Or "killed."

NEW INTERNATIONAL VERSION

worthy of them. They wandered in deserts and mountains,
and in caves and holes in the ground.
[39]These were all commended for their faith, yet none of
them received what had been promised. [40]God had planned
something better for us so that only together with us
would they be made perfect.

God Disciplines His Sons

12 Therefore, since we are surrounded by such a great
cloud of witnesses, let us throw off everything that
hinders and the sin that so easily entangles, and let us run
with perseverance the race marked out for us. [2]Let us fix
our eyes on Jesus, the author and perfecter of our faith,
who for the joy set before him endured the cross, scorning
its shame, and sat down at the right hand of the throne of
God. [3]Consider him who endured such opposition from sin-
ful men, so that you will not grow weary and lose heart.
[4]In your struggle against sin, you have not yet resisted
to the point of shedding your blood. [5]And you have forgot-
ten that word of encouragement that addresses you as
sons:

NEW LIVING TRANSLATION

for this world. They wandered over deserts and mountains,
hiding in caves and holes in the ground.
[39]All of these people we have mentioned received God's
approval because of their faith, yet none of them received
all that God had promised. [40]For God had far better things
in mind for us that would also benefit them, for they can't
receive the prize at the end of the race until we finish the
race.*

God's Discipline Proves His Love

12 Therefore, since we are surrounded by such a huge
crowd of witnesses to the life of faith, let us strip
off every weight that slows us down, especially the sin
that so easily hinders our progress. And let us run with
endurance the race that God has set before us. [2]We do this
by keeping our eyes on Jesus, on whom our faith depends
from start to finish.* He was willing to die a shameful
death on the cross because of the joy he knew would be his
afterward. Now he is seated in the place of highest honor
beside God's throne in heaven. [3]Think about all he
endured when sinful people did such terrible things to him,
so that you don't become weary and give up. [4]After all,
you have not yet given your lives in your struggle against
sin.
[5]And have you entirely forgotten the encouraging words
God spoke to you, his children? He said,

11:40 Greek *for us, for they apart from us can't finish.* 12:2 Or *Jesus, the Originator and Perfecter of our faith.*

NEW KING JAMES VERSION

tormented— [38]of whom the world was not worthy. They
wandered in deserts and mountains, *in* dens and caves of
the earth.
[39]And all these, having obtained a good testimony
through faith, did not receive the promise, [40]God having
provided something better for us, that they should not be
made perfect apart from us.

The Race of Faith

12 Therefore we also, since we are surrounded by so
great a cloud of witnesses, let us lay aside every
weight, and the sin which so easily ensnares *us,* and let us
run with endurance the race that is set before us, [2]looking
unto Jesus, the author and finisher of *our* faith, who for
the joy that was set before Him endured the cross, despis-
ing the shame, and has sat down at the right hand of the
throne of God.

The Discipline of God

[3]For consider Him who endured such hostility from sin-
ners against Himself, lest you become weary and discour-
aged in your souls. [4]You have not yet resisted to blood-
shed, striving against sin. [5]And you have forgotten the
exhortation which speaks to you as to sons:

THE MESSAGE

friendless, powerless—the world didn't deserve them!—making their way as best they could on the cruel edges of the world.

Not one of these people, even though their lives of faith were exemplary, got their hands on what was promised. God had a better plan for us: that their faith and our faith would come together to make one completed whole, their lives of faith not complete apart from ours.

Discipline in a Long-Distance Race

12 Do you see what this means—all these pioneers who blazed the way, all these veterans cheering us on? It means we'd better get on with it. Strip down, start running—and never quit! No extra spiritual fat, no parasitic sins. Keep your eyes on *Jesus,* who both began and finished this race we're in. Study how he did it. Because he never lost sight of where he was headed—that exhilarating finish in and with God—he could put up with anything along the way: cross, shame, whatever. And now he's *there,* in the place of honor, right alongside God. When you find yourselves flagging in your faith, go over that story again, item by item, that long litany of hostility he plowed through. *That* will shoot adrenaline into your souls!

In this all-out match against sin, others have suffered far worse than you, to say nothing of what Jesus went through—all that bloodshed! So don't feel sorry for yourselves. Or have you forgotten how good parents treat children, and that God regards you as *his* children?

KING JAMES VERSION

unto you as unto children, My son, despise not thou the
chastening of the Lord, nor faint when thou art rebuked of
him:

6 For whom the Lord loveth he chasteneth, and scourgeth every son whom he receiveth.

7 If ye endure chastening, God dealeth with you as with sons; for what son is he whom the father chasteneth not?

8 But if ye be without chastisement, whereof all are partakers, then are ye bastards, and not sons.

9 Furthermore we have had fathers of our flesh which corrected *us*, and we gave *them* reverence: shall we not much rather be in subjection unto the Father of spirits, and live?

10 For they verily for a few days chastened *us* after their own pleasure; but he for *our* profit, that *we* might be partakers of his holiness.

11 Now no chastening for the present seemeth to be joyous, but grievous: nevertheless afterward it yieldeth the peaceable fruit of righteousness unto them which are exercised thereby.

12 Wherefore lift up the hands which hang down, and the feeble knees;

13 And make straight paths for your feet, lest that which is lame be turned out of the way; but let it rather be healed.

NEW AMERICAN STANDARD BIBLE

"MY SON, DO NOT REGARD LIGHTLY THE DISCIPLINE OF THE
LORD,
NOR FAINT WHEN YOU ARE REPROVED BY HIM;
6 FOR THOSE WHOM THE LORD LOVES HE DISCIPLINES,
AND HE SCOURGES EVERY SON WHOM HE RECEIVES."

7 It is for discipline that you endure; God deals with you as with sons; for what son is there whom *his* father does not discipline?

8 But if you are without discipline, of which all have become partakers, then you are illegitimate children and not sons.

9 Furthermore, we had earthly fathers to discipline us, and we respected them; shall we not much rather be subject to the Father of spirits, and live?

10 For they disciplined us for a short time as seemed best to them, but He *disciplines us* for *our* good, so that we may share His holiness.

11 All discipline for the moment seems not to be joyful, but sorrowful; yet to those who have been trained by it, afterwards it yields the peaceful fruit of righteousness.

12 Therefore, strengthen the hands that are weak and the knees that are feeble,

13 and make straight paths for your feet, so that *the limb* which is lame may not be put out of joint, but rather be healed.

NEW CENTURY VERSION

"My child, don't think the Lord's discipline is worth
nothing,
and don't stop trying when he corrects you.
6 The Lord disciplines those he loves,
and he punishes everyone he accepts as his child."

Proverbs 3:11–12

7 So hold on through your sufferings, because they are
like a father's discipline. God is treating you as children.
All children are disciplined by their fathers. 8 If you are
never disciplined (and every child must be disciplined), you
are not true children. 9 We have all had fathers here on
earth who disciplined us, and we respected them. So it is
even more important that we accept discipline from the
Father of our spirits so we will have life. 10 Our fathers on
earth disciplined us for a short time in the way they
thought was best. But God disciplines us to help us, so we
can become holy as he is. 11 We do not enjoy being disci-
plined. It is painful, but later, after we have learned from
it, we have peace, because we start living in the right way.

Be Careful How You Live

12 You have become weak, so make yourselves strong
again. 13 Live in the right way so that you will be saved
and your weakness will not cause you to be lost.

CONTEMPORARY ENGLISH VERSION

"When the Lord punishes you,
don't make light of it,
and when he corrects you,
don't be discouraged.
6 The Lord corrects the people
he loves
and disciplines those
he calls his own."

7 Be patient when you are being corrected! This is how
God treats his children. Don't all parents correct their chil-
dren? 8 God corrects all of his children, and if he doesn't
correct you, then you don't really belong to him. 9 Our
earthly fathers correct us, and we still respect them. Isn't it
even better to be given true life by letting our spiritual
Father correct us?

10 Our human fathers correct us for a short time, and
they do it as they think best. But God corrects us for our
own good, because he wants us to be holy, as he is. 11 It is
never fun to be corrected. In fact, at the time it is always
painful. But if we learn to obey by being corrected, we will
do right and live at peace.

12 Now stand up straight! Stop your knees from shaking
13 and walk a straight path. Then lame people will be
healed, instead of getting worse.

NEW INTERNATIONAL VERSION

"My son, do not make light of the Lord's discipline,
and do not lose heart when he rebukes you,
6 because the Lord disciplines those he loves,
and he punishes everyone he accepts as a son."[a]

7 Endure hardship as discipline; God is treating you as
sons. For what son is not disciplined by his father? 8 If you
are not disciplined (and everyone undergoes discipline),
then you are illegitimate children and not true sons.
9 Moreover, we have all had human fathers who disciplined
us and we respected them for it. How much more should
we submit to the Father of our spirits and live! 10 Our
fathers disciplined us for a little while as they thought
best; but God disciplines us for our good, that we may
share in his holiness. 11 No discipline seems pleasant at the
time, but painful. Later on, however, it produces a harvest
of righteousness and peace for those who have been
trained by it.

12 Therefore, strengthen your feeble arms and weak
knees. 13 "Make level paths for your feet,"[b] so that the
lame may not be disabled, but rather healed.

[a] *6* Prov. 3:11,12 [b] *13* Prov. 4:26

NEW LIVING TRANSLATION

"My child, don't ignore it when the Lord disciplines you,
and don't be discouraged when he corrects you.
6 For the Lord disciplines those he loves,
and he punishes those he accepts as his children."*

7 As you endure this divine discipline, remember that God
is treating you as his own children. Whoever heard of a
child who was never disciplined? 8 If God doesn't discipline
you as he does all of his children, it means that you are
illegitimate and are not really his children after all. 9 Since
we respect our earthly fathers who disciplined us, should
we not all the more cheerfully submit to the discipline of
our heavenly Father and live forever*?

10 For our earthly fathers disciplined us for a few years,
doing the best they knew how. But God's discipline is
always right and good for us because it means we will
share in his holiness. 11 No discipline is enjoyable while it
is happening—it is painful! But afterward there will be a
quiet harvest of right living for those who are trained in
this way.

12 So take a new grip with your tired hands and stand
firm on your shaky legs. 13 Mark out a straight path for
your feet. Then those who follow you, though they are
weak and lame, will not stumble and fall but will become
strong.

12:5-6 Prov 3:11-12. **12:9** Or *really live.*

NEW KING JAMES VERSION

"My son, do not despise the chastening of the LORD,
Nor be discouraged when you are rebuked by Him;
6 *For whom the LORD loves He chastens,*
And scourges every son whom He receives."[a]

7 If[b] you endure chastening, God deals with you as with
sons; for what son is there whom a father does not chas-
ten? 8 But if you are without chastening, of which all have
become partakers, then you are illegitimate and not sons.
9 Furthermore, we have had human fathers who corrected
us, and we paid *them* respect. Shall we not much more
readily be in subjection to the Father of spirits and live?
10 For they indeed for a few days chastened *us* as seemed
best to them, but He for *our* profit, that *we* may be partak-
ers of His holiness. 11 Now no chastening seems to be joy-
ful for the present, but painful; nevertheless, afterward it
yields the peaceable fruit of righteousness to those who
have been trained by it.

Renew Your Spiritual Vitality

12 Therefore strengthen the hands which hang down, and
the feeble knees, 13 and make straight paths for your feet,
so that what is lame may not be *dislocated,* but rather be
healed.

12:6 [a] Proverbs 3:11, 12 **12:7** [b] NU-Text and M-Text read *It is for discipline that you endure; God . . . .*

THE MESSAGE

"My dear child, don't shrug off God's discipline,
but don't be crushed by it either.
It's the child he loves that he disciplines;
the child he embraces, he also corrects."

God is educating you; that's why you must never drop out.
He's treating you as dear children. This trouble you're in
isn't punishment; it's *training,* the normal experience of
children. Only irresponsible parents leave children to fend
for themselves. Would you prefer an irresponsible God? We
respect our own parents for training and not spoiling us,
so why not embrace God's training so we can truly *live*?
While we were children, our parents did what *seemed* best
to them. But God is doing what *is* best for us, training us
to live God's holy best. At the time, discipline isn't much
fun. It always feels like it's going against the grain. Later,
of course, it pays off handsomely, for it's the well-trained
who find themselves mature in their relationship with God.

So don't sit around on your hands! No more dragging
your feet! Clear the path for long-distance runners so no
one will trip and fall, so no one will step in a hole and
sprain an ankle. Help each other out. And run for it!

KING JAMES VERSION

14 Follow peace with all *men*, and holiness, without which no man shall see the Lord:

15 Looking diligently lest any man fail of the grace of God; lest any root of bitterness springing up trouble *you*, and thereby many be defiled;

16 Lest there *be* any fornicator, or profane person, as Esau, who for one morsel of meat sold his birthright.

17 For ye know how that afterward, when he would have inherited the blessing, he was rejected: for he found no place of repentance, though he sought it carefully with tears.

18 ¶ For ye are not come unto the mount that might be touched, and that burned with fire, nor unto blackness, and darkness, and tempest,

19 And the sound of a trumpet, and the voice of words; which *voice* they that heard intreated that the word should not be spoken to them any more:

20 (For they could not endure that which was commanded, And if so much as a beast touch the mountain, it shall be stoned, or thrust through with a dart:

21 And so terrible was the sight, *that* Moses said, I exceedingly fear and quake:)

22 But ye are come unto mount Sion, and unto the city of the living God, the heavenly Jerusalem, and to an innumerable company of angels,

NEW AMERICAN STANDARD BIBLE

14 Pursue peace with all men, and the sanctification without which no one will see the Lord.

15 See to it that no one comes short of the grace of God; that no root of bitterness springing up causes trouble, and by it many be defiled;

16 that *there be* no immoral or godless person like Esau, who sold his own birthright for a *single* meal.

17 For you know that even afterwards, when he desired to inherit the blessing, he was rejected, for he found no place for repentance, though he sought for it with tears.

Contrast of Sinai and Zion

18 For you have not come to *a mountain* that can be touched and to a blazing fire, and to darkness and gloom and whirlwind,

19 and to the blast of a trumpet and the sound of words which *sound was such that* those who heard begged that no further word be spoken to them.

20 For they could not bear the command, "IF EVEN A BEAST TOUCHES THE MOUNTAIN, IT WILL BE STONED."

21 And so terrible was the sight, *that* Moses said, "I AM FULL OF FEAR and trembling."

22 But you have come to Mount Zion and to the city of the living God, the heavenly Jerusalem, and to myriads of angels,

NEW CENTURY VERSION

14 Try to live in peace with all people, and try to live free
from sin. Anyone whose life is not holy will never see the
Lord. 15 Be careful that no one fails to receive God's grace
and begins to cause trouble among you. A person like that
can ruin many of you. 16 Be careful that no one takes part
in sexual sin or is like Esau and never thinks about God.
As the oldest son, Esau would have received everything
from his father, but he sold all that for a single meal.
17 You remember that after Esau did this, he wanted to get
his father's blessing, but his father refused. Esau could
find no way to change what he had done, even though he
wanted the blessing so much that he cried.

18 You have not come to a mountain that can be touched
and that is burning with fire. You have not come to dark-
ness, sadness, and storms. 19 You have not come to the
noise of a trumpet or to the sound of a voice like the one
the people of Israel heard and begged not to hear another
word. 20 They did not want to hear the command: "If any-
thing, even an animal, touches the mountain, it must be
put to death with stones."[a] 21 What they saw was so terri-
ble that Moses said, "I am shaking with fear."[b]

22 But you have come to Mount Zion,[c] to the city of the
living God, the heavenly Jerusalem. You have come to
thousands of angels gathered together with joy. 23 You

12:20 [a] "If...stones." Quotation from Exodus 19:12–13.
12:21 [b] "I...fear." Quotation from Deuteronomy 9:19. 12:22 [c] **Mount Zion** Another name for Jerusalem, here meaning the spiritual city of God's people.

CONTEMPORARY ENGLISH VERSION

Warning against Turning from God

14 Try to live at peace with everyone! Live a clean life. If
you don't, you will never see the Lord. 15 Make sure that no
one misses out on God's wonderful kindness. Don't let
anyone become bitter and cause trouble for the rest of you.
16 Watch out for immoral and ungodly people like Esau,
who sold his future blessing[c] for only one meal. 17 You
know how he later wanted it back. But there was nothing
he could do to change things, even though he begged his
father and cried.

18 You have not come to a place like Mount Sinai[d] that
can be seen and touched. There is no flaming fire or dark
cloud or storm 19 or trumpet sound. The people of Israel
heard a voice speak. But they begged it to stop, 20 because
they could not obey its commands. They were even told to
kill any animal that touched the mountain. 21 The sight
was so frightening that Moses said he shook with fear.

22 You have now come to Mount Zion and to the heavenly
Jerusalem. This is the city of the living God, where thousands
and thousands of angels have come to celebrate. 23 Here you

[c] 12.16 *sold his future blessing*: As the first-born son, Esau had certain privileges that were known as a "birthright." [d] 12.18 *a place like Mount Sinai*: The Greek text has "a place," but the writer is referring to the time that the Lord spoke to the people of Israel from Mount Sinai (see Exodus 19.16-25).

NEW INTERNATIONAL VERSION

Warning Against Refusing God

14 Make every effort to live in peace with all men and to be holy; without holiness no one will see the Lord. 15 See to it that no one misses the grace of God and that no bitter root grows up to cause trouble and defile many. 16 See that no one is sexually immoral, or is godless like Esau, who for a single meal sold his inheritance rights as the oldest son. 17 Afterward, as you know, when he wanted to inherit this blessing, he was rejected. He could bring about no change of mind, though he sought the blessing with tears.

18 You have not come to a mountain that can be touched and that is burning with fire; to darkness, gloom and storm; 19 to a trumpet blast or to such a voice speaking words that those who heard it begged that no further word be spoken to them, 20 because they could not bear what was commanded: "If even an animal touches the mountain, it must be stoned."[c] 21 The sight was so terrifying that Moses said, "I am trembling with fear."[d]

22 But you have come to Mount Zion, to the heavenly Jerusalem, the city of the living God. You have come to thousands upon thousands of angels in joyful assembly,

[c] *20* Exodus 19:12,13 [d] *21* Deut. 9:19

NEW LIVING TRANSLATION

A Call to Listen to God

14 Try to live in peace with everyone, and seek to live a clean and holy life, for those who are not holy will not see the Lord. 15 Look after each other so that none of you will miss out on the special favor of God. Watch out that no bitter root of unbelief rises up among you, for whenever it springs up, many are corrupted by its poison. 16 Make sure that no one is immoral or godless like Esau. He traded his birthright as the oldest son for a single meal. 17 And afterward, when he wanted his father's blessing, he was rejected. It was too late for repentance, even though he wept bitter tears.

18 You have not come to a physical mountain, to a place of flaming fire, darkness, gloom, and whirlwind, as the Israelites did at Mount Sinai when God gave them his laws. 19 For they heard an awesome trumpet blast and a voice with a message so terrible that they begged God to stop speaking. 20 They staggered back under God's command: "If even an animal touches the mountain, it must be stoned to death."* 21 Moses himself was so frightened at the sight that he said, "I am terrified and trembling."*

22 No, you have come to Mount Zion, to the city of the living God, the heavenly Jerusalem, and to thousands of angels

12:20 Exod 19:13. **12:21** Deut 9:19.

NEW KING JAMES VERSION

14 Pursue peace with all *people,* and holiness, without which no one will see the Lord: 15 looking carefully lest anyone fall short of the grace of God; lest any root of bitterness springing up cause trouble, and by this many become defiled; 16 lest there *be* any fornicator or profane person like Esau, who for one morsel of food sold his birthright. 17 For you know that afterward, when he wanted to inherit the blessing, he was rejected, for he found no place for repentance, though he sought it diligently with tears.

The Glorious Company

18 For you have not come to the mountain that[c] may be touched and that burned with fire, and to blackness and darkness[d] and tempest, 19 and the sound of a trumpet and the voice of words, so that those who heard *it* begged that the word should not be spoken to them anymore. 20 (For they could not endure what was commanded: *"And if so much as a beast touches the mountain, it shall be stoned*[e] *or shot with an arrow."*[f] 21 And so terrifying was the sight *that* Moses said, *"I am exceedingly afraid* and trembling."[g])

22 But you have come to Mount Zion and to the city of the living God, the heavenly Jerusalem, to an innumerable

12:18 [c] NU-Text reads *to that which.* [d] NU-Text reads *gloom.*
12:20 [e] NU-Text and M-Text omit the rest of this verse. [f] Exodus 19:12, 13 **12:21** [g] Deuteronomy 9:19

THE MESSAGE

Work at getting along with each other and with God. Otherwise you'll never get so much as a glimpse of God. Make sure no one gets left out of God's generosity. Keep a sharp eye out for weeds of bitter discontent. A thistle or two gone to seed can ruin a whole garden in no time. Watch out for the Esau syndrome: trading away God's lifelong gift in order to satisfy a short-term appetite. You well know how Esau later regretted that impulsive act and wanted God's blessing—but by then it was too late, tears or no tears.

An Unshakable Kingdom

Unlike your ancestors, you didn't come to Mount Sinai—all that volcanic blaze and earthshaking rumble—to hear God speak. The earsplitting words and soul-shaking message terrified them and they begged him to stop. When they heard the words—"If an animal touches the Mountain, it's as good as dead"—they were afraid to move. Even Moses was terrified.

No, that's not *your* experience at all. You've come to Mount Zion, the city where the living God resides. The invisible Jerusalem is populated by throngs of festive angels and Christian citizens. It is the city where God is

KING JAMES VERSION

23 To the general assembly and church of the firstborn, which are written in heaven, and to God the Judge of all, and to the spirits of just men made perfect,

24 And to Jesus the mediator of the new covenant, and to the blood of sprinkling, that speaketh better things than *that of* Abel.

25 See that ye refuse not him that speaketh. For if they escaped not who refused him that spake on earth, much more *shall not* we *escape*, if we turn away from him that *speaketh* from heaven:

26 Whose voice then shook the earth: but now he hath promised, saying, Yet once more I shake not the earth only, but also heaven.

27 And this *word*, Yet once more, signifieth the removing of those things that are shaken, as of things that are made, that those things which cannot be shaken may remain.

28 Wherefore we receiving a kingdom which cannot be moved, let us have grace, whereby we may serve God acceptably with reverence and godly fear:

29 For our God *is* a consuming fire.

13 Let brotherly love continue.

2 Be not forgetful to entertain strangers: for thereby some have entertained angels unawares.

NEW AMERICAN STANDARD BIBLE

23 to the general assembly and church of the firstborn who are enrolled in heaven, and to God, the Judge of all, and to the spirits of *the* righteous made perfect,

24 and to Jesus, the mediator of a new covenant, and to the sprinkled blood, which speaks better than *the blood* of Abel.

The Unshaken Kingdom

25 See to it that you do not refuse Him who is speaking. For if those did not escape when they refused him who warned *them* on earth, much less *will* we *escape* who turn away from Him who *warns* from heaven.

26 And His voice shook the earth then, but now He has promised, saying, "YET ONCE MORE I WILL SHAKE NOT ONLY THE EARTH, BUT ALSO THE HEAVEN."

27 This *expression*, "Yet once more," denotes the removing of those things which can be shaken, as of created things, so that those things which cannot be shaken may remain.

28 Therefore, since we receive a kingdom which cannot be shaken, let us show gratitude, by which we may offer to God an acceptable service with reverence and awe;

29 for our God is a consuming fire.

The Changeless Christ

13 Let love of the brethren continue.

2 Do not neglect to show hospitality to strangers, for by this some have entertained angels without knowing it.

NEW CENTURY VERSION

have come to the meeting of God's firstborn[d] children
whose names are written in heaven. You have come to
God, the judge of all people, and to the spirits of good peo-
ple who have been made perfect. 24You have come to Jesus,
the One who brought the new agreement from God to his
people, and you have come to the sprinkled blood[e] that
has a better message than the blood of Abel.[f]
25So be careful and do not refuse to listen when God
speaks. Others refused to listen to him when he warned
them on earth, and they did not escape. So it will be worse
for us if we refuse to listen to God who warns us from
heaven. 26When he spoke before, his voice shook the earth,
but now he has promised, "Once again I will shake not
only the earth but also the heavens."[g] 27The words "once
again" clearly show us that everything that was made—
things that can be shaken—will be destroyed. Only the
things that cannot be shaken will remain.
28So let us be thankful, because we have a kingdom that
cannot be shaken. We should worship God in a way that
pleases him with respect and fear, 29because our God is
like a fire that burns things up.
13 Keep on loving each other as brothers and sisters.
2Remember to welcome strangers, because some
who have done this have welcomed angels without knowing

12:23 [d] **firstborn** The first son born in a Jewish family was given the most important place in the family and received special blessings. All of God's children are like that. 12:24 [e] **sprinkled blood** The blood of Jesus' death. 12:24 [f] **Abel** The son of Adam and Eve, who was killed by his brother Cain (Genesis 4:8). 12:26 [g] **"Once...heavens."** Quotation from Haggai 2:6, 21.

CONTEMPORARY ENGLISH VERSION

will find all of God's dearest children,[e] whose names are
written in heaven. And you will find God himself, who judges
everyone. Here also are the spirits of those good people who
have been made perfect. 24And Jesus is here! He is the one
who makes God's new agreement with us, and his sprinkled
blood says much better things than the blood of Abel.[f]
25Make sure that you obey the one who speaks to you.
The people did not escape, when they refused to obey the
one who spoke to them at Mount Sinai. Do you think you
can possibly escape, if you refuse to obey the one who
speaks to you from heaven? 26When God spoke the first
time, his voice shook only the earth. This time he has
promised to shake the earth once again, and heaven too.
27The words "once again" mean that these created things
will someday be shaken and removed. Then what cannot be
shaken will last. 28We should be grateful that we were
given a kingdom that cannot be shaken. And in this king-
dom we please God by worshiping him and by showing him
great honor and respect. 29Our God is like a destructive fire!

Service That Pleases God

13 Keep being concerned about each other as the
Lord's followers should.
2Be sure to welcome strangers into your home. By doing
this, some people have welcomed angels as guests, with-
out even knowing it.

[e] 12.23 *all of God's dearest children*: The Greek text has "the gathering of the first-born children" (see the note at 1.6). [f] 12.24 *blood of Abel*: Cain and Abel were the two sons of Adam and Eve. Cain murdered Abel (see Genesis 4.1-16).

NEW INTERNATIONAL VERSION

23to the church of the firstborn, whose names are written
in heaven. You have come to God, the judge of all men, to
the spirits of righteous men made perfect, 24to Jesus the
mediator of a new covenant, and to the sprinkled blood
that speaks a better word than the blood of Abel.
25See to it that you do not refuse him who speaks. If
they did not escape when they refused him who warned
them on earth, how much less will we, if we turn away
from him who warns us from heaven? 26At that time his
voice shook the earth, but now he has promised, "Once
more I will shake not only the earth but also the
heavens."[e] 27The words "once more" indicate the removing
of what can be shaken—that is, created things—so that
what cannot be shaken may remain.
28Therefore, since we are receiving a kingdom that can-
not be shaken, let us be thankful, and so worship God
acceptably with reverence and awe, 29for our "God is a
consuming fire."[f]

Concluding Exhortations

13 Keep on loving each other as brothers. 2Do not for-
get to entertain strangers, for by so doing some
people have entertained angels without knowing it.

[e] *26* Haggai 2:6 [f] *29* Deut. 4:24

NEW LIVING TRANSLATION

in joyful assembly. 23You have come to the assembly of
God's firstborn children, whose names are written in heaven.
You have come to God himself, who is the judge of all people.
And you have come to the spirits of the redeemed in heaven
who have now been made perfect. 24You have come to Jesus,
the one who mediates the new covenant between God and
people, and to the sprinkled blood, which graciously forgives
instead of crying out for vengeance as the blood of Abel did.
25See to it that you obey God, the one who is speaking to
you. For if the people of Israel did not escape when they
refused to listen to Moses, the earthly messenger, how ter-
rible our danger if we reject the One who speaks to us from
heaven! 26When God spoke from Mount Sinai his voice
shook the earth, but now he makes another promise:
"Once again I will shake not only the earth but the heav-
ens also."* 27This means that the things on earth will be
shaken, so that only eternal things will be left.
28Since we are receiving a Kingdom that cannot be
destroyed, let us be thankful and please God by worshiping
him with holy fear and awe. 29For our God is a consuming
fire.

Concluding Words

13 Continue to love each other with true Christian
love.* 2Don't forget to show hospitality to
strangers, for some who have done this have entertained
angels without realizing it! 3Don't forget about those in

12:26 Hag 2:6. 13:1 Greek *with brotherly love.*

NEW KING JAMES VERSION

company of angels, 23to the general assembly and church
of the firstborn *who are* registered in heaven, to God the
Judge of all, to the spirits of just men made perfect, 24to
Jesus the Mediator of the new covenant, and to the blood
of sprinkling that speaks better things than *that of* Abel.

Hear the Heavenly Voice

25See that you do not refuse Him who speaks. For if they
did not escape who refused Him who spoke on earth, much
more *shall we not escape* if we turn away from Him who
speaks from heaven, 26whose voice then shook the earth;
but now He has promised, saying, *"Yet once more I shake*[h]
not only the earth, but also heaven."[i] 27Now this, *"Yet
once more,"* indicates the removal of those things that are
being shaken, as of things that are made, that the things
which cannot be shaken may remain.
28Therefore, since we are receiving a kingdom which
cannot be shaken, let us have grace, by which we may[j]
serve God acceptably with reverence and godly fear. 29For
our God *is* a consuming fire.

Concluding Moral Directions

13 Let brotherly love continue. 2Do not forget to
entertain strangers, for by so *doing* some have
unwittingly entertained angels. 3Remember the prisoners

12:26 [h] NU-Text reads *will shake.* [i] Haggai 2:6 12:28 [j] M-Text
omits *may.*

THE MESSAGE

Judge, with judgments that make us just. You've come to
Jesus, who presents us with a new covenant, a fresh char-
ter from God. He is the Mediator of this covenant. The
murder of Jesus, unlike Abel's—a homicide that cried out
for vengeance—became a proclamation of grace.
So don't turn a deaf ear to these gracious words. If those
who ignored earthly warnings didn't get away with it,
what will happen to us if we turn our backs on heavenly
warnings? His voice that time shook the earth to its foun-
dations; this time—he's told us this quite plainly—he'll
also rock the heavens: "One last shaking, from top to bot-
tom, stem to stern." The phrase "one last shaking" means
a thorough housecleaning, getting rid of all the historical
and religious junk so that the unshakable essentials stand
clear and uncluttered.
Do you see what we've got? An unshakable kingdom!
And do you see how thankful we must be? Not only thank-
ful, but brimming with worship, deeply reverent before
God. For God is not an indifferent bystander. He's actively
cleaning house, torching all that needs to burn, and he
won't quit until it's all cleansed. God himself is Fire!

Jesus Doesn't Change

13 Stay on good terms with each other, held together
by love. Be ready with a meal or a bed when it's
needed. Why, some have extended hospitality to angels
without ever knowing it! Regard prisoners as if you were

KING JAMES VERSION

3 Remember them that are in bonds, as bound with them; *and* them which suffer adversity, as being yourselves also in the body.

4 Marriage *is* honourable in all, and the bed undefiled: but whoremongers and adulterers God will judge.

5 *Let your* conversation *be* without covetousness; *and be* content with such things as ye have: for he hath said, I will never leave thee, nor forsake thee.

6 So that we may boldly say, The Lord *is* my helper, and I will not fear what man shall do unto me.

7 Remember them which have the rule over you, who have spoken unto you the word of God: whose faith follow, considering the end of *their* conversation.

8 Jesus Christ the same yesterday, and to day, and for ever.

9 Be not carried about with divers and strange doctrines. For *it is* a good thing that the heart be established with grace; not with meats, which have not profited them that have been occupied therein.

NEW AMERICAN STANDARD BIBLE

3 Remember the prisoners, as though in prison with them, *and* those who are ill-treated, since you yourselves also are in the body.

4 Marriage *is to be held* in honor among all, and the *marriage* bed *is to be* undefiled; for fornicators and adulterers God will judge.

5 *Make sure that* your character is free from the love of money, being content with what you have; for He Himself has said, "I WILL NEVER DESERT YOU, NOR WILL I EVER FORSAKE YOU,"

6 so that we confidently say,

"THE LORD IS MY HELPER, I WILL NOT BE AFRAID.
WHAT WILL MAN DO TO ME?"

7 Remember those who led you, who spoke the word of God to you; and considering the result of their conduct, imitate their faith.

8 Jesus Christ *is* the same yesterday and today and forever.

9 Do not be carried away by varied and strange teachings; for it is good for the heart to be strengthened by grace, not by foods, through which those who were so occupied were not benefited.

NEW CENTURY VERSION

it. 3 Remember those who are in prison as if you were in
prison with them. Remember those who are suffering as if
you were suffering with them.
4 Marriage should be honored by everyone, and husband
and wife should keep their marriage pure. God will judge
as guilty those who take part in sexual sins. 5 Keep your
lives free from the love of money, and be satisfied with
what you have. God has said,

"I will never leave you;
I will never forget you." *Deuteronomy 31:6*

6 So we can be sure when we say,

"I will not be afraid, because the Lord is my helper.
People can't do anything to me." *Psalm 118:6*

7 Remember your leaders who taught God's message to
you. Remember how they lived and died, and copy their
faith. 8 Jesus Christ is the same yesterday, today, and forever.
9 Do not let all kinds of strange teachings lead you into
the wrong way. Your hearts should be strengthened by
God's grace, not by obeying rules about foods, which do
not help those who obey them.

CONTEMPORARY ENGLISH VERSION

3 Remember the Lord's people who are in jail and be concerned for them. Don't forget those who are suffering, but
imagine that you are there with them.
4 Have respect for marriage. Always be faithful to your
partner, because God will punish anyone who is immoral
or unfaithful in marriage.
5 Don't fall in love with money. Be satisfied with what
you have. The Lord has promised that he will not leave us
or desert us. 6 That should make you feel like saying,

"The Lord helps me!
Why should I be afraid
of what people
can do to me?"

7 Don't forget about your leaders who taught you God's
message. Remember what kind of lives they lived and try
to have faith like theirs.
8 Jesus Christ never changes! He is the same yesterday,
today, and forever. 9 Don't be fooled by any kind of strange
teachings. It is better to receive strength from God's undeserved kindness than to depend on certain foods. After all,
these foods don't really help the people who eat them.

NEW INTERNATIONAL VERSION

3 Remember those in prison as if you were their fellow prisoners, and those who are mistreated as if you yourselves were suffering.

4 Marriage should be honored by all, and the marriage bed kept pure, for God will judge the adulterer and all the sexually immoral. 5 Keep your lives free from the love of money and be content with what you have, because God has said,

> "Never will I leave you;
> never will I forsake you."[a]

6 So we say with confidence,

> "The Lord is my helper; I will not be afraid.
> What can man do to me?"[b]

7 Remember your leaders, who spoke the word of God to you. Consider the outcome of their way of life and imitate their faith. 8 Jesus Christ is the same yesterday and today and forever.

9 Do not be carried away by all kinds of strange teachings. It is good for our hearts to be strengthened by grace, not by ceremonial foods, which are of no value to those

[a] *5* Deut. 31:6 [b] *6* Psalm 118:6,7

NEW LIVING TRANSLATION

prison. Suffer with them as though you were there yourself. Share the sorrow of those being mistreated, as though you feel their pain in your own bodies.

4 Give honor to marriage, and remain faithful to one another in marriage. God will surely judge people who are immoral and those who commit adultery.

5 Stay away from the love of money; be satisfied with what you have. For God has said,

> "I will never fail you.
> I will never forsake you."*

6 That is why we can say with confidence,

> "The Lord is my helper,
> so I will not be afraid.
> What can mere mortals do to me?"*

7 Remember your leaders who first taught you the word of God. Think of all the good that has come from their lives, and trust the Lord as they do.

8 Jesus Christ is the same yesterday, today, and forever. 9 So do not be attracted by strange, new ideas. Your spiritual strength comes from God's special favor, not from ceremonial rules about food, which don't help those who follow them.

13:5 Deut 31:6, 8. 13:6 Ps 118:6.

NEW KING JAMES VERSION

as if chained with them—those who are mistreated—since you yourselves are in the body also.

4 Marriage *is* honorable among all, and the bed undefiled; but fornicators and adulterers God will judge.

5 *Let your* conduct *be* without covetousness; *be* content with such things as you have. For He Himself has said, *"I will never leave you nor forsake you."*[a] 6 So we may boldly say:

> *"The LORD is my helper;*
> *I will not fear.*
> *What can man do to me?"*[b]

Concluding Religious Directions

7 Remember those who rule over you, who have spoken the word of God to you, whose faith follow, considering the outcome of *their* conduct. 8 Jesus Christ *is* the same yesterday, today, and forever. 9 Do not be carried about[c] with various and strange doctrines. For *it is* good that the heart be established by grace, not with foods which have not profited those who have been occupied with them.

13:5 [a] Deuteronomy 31:6, 8; Joshua 1:5 **13:6** [b] Psalm 118:6
13:9 [c] NU-Text and M-Text read *away.*

THE MESSAGE

in prison with them. Look on victims of abuse as if what happened to them had happened to you. Honor marriage, and guard the sacredness of sexual intimacy between wife and husband. God draws a firm line against casual and illicit sex.

Don't be obsessed with getting more material things. Be relaxed with what you have. Since God assured us, "I'll never let you down, never walk off and leave you," we can boldly quote,

> "God is there, ready to help;
> I'm fearless no matter what.
> Who or what can get to me?"

Appreciate your pastoral leaders who gave you the Word of God. Take a good look at the way they live, and let their faithfulness instruct you, as well as their truthfulness. There should be a consistency that runs through us all. For Jesus doesn't change—yesterday, today, tomorrow, he's always totally himself.

Don't be lured away from him by the latest speculations about him. The grace of Christ is the only good ground for life. Products named after Christ don't seem to do much for those who buy them.

KING JAMES VERSION

10 We have an altar, whereof they have no right to eat which serve the tabernacle.

11 For the bodies of those beasts, whose blood is brought into the sanctuary by the high priest for sin, are burned without the camp.

12 Wherefore Jesus also, that he might sanctify the people with his own blood, suffered without the gate.

13 Let us go forth therefore unto him without the camp, bearing his reproach.

14 For here have we no continuing city, but we seek one to come.

15 By him therefore let us offer the sacrifice of praise to God continually, that is, the fruit of *our* lips giving thanks to his name.

16 But to do good and to communicate forget not: for with such sacrifices God is well pleased.

17 Obey them that have the rule over you, and submit yourselves: for they watch for your souls, as they that must give account, that they may do it with joy, and not with grief: for that *is* unprofitable for you.

18 ¶ Pray for us: for we trust we have a good conscience, in all things willing to live honestly.

NEW AMERICAN STANDARD BIBLE

10 We have an altar from which those who serve the tabernacle have no right to eat.

11 For the bodies of those animals whose blood is brought into the holy place by the high priest *as an offering* for sin, are burned outside the camp.

12 Therefore Jesus also, that He might sanctify the people through His own blood, suffered outside the gate.

13 So, let us go out to Him outside the camp, bearing His reproach.

14 For here we do not have a lasting city, but we are seeking *the city* which is to come.

God-pleasing Sacrifices

15 Through Him then, let us continually offer up a sacrifice of praise to God, that is, the fruit of lips that give thanks to His name.

16 And do not neglect doing good and sharing, for with such sacrifices God is pleased.

17 Obey your leaders and submit *to them*, for they keep watch over your souls as those who will give an account. Let them do this with joy and not with grief, for this would be unprofitable for you.

18 Pray for us, for we are sure that we have a good conscience, desiring to conduct ourselves honorably in all things.

NEW CENTURY VERSION

10 We have a sacrifice, but the priests who serve in the
Holy Tent cannot eat from it. 11 The high priest carries the
blood of animals into the Most Holy Place where he offers
this blood for sins. But the bodies of the animals are
burned outside the camp. 12 So Jesus also suffered outside
the city to make his people holy with his own blood. 13 So
let us go to Jesus outside the camp, holding on as he did
when we are abused.

14 Here on earth we do not have a city that lasts forever,
but we are looking for the city that we will have in the
future. 15 So through Jesus let us always offer to God our
sacrifice of praise, coming from lips that speak his name.
16 Do not forget to do good to others, and share with them,
because such sacrifices please God.

17 Obey your leaders and act under their authority. They are watching over you, because they are responsible for your souls. Obey them so that they will do this work with joy, not sadness. It will not help you to make their work hard.

18 Pray for us. We are sure that we have a clear conscience, because we always want to do the right thing. 19 I

CONTEMPORARY ENGLISH VERSION

10 But we have an altar where even the priests who serve in the place of worship have no right to eat.

11 After the high priest offers the blood of animals as a
sin offering, the bodies of those animals are burned out-
side the camp. 12 Jesus himself suffered outside the city
gate, so that his blood would make people holy. 13 That's
why we should go outside the camp to Jesus and share in
his disgrace. 14 On this earth we don't have a city that lasts
forever, but we are waiting for such a city.

15 Our sacrifice is to keep offering praise to God in the
name of Jesus. 16 But don't forget to help others and to
share your possessions with them. This too is like offering
a sacrifice that pleases God.

17 Obey your leaders and do what they say. They are watching over you, and they must answer to God. So don't make them sad as they do their work. Make them happy. Otherwise, they won't be able to help you at all.

18 Pray for us. Our consciences are clear, and we always

NEW INTERNATIONAL VERSION

who eat them. 10We have an altar from which those who
minister at the tabernacle have no right to eat.
11The high priest carries the blood of animals into the
Most Holy Place as a sin offering, but the bodies are
burned outside the camp. 12And so Jesus also suffered out-
side the city gate to make the people holy through his own
blood. 13Let us, then, go to him outside the camp, bearing
the disgrace he bore. 14For here we do not have an endur-
ing city, but we are looking for the city that is to come.
15Through Jesus, therefore, let us continually offer to
God a sacrifice of praise—the fruit of lips that confess his
name. 16And do not forget to do good and to share with
others, for with such sacrifices God is pleased.
17Obey your leaders and submit to their authority. They
keep watch over you as men who must give an account.
Obey them so that their work will be a joy, not a burden,
for that would be of no advantage to you.
18Pray for us. We are sure that we have a clear conscience
and desire to live honorably in every way. 19I particularly

NEW LIVING TRANSLATION

10We have an altar from which the priests in the Temple
on earth have no right to eat. 11Under the system of Jewish
laws, the high priest brought the blood of animals into the
Holy Place as a sacrifice for sin, but the bodies of the ani-
mals were burned outside the camp. 12So also Jesus suf-
fered and died outside the city gates in order to make his
people holy by shedding his own blood. 13So let us go out
to him outside the camp and bear the disgrace he bore.
14For this world is not our home; we are looking forward
to our city in heaven, which is yet to come.
15With Jesus' help, let us continually offer our sacrifice
of praise to God by proclaiming the glory of his name.
16Don't forget to do good and to share what you have with
those in need, for such sacrifices are very pleasing to God.
17Obey your spiritual leaders and do what they say.
Their work is to watch over your souls, and they know
they are accountable to God. Give them reason to do this
joyfully and not with sorrow. That would certainly not be
for your benefit.
18Pray for us, for our conscience is clear and we want to
live honorably in everything we do. 19I especially need

NEW KING JAMES VERSION

10We have an altar from which those who serve the
tabernacle have no right to eat. 11For the bodies of those
animals, whose blood is brought into the sanctuary by the
high priest for sin, are burned outside the camp. 12There-
fore Jesus also, that He might sanctify the people with His
own blood, suffered outside the gate. 13Therefore let us go
forth to Him, outside the camp, bearing His reproach. 14For
here we have no continuing city, but we seek the one to
come. 15Therefore by Him let us continually offer the sacri-
fice of praise to God, that is, the fruit of *our* lips, giving
thanks to His name. 16But do not forget to do good and to
share, for with such sacrifices God is well pleased.
17Obey those who rule over you, and be submissive, for
they watch out for your souls, as those who must give
account. Let them do so with joy and not with grief, for
that would be unprofitable for you.

Prayer Requested

18Pray for us; for we are confident that we have a good
conscience, in all things desiring to live honorably. 19But I

THE MESSAGE

The altar from which God gives us the gift of himself is not for exploitation by insiders who grab and loot. In the old system, the animals are killed and the bodies disposed of outside the camp. The blood is then brought inside to the altar as a sacrifice for sin. It's the same with Jesus. He was crucified outside the city gates—*that* is where he poured out the sacrificial blood that was brought to God's altar to cleanse his people.

So let's go outside, where Jesus is, where the action is—not trying to be privileged insiders, but taking our share in the abuse of Jesus. This "insider world" is not our home. We have our eyes peeled for the City about to come. Let's take our place outside with Jesus, no longer pouring out the sacrificial blood of animals but pouring out sacrificial praises from our lips to God in Jesus' name.

✠

Make sure you don't take things for granted and go slack in working for the common good; share what you have with others. God takes particular pleasure in acts of worship—a different kind of "sacrifice"—that take place in kitchen and workplace and on the streets.

Be responsive to your pastoral leaders. Listen to their counsel. They are alert to the condition of your lives and work under the strict supervision of God. Contribute to the joy of their leadership, not its drudgery. Why would you want to make things harder for them?

Pray for us. We have no doubts about what we're doing or why, but it's hard going and we need your prayers. All

KING JAMES VERSION

19 But I beseech *you* the rather to do this, that I may be restored to you the sooner.

20 Now the God of peace, that brought again from the dead our Lord Jesus, that great shepherd of the sheep, through the blood of the everlasting covenant,

21 Make you perfect in every good work to do his will, working in you that which is wellpleasing in his sight, through Jesus Christ; to whom *be* glory for ever and ever. Amen.

22 And I beseech you, brethren, suffer the word of exhortation: for I have written a letter unto you in few words.

23 Know ye that *our* brother Timothy is set at liberty; with whom, if he come shortly, I will see you.

24 Salute all them that have the rule over you, and all the saints. They of Italy salute you.

25 Grace *be* with you all. Amen.

NEW AMERICAN STANDARD BIBLE

19 And I urge *you* all the more to do this, so that I may be restored to you the sooner.

Benediction

20 Now the God of peace, who brought up from the dead the great Shepherd of the sheep through the blood of the eternal covenant, *even* Jesus our Lord,

21 equip you in every good thing to do His will, working in us that which is pleasing in His sight, through Jesus Christ, to whom *be* the glory forever and ever. Amen.

22 But I urge you, brethren, bear with this word of exhortation, for I have written to you briefly.

23 Take notice that our brother Timothy has been released, with whom, if he comes soon, I will see you.

24 Greet all of your leaders and all the saints. Those from Italy greet you.

25 Grace be with you all.

NEW CENTURY VERSION

especially beg you to pray so that God will send me back to you soon.

20–21I pray that the God of peace will give you every good thing you need so you can do what he wants. God raised from the dead our Lord Jesus, the Great Shepherd of the sheep, because of the blood of his death. His blood began the eternal agreement that God made with his people. I pray that God will do in us what pleases him, through Jesus Christ, and to him be glory forever and ever. Amen.

22My brothers and sisters, I beg you to listen patiently to this message I have written to encourage you, because it is not very long. 23I want you to know that our brother Timothy has been let out of prison. If he arrives soon, we will both come to see you.

24Greet all your leaders and all of God's people. Those from Italy send greetings to you.

25Grace be with you all.

CONTEMPORARY ENGLISH VERSION

try to live right. 19I especially want you to pray that I can visit you again soon.

Final Prayers and Greetings

20God gives peace, and he raised our Lord Jesus Christ from death. Now Jesus is like a Great Shepherd whose blood was used to make God's eternal agreement with his flock.[a] 21I pray that God will make you ready to obey him and that you will always be eager to do right. May Jesus help you do what pleases God. To Jesus Christ be glory forever and ever! Amen.

22My friends, I have written only a short letter to encourage you, and I beg you to pay close attention to what I have said.

23By now you surely must know that our friend Timothy is out of jail. If he gets here in time, I will bring him with me when I come to visit you.

24Please give my greetings to your leaders and to the rest of the Lord's people.

His followers from Italy send you their greetings.

25I pray that God will be kind to all of you![b]

[a] **13.20** *whose blood was used to make God's eternal agreement with his flock*: See 9.18-22. [b] **13.25** *to all of you!*: Some manuscripts add "Amen."

NEW INTERNATIONAL VERSION

urge you to pray so that I may be restored to you soon.
[20]May the God of peace, who through the blood of the
eternal covenant brought back from the dead our Lord
Jesus, that great Shepherd of the sheep, [21]equip you with
everything good for doing his will, and may he work in us
what is pleasing to him, through Jesus Christ, to whom be
glory for ever and ever. Amen.

[22]Brothers, I urge you to bear with my word of exhorta-
tion, for I have written you only a short letter.
[23]I want you to know that our brother Timothy has been
released. If he arrives soon, I will come with him to see
you.
[24]Greet all your leaders and all God's people. Those from
Italy send you their greetings.
[25]Grace be with you all.

NEW LIVING TRANSLATION

your prayers right now so that I can come back to you
soon.
[20-21]And now, may the God of peace, who brought again
from the dead our Lord Jesus, equip you with all you need
for doing his will. May he produce in you, through the
power of Jesus Christ, all that is pleasing to him. Jesus is
the great Shepherd of the sheep by an everlasting cov-
enant, signed with his blood. To him be glory forever and
ever. Amen.
[22]I urge you, dear brothers and sisters,* please listen
carefully to what I have said in this brief letter.
[23]I want you to know that our brother Timothy is now
out of jail. If he comes here soon, I will bring him with me
to see you.
[24]Give my greetings to all your leaders and to the other
believers there. The Christians from Italy send you their
greetings.
[25]May God's grace be with you all.

13:22 Greek *brothers.*

NEW KING JAMES VERSION

especially urge *you* to do this, that I may be restored to
you the sooner.

Benediction, Final Exhortation, Farewell

[20]Now may the God of peace who brought up our Lord
Jesus from the dead, that great Shepherd of the sheep,
through the blood of the everlasting covenant, [21]make you
complete in every good work to do His will, working in
you[d] what is well pleasing in His sight, through Jesus
Christ, to whom *be* glory forever and ever. Amen.
[22]And I appeal to you, brethren, bear with the word of
exhortation, for I have written to you in few words.
[23]Know that *our* brother Timothy has been set free, with
whom I shall see you if he comes shortly.
[24]Greet all those who rule over you, and all the saints.
Those from Italy greet you.
[25]Grace *be* with you all. Amen.

13:21 [d] NU-Text and M-Text read *us.*

THE MESSAGE

we care about is living well before God. Pray that we may
be together soon.

May God, who puts all things together,
makes all things whole,
Who made a lasting mark through the sacrifice of Jesus,
the sacrifice of blood that sealed the eternal
covenant,
Who led Jesus, our Great Shepherd,
up and alive from the dead,
Now put you together, provide you
with everything you need to please him,
Make us into what gives him most pleasure,
by means of the sacrifice of Jesus, the Messiah.
All glory to Jesus forever and always!
Oh, yes, yes, yes.

Friends, please take what I've written most seriously. I've kept this as brief as possible; I haven't piled on a lot of extras. You'll be glad to know that Timothy has been let out of prison. If he leaves soon, I'll come with him and get to see you myself.

Say hello to your pastoral leaders and all the congregations. Everyone here in Italy wants to be remembered to you.

Grace be with you, every one.

KING JAMES VERSION

THE EPISTLE OF
ST. JAMES

1 James, a servant of God and of the Lord Jesus Christ, to the twelve tribes which are scattered abroad, greeting.

2 ¶ My brethren, count it all joy when ye fall into divers temptations;

3 Knowing *this*, that the trying of your faith worketh patience.

4 But let patience have *her* perfect work, that ye may be perfect and entire, wanting nothing.

5 If any of you lack wisdom, let him ask of God, that giveth to all *men* liberally, and upbraideth not; and it shall be given him.

6 But let him ask in faith, nothing wavering. For he that wavereth is like a wave of the sea driven with the wind and tossed.

7 For let not that man think that he shall receive any thing of the Lord.

8 A double minded man *is* unstable in all his ways.

NEW AMERICAN STANDARD BIBLE

THE LETTER OF
JAMES

Testing Your Faith

1 James, a bond-servant of God and of the Lord Jesus Christ,

To the twelve tribes who are dispersed abroad: Greetings.

2 Consider it all joy, my brethren, when you encounter various trials,

3 knowing that the testing of your faith produces endurance.

4 And let endurance have *its* perfect result, so that you may be perfect and complete, lacking in nothing.

5 But if any of you lacks wisdom, let him ask of God, who gives to all generously and without reproach, and it will be given to him.

6 But he must ask in faith without any doubting, for the one who doubts is like the surf of the sea, driven and tossed by the wind.

7 For that man ought not to expect that he will receive anything from the Lord,

8 *being* a double-minded man, unstable in all his ways.

NEW CENTURY VERSION

JAMES

1 From James, a servant of God and of the Lord Jesus Christ.

To all of God's people who are scattered everywhere in the world:

Greetings.

Faith and Wisdom

2My brothers and sisters,[a] when you have many kinds of troubles, you should be full of joy, 3because you know that these troubles test your faith, and this will give you patience. 4Let your patience show itself perfectly in what you do. Then you will be perfect and complete and will have everything you need. 5But if any of you needs wisdom, you should ask God for it. He is generous and enjoys giving to all people, so he will give you wisdom. 6But when you ask God, you must believe and not doubt. Anyone who doubts is like a wave in the sea, blown up and down by the wind. 7–8Such doubters are thinking two different things at the same time, and they cannot decide about anything they do. They should not think they will receive anything from the Lord.

1:2 [a] **brothers and sisters** Although the Greek text says "brothers" here and throughout this book, James' words were meant for the entire church, including men and women.

CONTEMPORARY ENGLISH VERSION

JAMES

1 From James, a servant of God and of our Lord Jesus Christ.

Greetings to the twelve tribes scattered all over the world.[a]

Faith and Wisdom

2My friends, be glad, even if you have a lot of trouble. 3You know that you learn to endure by having your faith tested. 4But you must learn to endure everything, so that you will be completely mature and not lacking in anything.

5If any of you need wisdom, you should ask God, and it will be given to you. God is generous and won't correct you for asking. 6But when you ask for something, you must have faith and not doubt. Anyone who doubts is like an ocean wave tossed around in a storm. 7–8If you are that kind of person, you can't make up your mind, and you surely can't be trusted. So don't expect the Lord to give you anything at all.

[a] 1.1 *twelve tribes scattered all over the world*: James is saying that the Lord's followers are like the tribes of Israel that were scattered everywhere by their enemies.

NEW INTERNATIONAL VERSION

JAMES

1 James, a servant of God and of the Lord Jesus Christ,

To the twelve tribes scattered among the nations:

Greetings.

Trials and Temptations

2 Consider it pure joy, my brothers, whenever you face
trials of many kinds, 3 because you know that the testing
of your faith develops perseverance. 4 Perseverance must
finish its work so that you may be mature and complete,
not lacking anything. 5 If any of you lacks wisdom, he
should ask God, who gives generously to all without finding fault, and it will be given to him. 6 But when he asks,
he must believe and not doubt, because he who doubts is
like a wave of the sea, blown and tossed by the wind.
7 That man should not think he will receive anything from
the Lord; 8 he is a double-minded man, unstable in all he
does.

NEW LIVING TRANSLATION

JAMES

Greetings from James

1 This letter is from James, a slave of God and of the Lord Jesus Christ.

It is written to Jewish Christians scattered among the nations.*

Greetings!

Faith and Endurance

2 Dear brothers and sisters,* whenever trouble comes
your way, let it be an opportunity for joy. 3 For when your
faith is tested, your endurance has a chance to grow. 4 So
let it grow, for when your endurance is fully developed,
you will be strong in character and ready for anything.
5 If you need wisdom—if you want to know what God
wants you to do—ask him, and he will gladly tell you. He
will not resent your asking. 6 But when you ask him, be
sure that you really expect him to answer, for a doubtful
mind is as unsettled as a wave of the sea that is driven and
tossed by the wind. 7 People like that should not expect to
receive anything from the Lord. 8 They can't make up their
minds. They waver back and forth in everything they do.

1:1 Greek *To the twelve tribes in the dispersion.* 1:2 Greek *brothers;* also in 1:16, 19.

NEW KING JAMES VERSION

THE EPISTLE OF

JAMES

Greeting to the Twelve Tribes

1 James, a bondservant of God and of the Lord Jesus Christ,

To the twelve tribes which are scattered abroad:

Greetings.

Profiting from Trials

2 My brethren, count it all joy when you fall into various
trials, 3 knowing that the testing of your faith produces patience. 4 But let patience have *its* perfect work, that you
may be perfect and complete, lacking nothing. 5 If any of
you lacks wisdom, let him ask of God, who gives to all liberally and without reproach, and it will be given to him.
6 But let him ask in faith, with no doubting, for he who
doubts is like a wave of the sea driven and tossed by the
wind. 7 For let not that man suppose that he will receive
anything from the Lord; 8 *he is* a double-minded man,
unstable in all his ways.

THE MESSAGE

JAMES

1 I, James, am a slave of God and the Master Jesus, writing to the twelve tribes scattered to Kingdom Come: Hello!

Faith Under Pressure

Consider it a sheer gift, friends, when tests and challenges come at you from all sides. You know that under pressure, your faith-life is forced into the open and shows its true colors. So don't try to get out of anything prematurely. Let it do its work so you become mature and well-developed, not deficient in any way.

If you don't know what you're doing, pray to the Father. He loves to help. You'll get his help, and won't be condescended to when you ask for it. Ask boldly, believingly, without a second thought. People who "worry their prayers" are like wind-whipped waves. Don't think you're going to get anything from the Master that way, adrift at sea, keeping all your options open.

KING JAMES VERSION

9 Let the brother of low degree rejoice in that he is exalted:

10 But the rich, in that he is made low: because as the flower of the grass he shall pass away.

11 For the sun is no sooner risen with a burning heat, but it withereth the grass, and the flower thereof falleth, and the grace of the fashion of it perisheth: so also shall the rich man fade away in his ways.

12 Blessed *is* the man that endureth temptation: for when he is tried, he shall receive the crown of life, which the Lord hath promised to them that love him.

13 ¶ Let no man say when he is tempted, I am tempted of God: for God cannot be tempted with evil, neither tempteth he any man:

14 But every man is tempted, when he is drawn away of his own lust, and enticed.

15 Then when lust hath conceived, it bringeth forth sin: and sin, when it is finished, bringeth forth death.

16 Do not err, my beloved brethren.

17 Every good gift and every perfect gift is from above, and cometh down from the Father of lights, with whom is no variableness, neither shadow of turning.

18 Of his own will begat he us with the word of truth, that we should be a kind of firstfruits of his creatures.

NEW AMERICAN STANDARD BIBLE

9 But the brother of humble circumstances is to glory in his high position;

10 and the rich man *is to glory* in his humiliation, because like flowering grass he will pass away.

11 For the sun rises with a scorching wind and withers the grass; and its flower falls off and the beauty of its appearance is destroyed; so too the rich man in the midst of his pursuits will fade away.

12 Blessed is a man who perseveres under trial; for once he has been approved, he will receive the crown of life which *the Lord* has promised to those who love Him.

13 Let no one say when he is tempted, "I am being tempted by God"; for God cannot be tempted by evil, and He Himself does not tempt anyone.

14 But each one is tempted when he is carried away and enticed by his own lust.

15 Then when lust has conceived, it gives birth to sin; and when sin is accomplished, it brings forth death.

16 Do not be deceived, my beloved brethren.

17 Every good thing given and every perfect gift is from above, coming down from the Father of lights, with whom there is no variation or shifting shadow.

18 In the exercise of His will He brought us forth by the word of truth, so that we would be a kind of first fruits among His creatures.

NEW CENTURY VERSION

True Riches

[9]Believers who are poor should be proud, because God
has made them spiritually rich. [10]Those who are rich
should be proud, because God has shown them that they
are spiritually poor. The rich will die like a wild flower in
the grass. [11]The sun rises with burning heat and dries up
the plants. The flower falls off, and its beauty is gone. In
the same way the rich will die while they are still taking
care of business.

Temptation Is Not from God

[12]When people are tempted and still continue strong,
they should be happy. After they have proved their faith,
God will reward them with life forever. God promised this
to all those who love him. [13]When people are tempted,
they should not say, "God is tempting me." Evil cannot
tempt God, and God himself does not tempt anyone. [14]But
people are tempted when their own evil desire leads them
away and traps them. [15]This desire leads to sin, and then
the sin grows and brings death.

[16]My dear brothers and sisters, do not be fooled about
this. [17]Every good action and every perfect gift is from
God. These good gifts come down from the Creator of the
sun, moon, and stars, who does not change like their shift-
ing shadows. [18]God decided to give us life through the
word of truth so we might be the most important of all the
things he made.

CONTEMPORARY ENGLISH VERSION

Poor People and Rich People

[9]Any of God's people who are poor should be glad that
he thinks so highly of them. [10]But any who are rich should
be glad when God makes them humble. Rich people will
disappear like wild flowers [11]scorched by the burning heat
of the sun. The flowers lose their blossoms, and their
beauty is destroyed. That is how the rich will disappear, as
they go about their business.

Trials and Temptations

[12]God will bless you, if you don't give up when your
faith is being tested. He will reward you with a glorious
life,[b] just as he rewards everyone who loves him.

[13]Don't blame God when you are tempted! God cannot
be tempted by evil, and he doesn't use evil to tempt others.
[14]We are tempted by our own desires that drag us off and
trap us. [15]Our desires make us sin, and when sin is fin-
ished with us, it leaves us dead.

[16]Don't be fooled, my dear friends. [17]Every good and
perfect gift comes down from the Father who created all
the lights in the heavens. He is always the same and never
makes dark shadows by changing. [18]He wanted us to be
his own special people,[c] and so he sent the true message
to give us new birth.

[b] 1.12 *a glorious life*: The Greek text has "the crown of life." In ancient times an athlete who had won a contest was rewarded with a crown of flowers as a sign of victory. [c] 1.18 *his own special people*: The Greek text has "the first of his creatures." The Law of Moses taught that the first-born of all animals and the first part of the harvest were special and belonged to the Lord.

NEW INTERNATIONAL VERSION

9The brother in humble circumstances ought to take
pride in his high position. 10But the one who is rich should
take pride in his low position, because he will pass away
like a wild flower. 11For the sun rises with scorching heat
and withers the plant; its blossom falls and its beauty is
destroyed. In the same way, the rich man will fade away
even while he goes about his business.

12Blessed is the man who perseveres under trial,
because when he has stood the test, he will receive the
crown of life that God has promised to those who love him.

13When tempted, no one should say, "God is tempting
me." For God cannot be tempted by evil, nor does he tempt
anyone; 14but each one is tempted when, by his own evil
desire, he is dragged away and enticed. 15Then, after
desire has conceived, it gives birth to sin; and sin, when it
is full-grown, gives birth to death.

16Don't be deceived, my dear brothers. 17Every good and
perfect gift is from above, coming down from the Father of
the heavenly lights, who does not change like shifting shad-
ows. 18He chose to give us birth through the word of truth,
that we might be a kind of firstfruits of all he created.

NEW LIVING TRANSLATION

9Christians who are* poor should be glad, for God has
honored them. 10And those who are rich should be glad,
for God has humbled them. They will fade away like a
flower in the field. 11The hot sun rises and dries up the
grass; the flower withers, and its beauty fades away. So
also, wealthy people will fade away with all of their
achievements.

12God blesses the people who patiently endure testing.
Afterward they will receive the crown of life that God has
promised to those who love him. 13And remember, no one
who wants to do wrong should ever say, "God is tempting
me." God is never tempted to do wrong, and he never
tempts anyone else either. 14Temptation comes from the
lure of our own evil desires. 15These evil desires lead to
evil actions, and evil actions lead to death. 16So don't be
misled, my dear brothers and sisters.

17Whatever is good and perfect comes to us from God
above, who created all heaven's lights.* Unlike them, he
never changes or casts shifting shadows. 18In his goodness
he chose to make us his own children by giving us his true
word. And we, out of all creation, became his choice pos-
session.

1:9 Greek *The brother who is.* **1:17** Greek *from above, from the Father of lights.*

NEW KING JAMES VERSION

The Perspective of Rich and Poor

9Let the lowly brother glory in his exaltation, 10but the
rich in his humiliation, because as a flower of the field he
will pass away. 11For no sooner has the sun risen with a
burning heat than it withers the grass; its flower falls, and
its beautiful appearance perishes. So the rich man also will
fade away in his pursuits.

Loving God Under Trials

12Blessed *is* the man who endures temptation; for when
he has been approved, he will receive the crown of life
which the Lord has promised to those who love Him. 13Let
no one say when he is tempted, "I am tempted by God"; for
God cannot be tempted by evil, nor does He Himself tempt
anyone. 14But each one is tempted when he is drawn away
by his own desires and enticed. 15Then, when desire has
conceived, it gives birth to sin; and sin, when it is full-
grown, brings forth death.

16Do not be deceived, my beloved brethren. 17Every good
gift and every perfect gift is from above, and comes down
from the Father of lights, with whom there is no variation
or shadow of turning. 18Of His own will He brought us
forth by the word of truth, that we might be a kind of first-
fruits of His creatures.

THE MESSAGE

When down-and-outers get a break, cheer! And when the arrogant rich are brought down to size, cheer! Prosperity is as short-lived as a wildflower, so don't ever count on it. You know that as soon as the sun rises, pouring down its scorching heat, the flower withers. Its petals wilt and, before you know it, that beautiful face is a barren stem. Well, that's a picture of the "prosperous life." At the very moment everyone is looking on in admiration, it fades away to nothing.

Anyone who meets a testing challenge head-on and manages to stick it out is mighty fortunate. For such persons loyally in love with God, the reward is life and more life.

Don't let anyone under pressure to give in to evil say, "God is trying to trip me up." God is impervious to evil, and puts evil in no one's way. The temptation to give in to evil comes from us and only us. We have no one to blame but the leering, seducing flare-up of our own lust. Lust gets pregnant, and has a baby: sin! Sin grows up to adulthood, and becomes a real killer.

So, my very dear friends, don't get thrown off course. Every desirable and beneficial gift comes out of heaven. The gifts are rivers of light cascading down from the Father of Light. There is nothing deceitful in God, nothing two-faced, nothing fickle. He brought us to life using the true Word, showing us off as the crown of all his creatures.

KING JAMES VERSION

19 ¶ Wherefore, my beloved brethren, let every man be swift to hear, slow to speak, slow to wrath:

20 For the wrath of man worketh not the righteousness of God.

21 Wherefore lay apart all filthiness and superfluity of naughtiness, and receive with meekness the engrafted word, which is able to save your souls.

22 But be ye doers of the word, and not hearers only, deceiving your own selves.

23 For if any be a hearer of the word, and not a doer, he is like unto a man beholding his natural face in a glass:

24 For he beholdeth himself, and goeth his way, and straightway forgetteth what manner of man he was.

25 But whoso looketh into the perfect law of liberty, and continueth *therein*, he being not a forgetful hearer, but a doer of the work, this man shall be blessed in his deed.

26 If any man among you seem to be religious, and bridleth not his tongue, but deceiveth his own heart, this man's religion *is* vain.

27 Pure religion and undefiled before God and the Father is this, To visit the fatherless and widows in their affliction, *and* to keep himself unspotted from the world.

NEW AMERICAN STANDARD BIBLE

19 [1]*This* you know, my beloved brethren. But everyone must be quick to hear, slow to speak *and* slow to anger;

20 for the anger of man does not achieve the righteousness of God.

21 Therefore, putting aside all filthiness and *all* that remains of wickedness, in humility receive the word implanted, which is able to save your souls.

22 But prove yourselves doers of the word, and not merely hearers who delude themselves.

23 For if anyone is a hearer of the word and not a doer, he is like a man who looks at his natural face in a mirror;

24 for *once* he has looked at himself and gone away, he has immediately forgotten what kind of person he was.

25 But one who looks intently at the perfect law, the *law* of liberty, and abides by it, not having become a forgetful hearer but an effectual doer, this man will be blessed in what he does.

26 If anyone thinks himself to be religious, and yet does not bridle his tongue but deceives his *own* heart, this man's religion is worthless.

27 Pure and undefiled religion in the sight of *our* God and Father is this: to visit orphans and widows in their distress, *and* to keep oneself unstained by the world.

1:19 [1] Or *Know* this

NEW CENTURY VERSION

Listening and Obeying

19My dear brothers and sisters, always be willing to lis-
ten and slow to speak. Do not become angry easily,
20because anger will not help you live the right kind of life
God wants. 21So put out of your life every evil thing and
every kind of wrong. Then in gentleness accept God's
teaching that is planted in your hearts, which can save
you.
22Do what God's teaching says; when you only listen
and do nothing, you are fooling yourselves. 23Those who
hear God's teaching and do nothing are like people who
look at themselves in a mirror. 24They see their faces and
then go away and quickly forget what they looked like.
25But the truly happy people are those who carefully study
God's perfect law that makes people free, and they contin-
ue to study it. They do not forget what they heard, but
they obey what God's teaching says. Those who do this
will be made happy.

The True Way to Worship God

26People who think they are religious but say things
they should not say are just fooling themselves. Their
"religion" is worth nothing. 27Religion that God accepts as
pure and without fault is this: caring for orphans or wid-
ows who need help, and keeping yourself free from the
world's evil influence.

CONTEMPORARY ENGLISH VERSION

Hearing and Obeying

19My dear friends, you should be quick to listen and
slow to speak or to get angry. 20If you are angry, you can-
not do any of the good things that God wants done. 21You
must stop doing anything immoral or evil. Instead be hum-
ble and accept the message that is planted in you to save
you.
22Obey God's message! Don't fool yourselves by just lis-
tening to it. 23If you hear the message and don't obey it,
you are like people who stare at themselves in a mirror
24and forget what they look like as soon as they leave.
25But you must never stop looking at the perfect law that
sets you free. God will bless you in everything you do, if
you listen and obey, and don't just hear and forget.
26If you think you are being religious, but can't control
your tongue, you are fooling yourself, and everything you
do is useless. 27Religion that pleases God the Father must
be pure and spotless. You must help needy orphans and
widows and not let this world make you evil.

NEW INTERNATIONAL VERSION

Listening and Doing

19 My dear brothers, take note of this: Everyone should be quick to listen, slow to speak and slow to become angry, 20 for man's anger does not bring about the righteous life that God desires. 21 Therefore, get rid of all moral filth and the evil that is so prevalent and humbly accept the word planted in you, which can save you.

22 Do not merely listen to the word, and so deceive yourselves. Do what it says. 23 Anyone who listens to the word but does not do what it says is like a man who looks at his face in a mirror 24 and, after looking at himself, goes away and immediately forgets what he looks like. 25 But the man who looks intently into the perfect law that gives freedom, and continues to do this, not forgetting what he has heard, but doing it—he will be blessed in what he does.

26 If anyone considers himself religious and yet does not keep a tight rein on his tongue, he deceives himself and his religion is worthless. 27 Religion that God our Father accepts as pure and faultless is this: to look after orphans and widows in their distress and to keep oneself from being polluted by the world.

NEW LIVING TRANSLATION

Listening and Doing

19 My dear brothers and sisters, be quick to listen, slow to speak, and slow to get angry. 20 Your anger can never make things right in God's sight.

21 So get rid of all the filth and evil in your lives, and humbly accept the message God has planted in your hearts, for it is strong enough to save your souls.

22 And remember, it is a message to obey, not just to listen to. If you don't obey, you are only fooling yourself. 23 For if you just listen and don't obey, it is like looking at your face in a mirror but doing nothing to improve your appearance. 24 You see yourself, walk away, and forget what you look like. 25 But if you keep looking steadily into God's perfect law—the law that sets you free—and if you do what it says and don't forget what you heard, then God will bless you for doing it.

26 If you claim to be religious but don't control your tongue, you are just fooling yourself, and your religion is worthless. 27 Pure and lasting religion in the sight of God our Father means that we must care for orphans and widows in their troubles, and refuse to let the world corrupt us.

NEW KING JAMES VERSION

Qualities Needed in Trials

19 So then,[a] my beloved brethren, let every man be swift to hear, slow to speak, slow to wrath; 20 for the wrath of man does not produce the righteousness of God.

Doers—Not Hearers Only

21 Therefore lay aside all filthiness and overflow of wickedness, and receive with meekness the implanted word, which is able to save your souls.

22 But be doers of the word, and not hearers only, deceiving yourselves. 23 For if anyone is a hearer of the word and not a doer, he is like a man observing his natural face in a mirror; 24 for he observes himself, goes away, and immediately forgets what kind of man he was. 25 But he who looks into the perfect law of liberty and continues *in it,* and is not a forgetful hearer but a doer of the work, this one will be blessed in what he does.

26 If anyone among you[b] thinks he is religious, and does not bridle his tongue but deceives his own heart, this one's religion *is* useless. 27 Pure and undefiled religion before God and the Father is this: to visit orphans and widows in their trouble, *and* to keep oneself unspotted from the world.

1:19 [a] NU-Text reads *Know this* or *This you know.* **1:26** [b] NU-Text omits *among you.*

THE MESSAGE

Act on What You Hear

Post this at all the intersections, dear friends: Lead with your ears, follow up with your tongue, and let anger straggle along in the rear. God's righteousness doesn't grow from human anger. So throw all spoiled virtue and cancerous evil in the garbage. In simple humility, let our gardener, God, landscape you with the Word, making a salvation-garden of your life.

Don't fool yourself into thinking that you are a listener when you are anything but, letting the Word go in one ear and out the other. *Act* on what you hear! Those who hear and don't act are like those who glance in the mirror, walk away, and two minutes later have no idea who they are, what they look like.

But whoever catches a glimpse of the revealed counsel of God—the free life!—even out of the corner of his eye, and sticks with it, is no distracted scatterbrain but a man or woman of action. That person will find delight and affirmation in the action.

Anyone who sets himself up as "religious" by talking a good game is self-deceived. This kind of religion is hot air and only hot air. Real religion, the kind that passes muster before God the Father, is this: Reach out to the homeless and loveless in their plight, and guard against corruption from the godless world.

KING JAMES VERSION

2 My brethren, have not the faith of our Lord Jesus Christ, *the Lord* of glory, with respect of persons.

2 For if there come unto your assembly a man with a gold ring, in goodly apparel, and there come in also a poor man in vile raiment;

3 And ye have respect to him that weareth the gay clothing, and say unto him, Sit thou here in a good place; and say to the poor, Stand thou there, or sit here under my footstool:

4 Are ye not then partial in yourselves, and are become judges of evil thoughts?

5 Hearken, my beloved brethren, Hath not God chosen the poor of this world rich in faith, and heirs of the kingdom which he hath promised to them that love him?

6 But ye have despised the poor. Do not rich men oppress you, and draw you before the judgment seats?

7 Do not they blaspheme that worthy name by the which ye are called?

8 ¶ If ye fulfil the royal law according to the scripture, Thou shalt love thy neighbour as thyself, ye do well:

NEW AMERICAN STANDARD BIBLE

The Sin of Partiality

2 My brethren, do not hold your faith in our glorious Lord Jesus Christ with *an attitude of* personal favoritism.

2 For if a man comes into your assembly with a gold ring and dressed in fine clothes, and there also comes in a poor man in dirty clothes,

3 and you pay special attention to the one who is wearing the fine clothes, and say, "You sit here in a good place," and you say to the poor man, "You stand over there, or sit down by my footstool,"

4 have you not made distinctions among yourselves, and become judges with evil motives?

5 Listen, my beloved brethren: did not God choose the poor of this world *to be* rich in faith and heirs of the kingdom which He promised to those who love Him?

6 But you have dishonored the poor man. Is it not the rich who oppress you and personally drag you into court?

7 Do they not blaspheme the fair name by which you have been called?

8 If, however, you are fulfilling the royal law according to the Scripture, "YOU SHALL LOVE YOUR NEIGHBOR AS YOURSELF," you are doing well.

NEW CENTURY VERSION

Love All People

2 My dear brothers and sisters, as believers in our glorious Lord Jesus Christ, never think some people are more important than others. 2Suppose someone comes into your church meeting wearing nice clothes and a gold ring. At the same time a poor person comes in wearing old, dirty clothes. 3You show special attention to the one wearing nice clothes and say, "Please, sit here in this good seat." But you say to the poor person, "Stand over there," or, "Sit on the floor by my feet." 4What are you doing? You are making some people more important than others, and with evil thoughts you are deciding that one person is better.

5Listen, my dear brothers and sisters! God chose the poor in the world to be rich with faith and to receive the kingdom God promised to those who love him. 6But you show no respect to the poor. The rich are always trying to control your lives. They are the ones who take you to court. 7And they are the ones who speak against Jesus, who owns you.

8This royal law is found in the Scriptures: "Love your neighbor as you love yourself."[a] If you obey this law, you

2:8 [a] "Love...yourself." Quotation from Leviticus 19:18.

CONTEMPORARY ENGLISH VERSION

Warning against Having Favorites

2 My friends, if you have faith in our glorious Lord Jesus Christ, you won't treat some people better than others. 2Suppose a rich person wearing fancy clothes and a gold ring comes to one of your meetings. And suppose a poor person dressed in worn-out clothes also comes. 3You must not give the best seat to the one in fancy clothes and tell the one who is poor to stand at the side or sit on the floor. 4That is the same as saying that some people are better than others, and you would be acting like a crooked judge.

5My dear friends, pay attention. God has given a lot of faith to the poor people in this world. He has also promised them a share in his kingdom that he will give to everyone who loves him. 6You mistreat the poor. But isn't it the rich who boss you around and drag you off to court? 7Aren't they the ones who make fun of your Lord?

8You will do all right, if you obey the most important law[a] in the Scriptures. It is the law that commands us to love others as much as we love ourselves. 9But if you treat

[a] 2.8 *most important law*: The Greek text has "royal law," meaning the one given by the king (that is, God).

NEW INTERNATIONAL VERSION

Favoritism Forbidden

2 My brothers, as believers in our glorious Lord Jesus
Christ, don't show favoritism. 2Suppose a man comes
into your meeting wearing a gold ring and fine clothes,
and a poor man in shabby clothes also comes in. 3If you
show special attention to the man wearing fine clothes and
say, "Here's a good seat for you," but say to the poor man,
"You stand there" or "Sit on the floor by my feet," 4have
you not discriminated among yourselves and become
judges with evil thoughts?
5Listen, my dear brothers: Has not God chosen those
who are poor in the eyes of the world to be rich in faith
and to inherit the kingdom he promised those who love
him? 6But you have insulted the poor. Is it not the rich
who are exploiting you? Are they not the ones who are
dragging you into court? 7Are they not the ones who are
slandering the noble name of him to whom you belong?
8If you really keep the royal law found in Scripture,
"Love your neighbor as yourself,"[a] you are doing right.

[a] *8* Lev. 19:18

NEW LIVING TRANSLATION

A Warning against Prejudice

2 My dear brothers and sisters,* how can you claim that
you have faith in our glorious Lord Jesus Christ if you
favor some people more than others?
2For instance, suppose someone comes into your meet-
ing* dressed in fancy clothes and expensive jewelry, and
another comes in who is poor and dressed in shabby
clothes. 3If you give special attention and a good seat to
the rich person, but you say to the poor one, "You can
stand over there, or else sit on the floor"—well, 4doesn't
this discrimination show that you are guided by wrong
motives?
5Listen to me, dear brothers and sisters. Hasn't God cho-
sen the poor in this world to be rich in faith? Aren't they
the ones who will inherit the Kingdom he promised to
those who love him? 6And yet, you insult the poor man!
Isn't it the rich who oppress you and drag you into court?
7Aren't they the ones who slander Jesus Christ, whose
noble name you bear?
8Yes indeed, it is good when you truly obey our Lord's
royal command found in the Scriptures: "Love your neigh-
bor as yourself."* 9But if you pay special attention to the

2:1 Greek *brothers;* also in 2:5, 14. 2:2 Greek *synagogue.*
2:8 Lev 19:18.

NEW KING JAMES VERSION

Beware of Personal Favoritism

2 My brethren, do not hold the faith of our Lord Jesus
Christ, *the Lord* of glory, with partiality. 2For if there
should come into your assembly a man with gold rings, in
fine apparel, and there should also come in a poor man in
filthy clothes, 3and you pay attention to the one wearing
the fine clothes and say to him, "You sit here in a good
place," and say to the poor man, "You stand there," or,
"Sit here at my footstool," 4have you not shown partiality
among yourselves, and become judges with evil thoughts?
5Listen, my beloved brethren: Has God not chosen the
poor of this world *to be* rich in faith and heirs of the king-
dom which He promised to those who love Him? 6But you
have dishonored the poor man. Do not the rich oppress you
and drag you into the courts? 7Do they not blaspheme that
noble name by which you are called?
8If you really fulfill *the* royal law according to the
Scripture, *"You shall love your neighbor as yourself,"*[a] you

2:8 [a] Leviticus 19:18

THE MESSAGE

The Royal Rule of Love

2 My dear friends, don't let public opinion influence
how you live out our glorious, Christ-originated faith.
If a man enters your church wearing an expensive suit,
and a street person wearing rags comes in right after him,
and you say to the man in the suit, "Sit here, sir; this is
the best seat in the house!" and either ignore the street
person or say, "Better sit here in the back row," haven't
you segregated God's children and proved that you are
judges who can't be trusted?
Listen, dear friends. Isn't it clear by now that God oper-
ates quite differently? He chose the world's down-and-out
as the kingdom's first citizens, with full rights and privi-
leges. This kingdom is promised to anyone who loves God.
And here you are abusing these same citizens! Isn't it the
high and mighty who exploit you, who use the courts to
rob you blind? Aren't they the ones who scorn the new
name—"Christian"—used in your baptisms?
You do well when you complete the Royal Rule of the
Scriptures: "Love others as you love yourself." But if you

KING JAMES VERSION

9 But if ye have respect to persons, ye commit sin, and are convinced of the law as transgressors.

10 For whosoever shall keep the whole law, and yet offend in one *point*, he is guilty of all.

11 For he that said, Do not commit adultery, said also, Do not kill. Now if thou commit no adultery, yet if thou kill, thou art become a transgressor of the law.

12 So speak ye, and so do, as they that shall be judged by the law of liberty.

13 For he shall have judgment without mercy, that hath shewed no mercy; and mercy rejoiceth against judgment.

14 ¶ What *doth it* profit, my brethren, though a man say he hath faith, and have not works? can faith save him?

15 If a brother or sister be naked, and destitute of daily food,

16 And one of you say unto them, Depart in peace, be *ye* warmed and filled; notwithstanding ye give them not those things which are needful to the body; what *doth it* profit?

17 Even so faith, if it hath not works, is dead, being alone.

NEW AMERICAN STANDARD BIBLE

9 But if you show partiality, you are committing sin *and* are convicted by the law as transgressors.

10 For whoever keeps the whole law and yet stumbles in one *point,* he has become guilty of all.

11 For He who said, "DO NOT COMMIT ADULTERY," also said, "DO NOT COMMIT MURDER." Now if you do not commit adultery, but do commit murder, you have become a transgressor of the law.

12 So speak and so act as those who are to be judged by *the* law of liberty.

13 For judgment *will be* merciless to one who has shown no mercy; mercy triumphs over judgment.

Faith and Works

14 What use is it, my brethren, if someone says he has faith but he has no works? Can that faith save him?

15 If a brother or sister is without clothing and in need of daily food,

16 and one of you says to them, "Go in peace, be warmed and be filled," and yet you do not give them what is necessary for *their* body, what use is that?

17 Even so faith, if it has no works, is dead, *being* by itself.

NEW CENTURY VERSION

are doing right. 9But if you treat one person as being more
important than another, you are sinning. You are guilty of
breaking God's law. 10A person who follows all of God's
law but fails to obey even one command is guilty of break-
ing all the commands in that law. 11The same God who
said, "You must not be guilty of adultery,"[b] also said, "You
must not murder anyone."[c] So if you do not take part in
adultery but you murder someone, you are guilty of break-
ing all of God's law. 12In everything you say and do,
remember that you will be judged by the law that makes
people free. 13So you must show mercy to others, or God
will not show mercy to you when he judges you. But the
person who shows mercy can stand without fear at the
judgment.

Faith and Good Works

14My brothers and sisters, if people say they have faith,
but do nothing, their faith is worth nothing. Can faith like
that save them? 15A brother or sister in Christ might need
clothes or food. 16If you say to that person, "God be with
you! I hope you stay warm and get plenty to eat," but you
do not give what that person needs, your words are worth
nothing. 17In the same way, faith that is alone—that does
nothing—is dead.

2:11 [b] **"You...adultery."** Quotation from Exodus 20:14 and Deuteronomy 5:18. 2:11 [c] **"You...anyone."** Quotation from Exodus 20:13 and Deuteronomy 5:17.

CONTEMPORARY ENGLISH VERSION

some people better than others, you have done wrong, and
the Scriptures teach that you have sinned.

10If you obey every law except one, you are still guilty of
breaking them all. 11The same God who told us to be faith-
ful in marriage also told us not to murder. So even if you
are faithful in marriage, but murder someone, you still
have broken God's Law.

12Speak and act like people who will be judged by the
law that sets us free. 13Do this, because on the day of
judgment there will be no pity for those who have not had
pity on others. But even in judgment, God is merciful![b]

Faith and Works

14My friends, what good is it to say you have faith,
when you don't do anything to show that you really do
have faith? Can that kind of faith save you? 15If you know
someone who doesn't have any clothes or food, 16you
shouldn't just say, "I hope all goes well for you. I hope you
will be warm and have plenty to eat." What good is it to
say this, unless you do something to help? 17Faith that
doesn't lead us to do good deeds is all alone and dead!

[b] 2.13 *But even in judgment, God is merciful!*: Or "So be merciful, and you will be shown mercy on the day of judgment."

NEW INTERNATIONAL VERSION

[9]But if you show favoritism, you sin and are convicted by the law as lawbreakers. [10]For whoever keeps the whole law and yet stumbles at just one point is guilty of breaking all of it. [11]For he who said, "Do not commit adultery,"[b] also said, "Do not murder."[c] If you do not commit adultery but do commit murder, you have become a lawbreaker.

[12]Speak and act as those who are going to be judged by the law that gives freedom, [13]because judgment without mercy will be shown to anyone who has not been merciful. Mercy triumphs over judgment!

Faith and Deeds

[14]What good is it, my brothers, if a man claims to have faith but has no deeds? Can such faith save him? [15]Suppose a brother or sister is without clothes and daily food. [16]If one of you says to him, "Go, I wish you well; keep warm and well fed," but does nothing about his physical needs, what good is it? [17]In the same way, faith by itself, if it is not accompanied by action, is dead.

[b] *11* Exodus 20:14; Deut. 5:18 [c] *11* Exodus 20:13; Deut. 5:17

NEW LIVING TRANSLATION

rich, you are committing a sin, for you are guilty of breaking that law.

[10]And the person who keeps all of the laws except one is as guilty as the person who has broken all of God's laws. [11]For the same God who said, "Do not commit adultery," also said, "Do not murder."* So if you murder someone, you have broken the entire law, even if you do not commit adultery.

[12]So whenever you speak, or whatever you do, remember that you will be judged by the law of love, the law that set you free. [13]For there will be no mercy for you if you have not been merciful to others. But if you have been merciful, then God's mercy toward you will win out over his judgment against you.

Faith without Good Deeds Is Dead

[14]Dear brothers and sisters, what's the use of saying you have faith if you don't prove it by your actions? That kind of faith can't save anyone. [15]Suppose you see a brother or sister who needs food or clothing, [16]and you say, "Well, good-bye and God bless you; stay warm and eat well"—but then you don't give that person any food or clothing. What good does that do?

[17]So you see, it isn't enough just to have faith. Faith that doesn't show itself by good deeds is no faith at all—it is dead and useless.

2:11 Exod 20:13-14; Deut 5:17-18.

NEW KING JAMES VERSION

do well; [9]but if you show partiality, you commit sin, and are convicted by the law as transgressors. [10]For whoever shall keep the whole law, and yet stumble in one *point,* he is guilty of all. [11]For He who said, *"Do not commit adultery,"*[b] also said, *"Do not murder."*[c] Now if you do not commit adultery, but you do murder, you have become a transgressor of the law. [12]So speak and so do as those who will be judged by the law of liberty. [13]For judgment is without mercy to the one who has shown no mercy. Mercy triumphs over judgment.

Faith Without Works Is Dead

[14]What *does it* profit, my brethren, if someone says he has faith but does not have works? Can faith save him? [15]If a brother or sister is naked and destitute of daily food, [16]and one of you says to them, "Depart in peace, be warmed and filled," but you do not give them the things which are needed for the body, what *does it* profit? [17]Thus also faith by itself, if it does not have works, is dead.

2:11 [b] Exodus 20:14; Deuteronomy 5:18 [c] Exodus 20:13; Deuteronomy 5:17

THE MESSAGE

play up to these so-called important people, you go against the Rule and stand convicted by it. You can't pick and choose in these things, specializing in keeping one or two things in God's law and ignoring others. The same God who said, "Don't commit adultery," also said, "Don't murder." If you don't commit adultery but go ahead and murder, do you think your non-adultery will cancel out your murder? No, you're a murderer, period.

Talk and act like a person expecting to be judged by the Rule that sets us free. For if you refuse to act kindly, you can hardly expect to be treated kindly. Kind mercy wins over harsh judgment every time.

Faith in Action

Dear friends, do you think you'll get anywhere in this if you learn all the right words but never do anything? Does merely talking about faith indicate that a person really has it? For instance, you come upon an old friend dressed in rags and half-starved and say, "Good morning, friend! Be clothed in Christ! Be filled with the Holy Spirit!" and walk off without providing so much as a coat or a cup of soup—where does that get you? Isn't it obvious that God-talk without God-acts is outrageous nonsense?

KING JAMES VERSION

18 Yea, a man may say, Thou hast faith, and I have works: shew me thy faith without thy works, and I will shew thee my faith by my works.

19 Thou believest that there is one God; thou doest well: the devils also believe, and tremble.

20 But wilt thou know, O vain man, that faith without works is dead?

21 Was not Abraham our father justified by works, when he had offered Isaac his son upon the altar?

22 Seest thou how faith wrought with his works, and by works was faith made perfect?

23 And the scripture was fulfilled which saith, Abraham believed God, and it was imputed unto him for righteousness: and he was called the Friend of God.

24 Ye see then how that by works a man is justified, and not by faith only.

25 Likewise also was not Rahab the harlot justified by works, when she had received the messengers, and had sent *them* out another way?

26 For as the body without the spirit is dead, so faith without works is dead also.

NEW AMERICAN STANDARD BIBLE

18 But someone may *well* say, "You have faith and I have works; show me your faith without the works, and I will show you my faith by my works."

19 You believe that [1]God is one. You do well; the demons also believe, and shudder.

20 But are you willing to recognize, you foolish fellow, that faith without works is useless?

21 Was not Abraham our father justified by works when he offered up Isaac his son on the altar?

22 You see that faith was working with his works, and as a result of the works, faith was perfected;

23 and the Scripture was fulfilled which says, "AND ABRAHAM BELIEVED GOD, AND IT WAS RECKONED TO HIM AS RIGHTEOUSNESS," and he was called the friend of God.

24 You see that a man is justified by works and not by faith alone.

25 In the same way, was not Rahab the harlot also justified by works when she received the messengers and sent them out by another way?

26 For just as the body without *the* spirit is dead, so also faith without works is dead.

2:19 [1] One early ms reads *there is one God*

NEW CENTURY VERSION

18 Someone might say, "You have faith, but I have
deeds." Show me your faith without doing anything, and I
will show you my faith by what I do. 19 You believe there is
one God. Good! But the demons believe that, too, and they
tremble with fear.
20 You foolish person! Must you be shown that faith that
does nothing is worth nothing? 21 Abraham, our ancestor,
was made right with God by what he did when he offered
his son Isaac on the altar. 22 So you see that Abraham's
faith and the things he did worked together. His faith was
made perfect by what he did. 23 This shows the full meaning of the Scripture that says: "Abraham believed God, and
God accepted Abraham's faith, and that faith made him
right with God."[d] And Abraham was called God's friend.[e]
24 So you see that people are made right with God by what
they do, not by faith only.
25 Another example is Rahab, a prostitute, who was
made right with God by something she did. She welcomed
the spies into her home and helped them escape by a different road.
26 Just as a person's body that does not have a spirit is
dead, so faith that does nothing is dead!

2:23 [d] **"Abraham...God."** Quotation from Genesis 15:6. **2:23** [e] **God's friend** These words about Abraham are found in 2 Chronicles 20:7 and Isaiah 41:8.

CONTEMPORARY ENGLISH VERSION

18 Suppose someone disagrees and says, "It is possible to
have faith without doing kind deeds."
I would answer, "Prove that you have faith without
doing kind deeds, and I will prove that I have faith by
doing them." 19 You surely believe there is only one God.
That's fine. Even demons believe this, and it makes them
shake with fear.
20 Does some stupid person want proof that faith without
deeds is useless? 21 Well, our ancestor Abraham pleased
God by putting his son Isaac on the altar to sacrifice him.
22 Now you see how Abraham's faith and deeds worked
together. He proved that his faith was real by what he did.
23 This is what the Scriptures mean by saying, "Abraham
had faith in God, and God was pleased with him." That's
how Abraham became God's friend.
24 You can now see that we please God by what we do
and not only by what we believe. 25 For example, Rahab
had been a prostitute. But she pleased God when she welcomed the spies and sent them home by another way.
26 Anyone who doesn't breathe is dead, and faith that
doesn't do anything is just as dead!

NEW INTERNATIONAL VERSION

18 But someone will say, "You have faith; I have deeds."
Show me your faith without deeds, and I will show you
my faith by what I do. 19 You believe that there is one God.
Good! Even the demons believe that—and shudder.

20 You foolish man, do you want evidence that faith
without deeds is useless[d]? 21 Was not our ancestor
Abraham considered righteous for what he did when he
offered his son Isaac on the altar? 22 You see that his faith
and his actions were working together, and his faith was
made complete by what he did. 23 And the scripture was
fulfilled that says, "Abraham believed God, and it was
credited to him as righteousness,"[e] and he was called
God's friend. 24 You see that a person is justified by what
he does and not by faith alone.

25 In the same way, was not even Rahab the prostitute
considered righteous for what she did when she gave lodg-
ing to the spies and sent them off in a different direction?
26 As the body without the spirit is dead, so faith without
deeds is dead.

[d] *20* Some early manuscripts *dead* [e] *23* Gen. 15:6

NEW LIVING TRANSLATION

18 Now someone may argue, "Some people have faith;
others have good deeds." I say, "I can't see your faith if
you don't have good deeds, but I will show you my faith
through my good deeds."

19 Do you still think it's enough just to believe that there
is one God? Well, even the demons believe this, and they
tremble in terror! 20 Fool! When will you ever learn that
faith that does not result in good deeds is useless?

21 Don't you remember that our ancestor Abraham was
declared right with God because of what he did when he
offered his son Isaac on the altar? 22 You see, he was trust-
ing God so much that he was willing to do whatever God
told him to do. His faith was made complete by what he
did—by his actions. 23 And so it happened just as the
Scriptures say: "Abraham believed God, so God declared
him to be righteous."* He was even called "the friend of
God."* 24 So you see, we are made right with God by what
we do, not by faith alone.

25 Rahab the prostitute is another example of this. She
was made right with God by her actions—when she hid
those messengers and sent them safely away by a different
road. 26 Just as the body is dead without a spirit, so also
faith is dead without good deeds.

2:23a Gen 15:6. **2:23b** See Isa 41:8.

NEW KING JAMES VERSION

18 But someone will say, "You have faith, and I have
works." Show me your faith without your[d] works, and I
will show you my faith by my[e] works. 19 You believe that
there is one God. You do well. Even the demons believe—
and tremble! 20 But do you want to know, O foolish man,
that faith without works is dead?[f] 21 Was not Abraham our
father justified by works when he offered Isaac his son on
the altar? 22 Do you see that faith was working together
with his works, and by works faith was made perfect?
23 And the Scripture was fulfilled which says, *"Abraham
believed God, and it was accounted to him for righteous-
ness."*[g] And he was called the friend of God. 24 You see
then that a man is justified by works, and not by faith
only.

25 Likewise, was not Rahab the harlot also justified by
works when she received the messengers and sent *them*
out another way?

26 For as the body without the spirit is dead, so faith
without works is dead also.

2:18 [d] NU-Text omits *your.* [e] NU-Text omits *my.* **2:20** [f] NU-Text reads *useless.* **2:23** [g] Genesis 15:6

THE MESSAGE

I can already hear one of you agreeing by saying, "Sounds good. You take care of the faith department, I'll handle the works department."

Not so fast. You can no more show me your works apart from your faith than I can show you my faith apart from my works. Faith and works, works and faith, fit together hand in glove.

Do I hear you professing to believe in the one and only God, but then observe you complacently sitting back as if you had done something wonderful? That's just great. Demons do that, but what good does it do them? Use your heads! Do you suppose for a minute that you can cut faith and works in two and not end up with a corpse on your hands?

Wasn't our ancestor Abraham "made right with God by works" when he placed his son Isaac on the sacrificial altar? Isn't it obvious that faith and works are yoked partners, that faith expresses itself in works? That the works are "works of faith"? The full meaning of "believe" in the Scripture sentence, "Abraham believed God and was set right with God," includes his action. It's that mesh of believing and acting that got Abraham named "God's friend." Is it not evident that a person is made right with God not by a barren faith but by faith fruitful in works?

The same with Rahab, the Jericho harlot. Wasn't her action in hiding God's spies and helping them escape—that seamless unity of *believing* and *doing*—what counted with God? The very moment you separate body and spirit, you end up with a corpse. Separate faith and works and you get the same thing: a corpse.

KING JAMES VERSION

3 My brethren, be not many masters, knowing that we shall receive the greater condemnation.

2 For in many things we offend all. If any man offend not in word, the same *is* a perfect man, *and* able also to bridle the whole body.

3 Behold, we put bits in the horses' mouths, that they may obey us; and we turn about their whole body.

4 Behold also the ships, which though *they be* so great, and *are* driven of fierce winds, yet are they turned about with a very small helm, whithersoever the governor listeth.

5 Even so the tongue is a little member, and boasteth great things. Behold, how great a matter a little fire kindleth!

6 And the tongue *is* a fire, a world of iniquity: so is the tongue among our members, that it defileth the whole body, and setteth on fire the course of nature; and it is set on fire of hell.

7 For every kind of beasts, and of birds, and of serpents, and of things in the sea, is tamed, and hath been tamed of mankind:

8 But the tongue can no man tame; *it is* an unruly evil, full of deadly poison.

9 Therewith bless we God, even the Father; and therewith curse we men, which are made after the similitude of God.

10 Out of the same mouth proceedeth blessing and cursing. My brethren, these things ought not so to be.

NEW AMERICAN STANDARD BIBLE

The Tongue Is a Fire

3 Let not many *of you* become teachers, my brethren, knowing that as such we will incur a stricter judgment.

2 For we all stumble in many *ways.* If anyone does not stumble in what he says, he is a perfect man, able to bridle the whole body as well.

3 Now if we put the bits into the horses' mouths so that they will obey us, we direct their entire body as well.

4 Look at the ships also, though they are so great and are driven by strong winds, are still directed by a very small rudder wherever the inclination of the pilot desires.

5 So also the tongue is a small part of the body, and *yet* it boasts of great things.

See how great a forest is set aflame by such a small fire!

6 And the tongue is a fire, the *very* world of iniquity; the tongue is set among our members as that which defiles the entire body, and sets on fire the course of *our* life, and is set on fire by hell.

7 For every species of beasts and birds, of reptiles and creatures of the sea, is tamed and has been tamed by the human race.

8 But no one can tame the tongue; *it is* a restless evil *and* full of deadly poison.

9 With it we bless *our* Lord and Father, and with it we curse men, who have been made in the likeness of God;

10 from the same mouth come *both* blessing and cursing. My brethren, these things ought not to be this way.

NEW CENTURY VERSION

Controlling the Things We Say

3 My brothers and sisters, not many of you should become teachers, because you know that we who teach will be judged more strictly. 2We all make many mistakes. If people never said anything wrong, they would be perfect and able to control their entire selves, too. 3When we put bits into the mouths of horses to make them obey us, we can control their whole bodies. 4Also a ship is very big, and it is pushed by strong winds. But a very small rudder controls that big ship, making it go wherever the pilot wants. 5It is the same with the tongue. It is a small part of the body, but it brags about great things.

A big forest fire can be started with only a little flame. 6And the tongue is like a fire. It is a whole world of evil among the parts of our bodies. The tongue spreads its evil through the whole body. The tongue is set on fire by hell, and it starts a fire that influences all of life. 7People can tame every kind of wild animal, bird, reptile, and fish, and they have tamed them, 8but no one can tame the tongue. It is wild and evil and full of deadly poison. 9We use our tongues to praise our Lord and Father, but then we curse people, whom God made like himself. 10Praises and curses come from the same mouth! My brothers and sisters, this

CONTEMPORARY ENGLISH VERSION

The Tongue

3 My friends, we should not all try to become teachers. In fact, teachers will be judged more strictly than others. 2All of us do many wrong things. But if you can control your tongue, you are mature and able to control your whole body.

3By putting a bit into the mouth of a horse, we can turn the horse in different directions. 4It takes strong winds to move a large sailing ship, but the captain uses only a small rudder to make it go in any direction. 5Our tongues are small too, and yet they brag about big things.

It takes only a spark to start a forest fire! 6The tongue is like a spark. It is an evil power that dirties the rest of the body and sets a person's entire life on fire with flames that come from hell itself. 7All kinds of animals, birds, reptiles, and sea creatures can be tamed and have been tamed. 8But our tongues get out of control. They are restless and evil, and always spreading deadly poison.

9-10My dear friends, with our tongues we speak both praises and curses. We praise our Lord and Father, and we curse people who were created to be like God, and this isn't

NEW INTERNATIONAL VERSION

Taming the Tongue

3 Not many of you should presume to be teachers, my
brothers, because you know that we who teach will be
judged more strictly. 2We all stumble in many ways. If
anyone is never at fault in what he says, he is a perfect
man, able to keep his whole body in check.
3When we put bits into the mouths of horses to make
them obey us, we can turn the whole animal. 4Or take
ships as an example. Although they are so large and are
driven by strong winds, they are steered by a very small
rudder wherever the pilot wants to go. 5Likewise the
tongue is a small part of the body, but it makes great
boasts. Consider what a great forest is set on fire by a
small spark. 6The tongue also is a fire, a world of evil
among the parts of the body. It corrupts the whole person,
sets the whole course of his life on fire, and is itself set on
fire by hell.
7All kinds of animals, birds, reptiles and creatures of the
sea are being tamed and have been tamed by man, 8but no
man can tame the tongue. It is a restless evil, full of dead-
ly poison.
9With the tongue we praise our Lord and Father, and
with it we curse men, who have been made in God's like-
ness. 10Out of the same mouth come praise and cursing.
My brothers, this should not be. 11Can both fresh water

NEW LIVING TRANSLATION

Controlling the Tongue

3 Dear brothers and sisters,* not many of you should
become teachers in the church, for we who teach will
be judged by God with greater strictness.
2We all make many mistakes, but those who control
their tongues can also control themselves in every other
way. 3We can make a large horse turn around and go
wherever we want by means of a small bit in its mouth.
4And a tiny rudder makes a huge ship turn wherever the
pilot wants it to go, even though the winds are strong. 5So
also, the tongue is a small thing, but what enormous dam-
age it can do. A tiny spark can set a great forest on fire.
6And the tongue is a flame of fire. It is full of wickedness
that can ruin your whole life. It can turn the entire course
of your life into a blazing flame of destruction, for it is set
on fire by hell itself.
7People can tame all kinds of animals and birds and rep-
tiles and fish, 8but no one can tame the tongue. It is an
uncontrollable evil, full of deadly poison. 9Sometimes it
praises our Lord and Father, and sometimes it breaks out
into curses against those who have been made in the
image of God. 10And so blessing and cursing come pouring
out of the same mouth. Surely, my brothers and sisters,

3:1 Greek *brothers;* also in 3:10.

NEW KING JAMES VERSION

The Untamable Tongue

3 My brethren, let not many of you become teachers,
knowing that we shall receive a stricter judgment.
2For we all stumble in many things. If anyone does not
stumble in word, he *is* a perfect man, able also to bridle
the whole body. 3Indeed,[a] we put bits in horses' mouths
that they may obey us, and we turn their whole body.
4Look also at ships: although they are so large and are
driven by fierce winds, they are turned by a very small rud-
der wherever the pilot desires. 5Even so the tongue is a lit-
tle member and boasts great things.
See how great a forest a little fire kindles! 6And the
tongue *is* a fire, a world of iniquity. The tongue is so set
among our members that it defiles the whole body, and
sets on fire the course of nature; and it is set on fire by
hell. 7For every kind of beast and bird, of reptile and crea-
ture of the sea, is tamed and has been tamed by mankind.
8But no man can tame the tongue. *It is* an unruly evil, full
of deadly poison. 9With it we bless our God and Father,
and with it we curse men, who have been made in the si-
militude of God. 10Out of the same mouth proceed blessing
and cursing. My brethren, these things ought not to be so.

3:3 [a] NU-Text reads *Now if.*

THE MESSAGE

When You Open Your Mouth

3 Don't be in any rush to become a teacher, my friends.
Teaching is highly responsible work. Teachers are
held to the strictest standards. And none of us are perfect-
ly qualified. We get it wrong nearly every time we open our
mouths. If you could find someone whose speech was per-
fectly true, you'd have a perfect person, in perfect control
of life.

A bit in the mouth of a horse controls the whole horse. A
small rudder on a huge ship in the hands of a skilled cap-
tain sets a course in the face of the strongest winds. A
word out of your mouth may seem of no account, but it
can accomplish nearly anything—or destroy it!

It only takes a spark, remember, to set off a forest fire. A
careless or wrongly placed word out of your mouth can do
that. By our speech we can ruin the world, turn harmony
to chaos, throw mud on a reputation, send the whole world
up in smoke and go up in smoke with it, smoke right from
the pit of hell.

This is scary: You can tame a tiger, but you can't tame a
tongue—it's never been done. The tongue runs wild, a
wanton killer. With our tongues we bless God our Father;
with the same tongues we curse the very men and women
he made in his image. Curses and blessings out of the
same mouth!

KING JAMES VERSION

11 Doth a fountain send forth at the same place sweet *water* and bitter?

12 Can the fig tree, my brethren, bear olive berries? either a vine, figs? so *can* no fountain both yield salt water and fresh.

13 ¶ Who *is* a wise man and endued with knowledge among you? let him shew out of a good conversation his works with meekness of wisdom.

14 But if ye have bitter envying and strife in your hearts, glory not, and lie not against the truth.

15 This wisdom descendeth not from above, but *is* earthly, sensual, devilish.

16 For where envying and strife *is*, there *is* confusion and every evil work.

17 But the wisdom that is from above is first pure, then peaceable, gentle, *and* easy to be intreated, full of mercy and good fruits, without partiality, and without hypocrisy.

18 And the fruit of righteousness is sown in peace of them that make peace.

4 From whence *come* wars and fightings among you? *come they* not hence, *even* of your lusts that war in your members?

NEW AMERICAN STANDARD BIBLE

11 Does a fountain send out from the same opening *both* fresh and bitter *water?*

12 Can a fig tree, my brethren, produce olives, or a vine produce figs? Nor *can* salt water produce fresh.

Wisdom from Above

13 Who among you is wise and understanding? Let him show by his good behavior his deeds in the gentleness of wisdom.

14 But if you have bitter jealousy and selfish ambition in your heart, do not be arrogant and *so* lie against the truth.

15 This wisdom is not that which comes down from above, but is earthly, natural, demonic.

16 For where jealousy and selfish ambition exist, there is disorder and every evil thing.

17 But the wisdom from above is first pure, then peaceable, gentle, reasonable, full of mercy and good fruits, unwavering, without hypocrisy.

18 And the seed whose fruit is righteousness is sown in peace by those who make peace.

Things to Avoid

4 What is the source of quarrels and conflicts among you? Is not the source your pleasures that wage war in your members?

NEW CENTURY VERSION

should not happen. 11Do good and bad water flow from the
same spring? 12My brothers and sisters, can a fig tree
make olives, or can a grapevine make figs? No! And a well
full of salty water cannot give good water.

True Wisdom

13Are there those among you who are truly wise and
understanding? Then they should show it by living right
and doing good things with a gentleness that comes from
wisdom. 14But if you are selfish and have bitter jealousy in
your hearts, do not brag. Your bragging is a lie that hides
the truth. 15That kind of "wisdom" does not come from
God but from the world. It is not spiritual; it is from the
devil. 16Where jealousy and selfishness are, there will be
confusion and every kind of evil. 17But the wisdom that
comes from God is first of all pure, then peaceful, gentle,
and easy to please. This wisdom is always ready to help
those who are troubled and to do good for others. It is
always fair and honest. 18People who work for peace in a
peaceful way plant a good crop of right-living.

Give Yourselves to God

4 Do you know where your fights and arguments come
from? They come from the selfish desires that war

CONTEMPORARY ENGLISH VERSION

right. 11Can clean water and dirty water both flow from the
same spring? 12Can a fig tree produce olives or a grapevine
produce figs? Does fresh water come from a well full of salt
water?

Wisdom from Above

13Are any of you wise or sensible? Then show it by living right and by being humble and wise in everything you
do. 14But if your heart is full of bitter jealousy and selfishness, don't brag or lie to cover up the truth. 15That kind of
wisdom doesn't come from above. It is earthly and selfish
and comes from the devil himself. 16Whenever people are
jealous or selfish, they cause trouble and do all sorts of
cruel things. 17But the wisdom that comes from above
leads us to be pure, friendly, gentle, sensible, kind, helpful,
genuine, and sincere. 18When peacemakers plant seeds of
peace, they will harvest justice.

Friendship with the World

4 Why do you fight and argue with each other? Isn't it
because you are full of selfish desires that fight to

NEW INTERNATIONAL VERSION

and salt[a] water flow from the same spring? 12 My brothers, can a fig tree bear olives, or a grapevine bear figs? Neither can a salt spring produce fresh water.

Two Kinds of Wisdom

13 Who is wise and understanding among you? Let him show it by his good life, by deeds done in the humility that comes from wisdom. 14 But if you harbor bitter envy and selfish ambition in your hearts, do not boast about it or deny the truth. 15 Such "wisdom" does not come down from heaven but is earthly, unspiritual, of the devil. 16 For where you have envy and selfish ambition, there you find disorder and every evil practice.

17 But the wisdom that comes from heaven is first of all pure; then peace-loving, considerate, submissive, full of mercy and good fruit, impartial and sincere. 18 Peacemakers who sow in peace raise a harvest of righteousness.

Submit Yourselves to God

4 What causes fights and quarrels among you? Don't they come from your desires that battle within you?

a *11* Greek *bitter* (see also verse 14)

NEW LIVING TRANSLATION

this is not right! 11 Does a spring of water bubble out with both fresh water and bitter water? 12 Can you pick olives from a fig tree or figs from a grapevine? No, and you can't draw fresh water from a salty pool.

True Wisdom Comes from God

13 If you are wise and understand God's ways, live a life of steady goodness so that only good deeds will pour forth. And if you don't brag about the good you do, then you will be truly wise! 14 But if you are bitterly jealous and there is selfish ambition in your hearts, don't brag about being wise. That is the worst kind of lie. 15 For jealousy and selfishness are not God's kind of wisdom. Such things are earthly, unspiritual, and motivated by the Devil. 16 For wherever there is jealousy and selfish ambition, there you will find disorder and every kind of evil.

17 But the wisdom that comes from heaven is first of all pure. It is also peace loving, gentle at all times, and willing to yield to others. It is full of mercy and good deeds. It shows no partiality and is always sincere. 18 And those who are peacemakers will plant seeds of peace and reap a harvest of goodness.

Drawing Close to God

4 What is causing the quarrels and fights among you? Isn't it the whole army of evil desires at war within

NEW KING JAMES VERSION

11 Does a spring send forth fresh *water* and bitter from the same opening? 12 Can a fig tree, my brethren, bear olives, or a grapevine bear figs? Thus no spring yields both salt water and fresh.[b]

Heavenly Versus Demonic Wisdom

13 Who *is* wise and understanding among you? Let him show by good conduct *that* his works *are done* in the meekness of wisdom. 14 But if you have bitter envy and self-seeking in your hearts, do not boast and lie against the truth. 15 This wisdom does not descend from above, but *is* earthly, sensual, demonic. 16 For where envy and self-seeking *exist,* confusion and every evil thing *are* there. 17 But the wisdom that is from above is first pure, then peaceable, gentle, willing to yield, full of mercy and good fruits, without partiality and without hypocrisy. 18 Now the fruit of righteousness is sown in peace by those who make peace.

Pride Promotes Strife

4 Where do wars and fights *come* from among you? Do *they* not *come* from your *desires for* pleasure that war

3:12 b NU-Text reads *Neither can a salty spring produce fresh water.*

THE MESSAGE

My friends, this can't go on. A spring doesn't gush fresh water one day and brackish the next, does it? Apple trees don't bear strawberries, do they? Raspberry bushes don't bear apples, do they? You're not going to dip into a polluted mud hole and get a cup of clear, cool water, are you?

Live Well, Live Wisely

Do you want to be counted wise, to build a reputation for wisdom? Here's what you do: Live well, live wisely, live humbly. It's the way you live, not the way you talk, that counts. Mean-spirited ambition isn't wisdom. Boasting that you are wise isn't wisdom. Twisting the truth to make yourselves sound wise isn't wisdom. It's the furthest thing from wisdom—it's animal cunning, devilish conniving. Whenever you're trying to look better than others or get the better of others, things fall apart and everyone ends up at the others' throats.

Real wisdom, God's wisdom, begins with a holy life and is characterized by getting along with others. It is gentle and reasonable, overflowing with mercy and blessings, not hot one day and cold the next, not two-faced. You can develop a healthy, robust community that lives right with God and enjoy its results *only* if you do the hard work of getting along with each other, treating each other with dignity and honor.

Get Serious

4 Where do you think all these appalling wars and quarrels come from? Do you think they just happen? Think again. They come about because you want your own

KING JAMES VERSION

2 Ye lust, and have not: ye kill, and desire to have, and cannot obtain: ye fight and war, yet ye have not, because ye ask not.

3 Ye ask, and receive not, because ye ask amiss, that ye may consume *it* upon your lusts.

4 Ye adulterers and adulteresses, know ye not that the friendship of the world is enmity with God? whosoever therefore will be a friend of the world is the enemy of God.

5 Do ye think that the scripture saith in vain, The spirit that dwelleth in us lusteth to envy?

6 But he giveth more grace. Wherefore he saith, God resisteth the proud, but giveth grace unto the humble.

7 Submit yourselves therefore to God. Resist the devil, and he will flee from you.

8 Draw nigh to God, and he will draw nigh to you. Cleanse *your* hands, *ye* sinners; and purify *your* hearts, *ye* double minded.

9 Be afflicted, and mourn, and weep: let your laughter be turned to mourning, and *your* joy to heaviness.

10 Humble yourselves in the sight of the Lord, and he shall lift you up.

NEW AMERICAN STANDARD BIBLE

2 You lust and do not have; *so* you commit murder. You are envious and cannot obtain; *so* you fight and quarrel. You do not have because you do not ask.

3 You ask and do not receive, because you ask with wrong motives, so that you may spend *it* on your pleasures.

4 You adulteresses, do you not know that friendship with the world is hostility toward God? Therefore whoever wishes to be a friend of the world makes himself an enemy of God.

5 Or do you think that the Scripture speaks to no purpose: "[1]He jealously desires the Spirit which He has made to dwell in us"?

6 But He gives a greater grace. Therefore *it* says, "GOD IS OPPOSED TO THE PROUD, BUT GIVES GRACE TO THE HUMBLE."

7 Submit therefore to God. Resist the devil and he will flee from you.

8 Draw near to God and He will draw near to you. Cleanse your hands, you sinners; and purify your hearts, you double-minded.

9 Be miserable and mourn and weep; let your laughter be turned into mourning and your joy to gloom.

10 Humble yourselves in the presence of the Lord, and He will exalt you.

4:5 [1] Or *The spirit which He has made to dwell in us lusts with envy*

NEW CENTURY VERSION

within you. 2You want things, but you do not have them.
So you are ready to kill and are jealous of other people, but
you still cannot get what you want. So you argue and
fight. You do not get what you want, because you do not
ask God. 3Or when you ask, you do not receive because the
reason you ask is wrong. You want things so you can use
them for your own pleasures.
4So, you are not loyal to God! You should know that lov-
ing the world is the same as hating God. Anyone who
wants to be a friend of the world becomes God's enemy.
5Do you think the Scripture means nothing that says, "The
Spirit that God made to live in us wants us for himself
alone."[a] 6But God gives us even more grace, as the
Scripture says,

"God is against the proud,
but he gives grace to the humble." *Proverbs 3:34*

7So give yourselves completely to God. Stand against the
devil, and the devil will run from you. 8Come near to God,
and God will come near to you. You sinners, clean sin out
of your lives. You who are trying to follow God and the
world at the same time, make your thinking pure. 9Be sad,
cry, and weep! Change your laughter into crying and your
joy into sadness. 10Don't be too proud in the Lord's pres-
ence, and he will make you great.

4:5 [a] **"The Spirit...alone."** These words may be from Exodus 20:5.

CONTEMPORARY ENGLISH VERSION

control your body? 2You want something you don't have,
and you will do anything to get it. You will even kill! But
you still cannot get what you want, and you won't get it
by fighting and arguing. You should pray for it. 3Yet even
when you do pray, your prayers are not answered, because
you pray just for selfish reasons.
4You people aren't faithful to God! Don't you know that
if you love the world, you are God's enemies? And if you
decide to be a friend of the world, you make yourself an
enemy of God. 5Do you doubt the Scriptures that say, "God
truly cares about the Spirit he has put in us"?[a] 6In fact,
God treats us with even greater kindness, just as the
Scriptures say,

"God opposes everyone
who is proud,
but he is kind to everyone
who is humble."

7Surrender to God! Resist the devil, and he will run from
you. 8Come near to God, and he will come near to you.
Clean up your lives, you sinners. Purify your hearts, you
people who can't make up your mind. 9Be sad and sorry
and weep. Stop laughing and start crying. Be gloomy
instead of glad. 10Be humble in the Lord's presence, and he
will honor you.

[a] 4.5 *God truly cares about the Spirit he has put in us*: One possible meaning for the difficult Greek text; other translations are possible, such as, "the Spirit that God put in us truly cares."

NEW INTERNATIONAL VERSION

[2]You want something but don't get it. You kill and covet,
but you cannot have what you want. You quarrel and
fight. You do not have, because you do not ask God.
[3]When you ask, you do not receive, because you ask with
wrong motives, that you may spend what you get on your
pleasures.

[4]You adulterous people, don't you know that friendship
with the world is hatred toward God? Anyone who chooses
to be a friend of the world becomes an enemy of God. [5]Or
do you think Scripture says without reason that the spirit
he caused to live in us envies intensely?[a] [6]But he gives us
more grace. That is why Scripture says:

"God opposes the proud
but gives grace to the humble."[b]

[7]Submit yourselves, then, to God. Resist the devil, and
he will flee from you. [8]Come near to God and he will come
near to you. Wash your hands, you sinners, and purify
your hearts, you double-minded. [9]Grieve, mourn and wail.
Change your laughter to mourning and your joy to gloom.
[10]Humble yourselves before the Lord, and he will lift
you up.

[a] *5* Or *that God jealously longs for the spirit that he made to live in us*; or *that the Spirit he caused to live in us longs jealously* [b] *6* Prov. 3:34

NEW LIVING TRANSLATION

you? [2]You want what you don't have, so you scheme and
kill to get it. You are jealous for what others have, and you
can't possess it, so you fight and quarrel to take it away
from them. And yet the reason you don't have what you
want is that you don't ask God for it. [3]And even when you
do ask, you don't get it because your whole motive is
wrong—you want only what will give you pleasure.

[4]You adulterers! Don't you realize that friendship with
this world makes you an enemy of God? I say it again, that
if your aim is to enjoy this world, you can't be a friend of
God. [5]What do you think the Scriptures mean when they
say that the Holy Spirit, whom God has placed within us,
jealously longs for us to be faithful*? [6]He gives us more
and more strength to stand against such evil desires. As
the Scriptures say,

"God sets himself against the proud,
but he shows favor to the humble."*

[7]So humble yourselves before God. Resist the Devil, and
he will flee from you. [8]Draw close to God, and God will draw
close to you. Wash your hands, you sinners; purify your
hearts, you hypocrites. [9]Let there be tears for the wrong
things you have done. Let there be sorrow and deep grief. Let
there be sadness instead of laughter, and gloom instead of
joy. [10]When you bow down before the Lord and admit your
dependence on him, he will lift you up and give you honor.

4:5 Or *the spirit that God placed within us tends to envy*, or *the Holy Spirit, whom God has placed within us, opposes our envy.* 4:6 Prov 3:34.

NEW KING JAMES VERSION

in your members? [2]You lust and do not have. You murder
and covet and cannot obtain. You fight and war. Yet[a] you
do not have because you do not ask. [3]You ask and do not
receive, because you ask amiss, that you may spend *it* on
your pleasures. [4]Adulterers and[b] adulteresses! Do you not
know that friendship with the world is enmity with God?
Whoever therefore wants to be a friend of the world makes
himself an enemy of God. [5]Or do you think that the
Scripture says in vain, "The Spirit who dwells in us yearns
jealously"?

[6]But He gives more grace. Therefore He says:

"*God resists the proud,*
But gives grace to the humble."[c]

Humility Cures Worldliness

[7]Therefore submit to God. Resist the devil and he will
flee from you. [8]Draw near to God and He will draw near to
you. Cleanse *your* hands, *you* sinners; and purify *your*
hearts, *you* double-minded. [9]Lament and mourn and weep!
Let your laughter be turned to mourning and *your* joy to
gloom. [10]Humble yourselves in the sight of the Lord, and
He will lift you up.

4:2 [a] NU-Text and M-Text omit *Yet.* 4:4 [b] NU-Text omits *Adulterers and.* 4:6 [c] Proverbs 3:34

THE MESSAGE

way, and fight for it deep inside yourselves. You lust for what you don't have and are willing to kill to get it. You want what isn't yours and will risk violence to get your hands on it.

You wouldn't think of just asking God for it, would you? And why not? Because you know you'd be asking for what you have no right to. You're spoiled children, each wanting your own way.

You're cheating on God. If all you want is your own way, flirting with the world every chance you get, you end up enemies of God and his way. And do you suppose God doesn't care? The proverb has it that "he's a fiercely jealous lover." And what he gives in love is far better than anything else you'll find. It's common knowledge that "God goes against the willful proud; God gives grace to the willing humble."

So let God work his will in you. Yell a loud *no* to the Devil and watch him scamper. Say a quiet *yes* to God and he'll be there in no time. Quit dabbling in sin. Purify your inner life. Quit playing the field. Hit bottom, and cry your eyes out. The fun and games are over. Get serious, really serious. Get down on your knees before the Master; it's the only way you'll get on your feet.

KING JAMES VERSION

11 ¶ Speak not evil one of another, brethren. He that speaketh evil of *his* brother, and judgeth his brother, speaketh evil of the law, and judgeth the law: but if thou judge the law, thou art not a doer of the law, but a judge.

12 There is one lawgiver, who is able to save and to destroy: who art thou that judgest another?

13 Go to now, ye that say, To day or to morrow we will go into such a city, and continue there a year, and buy and sell, and get gain:

14 Whereas ye know not what *shall be* on the morrow. For what *is* your life? It is even a vapour, that appeareth for a little time, and then vanisheth away.

15 For that ye *ought* to say, If the Lord will, we shall live, and do this, or that.

16 But now ye rejoice in your boastings: all such rejoicing is evil.

17 Therefore to him that knoweth to do good, and doeth *it* not, to him it is sin.

5 Go to now, *ye* rich men, weep and howl for your miseries that shall come upon *you*.

2 Your riches are corrupted, and your garments are motheaten.

NEW AMERICAN STANDARD BIBLE

11 Do not speak against one another, brethren. He who speaks against a brother or judges his brother, speaks against the law and judges the law; but if you judge the law, you are not a doer of the law but a judge *of it.*

12 There is *only* one Lawgiver and Judge, the One who is able to save and to destroy; but who are you who judge your neighbor?

13 Come now, you who say, "Today or tomorrow we will go to such and such a city, and spend a year there and engage in business and make a profit."

14 Yet you do not know what your life will be like tomorrow. You are *just* a vapor that appears for a little while and then vanishes away.

15 Instead, *you ought* to say, "If the Lord wills, we will live and also do this or that."

16 But as it is, you boast in your arrogance; all such boasting is evil.

17 Therefore, to one who knows *the* right thing to do and does not do it, to him it is sin.

Misuse of Riches

5 Come now, you rich, weep and howl for your miseries which are coming upon you.

2 Your riches have rotted and your garments have become moth-eaten.

NEW CENTURY VERSION

You Are Not the Judge

11 Brothers and sisters, do not tell evil lies about each
other. If you speak against your fellow believers or judge
them, you are judging and speaking against the law they
follow. And when you are judging the law, you are no
longer a follower of the law. You have become a judge.
12 God is the only Lawmaker and Judge. He is the only One
who can save and destroy. So it is not right for you to
judge your neighbor.

Let God Plan Your Life

13 Some of you say, "Today or tomorrow we will go to
some city. We will stay there a year, do business, and
make money." 14 But you do not know what will happen
tomorrow! Your life is like a mist. You can see it for a
short time, but then it goes away. 15 So you should say, "If
the Lord wants, we will live and do this or that." 16 But
now you are proud and you brag. All of this bragging is
wrong. 17 Anyone who knows the right thing to do, but
does not do it, is sinning.

A Warning to the Rich

5 You rich people, listen! Cry and be very sad because of
the troubles that are coming to you. 2 Your riches have
rotted, and your clothes have been eaten by moths. 3 Your

CONTEMPORARY ENGLISH VERSION

Saying Cruel Things about Others

11 My friends, don't say cruel things about others! If you
do, or if you condemn others, you are condemning God's
Law. And if you condemn the Law, you put yourself above
the Law and refuse to obey either it 12 or God who gave it.
God is our judge, and he can save or destroy us. What
right do you have to condemn anyone?

Warning against Bragging

13 You should know better than to say, "Today or tomor-
row we will go to the city. We will do business there for a
year and make a lot of money!" 14 What do you know about
tomorrow? How can you be so sure about your life? It is
nothing more than mist that appears for only a little while
before it disappears. 15 You should say, "If the Lord lets us
live, we will do these things." 16 Yet you are stupid enough
to brag, and it is wrong to be so proud. 17 If you don't do
what you know is right, you have sinned.

Warning to the Rich

5 You rich people should cry and weep! Terrible things
are going to happen to you. 2 Your treasures have
already rotted, and moths have eaten your clothes. 3 Your

NEW INTERNATIONAL VERSION

11 Brothers, do not slander one another. Anyone who speaks against his brother or judges him speaks against the law and judges it. When you judge the law, you are not keeping it, but sitting in judgment on it. 12 There is only one Lawgiver and Judge, the one who is able to save and destroy. But you—who are you to judge your neighbor?

Boasting About Tomorrow

13 Now listen, you who say, "Today or tomorrow we will go to this or that city, spend a year there, carry on business and make money." 14 Why, you do not even know what will happen tomorrow. What is your life? You are a mist that appears for a little while and then vanishes. 15 Instead, you ought to say, "If it is the Lord's will, we will live and do this or that." 16 As it is, you boast and brag. All such boasting is evil. 17 Anyone, then, who knows the good he ought to do and doesn't do it, sins.

Warning to Rich Oppressors

5 Now listen, you rich people, weep and wail because of the misery that is coming upon you. 2 Your wealth has rotted, and moths have eaten your clothes. 3 Your gold and

NEW LIVING TRANSLATION

Warning against Judging Others

11 Don't speak evil against each other, my dear brothers and sisters.* If you criticize each other and condemn each other, then you are criticizing and condemning God's law. But you are not a judge who can decide whether the law is right or wrong. Your job is to obey it. 12 God alone, who made the law, can rightly judge among us. He alone has the power to save or to destroy. So what right do you have to condemn your neighbor?

Warning about Self-Confidence

13 Look here, you people who say, "Today or tomorrow we are going to a certain town and will stay there a year. We will do business there and make a profit." 14 How do you know what will happen tomorrow? For your life is like the morning fog—it's here a little while, then it's gone. 15 What you ought to say is, "If the Lord wants us to, we will live and do this or that." 16 Otherwise you will be boasting about your own plans, and all such boasting is evil.

17 Remember, it is sin to know what you ought to do and then not do it.

Warning to the Rich

5 Look here, you rich people, weep and groan with anguish because of all the terrible troubles ahead of you. 2 Your wealth is rotting away, and your fine clothes are moth-eaten rags. 3 Your gold and silver have become

4:11 Greek *brothers.*

NEW KING JAMES VERSION

Do Not Judge a Brother

11 Do not speak evil of one another, brethren. He who speaks evil of a brother and judges his brother, speaks evil of the law and judges the law. But if you judge the law, you are not a doer of the law but a judge. 12 There is one Lawgiver,[d] who is able to save and to destroy. Who[e] are you to judge another?[f]

Do Not Boast About Tomorrow

13 Come now, you who say, "Today or tomorrow we will[g] go to such and such a city, spend a year there, buy and sell, and make a profit"; 14 whereas you do not know what *will happen* tomorrow. For what *is* your life? It is even a vapor that appears for a little time and then vanishes away. 15 Instead you *ought* to say, "If the Lord wills, we shall live and do this or that." 16 But now you boast in your arrogance. All such boasting is evil.

17 Therefore, to him who knows to do good and does not do *it,* to him it is sin.

Rich Oppressors Will Be Judged

5 Come now, *you* rich, weep and howl for your miseries that are coming upon *you!* 2 Your riches are corrupted, and your garments are moth-eaten. 3 Your gold and silver

4:12 [d] NU-Text adds *and Judge.* [e] NU-Text and M-Text read *But who.* [f] NU-Text reads *a neighbor.* 4:13 [g] M-Text reads *let us.*

THE MESSAGE

Don't bad-mouth each other, friends. It's God's Word, his Message, his Royal Rule, that takes a beating in that kind of talk. You're supposed to be honoring the Message, not writing graffiti all over it. God is in charge of deciding human destiny. Who do you think you are to meddle in the destiny of others?

Nothing But a Wisp of Fog

And now I have a word for you who brashly announce, "Today—at the latest, tomorrow—we're off to such and such a city for the year. We're going to start a business and make a lot of money." You don't know the first thing about tomorrow. You're nothing but a wisp of fog, catching a brief bit of sun before disappearing. Instead, make it a habit to say, "If the Master wills it and we're still alive, we'll do this or that."

As it is, you are full of your grandiose selves. All such vaunting self-importance is evil. In fact, if you know the right thing to do and don't do it, that, for you, *is* evil.

Destroying Your Life From Within

5 And a final word to you arrogant rich: Take some lessons in lament. You'll need buckets for the tears when the crash comes upon you. Your money is corrupt

KING JAMES VERSION

3 Your gold and silver is cankered; and the rust of them shall be a witness against you, and shall eat your flesh as it were fire. Ye have heaped treasure together for the last days.

4 Behold, the hire of the labourers who have reaped down your fields, which is of you kept back by fraud, crieth: and the cries of them which have reaped are entered into the ears of the Lord of sabaoth.

5 Ye have lived in pleasure on the earth, and been wanton; ye have nourished your hearts, as in a day of slaughter.

6 Ye have condemned *and* killed the just; *and* he doth not resist you.

7 Be patient therefore, brethren, unto the coming of the Lord. Behold, the husbandman waiteth for the precious fruit of the earth, and hath long patience for it, until he receive the early and latter rain.

8 Be ye also patient; stablish your hearts: for the coming of the Lord draweth nigh.

9 Grudge not one against another, brethren, lest ye be condemned: behold, the judge standeth before the door.

10 Take, my brethren, the prophets, who have spoken in the name of the Lord, for an example of suffering affliction, and of patience.

11 Behold, we count them happy which endure. Ye have

NEW AMERICAN STANDARD BIBLE

3 Your gold and your silver have rusted; and their rust will be a witness against you and will consume your flesh like fire. It is in the last days that you have stored up your treasure!

4 Behold, the pay of the laborers who mowed your fields, *and* which has been withheld by you, cries out *against you;* and the outcry of those who did the harvesting has reached the ears of the Lord of Sabaoth.

5 You have lived luxuriously on the earth and led a life of wanton pleasure; you have fattened your hearts in a day of slaughter.

6 You have condemned and put to death the righteous *man;* he does not resist you.

Exhortation

7 Therefore be patient, brethren, until the coming of the Lord. The farmer waits for the precious produce of the soil, being patient about it, until it gets the early and late rains.

8 You too be patient; strengthen your hearts, for the coming of the Lord is near.

9 Do not complain, brethren, against one another, so that you yourselves may not be judged; behold, the Judge is standing right at the door.

10 As an example, brethren, of suffering and patience, take the prophets who spoke in the name of the Lord.

11 We count those blessed who endured. You have

NEW CENTURY VERSION

gold and silver have rusted, and that rust will be a proof
that you were wrong. It will eat your bodies like fire. You
saved your treasure for the last days. 4 The pay you did not
give the workers who mowed your fields cries out against
you, and the cries of the workers have been heard by the
Lord All-Powerful. 5 Your life on earth was full of rich living and pleasing yourselves with everything you wanted.
You made yourselves fat, like an animal ready to be killed.
6 You have judged guilty and then murdered innocent people, who were not against you.

Be Patient

7 Brothers and sisters, be patient until the Lord comes
again. A farmer patiently waits for his valuable crop to
grow from the earth and for it to receive the autumn and
spring rains. 8 You, too, must be patient. Do not give up
hope, because the Lord is coming soon. 9 Brothers and sisters, do not complain against each other or you will be
judged guilty. And the Judge is ready to come! 10 Brothers
and sisters, follow the example of the prophets who spoke
for the Lord. They suffered many hard things, but they
were patient. 11 We say they are happy because they did

CONTEMPORARY ENGLISH VERSION

money has rusted, and the rust will be evidence against
you, as it burns your body like fire. Yet you keep on storing up wealth in these last days. 4 You refused to pay the
people who worked in your fields, and now their unpaid
wages are shouting out against you. The Lord All-Powerful
has surely heard the cries of the workers who harvested
your crops.

5 While here on earth, you have thought only of filling
your own stomachs and having a good time. But now you
are like fat cattle on their way to be butchered. 6 You have
condemned and murdered innocent people, who couldn't
even fight back.

Be Patient and Kind

7 My friends, be patient until the Lord returns. Think of
farmers who wait patiently for the spring and summer
rains to make their valuable crops grow. 8 Be patient like
those farmers and don't give up. The Lord will soon be
here! 9 Don't grumble about each other or you will be
judged, and the judge is right outside the door.

10 My friends, follow the example of the prophets who
spoke for the Lord. They were patient, even when they had
to suffer. 11 In fact, we praise the ones who endured the

NEW INTERNATIONAL VERSION

silver are corroded. Their corrosion will testify against you
and eat your flesh like fire. You have hoarded wealth in
the last days. 4Look! The wages you failed to pay the
workmen who mowed your fields are crying out against
you. The cries of the harvesters have reached the ears of
the Lord Almighty. 5You have lived on earth in luxury and
self-indulgence. You have fattened yourselves in the day of
slaughter.[a] 6You have condemned and murdered innocent
men, who were not opposing you.

Patience in Suffering

7Be patient, then, brothers, until the Lord's coming. See
how the farmer waits for the land to yield its valuable crop
and how patient he is for the autumn and spring rains.
8You too, be patient and stand firm, because the Lord's
coming is near. 9Don't grumble against each other, broth-
ers, or you will be judged. The Judge is standing at the
door!
10Brothers, as an example of patience in the face of suf-
fering, take the prophets who spoke in the name of the
Lord. 11As you know, we consider blessed those who have

[a] 5 Or *yourselves as in a day of feasting*

NEW LIVING TRANSLATION

worthless. The very wealth you were counting on will eat
away your flesh in hell.* This treasure you have accumu-
lated will stand as evidence against you on the day of
judgment. 4For listen! Hear the cries of the field workers
whom you have cheated of their pay. The wages you held
back cry out against you. The cries of the reapers have
reached the ears of the Lord Almighty.
5You have spent your years on earth in luxury, satisfy-
ing your every whim. Now your hearts are nice and fat,
ready for the slaughter. 6You have condemned and killed
good people who had no power to defend themselves
against you.

Patience in Suffering

7Dear brothers and sisters,* you must be patient as you
wait for the Lord's return. Consider the farmers who eager-
ly look for the rains in the fall and in the spring. They
patiently wait for the precious harvest to ripen. 8You, too,
must be patient. And take courage, for the coming of the
Lord is near.
9Don't grumble about each other, my brothers and sis-
ters, or God will judge you. For look! The great Judge is
coming. He is standing at the door!
10For examples of patience in suffering, dear brothers
and sisters, look at the prophets who spoke in the name of
the Lord. 11We give great honor to those who endure under

5:3 Or *will eat your flesh like fire.* 5:7 Greek *brothers;* also in 5:9, 10, 12, 19.

NEW KING JAMES VERSION

are corroded, and their corrosion will be a witness against
you and will eat your flesh like fire. You have heaped up
treasure in the last days. 4Indeed the wages of the laborers
who mowed your fields, which you kept back by fraud, cry
out; and the cries of the reapers have reached the ears of
the Lord of Sabaoth.[a] 5You have lived on the earth in plea-
sure and luxury; you have fattened your hearts as[b] in a
day of slaughter. 6You have condemned, you have mur-
dered the just; he does not resist you.

Be Patient and Persevering

7Therefore be patient, brethren, until the coming of the
Lord. See *how* the farmer waits for the precious fruit of the
earth, waiting patiently for it until it receives the early and
latter rain. 8You also be patient. Establish your hearts, for
the coming of the Lord is at hand.
9Do not grumble against one another, brethren, lest you
be condemned.[c] Behold, the Judge is standing at the door!
10My brethren, take the prophets, who spoke in the name of
the Lord, as an example of suffering and patience. 11Indeed
we count them blessed who endure. You have heard of the

5:4 [a] Literally, in Hebrew, *Hosts* 5:5 [b] NU-Text omits *as.*
5:9 [c] NU-Text and M-Text read *judged.*

THE MESSAGE

and your fine clothes stink. Your greedy luxuries are a can-
cer in your gut, destroying your life from within. You
thought you were piling up wealth. What you've piled up
is judgment.

All the workers you've exploited and cheated cry out for
judgment. The groans of the workers you used and abused
are a roar in the ears of the Master Avenger. You've looted
the earth and lived it up. But all you'll have to show for it
is a fatter than usual corpse. In fact, what you've done is
condemn and murder perfectly good persons, who stand
there and take it.

✢

Meanwhile, friends, wait patiently for the Master's
Arrival. You see farmers do this all the time, waiting for
their valuable crops to mature, patiently letting the rain do
its slow but sure work. Be patient like that. Stay steady
and strong. The Master could arrive at any time.

Friends, don't complain about each other. A far greater
complaint could be lodged against you, you know. The
Judge is standing just around the corner.

Take the old prophets as your mentors. They put up with
anything, went through everything, and never once quit,
all the time honoring God. What a gift life is to those who

KING JAMES VERSION

heard of the patience of Job, and have seen the end of the Lord; that the Lord is very pitiful, and of tender mercy.

12 ¶ But above all things, my brethren, swear not, neither by heaven, neither by the earth, neither by any other oath: but let your yea be yea; and *your* nay, nay; lest ye fall into condemnation.

13 Is any among you afflicted? let him pray. Is any merry? let him sing psalms.

14 Is any sick among you? let him call for the elders of the church; and let them pray over him, anointing him with oil in the name of the Lord:

15 And the prayer of faith shall save the sick, and the Lord shall raise him up; and if he have committed sins, they shall be forgiven him.

16 Confess *your* faults one to another, and pray one for another, that ye may be healed. The effectual fervent prayer of a righteous man availeth much.

17 Elias was a man subject to like passions as we are, and he prayed earnestly that it might not rain: and it rained not on the earth by the space of three years and six months.

18 And he prayed again, and the heaven gave rain, and the earth brought forth her fruit.

NEW AMERICAN STANDARD BIBLE

heard of the endurance of Job and have seen the outcome of the Lord's dealings, that the Lord is full of compassion and *is* merciful.

12 But above all, my brethren, do not swear, either by heaven or by earth or with any other oath; but your yes is to be yes, and your no, no, so that you may not fall under judgment.

13 Is anyone among you suffering? *Then* he must pray. Is anyone cheerful? He is to sing praises.

14 Is anyone among you sick? *Then* he must call for the elders of the church and they are to pray over him, anointing him with oil in the name of the Lord;

15 and the prayer offered in faith will [1]restore the one who is sick, and the Lord will raise him up, and if he has committed sins, they will be forgiven him.

16 Therefore, confess your sins to one another, and pray for one another so that you may be healed. The effective prayer of a righteous man can accomplish much.

17 Elijah was a man with a nature like ours, and he prayed earnestly that it would not rain, and it did not rain on the earth for three years and six months.

18 Then he prayed again, and the sky poured rain and the earth produced its fruit.

5:15 [1] Or *save*

NEW CENTURY VERSION

not give up. You have heard about Job's patience, and you know the Lord's purpose for him in the end. You know the Lord is full of mercy and is kind.

Be Careful What You Say

12My brothers and sisters, above all, do not use an oath when you make a promise. Don't use the name of heaven, earth, or anything else to prove what you say. When you mean yes, say only yes, and when you mean no, say only no so you will not be judged guilty.

The Power of Prayer

13Anyone who is having troubles should pray. Anyone
who is happy should sing praises. 14Anyone who is sick
should call the church's elders. They should pray for and
pour oil on the person[a] in the name of the Lord. 15And the
prayer that is said with faith will make the sick person
well; the Lord will heal that person. And if the person has
sinned, the sins will be forgiven. 16Confess your sins to
each other and pray for each other so God can heal you.
When a believing person prays, great things happen.
17Elijah was a human being just like us. He prayed that it
would not rain, and it did not rain on the land for three
and a half years! 18Then Elijah prayed again, and the rain
came down from the sky, and the land produced crops
again.

5:14 [a] **pour oil on the person** Oil was used in the name of the Lord as a sign that the person was now set apart for God's special attention and care.

CONTEMPORARY ENGLISH VERSION

most. You remember how patient Job was and how the Lord finally helped him. The Lord did this because he is so merciful and kind.

12My friends, above all else, don't take an oath. You must not swear by heaven or by earth or by anything else. "Yes" or "No" is all you need to say. If you say anything more, you will be condemned.

13If you are having trouble, you should pray. And if you
are feeling good, you should sing praises. 14If you are sick,
ask the church leaders[a] to come and pray for you. Ask
them to put olive oil[b] on you in the name of the Lord. 15If
you have faith when you pray for sick people, they will get
well. The Lord will heal them, and if they have sinned, he
will forgive them.

16If you have sinned, you should tell each other what
you have done. Then you can pray for one another and be
healed. The prayer of an innocent person is powerful, and
it can help a lot. 17Elijah was just as human as we are, and
for three and a half years his prayers kept the rain from
falling. 18But when he did pray for rain, it fell from the
skies and made the crops grow.

[a] 5.14 *church leaders*: Or "elders" or "presbyters" or "priests."

[b] 5.14 *olive oil*: The Jewish people used olive oil for healing.

NEW INTERNATIONAL VERSION

persevered. You have heard of Job's perseverance and have seen what the Lord finally brought about. The Lord is full of compassion and mercy.

12 Above all, my brothers, do not swear—not by heaven or by earth or by anything else. Let your "Yes" be yes, and your "No," no, or you will be condemned.

The Prayer of Faith

13 Is any one of you in trouble? He should pray. Is anyone happy? Let him sing songs of praise. 14 Is any one of you sick? He should call the elders of the church to pray over him and anoint him with oil in the name of the Lord. 15 And the prayer offered in faith will make the sick person well; the Lord will raise him up. If he has sinned, he will be forgiven. 16 Therefore confess your sins to each other and pray for each other so that you may be healed. The prayer of a righteous man is powerful and effective.

17 Elijah was a man just like us. He prayed earnestly that it would not rain, and it did not rain on the land for three and a half years. 18 Again he prayed, and the heavens gave rain, and the earth produced its crops.

NEW LIVING TRANSLATION

suffering. Job is an example of a man who endured patiently. From his experience we see how the Lord's plan finally ended in good, for he is full of tenderness and mercy.

12 But most of all, my brothers and sisters, never take an oath, by heaven or earth or anything else. Just say a simple yes or no, so that you will not sin and be condemned for it.

The Power of Prayer

13 Are any among you suffering? They should keep on praying about it. And those who have reason to be thankful should continually sing praises to the Lord.

14 Are any among you sick? They should call for the elders of the church and have them pray over them, anointing them with oil in the name of the Lord. 15 And their prayer offered in faith will heal the sick, and the Lord will make them well. And anyone who has committed sins will be forgiven.

16 Confess your sins to each other and pray for each other so that you may be healed. The earnest prayer of a righteous person has great power and wonderful results. 17 Elijah was as human as we are, and yet when he prayed earnestly that no rain would fall, none fell for the next three and a half years! 18 Then he prayed for rain, and down it poured. The grass turned green, and the crops began to grow again.

NEW KING JAMES VERSION

perseverance of Job and seen the end *intended by* the Lord—that the Lord is very compassionate and merciful.

12 But above all, my brethren, do not swear, either by heaven or by earth or with any other oath. But let your "Yes" be "Yes," and *your* "No," "No," lest you fall into judgment.[d]

Meeting Specific Needs

13 Is anyone among you suffering? Let him pray. Is anyone cheerful? Let him sing psalms. 14 Is anyone among you sick? Let him call for the elders of the church, and let them pray over him, anointing him with oil in the name of the Lord. 15 And the prayer of faith will save the sick, and the Lord will raise him up. And if he has committed sins, he will be forgiven. 16 Confess *your* trespasses[e] to one another, and pray for one another, that you may be healed. The effective, fervent prayer of a righteous man avails much. 17 Elijah was a man with a nature like ours, and he prayed earnestly that it would not rain; and it did not rain on the land for three years and six months. 18 And he prayed again, and the heaven gave rain, and the earth produced its fruit.

5:12 [d] M-Text reads *hypocrisy.* 5:16 [e] NU-Text reads *Therefore confess your sins.*

THE MESSAGE

stay the course! You've heard, of course, of Job's staying power, and you know how God brought it all together for him at the end. That's because God cares, cares right down to the last detail.

And since you know that he cares, let your language show it. Don't add words like "I swear to God" to your own words. Don't show your impatience by concocting oaths to hurry up God. Just say yes or no. Just say what is true. That way, your language can't be used against you.

Prayer to Be Reckoned With

Are you hurting? Pray. Do you feel great? Sing. Are you sick? Call the church leaders together to pray and anoint you with oil in the name of the Master. Believing-prayer will heal you, and Jesus will put you on your feet. And if you've sinned, you'll be forgiven—healed inside and out.

Make this your common practice: Confess your sins to each other and pray for each other so that you can live together whole and healed. The prayer of a person living right with God is something powerful to be reckoned with. Elijah, for instance, human just like us, prayed hard that it wouldn't rain, and it didn't—not a drop for three and a half years. Then he prayed that it would rain, and it did. The showers came and everything started growing again.

KING JAMES VERSION

19 Brethren, if any of you do err from the truth, and one convert him;

20 Let him know, that he which converteth the sinner from the error of his way shall save a soul from death, and shall hide a multitude of sins.

NEW AMERICAN STANDARD BIBLE

19 My brethren, if any among you strays from the truth and one turns him back,

20 let him know that he who turns a sinner from the error of his way will save his soul from death and will cover a multitude of sins.

NEW CENTURY VERSION

Saving a Soul

19My brothers and sisters, if one of you wanders away from the truth, and someone helps that person come back,
20remember this: Anyone who brings a sinner back from the wrong way will save that sinner's soul from death and will cause many sins to be forgiven.

CONTEMPORARY ENGLISH VERSION

19My friends, if any followers have wandered away from the truth, you should try to lead them back. 20If you turn sinners from the wrong way, you will save them from death, and many of their sins will be forgiven.

NEW INTERNATIONAL VERSION

19My brothers, if one of you should wander from the truth and someone should bring him back, 20remember this: Whoever turns a sinner from the error of his way will save him from death and cover over a multitude of sins.

NEW LIVING TRANSLATION

Restore Wandering Believers

19My dear brothers and sisters, if anyone among you wanders away from the truth and is brought back again, 20you can be sure that the one who brings that person back will save that sinner from death and bring about the forgiveness of many sins.

NEW KING JAMES VERSION

Bring Back the Erring One

19Brethren, if anyone among you wanders from the truth, and someone turns him back, 20let him know that he who turns a sinner from the error of his way will save a soul[f] from death and cover a multitude of sins.

5:20 [f] NU-Text reads *his soul.*

THE MESSAGE

My dear friends, if you know people who have wandered off from God's truth, don't write them off. Go after them. Get them back and you will have rescued precious lives from destruction and prevented an epidemic of wandering away from God.

KING JAMES VERSION

THE FIRST EPISTLE OF

ST. PETER

1 Peter, an apostle of Jesus Christ, to the strangers scattered throughout Pontus, Galatia, Cappadocia, Asia, and Bithynia,

2 Elect according to the foreknowledge of God the Father, through sanctification of the Spirit, unto obedience and sprinkling of the blood of Jesus Christ: Grace unto you, and peace, be multiplied.

3 ¶ Blessed *be* the God and Father of our Lord Jesus Christ, which according to his abundant mercy hath begotten us again unto a lively hope by the resurrection of Jesus Christ from the dead,

4 To an inheritance incorruptible, and undefiled, and that fadeth not away, reserved in heaven for you,

5 Who are kept by the power of God through faith unto salvation ready to be revealed in the last time.

6 ¶ Wherein ye greatly rejoice, though now for a season, if need be, ye are in heaviness through manifold temptations:

NEW AMERICAN STANDARD BIBLE

THE FIRST LETTER OF

PETER

A Living Hope, and a Sure Salvation

1 Peter, an apostle of Jesus Christ,

To those who reside as aliens, scattered throughout Pontus, Galatia, Cappadocia, Asia, and Bithynia, who are chosen

2 according to the foreknowledge of God the Father, by the sanctifying work of the Spirit, to obey Jesus Christ and be sprinkled with His blood: May grace and peace be yours in the fullest measure.

3 Blessed be the God and Father of our Lord Jesus Christ, who according to His great mercy has caused us to be born again to a living hope through the resurrection of Jesus Christ from the dead,

4 to *obtain* an inheritance *which is* imperishable and undefiled and will not fade away, reserved in heaven for you,

5 who are protected by the power of God through faith for a salvation ready to be revealed in the last time.

6 In this you greatly rejoice, even though now for a little while, if necessary, you have been distressed by various trials,

NEW CENTURY VERSION

1 PETER

1 From Peter, an apostle of Jesus Christ.

To God's chosen people who are away from their homes and are scattered all around the countries of Pontus, Galatia, Cappadocia, Asia, and Bithynia. 2God planned long ago to choose you by making you his holy people, which is the Spirit's work. God wanted you to obey him and to be made clean by the blood of the death of Jesus Christ.

Grace and peace be yours more and more.

We Have a Living Hope

3Praise be to the God and Father of our Lord Jesus Christ. In God's great mercy he has caused us to be born again into a living hope, because Jesus Christ rose from the dead. 4Now we hope for the blessings God has for his children. These blessings, which cannot be destroyed or be spoiled or lose their beauty, are kept in heaven for you. 5God's power protects you through your faith until salvation is shown to you at the end of time. 6This makes you very happy, even though now for a short time different kinds of troubles may make you sad. 7These troubles come

CONTEMPORARY ENGLISH VERSION

1 PETER

1 From Peter, an apostle of Jesus Christ.

To God's people who are scattered like foreigners in Pontus, Galatia, Cappadocia, Asia, and Bithynia.

2God the Father decided to choose you as his people, and his Spirit has made you holy. You have obeyed Jesus Christ and are sprinkled with his blood.[a]

I pray that God will be kind to you and will keep on giving you peace!

A Real Reason for Hope

3Praise God, the Father of our Lord Jesus Christ. God is so good, and by raising Jesus from death, he has given us new life and a hope that lives on. 4God has something stored up for you in heaven, where it will never decay or be ruined or disappear.

5You have faith in God, whose power will protect you until the last day.[b] Then he will save you, just as he has always planned to do. 6On that day you will be glad, even if you have to go through many hard trials for a while.

[a] 1.2 *sprinkled with his blood*: According to Exodus 24.3-8 the people of Israel were sprinkled with the blood of cows to show they would keep their agreement with God. Peter says that it is the blood of Jesus that seals the agreement between God and his people (see Hebrews 9.18-21).
[b] 1.5 *the last day*: When God will judge all people.

NEW INTERNATIONAL VERSION

1 PETER

1 Peter, an apostle of Jesus Christ,

To God's elect, strangers in the world, scattered through-
out Pontus, Galatia, Cappadocia, Asia and Bithynia, 2who
have been chosen according to the foreknowledge of God
the Father, through the sanctifying work of the Spirit, for
obedience to Jesus Christ and sprinkling by his blood:

Grace and peace be yours in abundance.

Praise to God for a Living Hope

3Praise be to the God and Father of our Lord Jesus
Christ! In his great mercy he has given us new birth into a
living hope through the resurrection of Jesus Christ from
the dead, 4and into an inheritance that can never perish,
spoil or fade—kept in heaven for you, 5who through faith
are shielded by God's power until the coming of the salva-
tion that is ready to be revealed in the last time. 6In this
you greatly rejoice, though now for a little while you may
have had to suffer grief in all kinds of trials. 7These have

NEW LIVING TRANSLATION

1 PETER

Greetings from Peter

1 This letter is from Peter, an apostle of Jesus Christ.
I am writing to God's chosen people who are living
as foreigners in the lands of Pontus, Galatia, Cappadocia,
the province of Asia, and Bithynia. 2God the Father chose
you long ago, and the Spirit has made you holy. As a result,
you have obeyed Jesus Christ and are cleansed by his blood.

May you have more and more of God's special favor and
wonderful peace.

The Hope of Eternal Life

3All honor to the God and Father of our Lord Jesus
Christ, for it is by his boundless mercy that God has given
us the privilege of being born again. Now we live with a
wonderful expectation because Jesus Christ rose again
from the dead. 4For God has reserved a priceless inheri-
tance for his children. It is kept in heaven for you, pure
and undefiled, beyond the reach of change and decay.
5And God, in his mighty power, will protect you until you
receive this salvation, because you are trusting him. It will
be revealed on the last day for all to see. 6So be truly
glad!* There is wonderful joy ahead, even though it is nec-
essary for you to endure many trials for a while.

1:6 Or *So you are truly glad.*

NEW KING JAMES VERSION

THE FIRST EPISTLE OF

PETER

Greeting to the Elect Pilgrims

1 Peter, an apostle of Jesus Christ,

To the pilgrims of the Dispersion in Pontus, Galatia, Cap-
padocia, Asia, and Bithynia, 2elect according to the
foreknowledge of God the Father, in sanctification of the
Spirit, for obedience and sprinkling of the blood of Jesus
Christ:

Grace to you and peace be multiplied.

A Heavenly Inheritance

3Blessed *be* the God and Father of our Lord Jesus Christ,
who according to His abundant mercy has begotten us
again to a living hope through the resurrection of Jesus
Christ from the dead, 4to an inheritance incorruptible and
undefiled and that does not fade away, reserved in heaven
for you, 5who are kept by the power of God through faith
for salvation ready to be revealed in the last time.

6In this you greatly rejoice, though now for a little while,
if need be, you have been grieved by various trials, 7that

THE MESSAGE

1 Peter

1 I, Peter, am an apostle on assignment by Jesus, the Messiah, writing to exiles scattered to the four winds. Not one is missing, not one forgotten. God the Father has his eye on each of you, and has determined by the work of the Spirit to keep you obedient through the sacrifice of Jesus. May everything good from God be yours!

A New Life

What a God we have! And how fortunate we are to have him, this Father of our Master Jesus! Because Jesus was raised from the dead, we've been given a brand-new life and have everything to live for, including a future in heaven—and the future starts now! God is keeping careful watch over us and the future. The Day is coming when you'll have it all—life healed and whole.

I know how great this makes you feel, even though you have to put up with every kind of aggravation in the mean-

KING JAMES VERSION

7 That the trial of your faith, being much more precious than of gold that perisheth, though it be tried with fire, might be found unto praise and honour and glory at the appearing of Jesus Christ:

8 Whom having not seen, ye love; in whom, though now ye see *him* not, yet believing, ye rejoice with joy unspeakable and full of glory:

9 Receiving the end of your faith, *even* the salvation of *your* souls.

10 ¶ Of which salvation the prophets have inquired and searched diligently, who prophesied of the grace *that should come* unto you:

11 Searching what, or what manner of time the Spirit of Christ which was in them did signify, when it testified beforehand the sufferings of Christ, and the glory that should follow.

12 Unto whom it was revealed, that not unto themselves, but unto us they did minister the things, which are now reported unto you by them that have preached the gospel unto you with the Holy Ghost sent down from heaven; which things the angels desire to look into.

13 ¶ Wherefore gird up the loins of your mind, be sober, and hope to the end for the grace that is to be brought unto you at the revelation of Jesus Christ;

NEW AMERICAN STANDARD BIBLE

7 so that the proof of your faith, *being* more precious than gold which is perishable, even though tested by fire, may be found to result in praise and glory and honor at the revelation of Jesus Christ;

8 and though you have not seen Him, you love Him, and though you do not see Him now, but believe in Him, you greatly rejoice with joy inexpressible and full of glory,

9 obtaining as the outcome of your faith the salvation of [1]your souls.

10 As to this salvation, the prophets who prophesied of the grace that *would come* to you made careful searches and inquiries,

11 seeking to know what person or time the Spirit of Christ within them was indicating as He predicted the sufferings of Christ and the glories to follow.

12 It was revealed to them that they were not serving themselves, but you, in these things which now have been announced to you through those who preached the gospel to you by the Holy Spirit sent from heaven—things into which angels long to look.

13 Therefore, prepare your minds for action, keep sober *in spirit,* fix your hope completely on the grace to be brought to you at the revelation of Jesus Christ.

1:9 [1] One early ms does not contain *your*

NEW CENTURY VERSION

to prove that your faith is pure. This purity of faith is
worth more than gold, which can be proved to be pure by
fire but will ruin. But the purity of your faith will bring
you praise and glory and honor when Jesus Christ is
shown to you. [8]You have not seen Christ, but still you love
him. You cannot see him now, but you believe in him. So
you are filled with a joy that cannot be explained, a joy full
of glory. [9]And you are receiving the goal of your faith—the
salvation of your souls.

[10]The prophets searched carefully and tried to learn
about this salvation. They prophesied about the grace that
was coming to you. [11]The Spirit of Christ was in the proph-
ets, telling in advance about the sufferings of Christ and
about the glory that would follow those sufferings. The
prophets tried to learn about what the Spirit was showing
them, when those things would happen, and what the
world would be like at that time. [12]It was shown them that
their service was not for themselves but for you, when they
told about the truths you have now heard. Those who
preached the Good News to you told you those things with
the help of the Holy Spirit who was sent from heaven—
things into which angels desire to look.

A Call to Holy Living

[13]So prepare your minds for service and have self-con-
trol. All your hope should be for the gift of grace that will
be yours when Jesus Christ is shown to you. [14]Now that

CONTEMPORARY ENGLISH VERSION

[7]Your faith will be like gold that has been tested in a fire.
And these trials will prove that your faith is worth much
more than gold that can be destroyed. They will show that
you will be given praise and honor and glory when Jesus
Christ returns.

[8]You have never seen Jesus, and you don't see him now.
But still you love him and have faith in him, and no words
can tell how glad and happy [9]you are to be saved. That's
why you have faith.

[10]Some prophets told how kind God would be to you,
and they searched hard to find out more about the way
you would be saved. [11]The Spirit of Christ was in them and
was telling them how Christ would suffer and would then
be given great honor. So they searched to find out exactly
who Christ would be and when this would happen. [12]But
they were told that they were serving you and not them-
selves. They preached to you by the power of the Holy
Spirit, who was sent from heaven. And their message was
only for you, even though angels would like to know more
about it.

Chosen To Live a Holy Life

[13]Be alert and think straight. Put all your hope in how
kind God will be to you when Jesus Christ appears.

NEW INTERNATIONAL VERSION

come so that your faith—of greater worth than gold, which perishes even though refined by fire—may be proved genuine and may result in praise, glory and honor when Jesus Christ is revealed. 8Though you have not seen him, you love him; and even though you do not see him now, you believe in him and are filled with an inexpressible and glorious joy, 9for you are receiving the goal of your faith, the salvation of your souls.

10Concerning this salvation, the prophets, who spoke of the grace that was to come to you, searched intently and with the greatest care, 11trying to find out the time and circumstances to which the Spirit of Christ in them was pointing when he predicted the sufferings of Christ and the glories that would follow. 12It was revealed to them that they were not serving themselves but you, when they spoke of the things that have now been told you by those who have preached the gospel to you by the Holy Spirit sent from heaven. Even angels long to look into these things.

Be Holy

13Therefore, prepare your minds for action; be self-controlled; set your hope fully on the grace to be given you when Jesus Christ is revealed. 14As obedient children, do

NEW LIVING TRANSLATION

7These trials are only to test your faith, to show that it is strong and pure. It is being tested as fire tests and purifies gold—and your faith is far more precious to God than mere gold. So if your faith remains strong after being tried by fiery trials, it will bring you much praise and glory and honor on the day when Jesus Christ is revealed to the whole world.

8You love him even though you have never seen him. Though you do not see him, you trust him; and even now you are happy with a glorious, inexpressible joy. 9Your reward for trusting him will be the salvation of your souls.

10This salvation was something the prophets wanted to know more about. They prophesied about this gracious salvation prepared for you, even though they had many questions as to what it all could mean. 11They wondered what the Spirit of Christ within them was talking about when he told them in advance about Christ's suffering and his great glory afterward. They wondered when and to whom all this would happen.

12They were told that these things would not happen during their lifetime, but many years later, during yours. And now this Good News has been announced by those who preached to you in the power of the Holy Spirit sent from heaven. It is all so wonderful that even the angels are eagerly watching these things happen.

A Call to Holy Living

13So think clearly and exercise self-control. Look forward to the special blessings that will come to you at the return of Jesus Christ. 14Obey God because you are his children.

NEW KING JAMES VERSION

the genuineness of your faith, *being* much more precious than gold that perishes, though it is tested by fire, may be found to praise, honor, and glory at the revelation of Jesus Christ, 8whom having not seen[a] you love. Though now you do not see *Him,* yet believing, you rejoice with joy inexpressible and full of glory, 9receiving the end of your faith—the salvation of *your* souls.

10Of this salvation the prophets have inquired and searched carefully, who prophesied of the grace *that would come* to you, 11searching what, or what manner of time, the Spirit of Christ who was in them was indicating when He testified beforehand the sufferings of Christ and the glories that would follow. 12To them it was revealed that, not to themselves, but to us[b] they were ministering the things which now have been reported to you through those who have preached the gospel to you by the Holy Spirit sent from heaven—things which angels desire to look into.

Living Before God Our Father

13Therefore gird up the loins of your mind, be sober, and rest *your* hope fully upon the grace that is to be brought to you at the revelation of Jesus Christ; 14as obedient children,

1:8 [a] M-Text reads *known.* 1:12 [b] NU-Text and M-Text read *you.*

THE MESSAGE

time. Pure gold put in the fire comes out of it *proved* pure; genuine faith put through this suffering comes out *proved* genuine. When Jesus wraps this all up, it's your faith, not your gold, that God will have on display as evidence of his victory.

You never saw him, yet you love him. You still don't see him, yet you trust him—with laughter and singing. Because you kept on believing, you'll get what you're looking forward to: total salvation.

The prophets who told us this was coming asked a lot of questions about this gift of life God was preparing. The Messiah's Spirit let them in on some of it—that the Messiah would experience suffering, followed by glory. They clamored to know who and when. All they were told was that they were serving you, you who by orders from heaven have now heard for yourselves—through the Holy Spirit—the Message of those prophecies fulfilled. Do you realize how fortunate you are? Angels would have given anything to be in on this!

A Future in God

So roll up your sleeves, put your mind in gear, be totally ready to receive the gift that's coming when Jesus arrives. Don't lazily slip back into those old grooves of evil, doing just what you feel like doing. You didn't know any better then; you do now. As obedient children, let yourselves be

KING JAMES VERSION

14 As obedient children, not fashioning yourselves according to the former lusts in your ignorance:

15 But as he which hath called you is holy, so be ye holy in all manner of conversation;

16 Because it is written, Be ye holy; for I am holy.

17 And if ye call on the Father, who without respect of persons judgeth according to every man's work, pass the time of your sojourning *here* in fear:

18 Forasmuch as ye know that ye were not redeemed with corruptible things, *as* silver and gold, from your vain conversation *received* by tradition from your fathers;

19 But with the precious blood of Christ, as of a lamb without blemish and without spot:

20 Who verily was foreordained before the foundation of the world, but was manifest in these last times for you,

21 Who by him do believe in God, that raised him up from the dead, and gave him glory; that your faith and hope might be in God.

22 Seeing ye have purified your souls in obeying the truth through the Spirit unto unfeigned love of the brethren, *see that ye* love one another with a pure heart fervently:

23 Being born again, not of corruptible seed, but of incorruptible, by the word of God, which liveth and abideth for ever.

NEW AMERICAN STANDARD BIBLE

14 As obedient children, do not be conformed to the former lusts *which were yours* in your ignorance,

15 but like the Holy One who called you, be holy yourselves also in all *your* behavior;

16 because it is written, "YOU SHALL BE HOLY, FOR I AM HOLY."

17 If you address as Father the One who impartially judges according to each one's work, conduct yourselves in fear during the time of your stay *on earth;*

18 knowing that you were not redeemed with perishable things like silver or gold from your futile way of life inherited from your forefathers,

19 but with precious blood, as of a lamb unblemished and spotless, *the blood* of Christ.

20 For He was foreknown before the foundation of the world, but has appeared in these last times for the sake of you

21 who through Him are believers in God, who raised Him from the dead and gave Him glory, so that your faith and hope are in God.

22 Since you have in obedience to the truth purified your souls for a sincere love of the brethren, fervently love one another from [2]the heart,

23 for you have been born again not of seed which is perishable but imperishable, *that is,* through the living and enduring word of God.

1:22 [2] Two early mss read *a clean heart*

NEW CENTURY VERSION

you are obedient children of God do not live as you did in
the past. You did not understand, so you did the evil
things you wanted. 15But be holy in all you do, just as
God, the One who called you, is holy. 16It is written in the
Scriptures: "You must be holy, because I am holy."[a]

17You pray to God and call him Father, and he judges
each person's work equally. So while you are here on
earth, you should live with respect for God. 18You know
that in the past you were living in a worthless way, a way
passed down from the people who lived before you. But
you were saved from that useless life. You were bought,
not with something that ruins like gold or silver, 19but
with the precious blood of Christ, who was like a pure and
perfect lamb. 20Christ was chosen before the world was
made, but he was shown to the world in these last times
for your sake. 21Through Christ you believe in God, who
raised Christ from the dead and gave him glory. So your
faith and your hope are in God.

22Now that you have made your souls pure by obeying
the truth, you can have true love for your Christian broth-
ers and sisters.[b] So love each other deeply with all your
heart. 23You have been born again, and this new life did
not come from something that dies, but from something
that cannot die. You were born again through God's living
message that continues forever. 24The Scripture says,

1:16 [a] **"You must be...holy."** Quotation from Leviticus 11:45; 19:2; 20:7.
1:22 [b] **brothers and sisters** Although the Greek text says "brothers" here and throughout this book, Peter's words were meant for the entire church, including men and women.

CONTEMPORARY ENGLISH VERSION

14Behave like obedient children. Don't let your lives be
controlled by your desires, as they used to be. 15Always
live as God's holy people should, because God is the one
who chose you, and he is holy. 16That's why the Scriptures
say, "I am the holy God, and you must be holy too."

17You say that God is your Father, but God doesn't have
favorites! He judges all people by what they do. So you
must honor God while you live as strangers here on earth.
18You were rescued[c] from the useless way of life that you
learned from your ancestors. But you know that you were
not rescued by such things as silver or gold that don't last
forever. 19You were rescued by the precious blood of Christ,
that spotless and innocent lamb. 20Christ was chosen even
before the world was created, but because of you, he did
not come until these last days. 21And when he did come, it
was to lead you to have faith in God, who raised him from
death and honored him in a glorious way. That's why you
have put your faith and hope in God.

22You obeyed the truth,[d] and your souls were made
pure. Now you sincerely love each other. But you must
keep on loving with all your heart. 23Do this because God
has given you new birth by his message that lives on for-
ever. 24The Scriptures say,

[c] **1.18** *rescued*: The Greek word often, though not always, means payment of a price to free a slave or prisoner. [d] **1.22** *You obeyed the truth*: Some manuscripts add "by the power of the Spirit."

NEW INTERNATIONAL VERSION

not conform to the evil desires you had when you lived in ignorance. 15But just as he who called you is holy, so be holy in all you do; 16for it is written: "Be holy, because I am holy."[a]

17Since you call on a Father who judges each man's work impartially, live your lives as strangers here in reverent fear. 18For you know that it was not with perishable things such as silver or gold that you were redeemed from the empty way of life handed down to you from your forefathers, 19but with the precious blood of Christ, a lamb without blemish or defect. 20He was chosen before the creation of the world, but was revealed in these last times for your sake. 21Through him you believe in God, who raised him from the dead and glorified him, and so your faith and hope are in God.

22Now that you have purified yourselves by obeying the truth so that you have sincere love for your brothers, love one another deeply, from the heart.[b] 23For you have been born again, not of perishable seed, but of imperishable, through the living and enduring word of God. 24For,

[a] *16* Lev. 11:44,45; 19:2; 20:7 [b] *22* Some early manuscripts *from a pure heart*

NEW LIVING TRANSLATION

Don't slip back into your old ways of doing evil; you didn't know any better then. 15But now you must be holy in everything you do, just as God—who chose you to be his children—is holy. 16For he himself has said, "You must be holy because I am holy."*

17And remember that the heavenly Father to whom you pray has no favorites when he judges. He will judge or reward you according to what you do. So you must live in reverent fear of him during your time as foreigners here on earth. 18For you know that God paid a ransom to save you from the empty life you inherited from your ancestors. And the ransom he paid was not mere gold or silver. 19He paid for you with the precious lifeblood of Christ, the sinless, spotless Lamb of God. 20God chose him for this purpose long before the world began, but now in these final days, he was sent to the earth for all to see. And he did this for you.

21Through Christ you have come to trust in God. And because God raised Christ from the dead and gave him great glory, your faith and hope can be placed confidently in God. 22Now you can have sincere love for each other as brothers and sisters* because you were cleansed from your sins when you accepted the truth of the Good News. So see to it that you really do love each other intensely with all your hearts.*

23For you have been born again. Your new life did not come from your earthly parents because the life they gave you will end in death. But this new life will last forever because it comes from the eternal, living word of God. 24As the prophet says,

1:16 Lev 11:44-45; 19:2; 20:7. **1:22a** Greek *can have brotherly love.* **1:22b** Some manuscripts read *with a pure heart.*

NEW KING JAMES VERSION

not conforming yourselves to the former lusts, *as* in your ignorance; 15but as He who called you *is* holy, you also be holy in all *your* conduct, 16because it is written, *"Be holy, for I am holy."*[c]

17And if you call on the Father, who without partiality judges according to each one's work, conduct yourselves throughout the time of your stay *here* in fear; 18knowing that you were not redeemed with corruptible things, *like* silver or gold, from your aimless conduct *received* by tradition from your fathers, 19but with the precious blood of Christ, as of a lamb without blemish and without spot. 20He indeed was foreordained before the foundation of the world, but was manifest in these last times for you 21who through Him believe in God, who raised Him from the dead and gave Him glory, so that your faith and hope are in God.

The Enduring Word

22Since you have purified your souls in obeying the truth through the Spirit[d] in sincere love of the brethren, love one another fervently with a pure heart, 23having been born again, not of corruptible seed but incorruptible, through the word of God which lives and abides forever,[e] 24because

1:16 [c] Leviticus 11:44, 45; 19:2; 20:7 **1:22** [d] NU-Text omits *through the Spirit.* **1:23** [e] NU-Text omits *forever.*

THE MESSAGE

pulled into a way of life shaped by God's life, a life energetic and blazing with holiness. God said, "I am holy; you be holy."

You call out to God for help and he helps—he's a good Father that way. But don't forget, he's also a responsible Father, and won't let you get by with sloppy living.

Your life is a journey you must travel with a deep consciousness of God. It cost God plenty to get you out of that dead-end, empty-headed life you grew up in. He paid with Christ's sacred blood, you know. He died like an unblemished, sacrificial lamb. And this was no afterthought. Even though it has only lately—at the end of the ages—become public knowledge, God always knew he was going to do this for you. It's because of this sacrificed Messiah, whom God then raised from the dead and glorified, that you trust God, that you know you have a future in God.

Now that you've cleaned up your lives by following the truth, love one another as if your lives depended on it. Your new life is not like your old life. Your old birth came from mortal sperm; your new birth comes from God's living Word. Just think: a life conceived by God himself! That's why the prophet said,

KING JAMES VERSION

24 ¶ For all flesh *is* as grass, and all the glory of man as the flower of grass. The grass withereth, and the flower thereof falleth away:

25 But the word of the Lord endureth for ever. And this is the word which by the gospel is preached unto you.

2 Wherefore laying aside all malice, and all guile, and hypocrisies, and envies, and all evil speakings,

2 As newborn babes, desire the sincere milk of the word, that ye may grow thereby:

3 If so be ye have tasted that the Lord *is* gracious.

4 ¶ To whom coming, *as unto* a living stone, disallowed indeed of men, but chosen of God, *and* precious,

5 Ye also, as lively stones, are built up a spiritual house, an holy priesthood, to offer up spiritual sacrifices, acceptable to God by Jesus Christ.

6 Wherefore also it is contained in the scripture, Behold, I lay in Sion a chief corner stone, elect, precious:

NEW AMERICAN STANDARD BIBLE

24 For,
"ALL FLESH IS LIKE GRASS,
AND ALL ITS GLORY LIKE THE FLOWER OF GRASS.
THE GRASS WITHERS,
AND THE FLOWER FALLS OFF,
25 BUT THE WORD OF THE LORD ENDURES FOREVER."
And this is the word which was preached to you.

As Newborn Babes

2 Therefore, putting aside all malice and all deceit and hypocrisy and envy and all slander,

2 like newborn babies, long for the pure milk of the word, so that by it you may grow in respect to salvation,

3 if you have tasted the kindness of the Lord.

As Living Stones

4 And coming to Him as to a living stone which has been rejected by men, but is choice and precious in the sight of God,

5 you also, as living stones, are being built up as a spiritual house for a holy priesthood, to offer up spiritual sacrifices acceptable to God through Jesus Christ.

6 For *this* is contained in Scripture:
"BEHOLD, I LAY IN ZION A CHOICE STONE, A PRECIOUS
CORNER *stone*,

NEW CENTURY VERSION

"All people are like the grass,
and all their glory is like the flowers of the field.
The grass dies and the flowers fall,
25 but the word of the Lord will live forever."
Isaiah 40:6–8

And this is the word that was preached to you.

Jesus Is the Living Stone

2 So then, rid yourselves of all evil, all lying, hypocrisy,
jealousy, and evil speech. 2As newborn babies want
milk, you should want the pure and simple teaching. By it
you can grow up and be saved, 3because you have already
examined and seen how good the Lord is.

4Come to the Lord Jesus, the "stone"[a] that lives. The
people of the world did not want this stone, but he was the
stone God chose, and he was precious. 5You also are like
living stones, so let yourselves be used to build a spiritual
temple—to be holy priests who offer spiritual sacrifices to
God. He will accept those sacrifices through Jesus Christ.
6The Scripture says:

"I will put a stone in the ground in Jerusalem.
Everything will be built on this important and
precious rock.

2:4 [a] **"stone"** The most important stone in God's spiritual temple or house (his people).

CONTEMPORARY ENGLISH VERSION

"Humans wither like grass,
and their glory fades
like wild flowers.
Grass dries up,
and flowers fall
to the ground.
25 But what the Lord has said
will stand forever."

Our good news to you is what the Lord has said.

A Living Stone and a Holy Nation

2 Stop being hateful! Quit trying to fool people, and
start being sincere. Don't be jealous or say cruel
things about others. 2Be like newborn babies who are
thirsty for the pure spiritual milk that will help you grow
and be saved. 3You have already found out how good the
Lord really is.

4Come to Jesus Christ. He is the living stone that people
have rejected, but which God has chosen and highly hon-
ored. 5And now you are living stones that are being used to
build a spiritual house. You are also a group of holy priests,
and with the help of Jesus Christ you will offer sacrifices
that please God. 6It is just as God says in the Scriptures,

"Look! I am placing in Zion
a choice and precious
cornerstone.

NEW INTERNATIONAL VERSION

"All men are like grass,
and all their glory is like the flowers of the field;
the grass withers and the flowers fall,
25 but the word of the Lord stands forever."[c]

And this is the word that was preached to you.
2 Therefore, rid yourselves of all malice and all deceit,
hypocrisy, envy, and slander of every kind. 2 Like new-
born babies, crave pure spiritual milk, so that by it you
may grow up in your salvation, 3 now that you have tasted
that the Lord is good.

The Living Stone and a Chosen People

4 As you come to him, the living Stone—rejected by men
but chosen by God and precious to him— 5 you also, like
living stones, are being built into a spiritual house to be a
holy priesthood, offering spiritual sacrifices acceptable to
God through Jesus Christ. 6 For in Scripture it says:

"See, I lay a stone in Zion,
a chosen and precious cornerstone,

[c] *25* Isaiah 40:6–8

NEW LIVING TRANSLATION

"People are like grass that dies away;
their beauty fades as quickly as the beauty of
wildflowers.
The grass withers,
and the flowers fall away.
25 But the word of the Lord will last forever."*

And that word is the Good News that was preached to you.
2 So get rid of all malicious behavior and deceit. Don't
just pretend to be good! Be done with hypocrisy and
jealousy and backstabbing. 2 You must crave pure spiritual
milk so that you can grow into the fullness of your salva-
tion. Cry out for this nourishment as a baby cries for milk,
3 now that you have had a taste of the Lord's kindness.

Living Stones for God's House

4 Come to Christ, who is the living cornerstone of God's
temple. He was rejected by the people, but he is precious to
God who chose him.
5 And now God is building you, as living stones, into his
spiritual temple. What's more, you are God's holy priests,
who offer the spiritual sacrifices that please him because
of Jesus Christ. 6 As the Scriptures express it,

"I am placing a stone in Jerusalem,*
a chosen cornerstone,

1:24-25 Isa 40:6-8. 2:6a Greek *in Zion.*

NEW KING JAMES VERSION

"*All flesh is as grass,*
And all the glory of man[f] *as the flower of the grass.*
The grass withers,
And its flower falls away,
25 *But the word of the* LORD *endures forever.*"[g]

Now this is the word which by the gospel was preached to
you.
2 Therefore, laying aside all malice, all deceit, hypocri-
sy, envy, and all evil speaking, 2 as newborn babes,
desire the pure milk of the word, that you may grow there-
by,[a] 3 if indeed you have tasted that the Lord *is* gracious.

The Chosen Stone and His Chosen People

4 Coming to Him *as to* a living stone, rejected indeed by
men, but chosen by God *and* precious, 5 you also, as living
stones, are being built up a spiritual house, a holy priest-
hood, to offer up spiritual sacrifices acceptable to God
through Jesus Christ. 6 Therefore it is also contained in the
Scripture,

"*Behold, I lay in Zion*
A chief cornerstone, elect, precious,

1:24 [f] NU-Text reads *all its glory.* 1:25 [g] Isaiah 40:6–8
2:2 [a] NU-Text adds *up to salvation.*

THE MESSAGE

"The old life is a grass life,
its beauty as short-lived as wildflowers;
Grass dries up, flowers droop,
God's Word goes on and on forever."

This is the Word that conceived the new life in you.
2 So clean house! Make a clean sweep of malice and
pretense, envy and hurtful talk. You've had a taste of
God. Now, like infants at the breast, drink deep of God's
pure kindness. Then you'll grow up mature and whole in
God.

The Stone

Welcome to the living Stone, the source of life. The
workmen took one look and threw it out; God set it in the
place of honor. Present yourselves as building stones for
the construction of a sanctuary vibrant with life, in which
you'll serve as holy priests offering Christ-approved lives
up to God. The Scriptures provide precedent:

"Look! I'm setting a stone in Zion,
a cornerstone in the place of honor.

KING JAMES VERSION

and he that believeth on him shall not be confounded.
7 Unto you therefore which believe *he is* precious: but
unto them which be disobedient, the stone which the
builders disallowed, the same is made the head of the cor-
ner,
8 And a stone of stumbling, and a rock of offence, *even*
to them which stumble at the word, being disobedient:
whereunto also they were appointed.
9 But ye *are* a chosen generation, a royal priesthood, an
holy nation, a peculiar people; that ye should shew forth
the praises of him who hath called you out of darkness
into his marvellous light:
10 Which in time past *were* not a people, but *are* now
the people of God: which had not obtained mercy, but now
have obtained mercy.

NEW AMERICAN STANDARD BIBLE

AND HE WHO BELIEVES IN HIM WILL NOT BE
DISAPPOINTED."
7 This precious value, then, is for you who believe; but
for those who disbelieve,
"THE STONE WHICH THE BUILDERS REJECTED,
THIS BECAME THE VERY CORNER *stone*,"
8 and,
"A STONE OF STUMBLING AND A ROCK OF OFFENSE";
for they stumble because they are disobedient to the word,
and to this *doom* they were also appointed.
9 But you are A CHOSEN RACE, A royal PRIESTHOOD, A HOLY
NATION, A PEOPLE FOR *God's* OWN POSSESSION, so that you
may proclaim the excellencies of Him who has called you
out of darkness into His marvelous light;
10 for you once were NOT A PEOPLE, but now you are THE
PEOPLE OF GOD; you had NOT RECEIVED MERCY, but now you
have RECEIVED MERCY.

NEW CENTURY VERSION

Anyone who trusts in him
will never be disappointed." *Isaiah 28:16*
7 This stone is worth much to you who believe. But to the
people who do not believe,
"the stone that the builders rejected
has become the cornerstone." *Psalm 118:22*
8 Also, he is
"a stone that causes people to stumble,
a rock that makes them fall." *Isaiah 8:14*
They stumble because they do not obey what God says,
which is what God planned to happen to them.
9 But you are a chosen people, royal priests, a holy
nation, a people for God's own possession. You were cho-
sen to tell about the wonderful acts of God, who called you
out of darkness into his wonderful light. 10 At one time you
were not a people, but now you are God's people. In the
past you had never received mercy, but now you have
received God's mercy.

CONTEMPORARY ENGLISH VERSION

No one who has faith
in that one
will be disappointed."

7 You are followers of the Lord, and that stone is pre-
cious to you. But it isn't precious to those who refuse to
follow him. They are the builders who tossed aside the
stone that turned out to be the most important one of all.
8 They disobeyed the message and stumbled and fell over
that stone, because they were doomed.
9 But you are God's chosen and special people. You are a
group of royal priests and a holy nation. God has brought
you out of darkness into his marvelous light. Now you
must tell all the wonderful things that he has done. The
Scriptures say,

10 "Once you were nobody.
Now you are God's people.
At one time no one
had pity on you.
Now God has treated you
with kindness.

NEW INTERNATIONAL VERSION

and the one who trusts in him
will never be put to shame."[a]

7 Now to you who believe, this stone is precious. But to
those who do not believe,

"The stone the builders rejected
has become the capstone,[b]"[c]

8 and,

"A stone that causes men to stumble
and a rock that makes them fall."[d]

They stumble because they disobey the message—which is
also what they were destined for.

9 But you are a chosen people, a royal priesthood, a holy
nation, a people belonging to God, that you may declare
the praises of him who called you out of darkness into his
wonderful light. 10 Once you were not a people, but now
you are the people of God; once you had not received
mercy, but now you have received mercy.

[a] *6* Isaiah 28:16 [b] *7* Or *cornerstone* [c] *7* Psalm 118:22
[d] *8* Isaiah 8:14

NEW LIVING TRANSLATION

and anyone who believes in him
will never be disappointed.*"

7 Yes, he is very precious to you who believe. But for those
who reject him,

"The stone that was rejected by the builders
has now become the cornerstone."*

8 And the Scriptures also say,

"He is the stone that makes people stumble,
the rock that will make them fall."*

They stumble because they do not listen to God's word or
obey it, and so they meet the fate that has been planned
for them.

9 But you are not like that, for you are a chosen people.
You are a kingdom of priests, God's holy nation, his very
own possession. This is so you can show others the good-
ness of God, for he called you out of the darkness into his
wonderful light.

10 "Once you were not a people;
now you are the people of God.
Once you received none of God's mercy;
now you have received his mercy."*

2:6b Or *will never be put to shame.* Isa 28:16. **2:7** Ps 118:22.
2:8 Isa 8:14. **2:10** Hos 1:6, 9; 2:23.

NEW KING JAMES VERSION

And he who believes on Him will by no means be put
to shame."[b]

7 Therefore, to you who believe, *He is* precious; but to
those who are disobedient,[c]

"The stone which the builders rejected
Has become the chief cornerstone,"[d]

8 and

"A stone of stumbling
And a rock of offense."[e]

They stumble, being disobedient to the word, to which they
also were appointed.

9 But you *are* a chosen generation, a royal priesthood, a
holy nation, His own special people, that you may pro-
claim the praises of Him who called you out of darkness
into His marvelous light; 10 who once *were* not a people but
are now the people of God, who had not obtained mercy
but now have obtained mercy.

2:6 [b] Isaiah 28:16 **2:7** [c] NU-Text reads *to those who disbelieve.*
[d] Psalm 118:22 **2:8** [e] Isaiah 8:14

THE MESSAGE

Whoever trusts in this stone as a foundation
will never have cause to regret it."

To you who trust him, he's a Stone to be proud of, but to
those who refuse to trust him,

"The stone the workmen threw out
is now the chief foundation stone."

For the untrusting it's

". . . a stone to trip over,
a boulder blocking the way."

They trip and fall because they refuse to obey, just as pre-
dicted.

But you are the ones chosen by God, chosen for the high
calling of priestly work, chosen to be a holy people, God's
instruments to do his work and speak out for him, to tell
others of the night-and-day difference he made for you—
from nothing to something, from rejected to accepted.

✠

KING JAMES VERSION

11 Dearly beloved, I beseech *you* as strangers and pilgrims, abstain from fleshly lusts, which war against the soul;

12 Having your conversation honest among the Gentiles: that, whereas they speak against you as evildoers, they may by *your* good works, which they shall behold, glorify God in the day of visitation.

13 ¶ Submit yourselves to every ordinance of man for the Lord's sake: whether it be to the king, as supreme;

14 Or unto governors, as unto them that are sent by him for the punishment of evildoers, and for the praise of them that do well.

15 For so is the will of God, that with well doing ye may put to silence the ignorance of foolish men:

16 As free, and not using *your* liberty for a cloke of maliciousness, but as the servants of God.

17 Honour all *men*. Love the brotherhood. Fear God. Honour the king.

18 Servants, *be* subject to *your* masters with all fear; not only to the good and gentle, but also to the froward.

19 For this *is* thankworthy, if a man for conscience toward God endure grief, suffering wrongfully.

20 For what glory *is it*, if, when ye be buffeted for your faults, ye shall take it patiently? but if, when ye do well,

NEW AMERICAN STANDARD BIBLE

11 Beloved, I urge you as aliens and strangers to abstain from fleshly lusts which wage war against the soul.

12 Keep your behavior excellent among the Gentiles, so that in the thing in which they slander you as evildoers, they may because of your good deeds, as they observe *them,* glorify God in the day of [l]visitation.

Honor Authority

13 Submit yourselves for the Lord's sake to every human institution, whether to a king as the one in authority,

14 or to governors as sent by him for the punishment of evildoers and the praise of those who do right.

15 For such is the will of God that by doing right you may silence the ignorance of foolish men.

16 *Act* as free men, and do not use your freedom as a covering for evil, but *use it* as bondslaves of God.

17 Honor all people, love the brotherhood, fear God, honor the king.

18 Servants, be submissive to your masters with all respect, not only to those who are good and gentle, but also to those who are unreasonable.

19 For this *finds* favor, if for the sake of conscience toward God a person bears up under sorrows when suffering unjustly.

20 For what credit is there if, when you sin and are harshly treated, you endure it with patience? But if when

2:12 [l] I.e. Christ's coming again in judgment

NEW CENTURY VERSION

Live for God

11Dear friends, you are like foreigners and strangers in this world. I beg you to avoid the evil things your bodies want to do that fight against your soul. 12People who do not believe are living all around you and might say that you are doing wrong. Live such good lives that they will see the good things you do and will give glory to God on the day when Christ comes again.

Yield to Every Human Authority

13For the Lord's sake, yield to the people who have authority in this world: the king, who is the highest authority, 14and the leaders who are sent by him to punish those who do wrong and to praise those who do right. 15It is God's desire that by doing good you should stop foolish people from saying stupid things about you. 16Live as free people, but do not use your freedom as an excuse to do evil. Live as servants of God. 17Show respect for all people: Love the brothers and sisters of God's family, respect God, honor the king.

Follow Christ's Example

18Slaves, yield to the authority of your masters with all respect, not only those who are good and kind, but also those who are dishonest. 19A person might have to suffer even when it is unfair, but if he thinks of God and stands the pain, God is pleased. 20If you are beaten for doing wrong, there is no reason to praise you for being patient in

CONTEMPORARY ENGLISH VERSION

Live as God's Servants Should

11Dear friends, you are foreigners and strangers on this earth. So I beg you not to surrender to those desires that fight against you. 12Always let others see you behaving properly, even though they may still accuse you of doing wrong. Then on the day of judgment, they will honor God by telling the good things they saw you do.

13The Lord wants you to obey all human authorities, especially the Emperor, who rules over everyone. 14You must also obey governors, because they are sent by the Emperor to punish criminals and to praise good citizens. 15God wants you to silence stupid and ignorant people by doing right. 16You are free, but still you are God's servants, and you must not use your freedom as an excuse for doing wrong. 17Respect everyone and show special love for God's people. Honor God and respect the Emperor.

The Example of Christ's Suffering

18Servants, you must obey your masters and always show respect to them. Do this, not only to those who are kind and thoughtful, but also to those who are cruel. 19God will bless you, even if others treat you unfairly for being loyal to him. 20You don't gain anything by being punished for some wrong you have done. But God will bless you, if

NEW INTERNATIONAL VERSION

[11]Dear friends, I urge you, as aliens and strangers in the world, to abstain from sinful desires, which war against your soul. [12]Live such good lives among the pagans that, though they accuse you of doing wrong, they may see your good deeds and glorify God on the day he visits us.

Submission to Rulers and Masters

[13]Submit yourselves for the Lord's sake to every authority instituted among men: whether to the king, as the supreme authority, [14]or to governors, who are sent by him to punish those who do wrong and to commend those who do right. [15]For it is God's will that by doing good you should silence the ignorant talk of foolish men. [16]Live as free men, but do not use your freedom as a cover-up for evil; live as servants of God. [17]Show proper respect to everyone: Love the brotherhood of believers, fear God, honor the king.

[18]Slaves, submit yourselves to your masters with all respect, not only to those who are good and considerate, but also to those who are harsh. [19]For it is commendable if a man bears up under the pain of unjust suffering because he is conscious of God. [20]But how is it to your credit if you receive a beating for doing wrong and endure it? But if you

NEW LIVING TRANSLATION

[11]Dear brothers and sisters, you are foreigners and aliens here. So I warn you to keep away from evil desires because they fight against your very souls. [12]Be careful how you live among your unbelieving neighbors. Even if they accuse you of doing wrong, they will see your honorable behavior, and they will believe and give honor to God when he comes to judge the world.*

Respecting People in Authority

[13]For the Lord's sake, accept all authority—the king as head of state, [14]and the officials he has appointed. For the king has sent them to punish all who do wrong and to honor those who do right.

[15]It is God's will that your good lives should silence those who make foolish accusations against you. [16]You are not slaves; you are free. But your freedom is not an excuse to do evil. You are free to live as God's slaves. [17]Show respect for everyone. Love your Christian brothers and sisters.* Fear God. Show respect for the king.

Slaves

[18]You who are slaves must accept the authority of your masters. Do whatever they tell you—not only if they are kind and reasonable, but even if they are harsh. [19]For God is pleased with you when, for the sake of your conscience, you patiently endure unfair treatment. [20]Of course, you get no credit for being patient if you are beaten for doing wrong.

2:12 Or *on the day of visitation.* 2:17 Greek *Love the brotherhood.*

NEW KING JAMES VERSION

Living Before the World

[11]Beloved, I beg *you* as sojourners and pilgrims, abstain from fleshly lusts which war against the soul, [12]having your conduct honorable among the Gentiles, that when they speak against you as evildoers, they may, by *your* good works which they observe, glorify God in the day of visitation.

Submission to Government

[13]Therefore submit yourselves to every ordinance of man for the Lord's sake, whether to the king as supreme, [14]or to governors, as to those who are sent by him for the punishment of evildoers and *for the* praise of those who do good. [15]For this is the will of God, that by doing good you may put to silence the ignorance of foolish men— [16]as free, yet not using liberty as a cloak for vice, but as bondservants of God. [17]Honor all *people.* Love the brotherhood. Fear God. Honor the king.

Submission to Masters

[18]Servants, *be* submissive to *your* masters with all fear, not only to the good and gentle, but also to the harsh. [19]For this *is* commendable, if because of conscience toward God one endures grief, suffering wrongfully. [20]For what credit *is it* if, when you are beaten for your faults, you take

THE MESSAGE

Friends, this world is not your home, so don't make yourselves cozy in it. Don't indulge your ego at the expense of your soul. Live an exemplary life among the natives so that your actions will refute their prejudices. Then they'll be won over to God's side and be there to join in the celebration when he arrives.

Make the Master proud of you by being good citizens. Respect the authorities, whatever their level; they are God's emissaries for keeping order. It is God's will that by doing good, you might cure the ignorance of the fools who think you're a danger to society. Exercise your freedom by serving God, not by breaking the rules. Treat everyone you meet with dignity. Love your spiritual family. Revere God. Respect the government.

The Kind of Life He Lived

You who are servants, be good servants to your masters—not just to good masters, but also to bad ones. What counts is that you put up with it for God's sake when you're treated badly for no good reason. There's no particular virtue in accepting punishment that you well deserve.

KING JAMES VERSION

and suffer *for it*, ye take it patiently, this *is* acceptable
with God.
21 For even hereunto were ye called: because Christ
also suffered for us, leaving us an example, that ye should
follow his steps:
22 Who did no sin, neither was guile found in his
mouth:
23 Who, when he was reviled, reviled not again; when
he suffered, he threatened not; but committed *himself* to
him that judgeth righteously:
24 Who his own self bare our sins in his own body on
the tree, that we, being dead to sins, should live unto righ-
teousness: by whose stripes ye were healed.
25 For ye were as sheep going astray; but are now
returned unto the Shepherd and Bishop of your souls.
3 Likewise, ye wives, *be* in subjection to your own hus-
bands; that, if any obey not the word, they also may
without the word be won by the conversation of the wives;

NEW AMERICAN STANDARD BIBLE

you do what is right and suffer *for it* you patiently endure
it, this *finds* favor with God.

Christ Is Our Example

21 For you have been called for this purpose, since
Christ also suffered for you, leaving you an example for
you to follow in His steps,
22 WHO COMMITTED NO SIN, NOR WAS ANY DECEIT FOUND IN
HIS MOUTH;
23 and while being reviled, He did not revile in return;
while suffering, He uttered no threats, but kept entrusting
Himself to Him who judges righteously;
24 and He Himself bore our sins in His body on the
cross, so that we might die to sin and live to righteous-
ness; for by His wounds you were healed.
25 For you were continually straying like sheep, but now
you have returned to the Shepherd and Guardian of your
souls.

Godly Living

3 In the same way, you wives, be submissive to your
own husbands so that even if any *of them* are disobe-
dient to the word, they may be won without a word by the
behavior of their wives,

NEW CENTURY VERSION

your punishment. But if you suffer for doing good, and you
are patient, then God is pleased. 21 This is what you were
called to do, because Christ suffered for you and gave you
an example to follow. So you should do as he did.
22 "He had never sinned,
and he had never lied." *Isaiah 53:9*
23 People insulted Christ, but he did not insult them in
return. Christ suffered, but he did not threaten. He let God,
the One who judges rightly, take care of him. 24 Christ car-
ried our sins in his body on the cross so we would stop liv-
ing for sin and start living for what is right. And you are
healed because of his wounds. 25 You were like sheep that
wandered away, but now you have come back to the
Shepherd and Protector of your souls.

Wives and Husbands

3 In the same way, you wives should yield to your hus-
bands. Then, if some husbands do not obey God's
teaching, they will be persuaded to believe without anyone's
saying a word to them. They will be persuaded by the way

CONTEMPORARY ENGLISH VERSION

you have to suffer for doing something good. 21 After all,
God chose you to suffer as you follow in the footsteps of
Christ, who set an example by suffering for you.

22 Christ did not sin
or ever tell a lie.
23 Although he was abused,
he never tried to get even.
And when he suffered,
he made no threats.
Instead, he had faith in God,
who judges fairly.
24 Christ carried the burden
of our sins.
He was nailed to the cross,
so that we would stop sinning
and start living right.
By his cuts and bruises
you are healed.
25 You had wandered away
like sheep.
Now you have returned
to the one
who is your shepherd
and protector.

Wives and Husbands

3 If you are a wife, you must put your husband first.
Even if he opposes our message, you will win him
over by what you do. No one else will have to say anything

NEW INTERNATIONAL VERSION

suffer for doing good and you endure it, this is commendable before God. 21 To this you were called, because Christ suffered for you, leaving you an example, that you should follow in his steps.

22 "He committed no sin,
and no deceit was found in his mouth."[e]

23 When they hurled their insults at him, he did not retaliate; when he suffered, he made no threats. Instead, he entrusted himself to him who judges justly. 24 He himself bore our sins in his body on the tree, so that we might die to sins and live for righteousness; by his wounds you have been healed. 25 For you were like sheep going astray, but now you have returned to the Shepherd and Overseer of your souls.

Wives and Husbands

3 Wives, in the same way be submissive to your husbands so that, if any of them do not believe the word, they may be won over without words by the behavior of

[e] *22* Isaiah 53:9

NEW LIVING TRANSLATION

But if you suffer for doing right and are patient beneath the blows, God is pleased with you.

21 This suffering is all part of what God has called you to. Christ, who suffered for you, is your example. Follow in his steps. 22 He never sinned, and he never deceived anyone. 23 He did not retaliate when he was insulted. When he suffered, he did not threaten to get even. He left his case in the hands of God, who always judges fairly. 24 He personally carried away our sins in his own body on the cross so we can be dead to sin and live for what is right. You have been healed by his wounds! 25 Once you were wandering like lost sheep. But now you have turned to your Shepherd, the Guardian of your souls.

Wives

3 In the same way, you wives must accept the authority of your husbands, even those who refuse to accept the Good News. Your godly lives will speak to them better than

NEW KING JAMES VERSION

it patiently? But when you do good and suffer, if you take it patiently, this *is* commendable before God. 21 For to this you were called, because Christ also suffered for us,[f] leaving us[g] an example, that you should follow His steps:

22 "*Who committed no sin,*
Nor was deceit found in His mouth";[h]

23 who, when He was reviled, did not revile in return; when He suffered, He did not threaten, but committed *Himself* to Him who judges righteously; 24 who Himself bore our sins in His own body on the tree, that we, having died to sins, might live for righteousness—by whose stripes you were healed. 25 For you were like sheep going astray, but have now returned to the Shepherd and Overseer[i] of your souls.

Submission to Husbands

3 Wives, likewise, *be* submissive to your own husbands, that even if some do not obey the word, they, without a word, may be won by the conduct of their wives, 2 when

2:21 [f] NU-Text reads *you.* [g] NU-Text and M-Text read *you.*
2:22 [h] Isaiah 53:9 2:25 [i] Greek *Episkopos*

THE MESSAGE

But if you're treated badly for good behavior and continue in spite of it to be a good servant, that is what counts with God.

This is the kind of life you've been invited into, the kind of life Christ lived. He suffered everything that came his way so you would know that it could be done, and also know how to do it, step by step.

"He never did one thing wrong,
Not once said anything amiss."

They called him every name in the book and he said nothing back. He suffered in silence, content to let God set things right. He used his servant body to carry our sins to the Cross so we could be rid of sin, free to live the right way. His wounds became your healing. You were lost sheep with no idea who you were or where you were going. Now you're named and kept for good by the Shepherd of your souls.

Cultivate Inner Beauty

3 The same goes for you wives: Be good wives to your husbands, responsive to their needs. There are husbands who, indifferent as they are to any words about

KING JAMES VERSION

2 While they behold your chaste conversation *coupled* with fear.

3 Whose adorning let it not be that outward *adorning* of plaiting the hair, and of wearing of gold, or of putting on of apparel;

4 But *let it be* the hidden man of the heart, in that which is not corruptible, *even the ornament* of a meek and quiet spirit, which is in the sight of God of great price.

5 For after this manner in the old time the holy women also, who trusted in God, adorned themselves, being in subjection unto their own husbands:

6 Even as Sara obeyed Abraham, calling him lord: whose daughters ye are, as long as ye do well, and are not afraid with any amazement.

7 Likewise, ye husbands, dwell with *them* according to knowledge, giving honour unto the wife, as unto the weaker vessel, and as being heirs together of the grace of life; that your prayers be not hindered.

8 ¶ Finally, *be ye* all of one mind, having compassion one of another, love as brethren, *be* pitiful, *be* courteous:

9 Not rendering evil for evil, or railing for railing: but contrariwise blessing; knowing that ye are thereunto called, that ye should inherit a blessing.

10 For he that will love life, and see good days, let him

NEW AMERICAN STANDARD BIBLE

2 as they observe your chaste and respectful behavior.

3 Your adornment must not be *merely* external—braiding the hair, and wearing gold jewelry, or putting on dresses;

4 but *let it be* the hidden person of the heart, with the imperishable quality of a gentle and quiet spirit, which is precious in the sight of God.

5 For in this way in former times the holy women also, who hoped in God, used to adorn themselves, being submissive to their own husbands;

6 just as Sarah obeyed Abraham, calling him lord, and you have become her children if you do what is right without being frightened by any fear.

7 You husbands in the same way, live with *your wives* in an understanding way, as with someone weaker, since she is a woman; and show her honor as a fellow heir of the grace of life, so that your prayers will not be hindered.

8 To sum up, all of you be harmonious, sympathetic, brotherly, kindhearted, and humble in spirit;

9 not returning evil for evil or insult for insult, but giving a blessing instead; for you were called for the very purpose that you might inherit a blessing.

10 For,

"THE ONE WHO DESIRES LIFE, TO LOVE AND SEE GOOD DAYS,

NEW CENTURY VERSION

their wives live. [2]Your husbands will see the pure lives you
live with your respect for God. [3]It is not fancy hair, gold jew-
elry, or fine clothes that should make you beautiful. [4]No,
your beauty should come from within you—the beauty of a
gentle and quiet spirit that will never be destroyed and is
very precious to God. [5]In this same way the holy women
who lived long ago and followed God made themselves
beautiful, yielding to their own husbands. [6]Sarah obeyed
Abraham, her husband, and called him her master. And you
women are true children of Sarah if you always do what is
right and are not afraid.

[7]In the same way, you husbands should live with your
wives in an understanding way, since they are weaker
than you. But show them respect, because God gives them
the same blessing he gives you—the grace that gives true
life. Do this so that nothing will stop your prayers.

Suffering for Doing Right

[8]Finally, all of you should be in agreement, understand-
ing each other, loving each other as family, being kind and
humble. [9]Do not do wrong to repay a wrong, and do not
insult to repay an insult. But repay with a blessing,
because you yourselves were called to do this so that you
might receive a blessing. [10]The Scripture says,

"A person must do these things
to enjoy life and have many happy days.

CONTEMPORARY ENGLISH VERSION

to him, [2]because he will see how you honor God and live a
pure life. [3]Don't depend on things like fancy hairdos or
gold jewelry or expensive clothes to make you look beauti-
ful. [4]Be beautiful in your heart by being gentle and quiet.
This kind of beauty will last, and God considers it very
special.

[5]Long ago those women who worshiped God and put
their hope in him made themselves beautiful by putting
their husbands first. [6]For example, Sarah obeyed Abraham
and called him her master. You are her true children, if you
do right and don't let anything frighten you.

[7]If you are a husband, you should be thoughtful of your
wife. Treat her with honor, because she isn't as strong as
you are, and she shares with you in the gift of life. Then
nothing will stand in the way of your prayers.

Suffering for Doing Right

[8]Finally, all of you should agree and have concern and
love for each other. You should also be kind and humble.
[9]Don't be hateful and insult people just because they are
hateful and insult you. Instead, treat everyone with kind-
ness. You are God's chosen ones, and he will bless you.
The Scriptures say,

[10]"Do you really love life?
Do you want to be happy?

NEW INTERNATIONAL VERSION

their wives, 2when they see the purity and reverence of your lives. 3Your beauty should not come from outward adornment, such as braided hair and the wearing of gold jewelry and fine clothes. 4Instead, it should be that of your inner self, the unfading beauty of a gentle and quiet spirit, which is of great worth in God's sight. 5For this is the way the holy women of the past who put their hope in God used to make themselves beautiful. They were submissive to their own husbands, 6like Sarah, who obeyed Abraham and called him her master. You are her daughters if you do what is right and do not give way to fear.

7Husbands, in the same way be considerate as you live with your wives, and treat them with respect as the weaker partner and as heirs with you of the gracious gift of life, so that nothing will hinder your prayers.

Suffering for Doing Good

8Finally, all of you, live in harmony with one another; be sympathetic, love as brothers, be compassionate and humble. 9Do not repay evil with evil or insult with insult, but with blessing, because to this you were called so that you may inherit a blessing. 10For,

"Whoever would love life
and see good days

NEW LIVING TRANSLATION

any words. They will be won over 2by watching your pure, godly behavior.

3Don't be concerned about the outward beauty that depends on fancy hairstyles, expensive jewelry, or beautiful clothes. 4You should be known for the beauty that comes from within, the unfading beauty of a gentle and quiet spirit, which is so precious to God. 5That is the way the holy women of old made themselves beautiful. They trusted God and accepted the authority of their husbands. 6For instance, Sarah obeyed her husband, Abraham, when she called him her master. You are her daughters when you do what is right without fear of what your husbands might do.

Husbands

7In the same way, you husbands must give honor to your wives. Treat her with understanding as you live together. She may be weaker than you are, but she is your equal partner in God's gift of new life. If you don't treat her as you should, your prayers will not be heard.

All Christians

8Finally, all of you should be of one mind, full of sympathy toward each other, loving one another with tender hearts and humble minds. 9Don't repay evil for evil. Don't retaliate when people say unkind things about you. Instead, pay them back with a blessing. That is what God wants you to do, and he will bless you for it. 10For the Scriptures say,

"If you want a happy life and good days,

NEW KING JAMES VERSION

they observe your chaste conduct *accompanied* by fear. 3Do not let your adornment be *merely* outward—arranging the hair, wearing gold, or putting on *fine* apparel— 4rather *let it be* the hidden person of the heart, with the incorruptible *beauty* of a gentle and quiet spirit, which is very precious in the sight of God. 5For in this manner, in former times, the holy women who trusted in God also adorned themselves, being submissive to their own husbands, 6as Sarah obeyed Abraham, calling him lord, whose daughters you are if you do good and are not afraid with any terror.

A Word to Husbands

7Husbands, likewise, dwell with *them* with understanding, giving honor to the wife, as to the weaker vessel, and as *being* heirs together of the grace of life, that your prayers may not be hindered.

Called to Blessing

8Finally, all *of you be* of one mind, having compassion for one another; love as brothers, *be* tenderhearted, *be* courteous;[a] 9not returning evil for evil or reviling for reviling, but on the contrary blessing, knowing that you were called to this, that you may inherit a blessing. 10For

"He who would love life
And see good days,

3:8 [a] NU-Text reads *humble.*

THE MESSAGE

God, will be captivated by your life of holy beauty. What matters is not your outer appearance—the styling of your hair, the jewelry you wear, the cut of your clothes—but your inner disposition.

Cultivate inner beauty, the gentle, gracious kind that God delights in. The holy women of old were beautiful before God that way, and were good, loyal wives to their husbands. Sarah, for instance, taking care of Abraham, would address him as "my dear husband." You'll be true daughters of Sarah if you do the same, unanxious and unintimidated.

The same goes for you husbands: Be good husbands to your wives. Honor them, delight in them. As women they lack some of your advantages. But in the new life of God's grace, you're equals. Treat your wives, then, as equals so your prayers don't run aground.

Suffering for Doing Good

Summing up: Be agreeable, be sympathetic, be loving, be compassionate, be humble. That goes for all of you, no exceptions. No retaliation. No sharp-tongued sarcasm. Instead, bless—that's your job, to bless. You'll be a blessing and also get a blessing.

"Whoever wants to embrace life
and see the day fill up with good,

KING JAMES VERSION

refrain his tongue from evil, and his lips that they speak
no guile:
11 Let him eschew evil, and do good; let him seek
peace, and ensue it.
12 For the eyes of the Lord *are* over the righteous, and
his ears *are open* unto their prayers: but the face of the
Lord *is* against them that do evil.
13 And who *is* he that will harm you, if ye be followers
of that which is good?
14 But and if ye suffer for righteousness' sake, happy
are ye: and be not afraid of their terror, neither be troubled;
15 But sanctify the Lord God in your hearts: and *be*
ready always to *give* an answer to every man that asketh
you a reason of the hope that is in you with meekness and
fear:
16 ¶ Having a good conscience; that, whereas they
speak evil of you, as of evildoers, they may be ashamed
that falsely accuse your good conversation in Christ.
17 For *it is* better, if the will of God be so, that ye suffer
for well doing, than for evil doing.
18 ¶ For Christ also hath once suffered for sins, the just

NEW AMERICAN STANDARD BIBLE

MUST KEEP HIS TONGUE FROM EVIL AND HIS LIPS FROM
SPEAKING DECEIT.
11 "HE MUST TURN AWAY FROM EVIL AND DO GOOD;
HE MUST SEEK PEACE AND PURSUE IT.
12 "FOR THE EYES OF THE LORD ARE TOWARD THE RIGHTEOUS,
AND HIS EARS ATTEND TO THEIR PRAYER,
BUT THE FACE OF THE LORD IS AGAINST THOSE WHO DO
EVIL."
13 Who is there to harm you if you prove zealous for
what is good?
14 But even if you should suffer for the sake of righteousness, *you are* blessed. AND DO NOT FEAR THEIR INTIMIDATION, AND DO NOT BE TROUBLED,
15 but [1]sanctify Christ as Lord in your hearts, always
being ready to make a defense to everyone who asks you
to give an account for the hope that is in you, yet with
gentleness and reverence;
16 and keep a good conscience so that in the thing in
which you are slandered, those who revile your good
behavior in Christ will be put to shame.
17 For it is better, if God should will it so, that you suffer for doing what is right rather than for doing what is
wrong.
18 For Christ also died for sins once for all, *the* just for

3:15 [1] I.e. set apart

NEW CENTURY VERSION

He must not say evil things,
and he must not tell lies.
11 He must stop doing evil and do good.
He must look for peace and work for it.
12 The Lord sees the good people
and listens to their prayers.
But the Lord is against
those who do evil." *Psalm 34:12–16*
13 If you are trying hard to do good, no one can really
hurt you. 14 But even if you suffer for doing right, you are
blessed.
"Don't be afraid of what they fear;
do not dread those things." *Isaiah 8:12–13*
15 But respect Christ as the holy Lord in your hearts.
Always be ready to answer everyone who asks you to
explain about the hope you have, 16 but answer in a gentle
way and with respect. Keep a clear conscience so that
those who speak evil of your good life in Christ will be
made ashamed. 17 It is better to suffer for doing good than
for doing wrong if that is what God wants. 18 Christ himself
suffered for sins once. He was not guilty, but he suffered

CONTEMPORARY ENGLISH VERSION

Then stop saying cruel things
and quit telling lies.
11 Give up your evil ways
and do right,
as you find and follow
the road that leads
to peace.
12 The Lord watches over
everyone who obeys him,
and he listens
to their prayers.
But he opposes everyone
who does evil."

13 Can anyone really harm you for being eager to do good
deeds? 14 Even if you have to suffer for doing good things,
God will bless you. So stop being afraid and don't worry
about what people might do. 15 Honor Christ and let him be
the Lord of your life.
Always be ready to give an answer when someone asks
you about your hope. 16 Give a kind and respectful answer
and keep your conscience clear. This way you will make
people ashamed for saying bad things about your good conduct as a follower of Christ. 17 You are better off to obey God
and suffer for doing right than to suffer for doing wrong.

18 Christ died once for our sins.
An innocent person died
for those who are guilty.

NEW INTERNATIONAL VERSION

must keep his tongue from evil
and his lips from deceitful speech.
11 He must turn from evil and do good;
he must seek peace and pursue it.
12 For the eyes of the Lord are on the righteous
and his ears are attentive to their prayer,
but the face of the Lord is against those who do evil."[a]

13 Who is going to harm you if you are eager to do good?
14 But even if you should suffer for what is right, you are
blessed. "Do not fear what they fear[b]; do not be fright-
ened."[c] 15 But in your hearts set apart Christ as Lord.
Always be prepared to give an answer to everyone who
asks you to give the reason for the hope that you have. But
do this with gentleness and respect, 16 keeping a clear con-
science, so that those who speak maliciously against your
good behavior in Christ may be ashamed of their slander.
17 It is better, if it is God's will, to suffer for doing good
than for doing evil. 18 For Christ died for sins once for all,
the righteous for the unrighteous, to bring you to God. He

[a] *12* Psalm 34:12–16 [b] *14* Or *not fear their threats*
[c] *14* Isaiah 8:12

NEW LIVING TRANSLATION

keep your tongue from speaking evil,
and keep your lips from telling lies.
11 Turn away from evil and do good.
Work hard at living in peace with others.
12 The eyes of the Lord watch over those who do right,
and his ears are open to their prayers.
But the Lord turns his face
against those who do evil."*

Suffering for Doing Good

13 Now, who will want to harm you if you are eager to do
good? 14 But even if you suffer for doing what is right, God
will reward you for it. So don't be afraid and don't worry.
15 Instead, you must worship Christ as Lord of your life.
And if you are asked about your Christian hope, always be
ready to explain it. 16 But you must do this in a gentle and
respectful way. Keep your conscience clear. Then if people
speak evil against you, they will be ashamed when they
see what a good life you live because you belong to Christ.
17 Remember, it is better to suffer for doing good, if that is
what God wants, than to suffer for doing wrong!
18 Christ also suffered when he died for our sins once for
all time. He never sinned, but he died for sinners that he

3:10-12 Ps 34:12-16.

NEW KING JAMES VERSION

Let him refrain his tongue from evil,
And his lips from speaking deceit.
11 *Let him turn away from evil and do good;*
Let him seek peace and pursue it.
12 *For the eyes of the* LORD *are on the righteous,*
And His ears are open to their prayers;
But the face of the LORD *is against those who do*
evil."[b]

Suffering for Right and Wrong

13 And who *is* he who will harm you if you become fol-
lowers of what is good? 14 But even if you should suffer for
righteousness' sake, *you are* blessed. *"And do not be afraid*
of their threats, nor be troubled."[c] 15 But sanctify the Lord
God[d] in your hearts, and always *be* ready to *give* a defense
to everyone who asks you a reason for the hope that is in
you, with meekness and fear; 16 having a good conscience,
that when they defame you as evildoers, those who revile
your good conduct in Christ may be ashamed. 17 For *it is*
better, if it is the will of God, to suffer for doing good than
for doing evil.

Christ's Suffering and Ours

18 For Christ also suffered once for sins, the just for the

3:12 [b] Psalm 34:12–16 3:14 [c] Isaiah 8:12 3:15 [d] NU-Text reads
Christ as Lord.

THE MESSAGE

Here's what you do:
Say nothing evil or hurtful;
Snub evil and cultivate good;
run after peace for all you're worth.
God looks on all this with approval,
listening and responding well to what he's asked;
But he turns his back
on those who do evil things."

If with heart and soul you're doing good, do you think
you can be stopped? Even if you suffer for it, you're still
better off. Don't give the opposition a second thought.
Through thick and thin, keep your hearts at attention, in
adoration before Christ, your Master. Be ready to speak up
and tell anyone who asks why you're living the way you
are, and always with the utmost courtesy. Keep a clear con-
science before God so that when people throw mud at you,
none of it will stick. They'll end up realizing that *they're* the
ones who need a bath. It's better to suffer for doing good, if
that's what God wants, than to be punished for doing bad.
That's what Christ did definitively: suffered because of oth-
ers' sins, the Righteous One for the unrighteous ones. He

KING JAMES VERSION

for the unjust, that he might bring us to God, being put to death in the flesh, but quickened by the Spirit:

19 By which also he went and preached unto the spirits in prison;

20 Which sometime were disobedient, when once the longsuffering of God waited in the days of Noah, while the ark was a preparing, wherein few, that is, eight souls were saved by water.

21 ¶ The like figure whereunto *even* baptism doth also now save us (not the putting away of the filth of the flesh, but the answer of a good conscience toward God,) by the resurrection of Jesus Christ:

22 Who is gone into heaven, and is on the right hand of God; angels and authorities and powers being made subject unto him.

4 Forasmuch then as Christ hath suffered for us in the flesh, arm yourselves likewise with the same mind: for he that hath suffered in the flesh hath ceased from sin;

2 That he no longer should live the rest of *his* time in the flesh to the lusts of men, but to the will of God.

3 For the time past of *our* life may suffice us to have wrought the will of the Gentiles, when we walked in lasciviousness, lusts, excess of wine, revellings, banquetings, and abominable idolatries:

NEW AMERICAN STANDARD BIBLE

the unjust, so that He might bring us to God, having been put to death in the flesh, but made alive in the spirit;

19 in which also He went and made proclamation to the spirits *now* in prison,

20 who once were disobedient, when the patience of God kept waiting in the days of Noah, during the construction of the ark, in which a few, that is, eight persons, were brought safely through *the* water.

21 Corresponding to that, baptism now saves you—not the removal of dirt from the flesh, but an appeal to God for a good conscience—through the resurrection of Jesus Christ,

22 who is at the right hand of God, having gone into heaven, after angels and authorities and powers had been subjected to Him.

Keep Fervent in Your Love

4 Therefore, since Christ has [1]suffered in the flesh, arm yourselves also with the same purpose, because he who has suffered in the flesh has ceased from sin,

2 so as to live the rest of the time in the flesh no longer for the lusts of men, but for the will of God.

3 For the time already past is sufficient *for you* to have carried out the desire of the Gentiles, having pursued a course of sensuality, lusts, drunkenness, carousing, drinking parties and abominable idolatries.

4:1 [1] I.e. suffered death

NEW CENTURY VERSION

for those who are guilty to bring you to God. His body was
killed, but he was made alive in the spirit. 19 And in the
spirit he went and preached to the spirits in prison 20 who
refused to obey God long ago in the time of Noah. God was
waiting patiently for them while Noah was building the
boat. Only a few people—eight in all—were saved by
water. 21 And that water is like baptism that now saves
you—not the washing of dirt from the body, but the promise made to God from a good conscience. And this is
because Jesus Christ was raised from the dead. 22 Now
Jesus has gone into heaven and is at God's right side ruling over angels, authorities, and powers.

Change Your Lives

4 Since Christ suffered while he was in his body, strengthen yourselves with the same way of thinking
Christ had. The person who has suffered in the body is finished with sin. 2 Strengthen yourselves so that you will live
here on earth doing what God wants, not the evil things
people want. 3 In the past you wasted too much time doing
what nonbelievers enjoy. You were guilty of sexual sins,
evil desires, drunkenness, wild and drunken parties, and

CONTEMPORARY ENGLISH VERSION

Christ did this
to bring you to God,
when his body
was put to death
and his spirit
was made alive.

19 Christ then preached to the spirits that were being kept
in prison. 20 They had disobeyed God while Noah was
building the boat, but God had been patient with them.
Eight people went into that boat and were brought safely
through the flood.

21 Those flood waters were like baptism that now saves
you. But baptism is more than just washing your body. It
means turning to God with a clear conscience, because
Jesus Christ was raised from death. 22 Christ is now in
heaven, where he sits at the right side[a] of God. All angels,
authorities, and powers are under his control.

Being Faithful to God

4 Christ suffered here on earth. Now you must be ready to suffer as he did, because suffering shows that you
have stopped sinning. 2 It means you have turned from
your own desires and want to obey God for the rest of your
life. 3 You have already lived long enough like people who
don't know God. You were immoral and followed your evil
desires. You went around drinking and partying and carrying on. In fact, you even worshiped disgusting idols. 4 Now

[a] 3.22 *right side*: The place of honor and power.

NEW INTERNATIONAL VERSION

was put to death in the body but made alive by the Spirit,
19through whom[d] also he went and preached to the spirits
in prison 20who disobeyed long ago when God waited
patiently in the days of Noah while the ark was being
built. In it only a few people, eight in all, were saved
through water, 21and this water symbolizes baptism that
now saves you also—not the removal of dirt from the body
but the pledge[e] of a good conscience toward God. It saves
you by the resurrection of Jesus Christ, 22who has gone
into heaven and is at God's right hand—with angels,
authorities and powers in submission to him.

Living for God

4 Therefore, since Christ suffered in his body, arm your-
selves also with the same attitude, because he who
has suffered in his body is done with sin. 2As a result, he
does not live the rest of his earthly life for evil human
desires, but rather for the will of God. 3For you have spent
enough time in the past doing what pagans choose to do—
living in debauchery, lust, drunkenness, orgies, carousing

[d] *18,19* Or *alive in the spirit,* [19]*through which* [e] *21* Or *response*

NEW LIVING TRANSLATION

might bring us safely home to God. He suffered physical
death, but he was raised to life in the Spirit.*
19So he went and preached to the spirits in prison—
20those who disobeyed God long ago when God waited
patiently while Noah was building his boat. Only eight
people were saved from drowning in that terrible flood.*
21And this is a picture of baptism, which now saves you by
the power of Jesus Christ's resurrection. Baptism is not a
removal of dirt from your body; it is an appeal to God
from* a clean conscience.
22Now Christ has gone to heaven. He is seated in the
place of honor next to God, and all the angels and authori-
ties and powers are bowing before him.

Living for God

4 So then, since Christ suffered physical pain, you must
arm yourselves with the same attitude he had, and be
ready to suffer, too. For if you are willing to suffer for
Christ, you have decided to stop sinning. 2And you won't
spend the rest of your life chasing after evil desires, but
you will be anxious to do the will of God. 3You have had
enough in the past of the evil things that godless people
enjoy—their immorality and lust, their feasting and drunk-
enness and wild parties, and their terrible worship of idols.

3:18 Or *spirit.* 3:20 Greek *saved through water.* 3:21 Or *for.*

NEW KING JAMES VERSION

unjust, that He might bring us[e] to God, being put to death
in the flesh but made alive by the Spirit, 19by whom also
He went and preached to the spirits in prison, 20who for-
merly were disobedient, when once the Divine longsuffer-
ing waited[f] in the days of Noah, while *the* ark was being
prepared, in which a few, that is, eight souls, were saved
through water. 21There is also an antitype which now
saves us—baptism (not the removal of the filth of the
flesh, but the answer of a good conscience toward God),
through the resurrection of Jesus Christ, 22who has gone
into heaven and is at the right hand of God, angels and
authorities and powers having been made subject to Him.

4 Therefore, since Christ suffered for us[a] in the flesh,
arm yourselves also with the same mind, for he who
has suffered in the flesh has ceased from sin, 2that he no
longer should live the rest of *his* time in the flesh for the
lusts of men, but for the will of God. 3For we *have spent*
enough of our past lifetime[b] in doing the will of the
Gentiles—when we walked in lewdness, lusts, drunken-
ness, revelries, drinking parties, and abominable idolatries.

3:18 [e] NU-Text and M-Text read *you.* 3:20 [f] NU-Text and M-Text read *when the longsuffering of God waited patiently.* 4:1 [a] NU-Text omits *for us.* 4:3 [b] NU-Text reads *time.*

THE MESSAGE

went through it all—was put to death and then made
alive—to bring us to God.

He went and proclaimed God's salvation to earlier gener-
ations who ended up in the prison of judgment because
they wouldn't listen. You know, even though God waited
patiently all the days that Noah built his ship, only a few
were saved then, eight to be exact—saved *from* the water
by the water. The waters of baptism do that for you, not by
washing away dirt from your skin but by presenting you
through Jesus' resurrection before God with a clear con-
science. Jesus has the last word on everything and every-
one, from angels to armies. He's standing right alongside
God, and what he says goes.

Learn to Think Like Him

4 Since Jesus went through everything you're going
through and more, learn to think like him. Think of
your sufferings as a weaning from that old sinful habit of
always expecting to get your own way. Then you'll be able
to live out your days free to pursue what God wants
instead of being tyrannized by what you want.

You've already put in your time in that God-ignorant way
of life, partying night after night, a drunken and profligate

KING JAMES VERSION

4 ¶ Wherein they think it strange that ye run not with *them* to the same excess of riot, speaking evil of *you*:

5 Who shall give account to him that is ready to judge the quick and the dead.

6 For for this cause was the gospel preached also to them that are dead, that they might be judged according to men in the flesh, but live according to God in the spirit.

7 ¶ But the end of all things is at hand: be ye therefore sober, and watch unto prayer.

8 And above all things have fervent charity among yourselves: for charity shall cover the multitude of sins.

9 Use hospitality one to another without grudging.

10 As every man hath received the gift, *even so* minister the same one to another, as good stewards of the manifold grace of God.

11 If any man speak, *let him speak* as the oracles of God; if any man minister, *let him do it* as of the ability which God giveth: that God in all things may be glorified through Jesus Christ, to whom be praise and dominion for ever and ever. Amen.

12 ¶ Beloved, think it not strange concerning the fiery trial which is to try you, as though some strange thing happened unto you:

13 But rejoice, inasmuch as ye are partakers of Christ's sufferings; that, when his glory shall be revealed, ye may be glad also with exceeding joy.

NEW AMERICAN STANDARD BIBLE

4 In *all* this, they are surprised that you do not run with *them* into the same excesses of dissipation, and they malign *you;*

5 but they will give account to Him who is ready to judge the living and the dead.

6 For the gospel has for this purpose been preached even to those who are dead, that though they are judged in the flesh as men, they may live in the spirit according to *the will of* God.

7 The end of all things is near; therefore, be of sound judgment and sober *spirit* for the purpose of prayer.

8 Above all, keep fervent in your love for one another, because love covers a multitude of sins.

9 Be hospitable to one another without complaint.

10 As each one has received a *special* gift, employ it in serving one another as good stewards of the manifold grace of God.

11 Whoever speaks, *is to do so* as one who is speaking the utterances of God; whoever serves *is to do so* as one who is serving by the strength which God supplies; so that in all things God may be glorified through Jesus Christ, to whom belongs the glory and dominion forever and ever. Amen.

Share the Sufferings of Christ

12 Beloved, do not be surprised at the fiery ordeal among you, which comes upon you for your testing, as though some strange thing were happening to you;

13 but to the degree that you share the sufferings of Christ, keep on rejoicing, so that also at the revelation of His glory you may rejoice with exultation.

NEW CENTURY VERSION

hateful idol worship. 4Nonbelievers think it is strange that you do not do the many wild and wasteful things they do, so they insult you. 5But they will have to explain this to God, who is ready to judge the living and the dead. 6For this reason the Good News was preached to those who are now dead. Even though they were judged like all people, the Good News was preached to them so they could live in the spirit as God lives.

Use God's Gifts Wisely

7The time is near when all things will end. So think clearly and control yourselves so you will be able to pray. 8Most importantly, love each other deeply, because love will cause many sins to be forgiven. 9Open your homes to each other, without complaining. 10Each of you has received a gift to use to serve others. Be good servants of God's various gifts of grace. 11Anyone who speaks should speak words from God. Anyone who serves should serve with the strength God gives so that in everything God will be praised through Jesus Christ. Power and glory belong to him forever and ever. Amen.

Suffering as a Christian

12My friends, do not be surprised at the terrible trouble which now comes to test you. Do not think that something strange is happening to you. 13But be happy that you are sharing in Christ's sufferings so that you will be happy and full of joy when Christ comes again in glory. 14When

CONTEMPORARY ENGLISH VERSION

your former friends wonder why you have stopped running around with them, and they curse you for it. 5But they will have to answer to God, who judges the living and the dead. 6The good news has even been preached to the dead,[a] so that after they have been judged for what they have done in this life, their spirits will live with God.

7Everything will soon come to an end. So be serious and be sensible enough to pray.

8Most important of all, you must sincerely love each other, because love wipes away many sins.

9Welcome people into your home and don't grumble about it.

10Each of you has been blessed with one of God's many wonderful gifts to be used in the service of others. So use your gift well. 11If you have the gift of speaking, preach God's message. If you have the gift of helping others, do it with the strength that God supplies. Everything should be done in a way that will bring honor to God because of Jesus Christ, who is glorious and powerful forever. Amen.

Suffering for Being a Christian

12Dear friends, don't be surprised or shocked that you are going through testing that is like walking through fire. 13Be glad for the chance to suffer as Christ suffered. It will prepare you for even greater happiness when he makes his glorious return.

[a] **4.6** *the dead*: Either people who died after becoming followers of Christ or the people of Noah's day (see 3.19).

NEW INTERNATIONAL VERSION

and detestable idolatry. 4They think it strange that you do not plunge with them into the same flood of dissipation, and they heap abuse on you. 5But they will have to give account to him who is ready to judge the living and the dead. 6For this is the reason the gospel was preached even to those who are now dead, so that they might be judged according to men in regard to the body, but live according to God in regard to the spirit.

7The end of all things is near. Therefore be clear minded and self-controlled so that you can pray. 8Above all, love each other deeply, because love covers over a multitude of sins. 9Offer hospitality to one another without grumbling. 10Each one should use whatever gift he has received to serve others, faithfully administering God's grace in its various forms. 11If anyone speaks, he should do it as one speaking the very words of God. If anyone serves, he should do it with the strength God provides, so that in all things God may be praised through Jesus Christ. To him be the glory and the power for ever and ever. Amen.

Suffering for Being a Christian

12Dear friends, do not be surprised at the painful trial you are suffering, as though something strange were happening to you. 13But rejoice that you participate in the sufferings of Christ, so that you may be overjoyed when his glory is

NEW LIVING TRANSLATION

4Of course, your former friends are very surprised when you no longer join them in the wicked things they do, and they say evil things about you. 5But just remember that they will have to face God, who will judge everyone, both the living and the dead. 6That is why the Good News was preached even to those who have died—so that although their bodies were punished with death, they could still live in the spirit as God does.

7The end of the world is coming soon. Therefore, be earnest and disciplined in your prayers. 8Most important of all, continue to show deep love for each other, for love covers a multitude of sins. 9Cheerfully share your home with those who need a meal or a place to stay.

10God has given gifts to each of you from his great variety of spiritual gifts. Manage them well so that God's generosity can flow through you. 11Are you called to be a speaker? Then speak as though God himself were speaking through you. Are you called to help others? Do it with all the strength and energy that God supplies. Then God will be given glory in everything through Jesus Christ. All glory and power belong to him forever and ever. Amen.

Suffering for Being a Christian

12Dear friends, don't be surprised at the fiery trials you are going through, as if something strange were happening to you. 13Instead, be very glad—because these trials will make you partners with Christ in his suffering, and afterward you will have the wonderful joy of sharing his glory when it is displayed to all the world.

NEW KING JAMES VERSION

4In regard to these, they think it strange that you do not run with *them* in the same flood of dissipation, speaking evil of *you.* 5They will give an account to Him who is ready to judge the living and the dead. 6For this reason the gospel was preached also to those who are dead, that they might be judged according to men in the flesh, but live according to God in the spirit.

Serving for God's Glory

7But the end of all things is at hand; therefore be serious and watchful in your prayers. 8And above all things have fervent love for one another, for *"love will cover a multitude of sins."*[c] 9*Be* hospitable to one another without grumbling. 10As each one has received a gift, minister it to one another, as good stewards of the manifold grace of God. 11If anyone speaks, *let him speak* as the oracles of God. If anyone ministers, *let him do it* as with the ability which God supplies, that in all things God may be glorified through Jesus Christ, to whom belong the glory and the dominion forever and ever. Amen.

Suffering for God's Glory

12Beloved, do not think it strange concerning the fiery trial which is to try you, as though some strange thing happened to you; 13but rejoice to the extent that you partake of Christ's sufferings, that when His glory is revealed, you may also be glad with exceeding joy. 14If you are

4:8 c Proverbs 10:12

THE MESSAGE

life. Now it's time to be done with it for good. Of course, your old friends don't understand why you don't join in with the old gang anymore. But you don't have to give an account to them. They're the ones who will be called on the carpet—and before God himself.

Listen to the Message. It was preached to those believers who are now dead, and yet even though they died (just as all people must), they will still get in on the *life* that God has given in Jesus.

Everything in the world is about to be wrapped up, so take nothing for granted. Stay wide-awake in prayer. Most of all, love each other as if your life depended on it. Love makes up for practically anything. Be quick to give a meal to the hungry, a bed to the homeless—cheerfully. Be generous with the different things God gave you, passing them around so all get in on it: if words, let it be God's words; if help, let it be God's hearty help. That way, God's bright presence will be evident in everything through Jesus, and *he'll* get all the credit as the One mighty in everything—encores to the end of time. Oh, yes!

Glory Just Around the Corner

Friends, when life gets really difficult, don't jump to the conclusion that God isn't on the job. Instead, be glad that you are in the very thick of what Christ experienced. This is a spiritual refining process, with glory just around the corner.

KING JAMES VERSION

14 If ye be reproached for the name of Christ, happy *are ye*; for the spirit of glory and of God resteth upon you: on their part he is evil spoken of, but on your part he is glorified.

15 But let none of you suffer as a murderer, or *as* a thief, or *as* an evildoer, or as a busybody in other men's matters.

16 Yet if *any man suffer* as a Christian, let him not be ashamed; but let him glorify God on this behalf.

17 For the time *is come* that judgment must begin at the house of God: and if *it* first *begin* at us, what shall the end *be* of them that obey not the gospel of God?

18 And if the righteous scarcely be saved, where shall the ungodly and the sinner appear?

19 Wherefore let them that suffer according to the will of God commit the keeping of their souls *to him* in well doing, as unto a faithful Creator.

5 The elders which are among you I exhort, who am also an elder, and a witness of the sufferings of Christ, and also a partaker of the glory that shall be revealed:

2 Feed the flock of God which is among you, taking the oversight *thereof*, not by constraint, but willingly; not for filthy lucre, but of a ready mind;

NEW AMERICAN STANDARD BIBLE

14 If you are reviled for the name of Christ, you are blessed, because the Spirit of glory and of God rests on you.

15 Make sure that none of you suffers as a murderer, or thief, or evildoer, or a troublesome meddler;

16 but if *anyone suffers* as a Christian, he is not to be ashamed, but is to glorify God in this name.

17 For *it is* time for judgment to begin with the household of God; and if *it begins* with us first, what *will be* the outcome for those who do not obey the gospel of God?

18 AND IF IT IS WITH DIFFICULTY THAT THE RIGHTEOUS IS SAVED, WHAT WILL BECOME OF THE GODLESS MAN AND THE SINNER?

19 Therefore, those also who suffer according to the will of God shall entrust their souls to a faithful Creator in doing what is right.

Serve God Willingly

5 Therefore, I exhort the elders among you, as *your* fellow elder and witness of the sufferings of Christ, and a partaker also of the glory that is to be revealed,

2 shepherd the flock of God among you, exercising oversight not under compulsion, but voluntarily, according to *the will of* God; and not for sordid gain, but with eagerness;

NEW CENTURY VERSION

people insult you because you follow Christ, you are
blessed, because the glorious Spirit, the Spirit of God, is
with you. 15Do not suffer for murder, theft, or any other
crime, nor because you trouble other people. 16But if you
suffer because you are a Christian, do not be ashamed.
Praise God because you wear that name. 17It is time for
judgment to begin with God's family. And if that judging
begins with us, what will happen to those people who do
not obey the Good News of God?

18 "If it is very hard for a good person to be saved,
the wicked person and the sinner will surely be
lost!"[a]

19So those who suffer as God wants should trust their
souls to the faithful Creator as they continue to do what is
right.

The Flock of God

5 Now I have something to say to the elders in your
group. I also am an elder. I have seen Christ's sufferings,
and I will share in the glory that will be shown to us.
I beg you to 2shepherd God's flock, for whom you are
responsible. Watch over them because you want to, not
because you are forced. That is how God wants it. Do it
because you are happy to serve, not because you want

4:18 [a] "If...lost!" Quotation from Proverbs 11:31 in the Septuagint, the Greek version of the Old Testament.

CONTEMPORARY ENGLISH VERSION

14Count it a blessing when you suffer for being a
Christian. This shows that God's glorious Spirit is with
you. 15But you deserve to suffer if you are a murderer, a
thief, a crook, or a busybody. 16Don't be ashamed to suffer
for being a Christian. Praise God that you belong to him.
17God has already begun judging his own people. And if
his judgment begins with us, imagine how terrible it will
be for those who refuse to obey his message. The
Scriptures say,

18 "If good people barely escape,
what will happen to sinners
and to others
who don't respect God?"

19If you suffer for obeying God, you must have complete
faith in your faithful Creator and keep on doing right.

Helping Christian Leaders

5 Church leaders,[a] I am writing to encourage you. I too
am a leader, as well as a witness to Christ's suffering,
and I will share in his glory when it is shown to us.

2Just as shepherds watch over their sheep, you must
watch over everyone God has placed in your care. Do it
willingly in order to please God, and not simply because
you think you must. Let it be something you want to do,
instead of something you do merely to make money.

[a] 5.1 *Church leaders*: Or "Elders" or "Presbyters" or "Priests."

NEW INTERNATIONAL VERSION

revealed. 14If you are insulted because of the name of Christ,
you are blessed, for the Spirit of glory and of God rests on
you. 15If you suffer, it should not be as a murderer or thief
or any other kind of criminal, or even as a meddler.
16However, if you suffer as a Christian, do not be ashamed,
but praise God that you bear that name. 17For it is time for
judgment to begin with the family of God; and if it begins
with us, what will the outcome be for those who do not obey
the gospel of God? 18And,

"If it is hard for the righteous to be saved,
what will become of the ungodly and the sinner?"[a]

19So then, those who suffer according to God's will
should commit themselves to their faithful Creator and
continue to do good.

To Elders and Young Men

5 To the elders among you, I appeal as a fellow elder, a
witness of Christ's sufferings and one who also will
share in the glory to be revealed: 2Be shepherds of God's
flock that is under your care, serving as overseers—not
because you must, but because you are willing, as God
wants you to be; not greedy for money, but eager to serve;

[a] *18* Prov. 11:31

NEW LIVING TRANSLATION

14Be happy if you are insulted for being a Christian, for
then the glorious Spirit of God will come upon you. 15If
you suffer, however, it must not be for murder, stealing,
making trouble, or prying into other people's affairs. 16But
it is no shame to suffer for being a Christian. Praise God
for the privilege of being called by his wonderful name!
17For the time has come for judgment, and it must begin
first among God's own children. And if even we Christians
must be judged, what terrible fate awaits those who have
never believed God's Good News? 18And

"If the righteous are barely saved,
what chance will the godless and sinners have?"*

19So if you are suffering according to God's will, keep on
doing what is right, and trust yourself to the God who
made you, for he will never fail you.

Advice for Elders and Young Men

5 And now, a word to you who are elders in the
churches. I, too, am an elder and a witness to the suf-
ferings of Christ. And I, too, will share his glory and his
honor when he returns. As a fellow elder, this is my appeal
to you: 2Care for the flock of God entrusted to you. Watch
over it willingly, not grudgingly—not for what you will get
out of it, but because you are eager to serve God. 3Don't

4:18 Prov 11:31.

NEW KING JAMES VERSION

reproached for the name of Christ, blessed *are you,* for the
Spirit of glory and of God rests upon you.[d] On their part He
is blasphemed, but on your part He is glorified. 15But let
none of you suffer as a murderer, a thief, an evildoer, or as
a busybody in other people's matters. 16Yet if *anyone suf-
fers* as a Christian, let him not be ashamed, but let him
glorify God in this matter.[e]

17For the time *has come* for judgment to begin at the
house of God; and if *it begins* with us first, what will *be*
the end of those who do not obey the gospel of God?
18Now

*"If the righteous one is scarcely saved,
Where will the ungodly and the sinner appear?"*[f]

19Therefore let those who suffer according to the will of
God commit their souls *to Him* in doing good, as to a faith-
ful Creator.

Shepherd the Flock

5 The elders who are among you I exhort, I who am a
fellow elder and a witness of the sufferings of Christ,
and also a partaker of the glory that will be revealed:
2Shepherd the flock of God which is among you, serving as
overseers, not by compulsion but willingly,[a] not for dis-
honest gain but eagerly; 3nor as being lords over those

4:14 [d] NU-Text omits the rest of this verse. 4:16 [e] NU-Text reads *name.* 4:18 [f] Proverbs 11:31 5:2 [a] NU-Text adds *according to God.*

THE MESSAGE

If you're abused because of Christ, count yourself fortu-
nate. It's the Spirit of God and his glory in you that
brought you to the notice of others. If they're on you
because you broke the law or disturbed the peace, that's a
different matter. But if it's because you're a Christian,
don't give it a second thought. Be proud of the distin-
guished status reflected in that name!

It's judgment time for Christians. We're first in line. If it
starts with us, think what it's going to be like for those
who refuse God's Message!

"If good people barely make it,
What's in store for the bad?"

So if you find life difficult because you're doing what God
said, take it in stride. Trust him. He knows what he's
doing, and he'll keep on doing it.

He'll Promote You at the Right Time

5 I have a special concern for you church leaders. I
know what it's like to be a leader, in on Christ's suf-
ferings as well as the coming glory. Here's my concern:
that you care for God's flock with all the diligence of a
shepherd. Not because you have to, but because you want
to please God. Not calculating what you can get out of it,

KING JAMES VERSION

3 Neither as being lords over *God's* heritage, but being ensamples to the flock.

4 And when the chief Shepherd shall appear, ye shall receive a crown of glory that fadeth not away.

5 ¶ Likewise, ye younger, submit yourselves unto the elder. Yea, all *of you* be subject one to another, and be clothed with humility: for God resisteth the proud, and giveth grace to the humble.

6 Humble yourselves therefore under the mighty hand of God, that he may exalt you in due time:

7 Casting all your care upon him; for he careth for you.

8 ¶ Be sober, be vigilant; because your adversary the devil, as a roaring lion, walketh about, seeking whom he may devour:

9 Whom resist stedfast in the faith, knowing that the same afflictions are accomplished in your brethren that are in the world.

10 ¶ But the God of all grace, who hath called us unto his eternal glory by Christ Jesus, after that ye have suffered a while, make you perfect, stablish, strengthen, settle *you*.

11 To him *be* glory and dominion for ever and ever. Amen.

NEW AMERICAN STANDARD BIBLE

3 nor yet as lording it over those allotted to your charge, but proving to be examples to the flock.

4 And when the Chief Shepherd appears, you will receive the unfading crown of glory.

5 You younger men, likewise, be subject to *your* elders; and all of you, clothe yourselves with humility toward one another, for GOD IS OPPOSED TO THE PROUD, BUT GIVES GRACE TO THE HUMBLE.

6 Therefore humble yourselves under the mighty hand of God, that He may exalt you at the proper time,

7 casting all your anxiety on Him, because He cares for you.

8 Be of sober *spirit,* be on the alert. Your adversary, the devil, prowls around like a roaring lion, seeking someone to devour.

9 But resist him, firm in *your* faith, knowing that the same experiences of suffering are being accomplished by your brethren who are in the world.

10 After you have suffered for a little while, the God of all grace, who called you to His eternal glory in Christ, will Himself perfect, confirm, strengthen *and* establish you.

11 To Him *be* dominion forever and ever. Amen.

NEW CENTURY VERSION

money. 3Do not be like a ruler over people you are responsible for, but be good examples to them. 4Then when Christ, the Chief Shepherd, comes, you will get a glorious crown that will never lose its beauty.

5In the same way, younger people should be willing to be under older people. And all of you should be very humble with each other.

"God is against the proud,
but he gives grace to the humble." *Proverbs 3:34*

6Be humble under God's powerful hand so he will lift you up when the right time comes. 7Give all your worries to him, because he cares about you.

8Control yourselves and be careful! The devil, your enemy, goes around like a roaring lion looking for someone to eat. 9Refuse to give in to him, by standing strong in your faith. You know that your Christian family all over the world is having the same kinds of suffering.

10And after you suffer for a short time, God, who gives all grace, will make everything right. He will make you strong and support you and keep you from falling. He called you to share in his glory in Christ, a glory that will continue forever. 11All power is his forever and ever. Amen.

CONTEMPORARY ENGLISH VERSION

3Don't be bossy to those people who are in your care, but set an example for them. 4Then when Christ the Chief Shepherd returns, you will be given a crown that will never lose its glory.

5All of you young people should obey your elders. In fact, everyone should be humble toward everyone else. The Scriptures say,

"God opposes proud people,
but he helps everyone
who is humble."

6Be humble in the presence of God's mighty power, and he will honor you when the time comes. 7God cares for you, so turn all your worries over to him.

8Be on your guard and stay awake. Your enemy, the devil, is like a roaring lion, sneaking around to find someone to attack. 9But you must resist the devil and stay strong in your faith. You know that all over the world the Lord's followers are suffering just as you are. 10But God shows undeserved kindness to everyone. That's why he appointed Christ Jesus to choose you to share in his eternal glory. You will suffer for a while, but God will make you complete, steady, strong, and firm. 11God will be in control forever! Amen.

NEW INTERNATIONAL VERSION

3 not lording it over those entrusted to you, but being
examples to the flock. 4 And when the Chief Shepherd
appears, you will receive the crown of glory that will never
fade away.
5 Young men, in the same way be submissive to those
who are older. All of you, clothe yourselves with humility
toward one another, because,

"God opposes the proud
but gives grace to the humble."[a]

6 Humble yourselves, therefore, under God's mighty hand,
that he may lift you up in due time. 7 Cast all your anxiety
on him because he cares for you.
8 Be self-controlled and alert. Your enemy the devil
prowls around like a roaring lion looking for someone to
devour. 9 Resist him, standing firm in the faith, because
you know that your brothers throughout the world are
undergoing the same kind of sufferings.
10 And the God of all grace, who called you to his eternal
glory in Christ, after you have suffered a little while, will
himself restore you and make you strong, firm and stead-
fast. 11 To him be the power for ever and ever. Amen.

[a] *5* Prov. 3:34

NEW LIVING TRANSLATION

lord it over the people assigned to your care, but lead them
by your good example. 4 And when the head Shepherd
comes, your reward will be a never-ending share in his
glory and honor.
5 You younger men, accept the authority of the elders.
And all of you, serve each other in humility, for

"God sets himself against the proud,
but he shows favor to the humble."*

6 So humble yourselves under the mighty power of God,
and in his good time he will honor you. 7 Give all your wor-
ries and cares to God, for he cares about what happens to
you.
8 Be careful! Watch out for attacks from the Devil, your
great enemy. He prowls around like a roaring lion, looking
for some victim to devour. 9 Take a firm stand against him,
and be strong in your faith. Remember that your Christian
brothers and sisters* all over the world are going through
the same kind of suffering you are.
10 In his kindness God called you to his eternal glory by
means of Jesus Christ. After you have suffered a little
while, he will restore, support, and strengthen you, and he
will place you on a firm foundation. 11 All power is his for-
ever and ever. Amen.

5:5 Prov 3:34. **5:9** Greek *your brothers.*

NEW KING JAMES VERSION

entrusted to you, but being examples to the flock; 4 and
when the Chief Shepherd appears, you will receive the
crown of glory that does not fade away.

Submit to God, Resist the Devil

5 Likewise you younger people, submit yourselves to
your elders. Yes, all of *you* be submissive to one another,
and be clothed with humility, for

"God resists the proud,
But gives grace to the humble."[b]

6 Therefore humble yourselves under the mighty hand of
God, that He may exalt you in due time, 7 casting all your
care upon Him, for He cares for you.
8 Be sober, be vigilant; because[c] your adversary the devil
walks about like a roaring lion, seeking whom he may
devour. 9 Resist him, steadfast in the faith, knowing that
the same sufferings are experienced by your brotherhood
in the world. 10 But may[d] the God of all grace, who called
us[e] to His eternal glory by Christ Jesus, after you have suf-
fered a while, perfect, establish, strengthen, and settle *you.*
11 To Him *be* the glory and the dominion forever and ever.
Amen.

5:5 [b] Proverbs 3:34 **5:8** [c] NU-Text and M-Text omit *because.*
5:10 [d] NU-Text reads *But the God of all grace . . . will perfect, establish, strengthen, and settle you.* [e] NU-Text and M-Text read *you.*

THE MESSAGE

but acting spontaneously. Not bossily telling others what
to do, but tenderly showing them the way.
When God, who is the best shepherd of all, comes out in
the open with his rule, he'll see that you've done it right
and commend you lavishly. And you who are younger
must follow your leaders. But all of you, leaders and fol-
lowers alike, are to be down to earth with each other, for—

"God has had it with the proud,
But takes delight in just plain people."

So be content with who you are, and don't put on airs.
God's strong hand is on you; he'll promote you at the right
time. Live carefree before God; he is most careful with you.

He Gets the Last Word

Keep a cool head. Stay alert. The Devil is poised to
pounce, and would like nothing better than to catch you
napping. Keep your guard up. You're not the only ones
plunged into these hard times. It's the same with
Christians all over the world. So keep a firm grip on the
faith. The suffering won't last forever. It won't be long
before this generous God who has great plans for us in
Christ—eternal and glorious plans they are!—will have
you put together and on your feet for good. He gets the
last word; yes, he does.

KING JAMES VERSION

12 By Silvanus, a faithful brother unto you, as I suppose, I have written briefly, exhorting, and testifying that this is the true grace of God wherein ye stand.

13 The *church that is* at Babylon, elected together with *you*, saluteth you; and *so doth* Marcus my son.

14 Greet ye one another with a kiss of charity. Peace *be* with you all that are in Christ Jesus. Amen.

NEW AMERICAN STANDARD BIBLE

12 Through Silvanus, our faithful brother (for so I regard *him),* I have written to you briefly, exhorting and testifying that this is the true grace of God. Stand firm in it!

13 She who is in Babylon, chosen together with you, sends you greetings, and *so does* my son, Mark.

14 Greet one another with a kiss of love.

Peace be to you all who are in Christ.

NEW CENTURY VERSION

Final Greetings

12I wrote this short letter with the help of Silas, who I know is a faithful brother in Christ. I wrote to encourage you and to tell you that this is the true grace of God. Stand strong in that grace.

13The church in Babylon, who was chosen like you, sends you greetings. Mark, my son in Christ, also greets you. 14Give each other a kiss of Christian love when you meet.

Peace to all of you who are in Christ.

CONTEMPORARY ENGLISH VERSION

Final Greetings

12Silvanus helped me write this short letter, and I consider him a faithful follower of the Lord. I wanted to encourage you and tell you how kind God really is, so that you will keep on having faith in him.

13Greetings from the Lord's followers in Babylon.[b] They are God's chosen ones.

Mark, who is like a son to me, sends his greetings too.

14Give each other a warm greeting. I pray that God will give peace to everyone who belongs to Christ.[c]

[b] 5.13 *Babylon*: This may be a secret name for the city of Rome.
[c] 5.14 *Christ*: Some manuscripts add "Amen."

NEW INTERNATIONAL VERSION

Final Greetings

12 With the help of Silas,[b] whom I regard as a faithful brother, I have written to you briefly, encouraging you and testifying that this is the true grace of God. Stand fast in it.

13 She who is in Babylon, chosen together with you, sends you her greetings, and so does my son Mark. 14 Greet one another with a kiss of love.

Peace to all of you who are in Christ.

b 12 Greek *Silvanus*, a variant of *Silas*

NEW LIVING TRANSLATION

Peter's Final Greetings

12 I have written this short letter to you with the help of Silas,* whom I consider a faithful brother. My purpose in writing is to encourage you and assure you that the grace of God is with you no matter what happens.

13 Your sister church here in Rome* sends you greetings, and so does my son Mark. 14 Greet each other in Christian love.*

Peace be to all of you who are in Christ.

5:12 Greek *Silvanus*. 5:13 Greek *The elect one in Babylon*. Babylon was probably a code name for Rome. 5:14 Greek *with a kiss of love*.

NEW KING JAMES VERSION

Farewell and Peace

12 By Silvanus, our faithful brother as I consider him, I have written to you briefly, exhorting and testifying that this is the true grace of God in which you stand.

13 She who is in Babylon, elect together with *you,* greets you; and *so does* Mark my son. 14 Greet one another with a kiss of love.

Peace to you all who are in Christ Jesus. Amen.

THE MESSAGE

I'm sending this brief letter to you by Silas, a most dependable brother. I have the highest regard for him.

I've written as urgently and accurately as I know how. This is God's generous truth; embrace it with both arms!

The church in exile here with me—but not for a moment forgotten by God—wants to be remembered to you. Mark, who is like a son to me, says hello. Give holy embraces all around! Peace to you—to all who walk in Christ's ways.

KING JAMES VERSION

THE SECOND EPISTLE OF
ST. PETER

1 Simon Peter, a servant and an apostle of Jesus Christ, to them that have obtained like precious faith with us through the righteousness of God and our Saviour Jesus Christ:

2 Grace and peace be multiplied unto you through the knowledge of God, and of Jesus our Lord,

3 According as his divine power hath given unto us all things that *pertain* unto life and godliness, through the knowledge of him that hath called us to glory and virtue:

4 Whereby are given unto us exceeding great and precious promises: that by these ye might be partakers of the divine nature, having escaped the corruption that is in the world through lust.

5 ¶ And beside this, giving all diligence, add to your faith virtue; and to virtue knowledge;

6 And to knowledge temperance; and to temperance patience; and to patience godliness;

NEW AMERICAN STANDARD BIBLE

THE SECOND LETTER OF
PETER

Growth in Christian Virtue

1 Simon Peter, a bond-servant and apostle of Jesus Christ,

To those who have received a faith of the same kind as ours, by the righteousness of our God and Savior, Jesus Christ:

2 Grace and peace be multiplied to you in the knowledge of God and of Jesus our Lord;

3 seeing that His divine power has granted to us everything pertaining to life and godliness, through the true knowledge of Him who called us by His own glory and excellence.

4 For by these He has granted to us His precious and magnificent promises, so that by them you may become partakers of *the* divine nature, having escaped the corruption that is in the world by lust.

5 Now for this very reason also, applying all diligence, in your faith supply moral excellence, and in *your* moral excellence, knowledge,

6 and in *your* knowledge, self-control, and in *your* self-control, perseverance, and in *your* perseverance, godliness,

NEW CENTURY VERSION

2 PETER

1 From Simon Peter, a servant and apostle of Jesus Christ.

To you who have received a faith as valuable as ours, because our God and Savior Jesus Christ does what is right.

2Grace and peace be given to you more and more, because you truly know God and Jesus our Lord.

God Has Given Us Blessings

3Jesus has the power of God, by which he has given us
everything we need to live and to serve God. We have these
things because we know him. Jesus called us by his glory
and goodness. 4Through these he gave us the very great
and precious promises. With these gifts you can share in
being like God, and the world will not ruin you with its evil
desires.

5Because you have these blessings, do your best to add
these things to your lives: to your faith, add goodness;
and to your goodness, add knowledge; 6and to your
knowledge, add self-control; and to your self-control, add
patience; and to your patience, add service for God; 7and

CONTEMPORARY ENGLISH VERSION

2 PETER

1 From Simon Peter, a servant and an apostle of Jesus Christ.

To everyone who shares with us in the privilege of believing that our God and Savior Jesus Christ will do what is just and fair.[a]

2I pray that God will be kind to you and will let you live in perfect peace! May you keep learning more and more about God and our Lord Jesus.

Living as the Lord's Followers

3We have everything we need to live a life that pleases
God. It was all given to us by God's own power, when we
learned that he had invited us to share in his wonderful
goodness. 4God made great and marvelous promises, so that
his nature would become part of us. Then we could escape
our evil desires and the corrupt influences of this world.

5Do your best to improve your faith. You can do this by
adding goodness, understanding, 6self-control, patience,

[a] 1.1 *To everyone who . . . just and fair*: Or "To everyone whose faith in the justice and fairness of our God and Savior Jesus Christ is as precious as our own faith."

NEW INTERNATIONAL VERSION

2 PETER

1 Simon Peter, a servant and apostle of Jesus Christ,

To those who through the righteousness of our God and
Savior Jesus Christ have received a faith as precious as
ours:

2Grace and peace be yours in abundance through the
knowledge of God and of Jesus our Lord.

Making One's Calling and Election Sure

3His divine power has given us everything we need for
life and godliness through our knowledge of him who
called us by his own glory and goodness. 4Through these
he has given us his very great and precious promises, so
that through them you may participate in the divine nature
and escape the corruption in the world caused by evil
desires.
5For this very reason, make every effort to add to your
faith goodness; and to goodness, knowledge; 6and to knowl-
edge, self-control; and to self-control, perseverance; and to

NEW LIVING TRANSLATION

2 PETER

Greetings from Peter

1 This letter is from Simon* Peter, a slave and apostle of
Jesus Christ.
I am writing to all of you who share the same precious
faith we have, faith given to us by Jesus Christ, our God
and Savior, who makes us right with God.
2May God bless you with his special favor and wonder-
ful peace as you come to know Jesus, our God and Lord,*
better and better.

Growing in the Knowledge of God

3As we know Jesus better, his divine power gives us
everything we need for living a godly life. He has called us
to receive his own glory and goodness! 4And by that same
mighty power, he has given us all of his rich and wonder-
ful promises. He has promised that you will escape the
decadence all around you caused by evil desires and that
you will share in his divine nature.
5So make every effort to apply the benefits of these prom-
ises to your life. Then your faith will produce a life of moral
excellence. A life of moral excellence leads to knowing God
better. 6Knowing God leads to self-control. Self-control
leads to patient endurance, and patient endurance leads to

1:1 Greek *Simeon.* 1:2 Or *come to know God and Jesus our Lord.*

NEW KING JAMES VERSION

THE SECOND EPISTLE OF

PETER

Greeting the Faithful

1 Simon Peter, a bondservant and apostle of Jesus
Christ,

To those who have obtained like precious faith with us
by the righteousness of our God and Savior Jesus Christ:

2Grace and peace be multiplied to you in the knowledge
of God and of Jesus our Lord, 3as His divine power has
given to us all things that *pertain* to life and godliness,
through the knowledge of Him who called us by glory and
virtue, 4by which have been given to us exceedingly great
and precious promises, that through these you may be par-
takers of the divine nature, having escaped the corruption
that is in the world through lust.

Fruitful Growth in the Faith

5But also for this very reason, giving all diligence, add
to your faith virtue, to virtue knowledge, 6to knowledge
self-control, to self-control perseverance, to perseverance

THE MESSAGE

2 PETER

1 I, Simon Peter, am a servant and apostle of Jesus
Christ. I write this to you whose experience with God
is as life-changing as ours, all due to our God's straight
dealing and the intervention of our God and Savior, Jesus
Christ. Grace and peace to you many times over as you
deepen in your experience with God and Jesus, our Master.

Don't Put It Off

Everything that goes into a life of pleasing God has been
miraculously given to us by getting to know, personally
and intimately, the One who invited us to God. The best
invitation we ever received! We were also given absolutely
terrific promises to pass on to you—your tickets to partici-
pation in the life of God after you turned your back on a
world corrupted by lust.
So don't lose a minute in building on what you've been
given, complementing your basic faith with good charac-
ter, spiritual understanding, alert discipline, passionate

KING JAMES VERSION

7 And to godliness brotherly kindness; and to brotherly kindness charity.

8 For if these things be in you, and abound, they make *you that ye shall* neither *be* barren nor unfruitful in the knowledge of our Lord Jesus Christ.

9 But he that lacketh these things is blind, and cannot see afar off, and hath forgotten that he was purged from his old sins.

10 Wherefore the rather, brethren, give diligence to make your calling and election sure: for if ye do these things, ye shall never fall:

11 For so an entrance shall be ministered unto you abundantly into the everlasting kingdom of our Lord and Saviour Jesus Christ.

12 ¶ Wherefore I will not be negligent to put you always in remembrance of these things, though ye know *them*, and be established in the present truth.

13 Yea, I think it meet, as long as I am in this tabernacle, to stir you up by putting *you* in remembrance;

14 Knowing that shortly I must put off *this* my tabernacle, even as our Lord Jesus Christ hath shewed me.

15 Moreover I will endeavour that ye may be able after my decease to have these things always in remembrance.

16 ¶ For we have not followed cunningly devised fables, when we made known unto you the power and coming of our Lord Jesus Christ, but were eyewitnesses of his majesty.

NEW AMERICAN STANDARD BIBLE

7 and in *your* godliness, brotherly kindness, and in *your* brotherly kindness, love.

8 For if these *qualities* are yours and are increasing, they render you neither useless nor unfruitful in the true knowledge of our Lord Jesus Christ.

9 For he who lacks these *qualities* is blind *or* short-sighted, having forgotten *his* purification from his former sins.

10 Therefore, brethren, be all the more diligent to make certain about His calling and choosing you; for as long as you practice these things, you will never stumble;

11 for in this way the entrance into the eternal kingdom of our Lord and Savior Jesus Christ will be abundantly supplied to you.

12 Therefore, I will always be ready to remind you of these things, even though you *already* know *them*, and have been established in the truth which is present with *you*.

13 I consider it right, as long as I am in this *earthly* dwelling, to stir you up by way of reminder,

14 knowing that the laying aside of my *earthly* dwelling is imminent, as also our Lord Jesus Christ has made clear to me.

15 And I will also be diligent that at any time after my departure you will be able to call these things to mind.

Eyewitnesses

16 For we did not follow cleverly devised tales when we made known to you the power and coming of our Lord Jesus Christ, but we were eyewitnesses of His majesty.

NEW CENTURY VERSION

to your service for God, add kindness for your brothers
and sisters in Christ; and to this kindness, add love. [8]If all
these things are in you and are growing, they will help
you to be useful and productive in your knowledge of our
Lord Jesus Christ. [9]But anyone who does not have these
things cannot see clearly. He is blind and has forgotten
that he was made clean from his past sins.

[10]My brothers and sisters,[a] try hard to be certain that
you really are called and chosen by God. If you do all these
things, you will never fall. [11]And you will be given a very
great welcome into the eternal kingdom of our Lord and
Savior Jesus Christ.

[12]You know these things, and you are very strong in the
truth, but I will always help you remember them. [13]I think
it is right for me to help you remember as long as I am in
this body. [14]I know I must soon leave this body, as our
Lord Jesus Christ has shown me. [15]I will try my best so
that you may be able to remember these things even after I
am gone.

We Saw Christ's Glory

[16]When we told you about the powerful coming of our
Lord Jesus Christ, we were not telling just smart stories that
someone invented. But we saw the greatness of Jesus with

1:10 [a] **brothers and sisters** Although the Greek text reads "brothers" here and throughout this book, Peter's words were meant for the entire church, including men and women.

CONTEMPORARY ENGLISH VERSION

devotion to God, [7]concern for others, and love. [8]If you keep
growing in this way, it will show that what you know
about our Lord Jesus Christ has made your lives useful and
meaningful. [9]But if you don't grow, you are like someone
who is nearsighted or blind, and you have forgotten that
your past sins are forgiven.

[10]My friends, you must do all you can to show that God
has really chosen and selected you. If you keep on doing
this, you won't stumble and fall. [11]Then our Lord and
Savior Jesus Christ will give you a glorious welcome into
his kingdom that will last forever.

[12]You are holding firmly to the truth that you were
given. But I am still going to remind you of these things.
[13]In fact, I think I should keep on reminding you until I
leave this body. [14]And our Lord Jesus Christ has already
told me that I will soon leave it behind. [15]That is why I am
doing my best to make sure that each of you remembers all
of this after I am gone.

The Message about the Glory of Christ

[16]When we told you about the power and the return of
our Lord Jesus Christ, we were not telling clever stories that
someone had made up. But with our own eyes we saw his

NEW INTERNATIONAL VERSION

perseverance, godliness; 7and to godliness, brotherly kind-
ness; and to brotherly kindness, love. 8For if you possess
these qualities in increasing measure, they will keep you
from being ineffective and unproductive in your knowledge
of our Lord Jesus Christ. 9But if anyone does not have them,
he is nearsighted and blind, and has forgotten that he has
been cleansed from his past sins.

10Therefore, my brothers, be all the more eager to make
your calling and election sure. For if you do these things,
you will never fall, 11and you will receive a rich welcome
into the eternal kingdom of our Lord and Savior Jesus
Christ.

Prophecy of Scripture

12So I will always remind you of these things, even
though you know them and are firmly established in the
truth you now have. 13I think it is right to refresh your
memory as long as I live in the tent of this body, 14because
I know that I will soon put it aside, as our Lord Jesus
Christ has made clear to me. 15And I will make every effort
to see that after my departure you will always be able to
remember these things.

16We did not follow cleverly invented stories when we
told you about the power and coming of our Lord Jesus
Christ, but we were eyewitnesses of his majesty. 17For he

NEW LIVING TRANSLATION

godliness. 7Godliness leads to love for other Christians,*
and finally you will grow to have genuine love for every-
one. 8The more you grow like this, the more you will
become productive and useful in your knowledge of our
Lord Jesus Christ. 9But those who fail to develop these vir-
tues are blind or, at least, very shortsighted. They have
already forgotten that God has cleansed them from their old
life of sin.

10So, dear brothers and sisters,* work hard to prove that
you really are among those God has called and chosen.
Doing this, you will never stumble or fall away. 11And God
will open wide the gates of heaven for you to enter into the
eternal Kingdom of our Lord and Savior Jesus Christ.

Paying Attention to Scripture

12I plan to keep on reminding you of these things—even
though you already know them and are standing firm in
the truth. 13Yes, I believe I should keep on reminding you
of these things as long as I live. 14But the Lord Jesus Christ
has shown me that my days here on earth are numbered
and I am soon to die.* 15So I will work hard to make these
things clear to you. I want you to remember them long
after I am gone.

16For we were not making up clever stories when we told
you about the power of our Lord Jesus Christ and his coming
again. We have seen his majestic splendor with our own

1:7 Greek *brotherly love.* 1:10 Greek *brothers.* 1:14 Greek *I must soon put off this earthly tent.*

NEW KING JAMES VERSION

godliness, 7to godliness brotherly kindness, and to broth-
erly kindness love. 8For if these things are yours and
abound, *you will be* neither barren nor unfruitful in the
knowledge of our Lord Jesus Christ. 9For he who lacks
these things is shortsighted, even to blindness, and has
forgotten that he was cleansed from his old sins.

10Therefore, brethren, be even more diligent to make
your call and election sure, for if you do these things you
will never stumble; 11for so an entrance will be supplied to
you abundantly into the everlasting kingdom of our Lord
and Savior Jesus Christ.

Peter's Approaching Death

12For this reason I will not be negligent to remind you
always of these things, though you know and are estab-
lished in the present truth. 13Yes, I think it is right, as long
as I am in this tent, to stir you up by reminding *you,*
14knowing that shortly I *must* put off my tent, just as our
Lord Jesus Christ showed me. 15Moreover I will be careful
to ensure that you always have a reminder of these things
after my decease.

The Trustworthy Prophetic Word

16For we did not follow cunningly devised fables when
we made known to you the power and coming of our Lord
Jesus Christ, but were eyewitnesses of His majesty. 17For

THE MESSAGE

patience, reverent wonder, warm friendliness, and gener-
ous love, each dimension fitting into and developing the
others. With these qualities active and growing in your
lives, no grass will grow under your feet, no day will pass
without its reward as you mature in your experience of our
Master Jesus. Without these qualities you can't see what's
right before you, oblivious that your old sinful life has
been wiped off the books.

So, friends, confirm God's invitation to you, his choice of
you. Don't put it off; do it now. Do this, and you'll have
your life on a firm footing, the streets paved and the way
wide open into the eternal kingdom of our Master and
Savior, Jesus Christ.

The One Light in a Dark Time

Because the stakes are so high, even though you're up-
to-date on all this truth and practice it inside and out, I'm
not going to let up for a minute in calling you to attention
before it. This is the post to which I've been assigned—
keeping you alert with frequent reminders—and I'm stick-
ing to it as long as I live. I know that I'm to die soon; the
Master has made that quite clear to me. And so I am espe-
cially eager that you have all this down in black and white
so that after I die, you'll have it for ready reference.

We weren't, you know, just wishing on a star when we
laid the facts out before you regarding the powerful return
of our Master, Jesus Christ. We were there for the preview!
We saw it with our own eyes: Jesus resplendent with light

KING JAMES VERSION

17 For he received from God the Father honour and glory, when there came such a voice to him from the excellent glory, This is my beloved Son, in whom I am well pleased.

18 And this voice which came from heaven we heard, when we were with him in the holy mount.

19 ¶ We have also a more sure word of prophecy; whereunto ye do well that ye take heed, as unto a light that shineth in a dark place, until the day dawn, and the day star arise in your hearts:

20 Knowing this first, that no prophecy of the scripture is of any private interpretation.

21 For the prophecy came not in old time by the will of man: but holy men of God spake *as they were* moved by the Holy Ghost.

2 But there were false prophets also among the people, even as there shall be false teachers among you, who privily shall bring in damnable heresies, even denying the Lord that bought them, and bring upon themselves swift destruction.

2 And many shall follow their pernicious ways; by reason of whom the way of truth shall be evil spoken of.

3 ¶ And through covetousness shall they with feigned words make merchandise of you: whose judgment now of a long time lingereth not, and their damnation slumbereth not.

NEW AMERICAN STANDARD BIBLE

17 For when He received honor and glory from God the Father, such an utterance as this was made to Him by the Majestic Glory, "This is My beloved Son with whom I am well-pleased"—

18 and we ourselves heard this utterance made from heaven when we were with Him on the holy mountain.

19 *So* we have the prophetic word *made* more sure, to which you do well to pay attention as to a lamp shining in a dark place, until the day dawns and the morning star arises in your hearts.

20 But know this first of all, that no prophecy of Scripture is *a matter* of one's own interpretation,

21 for no prophecy was ever made by an act of human will, but men moved by the Holy Spirit spoke from God.

The Rise of False Prophets

2 But false prophets also arose among the people, just as there will also be false teachers among you, who will secretly introduce destructive heresies, even denying the Master who bought them, bringing swift destruction upon themselves.

2 Many will follow their sensuality, and because of them the way of the truth will be maligned;

3 and in *their* greed they will exploit you with false words; their judgment from long ago is not idle, and their destruction is not asleep.

NEW CENTURY VERSION

our own eyes. 17 Jesus heard the voice of God, the Greatest
Glory, when he received honor and glory from God the
Father. The voice said, "This is my Son, whom I love, and I
am very pleased with him." 18 We heard that voice from
heaven while we were with Jesus on the holy mountain.
19 This makes us more sure about the message the
prophets gave. It is good for you to follow closely what
they said as you would follow a light shining in a dark
place, until the day begins and the morning star rises in
your hearts. 20 Most of all, you must understand this: No
prophecy in the Scriptures ever comes from the prophet's
own interpretation. 21 No prophecy ever came from what a
person wanted to say, but people led by the Holy Spirit
spoke words from God.

False Teachers

2 There used to be false prophets among God's people,
just as you will have some false teachers in your
group. They will secretly teach things that are wrong—
teachings that will cause people to be lost. They will even
refuse to accept the Master, Jesus, who bought their free-
dom. So they will bring quick ruin on themselves. 2 Many
will follow their evil ways and say evil things about the
way of truth. 3 Those false teachers only want your money,
so they will use you by telling you lies. Their judgment
spoken against them long ago is still coming, and their
ruin is certain.

CONTEMPORARY ENGLISH VERSION

true greatness. 17 God, our great and wonderful Father, truly
honored him by saying, "This is my own dear Son, and I
am pleased with him." 18 We were there with Jesus on the
holy mountain and heard this voice speak from heaven.
19 All of this makes us even more certain that what the
prophets said is true. So you should pay close attention to
their message, as you would to a lamp shining in some
dark place. You must keep on paying attention until day-
light comes and the morning star rises in your hearts.
20 But you need to realize that no one alone can under-
stand any of the prophecies in the Scriptures. 21 The proph-
ets did not think these things up on their own, but they
were guided by the Spirit of God.

False Prophets and Teachers

2 Sometimes false prophets spoke to the people of
Israel. False teachers will also sneak in and speak
harmful lies to you. But these teachers don't really belong
to the Master who paid a great price for them, and they
will quickly destroy themselves. 2 Many people will follow
their evil ways and cause others to tell lies about the true
way. 3 They will be greedy and cheat you with smooth talk.
But long ago God decided to punish them, and God doesn't
sleep.

NEW INTERNATIONAL VERSION

received honor and glory from God the Father when the
voice came to him from the Majestic Glory, saying, "This is
my Son, whom I love; with him I am well pleased."[a] 18We
ourselves heard this voice that came from heaven when we
were with him on the sacred mountain.

19And we have the word of the prophets made more cer-
tain, and you will do well to pay attention to it, as to a
light shining in a dark place, until the day dawns and the
morning star rises in your hearts. 20Above all, you must
understand that no prophecy of Scripture came about by
the prophet's own interpretation. 21For prophecy never had
its origin in the will of man, but men spoke from God as
they were carried along by the Holy Spirit.

False Teachers and Their Destruction

2 But there were also false prophets among the people,
just as there will be false teachers among you. They
will secretly introduce destructive heresies, even denying
the sovereign Lord who bought them—bringing swift
destruction on themselves. 2Many will follow their shame-
ful ways and will bring the way of truth into disrepute. 3In
their greed these teachers will exploit you with stories they
have made up. Their condemnation has long been hanging
over them, and their destruction has not been sleeping.

[a] *17* Matt. 17:5; Mark 9:7; Luke 9:35

NEW LIVING TRANSLATION

eyes. 17And he received honor and glory from God the Father
when God's glorious, majestic voice called down from heav-
en, "This is my beloved Son; I am fully pleased with him."
18We ourselves heard the voice when we were there with
him on the holy mountain.

19Because of that, we have even greater confidence in
the message proclaimed by the prophets. Pay close atten-
tion to what they wrote, for their words are like a light
shining in a dark place—until the day Christ appears and
his brilliant light shines in your hearts.* 20Above all, you
must understand that no prophecy in Scripture ever came
from the prophets themselves* 21or because they wanted to
prophesy. It was the Holy Spirit who moved the prophets
to speak from God.

The Danger of False Teachers

2 But there were also false prophets in Israel, just as
there will be false teachers among you. They will clev-
erly teach their destructive heresies about God and even
turn against their Master who bought them. Theirs will be
a swift and terrible end. 2Many will follow their evil teach-
ing and shameful immorality. And because of them, Christ
and his true way will be slandered. 3In their greed they
will make up clever lies to get hold of your money. But God
condemned them long ago, and their destruction is on the
way.

1:19 Or *until the day dawns and the morning star rises in your hearts.*
1:20 Or *is a matter of one's own interpretation.*

NEW KING JAMES VERSION

He received from God the Father honor and glory when
such a voice came to Him from the Excellent Glory: "This
is My beloved Son, in whom I am well pleased." 18And we
heard this voice which came from heaven when we were
with Him on the holy mountain.

19And so we have the prophetic word confirmed,[a] which
you do well to heed as a light that shines in a dark place,
until the day dawns and the morning star rises in your
hearts; 20knowing this first, that no prophecy of Scripture
is of any private interpretation,[b] 21for prophecy never came
by the will of man, but holy men of God[c] spoke *as they
were* moved by the Holy Spirit.

Destructive Doctrines

2 But there were also false prophets among the people,
even as there will be false teachers among you, who
will secretly bring in destructive heresies, even denying the
Lord who bought them, *and* bring on themselves swift
destruction. 2And many will follow their destructive ways,
because of whom the way of truth will be blasphemed. 3By
covetousness they will exploit you with deceptive words;
for a long time their judgment has not been idle, and their
destruction does[a] not slumber.

1:19 [a] Or *We also have the more sure prophetic word.* 1:20 [b] Or
origin 1:21 [c] NU-Text reads *but men spoke from God.* 2:3 [a] M-Text
reads *will not.*

THE MESSAGE

from God the Father as the voice of Majestic Glory spoke:
"This is my Son, marked by my love, focus of all my
delight." We were there on the holy mountain with him.
We heard the voice out of heaven with our very own ears.

We couldn't be more sure of what we saw and heard—
God's glory, *God's* voice. The prophetic Word was con-
firmed to us. You'll do well to keep focusing on it. It's the
one light you have in a dark time as you wait for daybreak
and the rising of the Morning Star in your hearts. The
main thing to keep in mind here is that no prophecy of
Scripture is a matter of private opinion. And why? Because
it's not something concocted in the human heart. Prophecy
resulted when the Holy Spirit prompted men and women to
speak God's Word.

Lying Religious Leaders

2 But there were also *lying* prophets among the people
then, just as there will be lying religious teachers
among you. They'll smuggle in destructive divisions, pit-
ting you against each other—biting the hand of the One
who gave them a chance to have their lives back! They've
put themselves on a fast downhill slide to destruction, but
not before they recruit a crowd of mixed-up followers who
can't tell right from wrong.

They give the way of truth a bad name. They're only out
for themselves. They'll say anything, *anything*, that
sounds good to exploit you. They won't, of course, get by
with it. They'll come to a bad end, for God has never just
stood by and let that kind of thing go on.

KING JAMES VERSION

4 For if God spared not the angels that sinned, but cast *them* down to hell, and delivered *them* into chains of darkness, to be reserved unto judgment;

5 And spared not the old world, but saved Noah the eighth *person*, a preacher of righteousness, bringing in the flood upon the world of the ungodly;

6 And turning the cities of Sodom and Gomorrha into ashes condemned *them* with an overthrow, making *them* an ensample unto those that after should live ungodly;

7 ¶ And delivered just Lot, vexed with the filthy conversation of the wicked:

8 (For that righteous man dwelling among them, in seeing and hearing, vexed *his* righteous soul from day to day with *their* unlawful deeds;)

9 The Lord knoweth how to deliver the godly out of temptations, and to reserve the unjust unto the day of judgment to be punished:

10 ¶ But chiefly them that walk after the flesh in the lust of uncleanness, and despise government. Presumptuous *are they*, selfwilled, they are not afraid to speak evil of dignities.

11 Whereas angels, which are greater in power and might, bring not railing accusation against them before the Lord.

12 But these, as natural brute beasts, made to be taken and destroyed, speak evil of the things that they understand not; and shall utterly perish in their own corruption;

NEW AMERICAN STANDARD BIBLE

4 For if God did not spare angels when they sinned, but cast them into hell and committed them to pits of darkness, reserved for judgment;

5 and did not spare the ancient world, but preserved Noah, a preacher of righteousness, with seven others, when He brought a flood upon the world of the ungodly;

6 and *if* He condemned the cities of Sodom and Gomorrah to destruction by reducing *them* to ashes, having made them an example to those who would live ungodly *lives* thereafter;

7 and *if* He rescued righteous Lot, oppressed by the sensual conduct of unprincipled men

8 (for by what he saw and heard *that* righteous man, while living among them, felt *his* righteous soul tormented day after day by *their* lawless deeds),

9 *then* the Lord knows how to rescue the godly from temptation, and to keep the unrighteous under punishment for the day of judgment,

10 and especially those who indulge the flesh in *its* corrupt desires and despise authority.

Daring, self-willed, they do not tremble when they revile angelic majesties,

11 whereas angels who are greater in might and power do not bring a reviling judgment against them before the Lord.

12 But these, like unreasoning animals, born as creatures of instinct to be captured and killed, reviling where they have no knowledge, will in the destruction of those creatures also be destroyed,

NEW CENTURY VERSION

4When angels sinned, God did not let them go free without punishment. He sent them to hell and put them in caves of darkness where they are being held for judgment.
5And God punished the world long ago when he brought a flood to the world that was full of people who were against him. But God saved Noah, who preached about being right with God, and seven other people with him. 6And God also destroyed the evil cities of Sodom and Gomorrah[a] by burning them until they were ashes. He made those cities an example of what will happen to those who are against God.
7But he saved Lot from those cities. Lot, a good man, was troubled because of the filthy lives of evil people. 8(Lot was a good man, but because he lived with evil people every day, his good heart was hurt by the evil things he saw and heard.) 9So the Lord knows how to save those who serve him when troubles come. He will hold evil people and punish them, while waiting for the Judgment Day. 10That punishment is especially for those who live by doing the evil things their sinful selves want and who hate authority.

These false teachers are bold and do anything they want. They are not afraid to speak against the angels.
11But even the angels, who are much stronger and more powerful than false teachers, do not accuse them with insults before the Lord. 12But these people speak against things they do not understand. They are like animals that act without thinking, animals born to be caught and killed. And, like animals, these false teachers will be destroyed.

2:6 [a] **Sodom and Gomorrah** Two cities God destroyed because the people were so evil.

CONTEMPORARY ENGLISH VERSION

4God did not have pity on the angels that sinned. He had them tied up and thrown into the dark pits of hell until the time of judgment. 5And during Noah's time, God did not have pity on the ungodly people of the world. He destroyed them with a flood, though he did save eight people, including Noah, who preached the truth.

6God punished the cities of Sodom and Gomorrah[a] by burning them to ashes, and this is a warning to anyone else who wants to sin.

7-8Lot lived right and was greatly troubled by the terrible way those wicked people were living. He was a good man, and day after day he suffered because of the evil things he saw and heard. So the Lord rescued him. 9This shows that the Lord knows how to rescue godly people from their sufferings and to punish evil people while they wait for the day of judgment.

10The Lord is especially hard on people who disobey him and don't think of anything except their own filthy desires. They are reckless and proud and are not afraid of cursing the glorious beings in heaven. 11Although angels are more powerful than these evil beings,[b] even the angels don't dare to accuse them to the Lord.

12These people are no better than senseless animals that live by their feelings and are born to be caught and killed. They speak evil of things they don't know anything about. But their own corrupt deeds will destroy them.

[a] **2.6** *Sodom and Gomorrah*: During the time of Abraham the Lord destroyed these cities because the people there were so evil (see Genesis 19.24). [b] **2.11** *evil beings*: Or "evil teachers."

NEW INTERNATIONAL VERSION

4For if God did not spare angels when they sinned, but
sent them to hell,[a] putting them into gloomy dungeons[b] to
be held for judgment; 5if he did not spare the ancient
world when he brought the flood on its ungodly people,
but protected Noah, a preacher of righteousness, and seven
others; 6if he condemned the cities of Sodom and
Gomorrah by burning them to ashes, and made them an
example of what is going to happen to the ungodly; 7and if
he rescued Lot, a righteous man, who was distressed by
the filthy lives of lawless men 8(for that righteous man,
living among them day after day, was tormented in his
righteous soul by the lawless deeds he saw and heard)—
9if this is so, then the Lord knows how to rescue godly
men from trials and to hold the unrighteous for the day of
judgment, while continuing their punishment.[c] 10This is
especially true of those who follow the corrupt desire of
the sinful nature[d] and despise authority.

Bold and arrogant, these men are not afraid to slander
celestial beings; 11yet even angels, although they are
stronger and more powerful, do not bring slanderous accu-
sations against such beings in the presence of the Lord.
12But these men blaspheme in matters they do not under-
stand. They are like brute beasts, creatures of instinct,
born only to be caught and destroyed, and like beasts they
too will perish.

[a] *4* Greek *Tartarus* [b] *4* Some manuscripts *into chains of darkness*
[c] *9* Or *unrighteous for punishment until the day of judgment*
[d] *10* Or *the flesh*

NEW LIVING TRANSLATION

4For God did not spare even the angels when they
sinned; he threw them into hell,* in gloomy caves* and
darkness until the judgment day. 5And God did not spare
the ancient world—except for Noah and his family of
seven. Noah warned the world of God's righteous judg-
ment. Then God destroyed the whole world of ungodly peo-
ple with a vast flood. 6Later, he turned the cities of Sodom
and Gomorrah into heaps of ashes and swept them off the
face of the earth. He made them an example of what will
happen to ungodly people. 7But at the same time, God res-
cued Lot out of Sodom because he was a good man who
was sick of all the immorality and wickedness around him.
8Yes, he was a righteous man who was distressed by the
wickedness he saw and heard day after day.

9So you see, the Lord knows how to rescue godly people
from their trials, even while punishing the wicked right up
until the day of judgment. 10He is especially hard on those
who follow their own evil, lustful desires and who despise
authority. These people are proud and arrogant, daring
even to scoff at the glorious ones* without so much as
trembling. 11But the angels, even though they are far
greater in power and strength than these false teachers,
never speak out disrespectfully against* the glorious ones.
12These false teachers are like unthinking animals, crea-
tures of instinct, who are born to be caught and killed. They
laugh at the terrifying powers they know so little about,

2:4a Greek *Tartaros.* 2:4b Some manuscripts read *chains of gloom.*
2:10 *The glorious ones* are probably evil angels; also in 2:11.
2:11 Greek *never bring blasphemous judgment from the Lord against.*

NEW KING JAMES VERSION

Doom of False Teachers

4For if God did not spare the angels who sinned, but cast
them down to hell and delivered *them* into chains of dark-
ness, to be reserved for judgment; 5and did not spare the
ancient world, but saved Noah, *one of* eight *people,* a
preacher of righteousness, bringing in the flood on the
world of the ungodly; 6and turning the cities of Sodom and
Gomorrah into ashes, condemned *them* to destruction,
making *them* an example to those who afterward would
live ungodly; 7and delivered righteous Lot, *who was*
oppressed by the filthy conduct of the wicked 8(for that
righteous man, dwelling among them, tormented *his* righ-
teous soul from day to day by seeing and hearing *their*
lawless deeds)— 9*then* the Lord knows how to deliver the
godly out of temptations and to reserve the unjust under
punishment for the day of judgment, 10and especially
those who walk according to the flesh in the lust of
uncleanness and despise authority. *They are* presumptu-
ous, self-willed. They are not afraid to speak evil of digni-
taries, 11whereas angels, who are greater in power and
might, do not bring a reviling accusation against them
before the Lord.

Depravity of False Teachers

12But these, like natural brute beasts made to be caught
and destroyed, speak evil of the things they do not under-
stand, and will utterly perish in their own corruption,

THE MESSAGE

God didn't let the rebel angels off the hook, but jailed them in hell till Judgment Day. Neither did he let the ancient ungodly world off. He wiped it out with a flood, rescuing only eight people—Noah, the sole voice of righteousness, was one of them.

God decreed destruction for the cities of Sodom and Gomorrah. A mound of ashes was all that was left—grim warning to anyone bent on an ungodly life. But that good man Lot, driven nearly out of his mind by the sexual filth and perversity, was rescued. Surrounded by moral rot day after day after day, that righteous man was in constant torment.

So God knows how to rescue the godly from evil trials. And he knows how to hold the feet of the wicked to the fire until Judgment Day.

Predators on the Prowl

God is especially incensed against these "teachers" who live by lust, addicted to a filthy existence. They despise interference from true authority, preferring to indulge in self-rule. Insolent egotists, they don't hesitate to speak evil against the most splendid of creatures. Even angels, their superiors in every way, wouldn't think of throwing their weight around like that, trying to slander others before God.

These people are nothing but brute beasts, born in the wild, predators on the prowl. In the very act of bringing down others with their ignorant blasphemies, they themselves will be brought down, losers in the end. Their evil

KING JAMES VERSION

13 And shall receive the reward of unrighteousness, *as* they that count it pleasure to riot in the day time. Spots *they are* and blemishes, sporting themselves with their own deceivings while they feast with you;

14 Having eyes full of adultery, and that cannot cease from sin; beguiling unstable souls: an heart they have exercised with covetous practices; cursed children:

15 Which have forsaken the right way, and are gone astray, following the way of Balaam *the son* of Bosor, who loved the wages of unrighteousness;

16 But was rebuked for his iniquity: the dumb ass speaking with man's voice forbad the madness of the prophet.

17 These are wells without water, clouds that are carried with a tempest; to whom the mist of darkness is reserved for ever.

18 For when they speak great swelling *words* of vanity, they allure through the lusts of the flesh, *through much* wantonness, those that were clean escaped from them who live in error.

19 While they promise them liberty, they themselves are the servants of corruption: for of whom a man is overcome, of the same is he brought in bondage.

20 For if after they have escaped the pollutions of the world through the knowledge of the Lord and Saviour Jesus Christ, they are again entangled therein, and overcome, the latter end is worse with them than the beginning.

NEW AMERICAN STANDARD BIBLE

13 suffering wrong as the wages of doing wrong. They count it a pleasure to revel in the daytime. They are stains and blemishes, reveling in their [1]deceptions, as they carouse with you,

14 having eyes full of adultery that never cease from sin, enticing unstable souls, having a heart trained in greed, accursed children;

15 forsaking the right way, they have gone astray, having followed the way of Balaam, the *son* of Beor, who loved the wages of unrighteousness;

16 but he received a rebuke for his own transgression, *for* a mute donkey, speaking with a voice of a man, restrained the madness of the prophet.

17 These are springs without water and mists driven by a storm, for whom the black darkness has been reserved.

18 For speaking out arrogant *words* of vanity they entice by fleshly desires, by sensuality, those who barely escape from the ones who live in error,

19 promising them freedom while they themselves are slaves of corruption; for by what a man is overcome, by this he is enslaved.

20 For if, after they have escaped the defilements of the world by the knowledge of the Lord and Savior Jesus Christ, they are again entangled in them and are overcome, the last state has become worse for them than the first.

2:13 [1] One early ms reads *love feasts*

NEW CENTURY VERSION

13They have caused many people to suffer, so they themselves will suffer. That is their pay for what they have done. They take pleasure in openly doing evil, so they are like dirty spots and stains among you. They delight in trickery while eating meals with you. 14Every time they look at a woman they want her, and their desire for sin is never satisfied. They lead weak people into the trap of sin, and they have taught their hearts to be greedy. God will punish them! 15These false teachers left the right road and lost their way, following the way Balaam went. Balaam was the son of Beor, who loved being paid for doing wrong. 16But a donkey, which cannot talk, told Balaam he was sinning. It spoke with a man's voice and stopped the prophet's crazy thinking.

17Those false teachers are like springs without water and clouds blown by a storm. A place in the blackest darkness has been kept for them. 18They brag with words that mean nothing. By their evil desires they lead people into the trap of sin—people who are just beginning to escape from others who live in error. 19They promise them freedom, but they themselves are not free. They are slaves of things that will be destroyed. For people are slaves of anything that controls them. 20They were made free from the evil in the world by knowing our Lord and Savior Jesus Christ. But if they return to evil things and those things control them, then it is worse for them than it was before.

CONTEMPORARY ENGLISH VERSION

13They have done evil, and they will be rewarded with evil.

They think it is fun to have wild parties during the day. They are immoral, and the meals they eat with you are spoiled by the shameful and selfish way they carry on.[c] 14All they think about is having sex with someone else's husband or wife. There is no end to their wicked deeds. They trick people who are easily fooled, and their minds are filled with greedy thoughts. But they are headed for trouble!

15They have left the true road and have gone down the wrong path by following the example of the prophet Balaam. He was the son of Beor and loved what he got from being a crook. 16But a donkey corrected him for this evil deed. It spoke to him with a human voice and made him stop his foolishness.

17These people are like dried up water holes and clouds blown by a windstorm. The darkest part of hell is waiting for them. 18They brag out loud about their stupid nonsense. And by being vulgar and crude, they trap people who have barely escaped from living the wrong kind of life. 19They promise freedom to everyone. But they are merely slaves of filthy living, because people are slaves of whatever controls them.

20When they learned about our Lord and Savior Jesus Christ, they escaped from the filthy things of this world. But they are again caught up and controlled by these filthy things, and now they are in worse shape than they were at

[c] 2.13 *and the meals they eat with you are spoiled by the shameful and selfish way they carry on*: Some manuscripts have "and the meals they eat with you are spoiled by the shameful way they carry on during your feasts of Christian love."

NEW INTERNATIONAL VERSION

[13]They will be paid back with harm for the harm they have done. Their idea of pleasure is to carouse in broad daylight. They are blots and blemishes, reveling in their pleasures while they feast with you.[e] [14]With eyes full of adultery, they never stop sinning; they seduce the unstable; they are experts in greed—an accursed brood! [15]They have left the straight way and wandered off to follow the way of Balaam son of Beor, who loved the wages of wickedness. [16]But he was rebuked for his wrongdoing by a donkey—a beast without speech—who spoke with a man's voice and restrained the prophet's madness.

[17]These men are springs without water and mists driven by a storm. Blackest darkness is reserved for them. [18]For they mouth empty, boastful words and, by appealing to the lustful desires of sinful human nature, they entice people who are just escaping from those who live in error. [19]They promise them freedom, while they themselves are slaves of depravity—for a man is a slave to whatever has mastered him. [20]If they have escaped the corruption of the world by knowing our Lord and Savior Jesus Christ and are again entangled in it and overcome, they are worse off at the end than they were at the beginning. [21]It would

[e] *13* Some manuscripts *in their love feasts*

NEW LIVING TRANSLATION

and they will be destroyed along with them. [13]Their destruction is their reward for the harm they have done. They love to indulge in evil pleasures in broad daylight. They are a disgrace and a stain among you. They revel in deceitfulness while they feast with you. [14]They commit adultery with their eyes, and their lust is never satisfied. They make a game of luring unstable people into sin. They train themselves to be greedy; they are doomed and cursed. [15]They have wandered off the right road and followed the way of Balaam son of Beor,* who loved to earn money by doing wrong. [16]But Balaam was stopped from his mad course when his donkey rebuked him with a human voice.

[17]These people are as useless as dried-up springs of water or as clouds blown away by the wind—promising much and delivering nothing. They are doomed to blackest darkness. [18]They brag about themselves with empty, foolish boasting. With lustful desire as their bait, they lure back into sin those who have just escaped from such wicked living. [19]They promise freedom, but they themselves are slaves to sin and corruption. For you are a slave to whatever controls you. [20]And when people escape from the wicked ways of the world by learning about our Lord and Savior Jesus Christ and then get tangled up with sin and become its slave again, they are worse off than before.

2:15 Other manuscripts read *Bosor*.

NEW KING JAMES VERSION

[13]*and* will receive the wages of unrighteousness, *as* those who count it pleasure to carouse in the daytime. *They are* spots and blemishes, carousing in their own deceptions while they feast with you, [14]having eyes full of adultery and that cannot cease from sin, enticing unstable souls. *They have* a heart trained in covetous practices, *and are* accursed children. [15]They have forsaken the right way and gone astray, following the way of Balaam the *son* of Beor, who loved the wages of unrighteousness; [16]but he was rebuked for his iniquity: a dumb donkey speaking with a man's voice restrained the madness of the prophet.

[17]These are wells without water, clouds[b] carried by a tempest, for whom is reserved the blackness of darkness forever.[c]

Deceptions of False Teachers

[18]For when they speak great swelling *words* of emptiness, they allure through the lusts of the flesh, through lewdness, the ones who have actually escaped[d] from those who live in error. [19]While they promise them liberty, they themselves are slaves of corruption; for by whom a person is overcome, by him also he is brought into bondage. [20]For if, after they have escaped the pollutions of the world through the knowledge of the Lord and Savior Jesus Christ, they are again entangled in them and overcome, the latter end is worse for them than the beginning. [21]For it would

2:17 [b] NU-Text reads *and mists.* [c] NU-Text omits *forever.*
2:18 [d] NU-Text reads *are barely escaping.*

THE MESSAGE

will boomerang on them. They're so despicable and addicted to pleasure that they indulge in wild parties, carousing in broad daylight. They're obsessed with adultery, compulsive in sin, seducing every vulnerable soul they come upon. Their specialty is greed, and they're experts at it. Dead souls!

They've left the main road and are directionless, having taken the way of Balaam, son of Beor, the prophet who turned profiteer, a connoisseur of evil. But Balaam was stopped in his wayward tracks: A dumb animal spoke in a human voice and prevented the prophet's craziness.

There's nothing to these people—they're dried-up fountains, storm-scattered clouds, headed for a black hole in hell. They are loudmouths, full of hot air, but still they're dangerous. Men and women who have recently escaped from a deviant life are most susceptible to their brand of seduction. They promise these newcomers freedom, but they themselves are slaves of corruption, for if they're addicted to corruption—and they are—they're *enslaved*.

If they've escaped from the slum of sin by experiencing our Master and Savior, Jesus Christ, and then slid back into that same old life again, they're worse than if they had

KING JAMES VERSION

21 For it had been better for them not to have known the way of righteousness, than, after they have known *it*, to turn from the holy commandment delivered unto them.

22 But it is happened unto them according to the true proverb, The dog *is* turned to his own vomit again; and the sow that was washed to her wallowing in the mire.

3 This second epistle, beloved, I now write unto you; in *both* which I stir up your pure minds by way of remembrance:

2 That ye may be mindful of the words which were spoken before by the holy prophets, and of the commandment of us the apostles of the Lord and Saviour:

3 ¶ Knowing this first, that there shall come in the last days scoffers, walking after their own lusts,

4 And saying, Where is the promise of his coming? for since the fathers fell asleep, all things continue as *they were* from the beginning of the creation.

5 For this they willingly are ignorant of, that by the word of God the heavens were of old, and the earth standing out of the water and in the water:

6 Whereby the world that then was, being overflowed with water, perished:

NEW AMERICAN STANDARD BIBLE

21 For it would be better for them not to have known the way of righteousness, than having known it, to turn away from the holy commandment handed on to them.

22 It has happened to them according to the true proverb, "A DOG RETURNS TO ITS OWN VOMIT," and, "A sow, after washing, *returns* to wallowing in the mire."

Purpose of This Letter

3 This is now, beloved, the second letter I am writing to you in which I am stirring up your sincere mind by way of reminder,

2 that you should remember the words spoken beforehand by the holy prophets and the commandment of the Lord and Savior *spoken* by your apostles.

The Coming Day of the Lord

3 Know this first of all, that in the last days mockers will come with *their* mocking, following after their own lusts,

4 and saying, "Where is the promise of His coming? For *ever* since the fathers fell asleep, all continues just as it was from the beginning of creation."

5 For when they maintain this, it escapes their notice that by the word of God *the* heavens existed long ago and *the* earth was formed out of water and by water,

6 through which the world at that time was destroyed, being flooded with water.

NEW CENTURY VERSION

21 Yes, it would be better for them to have never known the right way than to know it and to turn away from the holy teaching that was given to them. 22 What they did is like this true saying: "A dog goes back to what it has thrown up,"[b] and, "After a pig is washed, it goes back and rolls in the mud."

Jesus Will Come Again

3 My friends, this is the second letter I have written you to help your honest minds remember. 2 I want you to think about the words the holy prophets spoke in the past, and remember the command our Lord and Savior gave us through your apostles. 3 It is most important for you to understand what will happen in the last days. People will laugh at you. They will live doing the evil things they want to do. 4 They will say, "Jesus promised to come again. Where is he? Our fathers have died, but the world continues the way it has been since it was made." 5 But they do not want to remember what happened long ago. By the word of God heaven was made, and the earth was made from water and with water. 6 Then the world was flooded and destroyed with

2:22 [b] **"A dog...up"** Quotation from Proverbs 26:11.

CONTEMPORARY ENGLISH VERSION

first. 21 They would have been better off if they had never known about the right way. Even after they knew what was right, they turned their backs on the holy commandments that they were given. 22 What happened to them is just like the true saying,

"A dog will come back
to lick up its own vomit.
A pig that has been washed
will roll in the mud."

The Lord Will Return

3 My dear friends, this is the second letter I have written to encourage you to do some honest thinking. I don't want you to forget 2 what God's prophets said would happen. You must never forget what the holy prophets taught in the past. And you must remember what the apostles told you our Lord and Savior has commanded us to do.

3 But first you must realize that in the last days some people won't think about anything except their own selfish desires. They will make fun of you 4 and say, "Didn't your Lord promise to come back? Yet the first leaders have already died, and the world hasn't changed a bit."

5 They will say this because they want to forget that long ago the heavens and the earth were made at God's command. The earth came out of water and was made from water. 6 Later it was destroyed by the waters of a mighty

NEW INTERNATIONAL VERSION

have been better for them not to have known the way of
righteousness, than to have known it and then to turn
their backs on the sacred command that was passed on to
them. 22Of them the proverbs are true: "A dog returns to
its vomit,"[f] and, "A sow that is washed goes back to her
wallowing in the mud."

The Day of the Lord

3 Dear friends, this is now my second letter to you. I
have written both of them as reminders to stimulate
you to wholesome thinking. 2I want you to recall the words
spoken in the past by the holy prophets and the command
given by our Lord and Savior through your apostles.
3First of all, you must understand that in the last days
scoffers will come, scoffing and following their own evil
desires. 4They will say, "Where is this 'coming' he prom-
ised? Ever since our fathers died, everything goes on as it
has since the beginning of creation." 5But they deliberately
forget that long ago by God's word the heavens existed
and the earth was formed out of water and by water. 6By
these waters also the world of that time was deluged and

f 22 Prov. 26:11

NEW LIVING TRANSLATION

21It would be better if they had never known the right way
to live than to know it and then reject the holy command-
ments that were given to them. 22They make these prov-
erbs come true: "A dog returns to its vomit,"[*] and "A
washed pig returns to the mud."

The Day of the Lord Is Coming

3 This is my second letter to you, dear friends, and in
both of them I have tried to stimulate your wholesome
thinking and refresh your memory. 2I want you to remem-
ber and understand what the holy prophets said long ago
and what our Lord and Savior commanded through your
apostles.
3First, I want to remind you that in the last days there
will be scoffers who will laugh at the truth and do every
evil thing they desire. 4This will be their argument: "Jesus
promised to come back, did he? Then where is he? Why, as
far back as anyone can remember, everything has remained
exactly the same since the world was first created."
5They deliberately forget that God made the heavens by
the word of his command, and he brought the earth up
from the water and surrounded it with water. 6Then he
used the water to destroy the world with a mighty flood.

2:22 Prov 26:11.

NEW KING JAMES VERSION

have been better for them not to have known the way of
righteousness, than having known *it,* to turn from the holy
commandment delivered to them. 22But it has happened to
them according to the true proverb: *"A dog returns to his
own vomit,"*[e] and, "a sow, having washed, to her wal-
lowing in the mire."

God's Promise Is Not Slack

3 Beloved, I now write to you this second epistle (in
both of which I stir up your pure minds by way of
reminder), 2that you may be mindful of the words which
were spoken before by the holy prophets, and of the com-
mandment of us,[a] the apostles of the Lord and Savior,
3knowing this first: that scoffers will come in the last
days, walking according to their own lusts, 4and saying,
"Where is the promise of His coming? For since the fathers
fell asleep, all things continue as *they were* from the begin-
ning of creation." 5For this they willfully forget: that by
the word of God the heavens were of old, and the earth
standing out of water and in the water, 6by which the
world *that* then existed perished, being flooded with water.

2:22 [e] Proverbs 26:11 3:2 [a] NU-Text and M-Text read *commandment of the apostles of your Lord and Savior* or *commandment of your apostles of the Lord and Savior.*

THE MESSAGE

never left. Better not to have started out on the straight
road to God than to start out and then turn back, repudiat-
ing the experience and the holy command. They prove the
point of the proverbs, "A dog goes back to its own vomit,"
and, "A scrubbed-up pig heads for the mud."

In the Last Days

3 My dear friends, this is now the second time I've writ-
ten to you, both letters reminders to hold your minds
in a state of undistracted attention. Keep in mind what the
holy prophets said, and the command of our Master and
Savior that was passed on by your apostles.
First off, you need to know that in the last days, mock-
ers are going to have a heyday. Reducing everything to the
level of their puny feelings, they'll mock, "So what's hap-
pened to the promise of his Coming? Our ancestors are
dead and buried, and everything's going on just as it has
from the first day of creation. Nothing's changed."
They conveniently forget that long ago all the galaxies
and this very planet were brought into existence out of
watery chaos by God's word. Then God's word brought the
chaos back in a flood that destroyed the world. The current

KING JAMES VERSION

7 But the heavens and the earth, which are now, by the same word are kept in store, reserved unto fire against the day of judgment and perdition of ungodly men.

8 ¶ But, beloved, be not ignorant of this one thing, that one day *is* with the Lord as a thousand years, and a thousand years as one day.

9 ¶ The Lord is not slack concerning his promise, as some men count slackness; but is longsuffering to us-ward, not willing that any should perish, but that all should come to repentance.

10 But the day of the Lord will come as a thief in the night; in the which the heavens shall pass away with a great noise, and the elements shall melt with fervent heat, the earth also and the works that are therein shall be burned up.

11 ¶ *Seeing* then *that* all these things shall be dissolved, what manner *of persons* ought ye to be in *all* holy conversation and godliness,

12 Looking for and hasting unto the coming of the day of God, wherein the heavens being on fire shall be dissolved, and the elements shall melt with fervent heat?

13 Nevertheless we, according to his promise, look for new heavens and a new earth, wherein dwelleth righteousness.

14 Wherefore, beloved, seeing that ye look for such things, be diligent that ye may be found of him in peace, without spot, and blameless.

NEW AMERICAN STANDARD BIBLE

7 But by His word the present heavens and earth are being reserved for fire, kept for the day of judgment and destruction of ungodly men.

8 But do not let this one *fact* escape your notice, beloved, that with the Lord one day is like a thousand years, and a thousand years like one day.

9 The Lord is not slow about His promise, as some count slowness, but is patient toward you, not wishing for any to perish but for all to come to repentance.

A New Heaven and Earth

10 But the day of the Lord will come like a thief, in which the heavens will pass away with a roar and the elements will be destroyed with intense heat, and the earth and its works will be [l]burned up.

11 Since all these things are to be destroyed in this way, what sort of people ought you to be in holy conduct and godliness,

12 looking for and hastening the coming of the day of God, because of which the heavens will be destroyed by burning, and the elements will melt with intense heat!

13 But according to His promise we are looking for new heavens and a new earth, in which righteousness dwells.

14 Therefore, beloved, since you look for these things, be diligent to be found by Him in peace, spotless and blameless,

3:10 [l] Two early mss read *discovered*

NEW CENTURY VERSION

water. [7]And that same word of God is keeping heaven and earth that we now have in order to be destroyed by fire. They are being kept for the Judgment Day and the destruction of all who are against God.

[8]But do not forget this one thing, dear friends: To the Lord one day is as a thousand years, and a thousand years is as one day. [9]The Lord is not slow in doing what he promised—the way some people understand slowness. But God is being patient with you. He does not want anyone to be lost, but he wants all people to change their hearts and lives.

[10]But the day of the Lord will come like a thief. The skies will disappear with a loud noise. Everything in them will be destroyed by fire, and the earth and everything in it will be burned up.[a] [11]In that way everything will be destroyed. So what kind of people should you be? You should live holy lives and serve God, [12]as you wait for and look forward to the coming of the day of God. When that day comes, the skies will be destroyed with fire, and everything in them will melt with heat. [13]But God made a promise to us, and we are waiting for a new heaven and a new earth where goodness lives.

[14]Dear friends, since you are waiting for this to happen, do your best to be without sin and without fault. Try to be

3:10 [a] **will be burned up** Many Greek copies say, "will be found." One copy says, "will disappear."

CONTEMPORARY ENGLISH VERSION

flood. [7]But God has commanded the present heavens and earth to remain until the day of judgment. Then they will be set on fire, and ungodly people will be destroyed.

[8]Dear friends, don't forget that for the Lord one day is the same as a thousand years, and a thousand years is the same as one day. [9]The Lord isn't slow about keeping his promises, as some people think he is. In fact, God is patient, because he wants everyone to turn from sin and no one to be lost.

[10]The day of the Lord's return will surprise us like a thief. The heavens will disappear with a loud noise, and the heat will melt the whole universe.[a] Then the earth and everything on it will be seen for what they are.[b]

[11]Everything will be destroyed. So you should serve and honor God by the way you live. [12]You should look forward to the day when God judges everyone, and you should try to make it come soon.[c] On that day the heavens will be destroyed by fire, and everything else will melt in the heat. [13]But God has promised us a new heaven and a new earth, where justice will rule. We are really looking forward to that!

[14]My friends, while you are waiting, you should make certain that the Lord finds you pure, spotless, and living at

[a] **3.10** *the whole universe*: Probably the sun, moon, and stars, or the elements that everything in the universe is made of. [b] **3.10** *will be seen for what they are*: Some manuscripts have "will go up in flames." [c] **3.12** *and you should try to make it come soon*: Or "and you should eagerly desire for that day to come."

NEW INTERNATIONAL VERSION

destroyed. 7By the same word the present heavens and earth are reserved for fire, being kept for the day of judgment and destruction of ungodly men.

8But do not forget this one thing, dear friends: With the Lord a day is like a thousand years, and a thousand years are like a day. 9The Lord is not slow in keeping his promise, as some understand slowness. He is patient with you, not wanting anyone to perish, but everyone to come to repentance.

10But the day of the Lord will come like a thief. The heavens will disappear with a roar; the elements will be destroyed by fire, and the earth and everything in it will be laid bare.[a]

11Since everything will be destroyed in this way, what kind of people ought you to be? You ought to live holy and godly lives 12as you look forward to the day of God and speed its coming.[b] That day will bring about the destruction of the heavens by fire, and the elements will melt in the heat. 13But in keeping with his promise we are looking forward to a new heaven and a new earth, the home of righteousness.

14So then, dear friends, since you are looking forward to this, make every effort to be found spotless, blameless and

[a] *10* Some manuscripts *be burned up* [b] *12* Or *as you wait eagerly for the day of God to come*

NEW LIVING TRANSLATION

7And God has also commanded that the heavens and the earth will be consumed by fire on the day of judgment, when ungodly people will perish.

8But you must not forget, dear friends, that a day is like a thousand years to the Lord, and a thousand years is like a day. 9The Lord isn't really being slow about his promise to return, as some people think. No, he is being patient for your sake. He does not want anyone to perish, so he is giving more time for everyone to repent. 10But the day of the Lord will come as unexpectedly as a thief. Then the heavens will pass away with a terrible noise, and everything in them will disappear in fire, and the earth and everything on it will be exposed to judgment.*

11Since everything around us is going to melt away, what holy, godly lives you should be living! 12You should look forward to that day and hurry it along—the day when God will set the heavens on fire and the elements will melt away in the flames. 13But we are looking forward to the new heavens and new earth he has promised, a world where everyone is right with God.

14And so, dear friends, while you are waiting for these things to happen, make every effort to live a pure and blameless life. And be at peace with God.

3:10 Some manuscripts read *will be burned up.*

NEW KING JAMES VERSION

7But the heavens and the earth *which* are now preserved by the same word, are reserved for fire until the day of judgment and perdition of ungodly men.

8But, beloved, do not forget this one thing, that with the Lord one day *is* as a thousand years, and a thousand years as one day. 9The Lord is not slack concerning *His* promise, as some count slackness, but is longsuffering toward us,[b] not willing that any should perish but that all should come to repentance.

The Day of the Lord

10But the day of the Lord will come as a thief in the night, in which the heavens will pass away with a great noise, and the elements will melt with fervent heat; both the earth and the works that are in it will be burned up.[c] 11Therefore, since all these things will be dissolved, what manner *of persons* ought you to be in holy conduct and godliness, 12looking for and hastening the coming of the day of God, because of which the heavens will be dissolved, being on fire, and the elements will melt with fervent heat? 13Nevertheless we, according to His promise, look for new heavens and a new earth in which righteousness dwells.

Be Steadfast

14Therefore, beloved, looking forward to these things, be diligent to be found by Him in peace, without spot and

3:9 [b] NU-Text reads *you.* **3:10** [c] NU-Text reads *laid bare* (literally *found*).

THE MESSAGE

galaxies and earth are fuel for the final fire. God is poised, ready to speak his word again, ready to give the signal for the judgment and destruction of the desecrating skeptics.

The Day the Sky Will Collapse

Don't overlook the obvious here, friends. With God, one day is as good as a thousand years, a thousand years as a day. God isn't late with his promise as some measure lateness. He is restraining himself on account of you, holding back the End because he doesn't want anyone lost. He's giving everyone space and time to change.

But when the Day of God's Judgment does come, it will be unannounced, like a thief. The sky will collapse with a thunderous bang, everything disintegrating in a huge conflagration, earth and all its works exposed to the scrutiny of Judgment.

Since everything here today might well be gone tomorrow, do you see how essential it is to live a holy life? Daily expect the Day of God, eager for its arrival. The galaxies will burn up and the elements melt down that day—but *we'll* hardly notice. We'll be looking the other way, ready for the promised new heavens and the promised new earth, all landscaped with righteousness.

✠

So, my dear friends, since this is what you have to look forward to, do your very best to be found living at your best,

KING JAMES VERSION

15 And account *that* the longsuffering of our Lord *is* salvation; even as our beloved brother Paul also according to the wisdom given unto him hath written unto you;

16 As also in all *his* epistles, speaking in them of these things; in which are some things hard to be understood, which they that are unlearned and unstable wrest, as *they do* also the other scriptures, unto their own destruction.

17 Ye therefore, beloved, seeing ye know *these things* before, beware lest ye also, being led away with the error of the wicked, fall from your own stedfastness.

18 But grow in grace, and *in* the knowledge of our Lord and Saviour Jesus Christ. To him *be* glory both now and for ever. Amen.

NEW AMERICAN STANDARD BIBLE

15 and regard the patience of our Lord *as* salvation; just as also our beloved brother Paul, according to the wisdom given him, wrote to you,

16 as also in all *his* letters, speaking in them of these things, in which are some things hard to understand, which the untaught and unstable distort, as *they do* also the rest of the Scriptures, to their own destruction.

17 You therefore, beloved, knowing this beforehand, be on your guard so that you are not carried away by the error of unprincipled men and fall from your own steadfastness,

18 but grow in the grace and knowledge of our Lord and Savior Jesus Christ. To Him *be* the glory, both now and to the day of eternity. Amen.

NEW CENTURY VERSION

at peace with God. 15Remember that we are saved because our Lord is patient. Our dear brother Paul told you the same thing when he wrote to you with the wisdom that God gave him. 16He writes about this in all his letters. Some things in Paul's letters are hard to understand, and people who are ignorant and weak in faith explain these things falsely. They also falsely explain the other Scriptures, but they are destroying themselves by doing this.

17Dear friends, since you already know about this, be careful. Do not let those evil people lead you away by the wrong they do. Be careful so you will not fall from your strong faith. 18But grow in the grace and knowledge of our Lord and Savior Jesus Christ. Glory be to him now and forever! Amen.

CONTEMPORARY ENGLISH VERSION

peace. 15Don't forget that the Lord is patient because he wants people to be saved. This is also what our dear friend Paul said when he wrote you with the wisdom that God had given him. 16Paul talks about these same things in all his letters, but part of what he says is hard to understand. Some ignorant and unsteady people even destroy themselves by twisting what he said. They do the same thing with other Scriptures too.

17My dear friends, you have been warned ahead of time! So don't let the errors of evil people lead you down the wrong path and make you lose your balance. 18Let the wonderful kindness and the understanding that come from our Lord and Savior Jesus Christ help you to keep on growing. Praise Jesus now and forever! Amen.[d]

[d] 3.18 *Amen*: Some manuscripts do not have "Amen."

NEW INTERNATIONAL VERSION

at peace with him. 15 Bear in mind that our Lord's patience means salvation, just as our dear brother Paul also wrote you with the wisdom that God gave him. 16 He writes the same way in all his letters, speaking in them of these matters. His letters contain some things that are hard to understand, which ignorant and unstable people distort, as they do the other Scriptures, to their own destruction.

17 Therefore, dear friends, since you already know this, be on your guard so that you may not be carried away by the error of lawless men and fall from your secure position. 18 But grow in the grace and knowledge of our Lord and Savior Jesus Christ. To him be glory both now and forever! Amen.

NEW LIVING TRANSLATION

15 And remember, the Lord is waiting so that people have time to be saved. This is just as our beloved brother Paul wrote to you with the wisdom God gave him—16 speaking of these things in all of his letters. Some of his comments are hard to understand, and those who are ignorant and unstable have twisted his letters around to mean something quite different from what he meant, just as they do the other parts of Scripture—and the result is disaster for them.

Peter's Final Words

17 I am warning you ahead of time, dear friends, so that you can watch out and not be carried away by the errors of these wicked people. I don't want you to lose your own secure footing. 18 But grow in the special favor and knowledge of our Lord and Savior Jesus Christ.

To him be all glory and honor, both now and forevermore. Amen.

NEW KING JAMES VERSION

blameless; 15 and consider *that* the longsuffering of our Lord *is* salvation—as also our beloved brother Paul, according to the wisdom given to him, has written to you, 16 as also in all his epistles, speaking in them of these things, in which are some things hard to understand, which untaught and unstable *people* twist to their own destruction, as *they do* also the rest of the Scriptures.

17 You therefore, beloved, since you know *this* beforehand, beware lest you also fall from your own steadfastness, being led away with the error of the wicked; 18 but grow in the grace and knowledge of our Lord and Savior Jesus Christ.

To Him *be* the glory both now and forever. Amen.

THE MESSAGE

in purity and peace. Interpret our Master's patient restraint for what it is: salvation. Our good brother Paul, who was given much wisdom in these matters, refers to this in all his letters, and has written you essentially the same thing. Some things Paul writes are difficult to understand. Irresponsible people who don't know what they are talking about twist them every which way. They do it to the rest of the Scriptures, too, destroying themselves as they do it.

But you, friends, are well-warned. Be on guard lest you lose your footing and get swept off your feet by these lawless and loose-talking teachers. Grow in grace and understanding of our Master and Savior, Jesus Christ.

Glory to the Master, now and forever! Yes!

KING JAMES VERSION

THE FIRST EPISTLE OF
ST. JOHN

1 That which was from the beginning, which we have heard, which we have seen with our eyes, which we have looked upon, and our hands have handled, of the Word of life;

2 (For the life was manifested, and we have seen *it*, and bear witness, and shew unto you that eternal life, which was with the Father, and was manifested unto us;)

3 That which we have seen and heard declare we unto you, that ye also may have fellowship with us: and truly our fellowship *is* with the Father, and with his Son Jesus Christ.

4 And these things write we unto you, that your joy may be full.

5 ¶ This then is the message which we have heard of him, and declare unto you, that God is light, and in him is no darkness at all.

NEW AMERICAN STANDARD BIBLE

THE FIRST LETTER OF
JOHN

Introduction The Incarnate Word

1 What was from the beginning, what we have heard, what we have seen with our eyes, what we have looked at and touched with our hands, concerning the Word of Life—

2 and the life was manifested, and we have seen and testify and proclaim to you the eternal life, which was with the Father and was manifested to us—

3 what we have seen and heard we proclaim to you also, so that you too may have fellowship with us; and indeed our fellowship is with the Father, and with His Son Jesus Christ.

4 These things we write, so that our joy may be made complete.

God Is Light

5 This is the message we have heard from Him and announce to you, that God is Light, and in Him there is no darkness at all.

NEW CENTURY VERSION

1 JOHN

1 We write you now about what has always existed,
which we have heard, we have seen with our own
eyes, we have looked at, and we have touched with our
hands. We write to you about the Word[a] that gives life.
2He who gives life was shown to us. We saw him and can
give proof about it. And now we announce to you that he
has life that continues forever. He was with God the Father
and was shown to us. 3We announce to you what we have
seen and heard, because we want you also to have fellow-
ship with us. Our fellowship is with God the Father and
with his Son, Jesus Christ. 4We write this to you so you
can be full of joy with us.

God Forgives Our Sins

5Here is the message we have heard from Christ and
now announce to you: God is light,[b] and in him there is no

1:18 [a] **Word** The Greek word is "logos," meaning any kind of communication. Here, it means Christ, who was the way God told people about himself. 1:5 [b] **light** Here, this word is used as a symbol of God's goodness or truth.

CONTEMPORARY ENGLISH VERSION

1 JOHN

1 The Word that gives life
was from the beginning,
and this is the one
our message is about.

Our ears have heard,
our own eyes have seen,
and our hands touched
this Word.

2The one who gives life appeared! We saw it happen,
and we are witnesses to what we have seen. Now we are
telling you about this eternal life that was with the Father
and appeared to us. 3We are telling you what we have seen
and heard, so that you may share in this life with us. And
we share in it with the Father and with his Son Jesus
Christ. 4We are writing to tell you these things, because
this makes us[a] truly happy.

God Is Light

5Jesus told us that God is light and doesn't have any
darkness in him. Now we are telling you.

[a] 1.4 *us*: Some manuscripts have "you."

NEW INTERNATIONAL VERSION

1 JOHN

The Word of Life

1 That which was from the beginning, which we have
heard, which we have seen with our eyes, which we
have looked at and our hands have touched—this we pro-
claim concerning the Word of life. 2The life appeared; we
have seen it and testify to it, and we proclaim to you the
eternal life, which was with the Father and has appeared
to us. 3We proclaim to you what we have seen and heard,
so that you also may have fellowship with us. And our fel-
lowship is with the Father and with his Son, Jesus Christ.
4We write this to make our[a] joy complete.

Walking in the Light

5This is the message we have heard from him and
declare to you: God is light; in him there is no darkness at

[a] *4* Some manuscripts *your*

NEW LIVING TRANSLATION

1 JOHN

Introduction

1 The one who existed from the beginning* is the one
we have heard and seen. We saw him with our own
eyes and touched him with our own hands. He is Jesus
Christ, the Word of life. 2This one who is life from God was
shown to us, and we have seen him. And now we testify
and announce to you that he is the one who is eternal life.
He was with the Father, and then he was shown to us.
3We are telling you about what we ourselves have actually
seen and heard, so that you may have fellowship with us.
And our fellowship is with the Father and with his Son,
Jesus Christ.
4We are writing these things so that our* joy will be
complete.

Living in the Light

5This is the message he has given us to announce to
you: God is light and there is no darkness in him at all.

1:1 Greek *What was from the beginning.* 1:4 Some manuscripts read *your.*

NEW KING JAMES VERSION

THE FIRST EPISTLE OF JOHN

What Was Heard, Seen, and Touched

1 That which was from the beginning, which we have
heard, which we have seen with our eyes, which we
have looked upon, and our hands have handled, concern-
ing the Word of life— 2the life was manifested, and we
have seen, and bear witness, and declare to you that eter-
nal life which was with the Father and was manifested to
us— 3that which we have seen and heard we declare to
you, that you also may have fellowship with us; and truly
our fellowship *is* with the Father and with His Son Jesus
Christ. 4And these things we write to you that your[a] joy
may be full.

Fellowship with Him and One Another

5This is the message which we have heard from Him and
declare to you, that God is light and in Him is no darkness

1:4 [a] NU-Text and M-Text read *our.*

THE MESSAGE

1 JOHN

1 From the very first day, we were there, taking it all
in—we heard it with our own ears, saw it with our
own eyes, verified it with our own hands. The Word of Life
appeared right before our eyes; we saw it happen! And
now we're telling you in most sober prose that what we
witnessed was, incredibly, this: The infinite Life of God
himself took shape before us.

We saw it, we heard it, and now we're telling you so you
can experience it along with us, this experience of commu-
nion with the Father and his Son, Jesus Christ. Our motive
for writing is simply this: We want you to enjoy this, too.
Your joy will double our joy!

Walk in the Light

This, in essence, is the message we heard from Christ
and are passing on to you: God is light, pure light; there's
not a trace of darkness in him.

KING JAMES VERSION

6 If we say that we have fellowship with him, and walk in darkness, we lie, and do not the truth:

7 But if we walk in the light, as he is in the light, we have fellowship one with another, and the blood of Jesus Christ his Son cleanseth us from all sin.

8 ¶ If we say that we have no sin, we deceive ourselves, and the truth is not in us.

9 If we confess our sins, he is faithful and just to forgive us *our* sins, and to cleanse us from all unrighteousness.

10 If we say that we have not sinned, we make him a liar, and his word is not in us.

2 My little children, these things write I unto you, that ye sin not. And if any man sin, we have an advocate with the Father, Jesus Christ the righteous:

2 And he is the propitiation for our sins: and not for ours only, but also for *the sins of* the whole world.

3 ¶ And hereby we do know that we know him, if we keep his commandments.

4 He that saith, I know him, and keepeth not his commandments, is a liar, and the truth is not in him.

5 But whoso keepeth his word, in him verily is the love of God perfected: hereby know we that we are in him.

6 He that saith he abideth in him ought himself also so to walk, even as he walked.

NEW AMERICAN STANDARD BIBLE

6 If we say that we have fellowship with Him and *yet* walk in the darkness, we lie and do not practice the truth;

7 but if we walk in the Light as He Himself is in the Light, we have fellowship with one another, and the blood of Jesus His Son cleanses us from all sin.

8 If we say that we have no sin, we are deceiving ourselves and the truth is not in us.

9 If we confess our sins, He is faithful and righteous to forgive us our sins and to cleanse us from all unrighteousness.

10 If we say that we have not sinned, we make Him a liar and His word is not in us.

Christ Is Our Advocate

2 My little children, I am writing these things to you so that you may not sin. And if anyone sins, we have an [1]Advocate with the Father, Jesus Christ the righteous;

2 and He Himself is the propitiation for our sins; and not for ours only, but also for *those of* the whole world.

3 By this we know that we have come to know Him, if we keep His commandments.

4 The one who says, "I have come to know Him," and does not keep His commandments, is a liar, and the truth is not in him;

5 but whoever keeps His word, in him the love of God has truly been perfected. By this we know that we are in Him:

6 the one who says he abides in Him ought himself to walk in the same manner as He walked.

2:1 [1] Gr *Paracletos,* one called alongside to help; or *Intercessor*

NEW CENTURY VERSION

darkness at all. 6So if we say we have fellowship with God,
but we continue living in darkness, we are liars and do not
follow the truth. 7But if we live in the light, as God is in
the light, we can share fellowship with each other. Then
the blood of Jesus, God's Son, cleanses us from every sin.
8If we say we have no sin, we are fooling ourselves, and
the truth is not in us. 9But if we confess our sins, he will
forgive our sins, because we can trust God to do what is
right. He will cleanse us from all the wrongs we have
done. 10If we say we have not sinned, we make God a liar,
and we do not accept God's teaching.

Jesus Is Our Helper

2 My dear children, I write this letter to you so you will
not sin. But if anyone does sin, we have a helper in
the presence of the Father—Jesus Christ, the One who does
what is right. 2He is the way our sins are taken away, and
not only our sins but the sins of all people.
3We can be sure that we know God if we obey his com-
mands. 4Anyone who says, "I know God," but does not
obey God's commands is a liar, and the truth is not in that
person. 5But if someone obeys God's teaching, then in that
person God's love has truly reached its goal. This is how
we can be sure we are living in God: 6Whoever says that
he lives in God must live as Jesus lived.

CONTEMPORARY ENGLISH VERSION

6If we say that we share in life with God and keep on
living in the dark, we are lying and are not living by the
truth. 7But if we live in the light, as God does, we share in
life with each other. And the blood of his Son Jesus washes
all our sins away. 8If we say that we have not sinned, we
are fooling ourselves, and the truth isn't in our hearts.
9But if we confess our sins to God, he can always be trust-
ed to forgive us and take our sins away.
10If we say that we have not sinned, we make God a liar,
and his message isn't in our hearts.[b]

Christ Helps Us

2 My children, I am writing this so that you won't sin.
But if you do sin, Jesus Christ always does the right
thing, and he will speak to the Father for us. 2Christ is the
sacrifice that takes away our sins and the sins of all the
world's people.
3When we obey God, we are sure that we know him.
4But if we claim to know him and don't obey him, we are
lying and the truth isn't in our hearts. 5We truly love God
only when we obey him as we should, and then we know
that we belong to him. 6If we say we are his, we must fol-
low the example of Christ.

[b] 1.10 *and his message isn't in our hearts*: Or "because we have not accepted his message."

NEW INTERNATIONAL VERSION

all. 6If we claim to have fellowship with him yet walk in
the darkness, we lie and do not live by the truth. 7But if
we walk in the light, as he is in the light, we have fellow-
ship with one another, and the blood of Jesus, his Son,
purifies us from all[b] sin.
8If we claim to be without sin, we deceive ourselves and
the truth is not in us. 9If we confess our sins, he is faithful
and just and will forgive us our sins and purify us from all
unrighteousness. 10If we claim we have not sinned, we
make him out to be a liar and his word has no place in our
lives.

2 My dear children, I write this to you so that you will
not sin. But if anybody does sin, we have one who
speaks to the Father in our defense—Jesus Christ, the
Righteous One. 2He is the atoning sacrifice for our sins,
and not only for ours but also for[a] the sins of the whole
world.
3We know that we have come to know him if we obey
his commands. 4The man who says, "I know him," but
does not do what he commands is a liar, and the truth is
not in him. 5But if anyone obeys his word, God's love[b] is
truly made complete in him. This is how we know we are
in him: 6Whoever claims to live in him must walk as Jesus
did.

[b] 7 Or *every* [a] 2 Or *He is the one who turns aside God's wrath, taking away our sins, and not only ours but also* [b] 5 Or *word, love for God*

NEW LIVING TRANSLATION

6So we are lying if we say we have fellowship with God but
go on living in spiritual darkness. We are not living in the
truth. 7But if we are living in the light of God's presence,
just as Christ is, then we have fellowship with each other,
and the blood of Jesus, his Son, cleanses us from every sin.
8If we say we have no sin, we are only fooling ourselves
and refusing to accept the truth. 9But if we confess our
sins to him, he is faithful and just to forgive us and to
cleanse us from every wrong. 10If we claim we have not
sinned, we are calling God a liar and showing that his
word has no place in our hearts.

2 My dear children, I am writing this to you so that you
will not sin. But if you do sin, there is someone to
plead for you before the Father. He is Jesus Christ, the one
who pleases God completely.* 2He is the sacrifice for our
sins. He takes away not only our sins but the sins of all
the world.
3And how can we be sure that we belong to him? By
obeying his commandments. 4If someone says, "I belong to
God," but doesn't obey God's commandments, that person
is a liar and does not live in the truth. 5But those who
obey God's word really do love him. That is the way to
know whether or not we live in him. 6Those who say they
live in God should live their lives as Christ did.

2:1 Greek *Jesus Christ, the righteous.*

NEW KING JAMES VERSION

at all. 6If we say that we have fellowship with Him, and
walk in darkness, we lie and do not practice the truth. 7But
if we walk in the light as He is in the light, we have fellow-
ship with one another, and the blood of Jesus Christ His
Son cleanses us from all sin.
8If we say that we have no sin, we deceive ourselves,
and the truth is not in us. 9If we confess our sins, He is
faithful and just to forgive us *our* sins and to cleanse us
from all unrighteousness. 10If we say that we have not
sinned, we make Him a liar, and His word is not in us.

2 My little children, these things I write to you, so that
you may not sin. And if anyone sins, we have an
Advocate with the Father, Jesus Christ the righteous. 2And
He Himself is the propitiation for our sins, and not for ours
only but also for the whole world.

The Test of Knowing Him

3Now by this we know that we know Him, if we keep His
commandments. 4He who says, "I know Him," and does
not keep His commandments, is a liar, and the truth is not
in him. 5But whoever keeps His word, truly the love of God
is perfected in him. By this we know that we are in Him.
6He who says he abides in Him ought himself also to walk
just as He walked.

THE MESSAGE

If we claim that we experience a shared life with him
and continue to stumble around in the dark, we're obvi-
ously lying through our teeth—we're not *living* what we
claim. But if we walk in the light, God himself being the
light, we also experience a shared life with one another, as
the sacrificed blood of Jesus, God's Son, purges all our sin.
If we claim that we're free of sin, we're only fooling our-
selves. A claim like that is errant nonsense. On the other
hand, if we admit our sins—make a clean breast of them—
he won't let us down; he'll be true to himself. He'll forgive
our sins and purge us of all wrongdoing. If we claim that
we've never sinned, we out and out contradict God—make
a liar out of him. A claim like that only shows off our igno-
rance of God.

2 I write this, dear children, to guide you out of sin. But
if anyone does sin, we have a Priest-Friend in the
presence of the Father: Jesus Christ, righteous Jesus. When
he served as a sacrifice for our sins, he solved the sin prob-
lem for good—not only ours, but the whole world's.

The Only Way to Know We're in Him

Here's how we can be sure that we know God in the
right way: Keep his commandments.
If someone claims, "I know him well!" but doesn't keep
his commandments, he's obviously a liar. His life doesn't
match his words. But the one who keeps God's word is the
person in whom we see God's mature love. This is the only
way to be sure we're in God. Anyone who claims to be inti-
mate with God ought to live the same kind of life Jesus lived.

KING JAMES VERSION

7 ¶ Brethren, I write no new commandment unto you,
but an old commandment which ye had from the begin-
ning. The old commandment is the word which ye have
heard from the beginning.
8 Again, a new commandment I write unto you, which
thing is true in him and in you: because the darkness is
past, and the true light now shineth.
9 He that saith he is in the light, and hateth his broth-
er, is in darkness even until now.
10 He that loveth his brother abideth in the light, and
there is none occasion of stumbling in him.
11 But he that hateth his brother is in darkness, and
walketh in darkness, and knoweth not whither he goeth,
because that darkness hath blinded his eyes.
12 ¶ I write unto you, little children, because your sins
are forgiven you for his name's sake.
13 I write unto you, fathers, because ye have known him
that is from the beginning. I write unto you, young men,
because ye have overcome the wicked one. I write unto you,
little children, because ye have known the Father.

NEW AMERICAN STANDARD BIBLE

7 Beloved, I am not writing a new commandment to
you, but an old commandment which you have had from
the beginning; the old commandment is the word which
you have heard.
8 On the other hand, I am writing a new commandment
to you, which is true in Him and in you, because the dark-
ness is passing away and the true Light is already shining.
9 The one who says he is in the Light and *yet* hates his
brother is in the darkness until now.
10 The one who loves his brother abides in the Light
and there is no cause for stumbling in him.
11 But the one who hates his brother is in the darkness
and walks in the darkness, and does not know where he is
going because the darkness has blinded his eyes.
12 I am writing to you, little children, because your sins
have been forgiven you for His name's sake.
13 I am writing to you, fathers, because you know Him
who has been from the beginning. I am writing to you,
young men, because you have overcome the evil one. I have
written to you, children, because you know the Father.

NEW CENTURY VERSION

The Command to Love Others

7My dear friends, I am not writing a new command to
you but an old command you have had from the begin-
ning. It is the teaching you have already heard. 8But also I
am writing a new command to you, and you can see its
truth in Jesus and in you, because the darkness is passing
away, and the true light is already shining.
9Anyone who says, "I am in the light,"[a] but hates a
brother or sister,[b] is still in the darkness. 10Whoever loves
a brother or sister lives in the light and will not cause any-
one to stumble in his faith. 11But whoever hates a brother
or sister is in darkness, lives in darkness, and does not
know where to go, because the darkness has made that
person blind.

12 I write to you, dear children,
because your sins are forgiven through Christ.
13 I write to you, parents,
because you know the One who existed from the
beginning.
I write to you, young people,
because you have defeated the Evil One.
14 I write to you, children,
because you know the Father.

2:9 [a] **light** Here, this word is used as a symbol of God's goodness or truth. 2:9 [b] **brother or sister** Although the Greek text says "brother" here and throughout this book, the writer's words were meant for the entire church, including men and women.

CONTEMPORARY ENGLISH VERSION

The New Commandment

7My dear friends, I am not writing to give you a new
commandment. It is the same one that you were first
given, and it is the message you heard. 8But it really is a
new commandment, and you know its true meaning, just
as Christ does. You can see the darkness fading away and
the true light already shining.
9If we claim to be in the light and hate someone, we are
still in the dark. 10But if we love others, we are in the light,
and we don't cause problems for them.[a] 11If we hate others,
we are living and walking in the dark. We don't know
where we are going, because we can't see in the dark.

12 Children, I am writing you,
because your sins
have been forgiven
in the name of Christ.
13 Parents, I am writing you,
because you have known
the one who was there
from the beginning.
Young people, I am writing you,
because you have defeated
the evil one.
14 Children, I am writing you,
because you have known
the Father.

[a] 2.10 *and we don't cause problems for them*: Or "and we can see anything that might make us fall."

NEW INTERNATIONAL VERSION

7 Dear friends, I am not writing you a new command but
an old one, which you have had since the beginning. This
old command is the message you have heard. 8 Yet I am
writing you a new command; its truth is seen in him and
you, because the darkness is passing and the true light is
already shining.
9 Anyone who claims to be in the light but hates his
brother is still in the darkness. 10 Whoever loves his broth-
er lives in the light, and there is nothing in him[c] to make
him stumble. 11 But whoever hates his brother is in the
darkness and walks around in the darkness; he does not
know where he is going, because the darkness has blinded
him.

12 I write to you, dear children,
  because your sins have been forgiven on account of
    his name.
13 I write to you, fathers,
  because you have known him who is from the
    beginning.
I write to you, young men,
  because you have overcome the evil one.
I write to you, dear children,
  because you have known the Father.

[c] *10* Or *it*

NEW LIVING TRANSLATION

A New Commandment

7 Dear friends, I am not writing a new commandment, for
it is an old one you have always had, right from the begin-
ning. This commandment—to love one another—is the
same message you heard before. 8 Yet it is also new. This
commandment is true in Christ and is true among you,
because the darkness is disappearing and the true light is
already shining.
9 If anyone says, "I am living in the light," but hates a
Christian brother or sister,* that person is still living in
darkness. 10 Anyone who loves other Christians* is living in
the light and does not cause anyone to stumble. 11 Anyone
who hates a Christian brother or sister is living and walk-
ing in darkness. Such a person is lost, having been blinded
by the darkness.

12 I am writing to you, my dear children, because your
sins have been forgiven because of Jesus.

13 I am writing to you who are mature because you know
Christ, the one who is from the beginning.

I am writing to you who are young because you have
won your battle with Satan.

14 I have written to you, children, because you have
known the Father.

2:9 Greek *his brother;* also in 2:11. 2:10 Greek *his brother.*

NEW KING JAMES VERSION

7 Brethren,[a] I write no new commandment to you, but an
old commandment which you have had from the begin-
ning. The old commandment is the word which you heard
from the beginning.[b] 8 Again, a new commandment I write
to you, which thing is true in Him and in you, because the
darkness is passing away, and the true light is already
shining.
9 He who says he is in the light, and hates his brother, is
in darkness until now. 10 He who loves his brother abides
in the light, and there is no cause for stumbling in him.
11 But he who hates his brother is in darkness and walks in
darkness, and does not know where he is going, because
the darkness has blinded his eyes.

Their Spiritual State

12 I write to you, little children,
  Because your sins are forgiven you for His name's
    sake.
13 I write to you, fathers,
  Because you have known Him *who is* from the
    beginning.
I write to you, young men,
  Because you have overcome the wicked one.
I write to you, little children,
  Because you have known the Father.

2:7 [a] NU-Text reads *Beloved.* [b] NU-Text omits *from the beginning.*

THE MESSAGE

My dear friends, I'm not writing anything new here. This is the oldest commandment in the book, and you've known it from day one. It's always been implicit in the Message you've heard. On the other hand, perhaps it is new, freshly minted as it is in both Christ and you—the darkness on its way out and the True Light already blazing!

Anyone who claims to live in God's light and hates a brother or sister is still in the dark. It's the person who loves brother and sister who dwells in God's light and doesn't block the light from others. But whoever hates is still in the dark, stumbles around in the dark, doesn't know which end is up, blinded by the darkness.

Loving the World

I remind you, my dear children: Your sins are forgiven in Jesus' name. You veterans were in on the ground floor, and know the One who started all this; you newcomers have won a big victory over the Evil One.

And a second reminder, dear children: You know the Father from personal experience. You veterans know the

KING JAMES VERSION

14 I have written unto you, fathers, because ye have known him *that is* from the beginning. I have written unto you, young men, because ye are strong, and the word of God abideth in you, and ye have overcome the wicked one.

15 Love not the world, neither the things *that are* in the world. If any man love the world, the love of the Father is not in him.

16 For all that *is* in the world, the lust of the flesh, and the lust of the eyes, and the pride of life, is not of the Father, but is of the world.

17 And the world passeth away, and the lust thereof: but he that doeth the will of God abideth for ever.

18 ¶ Little children, it is the last time: and as ye have heard that antichrist shall come, even now are there many antichrists; whereby we know that it is the last time.

19 They went out from us, but they were not of us; for if they had been of us, they would *no doubt* have continued with us: but *they went out*, that they might be made manifest that they were not all of us.

NEW AMERICAN STANDARD BIBLE

14 I have written to you, fathers, because you know Him who has been from the beginning. I have written to you, young men, because you are strong, and the word of God abides in you, and you have overcome the evil one.

Do Not Love the World

15 Do not love the world nor the things in the world. If anyone loves the world, the love of the Father is not in him.

16 For all that is in the world, the lust of the flesh and the lust of the eyes and the boastful pride of life, is not from the Father, but is from the world.

17 The world is passing away, and *also* its lusts; but the one who does the will of God lives forever.

18 Children, it is the last hour; and just as you heard that antichrist is coming, even now many antichrists have appeared; from this we know that it is the last hour.

19 They went out from us, but they were not *really* of us; for if they had been of us, they would have remained with us; but *they went out,* so that it would be shown that they all are not of us.

NEW CENTURY VERSION

I write to you, parents,
because you know the One who existed from the beginning.
I write to you, young people,
because you are strong;
the teaching of God lives in you,
and you have defeated the Evil One.

15Do not love the world or the things in the world. If you love the world, the love of the Father is not in you. 16These are the ways of the world: wanting to please our sinful selves, wanting the sinful things we see, and being too proud of what we have. None of these come from the Father, but all of them come from the world. 17The world and everything that people want in it are passing away, but the person who does what God wants lives forever.

Reject the Enemies of Christ

18My dear children, these are the last days. You have heard that the enemy of Christ is coming, and now many enemies of Christ are already here. This is how we know that these are the last days. 19These enemies of Christ were in our fellowship, but they left us. They never really belonged to us; if they had been a part of us, they would have stayed with us. But they left, and this shows that none of them really belonged to us.

CONTEMPORARY ENGLISH VERSION

Parents, I am writing you,
because you have known
the one who was there
from the beginning.
Young people, I am writing you,
because you are strong.
God's message is firm
in your hearts,
and you have defeated
the evil one.

15Don't love the world or anything that belongs to the world. If you love the world, you cannot love the Father. 16Our foolish pride comes from this world, and so do our selfish desires and our desire to have everything we see. None of this comes from the Father. 17The world and the desires it causes are disappearing. But if we obey God, we will live forever.

The Enemy of Christ

18Children, this is the last hour. You heard that the enemy of Christ would appear at this time, and many of Christ's enemies have already appeared. So we know that the last hour is here. 19These people came from our own group, yet they were not part of us. If they had been part of us, they would have stayed with us. But they left, which proves that they did not belong to our group.

NEW INTERNATIONAL VERSION

14 I write to you, fathers,
because you have known him who is from the beginning.
I write to you, young men,
because you are strong,
and the word of God lives in you,
and you have overcome the evil one.

Do Not Love the World

15 Do not love the world or anything in the world. If any-
one loves the world, the love of the Father is not in him.
16 For everything in the world—the cravings of sinful man,
the lust of his eyes and the boasting of what he has and
does—comes not from the Father but from the world.
17 The world and its desires pass away, but the man who
does the will of God lives forever.

Warning Against Antichrists

18 Dear children, this is the last hour; and as you have
heard that the antichrist is coming, even now many
antichrists have come. This is how we know it is the last
hour. 19 They went out from us, but they did not really
belong to us. For if they had belonged to us, they would
have remained with us; but their going showed that none
of them belonged to us.

NEW LIVING TRANSLATION

I have written to you who are mature because you know Christ, the one who is from the beginning.

I have written to you who are young because you are strong with God's word living in your hearts, and you have won your battle with Satan.

15 Stop loving this evil world and all that it offers you, for
when you love the world, you show that you do not have
the love of the Father in you. 16 For the world offers only
the lust for physical pleasure, the lust for everything we
see, and pride in our possessions. These are not from the
Father. They are from this evil world. 17 And this world is
fading away, along with everything it craves. But if you do
the will of God, you will live forever.
18 Dear children, the last hour is here. You have heard
that the Antichrist is coming, and already many such
antichrists have appeared. From this we know that the end
of the world has come. 19 These people left our churches
because they never really belonged with us; otherwise they
would have stayed with us. When they left us, it proved
that they do not belong with us. 20 But you are not like

NEW KING JAMES VERSION

14 I have written to you, fathers,
Because you have known Him *who is* from the beginning.
I have written to you, young men,
Because you are strong, and the word of God abides in you,
And you have overcome the wicked one.

Do Not Love the World

15 Do not love the world or the things in the world. If
anyone loves the world, the love of the Father is not in
him. 16 For all that *is* in the world—the lust of the flesh,
the lust of the eyes, and the pride of life—is not of the
Father but is of the world. 17 And the world is passing
away, and the lust of it; but he who does the will of God
abides forever.

Deceptions of the Last Hour

18 Little children, it is the last hour; and as you have
heard that the[c] Antichrist is coming, even now many
antichrists have come, by which we know that it is the last
hour. 19 They went out from us, but they were not of us; for
if they had been of us, they would have continued with us;
but *they went out* that they might be made manifest, that
none of them were of us.

2:18 [c] NU-Text omits *the*.

THE MESSAGE

One who started it all; and you newcomers—such vitality and strength! God's word is so steady in you. Your fellowship with God enables you to gain a victory over the Evil One.

Don't love the world's ways. Don't love the world's goods. Love of the world squeezes out love for the Father. Practically everything that goes on in the world—wanting your own way, wanting everything for yourself, wanting to appear important—has nothing to do with the Father. It just isolates you from him. The world and all its wanting, wanting, wanting is on the way out—but whoever does what God wants is set for eternity.

Antichrists Everywhere You Look

Children, time is just about up. You heard that Antichrist is coming. Well, they're all over the place, antichrists everywhere you look. That's how we know that we're close to the end.

They left us, but they were never really with us. If they had been, they would have stuck it out with us, loyal to the end. In leaving, they showed their true colors, showed they never did belong.

KING JAMES VERSION

20 ¶ But ye have an unction from the Holy One, and ye know all things.

21 I have not written unto you because ye know not the truth, but because ye know it, and that no lie is of the truth.

22 Who is a liar but he that denieth that Jesus is the Christ? He is antichrist, that denieth the Father and the Son.

23 Whosoever denieth the Son, the same hath not the Father: *(but) he that acknowledgeth the Son hath the Father also*.

24 Let that therefore abide in you, which ye have heard from the beginning. If that which ye have heard from the beginning shall remain in you, ye also shall continue in the Son, and in the Father.

25 And this is the promise that he hath promised us, *even* eternal life.

26 These *things* have I written unto you concerning them that seduce you.

27 But the anointing which ye have received of him abideth in you, and ye need not that any man teach you: but as the same anointing teacheth you of all things, and is truth, and is no lie, and even as it hath taught you, ye shall abide in him.

NEW AMERICAN STANDARD BIBLE

20 But you have an anointing from the Holy One, and you all know.

21 I have not written to you because you do not know the truth, but because you do know it, and because no lie is of the truth.

22 Who is the liar but the one who denies that Jesus is the Christ? This is the antichrist, the one who denies the Father and the Son.

23 Whoever denies the Son does not have the Father; the one who confesses the Son has the Father also.

24 As for you, let that abide in you which you heard from the beginning. If what you heard from the beginning abides in you, you also will abide in the Son and in the Father.

The Promise Is Eternal Life

25 This is the promise which He Himself made to us: eternal life.

26 These things I have written to you concerning those who are trying to deceive you.

27 As for you, the anointing which you received from Him abides in you, and you have no need for anyone to teach you; but as His anointing teaches you about all things, and is true and is not a lie, and just as it has taught you, you abide in Him.

NEW CENTURY VERSION

20You have the gift[c] that the Holy One gave you, so you
all know the truth. 21I do not write to you because you do
not know the truth but because you do know the truth.
And you know that no lie comes from the truth.

22Who is the liar? It is the person who does not accept
Jesus as the Christ. This is the enemy of Christ: the person
who does not accept the Father and his Son. 23Whoever
does not accept the Son does not have the Father. But
whoever confesses the Son has the Father, too.

24Be sure you continue to follow the teaching you heard
from the beginning. If you continue to follow what you
heard from the beginning, you will stay in the Son and in
the Father. 25And this is what the Son promised to us—life
forever.

26I am writing this letter about those people who are try-
ing to lead you the wrong way. 27Christ gave you a special
gift that is still in you, so you do not need any other
teacher. His gift teaches you about everything, and it is
true, not false. So continue to live in Christ, as his gift
taught you.

2:20 [c] **gift** This might mean the Holy Spirit, or it might mean teaching or truth as in verse 24.

CONTEMPORARY ENGLISH VERSION

20Christ, the Holy One,[b] has blessed[c] you, and now all of
you understand.[d] 21I did not need to write you about the
truth, since you already know it. You also know that liars
do not belong to the truth. 22And a liar is anyone who says
that Jesus isn't truly Christ. Anyone who says this is an
enemy of Christ and rejects both the Father and the Son.
23If we reject the Son, we reject the Father. But if we say
that we accept the Son, we have the Father. 24Keep think-
ing about the message you first heard, and you will always
be one in your heart with the Son and with the Father.
25The Son[e] has promised us[f] eternal life.

26I am writing to warn you about those people who are
misleading you. 27But Christ has blessed you with the Holy
Spirit.[g] Now the Spirit stays in you, and you don't need
any teachers. The Spirit is truthful and teaches you every-
thing. So stay one in your heart with Christ, just as the
Spirit has taught you to do.

[b] **2.20** *Christ, the Holy One*: The Greek text has "the Holy One" which may refer either to Christ or to God the Father. [c] **2.20** *blessed*: This translates a word which means "to pour olive oil on (someone's head)." In Old Testament times it was the custom to pour olive oil on a person's head when that person was chosen to be a priest or a king. Here the meaning is not clear. It may refer to the ceremony of pouring olive oil on the followers of the Lord right before they were baptized or it may refer to the gift of the Holy Spirit which they were given at baptism (see verse 27). [d] **2.20** *now all of you understand*: Some manuscripts have "you understand all things." [e] **2.25** *The Son*: The Greek text has "he" and may refer to God the Father. [f] **2.25** *us*: Some manuscripts have "you." [g] **2.27** *Christ has blessed you with the Holy Spirit*: The Greek text has "You received a pouring on of olive oil from him" (see verse 20). The "pouring on of olive oil" is here taken to refer to the gift of the Holy Spirit, and "he" may refer either to Christ or to the Father.

NEW INTERNATIONAL VERSION

[20]But you have an anointing from the Holy One, and all of you know the truth.[d] [21]I do not write to you because you do not know the truth, but because you do know it and because no lie comes from the truth. [22]Who is the liar? It is the man who denies that Jesus is the Christ. Such a man is the antichrist—he denies the Father and the Son. [23]No one who denies the Son has the Father; whoever acknowledges the Son has the Father also.

[24]See that what you have heard from the beginning remains in you. If it does, you also will remain in the Son and in the Father. [25]And this is what he promised us—even eternal life.

[26]I am writing these things to you about those who are trying to lead you astray. [27]As for you, the anointing you received from him remains in you, and you do not need anyone to teach you. But as his anointing teaches you about all things and as that anointing is real, not counterfeit—just as it has taught you, remain in him.

[d] *20* Some manuscripts *and you know all things*

NEW LIVING TRANSLATION

that, for the Holy Spirit has come upon you,* and all of you know the truth. [21]So I am writing to you not because you don't know the truth but because you know the difference between truth and falsehood. [22]And who is the great liar? The one who says that Jesus is not the Christ. Such people are antichrists, for they have denied the Father and the Son. [23]Anyone who denies the Son doesn't have the Father either. But anyone who confesses the Son has the Father also.

[24]So you must remain faithful to what you have been taught from the beginning. If you do, you will continue to live in fellowship with the Son and with the Father. [25]And in this fellowship we enjoy the eternal life he promised us.

[26]I have written these things to you because you need to be aware of those who want to lead you astray. [27]But you have received the Holy Spirit,* and he lives within you, so you don't need anyone to teach you what is true. For the Spirit teaches you all things, and what he teaches is true—it is not a lie. So continue in what he has taught you, and continue to live in Christ.

2:20 Greek *But you have an anointing from the Holy One.* 2:27 Greek *the anointing.*

NEW KING JAMES VERSION

[20]But you have an anointing from the Holy One, and you know all things.[d] [21]I have not written to you because you do not know the truth, but because you know it, and that no lie is of the truth.

[22]Who is a liar but he who denies that Jesus is the Christ? He is antichrist who denies the Father and the Son. [23]Whoever denies the Son does not have the Father either; he who acknowledges the Son has the Father also.

Let Truth Abide in You

[24]Therefore let that abide in you which you heard from the beginning. If what you heard from the beginning abides in you, you also will abide in the Son and in the Father. [25]And this is the promise that He has promised us—eternal life.

[26]These things I have written to you concerning those who *try to* deceive you. [27]But the anointing which you have received from Him abides in you, and you do not need that anyone teach you; but as the same anointing teaches you concerning all things, and is true, and is not a lie, and just as it has taught you, you will[e] abide in Him.

2:20 [d] NU-Text reads *you all know.* 2:27 [e] NU-Text reads *you abide.*

THE MESSAGE

But you belong. The Holy One anointed you, and you all know it. I haven't been writing this to tell you something you don't know, but to confirm the truth you do know, and to remind you that the truth doesn't breed lies.

So who is lying here? It's the person who denies that Jesus is the Divine Christ, that's who. This is what makes an antichrist: denying the Father, denying the Son. No one who denies the Son has any part with the Father, but affirming the Son is an embrace of the Father as well.

Stay with what you heard from the beginning, the original message. Let it sink into your life. If what you heard from the beginning lives deeply in you, you will live deeply in both Son and Father. This is exactly what Christ promised: eternal life, real life!

I've written to warn you about those who are trying to deceive you. But they're no match for what is embedded deeply within you—Christ's anointing, no less! You don't need any of their so-called teaching. Christ's anointing teaches you the truth on everything you need to know about yourself and him, uncontaminated by a single lie. Live deeply in what you were taught.

KING JAMES VERSION

28 ¶ And now, little children, abide in him; that, when he shall appear, we may have confidence, and not be ashamed before him at his coming.

29 If ye know that he is righteous, ye know that every one that doeth righteousness is born of him.

3 Behold, what manner of love the Father hath bestowed upon us, that we should be called the sons of God: therefore the world knoweth us not, because it knew him not.

2 Beloved, now are we the sons of God, and it doth not yet appear what we shall be: but we know that, when he shall appear, we shall be like him; for we shall see him as he is.

3 And every man that hath this hope in him purifieth himself, even as he is pure.

4 ¶ Whosoever committeth sin transgresseth also the law: for sin is the transgression of the law.

5 And ye know that he was manifested to take away our sins; and in him is no sin.

6 Whosoever abideth in him sinneth not: whosoever sinneth hath not seen him, neither known him.

7 Little children, let no man deceive you: he that doeth righteousness is righteous, even as he is righteous.

NEW AMERICAN STANDARD BIBLE

28 Now, little children, abide in Him, so that when He appears, we may have confidence and not shrink away from Him in shame at His coming.

29 If you know that He is righteous, you know that everyone also who practices righteousness is born of Him.

Children of God Love One Another

3 See how great a love the Father has bestowed on us, that we would be called children of God; and *such* we are. For this reason the world does not know us, because it did not know Him.

2 Beloved, now we are children of God, and it has not appeared as yet what we will be. We know that when He appears, we will be like Him, because we will see Him just as He is.

3 And everyone who has this hope *fixed* on Him purifies himself, just as He is pure.

4 Everyone who practices sin also practices lawlessness; and sin is lawlessness.

5 You know that He appeared in order to take away sins; and in Him there is no sin.

6 No one who abides in Him sins; no one who sins has seen Him or knows Him.

7 Little children, make sure no one deceives you; the one who practices righteousness is righteous, just as He is righteous;

NEW CENTURY VERSION

28 Yes, my dear children, live in him so that when Christ
comes back, we can be without fear and not be ashamed in
his presence. 29 If you know that Christ is all that is right,
you know that all who do right are God's children.

We Are God's Children

3 The Father has loved us so much that we are called
children of God. And we really are his children. The
reason the people in the world do not know us is that they
have not known him. 2 Dear friends, now we are children of
God, and we have not yet been shown what we will be in
the future. But we know that when Christ comes again, we
will be like him, because we will see him as he really is.
3 Christ is pure, and all who have this hope in Christ keep
themselves pure like Christ.

4 The person who sins breaks God's law. Yes, sin is living
against God's law. 5 You know that Christ came to take
away sins and that there is no sin in Christ. 6 So anyone
who lives in Christ does not go on sinning. Anyone who
goes on sinning has never really understood Christ and
has never known him.

7 Dear children, do not let anyone lead you the wrong way.
Christ is all that is right. So to be like Christ a person must

CONTEMPORARY ENGLISH VERSION

Children of God

28 Children, stay one in your hearts with Christ. Then
when he returns, we will have confidence and won't have
to hide in shame. 29 You know that Christ always does
right and that everyone who does right is a child of God.

3 Think how much the Father loves us. He loves us so
much that he lets us be called his children, as we
truly are. But since the people of this world did not know
who Christ[a] is, they don't know who we are. 2 My dear
friends, we are already God's children, though what we
will be hasn't yet been seen. But we do know that when
Christ returns, we will be like him, because we will see him
as he truly is. 3 This hope makes us keep ourselves holy,
just as Christ[b] is holy.

4 Everyone who sins breaks God's law, because sin is the
same as breaking God's law. 5 You know that Christ came
to take away sins. He isn't sinful, 6 and people who stay
one in their hearts with him won't keep on sinning. If they
do keep on sinning, they don't know Christ, and they have
never seen him.

7 Children, don't be fooled. Anyone who does right is good,
just like Christ himself. 8 Anyone who keeps on sinning

[a] **3.1** *Christ*: The Greek text has "he" and may refer to God.
[b] **3.3** *Christ*: The Greek text has "that one" and may refer to God.

NEW INTERNATIONAL VERSION

Children of God

[28]And now, dear children, continue in him, so that when he appears we may be confident and unashamed before him at his coming.

[29]If you know that he is righteous, you know that everyone who does what is right has been born of him.

3 How great is the love the Father has lavished on us, that we should be called children of God! And that is what we are! The reason the world does not know us is that it did not know him. [2]Dear friends, now we are children of God, and what we will be has not yet been made known. But we know that when he appears,[a] we shall be like him, for we shall see him as he is. [3]Everyone who has this hope in him purifies himself, just as he is pure.

[4]Everyone who sins breaks the law; in fact, sin is lawlessness. [5]But you know that he appeared so that he might take away our sins. And in him is no sin. [6]No one who lives in him keeps on sinning. No one who continues to sin has either seen him or known him.

[7]Dear children, do not let anyone lead you astray. He who does what is right is righteous, just as he is righteous.

[a] 2 Or *when it is made known*

NEW LIVING TRANSLATION

[28]And now, dear children, continue to live in fellowship with Christ so that when he returns, you will be full of courage and not shrink back from him in shame. [29]Since we know that God is always right, we also know that all who do what is right are his children.

Living as Children of God

3 See how very much our heavenly Father loves us, for he allows us to be called his children, and we really are! But the people who belong to this world don't know God, so they don't understand that we are his children. [2]Yes, dear friends, we are already God's children, and we can't even imagine what we will be like when Christ returns. But we do know that when he comes we will be like him, for we will see him as he really is. [3]And all who believe this will keep themselves pure, just as Christ is pure.

[4]Those who sin are opposed to the law of God, for all sin opposes the law of God. [5]And you know that Jesus came to take away our sins, for there is no sin in him. [6]So if we continue to live in him, we won't sin either. But those who keep on sinning have never known him or understood who he is.

[7]Dear children, don't let anyone deceive you about this: When people do what is right, it is because they are righteous, even as Christ is righteous. [8]But when people keep

NEW KING JAMES VERSION

The Children of God

[28]And now, little children, abide in Him, that when[f] He appears, we may have confidence and not be ashamed before Him at His coming. [29]If you know that He is righteous, you know that everyone who practices righteousness is born of Him.

3 Behold what manner of love the Father has bestowed on us, that we should be called children of God![a] Therefore the world does not know us,[b] because it did not know Him. [2]Beloved, now we are children of God; and it has not yet been revealed what we shall be, but we know that when He is revealed, we shall be like Him, for we shall see Him as He is. [3]And everyone who has this hope in Him purifies himself, just as He is pure.

Sin and the Child of God

[4]Whoever commits sin also commits lawlessness, and sin is lawlessness. [5]And you know that He was manifested to take away our sins, and in Him there is no sin. [6]Whoever abides in Him does not sin. Whoever sins has neither seen Him nor known Him.

[7]Little children, let no one deceive you. He who practices righteousness is righteous, just as He is righteous. [8]He

2:28 [f] NU-Text reads *if.* 3:1 [a] NU-Text adds *And we are.*
[b] M-Text reads *you.*

THE MESSAGE

Live Deeply in Christ

And now, children, stay with Christ. Live deeply in Christ. Then we'll be ready for him when he appears, ready to receive him with open arms, with no cause for red-faced guilt or lame excuses when he arrives.

Once you're convinced that he is right and righteous, you'll recognize that all who practice righteousness are God's true children.

3 What marvelous love the Father has extended to us! Just look at it—we're called children of God! That's who we really are. But that's also why the world doesn't recognize us or take us seriously, because it has no idea who he is or what he's up to.

But friends, that's exactly who we are: children of God. And that's only the beginning. Who knows how we'll end up! What we know is that when Christ is openly revealed, we'll see him—and in seeing him, become like him. All of us who look forward to his Coming stay ready, with the glistening purity of Jesus' life as a model for our own.

All who indulge in a sinful life are dangerously lawless, for sin is a major disruption of God's order. Surely you know that Christ showed up in order to get rid of sin. There is no sin in him, and sin is not part of his program. No one who lives deeply in Christ makes a practice of sin. None of those who do practice sin have taken a good look at Christ. They've got him all backwards.

So, my dear children, don't let anyone divert you from the truth. It's the person who *acts* right who *is* right, just as we see it lived out in our righteous Messiah. Those who

KING JAMES VERSION

8 He that committeth sin is of the devil; for the devil sinneth from the beginning. For this purpose the Son of God was manifested, that he might destroy the works of the devil.

9 Whosoever is born of God doth not commit sin; for his seed remaineth in him: and he cannot sin, because he is born of God.

10 In this the children of God are manifest, and the children of the devil: whosoever doeth not righteousness is not of God, neither he that loveth not his brother.

11 ¶ For this is the message that ye heard from the beginning, that we should love one another.

12 Not as Cain, *who* was of that wicked one, and slew his brother. And wherefore slew he him? Because his own works were evil, and his brother's righteous.

13 Marvel not, my brethren, if the world hate you.

14 ¶ We know that we have passed from death unto life, because we love the brethren. He that loveth not *his* brother abideth in death.

15 Whosoever hateth his brother is a murderer: and ye know that no murderer hath eternal life abiding in him.

16 Hereby perceive we the love *of God*, because he laid down his life for us: and we ought to lay down *our* lives for the brethren.

NEW AMERICAN STANDARD BIBLE

8 the one who practices sin is of the devil; for the devil has sinned from the beginning. The Son of God appeared for this purpose, to destroy the works of the devil.

9 No one who is born of God practices sin, because His seed abides in him; and he cannot sin, because he is born of God.

10 By this the children of God and the children of the devil are obvious: anyone who does not practice righteousness is not of God, nor the one who does not love his brother.

11 For this is the message which you have heard from the beginning, that we should love one another;

12 not as Cain, *who* was of the evil one and slew his brother. And for what reason did he slay him? Because his deeds were evil, and his brother's were righteous.

13 Do not be surprised, brethren, if the world hates you.

14 We know that we have passed out of death into life, because we love the brethren. He who does not love abides in death.

15 Everyone who hates his brother is a murderer; and you know that no murderer has eternal life abiding in him.

16 We know love by this, that He laid down His life for us; and we ought to lay down our lives for the brethren.

NEW CENTURY VERSION

do what is right. 8The devil has been sinning since the
beginning, so anyone who continues to sin belongs to the
devil. The Son of God came for this purpose: to destroy
the devil's work.
9Those who are God's children do not continue sinning,
because the new life from God remains in them. They are
not able to go on sinning, because they have become children of God. 10So we can see who God's children are and
who the devil's children are: Those who do not do what is
right are not God's children, and those who do not love
their brothers and sisters are not God's children.

We Must Love Each Other

11This is the teaching you have heard from the beginning: We must love each other. 12Do not be like Cain who
belonged to the Evil One and killed his brother. And why
did he kill him? Because the things Cain did were evil, and
the things his brother did were good.
13Brothers and sisters, do not be surprised when the
people of the world hate you. 14We know we have left
death and have come into life because we love each other.
Whoever does not love is still dead. 15Everyone who hates
a brother or sister is a murderer,[a] and you know that no
murderers have eternal life in them. 16This is how we
know what real love is: Jesus gave his life for us. So we
should give our lives for our brothers and sisters.

3:15 [a] **Everyone...murderer** If one person hates a brother or sister, then in the heart that person has killed that brother or sister. Jesus taught about this sin to his followers (Matthew 5:21–26).

CONTEMPORARY ENGLISH VERSION

belongs to the devil. He has sinned from the beginning, but
the Son of God came to destroy all that he has done. 9God's
children cannot keep on being sinful. His life-giving power[c]
lives in them and makes them his children, so that they cannot keep on sinning. 10You can tell God's children from the
devil's children, because those who belong to the devil
refuse to do right or to love each other.

Love Each Other

11From the beginning you were told that we must love
each other. 12Don't be like Cain, who belonged to the devil
and murdered his own brother. Why did he murder him?
He did it because his brother was good, and he was evil.
13My friends, don't be surprised if the people of this world
hate you. 14Our love for each other proves that we have
gone from death to life. But if you don't love each other,
you are still under the power of death.
15If you hate each other, you are murderers, and we
know that murderers do not have eternal life. 16We know
what love is because Jesus gave his life for us. That's why
we must give our lives for each other. 17If we have all we

[c] 3.9 *His life-giving power*: The Greek text has "his seed."

NEW INTERNATIONAL VERSION

8He who does what is sinful is of the devil, because the
devil has been sinning from the beginning. The reason the
Son of God appeared was to destroy the devil's work. 9No
one who is born of God will continue to sin, because God's
seed remains in him; he cannot go on sinning, because he
has been born of God. 10This is how we know who the chil-
dren of God are and who the children of the devil are:
Anyone who does not do what is right is not a child of
God; nor is anyone who does not love his brother.

Love One Another

11This is the message you heard from the beginning: We
should love one another. 12Do not be like Cain, who
belonged to the evil one and murdered his brother. And
why did he murder him? Because his own actions were evil
and his brother's were righteous. 13Do not be surprised,
my brothers, if the world hates you. 14We know that we
have passed from death to life, because we love our broth-
ers. Anyone who does not love remains in death. 15Anyone
who hates his brother is a murderer, and you know that no
murderer has eternal life in him.

16This is how we know what love is: Jesus Christ laid
down his life for us. And we ought to lay down our lives for

NEW LIVING TRANSLATION

on sinning, it shows they belong to the Devil, who has
been sinning since the beginning. But the Son of God came
to destroy these works of the Devil. 9Those who have been
born into God's family do not sin, because God's life is in
them. So they can't keep on sinning, because they have
been born of God. 10So now we can tell who are children of
God and who are children of the Devil. Anyone who does
not obey God's commands and does not love other
Christians* does not belong to God.

Love One Another

11This is the message we have heard from the begin-
ning: We should love one another. 12We must not be like
Cain, who belonged to the evil one and killed his brother.
And why did he kill him? Because Cain had been doing
what was evil, and his brother had been doing what was
right. 13So don't be surprised, dear brothers and sisters,* if
the world hates you.

14If we love our Christian brothers and sisters, it proves
that we have passed from death to eternal life. But a per-
son who has no love is still dead. 15Anyone who hates
another Christian* is really a murderer at heart. And you
know that murderers don't have eternal life within them.
16We know what real love is because Christ gave up his life
for us. And so we also ought to give up our lives for our
Christian brothers and sisters. 17But if anyone has enough

3:10 Greek *his brother.* 3:13 Greek *brothers;* also in 3:14, 16.
3:15 Greek *his brother.*

NEW KING JAMES VERSION

who sins is of the devil, for the devil has sinned from the
beginning. For this purpose the Son of God was manifest-
ed, that He might destroy the works of the devil. 9Whoever
has been born of God does not sin, for His seed remains in
him; and he cannot sin, because he has been born of God.

The Imperative of Love

10In this the children of God and the children of the devil
are manifest: Whoever does not practice righteousness is
not of God, nor *is* he who does not love his brother. 11For
this is the message that you heard from the beginning,
that we should love one another, 12not as Cain *who* was of
the wicked one and murdered his brother. And why did he
murder him? Because his works were evil and his brother's
righteous.

13Do not marvel, my brethren, if the world hates you.
14We know that we have passed from death to life,
because we love the brethren. He who does not love *his*
brother[c] abides in death. 15Whoever hates his brother is a
murderer, and you know that no murderer has eternal life
abiding in him.

The Outworking of Love

16By this we know love, because He laid down His life
for us. And we also ought to lay down *our* lives for the

3:14 [c] NU-Text omits *his brother.*

THE MESSAGE

make a practice of sin are straight from the Devil, the pio-
neer in the practice of sin. The Son of God entered the
scene to abolish the Devil's ways.

People conceived and brought into life by God don't
make a practice of sin. How could they? God's seed is deep
within them, making them who they are. It's not in the
nature of the God-begotten to practice and parade sin.
Here's how you tell the difference between God's children
and the Devil's children: The one who won't practice righ-
teous ways isn't from God, nor is the one who won't love
brother or sister. A simple test.

✢

For this is the original message we heard: We should
love each other.

We must not be like Cain, who joined the Evil One and
then killed his brother. And why did he kill him? Because
he was deep in the practice of evil, while the acts of his
brother were righteous. So don't be surprised, friends,
when the world hates you. This has been going on a long
time.

The way we know we've been transferred from death to
life is that we love our brothers and sisters. Anyone who
doesn't love is as good as dead. Anyone who hates a
brother or sister is a murderer, and you know very well
that eternal life and murder don't go together.

This is how we've come to understand and experience
love: Christ sacrificed his life for us. This is why we ought
to live sacrificially for our fellow believers, and not just be

KING JAMES VERSION

17 But whoso hath this world's good, and seeth his brother have need, and shutteth up his bowels *of compassion* from him, how dwelleth the love of God in him?

18 My little children, let us not love in word, neither in tongue; but in deed and in truth.

19 And hereby we know that we are of the truth, and shall assure our hearts before him.

20 ¶ For if our heart condemn us, God is greater than our heart, and knoweth all things.

21 Beloved, if our heart condemn us not, *then* have we confidence toward God.

22 And whatsoever we ask, we receive of him, because we keep his commandments, and do those things that are pleasing in his sight.

23 ¶ And this is his commandment, That we should believe on the name of his Son Jesus Christ, and love one another, as he gave us commandment.

24 And he that keepeth his commandments dwelleth in him, and he in him. And hereby we know that he abideth in us, by the Spirit which he hath given us.

4 Beloved, believe not every spirit, but try the spirits whether they are of God: because many false prophets are gone out into the world.

NEW AMERICAN STANDARD BIBLE

17 But whoever has the world's goods, and sees his brother in need and closes his heart against him, how does the love of God abide in him?

18 Little children, let us not love with word or with tongue, but in deed and truth.

19 We will know by this that we are of the truth, and will assure our heart before Him

20 in whatever our heart condemns us; for God is greater than our heart and knows all things.

21 Beloved, if our heart does not condemn us, we have confidence before God;

22 and whatever we ask we receive from Him, because we keep His commandments and do the things that are pleasing in His sight.

23 This is His commandment, that we believe in the name of His Son Jesus Christ, and love one another, just as He commanded us.

24 The one who keeps His commandments abides in Him, and He in him. We know by this that He abides in us, by the Spirit whom He has given us.

Testing the Spirits

4 Beloved, do not believe every spirit, but test the spirits to see whether they are from God, because many false prophets have gone out into the world.

NEW CENTURY VERSION

17Suppose someone has enough to live and sees a brother
or sister in need, but does not help. Then God's love is not
living in that person. 18My children, we should love people
not only with words and talk, but by our actions and true
caring.
19–20This is the way we know that we belong to the way
of truth. When our hearts make us feel guilty, we can still
have peace before God. God is greater than our hearts, and
he knows everything. 21My dear friends, if our hearts do
not make us feel guilty, we can come without fear into
God's presence. 22And God gives us what we ask for
because we obey God's commands and do what pleases
him. 23This is what God commands: that we believe in his
Son, Jesus Christ, and that we love each other, just as he
commanded. 24The people who obey God's commands live
in God, and God lives in them. We know that God lives in
us because of the Spirit God gave us.

Warning Against False Teachers

4 My dear friends, many false prophets have gone out
into the world. So do not believe every spirit, but test
the spirits to see if they are from God. 2This is how you

CONTEMPORARY ENGLISH VERSION

need and see one of our own people in need, we must have
pity on that person, or else we cannot say we love God.
18Children, you show love for others by truly helping them,
and not merely by talking about it.
19When we love others, we know that we belong to the
truth, and we feel at ease in the presence of God. 20But
even if we don't feel at ease, God is greater than our feel-
ings, and he knows everything. 21Dear friends, if we feel at
ease in the presence of God, we will have the courage to
come near him. 22He will give us whatever we ask, because
we obey him and do what pleases him. 23God wants us to
have faith in his Son Jesus Christ and to love each other.
This is also what Jesus taught us to do. 24If we obey God's
commandments, we will stay one in our hearts with him,
and he will stay one with us. The Spirit that he has given
us is proof that we are one with him.

God Is Love

4 Dear friends, don't believe everyone who claims to
have the Spirit of God. Test them all to find out if they
really do come from God. Many false prophets have already
gone out into the world, 2and you can know which ones

NEW INTERNATIONAL VERSION

our brothers. [17]If anyone has material possessions and sees his brother in need but has no pity on him, how can the love of God be in him? [18]Dear children, let us not love with words or tongue but with actions and in truth. [19]This then is how we know that we belong to the truth, and how we set our hearts at rest in his presence [20]whenever our hearts condemn us. For God is greater than our hearts, and he knows everything.

[21]Dear friends, if our hearts do not condemn us, we have confidence before God [22]and receive from him anything we ask, because we obey his commands and do what pleases him. [23]And this is his command: to believe in the name of his Son, Jesus Christ, and to love one another as he commanded us. [24]Those who obey his commands live in him, and he in them. And this is how we know that he lives in us: We know it by the Spirit he gave us.

Test the Spirits

4 Dear friends, do not believe every spirit, but test the spirits to see whether they are from God, because many false prophets have gone out into the world. [2]This is

NEW LIVING TRANSLATION

money to live well and sees a brother or sister in need and refuses to help—how can God's love be in that person?

[18]Dear children, let us stop just saying we love each other; let us really show it by our actions. [19]It is by our actions that we know we are living in the truth, so we will be confident when we stand before the Lord, [20]even if our hearts condemn us. For God is greater than our hearts, and he knows everything.

[21]Dear friends, if our conscience is clear, we can come to God with bold confidence. [22]And we will receive whatever we request because we obey him and do the things that please him. [23]And this is his commandment: We must believe in the name of his Son, Jesus Christ, and love one another, just as he commanded us. [24]Those who obey God's commandments live in fellowship with him, and he with them. And we know he lives in us because the Holy Spirit lives in us.

Discerning False Prophets

4 Dear friends, do not believe everyone who claims to speak by the Spirit. You must test them to see if the spirit they have comes from God. For there are many false prophets in the world. [2]This is the way to find out if they

NEW KING JAMES VERSION

brethren. [17]But whoever has this world's goods, and sees his brother in need, and shuts up his heart from him, how does the love of God abide in him?

[18]My little children, let us not love in word or in tongue, but in deed and in truth. [19]And by this we know[d] that we are of the truth, and shall assure our hearts before Him. [20]For if our heart condemns us, God is greater than our heart, and knows all things. [21]Beloved, if our heart does not condemn us, we have confidence toward God. [22]And whatever we ask we receive from Him, because we keep His commandments and do those things that are pleasing in His sight. [23]And this is His commandment: that we should believe on the name of His Son Jesus Christ and love one another, as He gave us[e] commandment.

The Spirit of Truth and the Spirit of Error

[24]Now he who keeps His commandments abides in Him, and He in him. And by this we know that He abides in us, by the Spirit whom He has given us.

4 Beloved, do not believe every spirit, but test the spirits, whether they are of God; because many false prophets have gone out into the world. [2]By this you know

3:19 [d] NU-Text reads *we shall know.* 3:23 [e] M-Text omits *us.*

THE MESSAGE

out for ourselves. If you see some brother or sister in need and have the means to do something about it but turn a cold shoulder and do nothing, what happens to God's love? It disappears. And you made it disappear.

When We Practice Real Love

My dear children, let's not just talk about love; let's practice real love. This is the only way we'll know we're living truly, living in God's reality. It's also the way to shut down debilitating self-criticism, even when there is something to it. For God is greater than our worried hearts and knows more about us than we do ourselves.

And friends, once that's taken care of and we're no longer accusing or condemning ourselves, we're bold and free before God! We're able to stretch our hands out and receive what we asked for because we're doing what he said, doing what pleases him. Again, this is God's command: to believe in his personally named Son, Jesus Christ. He told us to love each other, in line with the original command. As we keep his commands, we live deeply and surely in him, and he lives in us. And this is how we experience his deep and abiding presence in us: by the Spirit he gave us.

Don't Believe Everything You Hear

4 My dear friends, don't believe everything you hear. Carefully weigh and examine what people tell you. Not everyone who talks about God comes from God. There are a lot of lying preachers loose in the world.

Here's how you test for the genuine Spirit of God.

KING JAMES VERSION

2 Hereby know ye the Spirit of God: Every spirit that confesseth that Jesus Christ is come in the flesh is of God:

3 And every spirit that confesseth not that Jesus Christ is come in the flesh is not of God: and this is that *spirit* of antichrist, whereof ye have heard that it should come; and even now already is it in the world.

4 ¶ Ye are of God, little children, and have overcome them: because greater is he that is in you, than he that is in the world.

5 They are of the world: therefore speak they of the world, and the world heareth them.

6 We are of God: he that knoweth God heareth us; he that is not of God heareth not us. Hereby know we the spirit of truth, and the spirit of error.

7 ¶ Beloved, let us love one another: for love is of God; and every one that loveth is born of God, and knoweth God.

8 He that loveth not knoweth not God; for God is love.

9 In this was manifested the love of God toward us, because that God sent his only begotten Son into the world, that we might live through him.

10 Herein is love, not that we loved God, but that he loved us, and sent his Son *to be* the propitiation for our sins.

11 Beloved, if God so loved us, we ought also to love one another.

NEW AMERICAN STANDARD BIBLE

2 By this you know the Spirit of God: every spirit that confesses that Jesus Christ has come in the flesh is from God;

3 and every spirit that does not confess Jesus is not from God; this is the *spirit* of the antichrist, of which you have heard that it is coming, and now it is already in the world.

4 You are from God, little children, and have overcome them; because greater is He who is in you than he who is in the world.

5 They are from the world; therefore they speak *as* from the world, and the world listens to them.

6 We are from God; he who knows God listens to us; he who is not from God does not listen to us. By this we know the spirit of truth and the spirit of error.

God Is Love

7 Beloved, let us love one another, for love is from God; and everyone who loves is born of God and knows God.

8 The one who does not love does not know God, for God is love.

9 By this the love of God was manifested in us, that God has sent His only begotten Son into the world so that we might live through Him.

10 In this is love, not that we loved God, but that He loved us and sent His Son *to be* the propitiation for our sins.

11 Beloved, if God so loved us, we also ought to love one another.

NEW CENTURY VERSION

can know God's Spirit: Every spirit who confesses that
Jesus Christ came to earth as a human is from God. 3And
every spirit who refuses to say this about Jesus is not from
God. It is the spirit of the enemy of Christ, which you have
heard is coming, and now he is already in the world.

4My dear children, you belong to God and have defeated
them; because God's Spirit, who is in you, is greater than
the devil, who is in the world. 5And they belong to the
world, so what they say is from the world, and the world
listens to them. 6But we belong to God, and those who
know God listen to us. But those who are not from God do
not listen to us. That is how we know the Spirit that is
true and the spirit that is false.

Love Comes from God

7Dear friends, we should love each other, because love
comes from God. Everyone who loves has become God's
child and knows God. 8Whoever does not love does not
know God, because God is love. 9This is how God showed
his love to us: He sent his one and only Son into the world
so that we could have life through him. 10This is what real
love is: It is not our love for God; it is God's love for us in
sending his Son to be the way to take away our sins.

11Dear friends, if God loved us that much we also should

CONTEMPORARY ENGLISH VERSION

come from God. His Spirit says that Jesus Christ had a truly
human body. 3But when someone doesn't say this about
Jesus, you know that person has a spirit that doesn't come
from God and is the enemy of Christ. You knew that this
enemy was coming into the world and now is already here.

4Children, you belong to God, and you have defeated
these enemies. God's Spirit[a] is in you and is more powerful
than the one that is in the world. 5These enemies belong to
this world, and the world listens to them, because they
speak its language. 6We belong to God, and everyone who
knows God will listen to us. But the people who don't
know God won't listen to us. That is how we can tell the
Spirit that speaks the truth from the one that tells lies.

7My dear friends, we must love each other. Love comes
from God, and when we love each other, it shows that we
have been given new life. We are now God's children, and
we know him. 8God is love, and anyone who doesn't love
others has never known him. 9God showed his love for us
when he sent his only Son into the world to give us life.
10Real love isn't our love for God, but his love for us. God
sent his Son to be the sacrifice by which our sins are for-
given. 11Dear friends, since God loved us this much, we
must love each other.

[a] 4.4 *God's Spirit*: The Greek text has "he" and may refer to the Spirit or to God or to Jesus.

NEW INTERNATIONAL VERSION

how you can recognize the Spirit of God: Every spirit that
acknowledges that Jesus Christ has come in the flesh is
from God, 3but every spirit that does not acknowledge
Jesus is not from God. This is the spirit of the antichrist,
which you have heard is coming and even now is already
in the world.

4You, dear children, are from God and have overcome
them, because the one who is in you is greater than the
one who is in the world. 5They are from the world and
therefore speak from the viewpoint of the world, and the
world listens to them. 6We are from God, and whoever
knows God listens to us; but whoever is not from God does
not listen to us. This is how we recognize the Spirit[a] of
truth and the spirit of falsehood.

God's Love and Ours

7Dear friends, let us love one another, for love comes
from God. Everyone who loves has been born of God and
knows God. 8Whoever does not love does not know God,
because God is love. 9This is how God showed his love
among us: He sent his one and only Son[b] into the world
that we might live through him. 10This is love: not that we
loved God, but that he loved us and sent his Son as an
atoning sacrifice for[c] our sins. 11Dear friends, since God so
loved us, we also ought to love one another. 12No one has

[a] 6 Or *spirit* [b] 9 Or *his only begotten Son* [c] 10 Or *as the one who would turn aside his wrath, taking away*

NEW LIVING TRANSLATION

have the Spirit of God: If a prophet acknowledges that
Jesus Christ became a human being, that person has the
Spirit of God. 3If a prophet does not acknowledge Jesus,
that person is not from God. Such a person has the spirit
of the Antichrist. You have heard that he is going to come
into the world, and he is already here.

4But you belong to God, my dear children. You have
already won your fight with these false prophets, because
the Spirit who lives in you is greater than the spirit who
lives in the world. 5These people belong to this world, so
they speak from the world's viewpoint, and the world lis-
tens to them. 6But we belong to God; that is why those
who know God listen to us. If they do not belong to God,
they do not listen to us. That is how we know if someone
has the Spirit of truth or the spirit of deception.

Loving One Another

7Dear friends, let us continue to love one another, for
love comes from God. Anyone who loves is born of God
and knows God. 8But anyone who does not love does not
know God—for God is love.

9God showed how much he loved us by sending his only
Son into the world so that we might have eternal life
through him. 10This is real love. It is not that we loved
God, but that he loved us and sent his Son as a sacrifice to
take away our sins.

11Dear friends, since God loved us that much, we surely

NEW KING JAMES VERSION

the Spirit of God: Every spirit that confesses that Jesus
Christ has come in the flesh is of God, 3and every spirit
that does not confess that[a] Jesus Christ has come in the
flesh is not of God. And this is the *spirit* of the Antichrist,
which you have heard was coming, and is now already in
the world.

4You are of God, little children, and have overcome
them, because He who is in you is greater than he who is
in the world. 5They are of the world. Therefore they speak
as of the world, and the world hears them. 6We are of God.
He who knows God hears us; he who is not of God does
not hear us. By this we know the spirit of truth and the
spirit of error.

Knowing God Through Love

7Beloved, let us love one another, for love is of God; and
everyone who loves is born of God and knows God. 8He
who does not love does not know God, for God is love. 9In
this the love of God was manifested toward us, that God
has sent His only begotten Son into the world, that we
might live through Him. 10In this is love, not that we loved
God, but that He loved us and sent His Son *to be* the propi-
tiation for our sins. 11Beloved, if God so loved us, we also
ought to love one another.

4:3 [a] NU-Text omits *that* and *Christ has come in the flesh.*

THE MESSAGE

Everyone who confesses openly his faith in Jesus Christ—the Son of God, who came as an actual flesh-and-blood person—comes from God and belongs to God. And everyone who refuses to confess faith in Jesus has nothing in common with God. This is the spirit of antichrist that you heard was coming. Well, here it is, sooner than we thought!

My dear children, you come from God and belong to God. You have already won a big victory over those false teachers, for the Spirit in you is far stronger than anything in the world. These people belong to the Christ-denying world. They talk the world's language and the world eats it up. But we come from God and belong to God. Anyone who knows God, understands us and listens. The person who has nothing to do with God will, of course, not listen to us. This is another test for telling the Spirit of Truth from the spirit of deception.

God Is Love

My beloved friends, let us continue to love each other since love comes from God. Everyone who loves is born of God and experiences a relationship with God. The person who refuses to love doesn't know the first thing about God, because God *is* love—so you can't know him if you don't love. This is how God showed his love for us: God sent his only Son into the world so we might live through him. This is the kind of love we are talking about—not that we once upon a time loved God, but that he loved us and sent his Son as a sacrifice to clear away our sins and the damage they've done to our relationship with God.

My dear, dear friends, if God loved us like this, we cer-

KING JAMES VERSION

12 No man hath seen God at any time. If we love one another, God dwelleth in us, and his love is perfected in us.

13 Hereby know we that we dwell in him, and he in us, because he hath given us of his Spirit.

14 ¶ And we have seen and do testify that the Father sent the Son *to be* the Saviour of the world.

15 Whosoever shall confess that Jesus is the Son of God, God dwelleth in him, and he in God.

16 And we have known and believed the love that God hath to us. God is love; and he that dwelleth in love dwelleth in God, and God in him.

17 ¶ Herein is our love made perfect, that we may have boldness in the day of judgment: because as he is, so are we in this world.

18 There is no fear in love; but perfect love casteth out fear: because fear hath torment. He that feareth is not made perfect in love.

19 We love him, because he first loved us.

20 If a man say, I love God, and hateth his brother, he is a liar: for he that loveth not his brother whom he hath seen, how can he love God whom he hath not seen?

21 And this commandment have we from him, That he who loveth God love his brother also.

NEW AMERICAN STANDARD BIBLE

12 No one has seen God at any time; if we love one another, God abides in us, and His love is perfected in us.

13 By this we know that we abide in Him and He in us, because He has given us of His Spirit.

14 We have seen and testify that the Father has sent the Son *to be* the Savior of the world.

15 Whoever confesses that Jesus is the Son of God, God abides in him, and he in God.

16 We have come to know and have believed the love which God has for us. God is love, and the one who abides in love abides in God, and God abides in him.

17 By this, love is perfected with us, so that we may have confidence in the day of judgment; because as He is, so also are we in this world.

18 There is no fear in love; but perfect love casts out fear, because fear involves punishment, and the one who fears is not perfected in love.

19 We love, because He first loved us.

20 If someone says, "I love God," and hates his brother, he is a liar; for the one who does not love his brother whom he has seen, cannot love God whom he has not seen.

21 And this commandment we have from Him, that the one who loves God should love his brother also.

NEW CENTURY VERSION

love each other. 12No one has ever seen God, but if we love
each other, God lives in us, and his love is made perfect
in us.
13We know that we live in God and he lives in us,
because he gave us his Spirit. 14We have seen and can tes-
tify that the Father sent his Son to be the Savior of the
world. 15Whoever confesses that Jesus is the Son of God
has God living inside, and that person lives in God. 16And
so we know the love that God has for us, and we trust that
love.

God is love. Those who live in love live in God, and God
lives in them. 17This is how love is made perfect in us: that
we can be without fear on the day God judges us, because
in this world we are like him. 18Where God's love is, there
is no fear, because God's perfect love drives out fear. It is
punishment that makes a person fear, so love is not made
perfect in the person who fears.
19We love because God first loved us. 20If people say, "I
love God," but hate their brothers or sisters, they are liars.
Those who do not love their brothers and sisters, whom
they have seen, cannot love God, whom they have never
seen. 21And God gave us this command: Those who love
God must also love their brothers and sisters.

CONTEMPORARY ENGLISH VERSION

12No one has ever seen God. But if we love each other,
God lives in us, and his love is truly in our hearts.
13God has given us his Spirit. That is how we know that
we are one with him, just as he is one with us. 14God sent
his Son to be the Savior of the world. We saw his Son and
are now telling others about him. 15God stays one with
everyone who openly says that Jesus is the Son of God.
That's how we stay one with God 16and are sure that God
loves us.

God is love. If we keep on loving others, we will stay one
in our hearts with God, and he will stay one with us. 17If
we truly love others and live as Christ did in this world, we
won't be worried about the day of judgment. 18A real love
for others will chase those worries away. The thought of
being punished is what makes us afraid. It shows that we
have not really learned to love.
19We love because God loved us first. 20But if we say we
love God and don't love each other, we are liars. We can-
not see God. So how can we love God, if we don't love the
people we can see? 21The commandment that God has
given us is: "Love God and love each other!"

NEW INTERNATIONAL VERSION

ever seen God; but if we love one another, God lives in us
and his love is made complete in us.
13We know that we live in him and he in us, because he
has given us of his Spirit. 14And we have seen and testify
that the Father has sent his Son to be the Savior of the
world. 15If anyone acknowledges that Jesus is the Son of
God, God lives in him and he in God. 16And so we know
and rely on the love God has for us.

God is love. Whoever lives in love lives in God, and God
in him. 17In this way, love is made complete among us so
that we will have confidence on the day of judgment,
because in this world we are like him. 18There is no fear in
love. But perfect love drives out fear, because fear has to
do with punishment. The one who fears is not made per-
fect in love.

19We love because he first loved us. 20If anyone says, "I
love God," yet hates his brother, he is a liar. For anyone
who does not love his brother, whom he has seen, cannot
love God, whom he has not seen. 21And he has given us
this command: Whoever loves God must also love his
brother.

NEW LIVING TRANSLATION

ought to love each other. 12No one has ever seen God. But
if we love each other, God lives in us, and his love has
been brought to full expression through us.
13And God has given us his Spirit as proof that we live
in him and he in us. 14Furthermore, we have seen with our
own eyes and now testify that the Father sent his Son to
be the Savior of the world. 15All who proclaim that Jesus is
the Son of God have God living in them, and they live in
God. 16We know how much God loves us, and we have put
our trust in him.

God is love, and all who live in love live in God, and God
lives in them. 17And as we live in God, our love grows
more perfect. So we will not be afraid on the day of judg-
ment, but we can face him with confidence because we are
like Christ here in this world.

18Such love has no fear because perfect love expels all
fear. If we are afraid, it is for fear of judgment, and this
shows that his love has not been perfected in us. 19We love
each other* as a result of his loving us first.

20If someone says, "I love God," but hates a Christian
brother or sister,* that person is a liar; for if we don't love
people we can see, how can we love God, whom we have
not seen? 21And God himself has commanded that we must
love not only him but our Christian brothers and sisters,
too.

4:19 Or *We love him;* Greek reads *We love.* 4:20 Greek *brother;* also in 4:21.

NEW KING JAMES VERSION

Seeing God Through Love

12No one has seen God at any time. If we love one
another, God abides in us, and His love has been perfected
in us. 13By this we know that we abide in Him, and He in
us, because He has given us of His Spirit. 14And we have
seen and testify that the Father has sent the Son *as* Savior
of the world. 15Whoever confesses that Jesus is the Son of
God, God abides in him, and he in God. 16And we have
known and believed the love that God has for us. God is
love, and he who abides in love abides in God, and God in
him.

The Consummation of Love

17Love has been perfected among us in this: that we
may have boldness in the day of judgment; because as He
is, so are we in this world. 18There is no fear in love; but
perfect love casts out fear, because fear involves torment.
But he who fears has not been made perfect in love. 19We
love Him[b] because He first loved us.

Obedience by Faith

20If someone says, "I love God," and hates his brother,
he is a liar; for he who does not love his brother whom he
has seen, how can[c] he love God whom he has not seen?
21And this commandment we have from Him: that he who
loves God *must* love his brother also.

4:19 [b] NU-Text omits *Him.* 4:20 [c] NU-Text reads *he cannot.*

THE MESSAGE

tainly ought to love each other. No one has seen God, ever.
But if we love one another, God dwells deeply within us,
and his love becomes complete in us—perfect love!

This is how we know we're living steadily and deeply in
him, and he in us: He's given us life from his life, from his
very own Spirit. Also, we've seen for ourselves and contin-
ue to state openly that the Father sent his Son as Savior of
the world. Everyone who confesses that Jesus is God's Son
participates continuously in an intimate relationship with
God. We know it so well, we've embraced it heart and soul,
this love that comes from God.

To Love, To Be Loved

God is love. When we take up permanent residence in a
life of love, we live in God and God lives in us. This way,
love has the run of the house, becomes at home and
mature in us, so that we're free of worry on Judgment
Day—our standing in the world is identical with Christ's.
There is no room in love for fear. Well-formed love banish-
es fear. Since fear is crippling, a fearful life—fear of death,
fear of judgment—is one not yet fully formed in love.

We, though, are going to love—love and be loved. First
we were loved, now we love. He loved us first.

If anyone boasts, "I love God," and goes right on hating
his brother or sister, thinking nothing of it, he is a liar. If
he won't love the person he can see, how can he love the
God he can't see? The command we have from Christ is
blunt: Loving God includes loving people. You've got to
love both.

KING JAMES VERSION

5 Whosoever believeth that Jesus is the Christ is born of God: and every one that loveth him that begat loveth him also that is begotten of him.

2 By this we know that we love the children of God, when we love God, and keep his commandments.

3 For this is the love of God, that we keep his commandments: and his commandments are not grievous.

4 For whatsoever is born of God overcometh the world: and this is the victory that overcometh the world, *even* our faith.

5 Who is he that overcometh the world, but he that believeth that Jesus is the Son of God?

6 ¶ This is he that came by water and blood, *even* Jesus Christ; not by water only, but by water and blood. And it is the Spirit that beareth witness, because the Spirit is truth.

7 For there are three that bear record in heaven, the Father, the Word, and the Holy Ghost: and these three are one.

8 And there are three that bear witness in earth, the Spirit, and the water, and the blood: and these three agree in one.

9 If we receive the witness of men, the witness of God is greater: for this is the witness of God which he hath testified of his Son.

10 ¶ He that believeth on the Son of God hath the witness in himself: he that believeth not God hath made him a liar; because he believeth not the record that God gave of his Son.

NEW AMERICAN STANDARD BIBLE

Overcoming the World

5 Whoever believes that Jesus is the [1]Christ is born of God, and whoever loves the Father loves the *child* born of Him.

2 By this we know that we love the children of God, when we love God and observe His commandments.

3 For this is the love of God, that we keep His commandments; and His commandments are not burdensome.

4 For whatever is born of God overcomes the world; and this is the victory that has overcome the world—our faith.

5 Who is the one who overcomes the world, but he who believes that Jesus is the Son of God?

6 This is the One who came by water and blood, Jesus Christ; not with the water only, but with the water and with the blood. It is the Spirit who testifies, because the Spirit is the truth.

7 For there are three that testify:

8 [2]the Spirit and the water and the blood; and the three are in agreement.

9 If we receive the testimony of men, the testimony of God is greater; for the testimony of God is this, that He has testified concerning His Son.

10 The one who believes in the Son of God has the testimony in himself; the one who does not believe God has made Him a liar, because he has not believed in the testimony that God has given concerning His Son.

5:1 [1] I.e. Messiah 5:8 [2] A few late mss add ...*in heaven, the Father, the Word, and the Holy Spirit, and these three are one. And there are three that testify on earth, the Spirit*

NEW CENTURY VERSION

Faith in the Son of God

5 Everyone who believes that Jesus is the Christ is God's
child, and whoever loves the Father also loves the
Father's children. 2This is how we know we love God's
children: when we love God and obey his commands.
3Loving God means obeying his commands. And God's
commands are not too hard for us, 4because everyone who
is a child of God conquers the world. And this is the victory
that conquers the world—our faith. 5So the one who wins
against the world is the person who believes that Jesus is
the Son of God.

6Jesus Christ is the One who came by water[a] and blood.[b]
He did not come by water only, but by water and blood. And
the Spirit says that this is true, because the Spirit is the
truth. 7So there are three witnesses that tell us about Jesus:
8the Spirit, the water, and the blood; and these three wit-
nesses agree. 9We believe people when they say something
is true. But what God says is more important, and he has
told us the truth about his own Son. 10Anyone who believes
in the Son of God has the truth that God told us. Anyone
who does not believe makes God a liar, because that person
does not believe what God told us about his Son. 11This is

5:6 [a] **water** This probably means the water of Jesus' baptism.
5:6 [b] **blood** This probably means the blood of Jesus' death.

CONTEMPORARY ENGLISH VERSION

Victory over the World

5 If we believe that Jesus is truly Christ, we are God's
children. Everyone who loves the Father will also love
his children. 2If we love and obey God, we know that we
will love his children. 3We show our love for God by obey-
ing his commandments, and they are not hard to follow.
4Every child of God can defeat the world, and our faith
is what gives us this victory. 5No one can defeat the world
without having faith in Jesus as the Son of God.

Who Jesus Is

6Water and blood came out from the side of Jesus Christ.
It wasn't just water, but water and blood.[a] The Spirit tells
about this, because the Spirit is truthful. 7In fact, there are
three who tell about it. 8They are the Spirit, the water, and
the blood, and they all agree.

9We believe what people tell us. But we can trust what
God says even more, and God is the one who has spoken
about his Son. 10If we have faith in God's Son, we have
believed what God has said. But if we don't believe what God
has said about his Son, it is the same as calling God a liar.

[a] **5.6** *Water and blood came out from the side of Jesus Christ. It wasn't just water, but water and blood*: See John 19.34. It is also possible to translate, "Jesus Christ came by the water of baptism and by the blood of his death! He was not only baptized, but he bled and died." The purpose of the verse is to tell that Jesus was truly human and that he really died.

NEW INTERNATIONAL VERSION

Faith in the Son of God

5 Everyone who believes that Jesus is the Christ is born of God, and everyone who loves the father loves his child as well. [2]This is how we know that we love the children of God: by loving God and carrying out his commands. [3]This is love for God: to obey his commands. And his commands are not burdensome, [4]for everyone born of God overcomes the world. This is the victory that has overcome the world, even our faith. [5]Who is it that overcomes the world? Only he who believes that Jesus is the Son of God.

[6]This is the one who came by water and blood—Jesus Christ. He did not come by water only, but by water and blood. And it is the Spirit who testifies, because the Spirit is the truth. [7]For there are three that testify: [8]the[a] Spirit, the water and the blood; and the three are in agreement. [9]We accept man's testimony, but God's testimony is greater because it is the testimony of God, which he has given about his Son. [10]Anyone who believes in the Son of God has this testimony in his heart. Anyone who does not believe God has made him out to be a liar, because he has not believed the testimony God has given about his Son.

[a] *7,8* Late manuscripts of the Vulgate *testify in heaven: the Father, the Word and the Holy Spirit, and these three are one. [8]And there are three that testify on earth: the* (not found in any Greek manuscript before the sixteenth century)

NEW LIVING TRANSLATION

Faith in the Son of God

5 Everyone who believes that Jesus is the Christ is a child of God. And everyone who loves the Father loves his children, too. [2]We know we love God's children if we love God and obey his commandments. [3]Loving God means keeping his commandments, and really, that isn't difficult. [4]For every child of God defeats this evil world by trusting Christ to give the victory. [5]And the ones who win this battle against the world are the ones who believe that Jesus is the Son of God.

[6]And Jesus Christ was revealed as God's Son by his baptism in water and by shedding his blood on the cross*—not by water only, but by water and blood. And the Spirit also gives us the testimony that this is true. [7]So we have these three witnesses*—[8]the Spirit, the water, and the blood—and all three agree. [9]Since we believe human testimony, surely we can believe the testimony that comes from God. And God has testified about his Son. [10]All who believe in the Son of God know that this is true. Those who don't believe this are actually calling God a liar because they don't believe what God has testified about his Son.

5:6 Greek *This is he who came by water and blood.* 5:7 Some very late manuscripts add *in heaven—the Father, the Word, and the Holy Spirit, and these three are one. And we have three witnesses on earth.*

NEW KING JAMES VERSION

5 Whoever believes that Jesus is the Christ is born of God, and everyone who loves Him who begot also loves him who is begotten of Him. [2]By this we know that we love the children of God, when we love God and keep His commandments. [3]For this is the love of God, that we keep His commandments. And His commandments are not burdensome. [4]For whatever is born of God overcomes the world. And this is the victory that has overcome the world—our[a] faith. [5]Who is he who overcomes the world, but he who believes that Jesus is the Son of God?

The Certainty of God's Witness

[6]This is He who came by water and blood—Jesus Christ; not only by water, but by water and blood. And it is the Spirit who bears witness, because the Spirit is truth. [7]For there are three that bear witness in heaven: the Father, the Word, and the Holy Spirit; and these three are one. [8]And there are three that bear witness on earth:[b] the Spirit, the water, and the blood; and these three agree as one.

[9]If we receive the witness of men, the witness of God is greater; for this is the witness of God which[c] He has testified of His Son. [10]He who believes in the Son of God has the witness in himself; he who does not believe God has made Him a liar, because he has not believed the testimony that God has given of His Son. [11]And this is the testimony:

5:4 [a] M-Text reads *your.* 5:8 [b] NU-Text and M-Text omit the words from *in heaven* (verse 7) through *on earth* (verse 8). Only four or five very late manuscripts contain these words in Greek. 5:9 [c] NU-Text reads *God, that.*

THE MESSAGE

5 Every person who believes that Jesus is, in fact, the Messiah, is God-begotten. If we love the One who conceives the child, we'll surely love the child who was conceived. The reality test on whether or not we love God's children is this: Do we love God? Do we keep his commands? The proof that we love God comes when we keep his commandments and they are not at all troublesome.

The Power That Brings the World to Its Knees

Every God-begotten person conquers the world's ways. The conquering power that brings the world to its knees is our faith. The person who wins out over the world's ways is simply the one who believes Jesus is the Son of God.

Jesus—the Divine Christ! He experienced a life-giving birth and a death-killing death. Not only birth from the womb, but baptismal birth of his ministry and sacrificial death. And all the while the Spirit is confirming the truth, the reality of God's presence at Jesus' baptism and crucifixion, bringing those occasions alive for us. A triple testimony: the Spirit, the Baptism, the Crucifixion. And the three in perfect agreement.

If we take human testimony at face value, how much more should we be reassured when God gives testimony as he does here, testifying concerning his Son. Whoever believes in the Son of God inwardly confirms God's testimony. Whoever refuses to believe in effect calls God a liar, refusing to believe God's own testimony regarding his Son.

KING JAMES VERSION

11 And this is the record, that God hath given to us eternal life, and this life is in his Son.

12 He that hath the Son hath life; *and* he that hath not the Son of God hath not life.

13 These things have I written unto you that believe on the name of the Son of God; that ye may know that ye have eternal life, and that ye may believe on the name of the Son of God.

14 ¶ And this is the confidence that we have in him, that, if we ask any thing according to his will, he heareth us:

15 And if we know that he hear us, whatsoever we ask, we know that we have the petitions that we desired of him.

16 If any man see his brother sin a sin *which is* not unto death, he shall ask, and he shall give him life for them that sin not unto death. There is a sin unto death: I do not say that he shall pray for it.

17 All unrighteousness is sin: and there is a sin not unto death.

18 ¶ We know that whosoever is born of God sinneth not; but he that is begotten of God keepeth himself, and that wicked one toucheth him not.

19 *And* we know that we are of God, and the whole world lieth in wickedness.

NEW AMERICAN STANDARD BIBLE

11 And the testimony is this, that God has given us eternal life, and this life is in His Son.

12 He who has the Son has the life; he who does not have the Son of God does not have the life.

This Is Written That You May Know

13 These things I have written to you who believe in the name of the Son of God, so that you may know that you have eternal life.

14 This is the confidence which we have before Him, that, if we ask anything according to His will, He hears us.

15 And if we know that He hears us *in* whatever we ask, we know that we have the requests which we have asked from Him.

16 If anyone sees his brother committing a sin not *leading* to death, he shall ask and *God* will for him give life to those who commit sin not *leading* to death. There is a sin *leading* to death; I do not say that he should make request for this.

17 All unrighteousness is sin, and there is a sin not *leading* to death.

18 We know that no one who is born of God sins; but He who was born of God keeps him, and the evil one does not touch him.

19 We know that we are of God, and that the whole world lies in *the power of* the evil one.

NEW CENTURY VERSION

what God told us: God has given us eternal life, and this life
is in his Son. 12 Whoever has the Son has life, but whoever
does not have the Son of God does not have life.

We Have Eternal Life Now

13 I write this letter to you who believe in the Son of God
so you will know you have eternal life. 14 And this is the
boldness we have in God's presence: that if we ask God for
anything that agrees with what he wants, he hears us. 15 If
we know he hears us every time we ask him, we know we
have what we ask from him.

16 If anyone sees a brother or sister sinning (sin that
does not lead to eternal death), that person should pray,
and God will give the sinner life. I am talking about people
whose sin does not lead to eternal death. There is sin that
leads to death. I do not mean that a person should pray
about that sin. 17 Doing wrong is always sin, but there is
sin that does not lead to eternal death.

18 We know that those who are God's children do not
continue to sin. The Son of God keeps them safe, and the
Evil One cannot touch them. 19 We know that we belong to
God, but the Evil One controls the whole world. 20 We also

CONTEMPORARY ENGLISH VERSION

11 God has also said that he gave us eternal life and that this
life comes to us from his Son. 12 And so, if we have God's
Son, we have this life. But if we don't have the Son, we don't
have this life.

Knowing about Eternal Life

13 All of you have faith in the Son of God, and I have
written to let you know that you have eternal life. 14 We are
certain that God will hear our prayers when we ask for
what pleases him. 15 And if we know that God listens when
we pray, we are sure that our prayers have already been
answered.

16 Suppose you see one of our people commit a sin that
isn't a deadly sin. You can pray, and that person will be
given eternal life. But the sin must not be one that is dead-
ly. 17 Everything that is wrong is sin, but not all sins are
deadly.

18 We are sure that God's children do not keep on sin-
ning. God's own Son protects them, and the devil cannot
harm them.

19 We are certain that we come from God and that the
rest of the world is under the power of the devil.

NEW INTERNATIONAL VERSION

11And this is the testimony: God has given us eternal life,
and this life is in his Son. 12He who has the Son has life;
he who does not have the Son of God does not have life.

Concluding Remarks

13I write these things to you who believe in the name of
the Son of God so that you may know that you have eter-
nal life. 14This is the confidence we have in approaching
God: that if we ask anything according to his will, he hears
us. 15And if we know that he hears us—whatever we
ask—we know that we have what we asked of him.

16If anyone sees his brother commit a sin that does not
lead to death, he should pray and God will give him life. I
refer to those whose sin does not lead to death. There is a
sin that leads to death. I am not saying that he should
pray about that. 17All wrongdoing is sin, and there is sin
that does not lead to death.

18We know that anyone born of God does not continue to
sin; the one who was born of God keeps him safe, and the
evil one cannot harm him. 19We know that we are children
of God, and that the whole world is under the control of the

NEW LIVING TRANSLATION

11And this is what God has testified: He has given us
eternal life, and this life is in his Son. 12So whoever has
God's Son has life; whoever does not have his Son does
not have life.

Conclusion

13I write this to you who believe in the Son of God, so
that you may know you have eternal life. 14And we can be
confident that he will listen to us whenever we ask him for
anything in line with his will. 15And if we know he is lis-
tening when we make our requests, we can be sure that he
will give us what we ask for.

16If you see a Christian brother or sister* sinning in a
way that does not lead to death, you should pray, and God
will give that person life. But there is a sin that leads to
death, and I am not saying you should pray for those who
commit it. 17Every wrong is sin, but not all sin leads to
death.

18We know that those who have become part of God's
family do not make a practice of sinning, for God's Son
holds them securely, and the evil one cannot get his hands
on them. 19We know that we are children of God and that
the world around us is under the power and control of the

5:16 Greek *your brother.*

NEW KING JAMES VERSION

that God has given us eternal life, and this life is in His
Son. 12He who has the Son has life; he who does not have
the Son of God does not have life. 13These things I have
written to you who believe in the name of the Son of God,
that you may know that you have eternal life,[d] and that
you may *continue to* believe in the name of the Son of God.

Confidence and Compassion in Prayer

14Now this is the confidence that we have in Him, that if
we ask anything according to His will, He hears us. 15And
if we know that He hears us, whatever we ask, we know
that we have the petitions that we have asked of Him.

16If anyone sees his brother sinning a sin *which does*
not *lead* to death, he will ask, and He will give him life for
those who commit sin not *leading* to death. There is sin
leading to death. I do not say that he should pray about
that. 17All unrighteousness is sin, and there is sin not
leading to death.

Knowing the True—Rejecting the False

18We know that whoever is born of God does not sin; but
he who has been born of God keeps himself,[e] and the
wicked one does not touch him.

19We know that we are of God, and the whole world lies
under the sway of the wicked one.

5:13 [d] NU-Text omits the rest of this verse. 5:18 [e] NU-Text reads *him.*

THE MESSAGE

This is the testimony in essence: God gave us eternal life; the life is in his Son. So, whoever has the Son, has life; whoever rejects the Son, rejects life.

The Reality, Not the Illusion

My purpose in writing is simply this: that you who believe in God's Son will know beyond the shadow of a doubt that you have eternal life, the reality and not the illusion. And how bold and free we then become in his presence, freely asking according to his will, sure that he's listening. And if we're confident that he's listening, we know that what we've asked for is as good as ours.

For instance, if we see a Christian believer sinning (clearly I'm not talking about those who make a practice of sin in a way that is "fatal," leading to eternal death), we ask for God's help and he gladly gives it, gives life to the sinner whose sin is not fatal. There is such a thing as a fatal sin, and I'm not urging you to pray about that. Everything we do wrong is sin, but not all sin is fatal.

We know that none of the God-begotten make a practice of sin—fatal sin. The God-begotten are also the God-protected. The Evil One can't lay a hand on them. We know that we are held firm by God; it's only the people of the world who continue in the grip of the Evil One. And we

KING JAMES VERSION

20 And we know that the Son of God is come, and hath given us an understanding, that we may know him that is true, and we are in him that is true, *even* in his Son Jesus Christ. This is the true God, and eternal life.
21 Little children, keep yourselves from idols. Amen.

NEW AMERICAN STANDARD BIBLE

20 And we know that the Son of God has come, and has given us understanding so that we may know Him who is true; and we are in Him who is true, in His Son Jesus Christ. This is the true God and eternal life.
21 Little children, guard yourselves from idols.

NEW CENTURY VERSION

know that the Son of God has come and has given us understanding so that we can know the True One. And our lives are in the True One and in his Son, Jesus Christ. He is the true God and the eternal life.
21 So, dear children, keep yourselves away from gods.

CONTEMPORARY ENGLISH VERSION

20 We know that Jesus Christ the Son of God has come and has shown us the true God. And because of Jesus, we now belong to the true God who gives eternal life.
21 Children, you must stay away from idols.

NEW INTERNATIONAL VERSION

evil one. 20We know also that the Son of God has come and has given us understanding, so that we may know him who is true. And we are in him who is true—even in his Son Jesus Christ. He is the true God and eternal life.

21Dear children, keep yourselves from idols.

NEW LIVING TRANSLATION

evil one. 20And we know that the Son of God has come, and he has given us understanding so that we can know the true God. And now we are in God because we are in his Son, Jesus Christ. He is the only true God, and he is eternal life.

21Dear children, keep away from anything that might take God's place in your hearts.*

5:21 Greek *keep yourselves from idols.*

NEW KING JAMES VERSION

20And we know that the Son of God has come and has given us an understanding, that we may know Him who is true; and we are in Him who is true, in His Son Jesus Christ. This is the true God and eternal life.

21Little children, keep yourselves from idols. Amen.

THE MESSAGE

know that the Son of God came so we could recognize and understand the truth of God—what a gift!—and we are living in the Truth itself, in God's Son, Jesus Christ. This Jesus is both True God and Real Life. Dear children, be on guard against all clever facsimiles.

KING JAMES VERSION

THE SECOND EPISTLE OF
ST. JOHN

1 ¶ The elder unto the elect lady and her children, whom I love in the truth; and not I only, but also all they that have known the truth;

2 For the truth's sake, which dwelleth in us, and shall be with us for ever.

3 Grace be with you, mercy, *and* peace, from God the Father, and from the Lord Jesus Christ, the Son of the Father, in truth and love.

4 I rejoiced greatly that I found of thy children walking in truth, as we have received a commandment from the Father.

5 ¶ And now I beseech thee, lady, not as though I wrote a new commandment unto thee, but that which we had from the beginning, that we love one another.

6 And this is love, that we walk after his commandments. This is the commandment, That, as ye have heard from the beginning, ye should walk in it.

NEW AMERICAN STANDARD BIBLE

THE SECOND LETTER OF
JOHN

Walk According to His Commandments

1 The elder to the chosen lady and her children, whom I love in truth; and not only I, but also all who know the truth,

2 for the sake of the truth which abides in us and will be with us forever:

3 Grace, mercy *and* peace will be with us, from God the Father and from Jesus Christ, the Son of the Father, in truth and love.

4 I was very glad to find *some* of your children walking in truth, just as we have received commandment *to do* from the Father.

5 Now I ask you, lady, not as though *I were* writing to you a new commandment, but the one which we have had from the beginning, that we love one another.

6 And this is love, that we walk according to His commandments. This is the commandment, just as you have heard from the beginning, that you should walk in it.

NEW CENTURY VERSION

2 JOHN

1From the Elder.[a]

To the chosen lady[b] and her children:

I love all of you in the truth,[c] and all those who know
the truth love you. 2We love you because of the truth that
lives in us and will be with us forever.

3Grace, mercy, and peace from God the Father and his Son, Jesus Christ, will be with us in truth and love.

4I was very happy to learn that some of your children
are following the way of truth, as the Father commanded
us. 5And now, dear lady, this is not a new command but is
the same command we have had from the beginning. I ask
you that we all love each other. 6And love means living the
way God commanded us to live. As you have heard from the beginning, his command is this: Live a life of love.

1 [a] **Elder** "Elder" means an older person. It can also mean a special leader in the church (as in Titus 1:5). 1 [b] **lady** This might mean a woman, or in this letter it might mean a church. If it is a church, then "her children" would be the people of the church. 1 [c] **truth** The truth or "Good News" about Jesus Christ that joins all believers together.

CONTEMPORARY ENGLISH VERSION

2 JOHN

1From the church leader.[a]

To a very special woman and her children.[b] I truly love all of you, and so does everyone else who knows the truth.
2We love you because the truth is now in our hearts, and it
will be there forever.

3I pray that God the Father and Jesus Christ his Son will be kind and merciful to us! May they give us peace and truth and love.

Truth and Love

4I was very glad to learn that some of your children are
obeying the truth, as the Father told us to do. 5Dear friend,
I am not writing to tell you and your children to do something you have not done before. I am writing to tell you to love each other, which is the first thing you were told to
do. 6Love means that we do what God tells us. And from the beginning, he told you to love him.

[a] 1 *church leader*: Or "elder" or "presbyter" or "priest." [b] 1 *very special woman and her children*: A group of the Lord's followers who met together for worship. "The children of your . . . sister" (see verse 13) is another group of followers. "Very special" (here and verse 13) probably means "chosen (by the Lord)."

NEW INTERNATIONAL VERSION

2 JOHN

1 The elder,

To the chosen lady and her children, whom I love in the
truth—and not I only, but also all who know the truth—
2 because of the truth, which lives in us and will be with us
forever:

3 Grace, mercy and peace from God the Father and from
Jesus Christ, the Father's Son, will be with us in truth and
love.

4 It has given me great joy to find some of your children
walking in the truth, just as the Father commanded us.
5 And now, dear lady, I am not writing you a new command
but one we have had from the beginning. I ask that we
love one another. 6 And this is love: that we walk in obedi-
ence to his commands. As you have heard from the begin-
ning, his command is that you walk in love.

NEW LIVING TRANSLATION

2 JOHN

Greetings

This letter is from John the Elder.*

It is written to the chosen lady and to her children,*
whom I love in the truth, as does everyone else who knows
God's truth—2 the truth that lives in us and will be in our
hearts forever.

3 May grace, mercy, and peace, which come from God our
Father and from Jesus Christ his Son, be with us who live
in truth and love.

Live in the Truth

4 How happy I was to meet some of your children and
find them living in the truth, just as we have been com-
manded by the Father.

5 And now I want to urge you, dear lady, that we should
love one another. This is not a new commandment, but
one we had from the beginning. 6 Love means doing what
God has commanded us, and he has commanded us to love
one another, just as you heard from the beginning.

1a Greek *From the elder.* **1b** Or *the church God has chosen and her members,* or *the chosen Kyria and her children.*

NEW KING JAMES VERSION

THE SECOND EPISTLE OF JOHN

Greeting the Elect Lady

1 The Elder,

To the elect lady and her children, whom I love in truth,
and not only I, but also all those who have known the
truth, 2 because of the truth which abides in us and will be
with us forever:

3 Grace, mercy, *and* peace will be with you[a] from God the
Father and from the Lord Jesus Christ, the Son of the
Father, in truth and love.

Walk in Christ's Commandments

4 I rejoiced greatly that I have found *some* of your chil-
dren walking in truth, as we received commandment from
the Father. 5 And now I plead with you, lady, not as though
I wrote a new commandment to you, but that which we
have had from the beginning: that we love one another.
6 This is love, that we walk according to His command-
ments. This is the commandment, that as you have heard
from the beginning, you should walk in it.

3 [a] NU-Text and M-Text read *us.*

THE MESSAGE

2 JOHN

My dear congregation, I, your pastor, love you in very truth. And I'm not alone—everyone who knows the Truth that has taken up permanent residence in us loves you.

Let grace, mercy, and peace be with us in truth and love from God the Father and from Jesus Christ, Son of the Father!

I can't tell you how happy I am to learn that many members of your congregation are diligent in living out the Truth, exactly as commanded by the Father. But permit me a reminder, friends, and this is not a new commandment but simply a repetition of our original and basic charter: that we love each other. Love means following his commandments, and his unifying commandment is that you conduct your lives in love. This is the first thing you heard, and nothing has changed.

KING JAMES VERSION

7 ¶ For many deceivers are entered into the world, who confess not that Jesus Christ is come in the flesh. This is a deceiver and an antichrist.

8 Look to yourselves, that we lose not those things which we have wrought, but that we receive a full reward.

9 Whosoever transgresseth, and abideth not in the doctrine of Christ, hath not God. He that abideth in the doctrine of Christ, he hath both the Father and the Son.

10 ¶ If there come any unto you, and bring not this doctrine, receive him not into *your* house, neither bid him God speed:

11 For he that biddeth him God speed is partaker of his evil deeds.

12 ¶ Having many things to write unto you, I would not *write* with paper and ink: but I trust to come unto you, and speak face to face, that our joy may be full.

13 The children of thy elect sister greet thee. Amen.

NEW AMERICAN STANDARD BIBLE

7 For many deceivers have gone out into the world, those who do not acknowledge Jesus Christ *as* coming in the flesh. This is the deceiver and the antichrist.

8 Watch yourselves, that you do not lose what we have accomplished, but that you may receive a full reward.

9 Anyone who goes too far and does not abide in the teaching of Christ, does not have God; the one who abides in the teaching, he has both the Father and the Son.

10 If anyone comes to you and does not bring this teaching, do not receive him into *your* house, and do not give him a greeting;

11 for the one who gives him a greeting participates in his evil deeds.

12 Though I have many things to write to you, I do not want to *do so* with paper and ink; but I hope to come to you and speak face to face, so that your joy may be made full.

13 The children of your chosen sister greet you.

NEW CENTURY VERSION

7Many false teachers are in the world now who do not confess that Jesus Christ came to earth as a human. Anyone who does not confess this is a false teacher and an enemy of Christ. 8Be careful yourselves that you do not lose everything you have worked for, but that you receive your full reward.

9Anyone who goes beyond Christ's teaching and does not continue to follow only his teaching does not have God. But whoever continues to follow the teaching of Christ has both the Father and the Son. 10If someone comes to you and does not bring this teaching, do not welcome or accept that person into your house. 11If you welcome such a person, you share in the evil work.

12I have many things to write to you, but I do not want to use paper and ink. Instead, I hope to come to you and talk face to face so we can be full of joy. 13The children of your chosen sister[d] greet you.

13 [d] **sister** Sister of the "lady" in verse 1. This might be another woman or another church.

CONTEMPORARY ENGLISH VERSION

7Many liars have gone out into the world. These deceitful liars are saying that Jesus Christ did not have a truly human body. But they are liars and the enemies of Christ. 8So be sure not to lose what we[c] have worked for. If you do, you won't be given your full reward. 9Don't keep changing what you were taught about Christ, or else God will no longer be with you. But if you hold firmly to what you were taught, both the Father and the Son will be with you. 10If people won't agree to this teaching, don't welcome them into your home or even greet them. 11Greeting them is the same as taking part in their evil deeds.

Final Greetings

12I have much more to tell you, but I don't want to write it with pen and ink. I want to come and talk to you in person, because that will make us[d] really happy.

13Greetings from the children of your very special sister.[e]

[c] **8** *we*: Some manuscripts have "you." [d] **12** *us*: Some manuscripts have "you." [e] **13** *sister*: See the note at verse 1.

NEW INTERNATIONAL VERSION

[7]Many deceivers, who do not acknowledge Jesus Christ as coming in the flesh, have gone out into the world. Any such person is the deceiver and the antichrist. [8]Watch out that you do not lose what you have worked for, but that you may be rewarded fully. [9]Anyone who runs ahead and does not continue in the teaching of Christ does not have God; whoever continues in the teaching has both the Father and the Son. [10]If anyone comes to you and does not bring this teaching, do not take him into your house or welcome him. [11]Anyone who welcomes him shares in his wicked work.

[12]I have much to write to you, but I do not want to use paper and ink. Instead, I hope to visit you and talk with you face to face, so that our joy may be complete.

[13]The children of your chosen sister send their greetings.

NEW LIVING TRANSLATION

[7]Many deceivers have gone out into the world. They do not believe that Jesus Christ came to earth in a real body. Such a person is a deceiver and an antichrist. [8]Watch out, so that you do not lose the prize for which we* have been working so hard. Be diligent so that you will receive your full reward. [9]For if you wander beyond the teaching of Christ, you will not have fellowship with God. But if you continue in the teaching of Christ, you will have fellowship with both the Father and the Son.

[10]If someone comes to your meeting and does not teach the truth about Christ, don't invite him into your house or encourage him in any way. [11]Anyone who encourages him becomes a partner in his evil work.

Conclusion

[12]Well, I have much more to say to you, but I don't want to say it in a letter. For I hope to visit you soon and to talk with you face to face. Then our joy will be complete.

[13]Greetings from the children of your sister,* chosen by God.

8 Some manuscripts read *you*. 13 Or *from the members of your sister church.*

NEW KING JAMES VERSION

Beware of Antichrist Deceivers

[7]For many deceivers have gone out into the world who do not confess Jesus Christ *as* coming in the flesh. This is a deceiver and an antichrist. [8]Look to yourselves, that we[b] do not lose those things we worked for, but *that* we[c] may receive a full reward.

[9]Whoever transgresses[d] and does not abide in the doctrine of Christ does not have God. He who abides in the doctrine of Christ has both the Father and the Son. [10]If anyone comes to you and does not bring this doctrine, do not receive him into your house nor greet him; [11]for he who greets him shares in his evil deeds.

John's Farewell Greeting

[12]Having many things to write to you, I did not wish *to do so* with paper and ink; but I hope to come to you and speak face to face, that our joy may be full.

[13]The children of your elect sister greet you. Amen.

8 [b] NU-Text reads *you*. [c] NU-Text reads *you*. 9 [d] NU-Text reads *goes ahead.*

THE MESSAGE

Don't Walk Out on God

There are a lot of smooth-talking charlatans loose in the world who refuse to believe that Jesus Christ was truly human, a flesh-and-blood human being. Give them their true title: Deceiver! Antichrist!

And be very careful around them so you don't lose out on what we've worked so diligently in together; I want you to get every reward you have coming to you. Anyone who gets so progressive in his thinking that he walks out on the teaching of Christ, walks out on God. But whoever stays with the teaching, stays faithful to both the Father and the Son.

If anyone shows up who doesn't hold to this teaching, don't invite him in and give him the run of the place. That would just give him a platform to perpetuate his evil ways, making you his partner.

I have a lot more things to tell you, but I'd rather not use paper and ink. I hope to be there soon in person and have a heart-to-heart talk. That will be far more satisfying to both you and me. Everyone here in your sister congregation sends greetings.

KING JAMES VERSION

THE THIRD EPISTLE OF
ST. JOHN

1 ¶ The elder unto the wellbeloved Gaius, whom I love in the truth.

2 Beloved, I wish above all things that thou mayest prosper and be in health, even as thy soul prospereth.

3 ¶ For I rejoiced greatly, when the brethren came and testified of the truth that is in thee, even as thou walkest in the truth.

4 I have no greater joy than to hear that my children walk in truth.

5 Beloved, thou doest faithfully whatsoever thou doest to the brethren, and to strangers;

6 Which have borne witness of thy charity before the church: whom if thou bring forward on their journey after a godly sort, thou shalt do well:

7 Because that for his name's sake they went forth, taking nothing of the Gentiles.

8 We therefore ought to receive such, that we might be fellowhelpers to the truth.

NEW AMERICAN STANDARD BIBLE

THE THIRD LETTER OF
JOHN

You Walk in the Truth

1 The elder to the beloved Gaius, whom I love in truth.

2 Beloved, I pray that in all respects you may prosper and be in good health, just as your soul prospers.

3 For I was very glad when brethren came and testified to your truth, *that is,* how you are walking in truth.

4 I have no greater joy than this, to hear of my children walking in the truth.

5 Beloved, you are acting faithfully in whatever you accomplish for the brethren, and especially *when they are* strangers;

6 and they have testified to your love before the church. You will do well to send them on their way in a manner worthy of God.

7 For they went out for the sake of the Name, accepting nothing from the Gentiles.

8 Therefore we ought to support such men, so that we may be fellow workers with the truth.

NEW CENTURY VERSION

3 JOHN

1 From the Elder.[a]

To my dear friend Gaius, whom I love in the truth:[b]

2 My dear friend, I know your soul is doing fine, and I pray that you are doing well in every way and that your health is good. 3 I was very happy when some brothers and sisters[c] came and told me about the truth in your life and how you are following the way of truth. 4 Nothing gives me greater joy than to hear that my children are following the way of truth.

5 My dear friend, it is good that you help the brothers and sisters, even those you do not know. 6 They told the church about your love. Please help them to continue their trip in a way worthy of God. 7 They started out in service to Christ, and they have been accepting nothing from nonbelievers. 8 So we should help such people; when we do, we share in their work for the truth.

1 [a] **Elder** "Elder" means an older person. It can also mean a special leader in the church (as Titus 1:5). 1 [b] **truth** The truth or "Good News" about Jesus Christ that joins all believers together. 3 [c] **brothers and sisters** Although the Greek text says "brothers" here and throughout this book, the writer's words were meant for the entire church, including men and women.

CONTEMPORARY ENGLISH VERSION

3 JOHN

1 From the church leader.[a]

To my dear friend Gaius.

I love you because we follow the truth, 2 dear friend, and I pray that all goes well for you. I hope that you are as strong in body, as I know you are in spirit. 3 It makes me very happy when the Lord's followers come by and speak openly of how you obey the truth. 4 Nothing brings me greater happiness than to hear that my children[b] are obeying the truth.

Working Together

5 Dear friend, you have always been faithful in helping other followers of the Lord, even the ones you didn't know before. 6 They have told the church about your love. They say you were good enough to welcome them and to send them on their mission in a way that God's servants deserve. 7 When they left to tell others about the Lord, they decided not to accept help from anyone who wasn't a follower. 8 We must support people like them, so that we can take part in what they are doing to spread the truth.

[a] 1 *church leader*: Or "elder" or "presbyter" or "priest." [b] 4 *children*: Probably persons that the leader had led to be followers of the Lord.

NEW INTERNATIONAL VERSION

3 JOHN

1The elder,

To my dear friend Gaius, whom I love in the truth.

2Dear friend, I pray that you may enjoy good health and that all may go well with you, even as your soul is getting along well. 3It gave me great joy to have some brothers come and tell about your faithfulness to the truth and how you continue to walk in the truth. 4I have no greater joy than to hear that my children are walking in the truth.

5Dear friend, you are faithful in what you are doing for the brothers, even though they are strangers to you. 6They have told the church about your love. You will do well to send them on their way in a manner worthy of God. 7It was for the sake of the Name that they went out, receiving no help from the pagans. 8We ought therefore to show hospitality to such men so that we may work together for the truth.

NEW LIVING TRANSLATION

3 JOHN

Greetings

This letter is from John the Elder.*

It is written to Gaius, my dear friend, whom I love in the truth.

2Dear friend, I am praying that all is well with you and that your body is as healthy as I know your soul is. 3Some of the brothers recently returned and made me very happy by telling me about your faithfulness and that you are living in the truth. 4I could have no greater joy than to hear that my children live in the truth.

Caring for the Lord's Workers

5Dear friend, you are doing a good work for God when you take care of the traveling teachers* who are passing through, even though they are strangers to you. 6They have told the church here of your friendship and your loving deeds. You do well to send them on their way in a manner that pleases God. 7For they are traveling for the Lord* and accept nothing from those who are not Christians.* 8So we ourselves should support them so that we may become partners with them for the truth.

1 Greek *From the elder.* 5 Greek *the brothers;* also in verse 10.
7a Greek *the Name.* 7b Greek *from Gentiles.*

NEW KING JAMES VERSION

THE THIRD EPISTLE OF

3 JOHN

Greeting to Gaius

1 The Elder,

To the beloved Gaius, whom I love in truth:

2Beloved, I pray that you may prosper in all things and be in health, just as your soul prospers. 3For I rejoiced greatly when brethren came and testified of the truth *that is* in you, just as you walk in the truth. 4I have no greater joy than to hear that my children walk in truth.[a]

Gaius Commended for Generosity

5Beloved, you do faithfully whatever you do for the brethren and[b] for strangers, 6who have borne witness of your love before the church. *If* you send them forward on their journey in a manner worthy of God, you will do well, 7because they went forth for His name's sake, taking nothing from the Gentiles. 8We therefore ought to receive[c] such, that we may become fellow workers for the truth.

4 [a] NU-Text reads *the truth.* 5 [b] NU-Text adds *especially.*
8 [c] NU-Text reads *support.*

THE MESSAGE

3 JOHN

The Pastor, to my good friend Gaius: How truly I love you! We're the best of friends, and I pray for good fortune in everything you do, and for your good health—that your everyday affairs prosper, as well as your soul! I was most happy when some friends arrived and brought the news that you persist in following the way of Truth. Nothing could make me happier than getting reports that my children continue diligently in the way of Truth!

Model the Good

Dear friend, when you extend hospitality to Christian brothers and sisters, even when they are strangers, you make the faith visible. They've made a full report back to the church here, a message about your love. It's good work you're doing, helping these travelers on their way, hospitality worthy of God himself! They set out under the banner of the Name, and get no help from unbelievers. So they deserve any support we can give them. In providing meals and a bed, we become their companions in spreading the Truth.

KING JAMES VERSION

9 ¶ I wrote unto the church: but Diotrephes, who loveth to have the preeminence among them, receiveth us not.

10 Wherefore, if I come, I will remember his deeds which he doeth, prating against us with malicious words: and not content therewith, neither doth he himself receive the brethren, and forbiddeth them that would, and casteth *them* out of the church.

11 Beloved, follow not that which is evil, but that which is good. He that doeth good is of God: but he that doeth evil hath not seen God.

12 ¶ Demetrius hath good report of all *men*, and of the truth itself: yea, and we *also* bear record; and ye know that our record is true.

13 I had many things to write, but I will not with ink and pen write unto thee:

14 But I trust I shall shortly see thee, and we shall speak face to face. Peace *be* to thee. *Our* friends salute thee. Greet the friends by name.

NEW AMERICAN STANDARD BIBLE

9 I wrote something to the church; but Diotrephes, who loves to be first among them, does not accept what we say.

10 For this reason, if I come, I will call attention to his deeds which he does, unjustly accusing us with wicked words; and not satisfied with this, he himself does not receive the brethren, either, and he forbids those who desire *to do so* and puts *them* out of the church.

11 Beloved, do not imitate what is evil, but what is good. The one who does good is of God; the one who does evil has not seen God.

12 Demetrius has received a *good* testimony from everyone, and from the truth itself; and we add our testimony, and you know that our testimony is true.

13 I had many things to write to you, but I am not willing to write *them* to you with pen and ink;

14 but I hope to see you shortly, and we will speak face to face.

Peace *be* to you. The friends greet you. Greet the friends by name.

NEW CENTURY VERSION

9 I wrote something to the church, but Diotrephes, who
loves to be their leader, will not listen to us. 10 So if I come,
I will talk about what Diotrephes is doing, about how he
lies and says evil things about us. But more than that, he
refuses to accept the other brothers and sisters; he even
stops those who do want to accept them and puts them out
of the church.

11 My dear friend, do not follow what is bad; follow what
is good. The one who does good belongs to God. But the
one who does evil has never known God.

12 Everyone says good things about Demetrius, and the
truth agrees with what they say. We also speak well of
him, and you know what we say is true.

13 I have many things I want to write you, but I do not
want to use pen and ink. 14 I hope to see you soon and talk
face to face. 15 Peace to you. The friends here greet you.
Please greet each friend there by name.

CONTEMPORARY ENGLISH VERSION

9 I wrote to the church. But Diotrephes likes to be the
number-one leader, and he won't pay any attention to us.
10 So if I come, I will remind him of how he has been
attacking us with gossip. Not only has he been doing this,
but he refuses to welcome any of the Lord's followers who
come by. And when other church members want to welcome them, he puts them out of the church.

11 Dear friend, don't copy the evil deeds of others! Follow
the example of people who do kind deeds. They are God's
children, but those who are always doing evil have never
seen God.

12 Everyone speaks well of Demetrius, and so does the
true message that he teaches. I also speak well of him, and
you know what I say is true.

Final Greetings

13 I have much more to say to you, but I don't want to
write it with pen and ink. 14 I hope to see you soon, and
then we can talk in person.

15 I pray that God will bless you with peace!

Your friends send their greetings. Please give a personal greeting to each of our friends.

NEW INTERNATIONAL VERSION

9I wrote to the church, but Diotrephes, who loves to be first, will have nothing to do with us. 10So if I come, I will call attention to what he is doing, gossiping maliciously about us. Not satisfied with that, he refuses to welcome the brothers. He also stops those who want to do so and puts them out of the church.

11Dear friend, do not imitate what is evil but what is good. Anyone who does what is good is from God. Anyone who does what is evil has not seen God. 12Demetrius is well spoken of by everyone—and even by the truth itself. We also speak well of him, and you know that our testimony is true.

13I have much to write you, but I do not want to do so with pen and ink. 14I hope to see you soon, and we will talk face to face.

Peace to you. The friends here send their greetings. Greet the friends there by name.

NEW LIVING TRANSLATION

9I sent a brief letter to the church about this, but Diotrephes, who loves to be the leader, does not acknowledge our authority. 10When I come, I will report some of the things he is doing and the wicked things he is saying about us. He not only refuses to welcome the traveling teachers, he also tells others not to help them. And when they do help, he puts them out of the church.

11Dear friend, don't let this bad example influence you. Follow only what is good. Remember that those who do good prove that they are God's children, and those who do evil prove that they do not know God. 12But everyone speaks highly of Demetrius, even truth itself. We ourselves can say the same for him, and you know we speak the truth.

Conclusion

13I have much to tell you, but I don't want to do it in a letter. 14For I hope to see you soon, and then we will talk face to face.

15May God's peace be with you.

Your friends here send you their greetings. Please give my personal greetings to each of our friends there.

NEW KING JAMES VERSION

Diotrephes and Demetrius

9I wrote to the church, but Diotrephes, who loves to have the preeminence among them, does not receive us. 10Therefore, if I come, I will call to mind his deeds which he does, prating against us with malicious words. And not content with that, he himself does not receive the brethren, and forbids those who wish to, putting *them* out of the church.

11Beloved, do not imitate what is evil, but what is good. He who does good is of God, but[d] he who does evil has not seen God.

12Demetrius has a *good* testimony from all, and from the truth itself. And we also bear witness, and you know that our testimony is true.

Farewell Greeting

13I had many things to write, but I do not wish to write to you with pen and ink; 14but I hope to see you shortly, and we shall speak face to face.

Peace to you. Our friends greet you. Greet the friends by name.

11 [d] NU-Text and M-Text omit *but.*

THE MESSAGE

Earlier I wrote something along this line to the church, but Diotrephes, who loves being in charge, denigrates my counsel. If I come, you can be sure I'll hold him to account for spreading vicious rumors about us.

As if that weren't bad enough, he not only refuses hospitality to traveling Christians but tries to stop others from welcoming them. Worse yet, instead of inviting them in he throws them out.

Friend, don't go along with evil. Model the good. The person who does good does God's work. The person who does evil falsifies God, doesn't know the first thing about God.

Everyone has a good word for Demetrius—the Truth itself stands up for Demetrius! We concur, and you know we don't hand out endorsements lightly.

I have a lot more things to tell you, but I'd rather not use pen and ink. I hope to be there soon in person and have a heart-to-heart talk.

Peace to you. The friends here say hello. Greet our friends there by name.

KING JAMES VERSION

THE EPISTLE OF
ST. JUDE

1 ¶ Jude, the servant of Jesus Christ, and brother of James, to them that are sanctified by God the Father, and preserved in Jesus Christ, *and* called:

2 Mercy unto you, and peace, and love, be multiplied.

3 ¶ Beloved, when I gave all diligence to write unto you of the common salvation, it was needful for me to write unto you, and exhort *you* that ye should earnestly contend for the faith which was once delivered unto the saints.

4 For there are certain men crept in unawares, who were before of old ordained to this condemnation, ungodly men, turning the grace of our God into lasciviousness, and denying the only Lord God, and our Lord Jesus Christ.

5 I will therefore put you in remembrance, though ye once knew this, how that the Lord, having saved the people out of the land of Egypt, afterward destroyed them that believed not.

NEW AMERICAN STANDARD BIBLE

THE LETTER OF
JUDE

The Warnings of History to the Ungodly

1 Jude, a bond-servant of Jesus Christ, and brother of James,

To those who are the called, beloved in God the Father, and kept for Jesus Christ:

2 May mercy and peace and love be multiplied to you.

3 Beloved, while I was making every effort to write you about our common salvation, I felt the necessity to write to you appealing that you contend earnestly for the faith which was once for all handed down to the saints.

4 For certain persons have crept in unnoticed, those who were long beforehand marked out for this condemnation, ungodly persons who turn the grace of our God into licentiousness and deny our only Master and Lord, Jesus Christ.

5 Now I desire to remind you, though you know all things once for all, that [1]the Lord, after saving a people out of the land of Egypt, subsequently destroyed those who did not believe.

5 [1] Two early mss read *Jesus*

NEW CENTURY VERSION

JUDE

1 From Jude, a servant of Jesus Christ and a brother of
James.
To all who have been called by God. God the Father
loves you, and you have been kept safe in Jesus Christ:
2 Mercy, peace, and love be yours richly.

God Will Punish Sinners

3 Dear friends, I wanted very much to write you about
the salvation we all share. But I felt the need to write you
about something else: I want to encourage you to fight
hard for the faith that was given the holy people of God
once and for all time. 4 Some people have secretly entered
your group. Long ago the prophets wrote about these peo-
ple who will be judged guilty. They are against God and
have changed the grace of our God into a reason for sexual
sin. They also refuse to accept Jesus Christ, our only
Master and Lord.
5 I want to remind you of some things you already know:
Remember that the Lord saved his people by bringing them
out of the land of Egypt. But later he destroyed all those
who did not believe. 6 And remember the angels who did

CONTEMPORARY ENGLISH VERSION

JUDE

1 From Jude, a servant of Jesus Christ and the brother of
James.
To all who are chosen and loved by God the Father and
are kept safe by Jesus Christ.
2 I pray that God will greatly bless you with kindness,
peace, and love!

False Teachers

3 My dear friends, I really wanted to write you about
God's saving power at work in our lives. But instead, I
must write and ask you to defend the faith that God has
once for all given to his people. 4 Some godless people have
sneaked in among us and are saying, "God treats us much
better than we deserve, and so it is all right to be
immoral." They even deny that we must obey Jesus Christ
as our only Master and Lord. But long ago the Scriptures
warned that these godless people were doomed.
5 Don't forget what happened to those people that the
Lord rescued from Egypt. Some of them did not have faith,
and he later destroyed them. 6 You also know about the

NEW INTERNATIONAL VERSION

JUDE

1 Jude, a servant of Jesus Christ and a brother of James,

To those who have been called, who are loved by God the Father and kept by[a] Jesus Christ:

2 Mercy, peace and love be yours in abundance.

The Sin and Doom of Godless Men

3 Dear friends, although I was very eager to write to you about the salvation we share, I felt I had to write and urge you to contend for the faith that was once for all entrusted to the saints. 4 For certain men whose condemnation was written about[b] long ago have secretly slipped in among you. They are godless men, who change the grace of our God into a license for immorality and deny Jesus Christ our only Sovereign and Lord.

5 Though you already know all this, I want to remind you that the Lord[c] delivered his people out of Egypt, but later destroyed those who did not believe. 6 And the angels who

[a] *1* Or *for*; or *in* [b] *4* Or *men who were marked out for condemnation*
[c] *5* Some early manuscripts *Jesus*

NEW LIVING TRANSLATION

JUDE

Greetings from Jude

This letter is from Jude, a slave of Jesus Christ and a brother of James.

I am writing to all who are called to live in the love of God the Father and the care of Jesus Christ.

2 May you receive more and more of God's mercy, peace, and love.

The Danger of False Teachers

3 Dearly loved friends, I had been eagerly planning to write to you about the salvation we all share. But now I find that I must write about something else, urging you to defend the truth of the Good News.* God gave this unchanging truth once for all time to his holy people. 4 I say this because some godless people have wormed their way in among you, saying that God's forgiveness allows us to live immoral lives. The fate of such people was determined long ago, for they have turned against our only Master and Lord, Jesus Christ.

5 I must remind you—and you know it well—that even though the Lord* rescued the whole nation of Israel from Egypt, he later destroyed every one of those who did not remain faithful. 6 And I remind you of the angels who did

3 Greek *to contend for the faith.* 5 Some manuscripts read *Jesus.*

NEW KING JAMES VERSION

THE EPISTLE OF

JUDE

Greeting to the Called

1 Jude, a bondservant of Jesus Christ, and brother of James,

To those who are called, sanctified[a] by God the Father, and preserved in Jesus Christ:

2 Mercy, peace, and love be multiplied to you.

Contend for the Faith

3 Beloved, while I was very diligent to write to you concerning our common salvation, I found it necessary to write to you exhorting you to contend earnestly for the faith which was once for all delivered to the saints. 4 For certain men have crept in unnoticed, who long ago were marked out for this condemnation, ungodly men, who turn the grace of our God into lewdness and deny the only Lord God[b] and our Lord Jesus Christ.

Old and New Apostates

5 But I want to remind you, though you once knew this, that the Lord, having saved the people out of the land of Egypt, afterward destroyed those who did not believe.

1 [a] NU-Text reads *beloved.* 4 [b] NU-Text omits *God.*

THE MESSAGE

JUDE

I, Jude, am a slave to Jesus Christ and brother to James, writing to those loved by God the Father, called and kept safe by Jesus Christ. Relax, everything's going to be all right; rest, everything's coming together; open your hearts, love is on the way!

Fight With All You Have in You

Dear friends, I've dropped everything to write you about this life of salvation that we have in common. I have to write insisting—begging!—that you fight with everything you have in you for this faith entrusted to us as a gift to guard and cherish. What has happened is that some people have infiltrated our ranks (our Scriptures warned us this would happen), who beneath their pious skin are shameless scoundrels. Their design is to replace the sheer grace of our God with sheer license—which means doing away with Jesus Christ, our one and only Master.

Lost Stars in Outer Space

I'm laying this out as clearly as I can, even though you once knew all this well enough and shouldn't need reminding. Here it is in brief: The Master saved a people out of the land of Egypt. Later he destroyed those who defected. And

KING JAMES VERSION

6 And the angels which kept not their first estate, but left their own habitation, he hath reserved in everlasting chains under darkness unto the judgment of the great day.

7 Even as Sodom and Gomorrha, and the cities about them in like manner, giving themselves over to fornication, and going after strange flesh, are set forth for an example, suffering the vengeance of eternal fire.

8 ¶ Likewise also these *filthy* dreamers defile the flesh, despise dominion, and speak evil of dignities.

9 Yet Michael the archangel, when contending with the devil he disputed about the body of Moses, durst not bring against him a railing accusation, but said, The Lord rebuke thee.

10 But these speak evil of those things which they know not: but what they know naturally, as brute beasts, in those things they corrupt themselves.

11 Woe unto them! for they have gone in the way of Cain, and ran greedily after the error of Balaam for reward, and perished in the gainsaying of Core.

NEW AMERICAN STANDARD BIBLE

6 And angels who did not keep their own domain, but abandoned their proper abode, He has kept in eternal bonds under darkness for the judgment of the great day,

7 just as Sodom and Gomorrah and the cities around them, since they in the same way as these indulged in gross immorality and went after strange flesh, are exhibited as an example in undergoing the punishment of eternal fire.

8 Yet in the same way these men, also by dreaming, defile the flesh, and reject authority, and revile angelic majesties.

9 But Michael the archangel, when he disputed with the devil and argued about the body of Moses, did not dare pronounce against him a railing judgment, but said, "The Lord rebuke you!"

10 But these men revile the things which they do not understand; and the things which they know by instinct, like unreasoning animals, by these things they are destroyed.

11 Woe to them! For they have gone the way of Cain, and for pay they have rushed headlong into the error of Balaam, and perished in the rebellion of Korah.

NEW CENTURY VERSION

not keep their place of power but left their proper home.
The Lord has kept these angels in darkness, bound with
everlasting chains, to be judged on the great day. 7Also
remember the cities of Sodom and Gomorrah[a] and the
other towns around them. In the same way they were full
of sexual sin and people who desired sexual relations that
God does not allow. They suffer the punishment of eternal
fire, as an example for all to see.

8It is the same with these people who have entered your
group. They are guided by dreams and make themselves
filthy with sin. They reject God's authority and speak
against the angels. 9Not even the archangel[b] Michael,
when he argued with the devil about who would have the
body of Moses, dared to judge the devil guilty. Instead, he
said, "The Lord punish you." 10But these people speak
against things they do not understand. And what they do
know, by feeling, as dumb animals know things, are the
very things that destroy them. 11It will be terrible for them.
They have followed the way of Cain, and for money they
have given themselves to doing the wrong that Balaam
did. They have fought against God as Korah did, and like

7 [a] **Sodom and Gomorrah** Two cities God destroyed because they were so evil. 9 [b] **archangel** The leader among God's angels or messengers.

CONTEMPORARY ENGLISH VERSION

angels[a] who didn't do their work and left their proper
places. God chained them with everlasting chains and is
now keeping them in dark pits until the great day of judg-
ment. 7We should also be warned by what happened to the
cities of Sodom and Gomorrah[b] and the nearby towns.
Their people became immoral and did all sorts of sexual
sins. Then God made an example of them and punished
them with eternal fire.

8The people I am talking about are behaving just like
those dreamers who destroyed their own bodies. They
reject all authority and insult angels. 9Even Michael, the
chief angel, didn't dare to insult the devil, when the two of
them were arguing about the body of Moses.[c] All Michael
said was, "The Lord will punish you!"

10But these people insult powers they don't know any-
thing about. They are like senseless animals that end up
getting destroyed, because they live only by their feelings.
11Now they are in for real trouble. They have followed
Cain's example[d] and have made the same mistake that
Balaam[e] did by caring only for money. They have also

[a] 6 *angels*: This may refer to the angels who liked the women on earth so much that they came down and married them (see Genesis 6.2).
[b] 7 *Sodom and Gomorrah*: During the time of Abraham the Lord destroyed these cities because the people there were so evil. [c] 9 *Michael . . . the body of Moses*: This refers to what was said in an ancient Jewish book about Moses. [d] 11 *Cain's example*: Cain murdered his brother Abel.
[e] 11 *Balaam*: According to the biblical account, Balaam refused to curse the people of Israel for profit (see Numbers 22.18; 24.13), though he led them to be unfaithful to the Lord (see Numbers 25.1-3; 31.16). But by New Testament times, some Jewish teachers taught that Balaam was greedy and did accept money to curse them.

NEW INTERNATIONAL VERSION

did not keep their positions of authority but abandoned
their own home—these he has kept in darkness, bound
with everlasting chains for judgment on the great Day. 7In
a similar way, Sodom and Gomorrah and the surrounding
towns gave themselves up to sexual immorality and per-
version. They serve as an example of those who suffer the
punishment of eternal fire.

8In the very same way, these dreamers pollute their own
bodies, reject authority and slander celestial beings. 9But
even the archangel Michael, when he was disputing with
the devil about the body of Moses, did not dare to bring a
slanderous accusation against him, but said, "The Lord
rebuke you!" 10Yet these men speak abusively against
whatever they do not understand; and what things they do
understand by instinct, like unreasoning animals—these
are the very things that destroy them.

11Woe to them! They have taken the way of Cain; they
have rushed for profit into Balaam's error; they have been
destroyed in Korah's rebellion.

NEW LIVING TRANSLATION

not stay within the limits of authority God gave them but
left the place where they belonged. God has kept them
chained in prisons of darkness, waiting for the day of judg-
ment. 7And don't forget the cities of Sodom and Gomorrah
and their neighboring towns, which were filled with sexual
immorality and every kind of sexual perversion. Those cit-
ies were destroyed by fire and are a warning of the eternal
fire that will punish all who are evil.

8Yet these false teachers, who claim authority from their
dreams, live immoral lives, defy authority, and scoff at the
power of the glorious ones.* 9But even Michael, one of the
mightiest of the angels, did not dare accuse Satan of blas-
phemy, but simply said, "The Lord rebuke you." (This took
place when Michael was arguing with Satan about Moses'
body.) 10But these people mock and curse the things they
do not understand. Like animals, they do whatever their
instincts tell them, and they bring about their own destruc-
tion. 11How terrible it will be for them! For they follow the
evil example of Cain, who killed his brother. Like Balaam,
they will do anything for money. And like Korah, they will
perish because of their rebellion.

8 *The glorious ones* are probably evil angels.

NEW KING JAMES VERSION

6And the angels who did not keep their proper domain, but
left their own abode, He has reserved in everlasting chains
under darkness for the judgment of the great day; 7as
Sodom and Gomorrah, and the cities around them in a
similar manner to these, having given themselves over to
sexual immorality and gone after strange flesh, are set
forth as an example, suffering the vengeance of eternal
fire.

8Likewise also these dreamers defile the flesh, reject
authority, and speak evil of dignitaries. 9Yet Michael the
archangel, in contending with the devil, when he disputed
about the body of Moses, dared not bring against him a
reviling accusation, but said, "The Lord rebuke you!" 10But
these speak evil of whatever they do not know; and what-
ever they know naturally, like brute beasts, in these things
they corrupt themselves. 11Woe to them! For they have
gone in the way of Cain, have run greedily in the error of
Balaam for profit, and perished in the rebellion of Korah.

THE MESSAGE

you know the story of the angels who didn't stick to their post, abandoning it for other, darker missions. But they are now chained and jailed in a black hole until the great Judgment Day. Sodom and Gomorrah, which went to sexual rack and ruin along with the surrounding cities that acted just like them, are another example. Burning and burning and never burning up, they serve still as a stock warning.

This is exactly the same program of these latest infiltrators: dirty sex, rule and rulers thrown out, glory dragged in the mud.

The Archangel Michael, who went to the mat with the Devil as they fought over the body of Moses, wouldn't have dared level him with a blasphemous curse, but said simply, "No you don't. *God* will take care of you!" But these people sneer at anything they can't understand, and by doing whatever they feel like doing—living by animal instinct only—they participate in their own destruction. I'm fed up with them! They've gone down Cain's road; they've been sucked into Balaam's error by greed; they're canceled out in Korah's rebellion.

KING JAMES VERSION

12 These are spots in your feasts of charity, when they feast with you, feeding themselves without fear: clouds *they are* without water, carried about of winds; trees whose fruit withereth, without fruit, twice dead, plucked up by the roots;

13 Raging waves of the sea, foaming out their own shame; wandering stars, to whom is reserved the blackness of darkness for ever.

14 And Enoch also, the seventh from Adam, prophesied of these, saying, Behold, the Lord cometh with ten thousands of his saints,

15 ¶ To execute judgment upon all, and to convince all that are ungodly among them of all their ungodly deeds which they have ungodly committed, and of all their hard *speeches* which ungodly sinners have spoken against him.

16 These are murmurers, complainers, walking after their own lusts; and their mouth speaketh great swelling *words*, having men's persons in admiration because of advantage.

NEW AMERICAN STANDARD BIBLE

12 These are the men who are hidden reefs in your love feasts when they feast with you without fear, caring for themselves; clouds without water, carried along by winds; autumn trees without fruit, doubly dead, uprooted;

13 wild waves of the sea, casting up their own shame like foam; wandering stars, for whom the black darkness has been reserved forever.

14 *It was* also about these men *that* Enoch, *in* the seventh *generation* from Adam, prophesied, saying, "Behold, the Lord came with many thousands of His holy ones,

15 to execute judgment upon all, and to convict all the ungodly of all their ungodly deeds which they have done in an ungodly way, and of all the harsh things which ungodly sinners have spoken against Him."

16 These are grumblers, finding fault, following after their *own* lusts; they speak arrogantly, flattering people for the sake of *gaining an* advantage.

NEW CENTURY VERSION

Korah, they surely will be destroyed. 12They are like dirty
spots in your special Christian meals you share. They eat
with you and have no fear, caring only for themselves.
They are clouds without rain, which the wind blows
around. They are autumn trees without fruit that are
pulled out of the ground. So they are twice dead. 13They
are like wild waves of the sea, tossing up their own
shameful actions like foam. They are like stars that wander in the sky. A place in the blackest darkness has been
kept for them forever.

14Enoch, the seventh descendant from Adam, said about
these people: "Look, the Lord is coming with many thousands of his holy angels to 15judge every person. He is
coming to punish all who are against God for all the evil
they have done against him. And he will punish the sinners who are against God for all the evil they have said
against him."

16These people complain and blame others, doing the
evil things they want to do. They brag about themselves,
and they flatter others to get what they want.

CONTEMPORARY ENGLISH VERSION

rebelled against God, just as Korah did.[f] Because of all
this, they will be destroyed.

12These people are filthy minded, and by their shameful
and selfish actions they spoil the meals you eat together.
They are like clouds blown along by the wind, but never
bringing any rain. They are like leafless trees, uprooted and
dead, and unable to produce fruit. 13Their shameful deeds
show up like foam on wild ocean waves. They are like wandering stars forever doomed to the darkest pits of hell.

14Enoch was the seventh person after Adam, and he was
talking about these people when he said:

> Look! The Lord is coming with thousands and thousands of holy angels 15to judge everyone. He will punish
> all those ungodly people for all the evil things they have
> done. The Lord will surely punish those ungodly sinners
> for every evil thing they have ever said about him.

16These people grumble and complain and live by their
own selfish desires. They brag about themselves and flatter others to get what they want.

[f] 11 *just as Korah did*: Together with Dathan and Abiram, Korah led a rebellion against Moses and Aaron (see Numbers 16.1-35; 26.9, 10).

NEW INTERNATIONAL VERSION

12These men are blemishes at your love feasts, eating with you without the slightest qualm—shepherds who feed only themselves. They are clouds without rain, blown along by the wind; autumn trees, without fruit and uprooted—twice dead. 13They are wild waves of the sea, foaming up their shame; wandering stars, for whom blackest darkness has been reserved forever.

14Enoch, the seventh from Adam, prophesied about these men: "See, the Lord is coming with thousands upon thousands of his holy ones 15to judge everyone, and to convict all the ungodly of all the ungodly acts they have done in the ungodly way, and of all the harsh words ungodly sinners have spoken against him." 16These men are grumblers and faultfinders; they follow their own evil desires; they boast about themselves and flatter others for their own advantage.

NEW LIVING TRANSLATION

12When these people join you in fellowship meals celebrating the love of the Lord, they are like dangerous reefs that can shipwreck you.* They are shameless in the way they care only about themselves. They are like clouds blowing over dry land without giving rain, promising much but producing nothing. They are like trees without fruit at harvesttime. They are not only dead but doubly dead, for they have been pulled out by the roots. 13They are like wild waves of the sea, churning up the dirty foam of their shameful deeds. They are wandering stars, heading for everlasting gloom and darkness.

14Now Enoch, who lived seven generations after Adam, prophesied about these people. He said,

"Look, the Lord is coming
with thousands of his holy ones.
15 He will bring the people of the world
to judgment.
He will convict the ungodly of all the evil things
they have done in rebellion
and of all the insults that godless sinners
have spoken against him."*

16These people are grumblers and complainers, doing whatever evil they feel like. They are loudmouthed braggarts, and they flatter others to get favors in return.

12 Or *they are contaminants among you,* or *they are stains.*
14-15 The quotation comes from the Apocrypha: Enoch 1:9.

NEW KING JAMES VERSION

Apostates Depraved and Doomed

12These are spots in your love feasts, while they feast with you without fear, serving *only* themselves. *They are* clouds without water, carried about[c] by the winds; late autumn trees without fruit, twice dead, pulled up by the roots; 13raging waves of the sea, foaming up their own shame; wandering stars for whom is reserved the blackness of darkness forever.

14Now Enoch, the seventh from Adam, prophesied about these men also, saying, "Behold, the Lord comes with ten thousands of His saints, 15to execute judgment on all, to convict all who are ungodly among them of all their ungodly deeds which they have committed in an ungodly way, and of all the harsh things which ungodly sinners have spoken against Him."

Apostates Predicted

16These are grumblers, complainers, walking according to their own lusts; and they mouth great swelling *words,* flattering people to gain advantage. 17But you, beloved,

12 [c] NU-Text and M-Text read *along.*

THE MESSAGE

These people are warts on your love feasts as you worship and eat together. They're giving you a black eye—carousing shamelessly, grabbing anything that isn't nailed down. They're—

Puffs of smoke pushed by gusts of wind;
late autumn trees stripped clean of leaf and fruit,
Doubly dead, pulled up by the roots;
wild ocean waves leaving nothing on the beach
but the foam of their shame;
Lost stars in outer space
on their way to the black hole.

Enoch, the seventh after Adam, prophesied of them: "Look! The Master comes with thousands of holy angels to bring judgment against them all, convicting each person of every defiling act of shameless sacrilege, of every dirty word they have spewed of their pious filth." These are the "grumpers," the bellyachers, grabbing for the biggest piece of the pie, talking big, saying anything they think will get them ahead.

KING JAMES VERSION

17 But, beloved, remember ye the words which were spoken before of the apostles of our Lord Jesus Christ;

18 How that they told you there should be mockers in the last time, who should walk after their own ungodly lusts.

19 These be they who separate themselves, sensual, having not the Spirit.

20 But ye, beloved, building up yourselves on your most holy faith, praying in the Holy Ghost,

21 Keep yourselves in the love of God, looking for the mercy of our Lord Jesus Christ unto eternal life.

22 And of some have compassion, making a difference:

23 And others save with fear, pulling *them* out of the fire; hating even the garment spotted by the flesh.

24 Now unto him that is able to keep you from falling, and to present *you* faultless before the presence of his glory with exceeding joy,

25 To the only wise God our Saviour, *be* glory and majesty, dominion and power, both now and ever. Amen.

NEW AMERICAN STANDARD BIBLE

Keep Yourselves in the Love of God

17 But you, beloved, ought to remember the words that were spoken beforehand by the apostles of our Lord Jesus Christ,

18 that they were saying to you, "In the last time there will be mockers, following after their own ungodly lusts."

19 These are the ones who cause divisions, worldly-minded, devoid of the Spirit.

20 But you, beloved, building yourselves up on your most holy faith, praying in the Holy Spirit,

21 keep yourselves in the love of God, waiting anxiously for the mercy of our Lord Jesus Christ to eternal life.

22 And have mercy on some, who are doubting;

23 save others, snatching them out of the fire; and on some have mercy with fear, hating even the garment polluted by the flesh.

24 Now to Him who is able to keep you from stumbling, and to make you stand in the presence of His glory blameless with great joy,

25 to the only God our Savior, through Jesus Christ our Lord, *be* glory, majesty, dominion and authority, before all time and now and forever. Amen.

NEW CENTURY VERSION

A Warning and Things to Do

[17]Dear friends, remember what the apostles of our Lord
Jesus Christ said before. [18]They said to you, "In the last
times there will be people who laugh about God, following
their own evil desires which are against God." [19]These are
the people who divide you, people whose thoughts are only
of this world, who do not have the Spirit.

[20]But dear friends, use your most holy faith to build
yourselves up, praying in the Holy Spirit. [21]Keep your-
selves in God's love as you wait for the Lord Jesus Christ
with his mercy to give you life forever.

[22]Show mercy to some people who have doubts. [23]Take
others out of the fire, and save them. Show mercy mixed
with fear to others, hating even their clothes which are
dirty from sin.

Praise God

[24]God is strong and can help you not to fall. He can
bring you before his glory without any wrong in you and
can give you great joy. [25]He is the only God, the One who
saves us. To him be glory, greatness, power, and authority
through Jesus Christ our Lord for all time past, now, and
forever. Amen.

CONTEMPORARY ENGLISH VERSION

More Warnings

[17]My dear friends, remember the warning you were
given by the apostles of our Lord Jesus Christ. [18]They told
you that near the end of time, selfish and godless people
would start making fun of God. [19]And now these people
are already making you turn against each other. They
think only about this life, and they don't have God's Spirit.

[20]Dear friends, keep building on the foundation of your
most holy faith, as the Holy Spirit helps you to pray. [21]And
keep in step with God's love, as you wait for our Lord
Jesus Christ to show how kind he is by giving you eternal
life. [22]Be helpful to[g] all who may have doubts. [23]Rescue
any who need to be saved, as you would rescue someone
from a fire. Then with fear in your own hearts, have mercy
on everyone who needs it. But hate even the clothes of
those who have been made dirty by their filthy deeds.

Final Prayer

[24-25]Offer praise to God our Savior because of our Lord
Jesus Christ! Only God can keep you from falling and make
you pure and joyful in his glorious presence. Before time
began and now and forevermore, God is worthy of glory,
honor, power, and authority. Amen.

g **22** ***Be helpful to***: Some manuscripts have "Correct."

NEW INTERNATIONAL VERSION

A Call to Persevere

17But, dear friends, remember what the apostles of our
Lord Jesus Christ foretold. 18They said to you, "In the last
times there will be scoffers who will follow their own
ungodly desires." 19These are the men who divide you,
who follow mere natural instincts and do not have the
Spirit.

20But you, dear friends, build yourselves up in your
most holy faith and pray in the Holy Spirit. 21Keep your-
selves in God's love as you wait for the mercy of our Lord
Jesus Christ to bring you to eternal life.

22Be merciful to those who doubt; 23snatch others from
the fire and save them; to others show mercy, mixed with
fear—hating even the clothing stained by corrupted flesh.

Doxology

24To him who is able to keep you from falling and to
present you before his glorious presence without fault and
with great joy— 25to the only God our Savior be glory,
majesty, power and authority, through Jesus Christ our
Lord, before all ages, now and forevermore! Amen.

NEW LIVING TRANSLATION

A Call to Remain Faithful

17But you, my dear friends, must remember what the
apostles of our Lord Jesus Christ told you, 18that in the last
times there would be scoffers whose purpose in life is to
enjoy themselves in every evil way imaginable. 19Now they
are here, and they are the ones who are creating divisions
among you. They live by natural instinct because they do
not have God's Spirit living in them.

20But you, dear friends, must continue to build your lives
on the foundation of your holy faith. And continue to pray
as you are directed by the Holy Spirit.* 21Live in such a way
that God's love can bless you as you wait for the eternal life
that our Lord Jesus Christ in his mercy is going to give you.
22Show mercy to those whose faith is wavering. 23Rescue
others by snatching them from the flames of judgment.
There are still others to whom you need to show mercy, but
be careful that you aren't contaminated by their sins.*

A Prayer of Praise

24And now, all glory to God, who is able to keep you
from stumbling, and who will bring you into his glorious
presence innocent of sin and with great joy. 25All glory to
him, who alone is God our Savior, through Jesus Christ our
Lord. Yes, glory, majesty, power, and authority belong to
him, in the beginning, now, and forevermore. Amen.

20 Greek *Pray in the Holy Spirit.* 23 Greek *mercy, hating even the clothing stained by the flesh.*

NEW KING JAMES VERSION

remember the words which were spoken before by the
apostles of our Lord Jesus Christ: 18how they told you that
there would be mockers in the last time who would walk
according to their own ungodly lusts. 19These are sensual
persons, who cause divisions, not having the Spirit.

Maintain Your Life with God

20But you, beloved, building yourselves up on your most
holy faith, praying in the Holy Spirit, 21keep yourselves in
the love of God, looking for the mercy of our Lord Jesus
Christ unto eternal life.

22And on some have compassion, making a distinction;[d]
23but others save with fear, pulling *them* out of the fire,[e]
hating even the garment defiled by the flesh.

Glory to God

24 Now to Him who is able to keep you[f] from stumbling,
And to present *you* faultless
Before the presence of His glory with exceeding joy,
25 To God our Savior,[g]
Who alone is wise,[h]
Be glory and majesty,
Dominion and power,[i]
Both now and forever.
Amen.

22 [d] NU-Text reads *who are doubting* (or *making distinctions*).
23 [e] NU-Text adds *and on some have mercy with fear* and omits *with fear* in first clause. 24 [f] M-Text reads *them.* 25 [g] NU-Text reads *To the only God our Savior.* [h] NU-Text omits *Who . . . is wise* and adds *Through Jesus Christ our Lord.* [i] NU-Text adds *Before all time.*

THE MESSAGE

But remember, dear friends, that the apostles of our Master, Jesus Christ, told us this would happen: "In the last days there will be people who don't take these things seriously anymore. They'll treat them like a joke, and make a religion of their own whims and lusts." These are the ones who split churches, thinking only of themselves. There's nothing to them, no sign of the Spirit!

✠

But you, dear friends, carefully build yourselves up in this most holy faith by praying in the Holy Spirit, staying right at the center of God's love, keeping your arms open and outstretched, ready for the mercy of our Master, Jesus Christ. This is the unending life, the *real* life!

Go easy on those who hesitate in the faith. Go after those who take the wrong way. Be tender with sinners, but not soft on sin. The sin itself stinks to high heaven.

And now to him who can keep you on your feet, standing tall in his bright presence, fresh and celebrating—to our one God, our only Savior, through Jesus Christ, our Master, be glory, majesty, strength, and rule before all time, and now, and to the end of all time. Yes.

KING JAMES VERSION

THE REVELATION
TO ST. JOHN

1 The Revelation of Jesus Christ, which God gave unto
him, to shew unto his servants things which must
shortly come to pass; and he sent and signified *it* by his
angel unto his servant John:
2 Who bare record of the word of God, and of the testi-
mony of Jesus Christ, and of all things that he saw.
3 ¶ Blessed *is* he that readeth, and they that hear the
words of this prophecy, and keep those things which are
written therein: for the time *is* at hand.
4 John to the seven churches which are in Asia: Grace
be unto you, and peace, from him which is, and which
was, and which is to come; and from the seven Spirits
which are before his throne;

NEW AMERICAN STANDARD BIBLE

THE REVELATION
TO JOHN

The Revelation of Jesus Christ

1 The Revelation of Jesus Christ, which God gave Him to
show to His bond-servants, the things which must
soon take place; and He sent and communicated *it* by His
angel to His bond-servant John,
2 who testified to the word of God and to the testimony
of Jesus Christ, *even* to all that he saw.
3 Blessed is he who reads and those who hear the
words of the prophecy, and heed the things which are writ-
ten in it; for the time is near.

Message to the Seven Churches

4 John to the seven churches that are in Asia: Grace to
you and peace, from Him who is and who was and who is
to come, and from the seven Spirits who are before His
throne,

NEW CENTURY VERSION

REVELATION

John Tells About This Book

1 This is the revelation[a] of Jesus Christ, which God gave
to him, to show his servants what must soon happen.
And Jesus sent his angel to show it to his servant John,
2 who has told everything he has seen. It is the word of
God; it is the message from Jesus Christ. 3 Happy is the one
who reads the words of God's message, and happy are the
people who hear this message and do what is written in it.
The time is near when all of this will happen.

Jesus' Message to the Churches

4 From John.
To the seven churches in the country of Asia:
Grace and peace to you from the One who is and was and
is coming, and from the seven spirits before his throne,

1:1 [a] **revelation** A making known of truth that has been hidden.

CONTEMPORARY ENGLISH VERSION

REVELATION

1 This is what God showed to Jesus Christ, so that he
could tell his servants what must happen soon. Christ
then sent his angel with the message to his servant John.
2 And John told everything that he had seen about God's
message and about what Jesus Christ had said and done.
3 God will bless everyone who reads this prophecy to oth-
ers,[a] and he will bless everyone who hears and obeys it.
The time is almost here.
4 From John to the seven churches in Asia.[b]

I pray that you
will be blessed
with kindness and peace
from God, who is and was
and is coming.
May you receive
kindness and peace
from the seven spirits
before the throne of God.

[a] 1.3 *who reads this prophecy to others*: A public reading, in a worship service. [b] 1.4 *Asia*: The section 1.4—3.22 is in the form of a letter. Asia was in the eastern part of the Roman Empire and is present day Turkey.

NEW INTERNATIONAL VERSION

REVELATION

Prologue

1 The revelation of Jesus Christ, which God gave him to show his servants what must soon take place. He made it known by sending his angel to his servant John, [2]who testifies to everything he saw—that is, the word of God and the testimony of Jesus Christ. [3]Blessed is the one who reads the words of this prophecy, and blessed are those who hear it and take to heart what is written in it, because the time is near.

Greetings and Doxology

[4]John,

To the seven churches in the province of Asia:

Grace and peace to you from him who is, and who was, and who is to come, and from the seven spirits[a] before his

[a] *4* Or *the sevenfold Spirit*

NEW LIVING TRANSLATION

REVELATION

Prologue

1 This is a revelation from* Jesus Christ, which God gave him concerning the events that will happen soon. An angel was sent to God's servant John so that John could share the revelation with God's other servants. [2]John faithfully reported the word of God and the testimony of Jesus Christ—everything he saw.

[3]God blesses the one who reads this prophecy to the church, and he blesses all who listen to it and obey what it says. For the time is near when these things will happen.

John's Greeting to the Seven Churches

[4]This letter is from John to the seven churches in the province of Asia. Grace and peace from the one who is, who always was, and who is still to come; from the sevenfold Spirit* before his throne; [5]and from Jesus Christ, who

1:1 Or *of.* 1:4 Greek *the seven spirits.*

NEW KING JAMES VERSION

REVELATION

OF JESUS CHRIST

Introduction and Benediction

1 The Revelation of Jesus Christ, which God gave Him to show His servants—things which must shortly take place. And He sent and signified *it* by His angel to His servant John, [2]who bore witness to the word of God, and to the testimony of Jesus Christ, to all things that he saw. [3]Blessed *is* he who reads and those who hear the words of this prophecy, and keep those things which are written in it; for the time *is* near.

Greeting the Seven Churches

[4]John, to the seven churches which are in Asia:

Grace to you and peace from Him who is and who was and who is to come, and from the seven Spirits who are

THE MESSAGE

REVELATION

1 A revealing of Jesus, the Messiah. God gave it to make plain to his servants what is about to happen. He published and delivered it by Angel to his servant John. And John told everything he saw: God's Word—the witness of Jesus Christ!

How blessed the reader! How blessed the hearers and keepers of these oracle words, all the words written in this book!

Time is just about up.

His Eyes Pouring Fire-Blaze

I, John, am writing this to the seven churches in Asia province: All the best to you from THE GOD WHO IS, THE GOD WHO WAS, AND THE GOD ABOUT TO ARRIVE, and from the Seven Spirits assembled before his throne, and from Jesus

KING JAMES VERSION

5 And from Jesus Christ, *who is* the faithful witness, *and* the first begotten of the dead, and the prince of the kings of the earth. Unto him that loved us, and washed us from our sins in his own blood,

6 And hath made us kings and priests unto God and his Father; to him *be* glory and dominion for ever and ever. Amen.

7 Behold, he cometh with clouds; and every eye shall see him, and they *also* which pierced him: and all kindreds of the earth shall wail because of him. Even so, Amen.

NEW AMERICAN STANDARD BIBLE

5 and from Jesus Christ, the faithful witness, the first-born of the dead, and the ruler of the kings of the earth. To Him who loves us and released us from our sins by His blood—

6 and He has made us *to be* a kingdom, priests to His God and Father—to Him *be* the glory and the dominion forever and ever. Amen.

7 BEHOLD, HE IS COMING WITH THE CLOUDS, and every eye will see Him, even those who pierced Him; and all the tribes of the earth will mourn over Him. So it is to be. Amen.

NEW CENTURY VERSION

5 and from Jesus Christ. Jesus is the faithful witness, the first among those raised from the dead. He is the ruler of the kings of the earth.

He is the One who loves us, who made us free from our sins with the blood of his death.
6 He made us to be a kingdom of priests who serve God his Father. To Jesus Christ be glory and power forever and ever! Amen.

7 Look, Jesus is coming with the clouds, and everyone will see him, even those who stabbed him. And all peoples of the earth will cry loudly because of him. Yes, this will happen! Amen.

CONTEMPORARY ENGLISH VERSION

5 May kindness and peace
be yours
from Jesus Christ,
the faithful witness.

Jesus was the first
to conquer death,
and he is the ruler
of all earthly kings.
Christ loves us,
and by his blood
he set us free
from our sins.
6 He lets us rule as kings
and serve God his Father
as priests.
To him be glory and power
forever and ever! Amen.
7 Look! He is coming
with the clouds.
Everyone will see him,
even the ones who stuck
a sword through him.
All people on earth
will weep because of him.
Yes, it will happen! Amen.

NEW INTERNATIONAL VERSION

throne, 5and from Jesus Christ, who is the faithful witness, the firstborn from the dead, and the ruler of the kings of the earth.

To him who loves us and has freed us from our sins by his blood, 6and has made us to be a kingdom and priests to serve his God and Father—to him be glory and power for ever and ever! Amen.

7Look, he is coming with the clouds,
and every eye will see him,
even those who pierced him;
and all the peoples of the earth will mourn
because of him.
So shall it be! Amen.

NEW LIVING TRANSLATION

is the faithful witness to these things, the first to rise from the dead, and the commander of all the rulers of the world.

All praise to him who loves us and has freed us from our sins by shedding his blood for us. 6He has made us his Kingdom and his priests who serve before God his Father. Give to him everlasting glory! He rules forever and ever! Amen!

7Look! He comes with the clouds of heaven. And everyone will see him—even those who pierced him. And all the nations of the earth will weep because of him. Yes! Amen!

NEW KING JAMES VERSION

before His throne, 5and from Jesus Christ, the faithful witness, the firstborn from the dead, and the ruler over the kings of the earth.

To Him who loved us and washed[a] us from our sins in His own blood, 6and has made us kings[b] and priests to His God and Father, to Him *be* glory and dominion forever and ever. Amen.

7Behold, He is coming with clouds, and every eye will see Him, even they who pierced Him. And all the tribes of the earth will mourn because of Him. Even so, Amen.

1:5 [a] NU-Text reads *loves us and freed;* M-Text reads *loves us and washed.* 1:6 [b] NU-Text and M-Text read *a kingdom.*

THE MESSAGE

Christ—Loyal Witness, Firstborn from the dead, Ruler of all earthly kings.

Glory and strength to Christ, who loves us,
who blood-washed our sins from our lives,
Who made us a Kingdom, Priests for his Father,
forever—and yes, he's on his way!
Riding the clouds, he'll be seen by every eye,
those who mocked and killed him will see him,
People from all nations and all times
will tear their clothes in lament.
Oh, Yes.

KING JAMES VERSION

8 I am Alpha and Omega, the beginning and the ending, saith the Lord, which is, and which was, and which is to come, the Almighty.

9 ¶ I John, who also am your brother, and companion in tribulation, and in the kingdom and patience of Jesus Christ, was in the isle that is called Patmos, for the word of God, and for the testimony of Jesus Christ.

10 I was in the Spirit on the Lord's day, and heard behind me a great voice, as of a trumpet,

11 Saying, I am Alpha and Omega, the first and the last: and, What thou seest, write in a book, and send *it* unto the seven churches which are in Asia; unto Ephesus, and unto Smyrna, and unto Pergamos, and unto Thyatira, and unto Sardis, and unto Philadelphia, and unto Laodicea.

12 And I turned to see the voice that spake with me. And being turned, I saw seven golden candlesticks;

13 And in the midst of the seven candlesticks *one* like unto the Son of man, clothed with a garment down to the foot, and girt about the paps with a golden girdle.

14 His head and *his* hairs *were* white like wool, as white as snow; and his eyes *were* as a flame of fire;

15 And his feet like unto fine brass, as if they burned in a furnace; and his voice as the sound of many waters.

16 And he had in his right hand seven stars: and out of his mouth went a sharp twoedged sword: and his countenance *was* as the sun shineth in his strength.

NEW AMERICAN STANDARD BIBLE

8 "I am the Alpha and the Omega," says the Lord God, "who is and who was and who is to come, the Almighty."

The Patmos Vision

9 I, John, your brother and fellow partaker in the tribulation and kingdom and perseverance *which are* in Jesus, was on the island called Patmos because of the word of God and the testimony of Jesus.

10 I was [1]in the Spirit on the Lord's day, and I heard behind me a loud voice like *the sound* of a trumpet,

11 saying, "Write in a book what you see, and send *it* to the seven churches: to Ephesus and to Smyrna and to Pergamum and to Thyatira and to Sardis and to Philadelphia and to Laodicea."

12 Then I turned to see the voice that was speaking with me. And having turned I saw seven golden lampstands;

13 and in the middle of the lampstands *I saw* one like [2]a son of man, clothed in a robe reaching to the feet, and girded across His chest with a golden sash.

14 His head and His hair were white like white wool, like snow; and His eyes were like a flame of fire.

15 His feet *were* like burnished bronze, when it has been made to glow in a furnace, and His voice *was* like the sound of many waters.

16 In His right hand He held seven stars, and out of His mouth came a sharp two-edged sword; and His face was like the sun shining in its strength.

1:10 [1] Or *in spirit*   1:13 [2] Or *the Son of Man*

NEW CENTURY VERSION

8 The Lord God says, "I am the Alpha and the Omega.[b] I am the One who is and was and is coming. I am the Almighty."

9 I, John, am your brother. All of us share with Christ in suffering, in the kingdom, and in patience to continue. I was on the island of Patmos,[c] because I had preached the word of God and the message about Jesus. 10 On the Lord's day I was in the Spirit, and I heard a loud voice behind me that sounded like a trumpet. 11 The voice said, "Write what you see in a book and send it to the seven churches: to Ephesus, Smyrna, Pergamum, Thyatira, Sardis, Philadelphia, and Laodicea."

12 I turned to see who was talking to me. When I turned, I saw seven golden lampstands 13 and someone among the lampstands who was "like a Son of Man."[d] He was dressed in a long robe and had a gold band around his chest. 14 His head and hair were white like wool, as white as snow, and his eyes were like flames of fire. 15 His feet were like bronze that glows hot in a furnace, and his voice was like the noise of flooding water. 16 He held seven stars in his right hand, and a sharp double-edged sword came out of his mouth. He looked like the sun shining at its brightest time.

1:8 [b] **Alpha and the Omega** The first and last letters of the Greek alphabet. This means "the beginning and the end."   1:9 [c] **Patmos** A small island in the Aegean Sea, near the coast of Asia Minor (modern Turkey).   1:13 [d] **"like...Man"** "Son of Man" is a name Jesus called himself. See dictionary.

CONTEMPORARY ENGLISH VERSION

8 The Lord God says, "I am Alpha and Omega,[c] the one who is and was and is coming. I am God All-Powerful!"

A Vision of the Risen Lord

9 I am John, a follower together with all of you. We suffer because Jesus is our king, but he gives us the strength to endure. I was sent to Patmos Island,[d] because I had preached God's message and had told about Jesus. 10 On the Lord's day the Spirit took control of me, and behind me I heard a loud voice that sounded like a trumpet. 11 The voice said, "Write in a book what you see. Then send it to the seven churches in Ephesus, Smyrna, Pergamum, Thyatira, Sardis, Philadelphia, and Laodicea."[e]

12 When I turned to see who was speaking to me, I saw seven gold lampstands. 13 There with the lampstands was someone who seemed to be the Son of Man.[f] He was wearing a robe that reached down to his feet, and a gold cloth was wrapped around his chest. 14 His head and his hair were white as wool or snow, and his eyes looked like flames of fire. 15 His feet were glowing like bronze being heated in a furnace, and his voice sounded like the roar of a waterfall. 16 He held seven stars in his right hand, and a sharp double-edged sword was coming from his mouth. His face was shining as bright as the sun at noon.

[c] **1.8** *Alpha and Omega*: The first and last letters of the Greek alphabet, which sometimes mean "first" and "last."   [d] **1.9** *Patmos Island*: A small island where prisoners were sometimes kept by the Romans.
[e] **1.11** *Ephesus . . . Laodicea*: Ephesus was in the center with the six other cities forming a half-circle around it.   [f] **1.13** *Son of Man*: That is, Jesus.

NEW INTERNATIONAL VERSION

8 "I am the Alpha and the Omega," says the Lord God, "who is, and who was, and who is to come, the Almighty."

One Like a Son of Man

9 I, John, your brother and companion in the suffering and kingdom and patient endurance that are ours in Jesus, was on the island of Patmos because of the word of God and the testimony of Jesus. 10 On the Lord's Day I was in the Spirit, and I heard behind me a loud voice like a trumpet, 11 which said: "Write on a scroll what you see and send it to the seven churches: to Ephesus, Smyrna, Pergamum, Thyatira, Sardis, Philadelphia and Laodicea."

12 I turned around to see the voice that was speaking to me. And when I turned I saw seven golden lampstands, 13 and among the lampstands was someone "like a son of man,"[b] dressed in a robe reaching down to his feet and with a golden sash around his chest. 14 His head and hair were white like wool, as white as snow, and his eyes were like blazing fire. 15 His feet were like bronze glowing in a furnace, and his voice was like the sound of rushing waters. 16 In his right hand he held seven stars, and out of his mouth came a sharp double-edged sword. His face was like the sun shining in all its brilliance.

[b] *13* Daniel 7:13

NEW LIVING TRANSLATION

8 "I am the Alpha and the Omega—the beginning and the end," says the Lord God. "I am the one who is, who always was, and who is still to come, the Almighty One."

Vision of the Son of Man

9 I am John, your brother. In Jesus we are partners in suffering and in the Kingdom and in patient endurance. I was exiled to the island of Patmos for preaching the word of God and speaking about Jesus. 10 It was the Lord's Day, and I was worshiping in the Spirit.* Suddenly, I heard a loud voice behind me, a voice that sounded like a trumpet blast. 11 It said, "Write down what you see, and send it to the seven churches: Ephesus, Smyrna, Pergamum, Thyatira, Sardis, Philadelphia, and Laodicea."

12 When I turned to see who was speaking to me, I saw seven gold lampstands. 13 And standing in the middle of the lampstands was the Son of Man.* He was wearing a long robe with a gold sash across his chest. 14 His head and his hair were white like wool, as white as snow. And his eyes were bright like flames of fire. 15 His feet were as bright as bronze refined in a furnace, and his voice thundered like mighty ocean waves. 16 He held seven stars in his right hand, and a sharp two-edged sword came from his mouth. And his face was as bright as the sun in all its brilliance.

1:10 Or *in spirit.* **1:13** Or *one who looked like a man;* Greek reads *one like a son of man.* See Dan 7:13.

NEW KING JAMES VERSION

8 "I am the Alpha and the Omega, *the* Beginning and *the* End,"[c] says the Lord,[d] "who is and who was and who is to come, the Almighty."

Vision of the Son of Man

9 I, John, both[e] your brother and companion in the tribulation and kingdom and patience of Jesus Christ, was on the island that is called Patmos for the word of God and for the testimony of Jesus Christ. 10 I was in the Spirit on the Lord's Day, and I heard behind me a loud voice, as of a trumpet, 11 saying, "I am the Alpha and the Omega, the First and the Last," and,[f] "What you see, write in a book and send *it* to the seven churches which are in Asia:[g] to Ephesus, to Smyrna, to Pergamos, to Thyatira, to Sardis, to Philadelphia, and to Laodicea."

12 Then I turned to see the voice that spoke with me. And having turned I saw seven golden lampstands, 13 and in the midst of the seven lampstands *One* like the Son of Man, clothed with a garment down to the feet and girded about the chest with a golden band. 14 His head and hair *were* white like wool, as white as snow, and His eyes like a flame of fire; 15 His feet *were* like fine brass, as if refined in a furnace, and His voice as the sound of many waters; 16 He had in His right hand seven stars, out of His mouth went a sharp two-edged sword, and His countenance *was* like the sun

1:8 [c] NU-Text and M-Text omit *the Beginning and the End.* [d] NU-Text and M-Text add *God.* **1:9** [e] NU-Text and M-Text omit *both.*
1:11 [f] NU-Text and M-Text omit *I am* through third *and.* [g] NU-Text and M-Text omit *which are in Asia.*

THE MESSAGE

The Master declares, "I'm A to Z. I'm THE GOD WHO IS, THE GOD WHO WAS, AND THE GOD ABOUT TO ARRIVE. I'm the Sovereign-Strong."

I, John, with you all the way in the trial and the Kingdom and the passion of patience in Jesus, was on the island called Patmos because of God's Word, the witness of Jesus. It was Sunday and I was in the Spirit, praying. I heard a loud voice behind me, trumpet-clear and piercing: "Write what you see into a book. Send it to the seven churches: to Ephesus, Smyrna, Pergamum, Thyatira, Sardis, Philadelphia, Laodicea." I turned and saw the voice.

I saw a gold menorah
  with seven branches,
And in the center, the Son of Man,
  in a robe and gold breastplate,
  hair a blizzard of white,
Eyes pouring fire-blaze,
  both feet furnace-fired bronze,
His voice a cataract,
  right hand holding the Seven Stars,
His mouth a sharp-biting sword,
  his face a perigee sun.

KING JAMES VERSION

17 And when I saw him, I fell at his feet as dead. And he laid his right hand upon me, saying unto me, Fear not; I am the first and the last:

18 I *am* he that liveth, and was dead; and, behold, I am alive for evermore, Amen; and have the keys of hell and of death.

19 Write the things which thou hast seen, and the things which are, and the things which shall be hereafter;

20 The mystery of the seven stars which thou sawest in my right hand, and the seven golden candlesticks. The seven stars are the angels of the seven churches: and the seven candlesticks which thou sawest are the seven churches.

2 Unto the angel of the church of Ephesus write; These things saith he that holdeth the seven stars in his right hand, who walketh in the midst of the seven golden candlesticks;

2 I know thy works, and thy labour, and thy patience, and how thou canst not bear them which are evil: and thou hast tried them which say they are apostles, and are not, and hast found them liars:

3 And hast borne, and hast patience, and for my name's sake hast laboured, and hast not fainted.

NEW AMERICAN STANDARD BIBLE

17 When I saw Him, I fell at His feet like a dead man. And He placed His right hand on me, saying, "Do not be afraid; I am the first and the last,

18 and the living One; and I was dead, and behold, I am alive forevermore, and I have the keys of death and of Hades.

19 "Therefore write the things which you have seen, and the things which are, and the things which will take place after these things.

20 "As for the mystery of the seven stars which you saw in My right hand, and the seven golden lampstands: the seven stars are the angels of the seven churches, and the seven lampstands are the seven churches.

Message to Ephesus

2 "To the angel of the church in Ephesus write:
The One who holds the seven stars in His right hand, the One who walks among the seven golden lampstands, says this:

2 'I know your deeds and your toil and perseverance, and that you cannot tolerate evil men, and you put to the test those who call themselves apostles, and they are not, and you found them *to be* false;

3 and you have perseverance and have endured for My name's sake, and have not grown weary.

NEW CENTURY VERSION

17When I saw him, I fell down at his feet like a dead
man. He put his right hand on me and said, "Do not be
afraid. I am the First and the Last. 18I am the One who
lives; I was dead, but look, I am alive forever and ever!
And I hold the keys to death and to the place of the dead.
19So write the things you see, what is now and what will
happen later. 20Here is the secret of the seven stars that
you saw in my right hand and the seven golden lamp-
stands: The seven lampstands are the seven churches, and
the seven stars are the angels of the seven churches.

To the Church in Ephesus

2 "Write this to the angel of the church in Ephesus:
"The One who holds the seven stars in his right hand
and walks among the seven golden lampstands says this:
2I know what you do, how you work hard and never give
up. I know you do not put up with the false teachings of
evil people. You have tested those who say they are apos-
tles but really are not, and you found they are liars. 3You
have patience and have suffered troubles for my name and
have not given up.

CONTEMPORARY ENGLISH VERSION

17When I saw him, I fell at his feet like a dead person.
But he put his right hand on me and said:

Don't be afraid! I am the first, the last, 18and the liv-
ing one. I died, but now I am alive forevermore, and I
have the keys to death and the world of the dead.[g]
19Write what you have seen and what is and what will
happen after these things. 20I will explain the mystery of
the seven stars that you saw at my right side and the
seven gold lampstands. The seven stars are the angels[h]
of the seven churches, and the lampstands are the seven
churches.

The Letter to Ephesus

2 This is what you must write to the angel of the church
in Ephesus:

I am the one who holds the seven stars in my right
hand, and I walk among the seven gold lampstands.
Listen to what I say.
2I know everything you have done, including your
hard work and how you have endured. I know you won't
put up with anyone who is evil. When some people pre-
tended to be apostles, you tested them and found out
that they were liars. 3You have endured and gone
through hard times because of me, and you have not
given up.

g 1.18 *keys to death and the world of the dead*: That is, power over death and the world of the dead. h 1.20 *angels*: Perhaps guardian angels that represent the churches, or they may be church leaders or messengers sent to the churches.

NEW INTERNATIONAL VERSION

[17]When I saw him, I fell at his feet as though dead. Then he placed his right hand on me and said: "Do not be afraid. I am the First and the Last. [18]I am the Living One; I was dead, and behold I am alive for ever and ever! And I hold the keys of death and Hades.

[19]"Write, therefore, what you have seen, what is now and what will take place later. [20]The mystery of the seven stars that you saw in my right hand and of the seven golden lampstands is this: The seven stars are the angels[c] of the seven churches, and the seven lampstands are the seven churches.

To the Church in Ephesus

2 "To the angel[a] of the church in Ephesus write:

These are the words of him who holds the seven stars in his right hand and walks among the seven golden lampstands: [2]I know your deeds, your hard work and your perseverance. I know that you cannot tolerate wicked men, that you have tested those who claim to be apostles but are not, and have found them false. [3]You have persevered and have endured hardships for my name, and have not grown weary.

[c] *20* Or *messengers*   [a] *1* Or *messenger*; also in verses 8, 12 and 18

NEW LIVING TRANSLATION

[17]When I saw him, I fell at his feet as dead. But he laid his right hand on me and said, "Don't be afraid! I am the First and the Last. [18]I am the living one who died. Look, I am alive forever and ever! And I hold the keys of death and the grave.* [19]Write down what you have seen—both the things that are now happening and the things that will happen later. [20]This is the meaning of the seven stars you saw in my right hand and the seven gold lampstands: The seven stars are the angels of* the seven churches, and the seven lampstands are the seven churches.

The Message to the Church in Ephesus

2 "Write this letter to the angel of* the church in Ephesus. This is the message from the one who holds the seven stars in his right hand, the one who walks among the seven gold lampstands:

[2]"I know all the things you do. I have seen your hard work and your patient endurance. I know you don't tolerate evil people. You have examined the claims of those who say they are apostles but are not. You have discovered they are liars. [3]You have patiently suffered for me

1:18 Greek *and Hades.*   1:20 Or *the messengers for.*   2:1 Or *the messenger for;* also in 2:8, 12, 18.

NEW KING JAMES VERSION

shining in its strength. [17]And when I saw Him, I fell at His feet as dead. But He laid His right hand on me, saying to me,[h] "Do not be afraid; I am the First and the Last. [18]I *am* He who lives, and was dead, and behold, I am alive forevermore. Amen. And I have the keys of Hades and of Death. [19]Write[i] the things which you have seen, and the things which are, and the things which will take place after this. [20]The mystery of the seven stars which you saw in My right hand, and the seven golden lampstands: The seven stars are the angels of the seven churches, and the seven lampstands which you saw[j] are the seven churches.

The Loveless Church

2 "To the angel of the church of Ephesus write,

'These things says He who holds the seven stars in His right hand, who walks in the midst of the seven golden lampstands: [2]"I know your works, your labor, your patience, and that you cannot bear those who are evil. And you have tested those who say they are apostles and are not, and have found them liars; [3]and you have persevered and have patience, and have labored for My name's sake and have not become weary. [4]Nevertheless I have *this*

1:17 [h] NU-Text and M-Text omit *to me.*   1:19 [i] NU-Text and M-Text read *Therefore, write.*   1:20 [j] NU-Text and M-Text omit *which you saw.*

THE MESSAGE

I saw this and fainted dead at his feet. His right hand pulled me upright, his voice reassured me:

"Don't fear: I am First, I am Last, I'm Alive. I died, but I came to life, and my life is now forever. See these keys in my hand? They open and lock Death's doors, they open and lock Hell's gates. Now write down everything you see: things that are, things about to be. The Seven Stars you saw in my right hand and the seven-branched gold menorah—do you want to know what's behind them? The Seven Stars are the Angels of the seven churches; the menorah's seven branches are the seven churches."

To Ephesus

2 Write this to Ephesus, to the Angel of the church. The One with Seven Stars in his right-fist grip, striding through the golden seven-lights' circle, speaks:

"I see what you've done, your hard, hard work, your refusal to quit. I know you can't stomach evil, that you weed out apostolic pretenders. I know your persistence, your courage in my cause, that you never wear out.

KING JAMES VERSION

4 Nevertheless I have *somewhat* against thee, because thou hast left thy first love.

5 Remember therefore from whence thou art fallen, and repent, and do the first works; or else I will come unto thee quickly, and will remove thy candlestick out of his place, except thou repent.

6 But this thou hast, that thou hatest the deeds of the Nicolaitans, which I also hate.

7 He that hath an ear, let him hear what the Spirit saith unto the churches; To him that overcometh will I give to eat of the tree of life, which is in the midst of the paradise of God.

8 ¶ And unto the angel of the church in Smyrna write; These things saith the first and the last, which was dead, and is alive;

9 I know thy works, and tribulation, and poverty, (but thou art rich) and *I know* the blasphemy of them which say they are Jews, and are not, but *are* the synagogue of Satan.

10 Fear none of those things which thou shalt suffer: behold, the devil shall cast *some* of you into prison, that ye may be tried; and ye shall have tribulation ten days: be thou faithful unto death, and I will give thee a crown of life.

NEW AMERICAN STANDARD BIBLE

4 'But I have *this* against you, that you have left your first love.

5 'Therefore remember from where you have fallen, and repent and do the deeds you did at first; or else I am coming to you and will remove your lampstand out of its place—unless you repent.

6 'Yet this you do have, that you hate the deeds of the Nicolaitans, which I also hate.

7 'He who has an ear, let him hear what the Spirit says to the churches. To him who overcomes, I will grant to eat of the tree of life which is in the Paradise of God.'

Message to Smyrna

8 "And to the angel of the church in Smyrna write:

The first and the last, who was dead, and has come to life, says this:

9 'I know your tribulation and your poverty (but you are rich), and the blasphemy by those who say they are Jews and are not, but are a synagogue of Satan.

10 'Do not fear what you are about to suffer. Behold, the devil is about to cast some of you into prison, so that you will be tested, and you will have tribulation for ten days. Be faithful until death, and I will give you the crown of life.

NEW CENTURY VERSION

4"But I have this against you: You have left the love you
had in the beginning. 5So remember where you were before
you fell. Change your hearts and do what you did at first.
If you do not change, I will come to you and will take away
your lampstand from its place. 6But there is something you
do that is right: You hate what the Nicolaitans[a] do, as
much as I.

7"Every person who has ears should listen to what the Spirit says to the churches. To those who win the victory I will give the right to eat the fruit from the tree of life, which is in the garden of God.

To the Church in Smyrna

8"Write this to the angel of the church in Smyrna:

"The One who is the First and the Last, who died and
came to life again, says this: 9I know your troubles and
that you are poor, but really you are rich! I know the bad
things some people say about you. They say they are Jews,
but they are not true Jews. They are a synagogue that
belongs to Satan. 10Do not be afraid of what you are about
to suffer. I tell you, the devil will put some of you in prison
to test you, and you will suffer for ten days. But be faithful, even if you have to die, and I will give you the crown of life.

2:6 [a] **Nicolaitans** This is the name of a religious group that followed false beliefs and ideas.

CONTEMPORARY ENGLISH VERSION

4But I do have something against you! And it is this:
You don't have as much love as you used to. 5Think
about where you have fallen from, and then turn back
and do as you did at first. If you don't turn back, I will
come and take away your lampstand. 6But there is one
thing you are doing right. You hate what the
Nicolaitans[a] are doing, and so do I.

7If you have ears, listen to what the Spirit says to the churches. I will let everyone who wins the victory eat from the life-giving tree in God's wonderful garden.

The Letter to Smyrna

8This is what you must write to the angel of the church in Smyrna:

I am the first and the last. I died, but now I am alive! Listen to what I say.

9I know how much you suffer and how poor you are, but you are rich. I also know the cruel things being said about you by people who claim to be Jews. But they are not really Jews. They are a group that belongs to Satan.

10Don't worry about what you will suffer. The devil will throw some of you into jail, and you will be tested and made to suffer for ten days. But if you are faithful until you die, I will reward you with a glorious life.[b]

[a] **2.6** *Nicolaitans*: Nothing else is known about these people, though it is possible that they claimed to be followers of Nicolaus from Antioch (see Acts 6.5). [b] **2.10** *a glorious life*: The Greek text has "a crown of life." In ancient times an athlete who had won a contest was rewarded with a crown of flowers as a sign of victory.

NEW INTERNATIONAL VERSION

4Yet I hold this against you: You have forsaken
your first love. 5Remember the height from which you
have fallen! Repent and do the things you did at first.
If you do not repent, I will come to you and remove
your lampstand from its place. 6But you have this in
your favor: You hate the practices of the Nicolaitans,
which I also hate.

7He who has an ear, let him hear what the Spirit
says to the churches. To him who overcomes, I will
give the right to eat from the tree of life, which is in
the paradise of God.

To the Church in Smyrna

8"To the angel of the church in Smyrna write:

These are the words of him who is the First and the
Last, who died and came to life again. 9I know your
afflictions and your poverty—yet you are rich! I know
the slander of those who say they are Jews and are
not, but are a synagogue of Satan. 10Do not be afraid
of what you are about to suffer. I tell you, the devil
will put some of you in prison to test you, and you
will suffer persecution for ten days. Be faithful, even
to the point of death, and I will give you the crown of
life.

NEW LIVING TRANSLATION

without quitting. 4But I have this complaint against you.
You don't love me or each other as you did at first!
5Look how far you have fallen from your first love! Turn
back to me again and work as you did at first. If you
don't, I will come and remove your lampstand from its
place among the churches. 6But there is this about you
that is good: You hate the deeds of the immoral
Nicolaitans, just as I do.
7"Anyone who is willing to hear should listen to the
Spirit and understand what the Spirit is saying to the
churches. Everyone who is victorious will eat from the
tree of life in the paradise of God.

The Message to the Church in Smyrna

8"Write this letter to the angel of the church in Smyrna.
This is the message from the one who is the First and the
Last, who died and is alive:

9"I know about your suffering and your poverty—but
you are rich! I know the slander of those opposing you.
They say they are Jews, but they really aren't because
theirs is a synagogue of Satan. 10Don't be afraid of what
you are about to suffer. The Devil will throw some of
you into prison and put you to the test. You will be persecuted for 'ten days.' Remain faithful even when facing
death, and I will give you the crown of life.

NEW KING JAMES VERSION

against you, that you have left your first love. 5Remember
therefore from where you have fallen; repent and do the
first works, or else I will come to you quickly and remove
your lampstand from its place—unless you repent. 6But
this you have, that you hate the deeds of the Nicolaitans,
which I also hate.

7"He who has an ear, let him hear what the Spirit says
to the churches. To him who overcomes I will give to eat
from the tree of life, which is in the midst of the Paradise
of God." '

The Persecuted Church

8"And to the angel of the church in Smyrna write,

'These things says the First and the Last, who was dead,
and came to life: 9"I know your works, tribulation, and
poverty (but you are rich); and *I know* the blasphemy of
those who say they are Jews and are not, but *are* a synagogue of Satan. 10Do not fear any of those things which
you are about to suffer. Indeed, the devil is about to throw
some of you into prison, that you may be tested, and you
will have tribulation ten days. Be faithful until death, and
I will give you the crown of life.

THE MESSAGE

"But you walked away from your first love—why? What's going on with you, anyway? Do you have any idea how far you've fallen? A Lucifer fall!

"Turn back! Recover your dear early love. No time to waste, for I'm well on my way to removing your light from the golden circle.

"You do have this to your credit: You hate the Nicolaitan business. I hate it, too.

"Are your ears awake? Listen. Listen to the Wind Words, the Spirit blowing through the churches. I'm about to call each conqueror to dinner. I'm spreading a banquet of Tree-of-Life fruit, a supper plucked from God's orchard."

To Smyrna

Write this to Smyrna, to the Angel of the church. The Beginning and Ending, the First and Final One, the Once Dead and Then Come Alive, speaks:

"I can see your pain and poverty—constant pain, dire poverty—but I also see your wealth. And I hear the lie in the claims of those who pretend to be good Jews, who in fact belong to Satan's crowd.

"Fear nothing in the things you're about to suffer—but stay on guard! Fear nothing! The Devil is about to throw you in jail for a time of testing—ten days. It won't last forever.

"Don't quit, even if it costs you your life. Stay there believing. I have a Life-Crown sized and ready for you.

KING JAMES VERSION

11 He that hath an ear, let him hear what the Spirit
saith unto the churches; He that overcometh shall not be
hurt of the second death.

12 ¶ And to the angel of the church in Pergamos write;
These things saith he which hath the sharp sword with
two edges;

13 I know thy works, and where thou dwellest, *even*
where Satan's seat *is*: and thou holdest fast my name, and
hast not denied my faith, even in those days wherein
Antipas *was* my faithful martyr, who was slain among
you, where Satan dwelleth.

14 But I have a few things against thee, because thou
hast there them that hold the doctrine of Balaam, who
taught Balac to cast a stumblingblock before the children
of Israel, to eat things sacrificed unto idols, and to commit
fornication.

15 So hast thou also them that hold the doctrine of the
Nicolaitans, which thing I hate.

16 Repent; or else I will come unto thee quickly, and
will fight against them with the sword of my mouth.

NEW AMERICAN STANDARD BIBLE

11 'He who has an ear, let him hear what the Spirit says
to the churches. He who overcomes will not be hurt by the
second death.'

Message to Pergamum

12 "And to the angel of the church in Pergamum write:
The One who has the sharp two-edged sword says this:

13 'I know where you dwell, where Satan's throne is; and
you hold fast My name, and did not deny My faith even in
the days of Antipas, My witness, My faithful one, who was
killed among you, where Satan dwells.

14 'But I have a few things against you, because you
have there some who hold the teaching of Balaam, who
kept teaching Balak to put a stumbling block before the
sons of Israel, to eat things sacrificed to idols and to com-
mit *acts of* immorality.

15 'So you also have some who in the same way hold the
teaching of the Nicolaitans.

16 'Therefore repent; or else I am coming to you quickly,
and I will make war against them with the sword of My
mouth.

NEW CENTURY VERSION

11 "Everyone who has ears should listen to what the
Spirit says to the churches. Those who win the victory will
not be hurt by the second death.

To the Church in Pergamum

12 "Write this to the angel of the church in Pergamum:
"The One who has the sharp, double-edged sword says
this: 13 I know where you live. It is where Satan has his
throne. But you are true to me. You did not refuse to tell
about your faith in me even during the time of Antipas, my
faithful witness who was killed in your city, where Satan
lives.

14 "But I have a few things against you: You have some
there who follow the teaching of Balaam. He taught Balak
how to cause the people of Israel to sin by eating food
offered to idols and by taking part in sexual sins. 15 You
also have some who follow the teaching of the Nicolaitans.[b]
16 So change your hearts and lives. If you do not, I will come
to you quickly and fight against them with the sword that
comes out of my mouth.

2:15 [b] **Nicolaitans** This is the name of a religious group that followed false beliefs and ideas.

CONTEMPORARY ENGLISH VERSION

11 If you have ears, listen to what the Spirit says to the
churches. Whoever wins the victory will not be hurt by
the second death.[c]

The Letter to Pergamum

12 This is what you must write to the angel of the church
in Pergamum:

I am the one who has the sharp double-edged sword!
Listen to what I say.

13 I know that you live where Satan has his throne.[d]
But you have kept true to my name. Right there where
Satan lives, my faithful witness Antipas[e] was taken
from you and put to death. Even then you did not give
up your faith in me.

14 I do have a few things against you. Some of you are
following the teaching of Balaam.[f] Long ago he told
Balak to teach the people of Israel to eat food that had
been offered to idols and to be immoral. 15 Now some of
you are following the teaching of the Nicolaitans.[g] 16 Turn
back! If you don't, I will come quickly and fight against
these people. And my words will cut like a sword.

[c] **2.11** *second death*: The first death is physical death, and the "second death" is eternal death. [d] **2.13** *where Satan has his throne*: The meaning is uncertain, but it may refer to the city as a center of pagan worship or of Emperor worship. [e] **2.13** *Antipas*: Nothing else is known about this man, who is mentioned only here in the New Testament. [f] **2.14** *Balaam*: According to Numbers 22–24, Balaam refused to disobey the Lord. But in other books of the Old Testament, he is spoken of as evil (see Deuteronomy 23.4, 5; Joshua 13.22; 24.9, 10; Nehemiah 13.2). [g] **2.15** *Nicolaitans*: See the note at 2.6.

NEW INTERNATIONAL VERSION

11 He who has an ear, let him hear what the Spirit
says to the churches. He who overcomes will not be
hurt at all by the second death.

To the Church in Pergamum

12 "To the angel of the church in Pergamum write:

These are the words of him who has the sharp, dou-
ble-edged sword. 13 I know where you live—where
Satan has his throne. Yet you remain true to my
name. You did not renounce your faith in me, even in
the days of Antipas, my faithful witness, who was put
to death in your city—where Satan lives.
14 Nevertheless, I have a few things against you:
You have people there who hold to the teaching of
Balaam, who taught Balak to entice the Israelites to
sin by eating food sacrificed to idols and by commit-
ting sexual immorality. 15 Likewise you also have
those who hold to the teaching of the Nicolaitans.
16 Repent therefore! Otherwise, I will soon come to you
and will fight against them with the sword of my
mouth.

NEW LIVING TRANSLATION

11 "Anyone who is willing to hear should listen to the
Spirit and understand what the Spirit is saying to the
churches. Whoever is victorious will not be hurt by the
second death.

The Message to the Church in Pergamum

12 "Write this letter to the angel of the church in Perga-
mum. This is the message from the one who has a sharp
two-edged sword:

13 "I know that you live in the city where that great
throne of Satan is located, and yet you have remained
loyal to me. And you refused to deny me even when
Antipas, my faithful witness, was martyred among you
by Satan's followers. 14 And yet I have a few complaints
against you. You tolerate some among you who are like
Balaam, who showed Balak how to trip up the people of
Israel. He taught them to worship idols by eating food
offered to idols and by committing sexual sin. 15 In the
same way, you have some Nicolaitans among you—peo-
ple who follow the same teaching and commit the same
sins. 16 Repent, or I will come to you suddenly and fight
against them with the sword of my mouth.

NEW KING JAMES VERSION

11 "He who has an ear, let him hear what the Spirit says
to the churches. He who overcomes shall not be hurt by
the second death." '

The Compromising Church

12 "And to the angel of the church in Pergamos write,
'These things says He who has the sharp two-edged
sword: 13 "I know your works, and where you dwell, where
Satan's throne *is.* And you hold fast to My name, and did
not deny My faith even in the days in which Antipas *was*
My faithful martyr, who was killed among you, where Sa-
tan dwells. 14 But I have a few things against you, because
you have there those who hold the doctrine of Balaam,
who taught Balak to put a stumbling block before the chil-
dren of Israel, to eat things sacrificed to idols, and to com-
mit sexual immorality. 15 Thus you also have those who
hold the doctrine of the Nicolaitans, which thing I hate.[a]
16 Repent, or else I will come to you quickly and will fight
against them with the sword of My mouth.

2:15 [a] NU-Text and M-Text read *likewise* for *which thing I hate.*

THE MESSAGE

"Are your ears awake? Listen. Listen to the Wind Words, the Spirit blowing through the churches. Christ-conquerors are safe from Devil-death."

To Pergamum

Write this to Pergamum, to the Angel of the church. The One with the sharp-biting sword draws from the sheath of his mouth—out come the sword words:

"I see where you live, right under the shadow of Satan's throne. But you continue boldly in my Name; you never once denied my Name, even when the pressure was worst, when they martyred Antipas, my witness who stayed faithful to me on Satan's turf.

"But why do you indulge that Balaam crowd? Don't you remember that Balaam was an enemy agent, seducing Balak and sabotaging Israel's holy pilgrimage by throwing unholy parties? And why do you put up with the Nicolaitans, who do the same thing?

"Enough! Don't give in to them; I'll be with you soon. I'm fed up and about to cut them to pieces with my sword-sharp words.

KING JAMES VERSION

17 He that hath an ear, let him hear what the Spirit saith unto the churches; To him that overcometh will I give to eat of the hidden manna, and will give him a white stone, and in the stone a new name written, which no man knoweth saving he that receiveth *it*.

18 ¶ And unto the angel of the church in Thyatira write; These things saith the Son of God, who hath his eyes like unto a flame of fire, and his feet *are* like fine brass;

19 I know thy works, and charity, and service, and faith, and thy patience, and thy works; and the last *to be* more than the first.

20 Notwithstanding I have a few things against thee, because thou sufferest that woman Jezebel, which calleth herself a prophetess, to teach and to seduce my servants to commit fornication, and to eat things sacrificed unto idols.

NEW AMERICAN STANDARD BIBLE

17 'He who has an ear, let him hear what the Spirit says to the churches. To him who overcomes, to him I will give *some* of the hidden manna, and I will give him a white stone, and a new name written on the stone which no one knows but he who receives it.'

Message to Thyatira

18 "And to the angel of the church in Thyatira write:

The Son of God, who has eyes like a flame of fire, and His feet are like burnished bronze, says this:

19 'I know your deeds, and your love and faith and service and perseverance, and that your deeds of late are greater than at first.

20 'But I have *this* against you, that you tolerate the woman Jezebel, who calls herself a prophetess, and she teaches and leads My bond-servants astray so that they commit *acts of* immorality and eat things sacrificed to idols.

NEW CENTURY VERSION

17 "Everyone who has ears should listen to what the Spirit says to the churches.

"I will give some of the hidden manna to everyone who wins the victory. I will also give to each one who wins the victory a white stone with a new name written on it. No one knows this new name except the one who receives it.

To the Church in Thyatira

18 "Write this to the angel of the church in Thyatira:

"The Son of God, who has eyes that blaze like fire and
feet like shining bronze, says this: 19 I know what you do. I
know about your love, your faith, your service, and your
patience. I know that you are doing more now than you
did at first.

20 "But I have this against you: You let that woman
Jezebel spread false teachings. She says she is a prophet-
ess, but by her teaching she leads my people to take part
in sexual sins and to eat food that is offered to idols. 21 I

CONTEMPORARY ENGLISH VERSION

17 If you have ears, listen to what the Spirit says to the churches. To everyone who wins the victory, I will give some of the hidden food.[h] I will also give each one a white stone[i] with a new name[j] written on it. No one will know that name except the one who is given the stone.

The Letter to Thyatira

18 This is what you must write to the angel of the church in Thyatira:

I am the Son of God! My eyes are like flames of fire, and my feet are like bronze. Listen to what I say.

19 I know everything about you, including your love,
your faith, your service, and how you have endured. I
know that you are doing more now than you have ever
done before. 20 But I still have something against you
because of that woman Jezebel.[k] She calls herself a
prophet, and you let her teach and mislead my servants
to do immoral things and to eat food offered to idols. 21 I

[h] 2.17 *hidden food*: When the people of Israel were going through the desert, the Lord provided a special food for them. Some of this was placed in a jar and stored in the sacred chest (see Exodus 16). According to later Jewish teaching, the prophet Jeremiah rescued the sacred chest when the temple was destroyed by the Babylonians. He hid the chest in a cave, where it would stay until God came to save his people. [i] 2.17 *white stone*: The meaning of this is uncertain, though it may be the same as a ticket that lets a person into God's banquet where the "hidden food" is eaten. Or it may be a symbol of victory. [j] 2.17 *a new name*: Either the name of Christ or God or the name of the follower who is given the stone. [k] 2.20 *Jezebel*: Nothing else is known about her. This may have been her real name or a name that was given to her because she was like Queen Jezebel, who opposed the Lord (see 1 Kings 19.1, 2; 21.1-26).

NEW INTERNATIONAL VERSION

17 He who has an ear, let him hear what the Spirit says to the churches. To him who overcomes, I will give some of the hidden manna. I will also give him a white stone with a new name written on it, known only to him who receives it.

To the Church in Thyatira

18 "To the angel of the church in Thyatira write:

These are the words of the Son of God, whose eyes are like blazing fire and whose feet are like burnished bronze. 19 I know your deeds, your love and faith, your service and perseverance, and that you are now doing more than you did at first.

20 Nevertheless, I have this against you: You tolerate that woman Jezebel, who calls herself a prophetess. By her teaching she misleads my servants into sexual immorality and the eating of food sacrificed to idols.

NEW LIVING TRANSLATION

17 "Anyone who is willing to hear should listen to the Spirit and understand what the Spirit is saying to the churches. Everyone who is victorious will eat of the manna that has been hidden away in heaven. And I will give to each one a white stone, and on the stone will be engraved a new name that no one knows except the one who receives it.

The Message to the Church in Thyatira

18 "Write this letter to the angel of the church in Thyatira. This is the message from the Son of God, whose eyes are bright like flames of fire, whose feet are like polished bronze:

19 "I know all the things you do—your love, your faith, your service, and your patient endurance. And I can see your constant improvement in all these things. 20 But I have this complaint against you. You are permitting that woman—that Jezebel who calls herself a prophet—to lead my servants astray. She is encouraging them to worship idols, eat food offered to idols, and commit sexual

NEW KING JAMES VERSION

17 "He who has an ear, let him hear what the Spirit says to the churches. To him who overcomes I will give some of the hidden manna to eat. And I will give him a white stone, and on the stone a new name written which no one knows except him who receives *it*." '

The Corrupt Church

18 "And to the angel of the church in Thyatira write,

'These things says the Son of God, who has eyes like a flame of fire, and His feet like fine brass: 19 "I know your works, love, service, faith,[b] and your patience; and *as* for your works, the last *are* more than the first. 20 Nevertheless I have a few things against you, because you allow[c] that woman[d] Jezebel, who calls herself a prophetess, to teach and seduce[e] My servants to commit sexual immorality and eat things sacrificed to idols. 21 And I gave her

2:19 [b] NU-Text and M-Text read *faith, service.* 2:20 [c] NU-Text and M-Text read *I have against you that you tolerate.* [d] M-Text reads *your wife Jezebel.* [e] NU-Text and M-Text read *and teaches and seduces.*

THE MESSAGE

"Are your ears awake? Listen. Listen to the Wind Words, the Spirit blowing through the churches. I'll give the sacred manna to every conqueror; I'll also give a clear, smooth stone inscribed with your new name, your secret new name."

To Thyatira

Write this to Thyatira, to the Angel of the church. God's Son, eyes pouring fire-blaze, standing on feet of furnace-fired bronze, says this:

"I see everything you're doing for me. Impressive! The love and the faith, the service and persistence. Yes, very impressive! You get better at it every day.

"But why do you let that Jezebel who calls herself a prophet mislead my dear servants into Cross-denying, self-indulging religion? I gave her a chance to change her

KING JAMES VERSION

21 And I gave her space to repent of her fornication; and she repented not.

22 Behold, I will cast her into a bed, and them that commit adultery with her into great tribulation, except they repent of their deeds.

23 And I will kill her children with death; and all the churches shall know that I am he which searcheth the reins and hearts: and I will give unto every one of you according to your works.

24 But unto you I say, and unto the rest in Thyatira, as many as have not this doctrine, and which have not known the depths of Satan, as they speak; I will put upon you none other burden.

25 But that which ye have *already* hold fast till I come.

26 And he that overcometh, and keepeth my works unto the end, to him will I give power over the nations:

27 And he shall rule them with a rod of iron; as the vessels of a potter shall they be broken to shivers: even as I received of my Father.

28 And I will give him the morning star.

29 He that hath an ear, let him hear what the Spirit saith unto the churches.

3 And unto the angel of the church in Sardis write; These things saith he that hath the seven Spirits of God, and

NEW AMERICAN STANDARD BIBLE

21 'I gave her time to repent, and she does not want to repent of her immorality.

22 'Behold, I will throw her on a bed *of sickness*, and those who commit adultery with her into great tribulation, unless they repent of [l]her deeds.

23 'And I will kill her children with pestilence, and all the churches will know that I am He who searches the minds and hearts; and I will give to each one of you according to your deeds.

24 'But I say to you, the rest who are in Thyatira, who do not hold this teaching, who have not known the deep things of Satan, as they call them—I place no other burden on you.

25 'Nevertheless what you have, hold fast until I come.

26 'He who overcomes, and he who keeps My deeds until the end, TO HIM I WILL GIVE AUTHORITY OVER THE NATIONS;

27 AND HE SHALL RULE THEM WITH A ROD OF IRON, AS THE VESSELS OF THE POTTER ARE BROKEN TO PIECES, as I also have received *authority* from My Father;

28 and I will give him the morning star.

29 'He who has an ear, let him hear what the Spirit says to the churches.'

Message to Sardis

3 "To the angel of the church in Sardis write:
He who has the seven Spirits of God and the seven

2:22 [l] One early ms reads *their*

NEW CENTURY VERSION

have given her time to change her heart and turn away
from her sin, but she does not want to change. 22So I will
throw her on a bed of suffering. And all those who take
part in adultery with her will suffer greatly if they do not
turn away from the wrongs she does. 23I will also kill her
followers. Then all the churches will know I am the One
who searches hearts and minds, and I will repay each of
you for what you have done.
24"But others of you in Thyatira have not followed her
teaching and have not learned what some call Satan's
deep secrets. I say to you that I will not put any other load
on you. 25Only continue in your loyalty until I come.
26"I will give power over the nations to everyone who
wins the victory and continues to be obedient to me until
the end.
27'You will rule over them with an iron rod,
as when pottery is broken into pieces.' *Psalm 2:9*
28This is the same power I received from my Father. I will
also give him the morning star. 29Everyone who has ears
should listen to what the Spirit says to the churches.

To the Church in Sardis

3 "Write this to the angel of the church in Sardis:
"The One who has the seven spirits and the seven stars

CONTEMPORARY ENGLISH VERSION

gave her a chance to turn from her sins, but she did not
want to stop doing these immoral things.
22I am going to strike down Jezebel. Everyone who does
these immoral things with her will also be punished, if
they don't stop. 23I will even kill her followers.[l] Then all
the churches will see that I know everyone's thoughts
and feelings. I will treat each of you as you deserve.
24Some of you in Thyatira don't follow Jezebel's teach-
ing. You don't know anything about what her followers
call the "deep secrets of Satan." So I won't burden you
down with any other commands. 25But until I come, you
must hold firmly to the teaching you have.
26I will give power over the nations to everyone who
wins the victory and keeps on obeying me until the end.
27-28I will give each of them the same power that my
Father has given me. They will rule the nations with an
iron rod and smash those nations to pieces like clay
pots. I will also give them the morning star.[m]
29If you have ears, listen to what the Spirit says to the
churches.

The Letter to Sardis

3 This is what you must write to the angel of the church
in Sardis:

I have the seven spirits of God and the seven stars.
Listen to what I say.

[l] 2.23 *her followers*: Or "her children." [m] 2.27,28 *the morning star*: Probably thought of as the star that signals the end of night and the beginning of day. In 22.16 Christ is called the "morning star."

NEW INTERNATIONAL VERSION

21 I have given her time to repent of her immorality,
but she is unwilling. 22 So I will cast her on a bed of
suffering, and I will make those who commit adultery
with her suffer intensely, unless they repent of her
ways. 23 I will strike her children dead. Then all the
churches will know that I am he who searches hearts
and minds, and I will repay each of you according to
your deeds. 24 Now I say to the rest of you in Thyatira,
to you who do not hold to her teaching and have not
learned Satan's so-called deep secrets (I will not
impose any other burden on you): 25 Only hold on to
what you have until I come.

26 To him who overcomes and does my will to the
end, I will give authority over the nations—

27 'He will rule them with an iron scepter;
he will dash them to pieces like pottery'[b]—

just as I have received authority from my Father. 28 I
will also give him the morning star. 29 He who has an
ear, let him hear what the Spirit says to the churches.

To the Church in Sardis

3 "To the angel[a] of the church in Sardis write:

These are the words of him who holds the seven
spirits[b] of God and the seven stars. I know your

[b] *27* Psalm 2:9 [a] *1* Or *messenger*; also in verses 7 and 14 [b] *1* Or *the sevenfold Spirit*

NEW LIVING TRANSLATION

sin. 21 I gave her time to repent, but she would not turn
away from her immorality. 22 Therefore, I will throw her
upon a sickbed, and she will suffer greatly with all who
commit adultery with her, unless they turn away from all
their evil deeds. 23 I will strike her children dead. And all
the churches will know that I am the one who searches
out the thoughts and intentions of every person. And I
will give to each of you whatever you deserve. 24 But I
also have a message for the rest of you in Thyatira who
have not followed this false teaching ('deeper truths,' as
they call them—depths of Satan, really). I will ask noth-
ing more of you 25 except that you hold tightly to what
you have until I come.

26 "To all who are victorious, who obey me to the very
end, I will give authority over all the nations. 27 They
will rule the nations with an iron rod and smash them
like clay pots. 28 They will have the same authority I
received from my Father, and I will also give them the
morning star! 29 Anyone who is willing to hear should
listen to the Spirit and understand what the Spirit is
saying to the churches.

The Message to the Church in Sardis

3 "Write this letter to the angel of* the church in Sardis.
This is the message from the one who has the seven-
fold Spirit* of God and the seven stars:

3:1a Or *the messenger for;* also in 3:7, 14. **3:1b** Greek *the seven spirits.*

NEW KING JAMES VERSION

time to repent of her sexual immorality, and she did not
repent.[f] 22 Indeed I will cast her into a sickbed, and those
who commit adultery with her into great tribulation,
unless they repent of their[g] deeds. 23 I will kill her children
with death, and all the churches shall know that I am He
who searches the minds and hearts. And I will give to
each one of you according to your works.

24 "Now to you I say, and[h] to the rest in Thyatira, as
many as do not have this doctrine, who have not known
the depths of Satan, as they say, I will[i] put on you no
other burden. 25 But hold fast what you have till I come.
26 And he who overcomes, and keeps My works until the
end, to him I will give power over the nations—

27 *'He shall rule them with a rod of iron;*
They shall be dashed to pieces like the potter's
vessels'[j]—

as I also have received from My Father; 28 and I will give
him the morning star.

29 "He who has an ear, let him hear what the Spirit says
to the churches." '

The Dead Church

3 "And to the angel of the church in Sardis write,
'These things says He who has the seven Spirits of

2:21 [f] NU-Text and M-Text read *time to repent, and she does not want to repent of her sexual immorality.* 2:22 [g] NU-Text and M-Text read *her.*
2:24 [h] NU-Text and M-Text omit *and.* [i] NU-Text and M-Text omit *will.*
2:27 [j] Psalm 2:9

THE MESSAGE

ways, but she has no intention of giving up a career in the
god-business. I'm about to lay her low, along with her
partners, as they play their sex-and-religion games. The
bastard offspring of their idol-whoring I'll kill. Then every
church will know that appearances don't impress me. I
X-ray every motive and make sure you get what's coming
to you.

"The rest of you Thyatirans, who have nothing to do
with this outrage, who scorn this playing around with the
Devil that gets paraded as profundity, be assured I'll not
make life any harder for you than it already is. Hold on to
the truth you have until I get there.

"Here's the reward I have for every conqueror, everyone
who keeps at it, refusing to give up: You'll rule the
nations, your Shepherd-King rule as firm as an iron staff,
their resistance fragile as clay pots. This was the gift my
Father gave me; I pass it along to you—and with it, the
Morning Star!

"Are your ears awake? Listen. Listen to the Wind Words,
the Spirit blowing through the churches."

To Sardis

3 Write this to Sardis, to the Angel of the church. The
One holding the Seven Spirits of God in one hand, a
firm grip on the Seven Stars with the other, speaks:

KING JAMES VERSION

the seven stars; I know thy works, that thou hast a name that thou livest, and art dead.

2 Be watchful, and strengthen the things which remain, that are ready to die: for I have not found thy works perfect before God.

3 Remember therefore how thou hast received and heard, and hold fast, and repent. If therefore thou shalt not watch, I will come on thee as a thief, and thou shalt not know what hour I will come upon thee.

4 Thou hast a few names even in Sardis which have not defiled their garments; and they shall walk with me in white: for they are worthy.

5 He that overcometh, the same shall be clothed in white raiment; and I will not blot out his name out of the book of life, but I will confess his name before my Father, and before his angels.

6 He that hath an ear, let him hear what the Spirit saith unto the churches.

7 ¶ And to the angel of the church in Philadelphia write; These things saith he that is holy, he that is true, he that hath the key of David, he that openeth, and no man shutteth; and shutteth, and no man openeth;

8 I know thy works: behold, I have set before thee an open door, and no man can shut it: for thou hast a little

NEW AMERICAN STANDARD BIBLE

stars, says this: 'I know your deeds, that you have a name that you are alive, but you are dead.

2 'Wake up, and strengthen the things that remain, which were about to die; for I have not found your deeds completed in the sight of My God.

3 'So remember what you have received and heard; and keep *it,* and repent. Therefore if you do not wake up, I will come like a thief, and you will not know at what hour I will come to you.

4 'But you have a few people in Sardis who have not soiled their garments; and they will walk with Me in white, for they are worthy.

5 'He who overcomes will thus be clothed in white garments; and I will not erase his name from the book of life, and I will confess his name before My Father and before His angels.

6 'He who has an ear, let him hear what the Spirit says to the churches.'

Message to Philadelphia

7 "And to the angel of the church in Philadelphia write:

He who is holy, who is true, who has the key of David, who opens and no one will shut, and who shuts and no one opens, says this:

8 'I know your [1]deeds. Behold, I have put before you an open door which no one can shut, because you have a little

3:8 [1] Or *deeds (behold...shut), that you have*

NEW CENTURY VERSION

says this: I know what you do. People say that you are alive,
but really you are dead. 2 Wake up! Make yourselves
stronger before what you have left dies completely. I have
found that what you are doing is less than what my God
wants. 3 So do not forget what you have received and heard.
Obey it, and change your hearts and lives. So you must
wake up, or I will come like a thief, and you will not know
when I will come to you. 4 But you have a few there in Sardis
who have kept their clothes unstained, so they will walk
with me and will wear white clothes, because they are worthy.
5 Those who win the victory will be dressed in white
clothes like them. And I will not erase their names from the
book of life, but I will say they belong to me before my
Father and before his angels. 6 Everyone who has ears
should listen to what the Spirit says to the churches.

To the Church in Philadelphia

7 "Write this to the angel of the church in Philadelphia:
"This is what the One who is holy and true, who holds
the key of David, says. When he opens a door, no one can
close it. And when he closes it, no one can open it. 8 I know
what you do. I have put an open door before you, which no

CONTEMPORARY ENGLISH VERSION

I know what you are doing. Everyone may think you
are alive, but you are dead. 2 Wake up! You have only a
little strength left, and it is almost gone. So try to
become stronger. I have found that you are not completely
obeying God. 3 Remember the teaching that you
were given and that you heard. Hold firmly to it and
turn from your sins. If you don't wake up, I will come
when you least expect it, just as a thief does.

4 A few of you in Sardis have not dirtied your clothes
with sin. You will walk with me in white clothes,
because you are worthy. 5 Everyone who wins the victory
will wear white clothes. Their names will not be erased
from the book of life,[a] and I will tell my Father and his
angels that they are my followers.

6 If you have ears, listen to what the Spirit says to the churches.

The Letter to Philadelphia

7 This is what you must write to the angel of the church in Philadelphia:

I am the one who is holy and true, and I have the keys that belonged to David.[b] When I open a door, no one can close it. And when I close a door, no one can open it. Listen to what I say.

8 I know everything you have done. And I have placed before you an open door that no one can close. You were

[a] 3.5 *book of life*: The book in which the names of God's people are written. [b] 3.7 *the keys that belonged to David*: The keys stand for authority over David's kingdom.

NEW INTERNATIONAL VERSION

deeds; you have a reputation of being alive, but you
are dead. 2Wake up! Strengthen what remains and is
about to die, for I have not found your deeds complete
in the sight of my God. 3Remember, therefore, what
you have received and heard; obey it, and repent. But
if you do not wake up, I will come like a thief, and you
will not know at what time I will come to you.
4Yet you have a few people in Sardis who have not
soiled their clothes. They will walk with me, dressed
in white, for they are worthy. 5He who overcomes will,
like them, be dressed in white. I will never blot out his
name from the book of life, but will acknowledge his
name before my Father and his angels. 6He who has
an ear, let him hear what the Spirit says to the
churches.

To the Church in Philadelphia

7"To the angel of the church in Philadelphia write:

These are the words of him who is holy and true,
who holds the key of David. What he opens no one
can shut, and what he shuts no one can open. 8I know
your deeds. See, I have placed before you an open
door that no one can shut. I know that you have little

NEW LIVING TRANSLATION

"I know all the things you do, and that you have a repu-
tation for being alive—but you are dead. 2Now wake up!
Strengthen what little remains, for even what is left is at
the point of death. Your deeds are far from right in the
sight of God. 3Go back to what you heard and believed
at first; hold to it firmly and turn to me again. Unless
you do, I will come upon you suddenly, as unexpected as
a thief.
4"Yet even in Sardis there are some who have not
soiled their garments with evil deeds. They will walk
with me in white, for they are worthy. 5All who are vic-
torious will be clothed in white. I will never erase their
names from the Book of Life, but I will announce before
my Father and his angels that they are mine. 6Anyone
who is willing to hear should listen to the Spirit and
understand what the Spirit is saying to the churches.

The Message to the Church in Philadelphia

7"Write this letter to the angel of the church in Phila-
delphia. This is the message from the one who is holy and
true. He is the one who has the key of David. He opens
doors, and no one can shut them; he shuts doors, and no
one can open them.

8"I know all the things you do, and I have opened a door
for you that no one can shut. You have little strength,

NEW KING JAMES VERSION

God and the seven stars: "I know your works, that you
have a name that you are alive, but you are dead. 2Be
watchful, and strengthen the things which remain, that are
ready to die, for I have not found your works perfect before
God.[a] 3Remember therefore how you have received and
heard; hold fast and repent. Therefore if you will not watch,
I will come upon you as a thief, and you will not know
what hour I will come upon you. 4You[b] have a few names
even in Sardis who have not defiled their garments; and
they shall walk with Me in white, for they are worthy. 5He
who overcomes shall be clothed in white garments, and I
will not blot out his name from the Book of Life; but I will
confess his name before My Father and before His angels.
6"He who has an ear, let him hear what the Spirit says
to the churches." '

The Faithful Church

7"And to the angel of the church in Philadelphia write,
'These things says He who is holy, He who is true, *"He
who has the key of David, He who opens and no one shuts,
and shuts and no one opens"*:[c] 8"I know your works. See, I
have set before you an open door, and no one can shut it;[d]

3:2 [a] NU-Text and M-Text read *My God.* 3:4 [b] NU-Text and M-Text
read *Nevertheless you have a few names in Sardis.* 3:7 [c] Isaiah 22:22
3:8 [d] NU-Text and M-Text read *which no one can shut.*

THE MESSAGE

"I see right through your work. You have a reputation
for vigor and zest, but you're dead, stone dead.

"Up on your feet! Take a deep breath! Maybe there's life
in you yet. But I wouldn't know it by looking at your busy-
work; nothing of *God's* work has been completed. Your
condition is desperate. Think of the gift you once had in
your hands, the Message you heard with your ears—grasp
it again and turn back to God.

"If you pull the covers back over your head and sleep on,
oblivious to God, I'll return when you least expect it, break
into your life like a thief in the night.

"You still have a few Christians in Sardis who haven't
ruined themselves wallowing in the muck of the world's
ways. They'll walk with me on parade! They've proved
their worth!

"Conquerors will march in the victory parade, their
names indelible in the Book of Life. I'll lead them up and
present them by name to my Father and his Angels.

"Are your ears awake? Listen. Listen to the Wind Words,
the Spirit blowing through the churches."

To Philadelphia

Write this to Philadelphia, to the Angel of the church.
The Holy, the True—David's key in his hand, opening
doors no one can lock, locking doors no one can open—
speaks:

"I see what you've done. Now see what *I've* done. I've
opened a door before you that no one can slam shut. You

KING JAMES VERSION

strength, and hast kept my word, and hast not denied my name.

9 Behold, I will make them of the synagogue of Satan, which say they are Jews, and are not, but do lie; behold, I will make them to come and worship before thy feet, and to know that I have loved thee.

10 Because thou hast kept the word of my patience, I also will keep thee from the hour of temptation, which shall come upon all the world, to try them that dwell upon the earth.

11 Behold, I come quickly: hold that fast which thou hast, that no man take thy crown.

12 Him that overcometh will I make a pillar in the temple of my God, and he shall go no more out: and I will write upon him the name of my God, and the name of the city of my God, *which is* new Jerusalem, which cometh down out of heaven from my God: and *I will write upon him* my new name.

13 He that hath an ear, let him hear what the Spirit saith unto the churches.

14 ¶ And unto the angel of the church of the Laodiceans write; These things saith the Amen, the faithful and true witness, the beginning of the creation of God;

NEW AMERICAN STANDARD BIBLE

power, and have kept My word, and have not denied My name.

9 'Behold, I will cause *those* of the synagogue of Satan, who say that they are Jews and are not, but lie—I will make them come and bow down at your feet, and *make them* know that I have loved you.

10 'Because you have kept the word of My perseverance, I also will keep you from the hour of testing, that *hour* which is about to come upon the whole world, to test those who dwell on the earth.

11 'I am coming quickly; hold fast what you have, so that no one will take your crown.

12 'He who overcomes, I will make him a pillar in the temple of My God, and he will not go out from it anymore; and I will write on him the name of My God, and the name of the city of My God, the new Jerusalem, which comes down out of heaven from My God, and My new name.

13 'He who has an ear, let him hear what the Spirit says to the churches.'

Message to Laodicea

14 "To the angel of the church in Laodicea write:

The Amen, the faithful and true Witness, the [2]Beginning of the creation of God, says this:

3:14 [2] I.e. Origin or Source

NEW CENTURY VERSION

one can close. I know you have a little strength, but you have obeyed my teaching and were not afraid to speak my name. 9Those in the synagogue that belongs to Satan say they are Jews, but they are not true Jews; they are liars. I will make them come before you and bow at your feet, and they will know that I have loved you. 10You have obeyed my teaching about not giving up your faith. So I will keep you from the time of trouble that will come to the whole world to test those who live on earth.

11"I am coming soon. Continue strong in your faith so no one will take away your crown. 12I will make those who win the victory pillars in the temple of my God, and they will never have to leave it. I will write on them the name of my God and the name of the city of my God, the new Jerusalem,[a] that comes down out of heaven from my God. I will also write on them my new name. 13Everyone who has ears should listen to what the Spirit says to the churches.

To the Church in Laodicea

14"Write this to the angel of the church in Laodicea:

"The Amen,[b] the faithful and true witness, the beginning of all God has made, says this: 15I know what you do,

3:12 [a] **Jerusalem** This name is used to mean the spiritual city God built for his people. See Revelation 21–22. 3:14 [b] **Amen** Used here as a name for Jesus; it means to agree fully that something is true.

CONTEMPORARY ENGLISH VERSION

not very strong, but you obeyed my message and did not deny that you are my followers.[c] 9Now you will see what I will do with those people who belong to Satan's group. They claim to be Jews, but they are liars. I will make them come and kneel down at your feet. Then they will know that I love you.

10You obeyed my message and endured. So I will protect you from the time of testing that everyone in all the world must go through. 11I am coming soon. So hold firmly to what you have, and no one will take away the crown that you will be given as your reward.

12Everyone who wins the victory will be made into a pillar in the temple of my God, and they will stay there forever. I will write on each of them the name of my God and the name of his city. It is the new Jerusalem that my God will send down from heaven. I will also write on them my own new name.

13If you have ears, listen to what the Spirit says to the churches.

The Letter to Laodicea

14This is what you must write to the angel of the church in Laodicea:

I am the one called Amen![d] I am the faithful and true witness and the source[e] of God's creation. Listen to what I say.

[c] 3.8 *did not deny that you are my followers*: Or "did not say evil things about me." [d] 3.14 *Amen*: Meaning "Trustworthy." [e] 3.14 *source*: Or "beginning."

NEW INTERNATIONAL VERSION

strength, yet you have kept my word and have not denied my name. [9]I will make those who are of the synagogue of Satan, who claim to be Jews though they are not, but are liars—I will make them come and fall down at your feet and acknowledge that I have loved you. [10]Since you have kept my command to endure patiently, I will also keep you from the hour of trial that is going to come upon the whole world to test those who live on the earth.

[11]I am coming soon. Hold on to what you have, so that no one will take your crown. [12]Him who overcomes I will make a pillar in the temple of my God. Never again will he leave it. I will write on him the name of my God and the name of the city of my God, the new Jerusalem, which is coming down out of heaven from my God; and I will also write on him my new name. [13]He who has an ear, let him hear what the Spirit says to the churches.

To the Church in Laodicea

[14]"To the angel of the church in Laodicea write:

These are the words of the Amen, the faithful and true witness, the ruler of God's creation. [15]I know

NEW LIVING TRANSLATION

yet you obeyed my word and did not deny me. [9]Look! I will force those who belong to Satan—those liars who say they are Jews but are not—to come and bow down at your feet. They will acknowledge that you are the ones I love.

[10]"Because you have obeyed my command to persevere, I will protect you from the great time of testing that will come upon the whole world to test those who belong to this world. [11]Look, I am coming quickly. Hold on to what you have, so that no one will take away your crown. [12]All who are victorious will become pillars in the Temple of my God, and they will never have to leave it. And I will write my God's name on them, and they will be citizens in the city of my God—the new Jerusalem that comes down from heaven from my God. And they will have my new name inscribed upon them. [13]Anyone who is willing to hear should listen to the Spirit and understand what the Spirit is saying to the churches.

The Message to the Church in Laodicea

[14]"Write this letter to the angel of the church in Laodicea. This is the message from the one who is the Amen—the faithful and true witness, the ruler* of God's creation:

3:14 Or *the source.*

NEW KING JAMES VERSION

for you have a little strength, have kept My word, and have not denied My name. [9]Indeed I will make *those* of the synagogue of Satan, who say they are Jews and are not, but lie—indeed I will make them come and worship before your feet, and to know that I have loved you. [10]Because you have kept My command to persevere, I also will keep you from the hour of trial which shall come upon the whole world, to test those who dwell on the earth. [11]Behold,[e] I am coming quickly! Hold fast what you have, that no one may take your crown. [12]He who overcomes, I will make him a pillar in the temple of My God, and he shall go out no more. I will write on him the name of My God and the name of the city of My God, the New Jerusalem, which comes down out of heaven from My God. And *I will write on him* My new name.

[13]"He who has an ear, let him hear what the Spirit says to the churches." '

The Lukewarm Church

[14]"And to the angel of the church of the Laodiceans[f] write,

'These things says the Amen, the Faithful and True Witness, the Beginning of the creation of God: [15]"I know

3:11 [e] NU-Text and M-Text omit *Behold.* 3:14 [f] NU-Text and M-Text read *in Laodicea.*

THE MESSAGE

don't have much strength, I know that; you used what you had to keep my Word. You didn't deny me when times were rough.

"And watch as I take those who call themselves true believers but are nothing of the kind, pretenders whose true membership is in the club of Satan—watch as I strip off their pretensions and they're forced to acknowledge it's you that I've loved.

"Because you kept my Word in passionate patience, I'll keep you safe in the time of testing that will be here soon, and all over the earth, every man, woman, and child put to the test.

"I'm on my way; I'll be there soon. Keep a tight grip on what you have so no one distracts you and steals your crown.

"I'll make each conqueror a pillar in the sanctuary of my God, a permanent position of honor. Then I'll write names on you, the pillars: the Name of my God, the Name of God's City—the new Jerusalem coming down out of Heaven—and my new Name.

"Are your ears awake? Listen. Listen to the Wind Words, the Spirit blowing through the churches."

To Laodicea

Write to Laodicea, to the Angel of the church. God's Yes, the Faithful and Accurate Witness, the First of God's creation, says:

KING JAMES VERSION

15 I know thy works, that thou art neither cold nor hot: I would thou wert cold or hot.

16 So then because thou art lukewarm, and neither cold nor hot, I will spue thee out of my mouth.

17 Because thou sayest, I am rich, and increased with goods, and have need of nothing; and knowest not that thou art wretched, and miserable, and poor, and blind, and naked:

18 I counsel thee to buy of me gold tried in the fire, that thou mayest be rich; and white raiment, that thou mayest be clothed, and *that* the shame of thy nakedness do not appear; and anoint thine eyes with eyesalve, that thou mayest see.

19 As many as I love, I rebuke and chasten: be zealous therefore, and repent.

20 Behold, I stand at the door, and knock: if any man hear my voice, and open the door, I will come in to him, and will sup with him, and he with me.

21 To him that overcometh will I grant to sit with me in my throne, even as I also overcame, and am set down with my Father in his throne.

22 He that hath an ear, let him hear what the Spirit saith unto the churches.

4 After this I looked, and, behold, a door *was* opened in heaven: and the first voice which I heard *was* as it were of a trumpet talking with me; which said, Come up hither, and I will shew thee things which must be hereafter.

NEW AMERICAN STANDARD BIBLE

15 'I know your deeds, that you are neither cold nor hot; I wish that you were cold or hot.

16 'So because you are lukewarm, and neither hot nor cold, I will spit you out of My mouth.

17 'Because you say, "I am rich, and have become wealthy, and have need of nothing," and you do not know that you are wretched and miserable and poor and blind and naked,

18 I advise you to buy from Me gold refined by fire so that you may become rich, and white garments so that you may clothe yourself, and *that* the shame of your nakedness will not be revealed; and eye salve to anoint your eyes so that you may see.

19 'Those whom I love, I reprove and discipline; therefore be zealous and repent.

20 'Behold, I stand at the door and knock; if anyone hears My voice and opens the door, I will come in to him and will dine with him, and he with Me.

21 'He who overcomes, I will grant to him to sit down with Me on My throne, as I also overcame and sat down with My Father on His throne.

22 'He who has an ear, let him hear what the Spirit says to the churches.' "

Scene in Heaven

4 After these things I looked, and behold, a door *standing* open in heaven, and the first voice which I had heard, like *the sound* of a trumpet speaking with me, said, "Come up here, and I will show you what must take place after these things."

NEW CENTURY VERSION

that you are not hot or cold. I wish that you were hot or
cold! 16But because you are lukewarm—neither hot, nor
cold—I am ready to spit you out of my mouth. 17You say,
'I am rich, and I have become wealthy and do not need
anything.' But you do not know that you are really miser-
able, pitiful, poor, blind, and naked. 18I advise you to buy
from me gold made pure in fire so you can be truly rich.
Buy from me white clothes so you can be clothed and so
you can cover your shameful nakedness. Buy from me
medicine to put on your eyes so you can truly see.

19"I correct and punish those whom I love. So be eager
to do right, and change your hearts and lives. 20Here I am!
I stand at the door and knock. If you hear my voice and
open the door, I will come in and eat with you, and you
will eat with me.

21"Those who win the victory will sit with me on my
throne in the same way that I won the victory and sat
down with my Father on his throne. 22Everyone who has
ears should listen to what the Spirit says to the churches."

John Sees Heaven

4 After the vision of these things I looked, and there
before me was an open door in heaven. And the same
voice that spoke to me before, that sounded like a trumpet,
said, "Come up here, and I will show you what must happen

CONTEMPORARY ENGLISH VERSION

15I know everything you have done, and you are not
cold or hot. I wish you were either one or the other.
16But since you are lukewarm and neither cold nor hot, I
will spit you out of my mouth. 17You claim to be rich
and successful and to have everything you need. But
you don't know how bad off you are. You are pitiful,
poor, blind, and naked.

18Buy your gold from me. It has been refined in a fire,
and it will make you rich. Buy white clothes from me.
Wear them and you can cover up your shameful naked-
ness. Buy medicine for your eyes, so that you will be
able to see.

19I correct and punish everyone I love. So make up
your minds to turn away from your sins. 20Listen! I am
standing and knocking at your door. If you hear my
voice and open the door, I will come in and we will eat
together. 21Everyone who wins the victory will sit with
me on my throne, just as I won the victory and sat with
my Father on his throne.

22If you have ears, listen to what the Spirit says to the
churches.

Worship in Heaven

4 After this, I looked and saw a door that opened into
heaven. Then the voice that had spoken to me at first
and that sounded like a trumpet said, "Come up here! I
will show you what must happen next." 2Right then the

NEW INTERNATIONAL VERSION

your deeds, that you are neither cold nor hot. I wish you were either one or the other! 16So, because you are lukewarm—neither hot nor cold—I am about to spit you out of my mouth. 17You say, 'I am rich; I have acquired wealth and do not need a thing.' But you do not realize that you are wretched, pitiful, poor, blind and naked. 18I counsel you to buy from me gold refined in the fire, so you can become rich; and white clothes to wear, so you can cover your shameful nakedness; and salve to put on your eyes, so you can see.

19Those whom I love I rebuke and discipline. So be earnest, and repent. 20Here I am! I stand at the door and knock. If anyone hears my voice and opens the door, I will come in and eat with him, and he with me.

21To him who overcomes, I will give the right to sit with me on my throne, just as I overcame and sat down with my Father on his throne. 22He who has an ear, let him hear what the Spirit says to the churches."

The Throne in Heaven

4 After this I looked, and there before me was a door standing open in heaven. And the voice I had first heard speaking to me like a trumpet said, "Come up here, and I will show you what must take place after this." 2At

NEW LIVING TRANSLATION

15"I know all the things you do, that you are neither hot nor cold. I wish you were one or the other! 16But since you are like lukewarm water, I will spit you out of my mouth! 17You say, 'I am rich. I have everything I want. I don't need a thing!' And you don't realize that you are wretched and miserable and poor and blind and naked. 18I advise you to buy gold from me—gold that has been purified by fire. Then you will be rich. And also buy white garments so you will not be shamed by your nakedness. And buy ointment for your eyes so you will be able to see. 19I am the one who corrects and disciplines everyone I love. Be diligent and turn from your indifference.

20"Look! Here I stand at the door and knock. If you hear me calling and open the door, I will come in, and we will share a meal as friends. 21I will invite everyone who is victorious to sit with me on my throne, just as I was victorious and sat with my Father on his throne. 22Anyone who is willing to hear should listen to the Spirit and understand what the Spirit is saying to the churches."

Worship in Heaven

4 Then as I looked, I saw a door standing open in heaven, and the same voice I had heard before spoke to me with the sound of a mighty trumpet blast. The voice said, "Come up here, and I will show you what must happen after these

NEW KING JAMES VERSION

your works, that you are neither cold nor hot. I could wish you were cold or hot. 16So then, because you are lukewarm, and neither cold nor hot,[g] I will vomit you out of My mouth. 17Because you say, 'I am rich, have become wealthy, and have need of nothing'—and do not know that you are wretched, miserable, poor, blind, and naked— 18I counsel you to buy from Me gold refined in the fire, that you may be rich; and white garments, that you may be clothed, *that* the shame of your nakedness may not be revealed; and anoint your eyes with eye salve, that you may see. 19As many as I love, I rebuke and chasten. Therefore be zealous and repent. 20Behold, I stand at the door and knock. If anyone hears My voice and opens the door, I will come in to him and dine with him, and he with Me. 21To him who overcomes I will grant to sit with Me on My throne, as I also overcame and sat down with My Father on His throne.

22"He who has an ear, let him hear what the Spirit says to the churches." ' "

The Throne Room of Heaven

4 After these things I looked, and behold, a door *standing* open in heaven. And the first voice which I heard *was* like a trumpet speaking with me, saying, "Come up here, and I will show you things which must take place after this."

3:16 [g] NU-Text and M-Text read *hot nor cold.*

THE MESSAGE

"I know you inside and out, and find little to my liking. You're not cold, you're not hot—far better to be either cold or hot! You're stale. You're stagnant. You make me want to vomit. You brag, 'I'm rich, I've got it made, I need nothing from anyone,' oblivious that in fact you're a pitiful, blind beggar, threadbare and homeless.

"Here's what I want you to do: Buy your gold from me, gold that's been through the refiner's fire. Then you'll be rich. Buy your clothes from me, clothes designed in Heaven. You've gone around half-naked long enough. And buy medicine for your eyes from me so you can see, *really* see.

"The people I love, I call to account—prod and correct and guide so that they'll live at their best. Up on your feet, then! About face! Run after God!

"Look at me. I stand at the door. I knock. If you hear me call and open the door, I'll come right in and sit down to supper with you. Conquerors will sit alongside me at the head table, just as I, having conquered, took the place of honor at the side of my Father. That's my gift to the conquerors!

"Are your ears awake? Listen. Listen to the Wind Words, the Spirit blowing through the churches."

A Door Into Heaven

4 Then I looked, and, oh!—a door open into Heaven. The trumpet-voice, the first voice in my vision, called out, "Ascend and enter. I'll show you what happens next."

KING JAMES VERSION

2 And immediately I was in the spirit: and, behold, a throne was set in heaven, and *one* sat on the throne.

3 And he that sat was to look upon like a jasper and a sardine stone: and *there was* a rainbow round about the throne, in sight like unto an emerald.

4 And round about the throne *were* four and twenty seats: and upon the seats I saw four and twenty elders sitting, clothed in white raiment; and they had on their heads crowns of gold.

5 And out of the throne proceeded lightnings and thunderings and voices: and *there were* seven lamps of fire burning before the throne, which are the seven Spirits of God.

6 And before the throne *there was* a sea of glass like unto crystal: and in the midst of the throne, and round about the throne, *were* four beasts full of eyes before and behind.

7 And the first beast *was* like a lion, and the second beast like a calf, and the third beast had a face as a man, and the fourth beast *was* like a flying eagle.

8 ¶ And the four beasts had each of them six wings about *him*; and *they were* full of eyes within: and they rest not day and night, saying, Holy, holy, holy, Lord God Almighty, which was, and is, and is to come.

NEW AMERICAN STANDARD BIBLE

2 Immediately I was [l]in the Spirit; and behold, a throne was standing in heaven, and One sitting on the throne.

3 And He who was sitting *was* like a jasper stone and a sardius in appearance; and *there was* a rainbow around the throne, like an emerald in appearance.

4 Around the throne *were* twenty-four thrones; and upon the thrones *I saw* twenty-four elders sitting, clothed in white garments, and golden crowns on their heads.

The Throne and Worship of the Creator

5 Out from the throne come flashes of lightning and sounds and peals of thunder. And *there were* seven lamps of fire burning before the throne, which are the seven Spirits of God;

6 and before the throne *there was something* like a sea of glass, like crystal; and in the center and around the throne, four living creatures full of eyes in front and behind.

7 The first creature *was* like a lion, and the second creature like a calf, and the third creature had a face like that of a man, and the fourth creature *was* like a flying eagle.

8 And the four living creatures, each one of them having six wings, are full of eyes around and within; and day and night they do not cease to say,

"HOLY, HOLY, HOLY *IS* THE LORD GOD, THE ALMIGHTY, WHO
WAS AND WHO IS AND WHO IS TO COME."

4:2 *l* Or *in spirit*

NEW CENTURY VERSION

after this." 2Immediately I was in the Spirit, and before me
was a throne in heaven, and someone was sitting on it. 3The
One who sat on the throne looked like precious stones, like
jasper and carnelian. All around the throne was a rainbow
the color of an emerald. 4Around the throne there were
twenty-four other thrones with twenty-four elders sitting on
them. They were dressed in white and had golden crowns on
their heads. 5Lightning flashes and noises and thundering
came from the throne. Before the throne seven lamps were
burning, which are the seven spirits of God. 6Also before the
throne there was something that looked like a sea of glass,
clear like crystal.

In the center and around the throne were four living
creatures with eyes all over them, in front and in back.
7The first living creature was like a lion. The second was
like a calf. The third had a face like a man. The fourth was
like a flying eagle. 8Each of these four living creatures had
six wings and was covered all over with eyes, inside and
out. Day and night they never stop saying:

"Holy, holy, holy is the Lord God Almighty.
He was, he is, and he is coming."

CONTEMPORARY ENGLISH VERSION

Spirit took control of me, and there in heaven I saw a
throne and someone sitting on it. 3The one who was sitting there sparkled like precious stones of jasper[a] and carnelian.[b] A rainbow that looked like an emerald[c] surrounded the throne.

4Twenty-four other thrones were in a circle around that
throne. And on each of these thrones there was an elder
dressed in white clothes and wearing a gold crown.
5Flashes of lightning and roars of thunder came out from
the throne in the center of the circle. Seven torches, which
are the seven spirits of God, were burning in front of the
throne. 6Also in front of the throne was something that
looked like a glass sea, clear as crystal.

Around the throne in the center were four living creatures covered front and back with eyes. 7The first creature
was like a lion, the second one was like a bull, the third
one had the face of a human, and the fourth was like a flying eagle. 8Each of the four living creatures had six wings,
and their bodies were covered with eyes. Day and night
they never stopped singing,

"Holy, holy, holy is the Lord,
the all-powerful God,
who was and is
and is coming!"

[a] 4.3 *jasper*: Usually green or clear. [b] 4.3 *carnelian*: Usually deep-red or reddish-white. [c] 4.3 *emerald*: A precious stone, usually green.

NEW INTERNATIONAL VERSION

once I was in the Spirit, and there before me was a throne in heaven with someone sitting on it. 3And the one who sat there had the appearance of jasper and carnelian. A rainbow, resembling an emerald, encircled the throne. 4Surrounding the throne were twenty-four other thrones, and seated on them were twenty-four elders. They were dressed in white and had crowns of gold on their heads. 5From the throne came flashes of lightning, rumblings and peals of thunder. Before the throne, seven lamps were blazing. These are the seven spirits[a] of God. 6Also before the throne there was what looked like a sea of glass, clear as crystal.

In the center, around the throne, were four living creatures, and they were covered with eyes, in front and in back. 7The first living creature was like a lion, the second was like an ox, the third had a face like a man, the fourth was like a flying eagle. 8Each of the four living creatures had six wings and was covered with eyes all around, even under his wings. Day and night they never stop saying:

"Holy, holy, holy
is the Lord God Almighty,
who was, and is, and is to come."

[a] *5* Or *the sevenfold Spirit*

NEW LIVING TRANSLATION

things." 2And instantly I was in the Spirit,* and I saw a throne in heaven and someone sitting on it! 3The one sitting on the throne was as brilliant as gemstones—jasper and carnelian. And the glow of an emerald circled his throne like a rainbow. 4Twenty-four thrones surrounded him, and twenty-four elders sat on them. They were all clothed in white and had gold crowns on their heads. 5And from the throne came flashes of lightning and the rumble of thunder. And in front of the throne were seven lampstands with burning flames. They are the seven spirits* of God. 6In front of the throne was a shiny sea of glass, sparkling like crystal.

In the center and around the throne were four living beings, each covered with eyes, front and back. 7The first of these living beings had the form of a lion; the second looked like an ox; the third had a human face; and the fourth had the form of an eagle with wings spread out as though in flight. 8Each of these living beings had six wings, and their wings were covered with eyes, inside and out. Day after day and night after night they keep on saying,

"Holy, holy, holy is the Lord God Almighty—
the one who always was, who is, and who is still to come."

4:2 Or *in spirit.* 4:5 See 1:4 and 3:1, where the same expression is translated *the sevenfold Spirit.*

NEW KING JAMES VERSION

2Immediately I was in the Spirit; and behold, a throne set in heaven, and *One* sat on the throne. 3And He who sat there was[a] like a jasper and a sardius stone in appearance; and *there was* a rainbow around the throne, in appearance like an emerald. 4Around the throne *were* twenty-four thrones, and on the thrones I saw twenty-four elders sitting, clothed in white robes; and they had crowns[b] of gold on their heads. 5And from the throne proceeded lightnings, thunderings, and voices.[c] Seven lamps of fire *were* burning before the throne, which are the[d] seven Spirits of God.

6Before the throne *there was*[e] a sea of glass, like crystal. And in the midst of the throne, and around the throne, *were* four living creatures full of eyes in front and in back. 7The first living creature *was* like a lion, the second living creature like a calf, the third living creature had a face like a man, and the fourth living creature *was* like a flying eagle. 8*The* four living creatures, each having six wings, were full of eyes around and within. And they do not rest day or night, saying:

"Holy, holy, holy,[f]
Lord God Almighty,
Who was and is and is to come!"

4:3 [a] M-Text omits *And He who sat there was* (which makes the description in verse 3 modify the throne rather than God). 4:4 [b] NU-Text and M-Text read *robes, with crowns.* 4:5 [c] NU-Text and M-Text read *voices, and thunderings.* [d] M-Text omits *the.* 4:6 [e] NU-Text and M-Text add *something like.* 4:8 [f] M-Text has *holy* nine times.

THE MESSAGE

I was caught up at once in deep worship and, oh!—a Throne set in Heaven with One Seated on the Throne, suffused in gem hues of amber and flame with a nimbus of emerald. Twenty-four thrones circled the Throne, with Twenty-four Elders seated, white-robed, gold-crowned. Lightning flash and thunder crash pulsed from the Throne. Seven fire-blazing torches fronted the Throne (these are the Sevenfold Spirit of God). Before the Throne it was like a clear crystal sea.

Prowling around the Throne were Four Animals, all eyes. Eyes to look ahead, eyes to look behind. The first Animal like a lion, the second like an ox, the third with a human face, the fourth like an eagle in flight. The Four Animals were winged, each with six wings. They were all eyes, seeing around and within. And they chanted night and day, never taking a break:

"Holy, holy, holy
Is God our Master, Sovereign-Strong,
THE WAS, THE IS, THE COMING."

KING JAMES VERSION

9 And when those beasts give glory and honour and thanks to him that sat on the throne, who liveth for ever and ever,

10 The four and twenty elders fall down before him that sat on the throne, and worship him that liveth for ever and ever, and cast their crowns before the throne, saying,

11 Thou art worthy, O Lord, to receive glory and honour and power: for thou hast created all things, and for thy pleasure they are and were created.

5 And I saw in the right hand of him that sat on the throne a book written within and on the backside, sealed with seven seals.

2 And I saw a strong angel proclaiming with a loud voice, Who is worthy to open the book, and to loose the seals thereof?

3 And no man in heaven, nor in earth, neither under the earth, was able to open the book, neither to look thereon.

4 And I wept much, because no man was found worthy to open and to read the book, neither to look thereon.

NEW AMERICAN STANDARD BIBLE

9 And when the living creatures give glory and honor and thanks to Him who sits on the throne, to Him who lives forever and ever,

10 the twenty-four elders will fall down before Him who sits on the throne, and will worship Him who lives forever and ever, and will cast their crowns before the throne, saying,

11 "Worthy are You, our Lord and our God, to receive
glory and honor and power; for You created all
things, and because of Your will they existed, and
were created."

The Book with Seven Seals

5 I saw in the right hand of Him who sat on the throne a book written inside and on the back, sealed up with seven seals.

2 And I saw a strong angel proclaiming with a loud voice, "Who is worthy to open the book and to break its seals?"

3 And no one in heaven or on the earth or under the earth was able to open the book or to look into it.

4 Then I *began* to weep greatly because no one was found worthy to open the book or to look into it;

NEW CENTURY VERSION

9These living creatures give glory, honor, and thanks to
the One who sits on the throne, who lives forever and ever.
10Then the twenty-four elders bow down before the One
who sits on the throne, and they worship him who lives
forever and ever. They put their crowns down before the
throne and say:

11 "You are worthy, our Lord and God,
to receive glory and honor and power,
because you made all things.
Everything existed and was made,
because you wanted it."

5 Then I saw a scroll in the right hand of the One sitting
on the throne. The scroll had writing on both sides
and was kept closed with seven seals. 2And I saw a power-
ful angel calling in a loud voice, "Who is worthy to break
the seals and open the scroll?" 3But there was no one in
heaven or on earth or under the earth who could open the
scroll or look inside it. 4I cried hard because there was no
one who was worthy to open the scroll or look inside. 5But

CONTEMPORARY ENGLISH VERSION

9The living creatures kept praising, honoring, and
thanking the one who sits on the throne and who lives for-
ever and ever. 10At the same time the twenty-four elders
knelt down before the one sitting on the throne. And as
they worshiped the one who lives forever, they placed their
crowns in front of the throne and said,

11 "Our Lord and God,
you are worthy
to receive glory,
honor, and power.
You created all things,
and by your decision they are
and were created."

The Scroll and the Lamb

5 In the right hand of the one sitting on the throne I
saw a scroll[a] that had writing on the inside and on
the outside. And it was sealed in seven places. 2I saw a
mighty angel ask with a loud voice, "Who is worthy to
open the scroll and break its seals?" 3No one in heaven or
on earth or under the earth was able to open the scroll or
see inside it.

4I cried hard because no one was found worthy to open
the scroll or see inside it. 5Then one of the elders said to

[a] 5.1 *scroll*: A roll of paper or special leather used for writing on. Sometimes a scroll would be sealed on the outside with one or more pieces of wax.

NEW INTERNATIONAL VERSION

[9]Whenever the living creatures give glory, honor and
thanks to him who sits on the throne and who lives for
ever and ever, [10]the twenty-four elders fall down before
him who sits on the throne, and worship him who lives for
ever and ever. They lay their crowns before the throne and
say:

[11]"You are worthy, our Lord and God,
to receive glory and honor and power,
for you created all things,
and by your will they were created
and have their being."

The Scroll and the Lamb

5 Then I saw in the right hand of him who sat on the
throne a scroll with writing on both sides and sealed
with seven seals. [2]And I saw a mighty angel proclaiming
in a loud voice, "Who is worthy to break the seals and
open the scroll?" [3]But no one in heaven or on earth or
under the earth could open the scroll or even look inside it.
[4]I wept and wept because no one was found who was wor-
thy to open the scroll or look inside. [5]Then one of the

NEW LIVING TRANSLATION

[9]Whenever the living beings give glory and honor and
thanks to the one sitting on the throne, the one who lives
forever and ever, [10]the twenty-four elders fall down and
worship the one who lives forever and ever. And they lay
their crowns before the throne and say,

[11]"You are worthy, O Lord our God,
to receive glory and honor and power.
For you created everything,
and it is for your pleasure that they exist and were
created."

The Lamb Opens the Scroll

5 And I saw a scroll in the right hand of the one who
was sitting on the throne. There was writing on the
inside and the outside of the scroll, and it was sealed with
seven seals. [2]And I saw a strong angel, who shouted with
a loud voice: "Who is worthy to break the seals on this
scroll and unroll it?" [3]But no one in heaven or on earth or
under the earth was able to open the scroll and read it.
[4]Then I wept because no one could be found who was
worthy to open the scroll and read it. [5]But one of the

NEW KING JAMES VERSION

[9]Whenever the living creatures give glory and honor and
thanks to Him who sits on the throne, who lives forever
and ever, [10]the twenty-four elders fall down before Him
who sits on the throne and worship Him who lives forever
and ever, and cast their crowns before the throne, saying:

[11]"You are worthy, O Lord,[g]
To receive glory and honor and power;
For You created all things,
And by Your will they exist[h] and were created."

The Lamb Takes the Scroll

5 And I saw in the right *hand* of Him who sat on the
throne a scroll written inside and on the back, sealed
with seven seals. [2]Then I saw a strong angel proclaiming
with a loud voice, "Who is worthy to open the scroll and to
loose its seals?" [3]And no one in heaven or on the earth or
under the earth was able to open the scroll, or to look at it.
[4]So I wept much, because no one was found worthy to
open and read[a] the scroll, or to look at it. [5]But one of the

4:11 [g] NU-Text and M-Text read *our Lord and God.* [h] NU-Text and M-Text read *existed.* 5:4 [a] NU-Text and M-Text omit *and read.*

THE MESSAGE

Every time the Animals gave glory and honor and
thanks to the One Seated on the Throne—the age-after-age
Living One—the Twenty-four Elders would fall prostrate
before the One Seated on the Throne. They worshiped the
age-after-age Living One. They threw their crowns at the
foot of the Throne, chanting,

"Worthy, Oh Master! Yes, our God!
Take the glory! the honor! the power!
You created it all;
It was created because you wanted it."

The Lion Is a Lamb

5 I saw a scroll in the right hand of the One Seated on
the Throne. It was written on both sides, fastened
with seven seals. I also saw a powerful Angel, calling out
in a voice like thunder, "Is there anyone who can open the
scroll, who can break its seals?"

There was no one—no one in Heaven, no one on earth,
no one from the underworld—able to break open the scroll
and read it.

I wept and wept and wept that no one was found able to
open the scroll, able to read it. One of the Elders said,

KING JAMES VERSION

5 And one of the elders saith unto me, Weep not: behold, the Lion of the tribe of Juda, the Root of David, hath prevailed to open the book, and to loose the seven seals thereof.

6 ¶ And I beheld, and, lo, in the midst of the throne and of the four beasts, and in the midst of the elders, stood a Lamb as it had been slain, having seven horns and seven eyes, which are the seven Spirits of God sent forth into all the earth.

7 And he came and took the book out of the right hand of him that sat upon the throne.

8 And when he had taken the book, the four beasts and four *and* twenty elders fell down before the Lamb, having every one of them harps, and golden vials full of odours, which are the prayers of saints.

9 And they sung a new song, saying, Thou art worthy to take the book, and to open the seals thereof: for thou wast slain, and hast redeemed us to God by thy blood out of

NEW AMERICAN STANDARD BIBLE

5 and one of the elders *said to me, "Stop weeping; behold, the Lion that is from the tribe of Judah, the Root of David, has overcome so as to open the book and its seven seals."

6 And I saw [1]between the throne (with the four living creatures) and the elders a Lamb standing, as if slain, having seven horns and seven eyes, which are the seven Spirits of God, sent out into all the earth.

7 And He came and took the book out of the right hand of Him who sat on the throne.

8 When He had taken the book, the four living creatures and the twenty-four elders fell down before the Lamb, each one holding a harp and golden bowls full of incense, which are the prayers of the saints.

9 And they *sang a new song, saying,

"Worthy are You to take the book and to break its
seals; for You were slain, and purchased for God with

5:6 [1] Lit *in the middle of the throne and of the four living creatures, and in the middle of the elders*

NEW CENTURY VERSION

one of the elders said to me, "Do not cry! The Lion[a] from
the tribe of Judah, David's descendant, has won the victory
so that he is able to open the scroll and its seven seals."
6Then I saw a Lamb standing in the center of the throne
and in the middle of the four living creatures and the
elders. The Lamb looked as if he had been killed. He had
seven horns and seven eyes, which are the seven spirits of
God that were sent into all the world. 7The Lamb came and
took the scroll from the right hand of the One sitting on
the throne. 8When he took the scroll, the four living crea-
tures and the twenty-four elders bowed down before the
Lamb. Each one of them had a harp and golden bowls full
of incense, which are the prayers of God's holy people.
9And they all sang a new song to the Lamb:

"You are worthy to take the scroll
and to open its seals,
because you were killed,
and with the blood of your death you bought people
for God

5:5 [a] **Lion** Here refers to Christ.

CONTEMPORARY ENGLISH VERSION

me, "Stop crying and look! The one who is called both the
'Lion from the Tribe of Judah'[b] and 'King David's Great
Descendant'[c] has won the victory. He will open the book
and its seven seals."
6Then I looked and saw a Lamb standing in the center of
the throne that was surrounded by the four living crea-
tures and the elders. The Lamb looked as if it had once
been killed. It had seven horns and seven eyes, which are
the seven spirits[d] of God, sent out to all the earth.
7The Lamb went over and took the scroll from the right
hand of the one who sat on the throne. 8After he had taken
it, the four living creatures and the twenty-four elders
knelt down before him. Each of them had a harp and a
gold bowl full of incense,[e] which are the prayers of God's
people. 9Then they sang a new song,

"You are worthy
to receive the scroll
and open its seals,
because you were killed.
And with your own blood
you bought for God

[b] **5.5** *'Lion from the Tribe of Judah'*: In Genesis 49.9 the tribe of Judah is called a young lion, and King David was from Judah. [c] **5.5** *'King David's Great Descendant'*: The Greek text has "the root of David" which is a title for the Messiah based on Isaiah 11.1, 10. [d] **5.6** *the seven spirits*: Some manuscripts have "the spirits." [e] **5.8** *incense*: A material that produces a sweet smell when burned. Sometimes it is a symbol for the prayers of God's people.

NEW INTERNATIONAL VERSION

elders said to me, "Do not weep! See, the Lion of the tribe
of Judah, the Root of David, has triumphed. He is able to
open the scroll and its seven seals."
6Then I saw a Lamb, looking as if it had been slain,
standing in the center of the throne, encircled by the four
living creatures and the elders. He had seven horns and
seven eyes, which are the seven spirits[a] of God sent out
into all the earth. 7He came and took the scroll from the
right hand of him who sat on the throne. 8And when he
had taken it, the four living creatures and the twenty-four
elders fell down before the Lamb. Each one had a harp and
they were holding golden bowls full of incense, which are
the prayers of the saints. 9And they sang a new song:

"You are worthy to take the scroll
  and to open its seals,
because you were slain,
  and with your blood you purchased men for God

[a] 6 Or *the sevenfold Spirit*

NEW LIVING TRANSLATION

twenty-four elders said to me, "Stop weeping! Look, the
Lion of the tribe of Judah, the heir to David's throne,* has
conquered. He is worthy to open the scroll and break its
seven seals."
6I looked and I saw a Lamb that had been killed but was
now standing between the throne and the four living
beings and among the twenty-four elders. He had seven
horns and seven eyes, which are the seven spirits* of God
that are sent out into every part of the earth. 7He stepped
forward and took the scroll from the right hand of the one
sitting on the throne. 8And as he took the scroll, the four
living beings and the twenty-four elders fell down before
the Lamb. Each one had a harp, and they held gold bowls
filled with incense—the prayers of God's people!
9And they sang a new song with these words:

"You are worthy to take the scroll
  and break its seals and open it.
For you were killed, and your blood has ransomed
    people for God

5:5 Greek *the root of David.* **5:6** See note on 4:5.

NEW KING JAMES VERSION

elders said to me, "Do not weep. Behold, the Lion of the
tribe of Judah, the Root of David, has prevailed to open the
scroll and to loose[b] its seven seals."
6And I looked, and behold,[c] in the midst of the throne
and of the four living creatures, and in the midst of the
elders, stood a Lamb as though it had been slain, having
seven horns and seven eyes, which are the seven Spirits of
God sent out into all the earth. 7Then He came and took the
scroll out of the right hand of Him who sat on the throne.

Worthy Is the Lamb

8Now when He had taken the scroll, the four living crea-
tures and the twenty-four elders fell down before the
Lamb, each having a harp, and golden bowls full of
incense, which are the prayers of the saints. 9And they
sang a new song, saying:

"You are worthy to take the scroll,
And to open its seals;
For You were slain,
And have redeemed us to God by Your blood

5:5 [b] NU-Text and M-Text omit *to loose.* **5:6** [c] NU-Text and M-Text read *I saw in the midst . . . a Lamb standing.*

THE MESSAGE

"Don't weep. Look—the Lion from Tribe Judah, the Root of David's Tree, has conquered. He can open the scroll, can rip through the seven seals."

So I looked, and there, surrounded by Throne, Animals, and Elders, was a Lamb, slaughtered but standing tall. Seven horns he had, and seven eyes, the Seven Spirits of God sent into all the earth. He came to the One Seated on the Throne and took the scroll from his right hand. The moment he took the scroll, the Four Animals and Twenty-four Elders fell down and worshiped the Lamb. Each had a harp and each had a bowl, a gold bowl filled with incense, the prayers of God's holy people. And they sang a new song:

"Worthy! Take the scroll, open its seals.
Slain! Paying in blood, you bought men and women,

KING JAMES VERSION

every kindred, and tongue, and people, and nation;
10 And hast made us unto our God kings and priests:
and we shall reign on the earth.
11 And I beheld, and I heard the voice of many angels
round about the throne and the beasts and the elders: and
the number of them was ten thousand times ten thousand,
and thousands of thousands;
12 Saying with a loud voice, Worthy is the Lamb that
was slain to receive power, and riches, and wisdom, and
strength, and honour, and glory, and blessing.
13 And every creature which is in heaven, and on the
earth, and under the earth, and such as are in the sea, and
all that are in them, heard I saying, Blessing, and honour,
and glory, and power, *be* unto him that sitteth upon the
throne, and unto the Lamb for ever and ever.
14 And the four beasts said, Amen. And the four *and*
twenty elders fell down and worshipped him that liveth for
ever and ever.

NEW AMERICAN STANDARD BIBLE

Your blood *men* from every tribe and tongue and people and nation.

10 "You have made them *to be* a kingdom and priests to our God; and they will reign upon the earth."

Angels Exalt the Lamb

11 Then I looked, and I heard the voice of many angels
around the throne and the living creatures and the elders;
and the number of them was myriads of myriads, and
thousands of thousands,
12 saying with a loud voice,

"Worthy is the Lamb that was slain to receive power and riches and wisdom and might and honor and glory and blessing."

13 And every created thing which is in heaven and on
the earth and under the earth and on the sea, and all
things in them, I heard saying,

"To Him who sits on the throne, and to the Lamb, *be* blessing and honor and glory and dominion forever and ever."

14 And the four living creatures kept saying, "Amen."
And the elders fell down and worshiped.

NEW CENTURY VERSION

from every tribe, language, people, and nation.
10 You made them to be a kingdom of priests for our God,
and they will rule on the earth."

11 Then I looked, and I heard the voices of many angels
around the throne, and the four living creatures, and the
elders. There were thousands and thousands of angels,
12 saying in a loud voice:
"The Lamb who was killed is worthy
to receive power, wealth, wisdom, and strength,
honor, glory, and praise!"

13 Then I heard all creatures in heaven and on earth and
under the earth and in the sea saying:
"To the One who sits on the throne
and to the Lamb
be praise and honor and glory and power
forever and ever."

14 The four living creatures said, "Amen," and the elders
bowed down and worshiped.

CONTEMPORARY ENGLISH VERSION

people from every tribe,
language, nation, and race.
10 You let them become kings
and serve God as priests,
and they will rule on earth."

11 As I looked, I heard the voices of a lot of angels
around the throne and the voices of the living creatures
and of the elders. There were millions and millions of
them, 12 and they were saying in a loud voice,

"The Lamb who was killed
is worthy to receive power,
riches, wisdom, strength,
honor, glory, and praise."

13 Then I heard all beings in heaven and on the earth and
under the earth and in the sea offer praise. Together, all of
them were saying,

"Praise, honor, glory,
and strength
forever and ever
to the one who sits
on the throne
and to the Lamb!"

14 The four living creatures said "Amen," while the elders
knelt down and worshiped.

NEW INTERNATIONAL VERSION

from every tribe and language and people and nation.
10 You have made them to be a kingdom and priests to serve our God,
and they will reign on the earth."

11 Then I looked and heard the voice of many angels, numbering thousands upon thousands, and ten thousand times ten thousand. They encircled the throne and the living creatures and the elders. 12 In a loud voice they sang:

"Worthy is the Lamb, who was slain,
to receive power and wealth and wisdom and strength
and honor and glory and praise!"

13 Then I heard every creature in heaven and on earth and under the earth and on the sea, and all that is in them, singing:

"To him who sits on the throne and to the Lamb
be praise and honor and glory and power,
for ever and ever!"

14 The four living creatures said, "Amen," and the elders fell down and worshiped.

NEW LIVING TRANSLATION

from every tribe and language and people and nation.
10 And you have caused them to become God's Kingdom
and his priests.
And they will reign* on the earth."

11 Then I looked again, and I heard the singing of thousands and millions of angels around the throne and the living beings and the elders. 12 And they sang in a mighty chorus:

"The Lamb is worthy—the Lamb who was killed.
He is worthy to receive power and riches
and wisdom and strength
and honor and glory and blessing."

13 And then I heard every creature in heaven and on earth and under the earth and in the sea. They also sang:

"Blessing and honor and glory and power
belong to the one sitting on the throne
and to the Lamb forever and ever."

14 And the four living beings said, "Amen!" And the twenty-four elders fell down and worshiped God and the Lamb.

5:10 Some manuscripts read *they are reigning.*

NEW KING JAMES VERSION

Out of every tribe and tongue and people and nation,
10 And have made us[d] kings[e] and priests to our God;
And we[f] shall reign on the earth."

11 Then I looked, and I heard the voice of many angels around the throne, the living creatures, and the elders; and the number of them was ten thousand times ten thousand, and thousands of thousands, 12 saying with a loud voice:

"Worthy is the Lamb who was slain
To receive power and riches and wisdom,
And strength and honor and glory and blessing!"

13 And every creature which is in heaven and on the earth and under the earth and such as are in the sea, and all that are in them, I heard saying:

"Blessing and honor and glory and power
Be to Him who sits on the throne,
And to the Lamb, forever and ever!"[g]

14 Then the four living creatures said, "Amen!" And the twenty-four[h] elders fell down and worshiped Him who lives forever and ever.[i]

5:10 [d] NU-Text and M-Text read *them.* [e] NU-Text reads *a kingdom.* [f] NU-Text and M-Text read *they.* 5:13 [g] M-Text adds *Amen.* 5:14 [h] NU-Text and M-Text omit *twenty-four.* [i] NU-Text and M-Text omit *Him who lives forever and ever.*

THE MESSAGE

Bought them back from all over the earth,
Bought them back for God.
Then you made them a Kingdom, Priests for our God,
Priest-kings to rule over the earth."

I looked again. I heard a company of Angels around the Throne, the Animals, and the Elders—ten thousand times ten thousand their number, thousand after thousand after thousand in full song:

"The slain Lamb is worthy!
Take the power, the wealth, the wisdom, the strength!
Take the honor, the glory, the blessing!"

Then I heard every creature in Heaven and earth, in underworld and sea, join in, all voices in all places, singing:

"To the One on the Throne! To the Lamb!
The blessing, the honor, the glory, the strength,
For age after age after age."

The Four Animals called out, "Oh, Yes!" The Elders fell to their knees and worshiped.

KING JAMES VERSION

6 And I saw when the Lamb opened one of the seals, and I heard, as it were the noise of thunder, one of the four beasts saying, Come and see.

2 And I saw, and behold a white horse: and he that sat on him had a bow; and a crown was given unto him: and he went forth conquering, and to conquer.

3 ¶ And when he had opened the second seal, I heard the second beast say, Come and see.

4 And there went out another horse *that was* red: and *power* was given to him that sat thereon to take peace from the earth, and that they should kill one another: and there was given unto him a great sword.

5 And when he had opened the third seal, I heard the third beast say, Come and see. And I beheld, and lo a black horse; and he that sat on him had a pair of balances in his hand.

6 And I heard a voice in the midst of the four beasts say, A measure of wheat for a penny, and three measures of barley for a penny; and *see* thou hurt not the oil and the wine.

NEW AMERICAN STANDARD BIBLE

The Book Opened; The First Seal—False Christ

6 Then I saw when the Lamb broke one of the seven seals, and I heard one of the four living creatures saying as with a voice of thunder, "Come."

2 I looked, and behold, a white horse, and he who sat on it had a bow; and a crown was given to him, and he went out conquering and to conquer.

The Second Seal—War

3 When He broke the second seal, I heard the second living creature saying, "Come."

4 And another, a red horse, went out; and to him who sat on it, it was granted to take peace from the earth, and that *men* would slay one another; and a great sword was given to him.

The Third Seal—Famine

5 When He broke the third seal, I heard the third living creature saying, "Come." I looked, and behold, a black horse; and he who sat on it had a pair of scales in his hand.

6 And I heard *something* like a voice in the center of the four living creatures saying, "A [1]quart of wheat for a [2]denarius, and three quarts of barley for a denarius; and do not damage the oil and the wine."

6:6 [1] Gr *choenix;* i.e. a dry measure almost equal to a qt **6:6** [2] The denarius was equivalent to a day's wages

NEW CENTURY VERSION

6 Then I watched while the Lamb opened the first of the
seven seals. I heard one of the four living creatures
say with a voice like thunder, "Come!" 2I looked, and there
before me was a white horse. The rider on the horse held a
bow, and he was given a crown, and he rode out, determined to win the victory.
3When the Lamb opened the second seal, I heard the
second living creature say, "Come!" 4Then another horse
came out, a red one. Its rider was given power to take
away peace from the earth and to make people kill each
other, and he was given a big sword.
5When the Lamb opened the third seal, I heard the third
living creature say, "Come!" I looked, and there before me
was a black horse, and its rider held a pair of scales in his
hand. 6Then I heard something that sounded like a voice
coming from the middle of the four living creatures. The
voice said, "A quart of wheat for a day's pay, and three
quarts of barley for a day's pay, and do not damage the
olive oil and wine!"

CONTEMPORARY ENGLISH VERSION

Opening the Seven Seals

6 At the same time that I saw the Lamb open the first of
the seven seals, I heard one of the four living creatures shout with a voice like thunder. It said, "Come out!"
2Then I saw a white horse. Its rider carried a bow and was
given a crown. He had already won some victories, and he
went out to win more.
3When the Lamb opened the second seal, I heard the
second living creature say, "Come out!" 4Then another
horse came out. It was fiery red. And its rider was given
the power to take away all peace from the earth, so that
people would slaughter one another. He was also given a
big sword.
5When the Lamb opened the third seal, I heard the third
living creature say, "Come out!" Then I saw a black horse,
and its rider had a balance scale in one hand. 6I heard
what sounded like a voice from somewhere among the four
living creatures. It said, "A quart of wheat will cost you a
whole day's wages! Three quarts of barley will cost you a
day's wages too. But don't ruin the olive oil or the wine."

NEW INTERNATIONAL VERSION

The Seals

6 I watched as the Lamb opened the first of the seven seals. Then I heard one of the four living creatures say in a voice like thunder, "Come!" 2 I looked, and there before me was a white horse! Its rider held a bow, and he was given a crown, and he rode out as a conqueror bent on conquest.

3 When the Lamb opened the second seal, I heard the second living creature say, "Come!" 4 Then another horse came out, a fiery red one. Its rider was given power to take peace from the earth and to make men slay each other. To him was given a large sword.

5 When the Lamb opened the third seal, I heard the third living creature say, "Come!" I looked, and there before me was a black horse! Its rider was holding a pair of scales in his hand. 6 Then I heard what sounded like a voice among the four living creatures, saying, "A quart[a] of wheat for a day's wages,[b] and three quarts of barley for a day's wages,[b] and do not damage the oil and the wine!"

[a] 6 Greek *a choinix* (probably about a liter) [b] 6 Greek *a denarius*

NEW LIVING TRANSLATION

The Lamb Breaks the First Six Seals

6 As I watched, the Lamb broke the first of the seven seals on the scroll. Then one of the four living beings called out with a voice that sounded like thunder, "Come!" 2 I looked up and saw a white horse. Its rider carried a bow, and a crown was placed on his head. He rode out to win many battles and gain the victory.

3 When the Lamb broke the second seal, I heard the second living being say, "Come!" 4 And another horse appeared, a red one. Its rider was given a mighty sword and the authority to remove peace from the earth. And there was war and slaughter everywhere.

5 When the Lamb broke the third seal, I heard the third living being say, "Come!" And I looked up and saw a black horse, and its rider was holding a pair of scales in his hand. 6 And a voice from among the four living beings said, "A loaf of wheat bread or three loaves of barley for a day's pay.* And don't waste* the olive oil and wine."

6:6a Greek *A choinix of wheat for a denarius, and 3 choinix of barley for a denarius.* **6:6b** Or *hurt.*

NEW KING JAMES VERSION

First Seal: The Conqueror

6 Now I saw when the Lamb opened one of the seals;[a] and I heard one of the four living creatures saying with a voice like thunder, "Come and see." 2 And I looked, and behold, a white horse. He who sat on it had a bow; and a crown was given to him, and he went out conquering and to conquer.

Second Seal: Conflict on Earth

3 When He opened the second seal, I heard the second living creature saying, "Come and see."[b] 4 Another horse, fiery red, went out. And it was granted to the one who sat on it to take peace from the earth, and that *people* should kill one another; and there was given to him a great sword.

Third Seal: Scarcity on Earth

5 When He opened the third seal, I heard the third living creature say, "Come and see." So I looked, and behold, a black horse, and he who sat on it had a pair of scales in his hand. 6 And I heard a voice in the midst of the four living creatures saying, "A quart[c] of wheat for a denarius,[d] and three quarts of barley for a denarius; and do not harm the oil and the wine."

6:1 [a] NU-Text and M-Text read *seven seals.* **6:3** [b] NU-Text and M-Text omit *and see.* **6:6** [c] Greek *choinix;* that is, approximately one quart [d] This was approximately one day's wage for a worker.

THE MESSAGE

Unsealing the Scroll

6 I watched while the Lamb ripped off the first of the seven seals. I heard one of the Animals roar, "Come out!" I looked—I saw a white horse. Its rider carried a bow and was given a victory garland. He rode off victorious, conquering right and left.

When the Lamb ripped off the second seal, I heard the second Animal cry, "Come out!" Another horse appeared, this one red. Its rider was off to take peace from the earth, setting people at each other's throats, killing one another. He was given a huge sword.

When he ripped off the third seal, I heard the third Animal cry, "Come out!" I looked. A black horse this time. Its rider carried a set of scales in his hand. I heard a message (it seemed to issue from the Four Animals): "A quart of wheat for a day's wages, or three quarts of barley, but all the oil and wine you want."

KING JAMES VERSION

7 And when he had opened the fourth seal, I heard the voice of the fourth beast say, Come and see.

8 And I looked, and behold a pale horse: and his name that sat on him was Death, and Hell followed with him. And power was given unto them over the fourth part of the earth, to kill with sword, and with hunger, and with death, and with the beasts of the earth.

9 ¶ And when he had opened the fifth seal, I saw under the altar the souls of them that were slain for the word of God, and for the testimony which they held:

10 And they cried with a loud voice, saying, How long, O Lord, holy and true, dost thou not judge and avenge our blood on them that dwell on the earth?

11 And white robes were given unto every one of them; and it was said unto them, that they should rest yet for a little season, until their fellowservants also and their brethren, that should be killed as they *were*, should be fulfilled.

12 And I beheld when he had opened the sixth seal, and, lo, there was a great earthquake; and the sun became black as sackcloth of hair, and the moon became as blood;

13 And the stars of heaven fell unto the earth, even as a fig tree casteth her untimely figs, when she is shaken of a mighty wind.

NEW AMERICAN STANDARD BIBLE

The Fourth Seal—Death

7 When the Lamb broke the fourth seal, I heard the voice of the fourth living creature saying, "Come."

8 I looked, and behold, an ashen horse; and he who sat on it had the name Death; and Hades was following with him. Authority was given to them over a fourth of the earth, to kill with sword and with famine and with pestilence and by the wild beasts of the earth.

The Fifth Seal—Martyrs

9 When the Lamb broke the fifth seal, I saw underneath the altar the souls of those who had been slain because of the word of God, and because of the testimony which they had maintained;

10 and they cried out with a loud voice, saying, "How long, O Lord, holy and true, will You refrain from judging and avenging our blood on those who dwell on the earth?"

11 And there was given to each of them a white robe; and they were told that they should rest for a little while longer, until *the number of* their fellow servants and their brethren who were to be killed even as they had been, would be completed also.

The Sixth Seal—Terror

12 I looked when He broke the sixth seal, and there was a great earthquake; and the sun became black as sackcloth *made* of hair, and the whole moon became like blood;

13 and the stars of the sky fell to the earth, as a fig tree casts its unripe figs when shaken by a great wind.

NEW CENTURY VERSION

7When the Lamb opened the fourth seal, I heard the
voice of the fourth living creature say, "Come!" 8I looked,
and there before me was a pale horse. Its rider was named
death, and Hades[a] was following close behind him. They
were given power over a fourth of the earth to kill people
by war, by starvation, by disease, and by the wild animals
of the earth.

9When the Lamb opened the fifth seal, I saw under the
altar the souls of those who had been killed because they
were faithful to the word of God and to the message they
had received. 10These souls shouted in a loud voice, "Holy
and true Lord, how long until you judge the people of the
earth and punish them for killing us?" 11Then each one of
them was given a white robe and was told to wait a short
time longer. There were still some of their fellow servants
and brothers and sisters[b] in the service of Christ who must
be killed as they were. They had to wait until all of this
was finished.

12Then I watched while the Lamb opened the sixth seal,
and there was a great earthquake. The sun became black
like rough black cloth, and the whole moon became red
like blood. 13And the stars in the sky fell to the earth like
figs falling from a fig tree when the wind blows. 14The sky

6:8 [a] **Hades** The unseen world of the dead. **6:11** [b] **brothers and sisters** Although the Greek text says "brothers" here and throughout this book, both men and women would have been included.

CONTEMPORARY ENGLISH VERSION

7When the Lamb opened the fourth seal, I heard the
voice of the fourth living creature say, "Come out!" 8Then I
saw a pale green horse. Its rider was named Death, and
Death's Kingdom followed behind. They were given power
over one fourth of the earth, and they could kill its people
with swords, famines, diseases, and wild animals.

9When the Lamb opened the fifth seal, I saw under the
altar the souls of everyone who had been killed for speak-
ing God's message and telling about their faith. 10They
shouted, "Master, you are holy and faithful! How long will
it be before you judge and punish the people of this earth
who killed us?"

11Then each of those who had been killed was given a
white robe and told to rest for a little while. They had to
wait until the complete number of the Lord's other ser-
vants and followers would be killed.

12When I saw the Lamb open the sixth seal, I looked and
saw a great earthquake. The sun turned as dark as sack-
cloth,[a] and the moon became as red as blood. 13The stars
in the sky fell to earth, just like figs shaken loose by a

[a] **6.12** *sackcloth*: A rough, dark-colored cloth made from goat or camel hair and used to make grain sacks. It was worn in times of trouble or sorrow.

NEW INTERNATIONAL VERSION

7When the Lamb opened the fourth seal, I heard the
voice of the fourth living creature say, "Come!" 8I looked,
and there before me was a pale horse! Its rider was named
Death, and Hades was following close behind him. They
were given power over a fourth of the earth to kill by
sword, famine and plague, and by the wild beasts of the
earth.
9When he opened the fifth seal, I saw under the altar the
souls of those who had been slain because of the word of
God and the testimony they had maintained. 10They called
out in a loud voice, "How long, Sovereign Lord, holy and
true, until you judge the inhabitants of the earth and
avenge our blood?" 11Then each of them was given a white
robe, and they were told to wait a little longer, until the
number of their fellow servants and brothers who were to
be killed as they had been was completed.
12I watched as he opened the sixth seal. There was a
great earthquake. The sun turned black like sackcloth
made of goat hair, the whole moon turned blood red, 13and
the stars in the sky fell to earth, as late figs drop from a fig
tree when shaken by a strong wind. 14The sky receded like

NEW LIVING TRANSLATION

7And when the Lamb broke the fourth seal, I heard the
fourth living being say, "Come!" 8And I looked up and saw
a horse whose color was pale green like a corpse. And
Death was the name of its rider, who was followed around
by the Grave.* They were given authority over one-fourth
of the earth, to kill with the sword and famine and dis-
ease* and wild animals.
9And when the Lamb broke the fifth seal, I saw under
the altar the souls of all who had been martyred for the
word of God and for being faithful in their witness. 10They
called loudly to the Lord and said, "O Sovereign Lord, holy
and true, how long will it be before you judge the people
who belong to this world for what they have done to us?
When will you avenge our blood against these people?"
11Then a white robe was given to each of them. And they
were told to rest a little longer until the full number of
their brothers and sisters*—their fellow servants of
Jesus—had been martyred.
12I watched as the Lamb broke the sixth seal, and there
was a great earthquake. The sun became as dark as black
cloth, and the moon became as red as blood. 13Then the
stars of the sky fell to the earth like green figs falling from
trees shaken by mighty winds. 14And the sky was rolled up

6:8a Greek *by Hades.* **6:8b** Greek *death.* **6:11** Greek *their brothers.*

NEW KING JAMES VERSION

Fourth Seal: Widespread Death on Earth

7When He opened the fourth seal, I heard the voice of
the fourth living creature saying, "Come and see." 8So I
looked, and behold, a pale horse. And the name of him
who sat on it was Death, and Hades followed with him.
And power was given to them over a fourth of the earth, to
kill with sword, with hunger, with death, and by the
beasts of the earth.

Fifth Seal: The Cry of the Martyrs

9When He opened the fifth seal, I saw under the altar the
souls of those who had been slain for the word of God and
for the testimony which they held. 10And they cried with a
loud voice, saying, "How long, O Lord, holy and true, until
You judge and avenge our blood on those who dwell on the
earth?" 11Then a white robe was given to each of them; and
it was said to them that they should rest a little while longer,
until both *the number of* their fellow servants and their
brethren, who would be killed as they *were,* was completed.

Sixth Seal: Cosmic Disturbances

12I looked when He opened the sixth seal, and behold,[e]
there was a great earthquake; and the sun became black
as sackcloth of hair, and the moon[f] became like blood.
13And the stars of heaven fell to the earth, as a fig tree
drops its late figs when it is shaken by a mighty wind.

6:12 [e] NU-Text and M-Text omit *behold.* [f] NU-Text and M-Text read *the whole moon.*

THE MESSAGE

When he ripped off the fourth seal, I heard the fourth
Animal cry, "Come out!" I looked. A colorless horse, sickly
pale. Its rider was Death, and Hell was close on its heels.
They were given power to destroy a fourth of the earth by
war, famine, disease, and wild beasts.

When he ripped off the fifth seal, I saw the souls of
those killed because they had held firm in their witness to
the Word of God. They were gathered under the Altar, and
cried out in loud prayers, "How long, Strong God, Holy and
True? How long before you step in and avenge our mur-
ders?" Then each martyr was given a white robe and told
to sit back and wait until the full number of martyrs was
filled from among their servant companions and friends in
the faith.

I watched while he ripped off the sixth seal: a bone-jar-
ring earthquake, sun turned black as ink, moon all bloody,
stars falling out of the sky like figs shaken from a tree in a

KING JAMES VERSION

14 And the heaven departed as a scroll when it is rolled
together; and every mountain and island were moved out
of their places.
15 And the kings of the earth, and the great men, and
the rich men, and the chief captains, and the mighty men,
and every bondman, and every free man, hid themselves in
the dens and in the rocks of the mountains;
16 And said to the mountains and rocks, Fall on us, and
hide us from the face of him that sitteth on the throne, and
from the wrath of the Lamb:
17 For the great day of his wrath is come; and who
shall be able to stand?
7 And after these things I saw four angels standing on
the four corners of the earth, holding the four winds
of the earth, that the wind should not blow on the earth,
nor on the sea, nor on any tree.
2 And I saw another angel ascending from the east,
having the seal of the living God: and he cried with a loud
voice to the four angels, to whom it was given to hurt the
earth and the sea,
3 Saying, Hurt not the earth, neither the sea, nor the
trees, till we have sealed the servants of our God in their
foreheads.

NEW AMERICAN STANDARD BIBLE

14 The sky was split apart like a scroll when it is rolled
up, and every mountain and island were moved out of
their places.
15 Then the kings of the earth and the great men and
the [3]commanders and the rich and the strong and every
slave and free man hid themselves in the caves and among
the rocks of the mountains;
16 and they *said to the mountains and to the rocks,
"Fall on us and hide us from the presence of Him who sits
on the throne, and from the wrath of the Lamb;
17 for the great day of their wrath has come, and who is
able to stand?"

An Interlude

7 After this I saw four angels standing at the four cor-
ners of the earth, holding back the four winds of the
earth, so that no wind would blow on the earth or on the
sea or on any tree.
2 And I saw another angel ascending from the rising of
the sun, having the seal of the living God; and he cried out
with a loud voice to the four angels to whom it was grant-
ed to harm the earth and the sea,
3 saying, "Do not harm the earth or the sea or the trees
until we have sealed the bond-servants of our God on their
foreheads."

6:15 [3] I.e. chiliarchs, in command of one thousand troops

NEW CENTURY VERSION

disappeared as a scroll when it is rolled up, and every
mountain and island was moved from its place.
15Then the kings of the earth, the rulers, the generals,
the rich people, the powerful people, the slaves, and the
free people hid themselves in caves and in the rocks on the
mountains. 16They called to the mountains and the rocks,
"Fall on us. Hide us from the face of the One who sits on
the throne and from the anger of the Lamb! 17The great
day for their anger has come, and who can stand against
it?"

The 144,000 People of Israel

7 After the vision of these things I saw four angels
standing at the four corners of the earth. The angels
were holding the four winds of the earth to keep them from
blowing on the land or on the sea or on any tree. 2Then I
saw another angel coming up from the east who had the
seal of the living God. And he called out in a loud voice to
the four angels to whom God had given power to harm the
earth and the sea. 3He said to them, "Do not harm the land
or the sea or the trees until we mark with a sign the fore-
heads of the people who serve our God." 4Then I heard

CONTEMPORARY ENGLISH VERSION

windstorm. 14Then the sky was rolled up like a scroll,[b] and
all mountains and islands were moved from their places.
15The kings of the earth, its famous people, and its mili-
tary leaders hid in caves or behind rocks on the moun-
tains. They hid there together with the rich and the power-
ful and with all the slaves and free people. 16Then they
shouted to the mountains and the rocks, "Fall on us! Hide
us from the one who sits on the throne and from the anger
of the Lamb. 17That terrible day has come! God and the
Lamb will show their anger, and who can face it?"

The 144,000 Are Marked for God

7 1-2After this I saw four angels. Each one was standing
on one of the earth's four corners. The angels held
back the four winds, so that no wind would blow on the
earth or on the sea or on any tree. These angels had also
been given the power to harm the earth and the sea. Then I
saw another angel come up from where the sun rises in the
east, and he was ready to put the mark of the living God
on people. He shouted to the four angels, 3"Don't harm the
earth or the sea or any tree! Wait until I have marked the
foreheads of the servants of our God."

[b] 6.14 *scroll*: See the note at 5.1.

NEW INTERNATIONAL VERSION

a scroll, rolling up, and every mountain and island was removed from its place.

15Then the kings of the earth, the princes, the generals, the rich, the mighty, and every slave and every free man hid in caves and among the rocks of the mountains. 16They called to the mountains and the rocks, "Fall on us and hide us from the face of him who sits on the throne and from the wrath of the Lamb! 17For the great day of their wrath has come, and who can stand?"

144,000 Sealed

7 After this I saw four angels standing at the four corners of the earth, holding back the four winds of the earth to prevent any wind from blowing on the land or on the sea or on any tree. 2Then I saw another angel coming up from the east, having the seal of the living God. He called out in a loud voice to the four angels who had been given power to harm the land and the sea: 3"Do not harm the land or the sea or the trees until we put a seal on the foreheads of the servants of our God." 4Then I heard the

NEW LIVING TRANSLATION

like a scroll and taken away. And all of the mountains and all of the islands disappeared. 15Then the kings of the earth, the rulers, the generals, the wealthy people, the people with great power, and every slave and every free person—all hid themselves in the caves and among the rocks of the mountains. 16And they cried to the mountains and the rocks, "Fall on us and hide us from the face of the one who sits on the throne and from the wrath of the Lamb. 17For the great day of their wrath has come, and who will be able to survive?"

God's People Will Be Preserved

7 Then I saw four angels standing at the four corners of the earth, holding back the four winds from blowing upon the earth. Not a leaf rustled in the trees, and the sea became as smooth as glass. 2And I saw another angel coming from the east, carrying the seal of the living God. And he shouted out to those four angels who had been given power to injure land and sea, 3"Wait! Don't hurt the land or the sea or the trees until we have placed the seal of God on the foreheads of his servants."

NEW KING JAMES VERSION

14Then the sky receded as a scroll when it is rolled up, and every mountain and island was moved out of its place. 15And the kings of the earth, the great men, the rich men, the commanders,[g] the mighty men, every slave and every free man, hid themselves in the caves and in the rocks of the mountains, 16and said to the mountains and rocks, "Fall on us and hide us from the face of Him who sits on the throne and from the wrath of the Lamb! 17For the great day of His wrath has come, and who is able to stand?"

The Sealed of Israel

7 After these things I saw four angels standing at the four corners of the earth, holding the four winds of the earth, that the wind should not blow on the earth, on the sea, or on any tree. 2Then I saw another angel ascending from the east, having the seal of the living God. And he cried with a loud voice to the four angels to whom it was granted to harm the earth and the sea, 3saying, "Do not harm the earth, the sea, or the trees till we have sealed the servants of our God on their foreheads." 4And I heard the

6:15 [g] NU-Text and M-Text read *the commanders, the rich men.*

THE MESSAGE

high wind, sky snapped shut like a book, islands and mountains sliding this way and that. And then pandemonium, everyone and his dog running for cover—kings, princes, generals, rich and strong, along with every commoner, slave or free. They hid in mountain caves and rocky dens, calling out to mountains and rocks, "Refuge! Hide us from the One Seated on the Throne and the wrath of the Lamb! The great Day of their wrath has come—who can stand it?"

The Servants of God

7 Immediately I saw Four Angels standing at the four corners of earth, standing steady with a firm grip on the four winds so no wind would blow on earth or sea, not even rustle a tree.

Then I saw another Angel rising from where the sun rose, carrying the seal of the Living God. He thundered to the Four Angels assigned the task of hurting earth and sea, "Don't hurt the earth! Don't hurt the sea! Don't so much as hurt a tree until I've sealed the servants of our God on their foreheads!"

KING JAMES VERSION

4 And I heard the number of them which were sealed: *and there were* sealed an hundred *and* forty *and* four thousand of all the tribes of the children of Israel.

5 Of the tribe of Juda *were* sealed twelve thousand. Of the tribe of Reuben *were* sealed twelve thousand. Of the tribe of Gad *were* sealed twelve thousand.

6 Of the tribe of Aser *were* sealed twelve thousand. Of the tribe of Nepthalim *were* sealed twelve thousand. Of the tribe of Manasses *were* sealed twelve thousand.

7 Of the tribe of Simeon *were* sealed twelve thousand. Of the tribe of Levi *were* sealed twelve thousand. Of the tribe of Issachar *were* sealed twelve thousand.

8 Of the tribe of Zabulon *were* sealed twelve thousand. Of the tribe of Joseph *were* sealed twelve thousand. Of the tribe of Benjamin *were* sealed twelve thousand.

9 After this I beheld, and, lo, a great multitude, which no man could number, of all nations, and kindreds, and people, and tongues, stood before the throne, and before the Lamb, clothed with white robes, and palms in their hands;

10 And cried with a loud voice, saying, Salvation to our God which sitteth upon the throne, and unto the Lamb.

NEW AMERICAN STANDARD BIBLE

A Remnant of Israel—144,000

4 And I heard the number of those who were sealed, one hundred and forty-four thousand sealed from every tribe of the sons of Israel:

5 From the tribe of Judah, twelve thousand *were* sealed, from the tribe of Reuben twelve thousand, from the tribe of Gad twelve thousand,

6 from the tribe of Asher twelve thousand, from the tribe of Naphtali twelve thousand, from the tribe of Manasseh twelve thousand,

7 from the tribe of Simeon twelve thousand, from the tribe of Levi twelve thousand, from the tribe of Issachar twelve thousand,

8 from the tribe of Zebulun twelve thousand, from the tribe of Joseph twelve thousand, from the tribe of Benjamin, twelve thousand *were* sealed.

A Multitude from the Tribulation

9 After these things I looked, and behold, a great multitude which no one could count, from every nation and *all* tribes and peoples and tongues, standing before the throne and before the Lamb, clothed in white robes, and palm branches *were* in their hands;

10 and they cry out with a loud voice, saying,

"Salvation to our God who sits on the throne, and to the Lamb."

NEW CENTURY VERSION

how many people were marked with the sign. There were one hundred forty-four thousand from every tribe of the people of Israel.

5 From the tribe of Judah twelve thousand were marked
with the sign,
from the tribe of Reuben twelve thousand,
from the tribe of Gad twelve thousand,
6 from the tribe of Asher twelve thousand,
from the tribe of Naphtali twelve thousand,
from the tribe of Manasseh twelve thousand,
7 from the tribe of Simeon twelve thousand,
from the tribe of Levi twelve thousand,
from the tribe of Issachar twelve thousand,
8 from the tribe of Zebulun twelve thousand,
from the tribe of Joseph twelve thousand,
and from the tribe of Benjamin twelve thousand were
marked with the sign.

The Great Crowd Worships God

9 After the vision of these things I looked, and there was a great number of people, so many that no one could count them. They were from every nation, tribe, people, and language of the earth. They were all standing before the throne and before the Lamb, wearing white robes and holding palm branches in their hands. 10 They were shouting in a loud voice, "Salvation belongs to our God, who sits on the throne, and to the Lamb." 11 All the angels were

CONTEMPORARY ENGLISH VERSION

4 Then I heard how many people had been marked on the forehead. There were one hundred forty-four thousand, and they came from every tribe of Israel:

5 12,000 from Judah,
12,000 from Reuben,
12,000 from Gad,
6 12,000 from Asher,
12,000 from Naphtali,
12,000 from Manasseh,
7 12,000 from Simeon,
12,000 from Levi,
12,000 from Issachar,
8 12,000 from Zebulun,
12,000 from Joseph, and
12,000 from Benjamin.

People from Every Nation

9 After this, I saw a large crowd with more people than could be counted. They were from every race, tribe, nation, and language, and they stood before the throne and before the Lamb. They wore white robes and held palm branches in their hands, 10 as they shouted,

"Our God, who sits
upon the throne,
has the power
to save his people,
and so does the Lamb."

NEW INTERNATIONAL VERSION

number of those who were sealed: 144,000 from all the tribes of Israel.

5 From the tribe of Judah 12,000 were sealed,
from the tribe of Reuben 12,000,
from the tribe of Gad 12,000,
6 from the tribe of Asher 12,000,
from the tribe of Naphtali 12,000,
from the tribe of Manasseh 12,000,
7 from the tribe of Simeon 12,000,
from the tribe of Levi 12,000,
from the tribe of Issachar 12,000,
8 from the tribe of Zebulun 12,000,
from the tribe of Joseph 12,000,
from the tribe of Benjamin 12,000.

The Great Multitude in White Robes

9 After this I looked and there before me was a great multitude that no one could count, from every nation, tribe, people and language, standing before the throne and in front of the Lamb. They were wearing white robes and were holding palm branches in their hands.
10 And they cried out in a loud voice:

"Salvation belongs to our God,
who sits on the throne,
and to the Lamb."

NEW LIVING TRANSLATION

4 And I heard how many were marked with the seal of God. There were 144,000 who were sealed from all the tribes of Israel:

5 from Judah .12,000
from Reuben 12,000
from Gad 12,000
6 from Asher .12,000
from Naphtali 12,000
from Manasseh 12,000
7 from Simeon 12,000
from Levi 12,000
from Issachar 12,000
8 from Zebulun 12,000
from Joseph .12,000
from Benjamin 12,000

Praise from the Great Multitude

9 After this I saw a vast crowd, too great to count, from every nation and tribe and people and language, standing in front of the throne and before the Lamb. They were clothed in white and held palm branches in their hands.
10 And they were shouting with a mighty shout, "Salvation comes from our God on the throne and from the Lamb!"

NEW KING JAMES VERSION

number of those who were sealed. One hundred *and* forty-four thousand of all the tribes of the children of Israel *were* sealed:

5 of the tribe of Judah twelve thousand *were* sealed;[a]
of the tribe of Reuben twelve thousand *were* sealed;
of the tribe of Gad twelve thousand *were* sealed;
6 of the tribe of Asher twelve thousand *were* sealed;
of the tribe of Naphtali twelve thousand *were* sealed;
of the tribe of Manasseh twelve thousand *were* sealed;
7 of the tribe of Simeon twelve thousand *were* sealed;
of the tribe of Levi twelve thousand *were* sealed;
of the tribe of Issachar twelve thousand *were* sealed;
8 of the tribe of Zebulun twelve thousand *were* sealed;
of the tribe of Joseph twelve thousand *were* sealed;
of the tribe of Benjamin twelve thousand *were* sealed.

A Multitude from the Great Tribulation

9 After these things I looked, and behold, a great multitude which no one could number, of all nations, tribes, peoples, and tongues, standing before the throne and before the Lamb, clothed with white robes, with palm branches in their hands,
10 and crying out with a loud voice, saying, "Salvation *belongs* to our God who sits on the throne, and to the Lamb!"
11 All the angels stood

7:5 [a] In NU-Text and M-Text *were sealed* is stated only in verses 5a and 8c; the words are understood in the remainder of the passage.

THE MESSAGE

I heard the count of those who were sealed: 144,000! They were sealed out of every Tribe of Israel: 12,000 sealed from Judah, 12,000 from Reuben, 12,000 from Gad, 12,000 from Asher, 12,000 from Naphtali, 12,000 from Manasseh, 12,000 from Simeon, 12,000 from Levi, 12,000 from Issachar, 12,000 from Zebulun, 12,000 from Joseph, 12,000 sealed from Benjamin.

✠

I looked again. I saw a huge crowd, too huge to count. Everyone was there—all nations and tribes, all races and languages. And they were *standing*, dressed in white robes and waving palm branches, standing before the Throne and the Lamb and heartily singing:

"Salvation to our God on his Throne!
Salvation to the Lamb!"

KING JAMES VERSION

11 And all the angels stood round about the throne, and *about* the elders and the four beasts, and fell before the throne on their faces, and worshipped God,

12 Saying, Amen: Blessing, and glory, and wisdom, and thanksgiving, and honour, and power, and might, *be* unto our God for ever and ever. Amen.

13 ¶ And one of the elders answered, saying unto me, What are these which are arrayed in white robes? and whence came they?

14 And I said unto him, Sir, thou knowest. And he said to me, These are they which came out of great tribulation, and have washed their robes, and made them white in the blood of the Lamb.

15 Therefore are they before the throne of God, and serve him day and night in his temple: and he that sitteth on the throne shall dwell among them.

NEW AMERICAN STANDARD BIBLE

11 And all the angels were standing around the throne and *around* the elders and the four living creatures; and they fell on their faces before the throne and worshiped God,

12 saying,

"Amen, blessing and glory and wisdom and thanksgiving and honor and power and might, *be* to our God forever and ever. Amen."

13 Then one of the elders answered, saying to me, "These who are clothed in the white robes, who are they, and where have they come from?"

14 I said to him, "My lord, you know." And he said to me, "These are the ones who come out of the great tribulation, and they have washed their robes and made them white in the blood of the Lamb.

15 "For this reason, they are before the throne of God; and they serve Him day and night in His temple; and He who sits on the throne will spread His tabernacle over them.

NEW CENTURY VERSION

standing around the throne and the elders and the four living creatures. They all bowed down on their faces before the throne and worshiped God, 12saying, "Amen! Praise, glory, wisdom, thanks, honor, power, and strength belong to our God forever and ever. Amen!"

13Then one of the elders asked me, "Who are these people dressed in white robes? Where did they come from?"

14I answered, "You know, sir."

And the elder said to me, "These are the people who have come out of the great distress. They have washed their robes[a] and made them white in the blood of the Lamb. 15Because of this, they are before the throne of God. They worship him day and night in his temple. And the One who sits on the throne will be present with them.

7:14 [a] **washed their robes** This means they believed in Jesus so that their sins could be forgiven by Christ's blood.

CONTEMPORARY ENGLISH VERSION

11The angels who stood around the throne knelt in front of it with their faces to the ground. The elders and the four living creatures knelt there with them. Then they all worshiped God 12and said,

"Amen! Praise, glory, wisdom,
thanks, honor, power,
and strength belong to our God
forever and ever! Amen!"

13One of the elders asked me, "Do you know who these people are that are dressed in white robes? Do you know where they come from?"

14"Sir," I answered, "you must know."
Then he told me:

"These are the ones
who have gone through
the great suffering.
They have washed their robes
in the blood of the Lamb
and have made them white.
15And so they stand
before the throne of God
and worship him in his temple
day and night.
The one who sits on the throne
will spread his tent
over them.

NEW INTERNATIONAL VERSION

11All the angels were standing around the throne and around the elders and the four living creatures. They fell down on their faces before the throne and worshiped God,
12saying:

"Amen!
Praise and glory
and wisdom and thanks and honor
and power and strength
be to our God for ever and ever.
Amen!"

13Then one of the elders asked me, "These in white robes—who are they, and where did they come from?"
14I answered, "Sir, you know."

And he said, "These are they who have come out of the great tribulation; they have washed their robes and made them white in the blood of the Lamb.
15Therefore,

"they are before the throne of God
and serve him day and night in his temple;
and he who sits on the throne will spread his tent over them.

NEW LIVING TRANSLATION

11And all the angels were standing around the throne and around the elders and the four living beings. And they fell face down before the throne and worshiped God.
12They said,

"Amen! Blessing and glory and wisdom
and thanksgiving and honor and power and strength
belong to our God forever and forever. Amen!"

13Then one of the twenty-four elders asked me, "Who are these who are clothed in white? Where do they come from?"
14And I said to him, "Sir, you are the one who knows."

Then he said to me, "These are the ones coming out of the great tribulation. They washed their robes in the blood of the Lamb and made them white.
15That is why they are standing in front of the throne of God, serving him day and night in his Temple. And he who sits on the throne will live among them and shelter them.
16They will never

NEW KING JAMES VERSION

around the throne and the elders and the four living creatures, and fell on their faces before the throne and worshiped God,
12saying:

"Amen! Blessing and glory and wisdom,
Thanksgiving and honor and power and might,
Be to our God forever and ever.
Amen."

13Then one of the elders answered, saying to me, "Who are these arrayed in white robes, and where did they come from?"
14And I said to him, "Sir,[b] you know."

So he said to me, "These are the ones who come out of the great tribulation, and washed their robes and made them white in the blood of the Lamb.
15Therefore they are before the throne of God, and serve Him day and night in His temple. And He who sits on the throne will dwell among

7:14 [b] NU-Text and M-Text read *My lord.*

THE MESSAGE

All who were standing around the Throne—Angels, Elders, Animals—fell on their faces before the Throne and worshiped God, singing:

"Oh, Yes!
The blessing and glory and wisdom and thanksgiving,
The honor and power and strength,
To our God forever and ever and ever!
Oh, Yes!"

Just then one of the Elders addressed me: "Who are these dressed in white robes, and where did they come from?" Taken aback, I said, "Oh, Sir, I have no idea—but you must know."

Then he told me, "These are those who come from the great tribulation, and they've washed their robes, scrubbed them clean in the blood of the Lamb. That's why they're standing before God's Throne. They serve him day and night in his Temple. The One on the Throne will pitch his tent

KING JAMES VERSION

16 They shall hunger no more, neither thirst any more; neither shall the sun light on them, nor any heat.

17 For the Lamb which is in the midst of the throne shall feed them, and shall lead them unto living fountains of waters: and God shall wipe away all tears from their eyes.

8 And when he had opened the seventh seal, there was silence in heaven about the space of half an hour.

2 And I saw the seven angels which stood before God; and to them were given seven trumpets.

3 And another angel came and stood at the altar, having a golden censer; and there was given unto him much incense, that he should offer *it* with the prayers of all saints upon the golden altar which was before the throne.

4 And the smoke of the incense, *which came* with the prayers of the saints, ascended up before God out of the angel's hand.

5 And the angel took the censer, and filled it with fire of the altar, and cast *it* into the earth: and there were voices, and thunderings, and lightnings, and an earthquake.

NEW AMERICAN STANDARD BIBLE

16 "They will hunger no longer, nor thirst anymore; nor will the sun beat down on them, nor any heat;

17 for the Lamb in the center of the throne will be their shepherd, and will guide them to springs of the water of life; and God will wipe every tear from their eyes."

The Seventh Seal—the Trumpets

8 When the Lamb broke the seventh seal, there was silence in heaven for about half an hour.

2 And I saw the seven angels who stand before God, and seven trumpets were given to them.

3 Another angel came and stood at the altar, holding a golden censer; and much incense was given to him, so that he might add it to the prayers of all the saints on the golden altar which was before the throne.

4 And the smoke of the incense, with the prayers of the saints, went up before God out of the angel's hand.

5 Then the angel took the censer and filled it with the fire of the altar, and threw it to the earth; and there followed peals of thunder and sounds and flashes of lightning and an earthquake.

NEW CENTURY VERSION

16 Those people will never be hungry again, and they will
never be thirsty again. The sun will not hurt them, and no
heat will burn them, 17 because the Lamb at the center of
the throne will be their shepherd. He will lead them to
springs of water that give life. And God will wipe away
every tear from their eyes."

The Seventh Seal

8 When the Lamb opened the seventh seal, there was
silence in heaven for about half an hour. 2 And I saw
the seven angels who stand before God and to whom were
given seven trumpets.
3 Another angel came and stood at the altar, holding a
golden pan for incense. He was given much incense to
offer with the prayers of all God's holy people. The angel
put this offering on the golden altar before the throne.
4 The smoke from the incense went up from the angel's
hand to God with the prayers of God's people. 5 Then the
angel filled the incense pan with fire from the altar and
threw it on the earth, and there were flashes of lightning,
thunder and loud noises, and an earthquake.

CONTEMPORARY ENGLISH VERSION

16 They will never hunger
or thirst again,
and they won't be troubled
by the sun
or any scorching heat.

17 The Lamb in the center
of the throne
will be their shepherd.
He will lead them to streams
of life-giving water,
and God will wipe all tears
from their eyes."

The Seventh Seal Is Opened

8 When the Lamb opened the seventh seal, there was
silence in heaven for about half an hour. 2 I noticed
that the seven angels who stood before God were each
given a trumpet.

3 Another angel, who had a gold container for incense,[a]
came and stood at the altar. This one was given a lot of
incense to offer with the prayers of God's people on the
gold altar in front of the throne. 4 Then the smoke of the
incense, together with the prayers of God's people, went up
to God from the hand of the angel.

5 After this, the angel filled the incense container with
fire from the altar and threw it on the earth. Thunder
roared, lightning flashed, and the earth shook.

[a] **8.3** *incense*: See the note at 5.8.

NEW INTERNATIONAL VERSION

16 Never again will they hunger;
never again will they thirst.
The sun will not beat upon them,
nor any scorching heat.
17 For the Lamb at the center of the throne will be their
shepherd;
he will lead them to springs of living water.
And God will wipe away every tear from their eyes."

The Seventh Seal and the Golden Censer

8 When he opened the seventh seal, there was silence in heaven for about half an hour.

2 And I saw the seven angels who stand before God, and to them were given seven trumpets.

3 Another angel, who had a golden censer, came and stood at the altar. He was given much incense to offer, with the prayers of all the saints, on the golden altar before the throne. 4 The smoke of the incense, together with the prayers of the saints, went up before God from the angel's hand. 5 Then the angel took the censer, filled it with fire from the altar, and hurled it on the earth; and there came peals of thunder, rumblings, flashes of lightning and an earthquake.

NEW LIVING TRANSLATION

again be hungry or thirsty, and they will be fully protected from the scorching noontime heat. 17 For the Lamb who stands in front of the throne will be their Shepherd. He will lead them to the springs of life-giving water. And God will wipe away all their tears."

The Lamb Breaks the Seventh Seal

8 When the Lamb broke the seventh seal, there was silence throughout heaven for about half an hour. 2 And I saw the seven angels who stand before God, and they were given seven trumpets.

3 Then another angel with a gold incense burner came and stood at the altar. And a great quantity of incense was given to him to mix with the prayers of God's people, to be offered on the gold altar before the throne. 4 The smoke of the incense, mixed with the prayers of the saints, ascended up to God from the altar where the angel had poured them out. 5 Then the angel filled the incense burner with fire from the altar and threw it down upon the earth; and thunder crashed, lightning flashed, and there was a terrible earthquake.

NEW KING JAMES VERSION

them. 16 They shall neither hunger anymore nor thirst anymore; the sun shall not strike them, nor any heat; 17 for the Lamb who is in the midst of the throne will shepherd them and lead them to living fountains of waters.[c] And God will wipe away every tear from their eyes."

Seventh Seal: Prelude to the Seven Trumpets

8 When He opened the seventh seal, there was silence in heaven for about half an hour. 2 And I saw the seven angels who stand before God, and to them were given seven trumpets. 3 Then another angel, having a golden censer, came and stood at the altar. He was given much incense, that he should offer *it* with the prayers of all the saints upon the golden altar which was before the throne. 4 And the smoke of the incense, with the prayers of the saints, ascended before God from the angel's hand. 5 Then the angel took the censer, filled it with fire from the altar, and threw *it* to the earth. And there were noises, thunderings, lightnings, and an earthquake.

7:17 [c] NU-Text and M-Text read *to fountains of the waters of life.*

THE MESSAGE

there for them: no more hunger, no more thirst, no more scorching heat. The Lamb on the Throne will shepherd them, will lead them to spring waters of Life. And God will wipe every last tear from their eyes."

8 When the Lamb ripped off the seventh seal, Heaven fell quiet—complete silence for about half an hour.

Blowing the Trumpets

I saw the Seven Angels who are always in readiness before God handed seven trumpets. Then another Angel, carrying a gold censer, came and stood at the Altar. He was given a great quantity of incense so that he could offer up the prayers of all the holy people of God on the Golden Altar before the Throne. Smoke billowed up from the incense-laced prayers of the holy ones, rose before God from the hand of the Angel.

Then the Angel filled the censer with fire from the Altar and heaved it to earth. It set off thunders, voices, lightnings, and an earthquake.

KING JAMES VERSION

6 And the seven angels which had the seven trumpets prepared themselves to sound.

7 ¶ The first angel sounded, and there followed hail and fire mingled with blood, and they were cast upon the earth: and the third part of trees was burnt up, and all green grass was burnt up.

8 And the second angel sounded, and as it were a great mountain burning with fire was cast into the sea: and the third part of the sea became blood;

9 And the third part of the creatures which were in the sea, and had life, died; and the third part of the ships were destroyed.

10 And the third angel sounded, and there fell a great star from heaven, burning as it were a lamp, and it fell upon the third part of the rivers, and upon the fountains of waters;

11 And the name of the star is called Wormwood: and the third part of the waters became wormwood; and many men died of the waters, because they were made bitter.

12 And the fourth angel sounded, and the third part of the sun was smitten, and the third part of the moon, and the third part of the stars; so as the third part of them was darkened, and the day shone not for a third part of it, and the night likewise.

NEW AMERICAN STANDARD BIBLE

6 And the seven angels who had the seven trumpets prepared themselves to sound them.

7 The first sounded, and there came hail and fire, mixed with blood, and they were thrown to the earth; and a third of the earth was burned up, and a third of the trees were burned up, and all the green grass was burned up.

8 The second angel sounded, and *something* like a great mountain burning with fire was thrown into the sea; and a third of the sea became blood,

9 and a third of the creatures which were in the sea and had life, died; and a third of the ships were destroyed.

10 The third angel sounded, and a great star fell from heaven, burning like a torch, and it fell on a third of the rivers and on the springs of waters.

11 The name of the star is called Wormwood; and a third of the waters became wormwood, and many men died from the waters, because they were made bitter.

12 The fourth angel sounded, and a third of the sun and a third of the moon and a third of the stars were struck, so that a third of them would be darkened and the day would not shine for a third of it, and the night in the same way.

NEW CENTURY VERSION

The Seven Angels and Trumpets

6Then the seven angels who had the seven trumpets prepared to blow them.

7The first angel blew his trumpet, and hail and fire mixed with blood were poured down on the earth. And a third of the earth, and all the green grass, and a third of the trees were burned up.

8Then the second angel blew his trumpet, and something that looked like a big mountain, burning with fire, was thrown into the sea. And a third of the sea became blood, 9a third of the living things in the sea died, and a third of the ships were destroyed.

10Then the third angel blew his trumpet, and a large star, burning like a torch, fell from the sky. It fell on a third of the rivers and on the springs of water. 11The name of the star is Wormwood.[a] And a third of all the water became bitter, and many people died from drinking the water that was bitter.

12Then the fourth angel blew his trumpet, and a third of the sun, and a third of the moon, and a third of the stars were struck. So a third of them became dark, and a third of the day was without light, and also the night.

8:11 [a] **Wormwood** Name of a very bitter plant; used here to give the idea of bitter sorrow.

CONTEMPORARY ENGLISH VERSION

The Trumpets

6The seven angels now got ready to blow their trumpets.

7When the first angel blew his trumpet, hail and fire mixed with blood were thrown down on the earth. A third of the earth, a third of the trees, and a third of all green plants were burned.

8When the second angel blew his trumpet, something like a great fiery mountain was thrown into the sea. A third of the sea turned to blood, 9a third of the living creatures in the sea died, and a third of the ships were destroyed.

10When the third angel blew his trumpet, a great star fell from heaven. It was burning like a torch, and it fell on a third of the rivers and on a third of the springs of water. 11The name of the star was Bitter, and a third of the water turned bitter. Many people died because the water was so bitter.

12When the fourth angel blew his trumpet, a third of the sun, a third of the moon, and a third of the stars were struck. They each lost a third of their light. So during a third of the day there was no light, and a third of the night was also without light.

NEW INTERNATIONAL VERSION

The Trumpets

6 Then the seven angels who had the seven trumpets pre-
pared to sound them.
7 The first angel sounded his trumpet, and there came
hail and fire mixed with blood, and it was hurled down
upon the earth. A third of the earth was burned up, a third
of the trees were burned up, and all the green grass was
burned up.
8 The second angel sounded his trumpet, and something
like a huge mountain, all ablaze, was thrown into the sea.
A third of the sea turned into blood,
9 a third of the living
creatures in the sea died, and a third of the ships were
destroyed.
10 The third angel sounded his trumpet, and a great star,
blazing like a torch, fell from the sky on a third of the
rivers and on the springs of water—
11 the name of the star
is Wormwood.[a] A third of the waters turned bitter, and
many people died from the waters that had become bitter.
12 The fourth angel sounded his trumpet, and a third of
the sun was struck, a third of the moon, and a third of the
stars, so that a third of them turned dark. A third of the
day was without light, and also a third of the night.

[a] *11* That is, Bitterness

NEW LIVING TRANSLATION

The First Four Trumpets

6 Then the seven angels with the seven trumpets pre-
pared to blow their mighty blasts.
7 The first angel blew his trumpet, and hail and fire
mixed with blood were thrown down upon the earth, and
one-third of the earth was set on fire. One-third of the
trees were burned, and all the grass was burned.
8 Then the second angel blew his trumpet, and a great
mountain of fire was thrown into the sea. And one-third of
the water in the sea became blood.
9 And one-third of all
things living in the sea died. And one-third of all the ships
on the sea were destroyed.
10 Then the third angel blew his trumpet, and a great
flaming star fell out of the sky, burning like a torch. It fell
upon one-third of the rivers and on the springs of water.
11 The name of the star was Bitterness.* It made one-third
of the water bitter, and many people died because the
water was so bitter.
12 Then the fourth angel blew his trumpet, and one-third
of the sun was struck, and one-third of the moon, and one-
third of the stars, and they became dark. And one-third of
the day was dark and one-third of the night also.

8:11 Greek *Wormwood.*

NEW KING JAMES VERSION

6 So the seven angels who had the seven trumpets pre-
pared themselves to sound.

First Trumpet: Vegetation Struck

7 The first angel sounded: And hail and fire followed,
mingled with blood, and they were thrown to the earth.[a]
And a third of the trees were burned up, and all green
grass was burned up.

Second Trumpet: The Seas Struck

8 Then the second angel sounded: And *something* like a
great mountain burning with fire was thrown into the sea,
and a third of the sea became blood.
9 And a third of the
living creatures in the sea died, and a third of the ships
were destroyed.

Third Trumpet: The Waters Struck

10 Then the third angel sounded: And a great star fell from
heaven, burning like a torch, and it fell on a third of the
rivers and on the springs of water.
11 The name of the star is
Wormwood. A third of the waters became wormwood, and
many men died from the water, because it was made bitter.

Fourth Trumpet: The Heavens Struck

12 Then the fourth angel sounded: And a third of the sun
was struck, a third of the moon, and a third of the stars, so
that a third of them were darkened. A third of the day did
not shine, and likewise the night.

8:7 [a] NU-Text and M-Text add *and a third of the earth was burned up.*

THE MESSAGE

The Seven Angels with the trumpets got ready to blow them. At the first trumpet blast, hail and fire mixed with blood were dumped on earth. A third of the earth was scorched, a third of the trees, and every blade of green grass—burned to a crisp.

The second Angel trumpeted. Something like a huge mountain blazing with fire was flung into the sea. A third of the sea turned to blood, a third of the living sea creatures died, and a third of the ships sank.

The third Angel trumpeted. A huge Star, blazing like a torch, fell from Heaven, wiping out a third of the rivers and a third of the springs. The Star's name was Wormwood. A third of the water turned bitter, and many people died from the poisoned water.

The fourth Angel trumpeted. A third of the sun, a third of the moon, and a third of the stars were hit, blacked out by a third, both day and night in one-third blackout.

KING JAMES VERSION

13 And I beheld, and heard an angel flying through the midst of heaven, saying with a loud voice, Woe, woe, woe, to the inhabiters of the earth by reason of the other voices of the trumpet of the three angels, which are yet to sound!

9 And the fifth angel sounded, and I saw a star fall from heaven unto the earth: and to him was given the key of the bottomless pit.

2 And he opened the bottomless pit; and there arose a smoke out of the pit, as the smoke of a great furnace; and the sun and the air were darkened by reason of the smoke of the pit.

3 And there came out of the smoke locusts upon the earth: and unto them was given power, as the scorpions of the earth have power.

4 And it was commanded them that they should not hurt the grass of the earth, neither any green thing, neither any tree; but only those men which have not the seal of God in their foreheads.

5 And to them it was given that they should not kill them, but that they should be tormented five months: and their torment *was* as the torment of a scorpion, when he striketh a man.

6 And in those days shall men seek death, and shall not find it; and shall desire to die, and death shall flee from them.

7 And the shapes of the locusts *were* like unto horses prepared unto battle; and on their heads *were* as it were crowns like gold, and their faces *were* as the faces of men.

NEW AMERICAN STANDARD BIBLE

13 Then I looked, and I heard an eagle flying in midheaven, saying with a loud voice, "Woe, woe, woe to those who dwell on the earth, because of the remaining blasts of the trumpet of the three angels who are about to sound!"

The Fifth Trumpet—the Bottomless Pit

9 Then the fifth angel sounded, and I saw a star from heaven which had fallen to the earth; and the key of the bottomless pit was given to him.

2 He opened the bottomless pit, and smoke went up out of the pit, like the smoke of a great furnace; and the sun and the air were darkened by the smoke of the pit.

3 Then out of the smoke came locusts upon the earth, and power was given them, as the scorpions of the earth have power.

4 They were told not to hurt the grass of the earth, nor any green thing, nor any tree, but only the men who do not have the seal of God on their foreheads.

5 And they were not permitted to kill anyone, but to torment for five months; and their torment was like the torment of a scorpion when it stings a man.

6 And in those days men will seek death and will not find it; they will long to die, and death flees from them.

7 The appearance of the locusts was like horses prepared for battle; and on their heads appeared to be crowns like gold, and their faces were like the faces of men.

NEW CENTURY VERSION

13 While I watched, I heard an eagle that was flying high
in the air cry out in a loud voice, "Trouble! Trouble!
Trouble for those who live on the earth because of the
remaining sounds of the trumpets that the other three
angels are about to blow!"

9 Then the fifth angel blew his trumpet, and I saw a
star fall from the sky to the earth. The star was given
the key to the deep hole that leads to the bottomless pit.
2 Then it opened up the hole that leads to the bottomless
pit, and smoke came up from the hole like smoke from a
big furnace. Then the sun and sky became dark because of
the smoke from the hole. 3 Then locusts came down to the
earth out of the smoke, and they were given the power to
sting like scorpions.[a] 4 They were told not to harm the
grass on the earth or any plant or tree. They could harm
only the people who did not have the sign of God on their
foreheads. 5 These locusts were not given the power to kill
anyone, but to cause pain to the people for five months.
And the pain they felt was like the pain a scorpion gives
when it stings someone. 6 During those days people will
look for a way to die, but they will not find it. They will
want to die, but death will run away from them.

7 The locusts looked like horses prepared for battle. On
their heads they wore what looked like crowns of gold, and
their faces looked like human faces. 8 Their hair was like

9:3 [a] **scorpions** A scorpion is an insect that stings with a bad poison.

CONTEMPORARY ENGLISH VERSION

13 Then I looked and saw a lone eagle flying across the
sky. It was shouting, "Trouble, trouble, trouble to everyone
who lives on earth! The other three angels are now going
to blow their trumpets."

9 When the fifth angel blew his trumpet, I saw a star[a]
fall from the sky to earth. It was given the key to the
tunnel that leads down to the deep pit. 2 As it opened the
tunnel, smoke poured out like the smoke of a great fur-
nace. The sun and the air turned dark because of the
smoke. 3 Locusts[b] came out of the smoke and covered the
earth. They were given the same power that scorpions
have.

4 The locusts were told not to harm the grass on the
earth or any plant or any tree. They were to punish only
those people who did not have God's mark on their fore-
heads. 5 The locusts were allowed to make them suffer for
five months, but not to kill them. The suffering they
caused was like the sting of a scorpion. 6 In those days peo-
ple will want to die, but they will not be able to. They will
hope for death, but it will escape from them.

7 These locusts looked like horses ready for battle. On
their heads they wore something like gold crowns, and
they had human faces. 8 Their hair was like a woman's

[a] 9.1 *star*: In the ancient world, stars were often thought of as living beings, such as angels. [b] 9.3 *Locusts*: A type of grasshopper that comes in swarms and causes great damage to crops.

NEW INTERNATIONAL VERSION

13 As I watched, I heard an eagle that was flying in
midair call out in a loud voice: "Woe! Woe! Woe to the
inhabitants of the earth, because of the trumpet blasts
about to be sounded by the other three angels!"
9 The fifth angel sounded his trumpet, and I saw a star
that had fallen from the sky to the earth. The star was
given the key to the shaft of the Abyss. 2 When he opened
the Abyss, smoke rose from it like the smoke from a gigan-
tic furnace. The sun and sky were darkened by the smoke
from the Abyss. 3 And out of the smoke locusts came down
upon the earth and were given power like that of scorpions
of the earth. 4 They were told not to harm the grass of the
earth or any plant or tree, but only those people who did
not have the seal of God on their foreheads. 5 They were
not given power to kill them, but only to torture them for
five months. And the agony they suffered was like that of
the sting of a scorpion when it strikes a man. 6 During
those days men will seek death, but will not find it; they
will long to die, but death will elude them.
7 The locusts looked like horses prepared for battle. On
their heads they wore something like crowns of gold, and
their faces resembled human faces. 8 Their hair was like

NEW LIVING TRANSLATION

13 Then I looked up. And I heard a single eagle crying
loudly as it flew through the air, "Terror, terror, terror to
all who belong to this world because of what will happen
when the last three angels blow their trumpets."

The Fifth Trumpet Brings the First Terror

9 Then the fifth angel blew his trumpet, and I saw a
star that had fallen to earth from the sky, and he was
given the key to the shaft of the bottomless pit. 2 When he
opened it, smoke poured out as though from a huge fur-
nace, and the sunlight and air were darkened by the
smoke.
3 Then locusts came from the smoke and descended on
the earth, and they were given power to sting like scorpi-
ons. 4 They were told not to hurt the grass or plants or
trees but to attack all the people who did not have the seal
of God on their foreheads. 5 They were told not to kill them
but to torture them for five months with agony like the
pain of scorpion stings. 6 In those days people will seek
death but will not find it. They will long to die, but death
will flee away!
7 The locusts looked like horses armed for battle. They
had gold crowns on their heads, and they had human faces.

NEW KING JAMES VERSION

13 And I looked, and I heard an angel[b] flying through the
midst of heaven, saying with a loud voice, "Woe, woe, woe
to the inhabitants of the earth, because of the remaining
blasts of the trumpet of the three angels who are about to
sound!"

Fifth Trumpet: The Locusts from the Bottomless Pit

9 Then the fifth angel sounded: And I saw a star fallen
from heaven to the earth. To him was given the key to
the bottomless pit. 2 And he opened the bottomless pit, and
smoke arose out of the pit like the smoke of a great fur-
nace. So the sun and the air were darkened because of the
smoke of the pit. 3 Then out of the smoke locusts came
upon the earth. And to them was given power, as the scor-
pions of the earth have power. 4 They were commanded not
to harm the grass of the earth, or any green thing, or any
tree, but only those men who do not have the seal of God
on their foreheads. 5 And they were not given *authority* to
kill them, but to torment them *for* five months. Their tor-
ment *was* like the torment of a scorpion when it strikes a
man. 6 In those days men will seek death and will not find
it; they will desire to die, and death will flee from them.
7 The shape of the locusts was like horses prepared for
battle. On their heads were crowns of something like gold,
and their faces *were* like the faces of men. 8 They had hair

8:13 [b] NU-Text and M-Text read *eagle*.

THE MESSAGE

I looked hard; I heard a lone eagle, flying through
Middle-Heaven, crying out ominously, "Doom! Doom!
Doom to everyone left on earth! There are three more
Angels about to blow their trumpets. Doom is on its way!"

9 The fifth Angel trumpeted. I saw a Star plummet from
Heaven to earth. The Star was handed a key to the
Well of the Abyss. He unlocked the Well of the Abyss—
smoke poured out of the Well, billows and billows of
smoke, sun and air in blackout from smoke pouring out of
the Well.
Then out of the smoke crawled locusts with the venom
of scorpions. They were given their orders: "Don't hurt the
grass, don't hurt anything green, don't hurt a single tree—
only men and women, and then only those who lack the
seal of God on their foreheads." They were ordered to tor-
ture but not kill, torture them for five months, the pain like
a scorpion sting. When this happens, people are going to
prefer death to torture, look for ways to kill themselves.
But they won't find a way—death will have gone into hid-
ing.
The locusts looked like horses ready for war. They had
gold crowns, human faces, women's hair, the teeth of

KING JAMES VERSION

8 And they had hair as the hair of women, and their teeth were as *the teeth* of lions.

9 And they had breastplates, as it were breastplates of iron; and the sound of their wings *was* as the sound of chariots of many horses running to battle.

10 And they had tails like unto scorpions, and there were stings in their tails: and their power *was* to hurt men five months.

11 And they had a king over them, *which is* the angel of the bottomless pit, whose name in the Hebrew tongue *is* Abaddon, but in the Greek tongue hath *his* name Apollyon.

12 One woe is past; *and*, behold, there come two woes more hereafter.

13 ¶ And the sixth angel sounded, and I heard a voice from the four horns of the golden altar which is before God,

14 Saying to the sixth angel which had the trumpet, Loose the four angels which are bound in the great river Euphrates.

15 And the four angels were loosed, which were prepared for an hour, and a day, and a month, and a year, for to slay the third part of men.

16 And the number of the army of the horsemen *were* two hundred thousand thousand: and I heard the number of them.

17 And thus I saw the horses in the vision, and them that sat on them, having breastplates of fire, and of jacinth, and brimstone: and the heads of the horses *were*

NEW AMERICAN STANDARD BIBLE

8 They had hair like the hair of women, and their teeth were like *the teeth* of lions.

9 They had breastplates like breastplates of iron; and the sound of their wings was like the sound of chariots, of many horses rushing to battle.

10 They have tails like scorpions, and stings; and in their tails is their power to hurt men for five months.

11 They have as king over them, the angel of the abyss; his name in Hebrew is [1]Abaddon, and in the Greek he has the name Apollyon.

12 The first woe is past; behold, two woes are still coming after these things.

The Sixth Trumpet—Army from the East

13 Then the sixth angel sounded, and I heard a voice from the [2]four horns of the golden altar which is before God,

14 one saying to the sixth angel who had the trumpet, "Release the four angels who are bound at the great river Euphrates."

15 And the four angels, who had been prepared for the hour and day and month and year, were released, so that they would kill a third of mankind.

16 The number of the armies of the horsemen was two hundred million; I heard the number of them.

17 And this is how I saw in the vision the horses and those who sat on them: *the riders* had breastplates *the color* of fire and of hyacinth and of brimstone; and the

9:11 [1] I.e. destruction 9:13 [2] Two early mss do not contain *four*

NEW CENTURY VERSION

women's hair, and their teeth were like lions' teeth. 9Their
chests looked like iron breastplates, and the sound of their
wings was like the noise of many horses and chariots hur-
rying into battle. 10The locusts had tails with stingers like
scorpions, and in their tails was their power to hurt people
for five months. 11The locusts had a king who was the
angel of the bottomless pit. His name in the Hebrew lan-
guage is Abaddon and in the Greek language is Apollyon.[b]
12The first trouble is past; there are still two other trou-
bles that will come.
13Then the sixth angel blew his trumpet, and I heard a
voice coming from the horns on the golden altar that is
before God. 14The voice said to the sixth angel who had
the trumpet, "Free the four angels who are tied at the great
river Euphrates." 15And they let loose the four angels who
had been kept ready for this hour and day and month and
year so they could kill a third of all people on the earth. 16I
heard how many troops on horses were in their army—two
hundred million.
17The horses and their riders I saw in the vision looked
like this: They had breastplates that were fiery red, dark
blue, and yellow like sulfur. The heads of the horses

9:11 [b] **Abaddon, Apollyon** Both names mean "Destroyer."

CONTEMPORARY ENGLISH VERSION

long hair, and their teeth were like those of a lion. 9On
their chests they wore armor made of iron. Their wings
roared like an army of horse-drawn chariots rushing into
battle. 10Their tails were like a scorpion's tail with a
stinger that had the power to hurt someone for five
months. 11Their king was the angel in charge of the deep
pit. In Hebrew his name was Abaddon, and in Greek it was
Apollyon.[c]
12The first horrible thing has now happened! But wait.
Two more horrible things will happen soon.
13Then the sixth angel blew his trumpet. I heard a voice
speak from the four corners of the gold altar that stands in
the presence of God. 14The voice spoke to this angel and
said, "Release the four angels who are tied up beside the
great Euphrates River." 15The four angels had been pre-
pared for this very hour and day and month and year. Now
they were set free to kill a third of all people.
16By listening, I could tell there were more than two
hundred million of these war horses. 17In my vision their
riders wore fiery-red, dark-blue, and yellow armor on their

[c] 9.11 *Abaddon . . . Apollyon*: The Hebrew word "Abaddon" and the Greek word "Apollyon" each mean "destruction."

NEW INTERNATIONAL VERSION

women's hair, and their teeth were like lions' teeth. 9They
had breastplates like breastplates of iron, and the sound of
their wings was like the thundering of many horses and
chariots rushing into battle. 10They had tails and stings
like scorpions, and in their tails they had power to torment
people for five months. 11They had as king over them the
angel of the Abyss, whose name in Hebrew is Abaddon,
and in Greek, Apollyon.[a]

12The first woe is past; two other woes are yet to come.

13The sixth angel sounded his trumpet, and I heard a
voice coming from the horns[b] of the golden altar that is
before God. 14It said to the sixth angel who had the trum-
pet, "Release the four angels who are bound at the great
river Euphrates." 15And the four angels who had been kept
ready for this very hour and day and month and year were
released to kill a third of mankind. 16The number of the
mounted troops was two hundred million. I heard their
number.

17The horses and riders I saw in my vision looked like
this: Their breastplates were fiery red, dark blue, and yellow

[a] *11 Abaddon* and *Apollyon* mean *Destroyer.* [b] *13* That is, projections

NEW LIVING TRANSLATION

8Their hair was long like the hair of a woman, and their
teeth were like the teeth of a lion. 9They wore armor made
of iron, and their wings roared like an army of chariots
rushing into battle. 10They had tails that stung like scorpi-
ons, with power to torture people. This power was given to
them for five months. 11Their king is the angel from the
bottomless pit; his name in Hebrew is *Abaddon,* and in
Greek, *Apollyon*—the Destroyer.

12The first terror is past, but look, two more terrors are
coming!

The Sixth Trumpet Brings the Second Terror

13Then the sixth angel blew his trumpet, and I heard a
voice speaking from the four horns of the gold altar that
stands in the presence of God. 14And the voice spoke to the
sixth angel who held the trumpet: "Release the four angels
who are bound at the great Euphrates River." 15And the
four angels who had been prepared for this hour and day
and month and year were turned loose to kill one-third of
all the people on earth. 16They led an army of 200 million
mounted troops—I heard an announcement of how many
there were.

17And in my vision, I saw the horses and the riders sit-
ting on them. The riders wore armor that was fiery red and

NEW KING JAMES VERSION

like women's hair, and their teeth were like lions' *teeth.*
9And they had breastplates like breastplates of iron, and
the sound of their wings *was* like the sound of chariots
with many horses running into battle. 10They had tails like
scorpions, and there were stings in their tails. Their power
was to hurt men five months. 11And they had as king over
them the angel of the bottomless pit, whose name in He-
brew *is* Abaddon, but in Greek he has the name Apollyon.

12One woe is past. Behold, still two more woes are com-
ing after these things.

Sixth Trumpet: The Angels from the Euphrates

13Then the sixth angel sounded: And I heard a voice
from the four horns of the golden altar which is before
God, 14saying to the sixth angel who had the trumpet, "Re-
lease the four angels who are bound at the great river Eu-
phrates." 15So the four angels, who had been prepared for
the hour and day and month and year, were released to
kill a third of mankind. 16Now the number of the army of
the horsemen *was* two hundred million; I heard the num-
ber of them. 17And thus I saw the horses in the vision:
those who sat on them had breastplates of fiery red,
hyacinth blue, and sulfur yellow; and the heads of the

THE MESSAGE

lions, and iron breastplates. The sound of their wings was
the sound of horse-drawn chariots charging into battle.
Their tails were equipped with stings, like scorpion tails.
With those tails they were ordered to torture the human
race for five months. They had a king over them, the Angel
of the Abyss. His name in Hebrew is *Abaddon*, in Greek,
Apollyon—"Destroyer."

The first doom is past. Two dooms yet to come.

The sixth Angel trumpeted. I heard a voice speaking to
the sixth Angel from the horns of the Golden Altar before
God: "Let the Four Angels loose, the Angels confined at the
great River Euphrates."

The Four Angels were untied and let loose, Four Angels
all prepared for the exact year, month, day, and even hour
when they were to kill a third of the human race. The num-
ber of the army of horsemen was twice ten thousand times
ten thousand. I heard the count and saw both horses and
riders in my vision: fiery breastplates on the riders, lion

KING JAMES VERSION

as the heads of lions; and out of their mouths issued fire and smoke and brimstone.

18 By these three was the third part of men killed, by the fire, and by the smoke, and by the brimstone, which issued out of their mouths.

19 For their power is in their mouth, and in their tails: for their tails *were* like unto serpents, and had heads, and with them they do hurt.

20 And the rest of the men which were not killed by these plagues yet repented not of the works of their hands, that they should not worship devils, and idols of gold, and silver, and brass, and stone, and of wood: which neither can see, nor hear, nor walk:

21 Neither repented they of their murders, nor of their sorceries, nor of their fornication, nor of their thefts.

10 And I saw another mighty angel come down from heaven, clothed with a cloud: and a rainbow *was* upon his head, and his face *was* as it were the sun, and his feet as pillars of fire:

2 And he had in his hand a little book open: and he set his right foot upon the sea, and *his* left *foot* on the earth,

3 And cried with a loud voice, as *when* a lion roareth: and when he had cried, seven thunders uttered their voices.

4 And when the seven thunders had uttered their voices, I was about to write: and I heard a voice from heaven saying unto me, Seal up those things which the seven thunders uttered, and write them not.

NEW AMERICAN STANDARD BIBLE

heads of the horses are like the heads of lions; and out of their mouths proceed fire and smoke and brimstone.

18 A third of mankind was killed by these three plagues, by the fire and the smoke and the brimstone which proceeded out of their mouths.

19 For the power of the horses is in their mouths and in their tails; for their tails are like serpents and have heads, and with them they do harm.

20 The rest of mankind, who were not killed by these plagues, did not repent of the works of their hands, so as not to worship demons, and the idols of gold and of silver and of brass and of stone and of wood, which can neither see nor hear nor walk;

21 and they did not repent of their murders nor of their sorceries nor of their immorality nor of their thefts.

The Angel and the Little Book

10 I saw another strong angel coming down out of heaven, clothed with a cloud; and the rainbow was upon his head, and his face was like the sun, and his feet like pillars of fire;

2 and he had in his hand a little book which was open. He placed his right foot on the sea and his left on the land;

3 and he cried out with a loud voice, as when a lion roars; and when he had cried out, the seven peals of thunder uttered their voices.

4 When the seven peals of thunder had spoken, I was about to write; and I heard a voice from heaven saying, "Seal up the things which the seven peals of thunder have spoken and do not write them."

NEW CENTURY VERSION

looked like heads of lions, with fire, smoke, and sulfur
coming out of their mouths. [18]A third of all the people on
earth were killed by these three terrible disasters coming
out of the horses' mouths: the fire, the smoke, and the sul-
fur. [19]The horses' power was in their mouths and in their
tails; their tails were like snakes with heads, and with
them they hurt people.

[20]The other people who were not killed by these terrible
disasters still did not change their hearts and turn away
from what they had made with their own hands. They did
not stop worshiping demons and idols made of gold, silver,
bronze, stone, and wood—things that cannot see or hear
or walk. [21]These people did not change their hearts and
turn away from murder or evil magic, from their sexual
sins or stealing.

The Angel and the Small Scroll

10 Then I saw another powerful angel coming down
from heaven dressed in a cloud with a rainbow
over his head. His face was like the sun, and his legs were
like pillars of fire. [2]The angel was holding a small scroll
open in his hand. He put his right foot on the sea and his
left foot on the land. [3]Then he shouted loudly like the roar-
ing of a lion. And when he shouted, the voices of seven
thunders spoke. [4]When the seven thunders spoke, I started
to write. But I heard a voice from heaven say, "Keep hid-
den what the seven thunders said, and do not write them
down."

CONTEMPORARY ENGLISH VERSION

chests. The heads of the horses looked like lions, with fire
and smoke and sulfur coming out of their mouths. [18]One-
third of all people were killed by the three terrible troubles
caused by the fire, the smoke, and the sulfur. [19]The horses
had powerful mouths, and their tails were like poisonous
snakes that bite and hurt.

[20]The people who lived through these terrible troubles
did not turn away from the idols they had made, and they
did not stop worshiping demons. They kept on worshiping
idols that were made of gold, silver, bronze, stone, and
wood. Not one of these idols could see, hear, or walk. [21]No
one stopped murdering or practicing witchcraft or being
immoral or stealing.

The Angel and the Little Scroll

10 I saw another powerful angel come down from
heaven. This one was covered with a cloud, and a
rainbow was over his head. His face was like the sun, his
legs were like columns of fire, [2]and with his hand he held
a little scroll[a] that had been unrolled. He stood there with
his right foot on the sea and his left foot on the land.
[3]Then he shouted with a voice that sounded like a growl-
ing lion. Thunder roared seven times.

[4]After the thunder stopped, I was about to write what it
had said. But a voice from heaven shouted, "Keep it secret!
Don't write these things."

[a] **10.2** *scroll*: See the note at 5.1.

NEW INTERNATIONAL VERSION

as sulfur. The heads of the horses resembled the heads of lions, and out of their mouths came fire, smoke and sulfur. [18]A third of mankind was killed by the three plagues of fire, smoke and sulfur that came out of their mouths. [19]The power of the horses was in their mouths and in their tails; for their tails were like snakes, having heads with which they inflict injury.

[20]The rest of mankind that were not killed by these plagues still did not repent of the work of their hands; they did not stop worshiping demons, and idols of gold, silver, bronze, stone and wood—idols that cannot see or hear or walk. [21]Nor did they repent of their murders, their magic arts, their sexual immorality or their thefts.

The Angel and the Little Scroll

10 Then I saw another mighty angel coming down from heaven. He was robed in a cloud, with a rainbow above his head; his face was like the sun, and his legs were like fiery pillars. [2]He was holding a little scroll, which lay open in his hand. He planted his right foot on the sea and his left foot on the land, [3]and he gave a loud shout like the roar of a lion. When he shouted, the voices of the seven thunders spoke. [4]And when the seven thunders spoke, I was about to write; but I heard a voice from heaven say, "Seal up what the seven thunders have said and do not write it down."

NEW LIVING TRANSLATION

sky blue and yellow. The horses' heads were like the heads of lions, and fire and smoke and burning sulfur billowed from their mouths. [18]One-third of all the people on earth were killed by these three plagues—by the fire and the smoke and burning sulfur that came from the mouths of the horses. [19]Their power was in their mouths, but also in their tails. For their tails had heads like snakes, with the power to injure people.

[20]But the people who did not die in these plagues still refused to turn from their evil deeds. They continued to worship demons and idols made of gold, silver, bronze, stone, and wood—idols that neither see nor hear nor walk! [21]And they did not repent of their murders or their witchcraft or their immorality or their thefts.

The Angel and the Small Scroll

10 Then I saw another mighty angel coming down from heaven, surrounded by a cloud, with a rainbow over his head. His face shone like the sun, and his feet were like pillars of fire. [2]And in his hand was a small scroll, which he had unrolled. He stood with his right foot on the sea and his left foot on the land. [3]And he gave a great shout, like the roar of a lion. And when he shouted, the seven thunders answered.

[4]When the seven thunders spoke, I was about to write. But a voice from heaven called to me: "Keep secret what the seven thunders said. Do not write it down."

NEW KING JAMES VERSION

horses *were* like the heads of lions; and out of their mouths came fire, smoke, and brimstone. [18]By these three *plagues* a third of mankind was killed—by the fire and the smoke and the brimstone which came out of their mouths. [19]For their power[a] is in their mouth and in their tails; for their tails *are* like serpents, having heads; and with them they do harm.

[20]But the rest of mankind, who were not killed by these plagues, did not repent of the works of their hands, that they should not worship demons, and idols of gold, silver, brass, stone, and wood, which can neither see nor hear nor walk. [21]And they did not repent of their murders or their sorceries[b] or their sexual immorality or their thefts.

The Mighty Angel with the Little Book

10 I saw still another mighty angel coming down from heaven, clothed with a cloud. And a rainbow *was* on his head, his face *was* like the sun, and his feet like pillars of fire. [2]He had a little book open in his hand. And he set his right foot on the sea and *his* left *foot* on the land, [3]and cried with a loud voice, as *when* a lion roars. When he cried out, seven thunders uttered their voices. [4]Now when the seven thunders uttered their voices,[a] I was about to write; but I heard a voice from heaven saying to me,[b] "Seal up the things which the seven thunders uttered, and do not write them."

9:19 [a] NU-Text and M-Text read *the power of the horses.*
9:21 [b] NU-Text and M-Text read *drugs.* 10:4 [a] NU-Text and M-Text read *sounded.* [b] NU-Text and M-Text omit *to me.*

THE MESSAGE

heads on the horses breathing out fire and smoke and brimstone. With these three weapons—fire and smoke and brimstone—they killed a third of the human race. The horses killed with their mouths and tails; their serpentlike tails also had heads that wreaked havoc.

The remaining men and women who weren't killed by these weapons went on their merry way—didn't change their way of life, didn't quit worshiping demons, didn't quit centering their lives around lumps of gold and silver and brass, hunks of stone and wood that couldn't see or hear or move. There wasn't a sign of a change of heart. They plunged right on in their murderous, occult, promiscuous, and thieving ways.

10 I saw another powerful Angel coming down out of Heaven wrapped in a cloud. There was a rainbow over his head, his face was sun-radiant, his legs pillars of fire. He had a small book open in his hand. He placed his right foot on the sea and his left foot on land, then called out thunderously, a lion roar. When he called out, the Seven Thunders called back. When the Seven Thunders spoke, I started to write it all down, but a voice out of Heaven stopped me, saying, "Seal with silence the Seven Thunders; don't write a word."

KING JAMES VERSION

5 And the angel which I saw stand upon the sea and upon the earth lifted up his hand to heaven,

6 And sware by him that liveth for ever and ever, who created heaven, and the things that therein are, and the earth, and the things that therein are, and the sea, and the things which are therein, that there should be time no longer:

7 But in the days of the voice of the seventh angel, when he shall begin to sound, the mystery of God should be finished, as he hath declared to his servants the prophets.

8 ¶ And the voice which I heard from heaven spake unto me again, and said, Go *and* take the little book which is open in the hand of the angel which standeth upon the sea and upon the earth.

9 And I went unto the angel, and said unto him, Give me the little book. And he said unto me, Take *it*, and eat it up; and it shall make thy belly bitter, but it shall be in thy mouth sweet as honey.

10 And I took the little book out of the angel's hand, and ate it up; and it was in my mouth sweet as honey: and as soon as I had eaten it, my belly was bitter.

11 And he said unto me, Thou must prophesy again before many peoples, and nations, and tongues, and kings.

NEW AMERICAN STANDARD BIBLE

5 Then the angel whom I saw standing on the sea and on the land lifted up his right hand to heaven,

6 and swore by Him who lives forever and ever, WHO CREATED HEAVEN AND THE THINGS IN IT, AND THE EARTH AND THE THINGS IN IT, AND THE SEA AND THE THINGS IN IT, that there will be delay no longer,

7 but in the days of the voice of the seventh angel, when he is about to sound, then the mystery of God is finished, as He preached to His servants the prophets.

8 Then the voice which I heard from heaven, *I heard* again speaking with me, and saying, "Go, take the book which is open in the hand of the angel who stands on the sea and on the land."

9 So I went to the angel, telling him to give me the little book. And he *said to me, "Take it and eat it; it will make your stomach bitter, but in your mouth it will be sweet as honey."

10 I took the little book out of the angel's hand and ate it, and in my mouth it was sweet as honey; and when I had eaten it, my stomach was made bitter.

11 And they *said to me, "You must prophesy again concerning many peoples and nations and tongues and kings."

NEW CENTURY VERSION

[5]Then the angel I saw standing on the sea and on the
land raised his right hand to heaven, [6]and he made a
promise by the power of the One who lives forever and
ever. He is the One who made the skies and all that is in
them, the earth and all that is in it, and the sea and all
that is in it. The angel promised, "There will be no more
waiting! [7]In the days when the seventh angel is ready to
blow his trumpet, God's secret will be finished. This secret
is the Good News God told to his servants, the prophets."
[8]Then I heard the same voice from heaven again, saying
to me: "Go and take the open scroll that is in the hand of
the angel that is standing on the sea and on the land."
[9]So I went to the angel and told him to give me the
small scroll. And he said to me, "Take the scroll and eat it.
It will be sour in your stomach, but in your mouth it will
be sweet as honey." [10]So I took the small scroll from the
angel's hand and ate it. In my mouth it tasted sweet as
honey, but after I ate it, it was sour in my stomach. [11]Then
I was told, "You must prophesy again about many peoples,
nations, languages, and kings."

CONTEMPORARY ENGLISH VERSION

[5]The angel I had seen standing on the sea and the land
then held his right hand up toward heaven. [6]He made a
promise in the name of God who lives forever and who cre-
ated heaven, earth, the sea, and every living creature. The
angel said, "You won't have to wait any longer. [7]God told
his secret plans to his servants the prophets, and it will all
happen by the time the seventh angel sounds his trumpet."
[8]Once again the voice from heaven spoke to me. It said,
"Go and take the open scroll from the hand of the angel
standing on the sea and the land."
[9]When I went over to ask the angel for the little scroll,
the angel said, "Take the scroll and eat it! Your stomach
will turn sour, but the taste in your mouth will be as sweet
as honey." [10]I took the little scroll from the hand of the
angel and ate it. The taste was as sweet as honey, but my
stomach turned sour.
[11]Then some voices said, "Keep on telling what will hap-
pen to the people of many nations, races, and languages,
and also to kings."

NEW INTERNATIONAL VERSION

[5]Then the angel I had seen standing on the sea and on the land raised his right hand to heaven. [6]And he swore by him who lives for ever and ever, who created the heavens and all that is in them, the earth and all that is in it, and the sea and all that is in it, and said, "There will be no more delay! [7]But in the days when the seventh angel is about to sound his trumpet, the mystery of God will be accomplished, just as he announced to his servants the prophets."

[8]Then the voice that I had heard from heaven spoke to me once more: "Go, take the scroll that lies open in the hand of the angel who is standing on the sea and on the land."

[9]So I went to the angel and asked him to give me the little scroll. He said to me, "Take it and eat it. It will turn your stomach sour, but in your mouth it will be as sweet as honey." [10]I took the little scroll from the angel's hand and ate it. It tasted as sweet as honey in my mouth, but when I had eaten it, my stomach turned sour. [11]Then I was told, "You must prophesy again about many peoples, nations, languages and kings."

NEW LIVING TRANSLATION

[5]Then the mighty angel standing on the sea and on the land lifted his right hand to heaven. [6]And he swore an oath in the name of the one who lives forever and ever, who created heaven and everything in it, the earth and everything in it, and the sea and everything in it. He said, "God will wait no longer. [7]But when the seventh angel blows his trumpet, God's mysterious plan will be fulfilled. It will happen just as he announced it to his servants the prophets."

[8]Then the voice from heaven called to me again: "Go and take the unrolled scroll from the angel who is standing on the sea and on the land."

[9]So I approached him and asked him to give me the little scroll. "Yes, take it and eat it," he said. "At first it will taste like honey, but when you swallow it, it will make your stomach sour!" [10]So I took the little scroll from the hands of the angel, and I ate it! It was sweet in my mouth, but it made my stomach sour. [11]Then he said to me, "You must prophesy again about many peoples, nations, languages, and kings."

NEW KING JAMES VERSION

[5]The angel whom I saw standing on the sea and on the land raised up his hand[c] to heaven [6]and swore by Him who lives forever and ever, who created heaven and the things that are in it, the earth and the things that are in it, and the sea and the things that are in it, that there should be delay no longer, [7]but in the days of the sounding of the seventh angel, when he is about to sound, the mystery of God would be finished, as He declared to His servants the prophets.

John Eats the Little Book

[8]Then the voice which I heard from heaven spoke to me again and said, "Go, take the little book which is open in the hand of the angel who stands on the sea and on the earth."

[9]So I went to the angel and said to him, "Give me the little book."

And he said to me, "Take and eat it; and it will make your stomach bitter, but it will be as sweet as honey in your mouth."

[10]Then I took the little book out of the angel's hand and ate it, and it was as sweet as honey in my mouth. But when I had eaten it, my stomach became bitter. [11]And he[d] said to me, "You must prophesy again about many peoples, nations, tongues, and kings."

10:5 [c] NU-Text and M-Text read *right hand.* 10:11 [d] NU-Text and M-Text read *they.*

THE MESSAGE

Then the Angel I saw astride sea and land lifted his right hand to Heaven and swore by the One Living Forever and Ever, who created Heaven and everything in it, earth and everything in it, sea and everything in it, that time was up—that when the seventh Angel blew his trumpet, which he was about to do, the Mystery of God, all the plans he had revealed to his servants, the prophets, would be completed.

The voice out of Heaven spoke to me again: "Go, take the book held open in the hand of the Angel astride sea and earth." I went up to the Angel and said, "Give me the little book." He said, "Take it, then eat it. It will taste sweet like honey, but turn sour in your stomach." I took the little book from the Angel's hand and it was sweet honey in my mouth, but when I swallowed, my stomach curdled. Then I was told, "You must go back and prophesy again over many peoples and nations and languages and kings."

KING JAMES VERSION

11 And there was given me a reed like unto a rod: and the angel stood, saying, Rise, and measure the temple of God, and the altar, and them that worship therein.

2 But the court which is without the temple leave out, and measure it not; for it is given unto the Gentiles: and the holy city shall they tread under foot forty *and* two months.

3 ¶ And I will give *power* unto my two witnesses, and they shall prophesy a thousand two hundred *and* threescore days, clothed in sackcloth.

4 These are the two olive trees, and the two candlesticks standing before the God of the earth.

5 And if any man will hurt them, fire proceedeth out of their mouth, and devoureth their enemies: and if any man will hurt them, he must in this manner be killed.

6 These have power to shut heaven, that it rain not in the days of their prophecy: and have power over waters to turn them to blood, and to smite the earth with all plagues, as often as they will.

7 And when they shall have finished their testimony, the beast that ascendeth out of the bottomless pit shall make war against them, and shall overcome them, and kill them.

8 And their dead bodies *shall lie* in the street of the great city, which spiritually is called Sodom and Egypt, where also our Lord was crucified.

NEW AMERICAN STANDARD BIBLE

The Two Witnesses

11 Then there was given me a measuring rod like a staff; and someone said, "Get up and measure the temple of God and the altar, and those who worship in it.

2 "Leave out the court which is outside the temple and do not measure it, for it has been given to the nations; and they will tread under foot the holy city for forty-two months.

3 "And I will grant *authority* to my two witnesses, and they will prophesy for twelve hundred and sixty days, clothed in sackcloth."

4 These are the two olive trees and the two lampstands that stand before the Lord of the earth.

5 And if anyone wants to harm them, fire flows out of their mouth and devours their enemies; so if anyone wants to harm them, he must be killed in this way.

6 These have the power to shut up the sky, so that rain will not fall during the days of their prophesying; and they have power over the waters to turn them into blood, and to strike the earth with every plague, as often as they desire.

7 When they have finished their testimony, the beast that comes up out of the abyss will make war with them, and overcome them and kill them.

8 And their dead bodies *will lie* in the street of the great city which [1]mystically is called Sodom and Egypt, where also their Lord was crucified.

11:8 [1] Lit *spiritually*

NEW CENTURY VERSION

The Two Witnesses

11 I was given a measuring stick like a rod, and I was
told, "Go and measure the temple of God and the
altar, and count the people worshiping there. 2But do not
measure the yard outside the temple. Leave it alone,
because it has been given to those who are not God's people. And they will trample on the holy city for forty-two
months. 3And I will give power to my two witnesses to
prophesy for one thousand two hundred sixty days, and
they will be dressed in rough cloth to show their sadness."
4These two witnesses are the two olive trees and the two
lampstands that stand before the Lord of the earth. 5And if
anyone tries to hurt them, fire comes from their mouths
and kills their enemies. And if anyone tries to hurt them in
whatever way, in that same way that person will die.
6These witnesses have the power to stop the sky from raining during the time they are prophesying. And they have
power to make the waters become blood, and they have
power to send every kind of trouble to the earth as many
times as they want.
7When the two witnesses have finished telling their
message, the beast that comes up from the bottomless pit
will fight a war against them. He will defeat them and kill
them. 8The bodies of the two witnesses will lie in the street
of the great city where the Lord was killed. This city is
named Sodom[a] and Egypt, which has a spiritual meaning.

11:8 [a] **Sodom** City that God destroyed because the people were so evil.

CONTEMPORARY ENGLISH VERSION

The Two Witnesses

11 An angel gave me a measuring stick and said:
Measure around God's temple. Be sure to
include the altar and everyone worshiping there. 2But
don't measure the courtyard outside the temple building.
Leave it out. It has been given to those people who don't
know God, and they will trample all over the holy city
for forty-two months. 3My two witnesses will wear sackcloth,[a] while I let them preach for one thousand two
hundred sixty days.
4These two witnesses are the two olive trees and the two
lampstands that stand in the presence of the Lord who
rules the earth. 5Any enemy who tries to harm them will
be destroyed by the fire that comes out of their mouths.
6They have the power to lock up the sky and to keep rain
from falling while they are prophesying. And whenever
they want to, they can turn water to blood and cause all
kinds of terrible troubles on earth.
7After the two witnesses have finished preaching God's
message, the beast that lives in the deep pit will come up
and fight against them. It will win the battle and kill them.
8Their bodies will be left lying in the streets of the same
great city where their Lord was nailed to a cross. And that
city is spiritually like the city of Sodom or the country of
Egypt.

[a] 11.3 *sackcloth*: See the note at 6.12.

NEW INTERNATIONAL VERSION

The Two Witnesses

11 I was given a reed like a measuring rod and was told, "Go and measure the temple of God and the altar, and count the worshipers there. 2But exclude the outer court; do not measure it, because it has been given to the Gentiles. They will trample on the holy city for 42 months. 3And I will give power to my two witnesses, and they will prophesy for 1,260 days, clothed in sackcloth." 4These are the two olive trees and the two lampstands that stand before the Lord of the earth. 5If anyone tries to harm them, fire comes from their mouths and devours their enemies. This is how anyone who wants to harm them must die. 6These men have power to shut up the sky so that it will not rain during the time they are prophesying; and they have power to turn the waters into blood and to strike the earth with every kind of plague as often as they want.

7Now when they have finished their testimony, the beast that comes up from the Abyss will attack them, and overpower and kill them. 8Their bodies will lie in the street of the great city, which is figuratively called Sodom and Egypt, where also their Lord was crucified. 9For three and

NEW LIVING TRANSLATION

The Two Witnesses

11 Then I was given a measuring stick, and I was told, "Go and measure the Temple of God and the altar, and count the number of worshipers. 2But do not measure the outer courtyard, for it has been turned over to the nations. They will trample the holy city for 42 months. 3And I will give power to my two witnesses, and they will be clothed in sackcloth and will prophesy during those 1,260 days."

4These two prophets are the two olive trees and the two lampstands that stand before the Lord of all the earth. 5If anyone tries to harm them, fire flashes from the mouths of the prophets and consumes their enemies. This is how anyone who tries to harm them must die. 6They have power to shut the skies so that no rain will fall for as long as they prophesy. And they have the power to turn the rivers and oceans into blood, and to send every kind of plague upon the earth as often as they wish.

7When they complete their testimony, the beast that comes up out of the bottomless pit will declare war against them. He will conquer them and kill them. 8And their bodies will lie in the main street of Jerusalem,* the city which is called "Sodom" and "Egypt," the city where their Lord

11:8 Greek *the great city.*

NEW KING JAMES VERSION

The Two Witnesses

11 Then I was given a reed like a measuring rod. And the angel stood,[a] saying, "Rise and measure the temple of God, the altar, and those who worship there. 2But leave out the court which is outside the temple, and do not measure it, for it has been given to the Gentiles. And they will tread the holy city underfoot *for* forty-two months. 3And I will give *power* to my two witnesses, and they will prophesy one thousand two hundred and sixty days, clothed in sackcloth."

4These are the two olive trees and the two lampstands standing before the God[b] of the earth. 5And if anyone wants to harm them, fire proceeds from their mouth and devours their enemies. And if anyone wants to harm them, he must be killed in this manner. 6These have power to shut heaven, so that no rain falls in the days of their prophecy; and they have power over waters to turn them to blood, and to strike the earth with all plagues, as often as they desire.

The Witnesses Killed

7When they finish their testimony, the beast that ascends out of the bottomless pit will make war against them, overcome them, and kill them. 8And their dead bodies *will lie* in the street of the great city which spiritually is called Sodom and Egypt, where also our[c] Lord was crucified. 9Then *those*

11:1 [a] NU-Text and M-Text omit *And the angel stood.* 11:4 [b] NU-Text and M-Text read *Lord.* 11:8 [c] NU-Text and M-Text read *their.*

THE MESSAGE

The Two Witnesses

11 I was given a stick for a measuring rod and told, "Get up and measure God's Temple and Altar and everyone worshiping in it. Exclude the outside court; don't measure it. It's been handed over to non-Jewish outsiders. They'll desecrate the Holy City for forty-two months.

"Meanwhile, I'll provide my two Witnesses. Dressed in sackcloth, they'll prophesy for one thousand two hundred sixty days. These are the two Olive Trees, the two Lampstands, standing at attention before God on earth. If anyone tries to hurt them, a blast of fire from their mouths will incinerate them—burn them to a crisp just like that. They'll have power to seal the sky so that it doesn't rain for the time of their prophesying, power to turn rivers and springs to blood, power to hit earth with any and every disaster as often as they want.

"When they've completed their witness, the Beast from the Abyss will emerge and fight them, conquer and kill them, leaving their corpses exposed on the street of the Great City spiritually called Sodom and Egypt, the same City where their Master was crucified. For three and a half

KING JAMES VERSION

9 And they of the people and kindreds and tongues and
nations shall see their dead bodies three days and an half,
and shall not suffer their dead bodies to be put in graves.
10 And they that dwell upon the earth shall rejoice over
them, and make merry, and shall send gifts one to anoth-
er; because these two prophets tormented them that dwelt
on the earth.
11 And after three days and an half the Spirit of life
from God entered into them, and they stood upon their
feet; and great fear fell upon them which saw them.
12 And they heard a great voice from heaven saying
unto them, Come up hither. And they ascended up to heav-
en in a cloud; and their enemies beheld them.
13 And the same hour was there a great earthquake,
and the tenth part of the city fell, and in the earthquake
were slain of men seven thousand: and the remnant were
affrighted, and gave glory to the God of heaven.
14 ¶ The second woe is past; *and*, behold, the third woe
cometh quickly.
15 And the seventh angel sounded; and there were
great voices in heaven, saying, The kingdoms of this world
are become *the kingdoms* of our Lord, and of his Christ;
and he shall reign for ever and ever.

NEW AMERICAN STANDARD BIBLE

9 Those from the peoples and tribes and tongues and
nations *will* look at their dead [2]bodies for three and a half
days, and will not permit their dead bodies to be laid in a
tomb.
10 And those who dwell on the earth *will* rejoice over
them and celebrate; and they will send gifts to one another,
because these two prophets tormented those who dwell on
the earth.
11 But after the three and a half days, the breath of life
from God came into them, and they stood on their feet;
and great fear fell upon those who were watching them.
12 And they heard a loud voice from heaven saying to
them, "Come up here." Then they went up into heaven in
the cloud, and their enemies watched them.
13 And in that hour there was a great earthquake, and a
tenth of the city fell; seven thousand people were killed in
the earthquake, and the rest were terrified and gave glory
to the God of heaven.
14 The second woe is past; behold, the third woe is com-
ing quickly.

The Seventh Trumpet—Christ's Reign Foreseen

15 Then the seventh angel sounded; and there were loud
voices in heaven, saying,
"The kingdom of the world has become *the kingdom* of
our Lord and of His [3]Christ; and He will reign forever and
ever."

11:9 [2] Lit *body* **11:15** [3] I.e. Messiah

NEW CENTURY VERSION

9 Those from every race of people, tribe, language, and
nation will look at the bodies of the two witnesses for
three and one-half days, and they will refuse to bury them.
10 People who live on the earth will rejoice and be happy
because these two are dead. They will send each other
gifts, because these two prophets brought much suffering
to those who live on the earth.
11 But after three and one-half days, God put the breath
of life into the two prophets again. They stood on their
feet, and everyone who saw them became very afraid.
12 Then the two prophets heard a loud voice from heaven
saying, "Come up here!" And they went up into heaven in
a cloud as their enemies watched.
13 In the same hour there was a great earthquake, and a
tenth of the city was destroyed. Seven thousand people
were killed in the earthquake, and those who did not die
were very afraid and gave glory to the God of heaven.
14 The second trouble is finished. Pay attention: The third
trouble is coming soon.

The Seventh Trumpet

15 Then the seventh angel blew his trumpet. And there
were loud voices in heaven, saying:
"The power to rule the world
now belongs to our Lord and his Christ,
and he will rule forever and ever."

CONTEMPORARY ENGLISH VERSION

9 For three and a half days the people of every nation,
tribe, language, and race will stare at the bodies of these
two witnesses and refuse to let them be buried. 10 Everyone
on earth will celebrate and be happy. They will give gifts to
each other, because of what happened to the two prophets
who caused them so much trouble. 11 But three and a half
days later, God will breathe life into their bodies. They will
stand up, and everyone who sees them will be terrified.
12 The witnesses then heard a loud voice from heaven,
saying, "Come up here." And while their enemies were
watching, they were taken up to heaven in a cloud. 13 At
that same moment there was a terrible earthquake that
destroyed a tenth of the city. Seven thousand people were
killed, and the rest were frightened and praised the God
who rules in heaven.
14 The second horrible thing has now happened! But the
third one will be here soon.

The Seventh Trumpet

15 At the sound of the seventh trumpet, loud voices were
heard in heaven. They said,

"Now the kingdom
of this world
belongs to our Lord
and to his Chosen One!
And he will rule
forever and ever!"

NEW INTERNATIONAL VERSION

a half days men from every people, tribe, language and
nation will gaze on their bodies and refuse them burial.
[10]The inhabitants of the earth will gloat over them and
will celebrate by sending each other gifts, because these
two prophets had tormented those who live on the earth.
[11]But after the three and a half days a breath of life
from God entered them, and they stood on their feet, and
terror struck those who saw them. [12]Then they heard a
loud voice from heaven saying to them, "Come up here."
And they went up to heaven in a cloud, while their ene-
mies looked on.
[13]At that very hour there was a severe earthquake and a
tenth of the city collapsed. Seven thousand people were
killed in the earthquake, and the survivors were terrified
and gave glory to the God of heaven.
[14]The second woe has passed; the third woe is coming
soon.

The Seventh Trumpet

[15]The seventh angel sounded his trumpet, and there
were loud voices in heaven, which said:

"The kingdom of the world has become the kingdom of
our Lord and of his Christ,
and he will reign for ever and ever."

NEW LIVING TRANSLATION

was crucified. [9]And for three and a half days, all peoples,
tribes, languages, and nations will come to stare at their
bodies. No one will be allowed to bury them. [10]All the peo-
ple who belong to this world will give presents to each
other to celebrate the death of the two prophets who had
tormented them.
[11]But after three and a half days, the spirit of life from
God entered them, and they stood up! And terror struck all
who were staring at them. [12]Then a loud voice shouted
from heaven, "Come up here!" And they rose to heaven in
a cloud as their enemies watched.
[13]And in the same hour there was a terrible earthquake
that destroyed a tenth of the city. Seven thousand people
died in that earthquake. And everyone who did not die was
terrified and gave glory to the God of heaven.
[14]The second terror is past, but look, now the third ter-
ror is coming quickly.

The Seventh Trumpet Brings the Third Terror

[15]Then the seventh angel blew his trumpet, and there
were loud voices shouting in heaven: "The whole world
has now become the Kingdom of our Lord and of his
Christ, and he will reign forever and ever."

NEW KING JAMES VERSION

from the peoples, tribes, tongues, and nations will see their
dead bodies three-and-a-half days, and not allow[d] their
dead bodies to be put into graves. [10]And those who dwell
on the earth will rejoice over them, make merry, and send
gifts to one another, because these two prophets tormented
those who dwell on the earth.

The Witnesses Resurrected

[11]Now after the three-and-a-half days the breath of life
from God entered them, and they stood on their feet, and
great fear fell on those who saw them. [12]And they[e] heard a
loud voice from heaven saying to them, "Come up here."
And they ascended to heaven in a cloud, and their enemies
saw them. [13]In the same hour there was a great earth-
quake, and a tenth of the city fell. In the earthquake seven
thousand people were killed, and the rest were afraid and
gave glory to the God of heaven.
[14]The second woe is past. Behold, the third woe is com-
ing quickly.

Seventh Trumpet: The Kingdom Proclaimed

[15]Then the seventh angel sounded: And there were loud
voices in heaven, saying, "The kingdoms[f] of this world
have become *the kingdoms* of our Lord and of His Christ,
and He shall reign forever and ever!" [16]And the twenty-four

11:9 [d] NU-Text and M-Text read *nations see . . . and will not allow.*
11:12 [e] M-Text reads *I.* **11:15** [f] NU-Text and M-Text read *kingdom . . . has become.*

THE MESSAGE

days they'll be there—exposed, prevented from getting a
decent burial, stared at by the curious from all over the
world. Those people will cheer at the spectacle, shouting
'Good riddance!' and calling for a celebration, for these
two prophets pricked the conscience of all the people on
earth, made it impossible for them to enjoy their sins.

"Then, after three and a half days, the Living Spirit of
God will enter them—they're on their feet!—and all those
gloating spectators will be scared to death."

I heard a strong voice out of Heaven calling, "Come up
here!" and up they went to Heaven, wrapped in a cloud,
their enemies watching it all. At that moment there was a
gigantic earthquake—a tenth of the city fell to ruin, seven
thousand perished in the earthquake, the rest frightened to
the core of their being, frightened into giving honor to the
God of Heaven.

The second doom is past, the third doom coming right
on its heels.

The Last Trumpet Sounds

The seventh Angel trumpeted. A crescendo of voices in
Heaven sang out,

"The kingdom of the world is now
the Kingdom of our God and his Messiah!
He will rule forever and ever!"

KING JAMES VERSION

16 And the four and twenty elders, which sat before God on their seats, fell upon their faces, and worshipped God,
17 Saying, We give thee thanks, O Lord God Almighty, which art, and wast, and art to come; because thou hast taken to thee thy great power, and hast reigned.
18 And the nations were angry, and thy wrath is come, and the time of the dead, that they should be judged, and that thou shouldest give reward unto thy servants the prophets, and to the saints, and them that fear thy name, small and great; and shouldest destroy them which destroy the earth.
19 And the temple of God was opened in heaven, and there was seen in his temple the ark of his testament: and there were lightnings, and voices, and thunderings, and an earthquake, and great hail.

NEW AMERICAN STANDARD BIBLE

16 And the twenty-four elders, who sit on their thrones before God, fell on their faces and worshiped God,
17 saying,
"We give You thanks, O Lord God, the Almighty, who are and who were, because You have taken Your great power and have begun to reign.
18 "And the nations were enraged, and Your wrath came, and the time *came* for the dead to be judged, and *the time* to reward Your bond-servants the prophets and the saints and those who fear Your name, the small and the great, and to destroy those who destroy the earth."
19 And the temple of God which is in heaven was opened; and the ark of His covenant appeared in His temple, and there were flashes of lightning and sounds and peals of thunder and an earthquake and a great hailstorm.

NEW CENTURY VERSION

16 Then the twenty-four elders, who sit on their thrones before God, bowed down on their faces and worshiped God.
17 They said:
"We give thanks to you, Lord God Almighty,
who is and who was,
because you have used your great power
and have begun to rule!
18 The people of the world were angry,
but your anger has come.
The time has come to judge the dead
and to reward your servants the prophets
and your holy people,
all who respect you, great and small.
The time has come to destroy those who destroy the earth!"
19 Then God's temple in heaven was opened. The Ark that holds the agreement God gave to his people could be seen in his temple. Then there were flashes of lightning, noises, thunder, an earthquake, and a great hailstorm.

CONTEMPORARY ENGLISH VERSION

16 Then the twenty-four elders, who were seated on thrones in God's presence, knelt down and worshiped him.
17 They said,

"Lord God All-Powerful,
you are and you were,
and we thank you.
You used your great power
and started ruling.
18 When the nations got angry,
you became angry too!
Now the time has come
for the dead
to be judged.
It is time for you to reward
your servants the prophets
and all of your people
who honor your name,
no matter who they are.
It is time to destroy everyone
who has destroyed
the earth."

19 The door to God's temple in heaven was then opened, and the sacred chest[b] could be seen inside the temple. I saw lightning and heard roars of thunder. The earth trembled and huge hailstones fell to the ground.

[b] 11.19 *sacred chest*: In Old Testament times the sacred chest was kept in the tent used for worship. It was the symbol of God's presence with his people and also of his agreement with them.

NEW INTERNATIONAL VERSION

16And the twenty-four elders, who were seated on their thrones before God, fell on their faces and worshiped God, 17saying:

"We give thanks to you, Lord God Almighty,
the One who is and who was,
because you have taken your great power
and have begun to reign.
18The nations were angry;
and your wrath has come.
The time has come for judging the dead,
and for rewarding your servants the prophets
and your saints and those who reverence your name,
both small and great—
and for destroying those who destroy the earth."

19Then God's temple in heaven was opened, and within his temple was seen the ark of his covenant. And there came flashes of lightning, rumblings, peals of thunder, an earthquake and a great hailstorm.

NEW LIVING TRANSLATION

16And the twenty-four elders sitting on their thrones before God fell on their faces and worshiped him. 17And they said,

"We give thanks to you, Lord God Almighty,
the one who is and who always was,
for now you have assumed your great power
and have begun to reign.
18 The nations were angry with you,
but now the time of your wrath has come.
It is time to judge the dead and reward your servants.
You will reward your prophets and your holy people,
all who fear your name, from the least to the greatest.
And you will destroy all who have caused destruction
on the earth."

19Then, in heaven, the Temple of God was opened and the Ark of his covenant could be seen inside the Temple. Lightning flashed, thunder crashed and roared; there was a great hailstorm, and the world was shaken by a mighty earthquake.

NEW KING JAMES VERSION

elders who sat before God on their thrones fell on their faces and worshiped God, 17saying:

"We give You thanks, O Lord God Almighty,
The One who is and who was and who is to come,[g]
Because You have taken Your great power and
reigned.
18 The nations were angry, and Your wrath has come,
And the time of the dead, that they should be judged,
And that You should reward Your servants the
prophets and the saints,
And those who fear Your name, small and great,
And should destroy those who destroy the earth."

19Then the temple of God was opened in heaven, and the ark of His covenant[h] was seen in His temple. And there were lightnings, noises, thunderings, an earthquake, and great hail.

11:17 [g] NU-Text and M-Text omit *and who is to come.*
11:19 [h] M-Text reads *the covenant of the Lord.*

THE MESSAGE

The Twenty-four Elders seated before God on their thrones fell to their knees, worshiped, and sang,

"We thank you, Oh God, Sovereign-Strong,
WHO IS AND WHO WAS.
You took your great power
and took over—reigned!
The angry nations now
get a taste of *your* anger.
The time has come to judge the dead,
to reward your servants, all prophets and saints,
Reward small and great who fear your Name,
and destroy the destroyers of earth."

The doors of God's Temple in Heaven flew open, and the Ark of his Covenant was clearly seen surrounded by flashes of lightning, loud shouts, peals of thunder, an earthquake, and a fierce hailstorm.

KING JAMES VERSION

12 And there appeared a great wonder in heaven; a woman clothed with the sun, and the moon under her feet, and upon her head a crown of twelve stars:

2 And she being with child cried, travailing in birth, and pained to be delivered.

3 And there appeared another wonder in heaven; and behold a great red dragon, having seven heads and ten horns, and seven crowns upon his heads.

4 And his tail drew the third part of the stars of heaven, and did cast them to the earth: and the dragon stood before the woman which was ready to be delivered, for to devour her child as soon as it was born.

5 And she brought forth a man child, who was to rule all nations with a rod of iron: and her child was caught up unto God, and *to* his throne.

6 And the woman fled into the wilderness, where she hath a place prepared of God, that they should feed her there a thousand two hundred *and* threescore days.

7 And there was war in heaven: Michael and his angels fought against the dragon; and the dragon fought and his angels,

NEW AMERICAN STANDARD BIBLE

The Woman, Israel

12 A great sign appeared in heaven: a woman clothed with the sun, and the moon under her feet, and on her head a crown of twelve stars;

2 and she was with child; and she *cried out, being in labor and in pain to give birth.

The Red Dragon, Satan

3 Then another sign appeared in heaven: and behold, a great red dragon having seven heads and ten horns, and on his heads *were* seven diadems.

4 And his tail *swept away a third of the stars of heaven and threw them to the earth. And the dragon stood before the woman who was about to give birth, so that when she gave birth he might devour her child.

The Male Child, Christ

5 And she gave birth to a son, a male *child*, who is to rule all the nations with a rod of iron; and her child was caught up to God and to His throne.

6 Then the woman fled into the wilderness where she *had a place prepared by God, so that there she would be nourished for one thousand two hundred and sixty days.

The Angel, Michael

7 And there was war in heaven, Michael and his angels waging war with the dragon. The dragon and his angels waged war,

NEW CENTURY VERSION

The Woman and the Dragon

12 And then a great wonder appeared in heaven: A woman was clothed with the sun, and the moon
was under her feet, and a crown of twelve stars was on her
head. 2She was pregnant and cried out with pain, because
she was about to give birth. 3Then another wonder
appeared in heaven: There was a giant red dragon with
seven heads and seven crowns on each head. He also had
ten horns. 4His tail swept a third of the stars out of the sky
and threw them down to the earth. He stood in front of the
woman who was ready to give birth so he could eat her
baby as soon as it was born. 5Then the woman gave birth
to a son who will rule all the nations with an iron rod. And
her child was taken up to God and to his throne. 6The
woman ran away into the desert to a place God prepared
for her where she would be taken care of for one thousand
two hundred sixty days.

7Then there was a war in heaven. Michael[a] and his angels
fought against the dragon, and the dragon and his angels

12:7 [a] **Michael** The archangel—leader among God's angels or messengers (Jude 9).

CONTEMPORARY ENGLISH VERSION

The Woman and the Dragon

12 Something important appeared in the sky. It was a woman whose clothes were the sun. The moon
was under her feet, and a crown made of twelve stars was
on her head. 2She was about to give birth, and she was
crying because of the great pain.

3Something else appeared in the sky. It was a huge red
dragon with seven heads and ten horns, and a crown on
each of its seven heads. 4With its tail, it dragged a third of
the stars from the sky and threw them down to the earth.
Then the dragon turned toward the woman, because it
wanted to eat her child as soon as it was born.

5The woman gave birth to a son, who would rule all
nations with an iron rod. The boy was snatched away. He
was taken to God and placed on his throne. 6The woman
ran into the desert to a place that God had prepared for
her. There she would be taken care of for one thousand
two hundred sixty days.

Michael Fights the Dragon

7A war broke out in heaven. Michael and his angels
were fighting against the dragon and its angels. 8But the

NEW INTERNATIONAL VERSION

The Woman and the Dragon

12 A great and wondrous sign appeared in heaven: a
woman clothed with the sun, with the moon under
her feet and a crown of twelve stars on her head. 2She was
pregnant and cried out in pain as she was about to give
birth. 3Then another sign appeared in heaven: an enor-
mous red dragon with seven heads and ten horns and
seven crowns on his heads. 4His tail swept a third of the
stars out of the sky and flung them to the earth. The drag-
on stood in front of the woman who was about to give
birth, so that he might devour her child the moment it was
born. 5She gave birth to a son, a male child, who will rule
all the nations with an iron scepter. And her child was
snatched up to God and to his throne. 6The woman fled
into the desert to a place prepared for her by God, where
she might be taken care of for 1,260 days.

7And there was war in heaven. Michael and his angels
fought against the dragon, and the dragon and his angels

NEW LIVING TRANSLATION

The Woman and the Dragon

12 Then I witnessed in heaven an event of great sig-
nificance. I saw a woman clothed with the sun,
with the moon beneath her feet, and a crown of twelve
stars on her head. 2She was pregnant, and she cried out in
the pain of labor as she awaited her delivery.

3Suddenly, I witnessed in heaven another significant
event. I saw a large red dragon with seven heads and ten
horns, with seven crowns on his heads. 4His tail dragged
down one-third of the stars, which he threw to the earth.
He stood before the woman as she was about to give birth
to her child, ready to devour the baby as soon as it was
born.

5She gave birth to a boy who was to rule all nations
with an iron rod. And the child was snatched away from
the dragon and was caught up to God and to his throne.
6And the woman fled into the wilderness, where God had
prepared a place to give her care for 1,260 days.

7Then there was war in heaven. Michael and the angels
under his command fought the dragon and his angels.

NEW KING JAMES VERSION

The Woman, the Child, and the Dragon

12 Now a great sign appeared in heaven: a woman
clothed with the sun, with the moon under her
feet, and on her head a garland of twelve stars. 2Then
being with child, she cried out in labor and in pain to give
birth.

3And another sign appeared in heaven: behold, a great,
fiery red dragon having seven heads and ten horns, and
seven diadems on his heads. 4His tail drew a third of the
stars of heaven and threw them to the earth. And the drag-
on stood before the woman who was ready to give birth, to
devour her Child as soon as it was born. 5She bore a male
Child who was to rule all nations with a rod of iron. And
her Child was caught up to God and His throne. 6Then the
woman fled into the wilderness, where she has a place pre-
pared by God, that they should feed her there one thou-
sand two hundred and sixty days.

Satan Thrown Out of Heaven

7And war broke out in heaven: Michael and his angels
fought with the dragon; and the dragon and his angels

THE MESSAGE

The Woman, Her Son, and the Dragon

12 A great Sign appeared in Heaven: a Woman dressed all in sunlight, standing on the moon, and crowned with Twelve Stars. She was giving birth to a Child and cried out in the pain of childbirth.

And then another Sign alongside the first: a huge and fiery Dragon! It had seven heads and ten horns, a crown on each of the seven heads. With one flick of its tail it knocked a third of the Stars from the sky and dumped them on earth. The Dragon crouched before the Woman in childbirth, poised to eat up the Child when it came.

The Woman gave birth to a Son who will shepherd all nations with an iron rod. Her Son was seized and placed safely before God on his Throne. The Woman herself escaped to the desert to a place of safety prepared by God, all comforts provided her for one thousand two hundred and sixty days.

War broke out in Heaven. Michael and his Angels fought the Dragon. The Dragon and his Angels fought back, but were no match for Michael. They were cleared out of

KING JAMES VERSION

8 And prevailed not; neither was their place found any
more in heaven.
9 And the great dragon was cast out, that old serpent,
called the Devil, and Satan, which deceiveth the whole
world: he was cast out into the earth, and his angels were
cast out with him.
10 And I heard a loud voice saying in heaven, Now is
come salvation, and strength, and the kingdom of our God,
and the power of his Christ: for the accuser of our brethren
is cast down, which accused them before our God day and
night.
11 And they overcame him by the blood of the Lamb,
and by the word of their testimony; and they loved not
their lives unto the death.
12 ¶ Therefore rejoice, *ye* heavens, and ye that dwell in

NEW AMERICAN STANDARD BIBLE

8 and they were not strong enough, and there was no
longer a place found for them in heaven.
9 And the great dragon was thrown down, the serpent
of old who is called the devil and Satan, who deceives the
whole world; he was thrown down to the earth, and his
angels were thrown down with him.
10 Then I heard a loud voice in heaven, saying,
"Now the salvation, and the power, and the kingdom of
our God and the authority of His Christ have come, for the
accuser of our brethren has been thrown down, he who
accuses them before our God day and night.
11 "And they overcame him because of the blood of the
Lamb and because of the word of their testimony, and they
did not love their life even when faced with death.
12 "For this reason, rejoice, O heavens and you who

NEW CENTURY VERSION

fought back. 8 But the dragon was not strong enough, and
he and his angels lost their place in heaven. 9 The giant
dragon was thrown down out of heaven. (He is that old
snake called the devil or Satan, who tricks the whole world.)
The dragon with his angels was thrown down to the earth.
10 Then I heard a loud voice in heaven saying:

"The salvation and the power and the kingdom of our
God
and the authority of his Christ have now come.
The accuser of our brothers and sisters,
who accused them day and night before our God,
has been thrown down.
11 And our brothers and sisters defeated him
by the blood of the Lamb's death
and by the message they preached.
They did not love their lives so much
that they were afraid of death.
12 So rejoice, you heavens
and all who live there!

CONTEMPORARY ENGLISH VERSION

dragon lost the battle. It and its angels were forced out of
their places in heaven 9 and were thrown down to the
earth. Yes, that old snake and his angels were thrown out
of heaven! That snake, who fools everyone on earth, is
known as the devil and Satan. 10 Then I heard a voice from
heaven shout,

"Our God has shown
his saving power,
and his kingdom has come!
God's own Chosen One
has shown his authority.
Satan accused our people
in the presence of God
day and night.
Now he has been thrown out!

11 Our people defeated Satan
because of the blood[a]
of the Lamb
and the message of God.
They were willing
to give up their lives.

12 The heavens should rejoice,
together with everyone
who lives there.

[a] 12.11 *blood*: Or "death."

NEW INTERNATIONAL VERSION

fought back. [8]But he was not strong enough, and they lost their place in heaven. [9]The great dragon was hurled down—that ancient serpent called the devil, or Satan, who leads the whole world astray. He was hurled to the earth, and his angels with him.

[10]Then I heard a loud voice in heaven say:

"Now have come the salvation and the power and the
kingdom of our God,
and the authority of his Christ.
For the accuser of our brothers,
who accuses them before our God day and night,
has been hurled down.
11 They overcame him
by the blood of the Lamb
and by the word of their testimony;
they did not love their lives so much
as to shrink from death.
12 Therefore rejoice, you heavens
and you who dwell in them!

NEW LIVING TRANSLATION

[8]And the dragon lost the battle and was forced out of heaven. [9]This great dragon—the ancient serpent called the Devil, or Satan, the one deceiving the whole world—was thrown down to the earth with all his angels.

[10]Then I heard a loud voice shouting across the heavens,

"It has happened at last—the salvation and power and kingdom of our God, and the authority of his Christ! For the Accuser has been thrown down to earth—the one who accused our brothers and sisters* before our God day and night. [11]And they have defeated him because of the blood of the Lamb and because of their testimony. And they were not afraid to die. [12]Rejoice, O heavens! And you who live in the heavens, rejoice! But terror will

12:10 Greek *brothers*.

NEW KING JAMES VERSION

fought, [8]but they did not prevail, nor was a place found for them[a] in heaven any longer. [9]So the great dragon was cast out, that serpent of old, called the Devil and Satan, who deceives the whole world; he was cast to the earth, and his angels were cast out with him.

[10]Then I heard a loud voice saying in heaven, "Now salvation, and strength, and the kingdom of our God, and the power of His Christ have come, for the accuser of our brethren, who accused them before our God day and night, has been cast down. [11]And they overcame him by the blood of the Lamb and by the word of their testimony, and they did not love their lives to the death. [12]Therefore rejoice, O heavens, and you who dwell in them! Woe to the

12:8 [a] M-Text reads *him.*

THE MESSAGE

Heaven, not a sign of them left. The great Dragon—ancient Serpent, the one called Devil and Satan, the one who led the whole earth astray—thrown out, and all his Angels thrown out with him, thrown down to earth. Then I heard a strong voice out of Heaven saying,

"Salvation and power are established!
Kingdom of our God, authority of his Messiah!
The Accuser of our brothers and sisters thrown out,
who accused them day and night before God.
They defeated him through the blood of the Lamb
and the bold word of their witness.
They weren't in love with themselves;
they were willing to die for Christ.
So rejoice, Oh Heavens, and all who live there,

KING JAMES VERSION

them. Woe to the inhabiters of the earth and of the sea! for the devil is come down unto you, having great wrath, because he knoweth that he hath but a short time.

13 And when the dragon saw that he was cast unto the earth, he persecuted the woman which brought forth the man *child*.

14 And to the woman were given two wings of a great eagle, that she might fly into the wilderness, into her place, where she is nourished for a time, and times, and half a time, from the face of the serpent.

15 And the serpent cast out of his mouth water as a flood after the woman, that he might cause her to be carried away of the flood.

16 And the earth helped the woman, and the earth opened her mouth, and swallowed up the flood which the dragon cast out of his mouth.

17 And the dragon was wroth with the woman, and went to make war with the remnant of her seed, which keep the commandments of God, and have the testimony of Jesus Christ.

13 And I stood upon the sand of the sea, and saw a beast rise up out of the sea, having seven heads and ten horns, and upon his horns ten crowns, and upon his heads the name of blasphemy.

NEW AMERICAN STANDARD BIBLE

dwell in them. Woe to the earth and the sea, because the devil has come down to you, having great wrath, knowing that he has *only* a short time."

13 And when the dragon saw that he was thrown down to the earth, he persecuted the woman who gave birth to the male *child*.

14 But the two wings of the great eagle were given to the woman, so that she could fly into the wilderness to her place, where she *was nourished for a time and times and half a time, from the presence of the serpent.

15 And the serpent poured water like a river out of his mouth after the woman, so that he might cause her to be swept away with the flood.

16 But the earth helped the woman, and the earth opened its mouth and drank up the river which the dragon poured out of his mouth.

17 So the dragon was enraged with the woman, and went off to make war with the rest of her children, who keep the commandments of God and hold to the testimony of Jesus.

The Beast from the Sea

13 And the dragon stood on the sand of the seashore. Then I saw a beast coming up out of the sea, having ten horns and seven heads, and on his horns *were* ten diadems, and on his heads *were* blasphemous names.

NEW CENTURY VERSION

But it will be terrible for the earth and the sea,
because the devil has come down to you!
He is filled with anger,
because he knows he does not have much time."
13When the dragon saw he had been thrown down to the
earth, he hunted for the woman who had given birth to the
son. 14But the woman was given the two wings of a great
eagle so she could fly to the place prepared for her in the
desert. There she would be taken care of for three and one-
half years, away from the snake. 15Then the snake poured
water out of its mouth like a river toward the woman so
the flood would carry her away. 16But the earth helped the
woman by opening its mouth and swallowing the river
that came from the mouth of the dragon. 17Then the drag-
on was very angry at the woman, and he went off to make
war against all her other children—those who obey God's
commands and who have the message Jesus taught.
18And the dragon stood on the seashore.

The Two Beasts

13 Then I saw a beast coming up out of the sea. It had ten horns and seven heads, and there was a crown on each horn. A name against God was written on

CONTEMPORARY ENGLISH VERSION

But pity the earth
and the sea,
because the devil
was thrown down
to the earth.
He knows his time is short,
and he is very angry."

13When the dragon realized that it had been thrown
down to the earth, it tried to make trouble for the woman
who had given birth to a son. 14But the woman was given
two wings like those of a huge eagle, so that she could fly
into the desert. There she would escape from the snake
and be taken care of for a time, two times, and half a time.
15The snake then spewed out water like a river to sweep
the woman away. 16But the earth helped her and swallowed
the water that had come from the dragon's mouth. 17This
made the dragon terribly angry with the woman. So it start-
ed a war against the rest of her children. They are the people
who obey God and are faithful to what Jesus did and taught.
18The dragon[b] stood on the beach beside the sea.

The Two Beasts

13 I looked and saw a beast coming up from the sea.
This one had ten horns and seven heads, and a
crown was on each of its ten horns. On each of its heads
were names that were an insult to God. 2The beast that I

[b] 12.18 *The dragon*: The text has "he," and some manuscripts have "I."

NEW INTERNATIONAL VERSION

But woe to the earth and the sea,
  because the devil has gone down to you!
He is filled with fury,
  because he knows that his time is short."

[13]When the dragon saw that he had been hurled to the earth, he pursued the woman who had given birth to the male child. [14]The woman was given the two wings of a great eagle, so that she might fly to the place prepared for her in the desert, where she would be taken care of for a time, times and half a time, out of the serpent's reach. [15]Then from his mouth the serpent spewed water like a river, to overtake the woman and sweep her away with the torrent. [16]But the earth helped the woman by opening its mouth and swallowing the river that the dragon had spewed out of his mouth. [17]Then the dragon was enraged at the woman and went off to make war against the rest of her offspring—those who obey God's commandments and hold to the testimony of Jesus. 13 [1]And the dragon[a] stood on the shore of the sea.

The Beast out of the Sea

And I saw a beast coming out of the sea. He had ten horns and seven heads, with ten crowns on his horns, and on each head a blasphemous name. [2]The beast I saw

[a] *1* Some late manuscripts *And I*

NEW LIVING TRANSLATION

come on the earth and the sea. For the Devil has come down to you in great anger, and he knows that he has little time."

[13]And when the dragon realized that he had been thrown down to the earth, he pursued the woman who had given birth to the child. [14]But she was given two wings like those of a great eagle. This allowed her to fly to a place prepared for her in the wilderness, where she would be cared for and protected from the dragon* for a time, times, and half a time.

[15]Then the dragon tried to drown the woman with a flood of water that flowed from its mouth. [16]But the earth helped her by opening its mouth and swallowing the river that gushed out from the mouth of the dragon. [17]Then the dragon became angry at the woman, and he declared war against the rest of her children—all who keep God's commandments and confess that they belong to Jesus.

The Beast out of the Sea

[18]Then he stood* waiting on the shore of the sea.

13 And now in my vision I saw a beast rising up out of the sea. It had seven heads and ten horns, with ten crowns on its horns. And written on each head were names that blasphemed God. [2]This beast looked like a

12:14 Greek *the serpent;* also in 12:15. See 12:9. 12:18 Some manuscripts read *Then I stood,* and some translations put this entire sentence into 13:1.

NEW KING JAMES VERSION

inhabitants of the earth and the sea! For the devil has come down to you, having great wrath, because he knows that he has a short time."

The Woman Persecuted

[13]Now when the dragon saw that he had been cast to the earth, he persecuted the woman who gave birth to the male *Child.* [14]But the woman was given two wings of a great eagle, that she might fly into the wilderness to her place, where she is nourished for a time and times and half a time, from the presence of the serpent. [15]So the serpent spewed water out of his mouth like a flood after the woman, that he might cause her to be carried away by the flood. [16]But the earth helped the woman, and the earth opened its mouth and swallowed up the flood which the dragon had spewed out of his mouth. [17]And the dragon was enraged with the woman, and he went to make war with the rest of her offspring, who keep the commandments of God and have the testimony of Jesus Christ.[b]

The Beast from the Sea

13 Then I[a] stood on the sand of the sea. And I saw a beast rising up out of the sea, having seven heads and ten horns,[b] and on his horns ten crowns, and on his heads a blasphemous name. [2]Now the beast which I saw

12:17 [b] NU-Text and M-Text omit *Christ.* 13:1 [a] NU-Text reads *he.* [b] NU-Text and M-Text read *ten horns and seven heads.*

THE MESSAGE

but doom to earth and sea,
For the Devil's come down on you with both feet;
  he's had a great fall;
He's wild and raging with anger;
  he hasn't much time and he knows it."

When the Dragon saw he'd been thrown to earth, he went after the Woman who had given birth to the Man-Child. The Woman was given wings of a great eagle to fly to a place in the desert to be kept in safety and comfort for a time and times and half a time, safe and sound from the Serpent. The Serpent vomited a river of water to swamp and drown her, but earth came to her help, swallowing the water the Dragon spewed from its mouth. Helpless with rage, the Dragon raged at the Woman, then went off to make war with the rest of her children, the children who keep God's commands and hold firm to the witness of Jesus. And the Dragon stood on the shore of the sea.

The Beast From the Sea

13 I saw a Beast rising from the sea. It had ten horns and seven heads—on each horn a crown, and each head inscribed with a blasphemous name. The Beast I saw

KING JAMES VERSION

2 And the beast which I saw was like unto a leopard, and his feet were as *the feet* of a bear, and his mouth as the mouth of a lion: and the dragon gave him his power, and his seat, and great authority.

3 And I saw one of his heads as it were wounded to death; and his deadly wound was healed: and all the world wondered after the beast.

4 And they worshipped the dragon which gave power unto the beast: and they worshipped the beast, saying, Who *is* like unto the beast? who is able to make war with him?

5 And there was given unto him a mouth speaking great things and blasphemies; and power was given unto him to continue forty *and* two months.

6 And he opened his mouth in blasphemy against God, to blaspheme his name, and his tabernacle, and them that dwell in heaven.

7 And it was given unto him to make war with the saints, and to overcome them: and power was given him over all kindreds, and tongues, and nations.

8 And all that dwell upon the earth shall worship him, whose names are not written in the book of life of the Lamb slain from the foundation of the world.

9 If any man have an ear, let him hear.

10 He that leadeth into captivity shall go into captivity:

NEW AMERICAN STANDARD BIBLE

2 And the beast which I saw was like a leopard, and his feet were like *those* of a bear, and his mouth like the mouth of a lion. And the dragon gave him his power and his throne and great authority.

3 *I saw* one of his heads as if it had been slain, and his fatal wound was healed. And the whole earth was amazed *and followed* after the beast;

4 they worshiped the dragon because he gave his authority to the beast; and they worshiped the beast, saying, "Who is like the beast, and who is able to wage war with him?"

5 There was given to him a mouth speaking arrogant words and blasphemies, and authority to act for forty-two months was given to him.

6 And he opened his mouth in blasphemies against God, to blaspheme His name and His tabernacle, *that is*, those who dwell in heaven.

7 It was also given to him to make war with the saints and to overcome them, and authority over every tribe and people and tongue and nation was given to him.

8 All who dwell on the earth will worship him, *everyone* whose name has not been [1]written from the foundation of the world in the book of life of the Lamb who has been slain.

9 If anyone has an ear, let him hear.

10 If anyone [2]*is destined* for captivity, to captivity he

13:8 [1] Or *written from the foundation of the world in the book...*
13:10 [2] Or leads *into captivity*

NEW CENTURY VERSION

each head. [2]This beast looked like a leopard, with feet like
a bear's feet and a mouth like a lion's mouth. And the
dragon gave the beast all of his power and his throne and
great authority. [3]One of the heads of the beast looked as if
it had been killed by a wound, but this death wound was
healed. Then the whole world was amazed and followed
the beast. [4]People worshiped the dragon because he had
given his power to the beast. And they also worshiped the
beast, asking, "Who is like the beast? Who can make war
against it?"
[5]The beast was allowed to say proud words and words
against God, and it was allowed to use its power for forty-
two months. [6]It used its mouth to speak against God,
against God's name, against the place where God lives,
and against all those who live in heaven. [7]It was given
power to make war against God's holy people and to defeat
them. It was given power over every tribe, people, lan-
guage, and nation. [8]And all who live on earth will worship
the beast—all the people since the beginning of the world
whose names are not written in the Lamb's book of life.
The Lamb is the One who was killed.
[9]Anyone who has ears should listen:
[10]If you are to be a prisoner,
then you will be a prisoner.

CONTEMPORARY ENGLISH VERSION

saw had the body of a leopard, the feet of a bear, and the
mouth of a lion. The dragon handed over its own power
and throne and great authority to this beast. [3]One of its
heads seemed to have been fatally wounded, but now it
was well. Everyone on earth marveled at this beast, [4]and
they worshiped the dragon who had given its authority to
the beast. They also worshiped the beast and said, "No one
is like this beast! No one can fight against it."
[5]The beast was allowed to brag and claim to be God, and
for forty-two months it was allowed to rule. [6]The beast
cursed God, and it cursed the name of God. It even cursed
the place where God lives, as well as everyone who lives in
heaven with God. [7]It was allowed to fight against God's
people and defeat them. It was also given authority over
the people of every tribe, nation, language, and race. [8]The
beast was worshiped by everyone whose name wasn't writ-
ten before the time of creation in the book of the Lamb
who was killed.[a]

[9]If you have ears,
then listen!
[10]If you are doomed
to be captured,
you will be captured.

[a] **13.8** *wasn't written . . . was killed*: Or "not written in the book of the Lamb who was killed before the time of creation."

NEW INTERNATIONAL VERSION

resembled a leopard, but had feet like those of a bear and a mouth like that of a lion. The dragon gave the beast his power and his throne and great authority. [3]One of the heads of the beast seemed to have had a fatal wound, but the fatal wound had been healed. The whole world was astonished and followed the beast. [4]Men worshiped the dragon because he had given authority to the beast, and they also worshiped the beast and asked, "Who is like the beast? Who can make war against him?"

[5]The beast was given a mouth to utter proud words and blasphemies and to exercise his authority for forty-two months. [6]He opened his mouth to blaspheme God, and to slander his name and his dwelling place and those who live in heaven. [7]He was given power to make war against the saints and to conquer them. And he was given authority over every tribe, people, language and nation. [8]All inhabitants of the earth will worship the beast—all whose names have not been written in the book of life belonging to the Lamb that was slain from the creation of the world.[b]

[9]He who has an ear, let him hear.

[10]If anyone is to go into captivity,
into captivity he will go.

[b] 8 Or *written from the creation of the world in the book of life belonging to the Lamb that was slain*

NEW LIVING TRANSLATION

leopard, but it had bear's feet and a lion's mouth! And the dragon gave him his own power and throne and great authority.

[3]I saw that one of the heads of the beast seemed wounded beyond recovery—but the fatal wound was healed! All the world marveled at this miracle and followed the beast in awe. [4]They worshiped the dragon for giving the beast such power, and they worshiped the beast. "Is there anyone as great as the beast?" they exclaimed. "Who is able to fight against him?"

[5]Then the beast was allowed to speak great blasphemies against God. And he was given authority to do what he wanted for forty-two months. [6]And he spoke terrible words of blasphemy against God, slandering his name and all who live in heaven, who are his temple. [7]And the beast was allowed to wage war against God's holy people and to overcome them. And he was given authority to rule over every tribe and people and language and nation. [8]And all the people who belong to this world worshiped the beast. They are the ones whose names were not written in the Book of Life, which belongs to the Lamb who was killed before the world was made.

[9]Anyone who is willing to hear should listen and understand. [10]The people who are destined for prison will be arrested and taken away. Those who are destined for death

NEW KING JAMES VERSION

was like a leopard, his feet were like *the feet of* a bear, and his mouth like the mouth of a lion. The dragon gave him his power, his throne, and great authority. [3]And *I saw* one of his heads as if it had been mortally wounded, and his deadly wound was healed. And all the world marveled and followed the beast. [4]So they worshiped the dragon who gave authority to the beast; and they worshiped the beast, saying, "Who *is* like the beast? Who is able to make war with him?"

[5]And he was given a mouth speaking great things and blasphemies, and he was given authority to continue[c] for forty-two months. [6]Then he opened his mouth in blasphemy against God, to blaspheme His name, His tabernacle, and those who dwell in heaven. [7]It was granted to him to make war with the saints and to overcome them. And authority was given him over every tribe,[d] tongue, and nation. [8]All who dwell on the earth will worship him, whose names have not been written in the Book of Life of the Lamb slain from the foundation of the world.

[9]If anyone has an ear, let him hear. [10]He who leads into captivity shall go into captivity; he who kills with the

13:5 [c] M-Text reads *make war.* 13:7 [d] NU-Text and M-Text add *and people.*

THE MESSAGE

looked like a leopard with bear paws and a lion's mouth. The Dragon turned over its power to it, its throne and great authority.

One of the Beast's heads looked as if it had been struck a deathblow, and then healed. The whole earth was agog, gaping at the Beast. They worshiped the Dragon who gave the Beast authority, and they worshiped the Beast, exclaiming, "There's never been anything like the Beast! No one would dare go to war with the Beast!"

The Beast had a loud mouth, boastful and blasphemous. It could do anything it wanted for forty-two months. It yelled blasphemies against God, blasphemed his Name, blasphemed his Church, especially those already dwelling with God in Heaven. It was permitted to make war on God's holy people and conquer them. It held absolute sway over all tribes and peoples, tongues and races. Everyone on earth whose name was not written from the world's foundation in the slaughtered Lamb's Book of Life will worship the Beast.

Are you listening to this? They've made their bed; now they must lie in it. Anyone marked for prison goes straight

KING JAMES VERSION

he that killeth with the sword must be killed with the sword. Here is the patience and the faith of the saints.

11 ¶ And I beheld another beast coming up out of the earth; and he had two horns like a lamb, and he spake as a dragon.

12 And he exerciseth all the power of the first beast before him, and causeth the earth and them which dwell therein to worship the first beast, whose deadly wound was healed.

13 And he doeth great wonders, so that he maketh fire come down from heaven on the earth in the sight of men,

14 And deceiveth them that dwell on the earth by *the means of* those miracles which he had power to do in the sight of the beast; saying to them that dwell on the earth, that they should make an image to the beast, which had the wound by a sword, and did live.

15 And he had power to give life unto the image of the beast, that the image of the beast should both speak, and cause that as many as would not worship the image of the beast should be killed.

16 And he causeth all, both small and great, rich and poor, free and bond, to receive a mark in their right hand, or in their foreheads:

17 And that no man might buy or sell, save he that had the mark, or the name of the beast, or the number of his name.

NEW AMERICAN STANDARD BIBLE

goes; if anyone kills with the sword, with the sword he must be killed. Here is the perseverance and the faith of the saints.

The Beast from the Earth

11 Then I saw another beast coming up out of the earth; and he had two horns like a lamb and he spoke as a dragon.

12 He exercises all the authority of the first beast in his presence. And he makes the earth and those who dwell in it to worship the first beast, whose fatal wound was healed.

13 He performs great signs, so that he even makes fire come down out of heaven to the earth in the presence of men.

14 And he deceives those who dwell on the earth because of the signs which it was given him to perform in the presence of the beast, telling those who dwell on the earth to make an image to the beast who *had the wound of the sword and has come to life.

15 And it was given to him to give breath to the image of the beast, so that the image of the beast would even [3]speak and cause as many as do not worship the image of the beast to be killed.

16 And he causes all, the small and the great, and the rich and the poor, and the free men and the slaves, to be given a mark on their right hand or on their forehead,

17 and *he provides* that no one will be able to buy or to sell, except the one who has the mark, *either* the name of the beast or the number of his name.

13:15 [3] One early ms reads *speak, and he will cause*

NEW CENTURY VERSION

If you are to be killed with the sword,
then you will be killed with the sword.
This means that God's holy people must have patience and faith.

11Then I saw another beast coming up out of the earth. It
had two horns like a lamb, but it spoke like a dragon.
12This beast stands before the first beast and uses the same
power the first beast has. By this power it makes everyone
living on earth worship the first beast, who had the death
wound that was healed. 13And the second beast does great
miracles so that it even makes fire come down from heaven
to earth while people are watching. 14It fools those who live
on earth by the miracles it has been given the power to do.
It does these miracles to serve the first beast. The second
beast orders people to make an idol to honor the first beast,
the one that was wounded by the deadly sword but sprang
to life again. 15The second beast was given power to give
life to the idol of the first one so that the idol could speak.
And the second beast was given power to command all who
will not worship the image of the beast to be killed. 16The
second beast also forced all people, small and great, rich
and poor, free and slave, to have a mark on their right hand
or on their forehead. 17No one could buy or sell without this
mark, which is the name of the beast or the number of its

CONTEMPORARY ENGLISH VERSION

If you are doomed
to be killed by a sword,
you will be killed
by a sword.

This means that God's people must learn to endure and be faithful!

11I now saw another beast. This one came out of the
ground. It had two horns like a lamb, but spoke like a
dragon. 12It worked for the beast whose fatal wound had
been healed. And it used all its authority to force the earth
and its people to worship that beast. 13It worked mighty
miracles, and while people watched, it even made fire
come down from the sky.

14This second beast fooled people on earth by working
miracles for the first one. Then it talked them into making
an idol in the form of the beast that did not die after being
wounded by a sword. 15It was allowed to put breath into
the idol, so that it could speak. Everyone who refused to
worship the idol of the beast was put to death. 16All people
were forced to put a mark on their right hand or forehead.
Whether they were powerful or weak, rich or poor, free
people or slaves, 17they all had to have this mark, or else
they could not buy or sell anything. This mark stood for
the name of the beast and for the number of its name.

NEW INTERNATIONAL VERSION

If anyone is to be killed[c] with the sword,
with the sword he will be killed.

This calls for patient endurance and faithfulness on the part of the saints.

The Beast out of the Earth

11 Then I saw another beast, coming out of the earth. He had two horns like a lamb, but he spoke like a dragon. 12 He exercised all the authority of the first beast on his behalf, and made the earth and its inhabitants worship the first beast, whose fatal wound had been healed. 13 And he performed great and miraculous signs, even causing fire to come down from heaven to earth in full view of men. 14 Because of the signs he was given power to do on behalf of the first beast, he deceived the inhabitants of the earth. He ordered them to set up an image in honor of the beast who was wounded by the sword and yet lived. 15 He was given power to give breath to the image of the first beast, so that it could speak and cause all who refused to worship the image to be killed. 16 He also forced everyone, small and great, rich and poor, free and slave, to receive a mark on his right hand or on his forehead, 17 so that no one could buy or sell unless he had the mark, which is the name of the beast or the number of his name.

[c] *10* Some manuscripts *anyone kills*

NEW LIVING TRANSLATION

will be killed. But do not be dismayed, for here is your opportunity to have endurance and faith.

The Beast out of the Earth

11 Then I saw another beast come up out of the earth. He had two horns like those of a lamb, and he spoke with the voice of a dragon. 12 He exercised all the authority of the first beast. And he required all the earth and those who belong to this world to worship the first beast, whose death-wound had been healed. 13 He did astounding miracles, such as making fire flash down to earth from heaven while everyone was watching. 14 And with all the miracles he was allowed to perform on behalf of the first beast, he deceived all the people who belong to this world. He ordered the people of the world to make a great statue of the first beast, who was fatally wounded and then came back to life. 15 He was permitted to give life to this statue so that it could speak. Then the statue commanded that anyone refusing to worship it must die.

16 He required everyone—great and small, rich and poor, slave and free—to be given a mark on the right hand or on the forehead. 17 And no one could buy or sell anything without that mark, which was either the name of the beast or the number representing his name. 18 Wisdom is needed

NEW KING JAMES VERSION

sword must be killed with the sword. Here is the patience and the faith of the saints.

The Beast from the Earth

11 Then I saw another beast coming up out of the earth, and he had two horns like a lamb and spoke like a dragon. 12 And he exercises all the authority of the first beast in his presence, and causes the earth and those who dwell in it to worship the first beast, whose deadly wound was healed. 13 He performs great signs, so that he even makes fire come down from heaven on the earth in the sight of men. 14 And he deceives those[e] who dwell on the earth by those signs which he was granted to do in the sight of the beast, telling those who dwell on the earth to make an image to the beast who was wounded by the sword and lived. 15 He was granted *power* to give breath to the image of the beast, that the image of the beast should both speak and cause as many as would not worship the image of the beast to be killed. 16 He causes all, both small and great, rich and poor, free and slave, to receive a mark on their right hand or on their foreheads, 17 and that no one may buy or sell except one who has the mark or[f] the name of the beast, or the number of his name.

13:14 [e] M-Text reads *my own people.* 13:17 [f] NU-Text and M-Text omit *or.*

THE MESSAGE

to prison; anyone pulling a sword goes down by the sword. Meanwhile, God's holy people passionately and faithfully stand their ground.

The Beast From Under the Ground

I saw another Beast rising out of the ground. It had two horns like a lamb but sounded like a dragon when it spoke. It was a puppet of the first Beast, made earth and everyone in it worship the first Beast, which had been healed of its deathblow.

This second Beast worked magical signs, dazzling people by making fire come down from Heaven. It used the magic it got from the Beast to dupe earth dwellers, getting them to make an image of the Beast that received the deathblow and lived. It was able to animate the image of the Beast so that it talked, and then arrange that anyone not worshiping the Beast would be killed. It forced all people, small and great, rich and poor, free and slave, to have a mark on the right hand or forehead. Without the mark of the name of the Beast or the number of its name, it was impossible to buy or sell anything.

KING JAMES VERSION

18 Here is wisdom. Let him that hath understanding count the number of the beast: for it is the number of a man; and his number *is* Six hundred threescore *and* six.

14 And I looked, and, lo, a Lamb stood on the mount Sion, and with him an hundred forty *and* four thousand, having his Father's name written in their foreheads.

2 And I heard a voice from heaven, as the voice of many waters, and as the voice of a great thunder: and I heard the voice of harpers harping with their harps:

3 And they sung as it were a new song before the throne, and before the four beasts, and the elders: and no man could learn that song but the hundred *and* forty *and* four thousand, which were redeemed from the earth.

4 These are they which were not defiled with women; for they are virgins. These are they which follow the Lamb whithersoever he goeth. These were redeemed from among men, *being* the firstfruits unto God and to the Lamb.

5 And in their mouth was found no guile: for they are without fault before the throne of God.

6 ¶ And I saw another angel fly in the midst of heaven,

NEW AMERICAN STANDARD BIBLE

18 Here is wisdom. Let him who has understanding calculate the number of the beast, for the number is that of a man; and his number is [4]six hundred and sixty-six.

The Lamb and the 144,000 on Mount Zion

14 Then I looked, and behold, the Lamb *was* standing on Mount Zion, and with Him one hundred and forty-four thousand, having His name and the name of His Father written on their foreheads.

2 And I heard a voice from heaven, like the sound of many waters and like the sound of loud thunder, and the voice which I heard *was* like *the sound* of harpists playing on their harps.

3 And they *sang a new song before the throne and before the four living creatures and the elders; and no one could learn the song except the one hundred and forty-four thousand who had been purchased from the earth.

4 These are the ones who have not been defiled with women, for they [1]have kept themselves chaste. These *are* the ones who follow the Lamb wherever He goes. These have been purchased from among men as first fruits to God and to the Lamb.

5 And no lie was found in their mouth; they are blameless.

Vision of the Angel with the Gospel

6 And I saw another angel flying in midheaven, having

13:18 [4] One early ms reads 616 14:4 [1] Lit *are chaste men*

NEW CENTURY VERSION

name. 18 This takes wisdom. Let the one who has understanding find the meaning of the number, which is the number of a person. Its number is six hundred sixty-six.

The Song of the Saved

14 Then I looked, and there before me was the Lamb standing on Mount Zion.[a] With him were one hundred forty-four thousand people who had his name and his Father's name written on their foreheads. 2 And I heard a sound from heaven like the noise of flooding water and like the sound of loud thunder. The sound I heard was like people playing harps. 3 And they sang a new song before the throne and before the four living creatures and the elders. No one could learn the new song except the one hundred forty-four thousand who had been bought from the earth. 4 These are the ones who did not do sinful things with women, because they kept themselves pure. They follow the Lamb every place he goes. These one hundred forty-four thousand were bought from among the people of the earth as people to be offered to God and the Lamb. 5 They were not guilty of telling lies; they are without fault.

The Three Angels

6 Then I saw another angel flying high in the air. He had

14:1 [a] **Mount Zion** Another name for Jerusalem; here meaning the spiritual city of God's people.

CONTEMPORARY ENGLISH VERSION

18 You need wisdom to understand the number of the beast! But if you are smart enough, you can figure this out. Its number is six hundred sixty-six, and it stands for a person.

The Lamb and His 144,000 Followers

14 I looked and saw the Lamb standing on Mount Zion![a] With him were a hundred forty-four thousand, who had his name and his Father's name written on their foreheads. 2 Then I heard a sound from heaven that was like a roaring flood or loud thunder or even like the music of harps. 3 And a new song was being sung in front of God's throne and in front of the four living creatures and the elders. No one could learn that song, except the one hundred forty-four thousand who had been rescued from the earth. 4 All of these are pure virgins, and they follow the Lamb wherever he leads. They have been rescued to be presented to God and the Lamb as the most precious people[b] on earth. 5 They never tell lies, and they are innocent.

The Messages of the Three Angels

6 I saw another angel. This one was flying across the sky

[a] **14.1** *Mount Zion*: Another name for Jerusalem. [b] **14.4** *the most precious people*: The Greek text has "the first people." The Law of Moses taught that the first-born of all animals and the first part of the harvest were special and belonged to the Lord.

NEW INTERNATIONAL VERSION

18 This calls for wisdom. If anyone has insight, let him calculate the number of the beast, for it is man's number. His number is 666.

The Lamb and the 144,000

14 Then I looked, and there before me was the Lamb, standing on Mount Zion, and with him 144,000 who had his name and his Father's name written on their foreheads. 2 And I heard a sound from heaven like the roar of rushing waters and like a loud peal of thunder. The sound I heard was like that of harpists playing their harps. 3 And they sang a new song before the throne and before the four living creatures and the elders. No one could learn the song except the 144,000 who had been redeemed from the earth. 4 These are those who did not defile themselves with women, for they kept themselves pure. They follow the Lamb wherever he goes. They were purchased from among men and offered as firstfruits to God and the Lamb. 5 No lie was found in their mouths; they are blameless.

The Three Angels

6 Then I saw another angel flying in midair, and he had

NEW LIVING TRANSLATION

to understand this. Let the one who has understanding solve the number of the beast, for it is the number of a man.* His number is 666.*

The Lamb and the 144,000

14 Then I saw the Lamb standing on Mount Zion, and with him were 144,000 who had his name and his Father's name written on their foreheads. 2 And I heard a sound from heaven like the roaring of a great waterfall or the rolling of mighty thunder. It was like the sound of many harpists playing together.

3 This great choir sang a wonderful new song in front of the throne of God and before the four living beings and the twenty-four elders. And no one could learn this song except those 144,000 who had been redeemed from the earth. 4 For they are spiritually undefiled, pure as virgins,* following the Lamb wherever he goes. They have been purchased from among the people on the earth as a special offering* to God and to the Lamb. 5 No falsehood can be charged against them; they are blameless.

The Three Angels

6 And I saw another angel flying through the heavens,

13:18a Or *of humanity.* **13:18b** Some manuscripts read *616.* **14:4a** Greek *they are virgins who have not defiled themselves with women.* **14:4b** Greek *as firstfruits.*

NEW KING JAMES VERSION

18 Here is wisdom. Let him who has understanding calculate the number of the beast, for it is the number of a man: His number *is* 666.

The Lamb and the 144,000

14 Then I looked, and behold, a[a] Lamb standing on Mount Zion, and with Him one hundred *and* forty-four thousand, having[b] His Father's name written on their foreheads. 2 And I heard a voice from heaven, like the voice of many waters, and like the voice of loud thunder. And I heard the sound of harpists playing their harps. 3 They sang as it were a new song before the throne, before the four living creatures, and the elders; and no one could learn that song except the hundred *and* forty-four thousand who were redeemed from the earth. 4 These are the ones who were not defiled with women, for they are virgins. These are the ones who follow the Lamb wherever He goes. These were redeemed[c] from *among* men, *being* firstfruits to God and to the Lamb. 5 And in their mouth was found no deceit,[d] for they are without fault before the throne of God.[e]

The Proclamations of Three Angels

6 Then I saw another angel flying in the midst of heaven,

14:1 [a] NU-Text and M-Text read *the.* [b] NU-Text and M-Text add *His name and.* **14:4** [c] M-Text adds *by Jesus.* **14:5** [d] NU-Text and M-Text read *falsehood.* [e] NU-Text and M-Text omit *before the throne of God.*

THE MESSAGE

Solve a riddle: Put your heads together and figure out the meaning of the number of the Beast. It's a human number: six hundred sixty-six.

A Perfect Offering

14 I saw—it took my breath away!—the Lamb standing on Mount Zion, One Hundred and Forty-four Thousand standing there with him, his Name and the Name of his Father inscribed on their foreheads. And I heard a voice out of Heaven, the sound like a cataract, like the crash of thunder.

And then I heard music, harp music and the harpists singing a new song before the Throne and the Four Animals and the Elders. Only the Hundred and Forty-four Thousand could learn to sing the song. They were bought from earth, lived without compromise, virgin-fresh before God. Wherever the Lamb went, they followed. They were bought from humankind, first fruits of the harvest for God and the Lamb. Not a false word in their mouths. A perfect offering.

Voices From Heaven

I saw another Angel soaring in Middle-Heaven. He had

KING JAMES VERSION

having the everlasting gospel to preach unto them that
dwell on the earth, and to every nation, and kindred, and
tongue, and people,
7 Saying with a loud voice, Fear God, and give glory to
him; for the hour of his judgment is come: and worship
him that made heaven, and earth, and the sea, and the
fountains of waters.
8 And there followed another angel, saying, Babylon is
fallen, is fallen, that great city, because she made all
nations drink of the wine of the wrath of her fornication.
9 And the third angel followed them, saying with a loud
voice, If any man worship the beast and his image, and
receive *his* mark in his forehead, or in his hand,
10 The same shall drink of the wine of the wrath of
God, which is poured out without mixture into the cup of
his indignation; and he shall be tormented with fire and
brimstone in the presence of the holy angels, and in the
presence of the Lamb:
11 And the smoke of their torment ascendeth up for
ever and ever: and they have no rest day nor night, who
worship the beast and his image, and whosoever receiveth
the mark of his name.
12 Here is the patience of the saints: here *are* they that
keep the commandments of God, and the faith of Jesus.
13 ¶ And I heard a voice from heaven saying unto me,
Write, Blessed *are* the dead which die in the Lord from
henceforth: Yea, saith the Spirit, that they may rest from
their labours; and their works do follow them.

NEW AMERICAN STANDARD BIBLE

an eternal gospel to preach to those who live on the earth,
and to every nation and tribe and tongue and people;
7 and he said with a loud voice, "Fear God, and give
Him glory, because the hour of His judgment has come;
worship Him who made the heaven and the earth and sea
and springs of waters."
8 And another angel, a second one, followed, saying,
"Fallen, fallen is Babylon the great, she who has made all
the nations drink of the wine of the passion of her
immorality."

Doom for Worshipers of the Beast

9 Then another angel, a third one, followed them, saying
with a loud voice, "If anyone worships the beast and his
image, and receives a mark on his forehead or on his hand,
10 he also will drink of the wine of the wrath of God,
which is mixed in full strength in the cup of His anger; and
he will be tormented with fire and brimstone in the presence of the holy angels and in the presence of the Lamb.
11 "And the smoke of their torment goes up forever and
ever; they have no rest day and night, those who worship
the beast and his image, and whoever receives the mark of
his name."
12 Here is the perseverance of the saints who keep the
commandments of God and their faith in Jesus.
13 And I heard a voice from heaven, saying, "Write,
'Blessed are the dead who die in the Lord from now on!' "
"Yes," says the Spirit, "so that they may rest from their
labors, for their deeds follow with them."

NEW CENTURY VERSION

the eternal Good News to preach to those who live on
earth—to every nation, tribe, language, and people. [7]He
preached in a loud voice, "Fear God and give him praise,
because the time has come for God to judge all people. So
worship God who made the heavens, and the earth, and
the sea, and the springs of water."
[8]Then the second angel followed the first angel and said,
"Ruined, ruined is the great city of Babylon! She made all
the nations drink the wine of the anger of her adultery."
[9]Then a third angel followed the first two angels, saying
in a loud voice: "If anyone worships the beast and his idol
and gets the beast's mark on the forehead or on the hand,
[10]that one also will drink the wine of God's anger, which is
prepared with all its strength in the cup of his anger. And
that person will be put in pain with burning sulfur before
the holy angels and the Lamb. [11]And the smoke from their
burning pain will rise forever and ever. There will be no
rest, day or night, for those who worship the beast and his
idol or who get the mark of his name." [12]This means God's
holy people must be patient. They must obey God's commands and keep their faith in Jesus.
[13]Then I heard a voice from heaven saying, "Write this:
Happy are the dead who die from now on in the Lord."
The Spirit says, "Yes, they will rest from their hard
work, and the reward of all they have done stays with
them."

CONTEMPORARY ENGLISH VERSION

and had the eternal good news to announce to the people
of every race, tribe, language, and nation on earth. [7]The
angel shouted, "Worship and honor God! The time has
come for him to judge everyone. Kneel down before the one
who created heaven and earth, the oceans, and every
stream."
[8]A second angel followed and said, "The great city of
Babylon has fallen! This is the city that made all nations
drunk and immoral. Now God is angry, and Babylon has
fallen."
[9]Finally, a third angel came and shouted:

Here is what will happen if you worship the beast and
the idol and have the mark of the beast on your hand or
forehead. [10]You will have to drink the wine that God gives
to everyone who makes him angry. You will feel his
mighty anger, and you will be tortured with fire and burning sulfur, while the holy angels and the Lamb look on.
[11]If you worship the beast and the idol and accept the
mark of its name, you will be tortured day and night.
The smoke from your torture will go up forever and ever,
and you will never be able to rest.

[12]God's people must learn to endure. They must also
obey his commands and have faith in Jesus.
[13]Then I heard a voice from heaven say, "Put this in
writing. From now on, the Lord will bless everyone who
has faith in him when they die."
The Spirit answered, "Yes, they will rest from their hard
work, and they will be rewarded for what they have done."

NEW INTERNATIONAL VERSION

the eternal gospel to proclaim to those who live on the
earth—to every nation, tribe, language and people. 7He
said in a loud voice, "Fear God and give him glory, because
the hour of his judgment has come. Worship him who
made the heavens, the earth, the sea and the springs of
water."
8A second angel followed and said, "Fallen! Fallen is
Babylon the Great, which made all the nations drink the
maddening wine of her adulteries."
9A third angel followed them and said in a loud voice:
"If anyone worships the beast and his image and receives
his mark on the forehead or on the hand, 10he, too, will
drink of the wine of God's fury, which has been poured full
strength into the cup of his wrath. He will be tormented
with burning sulfur in the presence of the holy angels and
of the Lamb. 11And the smoke of their torment rises for
ever and ever. There is no rest day or night for those who
worship the beast and his image, or for anyone who
receives the mark of his name." 12This calls for patient
endurance on the part of the saints who obey God's com-
mandments and remain faithful to Jesus.
13Then I heard a voice from heaven say, "Write: Blessed
are the dead who die in the Lord from now on."
"Yes," says the Spirit, "they will rest from their labor,
for their deeds will follow them."

NEW LIVING TRANSLATION

carrying the everlasting Good News to preach to the people
who belong to this world—to every nation, tribe, language,
and people. 7"Fear God," he shouted. "Give glory to him.
For the time has come when he will sit as judge. Worship
him who made heaven and earth, the sea, and all the
springs of water."
8Then another angel followed him through the skies,
shouting, "Babylon is fallen—that great city is fallen—
because she seduced the nations of the world and made
them drink the wine of her passionate immorality."
9Then a third angel followed them, shouting, "Anyone
who worships the beast and his statue or who accepts his
mark on the forehead or the hand 10must drink the wine of
God's wrath. It is poured out undiluted into God's cup of
wrath. And they will be tormented with fire and burning
sulfur in the presence of the holy angels and the Lamb.
11The smoke of their torment rises forever and ever, and
they will have no relief day or night, for they have wor-
shiped the beast and his statue and have accepted the
mark of his name. 12Let this encourage God's holy people
to endure persecution patiently and remain firm to the
end, obeying his commands and trusting in Jesus."
13And I heard a voice from heaven saying, "Write this
down: Blessed are those who die in the Lord from now on.
Yes, says the Spirit, they are blessed indeed, for they will
rest from all their toils and trials; for their good deeds fol-
low them!"

NEW KING JAMES VERSION

having the everlasting gospel to preach to those who dwell
on the earth—to every nation, tribe, tongue, and people—
7saying with a loud voice, "Fear God and give glory to Him,
for the hour of His judgment has come; and worship Him
who made heaven and earth, the sea and springs of water."
8And another angel followed, saying, "Babylon[f] is fallen,
is fallen, that great city, because she has made all nations
drink of the wine of the wrath of her fornication."
9Then a third angel followed them, saying with a loud
voice, "If anyone worships the beast and his image, and
receives *his* mark on his forehead or on his hand, 10he
himself shall also drink of the wine of the wrath of God,
which is poured out full strength into the cup of His
indignation. He shall be tormented with fire and brimstone
in the presence of the holy angels and in the presence of
the Lamb. 11And the smoke of their torment ascends forev-
er and ever; and they have no rest day or night, who wor-
ship the beast and his image, and whoever receives the
mark of his name."
12Here is the patience of the saints; here *are* those[g] who
keep the commandments of God and the faith of Jesus.
13Then I heard a voice from heaven saying to me,[h] "Write:
'Blessed *are* the dead who die in the Lord from now on.' "
"Yes," says the Spirit, "that they may rest from their
labors, and their works follow them."

14:8 [f] NU-Text reads *Babylon the great is fallen, is fallen, which has made;* M-Text reads *Babylon the great is fallen. She has made.*
14:12 [g] NU-Text and M-Text omit *here are those.* **14:13** [h] NU-Text and M-Text omit *to me.*

THE MESSAGE

an Eternal Message to preach to all who were still on
earth, every nation and tribe, every tongue and people. He
preached in a loud voice, "Fear God and give him glory!
His hour of judgment has come! Worship the Maker of
Heaven and earth, salt sea and fresh water!"

A second Angel followed, calling out, "Ruined, ruined, Great Babylon ruined! She made all the nations drunk on the wine of her whoring!"

A third Angel followed, shouting, warning, "If anyone worships the Beast and its image and takes the mark on forehead or hand, that person will drink the wine of God's wrath, prepared unmixed in his chalice of anger, and suffer torment from fire and brimstone in the presence of Holy Angels, in the presence of the Lamb. Smoke from their torment will rise age after age. No respite for those who worship the Beast and its image, who take the mark of its name."

Meanwhile, the saints stand passionately patient, keeping God's commands, staying faithful to Jesus.

I heard a voice out of Heaven, "Write this: Blessed are those who die in the Master from now on; how blessed to die that way!"

"Yes," says the Spirit, "and blessed rest from their hard, hard work. None of what they've done is wasted; God blesses them for it all in the end."

KING JAMES VERSION

14 And I looked, and behold a white cloud, and upon the cloud *one* sat like unto the Son of man, having on his head a golden crown, and in his hand a sharp sickle.

15 And another angel came out of the temple, crying with a loud voice to him that sat on the cloud, Thrust in thy sickle, and reap: for the time is come for thee to reap; for the harvest of the earth is ripe.

16 And he that sat on the cloud thrust in his sickle on the earth; and the earth was reaped.

17 And another angel came out of the temple which is in heaven, he also having a sharp sickle.

18 And another angel came out from the altar, which had power over fire; and cried with a loud cry to him that had the sharp sickle, saying, Thrust in thy sharp sickle, and gather the clusters of the vine of the earth; for her grapes are fully ripe.

19 And the angel thrust in his sickle into the earth, and gathered the vine of the earth, and cast *it* into the great winepress of the wrath of God.

20 And the winepress was trodden without the city, and blood came out of the winepress, even unto the horse bridles, by the space of a thousand *and* six hundred furlongs.

NEW AMERICAN STANDARD BIBLE

The Reapers

14 Then I looked, and behold, a white cloud, and sitting on the cloud *was* one like [2]a son of man, having a golden crown on His head and a sharp sickle in His hand.

15 And another angel came out of the temple, crying out with a loud voice to Him who sat on the cloud, "Put in your sickle and reap, for the hour to reap has come, because the harvest of the earth is ripe."

16 Then He who sat on the cloud swung His sickle over the earth, and the earth was reaped.

17 And another angel came out of the temple which is in heaven, and he also had a sharp sickle.

18 Then another angel, the one who has power over fire, came out from the altar; and he called with a loud voice to him who had the sharp sickle, saying, "Put in your sharp sickle and gather the clusters from the vine of the earth, because her grapes are ripe."

19 So the angel swung his sickle to the earth and gathered *the clusters from* the vine of the earth, and threw them into the great wine press of the wrath of God.

20 And the wine press was trodden outside the city, and blood came out from the wine press, up to the horses' bridles, for a distance of [3]two hundred miles.

14:14 [2] Or *the Son of Man* 14:20 [3] Lit *sixteen hundred stadia;* a stadion was approx 600 ft

NEW CENTURY VERSION

The Earth Is Harvested

14 Then I looked, and there before me was a white cloud,
and sitting on the white cloud was One who looked like a
Son of Man.[b] He had a gold crown on his head and a sharp
sickle[c] in his hand. 15 Then another angel came out of the
temple and called out in a loud voice to the One who was
sitting on the cloud, "Take your sickle and harvest from
the earth, because the time to harvest has come, and the
fruit of the earth is ripe." 16 So the One who was sitting on
the cloud swung his sickle over the earth, and the earth
was harvested.

17 Then another angel came out of the temple in heaven,
and he also had a sharp sickle. 18 And then another angel,
who has power over the fire, came from the altar. This
angel called to the angel with the sharp sickle, saying,
"Take your sharp sickle and gather the bunches of grapes
from the earth's vine, because its grapes are ripe." 19 Then
the angel swung his sickle over the earth. He gathered the
earth's grapes and threw them into the great winepress of
God's anger. 20 They were trampled in the winepress outside the city, and blood flowed out of the winepress as
high as horses' bridles for a distance of about one hundred
eighty miles.

14:14 [b] **Son of Man** "Son of Man" is a name Jesus called himself. See dictionary. 14:14 [c] **sickle** A farming tool with a curved blade. It was used to harvest grain.

CONTEMPORARY ENGLISH VERSION

The Earth Is Harvested

14 I looked and saw a bright cloud, and someone who
seemed to be the Son of Man[c] was sitting on the cloud. He
wore a gold crown on his head and held a sharp sickle[d] in
his hand. 15 An angel came out of the temple and shouted,
"Start cutting with your sickle! Harvest season is here, and
all crops on earth are ripe." 16 The one on the cloud swung
his sickle and harvested the crops.

17 Another angel with a sharp sickle then came out of the
temple in heaven. 18 After this, an angel with power over
fire came from the altar and shouted to the angel who had
the sickle. He said, "All grapes on earth are ripe! Harvest
them with your sharp sickle." 19 The angel swung his sickle
on earth and cut off its grapes. He threw them into a pit[e]
where they were trampled on as a sign of God's anger.
20 The pit was outside the city, and when the grapes were
mashed, blood flowed out. The blood turned into a river
that was about two hundred miles long and almost deep
enough to cover a horse.

[c] 14.14 *Son of Man*: See the note at 1.13. [d] 14.14 *sickle*: A knife with a long curved blade, used to cut grain and other crops. [e] 14.19 *pit*: It was the custom to put grapes in a pit (called a wine press) and stomp on them to make juice that would later turn to wine.

NEW INTERNATIONAL VERSION

The Harvest of the Earth

14 I looked, and there before me was a white cloud, and
seated on the cloud was one "like a son of man"[a] with a
crown of gold on his head and a sharp sickle in his hand.
15 Then another angel came out of the temple and called in
a loud voice to him who was sitting on the cloud, "Take
your sickle and reap, because the time to reap has come,
for the harvest of the earth is ripe." 16 So he who was seat-
ed on the cloud swung his sickle over the earth, and the
earth was harvested.

17 Another angel came out of the temple in heaven, and
he too had a sharp sickle. 18 Still another angel, who had
charge of the fire, came from the altar and called in a loud
voice to him who had the sharp sickle, "Take your sharp
sickle and gather the clusters of grapes from the earth's
vine, because its grapes are ripe." 19 The angel swung his
sickle on the earth, gathered its grapes and threw them
into the great winepress of God's wrath. 20 They were tram-
pled in the winepress outside the city, and blood flowed
out of the press, rising as high as the horses' bridles for a
distance of 1,600 stadia.[b]

[a] *14* Daniel 7:13 [b] *20* That is, about 180 miles (about 300 kilometers)

NEW LIVING TRANSLATION

The Harvest of the Earth

14 Then I saw the Son of Man* sitting on a white cloud.
He had a gold crown on his head and a sharp sickle in his
hand.

15 Then an angel came from the Temple and called out in
a loud voice to the one sitting on the cloud, "Use the sick-
le, for the time has come for you to harvest; the crop is ripe
on the earth." 16 So the one sitting on the cloud swung his
sickle over the earth, and the whole earth was harvested.

17 After that, another angel came from the Temple in
heaven, and he also had a sharp sickle. 18 Then another
angel, who has power to destroy the world with fire,
shouted to the angel with the sickle, "Use your sickle now
to gather the clusters of grapes from the vines of the earth,
for they are fully ripe for judgment." 19 So the angel swung
his sickle on the earth and loaded the grapes into the great
winepress of God's wrath. 20 And the grapes were trodden
in the winepress outside the city, and blood flowed from
the winepress in a stream about 180 miles* long and as
high as a horse's bridle.

14:14 Or *one who looked like a man;* Greek reads *one like a son of man.*
14:20 Greek *1,600 stadia* [296 kilometers].

NEW KING JAMES VERSION

Reaping the Earth's Harvest

14 Then I looked, and behold, a white cloud, and on the
cloud sat *One* like the Son of Man, having on His head a
golden crown, and in His hand a sharp sickle. 15 And
another angel came out of the temple, crying with a loud
voice to Him who sat on the cloud, "Thrust in Your sickle
and reap, for the time has come for You[i] to reap, for the
harvest of the earth is ripe." 16 So He who sat on the cloud
thrust in His sickle on the earth, and the earth was reaped.

Reaping the Grapes of Wrath

17 Then another angel came out of the temple which is in
heaven, he also having a sharp sickle.

18 And another angel came out from the altar, who had
power over fire, and he cried with a loud cry to him who
had the sharp sickle, saying, "Thrust in your sharp sickle
and gather the clusters of the vine of the earth, for her
grapes are fully ripe." 19 So the angel thrust his sickle into
the earth and gathered the vine of the earth, and threw *it*
into the great winepress of the wrath of God. 20 And the
winepress was trampled outside the city, and blood came
out of the winepress, up to the horses' bridles, for one
thousand six hundred furlongs.

14:15 [i] NU-Text and M-Text omit *for You.*

THE MESSAGE

Harvest Time

I looked up, I caught my breath!—a white cloud and one like the Son of Man sitting on it. He wore a gold crown and held a sharp sickle. Another Angel came out of the Temple, shouting to the Cloud-Enthroned, "Swing your sickle and reap. It's harvest time. Earth's harvest is ripe for reaping." The Cloud-Enthroned gave a mighty sweep of his sickle, began harvesting earth in a stroke.

Then another Angel came out of the Temple in Heaven. He also had a sharp sickle. Yet another Angel, the one in charge of tending the fire, came from the Altar. He thundered to the Angel who held the sharp sickle, "Swing your sharp sickle. Harvest earth's vineyard. The grapes are bursting with ripeness."

The Angel swung his sickle, harvested earth's vintage, and heaved it into the winepress, the giant winepress of God's wrath. The winepress was outside the City. As the vintage was trodden, blood poured from the winepress as high as a horse's bridle, a river of blood for two hundred miles.

KING JAMES VERSION

15 And I saw another sign in heaven, great and marvellous, seven angels having the seven last plagues; for in them is filled up the wrath of God.

2 And I saw as it were a sea of glass mingled with fire: and them that had gotten the victory over the beast, and over his image, and over his mark, *and* over the number of his name, stand on the sea of glass, having the harps of God.

3 And they sing the song of Moses the servant of God, and the song of the Lamb, saying, Great and marvellous *are* thy works, Lord God Almighty; just and true *are* thy ways, thou King of saints.

4 Who shall not fear thee, O Lord, and glorify thy name? for *thou* only *art* holy: for all nations shall come and worship before thee; for thy judgments are made manifest.

NEW AMERICAN STANDARD BIBLE

A Scene of Heaven

15 Then I saw another sign in heaven, great and marvelous, seven angels who had seven plagues, *which are* the last, because in them the wrath of God is finished.

2 And I saw something like a sea of glass mixed with fire, and those who had been victorious over the beast and his image and the number of his name, standing on the sea of glass, holding harps of God.

3 And they *sang the song of Moses, the bond-servant of God, and the song of the Lamb, saying,

"Great and marvelous are Your works,
O Lord God, the Almighty;
Righteous and true are Your ways,
King of the [1]nations!

4 "Who will not fear, O Lord, and glorify Your name?
For You alone are holy;
FOR ALL THE NATIONS WILL COME AND WORSHIP BEFORE
YOU,
FOR YOUR RIGHTEOUS ACTS HAVE BEEN REVEALED."

15:3 [1] Two early mss read *ages*

NEW CENTURY VERSION

The Last Troubles

15 Then I saw another wonder in heaven that was great and amazing. There were seven angels bringing seven disasters. These are the last disasters, because after them, God's anger is finished.

2 I saw what looked like a sea of glass mixed with fire. All of those who had won the victory over the beast and his idol and over the number of his name were standing by the sea of glass. They had harps that God had given them.
3 They sang the song of Moses, the servant of God, and the song of the Lamb:

"You do great and wonderful things, *Psalm 111:2*
Lord God Almighty. *Amos 3:13*
Everything the Lord does is right and true, *Psalm 145:17*
King of the nations.
4 Everyone will respect you, Lord, *Jeremiah 10:7*
and will honor you.
Only you are holy.
All the nations will come
and worship you, *Psalm 86:9–10*
because the right things you have done
are now made known." *Deuteronomy 32:4*

CONTEMPORARY ENGLISH VERSION

The Last of the Terrible Troubles

15 After this, I looked at the sky and saw something else that was strange and important. Seven angels were bringing the last seven terrible troubles. When these are ended, God will no longer be angry.
2 Then I saw something that looked like a glass sea mixed with fire, and people were standing on it. They were the ones who had defeated the beast and the idol and the number that tells the name of the beast. God had given them harps, 3 and they were singing the song that his servant Moses and the Lamb had sung. They were singing,

"Lord God All-Powerful,
you have done great
and marvelous things.
You are the ruler
of all nations,
and you do what is
right and fair.
4 Lord, who doesn't honor
and praise your name?
You alone are holy,
and all nations will come
and worship you,
because you have shown
that you judge
with fairness."

NEW INTERNATIONAL VERSION

Seven Angels With Seven Plagues

15 I saw in heaven another great and marvelous sign: seven angels with the seven last plagues—last, because with them God's wrath is completed. 2And I saw what looked like a sea of glass mixed with fire and, standing beside the sea, those who had been victorious over the beast and his image and over the number of his name. They held harps given them by God 3and sang the song of Moses the servant of God and the song of the Lamb:

"Great and marvelous are your deeds,
Lord God Almighty.
Just and true are your ways,
King of the ages.
4 Who will not fear you, O Lord,
and bring glory to your name?
For you alone are holy.
All nations will come
and worship before you,
for your righteous acts have been revealed."

NEW LIVING TRANSLATION

The Song of Moses and of the Lamb

15 Then I saw in heaven another significant event, and it was great and marvelous. Seven angels were holding the seven last plagues, which would bring God's wrath to completion. 2I saw before me what seemed to be a crystal sea mixed with fire. And on it stood all the people who had been victorious over the beast and his statue and the number representing his name. They were all holding harps that God had given them. 3And they were singing the song of Moses, the servant of God, and the song of the Lamb:

"Great and marvelous are your actions,
Lord God Almighty.
Just and true are your ways,
O King of the nations.*
4 Who will not fear, O Lord, and glorify your name?
For you alone are holy.
All nations will come and worship before you,
for your righteous deeds have been revealed."

15:3 Some manuscripts read *King of the ages;* other manuscripts read *King of the saints.*

NEW KING JAMES VERSION

Prelude to the Bowl Judgments

15 Then I saw another sign in heaven, great and marvelous: seven angels having the seven last plagues, for in them the wrath of God is complete.

2And I saw *something* like a sea of glass mingled with fire, and those who have the victory over the beast, over his image and over his mark[a] *and* over the number of his name, standing on the sea of glass, having harps of God. 3They sing the song of Moses, the servant of God, and the song of the Lamb, saying:

"Great and marvelous *are* Your works,
Lord God Almighty!
Just and true *are* Your ways,
O King of the saints![b]
4 Who shall not fear You, O Lord, and glorify Your name?
For *You* alone *are* holy.
For all nations shall come and worship before You,
For Your judgments have been manifested."

15:2 [a] NU-Text and M-Text omit *over his mark.* 15:3 [b] NU-Text and M-Text read *nations.*

THE MESSAGE

The Song of Moses, The Song of the Lamb

15 I saw another Sign in Heaven, huge and breathtaking: seven Angels with seven disasters. These are the final disasters, the wrap-up of God's wrath.

I saw something like a sea made of glass, the glass all shot through with fire. Carrying harps of God, triumphant over the Beast, its image, and the number of its name, the saved ones stood on the sea of glass. They sang the Song of Moses, servant of God; they sang the Song of the Lamb:

"Mighty your acts and marvelous,
Oh God, the Sovereign-Strong!
Righteous your ways and true,
King of the nations!
Who can fail to fear you, God,
give glory to your Name?
Because you and you only are holy,
all nations will come and worship you,
because they see your judgments are right."

KING JAMES VERSION

5 ¶ And after that I looked, and, behold, the temple of the tabernacle of the testimony in heaven was opened:
6 And the seven angels came out of the temple, having the seven plagues, clothed in pure and white linen, and having their breasts girded with golden girdles.
7 And one of the four beasts gave unto the seven angels seven golden vials full of the wrath of God, who liveth for ever and ever.
8 And the temple was filled with smoke from the glory of God, and from his power; and no man was able to enter into the temple, till the seven plagues of the seven angels were fulfilled.

16 And I heard a great voice out of the temple saying to the seven angels, Go your ways, and pour out the vials of the wrath of God upon the earth.
2 And the first went, and poured out his vial upon the earth; and there fell a noisome and grievous sore upon the men which had the mark of the beast, and *upon* them which worshipped his image.
3 And the second angel poured out his vial upon the sea; and it became as the blood of a dead *man*: and every living soul died in the sea.
4 And the third angel poured out his vial upon the rivers and fountains of waters; and they became blood.
5 And I heard the angel of the waters say, Thou art

NEW AMERICAN STANDARD BIBLE

5 After these things I looked, and the temple of the tabernacle of testimony in heaven was opened,
6 and the seven angels who had the seven plagues came out of the temple, clothed in [2]linen, clean *and* bright, and girded around their chests with golden sashes.
7 Then one of the four living creatures gave to the seven angels seven golden bowls full of the wrath of God, who lives forever and ever.
8 And the temple was filled with smoke from the glory of God and from His power; and no one was able to enter the temple until the seven plagues of the seven angels were finished.

Six Bowls of Wrath

16 Then I heard a loud voice from the temple, saying to the seven angels, "Go and pour out on the earth the seven bowls of the wrath of God."
2 So the first *angel* went and poured out his bowl on the earth; and it became a loathsome and malignant sore on the people who had the mark of the beast and who worshiped his image.
3 The second *angel* poured out his bowl into the sea, and it became blood like *that* of a dead man; and every living [1]thing in the sea died.
4 Then the third *angel* poured out his bowl into the rivers and the springs of waters; and they became blood.
5 And I heard the angel of the waters saying, "Righteous

15:6 [2] One early ms reads *stone* 16:3 [1] Lit *soul*

NEW CENTURY VERSION

5 After this I saw that the temple (the Tent of the
Agreement) in heaven was opened. 6 And the seven angels
bringing the seven disasters came out of the temple. They were dressed in clean, shining linen and wore golden
bands tied around their chests. 7 Then one of the four liv-
ing creatures gave to the seven angels seven golden bowls filled with the anger of God, who lives forever and ever.
8 The temple was filled with smoke from the glory and the power of God, and no one could enter the temple until the seven disasters of the seven angels were finished.

The Bowls of God's Anger

16 Then I heard a loud voice from the temple saying to the seven angels, "Go and pour out the seven bowls of God's anger on the earth."
2 The first angel left and poured out his bowl on the land. Then ugly and painful sores came upon all those who had the mark of the beast and who worshiped his idol.
3 The second angel poured out his bowl on the sea, and it became blood like that of a dead man, and every living thing in the sea died.
4 The third angel poured out his bowl on the rivers and
the springs of water, and they became blood. 5 Then I heard
the angel of the waters saying:

CONTEMPORARY ENGLISH VERSION

5 After this, I noticed something else in heaven. The sacred
tent used for a temple was open. 6 And the seven angels who were bringing the terrible troubles were coming out of it. They were dressed in robes of pure white linen and wore
belts made of pure gold. 7 One of the four living creatures
gave each of the seven angels a bowl made of gold. These bowls were filled with the anger of God who lives forever and
ever. 8 The temple quickly filled with smoke from the glory and power of God. No one could enter it until the seven angels had finished pouring out the seven last troubles.

The Bowls of God's Anger

16 From the temple I heard a voice shout to the seven angels, "Go and empty the seven bowls of God's anger on the earth."
2 The first angel emptied his bowl on the earth. At once ugly and painful sores broke out on everyone who had the mark of the beast and worshiped the idol.
3 The second angel emptied his bowl on the sea. Right away the sea turned into blood like that of a dead person, and every living thing in the sea died.
4 The third angel emptied his bowl into the rivers and
streams. At once they turned to blood. 5 Then I heard the
angel, who has power over water, say,

NEW INTERNATIONAL VERSION

5After this I looked and in heaven the temple, that is,
the tabernacle of the Testimony, was opened. 6Out of the
temple came the seven angels with the seven plagues.
They were dressed in clean, shining linen and wore golden
sashes around their chests. 7Then one of the four living
creatures gave to the seven angels seven golden bowls
filled with the wrath of God, who lives for ever and ever.
8And the temple was filled with smoke from the glory of
God and from his power, and no one could enter the tem-
ple until the seven plagues of the seven angels were com-
pleted.

The Seven Bowls of God's Wrath

16 Then I heard a loud voice from the temple saying
to the seven angels, "Go, pour out the seven bowls
of God's wrath on the earth."

2The first angel went and poured out his bowl on the
land, and ugly and painful sores broke out on the people
who had the mark of the beast and worshiped his image.

3The second angel poured out his bowl on the sea, and it
turned into blood like that of a dead man, and every living
thing in the sea died.

4The third angel poured out his bowl on the rivers and
springs of water, and they became blood. 5Then I heard the
angel in charge of the waters say:

NEW LIVING TRANSLATION

The Seven Bowls of the Seven Plagues

5Then I looked and saw that the Temple in heaven,
God's Tabernacle, was thrown wide open! 6The seven
angels who were holding the bowls of the seven plagues
came from the Temple, clothed in spotless white linen*
with gold belts across their chests. 7And one of the four
living beings handed each of the seven angels a gold bowl
filled with the terrible wrath of God, who lives forever and
forever. 8The Temple was filled with smoke from God's
glory and power. No one could enter the Temple until the
seven angels had completed pouring out the seven
plagues.

16 Then I heard a mighty voice shouting from the
Temple to the seven angels, "Now go your ways
and empty out the seven bowls of God's wrath on the
earth."

2So the first angel left the Temple and poured out his
bowl over the earth, and horrible, malignant sores broke
out on everyone who had the mark of the beast and who
worshiped his statue.

3Then the second angel poured out his bowl on the sea,
and it became like the blood of a corpse. And everything in
the sea died.

4Then the third angel poured out his bowl on the rivers
and springs, and they became blood. 5And I heard the
angel who had authority over all water saying, "You are

15:6 Some manuscripts read *in bright and sparkling stone.*

NEW KING JAMES VERSION

5After these things I looked, and behold,[c] the temple of
the tabernacle of the testimony in heaven was opened. 6And
out of the temple came the seven angels having the seven
plagues, clothed in pure bright linen, and having their
chests girded with golden bands. 7Then one of the four liv-
ing creatures gave to the seven angels seven golden bowls
full of the wrath of God who lives forever and ever. 8The
temple was filled with smoke from the glory of God and
from His power, and no one was able to enter the temple till
the seven plagues of the seven angels were completed.

16 Then I heard a loud voice from the temple saying
to the seven angels, "Go and pour out the bowls[a]
of the wrath of God on the earth."

First Bowl: Loathsome Sores

2So the first went and poured out his bowl upon the earth,
and a foul and loathsome sore came upon the men who had
the mark of the beast and those who worshiped his image.

Second Bowl: The Sea Turns to Blood

3Then the second angel poured out his bowl on the sea,
and it became blood as of a dead *man;* and every living
creature in the sea died.

Third Bowl: The Waters Turn to Blood

4Then the third angel poured out his bowl on the rivers
and springs of water, and they became blood. 5And I heard
the angel of the waters saying:

15:5 [c] NU-Text and M-Text omit *behold.* **16:1** [a] NU-Text and M-Text read *seven bowls.*

THE MESSAGE

Then I saw the doors of the Temple, the Tent of Witness
in Heaven, open wide. The Seven Angels carrying the
seven disasters came out of the Temple. They were dressed
in clean, bright linen and wore gold vests. One of the Four
Animals handed the Seven Angels seven gold bowls, brim-
ming with the wrath of God, who lives forever and ever.
Smoke from God's glory and power poured out of the
Temple. No one was permitted to enter the Temple until
the seven disasters of the Seven Angels were finished.

Pouring Out the Seven Disasters

16 I heard a shout of command from the Temple to
the Seven Angels: "Begin! Pour out the seven
bowls of God's wrath on earth!"

The first Angel stepped up and poured his bowl out on
earth: Loathsome, stinking sores erupted on all who had
taken the mark of the Beast and worshiped its image.

The second Angel poured his bowl on the sea: The sea
coagulated into blood, and everything in it died.

The third Angel poured his bowl on rivers and springs:
The waters turned to blood. I heard the Angel of Waters
say,

KING JAMES VERSION

righteous, O Lord, which art, and wast, and shalt be,
because thou hast judged thus.
6 For they have shed the blood of saints and prophets,
and thou hast given them blood to drink; for they are wor-
thy.
7 And I heard another out of the altar say, Even so,
Lord God Almighty, true and righteous *are* thy judgments.
8 ¶ And the fourth angel poured out his vial upon the
sun; and power was given unto him to scorch men with
fire.
9 And men were scorched with great heat, and blas-
phemed the name of God, which hath power over these
plagues: and they repented not to give him glory.
10 And the fifth angel poured out his vial upon the seat
of the beast; and his kingdom was full of darkness; and
they gnawed their tongues for pain,
11 And blasphemed the God of heaven because of their
pains and their sores, and repented not of their deeds.

NEW AMERICAN STANDARD BIBLE

are You, who are and who were, O Holy One, because You
judged these things;
6 for they poured out the blood of saints and prophets,
and You have given them blood to drink. They deserve it."
7 And I heard the altar saying, "Yes, O Lord God, the
Almighty, true and righteous are Your judgments."
8 The fourth *angel* poured out his bowl upon the sun,
and it was given to it to scorch men with fire.
9 Men were scorched with fierce heat; and they blas-
phemed the name of God who has the power over these
plagues, and they did not repent so as to give Him glory.
10 Then the fifth *angel* poured out his bowl on the
throne of the beast, and his kingdom became darkened;
and they gnawed their tongues because of pain,
11 and they blasphemed the God of heaven because of
their pains and their sores; and they did not repent of their
deeds.

NEW CENTURY VERSION

"Holy One, you are the One who is and who was.
You are right to decide to punish these evil people.
6 They have poured out the blood of your holy people and
your prophets.
So now you have given them blood to drink as they
deserve."
7 And I heard a voice coming from the altar saying:
"Yes, Lord God Almighty,
the way you punish evil people is right and fair."
8 The fourth angel poured out his bowl on the sun, and
he was given power to burn the people with fire. 9 They
were burned by the great heat, and they cursed the name
of God, who had control over these disasters. But the peo-
ple refused to change their hearts and lives and give glory
to God.
10 The fifth angel poured out his bowl on the throne of
the beast, and darkness covered its kingdom. People
gnawed their tongues because of the pain. 11 They also
cursed the God of heaven because of their pain and the
sores they had, but they refused to change their hearts and
turn away from the evil things they did.

CONTEMPORARY ENGLISH VERSION

"You have always been,
and you always will be
the holy God.
You had the right
to judge in this way.
6 They poured out the blood[a]
of your people
and your prophets.
So you gave them blood
to drink, as they deserve!"
7 After this, I heard
the altar shout,
"Yes, Lord God All-Powerful,
your judgments are honest
and fair."

8 The fourth angel emptied his bowl on the sun, and it
began to scorch people like fire. 9 Everyone was scorched
by its great heat, and all of them cursed the name of God
who had power over these terrible troubles. But no one
turned to God and praised him.
10 The fifth angel emptied his bowl on the throne of the
beast. At once darkness covered its kingdom, and its peo-
ple began biting their tongues in pain. 11 And because of
their painful sores, they cursed the God who rules in heav-
en. But still they did not stop doing evil things.

[a] **16.6** *They poured out the blood*: A way of saying, "They murdered."

NEW INTERNATIONAL VERSION

"You are just in these judgments,
you who are and who were, the Holy One,
because you have so judged;
6 for they have shed the blood of your saints and
prophets,
and you have given them blood to drink as they
deserve."

7 And I heard the altar respond:

"Yes, Lord God Almighty,
true and just are your judgments."

8 The fourth angel poured out his bowl on the sun, and
the sun was given power to scorch people with fire. 9 They
were seared by the intense heat and they cursed the name
of God, who had control over these plagues, but they
refused to repent and glorify him.
10 The fifth angel poured out his bowl on the throne of
the beast, and his kingdom was plunged into darkness.
Men gnawed their tongues in agony 11 and cursed the God
of heaven because of their pains and their sores, but they
refused to repent of what they had done.

NEW LIVING TRANSLATION

just in sending this judgment, O Holy One, who is and who
always was. 6 For your holy people and your prophets have
been killed, and their blood was poured out on the earth.
So you have given their murderers blood to drink. It is
their just reward." 7 And I heard a voice from the altar say-
ing, "Yes, Lord God Almighty, your punishments are true
and just."
8 Then the fourth angel poured out his bowl on the sun,
causing it to scorch everyone with its fire. 9 Everyone was
burned by this blast of heat, and they cursed the name of
God, who sent all of these plagues. They did not repent
and give him glory.
10 Then the fifth angel poured out his bowl on the throne
of the beast, and his kingdom was plunged into darkness.
And his subjects ground their teeth in anguish, 11 and they
cursed the God of heaven for their pains and sores. But
they refused to repent of all their evil deeds.

NEW KING JAMES VERSION

"You are righteous, O Lord,[b]
The One who is and who was and who is to be,[c]
Because You have judged these things.
6 For they have shed the blood of saints and prophets,
And You have given them blood to drink.
For[d] it is their just due."

7 And I heard another from[e] the altar saying, "Even so,
Lord God Almighty, true and righteous *are* Your judgments."

Fourth Bowl: Men Are Scorched

8 Then the fourth angel poured out his bowl on the sun,
and power was given to him to scorch men with fire. 9 And
men were scorched with great heat, and they blasphemed
the name of God who has power over these plagues; and
they did not repent and give Him glory.

Fifth Bowl: Darkness and Pain

10 Then the fifth angel poured out his bowl on the throne
of the beast, and his kingdom became full of darkness; and
they gnawed their tongues because of the pain. 11 They
blasphemed the God of heaven because of their pains and
their sores, and did not repent of their deeds.

16:5 [b] NU-Text and M-Text omit *O Lord.* [c] NU-Text and M-Text read *who was, the Holy One.* **16:6** [d] NU-Text and M-Text omit *For.*
16:7 [e] NU-Text and M-Text omit *another from.*

THE MESSAGE

"Righteous you are, and your judgments are righteous,
THE IS, THE WAS, THE HOLY.
They poured out the blood of saints and prophets
so you've given them blood to drink—
they've gotten what they deserve!"

Just then I heard the Altar chime in,

"Yes, Oh God, the Sovereign-Strong!
Your judgments are true and just!"

The fourth Angel poured his bowl on the sun: Fire blazed from the sun and scorched men and women. Burned and blistered, they cursed God's Name, the God behind these disasters. They refused to repent, refused to honor God.

The fifth Angel poured his bowl on the throne of the Beast: Its kingdom fell into sudden eclipse. Mad with pain, men and women bit and chewed their tongues, cursed the God of Heaven for their torment and sores, and refused to repent and change their ways.

KING JAMES VERSION

12 ¶ And the sixth angel poured out his vial upon the great river Euphrates; and the water thereof was dried up, that the way of the kings of the east might be prepared.

13 And I saw three unclean spirits like frogs *come* out of the mouth of the dragon, and out of the mouth of the beast, and out of the mouth of the false prophet.

14 For they are the spirits of devils, working miracles, *which* go forth unto the kings of the earth and of the whole world, to gather them to the battle of that great day of God Almighty.

15 Behold, I come as a thief. Blessed *is* he that watcheth, and keepeth his garments, lest he walk naked, and they see his shame.

16 And he gathered them together into a place called in the Hebrew tongue Armageddon.

17 ¶ And the seventh angel poured out his vial into the air; and there came a great voice out of the temple of heaven, from the throne, saying, It is done.

18 And there were voices, and thunders, and lightnings; and there was a great earthquake, such as was not since men were upon the earth, so mighty an earthquake, *and* so great.

NEW AMERICAN STANDARD BIBLE

12 The sixth *angel* poured out his bowl on the great river, the Euphrates; and its water was dried up, so that the way would be prepared for the kings from the east.

Armageddon

13 And I saw *coming* out of the mouth of the dragon and out of the mouth of the beast and out of the mouth of the false prophet, three unclean spirits like frogs;

14 for they are spirits of demons, performing signs, which go out to the kings of the whole world, to gather them together for the war of the great day of God, the Almighty.

15 ("Behold, I am coming like a thief. Blessed is the one who stays awake and keeps his clothes, so that he will not walk about naked and men will not see his shame.")

16 And they gathered them together to the place which in Hebrew is called [2]Har-Magedon.

Seventh Bowl of Wrath

17 Then the seventh *angel* poured out his bowl upon the air, and a loud voice came out of the temple from the throne, saying, "It is done."

18 And there were flashes of lightning and sounds and peals of thunder; and there was a great earthquake, such as there had not been since man came to be upon the earth, so great an earthquake *was it, and* so mighty.

16:16 [2] Two early mss read *Armagedon*

NEW CENTURY VERSION

12The sixth angel poured out his bowl on the great river
Euphrates so that the water in the river was dried up to
prepare the way for the kings from the east to come.
13Then I saw three evil spirits that looked like frogs coming out of the mouth of the dragon, out of the mouth of the
beast, and out of the mouth of the false prophet. 14These
evil spirits are the spirits of demons, which have power to do miracles. They go out to the kings of the whole world to gather them together for the battle on the great day of God Almighty.

15"Listen! I will come as a thief comes! Happy are those who stay awake and keep their clothes on so that they will not walk around naked and have people see their shame."

16Then the evil spirits gathered the kings together to the place that is called Armageddon in the Hebrew language.

17The seventh angel poured out his bowl into the air. Then a loud voice came out of the temple from the throne,
saying, "It is finished!" 18Then there were flashes of lightning, noises, thunder, and a big earthquake—the worst earthquake that has ever happened since people have been

CONTEMPORARY ENGLISH VERSION

12The sixth angel emptied his bowl on the great Euphrates River, and it completely dried up to make a road
for the kings from the east. 13An evil spirit that looked like
a frog came out of the mouth of the dragon. One also came out of the mouth of the beast, and another out of the
mouth of the false prophet. 14These evil spirits had the
power to work miracles. They went to every king on earth, to bring them together for a war against God All-Powerful. But that will be the day of God's great victory.

15Remember that Christ says, "When I come, it will surprise you like a thief! But God will bless you, if you are awake and ready. Then you won't have to walk around naked and be ashamed."

16Those armies came together in a place that in Hebrew is called Armagedon.[b]

17As soon as the seventh angel emptied his bowl in the air, a loud voice from the throne in the temple shouted,
"It's done!" 18There were flashes of lightning, roars of
thunder, and the worst earthquake in all history. 19The

[b] **16.16** *Armagedon*: The Hebrew form of the name would be "Har Megiddo," meaning "Hill of Megiddo," where many battles were fought in ancient times (see Judges 5.19; 2 Kings 23.29, 30).

NEW INTERNATIONAL VERSION

12The sixth angel poured out his bowl on the great river Euphrates, and its water was dried up to prepare the way for the kings from the East. 13Then I saw three evil[a] spirits that looked like frogs; they came out of the mouth of the dragon, out of the mouth of the beast and out of the mouth of the false prophet. 14They are spirits of demons performing miraculous signs, and they go out to the kings of the whole world, to gather them for the battle on the great day of God Almighty.

15"Behold, I come like a thief! Blessed is he who stays awake and keeps his clothes with him, so that he may not go naked and be shamefully exposed."

16Then they gathered the kings together to the place that in Hebrew is called Armageddon.

17The seventh angel poured out his bowl into the air, and out of the temple came a loud voice from the throne, saying, "It is done!" 18Then there came flashes of lightning, rumblings, peals of thunder and a severe earthquake. No earthquake like it has ever occurred since man has been on earth, so tremendous was the quake. 19The great

[a] *13* Greek *unclean*

NEW LIVING TRANSLATION

12Then the sixth angel poured out his bowl on the great Euphrates River, and it dried up so that the kings from the east could march their armies westward without hindrance. 13And I saw three evil spirits that looked like frogs leap from the mouth of the dragon, the beast, and the false prophet. 14These miracle-working demons caused all the rulers of the world to gather for battle against the Lord on that great judgment day of God Almighty.

15"Take note: I will come as unexpectedly as a thief!
Blessed are all who are watching for me, who keep their
robes ready so they will not need to walk naked and
ashamed."

16And they gathered all the rulers and their armies to a place called *Armageddon* in Hebrew.

17Then the seventh angel poured out his bowl into the air. And a mighty shout came from the throne of the Temple in heaven, saying, "It is finished!" 18Then the thunder crashed and rolled, and lightning flashed. And there was an earthquake greater than ever before in human history.

NEW KING JAMES VERSION

Sixth Bowl: Euphrates Dried Up

12Then the sixth angel poured out his bowl on the great river Euphrates, and its water was dried up, so that the way of the kings from the east might be prepared. 13And I saw three unclean spirits like frogs *coming* out of the mouth of the dragon, out of the mouth of the beast, and out of the mouth of the false prophet. 14For they are spirits of demons, performing signs, *which* go out to the kings of the earth and[f] of the whole world, to gather them to the battle of that great day of God Almighty.

15"Behold, I am coming as a thief. Blessed *is* he who watches, and keeps his garments, lest he walk naked and they see his shame."

16And they gathered them together to the place called in Hebrew, Armageddon.[g]

Seventh Bowl: The Earth Utterly Shaken

17Then the seventh angel poured out his bowl into the air, and a loud voice came out of the temple of heaven, from the throne, saying, "It is done!" 18And there were noises and thunderings and lightnings; and there was a great earthquake, such a mighty and great earthquake as had not occurred since men were on the earth. 19Now the

16:14 [f] NU-Text and M-Text omit *of the earth and.* **16:16** [g] M-Text reads *Megiddo.*

THE MESSAGE

The sixth Angel poured his bowl on the great Euphrates River: It dried up to nothing. The dry riverbed became a fine roadbed for the kings from the East. From the mouths of the Dragon, the Beast, and the False Prophet I saw three foul demons crawl out—they looked like frogs. These are demon spirits performing signs. They're after the kings of the whole world to get them gathered for battle on the Great Day of God, the Sovereign-Strong.

"Keep watch! I come unannounced, like a thief. You're blessed if, awake and dressed, you're ready for me. Too bad if you're found running through the streets, naked and ashamed."

The frog-demons gathered the kings together at the place called in Hebrew *Armageddon*.

The seventh Angel poured his bowl into the air: From the Throne in the Temple came a shout, "Done!" followed by lightning flashes and shouts, thunder crashes and a colossal earthquake—a huge and devastating earthquake, never an earthquake like it since time began. The Great

KING JAMES VERSION

19 And the great city was divided into three parts, and the cities of the nations fell: and great Babylon came in remembrance before God, to give unto her the cup of the wine of the fierceness of his wrath.

20 And every island fled away, and the mountains were not found.

21 And there fell upon men a great hail out of heaven, *every stone* about the weight of a talent: and men blasphemed God because of the plague of the hail; for the plague thereof was exceeding great.

17 And there came one of the seven angels which had the seven vials, and talked with me, saying unto me, Come hither; I will shew unto thee the judgment of the great whore that sitteth upon many waters:

2 With whom the kings of the earth have committed fornication, and the inhabitants of the earth have been made drunk with the wine of her fornication.

3 So he carried me away in the spirit into the wilderness: and I saw a woman sit upon a scarlet coloured beast, full of names of blasphemy, having seven heads and ten horns.

4 And the woman was arrayed in purple and scarlet colour, and decked with gold and precious stones and pearls, having a golden cup in her hand full of abominations and filthiness of her fornication:

5 And upon her forehead *was* a name written, MYSTERY,

NEW AMERICAN STANDARD BIBLE

19 The great city was split into three parts, and the cities of the nations fell. Babylon the great was remembered before God, to give her the cup of the wine of His fierce wrath.

20 And every island fled away, and the mountains were not found.

21 And huge hailstones, about [3]one hundred pounds each, *came down from heaven upon men; and men blasphemed God because of the plague of the hail, because its plague *was extremely severe.

The Doom of Babylon

17 Then one of the seven angels who had the seven bowls came and spoke with me, saying, "Come here, I will show you the judgment of the great harlot who sits on many waters,

2 with whom the kings of the earth committed *acts of* immorality, and those who dwell on the earth were made drunk with the wine of her immorality."

3 And he carried me away [1]in the Spirit into a wilderness; and I saw a woman sitting on a scarlet beast, full of blasphemous names, having seven heads and ten horns.

4 The woman was clothed in purple and scarlet, and adorned with gold and precious stones and pearls, having in her hand a gold cup full of abominations and of the unclean things of her immorality,

5 and on her forehead a name *was* written, a mystery,

16:21 [3] Lit *the weight of a talent* 17:3 [1] Or *in spirit*

NEW CENTURY VERSION

on earth. 19The great city split into three parts, and the cit-
ies of the nations were destroyed. And God remembered
the sins of Babylon the Great, so he gave that city the cup
filled with the wine of his terrible anger. 20Then every
island ran away, and mountains disappeared. 21Giant hail-
stones, each weighing about a hundred pounds, fell from
the sky upon people. People cursed God for the disaster of
the hail, because this disaster was so terrible.

The Woman on the Animal

17 Then one of the seven angels who had the seven
bowls came and spoke to me. He said, "Come, and
I will show you the punishment that will be given to the
great prostitute, the one sitting over many waters. 2The
kings of the earth sinned sexually with her, and the people
of the earth became drunk from the wine of her sexual
sin."

3Then the angel carried me away by the Spirit to the
desert. There I saw a woman sitting on a red beast. It was
covered with names against God written on it, and it had
seven heads and ten horns. 4The woman was dressed in
purple and red and was shining with the gold, precious
jewels, and pearls she was wearing. She had a golden cup
in her hand, a cup filled with evil things and the unclean-
ness of her sexual sin. 5On her forehead a title was written
that was secret. This is what was written:

CONTEMPORARY ENGLISH VERSION

great city of Babylon split into three parts, and the cities of
other nations fell. So God made Babylon drink from the
wine cup that was filled with his anger. 20Every island ran
away, and the mountains disappeared. 21Hailstones,
weighing about a hundred pounds each, fell from the sky
on people. Finally, the people cursed God, because the hail
was so terrible.

The Prostitute and the Beast

17 One of the seven angels who had emptied the
bowls came over and said to me, "Come on! I will
show you how God will punish that shameless prostitute
who sits on many oceans. 2Every king on earth has slept
with her, and her shameless ways are like wine that has
made everyone on earth drunk."

3With the help of the Spirit, the angel took me into the
desert, where I saw a woman sitting on a red beast. The
beast was covered with names that were an insult to God,
and it had seven heads and ten horns. 4The woman was
dressed in purple and scarlet robes, and she wore jewelry
made of gold, precious stones, and pearls. In her hand she
held a gold cup filled with the filthy and nasty things she
had done. 5On her forehead a mysterious name was written:

NEW INTERNATIONAL VERSION

city split into three parts, and the cities of the nations col-
lapsed. God remembered Babylon the Great and gave her
the cup filled with the wine of the fury of his wrath.
20Every island fled away and the mountains could not be
found. 21From the sky huge hailstones of about a hundred
pounds each fell upon men. And they cursed God on
account of the plague of hail, because the plague was so
terrible.

The Woman on the Beast

17 One of the seven angels who had the seven bowls
came and said to me, "Come, I will show you the
punishment of the great prostitute, who sits on many
waters. 2With her the kings of the earth committed adul-
tery and the inhabitants of the earth were intoxicated with
the wine of her adulteries."

3Then the angel carried me away in the Spirit into a
desert. There I saw a woman sitting on a scarlet beast that
was covered with blasphemous names and had seven
heads and ten horns. 4The woman was dressed in purple
and scarlet, and was glittering with gold, precious stones
and pearls. She held a golden cup in her hand, filled with
abominable things and the filth of her adulteries. 5This
title was written on her forehead:

NEW LIVING TRANSLATION

19The great city of Babylon split into three pieces, and cities
around the world fell into heaps of rubble. And so God
remembered all of Babylon's sins, and he made her drink
the cup that was filled with the wine of his fierce wrath.
20And every island disappeared, and all the mountains were
leveled. 21There was a terrible hailstorm, and hailstones
weighing seventy-five pounds* fell from the sky onto the
people below. They cursed God because of the hailstorm,
which was a very terrible plague.

The Great Prostitute

17 One of the seven angels who had poured out the
seven bowls came over and spoke to me. "Come
with me," he said, "and I will show you the judgment that
is going to come on the great prostitute, who sits on many
waters. 2The rulers of the world have had immoral rela-
tions with her, and the people who belong to this world
have been made drunk by the wine of her immorality."

3So the angel took me in spirit* into the wilderness. There
I saw a woman sitting on a scarlet beast that had seven
heads and ten horns, written all over with blasphemies
against God. 4The woman wore purple and scarlet clothing
and beautiful jewelry made of gold and precious gems and
pearls. She held in her hand a gold goblet full of obscenities
and the impurities of her immorality. 5A mysterious name

16:21 Greek *1 talent* [34 kilograms]. 17:3 Or *in the Spirit.*

NEW KING JAMES VERSION

great city was divided into three parts, and the cities of the
nations fell. And great Babylon was remembered before
God, to give her the cup of the wine of the fierceness of His
wrath. 20Then every island fled away, and the mountains
were not found. 21And great hail from heaven fell upon
men, *each hailstone* about the weight of a talent. Men
blasphemed God because of the plague of the hail, since
that plague was exceedingly great.

The Scarlet Woman and the Scarlet Beast

17 Then one of the seven angels who had the seven
bowls came and talked with me, saying to me,[a]
"Come, I will show you the judgment of the great harlot
who sits on many waters, 2with whom the kings of the
earth committed fornication, and the inhabitants of the
earth were made drunk with the wine of her fornication."

3So he carried me away in the Spirit into the wilderness.
And I saw a woman sitting on a scarlet beast *which was*
full of names of blasphemy, having seven heads and ten
horns. 4The woman was arrayed in purple and scarlet, and
adorned with gold and precious stones and pearls, having
in her hand a golden cup full of abominations and the
filthiness of her fornication.[b] 5And on her forehead a name
was written:

17:1 [a] NU-Text and M-Text omit *to me.* 17:4 [b] M-Text reads *the filthiness of the fornication of the earth.*

THE MESSAGE

City split three ways, the cities of the nations toppled to
ruin. Great Babylon had to drink the wine of God's raging
anger—God remembered to give her the cup! Every island
fled and not a mountain was to be found. Hailstones
weighing a ton plummeted, crushing and smashing men
and women as they cursed God for the hail, the epic disas-
ter of hail.

Great Babylon, Mother of Whores

17 One of the Seven Angels who carried the seven
bowls came and invited me, "Come, I'll show you
the judgment of the great Whore who sits enthroned over
many waters, the Whore with whom the kings of the earth
have gone whoring, show you the judgment on earth
dwellers drunk on her whorish lust."

In the Spirit he carried me out in the desert. I saw a
woman mounted on a Scarlet Beast. Stuffed with blasphe-
mies, the Beast had seven heads and ten horns. The
woman was dressed in purple and scarlet, festooned with
gold and gems and pearls. She held a gold chalice in her
hand, brimming with defiling obscenities, her foul fornica-
tions. A riddle-name was branded on her forehead: GREAT

KING JAMES VERSION

BABYLON THE GREAT, THE MOTHER OF HARLOTS AND ABOMINATIONS OF THE EARTH.

6 And I saw the woman drunken with the blood of the saints, and with the blood of the martyrs of Jesus: and when I saw her, I wondered with great admiration.

7 ¶ And the angel said unto me, Wherefore didst thou marvel? I will tell thee the mystery of the woman, and of the beast that carrieth her, which hath the seven heads and ten horns.

8 The beast that thou sawest was, and is not; and shall ascend out of the bottomless pit, and go into perdition: and they that dwell on the earth shall wonder, whose names were not written in the book of life from the foundation of the world, when they behold the beast that was, and is not, and yet is.

9 And here *is* the mind which hath wisdom. The seven heads are seven mountains, on which the woman sitteth.

10 And there are seven kings: five are fallen, and one is, *and* the other is not yet come; and when he cometh, he must continue a short space.

11 And the beast that was, and is not, even he is the eighth, and is of the seven, and goeth into perdition.

12 And the ten horns which thou sawest are ten kings, which have received no kingdom as yet; but receive power as kings one hour with the beast.

NEW AMERICAN STANDARD BIBLE

"BABYLON THE GREAT, THE MOTHER OF HARLOTS AND OF THE ABOMINATIONS OF THE EARTH."

6 And I saw the woman drunk with the blood of the saints, and with the blood of the witnesses of Jesus. When I saw her, I wondered greatly.

7 And the angel said to me, "Why do you wonder? I will tell you the mystery of the woman and of the beast that carries her, which has the seven heads and the ten horns.

8 "The beast that you saw was, and is not, and is about to come up out of the abyss and [2]go to destruction. And those who dwell on the earth, whose name has not been written in the book of life from the foundation of the world, will wonder when they see the beast, that he was and is not and will come.

9 "Here is the mind which has wisdom. The seven heads are seven mountains on which the woman sits,

10 and they are seven kings; five have fallen, one is, the other has not yet come; and when he comes, he must remain a little while.

11 "The beast which was and is not, is himself also an eighth and is *one* of the seven, and he goes to destruction.

12 "The ten horns which you saw are ten kings who have not yet received a kingdom, but they receive authority as kings with the beast for one hour.

17:8 [2] One early ms reads *is going*

NEW CENTURY VERSION

THE GREAT BABYLON
MOTHER OF PROSTITUTES
AND OF THE EVIL THINGS OF THE EARTH

6Then I saw that the woman was drunk with the blood of God's holy people and with the blood of those who were killed because of their faith in Jesus.

When I saw the woman, I was very amazed. 7Then the angel said to me, "Why are you amazed? I will tell you the secret of this woman and the beast she rides—the one with seven heads and ten horns. 8The beast you saw was once alive but is not alive now. But soon it will come up out of the bottomless pit and go away to be destroyed. There are people who live on earth whose names have not been written in the book of life since the beginning of the world. They will be amazed when they see the beast, because he was once alive, is not alive now, but will come again.

9"You need a wise mind to understand this. The seven heads on the beast are seven mountains where the woman sits. 10And they are seven kings. Five of the kings have already been destroyed, one of the kings lives now, and another has not yet come. When he comes, he must stay a short time. 11The beast that was once alive, but is not alive now, is also an eighth king. He belongs to the first seven kings, and he will go away to be destroyed.

12"The ten horns you saw are ten kings who have not yet begun to rule, but they will receive power to rule with the beast for one hour. 13All ten of these kings have the

CONTEMPORARY ENGLISH VERSION

I AM THE GREAT CITY OF BABYLON,
THE MOTHER OF EVERY IMMORAL
AND FILTHY THING ON EARTH.

6I could tell that the woman was drunk on the blood of God's people who had given their lives for Jesus. This surprising sight amazed me, 7and the angel said:

Why are you so amazed? I will explain the mystery about this woman and about the beast she is sitting on, with its seven heads and ten horns. 8The beast you saw is one that used to be and no longer is. It will come back from the deep pit, but only to be destroyed. Everyone on earth whose names were not written in the book of life[a] before the time of creation will be amazed. They will see this beast that used to be and no longer is, but will be once more.

9Anyone with wisdom can figure this out. The seven heads that the woman is sitting on stand for seven hills. These heads are also seven kings. 10Five of the kings are dead. One is ruling now, and the other one has not yet come. But when he does, he will rule for only a little while.

11You also saw a beast that used to be and no longer is. That beast is one of the seven kings who will return as the eighth king, but only to be destroyed.

12The ten horns that you saw are ten more kings, who have not yet come into power, and they will rule with the beast for only a short time. 13They all think alike and

[a] **17.8** *book of life*: See the note at 3.5.

NEW INTERNATIONAL VERSION

MYSTERY
BABYLON THE GREAT
THE MOTHER OF PROSTITUTES
AND OF THE ABOMINATIONS OF THE EARTH.

6I saw that the woman was drunk with the blood of the saints, the blood of those who bore testimony to Jesus.

When I saw her, I was greatly astonished. 7Then the angel said to me: "Why are you astonished? I will explain to you the mystery of the woman and of the beast she rides, which has the seven heads and ten horns. 8The beast, which you saw, once was, now is not, and will come up out of the Abyss and go to his destruction. The inhabitants of the earth whose names have not been written in the book of life from the creation of the world will be astonished when they see the beast, because he once was, now is not, and yet will come.

9"This calls for a mind with wisdom. The seven heads are seven hills on which the woman sits. 10They are also seven kings. Five have fallen, one is, the other has not yet come; but when he does come, he must remain for a little while. 11The beast who once was, and now is not, is an eighth king. He belongs to the seven and is going to his destruction.

12"The ten horns you saw are ten kings who have not yet received a kingdom, but who for one hour will receive authority as kings along with the beast. 13They have one

NEW LIVING TRANSLATION

was written on her forehead: "Babylon the Great, Mother of All Prostitutes and Obscenities in the World." 6I could see that she was drunk—drunk with the blood of God's holy people who were witnesses for Jesus. I stared at her completely amazed.

7"Why are you so amazed?" the angel asked. "I will tell you the mystery of this woman and of the beast with seven heads and ten horns. 8The beast you saw was alive but isn't now. And yet he will soon come up out of the bottomless pit and go to eternal destruction. And the people who belong to this world, whose names were not written in the Book of Life from before the world began, will be amazed at the reappearance of this beast who had died.

9"And now understand this: The seven heads of the beast represent the seven hills of the city where this woman rules. They also represent seven kings. 10Five kings have already fallen, the sixth now reigns, and the seventh is yet to come, but his reign will be brief. 11The scarlet beast that was alive and then died is the eighth king. He is like the other seven, and he, too, will go to his doom. 12His ten horns are ten kings who have not yet risen to power; they will be appointed to their kingdoms for one brief moment to reign with the beast. 13They will

NEW KING JAMES VERSION

MYSTERY,
BABYLON THE GREAT,
THE MOTHER OF HARLOTS
AND OF THE ABOMINATIONS OF THE EARTH.

6I saw the woman, drunk with the blood of the saints and with the blood of the martyrs of Jesus. And when I saw her, I marveled with great amazement.

The Meaning of the Woman and the Beast

7But the angel said to me, "Why did you marvel? I will tell you the mystery of the woman and of the beast that carries her, which has the seven heads and the ten horns. 8The beast that you saw was, and is not, and will ascend out of the bottomless pit and go to perdition. And those who dwell on the earth will marvel, whose names are not written in the Book of Life from the foundation of the world, when they see the beast that was, and is not, and yet is.[c]

9"Here *is* the mind which has wisdom: The seven heads are seven mountains on which the woman sits. 10There are also seven kings. Five have fallen, one is, *and* the other has not yet come. And when he comes, he must continue a short time. 11The beast that was, and is not, is himself also the eighth, and is of the seven, and is going to perdition.

12"The ten horns which you saw are ten kings who have received no kingdom as yet, but they receive authority for one hour as kings with the beast. 13These are of one mind,

17:8 [c] NU-Text and M-Text read *and shall be present.*

THE MESSAGE

BABYLON, MOTHER OF WHORES AND ABOMINATIONS OF THE EARTH. I could see that the woman was drunk, drunk on the blood of God's holy people, drunk on the blood of the martyrs of Jesus.

Astonished, I rubbed my eyes. I shook my head in wonder. The Angel said, "Does this surprise you? Let me tell you the riddle of the woman and the Beast she rides, the Beast with seven heads and ten horns. The Beast you saw once was, is no longer, and is about to ascend from the Abyss and head straight for Hell. Earth dwellers whose names weren't written in the Book of Life from the foundation of the world will be dazzled when they see the Beast that once was, is no longer, and is to come.

"But don't drop your guard. Use your head. The seven heads are seven hills; they are where the woman sits. They are also seven kings: five dead, one living, the other not yet here—and when he does come his time will be brief. The Beast that once was and is no longer is both an eighth and one of the seven—and headed for Hell.

"The ten horns you saw are ten kings, but they're not yet in power. They will come to power with the Scarlet Beast, but won't last long—a *very* brief reign. These kings

KING JAMES VERSION

13 These have one mind, and shall give their power and strength unto the beast.

14 ¶ These shall make war with the Lamb, and the Lamb shall overcome them: for he is Lord of lords, and King of kings: and they that are with him *are* called, and chosen, and faithful.

15 And he saith unto me, The waters which thou sawest, where the whore sitteth, are peoples, and multitudes, and nations, and tongues.

16 And the ten horns which thou sawest upon the beast, these shall hate the whore, and shall make her desolate and naked, and shall eat her flesh, and burn her with fire.

17 For God hath put in their hearts to fulfil his will, and to agree, and give their kingdom unto the beast, until the words of God shall be fulfilled.

18 And the woman which thou sawest is that great city, which reigneth over the kings of the earth.

18 And after these things I saw another angel come down from heaven, having great power; and the earth was lightened with his glory.

2 And he cried mightily with a strong voice, saying, Babylon the great is fallen, is fallen, and is become the habitation of devils, and the hold of every foul spirit, and a cage of every unclean and hateful bird.

NEW AMERICAN STANDARD BIBLE

13 "These have one purpose, and they give their power and authority to the beast.

Victory for the Lamb

14 "These will wage war against the Lamb, and the Lamb will overcome them, because He is Lord of lords and King of kings, and those who are with Him *are the* called and chosen and faithful."

15 And he *said to me, "The waters which you saw where the harlot sits, are peoples and multitudes and nations and tongues.

16 "And the ten horns which you saw, and the beast, these will hate the harlot and will make her desolate and naked, and will eat her flesh and will burn her up with fire.

17 "For God has put it in their hearts to execute His purpose by having a common purpose, and by giving their kingdom to the beast, until the words of God will be fulfilled.

18 "The woman whom you saw is the great city, which reigns over the kings of the earth."

Babylon Is Fallen

18 After these things I saw another angel coming down from heaven, having great authority, and the earth was illumined with his glory.

2 And he cried out with a mighty voice, saying, "Fallen, fallen is Babylon the great! She has become a dwelling place of demons and a prison of every unclean spirit, and a prison of every unclean and hateful bird.

NEW CENTURY VERSION

same purpose, and they will give their power and authority
to the beast. 14They will make war against the Lamb, but
the Lamb will defeat them, because he is Lord of lords and
King of kings. He will defeat them with his called, chosen,
and faithful followers."

15Then the angel said to me, "The waters that you saw,
where the prostitute sits, are peoples, races, nations, and
languages. 16The ten horns and the beast you saw will
hate the prostitute. They will take everything she has and
leave her naked. They will eat her body and burn her with
fire. 17God made the ten horns want to carry out his pur-
pose by agreeing to give the beast their power to rule, until
what God has said comes about. 18The woman you saw is
the great city that rules over the kings of the earth."

Babylon Is Destroyed

18 After the vision of these things, I saw another
angel coming down from heaven. This angel had
great power, and his glory made the earth bright. 2He
shouted in a powerful voice:

"Ruined, ruined is the great city of Babylon!
She has become a home for demons
and a prison for every evil spirit,
and a prison for every unclean bird and unclean
beast.

CONTEMPORARY ENGLISH VERSION

will give their power and authority to the beast. 14These
kings will go to war against the Lamb. But he will defeat
them, because he is Lord over all lords and King over all
kings. His followers are chosen and special and faithful.

15The oceans that you saw the prostitute sitting on are
crowds of people from all races and languages. 16The ten
horns and the beast will start hating the shameless
woman. They will strip off her clothes and leave her naked.
Then they will eat her flesh and throw the rest of her body
into a fire. 17God is the one who made these kings all think
alike and decide to give their power to the beast. And they
will do this until what God has said comes true.

18The woman you saw is the great city that rules over
all kings on earth.

The Fall of Babylon

18 I saw another angel come from heaven. This one
had great power, and the earth was bright because
of his glory. 2The angel shouted,

"Fallen! Powerful Babylon
has fallen
and is now the home
of demons.
It is the den
of every filthy spirit
and of all unclean birds,
and every dirty
and hated animal.

NEW INTERNATIONAL VERSION

purpose and will give their power and authority to the beast. 14 They will make war against the Lamb, but the Lamb will overcome them because he is Lord of lords and King of kings—and with him will be his called, chosen and faithful followers."

15 Then the angel said to me, "The waters you saw, where the prostitute sits, are peoples, multitudes, nations and languages. 16 The beast and the ten horns you saw will hate the prostitute. They will bring her to ruin and leave her naked; they will eat her flesh and burn her with fire. 17 For God has put it into their hearts to accomplish his purpose by agreeing to give the beast their power to rule, until God's words are fulfilled. 18 The woman you saw is the great city that rules over the kings of the earth."

The Fall of Babylon

18 After this I saw another angel coming down from heaven. He had great authority, and the earth was illuminated by his splendor. 2 With a mighty voice he shouted:

"Fallen! Fallen is Babylon the Great!
  She has become a home for demons
and a haunt for every evil[a] spirit,
  a haunt for every unclean and detestable bird.

[a] 2 Greek *unclean*

NEW LIVING TRANSLATION

all agree to give their power and authority to him. 14 Together they will wage war against the Lamb, but the Lamb will defeat them because he is Lord over all lords and King over all kings, and his people are the called and chosen and faithful ones."

15 And the angel said to me, "The waters where the prostitute is sitting represent masses of people of every nation and language. 16 The scarlet beast and his ten horns—which represent ten kings who will reign with him—all hate the prostitute. They will strip her naked, eat her flesh, and burn her remains with fire. 17 For God has put a plan into their minds, a plan that will carry out his purposes. They will mutually agree to give their authority to the scarlet beast, and so the words of God will be fulfilled. 18 And this woman you saw in your vision represents the great city that rules over the kings of the earth."

The Fall of Babylon

18 After all this I saw another angel come down from heaven with great authority, and the earth grew bright with his splendor. 2 He gave a mighty shout, "Babylon is fallen—that great city is fallen! She has become the hideout of demons and evil spirits, a nest for filthy buzzards, and a den for dreadful beasts. 3 For all the

NEW KING JAMES VERSION

and they will give their power and authority to the beast. 14 These will make war with the Lamb, and the Lamb will overcome them, for He is Lord of lords and King of kings; and those *who are* with Him *are* called, chosen, and faithful."

15 Then he said to me, "The waters which you saw, where the harlot sits, are peoples, multitudes, nations, and tongues. 16 And the ten horns which you saw on[d] the beast, these will hate the harlot, make her desolate and naked, eat her flesh and burn her with fire. 17 For God has put it into their hearts to fulfill His purpose, to be of one mind, and to give their kingdom to the beast, until the words of God are fulfilled. 18 And the woman whom you saw is that great city which reigns over the kings of the earth."

The Fall of Babylon the Great

18 After these things I saw another angel coming down from heaven, having great authority, and the earth was illuminated with his glory. 2 And he cried mightily[a] with a loud voice, saying, "Babylon the great is fallen, is fallen, and has become a dwelling place of demons, a prison for every foul spirit, and a cage for every unclean and hated

17:16 [d] NU-Text and M-Text read *saw, and the beast.* **18:2** [a] NU-Text and M-Text omit *mightily.*

THE MESSAGE

will agree to turn over their power and authority to the Beast. They will go to war against the Lamb but the Lamb will defeat them, proof that he is Lord over all lords, King over all kings, and those with him will be the called, chosen, and faithful."

The Angel continued, "The waters you saw on which the Whore was enthroned are peoples and crowds, nations and languages. And the ten horns you saw, together with the Beast, will turn on the Whore—they'll hate her, violate her, strip her naked, rip her apart with their teeth, then set fire to her. It was God who put the idea in their heads to turn over their rule to the Beast until the words of God are completed. The woman you saw is the great city, tyrannizing the kings of the earth."

Doom to the City of Darkness

18 Following this I saw another Angel descend from Heaven. His authority was immense, his glory flooded earth with brightness, his voice thunderous:

"Ruined, ruined, Great Babylon, ruined!
  A ghost town for demons is all that's left!
A garrison of carrion spirits,
  garrison of loathsome, carrion birds.

KING JAMES VERSION

3 For all nations have drunk of the wine of the wrath of
her fornication, and the kings of the earth have committed
fornication with her, and the merchants of the earth are
waxed rich through the abundance of her delicacies.
4 And I heard another voice from heaven, saying, Come
out of her, my people, that ye be not partakers of her sins,
and that ye receive not of her plagues.
5 For her sins have reached unto heaven, and God hath
remembered her iniquities.
6 Reward her even as she rewarded you, and double
unto her double according to her works: in the cup which
she hath filled fill to her double.
7 How much she hath glorified herself, and lived deli-
ciously, so much torment and sorrow give her: for she

NEW AMERICAN STANDARD BIBLE

3 "For all the nations [1]have drunk of the wine of the
passion of her immorality, and the kings of the earth have
committed *acts of* immorality with her, and the merchants
of the earth have become rich by the wealth of her sensual-
ity."
4 I heard another voice from heaven, saying, "Come out
of her, my people, so that you will not participate in her
sins and receive of her plagues;
5 for her sins have piled up as high as heaven, and God
has remembered her iniquities.
6 "Pay her back even as she has paid, and give back *to
her* double according to her deeds; in the cup which she
has mixed, mix twice as much for her.
7 "To the degree that she glorified herself and lived sen-
suously, to the same degree give her torment and mourning;

18:3 [1] Two early ancient mss read *have fallen by*

NEW CENTURY VERSION

3 She has been ruined, because all the peoples of the
earth
have drunk the wine of the desire of her sexual sin.
She has been ruined also because the kings of the earth
have sinned sexually with her,
and the merchants of the earth
have grown rich from the great wealth of her luxury."

4 Then I heard another voice from heaven saying:
"Come out of that city, my people,
so that you will not share in her sins,
so that you will not receive the disasters that will
come to her.
5 Her sins have piled up as high as the sky,
and God has not forgotten the wrongs she has done.
6 Give that city the same as she gave to others.
Pay her back twice as much as she did.
Prepare wine for her that is twice as strong
as the wine she prepared for others.
7 She gave herself much glory and rich living.
Give her that much suffering and sadness.

CONTEMPORARY ENGLISH VERSION

3 Babylon's evil and immoral wine
has made all nations drunk.
Every king on earth
has slept with her,
and every merchant on earth
is rich because of
her evil desires."

4 Then I heard another voice
from heaven shout,
"My people, you must escape
from Babylon.
Don't take part in her sins
and share her punishment.
5 Her sins are piled
as high as heaven.
God has remembered the evil
she has done.
6 Treat her as she
has treated others.
Make her pay double
for what she has done.
Make her drink twice as much
of what she mixed
for others.
7 That woman honored herself
with a life of luxury.
Reward her now
with suffering and pain.

NEW INTERNATIONAL VERSION

3 For all the nations have drunk
the maddening wine of her adulteries.
The kings of the earth committed adultery with her,
and the merchants of the earth grew rich from her
excessive luxuries."

4 Then I heard another voice from heaven say:

"Come out of her, my people,
so that you will not share in her sins,
so that you will not receive any of her plagues;
5 for her sins are piled up to heaven,
and God has remembered her crimes.
6 Give back to her as she has given;
pay her back double for what she has done.
Mix her a double portion from her own cup.
7 Give her as much torture and grief
as the glory and luxury she gave herself.

NEW LIVING TRANSLATION

nations have drunk the wine of her passionate immorality.
The rulers of the world have committed adultery with her,
and merchants throughout the world have grown rich as a
result of her luxurious living."
4 Then I heard another voice calling from heaven, "Come
away from her, my people. Do not take part in her sins, or
you will be punished with her. 5 For her sins are piled as
high as heaven, and God is ready to judge her for her evil
deeds. 6 Do to her as she has done to your people. Give her
a double penalty for all her evil deeds. She brewed a cup of
terror for others, so give her twice as much as she gave
out. 7 She has lived in luxury and pleasure, so match it
now with torments and sorrows. She boasts, 'I am queen

NEW KING JAMES VERSION

bird! 3 For all the nations have drunk of the wine of the
wrath of her fornication, the kings of the earth have com-
mitted fornication with her, and the merchants of the earth
have become rich through the abundance of her luxury."
4 And I heard another voice from heaven saying, "Come
out of her, my people, lest you share in her sins, and lest
you receive of her plagues. 5 For her sins have reached[b] to
heaven, and God has remembered her iniquities. 6 Render
to her just as she rendered to you,[c] and repay her double
according to her works; in the cup which she has mixed,
mix double for her. 7 In the measure that she glorified her-
self and lived luxuriously, in the same measure give her
torment and sorrow; for she says in her heart, 'I sit *as*

18:5 [b] NU-Text and M-Text read *have been heaped up.*
18:6 [c] NU-Text and M-Text omit *to you.*

THE MESSAGE

All nations drank the wild wine of her whoring;
kings of the earth went whoring with her;
entrepreneurs made millions exploiting her."

Just then I heard another shout out of Heaven:

"Get out, my people, as fast as you can,
so you don't get mixed up in her sins,
so you don't get caught in her doom.
Her sins stink to high Heaven;
God has remembered every evil she's done.
Give her back what she's given,
double what she's doubled in her works,
double the recipe in the cup she mixed;
Bring her flaunting and wild ways
to torment and tears.

KING JAMES VERSION

saith in her heart, I sit a queen, and am no widow, and
shall see no sorrow.
8 Therefore shall her plagues come in one day, death,
and mourning, and famine; and she shall be utterly burned
with fire: for strong *is* the Lord God who judgeth her.
9 ¶ And the kings of the earth, who have committed for-
nication and lived deliciously with her, shall bewail her,
and lament for her, when they shall see the smoke of her
burning,
10 Standing afar off for the fear of her torment, saying,
Alas, alas, that great city Babylon, that mighty city! for in
one hour is thy judgment come.
11 And the merchants of the earth shall weep and
mourn over her; for no man buyeth their merchandise any
more:
12 The merchandise of gold, and silver, and precious
stones, and of pearls, and fine linen, and purple, and silk,
and scarlet, and all thyine wood, and all manner vessels of
ivory, and all manner vessels of most precious wood, and
of brass, and iron, and marble,

NEW AMERICAN STANDARD BIBLE

for she says in her heart, 'I SIT *AS* A QUEEN AND I AM NOT A
WIDOW, and will never see mourning.'
8 "For this reason in one day her plagues will come,
pestilence and mourning and famine, and she will be
burned up with fire; for the Lord God who judges her is
strong.

Lament for Babylon

9 "And the kings of the earth, who committed *acts of*
immorality and lived sensuously with her, will weep and
lament over her when they see the smoke of her burning,
10 standing at a distance because of the fear of her tor-
ment, saying, 'Woe, woe, the great city, Babylon, the
strong city! For in one hour your judgment has come.'
11 "And the merchants of the earth weep and mourn over
her, because no one buys their cargoes any more—
12 cargoes of gold and silver and precious stones and
pearls and fine linen and purple and silk and scarlet, and
every *kind of* citron wood and every article of ivory
and every article *made* from very costly wood and bronze
and iron and marble,

NEW CENTURY VERSION

She says to herself, 'I am a queen sitting on my throne.
I am not a widow; I will never be sad.'
8 So these disasters will come to her in one day:
death, and crying, and great hunger,
and she will be destroyed by fire,
because the Lord God who judges her is powerful."
9 The kings of the earth who sinned sexually with her
and shared her wealth will see the smoke from her burn-
ing. Then they will cry and be sad because of her death.
10 They will be afraid of her suffering and stand far away
and say:
"Terrible! How terrible for you, great city,
powerful city of Babylon,
because your punishment has come in one hour!"
11 And the merchants of the earth will cry and be sad
about her, because now there is no one to buy their car-
goes— 12 cargoes of gold, silver, jewels, pearls, fine linen,
purple cloth, silk, red cloth; all kinds of citron wood and all
kinds of things made from ivory, expensive wood, bronze,

CONTEMPORARY ENGLISH VERSION

"Deep in her heart
Babylon said,
'I am the queen!
Never will I be a widow
or know what it means
to be sad.'
8 And so, in a single day
she will suffer the pain
of sorrow, hunger, and death.
Fire will destroy
her dead body,
because her judge
is the powerful Lord God."

9 Every king on earth who slept with her and shared in
her luxury will mourn. They will weep, when they see the
smoke from that fire. 10 Her sufferings will frighten them,
and they will stand at a distance and say,

"Pity that great
and powerful city!
Pity Babylon!
In a single hour
her judgment has come."

11 Every merchant on earth will mourn, because there is
no one to buy their goods. 12 There won't be anyone to buy
their gold, silver, jewels, pearls, fine linen, purple cloth, silk,
scarlet cloth, sweet-smelling wood, fancy carvings of ivory
and wood, as well as things made of bronze, iron, or marble.

NEW INTERNATIONAL VERSION

In her heart she boasts,
'I sit as queen; I am not a widow,
and I will never mourn.'
8 Therefore in one day her plagues will overtake her:
death, mourning and famine.
She will be consumed by fire,
for mighty is the Lord God who judges her.

9 "When the kings of the earth who committed adultery
with her and shared her luxury see the smoke of her burn-
ing, they will weep and mourn over her. 10 Terrified at her
torment, they will stand far off and cry:

" 'Woe! Woe, O great city,
O Babylon, city of power!
In one hour your doom has come!'

11 "The merchants of the earth will weep and mourn over
her because no one buys their cargoes any more— 12 car-
goes of gold, silver, precious stones and pearls; fine linen,
purple, silk and scarlet cloth; every sort of citron wood,
and articles of every kind made of ivory, costly wood,

NEW LIVING TRANSLATION

on my throne. I am no helpless widow. I will not experi-
ence sorrow.' 8 Therefore, the sorrows of death and mourn-
ing and famine will overtake her in a single day. She will
be utterly consumed by fire, for the Lord God who judges
her is mighty."

9 And the rulers of the world who took part in her
immoral acts and enjoyed her great luxury will mourn for
her as they see the smoke rising from her charred remains.
10 They will stand at a distance, terrified by her great tor-
ment. They will cry out, "How terrible, how terrible for
Babylon, that great city! In one single moment God's judg-
ment came on her."

11 The merchants of the world will weep and mourn for
her, for there is no one left to buy their goods. 12 She
bought great quantities of gold, silver, jewels, pearls, fine
linen, purple dye, silk, scarlet cloth, every kind of per-
fumed wood, ivory goods, objects made of expensive wood,

NEW KING JAMES VERSION

queen, and am no widow, and will not see sorrow.' 8 There-
fore her plagues will come in one day—death and mourn-
ing and famine. And she will be utterly burned with fire,
for strong *is* the Lord God who judges[d] her.

The World Mourns Babylon's Fall

9 "The kings of the earth who committed fornication and
lived luxuriously with her will weep and lament for her,
when they see the smoke of her burning, 10 standing at a
distance for fear of her torment, saying, 'Alas, alas, that
great city Babylon, that mighty city! For in one hour your
judgment has come.'

11 "And the merchants of the earth will weep and mourn
over her, for no one buys their merchandise anymore:
12 merchandise of gold and silver, precious stones and
pearls, fine linen and purple, silk and scarlet, every kind of
citron wood, every kind of object of ivory, every kind of
object of most precious wood, bronze, iron, and marble;

18:8 [d] NU-Text and M-Text read *has judged.*

THE MESSAGE

Because she gloated, 'I'm queen over all,
and no widow, never a tear on my face,'
In one day, disasters will crush her—
death, heartbreak, and famine—
Then she'll be burned by fire, because God,
the Strong God who judges her,
has had enough.

"The kings of the earth will see the smoke of her burning, and they'll cry and carry on, the kings who went night after night to her brothel. They'll keep their distance for fear they'll get burned, and they'll cry their lament:

'Doom, doom, the great city doomed!
City of Babylon, strong city!
In one hour it's over, your judgment come!'

"The traders will cry and carry on because the bottom dropped out of business, no more market for their goods: gold, silver, precious gems, pearls; fabrics of fine linen, purple, silk, scarlet; perfumed wood and vessels of ivory,

KING JAMES VERSION

13 And cinnamon, and odours, and ointments, and frankincense, and wine, and oil, and fine flour, and wheat, and beasts, and sheep, and horses, and chariots, and slaves, and souls of men.

14 And the fruits that thy soul lusted after are departed from thee, and all things which were dainty and goodly are departed from thee, and thou shalt find them no more at all.

15 The merchants of these things, which were made rich by her, shall stand afar off for the fear of her torment, weeping and wailing,

16 And saying, Alas, alas, that great city, that was clothed in fine linen, and purple, and scarlet, and decked with gold, and precious stones, and pearls!

NEW AMERICAN STANDARD BIBLE

13 and cinnamon and spice and incense and perfume and frankincense and wine and olive oil and fine flour and wheat and cattle and sheep, and *cargoes* of horses and chariots and slaves and human lives.

14 "The fruit you long for has gone from you, and all things that were luxurious and splendid have passed away from you and *men* will no longer find them.

15 "The merchants of these things, who became rich from her, will stand at a distance because of the fear of her torment, weeping and mourning,

16 saying, 'Woe, woe, the great city, she who was clothed in fine linen and purple and scarlet, and adorned with gold and precious stones and pearls;

NEW CENTURY VERSION

iron, and marble; 13cinnamon, spice, incense, myrrh, frankincense, wine, olive oil, fine flour, wheat, cattle, sheep, horses, carriages, slaves, and human lives.

14The merchants will say,

"Babylon, the good things you wanted are gone from
you.
All your rich and fancy things have disappeared.
You will never have them again."

15The merchants who became rich from selling to her will be afraid of her suffering and will stand far away. They will cry and be sad 16and say:

"Terrible! How terrible for the great city!
She was dressed in fine linen, purple and red cloth,
and she was shining with gold, precious jewels, and
pearls!

CONTEMPORARY ENGLISH VERSION

13No one will buy their cinnamon, spices, incense, myrrh, frankincense,[a] wine, olive oil, fine flour, wheat, cattle, sheep, horses, chariots, slaves, and other humans.

14 Babylon, the things
your heart desired
have all escaped
from you.
Every luxury
and all your glory
will be lost forever.
You will never
get them back.

15The merchants had become rich because of her. But when they saw her sufferings, they were terrified. They stood at a distance, crying and mourning. 16Then they shouted,

"Pity the great city
of Babylon!
She dressed in fine linen
and wore purple
and scarlet cloth.
She had jewelry
made of gold
and precious stones
and pearls.

[a] 18.13 *myrrh, frankincense*: Myrrh was a valuable sweet-smelling powder often used in perfume. Frankincense was a valuable powder that was burned to make a sweet smell.

NEW INTERNATIONAL VERSION

bronze, iron and marble; 13cargoes of cinnamon and spice,
of incense, myrrh and frankincense, of wine and olive oil,
of fine flour and wheat; cattle and sheep; horses and carriages; and bodies and souls of men.
14"They will say, 'The fruit you longed for is gone from you. All your riches and splendor have vanished, never to be recovered.'
15The merchants who sold these things and gained their wealth from her will stand far off, terrified at her torment. They will weep and mourn
16and cry out:

" 'Woe! Woe, O great city,
dressed in fine linen, purple and scarlet,
and glittering with gold, precious stones and pearls!

NEW LIVING TRANSLATION

bronze, iron, and marble.
13She also bought cinnamon, spice, incense, myrrh, frankincense, wine, olive oil, fine flour, wheat, cattle, sheep, horses, chariots, and slaves—yes, she even traded in human lives.
14"All the fancy things you loved so much are gone," they cry. "The luxuries and splendor that you prized so much will never be yours again. They are gone forever."
15The merchants who became wealthy by selling her these things will stand at a distance, terrified by her great torment. They will weep and cry.
16"How terrible, how terrible for that great city! She was so beautiful—like a woman clothed in finest purple and scarlet linens, decked out with gold and precious stones and pearls!

NEW KING JAMES VERSION

13and cinnamon and incense, fragrant oil and frankincense, wine and oil, fine flour and wheat, cattle and sheep, horses and chariots, and bodies and souls of men.
14The fruit that your soul longed for has gone from you, and all the things which are rich and splendid have gone from you,[e] and you shall find them no more at all.
15The merchants of these things, who became rich by her, will stand at a distance for fear of her torment, weeping and wailing,
16and saying, 'Alas, alas, that great city that was clothed in fine linen, purple, and scarlet, and adorned with gold and precious stones and pearls!
17For in one hour such

18:14 [e] NU-Text and M-Text read *been lost to you.*

THE MESSAGE

precious woods, bronze, iron, and marble; cinnamon and spice, incense, myrrh, and frankincense; wine and oil, flour and wheat; cattle, sheep, horses, and chariots. And slaves—their terrible traffic in human lives.

'Everything you've lived for, gone!
All delicate and delectable luxury, lost!
Not a scrap, not a thread to be found!'

The traders who made millions off her kept their distance for fear of getting burned, and cried and carried on all the more:

'Doom, doom, the great city doomed!
Dressed in the latest fashions,
adorned with the finest jewels,
in one hour such wealth wiped out!'

KING JAMES VERSION

17 For in one hour so great riches is come to nought. And every shipmaster, and all the company in ships, and sailors, and as many as trade by sea, stood afar off,

18 And cried when they saw the smoke of her burning, saying, What *city is* like unto this great city!

19 And they cast dust on their heads, and cried, weeping and wailing, saying, Alas, alas, that great city, wherein were made rich all that had ships in the sea by reason of her costliness! for in one hour is she made desolate.

20 Rejoice over her, *thou* heaven, and *ye* holy apostles and prophets; for God hath avenged you on her.

21 And a mighty angel took up a stone like a great millstone, and cast *it* into the sea, saying, Thus with violence shall that great city Babylon be thrown down, and shall be found no more at all.

NEW AMERICAN STANDARD BIBLE

17 for in one hour such great wealth has been laid waste!' And every shipmaster and every passenger and sailor, and as many as make their living by the sea, stood at a distance,

18 and were crying out as they saw the smoke of her burning, saying, 'What *city* is like the great city?'

19 "And they threw dust on their heads and were crying out, weeping and mourning, saying, 'Woe, woe, the great city, in which all who had ships at sea became rich by her wealth, for in one hour she has been laid waste!'

20 "Rejoice over her, O heaven, and you saints and apostles and prophets, because God has pronounced judgment for you against her."

21 Then a strong angel took up a stone like a great millstone and threw it into the sea, saying, "So will Babylon, the great city, be thrown down with violence, and will not be found any longer.

NEW CENTURY VERSION

17 All these riches have been destroyed in one hour!"
Every sea captain, every passenger, the sailors, and all those who earn their living from the sea stood far away
from Babylon. 18 As they saw the smoke from her burning, they cried out loudly, "There was never a city like this
great city!" 19 And they threw dust on their heads and cried out, weeping and being sad. They said:

"Terrible! How terrible for the great city!
All the people who had ships on the sea
became rich because of her wealth!
But she has been destroyed in one hour!
20 Be happy because of this, heaven!
Be happy, God's holy people and apostles and prophets!
God has punished her because of what she did to you."

21 Then a powerful angel picked up a large stone, like one used for grinding grain, and threw it into the sea. He said:

"In the same way, the great city of Babylon will be thrown down,
and it will never be found again.

CONTEMPORARY ENGLISH VERSION

17 Yet in a single hour
her riches disappeared."

Every ship captain and passenger and sailor stood at a distance, together with everyone who does business by
traveling on the sea. 18 When they saw the smoke from her fire, they shouted, "This was the greatest city ever!"
19 They cried loudly, and in their sorrow they threw dust on their heads, as they said,

"Pity the great city
of Babylon!
Everyone who sailed the seas
became rich
from her treasures.
But in a single hour
the city was destroyed.
20 The heavens should be happy
with God's people
and apostles and prophets.
God has punished her
for them."

21 A powerful angel then picked up a huge stone and threw it into the sea. The angel said,

"This is how the great city
of Babylon
will be thrown down,
never to rise again.

NEW INTERNATIONAL VERSION

[17]In one hour such great wealth has been brought to
ruin!'

"Every sea captain, and all who travel by ship, the
sailors, and all who earn their living from the sea, will
stand far off. [18]When they see the smoke of her burning,
they will exclaim, 'Was there ever a city like this great
city?' [19]They will throw dust on their heads, and with
weeping and mourning cry out:

" 'Woe! Woe, O great city,
where all who had ships on the sea
became rich through her wealth!
In one hour she has been brought to ruin!
[20]Rejoice over her, O heaven!
Rejoice, saints and apostles and prophets!
God has judged her for the way she treated you.' "

[21]Then a mighty angel picked up a boulder the size of a
large millstone and threw it into the sea, and said:

"With such violence
the great city of Babylon will be thrown down,
never to be found again.

NEW LIVING TRANSLATION

[17]And in one single moment all the wealth of the city is
gone!"

And all the shipowners and captains of the merchant
ships and their crews will stand at a distance. [18]They will
weep as they watch the smoke ascend, and they will say,
"Where in all the world is there another city like this?"
[19]And they will throw dust on their heads to show their
great sorrow. And they will say, "How terrible, how terrible
for the great city! She made us all rich from her great
wealth. And now in a single hour it is all gone."

[20]But you, O heaven, rejoice over her fate. And you also
rejoice, O holy people of God and apostles and prophets!
For at last God has judged her on your behalf.

[21]Then a mighty angel picked up a boulder as large as a
great millstone. He threw it into the ocean and shouted,
"Babylon, the great city, will be thrown down as violently
as I have thrown away this stone, and she will disappear

NEW KING JAMES VERSION

great riches came to nothing.' Every shipmaster, all who
travel by ship, sailors, and as many as trade on the sea,
stood at a distance [18]and cried out when they saw the
smoke of her burning, saying, 'What *is* like this great
city?'

[19]"They threw dust on their heads and cried out, weep-
ing and wailing, and saying, 'Alas, alas, that great city, in
which all who had ships on the sea became rich by her
wealth! For in one hour she is made desolate.'

[20]"Rejoice over her, O heaven, and *you* holy apostles[f]
and prophets, for God has avenged you on her!"

Finality of Babylon's Fall

[21]Then a mighty angel took up a stone like a great mill-
stone and threw *it* into the sea, saying, "Thus with violence
the great city Babylon shall be thrown down, and shall not

18:20 [f] NU-Text and M-Text read *saints and apostles.*

THE MESSAGE

"All the ship captains and travelers by sea, sailors and toilers of the sea, stood off at a distance and cried their lament when they saw the smoke from her burning: 'Oh, what a city! There was never a city like her!' They threw dust on their heads and cried as if the world had come to an end:

'Doom, doom, the great city doomed!
All who owned ships or did business by sea
Got rich on her getting and spending.
And now it's over—wiped out in one hour!'

"Oh Heaven, celebrate! And join in, saints, apostles, and prophets! God has judged her; every wrong you suffered from her has been judged."

A strong Angel reached for a boulder—huge, like a millstone—and heaved it into the sea, saying,

"Heaved and sunk, the great city Babylon,
sunk in the sea, not a sign of her ever again.

KING JAMES VERSION

22 And the voice of harpers, and musicians, and of pipers, and trumpeters, shall be heard no more at all in thee; and no craftsman, of whatsoever craft *he be*, shall be found any more in thee; and the sound of a millstone shall be heard no more at all in thee;
23 And the light of a candle shall shine no more at all in thee; and the voice of the bridegroom and of the bride shall be heard no more at all in thee: for thy merchants were the great men of the earth; for by thy sorceries were all nations deceived.
24 And in her was found the blood of prophets, and of saints, and of all that were slain upon the earth.
19 And after these things I heard a great voice of much people in heaven, saying, Alleluia; Salvation, and glory, and honour, and power, unto the Lord our God:

NEW AMERICAN STANDARD BIBLE

22 "And the sound of harpists and musicians and flute-players and trumpeters will not be heard in you any longer; and no craftsman of any craft will be found in you any longer; and the sound of a mill will not be heard in you any longer;
23 and the light of a lamp will not shine in you any longer; and the voice of the bridegroom and bride will not be heard in you any longer; for your merchants were the great men of the earth, because all the nations were deceived by your sorcery.
24 "And in her was found the blood of prophets and of saints and of all who have been slain on the earth."

The Fourfold Hallelujah

19 After these things I heard something like a loud voice of a great multitude in heaven, saying,
"Hallelujah! Salvation and glory and power belong to our God;

NEW CENTURY VERSION

22 The music of people playing harps and other
instruments, flutes, and trumpets,
will never be heard in you again.
No workman doing any job
will ever be found in you again.
The sound of grinding grain
will never be heard in you again.
23 The light of a lamp
will never shine in you again,
and the voices of a bridegroom and bride
will never be heard in you again.
Your merchants were the world's great people,
and all the nations were tricked by your magic.
24 You are guilty of the death of the prophets and God's
holy people
and all who have been killed on earth."

People in Heaven Praise God

19 After this vision and announcement I heard what sounded like a great many people in heaven saying:
"Hallelujah![a]
Salvation, glory, and power belong to our God,

19:1 [a] **Hallelujah** This means "praise God!"

CONTEMPORARY ENGLISH VERSION

22 The music of harps and singers
and of flutes and trumpets
will no longer be heard.
No workers will ever
set up shop in that city,
and the sound
of grinding grain
will be silenced forever.
23 Lamps will no longer shine
anywhere in Babylon,
and couples will never again
say wedding vows there.
Her merchants ruled
the earth,
and by her witchcraft
she fooled all nations.
24 On the streets of Babylon
is found the blood
of God's people
and of his prophets,
and everyone else."

19 After this, I heard what sounded like a lot of voices in heaven, and they were shouting,

"Praise the Lord!
To our God belongs
the glorious power to save,

NEW INTERNATIONAL VERSION

22 The music of harpists and musicians, flute players and trumpeters,
will never be heard in you again.
No workman of any trade
will ever be found in you again.
The sound of a millstone
will never be heard in you again.
23 The light of a lamp
will never shine in you again.
The voice of bridegroom and bride
will never be heard in you again.
Your merchants were the world's great men.
By your magic spell all the nations were led astray.
24 In her was found the blood of prophets and of the saints,
and of all who have been killed on the earth."

Hallelujah!

19 After this I heard what sounded like the roar of a great multitude in heaven shouting:

"Hallelujah!
Salvation and glory and power belong to our God,

NEW LIVING TRANSLATION

forever. 22Never again will the sound of music be heard
there—no more harps, songs, flutes, or trumpets. There
will be no industry of any kind, and no more milling of
grain. 23Her nights will be dark, without a single lamp.
There will be no happy voices of brides and grooms. This
will happen because her merchants, who were the greatest
in the world, deceived the nations with her sorceries. 24In
her streets the blood of the prophets was spilled. She was
the one who slaughtered God's people all over the world."

Songs of Victory in Heaven

19 After this, I heard the sound of a vast crowd in
heaven shouting, "Hallelujah! Salvation is from our
God. Glory and power belong to him alone. 2His judgments

NEW KING JAMES VERSION

be found anymore. 22The sound of harpists, musicians,
flutists, and trumpeters shall not be heard in you anymore.
No craftsman of any craft shall be found in you anymore,
and the sound of a millstone shall not be heard in you any-
more. 23The light of a lamp shall not shine in you anymore,
and the voice of bridegroom and bride shall not be heard in
you anymore. For your merchants were the great men of
the earth, for by your sorcery all the nations were deceived.
24And in her was found the blood of prophets and saints,
and of all who were slain on the earth."

Heaven Exults over Babylon

19 After these things I heard[a] a loud voice of a great
multitude in heaven, saying, "Alleluia! Salvation
and glory and honor and power *belong* to the Lord[b] our

19:1 [a] NU-Text and M-Text add *something like.* [b] NU-Text and M-Text omit *the Lord.*

THE MESSAGE

Silent the music of harpists and singers—
you'll never hear flutes and trumpets again.
Artisans of every kind—gone;
you'll never see their likes again.
The voice of a millstone grinding falls dumb;
you'll never hear that sound again.
The light from lamps, never again;
never again laughter of bride and groom.
Her traders robbed the whole earth blind,
and by black-magic arts deceived the nations.
The only thing left of Babylon is blood—
the blood of saints and prophets,
the murdered and the martyred."

The Sound of Hallelujahs

19 I heard a sound like massed choirs in Heaven singing,

"Hallelujah!
The salvation and glory and power are God's—

KING JAMES VERSION

2 For true and righteous *are* his judgments: for he hath judged the great whore, which did corrupt the earth with her fornication, and hath avenged the blood of his servants at her hand.
3 And again they said, Alleluia. And her smoke rose up for ever and ever.
4 And the four and twenty elders and the four beasts fell down and worshipped God that sat on the throne, saying, Amen; Alleluia.
5 ¶ And a voice came out of the throne, saying, Praise our God, all ye his servants, and ye that fear him, both small and great.
6 And I heard as it were the voice of a great multitude,

NEW AMERICAN STANDARD BIBLE

2 BECAUSE HIS JUDGMENTS ARE TRUE AND RIGHTEOUS; for He has judged the great harlot who was corrupting the earth with her immorality, and HE HAS AVENGED THE BLOOD OF HIS BOND-SERVANTS ON HER."
3 And a second time they said, "Hallelujah! HER SMOKE RISES UP FOREVER AND EVER."
4 And the twenty-four elders and the four living creatures fell down and worshiped God who sits on the throne saying, "Amen. Hallelujah!"
5 And a voice came from the throne, saying,
"Give praise to our God, all you His bond-servants, you who fear Him, the small and the great."
6 Then I heard *something* like the voice of a great mul-

NEW CENTURY VERSION

2 because his judgments are true and right.
He has punished the prostitute
who made the earth evil with her sexual sin.
He has paid her back for the death of his servants."
3 Again they said:
"Hallelujah!
She is burning, and her smoke will rise forever and ever."

4 Then the twenty-four elders and the four living creatures bowed down and worshiped God, who sits on the throne. They said:
"Amen, Hallelujah!"
5 Then a voice came from the throne, saying:
"Praise our God, all you who serve him
and all you who honor him, both small and great!"
6 Then I heard what sounded like a great many people,

CONTEMPORARY ENGLISH VERSION

2 because his judgments
are honest and fair.
That filthy prostitute
ruined the earth
with shameful deeds.
But God has judged her
and made her pay
the price for murdering
his servants."

3 Then the crowd shouted,

"Praise the Lord!
Smoke will never stop rising
from her burning body."

4 After this, the twenty-four elders and the four living creatures all knelt before the throne of God and worshiped him. They said, "Amen! Praise the Lord!"

The Marriage Supper of the Lamb

5 From the throne a voice said,

"If you worship
and fear our God,
give praise to him,
no matter who you are."

6 Then I heard what seemed to be a large crowd that

NEW INTERNATIONAL VERSION

2 for true and just are his judgments.
He has condemned the great prostitute
who corrupted the earth by her adulteries.
He has avenged on her the blood of his servants."

3And again they shouted:

"Hallelujah!
The smoke from her goes up for ever and ever."

4The twenty-four elders and the four living creatures fell
down and worshiped God, who was seated on the throne.
And they cried:

"Amen, Hallelujah!"

5Then a voice came from the throne, saying:

"Praise our God,
all you his servants,
you who fear him,
both small and great!"

6Then I heard what sounded like a great multitude, like

NEW LIVING TRANSLATION

are just and true. He has punished the great prostitute who
corrupted the earth with her immorality, and he has
avenged the murder of his servants." 3Again and again
their voices rang, "Hallelujah! The smoke from that city
ascends forever and forever!"
4Then the twenty-four elders and the four living beings
fell down and worshiped God, who was sitting on the
throne. They cried out, "Amen! Hallelujah!"
5And from the throne came a voice that said, "Praise our
God, all his servants, from the least to the greatest, all
who fear him."
6Then I heard again what sounded like the shout of a

NEW KING JAMES VERSION

God! 2For true and righteous *are* His judgments, because
He has judged the great harlot who corrupted the earth
with her fornication; and He has avenged on her the blood
of His servants *shed* by her." 3Again they said, "Alleluia!
Her smoke rises up forever and ever!" 4And the twenty-
four elders and the four living creatures fell down and wor-
shiped God who sat on the throne, saying, "Amen!
Alleluia!" 5Then a voice came from the throne, saying,
"Praise our God, all you His servants and those who fear
Him, both[c] small and great!"
6And I heard, as it were, the voice of a great multitude,

19:5 [c] NU-Text and M-Text omit *both.*

THE MESSAGE

his judgments true, his judgments just.
He judged the great Whore
who corrupted the earth with her lust.
He avenged on her the blood of his servants."

Then, more singing:
"Hallelujah!
The smoke from her burning billows up
to high Heaven forever and ever and ever."

The Twenty-four Elders and the Four Animals fell to
their knees and worshiped God on his Throne, praising,

"Amen! Yes! Hallelujah!"
From the Throne came a shout, a command:
"Praise our God, all you his servants,
All you who fear him, small and great!"

Then I heard the sound of massed choirs, the sound of a

KING JAMES VERSION

and as the voice of many waters, and as the voice of mighty thunderings, saying, Alleluia: for the Lord God omnipotent reigneth.
7 Let us be glad and rejoice, and give honour to him: for
the marriage of the Lamb is come, and his wife hath made herself ready.
8 And to her was granted that she should be arrayed in
fine linen, clean and white: for the fine linen is the righteousness of saints.
9 And he saith unto me, Write, Blessed *are* they which
are called unto the marriage supper of the Lamb. And he saith unto me, These are the true sayings of God.
10 And I fell at his feet to worship him. And he said
unto me, See *thou do it* not: I am thy fellowservant, and of thy brethren that have the testimony of Jesus: worship God: for the testimony of Jesus is the spirit of prophecy.

NEW AMERICAN STANDARD BIBLE

titude and like the sound of many waters and like the sound of mighty peals of thunder, saying,

"Hallelujah! For the Lord our God, the Almighty, reigns.

Marriage of the Lamb

7 "Let us rejoice and be glad and give the glory to Him,
for the marriage of the Lamb has come and His bride has made herself ready."
8 It was given to her to clothe herself in fine linen,
bright *and* clean; for the fine linen is the righteous acts of the saints.
9 Then he *said to me, "Write, 'Blessed are those who
are invited to the marriage supper of the Lamb.'" And he *said to me, "These are true words of God."
10 Then I fell at his feet to worship him. But he *said to
me, "Do not do that; I am a fellow servant of yours and your brethren who hold the testimony of Jesus; worship God. For the testimony of Jesus is the spirit of prophecy."

NEW CENTURY VERSION

like the noise of flooding water, and like the noise of loud thunder. The people were saying:

"Hallelujah!
Our Lord God, the Almighty, rules.
7 Let us rejoice and be happy
and give God glory,
because the wedding of the Lamb has come,
and the Lamb's bride has made herself ready.
8 Fine linen, bright and clean, was given to her to wear."

(The fine linen means the good things done by God's holy people.)
9 And the angel said to me, "Write this: Happy are those
who have been invited to the wedding meal of the Lamb!" And the angel said, "These are the true words of God."
10 Then I bowed down at the angel's feet to worship him,
but he said to me, "Do not worship me! I am a servant like you and your brothers and sisters who have the message of Jesus. Worship God, because the message about Jesus is the spirit that gives all prophecy."

CONTEMPORARY ENGLISH VERSION

sounded like a roaring flood and loud thunder all mixed together. They were saying,

"Praise the Lord!
Our Lord God All-Powerful
now rules as king.
7 So we will be glad and happy
and give him praise.
The wedding day of the Lamb
is here,
and his bride is ready.
8 She will be given
a wedding dress
made of pure
and shining linen.
This linen stands for
the good things
God's people have done."

9 Then the angel told me, "Put this in writing. God will
bless everyone who is invited to the wedding feast of the Lamb." The angel also said, "These things that God has said are true."
10 I knelt at the feet of the angel and began to worship
him. But the angel said, "Don't do that! I am a servant, just like you and everyone else who tells about Jesus. Don't worship anyone but God. Everyone who tells about Jesus does it by the power of the Spirit."

NEW INTERNATIONAL VERSION

the roar of rushing waters and like loud peals of thunder,
shouting:

"Hallelujah!
For our Lord God Almighty reigns.
7 Let us rejoice and be glad
and give him glory!
For the wedding of the Lamb has come,
and his bride has made herself ready.
8 Fine linen, bright and clean,
was given her to wear."
(Fine linen stands for the righteous acts of the saints.)

9Then the angel said to me, "Write: 'Blessed are those
who are invited to the wedding supper of the Lamb!' " And
he added, "These are the true words of God."
10At this I fell at his feet to worship him. But he said to
me, "Do not do it! I am a fellow servant with you and with
your brothers who hold to the testimony of Jesus. Worship
God! For the testimony of Jesus is the spirit of prophecy."

NEW LIVING TRANSLATION

huge crowd, or the roar of mighty ocean waves, or the
crash of loud thunder: "Hallelujah! For the Lord our God,
the Almighty, reigns. 7Let us be glad and rejoice and honor
him. For the time has come for the wedding feast of the
Lamb, and his bride has prepared herself. 8She is permit-
ted to wear the finest white linen." (Fine linen represents
the good deeds done by the people of God.)
9And the angel said, "Write this: Blessed are those who
are invited to the wedding feast of the Lamb." And he
added, "These are true words that come from God."
10Then I fell down at his feet to worship him, but he said,
"No, don't worship me. For I am a servant of God, just like
you and other brothers and sisters* who testify of their
faith in Jesus. Worship God. For the essence of prophecy is
to give a clear witness for Jesus.*"

19:10a Greek *brothers.* **19:10b** Or *is the message confirmed by Jesus.*

NEW KING JAMES VERSION

as the sound of many waters and as the sound of mighty
thunderings, saying, "Alleluia! For the[d] Lord God
Omnipotent reigns! 7Let us be glad and rejoice and give
Him glory, for the marriage of the Lamb has come, and His
wife has made herself ready." 8And to her it was granted
to be arrayed in fine linen, clean and bright, for the fine
linen is the righteous acts of the saints.
9Then he said to me, "Write: 'Blessed *are* those who are
called to the marriage supper of the Lamb!' " And he said
to me, "These are the true sayings of God." 10And I fell at
his feet to worship him. But he said to me, "See *that you
do* not *do that!* I am your fellow servant, and of your
brethren who have the testimony of Jesus. Worship God!
For the testimony of Jesus is the spirit of prophecy."

19:6 [d] NU-Text and M-Text read *our.*

THE MESSAGE

mighty cataract, the sound of strong thunder:

"Hallelujah!
The Master reigns,
our God, the Sovereign-Strong!
Let us celebrate, let us rejoice,
let us give him the glory!
The Marriage of the Lamb has come;
his Wife has made herself ready.
She was given a bridal gown
of bright and shining linen.
The linen is the righteousness of the saints."

The Angel said to me, "Write this: 'Blessed are those
invited to the Wedding Supper of the Lamb.' " He added,
"These are the true words of God!"
I fell at his feet to worship him, but he wouldn't let me.
"Don't do that," he said. "I'm a servant just like you, and
like your brothers and sisters who hold to the witness of
Jesus. The witness of Jesus is the spirit of prophecy."

KING JAMES VERSION

11 ¶ And I saw heaven opened, and behold a white horse; and he that sat upon him *was* called Faithful and True, and in righteousness he doth judge and make war.

12 His eyes *were* as a flame of fire, and on his head *were* many crowns; and he had a name written, that no man knew, but he himself.

13 And he *was* clothed with a vesture dipped in blood: and his name is called The Word of God.

14 And the armies *which were* in heaven followed him upon white horses, clothed in fine linen, white and clean.

15 And out of his mouth goeth a sharp sword, that with it he should smite the nations: and he shall rule them with a rod of iron: and he treadeth the winepress of the fierceness and wrath of Almighty God.

16 And he hath on *his* vesture and on his thigh a name written, KING OF KINGS, AND LORD OF LORDS.

17 And I saw an angel standing in the sun; and he cried with a loud voice, saying to all the fowls that fly in the midst of heaven, Come and gather yourselves together unto the supper of the great God;

18 That ye may eat the flesh of kings, and the flesh of captains, and the flesh of mighty men, and the flesh of horses, and of them that sit on them, and the flesh of all *men, both* free and bond, both small and great.

NEW AMERICAN STANDARD BIBLE

The Coming of Christ

11 And I saw heaven opened, and behold, a white horse, and He who sat on it *is* called Faithful and True, and in righteousness He judges and wages war.

12 His eyes *are* a flame of fire, and on His head *are* many diadems; and He has a name written *on Him* which no one knows except Himself.

13 *He is* clothed with a robe dipped in blood, and His name is called The Word of God.

14 And the armies which are in heaven, clothed in fine linen, white *and* clean, were following Him on white horses.

15 From His mouth comes a sharp sword, so that with it He may strike down the nations, and He will rule them with a rod of iron; and He treads the wine press of the fierce wrath of God, the Almighty.

16 And on His robe and on His thigh He has a name written, "KING OF KINGS, AND LORD OF LORDS."

17 Then I saw an angel standing in the sun, and he cried out with a loud voice, saying to all the birds which fly in midheaven, "Come, assemble for the great supper of God,

18 so that you may eat the flesh of kings and the flesh of [l]commanders and the flesh of mighty men and the flesh of horses and of those who sit on them and the flesh of all men, both free men and slaves, and small and great."

19:18 [l] I.e. chiliarchs, in command of one thousand troops

NEW CENTURY VERSION

The Rider on the White Horse

11 Then I saw heaven opened, and there before me was a
white horse. The rider on the horse is called Faithful and
True, and he is right when he judges and makes war. 12 His
eyes are like burning fire, and on his head are many
crowns. He has a name written on him, which no one but
himself knows. 13 He is dressed in a robe dipped in blood,
and his name is the Word of God. 14 The armies of heaven,
dressed in fine linen, white and clean, were following him
on white horses. 15 Out of the rider's mouth comes a sharp
sword that he will use to defeat the nations, and he will
rule them with a rod of iron. He will crush out the wine in
the winepress of the terrible anger of God the Almighty.
16 On his robe and on his upper leg was written this name:
KING OF KINGS AND LORD OF LORDS.

17 Then I saw an angel standing in the sun, and he called
with a loud voice to all the birds flying in the sky: "Come
and gather together for the great feast of God 18 so that you
can eat the bodies of kings, generals, mighty people,
horses and their riders, and the bodies of all people—free,
slave, small, and great."

CONTEMPORARY ENGLISH VERSION

The Rider on the White Horse

11 I looked and saw that heaven was open, and a white
horse was there. Its rider was called Faithful and True, and
he is always fair when he judges or goes to war. 12 He had
eyes like flames of fire, and he was wearing a lot of
crowns. His name was written on him, but he was the only
one who knew what the name meant.

13 The rider wore a robe that was covered with[a] blood,
and he was known as "The Word of God." 14 He was fol-
lowed by armies from heaven that rode on horses and were
dressed in pure white linen. 15 From his mouth a sharp
sword went out to attack the nations. He will rule them
with an iron rod and will show the fierce anger of God All-
Powerful by trampling the grapes in the pit where wine is
made. 16 On the part of the robe that covered his thigh was
written, "KING OF KINGS AND LORD OF LORDS."

17 I then saw an angel standing on the sun, and he
shouted to all the birds flying in the sky, "Come and join in
God's great feast! 18 You can eat the flesh of kings, rulers,
leaders, horses, riders, free people, slaves, important peo-
ple, and everyone else."

[a] **19.13** *covered with*: Some manuscripts have "sprinkled with."

NEW INTERNATIONAL VERSION

The Rider on the White Horse

11I saw heaven standing open and there before me was a white horse, whose rider is called Faithful and True. With justice he judges and makes war. 12His eyes are like blazing fire, and on his head are many crowns. He has a name written on him that no one knows but he himself. 13He is dressed in a robe dipped in blood, and his name is the Word of God. 14The armies of heaven were following him, riding on white horses and dressed in fine linen, white and clean. 15Out of his mouth comes a sharp sword with which to strike down the nations. "He will rule them with an iron scepter."[a] He treads the winepress of the fury of the wrath of God Almighty. 16On his robe and on his thigh he has this name written:

KING OF KINGS AND LORD OF LORDS.

17And I saw an angel standing in the sun, who cried in a loud voice to all the birds flying in midair, "Come, gather together for the great supper of God, 18so that you may eat the flesh of kings, generals, and mighty men, of horses and their riders, and the flesh of all people, free and slave, small and great."

[a] *15* Psalm 2:9

NEW LIVING TRANSLATION

The Rider on the White Horse

11Then I saw heaven opened, and a white horse was standing there. And the one sitting on the horse was named Faithful and True. For he judges fairly and then goes to war. 12His eyes were bright like flames of fire, and on his head were many crowns. A name was written on him, and only he knew what it meant. 13He was clothed with a robe dipped in blood, and his title was the Word of God. 14The armies of heaven, dressed in pure white linen, followed him on white horses. 15From his mouth came a sharp sword, and with it he struck down the nations. He ruled them with an iron rod, and he trod the winepress of the fierce wrath of almighty God. 16On his robe and thigh was written this title: King of kings and Lord of lords.

17Then I saw an angel standing in the sun, shouting to the vultures flying high in the sky: "Come! Gather together for the great banquet God has prepared. 18Come and eat the flesh of kings, captains, and strong warriors; of horses and their riders; and of all humanity, both free and slave, small and great."

NEW KING JAMES VERSION

Christ on a White Horse

11Now I saw heaven opened, and behold, a white horse. And He who sat on him *was* called Faithful and True, and in righteousness He judges and makes war. 12His eyes *were* like a flame of fire, and on His head *were* many crowns. He had[e] a name written that no one knew except Himself. 13He *was* clothed with a robe dipped in blood, and His name is called The Word of God. 14And the armies in heaven, clothed in fine linen, white and clean,[f] followed Him on white horses. 15Now out of His mouth goes a sharp[g] sword, that with it He should strike the nations. And He Himself will rule them with a rod of iron. He Himself treads the winepress of the fierceness and wrath of Almighty God. 16And He has on *His* robe and on His thigh a name written:

KING OF KINGS
AND LORD OF LORDS.

The Beast and His Armies Defeated

17Then I saw an angel standing in the sun; and he cried with a loud voice, saying to all the birds that fly in the midst of heaven, "Come and gather together for the supper of the great God,[h] 18that you may eat the flesh of kings, the flesh of captains, the flesh of mighty men, the flesh of horses and of those who sit on them, and the flesh of all *people,* free[i] and slave, both small and great."

19:12 [e] M-Text adds *names written, and.* 19:14 [f] NU-Text and M-Text read *pure white linen.* 19:15 [g] M-Text adds *two-edged.*
19:17 [h] NU-Text and M-Text read *the great supper of God.*
19:18 [i] NU-Text and M-Text read *both free.*

THE MESSAGE

A White Horse and Its Rider

Then I saw Heaven open wide—and oh! a white horse and its Rider. The Rider, named Faithful and True, judges and makes war in pure righteousness. His eyes are a blaze of fire, on his head many crowns. He has a Name inscribed that's known only to himself. He is dressed in a robe soaked with blood, and he is addressed as "Word of God." The armies of Heaven, mounted on white horses and dressed in dazzling white linen, follow him. A sharp sword comes out of his mouth so he can subdue the nations, then rule them with a rod of iron. He treads the winepress of the raging wrath of God, the Sovereign-Strong. On his robe and thigh is written, KING OF KINGS, LORD OF LORDS.

I saw an Angel standing in the sun, shouting to all flying birds in Middle-Heaven, "Come to the Great Supper of God! Feast on the flesh of kings and captains and champions, horses and their riders. Eat your fill of them all—free and slave, small and great!"

KING JAMES VERSION

19 And I saw the beast, and the kings of the earth, and their armies, gathered together to make war against him that sat on the horse, and against his army.

20 And the beast was taken, and with him the false prophet that wrought miracles before him, with which he deceived them that had received the mark of the beast, and them that worshipped his image. These both were cast alive into a lake of fire burning with brimstone.

21 And the remnant were slain with the sword of him that sat upon the horse, which *sword* proceeded out of his mouth: and all the fowls were filled with their flesh.

20 And I saw an angel come down from heaven, having the key of the bottomless pit and a great chain in his hand.

2 And he laid hold on the dragon, that old serpent, which is the Devil, and Satan, and bound him a thousand years,

3 And cast him into the bottomless pit, and shut him up, and set a seal upon him, that he should deceive the nations no more, till the thousand years should be fulfilled: and after that he must be loosed a little season.

4 And I saw thrones, and they sat upon them, and judgment was given unto them: and *I saw* the souls of them that were beheaded for the witness of Jesus, and for the word of God, and which had not worshipped the beast, neither his image, neither had received *his* mark upon their

NEW AMERICAN STANDARD BIBLE

19 And I saw the beast and the kings of the earth and their armies assembled to make war against Him who sat on the horse and against His army.

Doom of the Beast and False Prophet

20 And the beast was seized, and with him the false prophet who performed the signs in his presence, by which he deceived those who had received the mark of the beast and those who worshiped his image; these two were thrown alive into the lake of fire which burns with brimstone.

21 And the rest were killed with the sword which came from the mouth of Him who sat on the horse, and all the birds were filled with their flesh.

Satan Bound

20 Then I saw an angel coming down from heaven, holding the key of the abyss and a great chain in his hand.

2 And he laid hold of the dragon, the serpent of old, who is the devil and Satan, and bound him for a thousand years;

3 and he threw him into the abyss, and shut *it* and sealed *it* over him, so that he would not deceive the nations any longer, until the thousand years were completed; after these things he must be released for a short time.

4 Then I saw thrones, and they sat on them, and judgment was given to them. And I *saw* the souls of those who had been beheaded because of their testimony of Jesus and because of the word of God, and those who had not worshiped the beast or his image, and had not received the

NEW CENTURY VERSION

[19]Then I saw the beast and the kings of the earth. Their
armies were gathered together to make war against the
rider on the horse and his army. [20]But the beast was cap-
tured and with him the false prophet who did the miracles
for the beast. The false prophet had used these miracles to
trick those who had the mark of the beast and worshiped
his idol. The false prophet and the beast were thrown alive
into the lake of fire that burns with sulfur. [21]And their
armies were killed with the sword that came out of the
mouth of the rider on the horse, and all the birds ate the
bodies until they were full.

The Thousand Years

20 I saw an angel coming down from heaven. He had
the key to the bottomless pit and a large chain in
his hand. [2]The angel grabbed the dragon, that old snake
who is the devil and Satan, and tied him up for a thousand
years. [3]Then he threw him into the bottomless pit, closed
it, and locked it over him. The angel did this so he could
not trick the people of the earth anymore until the thou-
sand years were ended. After a thousand years he must be
set free for a short time.

[4]Then I saw some thrones and people sitting on them
who had been given the power to judge. And I saw the
souls of those who had been killed because they were faith-
ful to the message of Jesus and the message from God.
They had not worshiped the beast or his idol, and they had
not received the mark of the beast on their foreheads or on

CONTEMPORARY ENGLISH VERSION

[19]I also saw the beast and all kings of the earth come
together. They fought against the rider on the white horse
and against his army. [20]But the beast was captured and so
was the false prophet. This is the same prophet who had
worked miracles for the beast, so that he could fool every-
one who had the mark of the beast and worshiped the idol.
The beast and the false prophet were thrown alive into a
lake of burning sulfur. [21]But the rest of their army was
killed by the sword that came from the mouth of the rider
on the horse. Then birds stuffed themselves on the dead
bodies.

The Thousand Years

20 I saw an angel come down from heaven, carrying
the key to the deep pit and a big chain. [2]He
chained the dragon for a thousand years. It is that old
snake, who is also known as the devil and Satan. [3]Then
the angel threw the dragon into the pit. He locked and
sealed it, so that a thousand years would go by before the
dragon could fool the nations again. But after that, it
would have to be set free for a little while.

[4]I saw thrones, and sitting on those thrones were the
ones who had been given the right to judge. I also saw the
souls of the people who had their heads cut off because
they had told about Jesus and preached God's message.
They were the same ones who had not worshiped the beast
or the idol, and they had refused to let its mark be put on

NEW INTERNATIONAL VERSION

[19]Then I saw the beast and the kings of the earth and
their armies gathered together to make war against the
rider on the horse and his army. [20]But the beast was cap-
tured, and with him the false prophet who had performed
the miraculous signs on his behalf. With these signs he
had deluded those who had received the mark of the beast
and worshiped his image. The two of them were thrown
alive into the fiery lake of burning sulfur. [21]The rest of
them were killed with the sword that came out of the
mouth of the rider on the horse, and all the birds gorged
themselves on their flesh.

The Thousand Years

20 And I saw an angel coming down out of heaven,
having the key to the Abyss and holding in his
hand a great chain. [2]He seized the dragon, that ancient
serpent, who is the devil, or Satan, and bound him for a
thousand years. [3]He threw him into the Abyss, and locked
and sealed it over him, to keep him from deceiving the
nations anymore until the thousand years were ended.
After that, he must be set free for a short time.

[4]I saw thrones on which were seated those who had
been given authority to judge. And I saw the souls of those
who had been beheaded because of their testimony for
Jesus and because of the word of God. They had not wor-
shiped the beast or his image and had not received his

NEW LIVING TRANSLATION

[19]Then I saw the beast gathering the kings of the earth
and their armies in order to fight against the one sitting on
the horse and his army. [20]And the beast was captured, and
with him the false prophet who did mighty miracles on
behalf of the beast—miracles that deceived all who had
accepted the mark of the beast and who worshiped his
statue. Both the beast and his false prophet were thrown
alive into the lake of fire that burns with sulfur. [21]Their
entire army was killed by the sharp sword that came out of
the mouth of the one riding the white horse. And all the
vultures of the sky gorged themselves on the dead bodies.

The Thousand Years

20 Then I saw an angel come down from heaven with
the key to the bottomless pit and a heavy chain in
his hand. [2]He seized the dragon—that old serpent, the
Devil, Satan—and bound him in chains for a thousand
years. [3]The angel threw him into the bottomless pit, which
he then shut and locked so Satan could not deceive the
nations anymore until the thousand years were finished.
Afterward he would be released again for a little while.

[4]Then I saw thrones, and the people sitting on them had
been given the authority to judge. And I saw the souls of
those who had been beheaded for their testimony about
Jesus, for proclaiming the word of God. And I saw the
souls of those who had not worshiped the beast or his
statue, nor accepted his mark on their forehead or their

NEW KING JAMES VERSION

[19]And I saw the beast, the kings of the earth, and their
armies, gathered together to make war against Him who
sat on the horse and against His army. [20]Then the beast
was captured, and with him the false prophet who worked
signs in his presence, by which he deceived those who
received the mark of the beast and those who worshiped
his image. These two were cast alive into the lake of fire
burning with brimstone. [21]And the rest were killed with the
sword which proceeded from the mouth of Him who sat on
the horse. And all the birds were filled with their flesh.

Satan Bound 1000 Years

20 Then I saw an angel coming down from heaven,
having the key to the bottomless pit and a great
chain in his hand. [2]He laid hold of the dragon, that ser-
pent of old, who is *the* Devil and Satan, and bound him for
a thousand years; [3]and he cast him into the bottomless
pit, and shut him up, and set a seal on him, so that he
should deceive the nations no more till the thousand years
were finished. But after these things he must be released
for a little while.

The Saints Reign with Christ 1000 Years

[4]And I saw thrones, and they sat on them, and judgment
was committed to them. Then *I saw* the souls of those who
had been beheaded for their witness to Jesus and for the
word of God, who had not worshiped the beast or his
image, and had not received *his* mark on their foreheads or

THE MESSAGE

I saw the Beast and, assembled with him, earth's kings and their armies, ready to make war against the One on the horse and his army. The Beast was taken, and with him, his puppet, the False Prophet, who used signs to dazzle and deceive those who had taken the mark of the Beast and worshiped his image. They were thrown alive, those two, into Lake Fire and Brimstone. The rest were killed by the sword of the One on the horse, the sword that comes from his mouth. All the birds held a feast on their flesh.

A Thousand Years

20 I saw an Angel descending out of Heaven. He carried the key to the Abyss and a chain—a huge chain. He grabbed the Dragon, that old Snake—the very Devil, Satan himself!—chained him up for a thousand years, dumped him into the Abyss, slammed it shut and sealed it tight. No more trouble out of him, deceiving the nations—until the thousand years are up. After that he has to be let loose briefly.

I saw thrones. Those put in charge of judgment sat on the thrones. I also saw the souls of those beheaded because of their witness to Jesus and the Word of God, who refused to worship either the Beast or his image, refused to take his mark on forehead or hand—they lived

KING JAMES VERSION

foreheads, or in their hands; and they lived and reigned with Christ a thousand years.

5 But the rest of the dead lived not again until the thousand years were finished. This *is* the first resurrection.

6 Blessed and holy *is* he that hath part in the first resurrection: on such the second death hath no power, but they shall be priests of God and of Christ, and shall reign with him a thousand years.

7 And when the thousand years are expired, Satan shall be loosed out of his prison,

8 And shall go out to deceive the nations which are in the four quarters of the earth, Gog and Magog, to gather them together to battle: the number of whom *is* as the sand of the sea.

9 And they went up on the breadth of the earth, and compassed the camp of the saints about, and the beloved city: and fire came down from God out of heaven, and devoured them.

10 And the devil that deceived them was cast into the lake of fire and brimstone, where the beast and the false prophet *are*, and shall be tormented day and night for ever and ever.

11 ¶ And I saw a great white throne, and him that sat on it, from whose face the earth and the heaven fled away; and there was found no place for them.

NEW AMERICAN STANDARD BIBLE

mark on their forehead and on their hand; and they came to life and reigned with Christ for a thousand years.

5 The rest of the dead did not come to life until the thousand years were completed. This is the first resurrection.

6 Blessed and holy is the one who has a part in the first resurrection; over these the second death has no power, but they will be priests of God and of Christ and will reign with Him for a thousand years.

Satan Freed, Doomed

7 When the thousand years are completed, Satan will be released from his prison,

8 and will come out to deceive the nations which are in the four corners of the earth, Gog and Magog, to gather them together for the war; the number of them is like the sand of the seashore.

9 And they came up on the broad plain of the earth and surrounded the camp of the saints and the beloved city, and fire came down from heaven and devoured them.

10 And the devil who deceived them was thrown into the lake of fire and brimstone, where the beast and the false prophet are also; and they will be tormented day and night forever and ever.

Judgment at the Throne of God

11 Then I saw a great white throne and Him who sat upon it, from whose presence earth and heaven fled away, and no place was found for them.

NEW CENTURY VERSION

their hands. They came back to life and ruled with Christ for a thousand years. 5 (The others that were dead did not live again until the thousand years were ended.) This is the first raising of the dead. 6 Happy and holy are those who share in this first raising of the dead. The second death has no power over them. They will be priests for God and for Christ and will rule with him for a thousand years.

7 When the thousand years are over, Satan will be set free from his prison. 8 Then he will go out to trick the nations in all the earth—Gog and Magog—to gather them for battle. There are so many people they will be like sand on the seashore. 9 And Satan's army marched across the earth and gathered around the camp of God's people and the city God loves. But fire came down from heaven and burned them up. 10 And Satan, who tricked them, was thrown into the lake of burning sulfur with the beast and the false prophet. There they will be punished day and night forever and ever.

People of the World Are Judged

11 Then I saw a great white throne and the One who was sitting on it. Earth and sky ran away from him and disap-

CONTEMPORARY ENGLISH VERSION

their hands or foreheads. They will come to life and rule with Christ for a thousand years.

5-6 These people are the first to be raised to life, and they are especially blessed and holy. The second death[a] has no power over them. They will be priests for God and Christ and will rule with them for a thousand years.

No other dead people were raised to life until a thousand years later.

Satan Is Defeated

7 At the end of the thousand years, Satan will be set free. 8 He will fool the countries of Gog and Magog, which are at the far ends of the earth, and their people will follow him into battle. They will have as many followers as there are grains of sand along the beach, 9 and they will march all the way across the earth. They will surround the camp of God's people and the city that his people love. But fire will come down from heaven and destroy the whole army. 10 Then the devil who fooled them will be thrown into the lake of fire and burning sulfur. He will be there with the beast and the false prophet, and they will be in pain day and night forever and ever.

The Judgment at the Great White Throne

11 I saw a great white throne with someone sitting on it. Earth and heaven tried to run away, but there was no place

[a] 20.5,6 *second death*: See the note at 2.11.

NEW INTERNATIONAL VERSION

mark on their foreheads or their hands. They came to life and reigned with Christ a thousand years. 5(The rest of the dead did not come to life until the thousand years were ended.) This is the first resurrection. 6Blessed and holy are those who have part in the first resurrection. The second death has no power over them, but they will be priests of God and of Christ and will reign with him for a thousand years.

Satan's Doom

7When the thousand years are over, Satan will be released from his prison 8and will go out to deceive the nations in the four corners of the earth—Gog and Magog—to gather them for battle. In number they are like the sand on the seashore. 9They marched across the breadth of the earth and surrounded the camp of God's people, the city he loves. But fire came down from heaven and devoured them. 10And the devil, who deceived them, was thrown into the lake of burning sulfur, where the beast and the false prophet had been thrown. They will be tormented day and night for ever and ever.

The Dead Are Judged

11Then I saw a great white throne and him who was seated on it. Earth and sky fled from his presence, and there was no place for them. 12And I saw the dead, great

NEW LIVING TRANSLATION

hands. They came to life again, and they reigned with Christ for a thousand years. 5This is the first resurrection. (The rest of the dead did not come back to life until the thousand years had ended.) 6Blessed and holy are those who share in the first resurrection. For them the second death holds no power, but they will be priests of God and of Christ and will reign with him a thousand years.

The Defeat of Satan

7When the thousand years end, Satan will be let out of his prison. 8He will go out to deceive the nations from every corner of the earth, which are called Gog and Magog. He will gather them together for battle—a mighty host, as numberless as sand along the shore. 9And I saw them as they went up on the broad plain of the earth and surrounded God's people and the beloved city. But fire from heaven came down on the attacking armies and consumed them.

10Then the Devil, who betrayed them, was thrown into the lake of fire that burns with sulfur, joining the beast and the false prophet. There they will be tormented day and night forever and ever.

The Final Judgment

11And I saw a great white throne, and I saw the one who was sitting on it. The earth and sky fled from his presence, but they found no place to hide. 12I saw the dead, both

NEW KING JAMES VERSION

on their hands. And they lived and reigned with Christ for a[a] thousand years. 5But the rest of the dead did not live again until the thousand years were finished. This *is* the first resurrection. 6Blessed and holy *is* he who has part in the first resurrection. Over such the second death has no power, but they shall be priests of God and of Christ, and shall reign with Him a thousand years.

Satanic Rebellion Crushed

7Now when the thousand years have expired, Satan will be released from his prison 8and will go out to deceive the nations which are in the four corners of the earth, Gog and Magog, to gather them together to battle, whose number *is* as the sand of the sea. 9They went up on the breadth of the earth and surrounded the camp of the saints and the beloved city. And fire came down from God out of heaven and devoured them. 10The devil, who deceived them, was cast into the lake of fire and brimstone where[b] the beast and the false prophet *are.* And they will be tormented day and night forever and ever.

The Great White Throne Judgment

11Then I saw a great white throne and Him who sat on it, from whose face the earth and the heaven fled away. And there was found no place for them. 12And I saw the

20:4 [a] M-Text reads *the.* **20:10** [b] NU-Text and M-Text add *also.*

THE MESSAGE

and reigned with Christ for a thousand years! The rest of the dead did not live until the thousand years were up. This is the first resurrection—and those involved most blessed, most holy. No second death for them! They're priests of God and Christ; they'll reign with him a thousand years.

When the thousand years are up, Satan will be let loose from his cell, and will launch again his old work of deceiving the nations, searching out victims in every nook and cranny of earth, even Gog and Magog! He'll talk them into going to war and will gather a huge army, millions strong. They'll stream across the earth, surround and lay siege to the camp of God's holy people, the Beloved City. They'll no sooner get there than fire will pour out of Heaven and burn them up. The Devil who deceived them will be hurled into Lake Fire and Brimstone, joining the Beast and False Prophet, the three in torment around the clock for ages without end.

Judgment

I saw a Great White Throne and the One Enthroned. Nothing could stand before or against the Presence, nothing in Heaven, nothing on earth. And then I saw all the

KING JAMES VERSION

12 And I saw the dead, small and great, stand before God; and the books were opened: and another book was opened, which is *the book* of life: and the dead were judged out of those things which were written in the books, according to their works.

13 And the sea gave up the dead which were in it; and death and hell delivered up the dead which were in them: and they were judged every man according to their works.

14 And death and hell were cast into the lake of fire. This is the second death.

15 And whosoever was not found written in the book of life was cast into the lake of fire.

21 And I saw a new heaven and a new earth: for the first heaven and the first earth were passed away; and there was no more sea.

2 And I John saw the holy city, new Jerusalem, coming down from God out of heaven, prepared as a bride adorned for her husband.

3 And I heard a great voice out of heaven saying, Behold, the tabernacle of God *is* with men, and he will dwell with them, and they shall be his people, and God himself shall be with them, *and be* their God.

4 And God shall wipe away all tears from their eyes;

NEW AMERICAN STANDARD BIBLE

12 And I saw the dead, the great and the small, standing before the throne, and books were opened; and another book was opened, which is *the book* of life; and the dead were judged from the things which were written in the books, according to their deeds.

13 And the sea gave up the dead which were in it, and death and Hades gave up the dead which were in them; and they were judged, every one *of them* according to their deeds.

14 Then death and Hades were thrown into the lake of fire. This is the second death, the lake of fire.

15 And if anyone's name was not found written in the book of life, he was thrown into the lake of fire.

The New Heaven and Earth

21 Then I saw a new heaven and a new earth; for the first heaven and the first earth passed away, and there is no longer *any* sea.

2 And I saw the holy city, new Jerusalem, coming down out of heaven from God, made ready as a bride adorned for her husband.

3 And I heard a loud voice from the throne, saying, "Behold, the tabernacle of God is among men, and He will dwell among them, and they shall be His people, and God Himself will be among them,[1]

4 and He will wipe away every tear from their eyes;

21:3 [1] One early ms reads, and be *their God*

NEW CENTURY VERSION

peared. 12And I saw the dead, great and small, standing
before the throne. Then books were opened, and the book
of life was opened. The dead were judged by what they had
done, which was written in the books. 13The sea gave up
the dead who were in it, and Death and Hades[a] gave up
the dead who were in them. Each person was judged by
what he had done. 14And Death and Hades were thrown
into the lake of fire. The lake of fire is the second death.
15And anyone whose name was not found written in the
book of life was thrown into the lake of fire.

The New Jerusalem

21 Then I saw a new heaven and a new earth. The
first heaven and the first earth had disappeared,
and there was no sea anymore. 2And I saw the holy city,
the new Jerusalem,[a] coming down out of heaven from God.
It was prepared like a bride dressed for her husband. 3And
I heard a loud voice from the throne, saying, "Now God's
presence is with people, and he will live with them, and
they will be his people. God himself will be with them and
will be their God. 4He will wipe away every tear from their

20:13 [a] **Hades** The place of the dead. 21:2 [a] **new Jerusalem** The spiritual city where God's people live with him.

CONTEMPORARY ENGLISH VERSION

for them to go. 12I also saw all the dead people standing in
front of that throne. Every one of them was there, no mat-
ter who they had once been. Several books were opened,
and then the book of life[b] was opened. The dead were
judged by what those books said they had done.

13The sea gave up the dead people who were in it, and
death and its kingdom also gave up their dead. Then
everyone was judged by what they had done. 14Afterwards,
death and its kingdom were thrown into the lake of fire.
This is the second death.[c] 15Anyone whose name wasn't
written in the book of life was thrown into the lake of fire.

The New Heaven and the New Earth

21 I saw a new heaven and a new earth. The first
heaven and the first earth had disappeared, and so
had the sea. 2Then I saw New Jerusalem, that holy city,
coming down from God in heaven. It was like a bride
dressed in her wedding gown and ready to meet her hus-
band.

3I heard a loud voice shout from the throne:

God's home is now with his people. He will live with
them, and they will be his own. Yes, God will make his
home among his people. 4He will wipe all tears from

[b] 20.12 *book of life*: See the note at 3.5. [c] 20.14 *second death*: See the note at 2.11.

NEW INTERNATIONAL VERSION

and small, standing before the throne, and books were
opened. Another book was opened, which is the book of
life. The dead were judged according to what they had
done as recorded in the books. 13The sea gave up the dead
that were in it, and death and Hades gave up the dead that
were in them, and each person was judged according to
what he had done. 14Then death and Hades were thrown
into the lake of fire. The lake of fire is the second death.
15If anyone's name was not found written in the book of
life, he was thrown into the lake of fire.

The New Jerusalem

21 Then I saw a new heaven and a new earth, for the
first heaven and the first earth had passed away,
and there was no longer any sea. 2I saw the Holy City, the
new Jerusalem, coming down out of heaven from God, pre-
pared as a bride beautifully dressed for her husband. 3And
I heard a loud voice from the throne saying, "Now the
dwelling of God is with men, and he will live with them.
They will be his people, and God himself will be with them
and be their God. 4He will wipe every tear from their eyes.

NEW LIVING TRANSLATION

great and small, standing before God's throne. And the
books were opened, including the Book of Life. And the
dead were judged according to the things written in
the books, according to what they had done. 13The sea
gave up the dead in it, and death and the grave* gave up
the dead in them. They were all judged according to their
deeds. 14And death and the grave were thrown into the
lake of fire. This is the second death—the lake of fire.
15And anyone whose name was not found recorded in the
Book of Life was thrown into the lake of fire.

The New Jerusalem

21 Then I saw a new heaven and a new earth, for the
old heaven and the old earth had disappeared. And
the sea was also gone. 2And I saw the holy city, the new
Jerusalem, coming down from God out of heaven like a
beautiful bride prepared for her husband.
3I heard a loud shout from the throne, saying, "Look,
the home of God is now among his people! He will live
with them, and they will be his people. God himself will be
with them.* 4He will remove all of their sorrows, and there

20:13 Greek *and Hades;* also in 20:14. 21:3 Some manuscripts read *God himself will be with them, their God.*

NEW KING JAMES VERSION

dead, small and great, standing before God,[c] and books
were opened. And another book was opened, which is *the
Book* of Life. And the dead were judged according to their
works, by the things which were written in the books.
13The sea gave up the dead who were in it, and Death and
Hades delivered up the dead who were in them. And they
were judged, each one according to his works. 14Then
Death and Hades were cast into the lake of fire. This is the
second death.[d] 15And anyone not found written in the
Book of Life was cast into the lake of fire.

All Things Made New

21 Now I saw a new heaven and a new earth, for the
first heaven and the first earth had passed away.
Also there was no more sea. 2Then I, John,[a] saw the holy
city, New Jerusalem, coming down out of heaven from God,
prepared as a bride adorned for her husband. 3And I heard
a loud voice from heaven saying, "Behold, the tabernacle
of God *is* with men, and He will dwell with them, and they
shall be His people. God Himself will be with them *and be*
their God. 4And God will wipe away every tear from their

20:12 [c] NU-Text and M-Text read *the throne.* 20:14 [d] NU-Text and M-Text add *the lake of fire.* 21:2 [a] NU-Text and M-Text omit *John.*

THE MESSAGE

dead, great and small, standing there—before the Throne!
And books were opened. Then another book was opened:
the Book of Life. The dead were judged by what was writ-
ten in the books, by the way they had lived. Sea released
its dead, Death and Hell turned in their dead. Each man
and woman was judged by the way he or she had lived.
Then Death and Hell were hurled into Lake Fire. This is the
second death—Lake Fire. Anyone whose name was not
found inscribed in the Book of Life was hurled into Lake
Fire.

Everything New

21 I saw Heaven and earth new-created. Gone the
first Heaven, gone the first earth, gone the sea.
I saw Holy Jerusalem, new-created, descending resplen-
dent out of Heaven, as ready for God as a bride for her
husband.
I heard a voice thunder from the Throne: "Look! Look!
God has moved into the neighborhood, making his home
with men and women! They're his people, he's their God.
He'll wipe every tear from their eyes. Death is gone for

KING JAMES VERSION

and there shall be no more death, neither sorrow, nor crying, neither shall there be any more pain: for the former things are passed away.

5 And he that sat upon the throne said, Behold, I make all things new. And he said unto me, Write: for these words are true and faithful.

6 And he said unto me, It is done. I am Alpha and Omega, the beginning and the end. I will give unto him that is athirst of the fountain of the water of life freely.

7 He that overcometh shall inherit all things; and I will be his God, and he shall be my son.

8 But the fearful, and unbelieving, and the abominable, and murderers, and whoremongers, and sorcerers, and idolaters, and all liars, shall have their part in the lake which burneth with fire and brimstone: which is the second death.

9 ¶ And there came unto me one of the seven angels which had the seven vials full of the seven last plagues, and talked with me, saying, Come hither, I will shew thee the bride, the Lamb's wife.

10 And he carried me away in the spirit to a great and high mountain, and shewed me that great city, the holy Jerusalem, descending out of heaven from God,

NEW AMERICAN STANDARD BIBLE

and there will no longer be *any* death; there will no longer be *any* mourning, or crying, or pain; the first things have passed away."

5 And He who sits on the throne said, "Behold, I am making all things new." And He *said, "Write, for these words are faithful and true."

6 Then He said to me, "It is done. I am the Alpha and the Omega, the beginning and the end. I will give to the one who thirsts from the spring of the water of life without cost.

7 "He who overcomes will inherit these things, and I will be his God and he will be My son.

8 "But for the cowardly and unbelieving and abominable and murderers and immoral persons and sorcerers and idolaters and all liars, their part *will be* in the lake that burns with fire and brimstone, which is the second death."

9 Then one of the seven angels who had the seven bowls full of the seven last plagues came and spoke with me, saying, "Come here, I will show you the bride, the wife of the Lamb."

The New Jerusalem

10 And he carried me away [2]in the Spirit to a great and high mountain, and showed me the holy city, Jerusalem, coming down out of heaven from God,

21:10 [2] Or *in spirit*

NEW CENTURY VERSION

eyes, and there will be no more death, sadness, crying, or
pain, because all the old ways are gone."
5 The One who was sitting on the throne said, "Look! I
am making everything new!" Then he said, "Write this,
because these words are true and can be trusted."
6 The One on the throne said to me, "It is finished. I am
the Alpha and the Omega,[b] the Beginning and the End. I
will give free water from the spring of the water of life to
anyone who is thirsty. 7 Those who win the victory will
receive this, and I will be their God, and they will be my
children. 8 But cowards, those who refuse to believe, who
do evil things, who kill, who sin sexually, who do evil
magic, who worship idols, and who tell lies—all these will
have a place in the lake of burning sulfur. This is the second death."
9 Then one of the seven angels who had the seven bowls
full of the seven last troubles came to me, saying, "Come
with me, and I will show you the bride, the wife of the
Lamb." 10 And the angel carried me away by the Spirit to a
very large and high mountain. He showed me the holy city,
Jerusalem, coming down out of heaven from God. 11 It was

21:6 [b] **Alpha and the Omega** The first and last letters of the Greek alphabet. This means "the beginning and the end."

CONTEMPORARY ENGLISH VERSION

their eyes, and there will be no more death, suffering,
crying, or pain. These things of the past are gone forever.
5 Then the one sitting on the throne said:

I am making everything new. Write down what I have
said. My words are true and can be trusted. 6 Everything
is finished! I am Alpha and Omega,[a] the beginning and
the end. I will freely give water from the life-giving fountain to everyone who is thirsty. 7 All who win the victory
will be given these blessings. I will be their God, and
they will be my people.

8 But I will tell you what will happen to cowards and
to everyone who is unfaithful or dirty-minded or who
murders or is sexually immoral or uses witchcraft or
worships idols or tells lies. They will be thrown into that
lake of fire and burning sulfur. This is the second
death.[b]

The New Jerusalem

9 I saw one of the seven angels who had the bowls filled
with the seven last terrible troubles. The angel came to me
and said, "Come on! I will show you the one who will be
the bride and wife of the Lamb." 10 Then with the help of
the Spirit, he took me to the top of a very high mountain.
There he showed me the holy city of Jerusalem coming
down from God in heaven.

[a] **21.6** *Alpha and Omega*: See the note at 1.8. [b] **21.8** *second death*: See the note at 2.11.

NEW INTERNATIONAL VERSION

There will be no more death or mourning or crying or pain, for the old order of things has passed away."

5He who was seated on the throne said, "I am making everything new!" Then he said, "Write this down, for these words are trustworthy and true."

6He said to me: "It is done. I am the Alpha and the Omega, the Beginning and the End. To him who is thirsty I will give to drink without cost from the spring of the water of life. 7He who overcomes will inherit all this, and I will be his God and he will be my son. 8But the cowardly, the unbelieving, the vile, the murderers, the sexually immoral, those who practice magic arts, the idolaters and all liars—their place will be in the fiery lake of burning sulfur. This is the second death."

9One of the seven angels who had the seven bowls full of the seven last plagues came and said to me, "Come, I will show you the bride, the wife of the Lamb." 10And he carried me away in the Spirit to a mountain great and high, and showed me the Holy City, Jerusalem, coming down out of

NEW LIVING TRANSLATION

will be no more death or sorrow or crying or pain. For the old world and its evils are gone forever."

5And the one sitting on the throne said, "Look, I am making all things new!" And then he said to me, "Write this down, for what I tell you is trustworthy and true." 6And he also said, "It is finished! I am the Alpha and the Omega—the Beginning and the End. To all who are thirsty I will give the springs of the water of life without charge! 7All who are victorious will inherit all these blessings, and I will be their God, and they will be my children. 8But cowards who turn away from me, and unbelievers, and the corrupt, and murderers, and the immoral, and those who practice witchcraft, and idol worshipers, and all liars—their doom is in the lake that burns with fire and sulfur. This is the second death."

9Then one of the seven angels who held the seven bowls containing the seven last plagues came and said to me, "Come with me! I will show you the bride, the wife of the Lamb."

10So he took me in spirit* to a great, high mountain, and he showed me the holy city, Jerusalem, descending out of

21:10 Or *in the Spirit.*

NEW KING JAMES VERSION

eyes; there shall be no more death, nor sorrow, nor crying. There shall be no more pain, for the former things have passed away."

5Then He who sat on the throne said, "Behold, I make all things new." And He said to me,[b] "Write, for these words are true and faithful."

6And He said to me, "It is done![c] I am the Alpha and the Omega, the Beginning and the End. I will give of the fountain of the water of life freely to him who thirsts. 7He who overcomes shall inherit all things,[d] and I will be his God and he shall be My son. 8But the cowardly, unbelieving,[e] abominable, murderers, sexually immoral, sorcerers, idolaters, and all liars shall have their part in the lake which burns with fire and brimstone, which is the second death."

The New Jerusalem

9Then one of the seven angels who had the seven bowls filled with the seven last plagues came to me[f] and talked with me, saying, "Come, I will show you the bride, the Lamb's wife."[g] 10And he carried me away in the Spirit to a great and high mountain, and showed me the great city, the holy[h] Jerusalem, descending out of heaven from God,

21:5 [b] NU-Text and M-Text omit *to me.* 21:6 [c] M-Text omits *It is done.* 21:7 [d] M-Text reads *overcomes, I shall give him these things.* 21:8 [e] M-Text adds *and sinners.* 21:9 [f] NU-Text and M-Text omit *to me.* [g] M-Text reads *I will show you the woman, the Lamb's bride.* 21:10 [h] NU-Text and M-Text omit *the great* and read *the holy city, Jerusalem.*

THE MESSAGE

good—tears gone, crying gone, pain gone—all the first order of things gone." The Enthroned continued, "Look! I'm making everything new. Write it all down—each word dependable and accurate."

Then he said, "It's happened. I'm A to Z. I'm the Beginning, I'm the Conclusion. From Water-of-Life Well I give freely to the thirsty. Conquerors inherit all this. I'll be God to them, they'll be sons and daughters to me. But for the rest—the feckless and faithless, degenerates and murderers, sex peddlers and sorcerers, idolaters and all liars—for them it's Lake Fire and Brimstone. Second death!"

The City of Light

One of the Seven Angels who had carried the bowls filled with the seven final disasters spoke to me: "Come here. I'll show you the Bride, the Wife of the Lamb." He took me away in the Spirit to an enormous, high mountain and showed me Holy Jerusalem descending out of Heaven from

KING JAMES VERSION

11 Having the glory of God: and her light *was* like unto a stone most precious, even like a jasper stone, clear as crystal;

12 And had a wall great and high, *and* had twelve gates, and at the gates twelve angels, and names written thereon, which are *the names* of the twelve tribes of the children of Israel:

13 On the east three gates; on the north three gates; on the south three gates; and on the west three gates.

14 And the wall of the city had twelve foundations, and in them the names of the twelve apostles of the Lamb.

15 And he that talked with me had a golden reed to measure the city, and the gates thereof, and the wall thereof.

16 And the city lieth foursquare, and the length is as large as the breadth: and he measured the city with the reed, twelve thousand furlongs. The length and the breadth and the height of it are equal.

17 And he measured the wall thereof, an hundred *and* forty *and* four cubits, *according to* the measure of a man, that is, of the angel.

18 And the building of the wall of it was *of* jasper: and the city *was* pure gold, like unto clear glass.

19 And the foundations of the wall of the city *were* garnished with all manner of precious stones. The first foundation *was* jasper; the second, sapphire; the third, a chalcedony; the fourth, an emerald;

NEW AMERICAN STANDARD BIBLE

11 having the glory of God. Her brilliance was like a very costly stone, as a stone of crystal-clear jasper.

12 It had a great and high wall, with twelve gates, and at the gates twelve angels; and names *were* written on them, which are *the names* of the twelve tribes of the sons of Israel.

13 *There were* three gates on the east and three gates on the north and three gates on the south and three gates on the west.

14 And the wall of the city had twelve foundation stones, and on them *were* the twelve names of the twelve apostles of the Lamb.

15 The one who spoke with me had a gold measuring rod to measure the city, and its gates and its wall.

16 The city is laid out as a square, and its length is as great as the width; and he measured the city with the rod, [3]fifteen hundred miles; its length and width and height are equal.

17 And he measured its wall, [4]seventy-two yards, *according to* human measurements, which are *also* angelic *measurements.*

18 The material of the wall was jasper; and the city was pure gold, like clear glass.

19 The foundation stones of the city wall were adorned with every kind of precious stone. The first foundation stone was jasper; the second, sapphire; the third, chalcedony; the fourth, emerald;

21:16 [3] Lit *twelve thousand stadia;* a stadion was approx 600 ft
21:17 [4] Lit *one hundred forty-four cubits*

NEW CENTURY VERSION

shining with the glory of God and was bright like a very expensive jewel, like a jasper, clear as crystal. 12The city had a great high wall with twelve gates with twelve angels at the gates, and on each gate was written the name of one of the twelve tribes of Israel. 13There were three gates on the east, three on the north, three on the south, and three on the west. 14The walls of the city were built on twelve foundation stones, and on the stones were written the names of the twelve apostles of the Lamb.

15The angel who talked with me had a measuring rod made of gold to measure the city, its gates, and its wall. 16The city was built in a square, and its length was equal to its width. The angel measured the city with the rod. The city was twelve thousand stadia[c] long, twelve thousand stadia wide, and twelve thousand stadia high. 17The angel also measured the wall. It was one hundred forty-four cubits[d] high, by human measurements, which the angel was using. 18The wall was made of jasper, and the city was made of pure gold, as pure as glass. 19The foundation stones of the city walls were decorated with every kind of jewel. The first foundation was jasper, the second was sapphire, the third was chalcedony, the fourth was emerald,

21:16 [c] **stadia** One stadion was a distance of about two hundred yards; about one-eighth of a Roman mile. **21:17** [d] **cubits** A cubit is about half a yard, the length from the elbow to the tip of the little finger.

CONTEMPORARY ENGLISH VERSION

11The glory of God made the city bright. It was dazzling and crystal clear like a precious jasper stone. 12The city had a high and thick wall with twelve gates, and each one of them was guarded by an angel. On each of the gates was written the name of one of the twelve tribes of Israel. 13Three of these gates were on the east, three were on the north, three more were on the south, and the other three were on the west. 14The city was built on twelve foundation stones. On each of the stones was written the name of one of the Lamb's twelve apostles.

15The angel who spoke to me had a gold measuring stick to measure the city and its gates and its walls. 16The city was shaped like a cube, because it was just as high as it was wide. When the angel measured the city, it was about fifteen hundred miles high and fifteen hundred miles wide. 17Then the angel measured the wall, and by our measurements it was about two hundred sixteen feet high.

18The wall was built of jasper, and the city was made of pure gold, clear as crystal. 19Each of the twelve foundations was a precious stone. The first was jasper,[c] the second was sapphire, the third was agate, the fourth was emerald,

[c] **21.19** *jasper*: The precious and semi-precious stones mentioned in verses 19, 20 are of different colors. *Jasper* is usually green or clear; *sapphire* is blue; *agate* has circles of brown and white; *emerald* is green; *onyx* has different bands of color; *carnelian* is deep-red or reddish-white; *chrysolite* is olive-green; *beryl* is green or bluish-green; *topaz* is yellow; *chrysoprase* is apple-green; *jacinth* is reddish-orange; and *amethyst* is deep purple.

NEW INTERNATIONAL VERSION

heaven from God. 11 It shone with the glory of God, and its brilliance was like that of a very precious jewel, like a jasper, clear as crystal. 12 It had a great, high wall with twelve gates, and with twelve angels at the gates. On the gates were written the names of the twelve tribes of Israel. 13 There were three gates on the east, three on the north, three on the south and three on the west. 14 The wall of the city had twelve foundations, and on them were the names of the twelve apostles of the Lamb.

15 The angel who talked with me had a measuring rod of gold to measure the city, its gates and its walls. 16 The city was laid out like a square, as long as it was wide. He measured the city with the rod and found it to be 12,000 stadia[a] in length, and as wide and high as it is long. 17 He measured its wall and it was 144 cubits[b] thick,[c] by man's measurement, which the angel was using. 18 The wall was made of jasper, and the city of pure gold, as pure as glass. 19 The foundations of the city walls were decorated with every kind of precious stone. The first foundation was jasper, the second sapphire, the third chalcedony, the fourth emerald,

[a] *16* That is, about 1,400 miles (about 2,200 kilometers) [b] *17* That is, about 200 feet (about 65 meters) [c] *17* Or *high*

NEW LIVING TRANSLATION

heaven from God. 11 It was filled with the glory of God and sparkled like a precious gem, crystal clear like jasper. 12 Its walls were broad and high, with twelve gates guarded by twelve angels. And the names of the twelve tribes of Israel were written on the gates. 13 There were three gates on each side—east, north, south, and west. 14 The wall of the city had twelve foundation stones, and on them were written the names of the twelve apostles of the Lamb.

15 The angel who talked to me held in his hand a gold measuring stick to measure the city, its gates, and its wall. 16 When he measured it, he found it was a square, as wide as it was long. In fact, it was in the form of a cube, for its length and width and height were each 1,400 miles.* 17 Then he measured the walls and found them to be 216 feet thick* (the angel used a standard human measure).

18 The wall was made of jasper, and the city was pure gold, as clear as glass. 19 The wall of the city was built on foundation stones inlaid with twelve gems: the first was jasper, the second sapphire, the third agate, the fourth

21:16 Greek *12,000 stadia* [2,220 kilometers]. **21:17** Greek *144 cubits* [65 meters].

NEW KING JAMES VERSION

11 having the glory of God. Her light *was* like a most precious stone, like a jasper stone, clear as crystal. 12 Also she had a great and high wall with twelve gates, and twelve angels at the gates, and names written on them, which are *the names* of the twelve tribes of the children of Israel: 13 three gates on the east, three gates on the north, three gates on the south, and three gates on the west.

14 Now the wall of the city had twelve foundations, and on them were the names[i] of the twelve apostles of the Lamb. 15 And he who talked with me had a gold reed to measure the city, its gates, and its wall. 16 The city is laid out as a square; its length is as great as its breadth. And he measured the city with the reed: twelve thousand furlongs. Its length, breadth, and height are equal. 17 Then he measured its wall: one hundred *and* forty-four cubits, *according* to the measure of a man, that is, of an angel. 18 The construction of its wall was *of* jasper; and the city *was* pure gold, like clear glass. 19 The foundations of the wall of the city *were* adorned with all kinds of precious stones: the first foundation *was* jasper, the second sapphire, the third chalcedony, the fourth emerald, 20 the fifth sardonyx, the sixth

21:14 [i] NU-Text and M-Text read *twelve names.*

THE MESSAGE

God, resplendent in the bright glory of God.

The City shimmered like a precious gem, light-filled, pulsing light. She had a wall majestic and high with twelve gates. At each gate stood an Angel, and on the gates were inscribed the names of the Twelve Tribes of the sons of Israel: three gates on the east, three gates on the north, three gates on the south, three gates on the west. The wall was set on twelve foundations, the names of the Twelve Apostles of the Lamb inscribed on them.

The Angel speaking with me had a gold measuring stick to measure the City, its gates, and its wall. The City was laid out in a perfect square. He measured the City with the measuring stick: twelve thousand stadia, its length, width, and height all equal. Using the standard measure, the Angel measured the thickness of its wall: 144 cubits. The wall was jasper, the color of Glory, and the City was pure gold, translucent as glass. The foundations of the City walls were garnished with every precious gem imaginable: the first foundation jasper, the second sapphire, the third agate, the

KING JAMES VERSION

20 The fifth, sardonyx; the sixth, sardius; the seventh, chrysolite; the eighth, beryl; the ninth, a topaz; the tenth, a chrysoprasus; the eleventh, a jacinth; the twelfth, an amethyst.

21 And the twelve gates *were* twelve pearls; every several gate was of one pearl: and the street of the city *was* pure gold, as it were transparent glass.

22 And I saw no temple therein: for the Lord God Almighty and the Lamb are the temple of it.

23 And the city had no need of the sun, neither of the moon, to shine in it: for the glory of God did lighten it, and the Lamb *is* the light thereof.

24 And the nations of them which are saved shall walk in the light of it: and the kings of the earth do bring their glory and honour into it.

25 And the gates of it shall not be shut at all by day: for there shall be no night there.

26 And they shall bring the glory and honour of the nations into it.

27 And there shall in no wise enter into it any thing that defileth, neither *whatsoever* worketh abomination, or *maketh* a lie: but they which are written in the Lamb's book of life.

22 And he shewed me a pure river of water of life, clear as crystal, proceeding out of the throne of God and of the Lamb.

2 In the midst of the street of it, and on either side of the river, *was there* the tree of life, which bare twelve *manner*

NEW AMERICAN STANDARD BIBLE

20 the fifth, sardonyx; the sixth, sardius; the seventh, chrysolite; the eighth, beryl; the ninth, topaz; the tenth, chrysoprase; the eleventh, jacinth; the twelfth, amethyst.

21 And the twelve gates were twelve pearls; each one of the gates was a single pearl. And the street of the city was pure gold, like transparent glass.

22 I saw no temple in it, for the Lord God the Almighty and the Lamb are its temple.

23 And the city has no need of the sun or of the moon to shine on it, for the glory of God has illumined it, and its lamp *is* the Lamb.

24 The nations will walk by its light, and the kings of the earth will bring their glory into it.

25 In the daytime (for there will be no night there) its gates will never be closed;

26 and they will bring the glory and the honor of the nations into it;

27 and nothing unclean, and no one who practices abomination and lying, shall ever come into it, but only those whose names are written in the Lamb's book of life.

The River and the Tree of Life

22 Then he showed me a river of the water of life, clear as crystal, coming from the throne of God and of [1]the Lamb,

2 in the middle of its street. On either side of the river was the tree of life, bearing twelve [2]*kinds of* fruit, yielding

22:1 [1] Or *the Lamb. In the middle of its street, and on either side of the river, was* 22:2 [2] Or crops of *fruit*

NEW CENTURY VERSION

20the fifth was onyx, the sixth was carnelian, the seventh was chrysolite, the eighth was beryl, the ninth was topaz, the tenth was chrysoprase, the eleventh was jacinth, and the twelfth was amethyst.
21The twelve gates were twelve pearls, each gate having been made from a single pearl. And the street of the city was made of pure gold as clear as glass.

22I did not see a temple in the city, because the Lord God Almighty and the Lamb are the city's temple.
23The city does not need the sun or the moon to shine on it, because the glory of God is its light, and the Lamb is the city's lamp.
24By its light the people of the world will walk, and the kings of the earth will bring their glory into it.
25The city's gates will never be shut on any day, because there is no night there.
26The glory and the honor of the nations will be brought into it.
27Nothing unclean and no one who does shameful things or tells lies will ever go into it. Only those whose names are written in the Lamb's book of life will enter the city.

22 Then the angel showed me the river of the water of life. It was shining like crystal and was flowing from the throne of God and of the Lamb
2down the middle of the street of the city. The tree of life was on each side of the river. It produces fruit twelve times a year, once each

CONTEMPORARY ENGLISH VERSION

20the fifth was onyx, the sixth was carnelian, the seventh was chrysolite, the eighth was beryl, the ninth was topaz, the tenth was chrysoprase, the eleventh was jacinth, and the twelfth was amethyst.
21Each of the twelve gates was a solid pearl. The streets of the city were made of pure gold, clear as crystal.

22I did not see a temple there. The Lord God All-Powerful and the Lamb were its temple.
23And the city did not need the sun or the moon. The glory of God was shining on it, and the Lamb was its light.

24Nations will walk by the light of that city, and kings will bring their riches there.
25Its gates are always open during the day, and night never comes.
26The glorious treasures of nations will be brought into the city.
27But nothing unworthy will be allowed to enter. No one who is dirty-minded or who tells lies will be there. Only those whose names are written in the Lamb's book of life[d] will be in the city.

22 The angel showed me a river that was crystal clear, and its waters gave life. The river came from the throne where God and the Lamb were seated.
2Then it flowed down the middle of the city's main street. On each side of the river are trees[a] that grow a different kind of

[d] 21.27 *book of life*: See the note at 3.5. [a] 22.2 *trees*: The Greek has "tree," which is used in a collective sense of trees on both sides of the heavenly river.

NEW INTERNATIONAL VERSION

20the fifth sardonyx, the sixth carnelian, the seventh chrysolite, the eighth beryl, the ninth topaz, the tenth chrysoprase, the eleventh jacinth, and the twelfth amethyst.[d] 21The twelve gates were twelve pearls, each gate made of a single pearl. The great street of the city was of pure gold, like transparent glass.

22I did not see a temple in the city, because the Lord God Almighty and the Lamb are its temple. 23The city does not need the sun or the moon to shine on it, for the glory of God gives it light, and the Lamb is its lamp. 24The nations will walk by its light, and the kings of the earth will bring their splendor into it. 25On no day will its gates ever be shut, for there will be no night there. 26The glory and honor of the nations will be brought into it. 27Nothing impure will ever enter it, nor will anyone who does what is shameful or deceitful, but only those whose names are written in the Lamb's book of life.

The River of Life

22 Then the angel showed me the river of the water of life, as clear as crystal, flowing from the throne of God and of the Lamb 2down the middle of the great street of the city. On each side of the river stood the tree of life, bearing twelve crops of fruit, yielding its fruit every month.

[d] *20* The precise identification of some of these precious stones is uncertain.

NEW LIVING TRANSLATION

emerald, 20the fifth onyx, the sixth carnelian, the seventh chrysolite, the eighth beryl, the ninth topaz, the tenth chrysoprase, the eleventh jacinth, the twelfth amethyst.

21The twelve gates were made of pearls—each gate from a single pearl! And the main street was pure gold, as clear as glass.

22No temple could be seen in the city, for the Lord God Almighty and the Lamb are its temple. 23And the city has no need of sun or moon, for the glory of God illuminates the city, and the Lamb is its light. 24The nations of the earth will walk in its light, and the rulers of the world will come and bring their glory to it. 25Its gates never close at the end of day because there is no night. 26And all the nations will bring their glory and honor into the city. 27Nothing evil will be allowed to enter—no one who practices shameful idolatry and dishonesty—but only those whose names are written in the Lamb's Book of Life.

22 And the angel showed me a pure river with the water of life, clear as crystal, flowing from the throne of God and of the Lamb, 2coursing down the center of the main street. On each side of the river grew a tree of life, bearing twelve crops of fruit,* with a fresh crop each

22:2 Or *12 kinds of fruit.*

NEW KING JAMES VERSION

sardius, the seventh chrysolite, the eighth beryl, the ninth topaz, the tenth chrysoprase, the eleventh jacinth, and the twelfth amethyst. 21The twelve gates *were* twelve pearls: each individual gate was of one pearl. And the street of the city *was* pure gold, like transparent glass.

The Glory of the New Jerusalem

22But I saw no temple in it, for the Lord God Almighty and the Lamb are its temple. 23The city had no need of the sun or of the moon to shine in it,[j] for the glory[k] of God illuminated it. The Lamb *is* its light. 24And the nations of those who are saved[l] shall walk in its light, and the kings of the earth bring their glory and honor into it.[m] 25Its gates shall not be shut at all by day (there shall be no night there). 26And they shall bring the glory and the honor of the nations into it.[n] 27But there shall by no means enter it anything that defiles, or causes[o] an abomination or a lie, but only those who are written in the Lamb's Book of Life.

The River of Life

22 And he showed me a pure[a] river of water of life, clear as crystal, proceeding from the throne of God and of the Lamb. 2In the middle of its street, and on either side of the river, *was* the tree of life, which bore twelve fruits, each *tree* yielding its fruit every month. The leaves

21:23 [j] NU-Text and M-Text omit *in it.* [k] M-Text reads *the very glory.* 21:24 [l] NU-Text and M-Text omit *of those who are saved.* [m] M-Text reads *the glory and honor of the nations to Him.* 21:26 [n] M-Text adds *that they may enter in.* 21:27 [o] NU-Text and M-Text read *anything profane, nor one who causes.* 22:1 [a] NU-Text and M-Text omit *pure.*

THE MESSAGE

fourth emerald, the fifth onyx, the sixth carnelian, the seventh chrysolite, the eighth beryl, the ninth topaz, the tenth chrysoprase, the eleventh jacinth, the twelfth amethyst. The twelve gates were twelve pearls, each gate a single pearl.

The main street of the City was pure gold, translucent as glass. But there was no sign of a Temple, for the Lord God—the Sovereign-Strong—and the Lamb are the Temple. The City doesn't need sun or moon for light. God's Glory is its light, the Lamb its lamp! The nations will walk in its light and earth's kings bring in their splendor. Its gates will never be shut by day, and there won't be any night. They'll bring the glory and honor of the nations into the City. Nothing dirty or defiled will get into the City, and no one who defiles or deceives. Only those whose names are written in the Lamb's Book of Life will get in.

✠

22 Then the Angel showed me Water-of-Life River, crystal bright. It flowed from the Throne of God and the Lamb, right down the middle of the street. The Tree of Life was planted on each side of the River, producing twelve kinds of fruit, a ripe fruit each month. The

KING JAMES VERSION

of fruits, *and* yielded her fruit every month: and the leaves of the tree *were* for the healing of the nations.

3 And there shall be no more curse: but the throne of God and of the Lamb shall be in it; and his servants shall serve him:

4 And they shall see his face; and his name *shall be* in their foreheads.

5 And there shall be no night there; and they need no candle, neither light of the sun; for the Lord God giveth them light: and they shall reign for ever and ever.

6 ¶ And he said unto me, These sayings *are* faithful and true: and the Lord God of the holy prophets sent his angel to shew unto his servants the things which must shortly be done.

7 Behold, I come quickly: blessed *is* he that keepeth the sayings of the prophecy of this book.

8 And I John saw these things, and heard *them*. And when I had heard and seen, I fell down to worship before the feet of the angel which shewed me these things.

9 Then saith he unto me, See *thou do it* not: for I am thy fellowservant, and of thy brethren the prophets, and of them which keep the sayings of this book: worship God.

10 And he saith unto me, Seal not the sayings of the prophecy of this book: for the time is at hand.

NEW AMERICAN STANDARD BIBLE

its fruit every month; and the leaves of the tree were for the healing of the nations.

3 There will no longer be any curse; and the throne of God and of the Lamb will be in it, and His bond-servants will serve Him;

4 they will see His face, and His name *will be* on their foreheads.

5 And there will no longer be *any* night; and they will not have need of the light of a lamp nor the light of the sun, because the Lord God will illumine them; and they will reign forever and ever.

6 And he said to me, "These words are faithful and true"; and the Lord, the God of the spirits of the prophets, sent His angel to show to His bond-servants the things which must soon take place.

7 "And behold, I am coming quickly. Blessed is he who heeds the words of the prophecy of this book."

8 I, John, am the one who heard and saw these things. And when I heard and saw, I fell down to worship at the feet of the angel who showed me these things.

9 But he *said to me, "Do not do that. I am a fellow servant of yours and of your brethren the prophets and of those who heed the words of this book. Worship God."

The Final Message

10 And he *said to me, "Do not seal up the words of the prophecy of this book, for the time is near.

NEW CENTURY VERSION

month. The leaves of the tree are for the healing of all the
nations. 3Nothing that God judges guilty will be in that
city. The throne of God and of the Lamb will be there, and
God's servants will worship him. 4They will see his face,
and his name will be written on their foreheads. 5There
will never be night again. They will not need the light of a
lamp or the light of the sun, because the Lord God will give
them light. And they will rule as kings forever and ever.

6The angel said to me, "These words can be trusted and
are true." The Lord, the God of the spirits of the prophets,
sent his angel to show his servants the things that must
happen soon.

7"Listen! I am coming soon! Happy is the one who obeys
the words of prophecy in this book."

8I, John, am the one who heard and saw these things.
When I heard and saw them, I bowed down to worship at
the feet of the angel who showed these things to me. 9But
the angel said to me, "Do not worship me! I am a servant
like you, your brothers the prophets, and all those who
obey the words in this book. Worship God!"

10Then the angel told me, "Do not keep secret the words
of prophecy in this book, because the time is near for all

CONTEMPORARY ENGLISH VERSION

fruit each month of the year. The fruit gives life, and the leaves are used as medicine to heal the nations.

3God's curse will no longer be on the people of that city.
He and the Lamb will be seated there on their thrones, and
its people will worship God 4and will see him face to face.
God's name will be written on the foreheads of the people.
5Never again will night appear, and no one who lives there
will ever need a lamp or the sun. The Lord God will be
their light, and they will rule forever.

The Coming of Christ

6Then I was told:

These words are true and can be trusted. The Lord God
controls the spirits of his prophets, and he is the one
who sent his angel to show his servants what must hap-
pen right away. 7Remember, I am coming soon! God will
bless everyone who pays attention to the message of
this book.

8My name is John, and I am the one who heard and saw
these things. Then after I had heard and seen all this, I
knelt down and began to worship at the feet of the angel
who had shown it to me.

9But the angel said,

Don't do that! I am a servant, just like you. I am the
same as a follower or a prophet or anyone else who
obeys what is written in this book. God is the one you
should worship.

10Don't keep the prophecies in this book a secret.
These things will happen soon.

NEW INTERNATIONAL VERSION

And the leaves of the tree are for the healing of the nations. 3No longer will there be any curse. The throne of God and of the Lamb will be in the city, and his servants will serve him. 4They will see his face, and his name will be on their foreheads. 5There will be no more night. They will not need the light of a lamp or the light of the sun, for the Lord God will give them light. And they will reign for ever and ever.

6The angel said to me, "These words are trustworthy and true. The Lord, the God of the spirits of the prophets, sent his angel to show his servants the things that must soon take place."

Jesus Is Coming

7"Behold, I am coming soon! Blessed is he who keeps the words of the prophecy in this book."

8I, John, am the one who heard and saw these things. And when I had heard and seen them, I fell down to worship at the feet of the angel who had been showing them to me. 9But he said to me, "Do not do it! I am a fellow servant with you and with your brothers the prophets and of all who keep the words of this book. Worship God!"

10Then he told me, "Do not seal up the words of the prophecy of this book, because the time is near. 11Let him

NEW LIVING TRANSLATION

month. The leaves were used for medicine to heal the nations.

3No longer will anything be cursed. For the throne of God and of the Lamb will be there, and his servants will worship him. 4And they will see his face, and his name will be written on their foreheads. 5And there will be no night there—no need for lamps or sun—for the Lord God will shine on them. And they will reign forever and ever.

6Then the angel said to me, "These words are trustworthy and true: 'The Lord God, who tells his prophets what the future holds, has sent his angel to tell you what will happen soon.' "

Jesus Is Coming

7"Look, I am coming soon! Blessed are those who obey the prophecy written in this scroll."

8I, John, am the one who saw and heard all these things. And when I saw and heard these things, I fell down to worship the angel who showed them to me. 9But again he said, "No, don't worship me. I am a servant of God, just like you and your brothers the prophets, as well as all who obey what is written in this scroll. Worship God!"

10Then he instructed me, "Do not seal up the prophetic words you have written, for the time is near. 11Let the one

NEW KING JAMES VERSION

of the tree *were* for the healing of the nations. 3And there shall be no more curse, but the throne of God and of the Lamb shall be in it, and His servants shall serve Him. 4They shall see His face, and His name *shall be* on their foreheads. 5There shall be no night there: They need no lamp nor light of the sun, for the Lord God gives them light. And they shall reign forever and ever.

The Time Is Near

6Then he said to me, "These words *are* faithful and true." And the Lord God of the holy[b] prophets sent His angel to show His servants the things which must shortly take place.

7"Behold, I am coming quickly! Blessed *is* he who keeps the words of the prophecy of this book."

8Now I, John, saw and heard[c] these things. And when I heard and saw, I fell down to worship before the feet of the angel who showed me these things.

9Then he said to me, "See *that you do* not *do that.* For[d] I am your fellow servant, and of your brethren the prophets, and of those who keep the words of this book. Worship God." 10And he said to me, "Do not seal the words of the prophecy of this book, for the time is at hand. 11He who is

22:6 [b] NU-Text and M-Text read *spirits of the prophets.*
22:8 [c] NU-Text and M-Text read *am the one who heard and saw.*
22:9 [d] NU-Text and M-Text omit *For.*

THE MESSAGE

leaves of the Tree are for healing the nations. Never again will anything be cursed. The Throne of God and of the Lamb is at the center. His servants will offer God service—worshiping, they'll look on his face, their foreheads mirroring God. Never again will there be any night. No one will need lamplight or sunlight. The shining of God, the Master, is all the light anyone needs. And they will rule with him age after age after age.

Don't Put It Away on the Shelf

The Angel said to me, "These are dependable and accurate words, every one. The God and Master of the spirits of the prophets sent his Angel to show his servants what must take place, and soon. And tell them, 'Yes, I'm on my way!' Blessed be the one who keeps the words of the prophecy of this book."

I, John, saw all these things with my own eyes, heard them with my ears. Immediately when I heard and saw, I fell on my face to worship at the feet of the Angel who laid it all out before me. He objected, "No you don't! I'm a servant just like you and your companions, the prophets, and all who keep the words of this book. Worship God!"

The Angel continued, "Don't seal the words of the prophecy of this book; don't put it away on the shelf. Time is

KING JAMES VERSION

11 He that is unjust, let him be unjust still: and he which is filthy, let him be filthy still: and he that is righteous, let him be righteous still: and he that is holy, let him be holy still.

12 And, behold, I come quickly; and my reward *is* with me, to give every man according as his work shall be.

13 I am Alpha and Omega, the beginning and the end, the first and the last.

14 Blessed *are* they that do his commandments, that they may have right to the tree of life, and may enter in through the gates into the city.

15 For without *are* dogs, and sorcerers, and whoremongers, and murderers, and idolaters, and whosoever loveth and maketh a lie.

16 I Jesus have sent mine angel to testify unto you these things in the churches. I am the root and the offspring of David, *and* the bright and morning star.

17 And the Spirit and the bride say, Come. And let him that heareth say, Come. And let him that is athirst come. And whosoever will, let him take the water of life freely.

NEW AMERICAN STANDARD BIBLE

11 "Let the one who does wrong, still do wrong; and the one who is filthy, still be filthy; and let the one who is righteous, still practice righteousness; and the one who is holy, still keep himself holy."

12 "Behold, I am coming quickly, and My reward *is* with Me, to render to every man according to what he has done.

13 "I am the Alpha and the Omega, the first and the last, the beginning and the end."

14 Blessed are those who wash their robes, so that they may have the right to the tree of life, and may enter by the gates into the city.

15 Outside are the dogs and the sorcerers and the immoral persons and the murderers and the idolaters, and everyone who loves and practices lying.

16 "I, Jesus, have sent My angel to testify to you these things for the churches. I am the root and the descendant of David, the bright morning star."

17 The Spirit and the bride say, "Come." And let the one who hears say, "Come." And let the one who is thirsty come; let the one who wishes take the water of life without cost.

NEW CENTURY VERSION

this to happen. 11 Let whoever is doing evil continue to do
evil. Let whoever is unclean continue to be unclean. Let
whoever is doing right continue to do right. Let whoever is
holy continue to be holy."

12 "Listen! I am coming soon! I will bring my reward with
me, and I will repay each one of you for what you have
done. 13 I am the Alpha and the Omega,[a] the First and the
Last, the Beginning and the End.

14 "Happy are those who wash their robes[b] so that they
will receive the right to eat the fruit from the tree of life
and may go through the gates into the city. 15 Outside the
city are the evil people, those who do evil magic, who sin
sexually, who murder, who worship idols, and who love
lies and tell lies.

16 "I, Jesus, have sent my angel to tell you these things
for the churches. I am the descendant from the family of
David, and I am the bright morning star."

17 The Spirit and the bride say, "Come!" Let the one who
hears this say, "Come!" Let whoever is thirsty come; whoever wishes may have the water of life as a free gift.

22:13 [a] **Alpha and the Omega** The first and last letters of the Greek alphabet. This means "the beginning and the end." 22:14 [b] **wash their robes** This means they believed in Jesus so that their sins could be forgiven by Christ's blood.

CONTEMPORARY ENGLISH VERSION

11 Evil people will keep on being evil, and everyone
who is dirty-minded will still be dirty-minded. But good
people will keep on doing right, and God's people will
always be holy.

12 Then I was told:

I am coming soon! And when I come, I will reward
everyone for what they have done. 13 I am Alpha and
Omega,[b] the first and the last, the beginning and the
end.

14 God will bless all who have washed their robes.
They will each have the right to eat fruit from the tree
that gives life, and they can enter the gates of the city.
15 But outside the city will be dogs, witches, immoral
people, murderers, idol worshipers, and everyone who
loves to tell lies and do wrong.

16 I am Jesus! And I am the one who sent my angel to
tell all of you these things for the churches. I am David's
Great Descendant,[c] and I am also the bright morning
star.[d]

17 The Spirit and the bride say, "Come!"
Everyone who hears this[e] should say, "Come!"
If you are thirsty, come! If you want life-giving water,
come and take it. It's free!

[b] 22.13 *Alpha and Omega*: See the note at 1.8. [c] 22.16 *David's Great Descendant*: See the note at 5.5. [d] 22.16 *the bright morning star*: Probably thought of as the brightest star (see 2.27, 28). [e] 22.17 *who hears this*: The reading of the book of Revelation in a service of worship.

NEW INTERNATIONAL VERSION

who does wrong continue to do wrong; let him who is vile continue to be vile; let him who does right continue to do right; and let him who is holy continue to be holy."

12"Behold, I am coming soon! My reward is with me,
and I will give to everyone according to what he has done.
13I am the Alpha and the Omega, the First and the Last,
the Beginning and the End.

14"Blessed are those who wash their robes, that they
may have the right to the tree of life and may go through
the gates into the city. 15Outside are the dogs, those who
practice magic arts, the sexually immoral, the murderers,
the idolaters and everyone who loves and practices falsehood.

16"I, Jesus, have sent my angel to give you[a] this testimony for the churches. I am the Root and the Offspring of David, and the bright Morning Star."

17The Spirit and the bride say, "Come!" And let him who hears say, "Come!" Whoever is thirsty, let him come; and whoever wishes, let him take the free gift of the water of life.

[a] *16* The Greek is plural.

NEW LIVING TRANSLATION

who is doing wrong continue to do wrong; the one who is vile, continue to be vile; the one who is good, continue to do good; and the one who is holy, continue in holiness."

12"See, I am coming soon, and my reward is with me, to
repay all according to their deeds. 13I am the Alpha and
the Omega, the First and the Last, the Beginning and the End."

14Blessed are those who wash their robes so they can
enter through the gates of the city and eat the fruit from
the tree of life. 15Outside the city are the dogs—the sorcerers, the sexually immoral, the murderers, the idol worshipers, and all who love to live a lie.

16"I, Jesus, have sent my angel to give you this message for the churches. I am both the source of David and the heir to his throne.* I am the bright morning star."

17The Spirit and the bride say, "Come." Let each one who hears them say, "Come." Let the thirsty ones come—anyone who wants to. Let them come and drink the water of life

22:16 Greek *I am the root and offspring of David.*

NEW KING JAMES VERSION

unjust, let him be unjust still; he who is filthy, let him be filthy still; he who is righteous, let him be righteous[e] still; he who is holy, let him be holy still."

Jesus Testifies to the Churches

12"And behold, I am coming quickly, and My reward *is*
with Me, to give to every one according to his work. 13I am
the Alpha and the Omega, *the* Beginning and *the* End, the First and the Last."[f]

14Blessed *are* those who do His commandments,[g] that
they may have the right to the tree of life, and may enter
through the gates into the city. 15But[h] outside *are* dogs
and sorcerers and sexually immoral and murderers and idolaters, and whoever loves and practices a lie.

16"I, Jesus, have sent My angel to testify to you these things in the churches. I am the Root and the Offspring of David, the Bright and Morning Star."

17And the Spirit and the bride say, "Come!" And let him who hears say, "Come!" And let him who thirsts come. Whoever desires, let him take the water of life freely.

22:11 [e] NU-Text and M-Text read *do right.* **22:13** [f] NU-Text and M-Text read *the First and the Last, the Beginning and the End.*
22:14 [g] NU-Text reads *wash their robes.* **22:15** [h] NU-Text and M-Text omit *But.*

THE MESSAGE

just about up. Let evildoers do their worst and the dirty-minded go all out in pollution, but let the righteous maintain a straight course and the holy continue on in holiness."

✠

"Yes, I'm on my way! I'll be there soon! I'm bringing my payroll with me. I'll pay all people in full for their life's work. I'm A to Z, the First and the Final, Beginning and Conclusion.

"How blessed are those who wash their robes! The Tree of Life is theirs for good, and they'll walk through the gates to the City. But outside for good are the filthy curs: sorcerers, fornicators, murderers, idolaters—all who love and live lies.

"I, Jesus, sent my Angel to testify to these things for the churches. I'm the Root and Branch of David, the Bright Morning Star."

"Come!" say the Spirit and the Bride.
Whoever hears, echo, "Come!"
Is anyone thirsty? Come!
All who will, come and drink,
Drink freely of the Water of Life!

KING JAMES VERSION

18 For I testify unto every man that heareth the words of the prophecy of this book, If any man shall add unto these things, God shall add unto him the plagues that are written in this book:

19 And if any man shall take away from the words of the book of this prophecy, God shall take away his part out of the book of life, and out of the holy city, and *from* the things which are written in this book.

20 ¶ He which testifieth these things saith, Surely I come quickly. Amen. Even so, come, Lord Jesus.

21 The grace of our Lord Jesus Christ *be* with you all. Amen.

NEW AMERICAN STANDARD BIBLE

18 I testify to everyone who hears the words of the prophecy of this book: if anyone adds to them, God will add to him the plagues which are written in this book;

19 and if anyone takes away from the words of the book of this prophecy, God will take away his part from the tree of life and from the holy city, which are written in this book.

20 He who testifies to these things says, "Yes, I am coming quickly." Amen. Come, Lord Jesus.

21 The grace of the Lord Jesus be with [3]all. Amen.

22:21 [3] One early ms reads *the saints*

NEW CENTURY VERSION

18I warn everyone who hears the words of the prophecy of this book: If anyone adds anything to these words, God will add to that person the disasters written about in this book. 19And if anyone takes away from the words of this book of prophecy, God will take away that one's share of the tree of life and of the holy city, which are written about in this book.

20Jesus, the One who says these things are true, says, "Yes, I am coming soon."

Amen. Come, Lord Jesus!

21The grace of the Lord Jesus be with all. Amen.

CONTEMPORARY ENGLISH VERSION

18Here is my warning for everyone who hears the prophecies in this book:

If you add anything to them, God will make you suffer all the terrible troubles written in this book. 19If you take anything away from these prophecies, God will not let you have part in the life-giving tree and in the holy city described in this book.

20The one who has spoken these things says, "I am coming soon!"

So, Lord Jesus, please come soon!

21I pray that the Lord Jesus will be kind to all of you.

NEW INTERNATIONAL VERSION

[18]I warn everyone who hears the words of the prophecy of this book: If anyone adds anything to them, God will add to him the plagues described in this book. [19]And if anyone takes words away from this book of prophecy, God will take away from him his share in the tree of life and in the holy city, which are described in this book.

[20]He who testifies to these things says, "Yes, I am coming soon."

Amen. Come, Lord Jesus.

[21]The grace of the Lord Jesus be with God's people. Amen.

NEW LIVING TRANSLATION

without charge. [18]And I solemnly declare to everyone who hears the prophetic words of this book: If anyone adds anything to what is written here, God will add to that person the plagues described in this book. [19]And if anyone removes any of the words of this prophetic book, God will remove that person's share in the tree of life and in the holy city that are described in this book.

[20]He who is the faithful witness to all these things says, "Yes, I am coming soon!"

Amen! Come, Lord Jesus!

[21]The grace of the Lord Jesus be with you all.

NEW KING JAMES VERSION

A Warning

[18]For[i] I testify to everyone who hears the words of the prophecy of this book: If anyone adds to these things, God will add[j] to him the plagues that are written in this book; [19]and if anyone takes away from the words of the book of this prophecy, God shall take away[k] his part from the Book[l] of Life, from the holy city, and *from* the things which are written in this book.

I Am Coming Quickly

[20]He who testifies to these things says, "Surely I am coming quickly."

Amen. Even so, come, Lord Jesus!

[21]The grace of our Lord Jesus Christ *be* with you all.[m] Amen.

22:18 [i] NU-Text and M-Text omit *For.* [j] M-Text reads *may God add.* **22:19** [k] M-Text reads *may God take away.* [l] NU-Text and M-Text read *tree of life.* **22:21** [m] NU-Text reads *with all;* M-Text reads *with all the saints.*

THE MESSAGE

I give fair warning to all who hear the words of the prophecy of this book: If you add to the words of this prophecy, God will add to your life the disasters written in this book; if you subtract from the words of the book of this prophecy, God will subtract your part from the Tree of Life and the Holy City that are written in this book.

He who testifies to all these things says it again: "I'm on my way! I'll be there soon!"

Yes! Come, Master Jesus!

The grace of the Master Jesus be with all of you. Oh, Yes!

Common
English
Version